WHO'S WHO 2009
in
International
Affairs

WHO'S WHO
in
International Affairs

2009

6th Edition

Routledge
Taylor & Francis Group

LONDON AND NEW YORK

ISBN-10: 1-85743-479-X
ISBN-13: 978-185743-479-8
ISSN: 0956-7984

Editor: Robert J. Elster

Assistant Editors: Joanne Corsan, Amy Tyndall

Freelance Editorial Team: Gerard Delaney, Neil Higgins, Sue Leckey

Typeset by Data Standards Limited, Frome
Printed and bound in Great Britain by Polestar Wheatons, Exeter

FOREWORD

This sixth edition of WHO'S WHO IN INTERNATIONAL AFFAIRS provides, in one volume, biographical information on nearly 6,000 people prominent in the fields of international politics, diplomacy, law and economic affairs throughout the world. As well as politicians and diplomats, the book also includes academics, think tank analysts, and journalists, among others, who are active in, or relevant to, the world of foreign affairs.

WHO'S WHO IN INTERNATIONAL AFFAIRS is thus an invaluable guide to the lives and careers of the most important figures in international affairs today. Each entry is clearly laid out, with the international figure's personal details, education, career, publications and contact information conveniently divided into sections. In addition to the biographical information, an extensive index section is included, where entrants are listed once by nationality and for many by selected organizations for which they work. Thus it is possible to trace an entry for the occupant of a particular office without first having to know the incumbent's name. Explanatory notes on the structure and organization of the biographical entries and the indexes are provided overleaf.

Also provided is the Directory of Diplomatic Missions appendix that lists by country all embassies and diplomatic missions to other countries around the world, including missions to the United Nations. Listings include contact information and names of ambassador or head of mission.

Most of the entrants in this sixth edition have been mailed a questionnaire, in order that they may have the opportunity to make necessary additions and amendments. Many others have been contacted via e-mail. Supplementary research has been done by the Editor and the Europa editorial department to ensure that the listings are as up to date as possible on publication.

September 2008

EXPLANATORY NOTES

Each biographical entry in WHO'S WHO IN INTERNATIONAL AFFAIRS includes, where appropriate, the following details:

- Surname.
- Titles and first names.
- Academic degrees, professional qualifications and honours.
- Nationality.
- Job title and organization worked for.
- Date and place of birth.
- Name of spouse or partner, year of marriage and number of children.
- Educational establishments attended.
- Career history, including any honorary degrees, awards or prizes received.
- Titles of major publications with dates.
- Contact addresses with telephone and fax numbers, and e-mail and internet addresses.

Supplementary information is provided in the following sections of the book:

- An extensive list of ABBREVIATIONS (see pp vii–xiii).
- A guide to INTERNATIONAL TELEPHONE CODES (see pp xiv–xv).
- The appendix DIRECTORY OF DIPLOMATIC MISSIONS (see pp 651–832) lists by country all embassies and diplomatic missions to other countries around the world, including missions the the United Nations. Listings include contact information and name of ambassador or head of mission.
- The INDEX BY ORGANIZATION (see pp 833–855) provides access to the information in the book by listing alphabetically hundreds of important, primarily non-governmental organizations together with key entrants related to those organizations. Citations include entrant's name, job title, and number of the page where their entry can be found.
- The INDEX BY NATIONALITY (see pp 857–908) lists entrants alphabetically under the country of their nationality, giving their name, job title or profession, the organization for which they work, and the number of the page where their entry may be found.

Alphabetization Key:

- The list of names is alphabetical, with the entrants listed under surnames. If part of an entrant's first name is in parentheses, this will not affect his or her alphabetical listing.
- All names beginning with Mc and Mac are treated as though they began Mac, e.g. McEwan before Macfarlane, McHenry before Machungo.
- Names with Arabic prefixes are normally listed after the prefix. In the case ofsurnames beginning De, Des, Du, van or von the entries are normally found under the prefix.
- In the case of an entrant whose name is spelt in a variety of ways, who is known by a pseudonym or best known by another name, a cross reference will be provided, e.g. Kadhafi, Col. Mu'ammar Muhammed al- (see Gaddafi, Col. Mu'ammar Huhammed al-).

ABBREVIATIONS

AAA	Agricultural Adjustment Administration
AAAS	American Association for the Advancement of Science
AAF	Army Air Force
AASA	Associate of the Australian Society of Accountants
AB	Bachelor of Arts; Aktiebolag; Alberta
ABA	American Bar Association
AC	Companion of the Order of Australia
ACA	Associate of the Institute of Chartered Accountants
ACCA	Associate of the Association of Certified Accountants
Acad.	Academy; Académie
Accad.	Accademia
accred	accredited
ACIS	Associate of the Chartered Institute of Secretaries
ACP	American College of Physicians
ACS	American Chemical Society
ACT	Australian Capital Territory
ADC	Aide-de-camp
Adm.	Admiral
Admin(.)	Administrative; Administration; Administrator
AE	Air Efficiency Award
AERE	Atomic Energy Research Establishment
AF	Air Force
AFC	Air Force Cross
ADB	African Development Bank
affil.	affiliated
AFL	American Federation of Labor
AFM	Air Force Medal
AG	Aktiengesellschaft (Joint Stock Company)
Agric.	Agriculture
a.i.	ad interim
AIA	Associate of the Institute of Actuaries; American Institute of Architects
AIAA	American Institute of Aeronautics and Astronautics
AIB	Associate of the Institute of Bankers
AICC	All-India Congress Committee
AICE	Associate of the Institute of Civil Engineers
AIChE	American Institute of Chemical Engineers
AIDS	Acquired Immune Deficiency Syndrome
AIEE	American Institute of Electrical Engineers
AIME	American Institute of Mining Engineers; Associate of the Institution of Mining Engineers
AIMechE	Associate of the Institution of Mechanical Engineers
AIR	All-India Radio
AK	Alaska; Knight of the Order of Australia
Akad.	Akademie
AL	Alabama
Ala	Alabama
ALS	Associate of the Linnaean Society
Alt.	Alternate
AM	Alpes Maritimes; Albert Medal; Master of Arts; Member of the Order of Australia
Amb.	Ambassador
AMICE	Associate Member of the Institution of Civil Engineers
AMIEE	Associate Member of the Institution of Electrical Engineers
AMIMechE	Associate Member of the Institution of Mechanical Engineers
ANC	African National Congress
ANU	Australian National University
AO	Officer of the Order of Australia
AP	Andhra Pradesh
Apdo	Apartado
APEC	Asia and Pacific Economic Co-operation
approx.	approximately
appt	appointment
apptd	appointed
apt	apartment
AR	Arkansas
ARA	Associate of the Royal Academy
ARAM	Associate of the Royal Academy of Music
ARAS	Associate of the Royal Astronomical Society
ARC	Agriculture Research Council
ARCA	Associate of the Royal College of Art
ARCM	Associate of the Royal College of Music
ARCO	Associate of the Royal College of Organists
ARCS	Associate of the Royal College of Science
ARIBA	Associate of the Royal Institute of British Architects
Ariz.	Arizona
Ark.	Arkansas
ARSA	Associate of the Royal Scottish Academy; Associate of the Royal Society of Arts
ASEAN	Association of South-East Asian Nations
ASLIB	Association of Special Libraries and Information Bureaux
ASME	American Society of Mechanical Engineers
Asoc.	Asociación
Ass.	Assembly
Asscn	Association
Assoc.	Associate
ASSR	Autonomous Soviet Socialist Republic
Asst	Assistant
ATV	Associated Television
Aug.	August
autobiog.	autobiography
AZ	Arizona
b.	born
BA	Bachelor of Arts; British Airways
BAAS	British Association for the Advancement of Science
BAFTA	British Academy of Film and Television Arts
BAgr	Bachelor of Agriculture
BAgrSc	Bachelor of Agricultural Science
BAO	Bachelor of Obstetrics
BAOR	British Army of the Rhine
BArch	Bachelor of Architecture
Bart	Baronet
BAS	Bachelor in Agricultural Science
BASc	Bachelor of Applied Science
BBA	Bachelor of Business Administration
BBC	British Broadcasting Corporation
BC	British Columbia
BCC	British Council of Churches
BCE	Bachelor of Civil Engineering
BChir	Bachelor of Surgery
BCL	Bachelor of Civil Law; Bachelor of Canon Law
BCom(m)	Bachelor of Commerce
BCS	Bachelor of Commercial Sciences
BD	Bachelor of Divinity
Bd	Board
BDS	Bachelor of Dental Surgery
BE	Bachelor of Education; Bachelor of Engineering
BEA	British European Airways
BEcons	Bachelor of Economics
BEd	Bachelor of Education
Beds.	Bedfordshire
BEE	Bachelor of Electrical Engineering
BEM	British Empire Medal
BEng	Bachelor of Engineering
Berks.	Berkshire
BFA	Bachelor of Fine Arts
BFI	British Film Institute
BIM	British Institute of Management
biog.	biography
BIS	Bank for International Settlements
BL	Bachelor of Laws
BLA	Bachelor of Landscape Architecture
Bldg	Building
BLit(t)	Bachelor of Letters; Bachelor of Literature
BLL	Bachelor of Laws
BLS	Bachelor in Library Science
blvd	boulevard
BM	Bachelor of Medicine
BMA	British Medical Association
BMus	Bachelor of Music
Bn	Battalion
BNOC	British National Oil Corporation
BOAC	British Overseas Airways Corporation
BP	Boîte Postale
BPA	Bachelor of Public Administration
BPharm	Batchelor of Pharmacy
BPhil	Bachelor of Philosophy
Br.	Branch
Brig.	Brigadier
BS	Bachelor of Science; Bachelor of Surgery
BSA	Bachelor of Scientific Agriculture
BSc	Bachelor of Science
Bt	Baronet
Bucks.	Buckinghamshire
c.	child; children; circa
CA	California; Chartered Accountant
Calif.	California
Cambs.	Cambridgeshire
Cand.	Candidate; Candidature
Cantab.	of Cambridge University

ABBREVIATIONS

Capt.	Captain	CT	Connecticut
Cards.	Cardiganshire	Cttee	Committee
CB	Companion of the (Order of the) Bath	CUNY	City University of New York
CBC	Canadian Broadcasting Corporation	CV	Commandaitaire Vennootschap
CBE	Commander of the (Order of the) British Empire	CVO	Commander of the Royal Victorian Order
CBI	Confederation of British Industry		
CBiol	Chartered Biologist	d.	daughter(s)
CBIM	Companion of the British Institute of Management	DArch	Doctor of Architecture
CBS	Columbia Broadcasting System	DB	Bachelor of Divinity
CC	Companion of the Order of Canada	DBA	Doctor of Business Administration
CChem	Chartered Chemist	DBE	Dame Commander of (the Order of) the British Empire
CCMI	Companion of the Chartered Management Institute (formerly	DC	District of Columbia
	CIMgt)	DCE	Doctor of Civil Engineering
CCP	Chinese Communist Party	DCL	Doctor of Civil Law; Doctor of Canon Law
CD	Canadian Forces Decoration; Commander Order of Distinction	DCM	Distinguished Conduct Medal
Cdre	Commodore	DCMG	Dame Commander of (the Order of) St Michael and St George
CDU	Christlich-Demokratische Union	DCnL	Doctor of Canon Law
CE	Civil Engineer; Chartered Engineer	DComm	Doctor of Commerce
CEAO	Communauté Economique de l'Afrique de l'Ouest	DCS	Doctor of Commercial Sciences
Cen.	Central	DCT	Doctor of Christian Theology
CEng	Chartered Engineer	DCVO	Dame Commander of the Royal Victorian Order
CENTO	Central Treaty Organization	DD	Doctor of Divinity
CEO	Chief Executive Officer	DDR	Deutsche Demokratische Republik (German Democratic Republic)
CERN	Conseil (now Organisation) Européen(ne) pour la Recherche	DDS	Doctor of Dental Surgery
	Nucléaire	DE	Delaware
CFR	Commander of the Federal Republic of Nigeria	Dec.	December
CGM	Conspicuous Gallantry Medal	DEcon	Doctor of Economics
CGT	Confédération Général du Travail	DEd	Doctor of Education
CH	Companion of Honour	DEFRA	Department for Environment, Food and Rural Affairs
Chair.	Chairman; Chairwoman; Chairperson	Del.	Delegate; Delegation; Delaware
CHB	Companion of Honour of Barbados	Denbighs.	Denbighshire
ChB	Bachelor of Surgery	DenD	Docteur en Droit
Chem.	Chemistry	DenM	Docteur en Medicine
ChM	Master of Surgery	DEng	Doctor of Engineering
CI	Channel Islands	Dep.	Deputy
CIA	Central Intelligence Agency	Dept	Department
Cia	Compagnia (Company)	DES	Department of Education and Science
Cía	Compañia (Company)	Desig.	Designate
CID	Criminal Investigation Department	DèsL	Docteur ès Lettres
CIE	Companion of the (Order of the) Indian Empire	DèsSc	Docteur ès Sciences
Cie	Compagnie (Company)	Devt	Development
CIEE	Companion of the Institution of Electrical Engineers	DF	Distrito Federal
CIMgt	Companion of the Institute of Management (now CCMI)	DFA	Doctor of Fine Arts; Diploma of Fine Arts
C-in-C	Commander-in-Chief	DFC	Distinguished Flying Cross
CIO	Congress of Industrial Organizations	DFM	Distinguished Flying Medal
CIOMS	Council of International Organizations of Medical Science	DH	Doctor of Humanities
CIS	Commonwealth of Independent States	DHist	Doctor of History
CLD	Doctor of Civil Law (USA)	DHL	Doctor of Hebrew Literature
CLit	Companion of Literature	DHSS	Department of Health and Social Security
CM	Canada Medal; Master in Surgery	DHumLitt	Doctor of Humane Letters
CMEA	Council for Mutual Economic Assistance	DIC	Diploma of Imperial College
CMG	Companion of (the Order of) St Michael and St George	DipAD	Diploma in Art and Design
CNAA	Council for National Academic Awards	DipAgr	Diploma in Agriculture
CNRS	Centre National de la Recherche Scientifique	DipArch	Diploma in Architecture
CO	Colorado; Commanding Officer	DipEd	Diploma in Education
Co.	Company; County	DipEng	Diploma in Engineering
COI	Central Office of Information	DipMus	Diploma in Music
Col	Colonel	DipScEconSc	Diploma of Social and Economic Science
Coll.	College	DipTh	Doctor of Theology
Colo	Colorado	Dir	Director
COMECON	Council for Mutual Economic Assistance	Dist	District
COMESA	Common Market for Eastern and Southern Asia	DIur	Doctor of Law
Comm.	Commission	DIurUtr	Doctor of both Civil and Canon Law
Commdg	Commanding	Div.	Division; divisional
Commdr	Commander; Commandeur	DJur	Doctor of Law
Commdt	Commandant	DK	Most Esteemed Family (Malaysia)
Commr	Commissioner	DL	Deputy Lieutenant
CON	Commander of Order of Nigeria	DLit(t)	Doctor of Letters; Doctor of Literature
Conf.	Conference	DLS	Doctor of Library Science
Confed.	Confederation	DM	Doctor of Medicine (Oxford)
Conn.	Connecticut	DMD	Doctor of Dental Medicine
Contrib.	Contributor; contribution	DMedSc	Doctor of Medical Science
COO	Chief Operating Officer	DMilSc	Doctor of Military Science
Corp.	Corporate	DMunSci	Doctor of Municipal Science
Corpn	Corporation	DMS	Director of Medical Services
Corresp.	Correspondent; Corresponding	DMus	Doctor of Music
CP	Communist Party; Caixa Postal (Post Office Box)	DMV	Doctor of Veterinary Medicine
CPA	Certified Public Accountant; Commonwealth Parliamentary	DO	Doctor of Ophthalmology
	Association	DPH	Diploma in Public Health
CPhys	Chartered Physicist	DPhil	Doctor of Philosophy
CPP	Convention People's Party (Ghana)	DPM	Diploma in Psychological Medicine
CPPCC	Chinese People's Political Consultative Conference	DPS	Doctor of Public Service
CPSU	Communist Party of the Soviet Union	Dr	Doctor
cr.	created	DrAgr	Doctor of Agriculture
CSc	Candidate of Sciences	DrIng	Doctor of Engineering
CSCE	Conference on Security and Co-operation in Europe	DrIur	Doctor of Laws
CSI	Companion of the (Order of the) Star of India	DrMed	Doctor of Medicine
CSIRO	Commonwealth Scientific and Industrial Research Organization	DrOecPol	Doctor of Political Economy
CSSR	Czechoslovak Socialist Republic	DrOecPubl	Doctor of (Public) Economy
CStJ	Commander of (the Order of) St John of Jerusalem	DrPhilNat	Doctor of Natural Philosophy

ABBREVIATIONS

Dr rer. nat	Doctor of Natural Sciences	FCIA	Fellow of the Chartered Institute of Arbitrators
Dr rer. pol	Doctor of Political Science	FCIB	Fellow of the Chartered Institute of Bankers
DrSc(i)	Doctor of Sciences	FCIC	Fellow of the Chemical Institute of Canada
DrScNat	Doctor of Natural Sciences	FCIM	Fellow of the Chartered Institute of Management
DS	Doctor of Science	FCIS	Fellow of the Chartered Institute of Secretaries
DSC	Distinguished Service Cross	FCMA	Fellow of the Chartered Institute of Management Accountants
DSc(i)	Doctor of Sciences	FCO	Foreign and Commonwealth Office
DScS	Doctor of Social Science	FCSD	Fellow of the Chartered Society of Designers
DSM	Distinguished Service Medal	FCT	Federal Capital Territory
DSO	Companion of the Distinguished Service Order	FCWA	Fellow of the Institute of Cost and Works Accountants (now FCMA)
DSocSc	Doctor of Social Science	FDGB	Freier Deutscher Gewerkschaftsbund
DST	Doctor of Sacred Theology	FDP	Freier Demokratische Partei
DTech	Doctor of Technology	Feb.	February
DTechSc(i)	Doctor of Technical Sciences	Fed.	Federation; Federal
DTheol	Doctor of Theology	FEng	Fellow(ship) of Engineering
DTM	Diploma in Tropical Medicine	FFCM	Fellow of the Faculty of Community Medicine
DTM&H	Diploma in Tropical Medicine and Hygiene	FFPHM	Fellow of the Faculty of Public Health Medicine
DUP	Diploma of the University of Paris	FGS	Fellow of the Geological Society
DUniv	Doctor of the University	FGSM	Fellow of the Guildhall School of Music
		FIA	Fellow of the Institute of Actuaries
E	East; Eastern	FIAL	Fellow of the International Institute of Arts and Letters
EBRD	European Bank for Reconstruction and Development	FIAM	Fellow of the International Academy of Management
EC	European Commission; European Community	FIAMS	Fellow of the Indian Academy of Medical Sciences
ECA	Economic Co-operation Administration; Economic Commission for Africa	FIAP	Fellow of the Institution of Analysts and Programmers
		FIArb	Fellow of the Institute of Arbitrators
ECAFE	Economic Commission for Asia and the Far East	FIB	Fellow of the Institute of Bankers
ECE	Economic Commission for Europe	FIBA	Fellow of the Institute of Banking Associations
ECLA	Economic Commission for Latin America	FIBiol	Fellow of the Institute of Biologists
ECLAC	Economic Commission for Latin America and the Caribbean	FICE	Fellow of the Institution of Civil Engineers
ECO	Economic Co-operation Organization	FIChemE	Fellow of the Institute of Chemical Engineers
Econ.	Economic	FID	Fellow of the Institute of Directors
Econs	Economics	FIE	Fellow of the Institute of Engineers
ECOSOC	Economic and Social Council	FIEE	Fellow of the Institution of Electrical Engineers
ECSC	European Coal and Steel Community	FIEEE	Fellow of the Institute of Electrical and Electronics Engineers
ECWA	Economic Commission for Western Asia	FIFA	Fédération Internationale de Football Association
ed	educated; edited	FIJ	Fellow of the Institute of Journalists
Ed.	Editor	FilLic	Licentiate in Philosophy
ED	Efficiency Decoration; Doctor of Engineering (USA)	FIM	Fellow of the Institute of Metallurgists
EdD	Doctor of Education	FIME	Fellow of the Institute of Mining Engineers
Edin.	Edinburgh	FIMechE	Fellow of the Institute of Mechanical Engineers
EdM	Master of Education	FIMI	Fellow of the Institute of the Motor Industry
Edn	Edition	FInstF	Fellow of the Institute of Fuel
Educ.	Education	FInstM	Fellow of the Institute of Marketing
EEC	European Economic Community	FInstP	Fellow of the Institute of Physics
EFTA	European Free Trade Association	FInstPet	Fellow of the Institute of Petroleum
eh	Ehrenhalben (Honorary)	FIPM	Fellow of the Institute of Personnel Management
EIB	European Investment Bank	FIRE	Fellow of the Institution of Radio Engineers
EM	Edward Medal; Master of Engineering (USA)	FITD	Fellow of the Institute of Training and Development
Emer.	Emerita; Emeritus	FL	Florida
Eng	Engineering	Fla	Florida
EngD	Doctor of Engineering	FLA	Fellow of the Library Association
ENO	English National Opera	FLN	Front de Libération Nationale
EPLF	Eritrean People's Liberation Front	FLS	Fellow of the Linnaean Society
ESA	European Space Agency	FMedSci	Fellow of the Academy of Medical Sciences
ESCAP	Economic and Social Commission for Asia and the Pacific	fmr(ly)	former(ly)
ESCWA	Economic and Social Commission for Western Asia	FNI	Fellow of the National Institute of Sciences of India
est.	established	FNZIA	Fellow of the New Zealand Institute of Architects
ETH	Eidgenössische Technische Hochschule (Swiss Federal Institute of Technology)	FRACP	Fellow of the Royal Australasian College of Physicians
		FRACS	Fellow of the Royal Australasian College of Surgeons
Ets	Etablissements	FRAeS	Fellow of the Royal Aeronautical Society
EU	European Union	FRAI	Fellow of the Royal Anthropological Institute
EURATOM	European Atomic Energy Community	FRAIA	Fellow of the Royal Australian Institute of Architects
Exec.	Executive	FRAIC	Fellow of the Royal Architectural Institute of Canada
Exhbn	Exhibition	FRAM	Fellow of the Royal Academy of Music
Ext.	Extension	FRAS	Fellow of the Royal Astronomical Society; Fellow of the Royal Asiatic Society
f.	founded	FRBS	Fellow of the Royal Society of British Sculptors
FAA	Fellow of Australian Academy of Science	FRCA	Fellow of the Royal College of Anaesthetists
FAAS	Fellow of the American Association for the Advancement of Science	FRCM	Fellow of the Royal College of Music
FAATS	Fellow of the Australian Academy of Technological Sciences	FRCO	Fellow of the Royal College of Organists
FACC	Fellow of the American College of Cardiology	FRCOG	Fellow of the Royal College of Obstetricians and Gynaecologists
FACCA	Fellow of the Association of Certified and Corporate Accountants	FRCP	Fellow of the Royal College of Physicians
FACE	Fellow of the Australian College of Education	FRCPE	Fellow of the Royal College of Physicians, Edinburgh
FACP	Fellow of American College of Physicians	FRCPGlas	Fellow of the Royal College of Physicians (Glasgow)
FACS	Fellow of the American College of Surgeons	FRCPI	Fellow of the Royal College of Physicians of Ireland
FAHA	Fellow Australian Academy of the Humanities	FRCPath	Fellow Royal College of Pathologists
FAIA	Fellow of the American Institute of Architects	FRCR	Fellow Royal College of Radiology
FAIAS	Fellow of the Australian Institute of Agricultural Science	FRCS	Fellow of the Royal College of Surgeons
FAIM	Fellow of the Australian Institute of Management	FRCSE	Fellow of the Royal College of Surgeons, Edinburgh
FAO	Food and Agriculture Organization	FRCVS	Fellow of the Royal College of Veterinary Surgeons
FAS	Fellow of the Antiquarian Society	FREconS	Fellow of the Royal Economic Society
FASE	Fellow of Antiquarian Society, Edinburgh	FREng	Fellow of the Royal Academy of Engineering
FASSA	Fellow Academy of Social Sciences of Australia	FRES	Fellow of the Royal Entomological Society
FBA	Fellow of the British Academy	FRFPS	Fellow of the Royal Faculty of Physicians and Surgeons
FBI	Federal Bureau of Investigation	FRG	Federal Republic of Germany
FBIM	Fellow of the British Institute of Management	FRGS	Fellow of the Royal Geographical Society
FBIP	Fellow of the British Institute of Physics	FRHistS	Fellow of the Royal Historical Society
FCA	Fellow of the Institute of Chartered Accountants	FRHortS	Fellow of the Royal Horticultural Society
FCAE	Fellow Canadian Academy of Engineering	FRIBA	Fellow of the Royal Institute of British Architects
FCGI	Fellow of the City and Guilds of London Institute	FRIC	Fellow of the Royal Institute of Chemists

FRICS	Fellow of the Royal Institute of Chartered Surveyors	ICS	Indian Civil Service
FRMetS	Fellow of the Royal Meteorological Society	ICSID	International Centre for Settlement of Investment Disputes
FRNCM	Fellow of the Royal Northern College of Music	ICSU	International Council of Scientific Unions
FRPS	Fellow of the Royal Photographic Society	ID	Idaho
FRS	Fellow of the Royal Society	Ida	Idaho
FRSA	Fellow of the Royal Society of Arts	IDA	International Development Association
FRSAMD	Fellow of the Royal Scottish Academy of Music and Drama	IDB	Inter-American Development Bank
FRSC	Fellow of the Royal Society of Canada; Fellow of the Royal Society of Chemistry	IEA	International Energy Agency
		IEE	Institution of Electrical Engineers
FRSE	Fellow of the Royal Society of Edinburgh	IEEE	Institution of Electrical and Electronic Engineers
FRSL	Fellow of the Royal Society of Literature	IFAD	International Fund for Agricultural Development
FRSM	Fellow of the Royal Society of Medicine	IFC	International Finance Corporation
FRSNZ	Fellow of the Royal Society of New Zealand	IGAD	Intergovernmental Authority on Development
FRSS	Fellow of the Royal Statistical Society	IISS	International Institute for Strategic Studies
FRSSA	Fellow of the Royal Society of South Africa	IL	Illinois
FRTS	Fellow of the Royal Television Society	Ill.	Illinois
FSA	Fellow of the Society of Antiquaries	ILO	International Labour Organization
FSIAD	Fellow of the Society of Industrial Artists and Designers	IMCO	Inter-Governmental Maritime Consultative Organization
FTI	Fellow of the Textile Institute	IMechE	Institution of Mechanical Engineers
FTS	Fellow of Technological Sciences	IMF	International Monetary Fund
FWAAS	Fellow of the World Academy of Arts and Sciences	IMO	International Maritime Organization
FZS	Fellow of the Zoological Society	IN	Indiana
		Inc.	Incorporated
GA	Georgia	Ind.	Indiana; Independent
Ga	Georgia	Insp.	Inspector
GATT	General Agreement on Tariffs and Trade	Inst.	Institute; Institution
GB	Great Britain	Int.	International
GBE	Knight (or Dame) Grand Cross of (the Order of) the British Empire	INTERPOL	International Criminal Police Organization
GC	George Cross	INTUC	Indian National Trades Union Congress
GCB	Knight Grand Cross of (the Order of) the Bath	IOC	International Olympic Committee
GCIE	Knight Grand Commander of (the Order of) the Indian Empire	IPU	Inter-Parliamentary Union
GCMG	Knight (or Dame) Grand Cross of (the Order of) St Michael and St George	ISO	Companion of the Imperial Service Order
		ITA	Independent Television Authority
GCSI	Knight Grand Commander of (the Order of) the Star of India	ITU	International Telecommunications Union
GCVO	Knight (or Dame) Grand Cross of the Royal Victorian Order	ITV	Independent Television
GDR	German Democratic Republic	IUPAC	International Union of Pure and Applied Chemistry
Gen.	General	IUPAP	International Union of Pure and Applied Physics
GHQ	General Headquarters		
GLA	Greater London Authority	Jan.	January
Glam.	Glamorganshire	JCB	Bachelor of Canon Law
GLC	Greater London Council	JCD	Doctor of Canon Law
Glos.	Gloucestershire	JD	Doctor of Jurisprudence
GM	George Medal	JMK	Johan Mangku Negara (Malaysia)
GmbH	Gesellschaft mit beschränkter Haftung (Limited Liability Company)	JP	Justice of the Peace
GOC	General Officer Commanding	Jr	Junior
GOC-in-C	General Officer Commanding-in-Chief	JSD	Doctor of Juristic Science
Gov.	Governor	Jt(ly)	Joint(ly)
Govt	Government	JUD	Juris utriusque Doctor (Doctor of both Civil and Canon Law)
GPO	General Post Office	JuD	Doctor of Law
Grad.	Graduate	JUDr	Juris utriusque Doctor (Doctor of both Civil and Canon Law);
GRSM	Graduate of the Royal School of Music		Doctor of Law
GSO	General Staff Officer	Kan.	Kansas
		KBE	Knight Commander of (the Order of) the British Empire
Hants.	Hampshire	KC	King's Counsel
hc	honoris causa	KCB	Knight Commander of (the Order of) the Bath
HE	His Eminence; His (or Her) Excellency	KCIE	Knight Commander of (the Order of) the Indian Empire
Herefords.	Herefordshire	KCMG	Knight Commander of (the Order of) St Michael and St George
Herts.	Hertfordshire	KCSI	Knight Commander of (the Order of) the Star of India
HH	His (or Her) Highness	KCVO	Knight Commander of the Royal Victorian Order
HI	Hawaii	KG	Royal Knight of the Most Noble Order of the Garter
HIV	human immunodeficiency virus	KGB	Committee of State Security (USSR)
HLD	Doctor of Humane Letters	KK	Kaien Kaisha
HM	His (or Her) Majesty	KLM	Koninklijke Luchtvaart Maatschappij (Royal Dutch Airlines)
HMS	His (or Her) Majesty's Ship	KNZM	Knight of the New Zealand Order of Merit
Hon.	Honorary; Honourable	KP	Knight of (the Order of) St Patrick
Hons	Honours	KS	Kansas
Hosp.	Hospital	KStJ	Knight of (the Order of) St John of Jerusalem
HQ	Headquarters	KT	Knight of (the Order of) the Thistle
HRH	His (or Her) Royal Highness	Kt	Knight
HSH	His (or Her) Serene Highness	KY	Kentucky
HSP	Hungarian Socialist Party	Ky	Kentucky
HSWP	Hungarian Socialist Workers' Party		
Hunts.	Huntingdonshire	LA	Louisiana; Los Angeles
		La	Louisiana
IA	Iowa	Lab.	Laboratory
Ia	Iowa	Lancs.	Lancashire
IAAF	International Association of Athletics Federations	LDP	Liberal Democratic Party
IAEA	International Atomic Energy Agency	LDS	Licentiate in Dental Surgery
IATA	International Air Transport Association	Legis.	Legislative
IBA	Independent Broadcasting Authority	Leics.	Leicestershire
IBRD	International Bank for Reconstruction and Development (World Bank)	LenD	Licencié en Droit
		LèsL	Licencié ès Lettres
ICAO	International Civil Aviation Organization	LèsSc	Licencié ès Sciences
ICC	International Chamber of Commerce	LG	Lady of (the Order of) the Garter
ICE	Institution of Civil Engineers	LHD	Doctor of Humane Letters
ICEM	Intergovernmental Committee for European Migration	LI	Long Island
ICFTU	International Confederation of Free Trade Unions	LicenDer	Licenciado en Derecho
ICI	Imperial Chemical Industries	LicenFil	Licenciado en Filosofía
ICOM	International Council of Museums	LicMed	Licentiate in Medicine
ICRC	International Committee for the Red Cross	Lincs.	Lincolnshire

ABBREVIATIONS

LittD	Doctor of Letters	MPhil	Master of Philosophy
LLB	Bachelor of Laws	MPolSci	Master of Political Science
LLC	Limited Liability Company	MPP	Member of Provincial Parliament (Canada)
LLD	Doctor of Laws	MRAS	Member of the Royal Asiatic Society
LLL	Licentiate of Laws	MRC	Medical Research Council
LLM	Master of Laws	MRCP	Member of the Royal College of Physicians
LLP	Limited Liability Partnership	MRCPE	Member of the Royal College of Physicians, Edinburgh
LM	Licentiate of Medicine; Licentiate Midwifery	MRCS	Member of the Royal College of Surgeons
LN	League of Nations	MRCSE	Member of the Royal College of Surgeons, Edinburgh
LPh	Licentiate of Philosophy	MRCVS	Member of the Royal College of Veterinary Surgeons
LRAM	Licentiate of the Royal Academy of Music	MRI	Member of the Royal Institution
LRCP	Licentiate of the Royal College of Physicians	MRIA	Member of the Royal Irish Academy
LSE	London School of Economics and Political Science	MRIC	Member of the Royal Institute of Chemistry
Lt	Lieutenant	MRP	Mouvement Républicain Populaire
Ltd	Limited	MS	Mississippi; Master of Science; Master of Surgery
Ltda	Limitada	MSc	Master of Science
LTh	Licentiate in Theology	MScS	Master of Social Science
LVO	Lieutenant, Royal Victorian Order	MSP	Member Scottish Parliament
		MT	Montana
m.	married; marriage; metre(s)	MTS	Master of Theological Studies
MA	Massachusetts; Master of Arts	MUDr	Doctor of Medicine
MAgr	Master of Agriculture (USA)	MusB(ac)	Bachelor of Music
Maj.	Major	MusD(oc)	Doctor of Music
MALD	Master of Arts in Law and Diplomacy	MusM	Master of Music (Cambridge)
Man.	Management; Manager; Managing; Manitoba	MVD	Master of Veterinary Medicine
MArch	Master of Architecture	MVO	Member of the Royal Victorian Order
Mass	Massachusetts	MW	Master of Wine
Math.	Mathematics; Mathematical		
MB	Bachelor of Medicine; Manitoba	N	North; Northern
MBA	Master of Business Administration	NAS	National Academy of Sciences (USA)
MBE	Member of (the Order of) the British Empire	NASA	National Aeronautics and Space Administration
MBS	Master of Business Studies	Nat.	National
MC	Military Cross	NATO	North Atlantic Treaty Organization
MCC	Marylebone Cricket Club	Naz.	Nazionale
MCE	Master of Civil Engineering	NB	New Brunswick
MCh	Master of Surgery	NBC	National Broadcasting Corporation
MChD	Master of Dental Surgery	NC	North Carolina
MCL	Master of Civil Law	ND	North Dakota
MCom(m)	Master of Commerce	NE	Nebraska; North East
MCP	Master of City Planning	NEA	National Endowment for the Arts
MD	Maryland; Doctor of Medicine	Neb.	Nebraska
Md	Maryland	NEDC	National Economic Development Council
MDiv	Master of Divinity	NERC	Natural Environment Research Council
MDS	Master of Dental Surgery	Nev.	Nevada
ME	Maine; Myalgic Encephalomyelitis	NF	Newfoundland
Me	Maine	NGO	Non-Governmental Organization
MEconSc	Master of Economic Sciences	NH	New Hampshire
MEd	Master in Education	NHS	National Health Service
mem.	member	NI	Northern Ireland
MEng	Master of Engineering (Dublin)	NIH	National Institutes of Health
MEP	Member of European Parliament	NJ	New Jersey
MFA	Master of Fine Arts	NL	Newfoundland and Labrador
Mfg	Manufacturing	NM	New Mexico
Mfrs	Manufacturers	Northants.	Northamptonshire
Mgr	Monseigneur; Monsignor	Notts.	Nottinghamshire
MI	Michigan; Marshall Islands	Nov.	November
MIA	Master of International Affairs	NPC	National People's Congress
MICE	Member of the Institution of Civil Engineers	nr	near
MIChemE	Member of the Institution of Chemical Engineers	NRC	Nuclear Research Council
Mich.	Michigan	NS	Nova Scotia
Middx	Middlesex	NSF	National Science Foundation
MIEE	Member of the Institution of Electrical Engineers	NSW	New South Wales
Mil.	Military	NT	Northern Territory
MIMarE	Member of the Institute of Marine Engineers	NU	Nunavut Territory
MIMechE	Member of the Institution of Mechanical Engineers	NV	Naamloze Vennootschap; Nevada
MIMinE	Member of the Institution of Mining Engineers	NW	North West
Minn.	Minnesota	NWT	North West Territories
MInstT	Member of the Institute of Transport	NY	New York (State)
Miss.	Mississippi	NZ	New Zealand
MIStructE	Member of the Institution of Structural Engineers	NZIC	New Zealand Institute of Chemistry
MIT	Massachusetts Institute of Technology		
MJ	Master of Jurisprudence	O	Ohio
MLA	Member of the Legislative Assembly; Master of Landscape Architecture	OAPEC	Organization of Arab Petroleum Exporting Countries
		OAS	Organization of American States
MLC	Member of the Legislative Council	OAU	Organization of African Unity
MM	Military Medal	OBE	Officer of (the Order of) the British Empire
MLitt	Master in Letters	OC	Officer of the Order of Canada
MM	Military Medal	Oct.	October
MMus	Master of Music	OE	Order of Excellence (Guyana)
MN	Minnesota	OECD	Organisation for Economic Co-operation and Development
MNOC	Movement of Non-Aligned Countries	OEEC	Organization for European Economic Co-operation
MO	Missouri	OFS	Orange Free State
Mo.	Missouri	OH	Ohio
MOH	Medical Officer of Health	OHCHR	Office of the United Nations High Commissioner for Human Rights
Mon.	Monmouthshire	OIC	Organization of the Islamic Conference
Mont.	Montana	OJ	Order of Jamaica
Movt	Movement	OK	Oklahoma
MP	Member of Parliament; Madhya Pradesh	Okla	Oklahoma
MPA	Master of Public Administration (Harvard)	OM	Member of the Order of Merit
MPh	Master of Philosophy (USA)	ON	Ontario; Order of Nigeria

ABBREVIATIONS

Ont.	Ontario		RCP	Romanian Communist Party
ONZ	Order of New Zealand		RCP	Royal College of Physicians
OP	Ordo Praedicatorum (Dominicans)		RCPI	Royal College of Physicians of Ireland
OPCW	Organization for the Prohibition of Chemical Weapons		Regt	Regiment
OPEC	Organization of the Petroleum Exporting Countries		REME	Royal Electric and Mechanical Engineers
OPM	Office of Production Management		Rep.	Representative; represented
OQ	Officer National Order of Québec		Repub.	Republic
OR	Oregon		resgnd	resigned
Ore.	Oregon		retd	retired
Org.	Organization		Rev.	Reverend
OSB	Order of St Benedict		RI	Rhode Island
OSCE	Organization for Security and Co-operation in Europe		RIBA	Royal Institute of British Architects
Oxon.	of Oxford University; Oxfordshire		RMA	Royal Military Academy
			RN	Royal Navy
PA	Pennsylvania		RNR	Royal Naval Reserve
Pa	Pennsylvania		RNVR	Royal Naval Volunteer Reserve
Parl.	Parliament; Parliamentary		RNZAF	Royal New Zealand Air Force
PC	Privy Councillor		RP	Member Royal Society of Portrait Painters
PCC	Provincial Congress Committee		RPR	Rassemblement pour la République
PdB	Bachelor of Pedagogy		RSA	Royal Scottish Academy; Royal Society of Arts
PdD	Doctor of Pedagogy		RSC	Royal Shakespeare Company; Royal Society of Canada
PdM	Master of Pedagogy		RSDr	Doctor of Social Sciences
PDS	Partei des Demokratischen Sozialismus		RSFSR	Russian Soviet Federative Socialist Republic
PE	Prince Edward Island		RSL	Royal Society of Literature
PEI	Prince Edward Island		Rt Hon.	Right Honourable
Pembs.	Pembrokeshire		Rt Rev.	Right Reverend
PEN	Poets, Playwrights, Essayists and Novelists (Club)		RVO	Royal Victorian Order
Perm.	Permanent		RWS	Royal Society of Painters in Water Colours
PGCE	Postgraduate Certificate in Education			
PhB	Bachelor of Philosophy		s.	son(s)
PhD(r)	Doctor of Philosophy		S	South; Southern
PharmD	Docteur en Pharmacie		SA	Sociedad Anónima; Société Anonyme; South Africa; South Australia
Phila	Philadelphia		SAARC	South Asian Association for Regional Co-operation
PhL	Licentiate of Philosophy		SADC	South African Development Community
PLA	People's Liberation Army; Port of London Authority		SAE	Society of Aeronautical Engineers
PLC	Public Limited Company		Salop.	Shropshire
PLO	Palestine Liberation Organization		SALT	Strategic Arms Limitation Treaty
PMB	Private Mail Bag		Sask.	Saskatchewan
pnr	partner		SB	Bachelor of Science (USA)
PO(B)	Post Office (Box)		SC	Senior Counsel; South Carolina
POW	Prisoner of War		SCAP	Supreme Command Allied Powers
PPR	Polish Workers' Party		ScB	Bachelor of Science
PPRA	Past President of the Royal Academy		ScD	Doctor of Science
PQ	Province of Québec		SD	South Dakota
PR	Puerto Rico		SDak	South Dakota
PRA	President of the Royal Academy		SDLP	Social and Democratic Liberal Party
Pref.	Prefecture		SDP	Social Democratic Party
Prep.	Preparatory		SE	South East
Pres.	President		SEATO	South East Asia Treaty Organization
PRI	President of the Royal Institute (of Painters in Water Colours)		Sec.	Secretary
PRIBA	President of the Royal Institute of British Architects		SEC	Securities and Exchange Commission
Prin.	Principal		Secr.	Secretariat
Priv Doz	Privat Dozent (recognized teacher not on the regular staff)		SED	Sozialistische Einheitspartei Deutschlands (Socialist Unity Party of the German Democratic Republic)
PRO	Public Relations Officer			
Proc.	Proceedings		Sept.	September
prod.	producer		S-et-O	Seine-et-Oise
Prof.	Professor		SHAEF	Supreme Headquarters Allied Expeditionary Force
Propr	Proprietor		SHAPE	Supreme Headquarters Allied Powers in Europe
Prov.	Province; Provincial		SJ	Society of Jesus (Jesuits)
PRS	President of the Royal Society		SJD	Doctor of Juristic Science
PRSA	President of the Royal Scottish Academy		SK	Saskatchewan
PSM	Panglima Setia Mahota		SLD	Social and Liberal Democrats
Pty	Proprietary		SM	Master of Science
Publ.(s)	Publication(s)		SOAS	School of Oriental and African Studies
Publr	Publisher		Soc.	Society; Société
Pvt.	Private		SpA	Societá per Azioni
PZPR	Polish United Workers' Party		SPD	Sozialdemokratische Partei Deutschlands
			Sr	Senior
QC	Québec; Queen's Counsel		SRC	Science Research Council
QGM	Queen's Gallantry Medal		SRL	Societé a responsabilité
Qld	Queensland		SSM	Seria Seta Mahkota (Malaysia)
QPM	Queen's Police Medal		SSR	Soviet Socialist Republic
QSO	Queen's Service Order		St	Saint
q.v.	quod vide (to which refer)		Staffs.	Staffordshire
			STB	Bachelor of Sacred Theology
RA	Royal Academy; Royal Academician; Royal Artillery		STD	Doctor of Sacred Theology
RAAF	Royal Australian Air Force		STL	Licentiate of Sacred Theology
RAC	Royal Armoured Corps		STM	Master of Sacred Theology
RACP	Royal Australasian College of Physicians		str.	strasse
RADA	Royal Academy of Dramatic Art		Supt	Superintendent
RAF	Royal Air Force		SW	South West
RAFVR	Royal Air Force Volunteer Reserve		SWAPO	South West Africa People's Organization
RAM	Royal Academy of Music			
RAMC	Royal Army Medical Corps		TA	Territorial Army
RAOC	Royal Army Ordnance Corps		TD	Teachta Dála (member of the Dáil); Territorial Decoration
RC	Roman Catholic		Tech.	Technical; Technology
RCA	Radio Corporation of America; Royal Canadian Academy; Royal College of Art		Temp.	Temporary
			Tenn.	Tennessee
RCAF	Royal Canadian Air Force		Tex.	Texas
RCM	Royal College of Music		ThB	Bachelor of Theology

ABBREVIATIONS

ThD	Doctor of Theology	USAID	United States Agency for International Development
THDr	Doctor of Theology	USN	United States Navy
ThM	Master of Theology	USNR	United States Navy Reserve
TN	Tennessee	USPHS	United States Public Health Service
Trans.	Translation; Translator	USS	United States Ship
Treas.	Treasurer	USSR	Union of Soviet Socialist Republics
TU(C)	Trades Union (Congress)	UT	Utah
TV	television	UWI	University of the West Indies
TX	Texas		
		VA	Virginia
UAE	United Arab Emirates	Va	Virginia
UAR	United Arab Republic	VC	Victoria Cross
UCLA	University of California at Los Angeles	VI	(US) Virgin Islands
UDEAC	L'Union Douanière et Economique de l'Afrique Centrale	Vic.	Victoria
UDR	Union des Démocrates pour la République	Vol.(s)	Volume(s)
UED	University Education Diploma	VSO	Voluntary Services Overseas
UK	United Kingdom (of Great Britain and Northern Ireland)	VT	Vermont
UKAEA	United Kingdom Atomic Energy Authority	Vt	Vermont
UMIST	University of Manchester Institute of Science and Technology		
UMNO	United Malays National Organization	W	West; Western
UN(O)	United Nations (Organization)	WA	Washington (State); Western Australia
UNA	United Nations Association	Warwicks.	Warwickshire
UNCED	United Nations Council for Education and Development	Wash.	Washington (State)
UNCHS	United Nations Centre for Human Settlements (Habitat)	WCC	World Council of Churches
UNCTAD	United Nations Conference on Trade and Development	WCT	World Championship Tennis
UNDCP	United Nations International Drug Control Programme	WEU	Western European Union
UNDP	United Nations Development Programme	WFP	World Food Programme
UNDRO	United Nations Disaster Relief Office	WFTU	World Federation of Trade Unions
UNEF	United Nations Emergency Force	WHO	World Health Organization
UNEP	United Nations Environment Programme	WI	Wisconsin
UNESCO	United Nations Educational, Scientific and Cultural Organisation	Wilts.	Wiltshire
UNFPA	United Nations Population Fund	WIPO	World Intellectual Property Organization
UNHCR	United Nations High Commissioner for Refugees	Wis.	Wisconsin
UNICEF	United Nations International Children's Emergency Fund	WMO	World Meteorological Organization
UNIDO	United Nations Industrial Development Organization	WNO	Welsh National Opera
UNIFEM	United Nations Development Fund for Women	Worcs.	Worcestershire
UNITAR	United Nations Institute for Training and Research	WRAC	Women's Royal Army Corps
Univ.	University	WRNS	Women's Royal Naval Service
UNKRA	United Nations Korean Relief Administration	WTO	World Trade Organization
UNRRA	United Nations Relief and Rehabilitation Administration	WV	West Virginia
UNRWA	United Nations Relief and Works Agency	WVa	West Virginia
UNU	United Nations University	WWF	World Wildlife Fund
UP	United Provinces; Uttar Pradesh	WY	Wyoming
UPU	Universal Postal Union	Wyo.	Wyoming
Urb.	Urbanizacion		
US	United States	YMCA	Young Men's Christian Association
USA	United States of America	Yorks.	Yorkshire
USAAF	United States Army Air Force	YT	Yukon Territory
USAF	United States Air Force	YWCA	Young Women's Christian Association

INTERNATIONAL TELEPHONE CODES

To make international calls to telephone and fax numbers listed in the book, dial the international code of the country from which you are calling, followed by the appropriate code for the country you wish to call (listed below), followed by the area code (if applicable) and telephone or fax number listed in the entry.

	Country code	+ or − GMT*
Afghanistan	93	+4½
Albania	355	+1
Algeria	213	+1
Andorra	376	+1
Angola	244	+1
Antigua and Barbuda	1 268	−4
Argentina	54	−3
Armenia	374	+4
Australia	61	+8 to +10
Australian External Territories:		
Australian Antarctic Territory	672	+3 to +10
Christmas Island	61	+7
Cocos (Keeling) Islands	61	+6½
Norfolk Island	672	+11½
Austria	43	+1
Azerbaijan	994	+5
Bahamas	1 242	−5
Bahrain	973	+3
Bangladesh	880	+6
Barbados	1 246	−4
Belarus	375	+2
Belgium	32	+1
Belize	501	−6
Benin	229	+1
Bhutan	975	+6
Bolivia	591	−4
Bosnia and Herzegovina	387	+1
Botswana	267	+2
Brazil	55	−3 to −4
Brunei	673	+8
Bulgaria	359	+2
Burkina Faso	226	0
Burundi	257	+2
Cambodia	855	+7
Cameroon	237	+1
Canada	1	−3 to −8
Cape Verde	238	−1
Central African Republic	236	+1
Chad	235	+1
Chile	56	−4
China, People's Republic	86	+8
Special Administrative Regions:		
Hong Kong	852	+8
Macao	853	+8
China (Taiwan)	886	+8
Colombia	57	−5
Comoros	269	+3
Congo, Democratic Republic	243	+1
Congo, Republic	242	+1
Costa Rica	506	−6
Côte d'Ivoire	225	0
Croatia	385	+1
Cuba	53	−5
Cyprus	357	+2
'Turkish Republic of Northern Cyprus'	90 392	+2
Czech Republic	420	+1
Denmark	45	+1
Danish External Territories:		
Faroe Islands	298	0
Greenland	299	−1 to −4
Djibouti	253	+3
Dominica	1 767	−4
Dominican Republic	1 809	−4
Ecuador	593	−5
Egypt	20	+2
El Salvador	503	−6
Equatorial Guinea	240	+1
Eritrea	291	+3
Estonia	372	+2
Ethiopia	251	+3
Fiji	679	+12
Finland	358	+2
Finnish External Territory:		
Åland Islands	358	+2
France	33	+1
French Overseas Regions and Departments:		
French Guiana	594	−3
Guadeloupe	590	−4
Martinique	596	−4
Réunion	262	+4
French Overseas Collectivities:		
French Polynesia	689	−9 to −10
Mayotte	262	+3
Saint-Barthélemy	590	−4
Saint-Martin	590	−4
Saint Pierre and Miquelon	508	−3
Wallis and Futuna Islands	681	+12
Other French Overseas Territory:		
New Caledonia	687	+11
Gabon	241	+1
Gambia	220	0
Georgia	995	+4
Germany	49	+1
Ghana	233	0
Greece	30	+2
Grenada	1 473	−4
Guatemala	502	−6
Guinea	224	0
Guinea-Bissau	245	0
Guyana	592	−4
Haiti	509	−5
Honduras	504	−6
Hungary	36	+1
Iceland	354	0
India	91	+5½
Indonesia	62	+7 to +9
Iran	98	+3½
Iraq	964	+3
Ireland	353	0
Israel	972	+2
Italy	39	+1
Jamaica	1 876	−5
Japan	81	+9
Jordan	962	+2
Kazakhstan	7	+6
Kenya	254	+3
Kiribati	686	+12 to +13
Korea, Democratic People's Republic (North Korea)	850	+9
Korea, Republic (South Korea)	82	+9
Kosovo	381	+3
Kuwait	965	+3
Kyrgyzstan	996	+5
Laos	856	+7
Latvia	371	+2
Lebanon	961	+2
Lesotho	266	+2

INTERNATIONAL TELEPHONE CODES

	Country code	+ or – GMT*
Liberia	231	0
Libya	218	+1
Liechtenstein	423	+1
Lithuania	370	+2
Luxembourg	352	+1
Macedonia, former Yugoslav republic	389	+1
Madagascar	261	+3
Malawi	265	+2
Malaysia	60	+8
Maldives	960	+5
Mali	223	0
Malta	356	+1
Marshall Islands	692	+12
Mauritania	222	0
Mauritius	230	+4
Mexico	52	−6 to −7
Micronesia, Federated States	691	+10 to +11
Moldova	373	+2
Monaco	377	+1
Mongolia	976	+7 to +9
Montenegro	382	+1
Morocco	212	0
Mozambique	258	+2
Myanmar	95	$+6\frac{1}{2}$
Namibia	264	+2
Nauru	674	+12
Nepal	977	$+5\frac{3}{4}$
Netherlands	31	+1
Netherlands Dependencies:		
Aruba	297	−4
Netherlands Antilles	599	−4
New Zealand	64	+12
New Zealand's Dependent and Associated Territories:		
Tokelau	690	−10
Cook Islands	682	−10
Niue	683	−11
Nicaragua	505	−6
Niger	227	+1
Nigeria	234	+1
Norway	47	+1
Norwegian External Territory:		
Svalbard	47	+1
Oman	968	+4
Pakistan	92	+5
Palau	680	+9
Palestinian Autonomous Areas	970 or 972	+2
Panama	507	−5
Papua New Guinea	675	+10
Paraguay	595	−4
Peru	51	−5
Philippines	63	+8
Poland	48	+1
Portugal	351	0
Qatar	974	+3
Romania	40	+2
Russian Federation	7	+2 to +12
Rwanda	250	+2
Saint Christopher and Nevis	1 869	−4
Saint Lucia	1 758	−4
Saint Vincent and the Grenadines	1 784	−4
Samoa	685	−11
San Marino	378	+1
São Tomé and Príncipe	239	0
Saudi Arabia	966	+3
Senegal	221	0
Serbia	381	+1
Seychelles	248	+4
Sierra Leone	232	0
Singapore	65	+8
Slovakia	421	+1

	Country code	+ or – GMT*
Slovenia	386	+1
Solomon Islands	677	+11
Somalia	252	+3
South Africa	27	+2
Spain	34	+1
Sri Lanka	94	$+5\frac{1}{2}$
Sudan	249	+2
Suriname	597	−3
Swaziland	268	+2
Sweden	46	+1
Switzerland	41	+1
Syria	963	+2
Tajikistan	992	+5
Tanzania	255	+3
Thailand	66	+7
Timor-Leste	670	+9
Togo	228	0
Tonga	676	+13
Trinidad and Tobago	1 868	−4
Tunisia	216	+1
Turkey	90	+2
Turkmenistan	993	+5
Tuvalu	688	+12
Uganda	256	+3
Ukraine	380	+2
United Arab Emirates	971	+4
United Kingdom	44	0
United Kingdom Crown Dependencies	44	0
United Kingdom Overseas Territories:		
Anguilla	1 264	−4
Ascension Island	247	0
Bermuda	1 441	−4
British Virgin Islands	1 284	−4
Cayman Islands	1 345	−5
Diego Garcia (British Indian Ocean Territory)	246	+5
Falkland Islands	500	−4
Gibraltar	350	+1
Montserrat	1 664	−4
Pitcairn Islands	872	−8
Saint Helena	290	0
Tristan da Cunha	290	0
Turks and Caicos Islands	1 649	−5
United States of America	1	−5 to −10
United States Commonwealth Territories:		
Northern Mariana Islands	1 670	+10
Puerto Rico	1 787	−4
United States External Territories:		
American Samoa	1 684	−11
Guam	1 671	+10
United States Virgin Islands	1 340	−4
Uruguay	598	−3
Uzbekistan	998	+5
Vanuatu	678	+11
Vatican City	39	+1
Venezuela	58	$-4\frac{1}{2}$
Viet Nam	84	+7
Yemen	967	+3
Zambia	260	+2
Zimbabwe	263	+2

* The times listed compare the standard (winter) times in the various countries. Some countries adopt Summer (Daylight Saving) Time—i.e. +1 hour—for part of the year.

Mobile telephone numbers for Kosovo use the country code for Monaco (377).

A

AAVIKSOO, Jaak, PhD; Estonian politician, academic and government official; *Minister of Defence;* b. 11 Jan. 1954, Tartu; m.; three c. *Education:* Tartu Univ. and Inst. of Physics, Estonian Acad. of Science. *Career:* Jr, Sr and Chief Researcher, Inst. of Physics, Estonian Acad. of Science 1976–92; Prof. of Physics, Tartu Univ. 1992, First Pro-rector 1992–95, Head Inst. of Experimental Physics and Tech. 1996–98, Rector 1998–2007; Minister of Culture and Educ. 1995, of Educ. 1996, of Defence 2007–; mem. Estonian Acad. of Science 1994, Academia Europaea 2004, Estonian Physics Soc., American Physical Soc., American Optics Soc., European Physics Soc.; Order of the Nat. Coat of Arms (Estonia) 1999, Large Cross of Merit (Germany) 2000, Ordre nat. du Mérite 2001, Order of White Rose (Finland) 2001, Medal of Merit, City of Tartu 2002, Order of the White Star, Class Two (Estonia) 2006; Dr hc (Turku Univ.) 2003. *Publications include:* over 100 research papers.
Address: Ministry of Defence, Sakala 1, Tallinn 15094, Estonia (office). *Telephone:* 717-0010 (office). *Fax:* 717-0001 (office). *E-mail:* jaak .aaviksoo@kmin.ee (office). *Website:* www.mod.gov.ee (office).

ABAH ABAH, Polycarpe; Cameroonian politician. *Education:* Univ. of the Sorbonne, Paris, France. *Career:* Minister of the Economy and Finance 2004–07; Gov. for Cameroon, World Bank and IMF 2004–.
Address: c/o Ministry of the Economy and Finance, BP 13750, Quartier Administratif, Yaoundé, Cameroon (office).

A-BAKI, Ivonne, BA, BArch, MPA; Ecuadorean diplomatist and artist; b. Guayaquil; m. Sammi A-Baki; two s. one d. *Education:* Sorbonne Univ., Paris, France and Harvard Univ., USA. *Career:* fmr Dir Conflict Man. Group, Harvard Univ., del. to confs in Geneva 1984, Lausanne 1985; Adviser to Pres. on Ecuador–Peru peace negotiations –1998; Consul-Gen. then Hon. Consul in Lebanon; Consul-Gen. in Boston, Mass; apptd Amb. to USA 1999; Minister of Foreign Trade, Industrialization, Fishing and Competition –2005; painter, numerous exhbns in museums, galleries and pvt. collections in Europe, N and S America and Middle East; f. Harvard Foundation for the Arts; Artist-in-Residence, Harvard Univ. 1991–98; Pres. Arts and Community Renewal Coalition, Boston, Beyond Boundaries Foundation; Order of Merit; Honorato Vasquez Order; Keys of the City of Coral Gables, Florida; numerous other awards.
Address: 2535 15th Street NW, Washington, DC 20009, USA (office). *Telephone:* (202) 234-7200. *Fax:* (202) 667-3482.

ABAL, Sam; Papua New Guinea politician; *Minister for Foreign Affairs, Trade and Immigration; Career:* fmr Minister for Provincial Affairs, fmr Minister for Inter-Govt Relations, Minister for Foreign Affairs, Trade and Immigration 2007–; MP for Wabag; mem. Nat. Alliance Party.
Address: Department of Foreign Affairs, Central Government Offices, Kumul Ave, Post Office, Wards Strip, Waigani, National Capital District, Papua New Guinea (office). *Telephone:* 3271311 (office). *Fax:* 3254467 (office). *Website:* www.pngonline.gov.pg (office).

ABALKHAIL, Sheikh Mohamed Ali, BA; Saudi Arabian government official and financial executive; b. 1935, Buraida; m. 1966; two s. two d. *Education:* Cairo Univ. *Career:* began career as Asst Dir of Office of Minister of Communications, later Dir; Dir-Gen. of Inst. of Public Admin; Deputy Minister of Finance and Nat. Econ., then Vice-Minister, Minister of State, Minister for Finance and Nat. Econ. 1975–95; fmr Chair. Riyadh Bank, Riyadh; Chair. Centre for Econ. and Man. Studies; mem. JP Morgan Int. Council; decorations from Belgium, Egypt, France, Niger, Pakistan, Saudi Arabia, Sudan, Germany, Morocco, Spain.
Address: PO Box 287, Riyadh 11411, Saudi Arabia; J.P. Morgan Chase & Company, 270 Park Avenue, New York, NY 10017, USA (office). *Telephone:* (1) 478-1722; (1) 476-6965. *Fax:* (1) 478-1904. *E-mail:* abakhail@kfshhub.kfshrc.edu.sa (office).

ABALKIN, Leonid Ivanovich, PhD, DEcon; Russian economist; *Director of Science, Institute of Economics, Russian Academy of Sciences;* b. 5 May 1930, Moscow; m. Anna Vartanovna Abalkina (née Satarova) 1953; one s. one d. *Education:* Moscow Inst. of the Economy, State Econ. Inst. of Moscow. *Career:* teacher, Deputy Dir agricultural school 1953–58; Sr Teacher and Lecturer in Political Economy, Moscow Inst. of the Economy 1961–66, Chair holder 1966–76; Prof., Acad. of Social Sciences 1976–78,

Head, Faculty of Political Econ. 1978–86; Dir Inst. of Econs, USSR (now Russian) Acad. of Sciences 1986–2004, Dir of Science 2004–, Corresp. mem. USSR (now Russian) Acad. of Sciences 1984–87, mem. 1987–, mem. of Presidium 1988–; mem. CPSU 1956–91, mem. Cen. Cttee 1990–91; USSR People's Deputy 1989–91; Deputy Chair. State Comm. on Improving Man., Planning and Economy Mechanism, USSR Council of Ministers 1987–89; Deputy Prime Minister, Chair. State Comm. for Econ. Reforms 1989–91; adviser to Pres. Gorbachev 1991; mem. Bd Int. Foundation of Econ. and Social Reforms 1991–; mem. Govt's Econ. Crisis Group 1998–; Ed.-in-Chief Voprosy Ekonomiki 1992–, Ekonomicheskoe naslediye, Pamitniki ekonomicheskoi mysli; mem. New York Acad. of Sciences 1993–, Int. Acad. of Man. 1994–, Int. Econs Acad. of Eurasia 1997–; Pres. N. Kondratieff Int. Foundation 1992–; Vice-Pres. Int. Union of Economists, Free Econ. Soc. of Russia 1992–; columnist, Trud; mem. bds of EKO and Voprosy ekonomiki; Hon. mem. Moscow Intellectual Business Club 1992–; Order of People's Friendship 1986; Order for Distinguished Service to the Nation 2000. *Publications:* Political Economy and Economic Policy 1970, Final Economic Results 1978, Direction – Acceleration 1986, New Type of Economic Thinking 1987, Perestroika – Ways and Problems 1989, Missed Chance – A Year and a Half in the Soviet Union Government 1991, To the Goal Through Crisis: Destiny of Economic Reform 1992, At the Crossroads – Thoughts About Russia's Fate 1993, The Crisis Grip 1994, To Self-Perception of Russia 1995, Zigzags of Fate – Disappointments and Hopes 1996, Postponed Changes – The Lost Year 1997, Russia – The Choice 1998, Saving Russia 1999, Russian School of Economic Thought – In Search of Identity 2000, The New Century's Challenge 2001, The Logic of Economic Growth 2002, Russia: In Search of Identity (essays) 2002, Strategy: Choice of the Course 2003, Russia's Strategic Answer to the Calls of the New Era; numerous articles in Soviet press on theoretical problems of political economy under socialism.
Address: Institute of Economics, Academy of Sciences of Russia, Nakhimovsky Prospekt 32, 117218 Moscow; 38-8-89 Zelinskogo str., 117334 Moscow, Russia (home). *Telephone:* (495) 129-02-54 (office); (495) 135-10-85 (home). *Fax:* (495) 718-0511. *E-mail:* abalkin@inst-econ.org.ru (office). *Website:* www.inst-econ.org.ru (office).

ABANI, Aboubacar Ibrahim, BL; Niger diplomatist; *Permanent Representative, United Nations;* m.; two c. *Education:* Univ. of Niamey, School of Int. Service, American Univ., Washington, DC, USA. *Career:* Chief of Consular Office for Protection of Citizens of Niger, Foreign Ministry 1988–89, Chief of Section for UN Specialized Agencies 1989–90, Chief of Office for Inter-African Insts 1990–91; First Sec., Embassy in Ethiopia 1992–97, Mission to OAU, Addis Ababa 1992–97; Chief, Consular Div., Foreign Ministry's Directorate for Citizens of Niger Living Abroad 1997–98; internship, American Univ., Washington, DC 1998–99; Chief of Office, Multilateral Legal Affairs, Ministry of Foreign Affairs 2000–01; Diplomatic Adviser to Foreign Affairs Minister 2001–03; Perm. Rep. of Niger to UN, New York 2003–; named Hon. Citizen and Goodwill Amb., State of Ark., USA.
Address: Office of the Permanent Representative of Niger to the United Nations, 417 East 50th Street, New York, NY 10022, USA (office). *Telephone:* (212) 421-3260 (office). *Fax:* (212) 753-6931 (office). *E-mail:* nigerun@aol.com (office). *Website:* www.un.int/niger (office).

ABBAS, Mahmud, (Abu Mazen), PhD; Palestinian politician and head of state; *President;* b. 1935, Safad, Galilea. *Education:* Damascus Univ., Syria, Moscow Univ., Russia. *Career:* civil servant, UAE –1967; co-f. Fatah (largest political party in The Palestine Nat. Liberation Movt), mem. Cen. Cttee 1964–; elected to Palestine Liberation Org. (PLO) Exec. Cttee 1980, Head Pan-Arab and Int. Affairs Dept 1984, Sec.-Gen. PLO Exec. Cttee 1996–2004, Chair. 2004–; Exec. Pres. Palestinian Nat. Authority (PNA) known internationally as Palestinian Authority (PA) 2005–; participated in Middle East Peace Conf., Washington, DC and in Norwegian-mediated peace talks with Israel; Prime Minister, Palestinian Authority (PA) 2003.
Address: Office of the President, Ramallah, Palestinian Autonomous Areas. *E-mail:* fateh@fateh.org. *Website:* www.p-p-o.com; www.fateh.net.

ABBOTT, Roderick, BA; British international trade consultant; b. 1938, London. *Education:* Univ. of Oxford. *Career:* mem. staff, Bd of Trade, later

1

FCO 1962–73, with UK Del. to Geneva 1968–71; EC official 1973–2002, mem. EC Del. in Geneva for GATT Tokyo Round 1975–79, Dir Directorate-Gen. for External Trade 1982–2002, participated in GATT ministerial meetings 1982, 1984, mem. EC Steering Group for Uruguay Round and Lead Negotiator (tariffs) 1987–93, Amb. and Head of Del., Geneva 1996–2000, participant in all WTO ministerial meetings, Singapore, Seattle, Doha, Cancun 1996–2002; Deputy Dir-Gen. Directorate-Gen. for Trade 2000–02; Deputy Dir-Gen. WTO 2002–05; currently consultant on int. trade.
Telephone: (2) 762-0190 (home). *Fax:* (2) 762-0199 (home). *E-mail:* roderickabbott@compuserve.com (home).

ABBOUD, Farid, PhD; Lebanese diplomatist and civil servant; *Ambassador to Tunisia;* b. 1 July 1951, Beirut; m. Rim Hilal; one s. *Education:* Univ. of St Joseph, Beirut, Univ. of California, Los Angeles, USA. *Career:* Asst Prof. of Political Science, Univ. of St Joseph, Beirut 1973–77; with Cen. Admin govt office, Beirut 1974–77; served in embassies in Washington, DC, Moscow, London and Rome 1977–90, Gen. Counsel in LA 1990–95, Asst Dir-Gen. Dept of Political Affairs, Ministry of Foreign Affairs 1995, Del. to Monitoring Group of S Lebanon 1996 and int. confs including UN Gen. Ass. Sessions 1997–99, Non-Aligned Summit Meetings 1996, 1998, Amb. to USA 1999–2007, to Tunisia 2007–.
Address: Embassy of Lebanon, Les Berges du Lac, 2045 Tunis, Tunisia (office). *Telephone:* (1) 960001 (office). *Fax:* (1) 960001 (office). *E-mail:* ambassade.liban@planet.tn (office). *Website:* www.faridabboud.com (office).

ABDALLAH, Abdelwahab; Tunisian government official; *Minister of Foreign Affairs;* b. 14 Feb. 1940, Monastir. *Career:* fmr head several press agencies; Presidential Aide 1990–; Minister of Foreign Affairs 2005–.
Address: Ministry of Foreign Affairs, ave de la Ligue des états arabes, Tunis, Tunisia (office). *Telephone:* (71) 847-500 (office). *E-mail:* mae@ministeres.tn (office). *Website:* www.diplomatie.gov.tn (office).

ABDALLAHI, Sidi Ould Cheikh; Mauritanian politician and head of state; b. 1938, Aleg; m.; three s. one d. *Education:* William Ponty School, Senegal, Univ. of Dakar, Senegal and Univ. of Grenoble, France. *Career:* Dir of Planning, Second Plan for the Econ. and Social Devt of Mauritania 1968–71; served in several govt positions including Minister of State for Nat. Economy 1971–78; Econ. Adviser, Kuwait Fund for Arab Econ. Devt, Kuwait 1982–85, Head of Econs and Finance, Niger Div. 1989–2003; Minister of Hydraulics and Energy 1986–87, of Fisheries and Maritime Economy 1987–89; Pres. of Mauritania 2007–08 (ousted in coup).
Address: c/o Office of the President, National Assembly, BP 184, Nouakchott, Mauritania (office).

ABDEL-MALEK, Anouar I., DLit, PhD; Egyptian academic and writer; *Adviser, National Centre for Middle East Studies;* b. 23 Oct. 1924, Cairo; m. Karin Konigseider 1961; one d. *Education:* Coll. de la Sainte Famille, British Inst., Ain Shams Univ., Cairo and Univ. de Paris-Sorbonne. *Career:* leading mem. Egyptian Nat. and Progressive Movt 1941–; official, Nat. Bank of Egypt, Cairo 1941–42, Crédit Foncier Egyptien, Cairo 1943–46; Jt Ed. Actualité, Cairo 1950–59; journalist, Le Journal d'Egypte, Cairo 1950–59; contrib. to Rose el-Yusef, Al-Magallah, Al-Masa, Cairo 1950–59; teacher of philosophy, Lycée Al-Hurriya, Cairo 1958–59; Research Asst, Ecole Pratique des Hautes Etudes, Paris 1959–60; Research Lecturer, later Research Reader, Research Prof., CNRS, Paris 1960–, Dir of Research 1970–90, Hon. Dir 1990–; Project Co-ordinator, The UN Univ., Tokyo 1976–86; Prof! of Sociology and Politics, Faculty of Int. Relations, Ristumeikan Univ., Kyoto 1989–92; Prof. Emer. of Philosophy, Ain Shams Univ. 1998–; Adviser Nat. Centre for Middle East Studies, Cairo 1990–; mem. Bd and Adviser, Centre for Asian Studies, Cairo Univ. 1994–; writer, Al-Ahram 1995; mem. exec. cttee, EEC Int. Sociological Asscn 1970–74 (vice-pres. 1974–78), Egyptian Council for Foreign Affairs 2002–, IISS, Int. Political Science Asscn, Royal Inst. for Int. Affairs, Chatham House, London 2007–; Visiting Prof., Univ. of Santiago, Chile 1969, Ain Shams 1975, Québec 1986, Cairo 1992; Visiting Fellow, Clare Coll., Cambridge 1985, Life Assoc. 1986–; Ed. Library of the Contemporary Orient 1989, Ideas of the New World 1991; Prix du Jury de l'Amitié Franco-Arabe, Paris 1965, Gold Medal, Nasser Higher Mil. Acad. 1976, State Prize in the Social Sciences 1996, Prize for Best Book, Cairo 2001, Gold Medal, Faculty of Econs and Political Sciences, Cairo Univ. 2003. *Publications include:* Egypte, société militaire 1962, Studies on National Culture 1967, Idéologie et renaissance nationale: l'Egypte moderne 1969, La pensée politique arabe contemporaine 1970, Sociologie de l'impérialisme 1970, La dialectique sociale 1972, The Army and National Movements 1974, Spécificité et Théorie sociale 1977, Intellectual Creativity in Endogenous Culture 1983, East Wind 1983, The Transformation of the World 1985, The Egyptian Street and Thought 1989, Creativity and the Civilizational Project 1991, Endogenous Intellectual Creativity in the Arab World 1994, Towards a Civilizational Strategy 2005, On the Origins of the Civilizational Question 2005, Along the Path Towards a New Egypt 2005, China in the Eyes of Egyptians 2006, Patriotism is the Solution 2006.
Address: 48 Nehru Street, 11351 Heliopolis, Cairo, Egypt (home). *Telephone:* (2) 634-3977 (home). *Fax:* (2) 634-3977 (home). *E-mail:* anouarmalek@hotmail.com (home).

ABDEL-MEGUID, Ahmed Esmat, LLB, PhD; Egyptian diplomatist and lawyer; *President, Arab and African Arbitrators' Society;* b. 22 March 1923, Alexandria; m. Eglal Abou-Hamda 1950; three s. *Education:* Faculty of Law, Alexandria Univ. and Univ. of Paris. *Career:* Attaché and Sec., Embassy, London 1950–54; Head British Desk, Ministry of Foreign Affairs 1954–56, Asst Dir Legal Dept 1961–63, Head Cultural and Tech. Assistance Dept 1967–68; Counsellor, Perm. Mission to European Office of UN, Geneva 1957–61; Minister Counsellor, Embassy, Paris 1963–67; Official Spokesman of Govt and Head Information Dept 1968–69; Amb. to France 1969–70; Minister of State for Cabinet Affairs 1970–72; Head, Perm. Del. to UN 1972–83; Minister of Foreign Affairs 1984–91; Deputy Prime Minister 1985–91; Sec.-Gen. League of Arab States 1991–2001; pvt. law practice 2001–; Chair. Cairo Preparatory Conf. for Geneva Peace Conf. 1977; fmr Dir Cairo Int. Arbitration Centre, Pres. Arab and African Arbitrators' Soc. 2001–; mem. Politbureau, Nat. Democratic Party, Int. Law Asscn, Advisory Council of the Inst. for Int. Studies, took part in UN confs on the Law of the Sea 1959, on Consular Relations 1963 and on the Law of Treaties 1969; mem. Int. Center for Settlement of Investment Disputes, World Bank, Washington DC, High Level Advisory Panel of OAU; mem. Bd of Trustees, American Univ., Cairo (AUC), French Univ., Cairo; Ordre nat. du Mérite 1967, Grand Croix 1971, 1st Class Decoration, Arab Repub. of Egypt 1970 and numerous foreign decorations; Dr hc (Louvain) 1998, (Khartoum) 1998; Hon. PhD (American Univ., Cairo) 2002. *Publications:* Time of Defeat and Victory 1999, Positions and Challenges in the Arab World 2003; several articles in Revue Egyptienne de Droit International.
Address: 78 El Nile Street, Apt 23, Giza, Cairo, Egypt (home). *Telephone:* (202) 37489111 (also fax) (office); (202)37489001 (home).

ABDELA, Lesley Julia, MBE, FRSA, FRGS; British organization executive and consultant; *Chief Executive, Project Parity, and Senior Partner, Eyecatcher Associates/Shevolution;* b. 17 Nov. 1945, London; m. 1972 (divorced); one s. *Education:* Queen Anne's School, Caversham, Chatelard School Les Avants, Switzerland, Queen's Coll. Harley Street, Hammersmith Coll. of Art and Design, London School of Printing. *Career:* fmr advertising exec.; researcher House of Commons 1976–77; Parl. Cand. (Liberal) for Herts. E 1979; f. All-Party 300 Group 1980–95, Trustee –1995; UK Consultant, Project Liberty, Kennedy School of Govt, Harvard Univ., USA 1992–98; f. Project Parity (UK-based equivalent of Project Liberty) 1996, CEO 1996–; Sr Pnr, Eyecatcher Assocs 1986–, Shevolution Assocs 1998–; OSCE Deputy Dir for Democracy, UN Interim Admin in Kosovo 1999; has become an advocate for women and expert in post-conflict reconstruction, working in Kosovo, Iraq, Afghanistan, Aceh, Sierra Leone etc; Political Ed. Cosmopolitan 1993–96; consultant, BBC TV series Breaking Glass 1994; tutor to dels from Central Europe and Turkey on Beijing Express, train travelling from Warsaw, Poland to Beijing, People's Repub. of China for 4th UN World Conference on Women 1995; mem. Int. Inst. for Environment and Devt 1992–96, Global Bd British Council 1995–2000; Gov. Nottingham Trent Univ. 1997–2000; Hon. DLitt (Nottingham Trent) 1996; UK Woman of Europe 1996, Nancy Astor Media Award, one of New Statesman's 50 Heroes of our Time 2006. *Publications include:* Women With X Appeal, Breaking Through the Glass Ceilings, Do It! – Walk the Talk, What Women Want; contrib. to manuals, newspapers.
Address: Park Farm Oast, Bateman's Lane, Burwash, E Sussex, TN19 7DR, England (office). *Telephone:* (1435) 882655 (office). *Fax:* (1435) 882742 (office). *E-mail:* lesley.abdela@shevolution.com (office). *Website:* www.abdela.co.uk.

ABDELAZIZ, Maged Abdelfattah; Egyptian diplomatist; *Permanent Representative, United Nations;* b. 1954; m.; one d. *Education:* Ain Shams Univ. School of Law. *Career:* joined diplomatic service 1979; served in several positions in Ministry of Foreign Affairs including Int. Orgs Div., Legal and Treaties Dept 1979–83 (Head, 1987–89), Second and First Sec., Perm. Mission to UN, New York 1983–87, Political Counsellor in charge of Middle East, Arab-Soviet Relations, Int. Orgs and Disarmament, Embassy in Moscow 1989–93, Head, Specialized Agencies Dept, Multilateral Sector, Ministry of Foreign Affairs 1993–95; Political Counsellor, Office of Perm. Rep. to UN, New York 1995–97, Prin. Rep. in all disarmanent issues 1997–99, Deputy Perm. Rep. to UN 1997–99, Perm. Rep. 2005–, Coordinator, Del. during membership on Security Council 1996, 1997, Rep. in Expert Group, UN Sec.-Gen., UN Register for Conventional Arms 1997, Chair. Disarmanent Comm. 1999; Diplomatic Adviser and Official Spokesman of Pres. 1999–2005.

Address: Office of the Permanent Representative of Egypt to the United Nations, 304 East 44th Street, New York, NY 10017, USA (office). *Telephone:* (212) 503-0300 (office). *Fax:* (212) 949-5999 (office). *E-mail:* egypt@un.int (office).

ABDENUR, Roberto, BSc, LLB; Brazilian diplomatist; b. 5 May 1942, Rio de Janeiro; m.; three c. *Education:* LSE, UK, Pontifical Catholic Univ. of Rio de Janeiro. *Career:* joined Ministry of External Relations 1964, with Div. of Communications and Archives 1964–65, Trade Policy Div. 1966–67, Acting Head of Tech. Section of Analysis and Planning 1968, Sec. for Policy Planning 1968, Staff of Cabinet of Minister of External Relations 1969, Asst to Sec.-Gen. 1975–78, in charge of econ. and trade matters at Ministry 1979–84, Sec.-Gen. (Deputy Minister) of External Relations 1993–95; Deputy Consulate Gen. then Consulate Gen. in London, UK 1969–73; First Sec. Embassy in Washington, DC 1973–75; Amb. to Ecuador 1985–88, to China 1989–93, to Germany 1995–2002, to Austria 2002–03, to USA 2004–06. *Address:* c/o Ministério dos Assuntos Exteriores, Palácio do Itamaraty, Esplanada dos Ministérios, 70170–900 Brasília, DF, Brazil (office). *Website:* www.itamaraty.gov.br (office).

ABDIN, Hasan, PhD; Sudanese diplomatist; m. Manahil A. Abdin. *Career:* Under-Sec., Ministry of External Relations 1998; Amb. to UK 2000–06 (also accred to Ireland 2001–06); Patron Kids for Kids (charity). *Publication:* Early Sudanese Nationalism 1919–1925. *Address:* Ministry of Foreign Affairs, PO Box 873, Khartoum, Sudan (office). *Telephone:* (183) 773101 (office). *Fax:* (183) 772941 (office). *E-mail:* ministry@mfa.gov.sd (office). *Website:* www.sudanmfa.com (office).

ABDUL HADI, Mahdi, PhD; Palestinian research institute director; *Chairman, Palestinian Academic Society for the Study of International Affairs (PASSIA); Education:* Bradford Univ., UK. *Career:* Co-Founder and Ed. Al-Fajr daily newspaper 1972–74; Co-Founder and Gen. Sec. Council for Higher Educ. in the West Bank 1977–80; Founder and Pres. Arab Thought Forum, Jerusalem 1977–81; special adviser to Ministry of Occupied Land Affairs, Amman, Jordan 1985–86; Founder and Chair., Bd of Trustees, Palestinian Academic Soc. for Study of Int. Affairs (PASSIA) 1987–; mem. Arab Thought Forum, Amman 2002; occasional guest lecturer on Palestinian issues at local colls, univs and insts; mem. Jerusalem Arab Council, Palestinian Council for Justice and Peace, Assoc. of Palestinian Policy Research Insts; Fellow, Center for Int. Affairs, Harvard Univ. 1985, Salzburg Int. Seminar 1986; mem. Black Sea Univ. Foundation, Bucharest 1990, IISS, London, EuroMeSCo network, Arab Social Science Research Network. *Publications:* Awakening Sleeping Horses 2000; numerous articles, monographs and essays in newspapers and journals. *Address:* The Palestinian Academic Society for the Study of International Affairs, POB 19545, Jerusalem (office). *Telephone:* 2-6264426 (office). *Fax:* 2-6282819 (office). *E-mail:* passia@palnet.com (office). *Website:* www .passia.org (office).

ABDULAI, Yesufu Seyyid Momoh; Nigerian economist and international organization official; b. 19 June 1940, Auchi; m. Zene Makonnen Abdulai 1982; three s. one d. *Education:* Mount Allison Univ. and McGill Univ., Canada. *Career:* taught econs in Canada; Tech. Asst to Exec. Dir (Africa Group I), World Bank Group, Washington, DC 1971–73, Adviser to Exec. Dir 1973–78, Alternate Exec. Dir for Africa Group 1 1978–80, Exec. Dir 1980–82, Vice-Chair. Jt Audit Cttee Exec. Bd 1980–82; Chair. Jt Secr. African Exec. Dirs of the World Bank Group and the IMF 1975–77; Man. Dir and CEO Fed. Mortgage Bank of Nigeria 1982–83; Dir-Gen. OPEC Fund for Int. Devt 1983–2003; Grand Decoration of Honour (Austria) 2004. *Address:* c/o OPEC Fund for International Development, Parkring 8, PO Box 995, 1011 Vienna, Austria.

ABDULLAH, Abdul Samad; Maldivian international civil servant and diplomatist; *High Commissioner to Bangladesh; Career:* has served in Maldives Public Service as well as with WHO, has held several sr positions Maldives public health sector, including Dir-Gen. Health Services, Ministry of Health; first resident High Commr to Bangladesh 2008–. *Address:* High Commission of the Maldives, Dhaka, Bangladesh (office); Ministry of Foreign Affairs, Boduthakurufaanu Magu, Malé, Maldives. *Telephone:* (960) 3323400-7. *Fax:* (960)3323841. *E-mail:* info@foreign.gov .mv. *Website:* www.foreign.gov.mv.

ABDULLAH, Yousuf bin al-Alawi bin; Omani government minister and diplomatist; *Minister responsible for Foreign Affairs;* b. 1942, Salalah. *Education:* Egypt, univ. studies in political science, UK. *Career:* joined Diplomatic Service 1970, Second Sec. Ministry of Foreign Affairs 1972, postings to Cairo and Beirut; Amb. to Lebanon 1973; Under-Sec. Ministry of Foreign Affairs 1974, Minister of State 1982, Minister responsible for Foreign Affairs 1997–; First Grade Sultan Qaboos Decoration, Order of Merit, Egypt, Officier, Légion d'honneur, France, Grand Decoration of Honour, Austria, Cavaliere Grande Croce, Italy and other foreign decorations. *Address:* Ministry of Foreign Affairs, PO Box 252, Muscat 113, Oman (office). *Telephone:* 699500 (office). *Fax:* 699589 (office); 699531 (office). *E-mail:* mfaoman@omantel.net.om (office). *Website:* www.mofa.gov.om (office).

ABDULLAH II IBN AL-HUSSEIN, HM King of Jordan; head of state and army officer; b. 30 Jan. 1962, Amman; m. Rania al-Yassin 1993 (Queen Rania); two s. two d. *Education:* Islamic Educ. Coll., St Edmund's School, Surrey, UK, Deerfield Acad., USA, Sandhurst Mil. Acad. and Univ. of Oxford, UK. *Career:* succeeded to the throne 7 Feb. 1999; commissioned Second Lt 1981, Reconnaissance Troop Leader 13th/18th Bn Royal Hussars (British Army), FRG and England; rank of First Lt 1984; Platoon Commdr and Co. second-in-command 40th Armoured Brigade, Jordan, Commdr Tank Co. 91st Armoured Brigade 1985–86 (rank of Capt.); Tactics Instructor Helicopter Anti-Tank Wing, 1986–87; undertook advanced studies in int. affairs at School of Foreign Service, Georgetown Univ., Washington, DC 1987–88; Commdr of a co. 17th Tank Bn, 2nd Guards Brigade then Bn second-in-command (rank of Maj.) 1989; attended Command and Staff Coll., Camberley, UK 1990; Armour Rep. Office of the Insp. Gen. 1991, Commdr 2nd Armoured Car Regt, 40th Brigade (rank of Lt Col) 1992; promoted to rank of Col 1993; Deputy Commdr Jordanian Special Forces Jan.–June 1994; promoted to the rank of Brig. 1994 and assumed command of Royal Jordanian Special Forces; Commdr of Special Operations Command 1997–; Pres. Jordan Nat. Football Fed.; Hon. Pres. Int. Tourism Golden Rudder Soc.; Head Nat. Cttee for Tourism and Archaeological Film Production 1997–. *Address:* Royal Hashemite Court, Amman, Jordan. *Website:* www .kingabdullah.jo.

ABDULLATIF, Hussain Ali; Omani diplomatist; m. Fakhriya Hassan Makki. *Career:* Amb. to UK 1995–. *Address:* Embassy of The Sultanate of Oman, 167 Queen's Gate, London, SW7 5HE, England (office). *Telephone:* (20) 7225-0001 (office). *Fax:* (20) 7589-2505 (office). *E-mail:* theembassy@omanembassy.org.uk (office). *Website:* www.omanembassy.org.uk (office).

ABDYLDAEV, Erlan; Kyrgyzstani diplomatist and academic. *Education:* Moscow State Inst. of Int. Relations. *Career:* First Deputy Foreign Minister 1997–2001; Amb. to People's Repub. of China 2001–05 (also accred to Mongolia and Singapore); currently Expert, Inst. of Public Policy, Bishkek; Country Dir for Kyrgyzstan, Inst. for War and Peace Reporting 2007–. *Address:* Institute for Public Policy, 42/1 Isanov Str., Bishkek 720017, Kyrgyzstan (office). *Telephone:* (312) 90-62-40 (office). *E-mail:* office@ipp .kg (home); erlan200521@gmail.com (office). *Website:* www.ipp.kg (office).

ABE, Nobuyasu; Japanese diplomatist and fmr UN official; *Ambassador to Switzerland;* b. 9 Sept. 1945, Akita; m. Akiko Sugawara; two s. *Education:* Univ. of Tokyo, Amherst Coll., Mass, USA. *Career:* entered Foreign Service 1967, has held variety of positions in fields of arms control and disarmament; served in Perm. Missions to Int. Orgs, Geneva 1977–79, UN, New York 1987–90, 1996–97, Int. Orgs, Vienna 1999–2001; Pvt. Sec. to Foreign Minister Kiichi Miyazawa 1974–76; Dir of Policy Planning 1984–86; Sous-Sherpa for G7 Summits 1992–94; Consul-Gen. of Japan, Boston, Mass, USA 1994–96; Dir-Gen. for Arms Control and Science Affairs, Tokyo 1997–99; Amb. to Saudi Arabia 2001–03; UN Under-Sec.-Gen. for Disarmament Affairs, New York 2003–06; Amb. to Switzerland 2006–; Int. Fellow, Weatherhead Center for Int. Affairs, Harvard Univ. 1986–87. *Address:* Embassy of Japan, Engestr. 53, Postfach, 3000 Bern 9, Switzerland. *Telephone:* 313002222. *Fax:* 313002255. *E-mail:* eojs@bluewin.ch. *Website:* www.ch.emb-japan.go.jp.

ABE, Shinzo, LLB; Japanese politician; grandson of the late Nobusuke Kishi. *Education:* Faculty of Law, Seikei Univ., Univ. of Southern Calif., USA. *Career:* began career with Kobe Steel Ltd –1982; Exec. Asst to Minister for Foreign Affairs 1982–87; Pvt. Sec. to Chair. of Gen. Council, Liberal Democratic Party (LDP) 1987–87, Pvt. Sec. to Sec.-Gen. 1987–93, Dir of LDP Social Affairs Div. 1999–2000, Sec.-Gen. 2003–04, Acting Sec.-Gen. 2004, Pres. 2006–07; mem. House of Reps (Yamaguchi Pref., 4th Electoral Dist) 1993–, mem. Standing Cttee on Foreign Affairs 1993–99, on Health and Welfare 1999–2000, on Security 1999–2000; Deputy Chief Cabinet Sec. 2000–01, 2001–03, Chief Cabinet Sec. 2005–06, Prime Minister 2006–07 (resgnd). *Publications include:* Utsukushii Kuni E (Toward a Beautiful Country) 2006.

Address: Liberal-Democratic Party—LDP (Jiyu-Minshuto), 1-11-23, Nagata-cho, Chiyoda-ku, Tokyo 100-8910, Japan (office). *Telephone:* (3) 3581-6211 (office). *Website:* www.jimin.jp (office).

ABED, Ringo Festus; Namibian diplomatist; *Ambassador to Democratic Republic of the Congo;* m. Johanna Abed. *Career:* fmr Dir and Acting Chief of Protocol, Ministry of Foreign Affairs; High Commr to UK 2005–06; Amb. to Democratic Repub. of the Congo 2006–.
Address: Embassy of Namibia, 138 Boulevard du 30 Juin, PO Box 89, 34 Kinshasa 1, Democratic Republic of the Congo (office). *E-mail:* namembassy-drc@ic.cd (office).

ABELIAN, Movses, PhD; Armenian United Nations official, diplomatist and academic; *Secretary, Administrative and Budgetary Committee, General Assembly, United Nations;* b. 1964, Yerevan; m.; two s. *Education:* Yerevan Univ. and Moscow State Univ., New York Univ., USA. *Career:* Asst Prof. and Vice Dean, Dept of Applied Math., Yerevan State Univ. 1989–91, Assoc. Prof. 1991–93; joined UN 1993, Vice-Chair. Ad Hoc Intergovernmental Working Group (Financial and Legal Matters), Gen. Ass. 48th Session, Vice-Chair. Fifth Cttee (Admin and Budget), 50th Session, Sec. Admin. and Budgetary Cttee (Fifth Cttee), UN 2003–; Chargé d'affaires at UN, New York –1998, Perm. Rep. 1998–2003; mem. Strategic Planning Cttee UN Int. School, New York 2005–06; Spirit of Armenia Award 2003. *Address:* Administrative and Budgetary Committee, United Nations, S-2633A, New York, NY 10017, USA (office). *Telephone:* (212) 963-8255 (office). *Fax:* (212) 963-0360 (office). *Website:* abelian@un.org (office); www.un.org/ga/61/fifth (office).

ABIHAGGLE, Carlos Enrique; Argentine diplomatist; *Ambassador to Chile;* b. 20 March 1945, Mendoza. *Education:* Escuela Domingo Bombal, Escuela Superior de Comercio Martin Zapata, Universidad Naciónal de Cuyo, Univ. of Pa, USA. *Career:* Prov. Senator 1983–87; Nat. Del. 1993–97; Gen. Supt for Irrigation, Mendoza 1999; fmr Minister for Work and Public Services; Chair., Latin-American Network of Basin Orgs (LANBO) 1999–2000; Amb. to Chile 2003–.
Address: Embassy of Argentina, Miraflores 285, Santiago, Chile (office). *Telephone:* (2) 5822500 (office). *Fax:* (2) 6393321 (office). *E-mail:* embajador@embargentina.cl (office). *Website:* www.embargentina.cl (office).

ABIYEV, Col.-Gen. Safar Akhundbala oğlu; Azerbaijani politician and army officer; *Minister of Defence;* b. 27 June 1950, Baku. *Education:* Baku Troops Command Acad., Frunze Acad., Moscow. *Career:* served in Azerbaijani Army, attaining rank of Col-Gen.; currently Minister of Defence.
Address: Ministry of Defence, 1139 Baku, Azarbaycan pr, Azerbaijan (office). *Telephone:* (12) 439-41-89 (office). *Fax:* (12) 492-92-50 (office).

ABOLS, Col Gundars; Latvian military officer; *Deputy Assistant Chief of Staff of Joint Education and Training, NATO;* b. 9 July 1964, Riga; m. Liene Indriksone. *Education:* Latvian Agric. Acad., Defence Int. Mil. Coll. of France. *Career:* career in Latvian Armed Forces (LNAF) and Nat. Guard (NG), positions include Commdr of Mechanised Platoon of Fmr USSR Army, Asst to Commdr of NG Battalion, Chief of Staff of NG Battalion, Commdr of NG Battalion, Chief of G3 Dept at NG and LNAF HQ, Chief of Staff LNAF HQ 1997–2000, Acting Commdr LNAF 1998, Mil Rep. to NATO 2001, to the EU 2002, Deputy Asst of Chief of Staff, Jt Educ. and Training, HQ SACT 2004–; Latvian Minister of Defence's Hon. Medal, LNAF Commdr's Hon. Medal, Estonian Defence Forces Award, Achievement Medal of Lithuanian Armed Forces, Latvian Border Guard Anniversary Medal, Latvian NG Badge, LNAF Commdr's Medal For Services.
Address: NATO Headquarters, Blvd Leopold III, 1110 Brussels, Belgium (office); Ministry of Defence, K. Valdemāra iela 10–12, Rīga 1473, Latvia (office). *Telephone:* 721-0124 (office). *Fax:* 721-2307 (office). *E-mail:* natodoc@hq.nato.int (office); kanceleja@mod.lv (office). *Website:* www .nato.int (office); www.mod.lv (office).

ABOUD, Hon. Mahmoud Mohamed; Comoran diplomatist. *Career:* fmr Chargé d'affaires a.i., Perm. Mission to UN, New York, currently Minister-Counselor and Deputy Perm. Rep.
Address: Permanent Mission of the Islamic Federal Republic of Comoros to the United Nations, 420 East 50th Street, New York, NY 10022, USA (office). *Telephone:* (212) 972-8010 (office). *Fax:* (212) 983-4712 (office). *E-mail:* comoros@un.int (office). *Website:* www.un.int/comoros (office).

ABOUYOUB, Hassan; Moroccan diplomatist; b. 1952. *Career:* joined Ministry Commerce and Industry, then Dir of Int. Trade 1980, Minister External Trade and Minister Foreign Investment and Tourism 1990–93; elected mem. Parl. 1993; Amb. to Saudi Arabia 1994, to France –2004;

currently Sr Foreign Policy Adviser to King of Morocco; Minister Agric. 1995–97; Amb. responsible for trade negotiations 1998; directed Morocco's accession to GATT and its trade negotiations with EU, participated in conclusion of Uruguay Round, helped organise Marrakesh Ministerial Conf.; Hon. Chair. SIDA-Entreprises Maroc 2006–.
Address: c/o Ministry of Foreign Affairs and Co-operation, ave Franklin Roosevelt, Rabat, Morocco (office). *E-mail:* mail@maec.gov.ma (office). *Website:* www.maec.gov.ma (office).

ABRAHAM, Gen. Hérard; Haitian politician and army officer (retd); b. 28 July 1940. *Career:* enlisted in Haitian army, rose to rank of Lt-Gen.; supported coup against Duvalier 1986; Minister of Foreign Affairs 1987–88; Acting Pres. of Haiti after street protests forced Pres. Prosper Avril into exile 1990; helped to crush coup attempt by Roger Lafontant Jan. 1991; retd from army, settled in Miami, Fla 1991; made radio address from Fla calling on Pres. Jean-Bertrand Aristide to resign Feb. 2004; Minister of the Interior 2004–05, of Foreign Affairs and Religion 2005–06.
Address: c/o Ministry of Foreign Affairs and Religion, Blvd Harry S. Truman, Cité de l'Exposition, Port-au-Prince, Haiti (office).

ABRAMS, Hon. Elliott, MA, JD; American government official; *Deputy Assistant to the President and Deputy National Security Adviser for Global Democracy Strategy, National Security Council;* b. 24 Jan. 1948, New York, NY; m. Rachel Abrams; three c. *Education:* Harvard Coll., Harvard Law School, LSE, UK. *Career:* Chief of Staff, Special Counsel for Senator Daniel P. Moynihan 1977–79; Asst Sec. of State for Int. Org. Affairs 1981, for Human Rights and Humanitarian Affairs 1981–85, for Inter-American Affairs 1985–89; Sr Fellow, Hudson Inst. 1990–96; Pres. Ethics and Public Policy Center 1996–2001; mem. US Comm. on Int. Religious Freedom 1999–2001, Chair. 2000–01; Special Asst to Pres. and Sr Dir for Democracy, Human Rights and Int. Operations 2001–02, Special Asst to Pres. and Sr Dir for Near East and North African Affairs 2002–05, Deputy Asst to Pres. and Deputy Nat. Security Adviser for Global Democracy Strategy 2005–; mem. Council on Foreign Relations; Sec. of State's Distinguished Service Award 1988. *Publications:* Shield and Sword 1995, Security and Sacrifice: Isolation, Intervention, and American Foreign Policy 1995, Faith or Fear: How Jews Can Survive in a Christian America 1997, Honor Among Nations: Intangible Interests and Foreign Policy 1998, Undue Process: A Story of How Political Differences are Turned into Crimes 1998, Close Calls: Intervention, Terrorism, Missile Defense, and "Just War" Today 1998, Secularism, Spirituality, and the Future of American Jewry 1999, The Influence of Faith 2001, Democracy How Direct?: Views from the Founding Era and the Polling Era 2002.
Address: National Security Council, The White House, 1600 Pennsylvania Avenue, NW, Washington, DC 20500, USA (office). *Telephone:* (202) 456-9373 (office). *Fax:* (202) 456-7106 (office). *E-mail:* eabrams@nsc.eop.gov (office). *Website:* www.whitehouse.gov/nsc (office).

ABRASZEWSKI, Andrzej, MA, LLD; Polish diplomatist and international organization official; *Vice-Chairman, United Nations Advisory Committee on Administration and Budgetary Questions;* b. 4 Jan. 1938, Paradyz; m. Teresa Zagorska; one s. *Education:* Cen. School for Foreign Service, Warsaw and Copernicus Univ., Toruń. *Career:* researcher, Polish Inst. for Int. Affairs, Warsaw 1962–71; Sec. Polish Nat. Cttee on the 25th anniversary of the UN 1970; Counsellor to the Minister for Foreign Affairs, Dept of Int. Orgs, Ministry of Foreign Affairs, Warsaw 1971–83; mem. Polish del. to Gen. Ass. of the UN 1971–90, with rank of Amb. 2001–, mem. Ad Hoc Working Group on UN's programme and budget machinery 1975, mem. Advisory Cttee on Admin. and Budgetary Questions (ACABQ) 1977–82, 2001–, Vice-Chair. 2006–; Vice-Chair. Admin. and Budgetary Cttee of Gen. Ass. 1979, Chair. 1982; mem. Cttee on Contribs 1983–88 (Vice-Chair. 1987–88), mem. Cttee for Programmes and Co-ordination (Vice-Chair. 1989, Chair. 1990); Asst to Deputy Minister for Foreign Affairs 1984–90; mem. UN Jt Inspection Unit 1991–2000, Vice-Chair. 1993, 1998, Chair. 1994; Prize of the Minister for Foreign Affairs, Prize of the Minister of Finance. *Publications:* various publs on UN affairs.
Address: United Nations Advisory Committee on Administrative and Budgetary Questions, Room CB-60, New York, NY 10017 (office); 300 East 33rd Street, Apt. 19, New York, NY 10016, USA. *Telephone:* (212) 963-7456 (office). *Fax:* (212) 963-6943 (office). *E-mail:* abraszewski@un .org (office). *Website:* www.polandun.org (office); www.un.org/ga/acabq.

ABREHE, Berhane; Eritrean politician; *Minister of Finance; Career:* Acting Minister of Land, Water and Environment 1998; currently Minister of Finance; mem. Bd of Govs, African Devt Bank Group, Eritrea, Eastern and Southern African Trade and Devt Bank.
Address: Ministry of Finance, POB 896, Asmara, Eritrea (office). *Telephone:* (1) 118131 (office). *Fax:* (1) 127947 (office).

ABSHIRE, David Manker, PhD; American diplomatist and administrator; *President and CEO, Center for the Study of the Presidency;* b. 11 April 1926, Chattanooga, Tenn.; m. Carolyn Sample Abshire 1957; one s. four d. *Education:* Baylor School, Chattanooga, US Mil. Acad., West Point, NY, Georgetown Univ., Washington, DC. *Career:* co-f. Center for Strategic and Int. Studies, Georgetown Univ. 1962, Exec. Dir 1962–70, Chair. 1973–82, Pres. 1982–83, Vice-Chair. 1999–; Asst Sec. of State for Congressional Relations 1970–73; Perm. Rep. to NATO 1983–87; Special Counsellor to Pres. Jan.–April 1987; Chancellor Center for Strategic and Int. Studies (CSIS) April–Dec. 1987, Pres. 1988–, Vice-Chair. 1999–; Co-ed. Washington Quarterly 1977–83; Chair. US Bd for Int. Broadcasting 1974–77; Dir Nat. Security Group, Transition Office of Pres.-elect Reagan 1980–81; Pres. and CEO, Center for the Study of the Presidency 1999–; Pres. Richard Lounsbery Foundation of New York 2002–; mem. Congressional Cttee on the Org. of Govt for the Conduct of Foreign Policy 1973–75; mem. Bd Procter & Gamble 1987–96, Ogden Corpn, BP American Advisory Bd; mem. Advisory Bd Pres.'s Task Force on US Govt Int. Broadcasting 1991; Order of Crown (Belgium), Commdr Ordre de Léopold (Belgium), Order of the Lion of Finland (1st Class) 1994, Order of the Liberator (Argentina) 1999, Order of Sacred Treasure Gold and Silver Star (Japan) 2001; Pres. Civilian Service Award 1989, Medal of the Pres. of the Italian Repub., Senate, Parl. and Govt, Medal of Diplomatic Merit (Rep. of Korea) 1993, US Mil. Acad. Castle Award 1994, Distinguished Graduate Award, John Carroll Award for Outstanding Service by a Georgetown Univ. Alumnus. *Publications include:* International Broadcasting: A New Dimension of Western Diplomacy 1976, Foreign Policy Makers: President vs. Congress 1979, The Growing Power of Congress 1981, Preventing World War III: A Realistic Grand Strategy 1988, The Global Economy 1990, Putting America's House in Order: The Nation as a Family 1996, Report to the President-Elect 2000: Triumphs and Tragedies of the Modern Presidency 2000. *Address:* Center for Study of the Presidency, 1020 19th Street, NW, Suite 250, Washington, DC 20036 (office); 311 South St Asaph Street, Alexandria, VA 22314, USA (home). *Telephone:* (202) 872-9800 (office); (703) 836-2892 (home). *Fax:* (202) 872-9811 (office); (703) 836-2992 (home). *E-mail:* center@thepresidency.org (office). *Website:* www.thepresidency .org (office).

ABU GHAZALA, Field Marshal Muhammad Abd al-Halim (see Abd al-Halim Abu Ghazala, Field Marshal Muhammad).

ABU-HAMMOUR, Muhammed, MA, PhD; Jordanian politician; b. 1961, Salt; m.; two s. two d. *Education:* Yarmouk Univ., Univ. of Jordan, Univ. of Surrey, UK. *Career:* Researcher, Public Finance Div., Cen. Bank of Jordan 1987–91, Chief, External Economy and Balance of Payments Div. 1992–94, Chief, Public Finance Div. 1997–98; Advisor to Minister of Finance 1998–2000, Vice-Chair., Evaluation of Monetary, Financial and Econ. Situations Cttee 1999–; Chair., Fiscal Monitoring Unit 1999–, Sec. Gen., Ministry of Finance 2000–03; Minister of Industry and Trade July–Oct. 2003; Minister of Finance 2003–05; mem., Gen. Budget Cttee 1990, Evaluation of the Monetary, Financial and Econ. Situations Cttee 1992–93, Cttee Studying Priorities of Public Expenditure of Govt 1998, Cttee Evaluating Public Debt Management System 1998, Tech. Cttees 1998–99, Cttee Crystallizing and Formulating Nat. Strategy for Privatization and Privatization Law 1999, Jordanian delegation for negotiations on debt rescheduling 1999, Cttee following-up implementation of Nat. Information System on Jordanian Legislation 1999; mem. Cttee Guiding Plan for Econs Major, Al-Balqa' Applied Univ.; fmr mem. Bd of Dirs Jordan Telecom, Royal Jordanian, Arab Bank, Social Security Corpn, Nat. Resources Investment and Devt Corpn, Deposit Insurance Corpn, Jordan Petroleum Refinery Co. Ltd; part-time lecturer to grad. students in Econs, Univ. of Jordan 1999–; Best Minister of Finance of the Year in the Middle East, Euromoney Emerging Markets magazine, Washington, DC 2004. *Publications:* Property Tax in Jordan 1987, Factors Affecting Debt Service Ratio in Jordan 1988, The Impact of Financial Assistance and External Loans on Balance of Payments and Money Supply 1989, The Impact of Budget Deficit on GNP, BOP and Money Supply in Jordan 1990, The Instruments of Islamic Internal Debt 1992, Attracting Foreign Direct Investment in Jordan 1993, Measuring Taxable Capacity and Tax Effort in Jordan 1998. *Address:* c/o Ministry of Finance, POB 85, Amman 11118, Jordan (office).

ABU-NIMAH, Hasan; Jordanian diplomatist; *Director, Royal Institute for Inter-Faith Studies;* b. 11 Sept. 1935, Battir, Jerusalem; m. Samira Abu-Nimah; three c. *Education:* Al-Ummah Coll., Bethlehem, American Univ. of Beirut, Birkbeck Coll., London. *Career:* fmr political commentator, Amman Broadcasting Service and Lecturer, Teacher Training Centre, Ramallah, Jordan; Third Sec., Embassy, Kuwait 1965–67, Second Sec., Embassy, Iraq 1967–70, First Sec. in USA 1970–72, with Foreign Ministry, Amman 1972–73, Counsellor, Embassy, UK 1973–77, Amb. to Belgium (also accred to Netherlands and Luxembourg) 1978–90, to Italy 1990–95;

Perm. Rep. to UN 1995–2000; Dir Royal Inst. for Inter-Faith Studies; also currently adviser to Prince El-Hassan bin Talal; contribs to Electronic Intifada and Electronic Iraq (online publs), Green Left Weekly 2003, The Daily Star, Al-Rai; weekly articles in The Jordan Times and Al-Ghad; Order of Grand Cross of Crown of Belgium, Order of Independence of Jordan, Grade I, Order of Al-Kawkab of Jordan, Medal of Pope Paul VI, Order of Grand Cross of Merit, Italy. *Address:* PO Box 132, Jubeihah, Amman 11941, Jordan. *Telephone:* (9626) 461-8051 (office); (9626) 534-1360 (home). *Fax:* (9626) 461-8053 (office). *E-mail:* hasan.abunimah@riifs.org (office); abunimah@nol.com.jo (home).

ABU ZAYD, Karen Koning; American UN official; *Commissioner-General, United Nations Relief and Works Agency for Palestine Refugees in the Near East (UNRWA);* b. 21 Aug. 1941, Youngstown, Ohio; m. Abdul Abu Zayd 1969; two c. *Career:* fmr Lecturer in Political Science and Islamic Studies, Makerere Univ., Uganda and Jubu Univ., Sudan; joined UNHCR 1981, worked on various emergencies across Africa, served as UNHCR Chief of Mission during Bosnian war, Chef du Cabinet to High Commr Sadako Ogata, and Regional Rep. to USA and Caribbean 1981–2000; Deputy Commr-Gen. UNRWA 2000–05, Commr-Gen. 2005–. *Address:* UNWRA Headquarters Gaza, Gamal Abdul Nasser Street, Gaza City, Palestinian Autonomous Areas (office); PO Box 140157, Amman 11814, Jordan (office); UNWRA Liaison Office New York, Chief Liaison Officer Maher Nasser, One United Nations Plaza, Room DC1-1265, New York, NY 10017, USA (office). *Telephone:* (8) 677-7333 (office); (212) 963-2255 (NY) (office). *Fax:* (8) 677-7555 (office); (212) 935-7899 (NY) (office). *E-mail:* unrwa-pio@unrwa.org (office). *Website:* www.un.org/unrwa (office).

ABUBAKAR, Alhaji Atiku; Nigerian politician; *Vice-President;* b. 25 Nov. 1955, Jada, Adamawa State. *Education:* Adamawa Prov. Secondary School, Yola, Ahmadu Bello Univ., Zaira. *Career:* with Customs and Excise Dept 1969–89; joined People's Democratic Movt (PDM) 1989; fmr Gov. Adamawa State; mem. People's Democratic Party (PDP) 1998–2006; Chair. Nat. Econ. Council; Head Fed. Exec. Council meeting 1999; Vice-Pres. of Nigeria 1999–; mem. Action Congress (AC) Party 2006–; mem. Finance Cttee World Constitution and Parl. Asscn, World Citizens; Turaki Adamawa 1988. *Address:* Office of the Vice-President, New Federal Secretariat Complex, Shehu Shagari Way, Central Area, Abuja, Nigeria (office). *Website:* www .nigeria.gov.ng (office).

ABUSSEITOV, Kairat, PhD; Kazakhstani diplomatist; *Ambassador to UK.* *Education:* Univ. of Moscow. *Career:* fmr researcher in politics and history and Head of Foreign Policy and Nat. Security Programme, Centre of Strategic Research, Kazakhstan; joined Ministry of Foreign Affairs 1993, Deputy Minister, later First Deputy Minister of Foreign Affairs 1999–2007; Amb. to Switzerland 2007–08, to UK 2008–. *Address:* Embassy of Kazakhstan, 33 Thurloe Square, London, SW7 2SD, England (office). *Telephone:* (20) 7581-4646 (office). *Fax:* (20) 7584-8481 (office). *E-mail:* london@kazembassy.org.uk (office). *Website:* www .kazembassy.org.uk (office).

ABYKAYEV, Nurtai Abykayevich; Kazakhstani politician and diplomatist; *Ambassador to the Russian Federation;* b. 15 May 1947, Jambul (now Taraz); m.; three c. *Education:* S.M. Kirov Ural Polytech. Inst., Alma-Ata (Almaty) Higher CP School. *Career:* has rank of Amb.; engineer Almaty factory of heavy machine construction 1972–76; CP functionary 1976–88; First Sec. of Cen. Cttee 1988–89; Asst to First Sec. Cen. Cttee CP of Kazakh SSR 1989–90; Head Adm. of Pres. and Prime Minister Repub. of Kazakhstan, mem. Nat. Security Council 1990–95, also served as Chair.; Amb. to UK (also accred to Denmark, Norway and Sweden) 1995–96; First Asst to Pres. of Kazakhstan 1996–99, fmr Head of Presidential Admin; First Deputy Minister of Foreign Affairs 1999; Amb. to Russian Fed. 2002–03, 2007–; Chair. of Senate 2003–07. *Address:* Embassy of Kazakhstan, 101000 Moscow, Chistoprudnyi bulv. 3a, Russia (office). *Telephone:* (495) 927-17-15 (office). *Fax:* (495) 208-26-50 (office). *E-mail:* kazembassy@kazembassy.ru (office). *Website:* www .kazembassy.ru (office).

ACET, Ali Ahmet; Turkish diplomatist; *Ambassador to Germany;* b. 21 Feb. 1951, Helsinki, Finland. *Education:* American Univ., Beirut. *Career:* Third Sec., Political Dept, Ministry of Foreign Affairs 1973–74, Second Sec. 1974–75, Second Sec., Embassy in Vienna 1979–79, Second, then First Sec., Embassy in Baghdad 1979–81; Desk Officer, Dept for Security Affairs and Research, Ministry of Foreign Affairs 1981–83; First Sec. and Counsellor, Embassy in Bonn 1983–87; Head of Personnel Dept, Ministry of Foreign Affairs 1989–89; First Counsellor, Perm. Mission to UN, New York 1989–94; Envoy and Chief Adviser to State Pres. 1994–98; Amb. to Serbia

1998–2003; Deputy State Sec. for European Affairs 2005–08; Amb. to Germany 2008–.
Address: Embassy of Turkey, Rungestrasse 9, 10179 Berlin, Germany (office). *Telephone:* (30) 275850 (office). *Fax:* (30) 27590915 (office). *E-mail:* turk.em.berlin@t-online.de (office). *Website:* www.tuerkischebotschaft.de (office).

ACHARYA, Amitav, MA, PhD; Canadian academic and writer; *Professor, S. Rajaratnam School of International Studies, Nanyang Technological University;* b. Orissa, India; m. Dai Ying; one s. *Education:* Utkal Univ., Jawaharlal Nehru Univ., Murdoch Univ., Australia. *Career:* Fellow, Inst. of Southeast Asian Studies, Singapore 1987–89; Research Fellow, York Univ., Toronto 1989–90, later Prof. of Political Science; Lecturer, Dept of Political Science, Nat. Univ. of Singapore 1990–92; Visiting Lecturer, Sydney Univ. 1998; Fellow, Harvard Asia Center 2000–01, John F. Kennedy School of Govt, Harvard Univ. 2000–01 (later Sr Fellow, Asia Pacific Policy Program), Lecturer, Harvard Univ. 2001; Asia-Europe Meeting (ASEM) Chair in Regional Integration, Asia-Europe Inst., Univ. of Malaya 2003–04; Prof., S. Rajaratnam School of Int. Studies, Nanyang Tech. Univ., Singapore 2004–; Pres. Asian Political and Int. Studies Assocn 2003–05; mem. Editorial Bd Pacific Review, Pacific Affairs, European Journal of International Relations; Co-Ed. Asian Security monograph series, Stanford Univ. Press. *Publications:* U.S. Military Strategy in the Gulf: Origins and Evolution under the Carter and Reagan Administrations 1989, Cambodia: The 1989 Paris Peace Conference and After. Background and Documents (co-ed. with Pierre Lizze and Sorpong Peou) 1991, A New Regional Order in Southeast Asia: ASEAN in the Post-Cold War Era. Adelphi Paper No. 279 (monograph) 1993, An Arms Race in Post-Cold War Southeast Asia? Prospects for Control. Pacific Strategic Papers No. 8 (monograph) 1994, New Challenges for ASEAN: Emerging Policy Issues (co-ed. with Richard Stubbs and author of one chapter) 1995, The Next Stage: Preventive Diplomacy and Security Cooperation in the Asia-Pacific Region (co-ed. with Desmond Ball and author of two chapters) 1999, Democracy, Human Rights and Civil Society in Asia Pacific (co-ed. with Bernie Frolic and Richard Stubbs, co-author of introduction and author of one chapter) 2000, The Quest for Identity: International Relations of Southeast Asia 2000, Constructing a Security Community in Southeast Asia: ASEAN and the Problem of Regional Order 2001, Regionalism and Multilateralism: Essays on Cooperative Security in the Asia-Pacific 2002, 2nd revised and expanded edn 2003, Asia-Pacific Security Cooperation: Reconciling National Interest With Regional Order (co-ed. with Tan See Seng) 2004, The Age of Fear: Power Versus Principle in the War on Terror 2004, UN Peace Operations and Asian Security (co-ed. with Mely Caballero Anthony and author of final chapter) 2005, Reassessing Security Cooperation in Asia-Pacific (ed.) 2006, Crafting Cooperation: Regional International Institutions in Comparative Perspective (co-ed.) 2007, Why is There No Non-Western International Relations Theory? Reflections on and from Asia (co-ed.) 2007, Theorising Southeast Asian Relations: Emerging Debates 2006, and numerous other monographs, journal articles and book chapters.
Address: Institute of Defence and Strategic Studies, Nanyang Technological University, Block S4, Level B4, Nanyang Avenue, Singapore 639798 (office). *Telephone:* (65) 6790-6213 (office). *Fax:* (65) 6794-0617 (office). *E-mail:* isaacharya@ntu.edu.sg (office). *Website:* www.ntu.edu.sg/idss (office).

ACHARYA, Madhu Raman; Nepalese diplomatist; *Permanent Representative, United Nations;* b. 24 Feb. 1957, Udavapur; m.; two c. *Education:* Tribhuvan Univ., Kathmandu. *Career:* Asst Lecturer, Tribhuvan Univ. 1982–83; Section Officer, Ministry of Home Affairs 1983–90; Asst Sec., Ministry of Finance 1990–93, Under-Sec. of Finance 1993–96; Jt Sec., Ministry of Foreign Affairs 1996–97; Deputy Chief of Mission, New Delhi, India 1997–98; Amb. to Bangladesh 1998–2001; Foreign Sec. 2001–05; Perm. Rep. to UN, New York 2005–, Chair. Fourth Cttee (Special Political and Decolonization) for 61st session of Gen. Ass. 2006; participated in several UN missions in Cambodia, S Africa, Liberia in 1990s. *Publications:* several books, including Nepal Culture Shift!: Reinventing Culture in the Himalayan Kingdom 2002.
Address: Permanent Mission of Nepal to the United Nations, 820 Second Avenue, Suite 17B, New York, NY 10017, USA (office). *Telephone:* (212) 370-3988 (office). *Fax:* (212) 953-2038 (office). *E-mail:* nepal@un.int (office). *Website:* www.un.int/nepal (office).

ACOSTA ALVAREZ, María Cristina; Paraguayan diplomatist; *Chargé d'affaires a.i. in UK. Career:* fmr Acting Resident Rep. to IAEA; fmr Adviser to Dir-Gen. of Human Rights, Ministry of Foreign Affairs; currently Counsellor and Chargé d'affaires a.i. in UK (also accred to Norway, Sweden and Finland).
Address: Embassy of Paraguay, 3rd Floor, 344 Kensington High Street, London, W14 8NS, England (office). *Telephone:* (20) 7610-4180 (office).

Fax: (20) 7371-4279 (office). *E-mail:* embapar@btconnect.com (office). *Website:* www.paraguayembassy.co.uk (office).

ADADA, Rodolphe; Republic of the Congo politician; b. 1946. *Career:* fmr Minister of Economy, Finance and Budget, Repub. of the Congo; Minister of Foreign Affairs, Co-operation and Francophone Affairs 1997–2007; UN and African Union joint Special Rep. to Darfur 2007–.
Address: c/o Ministry of Foreign Affairs, Co-operation and Francophone Affairs, BP 2070, Brazzaville, Republic of the Congo (office). *Telephone:* 81-10-89 (office). *Fax:* 81-41-61 (office). *Website:* www.unamid.unmissions.org (office).

ADAM, Lt-Gen. Anbaree Abdul Sattar; Maldivian army officer (retd), politician and diplomatist; *High Commissioner to India; Career:* has served as Dir and Dir-Gen. of Nat. Security, Minister of State for Defence and Nat. Security, Chief of Staff of Nat. Security Services (NSS), and Deputy C-in-C of NSS and of Police since 1967; currently High Commr to India (also accred to Nepal and Bhutan).
Address: High Commission of the Maldives, E-45, Greater Kailash II, New Delhi 110 048, India (office). *Telephone:* (11) 51435701 (office). *Fax:* (11) 51435709 (office). *E-mail:* admin@maldiveshighcom.co.in (office). *Website:* www.maldiveshighcom.co.in (office).

ADAMIŠ, Miroslav; Slovak diplomat and economist; *Head of Cabinet of Commissioner Ján Figeľ, European Commission;* b. 26 June 1958. *Education:* Univ. of Economy, Bratislava, Covenant Coll. Chattanooga, Tenn., USA. *Career:* Asst, Univ. of Economy, Bratislava 1981–83; Head, Trade Section, Ministry of Commerce and Tourism 1983–93; Head, European Integration Dept Ministry of Economy 1993–96; First Sec. Mission to EU 1996–2000; Dir-Gen. Ministry of Foreign Affairs 2000–03; Amb. and Perm. Rep. to EU 2003–04, currently Head of Cabinet, Commr Ján Figeľ, EC, in charge of Educ., Training, Culture and Youth.
Address: Office of Commissioner Ján Figeľ, European Commission, Rue de la Loi 200, 1049 Brussels, Belgium (office). *Telephone:* (2) 292-08-36 (office). *E-mail:* miroslav.adamis@ec.europa.eu (office). *Website:* ec.europa.eu/commission_barroso/figel (office).

ADAMKUS, Valdas; Lithuanian politician and head of state; *President;* b. 3 Nov. 1926, Kaunas; m. Alma Adamkienė. *Education:* Munich Univ., Univ. of Ill., Ill. Inst. of Tech. *Career:* resistance movt, World War II; left Lithuania; on staff World YMCA, Sec.-Gen. and Chair. Chief Physical Training and Sports Cttee; emigrated to USA 1949; worked in Chicago sports cars factory, draftsman eng co.; f. Academic Sports Club of American Lithuanians 1951; Chair. Bd of Santara Cen. of Lithuanian Students in USA 1957–58; Vice-Chair., Chair. Santara-Sviesa Fed. of Lithuanian Émigrés 1958–67; mem. Bd Lithuanian Community in USA 1961–64; Deputy Chair. Cen. Bd, mem., Chair. American Lithuanian Community; Chair. Org. Cttee World Lithuanian Games 1983; fmr Head Scientific Research Cen. Environment Protection Agency, Admin. for Mid-W Regions Environment Protection Agency, USA, active participation in political life of Lithuania 1993–; Pres. of Lithuania 1998–2002, 2004–; UNESCO Goodwill Amb. for the Construction of Knowledge Socs 2003–; Grand Cross of the Order of Falcon, Iceland 1998, Grand Cross of the Order of St. Olof, Norway 1998, First Class, Order of Yaroslav the Wise, Ukraine 1998, Collar and Grand Cross of the Order of Mary's Land, Estonia 1999, Grand Cross of the Order of the Saviour, Greece 1999, Class Collar and Grand Cross of the Order for Service, Italy 1999, Order of the White Eagle, Poland 1999, Grand Cross of the Order for Service, Malta 1999, Grand Cross of the Order for Service, Hungary 1999, Grand Cross of the Order of Friendship, Kazakhstan 2000, Collar and Grand Cross of the Order of Three Stars, Latvia 2001, Grand Cross Légion d'Honneur, France 2001, Collar of the Order of the Star of Romania 2001, Order of St. Meshrop Mashtots, Armenia 2002, Collar and Grand Cross of the Order of the White Rose, Finland 2002, Order of Special Merit, Uzbekistan 2002, Order of Vytautas the Great with golden collar, Lithuania 2003, Golden Collar and Grand Cross of the Order of the White Star, Estonia 2004, Order of Isabel the Catholic with Collar, Spain 2005, Special Class of the Grand Cross of the Order for Service, Germany 2005, Grand Cross of the Order of Leopold, Belgium 2006; Dr hc (Vilnius) 1989, (Indiana St Joseph Coll.) 1991, (Northwestern Univ.) 1994, (Kaunas, American Catholic Univs) 1998, (Lithuanian Agricultural Univ., Ill. Inst. of Tech.) 1999, (Lev Gumilev Euro-Asian Univ. Kazakhstan) 2000, (De Paul Univ. Chicago, Law Univ. of Lithuania) 2001, (Vytautas Magnus Univ., Lithuania) 2002, (Lithuanian Acad. of Physical Educ.) 2004, (Yerevan State Univ., Armenia, Baku State Univ., Azerbaijan) 2006; Gold Medal, US Environment Protection Agency, US Distinguished Service Award, Int. Environmental Award 1988.
Address: Office of the President, S. Daukanto 3/8, Vilnius 01021, Lithuania (office). *Telephone:* (5) 266-4154 (office). *Fax:* (5) 266-4145 (office). *E-mail:*

bozena.krasovskaja@president.lt (office); info@president.lt (office). *Website:* www.president.lt (office); www.adamkus.lt (office).

ADAMOV, Yevgeny Olegovich, DTechSc; Russian politician, engineer and academic; *Research Supervisor, I. Kurchatovn Institute of Power Engineering;* b. 28 April 1939, Moscow; m.; two d. *Education:* Moscow Aviation Inst. *Career:* engineer, Deputy Dir I. Kurchatov Inst. of Power Eng. (NIKIET) 1962–86, Research Supervisor 1998–; Prof., Moscow Aviation Inst. 1965–; took part in Chernobyl Nuclear Power Station recovery work May–Aug. 1986; Dir Constructor-Gen. Research Inst. of Energy Tech. 1986–98, Scientific Dir 2001; Minister of Nuclear Energy 1998–2001; arrested in Switzerland 2005 on fraud charges at request of USA, won court decision to be extradited to Russia 2006; mem. Russian Acad. of Eng, New York Acad. of Sciences; Badge of Honour. *Publications:* over 100 books, papers and articles on man., econs of energy resources, nuclear energy, informatics.
Address: c/o NIKIET, Krasnoselskaya M. str. 2/8 a/y 788, 107140 Moscow, Russia. *Telephone:* (495) 264-46-10 (office). *Fax:* (495) 632-29-72 (office). *Website:* www.nikiet.ru/rus/index.html (office).

ADAMS, Geoffrey Doyne; British diplomatist; *Ambassador to Iran;* b. 11 June 1957; m. Mary Emma Baxter; two s. one d. *Education:* Univ. of Oxford and Ecole Nationale d'Admin, Paris. *Career:* joined FCO 1979, Southern African Dept 1979–80, Second Sec. Political, Jedda 1982–85, Econ. Relations Dept 1986-87, Pvt. Sec. to Perm. Under-Sec. 1987–91, First Sec. (Political), Cape Town/Pretoria 1991–94, EU Dept (External), FCO 1995–96, European Secr., Cabinet Office 1996–98, Deputy Head of Mission, Cairo 1998–2001, Consul-Gen. (Rep. to the Palestinian Authority), Jerusalem 2001–03, Prin. Pvt. Sec. to the Sec. of State, FCO 2003–05, Amb. to Iran 2006–.
Address: British Embassy, 198 Ferdowsi Avenue, PO Box 11365-4474, Tehran 11344, Iran (office). *Telephone:* (21) 6705011/7 (office). *Fax:* (21) 6710761 (office). *E-mail:* BritishEmbassyTehran@fco.gov.uk (office). *Website:* www.britishembassy.gov.uk/iran (office).

ADAMS, Gerard (Gerry); Northern Irish politician and author; *President, Sinn Féin;* b. 6 Oct. 1948, Falls Road, Belfast; m. Colette McCardle 1971; one s. *Education:* St Mary's Christian Brothers School, Belfast. *Career:* worked as a barman; Founder-mem. NI Civil Rights Assocn; mem. Belfast Housing Action Cttee; interned in Long Kesh under suspicion of being a terrorist March 1972; released to take part in secret London talks between Sec. of State for NI and Irish Republican Army (IRA) July 1972; re-arrested 1973, attempted to escape from Maze Prison, sentenced to 18 months' imprisonment, released Feb. 1977; charged with membership of Provisional IRA Feb. 1978, freed after seven months because of insufficient evidence for conviction; Vice-Pres. Sinn Féin 1978–83, Pres. 1983–; MP for Belfast West 1983–92, 1997–; mem. NI Ass. for Belfast West 1998– (Ass. suspended 11 Feb. 2000 and 14 Oct. 2002); involved in peace negotiations with British Govt; Thorr Award, Switzerland 1995. *Publications:* Falls Memory, Politics of Irish Freedom, Pathway to Peace 1988, Cage 11 (autobiog.) 1990, The Street and Other Stories 1992, Selected Writings 1994, Our Day Will Come (autobiog.) 1996, Before the Dawn (autobiog.) 1996, An Irish Voice 1997, An Irish Journal 2001.
Address: Sinn Féin, 51–55 Falls Road, Belfast, BT12 4PD, Northern Ireland (office). *Telephone:* (28) 9022-3000 (office). *Fax:* (28) 9022-0045 (office). *E-mail:* sfwestbelfast@talk21.com (office). *Website:* www.sinnfein.ie (office).

ADEDEJI, Adebayo, the Asiwaju of Ijebu and Olotu'fore of Ijebu-Ode, MPA, PhD; Nigerian economist; *Executive Director, African Centre for Development and Strategic Studies;* b. 21 Dec. 1930, Ijebu-Ode; m. Susan Aderinola Ogun 1957; eight s. three d. *Education:* Ijebu-Ode Grammar School, Univ. Coll., Ibadan, Univ. Coll., Leicester and Harvard Univs. *Career:* Asst Sec., Ministry of Econ. Planning, W Nigeria 1958–61, Principal Asst Sec. (Finance) 1962–63; Deputy Dir Inst. of Admin, Univ. of Ife 1963–66, Dir 1967– (on leave of absence 1971); Prof. of Public Admin, Univ. of Ife 1968– (on leave of absence 1971); Nat. Manpower Bd 1967–71; Fed. Commr for Econ. Devt and Reconstruction 1971–75; Chair. Directorate, Nigerian Youth Services Corps 1973–75; UN Under-Sec.-Gen. and Exec. Sec. UN Econ. Comm. for Africa 1975–91, Founder and Exec. Dir African Centre for Devt and Strategic Studies (ACDESS) 1992–; Chair. Senate of UN Inst. for Namibia 1975; Founder and Ed., Quarterly Journal of Administration 1967–75; Fellow, Nigerian Inst. of Man., Nigerian Econ. Soc., African Acad. of Sciences, African Assocn for Public Admin and Man.; Pres. Nigerian Econ. Soc. 1971–72; Pres. African Assocn for Public Admin and Man. 1974–83; Vice-Chair. Assocn of Schools and Inst. of Admin of Int. Inst. of Admin. Sciences 1970–; Head, Commonwealth Observer Group for Kenya's general elections Dec. 2002; Hon. DLitt (Ahmadu Bello Univ.); Hon. LLD (Dalhousie Univ., Univ. of Calabar, Univ. of Zambia); Hon. DSc (Obafemi Awolowo Univ.); numerous foreign decorations and awards. *Publications:* A Survey of Highway Development in Western Nigeria 1960, Nigerian Administration and its Political Setting (ed.) 1969, Nigerian Federal Finance: Its Development, Problems and Prospects 1969, Local Government Finance in Nigeria: Problems and Prospects (co-ed.) 1972, Management Problems and Rapid Urbanisation in Nigeria (co-ed.) 1973, The Tanzania Civil Service, A Decade After Independence 1974, Developing Research on African Administration: Some Methodological Issues (co-ed.) 1974, Africa, The Third World and the Search for a New Economic Order 1977, Africa and the New International Economic Order: A Reassessment 1979, The Indigenization of the African Economy 1981, Economic Crisis in Africa: African Perspectives on Development Problems and Potentials (co-ed.) 1985, Towards the Dawn of the Third Millennium and the Beginning of the Twenty-First Century 1986, Towards a Dynamic African Economy: Selected Speeches and Lectures 1975–1986 1989, African Within the World 1993, South Africa and Africa: Within or Apart? 1996, Nigeria: Renewal from the Roots? 1997, Comprehending and Mastering African Conflicts 1999.
Address: African Centre for Development and Strategic Studies (ACDESS), Obafemi Awolowo Way, POB 203, Molipa, Ijebu-Ode, Nigeria (office). *Telephone:* 37-432208 (office); 37-433000 (home). *Fax:* 1-269-1746 (office). *E-mail:* adebayo_adedeji@acdess.org (office). *Website:* www.acdess.org (office).

ADELMAN, Irma Glicman, PhD; American professor of economics and international consultant; *Professor Emerita of Economics and Agricultural and Resource Economics, University of California, Berkeley;* b. 14 March 1930, Romania; m. Frank Louis Adelman 1950 (divorced 1979); one s. *Education:* Univ. of Calif. at Berkeley. *Career:* Asst Prof., Stanford Univ. 1960–62; Assoc. Prof., Johns Hopkins Univ. 1962–66; Prof. of Econs, Northwestern Univ. 1967–72; Sr Economist, Devt Research Centre, IBRD 1971–72; Prof. of Econs, Univ. of Md 1972–79; Consultant, US Dept of State 1963–72, IBRD 1968–, ILO, Geneva 1973–; Fellow, Netherlands Inst. of Advanced Study, Cleveringa Chair, Leiden Univ. 1977–78; Prof. of Econs and Agric. and Resource Econs, Univ. of Calif. at Berkeley 1979–94, Prof. Emer. 1994–; Vice-Pres. American Econ. Asscn 1979–80; Fellow, American Acad. of Arts and Sciences, Econometric Soc., Royal Soc. for the Encouragement of the Arts, American Agricultural Econs Asscn; Order of the Bronze Tower (S Korea) 1971. *Publications:* Theories of Economic Growth and Development 1964, Society, Politics and Economic Development (with C.T. Morris) 1967, Economic Growth and Social Equity in Developing Countries (with C.T. Morris) 1973, Income Distribution Planning (with Sherman Robinson) 1978, Comparative Patterns of Economic Development: 1850–1914 (with C.T. Morris) 1988, Village Economies (with J. Edward Taylor) 1996, The Visible and Invisible Hand: The Case of Korea 2002.
Address: Agriculture and Resource Economics Department, 207 Gianninni Hall, University of California at Berkeley, Berkeley, CA 94720-3310 (office); 10 Rosemont Avenue, Berkeley, CA 94708, USA (home). *Telephone:* (510) 642-6417 (office); (510) 527-5280 (home). *Fax:* (510) 643-8911. *E-mail:* adelman@are.berkeley.edu (office). *Website:* are.berkeley.edu/~adelman (office).

ADELMAN, Kenneth Lee, PhD; American lobbyist and fmr government official; *Senior Counselor, Edelman Public Relations;* b. 9 June 1946, Chicago, Ill.; m. Carol Craigle 1971; two d. *Education:* Grinnell Coll., Georgetown Univ. *Career:* with US Dept of Commerce 1968–70; Special Asst, VISTA, Washington, DC 1970–72; Liaison Officer, AID 1975–76; Asst to Sec. of Defense 1975–77; Sr Political Scientist, Stanford Research Inst., Arlington, Va 1977–81; Amb. and Deputy Perm. Rep. to UN 1981–83; Dir Arms Control and Disarmament Agency (ACDA) 1983–88; Vice-Pres. Inst. of Contemporary Studies 1988–; mem. Defense Policy Bd. Advisory Cttee; Sr Counselor, Edelman Public Relations, Washington, DC; fmr Exec. Dir USA for Innovation; mem. Exec. Bd Noel Foundation; mem. Advisory Bd Princeton Review; Sec. Bd Trustees Freedom House; mem. Bd Shakespeare Theatre, Washington, DC; Instructor in Shakespeare, Georgetown Univ. 1977–79; taught at George Washington Univ.; Co-Host Tech Cen. Station. *Publications:* The Great Universal Embrace 1989, The Defense Revolution (with Norman Augustine) 1990, Shakespeare in Charge: The Bard's Guide to Leading and Succeeding on the Business Stage (with Norman Augustine) 1999, and articles in newspapers, magazines and professional journals.
Address: Edelman Public Relations, International Square, 1875 Eye Street, NW, Suite 900, Washington, DC 20006, USA (office). *Telephone:* (202) 371-0200 (office). *Fax:* (202) 371-2858 (office). *E-mail:* washington.dc@edelman.com (office). *Website:* www.edelman.com/offices/us/dc (office).

ADHIKARI, Karnadhoj; Nepalese diplomatist. *Career:* fmr Chief Sec., Govt of Nepal; Amb. to India 1990–2005, also to Bhutan 2004–05; Negotiator, Govt of Nepal-Maoist Peace Talks 2003.

Address: Ministry of Foreign Affairs, Shital Niwas, Maharajganj, Kathmandu, Nepal. *Telephone:* (1) 4416011. *Fax:* (1) 4416016. *E-mail:* mofa@mos.com.np. *Website:* www.mofa.gov.np.

ADING, Jack; Marshall Islands accountant and politician; *Minister of Finance; Career:* accountant, Pacific Resources for Educ. and Learning 1994–2007; Senator for Enewetak Atoll 2007–; Minister of Finance 2008–; mem. United People's Party (UPP).
Address: Ministry of Finance, POB D, Majuro MH 96960, Marshall Islands (office). *Telephone:* (625) 8320 (office). *Fax:* (625) 3607 (office). *E-mail:* secfin@ntamar.net (office).

ADONIS, Agnes; Dominican diplomatist; *Acting High Commissioner to UK. Career:* fmr Asst Sec., Govt of Dominica; Acting High Commr to UK and Perm. Rep. to UN and other Int. Orgs, Geneva 2004–.
Address: High Commission of Dominica, 1 Collingham Gardens, South Kensington, London, SW5 0HW, England (office). *Telephone:* (20) 7370-5194/5 (office). *Fax:* (20) 7373-8743 (office). *E-mail:* dominicahighcom@btconnect.com (office).

ADOUKI, Martin, DJur; Republic of the Congo diplomatist; *Ambassador and Diplomatic Adviser to the President;* b. 8 April 1942, Makoua. *Education:* Bordeaux and Paris Univs and Int. Inst. of Public Admin., Paris. *Career:* Information Officer for the Group of African, Caribbean and Pacific Countries (ACP) in Brussels and attended negotiations between the ACP and the EEC; fmrly Lecturer in Law at the Marien Ngouabi Univ., Brazzaville and later Special Adviser to the Prime Minister; Perm. Rep. to the UN 1985–94, to UN Security Council 1986–87, Pres. UN Security Council 1986–87, Chair. UN African Group Sept. 1986, Rep. of Chair. of OAU to UN 1986–87, Head Congo Del. to 43rd Session of Gen. Ass. 1988; mem. of the Zone of Peace and Co-operation in the South Atlantic 1988–90, mem. Del. of UN Special Cttee on the Verification of Elections in Namibia 1989, Vice-Pres. UN Gen. Ass. (44th Session) 1989; Observer on the Gen. Elections in Nicaragua Feb. 1990, Head Del. to World Summit for Children Sept. 1990; Chair. 4th Cttee of 45th Session of Gen. Ass. 1990–91; Amb. and Diplomatic Adviser to Pres. 1998–.
Address: c/o Ministry of Foreign Affairs and Co-operation, BP 2070, Brazzaville, Republic of the Congo.

ADOUM, Mahamat Ali; Chadian diplomatist; *Permanent Representative, United Nations;* b. 14 Nov. 1947, Michimeré; m.; six c. *Education:* Brazzaville Univ. (Congo), Laval Univ. Québec and Johns Hopkins School of Advanced Int. Studies, Washington, DC. *Career:* fmr school teacher, headmaster and educ. inspector; First Counsellor, Embassy of Chad, Washington, DC 1977–79, Chargé d'affaires 1979–81, 1982–83; Amb. to USA (also accred to Canada 1983); Perm. Rep. to UN 1985–92 and currently; mem. Chad del. to UN Gen. Ass. 1978, 1979, 1982, to meetings of IBRD and IMF 1977–84; Minister of Foreign Affairs 1992.
Address: Office of the Permanent Representative of Chad, 211 East 43rd Street, Suite 1703, New York, NY 10017, USA (office). *Telephone:* (212) 986-0980 (office). *Fax:* (212) 986-0152 (office). *E-mail:* chad@un.int (office).

ADVANI, Lal Krishna; Indian politician and fmr journalist and social worker; *Leader of the Opposition;* b. 8 Nov. 1927, Karachi (now in Pakistan); m. Kamala Jagtiani 1965; one s. one d. *Education:* St Patrick's High School, Karachi, D.G. Nat. Coll., Hyderabad, Sind, Govt Law Coll., Bombay (now Mumbai). *Career:* joined Rashtriya Swayam Sevak Sangh (RSS, social work org.) 1942, Sec. of Karachi br. 1947; joined Bharatiya Jana Sangh (BJS) 1951; party work in Rajasthan –1958, Sec. of Delhi State Jana Sangh 1958–63, Vice-Pres. 1965–67; mem. Cen. Exec. of BJS 1966; Jt Ed. BJS paper Organizer 1960–67; mem. interim Metropolitan Council, Delhi 1966, Leader of Jana Sangh Group 1966; Chair. Metropolitan Council 1967; mem. Rajya Sabha 1970, Head of Jana Sangh Parl. Group 1970; Pres. BJS 1973–77 (incorporated in Janata); detained during emergency 1975–77; Gen. Sec. Janata Party Jan.–May 1977; Minister of Information and Broadcasting 1977–79, of Home Affairs and of Kashmir Affairs 1998–99, of Home Affairs 1999–2004; Deputy Prime Minister of India 2002–04; Gen. Sec. Bharatiya Janata Party 1980–86, Pres. 1986–90, 1993–2005; Leader of Opposition, Lok Sabha 1990–91, 1991–96, 2004–. *Publications:* A Prisoner's Scrap-Book, The People Betrayed.
Address: 1835/16, Kasturbhai Block, Din Dayal Bhawan, J.P. Chowk, Khanpur, Ahmedabad (home); 30 Prithviraj Raj Road, New Delhi 110 003, India (home). *Telephone:* (11) 23794124 (New Delhi) (home). *Fax:* (11) 23017419 (New Delhi) (home). *E-mail:* advanilk@sansad.nic.in (office). *Website:* www.bjp.org (office).

ADYRBEKOV, Ikram; Kazakhstani business executive, politician and diplomatist; *Ambassador to People's Republic of China;* b. 8 July 1950, Tashkent, Uzbekistan; m.; three c. *Education:* Almaty Veterinary Inst.,

Experimental Biology Inst., Management and Marketing Inst. *Career:* Deputy Chair. Kazkarakul Industrial Science Unit 1988–90; Vice Pres. Kazrunokarakul Commercial Asscn 1990–92; Dir-Gen. Kazagrovneshtorg, foreign econ. assscn 1992–93; Pres. Agrosauda, foreign trade co. 1993–96; Deputy Minister of Foreign Affairs 1996–97; Amb. to Lithuania (also accred to Latvia and Estonia) 1997–2002, to Malaysia (also accred to Indonesia, Brunei Darussalam and the Philippines) 2002–04, to People's Repub. of China 2007–; Gov. Kyzylorda Region 2004–07.
Address: Embassy of Kazakhstan, 9 Dong Liu Jie, San Li Tun, Beijing 100600, People's Republic of China (office). *Telephone:* (10) 65324189 (office). *Fax:* (10) 65326183 (office). *E-mail:* kz@kazembchina.org (office). *Website:* www.kazembchina.org (office).

AFANASSIEVSKY, Nikolay Nikolayevich; Russian diplomatist; b. 1 Oct. 1940, Moscow; m.; one s. *Education:* Moscow Inst. of Int. Relations. *Career:* mem. CPSU 1968–91; Attaché, Embassy, Cameroon, 1964–66; with Ministry of Foreign Affairs 1966–76; del. to UN Gen. Ass. 1969; del. to CSCE, Geneva, Helsinki; 1973–75; Counsellor, Ministry Counsellor, Embassy, Paris 1976–83; Deputy Chief of First European Dept, Ministry of Foreign Affairs 1983–86, Chief 1986–90; Amb. to Belgium and liaison to NATO 1990–94; Deputy Minister of Foreign Affairs 1994–98; Amb. to France 1999–2002, to Poland 2002–06.
Address: c/o Ministry of Foreign Affairs, 119200 Moscow, Smolenskaya-Sennaya pl. 32/34, Russian Federation.

AFEWERKI, Issaias; Eritrean head of state; *President;* b. 2 Feb. 1946, Asmara. *Career:* trained as engineer; joined Eritrean Liberation Front (ELF) 1966, mil. training in China 1966, Leader fourth regional area ELF 1968, Gen. Commdr ELF 1969; Founding mem. Eritrean People's Liberation Front (now People's Front for Democracy and Justice— PFDJ 1977), fmr Asst Sec. Gen., Sec. Gen. 1987; Chair. State Council, Nat. Ass.; Sec. Gen. Provisional Govt of Eritrea 1991; assumed power May 1991; elected Pres. of Eritrea by Nat. Ass. 1993–.
Address: Office of the President, PO Box 257, Asmara, Eritrea. *Telephone:* (1) 122132. *Fax:* (1) 125123.

AGAKHANOV, Khalnazar Amannazarovich; Turkmenistan diplomatist and politician; *Ambassador to Russia;* b. 25 Feb. 1952, Ashgabat; m.; three c. *Education:* Samarkand State Inst. of Co-operation. *Career:* trader, Ashgabat 1969–87; First Deputy Chair. Turkmenpotrebsoyuz 1987–91; Minister of Trade 1991–94, of Trade and Resources 1994–98, of Trade and Foreign Econ. Relations 1998–99; Amb. to Kazakhstan 1999–2000, to Russia 2000–; Order of Galkynysh, For Love for Homeland and Gairat Medals.
Address: Embassy of Turkmenistan, Filippovskii per. 22, 121019 Moscow, Russia (office). *Telephone:* (095) 291-66-36 (office). *Fax:* (095) 291-09-35 (office).

AGAM, Tan Sri Hasmy, MA; Malaysian diplomatist; *Executive Chairman, Institute of Diplomacy and Foreign Relations, Ministry of Foreign Affairs;* b. 3 Feb. 1944, Malacca; m.; two d. *Education:* Univ. of Malaya, Kuala Lumpur, Fletcher School of Law and Diplomacy, Tufts Univ., USA. *Career:* joined Foreign Ministry as Asst Sec. 1968, various positions in Ministry and in missions in Saigon, Washington, DC, Hanoi and London; seconded to Nat. Inst. of Public Admin as Head, Centre for Int. Relations and Diplomacy 1981; Amb. to Libya (also accred to Malta) 1986–88, to France (also accred to Portugal) 1990–92; Alt. Perm. Rep. to UN, Alt. Del. to Security Council 1988–90; Dir-Gen. Relations with ASEAN, Foreign Ministry 1993, Deputy Sec.-Gen. for Int. Orgs and Multilateral Econs 1994–96; Alt. Perm. Rep. to UN 1996–98, apptd Perm. Rep. 1998; mem. Sec.-Gen.'s Advisory Bd on Disarmament Matters; currently Exec. Chair. Institute of Diplomacy and Foreign Relations (IDFR), Ministry of Foreign Affairs.
Address: Institute of Diplomacy and Foreign Relations, Ministry of Foreign Affairs, Jalan Wisma Putra, 50602 Kuala Lumpur, Malaysia (office). *Telephone:* (3) 21491001 (office). *Fax:* (3) 21445640 (office). *E-mail:* hasmy@idfr.gov.my (office). *Website:* www.idfr.gov.my (office).

AGARWAL, Bina, PhD; Indian economist and academic; *Professor of Economics, Institute of Economic Growth, University of Delhi;* b. Jabalpur, India. *Education:* Univ. of Delhi, Univ. of Cambridge, UK, Delhi School of Econs. *Career:* Research Assoc., Council for Social Devt 1972–74; Visiting Fellow, Inst. of Devt Studies, Univ. of Sussex, UK 1978–79, Research Fellow, Science Policy Research Unit 1979–80; Assoc. Prof. of Econs, Inst. of Econ. Growth, Univ. of Delhi 1981–88, Prof. 1988–, Head, Population Research Centre 1996–98; Fellow, Bunting Inst., Radcliffe Coll. 1989–91; mem. Harvard Center for Population and Devt Studies 1990–91; Visiting Prof., Harvard Univ. Cttee on Degrees in Women's Studies 1991–92, First Daniel H.H. Ingalls Visiting Prof. March–Sept. 1999; Visiting Scholar, Inst. for Advanced Study, Princeton 1995; Visiting Prof., Univ. of Michigan

2003; Visiting Prof. and Winton Chair Holder, Univ. of Minnesota 2004, Visiting Research Fellow, Ash Inst., Kennedy School of Govt, Harvard Univ. 2006; mem. numerous nat. and int. editorial bds, advisory cttees and consultancies; Padma Shri 2008; Dr hc (Inst. of Social Studies, The Hague) 2007; K.H. Batheja Award 1995–96, Edgar Graham Book Prize 1996, Ananda Kentish Coomaraswamy Book Prize 1996, Malcolm Adisheshiah Award for Distinguished Contributions to Development Studies 2002, Ramesh Chandra Award for Outstanding Contributions to Agricultural Economics 2005. *Publications:* Mechanization in Indian Agriculture 1983, Cold Hearths and Barren Slopes: The Woodfuel Crisis in the Third World 1986, A Field of One's Own: Gender and Land Rights in South Asia 1994, Structures of Patriarchy: State, Community and Household in Modernizing Asia (ed.) 1988, Women, Poverty and Ideology in Asia (co-ed.) 1989, Women and Work in the World Economy 1991; Psychology, Rationality and Economic Behaviour: Challenging Assumptions (co-ed.) 2005, Capabilities, Freedom and Equality: Amartyr Sen's Work from a Gender Perspective (co-ed.) 2006; numerous articles in learned journals on property rights, environment, agricultural technology, poverty, political economy of gender, and related topics.
Address: Institute of Economic Growth, University Enclave, University of Delhi, Delhi 110007, India (office). *Telephone:* (11) 27667101 (office). *Fax:* (11) 27667410 (office); (11) 24353393 (home). *E-mail:* bina@iegindia.org (office). *Website:* www.iegindia.org (office); www.binaagarwal.com (home).

AGATHOCLES, Aristides; Greek diplomatist. *Career:* fmr Perm. Rep. to EU; currently Sec. –Gen., Ministry of Foreign Affairs.
Address: Ministry for Foreign Affairs, Vasilissis Sophias Avenue, 5, Athens 106 71, Greece (office). *Telephone:* (21) 03681100 (office). *Fax:* (21) 3681364 (office). *E-mail:* sec.gen@mfa.gr (office). *Website:* www.mfa.gr (office).

AGUIRRE, Eduardo, Jr, BS; American banker, government official and diplomatist; *Ambassador to Spain;* b. 1946, Cuba; m. Maria Teresa Aguirre; one s. one d. *Education:* Louisiana State Univ., American Bankers Asscn's Nat. Commercial Lending Grad. School. *Career:* emigrated from Cuba aged 15; apptd to Nat. Comm. for Employment Policy; apptd to State Bar of Tex. as non-attorney Dir 1990; mem. Bd of Regents Univ. of Houston System for a six-year term, Chair. 1996–98; fmr Pres. Int. Pvt. Banking, Bank of America; fmr Vice-Chair. and COO Export-Import Bank of the United States (Ex-Im Bank), Acting Chair. for one year; Dir of US Citizenship and Immigration Services, Dept of Homeland Security 2003–05; has served on numerous professional and civic bds, including Tex. Children's Hosp., Tex. Bar Foundation, Operación Pedro Pan Foundation, Bankers Asscn for Finance and Trade, Houston chapters of the American Red Cross and the Salvation Army; Amb. to Spain (also accred to Andorra) 2005–; Dr hc (Univ. of Connecticut, Univ. of Houston, Universidad Tecnológica de Santiago, Dominican Repub.); Order of Hilal-i-Quaid-i-Azam (Pakistan), Grand Officer, Order of José Matías Delgado (El Salvador), Grand Officer, Order of Christopher Columbus (Dominican Repub.); Americanism Medal, The Daughters of the American Revolution 2004.
Address: Embassy of the USA, Serrano 75, 28006 Madrid, Spain (office). *Telephone:* (91) 5872200 (office). *Fax:* (91) 5872303 (office). *Website:* madrid.usembassy.gov (office).

AGUIRRE SACASA, Francisco Zavier, BSc, MA; Nicaraguan politician; *Secretary of International Relations, Partido Liberal Constitucionalista (PLC); Education:* Georgetown and Harvard Univs, USA. *Career:* mem. Int. Advisory Bd, Panamerican Agric. School; joined World Bank 1969, Chief of Chile, Ecuador and Peru Div., Latin America and Caribbean Region 1977–83, Chief of Trade, Finance and Industry Div., Eastern and Southern Africa Region 1983–86, Asst-Dir Agric. Projects, Latin America and Caribbean Region 1986–87, Sr Adviser to Vice-Pres., Latin America and Caribbean Region 1987–88, Dir External Affairs Dept 1988–90, Dir Cen. Africa and Indian Ocean Dept (Africa Regional Office) 1990–95, Dir Operations Evaluation Dept 1995–97; Amb. to USA and Canada 1997–2002; Minister of Foreign Affairs 1997–2002; currently Sec. of Int. Affairs, Constitutional Liberal Party (PLC), presidential cand. 2006.
Publications include: contribs to The Boston Globe, The Christian Science Monitor, The Wall Street Journal, The Washington Post, The Washington Times.
Address: Partido Liberal Constitucionalista (PLC), Semáforos Country Club 100 m al este, Apdo 4569, Managua, Nicaragua (office). *Telephone:* (2) 78-8705 (office). *Fax:* (2) 78-1800 (office). *E-mail:* plc@ibw.com.ni (office). *Website:* www.plc.org.ni (office).

ÁGÚSTSSON, Helgi; Icelandic diplomatist; b. 16 Oct. 1941, Reykjavik; m. Hervör Jónasdóttir 1963; three s. one d. *Education:* Commercial Coll. of Iceland and Univ. of Iceland. *Career:* joined Ministry for Foreign Affairs 1970; First Sec. and Counsellor, London 1973–77; Dir Defence Div.

Ministry for Foreign Affairs and Icelandic Chair. US-Icelandic Defence Council 1979; Minister-Counsellor, Washington, DC 1983–87; Deputy Perm. Sec., Ministry for Foreign Affairs 1987; Amb. to UK (also accred to Ireland, Netherlands and Nigeria) 1989–94; Perm. Sec., Ministry for Foreign Affairs 1995–99; Amb. to Denmark (also accred to Lithuania, Turkey, Israel and Romania) 1998–99, to USA (also accred to Argentina, Brazil, Chile, El Salvador, Guatemala, Mexico and Uruguay) 2002–06; fmr Pres. Icelandic Basketball Fed.; Hon. GCVO; Grand Cross of Dannebrog, Kt Commdr of White Rose, Grand Cross of Mérito Civil, Kt Commdr of Pole Star, Grand Cross of the Order of the Falcon, Grand Cross Oranje-Nassau Order, Grand Cross Norwegian Service Order, Grand Cross IMR.
Address: Ministry for Foreign Affairs, Rauarárstíg 25, 150 Reykjavík, Iceland (office). *Telephone:* 5459900 (office). *Fax:* 5622373 (office). *E-mail:* helgi.agustsson@utn.stjr.is (office). *Website:* www.utanrikisraduneyti.is (office).

AHERN, Dermot, BCL; Irish politician; *Minister for Justice, Equality and Law Reform;* b. Feb. 1955, Drogheda, Co. Louth; m. Maeve Coleman; two d. *Education:* Marist Coll., Dundalk, Univ. Coll., Dublin, Inc. Law Soc. of Ireland. *Career:* solicitor 1976–; mem. Louth Co. Council 1979–91; mem. Fianna Fáil 1987–; mem. various parl. cttees; Asst Govt Whip 1988–91; Minister of State at Depts of the Taoiseach and Defence, Govt Chief Whip 1991–92; Minister for Social, Community and Family Affairs 1997–2002, for Communications, Marine and Natural Resources 2002–04, Minister for Foreign Affairs 2004–08, Minister for Justice, Equality and Law Reform 2008–; mem. British-Irish Parl. Body 1991–97 (Co-Chair. 1993–95).
Address: Department of Justice, Equality and Law Reform, 94 St Stephen's Green, Dublin 2, Ireland (office). *Telephone:* (1) 6028202 (office). *Fax:* (1) 6615461 (office). *E-mail:* info@justice.ie (office). *Website:* www.justice.ie (office).

AHMAD, Shamshad, MA; Pakistani diplomatist; m.; two s. *Education:* Univ. of Punjab. *Career:* diplomatic postings to Tehran 1968–69, Dakar 1969–72, Paris 1972–74, Washington, DC 1977–80; with Mission to UN (Chair. Political Cttee UN Council for Namibia and mem. UN Cttee on Palestine) 1980–81, Consul Gen. 1981–85; Dir-Gen. Ministry of Foreign Affairs 1985–87; Amb. to Repub. of Korea 1987–90, to Iran 1990–92; Sec.-Gen. Econ. Cooperation Org., Tehran 1992–96; Special Sec., Ministry of Foreign Affairs 1996–97, Foreign Sec. 1997–2000; Perm. Rep. to UN, New York 2000–02; mem. ESCAP Panel of Eminent Persons on Human Resources Devt 1994.
Address: c/o Ministry of Foreign Affairs, Constitution Avenue, Islamabad, Pakistan (office).

AHMAD, Sufyan; Ethiopian politician. *Career:* currently Minister of Finance and Econ. Devt and Cooperation.
Address: Ministry of Finance and Economic Development and Cooperation, POB 1037, Addis Ababa, Ethiopia (office). *Telephone:* (11) 1552800 (office). *Fax:* (11) 1550118 (office). *E-mail:* media2@telecom.net.et.

AHMAD, Syed Hasan, MSc; Bangladeshi diplomatist; b. 1 Feb. 1936, Feni; m.; one s. two d. *Education:* Univ. of Dhaka, Imperial Coll. of Science and Tech., London, and London School of Econs, UK. *Career:* began career as exec. with Burmah Oil Co., Chittagong; Sr Exec. Pakistan Shell Oil Co., Karachi; joined Pakistan Civil Service 1960; Sec. E Pakistan Industrial Devt Corpn; Exec. Dir E Refinery, Titas Gas Transmission and Distribution Co.; Deputy Commr in Mymensing, Chittagong; Econ. and Commercial Counsellor in Bonn, FRG and Kuwait; Chair. Bangladesh Petroleum Corpn, Bangladesh Oil and Gas Corpn (Petrobangla), Tariff Comm.; Sec. in Ministries of Commerce, of Communications (Railway Div.), of Health and of Textiles; Dir-Gen. Bangladesh Railways; Prin. Sec. to the Prime Minister; Amb. to Belgium (also accred to Netherlands, Luxembourg, Switzerland and EU) 1992–96, to USA 2002–04; fmrly Ind. Consultant on Bangladesh Railway Reform project, Asian Devt Bank; mem. BNP Chair.'s Council of Advisers.
Address: c/o Ministry of Foreign Affairs, Segunbagicha, Dhaka 1000, Bangladesh (office).

AHMADINEJAD, Mahmoud, PhD; Iranian politician and head of state; *President;* b. 1956, Garmsar. *Education:* Iran Univ. of Science and Tech. (IUST). *Career:* joined Islamic Revolutionary Guards Corps 1986; Prof. of Civil Eng, IUST 1989–; Advisor for Cultural Affairs to Minister of Culture and Higher Educ. 1993; fmr Vice-Gov., then Gov. Maku and Khoy; Gov. –Gen. Ardabil prov. 1993–97; Mayor of Tehran 2003–05; Pres. of Iran 2005–; mem. Cen. Council, Islamic Soc. of Engineers; mem. Iran Tunnel Soc., Iran Civil Eng Soc. *Publications include:* numerous articles on political, social, cultural and economic topics.
Address: Office of the President, Palestine Avenue, Azerbaijan Intersection, Tehran, Iran (office). *E-mail:* webmaster@president.ir (office). *Website:* www.president.ir (office); www.mardomyar.com; www.ahmadinejad.ir.

AHMED, Iajuddin, BSc, MS, PhD; Bangladeshi soil scientist, academic, politician and head of state; *President;* b. 1 Feb. 1931, Nayagaon, Munshiganj Dist; m. Anwara Begum; three c. *Education:* Munshiganj Haraganga Coll., Dhaka Univ., Univ. of Wisconsin, USA. *Career:* Asst Prof., Dept of Soil Sciences, Dhaka Univ. 1963, Assoc. Prof. 1964–1973, Prof. 1973, Chair. of Dept 1968–69, 1976–79, Provost, Salimullah Muslim Hall 1975–1983, Dean, Faculty of Biological Sciences 1989–1990, 1990–91; Visiting Prof., Cornell Univ. 1983, German Tech. Univ., Berlin 1984, Gatinzens Univ., Germany 1984; adviser to caretaker govt 1991; Chair. Public Service Comm. 1991–93; Chair. Univ. Grants Comm. 1995–99; fmr Chancellor, State Univ. of Bangladesh; Pres. of Bangladesh 2002–, Chief Adviser (Head of Caretaker Govt), Minister of Foreign Affairs, of Defence, of Home Affairs 2006–07; mem. Bangladesh Jatiyabadi Dal (Bangladesh Nationalist Party); mem. Int. Soil Science Asscn, Indian Soil Science Asscn, Bangladesh Soil Science Asscn, Asiatic Soc.; Ibrahim Memorial Gold Medal 1987–88, Sri Gjyan Atish Dipanker Gold Medal 1990, Ekushey Award for Educ. 1995.
Address: President's Secretariat, Old Sansad Bhaban, Dhaka, Bangladesh (office).

AHMED, Imtiaz, PhD; Bangladeshi academic and diplomatist; *Ambassador to Nepal; Career:* fmr Asst Prof., Dept of Int. Relations, Univ. of Dhaka; fmr Minister and Deputy Chief of Mission, Washington, DC, currently Amb. to Nepal.
Address: Embassy of Bangladesh, Maharajgunj Ring Road, Kathmandu, Nepal (office). *Telephone:* (1) 4372843 (office). *Fax:* (1) 4373265 (office). *E-mail:* bdootktm@wlink.com.np (office).

AHMED, Khidir Haroun, BA, MA; Sudanese diplomatist; b. 1 Jan. 1951, Meroe Prov., Northern State; m. Howaida Abdulkarim Mahmoud; six c. *Career:* early career as press officer, trans. and cultural adviser; Counsellor, Algiers, Minister Plenipotentiary 1991, Chargé d'affaires a.i. 1991–96, Amb. to Algeria 1999, Head, American Affairs Dept, Ministry of Foreign Affairs, Khartoum 1996–99, Amb. to Japan 1999–2001, Chargé d'affaires a.i. in USA 2001–06.
Address: Ministry of Foreign Affairs, PO Box 873, Khartoum, Sudan (office). *Telephone:* (183) 773101 (office). *Fax:* (183) 772941 (office). *E-mail:* ministry@mfa.gov.sd (office). *Website:* www.sudanmfa.com (office).

AHMED, Mahmud Yayale, MA, BA; Nigerian civil servant and government official; *Minister of Defence;* b. 15 April 1952, Shira, Bauchi State; m.; c. *Education:* Ahmadu Bello Univ., Zaria. *Career:* began his civil service career, Bauchi State 1977; served as Vice Prin., Makurdi community secondary school; Deputy Sec., Ministry of Animal Health and Forestry Resources 1982–83; Acting Perm. Sec., Ministry of Rural Devt and Cooperatives 1983–84; based at Ministry of Finance and Econ. Planning 1984–86; joined Fed. Civil Service 1986, served in various posts including Admin. Officer I, Sec. CIPBS, Dir Finance and Accounts, Dir-Gen., Perm. Sec. and Head of Service of the Fed.; fmr mem. Council, Bauchi Coll. of Arts and Science, Coll. of Educ., Azare, Coll. of Legal and Islamic Studies, Misau; Minister of Defence 2007–; Ajiyan Katagum, Akowonio of Idanre Kingdom; Hon. LLD (Abuja), Hon. DLit (Bayero Univ., Kano).
Address: Ministry of Defence, Ship House, Central Area, Abuja, Nigeria (office). *Telephone:* (9) 2340534 (office). *Fax:* (9) 2340714 (office).

AHMED, Ougoureh Kifleh; Djibouti politician; *Minister of Defence; Career:* Leader Front pour la Restauration de l'Unité et de la Démocratie (FRUD– a splinter group in Afar guerilla movt) 1994, currently Sec.-Gen.; fmr Minister for the Public Office and Admin. Reforms; fmr Minister of Agric.; currently Minister of Defence.
Address: Ministry of Defence, BP 42, Djibouti (office). *Telephone:* 352034 (office).

AHMED, Sabihuddin, MEcon; Bangladeshi diplomatist; m. Rownak Ahmed; one s. one d. *Education:* Univ. of Dhaka. *Career:* served in various positions in Ministries of Information, Home, Land, Energy, Fisheries and Textiles, fmr Sec. Ministry of Environment and Forests; also worked in Foreign Ministry as Dir and in Bangladesh Consulate in Hong Kong; Pvt. Sec. to Prime Minister of Bangladesh 1991–95; Amb. to Sweden 2004–05, High Commr to UK 2005–07.
Address: Ministry of Foreign Affairs, Segunbagicha, Dhaka 1000, Bangladesh. *Telephone:* (2) 9562862. *Fax:* (2) 9555283. *E-mail:* info@mofabd.org. *Website:* www.mofa.gov.bd.

AHMED, Shafi U., BA, MA; Bangladeshi diplomatist; *High Commissioner to UK;* b. Nov. 1951; m. Sehelley Shafi; two s. *Education:* Univ. of Dhaka, Fletcher School, Tuffs Univ., USA. *Career:* joined Foreign Service 1979, Desk Officer, Ministry of Foreign Affairs 1980-85, Dir 1994–95, Dir-Gen. for Admin 2002–04; First Sec., High Comm. in Colombo 1987–90; First Sec., then Counsellor, Embassy in Riyadh, Counsellor, then Minister, High Comm. in London 1996–2000; Consul Gen. in Hong Kong 2000–02; High Commr to Malaysia 2004–07, to UK (also accred as Amb. to Ireland) 2007–.
Address: High Commission of Bangladesh, 28 Queen's Gate, London, SW7 5JA, England. *Telephone:* (20) 7584-0081 (office). *Fax:* (20) 7581-7477 (office). *E-mail:* bhclondon@btconnect.com (office). *Website:* www .bhclondon.org.uk (office).

AHMED, Shahabuddin, MA; Bangladeshi fmr head of state and judge; b. 1930, Pemai of Kendua, Greater Mymensingh Dist; two s. three d. *Education:* Dhaka Univ., Lahore Civil Service Acad., Univ. of Oxford, UK. *Career:* joined Civil Service of Pakistan 1954 as Sub-Div. Officer, later Additional Deputy Commr; transferred to Judicial Br. 1960; fmr Additional Dist and Sessions Judge, Dhaka and Barisal; fmr Dist and Sessions Judge, Comilla and Chittagong; fmr Registrar High Court of E Pakistan; elevated to High Court Bench 1972; apptd Judge of Appellate Div., Supreme Court of Bangladesh 1980; Chief Justice 1990, 1991–95; Chair. Labour Appellate Tribunal 1973–74, Bangladesh Red Cross Soc. 1978–82, Comm. of Inquiry into police shootings of students 1983, Nat. Pay Comm. 1984; Vice-Pres. League of Red Cross and Red Crescent Soc., Geneva, Switzerland; Acting Pres. of Bangladesh 1990–91, Pres. 1996–2001; Hon. Master Hon. Soc. of Gray's Inn, London.
Address: House Dal Motia, nr Mohammadpur, Dhaka, Bangladesh.

AHMETI, Ali; Macedonian politician; *President, Democratic Union for Integration;* b. 4 Jan. 1959, Zajas, Kičevo municipality; m.; one s. one d. *Education:* Prishtina Univ. *Career:* political activist as student; imprisoned for taking part in demonstrations by Kosovo Albanians 1981; granted asylum in Switzerland 1986; active in dissident People's Movt of Kosovo throughout 1980s; Founding mem. Kosovo Liberation Army 1996; Co-founder Democratic Union for Integration 1999, Pres. 2002–; elected mem. Parl. 2002; elected Supreme Commdr and Political Rep. of Nat. Liberation Army in Macedonia 2001; formed multi-ethnic coalition Govt with Prime Minister Branko Crvenkovski's Together for Macedonia coalition Oct. 2002.
Address: 1200 Tetova, Reçicë e vogël, Rruga 170 nr. 2 (office); Parliamentary Assembly Buildings, 1000 Skopje, Stojan Andov, 11 Oktomvri bb, Former Yugoslav Republic of Macedonia (office). *Telephone:* (4) 4334398 (office). *Fax:* (4) 4334397 (office). *E-mail:* bdi@bdi.org .mk (office). *Website:* www.bdi.org.mk (office).

AHO, Esko Tapani, MA; Finnish politician and organization executive; *President, Finnish National Fund for Research and Development (Sitra);* b. 20 May 1954, Veteli; m. Kirsti Hannele Söderkultalahti 1980; two s. one d. *Career:* Chair. Youth Org. of the Centre Party 1974–80, Chair. Finnish Centre Party (KESK) 1990–2002; Political Sec. to Minister of Foreign Affairs 1979–80; Trade Agent, Kannus 1980–; mem. Parl. 1983–; Prime Minister of Finland 1991–95; presidential cand. 2000; Lecturer, Harvard Univ., USA; currently Pres. Finnish Nat. Fund for Research and Development (Sitra).
Address: Sitra, Itämerentori 2, PL 160, 00181 Helsinki, Finland (office). *Telephone:* (9) 618991 (office). *Fax:* (9) 645072 (office). *E-mail:* aho.esko@ sitra.fi (office). *Website:* www.sitra.fi (office).

AHOOJA-PATEL, Krishna, PhD; Canadian international organization official and academic; *Adjunct Professor, International Development Programme, St Mary's University;* b. 15 March 1929, Amritsar, India; m. Surendra J. Patel 1950. *Career:* Legal Consultant, ECA, Addis Ababa, Ethiopia 1963–65; Research Scholar on Law and Devt, Univ. of Addis Ababa 1965; Corresp., Econ. and Political Weekly 1965–67; Employment and Devt Dept, Office for Women Workers' Questions and Ed. Women at Work, ILO 1976–86, Chief Research and Training Dept and Deputy Dir 1986–89; Deputy Dir INSTRAW 1986–90; fmr Nancy Rowell Jackman Chair., Dept of Women's Studies, Mount St Vincent Univ.; Pres. Women's Int. League for Peace and Freedom 2001-04; currently Adjunct Prof., Int. Devt Programme, St Mary's Univ., Nova Scotia; Dr hc (St Mary's Univ.) 2003. *Publications include:* Another Development with Women 1983, Women in Economic Activity: A Global Statistical Survey (ed.) 1985, World Economy in Transition (co-ed.) 1986, Women's Studies and Women in Development: Bridging the Gap (ed.) 1989.
Address: International Development Programme, St Mary's University, Robie Street, Halifax, NS B3H BC3, Canada (office). *Telephone:* (902) 420-5767 (office). *E-mail:* kahooja@smu.ca (office). *Website:* www.arts.smu.ca/ ids (office).

AHTISAARI, Martti; Finnish diplomatist and fmr head of state; *Chairman, Crisis Management Initiative;* b. 23 June 1937, Viipuri; m. Eeva Irmeli Hyvärinen 1968; one s. *Education:* Univ. of Oulu. *Career:* joined Finnish Ministry for Foreign Affairs 1965, worked in various positions in Ministry's Bureau for Tech. Cooperation 1965–72, Asst Dir 1971–72;

Deputy Dir Ministry for Foreign Affairs, Dept for Int. Devt Co-operation 1972–73; mem. Govt Advisory Cttee on Trade and Industrialisation Affairs of Developing Countries 1971–73; Amb. to Tanzania 1973–76 (also accred to Zambia, Somalia and Mozambique 1975–76); mem. Senate of UN Inst. for Namibia 1975–76; UN Commr for Namibia 1977–81, Special Rep. of Sec.-Gen. for Namibia 1978; Under-Sec. of State in charge of Int. Devt Co-operation, Ministry for Foreign Affairs 1984–86; UN Envoy, Head of operation monitoring Namibia's transition to independence 1989–90, Sr Envoy, participated in peace-making efforts in Fmr Yugoslavia 1992–93; Pres. of Finland 1994–2000; EU's Special Envoy on Crisis in Kosovo 1999, Special Envoy of the Sec.-Gen. of the UN for the Future Status Process for Kosovo 2005–08; mem. observer group on Austrian Govt's human rights record 2000; Co-Insp. of IRA arms dumps 2000–01; Head UN fact-finding mission into Israeli operation in Jenin refugee camp 2002; Chair. Int. Crisis Group –2004; mem. Bd War-torn Societies Project Int., Balkan Children and Youth Foundation; mem. Open Soc. Inst. Int. Adviser's Group, Exec. Bd of Int. Inst. for Democracy and Electoral Assistance –2003, Jt Advisers' Group Soros Foundations; Chair. Global Action Council of Int. Youth Foundation, Int. Bd WSP Int., founder and Chair. Crisis Man. Initiative, Helsinki 2000–; Chair. Int. Crisis Group –2004; Co-Chair. EastWest Inst. –2005; Chair. Supervisory Bd Finnish Nat. Opera; mem. Bd of Trustees Averett Univ., Inter Press Service Int. Asscn; Hon. Chair. Pro Baltica Forum, Advisory Cttee of Eurasia Foundation, Int. Cttee of Vyborg Library; Hon. Trustee American-Scandinavian Foundation; mem. Steering Cttee Northern Research Forum; Patron Koeppler Appeal; mem. Bd of Dirs Elcoteq SE, UPM-Kymmene, Naantali Music Festival, EUSTORY; Hon. AO 2002, Order of the Companion of Oliver Tambo 2004; Dr hc (Univ. of Oulu) 1959, 1989, (Bentley Coll., Waltham, Mass) 1990, (Kasetsart Univ., Bangkok) 1995, (Univ. of Turku) 1995, (Helsinki School of Econs and Business Admin) 1996, (Univ. of Palermo, Argentina) 1997, (Univ. of Helsinki) 1997, 2006, (Univ. of Moscow (MGIMO) 1997, (Kyiv) 1998, (Univ. of Tech., Espoo) 1998, (Univ. of Namibia) 2000, (Columbia Univ.) 2000, (Univ. of Jyväskylä) 2000, (Averett Coll.) 2001, (American Univ., Bulgaria) 2005; Franklin D. Roosevelt Four Freedoms Award 2000, Hessen Peace Prize 2000, J. William Fulbright Award for Int. Understanding 2000, European Centre for Common Ground European Peacebuilder Award 2003, European Foundation for Culture Euro-Atlantic Bridge Prize 2003, American-Scandinavian Foundation Golden Medal 2006, Friends of the UN Common Humanity Award 2006, Manfred Wörner Medal, German Ministry of Defence 2007, Geuzenmedal, Geuzen Resistance 1940–1945 Foundation 2008, Delta Prize for Global Understanding, Univ. of Georgia and Delta Air Lines 2008, Chair.'s Award of Int. Crisis Group for outstanding contributions to conflict prevention and resolution in Europe, Asia and Africa 2008, Félix Houphouët-Boigny Peace Prize, UNESCO 2008.
Address: Crisis Management Initiative, Pieni Roobertinkatu 13B, 00130 Helsinki, Finland (office). *Telephone:* (9) 4242810 (office). *Fax:* (9) 4242810 (office). *E-mail:* cmi.helsinki@cmi.fi (office). *Website:* www.cmi.fi (office).

AIMÉ, Jean-Claude C., MBA; Haitian international civil servant; b. 10 Sept. 1935, Port-au-Prince; m. 1st Elizabeth B. Bettison 1963 (divorced 1991); m. 2nd Lisa M. Buttenheim 1992. *Education:* Harvard Coll., Univ. of Pennsylvania, USA. *Career:* joined UN 1962, Programme Officer Tunis 1963–64, Asst Resident Rep. UNDP Algiers 1964–67, ILO Geneva 1967–69, Deputy Perm. Rep. UNDP Amman 1969–71, UN Relief Operation Dacca 1971–72, Rep. East African Community Arusha UNDP 1972–73, Resident Rep. UNDP Amman 1973–77, Sr Adviser UNIFIL Naqoura 1978, UN Sr Adviser in the Middle East 1979–82, Dir Office of Under-Secs-Gen. for Special Political Affairs 1982–88, Exec. Asst to Sec.-Gen. 1989–92, Asst Sec.-Gen., Chief of Staff 1992–96, Exec. Sec. UN Compensation Comm., Geneva 1997–2000.
Address: c/o Ministry of Foreign Affairs and Religion, blvd Harry S. Truman, Cité de l'Exposition, Port-au-Prince, Haiti. *Telephone:* 222-8482. *Fax:* 223-1668.

AISI, Robert Guba, LLB; Papua New Guinea diplomatist and lawyer; *Permanent Representative, United Nations;* m.; four c. *Education:* Armidale School, NSW, Australia, Univ. of Papua New Guinea. *Career:* postgraduate studies at Legal Training Inst.; studied human resources man. at Int. Inst. of Public Admin, France; admitted to Bar, Nat. and Supreme Courts 1980, Victorian Bar, Australia 1987, served with Australian law firms based in Papua New Guinea; served with Exec. Br. (Legal Affairs) of UNESCO; Prin. Legal Officer, City of Port Moresby Governing Authority 1986–90; Prin. Legal Officer and Deputy Comm. Sec., Electricity Comm. 1990–92; currently Perm. Rep. to UN, New York, Chair. Special Cttee on Decolonization 2004–, Chair. Asian States Regional Group 2004; fmr Councillor, Papua New Guinea Legal Training Inst. (later Visiting Lecturer); Founder and pnr, nat. corp. law firm; serves on several bds and orgs in business and pvt. sector; Pres. Business Council Papua New Guinea; mem. Australia-Papua New Guinea Business Council; founding mem. sports clubs, health clubs and professional club promoting int. linkages for youths; Hon. Consul to South Africa.
Address: Permanent Mission of Papua New Guinea, 210 East 42nd Street, Suite 405, New York, NY 10017, USA (office). *Telephone:* (212) 557-5001 (office). *Fax:* (212) 557-5009 (office). *E-mail:* pngmission@pngun.org (office).

AITIMOVA, Byrganym; Kazakhstani politician and diplomatist; *Permanent Representative, United Nations;* b. 1953; m.; two c. *Education:* Kazakh State Univ., Ural State Pedagogical Inst. *Career:* fmr Sec., Republican Youth Org.; Deputy Chair. Soviet Children's Fund 1988–90; mem. Parl. 1990–93; Minister for Youth Affairs, Tourism and Sport 1993–96; Amb. to Israel 1996–2002, to Italy 2002–04; Deputy Prime Minister 2004; Minister of Educ. and Science 2004–07; Perm. Rep. to UN, New York 2007–.
Address: Permanent Mission of Kazakhstan to the United Nations, 866 United Nations Plaza, Suite 586, New York, NY 10017, USA (office). *Telephone:* (212) 230-1900 (office). *Fax:* (212) 230-1172 (office). *E-mail:* kazakhstan@un.int (office). *Website:* www.un.int/kazakhstan (office).

AKASAKA, Kiyotaka, MA; Japanese diplomatist and UN official; *Under-Secretary-General, Department of Communications and Public Information, United Nations;* b. 1948, Osaka. *Education:* Kyoto Univ. and Trinity Coll., Cambridge, UK. *Career:* joined Foreign Ministry 1971; held several posts at Secr. of GATT 1988–91, WHO 1993–97; Deputy Dir-Gen. Multilateral Co-operation Dept, Ministry of Foreign Affairs 1997–2000; Perm. Rep., UN, New York 2000–01; Consul-Gen. Embassy in Sao Paulo 2001–03; Deputy Sec.-Gen. OECD 2003–07; Under-Sec.-Gen., Dept of Communications and Public Information, UN 2007–; Rep. to Kyoto Conf. on Climate Change 1997; Vice-Chair. Prep. Cttee World Summit on Sustainable Devt, Johannesburg 2002. *Publications:* The GATT and the Uruguay Round Negotiations; The Cartagena Protocol on Biosafety and numerous journal articles on trade, the environment and sustainable devt.
Address: Department of Communications and Public Information, United Nations, New York, NY, 10017, USA (office). *Telephone:* (212) 963-1234 (office). *Fax:* (212) 963-4879 (office). *Website:* www.un.org (office).

AKASHI, Yasushi; Japanese diplomatist; *Chairman, Japan Center for Conflict Prevention;* b. 19 Jan. 1931, Akita; m.; two c. *Education:* Univ. of Tokyo, Univ. of Virginia, Fletcher School of Law and Diplomacy and Columbia Univ. *Career:* Political Affairs Officer UN Secr. 1957–74; Chair. Univ. Seminar on Modern East Asia 1963–64; Amb. at Perm. Mission to UN, New York 1974–79; UN Under-Sec.-Gen. for Public Information 1979–87, for Disarmament Affairs 1987; UN Rep. in Cambodia 1992; Special Envoy to Fmr Yugoslavia 1994–95; UN Under-Sec. for Humanitarian Affairs 1996–97, UN Emergency Relief Co-ordinator 1997–98; Chair. Japan Center for Conflict Prevention 1999–, Int. Peace Co-operation Council 2002–; has represented Japan in Gen. Ass. and numerous UN confs and orgs; Chair. Budget and Finance Cttee Governing Council UNDP 1978; mem. Advisory Cttee on Admin. and Budgetary Questions 1974, 1977; Assoc. Columbia Univ. Seminars; Chair. Conf. of Mid-Career Asian Leaders on Devt 1967; Pres. Council on Population, Japan Asscn for the Study of the UN; Dir Int. Peace Acad., Better World Soc.; Sec. Founding Cttee UN International.; fmr Visiting Lecturer, Univ. of Tokyo, Int. Christian Univ., Tokyo and Sophia Univ.; currently Visiting Prof., Ritsumeikan Univ. *Publications:* The United Nations 1965, From the Windows of the United Nations 1984, The Lights and Shadows of the United Nations 1985 and numerous articles.
Address: Japan Center for Conflict Prevention, 2-14-11 Yushima, Bunkyo-ku, Tokyo 113-0034, Japan (office). *Telephone:* (3) 3834-2651 (office). *Fax:* (3) 3834-2652 (office). *E-mail:* contact@jccp.gr.jp (office). *Website:* www .jccp.gr.jp (office).

AKBAROV, Otabek Xamidullayevich; Uzbekistan diplomatist; *Ambassador to UK. Career:* helped establish Uzbekistan Embassy in Brussels during early years of independence; fmr Chief of Div., Dept of Co-operation with Countries of Europe, Ministry of Foreign Affairs, mem. team that put together Partnership and Co-operation Agreement between EU and Uzbekistan –1996, Amb. to UK 2007–.
Address: Embassy of Uzbekistan, 41 Holland Park, London, W11 2RP, England (office). *Telephone:* (20) 7229-7679 (office). *Fax:* (20) 7229-7029 (office). *E-mail:* info@uzbekembassy.org (office). *Website:* www .uzbekembassy.org (office).

AKERLOF, George Arthur, BA, PhD; American economist and academic; *Koshland Professor of Economics, University of California, Berkeley;* b. 17 June 1940, New Haven, Conn.; m. Janet L. Yellen; one s. *Education:* Massachusetts Inst. Tech., Yale Univ. *Career:* Asst Prof., Univ. of Calif., Berkeley 1966–70, Assoc. Prof. 1970–77, Prof. 1977–78, Koshland Prof. 1980–; Visiting Prof., Indian Statistical Inst. 1967–68; Research Assoc., Harvard Univ. 1969; Sr Staff Economist, Pres.'s Council of Econ. Advisers

1973–74; Visiting Research Economist, Special Studies Section, Bd of Govs of the Fed. Reserve System 1977–78; Cassel Prof. with respect to Money and Banking, LSE 1978–80; Sr Fellow, The Brookings Inst. 1994–; Vice-Pres. American Econ. Asscn; mem. Bd of Dirs Nat. Bureau for Economic Research 1997–; Assoc. Ed. several journals on econs; Guggenheim Fellow; Fellow Inst. for Policy Reform; numerous hon. lectureships; Nobel Prize in Econs 2001 (jt recipient); numerous other awards and prizes. *Publication:* An Economic Theorist's Book of Tales 1984.
Address: Department of Economics, 549 Evans Hall, #3880, University of California, Berkeley, CA 94720-3880, USA (office). *Telephone:* (510) 642-5837 (office). *Fax:* (510) 642-6615 (office). *E-mail:* akerlof@econ.berkeley.edu (office). *Website:* emlab.berkeley.edu/users/akerlof/index.shtml (office).

AKGÜNAY, Rafet; Turkish diplomatist; *Ambassador to Canada;* b. 1953. *Career:* joined Ministry of Foreign Affairs 1977, Section Head, Directorate-Gen. of Int. Security 1985–87, Dept Head 1991–93, Deputy Dir-Gen., Policy Planning Dept 1997–98, Chief of Cabinet for Pres. Süleyman Demirel 1998–2000, Sr Diplomatic Adviser to Prime Minister Recep Tayyip Erdoğan 2004–05, Deputy Under-Sec. 2006–08, Special Envoy for Counter-Terrorism Efforts 2007; overseas postings include Embassies in Lefkoaa, Athens and Tel-Aviv, Sr Rep., NATO Defense Coll., Rome 1987–91, at Embassy in Washington, DC 1993–97; Amb. to People's Repub. of China 2000–04, to Canada 2008–.
Address: Embassy of Turkey, 197 Wurtemburg Street, Ottawa, ON K1N 8L9, Canada (office). *Telephone:* (613) 789-4044 (office). *Fax:* (613) 789-3442 (office). *E-mail:* turkishottawa@mfa.gov.tr (office). *Website:* www.turkishembassy.com (office).

AKHMETOV, Danial Kenzhetayevich, BEng, BEcons; Kazakhstani politician; *Minister of Defence;* b. 15 June 1954, Pavlodar; m.; two c. *Education:* Pavlodar Industry Inst. *Career:* fmr racing cyclist; fmr Deputy Prime Minister and Minister of Industry, Energy, Transport and Communications; Akim (Gov.) Pavlodar Oblast 1995–97, 2001–03; Akim (Gov.) Northern Kazakhstan Oblast 1997–99; Deputy, then First Deputy Prime Minister, 1999–2001; Prime Minister of Kazakhstan 2003–07 (resgnd); Minister of Defence 2007–.
Address: Ministry of Defence, 010000 Astana, Beibitshilik 51a, Kazakhstan (office). *Telephone:* (7172) 33-78-89 (office). *Fax:* (7172) 33-78-89 (office). *Website:* www.mod.kz (office).

AKIHITO, Emperor of Japan; b. 23 Dec. 1933, Tokyo; m. Michiko Shoda 1959; two s. (including Crown Prince Naruhito) one d. *Education:* Gakushuin schools and Faculty of Politics and Econs Gakushuin Univ. *Career:* official investiture as Crown Prince 1952; succeeded 7 Jan. 1989; crowned 12 Nov. 1990; has undertaken visits to some 37 countries and travelled widely throughout Japan; Hon. Pres. or Patron, Asian Games 1958, Int. Sports Games for the Disabled 1964, Eleventh Pacific Science Congress 1966, Japan World Exposition 1970, Int. Skill Contest for the Disabled 1981; mem. Ichthyological Soc. of Japan; Hon. Sec. Int. Conf. on Indo-Pacific Fish 1985; Hon. mem. Linnean Soc. (London). *Publications:* 25 papers in journal of Ichthyological Soc. of Japan.
Address: The Imperial Palace, 1-1 Chiyoda, Chiyoda-ku, Tokyo 100, Japan. *Telephone:* (3) 32131111.

AKILOV, Akil Gaibullayevich; Tajikistan politician and engineer; *Chairman, Council of Ministers (Prime Minister) and Minister of Construction;* b. 2 Feb. 1944, Leninabad (now Khujand); m.; three c. *Education:* Moscow Inst. of Construction and Eng. *Career:* various posts in construction orgs, Leninabad (now Sogdh) Oblast 1960–76; worked for CP 1976–93; Minister of Construction of Tajikistan 1993–94; Deputy Prime Minister 1994–96; First Deputy Chair. Leninabad Oblast 1996–99; Chair. Council of Ministers (Prime Minister) and Minister of Construction 1999–.
Address: Secretariat of the Prime Minister, 734023 Dushanbe, Xiyoboni Rudaki 80, Tajikistan (office). *Telephone:* (372) 21-18-71 (office). *Fax:* (372) 21-51-10 (office).

AKOL, Lam; Sudanese politician; *Minister of Cabinet Affairs; Career:* fmr Sr mem. Sudan People's Liberation Army (SPLA) (Southern Sudanese opposition movt); participated in armed rebellion with Dr Riek Machar that split the rebel movt; signed Fashoda Agreement with Sudanese Govt 1997; Minister of Transport 1997; involved in peace process negotiations with ASAP 2003; Minister of Foreign Affairs 2005–07, of Cabinet Affairs 2007–; mem. Justice Party. *Publications:* SPLM/SPLA: Inside an African Revolution.
Address: Ministry of Cabinet Affairs, Khartoum, Sudan (office).

AKRAM, Munir, LLB, MA; Pakistani diplomatist and lawyer; *Permanent Representative, United Nations; Education:* Univ. of Karachi. *Career:* joined Foreign Service 1967, Section Officer, Ministry of Foreign Affairs

1968–69, Dir (UN) 1973–79, Dir-Gen. (UN, Econ. Co-operation and Policy Planning) 1985–88; Second Sec., Perm. Mission of Pakistan to UN, New York 1969–73, Councillor and Deputy Perm. Rep. to UN, Geneva 1979–82, Amb. and Perm. Rep., Geneva 1995–2002, Perm. Rep., New York 2002–; Minister/Counsellor, Embassy of Pakistan, Tokyo 1982–85; Amb. to EC, Belgium and Luxembourg 1988–92; Additional Foreign Sec. 1992–95; Chair. UN Cttee on Non-Governmental Orgs 1970, Special Group on Most Seriously Affected Countries by the Oil Crisis, UN Gen. Ass. Special Session on Raw Materials and Devt 1974, Group on Political Issues, Int. Women's Conf., Nairobi, Kenya 1985, Workshop on Fissile Materials and Tritium 1995, Trade Policy Review Body, Group of 77, Geneva 1997; Pres. Conf. on Disarmament 1996, UN Econ. and Social Council; mem. UN Sec.-Gen.'s Advisory Bd on Disarmament Matters.
Address: Permanent Mission of Pakistan to the UN, 8 East 65th Street, New York, NY 10021, USA (office). *Telephone:* (212) 879-8600 (office). *Fax:* (212) 744-7348 (office). *E-mail:* pakistan@un.int (office). *Website:* www.un.int/pakistan (office).

AKUFO-ADDO, Nano Addo Dankwa, BSc (Econs); Ghanaian politician and lawyer; m. Rebecca Akufo-Addo (née Griffiths-Randolph); five c. *Education:* Lancing Coll., Sussex, UK, Univ. of Ghana, Legon. *Career:* called to English Bar (Middle Temple) 1971, Ghanaian Bar 1975; Assoc. Counsel, Coudert Freres (US law firm), Paris office, France 1971–75; Jr mem. U. V. Campbell 1975–79; Sr Partner and Co-Founder Prempeh & Co.; Gen. Sec. People's Movt for Freedom and Justice 1977–78; Minister of Foreign Affairs 2000–07; mem. Gen. Legal Council 1991–96, Gen. Council, Ghana Bar Asscn 1991–96 (Vice-Pres. Greater Accra Regional Br. 1991–96); Founder and first Chair. Ghana Cttee on Human and People's Rights; mem. Nat. Council and Nat. Exec. Cttee, New Patriotic Party (NPP) 1992–2000; mem. Parl. (NPP) for Abuakwa constituency 1996–2000, Chair. NPP Internal Affairs Cttee, NPP Legal and Constitutional Affairs Cttee, Sec. NPP Political Cttee, Sec. NPP Policy Advisory Cttee 1996, Standing Cttee on Subsidiary Legislation 1997–2001; Ranking Minority mem. Parl.'s Select Cttee on Constitutional, Legal and Parl. Affairs 1997–2001; Chair. DHL, Ghana Ltd, Kinesec Communications Co. Ltd; Hon. Fellow Legon Hall, Univ. of Ghana.
Address: c/o Ministry of Foreign Affairs, Treasury Rd., POB M53, Accra, Ghana (office).

AKWA'A, Khaled Ismail al-; Yemeni diplomatist. *Career:* Gen. Coordinator, Supreme Nat. Cttee for Human Rights 1998; various positions in Ministry of Foreign Affairs, currently Dir European Dept; fmr Amb. to Saudi Arabia.
Address: Ministry of Foreign Affairs, POB 1994, San'a, Yemen. *Telephone:* (1) 276612. *Fax:* (1) 286618. *E-mail:* mofa1@mofa.gov.ye. *Website:* www.mofa.gov.ye.

ALABART, Manuel, BA, MA; Spanish diplomatist; *Ambassador to Saudi Arabia;* b. 1947, Madrid. *Education:* Univ. of Madrid. *Career:* fmr Dir-Gen. for Foreign Policy, Africa, Middle East and Asia, Ministry of Foreign Affairs; Dir-Gen. Dept of Mediterranean, Middle E and Africa, then Dept of Africa, Asia and Pacific, Ministry of Public Admin. –2000; Amb. to Argentina 2000–04, to Saudi Arabia 2005–.
Address: Embassy of Spain, POB 94347, Riyadh 11693, Saudi Arabia (office). *Telephone:* (1) 488-0606 (office). *Fax:* (1) 488-0420 (office). *E-mail:* embespsa@mail.mae.es (office).

ALAINI, Mohsin Ahmed; Yemeni politician and diplomatist; *Deputy Chairman, Consultative Council;* b. 20 Oct. 1932, Bani Bahloul, N Yemen; m. Aziza Abulahom 1962; two s. two d. *Education:* Faculty of Law, Cairo Univ. and the Sorbonne, Paris. *Career:* schoolteacher, Aden 1958–60; Int. Confed. of Arab Trade Unions 1960–62; Minister of Foreign Affairs, Yemeni Repub. Sept.–Dec. 1962, 1974–80; Perm. Rep. to UN 1962–65, 1965–66, 1967–69; Minister of Foreign Affairs May–July 1965; Prime Minister Nov.–Dec. 1967, 1974–80; Amb. to USSR 1968–70; Prime Minister, Minister of Foreign Affairs Feb. 1971, 1971–72, 1974–75; Amb. to France Aug.–Sept. 1974, 1975–76, to UK 1973–74, to FRG 1982–84, to USA 1984–97; Perm. Rep. to UN 1980–82; Deputy Chair. Consultative Council 1997–. *Publications include:* Battles and Conspiracies against Yemen 1957, Fifty Years of Mounting Sands (autobiog.) 2000.
Address: 8 Wissa Wassif Street, Giza, Cairo, Egypt (home); PO Box 72922, San'a, Yemen. *Telephone:* (1) 441185 (Yemen) (office); (2) 5702423 (Cairo). *Fax:* (2) 5762423 (Cairo) (home).

ALAOUI, Fatima; Moroccan politician and environmentalist; *President, National Green Party;* b. 27 March 1947, Marrakesh. *Education:* Univ. of Tunis. *Career:* founder and Dir Ere Nouvelle publrs; Pres. Comité des Femmes Marocaines pour le Développement 1987–; founder and Pres. Forum Maghrébin pour l'Environnement 1989; Pres. Agence de Recherches, d'Information et de Formation pour les Femmes; founder

and Pres. Parti Nat. des Verts pour le Développement (first female pres. of political party in Morocco) 1992–; Rep. of Southern NGOs to UN IFAD; has launched environmental and devt campaigns; helped draft charters for green parties across world including Nairobi 1998, Canberra 2001; FAO Ceres Medal 1991. *Publications include:* L'arbre sans racines ou je ne suis que journaliste 1981, Le rôle économique de la femme dans le milieu rural 1983, Le rôle et le statut de la femme dans le développement rural 1989, Dettes et crises quelles incidences sur l'environnement et le développement 1990, L'équation: paix droits de l'homme et son incidence sur l'environnement et le développement 1991, Parti de rien arrivée à zéro? 1996.
Address: Parti National des Verts pour le Développement, BP 403, 2 rue Zahla, Rabat, Morocco (office). *Telephone:* (7) 72-74-06 (office). *Fax:* (7) 73-74-06 (office).

ALARCÓN DE QUESADA, Ricardo; Cuban diplomatist and politician; *President of National Assembly;* b. 21 May 1937; m. Margarita Maza; one d. *Education:* Univ. de Habana. *Career:* Head of Student Section, Prov. Office of 26 July Revolutionary Movt 1957–59; Pres. Univ. Students' Fed., Sec. Union of Young Communists; Dir for Regional Policies (Latin America), Ministry of Foreign Affairs 1962–66; mem. Governing Council of Inst. for Int. Politics, Ministry of Foreign Affairs, Deputy Minister of Foreign Affairs 1978, mem. Tech. Advisory Council 1980; Perm. Rep. of Cuba to the UN 1966–78; Pres. UNDP 1976–77; Alt. mem. Cen. Cttee of CP of Cuba 1980–; mem. Politburo of CP 1992–; Perm Rep. to UN 1990; Minister of Foreign Affairs 1992–94; Pres. Nat. Ass. of People's Power 1993–.
Address: Asamblea Nacional del Poder Popular, Havana, Cuba; 42 Street No. 2308 e/23 and 25 Streets, Municipio Playa, Cuba.

ALASANIA, Irakli, LLB; Georgian diplomatist; *Permanent Representative, United Nations;* m.; two c. *Education:* Tbilisi State Univ. *Career:* with Ministry of State Security 1993–98; with Ministry of Foreign Affairs 1998–2001, postings include Embassies in USA, Canada and Mexico; Head, Directorate for Security Issues, Nat. Security Council 2001–02, Deputy Sec. 2004–05; First Deputy Minister of State Security 2002–04, of Defence 2004; Special Rep. for Abhkazia and Head of Govt, Abkhazia Autonomous Repub. 2005–06, Special Rep. for Abhkazia negotiations 2005–; adviser to Pres. of Georgia on Conflict Resolution 2006; Perm. Rep. to UN, New York 2006–.
Address: Permanent Mission of Georgia to the United Nations, 1 United Nations Plaza, 26th Floor, New York, NY 10021, USA (office). *Telephone:* (212) 759-1949 (office). *Fax:* (212) 759-1832 (office). *E-mail:* georgia@un .int (office). *Website:* www.un.int/georgia (office).

ALATAS, Ali, BA, LLM; Indonesian diplomatist; *Chairman, Advisory Council of the President;* b. 4 Nov. 1932, Jakarta; m. Yunisa Alatas 1956; three d. *Education:* Acad. for Foreign Affairs and School of Law, Univ. of Indonesia. *Career:* Financial and Econ. Ed. P.I.A. nat. news agency, Jakarta; joined Ministry of Foreign Affairs 1954; Second Sec. (later First Sec.), Bangkok, Thailand 1956–69; Dir Information and Cultural Affairs, Jakarta 1960–65, Dir 1965–66, 1970–72; Counsellor (later Minister Counsellor), Washington, DC 1966–70; Sec. Directorate Gen. for Political Affairs, Jakarta, Chef de Cabinet to Minister of Foreign Affairs 1972–75; Minister of Foreign Affairs 1988–99; Perm. Rep. to UN 1976–78, 1982–84, 1985–87; Sec. to the Vice-Pres. of Indonesia 1978–82; Chair. First Cttee, 40th UN Gen. Ass. 1985; Special Envoy UN Sec.-Gen. 2003–, in Myanmar Aug. 2005 to negotiate release of Aung San Suu Kyi; Chair. Advisory Council of the Pres. 2006–; Hon. Co-Chair. US–Indonesia Soc. Advisory Bd; Indonesian Order of Merit. *Publications:* A Voice for a Just Peace, The Pebble in the Shoe: The Diplomatic Struggle for East Timor; numerous articles and essays on Int. Relations.
Address: Office of the Advisory Council, Jalan Veteran III, Jakarta 10110 (office); Jalan Benda 19, Kemang Selatan, Jakarta 12560, Indonesia (home). *Telephone:* (21) 3447713 (office); (21) 7811195 (home). *Fax:* (21) 3866848 (office); (21) 7800487 (home). *E-mail:* ali.alatas@makarim.com (office).

ALBERDI, Inés, Doctorado en Ciencias Políticas y Sociología; Spanish sociologist, international organization official and academic; *Executive Director, United Nations Development Fund for Women (UNIFEM);* b. 11 Feb. 1948, Seville; m.; one s. one d. *Education:* Universidad Complutense de Madrid. *Career:* Asst Prof., Dept of Sociology, Universidad Complutense de Madrid 1971–75, Prof. Encargada 1975–78, Adjunct Prof. 1978, Adjunct Prof. of Sociology 1980–84, Titular Prof. of Sociology 1984–88, 1990–91, Prof. of Sociology 1993–2008; Visiting Scholar, Dept of Sociology, Georgetown Univ., Washington, DC 1978–79, Assoc. Researcher 1988–89; Univ. Prof. of Sociology, Univ. of Saragossa 1991–93; Dir for Research, Centre for Sociological Research 1992–93; Dir Masters programme 'Women's Studies and Equality Opportunity Policies' organized by School of Doctors and Lawyers in Political Sciences and Sociology and sponsored by Main Directorate of Woman of CAM 1994–96; Deputy

in Madrid Ass. 2003–07; Exec. Dir UNIFEM 2008–; Adviser for Women in Devt, IDB 1989–90; served as expert for Equal Opportunities Unit of EC on networks Family and Work and Diversification of Occupational Choices for Women 1998–2000; mem. Bd UN Int. Research and Training Inst. for Advancement of Women (INSTRAW) 1986–89; Eisenhower Fellowship 1998. *Publications include:* Guía didáctica para una orientación no sexista Ministerio de Educación y Ciencia 1988, Estudio Sociológico sobre las viudas en España (second edn; co-author) 1989, La situación social de las viudas en España. Aspectos Cuantitativos (co-author) 1990, Matrimonios y Parejas (co-author) 1994, Informe sobre la situación de la familia en España 1994, Lo personal es político. El movimiento feminista en la transición ((co-author) 1996, La nueva familia española 1999, Las mujeres jóvenes en España 2000, Les dones joves a Espanya Fundació 2001, Violencia: Tolerancia Cero (with Luis Rojas Marcos) 2005, Los hombres jóvenes y la paternidad 2007.
Address: UNIFEM Headquarters, 304 East 45th Street, 15th Floor, New York, NY 10017, USA (office). *Telephone:* (212) 906-6400 (office). *Fax:* (212) 906-6705 (office). *E-mail:* ines.alberdi@unifem.org (office). *Website:* www.unifem.org (office).

ALBERT II, HSH Prince of Monaco (Albert Alexandre Louis Pierre), BA; b. 14 March 1958. *Education:* Albert I High School, Amherst Coll., Mass, USA. *Career:* ranked as 1st Class Ensign (Sub-Capt.); Pres. Monegasque Del. to Gen. Ass., UN 1993–; Chair. of several sports feds and cttees; Chair. Organizing Cttee, Monte Carlo Int. Television Festival 1988–; Deputy Chair. Princess Grace Foundation of Monaco; named Prince Regent of Monaco 31 March 2005, became Sovereign Prince of Monaco upon death of father Prince Rainier III 6 April 2005, enthroned 12 July 2005; Hon. Pres. Int. Athletic Foundation, Int. Modern Pentathlon Union, World Beach Volleyball, hon. citizen of Forth Worth 2000, Hon. Chair. Jeune Chambre Economique, Monaco Aide et Présence, hon. mem. St Petersburg Naval Ass., Int. Inst. for Human Rights, Hon. Prof. of Int. Studies, Tarrant County Coll., Fort Worth 2000; Grand Cross, Order of Grimaldi 1958, Grand Officier, Nat. Order of the Lion of Senegal 1977, Grand Cross, Order of Saint-Charles 1979, Kt Grand Cross, Equestrian Order of the Holy Sepulchre of Jerusalem 1983, Grand Officer, Legion of Honour 1984, Col of the Carabineers 1986, Chevalier, Order of Malta 1989, Grand Officer, Merite Int. du Sang 1994, Grand Cross, National Order of Merit 1997, Grand Cross, Nat. Order of Niger 1998, Grand Cross of the Jordanian Renaissance (Nahdah medal) 2000, Grand Cross, Order of the Sun of Peru 2003, Grand Cross, Order Juan Mora Fernandez, Costa Rica 2003, Order of Stara Planina, Bulgaria 2004; Dr hc (Pontifical Univ., Maynooth) 1996.
Address: Palais Princier, BP 518, MC 98015, Monaco. *Website:* www.palais .mc.

ALBERT II, HM, King of the Belgians; b. 6 June 1934, Brussels; m. Donna Paola Ruffo di Calabria 1959; two s. Crown Prince Philippe, Prince Laurent, one d. Princess Astrid. *Career:* fmrly Prince of Liège; succeeded to the throne 9 Aug. 1993, on the death of his brother King Baudouin I; Pres. Caisse Générale d'Epargne et de Retraite 1954–92; Pres. Belgian Office of Foreign Trade 1962–93; Pres. Belgian Red Cross 1958–93.
Address: Office of HM the King, The Royal Palace, Rue Brederode 16, 1000 Brussels, Belgium (office). *Telephone:* (2) 551-20-20 (office). *Website:* www.monarchie.be.

ALBERT, Delia Domingo; Philippine politician and diplomatist; *Ambassador to Germany;* b. 11 Aug. 1942, Baguio City; m. Hans Albert; one d. *Education:* Univ. of the Philippines, Inst. for Int. Studies, Geneva, Switzerland, Diplomatic Inst., Salzburg, Austria, Boston Univ. Overseas, Bonn, Germany, Inst. for Political Science and Strategic Studies, Kiel, Germany, Kennedy School of Government, Harvard Univ., USA. *Career:* Asst, Office of Sec. of Foreign Affairs, Dept of Foreign Affairs 1967; assigned to Philippines Mission to UN, Geneva and attended confs of UN Specialized Agencies in Geneva and Vienna; rep. The Philippines in various diplomatic capacities in Romania, Hungary, FRG, GDR, Australia (also accred to Nauru, Tuvalu and Vanuatu); Dean of Diplomatic Corps, Australia 2001; Under-Sec. for Int. Econ. Relations and Philippine Sr Official for APEC 2001–03; Sec. of Foreign Affairs 2003–04; Presidential Adviser for Multilateral Cooperation and Devt 2004–05, concurrently Presidential Envoy for Mining 2005; Amb. to Germany 2005–; fmr Dir-Gen. ASEAN Nat. Secr. of the Philippines (served as Sec.-Gen. of Conf. Secr. of Fourth APEC Econ. Leaders' Meeting, The Philippines 1996); Kt Commdr's Cross of the Order of Merit with Star (FRG) 1992, Order of Sikatuna (rank of Datu); Dr hc (Philippine Women's Univ.) 2003; Outstanding Woman in Public Service, Nat. Council for Women of the Philippines 2005.
Address: Embassy of the Philippines, Uhlandstr. 97, 10715 Berlin, Germany (office); 306 University Avenue, Ayala Alabang, Muntinglupa, Metro Manila, The Philippines (home). *Telephone:* (30) 8649500 (office).

Fax: (30) 8732551 (office). *E-mail:* berlinpe@t-online.de (office). *Website:* www.philippine-embassy.com (office).

ALBRECHT, Ernst Carl Julius, Dr rer. pol; German politician and economist (retd); b. 29 June 1930, Heidelberg; m. Dr Heidi Adele Stromeyer 1953; five s. two d. *Education:* Univs of Tübingen, Cornell, Basle, Bonn. *Career:* Attaché to Council of Ministers, ECSC 1954; Sec. of Common Market section of Brussels conf. for preparation of Treaties of Rome 1956; CEO to EEC Commr Hans von der Groeben 1958; Deputy Head of Comm. del. at negotiations with Denmark, Ireland, Norway and UK for accession to EEC 1961–63; Dir-Gen. for Competition, EEC Comm. 1967–70; Financial Dir Bahlsens Keksfabrik, biscuit mfrs 1971–76; mem. Landtag (Parl.) for Lower Saxony 1970–90, Minister-Pres. of Lower Saxony 1976–90; personal consultant to Pres. and Prime Minister of Kyrgyzstan 1995–2005; mem. CDU; Grosskreuz der Bundesrepublik Deutschland. *Publication:* Der Staat – Idee und Wirklichkeit (The State – Idea and Reality) 1976–90, Erinnerungen (Memoirs) 1999.
Address: Am Brink 2B, 31303 Burgdorf, Germany. *Telephone:* (5136) 977900 (office); (5136) 977900 (home). *Fax:* (5136) 977901 (office).

ALBRIGHT, Madeleine Korbel, BA, MA, PhD; American fmr government official, diplomatist and international affairs adviser; *Principal, Albright Group LLC;* b. 15 May 1937, Prague, Czechoslovakia; m. Joseph Albright 1959 (divorced 1983); three d. *Education:* Wellesley Coll. and Columbia Univ. *Career:* Prof. of Int. Affairs, Georgetown Univ. 1982–83; Head, Center for Nat. Policy 1985–93; chief legis. asst to Democratic Senator Edmund Muskie 1976–78; mem. Nat. Security Council staff in Carter Admin 1978–81; adviser to Democrat cands Geraldine Ferraro 1984 and Michael Dukakis 1988; Perm. Rep. to UN 1993–97 (first foreign-born holder of this post); Sec. of State 1997–2001 (highest-ranking woman in history of US govt); Co-founder and Prin. The Albright Group LLC 2001–; Chair. Nat. Democratic Inst. for Int. Affairs, Washington, DC 2001–; Chair The PEW Global Attitudes Project; Pres. Truman Scholarship Foundation; mem. Bd NY Stock Exchange; mem. Council on Foreign Relations, American Political Science Asscn, American Asscn for Advancement of Slavic Studies. *Publications:* Poland: The Role of the Press in Political Change 1983, Madam Secretary: A Memoir 2003, The Mighty and the Almighty: Reflections on Faith, God and World Affairs 2006; numerous articles.
Address: The Albright Group LLC, 901 15th Street, NW, Suite 1000, Washington, DC 20005, USA (office). *Telephone:* (202) 842-7222 (office). *Fax:* (202) 354-3888 (office). *Website:* www.thealbrightgroupllc.com (office).

ALBURQUERQUE DE CASTRO, Rafael, DJur; Dominican Republic politician; *Vice-President;* b. 14 June 1940, Santo Domingo. *Education:* Univ. of Santo Domingo, Sorbonne, Université de Paris, France. *Career:* fmr Minister of Labour; Vice-Pres. of Dominican Repub. 2004–.
Address: Administrative Secretariat of the Presidency, Palacio Nacional, Avenida México, esq. Dr Delgado, Santo Domingo, DN, Dominican Republic (office). *Telephone:* 686-4771 (office). *Fax:* 688-2100 (office). *E-mail:* prensa@presidencia.gov.do (office). *Website:* www.presidencia.gov.do (office).

ALCALAY, Milos, LLB; Venezuelan diplomatist; b. 8 Nov. 1945; m.; three c. *Education:* Andres Bello Catholic Univ. School of Law, Univ. of Paris, Int. Public Admin. Inst., Paris, Int. Inst. of Human Rights, Strasbourg, France. *Career:* Head, Dept of Audiovisual Media and Communications, Ministry of Foreign Affairs 1969–70; Third Sec., Embassy in Paris 1970–71, Councillor 1978–79; Asst Dir-Gen. Ministry of Foreign Affairs 1971–72, Chief of Staff 1972–73; Minister Counsellor, Perm. Mission to EEC, Belgium 1979–83; Perm. Rep. of Latin American Parl. and Andean Parl., European Parl., Council of Europe 1983–97; Sec.-Gen. Andean Parl., Venezuela 1983–85, Exec. Sec., Andean Parl., Bogotá, Colombia 1985–90; Amb. to Romania 1990–92, to Israel 1992–95, to Brazil 1997–2000; Deputy Foreign Minister 1995–96; Perm. Rep. to UN, New York 2001–04 (resgnd), Chair. UN Cttee on Information 2001–02; Prof., Universidad Jose Maria Vargas de Caracas 2005–08, Universidad Catolica Cecilio Acosta, Maracaibo 2006–07; currently Co-ordinator, Int. Relations, Partido Social-Cristiano (Comité de Organización Política Electoral Independiente); columnist for Diario La Verdad, Analitica.com; Orden Rio Branco, Segunda Clase (Brazil) 1972, Orden Vladimir Teodorescu (Romania) 1973, Orden Heráldica Cristóbal Colón (Dominican Repub.) 1987, Orden Andrés Bello (Venezuela) 1988, Orden Libertador Simón Bolívar (Venezuela) 1988, Orden Rio Branco, Gran Comendador (Brazil) 1996, Orden El Sol de Perú 1996, Gran Cruz al Mérito (Germany) 1996, Cruz de las Fuerzas Armadas Terrestres (Venezuela) 1997, Orden De San Carlos (Colombia) 1971, Orden Almirante Brion (Venezuela) 1998, Orden Rio Branco (Brazil) 2001, Gran Cruz Orden Cruzeiro do Sul (Brazil) 2001; Medalla de la integración 1996.

Address: c/o Partido Social-Cristiano (Comité de Organización Política Electoral Independiente), esq. San Miguel, Avda Panteón cruce con Fuerzas Armadas, San José, Caracas 1010, Venezuela. *Telephone:* (212) 262-0792. *E-mail:* milosalcalay@yahoo.com. *Website:* www.partidocopei.org.ve; www.milosalcalay.com.

ALCHOURON, Guillermo E.; Argentine farmer, lawyer and politician; b. 4 Nov. 1933; m. María Elina Albin Etchart; two s. three d. *Education:* Univ. of Buenos Aires. *Career:* farmer specializing in breeding of Dutch, Argentine and Jersey dairy cattle and milk production at Coronel Brandsen Estate; mem. Bd of Dirs Argentine Rural Soc. 1969–96, Pres. 1984–90; Pres. Argentine Soc. of Jersey Dairy Cattle; Counsellor, Foundation for Latin American Econ. Research 1969–; Adviser, Argentine Council for Int. Relations 1987–; Deputy for Acción de la República 1999–; mem. Exec. Council, Int. Fed. of Agric. Producers; Gov. World Econ. Forum for Food and Farming Production; Pres. Agric. Soc.; mem. Acción por la República (AR); decorations from Spain, France, USA, Germany and Italy.
Address: Acción por la República (AR), Buenos Aires; La Juanita, Coronel Brandsen, Argentina.

ALDERDICE OF KNOCK, Baron (Life Peer), cr. 1996, of Knock, in the City of Belfast; **John Thomas Alderdice,** MB, BCh, BAO, FRCPsych, KCFO; British politician and psychiatrist; *Commissioner, Independent Monitoring Commission;* b. 28 March 1955, Lurgan, Co. Antrim; s. of Rev. David Alderdice and Helena Alderdice (née Sheilds); m. Joan Margaret (née Hill) 1977; two s. one d. *Education:* Ballymena Acad., Queen's Univ., Belfast; Royal Coll. of Psychiatrists. *Career:* apptd Consultant Psychotherapist, Eastern Health and Social Services Bd (EHSSB) 1988; Dir NI Inst. of Human Relations 1991–94; Exec. Medical Dir, S and E Belfast Health and Social Services Trust 1993–97; mem. Alliance Party of NI 1978–, mem. Exec. Cttee 1984–98, Chair. Policy Cttee 1985–87, Vice-Chair. 1987, Leader 1987–98; contested Belfast E 1987, 1992, NI European Parl. elections 1989; Councillor, Belfast City Council 1989–97; Leader of Del. to Inter-Party and Inter-Govt Talks on the Future of NI 1991–92; Leader of Del. at Forum for Peace and Reconciliation (Dublin Castle) 1994–96; mem. NI Forum for Political Dialogue 1996–98; Vice-Pres. European Liberal Democrat and Reform Party 1999–2003, Exec. Cttee mem. 1987–2003, Treas. 1995–99; Vice-Pres. Liberal Int. 1992–99, Deputy Pres. 1999–2005, Pres. 2005–, Chair. Human Rights Cttee 1999–2005; mem. House of Lords 1998–; mem. NI Ass. (Belfast E) 1998–2002, Speaker 1998–2004 (NI Ass. suspended Oct. 2002); Commr, Ind. Monitoring Comm. 2003–; mem. BMA, Asscn Psychoanalytic Psychotherapy; Trustee Ulster Museum 1993–97; Hon. Lecturer, Faculty of Medicine, Queen's Univ. Belfast 1991–99; Hon. Prof., Faculty of Medicine, Univ. of San Marcos, Lima (Peru) 1999; Hon. Fellow, Royal Coll. of Physicians of Ireland 1997, Royal Coll. of Psychiatrists 2001; W. Averell Harriman Award for Democracy 1998, John F. Kennedy Profiles in Courage Award 1998, Silver Medal of Congress of Peru 1999, Medal of Honour of Peru Coll. of Medicine 1999, Extraordinary Meritorious Service to Psychoanalysis, Int. Psychoanalytical Asscn 2005. *Publications include:* articles on psychology of violent conflict and terrorism.
Address: House of Lords, London, SW1A 0PW, England (office). *Telephone:* (20) 7219-5050 (office). *E-mail:* alderdicej@parliament.uk (office). *Website:* homepage.ntlworld.com/john.alderdice.

ALEKSEEV, Aleksander Yuryevich; Russian diplomatist and politician; *Permanent Representative to the Council of Europe;* b. 20 Aug. 1946, Moscow; m.; one d. *Education:* Moscow Inst. of Int. Relations. *Career:* diplomatic posts abroad, including in India and in Ministry of Foreign Affairs of USSR and Russia; Amb. to Pakistan 1993; Dir 3 Ascon Dept, Ministry of Foreign Affairs; Perm. Rep. to OSCE 2001–04; Deputy Minister of Foreign Affairs 2004–07; Perm. Rep.to Council of Europe 2007—.
Address: Office of the Permanent Representative to the Council of Europe, 75 allee de la Robertsau, 67000 Strasbourg, France (office). *Telephone:* (388) 24-20-15 (office). *Fax:* (388) 24-19-74 (office). *E-mail:* representationpermderussie@wanadoo.fr (office). *Website:* www.russiaeurope.mid.ru (office).

ALENCAR GOMES DA SILVA, José; Brazilian politician and business executive; *Vice-President;* b. 17 Oct. 1931, Muriaé; m. Mariza Campos Gomes da Silva; three c. *Career:* clerk, A Sedutora (textiles store), Muriaé 1946–48; salesperson, Casa Bonfim, Caratinga 1948–50; est. A Queimadeira (textiles store), Caratinga 1950–53; travelling salesman, Tecidos Fernandes SA 1953; co-f. Industria de Macarrão Santa Cruz (pasta factory) 1950s; inherited co. Uniãos dos Cometas from brother Geraldo Gomes da Silva 1959, renamed Geraldo Gomes da Silva Tecidos SA; f. Cia Industrial de Roupas União dos Cometas 1963, renamed Wembley Roupas SA; co-f. Companhia de Tecidos Norte de Minas—Coteminas, Montes Claros 1967; Senator for Tancredo Neves (Liberal Party) 1998–; Vice-Pres. of Brazil

2003–, Minister of Defence 2004–06; Hon. Prof., Fed. Univ. of Juiz de Fora 2003, Admin. Council of Senai/Cetiqt, Rio de Janeiro 2003; Legis. Order of Merit 1985, Cairu Badge of Merit 1985, Officer, Rio Branco Order 1989, Commdr Work Judiciary Merit Order 1991, Grand Cross, Mil. Merit Order 2003, Mil. Judiciary Merit Order 2003, Rio Branco Order 2003, Naval Merit Order 2003, Aviation Merit Order 2003, Defence Merit Order 2003; Dr hc (Fed. Univ. of Viçosa) 2002, (State Univ. of Minas Gerais Unimontes de Montes Claros) 2004; Prominent Businessman, Medal of the Trade Asscn of Minas Gerais 1970, 1975, Industrial Merit Badge 1976, Great Medal of the Inconfidência 1983, Santos Dumont Merit Medal 1985, Alferes Tiradentes Medal, Bicentennarian of the Inconfidência Mineira 1989, Commemorative Medal of the Day of the State of Minas Gerais 1989, Great Trade Merit Medal 1987, Municipal Merit Badge 2003, Public Prosecutor Ozanam Coelho Medal 2003, Great Necklace of Order of the Public Ministry of the Fed. Dist and Territories 2003, Legis. Municipal Great Merit Necklace, Municipal Chamber of Belo Horizonte 2003, Peacemaker's Medal 2003.
Address: Gabinete do Senador, Anexo II, 1 Andar, Gab. 57, Ala Senador Tancredo Neves, Senado Federal, 70165-900 Brasília (office); Companhia de Tecidos Norte de Minas—Coteminas, Matrix Unit, Av. Magalhaes Pinto, No. 4000, Bairro Planalto, 39404-166 Montes Claros, MG, Brazil (office). *Telephone:* (38) 3215-7777 (office). *Fax:* (38) 3217-1633 (office). *E-mail:* jose.alencar@senado.gov.br (office).

ALEXANDER, Héctor, MA, PhD; Panamanian economist and politician; *Minister of the Economy and Finance; Education:* Univ. of Panama, Univ. of Chicago and Univ. of St Thomas, Fla, USA, Catholic Univ. of Chile. *Career:* Prof. of Microeconomics, Analysis and Project Evaluation, Faculty of Econs, Univ. of Panama; Prof. of Accounting and Microeconomics, Panama Canal Coll.; mem. Tech. Comm. for Incentives to Exports, Ministry of Commerce and Industries; Expositor, Seminar on Economy for Journalists, organized by Repub. Nat. Bank 1976; fmr Minister of Planning and Political Economy; fmr Minister for External Relations; fmr Minister of Property and Treasury; fmr Minister in charge of Commerce and Industry; Sub-Gerente, Zona Libre de Colón; Minister of the Economy and Finance 2007–; Econ. Adviser, Superior Direction, Interoceanica Regional Authority (ARI), Dir of Tech. Planning; mem. of team that negotiated Torrijos-Carter Treaty concerning econ. position of Panama.
Address: Ministry of the Economy and Finance, Edif. Ogawa, Vía España, Apdo 5245, Panamá 5, Panama (office). *Telephone:* 507-7008 (office). *E-mail:* prensa@mef.gob.pa (office). *Website:* www.mef.gob.pa (office).

ALEXEEVA, Ludmilla; Russian human rights activist; *Chairwoman and President, Moscow Helsinki Group; Career:* forced to immigrate to USA in 1977, returned to Russia 1993; co-f. Moscow Helsinki Group, currently Chair. and Pres.; Pres. Int. Helsinki Fed. 1996–2004; mem. Presidential Council on Assistance of Insts of Civil Society and Human Rights; Co-Chair All-Russia Civil Congress; Olof Palme Prize (Jtly) 2004, Human Rights Award, Human Rights First 2005. *Publications include:* Soviet Dissent 1985.
Address: Moscow Helsinki Group, 107045 Moscow, Grand Golovin per, Bldg 22, p 1, Russia (office). *Telephone:* (495) 207-60-69 (office). *E-mail:* mhg-main@online.ptt.ru (office). *Website:* www.mhg.ru (office).

ALFARARGI, Saad; Egyptian diplomatist; *Head, Permanent Delegation and Permanent Observer of the League of Arab States, United Nations, Geneva; Career:* Personal Rep. of Pres. of Egypt to Group of Fifteen (G-15) and Adviser to Prime Minister 1990–95; Asst Admin. and Regional Dir of Regional Bureau for Arab States, UNDP, New York 1995–97; currently Head, Permanent Delegation and Permanent Observer of the League of Arab States, UN, Geneva.
Address: League of Arab States (LAS), rue du Valais 9, 1202 Geneva, Switzerland (office). *Telephone:* 227323030 (office). *Fax:* 227316947 (office). *E-mail:* delegation@bluewin.ch (office). *Website:* www.arableagueonline.org (office).

ALHEGELAN, Sheikh Faisal Abdul Aziz; Saudi Arabian diplomatist; b. 7 Oct. 1929, Jeddah; m. Nouha Tarazi 1961; three s. *Education:* Faculty of Law, Fouad Univ., Cairo. *Career:* Ministry of Foreign Affairs 1952–54; served in Embassy in Washington, DC 1954–58; Chief of Protocol in Ministry 1958–60; Political Adviser to HM King Sa'ud 1960–61; Amb. to Spain 1961–68, to Venezuela and Argentina 1968–75, to Denmark 1975–76, to UK 1976–79, to USA 1979–83, to France 1996–2003; Minister of State and mem. Council of Ministers (Saudi Arabia) April–Sept. 1984, of Health 1984–96, Chair. Bd of Dirs, Saudi Red Crescent Soc. 1984–, Saudi Anti-Smoking Soc. 1985–; Chair. Bd of Trustees, Saudi Council for Health Specialties 1992–; Order of King Abdulaziz, Gran Cruz Cordon of King Abdul Aziz, Order of Isabela la Católica (Spain), Gran Cordón, Orden del Libertador (Venezuela), Grande Oficial, Orden Riobranco (Brazil), May Grand Decoration (Argentina); Hon. KBE.

Address: PO Box 25557, Riyadh 11576, Saudi Arabia.

ALI, Ahmad Mohamed, LLB, DPA; Saudi Arabian development banker; *Chairman of the Board of Executive Directors and President, Islamic Development Bank;* b. 13 April 1934, Medina; m. Ghada Mahmood Masri 1968; one s. three d. *Education:* Cairo Univ., Univ. of Michigan, New York State Univ. *Career:* Dir Scientific and Islamic Inst., Aden 1958–59; Deputy Rector King Abdul Aziz Univ., Jeddah 1967–72; Deputy Minister of Educ. for Tech. Affairs 1972–75; Pres. Islamic Devt Bank 1975–93, 1995–, currently also Chair. Bd of Exec. Dirs; Sec.-Gen. Muslim World League 1993–95; mem. King Abdul Aziz Univ. Council, King Saud Univ., Oil and Minerals Univ., Islamic Univ., Imam Mohammed Ben Saud Univ.; mem. Admin. Bd Saudi Credit Bank, Saudi Fund for Devt. *Publications:* numerous articles and working papers on Islamic econs, banking and educ. *Address:* Islamic Development Bank, PO Box 5925, Jeddah 21432, Saudi Arabia (office). *Telephone:* (2) 6361400 (office). *Fax:* (2) 6366871 (office). *E-mail:* idbarchives@isdb.org.sa (office). *Website:* www.isdb.org (office).

ALI, Amadou; Cameroonian politician; *Deputy Prime Minister; Career:* Sr Minister in charge of Justice 2000–04; Deputy Prime Minister 2004–; mem. Rassemblement démocratique du peuple camerounais (RDPC).
Address: c/o Office of the Prime Minister, Yaoundé, Cameroon (office). *Telephone:* 223-8005 (office). *Fax:* 223-5735 (office). *Website:* www.spm.gov.cm (office).

ALI, Amina Salum, MBA; Tanzanian politician and diplomatist; *Permanent Representative, Representational Mission to the United States, African Union;* b. 24 Oct. 1956, Zanzibar; m. Alimansour Vuai 1982; one s. four d. *Education:* Univs of Delhi and Pune, India. *Career:* Asst Dir Ministry of State Planning and Dir Foreign Trade, Ministry of Trade 1981–82; Planning Officer, Perm. Planning Comm. 1984–85; Deputy Minister of Finance, Econ. Affairs and Planning 1985–88, Minister of State in charge of Int. and Regional Co-operation, Ministry of Foreign Affairs 1988–90; Minister of Finance, Zanzibar 1996–2000; cand. for presidency of Zanzibar (semi-autonomous) 2000; Minister of State in the Chief Minister's Office –2006 (resgnd); Perm. Rep. of African Union Mission to US, Washington, DC 2006–; Deputy Chair. Org. of Women in Tanzania –2006; mem. Cen. Cttee, Chama Cha Mapinduzi (CCM—Revolutionary Party of Tanzania), Deputy Chair. CCM Women's Wing –2006.
Address: Representational Mission of the African Union to the United States, 1875 I Street, NW, Suite 575, Washington, DC 20006, USA (office). *Telephone:* (202) 429-7136 (office). *Fax:* (202) 429-7130 (office). *Website:* www.africa-union.org (office).

ALI, Brig.-Gen. Muhammad Nasser Ahmad; Yemeni army officer and government official. *Career:* Minister of Defence 2006–.
Address: Ministry of Defence, POB 4131, San'a, Yemen (office). *Telephone:* (1) 252640 (office). *Fax:* (1) 252375 (office).

ALI, Zine al Abidine Ben; Tunisian politician and head of state; *President;* b. 3 Sept. 1936, Hammam Sousse; m. Leila Ben Ali; three c. *Education:* as grad. in electronics, Saint-Cyr Military Acad. (France), Chalons-sur-Marne School of Artillery (France), Special School of Intelligence and Security (USA). *Career:* Head of Mil. Security 1958–74; Mil. and Naval Attaché, Rabat, Morocco 1974–77; mem. of Cabinet for Minister of Nat. Defence, Dir-Gen. Nat. Security 1977–80; Amb. to Poland 1980–84; Sec. of State for Nat. Security 1984–85, Minister of the Interior 1986–87, Minister of State for the Interior May–Nov. 1987, Pres. of Tunisia Nov. 1987–; mem. politbureau of Parti Socialiste Destourien (PSD) 1986, Sec.-Gen. PSD 1986, Chair. Rassemblement Constitutionnel Démocratique (RCD); Order of Merit of Bourguiba, Order of Independence, Order of the Repub., several foreign orders.
Address: Présidence de la République, Palais de Carthage, Tunis, Tunisia. *Website:* www.carthage.tn (office).

ALIM, Abdullah bin Abd ar-Rahman; Saudi Arabian diplomatist; *Ambassador to Oman; Career:* fmr Amb. to Indonesia, currently Amb. to Oman. *Address:* Embassy of Saudi Arabia, Diplomatic City, Jamiat ad-Dowal al-Arabiya, POB 1411, Ruwi 112, Oman (office). *Telephone:* 24601744 (office). *Fax:* 24603540 (office). *E-mail:* omemb@mofa.gov.sa (office). *Website:* www.mofa.gov.sa (office).

ALITI, Abdiraman; Macedonian diplomatist; *Ambassador to Bulgaria; Career:* fmr mem. Parl., Deputy Speaker 1995; Leader, Albanian Party for Democratic Prosperity 1996–2003; Amb. to Bulgaria (also accred to Moldova) 2005–.
Address: Embassy of Former Yugoslav Republic of Macedonia, ul. F. Zh. Kyuri 17/2/1, 1113 Sofia, Bulgaria (office). *Telephone:* (2) 870-15-60 (office). *Fax:* (2) 971-28-32 (office). *E-mail:* todmak@bgnet.bg (office).

ALIYEV, İlham Heydar oğlu; Azerbaijani business executive, politician and head of state; *President;* b. 24 Dec. 1961, Baku; one s. two d. *Education:* Moscow State Univ. of Int. Relations. *Career:* teacher, Moscow State Univ. of Int. Relations 1985–90; engaged in commercial activity in Moscow and İstanbul following collapse of USSR 1991–94; First Vice-Pres. SOCAR (State Oil Co.) 1994–2003; mem. Parl. 1995–2003; Deputy Chair. Yeni Azerbaijan (New Azerbaijan Party) 1999–2001, First Deputy Chair. 2001–; Prime Minister of Azerbaijan Aug. 2003; Pres. of Azerbaijan Oct. 2003–; Pres. Nat. Olympic Cttee 1997–; Leader Del. to Council of Europe; Hon. Prof. L.N.Gumilev Eurasian Nat. Univ., Kazakhstan, Univ. of Nat. and World Economy, Bulgaria, Moscow State Univ. Order of Heydar Aliyev, of Sheikhulislam (Azerbaijan), Order of The Star of Romania, Order of King Abdul Aziz (Saudi Arabia), Order of Honour (Georgia), Grand Cross, Legion d'honneur, Grand Cross of Order of Merit (Poland); Dr hc (Lincoln Univ., USA, Moscow State Univ., Bilkent Univ., Turkey, Nat. Acad. of Taxes, Ukraine, Petroleum and Gas Univ. of Ploesti, Romania, Kyung Hee Univ., South Korea, Jordan Univ., Corvinus Univ., Hungary); PACE Medal 2004, Ihsan Dogramacı Prize for Int. Relations for Peace (Turkey). *Address:* Office of the President, 1066 Baku, İstiqlaliyet küç. 19, Azerbaijan (office). *Telephone:* (12) 492-17-26 (office). *Fax:* (12) 492-35-43 (office). *E-mail:* office@apparat.gov.az (office). *Website:* www.ilham-aliyev.com (office); www.president.az (office).

ALIYEV, Mukhu Gimbatovich, PhD; Russian/Dagestan politician; *President, Republic of Dagestan;* b. 6 Aug. 1940, Tanusi, Dagestan; m.; two c. *Education:* Dagestan State Univ. *Career:* began career as teacher, then Head Nizhne-Gakvarinskaya Secondary School; Sec. Comsomol Cttee, Dagestan State Univ. 1964–66; First Sec. Makhachkala City Comsomol Cttee 1969–72, Makhachkala Dist CPSU Cttee 1972–85; Bureau Head Dagestan Div. CPSU Cttee 1985–90; First Sec. Dagestan Repub. CPSU Cttee 1990–91; mem. Supreme Soviet of Dagestan (parl.), Vice-Chair. 1991–95; Chair. Econs Cttee, Repub. of Dagestan 1992–94; Chair. Peoples' Ass., Repub. of Dagestan 1999–2006, Pres. of Dagestan 2006–; mem. Council of Feds of Russia 1995–, Deputy Chair. Cttee on Foreign Affairs 1995–2001; fmr mem. Parl. Ass., CIS and Council of Europe; Labour Red Banner 1976, Badge of Honour 1981, For Services to Motherland, class IV 2000, class III 2005. *Publications:* Dagestan Republic: Priorities of National Policy 1996, Unity and Integrity of Dagestan Republic as a Constitutional Principle 1998, Searching for Consent 2002; numerous articles in magazines and journals. *Address:* House of Government, 1 Lenin Square, 367005 Makhachkala, Dagestan (office); 33/1a Korkmasov Street, 367005 Makhachkala, Dagestan, Russia (home). *Telephone:* (8722) 67-30-60 (office); (8722) 67-30-59 (office); (8722) 67-04-96 (home). *Fax:* (8722) 67-30-61 (office). *E-mail:* president@e-dag.ru (office). *Website:* www.president.e-dag.ru (office).

ALIYEV, Namiq, DSc; Azerbaijani diplomatist; *Ambassador to Georgia; Career:* fmr Counsellor, Ministry of Justice; Amb. to Georgia 2006–. *Address:* Embassy of Azerbaijan, 0177 Tbilisi, Nutsubidze 47, Georgia (office). *Telephone:* (32) 25-26-39 (office). *Fax:* (32) 25-00-13 (office). *E-mail:* secretariat@azembassy.ge (office). *Website:* www.azembassy.ge (office).

ALIYEV, Yashar Teymur oglu; Azerbaijani diplomatist; *Ambassador to USA;* b. Aug. 1955; m.; two c. *Education:* Azerbaijan State Univ., Russian Acad. of Sciences, Diplomatic Acad., Moscow. *Career:* Research Fellow, Oriental Studies Inst., Azerbaijan Acad. of Sciences 1979–89; joined Ministry of Foreign Affairs, Baku 1989, positions include Second Sec. 1989, First Sec. 1990, with Dept of Information and Political Analysis 1992, Head Dept of Int. Orgs 1992, joined Perm. Mission to UN, New York, USA 1992, served as Counsellor on Political Affairs 1992–93, 1994–2001, Chargé d'affaires a.i. 1993–94, 2001–02, Perm. Rep. 2002–06, Vice-Pres. UN Conf. on the Illicit Trade in Small Arms and Light Weapons in All Its Aspects 2001, Vice-Pres. 59th Session of Gen. Ass., Vice-Pres. Econ. and Social Council 2004–05, Chair. Fourth Cttee (Special Political and Decolonization) 2005–06, participated in Soviet trade and tech. missions to Iraq 1977–79, and Kuwait 1985–87, Amb. to USA 2006–. *Address:* Embassy of Azerbaijan, 2741 34th Street, NW, Washington DC, 20008, USA (office). *Telephone:* (202) 337-3500 (office). *Fax:* (202) 337-5911 (office). *E-mail:* azerbaijan@azembassy.com (office). *Website:* azembassy.com (office).

ALKALAJ, Sven, MS; Bosnia and Herzegovina diplomatist and politician; *Minister of Foreign Affairs;* b. 11 Nov. 1948, Sarajevo; m.; two c. *Education:* Univ. of Sarajevo and Harvard Univ. *Career:* Commercial Man., Petrolinvest, Sarajevo 1975–85; Regional Man. for Middle and Far East Energoinvest, Sarajevo 1985–88; Man. Dir Energoinvest–Thailand 1988–94; Amb. to USA 1994–2000, to OAS 2000–04, to Belgium 2004–07, to NATO 2004–07; Minister of Foreign Affairs 2007–; mem. Party for Bosnia-Herzegovina (SBiH); Silver Badge of Petrolinvest 1994, Sloboda Award. *Address:* Ministry of Foreign Affairs, 71000 Sarajevo, Musala 2, Bosnia and Herzegovina (office). *Telephone:* (33) 281100 (office). *Fax:* (33) 472188 (office). *E-mail:* info@mvp.gov.ba (office). *Website:* www.mvp.gov.ba (office).

ALLAF, Gen. Mohammed al-, BSc, MSc; Jordanian diplomatist and fmr army officer; *Permanent Representative, United Nations;* b. 1950, Amman; m.; five c. *Education:* Mu'ta Univ., Nat. Defense Univ., Washington, DC. *Career:* joined army 1969, Commdr Mil. contingent to UN Angola Verification Mission (UNAVEM I and II) 1989–91, Asst Chief of Staff and Chief of Strategic Planning 2006–2007; Commdt Royal Jordanian Nat. Defence Coll. 2002–06; Perm. Rep. to UN, New York 2007–. *Address:* Permanent Mission of Jordan to the United Nations, 866 United Nations Plaza, Suite 552, New York, NY 10017, USA (office). *Telephone:* (212) 832-9553 (office). *Fax:* (212) 832-5346 (office). *E-mail:* jordan@un.int (office).

ALLAWI, Ali Abdel-Amir, SB, MBA; Iraqi government official and business executive; b. 1947. *Education:* MIT, Harvard Business School, USA. *Career:* fmr consultant to World Bank and Head, Pan-Arab investment co.; Prof., Univ. of Oxford, UK –2003; Minister of Trade and Minister of Defence, Interim Iraq Governing Council 2003–04, Minister of Finance, Iraqi Transitional Govt 2005–06, then Sr Adviser to Prime Minister of Iraq; mem. United Iraqi Alliance. *Publication:* The Occupation of Iraq: Winning the War, Losing the Peace 2007. *Address:* c/o Ministry of Finance, Khulafa Street, nr ar-Russafi Square, Baghdad, Iraq (office).

ALLÈGRE, Maurice Marie, LenD; French research co-ordinator and business executive; b. 16 Feb. 1933, Antibes; m. Catherine Pierre 1962; one s. one d. *Education:* Ecole Polytechnique, Ecole Nat. Supérieure des Mines and Ecole Nat. Supérieure du Pétrole et des Moteurs, Faculté de Droit. *Career:* Engineer, Direction des Carburants, Ministry of Industry 1957–62; Dir Mines de l'Organisme Saharien 1962–64; Tech. Adviser to Ministry of Finance and Econ. Affairs 1965–67; Délégué à l'Informatique and Pres. Inst. de Recherche d'Informatique et d'Automatique 1968–74; Chief of Nickel Mission to New Caledonia 1975; Asst Dir-Gen. Inst. Français du Pétrole 1976–81; Pres. and Dir-Gen. ISIS 1976–81; Pres. FRANLAB, COFLEXIP 1976–81; Pres. Agence Nat. de Valorisation et de la Recherche (ANVAR) 1982–84; Dir Scientific and Tech. Devt, Ministry of Research and Tech. 1982–84; Dir-Gen. Bureau de Recherches Géologiques et Minières 1984–88, Pres. 1988–92; Pres. Nat. Agency for Man. of Radioactive Waste (ANDRA) 1993–98; Pres. Sicav Vauban 1998–2000; Pres. AGRER Asscn 1998–; consultant on energy policy and radioactive waste 1998–; Chevalier, Légion d'honneur; Officier Ordre Nat. du Mérite. *Address:* 85 rue de Sèvres, 75006 Paris; 50 boulevard d'Aguillon, 06600 Antibes, France. *Telephone:* 1-45-44-94-51 (office).

ALLEN, Bernadette Mary, BA, MA; American diplomatist; *Ambassador to Niger;* b. Washington, DC. *Education:* Central Coll., Pella, Ia, Univ. of Paris (Sorbonne), France, George Washington Univ. *Career:* career Foreign Service officer, State Dept since 1980, has served in Bureau for Asian and African Affairs, Bureau for Western Hemisphere Affairs, Bureau for the Americas, Gen. Services Officer/Vice-Consul, Embassy in Bujumbura, Burundi 1980–82, Consul, Embassy in Manila 1982–84, Consul, Consulate in Fukuoka, Japan 1984, Desk Officer, Africa Bureau's Regional Affairs Office 1985–87, Visa Officer, Visa Office Coordination Div. 1985–89, Mandarin language training, Nat. Foreign Affairs Training Center (NFATC) 1989, in Taipei, Taiwan 1990, Consular Section Chief, Consulate Gen., Guangzhou, China 1991–94, Deputy Dir Consular Training, NFATC 1994–96, Legis. Man. Officer 1996–98, Dir Visa Office Coordination Div. 1998–2000, Chief of Montreal Consular Section 2000–02, Consul Gen., Consulate Gen., Montreal 2002–05, Amb. to Niger 2006–; fmr volunteer, Big Sisters of the Washington, DC Metropolitan area; fmr Usher Bd Chair. Carmody Hills Baptist Church, Seat Pleasant, Md; fmr Pres. Central Coll. African-American Student Org.; Life mem. US Tennis Asscn; awards include Superior Honor Award for leadership as Consul Gen. in Montreal, Meritorious Honor Award for outstanding managerial and professional skills in Guangzhou, Superior Honor Award for outstanding leadership and performance as Visa Coordination Div. Dir. *Address:* Embassy of the USA, rue des Ambassades, BP 11201, Niamey, Niger (office). *Telephone:* 73-31-69 (office). *Fax:* 73-55-60 (office). *E-mail:* NiameyPASN@state.gov (office). *Website:* niamey.usembassy.gov (office).

ALLENDE KARAM, Isabel; Cuban diplomatist and academic; *Rector, El Instituto Superior de Relaciones Internacionales; Education:* Univ. of Havana. *Career:* joined Ministry of Foreign Relations 1963, held numerous positions including Czechoslovakia specialist 1967–69, Head, Socialist

Countries of Cen. Europe Dept 1969–79, USSR Dept 1979–82, Ministra Consejera, Embassy in Moscow 1986–88, Amb. to Poland 1988–91, to Spain 1999–2004; Rector, El Instituto Superior de Relaciones Internacionales, Havana 2005–; Medalla 40 Aniversario de las FAR, Medalla Enrique Hart, Medalla 23 de agosto, Medalla Felix Elmuza, Medalla por los 25 años de la Unión Arabe de Cuba, Medalla de la Ciudad de Guanabacoa. *Address:* El Instituto Superior de Relaciones Internacionales, Calzada no. 308, entre H e I, Vedado Municipio Plaza de la Revolución, 28036 Havana, Cuba (office). *Telephone:* (7) 55-1608 (office). *E-mail:* isabelallende@isri .minrex.gov.cu (office). *Website:* www.isri.cu (office).

ALLEYNE, Sir George, Kt, MD, FRCP; Barbadian physician; *Special Envoy of the Secretary-General for HIV/AIDS in the Caribbean, United Nations;* b. 7 Oct. 1932, Barbados; m. Sylvan I. Chen 1958; two s. one d. *Education:* Harrison Coll., Univ. of the West Indies. *Career:* Sr Resident, Univ. Hosp. of the W Indies 1963; Research Fellow, Tropical Metabolism Research Unit, Jamaica 1964–72. Prof. of Medicine, Univ. of the W Indies 1972–81, Chair. Dept of Medicine 1976–81; Head Research Unit, Pan American Health Org. 1981–83, Dir Health Programmes 1982–90, Asst Dir 1990–95, Dir 1995–2003, Dir Emer. 2003–; Special Envoy of the UN Sec.-Gen. for HIV/AIDS in the Caribbean 2003–; Chancellor Univ. of the West Indies 2003–; Order of the Caribbean Community 2001; Hon. DSc (Univ. of the W Indies) 1988. *Publications include:* The Importance of Health: A Caribbean Perspective 1989, Public Health for All 1991, Health and Tourism 1992; over 100 articles in major scientific research journals. *Address:* Pan American Health Organization, 525 23rd Street, NW, Washington, DC 20037, USA (office); Special Envoy of the UN Secretary-General for HIV/AIDS in the Caribbean, UNAIDS, 20 avenue Appia, 1211 Geneva 27, Switzerland (office). *Telephone:* (202) 974-3057 (Washington) (office). *Fax:* (202) 974-3677 (Washington) (office).

ALLIN, Dana H., BA, MA, PhD; American academic; *Carol Deane Senior Fellow for Transatlantic Affairs, International Institute for Strategic Studies (IISS); Education:* Yale Univ., Johns Hopkins Univ., Nitze School of Advanced Int. Studies (SAIS). *Career:* Visiting Asst Prof., European Studies and American Foreign Policy, SAIS centres, Bologna, Italy and Washington DC; Deputy Dir, Aspen Inst., Berlin, Deputy Dir, Int. Comm. on Balkans; Carol Deane Sr Fellow for Transatlantic Affairs, IISS 1997–, Ed. Survival (journal); Robert Bosch Foundation Fellow. *Publications include:* Cold War Illusions: America, Europe and Soviet Power 1969–1989 1994, NATO's Balkan Interventions, Adelphi Paper 347 2002, Unfinished Peace: Report of the International Commission on the Balkans (co-author); numerous articles in newspapers and journals, including commentary in The International Herald Tribune, Wall Street Journal, Financial Times and Frankfurter Allgemeine Zeitung. *Address:* International Institute for Strategic Studies (IISS), Arundel House, 13–15 Arundel Street, Temple Place, London, WC2R 3DX, England (office). *Telephone:* (20) 7379-7676 (office). *Fax:* (20) 7836-3108 (office). *E-mail:* allin@iiss.org (office); survival@iiss.org (office). *Website:* www.iiss.org (office); www.tandf.co.uk/journals/titles/00396338.asp.

ALLISON, Graham Tillett, Jr, AB, MA, PhD; American academic and government official; *Douglas Dillon Professor of Government and Director, Belfer Center for Science and International Affairs, Harvard University;* b. 23 March 1940, Charlotte, NC; m. Elisabeth K. Smith 1968. *Education:* Davidson Coll. and Harvard and Oxford Univs. *Career:* Instructor of Govt, Harvard Univ. 1967–68, Asst Prof. of Govt 1968–70, Assoc. Prof. of Politics 1970–72, Prof. of Politics 1972–93, Assoc. Dean and Chair. Public Policy Program, John F. Kennedy School of Govt 1975–77, Dean and Don K. Price Prof. of Politics, John F. Kennedy School of Govt 1977–89, Douglas Dillon Prof. of Govt, John F. Kennedy School of Govt 1989–; Asst Sec. of Defense for Policy and Plans, Dept of Defense, Washington, DC 1993–94; Dir Belfer Center for Science and Int. Affairs, John F. Kennedy School of Govt 1994–; numerous professional appointments; Hon. DPhil (Uppsala Univ.) 1979, Hon. DLaws (Davidson Coll.) 1985, (Univ. of NC at Wilmington) 1992. *Publications include:* Essence of Decision: Explaining the Cuban Missile Crisis 1971, Sharing International Responsibilities: A Report to the Trilateral Commission 1983; co-author: Hawks, Doves and Owls: An Agenda for Avoiding Nuclear War 1985, Fateful Visions: Avoiding Nuclear Catastrophe 1988, Windows of Opportunity: From Cold War to Peaceful Competition 1989, Window of Opportunity: The Grand Bargain for Democracy in the Soviet Union 1991, Beyond Cold War to Trilateral Cooperation in the Asia-Pacific Region 1992, Avoiding Nuclear Anarchy 1996, America's Achilles Heel: Nuclear, Biological, and Chemical Terrorism and Covert Attack 1998, Catastrophic Terrorism 1998, Realizing Human Rights: Moving from Inspiration to Impact 2000, Nuclear Terrorism: The Ultimate Preventable Catastrophe 2004. *Address:* Belfer Center for Science and International Affairs, 79 JFK Street, Cambridge, MA 02138 (office); 69 Pinehurst Road, Belmont, MA 02478-

1502, USA (home). *Telephone:* (617) 496-6099 (office). *Fax:* (617) 495-1905 (office). *E-mail:* graham_allison@harvard.edu (office). *Website:* bcsia.ksg .harvard.edu (office).

ALLISON, Roy, DPhil; British academic; *Senior Lecturer, Department of International Relations, London School of Economics;* b. London; m.; one d. *Education:* Univs of Exeter and Oxford. *Career:* Sr Assoc. Mem., St Antony's Coll., Oxford 1993–95, 2001–05; Sr Lecturer, Int. Security Policy, Centre for Russian and E European Studies, Univ. of Birmingham 1992–99; Head, Russia and Eurasia Programme, Royal Inst. of Int. Affairs (now Chatham House) 1993–2005; Sr Research Fellow, Centre for Int. Studies, Univ. of Oxford 2001–05; Sr Lecturer, Dept of Int. Relations, LSE 2005–; Kt (First Class), Order of the Lion of Finland 2002. *Publications include:* Finland's Relations with the Soviet Union, 1944–82 1983, The Soviet Union and the Strategy of Non-Alignment in the Third World 1988, Radical Reform in Soviet Defence Policy (ed.) 1991, Military Forces in the Soviet Successor States 1993, Peacekeeping in the Soviet Successor States 1994, Internal Factors in Russian Foreign Policy (co-author) 1996, Challenges for the Former Soviet Union (ed.) 1996, Security Dilemmas in Russia and Eurasia (co-ed.) 1998, Central Asian Security – The New International Context (co-ed.) 2001, Putin's Russia and the Enlarged Europe (co-author) 2006. *Address:* Department of International Relations, London School of Economics, Houghton Street, London, WC2A 2AE, England (office). *Telephone:* (20) 7955-7958 (office); (20) 7955-7561 (out of hours) (office). *Fax:* (20) 7955-7446 (office). *E-mail:* r.allison@lse.ac.uk (office). *Website:* www.lse.ac.uk/Depts/intrel (office).

ALMANSOOR, Tawfeeq Ahmed Khalil; Bahraini diplomatist; *Permanent Representative, United Nations;* b. 14 Nov. 1957; m.; three d. *Education:* St John's Univ., New York, Acad. of Int. Law, The Hague, Cairo Univ. *Career:* First Sec., Bahrain Embassy, Washington, DC 1990–94, First Sec. UN, New York 1995–99, Deputy Chief Bahrain Embassy, Cairo 1999–2001; Amb. to Russia 2001–03; Perm. Rep. to UN, New York 2003–. *Address:* Permanent Mission of Bahrain to the UN, 866 Second Avenue, 14th/15th Floor, New York, NY 10017, USA (office). *Telephone:* (212) 223-6200 (office). *Fax:* (212) 319-0687 (office). *E-mail:* bahrain@un.int (office). *Website:* www.un.int/bahrain (office).

ALMUNIA AMANN, Joaquín; Spanish politician; *Commissioner for Economic and Monetary Affairs, European Commission;* b. 1948, Bilbao; m.; two c. *Education:* Univ. of Deusto. *Career:* economist, various Spanish chambers of commerce in mem. countries of EEC; econ. adviser to Exec. Cttee, Unión General de Trabajo; Sec. for trade union relations, then Head of Dept of Research and Planning, then Head of Perm. Cttee for Political Man., Partido Socialista Obrero Español 1981, Sec.-Gen. 1997–2000; Minister of Labour and Social Security 1982–86; Minister of Public Admin 1987–91; Pres. Socialist Parl. Group 1994–2000, Budget Cttee Congreso de los Diputados 2000; EU Commr for Econ. and Monetary Affairs 2004–. *Publication:* Memorias Políticas 2001. *Address:* Rue de la Loi 200, 1049 Brussels, Belgium (office); Carrera de San Jerónimo, s/n 28014 Madrid, Spain (office). *E-mail:* joaquin.almunia@ diputado.congreso.esp (office). *Website:* europa.eu (office); www.almunia .com (office).

ALOBIDI, Abdulati Ibrahim; Libyan diplomatist. *Career:* Sec. (Amb.), People's Bureau in Rome, Italy –2006; Sec. for European Affairs Minister 2006. *Address:* c/o General People's Committee for Foreign Liaison and International Co-operation, Tripoli, Libya (office).

ALOGOSKOUFIS, Georgios, MSc, PhD; Greek politician; *Minister of the Economy and Finance;* b. 17 Oct. 1955, Athens; m. Dika Agapitidou; one s. two d. *Education:* Univ. of Athens, London School of Econs, UK. *Career:* Researcher Centre of Labour Finance, LSE and Centre for Econ. Policy Research, London 1981–82; Reader and Lecturer, Univ. of London 1984–92; Counsellor, EC 1989–90, World Bank 1991–92; Pres. Council of Financial Experts (SOE), Ministry of Nat. Economy 1992–93; Pres. Inst. of Econ. Studies 1994–96; elected mem. Parl. 1996, mem. Parl. Cttee for Econ. Relations 1996–2004, Parl. Speaker for Political Economy 1997–2004; Minister of the Economy and Finance 2004–; mem. Exec. Bd European Econ. Asscn 1994–98; Sayers Prize, Univ. of London 1981. *Publications:* La Drachme: du Phoenix à l'euro (Acad. of Athens Prize) 2002. *Address:* Ministry of the Economy and Finance, Odos Nikis 5–7, 101 80 Athens, Greece (office). *Telephone:* (210) 3332613 (office). *Fax:* (210) 3332611 (office). *E-mail:* minister@mnec.gr (office). *Website:* www.mnec .gr (office); www.alogoskoufis.gr (home).

ALOIS PHILIPP MARIA, Hereditary Prince, LLM; Liechtenstein royal; *Permanent Representative of the Head of State;* b. 11 June 1968, Zürich,

Switzerland; m. Duchess Sophie in Bavaria 1993; three s. one d. *Education:* Liechtenstein Grammar School, RMA, Sandhurst, England and Salzburg Univ., Austria. *Career:* heir to the throne of Liechtenstein; commissioned Second Lt, Coldstream Guards, Hong Kong and London 1988; swore Oath of Allegiance to Constitution alongside his father 1990; worked for auditing firm, London 1993–96; returned to live in Vaduz and given responsibility for various sections of the royal assets; apptd perm. rep. for exercising his father's sovereign powers 15 Aug. 2004.
Address: Fürstenhaus von Liechtenstein, Schloss Vaduz, Vaduz 9490, Liechtenstein (office). *Telephone:* 2381200 (office). *Fax:* 2381201 (office). *E-mail:* office@sfl.li (office). *Website:* www.fuerstenhaus.li (office).

ALOR KOL, Deng; Sudanese politician; *Minister of Foreign Affairs; Career:* fmr Commdr, Sudan People's Liberation Army (SPLA); attended peace talks in Nairobi 1994; fmr Minister of Cabinet Affairs, Minister of Foreign Affairs 2007–; mem. Sudan People's Liberation Movt (SPLM).
Address: Ministry of Foreign Affairs, POB 873, Khartoum, Sudan (office). *Telephone:* (183) 773101 (office). *Fax:* (183) 772941 (office). *E-mail:* ministry@mfa.gov.sd (office). *Website:* www.mfa.gov.sd (office).

ALPOGAN, Mehmet Yiğit; Turkish diplomatist; *Ambassador to UK;* b. 1945, Odemis township; m.; two c. *Education:* Ankara Univ. *Career:* joined Ministry of Foreign Affairs as diplomatic cand. 1968, worked at Embassy in Tokyo 1972, in Lefkose (Nicosia) 1975, Head of Cyprus Br., Cyprus-Greece Gen. Directorate 1977, Amb.-Under-Sec., Athens 1991, Amb. to Turkmenistan 1995, fmr Amb., Maritime and Aviation Gen. Directorate and dual political relations, Asst Adviser, Ministry of Foreign Affairs 2000, Amb. to Greece 2001–04, to UK 2007–; Sec.-Gen. Nat. Security Council (MGK) (first civilian) 2004–07.
Address: Embassy of Turkey, 43 Belgrave Square, London SW1X 8PA, England (office). *Telephone:* (20) 7393-0202 (office). *Fax:* (20) 7393-0066 (office). *E-mail:* turkish.emb@btclick.com (office). *Website:* www .turkishembassylondon.org (office).

ALPTUNA, Akin, BA, PhD; Turkish diplomatist; m. Esin Alptuna. *Education:* Ankara Univ. *Career:* Deputy Head of Mission, Turkish Perm. Del. to UN, returned to Ministry of Foreign Affairs, Ankara to become Dir-Gen. for the EU, Amb. to OECD –2000, Deputy Under-Sec. responsible for EU Affairs 2000–03, Amb. to UK 2003–07.
Address: Ministry of Foreign Affairs, Dişişleri Bakanlığı, Dr Sadık Ahmet Cad. 12, 06100, Balgat, Ankara, Turkey (office). *Telephone:* (312) 2921000 (office). *Fax:* (312) 2873869 (office). *E-mail:* webmaster@mfa.gov.tr (office). *Website:* www.mfa.gov.tr (office).

ALSTON, Philip, BComm, LLM, JSD; Australian academic; *Professor of Law, New York University;* b. 23 Jan. 1950, Melbourne. *Education:* Univ. of Melbourne, Univ. of California, Berkeley, USA. *Career:* Lecturer and Visiting Prof., Harvard Law School 1984–89, 1993; Assoc. Prof. of Int. Law, Fletcher School of Law and Diplomacy, Tufts Univ., Boston 1985–89; Prof. of Law and Foundation Dir, Centre for Int. and Public Law, ANU 1989–95; Helen L. Deroy Visiting Prof. of Law, Univ. of Mich. 1993; Prof. of Int. Law, European Univ. Inst. 1996–2001, Co-Dir Acad. of European Law 1996–2001, Head of Law Dept 1997–98; Visiting Prof., Woodruff Chair of Int. Law, Univ. of Georgia 2000–01; Prof. of Law, New York Univ. 2001–; Chief of Staff to Cabinet Minister, Australia, 1974–75; Human Rights Officer, UN Centre for Human Rights 1978–1984; Sr Legal Adviser to UNICEF 1984–92; Discrimination Commr for ACT 1992–94; rapporteur, UN Cttee on Econ., Social and Cultural Rights, 1987–90, Chair. 1991–98; UN Special Rapporteur on Extrajudicial, Summary or Arbitrary Executions 2004–; rapporteur, Meeting of Chairs of UN Human Rights Treaty Bodies, 1988, 1990, 1992, 1997–98, Chair. 1990, 1993, 1997–98; mem. Tech. Advisory Group, UN study on Impact of Armed Conflict on Children 1995–97; ind. expert reporting on effectiveness of UN Human Rights Bodies, reports submitted 1989, 1993, 1997; Co-Ed. Australian Yearbook of Int. Law 1991–96, Ed.-in-Chief European Journal of International Law 1996–; Series Co-Ed. Collected Courses of the Academy of European Law 1998–; mem. editorial and advisory bds of numerous int. journals on law and human rights; Chair. Coordinating Cttee for UN Human Rights Special Procedures 2005–06. *Publications include:* The Future of UN Human Rights Treaty Monitoring (co-ed.) 2000, International Human Rights in Context: Law, Politics, Morals (with H. Steiner) 2000, Peoples' Rights (ed. and contrib.) 2001, Economic and Social Rights: A Bibliography 2005, The United Nations and Human Rights: A Critical Appraisal (ed. and contrib.) 2005, Human Rights and Development (ed.) 2005, Neglected Rights 2006; over 100 articles in journals on law and human rights.
Address: New York University School of Law, Vanderbilt Hall, 40 Washington Square South, Room 305, New York, NY 10012-1099, USA (office). *Telephone:* (212) 998-6173 (office). *E-mail:* philip.alston@nyu.edu (office). *Website:* www.law.nyu.edu (office).

ALSTON, Hon. Richard Kenneth Robert, BA, BCom, MBA, LLM; Australian diplomatist, politician and business executive; b. 19 Dec. 1941, brother of Philip Alston; m. Margaret Mary Alston; two c. *Education:* Xavier Coll., Melbourne, Melbourne and Monash Univs. *Career:* Senator for Vic. 1986–2004; Shadow Minister for Communications 1989–90, for Social Security, Child Care and Retirement Incomes 1990–92, for Social Security, Child Care and Superannuation 1992, for Superannuation and Child Care and Shadow Minister Assisting Leader on Social Policy 1992–93, for Communications and the Arts 1994–96; Minister for Communications and the Arts 1996–2003, for Information Tech. 1998–2003; High Commr to UK 2005–08; Deputy Leader of Opposition in Senate 1993–96, of Govt in Senate 1996–2005; Deputy Chair. Senate Standing Cttee on Legal and Constitutional Affairs 1986, Jt Parl. Cttee on Nat. Crime Authority 1987; mem. Senate Standing Cttee on Finance and Public Admin 1987; State Pres. Liberal Party Vic. Div. 1979–82; mem. Amnesty Int. Parl. Group; Nat. Chair. Australian Council for Overseas Aid 1978–83; Chair. Afghan-Australia Council 1987–90; Fed. Pres. UNA of Australia 1977–79; Gov. Nat. Gallery of Australia Foundation; Adjunct Prof., Faculty of Information Tech., Bond Univ., Queensland; mem. Bell Shakespeare Foundation, Melba Foundation; Fellow, Inst. of Dirs 1983–88.
Address: c/o Department of Foreign Affairs and Trade, R. G. Casey Building, John McEwen Crescent, Barton, ACT 0221, Australia. *Telephone:* (2) 6261-1111.

ALTANGEREL, Bulgaa; Mongolian diplomatist; *Ambassador to UK;* m. Erdenee Chuluuntsetseg. *Career:* fmr Dir-Gen. Law and Treaty Dept, Ministry of Foreign Affairs; fmr Amb. to Belgium, Amb. to UK (also accred to Ireland) 2008–; mem. Bd of Dirs Trust Fund for Victims, Int. Criminal Court 2007–.
Address: Embassy of Mongolia, 7 Kensington Court, London, W8 5DL, England (office). *Telephone:* (20) 7937-0150 (office). *Fax:* (20) 7937-1117 (office). *E-mail:* office@embassyofmongolia.co.uk (office). *Website:* www .embassyofmongolia.co.uk (office).

ALTERMAN, Jon B., AB, PhD; American academic and research institute director; *Director and Senior Fellow, Middle East Program, Center for Strategic and International Studies; Education:* Woodrow Wilson School of Public and Int. Affairs, Princeton Univ., Harvard Univ. *Career:* teacher at Harvard 1993–97; fmr Legis. Aide to the late Senator Daniel P. Moynihan; Program Officer, Research and Studies, US Inst. of Peace; Soref Fellow, Washington Inst. for Near E Policy; mem. Policy Planning Staff, US State Dept, Special Asst to Sec. of State for Near Eastern Affairs; Dir and Sr Fellow, Middle East Program, Center for Strategic and Int. Studies 2002–; mem. Editorial Bds Middle East Journal, Transnational Broadcasting Studies; mem. Editorial Advisory Bd Arab Media and Society; fmr Int. Affairs fmr Int. Affairs Fellow, Council on Foreign Relations, now Life Mem. *Publications:* Sadat and his Legacy: Egypt and the World, 1977–1997 (ed.) 1998, New Media, New Politics? From Satellite Television to the Internet in the Arab World 1998, Hopes Dashed: Egypt and American Foreign Assistance, 1952–56 2002; numerous journal articles, book chapters and opinion pieces.
Address: Center for Strategic and International Studies (CSIS), 1800 K Street, NW, Suite 400, Washington, DC 20006, USA (office). *Telephone:* (202) 775-3295 (office). *Fax:* (202) 775-0199 (office). *E-mail:* jalterman@ csis.org (office). *Website:* www.csis.org (office).

ALTMANN, Rev. Walter, PhD; Brazilian ecclesiastic and international organization executive; *Moderator, Central Committee, World Council of Churches;* m.; four d. *Education:* studied theology in São Leopoldo, Buenos Aires, Argentina and Hamburg, Germany. *Career:* parish pastor, Ijui, southern Brazil 1972–74; teacher of systematic theology at Theological Coll., São Leopoldo 1974–, Head of Theological Coll. 1981–87; Dir Ecumenical Inst. for Postgraduate Studies 1989–94; Pres. Latin American Council of Churches 1995–2001; Vice-Pres. Evangelical Church of the Lutheran Confession in Brazil (IECLB) 1998–2002, Pres. 2002–; mem. Council of Lutheran World Fed. 2003–; Moderator Cen. Cttee, WCC 2006–. *Publications:* numerous theological articles on Martin Luther, Latin American liberation theology and ecumenism.
Address: World Council of Churches, PO Box 2100, 150 route de Ferney, 1211 Geneva 2, Switzerland (office). *Telephone:* (22) 791-6111 (office). *Fax:* (22) 791-0361 (office). *Website:* www.wcc-assembly.info (office).

ALTON, Roger Martin; British journalist; *Editor, The Independent;* b. 20 Dec. 1947, Oxford; m. (divorced); one d. *Education:* Clifton Coll., Exeter Coll., Oxford. *Career:* grad. trainee, Liverpool Post, then Gen. Reporter and Deputy Features Ed. 1969–74; Sub-Ed. News The Guardian 1974–76, Chief Sub-Ed. News 1976–81, Deputy Sports Ed. 1981–85, Arts Ed. 1985–90, Weekend Magazine Ed. 1990–93, Features Ed. 1993–96, Asst Ed. 1996–98, Ed. The Observer 1998–2007, The Independent 2008–; Editor of the Year, What the Papers Say Awards 2000, GQ Editor of the Year 2005.

Address: The Independent, Independent House, 191 Marsh Wall, London E14 9RS, England (office). *Telephone:* (20) 7005-2000 (office). *Fax:* (20) 7005-2999 (office). *Website:* www.independent.co.uk (office).

ALTYNBAYEV, General Mukhtar; Kazakhstani air force officer; b. 10 Dec. 1945, Karaganda; m. Gulbanu Rahimbaevna Altynbayeva; one s. *Education:* Karaganda Aviation Centre, Armavir Air Defence Mil. School, G.K. Jukov Air Defence Mil. Acad. *Career:* started career as miner, Karaganda 1962–66; graduated pilot school 1964; became pilot-cadet Kinnel-Cherkassy Aviation Training Centre 1965; held various military command positions including Flight Commdr, Squadron Commdr, Deputy Commdr of training regiment 1972–75, apptd Commdr of a fighter's regiment Ural District 1979; Deputy Div. Commdr then Commdr of Air Defence Div., Turkestan Mil. Dist. 1985–88, Commdr of Air Defence Corps 1992; apptd Air Defence Commdr and Deputy Defence Minister 1992, Air Forces Commdr 1993, Minister of Defence 1996, 2001–06. *Address:* c/o Ministry of Defence, Beibitshilik 51a, Astana 473000, Kazakhstan (office).

ALVARADO, José Arturo; Honduran banker and government official; b. 28 July 1944, San Pedro Sula; m. Maria Antonieta Arriaga Price de Alvarado. *Education:* Centro Universitario Regional de Norte. *Career:* Vice-Pres. Citibank NA; Pres., Gen. Man., Bank of Honduras; Exec. Vice-Pres. and Gen. Man., Ficensa Group; Supervisor for Cen. America and Panama, Pacific Financial Group –1990; Prof. of Banking Accountancy, Instituto José Trinidad Reyes; Pres., Honduran Asscn of Banking Insts; Minister of Finance –2004. *Address:* c/o Ministry of Finance, 5a Avda, 3a Calle, Tegucigalpa, Honduras (office).

ALVAREZ, Carlos Alberto (Chacho); Argentine politician; *President, Committee of Permanent Representatives, Mercosur;* b. 26 Dec. 1948, Balvanera; m. Liliana Chiernajowsky; one s. three d. *Education:* Mariano Acosta Coll., Univ. of Buenos Aires. *Career:* Assessor, Regional Econ. Cttee of Nat. Senate 1983–89; elected Deputy to Nat. Ass. for Fed. Capital 1989–93, 1997–99; left Partido Justicialista and f. Partido Movimiento por la Democracia y la Justicia Social (MODEJUSO) 1990; f. Frente Grande; Pres. Frente Grande Bloc in Nat. Constitutional Convention 1994; Founder, Leader Frente del País Solidario—FREPASO 1994–; Vice-Pres. of Argentina 1999–2000 (resgnd); Pres. Cttee of Perm. Reps, Mercosur 2006–. *Address:* Southern Common Market (MERCOSUR/MERCOSUL) (Mercado Común del Sur/Mercado Comum do Sul) Edif. Mercosur, Luis Piera 1992, 1°, 11200 Montevideo, Uruguay. *Telephone:* (2) 412-9024. *Fax:* (2) 418-0557. *E-mail:* sam@mercosur.org.uy. *Website:* www.mercosur.org.uy.

ALVAREZ HERRERA, Bernardo, MA; Venezuelan diplomatist, politician and academic; *Ambassador to USA;* b. 18 Aug. 1956, Carora, State of Lara; m. Margarete de Alvarez; one s. two d. *Education:* Univ. Cen. de Venezuela, Univ. of Sussex, UK. *Career:* Asst Prof., School of Political and Admin. Studies, Univ. Cen. de Venezuela 1977–80, Prof. 1982–, Dir of Cooperation 1993–94, mem. Profs' Asscn 1989–93; Chief of Research and Devt Div., Venezuelan Inst. of Foreign Trade 1986–87; Prof., Superior School of the Venezuelan Air Force 1990–92; Exec. Sec. Working Group on Political Reforms, Presidential Comm. for Reform of the State 1985–86; Exec. Sec. and Venezuelan Rep. to Forum on Debt and Devt (FONDAD) 1988–91; elected Deputy to Nat. Congress (Miranda State) 1994–99, also Vice-Pres. Defence Cttee and Pres. Energy and Mines Cttee, Chamber of Deputies; Dir-Gen. of Hydrocarbons, Ministry of Energy and Mines 1999–2000, Venezuelan Rep. to USA Energy Council 1999–; Vice-Minister of Hydrocarbons 2000–03, Head of Del. to OPEC Conf. of Ministers 2000–01, Co-ordinator Venezuelan-French Energy Task Force 2000–02, Co-operation Agreement between US Dept of Energy and Venezuelan Ministry of Energy and Mines 2000–02; Amb. to USA, Washington, DC 2003–. *Publications:* State Companies and Capitalist Development 1982, Venezuela: Foreign Debt and Crisis of the Developing Model 1989, Politics and the Process of Elaboration of Laws 1997. *Address:* Embassy of Venezuela, 1099 30th Street, NW, Washington, DC 20007, USA (office). *Telephone:* (202) 342-2214 (office). *Fax:* (202) 342-6820 (office). *E-mail:* apaiva@embavenez-us.org (office). *Website:* www .embavenez-us.org (office).

ALVEAR VALENZUELA, María Soledad; Chilean lawyer and politician; b. 17 Sept. 1950, Santiago; m. Gutenberg Martinez Ocamica 1973; two s. one d. *Education:* Univ. of Chile. *Career:* Prof., Faculty of Law and Social Sciences, Univ. of Chile 1973–75; pvt. practice 1973–90; Consultant to UN 1987–90; Dir Comisión Preparatoria, Servicio Nacional de la Mujer (women's org.) 1990; Minister, Dir Servicio Nacional de la Mujer 1991; Minister of Justice 1994–99; Leader of Pres. Ricardo Lagos Escobar election campaign 1999; Minister of Foreign Affairs 2000–04; mem. Exec.

Council Comisión Interamericana de Mujeres (women's org.) –1990; Orden al Mérito Institucional, Consejo Mundial de Educ. 1991; won nomination of Partido Demócrata Cristiano (PDC) to run for presidency of Chile (election Dec. 2005) but withdrew from race. *Publications:* Algunas Sugerencias de Modificaciones al Derecho de Familia 1984, Situación de la Mujer Campesina frente a la Legislación 1987, La Mujer Campesina y la Legislación en Colombia 1990. *Address:* c/o Partido Demócrata Cristiano (PDC), Alameda B. O'Higgins 1460, 2°, Santiago Chile (office). *Telephone:* (2) 757-4400 (office). *Fax:* (2) 757-4400 (office). *Website:* www.pdc.cl (office).

AMADO, André Mattoso Maia; Brazilian diplomatist and research institute director; *Ambassador to Japan; Career:* fmr Dir Inst. Rio Branco, Ministry of Foreign Relations, Brasilia; fmr Amb. to Peru, Amb. to Japan 2006–. *Address:* Embassy of Brazil, 2-11-12, Kita Aoyama, Minato-ku, Tokyo 107-8633, Japan (office). *Telephone:* (3) 3404-5211 (office). *Fax:* (3) 3405-5846 (office). *E-mail:* brasemb@brasemb.or.jp (office). *Website:* www .brasemb.or.jp (office).

AMADOU, Hama; Niger politician. *Career:* fmr Man. Dir Niger Broadcasting Bd; fmr Pvt. Sec. to Pres. Seyni Kountche and Pres. Ali Saibou; Prime Minister of Niger 1995, 2000–07; now Sec.-Gen. Mouvement national pour une société de développement—Nassara (MNSD). *Address:* c/o Office of the Prime Minister, BP 893, Niamey, Niger (office).

AMADUZZI, Luigi, KCVO; Italian diplomatist; b. 22 March 1937, Naples; m. Giovanna Amaduzzi; one s. one d. *Education:* Univ. of Rome. *Career:* joined diplomatic service 1963; Second Sec., London 1967; First Sec., Moscow 1969; First Sec., later Counsellor, Sec.-Gen.'s Office 1972, Head of Office 1983, 1991; Counsellor, Washington, DC 1975; Amb. to Jordan 1985–88, to Romania 1988; apptd Diplomatic Counsellor to the Pres. 1992; Amb. to UK 1999–2004. *Address:* c/o Ministry of Foreign Affairs, Piazzale della Farnesina 1, 00194 Rome, Italy. *Telephone:* (06) 36911. *Fax:* (06) 36918899. *E-mail:* relazioni .pubblico@esteri.it. *Website:* www.esteri.it.

AMAMOU, Mohamed; Tunisian diplomatist; b. 7 Oct. 1933, Kairouan; m. Beya Boujdaria; one s. one d. *Education:* Collège Sadiki and Inst. des Hautes Etudes. *Career:* Chargé d'affaires, Jordan 1969–71; Amb. to Zaïre 1972–73; Gen. Consul in Paris 1973–74; Amb. to Lebanon and Jordan 1974–78; Dir of Political Affairs for the Arab World, Ministry of Foreign Affairs 1978–81; Chargé de mission, Ministry of Foreign Affairs 1981–85; Amb. to Morocco and Portugal (resident in Rabat) 1985–87, to Syria 1987–89; Sec. of State for Maghreb Affairs 1989–90; Prin. Adviser to Pres. of Tunisia 1990–91, Minister Adviser 1991; Sec.-Gen. of Arab Maghreb Union 1991–2000; Grand Officier, Ordre de la République Tunisienne; Chevalier, Ordre Indépendance and several foreign decorations. *Address:* c/o Ministry of Foreign Affairs, place du Gouvernement, la Kasbah, 1006 Tunis, Tunisia. *Telephone:* (71) 660-088 (office).

AMANI, Michel N'Guessan; Côte d'Ivoirian politician; *Minister of Defence;* b. 1957, Messoukro. *Career:* fmr teacher of history and geography in various secondary schools in Bouaké, Botro and Bodokro; Sec.-Gen. Front Populaire Ivoirien (FPI) for Bouaké 1990–92, Fed.-Sec. for Centre region 1992; Minister of Nat. Educ. 2000–07, of Defence 2007–. *Address:* Ministry of Defence, Camp Galliéni, côté Bibliothèque nationale, PO Box V241, Abidjan, Côte d'Ivoire (office). *Telephone:* 20-21-02-88 (office). *Fax:* 20-22-41-75 (office).

AMANN, Ronald, MSocSc, PhD, FRSA, ACSS; British academic and civil servant (retd); *Emeritus Professor of Comparative Politics, University of Birmingham;* b. 21 Aug. 1943, North Shields; m. Susan Peters 1965; two s. one d. *Education:* Heaton Grammar School, Newcastle-upon-Tyne and Univ. of Birmingham. *Career:* Consultant, OECD and Research Assoc. 1965–69; Lecturer, Sr Lecturer in Soviet Science Policy, Univ. of Birmingham 1969–83, Dir Centre for Russian and East European Studies (CREES) 1983–89, Prof. of Comparative Politics 1986–, now Prof. Emer., Dean Faculty of Commerce and Social Science 1989–91, Pro-Vice-Chancellor 1991–94; Chief Exec. and Deputy Chair. Econ. and Social Science Research Council (ESRC) 1994–99; Dir Gen. Centre for Man. and Policy Studies, Cabinet Office 1999–2002; Chair. Centre for Research on Innovation and Competition, Univ. of Manchester; Visiting Fellow, Osteuropa Inst. Munich 1975; Specialist Adviser, House of Commons Select Cttee on Science and Tech. 1976, mem. Steering Cttee, Centre for the Analysis of Risk and Regulation, LSE; Founding Academician, Acad. of Learned Socs. for the Social Services 1999; ind. mem. West Midlands Police Authority 2007–. *Publications:* co-author: Science Policy in the USSR 1969, The Technological Level of Soviet Industry 1977, Industrial Innovation in the Soviet Union 1982, Technical Progress and Soviet Economic Development 1986.

Address: c/o Centre for Russian and East European Studies, University of Birmingham, Edgbaston, Birmingham, B15 2TT (office); 26 Spring Road, Edgbaston, Birmingham, B15 2HA, England. *Telephone:* (121) 440-6186.

AMANO, Mari; Japanese diplomatist and international organization executive; *Deputy Secretary-General, Organisation for Economic Co-operation and Development;* m.; three d. *Education:* Univ. of Tokyo, Hertford Coll., Oxford, UK. *Career:* career diplomat for over 30 years in Ministry of Foreign Affairs, posts have included service in Econ. Affairs Bureau, Ministry of Foreign Affairs 1980–84, Embassy in Kuwait 1984–87, Perm. Mission to OECD, Paris 1987–92, Minister at Embassies in Thailand 1994–96, USA 1996–98, Deputy Dir-Gen. in Multilateral Co-operation Dept, Ministry of Foreign Affairs 2000–01, Chief Negotiator for Trade Related Investment Measures in Uruguay Round 2000–03, Consul Gen., Houston, Tex. 2001–04; Deputy Exec. Dir Korean Peninsula Energy Devt Org. (KEDO) Secr. 2004–07; Deputy Sec.-Gen. OECD, in charge of Devt Cluster and Policy Coherence dossier 2007–.
Address: OECD, 2 rue André Pascal, 75775 Paris Cedex 16, France (office). *Telephone:* 1-45-24-82-00 (office). *Fax:* 1-45-24-85-00 (office). *E-mail:* webmaster@oecd.org (office). *Website:* www.oecd.org (office).

AMANPOUR, Christiane, CBE, AB; British broadcasting correspondent; *Chief International Correspondent, Cable News Network (CNN);* b. 12 Jan. 1958, London; m. James Rubin (q.v.) 1998; one s. *Education:* primary school in Tehran, Iran, Holy Cross Convent, UK, New Hall School, UK and Univ. of Rhode Island, USA. *Career:* radio producer/research asst, BBC Radio, London 1980–82; radio reporter, WBRU Brown Univ., USA 1981–83; electronic graphics designer, WJAR, Providence, RI 1983; Asst CNN int. assignment desk, Atlanta, GA 1983; news writer, CNN, Atlanta 1984–86; reporter/producer, CNN, New York 1987–90; Int. Corresp. CNN 1990, Sr Int. Corresp. 1994, Chief Int. Corresp. 1996–; assignments have included coverage of Gulf War 1990–91, break-up of USSR and subsequent war in Tbilisi 1991, extensive reports on conflict in Fmr Yugoslavia, Israel and Afghanistan and coverage of civil unrest and political crises in Haiti, Algeria, Somalia, Rwanda, Iran and Pakistan; Fellow, Soc. of Professional Journalists; several hon. degrees including Dr hc (Rhode Island); three Dupont-Columbia Awards 1986–96, nine Emmy Awards, Women, Men and Media Breakthrough Award 1991, named Woman of the Year by New York Chapter of Women in Cable and Telecommunications 1994, George Polk Award 1997, Nymphe d'Honneur, Monte Carlo Television Festival 1997, two News and Documentary Emmy Awards 1999, two George Foster Peabody Awards 1999, Univ. of Missouri Honor Award for Distinguished Service to Journalism 1999, Courage in Journalism Award, Worldfest-Houston Int. Film Festival Gold Award, Livingston Award for Young Journalists, Edward R. Murrow Award for Distinguished Achievement in Broadcast Journalism 2002, Sigma Chi Award, ranked by Forbes magazine amongst 100 Most Powerful Women (72nd) 2005, (79th) 2006, (74th) 2007.
Address: c/o CNN International, CNN House, 19–22 Rathbone Place, London, W1P 1DF, England. *Telephone:* (20) 7637-6800.

AMARAL, Diogo Freitas do, PhD; Portuguese politician and academic; b. 21 July 1941, Póvoa de Varzim; m. Maria José Salgado Sarmento de Matos 1965; two s. two d. *Career:* Prof. of Admin. Law, Lisbon Univ. 1968, Head Dept of Public Law, Prof., Portuguese Catholic Univ. 1978; mem. Council of State 1974–75, Parl. 1975–82, 1992–93; Pres. Centre Democrat Party (CDS) 1974–82, 1988–91; Pres. European Union of Christian Democrats 1981–82; Deputy Prime Minister and Minister for Foreign Affairs 1980–81, Deputy Prime Minister and Minister of Defence 1981–83; Presidential cand. 1986; Pres. 50th Gen. Ass. of UN 1995–96; Minister of Foreign Affairs and Portuguese Communities Abroad 2005–06 (resgnd); Founder, Chair. School of Law, New Univ. of Lisbon 1996–2001; Pres. Fundação Portugal Século XXI 1986–90, PETROCONTROL 1992–2000; Order of Christ, Order of Santiago, Order of Henry the Navigator; Calouste Gulbenkian Prize (twice), Henry the Navigator Prize. *Plays:* O Magnífico Reitor 2001, Viriato 2002. *Publications:* A Utilização do Domínio Público Pelos Particulares 1965, A Execução das Sentenças dos Tribunais Administrativos 1967, Conceito e natureza do recurso hierárquico 1981, Uma Solução para Portugal 1985, Curso de Direito Administrativo I, 1986, II 2001, O Antigo Regime e a Revolução (Memórias Políticas: 1941–76) 1995, História das Ideias Políticas, Vol. I 1998, D. Afonso Henriques. Biografia 2000, Estudios de Direito Público (two vols) 2004, Manual de Introdução ao direito (Vol. I) 2004.
Address: Av. Fontes Pereira de Melo 35, 12 B, 1050-118, Lisbon, Portugal.

AMARI, Akira; Japanese politician; *Minister of Economy, Trade and Industry;* b. 27 Aug. 1949. *Career:* worked for Sony Corpn 1972–74; mem. House of Reps of New Liberal Club for Ninami-Kanto, for Kanagawa Prefecture 13th Dist 1983–; subsequently joined LDP, Sr Dir LDP Commerce and Industry Panel 1990–95, Chair. 1995; Parl. Vice-Minister of Int. Trade and Industry 1989; Deputy Sec.-Gen. LDP 1999–2001, Chief Deputy Sec.-Gen. 2001; Minister of Labour 1998–99; Chair. House Budget Cttee 2004–05; Minister of Economy, Trade and Industry 2006–.
Address: Ministry of Economy, Trade and Industry, 1-3-1, Kasumigaseki, Chiyoda-ku, Tokyo 100-8901, Japan (office). *Telephone:* (3) 3501-1511 (office). *Fax:* (3) 3501-6942 (office). *E-mail:* webmail@meti.go.jp (office). *Website:* www.meti.go.jp (office).

AMARJARGAL, Rinchinnyamyn, MEcons; Mongolian politician; m.; one s. *Education:* Moscow Inst. of Econs, Univ. of Bradford, UK. *Career:* officer, Cen. Council of Mongolian Trade Unions 1982–83; Lecturer, Mil. Acad. and Tech. Univ. 1983–90; Dir Econs Coll., Ulan Bator 1991–96; MP 1996–99, Minister and Acting Minister of External Relations April–Dec. 1998, Prime Minister of Mongolia 1999–2000; mem. Mongolian Nat. Democratic Party (MNPP) Gen. Council; Dr hc (Bradford) 2000.
Address: c/o Office of the Prime Minister, Ulan Bator, Mongolia (office).

AMBARTSUMOV, Yevgeniy Arshakovich, CandHistSc; Russian politician, social scientist, political analyst and journalist; *Professor, Universidad La Salle;* b. 19 Aug. 1929, Moscow; m. Nina Ignatovskaia 1978; one s. *Education:* Moscow Inst. of Int. Relations. *Career:* with Novoye Vremya 1954–59, Problems of Peace and Socialism 1959–63; Sr Scientific Researcher, Inst. of World Econs and Int. Relations 1956–59, Head of Dept Inst. of World Int. Labour Movt 1966–69; Head of Dept, Inst. of Sociology 1969–73; Head of Dept of Politics, Inst. of Economics of World Socialist System (now Inst. of Int. Economic and Political Studies) 1973–90; Russian People's Deputy 1990–93; Chair. Foreign Affairs Cttee of Russian Supreme Soviet 1992–93; mem. State Duma (Parl.) 1993–94; mem. Presidential Council 1993–95; Amb. to Mexico, also accred to Belize 1994–99; Prof. Universidad La Salle, Mexico 1999–; Order of Aguila Azteca con banda Mexico 1999. *Publications include:* How Socialism Began: Russia under Lenin 1978, NEP: A Modern View 1988, Socialism: Past and Present (ed.) 1990.
Address: Universidad La Salle, Benjamin Franklin 47, Col Condesa, Del. Cuauhtémoc, 06140 México, DF, Mexico. *Telephone:* (55) 26-14-40-79 (Mexico) (home); (495) 332-64-25 (Russia) (home). *Website:* www.ulsa.edu .mx.

AMERASINGHE, Chittharanjan Felix, PhD, LLD; Sri Lankan judge and international lawyer; b. 2 March 1933, Colombo; m. Wimala Nalini Pieris 1964; one s. two d. *Education:* Royal Coll., Colombo, Trinity Hall, Univ. of Cambridge, UK, Harvard Univ. Law School, USA. *Career:* Supervisor in Law, Trinity Hall, Cambridge Univ. 1955–57; Jr Exec., Caltex Oil Co., Colombo 1959–61; Lecturer in Law, Univ. of Ceylon 1962–65, Sr Lecturer 1965–68, Reader 1968–69, Prof. of Law 1969–71; Counsel, World Bank 1970–75, Sr Counsel 1975–81, Exec. Sec., World Bank Admin. Tribunal 1981–96; Judge UN Tribunal, New York 1997–2000; Judge, Common-wealth Int. Arbitral Tribunal 1999–2002; Consultant in Int. Law, Govt of Ceylon 1963–70; mem. Ceylon Govt Comm. on Local Govt 1969; Adjunct Prof. of Int. Law, School of Law, American Univ. 1991–93; mem. Panel of Arbitrators and Conciliators, Law of the Sea Convention, Int. Centre for Settlement of Investment Disputes, Panel of UN Compensation Comm. for Kuwait; Exec. Council mem. American Soc. of Int. Law 1980–83; Assoc. mem. Inst. de Droit Int. 1981–87, mem. 1987–; mem. Int. Law Asscn 1986–; mem. Sr Editorial Bd, Project on Governing Rules of Int. Law, American Soc. of Int. Law; mem. Hon. Cttee Int. Inst. of Human Rights 1968–; mem. Advisory Bd Int. Inst. of Environmental Law 1987–98, Sri Lanka Journal of Int. Law 1989–, Int. Orgs Law Review 2004–; Sr Fellow (Visiting), Trinity Hall, Univ. of Cambridge 1996–97; Trinity Hall Law Studentship 1956–59, Research Fellowship, Harvard Univ. Law School 1957–58; Hon. Prof. of Int. Law, Univ. of Colombo 1991–94; Henry Arthur Thomas Classical Award, Univ. of Cambridge 1953, Angus Classical Prize 1953, Clement Davies Prize for Law 1955, Major Scholar and Prizeman, Trinity Hall, Cambridge 1953–56, Yorke Prize 1964, Certificate of Merit, American Soc. of Int. Law 1988–89. *Publications:* Some Aspects of the Actio Iniuriarum in Roman-Dutch Law 1966, Defamation and Other Injuries in Roman-Dutch Law 1968, State Responsibility for Injuries to Aliens 1967, Studies in International Law 1969, The Doctrines of Sovereignty and Separation of Powers in the Law of Ceylon 1970, The Law of the International Civil Service (two vols) 1988, Documents on International Administrative Tribunals 1989, Case Law of the World Bank Adminis-trative Tribunal (three vols) 1989, 1991, 1994, Local Remedies in International Law 1990, 2003, Principles of the Institutional Law of International Organizations 1996, 2005, Jurisdiction of International Tribunals 2003, Evidence in International Litigation 2005, Diplomatic Protection 2008; articles in leading law and int. law journals.
Address: 6100 Robinwood Road, Bethesda, MD 20817, USA (home). *Telephone:* (301) 229-2766 (home). *Fax:* (301) 229-4151 (home).

AMIN, Samir, DEcon; Egyptian economist; *Director (Africa Office), Third World Forum;* b. 4 Sept. 1931, Cairo; m. Isabelle Eynard 1957. *Education:* Univ. of Paris. *Career:* Sr Economist, Econ. Devt Org., Cairo 1957–60; Tech. Adviser for Planning to Govt of Mali 1960–63; Prof. of Econs, Univs of Poiters, Paris and Dakar; Dir UN African Inst. for Econ. Devt and Planning 1970–80; Dir Third World Forum (Africa Office), Senegal 1980–. *Publications include:* Trois expériences africaines de développement, Mali, Guinée, Ghana 1965, L'économie du Maghreb (2 vols) 1967, Le développement du capitalisme en Côte d'Ivoire 1968, Le monde des affaires sénégalais 1969, The Maghreb in the Modern World 1970, Neo-colonialism in West Africa 1973, Accumulation on a World Scale 1974, Unequal Development 1976, The Arab Nation 1978, Class and Nation 1980, The Arab Economy Today 1982, Eurocentrism 1989, Delinking: Towards a Polycentric World 1990, Maldevelopment: Anatomy of a Global Failure 1990, The Empire of Chaos 1992, Re-reading The Post War Period 1994, Capitalism in the Age of Globalisation 1996, Les défis de la mondialisation 1996, Spectres of Capitalism 1998, L'hégémonisme des Etats-Unis et l'effacement du projet européen 2000. *Address:* Third World Forum, B.P. 3501, Dakar, Senegal (office). *Telephone:* 821-11-44 (office). *Fax:* 821-11-44 (office). *E-mail:* ftm@refer.sn (office). *Website:* www.refer.sn/ftm.

AMINE SOUEF, Mohamed al-; Comoran politician and diplomatist. *Career:* apptd Amb. to Egypt (concurrently accred Amb. to the Arab League) 1995; Minister of Foreign Affairs 1999–2002, Minister of State, Minister of Foreign Affairs, Co-operation, Francophone Affairs, with responsibility for Comorans Abroad 2002–06. *Address:* c/o Représentation du Gouvernement, BP 20, Dzaoudzi 97610, Comoros (office).

AMMON, Peter; German diplomatist; *State Secretary, Federal Ministry of Foreign Affairs;* b. 23 Feb. 1952, Frankfurt; m.; two c. *Education:* Freie Universität Berlin, Inst. for Operations Research, Diplomatic School, Bonn. *Career:* joined Foreign Service 1978, served in Embassy in London 1980–82, in Dakar 1982–85, in New Delhi 1989–91; at Fed. Minister of Foreign Affairs, Bonn 1985–89, mem. Policy Planning Staff 1991–96, Head, Policy Planning Staff in Pres.'s Office 1996–99; Econ. Minister, Embassy in Washington, DC 1999–2001; Dir-Gen. for Econ. Affairs and Sustainable Devt, Fed. Ministry of Foreign Affairs, Berlin 2003–05, also G8-Sous Sherpa; Amb. to France 2007–2008; State Sec., Fed. Ministry of Foreign Affairs July 2008–. *Address:* Federal Ministry of Foreign Affairs, Werderscher Markt 1, 10117 Berlin, Germany (office). *Telephone:* (30) 18170 (office). *Fax:* (30) 18173402 (office). *Website:* www.auswaertiges-amt.de (office).

AMOAKO, Kingsley Y., BA, MA, PhD; Ghanaian economist; *President, African Center for Economic Transformation;* b. 1947. *Education:* Univ. of Ghana, Univ. of California, Berkeley, USA. *Career:* with IBRD from the 1970s, Dir Dept of Educ. and Social Policy 1993–95; UN Under-Sec.-Gen. and Exec. Sec. Econ. Comm. for Africa (ECA) 1995–2005; Distinguished African Scholar, Woodrow Wilson Int. Center 2006; Pres. African Center for Econ. Transformation, Accra 2006–; mem. Policy Advisory Bd DATA (debt, AIDS, trade, Africa); Dr hc (Addis Ababa Univ.) 2003, (Kwame Nkrumah Univ. of Science and Tech., Kumasi) 2005. *Address:* c/o DATA, 1400 Eye Street., NW, Suite 600, Washington, DC 20005, USA (office).

AMORIM, Celso Luiz Nunes; Brazilian diplomatist and politician; *Minister of Foreign Affairs;* b. 3 June 1942, Santos, São Paulo; m. Ana Maria Amorim; three s. one d. *Education:* Rio Branco Inst., Diplomatic Acad. Vienna and London School of Econs. *Career:* Lecturer in Portuguese, Rio Branco Inst. 1976; Lecturer, Dept of Political Science and Int. Relations, Univ. of Brasília 1977–; Dir-Gen. EMBRAFILME (Brazilian Film Corpn) 1979-1982; Deputy Head of Mission, The Hague 1982–85; Perm. Rep. to UN, GATT and Conf. on Disarmament, Geneva 1991–93 (Pres. 2000), to UN and WTO 1999–2001; Sec. for Int. Affairs, Ministry of Science and Tech. 1987–88; Dir–Gen. for Cultural Affairs, Ministry of Foreign Affairs 1989–90, for Econ. Affairs 1990–91, Sec.-Gen. 1993, Minister of Foreign Affairs 1993–94, 2003–; Perm. Rep. to UN, New York 1995–99; Amb. to UK 2001–02; Chair. UN Security Council Resolution Sanctions Cttee on Kosovo 1998–99, UN Security Council Panels on Iraq 1999, Governing Body ILO 2000, Council for Trade in Services, WTO 2001; Perm. mem. Dept of Int. Affairs, Inst. of Advanced Studies, Univ. of São Paulo; mem. Canberra Comm. on Elimination of Nuclear Weapons 1966, Int. Task Force on Security Council Peace Enforcement 1997; Foreign Policy Asscn Medal (USA) 1999. *Publications:* several works on political theory, int. relations, cultural policies and subjects connected with science and tech. *Address:* Ministry of Foreign Affairs, Palácio do Itamaraty, Esplanada dos Ministérios, Bloco H, 70170-900, Brasília DF, Brazil (office). *Telephone:* (61) 3411-6161 (office). *Fax:* (61) 3225-1272 (office). *Website:* www.mre.gov .br (office).

AMUNUGAMA, Sarath, PhD; Sri Lankan politician; *Minister of Enterprise Development and Investment Promotion;* b. 10 July 1939; m. *Career:* fmr Spokesman for People's Alliance (PA); elected mem. Parl. for Kandy Dist; Minister of Northern Rehabilitation 2000; Minister of Culture 2000; Minister of Finance –2005, of Public Admin and Home Affairs 2005–07, of Enterprise Devt and Investment Promotion 2007–. *Address:* Ministry of Enterprise Development and Investment Promotion, 25th Level, West Tower, World Trade Centre, Echelon Square, Colombo 1, Sri Lanka (office). *Telephone:* (11) 2394951 (office). *Fax:* (11) 2424960 (office). *E-mail:* secedip@sltnet.lk (office). *Website:* www.atned.lk (office).

ANAMARN, Chaisiri; Thai diplomatist; m.; two d. *Education:* Thammasat Univ., Eastern Mexico Univ., Mexico. *Career:* joined Ministry of Foreign Affairs 1975; postings include Brussels, Belgium, Philippines, Vietnam, Taipei; fmr Dir-Gen. Consular Affairs, Ministry of Foreign Affairs; Amb. to Malaysia –2005, to Denmark 2005–08. *Address:* c/o Ministry of Foreign Affairs, Thanon Sri Ayudhya, Bangkok 10400, Thailand. *Telephone:* (2) 643-5000. *Fax:* (2) 225-6155. *E-mail:* information@mfa.go.th. *Website:* www.mfa.go.th.

ANDELY, Roger Rigobert; Republic of the Congo politician. *Career:* fmr Minister of the Economy, Finance and the Budget. *Address:* c/o Ministry of the Economy, Finance and the Budget, Centre Administratif, Quartier Plateau, BP 2083, Brazzaville, Republic of the Congo (office).

ANDERSON, Anne; Irish diplomatist; *Ambassador to France; Career:* Rep. of Ireland to UN Conf. on Disarmament 1995–2001; Amb. to UN 2001–03, also Chair. UN Comm. on Human Rights; Perm. Rep. to EU 2003–05; Amb. to France 2005–. *Address:* Irish Embassy, 4 rue Rude, 75116 Paris, France (office). *Telephone:* 1-44-17-67-00 (office). *Fax:* 1-44-17-67-60 (office). *E-mail:* paris@dfa.ie (office).

ANDERSON, Jeffrey, PhD; American academic; *Graf Goltz Professor and Director, BMW Center for German and European Studies, Georgetown University; Education:* Pomona Coll., Yale Univ. *Career:* teacher, Emory Univ. 1988–90, Brown Univ. 1990–2002; Fellow, German Council on Foreign Relations and Minda de Gunzburg Center for European Studies, Harvard Univ.; Dir. of Studies, American Inst. for Contemporary German Studies; Visiting Prof., Georgetown Univ. 2000–01, Graf Goltz Prof. and Dir, BMW Center for German and European Studies 2002–; mem. Exec. Cttee European Union Studies Asscn 2003–05; DAAD Prize for Distinguished Scholarship 2000. *Publications:* The Territorial Imperative 1992, German Unification and the Union of Europe 1999, Regional Integration and Democracy (ed.) 1999. *Address:* BMW Center for German and European Studies, Intercultural Center, Room 505, Georgetown University, 7th and O Streets, NW, Washington, DC, 20057-1026, USA (office). *Telephone:* (202) 687-5602 (office). *Fax:* (202) 687-8359 (office). *E-mail:* jja5@georgetown.edu (office). *Website:* cges.georgetown.edu (office).

ANDERSON, Lisa, BA, MA, PhD; American academic; *James T. Shotwell Professor of International Relations and Dean, School of International and Public Affairs, Columbia University; Education:* Sarah Lawrence Coll., Fletcher School at Tufts Univ., Columbia Univ. *Career:* Asst Prof. of Govt and Social Studies, Harvard Univ. 1981–86; staff mem. Columbia Univ. 1986–, James T. Shotwell Prof. of Int. Relations, Dir Middle East Inst. 1990–93, Chair. Dept of Political Science 1994–96, Dean School of Int. and Public Affairs 1997–; mem. Bd Dirs Social Science Research Council, Human Rights Watch (Co-Chair. Middle East Program), Council on Foreign Relations; mem. Editorial Cttee Comparative Politics. *Publications include:* The State and Social Transformation in Tunisia and Libya, 1830–1980 1986, The Origins of Arab Nationalism (co-ed.) 1991, Transitions to Democracy (ed.) 1999; more than 35 scholarly articles; contribs to The New York Times, Washington Post and The Los Angeles Times. *Address:* Department of Political Science, Columbia University, 1414 International Affairs Building, Mailcode 3328, 420 West 118th Street, New York, NY 10027, USA (office). *Telephone:* (212) 854-4604 (office). *Fax:* (212) 854-4847 (office). *E-mail:* la8@columbia.edu (office). *Website:* www .columbia.edu/cu/polisci (office).

ANDINO-SALAZAR, José Roberto, BA; Salvadorean diplomatist; *Ambassador to Italy;* b. 10 July 1948; m.; four c. *Education:* Univ. of El Salvador, Universidad Nacional Autonoma de Mexico, UNAM. *Career:* Lecturer in Econs, Dept of Political Sciences and the Faculty of Law and Political

Science, Univ. of El Salvador 1974–75; joined Ministry of Foreign Affairs 1977 as Internal Dir responsible for Int. Orgs, held numerous other posts including Dir of American Affairs 1976–78, Alt. Rep. to Exec. Cttee of Salvadorean Foreign Trade Inst. 1978–79, Amb. and Alt. Rep. of Mission to UN, New York 1979–84, Dir-Gen. of Foreign Policy 1985, Amb. to Colombia and Barbados 1985–92, to OAS 1992–96, to Spain and Morocco 1996–2000, Perm. Rep. to UN, New York 2000–02, Amb. to Brazil 2002–04, to Italy (also accred to Greece, Switzerland and Cyprus) 2005–; Chair. Perm. Council, Cttee. on Hemispheric Security and Vice-Chair. Inter-American Econ. and Social Council, Rep. of El Salvador to Special Sessions of OAS Gen. Ass. 1992, 1993, 1996, 8th Session of UNCTAD 1992.
Address: Embassy of El Salvador, Via G. Castellini 13, 00197 Rome, Italy (office). *Telephone:* (06) 8076605 (office). *Fax:* (06) 8079726 (office). *E-mail:* embasalvaroma@iol.it (office). *Website:* www.embasalvaroma.com (office).

ANDJABA, Martin; Namibian diplomatist; b. 17 Dec. 1957, Ontokolo; m.; four c. *Education:* UN Inst. for Namibia, UN Econ. Comm. for Africa, Addis Ababa, Ethiopia, Foreign Service Acad., Lagos, Nigeria and Univ. of Namibia. *Career:* Gen. Service Officer, UN Inst. for Namibia 1981–83; Sr Coordinator, Dept of Foreign Affairs, SW Africa People's Org. (SWAPO), Luanda, Angola 1984–89; Sec. Africa Group of Ambs, Luanda 1986–89; repatriated to Namibia 1989; Chief of Protocol of Directorate of Elections of SWAPO, Windhoek 1989; Chief of Protocol 1990–96; Perm. Rep. to UN, New York 1996–2006; mem. Int. Advisory Bd Foundation for Post Conflict Devt.
Address: c/o International Advisory Board, Post Conflict Development, 1 River Place, Suite 2714, New York, NY 10036, USA.

ANDON, Nick Leon, BA, MSc; Micronesian politician and financial administrator; m. Marpellina Dereas; two c. *Education:* Truk High School, Univ. of Guam, Grossmont Coll. El Cajon CA, San Diego State Univ., United States Int. Univ. (USIU) San Diego. *Career:* Coordinator Territorial Econ. Opportunity Office 1977–78; Program Developer Office of Aging 1980–81, Trust Territory of Pacific Islands (TTPI) Saipan, Program Coordinator 1981–83; Man. Analysis Budget Office 1983–84; Admin. Div. Grants Man. 1990–97, FSM Nat. Govt; Dir Budget 1984–90, 1997–98, Dir Treasury 1998–2000, Chuuk State Govt; State Man. FSM Telecommunications Chuuk Station 2000–03; Sec. Dept of Finance and Admin, FSM Nat. Govt 2003–; Chair. Bd Chuuk Public Utility Corpn (CPUC) 1997–2001; Chair. Chuuk State Financial Control Comm. 2002–03; Sec. Bd Bank of FSM 1999–2007; Chair. Bd of Trustees Chuuk State Health Care Plan (CSHCP) 2001–.
Address: c/o Department of Finance and Administration, POB PS-158, Palikir, Pohnpei FM 96941, Federated States of Micronesia (office).

ANDRADE FALLA, Luis Fernando, BEcons; Guatemalan diplomatist; *Secretary General, Association of Caribbean States;* b. 10 July 1963; m. Irene Christine Ufer de Andrade; two d. *Education:* Francisco Marroquín Univ. *Career:* fmr banking exec.; fmr columnist and int. affairs adviser for Siglo XXI and Prensa Libre newspapers; fmr consultant on int. affairs, Facultad Latinoamericana de Ciencias Sociales (FLASCO); fmr consultant Netherlands Inst. for Multiparty Democracy; Minister Counsellor, Embassy in Cuba 1998–2000; fmr Vice-Minister for Foreign Affairs; Sec.-Gen. Asscn of Caribbean States 2008–; mem. Bd of Dirs Guatemalan Press Chamber.
Address: Association of Caribbean States, 5-7 Sweet Briar Road, St. Clair, PO Box 660, Port of Spain, Trinidad and Tobago (office). *Telephone:* 622-9575 (office). *Fax:* 622-1653 (office). *E-mail:* mail@acs-aec.org (office). *Website:* www.acs-aec.org (office).

ANDRESEN-GUIMARÃES, Fernando; Portuguese diplomatist; m. Graca Andresen-Guimarães; one s. *Career:* fmr Pres. Inter-ministerial Comm. on Macao (Head Portuguese–Chinese Jt Liaison Group); fmr Dir–Gen. of Devt Aid, Ministry of Foreign Affairs; fmr Amb. to Algeria and Iraq; fmr Consul-Gen. in Luanda, Angola; fmr Counsellor at Perm. Mission to UN, New York; fmr Auditor at NATO Defence Coll., Rome; Amb. to USA –1999; Amb. and Perm. Rep. to NATO and WEU 1999–2003; Amb. to UK 2003–06.
Address: Ministry of Foreign Affairs, Palácio das Necessidades, Largo do Rilvas, 1399-030 Lisbon, Portugal (office). *Telephone:* (213) 946000 (office). *Fax:* (213) 946053 (office). *E-mail:* gii@mne.gov.pt (office). *Website:* www .min-nestrangeiros.pt/ (office).

ANDRIANARIVELO-RAZAFY, Zina, MA, MBA; Malagasy diplomatist; *Permanent Representative, United Nations;* m.; two s. *Education:* Univs of Nantes and Angers, France and Ball State Univ., USA. *Career:* fmr Asst to Pres. HTR Enterprises Inc., Washington, DC; Sr. Man. Henri Fraise Sons

& Co. Group 1987–98; Amb. to USA 1999–2003; Perm. Rep. to UN, New York 2003–.
Address: Permanent Mission of Madagascar, 820 Second Avenue, Suite 800, New York, NY 10017, USA (office). *Telephone:* (212) 986-9491 (office). *Fax:* (212) 986-6271 (office). *E-mail:* repermad@ren.com (office). *Website:* www.un.int/madagascar (office).

ANDRIANARIVO, Tantely René Gabrio; Malagasy politician. *Career:* Prime Minister of Madagascar, Chief of Govt, Minister of Finances and Economy 1998–2002; sentenced to 12 years' hard labour for abuse of office Dec. 2003.

ANDRIKIENĖ, Laima Liucija, DEcon; Lithuanian politician and academic; b. 1 Jan. 1958, Druskininkai; m. (husband deceased); one s. *Education:* Druskininkai Secondary School, Druskininkai Seven-Year Music School, Vilnius State Univ., Univ. of Manchester, UK. *Career:* engineer, Computing Centre, Lithuanian Research Inst. of Agricultural Econs 1980–82, Researcher, Sr Researcher 1982–88; British Council Post-Doctoral Fellow, Univ. of Manchester 1988–89; Asst to Deputy Chair. Council of Ministers, Lithuanian SSR 1989–90; Deputy, Supreme Soviet 1990; signatory to Act on Re-establishment of Ind. State of Lithuania 1990; mem. Independence Party 1990–92; mem. Seimas (Parl.) (mem. Foreign Affairs Cttee, Vice-Chair. June–Oct. 2000, European Affairs Cttee 1998–2000) 1992–2000; Co-founder Homeland Union Party (Lithuanian Conservatives) 1993, mem. Bd 1993–98; Minister of Trade and Industry 1996, of European Affairs 1996–98; Head, Lithuanian Parl. Del. to Baltic Ass. 1998–2000 (Chair. Presidium 1998–99, 2000); Founder and Chair. Homeland People's Party 1999–2001; mem. Union of the Right 2001–03, Homeland Union 2003–; Chair. Bd Laitenis UAB, Vilnius 2001–03; consultant, Asscn of Lithuanian Chambers of Commerce, Industry and Crafts 2002–; Assoc. Prof., Dept of Political Science, Law Univ. of Lithuania 2002–04, Dir Inst. of EU Policy and Man. 2002–03, Dean Faculty of Public Man. 2003–04; mem. European Parl. (Group of the European People's Party (Christian Democrats) and European Democrats) 2004–, mem. Cttee on Budgets, Sub-cttee on Human Rights, Del. to EU-Moldova Parl. Co-operation Cttee; Pew Fellowship Scholar, School of Foreign Service, Georgetown Univ., Washington, DC 1996; Dr hc (Kingston Univ.) 2007; Grand Officier, l'Ordre nat. du Mérite 1997, Cross of Commdr of the Order of the Lithuanian Grand Duke Gediminas 2004; Independence Medal of Repub. of Lithuania 2000, Medal of the Baltic Ass. 2003. *Publications include:* more than 60 articles and academic monographs on foreign policy, EU policies and man., interest groups and lobbying, econ. reform, agricultural econs and human rights.
Address: European Parliament, Bâtiment Altiero Spinelli, ASP 11E153, 60 rue Wiertz, 1047 Brussels, Belgium (office); 8/26 Liejyklos Street, 01120 Vilnius, Lithuania. *Telephone:* (5) 212-2360; 699-05062 (Mobile). *Fax:* (2) 284-9858 (office). *E-mail:* llandrikiene@europarl.eu.int (office); info@ laimaandrikiene.lt. *Website:* www.europarl.eu.int (office); www .laimaandrikiene.lt; www.culture.lt/LLA.

ANEFAL, Sebastian L., BS; Micronesian politician; b. 21 Jan. 1952, Gurur, Gilman, State of Yap; m. Marita Phillip; two s. three d. *Education:* Yap High School, Sherwood High School, Ore., USA, Univ. of Guam, Agana, Guam, Eastern Ore. State Univ., La Grande, Ore., Micronesian Occupational Coll., Repub. of Palau, Ore. Coll. of Education, Univ. of Hawaii, Ore. State Univ., USA. *Career:* radio announcer/reporter, WSZA Radio Station, Yap 1970; Asst Dorm Man. Eastern Ore. State Univ. 1972–74; Sec. Educ. for Self-Governmental Task Force 1974; Classroom Instructor in Social Studies, Dept of Educ. 1975–80, Chief of Fed. Programs 1980–82, Chief of Community Outreach Aug.–Dec. 1982, ECIA (US Govt's Educ. Consolidation and Improvement Act of 1981) Chapter I Coordinator July–Sept. 1982, Man. and Support Admin. 1982–87; Public Information Program Coordinator, Office of the Plebiscite Commr, Yap Jan.–June 1982; Convention Sec., Yap Constitutional Convention March–Aug. 1982; Dir Dept of Public Affairs, Yap 1987–88, Dept of Resources and Devt 1988–91, Office of Planning and Budget 1991–95; Special Consultant to Gov. of State of Yap 1991–95, 2007–; Chief of Gilman (Municipality), Yap 1992–2007; Sec. of Dept of Resources and Devt, FSM Nat. Govt 1995–98, Dept of Econ. Affairs 1998–2003, Dept of Foreign Affairs 2003–07; Vice-Chair. Tourist Comm. 1975; mem. Nat. Disaster Control Bd 1976; Yap SPEA Coordinator, Festival of Arts, Papua New Guinea 1980; Chair. Elementary and Secondary Educ. Act (ESEA) Title IV State Advisory Council, Trust Territory of the Pacific Islands (TTPI) 1980; Chair. UN Day Cttee; Ed. 1981; mem. Old Age Program Advisory Bd 1983, COM Bd of Regents 1984–93, EPA Bd (TTPI/FSM) 1985–87; mem. Bd of Dirs Micronesia Maritime Authority 1989–95; Chair. Bd of Govs Pacific Island Development Bank 1989–95; Chair. Bd of Nat. Fisheries Corpn 1990–; Vice-Chair. Bd of Dirs Yap Econ. Devt Authority 1990–95; Pres. Yap Fishing Corpn 1990–95; Vice-Pres. Yap Purse Seiners Corpn 1990–95; mem. Bd of Dirs Yap Cooperative Asscn 1990–95, Micronesia Longline

Fishing Co. 1990–, FSM Development Bank 1990–; American Field Service Scholarship 1969–72, Trust Territory Social Sciences Scholarship 1972, UNESCO Fellowship in Ethnic Heritage to the Gilbert Islands 1978. *Publications include:* Social Studies Curriculum Guide (ed.) 1980, Tabina Rodad (social studies text book) (co-ed.) 1980. *Address:* c/o Government of Yap, POB 39, Colonia, Yap, FM 96943, The Federated States of Micronesia (office).

ANGELO, Victor da Silva, MA; Portuguese UN official and diplomatist; *Executive Representative for UN Integrated Force for Sierra Leone, United Nations;* b. 1949; m.; two d. *Education:* Instituto Superior Economico e Social, Univ. of Evora, Université Libre de Bruxelles, Belgium. *Career:* mem. Electoral Comm. of Portugal 1974–75; fmr Univ. Lecturer and Sr Statistician, Portuguese Nat. Inst. of Statistics (INE); UN Adviser in São Tome and Príncipe 1978–80; UN Population Fund (UNFPA) Rep. in Mozambique 1980–85; Resident Coordinator/Resident Rep. in Tanzania 1994–97; and The Gambia 1989–94; and Deputy Resident Rep. in Cen. African Repub.; Deputy Regional Dir for Africa at UNDP in New York 1998–99; UNDP Special Envoy for East Timor and Asia 1999–2000; UN Humanitarian and Resident Coordinator, and UNDP Resident Rep. in Zimbabwe 2000–04; Deputy Special Rep. of Sec.-Gen. for Sierra Leone 2004–06; UNDP Resident Rep. and UN Resident Coordinator in Sierra Leone 2004–06; Exec. Rep. for UN Integrated Office in Sierra Leone (UNIOSIL) 2006–. *Address:* UN Integrated Force for Sierra Leone (UNIOSIL), DSRSG, 76 Wilkinson Road, Freetown, Sierra Leone (office). *Telephone:* (22) 231311 (office). *E-mail:* registry.sl@undp.org (office). *Website:* www.undp.org (office).

ANGREMY, Jean-Pierre, (Pierre-Jean Rémy); French diplomatist and writer; b. 21 March 1937, Angoulême; m. 1st Odile Cail (divorced); one s. one d.; m. 2nd Sophie Schmit 1986 (divorced); one s. *Education:* Institut d'études politiques, Paris, Brandeis Univ., USA, Ecole nationale d'admin. *Career:* served in Hong Kong 1963–64, Beijing 1964–66, London 1966–71, 1975–79; Cultural, Scientific and Tech. Relations, Paris 1971–72; seconded to ORTF 1972–75; seconded to Ministry of Culture and Communication (Dir Theatre Dept) 1979–84; Consul, Florence 1984–87; Dir-Gen. Cultural, Scientific and Tech. Relations 1987–90; Amb. to UNESCO 1990–94; Dir Acad. de France, Rome 1994–97; Pres. Bibliothèque Nationale de France 1997–2002, Années France–Chine 2003–05, mem. Acad. française 1988; Commdr, Légion d'honneur, des Arts et Lettres; Officier, Ordre nat. du. Mérite. *Publications:* Désir d'Europe 1995, Le Rose et la Blanc 1997, Callas, une Vie 1997, Retour d'Hélène 1997, Aria Di Roma 1998, La Nuit de Ferrare 1999, Demi-Siècle 2000, Etat de Grâce et Dire Perdu 2001, Berlioz 2002, Chambre noire de Pekin 2004, Dictionnaire amoureux de l'Opéra 2004, and numerous other publs. *Address:* 63 Boulevard Saint-Michel, 75005 Paris, France (home). *Telephone:* 1-47-05-29-10 (home). *Fax:* 1-47-05-29-10 (home). *E-mail:* angremy@wanadoo.fr (home).

ANGULA, Nahas Gideon, BEd, MA, MEd; Namibian politician; *Prime Minister;* b. 22 Aug. 1943, Onyaanya; m. Katrina Tangeni Namalenga; four c. *Education:* Oniipa Boy's School, Engela Boy's School, Ongwediva Training Coll., Oshigambo Jr Secondary School, Nkumbi Int. Coll., Univ. of Zambia, Columbia Univ., New York, Univ. of Manchester, UK. *Career:* became active in SWAPO 1967, went into exile to Zambia 1967; Sec. for Educ., SWAPO Politburo; returned from exile 1989; Head of Dept, Voter Registration, SWAPO Election Directorate, Windhoek 1989; mem. Constituent Ass. 1989, Nat. Ass. 1990–; Minister of Educ., Sport and Culture 1990–95, of Higher Educ., Training and Employment Creation 1995–2005; nominated as one of three SWAPO presidential cands 2004; Prime Minister of Namibia 2005–. *Publication:* The African Origin of Civilisation and the Destiny of Africa (co-ed.) 2000. *Address:* Office of the Prime Minister, Robert Mugabe Avenue, PMB 13338, Windhoek, Namibia (office). *Telephone:* (61) 2879111 (office). *Fax:* (61) 230648 (office). *Website:* www.opm.gov.na (office).

ANGULO BARTUREN, Carmelo; Spanish diplomatist; *Ambassador to Argentina;* b. 23 May 1947, Bilbao; m. Ana María Ruiz Antelo. *Education:* Univ. of Pamplona, Navarra, Diplomatic School, Madrid. *Career:* fmr Dir-Gen. Ibero-American Inst. for Cooperation; fmr Amb. to Bolivia and Colombia, also postings in Tunisia, Canada and Mauritania; Resident Rep. in Argentina, UNDP –2004; Amb. to Argentina 2004–. *Address:* Embassy of Spain, Mariscal Ramón Castilla, 2720, 1425 Buenos Aires, Argentina (office). *Telephone:* (11) 4802-6031 (office). *Fax:* (11) 4802-0719 (office).

ANSARI, Gholamreza, BSc; Iranian diplomatist; *Ambassador to Russia;* b. 22 Nov. 1955, Shahrood; m. Shahih Shirazi; four d. *Education:* Allameh Tabatabaee Univ., Tehran. *Career:* Gov.-Gen. Piranshahr City, Deputy Gov.-Gen. Azarbayejan Prov., Supt of Gov.-Gen. of Azarbayejan Prov., Deputy Gen. Dir of Foreign Nationals and Refugees Dept 1980–88; Chargé d'Affaires, Embassy, London 1992–99, Amb. 1999–2000, to Russia (also accred to Turkmenistan) 2005–. *Address:* Embassy of Iran, 117292 Moscow, Pokrovskii bulv. 7, Russia (office). *Telephone:* (495) 917-72-82 (office). *Fax:* (495) 230-28-97 (office).

ANSI, Saud bin Salim al-, BA; Omani diplomatist; *Chief of Information Department, Ministry of Foreign Affairs;* b. 23 Dec. 1949, Salalah; m. 1976; two s. two d. *Education:* Beirut Univ. *Career:* with Ministry of Information and Culture and of Diwan Affairs 1974–75; Dir Dept of Research and Studies 1976–78; First Sec. Embassy, Tunis 1975–76, Consul-Gen., Karachi 1978–80, Amb. to Djibouti 1980–82, to Kuwait 1982–84; Perm. Rep. to the UN 1984–88; Under-Sec. and Dir-Gen. Council of Environment and Water Resources 1988–89; Sec.-Gen. Council of Educ. and Vocational Training 1990–92; Adviser to Ministry of Nat. Heritage and Culture 1993–94; Chief Information Dept, Ministry of Foreign Affairs 1995–; mem. Bd of Dirs Oman & Emirates Investment Holding Co. *Address:* PO Box 1128, Ruwi 112, Oman. *Telephone:* 701 207. *Fax:* 704 785.

ANSIP, Andrus; Estonian politician; *Prime Minister;* b. 1 Oct. 1956, Tartu; m.; three c. *Education:* Tartu Univ., Univ. of York. *Career:* Head of Regional Office, Joint Venture Estkompexim 1988–93; Chair. Radio Tartu Ltd 1994–99; Bankruptcy Trustee, Tartu Commercial Bank 1994–98; mem. Bd Dirs Rahvapank (People's Bank) 1993–95, Fondijuhtide AS 1995–96, Fundmanager Ltd; Chair. Livonia Privatization IF 1995–96; CEO Fondinvesteeringu Maakler AS 1995–96, Investment Fund Broker Ltd; Mayor City of Tartu 1998–2004; Minister of Econ. Affairs and Communications 2004–05; Prime Minister of Estonia 2005–; Officer, Nat. Order of Merit (Malta) 2001, Order of the White Star (Third Class) 2005. *Address:* Office of the Prime Minister, Stenbocki maja, Rahukohtu 3, Tallinn 15161, Estonia (office). *Telephone:* 693-5701 (office). *Fax:* 693-5704 (office). *E-mail:* peaminister@riik.ee (office). *Website:* www.peaminister.ee (office).

ANSTEE, Dame Margaret Joan, DCMG, BSc (Econ), MA; British/Bolivian international organization official, consultant, writer and lecturer; b. 25 June 1926, Writtle, Essex. *Education:* Chelmsford Co. High School for Girls, Newnham Coll. Cambridge and Univ. of London. *Career:* Lecturer in Spanish, Queen's Univ. Belfast 1947–48; Third Sec. Foreign Office 1948–52; UN Tech. Assistance Bd, Manila 1952–54; Spanish Supervisor, Univ. of Cambridge 1955–56; UN Tech. Assistance Bd, Colombia 1956–57, Uruguay 1957–59, Bolivia 1960–65; Resident Rep. UNDP, Ethiopia and UNDP Liaison Officer with ECA 1965–67; Sr Econ. Adviser, Office of Prime Minister, London 1967–68; Sr Asst to Commr in charge of study of Capacity of UN Devt System 1968–69; Resident Rep. UNDP, Morocco 1969–72, Chile (also UNDP Liaison Officer with ECLAC) 1972–74; Deputy to UN Under-Sec.-Gen. in charge of UN Relief Operation to Bangladesh and Deputy Co-ordinator of UN Emergency Assistance to Zambia 1973; with UNDP, New York 1974–78; Asst Sec.-Gen. of UN (Dept of Tech. Co-operation for Devt) 1978–87; Special Rep. of Sec.-Gen. to Bolivia 1982–92, for co-ordination of earthquake relief assistance to Mexico 1985–87; Under-Sec.-Gen. UN 1987–93, Dir-Gen. of UN office at Vienna, Head of Centre for Social Devt and Humanitarian Affairs 1987–92, Special Rep. of Sec.-Gen. for Angola and Head of Angolan Verification Mission 1992–93; Adviser to UN Sec.-Gen. on peacekeeping, post-conflict peacebuilding and training troops for UN peacekeeping missions 1994–; Chair. Advisory Group of Lessons Learned Unit, Dept of Peacekeeping Operations, UN 1996–2002; Co-ordinator of UN Drug Control Related Activities 1987–91, of Int. Co-operation for Chernobyl 1991–92 and for countering impact of burning oil wells in Gulf War 1991–92; Sec.-Gen. 8th UN Congress on Prevention of Crime and Treatment of Offenders Aug. 1990; writer, lecturer, consultant and adviser (ad honorem) to Bolivian Govt 1993–97, 2002–06 and to UN 1993–2001; Consultant to UN Dept of Political Affairs on post-conflict peacebuilding 1996–2001; mem. Advisory Bd UN Studies at Yale Univ. 1994–, Advisory Council Oxford Research Group 1997–, Advisory Bd UN Intellectual History Project 1999–; Trustee Helpage Int. 1994–97; Patron and Bd mem. British Angola Forum 1998–; mem. Pres. Carter's Int. Council for Conflict Resolution 2002–; Vice-Pres. UK/UN Asscn 2002–; mem. Editorial Bd Global Governance 2004–; Hon. Fellow Newnham Coll. Cambridge 1991; Commdr Ouissam Alaouite, Morocco 1972; Dama Gran Cruz Condor of the Andes, Bolivia 1986; Grosse Goldene Ehrenzeichen am Bande, Austria 1993, Grand Officer, Order of Bernardo O'Higgins, Chile 2006; Dr hc (Essex) 1994; Hon. LLD (Westminster) 1996; Hon. DSc (Econ) (London) 1998; Hon. DIur (Cambridge) 2004; Reves Peace Prize, William and Mary Coll., USA 1993. *Publications:* The Administration of International Development Aid 1969, Gate of the Sun: A Prospect of Bolivia 1970, Africa and the World (co-ed. with R. K. A. Gardiner and C. Patterson) 1970, Desarrollo Diferente para un Pais de Cambios: Salir del Circulo

Vicioso de la Riqueza Empobrecedura 1995, Orphan of the Cold War: The Inside Story of the Collapse of the Angolan Peace Process 1992–93 1996, Never Learn to Type: A Woman at the United Nations 2003, numerous articles on UN reforms and peacekeeping, Angola, econ. and social devt. *Address:* The Walled Garden, Knill, nr Presteigne, Powys, LD8 2PR, Wales (home); c/o PNUD, Casilla 9072, La Paz, Bolivia. *Telephone:* (1544) 267411 (Wales) (home); (1544) 260331 (Wales) (home).

ANTHONY, Kenny Davis, LLB, BSc, PhD; Saint Lucia politician; b. 8 Jan. 1951. *Education:* Univ. of Birmingham, Univ. of the West Indies. *Career:* Leader, Saint Lucia Labour Party; Prime Minister of Saint Lucia, Minister of Finance, Planning, Devt, Information and the Civil Service 1997–2001, Prime Minister, Minister of Finance, Int. Financial Services, Econ. Affairs and Information 2001–06.
Address: Tom Walcott Building, 2nd Floor, Jeremie Street, POB 427, Castries, Saint Lucia. *Telephone:* 451-8446. *Fax:* 451-9389. *Website:* www .geocities.com/~slp.

ANTOINE, Denis G., MA, MS, PhD; Grenadian diplomatist; *Ambassador to USA. Education:* DC Teachers Coll., Univ. of DC, LaSalle Univ. and Nat.-Louis Univ. *Career:* Educ. Coordinator for Catholic Charities 1982–87; Diplomatic Officer and Alt. Rep. to OAS 1986–90, Amb. and Perm. Rep. 1995–2002; Program Specialist, Govt of DC 1991–92, Educ. Supervisor DC Public Schools 1992–95; Amb. to USA and Perm. Rep. to OAS (also accred to Panama and Mexico) 1995–, Coordinator Caribbean Community (CARICOM) Corps of Ambs 1997–2004, Vice-Chair. OAS Fellowships Cttee 1998, Vice-Chair. Perm. Council of OAS 2001, Chair. 2002, Dean of Corps of Ambs of the Western Hemisphere; Chair. Exec. Cttee Inter-American Council for Integral Devt (CEPCIDI) 1999–2001; Chair. Young Americas Business Trust; Head of Del. for the Summit Implementation Review Group meetings; mem. Bd Dirs Inter-American Agency for Cooperation and Devt.
Address: Embassy of Grenada, 1701 New Hampshire Avenue, NW, Washington, DC 20009, USA (office). *Telephone:* (202) 265-2561 (office). *Fax:* (202) 265-2468 (office). *E-mail:* grenada@oas.org (office). *Website:* www.grenadaembassyusa.org (office).

ANTONAKOPOULOS, Gen. Georgios, LLB; Greek army officer; b. 5 Jan. 1943, Patra, Peloponnisos; m.; two c. *Education:* Aristotle Univ. of Thessaloniki, Hellenic Nat. Defence Coll., Hellenic Higher Army War Coll. *Career:* began career in Hellenic Armed Forces 1967, held positions successively as Artillery Battery Commdr, Instructor Artillery Schools, Staff Officer Infantry Div., Staff Officer Intelligence Div., Commdr Artillery Battalion, Commdr Field Artillery Command, Chief of Staff Mechanized Div., Dir 1st Staff Office Hellenic Army Gen. Staff, Brigade Commdg Gen., Dir. Operation Br. Hellenic Army Gen. Staff, Commdg Gen. XII Mechanized Infantry Div., Commdg Gen. D'Army Corps, Chief of Hellenic Army Gen. Staff, Chief of Hellenic Nat. Defence Gen. Staff 2002–05; Medal for Mil. Valour Class A and B, Chief of Hellenic Army Gen. Staff Commendation Medal, Star of Merit and Honour, Army Meritorious Command Commendation Medal Class A, Staff Officer Service Commendation Medal Class A, Golden Cross of the Order of Honour, Knight Commdr's Cross of Order of the Phoenix, Knight Commdr's Cross of Order of Honour.
Address: Ministry of Defence, Mesogeion 151, 15 500 Xolargos, Greece (office). *Telephone:* (210) 6598604 (office). *Fax:* (210) 6443832 (office). *E-mail:* minister@mod.gr (office). *Website:* www.mod.gr (office).

ANTONENKO, Oksana, BA, MA, PhD; Russian academic; *Senior Fellow, International Institute for Strategic Studies (IISS); Education:* Moscow State Univ., John F. Kennedy School of Govt, Harvard Univ., USA, LSE, UK. *Career:* Researcher, Strengthening Democratic Insts. Project, Harvard Univ. 1990–96; Leader and Research Fellow, Russian Mil. Reform Program, IISS 1996–2000, Dir Research and Seminar Program on Russian Regional Perspectives on Foreign and Security Policies, Sr Fellow, Russia and Eurasia 2000–. *Publications include:* Russia and the European Union: Prospects for a New Relationship (co-ed.) 2005; numerous scholarly reports and papers.
Address: International Institute for Strategic Studies, Arundel House, 13–15 Arundel Street, Temple Place, London, WC2R 3DX, England (office). *Telephone:* (20) 7379-7676 (office). *Fax:* (20) 7836-3108 (office). *E-mail:* Antonenko@iiss.org (office). *Website:* www.iiss.org (office).

ANTONIO, Joseph Philippe, LLB; Haitian politician and diplomatist; b. 22 July 1939, Saint-Marc; six c. *Education:* Port-au-Prince Univ., Ecole Normale Supérieure, Univ. of Geneva, Switzerland. *Career:* Prof. Nouveau Collège Bird, Haiti 1966–71; Dir-Co-ordinator Haitian Centre of Research and Documentation 1978–91; Chargé d'affaires, UN, New York 1991–94, Perm. Rep. 1995, 1998; Chargé d'affaires, Embassy in Germany 1992–94; Minister of Foreign Affairs and Religion 2001–04.

Address: c/o Ministry of Foreign Affairs and Religion, boulevard Harry S. Truman, Cité de l'Exposition, Port-au-Prince, Haiti (office).

ANTONSSON, Markús Örn; Icelandic diplomatist; *Ambassador to Canada;* b. 25 May 1943; m. Steinunn Ármannsdóttir; two c. *Education:* Reykjavík Coll., exchange student in USA. *Career:* part-time journalist and photographer, Morgunbladid (daily) 1961–65; trained in broadcasting journalism and TV production in UK and Sweden; reporter, newspresenter and programme producer, RUV TV 1965–70, Dir-Gen. Nat. Broadcasting Service, RUV TV and Radio 1985–91, Dir RUV Radio Div. 1995–98, Dir-Gen. RUV TV and Radio 1998–2005; mem. Broadcasting Council 1979–85, Chair. 1983–85; City Councillor, Reykjavík 1970–85, mem. Exec. Cttee Reykjavík City Council and Chair. several other cttees, Pres. City Council 1983–85, Chair. City Council Exec. Cttee and Leader of Independence Party Councillors' Group; Mayor of Reykjavík 1991–94; Amb. to Canada 2005–; mem. Bd Atlantic Alliance Asscn of Young Political Leaders 1971–75, Man. of Eurimages, European Film Fund 1994–99, Icelandic Symphony Orchestra 1995–98, Icelandic Nat. League 1997–2003 (Pres. 1998–2003); Ed. business and travel magazines with Frjálst framtak publishing house 1972–83; mem. Rotary 1983–, Jt-Ed. Rotary Norden (regional magazine for Rotary in the five Nordic countries) 1996–; mem. Exec. Cttee and Advisory Council European Cultural Foundation, Amsterdam 1994–.
Address: Embassy of Iceland, Constitution Square, 360 Albert Street, Suite 710, Ottawa, ON K1R 7X7, Canada (office). *Telephone:* (613) 482-1944 (office). *Fax:* (613) 482-1945 (office). *E-mail:* icemb.ottawa@utn.stjr.is (office). *Website:* www.iceland.org/ca (office).

ANTONY, Arackaparambil Kurian, BA, BL; Indian politician; *Minister of Defence;* b. 28 Dec. 1940, Cherthala, Alappuzha Dist, Kerala; m. Elizabeth Antony; two s. *Education:* Maharajas Coll., Government Law Coll., Ernakulam. *Career:* mem. Rajya Sabha (Parl.) from Kerala 1985–95, 2005–; fmr Minister of Civil Supplies, Consumer Affairs and Public Distribution; Chief Minister of Kerala 1977–78, 1995–96, 2001–04; Minister of Defence 2006–; Chair. Disciplinary Cttee of All India Congress Cttee.
Address: Ministry of Defence, South Block, New Delhi 110 011 (office); Anjanam, Easwara Vilasam Road, Thiruvananthapuram 695014, India (home). *Telephone:* (11) 23019030 (office). *Fax:* (11) 23015403 (office). *E-mail:* ak.antony@sansad.nic.in. *Website:* www.mod.nic.in (office).

ANWARZAI, Mohammad Anwar; Afghan civil servant and diplomatist; *Ambassador to Pakistan;* b. 1937, Kabul; m. Fauzia Asif Anwarzai; two s. two d. *Education:* Nejat (Amani) High School, Law Faculty, Kabul Univ., Univ. of Oxford, UK. *Career:* began career in civil service 1960; sr diplomat, served in various sections of Ministry of Foreign Affairs, including at Archives Dept, UN and Int. Confs Dept, Econ. Dept, Cultural Relations and at Political Div., first diplomatic assignment abroad as jr mem. in Perm. Mission of Afghanistan to UN, New York, Second Sec. 1964–69, represented Afghanistan on different cttees during 21st–24th Sessions of UN Gen. Ass., First Sec., Embassy in Moscow 1973–76, Chargé d'affaires a.i., Embassy in Tripoli 1976–78, forced with his family to become political refugees following Soviet invasion of Afghanistan, spent next 23 years in exile, returned to Afghanistan following Bonn Agreement Feb. 2002, assigned to Ministry of Foreign Affairs as Dir Fourth Political Dept responsible for European countries 2002–04, Minister Counsellor, Perm. Mission to UN, Geneva 2004–05, Amb. to Australia 2005–07, to Pakistan 2007–; Co-founder and fmr mem. Bd of Dirs Global Partnership for Afghanistan, Vice-Pres. and COO –2005.
Address: Embassy of Afghanistan, 8, Street 90, G-6/3, Islamabad 44000, Pakistan (office). *Telephone:* (51) 2824505 (office). *Fax:* (51) 2824504 (office). *E-mail:* contact@islamabad.mfa.gov.af (office). *Website:* www .islamabad.mfa.gov.af (office).

APARICIO OTERO, Jaime, LLB, MA; Bolivian international organization official and fmr diplomatist; *Vice-President, Inter-American Juridical Committee, Organization of American States; Education:* Univ. Mayor de San Andrés, Diplomatic Acad. of Bolivia. *Career:* career diplomat for Bolivian Foreign Office 1975–90, 1993–97; Prof. of Bolivian Diplomatic History and Law, Diplomatic Acad. of Bolivia 1985–92; Deputy Dir La Razón newspaper 1991–93; Prof. of Int. Law, Catholic Univ. of La Paz 1992–93; Vice-Minister then Acting Minister of Foreign Affairs 1993–97; Nat. Coordinator (first) Summit of the Americas, Miami and Santa Cruz 1993–97; Sr Adviser on Political Affairs to Sec.-Gen. of OAS 1997–98; Dir Office of Summits of the Americas Follow-Up, OAS 1998–2000, Exec. Sec. Summits of the Americas Secr. 2000–03; Amb. to USA 2003–06; Vice-Pres. OAS Inter-American Juridical Cttee, Rio de Janeiro, Brazil 2006–.
Address: Inter-American Juridical Committee, Avenida Marechal Floriano, 196-3 andar, Palacio de Itamaraty, Centro 20080-002, Rio de Janeiro,

R.J., Brazil (office). *Telephone:* (21) 2206-9903 (office). *Fax:* (21) 2203-2090 (office). *Website:* www.oas.org/cji (office).

APPLEBY, Scott, PhD; American research institute director, historian and academic; *John M. Regan Jr. Director of the Kroc Institute for International Peace Studies and Professor of History, University of Notre Dame; Education:* Univ. of Chicago. *Career:* Chair. Dept of Religious Studies, St. Xavier Coll., Chicago 1982–87; Co-Dir Fundamentalism Project, American Acad. of Arts and Sciences 1988–93; currently Prof. of History, Univ. of Notre Dame, Fellow, Joan B. Kroc Inst. for Int. Peace Studies 1996–, John M. Regan Jr Dir. 2000–. *Publications:* Transforming Parish Ministry: The Changing Roles of Clergy, Laity, and Religious Women (co-author) 1989, Church and Age Unite! The Modernist Impulse in American Catholicism 1992, Bring Right: Conservative Catholics in America (co-ed.) 1995, Spokesman for the Despised: Fundamentalist Leaders of the Middle East (ed.) 1997, The Ambivalence of the Sacred: Religion, Violence and Reconciliation 2000, Fundamentalism Project (five vols, co-ed. with Martin E. Marty).
Address: Joan B. Kroc Institute for International Peace Studies, 106 Hesburgh Center for International Studies, University of Notre Dame, Notre Dame, IN 46556, USA (office). *Telephone:* (574) 631-5665 (office). *Fax:* (574) 631-6973 (office). *E-mail:* Appleby.3@nd.edu (office). *Website:* www.nd.edu/~krocinst (office).

APPLEWHAITE, Lolita; Barbadian government official, international organization executive and academic; *Deputy Secretary-General, Caribbean Community and Common Market (CARICOM); Career:* fmr Perm. Sec., Ministry of Educ., Youth and Culture; fmr Dir Centre for Int. Services, Univ. of the West Indies, Mona, Jamaica; fmr Deputy Regional Authorising Officer, Caribbean Community (CARICOM) Secr., Georgetown, Guyana, currently Deputy Sec.-Gen.
Address: Caribbean Community Secretariat, PO Box 10827, Turkeyen Greater, Georgetown, Guyana (office). *Telephone:* (2) 222-0001 (office). *Fax:* (2) 222-0171 (office). *E-mail:* info@caricom.org (office). *Website:* www.caricom.org (office).

ARAGHCHI, (Seyed) Abbas, BA, MA, PhD; Iranian diplomatist; *Ambassador to Japan;* b. 1962, Tehran; m. Bahareh Araghchi; three c. *Education:* School of Int. Relations, Tehran, Azad Univ., Univ. of Kent, UK. *Career:* expert, Int. Affairs Div., Ministry of Foreign Affairs 1988–91, Deputy Dir for Islamic Forums, Regional and Non-Aligned Movt 1991–92, Chargé d' Affairs, Perm. Mission to Org. of Islamic Conf., Jeddah, Saudi Arabia 1992; Sr Researcher, Inst. for Political and Int. Studies (research inst. affiliated to Ministry of Foreign Affairs) 1995–97, Head, Center for Persian Gulf and Middle East Studies 1997–98, Dir Gen. 1998–2000, Editor in Chief Journal of Foreign Policy 1998–99; Lecturer, Faculty of International Relations 1995–99, Rector 2003–05; Amb. to Finland (also accred to Estonia) 1999-2003; Dir Western Europe Affairs, Foreign Ministry 2003–05; Deputy Foreign Minister for Legal and Int. Affairs 2005–08; Amb. to Japan 2008–.
Address: Embassy of Iran, 3-13-9, Minami Azabu, Minato-ku, Tokyo 106-0047, Japan (office). *Telephone:* (3) 3446-8011 (office). *Fax:* (3) 3446-9002 (office). *E-mail:* sjei@gol.com (office). *Website:* www.iranembassyjp.com (office).

ARAGONA, Giancarlo, LLB; Italian diplomatist; *Ambassador to UK;* b. 14 Nov. 1942, Messina. *Education:* Univ. of Messina. *Career:* joined Ministry of Foreign Affairs, Rome 1969, First Sec., Vienna 1972–74, Consul, Italian Consulate, Freiburg 1974–77, Counsellor, Lagos 1977–80, Directorate-Gen. for Political Affairs, Ministry of Foreign Affairs 1980, later Dept for Co-operation and Devt, First Counsellor, London 1984–87, First Counsellor, Perm. Mission of Italy to NATO, Brussels 1987–92, Diplomatic Adviser, Ministry of Defence 1992–94, Deputy Head of Staff to Foreign Minister 1994–95, Head of Staff 1995–96, Sec.-Gen. OSCE, Vienna 1996–99, Amb. to Russia 1999–2001, Dir-Gen. for Multilateral Political Affairs and Human Rights 2001–04, Amb. to UK 2004–; Hon. KCVO.
Address: Embassy of Italy, 14 Three Kings Yard, London, W1K 4EH, England (office). *Telephone:* (20) 7312-2200 (office). *Fax:* (20) 7313-2230 (office). *E-mail:* ambasciata.londra@esteri.it (office). *Website:* www .amblondra.esteri.it (office).

ARANDA DA SILVA, Manuel; Mozambican UN official and diplomatist; *Humanitarian Deputy Special Representative to the Secretary-General, United Nations;* b. 21 June 1951; m. Ana de Carvalho; one s. two d. *Education:* studies in econs in Portugal and France. *Career:* fmr activist in Mozambique liberation movt; fmr Minister of Trade and held several other govt posts, including in Ministry of Interior and Natural Disaster Prevention Comm.; has worked for UN World Food Programme in Sudan, Senegal, Rome and China, first ever Humanitarian Coordinator

(HC) in Angola during the country's civil war and ensuing humanitarian crisis, eventually taking on role of UN Resident Coordinator and Resident Rep. of UNDP, fmr Dir Div. on Complex Disasters, Dept of Humanitarian Affairs, UN HQ, New York, also served as HC for Horn of Africa, coordinating humanitarian response to drought of 2000, Deputy Special Rep. to Sec.-Gen. and UN HC and Resident Coordinator for Sudan 2004–.
Address: United Nations Mission in Sudan, House No 7, Block 5, R.F.E., Gama'a Avenue, POB 913, 11111 Khartoum, SudanTel: 1 83 783 820 Fax:; United Nations Mission in Sudan, PO Box 5013, Grand Central Station, New York, NY 10163-5013, USA (office). *Telephone:* 1 83 783 820 (Khartoum) (office). *Fax:* 1 83 783 764 (Khartoum) (office). *E-mail:* registry .sd@undp.org (office). *Website:* www.sd.undp.org (office).

ARANGIO-RUIZ, Gaetano; Italian professor of law; b. 10 July 1919, Milan. *Education:* Univ. of Naples. *Career:* Prof. of Int. Law, Univ. of Camerino 1952–54, Univ. of Padua 1955–67, Univ. of Bologna 1968–74; Prof. of Int. Law, Univ. of Rome 1974–, now Prof. Emer.; mem. Iran-United States Claims Tribunal, The Hague 1989–; Visiting Prof., Virginia Univ. Law School 1965, European Cen., Johns Hopkins School of Advanced Int. Studies 1967–75; Lecturer, Hague Acad. of Int. Law 1962, 1972, 1977, 1984; mem. UN Int. Law Comm. 1985–96; Special Rapporteur on State Responsibility 1987–96; mem. Int. Law Inst.; Dr hc (Univ. Panthéon-Assas, Paris II, France) 1997; Giuseppe Capograssi Prize 1990, Scanno Law Prize 2001. *Publications include:* Rapporti contrattuali fra Stati e organizzazione internazionale 1950, Gli enti soggetti 1951, Sula dinamica della base sociale 1954, The Normative Role of the UN General Assembly (Hague Rec.) Vol. III 1972, L'Etat dans le sens du droit des gens et la notion du droit international, 'Österreichische Zeitschrift für Öffentliches Recht' 1975–76, Human Rights and Non-Intervention in the Helsinki Final Act (Hague Rec.) Vol. IV 1977, The UN Declaration on Friendly Relations and the System of the Sources of International Law (Sijthoff and Noordhoff) 1979, le Domaine réservé, General Course in International Law (Hague Rec.) Vol. V 1990, Non-Appearance Before the International Court of Justice (report to the Int. Law Inst.) International Law Institute Yearbook 1991, On the Security Council's 'Law-Making', Rivista di Diritto Internazionale 2000, Dualism Revisited: International Law and Inter-individual Law, Rivista di Diritto Internazionale 2003, Article 39 of the ILC First-Reading Articles on State Responsibility, *ibidem,* The ICJ Statute, The Charter and Forms of Legality Review of Security Council Decisions, Liber Amicorum Cassese 2003, Customary Law, on the theory of 'spontaneous' international custom, Droit du Pouvoir, Pouvoir du Droit 2007, International Law and Interindividual Law: New Perspectives on the Divide Between National and International Law (co-eds J. Nijman and A. Nollkaemper) 2007.
Address: c/o Iran-United States Claims Tribunal, Parkweg 13, 2585 JH The Hague, Netherlands (office); Corso Trieste 51, interno 4, 00198 Rome, Italy (home). *Telephone:* (70) 3520064 (office); (06) 8559720 (home); (70) 3551371 (Netherlands) (home); (0564) 819200 (Italy) (home). *Fax:* (70) 3502456 (office).

ARÁOZ ESPARZA, Ántero Flores; Peruvian lawyer, politician and academic; *Minister of Defence;* b. 28 Feb. 1942, Lima. *Education:* Pontifical Catholic Univ. of Peru, Univ. of the Pacific, Nat. Univ. of San Marcos, Lima. *Career:* Univ. Prof., Faculty of Law, Univ. of Lima, Faculty of Law, Univ. of St Martín de Porres, Inst. of Govt, Univ. of St Martín de Porres; visiting prof. at numerous univs; Expository Pres. Peruvian Inst. of Humanistic Studies; Dir Estudio Flores-Aráoz & Asociados S.C. de R.L.; Vice-Pres. Sociedad de Beneficencia Pública de Lima 1980–85; Vice-Pres. and Pres. Caja de Ahorros de Lima (Savings Bank of Lima) 1980–85; Pres. Lotteries of Lima and Callao 1980–85; Metropolitan Regidor of Lima 1987–89, Dir Caja Municipal de Crédito Popular; Nat. Deputy 1990–92, mem. Constituent Congress 1993–95, Congressman of the Repub. 1995–, re-elected 2000, 2001, 2006, fmr mem. Consultative Comm., Ministry of Integration, Consultative Comm., Sec. of State of Integration, Consultative Comm. of Integration, Ministry of Industries, Tourism and Integration; mem. Consultative Cttee, Constitutional Comm. of Congress 2006–07, Consultative Comm., Ministry of Justice, Pres. Congress of the Repub. 2004–05, Pres. Constitutional Comm. Regulation of the Congress of the Repub. 2005–06; Minister of Defence 2007–; Rep. of Peru before the OAS 2007; Vice-Pres. Cttee against the Territory of the OAS 2007; mem. Peruvian Del. to Socio-Econ. Advisory Cttee (CAES) of Cartagena Agreement for several years; mem. and Pres. Partido Popular Cristiano –2007; mem. Unidad Nacional (Nat. Unity); columnist in various media; Hon. Prof. at several univs; Gran Cruz de la Orden José Gregorio Paz Soldán, Decoration 'Hipólito Unanue', Gran Cruz del Congreso de la República, Gran Cruz de la Orden del Sol; decorations from Colombia, Chile, Russian Fed. and Morocco; decorations of Peruvian Navy, Air Force, Nat. Police; Dr hc from several univs. *Publication:* Autoritarismo o Democracia 2006.

Address: Ministry of Defence, Avenida Arequipa 291, Lima 1, Peru (office). *Telephone:* (1) 6190600 (office); (1) 4335150 (office). *Fax:* (1) 4333636 (office). *E-mail:* webmaster@mindef.gob.pe (office). *Website:* www.mindef .gob.pe (office).

ARAÚJO, María Consuelo; Colombian politician; b. 1971, Cesar province; m.; one c. *Education:* Externado Univ. of Colombia, Columbia Univ., New York, Univ. of Milan, Sorbonne, Paris. *Career:* teaching asst, Externado Univ. of Colombia; Vice-Minister's Asst, Ministry of Law and Justice; Foreign Trade Adviser, Agricultural and Rural Devt Ministry; President's Asst, Communications Dept Chief, Housing Programme Dir, Rural and Industrial Bank; Commercial Dir Bermudez y Valenzuela Finance Co.; Botanic Garden Dir, Bogota; Recreation and Sports Inst. Dir, Bogota; Minister of Culture 2002–06, of Foreign Affairs 2006–07 (resgnd); mem., Bd of Dirs Bogota Aqueduct and Sewer Enterprise, Nat. Network of Botanical Gardens, Recreational and Sportive Local Inst., Capital Channel, Inst. for Childhood Protection; Ciudad de Bogota Civil Meritory Order. *Address:* c/o Ministry of Foreign Affairs, Palacio de San Carlos, Calle 10a, No 5-51, Bogotá, DC, Colombia (office).

ARAÚJO PERDOMO, Fernando, DEng; Colombian politician and engineer; b. 1955, Cartagena; m.; four s. *Education:* Javeriana Pontifical Univ. *Career:* Gen. Man. Empresas Públicas de Cartagena 1983–84; Dir Gen. Inmuebles Nacional 'MOPT' 1985–86; fmr Prof. of Engineering, Jorge Tadeo Lozano Univ., Univ. of Cartagena; Minister of Devt 1998–2000; captured and held hostage by Revolutionary Armed Forces of Colombia (FARC) 2000–06; Minister of Foreign Affairs 2007–08; unsuccessful cand. in Cartagena mayoral elections 1998; fmr Pres. Colombian Chamber of Construction (CAMACOL); fmr mem. Bd of Dirs El Universal (magazine), Hotel Las Américas Beach Resort. *Address:* c/o Ministry of Foreign Affairs, Palacio de San Carlos, Calle 10a, No 5-51, Bogotá, DC, Colombia (office).

ARBATOV, Aleksei Georgiyevich, DrHistSc; Russian politician; *Deputy Chairman, State Defence Committee;* b. 17 Jan. 1951, Moscow; m.; one d. *Education:* Moscow Inst. of Int. Relations. *Career:* researcher, then Head of Div., Inst. of World Econ. and Int. Relations (IMEMO), USSR (now Russian) Acad. of Sciences 1976–, Head Centre of Geopolitical and Mil. Prognoses 1992; Dir Centre on Disarmament and Strategic Stability of Asscn of Foreign Policy; adviser in different UN bodies; mem. State Duma (Parl.) 1993–99; Deputy Chair. State Defence Cttee 1994–; mem. faction Yabloko, mem. Cen. Council Yabloko Movt (now Yabloko Party). *Publications:* numerous papers and articles on problems with Russian foreign policy, int. relations and US political system. *Address:* State Duma of the Russian Federation, 1 Okhotny Ryad Street, 103265 Moscow, Russia (office). *Telephone:* (495) 292-80-23 (office). *Fax:* (495) 292-80-23 (office).

ARBOUR, Louise, CC, BA, LLL; Canadian judge (retd) and UN official; b. 10 Feb. 1947, Montréal; one s. two d. *Education:* Collège Regina Assumpta, Montréal, Université de Montréal. *Career:* articling, Legal Dept, City of Montréal 1970; called to Québec Bar 1971, Ont. Bar 1977; law clerk, Supreme Court of Canada 1971–72; Research Officer, Law Reform Comm. and mem. Criminal Procedure Project 1972; Lecturer in Criminal Procedure, Osgoode Hall Law School, York Univ., Toronto 1974, Asst Prof. 1975, Assoc. Prof. 1977–87, Assoc. Dean July–Dec. 1987; called to Bar, Ont. 1977; Judge, Supreme Court of Ont. (High Court of Justice) 1987–90; Judge, Court of Appeal for Ont. 1990–96; apptd by Order-in-Council as Commr to conduct inquiry into certain events at Prisons for Women, Kingston April 1995; Chief Prosecutor, Int. Criminal Tribunals for Fmr Yugoslavia and Rwanda, The Hague 1996–99; Puisne Judge, Supreme Court of Canada 1999–2004; UN High Commr for Human Rights 2004–08; Vice-Pres. Canadian Civil Liberties Asscn –1987; Lifetime mem. l'Asscn des jurists d'expression française de l'Ontario 1992–, Int. Council, Inst. for Global Legal Studies, Washington Univ. School of Law, Saint Louis, Mo. 2001; mem. Advisory Bd International Journal of Constitutional Law 2001–; mem. Bd of Eds Journal of International Criminal Justice 2003–; mem. Bd of Trustees, Int. Crisis Group 2000–; Hon. Prof., Univ. of Warwick, UK 1999–2004; Hon. mem. American Soc. of Int. Law 2000, Golden Key Nat. Honour Soc. 2000; Hon. Bencher Gray's Inn, London, England 2001; Hon. Fellow, American Coll. of Trial Lawyers 2003; Hon. LLD (York) 1995, (Law Soc. of Upper Canada, New Brunswick, Laurentian Univ., Université du Québec à Montréal) 1999, (Université Libre de Bruxelles, Univ. of Victoria, Kingston Royal Mil. Coll., Chicago-Kent Coll. of Law, Université de Montréal, McMaster Univ., Univ. of Western Ontario, Univ. of Toronto, Univ. of Glasgow, Queen's Univ., Carleton Univ.), (Mount Saint Vincent Univ., Univ. of King's Coll., Université de Moncton, Memorial Univ., St John's, Newfoundland, Windsor Univ., Concordia Univ., Univ. of British

Columbia) 2001, (Lakehead Univ.) 2002, (Université de Picardie Jules Verne, St Francis Xavier Univ., Antigonish, NS) 2003; Hon. DUniv (Ottawa) 1997; Médaille de l'Université de Montréal 1995, Achievement Award, Women's Law Asscn, Toronto 1996, G. Arthur Martin Award, Criminal Lawyers' Asscn 1998, First Recipient Toronto 1999 Medal of Honour, Int. Asscn of Prosecutors 1998, Medal of Honour, Int. Asscn of Prosecutors 1999, Médaille du Mérite, Institut de recherches cliniques de Montréal 1999, Fondation Louise Weiss Prize, Paris 1999, Second Annual Service to Humanity Award, Pennsylvania Bar Foundation 2000, Franklin and Eleanor Roosevelt Four Freedoms Medal (Freedom from Fear), Roosevelt Study Centre, Middleburg, Netherlands 2000, Women of Distinction Award, Toronto Hadassah-Wizo 2000, Peace Award, World Federalists of Canada 2000, Lord Reading Law Soc.'s Human Rights Award 2000, Wolfgang Freidman Memorial Award, Columbia Law School 2000, Eid-ul-Adha Award, Asscn of Progressive Muslims of Ontario 2000, Médaille du Barreau du Québec 2001, Nat. Achievement Award, Jewish Women Int. of Canada 2001, Stefan A. Riesenfeld Symposium Award, Berkeley Journal of International Law 2002, McGill Centre for Research and Teaching on Women Person of the Year 2002 Award 2002, 2002 Year Award, Prix de la Fondation Justice dans le Monde de l'Union internationale des Magistrats 2002, Médaille de la Faculté de droit de l'Université de Montréal 2003, inducted into Int. Hall of Fame – International Women's Forum 2003, Médaille 125e anniversaire, Faculté de droit, Asscn des diplômés en droit, Université de Montréal 2003. *Publications:* numerous articles on criminal procedure, human rights, civil liberties and gender issues. *Address:* c/o OHCHR-UNOG, 8–14 Avenue de la Paix, 1211 Geneva 10, Switzerland.

ARCAYA, Ignacio; Venezuelan diplomatist; b. 3 June 1939, Caracas; m.; two c. *Education:* Cen. Univ. of Venezuela. *Career:* Third Sec. Perm. Mission to UN in Geneva 1966–68, Second Sec., Ministry for Foreign Affairs 1968–69, First Sec., Mission to OAS, Washington, DC 1969–72, Counsellor Inst. of Foreign Trade, Ministry of Foreign Affairs 1972–75, Minister Counsellor of Econ. Affairs, Embassy in Paris 1975–78, Amb. to Australia (also accred to NZ, Fiji and the Philippines) 1978–84; Sec.-Gen. Asscn of Iron Ore Exporting Countries 1984–88; Amb.-at-Large, Ministry of Foreign Affairs 1988, Amb. to Chile 1989–92, to UK (also accred to Ireland) 1992–95, to Argentina 1995–98, to USA 2001–02; Minister of the Interior and Justice, then Acting Pres. 1999; Perm. Rep. to UN, New York 2000. *Address:* c/o Ministry of Foreign Affairs, Torre MRE, esq. Carmelitas, Avda Urdaneta, Caracas, 1010, Venezuela. *Telephone:* (212) 862-1085 (office). *Fax:* (212) 864-3633 (office). *E-mail:* criptogr@mre.gov.ve (office).

ARCE CATACORA, Luis Alberto, MSc; Bolivian government official; *Minister of Finance;* b. 28 Sept. 1963, La Paz; m.; three c. *Education:* Universidad Mayor de San Andrés, Univ. of Warwick, UK. *Career:* with Cen. Bank of Bolivia 1988–2006; fmr consultant Natsuky Co., Nacida Co., Centro de Estudios para el Desarrollo Laboral y Agrario, Sistema Contable Computarizado; Minister of Finance 2006–. *Publications include:* numerous journal articles. *Address:* Ministry of Finance, Edif. Palacio de Comunicaciones, Avda Mariscal Santa Cruz, La Paz, Bolivia (office). *Telephone:* (2) 237-7234 (office). *Fax:* (2) 235-9955 (office).

ARCHER, Nicholas Stewart, MVO; British diplomatist; *High Commissioner to Malta;* b. 24 Dec. 1960; m. Erica Power 1999; one s. *Education:* Univ. of Durham. *Career:* worked briefly at Sotheby's; joined FCO, studied Arabic and served in Jordan 1986–89, worked on Middle East Peace Process in London, representing the UK at Madrid Peace Conf., Pvt. Sec. to Minister of State, Douglas Hogg 1992–95, Head of Econ. and Commercial Section, Oslo 1995–97, Pvt. Sec. to HRH The Prince of Wales 1997–2001, Head of NE Asia and Pacific Dept 2001–02, Head of Near East and N Africa Dept 2002–05, worked with Nat. Audit Office on their report on the British consular response to the Tsunami 2005, High Commr to Malta 2006–. *Address:* British High Commission, Whitehall Mansions, Ta'Xbiex Seafront, Ta'Xbiex MSD 11, MaltaGC (office). *Telephone:* 23230000 (office). *Fax:* 23232216 (office). *E-mail:* bhcvalletta@fco.gov.uk (office). *Website:* www.britishhighcommission.gov.uk/malta (office).

ARDITO BARLETTA, Nicolás, PhD, MS; Panamanian politician and economist; b. 21 Aug. 1938, Aguadulce, Coclé; m. María Consuelo de Ardito Barletta; two s. one d. *Education:* Univ. of Chicago and N Carolina State Univ. *Career:* Cabinet mem. and Dir Planning 1968–70; Dir Econ. Affairs Org. of American States 1970–73; Minister of Planning 1973–78; Negotiator of econ. aspects of Panama Canal Treaties 1976–77; Vice-Pres. World Bank for Latin America and Caribbean 1978–84; Founder and first Pres. Latin American Export Bank (BLADEX) 1978; Pres. Latin American Econ. System (SELA) Constituent Ass.; Pres. of Panama 1984–85; Gen. Dir of Int. Centre for Econ. Growth 1986–95; Dir Autoridad de la Región

Interoceanía (ARI) 1995–2000; Chair. Asesores Estrategicos; mem. Bd of Dirs of several corpns, banks and policy insts. *Publications:* numerous publications on econ. and social devt issues.
Address: PO Box 0830, 00378 Panamá 9, Panama. *Telephone:* 264-6675. *Fax:* 223-6488. *E-mail:* asesores@cwpanama.net.

AREFI, Hamid Reza Nafez; Iranian diplomatist; m. Razieh Nafez Arefi. *Career:* Minister Counsellor, Embassy in London –2005, 2006–, Chargé d'affaires a.i. in UK 2006.
Address: Embassy of Iran, 16 Prince's Gate, London, SW7 1PT, England (office). *Telephone:* (20) 7225-3000 (office). *Fax:* (20) 7589-4440 (office). *E-mail:* info@iran-embassy.org.uk (office). *Website:* www.iran-embassy .org.uk (office).

ARENDARSKI, Andrzej, PhD; Polish politician, business executive and university lecturer; *President, Polish Chamber of Commerce;* b. 15 Nov. 1949, Warsaw; m. Agnieszka Łypacewicz; three s. one d. *Education:* Warsaw Univ. *Career:* teacher, East Dembowski Secondary School, Warsaw 1972–73, Inst. of Philosophy and Sociology of Polish Acad. of Sciences, Warsaw 1973–75; mem. Solidarity Trade Union 1980–; Ed.-in-Chief, underground journal Zeszyty Edukacji Narodowej 1981–82; co-f. Agric.-Industrial Soc., Konin 1988; mem. Soc. for Econ. and Econ. Action, Warsaw 1988–; co-f. Social Movt for Econ. Initiatives SPRING 1988; Deputy to Sejm (Parl.) 1989–93; mem. Liberal Democratic Congress (KLD) 1989–94, Deputy Chair. KLD 1989–94, mem. KLD Political Council 1991–94, now Chair.; Pres. Polish Chamber of Commerce 1990–; Minister of Foreign Econ. Co-operation 1992–93; Chair. Polish-Ukrainian Chamber of Commerce 1996–; Sec.-Gen. Polish Asscn Industry, Commerce and Finance 1997–; Chair. Polish-American Small Business Consultation Fund; CEO Tel-Emergo, Telephony Service Providers. *Publications:* contribs to underground journals 1981–89; co-author: Polska lat 80-tych: Analiza stanu obecnego i perspektywy rozwoju sytuacji politycznej w Polsce 1984, Stan środowiska przyrodniczego 1984.
Address: Krajowa Izba Gospodarcza, ul. Trębacka 4, 00-074 Warsaw, Poland. *Telephone:* (22) 630-96-00 (office). *Fax:* (22) 827-46-73 (office). *E-mail:* aarendarski@kig.pl (office). *Website:* www.kig.pl/english/index .htm (office).

ARENS, Moshe; Israeli politician, academic and diplomatist; b. 7 Dec. 1925, Lithuania. *Education:* Massachusetts and California Insts of Tech., USA. *Career:* Assoc. Prof. of Aeronautical Eng, Technion (Israel Inst. of Tech.), Haifa; Deputy Dir Israel Aircraft Industries, Lod; Amb. to USA 1982–83; Minister of Defence 1983–84, 1999, without Portfolio –1987, of Foreign Affairs 1988–90, of Defence 1990–92; Adviser to Prime Minister 2001; elected to Knesset (Likud), mem. Knesset Finance Cttee 1973; Israel Defence Prize 1971; Assoc. Fellow, AIAA. *Publications:* Broken Covenant 1994, several books on propulsion and flight mechanics.
Address: c/o Likud, 38 Rehov King George, Tel-Aviv 61231, Israel.

ARGÜELLO, Jorge Martín Arturo, MA; Argentine politician and diplomatist; *Permanent Representative, United Nations;* b. 20 April 1956, Buenos Aires. *Education:* San Andrés Univ. *Career:* mem. City Council, Buenos Aires 1987–91; mem. Nat. Congress 1991–95, 2003–07, Pres. Foreign Relations Cttee, Parl. Observatory of the Malvinas Question, Vice-Pres. Perm. Comm. on Int. Peace and Security with Inter-Parl. Union; mem. Constitutional Convention, Buenos Aires 1996–2003, Legislature 1997–2000, 2000–03; Latin America Rep. Parliamentarians for Global Action 1994–95; Perm. Rep. to UN, New York 2007–.
Address: Permanent Mission of Argentina to the United Nations, 1 United Nations Plaza, 25th Floor, New York, NY 10017, USA (office). *Telephone:* (212) 688-6300 (office). *Fax:* (212) 980-8395 (office). *E-mail:* argentina@un .int (office). *Website:* www.un.int/argentina (office).

ARGUETA DE BARILLAS, Marisol; Salvadorean lawyer and diplomatist; *Minister of Foreign Affairs;* b. 1968; m. Carlos R. Barillas; three d. *Education:* Univ. of Oxford, UK, New York Univ., USA. *Career:* fmr Asst Prof. of Constitutional Law and Political Law, El Salvador; Alt. Rep. to UN, New York 1990–97; Minister Counselor Embassy in Washington DC 1997–99; Gen. Dir of Foreign Policy, Ministry for Foreign Affairs –2004; Adviser to Minister of Foreign Affairs 2004–08, Minister of Foreign Affairs 2008–; fmr Vice-Pres. OAS Nat. Authorities Meeting for the Devt of Women; mem. Bd of Dirs Hogares CREA-El Salvador, Salvadorean Foundation for the Elderly, Int. Inst. for Women; mem. Oxford Union Soc.
Address: Ministry of Foreign Affairs, Calle El Pedregal, Blvd Cancillería, Ciudad Merliot, Antiguo Cuscatlan, El Salvador (office). *Telephone:* 2231-1000 (office). *Fax:* 2243-9656 (office). *E-mail:* webmaster@rree.gob.sv (office). *Website:* www.rree.gob.sv (office).

ARIAS, Inocencio F.; Spanish civil servant and diplomatist; *Consul General in Los Angeles;* b. 20 April 1940; m.; three c. *Career:* joined diplomatic service

1967; Dir of Diplomatic Information Office, Ministry of Foreign Affairs 1980–82, 1985–88, 1996–97; Under-Sec. Ministry of Foreign Affairs 1988–91; State Sec. for Int. Co-operation for Iberoamerican Affairs 1991–93; Gen. Dir Real Madrid 1993–95; Perm. Rep. to UN, New York 1998–2004; currently Consul Gen. Los Angeles, Calif.; fmr Prof. of Int. Relations, Univ. Complutense, Univ. Carlos III, Madrid. *Publications include:* numerous papers and contribs.
Address: Consulate of Spain, 5055 Wilshire Blvd., Suite 860, Los Angeles, CA 90054, USA (office). *Telephone:* (323) 938-0158 (office). *Fax:* (323) 938-0112 (office). *E-mail:* cog.losangeles@mae.es (office). *Website:* www.maec .es/Subwebs/Consulados/LosAngeles/en (office).

ARIAS, Ricardo Alberto, BS, LLB, LLM; Panamanian diplomatist and lawyer; *Permanent Representative, United Nations;* b. 11 Sept. 1939; m.; four c. *Education:* Edmund A. Walsh School of Foreign Service, Georgetown Univ., Univ. of Puerto Rico, Yale Univ. Law School. *Career:* Prof. of Fiscal Law and Admin Law, Santa Maria La Antigua Univ. 1973–78; Founding mem. and Pnr, Galindo, Arias and López (law firm), practised 1998–2004; Amb. to USA 1994–96; Foreign Minister 1996–98; Perm. Rep. to UN, New York 2004–; f. La Prensa newspaper; Founding Dir and fmr Pres. Panamanian Stock Exchange; mem. Panamanian Bar Asscn, Interamerican Bar Asscn, Int. Bar Asscn; mem. Bd of Dirs Banco Gen. SA, Copa Airlines 1985–; Hon. Pres., La Prensa.
Address: Office of the Permanent Representative of Panama to the United Nations, 866 United Nations Plaza, Suite 4030, New York, NY 10017, USA (office). *Telephone:* (212) 421-5420 (office). *Fax:* (212) 421-2694 (office). *E-mail:* emb@panama_msun.org (office).

ARIAS CÁRDENAS, Francisco Javier, BMASc; Venezuelan academic and diplomatist; *Permanent Representative, United Nations;* m.; two c. *Education:* Javeriana Univ., Colombia, Univ. of the Andes, Venezuelan Mil. Acad. *Career:* Prof., Venezuelan Mil. Acad. 1979–81, Venezuelan Army Artillery School 1981–82; Commdr Multiple Launch Rocket Group of José Gregorio Monagas 1989–92; Pres. Foundation for Mother and Child Food Programme 1992–95; Gov. Zulia State 1995–2000; Pres. Colombian-Venezuelan Council for Border Govs 1997–2000; Perm. Rep. to UN, New York 2006–; also currently Pres. Union for Progress (political movt), For a Praiseworthy Venezuela (civil asscn).
Address: Permanent Mission of Venezuela to the United Nations, 335 East 46th Street, New York, NY, 10017, USA (office). *Telephone:* (212) 557-2055 (office). *Fax:* (212) 557-3528 (office). *E-mail:* venezuela@un.int (office). *Website:* www.un.int/venezuela (office).

ARIETTI, Michael Ray; American diplomatist; *Ambassador to Rwanda;* m.; one d. *Career:* worked as Peace Corps volunteer in India; joined State Dept 1973, career mem. Sr Foreign Service, served in embassies in Sweden, Australia and Iran, Washington appointments have included Dir Office of UN Peacekeeping Operations, Dir Human Rights Office, and senior positions responsible for arms control negotiations, and Middle Eastern issues, Deputy Chief of Mission, Lusaka, Zambia, Deputy Perm. Rep., US Mission to UN, Geneva, Dir Office of W African Affairs –2005, Amb. to Rwanda 2005–.
Address: US Embassy, #2657 Avenue de la Gendarmerie (Kacyiru), Kigali, Rwanda (office). *Telephone:* 596400 (office). *Fax:* 596771 (office). *E-mail:* irckigali@state.gov (office). *Website:* rwanda.usembassy.gov (office).

ARISTIDE, Jean Bertrand, PhD; Haitian fmr head of state and fmr ecclesiastic; b. Salut; m. Mildred Trouillot 1996; one d. *Career:* Roman Catholic priest; expelled from Salesian Order 1988; resgnd from priesthood Nov. 1994; Pres. of Haiti Feb.–Oct. 1991, 1993–96, Feb. 2001–04; in exile in Caracas, Venezuela Oct. 1991; returned Oct. 1993 after resignation of junta; fled to Africa following civil unrest Feb. 2004; Research Fellow in African Languages, Univ. of SA 2004–07. *Publications:* Haiti and the New World Order 1995, Dignity 1996, Eyes of the Heart 2000.
Address: c/o Centre for African Renaissance Studies, PO Box 392, UNISA, 0003 Pretoria, South Africa.

ARLACCHI, Pino; Italian politician and international organization official; b. 21 Feb. 1951, Gioia Tauro, Reggio Calabria; m.; two c. *Career:* Assoc. Prof. of Applied Sociology, Univ. of Calabria 1982–85, Univ. of Florence 1988–94; apptd Prof. of Sociology, Univ. of Sassari 1994; elected to Chamber of Deputies 1994–95, to Senate 1995–97; Vice-Pres. Parl. Comm. on the Mafia; UN Under-Sec.-Gen. and Dir-Gen. UN Vienna Office 1997–2002; Exec. Dir UN Office for Drug Control and Crime Prevention 1997–2002; fmr Pres. Int. Asscn for the Study of Organized Crime; Hon. Pres. Giovanni Falcone Foundation 1992–; Fellow, Ford Foundation. *Publications:* numerous publs on int. organized crime.
Address: c/o Vienna International Centre, PO Box 500, 1400 Vienna, Austria (office).

ARMACOST, Michael Hayden, MA, PhD; American diplomatist, politician and administrator; *Shorenstein Distinguished Fellow, Asia Pacific Research Center, Institute for International Studies, Stanford University;* b. 15 April 1937, Cleveland, Ohio; brother of Samuel Henry Armacost; m. Roberta June Bray 1959; three s. *Education:* Carleton Coll., Friedrich Wilhelms Univ., Columbia Univ. *Career:* Assoc. Prof. of Govt, Pomona Coll., Claremont, Calif. 1962–70; Wig Distinguished Prof. 1966; Special Asst to Amb., American Embassy, Tokyo 1972–74, Amb. to Philippines 1982–84, to Japan 1989–93; mem. Policy Planning, Staff Dept, Washington, DC 1974–77; Sr Staff mem., Nat. Security Council, Washington, DC 1977–78; Dep. Asst Sec. Defence, Int. Security Affairs Defence Dept, Washington, DC 1978–79; Principal Deputy Asst Sec. E Asian and Pacific Affairs 1980–81; Undersec. Political Affairs 1984–89; mem. Council on Foreign Relations; Visiting Prof. of Int. Relations, Int. Christian Univ., Tokyo 1968–69; Pres. Brookings Inst., Washington, DC 1995–2002, Trustee 2002–, White House Fellow 1969–70; currently Shorenstein Distinguished Fellow, Asia Pacific Research Center, Stanford Institute for Int. Studies; Superior Honour Award, State Dept 1976; Distinguished Civilian Service Award, Defence Dept 1980; Presidential Distinguished Service Award; Sec. of State Distinguished Service Award. *Publications:* The Politics of Weapons Innovation 1969, The Foreign Relations of United States 1969, Friends or Rivals 1996.
Address: Asia Pacific Research Center, Stanford University, Encina Hall, Room E301, Stanford, CA 94305-6055, USA (office). *Telephone:* (650) 724-4002 (office). *Fax:* (650) 723-6530 (office). *E-mail:* armacost@stanford.edu (office). *Website:* fsi.stanford.edu/people/michaelharmacost (office).

ARMELLINI, Antonio; Italian diplomatist; *Ambassador to India;* b. 2 Aug. 1943, Rome; m.; two c. *Education:* Univ. of Rome La Sapienza, Stanford Univ., USA. *Career:* served as int. civil servant, Council of Europe, Strasbourg 1968–69; joined Ministry of Foreign Affairs 1969, assigned to Foreign Minister's Private Office 1969–72, 1974–75, assigned to Prime Minister's Office 1975–76, Head of Political Planning 1981–85, Head CSCE Dept 1988–92; foreign posts include Spokesman for EC Commr Altiero Spinelli, Brussels 1972–74, Commercial Counsellor and Head, Econ. Section, Embassy in Warsaw 1976–78, Political Counsellor and Deputy Head of Mission, Embassy in Addis Ababa 1978–80, Roving Amb. to CSCE (Vienna, Moscow, Helsinki) 1990–92, Minister-Counsellor and Deputy Head of Mission, Embassy in London 1993–98, Amb. to Algeria 1998–2000, Amb.-at-large, Special Italian Envoy in Iraq 2003–04, Amb. to India 2004–; Nat. Coordinator, Stability Pact for S-E Europe, Rome 2000–01; Int. Antiterrorism Coordinator, Rome 2001–2002; Diplomatic Adviser to Minister of Transport 1985–87, Chair. Quadripartite Tech. Comm. on transalpine tunnels, Ministry of Transport 1986–87; Adjunct Prof. of Comparative Politics, LUISS Univ., Rome 2003–04; Dir Venezia 2000 Foundation 2000–; mem. IISS, London, Istituto Affari Internazionali, Rome.
Address: Embassy of Italy, 50e Chandragupta Marg, Chanakyapuri, New Delhi 110 021, India (office). *Telephone:* (11) 26114355 (office). *Fax:* (11) 26873889 (office). *E-mail:* ambasciata.newdelhi@esteri.it (office). *Website:* www.ambnewdelhi.esteri.it (office).

ARMITAGE, Richard Lee; American fmr diplomatist; *President, Armitage International LC;* b. 1945. *Education:* US Naval Acad. *Career:* US naval officer served Viet Nam –1973; US Defense Attache Office Saigon 1973–75; consultant, Pentagon 1975, posted Tehran, Iran –1976; private sector 1976–78; Admin. Asst to Kan. Senator Robert Dole, 1978–80; Sr Advisor, Interim Foreign Policy Advisory Bd 1980; Deputy Asst Sec. of Defense, E Asia and Pacific Affairs 1981–83, Asst Sec. of Defense, Int. Security Affairs 1983–89; Presidential Special Negotiator, Philippines Mil. Bases Agreement and Special Mediator for Water, Middle East 1989–92; Special Emissary to King Hussein, Jordan 1991; Coordinator, Emergency Humanitarian Assistance 1992; Dir, assistance to new independent states (NIS), fmr Soviet Union 1992–93; Pres. Armitage Associates LLC 1993–2001; Deputy Sec. of State 2001–05; Pres. Armitage Int. LC 2005–; mem. Bd of Dirs ManTech Int. Corpn 2005–, ConocoPhillips Co. 2006–, Transcutaneous Technologies Inc. (TTI) 2006–; mem. Bd of Trustees Center for Strategic and Int. Studies (CSIS); Distinguished Public Service (four times), Outstanding Public Service, State Dept Distinguished Honor Award, numerous US mil. decorations, decorations from govts of Thailand, Repub. of Korea, Bahrain, Pakistan; Dept of Defense Medal, Sec. of Defense Medal, Presidential Citizens Medal.
Address: Armitage International LC, 2300 Clarendon Blvd, Suite 601, Arlington, VA 22201-3392, USA (office). *Telephone:* (703) 248-0344 (office). *Fax:* (703) 248-0166 (office). *Website:* www.armitageinternational .net (office).

ÁRNASON, Kristinn F., LLM; Icelandic diplomatist; *Director, Defence Department, Ministry of Foreign Affairs;* b. 5 Jan. 1954, Reykjavík; m.; three c. *Education:* Univ. of Iceland, Univ. of Exeter, UK, Univ. of Oslo,

Norway. *Career:* solicitor in pvt. attorney's office 1979–80, 1982, for Fed. of Employees 1983–85; First Sec. Ministry of Foreign Affairs 1985–87; Deputy Perm. Rep. to Int. Orgs, Geneva 1987–92; Chief Negotiator and Spokesman on Fisheries, Ministry of Foreign Affairs 1992–94, Dir for External Trade 1994–98; apptd Amb. 1997; Amb. to Slovakia and Poland 1999–2002, to Norway and Czech Repub. 1999–2003, to Egypt 2000–03; Dir Defence Dept, Ministry for Foreign Affairs 2003–.
Address: Department of Defence, Ministry of Foreign Affairs, Raudarárstíg 25, 150 Reykjavík, Iceland (office). *Telephone:* 5459900 (home). *Fax:* 5622373 (office). *E-mail:* external@utn.stjr.is (office). *Website:* www.mfa.is (office).

ARNAULT, Jean; French UN official and diplomatist; *Special Representative for Georgia, United Nations;* b. 1951; m.; one c. *Education:* Univ. of Sorbonne-Paris I, Polytechnic of Cen. London, UK. *Career:* fmr Sr Political Affairs Officer in Namibia and Afghanistan, Political Adviser to Special Rep. for Western Sahara 1991, Observer, then Mediator in Guatemala peace negotiations 1994–96, Special Rep. for Guatemala 1997–2000, Rep. of UN Sec.-Gen. in Burundi 2000–01, Deputy Head of UN Assistance Mission in Afghanistan 2002–04, Special Rep. for Afghanistan and Head of UN Assistance Mission 2004–06, Sec.-Gen.'s Special Rep. for Georgia and Head of UN Observer Mission in Georgia (UNOMIG) 2006–; Visiting Fellow, Center for Int. Studies, Princeton Univ., USA 2001.
Address: United Nations Observer Mission in Georgia, 38 Krtsanisi Street, 380060 Tbilisi, Georgia (office). *Telephone:* (32) 507200 (office). *E-mail:* unomig-pio@un.org (office); envera.selimovic@un.org (office). *Website:* www.unomig.org (office).

ARNOLD, Hans Redlef, PhD; German diplomatist (retd), writer and academic; *Lecturer, Academy of Political Science, Munich;* b. 14 Aug. 1923, Munich; m. Karin Baroness von Egloffstein 1954; three d. *Education:* Univ. of Munich. *Career:* joined Foreign Service, FRG; served Embassy, Paris 1952–55, Foreign Office, Bonn 1955–57, Embassy, Washington, DC 1957–61, Foreign Office 1961–68, sometime head of Foreign Minister Willy Brandt's office; Amb. to the Netherlands 1968–72; Head, Cultural Dept, Foreign Office 1972–77; Amb. to Italy 1977–81; Insp.-Gen. German Foreign Service 1981–82; Amb. and Perm. Rep. to UN and Int. Orgs, Geneva 1982–86; Lecturer, Acad. of Political Science, Munich; several nat. and foreign decorations. *Publications:* Cultural Export as Policy? 1976, Foreign Cultural Policy 1980, The March (co-author) 1990, Europe on the Decline? 1993, Germany's Power 1995, Europe To Be Thought Anew: Why and How Further Unification? 1999, Security for Europe (co-ed.) 2002, How Much Unification Does Europe Need? 2004; regular contribs to periodicals and newspapers.
Address: 83083 Riedering-Heft, Germany. *Telephone:* (8032) 5255. *E-mail:* hans.arnold@gmx.net (home).

ARON, Rachel Ann Golding; British diplomatist; *Ambassador to Belgium;* m. Michael Douglas Aron; two s. two d. *Career:* Desk Officer for Cyprus, FCO 1984–87, Desk Officer for Privileges and Immunities 1987–88, First Sec. (Political) and Head of Chancery, Brasilia 1988–90, Asst Head of Eastern Dept, FCO 1992–93, First Sec. (Sanctions), Perm. Mission to UN, New York 1993–96, Chair. Civil Service Selection Bd, FCO 1997–99, Counsellor (E-Guidance), Amman (remotely) 2000–02, Counsellor (E-Guidance), Brussels (remotely) 2002–04, Chair. Bd of Govs British School of Brussels 2005–07, Amb. to Belgium 2007–.
Address: British Embassy, Rue d'Arlon 85 Aarlenstraat, 1040 Brussels, Belgium (office). *Telephone:* (2) 287-62-11 (office). *Fax:* (2) 287-63-60 (office). *E-mail:* ppa@britain.be (office); info@britain.be (office). *Website:* www.britishembassy.gov.uk/belgium (office).

ARONSON, Geoffrey, BA, MLitt; American research institute director; *Director of Research and Publications, Foundation for Middle East Peace;* *Education:* Tufts Univ., St Antony's Coll., Univ. of Oxford, UK. *Career:* Visiting Scholar, Center for Contemporary Arab Studies, Georgetown Univ. 1984; Visiting Fellow, Inst. for Policy Studies 1985–87; fmr consultant, World Bank, UN; currently Dir of Research and Publs, Foundation for Middle East Peace, Washington DC, Ed. Report on Israeli Settlements in the Occupied Territories. *Publications:* From Sideshow to Center Stage: US Policy towards Egypt and Israel, Palestinians, and the Occupied Territories, Creating Facts: Israel, Palestinians, and the West Bank, Israel, Palestinians and the Intifada: Creating Facts on the West Bank; numerous articles in newspapers, magazines and journals.
Address: Foundation for Middle East Peace, 1761 N Street, NW, Washington, DC 20036, USA (office). *Telephone:* (202) 835-3650 (office). *Fax:* (202) 835-3651 (office). *E-mail:* info@fmep.org (office). *Website:* www .fmep.org (office).

ARROW, Kenneth Joseph, PhD; American economist and academic; *Professor Emeritus of Economics and Operations Research, Stanford University;* b. 23 Aug. 1921, New York; m. Selma Schweitzer 1947; two s. *Education:* The City College, Columbia Univ. *Career:* Capt. USAF 1942–46; Research Assoc. Cowles Comm. for Research in Econ., Univ. of Chicago 1947–49; Asst Assoc. and Prof. of Econs, Statistics and Operations Research, Stanford Univ., 1949–68; Prof. of Econs, Harvard Univ., 1968–79; Prof. of Econs and Operations Research, Stanford Univ., 1979–91, Prof. Emer. 1991–; mem. NAS, American Acad. of Arts and Sciences, American Philosophical Soc., Finnish Acad. of Sciences, British Acad., Inst. of Medicine, Pontifical Acad. of Social Sciences; Pres. Int. Soc. for Inventory Research 1983–90, Int. Econ. Asscn, Econometric Soc., American Econ. Asscn, Soc. for Social Choice and Welfare; Dir various cos; Order of the Rising Sun (Japan); Hon. LLD (City Univ., Univ. of Chicago, Washington Univ., Univ. of Pennsylvania, Ben-Gurion Univ., Harvard Univ., Univ. of Cyprus, Univ. of Buenos Aires); Hon. Dr of Social and Econ. Sciences (Vienna); Hon. ScD (Columbia Univ.) 1973; Hon. DSocSci (Yale) 1974; Hon. LLD (Hebrew Univ. Jerusalem) 1975, Hon. DPolSci (Helsinki) 1976; Hon. DLitt (Cambridge) 1985, (Harvard) 1999; Hon. DUniv (Uppsala) 1995; Hon. PhD (Univ. of Tel-Aviv) 2001; Dr hc (Univ. René Descartes) 1974, (Univ. Aix-Marseille III) 1985, (Univ. of Cyprus) 2000; Nobel Memorial Prize in Econ. Science 1972, John Bates Clark Medal, Von Neumann Prize, Medal of Univ. of Paris 1998, Nat. Medal of Science 2006. *Publications:* Social Choice and Individual Values 1951, 1963, Studies in the Mathematical Theory of Inventory and Production (with S. Karlin and H. Scarf) 1958, Studies in Linear and Nonlinear Programming (with L. Hurwicz and H. Uzawa) 1958, A Time Series Analysis of Inter-industry Demands (with M. Hoffenberg) 1959, Public Investment, The Rate of Return and Optimal Fiscal Policy (with M. Kurz) 1970, Essays in the Theory of Risk-Bearing 1971, General Competitive Analysis (with F. H. Hahn) 1971, The Limits of Organization 1973, Studies in Resource Allocation Processes (with L. Hurwicz) 1977, Collected Papers 1983–85, Social Choice and Multicriterion Decision Making (with H. Raynaud) 1985; more than 240 articles in learned journals. *Address:* Department of Economics, Stanford University, Stanford, CA 94305-6072 (office); 580 Constanzo Street, Stanford, CA 94305, USA (home). *Telephone:* (650) 723-9165 (office). *Fax:* (650) 725-5702 (office). *E-mail:* arrow@stanford.edu (office). *Website:* www-econ.stanford.edu/faculty/arrow.html (office).

ARSALA, Hedayat Amin, PhD; Afghan politician and economist; nephew of Pir Gailani. *Education:* high school in Kabul, George Washington Univ., Washington, DC, USA. *Career:* ethnic Pashtun descended from Jabar Khel tribe; foreign language trainer for three consecutive Peace Corps training programmes in USA; started his professional career at World Bank Youth Professional Program 1969, held various econ. and sr operational posts 1969–87; returned to Afghanistan to join Afghan resistance to Soviet occupation 1987–89, served as Sr Adviser and mem. Afghan Mujahideen Unity Council; Minister of Finance, Transitional Govt of Afghanistan 1989–92; Minister of Foreign Affairs 1993–96; Sr mem. Exec. Council of Loya Jirga (traditional council of Afghan tribal leaders) 1998–; played key role in Intra-Afghan Bonn Conf. following fall of the Taliban regime 2001; apptd Vice-Chair. and Minister of Finance of the interim admin 2001; named one of four Vice-Pres, Transitional Islamic State of Afghanistan 2001–04, Chair. Ind. Civil Services Admin Reform Comm., adviser to Cen. Statistics Office and Afghan Econ. Cooperation Cttee; mem. Afghan Nat. Security Council; Minister of Commerce and Sr Presidential Adviser 2004–06, Sr Minister in the Cabinet 2006–. *Address:* c/o Office of the President, Gul Khana Palace, Presidential Palace, Kabul, Afghanistan (office). *E-mail:* webmaster@afghanistangov.org (office). *Website:* www.president.gov.af (office).

ARTHUIS, Jean Raymond Francis Marcel; French politician; b. 7 Oct. 1944, Saint-Martin du Bois, Maine-et-Loire; m. Brigitte Lafont 1971; one s. one d. *Education:* Coll. Saint-Michel, Château-Gontier, Ecole Supérieure de Commerce, Nantes and Inst. d'Etudes Politiques, Paris. *Career:* chartered accountant, Paris 1971–86; Mayor of Château-Gontier 1971–2001; mem. Conseil, Gen., Mayenne, Château-Gontier canton 1976–, Pres. 1992–; Senator from Mayenne (Centrist Group) 1983–86, 1988–95; Sec. of State, Ministry of Social Affairs and Employment 1986–87, Ministry of Econ., Finance and Privatization 1987–88; Spokesman on Budget in Senate 1992–95; Minister of Econ. Devt and Planning May–Aug. 1995, of Econ. and Finance 1995–97; Vice-Pres. Force Démocrate (fmrly Centre des démocrates sociaux) 1995–; Vice-Pres. Nouvelle Union pour la Démocratie Française (UDF) 1998; Pres. Union centriste du Sénat 1998–2002, Financial Comm. in Senate 2002–; Chevalier du Mérite Agricole, Commandeur de l'Ordre du Mérite, Germany. *Publications:* Justice sinistrée, Démocratie en danger (co-author) 1991, Les Délocalisations et

l'emploi 1993, Dans les coulisses de Bercy, Le Cinquième pouvoir 1998, Mondialisation, la France à Contre Emploi 2007. *Address:* SENAT, Palais du Luxembourg, 75291 Paris Cedex 06 (office); Conseil général de la Mayenne, 39 rue Mazagran, BP 1429, 53014 Laval Cedex (office); 8 rue René Homo, 53200 Château-Gontier, France (home).

ARTHUR, Sir Michael Anthony, KCMG, BA; British diplomatist; *Ambassador to Germany;* b. 28 Aug. 1950; m. Plaxy Arthur; two s. two d. *Education:* St Anthony's Coll., Oxford. *Career:* entered Diplomatic Service 1972; served with Mission in New York and UN Dept, FCO 1972–74; Second Sec. in Brussels 1974–76, in Kinshasa 1976–78; Desk Officer, European Integration Dept 1978–80; Pvt. Sec. to Lord Privy Seal 1980–82; Pvt. Sec., Office of Minister of State 1982–84; First Sec. in Bonn 1984–88; Head of EC Dept 1988–93; Political Counsellor and Head of Chancery in Paris 1993–97; Dir of Resources, FCO 1997–99; Minister and Deputy Head of Mission in Washington, DC 1997–99; Dir-Gen. (EU and Econ.) FCO 2001–03; High Commr to India 2003–07; Amb. to Germany 2007–. *Address:* British Embassy, Wilhelmstrasse 70–71, 10117 Berlin, Germany (office). *Telephone:* (30) 204570 (office). *Fax:* (30) 20457594 (office). *E-mail:* info@britischebotschaft.de (office). *Website:* www.britischebotschaft.de (office).

ARTHUR, Rt Hon. Owen, PC; Barbadian politician and economist; b. 17 Oct. 1949; m. Beverley Jeanne Batchelor 1978. *Education:* Harrison Coll., Univ. of W Indies, Cave Hill, Univ. of W Indies, Mona. *Career:* Research Asst, Univ. of W Indies, Jamaica 1973; Asst Econ. Planner, Chief Econ. Planner Nat. Planning Agency, Jamaica 1974–79; Dir of Econs, Jamaica Bauxite Inst. 1979–81; Chief Project Analyst, Ministry of Finance, Barbados 1981–83; lecturer Dept of Man., Univ. of W Indies, Cave Hill 1986, Resident Fellow 1993; Senator 1983–84; Parl. Sec. Ministry of Finance 1985–86; mem. Barbados Labour Party (BLP), Chair. 1993–96; Prime Minister of Barbados, Minister of Defence and Security, Finance and Econ. Affairs and for the Civil Service Sept. 1994–2008. *Publications:* The Commercialisation of Technology in Jamaica 1979, Energy and Mineral Resource Development in the Jamaican Bauxite Industry 1981, The IMF and Economic Stabilisation Policies in Barbados 1984. *Address:* Barbados Labour Party, Grantley Adams House, 111 Roebuck Street, Bridgetown, Barbados (office). *Telephone:* 429-1990 (office). *Fax:* 427-8792. *E-mail:* will99@caribsurf.com (office). *Website:* labourparty.wordpress.com (office).

ARTUCIO RODRIGUEZ, Alejandro, DJur, DScS; Uruguayan diplomatist; *Permanent Representative, United Nations, Geneva;* b. 22 Aug. 1934; m.; two c. *Education:* Univ. of Repub. *Career:* Chief Counsel and Commr, Int. Comm. of Jurists, Geneva 1985–2005; Perm. Rep. of Uruguay to UN, New York 2004–06, to UN, Geneva 2007–; Special Rapporteur on Equatorial Guinea, UN High Comm. on Human Rights 1993–99; Chief Counsel for Human Rights, UN Verification Mission in Guatemala (MINUGUA) 1997; fmr mem. Governing Council, Inst. of Legal and Social Studies, Uruguay, Governing Council Assocn for Prevention of Torture, Geneva, Advice Council, Int. Service for Human Rights, Geneva, International Consulting Council, Legal and Social Studies Center, Argentina. *Address:* Office of the Permanent Representative of Uruguay to the United Nations, Rue de Lausanne 65 (4th Floor), 1202 Geneva, Switzerland (office). *Telephone:* 227318366 (office). *Fax:* 227315650 (office). *E-mail:* mission.uruguay@urugi.ch (office).

ARYSTANBEKOVA, Akmaral Khaudarovna, PhD; Kazakhstani politician and diplomatist; b. 12 May 1948, Alma-Ata (now Almaty). *Education:* Kazak State Univ. *Career:* mem. Staff Dept of Chem., Kazak State Univ. 1975–78; Chief of Dept and Sec. Cen. State Cttee, Kazak Komsomol 1978–83; mem. Supreme Council Kazakstan 1985–90, Praesidium 1987–90; Minister of Foreign Affairs 1989–91; Rep. of Kazakhstan at Perm. Mission of the fmr USSR 1991–92; Perm. Rep. and Amb., Perm. Mission of Kazakstan to UN 1992–99; Amb. to France 1999–2003; currently Amb.-at-Large, Ministry of Foreign Affairs; Deputy Chair. Kazak Friendship Soc. 1983–84; Chair. Presidium Kazakh Soc. for Friendship and Cultural Relations with Foreign Countries 1984–89; Medal of Supreme Soviet of USSR 1970, 1981, Kurmat Order 1996. *Publications:* United Nations and Kazakhstan 2002; numerous contribs to periodicals. *Address:* Ministry of Foreign Affairs, 010000 Astana, Beibitshilik 11, Kazakhstan (office). *Telephone:* (7172) 32-76-69 (office). *Fax:* (7172) 32-76-67 (home). *Website:* www.mfa.kz (office).

ASALI, Saif Mahyoub al-; Yemeni politician. *Career:* Minister of Finance 2006–07, of Industry and Commerce 2007–. *Address:* Ministry of Industry and Commerce, PO Box 22210, San'a, Yemen (office). *Telephone:* (1) 252345 (office). *Fax:* (1) 251557 (office). *E-mail:* most@y.net.ye (office). *Website:* www.most.org.ye (office).

ASAMOAH, Obed Y., JSD; Ghanaian politician and lawyer; b. 6 Feb. 1936, Likpe Bala, Volta Region; m. Yvonne Wood 1964; two s. one d. *Education:* Achimota Secondary School, Woolwich Polytechnic, London, King's Coll. London and Columbia Univ., New York. *Career:* called to the Bar, Middle Temple, London 1960; upon return to Ghana practised as solicitor and advocate of Supreme Court of Ghana; Lecturer, Faculty of Law, Univ. of Ghana, Legon 1965–69; fmr Chair. Bd of Dirs of Ghana Film Industry Corpn, Ghana Bauxite Co.; mem. Constituent Ass. which drafted Constitution for Second Repub. of Ghana 1969; elected to Parl. (Nat. Alliance of Liberals) 1969; mem. Constituent Ass. which drafted third Republican Constitution 1979; Gen. Sec. United Nat. Convention 1979, All People's Party 1981; Sec. for Foreign Affairs 1982–93; Minister of Foreign Affairs 1993–97; Attorney-Gen. and Minister of Justice 1993–2001; Chair. Nat. Democratic Congress 2002–05; mem. Ghana Bar Asscn; has served on several int. and public orgs; Patron Democratic Freedom Party; Order of the Star of Ghana 2001. *Publications:* The Legal Significance of the Declaration of the General Assembly of the United Nations 1967; articles in legal journals.
Address: PO Box 14581, Accra, Ghana. *Telephone:* (21) 668414 (home). *E-mail:* obed@obedasamoah.com.

ÁSGEIRSDÓTTIR, Berglind; Icelandic diplomatist and fmr international organization official; *Director General of External Trade, Ministry of Foreign Affairs; Education:* Boston Univ., US, Univ. of Iceland. *Career:* early career includes various positions in Ministry of Foreign Affairs from 1979 including service at embassies in Bonn and Stockholm; fmr Deputy Perm. Rep. to Council of Europe; Vice-Chair., Icelandic Del. to Conf. on Security and Confidence Bldg Measures in Europe, CSCE 1984–86; del. engaged in negotiations with EU on European Econ. Area in field of free movement of persons; Sec.-Gen., Ministry of Social Affairs 1988–96, 1999–2002; Sec.-Gen. Nordic Council, Copenhagen 1996–99; Deputy Sec.-Gen. OECD 2002–06; Dir Gen. of External Trade, Ministry for Foreign Affairs 2006–.
Address: Ministry for Foreign Affairs, Raudararstigur 25, 150 Reykjavik, Iceland (office). *Telephone:* 5459922 (office). *Fax:* 5622373 (office). *E-mail:* berglind.asgeirsdottir@utn.stjr.is (office). *Website:* www.mfa.is (office).

ÁSGRÍMSSON, Halldór; Icelandic politician; *Secretary General, Nordic Council of Ministers;* b. 8 Sept. 1947, Vopnafjörður; m. Sigurjóna Sigurðardóttir; three d. *Education:* Co-operative's Commercial Coll. and commerce univs in Bergen and Copenhagen. *Career:* Certified Public Accountant 1970; Lecturer in Auditing and Accounting, Univ. of Iceland 1973–75; mem. Parl. 1974–78, 1979–; mem. Bd Cen. Bank of Iceland 1976–83, Chair. 1981–83; mem. Nordic Council 1977–78, 1979–83, 1991–95, Chair. 1982–83, Chair. Icelandic Del. 1982–83, mem. Presidium 1991–94, Chair. Liberal Group 1992–94; Minister of Fisheries 1983–91, of Nordic Co-operation 1985–87, 1995, of Justice and Ecclesiastical Affairs 1988–89, of Foreign Affairs and External Trade 1995–2004; Prime Minister and Minister of the Statistical Bureau of Iceland 2004–06 (resgnd); Vice-Chair. Framsóknarflokkurinn (Progressive Party) 1980–94, Chair. 1994–2006; Vice-Pres. Liberal Int. 1994–99; Sec.-Gen. Nordic Council of Ministers 2007–; Kt of Order of Falcon of Iceland.
Address: Nordic Council of Ministers, Store Strandstraede 18, 1255 Copenhagen K, Denmark (office). *Telephone:* 33-96-03-22 (office). *E-mail:* ha@norden.org (office). *Website:* www.norden.org (office).

ASHCROFT, Andrew (Andy); British diplomatist. *Career:* career in British Diplomatic Service; overseas assignments include Commercial Sec., Embassy in Oman, various positions at Embassy in Israel; Pvt. Sec. to Minister of Foreign Affairs 1992–96; served in Embassy in Zimbabwe 1996; First Sec., Embassy in Harare 1996–99; Head of Caribbean Section, FCO 1999–2002; Amb. to Dominican Repub. and Haiti 2002–06.
Address: c/o Foreign and Commonwealth Office, King Charles Street, London, SW1A 2AH, England (office).

ASHDOWN OF NORTON SUB-HAMDON, Baron (Life Peer), cr. 2001, of Norton Sub-Hamdon in the County of Somerset; **Sir Jeremy John Durham (Paddy) Ashdown,** GCMG, KBE, PC; British politician; b. 27 Feb. 1941, Delhi, India; m. Jane Courtenay 1961; one s. one d. *Education:* Bedford School. *Career:* served in Royal Marines 1959–71, rank of Capt.; joined Diplomatic Service, First Sec. Mission to UN, Geneva 1971–76; Commercial Man.'s Dept, Westland Group 1976–78; Sr Man., Morlands Ltd 1978–81; employee, Dorset Co. Council 1982–83; Parl. Spokesman for Trade and Industry 1983–86; Liberal/SDP Alliance Spokesman on Education and Science 1987; Liberal MP for Yeovil 1983–88, Liberal Democrat MP for Yeovil 1988–2001; Leader Liberal Democrats 1988–99; UN Int. High Rep. to Bosnia and Herzegovina 2002–06. *Publications:* Citizen's Britain: A Radical Agenda for the 1990s 1989, Beyond Westminster 1994, The Ashdown Diaries 1988–1997 2000, The Ashdown Diaries Vol. II 1997–1999 2001, Swords and Ploughshares 2007.

Address: House of Lords, Westminster, London, SW1A 0PW, England (office). *Telephone:* (20) 7219-3000 (office). *Fax:* (20) 7219-5979 (office).

ASHE, John W., PhD; Antigua and Barbuda diplomatist; *Permanent Representative, United Nations;* m.; two c. *Education:* Univ. of Pennsylvania, USA. *Career:* Amb. to WTO; Minister responsible for Sustainable Devt Matters and WTO; Perm. Rep. to UN 2004–, Chair. Comm. on Sustainable Devt 2004–, fmr Vice-Chair. Exec. Bd UNDP/UNFPA, UNICEF, fmr Chair. UNFCCC subsidiary body on implementation; mem. and fmr Chair. Exec. Bd, Clean Devt Mechanism of Kyoto Protocol.
Address: Permanent Mission of Antigua and Barbuda, 610 Fifth Avenue, Suite 311, New York, NY 10020, USA (office). *Telephone:* (212) 541-4117 (office). *Fax:* (212) 757-1607 (office). *E-mail:* antigua@un.int (office). *Website:* www.un.int/antigua (office).

ASHE, Victor Henderson, BA, BL; American diplomatist; *Ambassador to Poland;* b. 1 Jan. 1945, Knoxville, Tenn.; m. Joan Plumlee; one s. one d. *Education:* Hotchkiss School, Lakeville, Conn., Yale Univ., Univ. of Tenn. Coll. of Law. *Career:* served 31 years in Tenn. state and city elective offices; intern in office of US Congressman Bill Brock 1965–67; mem. US Marine Corps Air Reserves 1967–1973; staff asst in office of US Senator Howard Baker 1967–68; mem. Tenn. House of Reps 1968–75, State Senate 1975–94; Exec. Dir Americans Outdoors Comm. 1985–87; Mayor of Knoxville 1987–2003; led del. of US mayors to Israel 1995 and to Uganda in 2003 to help combat HIV/AIDS; Pres. US Conf. of Mayors 1995, Tennessee Municipal League; fmr mem. Advisory Comm. on Intergovernmental Relations; fmr mem. Bd of Dirs Fannie Mae 2001–04; Amb. to Poland 2004–; Martin Luther King, Jr Holiday Comm. Chair. Award 2004, Cornelius Amory Pugsley Medal, American Acad. for Park and Recreation Admin in asscn with Nat. Park Foundation 2004.
Address: Embassy of the USA, Al. Ujazdowskie 29/31, 00-540 Warsaw, Poland (office). *Telephone:* (22) 6283041 (office). *Fax:* (22) 6288298 (office). *Website:* poland.usembassy.gov (office).

ASHEKH, Muhammad bin Ismaïl al-, DenD; Saudi Arabian diplomatist; *Ambassador to France;* b. Nov. 1964; m. Fadia El Bitar; two c. *Education:* King Saud Univ., Riyadh, Université d'Auvergne, Université de Rennes, France. *Career:* Asst, Law Dept, Univ. of Saudi Arabia, Riyadh 1986–87, Asst Head 1994–2003, Vice-Dean, Faculty of Admin Science 2000–03; Rep. of Minister of Higher Educ. and Minister of Interior in devt of nat. anti-drugs strategy 2000–03; Adviser to Minister of Foreign Affairs 2003; Amb. to France 2003–. *Publications:* numerous essays in journals.
Address: Embassy of Saudi Arabia, 5 avenue Hoche, 75008 Paris, France (office). *Telephone:* 1-56-79-40-00 (office). *Fax:* 1-56-79-40-01 (office). *E-mail:* ambsaudi@club-internet.fr (office). *Website:* www.mofa.gov.sa (office).

ASHMAWY, Muhammad Saïd al-, BA; Egyptian lawyer and writer; b. 1 Dec. 1932. *Career:* Asst of Dist Attorney, Alexandria 1954; Dist Attorney 1956; Judge 1961; Chief Prosecutor, Cairo 1973; Counsellor of State for Legislation 1977; Chief Justice High Criminal Court, Cairo 1985. *Publications:* Roots of Islamic Law 1979, Political Islam 1987, Islamic Caliphate 1990, Religion for the Future 1992, Veil and Tradition in Islam 1995, The Conflict between Arabs and Israel 1997, Reason in Islam 1998, Book of Ethics 1999, Egyptian Roots of Judaism 2001, Clash of Nations 2002.
Address: 9 Gezira al-Wosta Street, Zamalek, Cairo 11211, Egypt (home). *Telephone:* (2) 735-2060 (home). *Fax:* (2) 735-2060 (home). *E-mail:* ashmawy2@hotmail.com (home).

ASHRAWI, Hanan Daoud Khalil, BA, MA, PhD; Palestinian politician, organization executive and academic; *Media Director and Spokesperson, League of Arab States;* b. 8 Oct. 1946, Ramallah (then part of British Mandate of Palestine); m. Emile Ashrawi; two d. *Education:* American Univ. of Beirut, Univ. of Virginia, USA. *Career:* joined mainstream PLO Fatah faction; Prof. of English Literature, Birzeit Univ., West Bank 1973–90, mem. Faculty 1973–95, Chair. English Dept 1973–78, 1981–84, Dean of Faculty of Arts 1986–90; activist, Palestinian Women's Movt 1974–; f. Birzeit Univ. Legal Aid Cttee/Human Rights Action Project 1974; joined Intifada Political Cttee 1988, served on its Diplomatic Cttee 1988–93; official spokeswoman for Palestinian Del. to Middle East peace process 1991–93, mem. Leadership/Guidance Cttee and Exec. Cttee of del.; mem. Advisory Cttee Palestinian Del. at Madrid Peace Conf. on Middle East; mem. Palestinian Ind. Comm. for Palestinian Repub., Head 1993–95; Founder and Commr Gen. Palestinian Ind. Comm. for Citizens' Rights 1993–95; mem. Palestinian Legis. Council 1996– (re-elected on a nat. list, The Third Way 2006); Palestinian Authority Minister of Higher Educ. and Research 1996–98 (resgnd in protest against political corruption); f. MIFTAH (Palestinian Initiative for the Promotion of Global Dialogue and Democracy) 1998; currently Human Rights Commr (semi-official

ombudsman) and mem. Palestinian Council; Media Dir and Spokesperson Arab League 2001–; Olof Palme Prize 2002, Sydney Peace Prize 2003, ranked 96th by Forbes magazine amongst 100 Most Powerful Women 2004. *Publications:* numerous poems, short stories and papers and articles on Palestinian culture, literature and politics, including Anthology of Palestinian Literature (ed., The Modern Palestinian Short Story: An Introduction to Practical Criticism, Contemporary Palestinian Literature under Occupation, Contemporary Palestinian Poetry and Fiction, Literary Translation: Theory and Practice; A Passion for Peace 1994, This Side of Peace: A Personal Account (memoirs) 1995.
Address: Arab League, PO Box 11642, Arab League Building, Tahrir Square, Cairo, Egypt (office). *Telephone:* (2) 5750511 (office). *Fax:* (2) 5775726 (office). *Website:* www.arableagueonline.org (office); www.miftah .org (office).

ASHTAL, Abdalla Saleh al-, MA; Yemeni diplomatist; b. 5 Oct. 1940, Addis Ababa, Ethiopia; m. Vivian Eshoo al-Ashtal; one s. one d. *Education:* Menelik II Secondary School, American Univ. of Beirut and New York Univ. *Career:* Asst Dir Yemeni Bank for Reconstruction and Devt, San'a 1966–67; mem. Supreme People's Council, Hadramout Prov. 1967–68, Gen. Command Yemeni Nat. Liberation Front 1968–70; Political Adviser, Perm. Mission to UN 1970–72, Sr Counsellor 1972–73, Perm. Rep. 1973–2002; Non-Resident Amb. to Canada 1974, to Mexico 1975–79, to Brazil 1985–91 (Pres. Security Council 1991).
Address: c/o Ministry of Immigrants' and Foreign Affairs, PO Box 1994, San'a, Yemen.

ASIM, Mohamed, BA, MA, PhD; Maldivian diplomatist; *High Commissioner to UK;* b. 1960; m. Mariyam Ali Manik; one s. one d. *Education:* American Univ. of Beirut, Lebanon, California State Univ., Sacramento, USA, Australian Nat. Univ., Canberra, Australia. *Career:* early govt career as Admin. Officer, Ministry of Educ. 1982; Personnel Services Officer, Pres.'s Office 1983, then Sr Research Officer, Int. Div.; Presidential Aide 1990–92; Dir Employment Affairs 1992–96, Dir-Gen. 1996–99; Dir-Gen. Public Service Div. of Pres.'s Office 1999–2004; High Commr to Sri Lanka 2004–07, to UK 2007–; Pres. Colombo Plan Council 2004–; Grad. Asst, School of Business and Public Admin, Calif. State Univ. 1983–85; taught professional short courses in human resources man. at ANU, Canberra 1996–98; represented Maldives at numerous confs including Common-wealth Meeting of Small States, Windhoek, Namibia 1985, Third Asia Pacific Conf. on Public Admin, Katmandu, Nepal 1991; mem. Maldives del. to Commonwealth Heads of States and Govts Meeting, Kuala Lumpur, Malaysia 1989.
Address: High Commission of the Maldives, 22 Nottingham Place, London, W1U 5NJ, England (office). *Telephone:* (20) 7224-2135 (office). *Fax:* (20) 7224-2157 (office). *E-mail:* info@maldiveshighcommission.org (office). *Website:* www.maldiveshighcommission.org (office).

ASKEY, Thelma J., BA; American diplomatist and international organization executive; *Deputy Secretary-General, Organisation for Economic Co-operation and Development; Education:* Tennessee Technological Univ., Univ. of Tennessee, George Washington Univ. *Career:* worked for several years sr staffer and counsel on US House of Reps Committee on Ways and Means, Staff Dir Trade Sub-cttee, helped develop strategy for enactment and implementation of N America Free Trade Agreement (NAFTA), Uruguay Round of WTO, Africa Growth and Opportunity Act, and other trade agreements 1994–98; Commr US Int. Trade Comm. –2000; Dir US Trade and Devt Agency, Washington, DC 2001–07; Deputy Sec.-Gen. OECD in charge of Global Relations 2007–.
Address: OECD, 2 rue André Pascal, 75775 Paris Cedex 16, France (office). *Telephone:* 1-45-24-82-00 (office). *Fax:* 1-45-24-85-00 (office). *E-mail:* news .contact@oecd.org (office). *Website:* www.oecd.org (office).

ASLOV, Sirodjidin Mukhridinovich; Tajikistan diplomatist; *Permanent Representative, United Nations;* b. Feb. 1964; m.; four c. *Career:* worked in Ministry of Environment 1980–96, Deputy Chief, Hydrometeorogical Service 1995–96; Perm. Rep., Exec. Cttee, Aral Sea Fund 1996–2004; Chair., Exec. Cttee, Int. Fund for Saving Aral Sea 2002–04; First Deputy Foreign Minister 2004–05; Perm. Rep. to UN, New York 2005–.
Address: Office of the Permanent Representative of Tajikistan to the United Nations, 136 East 67th Street, New York, NY 10021, USA (office). *Telephone:* (212) 744-2196 (office). *Fax:* (212) 472-7645 (office). *E-mail:* tajikistan@un.int (office).

ASQUITH, Hon. Dominic Anthony Gerard, CMG; British diplomatist; *Ambassador to Egypt;* b. 7 Feb. 1957; m. Louise Asquith; two s. two d. *Career:* with Soviet Dept, FCO 1983–84, Southern European Dept 1984–85, Second Sec. and Head of Interests Section, Damascus 1986–87, First Sec. (Chancery), Muscat 1987–89, EC Dept (Internal), FCO 1989–90, Pvt. Sec. to Minister of State 1990–92, First Sec., Washington, DC 1992–96,

Drugs and Int. Crime Dept, FCO 1996, Minister and Deputy Head of Mission, Buenos Aires 1997–2001, Deputy Head of Mission and Chargé d'affaires a.i., Riyadh 2001–04, Deputy Special Rep. for Iraq and Deputy Head of Mission, Baghdad 2004, Dir Iraq, FCO 2004–06, Amb. to Iraq 2006–07, to Egypt 2007–.
Address: British Embassy, 7 Sharia Ahmad Ragheb, Cairo (Garden City), Egypt (office). *Telephone:* (2) 7940852 (office). *Fax:* (2) 7940859 (office). *E-mail:* info@britishembassy.org.eg (office). *Website:* www.britishembassy .org.eg (office).

ASSAD, Lt-Gen. Bashar al-; Syrian ophthalmologist, army officer and head of state; *President;* b. 11 Sept. 1965, Damascus; m. Asmaa al-Akhras 2001; one s. *Education:* Al-Huria High School, Damascus. *Career:* trained as an ophthalmologist; Capt., Medical Corps 1994, fmr commdr armoured div., Syrian Armed Forces, apptd. Col 1999; C-in-C Armed Forces 2000–; Pres. of Syria 2000–.
Address: Office of the President, Damascus, Syria (office). *Website:* www .assad.org (office).

ASSAF, Ibrahim ibn Abd al-Aziz al-, PhD; Saudi Arabian politician and economist; *Minister of Finance;* b. 28 Jan. 1949, Ayoun Al-Jawa, Qassim; m.; four c. *Education:* King Saud Univ. Riyadh, Univ. of Denver, Colo State Univ., USA. *Career:* Teaching Asst King Abdulaziz Mil. Acad. (KAMA) Riyadh 1971–82, Asst Prof. 1982–86, Head Dept of Admin. Sciences 1982–86; Visiting Lecturer Staff's Acad. 1982–83; Econ. Adviser Saudi Fund for Devt 1982–86; Alt. Exec. Dir IMF Saudi Arabia, Washington, DC 1986–89; Exec. Dir World Bank Saudi Arabia, Washington, DC 1989–95; Minister of Finance and Nat. Economy 1996–; Chair. Bd, Public Investment Fund, Pension and Retirement Fund, Saudi Fund Devt, Real Estate Devt Fund; Gov. for Saudi Arabia, Islamic Devt Bank, World Bank Group, IMF, Arab Funds and Financial Insts.; mem. Bd Supreme Econ. Council, Higher Advisory Council for Petroleum and Minerals, Saudi Arabian Oil Company (SAUDI ARA-MCO), Gen. Investment Authority, Supreme Tourism Authority, Higher Council Islamic Affairs, Higher Council for Univs, Civil Service Council, Manpower Council, Mil. Service Council, Higher Council for Civil Defense, Saudi Econ. Asscn.
Address: Ministry of Finance, Airport Road, Riyadh, 11177, Saudi Arabia (office). *Telephone:* (1) 405-0000 (office). *Fax:* (1) 401-0583 (office). *E-mail:* Minister@mof.gov.sa. *Website:* www.mof.gov.sa.

ASSAKER, Boutros; Lebanese diplomatist; *Ambassador to France; Career:* fmr Deputy Perm. Rep. to FAO; Amb. to Russian Fed. (also accred to Belarus) 2000–03; Acting Sec.-Gen. and Dir Political and Consular Affairs Dept, Ministry of Foreign Affairs and Emigrants 2004–06; Amb. to France 2006–.
Address: Embassy of Lebanon, 3 villa Copernic, 75116 Paris, France (office). *Telephone:* 1-40-67-75-75 (office). *Fax:* 1-40-67-16-42 (office). *E-mail:* na@ambliban.fr (office). *Website:* www.ambassadeliban.fr (office).

ASSEFA LEMMA, Samuel, PhD; Ethiopian diplomatist; *Ambassador to USA; Education:* Swarthmore Coll., Pa, Princeton Univ., NJ. *Career:* taught at Princeton Univ., Williams Coll. and Rutgers Univ.; Vice-Pres. Addis Ababa Univ. –2006; Amb. to USA 2006–; Founding mem. 'Ethiopia Past and Future' (ad hoc group of ambs from leading donor countries and mems of Ethiopian civil soc.) 2005; mem. Bd of Dirs Ethiopian Orthodox Church Devt Comm.; has also worked with several insts involved in strengthening civil society, including InterAfrica Group, Center for Peace, Democracy and Human Rights, African Initiative for a Democratic World Order, Heinrich Böll Foundation and Bonn Int. Centre for Conversion.
Address: Embassy of Ethiopia, 3506 International Drive, NW, Washington, DC 20008, USA (office). *Telephone:* (202) 364-1200 (office); (202) 274-4570 (Sec.) (office). *Fax:* (202) 587-0195 (office). *E-mail:* info@ ethiopianembassy.org (office). *Website:* www.ethiopianembassy.org (office).

ASSELBORN, Jean; Luxembourg politician; *Deputy Prime Minister and Minister of Foreign Affairs and Immigration;* b. 27 April 1949; m. Sylvie Hubert 1980; two d. *Education:* Athénée de Luxembourg and Univ. of Nancy. *Career:* left school to work for Uniroyal Labs 1967; became involved in trade-union movt, elected to post of Youth Rep. of Fed. of Luxembourg Workers (Lëtzebuerger Aarbechterverband, precursor to current OGB-L or Ind. Fed. of Trade Unions of Luxembourg); joined civil admin of Luxembourg City 1968–69; returned to Steinfort to serve in local admin 1969; Admin. Inter-municipal Hosp., Steinfort 1976; Mayor of Steinfort 1982–2004; elected to Luxembourg Parl. 1984–, Head, Parl. Group of Luxembourg Socialist Workers' Party (LSAP) 1989, Chair. LSAP 1997, Vice-Pres. Luxembourg Parl. 1999–2004, mem. Cttee of the Regions of the EU; Vice-Pres. European Socialist Party 2000–04; Deputy Prime Minister and Minister for Foreign Affairs and Immigration 2004–.

Address: Ministry of Foreign Affairs and Immigration, Hôtel St Maximin, 5 rue Notre-Dame, 2240 Luxembourg Ville, Luxembourg (office). *Telephone:* 478-1 (office). *Fax:* 22-31-44 (office). *E-mail:* officielle.boite@mae.etat.lu (office). *Website:* www.mae.lu (office).

ASSOWEH, Ali Farah; Djibouti politician; *Minister of Economy, Finance and Planning, in charge of Privatization; Career:* Minister of Economy, Finance and Planning, in charge of Privatization 2005–; Gov. for Djibouti IMF, World Bank, Int. Finance Corpn, Islamic Devt Bank 2005–. *Address:* Ministry of the Economy, Finance and Planning, BP 13, Djibouti, Djibouti (office). *Telephone:* 353331 (office). *Fax:* 356501 (office). *E-mail:* cabmefpp@intnet.dj (office); dfe@intnet.dj (office). *Website:* www.ministere-finances.dj (office).

ASTAKHOV, Yevgeny Mikhailovich, CandHist; Russian diplomatist; b. 9 March 1937, Moscow; m.; one d. *Education:* Tashkent Pedagogical Inst., Moscow State Inst. of Int. Relations, Diplomatic Acad., USSR Ministry of Foreign Affairs. *Career:* on staff USSR Embassy, Brazil 1963–65, Attaché 1965–68, Third Sec. 1968–69, Second Sec. 1971–73, First Sec. 1973–75; Third Sec., Div. of Latin America, USSR Ministry of Foreign Affairs 1969–71; First Sec., European Dept, USSR Ministry of Foreign Affairs 1977–78; First Sec. USSR Embassy, Spain 1979–80; Counsellor 1980–85; Head of Sector IEO 1985–87, Deputy Head 1987–90; Deputy Head, First European Dept, USSR Ministry of Foreign Affairs 1990; Amb. to Nicaragua 1990, to Honduras 1991, to El Salvador 1992; Russian Amb. to Uruguay 1999–2000, to Argentina 2000–04; observer at Latin America Asscn of Integration.

ASTBURY, Nicholas Paul; British diplomatist; b. 13 Aug. 1971. *Career:* joined FCO 1994, Desk Officer, EU Dept (External) 1994–95, Second Sec., Chancery, Colombo 1995–99, Head of Section, EU Dept (Internal), FCO 1999–2000, EU Spokesman, News Dept 2001, Pvt. Sec., Parl. Under-Sec. of State's Office 2001–02, Deputy Head of UK Visas 2002–04, Deputy Head of British Embassy Drugs Team, Kabul 2005, Amb. to Eritrea 2006–08. *Address:* Foreign and Commonwealth Office, King Charles Street, London, SW1A 2AH, England (office). *Telephone:* (20) 7008-1500 (office). *Website:* www.fco.gov.uk (office).

ASTORI, Danilo; Uruguayan economist and politician; *Minister of Economy and Finance;* b. 1940, Montevideo; m.; four c. *Education:* Univ. of the Repub., Montevideo. *Career:* econs researcher in govt agric. agencies and econ. consultant to UN agencies 1961–89; consultant to Head of Frente Amplio party 1984–; f. Asamblea Uruguay party 1994; elected as Senator 1995–2000, re-elected 2000–05; Minister of Economy and Finance 2005–. *Address:* Ministry of Finance and Economy, Colonia 1089, 3°, 11100 Montevideo, Uruguay (office). *Telephone:* (2) 9021017 (office). *Fax:* (2) 9021277 (office). *Website:* www.mef.gub.uy (office).

ASTURIAS, HRH The Prince of; Felipe de Borbón, (Prince of Girona, Prince of Viana, Duke of Montblanc, Count of Cervera, Lord of Balaguer), LLB, MA; Spanish; b. 30 Jan. 1968, Madrid; m. Letizia Ortiz Rocasolano 2004; two d. *Education:* Santa Maria de los Rosales, Madrid, Lakefield Coll., Canada, Gen. Mil. Acad., Zaragoza, Naval Coll., Marin, Air Force Gen. Acad., San Javier, Madrid Autonomous Univ., Georgetown Univ., USA. *Career:* heir to the throne; received dispatches as Infantry Lt, Sub-Lt and Lt of the Air Arm 1989, holds mil. ranks of Commdr of the General Land Army Corps (Infantry), Lt Commdr in the General Navy and Commdr of the General Air Force; qualified helicopter pilot; numerous official visits to countries in Europe, Latin America, Middle East, Asia and Australasia 1995–; named Eminent Person for UN Int. Year of Volunteers 2001; mem. Olympic sailing team, Barcelona 1992; established Prince of Asturias Foundation; Hon. Pres. Codespa Foundation, Asscn of European Journalists, Spain. *Address:* c/o The Royal Household of HM the King, La Zarzuela Palace, Madrid, Spain (office). *Website:* www.casareal.es.

ATACANLI, Sermet; Turkish diplomatist; *Ambassador to Japan; Career:* Amb. to South Africa 2000–03 (also accred to Botswana 2001–03); Chief Foreign Affairs Adviser to Presidency 2004; Deputy Spokesman, Ministry of Foreign Affairs 2005–07; Amb. to Japan 2007–; mem. EU–Japan Fest Cttee. *Address:* Embassy of Turkey, 2-33-6 Jingumae, Shibuya-ku, 150-0001 Tokyo, Japan (office). *Telephone:* (3) 3470-5131 (office). *Fax:* (3) 3470-5136 (office). *E-mail:* embassy@turkey.jp (office). *Website:* www.turkey.jp (office).

ATAEVA, Aksoltan Toreevna; Turkmenistan diplomatist, politician and medical practitioner; *Permanent Representative, United Nations;* b. 6 Nov. 1944, Ashgabat; m. Tchary Pirmoukhamedov 1969; one s. one d. *Education:* Turkmenistan State Medical Inst., Ashgabat. *Career:* doctor,

Hosp. No. 1, Ashgabat 1968–79, Asst to Chief Doctor 1979–80; Vice-Dir Regional Health Dept, Ashgabat 1980–85; Vice-Minister of Health 1985–90, Minister 1990–94; Minister of Social Security 1994–95; Amb. and Perm. Rep. to UN 1995–; mem. Democratic Party 1992–, Khalk Maslakhaty (Supreme People's Council of Turkmenistan) 1993–; Pres. Trade Unions of Turkmenistan 1994–95; Hon. Assoc. of Int. Acad. of Computer Sciences and Systems, Kiev, Ukraine 1993; Hon. Cand.Sci, Hon. DrMed (Russian Scientific Research Inst. for Social Hygiene and Health Care Man.) Neutrality Order, Gairat Medal 1992, Medal for Love of Motherland 1996, Order of Gurbansoltan Eje 1997, Order of Bitaraplyk 1999, Order for the Great of Independent Turkmenistan. *Publications:* 108 publs and two monographs on health and maternity care. *Address:* Permanent Mission of Turkmenistan to UN, 866 UN Plaza, Suite 424, New York, NY 10021, USA. *Telephone:* (212) 486-8908 (office). *Fax:* (212) 486-2521 (office). *E-mail:* turkmenistan@un.int (office).

ATALLAH, Hatem, MA; Tunisian diplomatist; *Ambassador to Ethiopioa;* m. Faika Atallah; two c. *Education:* Tunis Univ. of Arts and Univ. of Tunis. *Career:* Second Sec., Embassy in Washington, DC, USA 1983–87, Counsellor of Foreign Affairs 1988–90; Chief of Staff, Ministry of Foreign Affairs 1991, 1997; Amb. to S Africa, Mozambique, Zambia, Namibia, Angola and Zimbabwe 1994–96, to USA 2000–05, to Ethiopia 2008–; mem. Advisory Bd to Dean of Int. Studies, Univ. of Wisconsin, Madison. *Address:* Embassy of Tunisia, Wereda 17, Kebele 19, Bole Road, POB 100069, Addis Ababa, Ethiopia (office). *Telephone:* (11) 6612063 (office). *Fax:* (11) 6614568 (office). *E-mail:* embassy.tunisia@telecom.net.et (office).

ATIQUR RAHMAN, A. K. M., PhD; Bangladeshi economist, diplomatist and academic; *Ambassador to Bhutan; Career:* fought during war of independence in 1971; fmr Assoc. Prof., later Prof. and Chair. Dept of Econs, North South Univ., Dhaka, Head of Inst. of Devt, Environmental and Strategic Studies; fmrly with Centre for Studies in Int. Relations and Devt, Kolkata; joined Ministry of Foreign Affairs 1986; fmr Second Sec., later First Sec., Embassy in Rome; Consul-Gen. Embassy in Hong Kong 2003–04; Dir-Gen. Ministry of Foreign Affairs –2007; Amb. to Bhutan 2007–; Vice-Pres. Mercantile Bank Ltd. *Address:* Embassy of Bangladesh, PO Box 178, Upper Choubachu, Thimphu, Bhutan (office). *Telephone:* (2) 322539 (office). *Fax:* (2) 322629 (office). *E-mail:* bdoot@druknet.bt (office); akmatiq@northsouth.edu (office).

ATKINSON, Sir Anthony Barnes (Tony), Kt, MA, FBA; British economist and academic; *Warden, Nuffield College, University of Oxford;* b. 4 Sept. 1944, Caerleon; m. Judith Mary Mandeville 1965; two s. one d. *Education:* Cranbrook School, Kent and Churchill Coll., Cambridge. *Career:* Prof. of Econs, Univ. of Essex 1970–76; Head, Dept of Political Economy, Univ. Coll. London 1976–79; Prof. of Econs, LSE 1980–92; Prof. of Political Economy, Univ. of Cambridge, Fellow, Churchill Coll. 1992–94; Warden, Nuffield Coll. Oxford 1994–; Ed. Journal of Public Economics 1972–97; mem. Royal Comm. on Distribution of Income and Wealth 1978–79, Retail Prices Index Advisory Cttee 1984–90, Pension Law Review Cttee 1992–93, Conseil d'Analyse Economique 1997–2001; Fellow, St John's Coll., Cambridge 1967–70; Fellow, Econometric Soc. 1984, Pres. 1988; Vice-Pres. British Acad. 1988–90; Pres. of the European Econ. Asscn 1989; Pres. Int. Econ. Asscn 1989–92, Royal Econ. Soc. 1995–98; Hon. mem. American Econ. Asscn 1985; Chevalier Légion d'honneur; Hon. Dr rer. pol (Univ. of Frankfurt); hon. degrees from Univ. of Liège 1989, Athens Univ. of Econs 1991, Univ. of Stirling 1992, Univ. of Edin. 1994 and numerous others; UAP Prix Scientifique 1986, Frank E. Seidman Distinguished Award in Political Economy 1995. *Publications:* Poverty in Britain and the Reform of Social Security 1969, Unequal Shares 1972, The Economics of Inequality 1975, Distribution of Personal Wealth in Britain (with A. Harrison) 1978, Lectures on Public Economics (with J. E. Stiglitz) 1980, Social Justice and Public Policy 1983, Parents and Children (with A. Maynard and C. Trinder), Poverty and Social Security 1989, Economic Transformation in Eastern Europe and the Distribution of Income (with J. M. Micklewright) 1992, Public Economics in Action 1995, Incomes and the Welfare State 1996, Poverty in Europe 1998, The Economic Consequences of Rolling Back the Welfare State 1999, Social Indicators (jtly) 2002. *Address:* Nuffield College, Oxford, OX1 1NF (office); 39 Park Town, Oxford, OX2 6SL, England (home). *Telephone:* (1865) 278520 (office); (1865) 556064 (home). *E-mail:* tony.atkinson@nuf.ox.ac.uk (office).

ATOKI, Christian Ileka, BSc; Democratic Republic of the Congo diplomatist; *Permanent Representative, United Nations;* m.; five c. *Education:* Catholic Univ. of Louvain, Belgium. *Career:* First Sec. Embassy in Athens, Greece 1985–88; European Bureau Chief, Dept. of Foreign Affairs 1988; Vice-Chair. Social and Econ. Cttee., UN –1993, Human Rights Observer, Int. Civil Mission on Human Rights in Haiti (MICIVIH I) 1993, 1995–99, mem. Cttee. for New and Renewable Devt., New York 1993–96, Registration

Official and Press Officer for Asst. Special Rep. of the Sec.-Gen. and Pres. Identification Cttee. 1994; Minister Counsellor, Perm. Mission to UN, New York 1999–2001, Perm. Rep. to UN 2001–.
Address: Permanent Mission of Democratic Republic of the Congo, 866 United Nations Plaza, Suite 511, New York, NY 10017, USA (office). *Telephone:* (212) 319-8061 (office). *Fax:* (212) 319-8232 (office). *E-mail:* drcongo@un.int (office). *Website:* www.un.int/drcongo (office).

ATTAF, Ahmed; Algerian diplomatist and politician; b. 10 July 1953, Ain Defla. *Education:* Ecole Nationale d'Administration, Algiers. *Career:* fmr Amb. to India; Minister of Foreign Affairs 1996–99; Amb. to UK 2001–05. *Address:* c/o Ministry of Foreign Affairs, place Mohamed Seddik Benyahia, el-Mouradia, Algiers, Algeria (office). *Telephone:* (21) 69-23-33. *Fax:* (21) 69-21-61. *Website:* www.mae.dz.

ATTAKUROV, Raimkul A.; Kyrgyzstani diplomatist; *Ambassador to Russian Federation; Education:* Moscow Highway Inst., Russian Civil Service Acad. *Career:* Minister Counsellor, Embassy in Moscow 2005–07, Chargé d'affairs ad interim 2007, Amb. to Russian Fed. 2007–. *Address:* Embassy of Kyrgyzstan, 119017 Moscow, ul. B. Ordynka 64, Russian Federation (office). *Telephone:* (495) 237-48-82 (office). *Fax:* (495) 951-60-62 (office). *E-mail:* embassy@embas-kyrg.msk.ru (office).

ATTALIDES, Michalis A., PhD; Cypriot diplomatist, sociologist and academic; *Dean, School of Humanities, Social Sciences and Law, Intercollege, Nicosia;* b. 1941; m.; two c. *Education:* London School of Econs, UK and Princeton Univ., USA. *Career:* Lecturer in Sociology, Univ. of Leicester 1966–68; sociologist, Cyprus Town and Country Planning Project 1968–70; counterpart of UNESCO expert, Social Research Centre, Cyprus 1971, 1973–74; mil. service 1972; Guest Lecturer Otto Suhr Inst., Free Univ. of Berlin 1974–75; journalist 1975–76; worked in Int. Relations Service, House of Reps of Cyprus 1977–89, Dir 1979–89; Amb., Dir of Political Affairs Division B (Cyprus question), Ministry of Foreign Affairs 1989–91; Amb. of Cyprus to France (also accred to Morocco, Portugal and Spain) 1991–95, Amb. to Belgium (also accred to Luxembourg) and Perm. Del. of Cyprus to EU 1995–98, High Commr in UK 1998–2000; Perm. Sec., Ministry of Foreign Affairs 2000–01; Rep. of Govt of Cyprus Del. to Convention on the Future of Europe 2002–03; Dean, School of Humanities, Social Sciences and Law, Intercollege, Nicosia 2003–; Grand Officier, Ordre Nat. du Mérite. *Publications:* Cyprus: Nationalism and International Politics 1980, Social Change and Urbanization in Cyprus: A Study of Nicosia 1971. *Address:* 8 Sachtouris Street, Nicosia 1080, Cyprus (home). *E-mail:* mattali@spidernet.com.cy (home).

ATTIYA, Abdul Rahman bin Hamad al-, BA; Qatari diplomatist and international organization official; *Secretary-General, Co-operation Council for the Arab States of the Gulf (Gulf Co-operation Council);* b. 15 April 1950, Doha; m.; two s. four d. *Education:* Univ. of Miami, USA. *Career:* joined Ministry of Foreign Affairs 1972; Consul-Gen. in Geneva, Switzerland 1974–81, Perm. Rep. to UN and other Int. Orgs, Geneva 1975–81; Perm. Rep. to FAO, Rome 1975–81; Amb. to Saudi Arabia (also accred to Yemen and Djibouti) 1981–84; Amb. to Org. of the Islamic Conf. 1981–84; Perm. Rep. to UNESCO 1984–90; Amb. to France (also accred to Italy and Greece) 1984–92; Alt. Gov. IFAD 1985–92; Deputy Minister, Ministry Foreign Affairs 1988–2001, Minister of State 2001–; Secretary-General of the Cooperation Council for the Arab States of the Gulf 2002–; mem. Bd of Dirs Arab World Inst., Paris 1985–93. *Address:* Co-operation Council for the Arab States of the Gulf, POB 7153, Riyadh 11462, Saudi Arabia (office). *Telephone:* (1) 482-7777 (office). *Fax:* (1) 482-9089 (office). *Website:* www.gcc-sg.org (office).

AUBIN DE LA MESSUZIÈRE, Yves; French diplomatist; b. 7 Jan. 1942. *Education:* École Nationale des Langues Orientales. *Career:* joined Foreign Service 1968, worked in N Africa section 1970, 1975–76, Head, Office for Francophone Affairs 1987–88, Dir for Cultural Co-operation 1994, Head of Section 1994–97, Chief Adviser for French affairs in Baghdad 1997–99; Dir N Africa section 1999–2002; overseas posts include Second Sec., Embassy in Sanaa, Yemen 1971–74, First Sec., Damascus, Syria 1976–79, First Sec., Rabat, Morocco 1979–80, Second Counsellor, Cairo, Egypt 1983–87, Amb. to Chad 1991–94, to Tunisia 2002–05, to Italy 2005–07; envoy and adviser, SOFIRAD 1981–83; Officier de la Légion d'Honneur, Commdr de la Ordre National du Mérite. *Address:* c/o Ministry of Foreign and European Affairs, 37 quai d'Orsay, 75351 Paris Cedex 07, France (office).

AUJALI, Ali Suleiman; Libyan diplomatist; *Chief of the Libyan Interests Section, Washington, DC. Career:* Third Sec., Embassy in London 1971–76, First Sec., Embassy in Kuala Lumpur 1976–81, Amb. to Malaysia 1981–84, to Argentina 1984–88, to Brazil 1988–94, Deputy Dir-Gen. Americas Dept,

Ministry of Foreign Affairs 1994–98, Dir-Gen. N and S Americas Dept 1998–2000, Dir-Gen. European Affairs 2000–01, Chargé d'affaires a.i., Embassy in Ottawa 2001–04, Chief of Libyan Interests Section, Washington, DC 2004–; f. Libya-Canada Business Council. *Address:* Liaison Office, 2600 Virginia Avenue, NW, Suite 705, Washington, DC 20037, USA (office). *Telephone:* (202) 944-9601 (office). *Fax:* (202) 944-9606 (office). *E-mail:* libya@libyanbureau-dc.org (office).

AUNG SAN SUU KYI, BA; Myanma politician; b. 19 June 1945, Rangoon; m. Michael Aris 1972 (died 1999); two s. *Education:* St Francis Convent, Methodist English High School, Lady Shri Ram Coll., Delhi Univ., St Hugh's Coll., Oxford. *Career:* Asst Sec. Advisory Cttee on Admin. and Budgetary Questions UN Secr., New York 1969–71; Resident Officer, Ministry of Foreign Affairs, Bhutan 1972; Visiting Scholar Centre for SE Asian Studies, Kyoto Univ., Japan 1985–86; Fellow Indian Inst. of Advanced Studies 1987; Co-Founder, Gen. Sec. Nat. League for Democracy 1988 (expelled from party), reinstated as Gen. Sec. Oct. 1995; returned from UK 1988, under house arrest 1989–95, house arrest lifted July 1995, placed under de facto house arrest Sept. 2000, released unconditionally May 2002, placed under house arrest June 2003; Hon. mem. Bd Council Int. Inst. for Democracy and Electoral Assistance (IDEA) 2003; numerous hon. degrees; Rafto Prize 1990, Sakharov Prize 1990, European Parl. Human Rights Prize 1991, Nobel Peace Prize 1991, Simón Bolívar Prize 1992, Liberal Int. Prize for Freedom 1995, Jawaharlal Nehru Award for Int. Understanding 1995, Freedom Award of Int. Rescue Cttee 1995, Free Spirit Prize, Freedom Forum USA 2003, US Congressional Gold Medal 2008, ranked by Forbes magazine amongst 100 Most Powerful Women (45th) 2004, (15th) 2005, (47th) 2006, (71st) 2007. *Publications:* Aung San 1984, Burma and India: Some Aspects of Colonial Life Under Colonialism 1990, Freedom from Fear 1991, Towards a True Refuge 1993, Freedom from Fear and Other Writings 1995. *Address:* c/o National League for Democracy, 97B West Shwegondine Road, Bahan Township, Yangon, Myanmar.

AURE, Aud Inger, CandJur; Norwegian fmr politician; b. 12 Nov. 1942, Averøy; m.; three c. *Career:* mem. Kristiansund Municipal Council 1979–83; mem. Møre og Romsdal Co. Council 1984–95; mem. Cen. Exec. Cttee Women's Org. Christian Democratic Party 1982–, Deputy Chair. 1986–88, Chair. 1988–94; Deputy mem. Storting for Møre og Romsdal Co. 1985–93, mem. 1989–90; mem. Standing Cttee on Justice; Regional Employment Officer 1992–95; Mayor of Kristiansund 1995–99; mem. Cen. Exec. Cttee Christian Democratic Party 1995–99; Minister of Justice 1997–99.

AUSTEN, Richard, MBE; British diplomatist; *Ambassador to Panama;* b. 25 May 1955. *Career:* Desk Officer, Consular Dept, FCO 1981–82, Middle East Dept 1982–83, Attaché, Devt and Commercial Depts, Embassy in Dar es Salaam 1983–87, Third Sec., Embassy in Ottawa 1987–90, Desk Officer, Protocol Dept 1990–93, Deputy High Commr, Banjul 1993–96, Desk Officer, Perm. Under-Sec's Dept 1996–97, Deputy Head Conference Dept 1997–98, Head of Section, Latin America and Caribbean Dept 1998–2001, Deputy High Commr, Port Louis 2001–03, Amb. to Mongolia 2004–06, to Panama 2006–. *Address:* British Embassy, Torre Swiss Bank, 4°, Calle 53, Urb. Marbella, Apdo 0816-07946, Panamá 1, Panama (office). *Telephone:* 269-0866 (office). *Fax:* 223-0730 (office). *E-mail:* britemb@cwpanama.net (office). *Website:* www.britishembassy.gov.uk/panama (office).

AUSTIN, Roy Leslie, BA, MA, PhD; American academic and diplomatist; *Ambassador to Trinidad and Tobago;* b. 1939, Kingstown, Saint Vincent and the Grenadines; m. Glynis Sutherland Austin 1967; three c. *Education:* Yale Univ., Univ. of Washington. *Career:* worked as customs officer, secondary school teacher, carnival bandleader, capt. of nat. soccer team, and was selected for trials for nat. cricket squad; moved to USA to attend univ. 1964; Dir Crime, Law and Justice Program, Pennsylvania State Univ. 1994–98, Assoc. Prof. of Sociology, Justice and African American Studies 1998–2001, Dir Africana Research Center 2001; Amb. to Trinidad and Tobago 2001–. *Publications:* articles on the Caribbean and research publs on crime in several countries, including Trinidad and Tobago. *Address:* Embassy of the USA, 15 Queen's Park West, PO Box 752, Port of Spain, Trinidad and Tobago (office). *Telephone:* 622-6371 (office). *Fax:* 822-5905 (office). *E-mail:* ircpos@state.gov (office). *Website:* trinidad.usembassy.gov (office).

AVDEEV, Aleksander Alekseyevich; Russian politician and diplomatist; *Ambassador to France;* b. 8 Sept. 1946, Kremenchug, USSR (now Ukraine); m.; one s. *Education:* Moscow State Inst. of Int. Relations. *Career:* diplomatic service with USSR Ministry of Foreign Affairs 1968–; Second, First Sec., USSR Embassy, France 1977–85; Counsellor; Head of Sector, First European Dept, USSR Ministry of Foreign Affairs 1985–87; USSR

Amb. to Luxembourg 1987–90; First Deputy Head, First European Dept, Ministry of Foreign Affairs 1990–91; USSR Deputy Minister of Foreign Affairs 1991–92; Amb. at Large, Russian Ministry of Foreign Affairs 1992–; Amb. to Bulgaria 1992–96; Deputy Minister of Foreign Affairs 1996–98, First Deputy Minister 1998–2002, Amb. to France 2002–. *Address:* Embassy of Russia, 40–50 Boulevard Lannes, 75116 Paris, France (office). *Telephone:* 1-45-04-05-50 (office); 1-42-22-18-42 (home). *Fax:* 1-45-04-17-65 (office); 1-45-49-39-20 (home). *E-mail:* ambrus@wanadoo.fr (office). *Website:* www.france.mid.ru (office).

AVERCHENKO, Vladimir Alexandrovich, CandEcon; Russian politician and engineer; b. 23 July 1950, Belaya Kalitva, Rostov Region; m.; three c. *Education:* Novocherkassk Polytech. Inst., New York Univ. *Career:* army service 1969–71; on staff Belokalitvinsky City CPSU Cttee 1975–80; constructor major industrial sites Rostov Region; Head of Itominstroi, then Promstroi Rostov Region 1980–89; Deputy Chair. Novocherkassk City Exec. Cttee 1989–91; First Vice-Maj. Novocherkassk 1991–98; Deputy Gov., Minister of Econ., Int. and Foreign Relations, Rostov Region 1998–99; concurrently Head Econ. Council Asscn of Social-Econ. Devt N Caucasus; Deputy State Duma, People's Deputies Group 1999; Head Del. of Fed. Ass. in Parl. Ass. of Black Sea Econ. Co-operation (PACHES); Deputy Chair. State Duma 2000–03; Dir Fed. Agency for Construction and Housing Economy 2004–05; state awards and int. Award for contrib. to devt of free market relations between Russia and CIS countries 1994. *Publications:* numerous publs, eight books on man., investment policy, ecology. *Address:* c/o State Duma, Okhotny Ryad 1, 103265 Moscow, Russia (office). *Telephone:* (495) 292-84-40 (office). *Fax:* (495) 292-52-23 (office).

AVINERI, Shlomo; Israeli academic; *Professor of Political Science, Hebrew University of Jerusalem;* b. 20 Aug. 1933, Bielsko, Poland; m. Dvora Nadler 1957; one d. *Education:* Shalva Secondary School, Tel-Aviv, Hebrew Univ., Jerusalem and London School of Econs. *Career:* has lived in Israel since 1939; Prof. of Political Science, Hebrew Univ. Jerusalem 1971–, Dir Eshkol Research Inst. 1971–74, Dean of Faculty of Social Sciences 1974–76; Dir-Gen. Ministry of Foreign Affairs 1976–77; Dir Inst. for European Studies, Hebrew Univ. 1997–; visiting appointments at Yale Univ. 1966–67, Wesleyan Univ., Middletown, Conn. 1971–72, Research School of Social Sciences, ANU 1972, Cornell Univ. 1973, Univ. of California 1979, Queen's Coll., New York 1989, Univ. of Oxford 1989; mem. Int. Inst. of Philosophy 1980–; Fellow, Woodrow Wilson Center, Washington, DC 1983–84; Visiting Prof., Cardozo School of Law, New York 1996–97, 2000–01, Brookings Inst., Washington, DC 1991, Cen. European Univ., Budapest 1994, Northwestern Univ., Evanston 1997, Carnegie Endowment for Int. Peace, Washington, DC 2000–01; Fellow, Collegium Budapest 2002; British Council Scholarship 1961, Rubin Prize in the Social Sciences 1968, Naphtali Prize for study of Hegel 1977, Present Tense Award for Study of Zionism 1982, Carlyle Lecturer, Univ. of Oxford 1989, Israel Prize 1996, Life Award, Israel Political Science Asscn 2005. *Publications:* The Social and Political Thought of Karl Marx 1968, Karl Marx on Colonialism and Modernization 1968, Israel and the Palestinians 1971, Marx's Socialism 1972, Hegel's Theory of the Modern State 1973, Varieties of Marxism 1977, The Making of Modern Zionism 1981, Moses Hess – Prophet of Communism and Zionism 1985, Arlosoroff – A Political Biography 1989, Communitarianism and Individualism (co-author) 1992, Herzl's Diaries 1998, Identity and Integration 1999, The Law of Religious Identity (co-author) 1999, Identities in Transformation 2002, Herzl – An Intellectual Biography (in Hebrew) 2007. *Address:* Faculty of Social Sciences, Hebrew University of Jerusalem, Mount Scopus, Jerusalem (office); 10 Hagedud Ha-ivri Street, Jerusalem, Israel (home). *Telephone:* (2) 588-3286 (office); (2) 563-0862 (home). *Fax:* (2) 588-1333 (office). *E-mail:* shlomo.avineri@huji.ac.il (office).

AVOMO, Lino Sima Ekua; Equatorial Guinean politician and diplomatist; *Permanent Representative, United Nations;* b. 4 April 1957, Mongomo; m.; five c. *Career:* Sec., Embassy in USSR 1982, Mission to OAU (now the African Union) in Ethiopia 1984; fmr Amb. to People's Repub. of China; apptd Amb. to France 1995, to Switzerland 1998, to Portugal 1999; currently Perm. Rep. to UN, New York; Orden Nacional del Merito. *Address:* Permanent Mission of Equatorial Guinea, 57 Magnolia Avenue, Mount Vernon, NY 10553, USA (office). *Telephone:* (914) 667-8999 (office); (212) 223-2324 (office). *Fax:* (914) 667-8778 (office). *E-mail:* eqguinea@un.int (office). *Website:* www.un.int (office).

AWADALLAH, Bassem, PhD; Jordanian government official; b. 1964. *Education:* Georgetown Univ., USA, London School of Econs, UK. *Career:* worked in investment banking, UK 1986–91; Econ. Sec. to the Prime Minister of Jordan 1992–96, Econ. Adviser 1996–99; Dir Econ. Dept, Royal Hashemite Court 1999–2001; Minister of Planning and Int. Co-operation 2001–Feb. 2005; Minister of Finance April 2005–June 2005; Al

Kawkab and Al Istiqlal Decorations of the First Order of the Hashemite Kingdom of Jordan; Al Hussein Medal for Distinguished Service, Royal Hashemite Award for Distinguished Service 1995. *Address:* c/o Ministry of Finance, POB 85, Amman 11118, Jordan (office).

AWADHI, Badria A. al-, PhD; Kuwaiti academic and environmental consultant; *Director, Arab Regional Center for Environmental Law;* b. 20 April 1944, Kuwait City. *Education:* Cairo Univ., Egypt and Univ. Coll. London. *Career:* Dean, Faculty of Law and Sharia, Kuwait Univ. (first woman) 1979–83, later Prof. of Int. Law; Deputy Dir Regional Org. for the Protection of Marine Environment in the Arabian Gulf Region 1983–93; Dir Arab Regional Center for Environmental Law 2001–; mem. ILO Experts Group on Application of Labour Standards; Regional Vice-Chair. for West Asia, Comm. on Environmental Law –2003; consultant to Int. Red Cross on Application of Int. Humanitarian Law; mem. Int. Bar Asscn Task Force on Int. Terrorism 2002–, Int. Fed. of Women Lawyers, Int. Law Asscn, Int. Comm. of Jurists, Int. Council of Environmental Law, Arab Thought Forum; Founding mem. Kuwait Environment Protection Agency; currently practices law privately; Zayed Int. Prize for the Environment (Category III) 2004. *Publications include:* International Law in Times of Peace and War 1979, The Right of the Child in the Legal System of Kuwait 1980, Limitation Clauses of Human Rights in the Constitution of the State of the Gulf Co-operation Council 1984, Legal Status of Women in Kuwait 1985, Protection against Sex Discrimination – International and Comparative Law 1986, Women and the Law 1990. *Address:* Arab Regional Center for Environmental Law, Faculty of Law, Kuwait University, PO Box 5476, 13055 Safat; Al-Awadhi Towers, Tower 3, 3rd Floor, Ahmed Al-Jaber St, POB 27357 Safat, 13134 Safat, Kuwait City, Kuwait. *Telephone:* 2406882. *Fax:* 2406887. *E-mail:* arcel@kucol .kuniv.edu.kw.

AWORI, Arthur Moody; Kenyan politician and business executive; b. 5 Dec. 1927, Butere; m. *Education:* Chartered Inst. of Secretaries. *Career:* MP for Funyula constituency 1983–; numerous posts as Asst Minister under Pres. Daniel arap Moi, including Asst Minister for Educ.; left Kanu Party late 2002 to join new Narc alliance; Minister of Home Affairs 2002–05, Vice-Pres. 2003–05; fmr Chair. Western Province Kanu MPs Parl. Group; Chair. Francis Da Gama Rose Group 1981–; Dir East Africa Building Soc., Akiba Bank Ltd, Mercantile Life and General Insurance Co. Ltd, Macmillan Publrs Kenya Ltd, Securicor Security Services Ltd; Chair. Asscn for the Physically Disabled of Kenya; proprietor of Gulumwoyo Ltd, Western Sunrise Properties Ltd, Mocian Ltd, Rose Mareba Ltd, Mareba Enterprises Ltd; Sec. to the Bd of East African Industries (EAI); Elder of the Burning Spear. *Address:* c/o Office of the Vice President, Jogoo House 'A', Taifa Road, POB 30520, Nairobi, Kenya (office).

AYALA-LASSO, José; Ecuadorean diplomatist and international civil servant; b. 29 Jan. 1932, Quito; m.; four c. *Education:* Pontificia Universidad Católica del Ecuador, Universidad Cen. del Ecuador, Université Catholique de Louvain, Belgium. *Career:* several foreign affairs postings including at embassies in Tokyo, Seoul, Beijing, Rome; Minister of Foreign Affairs 1977, 1997–99; fmr Amb. to Belgium, Luxembourg, Peru, EEC; Lecturer, Int. Law Inst., Universidad Cen. del Ecuador; Deputy Legal Sec. Perm Comm. for the South Pacific; Perm. Rep. to UN, New York 1989–94, Chair. Security Council Cttee concerning Fmr Yugoslavia 1991; Chair. working group to establish post of High Commr for Human Rights 1993; UN High Commr for Human Rights 1994–97; Amb. to Holy See 1999–2002; Grand Cross, Nat. Order of Merit (Ecuador), numerous decorations from Japan, Belgium, Brazil, etc. *Address:* c/o Ministry of Foreign Affairs, Avda 10 de Agosto y Carrión, Quito, Ecuador.

AYASSOR, Adji Othèth, LLD; Togolese lawyer and politician; *Minister of Finance, Budget and Privatization;* b. 1952; m.; four c. *Education:* Univ. of Bordeaux, France, Univ. of Wisconsin, USA. *Career:* fmr Prof. of Law, Lomé Univ.; fmr Prof., École nationale d'administration (ENA), Lomé; int. consultant and expert on educ.; mem. Nat. Assembly (Parl.) for Doufelgou Préf.; Dir-Gen. Ministry of Educ. 1990–2006; Sec.-Gen. Cabinet Office 2006–07; Minister of Finance, Budget and Privatization 2007–. *Address:* Ministry of Finance, Budget and Privatization, Lomé, Togo (office).

AYED, Ali; Jordanian diplomatist; *Ambassador to Israel;* b. 1964. *Career:* fmr Chargé d'affairs, Embassy in Tel-Aviv, Embassy in Washington, DC 1997–2001; Foreign Ministry Spokesman 2001; Head of Political Office, Prime Minister's Office –2006; Amb to Israel 2006–. *Address:* Embassy of Jordan, 14 Abba Hillel, Ramat-Gan, Tel-Aviv, 52506, Israel (office). *Telephone:* 37517722 (office). *Fax:* 37517712 (office).

AYÉVA, Zarifou; Togolese politician; *President, Parti pour la démocratie et le renouveau (PDR);* b. 22 April 1942, Sokode; m. *Education:* Collège Moderne de Sokodé, Lycée Classique de COCODI, Abidjan, Univ. of Mons, Belgium. *Career:* Financial Dir SGGG, Lomé 1969–73, Head Sales Dept 1973–85; Lecturer Univ. of Lomé 1975–77; Asst Gen. Dir Société Nlle de Sidérurgie 1977–79, Gen. Dir 1979–82; Minister of Commerce and Transport 1978, of Information 1979; Dir CODIS 1983–, STOP-FEU-TOGO 1986–; Minister of State, Minister of Foreign Affairs and African Integration 2005–07; Pres. Parti pour la démocratie et le renouveau (PDR) 1991–.
Address: Parti pour la démocratie et le renouveau (PDR), Lomé, Togo (office).

AYISSI, Henri Eyebe, PhD; Cameroonian politician; *State Minister for External Relations; Education:* Nat. Advanced School of Admin and Magistracy. *Career:* Minister of Urban Affairs 1990–92; Inspector of Gen. Affairs, Ministry of Higher Educ. 1998; fmr mem. Nat. Census Comm. and Inspector-Gen. of elections; State Minister for External Relations 2007–.
Address: Ministry of External Relations, Yaoundé, Cameroon (office). *Telephone:* 2220-3850 (office). *Fax:* 2220-1133 (office). *Website:* www .diplocam.gov.cm (office).

AZIMOV, Rustam S., PhD; Uzbekistan economist and politician; *Deputy Prime Minister, responsible for the Economic Sector and Foreign Economic Relations and Minister of Finance;* b. 1958. *Education:* Tashkent Inst. of Agricultural Engineers. *Career:* Economist, Yulius Fuchik collective farm; Chief Economist of agricultural amalgamation in Djizak area; Chair. Nat. Bank for Foreign Econ. Activity 1991–98; mem. Oly Majlis (Supreme Ass.) 1994–; Minister of Finance 1998–2000, 2005–; Deputy Prime Minister and Minister of Macroeconomics and Statistics 2000–02; Deputy Prime Minister and Economy Minister 2002–05; Minister of Foreign Econ. Relations July–Nov. 2005; Deputy Prime Minister, responsible for the Econ. sector and Foreign Econ. Relations 2005–; Uzbekistan Del. to Asian Devt Bank; fmr lecturer in econs, Tashkent State Univ.; f. Ipak Yuli Bank.
Publications: numerous articles on econs.
Address: Ministry of Finance, 100008 Tashkent, Mustaqillik maydoni 5, Uzbekistan (office). *Telephone:* (71) 133-70-73 (office). *Fax:* (71) 144-56-43 (office). *E-mail:* info@mf.uz (office). *Website:* www.mf.uz (office).

AZIZ, Shaukat, BSc, MBA; Pakistani politician and banker; b. 6 March 1949, Karachi; m.; three c. *Education:* St Patrick's High School, Karachi, Abbottabad Public School, Abbottabad, Govt Islamia Coll., Kasur, Pakistani Business School Inst. of Business Admin, Karachi, Univ. of Karachi. *Career:* various posts with Citibank including Head of Corp. and Investment Banking, Asia Pacific Region, Head of Corp. and Investment Banking for Cen. and Eastern Europe, Middle East and Africa, Corp. Planning Officer, Citicorp, Man. Dir, Saudi American Bank, Global Head, Pvt. Banking, Vice-Pres. 1969–99; Minister of Finance and Revenue, Econ. Affairs and Statistics and of Planning and Econ. Devt 1999–2004; mem. Senate 2002–04; Prime Minister of Pakistan and Minister of Finance and Revenue, Econ. Affairs and Statistics 2004–07.
Address: c/o Office of the Prime Minister's Secretariat, Constitution Avenue, F-6/5, Cabinet Division, Cabinet Block, Islamabad, Pakistan. *Telephone:* (51) 9206111.

AZNAR LÓPEZ, José María; Spanish politician and academic; *President, FAES Fundación para el Análisis y los Estudios Sociales;* b. 1953, Madrid; m. Ana Botella; two s. one d. *Education:* Universidad Complutense, Madrid. *Career:* fmr tax inspector; fmr Chief Exec. Castile-Leon region; joined Rioja br. Alianza Popular 1978, Deputy Sec.-Gen. and mem. Cortes (Parl.) 1982; Premier Castilla y León Autonomous Region 1987; Pres. Partido Popular (PP, fmrly Alianza Popular) 1990–2004; Prime Minister of Spain and Pres. of the Council 1996–2004; currently Pres. FAES Fundación para el Análisis y los Estudios Sociales, Madrid; Distinguished Scholar in the Practice of Global Leadership Georgetown Univ., Washington DC 2004–; Vice-Pres. European Democratic Union (EDC); Pres. Int. Democratic Centre (IDC) 2001; mem. Bd of Dirs News Corp. 2006–; Pres.'s Medal Georgetown Univ. 2004. *Publication:* Ocho años de gobierno: una visión personal de España 2004.
Address: FAES Fundación para el Análisis y los Estudios Sociales, C/Juan Bravo, 3C, 7º, 28006 Madrid, Spain (office); Mortara Center for International Studies, Edmund A. Walsh School of Foreign Service, Georgetown University, ICC, Suite 304, 37th and O Streets, NW, Washington, DC 20057, USA (office). *Telephone:* (91) 5766857 (office). *Fax:* (91) 5754695 (office). *E-mail:* fundacionfaes@fundacionfaes.org (office); atencion@pp.es (office). *Website:* www.fundacionfaes.org (office); www.georgetown.edu/sfs/mortara (office); www.pp.es (office).

AZOUR, Jihad, MS, PhD; Lebanese economist and government official; b. 4 May 1964, Sir Denniye; m. Roula Rizk. *Education:* Assad Univ., Univ. of Paris, IEP Paris, France, Harvard Univ., USA. *Career:* with McKinsey, Lebanon 1989–93; Program Man. and Advisor to Dir Gen. Asscn d'Economie Financière 1993–94; Man. Pnr, AM&F Consulting 1996–98; consultant IMF and Booz Allen 2005; Prof., American Univ. Beirut; Dir UNDP/World Bank project 1999–2005; Adviser to Ministry of Finance 1999–2004; Minister of Finance 2005–08.
Address: c/o Ministry of Finance, 4e étage, Immeuble MOF, place Riad es-Solh, Beirut, Lebanon (office).

AZZIMAN, Omar; Moroccan academic, diplomatist and fmr government official; *Ambassador to Spain;* b. 17 Oct. 1947, Tetuán. *Education:* Univ. of Rabat, Univ. of Nice, France. *Career:* Prof., Faculty of Law, Univ. of Rabat 1972–; Founding mem. and fmr Pres. Organización Marroquí de Derechos Humanos (Moroccan Org. for Human Rights); Minister of Human Rights 1993–95, of Justice 1997–2002; Chair. Advisory Council for Human Rights 2002–04; Amb. to Spain 2004–; UNESCO Chair for Teaching, Training, and Research in the field of Human Rights, Mohammed V Univ. 1996–2006; Chair. Hassan II Foundation for Moroccans Living Abroad 1997–; mem. Academia del Reino de Marruecos 1996–; Grand Cordon Order of Merit (Portugal) 1988, Kt of the Order of the Ouissam of the Throne 1995, Commdr Légion d'honneur 1999, Grand Cross of Merit Order (Spain) 2000, Order of the Ouissam Al Arche 2006.
Address: Embassy of Morocco, Serrano 179, 28002 Madrid, Spain (office). *Telephone:* (91) 5631090 (office). *Fax:* (91) 5617887 (office). *E-mail:* correo@embajada-marruecos.es (office). *Website:* www.embajada -marruecos.es (office).

B

BA, Amadou Lamine, MSc, PhD; Senegalese development consultant and diplomatist; *Ambassador to USA. Education:* Ecole des Cadres Ruraux, Ohio State Univ., USA. *Career:* Dir Regional Educ. Centre, Crop Protection Directorate (Direction de la Protection des Végétaux/DPV), Dakar 1980–82; consultant in int. devt, USAID-Washington, in The Gambia 1981, in Guinea-Bissau 1981, in Niamey 1983; Research Asst, Coll. of Agric., Ohio State Univ., Columbus 1988–93, Researcher and Asst Prof. 1997–99; Consultant and Visiting Scholar, Dept of Int. Studies, Univ. of Vermont 1993; consultant in int. devt 1993–97; Jt Leader, Human Rights, Democracy and New Leadership in Africa (HDNA) 1995–97; mem. Exec. Bd US-Africa Inst. 1997–99; Prof. of Science, Bunker Hill Coll., Boston, Mass 1999–; Amb. to USA 2002–; mem. Forum des Citoyens pour l'Alternance, Asscn des Professeurs de Sciences, Int. Soc. of Quality Assurance. *Publications:* Integrated Pest Management and International Agriculture Development Policies: A Case Study of the United States and Africa 1993, Global Issues in Pesticides Regulation 1999.
Address: Embassy of Senegal, 2112 Wyoming Avenue, NW, Washington, DC 20008, USA (office). *Telephone:* (202) 234-0540 (office). *Fax:* (202) 332-6315 (office).

BAAH-WIREDU, Kwadwo; Ghanaian politician and chartered accountant; *Minister of Finance and Economic Planning; Education:* Kumasi High School, Prempeh Coll., Univ. of Ghana, Inst. of Chartered Accountants. *Career:* qualified as chartered accountant 1985; has worked for Ghana Airways Corpn, Volta River Authority; Finance Man. Ananse Systems; Pnr Asante Wiredu and Assocs accounting firm; mem. Parl. 1996–; Minister of Educ., Youth and Sports –2005, of Finance and Econ. Planning 2005–.
Address: Ministry of Finance and Economic Planning, POB M40, Accra, Ghana (office). *Telephone:* (21) 686204 (office). *Fax:* (21) 668879 (office). *Website:* www.finance.gov.gh (office).

BAALI, Abdallah; Algerian diplomatist; *Special Envoy of the President of Algeria;* b. 19 Oct. 1954, Guelma; m. Rafika Baali; one s. one d. *Education:* Ecole Nat. d'Admin., New York Univ. *Career:* Sec. of Foreign Affairs 1977–82, Head Dept of Communication and Documentation, Foreign Affairs Ministry 1990–92; mem. Perm. Mission to UN, New York 1982–89, Algeria's Alt. Rep. to Security Council 1988–89, Perm. Rep. to UN, New York 1996–2005, Rep. to Security Council 2004–05; Amb. to Indonesia (also accred to Australia, New Zealand and Brunei Darussalam) 1992–96; currently Special Envoy of the Pres. of Algeria; Pres. NPT Review Conf. 2000.
Address: c/o Office of the President, Présidence de la République, el-Mouradia, Algiers, Algeria (office). *Telephone:* (21) 69-15-15. *Fax:* (21) 69-15-95. *Website:* www.el-mouradia.dz.

BAARO, Makurita; I-Kiribati diplomatist; *Acting High Commissioner to UK. Career:* apptd Sec., Ministry of Foreign Affairs and Immigration 1994; Dir Political, Int. and Legal Affairs Div., Pacific Islands Forum Secr. 1996–2002; apptd Sec. to the Cabinet, Office of the Pres. 2002; currently Acting High Commr to UK (non-resident).
Address: c/o Office of the President (Beretitenti), PO Box 68, Bairiki, Tarawa, Kiribati (office). *Telephone:* 21183 (office). *Fax:* 21145 (office).

BAATAR, Choisürengiin; Mongolian diplomatist; b. 24 Dec. 1950, Tsakhir soum, Arkhangai Prov.; m. S. Tserenjargal 1975; two s. one d. *Education:* State Inst. of Int. Relations, Moscow. *Career:* Officer, Policy and Planning Dept, Ministry of Foreign Affairs 1975, 1985; Pvt. Sec. of Minister for Foreign Affairs 1977; served in embassies in Tokyo 1979–82, Vientiane 1982; Officer, Foreign Relations Dept, Cen. Cttee Mongolian People's Revolutionary Party (MPRP) 1986; mem. Presidium of State Great Hural (Parl.) 1980–; Head, Asia and Africa Dept 1990; Amb. to UK 1991–95; Deputy Minister of External Relations 1995–96; Exec. Sec. Nat. Security Council 1996; Perm. Rep. to UN, New York 2003–07.
Address: Ministry of Foreign Affairs, Enkh Taivny Örgön Chölöö 7a, Sükhbaatar District, Ulan Bator, Mongolia. *Telephone:* (11) 311311. *Fax:* (11) 322127. *E-mail:* mongmer@magicnet.mn. *Website:* www.mongolia-foreign-policy.net.

BABACAN, Ali, MBA, BSc; Turkish politician; *Minister of Foreign Affairs;* b. 1967, Ankara; m.; two c. *Education:* Middle East Tech. Univ., Ankara, Northwestern Univ., USA. *Career:* worked at QRM, Inc., Chicago, Ill. 1992–94; chief adviser to Mayor of Ankara 1994; ran family-owned textile co. 1994–2002; mem. of Grand Nat. Ass., representing Ankara 2002–; Minister of State for Economy 2002–05; Chief Negotiator in accession talks with EU 2005–; Minister of Foreign Affairs 2007–; Co-founder and Bd Mem., AKP (Adalet ve Kalkinma Partisi/Justice and Devt Party).
Address: Ministry of Foreign Affairs, Dışişleri Bakanliği, Dr Sadik Ahmet Cad. 12, 06100 Balgat, Ankara, Turkey (office). *Telephone:* (312) 2921000 (office). *Fax:* (312) 2873869 (office). *E-mail:* webmaster@mfa.gov.tr (office). *Website:* www.mfa.gov.tr (office).

BABUR, Alamgir; Pakistani diplomatist; *High Commissioner to Bangladesh; Career:* fmr Deputy Perm. Rep., later Acting Perm. Rep. to UN, New York; Dir-Gen. (Americas), Ministry of Foreign Affairs –2005; High Commr to Bangladesh 2005–.
Address: High Commission of Pakistan, House NE (C)-2, Road No. 71, Gulshan Avenue, Dhaka 1212, Bangladesh (office). *Telephone:* (2) 8825388 (office). *Fax:* (2) 8850673 (office). *E-mail:* parepdka@citech-bd.com (office).

BACELAR, Vice-Adm. José Carlos Lima; Portuguese naval officer; *Military Representative, NATO;* b. 11 May 1948, Arcos de Valdevez; m. Victória Bacelar; one s. *Education:* NATO Defence Coll. *Career:* joined officer training in Portuguese Navy 1966; promoted to Ensign 1966, Lt Jr Grade 1970, Lt 1974, Lt-Commdr 1980, Commdr 1989, Capt. 1997; posts at sea include Exec. Officer patrol ship Quanza (deployment in Cape Verde) 1970–72, served aboard hydrographic ship Carvalho Araújo, Angola 1973–75, corvette Oliveira e Carmo, East-Timor 1975–77, frigate Magalhães Corrêa, Standing Naval Force Atlantic 1981, Commdg Officer patrol ship Mandovi 1979–80, Exec. Officer frigate Hermenegildo Capelo 1984–86, CO corvette Afonso Cerqueira 1989–91; posts ashore have included Staff Officer, Operational Planning, Naval Command 1981–84, Navy Staff Officer, Org. Section 1986–89, Asst Officer to Navy Personnel Dir 1991–93, Naval Staff Officer PO MILREP, NATO HQ, Brussels 1993–96, Plans and Policy Div., Gen. Staff 1996, Head Personnel and Org. Div., Navy Staff 1997, Coordinator Strategy Studies area, Naval War Coll. 2001–02, Deputy Dir Naval War Coll. 2002, Deputy Vice-Chief of Navy Staff 2004; attended Gen., Flag Officers and Ambs Course, NATO Defence Coll., Rome 2005; Mil. Rep., NATO 2006–; promoted to Rear-Adm. 2002, Vice-Adm. 2006.
Address: NATO HQ, blvd Léopold III, 1110 Brussels, Belgium (office). *Telephone:* (2) 707-41-11 (office). *Fax:* (2) 707-45-79 (office). *E-mail:* natodoc@hq.nato.int (office). *Website:* www.nato.int (office).

BACHELET JERIA, Verónica Michelle; Chilean politician and head of state; *President;* b. 29 Sept. 1951, Santiago; m.; three c. *Education:* Universidad de Chile, Inter-American Coll. of Defense, Washington, DC, USA. *Career:* placed in Villa Grimaldi and Cuatro Alamos detention centres for father's resistance to Pinochet regime 1975; lived in Australia, then Germany 1975–80; trained as medical surgeon, podiatrist and epidemiologist, Universidad de Chile; Head of Medical Dept, PIDEE (NGO assisting the children of victims of the military regime); Consultant to Panamerican Health Org. and WHO 1990; mem. Cen. Cttee Socialist Party 1995–, Political Cttee 1998–; Adviser to Under-Sec. of Health 1994–97, to Ministry of Defence 1998–99; Minister of Health 2000–02, of Nat. Defence (first woman in position) 2002–04; Pres. of Chile (first woman) 2006–; ranked by Forbes magazine amongst 100 Most Powerful Women (17th) 2006, (27th) 2007.
Address: Office of the President, Moneda No. 1002, 1298, Santiago, Chile (office). *Telephone:* (2) 690-4000 (office). *E-mail:* contact@msgg.gov.cl (office). *Website:* www.presidencyofchile.cl (office).

BACHTIAR, Gen. D'ai, AO; Indonesian government official and diplomatist; *Ambassador to Malaysia;* b. 25 April 1951, Indramayu, W Java. *Career:* Chief of Nat. Police 2001–05; Amb. to Malaysia 2008–; Prof., Edith Cowan Univ., Australia; Presidium Chair. Indonesia Crime Prevention Foundation; Kt Order of Tan Sri (Malaysia).

Address: Embassy of Indonesia, 233 Jalan Tun Razak, POB 10889, 50400 Kuala Lumpur, Malaysia (office). *Telephone:* (3) 21452011 (office). *Fax:* (3) 21417908 (office). *E-mail:* dubresi_kul@kbrikl.org.my (office). *Website:* www.kbrikl.org.my (office).

BADAL, Parkash Singh, BA; Indian agriculturist and politician; *Chief Minister of Punjab;* b. 8 Dec. 1927, Abulkhurana, Punjab; m. Surinder Kaur; one s. one d. *Career:* entered politics 1947, first elected to Vidhan Sabha 1957; mem. and fmr Pres. Shiromani Akali Dal party; fmr mem. Shiromani Gurdwara Prabandhak Cttee; elected to Ass. 1957, re-elected 1969; Minister for Community Devt Panchayati Raj, Animal Husbandry, Dairying and Fisheries 1969–70; Chief Minister of Punjab 1970–71, 1977–80, 1997–2002, 2007–; imprisoned during State of Emergency 1975–77; elected to Lok Sabha 1977; Minister for Agric. 1977; Leader of Opposition 1980; imprisoned on corruption charges Dec. 2003; Chair. Punjab Arts Council; mem. Nankana Sahib Educational Trust, Ludhiana. *Address:* VPO Badal, Muktsar District (home); Office of the Chief Minister, Government of Punjab, 45, Sector 2, Chandigarh, India (office). *Telephone:* (172) 740737 (home); (172) 740325 (office). *E-mail:* pws@punjabmail.gov .in (office). *Website:* punjabgovt.nic.in (office).

BADAWI, Dato' Seri Abdullah Bin Haji Ahmad, BA; Malaysian politician; *Prime Minister and Minister of Finance;* b. 26 Nov. 1939, Pulau Pinang; m. Datin Endon bint Datuk Mahmud (died 2005). *Education:* Univ. of Malaya. *Career:* Asst Sec. Public Service Dept 1964; Asst Sec. MAGERAN 1969; Asst Sec. Nat. Security Council 1971; Dir (Youth), Ministry of Sport, Youth and Culture 1971–74, Deputy Sec.-Gen. 1974–78; Minister without Portfolio, Prime Minister's Dept 1982; Minister of Educ. 1984–86, of Defence 1986–87; mem. UMNO Supreme Council 1982–, Vice-Pres. 1984; Minister of Foreign Affairs 1991; Deputy Prime Minister and Minister of Home Affairs 1998–2003, Prime Minister and Minister of Finance 2003–. *Address:* Prime Minister's Office (Jabatan Perdana Menteri), Federal Government Administration Center, Bangunan Perdana Putra, 62502 Putrajaya, Malaysia (office). *Telephone:* (3) 88888000 (office). *Fax:* (3) 88883444 (office). *E-mail:* ppm@pmo.gov.my (office). *Website:* www.pmo .gov.my (office).

BADINTER, Robert, AM, LLD; French lawyer and professor of law; *President, Court of Conciliation and Arbitration, Organization for Security and Co-operation in Europe;* b. 30 March 1928, Paris; m. 1st Anne Vernon 1957; m. 2nd Elisabeth Bleustein-Blanchet 1966; two s. one d. *Education:* Univ. of Paris, Columbia Univ., New York. *Career:* Lawyer, Paris Court of Appeal 1951; Prof. of Law, Paris I (Sorbonne) 1974–81; Minister of Justice and Keeper of the Seals 1981–86; Pres. Constitutional Council 1986–95; currently Pres. Court of Conciliation and Arbitration, OSCE; Senator (Hauts de Seine) 1995–. *Play:* C.3.3., Paris 1995. *Publications:* L'exécution 1973, Liberté, libertés 1976, Condorcet (with Elisabeth Badinter) 1988, Libres et égaux: L'émancipation des juifs sous la révolution française 1989, La prison républicaine 1992, C.3.3. 1995, Un antisémitisme ordinaire: Vichy et les avocats juifs 1940–44 1997, L'abolition 2000, Une Constitution européenne 2002, Le plus grand bien 2004, Contre la peine de mort 2006. *Address:* Court of Conciliation and Arbitration within the OSCE, 266 route de Lausanne, PO Box 20, 1292 Chambesy, Geneva, Switzerland (office); 38 rue Guynemer, 75006 Paris, France (home). *Telephone:* 1-45-49-04-59 (home). *Fax:* 1-45-44-87-47 (home). *E-mail:* cca.osce@bluewin.ch (office); r.badinter@senat.fr (office). *Website:* www.osce (office); www.senat.fr (office).

BADJI, Paul, LLM; Senegalese diplomatist; *Permanent Representative, United Nations;* b. 28 April 1952, Zinguinchor; m.; four c. *Education:* Univ. of Dakar, Ecole Nat. d'Admin. et de Magistrateure (ENAM), The Hague Acad. of Int. Law, Netherlands. *Career:* joined Ministry of Foreign Affairs 1977, Deputy Head, UN and Int. Confs Div. 1977–79, Head 1979–85, First Counsellor, Perm. Mission of Senegal to UN 1985–88, Diplomatic Adviser to Pres. 1988–91, to Prime Minister 1991–2001, Amb. to Germany 2002–04, Perm. Rep. to UN 2004–. *Address:* Permanent Mission of Senegal, 238 East 68th Street, New York, NY 10021, USA (office). *Telephone:* (212) 517-9030 (office). *Fax:* (212) 517-3032 (office). *E-mail:* senegal@un.int (office). *Website:* www.un.int/senegal (office).

BADRAN, Adnan, PhD; Jordanian politician, university president and international organization official; m.; several c. *Education:* Oklahoma State Univ., Michigan State Univ. *Career:* Prof. of Science, Dean Faculty of Science, Univ. of Jordan 1971–76; Pres. Yarmouk Univ. 1976–86; Asst. Dir Gen. for Science, UNESCO 1990–93, Deputy Dir Gen. 1993–98; Pres. Philadelphia Univ., Jordan; fmr Minister of Agric. and Minister of Educ.; Prime Minister and Minister of Defence of Jordan April–Nov. 2005 (resgnd); fmr Sec.-Gen. Higher Council for Science and Tech.; Sec.-Gen. and Fellow Third World Acad. of Sciences; mem. Arab Thought Forum

1978–, World Affairs Council 1980–, Inst. of Biological Sciences, AAAS 1993–; Fellow Islamic Acad. of Sciences, mem. Council and Treas. 1999–; Dr hc (Sung Kyuakwan Univ., Seoul); Al-Nahda Medal (Jordan), Al-Yarmouk Medal (Jordan), Istilal Medal (Jordan) 1995, Alfonso X Medal (Spain). *Publications:* author and ed. of over 18 books and 90 research papers in the fields of botany, economic devt, educ. and int. co-operation. *Address:* PO Box 477, Amman 11941, Jordan (home). *Telephone:* (6) 5161880 (home). *Fax:* (6) 5165285 (home). *E-mail:* abadran@wanadoo .com (home).

BADUEL, Gen. Raúl; Venezuelan military officer and government official; b. Guárico State. *Education:* Mil. Acad. of Venezuela. *Career:* fmr Commdr 42nd Parachute Brigade; fmr Chief of Mil. Staff; Minister of Defence 2006–07; Co-founder Revolutionary Bolivarian Movt 200 (MBR-200). *Address:* c/o Ministry of National Defence, Edif.1, Piso 5, Fuerte Tiuna, El Valle, Caracas, CP-1090, Venezuela (office).

BAEHR, Peter, BSocSci, PhD, CertEd; Canadian academic; *Head, Department of Sociology and Social Policy and Fellow, Center for Asian Pacific Studies, Lingnan University;* b. 5 July 1953, Kuala Lumpur, Malaysia; m. Hedda Sies Schuurman; one s. one d. *Education:* St Peter's School, Bournemouth, Shelley Park, Bournemouth, Univ. of Leicester, Univ. of Manchester. *Career:* Lecturer, Dept of Social Science and Policy Studies, Coventry Polytechnic 1979–89; Visiting Fellow in Sociology, Univ. of Edinburgh 1989–90; Asst Prof. of Sociology, Memorial Univ. of Newfoundland, St John's, Canada 1990–94, Assoc. Prof. 1994–2000; Visiting Prof., Dept of Sociology, Hong Kong Baptist Univ. 1996–97; Assoc. Prof., Dept of Politics and Sociology (now Sociology and Social Policy), Lingnan Univ., Hong Kong 2000–03, Prof. 2003–, Head of Dept 2004–, Fellow, Center for Asian Pacific Studies 2003–; Co-Investigator, Hong Kong Transition Project; mem. Hong Kong Forum; mem. int. bd International Journal of Politics, Culture and Society, Max Weber Studies, Sociology, Canadian Journal of Sociology, Journal of Classical Sociology (journals); Exec. Council mem. Int. Sociological Asscn; contrib. Times Literary Supplement; Hon. Fellow, Dept of Sociology, Univ. of Edinburgh; Hon. Fellow, Univ. of Edinburgh. *Publications:* Max Weber: The Russian Revolutions (co-ed./ Trans.) 1997, Caesar and the Fading of the Roman World 1998 (Outstanding Academic Book 1998 by Choice), The Portable Hannah Arendt (Ed.) 2000, Founders, Classics and Canons 2002, The Protestant Ethic and the Spirit of Capitalism and Other Writings (co-ed./trans. with Gordon C. Wells) 2002, Dictatorship in History and Theory (co-ed.) 2004; numerous journal articles and reviews. *Address:* Room 321/1, Dorothy L. Wong Building, Department of Sociology and Social Policy, Lingnan University, Tuen Mun, Hong Kong Special Administrative Region, People's Republic of China (office). *Telephone:* (852) 2616-7185 (office). *Fax:* (852) 2891-7940 (office). *E-mail:* pbaehr@ln.edu.hk (office). *Website:* www.ln.edu.hk (office).

BAGABANDI, Natsagiin, PhD, ScD; Mongolian politician; b. 22 April 1950, Zavkhan Prov.; m. Azadsurengiin Oyunbileg 1971; one s. one d. *Education:* Refrigeration Jr Coll., Leningrad (now St Petersburg), USSR, Food Tech. Inst. of USSR, Odessa, Acad. of Social Science, Moscow, USSR. *Career:* machine operator, mechanic and engineer, Ulan Bator City Brewery and Distillery 1972–75; Chief of Dept Mongolian People's Revolutionary Party's (MPRP) Cttee of Tuv Aimag 1980–84; Chief of Div., Div. Moderator Cen. Cttee of MPRP 1987–90; Sec., Deputy Chair. Cen. Cttee of MPRP 1990–92, Chair. Feb.–June 1997; mem. of State Great Hural, Chair. 1992–96; Pres. of Mongolia and C-in-C of the Armed Forces 1997–2005; Hon. Prof., Mongolian Socio-Econ. Inst. 'Explorer XXI'; 70th Anniversary Order of the People's Revolution 1991, 'Golden Star' Olympic Order 1997, Academician Title 'Bilguun Nomch', Mongolian Nomadic Civilization Acad. and 'Ikh-Zasag' Univ. 2000, 'Peace' Order of Russian Fed. 2000, Order of Chinggis Khaan 2000; Dr hc (Nat. Food Tech. Acad. of Odessa, Ukraine) 1995, (Seng-Shui Univ., Japan) 1998, (Ankara Univ., Turkey) 1998, (Alma-Ata Univ., Kazakhstan) 1998, (Mongolian Admin Acad.) 1999, (Mongolian 'Otgontenger' Univ.) 2001, (Mongolian Defense Univ.) 2001, (Sougan Univ., S Korea) 2001, (Mongolian Science and Tech. Univ.) 2002, (Soka Univ., Japan), (Tokyo Univ. of Agric.), (Indiana Univ., USA) 2005, (Hokuriku Univ., Japan) 2007; Sukhbaatar Fund Prize 1996, Peter the Great Int. Prize 2001. *Publications include:* Mongolian Behaviour 1992, The President: Thought and Recommendation Before the New Century 1998, The President: Policy and Objectives Before the New Century 1998, Policy and Mind of the President 2000, Significance of Restoration and Tradition to the Development 2000, Mongolian Intelligence 2001, Policy and Diligence of the President 2001, Thought and Ideas of the President 2001, XXI Century Will Test You 2001, New Era and New Objectives of Mongolian Buddhist Religion 2001, Let Us Respect and Admire Elders 2001, Children, Youths and the President 2001, Multi-Sided National Security 2001, New Century: Adore Consent and Friendship, Develop the Country 2003, New Century: Meaning of Self-reliance upon Globalization,

and Globalization upon Self-reliance 2004, New Century: Meaning of Cherishing the Democracy 2005, Policy and Activity of President of Mongolia N. Bagabandi 2005.
Address: c/o Mr Ayursaikhan Tumurbaatar, Secretary to Former President N. Bagabandi, State Palace, Ulan Bator 12, Mongolia (office). *E-mail:* ayursaikhan@yahoo.com (office).

BÅGE, Lennart, MBA; Swedish diplomatist and international organization executive; *President, International Fund for Agricultural Development;* m.; two c. *Education:* Stockholm School of Econs. *Career:* Asst Under-Sec. Ministry of Foreign Affairs; Amb. to Zimbabwe; Head Dept for Int. Co-operation, Ministry of Foreign Affairs, Deputy Dir-Gen. Ministry of Foreign Affairs –2001; Pres. IFAD 2001– (re-elected 2005); Chair. UN High-Level Cttee on Programmes, mem. Sec.-Gen.'s High-Level Panel on UN Coherence 2007.
Address: International Fund for Agricultural Development, Via Paolo di Dono 44, 00142 Rome, Italy (office). *Telephone:* (06) 54591 (office). *Fax:* (06) 5043463 (office). *E-mail:* ifad@ifad.org (office). *Website:* www.ifad.org (office).

BAGIS, Egemen, MPA, BBA; Turkish politician; *Foreign Policy Advisor to the Prime Minister;* b. 1970, Bingol; m. Beyhan N. Bagis; two c. *Education:* Baruch Coll., City Univ. of New York, USA. *Career:* elected to Nat. Ass. for Istanbul 2002–, Foreign Policy Advisor to Prime Minister 2002–; mem. AK Party (Justice and Devt Party), serves as Deputy Chair. for Foreign Affairs; Chair. NATO Parl. Ass. on Transatlantic Relations; Chair. Turkey–USA Inter-Parl. Friendship Caucus; Chair. Advisory Cttee, Istanbul 2010 European Capital of Culture Initiative; Founding Patron, Istanbul Modern Museum, Santral Museum of Art and Industry; fmr Pres. Fed. of Turkish-American Asscns; Hon. mem. Bd of Dirs Siirt Solidarity Foundation.
Address: Turkish Grand National Assembly, A Blok, Alt Zemin, 3. Banko, No. 3, Bakanliklar, 06543 Ankara, Turkey (office). *Telephone:* (312) 4205908 (office). *Fax:* (312) 4206947 (office). *E-mail:* egemen@ egemenbagis.com (office). *Website:* www.egemenbagis.com (office).

BAHADIAN, Adhemar Gabriel; Brazilian diplomatist; *Ambassador to Italy;* b. 22 Oct. 1940, Rio de Janeiro. *Education:* Università Gama Filho, Istituto Rio Branco. *Career:* joined Ministry of Foreign Affairs 1967, Head Int. Commerce Div. 1987, Chief of Cabinet, Secr.-Gen. for Foreign Affairs 1994, Asst Sec.-Gen. 1995; First Sec., Perm. Mission to UN, Geneva 1976, Counsellor 1980, Minister Counsellor 1990, Alt. Perm. Rep. 2000; Consul-Gen. in Buenos Aires 2002; Amb. to Italy 2005–; fmr chief FTAA (Free Trade Area of the Americas) negotiator; Gran Croce, Ordine del Rio Branco 1994, Grande Ufficiale, Ordine al Merito Navale 1994, Grande Ufficiale, Ordine al Merito Militare 1995, Grande Ufficiale, Ordine al Merito dell'Aeronautica 1996, Commdr Legion d'Honneur (France) 1996, Ordine Francisco de Miranda (Venezuela) 1997, Cavalieri di Gran Croce (Italy) 1997, Gran Croce, Ordine di Bernardo O'Higgins (Chile) 1998, and other decorations from Germany, Finland, Portugal.
Address: Embassy of Brazil, Palazzo Pamphili, Piazza Navona 14, 00186 Rome, Italy (office). *Telephone:* (06) 683981 (office). *Fax:* (06) 6867858 (office). *E-mail:* info@ambrasile.it (office). *Website:* www .ambasciatadelbrasile.it (office).

BAHEMUKA, Judith Mbula, BA, MA, PhD; Kenyan sociologist, academic and diplomatist; *High Commissioner to Canada;* b. Makueni District. *Education:* Marygrove Coll., Detroit, USA, Univ. of Nairobi, Cornell Univ., Univ. of Minnesota. *Career:* worked with Kenya Nat. AIDS Secr. 1992–93; Chair. Cttee on Women, Children and AIDS 1995–97; Prof. and Chair. Dept of Sociology Univ. of Nairobi 1994–98, Founder and Dir Int. Learning Centre 1998–; Chair. Social and Human Sciences Nat. Cttee UNESCO –2003; Perm. Rep. to UN 2003–06; High Commr to Canada 2006–; mem Exec. Bd UNESCO, Chair. Women and Sustainable Devt; mem. Global Advisory Bd Devt Int. 2004–; fmr Visiting Scholar Catholic Univ., Washington Theological Union, Univ. of Leiden, Netherlands, Cornell Univ., Catholic Univ. of Eastern Africa; Dr hc (Kalamazoo Coll.), (Trinity Coll., Hartford, Conn.) 2005.
Address: Kenya High Commission, 415 Laurier Avenue East, Ottawa, ON K1N 6R4, Canada (office). *Telephone:* (613) 563-1773 (office). *Fax:* (613) 233-6599 (office). *E-mail:* kenyahighcommission@rogers.com (office). *Website:* www.kenyahighcommission.ca (office).

BAI, Keming; Chinese journalist and party official; *Vice-Chairman, Committee for Education, Science, Culture and Public Health, National People's Congress;* b. Oct. 1943, Jingbian, Shaanxi Prov. *Education:* Harbin Mil. Eng Inst. *Career:* joined CCP 1975; worker, Metallurgy and Geology Bureau, Harbin City, Heilongjiang Prov., Harbin Shipbuilding Inst., National Defence Industry Cttee, Shaanxi Prov.; fmr Deputy Div. Chief, Div. Chief then Deputy Dir of Gen. Office, Ministry of Educ.; fmr mem.

State Educ. Comm.; fmr Head Educ. Science, Culture and Public Health Group, Research Office of the State Council; fmr Sec.-Gen. Propaganda Dept of CCP Cen. Cttee, then Deputy Head 1993–2000; Del. 15th CCP Nat. Congress 1997–2002; Deputy Dir CCP Cen. Cttee Gen. Office 2000; Pres. CCP Cen. Cttee People's Daily (newspaper) 2000–01; Sec. CCP Hainan Prov. Cttee and Chair. Hainan People's Congress 2001–02; Sec. CCP Prov. Cttee, Hebei Prov. 2002–07; mem. 16th CCP Cen. Cttee 2002–; Vice-Chair. Cttee for Educ., Science, Culture and Public Health, Nat. People's Congress 2007–.
Address: National People's Congress, Beijing, People's Republic of China (office). *Website:* npc.people.com.cn (office).

BAIBOURTIAN, Armen, MA, PhD; Armenian academic and diplomatist; *Deputy Minister of Foreign Affairs;* b. 2 April 1964, Yerevan; m. three c. *Education:* Yerevan State Univ., Jawaharlal Nehru Univ., New Delhi-04. *Career:* Asst Prof., Yerevan State Univ. 1989–91; Special Asst to First Vice-Chair. of Parl, then Foreign Relations Adviser to Parl. 1991–92; Counselor, Dept of Int. Orgs, Foreign Ministery 1992; Counselor and Deputy Perm. Rep. to UN, New York 1993–95; Consul Gen., Los Angeles 1995–97; Amb. to India 2000–04, also accred to Sri Lanka, Indonesia, and Nepal 2002–04; Deputy Minister of Foreign Affairs, Ministry of Foreign Affairs 1997, 2004–.
Address: Ministry of Foreign Affairs, 0010 Yerevan, Republic Square, Government House 2, Armenia (office). *Telephone:* (10) 526909 (office). *Fax:* (10) 543925 (office). *E-mail:* a.baibourtian@mfa.am (office). *Website:* www.armeniaforeignministry.am (office).

BAILES, Alyson Judith Kirtley, CMG, MA; British diplomatist and academic; *Director, Stockholm International Peace Research Institute;* b. 6 April 1949. *Education:* Belvedere School, Liverpool, Somerville Coll., Oxford. *Career:* entered diplomatic service 1969; mem. staff, British Embassy in Budapest, Hungary 1970–74, FRG 1981–84, People's Repub. of China 1987–89; mem. UK Del. to NATO 1974–76; mem. staff, FCO 1976–79, 1984–86, 1994–96; Asst to EC Study Group 1979; seconded to Ministry of Defence 1979–81; Deputy Head of Mission, Norway 1990–93; on attachment to Royal Inst. of Int. Affairs 1990; Vice-Pres. Inst. for East-West Studies, New York 1996–97; Political Dir WEU, Brussels 1997–2000; Amb. to Finland 2000–02; Dir Stockholm Int. Peace Research Inst. 2002–.
Address: Stockholm International Peace Research Institute, Signalistgatan 9, 16970 Solna, Sweden (office). *Telephone:* (8) 6559751 (office). *Fax:* (8) 86559733 (office). *E-mail:* director@sipri.se (office). *Website:* www.sipri .org (office).

BAILEY, Catherine Todd; American diplomatist; b. Ind.; m. Irving W. Bailey, II; four c. *Career:* worked for eight years as an elementary school teacher; Co-founder Louisville Ronald McDonald House 1984; Founder Operation Open Arms charity, Pres. 2001–04; mem. from Ky, Republican Nat. Cttee 2000–04; Co-Chair. Republican Regents; fmr mem. Bd of Dirs PACA (Presidential Advisory Cttee), Kennedy Center, Washington, DC, McConnell Center for Political Leadership and Excellence, Univ. of Louisville 2000–04; Amb. to Latvia 2005–07; volunteered on Bd of Dirs Ky Opera, Ky Arts and Crafts Foundation; S. Tilford Payne, Jr Award for outstanding political volunteer services and contribs 2002, Unsung Heroine Award sponsored by Mitsubishi Motors 2003.
Address: US Department of State, 2201 C Street NW, Washington, DC 20520, USA (office). *Telephone:* (202) 647-4000 (office). *Fax:* (202) 647-6738 (office). *Website:* www.state.gov (office).

BAILEY, Norman A., PhD; American economist, academic and government official; *Mission Manager for Cuba and Venezuela, Office of the Director of National Intelligence; Education:* Oberlin Coll. and Columbia Univ. *Career:* fmr economist, Mobil Oil Co.; f. Overseas Equity Inc. .(later Bailey, Tondu, Warwick & Co., Inc.), Pres. 1980–84; fmr Prof. of Econs, CUNY; Prof., Center for Strategic and Int. Studies 1980–81; Dir Cttee for Monetary Research and Educ. 1980–81; Sr Dir of Econ. Affairs, Nat. Security Council 1981–83; Special Asst to Pres. Ronald Reagan 1983–89; Pres. Norman A. Bailey Inc. 1984–; Consultant Economist and Sr Fellow, Potomac Foundation, Inc. 2003–06; Adjunct Prof., Inst. of World Politics, Washington DC 2003–06; Mission Man. for Cuba and Venezuela, Office of the Dir of Nat. Intelligence 2006–; Kt Royal Order of Our Lady of the Conception of Vila Vicosa (Portugal); Nat. Security Award, Cold War Commemorative Medal, Medal of the Pan American Soc. *Publications:* The Strategic Plan that Won the Cold War 1999; numerous articles in professional journals.
Address: Mission for Cuba and Venezuela, Office of the Director of National Intelligence, Washington, DC, 20511 USA (office). *Telephone:* (202) 201-1111 (office). *Website:* www.dni.gov (office).

BAINIMARAMA, Cdre Josaia Voreqe, (Frank Bainimarama), OStJ; Fijian military officer; *Prime Minister, Minister of Home Affairs, Immigration and*

Information and Minister of Finance; b. 27 April 1954, Kiuva, Tailevu Province; m. Maria Makitalena; six c. *Education:* Maris Brothers High School, numerous mil. courses and insts. *Career:* enlisted in Fiji Navy as Ordinary Seaman 1975, commissioned as Ensign 1977, Navigation Officer Aug. 1978, Sub-Lt Nov. 1978, Exec. Officer HMFS Kiro 1979, Commdr HMFS Kikau 1982–84, HMFS Kula 1984–86, Lt Commdr 1986, served with Multinational Force and Observers in Sinai 1986–87, CO and Commdr Fiji Navy 1988, promoted to Capt. 1994, Chief of Staff 1997–99, Cdre and Commdr of Armed Forces 1999–; Head, Interim Mil. Govt of Fiji May–July 2000; Acting Pres. of Fiji (after mil. overthrow of govt of Prime Minister Laisenia Qarase) Dec. 2006–07, Interim Prime Minister Jan. 2007–, also Minister of Home Affairs, Immigration and Information 2007–, Minister of Finance 2008–; fmr Chair. Fiji Rugby Union; Meritorious Service Decoration, Peacekeeping Medal, General Service Medal, Fiji Republic Medal, 25 Anniversary Medal.
Address: Office of the Prime Minister, PO Box 2353, New Government Buildings, Suva, Fiji (office). *Telephone:* 3211201 (office). *Fax:* 3306034 (office). *E-mail:* pmsoffice@connect.com.fi (office). *Website:* www.fiji.gov.fj (office).

BAIRD, Nicholas Graham Faraday; British diplomatist; *Ambassador to Turkey;* b. 15 May 1962; m. Caroline; one s. two d. *Career:* Third, later Second Sec. (Chancery), Kuwait 1986–89, First Sec. (Econ./Finance), UK Representation to EU, Brussels 1989–93, Pvt. Sec. to Parl. Under-Sec. of State, FCO 1993–95, Head of Amsterdam IGC Unit, EU Dept (Internal) 1995–97, Deputy Head of Mission, Muscat 1997–98, Counsellor (Justice and Home Affairs), UK Representation to EU, Brussels 1998–2002, Head of EU Dept (Internal) 2002–03, on secondment to Immigration and Nationality Directorate at Home Office as Dir of Int. Delivery 2003–04, as Sr Policy Dir 2004–06, Amb. to Turkey 2006–.
Address: British Embassy, Şehit Ersan Caddesi 46/A, Cankaya, 06680 Ankara, Turkey (office). *Telephone:* (312) 455-3344 (office). *Fax:* (312) 455-3356 (office). *E-mail:* britembinf@turk.net (office). *Website:* www.britishembassy.org.tr (office).

BAJOLET, Bernard; French diplomatist; *Ambassador to Algeria;* b. 21 May 1949. *Education:* Institut d'études politiques de Paris and Ecole Nationale d'Admin. *Career:* Second Sec., then First Sec., Algiers 1975–79; mem. staff, Press Dept, Ministry of Foreign Affairs 1978–79; mem. Cabinet of Sec. of State for Foreign Affairs responsible for European Parl. relations 1979–81; Second Counsellor, Rome 1981–85, in Damascus 1986–90; Asst Dir for N Africa and the Middle East, Ministry of Foreign Affairs 1991–94; Amb. to Jordan 1994–98, to Bosnia and Herzegovina 1999–2003, to Iraq 2003–06, to Algeria 2006–.
Address: French Embassy, chemin Abd al-Kader Gadouche 25, Hydra, 16035 Algiers, Algeria (office). *Telephone:* (21) 69-24-88 (office). *Fax:* (21) 69-13-69 (office). *E-mail:* contact@ambafrance-dz.org (office). *Website:* www.ambafrance-dz.org (office).

BAJUK, Andrej, PhD; Slovenian politician and economist; *Minister of Finance;* b. 18 Oct. 1943, Ljubljana. *Education:* Universidad Nacional de Cuyo, Mendoza, Univs of Chicago and Calif., USA. *Career:* fmr Prof. Universidad Nacional de Cuyo, Mendoza; fmr mem. of staff, World Bank, Washington, DC; various positions at IDB including Exec. Vice-Pres., mem. Bd Dirs, apptd Rep. for Europe, Paris 1994; Prime Minister of Slovenia May–Nov. 2000; f. New Slovenia—Christian People's Party (NSi) (Nova Slovenija—Krščanska ljudska stranka) Aug. 2000, currently Pres.; Minister of Finance 2004–; Finance Minister of the Year, Financial Times and The Banker.
Address: Ministry of Finance, 1502 Ljubljana, Župančičeva 3, Slovenia (office). *Telephone:* (1) 3696601 (office). *Fax:* (1) 3696609 (office). *E-mail:* andrej.bajuk@mf-rs.si (office). *Website:* www.gov.si/mf (office).

BAKAYOKO, Youssouf; Côte d'Ivoirian politician and diplomatist; *Minister of Foreign Affairs;* b. 9 April 1943, Bouaké. *Career:* began diplomatic career 1973; Counsellor, Perm. Mission of Côte d'Ivoire to EU and Int. Orgs in Geneva 1973–83; Minister of Foreign Affairs 2006–.
Address: Ministry of Foreign Affairs, blvd Angoulvand, BP V109, Abidjan, Côte d'Ivoire (office). *Telephone:* 20-22-71-50 (office). *Fax:* 20-33-23-08 (office). *E-mail:* infos@mae.ci (office). *Website:* www.mae.ci (office).

BAKER, James Addison, III, LLB; American lawyer and fmr government official; *Senior Partner, Baker Botts LLP;* b. 28 April 1930, Texas; m. Susan Garrett 1973; eight c. *Education:* Princeton Univ. and Univ. of Texas Law School. *Career:* served in US Marine Corps 1952–54; with law firm Andrews, Kurth, Campbell and Jones, Houston, Tex. 1957–75; Under-Sec. of Commerce under Pres. Ford 1975; Nat. Chair. Ford's presidential campaign 1976; Campaign Dir for George Bush in primary campaign 1980, later joined Reagan campaign; White House Chief of Staff and on Nat. Security Council 1981–85; Trustee, Woodrow Wilson Int. Center for Scholars, Smithsonian Inst. 1977–; Sec. of the Treasury 1985–88, Sec. of State 1989–92; White House Chief of Staff and Sr Counsellor 1992–93; Gov. Rice Univ. 1993; Sr Pnr, Baker Botts LLP 1993–; also currently Sr Counselor, The Carlyle Group; Personal Envoy of UN Sec.-Gen., UN Mission for the Referendum in Western Sahara (MINURSO) 1997–2004 (resgnd); apptd special envoy on Middle East debt by US Pres. George W. Bush 2003; mem. Bd of Dirs Howard Hughes Medical Inst.; Hon. Chair. James A. Baker III Inst. for Public Policy, Rice Univ.; Co-Chair. Iraq Study Group, US Institute of Peace 2006–07. *Publication:* The Politics of Diplomacy 1995.
Address: Baker Botts LLP, The Warner, 1299 Pennsylvania Avenue, NW, Washington, DC 20004-2400, USA (office). *Telephone:* (202) 639-7778 (office). *E-mail:* james.baker@bakerbotts.com (office). *Website:* www.bakerbotts.com (office).

BAKER, Nigel Marcus, MVO; British diplomatist; *Ambassador to Bolivia;* m. Alexandra Baker. *Career:* Desk Officer for Libya and Tunisia, Near East and N Africa Dept, FCO 1990–91, Third, later Second Sec. (Econ.), Prague 1992–93, Deputy Head of Mission, Bratislava 1993–96, research sabbatical: Verona, Naples, Cambridge, Paris 1996–98, First Sec., UK EU Presidency, FCO 1998, Head of European Defence Section, Security Policy Dept 1998–2000, Asst Pvt. Sec. to HRH The Prince of Wales 2000–03, Deputy Head of Mission, Havana 2003–06, Amb. to Bolivia 2007–.
Address: British Embassy, Avda Sopocachi, Arce 2732, Casilla 694, La Paz, Bolivia (office). *Telephone:* (2) 243-3424 (office). *Fax:* (2) 243-1073 (office). *E-mail:* ppa@megalink.com (office). *Website:* www.britishembassy.gov.uk/bolivia (office).

BAKHIT, Maj.-Gen. Marouf al-, PhD; Jordanian government official and military officer (retd); b. 1947. *Education:* Univ. of Jordan, Univ. of Southern Calif., USA, Univ. of London, UK, Royal Jordanian Mil. Coll. *Career:* with Jordan Armed Forces 1964–1999, positions including Dir of Studies, Devt, and Procurement and Personnel Affairs; fmr Prof. of Political Science, Vice-Pres. for Mil. Affairs, Muta Univ.; fmr Amb. to Turkey, Israel; fmr Nat. Security Chief; Prime Minister of Jordan and Minister of Defence 2005–07; 14 Jordanian medals.
Address: c/o Office of the Prime Minister, POB 80, Amman 11180, Jordan (office).

BAKIYEV, Kurmanbek Saliyevich; Kyrgyzstani politician, engineer and head of state; *President;* b. 1 Aug. 1949, Masadan (now Teyyit), Suzdak Dist, Jalal-Abad; m. Tatyana Vasilyevna Bakiyeva; two s. *Education:* Kuibyshev (now Samara) Polytechnic Inst., Russia. *Career:* trained as electrical engineer 1972; served in Soviet Armed Forces 1974–86; electrical engineer Maslennikov Plant, Kuibyshev 1976–79; Sr Engineer, Head of VTs, then Deputy Chief Engineer, Jalal-Abad Electrical Factory 1979–85; Dir Profil Plant, Kok-Yangak 1985–90; First Sec. CP Kok-Yangak City Council 1990; Deputy Chair. W Jalal-Abad Council of People's Deputies 1991–92; Head of Toguz-Torou Regional Admin 1992–94; Deputy Chair. State Property Fund 1994–95; First Deputy Head, then Head W Jalal-Abad State Admin and Gov. of Jalal-Abad Duban 1995–97; Gov. of Chui Duban 1997–2000; Prime Minister of Kyrgyzstan 2000–02, Acting Prime Minister March–June 2005; mem. Zhogorku Kenesh (Parl.) 2003–05; Acting Pres. of Kyrgyzstan March–Aug. 2005, Pres. Aug. 2005–; Leader, People's Power Movt.
Address: Office of the President, 720003 Bishkek, Dom Pravitelstva, Kyrgyzstan (office). *Telephone:* (312) 21-24-66 (home). *Fax:* (312) 21-86-27 (office). *E-mail:* office@mail.gov.kg (office). *Website:* www.president.kg (office).

BAKOYANNIS, Dora; Greek politician; *Minister of Foreign Affairs;* b. 6 May 1954, Athens; m. 1st Pavlos Bakoyannis 1974 (assassinated 1989); one s. one d.; m. 2nd Isidoros Kouvelos 1998. *Education:* German School of Athens and Paris, France, Univ. of Munich, Germany, Univ. of Athens. *Career:* family fled to Paris to escape mil. dictatorship that ruled Greece 1967–74; worked at Ministry of Econ. Co-ordination and later Ministry of Foreign Affairs 1974–84; Chief of Staff, New Democratic Party 1984–1990; elected Deputy for Evrytania 1990, re-elected three times and later moved candidacy to central Athens; served as Under-Sec. of State 1990, later as Minister of Culture 1992–96; apptd shadow Foreign and Defence Minister 2000; Mayor of Athens (first woman) 2002–06; Minister of Foreign Affairs (first woman) 2006–; Int. Leadership Award, Women's Int. Center 1992, Fontana di Roma Award, 14th Int. Symposium 1993, World Mayor Award 2005, ranked by Forbes Magazine amongst 100 Most Powerful Women (66th) 2006, (67th) 2007.
Address: Ministry of Foreign Affairs, Odos Akadimias 3, 106 71 Athens, Greece (office). *Telephone:* (210) 3681800 (office). *Fax:* (210) 3681433 (office). *E-mail:* dorabakoyiannis@mfa.gr (office). *Website:* www.mfa.gr (office); www.dorabakoyannis.gr (home).

BAKRADZE, Davit, MPA, CandPhys-MathSci; Georgian physicist and politician; *Chairman, Sakartvelos Parlamenti;* b. 1 July 1972, Tbilisi; m.; two c. *Education:* Georgian Tech. Univ., Georgian-American Inst. of Public Admin, Tbilisi State Univ., Diplomats Training Course, Swiss Int. Relations Univ. Seminars (SIRUS), Geneva, Defence and Security Studies Course 'Leaders for the 21st Century', G. Marshall European Centre for Security Studies, Garmisch-Partenkirchen, Germany, Sr Course for Officers and Diplomats, NATO Defence Coll., Rome, Italy. *Career:* First Class State Counsellor; holds diplomatic rank of Chief Minister Counsellor; Deputy Head of Disarmament and Arms Control Div., Politico-Mil. Dept, Ministry of Foreign Affairs 1996–98, Head of Disarmament and Arms Control Div. 1998–2000, Deputy Dir Politico-Mil. Dept 2000–02, Head, Service for Security Issues, Nat. Security Council of Georgia 2002–03, Dir Dept for Int. Security and Conflict Man. 2003–04, Dir Dept for Political Security 2004; mem. Parl. 2004–, Chair. Cttee on European Integration 2004–07, Standing Del. to European Parl., Co-Chair. EU-Georgia Parl. Co-operation Cttee, mem. numerous dels; State Minister on Conflict Resolution Issues 2007–08; Minister of Foreign Affairs Feb.–May 2008; Chair. Sakartvelos Parlamenti (Parl.) June 2008–; mem. United Nat. Movement (UNP) Party; Special Prize of Pres. of Georgia: Prize for Academic Excellence to the Best Student of Inst. of Public Admin 1996, NATO/EAPC Research Fellowship 1998, Special Gratification from Minister of Foreign Affairs No. 53/2: For Active Participation in Drawing up Adapted Agreements on the Conventional Forces in Europe at OSCE Istanbul Summit 2000, Special Gratification for Significant Professional Achievements in Drawing up Significant Agreements between the States, Pres. of Georgia 2000, Swiss Leadership Award in Int. Relations, Special Award of Grad. Inst. of Int. Studies, Geneva 2005. *Address:* Sakartvelos Parlamenti, 0118 Tbilisi, Rustaveli 8, Georgia (office). *Telephone:* (32) 93-61-70 (office). *Fax:* (32) 99-93-86 (office). *E-mail:* hdstaff@parliament.ge (office). *Website:* www.parliament.ge (office).

BALA-GAYE, Mousa G., BA; Gambian politician; *Secretary of State for Finance and Economic Affairs;* b. 13 Aug. 1946. *Education:* Legon Univ., Univ. of Manchester, UK, IMF Inst. *Career:* Asst Sec., Ministry of Works and Communications 1971–73; Sec., Public Service Comm. 1973; Asst Sec., Ministry of Local Govt and Lands 1973; Sr Asst, Ministry of Finance and Trade 1976–79, Under-Sec. 1979–80, Deputy Perm. Sec. 1980–82, Perm. Sec. 1982–86; Exec. Dir African Devt Bank, Abidjan, Côte D'Ivoire 1986–89; Perm. Sec., Office of the Pres. 1989–90; Man. Dir Heron Ltd 1990; Chair. and Man. Dir Afri-Swiss Travel Ltd 1993; Vice-Chair. First Int. Bank Ltd 1999, Acting Chair. 2002; Alt. Dir Senegambia Beach Hotel 2000; Vice-Chair. Int. Trust Insurance Co. Ltd 2000; Sec. of State for Finance and Econ. Affairs 2003–05, for Foreign Affairs March–Oct. 2005, for Trade, Industry and Employment Oct.–Nov. 2005, for Finance and Econ. Affairs Nov. 2005–; fmr mem. Bd Dirs Cen. Bank of The Gambia, Gambia Produce Marketing Bd, Social Security and Housing Finance Corpn, Gambia Nat. Insurance Corpn; del. to numerous int. and multilateral confs and meetings of IMF, World Bank, OPEC Fund, the Commonwealth; Alt. Gov. African Devt Bank, Islamic Devt Bank, World Bank. *Address:* Ministry of Finance and Economic Affairs, The Quadrangle, PO Box 9686, Banjul, The Gambia (office). *Telephone:* 4228291 (office); 4393275 (home). *Fax:* 4227954 (office).

BALESTRA, Gian Nicola Filippi, MA; San Marino diplomatist; *Head of Mission to the European Communities;* b. 10 Dec. 1954. *Education:* Università degli Studi di Roma, Italy, New York Univ., USA and The Hague Acad. of Int. Law, Netherlands. *Career:* Programme Officer, Jr Professional Officers' Programme, UNDP, Addis Ababa, Ethiopia 1984–85, Perm. Observer of San Marino to UN, New York 1987–89, Amb. to Belgium and Head of Mission to EC (later EU) 1986–96, Perm. Rep. to Council of Europe, Strasbourg 1992–96, Perm. Rep. to UN 1997–2005; Head of Mission to EC 2005–. *Address:* Mission to the European Communities, 62, Av. Franklin Roosevelt, 1050 Brussels, Belgium (office). *Telephone:* (2) 644-22-24 (office). *Fax:* (2) 644-20-57 (office). *E-mail:* ambrsm.bxl@coditel.net (office).

BALKENENDE, Jan Pieter, DIur; Dutch politician; *Prime Minister;* b. 7 May 1956, Kapelle. *Education:* Free Univ. of Amsterdam. *Career:* Legal Affairs Policy Officer, Netherlands Univs Council 1982–84; mem. Amstelveen Municipal Council 1982–98, Leader, Council Christen-Democratisch Appèl (CDA) Group 1994–98; Prof. of Econs, Free Univ. of Amsterdam 1993–2002; mem. staff, Policy Inst. of the CDA 1984–98; elected mem. Parl. 1998, Parl. Leader CDA 2001–; Prime Minister of the Netherlands 2002–, also Minister of Gen. Affairs 2002–. *Publications include:* numerous articles on liberal individualism and communitarianism in Dutch society. *Address:* Office of the Prime Minister, Ministry of General Affairs, Binnenhof 20, POB 20001, 2500 EA The Hague (office); c/o Christen-Democratisch Appèl (CDA) (Christian Democratic Appeal), Dr Kuyper-

straat 5, POB 30453, 2500 GL The Hague, Netherlands. *Telephone:* (70) 3564100 (office). *Fax:* (70) 3564683 (office). *Website:* www.minaz.nl (office).

BALLADUR, Edouard, LenD; French politician; *Chairman, National Assembly Commission on Foreign Affairs;* b. 2 May 1929, Smyrna, Turkey; m. Marie-Josèphe Delacour 1957; four s. *Education:* Lycée Thiers, Marseilles, Faculté de Droit, Aix-en-Provence, Inst. d'Etudes Politiques, Paris and Ecole Nationale d'Admin. *Career:* auditor, Conseil d'Etat 1957, Maître des Requêtes 1963; adviser to Dir-Gen. of ORTF 1962–63; mem. Admin. Council of ORTF 1967–68; Tech. Adviser, Office of Prime Minister Georges Pompidou 1966–68; Pres. French soc. for Bldg and Devt of road tunnel under Mont Blanc 1968–81; mem. Admin. Council, Nat. Forestry Office 1968–73; Asst Sec.-Gen. Presidency of Repub. 1969, Sec.-Gen. 1974; Pres. Dir-Gen. Générale de Service Informatique 1977–86; Pres. Compagnie Européenne d'Accumulateurs 1980–86; mem. Conseil d'Etat 1984–88, 1988–; Minister of the Econ., of Finance and Privatization 1986–88; Prime Minister of France 1993–95; Presidential Cand. 1995; Comm. on Foreign Affairs, Nat. Ass. 2002–; mem. Nat. Ass.; Chevalier, Légion d'honneur; Grand-Croix Ordre Nat. du Mérite. *Publications:* l'Arbre de mai 1979, Je crois en l'homme plus qu'en l'Etat 1987, Passion et longueur de temps (with others) 1989, Douze Lettres aux français trop tranquilles 1990, Des Modes et des convictions 1992, Dictionnaire de la réforme 1992, L'Action pour la réforme 1995, Deux ans à Matignon 1995, Caractère de la France 1997, L'Avenir de la différence 1999, Renaissance de la droite, pour une alternance décomplexée 2000. *Address:* Conseil d'Etat, 75100 Paris; Assemblée Nationale, 126 rue de l'Université, 75355 Paris, France.

BALLANTYNE, Sir Frederick Nathaniel, Kt, GCMG, MD; Saint Vincent and the Grenadines cardiologist and government official; *Governor-General;* b. 5 July 1936; m. Sally Ann Ballantyne. *Education:* Howard Univ. and Syracuse Univ., USA. *Address:* Office of the Governor-General, Government Buildings, Kingstown, Saint Vincent and the Grenadines (office). *Telephone:* 456-1401 (office).

BALOI, Oldemiro; Mozambican economist, business executive and politician; *Minister of Foreign Affairs and Co-operation; Career:* Deputy Minister of Co-operation early 1990s; Minister of Industry and Trade and Tourism 1995–2000; active in pvt. business since leaving politics, notably as mem. Bd of Dirs and of Exec. Bd Millennium-BIM (Int. Bank of Mozambique); Minister of Foreign Affairs and Co-operation 2008–. *Address:* Ministry of Foreign Affairs and Co-operation, Av. Julius Nyerere 4, CP 2787, Maputo, Mozambique (office). *Telephone:* 21490222 (office). *Fax:* 21494070 (office). *E-mail:* minec@zebra.uem.mz (office).

BALUYEVSKII, Col-Gen. Yurii Nikolayevich; Russian army officer; *Chief of the General Staff, Russian Armed Forces;* b. 9 Jan. 1947, Trubavets, Drohobych Raion, Lviv Oblast, Ukrainian SSR. *Education:* Leningrad (now St Petersburg) Higher Mil. Command School of Gen. Army, M. Frunze Mil. Acad., Mil. Acad. of Gen. Staff. *Career:* infantry officer 1970–82; Sr Officer, Ooperator, and Head of Group Chief Operation Dept of Gen. Staff; First Deputy Commdr of Group, Russian Forces in Caucasus; Deputy Head Chief Operation Dept of Gen. Staff 1982–2001, First Deputy Chief of Gen. Staff 2001–04, Chief and First Deputy Minister of Defence 2004–; apptd to Security Council of Russian Fed. 2004; Order for Service to Motherland in Armed Forces, Order of Audacity; nine medals. *Address:* Ministry of Defence, 105175 Moscow, ul. Myasnitskaya 37, Russia (office). *Telephone:* (495) 293-38-54 (office). *Fax:* (495) 296-84-36 (office). *Website:* www.mil.ru (office).

BALZAN, Walter; Maltese diplomatist and civil servant; *Permanent Representative to the International Organizations, United Nations;* b. 1946; m.; two c. *Education:* The Lyceum, Malta. *Career:* joined civil service 1964, served in Ministries of Industrial Devt and Tourism, Trade and Industry and Finance; apptd govt mem. on Bd of Dirs Maritim Selmun Palace Hotel 1987–92, Malta Export Trade Corpn Ltd 1992–95; Personal Aide to Deputy Prime Minister, Minister of the Interior and Justice and Sec. of Airport Security Cttee of Directorate for Civil Aviation 1987–90, 1990–93, 1998–99; Perm. Rep. to Council of Europe on Relief in Major Natural and Technological Disasters 1987–90; mem. Cabinet of Pres., 45th Session on UN Gen. Ass. 1990–91; Rapporteur of Second Cttee (Econ. and Financial), 47th Session of UN Gen. Ass. 1992–93; Del. to CSCE summit meetings, Paris 1990, Helsinki 1992; Deputy Perm. Rep. to UN, New York 1993–96, Consul-Gen. in New York 1994–96, Perm. Rep. to UN 1999–2003; fmr Amb. to Austria and fmr Perm. Rep. to UN, Vienna, currently Perm. Rep. to Int. Orgs, Rome; Rep. to Preparatory Comm. for the Comprehensive

Nuclear-Test-Ban Treaty Org. (CTBTO Preparatory Comm.) 2003; Cavaliere dell'Ordine di San Gregorio Magno 1995.
Address: Permanent Representation of Malta, Via dei Somaschi 1, 00186 Rome, Italy (office). *Telephone:* (06) 6879990 (office). *Fax:* (06) 6892687 (office). *E-mail:* malta-un.rome@gov.mt (office).

BAMAKHRAMA, Dya-Eddine Said; Djibouti diplomatist. *Career:* Amb. to Saudi Arabia (also accred to Bahrain) and Perm. Rep. to OIC 2002–.
Address: Embassy of Djibouti, Salah Eddeen Quarter, PO Box 94340, Riyadh 11693, Saudi Arabia (office). *Telephone:* (1) 454-3182 (office); (1) 454-3583 (office). *Fax:* (1) 456-9068 (office); (1) 454-9168 (office). *E-mail:* dya_bamakhrama@hotmail.com (office).

BAMBA, Youssoufou; Côte d'Ivoirian diplomatist; *Ambassador to Austria;* b. 31 Dec. 1949, Abidjan; m. Marie-Madeleine Bamba; five c. *Career:* joined Ministry of Foreign Affairs in Abidjan as Asst Dir of Budget 1976, assigned to Perm. Mission to UN, Counsellor 1982–88, Asst Dir for Int. Co-operation 1988–90, Adviser to Minister for Foreign Affairs 1990–93, Amb. to Ethiopia and OAU, Addis Ababa 1993–94; Chief of Cabinet of Pres. of 49th Session of UN Gen. Ass. 1994–95, Amb. to Japan (also accred to S Korea) 1994–96, Perm. Rep. to UN, New York 1996–98, Deputy Minister for Foreign Co-operation, Ministry of Foreign Affairs 1998–99, Amb. to USA 2000–01, to UK 2001–07, to Austria 2007–, also Perm. Rep. to UN, Vienna and Comprehensive Nuclear-Test-Ban Treaty Org., Resident Rep. to IAEA and Perm. Rep. to UNIDO; fmr mem. Bd Africa Centre, London.
Address: Embassy of Côte d'Ivoire, Stadiongasse 4/5, 1010 Vienna, Austria (office). *Telephone:* (1) 406-50-51 (office). *Fax:* (1) 409-77-15 (office).

BAMBANG YUDHOYONO, Lt-Gen. Susilo, MA; Indonesian politician and head of state; *President;* b. 1949, East Java; m. Ani Herrawati; two s. *Education:* Indonesian Mil. Acad. and Webster Univ., USA. *Career:* participated in Operation Seroja (invasion of Timor Leste) and commanded Dili-based Battalion 744 1970s; spent much of mil. career with Kostrad airborne units; mil. training in USA and Europe 1980s–90s; lectured at Army Staff Command Coll . (Seskoad) 1980s; worked in territorial commands in Jakarta and S. Sumatra (Pangdam II/Sriwijaya) mid 1990s; Chief Mil. Observer in Bosnia 1995–96; Chief of the Armed Forces Social and Political Affairs Staff (Kassospol Abri) (renamed Chief of Territorial Affairs (Kaster) Nov. 1998) 1997–2000; retd from active mil. service 2000; Minister of Mines 1999–2000; Co-ordinating Minister for Political Affairs, Security and Social Welfare 2000–04 (resgnd); Pres. of Indonesia Oct. 2004–; UNPKF Medal; Mil. Service medals include Bintang Dharma, Bintang Mahaputera Adipurna, Bintang Republik Indonesia Adipurna.
Address: Office of the President, Instant Merdeka, Jakarta 10110, Indonesia (office). *Telephone:* (21) 3840946 (office). *Website:* www .presidensby.info (office).

BAMBASOVÁ, Helena; Czech politician and diplomatist; *Deputy Minister of Foreign Affairs;* b. 15 Sept. 1958, Chlumec nad Cidlinou; m.; two c. *Education:* Univ. of Econs, Prague. *Career:* with Centre for Commercial Research, Prague 1985–91, Head of Market Consumption Dept 1990–91; Deputy Dir Centre for Econ. Research and Grad. Educ., Charles Univ., Prague and Univ. of Pittsburgh, USA 1991–92; Dir-Gen. Admin. Section, Ministry of Foreign Affairs 1992–94, Man. Exec. Dir NATO Summit Czech Task Force 2001–02, Dir-Gen. Man. and Human Resources Section 2003–04, Dir-Gen. Bilateral Relations and Devt Co-operation 2004–06, Deputy Minister of Foreign Affairs 2006–; Amb. to the Netherlands 1997–2001.
Address: Ministry of Foreign Affairs, Loretánské náměstí 5, 118 00 Prague 1, Czech Republic (office). *Telephone:* (2) 24182449 (office). *Fax:* (2) 24183018 (office). *E-mail:* info@mzv.cz (office). *Website:* www.mzv.cz (office).

BAMIEH ABBASSI, Mayada, BA; Palestinian organization executive and diplomatist; *Vice-President, Women's International Democratic Federation;* b. 25 July 1945, Jaffa; m. Said Abbassi 1977; one d. *Education:* American Univ. of Beirut. *Career:* Asst Research Prof., American Univ. of Beirut 1969–70; mem. Leading Cttee Gen. Union of Palestinian Women (Lebanon) 1970–74; Founder and Head Int. Relations Dept, Palestinian Red Crescent 1973–75; responsible for social, econ. and political advancement of Palestinian women in refugee camps in S Lebanon 1974–77; First. Sec. Embassy of Palestine Liberation Org., Guinea 1977–78, Angola 1979–85; Co-ordinator Palestinian Women Asscns, Venezuela, Peru and Chile 1978; Dir Voice of Palestine, Radio Luanda, Angola 1979–85; mem. Palestinian Nat. Council (Parl.) 1985–; Head of Int. Relations, Palestinian Women Movt 1985–, mem. Tech. Cttee 1991–; mem. Gen. Secr. Gen. Union of Palestinian Women 1985–; co-founder Jerusalem Link project 1991; Vice-Pres. Women's Int. Democratic Fed. 1994–; mem. Palestinian

Human Rights Cttee; has attended numerous confs on women's issues and human rights.
Address: Women's International Democratic Federation, 25 rue du Charolais, 75012 Paris, France (office). *Fax:* 1-40-01-90-81 (office).

BAN, Ki-moon, BA, MPA; South Korean politician, diplomatist and UN official; *Secretary-General, United Nations;* b. 13 June 1944, Eumseong, North Chungcheong; m. Yoo Soon-taek; one s. two d. *Education:* Seoul Nat. Univ., Kennedy School of Govt, Harvard Univ., USA. *Career:* early postings include at Embassy in New Delhi, two terms at Embassy in Washington, DC, First Sec., Perm. Observer Mission to UN, New York; fmr Dir UN Div.; Amb. to Austria, also Chair. Preparatory Comm. for the Comprehensive Nuclear Test Ban Treaty Org. (CTBTO) 1999; Dir-Gen. of American Affairs 1990–92; Vice-Chair. South-North Jt Nuclear Control Comm. 1992; Deputy Minister for Policy Planning 1995–96; Nat. Security Adviser to the Pres. 1996–2000; Chef-de-Cabinet to Pres. of UN Gen. Ass. 2001; Vice-Minister 2000, then Foreign Policy Adviser to the Pres.; Minister of Foreign Affairs and Trade 2004–06; Sec.-Gen.-designate UN Oct.–Dec. 2006, Sec.-Gen. 2007–; Order of Service Merit 1975, 1986, Grand Decoration of Honour (Austria) 2001, Grand Cross of Rio Blanco (Brazil) 2002, Gran Cruz del Sol (Peru) 2006; Van Fleet Award, Korea Soc., New York 2005.
Address: Office of the Secretary-General, United Nations, New York, NY 10017, USA (office). *Telephone:* (212) 963-1234 (office). *Fax:* (212) 963-4879 (office). *Website:* www.un.org/sg (office).

BANDA, Joyce, BA; Malawi business executive and politician; *Minister of Foreign Affairs and International Cooperation;* b. 1952, Malemia, Zomba. *Career:* early career working as sec.; mem. Parl. for Zomba-Malosa constituency; Minister of Foreign Affairs and Int. Cooperation 2006–; mem. United Democratic Front; Chair., Malawi Housing Corpn; mem. Bd Malawi Entrepreneurs Devt Inst., Malawi Polytechnic; Founder and Chair. Nat. Asscn of Business Women 1989, now Exec. Dir; f. Hunger Project, Young Emerging Leader's Network, Joyce Banda Foundation; numerous awards including Africa Prize for Leadership 1997, 100 Heroines Award 1998.
Address: Ministry of Foreign Affairs and International Cooperation, POB 30315, Capital City, Lilongwe, Malawi (office). *Telephone:* 1789323 (office). *Fax:* 1788482 (office). *E-mail:* foreign@malawi.net (office). *Website:* www .malawi.gov.mw/foreign/foreign.htm (office).

BANGURA, Zainab Hawa, BA; Sierra Leone human rights activist and politician; *Minister of Foreign Affairs;* b. (Zainab Sesay), 18 Dec. 1959, Yonibana Chiefdom, Tonkolili Dist, Northern Prov. *Education:* schools in Magburaka and Freetown; diplomas in the UK on insurance studies and insurance management. *Career:* apptd Asst Reinsurance Man. Nat. Insurance Co. 1983; f. Women Organized for a Morally Enlightened Nation (WOMEN—first nonpartisan women's political rights org.) 1995; co-f. Campaign for Good Governance 1996; f. Nat. Accountability Group 2001; co-f. Movt for Progress (political party promoting good governance and empowerment of women, youth and the disabled) 2002, nominated Chair., ran as only female cand. in presidential elections May 2002; mem. Steering Cttee World Movt for Democracy; served as Chief Civil Affairs Officer to UN Mission in Liberia; Minister of Foreign Affairs 2007–; fmr Reagan-Fascell Democracy Fellow, The Nat. Endowment for Democracy; Assoc. and Fellow, Chartered Insurance Inst. (UK) 1991–.
Address: Ministry of Foreign Affairs, Gloucester Street, Freetown, Sierra Leone (office). *Telephone:* (22) 223260 (office). *Fax:* (22) 225615 (office). *E-mail:* mfaicsl@yahoo.com (office).

BANKS, Rosemary, MA, MSc; New Zealand diplomatist; *Permanent Representative, United Nations;* b. 1951, Christchurch; m. Brian Lockstone. *Education:* Univ. of Canterbury, LSE, UK. *Career:* various positions in Ministry of Foreign Affairs and Trade 1975–85 including in Devt, Econs, UN Divs; fmrly posted to NZ Mission to UN, Geneva and New York; Deputy High Commr, Honiara, Solomon Islands 1985–87; Dir Auckland Office, Ministry of Foreign Affairs and Trade 1987–88, Planning Unit, Ministry of Foreign Affairs 1988–90, Deputy Dir of Personnel 1990–92, Dir of Information and Public Affairs Div. 1996–97, Dir of N Asia Div. 1997–99, Dir of Devt Cooperation Div. 2000, Deputy Sec. of Multilateral Affairs 2000–05; Deputy High Commr, Canberra, Australia 1992–95; Perm. Rep. of NZ to UN, New York 2005–.
Address: Office of the Permanent Representative of New Zealand to the United Nations, 1 United Nations Plaza, 25th Floor, New York, NY 10017, USA (office). *Telephone:* (212) 317-3086 (office). *Fax:* (212) 758-0827 (office). *E-mail:* nzmissionny@earthlink.net (office). *Website:* www .nzmissionny.org (office).

BAPTISTA, Mawete João; Angolan diplomatist. *Career:* currently Amb. to the Democratic Repub. of Congo.

Address: Embassy of Angola, 4413–4429 blvd du 30 juin, BP 8625, Kinshasa, Democratic Republic of Congo (office). *Telephone:* (12) 33003 (office). *Fax:* (13) 98971 (office). *E-mail:* consangolakatanga@voila.fr (office).

BAR-ON, Ronnie; Israeli politician and lawyer; *Minister of Finance;* b. 1948, Tel-Aviv; m.; three c. *Education:* Hebrew Univ., Jerusalem. *Career:* completed mil. service with of Lt-Col, served as judge, Mil. Court of Appeals in Judea, Samaria, Gaza; mem. Cen. Cttee of Israel Bar 1995–2003, also served as mem. Jerusalem Regional Cttee of Israel Bar, Council for the Admin. Courts, Advisory Comm. to the Govt Cos Authority, Public Defenders Comm.; elected to 16th Knesset (parl.) 2003, re-elected 2006; Minister of Nat. Infrastructures and Minister of Science and Tech., January–May 2006, of the Interior 2006–07, of Finance 2007–. *Address:* Ministry of Finance, POB 13191, 1 Rehov Kaplan, Kiryat Ben-Gurion, Jerusalem 91008, Israel (office). *Telephone:* (2) 5317111 (office). *Fax:* (2) 5637891 (office). *E-mail:* webmaster@mof.gov.il (office). *Website:* www.mof.gov.il (office).

BAR-YAACOV, Nomi, LLM; Israeli lawyer, diplomatist and academic; *Research Fellow for Conflict Management, International Institute for Strategic Studies (IISS);* b. London, England. *Education:* Univ. of Cambridge, European Univ. Inst., Florence, Italy, Columbia Univ. NY, USA. *Career:* clerk, Israeli Supreme Court Justice Aharon Barak 1991; various UN posts in E. Asia Div. and Americas Div., including Dept Political Affairs, Assoc. Spokesperson for Sec. –Gen., UN, NY 1993–94, missions in Haiti 1993, S Africa 1994, Mozambique 1994, Guatemala 1995, Bosnia 1996–97; Legal Adviser OSCE 1997–98; corresp. Agence France-Presse 1998–2001; Visiting Fellow, IISS, London 2001–03, Research Fellow for Conflict Man. 2003–, advises Foreign Affairs Select Cttee Man. Programme; currently advises several European governments on foreign policy. *Publications include:* articles: Diplomacy and Human Rights: the Role of Human Rights in Conflict Resolution in El Salvador and Haiti, 1995; La lutte pour les droits de l'homme dans un conflit entre l'Etat et la nation, 1995; The Role of Human Rights Organsations in Ethnic and National Conflicts, 1998; Command Responsibility in Crimes of War, 1999; New Imperatives for Israeli-Palestinian Peace, 2003. *Address:* International Institute for Strategic Studies (IISS), Arundel House, 13–15 Arundel Street, Temple Place, London WC2R 3DX, England (office). *Telephone:* (20) 7379-7676 (office). *Fax:* (20) 7836-3108 (office). *E-mail:* Bar-Yaacov@iiss.org (office). *Website:* www.iiss.org (office).

BARADEI, Mohammad Mostafa el-, PhD; Egyptian international organization official and diplomatist; *Director-General, International Atomic Energy Agency;* b. 1942; m. Aida el-Kachef; one s. one d. *Education:* Univ. of Cairo, New York Univ., USA. *Career:* with Egyptian Ministry of Foreign Affairs, Dept of Int. Orgs 1964–67; mem. Perm. Mission to UN, New York 1967–71; Sr Fellow, Center for Int. Studies, New York Univ. 1973–74; Special Asst to Foreign Minister, Ministry of Foreign Affairs 1974–78; mem. Perm. Mission to UN, Geneva and Alt. Rep. Cttee on Disarmament 1978–80; Sr Fellow and Dir Int. Law and Orgs Programme, UN Inst. for Training and Research, New York 1980–84; Adjunct Prof. of Int. Law, New York Univ. 1981–87; Rep. of Dir-Gen. of IAEA to UN, New York 1984–87, Legal Adviser, then Dir Legal Div., IAEA, Vienna 1987–91, Dir of External Relations 1991–93, Asst Dir-Gen. for External Relations 1993–97, Dir-Gen. IAEA 1997– (re-appointed for third term 2005); mem. Int. Law Asscn, American Soc., of Int. Law, Nuclear Law Asscn; Nobel Peace Prize (jt winner with the IAEA) 2005. *Publications:* The International Law Commission: The Need for a New Direction 1981, Model Rules for Disaster Relief Operations 1982, The Role of International Atomic Energy Agency Safeguards in the Evolution of the Non-Proliferation Regime 1991, The International Law of Nuclear Energy 1993, On Compliance with Nuclear Non-Proliferation Obligations (Security Dialogue) 1996, and articles in int. law journals. *Address:* International Atomic Energy Agency, POB 100, Wagramerstrasse 5, 1400 Vienna, Austria (office). *Telephone:* (1) 26000 (office). *Fax:* (1) 26007 (office). *E-mail:* official.mail@iaea.org (office). *Website:* www.iaea .org (office).

BARAK, Lt-Gen. Ehud; Israeli politician and fmr army officer and business executive; *Deputy Prime Minister and Minister of Defence;* b. 12 Feb. 1942, Israel; m. Nava Cohen; three d. *Education:* Hebrew Univ. Jerusalem and Stanford Univ. Calif. *Career:* enlisted in Israeli Defence Force (IDF) 1959; grad. Infantry Officers' course 1962; commando course, France 1963; Armoured Corps Co. Commdrs. course 1968; various command roles; also served in operations br. of Gen. Staff; active service in Six Day War 1967 and Yom Kippur War 1973; Commdr Tank Commdrs' course 1974; Head, Gen. Staff Planning Dept 1982–83; Dir IDF Mil. Intelligence 1983–86; Commdr Cen. Command 1986–87; Deputy Chief of Gen. Staff Israeli Defence Force 1987–91, Chief of Gen. Staff 1991–94; Minister of Interior

July–Nov. 1995, of Foreign Affairs 1995–1996; Chair. Israel Labour Party 1997–2001, 2007–; Prime Minister of Israel 1999–2001; Deputy Prime Minister and Minister of Defence 2007–; mem. Knesset (Parl.) and of Parl. Security and Foreign Affairs Cttee 1996; Chair. Barak & Assocs LLC; most decorated soldier in history of IDF. *Address:* Ministry of Defence, Kaplan St, Hakirya, Tel-Aviv 67659 (office); Israel Labour Party, PO Box 62033, Tel-Aviv 61620 (office). *Telephone:* 3-5692010 (Ministry) (office); 3-6899444 (Labour Party) (office). *Fax:* 3-6916940 (Ministry) (office); 3-6899420 (Labour Party) (office). *E-mail:* public@mod.gov.il (Ministry) (office); inter@havoda.org.il (Labour Party) (office). *Website:* www.mod.gov.il (Ministry) (office); www.havoda.org.il (Labour Party) (office).

BARAK, Rafael, BA, MA; Israeli diplomatist; *Deputy Director General for Europe, Ministry of Foreign Affairs;* b. Montevido, Uruguay; m. Miriam Barak; three c. *Education:* Tel-Aviv Univ. *Career:* emigrated to Israel 1969; with Ministry of Foreign Affairs 1977–, Second, then First Sec., Peru –1987, Counsellor-Press Attaché to the EC, also Accred to Luxembourg 1987–91, Deputy Chief of Mission, Belgium and Luxembourg 1991–93, Chief Co-ordinator for negotiations with Palestinians 1993–96, Deputy Dir-Gen. Ministry of Foreign Affairs 1997–2000, Deputy Chief of Mission, USA 2000; currently Deputy Dir Gen. for Europe, Ministry of Foreign Affairs. *Address:* Ministry of Foreign Affairs, 9 Yitzhak Rabin Blvd, Kiryat Ben-Gurion, Jerusalem 91035, Israel (office). *Telephone:* 2-5303111 (office). *Fax:* 2-5303367 (office). *E-mail:* feedback@mfa.gov.il (office). *Website:* www.mfa.gov.il (office).

BARAMIDZE, Giorgi; Georgian politician; *Deputy Prime Minister and State Minister, responsible for Euro-Atlantic Integration;* b. 1968, Tbilisi; m. Eka Jafaridze; one d. *Education:* Polytechnic Inst. of Georgia, George C. Marshall Center for European Security Studies, Germany. *Career:* Founding mem. Green Party of Georgia 1990; commanded state centre responsible for the search for the missing and for freeing prisoners during war in Abkhazia 1992–93; Chair. Comm. for the Protection of Human Rights and Nat. Minorities 1992–94; mem. Parl. 1992–, Chair. Anti-Corruption Comm. 1996–98, Chair. Defence and Security Cttee 2000–03; Founding mem. Citizen's Union of Georgia 1995, Chair. Parl. Group 1996–98; Research Assoc., Georgetown Univ., Washington, DC 1998–99; Minister of Internal Affairs 2003–04, of Defence June–Dec. 2004; Deputy Prime Minister and State Minister, responsible for Euro-Atlantic Integration 2004–. *Address:* Office of the State Minister, responsible for Euro-Atlantic Integration, 0105 Tbilisi, P. Ingorovka 7, Georgia (office). *Telephone:* (32) 93-28-67 (office). *Fax:* (32) 93-27-22 (office). *Website:* www.eu-nato .gov.ge (office).

BARBOSA BORGES, Victor Manuel; Cape Verde politician; *Minister of Foreign Affairs, Co-operation and Communities; Career:* fmr Minister of Educ. with portfolio of Human Resources Devt; currently Minister of Foreign Affairs, Co-operation and Communities. *Address:* Ministry of Foreign Affairs, Co-operation and Communities, Palácio das Comunidades, Achada de Santo António, Praia, Santiago, Cape Verde (office). *Telephone:* 2615727 (office). *Fax:* 2616262 (office). *E-mail:* mne@gov.cv (office).

BARBOSA PEQUENO, Ovidio Manuel; São Tomé and Príncipe journalist, politician and diplomatist; b. 5 Nov. 1954; m. *Education:* Pacific Western Univ., Inst. of Tech. of New York, USA. *Career:* joined diplomatic service, overseas assignments included First Sec., Perm. Mission to UN, New York 1983–90; Sr Ed. Voice of America, Washington, DC 1990–99, headed Angola Bureau 1998–99; returned to diplomatic service and served as Amb. to Taiwan 1999–2004, Minister of Foreign Affairs and Co-operation 2004–06 (resgnd), 2007–08, Perm. Rep. to UN, New York and Amb. to USA (also accred to Canada and Brazil) 2006–07. *Address:* c/o Ministry of Foreign Affairs, Co-operation and Communities, Avda 12 de Julho, CP 111, São Tomé, São Tomé e Príncipe. *Telephone:* 221017.

BARBUT, Monique, MPhil(Econs), MA (Econs); French international organiza-tion official; *Chairperson and CEO, Global Environment Facility;* b. 22 Aug. 1956; m.; three c. *Education:* Univ. of Paris I, Grad. Inst. of Int. Studies, IHE, Paris II. *Career:* several internships in banking, including three months at Volksbank, Zürich, Switzerland 1979; Program Man. Saint-Denis La Réunion, Caisse Centrale de Cooperation Economique 1981–84, Head of Dept of sector-based policies and retrospective evaluation 1984–89, in charge of all public credit and housing cos in French Overseas Depts 1990, at Ministry of Cooperation and Devt 1990–93, in charge of Secr. of French Global Environment Fund (inter-ministerial field) 1994–96; Deputy Dir French Overseas Depts and Territories and Dir Div. in charge

of Devt inside same Dept, Agence Française de Développement (AFD) 1996–2000, Exec. Dir at AFD, especially in charge of all activities in French Overseas Depts and Territories, and responsible for all programmes for Pacific, Indian, Caribbean Ocean Islands 2000–02; Dir Div. of Tech., Industry and Econs, UNEP 2003–06; Chair. and CEO Global Environment Facility 2006–; mem. French Govt Del., Earth Summit, Rio de Janeiro, Brazil 1992.
Address: Global Environment Facility Secretariat, 1818 H Street, NW, Washington, DC 20433, USA (office); 1 rue Frédéric Bastiat, 75008 Paris, France. *Telephone:* (202) 473-3202 (US) (office); 1-42-89-42-33 (France). *Fax:* (202) 522-3240 (office); (202) 522-3245 (office). *E-mail:* mbarbut@ thegef.org (office). *Website:* www.thegef.org (office).

BÁRCENA IBARRA, Alicia, BSc, MSc, MPA; Mexican biologist and international organization official; *Executive Secretary, Economic Commission for Latin America and the Caribbean (ECLAC);* b. 5 March 1952. *Education:* Universidad Nacional Autónoma de Mexico (UNAM), Harvard Univ., USA, Instituto Miguel Angel, Mexico. *Career:* Research Asst, UNAM 1975-76, Assoc. Prof. of Botany, UNAM (Universidad Autónoma Metropolitana) 1976–78; Researcher on Ethnobotany, Instituto Nacional sobre Recursos Bióticos 1978–80; Regional Exec. Dir/Research Coordinator Instituto Nacional de Investigaciones sobre Recursos 1980–82; Under-Sec. of Ecology (Vice-Minister), Secretaría de Desarrollo Urbano y Ecología—SEDUE), Ministry of Urban Devt and Ecology 1982–86; consultant, IDB Aug.–Nov. 1987; Pres. Cultura Ecológica, Civil Soc. Org. in Mexico 1987–88; Dir Gen. Nat. Inst. of Fisheries, SEPESCA (Secretaría de Pesca) 1988-90; Prin. Officer, Programme Unit II, UN Conf. on Environment and Devt, Geneva, Switzerland 1990–92; Exec. Dir Earth Council Foundation, San Jose, Costa Rica 1992–95; Programme Coordinator Global Environmental Citizenship Programme, UNEP 1996–97; Chief Tech. Adviser on Environment and Devt, seconded by UNEP, Regional Bureau for Latin America and the Caribbean, UNDP 1998–99; Chief, Div. of Sustainable Devt and Human Settlements, ECLAC 1999–2003, Deputy Exec. Sec. 2003–06; Deputy Chef de Cabinet, UN, New York Feb.–March 2006, Acting Chef de Cabinet March 2006–07, Under-Sec.-Gen. for Man. 2007–08; Exec. Sec. ECLAC 2008–. *Publications:* The Millenium Development Goals: A Latin American and Caribbean Perspective 2005; numerous articles in professional journals.
Address: Economic Commission for Latin America and the Caribbean, Casilla de Correo 179-D, Av. Dag Hammarskjöld, 3477 Vitacura, Santiago, Chile (office). *Telephone:* (2) 471-2000 (office). *Fax:* (2) 208-0252 (office). *E-mail:* secretaria.se@cepal.org (office). *Website:* www.eclac .org (office).

BARCLAY, H(ugh) Douglas, BA, JD; American business executive and diplomatist; b. 5 July 1932, Pulaski, NY; m. Sara J. 'Dee Dee' Seiter; two s. three d. *Education:* Yale Univ. and Syracuse Univ. *Career:* Pnr, Hiscock & Barclay, NY 1961–2003; several sr advisory positions at KeyCorp; fmr mem. Bd of Dirs Overseas Private Investment Corpn, Mohawk Airlines, Syracuse China, Giant Portland & Masonry Cement Co., Coradian Corpn, Empire Airlines Inc., Excelsior Insurance Co.; fmr Chair. Panthus Corpn, QMP Enterprises Inc., Eagle Media Inc.; various positions, NY State Senate 1965–84, including Chair. Codes Cttee, Select Task Force on Court Reorganization, Senate Republican (Majority) Conf.; Amb. to El Salvador 2003–06; fmr mem. New York State Econ. Devt Power Allocation Bd; fmr Overseer Nelson A. Rockefeller Inst. of Govt, State Univ. of New York; Trustee Syracuse Univ. 1979–2003, Chair. Bd of Trustees 1992–98; fmr Trustee New York Racing Assen, Clarkson Univ.; several hon. doctorates; law library at Syracuse Univ. Coll. of Law is named in his honour; numerous prestigious academic awards.
Address: US Department of State, 2201 C Street NW, Washington, DC 20520, USA (office). *Telephone:* (202) 647-4000 (office). *Fax:* (202) 647-6738 (office). *Website:* www.state.gov (office).

BAREIRO SPAINI, Gen. (retd) Luis Nicanor; Paraguayan military officer and politician; *Minister of Defence; Career:* fmr Commdr Cadets Corps, Mil. Acad., Commdr Army Artillery Corps, Commdr Army Mil. Inst.; fmr Dir Inst. of High Strategic Studies, Ministry of Defence; fmr Dir Inspectorate Gen., Armed Forces; Minister of Defence 2008–.
Address: Ministry of National Defence, Avda Mariscal López y Vice-Presidente Sánchez, Asunción, Paraguay (office). *Telephone:* (21) 20-4771 (office). *Fax:* (21) 21-1583 (office). *E-mail:* ministro@mdn.gov.py (office). *Website:* www.mdn.gov.py (office).

BARING, Arnulf Martin, LLD; German academic; b. 8 May 1932, Dresden; m.; three d. one s. *Education:* Univs of Hamburg, Berlin, Freiburg, Columbia Univ., NY, USA, Freie Univ. Berlin, Inst. of Admin. Science, Speyer and Fondation Nat. des Sciences Politiques, Paris. *Career:* Lecturer, Inst. for Public and Admin. Law, Freie Univ. Berlin 1956–58, in Political Science and Int. Relations 1966–68, Univ. Lecturer, Faculty of Econ. and Social Sciences 1968, Prof. of Political Science, Otto-Suhr-Inst. and John F. Kennedy Inst. 1969–, of Contemporary History and Int. Relations, Dept of History 1976–98 (retd); Research Assoc., Center for Int. Affairs, Harvard Univ. 1968–69; Political Ed. Westdeutscher Rundfunk 1962–64; Guest Prof. Stiftung für Wissenschaft und Politik, Ebenhausen, Sr Research Assoc., Inst. for East-West Security Studies, New York, Fellow, Wilson Int. Center for Scholars, Washington, DC 1986–88; mem. Inst. for Advanced Study, Princeton, NJ 1992–93; Fellow, St Antony's Coll., Oxford 1993–94. *Publications include:* Charles de Gaulle: Grosse und Grenzen (with Christian Tautil) 1963, Aussenpolitik in Adenauers Kanzlerdemokratie 1969, Sehr verehrter Herr Bundeskanzler, Heinrich von Brentano im Briefwechsel mit Konrad Adenauer 1949–64, 1974, Zwei zaghafte Riesen? Deutschland und Japan nach 1945 (co-ed.) 1977, Machtwechsel, Die Ära Brandt-Scheel 1982, Unser neuer Grössenwahn, Deutschland zwischen Ost und West 1988, Deutschland, was nun? 1991, Scheitert Deutschland? 1997, Es lebe die Republik, es lebe Deutschland! 1999; contrib. to Frankfurter Allgemeine Zeitung, Westdeutscher und Norddeutscher Rundfunk, Sender Freies Berlin.
Address: Ahrenshooper Zeile 64, 14129 Berlin, Germany. *E-mail:* anfragen@arnulf-baring.de. *Website:* www.arnulf-baring.de.

BÄRLUND, Kaj-Ole Johannes, MSc (Econ); Finnish politician and international organization official; *Director, Environment and Human Settlements Division, Economic Commission for Europe, United Nations;* b. 9 Nov. 1945, Porvoo; m. Eeva-Kaisa Oksama 1972; one s. one d. *Career:* journalist, Finnish Broadcasting Co. 1967–71; Public Relations Officer, Cen. Org. of Finnish Trade Unions 1971–72; Legis. Sec. Ministry of Justice 1972–79; mem. Parl. 1979–91; Chair. Porvoo City Bd 1979–87, Nat. Cttee on Natural Resources 1979–83; Chair. Swedish Labour Union of Finland 1983–90; mem. Nordic Council, Vice-Chair. Nordic Council Social and Environment Cttee 1983–87; mem. Exec. Bd Finnish Broadcasting Co. 1982–83, Neste Oy 1983–90; Chair. Bureau of the Montreal Protocol 1989–90; Chair. UN/ECE Cttee on Environmental Policy 1991–95; Minister of the Environment 1987–91; Dir-Gen. Nat. Bd of Waters and the Environment 1990–95; Dir-Gen. Finnish Environment Inst. 1995–2001; Dir Environment and Human Settlements Div. UN/ECE 1995–; Chair. Consumers' Union of Finland 1983–90, Peoples of Finland and Russia Friendship Soc. 1991–95, Union of the Pulmonary Disabled in Finland 1993–95; mem. Party Exec., Finnish Social Democratic Party 1984–91, Chair. Environmental Working Group 1981–87; State Publicity Prize (Finland) 1972. *Publications:* Miksi Ei EEC 1971, Palkat Paketissa 1972.
Address: 229 rue de la Cité, 01220 Divonne-les-Bains, France (home). *Telephone:* (4) 50-20-44-93 (home).

BARNABY, Charles Frank, BSc, MSc, PhD; British physicist; *Consultant, Oxford Research Group;* b. 27 Sept. 1927, Andover, Hants.; m. Wendy Elizabeth Field 1972; one s. one d. *Education:* Andover Grammar School and Univ. of London. *Career:* Physicist, UK Atomic Energy Authority 1950–57; mem. Sr Scientific Staff, MRC, Univ. Coll. Medical School 1957–68; Exec. Sec. Pugwash Confs on Science and World Affairs 1968–70; Dir Stockholm Int. Peace Research Inst. (SIPRI) 1971–81; Prof. of Peace Studies, Free Univ., Amsterdam 1981–85; Dir and Scientific Adviser, World Disarmament Campaign (UK) 1982–; Consultant, Oxford Research Group 1998–; Ed. Int. Journal of Human Rights; Hon. DSc (Frei Univ., Amsterdam) 1982, (Southampton) 1996, (Bradford) 2007. *Publications:* Man and the Atom 1971, Preventing the Spread of Nuclear Weapons (ed.) 1971, Anti-ballistic Missile Systems (co-ed.) 1971, Disarmament and Arms Control 1973, Nuclear Energy 1975, The Nuclear Age 1976, Prospects for Peace 1980, Future Warfare (co-author and ed.) 1983, Space Weapons 1984, Star Wars Brought Down to Earth 1986, The Automated Battlefield 1986, The Invisible Bomb 1989, The Gaia Peace Atlas 1989, The Role and Control of Weapons in the 1990s 1992, How Nuclear Weapons Spread 1993, Instruments of Terror 1997, How to Build a Nuclear Bomb and Other Weapons of Mass Destruction 2003; articles in scientific journals.
Address: Brandreth, Chilbolton, Stockbridge, Hants., SO20 6HW, England (home). *Telephone:* (1264) 860423 (home). *Fax:* (1264) 860868 (home). *E-mail:* frank.barnaby@btinternet.com (home).

BARNALA, Surjit Singh, LLB; Indian politician and lawyer; *Governor of Tamil Nadu;* b. 21 Oct. 1925, Ateli, Gurgaon Dist (now in Haryana); m. Surjit Kaur 1954; three s. one d. *Education:* Lucknow Univ. *Career:* Shiromani Akali Dal MP for Barnala 1967–77; Educ. Minister of Punjab 1969–71; MP from Sangrur 1977; Union Agric., Irrigation and Food Minister in Janata Govt 1977–80; elected Pres. Shiromani Akali Dal 1985; Chief Minister of Punjab 1985–87; Gov. of Tamil Nadu 1990, 2004–, of Uttaranchal 2000–03, of Andhra Pradesh Jan. 2003–Nov. 04; Minister of Chemicals and Fertilizers 1998–99, of Food 1998–2001; represented India at FAO. *Publication:* Story of an Escape.

Address: Secretary to the Governor of Tamil Nadu, Chennai 600 009, India (office). *Telephone:* (44) 25671555 (office). *Fax:* (44) 25672304 (office). *E-mail:* governor@tn.nic.in (office). *Website:* www.tn.gov.in (office).

BARNES, Marsha E.; American diplomatist. *Education:* Lake Forest Coll., Nat. War Coll., Washington, DC. *Career:* joined State Dept in 1973, career mem. Sr Foreign Service with rank of Counselor, first appointment was as Vice-Consul in Georgetown, Guyana, has served abroad in Bonn, Berlin and Moscow, has served in State Dept as Dir Office of Caribbean Affairs 1999–2002, as Exec. Asst to Under-Sec. for Man., as Deputy Exec. Dir Bureau of Consular Affairs, as Chief of European Assignments Div., Bureau of Personnel, as Special Asst to Deputy Sec. of State, Amb. to Suriname 2003–06, Chargé d'affaires a.i. in Montenegro 2007.
Address: US Department of State, 2201 C Street NW, Washington, DC 20520, USA (office). *Telephone:* (202) 647-4000 (office). *Fax:* (202) 647-6738 (office). *Website:* www.state.gov (office).

BARNES, Nathaniel, BSc, MBA; Liberian business executive, politician and diplomatist; *Permanent Representative, United Nations;* b. 6 April 1954; m.; five c. *Education:* Pace Univ., New York, Rider Coll., NJ, USA. *Career:* early career as Underwriting Man. at Property and Casualty Dept, Insurance Co. of Africa 1979–81; sr positions at several cos in US, including NorTel, North American Wireless Inc. and Aurora Solutions Inc. 1981-1998; Co-ordinator Int. Econ. Cooperation and External Debt Man., Ministry of Finance 1988–99, Minister of Finance 1999–2002; Dir-Gen. Nat. Social Security and Welfare Corpn 1999; Founder and Leader, Destiny Party; cand. in presidential election 2005; Perm. Rep. to UN, New York 2006–.
Address: Permanent Mission of Liberia to the United Nations, 820 Second Avenue, 13th Floor, New York, NY 10017, USA (office). *Telephone:* (212) 687-1033 (office). *Fax:* (212) 687-1035 (office). *E-mail:* liberia@un.int (office).

BARNES JONES, Deborah Elizabeth Vavasseur, BA; British diplomatist; m. Richard Jones; twin d. *Education:* Benenden School and Univ. of Bristol. *Career:* joined FCO 1980, served in lower-ranking FCO posts in Moscow, Tel-Aviv and Montevideo, resgnd from FCO 1986, returned 1988, Amb. to Georgia 2001–04, Gov. of Montserrat (first female Gov. of Montserrat and first woman Gov. in British Overseas Territories) 2004–07.
Address: 4231 Marlboro Road SW, Topeka, KS 66610, USA (home).

BARNETT, Robin Anthony; British diplomatist; *Ambassador to Romania;* b. 8 March 1958; m. Tesca Barnett; one s. two step-s. one step-d. *Career:* Desk Officer for Indonesia and the Philippines, FCO 1980–81, Second Sec., Warsaw 1982–85, Desk Officer, EU Dept (Internal) and later in Security Policy Dept, FCO 1985–90, First Sec., UK Del. to Conventional Forces in Europe Negotiations, Vienna 1990–91, First Sec., Perm. Mission to UN, New York 1991–95, Deputy Head of Eastern Adriatic Dept, FCO 1996–98, Counsellor and Deputy Head of Mission, Warsaw 1998–2001, Dir UK Visas, FCO 2002–05, Amb. to Romania 2006–.
Address: British Embassy, Str. Jules Michelet 24, 010463 Bucharest, Romania (office). *Telephone:* (21) 2017200 (office). *Fax:* (21) 2017311 (office). *E-mail:* press.bucharest@fco.gov.uk (office). *Website:* www .britishembassy.gov.uk/romania (office).

BARR, Joyce Anne, BA, MPA, MS; American diplomatist; b. Tacoma, Wash. *Education:* Pacific Lutheran Univ., Harvard Univ., Industrial Coll. of the Armed Forces. *Career:* career mem. Foreign Service since 1979, overseas assignments have included Stockholm 1980, Budapest 1982, Nairobi 1985, Khartoum 1989, Ashgabat, Turkmenistan 1998, domestic assignments in Washington, DC have included Recruitment Officer, Bureau of Personnel, Human Rights Officer for the Middle East and South Asia, Bureau of Human Rights and Humanitarian Affairs, Desk Officer for US Industrial Devt Org. and WTO, Bureau of Int. Orgs, Post Man. Officer, Bureau of East Asia and Pacific Affairs, Sr Watch Officer, State Dept's Crisis Center, Counselor for Man. Affairs, Kuala Lumpur –2004, Amb. to Namibia 2004–07; participated in Pearson Program, which enabled her to work for one year in US Congress, worked as Legis. Asst to the late US Senator Daniel Patrick Moynihan and Miss. Congressman Bennie G. Thompson; three group Superior Honor Awards, Performance Pay Award, Dept of State.
Address: US Department of State, 2201 C Street NW, Washington, DC 20520, USA (office). *Telephone:* (202) 647-4000 (office). *Fax:* (202) 647-6738 (office). *Website:* www.state.gov (office).

BARREIRO FAJARDO, Georgina; Cuban politician, lawyer and banker; *Minister of Finance and Prices;* b. 1964. *Career:* lawyer in finance and credit; Vice-Pres. Cen. Bank of Cuba –2003; Minister of Finance and Prices 2003–; Head of Systems of Payment and Man., Risles; Dir Cen. Bank of Cuba.

Address: Ministry of Finance and Prices, Calle Obispo 211, Havana, Cuba (office). *Telephone:* (7) 867-1920 (office). *Fax:* (7) 33-8050 (office). *E-mail:* bhcifip@mfp.gov.cu (office). *Website:* www.mfp.cu (office).

BARRETO OTAZÚ, César Amado, MA; Paraguayan economist and politician; *Minister of Finance; Education:* Universidad Nacional de Asunción, Pontificia Universidad Católica de Chile. *Career:* with Entidad Binacional Itaipú 1988–94; Econ. Adviser, Nat. Econ. Equipment, Ministry of Finance 1997–98; Product Man., Cash Man. and Trade, Citibank NA, Paraguay Br. 1998–2000; Founding Pnr, Macroanálisis Consultora 1999; Project Man., Hutchison Telecom Paraguay SA Jan.–Oct. 2001, Gen. Man. 2001–02, Exec. Dir 2002–05; Exec. Dir Devt in Democracy 2004–05; Pres. Directory and Gen. Man. Agencia Financiera de Desarrollo 2005–07; Minister of Finance 2007–; fmr Prof. of Int. Economy and Master's Programme in Economy and Finances, Universidad Católica de Asunción. *Address:* Ministry of Finance, Sede Central: Chile 252, 1220 Asunción, Paraguay (office). *Telephone:* (21) 440010 (office). *Fax:* (21) 448283 (office). *E-mail:* info@hacienda.gov.py (office). *Website:* www.hacienda.gov.py (office).

BARRETT, Barbara McConnell, BA, MA; American lawyer and diplomatist; *Ambassador to Finland; Education:* Arizona State Univ. *Career:* intern, Ariz. State Legislature 1972; served as exec. of two Fortune 500 transportation cos; Vice-Chair. US Civil Aeronautics Bd 1980s; fmr pnr, Phoenix law firm; fmr Deputy Admin. Fed. Aviation Admin; fmr Pres. Ariz. World Affairs Council, Ariz. World Trade Asscn, Econ. Club of Phoenix; fmr Nat. Chair. Sec. of Commerce's Export Conf., Washington, DC; Pres. and CEO American Man. Asscn 1990s; Founding Chair. Valley Bank of Arizona; fmr Inst. of Politics Fellow, John F. Kennedy School of Govt, Harvard Univ.; fmr mem. Defense Advisory Cttee on Women in the Services; Republican cand. for Gov. of Ariz.; fmr Pres. Int. Women's Forum, led del. of women leaders to six cities in People's Repub. of China 2000; fmr Chair. US Advisory Comm. on Public Diplomacy and Sr Adviser to US Mission to UN; served in leadership roles at Freedom House, Center for Int. Pvt. Enterprise, Nat. Legal Center, Global Center for Dispute Resolution Research; fmr Pres. and CEO Triple Creek Guest Ranch, Darby, Mont.; fmr mem. Bd of Dirs Raytheon and Exponent, Inc.; fmr Trustee, Aerospace Corpn, Mayo Clinic, Thunderbird School of Global Man.; fmr mem. US-Afghan Women's Council, Horatio Alger Asscn Bd, Defense Business Bd, Smithsonian Nat. Bd, Sr Advisory Bd Inst. of Politics, Harvard; Amb. to Finland 2008–; Dr hc (Arizona State Univ., Embry-Riddle Aeronautical Univ., Thunderbird School of Global Man., Univ. of S Carolina); Horatio Alger Award, Woodrow Wilson Award for Corp. Citizenship, ABA Sandra Day O'Connor Excellence Award. *Achievements:* instrument-rated pilot; climbed Mount Kilimanjaro, Tanzania Aug. 2007.
Address: US Embassy, Itäinen puistotie 14B, 00140 Helsinki, Finland (office). *Telephone:* (9) 616250 (office). *Fax:* (9) 174681 (office). *Website:* www.helsinki.usembassy.gov (office).

BARRIE, George Napier, BA, LLD; South African professor and advocate; *Special Professor, Faculty of Law and Researcher, Centre for the Study of International Law in Africa, University of Johannesburg;* b. 10 Sept. 1940, Pietersburg; m. Marie Howell 1970; two s. one d. *Education:* Pretoria Univ., Univ. of S Africa and Univ. Coll., London, UK. *Career:* State Advocate, Supreme Court 1964–69; Sr Law Adviser, Dept of Foreign Affairs 1970–80; Prof. of Int. and Constitutional Law, Rand Afrikaans Univ. 1981–, Dean Faculty of Law 2001–04; Visiting Prof., Free Univ. of Brussels 1992; Leader of S African del. to numerous int. confs; mem. S African del. to Int. Bar Asscn Conf. 1984, Nat. Council on Correctional Services 1996–; Special Prof., Faculty of Law and Researcher, Centre for Study of Int. Law in Africa, Univ. of Johannesburg 2005–. *Publications include:* Topical International Law 1979, Self-Determination in Modern International Law 1995 and numerous works and articles on int. and constitutional law; co-author: Nuclear Non-Proliferation: The Why and the Wherefore 1985, Constitutions of Southern Africa 1985, Law of South Africa 1986, Law of the Sea 1987, Bill of Rights Compendium 1996, Managing African Conflicts 2000.
Address: Faculty of Law, University of Johannesburg, PO Box 524, Auckland Park, Johannesburg 2006, South Africa (office). *Telephone:* (11) 7044376 (home). *Fax:* (11) 4892049 (office); (11) 7044376 (home). *E-mail:* barriegm@telkomsa.net (home). *Website:* www.general.rau.ac.za/law (office).

BARROT, Jacques, LenD; French politician; *Vice-President and Commissioner for Justice, Freedom and Security, European Commission;* b. 3 Feb. 1937, Yssingeaux, Haute-Loire; one s. two d. *Education:* Coll. d'Yssingeaux and Faculté de Droit, Paris and Inst. d'Etudes Politiques, Paris. *Career:* Deputy to Nat. Ass. (Union Centriste) 1967–74, 1978, (Union pour la Démocratie Française) 1981–95, 1997–2002, (UMP) 2002–03, Pres. UMP

Group 2002–04; Councillor, Haute-Loire Regional Council 1966–2004, Pres. 1976–2004; Sec. of State, Ministry of Equipment 1974–78; Minister of Commerce and Working Classes 1978–79, of Health and Social Security 1979–81; Pres. Conseil-Gen. Haute-Loire 1976–2004; Mayor of Yssingeaux 1989–2001; Minister of Labour, Social Dialogue and Participation 1995–97, EU Commissioner for Regional Policy and Institutional Reform 2004, for Transport 2004–08, for Justice, Freedom and Security 2008–; Pres. Nat. Union for Environmental Improvement 1991–93; mem. Fondatems du "Dialogue et Initiations". *Publications:* Les Pierres de l'avenir 1978, Notre contrat pour l'alternance 2002, L'Europe n'est pas ce que vous croyez 2007.
Address: Rue de la Loi 200, 1049 Brussels, Belgium (office); Rue Beuve-Méry, 43200 Yssingeaux, France (home). *Telephone:* (2) 299-11-11 (office). *Fax:* (2) 295-01-38 (office). *Website:* europa.eu (office).

BARROW, Dean Oliver, MA, LLM; Belizean politician; *Prime Minister and Minister of Finance;* b. 2 March 1951, Belize City. *Education:* Univ. of West Indies and Center for Advanced Int. Studies, Univ. of Miami, USA. *Career:* elected (United Democratic Party—UDP)) to Belize City Council 1983; elected to Nat. Ass. (UDP) for Queen Square Div. 1984–89; Deputy Leader UDP 1990, currently Leader; Minister of Foreign Affairs and Econ. Devt 1984–86; Attorney-Gen. 1986–89; apptd Deputy Prime Minister, Minister of Foreign Affairs and Econ. Devt and Attorney-Gen. 1993, also Minister of Nat. Security, Immigration and Nationality Matters 1995; Prime Minister 2008–, Minister of Finance 2008–; Pnr, Barrow and Williams (law firm).
Address: Office of the Prime Minister, Sir Edney Cain Building, Belmopan (office); United Democratic Party, South End Bel-China Bridge, POB 1898, Belize City, Belize (office). *Telephone:* 822-2345 (office); 227-2576 (office). *Fax:* 822-3323 (office); 227-6441 (office). *E-mail:* primeministerbelize@btl.net (office); info@udp.org.bz (office). *Website:* www.udp.org.bz (office).

BARROW, Timothy Earle, CMG, LVO, MBE; British diplomatist; *Representative to the Political and Security Committee, European Union;* b. 15 Feb. 1964; m. Alison Earle; two s. one d. *Career:* Asst Desk Officer, Western European Dept, FCO 1987–88, Desk Officer, Soviet Dept 1988–89, Second Sec. (Chancery), Moscow 1989–93, Head of Russia Section, Eastern Dept, FCO 1993–94, Pvt. Sec., Minister of State's Office 1994–96, First Sec., External Relations, UK Representation to EU, Brussels 1996–98, Pvt. Sec., Sec. of State's Office, FCO 1998–2000, Head of Common Foreign and Security Policy Dept 2000–03, Deputy Political Dir and Asst Dir EU (External) 2003–06, Amb. to Ukraine 2006–08, UK Rep. to EU Political and Security Cttee, Brussels 2008–.
Address: Permanent Mission of UK to the European Union, 10 Avenue d'Auderghem/Oudergemselaan, 1040 Brussels, Belgium (office). *Telephone:* (2) 287-82-88 (office). *Fax:* (2) 287-83-98 (office). *E-mail:* Mary.Dawber@fco.gov.uk (office). *Website:* www.fco.gov.uk (office).

BARRY, Alpha Oumar Rafiou; Guinean diplomatist. *Career:* fmr Amb. to Japan, Amb. to USA 2002–07.
Address: Ministry of Foreign Affairs, Co-operation, African Integration and Guineans Abroad face au Port, ex-Primature, BP 2519, Conakry, Guinea (office). *Telephone:* 30-45-12-70 (office). *Fax:* 30-41-16-21 (office).

BARRY, Brian Michael, MA, DPhil, FBA.; British academic; *Professor Emeritus, Columbia University;* b. 7 Aug. 1936, London; m. 1st Joanna Hill 1960 (divorced 1988); one s.; m. 2nd Elizabeth Ann Parker 1991. *Education:* Taunton's School, Southampton and Queen's Coll., Oxford. *Career:* Fellow Nuffield Coll., Oxford 1966–69, 1972–75; Prof. of Govt, Univ. of Essex 1969–72; Prof. of Political Science and Philosophy, Univ. of Chicago 1977–82; Prof. of Philosophy, Calif. Inst. of Tech. 1982–86; Prof. European Univ. Inst. 1986–87; Prof. of Political Science, LSE 1987, now Prof. Emer.; Lieber Prof. of Political Philosophy, Columbia Univ., NY, USA, now Prof. Emer.; Fellow, British Acad., American Acad. of Arts and Sciences; Hon. DSc (Southampton); Dr hc (York) 2006; Johan Skytte Prize in Political Science 2001, Political Studies Asscn Lifetime Achievement Award 2001. *Publications:* Political Argument 1965, Sociologists, Economists and Democracy 1970, The Liberal Theory of Justice 1973, Theories of Justice (WJM Mackenzie Prize) 1989, Democracy, Power and Justice 1989, Democracy and Power 1991, Liberty and Justice 1991, Justice as Impartiality (WJM Mackenzie Prize) 1995, Culture and Equality: An Egalitarian Critique of Multiculturalism (WJM Mackenzie Prize) 2001, Why Social Justice Matters 2005.
Address: c/o Department of Political Science, Columbia University, 730 International Affairs Building, 420 West 118th Street, New York, NY 10027, USA.

BARTELS, Lt-Gen. Knud; Danish military officer; *Military Representative, NATO;* b. 8 April 1952, Copenhagen; m. Inge Vansteenkiste. *Education:* Royal Danish Army Acad., Ecole Supérieure de Guerre, Paris, US Army

War Coll. *Career:* promoted to First Lt 1977, Capt. 1982, Major 1987; regimental service 1977–80, UN Forces Cyprus 1980–81; Jr Army and Jt Staff Course 1981–82; Instructor in tactics, Army Combat School 1982–84, Instructor in tactics/operations, Royal Danish Defence Coll. 1986–87, 1988–90, Dir Army Command and Gen. Staff Course 1994–96; Co. Commdr, 2nd Armoured Bn Zealand Life Regt 1987–88, Staff Officer Danish Defence Command 1990–92, Commdg Officer 1st Bn Slesvig Foot Regt 1992–93, Commdr 3rd Jutland Brigade 1996–97, ACOS Plans Danish Defence Command 1997–99, Gen. Officer Commdg Danish Div. 2004–06; Sr Nat. Rep. KFOR/MNB (N) 1999, Deputy Mil. Rep., NATO 2001, Asst Dir for Operations, NATO Int. Mil. Staff 2002–04 Mil. Rep., NATO 2006–; promoted to Lt-Col 1992, Col 1996, Brig. 2001, Maj.-Gen. 2001, Lt-Gen. 2006; Commdr Order of Dannebrog, Ordre national du Mérite, Chevalier, Légion d'honneur; 25 Years Good Service Medal, UN Peace-keeping Force in Cyprus Medal, NATO KFOR Medal.
Address: NATO HQ, blvd Léopold III, 1110 Brussels, Belgium (office). *Telephone:* (2) 707-41-11 (office). *Fax:* (2) 707-45-79 (office). *E-mail:* natodoc@hq.nato.int (office). *Website:* www.nato.int (office).

BARTENSTEIN, Martin, PhD; Austrian politician and business executive; *Minister for Economic Affairs and Labour;* b. 3 June 1953, Graz; m.; five c. *Education:* Akademisches Gymnasium, Miami Univ., OH, USA, Karl Franzens Univ., Graz. *Career:* joined Lannacher Heilmittel GmbH (family-owned pharmaceutical co.) 1978, Man. Dir 1980–86; Chief Exec. Genericon Pharma GesmbH 1986–90; mem. Bd of Dirs Pharmavit AG, Budapest 1990; Chair. Asscn of Young Austrian Industrialists 1988; mem. Austrian People's Party (Österreichische Volkspartei—ÖVP), Party Spokesman on Industry 1991; Deputy Regional Chair. Styrian People's Party 1991; mem. (ÖVP) Nat. Ass. 1991–; State Sec., Fed. Ministry for Public Economy and Transport 1994; Minister for the Environment 1995, for Environment, Youth and Family Affairs 1996, for Econ. Affairs and Labour 2000–; Chair. Cancer Relief Fund for the Children of Styria 1988–92, Austrian Cancer Relief Fund for Children 1993–.
Address: Ministry of Economic Affairs and Labour, Stubenring 1, 1011 Vienna, Austria (office). *Telephone:* (1) 711-00-0 (office). *Fax:* (1) 713-79-95 (office). *E-mail:* service@bmwa.gv.at (office). *Website:* www.bmwa.gv.at (office).

BARTOLINI, Stefano; Italian academic and research institute director; *Director, Robert Schuman Centre for Advanced Studies, European University Institute;* b. 22 Jan. 1952, Florence; m.; two c. *Education:* Univ. of Florence. *Career:* Asst, Dept of Political History, Univ. of Bologna 1976; Asst Prof., Dept of Political and Social Sciences, European Univ. Inst., Florence 1979–85; Assoc. Prof. of Political Science, Univ. of Florence 1985–89; Prof. of Political Science, Univ. of Trieste 1990–91; Prof. of Political Behaviour, Univ. of Geneva 1991–94; Prof. of Comparative Political Insts, European Univ. Inst., Florence 1994–2004, Dir Robert Schuman Centre for Advanced Studies 2006–; Prof. of Political Science, Univ. of Bologna 2004–06; part-time Prof., Univ. of Geneva 1989–91, Institut d'Etudes Politiques, Paris 1991–93, 2004–06, Juan March Inst., Madrid 1999, Universitat Autonoma de Barcelona 2005; visiting lecturer at numerous insts including LSE, Nuffield Coll. Oxford, univs of Newcastle-upon-Tyne, Mannheim, Lausanne, Calif., Berkeley, Oslo, Hokkaido, Tokyo; mem. Editorial Bd Rivista Italiana di Scienza Politica; mem. Scientific Bd West European Politics, Swiss Review of Political Science, Acta Politica, European Journal of Political Research; UNESCO Stein Rokkan Prize 1990, Gregory Luebbert Award in Comparative Politics, American Political Science Asscn 2001. *Publications:* Progetto per l'Europa (jtly) 1978, Riforma Istituzionale e sistema politico: La Francia Gollista 1981, Party Politics in Contemporary Europe (co-ed) 1984, Manuale di Scienza Politica, Bologna (jtly) 1986, Identity, Competition, and Electoral Availability: The Stabilization of the European Electorate, 1885–1985 (with P. Mair) 1990, Maggioritario ma non troppo: Le elezioni politiche del 1994 (co-ed) 1995, Maggioritario per caso: Le elezioni politiche del 1996 (co-ed) 1997, Party and Party Systems: A Bibliographic Guide to the Literature on Parties and Party Systems in Europe since 1945 (jtly) 1998, The Class Cleavage: The Electoral Mobilisation of the European Left 1880–1980 2000, Maggioritario finalmente?: La transizione elettorale 1994–2001 (co-ed) 2002, Restructuring Europe: Centre Formation, System Building and Political Structuring between the Nation State and the EU 2005; numerous articles and chapters in journals and books.
Address: Robert Schuman Centre for Advanced Studies, European University Institute, Via Boccaccio 151, 50133 Florence, Italy (office). *Telephone:* (055) 4685792/796 (office). *Fax:* (055) 4685730 (office). *E-mail:* stefano.bartolini@eui.eu (office). *Website:* www.eui.eu (office).

BARZAGA NAVAS, Raùl; Cuban diplomatist; *Ambassador to Haiti; Career:* Amb. to Bolivia 1997–2005, to Haiti 2005–.

Address: Embassy of Cuba, 18 rue Marion, Peguy Ville, POB 15702, Port-au-Prince, Haiti (office). *Telephone:* 256-3812 (office). *Fax:* 257-8566 (office). *E-mail:* embacuba@hughes.net (office).

BARZANI, Masoud; Iraqi (Kurdish) politician; *President, Kurdistan Region and Leader, Kurdistan Democratic Party;* b. 16 Aug. 1946, Mahabad, Iran; m.; five s. three d. *Education:* Tehran Univ. *Career:* father forced to flee to USSR 1946, returned to Iraq following overthrow of Iraqi monarchy in 1958; reunited with his father, family returned to their home village of Barzan; KDP launched armed struggle to defend Kurdish people 1961, joined Peshmerga forces 1962; participated in del. that signed autonomy agreement with Govt in Baghdad March 1970; engaged in renewed Kurdish armed struggle 1970s; succeeded his father as Pres. of KDP 1979–; requested help from Iraqi Govt to capture city of Erbil from rival Patriotic Union of Kurdistan (PUK) 1995; led KDP in establishing a govt in Iraqi Kurdistan with PUK; mem. Iraqi Governing Council following invasion of Iraq 2003, Pres. Council April 2004; elected first Pres. Kurdistan Region in Iraq by Kurdistan Nat. Ass. June 2005–. *Publication:* Mustafa Barzani and the Kurdish Liberation Movement (with Ahmed Ferhani) (three vols in Arabic; first vol. also in English and Turkish).
Address: Office of the President, Kurdistan Regional Government, Erbil, Iraq (office). *E-mail:* info@krg.org (office); party@kdp.se (office). *Website:* www.krg.org (office); www.kdp.se (office).

BARZANI, Nechirvan Idris; Iraqi (Kurdish) politician; *Prime Minister, Kurdistan Regional Government;* b. 21 Sept. 1966, Barzan, southern Kurdistan; grandson of Mustafa Barzani, founder of Kurdistan Democratic Party (KDP), nephew of Masoud Barzani, Pres. of Kurdistan Region; m. Nabila Barzani; two c. *Education:* Tehran Univ. *Career:* family forced to flee to Iran 1975; often accompanied his father and sr KDP mem. Idris Barzani on his missions abroad; political science studies in Tehran cut short due to sudden death of his father 1987; took up active role in Kurdish politics, working in KDP youth orgs, rose rapidly through ranks of KDP; first elected to leadership of KDP in 1989, re-elected 1999; participated in negotiations with Iraqi Govt following Gulf War 1991; Deputy Prime Minister of KDP's controlled region in Iraqi Kurdistan 1996–99, Prime Minister 1999–2006, first Prime Minister of unified Govt of Kurdistan Region 2006–.
Address: Office of the Prime Minister, Council of Ministers Building, Kurdistan Regional Government, Erbil, Iraq (office). *E-mail:* info@krg .org (office). *Website:* www.krg.org (office).

BĂSESCU, Traian; Romanian politician, head of state and fmr naval officer; *President;* b. 4 Nov. 1951, Basarabi, Constanţa Co.; m.; two d. *Education:* Inst. of Civil Marine Mircea cel Bătrân and Norwegian Acad. *Career:* Officer Grades III, II and I, Romanian Navy 1976–81, Capt., Merchant Navy 1981–87; Head Navrom Agency, Antwerp 1987–89; Gen. Dir State Inspectorate of Civil Navigation, Ministry of Transportation 1989–90, Under-Sec. of State and Head of Naval Transportation Dept 1990–91, Minister of Transport 1991–92, 1996–2000; mem. Democratic Party (PD), Pres. 2001–04; mem. Chamber of Deputies 1992–96, 1996–2000; Vice-Pres. Chamber of Deputies Comm. for Industry and Services 1992–96; investigated for corruption and fraud 1996; Dir electoral campaign for Petre Roman (pres. cand.) 1996; Co-Pres. Justice and Truth Alliance (DA) 2003–; Mayor of Bucharest 2000–04; Pres. of Romania 2004– (suspended from post April–May 2007).
Address: Office of the President, 060116 Bucharest, Palatul Cotroceni, Str. Geniului 1–3, Sector 5, Romania (office). *Telephone:* (21) 4100581 (office). *Fax:* (21) 4103858 (office). *E-mail:* presedinte@basescu.ro (home); presedinte@presidency.ro (office). *Website:* www.basescu.ro (home); www .presidency.ro (office).

BASHA, Lulzim, LLM; Albanian politician; *Minister of Foreign Affairs;* b. 12 June 1974, Tirana; m. Aurela Basha; one d. *Education:* Utrecht Univ., Netherlands. *Career:* mem. war crimes investigation team of Serbian forces in Kosovo 1998–99; Legal Adviser, Justice Dept, UN Mission in Kosovo (UNMIK) 2000–01, Deputy Chief of Cabinet of Dir of Justice Dept 2001–02, Special Adviser for Transition, Justice Dept 2002–05; mem. Democratic Party of Albania (Partia Demokratike e Shqipërisë, PDSh) 2005–, Co-ordinator Cttee for Policy Orientation 2005–, Nat. Council 2005–, mem. Presidency 2005–, Spokesman of Gen. Election Campaign May–July 2005; mem. Parl. 2005–, Minister of Public Works, Transport and Telecommunications 2005–07, of Foreign Affairs 2007–.
Address: Ministry of Foreign Affairs, Bulevardi Gjergj Fishta 6, Tirana, Albania (office). *Telephone:* (4) 362170 (office). *Fax:* (4) 235899 (office). *E-mail:* ministri@mfa.gov.al (office). *Website:* www.mfa.gov.al (office).

BASHIR, Attalla Hamad, BSc, MA, PhD; Sudanese diplomatist and international organization official; *Executive Secretary, Intergovernmental Authority on Development;* b. 23 Aug. 1946, Dongola; m.; one s. one d. *Education:*

Khartoum Univ., Syracuse Univ., New York, USA, Acad. of Commerce, Bucharest, Romania. *Career:* joined diplomatic service 1971; served in Kuwait, Bahrain, Czechoslovakia, Hungary, Malta, Italy, Romania, Ethiopia; Amb. to GDR 1989–90, to Rep. of Korea 1990–93; Amb. to Saudi Arabia and Perm. Rep. to Islamic Devt Bank and Org. of the Islamic Conf. 1995–97; Amb. to Netherlands and Resident Rep. to Int. Court of Justice 1997–2000; Dir-Gen. Bilateral and Regional Relations, Ministry of External Relations –2000; Exec. Sec. Intergovernmental Authority on Devt (IGAD) 2000–; Guwang Hwa Medal for Merit for outstanding diplomatic service (Govt of S Korea) 1993.
Address: Intergovernmental Authority on Development, BP 2653, Djibouti (office). *Telephone:* 354050 (office). *Fax:* 356994 (office). *E-mail:* igad@ intnet.dj (office). *Website:* www.igad.org (office).

BASHIR, Lt-Gen. Omar Hassan Ahmad al-; Sudanese head of state and army officer; *President and Prime Minister;* b. 1 Jan. 1944, Hoshe Bannaga, Anglo-Egyptian Sudan. *Education:* Sudan Mil. Acad., Egyptian Mil. Acad., Cairo. *Career:* fought in Egyptian army during 1973 war with Israel; career army officer rising to rank of Brig., then Lt-Gen.; overthrew Govt of Sadiq al-Mahdi in coup 30 June 1989; Chair. Revolutionary Command Council for Nat. Salvation 1989–; Minister of Defence 1989–93; Pres. and Prime Minister of Sudan 1993–; Chair. Ass. Intergovernmental Authority on Devt 2000–01; charged with genocide by Int. Criminal Court 14 July 2008.
Address: Revolutionary Command Council, Khartoum, Sudan (office).

BASHIR, Salah ed-Din al-, MA, PhD; Jordanian lawyer, academic and politician; *Minister of Foreign Affairs;* b. 1966. *Education:* Univ. of Jordan, Harvard Law School, USA, McGill Univ., Canada. *Career:* Adjunct Prof. of Law, Univ. of Jordan 1996–, also Dir Centre for Strategic Studies 1999; fmr Minister of Industry and Trade, fmr Minister of State for Cabinet Affairs, fmr Minister of Justice; Minister of Foreign Affairs 2007–; Man. Pnr Abu Ghazaleh Legal Services; mem. Econ. Consultative Council 1999; Founder and Sr Man. Pnr Int. Business Legal Assocs (IBLAW); Co-Chair. Jordanian–American Comm. for Educational Exchange.
Address: Ministry of Foreign Affairs, POB 35217, Amman 11180, Jordan (office). *Telephone:* (6) 5735150 (office). *Fax:* (6) 5735163 (office). *E-mail:* inquiry@mfa.gov.jo (office). *Website:* www.mfa.gov.jo (office).

BASHIR, Salman, MA, LLB; Pakistani diplomatist; *Foreign Secretary;* b. 4 March 1952; m.; two s. one d. *Career:* joined Foreign Service 1976, assignments abroad in Geneva 1980–84, OIC Secr., Jeddah 1988–99, Section Officer, Ministry of Foreign Affairs 1976–80, Dir 1985–87, Dir-Gen. 1995–99, Amb. to Denmark 1999–2003, served as Additional Sec., Ministry of Foreign Affairs 2003–05, Amb. to People's Repub. of China 2005–08, Foreign Sec. 2008–.
Address: Ministry of Foreign Affairs, Constitution Ave, Islamabad, Pakistan (office). *Telephone:* (51) 9210335 (office). *Fax:* (51) 9207600 (office). *E-mail:* sadiq@mofa.gov.pk (office). *Website:* www.mofa.gov.pk (office).

BAŠKA, Jaroslav; Slovak politician; *Minister of Defence;* b. 5 April 1975, Považská Bystrica; m.; three c. *Education:* Electro-Technical Faculty, Žilina Univ. *Career:* Matador Púchov 1998–2000; Project Man. for information systems 1999–2000; Asst Dir for Econ 2001–02; mem. Parl. (Smer-Sociálna demokracia) 2002–06, mem. Perm Del. to Parl. Ass. of Council of Europe 2002–06; Mayor of Dohňany 2003–06; State Sec., Ministry of Defence 2006–08, Minister of Defence 2008–.
Address: Ministry of Defence, Kutuzovova 7, 832 47 Bratislava, Slovakia (office). *Telephone:* (2) 4425-0320 (office). *Fax:* (2) 4425-3242 (office). *E-mail:* kovacovaz@mod.gov.sk (office). *Website:* www.mosr.sk (office).

BASNET, Bhagirath, BA, BL, MA (Econs); Nepalese diplomatist; b. 17 Feb. 1951, Kathmandu; m.; one s. one d. *Education:* Univ. of Maryland, USA. *Career:* Section Officer, Supreme Court 1974–77, Ministry of Foreign Affairs 1977; First Sec., Royal Nepalese Embassy, Delhi 1981–88, Bonn 1988; Under-Sec., Ministry of Foreign Affairs 1988–92, Chief of Protocol 1999–2003; Deputy Chief of Mission, Brussels 1992–96, Beijing 1996–99; Amb. to Bangladesh 2003–07; Special Class Officer, Ministry of Foreign Affairs 2007–; decorations from Spain and UK.
Address: Ministry of Foreign Affairs, Shital Niwas, Maharajganj, Kathmandu (office); 15 Ta Dha Hiti Galli, Kathmandu, 6/5 Judha Road, Kathmandu, Nepal (home). *Telephone:* (1) 4416011 (office). *Fax:* (1) 4416016 (office). *E-mail:* adm@mofa.gov.np (office); rnedhaka@dbn-bd .net (office); bhagirath_51@hotmail.com (home). *Website:* www.mofa.gov .np (office).

BASSIOUNI, Muhammad Abd al-Aziz; Egyptian diplomatist; b. 31 July 1937, Cairo; m. Nagwa Elsabouny; one s. one d. *Education:* Egyptian Mil. Acad. *Career:* served in Egyptian Army 1956–80; mem. teaching staff, Mil.

Acad. 1959–66; Mil. Attaché to Syria 1968–76, Liaison Officer between Egyptian and Syrian Commands, War of Oct. 1973; Brig.-Gen. in Egyptian Army 1978; Mil. Attaché to Iran 1978–80; joined Foreign Service 1980; Counsellor, then Minister Plenipotentiary, Embassy, Tel-Aviv 1980, Amb. to Israel 1986–2000; participated in all Egyptian-Israeli talks on normalization of relations and on Taba dispute; twelve mil. decorations from Egyptian Army; High Medal of Honour for Bravery with rank of Kt, Syria; Dr hc (Ben Gurion Univ., Israel) 1995. *Publications:* several articles on Egyptian-Israeli relations, the peace process and the Taba talks.
Address: c/o Ministry of Foreign Affairs, Corniche en-Nil, Cairo, Egypt (office).

BASSOLE, Bazomboué Léandre, MA; Burkinabè diplomatist; b. 21 Sept. 1946, Koudougou; m. Louise Ouedraogo 1975; four s. one d. *Education:* Higher Educ. Centre, Ouagadougou, Univ. of Bordeaux and Int. Inst. for Public Admin., Paris. *Career:* Counsellor State Protocol Dept, Legal Affairs and Claims Dept and Int. Co-operation Dept of Ministry of Foreign Affairs 1975–76, Dir for Admin. and Consular Affairs 1976–77; Second Counsellor, later First Counsellor, Upper Volta Embassy, Paris 1977–81; First Counsellor, Perm. Mission of Upper Volta to the UN 1981–82, Chargé d'affaires 1982–83, Perm. Rep. of Upper Volta (now Burkina Faso) to the UN 1983–86; Amb. to USA March–Aug. 1986; Minister of External Affairs and Co-operation 1986–87; Amb. to Canada 1988–91, to Côte d'Ivoire 1991–2001.
Address: c/o Ministry of Foreign Affairs, 03 BP 7038, Ouagadougou 03, Burkina Faso (office).

BASSOLET, Djibril Ypéné; Burkinabé government official; *Joint United Nations-African Union Chief Mediator for Darfur;* b. 30 Nov. 1957, Nouna. *Education:* Collège Charles Luanga de Nouna, Prytanée Militaire de Kadiogo, Université de Ouagadougou, Académie Royale Militaire de Meknès, Ecole Nationale de la Gendarmerie, Abidjan, Côte d'Ivoire, Ecole Supérieure de la Gendarmerie, Maisons Alfort, France. *Career:* served as Commdt, Gendarmerie Nationale (nat. police force) 1983–95, served in various sr positions including Chef d'Etat-Major (head of police force) 1997–99; Minister-Del. for Security 1999–2000, Minister for Security 2000–07, Minister of Foreign Affairs and Regional Co-operation 2007–08; Jt UN —African Union Chief Mediator for Darfur 2008–; Officier et Commandeur de l'Ordre Nat. de Burkina Faso, Médaille d'honneur Militaire, Médaille d'honneur de la Police, Officier de l'Ordre Nat. du Lion (Senegal), Commandeur de l'Ordre du Mérite du Niger, Commandeur de l'Ordre du Mérite du Gabon, Officier de l'Ordre National du Mérite.
Address: Department of Peace-keeping Operations, Room S-3727-B, United Nations, New York, NY 10017, USA (office); UNAMID, El Fasher, Sudan (office). *Telephone:* (212) 963-8077 (office). *Fax:* (212) 963-9222 (office). *Website:* www.un.org/Depts/dpko (office); unamid .unmissions.org (office).

BAŠTA, Jaroslav; Czech diplomatist and politician; *Ambassador to Ukraine;* b. 15 May 1948, Plzen; m.; one s. *Education:* Charles Univ. *Career:* imprisoned for involvement in students' protest movement 1970; worked at Stavby silnic a zeleznic (civil eng co.); served at Fed. Ministry of Interior, Office for Protection of Constitution and Democracy 1990, later as Deputy Dir of Security and Information Service –1993; f. pvt. business 1993; Deputy Chamber of Deputies 1996–98, served as Chair. Information Security Service Activities Control Perm. Comm., Deputy Chair. Cttee for Defence and Security, mem. Perm. Del. of Czech Parl. to NATO, mem. Organizational Cttee; elected to Parl. 1998, Minister without Portfolio 1998–2000; Amb. to Russian Fed. 2000–05, to Ukraine 2007–; First Deputy Minister of Foreign Affairs 2005–07, Deputy Minister of Foreign Affairs 2007; mem. Social Democratic Party.
Address: Ministry of Foreign Affairs, Loretánské nám. 5, 118 00 Prague 1, Czech Republic (office); Embassy of the Czech Republic, Jaroslaviv Val, 34-A, Kiev 01901, Ukraine. *Telephone:* (44) 2722110 (Kiev) (office). *Fax:* (44) 2726204 (Kiev) (office). *E-mail:* kiev@embassy.mzv.cz (office). *Website:* www.mzv.cz/kiev (office).

BASTAGLI, Francesco; Italian fmr UN official and diplomatist; m.; two d. *Education:* State Univ. of Milan, Univ. of Georgia, USA. *Career:* began his int. career at UN HQ, working first in admin as Special Asst to Asst Sec.-Gen. for Personnel Services 1974–79, opened UNHCR office in Nicaragua and managed programme for 800,000 refugees and displaced persons 1979, moved to Secr. of Conf. for Int. Cooperation in Peaceful Uses of Nuclear Energy early 1980s, later became CEO UNRWA for Palestine Refugees in Near East –1991, transferred to UN Int. Drug Control Programme –1999, also in charge of Centre for Int. Crime Prevention –1999, UN Resident Coordinator and UNDP Resident Rep. in Iran 1999–2002, Deputy Special Rep. of Sec.-Gen. for Civil Admin, Kosovo 2002–05, Special Rep. of Sec.-Gen. for Western Sahara 2005–07.

Address: c/o Office of the Secretary-General, United Nations, New York, NY 10017, USA.

BASTARRECHE SAGUES, Carlos, LLB; Spanish diplomatist and academic; *Permanent Representative, European Union;* b. 1950, Madrid; m. Rosalía Gómez-Pineda Goizueta; four c. *Career:* entered diplomatic corps 1976; Spanish Embassy, Bucharest 1976–79, Sec., Conf. for Spanish Accession to EU, Perm. Mission of Spain to EU, Brussels 1979–84, Adviser to Sec. of State for EU Affairs, Madrid 1984–85, Asst Dir-Gen. for EU Co-ordination, Secr. of State for EU Affairs 1986–90, Dir-Gen. of Legal and Institutional Co-ordination 1990–91, Asst Perm. Rep. to EU 1991–96, Sec.-Gen. of Foreign Political and EU Affairs 1996–2000, Sec.-Gen. of European Affairs 2000–02, Perm. Rep. to EU 2002–; Prof. of Community Affairs, Escuela Diplomatica.
Address: Permanent Mission of Spain to the European Community, 52 blvd du Régent, 1000 Brussels, Belgium (office). *Telephone:* (2) 509-86-11 (office). *Fax:* (2) 511-19-40 (office). *E-mail:* carlos.bastarreche@reper.mae .es (office). *Website:* www.es-ue.org (office).

BASTIDAS CASTILLO, Adina Mercedes; Venezuelan economist and politician; *Executive Director, Inter-American Development Bank; Education:* Central Univ. of Venezuela. *Career:* Rep. of Venezuela to Inter-American Devt Bank, Washington, DC 1999–2000, currently Exec. Dir for Venezuela; Vice-Pres. of Venezuela 2000–04; Minister of Production and Commerce 2004.
Address: Inter-American Development Bank (IDB), 1300 New York Avenue, NW, Washington, DC 20577, USA (office). *Telephone:* (202) 623-1000 (office). *Fax:* (202) 623-3096 (office). *E-mail:* pic@iadb.org (office). *Website:* www.iadb.org (office).

BATEMAN, Peter; British diplomatist; *Ambassador to Luxembourg;* b. 23 Dec. 1955; m. Andrea Batemann; two s. one d. *Education:* St John's Comprehensive School, Episkopi, Cyprus, Carre's Grammar School, Sleaford, Lincs., St Peter's Coll., Oxford. *Career:* worked as civil servant at EC, Brussels 1979–84; joined FCO 1984, Asst Desk Officer, Uganda, Kenya and Tanzania, Japanese language training 1985, Second, later First Sec. (Political), Tokyo, Japan 1987–90, News Dept, FCO 1991, Head of Nuclear Non-Proliferation Section 1991–93, Head of Commercial Section, Berlin 1993–97, Dir of Trade and Investment Promotion, Tokyo 1998–2002, secondment to City of London as Deputy Chief Exec. Int. Financial Services London 2003–05, Amb. to Bolivia 2005–07, to Luxembourg 2007–.
Address: British Embassy, 5 Boulevard Joseph II, 1840 Luxembourg (office). *Telephone:* 22-98-64 (office). *Fax:* 22-98-67 (office). *E-mail:* britemb@pt.lu (office). *Website:* www.britain.lu (office).

BATKHUYAG, Jamyandorjiin, MA, PhD; Mongolian economist and politician; *Minister of Defence;* b. 1964. *Education:* , Univ. of Colorado at Denver, USA. *Career:* fmr Lecturer, Mongolian Nat. Univ. and Higher Polytechnic; fmr Sr Adviser on Econ. Policy to Prime Minister; fmr Learned Sec. and Dir Inst. of Finance and Econs; mem. Great Khural (Parl.) 2004–; Minister of Defence 2007–; mem. Nat. New Party.
Address: Ministry of Defence, Government Bldg 7, Dandaryn Gudamj, Bayanzürkh District, Ulan Bator, Mongolia (office). *Telephone:* (11) 458495 (office). *Fax:* (11) 451727 (office). *E-mail:* mdef@mongol.net (office). *Website:* www.pmis.gov.mn/mdef (office).

BATLINER, Gerard, DrIur; Liechtenstein lawyer; *Arbitrator, Court of Conciliation and Arbitration, Organization for Security and Co-operation in Europe;* b. 9 Dec. 1928, Eschen; m. Christina Negele 1965; two s. *Education:* Grammar School, Schwyz, Switzerland and Univs of Zürich, Fribourg, Paris and Freiburg im Breisgau. *Career:* practice at Co. Court of Principality of Liechtenstein 1954–55; lawyer, Vaduz 1956–62, 1970–; Vice-Pres. Fortschrittliche Bürgerpartei (Progressive Burgher Party) 1958–62; Deputy Mayor of commune of Eschen 1960–62; Head of Govt of Principality of Liechtenstein and Minister of Justice 1962–70; attorney-at-law 1970–; Pres. Liechtenstein Parl. 1974–77, Vice-Pres. 1978–81; Head of Liechtenstein Parl. Del. to the Council of Europe 1978–81; a Vice-Pres. Parl. Ass., Council of Europe 1981–82; mem. European Comm. on Human Rights 1983–90, European Comm. for Democracy Through Law (Venice Comm.) 1991–2003 (Vice-Pres. 1999–2001, Pres. Sub-comm. on Constitutional Reform); Arbitrator at Court of OSCE 1995–; merger and partnership, Batliner Wanger Batliner, Attorneys at Law 2002–; Chair. Scientific Council of Liechtenstein-Inst. 1987–97, mem. 1998–; Dir at Ed.'s Office, Liechtenstein Politische Schriften (Liechtenstein Political Publications) 1972–98; mem. Liecthensteinische Akademische Gesellschaft, Liechtensteinische Gesellschaft für Umweltschultz Historischer Verein, Liechtensteinische Kunstgesellschaft; Grand Cross of the Liechtenstein Order of Merit, Grand Silver Cross of Honour (Austria); Hon. DrIur (Basel) 1988, (Innsbruck) 2001; Fürstlicher Justizrat 1970. *Publications*

include: Grundlagen einer liechtensteinischen Politik: Kleinstaatliche Variationen zum Thema der Integration 1972, Denkmodelle: Die volkerrechtlichen und politischen Beziehungen zwischen dem Furstentum Liechtenstein und der Schweizerischen Eidgenossenschaft 1973, Zu heutigen Problemen unseres Staates – Gegebenheiten, Ziele und Strategien 1976, Zur heutigen Lage des liechtensteinischen Parlaments 1981, Liechtenstein und die europäische Integration 1989, Die Siechtensteinische Rechtsordnung und die Europaische Menschenrechtskonvention 1990, Schichten der liechtensteinischen Verfassung 1993, Einfuhrung in das liechtensteinische Verfassungsrecht 1994, Aktuelle Fragen des liechtensteinischen Verfassungsrechts 1998, Der konditionierte Verfassungsstaat 2001, and other publs, essays and speeches in the field of political science.
Address: Am Schrägen Weg 2, PO Box 185, 9490 Vaduz, Liechtenstein (office). *Telephone:* 239-78-78 (office). *Fax:* 239-78-79 (office). *E-mail:* office@bwb-law.li (office). *Website:* www.bwb-law.li (office).

BATUMUBWIRA, Antoinette, MA; Burundian government official; *Minister of External Relations and International Co-operation;* m. Jean-Marie Ngendahayo; two d. *Education:* Univ. of Bordeaux III, France. *Career:* emigrated to Finland as refugee 2003; fmr Planning Officer, Uudenmaa Employment and Econ. Devt Centre; returned to Burundi; Minister of External Relations and Int. Co-operation 2005–. *Publications:* The Route Towards Integration: The Share of Everyone 2004.
Address: Ministry of External Relations and International Co-operation, Bujumbura, Burundi (office). *Telephone:* 22222150 (office). *Fax:* 22223970 (office).

BATURIN, Yuri Mikhailovich, DJur; Russian politician, cosmonaut, lawyer and journalist; *Deputy Commander of the Cosmonaut Corps;* b. 12 June 1949, Moscow; m.; one d. *Education:* Moscow Inst. of Physics and Tech., All-Union Inst. of Law, Moscow State Univ. School of Journalism, Mil. Acad. of Gen. Staff. *Career:* worked in research production union Energia 1973–80; Inst. of State and Law USSR (now Russian) Acad. of Sciences 1980–91; Research Scholar, Kennan Inst. for Advanced Russian Studies, The Woodrow Wilson Center, Washington, DC, USA 1991; on staff of Pres. Mikhail Gorbachev Admin 1991; mem. Pres.'s Council 1993–; Asst to Pres. on legal problems 1993–94, on Nat. Security Problems 1994–96; mem. Council on Personnel Policy of Pres. 1994–97; Sec. Defence Council of Russian Fed. 1996–97; Asst to Pres., Chair. Cttee for Mil. Ranks and Posts 1995–97; columnist, Novaya Gazeta newspaper 1997–; cosmonaut and test pilot of the Cosmonaut Corps 1998–, Deputy Commr 2000–, participated in space flight to Mir Station Aug. 1998, second space flight to Int. Space Station 2001; Prof. of Computer Law, Moscow Inst. of Eng and Physics; Prof., Moscow Inst. of Physics and Tech.; Prof., School of Journalism, Moscow Univ., Pres. of the School, Media Law and Policy Center; Chair. Center for Anti-Corruption Research and Initiative Transparency Int. 2000–; Union of Journalists Prize 1990, Award for Outstanding Contribution to Mass-Media Law 1997, Themis Award 1998. *Exhibition:* Short Rendezvous with Earth (art photography) 1999. *Films:* documentaries: Tuch-and-go in Space 1997, Ladder to Heaven 2000. *Publications:* drafts of the laws on the freedom of the press of the USSR 1989 and of Russia 1991, Problems of Computer Law 1991.
Address: Y. Gagarin Centre for Cosmonaut Training, Zvezdny Gorodok, 141160 Shchelkovsky Raion, Moskovskaya oblast, Russia (office). *Telephone:* (495) 526-38-83 (office). *E-mail:* baturin@medialaw.ru (office); TIRussia@libfl.ru (office).

BAUCHARD, Denis M(ichel) B(ertrand), BA; French diplomatist; *Senior Fellow, Institut français des relations internationales;* b. 20 Sept. 1936, Paris; m. Geneviève Lanoë 1961; two s. two d. *Education:* Inst. of Political Studies, Ecole nat. d'administration. *Career:* Civil Admin., Ministry of Finance 1964–66, 1968–74; Financial Attaché Nr and Middle East, French Embassy, Beirut 1966–68; Asst to Minister 1974–76; Financial Counsellor, French Mission to UN 1977–81; Deputy Asst Sec., Ministry of Foreign Affairs 1981–85; Asst Sec. 1986–89; Amb. to Jordan 1989–93; Asst Sec. Ministry of Foreign Affairs (N Africa and Middle East) 1993–96; Chief of Staff to Minister of Foreign Affairs 1996–97; Amb. to Canada 1998–2001; Pres. Institut du Monde Arabe 2002–04; Sr Fellow, Institut Français de Relations Internationales 2004–; Adviser, Gen. Dir Agence française de Developpement 2005–; Officier, Légion d'honneur, Ordre nat. du Mérite. *Publications:* Le jeu mondial des pétroliers 1970, Economie financière des collectivités locales 1972.
Address: IFRI, 27 rue de la Procession, 75015 Paris (office); 91 rue de Rennes, 75006 Paris, France (home). *Telephone:* 1-40-61-60-82 (office); 1-45-44-18-05 (home). *Fax:* 1-40-61-60-82 (office). *E-mail:* bauchard@ifri.org (office); denis.bauchard@wanadoo.fr (home). *Website:* www.ifri.org (office).

BAUGH, Kenneth, MD; Jamaican politician and physician; *Deputy Prime Minister and Minister of Foreign Affairs and Foreign Trade;* b. Montego

Bay, St James; m. Vilma Baugh; two s. one d. *Education:* Univ. of W Indies, Royal Coll. of Surgeons. *Career:* MP for N W St James 1980–89, currently for St Catherine West Central; fmr Deputy Leader of the Opposition; fmr Minister of Health; Shadow Minister for Health and Environment –2007; Deputy Prime Minister and Minister of Foreign Affairs and Foreign Trade Sept. 2007–; mem. Jamaica Labour Party (currently Chair.).
Address: Office of the Deputy Prime Minister, 1 Devon Road, Kingston 10, Jamaica (office). *Telephone:* 929-8880 (office). *Fax:* 929-8459 (office). *E-mail:* info@cabinet.gov.jm (office); mfaftjam@cwjamaica.com (office). *Website:* www.cabinet.gov.jm (office); www.mfaft.gov.jm (office).

BAUMAN, Zygmunt, MA, PhD; British academic and writer; *Professor Emeritus of Sociology, University of Leeds;* b. 19 Nov. 1925, Poznań, Poland; m. Janina Bauman (née Lewinson) 1948; three d. *Education:* Univ. of Warsaw. *Career:* held Chair of Gen. Sociology, Univ. of Warsaw 1964–68, Prof. Emer. 1968–; Prof. of Sociology, Tel-Aviv Univ. 1968–71; Prof. of Sociology, Univ. of Leeds 1971–91, Prof. Emer. 1991–; mem. British Sociological Asscn, Polish Sociological Asscn; Dr hc (Oslo) 1997, (Lapland) 1999, (Uppsala) 2000, (Prague) 2001, (Copenhagen) 2001, (Sofia) 2001, (West of England) 2002, (London) 2003, (Leeds) 2004; Amalfi Prize for Sociology and Social Sciences 1989, Theodor W. Adorno Prize 1998. *Publications:* Culture as Praxis 1972, Hermeneutics and Social Science 1977, Memories of Class 1982, Legislators and Interpreters 1987, Modernity and the Holocaust 1989, Modernity and Ambivalence 1990, Intimations of Postmodernity 1991, Thinking Sociologically 1991, Mortality, Immortality and Other Life Strategies 1992, Postmodern Ethics 1993, Life in Fragments 1995, Postmodernity and Its Discontents 1996, Globalization: The Human Consequences 1998, Work, Consumerism and the New Poor 1998, In Search of Politics 1999, Liquid Modernity 2000, Individualized Society 2000, Community: Seeking Safety in an Uncertain World 2001, Society Under Siege 2002, Liquid Love: On the Frailty of Human Bonds 2003, Wasted Lives: Modernity and its Outcasts 2003, Europe: An Unfinished Adventure 2004, Liquid Life 2005, Liquid – Modern Fears 2006, The Art of Life 2008; contrib. to scholarly journals and general periodicals.
Address: 1 Lawnswood Gardens, Leeds, LS16 6HF, England (home). *Telephone:* (113) 267-8173 (home). *Fax:* (113) 267-8173 (home). *E-mail:* janzygbau@aol.com (home).

BAUMANN, Werner, LLD; Swiss lawyer and diplomatist; *Ambassador to Canada;* b. 26 May 1947, Altdorf, Uri; m. Susanna Ziegler. *Education:* Univs of Berne and Zurich. *Career:* pvt. law practice 1973–75; Law Dept, Allgemeinen Treuhand AG, Zurich 1976–78; Attaché, Swiss Del. to OECD, Paris 1979–80; Diplomatic Adviser, Law Dept, Ministry of Foreign Affairs 1980–84, Deputy Head, later Head 1987–91, Deputy Dir, later Dir 1993–98; Consul (legal and financial affairs), Swiss Gen. Consulate, New York 1984–87, First Sec., Swiss Embassy, Prague 1991–93, Amb. to the Philippines 1998–2002, to Germany 2002–06, to Canada 2006–.
Address: Embassy of Switzerland, 5 Marlborough Avenue, Ottawa, ON K1N 8E6, Canada (office). *Telephone:* (613) 235-1837 (office). *Fax:* (613) 563-1394 (office). *E-mail:* ott.vertretung@eda.admin.ch (office). *Website:* www.eda.admin.ch/canada (office).

BAWUAH-EDUSEI, Kwame, BSc, MD; Ghanaian physician and diplomatist; *Ambassador to USA;* m.; three c. *Education:* Univ. of Science and Tech., Kumasi. *Career:* Medical Officer, Okomfo Anokye Teaching Hosp., Kumasi 1983–85; Clinical Coordinator Nat. Clinical Research Center Inc., Bethesda, Md, USA 1986–93; residency in family medicine, Howard Univ. Hosp., Washington, DC 1993–96; coordinated Howard Univ. Medical Team visit to Ghana 1993; Physician Pnr, Greenbelt Medical Center, Md 1996–99; Physician Ind. Contractor via Goodwin Corpn, Dewitt Army Hosp., Fort Belvoir 1999–2003; opened own medical clinic and was Medical Dir Educe Medical Center, Alexandria, Va 2003–04; fmr Ghanaian community leader in N America, lobbyist of US Congress, Dept of State and World Bank 1996–2000; Amb. and Perm. Rep. to UN and other Int. Orgs in Geneva and Vienna (also accred to Switzerland and Austria) 2004–06, Head of Ghana's del. to Gen. Conf. of UNIDO, Vienna 2004, Alt. Leader Ghana's del. to World Summit on Information Society Summit, Tunis 2005, IAEA's multiple bd meetings in Vienna 2004–06, World Health Ass. 2004–06, WTO negotiations meetings, including Mutual Declaration Conf., Hong Kong 2005, Chair. African Ambs' Group of African Union, Geneva 2005, Amb. to USA (also accred to Mexico, Guatemala, Belize, Haiti and the Bahamas) 2006–.
Address: Embassy of Ghana, 3512 International Drive, NW, Washington, DC 20008, USA (office). *Telephone:* (202) 686-4520 (office). *Fax:* (202) 686-4527 (office). *E-mail:* info@ghanaembassy.org (office). *Website:* www.ghanaembassy.org (office).

BAXTER, Frank E., BA; American business executive and diplomatist; *Ambassador to Uruguay;* b. Northern Calif.; m. Kathy Baxter; three c.

Education: Univ. of California, Berkeley. *Career:* served in USAF for four years; worked at Bank of California, San Francisco; joined J.S. Strauss & Co., San Francisco 1963; employed by Jefferies & Co. (global investment bank) 1974–2002, moved to London as Man. Dir Jefferies International 1984, CEO Jefferies 1987, started Investment Technology Group (now Chair. Emer.); fmr mem. Bd of Dirs NASD, served as Chair. Cttee, which resulted in spin-off of NASDAQ, subsequently served on Bd of NASDAQ as mem. Exec. Cttee and Chair. CEO Search Cttee; fmr mem. Bd of Dirs Securities Industry Asscn; Amb. to Uruguay 2006–; Chair. Alliance for Coll.-Ready Public Schools, Los Angeles, After-School All Stars, Exec. Cttee Los Angeles Co. Museum of Art; Vice-Chair. Los Angeles Opera; mem. Bd California Inst. of the Arts, Gov. Schwarzenegger's Comm. for Jobs and Econ. Growth; Trustee, Univ. of California Berkeley Foundation, I Have A Dream Foundation (LA Chapter); Bet Tzedek Award, House of Justice Award, Getty House Foundation City of Angels Award.
Address: US Embassy, Lauro Muller 1776, Montevideo 11200, Uruguay (office). *Telephone:* (2) 4187777 (office). *Fax:* (2) 4188611 (office). *E-mail:* webmastermvd@state.gov (office). *Website:* uruguay.usembassy.gov (office).

BAYAR, Sanjaa; Mongolian politician and diplomatist; *Prime Minister;* b. 1956, Ulan Bator. *Education:* Moscow State Univ. *Career:* fmr officer, Ulaanbaatar City Ass. and Nairamdal Dist Office 1978–79; officer Gen. HQ Nat. Defence Army 1979–83; journalist and ed., Novosti Mongolii newspaper, Chief Ed. and Gen. Ed. Montsame news agency 1983–88; Deputy Head of Admin Agency, Mongolian Radio TV 1988–90; mem. Nat. Congress 1990–92; Head, Strategy and Research Center, Ministry of Defence 1992–97; Chief of Staff, Office of the Pres. 1997–2001; Amb. to Russian Fed. 2001–05; Chair. Mongolian People's Revolutionary Party 2005–07, Chair. 2007–; Prime Minister of Mongolia 2007–.
Address: State Palace, Sükhbaatayrn Talbai 1, Ulan Bator (office); Mongolian People's Revolutionary Party, Baga Toiruu 37/1, Ulan Bator, Mongolia (office). *Telephone:* (11) 320432 (office). *Fax:* (11) 323503 (office). *E-mail:* contact@mprp.mn (office). *Website:* www.mprp.mn (office).

BAYARDI, José, MD; Uruguayan physician and politician; *Minister of National Defence;* b. 30 June 1955, Montevideo. *Career:* Deputy (Vertiente Artiguista) Cámara de Representantes (Parl.) 1990–; Deputy Minister of Nat. Defence 2005–08, Minister of Nat. Defence 2008–; Chair. Vertiente Artiguista 1994–2001.
Address: Ministry of National Defence, Edif. General Artigas, Avda 8 de Octubre 2628 Montevideo, Uruguay (office). *Telephone:* (2) 4872828 (office). *Fax:* (2) 4809397 (office). *E-mail:* rrpp.secretaria@mdn.gub.uy (home). *Website:* www.mdn.gub.uy (office).

BAYATI, Hamid al-, BA, MA, PhD; Iraqi diplomatist; *Permanent Representative, United Nations;* b. 1952, Baghdad. *Education:* Baghdad Univ., Cairo Univ., Egypt, Manchester Univ., UK. *Career:* Dir World Charity Foundation, London 1992–2002; Ed. Iraq Update (weekly newsletter) 1992–2002; mem. Leadership Cttee Iraqi Nat. Congress, London 1992–98; mem. Bd INDICT (British based org. collecting evidence of alleged war crimes committed under regime of Saddam Hussein) 1995–2002; adviser to Iraqi Governing Council 2003–04; Deputy Minister of Foreign Affairs for Political Affairs and Bilateral Relations 2004–06, Head, Iraqi Centre for Strategic Studies 2004–; mem. Iraqi Del. to Iraqi Opposition Conf., Salah Al Deen 2003, to Int. Conf. for Econ. Cooperation, Iran 2004, to Islamic Conf. Org. Summit, Saudi Arabia 2005; Perm. Rep. to UN, New York 2006–. *Publications:* several books and articles on politics.
Address: Permanent Mission of Iraq to the United Nations, 14 East 79th Street, New York, NY 10021, USA (office). *Telephone:* (212) 737-4433 (office). *Fax:* (212) 772-1794 (office). *E-mail:* missionofiraq@nyc.rr.com (office). *Website:* www.iraqi-mission.org (office).

BAYNE, Sir Nicholas Peter, KCMG, MA, DPhil; British diplomatist (retd); *Fellow, International Trade Policy Unit, London School of Economics;* b. 15 Feb. 1937, London; m. Diana Wilde 1961; three s. (one deceased). *Education:* Eton Coll. and Christ Church, Oxford. *Career:* joined HM Diplomatic Service 1961; served in Manila 1963–66, Bonn 1969–72; seconded to HM Treasury 1974–75; Financial Counsellor, Paris 1975–79; Head of Econ. Relations Dept, FCO 1979–82; Royal Inst. of Int. Affairs 1982–83; Amb. to Zaïre, also accred to Congo, Rwanda, Burundi 1983–84; Amb. and Perm. Rep. to OECD 1985–88; Deputy Under-Sec. of State, FCO 1988–92; High Commr in Canada 1992–96; Fellow, Int. Trade Policy Unit, LSE 1997–. *Publications:* Hanging Together: The Seven-Power Summits (with R. Putnam) 1984, Hanging In There: The G7 and G8 Summit in Maturity and Renewal 2000, The Grey Wares of North-West Anatolia and their Relations to the Early Greek Settlements 2000, The New Economic Diplomacy (with S. Woolcock) 2003, Staying Together: The G8 Summit Confronts the 21st Century 2005.
Address: 2 Chetwynd House, Hampton Court, Surrey, KT8 9BS, England.

BAZHANOV, Yevgeny Petrovich, CSc, DHist; Russian diplomatist, scientist and journalist; *Vice-Rector for Research, Diplomatic Academy of the Ministry of Foreign Affairs;* b. 5 Nov. 1946, Lvov, Ukraine; m. *Education:* Nanyan Univ., Singapore, Moscow Inst. of Int. Relations, Inst. of the Far East, Diplomatic Acad., Inst. of Oriental Studies. *Career:* mem. staff, USSR Ministry of Foreign Affairs 1970–73; Vice-Consul, USSR Gen. Consulate, San Francisco 1973–79; Counsellor, USSR Embassy in Beijing 1981–85; consultant, Int. Dept, Cen. CPSU Cttee; mem. Exec. Cttee Asscn for Dialogue and Co-operation in Asian-Pacific Region 1991; mem. Nat. Cttee on Security, 1996; Vice-Rector for Research, Diplomatic Acad. of the Ministry of Foreign Affairs 1991–; Hon. Prof., People's Univ., Beijing, China 1999; mem. Int. Ecological Acad., Acad. of Humanitarian Research, Acad. of Political Sciences, USA, Asscn of Russian Sinologists 1986–, Nat. Cttee on Trade and Econ. Co-operation with the Pacific-Asian Countries, Asscn of Russian Diplomats 1999–, Political Science Asscn, Asscn of Asian Studies, Russia's Council on Foreign Policy; Distinguished Scholar of the Russian Fed. 1997; numerous prizes for journalistic and scholarly articles. *Publications:* China and the World 1990, Studies in Contemporary International Development. Vols I–III 2002 and 14 other books and over 1,000 articles and book chapters on world affairs, foreign policies and Russia's internal and foreign policy.
Address: Diplomatic Academy of the Ministry of Foreign Affairs, Moscow 119992, 53/2, Ostozhenka (office); 12165 Moscow, 30 Kutuzovsky Av. #462, Russia (home). *Telephone:* (495) 208-94-61 (office); (495) 249-15-60 (home). *Fax:* (495) 208-94-66 (office). *E-mail:* icipu@online.ru (office). *Website:* www.dipacademy.ru/english (office).

BEAN, Charles Richard, PhD; British economist; *Executive Director, Bank of England;* b. 16 Sept. 1953. *Education:* Brentwood School, Emmanuel Coll., Cambridge, Massachusetts Inst. of Tech., USA. *Career:* Econ. Asst, Short-Term Forecasting Div., HM Treasury 1975–79, Econ. Adviser, Monetary Policy Div. 1981–82; Lecturer in Econs, LSE 1982–86, Reader 1986–90, Prof. 1990–2000, Deputy Dir Centre for Econ. Performance 1990–94, Head of Econs Dept 1999–2000; Visiting Prof. Stanford Univ. 1990, Reserve Bank of Australia 1999; Exec. Dir, Chief Economist and mem. of Monetary Policy Cttee, Bank of England 2000–.
Address: Bank of England, Threadneedle Street, London, EC2R 8AH, England (office). *Telephone:* (20) 7601-4999 (office). *Fax:* (20) 7601-4112 (office). *Website:* www.bankofengland.co.uk (office).

BEATRIX WILHELMINA ARMGARD, HM Queen of The Netherlands; b. 31 Jan. 1938, Baarn; m. Claus George Willem Otto Frederik Geert Jonkheer von Amsberg 10 March 1966 (died 2002); children: Prince Willem-Alexander Claus George Ferdinand, Prince of Orange, b. 27 April 1967; Prince Johan Friso Bernhard Christiaan David, b. 25 Sept. 1968; Prince Constantijn Christof Frederik Aschwin, b. 11 Oct. 1969. *Education:* Baarn Grammar School, Leiden State Univ. *Career:* succeeded to the throne on abdication of her mother 30 April 1980; Hon. KG; ranked 35th by Forbes magazine amongst 100 Most Powerful Women 2004.
Address: c/o Government Information Service, Press and Publicity Department, Binnenhof 19, 2513 AA The Hague, Netherlands. *Telephone:* (70) 3564136. *Website:* www.koninklijkhuis.nl/english/.

BECHIR, Mahamoud Adam; Chadian diplomatist; *Ambassador to USA.* *Career:* fmr army officer with rank of Lt-Col; Co-ordinator High Cttee for Nat. Demining –2004; Amb. to USA 2004–.
Address: Embassy of Chad, 2002 R Street, NW, Washington, DC 20009, USA (office). *Telephone:* (202) 462-4009 (office). *Fax:* (202) 265-1937 (office).

BECK, Colin D., BA, MA; Solomon Islands diplomatist; *Ambassador to USA;* b. 1964; m. Helen Beck; two c. *Education:* Univ. of the South Pacific, Fiji, Univ. of Queensland, Australia, Univ. of Oxford, UK. *Career:* Perm. Rep. to Australia 1990–93, Counsellor, Perm. Mission to EU, Brussels, also attached to Embassies in Bonn, Brussels and The Hague 1993–95, Sr Civil Servant, Ministry of Foreign Affairs Gen. Secr. 1995–2002, Asst Sec., Asia Pacific Political Div., Ministry of Foreign Affairs 2002–03, Perm. Rep. to UN 2003–, Amb. to USA 2004–.
Address: Permanent Mission of the Solomon Islands to the United Nations, 800 Second Avenue, Suite 400L, New York, NY 10017, USA (office). *Telephone:* (212) 599-6192 (office). *Fax:* (212) 661-8925 (office). *E-mail:* simny@solomons.com (office).

BECK, Stuart; American diplomatist and lawyer; *Permanent Representative of Palau, United Nations;* b. 1946, New York; m. Mary Ebil Tulik Beck; four c. *Education:* Harvard Coll., Yale Law School. *Career:* early career as attorney Washington, DC and New York 1971–87; Chief Counsel, Palau Political Status Comm. 1977; Co-founder and Pres. Granite Broadcasting Corpn 1987–2004; Perm. Rep. of Palau to UN 2004–.

Address: Office of the Permanent Representative, 866 UN Plaza, Suite 575, New York, NY 10017, USA (office). *Telephone:* (212) 813-0310 (office). *Fax:* (212) 813-0317 (office). *E-mail:* mission@palauun.org (office). *Website:* www.palauun.org (office).

BECKETT, Rt Hon. Margaret (Mary), PC; British politician; *Chair, Intelligence and Security Committee;* b. 15 Jan. 1943, Ashton-under-Lyne, Lancs.; m. Leo Beckett 1979; two step-s. *Education:* Notre Dame High School, Manchester and Norwich, Manchester Coll. of Science and Tech., John Dalton Polytechnic. *Career:* eng apprentice (metallurgy), Associated Electrical Industries Ltd, Manchester, subsequently Experimental Officer, Univ. of Manchester; Sec. Trades Council and Labour Party 1968–70; researcher (Industrial Policy), Labour Party HQ 1970–74; Political Adviser to Minister of Overseas Devt Feb.–Oct. 1974; MP (Labour) for Lincoln 1974–79, for Derby S 1983–; Parl. Pvt. Sec., Minister for Overseas Devt 1974–75; Asst Govt Whip 1975–76; Minister, Dept of Educ. 1976–79; Prin. Researcher, Granada TV 1979–83; Opposition Spokeswoman with responsibility for Social Security 1984–89; Shadow Chief Sec. 1989–92; Shadow Leader of House, Campaigns Co-ordinator, Deputy Leader of Opposition 1992–94, Leader of Opposition May–July 1994; Shadow Sec. of State for Health 1994–95; Shadow Pres. Bd of Trade 1995–97, Pres. Bd of Trade and Sec. of State for Trade and Industry 1997–98; Pres. of Council and Leader House of Commons 1998–2001; Sec. of State for Environment, Food and Rural Affairs 2001–06, for Foreign and Commonwealth Affairs 2006–07; Chair. Intelligence and Security Cttee 2008–; Ministerial visits and trade missions to USA, Japan, Mexico, Netherlands, Australia, Paris, Brussels, Singapore, China, Hong Kong and Pakistan, India 1997–2001; mem. Labour Party 1963–, Nat. Exec. Cttee 1980–81, 1985–86, 1988–97, Transport & General Workers Union 1964–, T&GWU Parl. Labour Party Group; mem. Nat. Union of Journalists, BECTU, Fabian Soc., Anti-Apartheid Movt, Tribune Group, Socialist Educ. Cttee, Labour Women's Action Cttee, Derby Co-op Party, Socialist Environment & Resources Assen, Amnesty International, Council of St George's Coll., Windsor 1976–82; Privy Councillor 1993–; Hon. Pres. Labour Friends of India; ranked 29th by Forbes magazine amongst 100 Most Powerful Women 2006. *Publications:* Vision for Growth – A New Industrial Strategy for Britain 1996, Renewing the NHS 1995, relevant sections of Labour's Programme 1972, 1973, The Nationalisation of Shipbuilding, Ship Repair and Marine Engineering, The National Enterprise Board, The Need for Consumer Protection. *Address:* House of Commons, Westminster, London, SW1A 2NE, England (office). *Telephone:* (20) 7219-3000 (office); (1332) 345636 (constituency office) (office). *Fax:* www.parliament.uk (office).

BECKINGHAM, Peter, MA; British diplomatist; *Ambassador to the Philippines;* b. 1949, Essex; m. Jill Beckingham 1975; two d. *Education:* Selwyn Coll., Cambridge. *Career:* joined Argo Record Co. 1970; with British Overseas Trade Bd 1974–79, travelled with various business missions to Europe, SE Asia and the Middle East; joined FCO 1979, worked in News Dept, Head of Horn of Africa Section, Dir Dept overseeing Britain's commercial depts overseas, on short secondment to Cadbury Schweppes, was also attached to operations in Birmingham, London and Poland, overseas appointments have been in USA, Europe and Asia-Pacific, Dir British Information Services, New York, Head of Commercial Section, Stockholm, Head of Political Section, Canberra, later British Consul-Gen., Sydney and Dir-Gen. Trade and Investment, assisted the British team at Sydney Olympics 2000, Dean of the Diplomatic Corps for two years, Amb. to the Philippines 2005–; Nuffield Foundation Scholarship to teach in Zambia 1966. *Publication:* edited a collection of essays on British-Australian relations. *Address:* British Embassy, L.V. Locsin Building, 15th–17th Floors, 6752 Ayala Avenue, Makati City, 1226 Metro Manila, Philippines (office). *Telephone:* (2) 8167116 (office). *Fax:* (2) 8197206 (office). *E-mail:* uk@info.com.ph (office). *Website:* www.britishembassy.gov.uk/philippines (office).

BEDJAOUI, Mohammed; Algerian judge and diplomatist; b. 21 Sept. 1929, Sidi-Bel-Abbès; m. Leila Francis 1962; two d. *Education:* Univ. of Grenoble and Institut d'Etudes Politiques, Grenoble. *Career:* Lawyer, Court of Appeal, Grenoble 1951; research worker at CNRS, Paris 1955; Legal Counsellor of the Arab League in Geneva 1959–62; Legal Counsellor Provisional Republican Govt of Algeria in Exile 1958–61; Dir Office of the Pres. of Nat. Constituent Ass. 1962; mem. Del. to UN 1957, 1962, 1977, 1978–82; Sec.-Gen. Council of Ministers, Algiers 1962–63; Pres. Soc. Nat. des Chemins de Fer Algériens (SNCFA) 1964; Dean of the Faculty of Law, Algiers Univ. 1964; Minister of Justice and Keeper of the Seals 1964–70; mem., special reporter, Int. Law Comm. 1965–82; Amb. to France 1970–79; Perm. Rep. to UNESCO 1971–79, to UN 1979–82; Vice-Pres. UN Council on Namibia 1979–82; mem. UN Comm. of Inquiry (Iran) 1980; Pres. Group of 77 1981–82; Judge Int. Court of Justice 1982–2001 (Pres. 1994–97); Minister of State for Foreign Affairs 2005–07; fmr Pres. African

Soc. of Int. and Comparative Law; Head Algerian Del. to UN Conf. on Law of the Sea 1976–80; mem. Int. Inst. of Law; Carnegie Endowment for Int. Peace 1956; Ordre du Mérite Alaouite, Morocco, Order of the Repub., Egypt, Commdr Légion d'honneur (France), Ordre de la Résistance (Algeria). *Publications:* International Civil Service 1956, Fonction publique internationale et influences nationales 1958, La révolution algérienne et le droit 1961, Succession d'états 1970, Terra nullius, droits historiques et autodétermination 1975, Non-alignment et droit international 1976, Pour un nouvel ordre économique international 1979, Droit international: bilan et perspectives 1992. *Address:* c/o Ministry of Foreign Affairs, place Mohamed Seddik Benyahia, el-Mouradia, Algiers (office); 39 rue des Pins, Hydra, Algiers, Algeria. *Telephone:* (2) 60-30-89.

BEERLI, Christine, LicIur; Swiss politician, lawyer, university administrator and international organization official; *Vice-President, International Committee of the Red Cross;* b. 26 March 1953, Biel. *Education:* Univ. of Bern. *Career:* mem. Bern City Council 1980–83, Greater Bern Council 1986–91; Senator 1992–2003, Leader Parl. Group, Freisinnig-Demokratische Partei der Schweiz (Radical Democratic Party—FDP) 1996–2002; official FDP cand. for Bundesrat (Fed. Council) 2003; Dir School of Eng and Information Tech. (HTI), Berne Univ. of Applied Sciences 2003–07; Vice-Pres. Int. Cttee of the Red Cross, Geneva 2008–; mem. Bd of Dirs New Medical Tech., Annuity Bank; Pres. Bd of Dirs Dynamic Test Centre (Vauffelin); Pres. Alcohol Comm.; mem. Science, Health and Culture Comm., Social Security and Health Comm., Econs Comm. *Address:* International Committee of the Red Cross, 19 avenue de la Paix, 1202 Geneva, Switzerland (office). *Telephone:* 227346001 (office). *Fax:* 227332057 (home). *E-mail:* press.gva@icrc.org (office). *Website:* www.christine-beerli.ch.

BEHAJAINA, Maj.-Gen. Petera; Malagasy politician and army officer. *Education:* Asia-Pacific Center for Security Studies. *Career:* Chief of Staff of Madagascar Army 2003; Minister of Defence 2004–07. *Address:* c/o Ministry of Defence, BP 08, Ampahibe, 101 Antananarivo, Madagascar (office).

BEHBEHANI, Kazem, PhD, FRCPath; Kuwaiti international organization official; *Envoy, World Health Organization; Education:* Univs of Liverpool and London, UK. *Career:* fmr Deputy Dir Gen. Kuwait Inst. for Scientific Research; Prof. Kuwait Medical Faculty; Vice-Rector for Research, Kuwait Univ.; Programme Man., Special Programme for Research and Training, Tropical Diseases, WHO 1991–94, Dir of Tropical Diseases 1994–99, Dir Eastern Mediterranean Liaison Office and in charge of Resource Mobilization for the Eastern Mediterranean Region 1999–2003, Asst Dir Gen. WHO 2003–05, now Envoy; Visiting Prof./Scholar, Harvard Medical School, USA, currently Co-Chair. Scientific Advisory Bd for the Environment and Public Health; mem. British Soc. of Parasitology, American Soc. for Tropical Medicine and Hygiene, Electron Microscopy Soc. of America and European Acad. of Arts, Science and the Humanities; Fellow Islamic Acad. of Sciences; Award for Research in Medicine, Kuwait Foundation for the Advancement of Sciences. *Publications:* a book on science and tech. and more than 100 scientific papers. *Address:* Kuwait Mission, Geneva, Switzerland (office). *Telephone:* (22) 918-01-00 (office). *E-mail:* albader@kuwaitmission.ch (office). *Website:* www.kazembehbehani.com.

BEHMEN, Alija, PhD; Bosnia and Herzegovina politician and economist; b. 25 Dec. 1940, Split, Croatia; m.; two s. *Education:* Univ. of Sarajevo. *Career:* worked at Inst. of Econs, Sarajevo; mem. staff Railways Enterprise ŽTO Sarajevo, Deputy Pres., Pres. Exec. Bd 1970–78; Pres. Exec. Bd INTERŠPED 1978–80; Assoc. Prof., Faculty of Transportation and Communications 1980–; Vice-Pres. Social Democratic Party of Bosnia and Herzegovina; mem. Ass. of Sarajevo Canton; Deputy Chair. Parl. of Bosnia and Herzegovina 1998–2001; Prime Minister of the Fed. of Bosnia and Herzegovina 2001–03. *Address:* Social Democratic Party of Bosnia and Herzegovina, Alipašina 41, 71000 Sarajevo, Bosnia and Herzegovina (office). *Telephone:* (33) 663750 (office); (33) 663753 (office). *Fax:* (33) 213675 (office). *Website:* www.sdp-bih.org.ba (office).

BÉKÉSI, Maj.-Gen. István; Hungarian military officer; *Military Representative, NATO;* b. 27 Sept. 1954, Debrecen. *Education:* Lajos Kossuth Mil. Acad., Frunze Mil. Coll. Moscow, US Army War Coll. *Career:* joined Army 1973, commissioned Infantry officer 1977, Infantry Bn Commdr 1982–85, Deputy S-3 of Mechanized Infantry Brigade 1989–91, G-3 Planner of Land Forces Staff 1991–93, S-3 of Mechanized Infantry Brigade 1993–96, Deputy COS of Mechanized Infantry Brigade 1996–98, XO of Mechanized Infantry Brigade 1999–2000, Commdr 25 Brigade Mechanized

Infantry 2000–04; Deputy Head of Operational and Training Directorate, Ministry of Defence 2004–05, Deputy Dir Mil. Planning Directorate (including three-month tour in Baghdad as Chief of Training, NATO Training Mission Iraq) 2005–06, Head of Force Planning Dept 2006–07; Mil. Rep. to NATO and the EU 2007–.
Address: NATO HQ, blvd Léopold III, 1110 Brussels, Belgium (office). *Telephone:* (2) 707-41-11 (office). *Fax:* (2) 707-45-79 (office). *E-mail:* natodoc@hq.nato.int (office). *Website:* www.nato.int (office).

BEKHBAT, Khasbazar; Mongolian diplomatist; *Ambassador to USA. Career:* Perm. Rep. to UN, Geneva –2006; State Sec., Ministry of Foreign Affairs 2006–08; Amb. to USA 2008–.
Address: Embassy of Mongolia, 2833 M Street, NW, Washington, DC 20007, USA (office). *Telephone:* (202) 333-7117 (office). *Fax:* (202) 298-9227 (office). *E-mail:* esyam@mongolianembassy.us (office). *Website:* www .mongolianembassy.us (office).

BEKINK, Rudolf Simon, PhD; Dutch diplomatist; *Ambassador to People's Republic of China; Career:* career diplomat; fmr Amb. to Sweden; Amb. to Belgium 2004–08, to People's Repub. of China 2008–.
Address: Embassy of the Netherlands, 4 Liang Ma He Nan Lu, Beijing 100600, People's Republic of China (office). *Telephone:* (10) 65321131 (office). *Fax:* (10) 65324689 (office). *E-mail:* pek-cdp@minbuza.nl (office). *Website:* www.hollandinchina.org (office).

BELKA, Marek, MA, PhD; Polish politician, economist, academic and UN official; *Executive Secretary, United Nations Economic Commission for Europe (UNECE);* b. 9 Jan. 1952, Lodz; m.; two c. *Education:* Łódź Univ., Univ. of Chicago, USA, LSE, UK. *Career:* Master of Econs and Sociology Faculty, Łódź Univ. 1972, Asst Prof., then Prof. of Econs 1973–96; Visiting Scholar, Columbia Univ. (Fulbright Foundation), USA 1978–79; American Council of Scholarly Socs, Univ. of Chicago 1985–86; LSE 1990; Asst Prof., Inst. of Econs, Polish Acad. of Sciences (PAN) 1986–97, Dir 1993–97; adviser and consultant Finance Ministry, Privatisation Ministry and Cen. Planning Office 1990–96; Deputy Chair. Govt Council of Socio-Econ. Strategy 1994–96; Econ. Adviser to the Pres. of Poland 1996–97, 1997–2001; consultant to World Bank 1990–96; adviser to JP Morgan Chase; Deputy Prime Minister and Minister of Finance 1997, 2001–02; Head Coalition Council for Int. Co-ordination in Iraq 2003; Dir in charge of econ. policy, Coalition Provisional Authority 2003–04; Prime Minister of Poland 2004–05; Exec. Sec. UN Econ. Comm. for Europe (UNECE) 2005–. *Publications:* around a dozen books and over 100 articles in Polish and foreign press on anti-inflation policy in developed countries, the Milton Friedman socio-econ. doctrine and macroecon. policy in transition periods.
Address: UNECE, Palais des Nations, 1211, Geneva, Switzerland (office). *Telephone:* 229174444 (office). *Fax:* 229170505 (office). *E-mail:* info.ece@ unece.org (office). *Website:* www.unece.org (office).

BELKEZIZ, Abdellah, DEcon; Moroccan economist and diplomatist; *Ambassador to Algeria; Career:* worked as economist, various posts with nat. banks including Banque Nationale de Développement Economique, Banque Africaine de Développement; fmr Dir Société Nationale d'Investissement; Pres. Société des Ciments de Marrakech –2000; elected mem. of Parl., l'Union Constitutionnelle 1993; Regional Dir Assoc. Nationale pour la lutte contre l'Habitat Insalubre 1998; Regional Inspector Ministère de l'Amenagement du Territoire, de l'Urbanisme, de l'Habitat et de l'Environnement 2001; apptd Amb. to Tunisia 2001, currently Amb. to Algeria.
Address: Embassy of Morocco, Villa nos 21 et 22, Cité al-Fath, Sable Rouge, el-Biar, Algiers, Algeria (office). *Telephone:* (21) 69-14-08 (office). *Fax:* (21) 69-29-00 (office). *E-mail:* ambmaroc@wissal.dz (office); ambmaroc-alg@maec.gov.ma (office).

BELKHADEM, Abdelaziz; Algerian politician; b. 8 Nov. 1945, Aflou. *Career:* Deputy Dir of Int. Relations, Office of the Pres. 1972–77; Rapporteur, Planning and Finance Comm. 1978–87; mem. Front de Libération Nationale (FLN) 1977–, mem. Bureau Politique 1991–97, currently Sec.-Gen.; Deputy for Sougueur to Assemblée Populaire Nationale (APN) 1977–92, Vice-Pres. 1988–90, Pres. 1990–91, Pres. Educ., Training and Scientific Research Comm. 1987; Minister of State for Foreign Affairs 2000–05; Minister of State and Special Rep. of the Pres. 2005–06; Prime Minister 2006–08.
Address: Front de libération nationale (FLN), 7 rue du Stade, Hydra, Algiers, Algeria (office). *Telephone:* (21) 69-42-81 (office). *Fax:* (21) 69-47-07 (office). *E-mail:* pfln@wissal.dz (office). *Website:* www.pfln.dz (office).

BELLAL, Mohamed Vall Ould; Mauritanian politician; b. 1949, Maghtaa Lahjar (Brakna). *Education:* Univ. of Dakar. *Career:* civil admin. 1965; Head of Mission, Ministry of State for Nat. Orientation 1976–77, Sec.-Gen. 1977–78; Prefect, then Cen. Gov. 1979–81; political analyst, Paris 1993–95;

mem. Parl. for Maghtaa Lahjar 1996–2003; Minister of Foreign Affairs and Co-operation 2003–07.
Address: c/o Ministry of Foreign Affairs and Co-operation, BP 230, Nouakchott, Mauritania (office).

BELLAMY, Carol, JD; American international organization official; *President, School for International Training and President and CEO, World Learning;* b. 1942, Plainfield, NJ. *Education:* Gettysburg Coll. and New York Univ. *Career:* Peace Corps Volunteer, Guatemala 1963–65; Assoc., Cravath, Swaine & Moore, New York 1968–71; spent 13 years as elected public official including term as mem. New York State Senate 1973–77; Pres. New York City Council (first woman) 1978–85; Prin., Morgan Stanley and Co. 1986–90; Man. Dir Bear Stearns & Co. 1990–93; Prin. Morgan Stanley & Co. New York; Dir Peace Corps, Washington, DC 1993–95; Exec. Dir UNICEF 1995–2005; Pres. School for Int. Training and CEO World Learning 2005–; Chair. Bd of Dirs Fair Labor Foundation 2007–; fmr Fellow, Inst. of Politics, Kennedy School of Govt, Harvard Univ.; Hon. mem. Phi Alpha Alpha, the US Nat. Honor Soc. for Accomplishment and Scholarship in Public Affairs and Admin; Hon. LHD (Bates Coll.) 2003; ranked 95th by Forbes magazine amongst 100 Most Powerful Women 2004.
Address: World Learning, PO Box 676, Kipling Road, Brattleboro, VT 05302-0676, USA (office). *Telephone:* (802) 258-3100 (office). *Fax:* (802) 258-3248 (office). *E-mail:* carol.bellamy@worldlearning.org (office). *Website:* ourworld.worldlearning.org (office).

BELLAMY, William M., BA, MA; American diplomatist; *Senior Fellow in Residence, Africa Program and International Security Program, Center for Strategic and International Studies; m.* Pamela Bellamy; two c. *Education:* Occidental Coll., Los Angeles, Fletcher School of Law and Diplomacy, Tufts Univ., Institut Universitaire de Hautes Etudes Internationales, Geneva, Switzerland, Ecole Nationale d'Admin, Paris, France. *Career:* worked as journalist in San Francisco and as public relations officer for bank; career mem. Sr Foreign Service with rank of Minister-Counselor, posting to Embassy in Harare –1989, Head of Political Section, Embassy in Pretoria 1989–93, Chief of Political Section, Embassy in Paris 1993–97, Deputy Chief of Mission, Embassy in Canberra 1997–2000, Deputy Asst Sec. 2000–01, Prin. Deputy Asst Sec. for African Affairs 2001–03, Amb. to Kenya 2003–06; Sr Vice-Pres. Nat. Defense Univ., Washington, DC 2006–07; Sr Fellow in Residence, Africa Program and Int. Security Program, Center for Strategic and Int. Studies 2007–; Presidential Meritorious Service Award, Chair. of the Jt Chiefs of Staff Jt Distinguished Civilian Service Award, Distinguished Honor Award, two Superior Honor Awards conferred by US Sec. of State.
Address: Center for Strategic and International Studies, 1800 K Street, NW, Washington, DC 20006, USA (office). *Telephone:* (202)741-3925 (office). *Website:* www.csis.org (office).

BELMAHI, Muhammad; Moroccan diplomatist; *Ambassador to UK;* m. Ase Ask Belmahi. *Career:* fmr Minister of Tourism; Amb. to India 1997–99, to UK 1999–; Pres. Int. Conf. on Establishment of Supplementary Fund for Compensation for Oil Pollution Damage 2003; Kt Commdr, Royal Order of Francis I.
Address: Embassy of Morocco, 49 Queens Gate Gardens, London, SW7 5NE, England (office). *Telephone:* (20) 7581-5001 (office). *Fax:* (20) 7225-3862 (office). *E-mail:* ihilan@yahoo.co.uk (office); mail@sifamaldn.org (office).

BELOUS, Oleg Nikolayevich; Russian diplomatist; *Director, First European Department, Ministry of Foreign Affairs;* b. 18 Aug. 1951. *Education:* Moscow Inst. of Int. Relations. *Career:* on staff USSR (later Russian) Ministry of Foreign Affairs 1973–, Deputy Dir First European Dept 1994–96, Dir Dept of All-European Co-operation 1996–98, Dir First European Dept (Belgium, Vatican City, Italy, Spain, Luxembourg, Malta, Monaco, The Netherlands, Portugal, France) 2001–; Counsellor, Russian Embassy to Belgium 1991–94; Perm. Rep. of Russia to OSCE, Vienna 1998–2001.
Address: First European Department, Ministry of Foreign Affairs, Smolenskaya-Sennaya pl 32/34, Moscow 119200 Russia (office). *Telephone:* (495) 244-41-62 (office). *Fax:* (495) 244-31-87 (office). *E-mail:* ministry@ mid.ru (office). *Website:* www.mid.ru (office).

BELY, Mikhail M.; Russian diplomatist; *Ambassador to Japan; Education:* Moscow State Inst. of Int. Relations, Nanyang Univ., Singapore. *Career:* fmr Dir First Dept of Asia-Pacific Region, Ministry of Foreign Affairs; served as Attaché, Embassy in Singapore, First Sec. Embassy in Beijing, Counsellor, Perm. Mission to the UN, New York; Amb. to Singapore, Indonesia, Timor Leste, Papua New Guinea, Kiribati –2007, Amb. to Japan 2007–.

Address: Embassy of Russia, 2-1-1 Azabu-dai, Minato-ku, Tokyo 106-0041, Japan (office). *Telephone:* (3) 3583-4224 (office). *Fax:* (3) 3505-0593 (office). *E-mail:* rosconsl@ma.kcom.ne.jp (office). *Website:* www.russia-emb.jp (office).

BEN-AMI, Shlomo, BA, MA, PhD; Israeli academic and fmr politician; *Vice-President, Toledo International Centre for Peace;* b. 1943, Morocco; m.; three c. *Education:* Tel-Aviv Univ., Univ. of Oxford, UK. *Career:* Visiting Fellow, St Antony's Coll., Oxford 1980–82; Head, Grad. School of History, Tel-Aviv Univ. 1982–86, Elias Sourasky Chair for Spanish and Latin American Studies.1986–, Founder and Head, Curiel Center for Int. Studies 1993–96; Amb. to Spain 1987–91; mem. Knesset 1996–2001; fmr mem. Foreign Affairs and Defense Cttee; Minister of Public Security 1999–2001; Minister of Foreign Affairs 2000–01; currently Vice-Pres. Toledo International Centre for Peace (TICpax), Spain; mem. Bd of Dirs Int. Crisis Group 2006–. *Publications include:* Quel avenir pour Israel? 2001, A Front Without a Rearguard: A Voyage to the Boundaries of the Peace Process 2004, Scars of War, Wounds of Peace. The Arab-Israeli Tragedy 2006. *Address:* Toledo International Centre for Peace, Felipe IV, 5 Bajo Izq., 28014 Madrid, Spain (office). *Telephone:* (91) 5237452 (office). *Fax:* (91) 5227301 (office). *Website:* www.toledopax.org (home).

BEN BARKA, Lalla Aicha, PhD; Malian international organization official; *Director, Regional Office for Education in Africa, United Nations Educational, Scientific and Cultural Organization (UNESCO); Education:* Université de Paris X, France, Univ. of Southern Calif., USA. *Career:* with Gender Analysis and Research Devt Programme, West Africa 1991–93; Regional Coordinator, Educational Research Network for West and Cen. Africa 1993–96; Head Programme décennal développement de l'éducation team 1996–98; Deputy Exec. Sec., UN Econ. Comm. for Africa (UNECA), Ethiopia 1998–2004; currently Dir Regional Office for Educ. in Africa, UNESCO, Dakar, Senegal; has worked on projects with UNICEF, UNESCO, UNIFEM, UN Population Fund, African Asscn for Literacy and Adult Educ., Int. Council on Adult Educ.; mem. Bd of Govs, UNESCO Inst. for Statistics 1999–2001, Int. Devt Research Centre; UNESCO Literacy Prize 1993. *Address:* UNESCO Africa, 12 Avenue L. S. Senghor, BP 331, Dakar, Senegal (office). *Telephone:* 849-23-35 (office). *Fax:* 823-83-93 (office). *E-mail:* LA.Ben-Barka@unesco.org (office). *Website:* www.dakar.unesco.org (office).

BEN YAHIA, Habib; Tunisian politician; *Secretary General, Arab Maghreb Union;* b. 30 July 1938, Tunis; m. Naget Ben Yahia; one s. one d. *Education:* Univ. of Tunis, Columbia Univ., New York, USA. *Career:* fmr Dir African Div., Ministry of Foreign Affairs, then Dir Econ. Co-operation with the United States Div.; fmr Econ. Counsellor, Embassies of Tunisia, Paris and Washington, DC; fmr Chief of Staff, Ministry of Foreign Affairs; Amb. to UAE, Japan and Belgium –1981, apptd Amb. to USA 1981; Minister of Foreign Affairs 1991–97, of Defence and Foreign Affairs 1999–2004; Sec. Gen. Arab Maghreb Union 2006–. *Address:* Union du Maghreb Arabe, 14 Rue Zalagh Agdal, Rabat, Morocco (office). *Telephone:* (3) 7671274 (office); (3) 7671280 (office). *Fax:* (3) 7671253 (office). *E-mail:* sg.uma@maghrebarabe.org (office). *Website:* www.maghrebarabe.org (office).

BENACHENHOU, Abdellatif; Algerian economist and government official. *Career:* fmr financial consultant; worked for UNESCO; fmr econ. consultant for World Bank and UNEP; fmr chief consultant for Mediterranean Comm. on Sustainable Devt Working Group on Trade and Environment; Minister of Finance 1999–2001, 2003–05, currently econ. adviser to Pres. of Algeria. *Address:* c/o Office of the President, Présidence de la République, el-Mouradia, Algiers, Algeria. *Telephone:* (21) 69-15-15. *Fax:* (21) 69-15-95. *Website:* www.el-mouradia.dz.

BENAÏSSA, Muhammad, BA; Moroccan politician; b. 3 Jan. 1937, Asilah; m. Laila Hajoun-Benaissa; five c. *Education:* Univ. of Minnesota, Columbia Univ., USA. *Career:* Press Attaché, Perm. Mission of Morocco to UN, New York 1964–65; Information Officer, UN Dept of Information, 1965–67; Regional Information Adviser, FAO, Rome 1967–71, Head of Devt Support Communication 1971–73, Asst to Dir of Information 1973–74, Dir of Information Div. 1974–76; Asst Sec.-Gen. of UN, World Food Conf. 1975; elected to City Council of Asilah 1976–83, elected Mayor 1992; mem. Moroccan Parl. 1977–83; Co-Founder and Exec. mem. Moroccan Social Democratic Party (Rassemblement Nat. des Independents) 1978; consultant, UNDP, IFAD, UNFPA 1978–85; Chief Ed. Al-Mithak Al-Watani and Al-Maghrab publs 1980–85; apptd Amb. to USA 1993; Minister of Foreign Affairs and Co-operation 1999–2007. *Publications include:* Grains de Peau 1974.

Address: Rassemblement national des indépendants (RNI), 6 rue Laos, ave Hassan II, Rabat, Morocco (office). *Telephone:* (3) 7721420 (office). *Fax:* (3) 7733824 (office).

BÉNASSY-QUÉRÉ, Agnès, MBA, PhD; French economist and research institute director; *Director, Centre d'Etudes Prospectives et d'Informations Internationales;* b. 15 March 1966; m.; three c. *Education:* École Supérieure de Commerce de Paris, Univ. of Paris IX-Dauphine. *Career:* teaching asst, Univ. of Paris IX-Dauphine 1987–92; Lecturer, Univ. of Cergy-Pontoise 1992–96; Assoc. Researcher, Centre d'Etudes Prospectives et d'Informations Ints (CEPII) 1992–96, Scientific Adviser 1996–99, 2001–03, Deputy Dir 1999–2000, 2004–06, Dir 2006–; Prof., Univ. of Lille 2 1996–99; Prof., Univ. of Paris X 2001–03, 2004–06; Assoc. Prof., École Polytechnique 2006–; columnist for La Tribune 2006–; mem. Nat. Econ. Comm., Ministry of Economy and Finance 1999–, Cercle des Économistes 2001–, ECB Shadow Council 2005–; Best Young French Economist Award (Le Monde) 2000. *Publications:* Les Taux d'Intérêt 1998, Économie de l'Euro 2002, Politique Économique 2004; numerous articles in academic journals and policy papers. *Address:* Centre d'Etudes Prospectives et d'Informations Internationales, 9 rue Georges Pitard, 75015 Paris, France (office). *Telephone:* 1-53-68-55-47 (office). *E-mail:* agnes.benassy@cepii.fr (office). *Website:* www.cepii.fr (office).

BENAVIDES ORGAZ, Pablo; Spanish diplomatist; *Permanent Representative, NATO;* b. 6 July 1949, Madrid. *Education:* ICADE, Madrid. *Career:* Lecturer, Madrid Univ. 1970–73; attended Diplomatic School and joined Ministry of Foreign Affairs 1976, worked on Int. Security and Disarmament Affairs 1982, Deputy Dir Pvt. Office of the Minister 1983, Deputy Dir-Gen. European Political Co-operation 1987–89, Deputy Political Dir 1990, Adviser to Under-Sec. 1996, Chair. Higher Council of Foreign Affairs 2002–04; foreign posts include Sec., Embassy in Sweden 1977–79, Embassy in Senegal 1980–81, Deputy Chief of Mission to CSCE, Stockholm 1984, Counsellor, Mission to UN, New York 1985–86, Amb. to Libya 1991–92, to Hungary 1993–95, Deputy Perm. Rep. to UNESCO 1997–2001, Perm. Rep. to NATO 2004–; Officer, Order of Isabel the Catholic 1983, Commdr, Order of Civil Merit 1987, Commdr, Order of Isabel the Catholic 1990, Order of Trishakti-Patta, fourth class (Nepal), Grand Cross, Order Francisco de Miranda, first class (Venezuela), Grand-Cross, Order of Merit with Stars (Hungary). *Address:* Delegation of Spain, NATO Headquarters, Bld Léopold III, Brussels 1110, Belgium (office). *Telephone:* (2) 707-41-11 (office). *Fax:* (2) 707-45-79 (office). *E-mail:* natodoc@hq.nato.int (office). *Website:* www.nato.int (office).

BENBITOUR, Ahmed, MBA, PhD; Algerian economist, academic and fmr politician; b. 20 June 1946, Ghardaia; m.; four c. *Education:* Univ. of Algiers, Univ. of Montreal, Canada. *Career:* fmr CEO Nat. Co. of Studies and Processing, Nat. Co. of Juice and Tinned Fruits of Algeria; fmr Prof. of Business Man.; fmr mem. Parl., Chair.Econ. and Finance Comm. at Council of the Nation (Senate); fmr consultant at World Bank and IMF; fmr Minister of Finance, of Energy, of Treasury; Prime Minister of Algeria 1999–2000; currently Lecturer, African Inst. for Econ. Devt and Planning, Dakar, Senegal. *Publications:* several publs on econ. reforms and finance. *Address:* African Institute for Economic Development and Planning, POBox 3186, 18524 Dakar, Senegal (office). *Telephone:* 823-10-20 (office). *Fax:* 822-29-64 (office). *E-mail:* idep@unidep.org (office). *Website:* www.unidep.org (office).

BENDTSEN, Bendt; Danish politician; *Minister for Economic and Business Affairs;* b. 25 March 1954. *Education:* agricultural school, Danish Police Acad. *Career:* farm hand 1971–75; police constable 1980, Detective, Odense Criminal Investigation Dept 1984; mem. Bd local Conservative constituency org. 1982; his draft proposal for Party's official policy on legal issues approved by Conservative Nat. Congress 1987; mem. Odense City Council 1989, subsequently Political Spokesman; Deputy Chair. Odense Criminal Investigation Asscn 1989–92; parl. cand. (Conservative) 1990, 1992, 2001; substitute mem. Parl. April 1994, mem. Parl. Sept. 1994–; Leader, Conservative Party and Conservative Group in Danish Parl. 1999–; Minister for Econ. and Business Affairs 2001–, Minister for Nordic Cooperation 2001–02. *Address:* Ministry of Economic Affairs, Business and Trade, Slotsholmsgade 10–12, 1216 Copenhagen K, Denmark (office). *Telephone:* 33-92-33-50 (office). *Fax:* 33-12-37-78 (office). *E-mail:* oem@oem.dk (office). *Website:* www.oem.dk (office).

BENDUKIDZE, Kakha Avtandilovich, BSc; Georgian business executive, government official and scientist; *Head, Chancellery of the Government;* b. 20 April 1956, Tbilisi. *Education:* Tbilisi State Univ., Lomonosov State Univ., Moscow. *Career:* Sr Lab. Asst and Scientific Research Asst, USSR

Acad. of Sciences Inst. of Biochemistry and Physiology of Microorganisms 1981–85; Head, Molecular Genetics Lab., Scientific Research Inst. of Biotechnology 1985–92; f. Bioprocess Asscn 1988, Dir 1990–92; Chair. Bd of Dirs Promtorgbank (Industrial and Trade Bank) 1992–93; Chief Dir NIPEK (Nat. Oil Investment Corpn) 1993–95; co-f. Russian Business Round Table 1993; Chair. Uralmash-Izhora Group 1995–98, CEO 1998–2004; Prof., Higher School of Econs, Moscow 2002–; Minister of Econ. Devt June–Dec. 2004, State Minister, responsible for Econ. Reforms Dec. 2004–2007; Head, Chancellery of the Govt 2008–.
Address: Chancellery of the Government, 0105 Tbilisi, P. Ingorovka 7, Georgia (office). *Telephone:* (32) 92-26-87 (office). *Fax:* (32) 92-10-69 (office). *E-mail:* primeminister@geo.gov.ge (office). *Website:* www.government.gov.ge (office).

BENEDICT XVI, His Holiness Pope (Joseph Alois Ratzinger); German ecclesiastic; b. 16 April 1927, Marktl am Inn, Bavaria. *Education:* Univ. of Munich. *Career:* ordained Chaplain 1951; Prof. of Theology, Freising 1958, Bonn 1959–63, Münster 1963–66, Tübingen 1966–69, Regensburg 1969; co-f. Communio (theological journal) 1972; apptd Archbishop of Munich-Freising 1977–82; cr. Cardinal of Munich by Pope Paul VI 1977; Cardinal Bishop of the Episcopal See of Velletri-Segni 1993; fmr Chair. Bavarian Bishops' Conf.; Prefect, Sacred Congregation for the Doctrine of the Faith 1981–2005; Vice-Dean Coll. of Cardinals 1998–2002, Dean 2002–05; Titular Bishop of Ostia 2002; presided over funeral of Pope John Paul II and the Conclave which elected him April 2005; elected Pope 19 April 2005; Pres. Int. Theological Comm., Pontifical Biblical Comm.; mem. of the Congregations for the Oriental Churches, for the Divine Worship and the Discipline of the Sacrament, for the Bishops, for the Evangelization of Reapers, for Catholic Educ.; mem. Pontifical Council for the Promotion of Christian Unity; Dr hc (Navarra) 1998, numerous hon. doctorates.
Publications: books and articles on theological matters including Without Roots (with Marcello Pera) 2006.
Address: Palazzo Apostolico Vaticano, 00120 Città del Vaticano, Rome, Italy. *Website:* www.vatican.va.

BENGOA ALBIZU, Vicente, BSc; Dominican Republic economist; *Secretary of State for Finance; Education:* Univ. of Chile. *Career:* Prof. of Econs and Public Finance, Univ. of Santo Domingo 1973–94, Dir Econs Dept, Technological Inst. 1978–82; Superintendent of Banking 1997–2000; Deputy in Nat. Ass. 1982–86; Sec. of State for Finance 2004–.
Address: Secretariat of State for Finance, Avenida México 45, esq. Leopoldo Navarro, Apdo. 1478, Santo Domingo, DN, Dominican Republic (office). *Telephone:* 687-5131 (office). *Fax:* 682-0498 (office). *E-mail:* webmaster@finanzas.gov.do (office). *Website:* www.finanzas.gov.do (office).

BENHABIB, Seyla, MA, PhD; American political scientist, philosopher and academic; *Eugene Meyer Professor of Political Science and Professor of Philosophy, Yale University;* b. Istanbul, Turkey; m. James A. Sleeper; one d. *Education:* American Coll. for Girls, Istanbul, Brandeis and Yale Univs, USA. *Career:* Prof., New School for Social Research 1991–93; Prof., Dept of Govt and Sr Research Fellow, Center for European Studies, Harvard Univ. 1993–2000; Ed.-in-Chief Constellations: An International Journal of Critical and Democratic Theory 1993–97; Visiting Sr Fellow, Institut für Wissenschaft vom Menschen, Vienna, Austria 1996; Eugene Meyer Prof. of Political Science and Prof. of Philosophy, Yale Univ. 2000–; Baruch de Spinoza Distinguished Professorship, Univ. of Amsterdam 2000; Russell Sage Foundation Fellow 2000–01; Seeley Lectures, Cambridge 2002, Tanner Lectures, Berkeley 2004; Dr hc (Univ. of Utrecht) 2004.
Publications include: Critique, Norm and Utopia: A Study of the Foundations of Critical Theory 1986, Situating the Self: Gender, Community and Postmodernism in Contemporary Ethics 1992, The Reluctant Modernism of Hannah Arendt 1996, Feminist Contentions: A Philosophical Exchange 1996; (as ed.): Feminism as Critique: Essays on the Politics of Gender in Late-Capitalist Societies 1987, The Communicative Ethics Controversy (co-ed with Fred Dallmayr) 1990, On Max Horkheimer (co-ed. with Wolfgang Bonss and John McCole) 1993, The Philosophical Discourses of Modernity 1996, Democracy and Difference: Changes Boundaries of the Political 1996, Transformation of Citizenship – Dilemmas of the Nation-State in the Era of Globalization 2000, The Claims of Culture – Equality and Diversity in the Global Era 2002, The Rights of Others: The John Seeley Lectures 2004, Another Cosmopolitanism, with Responses by Jeremy Waldron, Bonnie Honig and Will Kymlicka; (trans.): Hegel's Ontology and the Theory of Historicity by Herbert Marcuse 1987; more than 100 articles on social and political thought, feminist theory and the history of modern political theory.
Address: Room 211, Department of Political Science, Yale University, PO Box 208301, 124 Prospect Street, New Haven, CT 06520-8301, USA (office). *Telephone:* (203) 436-3693 (office). *Fax:* (203) 432-6196 (office).

E-mail: seyla.benhabib@yale.edu (office). *Website:* www.yale.edu/polisci/people/sbenhabib.html (office).

BENHAMOUDA, Boualem, DIur; Algerian politician and lexicographer; b. (Boualem Benhamouda), 8 March 1933, Cherchell; m.; two s. one d. *Education:* Algiers Univ. *Career:* served with Army of Nat. Liberation 1956–62; mem. Parl. 1962–65; Minister of Ex-Combatants 1965–70, of Justice 1970–77, of Public Works 1977–80, of the Interior 1980–82, of Finance 1982–86; responsible for Inst. of Global Studies of Strategy 1986–90; mem. Political Bureau of Nat. Liberation Front (FLN) 1979–, Chair. FLN Cttee on Educ. Training and Culture 1979–80, Gen. Sec. FLN 1995–2001, currently mem. Exec. Organ; Medal of Liberation. *Publications:* The Keys of Arabic Language 1991, The Arabic Origin of Some Spanish Words 1991, The Democratic Practice of Power (Between Theory and Reality) 1992, Spanish-Arabic Pocket Dictionary 1993, The Arabic Origin of About 1000 French Words, General French-Arabic Dictionary 1996, General Arabic-French Dictionary 2000, 2001, Citizenship and Power 2006, Read and Understand The Coran 2006.
Address: Siege du Parti du FLN, Rue du Stade, Hydra, Algiers (office); 5 Rue de Frère Zennouch, El-Biar, Algiers, Algeria (home). *Telephone:* (21) 694701 (office). *Fax:* (21) 923538 (home).

BENJAMIN, John Oponjo; Sierra Leonean politician; b. 29 Nov. 1952, Segbwema. *Career:* Chief Sec. of State, Nat. Provisional Ruling Council (NPRC) 1992; Sec.-Gen. NPRC Govt 1993; Interim Chair. Nat. Unity Party 1997; Minister of Finance 2005–07; Exec. Dir African Information Tech. Holdings.
Address: c/o Ministry of Finance, Secretariat Building, George Street, Freetown, Sierra Leone (office).

BENN, Rt Hon. Anthony (Tony) Neil Wedgwood, PC, MA; British politician, writer and broadcaster; b. 3 April 1925, London; m. Caroline de Camp 1949 (died 2000); three s. one d. *Education:* Westminster School and New Coll., Oxford. *Career:* RAF pilot 1943–45; Univ. of Oxford 1946–49; Producer, BBC 1949–50; Labour MP for Bristol SE 1950–60, compelled to leave House of Commons on inheriting peerage 1960, re-elected and unseated 1961, renounced peerage and re-elected 1963, contested and lost Bristol E seat in 1983, re-elected as mem. for Chesterfield 1984–2001; Nat. Exec. Labour Party 1959–94; Chair. Fabian Soc. 1964; Postmaster-Gen. 1964–66; Minister of Tech. 1966–70, of Power 1969–70; Shadow Minister of Trade and Industry 1970–74; Sec. of State for Industry and Minister of Posts and Telecommunications 1974–75; Sec. of State for Energy 1975–79; Vice-Chair. Labour Party 1970, Chair. 1971–72; Chair. Labour Party Home Policy Cttee 1974–82; cand. for Leadership of Labour Party 1976, 1988, for Deputy Leadership 1971, 1981; Pres. Socialist Campaign Group of Labour MPs, EEC Energy Council 1977, Labour Action for Peace 1997–2007, currently Pres. Stop the War Coalition; Visiting Prof. of Politics, LSE 2001–02; fmr mem. Bureau Confed. of Socialist Parties of the European Community; numerous TV and radio broadcasts; Freeman of the City of Bristol 2003; Hon. Fellow, New Coll. Oxford 2005; Hon. LLD (Strathclyde, Williams Coll., USA, Brunel, Bristol, Univ. of West of England, Univ. of N London); Hon. DTech (Bradford); Hon. DSc (Aston); Dr hc (Paisley). *Television:* Speaking Up in Parliament 1993, Westminster Behind Closed Doors 1995, New Labour in Focus 1998, Tony Benn Speaks 2001. *Recordings:* The BBC Benn Tapes 1994, 1995, Writings on the Wall (with Roy Bailey) 1996, Tony Benn's Greatest Hits 2003, An Audience with Tony Benn 2003. *Publications:* The Privy Council as a Second Chamber 1957, The Regeneration of Britain 1964, The New Politics 1970, Speeches by Tony Benn 1974, Arguments for Socialism 1979, Arguments for Democracy 1981, Parliament, People and Power 1982, The Sizewell Syndrome 1984, Writings on the Wall: A Radical and Socialist Anthology 1215–1984 (ed.) 1984, Out of the Wilderness: Diaries 1963–67 1987, Office Without Power: Diaries 1968–72 1988, Fighting Back: Speaking Out for Socialism in the Eighties 1988, Against the Tide: Diaries 1973–76 1989, Conflicts of Interest: Diaries 1977–80 1990, A Future for Socialism 1991, End of an Era: Diaries 1980–90 1992, Common Sense: A New Constitution for Britain (with Andrew Hood) 1993, Years of Hope: Diaries 1940–1962 1994, The Benn Diaries 1940–1990 1995, Free at Last: Diaries 1991–2001 2002, Free Radical: New Century Essays 2003, Dare to be a Daniel (memoir) 2004, More Time for Politics: Diaries 2001–07 2007.
Address: 12 Holland Park Avenue, London, W11 3QU, England (office). *Telephone:* (20) 7229-0779 (office). *Fax:* (20) 7229-9693 (office). *E-mail:* tony@tbenn.fsnet.co.uk (office).

BENNETT, Brian Maurice; British diplomatist; b. 1 April 1948; m.; three s. *Career:* joined FCO 1971, Desk Officer, Western Orgs Dept 1971–73, Desk Officer, Personnel Policy Dept 1979–83, Desk Officer, Man. Review 1992–94, Desk Officer, Cen. European Dept 1994–97, Deputy Head, Personnel Services Dept 2001–02; Third Sec., Information, Prague, Czechoslovakia 1973–76; Third Sec., Chancery, Helskinki, Finland

1977–79; Second Sec., Commercial, Bridgetown, Barbados 1983–86; Second, later First, Sec., UK Del. to Mutual and Balanced Force Reductions Talks, Vienna, Austria 1986–88; First Sec., The Hague, Netherlands 1988–92; Deputy Head of Mission, Tunis, Tunisia 1997–2000; Amb. to Belarus 2003–07.
Address: Foreign and Commonwealth Office, King Charles Street, London, SW1A 2AH, England (office). *Telephone:* (20) 7008-1500 (office). *Website:* www.fco.gov.uk (office).

BENNOUNA, Mohamed, DIntLaw; Moroccan diplomatist, academic, lawyer and international judge; *Judge, International Court of Justice;* b. 29 April 1943, Marrakech; m.; three c. *Education:* Univ. of Nancy, Sorbonne Univ., Paris, France and The Hague Acad. of Int. Law, Netherlands. *Career:* Prof. of Public Law and Political Science, Univ. of the Sorbonne, Paris 1972–75; Prof., Faculty of Law, Mohammed V Univ. of Rabat and Casablanca 1975–79, Dean 1979–85; Dir-Gen. Arab World Inst. 1991–98; Judge, Int. Criminal Tribunal for the fmr Yugoslavia 1998–2001; Perm. Rep. of Morocco to UN, New York 1985–89, 2001–05; Judge, Int. Court of Justice 2006–, Judge ad hoc for dispute between Benin and Niger 2002; Chair. UN Compensation Comm., Geneva 1992–95, Group of 77 and China, UN 2003; mem. UNESCO Int. Panel on Democracy and Devt 1997–, UNESCO World Comm. on Ethics of Scientific Knowledge and Tech. (COMEST) 2002–, UNESCO Int. Bioethics Cttee 1992–98, UN Int. Law Comm., Geneva 1992–95; Nat. Prize for Culture, Morocco, Medal for Culture, Yemen; Chevalier de l'Ordre National de la Légion d'honneur.
Address: International Court of Justice, Peace Palace, 2517 KJ The Hague, Netherlands (office). *Telephone:* (70) 3022323 (office). *Fax:* (70) 3649928 (office). *Website:* www.icj-cij.org (office).

BENSAOU, Ben M., MA, MSc, PhD, DEA; French research institute director, professor of management and international business consultant; *Professor of Technology Management and Asian Business, Institut Européen d'Administration des Affaires (INSEAD);* m. Masako Bensaou; three s. *Education:* Institut Nat. Polytechnique de Grenoble, Ecole Nat. des TPE, Lyon, Hitotsubashi Univ., Tokyo, Massachusetts Inst. of Tech. Sloan School of Man. *Career:* consultant for int. corpns 1993–; Visiting Prof., Aoyama Gakuin Univ., Tokyo; teacher in Exec. Programs, Keio Business School, Tokyo; Visiting Assoc. Prof., Harvard Business School 1998–99; currently Prof. of Tech. Man. and Asian Business, INSEAD and Dir Euro-Asia Centre; developed two new MBA courses at INSEAD; mem. Editorial Bd Information Systems Research, MIS Quarterly, MISQ Executive. *Publications:* numerous papers in business and management journals.
Address: INSEAD, Boulevard de Constance, 77306 Fontainebleau Cedex, France (office). *Telephone:* 1-60-72-40-31 (office). *Fax:* 1-60-72-40-49 (office). *E-mail:* ben.bensaou@insead.edu (office). *Website:* www.insead.edu (office).

BENSBERG, Mark; British diplomatist; *High Commissioner to Namibia; Career:* joined FCO 1980, several postings in Africa, including Embassies and High Comms in Nigeria, Mozambique, Cameroon, Tanzania, Uganda and Ethiopia 1980s, Ghana and Togo 1990s, Democratic Repub. of the Congo and Repub. of Congo –2006, Sierra Leone 2007, High Commr to Namibia 2007–.
Address: British High Commission, 116 Robert Mugabe Avenue, PO Box 22202, Windhoek, Namibia (office). *Telephone:* (61) 274800 (office). *Fax:* (61) 228895 (office). *E-mail:* windhoek.general@fco.gov.uk (office). *Website:* www.britishhighcommission.gov.uk/namibia (office).

BENTÉGEAT, Gen. Henri; French army officer and diplomatist; *Chairman, Military Committee, European Union;* b. 27 May 1946, Talence; m.; four c. *Education:* Mil. Acad. of St Cyr, Institut d'Études Politiques de Paris. *Career:* jr officer in French Armed Forces, serving in Germany, Senegal, France and Djibouti 1968–73; as field grade officer, served in Army Public Information Service, Chief Operations of 9th Marine Div., Commdr Marine Infantry and Armoured Bn 1988–90; Asst Defence Attaché, Embassy in Washington, DC 1990–92; Asst to Chief of Mil. Staff of Pres. of Repub. 1993–96; Commdr French Forces in West Indies 1996–98; Asst to Dir for Strategic Affairs, Ministry of Defence 1998–99; Chief of Mil. Staff of Pres. of Repub. 1999–2002; Chief of Defence Staff 2002–06; Chair. EU Mil. Cttee 2006–; apptd Maj.-Gen. 1998, Lt-Gen. 1999, Gen. 2001; Chevalier, Ordre nat. du Mérit 1995, Légion d'honneur 2002.
Address: EU Military Committee, rue de la loi 175, 1048 Brussels, Belgium (office). *Telephone:* 22-81-96-92 (office). *Fax:* 22-81-96-93 (office). *E-mail:* henri.bentegeat@consilium.europa.eu (office). *Website:* consilium.europa.eu (office).

BENYAMINA, Ahmed; Algerian diplomatist; *Ambassador to Greece; Career:* past positions include Counsellor, Office of the Perm. Rep. to UN, New York and Sr Adviser to the Minister, Ministry of Foreign Office; fmr Amb. to UK, Amb. to Greece (also accred to Albania) 2005–.

Address: Embassy of Algeria, Leoforos Vassileos Konstantinou 14, 106 74 Athens, Greece (office). *Telephone:* (21) 07264191 (office). *Fax:* (21) 07018681 (office). *E-mail:* ambdzath@otenet.gr (office).

BERARDI, Fabio, BSc; San Marino geologist and politician; b. 26 May 1959, Borgo Maggiore; m. Emanuele Bollini; two s. *Education:* Liceo Classico, Univ. of Bologna. *Career:* began career with Sotecsa SA (Studio di Geologia Tecnica), San Marino 1984–86; mem. Council Borgo Maggiore 1984–89, 1995–98; Consultant, Studio Geotecnico Italiano, Milan 1986–89; pvt. practice as geologist 1989–95; Co-ordinator Dept of Territory, Environment and Agric. 1995–98; Pres. Admin. Council Azienda Autonoma di Stato per i Servizi Pubblici 1997–98; mem. Consiglio Grande Generale (Parl.) 1998–, Sec. of State for Territory, Environment and Agric. 2001–03, for Foreign and Political Affairs and Econ. Planning 2003–06; mem. Partito Socialista Sammarinese (PSS), mem. PSS Secr. 1999–; fmr Pres. Order of San Marino Geologists.
Address: c/o Secretariat of State for Foreign and Political Affairs and Economic Planning, Palazzo Begni, Contrada Omerelli, 47890 San Marino, San Marino (office).

BERDENNIKOV, Grigory Vitalievich; Russian diplomatist; b. 24 Dec. 1950, Moscow; m.; one d. *Education:* Moscow Inst. of Int. Relations. *Career:* diplomatic service 1973–, sec., attachè Mission in UN, New York 1973–78, Sec. of Div. USSR Ministry of Foreign Affairs 1978–81, Second then First Sec. Mission to UN, Geneva 1981–86, Counsellor, Chief of Div., Deputy Chief Dept of Armament Reduction and Disarmament, USSR (now Russian) Ministry of Foreign Affairs 1986–92, Deputy Minister of Foreign Affairs of Russia 1992–94, 1999–2001, Dir Dept of Security and Disarmament 1998–99; Perm. Rep. to Disarmament Conf. Geneva 1994–98; Perm. Rep. of Russia at Int. Orgs in Vienna 2001–06; Amb.-at-Large, Ministry of Foreign Affairs 2006–; Order of Friendship 1997; 850th Anniversary of Moscow Medal 1998, Presidential Letter of Gratitude 2000.
Address: Ministry of Foreign Affairs, 119200 Moscow, Smolenskaya-Sennaya pl. 32/34, Russia (office). *Telephone:* (495) 244-16-06 (office). *Fax:* (495) 230-21-30 (office). *E-mail:* ministry@mid.ru (office). *Website:* www.mid.ru (office).

BERDYMUKHAMMEDOV, Gurbanguly Myalikgulyyevich, PhD; Turkmenistan politician and head of state; *President and Prime Minister;* b. 1957, Babarab, Ahal Prov. *Education:* Turkmen State Medical Inst. *Career:* mem. Dentistry Faculty, Turkmen State Medical Inst. 1979–97, Assoc. Prof. and Dean 1995–97; Head of Dentistry Centre, Ministry of Health 1995–97; Minister of Health 1997–2001; Deputy Prime Minister 2001–06; acting Pres. (following death of Saparmurat Niyazov) 2006–07, Pres. and Prime Minister 2007–; Chair. Nat. Olympic Cttee 2007–.
Address: Office of the President and the Council of Ministers, 744000 Aşgabat, ul. 2001 24, Presidential Palace, Turkmenistan (office). *Telephone:* (12) 35-45-34 (office). *Fax:* (12) 35-51-12 (office). *Website:* www.turkmenistan.gov.tm (office).

BERE, Tchao Sotou; Togolese diplomatist; *Ambassador to France;* m. Bèindou Sotou Bere. *Career:* fmr Amb. to Libya, currently Amb. to France (also accred to UK, Spain and Italy 2003–).
Address: Embassy of Togo, 8 rue Alfred Roll, 75017 Paris, France (office). *Telephone:* 1-43-80-12-13 (office). *Fax:* 1-43-80-06-05 (office). *E-mail:* france@ambassadetogo.org (office). *Website:* www.ambassadetogo.org (office).

BEREND, T. Ivan, PhD, DEcon; American economic historian and academic; *Professor of History, University of California, Los Angeles;* b. 11 Dec. 1930, Budapest; two d. *Education:* Univ. of Economics and Univ. of Sciences, Faculty of Philosophy, Budapest. *Career:* Asst Lecturer, Karl Marx Univ. of Economics 1953, Sr Lecturer 1960, Prof. of Econ. History 1964–, Head of Dept 1967–85, Rector 1973–79; Prof. of History, UCLA 1990–, Dir Center for European and Eurasian Studies 1993–2005; Gen. Sec. Hungarian Historical Soc. 1966–72, Pres. 1975–79; Corresp. mem. Hungarian Acad. of Sciences 1973–79, mem. 1979–, Pres. 1985–90; Fellowship, Ford Foundation, New York 1966–67; Visiting Fellow, St Antony's Coll., Oxford 1972–73; Visiting Prof., Univ. of Calif., Berkeley 1978; Visiting Fellow, All Souls Coll., Oxford 1980; Fellow, Woodrow Wilson Int. Center for Scholars, Washington, DC 1982–83; Co-Chair. Bd of Dirs Inst. for East–West Security Studies 1986; mem. Exec. Cttee of Int. Econ. Soc. 1982–86, Vice-Pres. 1986–1994; First Vice-Pres. Int. Cttee of Historial Sciences 1990–95, Pres. 1995–2000; Corresp. mem. Royal Historical Soc. 1981, Academia Europaea 1987, Bulgarian Acad. of Sciences 1988, British Acad. 1989, Austrian Acad. of Sciences 1989, Czechoslovak Acad. of Sciences 1988; Hon. DLitt (St John's Univ., New York) 1986, (Glasgow) 1990, (Janus Pannonius Univ., Pécs) 1994; Kossuth Prize 1961, State Prize 1985. *Publications:* (with György Ránki) Magyarország gyáripara 1900–1914 1955, Magyarország gyáripara a II.

világháboru elött és a háboru idöszakában 1933–1944 1958, Magyarország a fasiszta Németország "életterében" 1960, Magyarország gazdasága az I. világháboru után 1919–1929 1966, Economic Development in East-Central Europe in the 19th and 20th Centuries 1974, Hungary—A Century of Economic Development, Underdevelopment and Economic Growth, The European Periphery and Industrialization 1780–1914 1982, The Hungarian Economy in the Twentieth Century 1985, The European Economy in the Nineteenth Century 1987; (as sole author): Ujjáépités és a nagytöke elleni harc Magyarországon 1945–1948 1962, Gazdaságpolitika az elsö ötéves terv meginditásakor 1948–1950 1964, Öt elöadás gazdaságról és oktatásról 1978, Napjaink a történelemben 1980, Válságos évtizedek 1982, Gazdasági utkeresés 1983, The Crisis Zone of Europe 1986, Szocializmus és reform 1986, The Hungarian Economic Reforms 1990, Central and Eastern Europe 1944–93 – Detour from the Periphery to the Periphery 1996, Decades of Crisis: Central and Eastern Europe Before World War II 1998, History Derailed: Central and Eastern Europe in the 'Long' 19th Century 2003.
Address: Department of History, UCLA, 405 Hildgard Avenue, Los Angeles, CA 90096, USA (office). *Telephone:* (310) 825-1178 (office). *Fax:* (310) 206-3556 (office); (310) 206-3556 (home). *E-mail:* iberend@history .ucla.edu (office). *Website:* www.history.ucla.edu/berend (office).

BEREWA, Solomon; Sierra Leonean politician. *Career:* Attorney-Gen., Sierra Leone 1996–97, 1998–2002; Vice-Pres. 2002–07.
Address: c/o Office of the Vice-President, State House, Freetown, Sierra Leone (office).

BERGEN SCHMIDT, Ernst Ferdinand; Paraguayan government official and business executive; b. 5 Oct. 1963, Colonia Fernheim (Chaco paraguayo); m. Lucía Ruth Giesbrecht; three c. *Career:* has held positions with Tecnoservice SAECA, Inverfin SAECA, Century System SRL, IMAG SRL, Mercotec SRL; fmr Pres. Récord Electric; Minister of Industry and Commerce –2005, of Finance 2005–07, Econ. Adviser to Pres. of Paraguay 2007–.
Address: Office of the President, Asunción, Paraguay.

BERGMANN, Barbara Rose, MA, PhD; American economist and academic; *Professor Emerita of Economics, American University;* b. 20 July 1927, New York; m. Fred H. Bergmann 1965; one s. one d. *Education:* Cornell and Harvard Univs. *Career:* economist, US Bureau of Statistics, New York 1949–53, New York Metropolitan Regional Study 1957–61; Instructor, Harvard Univ. 1958–61; Sr Research Assoc., Harvard Econ. Research Project 1960–61; Sr Staff Economist, Council of Econ. Advisers, Washington, DC 1961–62; Assoc. Prof., Brandeis Univ. 1962–64; mem. sr staff, Brookings Inst. Washington, DC 1963–65; Sr Econ. Adviser, AID, Washington, DC 1966–67; Prof. of Econs, Univ. of Maryland College Park 1971–88; Distinguished Prof. of Econs, American Univ. Washington, DC 1988–97, Prof. Emer. 1997–; Vice-Pres. American Econ. Assocn 1976; columnist on econ. affairs New York Times 1981–82, Los Angeles Times 1983–; Pres. American Assocn of Univ. Profs 1990–92, Int. Assocn for Feminist Economists 1999; Hon. PhD (De Montford Univ., UK) 1996, (Muhlenberg Coll.) 2000 Carolyn Shaw Bell Award 2004. *Publications:* Projection of a Metropolis (co-author) 1961, The Impact of Highway Investment on Development (co-author), A Microsimulated Transactions Model of the U.S. Economy (co-author) 1985, The Economic Emergence of Women 1986, Saving Our Children from Poverty: What the United States Can Learn From France 1995, In Defense of Affirmative Action 1996, Is Social Security Broke? A Cartoon Guide to the Issues 1999, America's Child Care Problem: The Way Out (co-author) 2002.
Address: Department of Economics, American University, Washington, DC 20016, USA (office). *E-mail:* bbergman@wam.umd.edu (office). *Website:* www.american.edu/cas/econ/faculty/bergmann.htm (office).

BERGQUIST, Mats, PhD; Swedish diplomatist; m. *Career:* Amb. to Israel 1987–92, to Finland 1992–97, to UK 1997–2004; currently Int. Adviser, Secr. of Nat. Linnaeus Comm.
Address: National Linnaeus Commission, Swedish Royal Academy of Sciences, Lilla Frescativägen 4A, Stockholm, Sweden (office). *Telephone:* (8) 673-95-00 (office). *E-mail:* mats.bergquist@kva.se (office).

BERGSTEN, C. Fred, MA, PhD; American economist and research institute director; *Director, Peterson Institute for International Economics;* b. 23 April 1941, New York, NY; m. Virginia W. Bergsten; one s. *Education:* Cen Methodist Coll, Fayette, Mo., Fletcher School of Law and Diplomacy, Boston, Mass. *Career:* Asst for Int. Econ. Affairs, US Nat. Security Council 1969–71; Asst Sec. for Int. Econ. Affairs, US Treasury 1977–81; Dir Inst. for Int. Econs (now Peterson Inst. for Int. Econs) 1981–; Chair. Competitiveness Policy Council 1991–95, Asia-Pacific Econ. Cooperation (APEC) Eminent Persons Group 1993–95; mem. Ind. Task Force on the Future Int. Financial Architecture 2000, Int. Financial Insts Advisory

Comm. 2000; Sr Fellow, Council on Foreign Relations 1967–68, Brookings Inst. 1972–76, Carnegie Endowment for Int. Peace 1981; Hon. Fellow, Chinese Acad. of Social Sciences 1997; Chevalier Légion d'honneur 1985; Dept of State Meritorious Honor Award 1965, Dept of Treasury Exceptional Service Award 1981. *Publications include:* America in the World Economy: A Strategy for the 1990s 1988, Pacific Dynamism and the International Economic System (with M. Noland) 1993, Reconcilable Differences? United States-Japan Economic Conflict (with M. Noland) 1993, The Dilemmas of the Dollar (second edn) 1996, Global Economic Leadership and the Group of Seven 1996; Whither APEC? The Progress to Date and Agenda for the Future 1997, No More Bashing: Building a New Japan-United States Economic Relationship 2001, The Korean Diaspora in the World Economy 2003, Dollar Overvaluation and the World Economy 2003, Dollar Adjustment: How Far? Against What? 2004, The United States and the World Economy (ed.) 2005, China: The Balance Sheet 2006; numerous other books and journal articles.
Address: Peterson Institute for International Economics, 1750 Massachusetts Avenue, NW, Washington, DC 20036-1903 (office); 4106 Sleepy Hollow Road, Annandale, VA 22003, USA (home). *Telephone:* (202) 328-9000 (office); (703) 256-3802 (home). *Fax:* (202) 659-3225 (office). *E-mail:* kkeenan@petersoninstitute.org (office). *Website:* www.iie.com (office).

BERISHA, Kolë; Kosovo politician; b. 26 Oct. 1947, Dobërdol; m.; two c. *Career:* fmr high school teacher in Klina; fmrly Sec., Democratic League of Kosovo (LDK), Vice-Pres. 1998–; Pres., Ass. of Kosovo 2006–07; mem. Parl. Group of LDK, Cttee for Rules of Procedure of Ass.
Address: Kodra e Diellit, Rruga Sali Nivica, 10000 Priština; c/o Office for Media and Publications, Assembly of Kosovo, Rruga Nëna Terezë, Kosovo, 10000 Priština, Serbia. *Telephone:* (38) 211186.

BERISHA, Sali, PhD; Albanian cardiologist and politician; *Prime Minister;* b. 15 Oct. 1944, Tropojë; m.; two c. *Education:* Univ. of Tirana and studies in Paris, France. *Career:* worked as cardiologist in Tirana Cardiology Clinic; taught at Univ. of Tirana 1980–90; fmr mem. Albanian Workers' Party; co-f. Democratic Party of Albania (Partia Demokratike e Shqipërisë), Leader 1991–97, Chair. 1991–; mem. Kuvendi Popullor (People's Ass.) 1991–; Pres. of Albania 1992–97; Prime Minister 2005–; mem. Nat. Medical Research Cttee, European Cttee on Medical Scientific Research 1968–. *Publications:* has published several textbooks and scientific articles on cardiology; numerous political articles in newspapers and magazines.
Address: Office of the Prime Minister, Office of the Council of Ministers, Bulevardi Dëshmorët e Kombit, Tirana, Albania (office). *Telephone:* (4) 229980 (office). *Fax:* (4) 234818 (office). *E-mail:* kryeministri@km.gov.al (office). *Website:* www.keshilliministrave.al (office).

BERKVENS, Arjen; Dutch research institute director and historian; *Director, Alfred Mozer Stichting;* b. (Adrianus Johannes Berkvens), 16 Oct. 1968, Alkmaar; m. *Education:* Atheneum, Petrus Canisus Coll., Alkmaar, Free Univ., Amsterdam. *Career:* Chair. and mem. Bd SRVU Student Union, Free Univ., Amsterdam 1991–93, Student Asst to Prof. Sutherland 1992–93; Scientific Asst, Leiden Koninklijk Instituut voor Taal Land, Volkenkunde 1994; Project Man. Alfred Mozer Stichting (Foundation for Cen. and Eastern Europe, Dutch Labour Party—PvdA) 1995–2002, Dir 2002–; Policy Officer, Int. Secr., Dutch Labour Party 1995–2000; freelance activities in training, chairing meetings, writing articles and editing 1998–2004; Election Campaign Man., Dutch Labour Party 2002–04; personal campaign adviser to Wouter Bos 2003, Max van den Berg 2004; Sec.-Gen. European Forum for Democracy and Solidarity 2002–; Project Man. Jt MATRA Project with Univ. of Amsterdam in Novosibirsk, Russian Fed., Ministry of Foreign Affairs 2002–; mem. Bd Milieukontakt Oost-Europa 2001–04.
Address: Alfred Mozer Stichting, PO Box 1310, 1000 BH Amsterdam, Netherlands (office). *Telephone:* (20) 5512121 (office); 650510206 (mobile). *Fax:* (20) 5512250 (office). *E-mail:* aberkvens@pvda.nl (office); ams@pvda .nl (office). *Website:* www.alfredmozerstichting.nl (office); www .effectivetraining.org; www.europeanforum.net.

BERLAKOVITS, Christian, JD; Austrian diplomatist; *Ambassador to Italy;* *Education:* Accademia Diplomatica, Vienna. *Career:* at Ministry of Foreign Affairs 1974–76; Sec., Embassy in Rome 1976–78, Embassy in Belgrade 1978–82; at Ministry of Foreign Affairs 1982–86; Minister Counsellor, Embassy in Madrid 1987–92; Amb. to Algeria 1992–94; at Ministry of Foreign Affairs 1994–96; Dir of IV.5, Crisis Unit, Ministry of Foreign Affairs 1996–97; Head, Office IV.2, Cross-Border Traffic of People and Policies, Migration and Deputy Dir Gen. for Legal Affairs, Ministry of Foreign Affairs 1997–2002, Dir. Gen. for Legal and Consular Affairs 2002–07; Amb.to Italy 2007–.

Address: Embassy of Austria, Via G. B. Pergolesi 3, 00198 Rome, Italy (office). *Telephone:* (06) 8440141 (office). *Fax:* (06) 8543286 (office). *E-mail:* rom-ob@bmaa.gv.at (office). *Website:* www.austria.it (office).

BERLIJN, Maj.-Gen. D. L.; Dutch military officer; b. 18 March 1950, Amsterdam; m. Elly M. A. Hermelink, two s. *Education:* Royal Mil. Acad., Breda, Air Force Staff Coll. *Career:* served as Operations Officer, later Commdr, Transition and Conversion Div., Leeuwarden Air Base 1983–85; Supervisor, Fighter Weapon Instruction Training, Denmark 1987; Head, Fighter Weapons Br., Tactical Air Command 1988; Head of Operations and Training, Royal Netherlands Air Force Staff 1991–92, Head, Fighter Operations Div. 1994, Deputy Chief (Operations) and Air Commodore 1995; Chief of Flying Operations, Twenthe Air Base 1992; Commdr first F-16 detachment to Italy 1993; apptd Commdr Tactical Air Force, rank Maj.-Gen. 1998; Commdr-in-Chief Royal Netherlands Air Force 2000–04; Chief of the Defence Staff 2004–08; Legion of Merit (USA), Légion d'honneur (France); Long Service Medal, NATO Medal, Multinational Peace Operations Medal.
Address: c/o Ministry of Defence, Plein 4, POB 20701, The Hague 2500, Netherlands (office).

BERLUSCONI, Silvio; Italian politician and business executive; *Prime Minister;* b. 29 Sept. 1936, Milan; m. 1st; one d. one s.; m. 2nd Veronica Lari; three c. *Education:* Univ. of Milan. *Career:* started building and property devt business aged 26; f. Elinord construction co. 1962; built up Fininvest, major conglomerate with interests in commercial TV, printed media, publishing, advertising, insurance and financial services, retailing and football; worked on Milan 2 Housing project 1969; Canale 5 network began broadcasting 1980; bought Italia 1 TV network 1983, Rete 4 TV network 1984; took stake in La Cinq commercial TV network 1985, Chain, Cinema 5 (largest in Italy); bought Estudios Roma 1986; Milan AC Football Club 1986; La Standa (Italy's largest Dept store chain) 1988; Chair. Arnoldo Mondadori Editore SpA Jan.–July 1990, (half-share) 1991; Founder and Pres. Forza Italia political movt 1993, began full-time political career 1994, declaring he had stepped down from exec. posts in Fininvest, owned 51% of Mediaset (Italy's largest pvt. TV network operator) through Fininvest, reduced stake by one-third 2005; led Forza Italia to win general elections in alliance with Lega Nord and Alleanza Nazionale parties 1994; Prime Minister of Italy April–Dec. 1994, 2001–06, 2008–, also Minister of Foreign Affairs 2002; Founder and Pres. Casa delle Libertà (House of Freedoms) 2002–07, replaced by Popolo della Libertà 2007–; Pres. EU Council July–Sept. 2003; MEP 1999. *Recording:* Meglio 'ne Canzone (album) 2003.
Address: Office of the Prime Minister, Palazzo Chigi, Piazza Colonna 370, 00187 Rome (office); Fininvest Spa, Via Paleocapa 3, 20121 Milan, Italy. *Telephone:* (06) 67791; (02) 85411. *Fax:* (06) 6788255 (office). *E-mail:* redazione.web@governo.it (office). *Website:* www.governo.it (office); www .fininvest.it; www.casadelleliberta.net.

BERMÚDEZ-AGUILAR, Hernán Antonio; Honduran diplomatist; *Ambassador to Ecuador; Career:* fmr Amb. to UK; currently Amb. to Ecuador.
Address: Embassy of Honduras, Edif. World Trade Centre, Torre A, 5°, Of. 501, Avda 12 de Octubre 1942 y Luis Cordero, Apdo 17-03-4753, Quito, Ecuador (office). *Telephone:* (2) 222-3985 (office). *Fax:* (2) 222-0441 (office). *E-mail:* embhquito@yahoo.com (office).

BERMÚDEZ AMADO, Brig. Gen. Francisco; Guatemalan military officer, government official and diplomatist; *Ambassador to Taiwan; Career:* fmr Brig. Gen., Guatemalan Armed Forces; Minister of Nat. Defence 2006–07; Amb. to Taiwan 2007–.
Address: Embassy of Guatemala 3/F, 9-1 Lane 62, Tien Mou West Rd, Taipei 11156, Taiwan (office). *Telephone:* (2) 28756952 (office). *Fax:* (2) 28740699 (office). *E-mail:* embaguat.tw@iname.com (office). *Website:* www.geocities.com/WallStreet/Floor/8227 (office).

BERMÚDEZ MERIZALDE, Jaime, PhD; Colombian lawyer, politician and diplomatist; *Minister of Foreign Affairs;* b. 1966, Bogotá; m.; two c. *Education:* Univ. de los Andes, Univ. of Oxford, UK. *Career:* with Human Rights Advisory Office 1991–93; Adviser to Minister of Foreign Affairs 1993–94, also coordinator Neighborhood Commissions; pvt communications consultant –2002; Dir Asociación Primero Colombia (political asscn) 2002–06; communications adviser during presidential election campaign of Alvaro Uribe 2002, Presidential Adviser in Communications 2002–06; Amb. to Argentina 2006–07; Minister of Foreign Affairs 2008–; served as UN observer during South African presidential elections 1994.
Address: Ministry of Foreign Affairs, Palacio de San Carlos, Calle 10a, No 5-51, Bogotá, DC Colombia (office). *Telephone:* (1) 282-7811 (office). *Fax:* (1) 341-6777 (office). *Website:* www.minrelext.gov.co (office).

BERNANKE, Ben S., PhD; American economist, academic and government official; *Chairman of the Board of Governors, Federal Reserve System;* b. 21 June 1953, Augusta, Ga; m. Anna; two c. *Education:* Harvard Univ., Massachusetts Inst. of Tech. *Career:* Prof. of Econs and Public Affairs, Princeton Univ. 1985–96, Howard Harrison and Gabrielle Snyder Beck Prof. of Econs and Public Affairs and Chair Econs Dept 1996–2002; fmr Dir Monetary Econs Program, Nat. Bureau of Econ. Research (NBER), fmr mem. Business Cycling Dating Cttee; mem. Bd of Govs, Fed. Reserve System –2005, Chair. 2006–; Chair. Pres.'s Council of Econ. Advisers 2005–06; fmr mem. Montgomery Township Bd of Educ.; Fellow, Econometric Soc., American Acad. of Arts and Sciences; Guggenheim Fellowship, Sloan Fellowship. *Publications:* Principles of Microeconomics (co-author), Principles of Economics (co-author), Macroeconomics (co-author); numerous articles.
Address: Board of Governors of the Federal Reserve, 20th Street and Constitution Avenue, NW, Washington, DC 20551, USA (office). *Telephone:* (202) 452-3000 (office). *Fax:* (202) 452-3819 (office). *Website:* www.federalreserve.gov (office).

BERNARD-MEUNIER, Marie, BA, MSc; Canadian diplomatist and academic; *Researcher, Centre d'études et de recherches internationales de l'Université de Montréal;* b. Noranda, Quebec; m. Pierre Bernard; one s. *Education:* Coll. de Rouyn, Univ. de Montréal, École Nat. d'Admin., Paris, France. *Career:* joined Dept of Foreign Affairs 1972; overseas assignments in New York, Bonn, Paris, The Hague; served as Asst Deputy Minister, Global Issues and Culture Br., and Dir-Gen. Int. Orgs, Dept of Foreign Affairs and Int. Trade, Ottawa; Amb. to Netherlands 1996–2000, to Germany 2000–04; Diplomat-in-Residence, Stiftung Wissenschaft und Politik, Deutsches Institut für Internationale Politik und Sicherheit 2005; currently Researcher, Centre d'études et de recherches internationales de l'Université de Montréal, also currently mem. Bd of Public Policy Forum; Chair. Atlantik Bruecke; Guest Prof. Univ. of Toronto; elected to Exec. Bd, UNESCO, Paris 1989, Pres. 1991–93. *Publications:* Canada Among Nations (co-author) 2006, Reconquerir le Canada (co-author) 2007; contrib.: La Presse (columnist), Policy Options.
Address: 30 Berlioz apt 1012, Verdun, QC H3E 1L3, Canada (home). *Telephone:* (514) 343-6111 (office). *Fax:* (514) 343-7348 (office). *E-mail:* marie.bernard-meunier@videotron.ca (home). *Website:* www.cerium.ca (office).

BERNES, Thomas Anthony, BA; Canadian international organization official; *Director, Independent Evaluation Office, International Monetary Fund;* b. 21 March 1946, Winnipeg; m. Ann Boyd 1974 (divorced 1997); one s. one d. *Education:* Univ. of Manitoba. *Career:* Dir Gen. Trade Policy, Dept of Industry, Trade and Commerce 1981–82, Economic Policy Planning Secr. 1982–83; Head Gen. Trade Policy Div., OECD 1983–85; Dir GATT Affairs, Dept of Foreign Affairs and Int. Trade, Govt of Canada 1985–87; Dir Internal Econ. Relations, Dept of Finance 1987–88, Gen. Dir Int. Trade and Finance Br. 1988–91, Exec. Dir Coordinating Secr. on Canadian Unity, Office of the Deputy Minister 1991–92, Asst Deputy Minister, Int. Trade and Finance Br. 1992–95; G7 Finance Deputy 1995–96; Alt. Gov. for Canada, IMF, Asia Devt Bank, African Devt Bank and Inter-American Devt Bank 1996; Dir Canadian Export Devt Corpn 1996; Exec. Dir IMF 1996–2001; Exec. Sec., Devt Cttee of Int. Bank for Reconstruction and Devt (World Bank) and IMF 2001–05, Dir Ind. Evaluation Office, IMF 2005–.
Address: Independent Evaluation Office, International Monetary Fund, 700 19th Street, NW, Washington, DC 20431, USA (office). *Telephone:* (202) 623-9980 (office). *Fax:* (202) 623-9990 (office). *E-mail:* tbernes@imf .org (office). *Website:* www.ieo-imf.org (office).

BERNS, Alphonse; Luxembourg diplomatist; *Ambassador to Belgium;* b. 9 April 1952; m. Christine Poeker; two c. *Education:* Univ. of Aix-en-Provence, European Univ. Center (Law), Nancy, France. *Career:* with Directorate for Political Affairs, Ministry of Foreign Affairs 1977–79; Deputy Perm. Rep. to Council of Europe, Strasbourg (non-resident) 1978–79; Deputy Perm. Rep. to NATO, Brussels 1979–86; Dir for Budget, Finance and Admin, Ministry of Foreign Affairs 1986–88, Dir for Int. Econ. Relations and Dir for Devt Co-operation 1988–91; Amb. to USA (also accred. to Canada and Mexico) 1991–98; Sec. Gen. Ministry of Foreign Affairs 1998–2002; Perm. Rep. to UN and Int. Orgs, Geneva 2002–05; Amb. to Belgium 2005–, also Perm. Rep. to NATO; Commdr Order of the Oak Crown (Luxembourg), Officer, Order of Merit (Luxembourg), Kt with Crown, Order of Civil and Mil. Merit of Adolphe of Nassau (Luxembourg), Grand Cross Order of Civil Merit (Spain), Grand Cross Order of the Aztec Eagle (Mexico), Grand Cross Order of the Phoenix (Greece), Grand Officer Order of the Crown (Belgium), Commdr with Star, Royal Norwegian Order of Merit, Commdr with Star, Order of the Falcon (Iceland), Commdr Order of Merit (Portugal), Commdr Order of Merit (Germany).

Address: Embassy of Luxembourg, 75 ave de Cortenbergh, 1000 Brussels, Belgium (office). *Telephone:* (2) 737-57-00 (office). *Fax:* (2) 737-57-10 (office). *E-mail:* bruxelles.amb@mae.etat.lu (office).

BERTHELOT, Yves M.; French statistician and economist; *Co-director, United Nations Intellectual History Project;* b. 15 Sept. 1937, Paris; m. Dosithée Yeatman 1961; three s. one d. *Education:* Ecole Polytechnique and Ecole Nationale de la Statistique et de l'Admin Economique. *Career:* Dir of Studies in the Ministry of Planning, Ivory Coast 1965–68; Chief of the Study of Enterprises Div., then Chief of Service of Programmes of INSEE (Institut Nat. de la Statistique et des Etudes Economiques) 1971–75; Chief, Service des Etudes et Questions Int., French Ministry of Co-operation 1976–78; Dir of Research, Devt Centre of OECD, Paris 1978–81; Dir CEPII (Prospective Studies and Int. Information Centre) 1981–85; Deputy Sec.-Gen. of UNCTAD 1985–93; Exec. Sec. UN Econ. Comm. for Europe 1993–2000; Vice-Pres. Fondation Européenne pour le Développement durable des Régions 1996–; Sr Research Fellow and Head, Geneva Liaison Office, City Univ. of New York Grad. Center 2000–, Co-dir UN Intellectual History Project, Geneva 2000–; mem. High Comm. Int. Co-operation 2001–; Pres. Comité Français de Solidarité Internationale 2002–, Political and Ethical Knowledge on Economic Activities 2003–; Chevalier Ordre Nat. du Mérite, Officier Ordre Nat. (Côte d'Ivoire). *Publications:* numerous articles on economics. *Address:* United Nations Intellectual History Project, Geneva Liaison Office, Palais des Nations, B 148, 1211 Geneva 10, Switzerland (office); City University of New York, 365 Fifth Avenue, New York, NY 10021, USA. *Telephone:* (22) 9072290 (office). *E-mail:* yberthelot@bluewin.ch (office); berthelotyd@wanadoo.fr. *Website:* www.unhistory.org (office).

BERTINI, Hon. ; Catherine Ann, BA; American international organization official and academic; *Professor of Public Administration, Maxwell School of Citizenship and Public Affairs, Syracuse University;* b. 30 March 1950, Syracuse, New York. *Education:* Cortland High School, NY, State Univ. of New York at Albany. *Career:* Youth Dir, New York Republican State Cttee 1971–74, Republican Nat. Cttee 1975–76; Man., Public Policy, Container Corpn of America 1977–87; Dir Office of Family Assistance, US Dept of Health and Human Services 1987–89; Acting Asst Sec., US Dept of Health and Human Services 1989, Asst Sec. US Dept of Agric. 1989–92; Exec. Dir World Food Programme of UN, Rome 1992–2002; mem. UN Sec.-Gen.'s Panel of High-Level Personalities on African Devt 1992–95; UN Sec.-Gen.'s Special Envoy on Drought in the Horn of Africa 2000–01; UN Sec.-Gen.'s Personal Humanitarian Envoy to Middle East 2002; Chair. UN System Standing Cttee on Nutrition 2002–06; UN Under-Sec.-Gen. for Man. 2002–05; Prof. of Public Admin, Maxwell School of Citizenship and Public Affairs, Syracuse Univ. 2005–; Fellow, Inst. of Politics, Harvard Univ. 1986; Commr Ill. State Scholarship Comm. 1979–84, Ill. Human Rights Comm. 1985–87; Towsley Foundation Policy Maker in Residence, Gerald R. Ford School of Public Policy, Univ. of Michigan 2002; Sr Fellow, Bill & Melinda Gates Foundation 2007–; Order of Merit (Italy) 2002; Hon. DSc (McGill Univ., Montreal) 1997, (Pine Major Coll.) 2000; Hon. DHL (State Univ. of New York, Cortland) 1999, (American Univ., Rome) 2001, (Loyola Univ., Chicago) 2002, (Dakota Wesleyan Univ., Mitchell, SDak) 2003; (Univ. of S Carolina, Spartanburg) 2003, (Colgate Univ.) 2004, Dr hc (Slovak Agricultural Univ., Nitra) 1999, Hon. DPS (John Cabot Univ., Rome) 2001; Leadership in Human Services Award, American Public Welfare Asscn 1990, Excellence in Public Service Award, American Acad. of Pediatrics 1991, Leadership Award, Nat. Asscn of WIC Dirs 1992, Quality of Life Award, Auburn School of Human Sciences 1996, Building World Citizenship Award, World Asscn of Girl Guides/Scouts 2001, Prize of Excellence, Asscn of African Journalists 2002, World Food Prize Laureate 2003, Univ. of Albany Medallion 2002, Leadership Award, Chicago Council on Foreign Relations 2004, Life Time Achievement in Child Nutrition Award, School Nutrition Asscn 2007. *Address:* Department of Public Administration, 351 Eggers Hall, The Maxwell School of Syracuse University, Syracuse, NY 13244, USA (office). *Telephone:* (315) 443-1341 (office). *Fax:* (315) 443-9085 (office). *E-mail:* cbertini@maxwell.syr.edu (office). *Website:* www.maxwell.syr.edu (office).

BERTONE, HE Cardinal Tarcisio, DCnL; Italian ecclesiastic and professor of canon law; *Secretary of State, Roman Curia;* b. 2 Dec. 1934, Romano Canavese. *Education:* Oratorio di Valdocco, Turin, Salesian novitiate of Monte Oliveto, Pinerolo, Pontifical Salesian Athenaeum (now Univ.), Rome. *Career:* entered Soc. of St Francis and St John (Salesian Order); made religious profession 1950; ordained priest by Albino Mensa, Bishop of Ivrea 1960; Prof. of Special Moral Theology, Pontifical Salesian Univ. 1967, Dir of Theologians 1974–76, Prof. of Canon Law 1976–91, Dean Faculty of Canon Law 1979–85, Vice-Rector 1987–89, apptd Rector 1989; Guest Prof. of Public Ecclesiastical Law, Pontifical Lateran Univ. 1978; collaborated in drafting revision of Code of Canon Law; Archbishop of Vercelli 1991–95; Sec. of Congregation of Doctrine of Faith 1995–2002;

entrusted with publ. of third secret of Fatima by Pope John Paul II 2000; Archbishop of Genoa 2002–06; Sec. of State, Roman Curia 2006–; cr. Cardinal Priest of S. Maria Ausiliatrice in via Tuscolana 2003–; consultant to several dicasteries of Roman Curia; Hon. PhD (Catholic Univ. of Salta, Argentina) 2005. *Address:* Office of the Secretary of State, 00120, Città del Vaticano, Italy (office). *Telephone:* (06) 69883913 (office). *Fax:* (06) 69885255 (office). *Website:* www.vatican.va/roman_curia/secretariat_state/index.htm (office).

BERTRAM, Christoph, DrJur; German research director, academic and journalist; *Chairman, Berlin Institute for Demography and Development;* b. 3 Sept. 1937, Kiel; m. 1st Renate Bertram (née Bergemann) (divorced 1980, died 1981); m. 2nd Ragnhild Bertram (née Lindemann); two s. two d. *Education:* Univs of Berlin and Bonn, Institut d'Etudes Politiques, Paris,France. *Career:* Dir Int. Inst. for Strategic Studies (IISS), London 1974–82; Foreign Policy Ed. Die Zeit, Hamburg 1982–98; Dir German Inst. for Int. and Security Affairs (SWP), Berlin 1998–2005; Steven Muller Chair for German Studies, Johns Hopkins Univ., Bologna Center 2005; Chair. Berlin Inst. for Demography and Devt 2006–. *Address:* Philosophenweg 27, 22763 Berlin, Germany (home). *Telephone:* (40) 881-89799 (home). *E-mail:* christoph.bertram@t-online.de (home).

BĒRZIŅŠ, Andris; Latvian politician and historian; b. 4 Aug. 1951, Riga; m.; two c. *Education:* Latvian State Univ. *Career:* teacher and admin. in several schools 1975–82; Head, Div. of Personnel Training Cttee for Vocational and Tech. Training 1982–86; Head, Div. State Cttee for Labour and Social Affairs 1986–90; Head, Div., Deputy Dir Welfare Dept Ministry of Econs 1990–92; Deputy Minister, concurrently Head, Labour Dept Ministry of Welfare 1992–93; State Minister of Labour 1993–94; Deputy Prime Minister, Minister of Welfare 1994–95; Minister of Labour 1995–97; Chair. Riga City Council 1997–2000; Prime Minister of Latvia 2000–02; Chair. Latvian Way (Latvijas ceļš) 2000–03; Strategic consultant for UNDP, Latvia 2004–. *Address:* Latvijas ceļš, Terbatas jela 4-9, 1001 Rīga (office); UNDP, 6 A/1 Ogres, 2015 Burmala, Latvia. *Telephone:* (2) 6728-5539 (office); 6781-1462. *Fax:* (2) 6728-1121 (office); 6703-5751. *E-mail:* lc@lc.lv (office); abkonsultants@apollo.lv. *Website:* www.lc.lv (office).

BĒRZIŅŠ, Indulis; Latvian politician and diplomatist; *Ambassador to UK;* b. 4 Dec. 1957, Madona; m. 1st Inese Bērziņš; one s. one d.; m. 2nd Ilze Gelnere. *Education:* Latvian State Univ. *Career:* Lecturer, Latvian State Univ. and Latvian Inst. of Agric. 1984–90; TV broadcaster 1988–89; Founder-mem. People's Front Movt for independence 1989; Deputy, Supreme Soviet Latvian Repub., Deputy Chair. Cttee on Foreign Affairs 1990–93, later Chair.; Dir Latvijas Ceļš Union 1993–; mem. People's Front of Latvia 1992–93, Latvia's Way Party 1993–; mem. Latvian del. to NATO 1993–95, Latvian Nat. Group to European Parl. 1995–97, 1998–99; Deputy Speaker of Saeima (Parl.) 1998–99; Minister of Foreign Affairs 1999–2002; Amb., State Sec.'s Bureau, Ministry of Foreign Affairs 2002–03; Amb. to Denmark 2003–05, to UK 2005–; Commdr, Ordre nat. du Mérite 1997, Commdr of the Three Stars Order (Latvia) 2000. *Address:* Embassy of Latvia, 45 Nottingham Place, London, W1U 5LY, England (office). *Telephone:* (20) 7312-0040 (office). *Fax:* (20) 7312-0042 (office). *E-mail:* embassy.uk@mfa.gov.lv (office). *Website:* www.london .mfa.gov.lv (office).

BESSMERTNYKH, Aleksandr Aleksandrovich, CandJurSc; Russian diplomatist; *President, International Foreign Policy Association;* b. 10 Nov. 1933, Biisk; m.; one s. one d. *Education:* Moscow State Inst. of Int. Relations. *Career:* joined Diplomatic Service 1957, with Embassy, Washington, DC 1970–83; fmr arms control negotiator; First Deputy Foreign Minister (with special responsibility for N America and the Middle East) 1987–90, Deputy 1986; Amb. to USA 1990–91; Minister of Foreign Affairs Jan.–Aug. 1991; mem. CP Cen. Cttee 1990–91; Head Policy Analysis Centre Soviet (now Russian) Foreign Policy Asscn 1991–92; Pres. Int. Foreign Policy Asscn 1992–, Chair. World Council of Fmr Foreign Ministers 1993–; Chair. Supervisory Bd Advanced Tech. Research Programs Foundation; Prof. Moscow Univ.; mem. Acad. of Social Sciences of Russian Fed.; Corresp. mem. Chilean Acad. of Social and Political Sciences; Order of Friendship of Peoples, Order of Peter the Great, Order of Lomonosov; Badge of Honour, various medals. *Publications:* numerous articles on foreign policy, diplomacy and military strategy. *Address:* International Foreign Policy Association, Yakovo-Apostolski per. 10, 105064 Moscow, Russia (office). *Telephone:* (495) 975-21-67 (office); (495) 698-50-08 (office). *Fax:* (495) 975-21-90 (office). *E-mail:* fpa .moscow@public.mtu.ru (office). *Website:* www.forpolicy.ru (office).

BETHEL, Paulette A., MA, PhD; Bahamian diplomatist and international official; *Permanent Representative, United Nations;* one d. *Education:*

Howard Univ., Univ. of Toronto, Canada, Univ. of Mass at Amherst, USA. *Career:* Lecturer in Sociology, Coll. of The Bahamas, Nassau 1976–77, Chair. Dept of Social Sciences 1977–78; Asst Social Affairs Officer, UN Centre for Social Devt and Humanitarian Affairs (CSDHA), Vienna 1980–83; Deputy Chief of Mission and Minister Counsellor, Perm. Mission to UN, New York 1983–88; Deputy Chief of Mission and Minister Counsellor, Embassy of the Bahamas and Perm. Mission to OAS, Washington, DC 1988–94; Dir Dept of Fellowships, OAS, Washington, DC 1994–97; Amb. and Perm. Rep. of The Bahamas to UN, New York 2003–; Vice-Pres. of Admin and Client Relations, Montaque Securities Int. (MSI), Nassau 1998–2000; Risk Man. and Compliance Man., Cardinal Int., Nassau 2000–02; head of dels to int. meetings; chair. numerous comms and cttees including UNIFEM 1994. *Publications:* Uneven Development in The Bahamas: Past and Present 1980.
Address: Permanent Mission of The Bahamas to the United Nations, 231 East 46th Street, New York, NY 10017, USA (office). *Telephone:* (212) 421-6925 (home). *Fax:* (212) 759-2135 (office). *E-mail:* bahamas@un.int (office). *Website:* www.un.int (office).

BEVANDA, Vjekoslav; Bosnia and Herzegovina politician. *Career:* currently Deputy Prime Minister and Minister of Finance, Fed. of Bosnia and Herzegovina.
Address: Ministry of Finance, Sarajevo, Mehmeda Spahe 5, Bosnia and Herzegovina (office). *Telephone:* (33) 203147 (office). *Fax:* (33) 203152 (office). *E-mail:* info@fmf.gov.ba (office). *Website:* www.fmf.gov.ba (office).

BEYER, John Charles; British diplomatist; *Ambassador to Moldova;* b. 29 April 1950; m. Letty Beyer; one s. one d. *Career:* Asia Researcher, Amnesty International 1981–82; Chinese language teacher, Univ. of Westminster 1982–84; Deputy Dir Sino-British Trade Council 1984–98, Dir China-Britain Trade Group 1991–98; joined FCO 1999, Head of Section, EU Dept 1999–2001, Deputy Head of Mission, Luxembourg 2002–05, Amb. to Moldova 2006–.
Address: British Embassy, str. N. Iorga 18, 2012 Chişinău, Moldova (office). *Telephone:* (22) 22-59-02 (office). *Fax:* (22) 24-25-00 (office). *E-mail:* enquiries.chisinau@fco.gov.uk (office). *Website:* www.britishembassy.md (office).

BEYRLE, John R., BA, MS; American diplomatist; *Ambassador to Bulgaria;* m. Jocelyn Greene; two d. *Education:* Grand Valley State Univ., Mich. and Nat. War Coll., Washington, DC. *Career:* career officer, Sr Foreign Service with rank of Minister-Counselor, overseas assignments have included postings to US Embassies in Moscow and Sofia as Political Officer and as Counselor for Political and Econ. Affairs at Embassy in Prague, has served as mem. US Delegation to Conventional Forces in Europe negotiations in Vienna, as staff officer to Secs of State George Shultz and James Baker, and as Pearson Fellow and Foreign Policy Adviser to the late Senator Paul Simon (Democrat, Ill.), Dir for Russian, Ukrainian and Eurasian Affairs, Nat. Security Council 1993–95, Deputy Special Adviser to Sec. of State for the New Independent States, US State Dept 1995, Acting Special Adviser –2002, Deputy Chief of Mission, Embassy in Moscow 2002–05, Amb. to Bulgaria 2005–; fmr Visiting Prof. of Nat. Security Studies, Nat. War Coll.
Address: Embassy of the USA, ul. Kozyak 16, Sofia 1407, Bulgaria (office). *Telephone:* (2) 937-51-00 (office). *Fax:* (2) 937-53-20 (office). *E-mail:* sofia@usembassy.bg (office). *Website:* bulgaria.usembassy.gov (office).

BEZHUASHVILI, Gela, LLM, MPA; Georgian politician, diplomatist and lawyer; *Head of Special Service, Foreign Intelligence Service;* b. 1 March 1967, Tetritskaro Region; m.; two s. one d. *Education:* Kyiv State Univ., Ukraine, Southern Methodist Univ. Law School and John F. Kennedy School of Govt, Harvard Univ., USA. *Career:* positions at Ministry of Foreign Affairs including Second Sec. of Int. Law Problems Div., Deputy Head of Dept then Deputy Head of Int. Law Bd 1991–93; Envoy, Embassy in Kazakhstan 1993–96; Dir Int. Law Dept 1997–2000; Deputy Minister of Defence 2000–04, Minister of Defence 2004; Asst to Pres. of Georgia on Nat. Security Issues and Sec. Nat. Security Council 2004–05; Minister of Foreign Affairs 2005–08; Head of Special Service, Foreign Intelligence Service 2008–; mem. Cttee on Int. Law, Cttee Against Corruption and Sub-Cttee on Protection of Nat. Minorities, European Council; Rep. of Georgia, Baku-Tbilisi-Ceyhan Law Documentation Package 1999–2000; Order of Merit, First Class (Ukraine) 2006, Order of Maarjamaa Rist III Class 2007; winner Edmund Mask Programe Nat. Competition (USA) 1995. *Publications:* International Law Aspects of the Foreign Policy of Georgia 2003; articles in professional journals of int. law, nat. minorities and self-determination.
Address: Foreign Intelligence Special Service, 4 Kekelidze Street Tbilisi, Georgia (office). *Telephone:* (32) 93-46-69 (ext. 101) (office). *Fax:* (32) 93-46-69 (office). *E-mail:* dir.int@fiss.gov.ge (office).

BHATTARAI, Krishna Prasad; Nepalese politician; b. 24 Dec. 1924, Banaras, India. *Career:* served 14 years' imprisonment for opposition to absolute monarchy in Nepal; Pres. Nepali Congress Party (banned for 29 years until 1990); Prime Minister of Nepal (presiding over interim multiparty Govt) 1990–91, 1999–2000, also Minister of Royal Palace Affairs, of Home Affairs, of Foreign Affairs, of Defence and of Women and Social Welfare.
Address: c/o Office of the Prime Minister, Central Secretariat, Singha Durbar, Kathmandu, Nepal.

BIANCHERI, Boris, BL, GCVO; Italian diplomatist; *President, Istituto per gli Studi di Politica Internazionale;* b. 3 Nov. 1930, Rome; m.; one s. one d. *Education:* Univ. of Rome. *Career:* entered diplomatic service 1956, Office of the Sec. of State, Ministry of Foreign Affairs 1956–58; Italian Embassy, Athens 1959; Econ. Affairs Dept, Ministry of Foreign Affairs 1964–67, Counsellor 1967–71; Sec.-Gen. of Govt Comm. for 1970 Universal Osaka Exhbn 1968; Political Counsellor, Italian Embassy, London 1972–75; Head of Office of Sec.-Gen. Ministry of Foreign Affairs 1975–78, Chef de Cabinet, Sec. of State for Foreign Affairs 1978, Minister Plenipotentiary 1979; Amb. to Japan 1980–84; Dir-Gen. Personnel and Admin., Ministry of Foreign Affairs 1984, Dir-Gen. Political Affairs 1985; Amb. to UK 1987–91, to USA 1991–95, Sec.-Gen. Ministry of Foreign Affairs 1995–97; Chair. Italian News Agency (Agenzia Nazionale Stampa Associata—ANSA) 1997–, MARSH (Gruppo MMC) 2001; Pres. Federazione Italiana Editori Giornali (Italian Fed. of Newspaper Publrs) 2004–; Pres. Istituto per gli Studi di Politica Internazionale (Inst. for Int. Studies) (ISPI), Milan 1997–; mem. Bd of Dirs M100 Sanssouci-Colloquium; Hon. LLD (St John, NY).
Address: Istituto per gli Studi di Politica Internazionale, Palazzo Clerici, Via Clerici 5, 20121 Milan, Italy (office). *Telephone:* (02) 8633131 (office). *Fax:* (02) 8692055 (office). *Website:* www.ispionline.it (office).

BIANCHI, Andrés, MA, PhD; Chilean diplomatist and banking executive; b. 12 Sept. 1935, Valdivia; m. Lily Urdinola; two s. one d. *Education:* Univ. of Chile, Yale Univ., USA. *Career:* Dir Int. Labor Office Regional Employment Program of Latin America and the Caribbean 1971–73; Visiting Research Assoc. Woodrow Wilson School of Public and Int. Affairs, Princeton Univ. 1973–75; Visiting Prof. Center for Latin American Devt Studies, Boston Univ. 1978; Dir Econ. Devt Div., UN Econ. Comm. for Latin America and the Caribbean 1981–88, Deputy Exec. Sec 1988–89; Gov. Cen. Bank of Chile 1989–91; Chair. Credit Lyonnais Chile 1992–96, Dresdner Banque Nationale de Paris, Chile 1996–2000; mem. External Advisory Group, Latin America and Caribbean Regional Office, World Bank 1994–2000; mem. Pres. of Chile's Nat. Savings Comm. 1997–98; Amb. to USA 2000–06; fmr adviser to cen. banks of Bolivia, Colombia, Mexico and Venezuela.
Address: Ministry of Foreign Affairs, Catedral 1158, Santiago, Chile. *Telephone:* (2) 679-4200. *Fax:* (2) 699-4202. *Website:* www.minrel.gov.cl.

BIAOU, Rogatien, CEPE, BEPC; Benin (b. Niger) politician and diplomatist; b. 19 May 1952, Niamey, Niger; m. Justine Atioukpe Biaou 1987; four c. *Education:* Cours Secondaire Protestant de Cotonou, Lycée Mathieu Bouké de Parakou, Nat. Univ. of Benin, Abomey-Calavi, Centre de Formation Admin. et de Perfectionnement, Cotonou, Institut Int. d'Admin Publique, Paris, France, Université Libre de Bruxelles, Brussels, Belgium. *Career:* Asst to Gen. Man., Ministry of Higher Educ. and Scientific Research 1980–82; Head of France Div., Direction Europe, Ministry of Foreign Affairs and Cooperation 1982–85, Head of Service, Western European Countries 1985–87, Head of Service, African Countries S of the Sahara, Direction Africa and Arab Countries 1987–90; First Counsellor, Perm. Mission of Benin to UN, New York 1990–93, Minister Counsellor 1993–97; Amb. and Deputy Dir of Cabinet, Ministry of Foreign Affairs 1997–98, Amb. and Dir of Europe Dept 1998–2000; Amb. and Sec.-Gen., Ministry of Foreign Affairs and African Integration 2000–03, Minister for Foreign Affairs and African Integration 2003–06; Pres. Fédération Nationale Béninoise de Scrabble 2003–06; Chevalier de l'Ordre Nat. du Bénin. *Publications:* Les Moyens de Communication en Masse et La Politique d'Information au Benin 1980, La Grève de la Faim en Ulster: Conséquences Biologiques et Politiques 1981, Essai d'Analyse du Code de la Citoyenneté de la CEDEAD 1982, An X du Plan d'Action de Lagos 1990, The Challenge of Poverty Eradication in Africa 1996; numerous articles on politics, econs and devt.
Address: c/o Zone Résidentielle, route de l'Aéroport, BP 318, Cotonou 06 (office); 03 BP 2752, Cotonou, Benin (home). *Telephone:* 21-36-08-96 (home). *E-mail:* rogasbiaou@yahoo.fr (home).

BIEGMAN, Nicolaas H., PhD; Dutch diplomatist and writer; *Chairman, Board of Trustees, East West Parliamentary Practice Project;* b. 23 Sept. 1936, Apeldoorn; m. Mirjana Cibilic; two s. *Education:* Univ. of Leiden. *Career:* Lecturer in Turkish and Persian, Univ. of Leiden 1960–62; various posts in Netherlands Foreign Service 1963–84; Amb. to Egypt 1984–88; Dir-Gen. for Int. Cooperation, Ministry of Foreign Affairs 1988–92; Perm. Rep. to UN 1992–97; Perm. Rep. to NATO 1998–2001 (retd from Dutch Foreign Service); Sr Civilian Rep. of NATO in Macedonia, Skopje 2002–04; currently Chair. Bd of Trustees East West Parl. Practice Project, Amsterdam; fmr mem. Bd of Dirs Int. Peace Acad.; Order of The Netherlands Lion, Order of Merit, UAR. *Publications:* The Turco-Ragusan Relationship 1967, Egypt-Moulids, Saints, Sufis 1990, Egypt's Sideshows 1992, An Island of Bliss 1993, Mainly Manhattan 1997, God's Lovers 2006. *Address:* c/o Board of Trustees, East West Parliamentary Practice Project, Roemer Visscherstraat 18-2, 1054 EX, Amsterdam, Netherlands. *Telephone:* (20) 6623664. *Fax:* (20) 6160892. *E-mail:* ewppp@ewppp.org. *Website:* www.ewppp.org.

BIERSTEKER, Thomas J., MS, PhD; American research institute director and professor of international relations; *Curt Gasteyger Professor of International Security, Graduate Institute, Geneva; Education:* Univ. of Chicago, Massachusetts Inst. of Tech. *Career:* Founding Dir Center for Int. Studies, Univ. of Southern California, also fmr Dir School of Int. Relations; Henry R. Luce Prof. of Transnational Orgs and Dir Watson Inst. for Int. Studies, Brown Univ. 1994–2006; currently Curt Gasteyger Prof. of Int. Security, The Graduate Inst., Geneva; fmr Chair. Global Security and Co-operation Cttee, Social Sciences Research Council; N American Ed. Oxford Development Studies; mem. Editorial Advisory Bd Cambridge Univ. Press, European Journal of International Relations, Japanese Journal of International Studies, Journal of Peace Research; fmr mem. Ind. Task Force on Terrorist Financing, Council on Foreign Relations; consultant to UN Secr., Govts of Switzerland, Sweden and Germany; Fellow, Club of Madrid; mem. Council on Foreign Relations; Hon. Fellow, Foreign Policy Asscn; Hon. Distinguished Prof., Ewha Univ., Korea; Helen Dwight Reid Award, American Political Science Asscn. *Publications include:* Distortion or Development? Contending Perspectives on the Multinational Corporation 1981, Multinationals, the State and Control of the Nigerian Economy 1987, Dealing With Debt: International Financial Negotiations and Adjustment Bargaining 1993, State Sovereignty As Social Construct (co-ed.) 1996; Argument Without End: Searching for Answers to the Vietnam Tragedy (co-author) 1999, The Emergence of Private Authority (co-author) 2002, The Rebordering of North America: Integration and Exclusion in a New Security Context (co-ed.) 2003, International Law and International Relations: Bridging Theory and Practice (co-ed.) 2006, Countering the Financing of Global Terrorism (co-ed.) 2007; numerous chapters in books and articles in professional journals. *Address:* The Graduate Institute, Rue de Lausanne 132, Case Postale 36, 1211 Geneva 21, Switzerland (office). *Telephone:* 229085807 (office). *Fax:* 229086271 (office). *E-mail:* thomas.biersteker@graduateinstitute.ch (office). *Website:* www.graduateinstitute.ch (office).

BILDT, Carl; Swedish politician and diplomatist; *Minister of Foreign Affairs;* b. 15 July 1949, Halmstad; m. Mia Bohman 1984; one s. one d. *Education:* Univ. of Stockholm. *Career:* Chair. Confed. of Liberal and Conservative Students 1973–74, European Democrat Students 1974–76; mem. Stockholm Co. Council 1974–77; Political Advisor on Policy Co-ordination Ministry of Econ. Affairs 1976–78; Under-Sec. of State for Co-ordination and Planning at the Cabinet Office 1979–81; mem. Parl. 1979–2001; mem. Exec. Cttee Moderate Party 1981, Leader 1986–99; mem. Advisory Council on Foreign Affairs 1982–99; mem. Submarine Defence Comm. 1982–83; mem. 1984 Defence Policy Comm. 1984–87; Prime Minister of Sweden 1991–94; EU Peace Envoy in Fmr Yugoslavia 1995; High Rep. of the Int. Community in Bosnia and Herzegovina 1995–97; Vice-Chair. Int. Democrat Union 1989–92, Chair. 1992–99; Special Envoy of Sec.-Gen. of the UN to the Balkans 1999–2001; Chair. At-Large-Membership Study Cttee Internet Corpn for Assigned Names and Numbers (ICANN) 2001–02; currently Chair. Bd of Dirs Kreab Group (public affairs and strategic communication cos), Nordic Venture Network, Teleoptimering AB; Minister of Foreign Affairs 2006–; mem. Bd of Dirs Centre for European Reform, Vostok Nafta, Lundin Petroleum, HiQ, Öhmans; Trustee RAND Corpn; Fellow, Inst. for the Study of Terrorism and Political Violence, Univ. of St Andrews, Scotland; mem. IISS, London. *Publications:* Landet som steg ut i kylan (The Country that Stepped Out into the Cold) 1972, Framtid i frihet (A Future in Freedom) 1976, Hallanning, svensk, europe (A Citizen of Holland, Sweden and Europe) 1991, Peace Journey 1997. *Address:* Ministry for Foreign Affairs, Gustav Adolfs torg 1, 103 39 Stockholm, Sweden (office). *Telephone:* (8) 405-10-00 (office). *Fax:* (8) 723-11-76 (office). *E-mail:* registrator@foreign.ministry.se (office); carl@bildt .net. *Website:* utrikes.regeringen.se (office); www.bildt.net.

BILE, Pastor Micha Ondo, MSc; Equatorial Guinean diplomatist and mining engineer; *Minister of Foreign Affairs, International Co-operation and Francophone Affairs;* b. 2 Dec. 1952, Nsinik-Esawong; m.; six c. *Education:*

Inst. of Mining, Krivoi-Rog Univ. *Career:* engineer, Mines and Quarries Section, Dept of Mines and Hydrocarbons, Ministry of Mines and Energy 1982, Chief of Section 1983–84, Dir-Gen. Dept 1984–94, Sec.-Gen. Ministry 1994–95; Perm. Rep. to UN 1995–2001; currently Minister of Foreign Affairs, International Co-operation and Francophone Affairs; Kt (Second Class), Order of Independence. *Address:* Ministry of Foreign Affairs, International Co-operation and Francophone Affairs, Malabo, Equatorial Guinea (office). *Telephone:* (09) 32-20. *Fax:* (09) 31-32.

BILOBLOTSKIY, Mykola P.; Ukrainian politician and diplomatist. *Career:* fmr Head, Admin. of Pres. of Ukraine; Deputy Prime Minister and Minister of Labour and Social Policy 1999; Amb. to Russian Fed. –2005. *Address:* c/o Ministry of Foreign Affairs, 01018 Kyiv, pl. Mykhailivska 1, Ukraine.

BIN LADEN, Osama; Saudi Arabia-born guerrilla leader; b. Jeddah; m. five wives including Najua Ghanem; three c.; Amal al-Sadah; one d.; (divorced from one wife); more than 20 c. *Education:* King Abdul-Aziz Univ., Jeddah. *Career:* funded and joined troops fighting against Soviet Union in Afghanistan 1979; co-f. group to send aid to Afghan resistance and establish recruitment centres mid-1980s; f. org. to support Islamist opposition movts 1988; expelled from Saudi Arabia for anti-govt activities 1991, Saudi Arabian citizenship removed for 'irresponsible activities' 1994; moved to Sudan 1991, expelled following pressure from USA and UN 1996; continued to support Islamist extremist activities from Afghanistan; as head of the al-Qa'ida org. believed to have masterminded attacks on World Trade Center, New York, and Pentagon, Washington, DC on 11 Sept. 2001.

BIN NAYAN, Hussin; Malaysian diplomatist; *Director-General, Southeast Asia Regional Center for Counter Terrorism; Career:* held several positions in Ministry of Foreign Affairs 1976–86 Second Sec., New York, First Sec. in High Comm., Bangladesh; Dir ASEAN II, Ministry of Foreign Affairs; Counsellor, Embassy in Vienna 1989–93; Prin. Asst Sec., Ministry of Foreign Affairs; Amb. to Bosnia and Herzegovina 1998–2003; High Commr to Australia 2003; currently Dir-Gen. Southeast Asia Regional Center for Counter Terrorism (SEARCCT), Kuala Lumpur. *Address:* Southeast Asia Regional Center for Counter Terrorism, No. 516, Persiaran Mahameru, 50480 Kuala Lumpur, Malaysia (office). *Telephone:* (3) 22611900, ext. 219 (office). *Fax:* (3) 22749487 (office). *E-mail:* hussin@ searcct.gov.my (office). *Website:* www.searcct.gov.my (office).

BINNS, Susan May, BSc; British diplomatist and European Union official; *Director, Directorate-General Information Society and Media, European Commission;* b. 22 April 1948, Keighley, Yorks.; partner, Muriel Gobiet. *Education:* Harrogate Coll., London School of Econs. *Career:* joined FCO 1968, worked in London 1968–70, 1975–78, Belgium 1970–75, India 1978–80; mem. staff EC 1981–84, mem. Del. of EC to Washington, DC, USA 1985–88, to Belgrade, Yugoslavia 1988, Deputy Chief of Cabinet, Cabinet of Bruce Millan (Commr responsible for Regional Policies) 1989, Chief of Cabinet 1991–95, Dir Directorate-Gen. Internal Market 1995–2004, Information Society and Media 2005–. *Address:* Directorate-General Information Society and Media, European Commission, 200 rue de la Loi, 1049 Brussels, Belgium (office). *Telephone:* (2) 296-3285 (office). *Fax:* (2) 299-0368 (office). *E-mail:* susan.binns@ec .europa.eu (office). *Website:* ec.europa.eu/dgs/information_society (office).

BIO-TCHANÉ, Abdoulaye, MA; Benin international organization official and economist; *President, West African Development Bank; Education:* Univ. of Dijon, France, Centre Ouest-Africain de Formation et d'Etudes, Dakar, Senegal. *Career:* economist, Cen. Bank for W African Countries (BCEAO), Dir Econ. and Monetary Survey Dept –1998; Minister of Finances and Economy 1998–2002; Dir IMF African Dept 2002–08; Pres. West African Devt Bank 2008–. *Address:* West African Development Bank, 68, Avenue de la Libération, BP 1172, Lomé, Togo (office). *Telephone:* 221-59-06 (office). *Fax:* 221-52-67 (office). *E-mail:* boadsiege@boad.org (office). *Website:* www.boad.org (office).

BIRDSALL, Nancy, MA, PhD; American research institute director; *President, Center for Global Development; Education:* Newton Coll. of the Sacred Heart, Paul H. Nitze School of Advanced Int. Studies (SAIS), Johns Hopkins Univ., Yale Univ. *Career:* joined World Bank (IBRD) 1979, various positions in research, policy and man. including Head of Team preparing World Devt Report 1983–84, Chief of Social Programs Operations in Brazil, Chief of Environmental Operations in Latin America, Dir Policy Research Dept –1993; Exec. Vice-Pres. IDB 1993–98; Sr Assoc. and Dir, Econ. Reform Project, Carnegie Endowment for Int. Peace 1998–2001; Sr Fellow (non-resident) Brookings Inst. 1998–; Founder and

Pres. Center for Global Devt, Washington, DC 2001–; Teacher SAIS, Johns Hopkins Univ.; fmr Adviser to Admin. of UNDP Rockefeller Foundation; fmr Consultant to Asia Soc., AAAS, UN Fund for Population Activities; fmr Chair. Int. Center for Research on Women; mem. Bd of Dir Population Council; fmr mem. Bd Social Science Research Council, Overseas Devt Council, cttees and working groups of Nat. Acad. of Sciences. *Publications include:* Population Growth and Economic Development 1986, Financing Health in Developing Countries: An Agenda for Reform (co-author) 1987, Unfair Advantage: Labor Market Discrimination in Developing Countries (co-ed.) 1991, The East Asian Miracle: Economic Growth and Public Policy (co-ed.) 1993, Opportunity Forgone: Education in Brazil (co-ed.) 1996, Pathways to Growth: Comparing East Asia and Latin America (co-ed.) 1997, Beyond Tradeoffs: Market Reform and Equitable Growth in Latin America (co-ed.) 1998, Population Matters: Demographic Change, Economic Growth and Poverty in the Developing World (co-author) 1999, Distributive Justice and Economic Development (co-ed.) 2000, New Markets, New Opportunities? Economic and Social Mobility in a Changing World 2000, Washington Contentious: Economic Policies for Social Equity in Latin American (co-author) 2001, Delivering on Debt Relief: From IMF Gold to a New Aid Architecture (co-author) 2002, Financing Development: The Power of Regionalism (co-ed.) 2004, Reality Check: The Distributional Impact of Privatization in Developing Countries (co-ed.) 2005; more than 75 articles in scholarly journals and chapters in books. *Address:* Center for Global Development, 1776 Massachusetts Avenue, NW, Suite 301, Washington, DC 20036, USA (office). *Telephone:* (202) 416-0700 (office). *Fax:* (202) 416-0750 (office). *E-mail:* cgd@cgdev.org (office). *Website:* www.cgdev.org (office).

BIRKE, Adolf Mathias, PhD, FRHistS; German historian and academic; b. 12 Oct. 1939, Wellingholzhausen; m. 1st Linde D. Birn 1968; m. 2nd Sabine Volk 1988; one s. two d. *Education:* Univ. of Berlin. *Career:* Prof. of Modern History, Free Univ. of Berlin 1979; Visiting Prof. of German and European Studies, Trinity Coll., Univ. of Toronto, Canada 1980–81; Asst St Antony's Coll., Oxford; Prof. of Modern History, Univ. of Bayreuth 1982–85, Univ. of Munich 1995–2000; Dir German Historical Inst., London 1985–94; Chair. Prince Albert Soc. 1983–95; Cusanuswerk Grant 1962; Heisenberg Fellow 1979; Fed. Cross of Merit 1996. *Publications:* Bischof Ketteler und der deutsche Liberalismus 1971, Pluralismus und Gewerkschaftsautonomie 1978, Britain and Germany 1987, Nation ohne Haus. Deutschland 1945–1961 1989, (4th edn) 1998, Prince Albert Studies (ed.) Vols I–XIII 1983–95, Die Herausforderung des europäischen Staatensystems 1989, Princes, Patronage and the Nobility (ed with R. Asch) 1991, The Quest for Stability (ed. with R. Ahmann and M. Howard) 1992, Control Commission for Germany (British Element) (11 vols) Inventory (with H. Booms and O. Merker) 1993, Die Bundesrepublik Deutschland. Verfassung: Parlament und Parteien 1997, Deutschland und Grossbritannien 1999, An Anglo-German Dialogue (co-ed. with Magnus Brechtken and Alaric Searle) 2000; numerous articles on 19th- and 20th-century German and English history. *Address:* Friedenstr. 16, 06114 Halle, Germany.

BISHOP, Clyde, BA, MA, PhD; American diplomatist; *Ambassador to the Marshall Islands;* b. Del.; m. Cynthia DePaulo; one s. one d. *Education:* Delaware State Univ., Univ. of Delaware. *Career:* career mem. Sr Foreign Service with rank of Minister Counsellor, began diplomatic career as Consular/Econ. Officer in Palermo, Italy, other Foreign Service postings have included Hong Kong, Mumbai, Rio de Janeiro and Korea, Consul Gen., Santo Domingo, Dominican Repub., also served as Prin. Officer, Naples, served as Diplomat in Residence, City Coll., New York, participated in Foreign Service Inst. Sr Seminar, Amb. to the Marshall Islands 2006–; two Meritorious Honor Awards, Superior Honor Award. *Address:* US Embassy, PO Box 1379, Majuro, MH 96960, Marshall Islands (office). *Telephone:* (247) 4011 (office). *Fax:* (247) 4012 (office). *E-mail:* publicmajuro@state.gov (office). *Website:* usembassy.state.gov/majuro (office).

BISOGNIERO, Claudio, BSc; Italian diplomatist; *Deputy Secretary-General, NATO;* b. 2 Aug. 1954, Rome; m. Laura Denise Noce Benigni Olivieri; one s. one d. *Education:* Univ. of Rome. *Career:* served in Italian army 1976–77; joined Foreign Service 1978, First Sec. for Econ. and Commercial Affairs, Embassy in Beijing 1981–84, Counsellor, Perm. Mission to NATO, Brussels 1984–89, with Office of Diplomatic Adviser to Pres., Rome 1989–92, First Counsellor for Econ. and Commercial Affairs, Embassy in Washington DC 1992–96, at Perm. Mission to UN, New York 1996–99, with Personnel Dept, Foreign Service 1999, with Office of Sec.-Gen., Ministry of Foreign Affairs 1999–2002, Deputy Dir-Gen. for Political Multilateral Affairs (Deputy Political Dir) 2002–05, Dir-Gen. for Americas 2005–07, Deputy Sec.-Gen. NATO 2007–.

Address: Office of the Deputy Secretary-General, North Atlantic Treaty Organization (NATO), blvd Léopold III, 1110 Brussels, Belgium (office). *Telephone:* (2) 707-41-11 (office). *Fax:* (2) 707-45-79 (office). *E-mail:* natodoc@hq.nato.int (office). *Website:* www.nato.int (office).

BIYA, Paul, LenD; Cameroonian politician and head of state; *President;* b. 13 Feb. 1933, Mvomeka'a; m. 1st Jeanne (née Atyam) Biya (deceased); one c.; m. 2nd Chantal Biya 1994. *Education:* Ndem Mission School, Edea and Akono Seminaries, Lycée Leclerc, Yaoundé, Univ. of Paris, Inst. d'Etudes Politiques, Inst. des Hautes Etudes d'Outre-Mer, Paris. *Career:* Head of Dept of Foreign Devt Aid 1962–63; Dir of Cabinet in Ministry of Nat. Educ., Youth and Culture 1964–65; on goodwill mission to Ghana and Nigeria 1965; Sec.-Gen. in Ministry of Educ., Youth and Culture 1965–67; Dir of Civil Cabinet of Head of State 1967–68; Minister of State, Sec.-Gen. to Pres. 1968–75; Prime Minister 1975–82; Pres. of Cameroon 1982–; Second Vice-Pres., Central Cttee, mem. Union Nationale Camerounaise (UNC), Pres. 1983–85; Pres. Rassemblement Démocratique du Peuple Camerounais (RDPC) 1985–; mem. Politbureau; Hon. Prof. (Univ. of Beijing); Commdr de l'Ordre de la Valeur Camerounaise, Commdr of Nat. Order of FRG and of Tunisia, Great Commdr of the Medal of St George UK, Great Commdr of Order of Nigeria, Grand Cross of Nat. Order of Merit of Senegal, Grand Officier, Légion d'honneur, Grand Collier of the Ordre of Ouissam Mohammadi, Morocco; Dr hc (Univ. of Maryland); Peace Laureate, Centre European Peace Studies 1988. *Publication:* Communal Liberalism 1987.
Address: Office of the President, Palais de l'Unité, Yaoundé, Cameroon (office). *Telephone:* 2223-4025 (office). *Website:* www.camnet.cm/celcom/homepr.htm (office).

BLACK, Peter; Jamaican diplomatist; *High Commissioner to Trinidad and Tobago; Career:* fmr Under-Sec. for Bilateral and Regional Affairs, Ministry of Foreign Affairs; fmr Amb. to Haiti; currently High Commr to Trinidad and Tobago.
Address: Jamaican High Commission, 2 Newbold Street, St Clair, Port of Spain, Trinidad and Tobago (office). *Telephone:* 622-4995 (office). *Fax:* 628-9043 (office). *E-mail:* jhctnt@tstt.net.tt (office).

BLACKBEARD, Roy; Botswana diplomatist; *High Commissioner to UK. Career:* Councillor, Cen. Dist 1979–89; mem. Parl. (Botswana Democratic Party) for Serowe N Constituency 1989–98, Asst Minister of Agric. 1992–94, Minister of Agric. 1994; High Commr to UK 1998– (also accred as Amb. to Ireland, Czech Repub., Slovakia and Romania); fmr Dir Air Botswana; fmr mem. Livestock Industry Advisory Cttee; fmr Treas. Botswana Democratic Party (youth wing).
Address: High Commission of Botswana, 6 Stratford Place, London, W1C 1AY, England (office). *Telephone:* (20) 7499-0031 (office). *Fax:* (20) 7495-8595 (office). *E-mail:* bohico@govbw.com (office).

BLACKER, Coit D., A, MS, PhD; American political scientist, academic, research institute director and international relations consultant; *Director and Senior Fellow, Freeman Spogli Institute for International Studies, Stanford University; Education:* Occidental Coll., Fletcher School of Law and Diplomacy, Tufts Univ. *Career:* Professor Stanford Univ. 1978–, and succession of other positions at Stanford, including Dir of Studies, Center for Int. Security and Arms Control, co-Chair. Int. Relations and Int. Policy Studies Programs, Olivier Nomellini Family Univ. Fellow in Undergraduate Educ., Deputy Dir, Freeman Spogli Inst. for Int. Studies, now Dir and Sr Fellow; Assoc. Prof. School of Int. Relations, Univ. of Southern Calif., Dir ad interim Peace and Conflict Studies Program; Special Asst for Nat. Security Affairs to US Senator Gary Hart, then to Pres. Clinton during first admin.; Sr Dir Russian, Ukrainian and Eurasian Affairs, Nat. Security Council; co-Dir Aspen Inst. US-Russia Dialogue 1998–2003; mem. study group US Comm. on Nat. Security in the 21st Century; mem. Council on Foreign Relations; mem. Bd of Dirs Int. Research and Exchanges Bd, Washington, DC; Chair. Exec. Cttee of the Int. Initiative 2005–; mem. Stanford Bd of Trustees Cttee on Devt 2004–07; Dr hc (Russian Acad. of Sciences Inst. of Far Eastern Studies) 1993; Laurance and Naomi Carpenter Hoagland Prize for Undergraduate Teaching 2001. *Publications include:* International Arms Control: Issues and Agreements (co-Ed.) 1984, Reluctant Warriors: the United States, The Soviet Union and Arms Control 1987, Hostage to Revolution: Gorbachev and Soviet Security Policy, 1985–91 1993, NATO After Madrid: Looking to the Future (Vol I) (co-Ed.) 1999, Belarus and the Flight from Sovereignty 2001, Arms Control 2002.
Address: Freeman Spogli Institute for International Studies, Stanford University, Encina Hall, C137, Stanford, CA 94305-6055, USA (office). *Telephone:* (650) 725-5368 (office). *Fax:* (650) 725-3435 (office). *E-mail:* cblacker@stanford.edu (office). *Website:* www.iis-db.stanford.edu (office).

BLACKWELL, Baron (Life Peer), cr. 1997, of Woodcote in the County of Surrey; **Norman Roy Blackwell,** MA, PhD, MBA; British business executive and fmr civil servant; *Chairman, Centre for Policy Studies;* b. 29 July 1952, London; m. Brenda Clucas 1974; three s. two d. *Education:* Latymer Upper School, Trinity Coll., Cambridge, Wharton Business School, Univ. of Pa (Thouron Scholar). *Career:* Jr Exhibitioner RAM 1963–69; Chair. Cambridge Univ. Conservative Asscn 1973; with Strategic Planning Unit, Plessey Co. 1976–78, McKinsey & Co. 1978–86, 1988–95 (partner 1984), Prime Minister's Policy Unit 1986–88, Head 1995–97; Dir of Group Devt NatWest Group 1997–2000; Dir Dixons Group 2000–03; Special Adviser KPMG Corp. Finance 2000–; Dir Corp. Services Group 2000–06, Slough Estates 2001–, Smartstream Technologies Group 2001–06, Standard Life 2003–; Chair. Interserve plc 2006–; Deputy Chair. British Urban Regeneration Asscn 1991–92; Chair. Centre for Policy Studies 2000–; mem. Bd Office of Fair Trading 2003–. *Address:* c/o House of Lords, London, SW1A 0PW; Centre For Policy Studies, 57 Tufton Street, London, SW1P 3QL, England (office). *Telephone:* (20) 7311-4997; (20) 7222-4488 (CPS) (office). *Fax:* (20) 7222-4388 (CPS) (office). *E-mail:* blackwelln@parliament.uk. *Website:* www.cps.org.uk (office).

BLAIR, Rt Hon. Anthony (Tony) Charles Lynton, BA, PC; British barrister and politician; *Special Envoy, Quartet on the Middle East;* b. 6 May 1953, Edinburgh; m. Cherie Booth 1980; three s. one d. *Education:* Fettes Coll., Edinburgh, St John's Coll., Oxford. *Career:* barrister, specializing in trade union and employment law; MP for Sedgefield 1983–2007; Shadow Spokesman on the Treasury 1984–87, on Trade and Industry 1987–88, on Energy 1988–89, on Employment 1989–92, on Home Affairs 1992–94; Leader of the Labour Party 1994–2007; Prime Minister, First Lord of the Treasury and Minister for the Civil Service 1997–2007 (re-elected 2001, 2005); Special Envoy to Middle East on behalf of USA, Russia, EU and UN 2007–; mem. Bd of Dirs World Econ. Forum Foundation Board 2007–; f. Tony Blair Sports Foundation 2007; Sr Adviser JP Morgan Chase & Co. 2008–; Howland Distinguished Fellow, Yale Univ. 2008–09; Hon. Bencher, Lincoln's Inn 1994; Hon. LLD (Northumbria) 1995; numerous awards including Charlemagne Prize 1999, Ellis Island Medal of Honor for Int. Leadership 2003, Congressional Gold Medal (US) 2003, Polio Eradication Champion, Rotary Int. 2006. *Publications:* New Britain: My Vision of a Young Country 1996, The Third Way 1998. *Address:* The Office of Tony Blair, PO Box 60519, London, W2 7JU (office); Myrobella, Trimdon Station, Co. Durham, TS29 6DU, England. *E-mail:* info@tonyblairoffice.org (office). *Website:* tonyblairoffice.org (office).

BLAIR, Bruce G., PhD, BS; American research institute director and academic; *President, World Security Insitute; Education:* Univ. of Ill., Yale Univ. *Career:* joined USAF, served as Minuteman ICBM launch control officer and support officer for the Strategic Air Command 1970–74; project dir Congressional Office of Tech. Assessment; Sr Fellow, Foreign Policy Studies Program, Brookings Inst. 1987–2000; Pres. World Security Inst. (fmly Center for Defense Information) 2000–; Visiting Prof. in security studies at Yale and Princeton Univs; MacArthur Fellowship Prize 1999. *Publications include:* Strategic Command and Control: Redefining the Nuclear Threat 1985, Crisis Stability and Nuclearwar (co-Ed.) 1988, The Logic of Accidental Nuclear War 1993, Global Zero Alert for Nuclear Forces 1995, De-Alerting Strategic Forces 2000; numerous articles in newspapers and journals. *Address:* World Security Institute, 1779 Massachusetts Avenue, NW, Suite 615, Washington, DC 20036, USA (office). *Telephone:* (202) 332-0900 (office). *Fax:* (202) 462-4559 (office). *E-mail:* info@worldsecurityinstitute.org (office). *Website:* www.worldsecurityinstitute.org (office).

BLAIR, Dennis Cutler, BA; American naval officer (retd); m. Diane Blair; one s. one d. *Education:* Univ. of Oxford, UK. *Career:* commissioned as ensign in USN; rank of Vice-Adm.; Commdr USS Cochrane 1984–86, Naval Staff Pearl Harbor 1988–89, Kittyhawk Battlegroup 1993–95; Assoc. Dir Cen. Intelligence Mil. Support 1995–96; Dir Jt Staff 1996–99; C-in-C US Pacific Command, Hawaii 1999–2002 (retd); Sr Fellow, Inst. for Defense Analyses 2002–03, Pres. 2003–07, now consultant; mem. IISS Council; White House Fellow, Naval Operations Fellow; Legion of Merit with three gold stars, Service Medal with two oak leaf clusters. *Address:* Institute for Defense Analyses, 4850 Mark Center Drive, Alexandria, VA 22311-1882, USA (office). *Telephone:* (703) 845-2000 (office). *Website:* www.ida.org (office).

BLAKE, Robert O., BA, MA; American diplomatist; *Ambassador to Sri Lanka;* m. Sofia Blake; three d. *Education:* Harvard Coll., Johns Hopkins School of Advanced Int. Studies. *Career:* career mem. Sr Foreign Service, entered Foreign Service 1985, has served at Embassies in Tunis, Algiers, Abuja and Cairo, has also held several positions at Dept of State, Washington, DC, Deputy Chief of Mission, New Delhi 2003–06, Amb. to Sri Lanka (also accred to the Maldives) 2006–. *Address:* US Embassy, PO Box 106, 210 Galle Road, Colombo 03, Sri Lanka (office). *Telephone:* (11) 2498500 (office). *E-mail:* consularcolombo@state.gov (office). *Website:* srilanka.usembassy.gov (office).

BLAKELOCK, Asi Tuiataga J. F.; Samoan diplomatist; *High Commissioner to New Zealand;* b. Moataa; m. Elena Blakelock; eight c. *Career:* served in Samoan Police Force for more than 40 years, Commr Samoa Police –2003 (retd), led contingent of 20 Samoan police officers on peacekeeping duties in Liberia 2003–04; Chair. South Pacific Chiefs of Police Conf. –2002; High Commr to NZ 2005–. *Address:* High Commission of Samoa, 1A Wesley Road, Kelburn, PO Box 1430, Wellington, New Zealand (office). *Telephone:* (4) 472-0953 (office). *Fax:* (4) 471-2479 (office). *E-mail:* shc@paradise.net.nz (office).

BLANCHARD, Olivier Jean, PhD; French economist and academic; *Economic Counsellor and Director of Research Department, International Monetary Fund;* b. 27 Dec. 1948, Amiens; m. Noelle Golinelli 1973; three d. *Education:* Univ. of Paris and Massachusetts Inst. of Tech. *Career:* Asst Prof., Harvard Univ., USA 1977–81, Assoc. Prof. 1981–83; Assoc. Prof., MIT, Cambridge, Mass, USA 1983–85, Prof. of Econs 1985–, Class of 1941 Prof. 1994–, Chair. Econs Dept 1998–2003; Econ. Counsellor and Dir Dept of Research, IMF 2008–; Vice-Pres. American Econ. Asscn 1995–96; Fellow, Econometric Soc.; mem. American Acad. of Arts and Sciences. *Publications:* Lectures on Macroeconomics (with S. Fischer) 1989, Reform in Eastern Europe 1991, Pour l'Emploi et Cohésion Sociale 1994, Spanish Unemployment: Is There a Solution? 1994, The Economics of Transition 1996, Macroeconomics 1997. *Address:* International Monetary Fund, 700 19th Street, N.W., Washington DC, 20431; Department of Economics, E52-357, Massachusetts Institute of Technology, Cambridge, MA 02139, USA (office). *Telephone:* (202) 623-7000 (office); (617) 253-8891 (office). *Fax:* (202) 623-4661 (office); (617) 258-8112 (office). *E-mail:* publicaffairs@imf.org (office); blanchar@mit.edu (office). *Website:* www.imf.org (office); econ-www.mit.edu (office).

BLANCHEMAISON, Claude Marie, LenD; French diplomatist; b. 6 March 1944, Loches, Indre et Loire; s. of Roger Blanchemaison and Louise Blanchemaison (née Lacour). *Education:* Faculté de Droit et de Sciences Economiques, Paris. *Career:* First Sec., then Counsellor to Perm. Rep. at EC 1978–82; Asst Gen. Sec. to the Interministerial Cttee for Questions of European Econ. Cooperation 1982–85; Chargé d'Affaires, SA 1985–86; Deputy Dir Centre Admin., Ministry of Foreign Affairs 1986–89; Amb. to Vietnam 1989–92; Dir for Europe, Ministry of Foreign Affairs 1992–93, for Asia and Oceania 1993–96; Amb. to India 1996–2000, to Russia 2000–04, to Spain 2005–07; Sec.-Gen. Presidency of the EU 2007–08; Chevalier Legion d'honneur, Ordre nat. du Mérite, Ordre du Mérite agricole. *Address:* Ministry of Foreign and European Affairs, 37 quai d'Orsay, 75351 Paris Cedex 07, France (office). *Telephone:* 1-43-17-53-53 (office). *Fax:* 1-43-17-52-03 (office). *Website:* www.diplomatie.gouv.fr (office).

BLANLOT SOZA, Vivianne, MA; Chilean engineer, economist and government official. *Education:* Pontificia Universidad Católica de Chile, American Univ., Washington, DC. *Career:* economist, Banco Interamericano de Desarrollo (BID) 1980–90; Dir Comisión Nacional de Medio Ambiente (Conama) 1995–97; Exec. Sec., Comisión Nacional de Energia (CNE) 2000–03; Minister of Nat. Defence 2006–07; mem. Exec. Council, BancoEstado 2005–. *Address:* Banco del Estado de Chile, Avenida B. O'Higgins 1111, Santiago, Chile (office). *Telephone:* (2) 970-7000 (office). *Fax:* (2) 970-5711 (office). *Website:* www.bancoestado.cl (office).

BLATHERWICK, Sir David (Elliott Spiby), KCMG, OBE, MA; British diplomatist (retd); *Chairman, Egyptian–British Chamber of Commerce;* b. 13 July 1941, Lincoln; m. (Margaret) Clare Crompton 1964; one s. one d. *Education:* Lincoln School and Wadham Coll. Oxford. *Career:* Foreign Office 1964; Second Sec., Kuwait 1968–70; First Sec. Dublin 1970–73; FCO 1973–77; Head of Chancery, Cairo 1977–80; NI Office, Belfast 1981–83; FCO 1983–85; sabbatical, Stanford Univ., USA 1985–86; Head of Chancery, Perm. Mission to UN, New York 1986–89; Prin. Finance Officer and Chief Insp., FCO 1989–91; Amb. to Ireland 1991–95, to Egypt 1995–99; Chair. Egyptian–British Chamber of Commerce 1999–; Jt Chair. Anglo-Irish Encounter 2003–08. *Publication:* The Politics of International Telecommunications 1987. *Address:* Egyptian–British Chamber of Commerce, PO Box 4EG, 299 Oxford Street, London, W1A 4EG, England (office). *Telephone:* (20) 7499-3100 (office). *Fax:* (20) 7499-1070 (office). *E-mail:* info@theebcc.com (office). *Website:* www.theebcc.com (office).

BLATOV, Igor; Russian diplomatist; *Ambassador to Turkmenistan; Education:* Moscow State Inst. of Int. Relations. *Career:* Deputy Dir European Co-operation Dept, Ministry of Foreign Affairs 1994–96, Deputy Dir Gen. Secr. 2000–06; Minister Counsellor, Embassy in Netherlands 1996–2000; Amb. to Turkmenistan 2006–.
Address: Embassy of Russia, ul. 1966, 11, Aşgabat 744004, Turkmenistan (office). *Telephone:* (12) 35-39-57 (office). *Fax:* (12) 39-84-66 (office). *E-mail:* emb-rus@online.tm (office).

BLATTMANN, René, LicIurU; Bolivian judge; *Second Vice-President, International Criminal Court;* b. 28 Jan. 1948, La Paz; m. Marianne Blattmann; one s. two d. *Education:* Bolivian Univ., La Paz, Univ. of Basle, Switzerland, Acad. of American and Int. Law, Dallas, TX, USA, Int. Faculty of Comparative Law, France and Italy. *Career:* Prof. of Criminal Law, San Andrés State Univ., La Paz 1973–94, Bolivian Catholic Univ., La Paz 1993–94; Attorney at Law 1975–93; Minister of Justice and Human Rights 1994–97; Chief of Human Rights and Justice Area, UN Human Rights Verification Mission in Guatemala 1998–2000; Dir Andrean Jurists Comm. (CAJ) 1997–2002; Judge, Int. Criminal Court 2003–, Second Vice-Pres. 2006–; mem. La Paz Bar Asscn, Bolivian Bar Asscn, Andrean Jurists Comm.; Hon. Life mem. Wilshire Bar Asscn, LA, USA 1977–; Hon. mem. Experts Asscn on Criminal Law of Bogota and Cundinamarca, Colombia 1995; Bundesverdienstkreuz 2005; Dr hc (Univ. of Basle) 1998; Robert J. Storey Int. Award of Leadership, Southwestern Legal Foundation, Univ. of Texas at Dallas 1995, Diosa Temis Medal, Nat. Foundation Fora and Interdisciplinary Studies of Colombia 1995, Monseñor Leonidas Proaño Latin American Prize of Human Rights, Latin American Asscn of Human Rights (ALDHU) 1995, Carl Bertelsmann Int. Prize 2001; distinctions from Bolivian Nat. Police 1995, Journalists Asscn of La Paz 1996, Superior Court of Justice of Santa Cruz 1997, Superior Court of Justice of Tarija 1997, Nat. Chamber of Commerce 1997, City Council of La Paz 2000.
Address: International Criminal Court, Maanweg 174, 2516 AB The Hague, Netherlands (office). *Telephone:* (70) 515-85-15 (office). *Fax:* (70) 515-87-89 (office). *E-mail:* pio@icc-cpi.int (office). *Website:* www.icc-cpi .int (office).

BLAY-AMIHERE, Kabral; Ghanaian diplomatist and journalist; *Ambassador to Côte d'Ivoire; Career:* fmr Ed. The Independent newspaper, Ghana, arrested for publishing criticism of mil. regime 2000; fmr Pres. West African Journalists' Asscn; High Commr to Sierra Leone 2001–05; Amb. to Côte d'Ivoire 2005–.
Address: Embassy of Ghana, Lot 2393, rue J 95, Cocody-Deux-Plateaux, 01 BP 1871, Abidjan 01, Côte d'Ivoire (office). *Telephone:* 20-33-11-24 (office). *Fax:* 20-22-33-57 (office). *E-mail:* ghembci@africaonline.co.ci (office).

BLICKENSTORFER, Christian, PhD; Swiss diplomatist; *Ambassador to Germany;* b. 1945, Horgen; m. Susanne Blickenstorfer; two c. *Education:* Univ. of Zurich. *Career:* Personal Asst. to Gen. Man., Swiss Textile Machine Producers, France and Spain 1972–74; joined Foreign Service 1974, Attaché at Embassy in Cairo, Egypt 1975–76, Diplomatic Collaborator with Ministry of Economy 1976–80; Deputy Chief of Mission in Bangkok, Thailand 1980–83, in Tehran, Iran 1983–85 (also Head of Foreign Interests Section in USA and S Africa); Deputy Chief of Mission and Head of Political Section, Washington, DC 1989–93; Amb. to Saudi Arabia, UAE, Oman and Yemen 1993–97; Deputy Head of Political Div. II (Africa, Asia, Latin America, Pacific Region), Amb. and Head of Political Div. II 1997–2000; Amb. and Head of Political Directorate 2000–01; Amb. to USA 2001–06, to Germany 2006–.
Address: Embassy of Switzerland, Otto-von-Bismarck-Allee 4a, 10557 Berlin, Germany (office). *Telephone:* (30) 3904000 (office). *Fax:* (30) 3911030 (office). *E-mail:* ber.vertretung@eda.admin.ch (office). *Website:* www.eda.admin.ch/berlin (office).

BLINDER, Alan Stuart, AB, MSc, PhD; American economist and academic; *Professor of Economics and Co-Director, Center for Economic Policy Studies, Princeton University;* b. 14 Oct. 1945, Brooklyn, New York; m. Madeline Schwartz 1967; two s. *Education:* Princeton Univ., LSE, MIT. *Career:* Deputy Asst Dir US Congressional Budget Office 1975; Gordon S. Rentschler Memorial Prof. of Econs, Princeton Univ., NJ 1982–, Dir Center for Econ. Policy Studies 1989–93, Co.-Dir 1996–; mem. Council of Econ. Advisers to Pres. Clinton 1993–94; Vice-Chair. Bd of Govs, Fed. Reserve System 1994–96; Vice-Chair., G7 Group 1997–; Fellow, American Acad. of Arts and Sciences 1991–; mem. American Philosophical Soc. 1996–; Pnr, Promotory Financial Group 2000–. *Publications include:* Growing Together: An Alternative Economic Strategy for the 1990s 1991, Central Banking in Theory and Practice 1998, Asking About Prices: A New Approach to Understanding Price Stickiness (jtly) 1998, Economics, Principles and Policy (jtly) 2000, The Fabulous Decade: Macroeconomic Lessons from the 1990s (jtly) 2001.

Address: Department of Economics, Princeton University, 105 Fisher Hall, Princeton, NJ 08544, USA (office). *Telephone:* (609) 258-3358 (office). *Fax:* (609) 258-5398 (office). *E-mail:* blinder@princeton.edu (office). *Website:* www.econ.princeton.edu (office).

BLIX, Hans Martin, LLD, PhD; Swedish lawyer and international official (retd); b. 28 June 1928, Uppsala; m. Eva Kettis 1962; two s. *Education:* Uppsala Univ., Univ. of Cambridge, UK, Columbia Univ., New York, USA, Univ. of Stockholm. *Career:* Asst Prof. of Int. Law, Univ. of Stockholm 1960–63; Legal Consultant on Int. Law, Foreign Ministry 1963–76; Under-Sec. of State for Int. Devt Co-operation, Foreign Ministry 1976–78, 1979–81; Minister for Foreign Affairs 1978–79; Dir-Gen. IAEA, Vienna 1981–97; mem. Swedish del. to UN Gen. Ass. 1961–81; mem. del. to Conf. on Disarmament, Geneva 1962–78; Exec. Chair. UN Monitoring, Verification and Inspection Comm. for Iraq 2000–03; Hon. Chair. World Nuclear Asscn; Commdr, Légion d'honneur 2004; Dr hc (Moscow State Univ.) 1987, (several other univs); Henry de Wolf Smyth Award 1988, Gold Medal, Uranium Inst. (now World Nuclear Asscn) 1997, Olof Palme Prize 2003. *Publications:* Treaty-Making Power (dissertation), Statsmyndigheternas Internationella Förbindelser (monograph) 1964, Sovereignty, Aggression and Neutrality 1970, The Treaty-Maker's Handbook 1973, Disarming Iraq: The Search for Weapons of Mass Destruction 2004; numerous articles in scientific journals.

BLIZNAKOV, Vesselin Vitanov; Bulgarian scientist and politician; b. 18 June 1944, Straldga, Yambol Dist; m. *Education:* Vassil Kkaragyizov High School, Yambol, Medical Acad., Sofia. *Career:* began career in general practice, Bourgas Dist 1972–75; Researcher Assoc. and Head of Lab., Nat. Centre for Radio-Biology and Radiation Protection, Sofia 1976–86, Head, Radiation Protection Dept 1986–99; Chair. Bulgarian Nuclear Soc. 1999–2001; fmr mem. Civil Cttee for Protection of Nuclear Power Plant Kozloduy; co-owner Dr. Atanas Shterev's Clinic; mem. Nat. Ass. for Vratsa 2001–05, for Haskovo 2005–, Chair. Energy Cttee 2001–05, mem. Foreign Policy, Defence and Security Cttees 2001–05; Deputy Chair. Parl. Group of Simeon II Nat. Movt 2001–03; mem. Del. to Jt Bulgarian-EU Parl. Cttee 2001; Minister of Defence 2005–08; mem. Governing Council, European Nuclear Soc. 1999–2001.
Address: c/o Ministry of Defence, 1000 Sofia, ul. Dyakon Ignatiy 3, Bulgaria. *Telephone:* (2) 922-09-22.

BLOKHIN, Alexander Victorovich; Russian politician and engineer; *Ambassador to Australia;* b. 12 Jan. 1951, Ivanovo, Russia; m.; one d. *Education:* Ivanovo Inst. of Energy. *Career:* sr engineer, deputy head of workshop, deputy chief energy expert factory Fizpribor, Leningrad 1974–77; with USSR Ministry of Defence in Mongolia 1977–78; chief mechanic, garment factory Ivanovo 1978–80; chief energy expert, State Schelkovo Biological Co., Moscow Region 1983–90; Chair. Sub-cttee, Sec. Cttee of Supreme Soviet on Devt of Self-govt, Moscow 1990–92; Counsellor of Minister of Foreign Affairs, Russian Fed. 1992–93; Dir Dept Ministry of Foreign Affairs, Russian Fed. 1993–95; Amb. for special missions 1995; Amb. to Azerbaijan 1995–2000; Minister for Nationalities and Regional Policy 2000–02; Amb. to Belarus 2002–05, to Australia 2005–.
Address: Embassy of the Russian Federation, 78 Canberra Avenue, Griffith, ACT 2603, Australia (office). *Telephone:* (2) 6295-9033 (office). *Fax:* (2) 6295-1847 (office). *E-mail:* rusembassy.australia@rambler.ru (office). *Website:* www.australia.mid.ru (office).

BLOOMFIELD, Keith; British diplomatist; b. 2 June 1947; m. Genevieve Bloomfield; three d. *Career:* served with Overseas Devt Admin, Ministry of Defence –1980; joined FCO 1980, with Office of Perm. Rep. to EC, Brussels 1980–85, Desk Officer, EC Dept, FCO 1985–87, Head of Chancery, Cairo 1987–90, Deputy Head of Mission, Algiers 1990–94, Counsellor, Rome 1994–98, Minister and Deputy Head of Mission 1998–99, Head of Counter-Terrorism Policy Dept, FCO 1999–2002, Amb. to Nepal 2002–06.
Address: c/o Foreign and Commonwealth Office, King Charles Street, London, SW1A 2AH, England. *Telephone:* (20) 7008-1500.

BLOOMFIELD, Lincoln P., Jr, AB, MALD; American government official and diplomatist; *Special Envoy for Man-Portable Air Defense Systems (MANPADS) Threat Reduction;* m. Rebecca Ann Meden; one d. *Education:* Harvard College, Coll. Fletcher School of Law and Diplomacy, Tufts Univ. *Career:* Dept of Defense Policy Dir for Lebanon, SE Asia, etc. 1981–87, Prin. Deputy Asst Sec. of Defense, Int. Security Affairs 1988–89; mem. US Water Meditation in the Middle East 1989–90; del., Philippine Base Negotiations 1990–91; Deputy Asst to Vice-Pres. for Nat. Security Affairs 1991–92, Deputy Asst Sec. of State for Near East Affairs 1992–93; Pnr, Armitage Associates LLC, Arlington Va 1993–2001; Asst Sec. of State for Political-Mil. Affairs 2001–05; Special Rep., Pres. and Sec. of State for Mine Action 2001–05; Sr adviser, Akin Gump Strauss Hauer & Feld LLP, Washington, DC 2005–, Center for Strategic and International Studies;

Founder and Pres. Palmer Coates LLC 2005–; Special Envoy for Man-Portable Air Defense Systems (MANPADS) Threat Reduction, US State Dept 2008–; Chair. Henry L. Stimson Center; mem. Bd Landmine Survivors' Network; Secretary of Defense Medal for Outstanding Public Service; Secretary of Defense Medal for Meritorious Civilian Service; State Department Superior Honor Award; Secretary of State Distinguished Honor Award. *Music:* Coalition of the Willing (charitable performances, diplomats, policy and security officials). *Publications:* Global Markets and National Interests: The New Geopolitics of Energy, Capital and Information (ed.) 2002.
Address: Palmer Coates LLC, PO Box 7406, Alexandria, VA 22307 (office); Akin Gump Strauss Hauer & Feld LLP, Robert S. Strauss Building, 1333 New Hampshire Avenue, NW, Washington, DC 20036-1564, USA (office). *Telephone:* (703) 960-4757 (Palmer Coates) (home); (202) 887-4351 (office). *Fax:* (703) 317-3339 (Palmer Coates) (office); (202) 887-4288 (office). *E-mail:* info@palmercoates.com (office); lbloomfield@akingump.com (office). *Website:* palmercoates.com (office); www.akingump.com (office); www.state.gov/t/pm/wra/c3670.htm.

BLUM, Yehuda Z., MJur, PhD; Israeli diplomatist, lawyer and academic; *Hersch Lauterpacht Professor of International Law, Hebrew University of Jerusalem;* b. 2 Oct. 1931, Bratislava; m. Moriah Rabinovitz-Teomim; two s. one d. *Education:* Hebrew Univ., Jerusalem, Univ. of London. *Career:* detained in Nazi concentration camp of Bergen-Belsen 1944; Asst to Judge Advocate-Gen. of Israel Defence Forces 1956–59; Sr Asst to Legal Adviser, Ministry for Foreign Affairs 1962–65; UNESCO Fellow, Univ. of Sydney July–Aug. 1968; Office of UN Legal Counsel Sept.–Dec. 1968; Sr Research Scholar, Univ. of Mich. Law School 1969; Visiting Prof., School of Law, Univ. of Tex. 1971, New York Univ. 1975–76, Univ. of Mich. Law School 1985, Cardozo School of Law, New York 1991, 2000, Univ. of Southern Calif., Los Angeles 1991–92, Tulane Univ., New Orleans 1994, 2003, Univ. of Miami 1999, Univ. of Calif., Berkeley 2002; Hersch Lauterpacht Prof. of Int. Law, Hebrew Univ. of Jerusalem 1991–; mem. Israeli del., Third UN Conf. on Law of the Sea 1973, 31st Session of UN Gen. Ass. 1976; Perm. Rep. to UN 1978–84; Law Ed. Encyclopedia Hebraica 1973–78; Hon. DJur (Yeshiva Univ.) 1981; Jabotinsky Prize 1984. *Publications:* Historic Titles in International Law 1965, Secure Boundaries and Middle East Peace 1971, For Zion's Sake 1987, Eroding the UN Charter 1993.
Address: Faculty of Law, Hebrew University, Mount Scopus, Jerusalem 91905, Israel (office). *Telephone:* 2-5882562 (office). *Fax:* 2-5823042. *E-mail:* msblumy@mscc.huji.ac.il (office). *Website:* law.mscc.huji.ac.il/law1/newsite/hebrew.html (office).

BLUM DE BARBERI, Claudia, MA; Colombian diplomatist, psychologist and journalist; *Permanent Representative, United Nations;* b. Cali; m. Francisco Barberi; two s. *Education:* Pontificia Universidad Javeriana, Harvard Law School, USA. *Career:* psychologist, Universidad del Valle; fmr Dir Proartes (foundation dedicated to promotion of culture); elected Councilwoman in her home city for two periods; mem. Senate 1991–2006, Pres. of Senate and Pres. Congress of the Repub. (first woman) 2005–06; Perm. Rep., UN, New York 2006–. *Publications:* Ministry of the Environment, Last Chance 1993, Corruption: Until When? 1995, Up Front 1997, For Truth 2001, The Reform Congress 2006.
Address: Permanent Mission of Colombia, 140 East 57th Street, 5th Floor, New York, NY 10022, USA (office). *Telephone:* (212) 355-7776 (ext. 223) (office). *Fax:* (212) 371-2813 (office). *E-mail:* cblum@colombiaun.org (office). *Website:* www.colombiaun.org (office).

BOATENG, Paul (Yaw), PC, LLB; British diplomatist, politician, lawyer and broadcaster; *High Commissioner to South Africa;* b. 14 June 1951, Hackney, London; m. Janet Alleyne 1980; two s. three d. *Education:* Ghana Int. School, Accra Acad., Apsley Grammar School and Univ. of Bristol. *Career:* solicitor, Paddington Law Centre 1976–79; solicitor and pnr, B. M. Birnberg & Co. 1979–87; called to Bar, Gray's Inn 1989; Legal Adviser, Scrap Sus Campaign 1977–81; mem. GLC (Labour) for Walthamstow 1981–86, Chair. Police Cttee 1981–86, Vice-Chair. Ethnic Minorities Cttee 1981–86; MP (Labour) for Brent S 1987–2005; Home Office mem. House of Commons Environment Cttee 1987–89; Opposition Frontbench Spokesman on Treasury and Econ. Affairs 1989–92, on Legal Affairs, Lord Chancellor's Dept 1992–97; Parl. Under-Sec. of State, Dept of Health 1997–98; Minister of State 1998–2001, Deputy Home Sec. 1999–2001; Minister for Young People 2000–01; Financial Sec. to HM Treasury 2001–02, Chief Sec. 2002–05; High Commr to S Africa 2005–; Chair. Afro-Caribbean Educ. Resource Project 1978–86, Westminster CRC 1979–81; Gov. Police Staff Coll., Bramshill 1981–84; mem. Home Sec.'s Advisory Council on Race Relations 1981–86, WCC Comm. on Programme to Combat Racism 1984–91, Police Training Council 1981–85; Exec. Nat. Council for Civil Liberties 1980–86; mem. Court of Univ. of Bristol 1994–; mem. Bd ENO 1984–97; Hon. LLD (Lincoln Univ., Pa) (Bristol). *Television work includes:* Behind the Hardlines (BBC), Nothing but the Truth

(Channel 4). *Publications include:* Reclaiming the Ground (contrib.) 1993, Introduction to Sense and Sensibility, The Complete Jane Austen 1993.
Address: British High Commission, 255 Hill Street, Arcadia, Pretoria 0002, South Africa (office). *Telephone:* (12) 4217500 (office). *Fax:* (12) 4217555 (office). *E-mail:* media.pretoria@fco.gov.uk (office). *Website:* www.britain.org.za (office).

BOATSWAIN, Anthony; Grenadian politician; *Minister of Economic Development and Planning; Career:* elected MP for St Patrick W 1999, re-elected 2003; currently Minister of Finance and Planning 2003–07, of Econ. Devt and Planning 2007–; mem. NNP.
Address: Ministry of Economic Development and Planning, Building 3, Financial Complex, The Carenage, St George's, Grenada (office). *Telephone:* 440-2214 (office). *Fax:* 440-0775 (office). *E-mail:* finance@gov.gd (office); director@economicaffairs.grenada.gd (office). *Website:* economicaffairs.grenada.gd (office).

BOBBITT, Philip Chase, JD, PhD; American academic and government official; *A. W. Walker Centennial Chair in Law, University of Texas;* b. 22 July 1948, Temple, Tex. *Education:* Princeton Univ., Yale Univ., Univ. of Oxford, UK. *Career:* Asst Prof. of Law, Univ. of Texas School of Law 1976–79, Prof. 1979–, A. W. Walker Centennial Chair 1996–; Jr Research Fellow, Nuffield Coll., Univ. of Oxford 1982–84, Research Fellow 1984–85, Anderson Sr Research Fellow 1985–91, mem. Modern History Faculty 1984–91; Sr Research Fellow, War Studies Dept, Kings Coll. London, UK 1994–97; Assoc. Counsel to Pres. of USA for Intelligence and Int. Security 1980–81; Legal Counsel to US Senate Intra-Contra Cttee 1987–88; Counsellor on Int. Law, US State Dept 1990–93; Dir for Intelligence, Nat. Security Council 1997–98, Sr Dir of Critical Infrastructure 1998–99, Sr Dir for Strategic Planning 1999; mem. American Law Inst., Council on Foreign Relations, Pacific Council on Int. Policy, Int. Inst. for Strategic Studies; fmr Trustee, Princeton Univ. *Publications include:* Tragic Choices (co-author) 1978, Constitutional Fate 1982, Democracy and Deterrence 1987, US Nuclear Strategy (co-author) 1989, Constitutional Interpretation 1991, The Shield of Achilles: War, Peace and the Course of History 2002, Terror and Consent: The Wars for the Twenty-First Century 2008.
Address: The University of Texas School of Law, TNH4.107, D1800, 727 East Dean Keeton Street, Austin, TX 78712, USA (office). *Telephone:* (512) 232-1376 (office); (512) 474-6460 (home). *Fax:* (512) 471-6988 (office). *E-mail:* pbobbitt@mail.law.utexas.edu (office). *Website:* www.utexas.edu (office).

BOBUŢAC, Valeriu; Moldovan politician and diplomatist; *Ambassador to Hungary;* b. 13 March 1945, Khankaun; m. Maria Bobutac; two c. *Education:* Lvov Trade-Econ. Inst., Ukraine, Higher CP School, Kiev, Ukraine. *Career:* worked in Comsomol, First-Sec. Cen. Cttee then Sec. Cen. Cttee Moldovan CP; Deputy Minister of Econs and Reforms; Amb. to Russia 1997–99, 2001; Prime Minister of Moldova 1999–2000; at Ministry of Foreign Affairs 2002–05; Amb. to Hungary (also accred. to Slovenia, Croatia, Bosnia and Herzegovina, Holy See) 2005–, also Rep. to Danube Comm. 2005–.
Address: Embassy of Hungary, 1024 Budapest, Ady Endre u. 16, Hungary (office). *Telephone:* (1) 336-3450 (office). *Fax:* (1) 209-1195 (office). *E-mail:* budapesta@mfa.md (office). *Website:* www.moldovaembassy.hu (office).

BOCAR BA, Ibrahim; Malian diplomatist; m. Ba Fanta Barry. *Career:* Amb. to Belgium and Perm. Rep. to EU (also accred to Luxembourg, Netherlands and UK) 2003–.
Address: Embassy of Mali, Avenue Molière 487, 1050 Brussels, Belgium (office). *Telephone:* (2) 345-74-32 (office). *Fax:* (2) 344-57-00 (office). *E-mail:* mali@skynet.be (office).

BOCHARNIKOV, Mikhail Nikolayevich; Russian diplomatist; *Ambassador to Kazakhstan;* b. 6 March 1948, Moscow; m.; one d. *Education:* Moscow Inst. of Int. Relations. *Career:* mem. staff Ministry of Foreign Affairs –1992; Amb. to Zambia 1992–96; Dir Dept of African Countries, Ministry of Foreign Affairs 1996–99; Amb. to Greece 1999–2003; Amb. for Special Missions of the Ministry of Foreign Affairs (Regulation of the Conflict between Abkhazia and Georgia); Amb. to Kazakhstan 2006–.
Address: Embassy of the Russian Federation, Barayev 4, Astana 010000, Kazakhstan. *Telephone:* (3272) 22-17-14 (office). *Fax:* (3172) 22-38-49 (office). *E-mail:* rfe@nursat.kz (office). *Website:* www.rfembassy.kz (office).

BOD, Péter Ákos, PhD; Hungarian economist, politician and academic; *Professor of Economic Policy, Budapest Corvinus University;* b. 28 July 1951, Szigetvár; divorced; one d. *Education:* high school, Miskolc, Univ. of Econ., Budapest. *Career:* worked as researcher, later Dept head, Inst. for Econ. Planning; UNDP adviser in Ghana; mem. of Parl. (Hungarian Democratic Forum) 1990–91; Minister of Industry and Trade 1990–91;

Pres. Nat. Bank of Hungary 1991–94; mem. Bd EBRD, London 1995–97; Prof. of Econ. Policy and Dept Chair., Budapest Corvinus Univ. 2001–; Personal Econ. Adviser to Pres. of the Repub. 2001–05; Medal of Merit, Pres. of the Repub. 2005. *Publications:* The Entrepreneurial State in the Contemporary Market Economy 1987, Foundations of Economic Theory and Policy 1999, The World of Money – The Money of the World 2001, Economic Policy 2002.
Address: Fövam tér 8, Budapest Corvinus University, 1093 Budapest, Hungary (office). *Telephone:* (1) 482-5370 (office). *Fax:* (1) 482-5034 (office). *E-mail:* petera.bod@uni-corvinus.hu (office). *Website:* www.corvinus.hu (office).

BODE, Ridvan, MSc; Albanian economist and politician; *Minister of Finance;* b. 26 May 1959, Korcë. *Education:* Higher Agricultural Inst., Tirana, Mediterranean Agricultural Inst. (DSPU), Montpellier, France. *Career:* Head, Finance Division, Perrenjas, Librazhd 1983–89; Lecturer on Financial Analysis and Accountability, Tirana Agrarian Univ. 1991–95; Dir-Gen. Albanian Customs Gen. Dept 1995–96; elected MP (Democratic Party—DP) for Devoli Dist 1996, Minister of Finance 1996–97, 2005–; mem. DP Nat. Council and Presidency 1997, Gen.-Sec. 1997–; Visiting Lecturer, Faculty of Econs, Tirana Univ. 2002–. *Publications:* numerous papers on financial analysis.
Address: Ministry of Finance, Bulevardi Dëshmorët e Kombit, Tirana, Albania (office). *Telephone:* (4) 267654 (office). *Fax:* (4) 226111 (office). *E-mail:* hvako@minfin.gov.al (office); secretary.minister@minfin.gov.al (office). *Website:* www.minfin.gov.al (office).

BODEN, Dieter, PhD; German diplomatist; b. 1940. *Education:* Münster and Hamburg Univs. *Career:* entered Foreign Service as career diplomat 1968; Head, OSCE Mission to Georgia 1995–96; Consul Gen. in St Petersburg, Russia –1999; Special Rep. of UN Sec.-Gen. (Asst Sec.-Gen.) to Georgia and Head of UN Observer Mission to Georgia (UNOMIG) 1999–2002; Head, Perm. Mission of FRG to OSCE 2002–05, then Chair. OSCE Office for Democracy and Human Rights (ODIHR), currently Head, OSCE/ODIHR Observation Mission in Georgia. *Publications:* The Image of the German in Soviet and Russian Literature 1982; numerous articles on political and literary topics.
Address: Krtsanisi Governmental Residence, Krtsanisi St. 0114 Tbilisi Georgia (office). *Telephone:* (32) 20-23-03 (office). *Fax:* (32) 20-23-04 (office). *Website:* www.osce.org/odihr-elections (office).

BODEWIG, Kurt; German politician; *Chairman, Baltic Sea Forum;* b. 26 April 1955, Rheinberg; m.; two s. *Education:* commercial coll. *Career:* joined SPD 1973, mem. Nat. Exec. Cttee 2000–05; held various party posts 1982–98; mem. Bundestag 1998–; Minister of Transport, Building and Housing 2000–02; Chair. Baltic Sea Forum e.V., Bd Trustees German-Lithuanian-Forum; Deputy Chair. Cttee on the Affairs of the EU; Pres. Deutsche Verkehrswacht e.V.; mem. European Council and Parl. Ass., Baltic Sea Parl. Conf.; Deputy mem. NATO Parl. Ass.
Address: Bundestag, Platz der Republik 1, 11011 Berlin, Germany (office). *Telephone:* (30) 22775313 (office). *Fax:* (30) 22776313 (office). *E-mail:* kurt.bodewig@bundestag.de (office). *Website:* www.kurt-bodewig.de.

BODINI, Daniele, MSc, MBA; San Marino diplomatist; *Permanent Representative, United Nations;* b. 20 Dec. 1945, Erba, Italy. *Education:* Univ. of Rome, Columbia Univ., New York. *Career:* attaché, Perm. Mission to UN, New York 1995–2004, Deputy Perm. Rep. 2004–05, Perm. Rep. 2005–; Chair. American-Italian Cancer Foundation, Foundation for Italian Art and Culture; Pres. New York's Friends of San Patrignano; Guarantor, Italian Acad., Columbia Univ.; mem. Bd of Advisers Columbia Univ. School of Business.
Address: Permanent Mission of San Marino to the United Nations, 327 East 50th Street, New York, NY 10022, USA (office). *Telephone:* (212) 751-1234 (office). *Fax:* (212) 751-1436 (office). *E-mail:* sanmarinoun@hotmail.com (office).

BOEL, Else Mariann Fischer; Danish politician; *Commissioner for Agriculture and Rural Development, European Commission;* b. 15 April 1943, Aasum, Funen. *Career:* Man. Sec. export co. Copenhagen 1965–67, Finance Man. 1967–71; mem. Munkebo Municipal Council 1982–91, 1994–97, Second Deputy Mayor 1986–90; Chair. Liberal Party Kerteminde constituency 1987–89; mem. Folketing for Funen County 1990–, Chair. Food, Agric. and Fisheries Cttee 1994–98, Trade and Industry Cttee 1998–99, Fiscal Affairs Cttee 1998–99; Minister of Food, Agric. and Fisheries 2001–04; EU Commr for Agric. and Rural Devt 2004–; mem. Cen. Bd, Liberal Party 1990–, mem. Man. Cttee Parl. Liberal Party 1990–; Chair. High Schools' Secr. 1993–; mem. Nat. Assessment Council 1994–98, Nat. Tax Tribunal 1998–2001; mem. Cttee of Reps Østifterne 1991–; mem. Bd of Govs Boel Fund 1992–.

Address: European Commission, 200 rue de la Loi, 1049 Brussels, Belgium (office); Dr. Tværgade 59, 3. sal, 1302 Copenhagen K, Denmark. *Telephone:* (2) 299-11-11 (office). *Fax:* (2) 295-01-38 (office). *Website:* europa.eu (office).

BOGDAN, Angela, BA, BEd, MA; Canadian diplomatist; *High Commissioner to Sri Lanka;* m.; two c. *Education:* York Univ. *Career:* joined Dept of External Affairs and Int. Trade 1984, overseas postings to Melbourne and Warsaw, fmr mem. Perm. Mission to NATO, Brussels; Amb. to Yugoslavia 2001–03; Dir Global Partnership Program, Dept of External Affairs and Int. Trade 2003–06; High Commr to Sri Lanka (also accred to the Maldives) 2007–.
Address: High Commission of Canada, 6 Gregory's Road, Cinnamon Gdns, POB 1006, Colombo, Sri Lanka (office). *Telephone:* (11) 5326232 (office). *Fax:* (11) 5226299 (office). *E-mail:* clmbo@international.gc.ca (office). *Website:* www.dfait-maeci.gc.ca/world/embassies/srilanka (office).

BOGDANOR, Vernon, CBE, MA, FRSA, FBA; British academic; *Professor of Government, University of Oxford;* b. 16 July 1943, London; m. Judith Beckett 1972 (divorced 2000); two s. *Education:* Queen's Coll. and Nuffield Coll. Oxford. *Career:* Fellow, Brasenose Coll. Oxford 1966–, Sr Tutor 1979–85, 1996–97; mem. Council of Hansard Soc. for Parl. Govt 1981–97; Special Adviser, House of Lords Select Cttee on European Communities 1982–83; adviser to Govts of Czech Repub., Slovakia, Hungary and Israel on constitutional and electoral matters 1988–; Reader in Govt Univ. of Oxford 1989–96, Prof. of Govt 1996–; Special Adviser, House of Commons Public Service Cttee 1996; Gresham Prof. of Law, Gresham Coll., London 2004–07; mem. UK del. to CSCE Conf. Oslo 1991; Mishcon Lecturer 1994; Magna Carta Lecturer 2006; Hon. Fellow Soc. for Advanced Legal Studies 1997. *Publications:* Devolution 1979, The People and the Party System 1981, Multi-party Politics and the Constitution 1983, What is Proportional Representation? 1984, The Blackwell Encyclopaedia of Political Institutions (ed.) 1987, Comparing Constitutions (co-author) 1995, The Monarchy and the Constitution 1995, Politics and the Constitution 1996, Power and the People 1997, Devolution in the United Kingdom 1999, The British Constitution in the Twentieth Century (ed.) 2003, Joined-Up Government (ed.) 2005.
Address: Brasenose College, Oxford, OX1 4AJ, England. *Telephone:* (1865) 277830. *Fax:* (1865) 277822.

BOGDANOV, Vsevolod Leonidovich; Russian journalist; *President, International Confederation of Journalists' Unions;* b. 6 Feb. 1944, Arkhangelsk Region; m.; three d. *Education:* Leningrad State Univ. *Career:* corresp., ed. in newspapers, radio and TV Magadan 1961–76; Head Chief Dept of Periodicals State Cttee of Publs 1976–89; Dir-Gen. TV programmes State Radio and TV Cttee 1989–92; Chair. Russian Union of Journalists 1992–; Pres. Nat. Journalist Trade Union 1999–; Pres. Int. Confed. of Journalists' Unions 1999–.
Address: Union of Journalists, Zubovsky blvd 4, 119021 Moscow, Russia (office). *Telephone:* (495) 201-51-01 (office). *E-mail:* ruj@ruj.ru (office). *Website:* www.ruj.ru (office).

BOGLE, Ellen Gray; Jamaican diplomatist and government official (retd); b. 9 Oct. 1941, St Andrew; one s. one d. *Education:* St Andrew High School, Univ. of the West Indies. *Career:* Dir Foreign Trade Div., Ministry of Foreign Affairs, with responsibility for formulation of Jamaica's Foreign Trade policy 1978–81; fmr Dir Jamaica Nat. Export Corpn; High Commr in Trinidad & Tobago 1981–89; High Commr in UK 1989–94; fmr Amb., Ministry of Foreign Affairs and Foreign Trade; Amb. and Special Envoy to the Asscn of Caribbean States and CARICOM 1997; fmr Under-Sec. Bilateral and Regional Affairs, Ministry of Foreign Affairs and Foreign Trade; represented Jamaica at numerous int. confs; Commdr Order of Distinction 1987.
Address: c/o Ministry of Foreign Affairs and Foreign Trade, 21 Dominica Drive, Kingston 5, Jamaica (office).

BOGOLLAGAMA, Rohitha; Sri Lankan lawyer and politician; *Minister of Foreign Affairs;* b. 5 Aug. 1954, Nikaweratiya; m.; two c. *Education:* Ananda Coll. and Sri Lanka Law Coll. *Career:* apptd attorney 1976; fmr Chair. Sri Lanka Cement Corpn, Sathosa Printers; fmr Dir Foreign Employment Bureau; Legal and Political Adviser to Voice of America project in Sri Lanka 1991–99; Chair. and Dir-Gen. Bd of Investment of Sri Lanka 1993–2000; mem. Parl. (United National Party—UNP) 2000–, served on Parl. Consultative Cttees on Finance, Foreign Affairs, Defence, Industrial Devt and Investment Promotion and Power and Energy 2000–05, Chair. Cttee on Public Enterprises 2005–07, Minister of Industrial Devt 2001–04, of Enterprise Devt and Investment Promotion 2004–07, of Foreign Affairs 2007–.

Address: Ministry of Foreign Affairs, Republic Building, Colombo 1, Sri Lanka (office). *Telephone:* (11) 2325371 (office). *Fax:* (11) 2446091 (office). *E-mail:* cypher@formin.gov.lk (office). *Website:* www.slmfa.gov.lk (office).

BOHATYROVA, Raisa Vasylivna; Ukrainian gynaecologist and politician; *Chairman, National Security and Defence Council; Career:* fmr Minister of Health; mem. Verkhovna Rada (Parl.) 2002–, mem. Party of Regions, fmr Leader Parl. faction; Chair. Nat. Security and Defence Council 2008–. *Address:* National Security and Defence Council, c/o Office of the President, 01021 Kyiv, vul. Shovkovichna 12, Ukraine (office). *Telephone:* (44) 226-20-77 (office). *Fax:* (44) 293-61-61 (office). *E-mail:* president@adm .gov.ua (office). *Website:* www.president.gov.ua (office).

BOIDEVAIX, Serge Marie-Germain, LèsL, LenD; French diplomatist; b. 15 Aug. 1928, Aurillac, Cantal; m. Francine Savard 1966; two d. *Education:* Lycée d'Aurillac, Lycée Louis-le-Grand, Faculté de Droit and Faculté des Lettres, Paris and Ecole Nat. d'Admin. *Career:* joined Ministry of Foreign Affairs 1954; served Vienna, Washington, DC and Bonn; Adviser, Pvt. Office of Minister of Defence 1969–73; Dir Office of Minister of Foreign Affairs 1973–74; Adviser on int. affairs and cooperation, Office of Prime Minister 1974–76; Amb. to Poland 1977–80, to India 1982–85, to Germany 1986–92; Deputy Sec.-Gen. Ministry of Foreign Affairs 1985–86; Sec. Gen. 1992–93; Sr mem. Council of State 1993–97; Chair. SB Consultants 1997–; Pres. Franco-Arab Chamber of Commerce 2002–06; Commdr, Légion d'honneur, Ordre Nat. du Mérite. *Address:* 5, Rue des Eaux, 75116 Paris, France (home).

BØJER, Jørgen R.H.; Danish diplomatist; *Chairman, Danish Centre for International Studies and Human Rights;* b. 5 March 1940, Hjørring; m. Lone Heilskov 1964; two d. *Education:* Univ. of Århus, Institut d'Etudes Politiques, Paris. *Career:* Foreign Service Officer 1967; Sec. of Embassy, Prague 1971; Head of Section, Ministry of Foreign Affairs, Copenhagen 1973, Dir 1982, Deputy Under-Sec. 1992; Visiting Fellow, Stanford Univ. 1978; Counsellor, Embassy, Washington, DC 1979; Amb. to Egypt (also accred to Sudan and Somalia), then to Austria, Slovenia, Bosnia and Herzegovina; Perm. Rep. to Int. Orgs in Vienna 1993; Perm. Rep. to UN, New York 1997–2001, Co-Chair. UN Int. Conf. on Financing for Devt 2001; Amb. to Czech Repub. 2001–07; Chair. Danish Centre for International Studies and Human Rights 2006–. *Address:* Danish Centre for International Studies and Human Rights, Strandgade 56, 1401 Copenhagen K, Denmark. *Telephone:* 32-69-86-86 (office). *Fax:* 32-69-86-00 (office). *E-mail:* dcism@dcism.dk (office). *Website:* www.dcism.dk (office).

BOKROS, Lajos, PhD; Hungarian economist, banker and academic; *Professor of Economics and Public Policy, Central European University;* b. 26 June 1954, Budapest; m. Maria Gyetuai; one s. one d. *Education:* Univ. of Econs, Budapest, Univ. of Panama. *Career:* Research Fellow, Financial Research Inst., Hungarian Ministry of Finance, Budapest 1980–86, Chief of Public Finance Div. 1986–87; Deputy Gen. Man. Econ. Dept, Nat. Bank of Hungary 1987–89, Man. Dir 1989, Dir Capital Market Dept 1989–91; Chair. Budapest Stock Exchange 1990–95; Chair. and CEO Budapest Bank 1991–95; Chair. Budapest Stock Exchange early 1990s; Minister of Finance 1995–96; Sr Advisor, Financial Sector Devt, IBRD 1996–97, Dir Pvt. and Financial Sector Devt, ECA 1997–99, Dir Financial Advisory Services, Europe and Cen. Asia 1999–2004; Prof. of Econs and Public Policy, Cen. European Univ. 2004–, also Sr Vice-Pres. for Research and Int. Projects and COO; Chief Econ. Adviser to Prime Minister of Croatia 2002–, to Deputy Prime Minister of Poland 2001–; mem. Bd of Dirs State Property Agency 1990–91. *Publications:* Development Commodity Production, Market Economy 1984, Market and Money in the Modern Economy 1985, Public Finance Reform during Transition – The Experience of Hungary (co-author) 1998, Visegrad Twins' Diverging Path to Relative Prosperity – Finance a Uver 2000, Financial Transition in Europe and Central Asia – The World Bank (co-author) 2001, Competition and Solidarity – Comparative Economic Studies 2004. *Address:* Department of Public Policy, Central European University, 1051 Budapest, Nador utca 9-11, Hungary. *Telephone:* (1) 328-3434 (office). *E-mail:* bokrosl@ceu.hu (office). *Website:* www.ceu.hu/dpp/people/bokros .htm (office).

BOLADUADUA, Emitai Lausiki, BSc, DipEd; Fijian diplomatist; *Chairman, Cakaudrove Provincial Council;* b. 13 April 1944; m. Asinate Boladuadua (née Taleaua); four c. *Education:* Queen Victoria School, Suva Grammar School, Univ. of New England, Armidale, NSW, Australia, Univ. of Reading, UK. *Career:* Asst Teacher, Ratu Kadavulevu School 1968–70, Head of Science Dept 1970–72, Vice-Prin. 1973–80, Prin. 1981–83; Prin. Labasa Coll. 1984–87, Fiji Inst. of Tech. 1988–90; Deputy Sec. for Educ., Youth and Sport 1990–93, for Foreign Affairs and Civil Aviation 1993–97; Perm. Sec. for Information, Broadcasting, TV and Telecommunications

1997, for Home Affairs and Immigration 1997–99, for Educ. and Tech. 1999, for Foreign Affairs and External Trade 1999–2000; with Ministry of Foreign Affairs and External Trade 2002; High Commr to UK (also accred as Amb. to Ireland, Denmark, Germany, Israel, Egypt and the Holy See) 2002–08; Chair. Cakaudrove Prov. Council 2008–; mem. Exec. Fijian Teachers Asscn 1969–72, Chemical Soc. for the S Pacific 1987–89, Fiji Govt Scholarship Cttee 1990–92, 1999, Land Transport Authority Bd 2002, Charter Preparation Cttee for Reorganization of Dept of Immigration 2002; rep. or del. to numerous nat. and int. confs and meetings, including World Confed. of Orgs of Teaching Profession, UNESCO, UNDP, Fed. of Island Nations for World Peace, Pacific Islands Devt Programme, IAEA; Civil Service Medal 1995. *Address:* Office of the Chairman, Cakaudrove Provincial Council, Savusavu, Fiji (office).

BOLAÑOS SUÁREZ, Jorge Alberto, MA; Cuban diplomatist and politician; *Head of Cuban Interests Section (Embassy of Switzerland) in USA;* b. 27 Nov. 1936, Las Tunas; m. Graciela Quercl Quercl; one s. one d. *Education:* Univ. of Havana, Univ. of London, UK. *Career:* Country Specialist, Chief of Dept, Ministry of Foreign Affairs 1963, Staff Dir 1964, First Sec., London 1965–68, Dir Western Europe Countries Div. 1968–71, Amb. to Poland 1971–74, to Czechoslovakia 1974–77, to UK 1977–81, to Brazil 1986–94, to Mexico 2001–07, Head of Cuban Interests Section (Embassy of Switzerland), Washington, DC, USA 2007–; Vice-Minister of Foreign Affairs 1981–86, 1994–95, First Vice-Minister 1995–2001, 2004–; mem. Nat. Bd Union of Banks and Insurance Cos 1959, 1963; Great Kt Commdr, Nat. Order of Merit (Poland), Order Julius Fucik, Friendship Medal, Army Medal and Militias Medal (Czechoslovakia), Queen Isabel II Jubilee Medal (UK), Great Kt Commdr, Order Cruzeiro do Sul, First Class Order of Merit of Brasilia and Medal of Merit Pedro Ernesto of State of Rio de Janeiro (Brazil), Underground Combatant Medal, 20th Anniversary of the Revolution Medal, Enrique Hart Order, 30th and 40th FAR Anniversary Medals. *Address:* Cuban Interests Section, c/o Embassy of Switzerland, 2630 16th Street, NW, Washington, DC 20009, USA (office). *Telephone:* (202) 797-8518 (office). *Fax:* (202) 797-8521 (office). *E-mail:* Informacion1@sicuw .org (office); Informacion2@sicuw.org (office). *Website:* www.eda.admin .ch/eda/en/arch/arcwas/repusa/wacuba.html (office).

BOLDYREV, Yuri Yuryevich; Russian politician; b. 29 May 1960, Leningrad; m. 1990; one s. *Education:* Leningrad Electrotech. Inst., Leningrad Inst. of Finance and Econs. *Career:* worked as engineer Cen. Research Inst. of Vessel Electronics and Tech. 1983–89; mem. CPSU 1987–90; USSR People's Deputy 1989–91; del. of 28 CPSU Congress; left CPSU 1990; mem. Council of Reps, then of Co-ordination Council of Democratic Russia Movt 1990–91; mem. Higher Advisory Council to Chair. of Russian Supreme Soviet (later to Pres. of Russian Fed.) 1990–92; consultant Russian Govt Feb.–March 1992; Chief State Inspector of Russian Fed., Chief Control Man. of Admin. of Presidency 1992–93; mem. Centre of Econ. and Political Research (Epicentre) 1993–94; mem. Duma (Parl.) 1993–95; Founder-mem. and Deputy Chair. Yabloko Movt 1993–95, left Party Sept. 1995; Deputy Chair. Accountant Chamber of Russian Fed. 1995–2001; Head of St Petersburg electoral candidates, Spravedlivaya Rossiya party (Fair Russia) 2007. *Address:* c/o B. Dmitrovka St 32/1, Moscow 107031, Russia (office). *Telephone:* (495) 650-38-80 (office). *E-mail:* info@spravedlivo.ru (office). *Website:* www.spravedlivo.ru (office).

BOLKIAH, HRH Prince Mohamed; Brunei politician; *Minister of Foreign Affairs;* b. 27 Aug. 1947, brother of Sultan Haji Hassanal Bolkiah Mu'izuddin Waddaulah of Brunei. *Education:* Royal Mil. Acad., Sandhurst, UK. *Career:* Minister of Foreign Affairs 1984–. *Address:* Ministry of Foreign Affairs, Jalan Subok, Bandar Seri Begawan (office); Hijau Baiduri, Bukit Kayangan, Jalan Tutong, Bandar Seri Begawan BD 2710, Brunei (home). *Telephone:* (2) 261177 (office); (2) 244101 (office). *Fax:* (2) 261709 (office); (2) 244659 (office).

BOLKIAH MU'IZUDDIN WADDAULAH, HM Sultan and Yang di-Pertuan of Brunei Darussalam, Haji Hassanal, DK, PSPNB, PSLI, SPBM, PANB; *Head of State, Prime Minister, Minister of Defence and Minister of Finance;* b. 15 July 1946; m. HM Raja Isteri Pengiran Anak Hajah Saleha 1965; two s. (including HRH Prince Haji al-Muhtadee Billah) four d.; also m. Mariam Abd Aziz 1981 (divorced 2003); two s. two d.; also m. HRH Pengiran Isteri Azrinaz Mazhar Hakim 2005; one s. *Education:* privately and Victoria Inst., Kuala Lumpur, Malaysia and Royal Mil. Acad., Sandhurst, UK. *Career:* appointed Crown Prince and Heir Apparent 1961; Ruler of State of Brunei Oct. 1967–; Prime Minister Jan. 1984–; Minister of Finance and Home Affairs 1984–86, of Defence Oct. 1986–, also of Finance; Hon. Marshal RAF 1992; Sovereign and Chief of Royal

Orders instituted by Sultans of Brunei; Head Dept of Islamic Religious Faith and Royal Custom and Tradition.
Address: Istana Nurul Iman, Bandar Seri Begawan, BA 1000, Brunei (office). *Telephone:* (2) 229988 (office). *Fax:* (2) 241717 (office). *E-mail:* info@jpm.gov.bn (office). *Website:* www.pmo.gov.bn.

BOLTEN, Joshua (Josh) B., BA, JD; American lawyer and government official; *White House Chief of Staff; Education:* Princeton Univ., Stanford Law School. *Career:* fmr Ed. Stanford Law Review; law clerk, US Dist Court, San Francisco 1980; Int. Trade Counsel to US Finance Cttee 1985–89, fmr Gen. Counsel to US Trade Rep.; Exec. Dir for Legal and Govt Affairs, Goldman Sachs Int., London 1994–99; Policy Dir Bush-Cheney presidential campaign 1999–2000; Asst to Pres., Deputy Chief of Staff for Policy 2001–03, Dir Office of Man. and Budget (OMB) 2003–06; White House Chief of Staff 2006–.
Address: Office of the Chief of Staff, The White House, 1600 Pennsylvania Avenue, NW, Washington, DC 20500, USA (office). *Telephone:* (202) 456-1414 (office). *Fax:* (202) 456-2461 (office). *Website:* www.whitehouse.gov/president (office).

BOLTON, John Robert, BA, JD; American lawyer, academic and fmr government official and fmr diplomatist; *Senior Fellow, American Enterprise Institute for Public Policy Research (AEI);* b. 20 Nov. 1948, Baltimore, Md; m. Gretchen Brainerd 1986; one d. *Education:* Yale Univ. *Career:* Assoc., Covington & Burling (law firm), Washington, DC 1974–81, Pnr 1983–85; Gen. Counsel, USAID 1981–82, Asst Admin. for Program and Policy Coordination 1982–83; Asst Attorney-Gen. for Legis. Affairs, US Dept of Justice 1985–88, Asst Attorney-Gen., Civil Div. 1988–89; Asst Sec. for Int. Org. Affairs, US State Dept 1989–93; Pnr, Lerner, Reed, Bolton & McManus LLP (law firm), Washington, DC 1993–99; Of Counsel, Kutak Rock 1999–2001; Sr Vice-Pres. American Enterprise Inst. (AEI), Washington, DC 1999–2001, Sr Fellow 2007–; Under-Sec. of State for Arms Control and Int. Security, US State Dept 2001–05; Perm. Rep. to UN, New York (recess appointment) 2005–06; Sr Adviser Kirkland & Ellis (law firm) 2008–; Sr Fellow, Manhattan Inst. 1993; Adjunct Prof., George Mason Univ. Law School 1994–2001; Pres. Nat. Policy Forum 1995–96; mem. US Comm. on Int. Religious Freedom 1999–2001. *Publication:* Surrender is not an Option: Defending America at the United Nations and Abroad 2008.
Address: American Enterprise Institute, 1150 Seventeenth Street, NW, Washington, DC 20036, USA (office). *Telephone:* (202) 862-5892 (office). *Fax:* (202) 862-7192 (office). *E-mail:* christine.samuelian@aei.org (office). *Website:* www.aei.org (office).

BOLY, Yéro; Burkinabè politician; *Minister of Defence;* b. 1954, Komki-Ipala; m. *Education:* Ecole Nat. d'Admin. *Career:* subprefect, Dori region 1978–80, l'Oudalan region 1980; civil servant, Ministry of the Interior 1983; Sec.-Gen. Namentenga Prov. and Prefect, Boulsa region 1983–84; Hiigh Commr, Gnagna Prov. 1984–86; Amb. to Côte-d'Ivoire 1986–88, to Libya 1988–95, to Iran 1990–92; Minister for Regional Affairs and Security 1995–2000; Head of Presidential Staff 2000–04; Minister of Defence 2004–; Grand Officier Ordre Nat. de Côte d'Ivoire 1988, Officier Ordre du Mérite (France) 2004, Commdr Ordre Nat. du Burkina Faso 2004; Médaille d'Honneur des Sapeurs Pompiers 2000, Médaille d'Honneur de la Police Nationale 2005.
Address: Ministry of Defence, 01 BP 496, Ouagadougou 01, Burkina Faso (office). *Telephone:* 50-30-72-14 (office). *Fax:* 50-31-36-10 (office). *E-mail:* yeo_boly@yahoo.fr (office). *Website:* www.defense.gov.bf.

BOND, Clifford G., MSc; American diplomatist; b. 23 Feb. 1948; m. Michele Thoren Bond; four c. *Education:* Georgetown Univ., LSE. *Career:* served in US Army in Germany; early career at Fed. Reserve Bank, New York then entered Foreign Service; Foreign Service Officer, Minister-Counselor, US Mission to EC; embassy postings in Belgrade, Stockholm, Prague; Special Adviser and Coordinator, Support East European Democracies (SEED) Program, Office of Deputy Sec. of State, Washington, DC 1990–92, Deputy Dir Office of Ind. States, Commonwealth Affairs 1992–95, Minister-Counsellor, Econ. Affairs, US Embassy in Moscow 1996–98, Head, Office of Caucasus and Cen. Asian Affairs 1998, Acting Prin. Deputy, Special Adviser, New Ind. States; Amb. to Bosnia and Herzegovina 2001–04; served as Sr Adviser to Congressional Comm. for Security and Cooperation in Europe; Assoc. Prof., Industrial Coll.of the Armed Forces, Nat. Defense Univ., Washington DC; High Rep. and EU Special Rep.'s Envoy to the Srebrenica Region 2007–; Recipient, Superior Honor, Meritorious Honor Awards.
Address: OHR Sarajevo, Emerika Bluma 1, 71 000 Sarajevo, Bosnia and Herzegovina (home). *Telephone:* (33) 283500 (office). *Fax:* (33) 283501 (office). *Website:* www.ohr.int (office).

BOND, Ian Andrew Minton, CVO, BA; British diplomatist; b. 19 April 1962, Birmingham; m. Kathryn Joan Bond; two s. one d. *Education:* King Edward's School, Birmingham, Phillips Acad., Andover, Mass, USA, Balliol Coll., Oxford. *Career:* joined FCO 1984, Soviet Dept 1984–85, Energy, Science and Space Dept 1986, Third Sec., UK Del. to NATO, Brussels 1987–89, Second Sec. 1990–90, Desk Officer, Security Policy Dept, FCO 1990–93, First Sec. (Political/Mil.), Moscow 1993–96, Desk Officer, Common Foreign and Security Policy, FCO 1996–97, Asst Head of Dept, Eastern Dept, FCO 1997–2000, Deputy Head of Mission, UK Del. to OSCE, Vienna 2000–04, Amb. to Latvia 2005–07; Counsellor Foreign Security and Policy Group, Embassy in Washington, DC 2007–.
Address: British Embassy, 3100 Massachusetts Avenue, NW, Washington, DC 20008, USA (office). *Telephone:* (202) 588-6500 (office). *Fax:* (202) 588-7870 (office). *E-mail:* washi@fco.gov.uk (office). *Website:* www.britainusa.com (office).

BONDEVIK, Kjell Magne; Norwegian politician and diplomatist; *Secretary-General's Special Humanitarian Envoy to the Horn of Africa, United Nations;* b. 3 Sept. 1947, Molde; m. Björg Bondevik 1970; two s. one d. *Education:* Free Faculty of Theology, Univ. of Oslo. *Career:* ordained minister 1979; Deputy Chair. Christian Democratic Youth Asscn 1968–70, Chair. 1970–73; Deputy mem. Storting 1969–73, mem. 1973–; Political Vice-Chair. Christian Democratic Party 1975–83, Chair. 1983–95; Minister of Church and Educ. 1983–86, Deputy Prime Minister 1985–86, Minister of Foreign Affairs 1989–90; Chair. Christian Democratic Party's Parl. Group 1981–83, 1986–89, 1993–97; Prime Minister of Norway 1997–2000, 2002–2005; UN Sec.-Gen.'s Special Humanitarian Envoy for the Horn of Africa 2006–; Founder and Pres. Oslo Center for Peace and Human Rights 2006–; mem. Club of Madrid; Hon. DTech (Brunel) 1997; Dr hc (Suffolk) 2000, (Wonkurang) 2000; Wittenberg Award, Luther Inst. 2000. *Publication:* Et liv i spenning 2006.
Address: Oslo Center for Peace and Human Rights, Postboks 2753 Solli, 0204 Oslo, Gange Rolvsgate 5, Norway (office). *Telephone:* 23-13-66-70 (office). *Fax:* 23-13-66-77 (office). *E-mail:* post@oslocenter.no (office). *Website:* www.oslocenter.no (office).

BONGO ONDIMBA, El Hadj Omar (Albert-Bernard); Gabonese politician and head of state; *President;* b. 30 Dec. 1935, Lewai, Franceville; m.; three c. *Education:* primary school at Bacongo (Congo–Brazzaville) and technical coll., Brazzaville. *Career:* civil servant; served in Air Force 1958–60; entered Ministry of Foreign Affairs 1960; Dir of Private Office of Pres. Léon Mba 1962, in charge of Information 1963–64, Nat. Defence 1964–65; Minister-Del. to Presidency in charge of Nat. Defence and Co-ordination, Information and Tourism 1965–66; Vice-Pres. of Govt, in charge of Co-ordination, Nat. Defence Planning, Information and Tourism 1966–67; Vice-Pres. of Gabon March–Nov. 1967, Pres. 1967–, Minister of Defence 1967–81, of Information 1967–80, of Planning 1967–77, Prime Minister 1967–75, Minister of the Interior 1967–70, of Devt 1970–77, of Women's Affairs 1976–77 and numerous other portfolios; Pres. UDEAC 1981; Founder and Sec.-Gen. Parti Démocratique Gabonais 1968; High Chancellor, Ordre Nat. de l'Etoile Equatoriale; decorations from the Ivory Coast, Niger, Chad, Cameroon, Central African Republic, Mauritius, Togo, Taiwan, Zaïre, France, UK and Guinea.
Address: Présidence de la République, Boîte Postale 546, Libreville, Gabon (office).

BONI, Yayi, PhD; Benin economist, banker and head of state; *President;* b. 1952, Tchaourou; m.; five c. *Education:* Nat. Univ. of Benin, Univ. of Dakar, Senegal, Univ. of Orleans and Paris Univ., France. *Career:* worked for Cen. Bank of the States of West Africa (BCEAO) becoming Deputy Dir 1980–88; Deputy Dir for Professional Devt, West African Centre for Banking Studies, Dakar 1988; worked in office of Pres. of Benin in charge of monetary and banking policies 1992–94; Pres. West African Devt Bank 1994–2006; Pres. of Benin 2006–; Chevalier de l'Ordre national de Mérite (France), Officier de l'Ordre National (Burkina Faso), Commdr, Ordre National of Benin, of Mali, of Niger, of Senegal.
Address: Office of the President, BP 1288, Cotonou, Benin (office). *Telephone:* 21-30-00-90 (office). *Fax:* 21-30-06-36 (office). *Website:* www.gouv.bj (office).

BONNELAME, Emile Patrick Jérémie; Seychelles politician and diplomatist; b. 24 Oct. 1938, Mahe. *Education:* Inst. Catholique de Paris, Inst. Ecuménique pour les Développement des Peuples, Paris, France, Sion School of Theology, Lucerne School of Theology, Switzerland, Univ. of Québec in Montréal, Canada. *Career:* teacher, Modern Secondary School of Seychelles 1967–75; Dir-Gen. of Information 1978–79; Prin.-Sec., Ministry of Educ. 1979–80, of External Relations 1981–83, of Educ. and Information 1983–86; Minister of Manpower 1986–88, of Transport 1988–89, of Agric. and Fisheries 1989–93, of Foreign Affairs 1997; Sec.-Gen. Indian Ocean Comm. 1993–97; Perm. Rep. to UN, New York

1997–2007, Amb. to USA 2005–07; Ed.-in-Chief L'Echo des Iles; Pres. Ministerial Council, Tuna Asscn; Co-ordinator Western Indian Ocean Tuna Org. (WIOTO); Gov. Int. Fund for Agricultural Devt; Head of Del. of Seychelles to numerous int. meetings of UN, OAU, ECA, FAO, UNESCO, EU, UNDP.
Address: Ministry of Foreign Affairs, Maison Queau de Quincy, PO Box 656, Mont Fleuri, Seychelles (office). *Telephone:* 283500 (office). *Fax:* 225398 (office). *E-mail:* dazemia@mfa.gov.sc (office). *Website:* seychelles .diplomacy.edu (office).

BONNICI, Ugo Mifsud (see Mifsud Bonnici, Ugo).

BONO MARTÍNEZ, José; Spanish politician; b. 14 Dec. 1950, Salobre; m.; four c. *Education:* Colegio de la Inmaculada, Alicante, Univ. of Deusto (ICADE). *Career:* lawyer –1979; fmr Prof. of Political Law, Universidad Complutense de Madrid; Pres. Castilla-La Mancha region 1983–; Minister of Defence 2004–06.
Address: c/o Ministry of Defence, Paseo de la Castellana 109, 28071 Madrid, Spain (office).

BOOS, Georgy Valentinovich, CandTechSc; Russian politician; b. 22 Jan. 1963, Moscow; m.; one d. *Education:* Moscow Energy Inst. *Career:* Sr Engineer, All-Union Research Inst. of Light Tech., also teacher of math., secondary school 1986–91; Founder, Dir-Gen., then Pres., Svetoservis Co. 1991–96; mem. State Duma 1996–98; Head, State Taxation Service of Russian Fed. Sept.–Dec. 1998; Minister of Revenue Dec. 1998–May 1999; Head, pre-election staff "Otechestvo-Vsya Rossiya" Movt; mem. State Duma 1999–, re-elected 2003 Yedinaya Rossiya party; Deputy Chair. 2000–; joined Yedinstvo and Otechestvo Union (later Yedibaya Rossiya) 2000–; Pres., Nat. Soc. of Light Tech.; designer of architectural illumination of Moscow 1996; State Prize 1996.
Address: State Duma, Okhotny Ryad 1, 103265 Moscow, Russia (office). *Telephone:* (495) 292-62-40 (office). *Fax:* (495) 292-80-07 (office).

BOOT, Max, BA, MA; American journalist; *Senior Fellow for National Security Studies, Council on Foreign Relations; Education:* Univ. of Calif., Berkeley, Yale Univ. *Career:* writer and ed. Christian Science Monitor 1992–94; writer and ed. Wall Street Journal 1994–97, Editorial Features Ed. 1997–02; currently Contrib. Ed. Weekly Standard, Foreign Affairs columnist Los Angeles Times newspaper; Sr Fellow for Nat. Security Studies, Council on Foreign Relations 2002–. *Publications:* Out of Order: Arrogance, Corruption and Incompetence on the Bench 1998, The Savage Wars of Peace: Small Wars and the Rise of American Power 2002, War Made New 2006.
Address: Council on Foreign Relations, Harold Pratt House, 58 East 68th Street, New York, NY 10021, USA (office). *Telephone:* (212) 434-9619 (office). *Fax:* (212) 434-9800 (office). *E-mail:* mboot@cfr.org (office). *Website:* www.cfr.org (office).

BOOTH, Donald E., BA, MA, MBA; American diplomatist; *Ambassador to Liberia;* m. Anita Booth; three c. *Education:* Georgetown Univ., Boston Univ., Nat. War Coll., Washington, DC. *Career:* career mem. Sr Foreign Service, Commercial Officer, Embassy in Monrovia 1979–81, was also stationed at embassies in Bucharest, Brussels and Libreville, has served as Int. Relations Officer, Office of Eastern European Affairs, as Desk Officer for Office of Egyptian Affairs and Office of E African Affairs, as Econ. Counselor in Athens, as Del. Chief for Bilateral Trade Affairs, Department of State, as Deputy Dir Office of Southern African Affairs, as Dir Office of W African Affairs, as Dir Office of Tech. and Specialized Agencies, Bureau of Int. Org. Affairs –2005, Amb. to Liberia 2005–.
Address: Embassy of the USA, 111 United Nations Drive, Mamba Point, PO Box 98, Monrovia, Liberia (office). *Telephone:* 226370 (office). *Fax:* 77010370 (office). *E-mail:* usvisamonrovia@state.gov (office). *Website:* monrovia.usembassy.gov (office).

BORDA, Dionisio, PhD; Paraguayan politician and economist; *Minister of Finance;* b. San Juan, Misiones. *Education:* Univs of Wis. and Mass, USA. *Career:* Prof. Catholic Univ. Nuestra Señora de la Asunción, Academic Dir, MA programme in Policy and Public Man.; Minister of Finance 2003–05 (resgnd), 2008–; currently Dir Center of Analysis and Diffusion, Economía Paraguaya (CADEP);. *Publications:* Presupuesto, Política Fiscal y Desempeño Económico en la Transición 2001, Globalización y Crisis fiscal (Ed.) 2003, Seguridad Social (Ed.) 2003.
Address: Ministry of Finance, Chile 128 esq. Palmas, Asunción, Paraguay (office). *Telephone:* (21) 44-0010 (office). *E-mail:* info@hacienda.gov.py (office). *Website:* www.hacienda.gov.py (office).

BORDEN, Anthony, BA; American journalist; *Executive Director, Institute for War and Peace Reporting; Education:* Yale Univ. *Career:* freelance and staff reporter, New York 1983–88; Staff Reporter, American Lawyer

(magazine), New York 1988–90; Launch Ed. Transitions, Inst. for Journalism, London/Prague 1998; Ed. War Report, London 1992–98; Consultant, Dept for Int. Devt, UK Govt 1999–2002; Founder and Exec. Dir Inst. for War and Peace Reporting 1991–; Assoc. Gov. New End Primary School, London; mem. Exec. Cttee New End Second Century Campaign; One World Media Awards, New Media Award 2004. *Publications:* Breakdown: War and Reconstruction in Yugoslavia (co-ed.) 1992, An Elections Handbook for Bosnian Journalists (co-ed.) 1996, Reporting Macedonia: The New Accommodation (co-ed.) 1998, Out of Time: Draskovic, Djindjic and Serbian Opposition Against Milosevic (co-ed.) 2000; numerous contribs to newpapers and journals.
Address: Institute for War and Peace Reporting, Lancaster House, 33 Islington High Street, London, N1 9LH, England (office). *Telephone:* (20) 7713-7130 (office). *Fax:* (20) 7713-7140 (office). *E-mail:* tony@iwpr.net (office). *Website:* www.iwpr.net (office).

BORDÓN GONZÁLEZ, José Octavio, MA; Argentine politician and diplomatist; m.; three c. *Education:* Universidad del Salvador, Buenos Aires. *Career:* mem. Partido Justicialista 1966–, elected Pres. Mendoza Br. of Party 1985, Foreign Affairs Sec. of Party 1987; elected Nat. Rep. 1983; Gov. Mendoza Prov. 1987–91; fmr Nat. Senator and Chair. Senate Foreign Relations Cttee; Founder FREPASO political coalition 1994 and cand. in presidential elections; fmr Pres. Peronist Party; fmr Int. Adviser to IDB; Amb. to USA 2003–07; Prof. of Govt and Political Science 1971–96; Fellow, Woodrow Wilson Center, Tinker Foundation and Visiting Prof., Georgetown Univ. 1992; lecturer at several univs, including LSE, Oxford, Salamanca, Bologna, Stanford, São Paulo, Fletcher School of Diplomacy; Pres. Andean Foundation 1990–, Instituto de Economia y Organizacion de Mendoza (INSTECO) 1992–; mem. Argentine Council on Int. Relations (CARI), Pacific Council on Int. Policies; Sr Fellow, Inter-American Dialogue. *Publications:* Immigration and Emigration of Professionals in Argentina 1972, La Racionalidad del Peronismo 1986, Political and Ethic Code for Argentina 1997; numerous articles and chapters in books.
Address: c/o Ministry of Foreign Affairs, International Trade and Worship, Esmeralda 1212, C1007ABR Buenos Aires, Argentina (office). *Website:* www.cancilleria.gov.ar (office).

BORDONARO, Molly Hering, BA; American diplomatist; *Ambassador to Malta;* b. Portland, Ore.; m. Matthew Bordonaro; three c. *Education:* Univ. of Colorado. *Career:* worked in commercial real estate in Portland; owned her own strategic consulting firm; fmr Prin., Portland office of The Gallatin Group; mem. Bd of Dirs Fannie Mae Corpn 2001–04; Co-founding Dir Portland Family of Funds; fmr mem. US Congress Comm. on Advancement of Women in Science and Tech.; fmr Sr Legis. Dir for American Legis. Exchange Council, Washington, DC; fmr Chair. Pacific states for Bush-Cheney presidential campaign 2000, Northwest regional chair. 2004; Republican nominee for Congress in Ore.'s First Dist 1998; has served on bds of numerous civic groups including Ore. Children's Scholarship Fund, Portland Center Stage; Amb. to Malta 2005–; recognized by Portland Business Journal as one of nine 'People of the Year' 2001, named as one of '40 under 40' leaders of the community 2002.
Address: PO Box 535, Valletta, CMR 01 (office); US Embassy, Development House, 3rd Floor, St Anne Street, Floriana VLT 01, Malta (office). *Telephone:* 25614000 (office). *Fax:* 21243229 (office). *E-mail:* usembmalta@state.gov (office). *Website:* malta.usembassy.gov (office).

BORDYUZHA, Gen. Nikolai Nikolayevich; Russian politician and diplomatist; *Secretary General, Collective Security Treaty Organization (CSTO);* b. 22 Oct. 1949, Orel; m.; one s. *Career:* service in army and state security forces 1972–91; First Deputy Head, Personnel Dept, Fed. Agency of Govt Communications and Information of Russian Presidency 1991–92; Deputy Commdr, Frontier Forces 1992–95; Deputy Dir, Fed. Frontier Service, C-in-C, Frontier Forces 1995–98; mem. Russian Security Council 1998–99, Sec. March 1999, Head Office of the Pres. 1998–99; Amb. to Denmark 2000–03; Sec. Gen. Collective Security Treaty Organization (CSTO) 2003–.
Address: Collective Security Treaty Organization (CSTO), 7 Varvarka, 103012 Moscow, Russia (office). *Telephone:* (495) 606-97-71 (office). *Fax:* (495) 625-76-20 (office). *E-mail:* odkb@gov.ru (office). *Website:* www.dkb .gov.ru (office).

BORG, Anders E.; Swedish economist and politician; *Minister of Finance;* b. 11 Jan. 1968, Stockholm; m. Sanna Borg; three c. *Education:* De Geer School, local authority adult secondary educ., Norrköping, Uppsala and Stockholm Univs. *Career:* Chair. Uppsala Univ. Student Union 1989, Föreningen Heimdal 1989; leader writer, Svenska Dagbladet 1990–91; Political Adviser, Prime Minister's Office, Coordination Secr., with responsibility for coordination of Ministry of Health and Social Affairs, Ministry of Public Admin, Ministry of Culture and Ministry of Educ. and Science 1991–93; Political Adviser to Carl Bildt at Prime Minister's Office 1993–93; Chief Economist, Transferator Alfred Berg 1995–98; Chief

Economist, ABN Amro Bank, Stockholm 1998–99; Head of Econ. Analysis Dept, Skandinaviska Enskilda Banken (SEB) 1999–2001; adviser on monetary policy issues to Exec. Bd Riksbank (Swedish Cen. Bank) 2001–02; Chief Economist and Admin. Dir Moderate Party 2002–06; Minister of Finance 2006–; mem. Expert Group on Public Finance 1992–96, Bd Swedish Labour Market Admin 2005.
Address: Ministry of Finance, Drottninggatan 21, 103 33 Stockholm, Sweden (office). *Telephone:* (8) 405-10-00 (office). *Fax:* (8) 21-73-86 (office). *E-mail:* registrator@finance.ministry.se (office). *Website:* finans.regeringen.se (office).

BORG, Joseph (Joe), LLD; Maltese politician and lawyer; *Commissioner for Fisheries and Maritime Affairs, European Commission;* b. 19 March 1952; m. Isabelle Agius; one s. one d. *Education:* Lyceum and Univ. of Malta. *Career:* practising lawyer 1976–; legal adviser to cos and corpns in Malta and abroad; Lecturer, Univ. of Malta 1979–88, Sr Lecturer 1988; adviser on EU matters to Minister of Foreign Affairs 1989–95; mem. Bd of Govs Malta Int. Business Authority 1989–92, Bd of Dirs of Cen. Bank 1992–95; MP 1995–; Shadow Minister for Industry and EU Impact on Malta; mem. Foreign Affairs Parl. Cttee, EU-Malta Jt Cttee 1996–98; Parl. Sec., Ministry of Foreign Affairs 1998–99; Minister of Foreign Affairs 1999–2004; EU Commr without Portfolio 2004, for Fisheries and Maritime Affairs 2004–; Int. Sec. Nationalist Party 1997–; Hon. LLM (Wales).
Address: European Commission, Rue de la Loi 200, 1049 Brussels, Belgium (office). *Telephone:* (2) 299-11-11 (office). *Fax:* (2) 295-01-38 (office). *Website:* europa.eu (office).

BORG, Saviour F., MPhil; Maltese diplomatist; *Permanent Representative, United Nations;* b. 12 Aug. 1945, Mosta; m.; three c. *Education:* Malta Coll. of Arts, Science and Tech., Univ. of Malta. *Career:* held numerous positions in health, agric. and fisheries ministries 1965–77; Deputy Perm. Rep. to UN, Geneva 1978–87; Head UN, Int. Orgs and Commonwealth Div., Ministry of Foreign Affairs 1988–92, Dir 1992–94, Dir Multilateral Affairs Dept 1994–97; Perm. Rep. to UNIDO 1994–99, serving concurrently as Perm. Rep. to UNEP, Org on Prohibition of Chemical Weapons, The Hague, Preparatory Comm. for Comprehensive Test-Ban Treaty Org, IAEA; Amb. to China, Japan, Repub. of Korea and Democratic People's Repub. of Korea 1999–2003; Perm. Rep. to UN, Geneva 2003–07, to UN, New York 2007–. *Publications:* numerous books and articles.
Address: Permanent Mission of Malta to the United Nations, 249 East 35th Street, New York, NY 10016, USA (office). *Telephone:* (212) 725-2345 (office). *Fax:* (212) 779-7097 (office). *E-mail:* mltun@un.int (office).

BORG, Tonio, LLD; Maltese politician and lawyer; *Deputy Prime Minister and Minister for Foreign Affairs;* b. 12 May 1957; m. Adele Galea 1982; one s. two d. *Education:* St Aloysius Coll. and Univ. of Malta. *Career:* Lecturer in Public Law, Univ. of Malta; exec. mem. of European Union Young Christian Democrats 1983–85; Dir Mid-Med Bank 1987–92; Pres. of Nationalist Party Gen. Council 1988–95; mem. of European Cttee for Prevention of Torture and Inhuman or Degrading Punishment or Treatment 1990–95; MP 1992–; mem. Planning Authority 1992–95; mem. of Council of Europe Ass. 1992–95; mem. Jt Parl. Cttee of the European Parl. and Maltese House of Reps 1992–95, 1996–98; Minister for Home Affairs 1995–96, 1998–2003, for Justice and Home Affairs 2003–08, for Foreign Affairs and Deputy Prime Minister 2008–; Nationalist Party.
Address: Ministry for Foreign Affairs, Palazzo Parisio, Merchants Street, Valletta, VLT 2000, Malta (office). *Telephone:* 22957000 (office). *Fax:* 22957348 (office). *E-mail:* mjha@gov.mt (office). *Website:* www.mjha.gov.mt (office).

BORGO BUSTAMANTE, Enrique, JD, MA; Salvadorean business executive, lawyer, politician and diplomatist; *Ambassador to Spain;* b. 1928. *Education:* Universidad de El Salvador, Rome Univ., Italy. *Career:* Judge, First Instance Criminal Court, San Vicente 1955–57; attorney: Salvadoran Social Security Inst. 1957–60; attorney Cen. Bank of El Salvador 1961–63; Dir Banco Cuscatlán 1975–79; Legal Adviseor, Taca Int. Airlines 1975–80, CEO 1981–94; Vice-Pres. of El Salvador 1994–99; Congressman, Cen. American Congress 1999–2000; Amb. to Spain 2004–.
Address: Embassy of El Salvador, General Oraá 9, 5° dcha, 28006 Madrid, Spain (office). *Telephone:* (91) 5628002 (office). *Fax:* (91) 5630584 (office). *E-mail:* embasalvamadrid@yahoo.com (office). *Website:* www.embasalva.com (office).

BORITH, Ouch; Cambodian diplomatist; *Secretary of State, Ministry of Foreign Affairs and International Cooperation;* b. 2 Nov. 1957, Phnom-Penh; m.; five c. *Education:* Medical Faculty, Phnom-Penh, Inst. of Sociology, Moscow. *Career:* French trans., Ministry of Foreign Affairs 1979–80, Dir Dept UN Humanitarian Org., Ministry of Foreign Affairs 1980–83, Dir Dept of Asia and Pacific Affairs 1987–90; Counsellor in charge of Political Affairs, Embassy, Moscow 1983–87; Amb. to Viet Nam

1990–92; Chargé d'affaires, Perm. Mission to UN 1992–93, Deputy Perm. Rep. 1993–97, Perm. Rep. 1998; currently Sec. of State, Ministry of Foreign Affairs and Int. Cooperation.
Address: Ministry of Foreign Affairs and International Cooperation, 3 rue Samdech Hun Sen, Khan Chamkarmon, Phnom-Penh, Cambodia (office). *Telephone:* (23) 214441 (office). *Fax:* (23) 216144 (office). *E-mail:* mfaicasean@online.com.kh (office). *Website:* www.mfaic.gov.kh (office).

BORKO, Yuri Antonovich, DEcon; Russian economist; *Head, Centre of European Documentation, Institute of Europe, Russian Academy of Sciences;* b. 6 Feb. 1929, Rostov-on-Don; m. Yelena Borisovna Borko; two s. *Education:* Moscow State Univ. *Career:* researcher, Inst. of World Econ. and Int. Relations USSR (now Russian) Acad. of Sciences 1962–63; Ed. and mem. of Bd journal World Econ. and Int. Relations 1963–69; Head of Div. Inst. of Information on Social Sciences, USSR (now Russian) Acad. of Sciences 1970–90; Head of Div., Deputy Dir, Head of Research Centre of European Integration, Head of Centre of European Documentation, Prof., Inst. of Europe, Russian Acad. of Sciences 1990–, Jean Monnet Chairholder 2001–; Pres. Asscn of European Studies 1992–. *Publications include:* works on problems of European integration, European Community policy and int. relations between Russia and European Community.
Address: Institute of Europe, Mokhovaya str. 11, stroenye 3B, 103873 Moscow (office); Sovetskoy Armii str. 13–43, 127018 Moscow, Russia (home). *Telephone:* (495) 292-10-23 (office); (495) 289-21-66 (home). *Fax:* (495) 200-42-98 (office). *E-mail:* aes@aes.org.ru (office); aes@centro.ru (office); yborko@aes.org.ru (home). *Website:* www.ieras.ru (office); www.aes.org.ru (office).

BORN, Wolf-Ruthart, DrJur; German diplomatist; *Ambassador to Spain;* b. 11 Aug. 1944, Görlitz; m. Valeria Born Sabena; two c. *Education:* in Saarbrücken, Amherst Coll. and Johns Hopkins Univ., USA, Royal Coll. of Defence Studies, London, UK. *Career:* mil. service 1965–67; attaché, Fed. Foreign Office 1975–77, Embassy in Khartoum 1977–79, in Buenos Aires 1980–82, Fed. Foreign Office 1983–85, Mediterranean and Turkey Dept 1987–89, Perm. Rep., Embassy in Pretoria 1989–92, Head of Ausländerrechts-und Schengenreferates, Fed. Foreign Office 1992–97, Head of Dept for Consular Affairs and for Political Affairs 1997–99, Amb. to Mexico 1999–2003, to Turkey 2003–06, to Spain (also accred to Andorra) 2006–.
Address: Embassy of Germany, Calle de Fortuny 8, 28010 Madrid, Spain (office). *Telephone:* (91) 5579000 (office). *Fax:* (91) 3102104 (office). *E-mail:* zreg@madri.diplo.de (office). *Website:* www.embajada-alemania.es (office); www.madrid.diplo.de (office).

BORNER, Silvio, DrOec; Swiss economist and academic; *Professor of Political Economics, University of Basle;* b. 24 April 1941; m. Verena Barth 1966; two d. *Education:* St Gall Grad. School and Yale Univ., USA. *Career:* Prof. of Econs, Univ. of St Gallen 1974–78, of Political Econs, Univ. of Basle 1978–. *Publications:* Die 'sechste Schweiz'—überleben auf dem Weltmarkt, New Forms of Internationalization: An Assessment, Einführung in die Volkswirtschaftslehre, International Finance and Trade in a Polycentric World.
Address: WWZ der Universität Basel, Angewandte Wirtschaftsforschung, Petersgraben 51, 4003 Basle, Switzerland (office). *Telephone:* (61) 267-33-46143 (office). *Fax:* (61) 267-33-46140 (office). *E-mail:* silvio.borner@unibas.ch (office).

BOROSS, Péter, PhD; Hungarian lawyer and politician; *Senior Counsellor and Adviser to Prime Minister;* b. 27 Aug. 1928, Nagybajom; m.; two c. *Education:* Eötvös Loránd Univ. of Budapest. *Career:* with Budapest Metropolitan Council 1951–56; dismissed for membership of revolutionary cttee and revolutionary council 1956; kept under police surveillance until 1959; employed as unskilled worker 1964; organized catering and tourist coll. training; catering chain dir 1971; mem. Council Coll. of Trade and Catering; mem. Hungarian League of Human Rights, Hungarian Chamber of Economy; Founder Nation Bldg Foundation 1988; Minister of State for the Office of Information and the Office of Nat. Security 1990–94; Minister of the Interior 1990–93; Prime Minister of Hungary 1993–94; mem. Parl. (Hungarian Democratic Forum—MDF) 1994–98; Chair. Nat. Security Cttee of Parl. 1994–96; Sr Counsellor and Adviser to Prime Minister 1998–; mem. Hungarian Democratic Forum Nat. Presidium 1993–.
Address: Kossuth Lajos tér 1–3, 1055 Budapest, Hungary. *Telephone:* (1) 441-3000. *Fax:* (1) 441-4888.

BORTNIKOV, Lt-Gen. Aleksander; Russian government official; *Head, Federal Security Service (FSB);* b. 1951, Perm Oblast; m.; one s. *Education:* Leningrad Inst. for Railway Eng. *Career:* joined Leningrad KGB (now Fed. Security Service—FSB) 1975, Deputy Head, FSB Directorate for St Petersburg and Leningrad Oblast in charge of counter-intelligence operations –2003, Head of Directorate 2003–04; Deputy Dir FSB and

Head, Econ. Security Service 2004–08, Head FSB 2008–; mem. Bd of Dirs Sovkomflot.
Address: Federal Security Service (FSB), Moscow, Bolshaya Lubyanka, Bldg 1/3, Russia (office). *Telephone:* (495) 914-43-69 (office). *E-mail:* fsb@ fsb.ru (office). *Website:* www.fsb.ru (office).

BORUBAYEV, Altai; Kyrgyzstani mathematician and politician; *Chairman (Speaker) of People's Assembly (Parliament);* b. 1950, Kara-oy, Kyrgyzia. *Education:* Kyrgyz State Univ. *Career:* teacher, Frunze Polytechnic Inst. 1975–76; teacher, Sr Teacher, Head of Chair., Dean, Pro-Rector Kyrgyz State Univ. 1976–92, Rector 1998–2000; Rector Kyrgyz State Pedagogical Inst. 1994–98; First Deputy Minister of Educ. 1992–94; Chair. (Speaker) Ass. of People's Reps Chamber of Zhogorku Kenesh (Parl.) 2000–; mem. Nat. Acad. of Sciences 2000, Russian Acad. of Social and Pedagogical Sciences. *Publications:* three monographs, over 100 articles.
Address: Zhogorku Kenesh, Assembly of People's Representatives, 720003 Bishkek, Kyrgyzstan (office). *Telephone:* (312) 27-17-19 (office).

BOS, Wouter; Dutch politician; *Deputy Prime Minister and Minister of Finance;* b. 14 July 1963, Vlaardingen. *Education:* Grammar School, Zeist and Free Univ. of Amsterdam. *Career:* Man. Consultant, Shell Netherlands Refinery BV 1988–90, Policy Adviser, Rotterdam 1990–92, Gen. Affairs Man. Shell Romania Exploration BV, Bucharest 1992–93, Staff Planning and Devt Man., Shell Cos in China, Hong Kong 1993–96, Consultant, New Markets, Shell Int. Oil Products, London 1996–98; mem. Parl. (Partij van de Arbeid) 1998–, Sec. of State for Finance (Taxes) 2002–02; Parl. Leader Partij van de Arbeid (PvdA) 2002–, Deputy Prime Minister and Minister of Finance 2007–.
Address: Ministry of Finance, Prinses Beatrixlaan 512, PO Box 20201, 2500 EE The Hague, Netherlands (office). *Telephone:* (70) 3428000 (office). *Fax:* 3427900 (office). *E-mail:* webmaster@minfin.nl (office). *Website:* www .minfin.nl (office).

BOSKIN, Michael Jay, MA, PhD; American economist, government official, academic and consultant; *Tim Friedman Professor of Economics and Hoover Institution Senior Fellow, Stanford University;* b. 23 Sept. 1945, New York; m. Chris Dornin 1981. *Education:* Univ. of California, Berkeley. *Career:* Asst Prof., Stanford Univ., Calif. 1970–75, Assoc. Prof. 1976–78, Prof. 1978–, Tim Friedman Prof. of Econs and Hoover Inst. Sr Fellow 1993–; Dir, Centre for Econ. Policy Research 1986–89; Wohlford Prof. of Econs 1987–89; Chair. Pres.'s Council of Econ. Advisers 1989–93; Chair. Congressional Comm. on the Consumer Price Index; Pres., Boskin & Co., Calif. 1993–; Research Assoc., Nat. Bureau of Econ. Research 1976–; Visiting Prof., Harvard Univ., Mass. 1977–78; Faculty Research Fellow, Mellon Foundation 1973; Distinguished Faculty Fellow, Yale Univ. 1993; Scholar, American Enterprise Inst.; mem. Bd of Dirs ExxonMobil Corpn (following merging of Exxon Corpn and Mobil Corpn), Oracle Corpn, Vodafone Group PLC, Shinsei Bank; several prizes and awards including Stanford's Distinguished Teaching Award 1987, Adam Smith Prize for Contribs to Econs 1998. *Publications:* Too Many Promises: The Uncertain Future of Social Security 1986, Reagan and the Economy: Successes, Failures, Unfinished Agenda 1987, Frontiers of Tax Reform 1996, Capital Technology and Growth 1996, Toward a More Accurate Measure of the Cost of Living 1996; contrib. articles in various professional journals.
Address: Stanford University, 213 HHMB, Stanford, CA 94305, USA. *Telephone:* (650) 723-6482. *Fax:* (650) 723-6494 (office). *E-mail:* boskin@ hoover.stanford.edu (office). *Website:* www-hoover.stanford.edu/bios/ boskin.html (office).

BOSSANO, Hon. Joseph J., BSc (Econ), BA; Gibraltarian politician; *Leader, Gibraltar Socialist Labour Party;* b. 10 June 1939; m. 1st Judith Baker 1967 (divorced 1988); three s. one d.; m. 2nd Rose Torilla 1988. *Education:* Gibraltar Grammar School, Birmingham Univ., Univ. of London. *Career:* factory worker 1958–60; merchant seaman 1960–64; Sec. Integration with Britain Movt 1964; mem. Man. Cttee Tottenham Constituency Labour Party 1965–68; fmr mem. IWBP Exec. Cttee; Leader Gibraltar Socialist Labour Party 1977–; Leader of the Opposition 1984–88, 1996–; Sec. Gibraltar Br. Commonwealth Parl. Asscn 1980–88; Br. Officer TGWU (Gibraltar) 1974–88; Chief Minister of Gibraltar, with responsibility for Information 1988–96.
Address: 2 Gowland's Ramp, Gibraltar (home); Gibraltar Socialist Labour Party, Suite 16, Watergardens 3, Gibraltar (office). *Telephone:* 50700 (office). *Fax:* 78983 (office). *E-mail:* hqgslp@gibtelecom.net (home). *Website:* www.gslp.gi (office).

BOST, Eric M., BA, MA; American diplomatist; *Ambassador to South Africa;* *Education:* Univ. of N Carolina, Univ. of S Florida. *Career:* served in a variety of positions in several state social welfare agenciesn and pvt. and non-profit orgs; Deputy Dir Ariz. Dept of Econ. Security 1994–97; Chief Exec. and Admin. Officer, Tex. Dept of Human Services 1997–2001;

Under-Sec. for Food, Nutrition, and Consumer Services 2001–06; Amb. to South Africa 2006–.
Address: Embassy of the USA, 877 Pretorius Street, Arcadia, Pretoria 0083 (office); Embassy of the USA, PO Box 9536, Pretoria 0001, South Africa (office). *Telephone:* (12) 4314000 (office). *Fax:* (12) 3422299 (office). *E-mail:* embassypretoria@state.gov (office). *Website:* southafrica.usembassy.gov (office).

BOSWORTH, Stephen Warren; American diplomatist; *Dean, The Fletcher School of Law and Diplomacy, Tufts University;* b. 4 Dec. 1939, Conn.; m. Christine Bosworth; two s. two d. *Education:* Dartmouth Coll. and George Washington Univ. *Career:* joined Foreign Service 1962, assignments in Paris, Madrid and Panama City, later Amb. to Tunisia 1979–81, the Philippines 1984–87, Repub. of Korea 1997–2001; various positions with Dept of State including Deputy Asst Sec. for Econ. Affairs and for Inter-American Affairs, Dir of Policy Planning and Head Office of Fuels and Energy; Pres. US-Japan Foundation 1988–96; Exec. Dir Korean Peninsula Energy Devt Corpn 1995–97; Dean, The Fletcher School of Law and Diplomacy, Tufts Univ. 2001–; Adjunct Prof., School of Int. and Public Affairs, Columbia Univ. 1990–94; Order of Rising Sun, Gold and Silver Star (Japan) 2006; Distinguished Service Award, Dept of State 1976, 1986, Distinguished Service Award, Dept of Energy 1979. *Publications:* articles: Why Do They Hate Us? The Reasons are Many, The History Long, Because We are Big, So Powerful, The Boston Globe 2001, Adjusting to the New Asia (with Morton Abramowitz), Foreign Affairs 2003.
Address: The Fletcher School of Law and Diplomacy, 160 Packard Avenue, Tufts University, Medford, MA 02155, USA (office). *Telephone:* (617) 627-3050 (office). *Fax:* (617) 627-3508 (office). *E-mail:* stephen.bosworth@tufts .edu (office). *Website:* www.fletcher.tufts.edu (office).

BOT, Bernard Rudolf (Ben), DJur; Dutch diplomatist and politician; b. 21 Nov. 1937, Jakarta, Indonesia; m. Christine Bot-Pathy 1962 (deceased); three c. *Education:* St Aloysius Coll., The Hague, Univ. of Leiden, Acad. of Int. Law, The Hague and Harvard Law School, USA. *Career:* Deputy Perm. Rep. of Netherlands to North Atlantic Council, Brussels 1982–86; Amb. to Turkey 1986–89; Sec.-Gen. Ministry of Foreign Affairs 1989–92; apptd Perm. Rep. to EU 1992; Minister of Foreign Affairs 2003–07; currently Pres. Netherlands Inst. of Int. Relations (Clingendael); Kt, Order of Netherlands Lion and other decorations. *Publications:* Non-recognition and Treaty Relations 1968; numerous articles on the Common Market, European political co-operation, NATO and other political matters.
Address: Clingendael, POB 93080, 2509 AB The Hague (office); c/o Ministry of Foreign Affairs, Bezuidenhoutseweg 67, POB 20061, 2500 EB The Hague, The Netherlands. *E-mail:* info@clingendael.nl (office). *Website:* www.clingendael.nl (office).

BOTCHWEY, Kwesi, LLB, LLM, SJD; Ghanaian academic and fmr government official; *Professor of Practice of Development Economics, The Fletcher School, Tufts University;* b. 13 Sept. 1942; m.; three c. *Education:* Univ. of Ghana, Legon and Yale Law School, and Univ. of Michigan Law School. *Career:* Lecturer, Univs of Zambia and Dar es Salaam; Sr Lecturer, Faculty of Law, Univ. of Ghana 1974; consultant, UN Univ. Project on Socio-Cultural Alternatives in the Transformation of the World; Sec. for Finance 1982–92; Minister of Finance and Economic Planning 1993–95; Devt Adviser, Harvard Inst. of Int. Devt, Harvard Univ., USA 1996–2000, Dir Africa Research and Programs, Center for Int. Devt 1998–2002; Exec. Chair. Africa Devt Policy Ownership Initiative 2003–; fmr Visiting Prof. of Int. Devt Econs, Fletcher School, Tufts Univ., now Prof. of Practice of Devt Econs; Chair. Econ. Cttee of the Global Coalition for Africa (GCA) 1991–2002; Chair. Exec. Bd, African Capacity Bldg 1998–2003; mem. Asscn of Third World Economists.
Address: Mugar 252E, The Fletcher School, Tufts University, 160 Packard Avenue, Medford, MA 02155, USA (office). *Telephone:* (617) 627-4926 (office). *E-mail:* kwesi.botchwey@tufts.edu (office). *Website:* fletcher.tufts .edu (office).

BOTHAMLEY, Arturo Guillermo; Argentine diplomatist; *Ambassador to Canada;* m. Maria Angélica Olmedo de Bothamley. *Career:* fmr Dir for Int. Negotiations, Ministry of Foreign Affairs; apptd Amb. to Jamaica 1992; Amb. to Canada 2007–; Hon. Pres., Canadian Argentine Chamber of Commerce.
Address: Embassy of the Argentine Republic, 81 Metcalfe Street, Suite 700, Ottawa, ON K1P 6K7, Canada (office). *Telephone:* (613) 236-2351 (office). *Fax:* (613) 235-2659 (office). *E-mail:* embargentina@argentina-canada.net (office). *Website:* www.argentina-canada.net (office).

BOTNARU, Ion, PhD; Moldovan diplomatist; *Ambassador to Turkey;* b. 19 Aug. 1954, Chişinău; m. 1979; one s. one d. *Education:* Inst. of Oriental Studies, Moscow, Moscow State Univ. *Career:* fmr translator and interpreter of Turkish and English; Sr Researcher, Inst. of History Studies,

Nat. Acad. of Science, Chişinău 1983–84; Prof. of Contemporary History of Asia and Africa, Chişinău State Univ. 1987–89; Deputy Dir-Gen. Dept of Protocol, Ministry of Foreign Affairs 1989–90, Dir-Gen. Dept of Political Affairs 1990–92, Deputy Minister 1992–93, Minister 1993–94; Amb. to Turkey (also accred to Kuwait and Egypt) 1994–98; Perm. Rep. to UN, New York 1998–2002; Amb. to Turkey 2002–; mem. Moldovan del. to UN Gen. Ass. 1992; Head Moldovan del. to UN World Conf. on Human Rights 1993; mem. Asscn of Orientalists 1985–. *Publications:* The Army and Politics in Turkey 1986, Islam and Political Parties in Turkey 1989, The Process of Democratisation in Moldova—Political Aspects 1993; numerous papers and articles.
Address: Embassy of Moldova, Kaptanpaşa Sok 49, Ankara, Turkey (office). *Telephone:* (312) 4465527 (office). *Fax:* (312) 4465816 (office).

BOUABRÉ BOHOUN, Paul-Antoine; Côte d'Ivoirian politician. *Career:* fmr Minister of State, Economy and Finance.
Address: c/o Ministry of the Economy and Finance, 16e étage, Immeuble SCIAM, avenue Marchand, BP V163, Abidjan, Côte d'Ivoire.

BOUASONE, (Bouasone Bouphavanh); Laotian politician; *Prime Minister;* b. 1954, Salavan Province. *Education:* in USSR. *Career:* student activist in 1970s; fmr Pres. State Planning Cttee; fmr Third Deputy Prime Minister, First Deputy Prime Minister 2003–06, Prime Minister 2006–.
Address: Office of the Prime Minister, Ban Sisavat, Vientiane, Laos (office). *Telephone:* (21) 213653 (office). *Fax:* (21) 213560 (office).

BOUCHER, Carlston B., BSc, MA; Barbadian diplomatist and international civil servant; b. 18 May 1933; m. *Education:* Univs of London and Sussex, UK. *Career:* govt appointments 1957–72; Research Economist, Econ. Programmes Dept, World Bank 1972–74, Country Economist for SA, Botswana, Lesotho and Swaziland, Africa Regional Dept 1974–78, Deputy Special Rep. of World Bank to UN 1978–83, Sr Economist, Strategic Planning and Review Dept 1983–87, Adviser, External Relations Dept 1987–90, Prin. Econ. Affairs Officer, Operations Policy Dept, Int. Econs Div. 1990–93, Special Rep. to UN, New York and Geneva 1993–95; Perm. Rep. to UN 1995–2001.
Address: c/o Ministry of Foreign Affairs and Foreign Trade, 1 Culloden Road, St Michael, Barbados (office).

BOUCHER, Richard A.; American diplomatist; *Assistant Secretary of State for South and Central Asian Affairs;* b. 1951, Bethesda, MD; m.; two c. *Education:* Tufts Univ., George Washington Univ. *Career:* entered Foreign Service 1977; early tours to Taiwan, Guangzhou then Econ. Bureau, China Desk, Washington, DC; Deputy Prin. Officer, US Consulate Gen., Shanghai, 1984–86; served in Operations Center of US State Dept; fmr Deputy Dir Office of European Security and Political Affairs; Deputy Spokesman for Sec. of State 1989–92, Spokesman 1992–93; Amb. to Cyprus 1993–96; Consul Gen., Hong Kong 1996–99; Sr Official, APEC 1999–2000; Asst Sec. for Public Affairs 2000–06, Spokesman 2000–05, Asst Sec. of State for S and Cen. Asian Affairs 2006–.
Address: Bureau of South and Central Asian Affairs, Department of State, Office 6254, Department of State, 2201 C Street, NW, Washington, DC 20520, USA (office). *Telephone:* (202) 736-4325 (office). *Website:* www.state .gov (office).

BOUH, Yacin Elmi; Djibouti politician; *Minister of the Interior and Decentralization;* b. 4 June 1962. *Education:* Univ. of Nantes, France. *Career:* Minister of the Economy, Finance and Planning, in charge of privatization 1997–2005; fmr mem. Bd of Govs Islamic Devt Bank; currently Minister of Interior and Decentralization.
Address: Ministry of the Interior and Decentralization, BP 33, Djibouti, Djibouti (office). *Telephone:* 352542 (office). *Fax:* 354862 (home). *Website:* www.elec.dj (office).

BOUKPESSI, Payadowa; Togolese government official. *Career:* Minister of the Economy, Finance and Privatization 2005–.
Address: Ministry of the Economy, Finance and Privatization, CASEF, ave Sarakawa, BP 387, Lomé, Togo (office). *Telephone:* 221-00-37 (office). *Fax:* 221-25-48 (office). *E-mail:* eco@republicoftogo.com (office).

BOULWARE, Mark, BA, MA; American diplomatist; *Ambassador to Mauritania;* b. 1948, Oklahoma City, Okla; m. Nora Jean Shay; three s. *Education:* Université Rennes 2, France, Midwestern State Univ., Wichita Falls, Tex., US Army War Coll., Carlisle, Pa. *Career:* commissioned officer, US Army, tours of duty in Pirmasens, Germany and Hawthorne, Nev., left active service with rank of Capt.; career mem. Sr Foreign Service with rank of Minister Counsellor, joined Foreign Service 1980, overseas postings as Gen. Services Officer, Jakarta, Indonesia 1980–82, Consular Officer, Maracaibo, Venezuela 1982–85, Supervisory Gen. Services Officer, Ouagadougou, Burkina Faso 1985–87, Admin. Officer, Banjul, The

Gambia 1987–89, Pearson Fellow, US House of Reps working for Congressman Dante Fascell 1989–90, Admin. Counsellor, Gaborone, Botswana 1990–93, and Bamako, Mali 1994–96, Deputy Chief of Mission, Yaoundé, Cameroon (concurrently accred to Equatorial Guinea) 1996–99, Deputy Chief of Mission, San Salvador 1999–2001, Consul Gen., Rio de Janeiro 2001–04, fmr Diplomat in Residence, Florida Int. Univ., Miami, Faculty Adviser, Nat. War Coll. –2007, Amb. to Mauritania 2007–; Hon. Citizen of Rio de Janeiro; Hon. Chief of the Nso people of Cameroon; Dept of State's Superior Honor Award, Sr Performance Pay Award, three Meritorious Honor Awards, NASA 'Silver Snoopy' Award, Pedro Ernesto Medal of Merit, City of Rio di Janeiro, Tamandaré Medal of Merit, Brazilian Navy.
Address: US Embassy, BP 222, 288 rue 41-100 (rue Abdallaye), Nouakchott, Mauritania (office). *Telephone:* 525-26-60 (office). *Fax:* 525-15-92 (office). *E-mail:* tayebho@state.gov (office). *Website:* mauritania .usembassy.gov (office).

BOUNGNANG, Volachit; Laotian politician and army officer; *Vice President;* b. 1936; m. Keosaychay Sayasone. *Career:* fmr army officer; fmr Gov. Savannaket, then Mayor Vientiane Municipality; apptd mem. Politburo 1996; Minister of Finance and Deputy Prime Minister 1999–2001; Prime Minister of Laos 2001–06; Vice Pres. 2006–.
Address: Office of the Vice President, rue Lane Xang, Vientiane, Laos. *Telephone:* (21) 214200 (office). *Fax:* (21) 214208 (office).

BOUNGOU, Carlos Victor, BA, MA; Gabonese diplomatist; *Ambassador to USA;* m.; five c. *Education:* Schiller Int. Univ., London and Polytechnic of Cen. London, UK. *Career:* Foreign Affairs Counsellor, Ministry of Foreign Affairs and Co-operation 1988–91, Head of Trans. and Integration Unit 1991–95, Tech. Advisor in charge of cultural matters for Sr Minister 1995–97, First Counsellor, Paris 1997–2000, Chargé d'affaires a.i., Embassy in London 2000–02, Amb. to Libya 2002–04, to Spain 2004–07, to USA 2008–.
Address: Embassy of Gabon, Suite 200, 2034 20th Street, NW, Washington, DC 20009, USA (office). *Telephone:* (202) 797-1000 (office). *Fax:* (202) 332-0668 (office).

BOURAN, Alia, BSc, MSc, PhD; Jordanian politician and diplomatist; *Ambassador to UK;* b. (Alia Hatoug), m. Ishaq Bouran; two c. *Education:* Moscow State Univ., Russian Acad. of Science, Novosibirsk Br. *Career:* Assoc. Prof. of Environmental Science, Faculty of Applied Sciences, Centre for Strategic Studies, Univ. of Jordan 1984–98; Sr Negotiating mem. on Environment Track during peace talks with Israel, Bilateral Negotiations 1993–94; Head of Jordanian Team on Environmental Multilateral Peace Talks 1998–99; Head of Environment Team of Free Trade Agreement between Jordan and USA 1999–2000; Head of Nat. Debt-for-Nature Swap Program with tech. assistance of Int. Union for Conservation of Nature and in partnership with UNDP, Amman 1995–2000; Sec.-Gen. Ministry of Tourism and Antiquities 1998–2001; Amb. to Belgium 2001–03 (also accred to the European Communities 2001–03, Luxembourg 2001–03, Norway 2002–03); Minister of Environment and Minister of Tourism and Antiquities 2003–04, of Tourism and Antiquities 2003–05; Amb. to UK (also accred to Ireland) 2006–; Independence Medal (First, Second and Third Degrees); Award by German-Mediterranean Council on Achievements and Excellence in the Field of Environment and Sustainable Devt.
Address: Embassy of Jordan, 6 Upper Phillimore Gardens, London, W8 7HA, England (office). *Telephone:* (20) 7937-3685 (office). *Fax:* (20) 7937-8795 (office). *E-mail:* info@jordanembassy.org (office). *Website:* www .jordanembassyuk.org (office).

BOURGES, Hervé; French administrator and journalist; *President, Union Internationale des Journalistes at de la Presse de Langue Française;* b. 2 May 1933, Rennes, Ile-et-Vilaine; m. Marie-Thérèse Lapouille 1966. *Education:* Lycée de Biarritz, Coll. Saint-Joseph, Reims, École supérieure de journalisme. *Career:* Ed. then Ed.-in-Chief Témoignage Chrétien 1956–62; attached to the Keeper of the Seals 1959–62, Dir Algerian Ministry of Youth and Popular Education, attached to Ministry of Information; Asst Lecturer Univ. de Paris II 1967–; Founder and Dir École supérieure de journalisme de Yaoundé, Cameroun 1970–76; Dir then Pres. Admin. Council École nat. supérieure de journalisme de Lille 1976–80; Dir Information Service and Dir-Gen.'s Messenger UNESCO 1980–81, Amb. to UNESCO 1994–95; Dir then Dir-Gen. Radio France Int. 1981–83; Chair. Dir-Gen. TV Française 1 (TF1) 1983–87, Hon. Pres. 1987–93; Hon. Pres. Admin. Council, Ecole Supérieure de Journalisme de Lille 1992–; Dir-Gen. Radio Monte Carlo (RMC) 1988; Pres., Dir-Gen. Société financière de radiodiffusion (Sofirad) 1989–91; Pres. Canal Horizon 1990–91, Conseil Supérieur de L'Audio-Visuel (CSA) 1995–2001; Pres. L'Union internationale des journalistes et de la presse de langue française (UIJPLF) 2001–; Docteur d'état en sciences politiques; Chevalier, Légion d'honneur; Croix de la Valeur Militaire. *Publications:* L'Algérie à l'épreuve du pouvoir 1967,

La Révolte étudiante 1968, Décoloniser l'information 1978, Les cinquante Afriques (jtly) 1979, Le village planétaire (jtly) 1986, Une Chaîne sur les bras 1987, Un amour de télévision (jtly) 1989, La Télévision du Public 1993, De mémoire d'éléphant (autobiog.) 2000, Le règne de la terreur sacrée (with Liess Boukra) 2001, Entretiens (with Jean-Michel Djian) 2003, Léopold Sédar Senghor, lumière noire 2006, Ma rue Montmartre 2006.
Address: UIJPLF, 3 cité Bergère, 74009 Paris (office); 12 rue Magellan, 75008 Paris, France. *Telephone:* 1-47-70-02-80 (office); 1-45-68-10-00. *Fax:* 1-48-24-26-32 (office); 1-45-67-16-90. *E-mail:* union@presse-francophone .org (office). *Website:* www.presse-francophone.org (office).

BOURGOIS, Joëlle Marie-Paule; French diplomatist; *Ambassador to Belgium;* b. 24 June 1945, Thaon-les-Vosges; d. of André Lombard-Platet and Paulette Lombard-Platet; m. Olivier Bourgois 1976; two d. *Education:* Inst. d'Etudes Politiques de Paris and Ecole Nat. d'Admin. *Career:* Sec. for Foreign Affairs, Ministry of Foreign Affairs 1970, Counsellor 1977, Rep. to Admin. and Finance Dir CNRS 1970–71, at European Directorate 1977, Deputy Dir for N Africa and the Middle East 1986–89, Deputy Dir for Econ. and Financial Affairs and Head, Dept for Int. Industrial Relations 1989–91; First Sec. Embassy in Vatican City 1976–77; Head, Int. Relations Div., Hydrocarbons Directorate, Ministry of Industry 1979–84; First Counsellor, Embassy in Mexico 1984–86; Minister Plenipotentiary, S Africa 1990, Amb. 1991–95, also accred to Lesotho 1994–95; Amb. to Disarmament Conf., Geneva, Switzerland 1995–99; Amb. and Perm. Rep. to OECD 1999, then Chair. Advisory Bd; currently Amb. to Belgium; Chevalier, Légion d'honneur, Ordre nat. du Mérite.
Address: Embassy of France, 65 rue Ducale, 1000 Brussels, Belgium (office). *Telephone:* (2) 548-87-11 (office). *Fax:* (2) 548-87-32 (office). *Website:* www.ambafrance-be.org (office).

BOURHANE, Ali; Comoran international civil servant; *Senior Adviser, African Development Bank;* b. 2 April 1946; m. Neila Bourhane; one s. one d. *Education:* Univ. of Bordeaux, Ecole Nationale d'Administration, Paris and Univ. of Toulouse. *Career:* Research Fellow, Univ. of Toulouse 1971; Prof. of Math., Comoros 1972–75; civil servant 1980–85; Sr Economist, IMF, Washington, DC 1985–90; Alt. Exec. Dir IBRD 1990–94, Exec. Dir 1994–99; currently Sr Adviser African Devt Bank, Tunis.
Address: African Development Bank, Angle des Trois Rues: Avenue du Ghana, Rue Pierre de Coubertin, Rue Hedi Nouira, POB 323, 1002 Tunis (office); Apartment A41, Venus, Rue Hedi Novira, Ennassa 2, 2037 Tunis, Tunisia (home). *Telephone:* (71) 102-686 (office); (71) 816-152 (home). *E-mail:* a.bourhane@afdb.org (office); alboucom@hotmail.com (home).

BOURJINI, Salah Amara, MA (Econs), PhD; Tunisian United Nations official; *Resident Representative and Co-ordinator for Libya, Development Programme, United Nations;* b. 17 Jan. 1938, Lekef; m. 1967; one s. two d. *Career:* engineer in planning and statistics, Tunis 1963–67; Lecturer in Econs, Univ. of Kansas, USA 1969–72; Prof., Univ. of Tunis 1972–80; Adviser to Minister of Economy 1972–76; Deputy Dir-Gen. Ministry of Foreign Affairs 1976–80; Deputy UN Resident Rep. and UN Co-ordinator, Algeria 1980–82; Chief, Div. for Regional Programme, Arab States, UNDP, New York 1982–87, UN Resident Rep. and UN Co-ordinator, Iraq 1987–92, UN Resident Rep. and UN Co-ordinator, Libya 1992–; Chevalier de la République; various UN service awards. *Publications:* Human Capital Investment and Economic Growth 1974, New International Economic Order 1978; articles on devt, educ. and trade.
Address: United Nations Development Programme, PO Box 358, Tripoli, Libya (office). *Telephone:* (21) 3330855 (office). *Fax:* (21) 3330856 (office).

BOUTEFLIKA, Abdul Aziz; Algerian head of state; *President and Minister of Defence;* b. 2 March 1937, Oujda. *Education:* Morocco. *Career:* Maj., Nat. Liberation Army and Sec. of Gen. Staff; mem. Parl. for Tlemcen 1962; Minister of Youth, Sports and Tourism 1962–63, of Foreign Affairs 1963–79; Counsellor to the Pres. March 1979–80; Pres. of Algeria and Minister of Defence 1999–; mem. FLN Political Bureau 1964–81, mem. Cen. Cttee 1989; mem. Revolutionary Council 1965–79; led negotiations with France 1963, 1966, for nationalization of hydrocarbons 1971; leader of dels to many confs of Arab League, OAU 1968, Group of 1977 1967, Non-aligned Countries 1973, Pres. Seventh Special Session of UN Gen. Ass. 1975, Int. Conf. on Econ. Co-operation, Paris 1975–76; Pres. 29th UN Gen. Ass. 1974; mem. Nat. Council Moujahidin (Nat. Liberation Army) 1990–.
Address: Office of the President, el-Mouradia, Algiers (office); 138 Chemin Bachir Brahimi, El Biar, Algiers, Algeria. *Telephone:* (21) 69-15-15 (office); (21) 60-34-59 (home). *Fax:* (21) 69-15-95 (office). *Website:* www.el -mouradia.dz (office).

BOUTROS GHALI, Boutros, LLB, PhD; Egyptian international civil servant and politician; *Secretary-General, Organisation Internationale de la Francophonie;* b. 14 Nov. 1922, Cairo; m. Leia Nadler. *Education:* Cairo Univ. and Paris Univ. *Career:* fmr Prof. of Int. Law and Int. Relations and

Head Dept of Political Sciences, Cairo Univ. 1949–77; fmr mem. Cen. Cttee Arab Socialist Union; Pres. Cen. of Political and Strategic Studies; f. Al Ahram Al Iktisadi, Ed. 1960–75, f. Al-Siyassa Ad-Dawlya, Ed.; Minister of State for Foreign Affairs 1977–91, Deputy Prime Minister for Foreign Affairs 1991–92; Sec.-Gen. of UN 1992–96; Sec.-Gen. Org. Int. de la Francophonie 1997–; Vice-Pres. Egyptian Soc. of Int. Law 1965–; mem. Cttee on Application of Conventions and Recommendations of Int. Labour Org. 1971–79; Pres. Centre of Political and Strategic Studies (Al-Ahram) 1975–; mem. Int. Comm. of Jurists, Geneva and Council and Exec. Cttee of Int. Inst. of Human Rights, Strasbourg; mem. UN Comm. of Int. Law 1979–92, Secretariat Nat. Democratic Party 1980–92, Parl. 1987–92; Onassis Foundation Prize 1995, recipient of honorary titles and awards from 24 countries. *Publications include:* Contribution à l'étude des ententes régionales 1949, Cours de diplomatie et de droit diplomatique et consulaire 1951, Le principe d'égalité des états et les organisations internationales 1961, Foreign Policies in World Change 1963, L'Organisation de l'unité africaine 1969, La ligue des états arabes 1972, Les Conflits des frontières en Afrique 1973; also numerous books in Arabic and contribs to periodicals.
Address: 2 avenue Epnipgiza, Cairo, Egypt (home).

BOUTROS-GHALI, Yousuf, BA, PhD; Egyptian politician and economist; *Minister of Finance; Education:* Cairo Univ., MIT, USA. *Career:* Sr Economist, IMF 1981–86; Econ. Adviser to Prime Minister and Gov. of Cen. Bank of Egypt 1986–93; Minister of State for Int. Cooperation 1993–95, Minister of State at Council of Ministers 1993–95; Minister of State for Econ. Affairs 1996–97, Minister of Economy 1997–99, Minister of Economy and Foreign Trade 1999–2001, of Foreign Trade 2001–2004, of Finance 2004–; fmr Lecturer of Econs, American Univ. in Cairo and MIT, Assoc. Prof. of Econs, Cairo Univ.; fmr Dir Centre for Econ. Analysis, Council of Ministers; mem. Bd of Dirs Nat. Bank of Egypt 1991–93. *Publications:* 22 papers and books on devt and theoretical issues in field of econs.
Address: Ministry of Finance, Ministry of Finance Towers Cairo (Nasr City), Egypt. *Telephone:* (2) 3428886 (office). *Fax:* (2) 6861861 (office). *E-mail:* finance@mof.gov.eg (office). *Website:* www.mof.gov.eg (office).

BOVA, Mario Salvatore, BSc; Italian diplomatist; *Ambassador to Japan;* b. 1 July 1945, Bivongi, Reggio Calabria. *Education:* Univ. of Rome. *Career:* entered diplomatic corps 1969, worked in Legal Dept 1969–73, First Sec., Embassy in Dar Es Salaam 1973–75, in Paris 1975–80, Dept of Econ. Affairs, Ministry of Foreign Affairs 1980–87, seconded to Ministry of Univs. and Scientific Research 1987–90, named Minister Plenipotentiary 1990, Dept of Cultural Relations 1994–96 (Deputy Dir 1995–96), Head of Performance Dept, Ministry of Culture 1996–99; Amb. to Albania 1999–2003, to Japan 2003–.
Address: Italian Embassy, 2-5-4 Mita, Minato-ku, Tokyo 108–8302, Japan (office). *Telephone:* (3) 34535291 (office). *Fax:* (3) 34562319 (office). *E-mail:* ambasciata.tokyo@esteri.it (office). *Website:* www.ambtokyo.esteri.it/ ambasciata_tokyo (office).

BOWDEN, Jamie Nicholas Geoffrey, OBE; British fmr army officer and diplomatist; *Ambassador to Bahrain;* b. 27 May 1960; m. Sarah Bowden; three s. two d. *Career:* army officer, Royal Green Jackets 1980–86; Desk Officer, Repub. of Ireland Dept, FCO 1987–88, Deputy, later Acting Consul Gen., Aden 1990–91, Second Sec. (Political and Information), Khartoum 1991–93, Head of Political Section, UN Dept, FCO 1993–96, First Sec. (Middle East Affairs and Counter-terrorism), Washington, DC 1996–99, First Sec. (Econ. and Commercial), Riyadh 1999–2000, seconded to Cabinet Office 2000–03, Deputy Head of Mission, Baghdad 2004–05, Kuwait 2005–06, Amb. to Bahrain 2006–.
Address: British Embassy, PO Box 114, 21 Government Avenue, Area 306, Manama, Bahrain (office). *Telephone:* 17574100 (office). *Fax:* 17574101 (office). *E-mail:* britemb@batelco.com.bh (office). *Website:* www .britishembassy.gov.uk/bahrain (office).

BOXHOORN, Bram, PhD; Dutch research institute director; *Director, Netherlands Atlantic Association;* b. 6 Oct. 1954, Amsterdam. *Education:* Montessori Lyceum Amsterdam, Univ. of Amsterdam. *Career:* Lecturer, Webster Univ., Leiden 1986–; Asst Prof. in History, Univ. of Amsterdam 1988–96; Visiting Prof., Univ. of Minn., USA 1992; Dir Netherlands Atlantic Asscn 1996–. *Publications include:* Europese integratie: een historische balans 2002; numerous articles on history and European integration, NATO and European Security and Defence Policy.
Address: Bezuidenhoutseweg 237–239, Den Haag, 2594 AM (office); Sandbergstraat 7, 1391 EJ, Abcoude, Netherlands (home). *Telephone:* (70) 3639495 (office). *Fax:* (70) 3646309 (office). *E-mail:* atlcom@xs4all.nl (office); boxhoorn@tele2.nl (home). *Website:* www.atlcom.nl (office).

BOYCE, Adm. The Lord Michael (Cecil), GCB, KStJ, OBE, DL; British naval officer; *Lord Warden and Admiral of the Cinque Ports and Constable of*

Dover Castle; b. 2 April 1943, Cape Town, SA; m. 1st Harriette Gail Fletcher 1971 (divorced 2005); one s. one d.; m. 2nd Fleur Margaret Ann Rutherford (née Smith). *Education:* Hurstpierpoint Coll., Royal Naval Coll., Dartmouth Royal Coll. of Defence Studies. *Career:* joined RN 1961; qualified submariner 1965, TAS 1970, served in HM submarines Anchorite, Valiant and Conqueror 1965–72, commanded HM submarines Oberon 1973–74, Opossum 1974–75, Superb 1979–81, frigate HMS Brilliant 1983–84, Capt. (SM) Submarine Sea Training 1984–86; Royal Coll. Defence Staff 1988; Sr Naval Officer ME 1989; Dir Naval Staff Duties 1989–91; Flag Officer, Sea Training 1991–92, Surface Flotilla 1992–95; Commdr Anti-Submarine Warfare Striking Force 1992–94; Second Sea Lord and C-in-C Naval Home Command 1995–97; Flag ADC to the Queen 1995–97; C-in-C Fleet, C-in-C Eastern Atlantic Area and Commdr Naval Forces NW Europe 1997–98; First Sea Lord 1998–2001; Chief of Defence Staff 2001–03; First and Prin. Naval ADC to the Queen 1998–2001, ADC 2001–03; Lord Warden and Adm. of the Cinque Ports and Constable of Dover Castle 2004–; Gov. Alleyn's School 1995–2005; mem. Bd Dirs W S Atkins 2004–, VT Group PLC 2004–; Pres. Officers Asscn 2003–, London Dist St John Ambulance 2003–, Submarine Museum 2005–; Patron Sail4Cancer 2003–, Submarine Asscn 2003–; mem. Council White Ensign Asscn 2003– (Chair. 2007–), Royal Nat. Lifeboat Inst. 2004– (Vice-Chair. 2006–); Trustee, Nat. Maritime Museum 2004–; Freeman City of London 1999, Younger Brother Trinity House 1999–2006, Elder Brother 2006–, DL Greater London 2003–, Hon. Freeman Drapers' Co. 2005; Commdr, Legion of Merit (USA) 1999, Bronze Oak Leaf (USA) 2003; Hon. LLD (Portsmouth) 2005.
Address: House of Lords, Westminster, London, SW1A 0PW, England (office).

BOYCE, Ralph, BA, MPA; American diplomatist; b. 1 Feb. 1952, Washington, DC; m. Kathryn Sligh; two c. *Education:* George Washington Univ., Princeton Univ. *Career:* joined Foreign Service 1976, Staff Asst to Amb., Tehran 1977–79, Commercial Attaché, Tunis 1979–81, Financial Econo- mist, Islamabad 1981–84, Special Asst, then Adviser to Deputy Sec. of State, State Dept 1984–88, Political Counsellor, Bangkok 1988–92, Deputy Chief of Mission, Singapore 1992–93, Chargé d'affaires a.i. 1993–94, Deputy Chief of Mission, Bangkok 1994–98, Deputy Asst Sec. for E Asia and Pacific Affairs 1998–2001, Amb. to Indonesia 2001–04, to Thailand 2004–07.
Address: US Department of State, 2201 C Street NW, Washington, DC 20520, USA (office). *Telephone:* (202) 647-4000 (office). *Fax:* (202) 647-6738 (office). *Website:* www.state.gov (office).

BOYD OF DUNCANSBY, Baron (Life Peer), cr. 2006, of Duncansby in the County of Caithness Colin Boyd, PC, QC, BA (Econ), LLB, FRSA, LARTPI; British lawyer; b. 7 June 1953, Falkirk; two s. one d. *Education:* Wick High School, George Watson's Coll., Edinburgh, Univ. of Manchester and Univ. of Edinburgh. *Career:* qualified as solicitor 1978; called to Bar 1983; Legal Assoc. Royal Town Planning Inst. 1990; Advocate Depute (prosecutor) 1993–95; QC 1995; Solicitor-Gen. for Scotland, UK Govt 1997; Solicitor-Gen., Scottish Exec. 1999–2000; Lord Advocate of Scotland 2000–06; Hon. Fellow, Inst. of Advanced Legal Studies 2001.
Address: House of Lords, London, SW1A 0PW, England (office). *Telephone:* (20) 7219-3000 (office). *E-mail:* boydcd@parliament.uk (office).

BOYE, Mame Madior; Senegalese politician and lawyer; b. 1940. *Education:* Faculty of Legal and Econ. Sciences, Dakar, Centre Nat. d'Etudes Judiciaires, Paris. *Career:* fmr Deputy Procurator of Repub.; Judge, First Vice-Pres. First Class Regional Court, Dakar; fmr Pres. Dakar Court of Appeal; Minister of Justice and Keeper of the Seals 2000–01; Prime Minister of Senegal 2001–02; Special Rep. for the Promotion of the Protection of Civilians in Armed Conflicts, African Union 2004–; mem. Parti Démocratique Sénégalais (PDS).
Address: Siege de L'Union Africaine, PO Box 3243, Addis Ababa, Ethiopia (office). *Telephone:* (1) 517700 (office). *Fax:* (1) 517844 (office). *Website:* www.africa-union.org (office).

BOYER, Yves, PhD; French research institute director; *Deputy Director, Fondation pour la Recherche Stratégique;* b. 9 Oct. 1950, Blois; m. Isabelle Kraft 1978; one s. one d. *Education:* Inst. d'Etudes Politiques, Paris and Paris-Panthéon Univ. *Career:* Deputy Gen. Sec. SOFRESA, Paris 1978–80; Bureau des Etudes Stratégiques et des Négociations Internationales, Secr. Gén. de la Défense Nationale 1980–82; Defence Consultant and Research Assoc., IISS, London 1982–83; Sr Researcher, Inst. Français des Relations Internationales 1983–88; Research Fellow, Woodrow Wilson Center 1986; fmr Deputy Dir CREST, Ecole Polytechnique; Prof., Army Acad. 1986–, Staff Coll. 1992–; currently Deputy Dir Fondation pour la Recherche Stratégique; Assoc. Prof., Institut d'Études Politiques de Paris, École Polytechnique; Chair. French Soc. for Mil. Studies (SFEM), Working Groups for the French Ministry of Defence's Scientific Advisers; mem.

Editorial Bd, Annuaire Français de Relations Internationales; Chevalier, Ordre des Palmes Académiques.
Address: Fondation pour la Recherche Stratégique, 27 rue Damesme, 75013 Paris (office); 2 rue de Haut Bourg, 41000 Blois, France (home). *Telephone:* (1) 43-13-77-66 (office). *Fax:* (1) 43-13-77-78 (office). *E-mail:* y.boyer@frstrategie.org (office).

BOZIZE YANGOVOUNDA, Gen. François; Central African Republic army officer and head of state; *President and Minister of Defence; Career:* opposition leader 1981–93, led unsuccessful coup 1983; spent many years in exile in Togo; presidential cand. 1993; supported Pres. Ange-Felix Patasse in suppressing coups 1996–97; sacked as Army Chief; participated in unsuccessful coup against Pres. 2001, took control of N Bangui before escaping to Chad with 300 supporters; launched several rebel attacks from base in Chad 2001–02; led successful coup March 2003, suspended constitution and dissolved Parl.; self-proclaimed Pres. of Cen. African Repub. 2003–05, elected 2005–, also currently Minister of Defence.
Address: Office of the President, Palais de la Renaissance, Bangui, Central African Republic (office). *Telephone:* 61-46-63 (office).

BOŽOVIĆ, Radoman, PhD; Serbian politician and economist; b. 1953, Sipcan, nr Niksic, Montenegro; m.; two c. *Education:* Belgrade Univ. *Career:* academic 1976–89; fmr deputy to Vojvodina Ass., later head of provincial Govt; mem. Socialist Party of Serbia (SPS) (fmrly League of Communists of Yugoslavia—LCY); Deputy, Serbian Ass. 1990–, Head SPS Parl. Group; Prime Minister of Serbia 1991–93; Chair. Council of Citizens, Fed. Ass. 1992–97; f. Bancor Group Sept. 1997; Prof., Univ. Subotica. *Publications:* numerous books and articles including Political Economy (two vols), Accumulation and Economic Development, Types of Prosperity in Socialism, Problems of Economic System Reform in Yugoslavia.

BRADLEY, Stephen Edward; British diplomatist; *Consul General, Hong Kong Special Administrative Region;* b. 4 April 1958; m. Elizabeth Bradley; one s. one d. *Education:* Balliol Coll., Oxford, Fudan Univ., Shanghai. *Career:* joined FCO 1981, Afghan/Pakistan Desk, S Asian Dept 1981–83; Second Sec., Econ., later First Sec., Chancery, British Embassy, Tokyo 1983–87; Deputy Political Adviser to Hong Kong Govt 1988–93; FCO French Desk, W European Dept 1995; Deputy Head of Near East and N Africa FCO Dept 1996–97; Head of W Indian Atlantic Dept 1997–98; Dir of Trade and Investment Promotion, British Embassy, Paris 1999–2002; Minister, Deputy Head of Mission and Consul Gen., British Embassy, Beijing 2002; Consul-Gen., Hong Kong Special Admin. Region 2003–; Marketing Dir, Guinness Peat Aviation, Hong Kong 1987–88, Assoc. Dir, Lloyd George Investment Man., Hong Kong 1993–95, New Millennium Experience Co. 1998–99.
Address: British Consulate-General, 1 Supreme Court Road, Hong Kong (office). *Telephone:* 29013000 (office). *Fax:* 29013066 (office).

BRADTKE, Robert Anthony, BA; American diplomatist; *Ambassador to Croatia;* b. Chicago, Ill.; m. Marsha Barnes. *Education:* Univ. of Notre Dame, Bologna Center, Johns Hopkins School of Advanced Int. Studies, Univ. of Virginia. *Career:* career Foreign Service Officer, joined Foreign Service 1973, first overseas assignments in Georgetown and Zagreb, served in Office of E European Affairs and as American Political Science Asscn Congressional Fellow, working in offices of Senator Mathias and Congressman Cheney 1978–83, posted to Moscow and then to Bonn 1983–90, worked in Bureau of Legis. Affairs, Dept of State 1990–94, Deputy Asst Sec. 1992, Acting Asst Sec. 1992–93, Exec. Asst to Sec. of State Warren Christopher 1994–96, Deputy Chief of Mission, London 1996–99, Exec. Sec. Nat. Security Council 1999–2001, Deputy Asst Sec. of State for European and Eurasian Affairs 2001–04, Prin. Deputy Asst Sec. of State for European and Eurasian Affairs July 2004, Amb. to Croatia 2006–; two Superior Honor Awards, Dept of State, Presidential Meritorious Service Award 2001.
Address: US Embassy, Ulica Thomasa Jeffersona 2, 10 010 Zagreb, Croatia (office). *Telephone:* (1) 661-2200 (office). *Fax:* (1) 661-2300 (office). *Website:* www.usembassy.hr (office).

BRADY, Sonia; Philippine diplomatist; *Ambassador to People's Republic of China; Career:* fmr Amb. to Myanmar, Amb. to Thailand 2002–03; Acting Foreign Sec. 2004, Foreign Under-Sec. 2004–06; Amb. to People's Repub. of China 2006–.
Address: Embassy of Philippines, 23 Xiu Shui Bei Jie, Jian Guo Men Wai, Beijing 100600, People's Republic of China (office). *Telephone:* (10) 65321872 (office). *Fax:* (10) 65323761 (office). *E-mail:* main@ philembassy-china.org (office). *Website:* www.philembassy-china.org (office).

BRAGHIŞ, Dumitru; Moldovan politician and business executive; *Co-Leader, Moldova Noastra Alliance;* b. 28 Dec. 1957, Grătieşti. *Education:* Institutul Politehnic din Chişinău. *Career:* First Sec. Komsomol, Moldovan SSR 1989–91; Dir-Gen. Dept Foreign Econ. Relations, Ministry of the Economy and Reform 1995; First Deputy Minister of Economy and Reform 1997–99; Prime Minister of Moldova 1999–2001; mem. Parl. 2000–; Leader Social-Democratic Alliance 2001–03; Co-Leader Moldova Noastra (AMN–Our Moldova) Alliance, following merger of Social-Democratic Alliance and two other centrist parties 2003–. *Address:* Alianţa Moldova Noastra, str. Puşkin A, Chişinău, Moldova (office). *Telephone:* (2) 54-85-38. *E-mail:* vitalia@ch.moldpac.md. *Website:* www.amn.md.

BRAHIMI, Lakhdar; Algerian UN official (retd), diplomatist and politician; b. 1 Jan. 1934; m.; three c. *Education:* in Algeria and France. *Career:* FLN Rep. in SE Asia 1956–61; Perm. Rep. to Arab League, Cairo 1963–70; Amb. to UK 1971–79, to Egypt and Sudan; Diplomatic Adviser to Pres. of Algeria 1982–84; Under-Sec.-Gen., League of Arab States 1984–91, Special Envoy Arab League Tripartite Cttee to Lebanon 1989–91; Minister of Foreign Affairs 1991–93; Rapporteur, UN Conf. on Environment and Devt (Earth Summit) 1992; Special Rep. of UN Sec.-Gen. in SA –1994, in Haiti 1994–96; Under-Sec.-Gen. for Special Assignments in Support of Preventive and Peacemaking Efforts of the Sec.-Gen. 1997; Special Envoy of UN Sec.-Gen. in Afghanistan, UN Special Mission to Afghanistan (UNSMA) 1997–99, Special Rep. 2001–04; Special Envoy of UN Sec.-Gen. in Angola 1998; Special Adviser to UN Sec.-Gen. 2004–05 (retd); Chair. UN panel for evaluation of peace-keeping operations March–Aug. 2000; other special missions to Zaïre (now Democratic Repub. of the Congo), Yemen, Liberia, and Iraq; Special Rep. of the UN Sec.-Gen. for Afghanistan and Head, UN Assistance Mission in Afghanistan 2001–03; Dir Visitor Inst. for Advanced Study, Princeton 2007; mem. Comm. on Legal Empowerment of the Poor (UNDP); Chair. Ind. Panel on Safety and Security of UN Personnel and Premises 2007–; Harvard Law School Great Negotiator Award 2002, Dag Hammarskjöld Hon. Medal, German UN Asscn 2004. *Address:* c/o Executive Office of the Secretary-General, Room 5-3860, United Nations, United Nations Plaza, New York, NY 10017, USA (office).

BRAKS, Gerrit J. M., MAgr; Dutch politician; b. 23 May 1933, Odiliapeel; m. Frens Bardoel 1965 (died 2000); two s. three d. *Education:* Agricultural Univ., Wageningen. *Career:* worked on parents' farm –1955; Asst Govt Agricultural Advisory Service, Eindhoven 1955–58; Directorate for Int. Econ. Co-operation, Ministry of Agric. and Fisheries 1965–66; Deputy Agricultural Attaché, Perm. Mission of Netherlands to EEC, Brussels 1966–67; Sec. North Brabant Christian Farmers' Union (NCB), Tilburg 1967–69; Agricultural Counsellor, Perm. Mission of Netherlands to EEC 1969–77; mem. Second Chamber of Parl. 1977–80, 1981–82; Chair. Standing Cttee on Agric., Second Chamber 1979–80 parl. year; Minister of Agric. and Fisheries 1980–81, 1982–90; mem. First Chamber of Parl. (Christian Democratic Appeal—CDA) 1991–; Pres. Catholic Broadcasting Org. 1991–96; Chair. and Pres. Céhavé Farmers Cooperative 1995–; mem. Interparl. Benelux Council 1996–2001; Pres. of Senate 2001–03; Govt Commr 'Floriade 2002'; currently ind. adviser; Commdr, Order of Netherlands Lion and other decorations. *Address:* Ruwenbergstraat 4, 5271 Sint-Michielsgestel AG, Netherlands. *Telephone:* (73) 5514759; (6) 52303360. *E-mail:* g.braks@planet.nl (home).

BRANCO, Joaquim Rafael; São Tome and Príncipe politician; *Prime Minister;* b. 1953. *Career:* Minister of Foreign Affairs 2000–01, of Public Works 2003; Prime Minister 2008–; Pres. Movt for the Liberation of São Tomé and Príncipe–Social Democratic Party. *Address:* Office of the Prime Minister, Rua do Município, CP 302, São Tomé, São Tomé and Príncipe (office). *Telephone:* 223913 (office). *Fax:* 224679 (office). *E-mail:* gpm@cstome.net (office).

BRANDENBURG, Ulrich; German diplomatist; *Permanent Representative, NATO;* b. 12 Oct. 1950, Münster, Westfalen; m. Barbara Brandenburg (née Tobias); two c. *Education:* Univ. of Münster, Univ. of Paris III, France. *Career:* Attaché, Ministry of Foreign Affairs 1980–82; Second, then First Sec., Embassy in Iraq 1982–84; Deputy Chief of Mission in Consulate Gen., Leningrad 1984–86; First Sec., Embassy in Moscow 1986–88; Counsellor, Ministry of Foreign Affairs 1988–91, Deputy Head OSCE Division 1992–95, Dir 1999; Head, Partnership and Cooperation Section, Political Affairs Div. NATO 1995–99, Head of Defence and Security Policy Div. 1999–2001; Commr for Russia, Caucasus and Cen. Asia, Ministry of Foreign Affairs 2001–03, Deputy Political Dir 2003–07; Perm. Rep. to NATO, Brussels 2007–; Fellow, Center for Int. Affairs, Harvard Univ. 1991–92. *Address:* North Atlantic Treaty Organization (NATO), boulevard Léopold III, 1110 Brussels, Belgium (office). *Telephone:* (2) 707-41-11 (office). *Fax:* (2) 707-45-79 (office). *E-mail:* natodoc@hq.nato.int (office). *Website:* www.nato.int (office).

BRANKOVIĆ, Nedžad, MSc, PhD; Bosnia and Herzegovina engineer and politician; *Prime Minister, Federation of Bosnia and Herzegovina;* b. 28 Dec. 1962, Višegrad; m.; two c. *Education:* Univ. of Sarajevo. *Career:* served with Bosnia-Herzegovina Army then apptd to head logistics team attached to Gen. Staff; with IPSI (Inst. for Transport and Communications), Sarajevo 1987–92; Dir-Gen. BiH Railways 1993–98; Dir-Gen. Energoinvest Co. (eng firm) 1998–2002; Sr Teaching Asst, Faculty for Transport and Communications, Univ. of Sarajevo; Minister of Transport and Communications, Fed. of Bosnia and Herzegovina 2003–07, Prime Minister 2007–; mem. Party of Democratic Action (SDA). *Address:* Office of the Prime Minister of the Federation of Bosnia and Herzegovina, 71000 Sarajevo, Alipašina 41, Bosnia and Herzegovina (office). *Telephone:* (33) 656679 (office). *Fax:* (33) 444718 (office). *E-mail:* kabprem@fbihvlada.gov.ba (office). *Website:* www.fbihvlada.gov.ba (office).

BRAUN, Maj.-Gen. László; Hungarian army officer; *First Deputy Chief of Defence Staff;* b. 1951, SE Hungary; m. Zsuzsa Braun; five c. *Education:* Máté Zalka Mil. Coll., Mil. Eng. Univ., Kiev, Zrinyi Miklós Mil. Acad. *Career:* began career in Hungarian Armed Forces 1973; training officer Air Defence Training Centre 1973–74; commdg officer of air defence missile battalion 1975–78; Sr Training Officer, 5th Army 1982–84, Chief of Training Cell 1984–86; Devt Officer, Directorate of Air Defence, Ministry of Defence 1986–93, Deputy Dir 1994–95; Dir Army and Home Defence Air Defence Forces 1996; Deputy Dir-Gen. Aviation and Air Defence 1997; Deputy Chief of Air Staff 1998–2000; Mil. Rep. to NATO, Brussels 2001; apptd Maj.-Gen. 2001; currently First Deputy Chief of Defence Staff, Ministry of Defence. *Address:* Ministry of Defence, 1055 Budapest, Balaton u. 7–11, Hungary (office). *Telephone:* (1) 236-5111 (office). *Fax:* (1) 311-0182 (office). *Website:* www.honvedelem.hu (office).

BRAUTASET, Tarald O., MSc; Norwegian diplomatist; b. 28 Sept. 1946. *Education:* Univ. of Oslo. *Career:* Ministry of Foreign Affairs 1973–75, Second Sec., Embassy in Abidjan 1975–77, First Sec., Embassy in Paris 1977–80; Exec. Officer, Ministry of Foreign Affairs 1981–84, Head of Div. (W European Affairs) 1985–88, Minister Counsellor, Perm Mission to EU, Brussels 1988–94, Deputy Dir Political Dept, Ministry of Foreign Affairs 1996–97, Asst Sec. Gen. for Political Affairs 1997–2000, Amb. to UK 2000–06. *Address:* c/o Ministry of Foreign Affairs, 7 juni pl. 1, POB 8114 Dep., 0032 Oslo, Norway.

BRAVO, Leopoldo Alfredo; Argentine diplomatist and fmr politician; *Ambassador to Russia; Career:* fmr Deputy, San Juan Prov. Ass. (elected three times); fmr mem. Nat. Congress (elected once); Head, Finance Section, Embassy in Moscow 2002–06, Amb. to Russia (also accred. to Armenia) 2006–. *Address:* Embassy of Argentina, 119017 Moscow, ul. Bolshaya Ordynka 72, Russia (office). *Telephone:* (495) 502-10-20 (office). *Fax:* (495) 502-10-21 (office). *E-mail:* efrus@mrecic.gov.ar (office). *Website:* www.mrecic.gov.ar (office).

BRECHER, Michael, PhD, FRSC; Canadian political scientist and academic; *R. B. Angus Professor of Political Science, McGill University;* b. 14 March 1925, Montreal; m. Eva Danon 1950; three d. *Education:* McGill and Yale Univs. *Career:* mem. Faculty, McGill Univ. 1952–, R. B. Angus Prof. of Political Science 1993–; Pres. Int. Studies Asscn 1999–2000; Visiting Prof., Univ. of Chicago 1963, Hebrew Univ., Jerusalem 1970–75, Univ. of Calif., Berkeley 1979, Stanford Univ. 1980; Nuffield Fellow 1955–56; Rockefeller Fellow 1964–65; Guggenheim Fellow 1965–66; f. Shashtri Indo-Canadian Inst. 1968; Watumull Prize (American Hist. Asscn) 1960, Killam Awards (Canada Council) 1970–74, 1976–79, Woodrow Wilson Award (American Political Science Asscn) 1973, Fieldhouse Award for Distinguished Teaching (McGill Univ.) 1986, Distinguished Scholar Award (Int. Studies Asscn) 1995, Léon-Gérin Quebec Prize 2000, Award for High Distinction in Research, McGill Univ. 2000. *Publications:* The Struggle for Kashmir 1953, Nehru: A Political Biography 1959, The New States of Asia 1963, Succession in India 1966, India and World Politics 1968, Political Leadership in India 1969, The Foreign Policy System of Israel 1972, Israel, the Korean War and China 1974, Decisions in Israel's Foreign Policy 1975, Studies in Crisis Behavior 1979, Decisions in Crisis 1980, Crisis and Change in World Politics 1986, Crises in the 20th Century (Vols I, II) 1988, Crisis, Conflict and Instability 1989, Crises in World Politics 1993, A Study of

Crisis 1997, 2000, Millennial Reflections on International Studies (Vols 1–5) 2002; over 85 articles in journals.
Address: Department of Political Science, McGill University, 855 Sherbrooke Street West, Montreal, PQ H3A 2T7, Canada (office); PO Box 4438, Jerusalem 91043, Israel (home). *Telephone:* (514) 398-4816 (office). *Fax:* (514) 398-1770 (office). *E-mail:* michael.brecher@mcgill.ca (office). *Website:* www.mcgill.ca/politicalscience (office).

BREMER DE MARTINO, Juan José, BL; Mexican diplomatist; *Ambassador to UK;* b. 1944, Mexico City. *Education:* Nat. Autonomous Univ. *Career:* Pvt. Sec. to Pres. of Mexico 1972–75, Deputy Sec., Ministry of the Presidency 1975–76; Head, Nat. Fine Arts Inst. 1976–82; Deputy Sec. for Cultural Affairs, Ministry of Educ. 1982; Amb. to Sweden 1982, to USSR 1988–90, to Germany 1990–98, to Spain 1998–2000, to USA 2000–04, to UK 2004–; Pres. Foreign Affairs Cttee of Chamber of Deputies 1985–88 (Co-Chair. Mexican Dels to XXVI and XXVII Mexico-US Inter-parl. Comm. meetings, Colorado Springs 1986, New Orleans 1988); mem. Ford Foundation Comm. to Study the Future of Mexican-American Relations 1986; Pres. Cervantino Int. Festival 1983.
Address: Embassy of Mexico, 16 St George Street, Hanover Square, London, W1S 1LX, England (office). *Telephone:* (20) 7499-8586 (office). *Fax:* (20) 7495-4035 (office). *E-mail:* mexuk@easynet.co.uk (office). *Website:* www.sre.gob.mx/reinounido (office).

BRENES ICABALCETA, Horacio; Nicaraguan politician and diplomatist; *Ambassador to Mexico;* b. 16 June 1949, Matagalpa; m.; four c. *Career:* Co-founder and Chair. Matagalpa Foundation for Business Devt (Fudemat) 1995–; mem. Partido Liberal Constitucionalista, then Frente Sandinista de Liberación Nacional; Minister of Devt, Industry and Trade 2006–07; Amb. to Mexico 2007–.
Address: Embassy of Nicaragua, Prado Norte 470, Col. Lomas de Chapultepec, Del. Miguel Hidalgo, 11000 México DF, Mexico (office). *Telephone:* (55) 5540-5625 (office). *Fax:* (55) 5520-6961 (office). *E-mail:* embanic@prodigy.net.mx (office).

BRENTON, Anthony; British diplomatist; b. 1 Jan. 1950; m. Susan Mary Penrose 1982; one s. two d. *Career:* joined FCO 1975, Far Eastern Dept 1975–76, language training (UK and Middle Eastern Centre for Arabic Studies) 1976–78, Second, later First Sec., Chancery, Cairo 1978–81, EC Dept, FCO 1981–85, First Sec. (Energy) and UK Rep., Brussels 1985–86, secondment to EC 1986–89, Counsellor (Head of UN Dept), FCO 1989–92, Career Devt Attachment, Harvard Univ. 1992–93, Counsellor (Econ., Aid and Scientific), Moscow 1994–98, Dir (Global Issues), FCO 1998–2001, Minister and Deputy Head of Mission, Washington, DC 2001–04, Amb. to Russia 2004–2008.
Address: Foreign and Commonwealth Office, King Charles St, London, SW1A 2AH, England (office). *Telephone:* (20) 7008-1500 (office). *Website:* www.fco.gov.uk (office).

BRICEÑO, Hon. John, BBA; Belizean politician; b. 17 July 1960, Orange Walk Town; m. Rossana Briceño; three s. *Education:* Muffles High School, St John's Coll., Belize City, Univ. of Texas at Austin, USA. *Career:* mem. Parl. for Orange Walk Cen. Div. (People's United Party) 1993–, currently Deputy Leader; Deputy Prime Minister 1998–2007, also Minister of Natural Resources and the Environment 1998–2007, of Commerce Trade and Industry 1999–2007, of Local Govt 2005–07.
Address: People's United Party (PUP), 3 Queen Street, Belize City, Belize (office). *Telephone:* 223-2428 (office). *Fax:* 223-3476 (office). *Website:* www.pupbelize.bz (office).

BRIDGEWATER, Pamela Ethel, BA, MA; American diplomatist; *Ambassador to Ghana; Education:* Walker-Grant High School, Fredericksburg, Va, Va State Univ., Univ. of Cincinnati, American Univ. School of Int. Service. *Career:* teaching career at Morgan State Univ. and Bowie State Univ., Md and Voorhees Coll., S Carolina –1980; joined Foreign Service in 1980, overseas postings have included Brussels, Kingston, Pretoria 1990–93, Durban 1993–96 (first African-American woman apptd Consul-Gen. in Durban), Deputy Chief of Mission, Embassy in Nassau, Bahamas 1996–99, Amb. to Benin 2000–02, Deputy Asst Sec. of State for African Affairs 2002–04 (named Special Coordinator for Peace in Liberia), Diplomat-in-Residence, Howard Univ. 2004–05, Amb. to Ghana 2005–; Hon. LLD (Va State Univ.) 1997; Nat. Order of Benin 2002; Charles E. Cobb, Jr Award for Initiative and Success in Trade Devt 2002, three Superior Honor Awards, Sr Presidential Performance Pay Award.
Address: Embassy of the USA, Ring Road East, PO Box GP 194, Accra, Ghana (office). *Telephone:* (21) 775348 (office). *Fax:* (21) 776008 (office). *E-mail:* prsaccra@pd.state.gov (office). *Website:* accra.usembassy.gov (office).

BRILL, Kenneth C., BA, MBA; American diplomatist and government official; *Director, National Counterproliferation Center;* b. 13 Oct. 1947, Fort Hood, Tex.; m. Mary Lee Brill; one s. one d. *Education:* Ohio Univ., Univ. of California, Berkeley. *Career:* joined State Dept 1975, overseas assignments included posts in Ghana, Jordan; Special Asst to Undersec. for Political Affairs, State Dept 1981–82, Deputy Dir then Dir Office of Egyptian Affairs 1982–84; Counsellor for Political Affairs, Embassy in Amman 1984–86; Consul Gen. in Calcutta 1986–89; Exec. Asst to Undersec. for Political Affairs 1989–91; Deputy Chief of Mission and Chargé d'Affaires, Embassy in India 1991–94; Exec. Sec. and Special Asst to Sec. of State 1994; Amb. to Cyprus 1996–99; Prin. Deputy Asst Sec. for Bureau of Oceans and Int. Environmental and Scientific Affairs 1999–2001, acting Asst Sec. 2001; US Rep. to IAEA, Vienna 2001–04, also Perm. Rep. to UN, Vienna; Int. Affairs Adviser to Commdt, Industrial Coll. of the Armed Forces, Washington, DC 2004–05; Dir Nat. Counterproliferation Center and Counter Proliferation Mission Man., Office of the Dir of Nat. Intelligence 2005–; Dept of State Distinguished, Superior and Meritorious Honor Awards.
Address: National Counterproliferation Center, c/o Office of the Director of National Intelligence, Washington, DC 20511, USA (office). *Telephone:* (202) 201-1111 (office). *Website:* www.dni.gov (office).

BRINKHORST, Laurens Jan, MA; Dutch politician and academic; *Professor of International and European Law and Governance, University of Leiden;* b. 18 March 1937, Zwolle. *Education:* Leiden Univ. and Columbia Univ., New York, USA. *Career:* worked for Shearman & Sterling law firm, New York; worked at Europe Inst., Leiden Univ., Dir Europe Inst. and Sr Lecturer in the Law of Int. Orgs 1965, later Extraordinary Prof. of Int. Environmental Law; Chair of European Law, Groningen Univ. 1967–73; State Sec. for Foreign Affairs with European Affairs portfolio 1973–77; mem. House of Reps of States Gen. 1977–82; mem. Democraten 66 (D66), Leader Parl. Party 1981–82, now Hon. mem.; Head, Del. of Comm. of European Communities in Japan 1982; Dir-Gen. of Environment, Consumer Protection and Nuclear Safety, EC 1987–89, of Environment, Nuclear Safety and Civil Protection 1989; mem. European Parl. 1994–99; Minister of Agric., Nature Man. and Fisheries 1999–2002; European Affairs Adviser, NautaDutilh law firm, Brussels 2002; Minister of Economic Affairs 2003–04; Deputy Prime Minister and Minister of Econ. Affairs 2004–06 (resgnd); mem. Bd of Dirs Salzburg Seminar, Int. Inst. of Sustainable Devt; currently Prof. of Int. and European Law and Governance, Univ. of Leiden; Coordinator EC for the Project No. 6 Trans-eur. Network; Sr Adviser to Dir-Gen. ESA; Dr hc (Sofia).
Address: Lange Voorhut 82, 2514 EJ The Hague, Netherlands (office). *Telephone:* (70) 30-20-165. *E-mail:* l.j.brinkhorst@gmail.com (office); office@voorhout82.nl (office).

BRINKLEY, Robert Edward, MA; British diplomatist; *High Commissioner to Pakistan;* b. 21 Jan. 1954; m. Mary Brinkley; three s. *Education:* Stonyhurst Coll., Lancs., Corpus Christi Coll., Oxford. *Career:* joined FCO, London 1977, mem. staff 1982–88, 1992–96; mem. UK Del. to Comprehensive Test Ban Negotiations, Geneva 1978; assigned to Embassy in Moscow 1979–82, 1996–99, to Embassy in Bonn 1988–92; with FCO/Home Office Jt Entry Clearance Unit 2000–02; Amb. to Ukraine 2002–06; High Commr to Pakistan 2006–.
Address: High Commission of the United Kingdom, Diplomatic Enclave, Ramna 5, POB 1122, Islamabad, Pakistan (office). *Telephone:* (51) 2012000 (office). *Fax:* (51) 2823439 (office). *E-mail:* bhcmedia@isb.comsats.net.pk (office). *Website:* www.britainonline.org.pk (office).

BRISTOW, Laurence Stanley, PhD; British diplomatist; b. 23 Nov. 1963; m. Fiona Bristow; two c. *Career:* joined FCO 1990, posted to Bucharest, Romania 1992–95; Pvt. Sec. to Minister of State for Europe 1996–98; Head of Political Section, Ankara, Turkey 1999–2002; worked at NATO Defence Coll., Rome, Italy 2002–03; Amb. to Azerbaijan 2003–07.
Address: c/o Foreign and Commonwealth Office, King Charles Street, London, SW1A 2AH, England (office). *Telephone:* (20) 7008-1500 (office). *Website:* www.fco.gov.uk (office).

BRITO, José, BA, MSc; Cape Verde diplomatist; *Minister of Economy, Growth and Competitiveness;* b. 19 March 1944; m. Maria de Lourdes Santos; two s. two d. *Education:* French Petroleum Inst. and Univ. of Abidjan. *Career:* Assoc. Prof., Abidjan Univ. of Science 1970–73; Chemical Engineer then Tech. Man. Abidjan Oil Refinery 1970–75; mem. Man. Team of Ruling Party in Cape Verde (including five years as mem. Parl.) 1981–91; Minister of Devt Planning and Foreign Aid 1977–91; worked on Strategic Devt Man. in Africa, UN 1992–96, ind. consultant 1997; Govt Relations Man., Ocean Energy Inc., Equatorial Guinea 1997–98, Vice-Pres. Govt Relations in Houston, Tex. 1999–2000, Govt Affairs Consultant in Côte d'Ivoire 2000–01; Amb. to USA (also accred to Canada and Mexico) 2001–06; Minister of Economy, Growth and Competitiveness 2007–.

Address: Ministry of the Economy, Growth and Competitiveness, Praia, Santiago, Cape Verde (office). *Telephone:* 2605300 (office). *Fax:* 2617299 (office). *E-mail:* jorge.borges@gov1.gov.cv (office).

BRITTAN, Sir Samuel, Kt, MA; British writer and journalist; *Columnist, Financial Times;* b. 29 Dec. 1933, London; brother of Lord Brittan of Spennithorne. *Education:* Kilburn Grammar School, Jesus Coll., Cambridge. *Career:* journalist on The Financial Times 1955–61, prin. economic commentator 1966–, Asst Ed. 1978–95; Econs Ed. The Observer 1961–64; Adviser, Dept of Econ. Affairs 1965; Research Fellow, Nuffield Coll., Oxford 1973–74, Visiting Fellow 1974–82; Visiting Prof., Chicago Law School, USA 1978; mem. Peacock Cttee on Finance of the BBC 1985–86; Hon. Prof. of Politics Univ. of Warwick 1987–92; Hon. Fellow Jesus Coll., Cambridge 1988; Chevalier, Légion d'honneur 1993; Hon. DLitt (Heriot-Watt) 1985; Hon. DUniv (Essex) 1995; first winner Sr Harold Wincott Award for financial journalists 1971, George Orwell Prize for political journalism 1980, Ludwig Erhard Prize 1987. *Publications:* Steering the Economy (3rd edn 1970), Left or Right: The Bogus Dilemma 1968, The Price of Economic Freedom: A Guide to Flexible Rates 1970, Is There an Economic Consensus? 1973, Capitalism and the Permissive Society 1973 (new edn A Restatement of Economic Liberalism 1988), The Delusion of Incomes Policy (with Peter Lilley) 1977, The Economic Consequences of Democracy 1977, How to End the 'Monetarist' Controversy 1981, Role and Limits of Government: Essays in Political Economy 1983, There Is No Such Thing As Society 1993, Capitalism with a Human Face 1995, Essays, Moral, Political and Economic 1998, Against the Flow 2005. *Address:* The Financial Times, Number 1 Southwark Bridge, London, SE1 9HL, England (office). *Telephone:* (20) 7873-3000 (office). *Fax:* (20) 7873-4343 (office). *E-mail:* samuel.brittan@ft.com (office). *Website:* www.samuelbrittan.co.uk.

BRIZ ABULARACH, Jorge; Guatemalan politician and businessman; b. 27 Sept. 1955, Guatemala City; m. *Education:* Univ. Rafael Landívar de Guatemala. *Career:* trained as lawyer; Dir Chamber of Commerce 1985–86, Vice-Pres. 1987–88, Pres. 1989–91, 1995–99, 2001–03; Leader Partido Movimiento Reformador (MR–Movt. for Reform Party) 2002–; elected mem. of Parl. 2003–; Minister of Foreign Affairs 2004–06; Pres. Coordinating Cttee, Asscn of Agric., Commerce, Industry and Finance (CACIF) 1990–96, Dir 2000–03; Pres. Perm. Secr. of Latin American Chambers of Commerce and Industry (CAMACOL) 1997–98; fmr Dir Fed. of Chambers of Commerce of Cen. America (CAMACOL); mem. Financial Bd of Guatemala 1992–2002; del. to IMF, World Bank, Inter-American Devt Bank and EU; Gran Oficial, Orden al Mérito Bernardo O'Higgins (Chile) 1997, Orden José Cecilio del Valle (Guatemala) 1999. *Address:* c/o Ministry of Foreign Affairs, 2a Avda La Reforma 4–47, Zona 10, Guatemala City, Guatemala (office).

BRIZUELA DE AVILA, María Eugenia; Salvadorean lawyer and politician; b. 31 Oct. 1945, San Salvador; m. Ricardo Antonio Avila Araujo; three c. *Education:* Geneva Univ., Switzerland, Sorbonne Univ., Paris, France, Dr. José Matías Delgado Univ. of El Salvador, Cen. American Inst. of Business (INCAE), Nicaragua. *Career:* Pres. Admin. Council for Int. Insurance, Salvadorean Asscn for the Study of Insurance Rights (AIDA) 1995–98, Salvador Foundation for the Devt of Women 1995–98; mem. Bd of Dirs Banco Salvadoreño; Co-ordinator 'The New Alliance', Govt of El Salvador 1999–; Minister of Foreign Affairs 1999–2004; mem. El Salvador Lawyers' Asscn 1985–, Chamber of Arbitration and Conciliation, Inst. of Notary Rights 1985–, Juridicial Studies Centre 1989–; Exec. mem. Social Security Inst. 1994, Social Investment Fund 1995. *Address:* c/o Ministry of Foreign Affairs, 5500 Alameda Dr Manuel Enrique Araújo, Km 6, Carretera a Santa Tecla, San Salvador, El Salvador (office).

BRÓDI, Gábor, MA, MB; Hungarian diplomatist; *Permanent Representative, United Nations;* b. 8 May 1953, Vértes; m.; one s. *Education:* Budapest Univ. of Econs, Eötvös Loránd Univ. Budapest. *Career:* Desk Officer, Euro-Atlantic Territorial Dept 1987; Deputy Head of Mission, London 1987–91, Deputy Head and Head of Security Policy and Cooperation in Europe Dept 1991–94; Chef de Cabinet, Minister of Foreign Affairs 1994–96; Amb. to OSCE, Vienna 1997–2001; Perm. Rep., NATO 1999–2001, Head of Policy Section, NATO-WEU Dept 2001–02; Deputy State Sec., Directorate for Multilateral Diplomacy 2002–05; Perm. Rep. to UN, New York 2005–; Commdr, Ordre National du Mérite 2004, Commdr's Cross, Order of Merit (Hungary) 2005. *Address:* Office of the Permanent Representative of Hungary to the United Nations, 227 East 52nd Street, New York, NY 10022, USA (office). *Telephone:* (212) 752-0209 (office). *Fax:* (212) 755-5395 (office). *E-mail:* hungary@un.int (office). *Website:* www.un.int/hungary (office).

BRONIAREK, Zygmunt; Polish journalist and broadcaster (retd); *Columnist, Trybuna;* b. 27 Aug. 1925, Warsaw; m. Elzbieta Sarcewicz 1972. *Education:* Warsaw School of Econs. *Career:* radiotelegraphic operator and stenographer, Czytelnik publrs, Warsaw 1945–48; Corresp. Trybuna Ludu 1950–90, Perm. Corresp. in USA 1985; in USA 1955, 1958, 1974, Latin America 1956, Paris 1959–60, 1969–73, Washington 1960–67, East Africa 1975, West Africa 1976, Nordic countries 1977–82; mem. Polish United Workers' Party (PZPR) 1956–90; Corresp., Polish Radio and TV, for Finland and Sweden; Chair. Polish Asscn of Int. Journalists and Writers 1974–77; mem. Bd of Foreign Press Asscn, Stockholm 1979–81; mem. Presidium of Journalists' Asscn Polish People's Repub. 1983–85; Vice-Pres. Polish Club of Int. Journalism 1984–85, 1991–; Corresp. Trybuna Ludu, LA Olympic Games 1984; Special Corresp. in Australia 1984; Corresp. Trybuna Ludu, USA 1985–90; presenter The Guests of Mr. Broniarek (TV), The Inner History of the Great Policy (TV) 1983, Behind the Scenes of Int. Politics (TV) 1983–85; retd 1990; columnist, Trybuna 1996–, Rynki Zagraniczne 1998–, Swiat Elit 2005–, Biznes Trendy 2006–; Gold Cross of Merit, Order of Banner of Labour (Second Class) 1984, Commdr's Cross with Star of Infante Dom Henrique the Navigator (Portugal), Commdr's Cross with Star of Polonia Restituta 2002; Int. Journalists Club of Polish Journalistic Asscn Prize 1978, Golden Screen Award of Weekly Ekran 1984, Victor Prize (TV) 1985, Polish Club of Int. Journalism (1st Prize) 1990, Bolesław Prus Award, First Class (SD PRL) 1984, Hon. Silver Ace of Polish Promotion Corpn 1995, City of Warsaw Award of Merit 2000, Gold Medal, Polish Acad. of Success 2000, Leader of Polish Journalism 2005. *Publications:* Od Hustonu do Mississipi 1956, Gorące dni Manhattanu 1960, Walka o Pałac Elizejski 1974, Kto się boi rewolucji (co-author) 1975, Angola zrodzona w walce 1977, Od Kissingera do Brzezińskiego 1980, Szaleństwo zbrojeń (co-author) 1982, Źródła spirali zbrojeń (co-author) 1985, Szczeble do Białego Domu 1986, Tajemnice Nagrody Nobla 1987, Ronald Reagan w Białym Domu 1989, Jak nauczyłem się ośmiu języków 1991, Biały Dom i Jego Prezydenci 1992, Wesoła spowiedź 1993, Książę Karol w Polsce 1994, Sekrety korespondenta zagranicznego 1995, Okiem światowca 1999, Kronika towarzyska Warszawy 2002, 365 dni z angielskim 2002, Kulisy polityki 2003, Papiez Pius X, syn Polaka a Pasja Mela Gibsona 2004, Broniarek o sobie, inni o Broniarku 2005. *Address:* ul. Gałczyńskiego 12 m. 9, 00-362 Warsaw, Poland (office). *Telephone:* (22) 8263304 (office). *Fax:* (22) 8276202 (home).

BRONSON, Rachel, BA, MA, PhD; American academic; *Vice President, Programs and Studies, Chicago Council on Global Affairs;* *Education:* Univ. of Pennsylvania, Columbia Univ., New York. *Career:* Fellow, Center for Science and Int. Affairs, Harvard Univ. 1994–96; Instructor and Adjunct Prof., Columbia Univ. 1995, 2005; Sr Fellow for Int. Security Affairs at Center for Strategic and Int. Studies 1997–99; Sr Fellow and Dir of Middle East Studies, Council on Foreign Relations 1999–2007; Vice Pres., Programs and Studies, Chicago Council on Global Affairs 2007–; consultant for Troy Systems 1998–2000, Center for Naval Analyses 1999–2001, CENTRA 2002–; has testified before US Congress' Jt Econ. Cttee, Pres.'s 9/11 Comm. and Congressional Anti-Terrorist Finance Task Force; Columbia Univ. Foreign Languages and Area Studies Fellowship 1994, Arabic Language Fellowship, Middlebury Coll. 1994, Women's Caucus of Political Science 1995, Alice Paul Dissertation Award 1995, Smith Richardson Pre-doctoral Fellowship 1996, Carnegie Scholar Award 2003. *Publications include:* Thicker than Oil: America's Uneasy Partnership with Saudi Arabia 2006; numerous articles in journals and newspapers. *Address:* Chicago Council on Global Affairs, 332 South Michigan Avenue, Suite 1100, Chicago, IL 60604-4416, USA (office). *Telephone:* (312)726-3860 (office). *Fax:* (312) 821-7555 (office). *E-mail:* (office). *Website:* www.thechicagocouncil.org (office).

BROWN, Hon. Ewart Frederick, Jr, BSc, MD, MPH, JP; Bermudian physician and politician; *Premier and Minister of Transport and Tourism;* b. 1946, Bermuda; m. Wanda Henton Brown; four s. from previous m. *Education:* Berkeley Inst., Howard Univ., Washington DC, USA, Howard Coll. of Medicine, UCLA. *Career:* represented Bermuda at Commonwealth Games, Kingston, Jamaica, where he ran the 400m and 1600m relay 1966; spent many years practising medicine in USA, including at Vermont-Century Medical Clinic, Los Angeles –1993; Medical Dir Bermuda HealthCare Services Ltd; MP for Warwick West 1993–98, for Warwick South Cen. 1998–; Minister of Transport 1998–2003; Deputy Premier and Minister of Transport 2003–04; Deputy Premier and Minister of Transport and Tourism 2004–06; Premier and Minister of Transport and Tourism 2006–; Leader Bermuda Progressive Labour Party 2006–; certified Diplomat of American Bd of Family Practice; Diplomat of American Bd of Quality Assurance and Utilization Review Physicians; fmr Vice-Pres. Union of American Physicians and Dentists; fmr Asst Prof., Dept of Family Practice, Charles R. Drew Univ. of Medicine and Science; fmr Dir, Marcus Garvey School, Los Angeles; fmr mem. Bd Union of American Physicians and Dentists (California Fed.); fmr mem. Editorial Bd Feeling

Good magazine; fmr mem. Bd Dirs Marina Hills Hosp., Los Angeles; fmr physician consultant of Rev. Jesse Jackson (1988 US presidential cand.); fmr mem. California State Comm. on Maternal, Child and Adolescent Health; founding Commr Bd of Prevention Commrs for South Cen. Los Angeles Regional Centre for Devt Disabilities; Founder and Chair. Western Park Hosp., Calif.; fmr Dir of Quality Assurance, Los Angeles Doctor's Hosp.; fmr Student Body Pres., Howard Univ.; fmr Chair. Minority Group Affairs, Student American Medical Asscn; fmr Coordinator Summer Health Task Force, Nat. Urban Coalition, Washington, DC; fmr Chair. Utilization Review Cttee, West Adams Hosp., Los Angeles; fmr Sec. Charles R. Drew Medical Soc., Los Angeles; mem. Nat. Medical Asscn, American Coll. of Utilization Review Physicians, Golden State Medical Asscn, American Medical Asscn, American Acad. of Family Physicians, American Public Health Asscn, Charles R. Drew Medical Soc.; fmr Trustee Howard Univ., Charles R. Drew Univ. of Medicine and Science; Howard Univ. Service Awards 1968, 1972, Physician's Recognition Award, American Medical Asscn 1977, Sons of Watts Grassroots Health Award 1979, Community Leadership Award, DuBois Academic Inst. 1982, Pacesetter Award, Nat. Asscn for the Advancement of Coloured People 1984, Humanitarian of the Year Award, Marcus Garvey School, Los Angeles 1991, Scroll Award, Union of American Physicians and Dentists 1993.
Address: Progressive Labour Party, Alaska Hall, 16 Court Street, Hamilton, HM 17, Bermuda (office). *Telephone:* 292-2264 (office). *Fax:* 295-7890 (office). *E-mail:* info@plp.bm (office). *Website:* www.plp.bm/ leadership/leader (office).

BROWN, Gayleatha B., BA, MA; American diplomatist; *Ambassador to Benin;* *Education:* high schools in Mingo Co., W Va, Edison Township High School, Edison, NJ, Howard Univ., John Hopkins Univ. School of Advanced Int. Studies, Washington, DC. *Career:* fmr Special Asst to USAID Asst Admin. for Africa and Legis. Asst in US House of Reps; Counsellor in Sr Foreign Service, served as Econ. Officer/Regional USAID Rep. and Finance and Devt Officer, Embassies in Paris and Abidjan, respectively, has rep. Dept of State at OECD Export Credit Arrangement negotiations as Desk Officer for US Export-Import Bank (EXIM) in Dept's Bureau of Econ. and Business Affairs, served as Counsellor for Political Affairs, Pretoria, as Consul Gen. at US Consulate Gen. and concurrently as US Deputy Perm. Observer to Council of Europe, Strasbourg, served as Chief of Econ. and Commercial Sections at Embassies in Harare and Dar es Salaam, other tours of duty have included Desk Officer for Canada and also Senegal, Guinea and Mauritania, Dept of State, Washington, DC, Amb. to Benin 2006–; Charter mem. New Jersey Edison Township High School Alumni Hall of Fame; mem. Shiloh Baptist Church (Pilgrim Circle), Washington, DC; Lady of the Golden Horseshoe (W Va state academic honour), Hon. mem. Sandown Rotary Club, Johannesburg, S Africa; two Dept of State Superior Honor Awards and a Meritorious Honor Award.
Address: US Embassy, Carré 125, rue Caporal Anani Bernard, 01 BP 2012, Cotonou, Benin (office). *Telephone:* 30-06-50 (office). *Fax:* 30-03-84 (office). *Website:* cotonou.usembassy.gov (office).

BROWN, Rt Hon. (James) Gordon, PC, MA, PhD; British politician; *Prime Minister;* b. 20 Feb. 1951, Glasgow; m. Sarah Macaulay 2000; one d. (deceased) two s. *Education:* Kirkcaldy High School and Univ. of Edinburgh. *Career:* Rector, Univ. of Edinburgh 1972–75, Temporary Lecturer 1976; Lecturer, Glasgow Coll. of Tech. 1976–80; journalist and Current Affairs Ed., Scottish TV 1980–83; MP (Labour) for Dunfermline East 1983–; Chair. Labour Party Scottish Council 1983–84; Opposition Chief Sec. to the Treasury 1987–89; Shadow Sec. of State for Trade and Industry 1989–92; Shadow Chancellor of the Exchequer 1992–97; Chancellor of the Exchequer 1997–07; Prime Minister 2007–; Leader, Labour Party 2007–; mem. Chair. Interim Cttee IMF 1999–; mem. Transport and Gen. Workers' Union; Hon. DCL (Newcastle) 2007. *Publications:* The Red Paper on Scotland (ed.) 1975, The Politics of Nationalism and Devolution (with H. M. Drucker) 1980, Scotland: The Real Divide (ed.) 1983, Maxton 1986, Where There is Greed 1989, John Smith: Life and Soul of the Party (with J. Naughtie) 1994, Values, Visions and Voices (with T. Wright) 1995, Speeches 1997–2006 2006, Courage: Eight Portraits 2007.
Address: Office of the Prime Minister, 10 Downing Street, London, SW1A 2AA, England (office). *Telephone:* (20) 7270-3000 (office); (1383) 611702 (Dunfermline East constituency) (office). *Fax:* (20) 7295-0918 (office). *Website:* www.number-10.gov.uk (office).

BROWN, Harold, PhD; American fmr government official and physicist; *Counsellor, Center for Strategic and International Studies;* b. 19 Sept. 1927, New York City; m. Colene McDowell 1953; two d. *Education:* New York City public schools and Columbia Univ. *Career:* Lecturer in Physics, Columbia Univ. 1947–48, Stevens Inst. of Tech. 1949–50; Univ. of Calif. Radiation Laboratory, Berkeley 1950–52; Livermore Radiation Labora-

tory, 1952–61, Dir 1960–61; mem. Polaris Steering Cttee, Dept of Defense 1956–58; Consultant to Air Force Scientific Advisory Bd 1956–57; mem. Scientific Advisory Cttee on Ballistic Missiles to Sec. of Defense 1958–61; mem. President's Science Advisory Cttee 1961; Sec. of Air Force 1965–69; Pres. Calif. Inst. of Tech. 1969–77; US Sec. of Defense 1977–81; Distinguished Visiting Prof. of Nat. Security Affairs, School of Advanced Int. Studies, Johns Hopkins Univ. 1981–84, Chair. Johns Hopkins Univ. Foreign Policy Inst. 1984–92; business consultant 1981–; Dir Philip Morris, Evergreen Holdings Inc., Mattel; Pnr Warburg, Pincus and Co. 1990–; Counsellor, Center for Strategic and Int. Studies 1992–; mem. Del. to Strategic Arms Limitation Talks 1969; mem. NAS; Hon. DEng (Stevens Inst. of Tech.); Hon. LLD (Long Island Univ., Gettysburg Coll., Occidental Coll., Univ. of Calif., Univ. of S Carolina, Franklin and Marshall Coll., Univ. of the Pacific, Brown Univ.); Hon. DSc (Univ. of Rochester); Presidential Medal of Freedom 1981, Fermi Award 1993. *Publications:* Thinking About National Security: Defense and Foreign Policy in a Dangerous World 1983, The Strategic Defense Initiative: Shield or Snare? (ed.) 1987.
Address: Center for Strategic and International Studies, 1800 K Street, Suite 400, NW, Washington, DC 20006, USA (office). *Telephone:* (202) 887-0200 (office). *Fax:* (202) 775-3199 (office). *E-mail:* webmaster@csis.org (office). *Website:* www.csis.org (office).

BROWN, Michael E., PhD; American academic and research institute director; *Dean of the Elliott School of International Affairs and Professor of International Affairs and Political Science, George Washington University; Education:* Cornell Univ. *Career:* mem. Directing Staff and Sr Fellow in US Security Policy, IISS, London 1988–94; Assoc. Dir Int. Security Program, Belfer Center for Science and Int. Affairs, John F. Kennedy School of Govt, Harvard Univ. 1994–98; Prof., Edmund A. Walsh School of Foreign Service, Georgetown Univ. 1998–2005, Founding Dir Security Studies Program and Center for Peace and Security Studies 2000–05; Dean, Elliott School of Int. Affairs and Prof. of Int. Affairs and Political Science, George Washington Univ., Washington, DC 2005–; Ed. Survival 1991–94; currently co-Ed. International Security 1994–2006. *Publications:* Flying Bird: the Politics of the US Strategic Bomber Program (Edgar Furniss Nat. Security Book Award); as ed.: The International Dimensions of Internal Conflict 1996, Nationalism and Ethnic Conflict 1997, America's Strategic Choices 1997, Theories of War and Peace 1998, The Rise of China 2000, Grave New World: Global Dangers in the 21st Century, Ethnic Conflict and International Security; as co-ed.: The Perils of Anarchy 1995, Debating the Democratic Peace 1996, East Asian Security 1996, Government Policies and Ethnic Relations in Asia and the Pacific 1997, Fighting Words: Language Policy and Ethnic Conflict in Asia 2003, Changing Dimensions of International Security 2004, Offense, Defense and War 2004, The Costs of Conflict.
Address: Elliott School of International Affairs, George Washington University, 1957 E Street, NW, Suite 401, Washington, DC 20052, USA (office). *Telephone:* (202) 994-6241 (office). *Fax:* (202) 994-0335 (office). *E-mail:* esiadean@gwu.edu (office). *Website:* www.gwu.edu/~elliott (office).

BROWNE, Carolyn, PhD; British diplomatist; *Ambassador to Azerbaijan;* b. 19 Oct. 1958. *Career:* Desk Officer, Repub. of Ireland Dept, FCO 1986–76, Second (later First) Sec., Embassy in Moscow 1988–91, European Union Dept 1991–93, mem. Mission to UN, New York 1993–97, Deputy Head, Southern European Dept 1997–99, Head, Human Rights Policy Dept 1999–2002, Rep. to Brussels 2002–04, Adviser to Dir of Int. Security 2005–07, Amb. to Azerbaijan 2007–.
Address: British Embassy, Khagani küç. 45, Baku 1010, Azerbaijan (office). *Telephone:* (12) 497-51-88 (office). *Fax:* (12) 497-24-74 (office). *E-mail:* office@britemb.baku.az (office). *Website:* www.britishembassy.az (office).

BROWNE, Rt Hon. Des, PC, LLB; British politician and lawyer; *Secretary of State for Defence and Secretary of State for Scotland;* b. 22 March 1952, Ayrshire; m.; two s. *Education:* St Michael's Acad., Kilwinning, Univ. of Glasgow. *Career:* admitted as solicitor 1976; joined Ross, Harper and Murphy (law firm), Kilmarnock; Co-founder McCluskey Browne (law firm)–1993; unsuccessful cand. for MP for Argyll and Bute 1992; called to the Bar 1993, served as specialist child law advocate; MP for Kilmarnock and Loudoun 1997–2005, for New Kilmarnock and Loudoun 2005–; Parl. Pvt. Sec. to Sec. of State for Scotland Donald Dewar 1998–99, for Adam Ingram 2000; Parl. Under-Sec. of State, NI Office 2001–03; Minister of State, Dept for Work and Pensions (Work) 2003–04; Minister of State, Home Office (Citizenship, Immigration and Nationality) 2004–05; Chief Sec. to Treasury 2005–06; Sec. of State for Defence 2006–, for Scotland 2007–; Sec. Scottish Labour Party Working Party on Prison System 1988–90; mem. Commons Select Cttees on NI Affairs 1997–98, Public Admin 1999–2000, Jt Cttee on Human rights 2001; mem. Labour Party

Departmental Cttees for NI, Treasury, Civil Liberties Group 1997–2001; Hon. Sec. Labour Party Departmental Cttee for Social Security 1997–2001. *Address:* 32 Grange Street, Kilmarnock, KA1 2DD, Scotland (office); House of Commons, London, SW1A 0AA (office); Ministry of Defence, Main Building, Whitehall, London, SW1A 2HB, England (office). *Telephone:* (1563) 520267 (constituency) (office); (20) 7218-9000 (office). *Fax:* (1563) 539439 (constituency) (office). *E-mail:* browned@parliament .uk (office); public@ministers.mod.uk (office). *Website:* www .kilmarnockandloudoun.co.uk (office); www.mod.uk (office).

BROWNE, Michael (Mike); Saint Vincent and the Grenadines government official. *Career:* Minister of Educ., Youth and Sport –2005, of Foreign Affairs and of Commerce and Trade May–Dec. 2005.
Address: c/o Ministry of Foreign Affairs, Administrative Centre, Kingstown, Saint Vincent and the Grenadines (office).

BROWNE, Sir Nicholas, KBE, CMG; British diplomatist; b. 17 Dec. 1947; m. Diana Browne (née Aldwinckle) 1969; two s. two d. *Education:* Cheltenham Coll., Univ. Coll., Oxford. *Career:* joined British Diplomatic Service 1969; with FCO, London 1969–71, Second, then First Sec. 1974–76, First Sec. 1981–84, Counsellor 1989–90; assigned to Embassy in Tehran, Iran 1971–84, Chargé d'affaires 1989, 1997–99; secondment to Cabinet Office 1976–80; First Sec. and Head of Chancery, Embassy in Salisbury, Zimbabwe 1980–81; First Sec., Mission to EC, Brussels 1984–89; Counsellor, Press and Public Affairs, Embassy in Washington, DC and Head of Br Information Services in New York, USA 1990–94; Head of Middle East Dept, FCO 1994–97; Amb. to Iran 1999–2001; apptd Sr Dir (Civil) Royal Coll. of Defence Studies 2002; Amb. to Denmark 2002–06. *Address:* c/o Foreign and Commonwealth Office, King Charles Street, London, SW1A 2AH, England.

BROWNFIELD, William R.; American diplomatist; *Ambassador to Colombia;* b. 1952, Lubbock, Tex.; m. Kristie Anne Kenney, US Amb. to the Philippines. *Education:* Cornell Univ., Univ. of Tex. School of Law, Nat. War Coll. *Career:* entered Foreign Service 1979; Deputy Consul, Maracaibo, Venezuela 1979–81; Special Asst. to Under Sec. for Political Affairs, San Salvador 1981–83; Exec. Asst., Bureau of Interamerican Affairs 1984–85; Special Asst. to Under Sec. for Political Affairs, also mem. of Sec.'s Policy Planning Staff, Buenos Aires, Argentina 1986–89; Political Adviser to Commdr-in-Chief, US Southern Command in Panama 1989–90; Counselor, Humanitarian Affairs, US Mission in Geneva, Switzerland 1993–98; Prin. Deputy Asst Sec. of State 1998–99; Bureau of Int. Narcotics and Law Enforcement Affairs 1998–99; Deputy Asst Sec., Bureau of Western Hemisphere Affairs 1999–2002; Amb. to Chile 2002–04, to Venezuela 2004–07, to Colombia 2007–; State Dept Superior Honor Awards (four times). *Address:* Embassy of the USA, Calle 22d-bis, No 47-51, Apdo Aéreo 3831, Bogotá, Colombia (office). *Telephone:* (1) 315-0811 (office). *Fax:* (1) 315-2197 (office). *E-mail:* AmbassadorB@state.gov (office). *Website:* bogota .usembassy.gov (office).

BROWNING, Steven A., BA, MA; American diplomatist; *Ambassador to Uganda;* m. Susan Browning; two c. *Education:* Baylor Univ. and Univ. of Houston. *Career:* career mem. Sr Foreign Service with rank of Minister-Counselor, overseas postings have included Dominican Repub., Kenya, Egypt and Sri Lanka, Special Asst to the Under-Sec. for Man., Dept of State 1992–93, Deputy Chief of Mission, Dar es Salaam 1993–96, Exec. Dir Bureau of African Affairs 1996–98, Dean of Foreign Service Inst. School of Professional and Area Studies 1998–2000, Diplomat-in-Residence, Univ. of Southern Calif. and Univ. of Calif., Davis 2000–03, Amb. to Malawi 2003–04, Minister-Counselor for Man., Embassy in Baghdad 2004–06, Amb. to Uganda 2006–. *Address:* Embassy of the USA, Plot 1577, Ggaba Road, PO Box 7007, Kampala, Uganda (office). *Telephone:* (41) 259791 (office). *Fax:* (41) 259794 (office). *E-mail:* ambkampala@state.gov (office). *Website:* kampala .usembassy.gov (office).

BRUBAKER, Rogers, MA, PhD; American academic; *Professor of Sociology, University of California, Los Angeles;* b. 1956, Evanston, Ill.; m. Zsuzsa Berend; two s. *Education:* Harvard Coll., Columbia Univ. and Univ. of Sussex, UK. *Career:* Jr Fellow, Soc. of Fellows of Harvard Univ. 1988–91; Assoc. Prof. of Sociology, UCLA 1991–94, Prof. 1994–; Recurring Visiting Prof., Nationalism Studies Program, Cen. European Univ., Budapest; Sr Ed. Theory and Society; Fellow Center for Advanced Study in Behavioral Sciences 1995–96; MacArthur Fellowship 1994–99, Presidential Young Investigator Award, NSF 1994–99, John Simon Guggenheim Memorial Foundation Fellowship 1999–2000. *Publications include:* The Limits of Rationality: An Essay on the Social and Moral Thought of Max Weber 1984, Immigration and the Politics of Citizenship in Europe and North America (ed.) 1989, Citizenship and Nationhood in France and Germany

1992, Nationalism Reframed: Nationhood and the National Question in the New Europe 1996; Ethnicity without Groups 2004; more than 24 articles on social theory, immigration, citizenship and nationalism. *Address:* Department of Sociology, UCLA, 264 Haines Hall, 375 Portola Plaza, Los Angeles, CA 90095-1551, USA (office). *Telephone:* (310) 825-1129 (office). *Fax:* (310) 206-9838 (office). *E-mail:* brubaker@soc.ucla.edu (office). *Website:* www.sscnet.ucla.edu/soc/faculty/brubaker (office).

BRUMMELL, Paul, BA; British diplomatist; *Ambassador to Kazakhstan and Non-Resident Ambassador to Kyrgyzstan;* b. 28 Aug. 1965, Harpenden. *Education:* St Albans School, St Catharine's Coll., Cambridge. *Career:* joined HM Diplomatic Service 1987; Third Sec., later Second Sec., Islamabad 1989–92; with FCO, London 1993–94; First Sec., Rome 1995–2000; Deputy Head Eastern Dept, FCO 2000–01; Amb. to Turkmenistan 2002–05, to Kazakhstan (and non-resident to Kyrgyzstan) 2005–. *Publications:* Turkmenistan: The Bradt Travel Guide 2005. *Address:* Embassy of the United Kingdom, 480062 Almaty, Furmanova 173, Kazakhstan (office); c/o Foreign and Commonwealth Office (Almaty), King Charles Street, London, SW1A 2AH, England (office). *Telephone:* (3272) 50-61-91 (office). *Fax:* (3272) 50-62-60 (office). *E-mail:* british -embassy@nursat.kz (office); paul.brummell@fco.gov.uk (office). *Website:* www.britishembassy.gov.uk/kazakhstan (office).

BRUNDTLAND, Gro Harlem, MD, MPH; Norwegian international organization official and physician; *United Nations Special Envoy for Climate Change;* b. 20 April 1939, Oslo; m. Arne Olav Brundtland 1960; three s. (one deceased) one d. *Education:* Oslo Univ. and Harvard Univ., USA. *Career:* Consultant, Ministry of Health and Social Affairs 1965–67; Medical Officer, Oslo City Health Dept 1968–69; Deputy Dir School Health Services, Oslo 1969; Minister of Environment 1974–79; Deputy Leader Labour Party 1975–81, Leader Labour Parl. Group 1981–92; Prime Minister of Norway Feb.–Oct. 1981, 1986–89, 1990–96; mem. Parl. Standing Cttee on Foreign Affairs, fmr mem. Parl. Standing Cttee on Finance; mem. of Storting (Parl.) 1977–97; Dir-Gen. WHO 1998–2003; Chair. UN World Comm. on Environment and Devt 2003–05; UN Special Envoy for Climate Change 2007–fmr Vice-Chair. Sr Secondary Schools' Socialist Asscn, Students' Asscn of Labour Party; Dr hc (Oxford) 2001; Third World Prize for Work on Environmental Issues 1989, Indira Gandhi Prize 1990, Onassis Foundation Award 1992, Scientific American Policy Leader of the Year Award 2003. *Publications:* articles on preventive medicine, school health and growth studies. *Address:* United Nations, New York NY, 10017, USA (office). *Telephone:* (212) 963-1234 (office). *Fax:* (212) 963-4879 (office). *Website:* www.un.org (office).

BRUNETTA, Renato; Italian politician, labour economist, academic and government official; *Minister for Public Administration and Innovation;* b. 26 May 1950, Venice. *Education:* Marco Foscarini Liceo Classico, Venice and Univs of Padua, Cambridge, UK and Rotterdam, Netherlands. *Career:* researcher in political sciences, Univ. of Padua 1975–77, Prof. of Labour Econs 1978–82; Gen. Sec. Fondazione G. Brodolini, Rome 1980–; Chief Consultant, Econ. Adviser to Ministry of Labour 1983–88; Sec., Italian Asscn of Labour Economists 1985–87; Vice-Pres., OECD Manpower and Social Affairs Cttee 1985–89; Prof. of Labour Econs, Rome Univ. II 'Tor Vergata' 1990–; mem. Scientific Cttee on European Integration, Ministry of Foreign Affairs 1990–92, Taskforce for Programming and Econ. Policy, Ministry of the Budget 1990–; mem. European Parl. 1999–; Econ. Adviser to Prime Minister 2004–06; Minister for Public Administration and Innovation 2008–; Ed. Economia & Lavoro (quarterly review), Rome 1980–; Founder and Ed. Labour (4-monthly journal) 1987–; Pres. Comm. on Information for CNEL (Nat. Council of Economy and Labour) 1989–94, Councillor 1995; mem. European Asscn of Labour Economists 1989–93, ASPEN-Italy 1989–; fmr Vice-Pres. Cttee on Industry, External Trade, Research and Energy; Premio St Vincent (for Econs) 1988, Premio Tarantelli (for Econs) 1993, Scanno Prize 1994, Rodolfo Valentino Int. Prize 2000. *Publications:* Economia del Lavoro 1981, Multilocalizzazione produttiva come strategia d'impresa 1983, Squilibri, conflitto, piena occupazione 1983, Spesa pubblica e conflitto 1987, Microeconomia del lavoro: Teorie e analisi empiriche 1987, Labour Relations and Economic Performance (ed.) 1990, Il Modello Italia 1991, Economics for the New Europe 1991, Il conflitto e le relazioni di lavoro negli anni '90 1992, Disoccupazione, Isteresi, Irreversibilità 1992, Retribuzione, costo del lavoro. Regolazione e deregolazione; il capital umano; la destrutturazione del mercato (ed.) 1992, La fine della società dei salariati 1994, Sud: Alcune idee perché il Mezzogiorno non resti com'è 1995, Venezia XXI, Cronache di una transizione difficile 2004, Quindici piu Direci: Il difficile cammino-dell'integrazaione europea (jt author) 2004, Il coraggio e la paura, Scritti de economia e politica 1999–2003 2004; articles and essays on labour econs and industrial relations; Columnist, Il Sole 24 ore, Il Giornale.

Address: Via dell'Umilta 36, 00187 Rome, Italy (office); Palais de l'Europe Louise Weiss, 67070 Strasbourg, France (office). *Telephone:* (66) 731234 (Italy) (office); (3) 88-17-53-93 (France) (office). *Fax:* (66) 731362 (Italy) (office); (3) 88-17-93-93 (France) (office). *E-mail:* rbrunetta@europarl.eu .int. *Website:* www.renatobrunetta.it.

BRUTON, John Gerard, BA, BL; Irish politician, barrister and farmer; *European Union Ambassador and Head, European Commission Delegation to USA;* b. 18 May 1947, Dublin; m. Finola Gill 1981; one s. three d. *Education:* Clongowes Wood Coll., Univ. Coll., Dublin, King's Inn, Dublin. *Career:* mem. Dáil Éireann (House of Reps) 1969–; Fine Gael Spokesman on Agric. 1972–73; Parl. Sec. to Minister for Educ. 1973–77, to Minister for Industry and Commerce 1975–77; Fine Gael Spokesman on Agric. 1977–81, on Finance Jan.–June 1981; Minister of Finance 1981–82, of Industry, Trade, Commerce and Tourism 1982–86, of Finance 1986–87; Deputy Leader of Fine Gael 1987–90, Leader 1990–2001, Fine Gael Spokesman on Industry and Commerce 1987–89, on Educ. 1989–90; mem. Parl. Ass., Council of Europe 1989–91, British-Irish Parl. Body 1993–94, Parl. Ass., WEU 1997–; Prime Minister of Ireland 1994–97; Leader of Opposition 1997–2001; EU Amb. and Head, EC Del. to USA 2004–; mem. Fine Gael Front Bench 2002–; Gov. Ditchley Foundation 1999–; Hon. Citizen, Sioux City, Iowa, USA; Hon. LLD (Memorial Univ., St John's, Newfoundland), (Nat. Univ. of Ireland). *Publications:* Reform of the Dail 1980, A Better Way to Plan the Nation's Finances 1981.
Address: European Union, Delegation of the European Commission to the United States, 2300 M Street, NW, Washington, DC 20037, USA (office); Cornelstown, Dunboyne, Co. Meath, Ireland (home). *Telephone:* (202) 862-9500 (office). *Fax:* (202) 429-1766 (office). *E-mail:* john.bruton@ec.europa .eu (office). *Website:* www.eurunion.org (office).

BRUZGA, Andrius, BA; Lithuanian diplomatist; *Ambassador to USA;* m. Imsre Darija Sabaliunas Bruzgiene; one s. one d. *Education:* Vilnius Univ., Union Coll., New York, USA, Univ. of Leeds, UK, George C. Marshall European Center for Security Studies, Germany, USIA Int. Visitor Program. *Career:* has held numerous posts in Dept of State and Diplomatic Protocol, Ministry of Foreign Affairs, including Second Sec. 1991–92, First Sec. 1992, Deputy Dir 1992–93, Acting Dir 1993–95, First Sec., Tel-Aviv 1995–96, Counsellor, later Minister-Counsellor of Political Affairs, London 1996–98, Head of West European Div. 1998–99, Dir First Bilateral Relations Dept, Ministry of Foreign Affairs 1999–2002, Amb. to Finland 2002–07, to USA 2007–.
Address: Embassy of Lithuania, 2622 16th Street, NW, Washington, DC 20009 (office); Embassy of Lithuania, 2300 Clarendon Blvd, Suite 302, Arlington, VA 22201, USA (temporary address from Dec. 2007) (office). *Telephone:* (202) 234-5860 (office). *Fax:* (202) 328-0466 (office). *E-mail:* info@ltembassyus.org (office). *Website:* www.ltembassyus.org (office).

BRYER, David, CMG, MA, DPhil; British charity administrator; *Chairman, Oxfam International;* b. 15 March 1944, Newbury, Berks.; s. of Ronald Bryer and Betty Bryer (née Rawlinson); m. Margaret Bowyer; one s. one d. *Education:* King's School, Worcs., Worcester Coll., Oxford, Manchester Univ. and Univ. of Oxford. *Career:* teaching in Lebanon and UK 1964–65, 1967–74 and 1979–81; Visiting Fellow, British Acad. 1972; Asst Keeper, Ashmolean Museum, Oxford 1972–74; Field Dir Oxfam, Middle East 1975–79, Co-ordinator of Africa Programme 1981–84, Overseas Dir (responsible for overseeing Oxfam's relief and dev't work) 1984–91, Dir 1992–2001, Chair. Oxfam Int. 2001–; Trustee, Voluntary Services Overseas, Save the Children; Chair. Eurostep 1993–94, Steering Cttee for Humanitarian Response, Geneva 1995–97, British Overseas Aid Group 1998–2000; mem. Wilton Park Acad. Council 1999–, Oxford Brookes Univ. Court 1999–.
Address: Oxfam International, Suite 20, 266 Banbury Road, Oxford, OX2 7DL, England (office). *Telephone:* (01865) 313939 (office). *Fax:* (01865) 313770 (office). *E-mail:* dbryer@oxfaminternational.org (office). *Website:* www.oxfaminternational.org (office).

BRYN, Kåre; Norwegian diplomatist; *Secretary-General, European Free Trade Association;* b. 12 March 1944; m.; four c. *Education:* Norwegian School of Econs and Business Admin. *Career:* Trainee Ministry of Foreign Affairs 1969, Attaché/Second Sec. Norwegian Embassy, London 1971–74, First Sec., Belgrade 1974–76, Exec. Officer Ministry of Foreign Affairs 1976–79, First Sec., later Counsellor, Perm. Mission of Norway, Geneva 1979–84, Head of Div., Ministry of Foreign Affairs 1984, Asst Dir-Gen. 1985–89, Dir-Gen. Dept for Natural Resources and Environmental Affairs 1989–99, Norwegian Rep. to Int. Whaling Comm. (IWC) 1995–99, Amb. and Perm. Rep. to European Free Trade Assen (EFTA) and WTO, Geneva 1999–2003 (Chair. WTO Gen. Council 2000–01), Amb. to the Netherlands 2003–06; Sec.-Gen. EFTA 2006–.
Address: European Free Trade Association (EFTA), 9–11 rue de Varembé, 1211 Geneva 20, Switzerland (office). *Telephone:* 223322626 (office). *Fax:* 223322677 (office). *E-mail:* mail.gva@efta.int (office). *Website:* www.efta .int (office).

BRYNEN, Rex Jeffrey, PhD; Canadian academic; *Professor of Political Science, McGill University;* b. 25 Nov. 1961, Hamilton, Ont.; m.; two c. *Education:* Univ. of Victoria, Univ. of Calgary. *Career:* Lecturer, Univ. of Calgary 1985–88; Research Fellow, American Univ., Cairo 1986–87; Asst Prof., McGill Univ. 1988–93, Assoc. Prof. 1993–2002, Prof. 2002–, Chair. Middle East Studies Program; mem. Policy Planning staff, Dept of Foreign Affairs 1994–95, Special Adviser on Peacebuilding 1995–96; Interdepartmental Experts Group, Privy Council 1994–96; consultant, World Bank 1999–2004, Canadian Int. Devt Agency and Int. Devt Research Centre 1997, 2001–; Pres. Canadian Middle East Studies Assen 1998–2000, Canadian Council of Area Studies Learned Socs 2000–01; mem. Nat. Advisory Bd, Canadian Consortium on Human Security 2002–03; Research Coordinator, Interuniversity Consortium for Arab and Middle East Studies; Coordinator Palestinian Refugee ResearchNet; SSHRC Doctoral Fellowship 1985–87, Jules Léger Fellowship 1994–95; Canadian Inst. of Int. Affairs Prize 1981, H. Noel Fieldhouse Award for Distinguished Teaching, McGill Univ. 2002, Prin.'s Award for Excellence in Teaching, McGill Univ. 2004. *Publications:* Sanctuary and Survival: The PLO in Lebanon 1990, Echoes of the Intifada (ed.) 1991, The Many Faces of National Security in the Arab World (co-ed.) 1993, Political Liberalization and Democratization in the Arab World (Vol. II): Arab Experiences (co-ed.) 1998, A Very Political Economy: Peacebuilding and Foreign Aid in the West Bank and Gaza 2000, Aid Effectiveness in the West Bank and Gaza 2000, Persistent Permeability? Regionalism, Localism and Globalization in the Middle East (co-ed.) 2004, Palestinian Refugees: Challenges of Repatriation and Development (co-ed.) 2007; numerous articles, book reviews, conf. papers and policy papers.
Address: Department of Political Science, McGill University, 855 Sherbrooke Street W, Montreal, PQ H9W 3C2, Canada (office). *Telephone:* (514) 398-5075 (office). *Fax:* (514) 398-1770 (office); (514) 457-8109 (home). *E-mail:* rex.brynen@mcgill.ca (office). *Website:* www.mcgill.ca/ politicalscience (office).

BRZEZINSKI, Zbigniew Kazimierz, PhD; American academic and fmr government official; *Counsellor, Center for Strategic and International Studies;* b. 28 March 1928, Warsaw, Poland; m. Emilie Anna (Muska) Benes 1955; two s. one d. *Education:* McGill and Harvard Univs. *Career:* settled in N America 1938; Instructor in Govt and Research Fellow, Russian Research Center, Harvard Univ. 1953–56; Asst Prof. of Govt, Research Assoc. of Russian Research Center and of Center for Int. Affairs, Harvard Univ. 1956–60; Assoc. Prof. of Public Law and Govt, Columbia Univ. 1960–62, Prof. 1962–89 (on leave 1966–68, 1977–81) and Dir Research Inst. on Communist Affairs 1961–77 (on leave 1966–68); mem. Policy Planning Council, Dept of State 1966–68; mem. Hon. Steering Cttee, Young Citizens for Johnson 1964; Dir Foreign Policy Task Force for Vice-Pres. Humphrey 1968; Asst to the Pres. for Nat. Security Affairs 1977–81; mem. Nat. Security Council 1977–81; Counsellor, Center for Strategic and Int. Studies, Washington, DC 1981–; Robert E. Osgood Prof. of American Foreign Policy, Paul Nitze School of Advanced Int. Studies, Johns Hopkins Univ. 1989–; Fellow, American Acad. of Arts and Sciences 1969–; mem. Council on Foreign Relations, New York, Bd of Trustees, Freedom House; Guggenheim Fellowship 1960, Ford Fellowship 1970; Dr hc (Alliance Coll.) 1966, (Coll. of the Holy Cross) 1971, (Fordham Univ.) 1979, (Williams Coll.) 1986, (Georgetown Univ.) 1987, (Catholic Univ. of Lublin) 1990, (Warsaw Univ.) 1991; Presidential Medal of Freedom 1981, Order of White Eagle (Poland) 1995, Order of Merit (Ukraine) 1996, Masaryk Order 1998, Gedymim Order 1998. *Publications include:* Political Controls in the Soviet Army 1954, The Permanent Purge–Politics in Soviet Totalitarianism 1956, Totalitarian Dictatorship and Autocracy (with Carl Joachim Friedrich) 1957, The Soviet Bloc–Unity and Conflict 1960, Ideology and Power in Soviet Politics 1962, Africa and the Communist World (ed. and contrib.) 1963, Political Power: USA/USSR (with Samuel P. Huntington) 1964, Alternative to Partition: For a Broader Conception of America's Role in Europe 1965, Dilemmas of Change in Soviet Politics (ed. and contrib.) 1969, Between Two Ages: America's Role in the Technetronic Era 1970, The Fragile Blossom: Crisis and Change in Japan 1972, The Relevance of Liberalism 1977, Power and Principle: Memoirs of the National Security Adviser 1977–1981 1983, Game Plan: A Geostrategic Framework for the Conduct of the US-Soviet Contest 1986, In Quest of National Security 1988, The Grand Failure: The Birth and Death of Communism in the 20th Century 1989, Out of Control: Global Turmoil on the Eve of the Twenty-First Century 1993, The Grand Chessboard: American Primacy and its Geostrategic Imperatives 1996; contrib. to many publications, journals and periodicals.
Address: Center for Strategic and International Studies, 1800 K Street NW, Washington, DC 20006, USA (office). *Telephone:* (202) 833-2408 (office).

Fax: (202) 833-2409 (office). *E-mail:* zb@csis.org (office). *Website:* www
.csis.org (office).

BUALLAY, Yassim Muhammad, BBA; Bahraini diplomatist; *Ambassador to
Tunisia;* b. 15 March 1942, Muharraq; m. Satia Buallay 1969; two s. two d.
Education: American Univ. of Beirut, Long Island Univ., NY. *Career:*
Supervisor, Bursaries Section, Ministry of Educ. 1963–69; int. civil servant,
UNESCO, Paris 1970–74; Amb. to France 1974–79, to Tunisia 1987–94,
2004–; Perm. Rep. to UN 1994–2004; Dir of Econ. Affairs, Ministry of
Foreign Affairs, Bahrain 1979–87; Ordre nat. du Mérite, France,
decorations of Morocco (Alawite, First Class) 1994 and Tunisia 1994
(First Class).
Address: Embassy of Bahrain, 72 rue Mouaouia ibn Soufiane, al-Menzah
VI, Tunis, Tunisia (office). *Telephone:* (71) 750-865 (office).

BUBALO, Predrag, LLM, LLD; Serbian politician; *Minister of Trade and
Services;* b. 14 Oct. 1954, Vladicin Han; m.; one s. one d. *Education:* Faculty
of Law, University of Novi Sad. *Career:* joined Livnica Kikinda (foundry
co.) as Adviser to Gen. Man. 1977, Eng Man. 1981–90, Financial Man.
1991–94, Head, office in Beijing 1994–2000, Man. AUTO-KUCA (Livnica
Kikinda subsidiary) 2000–02, Gen. Man. Livnica Kikinda 2002–04;
Minister of International Economic Relations March–Oct. 2004, Coordinator, Ministry of Economy July–Oct. 2004, Minister of the Economy
2004–06, of Trade and Services 2007–; mem. Democratic Party of Serbia
(DPS).
Address: Ministry of Trade and Services, 11000 Belgrade, Nemanjina
22–26, Serbia (office). *Telephone:* (11) 3618852 (office). *Fax:* (11) 3610258
(office). *E-mail:* kabinet@minttu.sr.gov.yu (office). *Website:* www.minttu
.sr.gov.yu (office).

BUCHANAN, James McGill, MA, PhD; American academic; *Professor
Emeritus of Economics, Center for the Study of Public Choice, George
Mason University;* b. 3 Oct. 1919, Murfreesboro, Tenn.; m. Anne Bakke
1945. *Education:* Middle Tenn. State Coll. and Univs of Tenn. and Chicago.
Career: Prof. of Econs Univ. of Tenn. 1950–51, Fla State Univ. 1951–56,
Univ. of Va 1956–62; Paul. G. McIntyre Prof. of Econs Univ. of Va
1962–68; Prof. of Econs Univ. of Calif. Los Angeles 1968–69; Univ.
Distinguished Prof. of Econs Va Polytechnic Inst. 1969–83, Dir Center for
Study of Public Choice 1969–88, Advisory Gen. Dir 1988–, Prof. Emer.
2000–; Univ. Distinguished Prof. of Econs George Mason Univ. 1983–99,
Prof. Emer. 1999–; Fulbright Research Scholar, Italy 1955–56; Ford
Faculty Research Fellow 1959–60; Fulbright Visiting Prof. Univ. of
Cambridge 1961–62; Assoc. Prof. Francesco Marroquin Univ., Guatemala
2001–; Fellow, American Acad. of Arts and Sciences; Distinguished Fellow,
American Econ. Asscn; Dr hc (Giessen) 1982, (Zürich) 1984, (Valencia)
1987, (Lisbon) 1987, (Fairfax) 1987, (London) 1988, (Rome) 1993,
(Bucharest) 1994, (Catania) 1994, (Valladolid) 1996; American Econ.
Asscn Seidman Award 1984, Nobel Prize for Econs 1986. *Publications:*
author and co-author of numerous books on financial policy and other
econ. matters; articles in professional journals.
Address: Center for the Study of Public Choice, George Mason University,
Buchanan House Mail Stop 1 E6, Fairfax, VA 22030-4443 (office); PO Box
G, Blacksburg, VA 24063-1021, USA (home).

BUCHER, Johann, PhD; Swiss diplomatist; b. 1942, Sarnen. *Education:* Univ.
Berne, Univ. of Vienna. *Career:* joined Swiss Diplomatic Corps 1973,
various roles including posts in Algiers and Berne, at Perm. Mission of
Switzerland to UN, NY 1982, Amb. to Costa Rica, Nicaragua and Panama
1986, Amb. to Russia 1995–99, Amb. to Czech Repub. 2000–01, Amb. to
Austria 2001–06.
Address: c/o Federal Department of Foreign Affairs (FDFA), Bundeshaus
West, 3003 Berne 7, Switzerland (office). *Telephone:* 313222111 (office).
Fax: 313234001 (office). *E-mail:* info@eda.admin.ch (office). *Website:*
www.eda.admin.ch (office).

BUDD, Sir Colin Richard, KCMG, BA; British diplomatist (retd); *Commis-
sioner, Commission for Racial Equality;* b. 31 Aug. 1945, Harpenden,
Herts.; m. Agnes Smit; one s. one d. *Education:* Univ. of Cambridge.
Career: entered British Diplomatic Service 1967; overseas assignments in
Warsaw, Islamabad, Bonn and Brussels; Head of Political Section,
Embassy in The Hague 1980–84; various positions in European Div.,
FCO, London; Deputy Sec., Cabinet Office 1996–97; Deputy Under-Sec. of
State and Dir of EU and Econ. Affairs 1997–2001; Amb. to Netherlands
2001–05; currently Commr, Comm. for Racial Equality.
Telephone: (20) 7223-7211 (home). *E-mail:* acbudd@hotmail.com (office).
Website: www.cre.gov.uk/about/commissioners.html.

BUERGENTHAL, Thomas, LLM, JD, SJD; American judge and academic;
Judge, International Court of Justice; b. 11 May 1934, Lubochna, Slovakia;
m. 2nd Marjorie Julia Buergenthal (née Bell); three s. from previous m.

Education: Bethany Coll., W Va, New York Univ. Law School (Root
Tilden Scholar), Harvard Law School. *Career:* became US citizen 1957;
mem. (Judge, then Pres.) Inter-American Court on Human Rights 1979–91;
mem. (Judge, then Pres.) Admin. Tribunal, IDB 1989–94; mem. UN
Human Rights Comm. 1995–99; mem. Claims Resolution Tribunal for
Dormant Accounts, Switzerland 1998–99, Vice-Chair. 1999; Judge, Int.
Court of Justice 2000–; Lobingier Prof. Emer. of Int. and Comparative
Law, George Washington Univ. Law School, Washington, DC; Dr hc
(Bethany Coll.) 1981, (Heidelberg Univ.) 1986, (Free Univ. of Brussels)
1994, (State Univ. of New York) 2000, (American Univ., Washington, DC)
2002, (Univ. of Minnesota) 2003, (George Washington Univ.) 2004;
Manley O. Hudson Medal, American Soc. of Int. Law 2002, and numerous
other awards. *Publications include:* Law-Making in the International Civil
Aviation Organization 1969, International Protection of Human Rights
(with L. B. Sohn) 1973, Protecting Human Rights in the Americas (with D.
Shelton, fourth edn) 1995, International Human Rights (with D. Shelton
and D. Stewart, third edn) 2002, Public International Law (with S. Murphy,
third edn) 2002.
Address: International Court of Justice, Peace Palace, Carnegieplein 2, 2517
KJ The Hague, Netherlands (office). *Telephone:* (70) 3022408 (office). *Fax:*
(70) 3022464 (office). *E-mail:* t.buergenthalon@icj-cij.org (office).

BUFFET, Marie-George; French politician; *National Secretary, Parti
Communiste Français;* b. 7 May 1949, Sceaux (Hauts-de-Seine); m. Jean-
Pierre Buffet 1972; two c. *Career:* joined Parti Communiste Français (PCF)
1969, elected to PCF Cen. Cttee 1987, mem. Nat. Bureau 1994, Head Nat.
Women's Cttee 1996, elected to Nat. Secr. 1997, Nat. Sec. 2001–; municipal
councillor, then Deputy Mayor Châtenay-Malabry (Hauts-de-Seine)
1977–83; Nat. Ass. Deputy for Seine-Saint-Denis 1997–; Minister for
Youth and Sport 1997–2002.
Address: Parti Communiste Français, 2 place du Colonel Fabien, 75940
Paris, France.

BUIRA, Ariel, MA; Mexican economist; *Director of the Secretariat,
Intergovernmental Group of Twenty-Four on International Monetary Affairs
and Development (G-24);* b. 20 Sept. 1940, Chihuahua; m. Janet Clark
1965; two s. *Education:* Univ. of Manchester, UK. *Career:* Lecturer, Centre
for Econ. and Demographic Studies, El Colegio de México 1966–68; Prof.
of Econs, Grad. School of Business, Instituto Tecnológico de Monterrey
1968–70; Economist, IMF 1970–74; Econ. Adviser to Gov., Man. for Int.
Research, Banco de México, SA 1975–78, Deputy Dir then Dir for Int. Orgs
and Agreements 1982–94, then Deputy Gov. and mem. Bd of Govs; Del. to
Conf. on Int. Econ. Co-operation (CIEC) (Financial Affairs Comm.)
1976–77; Alt. Exec. Dir, IMF 1978–80, Exec. Dir for Mexico, Spain,
Venezuela, Cen. America 1980–82; Chair. Bd of Dirs BLADEX 1985–94;
mem. Bd of Govs Bank of Mexico 1994–96; Amb. to Greece 1998–2001; Sr
mem., St Antony's Coll., Oxford 2001–02; Special Envoy of the Pres. of
Mexico and Chair. of the Panel, UN Int. Conf. on Financing for Devt 2002;
Dir Secretariat, Intergovernmental Group of Twenty Four on Int.
Monetary Affairs and Devt (G–24) 2002–; Order of the Phoenix 2001;
First Prize, Course on Econ. Integration, Coll. Européen des Sciences
Sociales et Economiques 1963, Medal of the City of Athens 2001.
Publications: 50 Años de Banca Central (jtly) 1976, LDC External Debt
and the World Economy 1978, Directions for Reform – The Future of the
International Monetary System (jtly) 1984, México: Crisis Financiera y
Programa de Ajuste in América Latina: Deuda, Crisis y Perspectivas 1984;
Is There a Need for Reform? 1984; contrib.: Politics and Economics of
External Debt Crisis – The Latin American Experience 1985, Incomes
Policy (ed. V. L. Urquidi) 1987, Money and Finance Vol. I (R. Tandon)
1987, Adjustment with Growth and the Role of the IMF 1987, La
Economía Mundial: Evolución y Perspectivas 1989, Una Evalución de la
Estrategia de la Deuda 1989, Los Determinantes del Ahorro en México
1990, Evolución de la Estrategia de la Deuda 1990, International Liquidity
and the Needs of the World Economy (Vol. IV) 1994, Reflections on the
International Monetary System 1995, Can Currency Crises be Prevented or
Better Managed? (co-ed. Jan Joost Teunissen) 1996, The Potential of the
SDR for Improving the International Monetary System 1996, Reflections
on the Mexican Crisis of 1994 1996; and numerous articles and essays; as
ed.: The IMF and the World Bank at Sixty 2005, Introduction (in The IMF
and the World at Sixty) 2005, The IMF at Sixty: An Unfulfilled Potential?
(in The IMF and the World at Sixty) 2005, Reforming the Governance of
the IMF and the World Bank 2005, The Bretton Woods Institutions:
Governance Without Legitimacy? (in Reforming the Governance of the
IMF and the World Bank) 2005; as contrib. and ed.: The Governance of the
IMF in a Global Economy, An Analysis of IMF Conditionality (in
Challenges to the World Bank and the IMF: Developing Country
Perspectives) 2003; as contrib.: Curbing the Impact of Shocks (in Protecting
the Poor; ed. Jan Joost Teunissen and Age Akkerman) 2005, Does the IMF
Need More Financial Resources? (in Reform of the IMF for the 21st
Century; ed. Edwin M. Truman) 2006.

Address: G24 Secretariat, 1875 I Street, Suite IS2-285, Washington, DC 20431, USA (office); Ruben Dario 45, piso 9, Col. Ricon del Bosque, México, DF 11560, Mexico (home). *Telephone:* (202) 623-6065 (office); (55) 5250-1711 (home). *Fax:* (202) 623-6000 (office). *E-mail:* buira@g24.org (office); abuiras@yahoo.com.mx (home). *Website:* www.g24.org (office).

BUITER, Willem Hendrik, CBE, PhD, FBA; American/British professor of economics; *Chief Economist and Special Counsellor to the President, European Bank for Reconstruction and Development;* b. 26 Sept. 1949, The Hague, Netherlands; m. 1st Jean Archer 1988; two c.; m. 2nd Anne C. Sibert 1998. *Education:* Univ. of Cambridge, Yale Univ. *Career:* Asst Prof. of Econs and Int. Affairs, Woodrow Wilson School, Princeton Univ. 1975–79; Prof. of Econs, Univ. of Bristol 1980–82; Cassel Prof. of Econs with Special Reference to Money and Banking, LSE 1982–85; Prof. of Econs, Yale Univ. 1985–94, Juan T. Trippe Prof. of Int. Econs 1990–94; Prof. of Int. Macroeconomics, Univ. of Cambridge 1994–; mem. Monetary Policy Cttee, Bank of England 1997–2000; Chief Economist and Special Counsellor to the Pres., EBRD 2000–; Consultant IMF, IBRD, IDB 1979–; Adviser House of Commons Treasury Select Cttee, UK 1980–82, Netherlands Ministry of Educ. 1985–86, EC, DGII 1982–85; Corresp. mem. Royal Netherlands Acad. of Sciences 1995–, Research Assoc. Nat. Bureau of Econ. Research, Research Fellow Centre for Econ. Policy Research; N. G. Pierson Medal (Netherlands) 2000. *Publications:* Temporary and Long-run Equilibrium 1979, Budgetary Policy, International and Intertemporal Trade in the Global Economy 1989, Macroeconomic Theory and Stabilization Policy 1989, Principles of Budgetary and Financial Policy 1990, International Macroeconomics 1990, Financial Markets and European Monetary Cooperation: The Lessons of the 92–93 ERM crisis (with Giancarlo Corsetti and Paolo Pesenti) 1997. *Address:* European Bank for Reconstruction and Development, One Exchange Square, London, EC2A 2JN (office); 2 St David's Square, London, E14 3WA, England (home). *Telephone:* (20) 7338-6805 (office); (20) 7517-9289 (home); (20) 7338-6037. *Fax:* (20) 7338-6110 (office). *E-mail:* buiterw@ebrd.com (office); willembuiter@whsmithnet.co.uk (home). *Website:* ebrdnet.ebrd.com (office); www.nber.org/wbuiter (home).

BUKAYEV, Gennadii Ivanovich; Russian politician and engineer; b. 15 Sept. 1947, Stepnoye, Orenburg Region; m.; one s. *Education:* Ufa Inst. Oil., Sverdlovsk Higher CPSU School. *Career:* Sr Engineer 1972–75; Head of Div. Ufa Inst. of Oil 1975–77; Deputy Chair. Ufa Regional Exec. Cttee 1977–78; Instructor Bashkiria Regional Exec. CPSU Cttee 1980–85; Chair. Belebelyevo City CP Exec. Cttee. 1985–90; Head Div. of Trade Council of Ministers Bashkiria Autonomous Repub. 1990–92; Head State Taxation Inspection Repub. of Bashkortostan 1992–99; mem. Exec. Bd Ministry of Taxes and Levies of Russian Fed. 1999–2000, Minister 2000–04; Presidential Aide 2004–. *Address:* c/o Office of the President, Kremlin, 103073 Moscow, Russia (office).

BUKENYA, Gilbert Balibaseka, MSc, MD, PhD; Ugandan politician and professor of public health; *Vice-President;* b. May 1949, Wakiso Dist; m.; three c. *Education:* Makerere Univ. Medical School, Royal Inst. of Public Health and Hygiene, London, UK, Ross Inst., London School of Hygiene and Tropical Medicine, Univ. of Queensland, Australia. *Career:* internship in Uganda; following studies in public health in London returned to Uganda in 1983; Lecturer, Inst. of Public Health, Makerere Univ. 1983–84, Dir 1989, Assoc. Prof. 1993, Dean Faculty of Medicine 1995; Lecturer, Dept of Community Medicine, Univ. of Papua New Guinea 1984–87, Head of Dept 1987–89; Assoc. Prof., Tulane Univ. School of Public Health, New Orleans, La, USA 1995–; Adjunct Prof. of Int. Health, Case Western Reserve Univ., Cleveland, OH, USA 2004–; MP for Busiro North 1996–, Chair. Movement Caucus; Minister of State for Trade and Minister in charge of the Presidency; Vice-Pres. of Uganda 2003–; Chair. Nat. Advisory Cttee on Environmental Health and Maternal and Child Health, Papua New Guinea 1985–91, Bd of Examiners, Coll. of Allied Health Sciences Health Inspectors' Programme 1985–91; Vice-Chair. Network of African Postgraduate Public Health Training Schools, WHO-Afro Region 1992–94, Chair. 1994–96. *Address:* c/o Office of the President, Parliament Building, POB 7168, Kampala, Uganda (office). *Telephone:* (41) 258441 (office). *Fax:* (41) 256143 (office). *E-mail:* vp@statehouse.go.ug (office). *Website:* www.statehouse.go.up (office).

BULAI, Igor Borisovich, CandHist; Russian diplomatist; b. 17 May 1947, Moscow; m.; two c. *Education:* Moscow State Inst. of Int. Relations, Inst. of USA and Canada Acad. of Sciences. *Career:* Jr Researcher, Inst. of USA and Canada 1973–79; Instructor, Div. of Information Cen. Cttee CPSU 1979–85; Counsellor, Embassy in Washington, DC, USA 1985–91; with Dept of Information, USSR Ministry of Foreign Affairs 1991–92; Head,

Dept of Information and Press, Ministry of Foreign Affairs of Russia 1992–98; Consul-Gen. in Edin. 1998–2001; mem. staff, Dept for Information and Press and Head, Press Centre, Ministry of Foreign Affairs 2001–05. *Address:* c/o Press Centre, Ministry of Foreign Affairs, Sadoraya-Sennaya 32/34, 119200 Moscow, Russia (office). *Telephone:* (495) 244-16-06 (office). *Fax:* (495) 230-21-30 (office). *E-mail:* ministry@mid.ru (office). *Website:* www.mid.ru (office).

BULAJICH, Borjana; Serbian United Nations official; *Social Affairs Officer, International Research and Training Institute for the Advancement of Women, United Nations;* b. 5 Nov. 1961, Belgrade. *Education:* Gymnasium, Belgrade, Carleton Univ., Ottawa and Concordia Univ., Montréal, Canada. *Career:* Social Affairs Officer, Liaison Office, UN Int. Research and Training Inst. for the Advancement of Women (INSTRAW), New York, USA 1987–; creates training packages on water supply, sanitation, energy and women's affairs for developing countries. *Address:* United Nations INSTRAW, César Nicolás Penson 102–A, Santo Domingo, Dominican Republic (office). *Telephone:* (212) 963-5684 (office). *Fax:* (212) 963-2978 (office). *E-mail:* comments@un-instraw.org (office). *Website:* www.un-instraw.org (office).

BULATOVIĆ, Momir, CandEconSc; Montenegrin politician; b. 21 Sept. 1956, Belgrade. *Education:* Titograd Univ. *Career:* fmr mem. League of Communists of Montenegro, then leader Republican League of Communists; Chair. Democratic Party of Socialists (DPS) 1990–98; Chair. Socialist People's Party of Montenegro (SNP) 1998–2001; Pres. of Montenegro 1990–98; Prime Minister of Yugoslavia 1998–2001. *Address:* Socialist People's Party of Montenegro, Podgorica, Montenegro (office).

BULGAK, Vladimir Borisovich, CandTechSc, DEconSc; Russian politician and business executive; b. 9 May 1941, Moscow; m.; one d. *Education:* Moscow Electrotech. Inst. of Communications, Inst. of Man. of Nat. Econ., USSR State Cttee on Science and Tech. *Career:* instructor, then sec. Moscow City Komsomol Cttee 1963–68; for 15 years worked in Moscow radio trans. network; head of depts USSR Ministry of Telecommunications 1983–90; Minister 1990–91; Minister of Telecommunications Russian Fed. 1991–97; Deputy Chair. Govt of Russian Fed. 1997–98, 1998–99; Minister of Science and Tech. April–Sept. 1998; Chair. TV-Holding Svyazinvest 1999–2001, Comincom-Combellga group 1999–2003; fmr Chair. Insurance Group Nasta; mem. Council of Dirs Sovintel (operating company of Golden Telecom) 2004–; mem. Int. Acad. of Informatization, Russian Acad. of Tech. Sciences, Russian Acad. of Natural Sciences; USSR State Prize. *Publications:* several textbooks on communication techniques; over 100 articles and papers. *Address:* Golden Telecom, 1 Kozhevnicheskii prospect, 115114 Moscow, Russia (office). *Telephone:* (495) 787-10-00 (office). *E-mail:* info@goldentelecom.ru (office). *Website:* www.goldentelecom.ru (office).

BULÍK, Gen. Lubomír, PhD; Slovak military officer; *Chief of the General Staff;* b. 22 Sept. 1957, Turzovka; m., two s. *Education:* Land Forces Mil. Acad., Vyškov na Morave, Bundeswehr Gen. Staff School, Germany. *Career:* worked as teacher and instructor at various mil. schools; has held various positions at Ministry of Defence 1993–2001, including Dir-Gen. Strategic Planning Dept; promoted to Maj.-Gen. 2000; Deputy Chief, Requirements and Long-Term Planning Staff, Gen. Staff of Slovak Armed Forces 2001–02, Chief of Operational Div. and Deputy Chief of Operation Co-ordination and Planning Staff 2002, Chief, Requirements and Long-Term Planning Staff 2003–04; apptd Dir-Gen. Defence Planning and Man. Resources, Ministry of Defence 2004; Chief of Gen. Staff, Slovak Armed Forces 2005–. *Address:* Ministry of Defence, Kutuzovova 7, Bratislava 832 28, Slovakia (office). *Telephone:* (2) 4425-0320 (office). *Fax:* (2) 4425-3242 (office). *E-mail:* linka.dovery@mod.gov.sk (office). *Website:* www.mod.gov.sk (office).

BULL, William V.S., MA; Liberian diplomatist; b. 1946, Monrovia. *Education:* Univ. of Liberia, Univ. of Pittsburgh, USA. *Career:* joined Bureau of African and Asian Affairs, Ministry of Foreign Affairs 1972; Counsellor and Deputy Chief of Mission, Washington, DC 1976, Chargé d'affaires 1980; Asst Minister for American Affairs, Monrovia 1981, for African and Asian Affairs 1982–86, Prin. Deputy to Minister of Foreign Affairs 1987–90; Amb. and Perm. Rep. to UN, New York 1990–98; Amb. to UK 1998–2000, to USA 2000–03. *Address:* c/o Embassy of Liberia, 5201 16th Street, NW, Washington, DC 20011, USA (office).

BULLEN, Roland W., BA, MA; American diplomatist; *Deputy Chief of Mission, Embassy in Santo Domingo;* b. Grenada; m. Hilda Cox-Bullen;

two s. from previous m. *Education:* San Diego State Univ. and US Int. Univ., San Diego. *Career:* came to USA in 1966; worked for City of San Diego –1977; career mem. Foreign Service since 1977, rank of Minister-Counsellor, has served in diplomatic missions in Belize, Costa Rica and Venezuela, as well as in Washington, DC, Sr Insp., Office of State Dept's Insp.-Gen., Washington, DC 1994–96, Deputy Chief of Mission, later Chargé d'affaires a.i., Embassy in Bridgetown, Barbados 1998–2001, Deputy Exec. Dir Bureau of Western Hemisphere Affairs 2001–03, Amb. to Guyana 2003–06, Deputy Chief of Mission, Embassy in Santo Domingo 2006–; Superior Honor Award, Meritorious Honor Award.
Address: US Embassy, César Nicolás Pensón, esq. Leopoldo Navarro, Santo Domingo, DN, Dominican Republic (office). *Telephone:* 221-2171 (office). *Fax:* 685-6959 (office). *E-mail:* irc@usemb.gov.do (office). *Website:* www.usemb.gov.do (office).

BULMER-THOMAS, Victor Gerald, OBE, MA, DPhil; British economist, academic and international consultant; *Visiting Professor, Department of History, Florida International University;* b. 23 March 1948, London; m. Barbara Swasey 1970; two s. one d. *Education:* Westminster School, New Coll. and St Antony's Coll., Oxford. *Career:* Research Fellow, Fraser of Allander Inst. 1975–78; Lecturer in Econs, Queen Mary Coll., Univ. of London 1978–87, Reader 1987–90, Prof. of Latin American Econs 1990–98, Prof. Emer. 1998–, Dir Inst. of Latin American Studies 1992–98, Sr Research Fellow 1998–2001; Dir Chatham House (Royal Inst. of Int. Affairs) 2001–06; Visiting Prof., Fla Int. Univ., Miami 2007–; Dir Schroders Emerging Countries Fund 1996–2003, Deutsche Latin America Companies Trust 2004, New India Investment Trust 2004–; fmr Dir Gartmore Latin America New Growth Fund SA; fmr consultant for EC, IDB; Order of San Carlos (Colombia) 1998, Order of the Southern Cross (Brazil) 1998. *Publications:* Input-Output Analysis for Developing Countries 1982, The Political Economy of Central America since 1920 1987, Studies in the Economics of Central America 1988, Britain and Latin America: A Changing Relationship (ed.) 1989, The Economic History of Latin America Since Independence 1994, The New Economic Model in Latin America and Its Impact on Income Distribution and Poverty (ed.) 1996, Thirty Years of Latin American Studies in the UK 1997, United States and Latin America: The New Agenda (ed.) 1999, Regional Integration in Latin America and the Caribbean: The Political Economy of Open Regionalism (ed.) 2001, The Cambridge Economic History of Latin America, Vol. I: The Colonial Era and the Short Nineteenth Century, Vol. II The Long Twentieth Century (co-ed.) 2005.
Address: Department of History, Florida International University, University Park (DM-397), Miami, FL 33199, USA (office). *Telephone:* (305) 348-3883 (office). *Fax:* (305) 348-3561 (office). *Website:* www.fiu.edu/~history (office).

BUNDHUN, Raouf; Mauritian politician and diplomatist; *Vice-President; Career:* fmr Amb. to France; Vice-Pres. of Mauritius 2002–; Officier, Ordre nationale du Mérite; Officier, Ordre de la Pleiade (Ordre de la Francophonie).
Address: Office of the Vice-President, State House, Port Louis, Mauritius (office). *Telephone:* 454-3021 (office). *Fax:* 564-5370 (office). *E-mail:* statepas@intnet.mu (office). *Website:* ncb.intnet.mu/president.htm (office).

BUNDU, Abass, PhD; Sierra Leonean diplomatist and lawyer; *Leader, People's Progressive Party;* b. 3 June 1948; m. Khadija Allie 1976; two s. three d. *Education:* Australian Nat. Univ., Canberra, Univ. of Cambridge, UK. *Career:* Asst Dir, Commonwealth Secr., London 1975–82; mem. of Parl. for Port Loko NE 1982–90; Minister of Agric., Natural Resources and Forestry 1982–85; Exec. Sec., Econ. Community of W African States (ECOWAS) 1989–93; Sec. of State for Foreign Affairs and Int. Co-operation 1993–95; presidential cand., People's Progressive Party 1996, currently Leader; Yorke Award, Univ. of Cambridge.
Address: c/o Department of Foreign Affairs, Gloucester Street, Freetown, Sierra Leone.

BUNE, Poseci Wagalevu; Fijian politician and diplomatist; *Minister for Public Service and Public Sector Reform; Education:* Queen Victoria School, Royal Coll. of Public Admin., London. *Career:* joined Public Service Dept 1966, apptd Sr Admin. Officer 1972, attached to Australian Embassy, Bangkok 1973, joined Perm. Mission to UN, New York 1973, apptd First Sec. 1973, Counsellor, Mission to EEC 1976–80; Western Divisional Commr, Ministry of Rural Devt 1981–85; Amb. to EEC (also accred to Belgium, Luxembourg, Netherlands, France and Italy) 1985–87; Perm. Sec. for Public Service 1987–95, Perm. Sec. to Govt and for Public Service 1990–95; Perm. Rep. to UN 1995–2000; mem. Parl. for Macuata 2001–; Leader, Veitokani ni Lewenivanua Vakarisito (Christian Democratic Alliance); Minister for Public Service and Public Sector Reform 2007–.

Address: Ministry of Public Service and Public Sector Reform, PO Box 2278, Government Buildings, Suva, Fiji (office). *Telephone:* 3314588 (office). *Fax:* 3302570 (office). *Website:* www.psc.gov.fj (office).

BUNROD, Gen. Somtad; Thai government official and army officer (retd); *Minister of Defence; Career:* served in special warfare unit of Thai army; fmr Army Jt Chief of Staff; Minister of Defence 2006–.
Address: Ministry of Defence, Thanon Sanamchai, Bangkok 10200, Thailand (office). *Telephone:* (2) 222-1121 (office). *Fax:* (2) 226-3117 (office). *E-mail:* webmaster@mod.go.th (office). *Website:* www.mod.go.th (office).

BURBULIS, Gennady Eduardovich; Russian politician; b. 4 Aug. 1945, Pervouralsk, Sverdlovsk (now Ekaterinburg); m. Natalia Kirsanova; one s. *Education:* Ural State Univ. *Career:* Lecturer Ural Polytechnic Inst. 1974–83; Head of Chair., Deputy Dir Inst. of Non-Ferrous Metals 1983–89; USSR People's Deputy 1989–90; formed Discussion Tribune, Sverdlovsk 1988; elected to Congress of People's Deputies 1989; mem. Inter-Regional Group; Chief of Staff to Boris Yeltsin 1991; State Sec. RSFSR (now Russian Fed.) 1991–92, State Council Sec. 1991–92; First Deputy Chair. Russian Govt 1991–92, Sec. of State May–Nov. 1992, Head of Advisors' Team Nov.–Dec. 1992; Founder and Pres. Int. Humanitarian and Political Cen. Strategy 1993–; mem. State Duma (Parl.) 1993–99, mem. Cttee for Geopolitics; Deputy Gov. Novgorod Region 1999–2001; Chair. Observational Bd Novotrubny factory, Pervouralsk 1997–98; Rep. of Novgorod Region to Council of Fed. 2002–; Chair. Fed. Council Comm. on Methodology of Exercising the Fed. Council's Constitutional Powers 2002–. *Publication:* Profession – Politician 1999.
Address: Council of Federation, B. Dmitrovca 26, 103426 Moscow, Russia (office). *Telephone:* (495) 292-61-23 (office). *Fax:* (495) 926-69-50 (office). *E-mail:* GEBurbulis@council.gov.ru (office).

BURELLI RIVAS, Miguel Angel, LLB, DrPolSc; Venezuelan diplomatist and lawyer; b. 8 July 1922. *Education:* Univ. de Los Andes, Bogotá, Univ. Cen. de Venezuela y de Ecuador, Univ. Nacional de Bogotá, Univ. de Madrid and Univ. di Firenze. *Career:* pre-seminary Prof. of Political Sociology and Chief Prof. of Mining and Agrarian Legislation, Faculty of Law, Univ. de Los Andes, Bogotá, Chief Prof. of Humanities I and II, Faculty of Civil Eng, Dir of Univ. Culture, Founder of School of Humanities, Founder-Dir of Univ. reviews, Bibliotheca and Universitas Emeritensis; Political Dir Ministry of the Interior; Dir-Gen. Ministry of Foreign Affairs (nine times Acting Minister); Interim Minister of Foreign Affairs; returned to legal profession 1961; mem. Venezuelan Supreme Electoral Council 1961; Minister of Justice 1964–65; Amb. to Colombia 1965–67, to UK 1967–69; presidential cand. 1968, 1973; Amb. to USA 1974–76; Minister of Foreign Affairs 1994–99; numerous decorations.
Address: c/o Ministry of Foreign Affairs, Casa Amarilla Biblioteca Central, esq. Principal, Caracas 1010, Venezuela.

BURGHARDT, Raymond F., BA; American diplomatist and organization executive; *Chairman, American Institute in Taiwan;* b. 1945, New York City; m. Susan Day; two d. *Education:* Columbia Coll. and Columbia Univ. School of Int. Public Affairs. *Career:* fmr Peace Corps volunteer in Colombia; Refugee Affairs Officer Gia Dinh Province Viet Nam 1970–71, Political Officer, US Embassy in Saigon 1971–73; worked for Agency for Int. Devt in Viet Nam, concerned with Vietnamese refugee issues Hong Kong 1977–80; Deputy Dir State Dept Office of Viet Nam, Laos and Cambodia Affairs 1980–82; Political Counselor, Beijing, China 1987–89; Deputy Chief Mission, Embassies in Seoul 1990–93, in Manila 1993–96; US Consul Gen. in Shanghai 1997–99; Dir American Inst. in Taiwan 1999–2001, Chair. 2006–; Amb. to Viet Nam 2001–04; Dir East-West Seminars, East-West Center, Honolulu 2005–06; fmr Special Asst to Pres. Reagan, Sr Dir Latin American Affairs, Nat. Security Council; also served at embassies in Honduras, Guatemala.
Address: American Institute in Taiwan, No. 7, Lane 134, Sec. 3, HsinYi Road, Da-an District, Taipei City 10659, Taiwan (office). *E-mail:* aitarc@mail.ait.org.tw (office). *Website:* www.ait.org.tw (office).

BURIAN, Peter, PhD; Slovak diplomatist; *Permanent Representative, United Nations;* b. 21 March 1959, Hlohovec; m. Nina Burianova; two s. *Education:* St Petersburg Univ., Russia, Comenius Univ., Bratislava, Diplomatic Acad., Moscow. *Career:* joined Middle East Dept, Czechoslovak Fed. Ministry of Foreign Affairs 1983–87, 1991; Deputy Chief of Mission, Embassy in Beirut 1987–89; Second Sec., then Deputy Chief of Mission, Embassy in Washington, DC 1992, Chargé d'affaires 1993, Minister Counsellor, Deputy Chief of Mission 1994; Dir Gen. for Human Dimension Affairs, Foreign Ministry 1997–99; Amb. to NATO and Western European Union, Brussels 1999–2003; worked at Policy, Planning and Analysis Dept, Foreign Ministry 2003–04; Amb.-at-Large and Special

Coordinator, UN Security Council 2003–04; Perm. Rep. to UN, New York 2004–.
Address: Office of the Permanent Representative of Slovakia to the United Nations, 801 Second Avenue, 12th Floor, New York, NY 10017, USA (office). *Telephone:* (212) 286-8418 (office). *Fax:* (212) 286-8419 (office). *E-mail:* slovakia@un.int (office). *Website:* www.un.int/slovakia (office).

BURKE, Nazim; Grenadian lawyer and politician; *Minister of Finance; Education:* Concordia Univ., Univ. of Windsor, York Univ., Queen's Univ., Canada. *Career:* Perm. Sec., Ministry of Trade 1979–83; lawyer, Burke, Sealy-Burke (law firm), Toronto 1992–2000; Founding Pnr Ciboney Chambers Law Firm 2000; mem. Grenada House of Reps 2003–; Minister of Finance 2008–; mem. Nat. Democratic Congress Party, fmr Public Relations Officer.
Address: Ministry of Finance, Financial Complex, The Carenage, St George's, Grenada (office). *Telephone:* 440-2741 (office). *Fax:* 440-4115 (office). *E-mail:* finance@gov.gd (office). *Website:* finance.gov.gd (office).

BURLEIGH, A. Peter; American diplomatist and government official; *Ambassador in Residence and Distinguished Visiting Professor, University of Miami;* b. 7 March 1942, Los Angeles. *Education:* Colgate Univ. *Career:* Teaching Fellow, Wharton School, Univ. of Pennsylvania; Deputy Asst Sec. of State, Bureau of Near Eastern and South Asian Affairs 1987–89, Prin. Deputy Asst Sec. of State for Intelligence and Research 1989–91; Co-ordinator Office of Counter-Terrorism 1991–92; Prin. Deputy Asst Sec. of State for Personnel 1992–95; Amb. to Sri Lanka (also accred to the Maldives) 1995–97; Deputy Rep. to UN 1997–99, Chargé de Mission 1998–99; Amb. to Repub. of Philippines (also accred to Palau) 1999–2000; currently Amb. in Residence and Distinguished Visiting Prof., Univ. of Miami; Fulbright Scholar; mem. Asia Soc., American Foreign Service Asscn; numerous Dept of State Superior Honor Awards, Sr Foreign Service Presidential Award, Meritorious Service Award, Sec. of State's Distinguished Service Medal 2000, Presidential Distinguished Service Award 2000.
Address: Master of Arts in International Administration (MAIA) Program, University of Miami, PO Box 248005, Coral Gables, FL 33124-1610 (office); 2300 Riverlane Terrace, Fort Lauderdale, FL 33312-4762, USA (home). *Telephone:* (305) 284-2211 (office). *E-mail:* apburl@bellsouth.net (home). *Website:* www.miami.edu/maia (office).

BURNHAM, Christopher Bancroft, BA, MPA; American international organization executive; *Under-Secretary-General for Management, United Nations;* b. 1956, New York City. *Education:* Washington & Lee Univ., Harvard Univ., Georgetown Univ. Nat. Security Studies Program. *Career:* served in US Marine Corps Reserve, veteran of first Gulf War, led one of the first infantry units to reach and liberate Kuwait City in 1991; elected to Conn. House of Reps three times, served as Asst Minority Leader; fmr investment banker with Credit Suisse First Boston and Advest Corp. Finance; Treas. of Conn. 1994; fmr CEO PIMCO's Columbus Circle Investors (asset man. and mutual fund co.), fmr Vice-Chair. PIMCO's mutual fund group; Asst Sec. for Resource Man. and Chief Financial Officer, State Dept 2002–05; UN Under-Sec.-Gen. for Man. 2005–; recipient of several accounting, leadership and civic awards.
Address: Office of the Secretary-General, UN Headquarters, First Avenue at 46th Street, New York, NY 10017, USA (office). *Telephone:* (212) 963-1234 (office). *Fax:* (212) 963-4879 (office). *Website:* www.un.org/News/ossg/sg/stories/burnham_bio.asp (office).

BURNS, R. Nicholas, MA; American diplomatist; b. 28 Jan. 1956, Buffalo, NY; m. Elizabeth Baylies; three d. *Education:* Univ. of Paris, Boston Coll., Johns Hopkins School of Advanced Int. Studies. *Career:* before entering Foreign Service worked in US Embassy in Mauritania and as programme officer for AT Int.; Vice-Consul and Staff Asst to Amb., Cairo 1983–85; political officer, Consulate-Gen., Jerusalem 1985–87; staff officer, Operations Center and Secr., Dept of State 1987–88, Special Asst to Counsellor 1989–90; Adviser to Pres. George Bush on Greece, Turkey and Cyprus and Dir for Soviet (later Russian) Affairs; Special Asst to Pres. Clinton and Sr Dir for Russia, Ukraine and Eurasia Affairs; Spokesman, Dept of State and Acting Asst Sec. for Public Affairs 1995–97; Amb. to Greece 1997–2001; Perm. Rep. to NATO, Brussels 2001–05; UnderSec. Of State for Political Affairs 2005–08 (resgnd); mem. Council on Foreign Relations, Order of St. John, Int. Inst. for Strategic Studies; Order of the Terra Mariana (Estonia); Dr hc (Worcester Polytechnic Inst.) 1997; Superior Honor Award (three times), James Clement Dunn Award for Excellence 1994, Charles E. Cobb Award for Trade Devt by an Amb. 2000, Woodrow Wilson Award for Distinguished Govt Service (Johns Hopkins Univ.) 2002.
Address: c/o Office of the Under Secretary for Political Affairs, US Department of State, 201 C Street, NW, Washington, DC 20520, USA (office).

BURNS, Sir Robert Andrew, KCMG, MA, FRSA; British diplomatist (retd); *Chairman of the Council, Royal Holloway, University of London;* b. 21 July 1943, London; m. Sarah Cadogan 1973; two s. one d. *Education:* Highgate School, Trinity Coll. Cambridge, School of Oriental and African Studies, Univ. of London. *Career:* joined Diplomatic Service 1965, served in New Delhi 1967–71, FCO, London and UK Del. to CSCE 1971–75, First Sec. and Head of Chancery, Bucharest 1976–78, Pvt. Sec. to Perm. Under-Sec. and Head of Diplomatic Service, FCO 1979–82, Fellow, Center for Int. Affairs, Harvard Univ., USA 1982–83, Counsellor (Information) and Head of British Information Services, Washington, DC and New York 1983–86, Head S Asian Dept, FCO 1986–88, Head News Dept 1988–90, Asst Under-Sec. of State (Asia), FCO 1990–92; Amb. to Israel 1992–95; Deputy Under-Sec. of State (non-Europe, Trade and Investment Promotion) 1995–97; British Consul-Gen., Hong Kong Special Admin. Region and Macao 1997–2000; High Commr in Canada 2000–03; Int. Gov. BBC 2005–06; Dir JP Morgan Chinese Investment Trust 2003–; Chair. Council, Royal Holloway, Univ. of London 2004–, Anglo-Israel Asscn 2004–05, Hestercombe Gardens Trust 2005–, Advisory Council British Expertise 2006–; Vice-Chair. Cttee of Univ. Chairmen 2007–; mem. British North America Cttee 2004–; Fellow, Portland Trust 2004–; Hon. Pres. Canada UK Colloquia 2003–. *Publication:* Diplomacy, War and Parliamentary Democracy 1989.
Address: Royal Holloway, University of London, Egham, Surrey, TW20 0EX, England (office). *Telephone:* (1784) 443011. *Fax:* (1784) 433619. *E-mail:* andrew.burns@rhul.ac.uk (office). *Website:* www.rhul.ac.uk (office).

BURNS, William Joseph, DPhil; American diplomatist; *Ambassador to Russia;* b. 11 April 1956; m. Lisa Carty; two d. *Education:* LaSalle Univ., Univ. of Oxford, UK. *Career:* entered Foreign Service 1982; Political Officer, US Embassy, Amman; mem. staff Bureau of Near East Affairs, Office of Deputy Sec. of State; Special Asst to the Pres., Sr Dir for Near East and S Asian Affairs, Nat. Security Council; Acting Dir and Prin. Deputy Dir State Dept's Policy Planning; Minister-Counsellor for Political Affairs, Moscow; Exec. Sec., State Dept and Special Asst to Sec. of State; Amb. to Jordan 1998–2001; Asst Sec. of State for Near Eastern Affairs 2001–05; Amb. to Russia 2005–; Marshall Scholarship, two Distinguished Honor Awards, James Clement Dunn Award, five Superior Honor Awards, two Presidential Distinguished Service Awards, Robert C. Frasure Memorial Award. *Publication:* Economic Aid and American Policy Toward Egypt, 1955–1981.
Address: Embassy of the United States, Bolshoy Devyatinskii per. 8, 121099 Moscow, Russia (office). *Telephone:* (495) 728-50-00 (office). *Fax:* (495) 728-50-90 (office). *E-mail:* pamoscow@pd.state.gov (office). *Website:* moscow.usembassy.gov (office).

BURTON, Hon. Mark; New Zealand politician; b. 16 Jan. 1956, Northampton, England; m. Carol Burton; two s. one d. *Education:* Wanganui Boys' Coll., Univ. of Waikato, Massey Univ., NZ Council of Recreation and Sport. *Career:* began career in community and social work, adult educ. and recreation; fmr employee Red Cross, Dept of Social Welfare, Palmerston North City Council; fmr Community Educ. Organiser, Cen. N Island; MP for Tongariro 1993–96, for Taupo 1996–; Sr Labour Party Whip 1996–99; Minister of Defence, State-Owned Enterprises and Tourism 1999–2005, also Minister of Internal Affairs and Veterans' Affairs 1999–2002; Deputy Leader of the House 1999–2007; Minister Responsible for Fire Service Comm. 2004–05; Minister of Justice and of Local Govt and in Charge of Treaty of Waitanagi Negotiations and Minister Responsible for Law Comm. 2005–07; Pres. Japan Karate NZ; NZ 1990 Medal.
Address: Parliament Buildings, PO Box 10–041, Wellington, New Zealand (office). *Telephone:* (4) 817-8134 (office). *E-mail:* Helen.Kennelly@parliament.govt.nz (office). *Website:* www.ps.parliament.govt.nz (office).

BURZAN, Dragiša, MS, PhD; Montenegrin politician and diplomatist; *Ambassador to UK;* b. 1950, Podgorica; m. Vesna Burzan; one s. two d. *Education:* Univ. of Montenegro, Univ. of Belgrade, Univ. of Essex, UK. *Career:* mem. staff, Dept of Natural Sciences, Univ. of Montenegro 1976–98; Founder Democratic Alternative 1989; mem. Reform Forces of Fmr Yugoslavia 1991; Co-founder Montenegro Party 1992, Int. Sec. 1992–; mem. Parl. (Montenegro) 1992–96; Deputy Prime Minister of Montenegro with portfolios of Educ., Labour and Welfare, Health, Culture, Sport, Secr. of Information, Secr. for Int. and Science Cooperation, Commissariat for Refugees, etc. 1998–2001; Minister of Labour and Social Welfare 2001–02, of Foreign Affairs 2003–04; Amb. of Serbia and Montenegro to UK 2004–06, Amb. of Montenegro to UK 2007–; Chair. Parl. Comm. investigating abduction of group of Muslims in Bosnia; Vice-Pres. SDP 1996–2000; Co-founder Monitor (weekly). *Publications:* numerous articles on physics in scientific journals.
Address: Embassy of Montenegro, 5th Floor, Trafalgar House, 11–12 Waterloo Place, London, SW1Y 4AU, England (office). *Telephone:* (20)

7863-8806 (office). *Fax:* (20) 7863-8807 (office). *E-mail:* dragisa_burzan@ yahoo.co.uk (office).

BUSEK, Erhard, DJur; Austrian politician; *Special Co-ordinator, Stability Pact for South Eastern Europe;* b. 25 March 1941, Vienna; m. Helga Busek. *Education:* Univ. of Vienna. *Career:* Second Sec. Parl. Austrian People's Party (ÖVP); joined Fed. Exec. Cttee of Austrian Econ. Fed. 1968, Deputy Sec.-Gen. 1969, Sec.-Gen. 1972–76; Gen. Sec. ÖVP 1975–76; mem. Parl. 1975–78; City Councillor, Vienna City Senate 1976–78, 1987–89; Deputy Mayor of Vienna 1978–87; Deputy Fed. Chair. ÖVP 1983–91, Chair. 1991–95; Pres. Austrian Research Community; Fed. Minister of Science and Research 1989–94, of Educ. and Culture 1994–95, Vice-Chancellor 1992–95; with Instituts für den Donauraum und Mitteleuropa (IDM) 1995–; Co-ordinator for Southeastern European Co-operative Initiative 1996–; Pres. European Forum Alpbach 2000–; Special Co-ordinator Stability Pact for SE Europe 2002–; Guest Prof., Duke Univ., USA 1995–; Perm. Sr Fellow Centre for Research into European Integration, Bonn; Pres. Gustav Mahler Youth Orchestra, Österreichischen Volkslied-werkes, Stipendienwerkes 'pro scientia'; Jt-Pres. Technologieforums Sloweniens; Dr hc (Univs of Kraków, Bratislava, Czernowitz and Ruse). *Publications:* Projekt Mitteleuropa 1986, Aufbruch nach Mitteleuropa (with G. Wilflinger) 1986, Wissenschaft, Ethik und Politik (with M. Peterlik) 1987, Wissenschaft und Freiheit – Ideen zu Universität und Universalität (with W. Mantl and M. Perterlik) 1989, Heimat – Politik mit sitz im Leben 1994, Mensch im Wort 1994, Mitteleuropa: Eine Spurensicherung 1997, Politik am Gängelband der Medien 1998, Österreich und der Balkan – Vom Umgang mit dem Pulverfass Europas 1999, Eine Reise ins Innere Europas – Protokoll eines Österreichers 2001, Offenes Tor nach Osten 2003, Die Europäische Union auf dem Weg nach Osten 2003. *Address:* Special Co-ordinator, Stability Pact for South Eastern Europe, rue Wiertz 50, 1050 Brussels, Belgium (office). *Telephone:* (2) 401-87-01 (office). *Fax:* (2) 401-87-12 (office). *E-mail:* erhard.busek@stabilitypact.org (office). *Website:* www.stabilitypact.org (office).

BUSH, George Herbert Walker, BA (Econs); American fmr head of state; b. 12 June 1924, Milton, Mass.; m. Barbara Bush (née Pierce) 1945; four s. (including George Walker Bush, John Ellis (Jeb) Bush) one d. *Education:* Phillips Acad., Andover, Mass. and Yale Univ. *Career:* naval carrier pilot USN 1942–45; Co-founder, Bush-Overbey Oil Devt Co. 1951; Co-founder, Dir Zapata Petroleum Corpn 1953–59; Founder, Pres. Zapata Offshore Co. 1956–64, Chair. 1964–66; mem. House of Reps for 7th Dist of Texas 1967–71; Perm. Rep. to UN 1971–72; Chair. Republican Nat. Cttee 1973–74; Head US Liaison Office, Peking (now Beijing) 1974–75; Dir CIA 1976–77; Vice-Pres. of USA 1981–89, Pres. of USA 1989–93; Republican; Sr Adviser, Asia Advisory Bd, Carlyle Group 1998–2003; apptd UN Special Envoy in Pakistan and Kashmir earthquake zone 2005; Hon. KBE (UK); DFC, three Air Medals; Hon. GCB 1993; numerous hon. degrees; Churchill Award 1991. *Publications:* Looking Forward: An Autobiography (with Victor Gold) 1988, A World Transformed (with Brent Scowcroft) 1998, All the Best, George Bush 1999. *Address:* Suite 900, 10000 Memorial Drive, Houston, TX 77024-3422, USA (office). *Telephone:* (713) 686-1188 (office).

BUSH, George Walker, BA, MBA; American business executive, politician and head of state; *President;* b. 6 July 1946, New Haven, Conn.; brother of John Ellis (Jeb) Bush; m. Laura Welch Bush; twin d. *Education:* Yale Univ. and Harvard Business School. *Career:* trained as F-102 fighter pilot, Tex. Air Nat. Guard 1968; CEO Bush Exploration, Midland, Tex. 1975–83; Chair. and CEO Spectrum 7 Energy Corpn (merged with Harken Energy Corpn 1986) 1983–87; worked in father's presidential campaign 1988; Man. Gen. Pnr, Tex. Rangers professional baseball team 1989–94; Gov. of Tex. 1995–2000; Pres. of USA 2001– (re-elected 2004). *Publication:* A Charge To Keep (with Karen Hughes) 2000. *Address:* The White House, 1600 Pennsylvania Avenue, NW, Washington, DC 20500, USA (office). *Telephone:* (202) 456-1414 (office). *Fax:* (202) 456-2461 (office). *E-mail:* president@whitehouse.gov (office). *Website:* www .whitehouse.gov (office).

BUSQUETS APARICIO, Gabriel, LicenDer; Spanish diplomatist; *Ambassador to Germany;* b. 10 April 1950, Inca, Majorca; m. *Education:* Univ. of Barcelona, Centre Européen Universitaire, Nancy, France, Escuela Diplomática, Madrid. *Career:* Third Sec. 1977, Second Sec., Embassy in Addis Ababa 1977–79, Asst Consul, Consulate Gen., Frankfurt 1979–83, Asst Consul, Antwerp and Consul in Liège 1983–86, Deputy Dir Gen. Action and Cultural Cooperation, Directorate Gen. of Cultural Relations, Ministry of Foreign Affairs 1986–87, Minister Counsellor, Embassy in Berlin 1987–92, Embassy in Rabat 1992–95, Coordinator Euro-Mediterranean Conf., Barcelona 1995–96, Coordinator for Mediterranean Affairs, Ministry of Foreign Affairs 1996–97, Amb. to Iran 1997–2000, Dir

Gen. Foreign Policy for Mediterranean, Middle East and Africa 2000–04, Amb. to Germany 2004–. *Address:* Embassy of Spain, Liechtensteinallee 1, 10787 Berlin, Germany (office). *Telephone:* (30) 2540070 (office). *Fax:* (30) 25799557 (office). *E-mail:* embespde@mail.mae.es (office). *Website:* www.spanischebotschaft .de (office).

BUSTANI, José Mauricio, LLB; Brazilian diplomatist and government official; *Ambassador to France;* b. 5 June 1945, Porto Velho, Rondônia; m. Janine-Monique Bustani; two s. one d. *Education:* Pontifício Uni-versidade Católica (Law School), Rio de Janeiro, Rio Branco Inst. *Career:* joined Ministry of Foreign Relations 1967, Asst to Assoc. Sec.-Gen. for Int. Orgs 1967–70, 1975–77; posted to Brazilian Embassy in Moscow 1970–73, Vienna 1973–75, Brazilian Mission to the UN 1977–84, Embassy in Montevideo 1984–86 Consulate-Gen. Montreal 1987–92; Head Dept for Tech., Financial and Devt Policy, Ministry of Foreign Relations 1992–93; Dir-Gen. Dept for Int. Orgs 1993–97; Dir-Gen. UN OPCW, The Hague 1997–2002; Amb. to UK 2003–08, to France 2008–; del. to numerous int. confs. including UNIDO, Vienna 1973–75, UN Conf. on the Law of the Sea (13 sessions 1974–93), UN Gen. Ass. 1977–83, UN Special Sessions on Disarmament 1978–82, UN Emergency Sessions on Afghanistan 1980, Namibia 1981. *Address:* Embassy of Brazil, 34 cours Albert 1er, 75008 Paris, France (office). *Telephone:* 1-45-61-63-00 (office). *Fax:* 1-42-89-03-45 (office). *E-mail:* imprensa@bresil.org (office). *Website:* www.bresil.org (office).

BUSTILLO BONASSO, Francisco; Uruguayan diplomatist; *Ambassador to Argentina;* m. María Cecilia Bauer Ormazabal; two c. *Career:* Amb. to Ecuador 2004–05, to Argentina 2005–. *Address:* Embassy of Uruguay, Las Heras 1907, 1128 Buenos Aires, Argentina (office). *Telephone:* (11) 4803-6030 (office). *Fax:* (11) 4807-3050 (office). *E-mail:* webmaster@embajadauruguay.com (office). *Website:* www.embajadadeluruguay.com.ar (office).

BUTAGIRA, Francis, LLB, LLM; Ugandan diplomatist; *Permanent Repre-sentative and Chairman, General Assembly Third Committee, United Nations;* b. 22 Nov. 1942, Bugamba; m.; seven c. *Education:* Dar es Sallaam Univ. Coll., Harvard Univ., USA, SOAS, London, UK. *Career:* State Attorney, Ministry of Justice 1967; Lecturer in Law, Nsamizi Law School 1968; Head, Law Dept, Law Devt Center 1969–70; Chief Magistrate of Buganda Road Law Courts 1973, of Mbarara 1974; High Court Judge 1974–79; mem. Nat. Consultative Council 1979–80; mem. Parl. 1980–85, also served as Pres. Jt. Ass. of the European Econ. Community and the African, Caribbean and Pacific Group of States (EEC/ACP) 1981–83; Chair. Legal and Security Affairs Cttee, Nat. Resistance Council (Parl.) 1989–96; Amb. to Ethiopia and Perm. Rep. to Org. of African Unity (OAU), Addis Ababa 1998; led team of Ugandan negotiators in talks leading to establishment of E African Community 1999; fmr High Commr to Kenya and Perm. Rep. to UNEP and UN–HABITAT, Nairobi; served as mediator in Sudanese peace talks sponsored by Intergovernmental Authority on Devt (IGAD) 2000–03; Perm. Rep. to UN 2003–, Chair UN Gen. Ass. Third Cttee (Social, Humanitarian and Cultural) 2005–; Sr Pnr Butagira and Co. (law firm) 1989–; Uganda Investment Authority Golden Award for Attraction of Investment 2002. *Address:* Permanent Mission of Uganda to the United Nations, 336 East Street, New York NY 10017, USA (office). *Telephone:* (212) 949-0110 (office); (212) 963-5722 (Third Cttee) (office). *Fax:* (212) 687-4517 (office); (212) 963-5935 (Third Cttee) (office). *E-mail:* ugandaunny@un.int (office); 3rdcommittee@un.org (office). *Website:* www.un.int/uganda (office); www .un.org/ga/60/third (office); www.butagiraadvocates.com.

BUTCHER, Peter Roderick; British diplomatist; *Ambassador to Turkmeni-stan;* b. 6 Aug. 1947. *Education:* Univ. of Bath. *Career:* joined FCO 1974, Desk Officer (E Africa), Research Dept 1974–78, Desk Officer, Cen. African Dept 1978–79, Second Sec. (Political and Aid), Lima 1979–83, Madrid 1983, Second Sec. (Commercial), Mumbai 1983–87, Econ. and Commercial Relations, S Asian Dept, FCO 1987–90, Deputy High Commr, Maseru 1990–93, St Vincent and the Grenadines 1994–94, Head of Southern Cone Section, Latin America Dept, FCO 1994–96, Deputy Gov., Port Stanley 1996, Head of Western Balkans Section, Know How Fund, Dept for Int. Devt 1997–99, Deputy Head of Mission, Maputo 2000–03, language training 2004, Amb. to Turkmenistan 2005–. *Address:* British Embassy, Four Points Ak Altin Hotel, 301–308 Office Building, Ashgabat, Turkmenistan (office). *Telephone:* (12) 36-34-62 (office). *Fax:* (12) 36-34-65 (office). *E-mail:* beasb@online.tm (office). *Website:* www.britishembassy.gov.uk/turkmenistan (office).

BUTENIS, Patricia A., BA, MA; American diplomatist; *Deputy Chief of Mission, Baghdad;* b. NJ. *Education:* Univ. of Pennsylvania, Columbia Univ., New York. *Career:* career mem. Sr Foreign Service with rank of

Minister-Counsellor, has served in Karachi, San Salvador, Bogota, Warsaw and Washington, DC, Deputy Chief of Mission, Islamabad 2004–06, Amb. to Bangladesh 2006–07, Deputy Chief of Mission, Baghdad 2007–.
Address: US Embassy, APO AE 09316, Baghdad, Iraq (office). *E-mail:* BaghdadPressOffice@state.gov (office). *Website:* iraq.usembassy.gov (office).

BUTHELEZI, Chief Mangosuthu Gatsha, BA; South African politician and Zulu leader; b. 27 Aug. 1928, Mahlabatini; m. Irene Audrey Thandekile Mzila 1952; three s. four d. *Education:* Adams Coll., Fort-Hare Univ. *Career:* installed as Chief of Buthelezi Tribe 1953; assisted King Cyprian in admin. of Zulu people 1953–68; elected leader of Zululand territorial authority 1970; Chief Minister of KwaZulu 1976–94; Minister of Home Affairs (in Gov. of Nat. Unity) 1994–2004; Pres. Inkatha Freedom Party; Hon. LLD (Zululand and Cape Town); George Meany Human Rights Award 1982; Kt Commdr Star of Africa (Liberia), Commdr Ordre Nat. du Mérite 1981 and numerous other awards. *Publication:* South Africa: My Vision of the Future 1990.
Address: c/o Ministry of Home Affairs, Private Bag X741, Pretoria 0001 (office); Inkatha Freedom Party, Albany House North, 4th Floor, Albany Grove, PO Box 443, Durban 4000, South Africa. *Telephone:* (31) 3074962. *Fax:* (12) 3074964. *Website:* www.fp.org.za.

BUTLER, Georgina, LLB; British diplomatist; *British Consul, Tangier;* b. Upavon, Wilts.; m. 1st Stephen John Leadbetter Wright 1970 (divorced 2000); one s. one d.; m. 2nd Robert Kelly 2003. *Education:* Univ. Coll. London. *Career:* worked for British Embassy in Paris 1969–70; Southern European Dept FCO 1971–75, Head, Information Dept 1985–87, Deputy Head of Latin America and Caribbean Dept 1999–2001; UN Secretariat, New York 1976–77; EU Comm., Brussels 1982–84; Forum Europe, Brussels 1992–94; EU Comm. Office London 1996–97; Amb. to Costa Rica and Nicaragua 2002–06; British Consul, Tangier 2007–; Order of Juan Mora Fernandez (Costa Rica) 2006.
Address: British Consulate Tangier, Trafalgar House 9 rue Amerique du Sud, Tangier 90000, Morocco (office). *Telephone:* (3) 936939 (office). *Fax:* (3) 936914 (office). *E-mail:* uktanger2@menara.ma (office). *Website:* www .britain.org.ma (office).

BUTLER, Hon. Richard William, AC, DUniv; Australian diplomatist; b. 13 May 1942; m. Barbara Evans 1974; three s. one d. *Education:* Randwick Boys High School, Univ. of Sydney, Australian Nat. Univ. *Career:* Second Sec., Embassy and Perm. Mission to UN, Deputy Perm. Rep. IAEA, Vienna 1966–69; First Sec. Mission to UN, New York 1970–73; Deputy High Commr, Singapore, 1975–76; Prin. Pvt. Sec. to Leader of Opposition 1976–77; Counsellor, Bonn Embassy 1978–81; Minister-Del. to OECD, Paris, Amb. and Perm. Rep. to UN (Disarmament Matters), Geneva 1983–88; Amb. to Thailand 1989–92; Amb. and Perm. Rep. to Supreme Nat. Council of Cambodia 1991–92; Amb. and Perm. Rep. to UN, New York 1992–97; Exec. Chair. UN Special Comm. on Iraqi Disarmament 1997–99; Diplomat-in-Residence, Council on Foreign Relations, New York 1999–; Gov. of Tasmania 2003–04 (resgnd). *Publications:* The Greatest Threat 2000, Saddam Defiant 2000.
Address: c/o Government House, Hobart, Tasmania 7000, Australia.

BUTLER, William Elliott, MA, JD, LLM, PhD, LLD, FRSA, FSA; American/British legal scholar and academic; *John Edward Fowler Distinguished Professor of Law, Dickinson School of Law, Pennsylvania State University;* b. 20 Oct. 1939, Minneapolis, Minn.; m. 1st Darlene Johnson (died 1989); two s.; m. 2nd Maryann Gashi 1991. *Education:* Hibbing Jr Coll., The American Univ., Harvard Law School, Russian Acad. of Sciences, Johns Hopkins School of Advanced Int. Studies, Univ. of London. *Career:* Research Asst, Washington Center for Foreign Policy Research, Johns Hopkins Univ. 1966–68; Research Assoc. in Law and Assoc., Russian Research Center, Harvard Univ. 1968–70; Reader in Comparative Law, Univ. of London 1970–76, Prof. of Comparative Law 1976–2005, Dean, Faculty of Laws 1988–90, Prof. Emer. 2005–; mem. Council, School of Slavonic and E European Studies 1973–93; Dean, Faculty of Laws, Univ. Coll. London 1977–79, Vice-Dean 1979–81; Dir Vinogradoff Inst. Univ. Coll. London 1982–2005; Dean, Faculty of Law and Speranskii Prof. of Int. and Comparative Law, Moscow Higher School of Social and Econ. Sciences 1995–; John Edward Fowler Distinguished Prof. of Law, Dickinson School of Law, Pa State Univ. 2005–, mem. Faculty Council, School of Int. Affairs 2007–; Professional Research Assoc., SOAS, Univ. of London 2006–; Pnr, White & Case 1994–96, Price Waterhouse Coopers 1997–2001; Sr Pnr, Phoenix Law Assocs, Moscow 2002–; Special Counsel, Comm. on Econ. Reform, USSR Council of Ministers 1989–91; consultant, IBRD; adviser and consultant, Russian Fed., Belarus, Ukraine, Kyrgyzstan, Repub. of Kazakhstan, Repub. of Tajikistan, Repub. of Uzbekistan; Visiting Scholar, Moscow State Univ. 1972, 1980, Mongolian State Univ. 1979, Inst. of State and Law, USSR Acad. of Sciences 1976, 1981, 1983, 1984, 1988, Harvard Law School 1982; Visiting Prof., New York Univ. Law School 1978, Ritsumeikan Univ. 1985, Harvard Law School 1986–87, Washington and Lee Univ. 2005; mem. Russian Court of Int. Commercial Arbitration 1995–, Expert Council on Reform of Corp. Man., Ministry of Econ. Devt and Trade of Russian Fed. 2004–; Academician, Russian Acad. of Natural Sciences, Nat. Acad. of Sciences of Ukraine, Int. Acad. of the Book and Art of the Book, Russian Acad. of Legal Sciences; mem. Sr Common Room, St Antony's Coll., Oxford 2004–; G.I.Tunkin Medal 2003, Ivan Fedorov Medal 2004. *Publications:* more than 900 books, articles, reviews and translations including Soviet Law 1983, The Non-Use of Force in Int. Law 1989, Perestroika and Int. Law 1990, The History of Int. Law in Russia 1647–1917 1990, Foreign Investment Legislation in the Republics of the Former Soviet Union 1993, Russian Law of Treaties 1997, Russian Legal Texts 1998, Russian Law 1999, 2003, Constitutional Foundations of the CIS Countries 2000, American Bookplates 2000, Russian Company Law 2000, Russian-English Legal Dictionary 2001, Foreign Investment Laws in the CIS 2002, The Law of Treaties in Russia and the CIS 2002, Civil Code of the Russian Fed. 2003, Russian Co. and Commercial Law 2003, Narcotics and HIV in Russia 2005, Russian Intellectual Property Law (fourth edn) 2005, Russian Foreign Relations and Investment Law 2006, Russian Legal Biography 2007 (with V. A. Tomsinov), Civil Code of Uzbekistan 2007, Civil Code of Kazakhstan 2008.
Address: 155 Mount Rock Road, Newville, PA 17241 (home); Dickinson School of Law, Penn State University, 150 South College Street, Carlisle, PA 17013, USA (office). *Telephone:* (717) 776-7359 (home); (717) 240-5227 (office). *Fax:* (717) 240-5126 (office). *E-mail:* webakademik@aol.com (home); web15@psu.edu (office). *Website:* www.dsl.psu.edu/faculty/butler (office).

BUTLER, William Joseph; American lawyer; *President, American Association of The International Commission of Jurists;* b. 22 March 1924, Brighton, Mass; m. Jane Hays 1945; one s. one d. *Education:* Harvard Univ. and New York Univ. School of Law. *Career:* mem. New York Bar 1950; Assoc. Hays, St John, Abramson & Schulman, New York 1949–53; partner Butler, Jablow & Geller, New York 1953–; special counsel American Civil Liberties Union; Attorney for petitioner in Engel v. Vitale (school prayer case, landmark case in history of US constitutional law), US Supreme Court 1962; Lecturer, Practising Law Inst. 1966; Sec., Dir, Cen. Counsel, Walco Nat. Corpn, FAO Schwarz, New York; mem. Comm. on Urban Affairs, American Jewish Congress 1965–70; mem. Bd of Dirs New York Civil Liberties Union, Int. League for Rights of Man; mem. Exec. Cttee League to Abolish Capital Punishment; mem. Standing Cttee on Human Rights, World Peace Through Law Center, Geneva; Chair. Advisory Cttee Morgan Inst. for Human Rights; mem. Int. Comm. of Jurists (Pres. American Asscn for the Int. Comm. of Jurists), American Bar Asscn, Council on Foreign Relations, Int. Law Asscn, American Soc. of Int. Law, etc.; int. legal observer, Int. Human Rights Org. at trials in Greece, Burundi, Iran, Nicaragua, S Korea, Philippines, Uruguay, Israel, at Int. Criminal Tribunal for fmr Yugoslavia, The Hague 1996–; Special Regional Adviser for N America on Human Rights to the UN High Comm. for Human Rights 1998; originator of Princeton Project on Universal Jurisdiction; Hon. DHumLitt (Cincinnati) 1988. *Publications include:* Human Rights and the Legal System in Iran 1976, The Decline of Democracy in the Philippines 1977, Human Rights in United States and United Kingdom Foreign Policy 1977, Guatemala, a New Beginning 1987, Palau: A Challenge to the Rule of Law in Micronesia 1988, The New South Africa – The Dawn of Democracy 1994; contribs to professional journals.
Address: 280 Madison Avenue, New York, NY 10016 (office); 24 E 10th Street, New York, NY 10003, USA. *E-mail:* wjb@iopener.net (office). *Website:* www.law.uc.edu/archives/index.html (office).

BUTT, Simon John; British diplomatist; *Ambassador to Lithuania; Career:* Asst Desk Officer, Eastern European and Soviet Dept, FCO 1979–80, Russian Language Training 1981, Third Sec. (Chancery), Moscow 1982–84, Second Sec. and Vice-Consul, Rangoon 1984–86, Head of Section, Soviet Dept, FCO 1986–88, Planning Staff, Ministerial Speech-writer 1988–90, First Sec. (External), UK Del. to EU, Brussels 1990–94, Deputy Head of Eastern Dept, FCO 1994–97, Deputy Head of Mission, Kiev 1997–2000, Head of Eastern Dept, FCO 2000–04, Deputy High Commr, Islamabad 2004–07, Amb. to Lithuania 2008–.
Address: British Embassy, Antakalnio g. 2, Vilnius 10308, Lithuania (office). *Telephone:* (5) 246-2900 (office). *Fax:* (5) 246-2901 (office). *E-mail:* be-vilnius@britain.lt (office). *Website:* www.britain.lt (office).

BÜTTNER LIMPRICH, José Ernesto, MA; Paraguayan politician, banker and international organization executive. *Education:* Pontificia Universidad Católica, Santiago de Chile. *Career:* fmr Vice-Minister of Economy and Integration; fmr Alt. Gov. for Paraguay, IMF; Dir Mercosur Secr. 2006–08.

Address: c/o Mercosur Secretariat, Edificio Mercosur, Dr Luis Piera 1992 piso 1, CP 11.200, Montevideo, Uruguay. *Telephone:* (2) 412-9024.

BUYOYA, Maj. Pierre; Burundian politician and fmr head of state; *President, Foundation for Unity, Peace and Democracy;* b. 24 Nov. 1949, Mutangaro, Rutovu; m. Sophie Buyoya 1978; one s. three d. *Education:* Royal Mil. Acad., Brussels, staff coll. in France, war coll. in Germany. *Career:* degree in social science and mil. affairs; mem. Cen. Cttee UPRONA Party 1979–87; fmr COO Ministry of Nat. Defence; led mil. coup against fmr Pres. Bagaza Sept. 1987; Pres. of Third Repub. and Minister of Nat. Defence 1987–92; Chair. Mil. Cttee for Nat. Salvation 1987–93; Pres. Foundation for Unity, Peace and Democracy 1994–; Pres. of Burundi 1987–93, 1996–2003; mem. Senate 2003–. *Publications:* Building Peace in Burundi – Mission Impossible 1998.
Address: BP 2006, Bujumbura, Burundi (office). *Telephone:* (2) 20796 (office); (2) 13208 (home). *Fax:* (2) 20816 (office). *E-mail:* fupd2003@yahoo .fr (office).

BÜYÜKANIT, Gen. (Mehmet) Yaşar; Turkish army officer; *Commander of the Turkish Armed Forces;* b. 1 Sept. 1940, Istanbul; m. Filiz Büyükanit; one d. *Education:* Mil. Acad., Infantry School, Army Staff Coll., NATO Defence Coll. *Career:* served in different units of Land Forces as Platoon and Commando Co. Commdr 1963–70, then numerous leadership positions including Chief of Operations, 6th Infantry Div., Instructor, Army Staff Coll., Intelligence Div. Basic Intelligence Br. Forces and Systems Section Chief, Supreme HQ Allied Powers Europe (SHAPE), Mons, Belgium, Section then Br. Chief of Gen.-Adm. Br. at Turkish Gen. Staff (TGS) HQ, Commdr of Kuleli Mil. High School and of Presidential Guard Regiment; 2nd Armored Brigade Commdr then Chief of Intelligence Dept, AFSOUTH HQ, Naples, Italy; Sec. Gen. of Turkish Gen. Staff then Supt Turkish Army Acad. 1992–96; 7th Army Corps Commdr 1996–98; Chief of Operations TGS 1998–2000, Deputy Chief 2000–03, Commdr of First Army 2003–04; Commdr Turkish Land Forces 2004-06; Commdr Turkish Armed Forces 2006–; Turkish Armed Forces (TAF) Medal of Distinguished Service, TAF Medal of Distinguished Courage and Self-Sacrifice, TAF Medal of Honor, Italian Medal of Honor, USA Legion of Merit, Pakistani Nishan-ı Imtiaz.
Address: Ministry of National Defence, Milli Savunma Bakanlığı, 06100 Ankara, Turkey (office). *Telephone:* (312) 4254596 (office). *Fax:* (312) 4184737 (office). *E-mail:* meb@meb.gov.tr (office). *Website:* www.msb.gov .tr (office); www.tsk.mil.tr (office).

BUZEK, Jerzy Karol; Polish politician and chemical engineer; b. 3 July 1940, Śmiłowice; m. Ludgarda Buzek; one d. *Education:* Silesian Tech. Univ., Gliwice. *Career:* Scientific Researcher and Prof., Chemical Eng Inst., Polish Acad. of Sciences, Gliwice 1963–97, Prof. of Tech. Science 1997–; mem. Solidarity Trade Union 1980–; organizer of Solidarity underground structures in Silesia; activist of union's regional and nat. leadership; Chair. 1st, 4th, 5th and 6th Nat. Congresses of Dels; expert and co-author economic program of the Solidarity Election Action (AWS), Chair. Nat. Bd of Social Movt of Solidarity Election Action 1999–2001, Chair. AWS coalition 2001–; Deputy to Sejm (Parl.) 1997–2001; Prime Minister of Poland 1997–2001; Researcher and Pro-Rector Polonia Univ., Częstochowa 2002–; Prof., Mechanical Div., Tech. Univ. of Opole; mem. European Parl. (Silesian Voivodship constituency) (Group of the European People's Party—Christian Democrats and European Democrats) 2004–, mem. Cttee on Industry, Research and Energy, Substitute mem Cttee on the Environment, Public Health and Food Safety, mem. Del. to EU-Ukraine Parl. Cooperation Cttee, Substitute mem. Del. for Relations with the Countries of Cen. America; f. Family Foundation together with his wife 1998; est. annual Pro Publico Bono Prize for the best national civic initiatives 1999;; Dr hc (Seoul, Dortmund); Laureate, Grzegorz Palka Award 1998. *Publications include:* several dozen articles and monographs on mathematical modelling, desulphurization of exhaust gases and optimization of processes.
Address: European Parliament, Bâtiment Altiero Spinelli, 05F243, 60 rue Wiertz, 1047 Brussels, Belgium (office); Puxaskiego 4/6, 42 200 Częstochowa, Poland. *Telephone:* (2) 284-96-31 (office). *E-mail:* jbuzek@europarl .eu.int (office). *Website:* wwwdb.europarl.eu.int (office).

BYAMBASUREN, Dashiyn; Mongolian politician; *Director, Centre for Development Strategy and System Research;* b. 20 June 1942, Binder somon Dist, Hentii Prov.; m. Sanjeen Dulamlkhand 1968; three s. three d. *Education:* Inst. of Economics and Statistics, Moscow, USSR. *Career:* apptd Dept Chief, State Statistics Bd; Deputy Chair., then Chair. State Cttee for Prices and Standardization 1970–76; Chair. Construction and Repair Work Trust for Auto Transport 1984, Chief Research Officer, Research Inst. of Project Drafts for Automated Man. Systems 1985, Dir Manager Training Inst., Council of Ministers 1986; Deputy Chair. Council of Ministers 1989–90, First Deputy Chair. March–Sept. 1990, Prime

Minister 1990–92; Pres. Mongolian Devt Foundation, World Mongolian Fed. 1993; fmr mem. Parl; Chair. Mongolian Democratic Renewal Party 1994–; Rector Inst. of Admin. and Man. 1998–2000; Rector Acad. of Man.; Dir Centre for Devt Strategy and System Research 2001–; Prof. and Academician, Nat. Acad. of Science. *Publications:* Orchlongiin hurd, Sergen mandakh ireedui, Uuriin javar.
Address: GPO Box 248, Ulan Bator, Mongolia (home). *Telephone:* 324167 (office). *Fax:* 320090 (office). *E-mail:* byambasuren@cdssr.mn (office). *Website:* www.cdssr.mn (office).

BYANYIMA, Winnie, MSc; Ugandan aeronautical engineer, politician and international organization official; *Director, Gender Team, United Nations Development Programme (UNDP);* m. Kizza Besigye 1999. *Education:* Cranfield Inst. of Tech. and Manchester Univ., UK. *Career:* first female flight engineer Uganda Airlines; joined Uganda Nat. Resistance Movement (NRM) 1982; Deputy Perm. Delegate of Uganda to UNESCO for five years; elected Delegate to Constituent Assembly and Chair. Assembly's Women's Caucus; MP for Mbarara Municipality, Western Uganda 1994–2005; Chair. FOWODE (Forum for Women in Democracy); Dir of Women, Gender and Devt, African Union 2004–06; Dir. UNDP Gender Team, Bureau for Devt Policy, New York 2006–; mem. Exec. Bd African Capacity-Bldg Foundation; fmr mem. Exec. Bd UN Univ. Inst. for New Technologies; mem. Bd UN Comm. on Science and Tech. for Devt (UNCSTD), UN Millennium Devt Goals Task Force on Gender Equality and Educ., Int. Centre for Research on Women (ICRW), Advisory Council of Equality Now, UNDP Ind. Comm. for Africa Millennium Project; Amelia Earhart Fellowship, Zonta Int.
Address: Gender Programme Team, Bureau for Development Policy, UNDP, One United Nations Plaza, New York, NY 10017, USA (office). *Telephone:* (212) 906-5000 (office). *Fax:* (212) 906-5364 (office). *E-mail:* gidp@undp.org (office). *Website:* www.undp.org/women (office).

BYCZEWSKI, Iwo, DrIur; Polish diplomatist and lawyer; *Ambassador to Belgium;* b. 29 Feb. 1948, Poznań; m.; two d. *Education:* Adam Mickiewicz Univ., Poznań and Collège d'Europe, Bruges. *Career:* mem. staff, Ministry of Justice 1977–82; researcher, Inst. of Econ. Sciences, Polish Acad. of Sciences (PAN) 1982–89; Prin. Expert, Sec. Comm. in Senate Chancellery; Ministerial Adviser, Vice-Dir Council of Minister's Office 1989–90; Dir Personnel Dept, Ministry of Foreign Affairs 1990–91, Under-Sec. of State 1991–95; Perm. Rep. to EU 2001–02; Amb. to Belgium and Luxembourg 2002–03, to Belgium 2005–; Chair. Supervisory Bd Alcatel Polska SA 1995–; consultant, Hogan and Hartson (American law firm) 1996–; Chair. Centre of Int. Affairs Foundation 1997–.
Address: Ambassade de la République de Pologne, Av. des Gaulois 29, 1040 Brussels, Belgium (office). *Telephone:* (2) 73-90-151 (office). *Fax:* (2) 73-61-881 (office). *E-mail:* polambbxl@skynet.be (office). *Website:* www .polembassy.be (office).

BYKOV, Oleg Nikolayevich, DrHist; Russian political scientist; *Counsellor, Russian Academy of Sciences;* b. 15 Oct. 1926, Tula; m.; one d. *Education:* Moscow State Inst. of Int. Relations. *Career:* mem. staff Soviet Cttee of Peace 1952–55, Deputy Exec. Sec. 1959–64; mem. staff World Peace Council, Vienna 1953–59; Sr Researcher, Head of Int. Relations Dept, Deputy Dir Inst. of World Econs and Int. Relations, Russian Acad. of Sciences 1964–98, Counsellor, Russian Acad. of Sciences 1998–; mem. UN Consultative Bd on Studies of Disarmament Problems; Govt expert UN Research Group on Measures of Confidence; Ed.-in-Chief Year of the Planet (yearly journal) 1992–; Corresp. Mem. USSR (now Russian) Acad. of Sciences 1987; Soviet Orders of Labour Red Banner (1981, 1986), Russian Fed. Order of Merit 1999; USSR State Prize; four medals. *Publications:* over 600 scientific pubs on contemporary int. relations, Russian foreign policy, mil. and political problems; monographs: Russia in the System of International Relations of the Coming 10 Years 1995, Russian and International Stability 1995, National Security of Russia 1997, International Relations: The Global Structure Transformed (two vols) 2003.
Address: Institute of World Economics and International Relations, Russian Academy of Sciences, Profsoyuznaya str. 23, Moscow 117997, Russia (office). *Telephone:* (495) 120-5236 (office); (495) 120-23-40 (office). *E-mail:* imemoran@imemo.ru (office). *Website:* www.imemo.ru (office).

BYMAN, Daniel L., BA, PhD; American policy analyst and academic; *Director, Center for Peace and Security Studies, Georgetown University;* *Education:* Massachusetts Inst. of Tech., Amherst Coll. *Career:* Political Analyst, CIA 1990–93; Policy Analyst and Dir for Research, Center for Middle East Public Policy, The RAND Corpn 1997–2002; professional staff mem. Jt 9/11 Inquiry, US House and Senate Intelligence Cttees 2001–02, Nat. Comm. on Terrorist Attacks on the US 2003–04; Sr Fellow, Saban Center for Middle East Policy, Brookings Inst. 2003–; Assoc. Prof., Security Studies Program, Edmund A. Walsh School of Foreign Service and Dept of Govt, Georgetown Univ. 2005–, Dir Center for Peace and Security Studies 2005–; Kellogg Prize, Moseley Prize. *Publications:* Keeping the Peace: Lasting Solutions to Ethnic Conflicts 2002, The Dynamics of Coercion: American Foreign Policy and the Limits of Military Might (with Matthew Waxman) 2002, Deadly Connections: States that Sponsor Terrorism 2005, Things Fall Apart: Containing the Spillover from an Iraqi Civil War (with Kenneth Pollack), The Five Front War: The Better Way to Fight Global Jihad 2007; contribs to journals.

Address: Center for Peace and Security Studies, Georgetown University, 3600 N Street, NW, Washington, DC, 20007, USA (office). *Telephone:* (202) 687-4095 (office). *E-mail:* dlb32@georgetown.edu (office). *Website:* cpass.georgetown.edu (office).

BYRNE, David, BA, BL, SC, FRCPI; Irish European Union official, politician and barrister; b. 26 April 1947; m.; three c. *Education:* Dominican Coll., Newbridge, Univ. Coll. Dublin, King's Inns, Dublin. *Career:* called to the Bar 1970; mem. Bar Council 1974–87; mem. Exec. Cttee, Irish Maritime Law Asscn 1974–92; called to Inner Bar 1985; mem. Nat. Cttee ICC 1988–97; mem. Govt Review Body on Social Welfare Law 1989; mem. ICC Int. Court of Arbitration, Paris 1990–97; mem. Constitution Review Group 1995–96; External Examiner for Arbitration and Competition Law, King's Inns 1995–97; Attorney-Gen. 1997–99; mem. Council of State, Cabinet Sub-cttees on Social Inclusion, European Affairs, Child Abuse; EU Commr for Health and Consumer Protection (with particular responsibility for Food Safety, Public Health and Consumer Protection) 1999–2004; mem. Barristers' Professional Practices and Ethics Cttee 1995–97; participated in negotiation of Good Friday Agreement April 1998; Fellow, Chartered Inst. of Arbitrators of England and Ireland 1998–; f. Free Legal Advice Centre, Dublin; Hon. Treasurer, Bar Council 1982–83. *Publications:* numerous papers on legal affairs.

Address: c/o European Commission, 200 rue de la Loi, 1049 Brussels, Belgium (office).

C

CABALLERO, Gladys Aida; Honduran politician. *Career:* Vice-Minister of Justice 1996; Vice-Pres. of Honduras 1998–2001.
Address: c/o Office of the Vice-President, Palacio José Cecilio del Valle, Boulevard Juan Pablo II, Tegucigalpa, Honduras (office).

CABANISS, William J., Jr, BA; American diplomatist and business executive; b. Ala; m. Catherine Cabaniss; two d. *Education:* Vanderbilt Univ. *Career:* Airborne Ranger, First Lt, US Army, tour of duty in Germany 1961–64; began business career with Southern Cement Co. Div. of Martin Marietta Corpn, Birmingham, Ala, Dir Market Devt, Southern Cement 1964–71 (resgnd); acquired Precision Grinding, Inc. 1971; fmr mem. Bd of Dirs AmSouth Bank, Birmingham Steel Corpn, Southern Co., Protective Life Corpn; served in Ala House of Reps 1978–82, Ala State Senate 1982–90; fmr mem. Metropolitan Devt Bd (Past Chair.), Bd Nat. Asscn of Mfrs, Bd Southern Research Inst., Birmingham Chamber of Commerce, Business Council of Ala, Asscn of Iron and Steel Engineers, Nat. Tooling and Machining Asscn; fmr mem. Bd A + (The Coalition for Better Educ.), Kings Ranch, Boy Scouts; fmr Chair. Jr Achievement of Jefferson Co.; mem. Birmingham Rotary Club (fmr mem. Bd); led Alexis de Toqueville Soc. of United Way in 2000 campaign; Amb. to Czech Repub. 2004–06; fmr Trustee Sweet Briar Coll.; fmr Sr Warden St Luke's Episcopal Church; Army Commendation Medal; Community Service Award, Rotary Club of Birmingham 1993, Distinguished Builders of Birmingham Award 2002, inducted into Ala Academy of Honor 2004.
Address: US Department of State, 2201 C Street NW, Washington, DC 20520, USA (office). *Telephone:* (202) 647-4000 (office). *Fax:* (202) 647-6738 (office). *Website:* www.state.gov (office).

CABEZAS MORALES, Rodrigo Eduardo; Venezuelan politician and economist; b. 19 June 1956, Valera, Trujillo state; m. *Education:* Univ. of Zulia. *Career:* mem. Faculty, Univ. of Zulia 1982–, currently Prof. and mem. Instituto de Investigaciones; Deputy Congreso de la República 1990–93, 1994–98; Deputy Asamblea Nacional 2000–04, then Vice-Chair. Asamblea Nacional Finance Comm. 2000–01, Chair. 2002–06; Minister of Finance 2007–08; Bd mem. Nat. Council on Culture 2002; mem. Por la Democracia Social (PODEMOS) party.
Address: Por la Democracia Social (PODEMOS), Caracas, Venezuela (office). *E-mail:* contacto@podemos.org.ve (office). *Website:* www.podemos.org.ve (office).

CABI, Martinho N'Dafa; Guinea-Bissau politician; b. 17 Sept. 1957, Nhacra, Oio Prov.. *Career:* belongs to Balanta ethnic group; joined Partido Africano da Independência da Guiné e Cabo Verde (PAIGC) 1974, various roles including Chair. Cttee for Autonomous Region of Guinea-Bissau, mem. Cen. Cttee 1999, Third Vice-Pres. 2002–07; fmr Minister of Energy; Minister of Nat. Defence 2004–05; Prime Minister 2007–08.
Address: Partido Africano da Independência da Guiné e Cabo Verde (PAIGC), CP 106, Bissau, Guinea-Bissau (office). *Website:* www.paigc.org (office).

CABRERA, Cesar Benito, BS; American business executive, politician and diplomatist; *Ambassador to Mauritius;* b. San Juan, Puerto Rico; m. Helvetia Barros; one d. *Education:* Univ. of Puerto Rico, Mayaguez campus. *Career:* involved in banking, devt and construction industries in Puerto Rico for over 35 years; fmr pres. three devt cos; fmr mem. Bd of Dirs Home Builders Puerto Rico (also Treas.), Fed. Home Loan Mortgage Corpn; Exec. Dir Republican Party of Puerto Rico 1992–2004, Chair. Puerto Rico del. to Republican Nat. Convention 2000; mem. US Presidential Del. at inauguration of Martin Torrijos, Pres. of Panama 2004; Amb. to Mauritius 2006–; Home Builder Multifamily Project of the Year (twice).
Address: US Embassy, PO Box 544, 4th Floor, Rogers House, John F. Kennedy Avenue, Port Louis, Mauritius (office). *Telephone:* 208-4400 (office). *Fax:* 208-9534 (office). *E-mail:* usembass@intnet.mu (office). *Website:* mauritius.usembassy.gov (office).

CÁCERES CARDOZO, Manuel María; Paraguayan diplomatist; *Permanent Representative, Organization of American States; Career:* fmrly Amb. to Belgium, to EU; fmr Amb. to Argentina; currently Perm Rep to OAS,

Chair. Perm. Council 2005, fmr Chair. Working Group to Prepare for the Meeting of Nat. Authorities on Trafficking in Persons.
Address: Office of the Permanent Representative of Paraguay to the OAS, 2022 Connecticut Avenue, NW, Washington, DC 20008, USA (office). *Telephone:* (202) 232-8020 (office). *Fax:* (202) 232-8023 (office).

CACHIA CARUANA, Richard, BA, MA; Maltese diplomatist and press officer; *Permanent Representative, European Union;* b. 11 Feb. 1955, Sliema. *Education:* St Edward's Coll., Univ. of Malta, London Business School, UK. *Career:* Asst Sec.-Gen. and Dir AIESEC International, Belgium 1976–78; Marketing Consultant, Maltatours (UK) Ltd 1980–81; Campaign Manager, Partit Nazzjonalista 1981–82, 1985–87, also Dir Press and Information Office 1985–87; Man. Dir Gallup Ltd, Malta 1983–85; Personal Asst to Prime Minister 1987–96, Head, Prime Minister's Secr. 1998–2004; Sr Consultant, KPMG 1996–98; Chief Negotiator for Malta's EU Accession negotiations 1999–2003; Perm. Rep., EU 2003–; mem. Bd of Dirs Nat. Student Travel Service 1976, 1979–80, Gallup Ltd 1983–85, Malta Devt Corpn 1987–92, External Trade Corpn 1989–92, Air Malta PLC 1992–97, Central Bank of Malta 1997–98; Sovereign Mil. Order of Malta, and decorations from Estonia, Italy, Latvia, Poland, Portugal.
Address: Permanent Representation of Malta, Council of the European Union, rue Belliard 65–67, Brussels 1040, Belgium (office). *Telephone:* (2) 343-01-95 (office). *Fax:* (2) 343-01-06 (office). *E-mail:* maltarep@gov.mt (office).

CADET, Jean, LLB; French diplomatist; b. 15 Oct. 1942. *Education:* Inst. d'études politiques de Paris, Ecole Nat. d'Admin., Paris. *Career:* Attaché Cen. Admin., Ministry of Justice 1968–70, Cen. Admin., Econ. and Financial Affairs 1972–75; apptd Minister Plenipotentiary 1977; Second Sec., Perm. Rep. to EC, Brussels 1978–82, Minister Counsellor 1986–92; First Sec. in Abidjan 1982–84, in Bonn 1984–86; Amb. to Greece 1992–94, to Austria 1997–2001, to S Africa 2001–03, Amb. (non-resident) to Lesotho 2002–03; to Russian Fed. 2003–06; Sec.-Gen. Inter-ministerial Cttee on European Econ. Cooperation 1995–97; Counsellor for European Affairs, Cabinet of the Prime Minister 1995–97; Conseiller Maitre, Cour des Comptes 2006–; Officier Légion d'honneur, Officier Ordre nat. du Mérite.
Address: Cour des comptes, 13 rue Cambon, 75001 Paris, France (office). *E-mail:* contact@ccomptes.fr (office). *Website:* www.ccomptes.fr (office).

ÇAĞLAYAN, Zafer; Turkish business executive and politician; *Minister of Industry and Trade;* b. 1957, Muş; m.; two c. *Education:* Gazi Univ., Ankara. *Career:* Chair. Ankara Chamber of Industry (ASO) 1995–2007; Deputy Chair. Turkish Union of Chambers and Commodities Exchanges (TOBB) 2005–07; mem. Parl. (AKP) 2007–, Minister of Industry and Trade 2007–; Chair. Çağlayanlar Alüminyum Ltd, Akel Alüminyum A.Ş.
Address: Ministry of Industry and Trade, Sanayi ve Ticaret Bakanliği, Eskişehir yolu üzeri 7 km, Ankara, Turkey (office). *Telephone:* (312) 2860365 (office). *E-mail:* zcaglayanailetin@zafercaglayan.com.tr; akel@akelmetal.com.tr. *Website:* www.sanayi.gov.tr; www.zafercaglayan.com; www.akelmetal.com.tr.

CAIN, James Palmer; American lawyer and diplomatist; *Ambassador to Denmark;* b. N Carolina; m. Helen Cain; two d. *Education:* Wake Forest Univ. *Career:* with Kilpatrick Stockton (law firm) for twenty years, Co-founder Research Triangle office 1985, leave of absence to serve as Pres. and COO Nat. Hockey League Carolina Hurricanes and their parent co., Gale Force Holdings 2000–02; fmr mem. Bd N Carolina Citizens for Business and Industry, Wake Leadership Acad., N Carolina Character Educ. Foundation; fmr regional Chair. American Red Cross, American Diabetes Asscn, Boy Scouts of America annual campaigns; fmr Chair. Food Bank of N Carolina, Communities in Schools of Wake Co., Eastern N Carolina Chamber of Commerce; mem. Republican Nat. Cttee for N Carolina 2003–05; Regional Chair. and State Finance Vice-Chair. for Bush-Cheney '04 campaign; Pres. Bush's Emissary to the Philippines for Inauguration of Pres. Gloria Macapagal-Arroyo 2004; Amb. to Denmark 2005–; chosen as Business Leader of the Year by Business Leader Magazine, John Ross Leadership Award, Greater Raleigh Convention and Visitors Bureau, National Outstanding Community Service Award, American Diabetes Asscn 2003.

Address: Embassy of the USA, Dag Hammarskjölds Allé 24, 2100 Copenhagen Ø, Denmark (office). *Telephone:* 33-41-71-00 (office). *Fax:* 35-43-02-23 (office). *E-mail:* usembassycopenhagen@state.gov (office). *Website:* www.usembassy.dk (office).

CALDERA CARDINAL, Norman José, DPhil; Nicaraguan politician, economist and consultant; b. 21 Oct. 1946, Managua; m. Nora Maria Mayorga Arg Üello; one s. two d. *Education:* Wentworth Mil. Acad., Lexington, Missouri, Univ. of Texas at Austin, Columbia Univ., New York, USA. *Career:* fmr Marketing Supervisor, then Product Man. Kimberley Clark Co.; Finance Gen. Empresas Universales SA 1972, Exports Man. 1975, Gen. Man. 1976; consultant to Agricultural Devt of Latin America (ADELA) Investment Co. 1979, to OAS 1979, to UNCTAD/GATT 1980–96, to GUATEXPRO 1980–84 (apptd Chief Adviser 1984); Adjunct Sec.-Gen. SIECA and COMIECO (Cabinet of Integration and Commerce of Cen. America) 1992–95; consultant to Inter-American Devt Bank 1995–96, UNCTAD 1996; Econ. Adviser to Pres. of Nicaragua 1996–97; Exec. Sec. Cttee to Reform the Public Admin (CERAP) 1997; Minister of Trade, Industry and Commerce 1999–2001, of Foreign Affairs 2002–06. *Address:* c/o Ministry of Foreign Affairs, Del Cine González al Sur sobre Avda Bolivar, Managua, Nicaragua (office).

CALDERÓN HINOJOSA, Felipe, MEcon, MPA; Mexican lawyer, politician and head of state; *President;* b. 18 Aug. 1962, Morelia, Michoacan; m. Margarita Zavala; two s. one d. *Education:* Escuela Libre de Derecho, Mexico City, Instituto Tecnológico Autónomo de México (ITAM), Kennedy School of Govt, Harvard Univ., USA. *Career:* Pres. Partido Acción Nacional (PAN) youth group 1986, Sec.-Gen. 1993, Nat. Pres. 1996–99, Leader Parl. Group 2000–03; Rep. to Mexico City Legis. Ass. 1988; mem. Cámara Federal de Diputados Mexico (Fed. Chamber of Deputies) 1991–94, 2000–03; Dir Banobras 2001–03; Sec. of Energy 2003–04 (resgnd); Pres. of Mexico 2006–; unsuccessful cand. for Gov. of Michoacan 1995; named as a Global Leader of Tomorrow, World Econ. Forum 1997. *Publication:* El Hijo Desobediente 2006. *Address:* Office of the President, Los Pinos, Col. San Miguel Chapultepec, 11850 México, DF, Mexico (office). *Telephone:* (55) 5091-1100 (office). *Fax:* (55) 5277-2376 (office). *E-mail:* felipe.calderon@presidencia.gob.mx (office). *Website:* www.presidencia.gob.mx (office).

CALDERÓN SOL, Armando; Salvadorean fmr head of state; b. 24 June 1948, San Salvador; m. Elisabeth Aguirre; three c. *Education:* Univ. of El Salvador. *Career:* f. Alianza Republicana Nacionalista (ARENA) 1981, elected leader 1988; deputy 1985–88; Mayor of San Salvador 1988–94; Pres. of El Salvador 1994–99. *Address:* c/o Ministry for the Presidency, Avda Cuba, Calle Darió González 806, Barrio San Jacinto, San Salvador, El Salvador.

CALLAHAN, Robert J., BA, MA; American diplomatist; *Ambassador to Nicaragua;* b. Va. *Education:* Loyola Univ., DePaul Univ. *Career:* career mem. Sr Foreign Service, served as Public Affairs Officer in Rome, Dir of Public Diplomacy, Office of Dir of Nat. Intelligence, joined School of Media and Public Affairs as its first Public Diplomacy Fellow 2005, Diplomatic Fellow, George Washington Univ. –2008, Amb. to Nicaragua 2008–. *Address:* US Embassy, Km 5½, Carretera Sur, Apdo 327, Managua, Nicaragua (office). *Telephone:* (2) 252-7100 (office). *Fax:* (2) 252-7304 (office). *E-mail:* consularmanagua@state.gov (office). *Website:* nicaragua.usembassy.gov (office).

CALMON DE SÁ, Angelo (see Sá, Angelo Calmon de).

CALMY-REY, Micheline; Swiss politician; *Minister of Foreign Affairs;* b. 8 July 1945, Sion, Valais canton; m. André Calmy; two c. *Education:* Ecole de commerce, St Maurice, Valais, Grad. Inst. of Int. Studies, Geneva. *Career:* ran family books business 1977–97; joined Social Democratic Party 1979, Pres. 1986–90; elected Deputy Geneva Grand Council 1981–97, fmr Pres. Finance Comm., fmr Pres. Grand Council; elected to Geneva Conseil d'Etat (Head Dept of Finances) 1997–, Vice-Pres. 2000–01, Pres. 2001–02; elected to Fed. Council 2002–; Minister of Foreign Affairs 2002–; Vice-Pres. of the Swiss Confed. 2006, Pres. 2007; mem. Bd of Dirs Caisse d'épargne, Geneva 1986–93, Geneva Int. Airport 1994–97; Vice-Pres., later Pres. Caisse de la pension des employées de la fonction publique 1998–2002; mem. Bd of Dirs Fonds d'équipement communal 1998–2002, Banque Nat. Suisse 2002–. *Address:* Federal Department of Foreign Affairs, Bundeshaus West, 3003 Bern, Switzerland (office). *Telephone:* (31) 3222111 (office). *Fax:* (31) 334001 (office). *E-mail:* micheline.calmy-rey@etat.ge.ch (office). *Website:* www.eda.admin.ch (office); www.calmy-rey.net (office).

CAMACHO-OMISTE, Edgar; Bolivian diplomatist and lawyer; m. Georgette Canedo de Camacho; three c. *Education:* Univ. de Cochabamba. *Career:* career in Bolivian Foreign Service, previous assignments include Amb. to India, Perm. Rep. to UN, New York, Rep. to Corpn Andina de Fomento (CAF), Amb. to ALALC; fmr Minister of Foreign Affairs; Amb. to Brazil 2004; Vice-Pres. Gen. Ass. of UN 1995; decorations from Argentina, Brazil, Peru, Venezuela. *Publications:* Bolivia: Convenio y declaraciones internacionales 1969, Bolivia y la integración andina (third edn) 1987, Política Exterior Independiente 1990. *Address:* Calle 1, No. 77, Obrajes, La Paz, Bolivia (home). *Telephone:* (61) 248-3625 (home). *E-mail:* drecamacho@hotmail.com (home).

CAMARA, Kabèlè Abdoul; Guinean politician and lawyer. *Career:* fmr lawyer, Court of Appeal, Conakry; Overseer of Senegal elections for Parl. Ass. of Francophone Countries 2000; Pres. Bar Asscn of Guinea 2000–06; Minister of Foreign Affairs, Int. Co-operation, African Integration and Guineans Abroad 2007–08. *Address:* c/o Ministry of Foreign Affairs, face au Port, ex-Primature, BP 2519, Conakry, Guinea (office).

CAMARA, Malam; Guinea-Bissau diplomatist. *Career:* currently Amb. to Guinea. *Address:* Embassy of Guinea-Bissau, Quartier Bellevue, Commune de Dixinn, BP 298, Conakry, Guinea (office).

CAMERON, Peter Duncanson, LLB, PhD; British academic; *Professor of International Energy Law and Policy, University of Dundee;* b. 21 June 1952, Glasgow; m. Qiumin Li 2004; one s. *Education:* Bishop Vesey Grammar School, High School of Stirling and Univ. of Edinburgh. *Career:* Lecturer in Law, Univ. of Dundee 1977–86; Visiting Research Assoc., Oxford Univ. Centre for Socio-Legal Studies 1980, Visiting Scholar, Stanford Law School 1985; Adviser, UN Centre on Transnational Corpns 1985–86; Dir Int. Inst. of Energy Law, Univ. of Leiden 1986–97; Prof. of Int. Energy Law and Policy, Univ. of Dundee 1997–; Chair. Academic Advisory Group and mem. Council, Int. Bar Asscn Section on Energy and Natural Resources Law 1996–2001; Jean Monnet Fellow, European Univ. Inst., Florence, Italy 2001–02, Prof. 2002–05; Adviser UN ESCAP 1988–89; Consultant, World Bank 1990–; Visiting Prof., Univ. Autónoma de Madrid 1997–2000; mem. Editorial Bd Oil and Gas Law and Taxation Review 1989–97; Assoc. Ed. Journal of Energy and Natural Resources Law 1990–97, Jt Ed. 1997–2002; Fellow, Energy Delta Inst., Netherlands 2006–; Research Awards from Asscn of Int. Petroleum Negotiators (AIPN) 1996, 2005. *Publications:* Property Rights and Sovereign Rights: The Case of North Sea Oil 1983, Petroleum Licensing 1984, The Oil Supplies Industry: A Comparative Study of Legislative Restrictions and Their Impact 1986, Nuclear Energy Law After Chernobyl (ed.) 1988, The Regulation of Gas in Europe 1995, Gas Regulation in Western and Central Europe 1998, Kyoto: From Principles to Practice (ed.) 2001, Competition in Energy Markets 2002, Legal Aspects of EU Energy Regulation (ed.) 2005. *Address:* Centre for Energy, Petroleum and Mineral Law and Policy, University of Dundee, Park Place, Dundee, DD1 4HN (office); 23 Ainslie Place, Edinburgh, EH3 6AJ, Scotland (home). *Telephone:* (1382) 344388 (office); (131) 226-6536 (home). *Fax:* (1382) 322578 (office); (131) 225-7793 (home). *E-mail:* p.d.cameron@dundee.ac.uk (office); peterdcameron@btinternet.com (home). *Website:* www.cepmlp.org (office).

CAMILIÓN, Oscar Héctor, PhD; Argentine politician and international official; b. 6 Jan. 1930, Buenos Aires; m. Susana María Lascano 1956; two s. two d. *Education:* Colegio San Salvador, Univ. Nacional de Buenos Aires. *Career:* Asst, then Head of Research, Inst. of Constitutional Law, Univ. Nacional de Buenos Aires, Sec.-Gen. 1955, Prof. of Constitutional Law, concurrently at Univ. Católica de La Plata 1957; Prof. of Int. Law, Argentine Inst. of Hispanic Culture; Prof. of Int. Politics, Argentine Nat. Coll. of Defence; entered Ministry of Foreign Affairs 1958, held posts of Minister, Chief of Cabinet, Dir of Personnel, Minister-Counsellor, Argentine Embassy, Brazil 1959–61, Under-Sec. 1961–62; mem. dels. to UN Gen. Assembly, Confs of OAS and other regional orgs, to Conf. of Guaranteeing Countries of Peru-Ecuador Peace Protocol 1960, 1981; Chief Ed. Clarin newspaper, Buenos Aires 1965–72; Amb. to Brazil 1976–81; Minister of Foreign Affairs and Worship March–Dec. 1981, of Defence 1993–96; f. Argentine Council of Int. Relations; mem. Interamerican Dialogue, Atlantic Confs.; decorations from Brazil, Peru, Bolivia, Venezuela, Colombia, Honduras, El Salvador. *Publications:* several papers on historical, political and diplomatic subjects. *Address:* Montevideo 1597-4°, Buenos Aires 42-9557, Argentina.

CAMILLERI, Victor; Maltese diplomatist; *Permanent Representative, United Nations, Geneva;* b. 8 Oct. 1942, St Venera; m. Elizabeth B. Heaney 1967; two s. *Education:* Lyceum, Malta, Univ. of Birmingham, UK, Columbia Univ., USA. *Career:* fmr teacher, Educ. Dept; joined External

Affairs Service, Ministry of Commonwealth and Foreign Affairs 1968; First Sec., Perm. Mission to UN, New York 1974–81; Perm. Rep. to UNIDO and UNESCO 1981–84; apptd Head Multilateral Section, Ministry of Foreign Affairs, Valletta 1984, Acting Sec. 1985–87; Amb. and Head Malta's del. to Stockholm Conf., CSCE on Confidence and Security Building Measures 1984–85; Deputy High Commr in London 1987–90, High Commr (also accred to Sweden) 1991; Chef de Cabinet, Office of Pres. of 45th Session of UN Gen. Ass. 1990; Perm. Rep. to UN, New York 1991–93, 2003–07, to UN, Geneva 2007–; Amb. to Belgium 1997.
Address: Permanent Mission of Malta to the UN, Parc du Château-Banquet 26, 1202 Geneva, Switzerland (office). *Telephone:* 229010580 (office). *Fax:* 227381120 (home). *E-mail:* malta-un.geneva@gov.mt (office).

CAMPBELL, Francis Martin-Xavier, BA, MA; British diplomatist; *Ambassador to Vatican City (Holy See);* b. 20 April 1970, Newry, NI. *Education:* Queen's Univ., Belfast, Catholic Univ. of Leuven, Belgium, Univ. of Pennsylvania, USA. *Career:* joined FCO 1997, EC Del. to New York during the British Presidency of EU (on secondment to EC) 1997–98, European Enlargement Unit, FCO 1998–99, on secondment to No. 10 Downing Street (Policy Adviser to the Prime Minister) 1999–2001, (Pvt. Sec. to the Prime Minister) 2001–03, First Sec. (External Affairs), Embassy in Rome 2003–05, on sabbatical (Sr Policy Dir Amnesty International) 2005, Amb. to Vatican City (Holy See) 2005–; Thouron Fellow, Univ. of Pennsylvania, USA 1996.
Address: British Embassy to the Holy See, Via XX Settembre 80A, 00187 Rome, Italy (office). *Telephone:* (06) 4220-4000 (office). *Fax:* (06) 4220-4205 (office). *E-mail:* holysee@fco.gov.uk (office). *Website:* www .britishembassy.gov.uk/vatican (office).

CAMPBELL, John, BA, MA, PhD; American diplomatist; b. 1944, Washington, DC. *Education:* Univs of Virginia and Wisconsin. *Career:* taught British and French history at Mary Baldwin Coll., Staunton, Va 1970–75; career mem. Foreign Service since 1975, overseas postings have included Lyon, Paris, Geneva, Political Counsellor, Lagos, Nigeria 1988–90, Pretoria/Cape Town 1993–96, assignments at State Dept have included Dean of School of Language Studies, Foreign Service Inst., Deputy Exec. Sec., Dir UN Political Affairs, Int. Orgs, Deputy Asst Sec., Bureau of Human Resources –2004, Amb. to Nigeria 2004–07; State Dept Sr Fellow, Woodrow Wilson School, Princeton Univ. 1990–91.
Address: US Department of State, 2201 C Street NW, Washington, DC 20520, USA (office). *Telephone:* (202) 647-4000 (office). *Fax:* (202) 647-6738 (office). *Website:* www.state.gov (office).

CAMPBELL, John, MA; Irish diplomatist; b. 23 June 1936, Dublin; m. Nicole Lafon 1964; two s. *Education:* Trinity Coll. Dublin, Yale Univ. *Career:* Amb. to People's Repub. of China 1980–83, to FRG 1983–86, to EC 1986–91, to France 1991–95, Perm. Rep. to UN, New York 1995–98, apptd Amb. to Portugal (also accred to Brazil and Morocco) 1999.
Address: c/o Department of Foreign Affairs, 80 St Stephen's Green, Dublin 2, Ireland (office).

CAMPBELL, Kurt, BA, PhD; American defence analyst; *CEO, Center for a New American Security;* m. Lael Brainard; one d. *Education:* Univ. of Calif., San Diego, Univ. of Oxford, UK, Harvard Univ. *Career:* fmr reserve officer, US Navy; Assoc. Prof. of Public Policy and Int. Relations, John F. Kennedy School of Govt, Harvard Univ. 1988–93, fmr Asst Dir, Center for Science and Int. Affairs; White House Fellow, Dept of the Treasury 1992–93; fmr Deputy Special Counsellor to the Pres. for NAFTA; Dir Nat. Security Staff 1994; Deputy Asst Sec. of Defense 1995–2000; joined Center for Strategic and Int. Studies (CSIS) 2000, Sr Vice-Pres., Dir Int. Security Program, Henry A. Kissinger Chair in Nat. Security Policy 2000–07, mem. Advisory Bd 2007–; Co-founder and CEO Center for a New American Security 2007–; Dir Aspen Strategy Group; Chair. Editorial Bd Washington Quarterly; Founder and Prin. StratAsia (advisory firm); mem Bd of Dirs Aegis Capital, Woods Hole Oceanographic Inst., US-Australian Leadership Dialogue, Reves Center at Coll. of William and Mary, STS Techs, Civitas, 9/11 Pentagon Memorial Fund, New Media Strategies; fmr consultant ABC News; contrib. to New York Times; on-air essayist, All Things Considered, Nat. Public Radio; mem. Int. Inst. for Strategic Studies (IISS), Council on Foreign Relations; Distinguished Public Service Medal, Medal for Outstanding Public Service, Dept of State Honor Award, Joint Service Commendation Medal, Repub. of Korea Nat. Security Medal.
Publications: Hard Power (co-author), To Prevail: An American Strategy for the Campaign against Terrorism (prin. author) 2001, The Power of Balance 2003, The Nuclear Tipping Point (co-ed.) 2004; numerous contribs to policy journals and newspapers.
Address: Center for a New American Security, 1301 Pennsylvania Avenue, NW, Suite 403, Washington, DC 20004, USA (office). *Telephone:* (202)

457-9400 (office). *Fax:* (202) 457-9401 (office). *E-mail:* info@cnas.org (office). *Website:* www.cnas.org (office).

CÁMPORA, Mario, PhD; Argentine diplomatist; b. 3 Aug. 1930, Mendoza; m. Magdalena Díaz Gavier 1972; one s. two d. *Education:* Nat. Univ. of Rosario. *Career:* joined Foreign Service 1955; served Geneva, Washington, DC, The Hague, New Delhi; active in politics as mem. Justicialist Party 1971–73; resgnd from diplomatic service 1975; following 1976 coup was active in opposition seeking restoration of civil liberties, law and order 1976–83; Amb. Argentine Special Mission for Disarmament, Geneva 1985; Asst to presidential cand., Dr Carlos Menem 1988; Sec. of State, Ministry of Foreign Affairs 1989; Amb. to UK 1990–94, to Belgium (also accred to Luxembourg) 1996–99.
Address: c/o Ministry of Foreign Affairs, International Trade and Worship, Esmeralda 1212, 1007 Buenos Aires, Argentina (office).

CAMPORINI, Gen. Vincenzo, FRAeS; Italian military officer; *Chief of Defence General Staff;* b. 1946. *Education:* Air Force Acad., NATO Defence Coll., ITAF Air War Coll. *Career:* Staff Officer Personnel Div., Air Staff 1982–83, Aide-de Camp to Chief of Staff 1983–85; Commdr Air Force Flight Test Centre and Rep. to Aerospace Application Study Cttee, Advisory Group for Aerospace Research and Devt, NATO 1988; Head of Plans, Operations and Training Div., Air Force Staff 1993–96; Aviation Insp., The Navy 1996–97; Dir Inspectorate for Flight Safety 1997–98; Head of Mil. Policy and Planning Div., Defence Gen. Staff 1998–2001; Deputy Chief of Defence, Gen. Staff 2001–04; Pres. Italian Centre for High Defence Studies 2004–06; Chief of Staff of Air Force 2006–08; Chief of Defence Gen. Staff 2008–; Grand Kt Cross, Order of Merit, Commdr, Ordre Nat. du Mérite (France); Gold Medal for Flying Merit, Command Gold Medal, Gold Cross for Mil. Service, Italian Defence Gen. Staff Medal of Honour, Santos Dumont Medal.
Address: Ministry of Defence, Palazzo Baracchini, Via XX Settembre 8, 00187 Rome, Italy (office). *Telephone:* (06) 46911 (office). *E-mail:* pi@smd .difesa.it (office). *Website:* www.difesa.it (office).

CAMPOS E CUNHA, Luis; Portuguese economist and government official; b. 1954; m.; three c. *Education:* Univ. Católica Portuguesa, Columbia Univ., USA. *Career:* Vice-Gov. Banco de Portugal 1996–2002; Dean, School of Econs, New Univ. of Lisbon 2002–04; Minister of Finance and Public Admin, Minister of State March–July 2005; mem. Int. Relations Cttee, European Cen. Bank, Frankfurt 1998–2002; mem. Econ. and Finance Cttee, Brussels 1998–2001; mem. Bd of Dirs (non-exec.) Serralves Foundation 2006–.
Address: c/o Board of Directors, Fundação Serralves, Rua Dom João de Castro, 210, 4150–500 Oporto, Portugal.

CANAVAN, Katherine H., BA; American diplomatist; *Ambassador to Botswana;* b. Southern Calif.; m. Lt-Gen. (retd) Michael A. Canavan. *Education:* Univ. of Calif., Santa Cruz and Nat. War Coll. *Career:* Peace Corps volunteer in Zaïre (now Democratic Repub. of the Congo) for three years; career mem. Sr Foreign Service, entered Foreign Service in 1976, served for three years in Bureau of African Affairs as Regional Affairs Officer, staff asst to Asst Sec., Desk Officer and Press Officer, overseas assignments have included Kingston, Jamaica and Tijuana, Mexico, Deputy Chief of Mission, Windhoek 1993–96, Man. Dir Overseas Citizen Services, Bureau of Consular Affairs 1996–98, Amb. to Lesotho 1998–2001, Dir Foreign Service Inst., Washington, DC 2001–05, Amb. to Botswana and Sec. of State's Special Rep. to SADC 2005–; numerous awards, including Sr Performance Pay, Superior Honor Awards and Meritorious Honor Award, Presidential Rank Award 2003.
Address: Embassy of the USA, Embassy Enclave, (off Khama Crescent), PO Box 90, Gaborone, Botswana (office). *Telephone:* 3953982 (office). *Fax:* 3956947 (office). *E-mail:* ircgaborone@state.gov (office). *Website:* gaborone.usembassy.gov (office).

CANETE, Alfredo; Paraguayan diplomatist; *Director of Diplomatic Academy, Ministry of Foreign Affairs;* b. 14 March 1942, Asunción; m.; one s. *Career:* Sec. in Paraguayan Mission to UN 1961–62, Perm. Rep. to UN 1983–91; Deputy Dir Econ. Dept, Ministry of Foreign Affairs, then Dir Dept of Foreign Trade; Alt. Rep. to Latin-American Trade Asscn 1973–78; Consul-Gen. and Chargé d'Affaires in UK 1978; Minister in Embassy, USA 1980–81; Amb. to Belgium, Netherlands and Luxembourg 1981–83, to Belgium 1992–96; Head of Mission to EEC (now EU) 1982–83, 1992–96; Exec. Dir Paraguayan Centre for Int. Studies 1997–; Dir Diplomatic Acad., Ministry of Foreign Affairs 1999–; Kt's Cross, Order of Civil Merit (Spain), Great Cross, Cóndor de Los Andes (Bolivia).
Address: c/o Ministry of Foreign Affairs, Juan E. O'Leary y Presidente Franco, Asunción, Paraguay.

CANGELOSI, Rocco Antonio; Italian diplomatist; *Permanent Representative, European Union;* b. 8 Oct. 1943, Palermo. *Education:* Univ. of Rome, European Coll. of Bruges, Univ. of Bologna. *Career:* Deputy Consul, Bern, Switzerland 1970; First Sec., Mogadishu, Somalia 1973–76; Counsellor, Perm. Mission to EEC 1976–78; Directorate-Gen., Econ. Affairs, EU Dept, Ministry of Foreign Affairs 1978–80; Gen. Consul, Basel, Switzerland 1981–84; Head EEC Affairs, Directorate-Gen., Econ. Affairs, EU Dept, Ministry of Foreign Affairs 1984–87; Diplomatic Adviser, Office of the Prime Minister 1987–89; Counsellor, Perm. Mission to EU 1989–92, Deputy Perm. Rep. 1992–94; Coordinator, EU Affairs, Directorate-Gen., Econ. Affairs, EU Dept, Ministry of Foreign Affairs 1994–96; Amb. to Tunisia 1996–98; Gen. Coordinator, European Integration, Ministry of Foreign Affairs 1998–2000, Dir-Gen. 2000–; Perm. Rep. to EU 2004–; Cavaliere Ufficiale dell'Ordine al Merito della Repubblica Italiana 1982, Commendatore dell'Ordine al Merito della Repubblica Italiana 1994, Grand Officier, Tunisia 1998. *Publications:* Dal Progetto di Trattato Spinelli all'Atto Unico Europeo 1987, Dalle Comunita' all'Unione 1996, Verso la Costituzione Europea: da Amsterdam a Laeken 2002. *Address:* Permanent Mission of Italy to the EU, 9–11 rue de Marteau, 1000 Brussels, Belgium (office). *Telephone:* (2) 220-04-11 (office). *Fax:* (2) 219-34-49 (office). *E-mail:* rpue@rpue.it (office). *Website:* www.ataliaue.it (office).

CANNABRAVA, Iván Oliveira; Brazilian diplomatist; *Ambassador to Mexico;* b. 1941. *Career:* joined Ministry of Foreign Affairs 1965, Asst to Chief, Americas Dept 1974, S America Div. 1975, Adviser to Chief, Americas Dept 1976, Head Cen. America Div. 1978, Asst Sec.-Gen. for Political Affairs 1995, fmr Under-Sec.-Gen. for Political Affairs; overseas postings include Second Sec., Embassy in Bonn 1967, Embassy n Assunção 1970, Counsellor, Embassy in Washington, DC 1979, Minister-Counsellor, Embassy in Tokyo 1983; Amb. to Angola 1989–91, to Israel 1991, to Japan 2001, to Mexico 2008–; del. to 13th Conf. of Non-Aligned Movt, Kuala Lumpur 2003; include: Official, Ordem Nacional do Mérito (Paraguay) 1976, Ordem do Rio Branco 1989, Ordem do Mérito Militar 1991, Ordem Francisco de Miranda (Venezuela) 1995, Grand Croix, Ordre national de la Légion d'honneur (France) 1997, Grande Oficial, Aeronáutica 2001. *Address:* 130 Calle Lope de Armendáriz, Lomas Virreyes, Delegación Miguel Hidalgo, México, DF 11000, Mexico (office). *Telephone:* (55) 5201-4531 (office). *Fax:* (55) 5520-4929 (office). *E-mail:* embrasil@brasil.org.mx (office). *Website:* www.brasil.org.mx (office).

CANNING, Mark; British diplomatist; *Ambassador to Myanmar;* b. 15 Dec. 1954; m. Cecilia Canning; one d. *Career:* Migration and Visa Dept, FCO 1974–76, Registry/Communications, Freetown 1976–78, Middle Eastern Dept, FCO 1978, Consular Dept 1981–82, Third Sec. (Chancery and Information), Georgetown 1982–85, Man. Review Staff, FCO 1985–86, Vice-Consul (Commercial), Chicago 1986–88, Counter-Terrorism Dept, FCO 1988–92, W Africa Dept 1992-93, First Sec. (Commercial), Jakarta 1993–97, Head of Personnel Div. 1 (Postings Div.), FCO 1997–2001, Deputy High Commr, Kuala Lumpur 2001–06, Amb. to Myanmar 2006–. *Address:* British Embassy, 80 Strand Road (Box No. 638), Kyauktada Township, Yangon, Myanmar (office). *Telephone:* (1) 370863 (office). *Fax:* (1) 370866 (office). *E-mail:* Consular.Rangoon@fco.gov.uk (office).

CANNON, Nicholas, OBE; British diplomatist; *Ambassador to Rwanda;* m. Alice Cannon; two s. *Career:* Desk Officer, Econ. Relations Dept, FCO 1988–88, Desk Officer, Hong Kong Dept 1989–89, Third, later Second Sec., Paris 1990–92, Desk Officer, EC Dept (External), FCO 1992–93, Turkish language training 1993–94, Second Sec., Nicosia 1994–97, Head of Gibraltar Section, Southern European Dept, FCO 1997–2000, First Sec. and Head of Political Section, Islamabad 2000–02, Asst Pvt. Sec., Prime Minister's Office 2003–04, Iraq Directorate, FCO 2004, Deputy Head, Africa Dept (Southern) 2004–07, Amb. to Rwanda 2008–. *Address:* British Embassy, Parcelle No 1131, Boulevard de l'Umuganda, Kacyiru-Sud, BP 576, Kigali, Rwanda (office). *Telephone:* 584098 (office). *Fax:* 582044 (office). *E-mail:* embassy.kigali@fco.gov.uk (office). *Website:* www.britishembassykigali.org.rw (office).

CANTOR, Anthony John James; British diplomatist (retd); b. 1 Feb. 1946; m. Patricia Cantor; one s. two d. *Career:* joined Diplomatic Service 1965, Desk Officer, Finance Dept 1966–68, Third Sec., Rangoon, Burma 1968–71, Third Sec., later Second Sec. (Commercial), Tokyo, Japan 1972–76, Second Sec. (Consular), Accra, Ghana 1977–80, Desk Officer, Aid Policy Dept, FCO 1980–82, Desk Officer, West Indian Atlantic Dept 1982–83, Consul (Commercial), Osaka, Japan 1983–89, Deputy Head of Mission, Hanoi, Viet Nam 1990–92, on loan to Dept of Trade and Industry 1992–94, First Sec. (Commercial), Tokyo 1994–95, Deputy Consul Gen., Osaka 1995–98, Desk Officer, EU Dept (Bilateral), FCO 1999–2000, Deputy Commr Gen., Expo 2000, Hanover, Germany 2000, Head of Expo Section, Public Diplomacy Dept, FCO 2000–01; Amb. to Paraguay 2001–05, to Armenia 2006–07; mem. Royal Commonwealth Soc., Britain-Burma Soc., Kobe Club (Japan); Hon. Pres. British Alumni Asscn of Armenia 2006–. *Address:* c/o Foreign and Commonwealth Office, King Charles Street, London, SW1A 2AH, England. *Telephone:* (20) 7008-1500.

CAPELLE, Alfred, MA; Marshall Islands civil servant and diplomatist; *Permanent Representative, United Nations;* b. 20 March 1940; m. Mwejo term; five s. three d. *Education:* Univ. of Hawaii at Manoa. *Career:* Admin. Aide, Global Assocs, Inc., Kwajalein 1964–66; Mayor, Likiep Atoll 1966–68; elementary school teacher 1968–77; Educ. Specialist, Dept of Educ. 1977–79; Continuing Educ. Programme Coordinator, Coll. of Micronesia 1979–82; Chief of Post-Secondary Educ., Ministry of Educ. 1982–83, Language Consultant and Researcher 1996; Dir of Assumption Schools, Assumption Parish, Majuro 1983–86; Resource Protection Officer and CEO, Alele Museum 1986–96; Pres. Coll. of Marshall Islands 1996–2002; Perm. Rep. to UN 2002–. *Address:* Permanent Mission of the Republic of the Marshall Islands to the UN, 800 Second Avenue, 18th Floor, New York, NY 10017, USA (office). *Telephone:* (212) 983-3040 (office). *Fax:* (212) 983-3202 (office). *E-mail:* marshallislands@un.int (office). *Website:* marshallislands.un.int.

CAPITANICH, Jorge Milton; Argentine politician and accountant; b. 28 Nov. 1964, Roque Saenz Peña. *Career:* Head, Under-Secr. of Social Planning, Ministry of Social Devt 1998; Senator for Chaco Dec. 2001–; Acting Minister of Trade 2001; apptd Cabinet Chief of Argentina 2002. *Publications:* Investigación Sobre El Orígen de las Crisis Provinciales, Federalismo Fiscal y Coparticipación, La Sumergida. Chaco, Propuestas para la Integración. *Address:* c/o General Secretariat to the Presidency, Balcarce 50, 1064 Buenos Aires, Argentina.

CAPPE, Mel, MA; Canadian diplomatist and economist; *President and CEO, Institute for Research on Public Policy;* b. 3 Dec. 1948, Toronto; m. Marline (Marni) Cappe (née Pliskin); one s. one d. *Education:* Univs of Toronto and Western Ontario. *Career:* joined Canadian public service as a policy analyst 1975; with Treasury Bd 1975–78, Deputy Sec. 1990–94; with Dept of Finance 1978–82; Deputy Dir Investigation and Research, Dept of Consumer and Corp. Affairs 1982–90; Deputy Asst Sec. Dept of Finance 1990, Deputy Sec. Program Br. 1990; fmr Asst Deputy Minister Competition Policy; fmr Asst Deputy Minister Policy Co-ordination; fmr Asst Deputy Minister Corp. Affairs and Legis. Policy; Deputy Minister of the Environment 1994–96; Deputy Minister of Human Resources Devt 1996–99; Chair. Employment Insurance Comm. 1996–99; Deputy Minister of Labour 1996–99; Clerk of the Privy Council, Sec. to Cabinet and Head of the Public Service 1999–2002; Special Adviser to Prime Minister 2002; High Commr to UK 2002–06; Pres. and CEO Inst. for Research on Public Policy, Montreal 2006–; Hon. PhD (Univ. of Western Ontario); Hon. LLD. *Address:* Institute for Research on Public Policy, 1470 Peel Street, Suite 200, Montreal, PQ H3A 1T1, Canada (office). *Telephone:* (514) 985-2461 (office). *Fax:* (514) 985-2559 (office). *E-mail:* irpp@irpp.org (office). *Website:* www.irpp.org (office).

CAPUÑAY, Juan Carlos, BEcons; Peruvian diplomatist and international organization official; *Executive Director, Asia-Pacific Economic Co-operation (APEC);* b. 1948. *Education:* Nat. Univ. of San Marcos. *Career:* joined Ministry of Foreign Affairs 1972, Third Sec. Embassy in Tokyo 1973–76, Second Sec. 1976, Second Sec. Perm. Mission to UN, New York 1976–79, First Sec. 1979–82, First Sec. Perm. Mission to OAS 1982–83, Counsellor 1983–86, Minister Counsellor and Alt. Rep. 1986–91, Minister, Embassy in Tokyo and Alt. Rep. to Int. Org. for Tropical Woods 1991–94, Minister, Embassy in Beijing 1994–97, Minister, Chargé d'Affaires to Singapore 1997–98, Amb. to Singapore and Brunei 1998–2003, Amb. and Dir-Gen. Asia-Pacific Econ. Co-operation (APEC) Div., also Sr Official of Peru in APEC Under-Secr. for Asia and Pacific Basin Affairs 2003–07, Amb., Deputy Exec. Dir APEC Secr. 2007, Exec. Dir 2008–; official decorations from Japan, Repub. of Korea and Chile. *Address:* APEC, 35 Heng Mui Keng Terrace, Singapore 119616, Singapore (office). *Telephone:* 67756012 (office). *Fax:* 6775603 (office). *E-mail:* info@apec.org (office). *Website:* www.apec.org (office).

CAPUTO, Dante; Argentine politician, diplomatist and academic; b. 25 Nov. 1943, Buenos Aires; m. Anne Morel; three s. *Education:* Salvador Univ. of Buenos Aires, Univ. of Paris, Tufts Univ. and Harvard, Boston. *Career:* Adjunct Prof. of Political Sociology, Salvador Univ., Buenos Aires; Adjunct Prof. of Public Services and State Enterprises, Univ. of Buenos Aires; Dir Center for Social Investigations on State and Admin. 1976; Adjunct Investigator, Nat. Center for Scientific Investigation, France; Minister of Foreign Affairs and of Worship 1983–88; Pres. UN Gen. Ass. 1988–89; fmr Sec. of State for Tech., Science and Useful Innovations; fmr Special Rep. of UN Sec.-Gen. in Haiti.

Address: c/o Ministerio de Relaciones Exteriores y Culto, Reconquista 1088 C.P. 1003, Buenos Aires, Argentina.

CARBONEZ, Luc, LLD; Belgian diplomatist; *Ambassador to the Netherlands;* b. 1946; m. Marie-Claire Carbonez-deJager; four d. *Education:* Univ. of Louvain. *Career:* joined Diplomatic Corps 1978, has served in numerous positions including Attaché, Embassy in Dublin 1979–80, Embassy Sec., Abidjan 1980–84, Consul, Lille 1984–88, Deputy Head of Mission, Vienna 1988–92; Counsellor for Foreign Affairs, Brussels 1992–94, Minister-Counsellor and Perm. Deputy Rep. of Belgium to EU 1994–97, Amb. to Canada 1997–2002; Dir European Security, Ministry of Foreign Affairs 2002–06; Amb. to Netherlands 2006–, also Perm. Rep. to Org. for the Prohibition of Chemical Weapons (OPCW). *Address:* Embassy of Belgium, Alexanderveld 97, 2585 DB The Hague, Netherlands (office). *Telephone:* (70) 3123456 (office). *Fax:* (70) 3645579 (office). *E-mail:* thehague@diplobel.org (office). *Website:* www.diplomatie .be/thehague (office).

CARDENAS CONDE, Victor Hugo, BA; Bolivian politician and academic; *Leader, Tupac Katari Revolutionary Liberation Movement Party;* b. 4 June 1951, Achica Abajo Aymara Indian community, Omasuyos Prov., Dept of La Paz; m. Lidia Katari 1980; one s. two d. *Education:* Ayacucho High School, Universidad Mayor de San Andrés (UMSA). *Career:* univ. lecturer, then Prof. in Educ. Sciences, Linguistics and Languages, Faculty of Humanities and Educ., UMSA State Univ. 1975–92; Chair. First Nat. Congress for Peasant Unity 1979; consultant on educational issues UNESCO and UNICEF 1990, various other orgs 1992; Prof., Latin American Coll. of Social Sciences 1992–93; Nat. Rep. Tupac Katari Revolutionary Liberation Movt party (MRTKL), Exec. Sec. (Nat. Exec. Cttee) 1993, currently Leader; Pres. Nat. Congress 1993–94, Andean Parl. 1993–94, Science and Tech. Nat. Council 1993–94; Vice-Pres. of Bolivia 1993–97; mem. Culture and Educ. Comm., Bolivian Workers Union 1979, Educ. and Culture Comm., House of Reps 1985–86, political forum of Latin American Inst. for Social Research 1992–93, Exec. Council UNESCO 1995–2000; Fray Bartolomé de las Casas Award (Spain) 1994. *Publications:* articles on culture, educ. and history in local and foreign books, journals and newspapers. *Address:* Avda Baptista 939, Casilla 9133, La Paz, Bolivia.

CÁRDENAS SANTAMARIA, Mauricio, BA, MA, PhD; Colombian academic, economist and politician; *Executive Director, Fedesarrollo;* b. 9 July 1962, Bogotá. *Education:* Univ. de los Andes, Univ. of California, Berkeley. *Career:* Assoc. Prof. of Econs, Univ. de los Andes 1981–84, Prof. 1985–87, Adjunct Prof. 1992–; Research Assoc., Centre for Econ. Devt Studies 1983; Researcher, Fedesarrollo (Foundation for Higher Educ. and Devt) 1985–87, Asst Dir 1992–93, Assoc. Researcher 1994–96, Exec. Dir 1996–98, 2003–; intern, Int. Debt and Finance Div., World Bank 1990; Gen. Man. Empresa de Energía de Bogotá 1993; Minister for Econ. Devt 1994; Minister for Transport 1998–99; Dir Nat. Planning Dept 1999–2000; consultant to IDB and IFC 2000–01; Visiting Prof., Centre for Int. Devt, Harvard Univ. 2001; Pres. Titularizadora Colombiana 2001–03; Pres. Latin American and Caribbean Econ. Asscn (LACEA) 2008–09; Order of the Aztec Eagle (Mexico); Lauchlin Currie Scholarship, Nat. Bank of Colombia 1987–89. . *Publications:* Diez Años de Reformas Tributarias en Colombia (co-author) 1986, Movimiento Internacional de Capitales en los Años Noventa: la experiencia colombiana bajo análisis (co-author) 1993, El Crecimiento Económico en América Latina (ed.) 1996, Inflación, Estabilización y Política Cambiaria en América Latina: Lecciones de los años noventa (co-author) 1997, Empleo y Distribución del Ingreso en América Latina: ¿Hemos avanzado? (ed.) 1997, La Tasa de Cambio en Colombia 1997, Corrupción, Crimen y Justicia (co-author) 1998, Pobreza y Desigualdad en América Latina (co-author) 1999, Reflexiones sobre el aporte social y económico del sector cooperativo colombiano (co-author) 2005, La infraestructura de transporte en Colombia (co-author) 2005, Un pacto nacional para Colombia: crecimiento, estabilidad y progreso social (co-author) 2005, Análisis del sistema tributario colombiano y su impacto sobre la competitividad (co-author) 2006, Introducción a la Economía Colombiana 2007; numerous journal articles. *Address:* Fedesarrollo, Calle 78 No. 9–91, Bogotá, Colombia (office). *Telephone:* (1) 312-5300 (office). *Fax:* (1) 212-6073 (office). *E-mail:* mcardenas@fedesarrollo.org.co. *Website:* www.fedesarrollo.org (office); www.cardenasmauricio.com.

CARDOSO, Eliana Anastasia, MA, PhD; Brazilian academic and international finance official; *Visiting Professor of Economics, Getúlio Vargas Foundation, São Paulo;* one s. *Education:* Pontificia Universidade Católica do Rio de Janeiro, Universidade de Brasília and MIT, USA. *Career:* fmr Lead Economist and Sector Man. World Bank and adviser at Research Dept IMF; fmr Sec. for Int. Affairs, Ministry of Finance; taught at Boston Univ. then Fletcher School (William Clayton Prof. 1993); fmr Visiting Assoc.

Prof. of Econs, MIT and Yale Univ.; Visiting Scholar, Brazilian Studies Program, Georgetown Univ., Distinguished Visiting Prof. 2001–2002; Prof. of Econs, Universidade de Sao Paulo and MIT 2002–06; Visiting Prof. of Econs, Getúlio Vargas Foundation, São Paulo 2006–; fmr Pres. New England Council of Latin American Studies; fmr mem. Advisory Bd Journal of Latin American Studies; fmr mem. Editorial Bd Nova Economia and The World Bank Research Observer; currently Dir Advisory Council, Global Devt Network, New Delhi; mem. Int. Advisory Bd Instituto de Empresa, Madrid; Exec. mem. Latin America and Caribbean Econ. Asscn, Int. Econ. Asscn; mem. Council Kellogg Inst.; columnist for Valor Econômico and O Estado de São Paulo; Forbes Prize for the Most Influential Woman Economist in Brazil 2005. *Publications include:* Latin America's Economy: Diversity, Trends and Conflicts (jtly) (Scholarly Publishing Award), Fábulas Econômicas 2006 (Rio Grande do Sul Prize); more than 150 papers on econ. devt, inflation and int. finance. *Address:* School of Economics, Fundação Getulio Vargas, Rua Itapeva, 474, 13° andar, São Paulo, 01332-000, Brazil (office). *Telephone:* (11) 3062-8984 (office). *Fax:* (11) 3854-6543 (office). *E-mail:* eliana.cardoso@fgv.br (office); eliana.anastasia@gmail.com (home). *Website:* www.elianacardoso .com (office).

CARDOSO, Fernando Henrique, DSc; Brazilian sociologist and fmr head of state; b. 18 June 1931, Rio de Janeiro; m. Ruth Corrêa Leite Cardoso (died 2008); three c. *Education:* Univs of São Paulo and Paris, France. *Career:* Prof., Latin American Inst. for Econ. and Social Planning (ILPES/CEPAL), Santiago 1964–67; Prof. of Sociological Theory, Univ. of Paris-Nanterre 1967–68; Prof. of Political Science, Univ. of São Paulo 1968–69; Visiting Prof., Stanford Univ., USA 1972, Inst. for Econ. and Social Devt Univ. of Paris 1977, Univ. of Calif. 1981; Simon Bolivar Prof., Univ. of Cambridge, UK 1976; Assoc. Dir of Studies, Inst. for Higher Studies in Social Sciences, Univ. of Paris 1980–81; Prof., Coll. de France 1981; Prof. at Large, Watson Institute for International Studies, Brown Univ., USA 2003–; Fed. Senator for State of São Paulo 1983–94; fmr Leader, Brazilian Social Democratic Party (PSDB) in Fed. Senate; Govt Leader in Congress 1985–86; Minister of Foreign Affairs 1992–93; Minister of Economy and Finance 1993–94; Pres. of Brazil 1995–2002; Founder, Pres. of Fernando Henrique Cardoso Institute 2004; Co-Pres. Inter-American Dialogue; mem. of consultative Comm. for Institute for Advanced Study, Princeton Univ. and Rockefeller Foundation, New York; Pres. of Fundação Osesp; Foreign Hon. mem. American Acad. of Arts and Sciences;; Grand Cross, Order of Rio Branco; Chevalier, Légion d'honneur; Grand Cross, Order of Merit of Portugal; Dr hc (Rutgers), (Notre Dame, Ill.) 1991, (Santiago) 1993, (Central de Caracas), (Porto and Coimbra), (Sofia, Japan), (Free Univ. of Berlin), (Lumière Lyon 2), (Bologna), (Cambridge), (London); Fulbright Award for International Understanding. *Publications:* (jtly) São Paulo Growth and Poverty 1978, Dependency and Development in Latin America 1979, The New Global Economy in the Information Age 1993, Charting a New Course (co-ed.) 2001, A Arte da Política 2006, Carta a jovem político 2006. *Address:* c/o Watson Institute for International Studies, Brown University, POB 1970, Providence, RI 02912, USA (office). *Website:* www .watsoninstitute.org (office).

CAREW, David Omashola, BSc (Econ); Sierra Leone chartered accountant and politician; *Minister of Finance and Development;* m.; two c. *Education:* Univ. of Sierra Leone. *Career:* joined KPMG accounting and man. consultancy firm as grad. accountant in 1979, seconded to KPMG Nigeria 1979–86, Audit Supervisor in charge of KPMG's clients in banking and financial institutions industry, Kanu, designated Training Man. for three northern states in Nigeria, Asst Man., KPMG, Freetown 1986, acted as Relief Man. during leave of Resident Man. in The Gambia, promoted to Asst Man., then Deputy Man., then Man. and later Sr Man. 1986–88, Pnr, KPMG-Sierra Leone 1989, Pnr, KPMG-Gambia 1991, set up Man. Consulting Services in Sierra Leone and The Gambia, assisted Sr Pnr and was also in charge of forensic work with Govt of Sierra Leone, Man. Pnr for KPMG-Sierra Leone and for delivering KPMG services to clients in The Gambia and Liberia –2007; Minister of Finance and Devt 2007–; Fellow, Inst. of Chartered Accountants (Nigeria); Fellow and Past Pres. Inst. of Chartered Accountants (Sierra Leone). *Address:* Ministry of Finance and Development, Secretariat Bldg, George Street, Freetown, Sierra Leone (office). *Telephone:* (22) 225612 (office). *Fax:* (22) 228472 (office).

CAREY, Merrick, BA; American research institute director; *CEO, Lexington Institute;* m. Melissa Coggeshall; two s. one d. *Education:* Drew Univ. *Career:* Press Sec. for US Congressman Jack Kemp 1982–84; Chief of Staff for Rep. James Courter 1985–87; Dir Intergovernmental Affairs for NJ Gov. Thomas Kean 1989; with US Naval Reserve 1989–96, Petty Officer 1989, Ensign 1990, Lt 1994, Intelligence Watch Officer, USN HQ, Europe

1990–91; Exec. Vice-Pres. Johnson Smick Int. 1990–93; Pres. Alexis de Tocqueville Inst. 1993–98; f. Lexington Inst. 1998, CEO 1998–.
Address: Lexington Institute, 1600 Wilson Boulevard, Suite 900, Arlington, VA 22209, USA (office). *Telephone:* (703) 522-5828 (office). *Fax:* (703) 522-5837 (office). *Website:* www.lexingtoninstitute.org (office).

CARL XVI GUSTAF, HM The King of Sweden (Carl Gustaf Folke Hubertus); b. 30 April 1946; m. Silvia Sommerlath (HM Queen Silvia) 1976; two d., Crown Princess Victoria Ingrid Alice Désirée b. 14 July 1977, Princess Madeleine Thérèse Amelie Josephine b. 10 June 1982; one s., Prince Carl Philip Edmund Bertil b. 13 May 1979. *Education:* studied in Sigtuna and Univs of Uppsala and Stockholm. *Career:* created Duke of Jämtland; became Crown Prince 1950; succeeded to the throne on death of his grandfather, King Gustaf VI Adolf 15 Sept. 1973; Chair. Swedish Branch, World Wide Fund for Nature; Hon. Pres. World Scout Foundation; Dr hc (Swedish Univ. of Agricultural Sciences, Stockholm Inst. of Tech., Åbo Acad., Finland); US Environmental Protection Agency Award.
Address: The Royal Palace, 111 30 Stockholm, Sweden (office). *Telephone:* (8) 402-60-00 (office). *Fax:* (8) 402-60-05 (office). *E-mail:* info@royalcourt .se (office). *Website:* www.royalcourt.se (office).

CARLOT KORMAN, Maxime; Ni-Vanuatu politician; *Minister of Land; Career:* fmr Minister of Foreign Affairs, of Public Service, Planning and Statistics, of Media and Language Services; Prime Minister of Vanuatu 1991–95, Feb.–Sept. 1996; currently Minister of Land; fmr Leader, Union of Moderate Parties; currently Leader Vanuatu Republikan Pati (VRP).
Address: Ministry of Energy, Lands, Mines and Rural Water Supply, PMB 007, Port Vila (office). *Telephone:* 27833 (office). *Fax:* 25165 (office).

CARLSSON, Gunilla; Swedish politician; *Minister for International Development Cooperation;* b. 1963. *Education:* accounting and auditing courses and non-degree courses at Linköping Univ. *Career:* mem. Vadstena Municipal Council 1989; accountant 1984–90, accounting man. 1990–94; co-opted to Bd of Moderate Party, mem. Moderate Party Programme Cttee, Political Admin. at Moderate Party Secr. of Riksdag 1994, Vice-Chair. Moderate Party Youth League 1992–95, mem. Bd of Moderate Party 1999–, Second Vice-Chair. Moderate Party 1999–2003, First Vice-Chair. 2003–; Vice-Chair. Nordic Young Conservative Union 1993–94; Vice-Chair. Int. Young Democratic Union 1994–98; mem. European Parl. (Group of the European People's Party (Christian Democrats) and European Democrats—EPP-ED) 1995–2002, Leader Moderate Party Del., mem. Cttee on Foreign Affairs, Human Rights, Common Security and Defence Policy 1999–2002, mem. Del. to EU-Lithuania Jt Parl. Cttee, Del. to EU-Poland Jt Parl., Substitute mem. Cttee on Industry, External Trade, Research and Energy, Vice-Chair. EPP 2004–06; mem. Parl. (Riksdag) 2002–, mem. War Del. 2002–, mem. Cttee on Educ. 2002–03, Cttee on EU Affairs 2002–04, Cttee on Foreign Affairs 2003–04, Deputy Chair. Cttee on Foreign Affairs 2004–, Deputy mem. Cttee on EU Affairs 2004–, Minister for Int. Devt Cooperation 2006–; Alt. mem. Swedish Del. to Nordic Council 2004–.
Address: Office of the Minister for International Development Cooperation, Ministry of Foreign Affairs, Gustav Adolfs torg 1, 103 39 Stockholm, Sweden (office). *Telephone:* (8) 405-10-00 (office). *Fax:* (8) 723-11-76 (office). *Website:* www.sweden.gov.se/sb/d/2085 (office).

CARLSSON, Staffan; Swedish diplomatist; *Ambassador to UK;* m. Marie Thofte. *Career:* served in Dhaka, Moscow and Washington, DC, fmr Amb. to Hungary, fmr Head of European Security Policy Dept, Ministry for Foreign Affairs, Amb. to UK 2004–.
Address: Embassy of Sweden, 11 Montagu Place, London, W1H 2AL, England (office). *Telephone:* (20) 7917-6400 (office). *Fax:* (20) 7724-4174 (office). *E-mail:* ambassaden.london@foreign.ministry.se (office). *Website:* www.swedenabroad.com/london (office).

CARMENT, David, BA, MA, PhD; Canadian academic; *Professor, Norman Paterson School of International Affairs, Carleton University;* b. 25 July 1959, Hamilton, Ont.; one d. *Education:* McMaster Univ., Int. Univ. of Japan, Niigata, Carleton Univ. *Career:* Researcher, Canadian Int. Devt Agency 1987–89; Assoc. Adviser, McGill Univ. 1989–93, Research Asst 1991–93, Lecturer, 1993; Research Fellow, Inst. For Southeast Asian Studies, Singapore 1993; Post Doctoral Research Fellow, Hoover Inst., Stanford Univ. 1993–94; Dir Centre for Security and Defence Studies, Carleton Univ., Ottawa 2002–04, Assoc. Prof. of Int. Affairs, Norman Paterson School of Int. Affairs 1994–2005, Full Prof. 2005–, Prin. Investigator, CIFP; Lecturer, Harvard Univ. HUDCE 2000–01, Fellow, Belfer Centre for Science and Int. Affairs, J.F. Kennedy School of Govt 2000–01; Fellow, McGill Centre for Developing Area Studies; Guest Lecturer, Inst. for S European Cooperation and Devt, American Univ., Bulgaria 1996; mem. Bd Dirs Forum on Early Warning and Early Response

2001–03; Advisor and Researcher, Dept of Nat. Defence, Criminal Intelligence Service of Canada, CIDA, EU for work on Failed States and Early Warning 2003–; mem. Editorial Advisory Bd Journal of South Asian Development 2005–; mem. Political Science Asscn, Int. Studies Asscn, Int. Political Science Asscn; Marcel Cadieux Fellowship, Fellow Canadian Defence and Foreign Affairs Inst.; Petro-Canada Young Innovator Award; Carleton Univ. Research Achievement Award, SSHRCC Awards, Teaching Achievement Award, grants for work related to Failed and Fragile States, Early Warning and Conflict Prevention. *Publications:* War in the Midst of Peace (co-ed.) 1997, Peace in the Midst of Wars (co-ed.) 1998, Political and Religious Transition in Medieval South India and Sri Lanka 1999, Using Force to Prevent Ethnic Violence (co-author) 2000, The International Politics of Quebec Secession (co-ed.) 2001, Conflict Prevention: From Rhetoric to Reality (co-ed.) 2003, Conflict Prevention: Path to Peace or Grand Illusion? (co-ed.) 2003, Canada Among Nations (co-ed.) 2003, 2004, Peacekeeping Intelligence: New Players, Extended Boundaries (co-ed.) 2005, Who Intervenes? Ethic Conflict and Crises (co-author) 2005, Canadian Foreign Policy and the New 3Ds: Diasporas, Demography and Domestic Politics 2007; numerous journal articles, reviews, book chapters.
Address: Norman Paterson School of International Affairs (NPSIA), Carleton University, 1125 Colonel By Drive, Ottawa, ON K1S 5B6, Canada (office). *Telephone:* (613) 520-2600 (office). *Fax:* (613) 520-2889 (office). *Website:* www.carleton.ca/cifp (office); www.carleton.ca/~dcarment (office).

CARNEIRO LEÃO NETO, Valdemar; Brazilian diplomatist; *Ambassador to Colombia; Career:* Dir-Gen. Econ. Dept, Ministry of Foreign Relations –2003; Amb. to Canada 2004–07, to Colombia 2007–.
Address: Embassy of Brazil, Calle 93, No 14-20, 8°, Bogotá, DC Colombia (office). *Telephone:* (1) 218-0800 (office). *Fax:* (1) 218-8393 (office). *Website:* www.brasil.org.co (office).

ČARNOGURSKÝ, Ján, LLD, DJur; Slovak politician and lawyer; b. 1 Jan. 1944, Bratislava; m. Marta Stachová 1970; two s. two d. *Education:* Charles Univ., Prague 1966–69. *Career:* lawyer, Bratislava 1970–81; mem. of Slovak Lawyers' Cen. Office and Czech Lawyers' Cen. Office; banned from legal profession after defence in a political trial 1981; driver, lawyer for a co. Bratislava 1982–86; unemployed, after expulsion from legal profession, continued giving legal advice to members of the political opposition and religious activists 1987–89; held in custody, released and pardoned, Aug.–Nov. 1989; First Deputy Premier, Govt of Czechoslovakia 1989–90, Deputy Premier June 1990; Chair. Legis. Council Feb.–Aug. 1990; Chair. Christian Democratic Movt 1990–2000; First Deputy Premier, Govt of Slovak Repub. 1990–91, Prime Minister of Slovak Govt 1991–92; mem. State Defence Council 1991–92; Deputy to Slovak Nat. Council (Slovak Parl.) for KDH (Christian Democratic Movt) 1992–98; Deputy Chair. Parl. Ass. of CSCE 1993–95; Minister of Justice 1998–2002; advocate in pvt sector 2002–; Trustee Order of the German Kts 1994–; Slovak Literary Fund Prize (Journalists' Section) 1992. *Publications:* The Bratislava Letters (samizdat), Suffered for the Faith 1987, Seen from Danube 1997.
Address: Kardla Adlera 10, 84102 Bratislava (home); Law Office, Dostojevského rad 1, 81109 Bratislava (office); Karola Adlera 10, 84102 Bratislava, Slovakia. *Telephone:* (2) 5263-6954 (office). *Fax:* (2) 5263-6955 (office). *E-mail:* jancarnogursky@slovanet.sk (home); carnogursky@ba .psg.sk.

CARON, Joseph, BA; Canadian diplomatist; *Ambassador to Japan; Education:* Univ. of Ottawa, US Foreign Language Inst., Yokohama. *Career:* joined Canadian Foreign Service 1972; with Dept of Labour and Immigration, Ottawa 1971–72, Int. Comm. for Control and Supervision, Saigon 1973; Second Sec. in Ankara 1973–75; Deputy Dir, Indochina and SE Asia Div., Dept of External Affairs 1980–82; Sec., Cabinet Cttee for Foreign Affairs and Nat. Defence Privy Council Office 1982–84; Man. for Asia, Tokyo Council of Forest Industries of BC (COFI) 1984–87; Counsellor, Embassy in Tokyo 1987–89, Minister and Head of Chancery 1994–98; Dir Int. Econ. Affairs Div., Finance and Investment, Dept of External Affairs 1989–90, and responsible for Canadian participation in G-8 econ. summits 1990–93; Dir N Asia Relations Div., Dept of Foreign Affairs and Int. Trade 1993–94, Asst Deputy Minister, Asia Pacific and Africa 1998–2001; Sr Official for APEC 1998–2001; Amb. to People's Repub. of China 2001–05, to Japan 2005–; mem. Bd of Dirs Potash Corpn, Sask. 1982.
Address: Embassy of Canada, 7-3-38, Akasaka, Minato-ku, Tokyo 107-8503, Japan (office). *Telephone:* (3) 5412-6200 (office). *Fax:* (3) 5412-6249 (office). *Website:* www.canadanet.or.jp (office).

CARPENTIER, Michel André Georges, LenD, LenSc (Econ); French international organization official and international science consultant; b. 23 Oct. 1930, Billy Montigny, Pas de Calais; m. Annick Puget 1956; four s. *Education:* Ecole des Hautes Etudes Commerciales, Ecole des Sciences

Politiques and Univ. of Paris. *Career:* Commissariat à l'Energie Atomique (CEA) 1958; EURATOM 1959; Head of Dept Industrial, Technological and Scientific Affairs, EC Comm. 1967, Dir-Gen. Environment 1977, Dir-Gen. Energy 1981; Dir-Gen. Task Force for Information Technologies and Telecommunications, EC Comm. 1984; Dir-Gen. Information Technologies and Telecommunications, EC Comm. 1986; Dir-Gen. DG XIII, Telecommunications, Information Markets and Exploitation of Research, EC Comm. 1993–95; Hon. Dir-Gen. and Special Adviser EU Comm. 1996–; industrial adviser 1996–97; Pres. Scientific Cttee Aquitaine Europe Communication 1997; mem. Econ. and Social Cttee, EC Comm., Paris 1995–96; Pres. Centre Informatique Documentaire (CID) 1997–98, Paris, Orientation Cttee, AEC 1998–2004; Vice-Pres. AIACE, Paris; Municipal Councillor for Montcaret 2002–; Hon. mem. IEEE (USA), Royal Swedish Acad. of Eng Science; Chevalier, Légion d'honneur, Ehrenkreuz für Wissenschaft und Forschung (Austria), Commdr, Ordre du Mérite (Luxembourg), Order of the Rising Sun, Japan; Dr hc (Loughborough, Madrid). *Publications:* Telecommunications in Transition (with others) 1992, The French Space Policy 1998.
Address: Domaine de Lespinassat, 24230 Montcaret, France (home). *Telephone:* (5) 53-58-66-05 (home). *Fax:* (5) 53-58-66-05 (home). *E-mail:* m.carpentier@wanadoo.fr.

CARRANZA UGARTE, Luis, DEcon; Peruvian politician; *Minister of Economy and Finance;* b. 1967. *Education:* Pontifical Catholic Univ. of Peru, Lima, Univ. of Minnesota, USA. *Career:* worked as official at IMF for several years 1990s; worked in Dept of Econ. Investigation, Fed. Reserve Bank of Minneapolis 1990s; apptd Deputy Finance Minister and Dir Cen. Bank by Pres. Alejandro Toledo 2004–05 (resgnd); Chief Economist for Latin America and Emerging Markets, Banco Bilbao Vizcaya Argentaria 2005–06; consultant, IDB; Minister of Economy and Finance 2006–.
Address: Ministry of Economy and Finance, Jirón Junín 339, 4°, Circado de Lima, Lima 1, Peru (office). *Telephone:* (1) 4273930 (office). *Fax:* (1) 4282509 (office). *E-mail:* postmaster@mef.gob.pe (office). *Website:* www.mef.gob.pe (office).

CARRARD, François Denis Etienne, LLD; Swiss lawyer and international organization official; b. 19 Jan. 1938, Lausanne. *Education:* Lausanne, John Muir High School, Pasadena, Calif., USA, Univ. of Lausanne. *Career:* with audit co., Lausanne 1962; with attorney's practice, Stockholm, Sweden 1963–64; Attorney, Lausanne 1965–, admitted to bar of Vaud (Swiss bar) 1967, Sr Partner Etude Carrard, Paschoud, Heim et Associés; Dir and Chair. of Bds. of several cos.; Dir-Gen. Int. Olympic Cttee Sept. 1989–2003, currently Sr Adviser in charge of legal affairs; Chair. Montreux Jazz Festival Foundation, Gabriella Giorgi-Cavaglieri Foundation; Pres. Automobile-Club de Suisse; fmr Vice-Pres. Bd of Vintage Brands of Vaud; fmr mem. Swiss Fed. Comm. of Foreign Indemnities; mem. Ordre des Avocats Vaudois, Fédération Suisse des Avocats, Int. Bar Asscn, Asscn Suisse de l'Arbitrage, Union Internationale des Avocats; Commdr Orden del Mérito Civil (Spain) 1992; Officier Ordre de Saint-Charles (Monaco) 1993.
Address: c/o International Olympic Committee, Château de Vidy, 1007 Lausanne, Switzerland (office).

CARRASQUILLA BARRERA, Alberto, MS, PhD; Colombian politician and economist; b. Bogotá. *Education:* Univ. of Los Andes, Univ. of Ill., USA. *Career:* Tech. Man., Banco de la República 1993–97; Prin. Economist, Investigation Div., IDB, Washington, DC 1997–99; Econ. Adviser, Gen. Repub. Controllership 1999–2000; fmr Assoc. Teacher, Univ. of Los Andes, Dean Faculty of Econs 2000–02; Deputy Minister of Finance 2002–03, Minister of Finance 2003–07; fmr Assoc. Investigator, Fedesarrollo.
Address: c/o Ministry of Finance and Public Credit, Carrera 8a, No 6–64, Of. 305, Bogotá, DC, Colombia (office).

CARRICK, Sir Roger John, Kt, KCMG, LVO; British international consultant and fmr diplomatist; *Chairman, Strategy International Ltd;* b. 13 Oct. 1937, Middx; m. Hilary E. Blinman 1962; two s. *Education:* Isleworth Grammar School, Jt Services School for Linguists and School of Slavonic and E European Studies, Univ. of London. *Career:* RN 1956–58; joined HM Diplomatic Service 1956; served in Sofia 1962, FCO 1965, Paris 1967, Singapore 1971, FCO 1973–77; Visiting Fellow, Inst. of Int. Affairs, Univ. of Calif., Berkeley 1977–78; Counsellor, Washington, DC 1978; Head, Overseas Estate Dept FCO 1982; Consul-Gen., Chicago 1985–88; Asst Under-Sec. of State (Econ.), FCO 1988–90; Amb. to Indonesia 1990–94; High Commr to Australia 1994–97; Deputy Chair. Britain-Australia Soc. 1998–99, Chair. 1999–2002, Vice-Pres. 2003–, Pres. West Country Br. 2003–; Dir (non-exec.) cmb technologies 2000–02; Chair. (non-exec.) Charteris Mackie & Baillie Ltd 2001–03; Deputy Chair. The D Group 1999–2007; Dir Strategy International Ltd 2001–07, Chair. 2007–; Trustee

Chevening Estate 1998–2003, Britain-Australia Bicentennial Trust; Churchill Fellow, Westminster Coll., Mo. 1986; Freeman of the City of London 2002. *Publications:* East-West Technology Transfer in Perspective 1978, RolleroundOz: Reflections on a Journey Around Australia 1998.
Address: c/o Britain-Australia Society, West Country Branch, The Clerk's House, Pound Lane, Martock, TA12 6LU, England (office). *Website:* www.britozwest.org.uk (office).

CARRILLO CORLETO, Hugo Roberto; Salvadorean diplomatist; *Ambassador to Mexico; Career:* fmr Vice-Pres. of El Salvador; fmr Amb. to Chile, Amb. to Costa Rica –2005, to Mexico 2005–; fmr Dir Diplomatic Acad. of El Salvador, now Dir ad-honorem.
Address: Embassy of El Salvador, Temístocles 88, Col. Polanco, Delegación Miguel Hidalgo, 11560 Mexico City, DF, Mexico (office). *Telephone:* (55) 5281-5725 (office). *Fax:* (55) 5280-0657 (office). *E-mail:* embesmex@webtelmex.net.mx (office); embesmex@prodigy.net.mx (office).

CARRILLO ZÜRCHER, Federico, LLB; Costa Rican lawyer, banker and fmr government official; *Vice President, Central American Bank for Economic Integration;* b. 29 Sept. 1964, San José; m.; four c. *Education:* Austin Community Coll. and Univ. of Texas, USA, Univ. of Costa Rica. *Career:* Fulbright-Hats Scholarship, Northwestern Univ., Evanston, Ill., USA 1990; worked in investment banks in New York 1992–2000, later Exec. Vice-Pres. Lehman Brothers, Inc. and Salomon Brothers; Man. Costa Rican Stock Exchange 2000–04; Dir Tech. Advisory Cttee on Civil Aviation 2004; Minister of Finance 2004–05; Vice-Pres. Cen. American Bank for Econ. Integration 2005–;.
Address: Central American Bank for Economic Integration, Headquarters Building, Boulevard Suyapa, Tegucigalpa, Honduras (office). *Telephone:* 240-2243 (office). *Fax:* 240-2185/87 (office). *Website:* www.bcie.org (office).

CARRINGTON, Edwin Wilberforce, MSc; Trinidad and Tobago economist and international organization official; *Secretary-General, Caribbean Community and Common Market (CARICOM);* b. 23 June 1938; m.; two s. one d. *Education:* Univ. of the West Indies, McGill Univ., Montreal, Canada. *Career:* Admin. Cadet, Cen. Planning Unit, Prime Minister's Office 1964; Chief of Econs and Statistics, Caribbean Community and Common Market (CARICOM) 1973–76, Dir Trade and Integration Div. 1973–76, Sec.-Gen. CARICOM 1992–; Deputy Sec.-Gen. African, Caribbean and Pacific (ACP) states 1976–85, Sec.-Gen. 1985; High Commr to Guyana 1991; Sec.-Gen. Caribbean Forum ACP states; Duarte Sanchez y Mella, Gran Cruz de Plata (Dominican Repub.) 1993, Trinity Cross (Trinidad and Tobago 2005, Chaconia Medal Gold (Trinidad and Tobago) 1987, Order of Distinction (Belize) 2001, Companion of Honour (Barbados) 2002, Order of Jamaica (Jamaica) 2003, Cacique Crown of Honour (Guyana) 2003, Cacique's Crown of Honour (Guyana) 2004; Dr hc (Univ. of the West Indies) 2005, (Medgar Evers Coll., CUNY) 1995; Pinnacle Award Nat. Coalition of Caribbean Affairs. *Publications:* Industrialization by Invitation: The Case of Trinidad and Tobago 1968, The Solution of Economic Problems through Regional Groupings (jtly), Tourism as a Vehicle for Economic Development 1975.
Address: Caribbean Community and Common Market, Bank of Guyana Building, PO Box 10827, Turkeyen, Greater Georgetown (office); Colgrain House 205 Camp Street, Georgetown, Guyana (home). *Telephone:* (2) 222-0001/75 (office). *Fax:* (2) 222-0171 (office). *E-mail:* osc@caricom.org (office). *Website:* www.caricom.org (office).

CARRIÓN MENA, Francisco, PhD; Ecuadorean diplomatist and academic; b. 8 April 1953, Quito. *Education:* Univ. Cen. del Ecuador, Quito. *Career:* joined Ecuadorian Foreign Service 1974; Counsellor, Embassy in Paris 1982–88; Diplomatic Adviser to Pres. of Repub. 1988–91; Minister, Embassy in London 1991–96; Under-Sec., Ministry of Foreign Affairs 1996–98; Vice-Minister of Foreign Affairs 1998–2000; Amb. to Spain 2000–05; Minister of Foreign Affairs 2005–07; Prof. of Int. Relations and Politics, Univ. Cen. del Ecuador and Diplomatic Acad. of Quito 1988–92; Guest Lecturer, Univ. de Salamanca, Spain 2001, Univ. de Alcalá de Henares 2002; mem. Cttee on Protection of Rights of all Migrant Workers and Mems of their Families, Int. Service for Human Rights 2004–07. *Publications:* articles in scholarly and popular journals.
Address: c/o Ministry of Foreign Affairs, Avda 10 de Agosto y Carrión, Quito, Ecuador (office).

CARSTENS, Augustín, BA, MA, PhD; Mexican economist and government official; *Secretary of Finance and Public Credit;* b. 1958, Mexico City; m. Catherine Mansell. *Education:* Instituto Tecnológico Autónomo de México, Univ. of Chicago, USA. *Career:* Intern, Banco de México 1983; left for studies in USA and rejoined Banco de México 1986, Treas. 1987, Dir-Gen. Econ. Research and Chief of Staff in Gov.'s office 1991–94, Chief Economist and Research Dir 1994–98; Alt. Gov. for Mexico at IDB and World Bank 1998–2000; Deputy Sec. of Finance 2000–03, organized UN

Conf. on Financing for Devt, Monterrey, meetings of Group of 20 2002; Second Deputy Man. Dir IMF 2003–06; Sec. of Finance and Public Credit 2006–. *Publications:* has published articles in collections edited by Fed. Reserve Bank of Boston, Univ. of London, OECD, IMF and World Bank and in journals including Columbia Journal of World Business, American Economic Review, Journal of Asian Economics, Journal of International Finance, Cuadernos Económicos del ICE (Spain) and Gaceta de Economía del ITAM (Mexico).
Address: Secretariat of State for Finance and Public Credit, Palacio Nacional, Primer Patio Mariano, 3°, Of. 3045, Col. Centro, Del. Cuauhtémoc, 06000 Mexico City, DF, Mexico (office). *Telephone:* (55) 9158-2000 (office). *Fax:* (55) 9158-1142 (office). *E-mail:* secretario@hacienda.gob.mx (office). *Website:* www.hacienda.gob.mx (office).

CARTER, Ashton B., BA, PhD; American academic; *Professor of Science and International Affairs, Harvard University; Education:* Yale Univ., Univ. of Oxford, UK. *Career:* early career positions at MIT, US Congressional Office of Tech. Assessment, Rockefeller Univ.; served as Asst Sec. of Defense for Int. Security Policy 1993–96, responsible for nat. security policy towards states of fmr Soviet Union, US nuclear missile defense programs and int. arms control; currently co-Dir. Preventive Defense Project and Prof. of Science and Int. Affairs, Harvard Univ; Sr Partner Global Technology Partners; Chair. Advisory Bd MIT Lincoln Laboratories; Chair. Ed. Bd International Security (journal); mem. Bd of Dirs Mitretek Systems; consultant to US Dept of Defense, Goldman Sachs, Mitre Corp.; mem. Defense Science Bd, Defense Policy Bd, Draper Laboratory Corp., Aspen Strategy Group, Council on Foreign Relations, American Physical Soc., IISS, Nat. Cttee on US-China Relations; Fellow, American Acad. of Arts and Sciences; Ten Outstanding Young Americans 1987, Dept of Defense Distinguished Service Medal (twice), Defense Intelligence Medal. *Publications:* Directed Energy Missile Defense in Space 1984, Ballistic Missile Defense 1984, Managing Nuclear Operations 1987, Soviet Nuclear Fusion: Control of the Nuclear Arsenal in a Disintegrating Soviet Union 1991, Beyond Spinoff: Military and Commercial Technologies in a Changing World 1992, A New Concept of Cooperative Security 1992, Cooperative Denuclearization: From Pledges to Deeds 1993, Preventive Defense (jtly) 1997, Keeping the Edge: Managing Defense for the Future (co-ed.) 2001.
Address: John F. Kennedy School of Government, Harvard University, Littauer 374, 79 John F. Kennedy Street, Cambridge, MA, 02138, USA (office). *Telephone:* (617) 495-1405 (office). *Fax:* (617) 495- 9250 (office). *E-mail:* ashton_carter@harvard.edu (office). *Website:* www.ksg.harvard.edu (office).

CARTER, James (Jimmy) Earl, Jr, BSc; American politician, international political consultant and farmer; *Chairman, Carter Center;* b. 1 Oct. 1924, Plains, GA; m. Eleanor Rosalynn Smith 1946; three s. one d. *Education:* Plains High School, Georgia Southwestern Coll., Georgia Inst. of Tech., US Naval Acad., Annapolis, Md, Union Coll., New York State. *Career:* served in USN 1946–53, attained rank of Lt (submarine service); peanut farmer, warehouseman 1953–77, businesses Carter Farms, Carter Warehouses, Ga; State Senator, Ga 1962–66; Gov. of Georgia 1971–74; Pres. of USA 1977–81; Distinguished Prof., Emory Univ., Atlanta 1982–; leader int. observer teams Panama 1989, Nicaragua 1990, Dominican Repub. 1990, Haiti 1990; host peace negotiations Ethiopia 1989; visit to Democratic People's Repub. of Korea (in pvt. capacity) June 1994; negotiator in Haitian crisis Sept. 1994; visit to Bosnia Dec. 1994; f. Carter Presidential Center 1982; Chair. Bd of Trustees, Carter Center Inc. 1986–, Carter-Menil Human Rights Foundation 1986–, Global 2000 Inc. 1986–, Council of Freely Elected Heads of Govt 1986–, Council of Int. Negotiation Network 1991–; mem. Sumter County, Ga, School Bd 1955–62 (Chair. 1960–62), Americus and Sumter County Hospital Authority 1956–70, Sumter County Library Bd 1961; Pres. Plains Devt Corpn 1963; Georgia Planning Asscn 1968; Dir Ga Crop Improvement Asscn 1957–63 (Pres. 1961); Chair. West Cen. Ga Area Planning and Devt Comm. 1964; State Chair. March of Dimes 1968–70; District Gov. Lions Club 1968–69; Chair. Congressional Campaign Cttee, Democratic Nat. Cttee 1974; Democrat; several hon. degrees; Ansel Adams Conservation Award, Wilderness Society 1982, World Methodist Peace Award 1984, Albert Schweitzer Prize for Humanitarianism 1987, Onassis Foundation Award 1991, Notre Dame Univ. Award 1992, Matsunaga Medal of Peace 1993, J. William Fulbright Prize for Int. Understanding 1994, shared Houphouët Boigny Peace Prize, UNESCO 1995, UNICEF Int. Child Survival Award (jtly with Rosalynn Carter) 1999, Presidential Medal of Freedom 1999, Eisenhower Medallion 2000, Nobel Peace Prize 2002. *Publications:* Why Not the Best? 1975, A Government as Good as Its People 1977, Keeping Faith: Memoirs of a President 1982, The Blood of Abraham: Insights into the Middle East 1985, Everything to Gain: Making the Most of the Rest of Your Life 1987, An Outdoor Journal 1988, Turning Point: A Candidate, a State and a Nation Come of Age 1992, Always a Reckoning (poems) 1995, Sources of Strength

1997, The Virtues of Ageing 1998, An Hour Before Daylight 2001, The Hornet's Nest (novel) 2003, Our Endangered Values 2005, Palestine: Peace Not Apartheid 2006.
Address: The Carter Center, 453 Freedom Parkway, 1 Copenhill Avenue NE, Atlanta, GA 30307, USA (office). *Telephone:* (404) 420-5100 (office). *Fax:* (404) 420-5196 (office). *E-mail:* carterweb@emory.edu (office). *Website:* www.cartercenter.org (office).

CARTER, Peter Leslie; British diplomatist; *Ambassador to Estonia;* one d. *Career:* with Maritime, Aviation and Environment Dept, FCO 1984–85, Second, later First Sec. (Political), New Delhi 1986–89, Head of Indo-China Section, SE Asia Dept, FCO 1989–91, Head of Recruitment, Personnel Policy Dept 1992–94, secondment to Gen. Secr. of EU Council of Ministers, Brussels 1994–98, Head of NE Asia and Pacific Dept, FCO 1998–2001, Deputy Head of Mission and Consul-Gen., Tel-Aviv 2001–05, Consul-Gen. and Dir-Gen. for Trade and Investment, Milan 2005–07, Amb. to Estonia 2007–.
Address: British Embassy, Wismari 6, Tallinn 10136, Estonia (office). *Telephone:* 6674700 (office). *Fax:* 6674756 (office). *E-mail:* information@britishembassy.ee (office). *Website:* www.britishembassy.ee (office).

CARTER, Philip, III, BA, MA; American economist and diplomatist; *Ambassador to Guinea; Education:* Yale Univ., Drew Univ. *Career:* career mem. Sr Foreign Service with rank of Counsellor, Deputy Prin. Officer, Consulate Gen., Winnipeg, and Vice-Consul, Mexico City 1982–86, Desk Officer responsible for bilateral matters concerning Dominican Repub., Haiti, and Eastern Caribbean, Office of Caribbean Affairs, Dept of State 1987–89, Econ. and Commercial Officer, Lilongwe 1989–92, Econ. and Commercial Counsellor, Dhaka 1992–94, int. financial economist, Office of Monetary Affairs, Bureau of Econ. and Business Affairs, Dept of State 1994–97, Deputy Chief of Mission, Antananarivo, later in Libreville 1997, later Deputy Dir Office for East African Affairs, Dept of State, Dir for West African Affairs –2007, Amb. to Guinea 2007–; Superior Honor Award, The Franklin Award, several individual and group Meritorious Honor Awards.
Address: US Embassy, PO Box 603, Transversale No. 2, Centre Administratif de Koloma, Commune de Ratoma, Conakry, Guinea (office). *Telephone:* 30-42-08 (office). *Fax:* 30-42-08-73 (office). *E-mail:* ConsularConakr@state.gov (office). *Website:* conakry.usembassy.gov (office).

CARTWRIGHT, Dame Silvia Rose, DBE, PCNZM; New Zealand judge; b. 7 Nov. 1943; m. Peter John Cartwright 1969. *Education:* Univ. of Otago. *Career:* Partner, Harkness Henry & Co. barristers and solicitors, Hamilton 1971–81; Dist Court and Family Court Judge 1981–89, Chief Dist Court Judge 1989–93; Judge High Court of NZ 1993–2001; Gov.-Gen. of NZ and C-in-C 2001–06; mem. Comm. for the Future 1975–80, Cttee UN Human Rights Convention to eliminate discrimination against women 1992–2000; Hon. LLD (Otago) 1993, (Waikato) 1994, (Canterbury) 2002.
Address: c/o Government House, Wellington, New Zealand (office).

CARUANA, Peter R., QC; Gibraltarian politician and lawyer; *Chief Minister;* b. 15 Oct. 1956; m.; six c. *Education:* Christian Brothers School, Grace Dieu Manor, Leicester, Ratcliffe Coll. Leicester, Queen Mary Coll., Univ. of London, Council of Legal Educ., London. *Career:* joined law firm Triay & Triay, Gibraltar 1979, partner (specializing in commercial and shipping law) 1990–95; joined Gibraltar Social Democrats 1990, Leader Feb. 1991–; elected in Gibraltar's first-ever by-election to House of Ass. May 1991; Leader of Opposition 1992–96; Queen's Counsel for Gibraltar 1998; Chief Minister of Gibraltar 1996–, (re-elected 2000, 2003); Hon. Fellow Queen Mary Coll., Univ. of London.
Address: 10/3 Irish Town (home); Office of the Chief Minister, 6 Convent Place, Gibraltar (office). *Telephone:* 70071 (office). *Fax:* 76396 (office). *E-mail:* govsec@gibnet.gi (office). *Website:* www.gibraltar.gov.gi/chief_minister (office).

CARVALHO, Evaristo de; São Tomé and Príncipe politician. *Career:* mem. Acção Democrática Independente; Prime Minister of São Tomé e Príncipe 2001–02.
Address: c/o Office of the Prime Minister, Rua Município, CP 302, São Tomé, São Tomé e Príncipe (office). *Telephone:* (12) 23913 (office). *Fax:* (12) 21670 (office).

CARY, Anthony Joyce, MA, CMG, MBA; British diplomatist; *High Commissioner to Canada;* b. 1 July 1951; m. Clare Cary; three s. one d. *Education:* Univ. of Oxford, Stanford Business School, USA. *Career:* entered British Diplomatic Service 1973; with British Mil. Govt in Berlin 1975–78; mem. Policy Planning Staff, FCO 1978–80, EC Dept 1982–84; Pvt. Sec. to Ministers of State Malcolm Rifkind, then Lynda Chalker 1984–86; Head of Chancery, Kuala Lumpur 1986–89; Deputy Chef de Cabinet to Leon

Brittan, EC, Brussels 1989–93; Head of EU Dept, FCO 1993–97; Counsellor, Political and Public Affairs, Embassy in Washington, DC 1997–99; Chef de Cabinet to Chris Patten, European Commr for External Relations 1999–2003; Amb. to Sweden 2003–07; High Commr to Canada 2007–; Harkness Fellow, Stanford Univ. 1980.
Address: British High Commission, 80 Elgin Street, Ottawa, Ont. K1P 5K7 Canada (office). *Telephone:* (613) 237-1530 (office). *Fax:* (613) 237-7980 (office). *E-mail:* generalenquiries@britainincanada.org (office). *Website:* www.britainincanada.org (office).

CASALE, Silvia, MA, PhD; British international criminologist; *President, European Committee for the Prevention of Torture, Council of Europe;* b. 15 Feb. 1945, London; m. Jerrold Katzman; one d. *Education:* Univ. of Oxford, Yale Univ. *Career:* Consultant to Prisons Inspectorate for England and Wales; Sentence Review Commr for NI; UK mem., European Cttee for the Prevention of Torture and Inhuman or Degrading Treatment or Punishment 1997, Pres. 2000– (re-elected 2002, 2004).
Address: Committee for the Prevention of Torture, Human Rights Building, Council of Europe, 67075 Strasbourg cedex, France (office). *Telephone:* (3) 88-41-39-25 (office). *Fax:* (3) 88-41-27-72 (office). *E-mail:* cptdoc@coe.int (office). *Website:* www.cpt.coe.int (office).

CASANOVA, Jean-Claude, DEcon; French economist and journalist; *Editor, Commentaire;* b. 11 June 1934, Ajaccio, Corsica; m. Marie-Thérèse Demargne 1962; two s. *Education:* Lycée Carnot, Inst. des Hautes Etudes, Tunis, Univ. of Paris, Harvard Univ. *Career:* Asst Fondation nat. des sciences politiques 1958; Chief of Staff to Minister of Industry 1958–61; Asst in Law Faculty, Univ. of Dijon 1963; Sr Lecturer then Prof. Faculty of Law and Econ. Sciences, Univ. of Nancy 1964–68; with Univ. of Paris-Nanterre 1968; with Inst. d'Etudes politiques, Paris 1969–; Dir of Studies and Research, Fondation nat. des Sciences politiques 1965–90; Tech. Adviser to Minister of Educ. 1972–74; Adviser to Prime Minister Raymond Barre 1976–81; Ed. Commentaire 1978–; leader writer, L'Express 1985–95; regular contrib. to Le Figaro 1996–2001; mem. Econ. and Social Council 1994–2004, Acad. des Sciences morales et politiques 1996–; columnist, Le Monde 2002–; Officier, Légion d'honneur 1994, Officier du Mérite 1996.
Address: Commentaire, 116 rue du Bac, 75007 Paris (office); Institut de France, quai Conti, 75270 Paris (office); 11-13, Rue de l'Aude, 75014 Paris, France (home). *Telephone:* 1-45-49-37-82; 1-43-26-51-95. *Fax:* 1-45-44-32-18. *E-mail:* jcc@commentaire.fr; jcc-1@wanadoo.fr. *Website:* www .commentaire.fr (office).

CASAS-GONZALEZ, Antonio; Venezuelan banker; b. 24 July 1933, Mérida; m. Carmen Elena Granadino de Casas; five s. one d. *Education:* George Washington Univ., Georgetown Univ. *Career:* fmrly Prof. of Econs at various insts; Adviser Venezuelan Petrochemical Inst. and Asst to Minister of Mines and Hydrocarbons 1957–59; Petroleum and Econ. Counsellor Washington Embassy 1959–61; with Interamerican Devt Bank 1961–69; Vice-Minister of Devt 1969; Minister for National Planning Office (CORDIPLAN) 1972; Man. Dir Petróleos de Venezuela (UK) SA 1990–94; Gov. Banco Cen. de Venezuela 1994–99; Vice-Pres. Intergovern-mental Group of Twenty-Four on Int. Monetary Affairs 1996–; mem. Bd Dirs Venezolana de Aviación (VIASA) 1970–73, Corp. Andina de Fomento 1970–73, Banco Cen. de Venezuela 1972–75, Corp. Venezolana de Guyana 1979–82, Petróleos de Venezuela SA 1979–90; currently Sr Adviser, Tecnoconsult, mem. Int. Bd Elliot School of Int. Affairs, George Washington Univ.; sixteen decorations from nine countries. *Publications:* América Latina y los problemas de Desarrollo (co-author) 1974, Venezuela y el CIAP (co-author) 1974, La planificación en América Latina (co-author) 1975, World Development (co-author) 1977; articles for various publs.
Address: c/o Banco Central de Venezuela, Av. Urdaneta, Esq. Las Carmelitas, Caracas 1010, Venezuela.

CASAS REGUEIRO, Gen. Julio; Cuban military officer and politician; *Vice-President and Minister of the Revolutionary Armed Forces;* b. 16 Feb. 1936, Santiago de Cuba, Oriente. *Education:* Escuela Superior de Guerra, Inst. of Advanced Mil. Studies, Havana. *Career:* joined rebel army 1956, mem. July 26th Movt and Co-founder Second East Front in Sierra Cristal Mountains during the guerrilla war against Fulgencio Batista 1958; Officer of Nat. Revolutionary Police 1959–61; Chief of Logistics and Services of Armed Forces 1961–69; Vice Minister of Armed Forces 1969–70, Brig. Gen. and Vice Minister of Armed Forces for Gen. Services 1971–77; Div. Gen., Chief of Rear Services (Logistics), Ministry of the Revolutionary Armed Forces (MINFAR) 1977–80; Chief Anti-Air Defences and Air Force (DAAFAR) 1980–87; mem. Cuban CP 1965–, alt. mem. Cen. Cttee 1975–80, full mem. Cen. Cttee 1980–87; mem. Politburo 1991–; Deputy Nat. Ass. 1981–86, 1993; mem. Council of State; Deputy Minister MINFAR in charge of econ. activity and Pres. GAE SA (holding co. for MINFAR commercial

activities) –2008; Vice-Pres. and Minister of the Revolutionary Armed Forces 2008–; served in mil. mission in Ethiopa 1972.
Address: Ministry of the Revolutionary Armed Forces, Plaza de la Revolución, Havana, Cuba (office). *Website:* www.cubagob.cu/ otras_info/minfar/far/minfar.htm (office).

CASON, James Caldwell, BA, MA; American diplomatist; *Ambassador to Paraguay;* b. NJ; m. Carmen Cason; two s. *Education:* Dartmouth Coll., Johns Hopkins School of Advanced Int. Studies, Nat. War Coll., Washington, DC. *Career:* early foreign service postings to US embassies in El Salvador, Bolivia, Panama, Uruguay, Italy, Venezuela and Portugal; fmr Political Adviser to Commr US Atlantic Comm. (USACOM) and to NATO Supreme Allied Commr Atlantic (SACLANT); fmr Deputy Chief of Mission, Kingston, Jamaica and Tegulcigalpa, Honduras; fmr Guate-mala Desk Officer, Dept of State, later Dir of Policy, Planning and Coordination, Bureau of Western Hemisphere Affairs –2002, Chief of Mission, US Interests Section, Havana 2002–05, Amb. to Paraguay 2005–; Fulbright Scholar in Uruguay; six Meritorious Honor Awards, Superior Honor Award, State Dept's Distinguished Honor Award, Jt Chiefs of Staff Best Essay Award, Defense Intelligence Agency's Writing Award, Chair. Jt Chief of Staff's Jt Meritorious Service Medal, Coast Guard's Distinguished Public Service.
Address: US Embassy, Avenida Mariscal López 1776, Casilla 402, Asunción, Paraguay (office). *Telephone:* (21) 21-3715 (office). *Fax:* (21) 21-3728 (office). *E-mail:* paraguayusembassy@state.gov (office). *Website:* asuncion.usembassy.gov (office).

CASSESE, Antonio; Italian academic and international organization official; *Professor of International Law, Robert Schuman Centre for Advanced Studies, European University Institute; Career:* fmr mem. of numerous int. tribunals including UN Sub-Comm. on Prevention of Discrimination and Protection of Minorities 1977, Council of Europe Cttee on Prevention of Torture; Prof. of Int. Law, Robert Schuman Centre for Advanced Studies, Univ. of Florence 1981–; mem. Italian Delegation, Council of Europe Steering Cttee for Human Rights 1984–88; Mem. Int. Comm. of Jurists 1990–; mem. Int. Criminal Tribunal for Fmr Yugoslavia 1993–2000 (Pres. 1993–97); Chair. UN Int. Comm. of Inquiry on Darfur 2004–05; visiting prof. at several int. univs including Oxford, Cambridge, Rotterdam, Sorbonne, Univ. of Paris; mem. Inst. de Droit Int.; Ed. Journal of Int. Criminal Justice; mem. Editorial Bd European Journal of Int. Law; numerous hon. docs; Man for Peace Award 1995, Robert G. Storey Award for Leadership 1997, Int. Acad. of Culture Prize 2002, Wolfgang Friedmann Memorial Award 2007. *Publications:* International Law 2001, The Rome Statute for an International Criminal Court.
Address: Robert Schumann Center for Advanced Studies, Villa Malafrasca, European University Institute, Via Boccaccio, 151, 50133 Florence, Italy (office). *Telephone:* (55) 4685-807 (office). *Fax:* (55) 4685-755 (office). *E-mail:* Antonio.Cassese@EUI.eu (office). *Website:* www.eui.eu (office).

CASTAÑEDA-CORNEJO, Ricardo Guillermo; Salvadorean public servant; b. 11 March 1938; m.; two c. *Education:* Nat. Univ. of El Salvador, Princeton Univ. and Univ. of Michigan, USA. *Career:* Deputy Minister for Foreign Affairs 1970–72; Head El Salvador's del. to UN Ass. 1972–76; External Dir Banco Cuscatlan SA 1980–81; Pres. Nat. Cttee and Dir for El Salvador, Cen. American Inst. of Business Man. 1981–88; Perm. Rep. to UN 1989–2000.
Address: c/o Ministry of Foreign Affairs, 5500 Alameda Dr Manuel Enrique Araújo, Km 6, Carretera a Santa Tecla, San Salvador, El Salvador.

CASTELLANETA, Giovanni; Italian diplomatist; *Ambassador to USA; Education:* Faculty of Law, Univ. of Rome 'La Sapienza'. *Career:* joined Foreign Service 1967, assigned to Embassy in Somalia 1969–72, Consul, Chambery, France 1972–74, Head of Econ. and Trade Office, Embassy in Lisbon 1974–76, European Affairs Desk, Ministry of Foreign Affairs 1976–78, Chief of Staff to Sec.-Gen., Ministry of Foreign Affairs 1978–81, Head of Press, Information and Cultural Office, Embassy in France 1981–84, on special assignment to Prime Minister's Office 1984–85, Deputy Perm. Rep., Mission to UN and Int. Orgs, Geneva 1985–89, Diplomatic Adviser to Treasury Minister, then Spokesman, Ministry of Foreign Affairs 1989–92, Amb. to Iran 1992–95, Head, Office for Coordination of Int. Activity of Italian Regions 1995–97, Special Coordinator, Italian Recon-struction Program for Albania 1997–98, Amb. to Australia (also accred to various insular States in Pacific Ocean) 1998–2001, Foreign Policy Adviser to Prime Minister 2001–05, rank of Amb. of Italy 2002, Personal Rep. of Prime Minister for G8 Summits, Amb. to USA 2005–; Deputy Chair. Finmeccanica Group 2002–05; Great Cross, Order of Merit of the Italian Repub.
Address: Embassy of Italy, 3000 Whitehaven Street, NW, Washington, DC 20008, USA (office). *Telephone:* (202) 612-4400 (office). *Fax:* (202) 518-

2154 (office). *E-mail:* stampa.washington@esteri.it (office). *Website:* www
.ambwashingtondc.esteri.it (office).

CASTELLI, Roberto; Italian politician and engineer; b. 12 July 1946, Lecco,
Lombardy; m.; one s. *Education:* Alessandro Manzoni School, Lecco,
Politecnico di Milano. *Career:* researcher developing a technological
system of electronic noise reduction; adviser to EC on environmental
affairs; joined Lega Nord 1986, elected Deputy for Lecco 1992, 1994, fmr
Vice-Pres. of Lega Nord in Chamber of Deputies; elected Senator for Lecco
e Bergamo 1996–, Pres. Lega Nord Parl. Group 1999–2001; Minister of
Justice 2001–06; Group Leader Transport Cttee; mem. Budget Cttee of
Senate, Parl. Cttee for Impeachments; mem. Jt Cttee on Regional Affairs,
Supervision over RAI TV and Radio, Investigations over Terrorism and
Massacres; fmr mem. Comm. for Regional Affairs, Comm. on Terrorism;
voluntary mem. Nat. Alpine and Speleological Rescue Corps; Hon. Pres.
Alpe (Asscn of Free Padan Hikers).
Address: c/o Lega Nord, Via C. Bellerio 41, 20161 Milan, Italy (office).
Telephone: (02) 66234236 (office). *Fax:* (02) 66234402 (office). *E-mail:*
webmaster@leganord.org (office). *Website:* www.leganord.org (office).

CASTELLINA, Luciana, LLB; Italian politician and journalist; b. 9 Aug.
1929, Rome; m. (divorced); one s. one d. *Education:* Univ. of Rome. *Career:*
Ed. Nuova Generazione (weekly) 1958–62, Il Manifesto (daily) 1972–78,
Pace e Guerra (weekly) then Liberazione (weekly) 1992–94; elected mem.
Parl. 1976, 1979, 1983; elected mem. European Parl. 1979, 1984, 1989, 1994,
Chair. Culture and Media Cttee 1994–96, later Chair. External Econ.
Relations Cttee; fmr mem. Presidence Italian Women's Union, directorate
Italian Communist Party; Pres. Italia Cinema Srl); Cineuropa.org,
Europacinema; Vice-Pres. Eurovisioni Bd; mem. Bd of Dirs Associazione
Di Promozione Sociale (ARCI), Lelio Basso Foundation; Kt Commdr of
the Argentine Repub. *Publications:* Che c'è in America (reports from
America) 1972, Family and Society in Marxist Analysis 1974, Il Commino
Dei Movimenti 2003, 50 Anni d'Europa 2007.
Address: Via di San Valentino 32, 00197 Rome (home); c/o Board of
Directors, ARCI, Via dei Monti di Pietralata 16, 00182 Rome, Italy (office).
E-mail: lcastellina@mclink.it (home).

CASTIGLIONI SORIA, Luis Alberto; Paraguayan politician; *Vice-
President;* b. 31 July 1962, Itacurubí del Rosario. *Career:* joined Partido
Colorado 1979; Perm. Mem. Colorado Nat. Constituent Convention
1991–92; Perm. Mem. Colorado Govt Bd 1992–95; Pres. Capital Sectional
Cttee No. 4 1996–2000; Vice-Pres. of Paraguay 2003–.
Address: c/o Office of the President, Palacio de Gobierno, Asunción,
Paraguay (office).

CASTILLO VILLACORTA, José Guillermo, BA, MBA; Guatemalan politician and diplomatist; b. 29 June 1960; m. Flor de María Palacios; four c.
Education: Universidad Francisco Marroquín, J.L. Kellogg Grad. School
of Man., Northwestern Univ., USA. *Career:* taught courses in business
strategy, world political and econ. order, and int. trade and marketing at
pvt. univs in Guatemala; worked in banking, insurance and bonds as well as
industrial and commercial sectors in both Guatemala and abroad; fmr
Vice-Pres. of Strategic Planning, Cervecería Centroamericana; fmr mem.
Bd Dirs various cos; fmr Vice-Chair., Dir and Treas. Guatemalan Chamber
of Industry; fmr Coordinator Econ. Comm.; fmr Dir Business Council for
the Int. Trade Negotiations; fmr mem. Exec. Cttee Nat. Competitiveness
Program; fmr Dir FUNDESA (Foundation for the Devt of Guatemala),
Mariano and Rafael Castillo Córdova Foundation; fmr Dir and Pres.
Fundes Guatemala; del. of Ministry of Economy 1996–2000, coordinated
and completed negotiations for free trade agreement with Mexico, Vice-
Minister of the Economy in charge of Trade Issues 1998–99, Minister of the
Economy 1999–2000; observer of electoral process in Guatemala and
presidential election 2003; Amb. to USA 2004–08; Fulbright scholarship
grantee.
Address: Ministry of Foreign Affairs, 2A Avenida La Reforma 4-47, Zona
10, Guatemala City, Guatemala (office). *Telephone:* 2331-8410 (office).
Fax: 2331-8510 (office). *E-mail:* webmaster@minex.gob.gt (office).
Website: www.minex.gob.gt (office).

CASTRO, Fidel (see Castro Ruz, Fidel).

CASTRO, Gen. Raúl (see Castro Ruz, Gen. Raúl).

CASTRO CALDAS, Júlio de Lemos de; Portuguese politician and lawyer; b.
19 Nov. 1943, Lisbon; m. Ana Cristina Ribeiro Sobral Cid; one s. two d.
Career: Leader Students' Asscn, Classical Univ. of Lisbon 1963; f.
Associação para o Desenvolvimento Económico e Social (SEDES) 1970,
Partido Popular Democrático 1974; Democratic Alliance mem. Parl. for
Viana do Castelo 1979; Leader Parl. Group of Democratic Alliance
1979–82; Minister of Defence, Socialist Party 1999–2001; mem. Supreme

Council of Public Prosecutor Dept 1980–92; Treas. Nat. Bars Asscn
1988–91, Dean 1993–98; Pres. European Bars Fed. 1997–99; Chair. Bilbao
Vizcaya Bank (Portugal) 1995–99; fmr chair. several cos; Dir (non-exec.)
Companhia le Seguros Global SA, Carrefour SA.
Address: Avenida Duque D'Avila, 66, 5º andar, 1069-075 Lisbon, Portugal
(office). *Telephone:* (213) 564300 (office). *Fax:* (213) 564350 (office).

CASTRO RUZ, Fidel, DIur; Cuban fmr head of state; b. 13 Aug. 1926,
brother of Raúl Castro Ruz; m. Mirta Diaz-Bilart 1948 (divorced 1955);
one s. *Education:* Jesuit schools in Santiago and Havana, Univ. de la
Habana. *Career:* law practice in Havana; began active opposition to Batista
regime by attack on Moncada barracks at Santiago 26th July 1953;
sentenced to 15 years' imprisonment 1953; amnestied 1956; went into exile
in Mexico and began to organize armed rebellion; landed in Oriente
Province with small force Dec. 1956; carried on armed struggle against
Batista regime until flight of Batista Jan. 1959; Prime Minister of Cuba
1959–76; Head of State and Pres. of Council of State 1976–2008 (resgnd),
Pres. of Council of Ministers 1976–2008; Chair. Agrarian Reform Inst.
1965; First Sec. Partido Unido de la Revolución Socialista (PURS)
1963–65, Partido Comunista 1965–2008 (mem. Political Bureau
1976–2008), Head Nat. Defence Council 1992–2008; Order of Lenin
1972, 1986, Order of the October Revolution 1976, Somali Order (1st Class)
1977, Order of Jamaica 1977, Gold Star (Vietnam) 1982; Lenin Peace Prize
1961, Hero of the Soviet Union 1963, Dimitrov Prize (Bulgaria) 1980,
Muammar Gaddafi Human Rights Prize 1998. *Publications:* Ten Years of
Revolution 1964, History Will Absolve Me 1968, Fidel (with Frei Betto)
1987, How Far We Slaves Have Come: South Africa and Cuba in Today's
World (with Nelson Mandela) 1991, Fidel Castro (autobiog.) 2007.
Address: c/o Palacio del Gobierno, Havana, Cuba.

CASTRO RUZ, Gen. Raúl; Cuban politician and head of state; *President,
Council of State;* b. 3 June 1931, brother of Fidel Castro Ruz; m. Vilma
Espín 1959 (died 2007); one d. *Education:* Jesuit School of Colegio Dolores,
Santiago, Colegio de Belén, Havana. *Career:* sentenced to 15 years'
imprisonment for insurrection 1953; amnestied 1954; assisted his brother's
movement in Mexico and in Cuba after Dec. 1956, made Commdt 1957;
First Vice-Pres. of the Councils of State and Ministers and Maximum Gen.
of the Revolutionary Armed Forces 1959–2008, Acting Pres. Council of
State 2006–08, Pres. 2008–; led Cuban mil. in repulsing exiles forces in Bay
of Pigs invasion 1961; Second Sec. CP Cen. Cttee 1965; Deputy, Asamblea
Nacional del Poder Popular 1976; Order of Lenin 1979, Order of the
October Revolution 1981, Orden Máximo Gómez 1998; Medal for
Strengthening of Brotherhood in Arms 1977.
Address: Palicio del Gobierno, Havana, Cuba (office). *Website:* www2.cuba
.cu/politica/webpcc (office).

CASTRO-VALLE KUEHNE, Jorge; Mexican diplomatist; *Ambassador to
Germany; Education:* Nat. Autonomous Univ. of Mexico, Univ. of Vienna,
Austria. *Career:* joined Foreign Service 1973, overseas postings include
Embassy in Vienna 1973–76, Minister and Head of Chancery, Embassy in
London 1989–90, Chargé d'affaires Embassy in GDR 1990, Minister and
Head of Chancery, Embassy in Ottawa 1991–93; Sec. to Under-Sec. of Int.
Econ. Affairs, Ministry of Foreign Affairs 1979–82, Sec. to Minister of
Foreign Affairs 1985–88, Dir-Gen. for N America 1994–98; Deputy Amb.
to USA 1998–2001, Amb. to Sweden (also accred to Latvia and Lithuania)
2001–03, to Germany 2003–.
Address: Embassy of Mexico, Klingelhöferstr. 3, 10785 Berlin, Germany
(office). *Telephone:* (30) 2693230 (office). *Fax:* (30) 269323700 (office).
Website: mail@embamexale.de.

CASULE, Slobodan; Macedonian politician and journalist; b. 27 Sept. 1945,
Skopje. *Education:* Pontifical Catholic Univ., Lima, Peru. *Career:* journal-
ist and interpreter, Skopje TV 1965–67, Ed., Foreign Corresp. 1967–74;
Latin America Corresp. Tanjung News Agency 1974–80, Chief Ed.
1980–90; Dir, Chief Ed. Macedonian Radio 1990–94, Ed., Commentator
1994–99; Dir-Gen. Nova Makedonija, 1999; govt adviser 2000–; Minister
of Foreign Affairs 2001–02; Founder and mem. Human Rights Forum of
Macedonia, Int. Relations Forum; mem. European Inst. of Media, Inst. of
East–West Dialogue, Int. Fund for Media, US Democratic Inst., Helsinki
Watch, Peace in the Country–Peace in the World Org., Journalists' Asscn
of Macedonia, Int. Journalists' Asscn.
Address: c/o Ministry of Foreign Affairs, Dame Gruev 6, Skopje 1000,
Macedonia (office).

CATARINO, Pedro Manuel; Portuguese diplomatist; b. 12 May 1941,
Lisbon; m. Cheryl A. Steyn 1969; one s. one d. *Education:* Univ. of Lisbon.
Career: joined Foreign Service in 1964, served in Embassy in Pretoria
1967–69, Defence Counsellor, Del. to NATO, Brussels 1974–79, Consul-
Gen., Hong Kong 1979–82, mem. int. staff, NATO, Brussels 1983–89, head
of del. to negotiations for a new defence and co-operation agreement with

USA 1989–92, Pres. Inter-ministerial Comm. of Macao and Head of Portuguese del. to Jt Luso-Chinese Liaison Group, Perm. Rep. to UN 1992–97, Amb. to China 1997–2002, to USA 2002–06; Silver Medal for Distinguished Services.
Address: Ministry of Foreign Affairs, Palácio das Necessidades, Largo do Rilvas, 1399-030 Lisbon, Portugal (office). *Telephone:* (21) 3946000 (office). *Fax:* (21) 3946053 (office). *E-mail:* gii@mne.gov.pt (office). *Website:* www .min-nestrangeiros.pt (office).

CATO, Annan Arkyin, BA (Hons); Ghanaian diplomatist; *High Commissioner to UK;* b. 6 May 1939; widower; three c. *Education:* Achimota Secondary School, Univ. of Ghana, Legon, Ghana Inst. of Man. and Public Admin. *Career:* joined Ghana Foreign Service 1964, served in different capacities in Missions in Addis Ababa, Rome, New York (UN), Geneva and London, Deputy High Commr, London –1985, Acting High Commr 1985–87, Chair. UN Ad Hoc Working Group of Experts on Southern Africa 1976–86, served at Africa Div. and as Chief of Protocol, Ministry of Foreign Affairs 1978–81, seconded to Office of Pres. as Dir of State Protocol 1987–92, High Commr to Canada 1992–97, Chief Dir, Ministry of Foreign Affairs 1997–2001 (retd), Sec. to Cabinet 2001–05 (retd from Public Service), High Commr to UK (also accred as Amb. to Ireland) 2006–; State Award of Companion of the Order of the Volta.
Address: Ghana High Commission, 13 Belgrave Square, London, SW1X 8PN, England (office). *Telephone:* (20) 7201-5921 (office). *Fax:* (20) 7245-9552 (office). *E-mail:* information@ghanahighcommissionuk.com (office). *Website:* www.ghanahighcommissionuk.com (office).

CATON, Valerie, MA, PhD; British diplomatist; *Ambassador to Finland;* m. David Harrison; one s. one d. *Education:* Blackburn High School for Girls, Univs of Bristol and Reading. *Career:* joined FCO 1980, UK Rep., Brussels, then Second, later First Sec., EC Affairs, Brussels 1982–84, Desk Officer, Southern Africa Dept, FCO 1984–86, Deputy Head of Policy Planners, FCO 1986–88, First Sec. (Political), Paris 1988–92, Deputy Head of Mission and Consul-Gen., Stockholm 1993–96, Counsellor (Financial and Econ.), Paris 1997–2001, Head of Environment Policy Department, FCO 2002–04, Head of Climate Change and Energy Group, FCO 2004–06, Amb. to Finland 2006–; Sr Assoc. mem. St Antony's Coll., Oxford 2001–02. *Publication:* France and the Politics of EMU 2002.
Address: British Embassy, Itäinen Puistotie 17, 00140 Helsinki, Finland (office). *Telephone:* (9) 2286-5222 (office). *Fax:* (9) 2286-5284 (office). *E-mail:* info.helsinki@fco.gov.uk (office). *Website:* www.britishembassy.fi (office).

CATTO, Henry Edward; American diplomatist, business executive and academic; *Chairman, Atlantic Council of the United States;* b. 6 Dec. 1930, Dallas; m. Jessica Oveta Hobby 1958; two s. two d. *Education:* Williams Coll. *Career:* Partner, Catto & Catto, San Antonio 1955–; Deputy Rep. Org. of American States 1969–71; Amb. to El Salvador 1971–73; Chief of Protocol, The White House 1974–76; Amb. to the UN Office, Geneva 1976–77; Asst Sec. of Defense, Pentagon, Washington 1981–83; Dir Cullen-Frost Bankers, San Antonio, Nat. Public Radio, Wash.; Amb. to the UK 1989–91; Dir US Information Agency 1991–93; Adjunct Prof. of Political Science Univ. of Texas, San Antonio 1993–; mem. Council on Foreign Relations 1979; Vice-Chair. Aspen Inst. 1993–, H and C Communications 1983–89; Chair. Atlantic Council of the US 1999–; mem. Int. Advisory Bd Direct Relief International 2001–; columnist San Antonio Light 1985–89; fmr Publr Washington Journalism Review, now Contributing Ed.; Hon. LLD (Aberdeen) 1990. *Publication:* Ambassador at Sea 1999.
Address: c/o Atlantic Council of the United States, 1101 15th Street, NW, 11th Floor, Washington, DC 20005 (office); 200 Navarro, San Antonio, TX 78205, USA (office). *Telephone:* (202) 778-4941 (DC) (office); (210) 222-2161 (office). *Fax:* (210) 228-0332 (office). *E-mail:* hecatto@acus.org (office). *Website:* www.acus.org (office).

CAVACO SILVA, Anibal, PhD; Portuguese politician, economist, academic and head of state; *President;* b. 15 July 1939, Loulé; m. Maria Cavaco Silva 1963; one s. one d. *Education:* Univ. of York, UK and Inst. of Econ. and Financial Studies. *Career:* taught Public Econs and Political Economy, Inst. of Econ. and Financial Studies 1965–67, then at Catholic Univ. 1975–2006 and New Univ. of Lisbon 1977–2002; Research Fellow, Calouste Gulbenkian Foundation 1967–77; Dir of Research and Statistical Dept, Bank of Portugal 1977–85; Minister of Finance and Planning 1980–81; Pres. Council for Nat. Planning 1981–84; Leader, PSD 1985–95; Prime Minister of Portugal 1985–95; mem. Real Academia de Ciencias Morales y Políticas, Spain; Econ. Adviser to Bank of Portugal (Cen. Bank) 1995–2004; Pres. of Portugal 2006–; Social Democrat (PSD) mem. Exec. Cttee Club of Madrid in Democratic Transition and Consolidation; Dr hc (Univ. of York, UK, Universidada de Coruña, Spain); Joseph Bech Prize 1991, Max Schmidleinz Foundation Prize, Carl Bertelsmann Prize. *Publications:* Budgetary Policy and Economic Stabilization 1976, Eco-

nomic Effects of Public Debt 1977, The Economic Policy of Sá Carneiro's Government 1982, Public Finance and Macroeconomic Policy 1992, A Decade of Reforms 1995, Portugal and the Single Currency 1997, European Monetary Union 1999, Political Autobiography 2002; over 20 articles on financial markets, public economics and Portuguese economic policy.
Address: Office of the President, Presidência da República, Palácio de Belém, Calçada da Ajuda, 1349-022 Lisbon, Portugal (office). *Telephone:* (21) 3614600 (office). *Fax:* (21) 3614611 (office). *E-mail:* presidente@ presidenciarepublica.pt (office). *Website:* www.presidenciarepublica.pt (office).

CAVALLO, Domingo Felipe, DEcon, PhD; Argentine politician and economist; b. 21 July 1946, San Francisco, Córdoba; m. Sonia Abrazián; three s. *Education:* Nat. Univ. of Córdoba and Harvard Univ. *Career:* Under-Sec. for Devt Govt of Prov. of Córdoba 1969–70; Vice-Pres. Bd of Dirs. Banco de la Provincia de Córdoba 1971–72; Titular lecturer, Nat. and Catholic Univs. 1970–83; founding Dir Inst. for Econ. Studies of Mediterranean Found. 1977–87; fmr Pres., then Gov. Argentine Cen. Bank; mem. Advisory Cttee Inst. for Econ. Devt of World Bank (IBRD) 1988, Nat. Deputy for Córdoba 1987–91; Minister of Foreign Affairs and Worship 1989–91, of the Economy 1991–92, of the Economy and Public Works 1992–96, 2001; Visiting Prof., Stern School of Business, New York Univ. 1996–97; elected Nat. Deputy for Buenos Aires 1997; f. Acción por la República Party 1997; arrested for alleged involvement in arms smuggling April 2002, released June 2002. *Publications:* Volver a Crecer 1986, El Desafío Federal 1986, Economía en Tiempos de Crisis 1989, La Argentina que pudo ser 1989, El Peso de la Verdad 1997; numerous tech. publs and articles in Argentine and foreign newspapers.
Address: Acción por la República, Buenos Aires (office); Hipólito Yrigoyen 250, 1310 Buenos Aires, Argentina. *Telephone:* (11) 4349-5000. *E-mail:* edinfpub@mecon.gov.ar (office). *Website:* www.mecon.gov.ar (office).

CAVARAI, Gian Paolo, LLB; Italian diplomatist; *Diplomatic Adviser to President Emeritus Carlo Azeglio Ciampi;* b. 27 Aug. 1939, Gimma, Ethiopia. *Education:* Univ. of Rome. *Career:* entered diplomatic corps 1967; served in Dept of Econ. Affairs, Ministry of Foreign Affairs 1967–70, 1988–91, Deputy Dir-Gen. 1993–98; posting to Embassy in Ottawa 1970–73, First Sec., Embassy in Dublin 1973–78; Dept of Emigration and Social Affairs, Ministry of Foreign Affairs 1978–80; Counsellor, Embassy in Belgrade 1980–84, First Counsellor, Perm. Mission to EU, Brussels 1984–88, Minister Plenipotentiary 1991–; Diplomatic Adviser, Finance Ministry 1992–94; Amb. to Israel 1998–2002; Council of Ministers Rep. to Marshall Plan for Palestine 2002; Amb. to Greece 2003–06; Diplomatic Adviser to Pres. Emer. Carlo Azeglio Ciampi 2006–.
Address: Office of President Emeritus Carlo Azeglio Ciampi, Palazzo Giustiniani, Via Della Dogana Vecchia 29, 00186 Rome, Italy (office). *Telephone:* (06) 67065558 (office). *Fax:* (06) 67065056 (office). *E-mail:* gianpaolo.cavari@senato.it (office).

CEJAS, Paul L., BBA, CPA; American diplomatist and business executive; b. 4 Jan. 1943, Havana, Cuba. *Education:* Univ. of Miami. *Career:* founder, fmr Chair. and CEO CareFlorida Health Systems Inc. –1984; Amb. to Belgium 1998–2001; currently Chair. and CEO PLC Investments, Inc.; mem. Bd of Dirs Mellon Financial Corpn, Ivax Corpn; Chair. Dade Co. School Bd; Trustee Univ. of Miami; mem. Nat. Bd Smithsonian Inst.; mem. Latin American Advisory Bd, Tate Museum, London; mem. Bd of Regents, Fla Univ. System 1994; Chair. Post-Summit Cttee, Hemispheric Summit of the Americas 1994, Fla Partnership of the Americas 1994–97; Rep. US Del. to Gen. Ass., OAS 1996; fmr Dir Miami Art Museum of Dade County; fmr Trustee Fla Int. Univ.; Hon. PhD (Florida Int. Univ.) 1988.
Address: c/o Board of Directors, Mellon Financial Corporation, One Mellon Center, Pittsburgh, PA 15258-0001, USA.

ÇEKU, Agim; Kosovo politician and military officer; b. 29 Oct. 1960, Qyshk; m.; two s. one d. *Education:* Mil. High School, Belgrade and Zadar Mil. Acad. *Career:* began career as Platoon Commdr, Yugoslav People's Army 1984; joined newly formed Croatian Army as Capt. 1991, and rose to rank of Brig. Gen. 1995; joined Kosovo Liberation Army (KLA) and apptd Chief of Gen. Staff 1999, oversaw KLA demilitarisation and formation of Kosovo Protection Corps, Commdr 2000–06; Prime Minister 2006–08; nine Croatian army decorations.
Address: c/o Office of the Prime Minister, 10000 Priština, Government Building, Rruga Nëna Terezë, Kosovo (office). *Telephone:* (38) 211567 (office). *Fax:* (38) 20014612 (office). *E-mail:* info@ks-gov.net (office). *Website:* www.ks-gov.net/pm (office).

ČEKUOLIS, Dalius; Lithuanian diplomatist; *Permanent Representative, United Nations;* b. 29 March 1959, Vilnius; m. Jūratė Čekuolienė; one d. *Education:* Inst. of Int. Relations, Moscow. *Career:* Head of Press and Information Dept, Ministry of Foreign Affairs 1990–92; Amb. to

Denmark, Norway and Iceland 1992–94, to Belgium, the Netherlands and Luxembourg 1994–98, to Portugal 1999–2004; Rep. to WEU and NATO 1994–98; Head of Cttee of Sr Officials of the Council of the Baltic States 1998–99; Sec., Ministry of Foreign Affairs 2004–06; Perm. Rep. to UN, New York 2006–, Vice-Chair. ECOSOC 2006–07, Pres. 2007–.
Address: Office of the Permanent Representative of Lithuania, United Nations, 420 Fifth Avenue, 3rd Floor, New York, NY 10018, USA (office). *Telephone:* (212) 354-7820 (office). *Fax:* (212) 354-7833 (office). *E-mail:* lithuania@un.int (office). *Website:* www.un.int/lithuania (office).

CELIKKOL, Oguz; Turkish diplomatist; *Ambassador to Greece; Career:* served as First Sec., Embassy in Washington, DC, fmr Consul-Gen. in Calif., USA; fmr Dir-Gen. Ministry of Foreign Affairs; Amb. to Syria –2004; Ministry of Foreign Affairs Special Rep. to Iraq 2006–08; Amb. to Greece 2008–.
Address: Embassy of Turkey, Odos Vassileos Gheorghiou 8b, 106 74 Athens, Greece (office). *Telephone:* (210) 7263000 (office). *Fax:* (210) 7229597 (office). *E-mail:* atina.be@mfa.gov.tr (office).

CERAR, Božo, PhD; Slovenian diplomatist; *Permanent Representative, NATO;* b. 16 Oct. 1949, Ljubljana; m.; three c. *Education:* Univ. of Ljubljana, Univ. of Westminster, UK. *Career:* trainee, Fed. Secr. of Foreign Affairs, Socialist Fed. Repub. of Yugoslavia (SFRY) 1974; Vice Consul, Consulate Gen. in Sydney 1977–81; Sec., Slovenian Trade Unions Cttee for Int. Co-operation 1981–84; First Sec., Embassy in Athens 1985–89; Head of Dept for Western Europe, Fed. Secr. of Foreign Affairs 1990; Coordinator apptd by Govt of Slovenia concerning activities of EU observers who monitored ceasefire between Slovenian Territorial Defence and Yugoslav Army 1991; Head of Dept for Europe and N America, Ministry of Foreign Affairs of Slovenia 1991–92; Chargé d'Affaires a.i., Embassy in London 1992–96; State Under-Sec. and Head of Office of Minister of Foreign Affairs 1996–97; Amb. to Canada 1997–2001; State Under-Sec. and Head of Dept for Multilateral Relations, Ministry of Foreign Affairs 2001, State Under-Sec. and Head of Dept for NATO 2002–03; Amb. to Poland 2004; Deputy Minister, Ministry of Foreign Affairs 2004–06; Perm. Rep. to NATO, Brussels 2006–.
Address: North Atlantic Treaty Organization, blvd Léopold III, 1110 Brussels, Belgium (office). *Telephone:* (2) 707-41-11 (office). *Fax:* (2) 707-45-79 (office). *E-mail:* natodoc@hq.nato.int (office). *Website:* www.nato .int (office).

CÉSAR, Carlos Manuel Martins do Vale; Portuguese politician; *President, Regional Government of the Azores;* b. 30 Oct. 1956, Ponta Delgada; m. Luísa Maria Assís Vital Gomes; one s. *Education:* Antero de Quental High School, Faculty of Law, Lisbon. *Career:* f. Socialist Youth and Socialist Party 1974, mem. Nat. Exec. Socialist Party 1975–; Asst to State Sec. for Public Admin 1977–78; Deputy, Regional Ass. 1980–96, Vice-Pres. –1996; Pres. Regional Govt of the Azores 1996–; mem. State Council, Higher Nat. Defence Council, Higher Internal Security Council, Cttee of the Regions, Ass. of European Regions, Conf. of Presidents of Ultra-peripheral Regions, Conf. of Peripheral Maritime Regions of Europe, Congress of Local Regional Authorities of Europe.
Address: Residência do Presidente, Governo Regional, Palácio de Santana, 9500-077 Ponta Delgada, The Azores (office). *Telephone:* (296) 301000 (office). *Fax:* (296) 628890 (office). *E-mail:* presidencia@azores.gov.pt (office). *Website:* www.azores.gov.pt (office).

CEVIK, Bashar Khaled; Turkish diplomatist. *Career:* Amb. to Syria 2004–.
Address: Embassy of Turkey, BP 3738, 56–58 avenue Ziad bin Abou Soufian, Damascus, Syria (office). *Telephone:* (11) 33501930 (office). *Fax:* (11) 3339243 (office). *E-mail:* sambe@mfa.gov.tr (office).

CHAABANE, Sadok; Tunisian politician and professor of law; *Minister of Higher Education, Scientific Research and Technology;* b. (Sadok Chaabane), 23 Feb. 1950, Sfax; m. Dalenda Nouri 1974; one s. two d. *Career:* Prof. of Law, Univ. of Tunis 1973–; Dir of Studies, Research and Publ Centre 1975–82; Perm. Sec. of RCD 1988; Sec. of State for Higher Educ. and Scientific Research 1989; Adviser to the Pres. on Political Affairs 1990; Sec. of State for Scientific Research 1991; Prin. Adviser to the Pres. on Human Rights 1991; Minister of Justice 1992–97, of Higher Educ., Scientific Research and Tech. 1999–; Founder-mem. Int. Acad. of Constitutional Law, Int. Law Asscn; Commdr Order of Nov. 7; Great Cordon of Order of the Repub. *Publications:* The Law of International Institutions 1985, Ben Ali and The Way to Pluralism in Tunisia 1997, The Challenges of Ben Ali 1999, Hannibal Redux: The Renewal of Modern Tunisia 1977.
Address: Ministry of Higher Education, Scientific Research and Technology, Avenue Ouled Haffouz, 1030 Tunis (office); 30 Rue Mannoubia Ben Nasr, Manar 3, 2092 Tunis, Tunisia (home). *Telephone:* (71) 784-170

(office); (71) 889-690 (home); (98) 315-050. *Fax:* (71) 786-711 (office). *E-mail:* sadok.chaabane@mes.rnu.tn (office).

CHACÓN PIQUERAS, Carme, LLD; Spanish politician; *Minister of Defence;* b. 13 March 1971, Esplugues de Llobregat, Barcelona; m.; one s. *Education:* Univ. of Barcelona, Osgoode Hall Law School, Toronto, Univ. of Kingston, Univ. of Montreal, Canada. *Career:* Prof. of Constitutional Law, Univ. of Girona 1994–2004; Sec. of Educ., Culture and Research, Exec. Comm., Spanish Socialist Workers' Party (PSOE) 2000–04, mem. Fed. Exec. Comm. 2000–; MP (PSOE) for Barcelona 2000–, Vice-Pres. Congress of Deputies (Lower House) 2004–07; Minister of Housing 2007–08, of Defence 2008–.
Address: Ministry of Defence, Paseo de la Castellana 109, 28071 Madrid, Spain (office). *Telephone:* (91) 3955000 (office). *E-mail:* infodefensa@mde .es (office). *Website:* www.mde.es (office).

CHADERTON MATOS, Roy; Venezuelan politician and diplomatist; *Ambassador to France;* b. 17 Aug. 1942. *Education:* Cen. Univ. of Venezuela, Instituto de Altos Estudios de Defensa Nacional. *Career:* Second Sec. Embassy in Poland 1969–72; First Sec. Embassy in FRG 1973, Embassy in Canada 1975, in Ministry of Foreign Affairs 1973–75, Counsellor 1979, Minister Counsellor 1979–82, Amb. 1983–85, Gen. Dir of Int. Political Affairs 1990–93, Gen. Dir (Vice-Pres.) 1994–95; Counsellor Embassy in Belgium 1977–78; Counsellor Perm. Mission to UN, New York 1978–79, Deputy Perm. Rep. 1982–83; Amb. to Gabon 1985–87, to Norway and Iceland 1987–90, to Canada 1993–94, to UK and Ireland 1996–2000, to Colombia 2000–02, to USA 2002, to France 2004–; Minister of Foreign Affairs 2002–04; mem. Social Christian Party of Venezuela (COPEI) 1958–, Official Rep. 1994; Caballero de Madara Order (Bulgaria), Francisco de Miranda Order, First Class (Venezuela), Bernardo O'Higgins Order (Chile), Great Cross, May Order (Argentina), Great Cross, San Olav Order (Norway), Great Cross, Cruceiro do Sul National Order (Brazil), Great Cord Libertador Order (Venezuela).
Address: 11 rue Copernic, 75116 Paris, France (office). *Telephone:* 1-45-53-29-98 (office). *Fax:* 1-47-55-64-56 (office). *E-mail:* info@amb-venezuela.fr (office). *Website:* www.embavenez-paris.com (office).

CHAE, Tae-bok; North Korean politician and fmr professor of chemical engineering; *Chairman of Supreme People's Assembly;* b. 1929, N. Hamgyong Prov. *Education:* Mangyongdae Revolutionary School and studies in E. Germany. *Career:* Prof. of Chem. Eng., Hamhung Tech. Eng. Coll. 1961; Dean of Kimcahek Eng. Coll. 1978, Chair. Educ. Comm. 1981; Minister of Higher Educ. 1985; Sec. Worker's Party Cen. Cttee. 1986–; Assoc. mem. Politburo 1990–; elected Chair. Supreme People's Ass. 1998–.
Address: Choe Ko In Min Hoe Ui, Pyongyang, Democratic People's Republic of Korea (office).

CHAIGNEAU, Pascal Gérard Joël, DèsSc, DenScPol, DenScEcon, DenD; French academic; *Director, Centre d'Etudes Diplomatiques et Stratégiques;* b. 8 Feb. 1956, Paris; m. Marie-Claude Ratsarazaka-Ratsimandresy 1983; three s. *Education:* Coll. St Michel de Picpus and Facultés de Droit et des Lettres, Paris. *Career:* practical work 1974–75; Asst 1976–78, Prof. Ecole des Hautes Etudes Internationales and Ecole Supérieure de Journalisme 1978–, Dir of Studies 1984–85, Dir-Gen. 1985–90, Admin.-Gen. 1990–; Research, Fondation pour les Etudes de Défense Nationale 1980–82; in charge of course, Univ. de Paris II 1982–90; Maître de conférences, Univ. de Paris V 1990–2000, Professeur des universités 2000–;,; Sec.-Gen. Centre de Recherches Droit et Défense, Univ. de Paris V 1985–; Founder and Dir Centre d'Etudes Diplomatiques et Stratégiques 1986–; Advocate, Court of Appeal, Paris 1990–; Prof. Centre des Hautes Etudes sur l'Afrique et l'Asie Modernes; Lecturer, Inst. des Hautes Etudes de Défense Nationale; in charge of course, Ecole des Hautes Etudes Commerciales 1990–92, Prof. 1992–; Prof. Collège Interarmes de Défense 1994–; with Bolivian Consulate in France 1994–97; Foreign Trade Counsellor 1995–; many other public appointments; mem. Acad. des Sciences d'Outre-mer, Soc. d'Economie Politique; Chevalier, Légion d'honneur; Officier, Ordre nat. du mérite, Commdr, Ordre des Palmes Académiques; Commdr des Arts et des Lettres; decorations from Bolivia, Burkina Faso, Belgium, Honduras, Chad, Madagascar, Niger, etc.; Hon. LLD (Richmond, USA); Dr hc (Nat. Univ. of Bolivia); Grand Prix de l'Asscn des Ecrivains de Langue Française 1987, Prix de l'Acad. des Sciences Morales et Politiques 1993 and other prizes, awards and distinctions. *Publications:* La Stratégie soviétique 1978, La Politique militaire de la France en Afrique 1984, Rivalités politiques et socialisme à Madagascar 1985, Les Pays de l'Est et l'Afrique 1985, France-océan indien-mer rouge (with others) 1986, Pour une analyse du commerce international 1987, La Guerre du Golfe 1991, Europe: la nouvelle donne stratégique 1993, Les grands Enjeux du monde contemporain 1997, Dictionnaire des Relations Internationales 1998, Gestion des Risques internationaux 2001.

Address: Centre d'Etudes Diplomatiques et Stratégiques, 54 avenue Marceau, 75008 Paris (office); 68 avenue de Gravelle, 94220 Charenton-le-Pont, France (home). *Telephone:* 1-47-20-57-47 (office). *Fax:* 1-47-20-57-30 (office). *E-mail:* contact@ceds-fr.com (office). *Website:* www.ceds-fr.com.

CHAKRAVARTY, Pinak Ranjan; Indian diplomatist; *High Commissioner to Bangladesh;* m. Radha Chakravarty. *Career:* Chief of Protocol, Ministry of Foreign Affairs 2003–05, Jt Sec. 2005; Amb. to the Philippines 2005–06; High Commr to Bangladesh 2007–.
Address: High Commission of India, House No. 2, Road No. 142, Gulshan-1, Dhaka, Bangladesh (office). *Telephone:* (2) 9889339 (office). *Fax:* (2) 8817487 (office). *E-mail:* hc@hcidhaka.org (office). *Website:* www.hcidhaka.org (office).

CHALABI, Ahmad, PhD; Iraqi politician; *Leader, Iraqi National Congress;* b. 1945, Baghdad; m.; four c. *Education:* in UK, MIT and Univ. of Chicago, USA. *Career:* family moved to England following coup d'état and assassination of King of Iraq 1958; fmr Prof. of Math., American Univ. of Beirut; f. Bank of Petra, Jordan 1980, taken over by mil. decree 1989, charged with embezzlement, fraud and misuse of depositor funds by Jordanian court 1991, sentenced in absentia to 22 years' imprisonment 1992; organized conf. of 400 opposition leaders in Northern Iraq 1992; Chair. Exec. Council and Leader, Iraqi Nat. Congress 1992–; survived failed coup 1995; lived in exile in London 1996–2003; returned to Iraq to help establish an interim govt following overthrow of Saddam Hussein's regime April 2003; Deputy Prime Minister 2005–06, Acting Minister of Oil 2005.
Address: Iraqi National Congress, Baghdad, Iraq (office). *E-mail:* info@inciraq.com (office). *Website:* inciraq.com (office).

CHALIAND, Gérard, PhD; French academic and writer. *Education:* Institut National des Langues et Civilisations Orientales, Univ. of Paris V. *Career:* f. magazine Partisans during Algerian war;; Prof., Ecole nat. d'admin (ENA), Collège interarmes de défense 1980–89; taught at l'École Supérieure de Guerre 1993–99; Visiting Prof., Harvard Univ., Univ. of Calif., Berkeley, Military Acad., Bogota, Colombia, Univ. of Capetown, SA, Univ. of Salamanca, Spain, Univ. of Manchester, UK; Visiting Fellow, Centre for Conflict and Peace studies; advisor to Centre for Analysis and Planning, Ministry of Foreign Affairs 1984–94; Dir Centre européen d'étude des conflits 1997–2000. *Publications include:* Armed Struggle in Africa 1969, Mythes révolutionnaires du tiers-monde 1977, Atlas stratégique (with J.-P. Rageau) 1987, Anthologie mondiale de la stratégie 1996, Voyage dans le demi-siècle (with Jean Lacouture) 2001, Atlas du nouvel ordre mondial 2003, Histoire du terrorisme: de l'Antiquité à Al-Qaïda 2004, Guerres et civilisations. De l'Assyrie à l'époque contemporaine 2005, L'Amérique en guerre. Irak-Afghanistan 2007.
Address: 63 Rue Pascal, 75013 Paris, France (home). *Telephone:* 1-43-31-09-12 (home). *E-mail:* gchaliand@aol.com (home).

CHALISE, Suresh Chandra, PhD; Nepalese diplomatist; *Ambassador to USA.* *Education:* Justus-Liebig-Universität, Giessen, Germany, Banaras Hindu Univ., India. *Career:* fmr consultant for Nat. Democratic Inst., Dept for Int. Devt, UNDP, South Asia Regional Initiative, WHO; represented Nepal at UN, led del. at Annual Conf. of Labour Party, UK 2005, Special Envoy of Prime Minister to China 2006, assisted in various peacekeeping efforts with Maoists in Nepal 2006, Foreign Affairs Adviser to Prime Minister –2007, Amb. to USA 2007–; fellowships and grants from India and Germany. *Publications:* Nepal Human Development Report 2004: Empowerment and Poverty Reduction, Coalition Governments and Political Acculturation in Germany, Women in Politics in Nepal: Their Socio-Economic, Health, Legal and Political Constraints, Sociology of the Legislative Elite in Development Society.
Address: Embassy of Nepal, 2131 Leroy Place, NW, Washington, DC 20008, USA (office). *Telephone:* (202) 667-4550 (office). *Fax:* (202) 667-5534 (office). *E-mail:* info@nepalembassyusa.org (office). *Website:* www.nepalembassyusa.org (office).

CHALKER OF WALLASEY, Baroness (Life Peer), cr. 1992, of Leigh-on-Sea in the County of Essex; **Lynda Chalker,** PC; British politician and consultant on African business and development; *Chairman, Africa Matters Ltd;* b. 29 April 1942, Hitchin, Herts.; m. 1st Eric Robert Chalker 1967 (divorced 1973); m. 2nd Clive Landa 1981 (divorced 2003). *Education:* Heidelberg Univ., Germany, London Univ., Cen. London Polytechnic. *Career:* statistician with Research Bureau Ltd (Unilever) 1963–69; Deputy Market Research Man., Shell Mex & BP Ltd 1969–72; Chief Exec. Int. Div. of Louis Harris Int. 1972–74; MP for Wallasey 1974–92; Parl. Under-Sec. of State, Dept of Health and Social Security 1979–82, Dept of Transport 1982–83; Minister of State, Dept of Transport 1983–86, FCO 1986–97, Minister for Overseas Devt 1989–97; ind. consultant on Africa and Devt

1997–; Chair. Africa Matters Ltd 1998–; Dir (non-exec.) Capital Shopping Centres 1997–2000, Unilever PLC and NV 1998–, Landell Mills Ltd 1999–2001, Ashanti Goldfields Co. 2000–04, Group 5 (Pty) Ltd 2001–, Devt Consultants Int. 2001–, Equator Exploration Ltd 2005–; Chair. Greater London Young Conservatives (GLYC) 1969–70; Nat. Vice-Chair. Young Conservatives 1970–71; Chair. London School of Hygiene and Tropical Medicine 1998–; mem. Advisory Bd, Lafarge et Cie 2003–; mem. BBC Gen. Advisory Cttee 1975–79; Hon. Fellow Queen Mary and Westfield Coll.; Dr hc (Bradford) 1995, (Liverpool), (John Moores), (Cranfield), (Warwick), (Westminster), (East London). *Publications:* We Are Richer Than We Think 1978 (co-author), Africa: Turning the Tide 1989.
Address: 51 Causton Street, London, SW1P 4AT (office); House of Lords, London, SW1A 0PW, England. *Telephone:* (20) 7976-6850 (office). *Fax:* (20) 7976-4999 (office). *E-mail:* lchalker@africamatters.com (office). *Website:* www.africamatters.com (office).

CHALOBAH, Melvin Humpah, BEcons; Sierra Leonean banker and diplomatist; *High Commissioner to UK;* b. 1944. *Career:* early career with African Devt Bank; served as Sierra Leone's Rep. at Comm. of African Union (AU), Addis Ababa, Ethiopia; Acting Minister of Foreign Affairs during transition to multi-party democracy; then f. his own business; moved to Addis Ababa where he served as Chief Tech. Adviser on UNDP/OAU project to enhance OAU Conflict Man. Centre; Amb. to Ethiopia and Perm. Rep. to AU –2006, Amb. to UK 2006– (also accred to Ireland 2007–, to Sweden 2008–).
Address: Sierra Leone High Commission, 41 Eagle Street, Holborn, London, WC1R 4TL, England (office). *Telephone:* (20) 7404-0140 (office). *Fax:* (20) 7430-9862 (office). *E-mail:* info@slhc-uk.org.uk (office). *Website:* www.slhc-uk.org.uk (office).

CHAM, Prasidh; Cambodian politician; *Senior Minister and Minister of Commerce;* b. 15 May 1951, Phnom Penh; m. Tep Bopha Prasidh; one s. two d. *Education:* Lycée Descartes, Phnom Penh. *Career:* mem. Cambodian People's Party (CPP); currently Sr Minister and Minister of Commerce; Sr Adviser to His Holiness Samdech Preah Sometheatheppadey Tep Vong, Supreme Patriarch of the Mohanjkhay Buddhist Clergy 2004–; Order of the Sowathara, Moha Sereywadaan class, Order of the Kingdom of Cambodia Assarith Class 1998, Thipadin Class 2001, Oknha 2002.
Address: Ministry of Commerce, 20a–b Norodom blvd, Phnom-Penh, Cambodia (office). *Telephone:* (23) 991708 (office). *Fax:* (23) 213288 (office). *E-mail:* moccabdir@yahoo.com (office). *Website:* www.moc.gov.kh (office).

CHAMBAS, Mohamed Ibn, BA, MA, JD, PhD; Ghanaian lawyer, diplomatist, political scientist and international organization official; *President, Executive Secretariat, Economic Community of West African States (ECOWAS) Commission;* b. 12 July 1950; m. *Education:* Mfantsipim School, Cape Coast and Govt Secondary School, Tamale, Univ. of Ghana, Legon, Cornell Univ., New York, Case Western Reserve Univ., Cleveland, USA. *Career:* teacher, Oberlin Coll., Ohio; practised law with Forbes, Forbes and Teamor Legal Practice, Ohio; Deputy Foreign Minister 1987; MP for Bimbilla 1993–96, 2000–; First Deputy Speaker of Parl. 1993–94; Deputy Foreign Minister 1994–, Chair. Foreign Affairs Cttee 1993–94; Deputy Minister of Educ. 1997–2000; Exec. Sec. Econ. Community of West African States (ECOWAS) 2001–06, Pres. Exec. Secr. ECOWAS Comm. (after restructuring of ECOWAS insts) 2007–; fmr Del. to UN Gen. Ass., OAU, Non-aligned Movt, Commonwealth; mem. Nat. Democratic Congress; mem. Cornell Univ. Council 1997–2001, 2003–07.
Address: ECOWAS Executive Secretariat, 60 Yakubu Gowon Crescent, PMB 401, Asokoro, Abuja, Nigeria (office). *Telephone:* (9) 3147647 (office). *Fax:* (9) 3147646 (office). *E-mail:* info@ecowas.int (office). *Website:* www.ecowas.int (office).

CHAMBERLIN, Wendy J., MS; American diplomatist, international organization official and fmr United Nations official; *President, Middle East Institute;* b. 12 Oct. 1948, Bethesda, Md. *Education:* Northwestern, Boston and Harvard Univs. *Career:* joined Foreign Service, Dept of State, Washington, DC 1975; Consular and Econ. Officer, Vientiane 1976–78; Staff Aide E Asia Bureau, Washington, DC 1978–79; Special Asst to Deputy Sec. of State 1979; Political Officer, Kinshasa 1980–82; Pearson Fellow, US Senate, Washington, DC 1982–83; Political-Mil. Officer, Office of Israel Affairs, Dept of State 1983–85; Dir (acting) Office of Regional Affairs, Bureau of Near East–S Asian Affairs 1985–87; Asst Gen. Service Officer, Rabat 1988–89; Special Asst to Under-Sec. for Political Affairs, Dept of State 1989–90; Dir of Counter-Terrorism, Nat. Security Council, Washington, DC 1990–91; Dir Office of Press–Public Affairs, Bureau of Near East–S Asian Affairs 1991–93; Deputy Chief of Mission, Kuala Lumpur 1993–96; Amb. to Laos 1996–99; Prin. Deputy Asst Bureau of Int. Narcotics and Law Enforcement Programs, Washington, DC 1999–2001;

Amb. to Pakistan 2001–02; Asst Admin. for Asia and Near East, USAID 2002–04; Deputy UN High Commr for Refugees 2004–Feb. 2005, June 2005–06, Acting High Commr Feb.–June 2005; Pres. Middle East Inst. 2007–; Nat. Security Fellow 1984; Dr hc (Northwestern Univ.); numerous meritorious awards from US State Dept.
Address: Middle East Institute, 1761 N Street, NW, Washington, DC 20036-2882, USA (office). *Telephone:* (202) 785-1141 (office). *Fax:* (202) 331-8861 (office). *E-mail:* mideasti@mideasti.org (office). *Website:* www .mideasti.org (office).

CHAMLING, Pawan Kumar; Indian politician, poet and writer; *Chief Minister of Sikkim;* b. 22 Sept. 1950, Yangang Busty, South Sikkim; m. Tika Maya Chamling; four s. four d. *Career:* began career as ind. farmer; entered politics in 1973; Vice-Pres. Dist Youth Congress 1975; Pres. Sikkim Handicapped Persons Welfare Mission 1976–77; Ed. Nava Jyoti 1976–77, Founder Nirman Prakashan 1977, Ed. Nirman (quarterly literary magazine) 1977–; Gen. Sec. and Vice-Pres. Sikkim Prajatantra Congress 1978–84; Pres. of Yangang Gram Panchayat 1982; mem. Sikkim Legis. Ass. 1985–; Minister for Industries, Printing and Information and Public Relations 1989–92; formed Sikkim Democratic Front Party 1993, Leader 1993–; Chief Minister of Sikkim 1994–; Chair. Sikkim Distilleries Ltd 1985–; Hon. PhD (Manipal Univ.) 2003; numerous awards including Chinton Puraskar 1987, Bharat Shiromani 1996, Man of the Year 1998, The Greenest Chief Minister of India 1998, Man of Dedication 1999, Secular India Harmony Award 1998, Manav Sewa Puraskar 1999, Pride of India Gold Award 1999, Best Citizen of India 1999, Poets' Foundation Award 2001, Nat. Citizens of India Award 2002. *Publications include:* Veer koh Parichaya (poem) 1967, Antahin Sapana Meroh Bipana 1985, Perennial Dreams and My Reality, Prarambhek Kabitaharu 1991, Pratiwad 1992, Damthang Heejah ra Aajah 1992, Ma koh Hun 1992, Prarambheek Kabitaharu 1993, Sikkim ra Narikon Maryadha 1994, Crucified Prashna Aur Anya Kabitaye 1996, Sikkim ra Prajatantra 1996, Democracy Redeemed 1997, Prajatantra koh Mirmireymah 1997, Meroh Sapana Ko Sikkim 2002, Perspectives and Vision 2002.
Address: CM Secretariat, Tashiling, Gangtok, Sikkim 737 101 (office); Ghurpisay, Namchi, South Sikkim 737 126, India (home). *Telephone:* (3592) 222263 (office); (3592) 228200 (office); (3595) 263748 (home); (3592) 222536 (home). *Fax:* (3592) 222245 (office); (3592) 224710 (home). *E-mail:* cm-skm@nic.in (office). *Website:* sikkim.nic.in (office).

CHAN, Florinda da Rosa Silva, MBA; Chinese politician; *Secretary for Administration and Justice, Macao Special Administrative Region;* b. June 1954, Macao. *Education:* Int. Open Univ. of Asia (Macao), Univ. of Languages and Culture, Beijing, Nat. Inst. of Public Admin., Beijing. *Career:* joined Macao Govt 1974, Dir Macao Economic Services Bureau 1998, Sec. for Admin. and Justice, Macao Special Admin. Region 1999–; Medal of Professional Merit 1987, Medal of Dedication 1988.
Address: Office of the Secretary for Administration and Justice, Head-quarters of the Government, Avenida de Praia Grande, Macao Special Administrative Region, People's Republic of China (office). *Telephone:* 89895179 (office). *Fax:* 28726880 (office). *E-mail:* florindachan.saj@raem .gov.mo (office). *Website:* www.gov.mo (office).

CHAN, Heng Chee, MA, PhD; Singaporean diplomatist and professor of political science; *Ambassador to USA;* b. 19 April 1942, Singapore. *Education:* Nat. Univ. of Singapore, Cornell Univ., USA. *Career:* Asst Lecturer, Nat. Univ. of Singapore 1967–70, Lecturer 1970–75, Sr Lecturer 1976–80, Assoc. Prof. of Political Science 1981–, Head, Dept of Political Science 1985–88, Prof. 1990; Dir Inst. of Policy Studies, Singapore Jan.–Dec. 1988; Perm Rep. to UN 1989–91, Amb. to Mexico 1989–91, High Commr to Canada 1989–91; Exec. Dir Singapore Int. Foundation 1991–96; Amb. to USA 1996–; Dir Inst. of SE Asian Studies 1993; mem. Int. Council of Asia Soc. 1991–, Singapore Nat. Cttee of Council for Security Co-operation in the Asia-Pacific 1993–, IISS Council, Hong Kong, 1995–, Int. Advisory Bd of Council on Foreign Relations, New York 1995–; Hon. DLit (Newcastle, Australia) 1994, (Buckingham, UK) 1998; Nat. Book Award (non-fiction) 1978, 1986, Woman of the Year (Singapore) 1991. *Publications:* The Dynamics of One Party Dominance: The PAP at the Grassroots 1976, A Sensation of Independence 1984, Government and Politics of Singapore (co-ed.), The Prophetic and the Political 1987.
Address: Embassy of Singapore, 3501 International Place, NW, Washington, DC 20008, USA (office); Singapore International Foundation, 111 Somerset Road, 11-07 Devonshire Wing, Singapore 238164. *Telephone:* (202) 537-3100 (office). *Fax:* (202) 537-0876 (office). *E-mail:* singemb_was@sgmfa.gov.sg (office). *Website:* www.mfa.gov.sg/ washington (office).

CHAN, Rt Hon. Sir Julius, GCMG, KBE, PC; Papua New Guinea politician; b. 29 Aug. 1939, Tanga, New Ireland; m. Stella Ahmat 1966; one d. three s. *Education:* Marist Brothers Coll., Ashgrove, Queensland and Univ. of

Queensland, Australia. *Career:* Co-operative Officer, Papua New Guinea Admin. 1960–62; Man. Dir Coastal Shipping Co. Pty Ltd; mem. House of Ass. 1968–75, 1982–97, Deputy Speaker, Vice-Chair. Public Accounts Cttee 1968–72; Parl. Leader, People's Progress Party 1970–97; Minister of Finance and Parl. Leader of Govt Business 1972–77; Deputy Prime Minister and Minister for Primary Industry 1977–78, Prime Minister 1980–82, Deputy Prime Minister 1986–88, Minister of Trade and Industry 1986–88, Deputy Prime Minister 1992–94, Minister for Finance and Planning 1992–94, for Foreign Affairs and Trade 1994–96; Prime Minister 1994–97; Gov. of Papua New Guinea and Vice-Chair. Asian Devt Bank 1975–77; Fellowship mem. Int. Bankers' Asscn Inc., USA 1976; fmr Gov. IBRD/IMF; Hon. DEcon (Dankook Univ., Seoul) 1978; Hon. DTech (Univ. of Tech., Papua New Guinea) 1983.
Address: PO Box 6030, Boroko, Papua New Guinea.

CHAN, Laurie; Solomon Islands politician. *Career:* Minister of Finance –2002; Minister of Foreign Affairs, Commerce and Tourism 2002–06.
Address: c/o Ministry of Foreign Affairs, Commerce and Tourism, POB G10, Honiara, Solomon Islands (office).

CHAN, Margaret F. C., OBE, MSc, MScPH, MD, DSc, FFPHM; Chinese physician and international organization executive; *Director-General, World Health Organization;* b. 1947, Hong Kong; m.; one s. *Education:* Northcote Coll. of Educ., Hong Kong, Univ. of Western Ontario, Canada, Nat. Univ. of Singapore, Harvard Business School, USA, Tsinghua Univ., Beijing, Nat. School of Admin., Beijing. *Career:* Rotating Internship, Victoria Hosp., London, Ont. 1977–78; Medical Officer (Maternal and Child Health Services), Dept of Health, Hong Kong 1978–85, Sr Medical Officer (Family Health Services) 1985–78, Prin. Medical Officer (Health Admin) 1987–89, Asst Dir (Personal Health Services) 1989–92, Deputy Dir 1992–94, Dir Dept of Health, Hong Kong Special Admin. Region 1994–2003; Dir Dept of Protection of the Human Environment, WHO 2003–05, Asst Dir-Gen. of Communicable Diseases and Rep. of Dir-Gen. for Pandemic Influenza 2005–06, Dir-Gen. WHO 2006–, Organizer 43rd Session WHO Regional Cttee for the Western Pacific 1992, Chair. 49th Session WHO Regional Cttee for the Western Pacific 1998, WHO Guidelines on Methodologies for Research and Evaluation of Traditional Medicine 2000, WHO Int. Conf. for Drug Regulatory Authorities 2001 Planning Cttee 2000–02, Vice-Chair. WHO Working Group on Framework Convention on Tobacco Control 1999–2000, Moderator WHO Western Pacific Region Ministerial Round-table on Social Safety Net 1999; Prince Mahidol Award in Public Health (Thailand) 1999, ranked by Forbes magazine amongst 100 Most Powerful Women (37th) 2007.
Address: World Health Organization (WHO), Ave Appia 20, 1211 Geneva 27, Switzerland (office). *Telephone:* 227912111 (office). *Fax:* 227913111 (office). *E-mail:* info@who.int (office). *Website:* www.who.int (office).

CHAN TUNG, Tuala Falani, BA, MA; Samoan diplomatist; *Ambassador to Belgium;* m. Louisa Chan Tung. *Career:* began career in Dept of Econ. Devt (renamed Dept of Trade, Commerce and Industry), Sec. –2003; Special Consultant on Trade Matters, Ministry of Foreign Affairs and Trade 2003–05, Amb. to Belgium and EU 2005– (accred as High Commr to UK 2006–); holds the matai title Tuala from the village of Leauvaa.
Address: Embassy of Samoa, 20 Avenue de l'Orée, 1000 Brussels, Belgium (office). *Telephone:* (2) 660-84-54 (office). *Fax:* (2) 675-03-36 (office). *E-mail:* samoanembassy@skynet.be (office).

CHANDRA MUNGRA, Subhas, MA; Suriname diplomatist, international organization official and economist; b. 2 Sept. 1945, Paramaribo; m.; three c. *Education:* Municipal Univ. of Amsterdam. *Career:* Lecturer in Finance and Banking, Monetary Theory, Anton de Kom Univ. of Suriname 1976–86; Chair. Nat. Cardboard Industry 1985–86; Dir Nat. Devt Bank 1983; Minister of Foreign Affairs 1991–96, of Finance 1986–90; Chair. Jt Governing Bd of Centre for the Devt of Industry on behalf of the African, Caribbean and Pacific Group in Brussels 1988–90; apptd Perm. Rep. to UN 1997; Vice-Chair. Third UN Conf. on Least Developed Countries 2000; Pres. (Acting) UN Gen. Ass. Jan. 2001. *Publications:* numerous articles on econ. issues.
Address: c/o Permanent Mission of Suriname to the United Nations, 866 United Nations Plaza, Suite 320, New York, NY 10017, USA (office).

CHANET, Christine Simone; French lawyer, civil servant and UN official; *Personal Representative on the Situation of Human Rights in Cuba, United Nations Office of the High Commissioner for Human Rights;* b. 23 Feb. 1944, Paris. *Education:* Lycée La Fontaine, Paris and Univ. of Paris. *Career:* auditor, Ecole nat. de la Magistrature 1968–70; magistrate, Cen. Admin, Ministry of Justice 1970–74; Tech. Adviser, then Rep. to Secr. of State for Women's Affairs 1974–76; Rep. to Secr. of State for Culture 1976–77; Rep. to Judicial Affairs Section, Ministry of Foreign Affairs 1981–88; Sub-Dir for Human Rights and Int. Civil and Penal Affairs 1983; Tech. Adviser

Cabinet of the Minister of Justice, Keeper of the Seals 1988–90; Deputy Attorney-Gen. Cour d'Appel de Paris (Court of Appeal) 1992–96; Counsel Cour de Cassation 1996–; mem. UN Cttee against Torture 1988–1990, UN Cttee on Human Rights 1996– (Chair. 1997–98, 2005), Personal Rep. of UN High Commr on Human Rights on the Situation of Human Rights in Cuba 2003–; mem. Int. Comm. of Jurists 2003–; mem. Advisory Cttee on Human Rights in France, French Int. Law Soc., Int. Law Asscn (French br.); Chevalier de l'Ordre nat. du Mérite 1988; Laureate of Faculty of Law and Econs, Paris 1967. *Publications:* articles in law journals.
Address: Office of the High Commissioner for Human Rights, 1211 Geneva 10, Switzerland (office). *Telephone:* (22) 917-9011 (office). *E-mail:* ngochr@ ohchr.org (office). *Website:* www.ohchr.org (office).

CHANG, Chun-hsiung, LLB; Taiwanese politician; b. 23 March 1938; m.; three s. one d. *Education:* Nat. Taiwan Univ. *Career:* defence lawyer in mil. trial following Kaohsiung Incident 1980; mem. Legis. Yuan 1983–; a Founder-mem. Democratic Progressive Party (DPP) 1986–, mem. Cen. Standing Cttee and Cen. Exec. Cttee DPP 1986–2000, Exec. Dir DPP Caucus in Legis. Yuan 1987–88, Gen. Convenor 1990, 1998–99, Sec.-Gen. DPP 2002–07; Sec.-Gen. Office of Pres. 2000; Vice-Premier 2000; Premier 2000–02, 2007–08.
Address: Democratic Progressive Party, 10/F, 30 Beiping East Road, Taipei, 10051, Taiwan (office). *Telephone:* (2) 23929989 (office). *Fax:* (2) 23929989 (office). *E-mail:* foreign@dpp.org.tw (office). *Website:* www.dpp .org.tw (office).

CHANG, Manuel, MPhil; Mozambican government official; *Minister of Finance;* b. 22 Aug. 1955, Gaza; m. Lizete Izilda Adriano Simões Maia; three c. *Education:* Escola Industrial Mouzinho de Albuquerque, Universidade Eduardo Mondlane, Univ. of London, UK. *Career:* joined Ministry of Finance 1974, Section Head 1977, Section Head, Service Comm. 1979, Acting Head, Dept of the Treasury 1987, Head, Dept of the Treasury 1988–89, Adjunct Nat. Dir of the Treasury 1989–93, Dir of Nat. Budget 1993–96, Vice-Minister of Planning and Finance –2005, Minister of Finance 2005–; mem. Frente de Libertação de Moçambique (Frelimo) party; Vice-Pres. Fund for the Promotion of Fishing; Pres. of audit council Banco de Moçambique; mem. Bd of Dirs Pipeline Mozambique-Zimbabwe; mem. Admin. Council Correios de Moçambique 1994–96, Silos Granoleiros de Matola.
Address: Ministério do Plano e Finanças, Praça da Marinha Popular, CP 272, Maputo, Mozambique. *Telephone:* 21306808. *Fax:* 21306261. *E-mail:* dnpo@dnpo.uem.mz. *Website:* www.mozambique.mz/governo/mpf/dnpo.

CHANG, Sang, BSc, MDiv, DPhil; South Korean politician, theologist and academic; b. 9 Oct. 1939. *Education:* Ewha Women's Univ., Yonsei Univ., Yale Univ. and Princeton Theological Seminary, USA. *Career:* Prof. of New Testament Theology, Dept of Christian Studies, Ewha Women's Univ. (EWU) 1977–2002, Dir of Academic Affairs, Grad. School 1980, Chair. Dept of Christian Studies 1988, Dir Korea Cultural Research Inst., EWU 1989, Dean Student Affairs 1990, Dean Coll. of Liberal Arts 1993, Dean Grad. School of Information Science 1995, Vice-Pres. EWU 1996, Pres. 1996–2002; ordained to the Ministry of the Word 1988; mem. Exec. Cttee YWCA Korea 1979–97 (Vice-Pres. 1983–97), Exec. Cttee World Alliance of Reformed Churches (WARC) 1982–89 (Moderator Dept of Co-operation and Witness 1989–97), Exec. Cttee World YWCA 1987–91; mem. Public Official Ethics Cttee, Ministry of Admin. and Home Affairs 1997–99, Women's Policies Cttee 1997–2002; mem. Advisory Council on Korean Unification 1998–2002; Vice-Pres. Advisory Council on Democratic and Peaceful Unification 1998–2002; mem. Presidential Comm. for the New Millennium 1999–2002, Admin. Negotiating Cttee 2000–02; nominated Prime Minister of S. Korea July 2002, appointment vetoed by Parl.; Chair. Press Asscn of Pvt. Univs 1999–2002; Vice-Pres. Korean Council for Univ. Educ. 1999–2002; Chair. Korean Council for Pres. of Pvt. Univs 1999–2002; Trustee United Bd for Christian Higher Educ. in Asia 1995–2002, Int. Women's Univ., Hanover, Germany 2000–02, Bd Korea Research Foundation 2000–02, Korea Inst. of Science and Tech. Evaluation and Planning 2001–02; Order of Civil Merit 1999, Moran Medal 1999. *Publications include:* On Interpretation of Paul's Thoughts, Women's Status and Role in First Christian Movement, Paul's Somatic Understanding of Human Beings, The Origin and Development of Feminist Theology, Christianity and World Korean Theology in Transition, Korean Women's Studies, Paul's Understanding of History and Gospel.
Address: c/o National Assembly, 1 Yeouido-dong, Yeongdeungpo-gu, Seoul (office); 1901, Samdok Ever Villa, 105-1, Namgajwa-dong, Seodae-mun-gu, Seoul, Republic of Korea (home).

CHANG, (Katherine) Siao-Yue, MA, BA; Taiwanese politician and diplomatist; *Deputy Minister of Foreign Affairs;* b. 12 Feb. 1953. *Education:* Nat. Chengchi Univ., Foreign Service Inst., Long Island Univ., USA. *Career:*

Desk Officer, Dept of Int. Orgs, Ministry of Foreign Affairs 1976–77, Staff Officer, Secretariat, 1977–80; Vice-Consul, Taipei Econ. and Cultural Office, New York 1980–84, Consul 1984–89; Sec. on Home Assignment and Section Chief, Fourth Section, Dept of N American Affairs 1989–91, Deputy Dir-Gen. 1993–95; Asst Dir-Gen. and Section Chief, Ministry of Foreign Affairs 1991–93; Dir Taipei Econ. and Cultural Office, Seattle 1995–97; Amb. to St Kitts and Nevis 1997–2001; Dir-Gen., Dept of Information and Culture Affairs 2001–03; Rep. Taipei Rep. Office in the Netherlands 2003–06; Deputy Minister of Foreign Affairs 2006–.
Address: Ministry of Foreign Affairs, Kaitakelan Boulevard, Taipei 100, Taiwan (office). *Website:* www.mofa.gov.tw.

CHAPLIN, Edward Graham Mellish, CMG, OBE, BA; British diplomatist; *Ambassador to Italy;* b. 21 Feb. 1951; m. Nicola Chaplin; one s. two d. *Education:* Univ. of Cambridge and Ecole Nationale d'Admin, Paris. *Career:* entered FCO 1973; served with Middle East Dept 1973–74, Third Sec., Chancery, Oman 1975–77, Second Sec., Chancery, Brussels 1977–78; on secondment as Pvt. Sec. to Lord Pres. of the Council and Leader of the House of Lords 1979–81; Near East and N Africa Dept, FCO 1981–85, Head of Chancery, Tehran, Iran 1985–87, Personnel Operations Dept 1987–89; on secondment with Price Waterhouse as man. consultant 1990–92; Deputy Head of Perm. Mission to UN and Int. Orgs, Geneva 1992–96; Head of Middle East Dept, FCO 1996–99; Amb. to Jordan 2000–02; Dir Middle East and N Africa, FCO 2002–04; Amb. to Iraq 2004–05, to Italy 2006–; Visiting Fellow, Centre for Int. Studies, Univ. of Cambridge 2005–06.
Address: British Embassy, Via XX Settembre 80a, 00187, Rome, Italy (office). *Telephone:* (06) 42200001 (office). *Fax:* (06) 42202333 (office). *E-mail:* romepoliticalsection@fco.gov.uk (office). *Website:* www.britain.it (office).

CHARKVIANI, Gela; Georgian politician and diplomatist; *Ambassador to UK;* b. 1 March 1939, Tbilisi, Georgia; m. Nana Toidze-Charkviani; one s. one d. *Education:* Tbilisi Inst. of Foreign Languages, Univ. of Mich., USA. *Career:* teacher Tbilisi Inst. of Foreign Languages; author and narrator TV monthly programme Globe, Georgian TV 1976–94; Vice-Pres. Georgian Soc. for Cultural Relations with Foreign Countries 1984–92; apptd Chief Adviser to Pres. Shevardnadze on Foreign Affairs, Head of Int. Relations Georgian State Chancellery 1992; taught sociology at Tbilisi State Univ. 1982–; Asst to Pres. Saakashvili of Georgia and Presidential Spokesperson 2005–06; Amb. to UK (also accred to Ireland) 2006–; Chair. Presidential Comm. on Peaceful Caucasus; has lectured in Austria, Germany, Sweden, UK and USA; Order of Honour 1998. *Television:* author and dir of five-part documentary The Georgians in the Kremlin (Rustavi-II TV) 2004. *Publications include:* trans. of King Lear; Georgia, Transcaucasus and Beyond 1996; articles in numerous journals.
Address: Embassy of Georgia, 4 Russell Gardens, London, W14 8EZ, England (office); Gamsakhurdia str. 14, Tbilisi, Georgia (home). *Telephone:* (20) 7603-7799 (office); (32) 989679 (home). *Fax:* (20) 7603-6682 (office). *E-mail:* embassy@geoemb.plus.com (office). *Website:* www .geoemb.org.uk (office).

CHARLTON, Alan, CMG, CVO; British diplomatist; *Ambassador to Brazil;* m. Judith Charlton; two s. one d. *Career:* Desk Officer, West Africa Dept, FCO 1978–79, Arabic language training 1979–80, Second, later First Sec., Amman 1981–84, Desk Officer for Israel and Lebanon, Near East and N Africa Dept, FCO 1984–86, Deputy Political Adviser, British Mil. Govt (later British Mission), Berlin 1986–90, Deputy Chief of Assessments Staff, Cabinet Office 1991–92, Head of East Adriatic Unit and UK mem. of Bosnia Contact Group, FCO 1993–96, Counsellor, then Deputy Head of Mission, Bonn (later Berlin) 1996–2001, Dir SE Europe, FCO 2001, Dir of Human Resources 2001–04, Deputy Head of Mission, Washington, DC 2004–07, Amb. to Brazil 2008–.
Address: British Embassy, SES, Quadra 801, Conj. K, Lote 08, 70408-900 Brasília, DF, Brazil (office). *Telephone:* (61) 3329-2300 (office). *Fax:* (61) 3329-2369 (office). *E-mail:* contato@reinounido.org.br (office). *Website:* www.reinounido.org.br (office).

CHARTER, Joseph Stephen; Grenadian diplomatist; *High Commissioner to UK;* m. Aileen Valerie Charter. *Career:* Amb. to Libya 1979–83; fmr Lecturer in Caribbean Studies, St George's Univ.; fmr Perm. Sec., Ministry of Culture, Ministry of Health –2005; High Commr to UK 2005–; fmr mem. Bd of Dirs Nat. Telecommunications Regulatory Comm.
Address: High Commission of Grenada, The Chapel, Archel Road, London, W14 9QH, England (office). *Telephone:* (20) 7385-4415 (office). *Fax:* (20) 7381-4807 (office). *E-mail:* grenada@high-commission.demon.co .uk (office).

CHATAH, Mohamad, BA, PhD; Lebanese economist, academic, diplomatist and government official; *Minister of Finance;* b. March 1951, Tripoli; m.;

two c. *Education:* American Univ. of Beirut, Univ. of Texas, USA. *Career:* Instructor, Dept of Econs, Univ. of Texas 1977–92; advisor to Exec. Dir, IMF 1983–93, advisor on external relations 2000–02, 2003–05, Alt. Exec. Dir 2002–03; Vice-Gov. Cen. Bank of Lebanon 1993–97; Amb. to USA 1997–99; Chief Advisor to Pres. of Council of Ministers 2005–08; Minister of Finance 2008–.
Address: Ministry of Finance, 4e étage, Immeuble MOF, place Riad es-Solh, Beirut, Lebanon (office). *Telephone:* (1) 981001 (office). *Fax:* (1) 981059 (office). *E-mail:* infocenter@finance.gov.lb (office). *Website:* www .finance.gov.lb (office).

CHATTERTON DICKSON, Robert Maurice French, BA, MA; British diplomatist; b. 1 Feb. 1962, Plymouth; m. Teresa Albor; two d. one step-s. and one step-d. *Education:* Wellington Coll., Berks., Magdalene Coll., Cambridge (Exhibitioner). *Career:* investment analyst and portfolio man., Morgan Grenfell Asset Man. Ltd 1984–90; joined FCO 1990, Security Policy Dept 1990–91, Second Sec., Chancery/Information, Manila 1991–94, SE Asian Dept, FCO 1994–95, UN Dept 1995–96, First Sec., Press/Public Affairs, Washington, DC 1997–98, Pvt. Sec. to HM Amb., Washington, DC 1998–2000, Security Policy Dept, FCO 2000–03, Iraq Policy Unit, March–Nov. 2003, Review of Travel Advice 2003–04, Amb. to Fmr Yugoslav Repub. of Macedonia 2004–07.
Address: Foreign and Commonwealth Office, King Charles Street, London, SW1A 2AH, England (office). *Telephone:* (20) 7008-1500 (office). *Website:* www.fco.gov.uk (office).

CHAU, Nguyen Thanh, MA; Vietnamese diplomatist; b. 17 Sept. 1945, Phu Tho; m.; two c. *Education:* Australian Nat. Univ. *Career:* Lecturer Inst. of Int. Relations, Ministry of Foreign Affairs, Hanoi; Second Sec., Perm. Mission to UN 1983–86; various positions with Viet Nam Comm. for UNESCO including Sec.-Gen. 1987–92; Amb. to Australia (also accred to NZ, Papua New Guinea, Vanuatu and Fiji) 1992–96; Dir Int. Orgs Div., Ministry of Foreign Affairs 1996–2000; Perm. Rep. to UN 2000–04.
Address: c/o Permanent Mission of Viet Nam to the United Nations, 866 United Nations Plaza, Suite 435, New York, NY 10017, USA (office).

CHAUDHRY, Mahendra Pal; Fijian politician; *Secretary General, Fiji Labour Party;* b. 2 Sept. 1942, Ba, Fiji; two s. one d. *Career:* Sr Auditor, Office of the Auditor Gen. 1960–75; Gen. Sec. Nat. Farmers' Union 1978–; Gen. Sec. Fiji Public Service Asscn 1970–99; Nat. Sec. Fiji Trades Union Congress 1988–92; Minister of Finance April–May 1987 (ousted in May 1987 coup), Founding mem. Fiji Labour Party 1985, Parliamentary Leader 1992, Sec.-Gen. 1994–; Prime Minister and Minister of Finance, Public Enterprise, Sugar Industry and Information 1999–2000; ousted in coup by George Speight May 2000; reassumed post of Prime Minister 1 March 2001, dismissed 14 March 2001 by Pres. of Fiji; Leader of the Opposition 2004–; Minister of Finance, National Planning, Public Enterprise and Sugar Reform (in Cdre Josaia Bainimarama's interim govt) Jan. 2007–08 (resgnd); Bharatiya Samman Award, Govt of India 2004.
Address: Fiji Labour Party, PO Box 2162, Suva; 74 Augustus Street, Suva (office); 3 Hutson Street, Suva, Fiji (home). *Telephone:* 3305811 ext. 405 (office); 301875 (home). *Fax:* 3305317 (office). *E-mail:* flp@connect.com.fj (office); mahendrachaudhry42@hotmail.com (home). *Website:* www.flp .org.fj (office).

CHAUDHRY, Air Vice-Marshal Shahzad Aslam, MSc; Pakistani air force officer (retd) and diplomatist; *High Commissioner to Sri Lanka;* m.; five c. *Education:* Air Command and Staff Coll., USA, Nat. Defence Coll., Islamabad. *Career:* served in various command/staff and instructional roles during air force career including Officer Commanding F-16 Squadron 1987–89, Officer Commanding F-16 Wing 1996–97, Base Commdr, Pakistan Air Force Base, Rafiqui 2000–02, Air Officer Commanding Southern Air Command 2003, Deputy Chief of Air Staff (Operations), Pakistan Air Force 2003–06; Air Attaché, Pakistan High Comm., London 1992–96; High Commr to Sri Lanka 2006–; mem. UN Asscn of Sri Lanka; Hilal-e-Imtiaz (Mil.), Sitara-e-Imtiaz (Mil.), Tamgha-e-Basalat, Professional Efficiency Badge.
Address: High Commission of Pakistan, No. 211 De Saram Place, Colombo 10, Sri Lanka (office). *Telephone:* (11) 2696301 (office). *Fax:* (11) 2695780 (office). *E-mail:* parepcolombo@sltnet.lk (office). *Website:* www.mfa.gov .pk/Green_Book/Srilanka_GB.htm (office).

CHAVALIT, Gen. Yongchaiyudh; Thai politician; *Deputy Prime Minister;* b. 15 May 1932; m. Khunying Phankrua Yongchaiyudh. *Education:* Chulachomklao Royal Mil. Acad., Army Command and Gen. Staff Coll., Fort Leavenworth, USA. *Career:* Dir of Operations 1981, Chief of Staff 1985, C-in-C 1986–90, Acting Supreme Commdr 1987–90; Deputy Prime Minister March–June 1990, 1995–1996, 2001–, concurrently Minister of Defence March–June 1990, 1995–1996, 2001; Minister of the

Interior 1992–94, of Labour and Social Welfare 1993–94; Leader New Aspiration Party.
Address: New Aspiration Party, Ban Mittraphap, Thanon Rama IV, Bangkok, Thailand (office). *Telephone:* (2) 243-5000 (office).

CHÁVEZ FRÍAS, Lt-Col Hugo Rafael, MA; Venezuelan politician and head of state; *President;* b. 28 July 1954, Sabaneta, Barinas State; m. 1st (divorced); three d.; m. 2nd María Isabel Rodríguez (divorced); one d. *Education:* Liceo O'Leary, Barinas State, Mil. Acad., Univ. Simón Bolívar, Caracas. *Career:* f. Movimiento Bolivariano Revolucionario 1982; Lt-Col Venezuelan Paratroops 1990; led failed mil. coup against Pres. Carlos Pérez 1992; f. Movimiento Revolucionario V República 1998; represents Patriotic Pole coalition; Pres. of Venezuela 1999–12 April 2002, 14 April 2002–; Estrella de Carabobo Cruz de las Fuerzas Terrestres, Orden Militar Francisco de Miranda, Orden Militar Rafael Urdaneta, Orden Militar Libertador V Clase. *Film appearance:* The War on Democracy (documentary) 2007. *Publication:* Cómo salir del Laberinto? (co-author) 1992.
Address: Central Information Office of the Presidency, Torre Oeste 18°, Parque Central, Caracas 1010, Venezuela. *Telephone:* (2) 572-7110. *Fax:* (2) 572-2675.

CHECHELASHVILI, Valeri, PhD; Georgian diplomatist and international organization official; *Minister of Finance;* b. 17 March 1961, Tbilisi; m. Marine Neparidze; two s. one d. *Education:* Kiev State Univ., Ukraine. *Career:* mem. staff, Foreign Econ. Relations Dept, Ministry of Light Industry 1987–88; Deputy Head of Foreign Econ. Relations section, Jt Stock Co. Gruzkurort 1988–89; First Sec. Dept of Int. Econ. Relations, Ministry of Foreign Affairs 1989–90, Deputy Dir 1990–91, First Deputy Dir 1991–92, Dir 1992–94, Deputy Minister of Foreign Affairs 1998–2000; Amb. to Ukraine 1994–98, to Moldova 1996–98; Sec.-Gen. Black Sea Econ. Co-operation (BSEC) 2000–04; Amb. to Russian Fed. 2004–05; Minister of Finance 2005–; Second Degree Order for Service, Ukraine 1998. *Publications:* several articles on econ. co-operation in learned journals.
Address: Ministry of Finance, Abashidze 70, 0168 Tbilisi, Georgia (office). *Telephone:* (32) 22-68-05 (office). *Fax:* (32) 93-19-22 (office). *E-mail:* minister@mof.ge (office). *Website:* www.mof.ge (office).

CHEDID, Antoine, BA; Lebanese diplomatist; *Ambassador to USA;* b. 1951, Zahle; m. Nicole Saba; two s. one d. *Education:* School of Law, French Univ. of St Joseph. *Career:* sr career diplomat, entered Foreign Service in 1978, posted overseas to USA and Greece, held positions of Asst to Sec. Gen. of Ministry of Foreign Affairs; Consul, Press Attaché and Political Officer, Embassy in Washington, DC 1979–84; mem. Lebanese dels to 12 Sessions of UN Gen. Ass., New York; Presidential Adviser for American Affairs 1989–91, Head of America Desk Office, Ministry of Foreign Affairs; Consul Gen. in Los Angeles 1984–86, in New York and eastern States 1991–98, Amb. to Greece 1998–2000; Head of Bureau of Int. Orgs, Confs and Cultural Relations, Ministry of Foreign Affairs 2001–07; Chargé d'affaires a.i., Washington, DC 2007–08, Amb. to USA 2008–.
Address: Embassy of Lebanon, 2560 28th Street, NW, Washington, DC 20008, USA (office). *Telephone:* (202) 939-6300 (office). *Fax:* (202) 939-6324 (office). *E-mail:* info@lebanonembassyus.org (office). *Website:* www .lebanonembassyus.org (office).

CHEN, Lt-Gen. Bingde; Chinese army officer and politician; *Commander-in-Chief, Jinan Military Region, People's Liberation Army;* b. July 1941, Nantong City, Jiangsu Prov. *Education:* Mil. Acad. of the Chinese PLA. *Career:* joined PLA 1961, then Squadron Leader, Platoon Leader, Staff mem. PLA Services and Arms, Army (or Ground Force), Combat Training Section, Regt Chief of Staff, Div. Deputy Chief of Staff, Div. Chief of Staff 1979–81, Div. Commdr 1981–83, Deputy Commdr PLA Services and Arms, Army (or Ground Force) 1983, Maj.-Gen. 1988–95, Lt-Gen. 1995–99, Chief of Staff, PLA, Nanjing Mil. Region 1985, C-in-C 1996–99, C-in-C Jinan Mil. Region 1999–, Pres. PLA Nanchang Infantry Acad.; joined CCP 1962, Deputy Sec. CCP Party Cttee PLA, Nanjing Mil. Region; mem. 15th CCP Cen. Cttee 1997–2002, 16th CCP Cen. Cttee 2002– (mem. Cen. Mil. Comm. 2004–).
Address: Jinan Military Area Command, Jinan, Shandong Province, People's Republic of China.

CHEN, Deming, BA, PhD; Chinese government official; *Minister of Commerce;* b. July 1949, Shanghai. *Education:* Jiangxi Communist Labor Univ. (now Jiangxi Agricultural Univ.). *Career:* began career in 1969 in Jiangxi working five years for production team; joined CCP 1974; worked for three years for Jiangxi Agricultural Machinery Bureau, then worked for Jiangsu Food Products Corpn; Asst Dir, Gen. Office, Jiangsu Bureau of Commerce 1984, Deputy Dir 1985; fmr Sec.-Gen., Gen. Office Jiangsu prov. govt; Mayor of Suzhou City 1998–2003; Vice-Gov. Shaanxi Prov. 1998–2003, Acting Gov. 2004–05, Gov. 2005–06; Vice-Chair. State Devt and Reform Comm. 2006–07; Vice-Minister of Commerce 2007, Minister of Commerce

2007–; Deputy to 9th NPC 1998–2003, Del. to 16th CPC, Nat. Congress 2002–07, Alt. mem. 17th CPC, Cen. Cttee 2007–.
Address: Ministry of Commerce, 2 Dongchangan Jie, Dongcheng Qu, Beijing 100731, People's Republic of China (office). *Telephone:* (10) 65121919 (office). *Fax:* (10) 65599340 (office). *E-mail:* webmaster@ mofcom.gov.cn (office). *Website:* www.mofcom.gov.cn (office).

CHEN, Kuiyuan; Chinese party official; *Vice-Chairman, 10th Chinese People's Political Consultative Conference National Committee; Education:* Inner Mongolia Teachers' Univ. *Career:* joined CCP 1965; fmr mem., Deputy Sec.-Gen., Sec.-Gen. CCP League Cttee Standing Cttee, Hulun Buir League, Inner Mongolia Autonomous Region, Deputy Sec. and Sec. 1983–89; mem. CCP Autonomous Regional Cttee Standing Cttee, Inner Mongolia Autonomous Region 1989–92: Vice-Chair. Inner Mongolia Autonomous Regional People's Congress 1989–92; Deputy Sec. CCP Tibet Autonomous Region Cttee 1992, Sec. 1992–2000; mem. 14th CCP Cen. Cttee 1992–97, 15th CCP Cen. Cttee 1997–2002, 16th CCP Cen. Cttee 2002–; apptd First Sec. CCP Party Cttee PLA, Tibet Mil. Region 1996; Sec. CCP Henan Prov. Cttee 2000–; Pres. Chinese Acad. of Social Sciences 2002–; Vice-Chair. 10th CPPCC Nat. Cttee 2003–.
Address: Chinese Communist Party Henan Provincial Committee, Zhengzhou, Henan Province, People's Republic of China.

CHEN, Yuan, BS, MA; Chinese banker; *Governor, China Development Bank;* b. 13 Jan. 1945, Shanghai. *Education:* China Acad. of Social Sciences, Tsinghua Univ., Beijing. *Career:* Sec. CCP Cttee of Xicheng Dist, Beijing 1982–84; Dir-Gen. Dept of Commerce and Trade, Beijing Municipal Govt 1984–88; Vice-Gov. People's Bank of China 1988–98; Gov. China Devt Bank 1998–; mem. Preparatory Cttee of Hong Kong Special Admin. Region, Vice-Pres. Financial Soc.; mem. Securities Comm. of the State Council; Sec. CCP Xicheng Dist Cttee, Beijing; mem. Standing Cttee CCP Beijing Municipal Cttee; Dir Inst. for Int. Econs, USA (mem. Advisory Cttee and the Financial Stability Inst.); Deputy Gov., Dir Business and Trade Activities Dept, and Advisor to Postgraduates, People's Bank of China (also Deputy Sec. CCP Party Cttee). *Publications:* The Underlying Problems and Options in China's Economy, Macroeconomic Management: The Need for Deepening Reform, Collected Works.
Address: China Development Bank, 29 Fuchengmenwai Lu, Xicheng Qu, Beijing 100037, People's Republic of China (office). *Telephone:* (10) 68307608 (office). *Fax:* (10) 68306541 (office). *Website:* cdb.com.cn (office).

CHEN, Zhili; Chinese politician, academic and fmr physicist; *State Councillor;* b. 21 Nov. 1942, Xianyou Co., Fujian Prov. *Education:* Fudan Univ., Shanghai Inst. of Ceramics, Chinese Acad. of Sciences. *Career:* joined CCP 1961; served in People's Liberation Armym No. 6409 Army Unit, Danyang Lake Farm 1968–70; Assoc. Research Fellow, Chinese Acad. of Sciences 1970–80, 1982–84, Deputy Sec., CP Cttee of the Inst. 1982–84; Visiting Scholar, Materials Research Lab., Pa State Univ., USA 1980–82; Deputy Sec. CCP Party Cttee, Shanghai Inst. of Ceramics 1983–84; Deputy Sec. and Sec. Science and Tech. Work Cttee, Shanghai CCP Municipal Cttee 1984–86; Alt. mem. 13th CCP Cen. Cttee 1987–92, 14th CCP Cen. Cttee 1992–97; mem. Standing Cttee, Shanghai CCP Municipal Cttee 1988–89, Head Publicity Dept 1988–91, Deputy Sec. Publicity Dept 1991–97; Deputy Sec. CCP Shanghai Municipal Cttee 1991–97; Vice-Minister and Sec. CCP Leading Party Group, State Educ. Comm. 1997–98; Minister of Educ. 1998–2003; apptd mem. State Steering Group of Science, Tech. and Educ. 1998; apptd Vice-Chair. State Academic Degree Cttee 1999; State Councillor 2003–; mem. 15th CCP Cen. Cttee 1997–2002, 16th CCP Cen. Cttee 2002–; Hon. Pres. Shanghai Inst. of Int. Friendship.
Address: c/o Zhongguo Gongchan Dang (Chinese Communist Party), Beijing, People's Republic of China (office).

CHEN CHARPENTIER, Jorge Eduardo; Mexican diplomatist; *Ambassador to Italy;* b. June 1950, Mexico City; m.; two c. *Education:* El Colegio de Mexico. *Career:* joined Ministry of Foreign Affairs 1979, held several positions including Adviser to Sec. for Foreign Affairs 1985–92, Dir-Gen. of Diplomatic Archives 1992–93, Dir-Gen. for Asia and Africa 1993–95, Dir-Gen. for Europe 1995–97, Under-Sec. for Latin America and the Caribbean 2005–06; overseas postings include at Perm. Mission to UN, New York 1979–85, Chargé d'affaires Embassy in Chile 1990; Amb. to Hungary 1998–2001; Alt. Rep. to European Insts, Brussels 2001–04; Alt. Rep. to OAS 2004–05, Amb. to Italy (also accred. to Malta) 2007–, also Perm. Rep. to FAO, IFAD and PMA (WFP); fmr Prof., Americas Univ., Inst. of Tech. in Mexico, Nat. Univ. of Mexico.
Address: Embassy of Mexico, Via Lazzaro Spallanzani 16, 00161 Rome, Italy. *Telephone:* (06) 44115204 (office). *Fax:* (06) 4403876 (office). *E-mail:* ofna.embajador@emexitalia.it (office). *Website:* www.sre.gob.mx/italia (office).

CHENEY, Richard (Dick) B., BA, MA; American politician and fmr business executive; *Vice-President;* b. 30 Jan. 1941, Lincoln, Neb.; m. Lynne Vincent Cheney; two d. *Education:* Univ. of Wyoming, Univ. of Wisconsin. *Career:* engaged on staff of Gov. of Wis.; Special Asst to Dir White House Office of Econ. Opportunity 1969–70; Deputy to White House Presidential Counselor 1970–71; Asst Dir of Operations, White House Cost of Living Council 1971–73; partner, Bradley, Woods & Co. 1973–74; Deputy Asst to the Pres. 1974–75, White House Chief of Staff 1975–77; Congressman, At-large District, Wyoming, 1978–89; Chair. Republican Policy Cttee 1981–87; Chair. House Republican Conf. 1987; House Minority Whip 1988; Sec. of Defense 1989–93; Sr Fellow American Enterprise Inst. 1993–95; Chair. Bd and CEO Halliburton Co., Dallas, Tex. 1995–2000 (Pres. 1997); Vice-Pres. of USA Jan. 2001–; Presidential Medal of Freedom 1991.
Address: Office of the Vice-President, Eisenhower Executive Office Building, 1650 Pennsylvania Avenue, NW, Washington, DC 20502, USA (office). *Telephone:* (202) 456-7459 (office). *Fax:* (202) 456-1798 (office). *E-mail:* vice.president@whitehouse.gov (office). *Website:* www.whitehouse .gov/vicepresident/ (office).

CHENG, Tuan Y., BA, MA, PhD; Taiwanese academic; *Director, Institute of International Relations, National Chengchi University; Education:* Tunghai Univ., Nat. Chengchi Univ., State Univ. of New York at Albany, Univ. of Georgia, USA. *Career:* Deputy Chief and Chief of Cooperation and Exchange Section, Inst. of Int. Relations, Nat. Chengchi Univ. 1990–1993, Deputy Dir Inst. of Int. Relations 2006–07, Dir 2007–, also currently Assoc. Research Fellow (Div. 1); Ed. Meiguo yuekan (American Monthly) 1994–96. *Publications:* numerous articles in academic journals.
Address: Institute of International Relations, National Chengchi University, 64 Wan Shou Road, Taipei City, Taiwan (home). *Telephone:* (2) 82377277 (office). *E-mail:* tycheng@nccu.edu.tw (office). *Website:* iir.nccu .edu.tw (office).

CHEPURIN, Aleksandr Vasilyevich; Russian diplomatist; *Director, Department of Interaction with Compatriots Abroad, Ministry of Foreign Affairs;* b. 1952. *Education:* Moscow Inst. of Int. Relations. *Career:* on staff Ministry of Foreign Affairs 1975–; various diplomatic posts abroad and in USSR Ministry of Foreign Affairs; Deputy Head, First Deputy Head Personnel Service, Ministry of Foreign Affairs of Russia 1992–93, Dir Dept of Personnel 1994–96; Amb. to Denmark 1996–99; staff mem. Ministry of Foreign Affairs 1999–2005, Dir Dept of Interaction with Compatriots Abroad 2005–.
Address: Department of Interaction with Compatriots Abroad, Ministry of Foreign Affairs, Smolenskaya-Sennaya 32/34, 119200 Moscow, Russia (office). *Telephone:* (8) 305-244-43-51 (office). *Fax:* (8) 305-244-38-17 (office). *E-mail:* drs@mid.ru (office). *Website:* www.mid.ru (office).

CHERIF, Moustafa; Algerian diplomatist and academic; *Professor of Political Science, University of Algiers; Education:* Toulouse Univ, Sorbonne Univ., Paris. *Career:* fmr Minister of Educ.; fmr Amb. to Egypt; currently Prof. of Political Science, Univ. of Algiers; Visiting Prof., Coll. de France, Paris; Perm. Del., Arab States League. *Publications include:* L'islam, l'autre et la mondialisation 2005.
Address: Department of Political Sciences and International Relations, University of Algiers, 11 Rue Doudou Mokhtar, Ben Aknoun, Algiers, Algieria (office). *Telephone:* (21) 91-25-12 (office). *Website:* www.univ-alger .dz/ang/isic.html (office).

CHERIF, Taïeb, MSc, PhD; Algerian aviation official; *Secretary General, International Civil Aviation Organization;* b. 29 Dec. 1941, Kasr El Boukhari; m.; three c. *Education:* Univ. of Algiers, Ecole Nationale de l'aviation civile, France, Cranfield Inst. of Tech., UK. *Career:* Eng Officer, Civil Aviation Directorate, Ministry of Transport, Algiers 1970–71, Deputy Dir of Transport and Aerial Activities 1971–74, Deputy Dir of Air Navigation 1974–75, Dir of Air Transport 1985–87, Dir aeronautical construction project 1987–92; State Sec. for Higher Educ. 1992–94; Algerian Rep., ICAO Council 1998–2003, Sec.-Gen. ICAO 2003–; Dir Algiers Int. Airport 1975–76; Civil Aviation Consultant 1982–85, 1995–97; Visiting Lecturer, Inst. for Civil Aviation and Meteorology, Algiers 1970–71, Ecole Nationale des Techniciens de l'Aéronautique, Blida 1973–74, Econ. Science Inst., Algiers 1984–85.
Address: International Civil Aviation Organization, External Relations and Public Information Office, 999 University Street, Montreal, H3C 5H7, Canada (office). *Telephone:* (514) 954 8219 (office). *Fax:* (514) 954 6077 (office). *E-mail:* icaohq@icao.int (office). *Website:* www.icao.int (office).

CHERKESOV, Col.-Gen. Victor Vasilejvich; Russian security officer and lawyer; *Director, Federal Service for Control over Drugs and Psychotropic Substances;* b. 13 July 1950, Leningrad; m. Natalya Sergejvna Cherkesova (née Chaplina); two d. *Education:* Leningrad State Univ. *Career:* investigator Leningrad KGB Dept 1975–; Head Dept of Fed. Security

Service St Petersburg and Leningrad Region 1992–98; First Deputy Dir Russian Fed. Security Service 1998–2000; Rep. of Russian Pres. to NW Fed. Dist 2000–2003; mem. Russian Federation Security Council; Dir Fed. Service for Control over Drugs and Psychotropic Substances 2003–; Order of the Red Star 1985, Order of Honour 2000; 14 medals, Honoured Lawyer of the Russian Federation, Honourable Domestic Intelligence Officer of the Russian Federation, Honourable External Intelligence Officer of the Russian Federation.
Address: c/o Office of the Government, Krasnopresnenskaya nab. 2, 103274 Moscow, Russia (office). *Telephone:* (495) 205-57-35 (office). *Fax:* (495) 205-42-19 (office).

CHERNOMYRDIN, Viktor Stepanovich, CandTechSc; Russian politician and diplomatist; *Ambassador to Ukraine;* b. 9 April 1938, Cherny-Otrog, Orenburg Dist; m.; two s. *Education:* Kuibyshev Polytechnic Inst., All-Union Correspondence Polytechnic. *Career:* served in Soviet Army 1957–60; operator in oil refinery 1960–67; mem. CPSU 1961–91 (mem. Cen. Cttee 1986–90); work with Orsk City Cttee 1967–73; deputy chief engineer, Dir of Orenburg gas plant 1973–78; work with CPSU Cen. Cttee 1978–82; USSR Deputy Minister of Gas Industry, Chief of All-Union production unit for gas exploitation in Tyumen Dist 1982–85; USSR Minister of Gas 1985–89; Chair. Bd Gasprom 1989–92, 1999–2000; Deputy Prime Minister, Minister of Fuel and Energy June–Dec. 1992; Chair. Council of Ministers 1992–98; Acting Prime Minister Aug.–Sept. 1998; Deputy to USSR Supreme Soviet 1987–89; Chair. Bd All-Russian Movt Our Home–Russia 1995–2000; apptd Special Rep. of Pres. Yeltsin on Kosovo conflict settlement April 1999; mem. State Duma 1999; joined Yedinstvo (Unity) Movt 2000; Amb. to Ukraine and Special Rep. of Pres. of Russian Fed. for Devt of Trade and Econ. Relations 2001–; mem. Russian Eng Acad.; Hon. Prof. (Moscow State Univ.); numerous orders and medals including Order of October Revolution, Order of Labour Red Banner, Order for Services to the Motherland. *Publications:* Challenge 2004.
Address: Embassy of Russia, Povitroflotskyi pr. 27, 03049 Kiev, Ukraine. *Telephone:* (44) 244-09-63 (office). *Fax:* (44) 246-34-69 (office). *E-mail:* embrus@public.icyb.kiev.ua (office). *Website:* www.embrus.org.ua (office).

CHERNYSHOV, Albert Sergeyevich; Russian diplomatist; b. 18 Aug. 1936, Voronezh; m.; one d. *Education:* Moscow Inst. of Int. Relations. *Career:* diplomatic service 1959–; Asst man., attaché, Sec. Dept of External Policy Information, USSR Ministry of Foreign Affairs 1959–67; Second, First Sec. Embassy Vietnam 1967–71; Counsellor of Minister of Foreign Affairs 1973–76, Chief Counsellor 1976–81, Asst Minister 1982–87, Chief Gen. Secretariat, mem. of Bd 1987; USSR (later Russian) Amb. to Turkey 1987–94; Deputy Minister of Foreign Affairs 1994–96; Amb. to India 1996–2001; mem. staff, Ministry of Foreign Affairs 2001–.
Address: Ministry of Foreign Affairs, Smolenskaya Sennaya 32/34, 119200 Moscow, Russia (office).

CHERTOFF, Michael, BA, JD; American government official and judge; *Secretary of Homeland Security;* b. 28 Nov. 1953, Elizabeth, NJ. *Education:* Harvard Univ. *Career:* Summer Assoc., Miller, Cassidy, Larroca & Lewin (law firm) 1978; Law Clerk, Court of Appeals Second Circuit 1978–79, Supreme Court 1979–80; Assoc., Latham & Watkins 1980–83, Pnr 1994–2001; Asst US Attorney, Attorney's Office, S Dist of NY 1983–87, First Asst US Attorney, Dist of NJ 1987–90, US Attorney 1990–94; Special Counsel, Whitewater Cttee, US Senate 1994–96; Asst Attorney-Gen., Criminal Div., Dept of Justice 2001–03; Judge, Court of Appeals Third Circuit 2003–05; Sec. of Homeland Security 2005–.
Address: Department of Homeland Security, Washington, DC 20528, USA (office). *Telephone:* (202) 282-8000 (office). *Website:* www.dhs.gov/dhspublic (office).

CHESNAKOV, Aleksei Aleksandrovich, PhD; Russian political scientist; *Director, Centre of Social-Political Information, Institute of Social-Political Studies, Russian Academy of Sciences;* b. 1 Sept. 1970, Baku, Azerbaijan; m.; one d. *Education:* Moscow State Univ. *Career:* Jr, then Sr Researcher Inst. of Mass Political Movements, Russian-American Univ. 1991–93; researcher, then Head of Collective of Political Lectures, Centre of Political Conjunction of Russia 1993–97, Dir 1997–; Dir Centre of Social-Political Information, Inst. of Social-Political Studies, Russian Acad. of Sciences 1997–mem. Presidium Ind. Assoc. Civil Soc. *Publications:* numerous scientific pubs on social and political problems; monographs: One Hundred Political Leaders of Russia 1993, Azerbaijan: Political Parties and Organizations 1993, Russia: Power and Elections 1996, Social and Political Situation in Russia in 1996 1997, Russia: New Stage of Neo-liberal Reforms 1998.

Address: Institute of Social-Political Studies, Russian Academy of Sciences, Leninsky prosp. 32A, 117334 Moscow, Russia (office). *Telephone:* (495) 938-19-10 (office).

CHI, Gen. Haotian; Chinese politician and army officer; b. 1929, Zhaoyuan Co., Shandong Prov.; m. Jiang Qingping. *Education:* Anti-Japanese Mil. and Political Coll., Nanjing Mil. Acad., Political Acad. of the Chinese PLA, PLA High Infantry School, Mil. Acad. of the Chinese PLA. *Career:* joined PLA 1945, CCP 1946; Company Instructor, Field Army, PLA Services and Arms 1946–49; joined Chinese People's Volunteers during Korean War 1951, bn instructor and Deputy Dir PLA Regimental Political Dept; Maj., unit, Nanjing Mil. Region 1958; Deputy Political Commissar, Beijing Mil. Region 1975–77; Deputy Ed.-in-Chief, People's Daily 1977–82; Deputy Chief of Staff PLA 1977–82; Political Commissar, Jinan Mil. Region 1985–87; PLA Chief of Staff Dec. 1987–; Minister of Nat. Defence 1993–1998, 1998–2003, State Councillor 2000–03; Chair. Drafting Cttee for Nat. Defence Law of People's Repub. of China; mem. CCP Cen. Cttee 1985–; mem. PRC Cen. Mil. Cttee 1988–; rank of Gen. 1988; mem. 14th CCP Cen. Cttee 1992–97, 15th CCP Cen. Cttee 1997–2002, 16th CCP Cen. Cttee 2002–; mem. Cen. Mil. Comm. CCP 1992–, Vice-Chair. 1995–; mem. 8th NPC 1993–, Politburo; State Councillor 1993–; mem. Macao Special Admin. Region Preparatory Cttee, Govt Del., Macao Hand-Over Ceremony 1999; Hon. Pres. Wrestling Asscn of China; Third-Class People's Hero of East China.
Address: c/o Ministry of National Defence, Jingshanqian Jie, Beijing 100009, People's Republic of China (office).

CHIABRA LEÓN, Gen. Roberto; Peruvian army officer (retd) and politician; b. 1950, Callao. *Education:* Escuela Militar de Chorrillos, Inst. Int. de Derechos Humanos, Costa Rica, Univ. of Piura. *Career:* fmr instructor, Escuela Militar de Chorrillos, Escuela Superior de Guerra, Centro de Altos Estudios Militares (CAEM); Commdr-in-Chief, Cenepa conflict 1995 (rank of Col, later Brig.-Gen., Gen. Commdr Second Mil. Region 2002, Commdr Gen. of Armed Forces 2002–03; Minister of Defence 2003–07; numerous mil. awards including Medalla Académica del Ejército (Merit, Honour and Distinction), Peruvian Cross of Merit, Marshal Andrés Avelino Cáceres Medal, Grand Cross of Mil. Order Francisco Bolognesi.
Address: c/o Ministry of Defence, Avda Arequopa 291, Lima 1, Peru (office).

CHIBESAKUNDA, Hon. Justice Lombe Phyllis, BL; Zambian judge and diplomatist; *Chairwoman, Permanent Human Rights Commission;* b. 5 May 1944. *Education:* Chipembi Girls' School, Nat. Inst. of Public Admin, Lusaka. *Career:* called to the Bar, Gray's Inn, UK; State Advocate Ministry of Legal Affairs 1969–72; pvt legal practice with Jacques and Partners 1972–73; mem. Nat. Ass. (Parl.) for Matero 1973; Minister of Legal Affairs and Justice 1974–75; Minister of State and Solicitor-Gen. 1975–77; Amb. to Japan 1975–77; High Commr in UK, also accred Amb. to FRG, the Netherlands and the Holy See 1977–81, Chief Justice 1981–82; Judge, High Court, Lusaka 1982–; Chair. Industrial Court of Zambia, Perm. Human Rights Comm. (PHRC) 1998–; Chief Zambian Del., UN Law of the Sea Conf. 1975, Rep. UN Comm. on the Status of Women; Chair. Equality Cttee Sub-Cttee UN Independence Party's Women's League; f. Social Action Charity, Lusaka; Founder-mem. Link Voluntary Org.; Life mem. Commonwealth Parl. Asscn; Kt Grand Cross of the Order of Pope Pius IX 1979.
Address: Permanent Human Rights Commission, POB 33812, Lusaka (office); High Court of Zambia, POB 50067, Lusaka, Zambia (office). *Telephone:* (1) 251347 (office). *Fax:* (1) 251342 (office). *E-mail:* phrc@zamnet.zm (office).

CHIBWA, Anderson Kaseba, BA, MA; Zambian diplomatist; *High Commissioner to UK;* b. March 1950, Kabwe; m. Grace Chibwa; six c. *Education:* Univ. of Zambia, Lusaka, Univ. of Miami, USA. *Career:* Sr Scientific Officer, Nat. Council for Scientific Research, Lusaka 1974–82; Sr Researcher and Lecturer, Pan African Inst. of Devt 1983; fmr Project Man. Care International; High Commr to UK (also accred to the Holy See) 2003–.
Address: High Commission of Zambia, Zambia House, 2 Palace Gate, London, W8 5NG, England (office). *Telephone:* (20) 7589-6655 (office). *Fax:* (20) 7581-0546 (office); (20) 7581-1353 (office). *E-mail:* zhcl@btconnect.com (office); immzhcl@btconnect.com (office). *Website:* www.zhcl.org.uk (office).

CHICOLA, Phillip T., BA, MA; American diplomatist; *Chargé d'affaires in Brazil;* b. Cuba; m.; three c. *Education:* Florida Atlantic Univ., Florida State Univ., Army War Coll. *Career:* came to USA 1961, naturalized 1968, joined US State Dept in 1979 as civil service employee; career officer, Foreign Service since 1983 with rank of Minister Counselor, Officer for Latin America, Bureau of Refugee Affairs 1979–84, Deputy Political

Counselor, Embassy in Guatemala City 1984–86, Political Counselor and Deputy Chief of Mission, Embassy in San Salvador 1988–93, Econ.-Political Counselor, Embassy in Santiago 1994–96, Acting Dir Office of Policy Planning and Coordination, Bureau of Inter-American Affairs, Washington, DC 1996–97, Sr Advisor to UN Transitional Admin. for Eastern Slavonia, Croatia 1997–98, Dir Office of Andean Affairs, Bureau of Western Hemisphere Affairs, State Dept 1998–2004, Deputy Chief of Mission, Embassy in Brasília 2004–05, Chargé d'affaires a.i. 2005–; Superior Honor Awards 1984, 1993, 2000, Meritorious Honor Award 1989, Intelligence Collector of the Year Award 1991, James Clement Dunn Award for Excellence 1993.
Address: Embassy of the USA, SES, Av. das Nações, Quadra 801, Lote 03, 70403-900 Brasília, DF, Brazil (office). *Telephone:* (61) 3312-7000 (office). *Fax:* (61) 3225-9136 (office). *E-mail:* contact@embaixadaamericana.org.br (office). *Website:* brasilia.usembassy.gov (office).

CHIDAMBARAM, Palaniappan, BSc, LLB, MBA; Indian politician; *Minister of Finance;* b. 16 Sept. 1956, Kanadukathan, Tamil Nadu; m. Nalini Chidambaram; one c. *Education:* Presidency Coll., Madras Univ., Harvard Business School, USA. *Career:* first elected to Parl. 1984; Deputy Minister, Dept of Commerce and Dept of Personnel 1985; Minister of State, Depts of Personnel and Home Affairs 1986–89; Minister of State, Dept of Commerce 1991–92, 1995–96; Minister of Finance 1996–98, 2004–; Trustee Rajiv Gandhi Foundation, Indian Asscn of Literature.
Address: Ministry of Finance, North Block, New Delhi 110 001, India (office). *Telephone:* (11) 23094905 (office). *Fax:* (11) 23093422 (office). *E-mail:* mprasad@nic.in (office). *Website:* www.finmin.nic.in (office).

CHIDUMO, Filipe; Mozambican diplomatist; *Permanent Representative, United Nations;* b. 1957. *Career:* Cabinet Dir, Ministry of Foreign Affairs and Devt 1992–99; fmr Amb. to Spain; fmr Nat. Dir of Int. Orgs and Co-operation; Perm. Rep. to UN 2003–.
Address: Permanent Mission of Mozambique to the UN, 420 East 50th Street, New York, NY 10022, USA (office). *Telephone:* (212) 644-5965 (office). *Fax:* (212) 644-5972 (office). *E-mail:* mozambique@un.int (office). *Website:* www.un.int/mozambique (office).

CHIDYAUSIKU, Boniface Guwa, BA, MSc; Zimbabwean diplomatist; *Permanent Representative, United Nations;* b. 29 Dec. 1950, Goromonzi; m. Evelyn Gurupira 1983; one s. two d. *Education:* Univ. of Zimbabwe. *Career:* military service, Zimbabwe Nat. Army, rank of Lt-Col 1975–80, 1985; Research Officer, Dept of Prime Minister 1980–84; Defence Attaché, Embassy of Zimbabwe, Washington DC 1986–88; Deputy Sec., Ministry of Defence 1988–90, Ministry of Foreign Affairs 1990; Amb. to People's Repub. of China 1990–96, to Angola 1996–99; Perm. Rep. to UN, Geneva 1999–2002; Chair. Cttee on Regional Trade Agreements (CRTA), WTO 2002; Perm. Rep. to UN, New York 2003–; Zimbabwe Liberation Medal 1980. *Publications:* articles: A Reconciliation Process as a Component of Conflict Resolution in Zimbabwe 1990, Effective Participation of Developing Countries in the WTO 2001, The Review Process in the WTO and the Development of Regional/National Levels 2001; contrib. to TRIPS Agreement 2001.
Address: Permanent Mission of Zimbabwe to the UN, 128 East 56th Street, New York, NY 10022, USA (office). *Telephone:* (212) 980-9511 (office). *Fax:* (212) 308-6705 (office). *E-mail:* zimbabwe@un.int (office); bgchid@yahoo.com (home). *Website:* www.un.int (office).

CHIDYAUSIKU, Godfrey; Zimbabwean judge; *Chief Justice;* b. 1947. *Career:* MP (Ind.) 1974–77, elected Zimbabwe African Nat. Union-Patriotic Front (ZANU-PF) MP 1980; Deputy Minister of Local Govt 1980, of Justice 1981; Attorney-Gen. 1982, apptd High Court Judge 1987; Chief Justice of Zimbabwe 2001–; Chair. Constitutional Comm. 2000.
Address: Chief Justice Chambers, CY 870, Causeway, Zimbabwe (office). *Fax:* (4) 731867 (office).

CHIEN, Eugene Y. H., BS, MS, PhD; Taiwanese politician and professor of engineering; *Chairman, Taiwan Institute for Sustainable Energy;* b. 4 Feb. 1946, Taoyuan Co.; m. Wang Kuei-Jung (Gwendolyn Chien); two s. one d. *Education:* Nat. Taiwan Univ. and New York Univ., USA. *Career:* Assoc. Prof., Tamkang Univ. 1973–76, Prof. and Chair. Dept of Aeronautical Eng 1976–78, Prof. and Dean Coll. of Eng 1978–84; mem. Legis. Yuan 1984–87, Chair. Nat. Defense Cttee 1984–85, Educ. Cttee 1986; Minister of State, Environmental Protection Admin. 1987–91; Minister of Transportation and Communications 1991–93; Nat. Policy Adviser to Pres. 1993–96; Rep., Taipei Rep. Office, UK 1993–97; Project Consultant EBRD 1997; Sr Adviser, Nat. Security Council 1997–2000; Deputy Sec.-Gen., Office of the Pres. 2000–02; Minister of Foreign Affairs 2002–04; Chair. Int. Co-operation and Devt Fund 2002–; consultant to various hi-tech cos 2004–; Chair. Taiwan Inst. for Sustainable Energy 2007–; Pres. Chinese Inst. of Environmental Eng 1988–91, Sino-British Cultural and Econ. Asscn 1998–;

Prof. Emer., Catholic Univ. of Honduras 2002; Hon. Fellow, Cardiff Univ., UK 1998; Ten Outstanding Young Persons of the World, Jaycees Int. 1985, Chinese Inst. of Environmental Eng Award 1991, Environment Protection Admin Medal 1998. *Publications:* The Asian Regional Economy (co-ed.) 1993.
Address: 5F, No. 35, Kwang Fu N. Road, Taipei, Taiwan (office); 7F, No. 61 Ching-Chong Street, Taipei 105, Taiwan (home). *Telephone:* (2) 2768-2655 (office); (2) 2718-4172 (home). *Fax:* (2) 2719-0733 (home). *E-mail:* chieneugene@yahoo.com.tw.

CHIEN, Nguyen Tam, MA; Vietnamese diplomatist; b. 20 Jan. 1948, Nghe An Prov.; m. Nguyen Thi Lien Huong; three c. *Education:* Eng Eng Univ., Moscow Diplomacy Acad., Russia. *Career:* joined Ministry of Foreign Affairs 1972, staff mem., Embassy in Moscow 1972–73, Desk Officer, Soviet Union Dept, Hanoi 1973–85, Attaché in Moscow 1975–79, returned to Soviet Union Dept 1979, with Policy Planning Dept 1984–88, Deputy Dir-Gen. 1988–90, Dir-Gen. 1990–92, Amb. to Japan 1992–96, Asst Minister of Foreign Affairs 1996–97, Vice-Minister 1997–2001, Amb. to USA 2001–07.
Address: Ministry of Foreign Affairs, 1 Ton That Dam, Ba Dinh District, Hanoi, Viet Nam (office). *Telephone:* (4) 8452980 (office). *Fax:* (4) 82318725 (office). *E-mail:* banbientap@mofa.gov.vn (office). *Website:* www.mofa.gov.vn (office).

CHIKÁN, Attila, PhD; Hungarian politician and economist; *Rector, Budapest University of Economic Sciences and Public Administration;* b. 4 April 1944, Budapest; m. Márta Nagy; one s. one d. *Education:* Karl Marx Univ. of Econ. Sciences, Budapest, Grad. School of Business, Stanford Univ. *Career:* Prof., Budapest Univ. of Econ. Sciences and Public Admin 1968–, Prof. and Chair. 1990–, Rector 2000–; Minister of Econ. Affairs 1998–99; Chair. Council of Econ. Advisers of the Prime Minister 2000–; First Vice-Pres., Sec.-Gen. Int. Soc. for Inventory Research; Pres. Fed. of European Production and Industrial Man. Societies 1996–; Pres. Int. Fed. of Purchasing Materials and Man. 2000–01; mem. editorial bds Int. Journal of Purchasing and Materials Man., Int. Journal of Logistics 1997–, Int. Journal of Quantitative and Operations Man. 1998–. *Publications:* author or ed. of several books, including Current Trends in Inventory Research: A Selection of Papers Presented at the Sixth International Symposium on Inventories, Budapest, August 1990, Inventory Models (co-ed.) 1991, Erzsebet Czako Zoltay-Paprika 2002.
Address: Budapest University of Economic Sciences and Public Administration, 1093 Budapest, Fovám tér 9, Hungary (office). *Telephone:* (1) 217-62-68 (office). *Fax:* (1) 217-88-83 (office). *E-mail:* chikan@rektor.bke.hu (office).

CHIKVAIDZE, Alexander Davidovich; Georgian diplomatist; *Ambassador to Switzerland;* b. 19 Jan. 1932, T'bilisi; m.; two s. *Education:* Moscow State Univ., Acad. of Political Sciences, Diplomatic Acad. *Career:* taught int. law, Moscow State Univ., headed youth orgs in Georgian Repub., then Head T'bilisi Region Cttee of CPSU; Chair. Rep. Cttee for Publishing and Book Trade 1976–79; fmr Vice-Consul (Cultural Affairs), Mumbai, First Sec. (Cultural Dept), Embassy of USSR in London; Consul-Gen., San Francisco 1979–83; Amb. to Kenya and to UNEP and Habitat 1983–85; Head of Sector, CPSU Cen. Cttee 1985–88; USSR Amb. to Netherlands 1988–91, Russian Amb. to the Netherlands 1991–92; Minister of Foreign Affairs of Georgia 1992–95; Amb. to Greece –2003, to Switzerland 2003–; fmr Chair. USSR Chess Fed.; Lenin Centenary Medal. *Publication:* Western Countries' Foreign Policy on the Eve of the Second World War 1976.
Address: Embassy of Georgia, rue Richard Wagner 1, 1202 Geneva, Switzerland. *Telephone:* 229191010 (office). *Fax:* 227339033 (office). *E-mail:* geomission.geneva@bluewin.ch (office).

CHILCOTT, Dominick John; British diplomatist; *High Commissioner to Sri Lanka;* b. 17 Nov. 1959; m. Jane Chilcott; three s. one d. *Career:* Asst Desk Officer, Southern African Dept, FCO 1982–83, Third, later Second Sec. (Chancery), Ankara 1985–88, Head of Section, Cen. African Dept 1988–89, Head of Section, EU Dept (Internal), FCO 1990–92, Head of Political Section, Lisbon 1993–95, Pvt. Sec. to the Foreign Sec., FCO 1996–98, Head of External Relations Section, UK Rep. to the EU, Brussels 1998–2002, Dir Iraqi Planning (later Policy) Unit 2002–03, Dir Europe (Bilateral Relations, Resources and Mediterranean Issues), FCO 2003–05, High Commr to Sri Lanka (also accred to the Maldives) 2006–.
Address: British High Commission, PO Box 1433, 190 Galle Road, Kollupitiya, Colombo 3, Sri Lanka (office). *Telephone:* (11) 2437336 (office). *Fax:* (11) 2430308 (office). *E-mail:* colombo.general@fco.gov.lk (office). *Website:* www.britishhighcommission.gov.uk/srilanka (office).

CHILUBA, Frederick J.T., MPhil; Zambian fmr politician; b. 30 April 1943, Wusakile; m. 1st Vera Chiluba (divorced); nine c.; m. 2nd Regina Mwanza.

Education: Kawambwa Secondary School, and later in USA and fmr Soviet Bloc countries, Univ. of Warwick (UK). *Career:* shop steward 1967; fmr Chair. Zambian Congress of Trades Unions 1987–91; mem. Parl. for Nkana; Pres. of Zambia 1991–2001; Co-Founder and Leader Movt for Multiparty Democracy (MMD); Chair. African Union (AV) 2001–2003; charged with theft of public money Feb. 2003, trial 2004–.
Address: c/o Office of the President, PO Box 30208, Lusaka, Zambia (office).

CHILUMPHA, Cassim; Malawi politician; *Vice-President and Minister responsible for Statutory Corporations; Career:* Minister of Finance 1998–2000; Vice-Pres. and Minister responsible for Statutory Corpns 2004–.
Address: Office of the President and Cabinet, Private Bag 301, Capital City, Lilongwe 3, Malawi (office). *Telephone:* 1782655 (office). *Fax:* 1783654 (office).

CHIMAMBO, Zililo Q. Y.; Malawi diplomatist. *Career:* currently High Commr in Maputo, Mozambique.
Address: High Commission of Malawi, Avda Kenneth Kaunda 75, Maputo, CP 4148, Mozambique (office). *Telephone:* 21491468 (office). *Fax:* 21490224 (office). *E-mail:* malawmoz@virconn.com (office). *Website:* www.malawi.gov.mw (office).

CHIMPHAMBA, Brown B., BSc, MSc, PhD; Malawi diplomatist and fmr academic; b. 1939, Ntcheu; m.; four c. *Education:* Fourah Bay Coll., Univ. of Sierra Leone, Univ. Coll. London. *Career:* various positions at Bunda Coll. of Agric., Univ. of Malawi 1961–81, including Research Assoc., Sr Lecturer, Prof. of Biology, Dean of Faculty of Science, Prin. 1981–90; Prin., Malawi Polytechnic 1991–92; Acting Vice-Chancellor, Univ. of Malawi 1991–92, Vice-Chancellor 1992–2000; Presidential Advisor on Educ. 2000–04; Chair. Nat. AIDS Comm. 2000–04; Perm. Rep. to UN, New York 2004–06; Fulbright Hayes Fellow; Hon. DLitt (Univ. of Malawi); Certificate of Merit for Devt Work. *Publications include:* numerous scientific publs.
Address: c/o Ministry of Foreign Affairs, POB 30315, Lilongwe 3, Malawi (office). *Website:* www.malawi.gov.mw (office).

CHIMUTENGWENDE, Chen (Chenhamo), MA; Zimbabwean writer, activist and politician; *President, United New Africa Global Network;* b. 28 Aug. 1943, Mazowe Dist; m. Edith Matore; three s. two d. *Education:* Univ. of Bradford, UK. *Career:* Exec. Dir Europe–Third World Research Centre, London 1969–74; Pres. Kwame Nkrumah Inst. of Writers and Journalists, London 1969–77; Deputy Dir and Sr Lecturer in Mass Communications and Int. Affairs, City Univ., London 1978–79; UNESCO Consultant on Mass Communications (Broadcasting) 1979–80; Corresp. for East and Southern Africa, Inter Press Service, Rome 1980–83; Sr Lecturer and Head, School of Journalism, Univ. of Nairobi 1980–82; MP 1985–; fmr Minister of Information, Posts and Telecommunications, Environment and Tourism; Pres. United New Africa Global Network (UNAGN) 1997–; Corresp. UNESCO's Int. Social Science Journal 1980–2003; Chair. Africa Star Holdings Ltd 1986–; Pres. UN Convention on Climate Change 1996–98; Chair. UN High Level Cttee of Ministers and Sr Officials 1997–98. *Publication:* South Africa: The Press and the Politics of Liberation 1978.
Address: United New Africa Global Network, 8 San Fernando, 130 Fife Avenue, Corner 5th Street, Harare (office); 6 Duthie Road, Belgravia, Harare, Zimbabwe (home). *Telephone:* (4) 253296/7 (office); (4) 704586 (home). *Fax:* (4) 707771 (office); (4) 253298 (office). *E-mail:* info@unitednewafrica.com (office); chenchim@yahoo.com (home). *Website:* www.unitednewafrica.com (office).

CHINKIN, Christine, LLM, PhD; British academic; *Professor of International Law, London School of Economics; Education:* Queen Mary Coll., Univ. of London, Yale Univ., USA, Univ. of Sydney, Australia. *Career:* Lecturer, Queen Mary Coll., Univ. of London 1975–78, New York Univ. Law School 1978–80, Nat. Univ. of Singapore 1981–84, Univ. of Sydney Law School 1984–92; Dean and Head of Dept of Law, Univ. of Southampton 1993–97; Prof of Int. Law, LSE 1997–; Affiliated Overseas Faculty Mem., Univ. of Mich, USA; Consultant on Int. Law, Asian Devt Bank; visiting lecturer at numerous univs including Hong Kong Univ. Law School, Int. Law Inst. of China, European Univ. Inst.; mem. Advisory Bd British Inst. of Int. and Comparative Law; mem. Editorial Bd American Journal of International Law, Leiden Journal of International Law; Certificate of Merit, American Soc. of Int. Law 2001. *Publications:* Dispute Resolution in Australia (co-author) 1992, Third Parties in International Law 1993, The Boundaries of International Law: A Feminist Analysis (co-author) 2000; numerous articles in legal journals.
Address: Law Department, London School of Economics, Houghton Street, London, WC2A 2AE, England (office). *Telephone:* (20) 7955-6393 (office). *Fax:* (20) 7955-7366 (office). *E-mail:* c.chinkin@lse.ac.uk (office). *Website:* www.lse.ac.uk (office).

CHINO, Tadao, BA; Japanese international banker; b. 1934; m.; two d. *Education:* Stanford Univ., Tokyo Univ. *Career:* joined Ministry of Finance 1960, jr official at UN Econ. Comm. for Asia and Far East (ECAFE) 1964, numerous sr posts in banking, budget and int. finance bureaux, Deputy Dir-Gen. Banking Bureau 1987–89, Dir-Gen. Int. Finance Bureau 1989, Vice-Minister of Finance for Int. Affairs 1991–93, Special Adviser to Finance Minister 1993; Deputy Gov. Agric., Forestry and Fisheries Finance Corpn 1994; now Chair. Bd of Advisers, Nomura Research Inst. Ltd; Chair. Bd and Pres. Asian Devt Bank 1999–2005.
Address: c/o Asian Development Bank, 6 Asian Development Bank Avenue, Mandaluyong City 0401, Metro Manila, Philippines (office). *Telephone:* (2) 6324444 (office).

CHIPMAN, John Miguel Warwick, CMG, MA, DPhil; British administrator and academic; *Director, International Institute for Strategic Studies (IISS);* b. 10 Feb. 1957, Montreal; m. Lady Theresa Manners 1997; two s. *Education:* Westmount High School, Montreal, El Estudio, Madrid, Harvard Univ., USA, London School of Econs and Balliol Coll. Oxford. *Career:* Research Assoc. IISS, London 1983–84; Asst Dir for Regional Security, IISS 1987–91, Dir of Studies 1991–93, Dir IISS 1993–, Founder IISS Publ Strategic Comments; Research Assoc. Atlantic Inst. for Int. Affairs, Paris 1985–87; Dir Arundel House Enterprises, US Office IISS, Washington, DC, Asia Office IISS, Singapore; mem. Bd Aspen Inst. Italia; regular broadcaster on int. affairs; NATO Fellowship 1983. *Publications:* Cinquième République et Défense de l'Afrique 1986, French Power in Africa 1989; ed. and prin. contrib. to NATO's Southern Allies: Internal and External Challenges 1988; articles in journals and book chapters.
Address: International Institute for Strategic Studies, Arundel House, 13–15 Arundel Street, London, WC2R 3DX, England (office). *Telephone:* (20) 7379-7676 (office). *Fax:* (20) 7836-3108 (office). *E-mail:* iiss@iiss.org (office). *Website:* www.iiss.org (office).

CHIRAC, Jacques René; French politician and fmr head of state; b. 29 Nov. 1932, Paris; m. Bernadette Chodron de Courcel 1956; two d. *Education:* Lycée Carnot, Lycée Louis-le-Grand, Ecole Nationale d'Admin and Inst. d'Etudes Politiques, Paris. *Career:* mil. service in Algeria; auditor, Cour des Comptes 1959–62; Special Asst, Secr.-Gen. of Govt 1962; Special Asst, Pvt. Office of M. Pompidou 1962–65; Counsellor, Cour des Comptes 1965–94; Sec. of State for Employment Problems 1967–68; Sec. of State for Economy and Finance 1968–71; Minister for Parl. Relations 1971–72, of Agriculture and Rural Devt 1972–73, 1973–74, of the Interior March–May 1974; Prime Minister of France 1974–1976, 1986–88; Sec.-Gen. UDR 1974–75, Hon. Sec.-Gen. 1975–76; Pres. RPR (fmrly UDR) 1976–94, Hon. Sec.-Gen. 1977–80; mem. European Parl. 1979; Pres. Regional Council, La Corrèze 1970–79; Municipal Counsellor, Sainte-Féréole 1965–77; Mayor of Paris 1977–95; Pres. of France May 1995–2007; Deputy for Corrèze March–May 1967, June–Aug. 1968, March–May 1973, 1976–79, 1981–86, 1988–95; mem. Comm. on Nat. Defence, Nat. Assembly 1980–86; mem. (ex officio) Conseil Constitutionnel 2007–; Grand-Croix, Légion d'honneur; Ordre nat. du Mérite; Croix de la Valeur Militaire; Chevalier du Mérite agricole, des Arts et Lettres, de l'Étoile noire, du Mérite sportif, du Mérite touristique; Grand Cross Merit of the Sovereign Order of Malta; Prix Louise Michel 1986, Médaille de l'Aéronautique, State Prize of the Russian Federation 2008. *Publications:* Discours pour la France à l'heure du choix, La lueur de l'espérance: réflexion du soir pour le matin 1978, Une Nouvelle France, Réflexions 1 1994, La France pour Tous 1995.
Address: c/o Conseil Constitutionnel, 2 rue de Montpensier, 75001 Paris, France. *Telephone:* 1-40-15-30-00. *Fax:* 1-40-20-93-27. *E-mail:* relations-exterieures@conseil-constitutionnel.fr. *Website:* www.conseil-constitutionnel.fr.

CHIRTOACA, Nicolae; Moldovan politician, diplomatist and fmr army officer; *Ambassador to USA. Education:* Polytechnic Inst. of Chisinau. *Career:* mil. service 1977–90, served in different structures of armed forces of fmr Soviet Union; joined Movt for Democracy and Nat. Liberation of Moldova 1990; apptd Dir-Gen. Dept of State for Mil. Problems of Moldova (became Ministry of Defence 1991) 1991–94, active role in creation of Nat. Army of Moldova with rank of Col, Nat. Security Adviser to Pres. of Moldova 1992–94, Rep. of Moldova at ambassadorial level at meetings of N Atlantic Co-operation Council at NATO; Co-founder Liberal Party of Moldova, Vice-Chair. and mem. Man. Bd 1994–98; Sr State Adviser to Prime Minister (Press Sec. of Govt) 1999–2006; Amb. to USA 2006–; mem. Man. Bd Soros Foundation Moldova; Dir Invisible Coll. of Moldova; Pres. Man. Bd Euro-Atlantic Center of Moldova 1994–2006; Hon. Pres. European Movt of Moldova 2003.

Address: Embassy of Moldova, 2101 S Street, NW, Washington, DC 20008, USA (office). *Telephone:* (202) 667-1130 (office). *Fax:* (202) 667-1204 (office). *Website:* www.embassyrm.org (office).

CHISSANO, Joaquim Alberto; Mozambican politician; *Special Envoy to Northern Uganda, United Nations;* b. 2 Oct. 1939, Chibuto; m. Marcelina Rafael Chissano; four c. *Career:* faculty of medicine in Lisbon, Portugal and Poitiers, France; Founding mem. Frente de Libertação de Mozambique (FRELIMO), Asst Sec. to Pres., FRELIMO in charge of Educ. 1963–66, Sec. to Pres., FRELIMO 1966–69; Chief Rep. FRELIMO in Dar es Salaam 1969–74; Prime Minister, Transitional Govt of Mozambique 1974–75, Minister of Foreign Affairs 1975–86, Pres. of Mozambique and C-in-C of Armed Forces 1986–2005; Pres. FRELIMO 1991–2004; Chair. African Union 2002–04; UN Special Envoy to N Uganda 2006–; Order, Augusto César Sandino (Nicaragua) 1988; numerous awards including Chatham House Prize 2006, Mo Ibrahim Prize for Achievement in African Leadership (first recipient) 2007.
Address: c/o United Nations Peace-Building and Special Missions, Department of Political Affairs, United Nations, New York, NY, 10017 USA.

CHITANAVA, Nodari Amrosievich, PhD; Georgian politician, agricultural specialist and macroeconomist; *Director, Economic and Social Problems Research Institute;* b. 10 March 1936, Zugdidi Region, Georgia; m. Keto Dimitrovna 1964; two d. *Education:* Georgian Polytechnic Inst., Moscow High Political School. *Career:* mem. CPSU 1958–91; komsomol and party work 1959–; Second Sec. Adzhar obkom 1973–74; Minister of Agric. for Georgian SSR 1974–79; First Deputy Chair., Georgian Council of Ministers 1979–85; Party Sec. for Agric. 1985–89; Chair. Council of Ministers, Georgian SSR 1989–90; Minister of Agric. 1991–93; Dir Econ. and Social Problems Research Inst. 1993–; Chair. Georgian Economists' Soc. *Publications:* 70 scientific works of which there are seven monographs including Social-Economic Pproblems During Transition Perios (three vols).
Address: Institute for Macroeconomics, 16 Zandukeli Str., 380008 Tbilisi; Atheni Str. 16, Tbilisi, Georgia (home). *Telephone:* (32) 93-12-55; (32) 99-75-15 (office); (32) 23-37-53 (home).

CHIZHOV, Ludvig Aleksandrovich; Russian diplomatist; b. 25 April 1936, Radornishl, Zhitomir Region; m.; one s. one d. *Education:* Moscow Inst. of Int. Relations. *Career:* fmr mem. CPSU; attaché, Embassy, Japan 1960–65, First Sec., Counsellor, 1971–77; Third Sec., Second Sec., Second Far Eastern Dept, Ministry of Foreign Affairs 1966–70; Counsellor, Second Far Eastern Dept 1978–80; Minister Counsellor, Embassy, Japan 1980–86; Head of Pacific Ocean Countries Dept, Ministry of Foreign Affairs 1986–89; Russian Amb. to Japan 1990–96; Amb.-at-Large 1996–98; Dir 3rd European Dept, Ministry of Foreign Affairs 1998–2001, on staff of Ministry 2001–2003, Deputy Minister 2003–.
Address: Ministry of Foreign Affairs, Smolenskaya-Sennaya pl. 32/34, 119200 Moscow, Russia (office). *Telephone:* (495) 244-16-06 (office). *Fax:* (495) 230-21-30 (office). *E-mail:* ministry@mid.ru (office). *Website:* www.mid.ru (office).

CHIZHOV, Vladimir; Russian diplomatist; *Permanent Representative, European Union;* b. 3 Dec. 1953, Moscow; m., two c. *Education:* Moscow State Inst. of Int. Relations. *Career:* joined diplomatic service 1976, numerous posts with Ministry of Foreign Affairs, Moscow including at 5th European Dept 1981, Counsellor, 2nd European Dept 1992, Head UK and Ireland Div. 1992, Deputy Dir 2nd European Dept 1993, Dir 3rd European Dept 1997, Dir European Multilateral Co-operation Dept 1999, Deputy Minister of Foreign Affairs 2002; served at Embassy in Athens, Greece 1976, Embassy in Nicosia, Cyprus 1985, Deputy Head of Del. to OSCE, Vienna, Austria 1995, Deputy High Rep. for Bosnia Peace Implementation, Sarajevo 1996, Perm. Rep. to EU 2005–; Order of Friendship 2003, Order of Merit (Luxembourg) 2006.
Address: Mission of the Russian Federation to the European Union, 31–33 Blvd du Regent, 1000 Brussels, Belgium (office). *Telephone:* (2) 502-17-91 (office). *Fax:* (2) 513-76-49 (office). *E-mail:* misruscel@coditel.net (office). *Website:* www.russiaeu.mid.ru (office).

CHKHEIDZE, Peter, PhD; Georgian diplomatist; *Ambassador to Turkmenistan;* b. 22 Oct. 1941, Tbilisi; m. Manana Chkheidze 1963; two s. *Education:* Tbilisi Nat. Univ., Diplomatic Acad. of USSR Ministry of Foreign Affairs and Inst. of State and Law, USSR Acad. of Sciences. *Career:* various positions, Attorney Service of Repub. of Georgia 1963–75; First Sec., Dept of Int. Orgs, Ministry of Foreign Affairs of USSR 1978; First Sec., Counsellor, then Chief of Dept Perm. Mission of USSR to UN 1978–84; leading posts in nat. state and public insts 1984–89; Chair. Ind. Trade Unions Confed. of Repub. of Georgia 1989–91; Deputy Prime Minister of Repub. of Georgia and Perm. Rep. of Govt of Georgia to USSR, later

Russian Fed. 1991–92; Chargé d'Affaires in Russian Fed. 1992–93; Amb. to USA 1993–94; Perm. Rep. to UN 1993–2002; Amb. to Turkmenistan (also accred to Afghanistan) 2002–; Corresp. mem. Int. Informatization Acad. 1994–. *Publications:* various publs in fields of law and int. relations 1975–95.
Address: 139A, Azadi str., Ashgabat 744000, Turkmenistan (office); Inguri St 3, Apt. 52, Tbilisi 380071, Georgia (home). *Telephone:* (12) 344838 (Ashgabat) (office); (12) 343568 (Ashgabat) (home); 33-7056 (Tbilisi). *Fax:* (12) 343248 (Ashgabat) (office). *E-mail:* georgia@online.tm (office).

CHKHIKVISHVILI, Vladimir I.; Georgian diplomatist; b. Tbilisi. *Career:* fmr Dir N American Dept, Russian Ministry of Foreign Affairs; Russian Amb. to Georgia 2002–06.
Address: Ministry of Foreign Affairs, 119200 Moscow, Smolenskaya-Sennaya pl. 32/34, Russia. *Telephone:* (495) 244-16-06. *Fax:* (495) 230-21-30. *E-mail:* ministry@mid.ru. *Website:* www.mid.ru.

CHO, Il-hwan; South Korean diplomatist; *Ambassador to France; Career:* joined Ministry of Foreign Affairs 1973, served as Counsellor in various countries including Zaire 1982, France 1985, USA 1991; Minister, Embassy in Moscow 1996–97, Embassy in Germany 1999–2001; Amb. to Senegal 2001–04; Dir-Gen., European Affairs Bureau, Ministry of Foreign Affairs and Trade 1997–99, Amb. for Counter-Terrorism 2004; Amb. to France (also accred to Monaco) 2006–, Del. Mission to UNESCO; Fellow, Center for Int. Affairs, Harvard Univ. 1994–95; Hon. mem., Asscn Jung-Hun Mécénat.
Address: Embassy of The Republic of Korea, 125 rue de Grenelle, 75007 Paris, France (office). *Telephone:* 1-47-53-01-01 (office). *Fax:* 1-47-53-00-41 (office). *E-mail:* koremb-fr@mofat.go.kr (office). *Website:* www.amb-coreesud.fr (office).

CHO, Vice-Marshal Myong–rok; North Korean army officer and government official; *First Vice-Chairman, National Defence Committee;* b. 1930, Manchuria. *Education:* Mangyong-dae Revolutionary School. *Career:* returned from Soviet Union 1959; began his career as fighter pilot; well known for commanding N Korean mil. advisers directing surprise air attacks on Israeli air fields during Middle East War 1973; N Korean Air Force Commdr 1979; elected mem. Cen. Cttee of Korean Worker's Party (KWP) 1980, KWP Cen. Mil. Comm. 1980; mem. 7–10th Supreme People's Ass.; rank of Gen. and Alt. mem. Supreme Council 1980; rank of Vice-Marshal 1995; Dir-Gen., Gen. Political Bureau of the People's Army 1995–; close confidante of Pres. Kim Jong-il; First Vice-Chair. Nat. Defence Comm. 1998–; Special Envoy of Kim Jong-il to USA for talks with Pres. Clinton and Sec. of State Madeleine Albright 2000.
Address: National Defence Commission, Pyongyang, Democratic People's Republic of Korea (office).

CHO, Yoon-je; South Korean economist and diplomatist; m. Cho Sun-ae; one s. one d. *Career:* Jt Pres. Anglo-Korean Soc.; Amb. to UK 2005–08. *Publications include:* Credit Policies and the Industrialization of Korea (co-author), Lessons of Financial Liberalization in Asia: A Comparative Study (co-author).
Address: Ministry of Foreign Affairs and Trade 95-1, Doryeom-dong, Jongno-gu, Seoul 110-787, Republic of Korea (office). *Telephone:* (2) 3703-2114 (office). *Fax:* (2) 2100-7999 (office). *E-mail:* web@mofat.go.kr (office). *Website:* www.mofat.go.kr (office).

CHO, Yung-kil; South Korean politician and army general; b. 9 May 1940, Yongkwangkun, Chollanamdo Prov.; m. Kang Suk; one s. two d. *Education:* Kwangju Soongil High School, Army Coll., Nat. Defence Coll., Grad. School of Public Admin, Dongkuk Univ. *Career:* commissioned Second Lt 1962; Co. Commdr Tiger Unit, Vietnam War 1962–70; Commdr 26th Brigade, Capital Mechanized Div. 1983–84; Chief of Strategic Planning, Policy Planning Office, Army HQ 1984–87, Dir Special Inspection Group 1987–88, Dir of Strategic Planning 1989–91; Dean of Faculty, Nat. Defence Univ. 1988–89; Commdg Gen. 2nd Corps 1995–97, 2nd Repub. of Korea Army 1998–99; Chair. of Jt Chiefs of Staff 1999–2001; Minister of Nat. Defence 2003–04 (resgnd); United States Legion of Merit 2000, 2001 Order of Mil. Merit Hwarang Medal 1970, Vietnam Hero Medal (Silver) and Bronze Star 1970, United States Bronze Star 1970, Order of Nat. Security Medal (Cheonsu) 1987, (Gukson) 1996, (Tongil) 1999.
Address: c/o Ministry of National Defence, 1, 3-ga, Yonsan-dong, Yeongsan-gu, Seoul, Republic of Korea (office).

CHOE, Jin-su; North Korean diplomatist; *Ambassador to China;* b. 1941, S Hwanghae Prov. *Education:* Univ. of Int. Affairs, Pyongyang. *Career:* began career in Ministry of Foreign Affairs, posted to Embassy, Brunei 1969, Burkina Faso 1974, to Trade Rep. Office, Paris 1978; later Head of W European Affairs, Ministry of Foreign Affairs, Pyongyang; Amb. to

Switzerland 1986–89, to China 2000–; Deputy Chief, Workers' Party Cen. Cttee Int. Dept 1995–2000.
Address: Embassy of the Democratic People's Republic of Korea, Ki Tan Bei Lu, Jian Guo Men Wai, Beijing 100600, People's Republic of China (office). *Telephone:* (10) 65321186 (office). *Fax:* (10) 65326056 (office).

CHOHAN, Muhammad Anwar; Pakistani diplomatist; *High Commissioner to the Maldives; Education:* Asia-Pacific Center for Security Studies. *Career:* High Commr to the Maldives 2006–.
Address: High Commission of Pakistan, G. Helengely, Lily Magu, Malé, Maldives (office). *Telephone:* 3323005 (office). *Fax:* 3321832 (office). *E-mail:* pahicmale@hotmail.com (office). *Website:* www.mofa.gov.pk/Green_Book/Maldives_GB.htm.

CHOI, Jung-il; South Korean diplomatist; *Ambassador to Germany; Education:* Seoul Nat. Univ., Royal Inst. of Int. Affairs, London. *Career:* joined Ministry of Foreign Affairs 1975, overseas postings include Third Sec., Embassy in Copenhagen 1978, Second Sec., Embassy in Mauritania 1980, First Sec., Embassy in Singapore 1985, Counsellor, Embassy in Washington, DC 1994; Dir Int. Legal Affairs Div., Ministry of Foreign Affairs 1991, Prin. Sec. to Minister of Foreign Affairs 1993, Deputy Dir-Gen., N American Affairs Bureau 1997, Aide to Minister of Foreign Affairs and Trade 1998, Dir-Gen. Treaties Bureau, Ministry of Foreign Affairs and Trade 2000, Chief of Protocol 2002; Asst Sec., Office of the Pres. 1988, Protocol Sec. to Pres. 2000; Amb. to India 2004–07, to Germany 2007–.
Address: Embassy of The Republic of Korea, Stülerstr. 8–10, 10787 Berlin, Germany (office). *Telephone:* (30) 260650 (office). *Fax:* (30) 2606551 (office). *E-mail:* koremb-ge@mofat.go.kr (office). *Website:* www.koreaemb.de (office).

CHOI, Seok-young, BA, MBA; South Korean diplomatist and international organization official; *Minister of Economic Affairs, Embassy of South Korea, Washington, DC;* b. 1955, Kangleung; m. Kim Young In; one s. one d. *Education:* Seoul Nat. Univ., Univ. of Heidelberg, Germany, Korea Devt Inst. School of Public Policy and Man. *Career:* joined Ministry of Foreign Affairs (MOF) 1979; Consul in Hamburg, Germany 1986–88; First Sec. in Nairobi, Kenya 1988–91; Asst Dir Environmental Cooperation Div., MOF 1991–94; Counsellor for Econ. and Trade Affairs, Perm. Mission to UN, Geneva 1994–97; Dir for Environment and Science and Chief Negotiator for 1997 UNGA Special Session, MOF 1997–99; Counsellor and Chief of Econ. Section, Perm. Mission to UN, New York 1999–2002; Adviser to Pres. of UN Gen. Ass. 2001; Deputy Dir-Gen. Multilateral Trade Bureau, MOF 2002–03; Deputy Sr Official to APEC 2002–03; Deputy Exec.-Dir, APEC Secr. 2004, Exec.-Dir 2005; Minister of Econ. Affairs, Embassy of South Korea, Washington, DC 2006–; del. to numerous int. and multilateral forums including UN, WTO and APEC. *Publications:* numerous articles on trade, environmental issues and climate change negotiations.
Address: Embassy of the Republic of Korea, 2450 Massachusetts Avenue, NW, Washington, DC 20008, USA (office). *Telephone:* (202) 939-5600 (office). *Fax:* (202) 797-0595 (office). *E-mail:* information-usa@mofat.go.kr (office). *Website:* emb.dsdn.net (office).

CHOI, Young-jin; South Korean diplomatist; *Special Representative for Côte d'Ivoire, United Nations;* b. 29 March 1948, Seoul; m.; two s. *Education:* Dept of Int. Relations, Yonsei Univ., Univ. of Paris I (Panthéon-Sorbonne), Fletcher School of Law, Tufts Univ., Boston. *Career:* Political Officer, Embassy in Dakar, Senegal 1977–78, in Paris, France 1979–81; Dir Cultural Exchanges Div., Ministry of Foreign Affairs, Seoul 1981; Political Counsellor, Embassy in Tunis 1983–85; Dir Int. Orgs Div., Ministry of Foreign Affairs, Seoul 1986, Sr Asst to Minister for Foreign Affairs 1987; Econ. Counsellor, Embassy in Washington DC 1988–90; First Sr Coordinator, Office of Policy Planning, Ministry of Foreign Affairs, Seoul 1991–93, Dir-Gen. Int. Econ. Affairs Bureau 1994–95; Deputy Exec. Dir, Korean Peninsula Energy Devt Org., New York 1995–97; UN Asst Sec.-Gen. for Peacekeeping Operations 1998–99; Deputy Minister for Policy Planning and Int. Orgs, Seoul 2000–01; Amb. to Austria and Solvenia 2002, also Perm. Rep. to all int. orgs in Vienna 2002; Chancellor, Inst. of Foreign Affairs and Nat. Security (IFANS), Ministry of Foreign Affairs and Trade 2003; Vice Minister for Foreign Affairs and Trade 2004–05; Perm. Rep. to UN, New York 2005–07; UN Special Rep. for Côte d'Ivoire 2007–.
Address: United Nations Operation in Côte d'Ivoire, Abidjan, Côte d'Ivoire (office). *Website:* www.un.org/Depts/dpko/missions/unoci (office).

CHOLCHINEEPAN, Chiranond; Thai diplomatist; *Ambassador to Denmark;* m.; c. *Education:* Cornell Univ., Fletcher School of Law and Diplomacy, Tufts Univ., USA. *Career:* joined Ministry of Foreign Affairs 1975; served in Embassies in Kuala Lumpur, Rome, Ottawa; fmr Dir European Affairs Dept, Ministry of Foreign Affairs, fmr Dir Gen. Dept of Int. Orgs; fmr Amb. to Germany; Deputy Perm. Sec., Ministry of Foreign Affairs –2007; Amb. to Denmark 2008–.
Address: Embassy of Thailand, Norgesmindevej 18, 2900 Hellerup, Denmark (office). *Telephone:* 39-62-50-10 (office). *Fax:* 39-62-50-59 (office). *E-mail:* mail@thai-embassy.dk (office).

CHOMSKY, (Avram) Noam, MA, PhD; American theoretical linguist and writer; *Professor Emeritus, Department of Linguistics, Massachusetts Institute of Technology;* b. 7 Dec. 1928, Philadelphia, PA; m. Carol Schatz 1949; one s. two d. *Education:* Univ. of Pennsylvania. *Career:* Asst Prof., MIT 1955–58, Assoc. Prof. 1958–61, Prof. of Modern Languages 1961–66, Ferrari P. Ward Prof. of Modern Languages and Linguistics 1966–76, Institute Prof. 1976–; Visiting Prof., Columbia Univ. 1957–58; NSF Fellow, Princeton Inst. for Advanced Study 1958–59; American Council of Learned Socs Fellow, Center for Cognitive Studies, Harvard Univ. 1964–65; Linguistics Soc. of America Prof., Univ. of California at Los Angeles 1966; Beckman Prof., Univ. of California at Berkeley 1966–67; John Locke Lecturer, Univ. of Oxford 1969; Shearman Lecturer, Univ. Coll. London 1969; Bertrand Russell Memorial Lecturer, Univ. of Cambridge 1971; Nehru Memorial Lecturer, Univ. of New Delhi 1972; Whidden Lecturer, McMaster Univ. 1975; Huizinga Memorial Lecturer, Univ. of Leiden 1977; Woodbridge Lecturer, Columbia Univ. 1978; Kant Lecturer, Stanford Univ. 1979; Jeanette K. Watson Distinguished Visiting Prof., Syracuse Univ. 1982; Pauling Memorial Lecturer, Oregon State Univ. 1995; mem. American Acad. of Arts and Sciences, Linguistic Soc. of America, American Philosophical Asscn, American Acad. of Political and Social Science, NAS, Bertrand Russell Peace Foundation, Deutsche Akademie der Naturforscher Leopoldina, Nat. Acad. of Sciences, Royal Anthropological Inst., Utrecht Soc. of Arts and Sciences; Fellow, American Asscn for the Advancement of Science; Corresp. Fellow, British Acad.; Hon. Fellow, British Psychological Soc. 1985, Royal Anthropological Inst.; Hon. DHL (Chicago) 1967, (Loyola Univ., Swarthmore Coll.) 1970, (Bard Coll.) 1971, (Mass.) 1973, (Maine, Gettysburg Coll.) 1992, (Amherst Coll.) 1995, (Buenos Aires) 1996; Hon. DLitt (London) 1967, (Delhi) 1972, Visva-Bharati (West Bengal) 1980, (Pa) 1984, (Cambridge) 1995; hon. degrees (Tarragona) 1998, (Guelph) 1999, (Columbia) 1999, (Connecticut) 1999, (Pisa) 1999, (Harvard) 2000, (Toronto) 2000, (Western Ontario) 2000, Kolkata (2001); George Orwell Award, Nat. Council of Teachers of English 1987, Kyoto Prize in Basic Sciences 1988, James Killian Award, MIT 1992, Helmholtz Medal, Berlin Brandenburgische Akad. Wissenschaften 1996, Benjamin Franklin Medal, Franklin Inst., Philadelphia 1999, Rabindranath Tagore Centenary Award, Asiatic Soc. 2000, Peace Award, Turkish Publrs Asscn 2002. *Publications include:* Syntactic Structures 1957, Current Issues in Linguistic Theory 1964, Aspects of the Theory of Syntax 1965, Cartesian Linguistics 1966, Topics in the Theory of Generative Grammar 1966, Language and Mind 1968, The Sound Pattern of English (with Morris Halle) 1968, American Power and the New Mandarins 1969, At War with Asia 1970, Problems of Knowledge and Freedom 1971, Studies on Semantics in Generative Grammar 1972, For Reasons of State 1973, The Backroom Boys 1973, Counter-revolutionary Violence (with Edward Herman) 1973, Peace in the Middle East? 1974, Reflections on Language 1975, The Logical Structure of Linguistic Theory 1975, Essays on Form and Interpretation 1977, Human Rights and American Foreign Policy 1978, Language and Responsibility 1979, The Political Economy of Human Rights (two vols, with Edward Herman) 1979, Rules and Representations 1980, Lectures on Government and Binding 1981, Radical Priorities 1981, Towards a New Cold War 1982, Concepts and Consequences of the Theory of Government and Binding 1982, Fateful Triangle: The United States, Israel and the Palestinians 1983, Modular Approaches to the Study of the Mind 1984, Turning the Tide 1985, Knowledge of Language: Its Nature, Origins and Use 1986, Barriers 1986, Pirates and Emperors 1986, Generative Grammar: Its Basis, Development and Prospects 1987, On Power and Ideology 1987, Language and Problems of Knowledge 1987, Language in a Psychological Setting 1987, The Chomsky Reader 1987, The Culture of Terrorism 1988, Manufacturing Consent (with Edward Herman) 1988, Language and Politics 1988, Necessary Illusions 1989, Deterring Democracy 1991, What Uncle Sam Really Wants 1992, Chronicles of Dissent 1992, Year 501: The Conquest Continues 1993, Rethinking Camelot: JFK, the Vietnam War and US Political Culture 1993, Letters from Lexington: Reflections on Propaganda 1993, The Prosperous Few and the Restless Many 1993, Language and Thought 1994, World Orders, Old and New 1994, The Minimalist Program 1995, Powers and Prospects 1996, Class Warfare 1996, The Common Good 1998, Profit over People 1998, The New Military Humanism 1999, New Horizons in the Study of Language and Mind 2000, Rogue States: The Rule of Force in World Affairs 2000, A New Generation Draws the Line 2000, Architecture of Language 2000, Propaganda and the Public Mind 2001, 9-11 2001, Understanding Power 2002, On Nature and Language 2002, Middle East Illusions 2003, Hegemony or Survival: America's Quest for Global Dominance 2003, Failed States: America 2006, Interventions 2007, What

We Say Goes 2008, Perilous Power (with Gilbert Achcar) 2008; numerous lectures, contribs. to scholarly journals.
Address: Department of Linguistics and Philosophy, Massachusetts Institute of Technology, 77 Massachusetts Avenue, Bldg. 32-D808, Cambridge, MA 02139 (office); 15 Suzanne Road, Lexington, MA 02420, USA (home). *Telephone:* (617) 253-7819 (office); (781) 862-6160 (home). *Fax:* (617) 253-9425 (office). *E-mail:* chomsky@mit.edu (office). *Website:* web.mit.edu/linguistics/www (office).

CHON, Chol-hwan, MA; South Korean banker, economist and academic; b. 6 Aug. 1938, Jeolla Buk-do Prov. *Education:* Seoul Nat. Univ., Victoria Univ. of Manchester, UK. *Career:* Prof., Dept of Econs, Chungnam Nat. Univ. 1976–98, Dean Coll. of Econs and Man. 1991–93; mem. Monetary Bd, Bank of Korea 1983–89, Gov. Bank of Korea (Chair. Monetary Policy Cttee) 1998–2002; Pres. Soc. for Korean Econ. Devt 1995–96; Hon. PhD (Kunsan Nat. Univ.); 12th Dasan Econs Prize 1993. *Publications:* Social Justice and Economic Logic 1980, The Korean Economy 1986, An Introduction to International Economic Co-operation 1987, The Monetary History of Korea (1961–1990) 1991, Economics 1993.
Address: c/o The Bank of Korea, 110, 3-ga, Namdaemun-no, Jung-gu, Seoul 100-794, Republic of Korea (office).

CHONG WONG, William, DrLic; Honduran politician. *Career:* fmr Prof. and Vice-Pres. La Universidad Tecnologica Centroamericana (UNITEC); Deputy Minister of Finance 2002–04, Minister of Finance 2004–06; Gov. for Honduras World Bank, IMF, IDB.
Address: c/o Ministry of Finance, 5a Avda, 3a Calle, Tegucigalpa, Honduras (office).

CHOONG, Yong-ahn, MA, PhD; South Korean economist; *President, Korea Institute for International Economic Policy; Education:* Kyung-Pook Nat. Univ., Univ. of Hawaii, Ohio State Univ., USA. *Career:* advisor to Fed. of Korean Industries 1980–, to Bank of Korea 1984–87; Pres. Korea Econometric Soc. 1991–93, Int. Econs Asscn 1995–96, Devt Econs Asscn 1997–98, Asscn of Trade and Industry Studies 2000–01; Advisory Prof., Ministry of Foreign Affairs and Trade 1999–; mem. Presidential Econ. Advisory Council 2000–02; Chair. Korean Nat. Cttee for Pacific Econ. Cooperation (KOPEC) 2001–, APEC Econ. Cttee 2002–; Pres. Korea Inst. for Int. Econ. Policy (KIEP) 2002–. *Publications:* numerous articles and newspapers in journals.
Address: Korea Institute for International Economic Policy, 300-4, Yomgok-Dong, Seocho-Gu, Seoul, 137-747, Republic of Korea (office). *Telephone:* (23) 460-1001 (office). *Fax:* (23) 460-1199 (office). *E-mail:* cyahn@kiep.go.kr (office). *Website:* www.kiep.go.kr (office).

CHOQUEHUANCA CÉSPEDES, David; Bolivian government official; *Minister of Foreign Affairs and Worship;* b. 7 May 1961, Cota Cota Baja. *Education:* Colegio General José Miguel Lanza, Escuela Nacional de Formación de Cuadros Niceto Pérez, Cuba, Universidad Cordillera. *Career:* Nat. Co-ordinator NINA 1998; Minister of Foreign Affairs and Worship 2006–.
Address: Ministry of Foreign Affairs and Worship, Calle Ingavi, esq. Junín, La Paz, Bolivia (office). *Telephone:* (2) 237-1150 (office). *Fax:* (2) 237-1155 (office). *E-mail:* mreuno@rree.gov.bo (office). *Website:* www.rree.gov.bo (office).

CHOSSUDOVSKY, Michel, PhD; Canadian economist and academic; *Director, Centre for Research on Globalization; Education:* Univ. of Manchester, UK and Univ. of N Carolina, USA. *Career:* currently Prof. of Econs, Univ. of Ottawa; Dir Centre for Research on Globalization, Montréal 2001–, Adviser to The Transnational Foundation 1999–; visiting prof. at academic insts in Western Europe, Latin America and SE Asia; fmr Pres. Canadian Asscn of Latin American and Caribbean Studies; fmr econ. adviser to govts of developing countries and consultant to UNDP, African Devt Bank, UN African Inst. for Econ. Devt and Planning, UN Population Fund, ILO, WHO, UN ECLAC; mem. Cttee on Monetary and Econ. Reform, Geopolitical Drug Watch, Paris, Int. People's Health Council; active mem. anti-war movt in Canada; Human Rights Award, Berlin, Best Books in Germany (Non-Fiction). *Publications include:* America's "War on Terrorism" 2005, The Globalization of Poverty and the New World Order (published in 11 languages) 2005; contrib. to Encyclopaedia Britannica; has written extensively on int. financial issues, macro-economic reform in developing countries, and the wars in the Middle East and the Balkans.
Address: Centre for Research on Globalization, PO Box 55019, 11 Notre-Dame Ouest, Montreal, PQ H2Y 4A7, Canada (office). *Telephone:* (450) 510-0720 (office). *E-mail:* crgeditor@yahoo.com (office). *Website:* www.globalresearch.ca (office).

CHOUDHURY, Anwar, BSc, MBA; British diplomatist; b. 1959, Sunamganj, Bangladesh; m. Momina Choudhury; one s. two d. *Education:* Univs of

Salford and Durham. *Career:* Consultant Engineer, Siemens Plessey 1986–92; Strategist in Signal Eng, RAF 1993–95; Asst Dir, Ministry of Defence 1995–2000; apptd Dir of Cabinet Office 2000; transferred to FCO, High Commr to Bangladesh 2004–08.
Address: Foreign and Commonwealth Office, King Charles Street, London, SW1A 2AH, England (office). *Telephone:* (20) 7008-1500 (office). *Website:* www.fco.gov.uk (office).

CHOUDHURY, Liaquat Ali; Bangladeshi diplomatist; *High Commissioner to India;* m. Homaira Choudhury; one s. one d. *Education:* Dhaka Univ. and in Paris. *Career:* career diplomat with Bangladesh Foreign Service, served abroad in Perm. Missions to UN, New York and Geneva, Bangladesh High Comm., New Delhi, seconded to S Asian Asscn for Regional Cooperation (SAARC) Secr. as Dir and Head of Poverty Eradication Div., Kathmandu, Nepal 1995–99, Dir-Gen. Multilateral Econ. Affairs, UN, Int. Orgs, S Asia and SAARC Divs, Ministry of Foreign Affairs 2001–03, Amb. to the Netherlands 2003–05, promoted to rank of Sec. and Grade A Amb. 2005, High Commr to India 2005–.
Address: High Commission of Bangladesh, EP-39 Dr S. Radhakrishnan Marg, Chanakyapuri, New Delhi 110 021, India (office). *Telephone:* (11) 24121389 (office). *Fax:* (11) 26878953 (office). *E-mail:* bhcdelhi@mantraonline.com (office). *Website:* www.bhcdelhi.org (office).

CHOUMMALI, Lt-Gen. Saignason; Laotian army officer, politician and head of state; *President;* b. 6 March 1936, Attapu. *Career:* mem. Nat. Ass.; Deputy Prime Minister and Minister of Nat. Defence –2001; Vice-Pres. of Laos 2001–06, Pres. 2006–; elected Gen. Sec. Phak Pasason Pativat Lao (Lao People's Revolutionary Party) 2006–.
Address: Office of the President, Vientiane, Laos (office). *Telephone:* (21) 214200 (office). *Fax:* (21) 214208 (office).

CHOWDHURY, Anwarul Karim, MA; Bangladeshi diplomatist and international organization official (retd); b. 5 Feb. 1943, Dhaka; m.; three c. *Education:* Univ. of Dhaka. *Career:* Dir-Gen. for S and SE Asia, Foreign Ministry 1979–80, for Multilateral Econ. Co-operation 1986–90; Deputy Perm. Rep. to UN 1980–86, Perm. Rep. 1996–2001, Chair. Fifth Cttee (Admin. and Budgetary) of UN 1997–98); UNICEF Dir for Japan, Australia and NZ 1990–93, Sec. Exec. Bd UNICEF, New York 1993–96 (Chair. Bd 1985–86), UN Under-Sec.-Gen. for Least Developed Countries, Landlocked Developing Countries and Small Island Developing States 2002–07 (retd); Dr hc (Soka Univ., Tokyo); U Thant Peace Award, UNESCO Gandhi Gold Medal for Culture and Peace. *Publications:* contribs to journals on devt and human rights issues.
Address: c/o OHRLLS, United Nations Headquarters, Room S-770, New York, NY 10017. *Telephone:* (212) 963-9078.

CHOWDHURY, Iftekhar Ahmed, BA, MA, PhD; Bangladeshi diplomatist; *Adviser (Minister) for Foreign Affairs and for Expatriates' Welfare and Overseas Employment;* b. 25 Oct. 1946, British India; m. Nicole Chowdhury; one d. *Education:* Dhaka Univ., Australian Nat. Univ., Canberra. *Career:* began diplomatic career 1969; Deputy Sec., Ministry of Shipping and Aviation 1972–74; Deputy Chief of External Resources Div., Planning Comm. 1974–76; Counsellor, Embassy in Bonn, FRG 1983–86; First Counsellor, Perm. Mission to UN, New York 1986–88, Deputy Perm. Rep. 1988–91, Perm. Rep. 2001–07, Vice-Chair. Exec. Bd UNICEF 1998–99, 2005–06, Pres. Conf. on Disarmament 1999, Special Adviser to Sec.-Gen. of UNCTAD 2001, Vice-Pres. 59th UN Gen. Ass., Chair. Comm. for Social Devt 2002–03, Chair. Second Cttee of UN Gen. Ass. (Econ. and Financial) 2003–04, Chair. Comm. on Population and Devt 2005–06; Dir-Gen. Econ. Affairs, Ministry of Foreign Affairs 1991–94; Amb. to Qatar 1994–96; Amb. and Perm. Rep. to UN, Geneva 1996–2000; Adviser (Minister) for Foreign Affairs to Caretaker Govt of Bangladesh, with responsibility for Ministry of Expatriates' Welfare and for Ministry for Chittagong Hill Tracts Affairs 2007–08, for Foreign Affairs and for Expatriates' Welfare and Overseas Employment 2008–; Kt Order of St Gregory the Great (Vatican) 1999; named by New York City Council "one of the world's leading diplomatic leaders" 2003.
Address: Ministry of Foreign Affairs, Segunbagicha, Dhaka 1000, Bangladesh (office). *Telephone:* (2) 9562862 (office). *Fax:* (2) 9555283 (office). *E-mail:* webmaster@mofabd.org (office). *Website:* www.mofa.gov.bd (office).

CHOWDHURY, Shamsher Mobin, BA; Bangladeshi diplomatist. *Education:* Pakistan Mil. Acad. *Career:* joined Pakistan army 1969, promoted to rank of Maj. 1973; joined Bangladesh Civil Service 1975; Deputy Chief of Protocol and Dir West Europe, Ministry of Foreign Affairs 1975–77, with Embassy in Rome 1977–81, Counsellor, Embassy in Washington, DC 1981–83, Counsellor and Minister, High Comm. in Ottawa 1983–86, Deputy Chief of Mission, Embassy in Beijing 1986–88, Dir-Gen. SAARC Div., Ministry of Foreign Affairs 1988–91, High Commr to Sri Lanka

1991–95, Amb. to Germany 1995–98, to Viet Nam 1998–2001, Foreign Sec. 2001–05, Amb. to USA 2005–07; Gallantry Award Bir Bikram (BB). *Address:* Ministry of Foreign Affairs, Segunbagicha, Dhaka 1000, Bangladesh (office). *Telephone:* (2) 9562862 (office). *Fax:* (2) 9555283 (office). *E-mail:* info@mofabd.org (office). *Website:* www.mofa.gov.bd (office).

CHRISTENSEN, Søren, LLB; Danish civil servant; *Head, Department for Nordic Cooperation, Faroe Islands and Greenland, Ministry of Foreign Affairs;* b. 31 Oct. 1940, Copenhagen; m. Inge Rudbeck 1964. *Education:* Univ. of Copenhagen. *Career:* sec. Secr. of Lord Mayor, Municipality of Copenhagen 1968–71, deputy office man. 1971–73; Head of Secr. Municipality of Randers 1973–78, CEO 1978–86; Perm. Under-Sec. Ministry of Finance 1986–94; Head of Danish Supreme Admin. Authority, Copenhagen 1994–97; Sec.-Gen. Nordic Council of Ministers 1997–2002; Head of Dept for Nordic Cooperation, Faroe Islands and Greenland, Ministry of Foreign Affairs 2003–. *Publication:* Info Society Year 2000 1994. *Address:* c/o Ministry of Foreign Affairs, Asiatisk Plads 2, 1448 Copenhagen K, Denmark.

CHRISTIAN, Leslie Kojo, BA; Ghanaian diplomatist; *Permanent Representative, United Nations;* b. 1951, London, UK; m.; three c. *Education:* Univ. of Ghana. *Career:* Desk Officer Africa Div., Ministry of Foreign Affairs 1975–76, with Int. Orgs and Confs Bureau 1977–81; First Sec., Perm. Mission to UN, Geneva 1981–86; Desk Officer Protocol Div., Ministry of Foreign Affairs 1986–89, Finance and Accounts Div. 1989, Africa and OAU Bureau 1989–90; Counsellor, then Minister Counsellor, Embassy in Rome 1990–94; Deputy Chief of Protocol, Ministry of Foreign Affairs 1994–95, Acting Dir Finance and Accounts Bureau 1995–97; Deputy Perm. Rep. to UN, New York 1997–2001, 2006–07, Perm. Rep. 2007–; Dir OAU Bureau, Ministry of Foreign Affairs 2001–02, Supervising Dir Political and Econ. Dept 2003–06. *Address:* Permanent Mission of Ghana to the United Nations, 19 East 47th Street, New York, NY 10017, USA (office). *Telephone:* (212) 832-1300 (office). *Fax:* (212) 751-6743 (office). *E-mail:* ghanaperm@aol.com (office).

CHRISTIE, Rt Hon. Perry Gladstone, LLB; Bahamian politician; b. 21 Aug. 1943, Nassau; m. Bernadette Hanna; two s. one d. *Education:* Eastern Senior School, New Providence, Univ. of London and Univ. of Birmingham, UK. *Career:* attorney with McKinney Bancroft and Hughes; f. own law practice Christie Ingraham & Co. (now Christie Davis & Co.); mem. Bd Dirs Broadcasting Corpn of The Bahamas 1973; mem. Progressive Liberal Party (PLP), Co-Deputy Leader 1993–97, Leader 1997–; Senator 1974; mem. House of Ass. (PLP) for Centerville and Farm Road, New Providence 1977–; Minister of Health and Nat. Insurance 1977–82, of Tourism 1977–82, of Agric., Trade and Industry 1990–93; Prime Minister and Minister of Finance 2002–07. *Address:* c/o Office of the Prime Minister, Sir Cecil V. Wallace-Whitfield Centre, POB CB-10980, Nassau, Bahamas (office).

CHRISTMAS, Joseph R., MSC, PhD; Saint Christopher and Nevis diplomatist; b. 7 Feb. 1940, Saint Christopher. *Education:* Erdiston Coll., Barbados, Univ. of London, UK, Univ. of N. Carolina, USA and Univ. of West Indies (UWI). *Career:* Man. Nat. Water Dept 1972–77; Sr. Project Officer for Water and Environmental Sanitation, UNICEF, Mozambique 1978–83, Sr Program Officer and later Global Chief of Water Supply and Environmental Sanitation Section 1984–92, Resident Rep. in Angola and later in Kenya 1992–96; retd 1996; Foreign Policy Adviser to Prime Minister 1996–2000; Perm. Rep. to UN, New York 2000–06. *Address:* c/o Ministry of Foreign Affairs, Church Street, POB 186, Basseterre, Saint Christopher and Nevis (office). *Website:* www.mofa.gov .kn (office).

CHRISTODOULAKIS, Nikos M., EngDipl, MPhil, PhD; Greek politician and academic; *Professor of Economic Analysis, Athens University of Economics;* b. 27 Oct. 1952, Chania, Crete. *Education:* Nat. Tech. Univ. of Athens and Univ. of Cambridge, UK. *Career:* fmr mem. Euro-Communist party, linked with student uprising at Athens polytechnic 1973; Sr Research Officer, Dept of Applied Econs, Univ. of Cambridge 1984–86; Fellow, European Univ. of Florence 1989–90; apptd Prof. of Econ. Analysis, Athens Univ. of Econs 1990, Vice-Rector 1992–94, Prof. of Econ. Analysis 2007–; fmr Visiting Research Fellow, London Business School, Tinbergen Inst.; Prof. of Econs, Grad. School, Charles Univ., Prague 1992–93, Univ. of Cyprus 1996; Sec.-Gen. Research and Tech. 1993–96; Econ. Adviser to Prime Minister 1996; Deputy Minister of Finance 1996–2000; Minister of Devt with portfolios of Energy, Industry, Tech., Tourism and Commerce 2000–01; Minister of Economy and Finance 2001–04; mem. Parl. (Socialist Party) for Chania, Crete 2004–07; First Prize, Greek Math. Soc. 1970, Winbolt Prize 1985. *Publications include:* The New Terrain for Growth (in

Greek) 1998, Growth, Employment and the Environment 2002, The Pendulum of Convergence (in Greek) 2006, several books and articles on econ. policy, business cycles, growth, forecasting and econ. models. *Address:* 9 Kolokotroni Street, 10562 Athens, Greece (office). *Telephone:* (21) 03313488 (office). *Fax:* (21) 03313428 (office). *E-mail:* christodoulakis@parliament.gr (office). *Website:* www.christodoulakis.gr (office).

CHRISTOFFERSEN, Poul Skytte; Danish diplomatist; *Head of Cabinet, European Commissioner for Agriculture and Rural Development; Education:* Copenhagen Univ., European Coll., Bruges, Belgium. *Career:* Lecturer, Copenhagen Univ. 1973–77; with Ministry of Foreign Affairs 1973–77; First Sec., Perm. Rep. to EC, Brussels 1977–80; Head of Cabinet to Sec.-Gen. Council of EU 1980–94; at Ministry of Foreign Affairs 1994; Perm. Rep. to EU, Brussels 1995–2003; Perm. Rep. to FAO, WFP and IFAD, Rome 2003–05; currently Head of Cabinet, European Commr for Agric. and Rural Devt Mariann Fischer Boel; Prof., Copenhagen Business School 2004–; Pres. WFP Exec. Bd 2005; Alumnus of the Year Award, Alumni Asscn of the Coll. of Europe 2003. *Address:* Office of Commissioner Mariann Fischer Boel, European Commission, 200, Rue de la Loi, 1049 Brussels, Belgium (office). *Telephone:* (2) 296-35-32 (office). *E-mail:* poul-skytte.christoffersen@ec .europa.eu (office). *Website:* ec.europa.eu/commission_barroso/fischer -boel (office).

CHRISTOFIAS, Demetris, PhD; Cypriot politician and head of state; *President;* b. 29 Aug. 1946, Kyrenia. *Education:* Nicosia Commercial Lyceum, Inst. of Social Sciences and Acad. of Social Sciences, Moscow. *Career:* joined United Democratic Youth Org. (EDON) 1964, elected mem. Central Council 1969, Cen. Organisational Sec. 1974–77, Sec.-Gen. 1977–87; mem. Anorthotiko Komma Ergazomenou Laou (AKEL) 1964–, Sec.-Gen. 1988–; mem. House of Reps representing Kyrenia 1991–, Pres. House of Reps 2001–08; Pres. of Cyprus 2008–; Dr hc (Univ. of Macedonia) 2004. *Address:* Office of the President, Presidential Palace, Dem. Severis Avenue, 1400 Nicosia, Cyprus (office). *Telephone:* 22867400 (office). *Fax:* 22867594 (office). *E-mail:* president@presidency.gov.cy (office). *Website:* www .cyprus.gov.cy (office).

CHRISTOFIDES, Manolis; Cypriot government official and lawyer; *Presidential Commissioner;* b. 1 Feb. 1941, Lefka; m.; two d. *Education:* Pancyprian Gymnasium and Univ. of Athens. *Career:* leading mem. of Youth Org. of EOKA during Cyprus liberation struggle 1955–59; reserve officer with rank of Lt; served in area of Morphou-Lefka during Turkish invasion 1974; fmr Chair. Nicosia Bar Asscn; Chair. Cyprus Bar Council 1982–88; mem. Bd Cyprus Broadcasting Corpn 1971–79; Founding mem. Democratic Rally Party, f. party's youth org. NEDISY, Chair. for 10 years, now Hon. Pres.; mem. Parl. 1981–91; Minister of Health 1993–97; Govt Spokesperson 1997–98; Presidential Commr 1998–; Grand Commdr of Honour (Hellenic Repub.), Grand Commdr Order of the Orthodox Kts of the Holy Sepulchre (Patriarch of Jerusalem). *Address:* Presidential Palace, Nicosia (office); 23 Armenias Street, Flat 502, Strovolos, Nicosia, Cyprus (home). *Telephone:* 867429 (office); 312312 (home). *Fax:* 513605 (office); 513110 (home).

CHRISTOPHER, Sir (Duncan) Robin Carmichael, Kt, KBE, CMG; British diplomatist (retd) and international organization executive; *Secretary-General, GLF Global Leadership Foundation;* b. 13 Oct. 1944, Sussex; m. Merril Stevenson 1980; two d. *Education:* Keble Coll., Oxford and Fletcher School, Tufts Univ., USA. *Career:* VSO volunteer in Bolivia; philosophy teacher, Univ. of Sussex 1969; joined FCO 1970, New Delhi 1972–76, FCO 1976, Deputy High Commr, Lusaka 1980–83, FCO and Cabinet Office 1983–87, Counsellor, Madrid 1987–91, Head Southern African Dept, FCO 1991–94, Amb. to Ethiopia 1994–97, to Indonesia 1997–2000, to Argentina 2000–04; Sec.-Gen. GLF Global Leadership Foundation 2007–; Dir Rurelec PLC; Trustee, The Brooke, Prospect Burma, St Matthew's Children's Fund (Ethiopia), Redress; Fellow, Univ. of London Inst. for the Study of the Americas. *Publications:* Indonesia in Transition: Democracy or Disintegration? 2000, Justice and Peace 2000 (Czech edn 2007), Remembrance Day 2007. *Address:* GLF Global Leadership Foundation, 14 Curzon Street, London, W1J 5HN, England (office). *Telephone:* (20) 7861-8855 (office). *Fax:* (20) 7861-8856 (office). *E-mail:* Secretariat@g-l-f.org (office); rchristopher2@ yahoo.co.uk (home). *Website:* www.g-l-f.org (office).

CHRISTOPHER, Warren M.; American fmr. government official and lawyer; *Senior Partner, O'Melveny and Myers LLP;* b. 27 Oct. 1925, Scranton, ND; m. Marie Wyllis 1956; three s. one d. *Education:* Univ. of Southern California, Stanford Univ. Law School. *Career:* served in USNR 1943–45; Law Clerk, Justice William O. Douglas, US Supreme Court;

mem. O'Melveny and Myers law firm, LA 1950–67, 1969, Pnr 1958–67, 1969–76, 1981–93, Sr Pnr 1997–; special consultant on foreign econ. problems to Under-Sec. of State George Ball 1961–65; a trade negotiator in Kennedy Admin.; Deputy Attorney-Gen. in Johnson Admin.; Deputy Sec. of State in Carter Admin. (chief negotiator for Panama Canal treaties, supervisor human rights policies abroad, negotiated for release of US hostages in Iran 1980) 1977–81; Chair. comm. to review conduct of LA Police Dept in Rodney King case 1991; US Sec. of State 1993–97; Past-Pres. LA Co. Bar Asscn; fmr Chair. Federal Judiciary Cttee, American Bar Asscn; fmr Dir LA World Affairs Council; fmr mem. Trilateral Comm.; several hon. degrees; Medal of Freedom 1981, Los Angeles Chamber of Commerce, First Civic Medal of Honor 2003. *Publications:* In the Stream of History 1998, Chances of a Lifetime 2000.
Address: O'Melveny and Myers, 1999 Avenue of the Stars, Floor 7, Los Angeles, CA 90067-6035, USA. *Telephone:* (310) 246-6750. *Fax:* (310) 246-6779. *E-mail:* wchristopher@omm.com. *Website:* www.omm.com.

CHRISTOPHERSEN, Henning, MEcon; Danish politician; *Chairman, European Institute of Public Administration;* b. 8 Nov. 1939, Copenhagen; m. Jytte Risbjerg Nielsen 1961; one s. two d. *Education:* Univ. of Copenhagen. *Career:* Head of the Economic Section of the Handicrafts Council 1965–70; mem. Folketing 1971–84, mem. of Parl. Finance Cttee 1972–76, Vice-Chair. 1976–78, Minister of Foreign Affairs 1978–79; Deputy Leader, Danish Liberal Party 1972, Acting Party Leader 1977–78, Party Leader 1978–84; Deputy Prime Minister and Minister of Finance 1982–84; Vice-Pres. Comm. responsible for Budget, Financial Control, Personnel and Admin., Comm. of EC (now European Comm.) 1985–89, Econ. and Financial Affairs 1989–95, Co-ordination of Structural Funds 1989–92; a Vice Pres. of EC (now EU) 1993–95; Swedish Prime Minister's Adviser, Council for Baltic Sea Cooperation 1996–2000; Danish Prime Minister's Personal Rep. to European Convention and mem. Presidium 2002–03; Chair. European Inst. of Public Admin., Netherlands 1996–; Pres. The Energy Charter Treaty Conf., Brussels 1998–2007; Chair. Supervisory Bd of Dirs Örestad Devt Cooperation, Copenhagen 1999–; Vice-Chair. Supervisory Bd of Dirs Scania Danmark A/S, Herlev, Denmark 2000–; Sr Partner, Kreab A/B, Brussels 2002–; mem. Bd of Dirs Den Danske Bank 1996–, Int. Advisory Bd Creditanstalt-Bankverein, Austria, European Advisory Cttee on the Opening-up of Public Procurement, Danish Council for European Policy and the Baltic Sea Council, Sweden; Nat. Order of Merit. *Publications:* En udfordring for de Liberale, Taenker om Danmark i Det Nye Europa 1989 and numerous articles on econs.
Address: Kreab A/B, Av. de Tervueren 2, 1040 Brussels, Belgium.

CHRYSANTHOPOULOS, Leonidas T.; Greek diplomatist and international organization executive; *Secretary-General, Organization of the Black Sea Economic Cooperation;* b. 1946, Athens. *Education:* Univ. of Athens. *Career:* joined Greek Foreign Ministry in 1972, served as Vice-Consul in Toronto, as Second Sec. at Perm. Mission of Greece to EEC, as Dir Diplomatic Cabinet of the Minister in Charge of EEC Affairs, as Consul-Gen. in Istanbul, as Rep. of Greece in Charge of Third Cttee Questions (UN), as Deputy Perm. Rep. of Greece to the UN, as Minister-Counsellor in Beijing, as Amb. of Greece to Armenia 1993, as Alt. Dir-Gen. for EU Affairs, as Amb. to Poland, to Canada 2000–04, as Dir-Gen. for EU Affairs, as Dir-Gen. for Bilateral Econ. Relations and Multilateral Econ. Cooperation; Sec.-Gen. Org. of Black Sea Econ. Cooperation 2006–. *Publication:* Caucasus Chronicles: Nation-Building and Diplomacy in Armenia, 1993–1994 2002.
Address: Permanent International Secretariat, Black Sea Economic Cooperation, Sakıp Sabancı Caddesi, Müşir Fuad Paşa Yalısı, Eski Tersane, 34460 İstanbul, Turkey (office). *Telephone:* (212) 229-63-30-35 (office). *Fax:* (212) 229-63-36 (office). *E-mail:* info@bsec-organization.org (office). *Website:* www.bsec-organization.org (office).

CHSHMARITIAN, Karen, PhD; Armenian politician and economist; b. 12 Sept. 1959, Yerevan; m.; two c. *Education:* Yerevan Inst. of Nat. Economy. *Career:* trained as economist, Georgetown Univ. and USAID Tech. Cooperation Program, Int. Law Acad. for Educational Devt, Washington, DC, USA 1995; economist, Armenian Br., Research Inst. of Standards and State Planning, USSR 1980; mil. service, Soviet Army 1981–82; Sr Economist, Chief Specialist and Head of Financial Sub-Div., State Supply, Armenia 1985–90; Vice-Pres. Haielectramekenametzar (state co.), Armenia 1990–91; Head of Dept, State Supply 1991–93; Deputy Minister, Ministry of Material Resources, Repub. of Armenia 1993–96; Head of Foreign Trade Dept, Ministry of Trade, Services and Tourism 1996–97; First Deputy Minister, Ministry of Industry and Trade 1997–98; Minister of Industry and Trade 1999–2000; Minister of Trade and Econ. Devt 2002–07; mem. Republican Party of Armenia.
Address: c/o Ministry of Industry and Trade, 5 M. Mkrtchian, Yerevan 375050, Armenia (office).

CHU, Bo; Chinese politician; *Secretary, Committee of Inner Mongolian Autonomous Region, Chinese Communist Party;* b. Oct. 1944, Tongcheng, Anhui Prov. *Education:* Tianjin Univ. *Career:* joined CCP 1969; fmr Deputy Dir and Deputy Sec. CCP Party Cttee, Yueyang Chemical Works; fmr Deputy Sec. and Sec. CCP City Cttee, Yueyang Co., Hunan Prov.; fmr Mayor Yueyang Co.; Del., 13th CCP Nat. Congress 1987–92; mem. Standing Cttee, CCP Hunan Prov. Cttee 1990, Deputy Sec. CCP Hunan Prov. Cttee 1994–99; Exec. Vice-Gov. Hunan Prov. 1993–94, Vice-Gov. (also Acting Gov.) 1998–99, Gov. 1999–2001; Deputy, 9th NPC 1998–2003; Sec. CCP Cttee of Inner Mongolian Autonomous Region 2001–; Alt. mem. 15th CCP Cen. Cttee 1997–2002, mem. 16th CCP Cen. Cttee 2002–; Hon. Pres. Hunan Prov. Merchants' Asscn.
Address: Chinese Communist Party Committee of Inner Mongolian Autonomous Region, Huhot, Inner Mongolia, People's Republic of China (office).

CHUAN, Leekpai, LLB; Thai politician; *President of the Advisory Council, Democrat Party;* b. 28 July 1938, Muang Dist, Trang Prov. *Education:* Trang Wittaya School, Silapakorn Pre-Univ. and Thammasat Univ. *Career:* studied for two years with Bar Asscn of Thailand; mem. Parl. for Trang Prov. 1969–; Deputy Minister of Justice 1975; Deputy Minister of Justice and Minister, Prime Minister's Office 1976; Minister of Justice 1980; Minister of Commerce 1981, of Agric. and Co-operatives 1982–83, of Educ. 1983–86; Speaker of House of Reps 1986–88; Minister of Public Health 1988–89, of Agric. and Co-operatives 1990–91; Deputy Prime Minister 1990, Prime Minister of Thailand 1992–95, 1997–2001; Leader Prachatipat (Democrat Party—DP); Leader of Opposition 1995–96, 1996–97, 2001–; Minister of Defence 1997–2001; Vice-Pres. Prince of Songkhla Univ. Council; 6 hon. degrees; Kt Grand Cordon of the Most Noble Order of the Crown of Thailand 1981, Kt Grand Cordon (Special Class) of the Most Exalted Order of the White Elephant 1982, Order of Sukatuna (Special Class), Raja, Philippines 1993, Kt Grand Commdr (2nd Class, Higher Grade) of the Most Illustrious Order of Chula Chom Klao 1998, Order of the Sun (Grand Cross), Peru 1999.
Address: Prachatipat (Democrat Party), 67 Thanon Setsiri, Samsen Nai, Phyathai, 10400, Bangkok 10300 (office); 471/2 Rajaprasop Road, Magasasam, Rajatheri District, Metropolitan 10400, Bangkok, Thailand (home). *Telephone:* (2) 278-4042 (office); (2) 245-4415 (home). *Fax:* (2) 279-6086; (2) 278-4218 (office). *E-mail:* admin@democrat.or.th (office). *Website:* www.democrat.or.th (office); www.chuan.org (office).

CHUBUK, Ion, DrEcon; Moldovan politician; b. 20 May 1943. *Education:* Odessa Inst. of Agric. *Career:* First Deputy Chair. Moldovan State Planning Cttee 1984–86; Head of Div. Research Inst. of Agric. 1986–89; Deputy Chair. Moldovan Agricultural-Industrial Council 1989–90; First Deputy Minister of Econs 1990–91; Deputy Prime Minister, Perm. Rep. of Moldovan Govt in USSR Council of Ministers 1991–92; First Deputy Minister of Foreign Affairs 1992–94; First Deputy Minister of Econs April–Dec. 1994; Chair. Moldovan Accountant Chamber 1994–97, Deputy Chair. Accountant Chamber 1999–; Prime Minister of Moldova 1997–99; Deputy Chair. Centrists Union 2000–.
Address: c/o Office of the Prime Minister, Piata Marii Adunari Nationale 1, 277033 Chisinau, Moldova (office).

CHUDINOV, Igor Vitalyevich; Kyrgyzstani politician; *Prime Minister;* b. 21 Aug. 1961. *Education:* Kyrgyz State Univ., Int. Business School, Moscow. *Career:* held high-ranking positions in Komsomol (Soviet-era youth org.); early career as computer programmer; worked in a variety of positions as business exec. 1991–2005; Dir-Gen. Kyrgyzgaz (state co. that procures gas supplies for Kyrgyzstan) 2005–07; Minister of Industry, Energy and Fuel Resources Feb.–Dec. 2007; Prime Minister Dec. 2007–; mem. Ak Zhol party.
Address: Office of the Prime Minister, 720003 Bishkek, Dom Pravitelstv, Kyrgyzstan (office). *Telephone:* (312) 66-12-20 (office). *Fax:* (312) 66-66-58 (office). *E-mail:* pmoffice@mail.gov.kg (office). *Website:* www.government.gov.kg (office).

CHUN, Yung-woo, BA, MIA; South Korean diplomatist; *Ambassador to UK;* b. 27 Jan. 1952; m.; two s. *Education:* Pusan Nat. Univ., Columbia Univ., USA. *Career:* joined Ministry of Foreign Affairs 1977, overseas postings include Embassy in Paris 1981–84, in Rabat 1987–90, in Vienna 1994–95; Counsellor, Perm. Mission to UN, New York, Alternate Rep. to UN Security Council 1995–98, Deputy Perm. Rep. to UN 2003–05, Chair. Nuclear Suppliers Group 2003, mem. UN Missile Panel 2004; Dir for Policy Planning, Minstry of Foreign Affairs and Trade 1990–92, Deputy Dir-Gen. for Int. Econ. Co-operation, in charge of Science and Environmental Affairs 1998–99, Dir-Gen. for Int. Co-operation, Office of Light Water Reactor Project 1999–2001, Aide to Minister of Foreign Affairs and Trade 2001–02, Dir-Gen. for Int. Orgs 2002–03, Deputy Minister for Policy

Planning and Int. Orgs 2005–06, Special Rep. for Korean Peninsula Peace and Security Affairs 2006–08; Amb. to UK 2008–.
Address: Embassy of The Republic of Korea, 60 Buckingham Gate, London, SW1E 6AJ, England (office). *Telephone:* (20) 7227-5500 (office). *Fax:* (20) 7227-5503 (office). *E-mail:* koreanembinuk@mofat.go.kr (office). *Website:* www.koreanembassy.org.uk (office).

CHUNG, Shui-ming, BSc, MBA; Hong Kong government official; *Chief Executive, Hong Kong Special Administrative Region Land Fund;* b. 23 Nov. 1951, Hong Kong; two c. *Education:* Univ. of Hong Kong, Chinese Univ. of Hong Kong. *Career:* fmr Hong Kong Affairs Adviser to Chinese Govt; Fellow Hong Kong Soc. of Accountants; mem. Exec. Council, Hong Kong Special Admin. Region July 1997–, Hong Kong Housing Soc. Exec. Cttee, Housing Authority Finance Cttee; currently Chief Exec. Hong Kong Special Admin. Region Land Fund; fmr Chinese mem. Sino-British Land Comm.
Address: Executive Council Secretariat, First Floor, Main Wing, Central Government Offices, Lower Albert Road, Central, Hong Kong Special Administrative Region, People's Republic of China.

CHURKIN, Vitaly Ivanovich, PhD; Russian diplomatist; *Permanent Representative, United Nations;* b. 21 Feb. 1952; m.; one s. one d. *Education:* Moscow State Inst. of Int. Relations. *Career:* attaché, Translations Dept, Ministry of Foreign Affairs, Interpreter of USSR del. to SALT II Negotiations 1974–79; Third Sec. USA Dept of Ministry of Foreign Affairs 1979–82; Second Sec., First Sec., USSR Embassy, Washington, DC 1982–87; expert, Int. Dept of Cen. Cttee CPSU 1987–89; Counsellor of Ministry of Foreign Affairs 1989–90; Dir Information and Press Dept 1990–92; rank of Amb. Extraordinary and Plenipotentiary 1990; Deputy Minister of Foreign Affairs of Russia 1992–94; Amb. to Belgium 1994–97, to Canada 1998–2003; on staff, Ministry of Foreign Affairs 2003–, Chair. Sr Arctic Officials Cttee 2004–06; Perm. Rep. to UN, New York 2006–.
Address: Office of the Permanent Representative of the Russian Federation to the United Nations, 136 East 67th Street, New York, NY 10021, USA (office). *Telephone:* (212) 861-4900 (office). *Fax:* (212) 628-0252 (office). *E-mail:* rusun@un.int (office). *Website:* www.un.int/russia (office).

CIAMPI, Carlo Azeglio, LLB; Italian fmr head of state; b. 9 Dec. 1920, Livorno; m. Franca Pilla 1946; one s. one d. *Education:* Scuola Normale Superiore di Pisa, Pisa Univ. *Career:* served in Italian Army 1941–44; with Banca d'Italia 1946, economist, Research Dept 1960–70, Head Research Dept 1970–73, Sec.-Gen. 1973–76, Deputy Dir-Gen. 1976–78, Dir-Gen. 1978–79, Gov. 1979–93, Chair. Ufficio Italiano dei Cambi, 1979–83 (Hon. Gov. 1994–); Prime Minister 1993–94; Minister of the Treasury and the Budget 1996–98; Pres. of Italy 1999–2006 (retd); Chair. IMF Interim Cttee 1998–99; fmr mem. Bd of Govs for Italy IBRD, IDA, IFC; fmr mem. Cttee of Govs EEC; fmr mem. Bd of Dirs Consiglio Nazionale delle Ricerche, BIS; mem. Istituto Adriano Olivetti di Studi per la Gestione dell'Economia e delle Aziende; Mil. Cross, Grand Officer, Order of Merit of the Italian Repub. *Publications:* Un metodo per Governare 1996.
Address: c/o Office of the President, Palazzo del Quirinale, 00187 Rome, Italy (office).

CIANCHETTE, Peter, BS; American business executive, politician and diplomatist; *Ambassador to Costa Rica;* m. Carolyn Cianchette; two c. *Education:* Univ. of Maine. *Career:* more than 20 years of business experience, from serving as sr exec. in Dragon Products Co., to running his own business, Cianchette Enterprises, Inc.; joined consulting firm Pierce Atwood Consulting 1998, served as COO and Exec. Vice-Pres.; Pres. The Cianchette Group (public affairs man. and business consulting firm); Pnr, CHK Capital Partners, Portland; served in Maine's State Legislature representing South Portland and Cape Elizabeth in Maine's House of Reps 1996–2000, mem. Jt Standing Cttee on Taxation; Republican nominee for Gov. of Maine 2002; currently Maine's Nat. Republican Committeeman, served as Maine Gen. Chair. of Bush-Cheney 2004 campaign; mem. Bd of Dirs Make-A-Wish Foundation of Maine and YES! to Youth; mem. George and Barbara Bush Maine Cultural Center Cttee, Finance Cttee of American Lighthouse Foundation, MaineHealth Corporator; fmr mem. Bd of Dirs Greater Portland Big Brothers/Big Sisters, Boy Scouts of America/ Pine Tree Council, Portland Chamber of Commerce, Southern Maine Community Coll. Foundation; fmr Pres. Maine Better Transportation Asscn; fmr Chair. Maine Advancement Program; Amb. to Costa Rica 2008–.
Address: US Embassy, Calle 120 Avenida 0, Pavas, Apdo 920, 1200 San José, Costa Rica (office). *Telephone:* 519-2000 (office). *Fax:* 220-2305 (office). *E-mail:* info@usembassy.or.cr (office). *Website:* sanjose .usembassy.gov (office).

CIENIUCH, Lt-Gen. Mieczyslaw; Polish military officer; *Military Representative, NATO;* b. 24 Jan. 1951; m. Danuta Cieniuch, one s. *Education:*

Armour Office Coll., Nat. Defence Univ., Moscow, Nat. Defense Univ., Washington, DC. *Career:* several positions in mil. including MBT Platoon Leader, Tank Regt, Coy Ccommdr, Staff Officer, Chief of Training, Chief of Staff 1974–89, fmr Commdr 68th Tank Regiment, Budowo, served as Chief of Staff and Deputy Commdr 2nd Mechanized Div., subsequently Chief of Operations and Deputy Chief of Staff for Operations, Pomeranian Dist 1989–95, Commdr 8th Coast Defence Div. 1995–97, promoted to Brig.-Gen. 1996, Chief, Command and Control Div., later Chief J5, Gen. Staff, Warsaw 1997–2003, promoted to Maj.-Gen. 2003, apptd 1st Deputy Chief, Gen. Staff and promoted to Lt-Gen. 2003; Mil. Rep. to NATO 2006–; Cavalier's Cross of the Order of Polonia Restituta, Golden Cross of Merits.
Address: Delegation of Poland, NATO Headquarters, Bld Léopold III, Brussels 1110, Belgium (office). *Telephone:* (2) 707-14-56 (office). *Fax:* (2) 707-13-89 (office). *Website:* users.skynet.be/pldel/index.html (office).

CIKOTIĆ, Brig.-Gen. Selmo, MA; Bosnia and Herzegovina government official and army officer (retd); *Minister of Defence;* b. 25 Jan. 1964, Berane-Ivangrad, Montenegro; m. Tanja Cikotić; one s. one d. *Education:* Bratstvo i Jedinstvo Mil. High School, Belgrade, Zadar Mil. Acad., Sarajevo Univ. *Career:* PhD cand., Sarajevo Univ.; Duty Officer, Air Defence Educ. Centre, Zadar 1986–92; mem. Bosnia and Herzegovina Army 1992–94; Defence Attaché in Washington, DC 1994–97; Head of Training and Educ. Centre, Joint Command of Fed. of Bosnia and Herzegovina Army 1997–99; Head of Cabinet, Deputy Minister of Defence of Fed. of Bosnia and Herzegovina 1999–2000; Deputy Commdr of 1st Corps, Fed. of Bosnia and Herzegovina Army 2000–01, Commdr 2001–04; retd from active mil. duty 2004; CEO OKI Ltd, Sarajevo 2004–07; Minister of Defence 2007–; mem. Party of Democratic Action (SDA). *Publications:* several articles on defence and security.
Address: Ministry of Defence, 71000 Sarajevo, Bistrik 5, Bosnia and Herzegovina (office). *Telephone:* (33) 286500 (office). *Fax:* (33) 206094 (office). *E-mail:* mod@mod.gov.ba (office). *Website:* www.mod.gov.ba (office).

CIMOSZEWICZ, Włodzimierz, MA, PhD, DJur; Polish politician, lawyer and farmer; *Marshal (Speaker) of the Sejm;* b. 13 Sept. 1950, Warsaw; m.; one s. one d. *Education:* Warsaw Univ. *Career:* Asst. and Lecturer, Inst. of Int. Law, Warsaw Univ. 1972–78; Fullbright Scholar, Columbia Univ., New York, USA 1980–81; farmer 1985–; mem. Union of Socialist Youth 1968–73 (Chair. Bd, Warsaw Univ. 1972–73), Union of Polish Students/ Socialist Union of Polish Students 1968–75 (Chair. Univ. Council 1973), PZPR 1971–90; Deputy to Sejm (Parl.) 1989– (mem. PZPR caucus 1989–90, Chair. SLD Parl. Group 1990–93, Vice-Chair. Nat. and Ethnic Minorities Comm. 1989–91, mem. Parl. Foreign Affairs Comm. 1989, Special Comm. on Territorial Self-Government 1990, Chair. Constitutional Cttee 1995–96), Deputy Speaker 1995–96; mem. Bd Interparliamentary Union 1989–91; presidential cand. for Democratic Left Alliance (SLD) 1990; mem. Parl. Ass. Council of Europe 1992–96; Deputy Chair. Council of Ministers and Minister of Justice and Attorney-Gen. 1993–95; Prime Minister of Poland 1996–97; Chair. European Integration Cttee 1996–97; mem. Podlaskie Prov. Council 1998–2001; Minister of Foreign Affairs 2001–04; elected Marshal (Speaker) Sejm 2004–; Chevalier Ordre nat. du Mérite 1997; Kt Order of the Greek Repub. 1997; Dr hc (South Carolina Univ.) 1997, (Appalachian Univ.) 1998.
Address: Sejm, ul. Wiejska 4/6, 00-902 Warsaw, Poland (office). *Telephone:* (22) 285927 (office). *Website:* www.sejm.gov.pl (office).

CIOCCA, Pierluigi, DIur; Italian banker; *Deputy Director-General, Banca d'Italia;* b. 17 Oct. 1941, Pescara. *Education:* Univ. of Rome, Fondazione Einaudi (Univ. of Turin) and Balliol Coll., Oxford, UK. *Career:* economist, Research Dept Banca d'Italia (Bank of Italy) 1969–82; Cen. Man. for Cen. Bank Operations, Bank of Italy 1985–88, Cen. Man. for Econ. Research 1988–95; Deputy Dir-Gen. Bank of Italy 1995–; mem. Working Party 3 OECD Econ. Policy Cttee 1997–; substitute for Gov. Bank of Italy, Governing Council, European Cen. Bank 1998; mem. Financial Stability Forum 1999–, EU Econ. and Financial Cttee 2003–. *Publications:* La nuova finanza in Italia, Una difficile metamorfosi (1980–2000) 2000.
Address: Banca d'Italia, Via Nazionale 91, 00184 Rome, Italy. *Telephone:* (06) 47921. *Fax:* (06) 47922983. *Website:* www.bancaditalia.it (office).

CIORBEA, Victor; Romanian politician and jurist; *Chairman, Christian Democratic National Peasants' Party;* b. 26 Oct. 1954, Ponor Village; m. 1977; one d. *Education:* Law School, Cluj-Napoca, Case Western Reserve Univ., Cleveland, Ohio, USA. *Career:* judge, Court of Bucharest 1979–84; Prosecutor, Dept Civil Cases, Gen. Prosecutor's Office 1984–87; Asst to Lecturer Law School, Bucharest 1987–90; Pres. Free Trade Unions Fed. in Educ. 1990–96, CNSLR 1990–93, CNSLR-FRĂTIA 1993–94, Democratic Union Confed., Romania 1994–96; Prime Minister of Romania 1996–98; mem. Exec. Bd ICFTU, ETUC, CES 1993–94, Congress of Local and

Regional Powers, Council of Europe, Strasbourg 1996– European Hon. Senate 1999–; rep. of Romania at OIM confs; Vice-Pres. PNTCD 1997–99, Pres. 2001–; Mayor of Bucharest 1996–98; Vice-Pres. Christian Democratic Nat. Peasants' Party (CDNPP) 1999, now Chair.; mem. Bd Alianta Civica 1996; Founding mem. Int. Christian Coalition 1999–.
Address: CDNPP, Boulevard Carol I 34, 73231 Bucharest, Romania (office). *Telephone:* (1) 6154533 (office). *Fax:* (1) 6143277 (office). *E-mail:* president@pntcd.ro (office). *Website:* www.pntcd.ro (office).

CIOSEK, Stanisław, MA; Polish politician; b. 2 May 1939, Pawłowice, Radom Prov.; m. Anna Ciosek 1969; two d. *Education:* Higher School of Econs, Sopot. *Career:* activist in youth orgs. 1957–75; Chair. Regional Council of Polish Students' Asscn (ZSP), Gdańsk, Deputy Chair. and Chair. Chief Council, ZSP 1957–73; Chair. Chief Council of Fed. of Socialist Unions of Polish Youth (FSZMP) 1974–75; mem. Polish United Workers' Party (PZPR) 1959–90, Deputy mem. PZPR Cen. Cttee 1971–80, First Sec. Voivodship Cttee PZPR and Chair. Presidium of Voivodship Nat. Council, Jelenia Góra 1975–80, mem. PZPR Cen. Cttee 1980–81, 1986–90; Deputy to Sejm 1972–85; Minister for Co-operation with Trade Unions 1980–85, for Labour, Wages and Social Affairs 1983–84, Vice-Chair. Cttee of Council of Ministers for Co-operation with Trade Unions 1983–85; Sec. Socio-Political Cttee of Council of Ministers 1981–85; Sec. PZPR Cen. Cttee 1986–88; Alt. mem. Political Bureau of PZPR Cen. Cttee 1988, mem. Political Bureau 1988–89; Sec.-Gen. Nat. Council of Patriotic Movt for Rebirth (PRON) 1988–89; Co-organizer and participant, Round Table debates 1989; Amb. to USSR 1989–91, to Russia 1991–96; Foreign Policy Adviser to Pres. of Poland 1997–2005; Sec.-Gen. Eastern Club; Commdr's Cross, Order of Polonia Restituta.
Address: ul. Belgijska 11/11, 02-511 Warsaw, Poland (office). *Telephone:* (22) 542-8240 (office). *Fax:* (22) 542-8244 (office). *E-mail:* ciosek@ipgroup.pl (office).

CISSE, Gen. Lamine; Senegalese politician and UN official; b. 1939. *Education:* Nat. Defense Univ., USA, Center for Higher Studies in Nat. Defence, Paris, Command and Gen. Staff Coll., Fort Leavenworth, Kan., USA, University of Rennes, Special Mil. Acad. of Saint Cyr, France. *Career:* fmr. Gen.-Insp. of Senegalese Armed Forces and Head of Gen. Staff of the Army; chief of observers supervising ceasefire between MORO Liberation Front and Philippine armed forces 1976–78; Minister of the Interior 1998–2000, organised Parl. elections of May 1998 and presidential elections of Feb. and March 2000; Rep. of the Sec.-Gen. and Head of the UN Peace-building Office in the Cen. African Repub. (BONUCA) 2001–09, Officer-in-Charge, UN Office in W Africa 2007–08; Founder and Pres. Observatoire Int. de la Démocratie et de la Gestion des Crises et Conflits (OIDEC), Dakar 2000–; Commdr, Nat. Order of Lion (Senegal), Grand Croix of the Order of Merit (Senegal), Officier, Légion d'honneur, Grand Officier, Ordre national du Mérite, Chevalier, Nat. Order (Nigeria), Grand Officier, Order of Malta. *Publication:* Secret Memoirs of a Regime Change: A Soldier in the Midst of Democracy 2001.
Address: Observatoire Int. de la Démocratie et de la Gestion des Crises et Conflits, Dakar, Senegal.

CIVILI, Patrizio M.; Italian United Nations official; *Assistant Secretary-General for Policy Coordination and Inter-Agency Affairs, United Nations Department of Economic and Social Affairs; Career:* joined UN Secr. in Office for Inter-Agency Affairs and Co-ordination 1969, positions held include Deputy Sec. High-Level Group on Restructuring the Econ. and Social Sectors of UN System 1975, sr mem. Cabinet of Sec.-Gen. of UNCTAD 1986–92, Dir Exec. Office of Sec.-Gen. –1998, Sec. Chief Execs' Bd for Coordination, Asst Sec.-Gen. for Policy Coordination and Inter-Agency Affairs, Dept of Econ. and Social Affairs 1998–.
Address: Department of Economic and Social Affairs, United Nations, New York, NY 10017, USA (office). *Telephone:* (212) 963-5064 (office). *Fax:* (212) 963-4324 (office). *Website:* www.un.org (office).

CLARK, Rt Hon. Helen Elizabeth, PC, MA; New Zealand politician; *Prime Minister and Minister for Arts, Culture and Heritage;* b. 26 Feb. 1950, Hamilton; m. Peter Davis. *Education:* Epsom Girls' Grammar School and Auckland Univ. *Career:* fmr Lecturer, Dept of Political Studies, Auckland Univ. 1973–81; MP for Mount Albert 1981–96, 1999–, for Owairaka 1996–99; Minister of Housing and Minister of Conservation 1987–89, of Health 1989–90, of Labour 1989–90; Deputy Prime Minister 1989–90, Prime Minister of New Zealand Nov. 1999–, also Minister for Arts, Culture and Heritage; Deputy Leader of the Opposition 1990–93; Leader NZ Labour Party and Leader of the Opposition 1993–99; Spokesperson on Health and Labour 1990–93; mem. Labour Party 1971–; Danish Peace Foundation's Peace Prize 1986, ranked by Forbes magazine amongst 100 Most Powerful Women (43rd) 2004, (24th) 2005, (20th) 2006, (38th) 2007.

Address: Parliament House, Wellington, New Zealand (office). *Website:* www.primeminister.govt.nz (office).

CLARK, James; British diplomatist; b. 12 March 1963; partner Anthony Stewart. *Education:* Univ. of Edinburgh. *Career:* joined British Diplomatic Service 1988; with Mexico and Cen. America Dept, FCO 1988–90; language training in Cairo, Egypt 1990–91; Second Sec., External Relations, Rep. to EU, Brussels 1991–93; with Repub. of Ireland Dept, FCO 1993–94, Econ. Relations Dept 1994–95, Press Office 1995–97, secondment to German Ministry of Foreign Affairs, Bonn 1997–98, First Sec., EU, Embassy in Bonn 1998–99, with Head of Conf. and Visits Group, FCO 1999–2003, Commercial Dir and Head of Client Services Project Team, FCO Services 2003–04, Amb. to Luxembourg 2004–07.
Address: Foreign and Commonwealth Office, King Charles Street, London, SW1A 2AH, England (office). *Telephone:* (20) 7008-1500 (office). *Website:* www.fco.gov.uk (office).

CLARK, Maureen Harding, BCL; Irish criminal lawyer and judge; *Judge, International Criminal Court;* b. 3 Jan. 1946. *Education:* Bukit Nanas School, Kuala Lumpur, Malaysia, Muckross Park School, Dublin, Trinity Coll. Dublin, Univ. Coll. Dublin, Univ. of Lyons, France. *Career:* called to Irish Bar 1975, Irish Inner Bar 1991; criminal defence practice 1976–2001; Regional State Prosecutor 1985–91; Lead Counsel, Court of Criminal Appeal, Dublin 1991–2001; elected Judge Int. Criminal Tribunal for the Fmr Yugoslavia (ICTY) 2001; elected Judge Int. Criminal Court 2003–; governmental adviser on issues relating to victims' rights in sexual offence cases; Sec. and elected mem. Bar Council of Ireland; mem. Int. Asscn of Prosecutors, Irish Women Lawyers Asscn, Irish Human Rights Comm. 2004–; Assoc. mem. American Bar Asscn; Rep. of Irish Bar to numerous int. legal confs.
Address: International Criminal Court, Maanweg 174, 2516 AB The Hague, The Netherlands (office). *Telephone:* (70) 5158515 (office). *Fax:* (70) 5158555 (office). *E-mail:* pio@icc-cpi.int (office). *Website:* www.icp-cpi.int (office).

CLARK, Gen. Wesley, KBE; American fmr army officer and politician; *Strategic Adviser, Center for Strategic and International Studies; Education:* US Mil. Acad., Univ. of Oxford (Rhodes Scholar). *Career:* served in Viet Nam, awarded silver and bronze stars; fmr Sr mil. Asst to Gen. Alexander Haig; fmr Head Nat. Army Training Center; fmr Dir of Strategy Dept of Defense; Sr mem. American negotiating team at Bosnian peace negotiations, Dayton, OH 1995; fmr Head US Southern Command, Panama; NATO Supreme Allied Commdr in Europe (SACEUR) 1997–2000; Head US Forces in Europe 1997–2000; Consultant Stephens Group Inc. 2000–; Sr Adviser Center for Strategic and Int. Studies, Washington, DC 2000–; ran for Democratic presidential candidacy 2003. *Publication:* Waging Modern War: Bosnia, Kosovo and the Future of Combat 2001, Winning Modern Wars 2003.
Address: Stephens Group Inc., 111 Center Street, Little Rock, AR 72201, USA. *Website:* www.stephens.com.

CLARK, William, Jr, BA; American diplomatist; b. 12 Oct. 1930, Oakland, Calif.; m. Judith Lee Riley 1954; one s. *Education:* San Jose State Univ., Columbia Univ., Nat. War Coll. *Career:* Dir Liaison Dept US Civil Admin, Naha, Japan 1970–72; US-Japan Trade Officer, Embassy in Tokyo 1972–74; Dir Special Trade Activities, State Dept, Washington, DC 1974–76; served at Nat. War Coll. 1976–77, Political Counsellor, Embassy in Seoul 1977–80; Dir Japanese Affairs, State Dept, Washington, DC 1980–81; Minister, Embassy in Tokyo 1981–85, in Cairo 1985–86; Chargé d'affaires 1986; Deputy Asst Sec. of State 1986–89; Amb. to India 1989–92; Asst Sec. of State for East Asian and Pacific Affairs 1992–93; Sr Advisor and Japan Chair, Center for Strategic and Int. Studies, Washington, DC 1993–95, adviser on India program 1996–; Pres. Japan Soc. 1996–2003; mem. Bd of Advisors Transclick Inc. 2003–; Order of the Sacred Treasure Gold and Silver Star (Japan) 2000; Hon. DLitt (Calif. State Univ.) 1992; Superior Service Award 1971, Outstanding Service Award 1972, Distinguished Service Award 1985, Meritorious Service Award 1987, Distinguished Honor Award 1989.
Address: c/o Board of Advisors, Transclick Inc., 99 Spring Street, 3rd Floor, New York, NY 10012; 420 E 54th Street, Apartment 5-J, New York, NY 10022; 4845 W Street NW, Washington, DC 20007, USA (home). *Telephone:* (212) 319-4927 (home); (202) 398-7160.

CLAY, Sir Edward, CMG; British diplomatist (retd); b. 21 July 1945; m. Ann Clay; three c. *Career:* joined British Diplomatic Service 1968, Desk Officer, N and E Africa Dept 1968–70, Third Sec., Nairobi 1970–71, Second Sec. 1971–72, Second Sec., Sofia 1973–74, First Sec. 1974–75, Desk Officer, Dept of Defence, FCO 1975–78, First Sec., Budapest 1979–82, Area Officer, Personnel Dept, FCO 1982–84, Asst 1984–85, Head of Dept 1989–93, Deputy High Commr, Nicosia 1985–89, High Commr to Cyprus

1999–2001, to Uganda 1993–97, Dir of Public Services, FCO 1997–99, High Commr to Kenya 2002–05.
Address: c/o Foreign & Commonwealth Office, King Charles Street, London, SW1A 2AH, England. *Telephone:* (20) 7008-1500.

CLERIDES, Glafcos, BA, LLB; Cypriot fmr head of state and lawyer; b. 24 April 1919, Nicosia; m. Lilla-Irene Erulkar 1946; one d. *Education:* Pancyprian Gymnasium, Nicosia, King's Coll., London, UK. *Career:* served with RAF 1939–45, POW 1942–45; called to Bar, Gray's Inn 1951; practised law in Cyprus 1951–60; Minister of Justice 1959–60; Head Greek Cypriot Del., Jt Constitutional Comm. 1959–60, Greek Cypriot Del., London Conf. 1964, Rep. Negotiator Greek Cypriot Community Intercommunal Talks 1968; mem. House of Reps. 1960–76, 1981–93, Pres. 1960–76; Acting Pres. of Cyprus July–Dec. 1974, Pres. 1993–2003; Pres. Red Cross 1961–63 (Hon. Certificate and Hon. Life mem., Recognition of Distinguished Service); f. Unified Party 1969, Democratic Rally 1976; leading mem. Unified Party, Progressive Front and Democratic Nat. Front 1976; Grand Cross of the Saviour (Greece); Gold Medal (Order of Holy Sepulchre), Recognized Services and Understanding of Roman Catholic Religious Group (by approval of His Holiness Pope John XXIII). *Publications:* My Deposition (four vols).
Address: PO Box 28560, 2080 Nicosia (office); 5 Ioannis Clerides Street, Nicosia, Cyprus (home). *Telephone:* (22) 444400 (office). *Fax:* (22) 341777 (office). *E-mail:* grafio.proedrou@cytanet.com.cy (office).

CLERISME, Jean Renald, BA, MA, MPhil, PhD; Haitian anthropologist, politician and diplomatist; *Minister of Foreign Affairs;* b. 7 Nov. 1937, Arniquet; m. Dr Linda Geralde; three s. *Education:* Université d'Haiti, New York Univ. and Yale Univ., USA. *Career:* Amb. of Haiti to WTO, Int. Trade Center, UNCTAD, ITU, Geneva, Switzerland 2001–03; Del. Plenipotentiary to IAEA, Vienna 2001–03; Del. to Gen. Ass., Complete Test Ban Treaty Org. (CTBTO), Vienna 2003; Minister of Foreign Affairs 2006–; past positions include Pres. and Co-Pres. of Task Forces, WTO on Budget, Finances and Admin Cttee, Minister Counsellor to Perm. Mission to UN Office, Geneva, Rep. to UNIDO, Vienna; fmr Del. to WTO Confs. Singapore, Geneva, Seattle, Cancun, to UNCTAD Confs in Geneva, Bangkok, Brussels, to WIPO, Lisbon; Fulbright/LASPAU Scholarship, Mellon Fondation Grant. *Publication:* Main-d'oeuvre haïtienne and capital dominicain (Haitian Labor and Dominican Capital) 2003.
Address: Ministry of Foreign Affairs, Blvd Harry S. Truman, Cité de l'Exposition, Port-au-Prince, Haiti (office). *Telephone:* 2983768 (office). *Fax:* 2231668 (office). *E-mail:* rclerisme@yahoo.fr (home).

CLIFF, Ian Cameron, OBE, MA; British diplomatist; *Ambassador and Head of Delegation to the Organization for Security and Co-operation in Europe (OSCE);* b. 11 Sept. 1952, Twickenham; m. Caroline Redman 1988; one s. two d. *Education:* Hampton Grammar School and Univ. of Oxford. *Career:* history teacher, Dr Challoner's Grammar School, Amersham 1975–79; joined FCO Office 1979; First Sec., Khartoum 1982–85, FCO 1985–89, UK Mission to UN, New York 1989–93; Dir Exports to Middle East, Near East and N Africa, Dept of Trade and Industry 1993–96; Deputy Head of Mission, Embassy in Vienna 1995–2001; Amb. to Bosnia and Herzegovina 2001–05, to Sudan 2005–07, Amb. and Head of Del. to OSCE, Vienna 2007–.
Address: UK Delegation to the OSCE, Jauresgasse 12, 1030 Vienna, Austria (office). *Telephone:* (1) 716133304 (office). *Fax:* (1) 716133900 (office). *E-mail:* ian.cliff@fco.gov.uk (office). *Website:* www .britishembassy.gov.uk/austria (office).

CLINTON, Hillary Rodham, MA, DJur; American politician and lawyer; *Senator from New York;* b. 26 Oct. 1947, Chicago, Ill.; m. William (Bill) Jefferson Clinton (q.v.) (fmr President of USA), 1975; one d. *Education:* Wellesley Coll. and Yale Univ. *Career:* joined Rose Law Firm 1977, fmr Sr Pnr; Legal Counsel, Nixon impeachment staff, US House Judiciary Cttee 1974; Asst Prof. of Law, Univ. of Ark., Fayetteville and Dir Legal Aid Clinic 1974–77; Lecturer in Law, Univ. of Ark., Little Rock 1979–80; Chair. Comm. on Women in the Profession, ABA 1987–91; First Lady of USA 1993–2001; Head, Pres.'s Task Force on Nat. Health Reform 1993–94; newspaper columnist 1995; Senator from New York 2001–, mem. Armed Services Cttee, Environment and Public Works Cttee, Health, Educ., Labor and Pensions Cttee, Special Cttee on Aging; Co-Chair. Children's Defense Fund 1973–74; cand. for Democratic nomination for US Pres. 2007–08; mem. Bd of Dirs Southern Devt Bancorpn 1986, Nat. Center on Educ. and the Economy 1987, Franklin and Eleanor Roosevelt Inst. 1988, Children's TV Workshop 1989, Public/Pvt. Ventures 1990, Ark. Single Parent Scholarship Fund Program 1990; Hon. LLD (Arkansas, Little Rock) 1985, (Arkansas Coll.) 1988, (Hendrix Coll.) 1992; Hon. DHL (Drew) 1996; numerous awards and distinctions including One of Most Influential Lawyers in America (Nat. Law Journal) 1988, 1991, Outstanding Lawyer-Citizen Award (Arkansas Bar Asscn) 1992, Lewis Hine

Award, Nat. Child Labor Law Comm. 1993, Friend of Family Award, American Home Econs Foundation 1993, Humanitarian Award, Alzheimer's Asscn 1994, Elie Wiesel Foundation 1994, AIDS Awareness Award 1994, Grammy Award 1996, ranked by Forbes magazine amongst 100 Most Powerful Women (fifth) 2004, (26th) 2005, (18th) 2006, (25th) 2007, numerous other awards and prizes. *Publications:* It Takes a Village 1996, Dear Socks, Dear Buddy 1998, An Invitation to the White House 2000, Living History (memoirs) 2003; numerous contribs to professional journals.
Address: 476 Russell Senate Office Building, Washington, DC 20510, USA (office). *Telephone:* (202) 224-4451 (office). *Fax:* (202) 228-0282 (office). *Website:* clinton.senate.gov (office).

CLINTON, William (Bill) Jefferson, JD; American lawyer, fmr politician and fmr head of state; b. 19 Aug. 1946, Hope, Ark.; m. Hillary Rodham Clinton (q.v.) 1975; one d. *Education:* Hot Springs High School, Ark., Georgetown Univ., Univ. Coll., Oxford UK, Yale Law School. *Career:* Professor, Univ. of Ark. Law School 1974–76; Democratic Nominee, US House Third Dist., Ark. 1974; Attorney-Gen., Ark. 1977–79, Gov. of Ark. 1979–81, 1983–93; Pres. of USA 1993–2001; impeached by US House of Reps for perjury and obstruction of justice Dec. 1998, acquitted in Senate on both counts Jan. 1999; suspended from practising law in Supreme Court 2001–06; mem. counsel firm Wright, Lindsey & Jennings 1981–83; UN Special Envoy for Tsunami Recovery 2005–; Chair. Southern Growth Policies Bd 1985–86; Chair. Nat. Govs.' Asscn 1987, Co-Chair. Task Force on Educ. 1990–91; Vice-Chair. Democratic Govs' Asscn 1987–88, Chair. (elect) 1988–89, Chair. 1989–90; Chair. Educ. Comm. of the States 1987; Chair. Democratic Party Affirmative Action 1975, Southern Growth Policies Bd 1980; Chair. Democratic Leadership Council 1990–91; mem. US Supreme Court Bar, Bd of Trustees, Southern Center for Int. Studies of Atlanta, Ga; Chair. Bd of Dirs Global Fairness Initiative; Founder William J. Clinton Foundation, NY and Clinton Presidential Center, Ark.; Hon. Co-Chair. Club of Madrid; Hon. Fellow, Univ. Coll. Oxford 1992; Hon. DCL (Oxford) 1994; Hon. DLitt (Ulster) 1995; TED (Tech. Entertainment Design) Prize (co–recipient) 2007. *Recordings include:* Peter and the Wolf: Wolf Tracks (Grammy Award, Best Spoken Word Album for Children (jtly) 2004) 2003, My Life (Grammy Award, Best Spoken Word Album) 2005. *Publication:* Between Hope and History 1996, My Life (memoir) (British Book Award for Biography of the Year 2005) 2004.
Address: William J. Clinton Foundation, 55 West 125th Street, New York, NY 10027; Clinton Presidential Center, 1200 President Clinton Avenue, Little Rock, AR 72201, USA. *Website:* www.clintonpresidentialcenter.org; www.clintonfoundation.org.

CLODUMAR, Kinza (Godfrey); Nauruan politician; b. 1944. *Career:* entered parl. 1977; prin. financial adviser to Pres. 1992–95; Pres. of Nauru 1997–98, Jan.–May 2003; Minister of Finance several times between 1977–92, also 2003–04; Minister of the Environment 2004; fmr Chair. Nauru Insurance Corpn.

CLODUMAR, Vinci Neil; Nauruan diplomatist; b. 23 March 1951; m. *Career:* MP for Meneng 1987–97, Minister for Justice 1989, for Health and Educ. 1989–92, for Finance 1992–94, for Works and Community Service 1994–95; Chair. Nauru Phosphates Royalties Trust 1997–99; Mining Engineer, Supt, Operations Man., Production Man. and Gen. Man., Nauru Phosphate Corpn 1982–89, Chair. 1997–99; Dir Nauru Rehabilitation Corpn –1999; Perm. Rep. to UN, New York 1999–2005; Grad. Mem., Inst. of Engineers (Australia).
Address: c/o Ministry of Foreign Affairs, Nauru (office).

CLOUD, John A., BA, MA; American diplomatist; *Ambassador to Lithuania;* m.; two c. *Education:* Univ. of Connecticut and George Washington Univ. *Career:* Foreign Service assignments in Mexico and Warsaw, served at State Dept 1988–91, Econ. Counselor, Embassy in Bonn 1991–95, Deputy Chief of Mission, Embassy in Warsaw 1996–99, Deputy Chief of Mission, US Mission to EU 1999–2001, Special Asst to Pres. and Sr Dir for Int. Econ. Affairs, Nat. Security Council 2001–03, Chargé d'affaires a.i., Embassy in Berlin Feb.–Sept. 2005, Deputy Chief of Mission 2005–06, Amb. to Lithuania 2006–; three Superior Honor Awards.
Address: Embassy of the USA, Akmenų gatvė 6, Vilnius 03106, Lithuania (office). *Telephone:* (5) 266-5500 (office). *Fax:* (5) 266-5510 (office). *E-mail:* WebEmailVilnius@state.gov (office). *Website:* vilnius.usembassy.gov (office).

COBBOLD, Rear Adm. Richard, CB, FRAeS; British research institute director and military analyst; *Director, Royal United Services Institute; Career:* served in RN 1961–94, first as seaman officer and helicopter observer, commanded frigates HMS Mohawk and HMS Brazen, then Capt. of 2nd Frigate Squadron in HMS Brilliant; promoted Rear Adm. 1991; Asst Chief Defence Staff Operational Requirements for Sea Systems –1994, ACDS (Jt

Systems) 1992–94; mem. Royal Coll. of Defence Studies 1984; Dir of Defence Concepts, Ministry of Defence 1987; Dir Royal United Services Inst. for Defence Studies 1994–; specialist adviser to House of Commons Defence Cttee 1997–; Gov., London Nautical School. *Publications:* numerous articles on defence and security issues.
Address: Royal United Services Institute for Defence Studies, Whitehall, London, SW1 2ET, England (office). *Telephone:* (20) 7747-2602 (office). *Fax:* (20) 7321-0943 (office). *E-mail:* director@rusi.org (office). *Website:* www.rusi.org (office).

COCHRANE-DYET, Fergus; British diplomatist; *High Commissioner to the Seychelles;* m. Susie Cochrane-Dyet; three s. *Career:* Asst Desk Officer for Zimbabwe/Desk Officer for Libya/Tunisia, FCO 1987–90, Political Officer, Lagos and Abuja 1990–94, Head of N Africa Section, FCO 1994–96, Head of British Interests Section, Tripoli 1996–97, Head of Commercial Section, Jakarta 1998, Deputy Consul Gen./Dir of Trade and Investment, Sydney 1998–2001, Chargé d'Affaires, Conakry 2001–02, Chargé d'Affaires, later Deputy Head of Mission, Kabul 2002, Deputy Head of Africa Dept (Southern), FCO 2002–04, Deputy High Commr, Lusaka 2004–07, Deputy Head of Prov. Reconstruction Team, Helmand, Afghanistan 2007, High Commr to the Seychelles 2007–.
Address: British High Commission, Third Floor, Oliaji Trade Centre, Francis Rachel Street, PO Box 161, Victoria, Mahé, Seychelles (office). *Telephone:* 283666 (office). *Fax:* 283657 (office). *E-mail:* bhcvictoria@fco.gov.uk (office). *Website:* www.bhcvictoria.sc (office).

CODNER, Michael; British defence analyst; *Director of Military Sciences, Royal United Services Institute; Career:* Seaman Officer, RN –1995; Dir of Mil. Sciences, Royal United Services Inst. (RUSI); fmr Lecturer, US Naval War Coll.; Defence Fellow, Centre for Defence Studies, King's Coll., London; fmr NATO Fellow; Visiting Lecturer, Univ. Coll., London, Southampton Univ., Univ. of St Andrews. *Publications:* The Fundamentals of British Maritime Doctrine (ed. and prin. author); numerous journal articles, papers and chapters on defence policy and strategic theory.
Address: Royal United Services Institute for Defence & Security Studies (RUSI), Whitehall, London, SW1A 2ET, England (office). *Telephone:* (20) 7747-2621 (office). *E-mail:* codner@rusi.org (office). *Website:* www.rusi.org (office).

COEN UBILLA, Piero Paolo; Nicaraguan diplomatist; *Ambassador to UK;* m. Jaffa Coen. *Career:* Amb. to Russian Fed. –2005, to UK 2005–.
Address: Embassy of Nicaragua, Suite 31, Vicarage House, 58–60 Kensington Church Street, London, W8 4DP, England (office). *Telephone:* (20) 7938-2373 (office). *Fax:* (20) 7937-0952 (office). *E-mail:* embaniclondon@btconnect.com (office).

COGAN, John Francis (Frank); Irish diplomatist; *Ambassador to Austria;* b. Clonsilla, Carnaross, County Meath; m. Pauline Cogan. *Education:* St Patrick's Coll., Cavan. *Career:* Asst Sec.-Gen. Dept of Foreign Affairs, Dublin 1999; fmr Amb. to Iran; Amb. to Italy 2002–06, to Austria 2006–, also Resident Rep. to IAEA, Perm. Rep. to UN, Vienna, UNIDO and CTBTO.
Address: Embassy of Ireland, Rotenturmstr. 16–18, 5th Floor, 1010 Vienna, Austria (office). *Telephone:* (1) 715-42-46 (office). *Fax:* (1) 713-60-04 (office). *E-mail:* vienna@dfa.ie (office).

COHEN, Ra'anan, PhD; Israeli politician; b. 1941, Iraq; m.; four c. *Education:* Tel-Aviv Univ. *Career:* moved to Israel 1951; army service; mem. Knesset 1988–; served on Immigration and Absorption, Labour and Welfare, State Control, Finance, Anti-Drug Abuse, Knesset, Foreign Affairs and Defence Cttees; Chair. Meretz Parl. Group 1992–99; Chair. of House of Reps of Histadrut 1994–98; Sec.-Gen. Labor Party 1998–; mem. Meretz leadership; Sec. Israel Ahat; Chair. Beit Or Aviva (org. for the rehabilitation of drug addicts); Minister of Labor and Social Welfare 2000–2001, Minister without Portfolio 2001–; Chair. Industrial Devt Bank of Israel Ltd.
Address: The Knesset, Jerusalem, Israel (office); Israel Ahat, Ramat-Gan, Tel-Aviv. *E-mail:* amuta@ehudbarak.co.il (office).

COHEN, Shalom; Israeli diplomatist; *Ambassador to Egypt; Career:* Chair. Israeli interest section in Tunisia in 1996–2000; Counsellor for Maghreb Affairs, Ministry of Foreign Affairs 2003–05; Amb. to Egypt 2005–.
Address: Embassy of Israel, 6 Sharia Ibn el-Malek, Cairo (Giza), Egypt (office). *Telephone:* (2) 33321500 (office). *Fax:* (2) 33321555 (office). *E-mail:* info@cairo.mfa.gov.il (home).

COHEN, Stephen S., BA, PhD; American economist, academic and consultant; *Professor of Regional Planning and Co-Director, Berkeley Roundtable on the International Economy, University of California, Berkeley; Education:* Williams Coll., London School of Econs, UK. *Career:* faculty mem. Univ. of Calif. Berkeley 1968–, now Prof. of Regional Planning, also Dir

Berkeley Roundtable on the Int.Economy; consultant to OECD, UN, govts including France, Denmark, Columbia and Spain; The Medal of Paris. *Publications include:* The New Global Economy in the Information Age (jtly), Reading Our Times (co-ed. with J.K. Galbraith and others), Manufacturing Matters: the Myth of the Post Industrial Economy (with J. Zysman), France in the Troubled World Economy (with P. Gourevitch), Modern Capitalist Planning: the French Model.
Address: Berkeley Roundtable on the International Economy, 2234 Piedmont Avenue, No 2322, University of California, Berkeley, CA, 94720, USA (office). *Telephone:* (510) 642-3067 (office). *Fax:* (510) 643-6617 (office). *E-mail:* brie@socrates.berkeley.edu (office). *Website:* brie.berkeley.edu/BRIE (office).

COHEN, William Sebastian, BA, LLB; American fmr politician and consultant; *Chairman and CEO, Cohen Group;* b. 28 Aug. 1940, Bangor, Maine; two s. *Education:* Bangor High School, Bowdoin Coll., Boston Univ. Law School. *Career:* admitted to Maine Bar, Mass. Bar, Dist of Columbia Bar; partner Prairie, Cohen, Lynch, Weatherbee and Kobritz 1966–72; Asst Attorney, Penobscot County, Maine 1968–70, instructor Univ. of Maine at Orono 1968–72; mem. Bd of Overseers, Bowdoin Coll. 1973–85; City Councillor, Bangor 1969–72, Mayor 1971–72; elected to Congress 1972, re-elected 1974, 1976, Senator from Maine 1979–96; fmr mem. numerous cttees and sub-cttees; Sec. of Defense 1997–2001; founder and CEO The Cohen Group 2001–; Fellow of John F. Kennedy Inst. of Politics, Harvard Univ. 1972; mem. Bd of Dirs AIG –2006; Distinguished Public Service, Boston Univ. Alumni Asscn 1976, L. Mendel Rivers Award, Non-Commissioned Officers' Asscn 1983, Pres.'s Award, New England Asscn of School Superintendents 1984, Silver Anniversary Award, Nat. Collegiate Athletic Asscn 1987, Nat. Asscn Basketball Coaches, US 1987, numerous other awards. *Publications:* Of Sons and Seasons 1978, Roll Call 1981, Getting the Most Out of Washington 1982 (with Prof. Kenneth Lasson), The Double Man 1985 (with Senator Gary Hart), A Baker's Nickel 1986, Men of Zeal (with Senator George Mitchell) 1988, One-Eyed Kings 1991, Murder in the Senate (with Thomas B. Allen) 1993.
Address: The Cohen Group, 1200 19th Street, NW, Suite 400, Washington, DC 20036, USA (office). *Telephone:* (202) 689-7900 (office). *Fax:* (202) 689-7910 (office). *E-mail:* wsc@cohengroup.net (office). *Website:* www.cohengroup.net (office).

COHEN, Yitzhak; Israeli politician; b. 2 Dec. 1951; m.; ten c. *Career:* army service; fmr Deputy Mayor of Ashkelon and Sec.-Gen. of El Hama'ayan (Shas-affiliated educational inst.); mem. Knesset (Parl.) 1996–; mem. of Labour and Social Affairs and Finance Cttees; Minister of Religious Affairs 1999–2000; Deputy Minister of Finance 2001–03; Minister without Portfolio (responsible for religious councils) 2006–.
Address: The Knesset, HaKiryah, Jerusalem, 91950, Israel (office). *Telephone:* (2) 5311170 (office). *Fax:* (2) 6535469 (office).

COKER, Christopher; British academic and writer; *Professor of International Relations, London School of Economics; Career:* NATO Fellow 1981–; currently Prof. of Int. Relations, LSE; adviser to several UK Conservative Party think tanks including Inst. for European Defence and Strategic Studies and Centre for Policy Studies; visiting lecturer, Jt Staff Coll., Royal Coll. of Defence Studies, London, NATO Coll., Rome, Centre for Int. Security, Geneva, Nat. Inst. for Defence Studies, Tokyo; mem. Washington Strategy Seminar, Inst. for Foreign Policy Analysis, Cambridge, MA, Black Sea Univ. Foundation, Moscow School of Politics; fmr Ed. Atlantic Quarterly; fmr mem. Council of Royal United Services Inst. *Publications:* A Nation in Retreat 1991, Britain's Defence Policy in the 1990s: An Intelligent Person's Guide to the Defence Debate 1992, War and the Twentieth Century 1994, Twilight of the West 1997, War and the Illiberal Conscience 1998, Humane Warfare 2001, Waging War without Warriors 2002, The Future of War: the Re-enchantment of War in the Early 21st Century 2004; numerous contribs to books, newspapers and journals, including Wall Street Journal, The Times, Independent, The Spectator, The Times Literary Supplement.
Address: Department of International Relations, London School of Economics, Houghton Street, London, WC2A 2AE, England (office). *Telephone:* (20) 7955-7387 (office). *E-mail:* c.coker@lse.ac.uk (office). *Website:* www.lse.ac.uk/Depts/intrel/ (office).

COLEMAN, Sir Robert John, MA, JD, KCMG; British academic, lawyer and EU official; *Visiting Research Fellow, Institute of Governance, Queen's University, Belfast;* b. 8 Sept. 1943; m. Malinda Tigay Cutler 1966; two d. *Education:* Devonport High School for Boys, Plymouth, Jesus Coll. Oxford and Univ. of Chicago Law School. *Career:* Lecturer in Law, Univ. of Birmingham 1967–70; called to the Bar 1969; in practice as barrister-at-law, London 1970–73; Admin., subsequently Prin. Admin., EC 1974–82, Deputy Head of Div. 1983, Head of Div. 1984–87, Dir Public Procurement 1987–90, Dir Approximation of Laws, Freedom of Establishment and

Freedom to Provide Services, the Professions 1990–91, Dir-Gen. Transport, European Comm. 1991–99; Dir-Gen. Health and Consumer Protection 1999–2003; Sr Practitioner Fellow, Inst. of Governance, Queen's Univ., Belfast 2003–04, Visiting Research Fellow 2004–; mem. School of Man. Advisory Bd, Univ. of Bath 2001–. *Publications:* articles in professional journals.
Address: Institute of Governance, 29 University Square, Belfast BT7 1NN, Northern Ireland (office). *Telephone:* (1297) 560175 (home). *E-mail:* r.coleman@qub.ac.uk (office).

COLIN DE VERDIÈRE, Hubert; French diplomatist; b. 31 Oct. 1941; m. 1969; three c. *Education:* Ecole Nationale d'Admin. *Career:* Sec. of Foreign Affairs 1970–71; with Ministry of Public Health and Social Security 1970–71; at Cen. Admin, Econ. and Financial Affairs 1971–73, N Africa and Middle East Affairs 1980–83; First Sec., Embassy in Australia 1973–75; First Sec., Embassy in Algeria 1975–77, Second Counsellor 1977–79; Second Counsellor, Embassy in Spain 1983–84, First Counsellor 1984–87; Amb. to UAE 1987–91, to Iran 1991–94; Dir UN and Int. Orgs 1994–95; Dir Cabinet of the Minister 1995–96; Amb. to Russia 1996 (also accred to Tajikistan) 1997, to Algeria 2000–02, 2004–06; Sec.-Gen., Ministry of Foreign Affairs 2002–04; Commdr de la Légion d'honneur, Officier de l'ordre national du Mérite.
Address: c/o Ministry of Foreign Affairs, 37 quai d'Orsay, 75351 Paris (office); 1 rue Admiral Cloué, 75016 Paris, France. *E-mail:* hdeverdiere@yahoo.fr (home). *Website:* www.diplomatie.gouv.fr (office).

COLL, Alberto R., BA, JD, PhD; American lawyer and academic; *Director, European Legal Studies Program and Associate Professor of Law, DePaul University;* b. Havana, Cuba. *Education:* Princeton Univ., Univ. of Virginia. *Career:* joined Georgetown Univ. as teacher of int. relations, law and org. 1982; apptd Sec. of Navy Sr Research Fellow, Strategy, Naval War Coll. 1986, Charles H. Stockton Chair. 1989, Prof. of Strategy 1993–99, then Dean, Center for Naval Warfare Studies, then Chair. Strategic Research Dept; Deputy Asst Sec. of Defense 1990–93; currently Dir European Legal Studies Program and Assoc. Prof. of Law, DePaul Univ., Chicago; consultant to US Inst. of Peace, Center for Strategic and Int. Studies, Ethics and Public Policy Inst., Foreign Service Inst., US Information Agency, Defense Dept, RAND Corpn. *Publications include:* The Wisdom of Statecraft, The Western Heritage and American Values, The Falklands War (co-ed.), Legal and Moral Constraints on Low-Intensity Conflict.
Address: Office of the Director, European Legal Studies Program, College of Law, Depaul University, 25 East Jackson Blvd, Chicago, IL 60604, USA (office). *Telephone:* (312) 362-5663 (office). *Fax:* (312) 362-5923 (office). *E-mail:* acoll@depaul.edu (office). *Website:* www.law.depaul.edu (office).

COLLAKU, Kreshnik; Albanian diplomatist; *Chargé d'affaires a.i. in USA.* *Career:* fmr Prof., Univ. of Tirana; fmr Sec.-Gen. Renovated Democratic Party; Minister Counselor, Deputy Chief of Mission and Chargé d'affaires a.i. in USA 2006–.
Address: Embassy of Albania, 2100 S Street, NW, Washington, DC 20008, USA (office). *Telephone:* (202) 223-4942 (office). *Fax:* (202) 628-7342 (office).

COLLECOTT, Peter Salmon, CMG, PhD; British diplomatist; b. 8 Oct. 1950; m. Judith Patricia Pead 1982. *Education:* St John's Coll., Cambridge. *Career:* entered Diplomatic Service 1977; studied Arabic before a posting as First Sec., Khartoum, Sudan 1980–82; First Sec. (Econ./Commercial), Canberra, Australia 1982–86; Head, Iran/Iraq Section, FCO 1986–88, Asst Head, EC Dept (External) 1988–89; Counsellor, later Deputy Head of Mission, Jakarta, Indonesia 1989–94; Counsellor (EU and Econ.), Bonn, Germany 1994–99; Dir Resources, FCO 1999–2001, Chief Clerk, later Dir Gen. Corp. Affairs 2001–04; Amb. to Brazil 2004–08.
Address: Foreign and Commonwealth Office, King Charles Street, London, SW1A 2AH, England (office). *Telephone:* (20) 7008-1500 (office). *Website:* www.fco.gov.uk (office).

COLLIGNON, Stefan Colin, PhD; German economist; *Professor of Political Economy, London School of Economics;* b. 11 Dec. 1951, Munich; m. Judith Zahler 1984. *Education:* Institut d'Etudes Politiques, Paris, Free Univ. of Berlin, Univ. of Dar es Salaam, Tanzania, Queen Elizabeth House, Oxford, UK, London School of Econs. *Career:* financial analyst, First Nat. Bank in Dallas, Paris 1975–76; teacher, Lindi Secondary School, Deutscher Entwicklungsdienst (German Volunteer Service), Tanzania 1977–79; Man. Dir and Chair. Dorcas Ltd, London 1981–88; Dir Research and Communication, Asscn for the Monetary Union of Europe, Paris 1989–98; Lecturer, Institut d'Etudes Politiques, Paris 1990–95, Free Univ. of Berlin 1997–2000; Pres. Asscn France-Birmanie 1990–; Prof. of European Political Economy, LSE 2001–; Prix du meilleur livre politique, Paris 2004. *Publications:* Europe's Monetary Future (Vol. I) 1994, The Monetary Economics of Europe: Causes of the EMS Crisis (Vol. II) 1994, European Monetary Policy (ed.) 1997, Exchange Rate Policies in Emerging Asian Countries 1999, Monetary Stability in Europe 2002, Private Sector Involvement in the Euro 2003, The European Republic 2003; numerous articles and book chapters on monetary union.
Address: London School of Economics, Houghton Street, London, WC2A 2AE, England. *Telephone:* (20) 7955-6823 (office). *Website:* www.stefancollignon.de (home).

COLLINS, Sir Alan Stanley, CMG; British diplomatist; *Consul–General in New York;* m. Ann Collins; two s. one d. *Career:* joined FCO 1981, Officer, Western European Dept 1981–83, Desk Officer, Middle East Dept 1983–86, Deputy Head of Mission, Addis Ababa 1986–90, Deputy Head of Mission, Manila 1990–93, Head of Aviation and Maritime Dept, FCO 1993–95, Dir-Gen. British Trade and Cultural Office, Taipei 1995–98, Amb. to the Philippines 1998–2002, on loan to Shell International (Vice-Pres. for Int. Relations) 2002, High Commr to Singapore 2003–07, Consul-Gen. in New York, USA 2007–.
Address: British Consulate-General, 845 Third Avenue, New York, NY 10022, USA (office). *Telephone:* (212) 745-0200 (office). *Fax:* (212) 754-3062 (office). *Website:* www.britainusa.com/ny (office).

COLLINS, Gerard; Irish politician; b. 16 Oct. 1938, Abbeyfeale, Co. Limerick; m. Hilary Tattan. *Education:* Univ. Coll. Dublin. *Career:* fmr vocational teacher; mem. Dáil 1967–; Acting Gen. Sec. Fianna Fáil Party 1964–67; Parl. Sec. to Minister for Industry and Commerce and to Minister for the Gaeltacht 1969–70; Minister for Posts and Telegraphs 1970–73; mem. Consultative Ass. of Council of Europe 1973–75; Limerick Co. Council 1974–77; Minister for Justice 1977–81, 1987–89, for Foreign Affairs March–Dec. 1982, 1989–93; Chair. Parl. Cttee on EEC Affairs 1983–87; mem. European Parl. 1994–, Leader Fianna Fáil Group, Vice-Pres. Union for Europe Group, Pres. European Parl. Del. to S. Asia and South Asian Asscn for Regional Co-operation (SAARC); Chair. of the EU-South Africa Interparliamentary Del.
Address: The Hill, Abbeyfeale, Co. Limerick, Ireland (home); 6F 365, European Parliament, 97–113 rue Wiertz, 1047 Brussels, Belgium (office). *Telephone:* (2) 284-56-22 (office); (68) 32441. *Fax:* (2) 284-96-22 (office). *E-mail:* gcollins@europarl.eu.int (office). *Website:* www.europarl.ep.ec (office).

COLLINS, Michael, BSc; Irish diplomatist; *Ambassador to USA;* m. Marie Collins; three s. *Education:* Inst. of Public Admin, Blackrock Coll., Trinity Coll., Dublin. *Career:* joined Foreign Service in 1974, First Sec., Anglo-Irish Div. HQ 1977–82, First Sec., Consulate-Gen., New York 1982–86, First Sec., Political Div. HQ 1986–90, Counsellor, Dept of Foreign Affairs, Anglo-Irish Div. HQ 1990 and in Press Section HQ 1990–93; Counsellor, Embassy in Washington, DC 1993–95; Amb. to Saudi Arabia (also accred to Bahrain, Kuwait, Oman, Qatar and UAE) 1995–99, to Czech Repub. (also accred to Ukraine) 1999–2001; Second Sec.-Gen., Dept of the Taoiseach, responsible for int. and EU affairs, particularly the NI Peace Process 2001–07; Amb. to USA 2007–.
Address: Embassy of Ireland, 2234 Massachusetts Avenue, NW, Washington, DC 20008, USA (office). *Telephone:* (202) 462-3939 (office). *Fax:* (202) 232-5993 (office). *Website:* www.irelandemb.org (office).

COLLIS, Simon Paul; British diplomatist; *Ambassador to Syria;* b. 23 Feb. 1956; partner Sandra Kelly; one s. one d. *Career:* joined FCO 1978, Southern European Dept 1978–79, full-time language training 1980–81, Second Sec., Chancery, Bahrain 1981-83, Press Office, FCO 1984–86, First Sec., UK Mission to the UN, New York 1986, South Asian Dept, FCO 1987–88, Deputy Head of Mission, Tunis 1988–90, Emergency Unit, FCO 1990–91, First Sec. (Political), New Delhi 1991–94, Deputy Head of Near East and North African Dept, FCO 1994–96, Deputy Head of Mission and Consul-Gen., Amman 1996–99, on secondment to BP 1999–2000, Consul-Gen., Dubai 2000–04, Basra 2004, Amb. to Qatar 2004–07, to Syria 2007–.
Address: British Embassy, BP 37, Immeuble Kotob, 11 rue Muhammad Kurd Ali, Malki, Damascus, Syria (office). *Telephone:* (11) 3739241 (office). *Fax:* (11) 3731600 (office). *E-mail:* british.embassy.damascus@fco.gov.uk (office). *Website:* www.britishembassy.gov.uk/syria (office).

COLOM CABALLEROS, Álvaro, BEng; Guatemalan industrial engineer, business executive, politician and head of state; *President;* b. 15 June 1951, Guatemala City; m. *Education:* Univ. de San Carlos. *Career:* Deputy Minister for the Economy 1991; Founder and Pres., Unidad Nacional de la Esperanza (UNE) 2001–, runner up in primary elections for Pres. 2003, Pres. 2008–; Founder and Pres. Grupo Mega; Exec. Dir Dependencia Presidencial de Asistencia Legal y Resolución de Conflictors sobre la Tierra (CONTIERRA); Founder, Pnr and Production Man. Roprisma, Intraexsa; Man. Dept Industrial de DINAH SA; Dir Clothing Comm., Chamber of Industry and Commerce 1977–82; Vice Pres. Asscn of Guatemalan

Exporters 1990–; Dir Fundación para el Análisis y Desarollo de Centroamérica (FADES) 1999–; Adviser, Consejo Nacional de Ancianos Mayas (Mayan Council) 1996–; mem. Consultative Bd, AGEXPRONT 1977–82, Dir 1982–90; Founder and Pres. Nat. Comm. for the Clothing Industry 1984; Adviser, Secretaría de la Paz (SEPAZ) 1997; serves as an ordained Mayan minister.
Address: Office of the President, Guatemala City; Unidad Nacional de la Esperanza (UNE), 2a Avenida 5-11, Zona 9, Guatemala City, Guatemala (office). *Telephone:* 232-4685 (office). *E-mail:* ideas@une.org.gt (office). *Website:* www.une.org.gt (office).

COLOMBANI, Jean-Marie; French journalist; b. 7 July 1948, Dakar, Senegal; m. Catherine Sénès 1976; five c. *Education:* Lycée Hoche, Versailles, Lycée La Pérouse, Nouméa, New Caledonia, Univ. of Paris II-Assas, Univ. of Paris I Panthéon-Sorbonne, Inst. d'Etudes Politiques, Paris and Inst. d'Etudes Supérieures de Droit Public. *Career:* journalist, ORTF, later Office of FR3, Nouméa 1973; Ed. Political Service, Le Monde 1977, Head of Political Service 1983, Ed.-in-Chief 1990, Deputy Editorial Dir 1991; Man. Dir S.A.–Le Monde March–Dec. 1994, Chair. of Bd and Dir of Publs 1994–2007, mem. Bd Dirs 2007–; Chair. Advisory Council, Midi-Libre Group 2000–. *Publications:* Contradictions: entretiens avec Anicet Le Poro 1984, L'utopie calédonienne 1985, Portrait du président ou le monarque imaginaire 1985, Le mariage blanc (co-author) 1986, Questions de confiance: entretiens avec Raymond Barre 1987, Les héritiers (co-author), La France sans Mitterrand 1992, La gauche survivra-t-elle aux socialistes? 1994, Le Double Septennat de François Mitterrand, Dernier Inventaire (jtly) 1995, De la France en général et de ses dirigeants en particulier 1996, Le Résident de la République 1998, La Cinquième ou la République des phratries (co-author) 1999, Les infortunes de la Republique 2000, Tous Américains? 2002.
Address: c/o Le Monde, 21 bis rue Claude Bernard, 75242 Paris cedex 05 (office); 5 rue Joseph Bara, 75006 Paris, France (home).

COLVILLE OF CULROSS, 4th Viscount, cr. 1902; 14th Baron (Scotland), cr. 1604; 4th Baron (UK), cr. 1885; **John Mark Alexander Colville,** QC, MA; British judge; *Assistant Surveillance Commissioner;* b. 19 July 1933; m. 1st Mary Elizabeth Webb-Bowen 1958 (divorced 1973); four s.; m. 2nd Margaret Birgitta, Viscountess Davidson (née Norton) 1974; one s. *Education:* Rugby School, New Coll. Oxford. *Career:* called to Bar, Lincoln's Inn 1960, QC 1978, Bencher 1986, a Recorder 1990–93, Judge, South Eastern Circuit 1993–99; Minister of State, Home Office 1972–74; UK Rep., UN Human Rights Comm. 1980–83, mem. UN Working Group on Disappeared Persons 1980–84 (Chair. 1981–84), Special Rapporteur on Human Rights in Guatemala 1983–87, mem. UN Human Rights Cttee 1996–2000; Asst Surveillance Commr 2001–; Dir Securities and Futures Authority (fmrly Securities Asscn) 1987–93; Chair. Mental Health Act Comm. 1983–88, Alcohol Educ. and Research Council 1984–90, Parole Bd for England and Wales 1988–92; author of reports for Govt on Prevention of Terrorism Act and Northern Ireland Emergency Powers Act 1986–93; Chair. Norwich Information and Tech. Centre 1983–85; Dir Rediffusion TV Ltd 1961–68, British Electric Traction Co. Ltd 1968–72, 1974–84 (Deputy Chair. 1980–81); mem. CBI Council 1982–84; Gov. BUPA 1990–93; mem. Royal Co. of Archers (Queen's Body Guard for Scotland); Hon. Fellow New Coll. Oxford; Hon. DCL (East Anglia).
Address: House of Lords, Westminster, London, SW1A 0PW (office); West Lexham Manor, King's Lynn, Norfolk, PE32 2QN, England (home).

COLVIN, Marie Catherine, BA; American journalist; *Foreign Affairs Correspondent, The Sunday Times (UK);* b. 12 Jan. 1956, New York; m. Patrick Bishop 1989 (divorced). *Education:* Yale Univ. *Career:* with United Press Int. (UPI), New York and Washington, DC 1982–84, Paris Bureau Chief 1984–86; Middle East Corresp., The Sunday Times, London 1986–96, Foreign Affairs Corresp. 1996–; Woman of the Year (for work in Timor-Leste), Women of the Year Foundation, London 2000, Courage in Journalism Award, Int. Women's Media Foundation, USA 2000, Journalist of the Year, USA Foreign Corresps' Asscn 2001, Foreign Reporter of the Year, UK Press Awards 2001. *Television:* Behind the Myth: Yasser Arafat (BBC documentary), Martha Gelhorn (BBC documentary).
Address: c/o Sunday Times Foreign Desk, 1 Pennington Street, London, E1 9XW, England (office). *Telephone:* (20) 7782-5701 (office). *Fax:* (20) 7782-5050 (office). *E-mail:* mariecolvin@hotmail.com (home).

COMĂNESCU, Lazăr, PhD; Romanian diplomatist and politician; *Minister of Foreign Affairs;* b. 4 June 1949, Horezu (Ursani), Vâlcea; m. Mihaela Comănescu; one d. *Education:* Acad. of Econ. Studies, Bucharest, Sorbonne, Paris. *Career:* Jr Diplomat, Ministry of Foreign Affairs 1972–82, Counsellor, later Minister-Counsellor, Mission to EU, Brussels 1990–94, Dir EU Directorate, Ministry of Foreign Affairs 1994–95, Dir-Gen. and Adviser to Minister of Foreign Affairs, also Head of Minister's office 1995, State Sec., Ministry of Foreign Affairs 1995–98, Amb. and Head, Mission to NATO and WEU 1998–2001, Amb. and Head of Mission to EU 2001–07, Perm. Rep., EU, Brussels 2007–08; Minister of Foreign Affairs 2008–; Prof. of Int. Econs, Acad. of Econ. Studies, Bucharest 1982–90; mem. Scientific Consultative Bd European Inst. in Romania; mem. Scientific Bd Romanian Inst. for Int. Studies; Founding mem. Warsaw Cen. European Forum; Grand Officer, Romanian Nat. Order of Loyal Service 2000, Romanian Nat. Order of Loyal Service with Great Cross 2007. *Publications:* author of several univ. courses and books; numerous articles in journals.
Address: Ministry of Foreign Affairs, Al. Alexandru 31, 011822 Bucharest, Romania (office). *Telephone:* (21) 3192108 (office). *Fax:* (21) 3196862 (office). *E-mail:* mae@mae.ro (office). *Website:* www.mae.ro (office).

COMPAORÉ, Blaise; Burkinabè head of state and fmr army officer; *President;* b. 3 Feb. 1951, Ouagadougou; m. Chantal K. Terrasson; one d. *Career:* trained as soldier in Cameroon and Morocco; fmr second in command to Capt. Thomas Sankara whom he overthrew in a coup in Oct. 1987; Minister of State to the Pres., then Minister for Justice 1983–87; Chair. Popular Front of Burkina Faso and Head of Govt Oct. 1987–, Interim Head of State June–Dec. 1991, Pres. of Burkina Faso Dec. 1991–; Assoc. mem. Overseas Acad. of Sciences, France 1995–; Commdr, Ordre Int. des Palmes académiques 2005; Dr hc (Ecole des Hautes Etudes Ints de Paris) 1992, (Soka Univ., Japan) 1995, (Jean-Moulin de Lyon 3 Univ., France) 2004, (Ramkhamaeng Univ., Thailand) 2005.
Address: Office of the President, 03 BP 7030, Ouagadougou 03, Burkina Faso (office). *Telephone:* 30-66-30 (office). *Fax:* 31-49-26 (office). *Website:* www.primature.gov.bf (office).

COMPAORE, Jean-Baptiste Marie Pascal, MEconSc; Burkinabè politician; *Minister of Finance and the Budget;* m.; four c. *Education:* Phillipe Zinda Kabore Coll., Ouagadougou, Univ. of Benin, Lome, Togo. *Career:* joined Bank of the States of W Africa (BCEAO), Dakar 1981, served in Credit and Inspection Divs; Inspector of Banks, Banking Comm. of W Africa Monetary Union 1990–95; Counsellor, Dir of Econ. and Social Affairs, Office of the Pres. 1995–96, Sec.-Gen. of Ministry 1996–2000; Minister to the Prime Minister, responsible for Finance and the Budget 2000–02; Minister of Finance and the Budget 2002–; fmr Lecturer (part-time) Lome Tech. School, Togo; Coordinator Program of Admin. Support 1997–; fmr Chair. Inter-Departmental Cttee to Follow-up Recommendations of Arbitrator of Faso; Officier, Ordre Nat.
Address: Ministry of Finance and the Budget, 03 BP 7050, Ouagadougou 03, Burkina Faso (office). *Telephone:* 50-32-42-11 (office). *Fax:* 50-31-27-15 (office). *E-mail:* finances@cenatrin.bf (office). *Website:* www.finances.gov .bf (office).

CONDE de SARO, Francisco Javier, M.L.; Spanish diplomatist; *Ambassador to Japan;* b. 13 March 1946, Madrid; m. Ana Martínez de Irujo; one s. two d. *Education:* Univ. of Madrid, Diplomatic School, Madrid. *Career:* Dir-Gen. for Int. Econ. Relations, Ministry of Foreign Affairs 1971; Asst Dir-Gen. for Int. Relations, Directorate of Maritime Fisheries 1976; Dir of Political Affairs for Africa and Asia, Ministry of Foreign Affairs 1978; counsellor Ministry of Transport, Tourism and Communications 1978; Econ. and Commercial Counsellor, Spanish Embassy, Rabat 1979–83, Buenos Aires 1983–86; Dir-Gen. Juridical and Institutional Co-ordination, Sec. of State for EU, Ministry of Foreign Affairs 1986–90, Sec.-Gen. 1994; Amb. of Spain to Algeria 1990–94; Perm. Rep. to NATO 1996–2000; Perm. Rep. to EU 2000–04; Amb. to Japan 2004–; Kt Commdr of Civil Merit (Spain), of Isabel la Católica (Spain), of Mayo Order (Argentina), of Order of the Lion (Senegal); Kt of Order of El Ouissam El Mohammadi (Morocco); Grand Cross for Naval Merit (Spain), Grand Cross of Merit (Austria).
Address: Embassy of Spain, 1-3-29, Roppongi, Minato-ku, Tokyo, 106-0032, Japan (office). *Telephone:* (3) 3583-8531 (office). *Fax:* (3) 3582-8627 (office). *E-mail:* embspjp@mail.mae.es (office).

CONDOR, Sam Terence, BA; Saint Christopher and Nevis politician and businessman; *Deputy Prime Minister and Minister of Education, Youth, Social and Community Development and Gender Affairs;* b. 4 Nov. 1949; m.; one s. two d. *Education:* Ruskin Coll., Oxford, Univ. of Sussex, UK. *Career:* printer, Saint Christopher and Nevis Govt Printery 1967–82; Sr Clerk, Inland Revenue Dept 1980–82; Man. Dir Quality Foods Ltd 1986–95; MP 1989–; Deputy Prime Minister, Minister of Trade, Industry, Caricom Affairs, Youth, Sports and Community Devt 1995–99, Deputy Prime Minister, Minister of Foreign Affairs, Int. Trade and Caricom Affairs, Community and Social Devt and Gender Affairs 2000–01; apptd Deputy Prime Minister and Minister of CARICOM Affairs, Int. Trade, Labour, Social Security, Telecommunications and Tech. 2001; currently Deputy Prime Minister and Minister of Educ., Youth, Social and Community Devt and Gender Affairs; Vice-Chair. Young Labour 1980–82, Deputy Leader Saint Christopher and Nevis Labour Party

1990–; mem. Saint Christopher and Nevis Tourist Bd 1975–78; Nat. Football Player 1969–72, Man. and Coach Nat. Football Team 1986–88; Margaret Marsh Prize for Most Outstanding Overseas Student, Ruskin Coll. 1979–80.
Address: Ministry of Education, Youth, Social and Community Development and Gender, Church Street, PO Box 186, Basseterre (office); North Pelican Drive, Bird Rock, Saint Christopher, Saint Christopher and Nevis, West Indies (home). *Telephone:* 465-2521 (office); 465-1545 (home). *Fax:* 465-2556 (office). *E-mail:* dpmin@caribsurf.com (office).

CONEWAY, Peter R., MBA; American business executive and diplomatist; *Ambassador to Switzerland and Liechtenstein;* m. Lynn Coneway; two c. *Education:* Coll. of Business Admin, Univ. of Texas, Stanford Univ. *Career:* joined Goldman, Sachs & Co. 1969, later fmr Advisory Dir, f. Houston office for Goldman Sachs 1975, named Gen. Pnr 1978, est. firm's equities sales, trading and research div., Tokyo 1987–88, returned to manage Houston office; Amb. to Switzerland (also accred to Liechtenstein) 2006–; immediate past Chair. and mem. Bd of Visitors for Univ. of Texas M. D. Anderson Cancer Center; apptd to UT System Bd of Regents 1993; fmr mem. Nat. Bd Smithsonian Inst.; fmr Chair. Stanford Business School Trust, Houston/Harris County Sports Facility Public Advisory Cttee; fmr Dir Greater Houston Partnership; Trustee, Tex. Heart Inst., Houston Museum of Fine Arts; Outstanding Young Tex. Ex Award 1983, named a Distinguished Alumnus 2003, McCombs Business School Hall of Fame Award 2004.
Address: US Embassy, Sulgeneckstrasse 19, 3007 Bern, Switzerland (office). *Telephone:* (31) 357-70-11 (office). *Fax:* (31) 357-73-44 (office). *Website:* bern.usembassy.gov (office).

CONLEY TYLER, Melissa, BA, LLB, MALD; Australian lawyer and research institute director; *Executive Director, Australian Institute of International Affairs;* b. 1970, Melbourne; m. Dr Simon Evans; two d. *Education:* Univ. of Melbourne, Fletcher School of Law and Diplomacy, USA. *Career:* solicitor, Freehill Hollingdale & Page 1993–94; Legal Policy Officer, Dept of the Premier and Cabinet, Victoria 1994; Mediator, IMCR Dispute Resolution Center, New York 1995; Project Officer, Int. Peace Acad., African Conflict Resolution Program and Human Rights Watch, Children's Rights Project, New York 1995; trainer and evaluator, Centre for the Study of Violence and Reconciliation, Univ. of Witwatersrand, Johannesburg, SA 1996; negotiation and communication trainer, Conflict Man. Australasia 1997; CEO Int. Inst. for Negotiation and Conflict Man. 1997–98; Nat. Corp. Partnerships Exec., Mission Australia 1998–2000; Sr Policy Officer, Victorian Community Council Against Violence 2000–01; Corp. and Community Partnerships Man., Reconciliation Australia 2001–02; researcher and teacher, Univ. of Melbourne 2002–05, also Programme Man., Int. Conflict Resolutions Centre, Sr Fellow, Faculty of Law and Assoc., Centre for Programme Evaluation; Exec. Dir Australian Inst. of Int. Affairs 2006–; Dir Charities Aid Foundation 2000–; mem. UN Expert Working Group on Online Dispute Resolution 2003–, Conflict Resolution Educ. Working Group, Global Partnership on Prevention of Armed Conflict 2005–, World Mediation Forum 2005–; Convenor, UN ESCAP Forum on Online Dispute Resolution 2003–04, Fulbright Symposium on Peace and Human Rights Educ. 2005. *Publications:* Proceedings of the Third Annual Forum on Online Dispute Resolution (co-ed.) 2005; numerous journal articles.
Address: Australian Institute of International Affairs, Stephen House, 32 Thesiger Court, Deakin, ACT 2600 (office); 10 Sturrock Street, Brunswick East, Vic. 3057, Australia (home). *Telephone:* (2) 6282-2133 (office); (3) 9386-5888 (home). *Fax:* (2) 6585-2334 (office); (3) 9386-5888 (home). *E-mail:* ceo@aiia.asn.au (office); m.conleytyler@gmail.com (home). *Website:* www.aiia.asn.au.

CONSTAS, Dimitri, LLB, PhD; Greek government official and research institute director; *Director, Institute of International Relations, Athens; Education:* Panteion Univ., Univ. of Thessaloniki, Carleton Univ., Canada, Tufts Univ., USA. *Career:* Interim Minister for Press and Mass Media 1996; Perm. Rep. to Council of Europe 1997–99; Head of Task Forces on Euro-Mediterranean Cooperation, Middle East Peace Process, Greek role in Int. Conflict Resolution 2000; currently Dir Inst. of Int. Relations, Athens; Fellow, Woodrow Wilson Int. Center for Scholars 1998; Fulbright Scholar 1976–79, MacJannet Fellow, Institut des Hautes Etudes Internationaux 1978, Robert Schumann Fellow in European Integration 1979, Noted Scholar, Univ. of British Columbia 1996, Sr Fulbright Scholar, Princeton Univ. 1996. *Publications include:* The Greek–Turkish Conflict in the 1990s (ed.) 1991, Modern Diasporas in World Politics: the Greeks in Comparative Perspective (co-ed.) 1993, Greece Prepares for the Twenty-First Century (co-ed.) 1995, Greek and European Foreign Policy (1991–99), Diplomacy and Politics 2003.

Address: Institute of International Relations, 3–5 Hill Street, Athens 10558, Greece (office). *Telephone:* (21) 13312325 (office). *Fax:* (21) 13313575 (office). *E-mail:* constas@idis.gr (office). *Website:* www.idis.gr (office).

CONTÉ, Gen. Lansana; Guinean army officer and head of state; *President;* b. 1934, Moussayah Loumbaya; m. *Career:* fmr mil. commdr of Boké Region, W Guinea; mem. Parti de l'unité et du progrès; Pres. Repub. of Guinea after mil. coup April 1984–, fmrly Minister of Defence, Security, Planning Co-operation and Information and Pres. Council of Ministers; Chair. Comité militaire de redressement nat. (CMRN) April 1984–90, Comité transitoire de redressement nat. (CTRN) 1991–92.
Address: Office du Président, BP 5141, Conakry, Guinea (office). *Telephone:* 30-41-51-19 (office). *Fax:* 30-41-52-82 (office). *Website:* www.guinee.gov.gn (office).

CONTEH, Maj. (Alfred) Paolo, LLB (Hons), LLM; Sierra Leone army officer (retd) and government official; *Minister of Defence; Education:* Univs of London and East London, UK. *Career:* served in Sierra Leone army 1976–92, rose to rank of Maj. and CO of the Mil. Police; went to UK on leave to pursue legal studies 1986; Court Liaison Officer and Prosecution Sec., Dept for Work and Pensions for the investigation service in London –2007; Minister of Defence 2007–.
Address: Ministry of Defence, State Avenue, Freetown, Sierra Leone (office). *Telephone:* (22) 227369 (office). *Fax:* (22) 229380 (office).

CONTOGEORGIS, George, MA, PhD; Greek academic; *Professor of Political Science, Panteion University of Athens;* b. 14 Feb. 1947, Letkas; m. Catherine Kampourgiannidou 1972; two d. *Education:* Univ. of Athens, Univ. of Paris II, Ecole Pratique des Hautes Etudes, Ecole des Hautes Etudes en Sciences Sociales. *Career:* Prof. of Political Science, Panteion Univ. Athens 1983–, Rector 1984–90; Gen. Dir ERT SA (Hellenic Broadcasting Corpn) 1985, Pres.-Gen. Dir 1989; Minister, Ministry of the Presidency (State Admin., Communication, Media), Govt Spokesman 1993; Founding mem. European Political Science Network (EPSNET); Dir European Masters Programme in Political Science; Founder-mem. and Sec.-Gen. Greek Political Sciences Asscn 1975–80; leader writer in Athenian daily newspapers; mem. High Council and Research Council, European Univ. Florence 1986–94; mem. High Council, Univ. of Europe, Paris and Centre of Regional Studies, Montpellier; Visiting Prof., Inst. d'Etudes Politiques, Paris, Univ. Libre de Bruxelles, Univ. Catholique de Louvain, Univs of Montpellier, Tokyo, IEP Bordeaux, Lille etc.; Prof., Franqui Chair., Univ. of Brussels; Prof. of European Studies, Univ. of Siena; mem. Council Pôle Sud, Political Science Review, Revue Inter-nationale de Politique Comparée; corresponding mem. Int. Acad. of Culture, Portugal; mem. French Political Science Asscn, IPSA and other int. asscns; Chevalier, des Palmes Academiques. *Publications:* The Theory of Revolution in Aristotle 1975, The Popular Ideology: Socio-political Study of the Greek Folk Song 1979, Political System and Politics 1985, Social Process and Political Self-government: The Greek City-State Under the Ottoman Empire 1982, The Local Government in the State 1985, Nuclear Energy and Public Opinion in Europe 1991, History of Greece 1992, Système de communication et système d'échange: La télévision 1993, After Communism (in collaboration) 1993, Greek Society in the 20th Century 1995, Democracy in the Technological Society 1995, Society and Politics 1996, The Greek Cosmosystem 1997, New World Order 1998, Identité cosmosystémique ou identité nationale? Le Paradigme hellénique 1999, Le Citoyen dans la cité 2000, Religion and Politics 2000, Modernity and Progress 2001, State and Globalization 2003, Work and Freedom 2003, Citizenship and State, Concept and Typology of Citizenship 2004, The Authoritarian Phenomenon 2004, Nation and Modernity 2006, The Hellenic Cosmosystem: Vol. 1, The Statocentric Period 2006, Democracy as Freedom 2007, Nation and Modernity 2007.
Address: Panteion University of Athens, 136 Sygrou Avenue, Athens 176 71 (office); 7 Tassopoulou Street, Athens 153 42, Greece (home). *Telephone:* (210) 9201743 (office); (210) 6399662 (home); (210) 6081780 (home). *Fax:* (210) 9201743 (office); (210) 6081780. *E-mail:* contogeo@panteion.gr (office). *Website:* www.panteion.gr (office).

CONZEMIUS-PACCOUD, Arlette, MA; Luxembourg diplomatist; *Director for International and Economic European Affairs;* m.; two c. *Education:* Grad. Inst. of Int. Studies, Geneva and Fletcher School of Law and Diplomacy, USA. *Career:* joined Directorate for Int. Econ. Relations, Ministry of Foreign Affairs 1981–83; Perm. Rep. to EC, Brussels 1983–88; Deputy Chief of Mission, Washington, DC 1989–93; Amb. and Perm. Rep. to Council of Europe, Strasbourg 1993–98; Amb. to USA 1998–2005; currently Dir for Int. and Econ. European Affairs, Ministry of Foreign Affairs and Immigration.
Address: Ministry of Foreign Affairs and Immigration, 5 rue Notre-Dame, 2240 Luxembourg (office). *Telephone:* 478-1 (office). *Fax:* 22-31-44 (office). *E-mail:* officielle.boite@mae.etat.lu (office). *Website:* www.mae.lu (office).

COOK, Frederick B., BA; American diplomatist; *Ambassador to Central African Republic;* b. Washington, DC. *Education:* Tufts Univ., Medford, Mass. *Career:* raised in Foreign Service, living in India, Jordan, the Philippines and Indonesia; joined Foreign Service 1972, has served in Africa, Western Hemisphere, Washington, DC, has served as Man. Officer in La Paz, Havana, Gaborone and Monrovia; State Dept assignments have included Deputy Dir Information Resources Man., Exec. Secr., Labor Advisor for Bureau of African Affairs, and Systems Devt Officer for Office of Overseas Buildings, previous overseas assignment as Deputy Chief of Mission, Caracas, most recently served as Foreign Policy Adviser to Combined Jt Task Force – Horn of Africa (US mil. force based at Camp Lemonier, Djibouti) –2007, Amb. to Cen. African Repub. 2007–.
Address: US Embassy, avenue David Dacko, BP 924, Bangui, Central African Republic (office). *Telephone:* 61-02-00 (office). *Fax:* 61-44-94 (office).

COOKE, Sir Howard (Felix Hanlan), ON, GCMG, GCVO, CD; Jamaican politician, schoolteacher and insurance company executive; b. 13 Nov. 1915, Goodwill; m. Ivy Sylvia Lucille Tai 1939; two s. one d. *Career:* teacher, Mico Training Coll. 1936–38; Headmaster, Belle-Castle All-Age School 1939–50; teacher, Port Antonio Upper School 1951, Montego Bay Boys' School 1952–58; Br. Man. Standard Life Insurance Co. Ltd 1960–71; Unit Man. Jamaica Mutual Life Assurance Co. Ltd 1971–81; Br. Man. Alico Jamaica 1982–91; mem. West Indies Fed. Parl. 1958–62, Senate 1962–67, House of Reps 1967–80; Govt Minister 1972–80; Gov.-Gen. of Jamaica 1991–2006; Sr Elder United Church of Jamaica and Grand Cayman; lay pastor and fmr Chair. Cornwall Council of Churches; mem. Ancient and Accepted Order of Masons; Kt of St John (St John's Council) 1993; Jamaica Independence Medal 1962, Special Plaque for Distinguished Services (CPA) 1980.
Address: c/o Office of the Governor-General, King's House, Hope Road, Kingston 10, Jamaica, West Indies (office).

COOMARASWAMY, Radhika, BA, LLM, JD; Sri Lankan lawyer and international organization executive; *Special Representative of the Secretary-General, Office of the Special Representative of the Secretary-General for Children and Armed Conflict, United Nations; Education:* Yale, Columbia and Harvard Univs and UN Int. School, New York, USA. *Career:* Special Rapporteur on Violence Against Women 1994–2003; Chair. Sri Lanka Human Rights Comm. 2003–; Dir Int. Centre for Ethnic Studies, Colombo; Special Rep. of the Sec.-Gen., UN Office of the Special Rep. of the Sec.-Gen. for Children and Armed Conflict 2006–; mem. Global Faculty, New York Univ. School of Law; teaches a summer course at New Coll., Oxford, UK every July; title of 'Deshamanya' conferred on her by Pres. of Sri Lanka 2005 (only female recipient); Hon. PhD (Amherst Coll., Univ. of Edinburgh, Univ. of Essex); ABA Int. Law Award, Human Rights Award, Int. Human Rights Law Group, Bruno Kreisky Award 2000, Leo Ettinger Human Rights Prize, Univ. of Oslo, Cesar Romero Award, Univ. of Dayton, William J. Butler Award, Univ. of Cincinnati, Robert S. Litvack Award, McGill Univ. *Publications:* two books on constitutional law and numerous articles on ethnic studies and the status of women.
Address: Office of the Special Representative of the Secretary-General for Children and Armed Conflict, United Nations, Room S-3161, New York, NY 10017, USA (office). *Telephone:* (212) 963-3178 (office). *Fax:* (212) 963-0807 (office). *Website:* www.un.org/special-rep/children-armed-conflict (office).

COONEY, David, BA; Irish diplomatist; *Ambassador to UK;* b. 29 April 1954, London, England; m.; four c. *Education:* Univ. of Keele, UK. *Career:* Officer, Dept of Agric., then Dept of Public Service, Dublin 1976–79; Perm. Rep. of Ireland to Holy See 1981–85, Vienna 1988–89, EU 1990–93, Counsellor and European Corresp., Dept of Foreign Affairs 1994, Coordinator of White Paper on Irish Foreign Policy 1994–95, Counsellor and Head of Political Section, Anglo-Irish Div. 1995–98, Counsellor and Deputy Perm. Rep. to OECD, Paris 1998–2000, Deputy Perm. Rep. to UN, New York 2000–01, Perm. Rep. 2005–07, Political Dir and Asst Sec.-Gen., Dept of Foreign Affairs, Dublin 2001–05, Amb. to UK 2007–.
Address: Embassy of Ireland, 17 Grosvenor Place, London, SW1X 7HR, England (office). *Telephone:* (20) 7235-2171 (office). *Fax:* (20) 7245-6961 (office). *E-mail:* info@embassyofireland.co.uk (office). *Website:* www.embassyofireland.co.uk (office).

COOPER, Katrina, BA, BLL; Australian diplomatist; *Ambassador to Mexico;* m.; two c. *Education:* Australian Nat. Univ. *Career:* numerous postings with Department of Foreign Affairs and Trade including with Canada, Latin America and Caribbean Section 1993–94, Dir, Admin. and Domestic Law Group 2000–01, Dir, Biological Disarmament Unit 1999–2000, Asst Sec., Domestic Legal Branch 2006–07, Legal Adviser, Int. Orgs and Legal Div. 2007; foreign postings include Third, later Second Sec., Embassy in

Santiago de Chile 1995–98, Counsellor, Embassy in Port Moresby 2002–05; Amb. to Mexico 2007–.
Address: Embassy of Australia, Ruben Dario 55, Col. Polanco, México 11580, DF, Mexico (office). *Telephone:* (55) 1101-2200 (office). *Fax:* (55) 1101-2201 (office). *E-mail:* embaustmex@yahoo.com.mx (office). *Website:* www.mexico.embassy.gov.au (office).

COOPER, Richard Newell, PhD; American economist, academic and fmr public official; *Maurits C. Boas Professor of International Economics, Harvard University;* b. 14 June 1934, Seattle, Wash.; m. 1st Carolyn Cahalan 1956 (divorced 1980); m. 2nd Ann Lorraine Hollick 1982 (divorced 1994); m. 3rd Jin Chen 2000; two s. two d. *Education:* Oberlin Coll., London School of Econs, UK, Harvard Univ. *Career:* Sr Staff Economist, Council of Econ. Advisers 1961–63; Deputy Asst Sec. of State for Monetary Affairs 1965–66; Prof. of Econs, Yale Univ. 1966–77, Provost 1972–74; Under-Sec. of State for Econ. Affairs 1977–81; Maurits C. Boas Prof. of Int. Econs, Harvard Univ. 1981–; Dir Rockefeller Bros Fund 1975–77, Schroders Bank and Trust Co. 1975–77, Warburg-Pincus Funds 1986–98, Center for Naval Analysis 1992–95, Phoenix Cos 1983–2005, Circuit City Stores 1983–2004, CNA Corpn 1997–, Inst. for Int. Econs 1983–, Fed. Reserve Bank of Boston 1987–92 (Chair. 1990–92); Chair. Nat. Intelligence Council 1995–97; consultant to US Treasury, Nat. Security Council, World Bank, IMF, USN; Marshall Scholarship (UK) 1956–58; Fellow American Acad. of Sciences 1974; Hon. LLD (Oberlin Coll.) 1958; Dr hc (Paris II) 2000; Nat. Intelligence Medal 1996. *Publications:* The Economics of Interdependence 1968, Economic Policy in an Interdependent World 1986, The International Monetary System 1987, Stabilization and Debt in Developing Countries 1992, Boom, Crisis and Adjustment (co-author) 1993, Environment and Resource Policies for the World Economy 1994, Trade Growth in Transition Economies (ed.) 1997, What The Future Holds (ed.) 2002; more than 300 articles.
Address: Center for International Affairs, Harvard University, 1737 Cambridge Street, Cambridge, MA 02138 (office); 33 Washington Avenue, Cambridge, MA 02140, USA (home). *Telephone:* (617) 495-5076 (office). *Fax:* (617) 495-8292 (office). *E-mail:* rcooper@fas.harvard.edu (office). *Website:* www.economics.harvard.edu (office).

COOPER, Robert, BA, MA, MVO, CMG; British diplomatist; *Director General, External and Politico-Military Affairs, Council of the European Union;* b. 28 Aug. 1947, Brentwood, Essex. *Education:* Delamere School, Nairobi, Worcester Coll. Univ. of Oxford, Univ. of Pennsylvania, USA. *Career:* fmr Adviser to UK Prime Minister Tony Blair; currently Dir-Gen. External and Politico-Mil. Affairs, Council of the EU; Orwell Prize for Political Writing 2003. *Publication:* Breaking of Nations 2003.
Address: Council of the EU, Directorate-General E, 175 rue de la Loi, 1048 Brussels, Belgium (office). *Telephone:* (2) 281-85-52 (office). *Fax:* (2) 281-62-18 (office). *E-mail:* robert.cooper@consilium.europa.eu (office).

CORDEN, Warner Max, AC, MComm, MA, PhD, FBA, FASSA; Australian economist and academic; *Professorial Fellow, Department of Economics, University of Melbourne;* b. 13 Aug. 1927, Breslau, Germany (now Wrocław, Poland); m. Dorothy Martin 1957; one d. *Education:* Melbourne Boys High School, Univ. of Melbourne and London School of Econs. *Career:* Lecturer, Univ. of Melbourne 1958–61, Professorial Fellow 2002–; Nuffield Reader in Int. Econs and Fellow of Nuffield Coll., Oxford 1967–76; Professorial Fellow, ANU 1962–67, Prof. of Econs 1976–88; Chung Ju Yung Prof. of Int. Econs, Paul H. Nitze School of Advanced Int. Studies, Johns Hopkins Univ., Washington, DC, USA 1989–2002, Prof. Emer. of Int. Econs 2002–; Visiting Prof., Univ. of California, Berkeley 1965, Univ. of Minnesota 1971, Princeton Univ. 1973, Harvard Univ. 1986; Sr Adviser, IMF 1986–88; Pres. Econ. Soc. of Australia and New Zealand 1977–80; mem. Group of Thirty 1982–90; Foreign Hon. mem. American Econ. Asscn 1986; Distinguished Fellow, Econ. Soc. of Australia 1995; Dr hc (Melbourne) 1995; Bernard Harms Prize 1986. *Publications:* The Theory of Protection 1971, Trade Policy and Economic Welfare 1974, 1997, Inflation, Exchange Rates and the World Economy 1977, 1985, Protection, Growth and Trade 1985, International Trade Theory and Policy 1992, Economic Policy, Exchange Rates and the International System 1994, The Road to Reform 1997, Too Sensational: On the Choice of Exchange Rate Regimes 2002.
Address: Department of Economics, University of Melbourne, Melbourne, Victoria 3010, Australia (office). *Telephone:* (3) 8344-5296 (office). *Fax:* (3) 8344-6899 (office). *E-mail:* m.corden@unimelb.edu.au (office). *Website:* www.economics.unimelb.edu.au (office).

CORDESMAN, Anthony H.; American fmr government official and academic; *Arleigh A. Burke Chair in Strategy, Center for Strategic and International Studies; Career:* numerous positions in US Govt, including Dir of Intelligence Assessment, Office of Sec. of Defense, Civilian Asst to Deputy Sec. of Defense, and positions in State Dept, NATO Int. Staff and

in Dept of Energy; overseas posts in Lebanon, Egypt, Iran and Saudi Arabia; currently Arleigh A. Burke Chair in Strategy, Center for Strategic and Int. Studies, Washington, DC, projects directed include Gulf Net Assessment Project, Middle East Net Assessment Project, Gulf in Transition Study, Prin. Investigator, Homeland Defense Project, Co-Dir Strategic Energy Initiative; Dept of Defense Distinguished Service Medal. *Publications include:* The Iraq War – Saudi Arabia Enters the 21st Century, The Lessons of Afghanistan, Terrorism, Asymmetric Warfare and Weapons of Mass Destruction, Cyberthreats – Information Warfare and Critical Infrastructure Protection, Strategic Threats and National Missile Defenses, The Lessons and Non-Lessons of the Air and Missile Campaign in Kosovo.
Address: Center for Strategic and International Studies, 1800 K Street, NW, Suite 400, Washington, DC 20006, USA (office). *Telephone:* (202) 775-3270 (office). *Fax:* (202) 457-8746 (office). *E-mail:* acordesman@aol .com (office). *Website:* www.csis.org (office).

CORDOVEZ, Diego; Ecuadorean diplomatist and lawyer; b. 3 Nov. 1935, Quito; m. Maria Teresa Somavia 1960; one s. *Education:* Univ. of Chile. *Career:* admitted to Bar 1962; served in Foreign Service of Ecuador until 1963; joined UN as Econ. Affairs Officer 1963; Political Officer on special missions to Dominican Repub. 1965, Pakistan 1971; Dir UN Econ. and Social Council Secr. 1973–78, Asst Sec.-Gen. for Econ. and Social Matters, UN 1978–81; Special Rep. of UN Sec.-Gen. on Libya–Malta dispute 1980–82; Sec.-Gen.'s rep. on UN Comm. of Inquiry on hostage crisis in Tehran 1980; Sr officer responsible for efforts to resolve Iran/Iraq war 1980–88; Under-Sec.-Gen. for Special Political Affairs 1981–1988; Special Envoy to Grenada 1983; UN Mediator, Afghanistan 1982–88, Rep. for implementation of Geneva Accords 1988–89; Minister for Foreign Affairs 1988–92; Pres. World Trade Center (Ecuador) 1993–98; Special Counsel LeBoeuf, Lamb, Greene and Macrae 1993–98; Special Adviser to UN Sec.-Gen. for Cyprus 1997–99, for Latin American Affairs 1999–2005; Perm. Rep. to UN, New York 2005–08; Pres. Andean Centre for Int. Studies 2000; mem. American Soc. of Int. Law; Order of Merit (Ecuador), Légion d'honneur, Grand Cross (Spain, Portugal, Brazil, Argentina, Chile, Peru, Colombia, Venezuela). *Publications:* UNCTAD and Development Diplomacy 1971, Out of Afghanistan: The Inside Story of the Soviet Withdrawal (with Selig S. Harrison) 1995, Nuestra Propuesta Inconclusa (Ecuador–Perú: Del Inmovilismo al Acuerdo de Brasilia) 2000.
Address: c/o Ministry of External Relations, Trade and Integration, Avda 10 de Agosto y Carrión, Quito (office); Calle Afganistán N41–90, El Bosque, Quito, Ecuador (office).

CORELL, Hans, LLB; Swedish diplomatist and lawyer; b. 7 July 1939, Västermo; m. Inger Peijfors 1964; one s. one d. *Education:* Univ. of Uppsala. *Career:* court clerk, Eksjö Dist Court and Göta Court of Appeal 1962–67; Asst Judge, Västervik Dist Court 1968–72; Legal Adviser, Ministry of Justice 1972, 1974–79; Additional mem. and Assoc. Judge of Appeal, Svea Court of Appeal 1973; Asst Under-Sec. Div. for Constitutional and Admin. Law, Ministry of Justice 1979–81; Judge of Appeal 1980; Under-Sec. for Legal Affairs, Ministry of Justice 1981–84; Amb. and Under-Sec. for Legal and Consular Affairs, Ministry of Foreign Affairs 1984–94; mem. Perm. Court of Arbitration, The Hague 1990–; Under-Sec.-Gen. for Legal Affairs, The Legal Counsel of the UN 1994–2004; Hon. LLD (Stockholm) 1997; William J. Butler Human Rights Medal (Cincinnati) 2001. *Publications:* Sekretesslagen (co-author) 1992, Proposal for an International War Crimes Tribunal for the Former Yugoslavia (CSCE Report) (co-author) 1993; various legal publs.
Address: Norr Mälarstrand 70, 112 35 Stockholm, Sweden. *Telephone:* (8) 473-0753. *Fax:* (8) 473-0753 (office). *E-mail:* hans.corell@tele2.se.

CORNISH, Paul, PhD; British research institute director and university lecturer; *Head, International Security Programme and Carrington Chair in International Security, Chatham House; Education:* Univ. of St Andrews, London School of Econs, Royal Mil. Acad. Sandhurst, Univ. of Cambridge. *Career:* served in British Army, Royal Tank Regiment 1983–89; Arms Control and Disarmament Analyst, FCO, London 1991–93; Sr Research Fellow, Int. Security Programme, Royal Inst. of Int. Affairs 1993–96; Visiting Fellow, Centre of Int. Studies, Univ. of Cambridge 1996–97, Lecturer in Int. Relations 1998–2001; Lecturer in Defence Studies, Jt Service Command and Staff Coll., King's Coll. London 1997–98, Dir of Conflict, Security and Devt Group 2001, Research Dir Centre for Defence Studies (CDS) Jan.–Sept. 2002, Dir 2002–05; Head, Int. Security Programme and Carrington Chair in Int. Security, Chatham House, London 2005–; NATO Research Fellow 2000–02; Expert, Strengthening the Global Partnership Project (SGPP), Center for Strategic and Int. Studies, Washington, DC. *Publications include:* The Arms Trade and Europe 1995, British Military Planning and the Defence of Germany 1945–50 1996, Controlling the Arms Trade: the West versus the Rest 1996, Partnership in Crisis: the US, Europe and the Fall and Rise of NATO 1997.

Address: Chatham House, 10 St James's Square, London, SW1Y 4LE, England (office). *Telephone:* (20) 7957-5726 (office). *Fax:* (20) 7957-5710 (office). *E-mail:* contact@chathamhouse.org.uk (office). *Website:* www .chathamhouse.org.uk (office).

COROPCEAN, Brig. Gen. Ion; Moldovan army officer; *Chief of General Staff, Commander of the National Army of the Republic;* b. 11 March 1960, Liveden' vill; m. Valentina Coropcean; one s. one d. *Education:* Poltava Mil. Air Defence High School, Mil. Air Defence Acad. *Career:* cadet 1977–81, Air Defence Platoon Commdr 1981–84, Air Defence Battery Commdr 1984–87, Air Defence Bn Commdr, Air Defence Acad. 1987–88, Chief of Staff and Deputy Commdr Air Defence Regt 1991–92, Deputy Commdr Air Defence Brigade 1992–97, Commdr Mil. Coll. 1997–98, Chief of Gen. Staff Nat. Army and Deputy Minister of Defence 1998–2006, Chief of Gen. Staff, Commdr Nat. Army 2006–; Medal of Courage, Medal of Mil. Merit, Award for Allegiance to the Motherland.
Address: ŞOS. Hinceşti 84, 2021 Chişinău (office); str. Alba Julia 200/1, Ap. 100, 2071 Chişinău, Republic of Moldova (home). *Telephone:* (2) 252444 (office); (2) 514874 (home). *Fax:* (2) 234434 (office). *E-mail:* coropcei@md .pims.org (office); ion.coropcean@army.md (office). *Website:* www.army .md (office).

CORREA DELGADO, Rafael, MSc, PhD; Ecuadorean economist, politician and head of state; *President;* b. 6 April 1963, Guayaquil. *Education:* Universidad Católica de Santiago de Guayaquil, Catholic Univ. of Louvain, Belgium, Univ. of Illinois, USA. *Career:* teaching asst, Econs Faculty, Universidad Católica de Santiago de Guayaquil 1983–85, Assoc. Prof. 1988–1989; Industrial Specialist, Centre of Industrial Devt 1984–87; volunteer in Mission of the Salesian Fathers, Zumbahua, Cotopaxi 1987–88; Admin. Dir in charge of educational projects financed by IDB 1992–93; Head Prof., Dept of Econs, Universidad San Francisco de Quito 1993–2005; Minister of the Economy following overthrow of Lucio Gutierrez April–Aug. 2005 (resgnd); Founder,Alianza PAIS (Patria Altiva i Soberana); Pres. of Ecuador 2007–. *Publications:* El Reto del Desarrollo: ¿Estamos Preparados para el Futuro? 1996, La Vulnerabilidad de la Economía Ecuatoriana 2004; numerous journal Contribs.
Address: Office of the President, Palacio Nacional, García Moreno 1043, Quito (office); Diego de Almagro N32-27 y Whimper, Edif. Torres Whimper, Of. 501, Quito, Ecuador. *Telephone:* (2) 221-6300 (office); (2) 600-0630; (2) 600-1029. *E-mail:* info@rafaelcorrea.com. *Website:* www .presidencia.gov.ec (office); www.rafaelcorrea.com.

CORREIA, Carlos; Guinea-Bissau politician; *Prime Minister; Career:* mem. Partido Africano da Independência da Guiné e Cabo Verde (PAIGC); fmr Minister of State for Rural Devt and Agric.; Prime Minister of Guinea-Bissau 1991–94, 1997–98, 2008–; fmr Perm. Sec. Council of State; fmr Gov. for Guinea Bissau, African Devt Bank.
Address: Office of the Prime Minister, Av. Unidade Africana, CP 137, Bissau, Guinea-Bissau. *Telephone:* 211308 (office). *Fax:* 201671 (office).

CORT, Errol; Antigua and Barbuda politician, economist and lawyer; *Minister of Finance, Economic Development and Planning;* m.; c. *Education:* trained as economist and attorney; Attorney-Gen. of Antigua and Barbuda 1999–2001; elected mem. Parl. for St John's E; Minister of Finance, Econ. Devt and Planning 2004–.
Address: Ministry of Finance, Economic Development and Planning, Government Office Complex, Parliament Drive, St John's, Antigua (office). *Telephone:* 462-5015 (office). *Fax:* 462-4260 (office). *E-mail:* budget@ candw.ag (office).

COŞKUN, Ali, MSc; Turkish politician and business executive; *Minister of Industry and Commerce;* b. 1939, Kemaliye, Erzincan; m.; two c. *Education:* Faculty of Electrical Eng, Yildiz Tech. Univ., Wirtschaft Academie, Hamburg, Germany. *Career:* fmr Pres. Admin. Bd, Ihlas Finance Inst. and Bisan Bicycle Industry and Commerce; fmr Deputy Pres. Istanbul Chamber of Commerce; fmr Pres. Turkish Union of Chambers and Commodities Exchanges (TOBB); fmr Deputy Pres. Islamic Countries Union of Chambers; elected mem. of Parl. (ANAP) for Istanbul Constituency 1995; joined Welfare Party; currently Minister of Industry and Commerce.
Address: Ministry of Trade and Industry, Sanayi ve Ticaret Bakanliği, Eskişehir, yolu üzeri 7 km, Ankara, Turkey (office). *Telephone:* (312) 2860365 (office). *Website:* www.sanayi.gov.tr (office).

COSTA, Antonio; Portuguese politician; *Minister of Internal Affairs, Minister of State;* b. 17 July 1961; m.; two c. *Education:* Univ. of Lisbon. *Career:* mem. Municipal Ass. of Lisbon 1982–93; Deputy Ass. of Repub. 1991–; Sec. of State for Parl. Affairs 1995–97; Govt Rep. Expo '98 1997–98; Minister of Justice 1999–2002; MEP 2004–05; Minister of Internal Affairs, Minister of State 2005–; mem. Partido Socialista 1994–, Pres. 2002–04.

Address: Ministry of Internal Affairs, Praça do Comércio, 1149-015 Lisbon, Portugal. *Telephone:* (21) 3233000 (office). *Fax:* (21) 2468031 (office). *E-mail:* dirp@sg.mai.gov.pt (office). *Website:* www.mai.gov.pt (office).

COSTA, Antonio Maria, PhD; Italian UN official and economist; *Executive Director, Office on Drugs and Crime and Director-General, United Nations, Vienna;* b. 16 June 1941, Mondovi; m. Patricia Agnes Wallace 1971; two s. one d. *Education:* Univ. of California, Berkeley, Acad. of Sciences of the USSR and Univ. of Turin. *Career:* Visiting Prof. of Econs, Moscow Univ. and Acad. of Sciences of the USSR 1965–67; Instructor of Econs, Univ. of Calif., Berkeley 1968–70; Prof. of Econs, New York Univ., 1976–83; Sr Econ. Adviser to the UN 1970–83; Special Counsellor in Econs to the Sec.-Gen. of OECD 1983–87; Dir Gen. Econ. and Financial Affairs, EC 1987–92; Sec.-Gen. EBRD, London, UK 1992–2001; Dir-Gen. UN Office on Drugs and Crime (fmrly UN Office for Drug Control and Crime Prevention), Vienna, Austria 2002–. *Publications:* articles on econs and politics.
Address: United Nations Office on Drugs and Crime, Vienna International Centre, PO Box 500, 1400 Vienna, Austria. *Telephone:* (1) 26060-0 (office). *Fax:* (1) 26060-5819 (office). *E-mail:* unodc@unodc.org (office). *Website:* www.unodc.org (office).

COSTA, Constantino; Guinea-Bissau diplomatist; *Ambassador to Portugal;* *Career:* fmr Amb. to Cuba; Amb. to Portugal 2006–.
Address: Embassy of Guinea-Bissau, Rua de Alcolena 17, 1400-004 Lisbon, Portugal (office). *Telephone:* (21) 3030440 (office). *Fax:* (21) 3019653 (office).

COSTA, Gabriel Arcanjo Ferreira da, BLL; São Tomé and Príncipe politician and lawyer; b. 11 Dec. 1954. *Career:* lawyer and magistrate; mem. Parl. (Juventude Movimento Libertação de São Tomé e Príncipe) in first Ass. following nat. independence 1975–98; Counsellor for Legal and Political Affairs to Pres. Trovoada 1991–95, Head of Cabinet of Pres. 1996–98; State Minister of Justice, Admin. Reform and Local Admin. –1998; Special Rep. of Exec. of CPLP for Guinea-Bissau 1998–2000; Amb. to Portugal, Morocco and Spain 2000–02; Prime Minister of São Tomé e Príncipe 2002.
Address: c/o Office of the Prime Minister, Rua Município, CP 302, São Tomé, São Tomé e Príncipe (office).

COSTA, Jean-Paul, LLM, PhD; French judge; *President, European Court of Human Rights;* b. 3 Nov. 1941, Tunis, Tunisia. *Education:* Inst. of Political Studies, Nat. School of Man., Paris. *Career:* clerk, Council of State 1966, Advisor, Judicial Section 1966–71, 1977–80, 1987–89, Assessor of Sub-section of Judicial Section 1989–93, Pres. of Sub-section of Judicial Section 1993–98; Political Sec. to Minister of Educ. 1981–84; Assoc. Prof., Orléans Univ. 1989–98, Panthéon-Sorbonne Univ. 1992–98; Judge, European Court of Human Rights 1998–, Vice-Pres. 2001–07, Pres. 2007–.
Address: Office of the President, European Court of Human Rights, Council of Europe, 67075 Strasbourg, France (office). *Telephone:* 3-88-41-38-24 (office). *Fax:* 3-88-41-27-91 (office). *Website:* www.echr.coe.int (office).

COSTEDOAT, Lt-Gen. Pierre-Jacques; French army officer and consultant; b. 27 Jan. 1942, Casablanca, Morocco; m. Anne-Marie Delamare 1965; four d. *Education:* Saint-Cyr-Coëtquidan Mil. Acad. *Career:* Second Lt, 74th Artillery Regt 1964, Lt 1966; Capt., 1st Artillery Regt 1972, then Battery CO; Maj., 11th Artillery Regt 1977, Lt-Col 1981, Col 1984; attended as auditeur Centre des hautes études militaires and Institut des hautes études de défense nationale 1987–88; CO 93rd Mountain Artillery Regt, then Staff 1988–89, at Direction Générale de la Sécurité extérieure 1989–95; Brig. 1992; CO Saint-Cyr Coëtquidan Mil. Acad. 1995–98; rank of Maj.-Gen. 1995, later Lt-Gen.; Asst Gen. Sec. of Nat. Defence 1998–2000; Gen. de corps 1998–; Mil. Gov. of Paris, Commdr of Ile-de-France, Officer Gen. Paris Zone of Defence 2000–02; Advisor to Pres. of Sécurité Sans Frontières (risk prevention and man. consultancy) 2003–; Officier Légion d'honneur, Commdr Ordre nat. du Mérite.
Address: c/o Office of the President, Sécurité Sans Frontières, Sofema Groupe, 58 avenue Marceau, 75008 Paris France.

COSTELLO, Peter Howard, BA, LLB; Australian politician; b. 14 Aug. 1957; m. Tanya Costello 1982; one s. two d. *Education:* Carey Grammar School, Monash Univ. *Career:* solicitor, Mallesons, Melbourne 1981–84; tutor (part-time) Monash Univ. 1984–86; mem. Victorian Bar 1984–90; MP for Higgins, Victoria, 1990–2007; Shadow Minister for Corp. Law Reform and Consumer Affairs 1990–92; Shadow Attorney-Gen. and Shadow Minister for Justice 1992–93, for Finance 1993–94; Deputy Leader of the Opposition and Shadow Treas. 1994–96; Deputy Leader Liberal Party 1996–2007, Commonwealth of Australia Treas. 1996–2007; mem. Liberal Party.

Publication: Arbitration in Contempt (jtly) 1986; articles for periodicals and journals.
Address: c/o Liberal Party of Australia, Federal Secretariat, cnr Blackall and Macquarie Streets, Barton, ACT 2600, Australia.

COT, Jean-Pierre; French politician, international organization official and academic; *Judge, International Tribunal for the Law of the Sea;* b. 23 Oct. 1937, Geneva, Switzerland; m.; three c. *Career:* Prof., then Dean, Faculty of Law, Amiens 1968; Prof. of Int. Law and Political Sociology, Univ. of Paris I (Panthéon-Sorbonne) 1969, Dir Disarmament Research and Study Centre (CEREDE); mem. Steering Cttee, Parti Socialiste (PS) 1970, 1973, mem. Exec. Bureau 1976; Mayor of Coise-Saint-Jean-Pied-Gauthier 1971–95; Deputy (Savoie) to Nat. Ass. 1973–81; Gen. Councillor, Savoie 1973–81; PS Nat. Del. for matters relating to the EC 1976–79; mem. European Parl. 1978–79, 1984–99, Pres. Budget Cttee 1984–87, Chair. Socialist Group 1989–94, Vice-Pres. 1997–99; Judge, Int. Tribunal for the Law of the Sea 2002–; Minister-Del. for Co-operation, attached to Minister for External Relations 1981–82; mem. Exec. Council UNESCO 1983–84. *Publication:* A l'épreuve du pouvoir: le tiers-mondisme, pour quoi faire? 1984 and numerous works on int. law and political science.
Address: Coise-Saint-Jean-Pied-Gauthier, 73800 Montmélian, France (home).

COTAN, Imron; Indonesian diplomatist; *Secretary General, Ministry of Foreign Affairs;* b. 21 Dec. 1954; m. Sri Nuraeni Cotan; three c. *Education:* Gadjah Mada Univ. *Career:* joined Dept of Foreign Affairs 1983; Third Sec., Perm. Mission to UN, Geneva 1986, Second then First Sec. 1992–97; Chief of Disarmament Section, Dept of Foreign Affairs 1989–91, Deputy Dir for Mass Media 1997; Deputy Asst to Minister State Sec. for Political Affairs 1998–200; Dir Bureau for Int. Studies 2000–02; Minister, Embassy in Canberra, Australia 2002, Amb. to Australia 2003–05; Sec. Gen., Ministry of Foreign Affairs 2005–; Satya Wirakarya Medal.
Address: Ministry of Foreign Affairs, Jalan Taman Pejambon 6, 10th Floor, Jakarta 10110, Indonesia (office). *Telephone:* (21) 3813453 (office). *Fax:* (21) 3857316 (office). *E-mail:* ditpen1@deplu.go.id (office). *Website:* www.deplu.go.id (office).

COTTE, Bruno; French judge; *Judge, International Criminal Court;* b. 10 June 1945, Lyons; m.; three c. *Education:* Univ. of Lyons, Ecole Nationale de la Magistrature, Bordeaux; studies in Paris. *Career:* Teaching Asst in Criminology, Faculty of Law, Univ. of Paris II 1970; Magistrate in Ministry of Justice and Head, Office of Dir of Criminal Affairs and Pardons 1970–73; Deputy Public Prosecutor, Tribunal de Grande Instance de Lyon (Lyons Dist Court) 1973–75; Head of Prosecution Bureau, Directorate of Criminal Affairs and Pardons, Ministry of Justice with competence in econ., financial and social criminal matters 1975–80; Lecturer, French Nat. School for Judiciary, Bordeaux 1975–80; Special Asst to First Pres. of Supreme Court of Appeal (judicial competence of First Pres.) 1980–81; Special Asst to Attorney Gen., Paris Court of Appeal, serving as Sec.-Gen. of Public Prosecutor's Dept 1981–84; Deputy Dir of Criminal Justice, Directorate of Criminal Affairs and Pardons, Ministry of Justice 1983–84, Dir for Criminal Affairs and Pardons 1984–90; Attorney Gen. to Versailles Court of Appeal May–Sept. 1990; Public Prosecutor in Tribunal de Grande Instance de Paris (Paris Dist Court) 1990–95; Counsel for Prosecution to Supreme Court of Appeal (Criminal Chamber) 1995–2000; Lecturer in Criminal Procedure to mems of Prefectural Police, Ministry of the Interior 1995–2000; Pres. of jury that confers rank of judicial police officers to student inspectors of Nat. Police Force, Ministry of the Interior 1996–2000; Pres. Criminal Chamber of Supreme Court of Appeal 2000–08; Lecturer in Criminal Procedure, Nat. School for the Judiciary, Paris 2000–07; Acting First Pres. Cour de Cassation (Supreme Court of Appeal) March–May 2007; Judge, Int. Criminal Court, The Hague 2008–; mem. Paris Aide aux Victimes, amongst others; Chevalier du Mérite agricole 1979, Commdr Ordre nat. du Mérite 2001, Commdr Légion d'honneur 2005; Penitentiary Medal.
Address: International Criminal Court, PO Box 19519, 2500 CM The Hague, The Netherlands (office). *Telephone:* (70) 515-8515 (office). *Fax:* (70) 515-8555 (office). *E-mail:* info@icc-cpi.int (office). *Website:* www.icc-cpi.int (office).

COTTER, Emmanuel H., MBE; Saint Lucia diplomatist; m. Stephanie Cotter. *Career:* High Commr to UK 1998–2008.
Address: Ministry of External Affairs, International Financial Services, Information and Broadcasting, Conway Business Centre, Waterfront, Castries, Saint Lucia (office). *Telephone:* 468-4501 (office). *Fax:* 468-4501 (office). *E-mail:* foreign@candw.lc (office).

COUCHEPIN, Pascal; Swiss politician and fmr head of state; *President of the Swiss Confederation and Head, Federal Department of Home Affairs;* b. 5 April 1942, Martigny; m.; three c. *Education:* Lausanne Univ. *Career:*

elected mem. local council Martigny 1968; Deputy Mayor of Martigny 1976, Mayor 1984–98; elected to the Nat. Council 1979; Chair. Parl. Group, Liberal Democrat Party (LDP) 1989–96; fmr Chair. Nat. Council's Cttee for Science and Research; fmr Chair. Fed. Dept of Justice and Police section of the Control Cttee; elected to Federal Council 1998; Vice-Pres. of the Swiss Confederation 2002, 2007, Pres. of the Swiss Confederation 2003, 2008; Head of Fed. Dept of Econ. Affairs 1998–2002, of Home Affairs 2003–; fmr Gov. IBRD, EBRD.
Address: Federal Department of Home Affairs, Bundeshaus, Inselgasse, 3003 Bern, Switzerland (office). *Telephone:* (31) 3228001 (office). *Fax:* (31) 3227901 (office). *E-mail:* info@gs-edi.admin.ch. *Website:* www.edi.admin .ch (office).

COURVILLE, Cindy Lou, BA, MA, PhD; American diplomatist; *Permanent Representative, African Union; Education:* Univ. of Louisiana at Lafayette, Univ. of Denver Grad. School of Int. Studies. *Career:* fmr mem. Political Science Faculty, Hanover Coll., Ind. and Occidental Coll., Los Angeles; fmr Hon. Research Fellow, Univ. of Zimbabwe; fmr Shell Oil Fellow, Univ. of Denver; fmr Ford Minority Post-Doctoral Fellow, UCLA; fmr Sr Intelligence Officer, Office of Chief of Staff, Defense Intelligence Agency, also served the Deputy Asst Defense Intelligence Office for Africa Policy as liaison to Office of Sec. of Defense for Africa, Nat. Security Council, Dept of State, and Office of Sec. of Defense, was also Dir for East African Affairs in Office of Sec. of Defense, Dir for African Affairs, Nat. Security Council 2001–03, Special Asst to Pres. and Sr Dir for African Affairs, Nat. Security Council 2003–06, Amb. and Perm. Rep. to African Union, Addis Ababa 2006–.
Address: US Mission to the African Union, Entoto Street, Addis Ababa, Ethiopia (office). *E-mail:* USAU@state.gov (office). *Website:* www.usau .usmission.gov (office).

COUTURIER MARIÁTEGUI, Hernán, BA; Peruvian diplomatist; b. 9 Dec. 1943; m.; four c. *Education:* Faculty of Humanities and Law, Catholic Univ., Nat. Univ. of San Marcos, Diplomatic Acad. of Peru. *Career:* joined Ministry of Foreign Affairs 1964, overseas positions include Third Sec., Embassy in Chile 1968, Second Sec., Perm. Mission to OAS 1971; Second Sec., Embassy in Washington, DC 1973, First Sec., 1974; First Sec., Embassy in Colombia 1977, Counsellor 1978; Counsellor, Perm. Mission to UN, New York 1980, Minister Counsellor and Deputy Perm. Rep. 1981; Amb. to Zimbabwe (also accred. to Angola, Mozambique, Tanzania) 1987–89; Consul Gen. in New York 1989–92; Amb. to Canada 1994; fmr Under-Sec. for Multilateral and Special Affairs; fmr Amb. to Bolivia, to Brazil; Co-ordinator General de la V Cumbre de Jefes de Estado y de Gobierno de América Latina, el Caribe y la Unión Europea 2008; Order of the Condor of the Andes, Degree of the Great Cross.
Address: Ministry of Foreign Affairs, Jirón Lampa 535, Lima 1, Peru. *Telephone:* (1) 3112402. *Fax:* (1) 3112406. *E-mail:* . *Website:* www.rree.gob .pe.

COUVREUR, Philippe; Belgian lawyer and international organization official; *Registrar, International Court of Justice;* b. 29 Nov. 1951, Schaerbeek. *Education:* Collège Jean XXIII, Brussels, Facultés Notre-Dame de la Paix, Namur, Université Catholique de Louvain, King's Coll., London, UK, Universidad Complutense de Madrid, Spain. *Career:* Intern, Legal Service, Comm. of EC 1978–79 (worked on accessions of Spain and Portugal to join EC); Special Asst in offices Registrar and Deputy-Registrar, Int. Court of Justice 1982–86, Sec. 1986–94, First Sec. 1994–95, Prin. Legal Sec. 1995–2000; Registrar Int. Court of Justice 2000– (re-elected 2007); Asst Prof., Centre d'études européennes and in Law Faculty of Université Catholique de Louvain 1976–82; Visiting Prof. in the Law of Int. Orgs, Univ. of Ouagadougou, Burkina Faso 1980–82; Professeur extra-ordinaire in Law of Nations and Comparative Constitutional Law, Ecole des Hautes études commerciales Saint-Louis, Brussels 1986–96; Guest Lecturer in Public Int. Law, Université Catholique de Louvain 1997–; Corresp. mem. Spanish Royal Acad. of Moral and Political Sciences; mem. various other learned socs; Netherlands Embassy Prize 1969. *Publications:* numerous publs and articles.
Address: International Court of Justice, Peace Palace, Carnegieplein 2, 2517 KJ The Hague, The Netherlands (office). *Telephone:* (70) 302-23-23 (office). *Fax:* (70) 364-99-28 (office). *E-mail:* info@icj-cij.org (office). *Website:* www .icj-cij.org (office).

ČOVIĆ, Dragan, PhD; Bosnia and Herzegovina politician; *President, Croatian Democratic Union of Bosnia and Herzegovina;* b. 20 Aug. 1956, Mostar; m.; two d. *Education:* Univ. of Mostar, Sarajevo Univ. *Career:* with SOKO co., Mostar, holding sr managerial positions 1977–98; Assoc. Prof., then Prof., Univ. of Mostar 1996–; mem. Croat Democratic Union; Deputy Prime Minister and Minister of Finance, Fed. of Bosnia and Herzegovina 1998–2001; elected to Tripartite Presidency 2002, Leader of Presidency 2003–04, dismissed by High Rep. of the Int. Community in

Bosnia and Herzegovina Paddy Ashdown following indictment for financial corruption, before trial took place 29 March 2005; Vice-Pres., Croatian Democratic Union of Bosnia and Herzegovina 1998–2005, Pres. 2005–.
Address: Croatian Democratic Union of Bosnia and Herzegovina, 88000 Mostar, Mostar-Zapad, Kneza Domagoja b.b, Bosnia and Herzegovina. *Telephone:* (36) 310701. *Fax:* (36) 315024. *E-mail:* hdzbih@hdzbih.org. *Website:* www.hdzbih.org.

COWEN, Brian, BCL; Irish solicitor and politician; *Taoiseach (Prime Minister);* b. 10 Jan. 1960, Tullamore; m. Mary Molloy 1990; two d. *Education:* Univ. Coll. Dublin and Inc. Law Soc. of Ireland. *Career:* mem. Offaly Co. Council 1984–93; mem. Dáil for Laois-Offaly 1984–; Minister for Labour 1991–92, for Transport, Energy and Communications 1992–94, for Health and Children 1997–2000, for Foreign Affairs 2000–04, for Finance 2004–08 (also Deputy Prime Minister), Taoiseach (Prime Minister) 2008–, Leader, Fianna Fáil 2008, Leader Parl. Party 2008–; fmr Opposition Spokesperson on Agric. and Food.
Address: Department of the Taoiseach, Government Bldgs, Upper Merrion Street, Dublin 2; Ballard, Tullamore, Co. Offaly, Ireland. *Telephone:* (1) 6194000. *Fax:* (1) 6194297. *E-mail:* webmaster@taoiseach.gov.ie. *Website:* www.taoiseach.gov.ie.

COWPER-COLES, Sir Sherard Louis, Kt, KCMG, LVO; British diplomatist; *Ambassador to Afghanistan;* b. 8 Jan. 1955, London; m. Bridget Cowper-Coles; four s. one d. *Education:* Tonbridge School, Hertford Coll., Oxford. *Career:* joined FCO 1977; Third, then Second Sec., Cairo 1980–83; First Sec. Planning Office, FCO 1983–85, Pvt. Sec. to Perm. Under-Sec. of State 1985–87; First Sec., Washington, DC 1987–91; Asst Security Policy Dept, FCO 1991–93, Head Hong Kong Dept 1994–97; Counsellor, Paris 1997–99; Prin. Pvt. Sec. to Sec. of State for Foreign and Commonwealth Affairs 1999–2001; Amb. to Israel 2001–03, to Saudi Arabia 2003–07, to Afghanistan 2007–; Hon. Fellow, Hertford Coll. Oxford 2002. *Publication:* From Defence to Security 2004.
Address: BFPO 5426, HA4 6EP, England (office). *Telephone:* 70-102201 (Afghanistan, mobile) (office). *E-mail:* sherard.cowper-coles@fco.gov.uk (office). *Website:* www.britishembassy.gov.uk/afghanistan (office).

COX, Michael; British academic; *Professor of International Relations, London School of Economics; Career:* Research Fellow, Royal Inst. of Int. Affairs 1994–; Sr Lecturer in Int. Politics, Univ. of Wales at Aberystwyth 1995–99, Prof. of Int. Politics, 1996–; Visiting Prof. CERIS, Free Univ. of Brussels 1999–; Sr Fellow, Norwegian Nobel Inst. 2001–02; Visiting Prof., Catholic Univ. Milan 2003–; Prof. of Int. Relations, London School of Econs 2003–, Dir Centre for Cold War Studies 2004–; Dir David Davies Memorial Inst. 2000–02; Ed. Review of Int. Studies 1998, Int. Relations 2001–; mem. Irish Nat. Cttee for the Study of Int. Affairs (Royal Irish Acad.) 1993–, Exec. Cttee European Consortium of Political Research 2003–; mem. Exec., British Int. Studies Asscn 1996–. *Publications:* America at War: American Foreign Policy after September 11 2004, The 'New' American Empire 2004.
Address: International Relations Department, London School of Economics & Political Science, Houghton Street, London, WC2A 2AE; Royal Institute of International Affairs, Chatham House, 10 St James's Square, London, SW1Y 4LE, England (office). *Telephone:* (20) 7955-7404 (office); (20) 7957-5700 (office). *Fax:* (20) 7955-7446 (office); (20) 7957-5710 (office). *E-mail:* m.e.cox@lse.ac.uk (office); contact@riia.org (office). *Website:* www.lse.ac.uk/people/m.e.cox@lse.ac.uk (office); www.riia.org (office).

COX, Hon. Paula Ann, JP, BA; Bermudian politician and lawyer; *Minister of Finance; Education:* McGill Univ., Canada, Univ. of Manchester, UK. *Career:* fmr Vice Pres. and Sr Legal Counsel, Global Funds Bank of Bermuda Ltd; Corp. Counsel, ACE Ltd 1996; mem. of Parl. 1998–, Minister of Labour, Home Affairs and Public Safety 1998–2001, Minister of Educ. and Devt 2001–02, Attorney-Gen. and Minister of Educ. 2003–04, Minister of Finance 2004–; Dr hc (Wheelock Coll.) 2004; Most Effective Politician 2001, 2003.
Address: Ministry of Finance, Government Administration Building, 30 Parliament Street, Hamilton, HM 12, Bermuda (office). *Telephone:* 295-5151 (office). *Fax:* 296-5727 (office). *E-mail:* pcox@gov.bm (office).

COX, Robert W., MA, FRSC; Canadian academic, political scientist and international civil servant; *Professor Emeritus, Department of Political Science, York University;* b. 18 Sept. 1926, Montreal. *Education:* McGill Univ. *Career:* fmr Asst Dir-Gen. ILO; fmr Dir Int. Inst. for Labour Studies, Geneva, Switzerland; fmr Prof. of Political Science, Grad. Inst. of Int. Studies, Geneva; Prof. of Int. Org., Columbia Univ., New York 1972–77; Visiting Prof., Yale Univ., Univ. de Laval, Québec, Univ. of Toronto, Univ. of Denver; Programme Co-ordinator on Multilateralism and the UN System, UN Univ., Tokyo; currently Prof. Emer., Dept of Political Science, York Univ., Toronto. *Publications include:* The Anatomy of Influence 1975, Production, Power and World Order 1987, International Political Economy: Understanding Global Disorder 1995, Approaches to World Order 1996, The New Realism (ed.) 1997, Political Economy of a Plural World: Critical Reflections on Power, Morals and Civilizations 2002. *Address:* Department of Political Science, Faculty of Arts, S652 Ross Building, York University, 4700 Keele Street, Toronto, ON M3J 1P3 (office); 5 Metcalfe Street, Toronto, ON M4X 1R5, Canada (home). *Telephone:* (416) 736-5265 (office); (416) 925-7307 (home). *Fax:* (416) 736-5700 (office); (416) 925-8892 (home). *E-mail:* rwcox@yorku.ca (office). *Website:* www.yorku.ca/polisci (office).

COX, Winston A., MSc (Econs); Barbadian banker and international organization official; *Alternate Executive Director for the Bahamas, Barbados, Guyana, Jamaica, and Trinidad and Tobago, Inter-American Development Bank;* m.; five c. *Education:* Univ. of the West Indies, Inst. of Social Studies, Netherlands. *Career:* joined Cen. Bank of Barbados 1974, Adviser to Gov. 1982–87, Gov. 1997; Dir of Finance, Ministry of Finance 1987–91; mem. Exec. Bd IBRD 1994–97; Gov. Cen. Bank of Barbados 1997–99; Deputy Sec.-Gen. (for Devt Co-operation) of the Commonwealth 2000–06; Alt. Exec. Dir for the Bahamas, Barbados, Guyana, Jamaica, and Trinidad and Tobago, IDB 2006–. *Address:* Inter-American Development Bank, 1300 New York Avenue, NW, Washington, DC 20577, USA (office). *Telephone:* (202) 942-8211 (office). *Fax:* (202) 942-8100 (office). *E-mail:* mifcontact@iadb.org (office). *Website:* www.iadb.org (office).

CRADDOCK, Gen. (Bantz) John, BA, MA; American army officer; *Supreme Allied Commander Europe and Commander of US European Command, NATO;* b. 1950, West Union, Doddridge Co., W Va; m. Linda Craddock; one s. one d. *Education:* West Virginia Univ., Command and Gen. Staff Coll., US Army War Coll. *Career:* commissioned as Armour Officer; Tank Co. Commdr, 3rd Armoured Div.; Systems Analyst then Exec. Officer, Office of Program Man., Abrams Tank System, Warren, Mich. 1981; assumed command of 4th Bn 64th Armour 24th Infantry Div. (Mechanised), Fort Stewart, Ga 1989; Asst Chief of Staff, (Operations) for 24th Div.; assumed command of 194th Separate Armoured Brigade 1993–95, then Asst Chief of Staff (Operations) for III Corps, Fort Hood, Tex.; Asst Deputy Dir (Plans and Policy), Jt Staff at Pentagon 1996–98; Asst Divisional Commdr for Manoeuvre of 1st Infantry Div. (Mechanised), Germany 1998; Commanding Gen. 7th Army Training Command, US Army Europe, then assumed command of 1st Infantry Div. (Mechanised); Sr Mil. Asst to Sec. of Defense; Combatant Commdr US Southern Command –2004, led US Southern Command 2004–06; Supreme Allied Commdr Europe and Commdr US European Command, NATO 2006–; served in Operation Desert Storm and Kosovo War; Valorous Unit Award, Defense Distinguished Service Medal, Distinguished Service Medal, Silver Star, Defense Superior Service Medal with 1 Oak Leaf Cluster, Legion of Merit with 2 Oak Leaf Clusters, Bronze Star. *Address:* NATO Allied Commander Europe, NATO Headquarters, boulevard Léopold III, 1110 Brussels, Belgium (office). *E-mail:* natodoc@hq.nato.int (office). *Website:* www.nato.int/shape (office); www.eucom.mil/english/index.asp (office).

CRADOCK, Rt Hon. Sir Percy, PC, GCMG; British diplomatist; b. 26 Oct. 1923; m. Birthe Marie Dyrlund 1953. *Career:* joined FCO 1954; First Sec. Kuala Lumpur, Malaya 1957–61, Hong Kong 1961–62, Beijing 1962–63; Foreign Office 1963–66; Counsellor and Head of Chancery, Beijing 1966–68, Chargé d'affaires 1968–69; Head of FCO Planning Staff 1969–71; Asst Under-Sec. of State and Head of Cabinet Office Assessments Staff 1971–76; Amb. to GDR 1976–78, concurrently Leader UK Mission to Comprehensive Test Ban Negotiations, Geneva 1977–78; Amb. to People's Repub. of China 1978–83: Leader of Negotiating Team with China over Hong Kong 1982–83; Deputy Under-Sec. with special responsibility for negotiations with China over Hong Kong 1983–85; Foreign Policy Adviser to the Prime Minister 1984–92; Chair. Jt Intelligence Cttee 1985–92; Dir South China Morning Post 1996–2000; Hon. Fellow St John's, Cambridge 1982. *Publications:* Experiences of China 1993, In Pursuit of British Interests 1997, Know Your Enemy: How the Joint Intelligence Committee Saw the World 2002. *Address:* c/o The Reform Club, 104 Pall Mall, London, SW1Y 5EW, England.

CRANFIELD, Thomas L., BA; Irish banker and civil servant; *Director-General, Office for Official Publications, European Union;* b. 3 Feb. 1945, Dublin; m.; three d. *Education:* Univ. Coll. Dublin. *Career:* personal admin. in American biomedical eng co., Dublin 1970–73; Head of Div. EIB (Luxembourg) 1973–90; Deputy Registrar European Court of Justice (Luxembourg) 1990–2000; Dir-Gen. Office for Official Publs of the EU 2000–. *Address:* Office for Official Publications of the European Union, 2 rue Mercier, 2985 Luxembourg (office). *Telephone:* 2929-1 (office). *Fax:* 2929-44691 (office). *E-mail:* ThomasL.Cranfield@publications.europa.eu (office). *Website:* www.publications.europa.eu (office).

CRAWFORD, Beverly, PhD; American academic; *Associate Director and Associate Research Political Scientist, Center for German and European Studies, University of California, Berkeley;* *Education:* Chapman Coll., Calif., Boston Univ., Univ. of Calif., Berkeley. *Career:* Acting Instructor in Politics, Univ. of Calif., Santa Cruz 1980–81, Visting Asst Prof 1987–89; Instructor, Int. Relations, Mills Coll. 1981–82; Asst Prof. of Int. Affairs, Univ. of Pittsburgh 1983–88; Sr Lecturer, Political Economy of Industrial Socs, Univ. of Calif., Berkeley 1989–, also Assoc. Dir and Assoc. Research Political Scientist, Center for German and European Studies; Sr Research Assoc., Center for Int. Trade and Security, Univ. of Georgia 1994–; mem. Fellowship Inst. for the Study of World Politics 1979–80, Danforth Foundation 1980–82, Friedrich Ebert Foundation 1986, 1996, Hoover Inst. 1987; Fulbright Fellow (Sofia, Bulgaria) 1994; DAAD Prof., Free Univ. of Berlin 2000; Visiting Prof., MIEM—SDA Bocconi, Bocconi Univ., Milan, Italy 2000, 2003; mem. American Political Science Asscn, Int. Studies Asscn, Soc. for Values in Higher Educ. *Publications include:* Economic Vulnerability in International Relations 1993; as ed. or co-ed.: A New Europe Asserts Itself: Europe's Changing Role in International Relations 1991, Progress in Post-War International Relations 1991, The Future of European Security 1992, European Dilemmas after Maastricht 1993, Markets, States and Democracy: the Political Economy of Post-Communist Transformation 1995, Liberalization and Leninist Legacies 1997, Myth of "Ethnic Conflict": Politics, Economics and Cultural Violence 1998, Post-War Transformation of Germany: Democracy, Prosperity and Nationhood 1999. *Address:* Institute of European Studies, International and Area Studies, 202 Moses Hall, University of California, Berkeley, CA 94720 (office); 1604 Addison, Berkeley, CA 94703, USA (home). *Telephone:* (510) 549-2018 (home); (501) 642-0210 (office). *Fax:* (510) 643-3372 (office). *E-mail:* bev@berkeley.edu (office). *Website:* ies.berkeley.edu (office).

CRAWFORD, Charles Graham, CMG, MA; British diplomatist; b. 2 May 1954, Liss; m. Helen Crawford; three c. *Education:* Univ. of Oxford, Fletcher School of Law and Diplomacy, Tufts Univ., USA. *Career:* trained as barrister; began diplomatic career with FCO with Embassy posting in Belgrade 1981–84, in Pretoria, SA 1987–91, Asst Head of Soviet Dept, FCO 1991–93, Counsellor, Embassy in Moscow 1993–96, Amb. in Sarajevo 1996–98, directed UK policy towards Fmr Yugoslavia 1999–2000, Amb. to Serbia and Montenegro 2001–03, to Poland 2003–07; in pvt. business 2007–. *Address:* c/o Foreign and Commonwealth Office, King Charles Street, London, SW1A 2AH, England. *Telephone:* (20) 7008-1500.

CRAWFORD, James Richard, SC, DPhil, FBA; Australian academic; *Whewell Professor of International Law, University of Cambridge;* b. 14 Nov. 1948, Adelaide; m. 1st Marisa Luigina Ballini 1971 (divorced 1990); four d.; m. 2nd Patricia Hyndman 1992 (divorced 1998); m. 3rd Joanna Gomula 1998; one s. *Education:* Brighton High School and Univs of Adelaide and Oxford. *Career:* Lecturer, Sr Lecturer, Reader, Prof. of Law, Univ. of Adelaide 1974–86; mem. Australian Law Reform Comm. 1982–84, part-time 1984–90; Challis Prof. of Int. Law, Univ. of Sydney 1986–92, Dean, Faculty of Law 1990–92; Whewell Prof. of Int. Law, Univ. of Cambridge 1992–; Dir Lauterpacht Research Centre for Int. Law 1997–2003, Chair. Faculty Bd of Law 2003–06; barrister, SC (NSW, Australia) 1997; mem. UN Int. Law Comm. 1992–2001; mem. Matrix Chambers. *Publications:* The Creation of States in International Law 1979, The Rights of Peoples (ed.) 1988, Australian Courts of Law (third edn) 1993, The International Law Commission Articles on State Responsibility 2002, International Law as an Open System 2002. *Address:* Lauterpacht Research Centre for International Law, 5 Cranmer Road, Cambridge, CB3 8BL (office); 7 Archway Court, Barton Road, Cambridge, CB3 9LW, England (home). *Telephone:* (1223) 335358 (office). *Fax:* (1223) 311668 (office). *E-mail:* jrc1000@hermes.cam.ac.uk (office). *Website:* www.law.cam.ac.uk\rcil (office).

CREECH, Rt Hon. Wyatt (W. B.), BA; New Zealand politician, accountant and vineyard developer; *Shadow Minister of State;* b. Oct. 1946, Oceanside, Calif., USA; m. Danny (Diana) Creech; three s. *Education:* Massey and Victoria Univs. *Career:* mem. Martinborough Council 1980–86; MP for Wairarapa 1988–; Minister of Revenue, Customs, in Charge of the Public Trust Office and responsible for Govt Superannuation Fund 1990–91, Minister of Revenue, in Charge of the Public Trust Office and responsible for Govt Superannuation Fund and Sr Citizens, Assoc. Minister of Finance and Social Welfare 1991–93, Minister of Revenue and Employment, Deputy Minister of Finance 1993–96, Minister of Educ., for Courts, for

Ministerial Services and Leader of the House 1996–98, Deputy Prime Minister 1998–99; Shadow Minister of State 2001–; Assoc. Spokesperson for Foreign Affairs and Trade; Deputy Leader Nat. Party 1997–2001; Chair. Cabinet Social Policy Cttee, Cabinet Legislation Cttee; mem. Nat. Party.

Address: Parliament Buildings, Wellington, New Zealand (office).

CRESSWELL, Jeremy Michael; British diplomatist; *High Commissioner to Jamaica;* b. 1 Oct. 1949; partner Dr Barbara Munske; one s. one d. *Education:* Exeter Coll., Oxford and Johannes Gutenberg Univ., Mainz, Germany. *Career:* joined FCO 1972, Desk Officer, West African Dept 1972–73, Third, later Second Sec., Chancery, Brussels 1973–77, Second, later First Sec., Chancery, Kuala Lumpur 1977–78, Desk Officer, Trade Relations and Export Dept, FCO 1978–81, Pvt. Sec., Parl. Under-Sec.'s Office 1981, Pvt. Sec., Minister of State's Office 1982, Deputy Political Adviser, British Mil. Govt, Berlin 1982–86, Deputy Head of Dept, Press Office, FCO 1986–88, Asst Head of Dept, S America Dept 1988–90, Counsellor/Head of Chancery, UK Del. to NATO, Brussels 1990–94, Deputy Head of Mission, Prague 1995–98, Head of Dept, Western European Dept, FCO 1998–99, Head of Dept, EU (Bilateral) Dept 1999–2001, Minister and Deputy Head of Mission, Berlin 2001–05, High Commr to Jamaica 2005–; Sr Dir Royal Coll. of Defence Studies, London 1998.

Address: British High Commission, PO Box 575, 28 Trafalgar Road, Kingston 10, Jamaica (office). *Telephone:* 510-0700 (office). *Fax:* 510-0737 (office). *E-mail:* bhckingston@cwjamaica.com (office). *Website:* www .britishhighcommission.gov.uk/jamaica (office).

CROCKER, Chester Arthur, PhD; American academic and fmr government official; *James R. Schlesinger Professor of Strategic Studies, Edmund A. Walsh School of Foreign Service, Georgetown University;* b. 29 Oct. 1941, New York; m. Saone Baron 1965; three d. *Education:* Ohio State Univ., Johns Hopkins Univ. *Career:* editorial asst, Africa Report 1965–66, News Ed. 1968–69; Lecturer, American Univ. 1969–70; staff officer, Nat. Security Council 1970–72; Dir Master of Science, Foreign Service Program, Georgetown Univ. 1972–78, James R. Schlesinger Prof. of Strategic Studies 1989–; Dir African Studies, Center for Strategic and Inst. Studies 1976–81; Asst Sec. of State for African Affairs 1981–89; Chair. African Working Group, Reagan Campaign 1980; Chair. US Inst. of Peace 1992–2004; work as int. consultant; mem. Bd of Dirs ASA Ltd, Nat. Defense Univ., US Inst. of Peace, Universal Corpn, Bell Pottinger Communications USA LLC, First Africa Holdings Ltd, G3 Good Governance Group Holdings Ltd; Presidential Citizen's Medal, Sec. of State's Distinguished Service Award, Vicennial Award for Service and John Carroll Medal, Georgetown Univ., Woodrow Wilson Award for Distinguished Public Service, Johns Hopkins Univ. *Publications:* South Africa's Defense Posture 1982, South Africa into the 1980s 1979, High Noon in Southern Africa 1992, African Conflict Resolution 1995, Managing Global Chaos 1996, Herding Cats: Multiparty Mediation in a Complex World 1999, Turbulent Peace: The Challenges of Managing International Conflict 2001, Taming Intractable Conflicts 2004, Grasping the Nettle: Analysing Cases of Intractable Conflict 2005, Leashing the Dogs of War: Conflict Management in a Divided World 2007; numerous articles.

Address: Room 801, Intercultural Center, School of Foreign Service, Georgetown University, Washington, DC 20057, USA (office). *Telephone:* (202) 687-5074 (office). *Fax:* (202) 687-2315 (office). *E-mail:* crockerc@ georgetown.edu (office). *Website:* www.georgetown.edu/sfs (office).

CROCKER, Ryan C., BA; American diplomatist; *Ambassador to Iraq;* b. 19 June 1949, Spokane, Wash.; m. Christine Barnes. *Education:* schools in Morocco, Canada, Turkey and USA, Univ. Coll. Dublin, Ireland, Whitman Coll., Walla Walla, Wash., Princeton Univ. *Career:* joined Foreign Service in 1971, diplomatic positions in Iran 1972–74, Qatar 1974–76, Iraq 1978–80, Lebanon 1981–84; Deputy Dir Office of Arab-Israeli Affairs 1985–87; Political Counselor, Embassy in Cairo 1987–90; Dir State Dept's Iraq-Kuwait Task Force Aug. 1990; Amb. to Lebanon 1990–93, to Kuwait 1994–97, to Syria 1998–2001; Deputy Asst Sec. of State for Near Eastern Affairs 2001–03; Interim Envoy to new Govt of Afghanistan 2002–04; Int. Affairs Advisor, Nat. War Coll., Washington, DC 2003–04; Amb. to Pakistan 2004–07, to Iraq 2007–, rank of Career Amb. 2004; Hon. LLD (Whitman Coll.) 2001; Presidential Distinguished Service Award 1994, Dept of Defense Medal for Distinguished Civilian Service 1997, Presidential Meritorious Service Award 1999, 2003, State Dept Award for Valor, Three Superior Honor Awards, American Foreign Service Asscn Rivkin Award, State Dept Distinguished Honor Award 2004.

Address: Embassy of the United States, APO AE 09316, Baghdad, Iraq (office). *E-mail:* BaghdadPressOffice@state.gov (office). *Website:* iraq .usembassy.gov (office).

CROPPER, Angela, BSc, LLB; Trinidad and Tobago economist, international organization official and foundation executive; *Deputy Executive Director, United Nations Environment Programme;* b. (Sarojini Persad), Port-of-Spain; m. John Cropper (died 2001); one s. (died 1998). *Education:* Univ. of the West Indies. *Career:* fmr Project Man., Eastern Caribbean Office, Int. Planned Parenthood Fed., Western Hemisphere Region (IPPF/WHR); Adviser on Environment and Educ., Caribbean Community Secr. (CARICOM), fmrly Dir of Functional Co-operation; Exec. Sec. Interim UN Convention on Biological Diversity (CBD) 1993–95; Sr Adviser on Environment and Devt, UNDP; mem. External Advisory Group on Forest Policy Implementation, World Bank (IBRD); Co-Founder and Pres. The Cropper Foundation (NGO active in sustainable devt issues, environmental awareness and Caribbean writing) 1999–; Co-Chair. Millennium Ecosystem Assessment (MA) 2001–; mem. Bd Int. Inst. for Sustainable Devt (IISD); Chair. Ed. Cttee and Ed. World Comm. on Forests and Sustainable Devt, also fmr Comm. mem.; fmr Chair. Bd of Trustees Iwokrama Int. Centre for Rainforest Conservation and Devt, Guyana; Chair. Bd of Trustees Centre for Int. Forestry Research (CIFOR); mem. Bd of Trustees Environmental Man. Authority, Environmental Trust Fund; Winslow Visiting Distinguished Scientist, Woods Hole Research Center 2000, McCluskey Fellow, Yale School of Forestry and Environmental Studies 2006; Deputy Exec. Dir UN Environment Programme and UN Asst Sec. Gen. 2008–.

Address: United Nations Environment Programme, United Nations Avenue, Gigiri, PO Box 30552, 00100 Nairobi, Kenya (office); The Cropper Foundation, Building 7, Fernandes Industrial Centre, Laventille, Port-of-Spain, Trinidad and Tobago (office). *Telephone:* (868) 626-2628 (office). *Fax:* (868) 626-2564 (office). *E-mail:* executiveoffice@unep.org (office); acropper@thecropperfoundation.org (office); info@thecropperfoundation .org (office). *Website:* www.unep.org (office); www.thecropperfoundation .org (office).

CRUMPTON, Henry A., BA; American academic and fmr government official; *Distinguished Fellow, Global Security Program, EastWest Institute;* b. 1957, Athens, Ga; m.; three s. *Education:* Univ. of New Mexico, School of Advanced Int. Studies, Johns Hopkins Univ. *Career:* joined CIA 1981, served as operations officer at HQ and abroad and in several foreign field assignments, including two as Chief of Station; Deputy Chief Int. Terrorism Operations Section, FBI 1998–99; Deputy Chief of Operations, Counterterrorist Centre, CIA 1999–2001, Leader, Afghan Campaign 2001–02, Chief Nat. Resources Div. 2003–05; Amb.-at-Large and Coordinator for Counterterrorism, US State Dept 2005–07; Distinguished Fellow, Global Security Program, EastWest Inst. 2007–; consultant to cos on global risk; fmr mem. Advisory Bd to Study of Terrorism and Responses to Terrorism (START), US Dept of Homeland Security; Intelligence Commendation Medal, Distinguished Intelligence Medal, CIA, George H.W. Bush Award for Excellence in Counterterrorism, Sherman Kent Award, Donovan Award. *Publications:* contrib. to: Transforming US Intelligence 2005.

Address: Global Security Program, EastWest Institute, 700 Broadway, New York, NY 10003, USA (office). *Telephone:* (212) 824-4100 (office). *Website:* www.iews.org (office).

CRUZ SEQUEIRA, Arturo José, MA, DPhil; Nicaraguan economist, politician, academic and diplomatist; *Ambassador to USA;* b. 1954. *Education:* American Univ., Washington, DC and Paul H. Nitze School of Advanced Int. Studies, Johns Hopkins Univ., Univ. of Oxford, UK. *Career:* supported Edén Pastora (fmr Sandinista commdr starting up rebel Democratic Revolutionary Alliance) 1982, then became involved with United Nicaraguan Opposition (rebel umbrella group) 1985, involved in exile politics of Contra rebels opposing Sandinista (FSLN) Govt 1987; Prof., INCAE Business School, Managua –2007; Visiting Prof., Advanced School of Econs and Business, San Salvador, El Salvador 2007; Amb. to USA 2007–; fmr Bradley Fellow, Hudson Inst., Washington, DC. *Publication:* Memoirs of a Counter-Revolutionary, Nicaragua's Conservative Republic 1853–1893 2002 (translated and published in Spanish 2003), Varieties of Liberalism in Central America: Nation-States as Works in Progress (with Forrest Colburn) 2007; articles on the analysis of social, econ. and political trends in Latin America.

Address: Embassy of Nicaragua, 1627 New Hampshire Avenue, NW, Washington, DC 20009, USA (office). *Telephone:* (202) 939-6570 (office). *Fax:* (202) 939-6545 (office). *E-mail:* nicaraguan.embassy@embanic.org (office).

CRVENKOVSKI, Branko; Macedonian politician, engineer and head of state; *President;* b. 12 Oct. 1962, Sarajevo, Bosnia and Herzegovina; m. Jasmina Crvenkovska; one s. one d. *Education:* Skopje Univ. *Career:* computer engineer, SEMOS Co. 1987–90; mem. Nat. Ass. 1990–2004; Chair. Social-Democratic Union of Macedonia (SDUM) 1990–92, Pres.

1991–2004; Chair. Cabinet of Ministers (Prime Minister) 1992–98, 2002–04; Pres. 2004–.
Address: Office of the President, 1000 Skopje, 11 Oktomvri bb, Former Yugoslav Republic of Macedonia (office). *Telephone:* (2) 3113318 (office). *Fax:* (2) 3112147 (office). *Website:* www.president.gov.mk (office).

CSABA, László, PhD, DrSci, DrHab; Hungarian economist and academic; *Professor of Economics and European Studies, Central European University;* b. 27 March 1954, Budapest; m. Gabriella Ónody 1980; one s. one d. *Education:* Univ. of Budapest, Hungarian Acad. of Sciences. *Career:* Fellow, Inst. for World Econs, Budapest 1976–87; economist/researcher, then Sr Economist, Kopint-Datorg Econ. Research 1988–2000; Hon. Prof. of Int. Econs, Coll. of Foreign Trade, Budapest Univ. of Econs 1991–97, Prof. 1997–; Prof. of Econs and European Studies, Cen. European Univ. 2000–; Head Doctoral Programme, Univ. of Debrecen 1999–2004; Vice-Pres. European Asscn for Comparative Econs 1990–94, 1996–98, Pres. 1999–2000; mem. Econs Cttee Hungarian Acad. of Sciences 1986–, Co-Chair. 1996–99, 2000–02, Chair. 2003–05; Visiting Prof., Bocconi Univ., Milan 1991, Helsinki Univ. 1993, Europa Univ., Viadrina, Frankfurt 1997, Freie Univ., Berlin 1998–2000, Cen. European Univ. 1998; mem. Bd TIGER Inst., Poland, NORDI Inst., Finland; mem. editorial bd of various journals; Ministry of External Econ. Affairs Prize 1994, Bezeredi Prize for European Integration 2003, Nat. Bank of Hungary Prize 2004, Akademia Publishing House Best Economics Book Award 2005. *Publications:* Eastern Europe in the World Economy 1990, The Capitalist Revolution in Eastern Europe 1995, The New Political Economy of Emerging Europe 2005; ed. six books; over 190 articles and chapters in books published in 18 countries. *Address:* Department of International Relations and European Studies, Central European University, Nador u. 9, 1051 Budapest (office); Dohány u. 94, 1074 Budapest, Hungary (home). *Telephone:* (1) 327-30-80 (office); (1) 327-30-17 (office); (1) 322-05-19 (home). *Fax:* (1) 327-32-43 (office). *E-mail:* csabal@ceu.hu (office). *Website:* www.ceu.hu (office).

CUEVAS ARGOTE, Javier Gonzalo, MBS; Bolivian government official; b. 1955, La Paz. *Education:* Universidad Mayor de san Andrés, Universidad de Chile, Universidad Privada Boliviana, Florida Int. Univ., USA. *Career:* director of numerous public and private finance insts; adviser to Pres. of Central Bank; Vice-Minister, Ministry of Finance, Minister of Finance 2003–06.
Address: c/o Ministry of Finance, Edif. Palacio de Communicaciones, Avda. Mariscal Santa Cruz, La Paz, Bolivia (office).

CUI, Tiankai; Chinese diplomatist; *Ambassador to Japan;* b. Oct. 1952, Shanghai; m.; one d. *Career:* interpreter, UN HQ, New York 1981–84; began career at Ministry of Foreign Affairs with Dept of Int. Orgs and Confs, serving successively as Attaché, Third Sec., Deputy Dir, Dir, Counsellor 1984–96, Deputy Dir-Gen. Information Dept 1996–97, Deputy Exec. Dir-Gen. Policy Research Office 1999–2001, Dir-Gen. Policy Research Office 2001–03, Dir-Gen. Dept of Asian Affairs 2003–06, Asst Minister of Foreign Affairs, responsible for Asian Affairs, Int. Orgs and Confs and Arms Control 2006–07; Counsellor with ministerial rank, Perm. Rep to UN, New York 1997–99; Amb. to Japan 2007–.
Address: Embassy of the People's Republic of China, 3-4-33 Moto Azabu, Minato-ku, Tokyo 106-0046, Japan (office). *Telephone:* (3) 3403-3380 (office). *Fax:* (3) 3403-3345 (office). *E-mail:* lsb@china-embassy.or.jp (office). *Website:* www.china-embassy.or.jp/chn (office).

CULLEN, Michael John, MA, PhD; New Zealand politician; *Deputy Prime Minister, Attorney-General, Minister of Finance, Minister for Treaty of Waitingi Negotiations and Leader of the House;* b. 1945, London, England; m. 1st Rowena Joy Knight; two d.; m. 2nd Anne Lowson Collins. *Education:* Christ's Coll. Christchurch, Univ. of Canterbury and Univ. of Edinburgh, UK. *Career:* Asst Lecturer, Univ. of Canterbury, Tutor Univ. of Stirling, Sr Lecturer in History, Univ. of Otago, Dunedin and Visiting Fellow, ANU 1968–81; MP 1981–; Minister of Social Welfare 1987–90; Assoc. Minister of Finance 1987–88, of Health 1988–90, of Labour 1989–90; Opposition Spokesperson on Finance 1991, apptd Deputy Leader of Opposition 1996; fmr Minister for Accident Insurance, Leader of the House; Treas., Minister of Finance 1999–, of Revenue 1999–2005; Deputy Prime Minister 2002–, Minister of Tertiary Educ. 2005–07, Minister in charge of Treaty of Waitingi Negotiations–, also Attorney-Gen; mem. Labour Party.
Address: Executive Wing, Parliament Buildings, Wellington, New Zealand (office). *Telephone:* 470-6551 (office). *Fax:* 495-8442 (office). *E-mail:* michael.cullen@parliament.govt.nz (office). *Website:* www.beehive.govt.nz (office).

CUNTZ, Eckart; German lawyer and diplomatist; *Ambassador to Turkey;* b. 3 April 1950, Mannheim; m. Ursula Cuntz; three c. *Career:* early career as lawyer; joined Ministry of Foreign Affairs 1975, worked in NATO Dept 1983–85, Head, Maastricht Treaty Negotiations Div. 1991–93, Deputy Head Europe Dept 2001–03, Head 2003–06; served in embassies in Kabul, Kuala Lumpur and Luanda 1977–82; Amb. to Brunei 1985; at Perm. Mission to EEC, Brussels 1988–90, Embassy in Tehran 1993–94; Chef de Cabinet to Sec.-Gen., Council of the EU, Brussels 1994–99; Amb. to Turkey 2006–.
Address: Embassy of Germany, Ataturk Bul. 114, 06690 Kavaklıdere, Ankara, Turkey (office). *Telephone:* (312) 4555100 (office). *Fax:* (312) 4266959 (office). *E-mail:* infomail@germanembassyank.com (office). *Website:* www.ankara.diplo.de (office).

CUTILEIRO, Jose; Portuguese academic, international organization official and fmr diplomatist. *Education:* Univ. of Oxford. *Career:* fmr diplomatist; EU negotiator, Sarajevo 1992; Sec.-Gen. WEU 1994–99; Special Counsellor, Portuguese Presidency of EU 2000; Special Rep. UN Comm. on Human Rights for Bosnia-Herzegovina and Fed. Repub. of Yugoslavia 2001–03; George F. Kennan Prof., Inst. for Advanced Study, Princeton Univ. 2001–04; contrib. to Expresso weekly. *Publications:* A Portuguese Rural Society 1971; numerous essays and articles in newspapers and periodicals.
Address: c/o Expresso, Edifício S. Francisco de Sales, Rua Calvet de Magalhães, 242, Paço de Arcos, 2770-022 Lisbon, Portugal (office). *Website:* www.expresso.dix.pt (office).

CUTLER, Walter Leon, MA; American diplomatist; *President, Meridian International Center;* b. 25 Nov. 1931, Boston, Mass.; m. 1st Sarah Gerard Beeson 1957 (divorced 1981); two s.; m. 2nd Isabel Kugel Brookfield 1981. *Education:* Wesleyan Univ. and Fletcher School of Int. Law and Diplomacy. *Career:* Vice-Consul, Yaoundé, Cameroon 1957–59; Staff Asst to Sec. of State 1960–62; Political-Econ. Officer, Algiers 1962–65; Consul, Tabriz, Iran 1965–67; Political-Mil. Officer, Seoul, Repub. of Korea 1967–69; Political Officer, Saigon, Repub. of Viet Nam 1969–71; Special Asst, Bureau of Far Eastern Affairs, Dept of State 1971–73, mem. Sr Seminar on Foreign Policy 1973–74, Dir Office of Cen. Africa 1974–75; Amb. to Zaïre 1975–79, to Iran 1979; Deputy Asst Sec. of State for Congressional Relations 1979–81; Amb. to Tunisia 1981–83, to Saudi Arabia 1983–87, 1988–89; Pres. Meridian Int. Center, Washington, DC 1989–; Sr Advisor Trust Co. of the West, LA 1990–; Research Prof. of Diplomacy, Georgetown Univ. 1987–88; Special Emissary for Sec.-Gen. of UN, New York 1994; mem. Council on Foreign Relations, New York, American Acad. of Diplomacy, Washington Inst. of Foreign Affairs; Wilbur J. Carr Award 1989, Dir-Gen.'s Cup, Dept of State 1993; Order of the Leopard (Repub. of Zaïre) 1979; King Abdulaziz Decoration (Saudi Arabia) 1985.
Address: Meridian International Center, 1630 Crescent Place, NW, Washington, DC 20009-4004, USA. *Telephone:* (202) 667-6800 (office). *Fax:* (202) 667-1475 (office). *E-mail:* info@meridian.org (office). *Website:* www.meridian.org (office).

CUTTAREE, Hon. Jayakrishna, MSc, PhD; Mauritian politician and lawyer; *Minister of Foreign Affairs, International Trade and Regional Co-operation;* *Education:* Univ. of Edinburgh, UK, Uppsala Univ., Sweden, Univ. of Cambridge, UK. *Career:* called to the Bar, Lincoln's Inn, London, UK; fmr Asst Conservator of Forests, Ministry of Agric. and Natural Resources; fmr Gen. Man. Sugar Planters' Mechanical Pool Corpn; fmr Chief of Natural Resources Div., OAU, Addis Ababa, Ethiopia; fmr Programme Specialist (Research and Devt in Natural Resources), UNESCO, Paris, France; Deputy Leader Mouvement Militant Mauricien; mem. Legis. Ass. 1982–; Minister of Labour and Industrial Relations 1982–83, Attorney-Gen. and Minister of Housing, Lands, Town and Country Planning 1991, of Industry, Industrial Tech., Scientific Research and Handicraft 1996, of Industry and Commerce 1996–97, of Industry, Commerce and Int. Trade 2000–03, of Foreign Affairs, Int. Trade and Regional Co-operation 2003–; Spokesman, Pacific Common Market, Indian Ocean Comm. and Pacific Forum at WTO meeting, Doha, Qatar 2001; led negotiations between EU and African Pacific Caribbean countries under Cotonou Agreement 2002; Spokesman of African Union at WTO meeting, Cancun, Mexico 2003; Head of Mauritian Del. and Spokesman of the African Union at Africa Growth and Opportunity Act (AGOA) Conf., Washington, DC, 2003.
Address: Ministry of Foreign Affairs, International Trade and Regional Co-operation, New Government Centre, 5th Floor, Port Louis, Mauritius (office). *Telephone:* 201-1648 (office). *Fax:* 208-8087 (office). *E-mail:* mfa@mail.gov.mu (office). *Website:* foreign.gov.mu (office).

CVETKOVIĆ, Mirko, MA, PhD; Serbian economist and politician; *Prime Minister;* b. 1950, Zaječar; m.; two c. *Education:* Faculty of Econs, Univ. of Belgrade. *Career:* began career as Economist, Inst. of Mining and Inst. of

Econs; consultant, CES MECON (advisory and research co.); fmr foreign consultant on World Bank projects in Pakistan, India and Turkey; Econ. Adviser, Inst. of Mining 1998–2001; Deputy Minister of Economy and Privatization 2001–04; Dir Privatization Agency 2003–04; Special Adviser to CEO Intercom Consulting/CES MECON 2005–; Minister of Finance 2007–08; Prime Minister 2008–.
Address: Office of the Prime Minister, 11000 Belgrade, Nemanjina 11, Serbia (office). *Telephone:* (11) 3617719 (office). *Fax:* (11) 3617609 (office). *E-mail:* predsednikvladesrbije@srbija.sr.gov.yu (office).

CZAKÓ, Borbála; Hungarian business executive and diplomatist; *Ambassador to UK. Career:* fmr Country Man. Pnr, Ernst & Young (Hungary); Investment Officer, later Chief of Mission, International Finance Corpn (with investment banking responsibilities in Hungary and the region), World Bank Group 1992–2002, also worked on special assignments in Washington, DC and in Africa; fmr Chair. British-Hungarian Business Leaders Forum; Amb. to UK 2007–.
Address: Embassy of Hungary, 35 Eaton Place, London, SW1X 8BY, England (office). *Telephone:* (20) 7201-3440 (office). *Fax:* (20) 7823-1348 (office). *E-mail:* office@huemblon.org.uk (office). *Website:* www.mfa.gov.hu/emb/london (office).

D

D'ABOVILLE, Benoît; French diplomatist and international organization official; *Senior Auditor, Cour des Comptes;* b. 14 May 1942, Rabat, Morocco; m. Benedetta Craveri; one d. *Education:* Institut d'Etudes Politiques, Paris, Ecole Nat. d'Admin. *Career:* joined Ministry of Foreign Affairs 1968, assigned to Embassy in Washington, DC, USA 1969–73, in Moscow 1973–76, Desk Officer for Political-Mil. Affairs, Quai d'Orsay 1976–77, Adviser, Office of the Minister 1977–78; Deputy Head of Mission, Geneva Cttee on Disarmament 1979; Deputy Under-Sec., Political Affairs Bureau, Ministry of Foreign Affairs 1980–86; Deputy Head of French Del. to CSCE Conf., Madrid 1980; Deputy Dir for Political Affairs 1987–89; Consul Gen. in New York 1989–93; Amb. to Czech Repub. 1994–97, to Poland 1997–2001; Perm. Rep. to NATO, Brussels 2001–05; Sr Auditor, Cour des Comptes 2006–; Chevalier de la Légion d'honneur, Officer, Ordre nat. du Mérite, Grand Cross, German Fed. Order of Merit, Grand Cross, Polish Order of Merit. *Publications include:* contribs to various books and publs. *Address:* Cour des Comptes, 13 rue Cambon, Paris 75001 (office); 34 rue de Pentherie, Paris 75008, France (home). *Telephone:* 1-42-98-91-04 (office). *Fax:* 1-42-98-59-75 (office). *E-mail:* bdaboville@ccomptes.fr (office). *Website:* www.ccomptes.fr (office).

DA COSTA, Luis Carlos, MA; Brazilian diplomatist and UN official; *Principal Deputy Special Representative of the Secretary-General for Haiti (MINUSTAH), United Nations;* b. 4 June 1949; m.; two d. *Education:* New York Univ. *Career:* joined UN 1969, served in various positions at UN HQ, including with Office of Human Resources Man. and then Dept of Conf. Services 1969–92, Chief of Personnel Man. and Support Service, Field Admin and Logistics Div., Dept of Peacekeeping Operations, New York 1992–2000, Dir Admin, UN Mission in Kosovo (UNMIK) 2000–01, 2002–03, Prin. Officer for Change Man., Office of Under-Sec.-Gen. for Peacekeeping Operations 2001–02, Dir Logistics Support Div., Office of Mission Support, Dept of Peacekeeping Operations 2003–05, Deputy Special Rep. of UN Sec.-Gen for Operations and Rule of Law for Liberia 2005–06; Prin. Deputy Special Rep. of the Sec.-Gen. for UN Stabilization Mission in Haiti (MINUSTAH), Port-au-Prince 2006–. *Address:* Office of the Secretary-General, UN Headquarters, First Avenue at 46th Street, New York, NY 10017, USA (office); MINUSTAH 11, Impasse Théodule Bourdon, Port-au-Prince, Haïti (office). *Telephone:* 244-2050 (Haiti) (office). *E-mail:* press@minustah.org (office). *Website:* www .un.org/Depts/dpko/missions/minustah (office); www.minustah.org (office).

DA COSTA, Zacarias; Timor-Leste politician; *Minister of Foreign Affairs;* m. Milena Pires. *Career:* served as Conselho Nacional da Resistência Timorense (CNRT) rep. to EU in Brussels, UN in Geneva –1999; fmr Vice-Pres. União Democrática Timorense; Co-founder Partido Social Demo-crata (PSD) 2000, held several posts including Gen.-Sec., Pres. Nat. Congress and Nat. Chair.; consultant for Asian Bank of Devt; Minister of Foreign Affairs 2007–. *Address:* Ministry of Foreign Affairs and Cooperation, GPA Building 1, Ground Floor, Rua Avenida Presidente Nicolau Lobato, PO BOX 6, Dili, Timor-Leste (office). *Telephone:* 3339600 (office). *Fax:* 3339025 (office). *E-mail:* administration@mnec.gov-tl.net (office). *Website:* www.mfac.gov .tp (office).

DA COSTA FERNANDES, António, BA; Angolan diplomatist; b. 26 April 1942, Cabinda; m. *Education:* Univ. of Fribourg, Switzerland. *Career:* Amb. to UK –2005, to India (also accred to Thailand and Malaysia) 2005–; Gold Medal of Nat. Hero, Angola 2005. *Address:* 5 Poorvi Marg, New Delhi 110 057 (office); 2A Cassia Avenue, Westend Greens, Rajokry 110 058, India (home). *Telephone:* (11) 26146195; (11) 26146197 (home). *Fax:* (11) 26146184; (11) 26146190 (home). *E-mail:* enquiry@angolaembassyindia.com; mwanami@hotmail.com (home). *Website:* www.angolaembassyindia.com.

DA FONSECA, Luis de Matos Monteiro; Cape Verde diplomatist and politician; *Executive Secretary, Community of Portuguese Speaking Countries;* b. 17 May 1944, Santo Antao; m. Maria Fernanda Benros Lima da Fonseca; two c. *Education:* Instituto Superior de Ciencias Economicas e Financas, Lisbon, Portugal. *Career:* young leader of independence movt., imprisoned in Mindelo, Praia and Tarrafal 1967–73; Regional Co-ordinator for St. Vincent Islands transition to independence 1974–75; First Sec., Chair. of the Nat. Ass. 1975–78; Nat. Sec. Cape Verdean Youth Org. 1978–84; Head of Town Cttee. 1984–86; Minister Plenipotentiary, Minister of Foreign Affairs 1986; Amb. to Netherlands (also accred. to EC, U.K., Belgium, Luxembourg and Nordic countries) 1987–91, to Russia (later also Ukraine, Belarus, Kazakhstan, Estonia and Lithuania) 1991–94, to Austria (concurrently Perm. Rep. to UN Industrial Devt. Org. and Comprehensive Nuclear Test-Ban Treaty Org., Vienna) 1999–2001; Dir.-Gen. for Political and Cultural Affairs 1995–97, for Foreign Policy 1997–99; Perm. Rep. to UN, New York Sept. 2001–04; Exec.-Sec. Community of Portuguese Speaking Countries 2004–; fmr. Del. of Cape Verde to UN Gen. Ass., Head of Del. to UN Comm. on Human Rights, Geneva 1997. *Address:* Community of Portuguese Speaking Countries, Rua de São Caetano 32, 1200-829 Lisbon, Portugal (office). *Telephone:* (21) 3928560 (office). *Fax:* (21) 3928588 (office). *Website:* ww.cplp.org (office).

DA SILVA, Henrique Adriano; Guinea-Bissau diplomatist. *Career:* currently Chargé d'affaires in USA. *Address:* Embassy of Guinea-Bissau, 1511 K Street, Suite 519, NW, Washington, DC 20005 (office); Embassy of Guinea-Bissau, 15929 Yukon Lane, Rockville MD 20855, USA. *Telephone:* (202) 872-4222 (office); (301) 947-3958. *Fax:* (202) 872-4226 (office). *Website:* www.embassy.org/ embassies/gw.html (office).

DA SILVA, Luis Inácio (Lula) (see LULA DA SILVA, Inácio).

DA VEIGA, Marias de Fátima Lima; Cape Verde politician and diplomatist; *Ambassador to USA;* b. 22 June 1957, São Vicente; m.; two c. *Education:* Univ. of Aix-ex-Provence, France. *Career:* Amb. to Cuba 1999–2001; fmr adviser, Ministry of Foreign Affairs, Chief of Staff, Office of the Minister for Foreign Affairs 1995–99, Sec. of State for Foreign Affairs 2001–02, Minister of Foreign Affairs, Co-operation and Communities 2002–04, Perm. Rep. to UN, New York 2004–07, Amb. to USA 2007–; mem. Nat. Comm. CILSS. *Address:* Embassy of Cape Verde, 3415 Massachusetts Avenue, NW, Washington DC, 20007, USA (office). *Telephone:* (202) 965-6820 (office). *Fax:* (202) 965-1207 (office). *E-mail:* ambacvus@sysnet.net (office). *Website:* www.virtualcapeverde.net (office).

DAALDER, Ivo H., BA, MA, MLitt, PhD; American academic and fmr government official; *Senior Fellow, Foreign Policy Studies, Brookings Institution;* b. 1960, The Hague, Netherlands; m. Elisa D. Harris; two s. *Education:* Univs of Kent and Oxford, UK, Georgetown Univ., MIT. *Career:* fmr Assoc. Prof. and Dir of Research Center for Int. and Security Studies, Univ. of Maryland; served as Dir European Affairs in Pres. Clinton's Nat. Security Council 1995–96; mem. Study Group US Comm. on Nat. Security 1998–2001; currently Sr Fellow, Foreign Policy Studies and Sydney Stein Jr Chair in Int. Security, Brookings Inst.; mem. Acad. of Political Science, Council on Foreign Relations, IISS. *Publications:* The SDI Challenge to Europe 1986, Strategic Defenses in the 1990s 1991, Nature and Practice of Flexible Response: NATO Strategy and Theater Nuclear Forces since 1967 1991, Rethinking the Unthinkable: New Directions for Nuclear Arms Control (co-ed.) 1993, The United States and Europe in the Global Arena (co-ed.) 1999, Getting to Dayton: The Making of America's Bosnia Policy 2000, Winning Ugly: NATO's War to Save Kosovo (jtly) 2000, Protecting the American Homeland (jtly) 2002, America Unbound: The Bush Revolution in Foreign Policy (jtly; Lionel Gelber Prize for Best Book in Int. Affairs 2003) 2003, Beyond Preemption: Force and Legitimacy in a Changing World (ed) 2007; numerous articles in journals and newspapers. *Address:* Foreign Policy Studies Program, Brookings Institution, 1775 Massachusetts Avenue, NW, Washington, DC 20036, USA (office). *Telephone:* (202) 797-6058 (office). *Fax:* (202) 797-6003 (office). *E-mail:* idaalder@brookings.edu (office). *Website:* www.brookings.edu/experts/ daalderi.aspx (office).

DABOUB, Juan José; Salvadorean politician and international organization official; *Managing Director, World Bank Group;* Career: led family-owned

businesses for nearly a decade before joining Bd of CEL (electricity utility); fmr Pres. ANTEL (state-owned telecommunications co. which he privatized); served three different govts for 12 years and then returned to pvt. sector; fmr Chief of Staff to Pres. of El Salvador, co-ordinated donors and oversaw reconstruction of El Salvador after two earthquakes of 2001; Minister of Finance –2006; Man. Dir World Bank Group 2006–.
Address: The World Bank Group, 1818 H Street, NW, Washington, DC 20433, USA (office). *Telephone:* (202) 473-1000 (office). *Fax:* (202) 477-6391 (office). *E-mail:* webmaster@worldbank.org (office). *Website:* www.worldbank.org (office).

DACI, Nexhat, MA, PhD; Kosovo politician and academic; *University Professor, University of Priština;* b. 26 July 1944, Tërnoc, Serbia and Montenegro (now in Kosovo); m. Zineta Daci; two s. one d. *Education:* Univ. of Priština, also educated in UK and Belgium. *Career:* Univ. Prof., Univ. of Priština 1983–; Pres. and Sec., Kosovo Acad. of Sciences and Arts 1995–2002; Pres. of Kosovo Ass. 2001–06; Acting Pres. of Kosovo Jan.-Feb. 2006; mem. Democratic League of Kosovo, European Acad. for the Environment, American Chem. Asscn. *Publications:* author of four text books.
Address: Velania 18/IV, Priština, Kosovo (home). *E-mail:* nexhat.daci@assembly-kosova.org (office). *Website:* www.kuvendikosoves.org (office).

DADAE, Bob; Papua New Guinea politician; *Minister of Defence; Career:* fmr Deputy Speaker of Parl.; Minister of Defence 2007–; MP for Kabwum; Leader, United Party 2007–.
Address: Department of Defence, Murray Barracks, Free Mail Bag, Boroko 111, National Capital District, Papua New Guinea (office). *Telephone:* 3242480 (office). *Fax:* 3256117 (office). *Website:* www.defence.gov.pg (office).

DADE, Arta, PhD; Albanian politician; b. 15 March 1953, Tirana; two s. *Education:* Tirana Univ. *Career:* teacher Foreign Languages School, Tirana 1977–85, Prof. of English, Tirana Univ. 1985–97; mem. Socialist Party 1991–, mem. Presidency 1992, Foreign Relations Sec. 1996, MP Socialist Group 1997–2001; Minister of Culture, Youth and Sport 1997–98; Vice-Chair. Foreign Policy Cttee, Albanian Parl. 1998–2001; Minister of Foreign Affairs 2001–02, of Culture, Youth and Sports 2002; currently mem. Kuvendi Popullor (Parl.); fmr head of Albanian Delegation to OSCE; mem. Parl. Ass. Council of Europe; mem. Socialist Women Forum 1991, European Forum of the Left Women 1993, Global Forum of Leading Women; H. H. Humphrey Fellowship, Rutgers Univ. 1997. *Publications include:* many politicial, social and scientific articles.
Address: Kuvendi Popullor (People's Assembly), Bulevardi Dëshmorët e Kombit 4, Tirana, Albania. *Telephone:* (4) 237418. *Fax:* (4) 227949. *E-mail:* marlind@parlament.al. *Website:* www.parlament.al.

DADONN, David; Israeli diplomatist; m. Karen Dadonn. *Career:* fmr Head, Dept of the Maghreb, Syria and Lebanon, Ministry of Foreign Affairs; fmr Amb. to Morocco; Amb. to Jordan –2003, to Mexico 2003–06; at Ministry of Foreign Affairs 2006–.
Address: Ministry of Foreign Affairs, 9 Yitzhak Rabin Blvd, Kiryat Ben-Gurion, Jerusalem 91035, Israel (office). *Telephone:* 2-5303111 (office). *Fax:* 2-5303367 (office). *E-mail:* feedback@mfa.gov.il (office). *Website:* www.mfa.gov.il (office).

DAERR, Hans-Joachim; German diplomatist; *Ambassador to Japan;* b. 22 Dec. 1943, Frankenstein/Schlesien; m. Alexa Daer; two s. *Education:* Baccalauréat in Paris. *Career:* nat. service in navy 1962–64, law studies in Tübingen, Bonn and Berlin 1964–68, Japanese studies, Tübingen 1969, joined Foreign Service 1970, Rep. to EC, Brussels 1970–71, posted to Consulate Gen., Osaka-Kobe 1973–76, NATO Dept, Foreign Office, Bonn 1976–79, Embassy in Tokyo 1979–83, Planning Staff, Foreign Office 1983–86, Head of Strategic Issues Opertions Staff 1986–87, Perm. Rep., Embassy in Lagos 1988–91, Head of S Africa Dept, Foreign Office 1991–95, Head of Subdivision 20 (NATO, WEU, OSCE, GASP, N America) and Deputy Political Dir 1995–98, Amb. to Pakistan 1998–2001, Rep. of Fed. Govt for Issues on Disarmament and Arms Control, Berlin 2001–02, Amb.-at-Large for Afghanistan 2001–02, Head of Dept for Global Issues, UN, Human Rights and Humanitarian Aid, Foreign Office, Berlin 2003–06, Amb. to Japan 2006–.
Address: Embassy of Germany, 4-5-10, Minami Azabu, Minato-ku, Tokyo, 106-0047, Japan (office). *Telephone:* (3) 5791-7700 (office). *Fax:* (3) 3473-4243 (office). *E-mail:* germtoky@ma.rosenet.ne.jp (office). *Website:* www.tokyo.diplo.de (office).

DAFA, Bader Omar ad-, MA; Qatari UN official and diplomatist; *Executive Secretary, United Nations Economic and Social Commission for Western Asia (ESCWA);* b. 2 Oct. 1950; m. Awatef Mohamed Al-Dafa; one s. two d. *Education:* Kalamazoo Community Coll., Western Michigan Univ.,

School of Advanced Int. Studies, Johns Hopkins Univ., USA. *Career:* diplomatic attaché, Ministry of Foreign Affairs 1976–77, 1981–82; First Sec., Qatar Embassy, Washington, DC 1977–81; Amb. to Spain 1982–88, to Egypt (also Perm. Rep. to Arab League) 1988–93, to France (also accred to Greece and Switzerland) 1993–95, to Russia (also accred to Finland, Latvia, Lithuania and Estonia) 1995–98; Dir of European and American Affairs, Ministry of Foreign Affairs 1998–2000; Amb. to USA and Perm. Observer to OAS 2000–05, non-resident Amb. . to Mexico 2002–07; Exec. Sec. UN Econ. and Social Comm. for Western Asia (ESCWA) 2007–; Ordre nat. du Mérite.
Address: Economic and Social Commission for Western Asia, Riad es-Solh Square, PO Box 11-8575, Beirut, Lebanon (office). *Telephone:* (1) 981301 (office). *Fax:* (1) 981510 (office). *E-mail:* webmaster-escwa@un.org (office). *Website:* www.escwa.org.lb (office); al-dafa.com/bader (office).

DAHABI, Nader al-, MSc, MPA; Jordanian politician; *Prime Minister and Minister of Defence;* b. 1946, Amman; m.; two s. one d. *Education:* Al Hussein Coll., Amman, Hellenic Air Force Acad., Tatoi, Greece, Cranfield Inst. of Tech., UK, Auburn Univ., USA. *Career:* cadet in Royal Jordanian Air Force 1964, served 30 years becoming Asst Commdr for Logistics 1992–94; CEO Royal Jordanian Airlines 1994–2001; Minister of Transport 2001–03; Chief Commr Aqaba Special Econ. Zone Authority 2004–07; Prime Minister and Minister of Defence 2007–; mem. Exec. Cttee Arab Air Carriers Org. (AACO), Chair. 1994–95; Chair. Royal Jordanian Air Falcons 1994–; Dir Royal Jordanian Acad.; mem. Higher Cttee Jerash Festival for Culture and Arts; mem. Higher Council of Tourism; Pres. IATA 1996–97, mem. Bd of Govs 1995–98.
Address: Office of the Prime Minister, POB 80, Amman 11180, Jordan (office). *Telephone:* (6) 4641211 (office). *Fax:* (6) 5695541 (office). *E-mail:* info@pm.gov.jo (office). *Website:* www.pm.gov.jo (office).

DAHL, Birgitta, BA; Swedish politician; b. 20 Sept. 1937, Råda; m. Enn Kokk; one s. two d. *Education:* Univ. of Uppsala. *Career:* teacher, clerical officer, Scandinavian Inst. of African Studies, Uppsala 1960–65; Sr Admin. Officer, Dag Hammarskjöld Foundation 1965–68, Swedish Int. Devt Authority 1965–82; mem. Parl. 1968–2002; mem. Advisory Council of Foreign Affairs; del. to UN Gen. Ass.; mem. Exec. Cttee Social Democratic Party 1975–96; Minister with special responsibility for Energy Issues, Ministry of Energy 1982–86, for the Environment and Energy 1987–90, for the Environment 1990–91; Spokesperson on Social Welfare; Chair. Environment Cttee of Socialist Int. 1986–93, Confed. of Socialist Parties of EC 1990–94, Chair. High Level Advisory Bd on Sustainable Devt to Sec.-Gen. 1996–97; Speaker of Riksdag (Swedish Parl.) 1994–2002; Chair. Bd Swedish Coral Asscn 2002–05, Nat. Museum of Cultural History, Centre for Gender Research, Uppsala Univ.; Pres. UNICEF Sweden World Infections Foundation; Sr Adviser Global Environment Facility 1998–; mem. Panel of Eminent Persons on United Nations-Civil Society; mem. Bd Stockholm Environment Inst., Int. Inst. for Industrial Environment Econs, Lund Univ.; fmr mem. Bd of Dirs Nat. Housing Bd; Gran Condecoración de Honor del Senado (Chile) 2000, Grand Cross Order of the White Rose (Finland) 2002; Cross of Terra Mariana (Estonia) 2002, Das Grosse Goldene Ehrenzeichens am Bande für Verdienste (Austria) 2002, Illis Quorum Meruere Labores (Sweden) 2003, Medal of Merit (Algeria) 2006. *Publications:* contrib. numerous articles and chapters to magazines and books on democracy and human rights, peace and int. cooperation, sexual equality, children's rights, education and science, the environment and sustainable devt.
Address: Idrottsgatan 12, 753 35 Uppsala, Sweden (home). *Telephone:* (18) 211793 (home). *Fax:* (18) 211793 (home). *E-mail:* 34dahl@telia.com.

DAHL, Robert Alan, PhD; American academic and political scientist; *Sterling Professor Emeritus of Political Science, Yale University;* b. 17 Dec. 1915, Inwood, Ia; m. 1st Mary Louise Barlett 1940 (died 1970); three s. one d.; m. 2nd Ann Goodrich Sale 1973. *Education:* Univ. of Washington, Div. of Econ. Research, Nat. Labor Relations Bd and Yale Univ. *Career:* Man. Analyst, US Dept of Agric. 1940; Economist, Office of Production Man., OPACS and War Production Bd 1940–42; US Army 1943–45; with Yale Univ., successively Instructor, Asst Prof., Assoc. Prof. and Sterling Prof. of Political Science 1964–86, Sterling Prof. Emer. of Political Science 1986–, fmr Sr Research Scientist in Sociology; Chair. Dept of Political Science 1957–62; Ford Research Prof. 1957; Lecturer in Political Science, Flacso, Santiago, Chile 1967; Guggenheim Fellow 1950 and 1978; Fellow, Center for Advanced Study in the Behavioral Sciences 1955–56, 1967; Pres. American Political Science Asscn 1967; mem. American Acad. of Arts and Sciences, American Philosophical Soc., NAS; Corresp. mem. British Acad.; fmr Trustee, Center for Advanced Study in the Behavioral Sciences; fmr mem. Educ. Advisory Bd, Guggenheim Foundation; Bronze Star Medal with Cluster, Cavaliere of Repub. of Italy; Hon. LLD (Mich.) 1983, (Alaska) 1987, (Harvard) 1996; Hon. DHumLitt (Georgetown) 1993; Woodrow Wilson Prize 1963, Talcott Parsons Prize 1977 and other prizes.

Publications: Congress and Foreign Policy 1950, Domestic Control of Atomic Energy (with R. Brown) 1951, Politics, Economics and Welfare (with C. E. Lindblom) 1953, A Preface to Democratic Theory 1956, Social Science Research on Business (with Haire and Lazarsfeld) 1959, Who Governs? 1961, Modern Political Analysis 1963, Political Oppositions in Western Democracies 1966, Pluralist Democracy in the United States 1967, After the Revolution 1970, Polyarchy: Participation and Opposition 1971, Regimes and Opposition 1972, Democracy in the United States 1972, Size and Democracy (with E. R. Tufte) 1973, Dilemmas of Pluralist Democracy 1982, A Preface to Economic Democracy 1985, The Control of Nuclear Weapons: Democracy v. Guardianship 1985, Democracy, Liberty and Equality 1986, Democracy and the Critics 1989, Towards Democracy: A Journey 1997, Reflections (1940–1997) 1997, On Democracy 1999, Politica e Virtú 2001: La teoria democratica di nuovo secolo, How Democratic is the American Constitution? 2002, Intervista sul Pluralismo 2002.
Address: 124 Prospect Street, Room 209, Yale University, North Haven, CT 06520 (office); 17 Cooper Road, North Haven, CT 06473, USA (home). *Telephone:* (203) 432-5283 (office); (203) 288-3126 (home). *Fax:* (203) 432-6196 (home). *E-mail:* robert.dahl@yale.edu (office). *Website:* www.yale.edu/polisci/dahl/index.htm (office).

DAI, Bingguo; Chinese politician and diplomatist; b. 1941, Yinjiang Co., Guizhou Prov. *Education:* Foreign Affairs Coll., Sichuan Univ. *Career:* joined CCP 1973; Deputy Div. Chief, later Div. Chief, later Deputy Dir, later Dir Dept of USSR and Eastern European Affairs, Ministry of Foreign Affairs, later Amb. to Hungary, later Asst Minister of Foreign Affairs, Deputy Minister of Foreign Affairs 1994–95; Deputy Head Int. Liaison Dept of CCP Cen. Cttee 1995–97, Head 1997–2003; mem. 15th CCP Cen. Cttee 1997–2002, 16th CCP Cen. Cttee 2002–.
Address: c/o International Liaison Department of Chinese Communist Party Central Committee, Beijing, People's Republic of China.

DAI, Gen. (retd) Tobias Joaquim; Mozambican politician and fmr army officer; *Minister of National Defence;* b. 25 Nov. 1950, Manica City; m.; two c. *Education:* João XXII and Pêro de Anaia Secondary Schools. *Career:* joined Mozambique Armed Forces 1971; instructor and Commdr, Nachingweia 1971–76; Weapons Commdr, Vestrel de Moscovo Mil. Acad., USSR 1976–78; Commdr Mil. Garrison, City of Maputo 1978–80; several sr mil. positions including Vice-Commdt and Head of Mil. House of Pres. of the Repub., Prov. Mil. Commdr in Manica, Head of Directorate of Operations, and Commdr-in-Chief of Armed Forces 1980–95; Sec.-Gen. Ministry of Nat. Defence 1995–2000; Minister of Nat. Defence 2000–; participated in Peace Negotiations 1993–94; elected to House of Reps 1987–94; mem. Frelimo Party; Veteran of the Struggle for Nat. Independence of Mozambique Medal.
Address: Ministry of National Defence, Avda Mártires de Mueda 280, CP 3216, Maputo, Mozambique (office). *Telephone:* 21492081 (office). *Fax:* 21491619 (office).

DAIANU, Daniel, PhD; Romanian economist and politician; *Professor of Economics, Academy of Economic Studies, Bucharest;* b. 30 Aug. 1952, Bucharest. *Education:* Acad. of Econ. Studies, Bucharest, Acad. of Sciences, Bucharest and Harvard Business School, USA. *Career:* Visiting Scholar, Russian Research Center, Harvard Univ. 1990–92; Deputy Minister of Finance Feb.–Aug. 1992; Chief Economist, Nat. Bank of Romania 1992–97; Minister of Finance 1997–98; currently Prof. of Econs, Acad. of Econ. Studies, Bucharest; Visiting Scholar, Woodrow Wilson Center, Washington, DC 1992, IMF, Washington, DC 1993, UN/ECE; Visiting Sr Fellow NATO Defense Coll., Rome 1995; Visiting Prof., Univ. of California, Berkeley 1999, Anderson School of Man., UCLA 1999–2002, Univ. of Bologna 2000–02; Fellow, William Davidson Inst., Univ. of Michigan Business School; Chair. Romanian Econ. Soc.; Pres. European Asscn for Comparative Econ. Studies, OSCE Econ. Forum 2001; Acad. of Sciences Highest Award for Econs 1994. *Publications:* Transformation of Economies as a Real Process – An Insider's Perspective 1998, Economic Vitality and Viability – A Dual Challenge for European Security 1996, Romania—Winners and Losers: The Impact of Reform of Intergovernmental Transfers (research report, co-author) 1999, Balkan Reconstruction (co-ed.) 2001.
Address: Academia de Studii Economice, Piata Romana nr 6, Sector 1, Bucharest 7000 (office); Negro Voda Street, Block C3, Floor 3, Apt 9, Sector 3, Bucharest, Romania. *Telephone:* (21) 2112650 (office); (21) 2300723 (home). *Fax:* (21) 3129549 (office); (21) 2315530 (home). *E-mail:* ddaianu@rnc.ro (office). *Website:* www.ase.ro (office).

DALAI LAMA, The, temporal and spiritual head of Tibet; Fourteenth Incarnation (Tenzin Gyatso); Tibetan; b. 6 July 1935, Taktser, Amdo Prov., NE Tibet. *Career:* born of Tibetan peasant family in Amdo Prov.; enthroned at Lhasa 1940; rights exercised by regency 1934–50; assumed political power 1950; fled to Chumbi in S Tibet after abortive resistance to

Chinese State 1950; negotiated agreement with China 1951; Vice-Chair. Standing Cttee CPPCC, mem. Nat. Cttee 1951–59; Hon. Chair. Chinese Buddhist Asscn 1953–59; Del. to Nat. People's Congress 1954–59; Chair. Preparatory Cttee for the 'Autonomous Region of Tibet' 1955–59; fled Tibet to India after suppression of Tibetan national uprising 1959; Dr of Buddhist Philosophy (Monasteries of Sera, Drepung and Gaden, Lhasa) 1959; Supreme Head of all Buddhist sects in Tibet (Xizang); Presidential Distinguished Prof., Emory Univ., USA 2007–; Hon. Citizen of Paris 2008; Memory Prize 1989, Congressional Human Rights Award 1989, Nobel Peace Prize 1989, Freedom Award (USA) 1991, Presidential Congressional Gold Medal (USA) 2007. *Publications:* My Land and People 1962, The Opening of the Wisdom Eye 1963, The Buddhism of Tibet and the Key to the Middle Way 1975, Kindness, Clarity and Insight 1984, A Human Approach to World Peace 1984, Freedom in Exile (autobiog.) 1990, My Tibet 1990, The Way to Freedom 1995, The Good Heart 1996, Beyond Dogma 1996, Ethics for the New Millennium 1998, Violence and Compassion 1998, Art of Happiness (co-author) 1999, Ancient Wisdom, Modern World 1999, The Path to Tranquility: Daily Wisdom 1999, Transforming the Mind: Eight Verses on Generating Compassion and Transforming Your Life 2000, A Simple Path: Basic Buddhist Teachings by His Holiness the Dalai Lama 2000, The Art of Living: A Guide to Contentment, Joy and Fulfillment 2001, Stages of Meditation: Training the Mind for Wisdom 2001, Compassionate Life 2001, His Holiness the Dalai Lama: In My Own Words 2001, Essence of the Heart Sutra 2002, How to Practice 2002, The Spirit of Peace 2002, How to See Yourself As You Really Are 2007, Comfort, Ease and Enlightenment: Living the Great Perfection 2007.
Address: Thekchen Choeling, McLeod Ganj 176219, Dharamsala, Himachal Pradesh, India.

DALES, Sir Richard Nigel, Kt, KCVO, CMG, MA; British diplomatist; b. 26 Aug. 1942, Woodford, Essex; m. Elizabeth M. Martin 1966; one s. one d. *Education:* Chigwell School, Essex and St Catharine's Coll. Cambridge. *Career:* joined Foreign Office 1964; Third Sec. Yaoundé, Cameroon 1965–67; with FCO, London 1968–70; Second Sec., later First Sec., Copenhagen 1970–73; Asst Pvt. Sec. to Sec. of State for Foreign and Commonwealth Affairs 1974–77; Head of Chancery, Sofia 1977–81; FCO 1981–82; Head of Chancery, Copenhagen 1982–86; Deputy High Commr in Zimbabwe 1986–89; Head of Southern Africa Dept FCO 1989–91; seconded to Civil Service Comm. 1991–92; High Commr in Zimbabwe 1992–95; Dir (Africa and Commonwealth), FCO 1995–98; Amb. to Norway 1998–2002; Chair. Anglo-Norse Soc. 2003–; mem. Bd Norfolk and Norwich Festival 2003–; mem. Council of Univ. of East Anglia 2004–; Vice Chair. International Alert 2005–.
Address: 521 Bunyan Court, Barbican, London, EC2Y 8DH, England.

DALHALYOV, Vasil; Belarusian politician and diplomatist; *Ambassador to Russian Federation;* b. 25 May 1951, Rogatchyov. *Education:* Belarus State Econ. Univ. *Career:* Vice-Pres. State Control Cttee 1992–94; Asst to Prime Minister 1995–97, First Deputy Prime Minister 1998–2000; Chair. Brest Exec. Cttee 2000–04; Deputy Prime Minister 2004–06; Amb. to Russian Fed. 2006–, concurrently Perm. Rep. to Eurasian Econ. Community.
Address: Embassy of Belarus, 101990 Moscow, ul. Maroseika 17/6, Russian Federation (office). *Telephone:* (495) 777-66-44 (office). *Fax:* (495) 777-66-33 (office). *E-mail:* mail@embassybel.ru (office). *Website:* www.embassybel.ru (office).

DALLARA, Charles H., MA, PhD, MALD; American fmr government official and international organization official; *Managing Director, Institute of International Finance;* b. 1948, Spartanburg, NC; m. 1st Carolyn Gault; one s. one d.; m. 2nd Peixin Li. *Education:* Univ. of S Carolina and Fletcher School of Law and Diplomacy. *Career:* int. economist, US Treasury Dept 1976–79; Special Asst to Under-Sec. for Monetary Affairs 1979–80; Guest Scholar Brookings Inst. 1980–81; Special Asst to Asst Sec. for Int. Affairs 1981–82; Alt. Exec. Dir IMF 1982–83; Deputy Asst Sec. for Int. Monetary Affairs, US Treasury Dept 1983–85; Exec. Dir IMF 1984–89; Asst Sec. for Policy Devt and Sr Adviser for Policy 1988–89; Asst Sec. for Internal Affairs 1989–93; Man. Dir JP Morgan 1991–93; Man. Dir Inst. of Int. Finance 1993–.
Address: Institute of International Finance, Inc., 1333 H Street, NW, Suite 800E, Washington, DC 20005-4770 (office); 12196 Goldenchair Court, Oak Hill, VA 20171, USA (home). *Telephone:* (202) 857-3604 (office). *Fax:* (202) 833-1194 (office). *E-mail:* cdallara@iif.com (office). *Website:* www.iif.com (office).

DALLI, Hon. John, FCCA, CPA, CIM; Maltese politician and accountant; *Executive Chairman, John Dalli and Associates;* b. 5 Oct. 1948, Qormi; m. Josette Callus; two d. *Education:* Malta Coll. of Arts, Science and Tech. *Career:* posts in financial admin and gen. man., Malta and Brussels; Man. Consultant; MP, Nationalist Party 1987–; Parl. Sec. for Industry 1987–90;

Minister for Econ. Affairs 1990–92, of Finance 1992–96, 1998–2003, of Finance and Econ. Affairs 2003–04, of Foreign Affairs and Investment Promotion 2004 (resgnd); Shadow Minister and Opposition Spokesman for Finance 1996–98; currently Exec. Chair. John Dalli and Assocs; mem. Inst. of Man., Malta, Nat. Asscn of Accountants, USA.
Address: 1400 Blk 14, Portohaso, St Julians PTH01 (office); 2461 Blk 24, Portohaso, St Julians PTH01, Malta (home). *Telephone:* 377948 (office). *Fax:* 377187 (office). *E-mail:* jd@dbms.com.mt (office). *Website:* www .dbms.com.mt (office); www.johndalli.com (home).

D'ALMEIDA, Damião Vaz; São Tomé and Príncipe politician. *Career:* fmr Pres. Pagué Dist Ass.; Pres. Príncipe regional govt 1995–2002; fmr Minister of Labour, Employment and Solidarity; Prime Minister of São Tomé e Príncipe 2004–05 (resgnd); Vice-Pres. Movimento de Libertação de São Tomé e Príncipe–Partido Social Democrata (MLSTP–PSD).
Address: c/o Office of the Prime Minister, Rua do Município, CP 302, São Tomé, São Tomé e Príncipe (office).

DALRYMPLE, Frederick Rawdon, AO; Australian diplomatist; b. 6 Nov. 1930, Sydney; m. Ross E. Williams 1957; one s. one d. *Education:* Sydney Church of England Grammar School and Univs of Sydney and Oxford. *Career:* Lecturer in Philosophy, Univ. of Sydney 1955–57; joined Dept of External Affairs 1957, served in Bonn, London 1959–64; Alt. Dir Asian Devt Bank, Manila 1967–69; Minister, Djakarta 1969–71; Amb. to Israel 1972–75, to Indonesia 1981–85, to USA 1985–89, to Japan 1989–93; Chair. ASEAN Focus Group Pty Ltd 1994–2001; Visiting Prof., Univ. of Sydney 1994–2002; Hon. Fellow Univ. of Sydney 2003. *Publications:* Looking East and West from Down Under 1992; Continental Drift: Australia's Search for a Regional Identity 2003.
Address: 34 Glenmore Road, Paddington, NSW 2021, Australia (home). *E-mail:* rdalrymple@econ.usyd.edu.au (office); rdalrymp@ozemail.com.au (home). *Website:* www.usyd.edu.au (office); aseanfocus.com (office).

DALTON, Sir Richard John, Kt, KCMG; British former diplomatist and business consultant; *Director-General, British-Libyan Business Council;* b. 10 Oct. 1948; m. Elisabeth Dalton; two s. two d. *Career:* joined FCO 1970, Reporting Officer, UK Mission, New York 1970, Asst Desk Officer, Cen. and Southern Africa Dept, FCO 1971, full-time overseas language training 1971–73, Third, later Second Sec., Chancery, Amman 1973–75, Second, later First Sec., UK Mission, New York 1975–79, Desk Officer, Cen. and Southern Africa Dept, FCO 1979–81, Desk Officer, Personnel Operations Dept, FCO 1981–83, Deputy Head of Mission, Muscat 1983–87, Deputy Head of Southern Africa Dept, FCO 1987–88, on loan to Ministry of Agric., Fisheries and Food as Head of Tropical Foods and External Relations Dept 1988–91, Head of CSCE Unit, FCO 1992–93, Consul-Gen., Jerusalem 1993–97, Dir of Personnel, FCO 1998–99, Amb. to Libya 1999–2002, to Iran 2003–06; Visiting Research Fellow, Chatham House 1991–92; currently Dir-Gen. British-Libyan Business Council.
Address: Rossetti House, Erasmus Street, London, SW1P 4HT, England (office). *Telephone:* (20) 7828-2215 (office). *E-mail:* rjdalton@mac.com (office).

DALY, Brendan; Irish politician; b. 2 Feb. 1940, Cooraclare, Co. Clare; m. Patricia Carmody; two s. one d. *Education:* Kilrush Co. Boys' School. *Career:* mem. Dáil 1973–; Minister of State, Dept of Labour 1980–81; Minister for Fisheries and Forestry March–Dec. 1982, for the Marine 1987–89, for Defence Feb.–Nov. 1991, for Social Welfare 1991–92; Minister of State, Dept of Foreign Affairs 1992–93; elected to Seanad Éireann 1993, re-elected 1997, 2002; mem. Northern Ireland Peace Forum 1994; mem. Irish Parl. Foreign Affairs Cttee 1993–; mem. Fianna Fáil.
Address: Cooraclare, Kilrush, Co. Clare, Republic of Ireland (home). *Telephone:* (65) 9059040 (home). *Fax:* (65) 9059218 (home). *E-mail:* brendan.daly@oireachtas.irlgov.ie (office).

DAMUŠIS, Gintė Bernadeta; Lithuanian diplomatist; *Ambassador to Canada; Career:* fmr freelance journalist Radio Free Europe and Vatican Radio; Dir Lithuanian Information Center, New York 1979–91; Visiting Researcher, Keston Coll., UK 1981; joined Lithuanian Foreign Service 1992; Counsellor, Perm. Mission to UN, New York 1992–96; Head of Del. to OSCE and Perm. Rep. to Conventional Test Ban Treaty Org., Vienna 1996–99; Amb. to Austria 1998–2000 (also accred to Slovenia and Slovakia 1999–2001), to Croatia 2000–01; Head of Mission to NATO, Brussels 2001–03, Perm. Rep. to NATO 2003–05; fmr mem. Advisory Bd US–Baltic Foundation, Washington, DC, Lithuanian Catholic Religious Aid, New York; Founding mem. Citizens Alliance (Pilieciu santalka) 2006; Amb. to Canada 2008–; Commdr Cross of the Order of Merit of Lithuania 2003. *Publications:* articles on Lithuanian foreign policy and diplomatic relations. *Address:* Embassy of Lithuania, 130 Albert St, Suite 204, Ottawa, ON K1P 5G4, Canada (office). *Telephone:* (613) 567-5458 (office). *Fax:* (613) 567-5315 (office). *E-mail:* litemb@storm.ca (office). *Website:* www .lithuanianembassy.ca (office).

DAN, Zeng; Chinese politician, journalist and writer; *Vice-General Manager, Chinese Centre for Tibet Research;* b. 1946, Tibet. *Education:* Fudan Univ., Shanghai. *Career:* began publishing career 1980; reporter, Tibet Daily, later Assoc. Chief Ed.; Dir Bureau of Culture, Tibet Autonomous Region, Vice-Sec. CCP Tibet Autonomous Region Cttee; Vice-Chair. China Fed. of Literary and Arts Circles, Vice-Chair. Chinese Writers' Asscn; Alt. mem. 12th CCP Cen. Cttee. 1982–87, 13th CCP Cen. Cttee. 1987–92, 14th CCP Cen. Cttee. 1992–97, 15th CCP Cen. Cttee. 1997–2002; currently Vice-Gen. Man. Chinese Centre for Tibet Research; Tibet Autonomous Region Newspaper of the Year Award 1979, Tibet Autonomous Region Best Short Story Award 1980. *Publications include:* Report from the Roof of the World, The Blessing of the Deity.
Address: c/o Chinese Communist Party Tibetan Autonomous Region Committee, Lhasa, Tibet, People's Republic of China (office).

DANELIUS, Hans Carl Yngve; Swedish judge and diplomatist; b. 2 April 1934, Stockholm; m. Hannah Schadee 1961; three s. one d. *Education:* Dept of Legal Studies, Stockholm Univ. *Career:* law practice in Swedish courts 1957–64; mem. Secr., European Comm. of Human Rights, Strasbourg 1964–67, mem. European Comm. of Human Rights 1983–99; Asst Judge, Svea Court of Appeal 1967–68; Adviser, Ministry of Justice 1968–71; Deputy Head, Legal Dept, Ministry for Foreign Affairs 1971–75, Head 1975–84, rank of Amb. 1977–84; Amb. to Netherlands 1984–88; Judge, Supreme Court of Sweden 1988–2001; Pres. Council on Legislation 2001–03; Arbitrator, ICSID 1999–2005; mem. Perm. Court of Arbitration at The Hague 1982–; mem. Court of Conciliation and Arbitration, OSCE 1995–2007; mem. Constitutional Court of Bosnia and Herzegovina 1996–2002; Chief Ed. Svensk Juristtidning (Swedish Law Journal) 1973–84; Swedish and foreign decorations; Dr hc (Stockholm) 1988. *Publications:* The United Nations Convention Against Torture 1988, Mänskliga Rättigheter (Human Rights) (5th edn) 1993, Mänskliga Rättigheter i Europeisk Praxis (Human Rights in European Practice) (3rd edn) 2007; numerous articles in Swedish and foreign journals. *Address:* Roslinvägen 33, 16851 Bromma, Sweden (home). *Telephone:* (8) 37-34-91 (home). *Fax:* (8) 37-34-91 (home). *E-mail:* hans.danelius@telia .com (home).

DANIEL, Sir John Sagar, Kt, MA, MAEd.Tech, ATh, DèsSc; British/Canadian academic and university administrator; *President and CEO, Commonwealth of Learning;* b. 31 May 1942, Banstead, Surrey, UK; m. Kristin Anne Swanson 1966; one s. two d. *Education:* Christ's Hosp., Sussex, St Edmund Hall, Oxford, Univ. of Paris, Concordia Univ., Montréal. *Career:* Assoc. Prof. Ecole Polytechnique, Univ. de Montréal 1969–73; Dir des Etudes, Télé-Univ., Univ. de Québec 1973–77; Vice-Pres. Athabasca Univ., Alberta 1977–80; Academic Vice-Rector Concordia Univ. 1980–84; Pres. Laurentian Univ., Sudbury 1984–90; Vice-Chancellor Open Univ., UK 1990–2001; Pres. Open Univ., USA 1999–2001; Asst Dir-Gen. for Educ., UNESCO 2001–04; Pres. and CEO Commonwealth of Learning 2004–; mem. Council of Foundation, Int. Baccalaureate 1992– (Vice-Pres. 1996–99), British North American Cttee 1995–; mem. Council Open Univ., Hong Kong 1996–, CBI 1996–; mem. Bd Canadian Council on Learning 2005–; Trustee Carnegie Foundation for the Advancement of Teaching 1993–; Forum Fellow, World Econ. Forum, Switzerland 1998; Fellow, Open Univ. (UK); Senior Fellow, European Distance Educ. Network 2007; Hon. Fellow, St Edmund Hall, Oxford; Officier, Ordre des Palmes Académiques; Hon. DLitt (Deakin Univ., Australia), (Univ. of Lincs. and Humberside) 1996, (Indira Gandhi Nat. Open, India) 2003, (Thompson Rivers, Canada) 2005, (Netaji Subhas Open, India) 2005, (Kota Open, India), (McGill Univ., Canada), Hon. DSc (Coll. Mil. Royal, Saint-Jean) 1988, (Open Univ. of Sri Lanka) 1994, (Univ. de Paris VI) 2001 (Univ. of Winneba, Ghana) 2006, Hon. D.Ed. (CNAA) 1992, Hon. LLD (Waterloo, Canada) 1993, (Univ. of Wales) 2002, (Laurentian Univ. Canada) 2006, Hon. DUniv (Univs of Athabasca, Portugal, Humberside, Anadolu Univ., Turkey, Sukhothai Thammathirat Open Univ., Thailand, Télé-université, Université du Québec, Canada, Univ. of Derby, Open Univ., Hong Kong, New Bulgarian Univ.); Hon. D.Hum.Lit. (Thomas Edison State Coll., USA, Richmond, American Int. Univ. in London); Individual Award of Excellence, Commonwealth of Learning 1995, Morris T. Keeton Award, Council for Adult and Experiential Learning (USA) 1999; Queen's Jubilee Medal (Canada). *Publications:* over 200 articles and books including Learning at a Distance: A World Perspective 1982, Developing Distance Education (jtly) 1988, Mega-universities and Knowledge Media: Technology Strategies for Higher Education 1996.
Address: Commonwealth of Learning, 1055 West Hastings #1200, Vancouver, BC V6E 3E9, Canada (office). *Telephone:* (604) 775-8200 (office). *Fax:* (604) 775-8210 (office). *E-mail:* jdaniel@col.org (office). *Website:* www.col.org (office).

DANILOV-DANILYAN, Victor Ivanovich, DEcon; Russian politician; *Director, Institute of Aquatic Studies, Russian Academy of Sciences;* b. 9 May 1938, Moscow; m.; three s. *Education:* Moscow State Univ. *Career:* jr researcher, engineer, sr engineer, Computation Cen., Moscow State Univ. 1960–64; researcher, leading engineer, Head of lab., Cen. Inst. of Math. and Econs, USSR Acad. of Sciences 1964–76; Head of Lab., Prof., All-Union Research Inst. of System Studies, USSR Acad. of Sciences 1976–80; Head of lab., Chair. Acad. of Nat. Econ., USSR Council of Ministers 1980–91; Deputy Minister of Nature Man. and Environmental Control of USSR Aug.–Nov. 1991, Minister of Ecology and Natural Resources, Russian Fed. 1991–92, of Environmental Control and Natural Resources 1992–96; Chair. State Cttee for Environmental Control 1996–; Pres.-Rector Int. Industrial Ecology and Political Univ. (MNEPU) 1991–; mem. State Duma (parl.) 1993–96; founder and author, ecological programme of Kedr (Cedar) Movt 1994; Dir and corresponding mem., Inst. of Aquatic Studies, Russian Acad. of Sciences 2003–; mem. Russian Acad. of Natural Sciences. *Address:* Institute of Aquatic Studies, Russian Academy of Sciences, 3 Gubkina Street, 119333 Moscow (office); MNEPU, Krasnokazarmennaya str. 14, 111250 Moscow, Russia (office). *Telephone:* (499) 135-54-56 (office); (495) 273-55-48 (office). *Fax:* (499) 135- 54-15 (office). *E-mail:* vidd@aqua .laser.ru (office). *Website:* www.iwp.ru (office).

DANNATT, Gen. Sir Richard, Kt, KCB, CBE, MC; British army officer; *Chief of the General Staff;* b. 23 Dec. 1950. *Education:* Felsted School, St Lawrence Coll. *Career:* commissioned into The Green Howards 1971; has served with 1st Battalioin in NI, Cyprus and Germany, Commdr in Airmobile role 1989–91; Commdr 4th Armoured Brigade in Germany and Bosnia 1994–96; Commdr 3rd (UK) Div. and Commdr British Forces in Kosovo 1999, Deputy Commdr, Operations of the Stabilisation Force (SFOR) 2000; Asst Chief of Gen. Staff, Ministry of Defence 2001–02; Commdr NATO Allied Rapid Reaction Corps 2002–05; C-in-C Land Command 2005–06; Chief of the Gen. Staff 2006–; Pres. Army Rifle Asscn, Army Rugby Union, Army Winter Sports Asscn, Soldiers' and Airmen's Scripture Readers Asscn; Vice-Pres. Armed Forces Christian Union. *Address:* Office of the Chief of the General Staff, Ministry of Defence, Main Building, Whitehall, London, SW1A 2HB, England (office). *Telephone:* (20) 7218-9000 (office). *Fax:* (20) 7218-2340 (office). *E-mail:* webmaster@ dgics.mod.uk (office). *Website:* www.mod.uk (office).

DANYLYSHYN, Bohdan Myhaylovich, DEcon; Ukrainian economist, academic and government official; *Minister of the Economy;* b. 6 June 1965, Tserkivna, Dolyn dist. *Education:* Ternopil State Pedagogical Inst. *Career:* Prof. of Econs 2003–; fmr Head, Council on Productive Forces Research, Nat. Acad. of Sciences of Ukraine; Minister of the Economy 2007–; Corresp. mem. Nat. Acad. of Sciences of Ukraine 2004–; State Prize of Ukraine in of science and technology. *Publications include:* more than 150 scientific papers on regional policy, economics and exploration of nature resources. *Address:* Ministry of the Economy, 01008 Kiev, vul. M. Hrushevskoho 12/2, Ukraine (office). *Telephone:* (44) 253-93-94 (office). *Fax:* (44) 226-31-81 (office). *E-mail:* meconomy@me.gov.ua (office). *Website:* www.me.gov.ua (office).

DAOU, Omar; Malian diplomatist; *Permanent Representative, United Nations;* b. 13 May 1955; m.; three c. *Education:* Univ. of Beijing, Cairo Inst. of Diplomatic Studies, UNITAR. *Career:* Head, Africa-OAU Desk, Ministry of Foreign Affairs 1980–1986, Head, Africa-OAU Div. 1986–89; Counsellor, Embassy in Cairo 1989–95, also acting Charge d'Affaires for Liaison Office in Addis Ababa; served in Office of OAU Sec.-Gen. 1996–98, OAU Observer for the implementation of the UN project for Western Sahara in Laayoune 1998–2001; Head, Int. Orgs Dept, Ministry of Foreign Affairs 2001–03, Deputy Dir of Political Affairs, 2003–04, Dir of Political Affairs 2004–08; Perm. Rep. to UN, New York 2008–; Chevalier de l'Ordre national du Mali 2006; UN Disarmament Scholarship 1987, Friendship Citizen of Nagasaki, Japan 1987. *Address:* Permanent Mission of Mali to the United Nations, 111 East 69th Street, New York, NY 10021, USA (office). *Telephone:* (212) 737-4150 (office). *Fax:* (212) 472-3778 (office). *E-mail:* malionu@aol.com (office).

DAOUDI, Riad Rashad ad-, PhD; Syrian lawyer, professor of law and international arbitrator; *Registrar, Organization of Arab Petroleum Exporting Countries;* b. 22 July 1942, Damascus; m. Viviane Collin 1978; two s. one d. *Education:* Institut des Hautes Etudes Internationales, Paris. *Career:* Prof. of Int. Law, Damascus Law School 1978–91; Asst Dean for Academic Affairs, Faculty of Law, Univ. of Damascus 1980–82; lawyer, mem. Syrian Bar 1982–; Registrar, Judicial Tribunal OAPEC 1983–, now lawyer, legal adviser, Registrar Judicial Tribunal OAPEC; Legal Adviser to Ministry of Foreign Affairs 1991–; mem. UN Int. Law Comm. 2002–(07); Lauréat, best doctoral thesis, Univ. of Paris 1977–78. *Publications:* Parliamentary Immunities: Comparative Study in Arab Constitutions (in Arabic) 1982, Peace Negotiations – Treaty of Versailles (textbook for law students, in Arabic) 1983, Arab Commission for Human Rights, An Encyclopedia of Public International Law (in English) 1985; articles and contribs to books on int. affairs and int. law. *Address:* The Judicial Tribunal of the OAPEC, PO Box 20501, Safat 13066, Kuwait (office); Dam Zoukak Al Sakhar Salim Al Sharah Street, Hadjar Building, 3rd Floor, Syria (home). *Telephone:* 4844500 (office); (11) 6622266 (home). *Fax:* 4815747 (office); (11) 3319229 (home). *E-mail:* oapec@qualitynet.net (office). *Website:* www.oapecorg.org (office).

DAPKIUNAS, Andrei, PhD; Belarusian diplomatist; *Permanent Representative, United Nations;* b. 11 April 1963, Minsk; m.; one s. one d. *Education:* Minsk State Inst. for Foreign Languages, Belarusian State Univ., London School of Econs. *Career:* Lecturer, Interpretation Dept, Minsk State Inst. for Foreign Languages 1985–88; Second Sec., Chernobyl Int. Cooperation Dept, Ministry of Foreign Affairs 1992; Second Sec., Perm. Mission to UN, New York 1992–94; Asst to Minister 1994; Head, Office for USA and Canada 1995–97, Dir Americas Dept 1997–2004, Deputy Head, Recruitment and Postings Comm., Ministry of Foreign Affairs 2001–04; Perm. Rep. to UN, New York 2004–; mem. Personnel Assessment Comm. 2002–04, Bd of Ministry of Foreign Affairs 2002–05; Pres. Exec. Bd UNICEF 2006; Vice-Pres. UN Econ. and Social Council 2008. *Address:* Permanent Mission of Belarus to the United Nations, 136 East 67th Street, 4th Floor, New York, NY 10065, USA (office). *Telephone:* (212) 535-3420 (office). *Fax:* (212) 734-4810 (office). *E-mail:* belarus@un .int (office). *Website:* www.un.int/belarus (office).

DAR, Muhammad Ishaq, BCom; Pakistani economist and politician; *Minister of Finance and Minister for Economic Affairs and Statistics;* *Education:* Hailey Coll. of Commerce, Univ. of Punjab, Lahore. *Career:* Minister of Commerce 1997–99, of Finance 1998–99; Chair. Bd of Govs Islamic Devt Bank 1998–99; Senator (Pakistan Muslim League—Nawaz (PML—N)) 2006–, also PML—N Parl. Leader; Minister of Finance and Minister for Econ. Affairs and Statistics 2008–; President, Int. Affairs, PML—N; fmr Pres. Lahore Chamber of Commerce and Industry; fmr Dir IMF, Asian Devt Bank, Islamic Devt Bank.; Fellow, Inst. of Chartered Accountants in England and Wales, Inst. of Chartered Accountants of Pakistan, Inst. of Public Finance Accountants of Pakistan. *Address:* Ministry of Finance, Block Q, Pakistan Secretariat, Islamabad (office); 7-H, Gulberg-III, Lahore, Pakistan. *Telephone:* (51) 9201941 (office); (42) 5881594 (home). *Fax:* (51) 9202640 (office). *E-mail:* webmaster@finance.gov.pk (office); midar50@hotmail.com. *Website:* www.finance.gov.pk (office).

DARABOS, Norbert, MA; Austrian politician; *Minister of Defence;* b. 31 May 1964, Vienna; m.; one s. one d. *Education:* Univ. of Vienna. *Career:* Chief Exec. Dr.-Karl-Renner-Inst., Burgenland 1988–91; mem. Municipal Council of Nikitsch/Burgenland 1987–2003; Press Speaker for Gov. of Prov. of Burgenland Karl Stix 1991–98; mem. Diet of Burgenland 1999–2004, Pres. SPÖ Club 2000–03; Leader of Burgenland Prov. Social-Democratic Party of Austria—SPÖ 1998–2003, Sec.-Gen. Social Democratic Party of Austria 2003–; mem. Austrian Parl. 2004–; Minister of Defence 2007–; Supreme Commdr, Austrian Armed Forces 2007–. *Address:* Ministry of Defence, Roßauer Lände 1, Vienna 1090, Austria (office). *Telephone:* (1) 5200-21160 (office). *Fax:* (1) 520-17111 (office). *E-mail:* norbert.darabos@bmlv.gv.at (office); buergerservice@bmlv.gv.at (office). *Website:* www.bmlv.gv.at (office).

DARAJA, Andrew Mhando; Tanzanian diplomatist. *Career:* various posts serving in Ministry of Foreign Affairs, Perm. Mission to UN, New York, Amb. with Special Duties 1991–95, Amb. to Germany (also accred to Austria, Poland, Switzerland and the Holy See) 1995–2002, to USA (also accred to Brazil, Mexico and Venezuela) 2002–07; Personal Asst to Pres. 1991–94, Sec. to Pres. 1994–95. *Address:* Ministry of Foreign Affairs and International Co-operation, Kivukoni Front, PO Box 9000, postcode Dar es Salaam, Tanzania (office). *Telephone:* (22) 2111906 (office). *Fax:* (22) 2116600 (office). *E-mail:* nje@ foreign.go.tz (office). *Website:* www.mfaic.go.tz (office).

DARBINYAN, Armen Razmikovich, CandEcon; Armenian politician and university rector; *Rector and President, Russian-Armenian State University;* b. 23 Jan. 1965, Gyumri, Armenia; m.; one d. *Education:* Moscow State Univ. *Career:* Lecturer, Moscow State Univ. 1986–89; Sr Expert, Head of Dept, Perm. Mission of Armenia to Russian Fed., Plenipotentiary Rep., Intergovt Comm. on Debts of Vnesheconombank 1989–92; Dir-Gen. Armenian Foreign Trade Co. Armenintorg 1992–94; First Deputy Chair. Cen. Bank of Armenia 1994–97; Minister of Finance 1997, of Finance and Econs 1997–98; Prime Minister of Armenia 1998–99; Minister of Nat. Economy 1999–2000; Chair. Fund for Devt, Yerevan 2000–; Chair. Bd Trustees, Int. Center for Human Devt 2000–; Rector and Pres., Russian-

Armenian State Univ. 2001–; mem. Russian Acad. of Natural Sciences; Commdr World Order of Science, Education and Culture 2002; Int. Socrates Award 2006. *Publications:* over 40 publs including Role of the State in Countries with Transition Economies, Economic Development: Prospects and Role of the Diaspora, From Stability to Economic Growth. *Address:* 19 str. Sayat Nova, 375001 Yerevan, Armenia. *Telephone:* (10) 28-97-00 (office). *Fax:* (10) 22-14-63 (office). *E-mail:* adarbinian@ichd.org (office). *Website:* www.ichd.org (office).

DARDARI, Abdullah ad-, DEcon; Syrian politician and fmr journalist; *Deputy Prime Minister, responsible for Economic Affairs;* b. Damascus. *Career:* fmr journalist; fmr Chair. State Planning Comm.; Deputy Prime Minister, responsible for Econ. Affairs 2005–.
Address: State Planning Commission, Ibn Alnafees, Rukin Al Deen, Damascus, Syria (office). *Telephone:* (11) 5161015 (office). *Fax:* (11) 5161011 (office). *E-mail:* info@planning.gov.sy (office). *Website:* www.planning.gov.sy (office).

DAREMBLUM, Jaime, MA, PhD; Costa Rican diplomatist; *Director, Center for Latin American Studies and Senior Fellow, Hudson Institute;* b. 11 Oct. 1940, San Jose; m.; two c. *Education:* Univ. of Costa Rica, Fletcher School of Law and Diplomacy, USA. *Career:* economist, IMF, Washington, DC 1965–68; Sr Partner, Daremblum Asociados Abogados; Prof. of Int. Politics and Econs, Univ. of Costa Rica 1971–90, Autonomous Univ. of Cen. America 1990–94; Prof. and Sr Research Fellow, Center for Political and Admin. Research, Tulane Univ. 1975–; Pres. Jewish Community of Costa Rica 1986–88; Amb. to USA 1998–2004; Dir Center for Latin American Studies and Sr Fellow, Hudson Inst., Washington, DC 2004–; Guest Speaker at White House, Washington, DC, French Nat. Ass., Paris, France, Heritage Foundation, several univs, and other forums in USA, Europe and Latin America; Fulbright–Hayes Fellow 1963–64, William Clayton Fellow 1964–65, Fletcher School Fellow 1968–69; Dr hc (Univ. of Costa Rica) 1963. *Publications include:* several books and numerous articles for The Wall Street Journal.
Address: Hudson Institute, Inc., 1015 15th Street, NW, 6th Floor, Washington, DC 20005, USA (office). *Telephone:* (202) 974-2400 (office). *Fax:* (202) 974-2410 (office). *E-mail:* jaime@hudson.org (office). *Website:* www.hudson.org (office).

DAROUKI, Saleh Omar ad-; Libyan diplomatist; m. Soheila Al-Darouki. *Career:* fmr Amb. to USA, currently Amb. to Egypt.
Address: Embassy of Libya, 7 Sharia as-Saleh Ayoub, Zamalek, Cairo, Egypt (office). *Telephone:* (2) 3401864 (office).

DARROCH, Kim, BSc; British diplomatist; *Permanent Representative, European Union;* b. 30 April 1954, South Stanley, Co. Durham; m.; one s. one d. *Education:* Univ. of Durham. *Career:* joined FCO 1976, served in Protocol Dept, Planning Staff and News Dept 1976–80, Desk Officer Channel Tunnel Project and Law of the Sea, Maritime, Aviation and Environment Dept 1985–86, Pvt. Sec. to Minister of State dealing with Middle East, Arms Control, Eastern Europe 1987–89, Asst then Deputy Head of EU Dept 1993–95, Head of Eastern Adriatic Dept 1995–97, Head of News Dept 1998, Dir EU Affairs 2000, Dir-Gen. EU Affairs 2003; EU Adviser to Prime Minister and Head of Cabinet Office European Secr. 2004; overseas postings include Third, then Second, then First Sec., Embassy in Tokyo 1980–84, First Sec., Embassy in Rome 1989–92, Counsellor, Perm. Mission to EU, Brussels 1997–98, Perm. Rep. to EU 2007–.
Address: Permanent Representation of the UK to the European Union, 10 Avenue d'Auderghem, 1040 Brussels, Belgium (office). *Telephone:* (2) 287-82-11 (office). *Fax:* (2) 287-83-98 (office). *E-mail:* debbie.chilcott@fco.gov.uk (office). *Website:* www.ukrep.be (office).

DAS NEVES CEITA BAPTISTA DE SOUSA, Maria; São Tomé and Príncipe politician and economist; b. 1958; two c. *Education:* Univ. of the East, Santiago de Cuba, Cuba. *Career:* fmr economist World Bank and UNICEF; mem. Movimento Democrático das Forças para a Mudança–Partido de Convergência Democrática (Democratic Movement of Forces for Change–Party for Democratic Convergence); Minister of Trade, Industry and Tourism and Minister of the Economy –2002; Prime Minister of São Tomé e Príncipe (first woman premier in W Africa) 2002–04.
Address: c/o Office of the Prime Minister, Rua do Municipío, CP 302, São Tomé, São Tomé e Príncipe (office).

DASGUPTA, Sir Partha Sarathi, Kt, PhD, FBA; Indian/British professor of economics and philosophy; *Frank Ramsey Professor of Economics, University of Cambridge;* b. 17 Nov. 1942, Dacca; m. Carol M. Meade 1968; one s. two d. *Education:* Univs of Delhi and Cambridge. *Career:* Lecturer in Econs, LSE 1971–75, Reader 1975–78, Prof. of Econs 1978–85; Prof. of Econs, Univ. of Cambridge and Fellow St John's Coll. Cambridge

1985– (Frank Ramsey Prof. of Econs 1994–); Prof. of Econs and Prof. of Philosophy and Dir of Program on Ethics in Society, Stanford Univ., Calif., USA 1989–92; Chair. Beijer Int. Inst. of Ecological Econs, Stockholm; Pres. European Econ. Asscn 1999, Royal Econ. Soc. 1998–2001; mem. Pontifical Acad. of Social Science; Foreign mem. Royal Swedish Acad. of Sciences, American Philosophical Soc. 2005; Foreign Assoc. NAS; Fellow, Third World Acad. of Sciences, Econometric Soc.; Hon. mem. American Econ. Asscn; Foreign Hon. mem. American Acad. of Arts and Sciences; Hon. Fellow LSE; Dr hc (Wageningen Univ.) 2000, (Catholic Univ. of Louvain) 2007; Volvo Environment Prize 2002, John Kenneth Galbraith Award, American Agricultural Econs Asscn 2007. *Publications:* An Inquiry into Well-Being and Destitution 1993, Human Well-Being and the Natural Environment 2001, Economics: A Very Short Introduction 2007; books and articles on econs of environmental and natural resources, technological change, normative population theory, political philosophy, devt planning and the political economy of destitution.
Address: Faculty of Economics and Politics, Sidgwick Avenue, Cambridge, CB3 9DD (office); 1 Dean Drive, Holbrook Road, Cambridge, England. *Telephone:* (1223) 212179 (office). *Website:* www.econ.cam.ac.uk/faculty/dasgupta (office).

DAUBENFELD, Lt-Col. Mario; Luxembourg army officer; *Military Representative, NATO;* b. 16 Jan. 1958; m. Georgette Freimann; one d. *Education:* Royal Mil. Acad., Belgium, Montpellier Infantry School and Compiègne Ecole d'Etat-major, France. *Career:* served at Mil. Training Centre, Diekirch 1984–96, held positions successively as Infantry Platoon Leader, Co. Commdr, Personnel Officer, Chief of Logistics; Commdr 1st Luxembourg UNPROFOR contingent in Fmr Yugoslavia 1992–97; Staff mem. EC Monitoring Mission (ECMM), Sarajevo 1997–98; Nat. Mil. Rep. to SHAPE, Deputy Mil. Rep. to NATO Mil. Cttee and Mil. Adviser to NATO Perm. Rep., Brussels 1998–2002; Mil. Rep. to NATO 2002–; Cavalheiro da Ordem do Infante Dom Henrique (Portugal); UN Medal for Participation in UNPORFOR Mission, EU Medal for Participation in ECMM Mission in Bosnia.
Address: NATO Headquarters, Blvd Leopold III, 1110 Brussels, Belgium (office); Ministry of Foreign Affairs, Trade, Cooperation, Humanitarian Action and Defence, 5 rue Notre Dame, 2240 Luxembourg, Luxembourg (office). *Telephone:* 478-23-00 (home). *Fax:* 22-31-44 (office). *E-mail:* natodoc@hq.nato.int (office); officielle.boite@mae.etat.lu (office). *Website:* www.nato.int (office); www.mae.lu (office).

DAUDA, Joseph B., LLB; Sierra Leonean lawyer and politician. *Career:* began career as teacher; pvt. legal practice 1972–86, 1992–99; active in politics from 1986 holding various govt positions including Deputy Attorney-Gen., Minister of Trade and Industry –1992, Second Vice-Pres. 1991–92, Minister of Rural Devt and Local Govt 1999–2002, Minister of Finance 2002–05; Gov. for Sierra Leone, IBRD, IDA, IFC.
Address: c/o Ministry of Finance, Secretariat Building, George Street, Freetown, Sierra Leone (office).

DAUKŠYS, Kęstutis; Lithuanian politician; *Minister of the Economy;* b. 31 Jan. 1960, Alytus. *Education:* Univ. of Vilnius and G. Plechanov Russian Acad. of Econs, Moscow. *Career:* Asst, Political Economy Dept, Univ. of Vilnius 1983–85; Deputy Head of Planning Div., Furniture Design Construction Bureau 1985–87, Specialist of Foreign Trade Div. 1989–90; mil. service 1987–89; Dir UAB 'Balticum' 1990–95, UAB 'Balticum grupė' 1995–98, 2004; Dir Gen. AB 'Kilimai' 1998–2003, Chair. 1999–2004; mem. Darbo Partija (Lithuanian Labour Party—LLP); mem. Seimas (Parl.) 2004–; Minister of the Economy 2005–.
Address: Ministry of the Economy, Gedimino pr. 38/2, 01104 Vilnius, Lithuania (office). *Telephone:* (5) 262-2416 (office). *Fax:* (5) 262-3974 (office). *E-mail:* kanc@ukmin.lt (office). *Website:* www.ukmin.lt (office).

DAUNT, Sir Timothy Lewis Achilles, KCMG; British diplomatist; *Chairman, Anglo-Turkish Society;* b. 11 Oct. 1935; m. Patricia Susan Knight 1962; one s. two d. *Education:* Sherborne School, St Catharine's Coll., Cambridge. *Career:* mil. service with King's Royal Irish Hussars 1954–56; entered diplomatic service 1959; Ankara 1960; Foreign Office 1964; Nicosia 1967; Pvt. Sec. to Perm. Under-Sec. of State, FCO 1970; with Bank of England 1972; mem. UK Mission, New York 1973; Counsellor OECD, Paris 1975; Head of S European Dept, FCO 1978–81; Assoc. Centre d'études et de recherches internationales, Paris 1982; Minister and Deputy Perm. Rep. to NATO, Brussels 1982–85; Asst Under-Sec. of State (Defence), FCO 1985–86; Amb. to Turkey 1986–92; Deputy Under-Sec. of State (Defence), FCO 1992–95; Lt-Gov. Isle of Man 1995–2000; Chair. British Inst. of Archaeology, Ankara 1995–2006, Anglo-Turkish Soc. 2001–, The Ottoman Fund Ltd 2005–.
Address: 20 Ripplevale Grove, London, N1 1HU, England (home). *Telephone:* (20) 7697-8177. *E-mail:* daunt@ripplevale.fsnet.co.uk.

DAUTH, John, LVO; Australian diplomatist; *High Commissioner to New Zealand;* b. 9 April 1947, Brisbane, Queensland. *Education:* Univ. of Sydney. *Career:* joined Dept of External Affairs 1969, External Affairs Officer, Foreign Affairs Officer, Lagos, First Sec. and Deputy Head of Mission, Islamabad 1977; Asst Press Sec. to Queen Elizabeth II, then Press Sec. to Prince of Wales 1977–80; fmr Chargé d'affaires, Embassy in Tehran; Consul-Gen. in Noumea 1986–87; fmr Head of Commonwealth and Multilateral Org. Section, Dept of Foreign Affairs, Asst Sec., Public Affairs Br. 1987–89, Sr Private Sec. to Foreign Minister Gareth Evans, First Asst Sec. Int. Security Div. –1993, First Asst Sec., S and SE Asia Div. 1996–98, Deputy Sec. 1998–2001; High Commr to Malaysia 1993–96; Amb. and Perm. Rep. to UN, New York 2001–06; High Commr to New Zealand 2006–.
Address: Australian High Commission, Wellington, New Zealand (office). *Telephone:* (4) 473-6411 (office). *Fax:* (4) 498-7135 (office). *E-mail:* john .dauth@dfat.gov.au (office). *Website:* www.australia.org.nz (office).

DAVAASAMBUU, Dalrain; Mongolian diplomatist; m. Pagma Davasambuu. *Career:* Amb. to UK 2001–08.
Address: Ministry of Foreign Affairs, Enkh Taivny Örgön Chölöö 7A, Sükhbaatar District, Ulan Bator, Mongolia (office). *Telephone:* (11) 262788 (office). *Fax:* (11) 322127 (office). *E-mail:* mongmer@magicnet.mn (office). *Website:* www.mongolia-foreign-policy.net (office).

DAVID, Adelino Castelo; São Tomé and Príncipe politician; *Minister of Planning and Finance; Career:* Gov. Banco Central de São Tomé e Príncipe 1992–94; Minister of Planning and Finance 1999–2001, 2004–.
Address: Ministry of Planning and Finance, Largo Alfândega, CP 168, São Tomé, São Tomé e Príncipe (office). *Telephone:* 224173 (office). *Fax:* 222683 (office). *E-mail:* mpfc@cstome.net (office).

DAVID, Peter; Grenadian/Canadian politician; *Minister of Foreign Affairs; Career:* mem. House of Reps for St George 2003–; Gen. Sec., Nat. Democratic Congress Party; Minister of Foreign Affairs 2008–.
Address: Ministry of Foreign Affairs, Ministerial Complex, 4th Floor, Botanical Gardens, St St George's, Grenada (office). *Telephone:* 440-2640 (office). *Fax:* 440-4184 (office). *E-mail:* foreignaffairs@gov.gd (office).

DAVID, Ruth, MS, PhD; American research institute executive, intelligence officer and engineer; *President and CEO, Analytic Services Inc. (ANSER); Education:* Wichita State Univ., Stanford Univ. *Career:* several sr positions including Dir of Advanced Information Tech., Sandia Nat. Labs 1975–1991, Dir of Devt Testing Center 1991–94; Tech. Adviser to Dir of Cen. Intelligence, CIA 1994–95; Deputy Dir for Science and Tech., CIA 1995–98, rep. to numerous bodies including Nat. Science and Tech. Council and Cttee on Nat. Security; Pres. and CEO Analytic Services Inc. (ANSER) 1998–, est. ANSER Homeland Defence Strategic Thrust 1999, ANSER Inst. for Homeland Security 2001; fmr Adjunct Prof., Univ. of New Mexico; mem. Pres.'s Homeland Security Advisory Council, Nat. Acad. of Eng. (NAE), Corpn for Charles Stark Draper Lab. Inc.; mem. Advisory Bd Nat. Security Agency, Nat. Research Council Naval Studies Bd, Senate Select Cttee on Intelligence Tech. Advisory Group; fmr mem. Defense Science Bd, Dept of Energy Non-Proliferation, Nat. Security Advisory Cttee, Securities and Exchange Comm. Tech. Advisory Group; Assoc. Fellow, AIAA; Prin. Council for Excellence in Govt; Class Dir AFCEA Int. Bd of Dirs; mem. Tau Beta Pi Eng. Honor Soc., Eta Kappa Nu Electrical Eng. Soc.; CIA Distinguished Intelligence Medal, CIA Dir's Award, Dir of Nat. Security Agency Distinguished Service Medal, Nat. Reconnaisance Officer's Award for Distinguished Service, Defence Intelligence Dir's Award. *Publications:* co-author of 3 books on signal processing algorithms; numerous scholarly articles.
Address: ANSER Homeland Security Institute, 2900 South Quincy Street, Suite 800, Arlington, VA 22206, USA (office). *Telephone:* (703) 416-2000 (office). *Fax:* (703) 416-4173 (office). *Website:* www.anser.org (office); www .homelandsecurity.org (office).

DAVIDOVIĆ, Igor, BA; Bosnia and Herzegovina lawyer and diplomatist; b. 21 Jan. 1960, Tuzla; m. Tatjana Davidović; two d. *Education:* Banja Luka Univ. Law School, Belgrade Univ. Law School. *Career:* fmr staff mem. Meridian (foreign trade firm), positions include Legal Adviser, Br. Office Gen. Man., Gen. Man. of Head Office –1998; Chief of Staff and Spokesperson, Office of the Prime Minister of Bosnia and Herzegovina 1998–2000; Amb. to USA 2000–05; Chief Negotiator, Stabilization and Asscn Agreement Talks with EU 2005–.
Address: Ministry of Foreign Affairs, 71000 Sarajevo, Musala 2, Bosnia and Herzegovina. *Telephone:* (33) 281100. *Fax:* (33) 472188. *E-mail:* info@ mvp.gov.ba. *Website:* www.mvp.gov.ba.

DAVIDSON, Vice-Adm. Glenn V., CMM, CD; Canadian naval officer; *Military Representative, NATO;* b. 1952, Truro, Nova Scotia. *Education:*

Univ. of King's Coll., Halifax. *Career:* enrolled in Naval Reserves 1970, joined regular force 1974, served on naval vessels Nipigon, Fraser, Athabaskan and Venture, naval officers' training centre 1974–1980, promoted to Lt-Commdr 1982, Commdr 1986, Capt. 1991, Commodore 1997, Rear-Adm. 2000, Vice-Adm. 2004; fmr Operations Officer HMCS Annapolis, Operations Officer and Combat Officer/Chief Staff Officer First Canadian Destroyer Squadron 1982–84, attended Command and Staff Coll. 1984–85, served on naval planning staff 1985–86; assigned to Directorate of Naval Requirements 1986, Section Head, naval command and control and surface ships sections and Project Dir NATO Improved Link 11 and NFR-90 projects; Exec. Officer HMCS Provider 1988–89; Commdr HMCS Kootenay 1989–91; Canadian Forces Attaché, Embassy in Japan 1992–95; Commdr Maritime Operations Group Two 1995–97; Dir-Gen. Naval Personnel, Chief of Maritime Staff, Ottawa 1997–2000; Chief of Staff, Asst Deputy Minister (Human Resources–Mil.) 2000–02; Commdr Maritime Force Atlantic HQ, Halifax 2002–04; Mil. Rep. to NATO, Brussels 2004–; Dr hc (King's Coll. Univ.) 2007.
Address: Delegation of Canada, NATO Headquarters, Bld Léopold III, Brussels 1110, Belgium (office). *Telephone:* (2) 707-41-11 (office). *Fax:* (2) 707-45-79 (office). *E-mail:* natodoc@hq.nato.int (office). *Website:* www .nato.int (home).

DAVIES, Sir Howard John, Kt, MA, MSc; British academic administrator and business executive; *Director, London School of Economics;* b. 12 Feb. 1951; m. Prudence Keely 1984; two s. *Education:* Manchester Grammar School, Merton Coll., Oxford and Stanford Grad. School of Business. *Career:* Foreign Office 1973–74; Pvt. Sec. to British Amb. in Paris 1974–76; HM Treasury 1976–82; McKinsey & Co. Inc. 1982–87; Controller, Audit Comm. 1987–92; Dir GKN PLC 1990–95; Dir-Gen. Confed. of British Industry (CBI) 1992–95; Deputy Gov., Bank of England 1995–97, Dir (non-exec.) 1998–2003; Chair. Financial Services Authority (fmrly Securities and Investments Bd) 1997–2003; Dir LSE 2003–; mem. NatWest Int. Advisory Bd 1992–95; mem. Bd Morgan Stanley 2004–, Paternoster UK Ltd 2006–; Deputy Chair. Rowntree Cttee Enquiry 1993; Pres. Age Concern England 1994–98; Chair. Employers' Forum on Age 1996–2004; Chair. panel of judges Man Booker Prize 2007; Trustee, Tate 2002–; Gov. RAM 2004–.
Address: London School of Economics, Houghton Street, London, WC2A 2AE, England. *Telephone:* (20) 7405-7686 (office). *Website:* www.lse.ac.uk (office).

DAVIES, Omar, DEcon; Jamaican economist and academic; b. 28 May 1947, Clarendon; m.; three c. *Education:* Univ. of the West Indies, Northwestern Univ. USA. *Career:* Asst Prof. Stanford Univ. 1973–76; sr lecturer Univ. of the West Indies 1981–89; Dir Gen. Planning Inst. of Jamaica 1989–93; mem. People's National Party; previously Minister without Portfolio responsible for Planning Devt Project Implementation, Minister of Finance and Planning 1993–2007.
Address: People's National Party, 89 Old Hope Road, Kingston, 5, Jamaica (office). *Telephone:* 978-1337 (office). *Fax:* 927-4389 (office). *E-mail:* information@pnpjamaica.com (office). *Website:* www.pnpjamaica.com (office).

DAVINIĆ, Prvoslav, MA, PhD; Serbian politician; b. July 1938, Belgrade. *Education:* Univ. of Belgrade. *Career:* Research Asst, Inst. for Int. Relations and Econs 1965–66, Research Fellow 1973–76; Research Fellow, Stockholm Peace Research Inst. 1967–1973; Special Asst to UN Under-Sec., Dept for Disarmament (DDA) 1979–86, Head of DDA 1991–98; Amb., Ministry of Foreign Affairs 1999–2003; Minister of Defence 2004–05 (resgnd). *Publications:* numerous articles on arms control and int. security issues.
Address: c/o Ministry of Defence, Birčaninova 5, 11000 Belgrade, Serbia (office).

DAVIS, Ruth A., BA, MA; American diplomatist; *Distinguished Visitor, Ralph J. Bunche International Affairs Center, Howard University;* b. 28 May 1943, Phoenix, AZ. *Education:* Spelman Coll. and Univ. of California at Berkeley. *Career:* Consular Officer Kinshasa, Zaire 1969–71, Nairobi, Kenya 1971–73, Tokyo 1973–76, Naples, Italy 1976–80; Special Asst on Int. Affairs to Mayor of Washington 1980–82; Sr Watch Officer Operations Centre, Dept of State 1982–84, Chief of Training and Liaison Bureau Personnel 1984–86; Consul-Gen. Barcelona, Spain 1987–91; Amb. to Benin 1992–96; Prin. Dept Asst Sec. of State for Consular Affairs, Dept of State 1995–97; Dir Nat. Foreign Affairs Training Center 1997–2001; Dir-Gen. Foreign Service, Dir Human Resources, Dept of State 2001–03; currently Distinguished Visitor, Ralph J. Bunche Int. Affairs Center, Howard Univ., Washington DC; mem. sr seminar Foreign Service Inst. 1992; Dr hc (Spelman Coll.) 1998, (Middlebury Coll.) 2000; Presidential Distinguished Service Award 1999, 2002, Arnold L. Raphel Memorial Award, US State

Dept 1999, Superior Honor Award, US Dept of State, Sec.'s Distinguished Award 2003.
Address: Ralph J. Bunche International Affairs Center, Howard University, 2218 6th Street, NW, Washington, DC 20059, USA (office). *Telephone:* (202) 805-0034 (office). *Fax:* (202) 387-6951 (office). *E-mail:* Rdavis@howard.edu (office). *Website:* www.howard.edu/rjb (office).

DAVIS, Terence (Terry), PC, LLB, MBA; British politician and international organisation official; *Secretary General, Council of Europe;* b. 5 Jan. 1938; m. Anne Davis 1963; one s. one d. *Education:* Univ. Coll., London, Univ. of Michigan, USA. *Career:* Internal Auditor, Esso Oil Co. 1962–65; Man. Clarks Shoes 1965–68; Man. Chrysler Parts UK 1968–71; Sr Man. Leyland Cars 1974–79; joined Labour Party 1965; fmr local govt councillor; MP 1971–74, 1979–83, 1983–2004, Opposition Whip 1979–80, Opposition Spokesman for Health, Finance and Economic Affairs, then for Trade and Industry 1980–87, mem. Public Accounts Cttee 1987–94, Public Records Advisory Cttee, Special Cttee of PCs; mem. WEU Ass. 1992–2004, Leader British Del. 1997–2002, Vice-Pres. 1997–2001; mem. Parl. Ass. of Council of Europe 1992–2004, Leader British Del. 1997–2002, Vice-Pres. Ass., mem. Bureau, Pres. Socialist Group 2002–04, Sec.-Gen. Council of Europe 2004–; fmr Rapporteur, EBRD, North South Centre, OECD, Georgia's admission to Council of Europe; fmr Leader and mem. UK Del. to WEU Ass., fmr Vice-Pres. Ass., fmr Pres. Socialist Group, Rapporteur for several reports on defence and security issues; fmr mem. UK Del. to OSCE Ass., Leader of UK Del. to Parl. Ass.; fmr mem. Exec. Cttee of UK Br., IPU; fmr mem. UK Del. to UN Gen. Ass.; fmr Visiting Lecturer, Civil Service Coll.; Chair. Ind. Comm. of Inquiry into the Treatment of Elderly People in Birmingham 2001–02; attended two Parl. Confs for South East Europe Stability Pact; observed elections in Albania, Georgia, Latvia and Ukraine; mem. Amnesty International, UNA, Links Europa.
Address: Office of the Secretary General, Council of Europe, 67075 Strasbourg Cedex, France (office). *Telephone:* (3) 88-41-20-50 (office). *Fax:* (3) 88-41-27-99 (office). *E-mail:* private.office@coe.int (office). *Website:* www.coe.int (office).

DAVYDOV, Oleg Dmitriyevich; Russian politician; *Chief Consultant, Moscow Centre for Applied Social, Political and Economic Studies;* b. 25 May 1940, Moscow; m.; three c. *Education:* Moscow Inst. of Construction Eng. *Career:* staff mem. Inst. Hydroproject 1953–63; counsellor on foreign econ. activities in USSR Trade Missions in Finland, Libya and other countries, supervised construction of energy plants abroad; Deputy Chair. USSR State Cttee on Econ. Relations 1985–88, Deputy Minister of Foreign Econ. Relations 1988–91; mem. Bd of Dirs and Exec. Bd NIPEC Oil Corpn, consultant Dagwig Bureau Consulting Co. 1991–92; First Deputy Minister of Foreign Econ. Relations of Russia Jan.–Sept. 1993, Minister 1993–97; Deputy Prime Minister 1994–97; First Deputy Chair. Co-ordinating Cttee, Interdepartmental Council for Mil. Tech. Policy (KMS) 1996–97; Counsellor Immatrom Voyma Co. 1997–; Chief Consultant, Moscow Centre for Applied Social, Political and Econ. Studies 1998–.

DAWAGIV, Luvsandorj; Mongolian diplomatist; *Ambassador to Thailand;* b. 15 May 1943, Uyanga soum, Uburkhangai aimak (Prov.); m. Maya Jagdal 1971; one s. two d. *Education:* Moscow State Inst. of Int. Relations, Diplomatic Acad., Moscow. *Career:* joined Foreign Service of Mongolia in 1971; Attaché, London 1974; Deputy Head, Head of Dept 1984–90; Head of European and American Dept 1990–; Amb. to USA 1991–95; Head of Law, Treaty and Archives Dept 1995–; Deputy Dir First Dept (Asia and America) 1996–97, Ministry of External Relations, Dir 1997–2001; Amb. to Thailand 2001–, concurrently to Malaysia 2002–, to Indonesia 2002–; Order of Polar Star (Mongolia) 1991.
Address: Embassy of Mongolia, 251 Soi Rojana, Sukhumvit Road 21, Klongtoey–Nua, Wattana, Bangkok 10110, Thailand (office); Peace Avenue 7A, Ulan Bator 13, Mongolia (home). *Telephone:* (2) 640-8018 (office); (11) 311311. *Fax:* (2) 258-38492 (office); (11) 322127. *E-mail:* mongemb@loxinfo.co.th (office).

DAWSON, Thomas C., II, AB (Econs), MBA; American economist; *Director, External Relations Department, International Monetary Fund;* b. 9 March 1948, Washington, DC; m. Moira Jane Haley 1974; two s. one d. *Education:* Stanford Univ., Woodrow Wilson School of Public and Int. Affairs, Princeton Univ. *Career:* fmrly economist, US Consulate Gen., Rio de Janeiro for US State Dept; fmr Consultant, McKinsey and Co.; Deputy Asst Sec. for Developing Nations, Treasury Dept 1981–84; Asst Sec. for Business and Consumer Affairs, Treasury Dept 1984–85; fmr Deputy Asst to the Pres. and Exec. Asst to Chief of Staff, the White House; fmr Special Asst to Asst Sec. for Int. Affairs, Treasury Dept; Exec. Dir IMF 1989–93, Dir External Relations Dept 1999–; First Vice-Pres. Merrill Lynch and Co. 1993–94, Dir 1995–.
Address: International Monetary Fund, 700 19th Street, NW, Washington, DC 20431 (office); 50 Portland Road, Summit, NJ 07901, USA (home).

Telephone: (202) 623-7300 (office). *Fax:* (202) 623-6278 (office). *E-mail:* publicaffairs@imf.org (office). *Website:* www.imf.org (office).

DAY, Catherine, MA; Irish European Union official; *Secretary-General, European Commission;* b. Dublin. *Education:* Univ. Coll., Dublin. *Career:* loan officer, Investment Bank of Ireland 1974–75; EC Information Officer, Confed. of Irish Industry 1975–79; Admin., Directorate Gen. (DG) III 1979–82, mem. Cabinet of Richard Burke, in charge of Personnel and Admin 1982–84, Cabinet of Peter Sutherland, in charge of Competition 1985–89, Cabinet of Sir Leon Brittan, in charge of Competition and External Relations 1989–95, Deputy Chef de Cabinet to Sir Leon Brittan, in charge of External Relations 1995–96, Dir DG IA responsible for relations with the Balkans, Turkey and Cyprus 1996–97, Dir DG IA, subsequently DG Enlargement, responsible for relations with cand. countries of Cen. and Eastern Europe 1997–2000, Deputy Dir-Gen. DG for External Relations, responsible for relations with the Western Balkans, NIS, Mediterranean including the Middle East 2000–02, Dir-Gen. DG Environment 2002–05, Sec.-Gen. EC 2005–; Hon. LLD (Nat. Univ. of Ireland) 2003.
Address: Secretariat-General, European Commission, 1049 Brussels, Belgium (office). *Telephone:* (2) 2958312 (office). *Fax:* (2) 2993229 (office). *E-mail:* staffdir@ec.europa.eu (office). *Website:* (office).

DE AGUIAR PATRIOTA, Antonio; Brazilian diplomatist; *Ambassador to USA;* b. 27 April 1954, Rio de Janeiro; m. Tania Cooper Patriota; two s. *Education:* Univ. of Geneva, Switzerland and Rio Branco Inst. *Career:* Adviser to Head UN Div., Ministry of Foreign Affairs 1980–82; mem. Perm. Mission to Int. Orgs, Geneva 1983–86; Political Counsellor, Embassy in Beijing 1987–88; Head Econ. Section, Embassy in Caracas 1988–90; Adviser to Sec.-Gen. for Political Affairs, Ministry of Foreign Affairs 1990–92; Deputy Diplomatic Advisor to Pres. of Brazil 1992–94; Political Counsellor, Perm. Mission to UN, New York 1994–99, mem. Brazilian delegation to UN Security Council 1995, 1998–99; Minister Counsellor, Perm. Mission to Int. Orgs, Geneva 1999–2003; Deputy Perm. Rep. to WTO 2001–02; Sec. for Diplomatic Planning, Office of the Minister of Foreign Affairs 2002–04, Chief of Staff 2004–05, Under-Sec.-Gen. for Political Affairs, 2005–07; Amb. to USA 2007–; several decorations from Brazil, France, Norway and Morocco.
Address: Brazilian Embassy, 3006 Massachusetts Avenue, NW, Washington DC 20008, USA (office). *Telephone:* (202) 238-2700 (office). *Fax:* (202) 238-2827 (office). *E-mail:* ambassador@brasilemb.org (office). *Website:* www.brasilemb.org (office).

DE ANDRADE, António Paes; Brazilian diplomatist; *Ambassador to Portugal;* b. 18 May 1927, Mombaça, Ceará; m. Zilda Maria Martins Rodrigues de Andrade; four d. *Education:* Univ. of Rio de Janeiro and Univ. of Ceará. *Career:* State Deputy of Ceará 1951–63; Fed. Deputy of Ceará 1967–99; fmr Pres., Chamber of Deputies; fmr Pres. Brazilian Democratic Movement Party (PMDB); Amb. to Portugal 2003–; Dr hc (Coimbra and Lusíada) 2006.
Address: Embassy of Brazil, Quinta de Milflores, Estrada das Laranjeiras 144, 1649-021 Lisbon, Portugal (office). *Telephone:* (21) 7248510 (office). *Fax:* (21) 7267623 (office). *E-mail:* geral@embaixadadobrasil.pt (office). *Website:* www.embaixadadobrasil.pt (office).

DE ARAUJO, Fernando; Timor-Leste politician and acting head of state; *Leader, Democratic Party; Career:* fmr youth resistance leader; arrested for subversion 1991, imprisoned (with collaborator Xanana Gusmao) for six years in Cipinang Prison, Jakarta; f. Resistencia Nacional dos Estudantes de Timor-Leste (RENETIL); Founder and Leader Democratic Party (PD); current Pres. Nat. Parl.; Acting Pres. Feb.–April 2008.
Address: Partido Democrático, 1 Rua Democracia, Pantai Kelapa, Dili, Timor-Leste (office). *Telephone:* 3608421 (office). *E-mail:* flazama@ hotmail.com (office).

DE AZEVEDO RODRIGUES, Maria Celina; Brazilian diplomatist; *Permanent Representative, European Union;* b. Rio de Janeiro. *Education:* Pontifícia Universidade Católica de Rio de Janeiro, Univ. of Cambridge, UK. *Career:* entered Brazilian Diplomatic Service 1970; overseas assignments to Brussels 1973, 1992–99, Helsinki 1974, Bogotá 1977–82, Vienna 1984–88, Cairo 1988; Asst to Head of Commerce and Politics Div., Ministry of External Relations 1970–73; Asst to Head of Regional Office of Rio de Janeiro 1982–83; Expert, Dept of Cultural Cooperation 1983–84; Head of Industry Div. 199–92; Head of Inter-American Coordination 1999–2000; Dir-Gen. Cultural Dept 2000–02; Amb. to Colombia 2002–05; Perm. Rep. to European Communities, Brussels 2005–; Gran Cruz, Orden de Rio Branco (Brazil).
Address: Permanent Mission of Brazil to the European Union, Avenue F.D. Roosevelt 30, 1050 Brussels, Belgium (office). *Telephone:* (2) 640-20-

40 (office). *Fax:* (2) 648-80-40 (office). *E-mail:* missao@braseuropa.be (office).

DE BOCK, Jan; Belgian diplomatist; *Permanent Representative, European Union; Career:* fmr Chancellor on Political Consultations and Sec.-Gen., Ministry of Foreign Affairs; Perm. Rep. to EU 2002–07.
Address: Permanent Mission of Belgium to the European Union, Rondpoint Schuman 6, 1040 Brussels, Belgium (office). *Telephone:* (2) 233-21-11 (office). *Fax:* (2) 231-10-75 (office). *E-mail:* belrep@belgoeurope.diplobel .fgov.be (office).

DE BRICHAMBAUT, Marc Perrin; French international organization executive; *Secretary General, Organization for Security and Co-operation in Europe;* b. 29 Oct. 1948, Rabat, Morocco; m.; two c. *Education:* Ecole Normale Supérieur de Saint-Cloud, Institut d'Etudes Politiques and Ecole Nationale d'Admin, Paris. *Career:* began his career at Conseil d'Etat, first as admin. judge, later as Conseiller d'Etat; posted to New York as Special Asst to UN Under-Sec.-Gen. for Int. Econ. and Social Affairs 1978; adviser to French Foreign Minister 1981–83; Chief of Staff, Ministry of European Affairs 1983–86, Ministry of Foreign Affairs 1984–86; Counsellor, French Embassy, Washington, DC, USA 1986–88; Prin. Adviser to Minister of Defence 1988–91; Head of French Del., CSCE (later became OSCE), Vienna 1991–94; Head, Legal Div., Ministry of Foreign Affairs 1994–98; Dir for Strategic Affairs, Ministry of Defence 1998–2005; Sec. Gen. OSCE 2005–.
Address: OSCE, Kärtner Ring 5–7, 1010 Vienna, Austria (office). *Telephone:* (1) 514-36-180 (office). *Fax:* (1) 514-36-105 (office). *E-mail:* info@osce.org (office). *Website:* www.osce.org/secretariat (office).

DE BRITO FERNANDES, Armindo; São Tomé and Príncipe diplomatist; *Chargé d'affaires a.i. in Belgium;* m. Madame de Brito Fernandes. *Career:* currently Perm. Rep. to UNESCO and Chargé d'affaires a.i. in Belgium (also accred to UK).
Address: Embassy of São Tomé and Príncipe, Square Montgomery, 175 avenue de Tervueren, 1150 Brussels, Belgium (office). *Telephone:* (2) 734-89-66 (office). *Fax:* (2) 734-88-15 (office). *E-mail:* ambassade.saotome@fri .be (office).

DE BRUIJN, Thom; Dutch diplomatist; *Permanent Representative, European Union; Career:* fmr Dir Gen. for EU Affairs, Ministry of Foreign Affairs, The Hague; currently Perm. Rep. to EU, Brussels.
Address: Permanent Mission of the Netherlands to the European Union, 48 Avenue Herrmann Debroux, 1160 Brussels, Belgium (office). *Telephone:* (2) 679-15-11 (office). *Fax:* (2) 679-17-75 (office).

DE BRUM, Banny, BA; Marshall Islands diplomatist; b. 1956; m. Honor Note; four c. *Education:* Regis Univ., Denver, USA. *Career:* Legis. Liaison Officer, Govt of the Marshall Islands 1982–85; Deputy Chief of Mission, Embassy in Washington, DC 1985–1992, Chargé d'affaires a.i. 1995–96, Amb. to USA 1996–2008, Chargé d'affaires a.i., Perm. Mission to UN, New York 1992–93, Chair. Washington Pacific Cttee 1994–95.
Address: Ministry of Foreign Affairs, PO Box 1349, Majuro, MH 96960, Marshall Islands (office). *Telephone:* (625) 3181 (office). *Fax:* (623) 4979 (office). *E-mail:* mofasec@ntamar.net (office).

DE BRUM, Tony A.; Marshall Islands business executive and politician; *Minister of Foreign Affairs;* b. 1945, Likiep Atoll. *Education:* Xavier High School, Micronesia. *Career:* fmr mem. Ralik-Ratak Democratic Party; mem. Parl. for Majuro 1984–2000; fmr Minister of Health and Environment; Minister of Finance 1998–99; mem. Aelon Kein Ad (AKA) coalition 2007–; Senator for Kwajalein Atoll 2007–; Minister of Foreign Affairs 2008–.
Address: Ministry of Foreign Affairs, POB 1349, Majuro MH 96960, Marshall Islands (office). *Telephone:* (625) 3181 (office). *Fax:* (623) 4979 (office).

DE CARVAJAL SALIDO, José; Spanish lawyer and diplomatist; *Ambassador to Ireland;* b. 3 June 1945; m. *Career:* joined diplomatic corps 1971; overseas posts include Embassies in Philippines, Japan and Switzerland; Deputy Dir Gen. of the Budget Office, Ministry of Foreign Affairs 1981, also Deputy Gen. Admin.; Consul Gen. in Cape Town 1982; fmr Minister Counsellor, Perm. Mission to NATO, Brussels; Pres. Spanish Nat. Authority 1999; Dir Gen. Int. Affairs regarding Security and Disarmament, Ministry of Foreign Affairs 1991–96, Deputy Minister of Foreign Affairs 1996–2000; Amb. to Italy (also accred. to Malta, Albania, San Marino) 2000–04, to Ireland 2005–; fmr Pres. Spanish Nat. Authority.
Address: Embassy of Spain, 17a Merlyn Park, Dublin 4, Ireland (office). *Telephone:* (1) 2691640 (office). *Fax:* (1) 2691854 (office). *E-mail:* emb .dublin.inf@maec.es (office).

DE CASTRO, Anibal, BA; Dominican Republic business executive and diplomatist; *Ambassador to UK;* m. Manuela de Castro. *Education:* Universidad Autonoma de Santo Domingo, Univ. of East Anglia, UK. *Career:* Pres. Editorial AA (subsidiary of GFN) 1994–; mem. Bd Dirs Corporacion Dominicana de Electricidad (state-owned utility electricity co.) 1979–82, Tricom SA 1998–, Banco de la Pequena Empresa, several other Dominican cos; mem. Bd Dirs several professional asscns, including Fondo de Financiamiento de la Micro-Empresa; Amb. to UK 2005–.
Address: Embassy of the Dominican Republic, 139 Inverness Terrace, London, W2 6JF, England (office). *Telephone:* (20) 7727-6285 (office). *Fax:* (20) 7727-3693 (office). *E-mail:* embassy@dominicanembassy.org.uk (office). *Website:* www.dominicanembassy.org.uk (office).

DE CASTRO NEVES, Luiz Augusto; Brazilian diplomatist; *Ambassador to The People's Republic of China;* b. 29 Oct. 1943. *Education:* Fed. Univ. of Rio de Janeiro, Univ. of London. *Career:* joined Ministry of Foreign Affairs as Third Sec. 1968; Third, later Second Sec., Embassy in Buenos Aires 1972, Second Sec., Embassy in London 1974, del. to OAS, Washington, DC 1987, Minister-Counsellor, Embassy in Ottawa 1990; Amb. to Paraguay 2000–04, to The People's Repub. of China 2004–; Nat. Security Adviser, Office of Pres. 1985, Sec. of Strategic Affairs 1992; Sec.-Gen. of External Relations 1998; Prof., Univ. of Brasilia 1979, fmr Prof. of Econs, Instituto Rio Branco.
Address: Embassy of Brazil, 27 Guang Hua Lu, Jian Guo Men Wai, Beijing 100600, People's Republic of China (office). *Telephone:* (10) 65322881 (office). *Fax:* (10) 65322751 (office). *E-mail:* empequim@public.bta.net.cn (office). *Website:* www.brazil.org.cn (office).

DE CECCO, Marcello, BA, LLB; Italian economist; *Professor of Monetary Economics, University of Rome 'La Sapienza';* b. 17 Sept. 1939, Rome; m. Julia Maud Bamford; two s. *Education:* Univ. of Parma, Univ. of Cambridge, UK. *Career:* Asst Lecturer, Univ. of East Anglia, England 1967–68; Prof. of Econs, Univ. of Siena 1968–79, European Univ. Inst., Florence 1979–86, Univ. of Rome 'La Sapienza' 1986–, Prof. of Monetary Econs 1989–; Exec. Dir Monte dei Paschi di Siena 1978–83; Dir Crediop, Rome 1979–81, Italian Int. Bank, London 1980–83; Visiting Scholar, IMF 1994; fmr mem. Inst. for Advanced Study, Princeton Univ., Center for Int. Affairs and Center for European Studies, Harvard Univ. *Publications:* Money and Empire: International Gold Standard, 1890–1914 1975, International Economic Adjustment: Small Countries and the European Monetary System 1983, The International Gold Standard 1983, Changing Money 1985, Monetary Theory and Economic Institutions: Proceedings of a Conference Held by the International Economic Association at Fiesole, Florence, Italy (co-author) 1987, Changing Money 1987, A European Central Bank: Perspectives on Monetary Unification After Ten Years of the E.M.S. (co-author) 1989, Managing Public Debt: Index-linked Bonds in Theory and Practice 1997, Markets and Authorities: Global Finance and Human Choice (co-author) 2002.
Address: Dipartimento di Economia Pubblica, Via Castro Laurenziano 9, 00161 Rome, Italy (office). *Telephone:* (06) 49766358 (office).

DE CHASTELAIN, Gen. Alfred John Gardyne Drummond, OC, CMM, CH, CD, BA; Canadian army officer and diplomatist; *Chairman, Independent International Commission on Decommissioning (Northern Ireland);* b. 30 July 1937, Bucharest, Romania; emigrated to Canada 1955, naturalized 1962; m. Mary Ann Laverty 1961; one s. one d. *Education:* Fettes Coll., Edin., UK, Mount Royal Coll., Calgary, Royal Mil. Coll. of Canada, Kingston, British Army Staff Coll., Camberley. *Career:* commissioned 2nd Lt, 2nd Bn, Princess Patricia's Canadian Light Infantry (PPCLI) 1960, Capt., aide-de-camp to Chief of Gen. Staff, Army HQ 1962–64, Co. Commdr, 1st Bn, PPCLI, FRG 1964–65, Co. Commdr, Edmonton, rank of Maj., later with 1st Bn, UN Force, Cyprus 1968; Brigade Maj., 1st Combat Group, Calgary 1968–70, Commdg Officer, 2nd Bn, PPCLI, Winnipeg 1970–72, rank of Lt-Col, Sr Staff Officer, Quartier Gen. Dist, Québec 1973–74, rank of Col, Commdr Canadian Forces Base, Montréal 1974–76, Deputy Chief of Staff, HQ UN Forces, Cyprus and Commdr Canadian Contingent 1976–77, rank of Brig.-Gen. and apptd Commdt Royal Mil. Coll. of Canada, Kingston 1977–80, command of 4th Canadian Mechanized Brigade Group, FRG 1980–82, Dir.-Gen. Land Doctrine and Operations, Nat. Defence Headquarters, Ottawa 1982–83, rank of Maj.-Gen. 1983, Deputy Commdr Mobile Command, St Hubert, Québec 1983–86, rank of Lt-Gen. and apptd Asst Deputy Minister (Personnel) Nat. Defence HQ, Ottawa 1986–88, Vice-Chief, Defence Staff 1988–89, rank of Gen. and apptd Chief of the Defence Staff 1989–93; Amb. to USA 1993; reapptd Chief of the Defence Staff 1994–95; mem. Int. Body on the Decommissioning of Arms in NI 1995–96, Chair. Business Cttee and Co-Chair. Strand Two Talks, NI Peace Process (leading to the Good Friday Agreement) 1996–98, Chair. Independent Int. Comm. on Decommissioning, 1997–; Col of the Regt PPCLI 2000–03; Pres. Dominion of Canada Rifle Asscn 1986–93; mem. Royal Canadian Legion, Royal Canadian Mil.

Inst.; Past First Nat. Vice-Pres. Boy Scouts of Canada; mem. St Andrews Soc. of Montreal, Royal Scottish Country Dance Soc.; Hon. Fellow, Lady Margaret Hall, Univ. of Oxford 2006; Canadian Forces Decoration 1968, Commdr Order of Mil. Merit 1985, Commdr OSJ 1991, US Legion of Merit 1995, Companion of Honour, UK 1998; Hon. DMilSc (Royal Mil. Coll. of Canada) 1996, Hon. LLD (Royal Roads Univ.) 2002, (Nipissing) 2006, (Carleton) 2006, (Queen's Univ., Kingston) 2007; Commendation Medal of Merit and Honour (Greece) 1991, Vimy Award 1992. *Publications:* articles on mil. affairs and int. diplomacy.
Address: Independent International Commission on Decommissioning, Block 1, Knockview Buildings, Stormont Estate, Belfast, BT4 3SL, Northern Ireland (office); 170 Acacia Avenue, Ottawa, ON K1M 0R3, Canada (home). *Telephone:* (28) 9048-8600 (office). *Fax:* (28) 9048-8601 (office); (613) 744-0777 (home). *E-mail:* chairman@iol.ie (office).

DE CLERCK, Stefaan; Belgian politician; *Mayor of Kortryk;* b. 12 Dec. 1951, Kortryk; two s. three d. *Career:* mem. Parl. 1991, 1998–2001; Minister of Justice 1995; Pres. Christelijke Volksparteit (CVP) (renamed Christen-Democratisch en Vlaams Partij—CD&V 2001) 1999–2004; Mayor of Kortryk 2001–.
Address: Damkaai, 8500 Kortryk, Belgium (home). *Telephone:* (56) 20-46-33 (home). *Fax:* (56) 25-89-99 (home). *E-mail:* stefaan.d.clerck@pandora.be (home). *Website:* www.stef-kortryk.com (home).

DE CREM, Pieter Frans Norbert Jozef Raymond; Belgian politician; *Minister of Defence;* m. Caroline Bergez; three c. *Education:* Université Catholique de Louvain, Université Libre de Bruxelles. *Career:* worked for Roularta Media Group 1987–89; Pres. youth section of CVP (Christelijke Volkspartij), Gand-Eeklo 1989–95; Attaché, Cabinet of Prime Minister Wilfried Martens 1989–92, Cabinet of Minister of Defence 1992–93; Adviser to De fabrieken van de Gebroeders De Beukelaar 1993–94; elected Mayor of Aalter 1995, re-elected 2000, 2006; elected to Chamber of Reps for Gand-Eeklo (CVP) 1995, re-elected 1999, elected to Chamber of Reps for Flanders East (party renamed Christen-Democratisch en Vlaams—CD&V) 2003, re-elected 2007, Head, CD&V parl. group 2003–07, Pres. Interior Comm. 2007, mem. OSCE parl. cttee; Minister of Defence 2007–; Officier de l'Ordre de Léopold.
Address: Office of the Minister of Defence, Lambermont straat 8, 1000 Brussels (office); Bosvijverdreef 2, 9880 Aalter, Belgium (home). *Telephone:* (2) 550-28-11 (office). *E-mail:* info@mod.mil.be (office). *Website:* www.pieterdecrem.be (office).

DE ESCOBAR, Ana Vilma Albanez; Salvadorean politician and economist; *Vice-President;* b. 2 March 1954; m. Carlos Patricio Escobar; one d. *Education:* Universidad Centroamericana "José Simeón Cañas". *Career:* fmr Project Man. USAID; fmr Prof. of French; Pres. Salvadorean Inst. of Social Security 1999–2003; Vice-Pres. of El Salvador 2004–.
Address: Ministry for the Presidency, Avenida Cuba, Calle Darió González 806, Barrio San Jacinto, San Salvador, El Salvador (office). *Telephone:* 221-8483 (office). *Fax:* 771-0950 (office). *Website:* www.casapres.gob.sv (office).

DE FONBLANQUE, John, CMG, MA, MSc.; British diplomatist; *Director, Office of High Commissioner on National Minorities, Organization for Security and Co-operation in Europe;* b. 20 Dec. 1943, Fleet, Hants; m. Margaret Prest 1984; one s. *Education:* Ampleforth School, King's Coll., Cambridge, London School of Econs. *Career:* joined FCO 1968, Second Sec. Jakarta 1969–72, Second, later First Sec. to EC, Brussels 1972–77; Prin. HM Treasury 1977–80; FCO 1980–83; Asst Sec. Cabinet Office 1983–86; Head of Chancery, New Delhi 1986, Counsellor (Political and Institutional) Mission to EC, Brussels 1988, Asst Under-Sec. of State Int. Orgs, then Dir Global Issues 1994–98, Dir (Europe) FCO 1998–99, Head Del. to OSCE with rank of Amb. 1999–2003; Dir Office of OSCE High Commr on Nat. Minorities 2004–.
Address: Office of High Commissioner on National Minorities, Organisation for Security and Co-operation in Europe Secretariat, Kärntner Ring 5–7, 4th Floor, 1010 Vienna (office); Van Moersselestraat 5, 2596 PD The Hague, Netherlands (home). *Telephone:* (70) 3125512 (office); (70) 3249081 (home). *E-mail:* john.defonblanque@osce.org (office); jdefonblanque@hotmail.com (home). *Website:* www.osce.org (office).

DE FRANCHIS, Amedeo; Italian diplomatist; b. 9 Aug. 1939, Naples; m. Ilaria Nuti de Franchis; four c. *Education:* Univ. of Rome School of Law. *Career:* Army Lt Alpine Forces 1965–67; entered diplomatic service 1962, served at East-West Desk, Political Affairs Gen. Directorate, Ministry of Foreign Affairs 1962–65; Vice Consul then Deputy Consul Gen., Italian Consulate in New York 1967–70; Counsellor then Chargé d'affaires, Embassy in Tehran 1970–76; Deputy Head then Head, NATO Desk, Ministry of Foreign Affairs 1976–79, Dir-Gen. of Political Affairs 1995–98; First Counsellor for Political-Mil. Affairs, Perm. Del. to NATO 1979–83,

Deputy Perm. Rep. 1983–84, Deputy Sec.-Gen. 1989–94, Perm. Rep. 1998–2002; Amb. to Pakistan 1984–88, Amb. to Spain –2006.
Address: Ministry of Foreign Affairs, Piazzale della Farnesina 1, 00194 Rome, Italy. *Telephone:* (06) 36911. *Fax:* (06) 36918899. *E-mail:* relazioni.pubblico@esteri.it. *Website:* www.esteri.it.

DE FRANCIS, Maria Rosa Picart Sánchez; Andorran diplomatist; *Ambassador to UK;* m. Reginald Francis. *Career:* Chargé d'affaires a.i. in UK –2007, Amb. to UK (also accred to Ireland) 2007–.
Address: Embassy of Andorra, London Office, 63 Westover Road, London, SW18 2RF, England (office). *Telephone:* (20) 8874-4806 (office). *Fax:* (20) 8874-4902 (office).

DE GEUS, Aart; Dutch lawyer and international organization executive; *Deputy Secretary-General, Organisation for Economic Co-operation and Development;* m.; three c. *Education:* Erasmus Univ., Rotterdam, Nijmegen Univ. *Career:* worked as lawyer in industry sector of Christian Trade Union –1988; mem. Exec. Bd Nat. Fed. of Christian Trade Unions 1988–98, Vice-Chair. Exec. Bd 1993–98; pnr in Amsterdam-based co. for strategy and man. 1998–2002; Minister of Social Affairs and Employment 2002–07; Chair. OECD Social Policy Ministerial Meeting 2005, has served in various functions at local, nat. and int. level, Deputy Sec.-Gen. OECD 2007–, in charge of Political Economy of Reform, and preparations for Ministerial Council Meeting and Exec. Cttee in Special Session.
Address: OECD, 2 rue André Pascal, 75775 Paris Cedex 16, France (office). *Telephone:* 1-45-24-82-00 (office). *Fax:* 1-45-24-85-00 (office). *E-mail:* webmaster@oecd.org (office). *Website:* www.oecd.org (office).

DE GRAVE, Franciscus (Frank) Hendrikus Gerardus, DJur; Dutch politician; b. 27 June 1955, Amsterdam; m.; two c. *Education:* Univ. of Groningen. *Career:* Int. Sec. JOVD youth org. 1977–78, Nat. Pres. 1978–80; mem. Volkspartij voor Vrihoid en Democratie (VVD) Parl. group 1977–81; Asst Sec. to Man. Bd AMRO bank 1980–82; Amsterdam City Councillor 1982–86; mem. First Chamber of Parl. 1982–90; Councillor for Finances and Deputy Mayor, Amsterdam City Council 1990–94, Acting Mayor Jan.–June 1994; Sec. of State for Social Security and Employment 1996–98; Minister of Defence 1998–2002; mem. Vaste Comm. for Defence 1982–86, Bd Vereniging Nederlandse Gemeenten; Commr RAI, Bank Nederlandse Gemeenten and Amsterdam Arena.
Address: c/o Ministry of Defence, Plein 4, PO Box 20701, 2500 ES The Hague, Netherlands (office). *Telephone:* (70) 3187320 (office). *Fax:* (70) 3187264 (office). *Website:* www.mindef.nl (office).

DE GRUBEN, Baron Thierry, PhD; Belgian diplomatist; b. 17 Nov. 1941, Antwerp; m. Françoise Francq; one s. *Career:* with Belgian Del. to NATO 1969–70; Embassy Sec., Moscow 1971–76; Second, then First Sec., London, Econ. Attaché 1976–80; Consul-Gen., Bombay 1980–82; Counsellor in Pvt. Office, Ministry of Foreign Affairs 1982–85; Amb. to Poland 1985–90, to Russia 1990–95; Deputy Dir-Gen. of Political Affairs, Special Envoy to Eastern Slavonia 1996–97; Perm. Rep. to NATO, Brussels 1997–2002; Amb. to UK 2002–06.
Address: c/o Belgian Federal Foreign Office, Karmelietenstraat 15, 1000 Brussels, Belgium (office). *Telephone:* (2) 501-81-11 (office). *Website:* www.diplomatie.be (office).

DE GUCHT, Karel; Belgian politician; *Minister of Foreign Affairs;* b. 27 Jan. 1954, Overmere; m. Mireille Schreurs; two s. *Education:* Koninlijk Atheneum Aalst, Free Univ. Brussels. *Career:* Chair. Liberal Students' Union Brussels 1974–75, Nat. Chair. 1975–77; MEP 1980–94; Vice-Chair. PVV party 1985–88; Senator 1994–95; Nat. Chair. Flemish Liberals and Democrats–Citizens' Party (VLD) 1999; Minister of State 2002–04; Minister of Foreign Affairs 2004–07 (resgnd), reappointed Dec. 2007. *Publications:* De Tijd Wacht op Niemand (co-author; trans. Time and Tide Wait for No Man) 1990, Er Zijn Geen Eilanden Meer: Over Democratie, Vrijheid en Mensenrechten (co-author) 1999, Het Einde der Pilaren: Een Toscaans Gesprek (co-author) 2001, De Toekomst is Vrij 2002.
Address: Federal Public Service of Foreign Affairs, Foreign Trade and Development Co-operation, 15 rue des Petits Carmes, 1000 Brussels, Belgium (office). *Telephone:* (2) 501-81-11 (office). *Fax:* (2) 501-81-70 (office). *E-mail:* info@diplobel.fed.be (office). *Website:* www.diplomatie.be (office).

DE HAAN, Hendrik, PhD; Dutch academic; *Professor of International Economics, University of Groningen;* b. 8 April 1941, Nijmegen; m. Adriana Annie Kramer 1966; two s. one d. *Education:* Univ. of Groningen, Netherlands, Catholic Univ. of Louvain, Belgium. *Career:* Prof. of Int. Econs, Univ. of Groningen 1971–; consultant to UNCTAD 1975; consultant-expert to UN on econ. and social consequences of the arms race 1977, 1982, 1987; consultant to UN on relationship between disarmament and devt 1985–87; Foreign Policy Adviser to Christian

Democratic Party 1989–. *Publications:* Het Moderne Geldwezen (Modern Money), several other books on econ. topics, numerous articles in scientific journals.
Address: Department of Economics, PO Box 800, 9700 AV Groningen (office); Hoofdstraat 173, 9827 PB Lettelbert, Netherlands (home). *Telephone:* (50) 633710 (office). *Fax:* (50) 637337.

DE HOOP SCHEFFER, Jaap; Dutch politician and international organization official; *Secretary-General, NATO;* b. 3 April 1948; m. Jeannine de Hoop Scheffer-van Oorschot; two c. *Education:* Leiden Univ. *Career:* fmr Reserve Officer in Air Force; fmr Sec. Del. of Netherlands to NATO, Brussels; Deputy Parl. Leader Christen-Democratisch Appèl (CDA – Christian Democrats) 1995–97, Leader 1997–2001; Minister of Foreign Affairs 2002–03; Sec.-Gen. NATO 2004–.
Address: NATO Headquarters, Boulevard Leopold III, 1110 Brussels, Belgium (office). *Telephone:* (2) 707-4917 (office). *Fax:* (2) 707-4666 (office). *Website:* www.nato.int (office).

DE ICAZA GONZÁLEZ, Carlos Alberto; Mexican diplomatist; *Ambassador to France;* b. 1948. *Career:* joined Foreign Service 1970, Third Sec., Panama City 1971–73, Pvt. Sec. to Under-Sec. of Foreign Relations 1973–77, Dir Information and Documentation Centre, Under-Sec. of Culture, Secr. of Public Educ. 1977–78, Minister, Perm. Mission to UN, Geneva and Rep. to ILO 1979–80, Dir-Gen. Foreign Service 1980–83, Dir-Gen. for Latin American Affairs 1983–86, Amb. to Ecuador 1986–88, Pvt. Sec. to Sec. of Foreign Relations 1988–91, Under-Sec. for Man., Secr. for Foreign Relations 1991–93, for Public Educ. 1994, Amb. to Argentina 1995–96, to Belgium and Luxembourg 1996–98, Under-Sec. of Foreign Relations for Latin American and Asia Pacific 1998–2000, Amb. to Japan 2001–04, to USA 2004–07, to France 2007–, del. to several multilateral meetings of UN, OAS, ILO and APEC; recipient of decorations from 17 countries. *Publications:* La Diplomacia Contemporánea (Contemporary Diplomacy), El Orden Mundial Emergente (The Emerging World Order).
Address: Embassy of Mexico, 9 rue de Longchamp, 75116 Paris, France (office). *Telephone:* 1-53-70-27-70 (office). *Fax:* 1-47-55-65-29 (office). *E-mail:* embfrancia@sre.gob.mx (office). *Website:* www.sre.gob.mx/francia (office).

DE JESUS AMARAL, Ovidio, BEng; Timor-Leste engineeer, politician and diplomatist; *Ambassador to Indonesia;* b. Viqueque. *Education:* Nat. Inst. of Tech., Indonesia. *Career:* Cabinet Mem. for Infrastructure, East Timor Transitional Cabinet 2001, Minister for Transport, Communications and Public Works 2002–06; Amb. to Indonesia 2007–.
Address: Embassy of Timor Leste, Gedung Surya, 11th Floor, Jalan M. H. Thamrin, Kav. 9, Jakarta, Indonesia (office). *Telephone:* (21) 3902678 (office). *Fax:* (21) 3902660 (office).

DE JONGH-ELHAGE, Emily Saïdy; Netherlands Antilles politician; *Prime Minister and Minister of General Affairs and Foreign Relations;* b. 7 Dec. 1946. *Career:* Commr of Public Works and Public Housing of Curaçao 1998–99; Commr of Educ., Sport and Cultural Affairs 1999–2002; Minister of Educ. and Culture 2002–03; Commr of Public Enterprises and Public Housing of Curaçao 2004–05; Prime Minister and Minister of Gen. Affairs and Foreign Relations 2006–; Leader Partido Antia Restrukturá (Party for the Restructured Antilles—PAR) 2005–.
Address: Ministry of General Affairs and Foreign Relations, Plasa Horacio Hoyer 9, Willemstad, Curaçao, Netherlands Antilles (office). *Telephone:* (9) 461-1866 (office). *Fax:* (9) 461-1268 (office).

DE LA GARZA SANDOVAL, Maria Cristina; Mexican diplomatist; *Ambassador to Argentina;* b. 1951, Ciudad Juarez, Chihuahua. *Education:* Universidad de Brasilia. *Career:* Vice Consul, Ministry of Foreign Affairs 1973; fmr Sec. of Foreign Relations; Amb. to Jamaica 1994–95, to Finland 1999, to Estonia –2004, to Argentina 2004–; fmr Alt. Rep., Perm. Missions to ICAO, UNESCO.
Address: Embassy of Mexico, Acros 1650, Belgrano, 1426 Buenos Aires, Argentina (office). *Telephone:* (11) 4789-8800 (office). *Fax:* (11) 4789-8836 (office). *Website:* www.embamex.int.ar (office).

DE LA NUEZ RAMÍREZ, Raúl; Cuban politician; *Minister of Foreign Trade; Career:* fmr Vice-Minister, Basic Industry Ministry; Minister of Foreign Trade 2000–.
Address: Ministry of Foreign Trade, Infanta 16, esquina 23, Vedado, Havana, Cuba (office). *Telephone:* (7) 55-0428 (office). *Fax:* (7) 55-0376 (office). *E-mail:* cepecdir@infocex.cu (office). *Website:* www.infocex.cu/cepec (office).

DE LA SABLIÈRE, Jean-Marc Rochereau, LenD; French diplomatist; *Ambassador to Italy;* b. 8 Nov. 1946, Athens, Greece; m. Sylvie Laussel 1971; three c. *Education:* Lyceé Louis-le-Grand, Faculty of Law, Paris, Inst.

d'études politiques and École nat. d'admin, Paris. *Career:* Dir Econ. and Financial Affairs, Ministry of Foreign Affairs 1973–77, Tech. Sec. 1977–78; Chargé de mission (Culture and Communication), Office of the Prime Minister 1978–81; Admin. Sofirad, Radio Monte Carlo 1979–81; Second Sec. Perm. Mission to UN, New York 1981–84, Jt Perm. Rep. 1990–92, Perm. Rep. to UN, New York 2002–07; Asst Dir of African Affairs, Ministry of Foreign Affairs 1985–86, 1992–96, Co-Dir UN and Int. Orgs Section 1986–90; Minister Plenipotentiary 1991; Amb. to Egypt 1996–2000, to Italy 2007–; Diplomatic Adviser to Pres. of France 2000–02; Chevalier légion d'honneur, Ordre nat. du merite.
Address: Embassy of France, Piazza Farnese 67, 00186 Rome, Italy (office). *Telephone:* (06) 686011 (office). *Fax:* (06) 68601418 (office). *E-mail:* fatima.madjer@diplomatie.gouv.fr (office). *Website:* www.ambafrance-it.org (office).

DE LABOULAYE, Stanislas; French diplomatist; *Ambassador to Russia;* b. 12 Dec. 1946, Beyrouth; m.; four c. *Education:* Univ. of Paris, Sorbonne, Vincennes Univ., Ecole Nationale d'Administration. *Career:* held teaching posts at Lycée de Garçons de Sfax, Tunisia 1970–72, Univ. of Manchester, UK 1972–76; began diplomatic career as Sec. of Foreign Affairs, Ministry of Foreign Affairs 1980, with Asia Div. 1980–81, Econ. Div. 1981–84, Communications Dir 1991–95, Asst Sec.-Gen. and Political Dir 2002; First Sec., then Second Counsellor Perm. Mission to EU, Brussels 1984–87, Second Counsellor, Embassy in Madrid 1987–91, Consul-Gen. in Jerusalem 1996–99; Amb. to Madagascar 2000–02; Sec.-Gen. and Dir-Gen. Political Affairs and Security 2002–06; Amb. to Russia 2006–; Officier de l'Ordre National du Mérite, Chevalier de la Légion d'Honneur.
Address: Embassy of France, 119049 Moscow, ul. B. Yakimanka 45, Russia (office). *Telephone:* (495) 937-15-00 (office). *Fax:* (495) 937-14-46 (office). *E-mail:* amba@ambafrance.ru (office). *Website:* www.ambafrance.org/russie (office).

DE LEON, Ernesto H.; Philippine diplomatist; *Ambassador to Australia;* m. Emilie A de Leon. *Education:* Nat. Defense Coll. of the Philippines, Ecole Militaire, France. *Career:* Armed Forces of the Philippines (AFP) Deputy Chief for Plans –2003; Navy Vice Adm. and Flag Officer-in-Command of Philippine Navy 2003-05 (retd); Amb. to Australia (also accred to Nauru, Vanuatu and Tuvalu) 2006–; Officer Légion d'honneur.
Address: Embassy of the Philippines, 1 Moonah Place, Yarralumla, Canberra, ACT 2600, Australia (office). *Telephone:* (2) 6273-2535 (office). *Fax:* (2) 6273-3984 (office). *E-mail:* cbrpe@philembassy.au.com (office). *Website:* www.philembassy.au.com (office).

DE MARCHANT ET D'ANSEMBOURG, Count Jan Mark V. A., MA; Dutch diplomatist; b. 9 Oct. 1941, Croatia; m. Countess Nicole de Marchant et d'Ansembourg-Rougé 1979; one s. *Education:* Univ. of Leiden. *Career:* mil. service (rank of Lt) 1961–63; diplomatic postings to Damascus, New York, The Hague, Paris 1970–86, to CSCE, Vienna 1986, Head of UN Political Affairs Dept, The Hague 1989, New York 1990, Roving Amb. 1996–97, Deputy Political Dir 1997–98, Amb. to Spain 1998–2003, to UK 2003–06.
Address: Ministry of Foreign Affairs, Bezuidenhoutseweg 67, PO Box 20061, 2500 EB The Hague, Netherlands (office). *Telephone:* (70) 3486486 (office). *Fax:* (70) 3484848 (office). *E-mail:* minbuza@buza.minbuza.nl (office). *Website:* www.minbuza.nl (office).

DE MARCO, Guido, KUOM, BA, LLD; Maltese fmr head of state; b. 22 July 1931, Valletta; m. Violet Saliba; one s. two d. *Education:* St Aloysius Coll. and Royal Univ. of Malta. *Career:* Crown Counsel 1964–66; MP (Nationalist Party) 1966–99; Deputy Prime Minister 1987–96, Minister for Internal Affairs and Justice 1987–91, of Foreign Affairs 1991–96, 1998–99; Shadow Minister and Opposition Spokesman on Foreign Affairs 1996–98; Pres. of Malta 1999–2004; Pres. Gen. Ass. of UN 1990–91; Lecturer, later Prof. of Criminal Law, Univ. of Malta 1967–; Medal Order of Diplomatic Service Merit 1991, Grand Cross Order of Merit (Portugal) 1994, Chevalier Grand Cross Order of Merit (Italy) 1995, Hon. mem. Most Distinguished Order of St Michael and St George 2000, Collare dell'Ordine al Merito Melitense, Order Stara Planina with Ribbon (Bulgaria) 2001, Collar Estoniani Order of the Cross of Terra Mariana 2001, Grand Cross Special Class Order of Merit (FRG) 2001. *Publications:* A Presidency With a Purpose 1991, A Second Generation United Nations 1995, Malta's Foreign Policy in the Nineties 1996, Momentum I 2002, Momentum II 2004.
Address: c/o Office of the President, The Palace, Valletta CMR 02, Malta (office). *Telephone:* 21221221 (office). *Fax:* 21241241 (office).

DE MARIA Y CAMPOS, Mauricio, MA; Mexican diplomatist and economist; b. 13 Oct. 1943, Mexico DF; m. Patricia Meade 1981; two s. one d. *Education:* Nat. Univ. of Mexico, Univ. of Sussex, UK. *Career:* Head Planning and Policy Unit Mexican Nat. Science and Tech. Council

1971–72; Deputy Dir Evaluation Dept Tech. Transfer Ministry of Trade and Industry 1973–74, Dir Gen. Foreign Investment 1974–77, Vice-Minister Industrial Devt 1982–89; Dir Gen. Tax Incentives and Fiscal Promotion Ministry of Finance 1977–82; Exec. Vice-Pres. Banco Mexicano SOMEX 1989–92; Deputy Dir Gen. UNIDO 1992–93, Dir Gen. 1993–97; Amb. at Large and Special Adviser on UN Affairs, Ministry of Foreign Affairs 1998–2001; Amb. to Southern Africa 2002–07; mem. Int. Club of Rome 1998– (Pres. of Mexican Chapter 1998–); Grand Commendateur Ordre nat. du Mérite, Order of Francisco de Miranda (Venezuela); Great Decoration in Gold on the Sash (Austria); Grand Ordre du Mono (Togo). *Publications:* Challenges and Opportunities for Scientific and Technological Collaboration between the EEC and Mexico 1990, The Transformation of the Mexican Automobile Industry during the 1980s 1992; various publs on industrial and technological policy and on regional devt. *Address:* c/o Secretariat of State for Foreign Affairs, Avenida Ricardo Flores Magón 2, Col. Guerrero, Del. Cuauhtémoc, 06995 México, DF, México.

DE MELO DOS SANTOS, Alda Alves, PhD; São Tomé and Príncipe politician and diplomatist; *Ambassador to Portugal; Career:* Minister of Justice, State Reform and Public Admin. 2002; Amb. to Portugal 2003–. *Address:* Embassy of São Tomé e Príncipe, Av. Gago Coutinho 26-6°, Edif. EPAC, Areeiro, 1000-017 Lisbon, Portugal (office). *Telephone:* (21) 8461917 (office). *Fax:* (21) 8461895 (office). *E-mail:* embstp@mail.telepac .pt (office).

DE MIRANDA, João Bernardo; Angolan politician; *Minister of Foreign Affairs;* b. 18 July 1951; m. *Career:* Dir of Information, Rádio Nacional de Angola 1977–80; Ed.-in-Chief Jornal de Angola newspaper 1980–84; Sec. Movimento Popular de Libertação de Angola (MPLA) Ideological Area (Prov. of Luanda); Head of Political and Legal Affairs Div., MPLA Cen. Cttee 1985–89, Head of Information and Propaganda Dept 1989–91; Vice-Minister of Information 1991; Vice-Minister of Foreign Relations 1991–99, Minister of Foreign Affairs 1999–. *Publications include:* Nambuangongo. *Address:* Ministry of Foreign Affairs, Rua Major Kanhangulo, Luanda, Angola (office). *Telephone:* 222397490 (office). *Fax:* 222393246 (office). *E-mail:* webdesigner@mirex.ebonet.net (office). *Website:* www.angola -portal.ao/MIREX (office).

DE MISTURA, Stefan; Swedish United Nations official; *Special Representative of the Secretary-General for Iraq, United Nations;* b. 1947, Stockholm; m.; two d. *Education:* Univ. of Rome. *Career:* joined UN 1970; Deputy Chef de Cabinet, FAO 1976–85; Dir WFP Operations in Sudan 1987; Dir of Fund-Raising and External Relations, UN Office of the Co-ordinator for Afghanistan 1988–91; Special Envoy of UN Sec.-Gen. to Albania 1990; UN Humanitarian Co-ordinator for Iraq 1997; Dir UN Information Centre, Rome –2000; Personal Rep. of UN Sec.-Gen. in South Lebanon 2001–05; Deputy Special Rep. of UN Sec.-Gen. in Iraq 2005–06, Special Rep. 2007–; Dir UN Systems Staff Coll., Turin, Italy 2006–07. *Address:* United Nations Assistance Mission for Iraq (UNAMI), c/o Office of the Secretary-General, United Nations, New York, NY 10017, USA (office). *Telephone:* (212) 963-1234 (office). *Fax:* (212) 963-4879 (office). *Website:* www.uniraq.org (office).

DE MONTBRIAL, Thierry, PhD; French academic; *Director, French Institute for International Relations (IFRI); Education:* Ecole Polytechnique, Ecole des Mines, Univ. of Calif. Berkeley, USA. *Career:* Dir Policy Planning Staff, Ministry of Foreign Affairs 1973–79; Founder and Dir French Inst. for Int. Relations (Institut français des relations internationales—IFRI) 1979–; Chair. Foundation for Strategic Research 1993–2001; Prof. of Econs, Ecole Polytechnique 1974–, Chair. Dept of Econs 1974–92; Prof. of Econs and Int. Relations, Conservatoire Nat. des Arts et Métiers 1995–; mem. Inst. de France (Acad. des Sciences Morales et Politiques) 1992–, Pres. 2001; Chair. Franco–Austrian Center for European Econ. Convergence; mem. Acad. des Technologies, Acad. Europaea 1993–, Acad. Royale de Belgique 1996–, Royal Swedish Acad. of Eng. Sciences 1999–, Romanian Acad. 1999–, Russian Acad. of Sciences 2003–; columnist, Le Figaro 1989–2001, Le Monde 2002–; mem. bd of dirs of several int. research insts; orders of state from Austria, Belgium, Brazil, Germany, Netherlands, Poland and Romania; Dr hc (Romanian Acad. of Econ. Studies) 1996, (Acad. of Sciences of Azerbaijan) 2002. *Publications:* Economie Théorique 1971, Essais d'économie parétienne 1974, Le désordre économique mondial 1974, L'energie: le compte à rebours 1978, La revanche de l'histoire 1985, Que faire? Les grands manoeuvres du monde 1990, Mémoire du temps présent (Prix des Ambassadeurs) 1996, Introduction à l'économie 1999, Pour combattre les pensées uniques 2000, Dictionnaire de Stratégie (jt Ed.) 2000, La France du nouveau siècle 2002, L'action et le système du monde (Prix Georges Pompidou) 2002, Quinze ans qui bouleverserent le monde 2003; numerous articles in learned journals.

Address: Institut français des relations internationales, 27 rue de la Procession, Paris 75740, France (office). *Telephone:* 1-40-61-60-00 (office). *Fax:* 1-40-61-60-60 (office). *E-mail:* accueil@ifri.org (office). *Website:* www .ifri.org (office).

DE MONTFERRAND, Bernard, LLB; French diplomatist; *Ambassador to Germany;* b. 6 Aug. 1945, Cauderan, Gironde; m. Catherine de Tavernost; three c. *Education:* Faculty of Law, Paris, Inst. of Political Studies, Paris, Ecole Nat. d'Admin. *Career:* Sec. of Foreign Affairs, Econ. and Financial Affairs Div., Ministry of Foreign Affairs 1974–79; Lecturer, then Dir of Studies, Inst. of Political Studies, Paris 1975–79; Counsellor for Econ., Financial and Admin. Affairs, French Mil. Govt in Berlin 1979–82; Deputy Dir and Jt Head of Personnel and Gen. Admin., Ministry of Foreign Affairs 1982–85; Consul-Gen. in San Francisco, USA 1985–86; Dir of Cabinet for Minister of Cooperation Michel Aurillac 1986–88; Amb. to Singapore 1989–93, to The Netherlands 1995–2000, to India 2000–02, to Japan 2002–06, to Germany 2007–; Diplomatic Adviser to Prime Minister Edouard Balladur 1993–95; Chevalier Légion d'Honneur, Ordre Nat. du Mérite. *Publications:* La France et l'Etranger 1987, La vertu des Nations 1993, Défendre l'Europe: la tentation suisse 1999. *Address:* Embassy of France, Pariser Platz 5, 10117 Berlin, Germany (office). *Telephone:* (30) 590039000 (office). *Fax:* (30) 590039110 (office). *E-mail:* info@botschaft-frankreich.de (office). *Website:* www.ambafrance -de.org (office).

DE OLIVEIRA MACIEL, Marco Antônio, LLB, MA; Brazilian politician and lawyer; *Minority Leader in Senate;* b. 21 July 1940, Recife; m. Anna Maria Ferreira; one s. two d. *Education:* Catholic Univ. of Pernambuco, Pernambuco Univ. *Career:* adviser to Pernambuco State Govt 1964–66; Prof. of Public and Int. Law, Catholic Univ. of Pernambuco 1966–; State Deputy, Pernambuco Legis. Ass., Govt Leader 1967–71; Regional Sec. ARENA Party 1969–70, Second Nat. Sec. 1972, First Sec. 1974–75; Fed. Deputy 1971–79, Pres. Chamber of Deputies 1977–79; Gov. Pernambuco State 1979–82; Fed. Senator for PDS Party 1982; Minister for Educ. 1985–86; Minister Chief of Staff of Pres. 1986; Pres. Provisional Nat. Comm. Partido da Frente Liberal (PFL) 1984–85, Nat. Pres. 1987, Fed. Senator for PFL 1990, mem. Nat. Council, Leader PFL in Senate 1990; Minority Leader in Senate 1990–, Govt Leader 1991–92; Vice-Pres. of Brazil 1994–2003; mem. Pernambuco Section Brazilian Bar Asscn, Brazilian Acad. of Political and Moral Sciences 1993–, Argentinian Law Asscn; numerous honours including Grand Cross, Order of Rio Branco, Brasilia Order of Merit, Légion d'honneur (France), Grand Cross, Order of Infante Dom Henrique (Portugal), Grand Cross, Order of May (Argentina) 1979, Cross of Merit (FRG), Ordre nat. du Mérite (France), City of Recife Medal of Merit. *Publications:* numerous publs on politics and educ. *Address:* c/o Office of the Vice-President, Palácio do Planalto, 4° andar, 70150-900 Brasília, DF, Brasil (office). *Telephone:* (61) 411-1573 (office). *Fax:* (61) 323-1461 (office). *E-mail:* vpr@planalto.gov.br.

DE PERIO-SANTOS, Rosalinda, BS, LLB; Philippine diplomatist and lawyer; b. 18 Oct. 1939; d. of José T. De Perio and Soledad M. Molina; m. (husband deceased); one d. *Education:* Univ. of the Philippines, Far Eastern Univ., Columbia Univ., New York and Northwestern Univ., IL, USA. *Career:* Adviser Philippines Mission to UN, New York 1962–64; Vice-Consul Consulate-Gen., New York 1964–66; Consul Consulate-Gen., Chicago 1966–72; Minister Counsellor and Consul-Gen. Brasilia, Brazil 1981–83; Perm. Rep. to UN (and other int. orgs) Geneva, Switzerland 1986–89; Amb. to Israel and Amb. (non-resident) to Cyprus and Jordan 1993–2000; Colombo Plan Fellow 1961, Rockefeller Fellow, Carnegie Endowment for Int. Peace, Columbia Univ., NY 1961–62, Hague Acad. Int. Fellow 1974; Outstanding Zambaleña 1986, Outstanding Woman Lawyer, CIRDA 1987. *Address:* c/o Department of Foreign Affairs, DFA Building, 2330 Roxas Boulevard, Pasay City, Metro Manila, Philippines (office). *Telephone:* (2) 8344000 (office).

DE PIERREBOURG, Muriel, LèsL; French journalist and UN official; *Spokesperson for Director-General, United Nations Educational, Scientific and Cultural Organization (UNESCO);* b. (Muriel Morra), 20 Oct. 1950, Monaco; m. Olivier de Pierrebourg 1970; three s. *Education:* Lycée Albert I, Monaco, Univs of Nice and Paris II (Panthéon-Assas). *Career:* freelance journalist 1975–81; Information Officer and External Relations Officer Fondation Delta 7 1980–81; Press Officer Radio Monte-Carlo 1981–84, Head Press Dept 1984–87; Pvt Sec. to Chair. La Sept (TV station) 1987–88; Official Rep. to Presidency of the French Repub. 1988–91, Press Attaché 1991–95; Head of Press and Communications, Cour des Comptes 1995–2001; Spokesperson for Dir-Gen. UNESCO 2001–; Chevalier de la Légion d'honneur 2001. *Address:* UNESCO, 7 place de Fontenoy, 75352 Paris, France (office). *Telephone:* 1-45-68-13-26 (office). *Fax:* 1-45-68-55-66 (office). *E-mail:* m.de -pierrebourg@unesco.org (office). *Website:* www.unesco.org (office).

DE QUEIROZ DUARTE, Sergio; Brazilian diplomatist and UN official; *Under-Secretary-General and High Representative for Disarmament Affairs, United Nations;* b. Rio de Janeiro. *Education:* Fed. Fluminense Univ., Rio de Janeiro, Brazilian School of Public Admin (Getúlio Vargas Foundation), Rio de Janeiro, Brazilian Diplomatic Acad. (Instituto Rio Branco), Rio de Janeiro. *Career:* career diplomat with rank of Amb. in Brazilian Foreign Service, apptd Third Sec. 1957, diplomatic appointments have included Embassies in Rome 1961–63, in Buenos Aires 1963–66, in Washington, DC 1970–74, Perm. Mission to UN, Geneva 1966–68 (mem. Brazilian del. to 18-nation Disarmament Cttee); Alt. Rep., Office of Special Rep. of Brazil for Disarmament Affairs, Geneva 1979–86, Amb. to Nicaragua 1986–91, to Canada 1993–96, to People's Repub. of China 1996–99, to Austria 1999–2002 (also accred to Slovakia, Slovenia and Croatia and as Rep. to Int. Orgs, Vienna); Gov. for Brazil at Bd Govs, IAEA, Chair. Bd Govs 1999–2000; Head of Personnel, Ministry of Foreign Affairs, Brasilia 1975–79, Sec.-Gen. for Budget Control and Insp.-Gen. 1991, Exec. Sec.-Gen. 1991–92, Under-Sec.-Gen. for Foreign Service 1992–93, Amb.-at-Large for Disarmament and Non-Proliferation 2003–04; UN Under-Sec.-Gen. and High Rep. for Disarmament Affairs 2007–; elected Pres. Review Conf. of Parties to Treaty Prohibiting the Emplacement of Nuclear Weapons on the Seabed and the Subsoil Thereof, Geneva 1988, VII Review Conf. of Parties to Treaty on the Non-proliferation of Nuclear Weapons, New York 2005. *Address:* Office of the High Representative for Disarmament Affairs, Room S-3170, United Nations, New York, NY 10017, USA (office). *E-mail:* ddaweb@un.org (office). *Website:* disarmament.un.org (office).

DE RAAD, Ad, MSc; Dutch UN official; *Executive Coordinator, United Nations Volunteers;* b. 7 Dec. 1952. *Education:* Delft Univ. of Tech. *Career:* sr positions, UNDP Country Offices in Bangladesh 1980–84, Tanzania 1984–87; various posts, Bureau for Finance and Admin, UNDP, New York 1987–93; Dir of Budget, UNDP, New York 1993–98; Deputy Exec. Coordinator UN Volunteers (UNV) programme, Bonn, Germany 1998–2003, Acting Exec. Coordinator 2003–04, Exec. Coordinator 2004–. *Address:* United Nations Volunteers, Postfach 260 111, 53153 Bonn, Germany (office). *Telephone:* (228) 8152000 (office). *Fax:* (228) 8152001 (office). *E-mail:* information@unvolunteers.org (office). *Website:* www .unvolunteers.org (office).

DE RIVERO, Oswaldo, LLB; Peruvian diplomatist; b. 1936, Lima. *Education:* Catholic Univ. of Lima. *Career:* entered diplomatic service and held several posts including Amb. to UK, to Russia, Pres. Econ. Comm. of Non-Aligned Countries, Pres. Group of 77 Countries, Chair. Latin American Econ. System (SELA); Leader, Peruvian Delegation to GATT Uruguay Round of negotiations; Pres. Review Conf. of Nuclear Non-Proliferation Treaty 1990; fmr Perm. Rep to UN; contrib. La República (daily newspaper). *Publications:* El mito de desarrollo 1999 (translated as The Myth of Development: The Non-Viable Economies of the 21st Century). *Address:* c/o Ministry of Foreign Affairs, Jirón Lampa 535, Lima 1, Peru (office). *Website:* www.rree.gob.pe (office).

DE RUYT, Jean, DrJur; Belgian diplomatist; *Permanent Representative, European Union;* b. 14 Sept. 1947, Louvain; m. Sheila Arora; four c. *Education:* Univ. of Louvain, Johns Hopkins Univ., Bologna, Italy. *Career:* joined diplomatic service early 1970s, Press Attaché, Embassy in Kinshasa 1973–74, Embassy Sec. and Deputy Head of Mission in Algiers 1975–78, Dir Investment Promotion Dept, New York 1978–81; Deputy, Middle East Dept, Ministry of Foreign Affairs 1982, Dir of Politico-Mil. Affairs 1991–94, Dir for Political Affairs 1997–2001; Perm. Rep. of Belgium to EU 1982–87; Minister-Counsellor and Deputy Head of Mission in Washington, DC 1987–91; Perm. Rep. to WEU 1993–94; Amb. to Poland 1994–96; Perm. Rep. to NATO 1996–97, to UN, New York 2001–04; Amb. to Italy 2004–07; Perm. Rep. to EU 2007–. *Publications include:* various articles on European institutions and defence policy. *Address:* Rue de la Loi 61-63, 1040 Brussels, Belgium (office). *Telephone:* (02) 233-21-11 (office). *Fax:* (02) 231-10-75 (office). *E-mail:* dispatch .belgoeurop@diplobel.fed.be (office). *Website:* www.diplomatie.be/ belgoeurop (office).

DE SCHOUTHEETE DE TERVARENT, Baron Philippe; Belgian diplomatist; *Representative of Order of Malta, European Commission;* b. 21 May 1932, Berlin, Germany; m. Bernadette Joos de Ter Beerst 1956; two s. *Education:* Beaumont Coll., UK, Univ. of Louvain, Belgium. *Career:* joined Belgian diplomatic service; served in Paris 1959–61, Cairo 1962–65, Madrid 1968–72, Bonn 1972–76; Chef de Cabinet to Minister of Foreign Affairs 1980–81; Amb. to Spain 1981–85; Political Dir 1985–87; Perm. Rep. to EU 1987–97; Guest Prof., Univ. of Louvain la Neuve 1990–2000; Rep. of Order of Malta to EC 2000–; Special Adviser EC 2000–04; Dir European Studies, Royal Inst. for Int. Relations, Brussels; Pres. Fund Inbev Baillet Latour 1999–; mem. Bd of Dirs Centre for European Policy Studies, Acad.

Royale de Belgique; Grand Officer, Order of Leopold; Adolphe Bentinck Prize 1997. *Publications:* La coopération politique européenne 1986, Une Europe pour tous 1997, The Case for Europe 2000. *Address:* Avenue de Broqueville 99, 1200 Brussels, Belgium. *E-mail:* deschoutheete@skynet.be (home).

DE SEIXAS CORRÊA, Luiz Felipe; Brazilian diplomatist; *Ambassador to Germany;* b. 16 July 1945, Rio de Janeiro; m. Marilu Gurgel Valente de Seixas Corrêa. *Education:* Candido Mendes Univ., Rio Branco Inst. *Career:* joined Foreign Service as Third Sec. 1967, served in Dept of the Americas, Ministry of External Relations 1967–69, Dept for Int. Orgs 1977–78, Dept for Asia, Africa and Oceania 1978–79, Sec.-Gen. of Ministry 1992–93, 1999–2001; Special Adviser to Minister Chief of Civilian Household 1983–85, Chief Foreign Affairs Adviser to Pres. 1987–89; overseas postings include Second Sec., Embassy in Bonn 1970–71, served at Perm. Mission to UN, New York 1971–74, Embassy in Buenos Aires 1974–76, Counsellor, Embassy in Washington, DC 1979–83, Minister-Counsellor, Perm. Mission to UNESCO, Paris 1985–87, Chief of Mission, Embassy in Mexico 1989–92; Amb. to Spain 1993–97, to Argentina 1997–98; Perm. Rep. to WTO, Geneva 2002–05, Chair. Working Group on Investment 2002–03; Chair. Intergovernmental Negotiating Body on WHO Framework Convention on Tobacco Control 2002–03; Amb. to Germany 2005–. *Address:* Embassy of Brazil, Wallstrasse 57, 10179 Berlin, Germany (office). *Telephone:* (30) 726280 (office). *Fax:* (30) 72628320 (office). *E-mail:* brasil@ brasemberlim.de (office). *Website:* brasilianische-botschaft.de (office).

DE SILVA, Kingsley M., DLitt, PhD; Sri Lankan academic; *Chairman, International Centre for Ethnic Studies; Education:* Univ. of Ceylon, Peradeniya, Univ. of London, UK. *Career:* Smuts Visiting Fellow in Commonwealth Studies and Visiting Fellow, Clare Hall, Cambridge, UK 1968–69; Foundation Prof. of Sri Lankan History, Univ. of Peradeniya 1969–95; Commonwealth Visiting Prof., Dept of Govt, Univ. of Manchester, UK 1976–77; mem. Univ. Grants Comm., Colombo 1979–89, Vice-Chair. 1985–89; Fulbright Scholar in Residence and Visiting Prof. of History, Bowdoin Coll., Me, USA 1985–86; Fellow, Woodrow Wilson Center for Scholars, Washington, DC, USA 1991–92; Exec. Dir Int. Centre for Ethnic Studies, Sri Lanka 1982–2005, Chair. 2005–; Academic Prize Laureate, Fukuoka Asian Cultural Prize 2002. *Publications:* A History of Sri Lanka 1981, Regional Powers and Small State Security: India and Sri Lanka 1977–1990 1995, Reaping the Whirlwind: Ethnic Politics, Ethnic Conflict in Sri Lanka 1998, Sri Lanka's Troubled Inheritance 2007. *Address:* International Centre for Ethnic Studies, 554/6A Peradeniya Road, Kandy (office); 50 Deveni Rajasingha Mawatha, Kandy, Sri Lanka (home). *Telephone:* (8) 234892 (office); (8) 225040 (home). *Fax:* (8) 234-892 (office). *E-mail:* icesk@sltnet.lk (office). *Website:* www.ices.lk (office).

DE SOTO, Alvaro; Peruvian diplomatist; b. 16 March 1943, Argentina; divorced; two s. one d. *Education:* Int. School, Geneva, Catholic Univ. Lima, San Marcos Univ. Lima, Diplomatic Acad. Lima and Inst. of Int. Studies, Geneva. *Career:* Acting Dir Maritime Sovereignty Div. Ministry of Foreign Affairs 1975–78; Deputy Perm. Rep. of Peru at UN, Geneva 1978–82; Special Asst to UN Sec.-Gen. 1982–86; Asst Sec.-Gen. and Exec. Asst to UN Sec.-Gen. 1987–91; Personal Rep. of UN Sec.-Gen. in El Salvador Peace Negotiations 1990–91; Asst Sec.-Gen. UN Office for Research and Collection of Information 1991; Sr Political Adviser to UN Sec.-Gen. 1992–94; Asst Sec.-Gen. for Political Affairs 1995–99, Under-Sec.-Gen., Special Adviser to Sec.-Gen. on Cyprus 1999–2000; UN Special Envoy for Myanmar 1997–99; Special Rep. of the Sec.-Gen. for Cyprus and Chief of Mission UNFICYP (UN Peace-Keeping Force in Cyprus) 2000–03; Special Rep. of the Sec.-Gen. for Western Sahara and Chief of the UN Mission for the Referendum in Western Sahara (MINURSO) 2003–05; UN Special Coordinator for the Middle East Peace Process and Personal Rep. of the Sec.-Gen. to the Palestine Liberation Org. and the Palestinian Authority 2005–07. *Address:* c/o Executive Office of the UN Secretary-General, United Nations Plaza, New York, NY 10017, USA (office).

DE SOTO, Guillermo Fernández; Colombian politician and international organization official; b. 1956. *Education:* Univ. of Bogotá, Georgetown Univ., USA. *Career:* Under-Minister of Foreign Affairs 1980, Minister 1998–2002; f. Groupe de Contadora; Intermediate Sec. Groupe de Rio; Dir Chamber of Commerce, Bogotá 1993–98; Sec.-Gen. Andean Community of Nations 2002–03. *Address:* c/o Andean Community of Nations, Avda Paseo de la República 3895, esq. Aramburú, San Isidro, Lima 27, Peru (office).

DE SOTO, Hernando; Peruvian economist; *President, Institute for Liberty and Democracy;* b. 2 June 1941, Arequipa. *Education:* Institut Universitaire de Hautes Etudes Internationales, Geneva, Switzerland. *Career:* fmr economist for GATT; fmr Pres. Exec. Cttee, Copper Exporting Countries Org. (CIPEC); fmr Man. Dir Universal Eng Corpn; fmr Prin. Swiss Bank Corpn Consultant Group; fmr Gov. Cen. Reserve Bank, Peru; Personal Rep. and Chief Adviser to Pres. Alberto Fujimori; currently Pres. Inst. for Liberty and Democracy, Lima; apptd rep. of Pres. to USA on free trade agreement 2006; Co-Chair. UN High Level Comm. on Legal Empowerment for the Poor; Downey Fellow, Yale Univ., USA 2003; Most Admirable Order of the Direkgunabhorn (Fifth Class), Thailand 2004; Hon. DLitt (Buckingham, UK) 2005; Sir Antony Fisher Int. Memorial Award – Atlas 1990, 2001, one of five Leaders for the New Millennium chosen by Time magazine 1999, The Freedom Prize (Switzerland), Goldwater Award (USA) 2002, Adam Smith Award, Asscn of Pvt. Enterprise Educ. (USA) 2002, CARE Canada Award for Outstanding Devt Thinking 2002, inducted into Democracy Hall of Fame Int., Nat. Grad. Univ. 2003, Templeton Freedom Prize (USA) 2004, Milton Friedman Prize for Advancing Liberty (USA) 2004, Deutsche Stiftung Eigentum prize for Property Rights Theory 2004, IPAE Award, Peruvian Inst. of Business Admin 2004, Americas Award 2005, Acad. of Achievement Golden Plate Award, USA 2005, Forbes' Compass Award for Strategic Direction 2005. *Publications:* The Other Path 1986, The Mystery of Capital: Why Capitalism Triumphs in the West and Fails Everywhere Else 2000. *Address:* Instituto Libertad y Democracia, Av. Las Begonias 441, Piso 9, San Isidro, Lima 27, Peru (office). *Telephone:* (1) 222-6800 (office). *Fax:* (1) 221-6949 (office). *E-mail:* hds@ild.org.pe (office). *Website:* www.ild.org.pe (office).

DE SOUSA RODRIGUES, Lt-Gen. Fernando; Portuguese air force general; b. 8 Feb. 1946; m. Maria José de Sousa Rodrigues; one d. *Education:* Lisbon Mil. Acad. *Career:* began career in Portuguese Air Force (PoAF) 1964; Instructor Pilot 1968–73; Fighter Pilot, Guinea-Bissau and Montijo 1973–76; Transport Pilot, Azores and Montijo 1978–88; 503 Squadron Commdr, Azores 1978–80; 501 Squadron Commdr, Montijo 1983–86; 61 Operations Group Commdr, Montijo 1986–88; Planning and Org. Br. Chief, Operations Div. 1990; Dir of Staff Training, PoAF Staff Coll., Sintra 1991–93; Air Base Commdr, Montijo 1994–95; Chief of Operations Div, PoAF HQ 1996–97; Dir of Training 1997–2000; PoAF Del. to Mil. Cooperation with African Countries 1997–2000; Dir of F-16/MLU Transformation Programme 1998–2001; Prin. of Portugal to Multi-National Fighter Programme (MNFP) 2000–01; Insp.-Gen. of the Air Force 2000–03; Pres. PoAF Cultural and Historic Comm. 2001–03; Mil. Rep. to NATO, Brussels 2003–06; apptd Maj.-Gen. 1997, Lt-Gen. 2000; Mil. Merit 1st and 2nd Class, Aeronautical Merit 1st Class; Distinguished Service Silver and Gold Medals, War Campaign Medal. *Address:* Ministry of National Defence, Av. Ilha de Madeira, 1400-204 Lisbon, Portugal (office). *Website:* www.mdn.gov.pt (office).

DE SOUZA-GOMES, João Carlos; Brazilian diplomatist; *Permanent Representative, United Nations Educational, Scientific and Cultural Organization (UNESCO); Career:* fmr Amb. to Costa Rica, to USA; apptd. Amb. to Venezuela 2003; Perm. Rep. to UNESCO, Paris 2007–; Del. to Intergovernmental Oceanographic Comm. Exec. Council 2008. *Address:* Permanent Delegation of Brazil to UNESCO, Maison de l'UNESCO Bureau MR.07, 1, rue Miollis, 75732 Paris Cedex 15, France. *Telephone:* 1-45-68-29-01. *Fax:* 1-47-83-28-40. *E-mail:* dl.brasil@unesco .org.

DE VALLERA, João; Portuguese diplomatist; *Ambassador to USA. Career:* joined Diplomatic Service 1974, served at Embassy in Madrid, as Deputy Perm. Rep. and Perm. Rep. at Perm. Representation to European Communities, Brussels; Amb. to Ireland 1998–2001; Dir Gen. of European Affairs, Ministry of Foreign Affairs 2001–02, Del. to Convention on the Future of Europe Feb.–May 2002; Amb. to Germany 2002–07, to USA 2007–. *Address:* Embassy of Portugal, 2125 Kalorama Road, NW, Washington, DC 20008, USA (office). *Telephone:* (202) 328-8610 (office). *Fax:* (202) 462-3726 (office). *E-mail:* portugal@portugalemb.org (office); embportwash@ mindspring.com (office). *Website:* www.portugalemb.org (office).

DE WITTE, Bruno, LLB, PhD; Belgian academic; *Professor of European Law, European University Institute;* b. 1955, Kortrujk; m.; two c. *Education:* Univ. of Leuven, Coll. of Europe, Bruges, European Univ. Inst., Florence. *Career:* Researcher, Law Dept, European Univ. Inst. (EUI) 1979–82, Assoc. Prof. 1985–89, Prof. of European Law 2000–, also Jt Chair. Law Dept and Robert Schuman Centre, Co-Dir EUI Acad. of European Law; Prof. of European Law, Univ. of Maastricht 1989–2000; mem. Bd of Eds European Law Journal; mem. Advisory Bd European Journal of International Law, Maastricht Journal of European and Comparative Law; contrib. Rivista Italiana di Diritto Pubblico Comunitario. *Publications:* European Community Law of Education (ed.) 1989, The Common Law of Europe and the Future of Legal Education (jt ed.) 1992, The Many Faces of Differentiation in EU Law (jt ed.) 2001; numerous articles in legal journals and contributions to legal publs. *Address:* European University Institute, Law Department, Badia Fiesolana, Via dei Roccettini 9, 50016 San Domenico di Fiesole, Italy (office). *Telephone:* (055) 4685728 (office). *E-mail:* Bruno.DeWitte@eui.eu (office). *Website:* www.iue.it/LAW (office).

DE ZELA MARTÍNEZ, Hugo Claudio; Peruvian diplomatist; *Ambassador to Brazil; Education:* Academia Diplomática del Perú. *Career:* joined Foreign Service 1975; mem. and fmr Chair. Instituto Antártico Peruano; fmr Amb. to Argentina, Amb. to Brazil 2007–. *Address:* Embassy of Peru, SES, Av. das Nações, Quadra 811, Lote 43, 70428-900, Brasília, DF, Brazil (office). *Telephone:* (61) 3242-9933 (office). *Fax:* (61) 3244-9344 (office). *E-mail:* embperu@embperu.org.br (office); hdezela@rree.gob.pe (office). *Website:* www.embperu.org.br (office).

DE ZWAAN, Jaap W., PhD; Dutch diplomatist; *Director, Clingendael Institute;* b. 1949, Amsterdam; m.; three c. *Education:* Leiden Univ., Coll. of Europe, Bruges, Belgium, Groningen Univ. *Career:* mem. The Hague Bar 1973; worked for Ministry of Foreign Affairs, The Hague (European Integration Dept and Legal Service), acted as Agent for Netherlands Govt in numerous cases before the Court of Justice of the European Communities, Luxembourg 1979–83, 1988–95, acted as Legal Adviser of Perm. Representation of the Netherlands at EU, Brussels 1983–88, 1995–98; Prof. of the Law of the EU and Jean Monnet Chairholder 'Future Developments of the European Union', Erasmus Univ., Rotterdam 1998–2005, part-time 2005–, Dean of Faculty 2001–04; Dir Clingendael (Netherlands Inst. of Int. Relations), The Hague 2005–; Ed.-in-Chief Internationale Spectator; mem. Comm. on European Integration, Advisory Council on Int. Affairs, Minister of Foreign Affairs, Gen. Bd, European Movt (Netherlands section), French-Dutch Co-operation Council, Bd of Rotterdams Juridisch Genootschap (Rotterdam Law Asscn), Bd of Foundation Nederland-Roemenië. *Publications include:* articles on law and policy of the European Union, notably institutional aspects, justice and homes affairs, and external relations. *Address:* Clingendael Institute, PO Box 93080, 2509 AB The Hague, The Netherlands (office). *Telephone:* (70) 324-53-84 (office). *Fax:* (70) 328-20-02 (office). *E-mail:* jzwaan@clingendael.nl (office). *Website:* www.clingendael .nl (office).

DEANE, Hon. Sir William Patrick, AC, KBE, BA, LLB, QC; Australian fmr Governor-General and judge; b. 4 Jan. 1931, St Kilda; m. Helen Russell 1965; one s. one d. *Education:* St Joseph's Coll. Sydney, Sydney Univ. and Trinity Coll. Dublin, Ireland. *Career:* Teaching Fellow in Equity, Univ. of Sydney 1956–61; barrister 1957; Justice, Supreme Court, NSW 1977, Fed. Court of Australia 1977–82; Pres. Australian Trade Practices Tribunal 1977–82; Justice, High Court of Australia 1982–95; Gov.-Gen. of Australia 1996–2001; KStJ; Hon. LLD (Sydney, Griffith, Notre Dame, Trinity Coll., Univ. of NSW, Univ. of Tech. of Sydney, Univ. of Queensland); Hon. DUniv (Southern Cross, Australian Catholic Univ., Queensland Univ. of Tech., Univ. of W Sydney); Hon. DSacredTheol (Melbourne Coll. of Divinity). *Address:* c/o PO Box 4168, Manuka 2603, Australia. *Telephone:* (2) 6239-4716 (office). *Fax:* (2) 6239-4916 (office).

DEASY, Austin, TD; Irish politician (retd); b. 26 Aug. 1936, Dungarvan, Co. Waterford; m. Catherine Keating 1961; two s. two d. *Education:* Dungarvan Christian Brothers' School and Univ. Coll., Cork. *Career:* fmr secondary school teacher; mem. Waterford Co. Council and Dungarvan Urban Council 1967–2002; mem. Seanad Éireann 1973–77; mem. Dáil Éireann (Parl.) 1977–2002, Vice-Chair. Foreign Affairs Cttee 1997–2002; Minister for Agric. 1982–87; Leader, Irish Del. to Council of Europe 1997–2002; mem. Fine Gael. *Address:* Kilrush, Dungarvan, Co. Waterford, Ireland. *Telephone:* (58) 20760. *Fax:* (58) 45315.

DEBONO, Giovanna, BA; Maltese politician; *Minister for Gozo;* b. (Giovanna Attard), 25 Nov. 1956, Gozo; m. Anthony Debono; one s. one d. *Education:* Univ. of Malta. *Career:* teacher Educ. Dept 1981–87; MP, Nationalist Party 1987–; Parl. Sec. Ministry for Social Devt 1995–96; Minister for Gozo 1998–. *Address:* Ministry for Gozo, St Francis Square, Victoria, Gozo, Malta (office). *Telephone:* (21) 561482 (office). *Fax:* (21) 559360 (office). *E-mail:* giovanna.debono@gov.mt (office). *Website:* www.gozo.gov.mt (office).

DEBRÉ, Jean-Louis, DenD; French magistrate and politician; *President, Conseil Constitutionnel;* b. 30 Sept. 1944, Toulouse; m. Ann-Marie Engel 1971; two s. one d. *Education:* Lycée Janson-de-Sailly, Inst. d'Etudes Politiques, Faculté de Droit, Paris and Ecole Nat. de la Magistrature. *Career:* Asst Faculté de Droit, Paris 1972–75; Adviser, Office of Jacques

Chirac 1974–76; Deputy Public Prosecutor, Tribunal de Grande Instance, Evry 1976–78; Magistrate, Cen. Admin. of Ministry of Justice 1978; Chef de Cabinet to Minister of Budget 1978; Examining Magistrate, Tribunal de Grande Instance, Paris 1979; RPR Deputy to Nat. Ass. 1986–95, 1997–2002, Pres. RPR Group 1997–2002; Town Councillor, Evreux 1989; Conseiller Général, Canton de Nonancourt 1992–2001; Deputy Sec.-Gen. and Spokesman for Gaullist Party 1993; Minister of the Interior 1995–97; Vice-Pres. Gen. Council of the Euro 1998–; Mayor of Evreux 2001–07; Pres. Nat. Ass. 2002–07; Pres. Conseil Constitutionnel 2007–; Chevalier du Mérite Agricole, Grand-Croix l'Ordre d'Isabelle la catholique (Spain), Prix du Trombinoscope 2003, Marianne d'Or 2004,. *Publications:* Les idées constitutionnelles du Général de Gaulle 1974, La constitution de la Ve République 1974, Le pouvoir politique 1977, Le Gaullisme 1978, La justice au XIXe 1981, Les républiques des avocats 1984, Le curieux 1986, En mon for intérieur 1997, Pièges 1998, Le Gaulisme n'est pas une nostalgie 1999, Qu'est-ce que l'Assemblée nationale? 2006.
Address: Conseil Constitutionnel, 2 Rue de Montpensier, 75001 Paris (office); 126 rue de l'Université, 75007 Paris, France (home). *Telephone:* 1-40-15-30-00 (office). *Fax:* 1-40-20-93-27 (office). *E-mail:* administration@ conseil-constitutionnel.fr (office). *Website:* www.conseil-constitutionnel.fr (office).

DÉBY ITNO, Gen. Idriss; Chadian head of state; *President;* b. 1952, Zaghawa community. *Career:* served in Army, trained as helicoptor pilot; fmr C-in-C of Armed Forces; fmr mil. adviser to Pres. Hissène Habré, overthrew him in coup Dec. 1990; Chair. Interim Council of State, Head of State 1990–91; Pres. of Chad March 1991–, also C-in-C of Armed Forces; mem. Mouvement patriotique du salut (MPS).
Address: Office of the President, Palais rose, BP 74, N'Djamena, Chad (office). *Telephone:* 51-44-37 (office). *Fax:* 51-45-01 (office). *E-mail:* presidence@tchad.td (office).

DEDDACH, Mahfoudh Ould, LLM; Mauritanian diplomatist, politician and academic; b. 1954, Bassikounou; m.; seven c. *Education:* Catholic Univ. of Louvain, Belgium, Meknès Mil. Acad., Morocco. *Career:* Asst Lecturer, Faculty of Law, Univ. of Nouakchott 1984–92, also Dir Centre of Studies and Research; Tech. Adviser to Minister of Trade 1989–92; elected Senator of Dept of Bassikounou 1992; Minister of Rural Devt and the Environment 1992–93; Amb. to Senegal 1993–96; fmr Perm. Rep. to UN, New York.
Address: c/o Ministry of Foreign Affairs and Co-operation, BP 230, Nouakchott, Mauritania (office).

DEGUARA, Louis, MD; Maltese politician and doctor; *Minister of Health, the Elderly and Community Care;* b. 18 Sept. 1947, Naxxar; m. Maria Fatima Mallia; one s. one d. *Education:* St Aloysius Coll., Birkikara, Univ. of Malta. *Career:* medical practitioner 1973; fmrly houseman, St Luke's, Sir Paul Boffa and Gozo Gen. Hosps, Prin. Medical Officer of Health, Northern Region; Gen. Practitioner 1977–; MP, Nationalist Party 1981–; Parl. Sec. Ministry for Social Devt 1995–96; Shadow Minister and Opposition Spokesman for Health 1996–98; Minister of Health 1998–.
Address: Ministry of Health, the Elderly and Community Care, Palazzo Castellania, 15 Merchant Street, Valletta, CMR 02, Malta. *Telephone:* 21224071. *Fax:* 21252574.

DEGUTIS, Darius; Lithuanian diplomatist; *Ambassador for Special Assignments;* b. 1964. *Career:* career diplomat; Chargé d'Affaires, Embassy in Washington, DC 1998–2001, Amb. to Poland 2001–04; currently Amb. for Special Assignments, Ministry of Foreign Affairs; instructor, Vilnius Univ. Int. Business School; Commdr, Order for Merits to Lithuania 2003.
Address: Ministry of Foreign Affairs, J. Tumo-Vaižganto 2, Vilnius 01511, Lithuania (office). *Telephone:* (5) 236-2553 (office). *Fax:* (5) 231-3090 (office). *E-mail:* urm@urm.lt (office). *Website:* www.urm.lt (office).

DEHAENE, Jean-Luc; Belgian (b. French) politician; *Vice-President, Special Convention on a European Constitution, European Union;* b. 7 Aug. 1940, Montpellier, France; m. Celie Verbeke 1965; four c. *Education:* Univ. of Namur. *Career:* adviser to various govt ministries 1972–81; Minister of Social Affairs and Institutional Reforms 1981–88; Deputy Prime Minister and Minister of Communications and Institutional Reforms 1988–92; Prime Minister of Belgium 1992–99; Vice-Pres. of EU Special Convention on a European Constitution 2001–; cand. (Christen-Democratisch en Vlaams Partij—CD&V) in 2003 Belgian elections.
Address: Special Convention on a European Constitution, European Union, 200 rue de la Loi, 1049 Brussels, Belgium.

DEISS, Joseph; Swiss politician; b. 18 Jan. 1946, Fribourg; m. Elizabeth Mueller; three s. *Education:* Coll. Saint-Michel, Fribourg, Univ. of Fribourg, King's Coll., Cambridge, UK. *Career:* Lecturer (part-time) in Political Economy, Univ. of Fribourg 1973–83, Prof. Extraordinary 1984–99, Sr Faculty mem. Dept of Social and Econ. Science 1996–98;

Deputy, Great Council of Fribourg 1981–91, Pres. 1991, Nat. Adviser 1991–99; Vice-Pres. Comm. on Foreign Policy, Nat. Council 1995–96; Pres. Comm. on Revision of the Fed. Constitution 1996; Head of Fed. Dept of Foreign Affairs 1999–2002; Head of Fed. Dept of Econ. Affairs 2003–06 (resgnd); Pres. of the Swiss Confed. 2004; Pres. Banque Raiffaisen du Haut-Lac 1996–99; Chair. of Bd Schuhmacher AG, Schmitten 1996–99.
Address: c/o Federal Department of Economic Affairs, Bundeshaus Ost, 3003 Bern, Switzerland (office).

DEL CASTILLO GÁLVES, Jorge Alfonso Alejandro; Peruvian lawyer and politician; *President of the Council of Ministers (Prime Minister);* b. 2 July 1950, Lima. *Education:* Nat. Univ. of San Marcos, Lima, Pontifical Catholic Univ. of Peru. *Career:* Mayor of Barranco Ward, Lima 1984–86, apptd Prefect of Lima 1985; mem. Partido Aprista Peruano—PAP, Sec.-Gen. PAP 1999–, Rep. of PAP before OAS; Mayor of Metropolitan Lima Co. 1987–89; elected to Peruvian Congress of the Repub. for Lima 1995–, re-elected 2000, 2001, 2006; Pres. Council of Ministers (Prime Minister of Peru) 2006–.
Address: Office of the President of the Council of Ministers, Avenida 28 de Julio 878, Miraflores, Lima, Peru (office). *Telephone:* (1) 6109800 (office). *Fax:* (1) 4449168 (office). *E-mail:* webmaster@pcm.gob.pe (office). *Website:* www.pcm.gob.pe (office).

DEL CASTILLO VERA, Pilar; Spanish politician and academic; b. 31 July 1952, Nador, Morocco; m. Guillermo Gortázar; two c. *Education:* Universidad Complutense de Madrid, Univ. of Ohio, USA. *Career:* Lecturer in Constitutional Law, subsequently Prof. of Political Science and Admin, Universidad Nacional de Educación a Distancia (UNED) 1986–; wrote policy papers for Fundación para el Análisis y los Estudios Sociales (FAES); Tech. Adviser Centro de Investigaciones Sociológicas (CIS) 1987–88, Pres. 1996–2000; Minister of Educ., Culture and Sport 2000–04; fmr Ed. Nueva Revista de Política, Cultura y Arte; mem. Associación Nacional e Internacional de Ciencia Política; Fulbright Scholar. *Publications:* Financiación de los partidos y candidatos en las democracias occidentales, Cultura Política, Comportamiento político y electoral.
Address: c/o Ministry of Education, Culture and Sport, Alcala 34, 28071 Madrid, Spain (office).

DEL CID DE BONILLA, María Antonieta; Guatemalan politician and banking executive; *Minister of Public Finance; Career:* Exec. Dir for Guatemala, Inter-American Devt Bank 1998; fmr Vice-Pres. Bank of Guatemala; Minister of Public Finance 2004–.
Address: Ministry of Public Finance, Centro Cívico, 8a Avda y 21 Calle, Zona 1, Guatemala City, Guatemala (office). *Telephone:* 2248-5053 (office). *Fax:* 2248-5054 (office). *E-mail:* info@minfin.gob.gt. *Website:* www.minfin .gob.gt (office).

DEL PONTE, Carla, LLM; Swiss lawyer, international organization official and diplomatist; *Ambassador to Argentina;* b. 9 Feb. 1947, Lugano; one s. *Education:* Univs of Berne and Geneva. *Career:* in pvt. practice, Lugano 1975–81; Investigating Magistrate, then Public Prosecutor, Lugano 1981–94; Attorney-Gen. and Chief Prosecutor of Switzerland 1994–2000, mem. Fed. Comm. on White-Collar Crime 1994–99; Chief Prosecutor, Int. Criminal Tribunals of Rwanda 1999–2003, of the Fmr Yugoslavia 1999–2007; Amb. to Argentina 2008–; Dr hc (Liège) 2002, (Wales, Bangor) 2003, Hon. Dottore in Giurisprudenza (Genoa) 2004; 22nd Peace Prize, UNA (Spain) 2002, Goler T. Butcher Prize 2004.
Address: Embassy of Switzerland, Santa Fe 846, 10°, C1059ABP, Buenos Aires Argentina (office). *Telephone:* (11) 4311-6491 (office). *Fax:* (11) 4313-2998 (office). *E-mail:* vertretung@bue.rep.admin.ch (office). *Website:* www .eda.admin.ch/buenosaires_emb/s/home.html (office).

DEL ROSARIO, Albert F., BSc; Philippine diplomatist; b. 1939, Manila; m. Gretchen de Venecia; five c. *Education:* New York Univ., USA. *Career:* business career has spanned insurance, banking, real estate, shipping, telecommunications, consumer products, retail, pharmaceutical and food industries; fmr Chair./Dir Metro Pacific Corpn, Philippine Indocoil Corpn, Fort Bonifacio Devt Corpn, Philippine Long Distance Telephone Co.; currently Chair. Philippine Cancer Soc. Nat. Fund Drive, Free Rural Eye Clinic, Makati Foundation for Educ., Korean Hwa Rang Do Martial Arts Asscn; mem. Del. of the Philippines to USA and Indonesia; Amb. to USA 2001–06; Philippine Army Award 1991, Edsa II Heros Award 2001.
Address: Department of Foreign Affairs, DFA Bldg, 2330 Roxas Blvd, Pasay City, 1330 Metro Manila, The Philippines (office). *Telephone:* (2) 8344000 (office). *Fax:* (2) 8321597 (office). *E-mail:* webmaster@dfa.gov.ph (office). *Website:* www.dfa.gov.ph (office).

DELAYE, Bruno; French diplomatist; *Ambassador to Spain;* b. 8 May 1952. *Education:* Institut d'Études Politiques, Ecole Nat. d'Administration. *Career:* chargé de mission to Dir-Gen. of Energy and Raw Materials,

Ministry of Industry 1979–81, Tech. Advisor to Office of the Minister 1981; Tech. Advisor to Office of Minister of Foreign Affairs 1981–84; Int. Affairs Del., Ministry of Industry and Research 1985–86; First Counsellor, Embassy in Cairo 1987–91; Advisor to Pres. 1992–95; Dir Gen. for Int. Co-operation and Devt, Ministry of Foreign Affairs 2000–03; Amb. to Togo 1991–92, to Mexico 1995–2000, to Greece 2003–07, to Spain 2007–; Chair. Agency for French Teaching Abroad 2000, Coopération Int.; mem. Supervisory Bd French Devt Agency 2000–; mem. Comm. for Educ., Science and Culture; Chevalier, Légion d'honneur, Ordre Nat. du Mérite. *Address:* Embassy of France, Salustiano Olózaga 9, 28001 Madrid, Spain (office). *Telephone:* (91) 4238900 (office). *Fax:* (91) 4238908 (office). *E-mail:* chancellerie@ctv.es (office). *Website:* www.ambafrance-es.org (office).

DeLISI, Scott H.; American diplomatist; b. St Paul, Minn.; m. Leija DeLisi; three c. *Education:* Univ. of Minn. and Univ. of Minn. Law School. *Career:* career mem. Sr Foreign Service since 1981, rank of Counselor, overseas postings have included Vice-Consul, Bombay, Econ./Commercial Officer, Antananarivo, Madagascar, Political Officer, Islamabad, Chief of Political Section, Colombo, Sri Lanka, positions in Washington, DC in Bureau for S Asian Affairs and in Bureau for Intelligence and Research, Deputy Chief of Mission, Gaborone, Botswana 1997–2001, Dir for Southern African Affairs 2001–04, Amb. to Eritrea 2004–07; Humphrey Fellow, Hubert H. Humphrey Inst. of Public Affairs; James Clement Dunn Award for Excellence, Dir's Award, Defense Intelligence Agency, four Superior Honor Awards, two Meritorious Honor Awards. *Address:* US Department of State, 2201 C Street NW, Washington, DC 20520, USA (office). *Telephone:* (202) 647-4000 (office). *Fax:* (202) 647-6738 (office). *Website:* www.state.gov (office).

DELL, Christopher William, BA, MPhil; American diplomatist; *Deputy Chief of Mission, Kabul;* m. Theodora Galabora 2006; two c. from previous m. *Education:* Columbia Coll. and Balliol Coll., Oxford, UK. *Career:* career mem. Sr Foreign Service, served as Vice-Consul, Matamoros, Mexico 1981–83, Oporto, Portugal 1983–84, Political Officer, Embassy in Lisbon 1984–85, Staff Asst, Bureau of Political-Mil. Affairs 1985–86, Desk Officer for Spain and Portugal, Bureau of European and Canadian Affairs 1986–87, Exec. Asst to Special Negotiator for Greek Bases Agreement, Bureau of European and Canadian Affairs 1987–89, Special Asst to Under-Sec. for Int. Security Affairs 1989–91, Chief of Mission, US Office, Pristina, Kosovo 2000–01, Deputy Chief of Mission, Maputo 1991–94, Deputy Dir Office of Regional Political Affairs, Bureau of European and Canadian Affairs, Dept of State 1994–96, Deputy Chief of Mission, Sofia 1997–2000, Amb. to Angola 2001–04, to Zimbabwe 2004–07, Deputy Chief of Mission, Kabul 2007–; Order of the Madara Horseman, First Degree (Bulgaria) 2000; Columbia Univ. Kellett Fellowship for study at Univ. of Oxford 1978, numerous awards, including Presidential Distinguished Service Award 2004. *Publication:* article 'The Fork in the Road', Kosovo & Balkan Observer 2001.

DELORS, Jacques Lucien Jean; French politician and economist; *President, Conseil de l'emploi, des revenus et de la cohésion sociale;* b. 20 July 1925, Paris; m. Marie Lephaille 1948; one s. (deceased) one d. (Martine Aubry). *Education:* Lycée Voltaire, Paris, Lycée Blaise-Pascal, Clermont-Ferrand, Univ. of Paris, Centre d'Etudes Supérieur de Banque (IEP). *Career:* Head of Dept, Banque de France 1945–62, attached to staff of Dir-Gen. of Securities and Financial Market 1950–62, mem. Gen. Council 1973–79; mem. Planning and Investments Section, Econ. and Social Council 1959–61; Head of Social Affairs Section, Commissariat général du Plan 1962–69; Sec.-Gen. Interministerial Cttee for Vocational Training and Social Promotion 1969–72; Adviser to Jacques Chaban-Delmas 1969, Chargé de mission 1971–72; Assoc. Prof. of Co. Man., Univ. of Paris IX 1973–79; f. Club Echange et Projets 1974; Dir Labour and Soc. Research Centre 1975–79; Parti Socialiste Nat. Del. for int. econ. relations 1976–81; elected mem. European Parl. 1979, Chair. Econ. and Monetary Cttee 1979–81; Minister for the Economy and Finance 1981–84, for the Economy, Finance and Budget 1983–84; Mayor of Clichy 1983–84; Pres. Comm. of the European Communities (now European Commission) 1985–94; Pres. EMU Comm. 1988–89, Int. Comm. on Educ. for the Twenty-First Century, UNESCO 1992–99; Pres. Conseil d'admin. Collège d'Europe, Bruges 1995–99, Conseil de l'emploi, des revenus et de la cohésion sociale (CERC) 2000–08; f. Notre Europe 1996–2004; Officier, Légion d'honneur; hon. degrees from 24 univs in Europe, USA and Canada. *Publications:* Les indicateurs sociaux 1971, Changer 1975, En sortir ou pas (jtly) 1985, La France par l'Europe (jtly) 1988, Le Nouveau concert Européen 1992, Our Europe 1993, L'Unité d'un homme 1994, Combats pour l'Europe 1996, Mémoires 2004; numerous articles; reports for UN on French planning (1966) and long-term planning (1969). *Address:* Conseil de l'emploi, des revenus et de la cohésion sociale, 113 rue de Grenelle, 75007 Paris, France (office). *Telephone:* 1-53-85-15-16 (office).

Fax: 1-53-85-15-21 (office). *E-mail:* jacques.delors@cerc.gouv.fr (office). *Website:* www.cerc.gouv.fr (office).

DEMBRI, Muhammad Salah; Algerian diplomatist; *Ambassador to UK;* m. Monique Dembri. *Career:* fmr Minister of Foreign Affairs; fmr Amb. and Perm. Rep. to the UN, Geneva; Amb. to UK (also accred to Ireland) 2005–; fmr Pres. Conf. on Disarmament, Open-Ended Working Group on Right to Devt, UNHCR. *Address:* Algerian Embassy, 54 Holland Park, London, W11 3RS, England (office). *Telephone:* (20) 7221-7800 (office). *Fax:* (20) 7221-0448 (office). *E-mail:* info@algerianembassy.org.uk (office). *Website:* www .algerianembassy.org.uk (office).

DEMEKSA, Kuma; Ethiopian politician; *Minister of National Defence; Career:* fmr Minister of Internal Affairs; officially removed from presidency of Oromia State after he was dismissed from Oromo People's Democratic Org. for "abuse of power, corruption and anti-democratic practices"; absent from political scene until apptd State Minister of Capacity Building; Minister of Nat. Defence 2005–. *Address:* Ministry of National Defence, PO Box 1373, Addis Ababa, Ethiopia (office). *Telephone:* (11) 5511777 (office). *Fax:* (11) 5516053 (office).

DEMESSINE, Michelle; French politician; b. 18 June 1947, Frelinghien (Nord); m.; one c. *Education:* Valentine Labbé Tech. Lycée, Lille. *Career:* worked as sec. 1964–75; elected as union del. 1968, apptd mem. Département Exec. Cttee of Conféd. Générale du Travail 1973; Dept Br. Sec. Union des Femmes Françaises 1976–90, now Hon. Chair.; joined Parti Communiste Français (PCF) 1970, elected mem. Nord Département Cttee 1977, mem. PCF Bureau 1977–; mem. Regional Econ. and Social Cttee 1983–95; Senator for Nord 1992–97; Vice-Chair. Social Affairs Cttee, study group on combating drug trafficking and addiction, fact-finding mission on women in public life; municipal councillor for Houplines 1995–; Sec. of State for Tourism 1997–2002; elected to Senate 2001–; Prix Jean Faucher 2002. *Publication:* Femmes d'ici (co-author) 1985. *Address:* Sénat, 15 rue de Vaugirard, 75291 Paris Cedex 0, France (office). *Website:* www.senat.fr (office).

DEMON-BELGRAEF, Georgine Mavis; Suriname diplomatist; *Career:* Amb. to Brazil 2006–. *Address:* Embassy of Suriname, SHIS, QI 09, Conj. 08, Casa 24, 71625-080 Brasília, DF Brazil (office). *Telephone:* (61) 3248-6706 (office). *Fax:* (61) 3248-3791 (office). *E-mail:* surinameemb@terra.com.br (office).

DEMUTH, Christopher, JD, AB; American lawyer; *President, American Enterprise Institute for Public Policy Research (AEI); Education:* Univ. of Chicago Law School, Harvard Univ. *Career:* Staff Asst to Pres.Richard Nixon, White House 1969–70; Attorney, Sidley & Austin 1973–76; Assoc. Gen. Counsel, Consolidated Rail Corpn 1976–77; Dir Harvard Faculty Project on Regulation, also Lecturer on Public Policy, Kennedy School of Govt 1977–81; Exec. Dir Presidential Task Force on Regulatory Relief, White House 1981–83; Administrator, Office of Information and Regulatory Affairs, US Office of Man. and Budget 1981–84; Man. Dir Lexecon Inc. 1984–86; Pres. American Enterprise Inst. for Public Policy Research (AEI) 1986–. *Publications:* An Agenda for Federal Regulatory Reform, The Neoconservative Imagination. *Address:* American Enterprise Institute for Public Policy Research (AEI), 1150 17th Street, NW, Washington, DC, 20036, USA (office). *Telephone:* (202) 862-5800 (office). *Fax:* (202) 862-7177 (office). *E-mail:* CDemuth@aei .org (office). *Website:* www.aei.org (office).

DENG, Francis Mading, LLB, LLM, JSD; Sudanese diplomatist, academic and UN official; *Secretary-General's Special Adviser for the Prevention of Genocide, United Nations;* b. 1938. *Education:* Khartoum Univ., Yale Univ. Law School USA, and post-grad. educ. in UK. *Career:* fmr Human Rights Officer, UN Secr., New York; fmr Amb. to Canada, USA and Scandinavian countries; fmr Minister of State for Foreign Affairs; Guest Scholar, Woodrow Wilson Int. Center for Scholars 1983, later Sr Research Assoc; Sr Fellow (non-resident), Brookings Inst., est. African Studies Br. of Foreign Policy Studies Program 1989, Co-Founder and Co-Dir (with Roberta Cohen) Brookings Project on Internal Displacement, Ralph Bunche Inst. for Int. Studies, Grad. Center, CUNY 1992, Prof. of Political Science 2001; Special Rep. of the Sec.-Gen. on Internally Displaced Persons, Office of the High Commr. for Human Rights, Geneva 1992–2004; Research Prof. of Int. Politics, Law and Soc. and Dir Center for Displacement Studies, Nitze School for Advanced Int. Studies, Johns Hopkins Univ., Washington, DC 2003–; Distinguished Visiting Scholar, Kluge Center, US Library of Congress, Washington, DC 2005–06; Wilhelm Fellow, Center for Int. Studies, MIT 2006–07;; UN Sec.Gen.'s Special Adviser for the Prevention of Genocide 2007–; Sr Fellow, US Inst. of Peace

2002–03, now Dir Sudan Peace Support Project; fmr Visiting Lecturer, Yale Univ. School of Law, New York Univ.; Acting Chair. African Leadership Forum 1996; fmr Distinguished Fellow, Rockefeller Brothers Fund; Grawemeyer Award for Ideas Improving World (with Roberta Cohen), Univ. of Lousiville 2005, Merage Foundation American Dream Leadership Award 2007. *Publications include:* Tradition and Modernization: A Challenge for Law Amongst the Dinka of the Sudan 1971, The Man Called Majok: A Biography of Power, Polygamy and Change 1986; (as co-author): Human Rights in Africa: Cross-Cultural Perspectives 1990, Conflict Resolution in Africa 1991, The Challenges of Famine Relief: Emergency Operations in the Sudan 1992, Protecting the Dispossessed: A Challenge for the International Community 1993, War of Visions: Conflict Identities in the Sudan 1995, Masses in Flight: The Global Crisis of Internal Displacement 1998, A Strategic Vision for Africa 2001; (as co-ed.): Sovereignty as Responsibility: Conflict Management in Africa 1996, African Reckoning: A Quest for Good Governance 1998.
Address: Paul H. Nitze School of Advanced International Studies (SAIS), The Johns Hopkins University, 1740 Massachusetts Avenue, NW, Washington, DC 20036, USA (office). *Telephone:* (202) 663-5871 (office). *E-mail:* fdeng1@mail.jhuwash.jhu.edu (office). *Website:* www.sais-jhu.edu (office).

DENISOV, Andrei Ivanovich; Russian politician and diplomatist; *First Deputy Minister of Foreign Affairs;* b. 3 Oct. 1952, Kharkov, Ukraine; m. Natalya Denisova; one d. *Education:* Moscow Inst. of Int. Relations. *Career:* joined Ministry of Foreign Affairs 1992, various diplomatic posts in ministry and abroad, Dir Dept of Econ. Co-operation 1997–2000, Deputy Minister of Foreign Affairs responsible for int. econ. co-operation 2001–04; Amb. to Egypt 2000–01; Perm. Rep. to UN 2004–06; First Deputy Minister of Foreign Affairs 2006–.
Address: Ministry of Foreign Affairs, 119200 Moscow, Smolenskaya-Sennaya pl. 32/34, Russian Federation (office). *Telephone:* (495) 244-16-06 (office). *Fax:* (495) 230-21-30 (office). *E-mail:* ministry@mid.ru (office). *Website:* www.mid.ru (office).

DENKTAŞ, Rauf R.; Turkish Cypriot politician and barrister; b. 27 Jan. 1924, Baf; m. Aydin Munir 1949; two s. (one deceased) two d. *Education:* The English School, Nicosia and Lincoln's Inn, London. *Career:* law practice in Nicosia 1947–49; Jr Crown Counsel 1949, Crown Counsel 1952; Acting Solicitor-Gen. 1956–58; Pres. Fed. of Turkish Cypriot Asscns 1958–60; Pres. Turkish Communal Chamber 1960, re-elected 1970; Pres. 'Turkish Federated State of Cyprus' 1975–83; elected Pres. 'Turkish Repub. of Northern Cyprus' (TRNC) Nov. 1983–2005; radio and TV broadcasts on Cyprus; Dr hc (Middle East Tech. Univ., Ankara) 1984, (Southeastern Univ., Washington, DC) 1989, (Eastern Mediterranean Univ., TRNC) 1990, (Black Sea Tech. Univ., Turkey) 1991. *Publications:* Secrets of Happiness 1941, Hell Without Fire 1944, A Handbook of Criminal Cases 1955, Five Minutes to Twelve 1966, The AKRITAS Plan 1972, A Short Discourse on Cyprus 1972, The Cyprus Problem 1973, A Discourse with Youth 1981, The Cyprus Triangle 1982, Woman and the World 1985, Inspirations from the Koran 1986, Examination World 1986, For Tomorrows 1986, UN Speeches on Cyprus 1986, Cyprus, An Indictment and Defence 1987, Ataturk, Religion and Secularism 1989, A Challenge on Cyprus 1990, Denktas As A Photographer, Images from Northern Cyprus 1991, The Cyprus Problem and the Remedy 1992, Karkot Stream 1993, Those Days 1993, Lest Cyprus Becomes Crete 2005, 10 vols of memoirs 1963–74, The Cyprus Problem 2005.
Address: c/o The Office of the President, 'Turkish Republic of Northern Cyprus', via Mersin 10, Lefkoşa, Turkey (office). *Telephone:* (22) 83141 (office); (81) 53190 (home). *Fax:* (22) 75281 (office); (81) 58167 (home). *E-mail:* pressdpt@brimnet.com (office).

DENKTAŞ, Serdar; Turkish Cypriot politician; *Deputy Prime Minister and Minister of Foreign Affairs;* b. 1959, Lefkoşa; m.; three c. *Education:* Cardiff Coll., UK. *Career:* est. Turkish Students Asscn of Cardiff Coll., N Cyprus Cultural Asscn 1986, Young Businessman Asscn 1989; Dir-Gen. Cyprus Credit Bank –1990; elected mem. of Parl. for Lefkoşa 1990; Minister of Interior, Rural Affairs and Environment 1990–92; Leader Nine Movt (now Democracy Party) 1992; Dist Chair. for Lefkoşa, then Sec.-Gen. of Democracy Party 1992–93, Leader 1996–2000, 2002–; elected mem. of Parl. for Lefkoşa (Democracy Party) 1993; Minister of Youth and Sports 1994–95; Minister of Tourism and Environment 2001–03; Deputy Prime Minister and Minister of Foreign Affairs 2003–.
Address: Office of the Deputy Prime Minister, Selcuklu Road, Lefkoşa (Nicosia), Mersin 10, Turkey (office). *Telephone:* (22) 83241 (office). *Fax:* (22) 84290 (office). *E-mail:* pubinfo@trncinfo.org (office). *Website:* www.trncinfo.org (home).

DENT, Alberto; Costa Rican politician and banker; b. 11 Dec. 1945; m.; four c. *Education:* Calif. State Polytech. Univ., USA. *Career:* Gen. Man. Dent and Sons Ltd 1973–84; Pres. Banex Bank Ltd 1980–84; Exec. Pres. BFA Financial Group 1984–96; Dir Costa Rican Bankers' Asscn 1985–96, Pres. 1986–90; Adviser to Pres. of Costa Rica 1998–2000; Vice-Pres. Cen. Bank of Costa Rica 1998–2000; Minister of Agric. and Livestock 2000–01; Minister of Finance 2001–02, 2003–04 (resgnd); Pres. Financial Supervision Council 2003.
Address: c/o Ministry of Finance, Diagonal al Teatro Nacional, San José, Costa Rica (office).

DERBEZ BAUTISTA, Luis Ernesto, PhD; Mexican politician and economist; b. 1 April 1947, Mexico City. *Education:* San Luis Potosí Autonomous Univ., Univ. of Oregon and Iowa State Univ., USA. *Career:* economist, IBRD (World Bank), responsible for regional areas including Chile 1983–86, Cen. America 1986–89, Africa 1989–92, Western and Cen. Africa 1992–94, India, Nepal and Bhutan 1994–97 (also dir multilateral econ. assistance and structural adjustment programmes in Chile, Costa Rica, Honduras and Guatemala); ind. consultant, World Bank, Mexico City Office and IDB, Washington, DC 1997–2000; Econ. Adviser and Co-ordinator of Econ. Affairs to Pres.-Elect of Mexico 2000; fmr Sec. for Economy; Sec. of State for Foreign Affairs 2003–06; fmr Prof., Grad. School of Business Man., Instituto Tecnológico y de Estudios Superiores de Monterrey (also Dir Econometric Studies Unit and Econs Dept); fmr Vice-Rector Univ. of the Americas, Cholula, Mexico; fmr Visiting Prof., Johns Hopkins Univ. School of Int. Studies, USA.
Address: c/o Secretariat of State for Foreign Affairs, Avda Ricardo Flores Magón 2, Col. Guerrero, Del. Cuauhtémoc, 06995, Mexico, Mexico (office).

DERBY, Susan Meredith; Suriname diplomatist. *Career:* fmr Amb. to Netherlands; Chargé d'affaires a.i. in UK (non-resident) –2008, Counsellor, The Hague 2008–.
Address: Embassy of Suriname, Alexander Gogelweg 2, 2517 JH The Hague, Netherlands (office). *Telephone:* (70) 365-08-44 (office). *Fax:* (70) 361-74-45 (office). *E-mail:* ambassade.suriname@wxs.nl (office).

DERHAM, James M., MEcons, MPA; American diplomatist; *Ambassador to Guatemala; Education:* Fordham Univ., George Washington Univ., Harvard Univ. *Career:* served in US Army overseas in Germany; Foreign Service overseas assignments have been to Argentina, Brazil (tours as Consul-Gen. in Rio de Janeiro and Prin. Officer in Salvador da Bahia), Italy and as Chargé d'affaires a.i. and Deputy Chief of Mission in Brasília, Washington assignments in Econ. Bureau and in Office of Japanese Affairs, US State Dept, also spent a year on Capitol Hill as a legis. fellow, Deputy Chief of Mission, Embassy in Mexico City –2002, Prin. Deputy Asst Sec. of State, Bureau of Western Hemisphere Affairs 2002–05, Amb. to Guatemala 2005–.
Address: Embassy of the USA, Avenida de la Reforma 7-01, Zona 10, Guatemala City, Guatemala (office). *Telephone:* 2326-4000 (office). *Fax:* 2326-4654 (office). *E-mail:* AmCitsGuatemala@state.gov (office). *Website:* guatemala.usembassy.gov (office).

DERRYCK, Vivian Lowery, MIA; American organization official; *Senior Vice-President and Director of Public-Private Partnerships, Academy for Education Development;* b. 30 Jan. 1945, Cleveland, OH; m. Robert Berg 1989; one s. one d. *Education:* Columbia Univ., New York. *Career:* Sr Assoc. Vice-Pres.'s Task Force on Youth Employment 1979; Dir US Secr. World Conf. of UN Decade for Women 1979–80; Deputy Asst Sec. Dept of State 1980–82; Exec. Vice-Pres. and Dir Int. Div., Nat. Council of Negro Women 1982–84; Consultant Advisory Comm. on Voluntary Foreign Aid and Agency for Int. Affairs 1984; Vice-Pres. Nat. Democratic Inst. for Int. Affairs 1984–88; Exec. Dir Washington Int. Center and Vice-Pres. Meridian House 1988–89; Chair. African-American Inst. 1989; mem. Int. Devt Conf., Washington, DC 1983, Vice-Pres., mem. Bd of Dirs 1983–89; Sec. Bd, mem. Exec. Comm. InterAction, Washington, DC 1990; fmr Asst Admin. for Africa, United States Agency for Int. Devt (USAID); fmr Sr Vice-Pres. and Dir Public Policy Acad. for Educ. Devt (AED), Sr Vice-Pres. and Dir Public–Pvt Partnerships 2001–; mem. bd dirs GlobalRights.org; Woman of the Year, Freetown, Sierra Leone 1990.
Address: Academy for Educational Development, 1825 Connecticut Avenue, Washington, DC 20009, USA (office). *Telephone:* (202) 884-8000 (office). *Fax:* (202) 884-8000 (office). *Website:* www.aed.org (office).

DERSE, Anne Elizabeth, BA, MA; American diplomatist; *Ambassador to Azerbaijan;* b. 1954, Lakewood, Ohio; m. E. Mason Hendrickson, Jr; four c. *Education:* Macalester Coll., St Paul, Minnesota, Paul H. Nitze School of Advanced Int. Studies, Johns Hopkins Univ., Econ. and Commercial Studies Program, Dept of State. *Career:* career mem. Sr Foreign Service with rank of Minister Counselor, joined Dept of State in 1981, overseas assignments have included Vice-Consul, Trinidad and Tobago 1981–83, staff asst to Counselor of Dept of State 1983–84, trade officer, Singapore

1985–88, Finance and Devt Officer and Deputy Econ. Counselor, Seoul 1989–93, Special Asst for Asian Affairs 1993–95, Econ. Counselor and Deputy Counselor, Manila 1995–97, Econ. Counselor, Brussels 1997–99, served as last US Commr on Tripartite Gold Comm. (as it completed adjudication of sovereign claims for gold seized by Nazis and recovered by Allies during World War II), Minister Counselor for Econ. Affairs, Mission to EU 1999–2003, Exec. Asst to Under-Sec. for Econ., Business and Agricultural Affairs 2003–04, assisted in establishing the new US Embassy in Baghdad, serving there as Minister Counselor for Econ. Affairs 2004–05, Dir for Biodefense Policy, Homeland Security Council 2005–06, helped develop Implementation Plan for Pres. Bush's Nat. Strategy for Pandemic Influenza 2005–06, Amb. to Azerbaijan 2006–; Herbert Salzman Award for Excellence in Int. Econ. Performance 1986, Superior Honor Awards 1994, 1996, 2002, 2004, 2006, Cordell Hull Award for Sr Econ. Achievement, Dept of State 2004, Presidential Meritorious Service Award 2006.
Address: US Embassy, Azadlıq pr. 83, 1007 Baku, Azerbaijan (office). *Telephone:* (12) 498-03-35 (office). *Fax:* (12) 465-66-71 (office). *E-mail:* consularbaku@state.gov (office). *Website:* www.usembassybaku.org (office).

DERVIŞ, Kemal, BSc, PhD; Turkish economist and international organization official; *Administrator, United Nations Development Programme (UNDP);* b. 1949, Istanbul; m. Catherine Anne Derviş. *Education:* London School of Econs, UK, Princeton Univ., USA. *Career:* Lecturer in Econs, Middle Eastern Tech. Univ. 1973; Adviser on issues of econ. and int. relations to Prime Minister Bülent Ecevit 1973–76; Lecturer in Int. Relations and Econs, Princeton Univ. 1977; mem. Research Dept, World Bank 1978–82, Head of Industrial Strategy and Policy, Global Industry Dept 1982–86, Sr Economist for Europe, Middle East and N African Affairs 1986–87, Head of Cen. Europe Div. 1987–96, Vice-Pres. in charge of Middle East and Africa Region 1996–2000, Vice-Pres. in charge of Poverty Reduction and Econ. Man. 2000–01; Minister of Econ. Affairs 2001–02; Minister of State responsible for the Economy 2002; Admin. UNDP 2005–; mem. Cumhuriyet Halk Partisi–CHP (Republican People's Party) 2002–; Senator, Turkish Parl. 2002. *Publications include:* General Equilibrium Models for Development Policy (co-author); numerous articles on econ. policy and devt econs.
Address: United Nations Development Programme, Wisma UN, Block C, Kompleks Pejabat Damansara, Jalan Dungun, Damansara Heights, 50490 Kuala Lumpur, Malaysia (office); Türkiye Büyük Millet Meclisi, 06543 Ankara, Turkey (home). *Telephone:* (603) 2095-9122 (office); (312) 468-8901 (office). *Fax:* (603) 2095-2870 (office). *E-mail:* registry.my@undp.org (office); kdervis@chp.org.tr (home). *Website:* www.undp.org (office).

DERYABIN, Yuri Stepanovich; Russian diplomatist (retd); *Director, Centre for North European Research, Institute of Europe, Russian Academy of Sciences;* b. 3 Jan. 1932, Karachelka, Kurgan Region; m.; two d. *Education:* Moscow Inst. of Int. Relations. *Career:* diplomatic service 1954–; Third, then Second Sec., Dept of Scandinavian Countries, Ministry of Foreign Affairs 1959–62; Second Sec., Embassy in Oslo 1962–65, First Sec., Embassy in Finland 1968–73, Counsellor 1973–75; Counsellor-Envoy 1980–83; Deputy Chief Second, European Dept, Ministry of Foreign Affairs 1986–87; Chief Dept of Problems of Security and Cooperation in Europe 1987–90; Deputy Minister of Foreign Affairs 1991–92; Amb. to Finland 1992–96; Deputy Sec., Security Council of Russia 1997–98; Dir Centre for N European Research, Inst. of Europe, Russian Acad. of Sciences 1999–. *Publications:* various articles for newspapers and journals, mainly concerning the Northern European model of social-economic and socio-political devt.
Address: Institute of Europe, Centre for North European Research, Mokhovaya Str. 11, Korp. 38, 103873 Moscow, Russia (office). *Telephone:* (095) 692-04-86 (office); (495) 203-41-87 (office); (095) 931-22-96 (home). *Fax:* (095) 299-42-98 (office); (495) 200-42-98 (office). *E-mail:* namiant@list .ru (office); europe@ieras.ru (office); deryabin@newolymp.net (home). *Website:* www.ieras.ru/centrseurope.htm (office).

DESAI, Baron (Life Peer), cr. 1991, of St Clement Danes in the City of Westminster; **Meghnad Jagdishchandra Desai,** PhD; British economist and academic; *Professor Emeritus of Economics, London School of Economics;* b. 10 July 1940, Baroda, India; m. 1st Gail Wilson 1970 (divorced 2004); one s. two d.; m. 2nd Kishwar Rusha 2004. *Education:* Univ. of Bombay, Univ. of Pennsylvania, USA. *Career:* Assoc. Specialist, Dept of Agricultural Econs, Univ. of Calif., Berkeley, USA 1963–65; Lecturer, LSE 1965–77, Sr Lecturer 1977–80, Reader 1980–83, Prof. of Econs 1983–, now Prof. Emer., Head Devt Studies Inst. 1990–95, Dir Centre for the Study of Global Governance 1992–2003, Chair. Econ. Research Div. 1983–95; consultant at various times to FAO, UNCTAD, Int. Coffee Org., World Bank, UNIDO, Ministries of Industrial Devt and Educ., Algeria, British Airports Authority and other bodies; Co-Ed. Journal of Applied Econometrics 1984–; mem. Editorial Bds Int. Review of Applied Econs

and several other journals; mem. Council, Royal Econ. Soc. 1988; mem. Exec. Cttee Asscn of Univ. Teachers in Econs 1987– (Pres. 1987–90); mem. Univ. of London Senate representing LSE 1981–89; mem. Nat. Exec. of Council for Academic Freedom and Democracy 1972–83, Speaker's Comm. on Citizenship 1989–; Berndt Carlson Trust; mem. or fmr mem. Governing Body of Courtauld Inst., British Inst. in Paris, Cen. School of Arts, Polytechnic of N London; Chair. Holloway Ward (Islington Cen.) Labour Party 1977–80; Chair. Islington S and Finsbury Labour Party 1986–92, Pres. 1992–; Dr hc (Kingston Univ.) 1992; Hon. DSc (Econs) (E London) 1994; Hon. DPhil (London Guildhall) 1996; Hon. LLD (Monash Univ.) 2005; Pravasi Phraskar (Distinguished Diaspora Indian Award) 2004, Distinguished Alumnus Award, Martin School of Finance 2004. *Publications:* Marxian Economic Theory 1974 (trans. in several languages), Applied Econometrics 1976, Marxian Economics 1979, Testing Monetarism 1981, Marx's Revenge 2001, Nehru's Hero: Dilip Kumar in the Life of India 2004, Development and Nationhood 2004, Nehru's Hero 2005, Development and Nationhood 2005, The Route of All Evil: Political Economy of Ezra Pound 2006, Rethinking Islamism 2006; ed. several books; numerous papers and contribs to books and journals.
Address: House of Lords, London, SW1A 0AA (office); 3 Deepdene Road, London, SE5 8EG, England (home). *Telephone:* (20) 7219-5066 (office); (20) 7274-5561 (home). *Fax:* (20) 7219-5979 (office). *E-mail:* m.desai@lse .ac.uk (office). *Website:* www.lse.ac.uk/Depts/global (office).

DESAI, Nitin Dayalji, BA, MSc; Indian international official, economist and civil servant; *Under-Secretary-General of the Johannesburg Summit, United Nations;* b. 5 July 1941, Bombay; m. Aditi Gupta 1979; two s. *Education:* Univ. of Bombay and London School of Econs, UK. *Career:* Lecturer in Econs, Univ. of Liverpool, UK 1965–67, Univ. of Southampton, UK 1967–70; consultant, Tata (India) Econ. Consultancy Services 1970–73; consultant/adviser, Planning Comm. Govt of India 1973–85; Sr Adviser, Brundtland Comm. 1985–87; Special Sec. Planning Comm. India 1987–88; Sec./Chief Econ. Adviser, Ministry of Finance 1988–90; Deputy Under-Sec.-Gen. UNCED, Geneva 1990–92; UN Under-Sec.-Gen. for Econ. and Social Affairs 1992–2003, Under-Sec.-Gen. of Dept for Policy Co-ordination and Sustainable Devt 1993–97, Sec.-Gen. of Johannesburg Summit 2002, Sec.-Gen's Special Adviser for World Summit on the Information Society 2003–; Hon. Fellow LSE 2004.
Address: United Nations, New York, NY 10017 (office); 330 East 33 Street Apt. 12M, New York, NY 10016, USA (home). *Telephone:* (212) 532-0028 (home). *E-mail:* dsd@un.org (office). *Website:* www.un.org/esa/sustdev/ (office).

DESCOUEYTE, François, BA, LLM; French diplomatist; *Ambassador to Australia;* b. 1949, Paris; m., three c. *Education:* Institut d'Études Politiques, Paris, Paris Univ., Special Mil. School of Saint-Cyr. *Career:* served in Bureau of Econ. and Financial Affairs, Ministry of Foreign Affairs 1975–77, Diplomatic Adviser to Minister for Co-operation and Devt 1985–86, Deputy Dir for Western Europe, Bureau of European Affairs 1988–91, Inspector of Foreign Affairs 1998–2001; Sec. Embassy in Tokyo 1977–81, Counsellor for Cultural, Scientific and Tech. Co-operation, New Delhi 1981–85, Consul-Gen. for Western Japan, Osaka 1986–88, Amb. to Uganda 1994–97, to Korea 2001–05, to Australia 2005–; Head of Int. Affairs, French Planning Comm. 1991–93; Kt, Légion d'honneur, Kt Order of Merit, Officer of the Sacred Treasure (Japan), Officer of the Orange-Nassau (Netherlands), Grand Cross of Diplomatic Merit (Korea).
Address: Embassy of France, 6 Perth Avenue, Yarralumla, ACT 2600, Australia (office). *Telephone:* (2) 6216-0100 (office). *Fax:* (2) 6216-0127 (office). *E-mail:* embassy@ambafrance-au.org (office). *Website:* www .ambafrance-au.org (office).

DESKER, Barry, MA; Singaporean academic and fmr diplomatist; *Dean, S. Rajaratnam School of International Studies, Nanyang Technological University; Education:* Univ. of Singapore, Univ.of London, UK, Cornell Univ., Ithaca, NY. *Career:* joined Singapore Admin. Service (Foreign Service Br.) 1970, Deputy Perm. Rep. to UN, New York 1982–84, Dir Policy, Planning and Analysis Div., Ministry of Foreign Affairs 1984–86, Amb. to Indonesia 1986–93; CEO Singapore Trade Devt Bd 1994–2000; Dir Inst. of Defence and Strategic Studies (IDSS), Nanyang Tech. Univ. 2000–07, Dean, S. Rajaratnam School of Int. Studies 2007–; Chair. Singapore Network Services 1995–2002, CrimsonLogic 2000–02, TDB Holdings 1994–2000; Co-Chair. Steering Cttee, Council for Security Co-operation in the Asia Pacific (CSCAP) 2001–03; Chair. Singapore Int. Foundation, Jurong Port Pvt Ltd, Singapore Technologies Marine; Dir Singapore Airport Terminal Services, SembCorp Logistics, Cordell Hull Inst., Washington, DC; fmr Dir Econ. Devt Bd, Maritime and Port Authority, Nat. Library Bd, Sembawang Engineering, Sime SembCorp Engineering, Malaysia; fmr Trustee and mem. Exec. Cttee, Inst. of SE Asian Studies (ISEAS); Life Trustee Singapore Eurasian Community Fund; Hon.

Adviser to Minister for Trade and Industry, Hon. Adviser UN Asscn of Singapore; Singapore Expert, ASEAN Regional Forum Register of Experts/Eminent Persons; Vice-Chair. Singapore Business Fed.; mem. Trilateral Comm.; Public Admin. Medal (Gold) 1992. *Publications:* numerous articles in specialist journals.
Address: S. Rajaratnam School of International Studies, Nanyang Technological University, Blk S4, Level B4, Nanyang Avenue, Singapore 639798 (office). *Telephone:* (65) 6790-6982 (office). *Fax:* (65) 6793-2991 (office). *E-mail:* wwwidss@ntu.sg (office). *Website:* www.rsis.edu.sg (office).

DESTA, Araya, BSc, MSc; Eritrean diplomatist; *Permanent Representative, United Nations;* b. 1945, Senafe; m.; five c. *Education:* Stanmore Meteorological Training Centre, London, Univ. of Nairobi, Kenya, Univ. of Toronto, Canada. *Career:* Weather Forecaster, Civil Aviation Admin, Asmara, Eritrea 1963–72; Head, Meteorological Application Section, Ethiopian Meteorological Services, Addis Ababa 1972–76; Computer Programmer, Amoco Canada Petroleum Co., Calgary 1980–82; Exec. Dir and Chair. Eritrean Relief Asscn-Canada, Ottawa 1982–93; First Sec. and Consul, Consulate of Eritrea, Ottawa 1993–94; Minister Counsellor, Embassy in Beijing, China 1994–2001; Amb. to Nordic countries, Stockholm, Sweden 2002–05; Perm. Rep. to UN, New York 2005–; mem. Bd Eritrean Relief Asscn, Khartoum, Sudan 1982–91.
Address: Office of the Permanent Representative of Eritrea to the United Nations, 800 Second Avenue, 18th Floor, New York, NY 10017, USA (office). *Telephone:* (212) 687-3390 (office). *Fax:* (212) 687-3138 (office). *E-mail:* eritrea@un.int (office). *Website:* www.un.int/eritrea (office).

DeTRANI, Joseph, BA; American economist and diplomatist; *Mission Manager for North Korea, Office of the Director of National Intelligence; Education:* New York Univ., New York Grad. School of Business Admin. *Career:* spent several years living in East Asia and the Middle East; served as officer in USAF; worked as economist in pvt. sector; fmr econ. analyst at CIA, fmr Exec. Asst to Dir of Cen. Intelligence, fmr Dir European Operations, fmr Dir Tech. Services, fmr Dir Public Affairs, fmr Dir Crime and Narcotics Center, fmr Dir East Asia Operations; Special Envoy for the Six-Party Talks with rank of Amb. –2005; Mission Man. for N Korea, Office of Dir of Nat. Intelligence 2005–.
Address: Office of the Mission Manager for North Korea, Office of the Director of National Intelligence, Washington, DC 20511, USA (office). *Telephone:* (202) 201-1111 (office). *Website:* www.dni.gov (office).

DEUBA, Sher Bahadur, MA; Nepalese politician; b. 12 June 1946, Angra, Dadeldhura Dist; m. Arju Deuba; one s. *Education:* Tribhuvan Univ. *Career:* Chair. Far Western Students Cttee, Kathmandu 1965; served a total of nine years' imprisonment for political activities 1966–85; Founder-mem. Nepal Students' Union 1970; Research Fellow, LSE 1988–90; active in Popular Movt for Restoration of Democracy in Nepal 1991; mem. Parl. 1991–; Minister of Home Affairs; Leader Parl. Party, Nepali Congress 1994; Prime Minister 1995–97, 2001–02, 2004–05; Minister of Foreign Affairs and Defence 2001–02; sentenced to two-year jail term for graft July 2005, released Feb. 2006; fmr Pres. Nepali Congress Party (Democratic) (merged again with Nepali Congress under Girja Prasad Koirala as Nepali Congress 2007).
Address: Parliament of Nepal, Singha Durbar, Kathmandu, Nepal (office). *Telephone:* (1) 227480 (office). *Fax:* (1) 4222923 (office). *E-mail:* nparl@ntc .net.np (office). *Website:* www.parliament.gov.np (office).

DEVECCHI, Robert P., BA, MBA; American international organization official; *Adjunct Senior Fellow, Council on Foreign Relations; Education:* Yale Univ., Harvard Univ. *Career:* served as Foreign Service Officer posted in Washington, DC, NATO in Paris, embassies in Warsaw and Rome 1956–67; European Dir The Conference Board 1968–72; with Save the Children Fed. 1972–75; Indochina Dir., Int. Rescue Cttee 1975–80, Exec. Dir 1985–92, Pres. 1992–97, currently Pres. Emeritus; Adjunct Sr Fellow, Council on Foreign Relations 1997–; mem. Bd of Dirs Refugees Int.
Address: Council on Foreign Relations, The Harold Pratt House, 58 East 68th Street, New York, NY, USA (office). *Telephone:* (212) 434-9664. *Fax:* (212) 434-9800 (office). *E-mail:* rdevecchi@cfr.org (office). *Website:* www .cfr.org (office).

DEVI, V.S. Rama, MA, LLM; Indian politician and lawyer; b. 15 Jan. 1934, Chebrolu; m. V. S. Ramavatar; one s. two d. *Career:* advocate, Andhra Pradesh High Court 1959, various roles in Legis. Dept, then Special Sec. 1985; mem. Secr. of Law Comm. and Indian Govt 1985; Sec. Legis. Dept, Ministry of Law 1989–92; officiating Chief Election Commr 1990; Gov. of Himachal Pradesh 1997–1999 of Karnataka 1999–2002; Judicial mem. Customs, Excise and Gold Control Appellate Tribunal 1982–83; Sec.-Gen. Rajya Sabha. *Publications:* 20 books.

Address: Raj Bhavan, Bangalore, India (office). *Telephone:* (80) 2254101 (office). *Fax:* (80) 2258150 (office).

DEW, John Anthony; British diplomatist; *Ambassador to Colombia;* b. 1952; m. Marion Bewley Kirkwood 1975; three d. *Education:* Univ. of Oxford. *Career:* joined FCO 1973, Second Sec., British Embassy, Caracas 1975–78, worked in Perm. Under-Sec.'s Dept and EC Dept, FCO early 1980s, Falkland Islands Dept 1982–83, 1988–1990, UK Perm. Del. to OECD, Paris 1983–87, Repub. of Ireland Dept, FCO 1987–88, British Embassy, Dublin 1992–96, Minister and Deputy Head of Mission, Madrid 1996–2000, Head of Latin America and Caribbean Dept 2000–03, Amb. to Cuba 2004–08, to Colombia 2008–; worked for Lehman Brothers, London 2003.
Address: British Embassy, Carrera 9, No. 76-49, Floors 8 and 9, Bogotá, Colombia (office). *Telephone:* (1) 326-8300 (office). *Fax:* (1) 326-8302 (office). *E-mail:* britain@cable.net.co (office). *Website:* www.britain.gov.co (office).

DEWAR, Robert (Bob) Scott; British diplomatist; *High Commissioner to Nigeria;* b. 10 June 1949; m. Jennifer Dewar; one s. one d. *Career:* joined FCO 1973, Near East/N Africa Dept 1973–74, Third Sec., Chancery (Information), Colombo 1974–78, Rhodesia Dept, FCO 1978, Common-wealth Co-ordination Dept 1978–79, West African Dept 1980–81, First Sec. (Commercial) and Head of Chancery, Luanda 1981–84, South Asian Dept, FCO 1984–87, Deputy Head of Mission, Dakar 1988–92, Deputy High Commr, Harare 1992–96, Amb. to Madagascar 1996–99, High Commr to Mozambique 2000–03, Amb. to Ethiopia 2003–07, High Commr to Nigeria (also accred as Amb. to Equatorial Guinea and Benin and Perm. Rep. to Econ. Community of West African States—ECOWAS) 2008–.
Address: British High Commission, 19 Torren Close, off Mississippi Street, Shehu Shagari Way, Maitama, Abuja, Nigeria (office). *Telephone:* (9) 4132010 (office). *Fax:* (9) 4133552 (office). *E-mail:* information.abuja@fco .gov.uk (office). *Website:* www.ukinnigeria.com (office).

DEWOST, Jean-Louis; French academic and government official; *President, Commission nationale de contrôle des interceptions de sécurité (CNCIS);* b. 6 Sept. 1937, Dunkirk; m. Agnès Huet 1967; one s. two d. *Education:* Univ. de Paris, Inst. d'Etudes Politiques de Paris and Ecole Nat. d'Admin. *Career:* jr official, Conseil d'Etat 1967–69; Asst Man. Industrial Affairs, European Org. for Devt and Construction of Space Vehicle Launchers (CECLES/ELDO) 1962–72, Dir Finance and Econ. Planning 1972–73; Maître des Requêtes, Conseil d'Etat 1972, Conseiller d'Etat 1986, Pres. de la Section Sociale, 2001–03; legal adviser EC Council Legal Service 1973–85, Jurisconsulte 1986–87; Dir-Gen. EC Legal Service 1987–2001; Pres. Comm. Nat. de contrôle des interceptions de sécurité (govt. admin. authority) 2003–; Prof., Inst. d'Etudes Politiques (Sciences Po), Paris; Officier, Légion d'honneur, Officier, Ordre nat. du Mérite, Grand Officier, Order of White Rose of Finland, Grand Officier Order of the Falcon of Iceland. *Publications:* several publs on French public law and EU law.
Address: Commission nationale de contrôle des interceptions de sécurité, 35 rue Saint-Dominique, 75007 Paris (office); Sciences Po, 27 rue Saint-Guillaume, 75337 Paris Cedex 07 (office); 11 rue Sainte Anne, 75000, Paris, France (home). *Telephone:* 1-45-55-70-20 (office); 1-45-49-50-50 (office). *Fax:* 1-45-55-71-15 (office); 1-42-22-31-26 (office).

DEZCALLAR MAZARREDO, Jorge; Spanish lawyer and diplomatist; *Ambassador to USA;* b. 3 Nov. 1945, Palma de Mallorca; m. Pilar Lopez Chicheri; two s. one d. *Education:* Coll. of the Franciscan Fathers, Palma de Mallorca, Complutense Univ. of Madrid. *Career:* joined Ministry of Foreign Affairs 1971, stationed in Poland 1972–74, held several positions in Consulate Gen., New York 1974–78, Counsellor, Embassy in Montevideo 1978–81, Dir of Tech. Agencies and Devt, Directorate Gen. of Int. Orgs and Confs, Ministry of Foreign Affairs 1981–82, seconded as vocal adviser to Cabinet Office 1982, later as vocal adviser in Dept of Int. Affairs 1982–83, served in Moncloa Palace in Exec. chaired by Felipe González 1983–85, Gen. Dir Foreign Policy for Africa and Middle East, Ministry of Foreign Affairs 1985–93; played role in organizing Madrid Peace Conf. between PLA Chair. Yasser Arafat and Israeli Prime Minister, Yitzhak Shamir 1991; Dir-Gen. for Political Affairs 1993–96; Amb. to Special Mission for Common Foreign and Security Policy 1996–97, to OSCE 1997, to Morocco 1997–2001; Dir Cesid with rank of Sec. of State 2001–08 (first civilian in charge of Spanish secret services); Amb. to USA 2008–; Officer of the Order of Isabel the Catholic, Order of Civil Merit, Grand Cross of Wissam Alawites and many other foreign decorations. *Publications:* Racismo y xenofobia: búsqueda de las raíces (co-author); numerous newspaper articles.
Address: Embassy of Spain, 2375 Pennsylvania Avenue, NW, Washington, DC 20037, USA (office). *Telephone:* (202) 452-0100 (office). *Fax:* (202) 833-5670 (office). *E-mail:* emb.wash@maec.es (office). *Website:* www.maec.es/ Subwebs/Embajadas/washington/es/home/Paginas/Home.aspx (office).

DHAHIRI, Al Asri Saeed Ahmed Al-; United Arab Emirates diplomatist; *Ambassador to USA;* b. 30 April 1962, Al Ain; m.; six c. *Career:* began career with Foreign Service 1978 holding various positions including Third Sec. 1981, Acting Charge d'Affaires in Geneva 1987–89, First Sec. 1989–92, Counselor 1992–93, Amb. 1993, Amb. to Bahrain 1993–99, served with UAE Foreign Ministry 1999–2000; Amb. to USA (also non-resident Amb. to Mexico), Washington, DC 2000–; fmr Head UAE negotiating team for delineating border with Saudi Arabia; served as coordinator UAE governmental cttees at multilateral peace talks; del. to confs of ILO, WHO, GATT and UNESCO; Medal of Hon. (First Class) of Bahrain. *Address:* Embassy of the United Arab Emirates, 3522 International Court, NW, Washington, DC 20008-3022, USA (office). *Telephone:* (202) 243-2400 (office). *Fax:* (202) 243-2432 (office).

DHANAPALA, Jayantha, MA; Sri Lankan diplomatist and consultant; *Chairman, United Nations University Council;* b. 30 Dec. 1938, Colombo; m. Maureen Elhart; one s. one d. *Education:* Univ. of Peradeniya, Univ. of London, UK, American Univ., Washington, DC, USA. *Career:* corp. exec. in pvt. sector 1962–65; joined Sri Lankan Foreign Service 1965, diplomatic appointments in People's Repub. of China, UK and USA 1965–77; Dir Non-Aligned Movt Div., Ministry of Foreign Affairs 1978–80, Additional Foreign Sec. 1992–95; Deputy High Commr to India 1981–83; Amb. and Perm. Rep. to UN, Geneva, Switzerland 1984-87, Dir UN Inst. for Disarmament Research 1987–92; Amb. to USA (also accred to Mexico) 1995–97; UN Under-Sec.-Gen. for Disarmament Affairs 1998–2003; Sec.-Gen. Secr. for Co-ordinating the Peace Process 2004–05 (resgnd); Chief Negotiator in talks with LTTE 2004–05, Sr Adviser to Pres. 2004–05; Visiting Simons Prof., Simon Fraser Univ., Vancouver, Canada 2008; Pres. Review and Extension Conf. of Treaty on the Non-Proliferation of Nuclear Weapons 1995, Pugwash Confs on Science and World Affairs 2007–; Rep. of UN to Conf. on Disarmament; mem. Canberra Comm., Australia; Diplomat-in-Residence, Center for Non-Proliferation Studies, Monterey Inst. of Int. Studies, Calif., USA; Chair. UN Univ. Council, Governing Bd Stockholm Int. Peace Research Inst. (SIPRI); mem. Int. Weapons of Mass Destruction Comm., Int. Advisory Group ICRC, Geneva Centre for Democratic Control of Armed Forces, Advisory Council of Stanford Inst. for Int. Studies, Int. Bd of Bonn Int. Center for Conversion, Int. Advisory Bd Center for Nonproliferation Studies, Monterey Inst. of Int. Studies; Hon. Pres. Int. Peace Bureau; Dr hc (Univ. of Peradeniya) 2000, (Sabaragamuwa Univ.) 2003; Hon. DHumLitt (Monterey Inst. of Int. Studies) 2001; Hon. DSc in Social Sciences (Univ. of Southampton) 2003; 'Jit' Trainor Award for Distinction in the Conduct of Diplomacy, Sri Lankan of the Year, (Lanka Monthly Digest) 2006, Sean MacBride Peace Prize 2007. *Publications include:* China and the Third World 1984, Nuclear War, Nuclear Proliferation and Their Consequences (co-author) 1985, Multilateral Diplomacy and the NPT: An Insider's Account 2005. *Address:* 25/6 Pepiliyana Road, Nugegoda, Sri Lanka (home). *Telephone:* (11) 2856297 (home). *E-mail:* jdhanapala@yahoo.co.uk (office). *Website:* www.jayanthadhanapala.com.

DI PAOLA, Adm. Giampaolo; Italian naval officer; *Chairman of the Military Committee, NATO;* b. 15 Aug. 1944, Torre Annunziata, Naples; m. Roberta di Paola; two d. *Education:* Naval Acad., Submarine School, NATO Defence Coll., Rome. *Career:* served aboard conventional submarines Gazzana and Piomarta 1968–74; Commdr submarines Cappellini 1974–75, Sauro 1980–81; served as ASW and Undersea Warfare Programme Officer, Long Term Planning Br., SACLANT, Norfolk, Va, USA 1981–84; CO frigate Grecale 1984–86; Plans and Programmes Br. Chief, Gen. and Financial Planning Div., Navy Staff, Rome 1986–89; Capt. CO aircraft carrier Garibaldi 1989–90; Exec. Asst. to Deputy Chief of Staff 1990–91; Chief of Naval Plans and Policy Br., Plans and Operations Div. 1991–92; Asst Chief of Staff for Plans and Operations 1993–94; Chief of Mil. Policy Div. 1994–98; Chief of the Cabinet, Ministry of Defence 1998–2001; Sec.-Gen. of Defence and Nat. Armaments Dir 2001–04; Chief of Defence Staff March 2004–08; Chair. NATO Mil. Cttee, Brussels 2008–; apptd Rear Adm. 1997, Adm. 2004; Kt Grand Cross Order of Merit (Italy), Commdr Ordre Nat. du Mérite (France), Kt Commdr Order of St Gregory the Great, Grand Cross with Swords Order of Merit of Malta, Kt of the Grand Cross of Merit of the Sacred Constantine Mil. Order of San Giorgio, Grand Officer Order of Infante Don Enrico (Portugal), Commdr Legion of Merit (USA), Commdr de la Légion d'honneur (France); Medal of the Order of St Maurice, Meritorious Long Command Gold Medal, Distinguished Award for Submariners, Sr Service Gold Cross, Bronze Medal for Sea-Duty Service in the Navy, Commemorative Medal of Sovereign Mil. Hospitaller Order of St John of Jerusalem, of Rhodes and of Malta, UN Medal for UN Peacekeeping Mission in Kosovo. *Address:* Office of the Chairman of the Military Committee, NATO Headquarters, Blvd Leopold III, 1110 Brussels, Belgium (office). *Telephone:* (2) 707-41-11 (office). *Fax:* (2) 707-45-79 (office). *E-mail:* natodoc@hq.nato.int (office). *Website:* www.nato.int (office).

DI RUPO, Elio, DSc; Belgian politician; *President, Socialist Party and Minister-President of Wallonia;* b. 1951, Morlanwelz. *Education:* Univ. of Mons. *Career:* researcher, Chef de Cabinet, Budget and Energy Minister, Walloon Region 1982–85; Communal Councillor, Mons 1982–2000; MP 1987–89, MEP 1989–1991; Pres. of Energy Comm.; Senator 1991–95; Minister of Educ. 1992–94, Deputy Prime Minister and Minister of Communications and Public Enterprises 1994–95, Deputy Prime Minister and Minister for Economy and Telecommunications 1995–99; Minister-Pres. of Wallonia 1999–2000, 2005–; Mayor of Mons 2001–; Pres. Socialist Party (PS) 2000–. *Address:* Parti Socialiste, 13 boulevard de l'Empereur, 1000 Brussels, Belgium (office). *Telephone:* (2) 548-32-11 (office). *Fax:* (2) 548-33-90 (office). *E-mail:* elio@dirupo.net (office). *Website:* www.ps.be (office).

DIA, Ibrahima, PhD; Mauritanian diplomatist; *Ambassador to USA;* m.; one c. *Education:* Nat. Coll. of Admin, Tunis, Coll. of Diplomatic and Strategic Studies, Paris, Univ. of Paris I, Pantheon-Sorbonne, France. *Career:* legal officer, law office, Vaires-sur-Marne, France 1992–96; legal officer, ICRC Perm. Mission to OAU, Addis Ababa, Ethiopia 1997–99; Research Officer, Office of the Prosecutor, UN Criminal Tribunal for Rwanda 1999–2001, Human Rights Officer, UN Mission in Democratic Repub. of the Congo, Kinshasa April–Aug. 2001, Political Affairs Officer 2001–02, Disarmament Expert 2002–03, Regional Liaison Officer, Bujumbura, Burundi 2003–04, Political Affairs Officer, UN Mission in Ivory Coast 2004–07, Sr Governance Expert, UN Office for West Africa, Dakar, Senegal April–June 2007; Amb. to USA 2007–. *Address:* Embassy of Mauritania, 2129 Leroy Place, NW, Washington, DC 20008, USA (office). *Telephone:* (202) 232-5700 (office). *Fax:* (202) 319-2623 (office). *E-mail:* info@mauritaniembassy-usa.org (office). *Website:* mauritania-usa.org (office).

DIALLO, Cellou Dalein; Guinean economist and politician; b. 1953. *Career:* worked at Cen. Bank of Guinea before joining ministerial cabinet of Pres. Lansan Conté in 1995; served for several years as Minister of Public Works, later Minister of Fisheries –2004; Prime Minister of Guinea 2004–06. *Address:* c/o Office of the Prime Minister, Conakry, Guinea (office).

DIALLO, Claude Absa, BA; Senegalese diplomatist; *Ambassador and Permanent Representative, United Nations, Geneva;* b. 1942, Hanoi, Vietnam. *Education:* Univ. of Dakar and Nat. School of Admin. Senegal. *Career:* Head Geographical Div. Office of Political, Cultural and Social Affairs, Ministry of Foreign Affairs 1964; Adviser Office of Minister for Foreign Affairs 1965–72; Minister-Counsellor, Bonn (also accred to Austria and Switzerland) 1972–77; Perm. Del. of Senegal at UNESCO 1977–80; roving Amb. 1980–81; Dir of Political and Cultural Affairs, Ministry of Foreign Affairs 1981–88; Perm. Rep. to UN 1988–91, to UN Security Council 1988–89; Chair. UN Cttee on the Exercise of the Inalienable Rights of the Palestinian People 1988–91; UN ad hoc Cttee on Cambodia 1988–90; Amb. to Sweden 1992–93, to Norway 1993, to Russia 1993–95 (also accred to Bulgaria, Romania, Hungary, Ukraine, Poland, Czech Repub., Slovakia); Amb. and Perm. Rep. to UN and other int. orgs in Geneva 1996–; Chair. Bureau, World Conference Against Racism 2000. *Address:* c/o Ministry of Foreign Affairs and Sengalese Abroad, place de l'Indépendance, Dakar, Senegal.

DIALLO, Gen. Mamadou Bailo; Guinean army officer. *Career:* fmr Head of Ground Forces, Nat. Army of Guinea; Minister of Nat. Defence 2007–08. *Address:* c/o Ministry of National Defence, Camp Samory-Touré, Conakry, Guinea (office).

DIALLO, Marian Aladji Boni; Benin politician. *Career:* Minister of Foreign Affairs (first woman) 2006–07. *Address:* c/o Ministry of Foreign Affairs, Zone Résidentielle, route de l'Aéroport, 06 BP 318, Cotonou, Benin (office).

DIAMANTOPOULOU, Anna; Greek politician and European Union official; b. 1959, Kozani; m.; one c. *Education:* Aristotle Univ. of Thessaloniki, Panteion Univ. of Athens. *Career:* civil engineer 1981–85; Lecturer, Insts of Higher Technological Educ. 1983–85; Man. Dir of regional devt co.; Prefect of Kastoria 1985–86; Sec.-Gen. for Adult Educ. 1987–88; Sec.-Gen. for Youth 1988–89; mem. Cen. Cttee of PASOK 1991–99; Pres. of Hellenic Org. of Small and Medium-Sized Enterprises and Handicrafts (EOMMEX); Sec.-Gen. for Industry 1994–96; mem. of Parl. 1996–99, 2004–; Deputy Minister for Devt 1996–99; EU Commr for Employment and Social Affairs 1999–2004; mem. Forum for Co-operation of Balkan Peoples, Int. Women's Network; Chevalier, Légion d'Honneur 2002. *Address:* Parliament Building, Syntagma Square, 101 80 Athens, Greece (office). *Telephone:* (21) 03288434 (office). *Fax:* (21) 03310013 (office).

E-mail: infopar@parliament.gr (office). *Website:* www.parliament.gr (office).

DIARRA, Cheick Sidi; Malian diplomatist and UN official; *Under-Secretary-General and High Representative for the Least Developed Countries, Landlocked Developing Countries and Small Island Developing States, United Nations;* b. 31 May 1957, Kayes; m.; two c. *Education:* Dakar Univ. *Career:* joined civil service in 1981, assigned to Ministry of Foreign Affairs and Int. Co-operation, Legal Adviser 1987–88; First Counsellor, Perm. Mission to UN, New York 1989–93, Perm. Rep. to UN, New York 1993–2007; UN Under-Sec.-Gen. and High Rep. for the Least Developed Countries, Landlocked Developing Countries and Small Island Developing States; Chevalier de l'Ordre Nat. du Mali. *Address:* Office of the High Representative for the Least Developed Countries, Landlocked Developing Countries and Small Island Developing States, United Nations, Room S-770, New York, NY 10017, USA (office). *Telephone:* (212) 963-7778 (office). *Fax:* (917) 367-3415 (office). *E-mail:* OHRLLS-UNHQ@un.org (office). *Website:* unohrlls.expressiondev.com (office).

DIARRA, Fatoumata Dembele, LLB; Malian judge and professor of law; *Judge, International Criminal Court;* b. 15 Feb. 1949, Koulikoro; m.; six c. *Education:* Ecole Nat. de la Magistrature, Paris, France, Ecole Nat. d'Admin, Bamako, Dakar Univ., Senegal. *Career:* Investigative Judge, Jr Admin. Office, First Instance Tribunal of Bamako 1977–80; Trial Attorney, Office of the Prosecutor, Tribunal of Bamako 1980–81; Vice-Pres. Labour Court of Bamako 1981–82; Investigative Judge, Sr Investigation Office, Bamako 1984–86; Legis. Sec. Nat. Ass. of Mali 1986–91; Legal Adviser to Transition Cttee for the Reinstallation of Republican Inst., Office of the Head of State 1991; Gen.-Dir Malian Office for Intellectual Property and Copyright 1991–93; Official Rep. of Office of the Commr for the Promotion of Women 1993–94; Appeal Court Adviser, Criminal Chamber 1994–96; Pres. Criminal Chamber, Bamako Appeal Court 1996–99; Nat. Dir Justice Admin 1999–2001; elected Judge Int. Criminal Tribunal for the Fmr Yugoslavia (ICTY) 2001; elected Judge Int. Criminal Court (ICC) 2003–; Prof. of Constitutional Law, Civil Law and Criminal Law, Cen. School for Industry, Trade and Admin (ECICA) 1986–91; Gen.-Sec. Asscn of Malian Women Lawyers 1986–88, Pres. 1988–95; Founding Pres. Legal Clinic for Women and Children Without Means 1993; Pres. Support Group for Legal Reform 1994, Observatory for the Rights of Women and Children (ODEF) 1995–, Legal Br. of Int. Council for French-speaking Women (CIFF) 1996–, Malian Electoral Support Network 1997–; Vice-Pres. Int. Fed. of Women with Legal Careers (FIFCJ) 1994–97, Fed. of African Women Lawyers (FJA) 1995–; mem. numerous working groups and parl. cttee on legal reform; Officier, Ordre nat. du Mali 2001. *Publications include:* numerous articles in professional journals on women's rights and int. law. *Address:* International Criminal Court, Maanweg 174, 2516 AB, The Hague, The Netherlands (office). *Telephone:* (70) 5158515 (office). *Fax:* (70) 5158555 (office). *E-mail:* pio@icc-cpi.int (office). *Website:* www.icc-cpi.int (office).

DIARRA, Seydou Elimane; Côte d'Ivoirian politician and diplomatist; b. 23 Nov. 1933; m. *Education:* Lycée Fénelon, La Rochelle, France. *Career:* won scholarship to study agric. in France; researcher, Office de la recherche scientifique et technique d'outre-mer (Orstom) 1961; apptd Dir Centre national de la mutualité agricole 1962; Commercial Dir Caisse de stabilisation du café et du cacao (Caistab) 1965, Rep. of Caistab in London; fmr head of state-run agric. co-operation and insurance body, Abidjan; Pres., Dir-Gen. Saco et Chocodi 1985; fmr head of govt org. in charge of cocoa; fmr African Rep. to Int. Coffee Org.; fmr Amb. to Brazil, EU and UK; Chair. Chamber of Commerce and Industry, Côte d'Ivoire 1992; Minister of State, responsible for Governmental Co-ordination and the Planning of Devt Jan.–May 2000; Prime Minister of Côte d'Ivoire May–Oct. 2000 (resgnd), Jan. 2003–05. *Address:* c/o Office of the Prime Minister, Blvd Angoulvant, 01 BP 1533, Abidjan 01, Côte d'Ivoire (office).

DIAS DIOGO, Luisa, MEconSc; Mozambican politician; *Prime Minister;* b. 11 April 1958, Dist of Mágoè, Tete; m. António Albana Silva; two s. one d. *Education:* Univ. Eduardo Mondlane, Univ. of London, UK. *Career:* joined Ministry of Planning and Finance 1980, with Dept of Econs and Investment 1980–84, Assoc. Head of Dept 1984–86, Programme Officer Study Dept 1986–89, Head, Dept of Budget 1989–92, Nat. Dir of Budget 1993–94; Programme Officer IBRD, Maputo 1994; Vice-Minister of Planning and Finance 1994–2000; Minister of Planning and Finance 2000–05; Prime Minister of Mozambique 2004–; mem. Comm. on Political Information 2000–; Alt. Gov. for the IMF and World Bank 1991; del. to numerous int. confs; ranked by Forbes magazine amongst 100 Most Powerful Women (73rd) 2004, (96th) 2005, (83rd) 2006, (89th) 2007.

Address: Office of the Prime Minister, Praça da Marinha Popular, Maputo, Mozambique (office). *Telephone:* (1) 426861 (office). *Fax:* (1) 426881 (office). *E-mail:* dgpm.gov@teledata.mz (office). *Website:* www.mozambique.mz/governo/dnpo (office).

DÍAZ, Francisco Gil, BSc, PhD; Mexican economist and government official; b. 2 Sept. 1943, Mexico City. *Education:* Instituto Tecnológico Autónomo de México (ITAM), Univ. of Chicago, USA. *Career:* Prof. and Co-ordinator, ITAM Econs Program 1970–76; Prof., Colegio de México 1970–84; 20 years as economist, Bank of Mexico, becoming Asst Dir and later Dir of Econ. Research; fmr Chief of Econ. Projections, Pres.'s Secr.; fmr Under-Sec. for Revenue and later Gen. Man. for Econ. and Financial Studies, Finance and Public Credit Secr., then Gen. Dir of Revenue Policy; fmr Gen. Man. Avantel SA (telecommunications co.); Sec. of State for Finance and Public Credit –2006. *Address:* c/o Secretariat of State for Finance and Public Credit, Palacio Nacional, Primer Patio Mariano, 3°, Of. 3045, Col. Centro, Del. Cuauhtémoc, 06000 Mexico DF, Mexico (office).

DÍAZ, Nelson Merentes, PhD; Venezuelan politician and banker. *Education:* Central Univ. of Venezuela and Univ. of Budapest, Hungary. *Career:* Minister of Science and Tech. Feb.–Nov. 2002, of State for Devt and Econs 2002–04, of State for Financial Devt Sept.–Dec. 2004, of Finance 2004–07; Pres. Nat. Bank for Econ. and Social Devt 2002–04; fmr Gov. for Venezuela World Bank, IMF, Caribbean Devt Bank; mem. Bd of Dirs, Venezuela Cen. Bank 2007–. *Address:* c/o Board of Directors, Banco Central de Venezuela, Apartado 2017, Carmelitas, Caracas 1010, Venezuela (office). *Telephone:* (212) 801-5111 (office). *Fax:* (212) 861-1649 (office). *Website:* www.bcv.org.ve (office).

DÍAZ PÉREZ, Álvaro Humberto Abel, BA; Chilean economist and diplomatist; *Ambassador to Brazil; Career:* researcher, Centro de Estudios Sociales SUR –1991; Sec., Presidential Comm. on New Information and Communication Techs 1998–99; Head of Profitable Devt Div., Ministry of Finance 1999–2000; Under-Sec. for Economy 2000–03, Chair. Biotechnology Comm.; Regional Econ. Consultant, ECLAC 2004–07; Amb. to Brazil 2007–; fmr consultant to UNDP and IDB. *Publications:* numerous works on econ. devt. *Address:* Embassy of Chile, SES, Av. das Nações, Quadra 803, Lote 11, 70407-900 Brasília, DF Brazil (office). *Telephone:* (61) 2103-5151 (office). *Fax:* (61) 3322-0714 (office). *E-mail:* embchile@embchile.org.br (office).

DIBY, Charles Koffi; Côte d'Ivoirian economist and politician; *Minister of the Economy and Finance;* b. 7 Sept. 1957, Bouaké; m.; five c. *Education:* Nat. School of Man. and Int. Inst. of Public Admin, Paris. *Career:* began career at Treasury 1984, responsible for Nat. Inst. for the Youth and Sports 1985–90, for Nat. Inst. for Professional Training 1990–91, Rep. for Cen. Agency for Public Spending 1991–93, Treasurer for Bondoukou Prov. 1993–94, Treas. for Daoukro Prov. 1994–97, Accountant, Central Agency for Public Spending 1997–98, Paymaster-Gen. 1998–99, Deputy Dir-Gen. of the Treasury 1999–2000, Dir-Gen. 2001–07; Counsellor to Minister of the Economy and Finance 2000–01; Minister Del. of the Economy and Finance 2006–07; Minister of the Economy and Finance 2007–. *Address:* Ministry of the Economy and Finance, 16e étage, Immeuble SCIAM, avenue Marchand, PO Box V163, Abidjan, Côte d'Ivoire (office). *Telephone:* 20-20-08-42 (office). *Fax:* 20-21-32-08 (office).

DICENTA BALLESTER, José Luis; Spanish diplomatist; *Ambassador to Italy;* b. 24 Dec. 1937, Palma de Mallorca. *Education:* Univ. of Madrid, Spanish Diplomatic School. *Career:* began his diplomatic career in 1966, served in various posts including in Dominican Repub., Libya, France, Argentina, USA; Consul-Gen. in Zürich 2001, in Calif. 2002; fmr Amb. to Peru, Czechoslovakia, Colombia, Mexico, Amb. to Italy 2006–; Sec. of State for Int. Co-operation and Iberoamerica 1993–96. *Address:* Embassy of Spain, Palazzo Borghese, Largo Fontanella Borghese 19, Rome 00186, Italy (office). *Telephone:* (06) 6840401 (office). *Fax:* (06) 6872256 (office). *E-mail:* ambespit@mail.mae.es (office). *Website:* www.amba.spagna.com.

DICHTER, Avraham (Avi), BA, MBA; Israeli government official; *Minister of Public Security;* b. 1952. *Education:* Bar Ilan Univ., Tel-Aviv Univ. *Career:* mil. service 1971–90, served in Sayeret Matkal commando unit; Head, Southern Dist (ISA), Israel Security Agency—ISA (Shabak) 1992–96, Head, Security and Protection Div. 1996–99, Deputy Dir ISA 1999–2000, Dir 2000–05; elected to Knessett 2006, Minister of Public Security 2006–; Research Fellow, Brookings Inst., Washington, DC 2005; mem. Kadima party. *Address:* Ministry of Public Security, POB 91181, Bldg 3, Kiryat Hamemshala (East), Jerusalem 91181, Israel (office). *Telephone:* 2-

5308003 (office). *Fax:* 2-5847872 (office). *E-mail:* sar@mops.gov.il (office). *Website:* www.mops.gov.il (office).

DIDI, Ali Hussain; Maldivian civil servant and diplomatist; *High Commissioner to Sri Lanka; Career:* joined civil service 1983, Dir Passport Office 2001–03, Controller of Immigration and Emigration March–Dec. 2003, Dir-Gen. Dept of Penitentiary and Rehabilitation, Ministry of Home Affairs and Environment 2004; Chair. Malé Municipality 2004–07; CEO Maldives Airports Co. 2007–08; High Commr to Sri Lanka 2008–. *Address:* Maldives High Commission, 23 Kaviratne Place, Colombo 6, Sri Lanka (office). *Telephone:* (11) 2365686 (office); (11) 2587827 (office); (11) 5516302 (office). *Fax:* (11) 2581200 (office). *E-mail:* info@maldiveshighcom.lk (office). *Website:* www.maldiveshighcom.lk (office).

DIEMU, Chikez; Democratic Republic of the Congo politician; *Minister of Defence, Demobilization and War Veterans' Affairs; Career:* mem. Parl. 1997–; Sec. for Strategic Planning 1997–99; Vice-Pres. in charge of organization of Govt 1999–2001; Vice-Minister of Interior 2001–04; Gen.-Sec. People's Party for Reconstruction and Democracy 2001–05; Vice-Gov. Katanga Prov. 2004–07; Minister of Defence, Demobilization and War Veterans' Affairs 2007–. *Address:* Ministry of Defence, Demobilization and War Veterans' Affairs, BP 4111, Kinshasa-Gombe, Democratic Republic of the Congo (office). *Telephone:* (12) 59375 (office).

DIENG, Adama; Senegalese registrar, lecturer and United Nations consultant; *Assistant Secretary-General and Registrar, International Criminal Tribunal for Rwanda, United Nations;* b. 22 May 1950, Dakar; m. Aissatou Dieng; two one c. *Education:* Training Inst. in Law and Admin, Centre de Formation et de Perfectionnement Administratifs, Dakar, Research Centre of The Hague Acad. of Int. Law, Netherlands. *Career:* Registrar, Regional and Labour Courts of Senegal 1973; Registrar of the Supreme Court 1974–80; Legal Officer, Int. Comm. of Jurists 1982–89, Exec. Sec. 1989–90, Sec.-Gen. 1990–2000; apptd UN Ind. Expert for Haiti 1985; Asst Sec.-Gen. and Registrar for Int. Criminal Tribunal for Rwanda (ICTR) 2001–; mem. Bd Dirs Int. Inst. for Human Rights (Institut René Cassin); mem. Exec. Bd Africa Leadership Forum; Pres. Int. Jury, UNESCO Human Rights Educ. Prize; lecturer on int. law at various univs and insts; consultant for numerous orgs., including UNESCO, UN Inst. for Training (UNITAR), Ford Foundation, UNCHR, OAU; Hon. Chair. African Centre for Human Rights and Democratic Studies. *Publications:* more than 60 publs on human rights, democracy in Africa, int. law, the judicial system etc. *Address:* International Criminal Tribunal for Rwanda, Arusha International Conference Centre, PO Box 6016, Arusha, Tanzania (office). *Telephone:* (27) 256-5008 (office). *Fax:* (27) 256-4000 (office). *E-mail:* dieng1@un.org (office). *Website:* www.ictr.org (office).

DIENSTBIER, Jiří; Czech politician, journalist and writer; *Ambassador-at-Large and Director and Trustee, Reuters Founders Share Company;* b. 20 April 1937, Kladno; m. 4th J. Melenová 1999; one s. three d. *Education:* Charles Univ., Prague. *Career:* Czechoslovak Broadcasting 1959, foreign correspondent in Far East, USSR, Germany, France, UK, Yugoslavia 1960–68, USA 1968–69; dismissed from broadcasting 1970; worked in archives of an eng company; expelled from Czechoslovak CP and Journalists' Union 1969; signed Charter 1977, spokesman 1979; sentenced to three years in prison 1979–82; boilerman 1982–89; spokesman for Charter 77 1985–86; ed. of Čtverec (The Square), a periodical on int. politics 1979–; Co-Founder of Lidové Noviny (The People's Newspaper) 1988–; Czechoslovak Minister for Foreign Affairs 1989–92; mem. Council of State 1990–92, Deputy Prime Minister CFSR 1990–92, Deputy to House of People Fed. Ass. 1990–92, Chair. Council of the Civic Movt 1991–; Chair. Free Democrats Party (fmrly Civic Movt) 1993–95 (merged with Liberal Nat. Social Party 1995); Chair. Liberal Nat. Social Party 1995–96 (left Party 1997); Chair. Czech Council on Foreign Relations; mem. Comm. on Global Governance; mem. UN Cttee for Solving Global Problems 1995–; Special Envoy to Gen. Ass. of UN 1995; lecturer 1998–; Special Rapporteur of the UN Comm. on Human Rights for Bosnia and Herzegovina, Croatia and Yugoslavia 1998–2001; Dir and Trustee, Reuters Founders Share Co. 2005–; Visiting Prof., Claremont Grad. Univ., Calif. 1997–98, Univ. of North Carolina, Chapel Hill 1999, Charles Univ., Prague 2001, 2003, Watson Inst., Brown Univ. 2003; Grand Cross of Order for Merit (Order of Kts of Malta) 1990; Das Grosse Verdienstkreuz mit Stern und Schulterband (Germany) 2002, Officier Légion d'honneur 2005; Dr hc (Univ. de Bourgogne) 1993; Humanist of the Year (USA) 1979, Francesco Cossiga Medal (Italy) 1991, Pro Merito Medal, Parl. Ass. Council of Europe 1991, Hero of Freedom of the Press in the World, IPI (Boston, USA) 2000. *Publications include:* The Night Began at Three in the Morning 1967, Before We Roast Young Pigs 1976, Christmas Present 1977, Guests 1978, Charter 77 – Human Rights and Socialism 1981, Radio Against Tanks 1988, Dreaming of Europe 1990, From Dreams to Reality 1999;

Kosovo Shades over Balkans 2002, Tax on Blood 2002, stage plays, articles and essays in Samizdat. *Address:* Rytířská 31, 11000 Prague (office); Apolinářská 6, 12800 Prague 2, Czech Republic (home). *Telephone:* (2) 2161-0109; (2) 2492-3321 (home). *E-mail:* jiri_dienstbier@mzv.cz (office); j@dienstbier.cz (home).

DIESEN, Gen. Sverre, MSc; Norwegian military officer; *Chief of Defence;* b. 1949, Oslo. *Education:* Officer Candidate School, Univ. of Tech. and Science, Trondheim, Norwegian Mil. Acad., Army Staff Coll. I and II, Staff Coll., Camberley, UK. *Career:* Anti-tank Detachment Commdr, Recce Squadron 1970–71; Platoon Commdr, HM the King's Guards 1979–80; Co. Second in Command, First Bn, Worcs. and Sherwood Foresters, British Army of the Rhine 1980–81; Platoon Commdr, Second Infantry Bn, Bde N Norway 1982, Co. Commdr 1982–84; Instructor, School of Infantry and Winter Warfare 1984–86; promoted to Maj. 1987, Project Officer, Systems Analysis Div., Norwegian Defence Research Establishment 1987, 1991–92; Staff Officer, Army Staff, Defence Command HQ 1988–89, promoted to Lt-Col 1991, Staff Officer, Plans and Operation Staff 1992–93; OC Tactics Wing, Mil. Acad. 1993–94; CO HM the King's Guards 1994–96; promoted to Col 1996; Chief of Staff, Six Div. 1996–98; promoted to Brig. 1998; with ACOS Strategy and Long-Term Planning, Defence Command HQ 1998–2001; promoted to Maj.-Gen. (acting) 2001, Maj.-Gen. (substantive) 2002, Commdr Land Forces, N Norway 2001–02, Norway 2002; promoted to Lt-Gen. 2003; Deputy Sec.-Gen. (Mil.), Ministry of Defence 2003; promoted to Gen. 2005; Chief of Defence 2005–; Nat. Service Medal with three stars 1988, Defence Service Medal 1995, Defence Service Medal with Laurel Branch 2005, Commdr with Star of the Royal Norwegian Order of St. Olav 2005, Légion d'Honneur 2006. *Address:* Ministry of Defence, Myntgt. 1, POB 8126 Dep., Oslo 0032, Norway (office). *Telephone:* 23-09-80-00 (office). *Fax:* 23-09-60-51 (office). *E-mail:* postmottak@fd.dep.no (office). *Website:* www.mod.no (office).

DIETER, Robert J., BL, BA; American lawyer, diplomatist and academic; *Ambassador to Belize;* m.; three c. *Education:* Univ. of Denver Coll. of Law and Yale Univ. *Career:* early legal career as Deputy Dist Attorney and in pvt. practice; on staff, School of Law, Univ. of Colo since 1979, Clinical Prof. of Law and Dir of Clinical Programs –2005; Presidential Elector for the State of Colo 2000; mem. Bd of Dirs Legal Services Corpn, Washington, DC 2003, Chair. Finance Cttee; Amb. to Belize 2005–; fmr mem. Exec. Council, Criminal Law Section, Colo Bar Asscn; fmr Co-Chair. Criminal Section, Boulder Co. Bar Asscn. *Publication:* Colorado Criminal Practice and Procedure (two vols) 1996. *Address:* Embassy of the USA, 29 Gabourel Lane, PO Box 286, Belize City, Belize (office). *Telephone:* 227-7161 (office). *Fax:* 223-0802 (office). *E-mail:* embbelize@state.gov (office). *Website:* belize.usembassy.gov (office).

DIEZ CANSECO TERRY, Raúl; Peruvian politician; b. 23 Jan. 1948, Lima. *Education:* San Ignacio de Loyola Univ. *Career:* fmr Pres. Foptur, Dir Corpac; elected Frente Democrático mem. Parl. for Lima 1990; cand. for Mayor of Lima 1993; Acción Popular Party cand. for Pres. 1995; fmr Vice-Minister of Tourism; First Vice-Pres. 2001–04, concurrently Minister of Industry, Tourism, Integration and Int. Trade Negotiations 2001–03. *Address:* c/o Ministry of Industry, Tourism, Integration and International Trade Negotiations, Calle 1 Oeste, Urb. Corpac, San Isidro, Lima 27, Peru (office).

DIJOUD, Paul Charles Louis; French politician; *Conseiller d'Enterprises;* b. 25 July 1938, Neuilly-sur-Seine; m. Catherine Cochaux 1968 (divorced 1983); one s. one d.; m. 2nd Maryse Dolivot 1988. *Education:* Lycée Condorcet, Faculté de Droit de Paris, Ecole Nationale d'Administration Inst. d'Etudes politiques de Paris. *Career:* commercial attaché, Dept of External Econ. Relations in Ministry of Econ. and Finance; elected to Nat. Ass. 1967, 1968, 1973, 1978, defeated 1981; Asst Sec.-Gen. Ind. Republican Party 1967–69; Conseiller Général for Canton of Embrun 1968–88; Pres. Ind. Republican Exec. Cttee for Provence-Côte d'Azur 1968–88; Mayor of Briançon 1971–83; Sec. of State attached to Prime Minister's Office 1973–74, later to Minister of Cultural Affairs and the Environment, to Minister of Employment with Responsibility for Immigrant Workers 1974, Secretary of State for Sport 1977, for Overseas Depts and Territories 1978; Commercial Adviser to Cen. Admin., Ministry of Economy and Finance 1981; Man. Dir Cie Commerciale Sucres et Denrées 1982–84; Pres. Comidex 1984; Pres. Conseil d'admin du parc nat. des Ecrins 1973; Plenipotentiary Minister 1988; Amb. to Colombia 1988–91, to Mexico 1992–94; Minister of State with responsibility for the principality of Monaco 1994–97; Amb. to Argentina 1997–2003; Conseiller d'Enterprises 2003–; Officier de la Légion d'honneur. *Address:* 27 Rue de la Ferme, 92200 Neuilly, France (office). *Telephone:* 1-46-40-06-68 (office); (06) 21725701 (mobile). *Fax:* 1-46-40-06-68 (office). *E-mail:* pauldijoudfr@hotmail.com (office).

DILEITA, Dileita Mohamed; Djibouti politician and diplomatist; *Prime Minister;* b. 12 March 1958, Tadjourahle. *Education:* Centre for Vocational Training (CFA), Médéa, Algeria. *Career:* fmr Amb. to Ethiopia; Prime Minister of Djibouti 2001–.
Address: Office of the Prime Minister, BP 2086, Djibouti (office). *Telephone:* 351494 (office). *Fax:* 355049 (office).

DIMAS, Stavros, LLM; Greek politician and lawyer; *Commissioner for the Environment, European Commission;* b. 30 April 1941, Athens. *Education:* Univ. of Athens, New York Univ. *Career:* lawyer private firm Sullivan and Cromwell 1969–70; World Bank 1970–75; Deputy Gov. Hellenic Industrial Bank 1975–77; elected mem. of Parl. 1977; Deputy Minister of Econ. Coordination 1977–80; Minister of Trade 1980–81; parl. spokesman for New Democracy party 1985–89; Minister for Agriculture 1989–90, for Industry, Energy and Tech. 1990–91; Sec.–Gen. New Democracy party 1995–2000, Sr Mem. Political Analysis Steering Cttee 2000–03; Head Del. to Council of Europe 2000–04; EU Commr for Employment and Social Affairs –2004, for Environment 2004–.
Address: European Commission, Rue de la Loi 200, 1049 Brussels, Belgium (office). *Telephone:* (2) 299-11-11 (office). *Fax:* (2) 295-01-38 (office). *Website:* europa.eu (office).

DIMITROV, Aleksander; Macedonian politician and lawyer; b. 29 Nov. 1949, Skopje. *Education:* Skopje Univ. *Career:* mem. Man. Bd, Air Service Skopje, Sec. Forum for Int. Relations; ed. Forum (newspaper) 1969–72; ed. Mlad Borac (newspaper) 1972–78; Sec. Council for Foreign Relations 1979–82; Under-Sec. Cttee for Int. Relations 1982–92; Dir for Int. Affairs, Dir Office of Palair 1993–96; Minister of Foreign Affairs 1998–2001.
Address: c/o Ministry of Foreign Affairs, Dame Grueva 14, 9100 Skopje, Macedonia.

DIMITROV, Nikola, LLM; Macedonian diplomatist; m.; one c. *Education:* SS Cyril and Methodius Univ., Skopje, King's Coll., Cambridge, UK. *Career:* Human Rights Officer, Ministry of Foreign Affairs 1996–2000, Deputy Minister of Foreign Affairs 2000, Nat. Security Adviser to Pres. of Macedonia 2000–01; Amb. to USA and Perm. Rep. to UN 2001–06; Nat. Coordinator for NATO Integration 2006, Chief Negotiator in talks with Greece about use of name Macedonia 2008.
Address: Ministry of Foreign Affairs, Dame Gruev 6, 1000 Skopje, Former Yugoslav Republic of Macedonia (office). *Telephone:* (2) 3115266 (office). *Fax:* (2) 3115790 (office). *E-mail:* mailmnr@mfa.gov.mk (office). *Website:* www.mfa.gov.mk (office).

DIMITROV, Philip, JD; Bulgarian lawyer, politician, diplomatist, academic and author; *Deputy Speaker, National Assembly;* b. 31 March 1955, Sofia; m. Elena Valentinova Gueorgieva-Dimitrova 1988. *Education:* St Kliment Ohridsky Univ., Sofia. *Career:* attorney 1979–1991, 2002–05;Vice-Pres. Union of Democratic Forces 1990, Pres. 1990–94; Prime Minister of Bulgaria 1991–92; mem. Parl. 1991–97; Vice-Chair. Jt Parl. Cttee, EU–Bulgaria 1995–97; Perm. Rep. to UN, New York 1997–98; Amb. to USA 1998–2002; Special Envoy of OSCE Pres. for Armenia and Azerbaijan 2004; Deputy Speaker, Nat. Ass. (Parl.) 2005–; MEP 2007–; Woodrow Wilson Center Public Policy Scholar, Washington, DC 2003; Adjunct Prof., American Univ. in Bulgaria 2003–; mem. Sofia Bar Asscn; Truman-Reagan Freedom Award for contrib. to overcoming communism 1999; Dimitrov Scholarships and Lectures, American Univ. in Bulgaria, Sofia inaugurated 2002. *Publications include:* The Myths of the Bulgarian Transition 2003, The New Democracies and the Transatlantic Link 2003; three historical novels, For They Lived, O Lord 1991, The True Story of the Round Table Knights 1996, Light of Men 2003.
Address: Bulgarian National Assembly, 1 Batemberg Square, Sofia 1000 (office); American University in Bulgaria, 2700 Blagoevgrad, Bulgaria. *Telephone:* (2) 9873238 (office); (73) 888456. *Fax:* (2) 9805358 (office). *E-mail:* phd@parliament.bg (office). *Website:* www.parliament.bg (office).

DINGER, Larry Miles, BA, MA, JD; American diplomatist; *Ambassador to Fiji;* b. Riceville, Ia; m. Paula Dinger; three c. *Education:* Macalester Coll., Officer Candidate School, Harvard Law School, Nat. War Coll., Washington, DC. *Career:* officer, USN 1968–72, served in Nha Be, Viet Nam 1969–70, in London, UK as intelligence watch officer 1970–72; worked on staff of US Senate Judiciary Cttee, ran for office in Ia; briefly practised law before entering Foreign Service in 1983, Consular/Narcotics Affairs Officer, Embassy in Mexico City 1983–85, Staff Asst, Bureau of E Asian and Pacific Affairs 1985–86, Political Officer, Embassy in Jakarta 1987–90, Indonesia Desk Officer 1990–92, Political Officer, Embassy in Canberra 1992–95, Special Asst to Asst Sec. of State for E Asian and Pacific Affairs 1995–96, Deputy Chief of Mission, Embassy in Suva, Fiji 1996–99, Embassy in Kathmandu, Nepal 2001–02, Amb. to Federated States of Micronesia 2002–04, Sr Advisor, Naval War Coll., Newport, RI 2004–05, Amb. to Fiji (also accred to Kiribati, Nauru, Tonga and Tuvalu) 2005–.

Address: Embassy of the USA, 31 Loftus Street, PO Box 218, Suva, Fiji (office). *Telephone:* 3314466 (office). *Fax:* 3300081 (office). *E-mail:* usembsuva@is.com.fj (office). *Website:* suva.usembassy.gov (office).

DINKA, Berhanu; Ethiopian UN official; b. 4 June 1935, Wollega prov. *Career:* joined Foreign Service in 1959, served in various positions including Dir for Africa and Middle East 1975; overseas assignments included Amb. to Djibouti, Perm. Rep. to UN, New York, Amb. to Canada and Chair. UN Cttee on the Implementation of Declaration on Granting of Independence to Colonial Countries and Peoples (Special Committee of 24); consultant for Int. Livestock Centre, ECA, UNDP and Int. Peace Acad. 1989–92; fmr Special Envoy of the UN Sec.-Gen. to Sierra Leone; Special Rep. of the UN Sec.-Gen. for the Great Lakes Region 1997; Chair. Implementation Monitoring Cttee for Burundi Peace Process 2000–02; Personal Rep. of the Sec.-Gen. at Arusha Peace Talks; Sec.-Gen.'s Special Rep. of the Sec.Gen. for Burundi 2002–04, Head, UN Operation in Burundi 2004; Chair. Power Sharing Comm., Sudan 2006; Co-founder Sub-Saharan Africa Consultative Support Forum; Co-founder Forum for the Study of Foreign Policy, Addis Ababa.
Address: c/o Ministry of Foreign Affairs, POB 393, Addis Ababa, Ethiopia. *Telephone:* (11) 5517345. *Fax:* (11) 5514300. *E-mail:* mfa.addis@telecom .net.et. *Website:* www.mfa.gov.et.

DINWIDDY, Bruce Harry, CMG, MA; British diplomatist; b. 1 Feb. 1946, Epsom; m. Emma Victoria Llewellyn 1974; one s. one d. *Education:* Winchester Coll., New Coll. Oxford. *Career:* economist, Govt of Swaziland, Overseas Devt Inst. (ODI) Nuffield Fellow 1967–70, Research Officer 1970–73; entered FCO 1973, Cen. and Southern African Dept 1973–4, Second Sec. Mission CSCE, Geneva 1974, Hong Kong and Indian Ocean Dept 1974–75; Del. to Mutual and Balanced Force Reductions (MBFR) negotiations, Vienna 1975–77; Perm. Under Sec.'s Dept, FCO London 1977–81, Personnel Operations Dept 1983–84, Asst Head, Personnel Policy Dept 1985–86, 2001–02; Head of Chancery in Cairo, Egypt 1981–83; Counsellor on loan to Cabinet Office 1986–88; CDA/SWP, Ebenhausen 1989; Embassy Counsellor in Bonn, Germany 1989–91; Deputy High Commr in Ottawa, Canada 1992–95; Head of African Dept (Southern) FCO 1995–98; Commr (non-resident) British Indian Ocean Territory 1996–98; High Commr in Dar es Salaam, Tanzania 1998–2001; secondment to Standard Chartered Bank 2001–02; Gov. of Cayman Islands 2002–05. *Publication:* Promoting African Enterprise 1974.

DIOP, Abdoulaye, BA, MA; Malian (b. Congolese) diplomatist; *Ambassador to USA;* b. 17 Sept. 1965, Brazzaville, Repub. of Congo; m.; four c. *Education:* Nat. School of Admin of Algeria, Univ. of Paris XI and Int. Inst. of Public Admin, Paris. *Career:* intern, Ministry of Foreign Affairs 1988, recruited 1990, Counsellor, Embassy in Brussels in charge of multilateral cooperation issues 1998–99, Adviser to Minister of Foreign Affairs in charge of political and diplomatic issues 1999–2000, Diplomatic Adviser to Pres. Alpha Oumar Konaré and Pres. Amadou Toumani Touré 2000–03, Amb. to USA 2003–; mem. several nat. dels that attended regional and int. confs to discuss regional integration, econ. devt, peace and security; spent several years at Direction of Int. Cooperation, Ministry of Foreign Affairs implementing and monitoring European Devt Fund's financial programs in Mali; took part in negotiations between African, Caribbean and Pacific States and EU with regard to Partnership Agreement for Devt signed in Cotonou 2000; oversaw Mali's participation in UN Security Council 2000–01; mem. Steering Cttee New Partnership for Africa's Devt (NEPAD) process 2000–01.
Address: Embassy of Mali, 2130 R Street, NW, Washington, DC 20008, USA (office). *Telephone:* (202) 332-2249 (office). *Fax:* (202) 332-6603 (office). *E-mail:* info@maliembassy.us (office). *Website:* www.maliembassy .us (office).

DIOP, Abdoulaye; Senegalese politician; *Minister of State, Minister of the Economy and Finance; Education:* Lycée El Hadj Malick Sy de Thiès, Univ. of Dakar and Ecole Nat. d'Admin et de Magistrature. *Career:* asst to Prin. Paymaster, Thiès 1980–81; rate collector, Commune de Fatick 1981–84, Commune de Mbour 1984–87, Commune de Pikine 1987–90; tax collector, Dakar Centre 1990–93; tax and rate collector, Ville de Dakar 1993–95, Dakar Urban Community 1993–95; Sr Banking Exec., Treasurer-Gen. and Dir of Treasury and Public Finance 1995–98; Minister Del., Ministry of Economy and Finance 2000; Minister of State, Minister of Economy and Finance 2001–; mem. Observatoire des finances locales de Cotonou 1996–, Comm. de réforme des textes de la décentralisation; Pres. Tech. Cttee responsible for Reform of Local Finance in Senegal; Chevalier, Ordre nat. du Lion de la République du Sénégal 1996.
Address: Ministry of the Economy and Finance, rue René Ndiaye, BP 4017, Dakar, Senegal (office). *Telephone:* 822-11-06 (office). *Fax:* 822-41-95 (office). *E-mail:* cthiam@minfinances.sn (office). *Website:* www.finances .gouv.sn (office).

DIOP, Bécaye; Senegalese politician; *Minister of the Armed Forces; Career:* Minister of Tech. and Professional Training in charge of Literacy and Promotion of Nat. Languages –2002; Minister of the Armed Forces 2002–; mem. Parti Démocratique Sénégalais (PDS).
Address: Ministry of the Armed Forces, Bldg Administratif, avenue Léopold Sédar Senghor, BP 4041, Dakar, Senegal (office). *Telephone:* 849-75-44 (office). *Fax:* 823-63-38 (office). *Website:* www.forcesarmees.gouv.sn.

DIOP, Majmout; Senegalese politician and pharmacist; *Secretary-General, Parti africain de l'indépendance;* b. 30 Sept. 1922, St Louis. *Education:* Ecole Africaine de Médecine et de Pharmacie, Dakar, Paris Univ. and African Inst., Univ. of Moscow. *Career:* hosp. pharmacist, Senegal and Gabon 1947–50; Pres. Senegalese Students' Asscn in France 1951; studied Marxism at Bucharest 1953–56; Sec.-Gen. Parti africain de l'indépendance (PAI) 1957–; exiled from Senegal 1961–76; engaged in research in political sociology at Inst. of Human Sciences, Mali 1968–76; dispensary pharmacist, Dakar 1977–. *Publications:* Contribution à l'Etude des problèmes politiques en Afrique Noire 1959, Classes et idéologies de classe au Sénégal 1963, Notes sur la classe ouvrière sénégalaise 1965, Histoire des classes sociales dans l'Afrique de l'Ouest (Vol. I) 1971, (Vol. II) 1972, Etude sur le Salariat 1975, Essai sur l'esclavage en Afrique de l'Ouest (to be published); and many articles in reviews and journals.
Address: Parti africain de l'indépendance (PAI), PO Box 820, Maison du Peuple Guediewaye, Dakar (office); 153 Avenue du Président Lamine Gueye, Dakar (office); 210 HCM, Guediawaye, Dakar, Senegal (home). *Telephone:* 837-01-36 (office).

DIOP SALLA, Doudou; Senegalese diplomatist; *Ambassador to France; Career:* fmr Amb. to Morocco, Amb. to France 2001–.
Address: Embassy of Senegal, 14 avenue Robert Schuman, 75007 Paris, France (office). *Telephone:* 1-47-05-39-45 (office). *Fax:* 1-45-56-04-30 (office). *E-mail:* repsen@wanadoo.fr (office). *Website:* www.ambassenparis.com (office).

DIOUF, Abdou, LenD, LèsL; Senegalese fmr head of state; *Secretary-General, La Francophonie;* b. 7 Sept. 1935, Louga; m. 1963. *Education:* Lycée Faidherbe, St Louis, Dakar and Paris Univs. *Career:* Dir of Tech. Co-operation and Minister of Planning Sept.–Nov. 1960; Asst Sec.-Gen. to Govt 1960–61; Sec.-Gen. Ministry of Defence June–Dec. 1961; Gov. Sine-Saloum Region 1961–62; Dir de Cabinet of Minister of Foreign Affairs 1962–63, of Pres. of Repub. 1963–65; Sec.-Gen. to Pres.'s Office 1964–68; Minister of Planning and Industry 1968–70; Prime Minister 1970–80; Pres. of Senegal 1981–2000, of Confed. of Senegambia 1982–89; Chair. OAU 1985–86; mem. Nat. Ass. for Longa Département 1973–; mem. Senegalese Progressive Union (UPS) 1961–, later Asst Sec.-Gen.; fmr Asst Sec.-Gen. Parti socialiste sénégalais (PS), now Chair.; currently Sec.-Gen. La Francophonie, Paris; Jt Winner Africa Prize for Leadership 1987.
Address: La Francophonie, 28 rue de Bourgogne, 75007 Paris, France (office). *Telephone:* 1-44-11-12-50 (office). *Fax:* 1-44-11-12-76 (office). *E-mail:* oif@francophonie.org (office). *Website:* www.francophonie.org (office).

DIOUF, Jacques, PhD; Senegalese international civil servant and agronomist; *Director-General, United Nations Food and Agriculture Organization;* b. 1 Aug. 1938, Saint-Louis; m. Aïssatou Seye 1963; one s. four d. *Education:* Lycée Faidherbe, Saint-Louis, Ecole Nat. d'Agriculture, Paris/Grignon, Ecole Nat. d'Application d'Agronomie Tropicale, Paris/Nogent and Sorbonne, Paris. *Career:* Exec. Sec. African Groundnut Council, Lagos 1965–71; Exec. Sec. West African Rice Devt Asscn, Monrovia 1971–77; Sec. of State for Science and Tech., Govt of Senegal, Dakar 1978–83; mem. Nat. Ass., Chair. Foreign Relations Cttee and elected Sec., Dakar 1983–84; Sec.-Gen. Banque centrale des états de l'Afrique de l'ouest, Dakar 1985–90; Perm. Rep. of Senegal to UN 1991–93; Dir-Gen. FAO 1994–; led Senegalese dels to UN Confs on Science and Tech., Vienna 1979 (Chair. of 1st Comm.), Industrial Devt, New Delhi 1980, New and Renewable Energy Sources, Nairobi (Vice-Chair.) 1981, Peaceful Use of Space, Vienna 1982; African Rep., Consultative Group on Int. Agricultural Research, Washington; mem. Bd of Dirs ISNAR, The Hague, IITA Lagos, IIRSDA Abidjan, ICRAF, Nairobi, Int. Foundation for Science, Stockholm, African Capacity Building Foundation, Harare, World Inst. for Devt Econs Research, Helsinki, Council of African Advisers of the World Bank, Washington DC; Chair. SINAES, Dakar; mem. Consultative Cttee on Medical Research, WHO, Geneva; Grand Commdr, Order of the Star of Africa (Liberia) 1977, Commdr, Order of Agricultural Merit (Canada) 1995, Grand Cross, Order of Merit in Agric., Fisheries and Food (Spain) 1996, Order of Solidarity (Cuba) 1998, Commdr, Légion d'honneur 1998, Grand Cross, Order of May for Merit (Argentina) 1998, Two Niles Decoration (Sudan), 2000, Nat. Order of Merit for Co-Operation and Devt (Guinea Bissau) 2001, Distinguished Cross, Order of the Quetzal (Guatemala) 2001, Commdr, Order of St Charles (Monaco) 2002,

Distinguished Cross (Peru) 2002, Kt Grand Cross (First Class) of the Most Exalted Order of the White Elephant (Thailand) 2003, Order of the Golden Fleece (Georgia) 2003, Golden Fortune Saint George Award 'Honour, Eminence, Labour' (First Grade) (Ukraine) 2003, Medal of Commdr, Nat. Order of Merit (Mauritania) 2003, Congressional Medal of Achievement (Philippines) 2004, Order of Vasco Nuñez de Balboa (Panama) 2004, Order of Ulises Rojas (Guatemala) 2004, Order of the Golden Heart, Rank of Grand Cross (Philippines) 2004, Grand Master Nat. Order (Madagascar) 2005, Order of Malta 2006, Commdr Grand Cross, Order of Merit of Repub. of Hungary 2007; numerous hon. doctorates; Award for Services to Educ. (France) 1979, Hilal Award (Pakistan) 2005. *Publications:* La détérioration du pouvoir d'achat de l'Arachide 1972, Les fondements du dialogue scientifique entre les civilisations Euro-occidentale et Négro-Africaine 1979, The Challenge of Agricultural Development in Africa 1989.
Address: Food and Agriculture Organization of the United Nations, Viale delle Terme di Caracalla, 00153 Rome, Italy (office). *Telephone:* (06) 57051 (office). *Fax:* (06) 57053152 (office). *E-mail:* fao-hq@fao.org (office). *Website:* www.fao.org (office).

DIPICO, Manne Emsley, BA; South African civil servant and trade unionist; *Regional Chairman, African National Congress, Northern Cape;* b. 21 April 1959, Kimberley. *Education:* Univ. of Fort Hare. *Career:* joined African Nat. Congress (ANC) 1982; Nat. Educ. Co-ordinator Nat. Union of Mineworkers; Azanian Students' Org. (AZASO) rep. for United Democratic Front (UDF) Exec. Border Region, AZASO Treas. Univ. of Fort Hare; mem. UDF N Cape 1985–86; detained Ciskei 1984, detained under state of emergency Kimberley 1986, arrested and sentenced to five years for furthering the aims of a banned org. through terrorist activities 1987–90, released before end of sentence; Regional Sec. ANC 1991–92, Regional Chair. N Cape 1992–; Regional Elections Co-ordinator 1993–94; Premier N Cape Prov. Legislature 1994–2004.
Address: c/o Private Bag X5016, Kimberley 8301 (office); 5248 Magashula Street, PO Mankurwane, Galeshawe-Kimberley 8345, South Africa (home). *Telephone:* (53) 8309300 (home). *Fax:* (53) 8332122 (office). *E-mail:* cmatlhacko@pancmail.ncape.gov.za (office).

DITLHABI OLIPHANT, Tuelonyana Rosemary, BA, MPA; Botswana diplomatist; *High Commissioner to Zambia;* b. 13 Sept. 1954; m. Clement S Oliphant; one s. *Education:* Univ. of Botswana, Univ. of Pennsylvania, USA. *Career:* at Ministry of Resources and Water Affairs 1977–85, of Foreign Affairs 1985; Counsellor, Embassy in Washington, DC 1988–90; Amb. to Angola 1990–96; High Comm. to UK 1996–98; Deputy Perm. Sec.for Political Affairs, Office of the Pres. 1998–99, Perm. Sec. for Political Affairs, Office of the Pres. 1999–2005; High Commr to Zambia 2005–.
Address: High Commission of Botswana, 5201 Pandit Nehru Road, Diplomatic Triangle, POB 31910, 10101 Lusaka, Zambia (office). *Telephone:* (1) 250555 (office). *Fax:* (1) 250804 (office).

DITTUS, Peter, DEcon; German economist; *Secretary-General, Bank for International Settlements;* m., three c. *Education:* Saarbrücken Univ., Univ. of Mich. *Career:* worked as economist at World Bank and OECD; joined BIS as economist 1992, apptd Deputy Sec.-Gen. 2000, Sec.-Gen. 2005–, mem. Exec. Cttee. *Publications include:* Die Wahl der Geldverfassung 1987, A Macroeconomic Model for Debt Analysis of the Latin America Region and Debt Accounting Models for the Highly Indebted Countries (jtly) 1991, Trade and Employment: Can We Afford Better Market Access for Eastern Europe? (jtly) 1994, Corporate Governance in Central Europe: The Role of Banks 1994, Corporate Control in Central Europe and Russia: Should Banks Own Shares? (jtly) 1995, numerous papers on int. econs.
Address: Bank for International Settlements, Centralbahnplatz 2, Basel 4002, Switzerland (office). *Telephone:* (61) 2808080 (office). *Fax:* (61) 2809100 (office). *E-mail:* peter.dittus@bis.org (office). *Website:* www.bis.org (office).

DIVUNGUI-DI-N'DINGE, Didjob; Gabonese politician and engineer; *Vice-President;* b. 5 May 1946, Alombié; m.; six c. *Education:* Ecole Nat. Supérieure des Arts et Métiers, Paris, France, Institut Nat. Polytechnique, Grenoble, France. *Career:* fmr employers' rep. and Vice-Chair. Perm. Comm. to the Econ. and Social Council; Dir-Gen. Soc. d'Energie et d'Eau du Gabon 1974; Adviser to Pres. of Gabon for Electrical Energy and Water Resources 1975; Minister of Energy and Water Resources 1983; presidential cand. 1993; currently Vice-Pres. of Gabon; Grand Croix de l'Ordre National de l'Etoile Equatoriale, Grand Croix de l'Ordre National du Mérite Gabonais, Grand Officer dans l'Ordre National du Mérite Français, Commandeur dans l'Ordre National de Côte d'Ivoire.
Address: Office of the Vice-President, Libreville, Gabon (office).

DIŽDAREVIĆ, Zlatko; Bosnia and Herzegovina diplomatist and journalist. *Career:* fmr Ed.-in-Chief Svijet (weekly magazine); Amb. to Croatia –2006;

currently Amb.-at-Large, Ministry of Foreign Affairs; Reporters Without Borders-Fondation de France Prize 1992. *Publications:* Sarajevo: A War Journal 1994, Portraits of Sarajevo 1995, Feral Tribune, Lords of War and Peace 1996.
Address: Ministry of Foreign Affairs, 71000 Sarajevo, Musala 2, Bosnia and Herzegovina (office). *Telephone:* (33) 281100 (office). *Fax:* (33) 472188 (office). *E-mail:* info@mvp.gov.ba (office). *Website:* www.mvp.gov.ba (office).

DJAFFAR, Ahmed Ben Saïd; Comoran politician; *Minister of Foreign Affairs; Career:* fmr head of local devt charity funded by EU; Minister of Foreign Affairs 2006–.
Address: Ministry of Foreign Affairs, Co-operation, the Francophonie and Comorans Abroad, BP 428, Moroni, The Comoros (office). *Telephone:* (74) 4100 (office). *Fax:* (74) 4111 (office).

DJANGONÉ-BI, Djessan Philippe, MA, PhD; Côte d'Ivoirian academic and diplomatist; *Ambassador to UK and Ireland;* b. 1 Jan. 1946; m. Martine Djangoné-Bi; two c. *Education:* Brandeis Univ., USA, Univ. of Abidjan, Sorbonne Univ., Paris, Univ. of Paris III, France. *Career:* Second Asst to Dean of Faculty of Arts and Humanities, Nat. Univ. of Côte d'Ivoire 1979–82, Dir of English Dept 1980–82; currently Sr Lecturer, Dept of English, Univ. of Cocody, Abidjan; Head of Int. Co-operation Div., Ministry of Higher Educ. and Scientific Research 2000–01; Perm. Rep. to UN, New York 2001–07, Amb. to UK 2007– (also accred to Ireland 2008–).
Address: Embassy of Côte d'Ivoire 2 Upper Belgrave Street, London, SW1X 8BJ, England (office). *Telephone:* (20) 7235-6991 (office). *Fax:* (20) 7259-5320 (office).

DJÉDJÉ, Ilahiri A.; Côte d'Ivoirian diplomatist; *Permanent Representative, United Nations;* b. 1956; m.; three c. *Education:* Nat. School of Admin, Abidjan, Univ. of Lyon II, France. *Career:* several early positions with Ministry of Foreign Affairs including Head, co-operation with Africa, Chief of African Div. and Head, co-operation with UN and ECE 1987–89, Chief of UN Div. and ECE 1989–91, Chargé d'études 1991–94; First Sec. and Consul, Embassy in South Africa 1994–2000; Asst Dir of Diplomatic Privileges and Immunities, Ministry of Foreign Affairs 2002–05; Special Advisor to Pres. and Chargé d'affaires 2005–07; Perm. Rep. to UN, New York 2007–.
Address: Permanent Mission of Côte d'Ivoire to the United Nations, 46 East 74th Street, New York, NY 10021, USA (office). *Telephone:* (212) 717-5555 (office). *Fax:* (212) 717-4492 (office). *E-mail:* ivorycoast@un.int (office). *Website:* www.un.int/cotedivoire (office).

DJOUDI, Karim, BSc, MSc; Algerian banker and government official; *Minister of Finance;* b. 13 July 1958, Montpellier, France. *Education:* Louis Pasteur Univ., Strasbourg and Univ. of Paris, Sorbonne, France. *Career:* joined Cen. Bank of Algeria 1988, Cen. Dir 1990; Dir-Gen. of the Treasury, Ministry of Finance 1999–2003; Minister Del. responsible for Promotion of Investment 2003–05, responsible for Financial Reform 2005–07; Minister of Finance 2007–.
Address: Ministry of Finance, Immeuble Maurétania, place du Pérou, Algiers, Algeria (office). *Telephone:* (21) 71-13-66 (office). *Fax:* (21) 73-42-76 (office). *E-mail:* algeriafinance@multimania.com (office). *Website:* www.finances-algeria.org (office).

DJOUMBE, Maïtine; Chadian diplomatist; *Ambassador to Belgium; Career:* Amb. to Ethiopia 2003–08, to Belgium (also accred to UK and African Union) and Perm. Rep. to EU, Brussels 2008–; mem. N'djamena Ceasefire Comm. 2004.
Address: Embassy of Chad, 52 Boulevard Lambermont, 1030 Brussels, Belgium (office). *Telephone:* (2) 215-19-71 (office). *Fax:* (2) 216-35-26 (office). *E-mail:* ambassade.tchad@chello.be (office).

DLAMINI, Absalom Themba; Swazi politician; *Prime Minister; Career:* Prime Minister of Swaziland 2003–.
Address: Office of the Prime Minister, Government House, POB 395, Mbabane, Swaziland (office). *Telephone:* 4042251 (office). *Fax:* 4043943 (office). *E-mail:* ppcu@realnet.co.sz (office).

DLAMINI, Barnabas Sibusiso; Swazi politician. *Career:* Minister of Finance 1984–93; fmr Exec. Dir IMF; Prime Minister of Swaziland July 1996–2003.
Address: c/o Office of the Prime Minister, Government House, PO Box 395, Mbabane, Swaziland (office).

DLAMINI, Mabili, BA; Swazi politician and diplomatist; b. 10 April 1957, Mankayane; m.; three s. *Education:* Univ. of Botswana and Swaziland. *Career:* fmr Amb. to Malaysia and Singapore; Minister of Foreign Affairs and Trade 2003–06.

Address: c/o Ministry of Foreign Affairs and Trade, PO Box 518, Mbabane, Swaziland (office).

DLAMINI, Mbongeni, BA, MA; Swazi diplomatist; *Permanent Representative, United Nations;* b. 1 Jan. 1966, Lobamba; m.; four c. *Education:* Univ. of Swaziland, Univ. of Witwatersrand, S Africa, Univ. of London, UK, Georgetown Univ., Washington DC. *Career:* Counsellor, Univ. of Witwatersrand 1993; served as Crown Prosecutor, Ministry of Justice 1993–94; Clerk and Attorney, Millin and Currie Attorneys 1994–98; Attorney-Gen., Ministry of Justice and Constitutional Devt 1999–2005; Perm. Rep. to UN, New York 2005–; Chair. Legal Group of Eastern and Southern African Anti-Money Laundering Group 2003–05; ex-oficio MP; ex-oficio mem. of Council, Univ. of Swaziland; mem. Constitutional Review Comm., Constitutional Drafting Cttee; Dir Swaziland Devt and Savings Bank, Swaziland Liquor Distribution.
Address: Office of the Permanent Representative of Swaziland to the United Nations, 408 East 50th Street, New York, NY 10022, USA (office). *Telephone:* (212) 371-8910 (office). *Fax:* (212) 754-2755 (office). *E-mail:* swaziland@un.int (office).

DLAMINI, Moses Mathendele; Swazi politician and diplomatist; *Minister of Foreign Affairs and Trade; Career:* fmr Amb. to Taiwan; fmr Pres. of the Senate; fmr Chair. Parl. Del. to UN; Minister of Foreign Affairs and Trade 2006–; Order of Brilliant Star with Grand Cordon (Taiwan).
Address: Ministry of Foreign Affairs and Trade, POB 518, Mbabane, Swaziland (office). *Telephone:* 4042661 (office). *Fax:* 4042669 (office).

DLAMINI, Obed Mfanyana; Swazi politician; *President, Ngwane National Liberatory Congress;* b. 4 April 1937, Mhlosheni Area, Shiselweni Dist. *Education:* Swaziland Nat. High School, UNISA. *Career:* teacher and Boarding Master, Manzini Nazarene High School 1961–64; cost clerk, later Asst Personnel Officer, Roberts Construction (Swaziland) (Pty) Ltd 1964–66; clerk, Standard Chartered Bank of Swaziland 1966, Asst Man. Admin. –1981; fmr Training and Ind. Relations Man. Swaziland Fruit Canners (Pty) Ltd; fmr Gen. Sec. Swaziland Fed. of Trade Unions, mem. Labour Advisory Bd, Training and Localization Council, Wages Advisory Bd, Man. Training Council, Regional Educ. Advisory Bd, Workers' Educ. Group; Prime Minister of Swaziland 1989–93; Senator 1993–; Pres. Ngwane Nat. Liberatory Congress (CNNLC); Chair. Swazi Democratic Alliance 1999–.
Address: Ngwane National Liberatory Congress, Ilanga Centre, Martin Street, Manzini; The Senate, Mbabane, Swaziland. *Telephone:* 5053935 (office).

DLAMINI-ZUMA, Nkosazana C., MB, ChB; South African politician and medical doctor; *Minister of Foreign Affairs;* b. 27 Jan. 1949; m. Jacob Zuma (divorced); four c. *Education:* Amanzintoti Training Coll., Univ. of Zululand, Univ. of Natal, Univ. of Bristol, Univ. of Liverpool. *Career:* Research Technician Medical School, Univ. of Natal 1972; Vice-Pres. SA Students Org. 1975–76; Chair. ANC Youth Section GB 1977–78; House Officer Frenchay Hosp. Bristol 1978–79; House Officer Canadian Red Cross Memorial Hosp., Berks. 1979–80; Medical Officer-Pediatrics Mbabane Govt Hosp. Swaziland 1980–85; Pediatric attachment Wittington Hosp. 1987–89; Vice Chair. Regional Political Cttee of ANC GB 1978–88, Chair. 1988–89; ANC Health Dept Lusaka 1989–90; Research Scientist Medical Research Council, Durban 1991–94; Minister of Health 1994–99, of Foreign Affairs 1999–; Dir Health Refugee Trust, Health and Devt Org., England 1988–90; Chair. S Natal Region Health Cttee of ANC 1990–92; mem. Exec. Cttee S Natal Region of ANC 1990–93; Chair. S Natal Region ANC Women's League 1991–93; Pres. World Conf. Against Racism 2001; mem. Steering Cttee Nat. AIDS Co-ordinating Cttee 1992–; mem. Bd Centre for Social Devt Studies Univ. of Natal, Durban 1992–; Trustee Health Systems Trust 1992–; Dr hc (Natal) 1995, (Bristol) 1996.
Address: 602 Stretten Bay, St Andrews Street, Durban 4001 (home); Department of Foreign Affairs, Union Buildings, East Wing, Government Avenue, Pretoria 0002, South Africa (office). *Telephone:* (12) 3511000 (office). *Fax:* (12) 3510253 (office). *E-mail:* minister@foreign.gov.za (office). *Website:* www.dfa.gov.za (office).

DLHOPOLČEK, František, PhD; Slovak diplomatist; *Director, Department of Central and Northern Europe, Ministry of Foreign Affairs;* b. 13 Sept. 1953, Turzovka; m.; two c. *Education:* School of Econs, Banska Bystrica, Diplomatic Acad., Moscow. *Career:* Univ. Asst Lecturer, School of Econs 1977–79; joined Fed. Ministry of Foreign Affairs (FMFA) of Czechoslovakia 1979; Diplomatic Officer at Embassy in Nairobi, Kenya 1979–80, African Dept FMFA 1983–84, Office of the Minister of Foreign Affairs 1984–87, Dept of Arab and African Countries FMFA 1989–90, Dir African Dept FMFA 1990–91; Consul-Gen. in Pretoria 1991–92, Amb. of Czech and Slovak Fed. Repub., later Amb. of Slovak Repub. to S Africa 1992–93; Dir-Gen., Political Affairs, Ministry of Foreign Affairs, Slovak Repub.

1993, Political Dir-Gen. 1998, Dir-Gen. of Bilateral Co-operation 2000, currently Dir, Dept of Cen. and Northern Europe; Amb. to Israel 1994–98, Amb. to UK –2005.
Address: c/o Ministry of Foreign Affairs, Hlboká cesta 2, 833 36 Bratislava, Slovakia (office). *Telephone:* 259783441 (office). *Fax:* 259783459 (office). *E-mail:* frantisek_dlhopolcek@foreign.gov.sk (office).

DMITRIEV, Andrey Viktorovich; Russian diplomatist; *Ambassador to Cuba;* b. 10 April 1941, Moscow; m.; one s. one d. *Education:* Moscow State Pedagogic Inst. of Foreign Languages, Diplomatic Acad. *Career:* mem. staff UN Secr., New York 1969–76, USSR Embassy, Brazil 1978–82, Peru 1987–89, USSR then Russian Embassy, Nicaragua 1989–92, Amb. to Nicaragua 1995–99, Dir Latin American Dept Ministry of Foreign Affairs, Moscow 1999–2001, Amb. to Cuba (also accred to Barbados) 2000–.
Address: Embassy of Russia, 5A Avenida, N6402, entre 62–66, Miramar, Havana, Cuba (office). *Telephone:* (7) 204-10-85 (office). *Fax:* (7) 204-10-38 (office). *E-mail:* embrusia@ceniai.inf.cu (office). *Website:* www.cuba.mid.ru (office).

DO SACRAMENTO E SOUSA, Lt-Col. Óscar Aguiar; São Tomé and Príncipe politician. *Career:* Vice-Pres. Chamber of Commerce 2002; Minister of Defence and Internal Order 2003–08; Minister of Foreign Affairs 2004, 2006.
Address: c/o Ministry of Defence and Internal Order, Av. 12 de Julho, CP427, São Tomé (office).

DOBBINS, James F., BA; American diplomatist; *Director, International Security and Defense Policy Center, RAND Corporation;* b. 1942, New York; m. Toril Kleivdal; two s. *Education:* Georgetown Univ. School of Foreign Service. *Career:* US naval officer; mem. Policy Planning Staff, State Dept, Washington DC 1969–71, Deputy Asst Sec. 1982–85, Prin. Deputy Asst Sec. 1989–90, Acting Asst Sec. for European and Canadian Affairs 1991, Special Asst to Pres., Nat. Security Council Staff 1996–99, Special Adviser to Pres. for Kosovo and Dayton Implementation 1999–2000, Asst Sec. of State for European Affairs 2000–01; mem. US Mission to OECD 1967–68, US Del. to Vietnam Peace Talks 1968; Political Officer, US Embassy, Paris 1969; mem. US Mission to UN 1973–75, Political-Mil. Officer US Embassy, London 1978–81; Deputy Chief of Mission, Bonn, FRG 1985–89; Amb. to the EC 1991–93; Special Envoy to Afghanistan 2001–03; Sr Fellow, RAND Corpn 1993, Dir Int. Security and Defense Policy Center 2003–; mem. Council on Foreign Relations 1995–96; two Superior Honor Awards, three Presidential Awards, six Sr Performance Awards, Dept of the Army Decoration for Dist Civilian Service, Armed Forces Expeditionary Medal, Nat. Defense Service Medal, Expeditionary Medal, Repub. of Viet Nam. *Publication:* America's Role in Nation-Building: From Germany to Iraq (co-author) 2003, The UN's Role in Nation-Building: From the Congo to Iraq (co-author) 2005, The Beginner's Guide to Nation-Building (co-author) 2007.
Address: International Security and Defense Policy Center, RAND Corporation, 1200 South Hayes Street, Arlington, VA 22202, USA (office). *Telephone:* (703) 413-1100, ext. 5286 (office). *E-mail:* James_Dobbins@rand.org (office). *Website:* www.rand.org (office).

DOBRIANSKY, Paula J., MA, PhD, BSFS; American diplomatist; *Under-Secretary for Democracy and Global Affairs;* b. 14 Sept. 1955, Alexandria, VA. *Education:* Harvard Univ., Georgetown Univ. School of Foreign Service. *Career:* early career positions include Dir European and Soviet Affairs, Nat. Security Council, The White House; Deputy Asst Sec. of State, Human Rights and Humanitarian Affairs; Assoc. Dir Policy and Programs, US Information Agency; Co-Chair Int. TV Council, Corpn for Public Broadcasting Sr Int. Affairs and Trade Advisor, Hunton and Williams; Sr Vice-Pres. and Dir, George F. Kennan Sr Fellow for Russian and Eurasian Studies, Washington Office, Council of Foreign Relations; Under-Sec. for Democracy and Global Affairs 2001–, Special Envoy for NI 2007–; mem. Bd Western NIS Enterprise Fund, Nat. Endowment for Democracy (NED) (also Vice-Chair.), Freedom House, American Council of Young Political Leaders, ABA Cen. and E European Law Initiative, US Advisory Comm. on Public Diplomacy; Host, Freedom's Challenge (three years); Co-host Worldwise (Nat. Empowerment TV); Ford and Rotary Foundation Fellow; Poland's Highest Medal of Merit, Grand Cross, Commdr of Order of Lithuanian Grand Duke Gediminas; Dr hc (Fairleigh Dickinson Univ.), (Flagler Coll.); State Dept Superior Honor Award, Dialogue on Diversity's Int. Award 2001, NED Service Medal, Georgetown Univ. Annual Alumni Achievement Award.
Address: US Department of State, Office 7250, 2201 Central Street, NW, Washington, DC 20520, USA (office). *Telephone:* (202) 647-6240 (office). *Website:* www.state.gov (office).

DOCKRILL, Saki Ruth, LLM, MA, PhD, FRHistS; British academic; *Professor, Department of War Studies, King's College London;* b. 14 Dec. 1952, Osaka, Japan. *Education:* Kyoto Univ., Japan, Univ. of Sussex, King's Coll. London. *Career:* joined King's Coll., London as Lecturer 1990, currently Prof. of Contemporary History and Int. Security; Teaching Fellow, Inst. of US Studies, Univ. of London –1998, mem. Advisory Bd 2002–; John M. Olin Fellow, Yale Univ. 1988–89; Co-Ed. Journal of Cold War History; Academic Coordinator, Tempes-Tacis programme 1996–2001; Sr Research Fellow, Nobel Inst., Oslo 2002; mem. Ed. Bd Journal of Transatlantic Studies 2003–; Fellow, Royal Historical Soc. 1992; mem. Soc. of Historians of American Foreign Relations, IISS, British Int. Studies Assoc., Political Studies Asscn; John M. Olin Fellowship 1988–89, MacArthur Fellowship, King's Coll., London 1990–91. *Television films:* The Fall of Singapore 2004, 1945: A Year that Shaped the World 2005. *Publications:* Britain's Policy for West German Rearmament, 1950–55 1991, From Pearl Harbour to Hiroshima: the Second World War in Asia and the Pacific, 1941–45 (ed.) 1994, Eisenhower's New Look National Security Police, 1953–1961 1996, Controversy and Compromise: Alliance Politics Between Britain, the Federal Republic of Germany and the United States (ed.) 1998, Cold War Respite: The Geneva Summit of July 1955 (co-ed.) 2000, Britain's Retreat from the East of Suez: The Choice Between Europe and the World? 2002, L'Europe de l'Est et de l'Ouest dans la Guerre Froide 1948–53 (co-ed.) 2002, The End of the Cold War: The Transformation of the Global Security Order 2005, Gen. Ed., Cold War History series1996–, Palgrave Advances in Cold War History (co-ed) 2006.
Address: Department of War Studies, King's College London, Strand, London, WC2R 2LS, England (office). *Telephone:* (20) 7848-2397 (office). *Fax:* (20) 7848-2026 (office). *E-mail:* saki.dockrill@kcl.ac.uk (office); sakidock@kukonline.co.uk (home). *Website:* www.kcl.ac.uk (office).

DODGE, Toby, BA, MSc, PhD; British research institute director and academic; *Reader in International Politics, Department of Politics, Queen Mary, University of London;* *Education:* SOAS, Univ. of London. *Career:* fmr Lecturer on Int. Relations and Middle Eastern Politics, Dept of Political Studies, SOAS; Researcher, Middle E Programme, Royal Inst. of Int. Affairs (RIIA); currently Sr Research Fellow, Centre for the Study of Globalisation and Regionalisation, Univ. of Warwick; Dir of Gulf States Programme and Consulting Sr Fellow for Middle E, IISS, London 2003–; also currently Reader in Int. Politics, Dept of Politics, Queen Mary, Univ. of London. *Publications:* Globalisation and the Middle East, Islam, Economics, Culture and Politics (co-Ed.) 2002, Inventing Iraq: The Failure of Nation Building and a History Denied 2003; numerous research papers and scholarly articles.
Address: Department of Politics, Queen Mary, University of London, Mile End Road, London, E1 4NS, England (office). *Telephone:* (20) 7882-8600 (office). *Fax:* (20) 7882-7855 (office). *E-mail:* t.dodge@qmul.ac.uk (office). *Website:* www.politics.qmul.ac.uk (office).

DODIK, Milorad; Bosnia and Herzegovina politician; *Prime Minister, Republika Srpska;* b. 1959, Banja Luka; m.; two c. *Education:* Univ. of Belgrade. *Career:* Pres. of Exec. Bd, Municipal Ass. of Laktaši 1986–90; mem. Parl. Socialist Repub. of Bosnia and Herzegovina 1990; Rep. Nat. Ass. of Republika Srpska; Prime Minister 1998–2001, 2006–; Founder and Chair. Alliance of Ind. Social Democrats.
Address: Office of the Prime Minister of Republika Srpska, 78000 Banja Luka, trg Republike Srpske 1, Bosnia and Herzegovina (office). *Telephone:* (51) 331333 (office). *Fax:* (51) 331366 (office). *E-mail:* kabinet@vladars.net (office). *Website:* www.vladars.net (office).

DODON, Igor, DEcon; Moldovan economist, academic and government official; *First Deputy Prime Minister and Minister of the Economy and Trade;* b. 18 Feb. 1975, Sadova, Straseni Dist; m.; one c. *Education:* Agrarian Univ. of Moldova, Acad. of Econ. Studies, Int. Inst. of Man. *Career:* worked at Moldovan Stock Exchange 1997–2005, positions included Sr Specialist in Clearing and Listing Depts, Man. of Electronic Systems of Negotiation, Dir of Marketing, Listing and Quotations Dept; Chair. Nat. Securities Depository 2001–05; Chair. Moldovan Commodity Exchange 2003–05; Deputy Minister of Economy and Trade 2005–06, Minister of Economy and Trade 2006–08, First Deputy Prime Minister and Minister of Economy and Trade 2008–; fmr Prof., Acad. of Econ. Studies, Free Int. Univ. of Moldova, Int. Inst. of Man., State Univ. of Moldova.
Address: Ministry of the Economy and Trade, 2033 Chişinău, Piaţa Marii Adunări Naţionale 1, Moldova (office). *Telephone:* (22) 23-74-48 (office). *Fax:* (22) 23-40-64 (office). *E-mail:* mineconcom@mec.gov.md (office). *Website:* www.mec.gov.md (office).

D'OFFAY, Callixte François-Xavier; Seychelles diplomatist; m. Barbra d'Offay. *Career:* Amb. to France (also accred as High Commr to UK 2004–07) –2007, also Perm. Rep. to EU.
Address: Embassy of the Seychelles, 51 avenue Mozart, 75016 Paris, France (office). *Telephone:* 1-42-30-57-47 (office). *Fax:* 1-42-30-57-40 (office). *E-mail:* ambsey@aol.com (office).

DOGRA, Rajiv; Indian diplomatist and author; *Ambassador to Italy; Career:* joined Ministry of External Affairs 1974; has served at Embassies in Stockholm, Rome, Doha, Karachi, London, Bucharest; fmr Perm. Rep. to FAO, Rome; fmr Amb. to Romania; Additional Sec. (Eurasia) –2005; Amb. to Italy 2005–. *Publications include:* Footprints in Foreign Sands (novel) 1997, Almost an Ambassador (novel) 2005; several short stories and essays on int. affairs.
Address: Embassy of India, Via XX Settembre 5, 00187 Rome, Italy (office). *Telephone:* (06) 4884642 (office). *Fax:* (06) 4819539 (office). *E-mail:* gen.email@indianembassy.it (office). *Website:* www.indianembassy.it (office).

DOJE, Cering; Chinese government official; *Chairman, Ethnic Affairs Committee, 10th National People's Congress;* b. 1939, Xiahe Co., Gansu Prov. *Career:* worked as clerk in Tibet 1959; joined CCP 1960; magistrate, Co. (Dist) People's Court, Nagarze Co. and Gyaca Co., Tibet 1962; mem. Tibet Autonomous Region CCP 1974–90; mem. Standing Cttee Tibet CCP 1977–90; First Sec. Xigaze Municipality CCP 1979–82; Vice-Chair. Tibet Autonomous Region 1983–85, Acting Admin. Head 1986–88, Chair. 1988–90; Deputy for Tibet Autonomous Region, 7th NPC 1988–; Vice-Minister of Civil Affairs 1990–93, Minister 1993–2003; Chair. 10th NPC Ethnic Affairs Cttee 2003–; Vice-Chair. China Cttee Int. Decade for Nat. Disaster Reduction 1998–; mem. 8th NPC 1993; mem. 14th CCP Cen. Cttee 1992–97, 15th CCP Cen. Cttee 1997–2002, 16th CCP Cen. Cttee 2002–; Dir Leading Group for Placement of Demobilized Army Officers 1993–; Deputy Head Leading Group for the Work of Supporting the Army, Giving Preferential Treatment to the Families of Armymen and Martyrs, supporting the Govt and Cherishing the People, State Council Leading Group on Boundary Delimitation.
Address: c/o Ministry of Civil Affairs, 147 Beiheyan Dajie, Dongcheng Qu, Beijing 100721, People's Republic of China (office). *Telephone:* (10) 65135333 (office). *Fax:* (10) 65135332 (office).

DOLOGUELE, Anicet G.; Central African Republic politician; *Chairman, Banque de Développement des Etats de l'Afrique Centrale;* b. 17 April 1957, Bozoum; m.; three c. *Education:* Univ. de Bangui, Bordeaux Univ., France. *Career:* fmr Finance and Budget Minister; Prime Minister, Minister of the Economy, Finance, Planning and Int. Co-operation 1999–2001; currently Chair. Banque de Développement des Etats de l'Afrique Centrale; Grand Officier Ordre du Mérite Centrafricain, Commdr Ordre du Mérite Centrafricain, Médaille d'or Ordre du Mérite Centrafricain.
Address: Banque de Développement des Etats de l'Afrique Centrale, Place du Gouvernement, BP 1177, Brazzaville, Republic of the Congo (office). *Telephone:* (242) 81-18-85 (office). *Fax:* (242) 81-18-80 (office). *E-mail:* bdeac@bdeac.org (office). *Website:* www.bdeac.org (office).

DOMICHI, Hideaki, LLB; Japanese diplomatist; *Ambassador to India;* m. Noriko Domichi. *Education:* Tokyo Univ. *Career:* joined Ministry of Foreign Affairs 1988, served as Dir Second Africa Div. 1988–90, Dir Eastern Europe Div. 1990–92, Dir Gen. Affairs Div. 1996–98, Deputy Dir-Gen. Econ. Co-operation Bureau 1998–99, Dir-Gen. Sub-Saharan African Affairs 2002, Dir-Gen. Middle Eastern and African Affairs Bureau 2004; served abroad as Counsellor, Embassy in Washington, DC 1992–95, Minister, Embassy in Cairo 1995–96, Minister, Embassy in Jakarta 1999–2002; fmr Amb. to Iran, Amb. to India (also accred to Bhutan) 2007–; Personal Rep. for Africa, G8 2003.
Address: Embassy of Japan, Plot No. 4&5, 50-G Shantipath, Chanakya-puri, New Delhi 110021, India (office). *Telephone:* (11) 26876581 (office). *Fax:* (11) 26885587 (office). *Website:* www.in.emb-japan.go.jp (office).

DOMINGO SOLANS, Eugenio, DEcon; Spanish international banker, economist and university professor; b. 26 Nov. 1945, Barcelona. *Education:* Univ. of Barcelona, Autonomous Univ. of Madrid. *Career:* Prof. of Public Finance, Univ. of Barcelona 1968–70, Autonomous Univ. of Madrid 1970–; economist, Banco Atlántico 1970, 1973–77, 1978–79; economist, Research Group, Econ. and Social Devt Plan 1970–73; Econ. Adviser, Ministry of Econs 1977–78; Man. Research Dept, Inst. of Econ. Studies 1979–86; Asst Pres. Banco Zaragozano 1986–91; mem. Bd BZ Gestión 1987–91, Banco Zaragozano 1988–94, Banco de Toledo 1988–94 (Sec. Bd 1990–94); mem. Governing Council and Exec. Comm., Banco de España 1994–98; Prof. of Monetary Policy and Spanish Tax System, Univ. Coll. of Financial Studies, Madrid 1996–; mem. Exec. Bd and Governing Council, European Cen. Bank 1998–; Businessmen's Soc. Award 1994.
Address: Universidad Autónoma de Madrid, Carretera de Colmenar Km. 15, Cantoblanco, 28049 Madrid, Spain (office). *Telephone:* (91) 3975000 (office). *Fax:* (91) 3974123 (office). *Website:* www.uam.es (office).

DON MALAVO, Estanislao; Equatorial Guinean politician. *Career:* Deputy Minister of Finance and the Budget 2006–08, Minister of Finance and the Budget 2008–.
Address: Ministry of Finance and the Budget, Malabo, Equatorial Guinea (office). *Website:* www.ceiba-guinea-ecuatorial.org/guineees/indexbienv1.htm (office).

DONCA, Ioan; Romanian diplomatist; *Ambassador to Russian Federation;* b. 14 March 1940. *Education:* Univ. 'Babes Bolyai', Cluj-Napoca, Bucharest Univ. *Career:* fmr senator; Amb. to Hungary 1995–98, Dir-Gen. Ministry of Foreign Affairs 1998–99, Amb. to People's Repub. of China 1999–2000, Dir European Enlargement, Ministry of Foreign Affairs 2002–05, Amb. to Russian Fed. 2005–; Commdr Ordinului pentru Merit 2000, and decorations from Germany, Tunisia, Jordan, Brazil, Lebanon, Bolivia.
Address: Embassy of Romania, ul. Mosfilmovskaya 64, 119590 Moscow, Russian Federation (office). *Telephone:* (495) 143-04-24 (office). *Fax:* (495) 143-04-49 (office). *E-mail:* ambasada@orc.ru (office).

DONDUKOV, Alexander Nikolayevich, DTechSc; Russian politician and engineer; *Member, Federation Council;* b. 29 March 1954, Kuybyshev (now Samara). *Career:* engineer, Sr engineer, leading constructor Moscow Machine Construction Bureau (designers' office), Moscow 1977–85; Deputy Chief Constructor 1985, Chief Constructor 1991, Head, Gen. Constructor Moscow Machine Construction factory Skorost' 1991–93; Chair. Bd of Dirs, Gen. Constructor A. S. Yakovlev Machine Designers' Office 1993–2000, 2001–; mem. Govt Council for Industrial Policy 1994–; mem. Congress of Russian Intelligentsia 1994–; Minister of Industry, Science and Tech., Russian Fed. 2000–02; mem. Fed. Council (representing Belgorod) 2002–.
Address: A. S. Yakovlev Machine Designers' Bureau, Leningradsky prosp. 68, 123315 Moscow A–47 (office); Federation Council, ul. B. Dmitrovka 26, 103426 Moscow, Russia. *Telephone:* (495) 157-57-37 (office); (495) 203-90-74 (office). *Fax:* (495) 203-46-17 (office). *E-mail:* post_sf@gov.ru (office). *Website:* www.council.gov.ru (office).

DONIGI, Peter Dickson, CBE, LLB; Papua New Guinea diplomatist and lawyer; b. 19 Dec. 1950; m.; five c. *Education:* Univ. of Papua New Guinea. *Career:* pvt. legal practice 1981–98; Amb. and Special Envoy to UN 1991–92, apptd Perm. Rep. to UN 1998; Amb. to Germany (also accred to Holy See) 1992–95; mem. Council Commonwealth Lawyers' Asscn 1991–; fmr Pres. Papua New Guinea Law Soc.; Commonwealth Fellow 1991. *Publications:* Indigenous or Aboriginal Rights to Property: A Papua New Guinea Experience.
Address: c/o Permanent Mission of Papua New Guinea to the United Nations, 201 East 42nd Street, Suite 405, New York, NY 10017, USA (office).

DONNELLY, Sir Brian, Kt, KBE, CMG; British diplomatist (retd); b. 24 April 1945, Workington, Cumbria; m. 1st Susanne Gibb 1994 (divorced); m. 2nd Julia Mary Newsome; one d. one step-s. one step-d. *Career:* joined British Diplomatic Service 1973; served in FCO, London then Perm. Mission to UN, New York 1973–79; posted to Singapore 1979–82; with Personnel Dept, FCO 1982–84; secondment to Cabinet Office, Asst to Chief Scientific Adviser 1985–88; Political Counsellor and Consul-Gen., Embassy in Athens 1988–91; Head of Non-Proliferation Dept 1992–95; Deputy Perm. Rep. to NATO, Brussels 1995–97; Amb. to Yugoslavia 1997–99; Dir FCO 1999–2000; Amb. to Zimbabwe 2001–04.
Address: c/o Foreign and Commonwealth Office, King Charles Street, London, SW1A 2AH, England (office).

DONNELLY, Christopher Nigel, CMG, TD, BA; British defence, security and foreign affairs specialist and academic; *Senior Fellow, Defence Academy of the United Kingdom;* b. 10 Nov. 1946, Rochdale, Lancs.; m. Jill Norris 1971; one s. one d. *Education:* Cardinal Langley School, Middleton, Lancs. and Univ. of Manchester. *Career:* Instructor, Royal Mil. Acad. Sandhurst (RMAS) 1969–72; Sr Lecturer, Soviet Studies Research Centre, RMAS 1972–79, Dir 1979–89; TA (Int. Corps) 1970–93; Adjunct Prof., Carnegie Mellon Univ. 1985–89, Georgia Tech. Univ. 1989–93; Special Adviser for Cen. and E European Affairs to Sec.-Gen. of NATO 1989–2003; Sr Fellow, Defence Acad. of the UK 2003–, Founder and Head of Advanced Research and Assessment Group 2003–07; Dir Inst. for Statecraft and Governance, Oxford 2007–; Jt Chief Ed. The Journal of Slavic Military Studies; Grand Cross of Commdr, Order of the Lithuanian Grand Duke Gediminas. *Publications:* Red Banner 1989, War and the Soviet Union 1990, Gorbachev's Revolution 1991, Nations, Alliances and Security 2004; numerous articles on Russian and Eastern European defence and security issues.
Address: Headquarters, Defence Academy of the United Kingdom, Shrivenham, Swindon, Wilts., SN6 8LA, England (office). *Telephone:* (1793) 785075 (office). *Fax:* (1793) 785072 (office). *E-mail:* cdonnelly.hq@da.mod.uk (office). *Website:* www.defac.ac.uk (office); www.tandf.co.uk/journals/titles/13518046.asp.

DOOKERAN, Winston, BA, MSc; Trinidad and Tobago economist; *Leader, Congress of the People;* b. 24 June 1943, Trinidad and Tobago; m. Shirley Dookeran; one s. *Education:* Univ. of Manitoba, Canada, London School of Econs. *Career:* Lecturer in Econs, Univ. of the West Indies 1971–81, 1981–86; MP for Chaguanas constituency 1981–91, MP for St Augustine 2002–; Minister of Planning and Mobilization, Vice-Chair. Nat. Planning Comm. 1986–91; Dir Price-Waterhouse Man. Consultants and to the Caribbean Govs 1992–95; Fellow, Center for Int. Affairs, Harvard Univ. 1993–95; Sr Economist UN ECLAC 1995–97; fmr Gov. Cen. Bank of Trinidad and Tobago 1997–2002; Visiting Scholar, Weatherhead Center for Int. Affairs Harvard Univ. 2002–03; Leader, United Nat. Congress 2005–06, Congress of the People 2006–; Hon. LLD (Univ. of Manitoba) 1991. *Publications:* Choices and Change: Reflections on the Caribbean (ed.) 1996, The Caribbean Quest: Directions for Structural Reforms in a Global Economy (co-ed.) 1999, Uncertainty, Stability and Challenges 2006. *Address:* Systematics Studies Ltd, St Augustine, Trinidad (office). *Telephone:* (868) 645-8466 (office); (868) 640-5694 (home). *Fax:* (868) 645-8467 (office). *E-mail:* wdookeran@tstt.net.tt (home). *Website:* www .winstondookeran.com (home).

DORAKUMBURE, Wijeratne Bandara; Sri Lankan diplomatist. *Career:* High Commr to Pakistan 2007–. *Address:* High Commission of Sri Lanka, 2c, St 55, F-6/4, Islamabad, Pakistan (office). *Telephone:* (51) 2828723 (office). *Fax:* (51) 2828751 (office). *E-mail:* srilanka@isb.comsats.net.pk (office).

DORCHEH, Ali Jazini; Iranian diplomatist. *Career:* Head of Iranian Interests Section in USA, Embassy of Pakistan 2001–07. *Address:* Ministry of Foreign Affairs, Shahid Abd al-Hamid Mesri Street, Ferdowsi Avenue, Tehran, Iran (office). *Telephone:* (21) 61151 (office). *Fax:* (21) 66743149 (office). *E-mail:* matbuat@mfa.gov.ir (office). *Website:* www .mfa.gov.ir (office).

DORDA, Abuzed Omar, BA; Libyan politician and diplomatist; b. 4 April 1944, Rhebat; m.; six c. *Education:* Benghazi Univ. *Career:* teacher 1965–70; Gov. Misurata Prov. 1970–72; Minister of Information and Culture 1972–74, Under-Sec., Ministry of Foreign Affairs 1974–76, Minister of Municipalities 1976–79, Sec.-Gen. People's Cttee for Economy 1979–82, for Agric. 1982–86, for the Municipality of Al-Jabal Al-Gharbi 1986–90, Sec. of the Gen. People's Cttee (Prime Minister) 1990–94, Asst Sec. 1994–95; Perm. Rep. to UN 1997–2003. *Address:* c/o Permanent Mission of Libya to the UN, 309–315 East 48th Street, New York, NY 10017, USA (office).

DORÉ, Ousmane; Guinean economist and politician; *Minister of the Economy, Finance and Planning; Career:* fmr Sr Economist, IMF Africa Dept, fmr IMF Rep. to Senegal and Guinea-Bissau; Minister of the Economy, Finance and Planning 2007–. *Address:* Ministry of the Economy and Finance, Boulbinet, BP 221, Conakry, Guinea (office). *Telephone:* 30-45-17-95 (office). *Fax:* 30-41-30-59 (office).

DORE, Ronald Philip, CBE, BA; British university professor; *Research Associate, London School of Economics;* b. 1 Feb. 1925, Bournemouth; m. Nancy MacDonald 1957; one s. one d.; one s. with Maria Paisley. *Education:* School of Oriental and African Studies, London Univ. *Career:* Asst Prof. then Assoc. Prof., Univ. of BC 1956–60; Reader, LSE 1961, Hon. Fellow 1980; Prof., LSE and SOAS 1964–69; Prof. and Fellow, Inst. of Devt Studies, Sussex Univ. 1970–81; Tech. Change Centre, London 1982–86; Dir Japan-Europe Industry Research Centre, Imperial Coll., London 1986–91; Research Assoc., Centre for Econ. Performance, LSE and Political Science 1991–; Visiting Prof. Imperial Coll. of Science, Tech. and Medicine, London Univ. 1982, of Sociology, Harvard Univ. 1987; Adjunct Prof., MIT 1989–94; mem. British Acad. 1975–; Foreign Hon. Fellow, American Acad. of Arts and Sciences 1978, Hon. Foreign Fellow Japan Acad. 1986–; Order of the Rising Sun (Third Class) Japan; Japan Foundation Prize 1977. *Publications:* City Life in Japan 1958, Land Reform in Japan 1959, Education in Tokugawa Japan 1965, British Factory/Japanese Factory 1973, The Diploma Disease 1976, Shinohata Portrait of a Japanese Village 1978, Flexible Rigidities, Industrial Policy and Structural Adjustment in Japanese Economy 1986, Taking Japan Seriously: A Confucian Perspective on Leading Economic Issues 1987, Japan and World Depression, Then and Now (Essays) (Jt Ed.) 1987, How the Japanese Learn to Work (with Mari Sako) 1988, Corporatism and Accountability: Organized Interests in British Public Life (Jt Ed.) 1990, Will the 21st Century be the Age of Individualism? 1991, The Japanese Firm: the Source of Competitive Strength (Jt Ed.) 1994, Japan, Internationalism and the UN 1997, Stockmarket Capitalism, Welfare Capitalism: Japan and Germany versus the Anglo-Saxons 2000, Social Evolution, Economic Development and Culture 2001, Selected Writings of Ronald Dore 2002, New Forms and Meanings of Work in an Increasingly Globalised World 2004, Dare No Tame No Kaisha Ni Suru Ka? (Whom Should Corporations Serve?). *Address:* 157 Surrenden Road, Brighton, East Sussex, BN1 6ZA, England. *Telephone:* (1273) 501-370 (home).

DOREY, Gregory John, CVO; British diplomatist; *Ambassador to Hungary;* m. Alison; two s. one d. *Career:* with Ministry of Defence 1977–81, 1984–86; Second Sec., UK Del. to NATO, Brussels 1982–84, FCO 1986–89, First Sec. (Political/Econ.), Budapest 1989–92, FCO 1992–96, Counsellor (Econ., Commercial, Econ., Media), then Deputy High Commr, Islamabad 1996–99, secondment to HSBC, London 2000, Deputy Head of Mission, Hong Kong 2000–04, Asst Dir Human Resources Directorate, FCO 2004–07, Amb. to Hungary 2007–. *Address:* British Embassy, Harmincad Utca 6, Budapest 1051, Hungary (office). *Telephone:* (1) 266-2888 (office). *Fax:* (1) 266-0907 (office). *E-mail:* info@britemb.hu (office). *Website:* www.britishembassy.hu (office).

DORJI, Lyonpo Chenkyab, MSc; Bhutanese diplomatist and international organization official; b. 1943, Haa Dist, western Bhutan; m.; three c. *Education:* Forestry Research Inst., Dehra Dun, Swiss Technical Inst., Zurich, Switzerland, Wood Tech. and Transport, Austria. *Career:* joined Dept of Forests 1961, Dir –1984; Dir Bd of Int. Center for Integrated Mountain Devt (ICIMOD), Kathmandu, Nepal 1983–85; Jt Sec. Dept of Trade, Commerce, and Industry and Mines 1984–85; Sec. Ministry of Trade, Industries and Forests 1985–86; Sec. Nat. Planning Comm. 1986–88; Sec. Dept of Agric. 1986–88; Vice-Chair. and Deputy Minister of Planning Comm. (ind. charge) 1988–91; Cabinet Minister for Planning 1991, Chair. 1991–98; Chair. Nat. Environment Comm. 1992–98; served as mem. of several key insts of Royal Govt of Bhutan; Amb. to Thailand (also accred to Singapore and Australia, and responsible for Bhutan's relations with other SE Asian countries) –2005; Sec.-Gen. South Asian Asscn for Regional Cooperation (SAARC) 2005–08. *Publications:* The Bhutan Forest Act 1969, The National Forest Policy 1974. *Address:* c/o Ministry of Foreign Affairs, Convention Centre, PO Box 103, Thimphu, Bhutan. *Telephone:* (2) 321413.

DORJI, Dasho Tshering; Bhutanese government official and diplomatist; *Ambassador to Bangladesh; Career:* fmr Sec.-Gen. Bhutan Chamber of Commerce and Industry; fmr Sec., Ministry of Works and Human Settlements; Amb. to Bangladesh 2008–. *Address:* Embassy of Bhutan, House 12, Road 107, Gulshan 2, Dhaka 1212, Bangladesh (office). *Telephone:* (2) 8826863 (office). *Fax:* (2) 8823939 (office). *E-mail:* bhtemb@bdmail.net (office).

DORR, Noel, MA, BComm; Irish diplomatist; b. 1 Nov. 1933, Limerick; m. Caitríona Doran 1983. *Education:* St Nathy's Coll., Ballaghderreen, Nat. Univ. of Ireland, Georgetown Univ., Washington, DC, USA. *Career:* Third Sec., Dept of Foreign Affairs, Dublin 1960–62, Embassy, Brussels 1962–64, First Sec., Embassy, Washington, DC 1964–70, Dept of Foreign Affairs, Dublin 1970–72, Counsellor (Press and Information) 1972–74, Asst Sec. and Political Dir 1974-77, Deputy Sec. and Political Dir 1977–80, Perm. Rep. to UN 1980–83; Amb. to UK 1983–87; Sec. Dept of Foreign Affairs 1987–95; Personal Rep. of Minister for Foreign Affairs, EU Intergovernmental Conf. 1996–97, 2000. *Address:* 19 Whitebeam Avenue, Clonskeagh, Dublin 14, Ireland (home). *Telephone:* (1) 2694086 (home). *Fax:* (1) 2603430 (home). *E-mail:* ndorr@eircom.net (home).

DORSAINVIL, Daniel, PhD; Haitian economist and government official; *Minister of the Economy and Finance;* b. 25 Aug. 1959, Port-au-Prince. *Education:* Univ. of Pennsylvania, USA. *Career:* fmr official, USAID; Econ. Advisor to Pres. Préval –2006; Minister of the Economy and Finance 2006–. *Address:* Ministry of Economy and Finance, Palais des Ministères, rue Monseigneur Guilloux, Port-au-Prince, Haiti (office). *Telephone:* 2227113 (office). *Fax:* 2231247 (office).

DOS ANJOS, Assunção Afonso Sousa, LLB; Angolan diplomatist; *Ambassador to Portugal;* b. 13 Feb. 1946, Luanda; m. Maria Antonieta Azancot de Menezes Medeiros dos Anjos; two c. *Education:* Univ. de Coimbra and Univ. Clássica de Lisboa, Portugal. *Career:* Dir Africa and Middle E Dept, Ministry of External Relations 1975–78; Dir Cabinet of Vice-Prime Minister 1978–79, Cabinet of Minister of Planning 1979, Cabinet of Pres. of the Repub. 1979–93; Amb. to Spain 1993–2000, to France 2000–03, to Portugal 2003–; del. to numerous int. meetings and orgs including UN Gen. Ass., OAU, EU; Hon. mem. Notre Dame Univ. of Africa, Spain; Hon. Prof., Soc. of Int. Studies, Spain; Kt of Merit Order of San Lazaro of Jerusalem; Commdr, Ordre national du Mérite.

Address: Embassy of Angola, Av. da República 68, 1069-213 Lisbon, Portugal (office). *Telephone:* (21) 7961830 (office). *Fax:* (21) 7971238 (office). *E-mail:* embaixadadeangola@mail.telepac.pt (office). *Website:* www.embaixadadeangola.org (office).

DOS SANTOS, Fernando (Nandó) da Piedade Dias; Angolan politician; *Prime Minister;* b. 1952, Luanda. *Education:* Instituto Industrial de Luanda. *Career:* involved with Grupo Boa Esperança from 1970 (pro-independence); nat. service, Portuguese colonial army 1973–74, deserted to join guerilla forces of Movimento Popular de Libertação de Angola (MPLA); mem. staff FAPLA (Armed Forces of MPLA), rank of Maj. 1984, Col 1986, Maj.-Gen. 1992; Insp., Corpo do Polícia Popular de Angola—CPPA (People's Police Force of Angola) 1976–78, Head of 1st Command Div. 1978–79, Head of Political Dept and Personnel Section in Nat. Directorate 1979–81, Nat. Dir of People's Police 1984–86; Deputy Head Nat. Political Directorate, Ministry of the Interior 1981–84, Nat. Dir of Personnel 1982–84, Deputy Minister of State Security 1984, Deputy Minister of the Interior 1984, also Head of Information Services 1990, Deputy Minister of the Interior responsible for Internal Order 1995–99, Minister of the Interior 1999–2002; elected Deputy People's Ass. 1986–; Commdr-Gen. and Gen. Commr of Nat. Police (Polícia Nacional) 1995–; Co-ordinator Exec. Cttee of Inter-Ministerial Comm. of Process of Peace and Reconciliation 2001, Nat. Comm. for Social and Productive Reintegration of Demobilized Troops and Displaced Persons 2002; Prime Minister of Angola 2002–. *Address:* Office of the Prime Minister, c/o Ministry of the Interior, Avda 4 de Fevereiro, Luanda, CP 2723, Angola (office).

DOS SANTOS, José Eduardo; Angolan head of state; *President;* b. 28 Aug. 1942, Luanda. *Education:* Liceu Salvador Correia. *Career:* joined Movimento Popular de Libertação de Angola (MPLA) 1961; went into exile 1961 and was a founder mem. and Vice-Pres. of MPLA Youth based in Léopoldville, Congo (now Kinshasa, Democratic Repub. of Congo); first Rep., MPLA, Brazzaville 1961; sent with group of students for training in Moscow 1963; graduated as Petroleum Engineer, Inst. of Oil and Gas, Baku 1969; then mil. course in telecommunications; returned to Angola and participated in war against Portuguese 1970–74; Second in Command of Telecommunications Services, MPLA Second Politico-Military Region, Cabinda; mem. Provisional Readjustment Cttee, Northern Front 1974; mem. MPLA Cen. Cttee and Political Bureau 1974–; Chair. MPLA; Minister of Foreign Affairs, Angola 1975; Co-ordinator, MPLA Foreign Relations Dept 1975; Sec. Cen. Cttee for Educ., Culture and Sport, then for Nat. Reconstruction, then Economic Devt and Planning 1977–79; First Deputy Prime Minister, Minister of Planning and Head of Nat. Planning Comm. 1978–79; Pres. of Angola 1979– and Chair. of Council of Ministers 1979–, also Prime Minister 1999–2002; C-in-C of FAPLA (Armed Forces of MPLA). *Address:* Office of the President, Protocolo de Estado, Futungo de Belas, Luanda, Angola (office). *Telephone:* 222370150 (office). *Fax:* 222370366 (office).

DOSERI, Rashid Saad ad-; Bahraini diplomatist. *Career:* fmr Second Sec., Perm. Mission to UN, currently Amb. to Saudi Arabia. *Address:* Embassy of Bahrain, PO Box 94371, Riyadh 11693, Saudi Arabia (office). *Telephone:* (1) 4880044 (office). *Fax:* (1) 4880208 (office).

DOSS, Alan; British United Nations official; *Special Representative of the Secretary-General for Liberia, United Nations;* b. 7 Jan. 1945, Cardiff, Wales; m. Soheir Doss; three d. *Education:* London School of Econs. *Career:* held posts with UN in China, Kenya, Niger, Zaïre and Benin; fmr UN Resident Co-ordinator Regional Rep. of UNDP in Bangkok, Thailand; fmr Dir UN Border Relief Operation (Thai–Cambodia border); fmr Dir UNDP European Office, Geneva, Switzerland; Rep. of UNDP to Devt Assistance Cttee and OECD; Dir UN Devt Group (UNDG) –2001; Deputy Special Rep.of Sec.-Gen., UN Mission in Sierra Leone (UNAMSIL) 2001–04, Prin. Deputy Special Rep. of Sec.-Gen for Côte d'Ivoire 2004–05, Special Rep. of Sec.-Gen. for Liberia 2005–. *Address:* United Nations Mission in Liberia (UNMIL), Pan African Plaza, Tubman Boulevard, 1st Street, Monrovia, Liberia (office). *Telephone:* (212) 963-9926 (NY) (office). *Website:* www.unmil.org (office).

DOSTAM, Gen. Abdul Rashid; Afghan politician and militant leader; *Chief of Staff to Commander-in-Chief of Armed Forces;* b. 1954, Khowja Dokoh, Juzjan Prov. *Career:* fmr plumber; with Oil and Gas Exploration Enterprise 1979; undertook mil. training in USSR 1980; Commdr pro-Soviet Jozjani Dostum Militia, N Afghanistan 1980–92; Defence Minister in Pres. Najibullah's Govt (1986–92); allied with Gulbuddin Hekmatyar's Pashtun warriors and Shi'a guerrillas following transition of power 1992; est. Itehad Shamal/Northern Unity org. which controlled most N Afghanistan provs 1993–97; fled to Turkey when Taliban occupied Mazar-i-Sharif 1997;

returned to fight with Northern Alliance (NA) against Taliban 2001; Deputy Minister of Defence 2001–04; presidential cand. 2004; Chief of Staff to C-in-C of Armed Forces 2005–; Leader, Junbesh-i Melli-i Islami (Nat. Islamic Movt), Uzbek mil. wing of NA –2005; mem. Jabhe-ye-Motahed-e-Milli (United Nat. Front) 2007–; f. Balkh Air (airline); awarded Hero of the Repub. of Afghanistan Medal by Pres. Najibullah. *Address:* c/o Ministry of Defence, Shash Darak, Kabul, Afghanistan.

DOSTIYEV, Abdulmajid, DIur; Tajikistan diplomatist and fmr army officer; *Ambassador to Russian Federation;* b. 10 May 1946, Khatlon. *Education:* Tajik Agric. Inst. *Career:* served in USSR Armed Forces 1965–68; Chair. Agric. Exec. Cttee, Khatlon 1974–77; First Vice-Pres. Supreme Council 1993–95; First Deputy Chair. Nat. Ass. 1995–2000; First Vice-Chair. Ass. of Reps 2000–07; Amb. to Russian Fed. 2007–. *Address:* Embassy of Tajikstan, Granatnyi per. 13, 103001 Moscow, Russian Federation (office). *Telephone:* (495) 290-38-46 (office). *Fax:* (495) 291-89-98 (office). *E-mail:* embassy_moscow@tajikistan.ru (office). *Website:* www.tajikistan.ru (office).

DOUGLAS, Denzil Llewellyn; Saint Christopher and Nevis politician; *Prime Minister and Minister of Finance, Sustainable Development, Information and Technology and Minister of Tourism, Sports and Culture; Career:* Leader Saint Kitts-Nevis Labour Party; Prime Minister of Saint Christopher and Nevis, Minister of Finance, of Nat. Security, of Information, of Planning and of Foreign Affairs 1995–2001; Prime Minister and Minister of Finance, Devt Planning and Nat. Security 2001–04; Prime Minister, Minister of Finance, Sustainable Development, Information and Technology and Minister of Tourism, Sports and Culture 2004–; Chair. Bd Caribbean Devt Bank 2002–. *Address:* Office of the Prime Minister, Basseterre, Saint Christopher and Nevis (office).

DOUTOUM, Mahamat Habib; Chadian diplomatist; *Ambassador to Nigeria; Career:* Asst Sec.-Gen. for Educ., Scientific, Cultural and Social Affairs, OAU 2000–02; Commr for Social Affairs and Afro-Arab Cooperation, African Union 2003–07; Amb. to Nigeria 2007–. *Address:* Embassy of Chad, Goriola Street, Victoria Island, PMB 70662, Lagos, Nigeria (office). *Telephone:* (1) 2622590 (office). *Fax:* (1) 2618314 (office).

DOVE, Fiona Beck, MA; South African campaigner; *Executive Director, Transnational Institute;* b. 4 July 1961, Zambia. *Education:* Inst. of Social Studies. *Career:* active in feminist and anti-apartheid orgs 1980s; organiser and research co-ordinator, S African Commercial, Catering and Allied Workers' Union 1985–94; Ed. The Shopsteward magazine, Congress of S African Trade Unions 1992–94; Dir Transnational Inst., Amsterdam, Netherlands 1995–. *Address:* Transnational Institute, de Wittenstraat 25, 1052 AK, Amsterdam, Netherlands (office). *Telephone:* (20) 662-6608 (office). *Fax:* (20) 675-7176 (office). *E-mail:* fdove@tni.org (office). *Website:* www.tni.org (office).

DOYLE, Noreen, MBA; American banker and international finance official; *First Vice-President, European Bank for Reconstruction and Development;* b. 1949. *Education:* Coll. of Mount St Vincent, Tuck School of Business, Dartmouth Coll. *Career:* began career with Morgan Guaranty Trust; joined Bankers Trust 1974, Client Man., New York and Houston, Div. Man. for multinat. cos, New York, Man. Dir for distribution of structured financings, New York, responsible for European affairs, London 1990–92; joined EBRD and set up syndication business 1992, responsible for credit and market risks 1997–2001, First Vice-Pres. and Head of Banking 2001–, mem. Exec. Cttee. *Address:* c/o EBRD, One Exchange Square, London, EC2A 2EH, England (office). *Website:* www.ebrd.com (office).

DRACH, Ivan Fyodorovich; Ukrainian politician and writer; b. 17 Oct. 1936, Telizhentsy, Kiev Oblast; m. Mariya Drach; one s. one d. *Education:* Univ. of Kiev, Moscow State Univ. *Career:* worked as school teacher; Corresp. for Literaturnaya Ukraina and Witczyna newspapers 1961–87; scriptwriter Dovzheniev Studio 1964–87; mem. Bd, Sec. Union of Ukrainian Writers 1989–92; joined CP 1959, resgnd 1990; Founder mem. Narodny Rukh (Ukrainian nationalist opposition Movt), Leader, then co-Chair. 1989–92; Chair. Bd Ukraina Soc. 1992–; mem. Ukrainian Supreme Soviet 1990–; mem. Ukrainian World Co-ordination Council 1992–99; Chair. State Cttee of Information Policy, TV and Radio 2001; Ukrainian State Prize 1976, USSR State Prize 1983, Yaroslav Mudry Order 1996. *Publications include:* Sun Flower 1962, Ballads of Everyday Life 1967, I Come to You 1970, Poems 1972, The Kievan Sky 1976, The Sun and the Word (poetry) 1978, Green Gates 1980, Dramatic Poems 1982, Grigory Skovoroda 1984, Temple of Sun 1988.

Address: Gorky str. 18, Apt 7, 252005 Kiev, Ukraine. *Telephone:* (44) 228-87-69.

DRAKE, Howard Ronald, OBE; British diplomatist; *Ambassador to Chile;* b. 13 Aug. 1956; m. Gillian Drake; one s. one d. *Career:* Vice-Consul (Commercial), Los Angeles, USA 1981–83; Second Sec. (Political), Santiago, Chile 1985–88; Head of Chancery, Singapore early 1990s; Deputy Consul-Gen. and Dir of Inward Investment, New York 1997–2002; worked on EU Affairs, Cyprus, Counter-proliferation, Human Resources, FCO, London 2002–05; Amb. to Chile 2005–.
Address: British Embassy, Avda El Bosque Norte 0125, Las Condes, Santiago, Chile (office). *Telephone:* (2) 370-4100 (office). *Fax:* (2) 370-4180 (office). *E-mail:* chancery.santiago@fco.gov.uk (office). *Website:* www .britemb.cl (office).

DRASKOVICS, Tibor, LLB; Hungarian banking and finance executive and fmr government official; b. 26 June 1955, Budapest. *Education:* Eötvös Lóránd Univ. of Budapest. *Career:* started career as legal expert Ministry of Finance 1979–84, Sec. to Minister 1984–86, Head of Legal Dept 1986, Head of Legal Div. 1988, Deputy State Sec. 1990–91, Admin. State Sec. 1994–98; Man. Dir Concordia Biztosítási (insurance brokers) 1991–93; tax consulting man. Arthur Andersen Ltd 1993–94; mem. Monetary Council, Nat. Bank of Hungary 1995–98; CEO ABN-AMRO 1999; Deputy CEO K&H Bank 2001; Chief of Cabinet of the Prime Minister 2002; Minister of Finance 2004–05; Order of Merit of the Hungarian Republic's Middle Cross.

DREIFUSS, Ruth; Swiss politician; *Chairperson of Commission on Intellectual Property Rights, Innovation and Public Health, World Health Organization;* b. 9 Jan. 1940, St Gall. *Education:* Ecole d'Etudes Sociales, Geneva and Univ. of Geneva. *Career:* Sec. 1958–59; Ed. Coopération, Swiss Union of Cooperatives, Basle 1961–64; Asst Sociologist, Centre Psycho-Social Universitaire, Geneva 1965–68; Asst in Nat. Accounting, Faculty of Econ. and Social Sciences, Univ. of Geneva 1970–72; civil servant, Swiss Devt Agency Fed. Ministry of Foreign Affairs 1972–81; Sec. Swiss Fed. of Trade Unions 1981–93; elected to Swiss Fed. Council 1993, Vice-Pres. 1998, Pres. of Swiss Confed. 1999; Head, Fed. Dept of Home Affairs 1994–2002; Chair. Comm. on Intellectual Property Rights, Innovation and Public Health, WHO; mem. Social Democratic Party; Dr hc (Haifa) 1999, (Jerusalem) 2000.
Address: Secretariat for the Commission on Intellectual Property Rights, Innovation and Public Health, World Health Organization, 20 avenue Appia, 1211 Geneva 27, Switzerland (office). *Telephone:* (22) 7912764 (office). *Fax:* (22) 7914852 (office). *E-mail:* cipih@who.int (office). *Website:* www.who.int (office).

DRESSER GUERRA, Denise Eugenia, PhD; Mexican political scientist and academic; *Professor of Political Science, Instituto Tecnológico Autónomo de México (ITAM);* b. 22 Jan. 1963. *Education:* Colegio de México, Princeton Univ., USA. *Career:* post-doctoral fellow Center for Int. Studies, Univ. of Southern California; Prof. of Political Science, Instituto Tecnológico Autónomo de México (ITAM) 1991–; Dir North American Futures Project, Pacific Council on Int. Policy 1999–; Visting Prof., Univ. of California, Berkeley 2002; fmr Visiting Research Fellow, Center for US-Mexican Studies, University of California, San Diego; fmr Sr Visiting Fellow, Inter-American Dialogue, Washington DC; writes political column for Reforma (newspaper) and Proceso (news weekly); host political talk show Entre Versiones on Mexican TV 1998–99; fmr host weekly radio commentary on US-Mexico relations for W Radio, Mexico City; political consultant Baring Research 1993–95, Bank of Montreal 1996–99; mem. editorial bd Latin American Research Review; mem. Human Rights Watch Americas Advisory Cttee, Research Council of the Forum for Democratic Studies, Nat. Endowment for Democracy, World Acad. of Arts and Science.
Address: Río Hondo No. 1, Tizapán San Angel, México City 01000, D.F., Mexico. *Telephone:* (55) 5628-4000, Ext. 3761. *Fax:* (55) 5490-4672. *E-mail:* denise.dresser@attglobal.net. *Website:* politica.itam.mx.

DRISS, Rachid; Tunisian diplomatist and journalist; *President, Association des études internationales;* b. 27 Jan. 1917, Tunis; m. Jeanine Driss 1953; one s. *Education:* Sadiki Coll., Tunis. *Career:* joined Neo-Destour party 1934; journalist exiled in Cairo and, with Pres. Bourguiba, Founder mem. Bureau du Maghreb Arabe; returned to Tunisia 1955; Ed. El Amal; Deputy, Constitutional Ass. 1956; Minister of Posts, Telegraph and Telephones 1957–64; mem. Nat. Ass. 1959, 1969; Amb. to USA and Mexico 1964–69; mem. Political Bureau of Council of the Repub. 1969–; Perm. Rep. to UN 1970–76; Vice-Pres. Econ. and Soc. Council 1970, Pres. 1971, 1972; mem. Conseil Constitutionnel 1987–92; Special Emissary of Arab League to Kuwait and Iraq 1992; Founder, Pres. Asscn des études internationales 1981–, Arab Bd for Child Devt; Pres. Higher Comm. on Human Rights and

Fundamental Freedoms 1991–2000; Dir Etudes Internationales (quarterly); Grand Cordon de l'Ordre de l'Indépendance de la République Tunisienne and many foreign decorations. *Publications:* From Bab Souika to Manhattan 1980, Diaries from the Maghreb Office in Cairo 1981, A l'aube la lanterne 1981, From Djakarta to Carthage 1985, Errances (poems) 1990, Feuilles d'insomnie (novel) 1990, Report on Human Rights in Tunisia 1992, Au gré du Calame (poems) 1996, Reflets d'un combat (history of Tunisian Nat. Movt) 1997.
Address: Rue St Cyprien, 2016 Carthage, Tunisia (home). *Telephone:* (71) 791663 (office); (71) 746846 (home). *Fax:* (71) 796593 (office). *E-mail:* aeitunis@planet.tn (office).

DROBNJAK, Vladimir, JD, PhD; Croatian diplomatist; *Chief Negotiator for Accession Negotiations with EU;* b. 5 March 1956, Zagreb. *Education:* Univ. of Zagreb. *Career:* journalist, Vjesnik (daily newspaper) 1980–86, Ed.-in-Chief 1986–88, USA and UN corresp. 1988–92; Deputy Perm. Rep. to UN, New York 1992–97; Asst Minister, Ministry of Foreign Affairs, Head of Div. for Multilateral Affairs, 1997–2000; Nat. Co-ordinator for Stability Pact for S Eastern Europe 1999–2000, Chair. Third Working Table 2002–03; mem. Negotiating Team for Stabilization and Asscn Agreement with EU 2000–01; Head, Perm. Mission to EU, Brussels 2000–03; Perm. Rep. to UN, New York, 2003–05, also Scientific and Tech. Counsellor; Chief Negotiator for Accession Negotiations with EU and Deputy Head of State Del. 2005–; Order of the Croatian Trefoil 1996, Order of the Homeland Gratitude 1996; Young Journalist of the Year 1982, Golden Pen Award of the Croatian Journalist Association 1984, Memorial Medal Vukovar 1998.
Address: Office of the Chief Negotiator, Trg Sv. Marka 2, Zagreb, Croatia (office). *Telephone:* (1) 4569333 (office). *Fax:* (1) 4569325 (office).

DRYUKOV, Anatoly Matveyevich; Russian diplomatist; b. 4 Sept. 1936, Voronezh; m.; two d. *Education:* Moscow Inst. of Int. Relations. *Career:* diplomatic service 1960–; Attaché, Embassy in Karachi 1962–64; mem. Dept of S East Asia, USSR Ministry of Foreign Affairs 1964–66; mem. Secr. of Deputy Minister 1966–69; First Sec., Embassy in Lusaka 1969–73; Asst Deputy Minister 1973–78, expert, Deputy Chief Dept of S East Asia 1978–86, Deputy Chief Dept of Socialist Countries of Asia 1986–87; with Embassy in Singapore 1987–90; Chief, Main Dept of Staff and higher educ. establishments of USSR Ministry of Foreign Affairs 1990–91; Amb. to India 1991–96; Gen. Insp., Ministry of Foreign Affairs 1996–98; Amb. to Armenia 1998–2005.
Address: c/o Ministry of Foreign Affairs, 119200 Moscow, Smolenskaya-Sennaya pl. 32/34, Russian Federation.

DU, Gen. Tiehuan; Chinese government official; *Political Commissar, Beijing Military Area Command, People's Liberation Army;* *Career:* Asst Dir PLA Gen. Political Dept 1993–94; Political Commissar Ji'nan Mil. Region 1994–96; Political Commissar, Beijing Mil. Area Command 1996–; mem. 15th CCP Cen. Cttee 1997–2002; rank of Gen. 2000–.
Address: Political Commissar's Office, Beijing Military Area Command, Beijing, People's Republic of China (office).

DU, Trinh Duc, BA; Vietnamese diplomatist; b. 1949, Phu Tho Prov.; m. Ta Kim Son; two s. *Career:* Desk Officer, Ministry of Foreign Affairs 1974, Deputy Dir Northwest European Dept 1993–94, Dir-Gen. 1994–95, 2000–03, Minister Counsellor, Paris 1989–91, Chargé d'affairs a.i. 1992, Amb. to Francophone Community and to UNESCO, Paris 1996–99, Chair. Francophone Community 1997, Amb. to UK 2003–07 (also accred to Ireland 2004–07).
Address: Ministry of Foreign Affairs, 1 Ton That Dam, Ba Dinh District, Hanoi, Viet Nam (office). *Telephone:* (4) 8452980 (office). *Fax:* (4) 82318725 (office). *E-mail:* banbientap@mofa.gov.vn (office). *Website:* www.mofa.gov.vn (office).

DUALE, Elmi Ahmed; Somali diplomatist; *Permanent Representative, United Nations;* *Education:* Faculty of Medicine and Surgery, Univ. of Rome, Univ. of Edinburgh. *Career:* worked as clinical physician, DeMartino Gen. Hospital, Mogadishu and Medical Officer, Dept of Health, Mogadishu 1960–62; Dir Gen. Ministry of Health 1963–68; mem. Parl., then Minister of State for Foreign Affairs 1969; political detainee at fmr Presidential Villa 1970–73; worked for Medical Officer and Team Leader, WHO, North-Western State, Nigeria 1974–77, Team Leader, Programme Coordinator, Nigeria 1977–83, Rep. for Tanzania 1983–94, Rep. for Eritrea 1994–99, Public Health Consultant, Dar es Salaam 1999–2005; Perm. Rep. to UN, New York 2005–.
Address: Office of the Permanent Representative of Somalia to the United Nations, 425 East 61st Street, New York, NY 10021, USA (office). *Telephone:* (212) 688-9410 (office). *Fax:* (212) 759-0651 (office). *E-mail:* somalianet@hotmail.com (office). *Website:* www.iaed.org/somalia (office).

DUANGDY, Somdy; Laotian government official; *Minister of Finance;* Career: fmr Vice-Minister of Finance, Minister of Finance 2007–; fmr Vice-Chair. and Standing Mem. Poverty Reduction Fund Admin. Bd.
Address: Ministry of Finance, rue That Luang, Ban Phonxay, Vientiane, Laos (office). *Telephone:* (21) 412401 (office). *Fax:* (21) 412415 (office).

DUARTE, Cristina; Cape Verde politician, economist and international banker; *Minister of Finance and Public Administration; Career:* Co-ordinator World Bank Growth and Competitiveness Project 2005–06; Minister of Finance and Public Admin 2006–.
Address: Ministry of Finances and Public Administration, 107 Av. Amílcar Cabral, CP 30, Praia, Santiago, Cape Verde (office). *Telephone:* 2607400 (office). *E-mail:* aliciab@gov1.gov.cv (office). *Website:* www.mf.cv (office).

DUARTE, Yasmin Jessie; South African diplomatist; *Deputy Director-General for African Multilateral Affairs;* b. 19 Sept. 1953, Johannesburg; m. John Duarte; one s. one d. *Career:* began career at Raven Press 1985; restricted in terms of State of Emergency 1985–86, 1986–87, detained without trial 1988 and released and placed under restriction orders until State of Emergency was lifted; Special Asst to Pres. Nelson Mandela 1990; mem. Exec. Council, Safety and Security, Gauteng Prov. Govt 1994–98 (resgnd); High Commr to Mozambique 1999–2003; Deputy Dir.-Gen. of Africa Multilateral Affairs, Ministry of Foreign Affairs 2002–; mem. ANC Regional Exec. Council 1991, 1993; mem. ANC Nat. Exec. Council 1997–99; Gen.-Sec. Fed. of Transvaal Women 1985–91;.
Address: Ministry of Foreign Affairs, Union Bldgs, East Wing, 1 Government Avenue, Arcadia, Pretoria 0002, South Africa (office). *Telephone:* (12) 3511000 (office). *Fax:* (12) 3510253 (office). *E-mail:* minister@foreign.gov.za (office). *Website:* www.dfa.gov.za (office).

DUBAI, Ruler of (see MAKTOUM, Rashid al-).

DUBININ, Yuri Vladimirovich, DHistSc; Russian diplomatist (retd) and academic; *Professor of International Politics, Moscow State Institute of International Relations, Ministry of Foreign Affairs;* b. 7 Oct. 1930, Nalchik; m. Liana Khatchatrian 1953; three d. *Education:* Moscow Inst. for Int. Relations. *Career:* mem. CPSU 1954–91; Asst at Embassy in Paris 1955–56; with UNESCO Secr., Paris 1956–59; mem. Apparat USSR Ministry of Foreign Affairs 1959–63, 1969–78; First Sec., Embassy Counsellor, Embassy in Paris 1963–69; Amb. to Spain 1978–86, to USA 1986–90, to France 1990–91; Perm. Rep. to UN, New York 1986; Prof. of Political Science, George Washington Univ., USA 1991; Visiting Prof. of Politics and History, Washington and Lee Univ. 1993; Amb.-at-Large 1991–94; Deputy Minister of Foreign Affairs 1994–99; Amb. to Ukraine 1996–99; Head of Russian Del. on negotiations with Estonia 1991, with Ukraine 1992–94; mem. Int. Ecological Acad. Kiev 1997, Int. Acad. of Spiritual Unity of Peoples of the World 2001; currently Prof. of Int. Politics, Moscow State Inst. of Int. Relations, Ministry of Foreign Affairs; also currently Prof. of Int. Politics, Moscow Int. Higher Business School (MIRBIS) Inst.; Hon. Prof., Slaviansky Univ., Kiev, Ukraine 1999; numerous honours and awards including Orders of the Red Banner 1971, 1980, 1988, Order of Honour 1996, Order of Merit (Ukraine); planet named Dubinin by Int. Astronomical Soc. 1999. *Publications:* USSR–France: Experience of Co-operation 1979, Soviet-Spanish Relations 1983, Representing Perestroika in the West 1989, Diplomatic Truth: Memoirs of the Ambassador to France 1997, Ambassador, Ambassador!: Memoirs of the Ambassador to Spain 1999, Time of Change: Notes of the Ambassador to the US 2003.
Address: Moscow State Institute for International Affairs, 119454 Moscow, prospekt Vernadskogo, 76 (office); Bolshoi Palashevsky per. 3, App. 34, 123104 Moscow, Russia. *Telephone:* (495) 434- 00-89 (office); (495) 203-27-49 (office). *Fax:* (495) 434-90-66 (office); (495) 203-27-49 (office). *Website:* www .mgimo.ru (office).

DUBOIS, Paul; Canadian diplomatist; *Ambassador to Germany; Career:* joined Dept of External Affairs 1973, served abroad at Canadian embassies in Bangkok, Abidjan, Bonn; Dir Econ. and Trade Law Div., Legal Bureau, Ottawa 1986–90; Minister and Deputy Perm. Rep. to UN, Geneva 1990–94; Deputy Perm. Rep. to Conf. on Disarmament 1992–94; Dir Gen. of Western Europe Bureau 1994–97; Amb. to Austria 1997–2001; Asst Deputy Minister, Europe, Middle E and N Africa –2001, Asst Deputy Minister, Europe 2001–04; Amb. to Germany 2004–.
Address: Embassy of Canada, Leipziger Pl., 10117, Berlin, Germany (office). *Telephone:* (30) 203120 (office). *Fax:* (30) 20312590 (office). *E-mail:* brlin@international.gc.ca (office). *Website:* www.kanada-info.de (office).

DUBYNA, Oleh; Ukrainian politician and engineer; *President, Ukrainian National Energy Company (Ukrenergo);* b. 20 March 1959, Elizavetovka, Dnepropetrovsk region; m.; one s. *Education:* Dnieprodzerzhinsk Indus-trial Inst., Dnieprodzerzhinsk State Tech. Univ. *Career:* employee Dniepr Metallurgic plant 1976, master, Sr master, then engineer 1986–93, Head of Bureau, Deputy Head of Div., First Deputy Dir-Gen. 1996–98; teacher Dnieprodzerzhinsk Polytechnical Higher School 1985–86; Asst to Dir, then Deputy Dir-Gen. Dniepr br. of Intermontage Kam – Soviet-Swiss Joint Venture DEMOS 1993–96; Deputy Head, Chair. Bd of Dirs, Dir-Gen. Alchevsk Metallurgic plant 1998–99; Dir-Gen. Kryvoy Rog State Ore-Metallurgic plant, Krivorozhstal 1999–; Deputy Prime Minister for Econ. Policy 2000–01; First Deputy Prime Minister 2001–02; Adviser to Pres. Leonid Kuchma 2002–04; Pres. Ukrainian Nat. Energy Co. (Ukrenergo) 2004–.
Address: Ukrainian National Energy Company (Ukrenergo), Kiev, Ukraine (office). *Website:* www.ukrenergo.energy.gov.ua (office).

DUCARU, Sorin Dumitru, MSc, PhD; Romanian diplomatist; *Permanent Representative, NATO;* b. 22 June 1964, Baia-Mare; m. Carmen Ducaru; two c. *Education:* Polytechnic Inst. of Bucharest, Romanian Nat. School of Political Science and Public Admin, Amsterdam School of Int. Relations, Univ. of Amsterdam, Netherlands. *Career:* Ed.-in-Chief ING (student magazine) 1985–88; engineer, Brasov Telecommunications Co. 1988–90; Researcher, Inst. for Automation, Bucharest 1990–91; joined Ministry of Foreign Affairs 1993, has held several positions including Expert in Policy Planning Div. on Euro-Atlantic Integration Issues 1993–94, Counsellor to the Minister 1994–95, Dir of Minister's Office and Spokesman 1995–96, Head of Div. for Nat., WEU and Strategic Issues 1996–97, Deputy Chief of Mission, Washington, DC 1998–2000, Perm. Rep. to UN, New York 2000–01, Amb. to USA 2001–06, Perm. Rep. to NATO, Brussels 2006–; Assoc. Lecturer in European Studies, Romanian Nat. School for Political Studies and Public Admin, Dept of Int. Relations 1993–.
Address: Office of the Permanent Representative of Romania, Blvd Léopold III, 1110 Brussels, Belgium (office). *Telephone:* (2) 707-41-11 (office). *Fax:* (2) 707-45-79 (office). *E-mail:* natodoc@hq.nato.int (office). *Website:* www.nato.int (office).

DUCKWITZ, Edmund, DJur; German diplomatist; *Permanent Representative, European Union;* b. 8 March 1949, Bremen; m. Joke Duckwitz (née Aten); three c. *Education:* Univ. of Heidelberg, Univ. of Geneva. *Career:* scientific collaborator, Max Planck Inst., Heidelberg 1974–76; joined Foreign Service 1976, served in Fed. Foreign Office, Bonn 1981–85, Deputy Head of Section in Directorate-Gen. for Econ. and European Affairs 1989–92; Deputy Dir-Gen. of Foreign, Security and Devt Policy, Office of the Chancellor 1996–99; overseas postings include Embassy in Belgrade 1978–81, Counsellor, then Deputy Chief of Mission, Embassy in Manila 1985–89; Amb. to Dominican Repub. 1992–96, to Venezuela 1999–2001, to Netherlands 2001–06; Perm. Rep. to NATO, Brussels 2006–07; Perm. Rep. to EU, Brussels 2007–.
Address: Permanent Representation of Germany to the EU, 8-14 rue Jacques de Lalaing, 1040 Brussels, Belgium (office). *Telephone:* (2) 787-10-00 (office). *Fax:* (2) 787-20-00 (office). *E-mail:* Eurogerma.eu@bruessel .auswaertiges-amt.de (office). *Website:* www.eu-vertretung.de (office).

DUDAU, Nicolae; Moldovan politician and diplomatist; *Ambassador to Italy;* b. 19 Dec. 1945, Grineuts; m. Galina Dudau; one d. *Education:* Higher CPSU School, Moscow, Chişinău Tech. Univ. *Career:* employee Chişinău tractor mfg factory 1963–75; army service 1964–67; various admin. posts in orgs in Chişinău 1975–90; Deputy Chair. Chişinău City Planning Cttee 1990–91; First Sec. Chişinău City CP Cttee 1990–91; Exec. Dir Int. Charity Foundation 1991–93; Minister-Counsellor Moldovan Embassy in Russia 1993–94; First Deputy Minister of Foreign Affairs 1997–98, Minister of Foreign Affairs 2001–04; Amb. to Belarus 1998–2001, to Italy 2004–.
Address: Embassy of the Republic of Moldova, 8 Strada Monte Bello Rome, Italy (office).

DUDDY, Patrick Dennis; American diplomatist; *Ambassador to Venezuela;* b. Bangor, Maine; m. Mary Huband; two c. *Education:* Colby Coll., Northeastern Univ., Nat. War Coll. *Career:* career diplomatist, has served in embassies in Chile, Dominican Repub., Costa Rica, Paraguay and Panama, fmr Deputy Chief of Mission, La Paz, fmr Consul Gen., São Paulo, Deputy Asst Sec., Bureau of Western Hemisphere Affairs, Dept of State –2007, Amb. to Venezuela 2007–.
Address: US Embassy, Calle F con Calle Suapure, Urb. Colinas de Valle Arriba, Caracas 1080, USA (office). *Telephone:* (212) 975-6411 (office). *Fax:* (212) 975-6710 (office). *E-mail:* embajada@state.gov (office). *Website:* caracas.usembassy.gov (office).

DUEÑAS, F. Tomás; Costa Rican business executive, politician and diplomatist; *Ambassador to USA;* m. Diana Chavarría. *Education:* Univ. of Miami, Columbia Univ., Stanford Univ., Univ. of Pennsylvania. *Career:* fmr CEO ESCO InterAmerica; fmr Chair. Bd of Dirs and Exec. Cttee Costa Rica Investment and Devt Bank; fmr Chair. Procomer; Minister of Econs 2000, of Foreign Trade 2000–02, mem. Econ. Council; mem. Bd of Dirs La

Nación newspaper and publishing group; fmr Chair. Bd of Trustees Costa Rican Cen. Bank Museums; Vice-Chair. WTO Ministerial Meeting, Doha 2001; fmr Chief Negotiating Minister for a Free Trade Agreement of the Americas, as well as various other free trade agreements, credited with initiating process that led to Cen. American Free Trade Agreement with USA; Amb. to USA 2004–; fmr Fellow, Aspen Inst. Leadership Program. *Address:* Embassy of Costa Rica, 2114 S Street, NW, Washington, DC 20008, USA (office). *Telephone:* (202) 234-2945 (office). *Fax:* (202) 265-4795 (office). *Website:* www.costarica-embassy.org (office).

DUFFIELD, Linda Joy, CMG, BA; British diplomatist; *Ambassador to the Czech Republic;* b. 18 April 1953. *Education:* Univ. of Exeter, Ecole Nat. d'Admin, Paris. *Career:* joined FCO 1987, EU Dept 1987–88, full-time language training 1988, First Sec. (Commercial), Moscow 1989–92, Deputy Head of Eastern Dept, FCO 1993–94, Deputy High Commr, Ottawa 1995–99, High Commr to Sri Lanka 1999–2002, Dir Wider Europe, FCO 2002–04, Amb. to Czech Repub. 2004–. *Address:* British Embassy, Thunovska 14, 118 00 Prague 1, Czech Republic (office). *Telephone:* (2) 57402111 (office). *Fax:* (2) 57402296 (office). *E-mail:* info@britain.cz (office). *Website:* www.britain.cz (office).

DUHALDE MALDONADO, Eduardo Alberto; Argentine fmr head of state; b. 5 Oct. 1941, Lomas de Zamora, Prov. of Buenos Aires; m. Hilda Beatriz González 1971; one s. four d. *Career:* fmr mem. staff Legal Dept Lomas de Zamora Town Council; Pres. Exec. Cttee Partido Justicialista of Lomas de Zamora 1973; Mayor Lomas de Zamora 1974–76, removed from post following mil. coup, re-elected 1983; elected Nat. Deputy for Prov. of Buenos Aires 1987, First Vice-Pres. Chamber of Deputies 1987–89; Vice-Pres. of Argentina, Pres. Senate 1989–91; Gov. Prov. of Buenos Aires 1991–99; Partido Justicialista cand. presidential elections 1999; Pres. Congreso Nacional del Partido Justicialista; Pres. of Argentina 2002–03; f. Office for Drug Addiction Prevention and Assistance, Lomas de Zamora 1984, Comm. on Drug Addiction, Chamber of Deputies; Orden de Boyacá, Colombia, Orden Cruceiro do Sul, Brazil, Orden del Quetzal, Guatemala, Orden de Bernardo O'Higgins, Chile; Dr hc (Genoa) 1992, (Universidad Hebrea Argentina) 1999, (Universidad del Salvador) 1999. *Publications:* La revolución productiva (with Carlos Saúl Menem) 1987, Los políticos y las drogas 1988, Hacía un mundo sin drogas 1994, Política, familia, sociedad y drogas 1997. *Address:* c/o Office of the President, Balcarce 50, 1064 Buenos Aires, Argentina (office).

DUKE, Robin Chandler; American diplomatist; b. 1923; m. Angier Biddle Duke (deceased). *Career:* writer New York Journal American newspaper 1940s; fmr mem. Bd of Dirs American Home Products, Rockwell Int., Int. Flavors and Fragrances; mem. Bd of Trustees US –Japan Foundation; mem. Bd of Dirs Lucile and David Packard Foundation, UN Asscn of USA 2000–, The Worldwatch Institute 2005–; fmr Vice-Chair. and mem. Advisory Bd Inst. of Int. Educ.; Chair. Del. to 21st Session of UNESCO 1980, Amb. 1980; Amb. to Norway 2000–01; fmr Pres. NARAL Pro-Choice America; mem. Council on Foreign Relations; Fellow Acad. of Arts and Social Sciences; f. Population Action Int. *Address:* c/o Board of Trustees, United States-Japan Foundation, 45 East 32nd Street, New York, NY 10016 New York, NY 10016, USA.

DUKES, Alan M., MA; Irish politician; *Director-General, Institute of European Affairs;* b. 22 April 1945, Dublin; m. Fionnuala Corcoran 1968; two d. *Education:* Scoil Colmcille and Colaiste Mhuire, Dublin and Univ. Coll., Dublin. *Career:* Chief Econ., Irish Farmers Asscn 1967–72; Dir Irish Farmers Asscn, Brussels 1973–76; Personal Adviser to Commr of EEC 1977–80; TD (Fine Gael) for Kildare 1981–2002; Opposition Spokesperson on Agric. March–Dec. 1982; Minister of Agric. 1981–82, for Finance 1982–86, for Justice 1986–87; Leader and Pres. Fine Gael 1987–90; mem. Council of State 1987–90; Minister for Transport, Energy and Communications 1996–97; Opposition Spokesperson on Environment and Local Govt; Pres. Irish Council of the European Movt 1987–91, Chair. 1997–2000; Vice-Pres. Int. European Movt 1991–96; Adjunct Prof. of Public Admin, Man. Univ. of Limerick 1991–; Dir-Gen. Inst. of European Affairs 2003–; Public Affairs Consultant, WHPR, Dublin; Vice-Pres. European People's Party 1987–96; Chair. Jt Oireachtas Cttee on Foreign Affairs 1995–96; Officier de la Légion d'honneur 2004, Commdr's Cross of the Order of Merit (Poland) 2004. *Address:* Institute of European Affairs, Europe House, 8 North Great Georges Street, Dublin 1, Ireland (office). *Telephone:* (1) 8746756 (office); 876846274 (mobile) (home). *Fax:* (1) 8786880 (office); (45) 520306 (home). *E-mail:* info@iiea.com (office); alandukes@eircom.net (home). *Website:* www.iiea.com (office).

DULAIMI, Saadoun ad-, PhD; Iraqi government official, psychologist and statistician; b. 1954, Ramadi. *Education:* Univ. of Keele, UK. *Career:* fmr army reserve officer; emigrated 1980s; has taught in Jordan and USA; returned to Iraq 2003; est. Centre for Research and Strategic Studies; Minister of Defence 2005–06. *Address:* c/o Ministry of Defence, Baghdad, Iraq (office).

DUMONT, Dame Ivy Leona, DBE, DPA; Bahamian public servant and politician; b. 1930, Roses, Long Island; m. Reginald Dumont; two c. *Career:* fmr teacher; worked in public admin then in human resources devt in pvt. sector; fmr Sec.-Gen. Free Nat. Movt; Senator and Cabinet Minister 1992–2000; Chair. Public Service Comm. –2001; Acting Gov.-Gen. Nov.–Dec. 2001, Gov.-Gen. of the Bahamas 2002–05; Founding mem. Bahamas Union of Teachers. *Address:* c/o Government House, PO Box N-8301, Nassau, The Bahamas (office).

DUNAYEV, Arman G., PhD; Kazakhstani politician and economist; b. 1967. *Education:* Kazakh State Univ. *Career:* economist for various financial and investments cos; joined Ministry of Finance 2000, Vice-Minister of Finance 2001–04, Minister 2004–06. *Address:* c/o Ministry of Finance, pl. Respubiliki 60, 473000 Astana, Kazakhstan (office).

DUNCAN, Daniel Kablan; Côte d'Ivoirian politician; b. 1943, Ouelle. *Education:* Inst. Commercial, Nancy and Inst. de Commerce Int. Paris. *Career:* Ministry of Economy and Finance 1970; in-house training, IMF, Washington, DC 1973; joined Cen. Bank of W African States (BCEAO); with Caisse Nat. de Prévoyance Sociale; returned to BCEAO HQ, Dakar 1989; Minister Del. responsible for Econ., Finance and Planning, Office of Prime Minister 1990–93; Prime Minister of Côte d'Ivoire 1993–2000; also fmr Minister of Economy, Finance and Planning, Minister of Planning and Industrial Devt; mem. Parti démocratique de la Côte d'Ivoire—Rassemblement démocratique africain (PDCI—RDA). *Address:* c/o Office of the Prime Minister, boulevard Angoulvant, 01 BP 1533, Abidjan 01, Côte d'Ivoire.

DUNG, Nguyen Tan, LLB; Vietnamese politician; *Prime Minister;* b. 17 Nov. 1949, Ca Mau Town; m.; one d. one s. *Career:* served in Viet Nam People's Army 1961–81; mem. Communist Party of Viet Nam 1967–, mem. Central Police Party Cttee 1995–96, mem. Politburo 1997–; Deputy Interior Minister 1995–96; First Deputy Prime Minister of Viet Nam 1997–2006, Prime Minister 2006–; Gov. State Bank of Viet Nam 1998–06. *Address:* Office of the Prime Minister, Hanoi (office); c/o State Bank of Viet Nam, 47–49 Ly Thai To, Hanoi, Viet Nam (office). *Telephone:* (4) 9342524 (State Bank) (office). *Fax:* (4) 8268765 (State Bank) (office). *E-mail:* sf-sbv@hn.hnn.vn (office).

DUNN, David; British diplomatist; *High Commissioner to Papua New Guinea;* b. 21 Sept. 1968. *Career:* Desk Officer, South East Asia Dept 1991–92, Political Section, Embassy in Oslo 1992–94, Worldwide Floater 1994–96, Political Section, Embassy in Suva 1996–97, Third Sec., Mission to UN 1997–98, Special Advisor to UN 1998–2000, First Sec., Political Section, Embassy in Stockholm 2000–01, Private Sec. to Minister for Europe 2001–03, Deputy High Commr Sierra Leone 2004–07, High Commr to Papua New Guinea 2007–. *Address:* British High Commission, Kiroki Street, Locked Bag 212, Waigani 131, NCD Papua New Guinea (office). *Telephone:* 3251677 (office). *Fax:* 3253547 (office). *E-mail:* bhcpng@datec.net.pg (office). *Website:* www.britishhighcommission.gov.uk/papuanewguinea (office).

DUNN, David Bernard, BA, MA; American diplomatist; *Ambassador to Togo;* b. Great Falls, Mont.; m. Maria-Elena Dubourt; two s. *Education:* Occidental Coll., American Univ., Nat. War Coll., Washington, DC. *Career:* worked for City of Escondido, San Diego Co., Calif.; entered Foreign Service in 1978, career mem. Sr Foreign Service with rank of Minister-Counselor, overseas postings have included Jamaica, Tunisia, France, Burundi, Mauritius and Tanzania, Washington assignments as Deputy Dir and Dir Office of East African Affairs, Amb. to Zambia 1999–2002, Prin. Officer, Consulate Gen. in Johannesburg 2002–05, Amb. to Togo 2006–. *Address:* US Embassy, BP 852, Boulevard Eyadema, Lomé, Togo (office). *Telephone:* 261-54-70 (office). *Fax:* 261-55-01 (office). *E-mail:* RobertsonJJ2@state.gov (office). *Website:* togo.usembassy.gov (office).

DUNN, John Montfort, BA, FBA, FSA; British political theorist; *Professor of Political Theory, University of Cambridge;* b. 9 Sept. 1940, Fulmer; m. 1st Susan D. Fyvel 1965; m. 2nd Judith F. Bernal 1971; m. 3rd Ruth Ginette Scurr 1997; two s. (one deceased) two d. *Education:* Winchester Coll., Millfield School, King's Coll., Cambridge and Harvard Univ., USA. *Career:* Grad. School of Arts and Sciences; Official Fellow in History, Jesus Coll., Cambridge 1965–66; Fellow, King's Coll., Cambridge 1966–, Coll.

Lecturer, Dir of Studies in History 1966–72; Lecturer in Political Science, Univ. of Cambridge 1972–77, Reader in Politics 1977–87, Prof. of Political Theory 1987–; Visiting Lecturer, Univ. of Ghana 1968–69; Chair. Section P. (Political Studies), British Acad. 1994–97, Bd of Consultants, Kim Dae-Jung Peace Foundation for the Asia-Pacific Region 1994–; Distinguished Visiting Prof., Univs of Tulane, Minnesota, Yale; mem. Council of British Acad. 2004–07; hon. foreign mem. American Acad. of Arts and Sciences 1991. *Publications:* The Political Thought of John Locke 1969, Modern Revolutions 1972, Dependence and Opportunity (with A. F. Robertson) 1973, Western Political Theory in the Face of the Future 1979, Political Obligation in its Historical Context 1980, Locke 1984, The Politics of Socialism 1984, Rethinking Modern Political Theory 1985, The Economic Limits to Modern Politics (ed.) 1990, Interpreting Political Responsibility 1990, Storia delle dottrine politiche 1992, Democracy: The Unfinished Journey (ed.) 1992, Contemporary Crisis of the Nation State? (ed.) 1994, The History of Political Theory 1995, Great Political Thinkers (21 vols, co-ed.) 1997, The Cunning of Unreason 2000, Pensare la Politica 2002, Locke: A Very Short Introduction 2003, Setting the People Free: The Story of Democracy 2005.
Address: King's College, Cambridge, CB2 1ST (office); The Merchant's House, 31 Station Road, Swavesey, Cambridge, CB4 5QJ, England (home). *Telephone:* (1223) 331258 (office); (1954) 231451 (home). *Fax:* (1223) 331315 (office). *E-mail:* jmd24@cam.ac.uk (office).

DUQUÉ, Richard; French diplomatist; *Permanent Representative, NATO;* b. 12 Dec. 1947; m. Caridad Duqué; three c. *Education:* Institut d'Etudes politiques, Ecole Nationale d'Administration. *Career:* Second Sec., Perm. Mission to UN, New York 1975–76, First Sec. 1976–79; Second Counsellor to Perm. Rep. to NATO, Brussels 1982–85, First Counsellor 1989–92, Chargé de mission to Sec.-Gen. 1985–86; Tech. Advisor to Prime Minister's Office 1986–88; Perm. Rep. to WEU 1993; Dir of Press, Information and Communications and Govt Spokesman 1993–95; Diplomatic Advisor to Prime Minister 1995–97; Consul Gen. in New York 1998–2004; Amb. to Mexico 2004–05; Perm. Rep. to NATO, Brussels 2005–; Chevalier, Légion d'Honneur, Officier, Ordre Nat. du mérite.
Address: North Atlantic Treaty Organization (NATO), boulevard Léopold III, 1110 Brussels, Belgium (office). *Telephone:* (2) 707-41-11 (office). *Fax:* (2) 707-45-79 (office). *E-mail:* natodoc@hq.nato.int (office). *Website:* www .nato.int (office).

DUQUESNE, Antoine; Belgian politician and barrister; b. 3 Feb. 1941, Ixelles. *Education:* Athénée Royal of Liège, Univ. of Liège. *Career:* Asst Lecturer in Law, State Univ. of Liège 1965–71; barrister in Liège 1965–75; Chef de Cabinet for various ministers 1973–87; Asst Gen. Sec. of Comité Nat. de Formation et de Perfectionnement Professionel dans les Métiers et Négoces 1975–77; Gen. Admin. of Comité Nat. de Coordination et de Concertation de la Formation Permanente des Classes moyennes 1977–82; Man. of Caisse Nat. de Crédit Professionel (CNCP) 1983–88; Minister of Nat. Educ. 1987–88; Barrister in Marche-en-Famenne 1988–; Senator and mem. Comms on Social Affairs, Educ. and Science and Chair. Comm. of Agric. and the Self-Employed 1988–91; town councillor, Manhay 1989–, Mayor 1995–; Chair. Parti Réformateur Libéral (PRL) 1990–92; Deputy and mem. of Comms of Revision of the Constitution and of Justice 1991–99; Prov. Chair. PRL for Luxembourg 1994–; Vice-Chair. of House of Reps 1995–99; Chair. Comm. of Justice 1996–98; Chair. Comm. for Foreign Relations 1999; Minister of the Interior 1999–2004; mem. Conseil régional wallon 1991–95, Conseil de la Communauté française 1991–95; Grand Officer, Order of Leopold 1999. *Publications:* numerous legal articles.
Address: c/o Ministry of the Interior, 60–62 rue Royale, 1000 Brussels, Belgium (office); Al Maison 3, 6960 Harre-Manhay, Belgium (home). *Telephone:* (2) 504-85-11 (office). *Fax:* (2) 504-85-00 (office).

DURÁN-BALLÉN, Sixto; Ecuadorean fmr head of state and diplomatist; *Leader, Partido Conservador;* b. 14 July 1921, Boston, Mass, USA; m. Josephine Villa Lobos 1945; three s. six d. *Education:* Sturens Inst. of Tech., NJ, Columbia Univ. and Univ. of Wisconsin. *Career:* practised as architect; Sub-Dir of Regional Planning for Tungurahua 1949–68; fmr Mayor of Quito; official of Inter-American Devt Bank, Washington, DC 1956; mem. Chamber of Deputies 1984–; f. Partido Unidad Republicana 1992; Pres. of Ecuador 1992–96; mem. Partido Conservador Ecuatoriano (PCE), mem. Parl. 1998–; Amb. to UK 2001–03; Leader Partido Conservador; Chevalier Légion d'honneur, Commdr Order of Orange-Nassau (Netherlands), Order of San Carlos (Colombia), Order of Tidor Vladimirescu (First Class) (Romania), Order of Francisco Miranda (Venezuela).
Address: Partido Conservador, Wilsón 578, Quito, Ecuador (office). *Telephone:* (2) 250-5061 (office).

DURANT, Isabelle; Belgian politician; b. 4 Sept. 1954, Brussels. *Education:* Univ. Coll. London. *Career:* registered nurse; teacher 1981–89; mem. of

Ecologist Party (ECOLO) 1989–, Attaché of Ecologist Party Parl. Group at Regional Council of Brussels 1992–94, Fed. Sec. and Spokeswoman for ECOLO 1994–99, mem. Fed. Office of ECOLO-AGALEV 1995–99, Co-Pres. ECOLO 2004–; Co-ordinator of Etats généraux de l'Ecologie politique (EGEP) 1996–; Deputy Prime Minister and Minister for Mobility and Transport 1999–2003 (resgnd); Senator 2003–.
Address: Maison des Parlementaires, 21 rue de Louvain, Bureau 3213, 1009 Brussels, Belgium (office). *Telephone:* (2) 5499059 (office). *E-mail:* isabelle .durant@ecolo.be (home). *Website:* www.isabelledurant.be (office).

DURÃO BARROSO, José Manuel, MPolSci; Portuguese politician; *President, European Commission;* b. 23 March 1956, Lisbon; m. Margarida Sousa Uva; three s. *Education:* Univs of Lisbon and Geneva. *Career:* mem. Maoist party after revolution in Portugal 1974; Lecturer, Faculty of Law, Univ. of Lisbon, Dept of Political Science, Univ. of Geneva; mem. Parl. 1985–; fmr Sec. of State for Home Affairs and for Foreign Affairs and Co-operation; Minister of Foreign Affairs 1992–95; mem. Nat. Council Social Democratic Party (PSD), Leader 1999–; Vice-Pres. EPP 1999–; Prime Minister of Portugal 2002–04 (resgnd); Chair. Comm. for Foreign Affairs 1995–96; Pres. European Comm. 2004–; Head, Dept of Int. Relations, Univ. Lusíada 1995–99; Visiting Scholar, Georgetown Univ., Washington, DC, Visiting Prof. 1996–98; decorations from Brazil, Germany, Japan, Morocco, Netherlands, Portugal, Spain, UK; Hon. DUniv (Rhode Island) 2005, Hon. DH (Georgetown Univ.) 2006, Hon. Dr rer. pol (Genoa Univ.) 2006, Hon. DIur (Kobe Univ.) 2006. *Publications:* Governmental System and Party System (co-author) 1980, Le Système Politique Portugais face à l'Intégration Européenne 1983, Política de Cooperação 1990, A Política Externa Portuguesa 1992–93, A Política Externa Portuguesa 1994–95, Uma Certa Ideia de Europa 1999, Uma Ideia para Portugal 2000; several studies on political science and constitutional law in collective works, encyclopae-dias and int. journals.
Address: European Commission, 200 rue de la Loi, 1049 Brussels, Belgium (office); Social Democratic Party, Rua de São Caetano 9, 1249-087 Lisbon Codex, Portugal (office). *Telephone:* (2) 298-18-00 (office); (21) 3952140 (Lisbon) (office). *Fax:* (2) 295-01-38 (office); (21) 3976967 (Lisbon) (office). *E-mail:* psd@psd.pt (office). *Website:* europa.eu (office); www.psd.pt (office).

DURDYNETS, Gen. Vasyl Vasylyevich; Ukrainian lawyer and army officer; b. 27 Sept. 1937, Romochevytsya; m.; one d. *Education:* Lvov State Univ. *Career:* Sec., First Sec. Lvov Regional Comsomol Cttee, Deputy Head of Section Central Comsomol Cttee, Moscow, Head of Section Central Cttee of Lviv Regional CP 1960–73; Deputy Head of Dept of Admin., CP Cen. Cttee 1973–78; Deputy Minister, then First Deputy Minister of Internal Affairs 1978–91; People's Deputy 1991–94, Head Cttee of Defence and Nat. Safety 1991–92, mem. 1997–, First Deputy Speaker of Parl. 1992–94; First Deputy Head Co-ordination Cttee for Fighting Corruption and Organized Crime 1994–95, Head 1995–99; Vice-Prime Minister, First Vice-Prime Minister 1995–99, Acting Prime Minister June–July 1997; Dir Nat. Bureau of Investigations 1997–99; Minister for Emergency Situations and Protection of the Population from the Consequences of the Chernobyl Catastrophe 1999–2002; mem. Supreme Econ. Council 1997; Hon. Prof. Acad. of Internal Affairs 1997; ICDO Medal, Int. Civil Defence Org. (Switzerland) 2000, 14 nat. awards.
Address: c/o Ministry for Emergency Situations and Protection of the Population from the Consequences of Chernobyl, 01030 Kiev, 55 O. Gonchara Str., Ukraine (office). *Telephone:* (44) 247-30-01 (office). *Fax:* (44) 226-34-37 (office).

DURLEŞTEANU, Mariana; Moldovan diplomatist and government official; *Minister of Finance;* b. 5 Sept. 1971; m.; two c. *Education:* Univ. of Cluj-Napoca, Romania. *Career:* fmr nat. gymnast; joined Foreign Financing and External Debt Dept, Ministry of Finance 1995, Head of Dept 1997–2001, Deputy Minister of Finance 2001–02, First Deputy Minister of Finance 2002–05; Amb. to UK 2004–08; Minister of Finance 2008–.
Address: Ministry of Finance, 2005 Chişinău, str. Cosmonauţilor 7, Moldova (office). *Telephone:* (22) 23-35-75 (office). *Fax:* (22) 22-13-07 (office). *E-mail:* protocol@minfin.moldova.md (office). *Website:* www .minfin.md (office).

ĐUROVIĆ, Gordana, MA, PhD; Montenegrin (b. Serbian) academic and politician; *Deputy Prime Minister, responsible for European Integration;* b. 1964, Novi Kneževac, Vojvodina; m.; two c. *Education:* Herceg-Novi Secondary School of Econs, Faculty of Econs, Univ. of Belgrade and Univ. of Montenegro, Podgorica. *Career:* Assoc. Prof., Faculty of Econs, Univ. of Montenegro, Podgorica, Assoc. Vice-Dean for scientific research 1998–2000, Head Dept of Econ. Policy 2000–; project manager and assoc., Regional Devt in Montenegro 1998, Programme on Utility Services Usurpation in Montenegro 1999, Devt Strategy and Poverty Reduction in Montenegro 2000; Minister for Int. Econ. Relations and European

Integration, Ass. of the Repub. of Montenegro 2004–06; Deputy Prime Minister with responsibility for European Integration 2006–. *Publications:* Economic Development 1996, Alternative Development Draft Lines of the Economy of Montenegro (co-author) 2002; more than 40 articles and 15 research papers.
Address: Office of the Deputy Prime Minister, Government of Montenegro, 81000 Podgorica, Jovana Tomaševića bb, Montenegro (office). *Telephone:* (81) 242552 (office). *Fax:* (81) 224552 (office). *E-mail:* gordanadjurovic@ mn.yu (office). *Website:* www.vlada.cg.yu (office).

DURRANT, (Mignonette) Patricia, CD, OJ, BA; Jamaican diplomatist and United Nations official; *Ombudsman, United Nations;* b. 30 May 1943. *Education:* Univ. of West Indies, Univ. of Cambridge, UK. *Career:* Admin. Officer, Ministry of Agric. 1964–70; First Sec. Ministry of Foreign Affairs 1971–72, Prin. Asst Sec. 1972–74; Minister-Counsellor, Mission to OAS, Washington, DC 1974–77; Asst Dir Political Div., Ministry of Foreign Affairs 1977–81, Deputy Dir 1981–83; Deputy Perm. Rep. to UN, New York 1983–87, Perm. Rep. 1995–2002, Pres. UN High-Level Cttee on Tech. Co-operation among Developing Countries 1999–2001, Rep. of Jamaica to UN Security Council 2000–01, UN Ombudsman 2002–; Chair. UN Preparatory Cttee for the Special Session on Children, Chair. Consultative Cttee for the UN Devt Fund for Women (UNIFEM), Vice-Chair. Preparatory Cttee for Special Session on Population and Devt 1999 and Vice-Chair. Open-Ended Working Group on the Reform of the UN Security Council; Amb. to FRG (and non-resident Amb. to Israel, the Netherlands, Switzerland and the Holy See) 1987–92; Dir-Gen. Ministry of Foreign Affairs and Foreign Trade 1992–95; Distinguished Grad. Award, Univ. of West Indies 1998, Distinguished Achievement Award, World Asscn of fmr UN Interns and Fellows (WAFUNI).
Address: Permanent Mission of Jamaica to the United Nations, 767 Third Avenue, 9th Floor, New York, NY 10017, USA (office). *Telephone:* (212) 935-7509 (office). *Fax:* (212) 935-7607 (office). *E-mail:* jamaica@un.int (office). *Website:* www.un.int/jamaica (office).

DUVERGER, Maurice; French political scientist; *Professor Emeritus of Political Sociology, University of Paris;* b. 5 June 1917, Angoulême; m. Odile Batt 1949. *Education:* Bordeaux Univ. *Career:* contrib. to Le Monde 1946–, El País (Spain), Il Corriere della Sera (Italy); Prof. of Political Sociology, Univ. of Paris 1955–85, Prof. Emer. 1985–; Founder and Pres. Inst. of Research into Insts and Cultures of Europe (IRICE); mem. European Parl. 1989–95; mem. American Acad. of Arts and Sciences, Finnish Acad. of Sciences; Grand Officier Légion d'honneur, Commdr ordre nat. du Mérite; Dr hc (Siena, Geneva, New Jersey, Milan, Barcelona, Warsaw, Sofia, Prague, Athens). *Publications:* Les partis politiques 1951, Demain, la république… 1959, De la dictature 1961, La Sixième république et le régime présidentiel 1961, Introduction to the Social Sciences 1964, Introduction à la politique 1964, La démocratie sans le peuple 1967, Institutions politiques 1970, Janus: les deux faces de l'Occident 1972, Sociologie de la politique 1973, La monarchie républicaine 1974, Lettre ouverte aux socialistes 1976, L'autre coté des choses 1977, Echec au roi 1978, Les orangers du lac Balaton 1980, La République des Citoyens 1982, Bréviaire de la cohabitation 1986, La Cohabitation des Français 1987, La nostalgie de l'impuissance 1988, Le Lièvre libéral et la tortue européenne 1990, Europe des hommes 1994, L'Europe dans tous ses Etats 1995, A la recherche du droit perdu 2001.
Address: Presses universitaires de France, 6 avenue Reille, 75014 Paris (office); IRICE, 1 rue Descartes, 75005 Paris; Mas du Grand Côté, 13100 Le Tholonet, France (home); 24 rue des Fossés-Saint-Jacques, 75005 Paris (home).

DUWAISAN, Khalid Abdulaziz ad-, BA (Comm); Kuwaiti diplomatist; *Ambassador to UK;* b. 15 Aug. 1947; m. Dalal Al-Humaizi 1980; one s. one d. *Education:* Cairo Univ., Univ. of Kuwait. *Career:* joined Ministry of Foreign Affairs 1970, Diplomatic Attaché 1974, Embassy, Washington, DC 1975; Amb. to Netherlands 1984 (also accred to Romania 1988); Chair. Kuwaiti del. for supervision of demilitarized zone between Iraq and Kuwait and Chief Co-ordinator Comm. for Return of Stolen Property 1991; Amb. to UK (also accred to Ireland, Norway, Sweden and Denmark) 1993–; Hon. GCVO (UK).
Address: Kuwaiti Embassy, 2 Albert Gate, London, SW1X 7JU (office); 22 Kensington Palace Gardens, London, W8, England (home). *Telephone:* (20) 7590-3400 (office); (20) 7221-7374 (home). *Fax:* (20) 7823-1712 (office). *E-mail:* Kuwait@dircon.co.uk (office); enquiries@kuwaitinfo.org.uk (office). *Website:* www.kuwaitinfo.org.uk (office).

DYMOCK, Vice-Adm. Anthony K., CB, FRSA; British naval officer; *Military Representative, NATO;* b. 1949, Liverpool; m. Lizzie Frewer. *Education:* Univ. of E Anglia, Britannia Royal Naval Coll., Dartmouth, Greenwich Naval Coll., Harvard Univ., USA. *Career:* joined the Royal Navy 1969, served on HMS Antrim during Falklands War, promoted to Commdr 1985,

Commodore, Rear-Adm. 2000, currently Vice-Adm.; has served as Commdr HMS Plymouth, HMS Campbeltown, HMS Cornwall, HMS Invincible, served on USS Midway during Gulf War 1991, commanded a battle force during Operation Southern Watch, Iraq 1992 and operations in the Adriatic during Kosovo air campaign; NATO experience includes SNFL tour as Flag Captain, NATO course dir, Maritime Tactical School, Commdr UK Maritime Task Group in its ASWSTRIKFOR role, apptd Deputy Commdr STRIKFORSOUTH 2000, conducted NATO amphibious exercises around Mediterranean and Black Seas onboard USS Lasalle, Military Rep. 2006–; posts with Ministry of Defence include Commdr on Cen. Jt Staff, Capt. First Sea Lord's staff, Defence Attaché in Naples, Italy and Washington, DC 2002–05; has lectured on security at Nat. Defense Univ., Washington, DC, MIT; mem. Nautical Inst.; Freeman, City of London.
Address: UK Delegation to NATO, Autoroute Brussels–Zaventem, Brussels 1110, Belgium (office). *Telephone:* (2) 707-72-11 (office). *Fax:* (2) 707-75-96 (office). *E-mail:* ukdelnato@skynet.be (office). *Website:* www .britishembassy.gov.uk (office).

DYOMIN, Oleh O.; Ukrainian diplomatist and politician; b. 1947, Russia. *Education:* Kharkiv Inst. of Radio Electronics, Advanced School of Politics. *Career:* early career working in radio electronics; Deputy Speaker, Verkhovna Rada (Parl.) 1994–96; Chair. Kharkiv Regional State Admin 1996–2000; First Deputy Head Presidential Admin 2000–05; Deputy Head, People's Democratic Party, Head, Kharkiv br; Amb. to Russia 2006–08.
Address: Ministry of Foreign Affairs, 01018 Kyiv, pl. Mykhailivska 1, Ukraine. *Telephone:* (44) 238-15-06. *Fax:* (44) 226-31-69. *Website:* www .mfa.gov.ua.

DYSON, John, MVO; British diplomatist; b. 15 April 1949; m. Deidre Dyson; two s. *Career:* Desk Officer, FCO 1966–70, Attaché High Comm. in Port of Spain 1970–73, Attaché Embassy in Geneva 1973–76, Third Sec. Embassy in Yaounde 1976–78, Personnel Dept, FCO 1978–92, 1985–87, Third Sec. Embassy in Nuku'alofa 1982–84, Second Sec. Embassy in Jeddah 1987–90, Second Sec. Embassy in Cape Town 1991–95, Jt Assistance Unit, FCO 1996–98, Deputy Head of Crisis Man. 1998–2000, Chargé d'Affaires, Asmara 2001–02, Deputy High Commr, Suva 2002–03, Deputy High Commr, Bandar Seri Bagawan 2003, Deputy Chief of Staff, Basra 2003–04, Finance Directorate, FCO 2005–06, Amb. to Montenegro 2006–07; Iraq Reconstruction Medal.
Address: c/o Foreign and Commonwealth Office, King Charles Street, London, SW1A 2AH, England (office). *Telephone:* (20) 7008-1500 (office). *Website:* www.fco.gov.uk (home).

DZAIDDIN BIN HAJI ABDULLAH, Rt Hon Tun Sri Dato' Seri Mohamed; Malaysian judge; *Chairman, Bursa Malaysia Berhad;* b. 16 Sept. 1937, Arau, Perlis; m. Puan Noriah Binti Tengku Ismael; two c. *Education:* Sultan Abdul Hamid Coll. Alor Setar. *Career:* journalist The Malay Mail 1956; joined police service as Insp.; called to Bar, Middle Temple, London, UK 1966; admitted as advocate and solicitor in Kota Bharu and Kuala Lumpur 1967; juridical commr (part-time) 1979–82; apptd High Court Judge, Criminal Div. of Kuala Lumpur High Court 1982–84, Penang High Court 1984–92; Supreme Court Judge (renamed Fed. Court Judge) 1992–2000; Chief Justice of the Fed. Court 2000–03; Chair. Bursa Malaysia Berhad (fmrly Kuala Lumpur Stock Exchange) 2004–; apptd Dir (non-exec.) and Public Interest Dir by Minister of Finance 2004–; fmr Chair. Kelantan Bar Cttee; Vice-Pres. Malaysian Bar 1981–82; Chair. Tun Mohamad Suffian Foundation, Deutsche Bank (Malaysia), Advisory Council Business Ethics Inst. of Malaysia, Royal Comm. to Enhance the Operation and Man. of the Royal Police Force; Life mem. ASEAN Law Asscn of Malaysia, Pres. 1994–97; Pres. ASEAN Law Asscn 1997–; Hon. LLD (San Beda Coll.) 2002; several awards including Seri Paduka Baginda Yang DiPertuan Agong of the Most Esteemed Order of Seri Setia Mahkota Malaysia.
Address: The Special Commission to Enhance the Operation and Management of The Royal Police Force, PO Box 10840, 50726 Kuala Lumpur, Malaysia (office). *E-mail:* dzaiddin@suruhanjayakhaspolis.gov.my (office). *Website:* www.suruhanjayakhaspolis.gov.my (office).

DZHEMILEV, Mustafa (Abdul-Dzhemil); Ukrainian activist; b. 14 Nov. 1943, Ayserez, Crimea; m. Safinar Dzhemileva; two s. one d. *Career:* suffered continual harassment from Soviet authorities when he attempted to form a youth movt in Tashkent 1962–; subsequently, imprisonment or exile for activity: 1966–67, 1969–72, 1974–75, 1975–77, 1979–82, 1983–86; continued to organize Crimean Tatar protest actions in Cen. Asia and Moscow; returned to Crimea 1989; Chair. Crimean Tatar Majlis 1991–; Pres. Crimea Foundation 1991–; mem. Ukrainian Parl. 1998–, Chair. Council of Reps 1999–; political observer Business magazine; Dr hc (Seljuk Univ., Higher Tech. Inst. Gebze, Turkey); Nansen Medal UNHCR 1998,

Pylyp Orlyk Int. Award 2000, Yaroslav Mudryi Medal 2001, Hon. Prize of Parliament of Ukraine 2002.
Address: ul. Shmidta 25, Simferopol, Crimea (office); 6th Microrayon 100, Bakhchesaray, Crimea, Ukraine (home). *Telephone:* (652) 2275259 (office); (652) 5443758 (home). *Fax:* (652) 2274372 (office). *E-mail:* MCemiloglu@ttt.Crimea.com (home).

DZHORBENADZE, Avtandil Khristoforovich, DrMed; Georgian politician; b. 1951, Chibati, Lanchkhut region; m. Nino Vepkhadze; two s. *Education:* Tbilisi State Inst. of Med. 1974. *Career:* intern, Tbilisi Clinical Hosp. #1 1975, roentgenologist, Sec. CP Cttee, Deputy Chief Doctor 1978–86; therapeutist, Tbilisi Polyclinic #29 1975–76; practitioner mil. unit in Georgia 1976–78; First Deputy Head, then Head Tbilisi City Dept of Public Health 1986–92; Deputy Minister of Public Health and Social Security 1992–93; Minister of Public Health 1993–99, of Labour, Public Health and Social Security 1999–2001; Minister of State and Head of the State Chancellery of Georgia 2001–03; Chair. Citizens' Union of Georgia. *Publications:* over 30 scientific publs.
Address: c/o Office of State Minister, Ingorkva 7, 380034 Tbilisi, Georgia (office).

DZHUMALIYEV, Kubanychbek; Kyrgyzstani politician. *Career:* First Deputy Prime Minister and Minister of Transport and Communications 2005–06 (resgnd).
Address: c/o Ministry of Transport and Communications, 42 Isanova Street, 720017 Bishkek, Kyrgyzstan (office).

DZOMBIĆ, Aleksandar; Bosnia and Herzegovina banking executive and government official; *Minister of Finance, Republika Srpska;* b. 1968, Banja Luka; m.; one c. *Education:* Univ. of Banja Luka, Belgrade Univ. *Career:* worked in Banja Luka City Admin; Head, Dept and Project Man., Kristal Bank, Banja Luka; Dir Agroprom Bank, Banja Luka; Exec. Dir Nova Banka, Bijeljina; Minister of Finance 2006–.
Address: Ministry of Finance of Republika Srpska, Banja Luka, trg Republike Srpske 1, 78000 Bosnia and Herzegovina (office). *Telephone:* (51) 331350 (office). *Fax:* (51) 331351 (office). *E-mail:* mf@mf.vladars.net (office). *Website:* www.vladars.net (office).

DZUMAGULOV, Apas Dzumagulovich; Kyrgyzstani politician and diplomatist; b. 19 Sept. 1934, Arashan, Kyrgyz SSR; m.; three s. *Education:* Moscow Gubkin Inst. of Oil. *Career:* mem. CPSU 1962–91; worked at Complex S., Geological Expedition USSR Acad. of Sciences 1958–59; Sr geologist oil field Changar-Tash, Head. Cen. Research Lab., Chief Geologist Drilling Div., Chief Engineer Oil Co. Kyrghizneft Osh Dist 1959–73; Head Industrial-Transport Div. Cen. Cttee CP of Kyrgyz SSR 1973–79; Sec. Cen. Cttee CP of Kirgyzia 1979–85; First Sec. Issyk-Kul Dist Cttee 1985–86; Chair. Council of Ministers Kyrgyz SSR 1986–91; Chair. Org. Cttee, then Chair. Regional Soviet of Deputies, Head of Admin. Chuysk Region 1991–93; Deputy to USSR Supreme Soviet 1984–89; USSR People's Deputy 1989–91; People's Deputy of Kyrgyzstan; mem. Revision Comm. CPSU 1986–91; Prime Minister of Kyrgyz Repub. 1993–97; Amb. to Germany, Scandinavian countries and the Holy See 1998–2003.
Address: c/o Ministry of Foriegn Affairs, 59 Razzakov str., Bishkek 720040, Kyrgyzstan (office). *Telephone:* (312) 620545 (office). *Fax:* (312) 660501. *E-mail:* gendep@mfa.gov.kg (office).

DZUNDEV, Igor; Macedonian diplomatist; b. 12 June 1963; m.; two c. *Education:* Vienna Diplomatic Acad., Cyril and Methodius Univ., Skopje. *Career:* worked on commercial export issues, chemical factory in Skopje 1989–90; Attaché, Dept for Multilateral Econ. Affairs 1990; fmr Second Sec., UN Dept, Ministry of Foreign Affairs; First Sec., then Counsellor, Perm. Mission to UN, New York 1994–98; Head, Directorate for Political Relations with UN, OSCE and Council of Europe Affairs, Multilateral Affairs Dept 1998–2000, State Sec. 2000–04; Perm. Rep. to UN, New York 2004–08.
Address: c/o Ministry of Foreign Affairs, 1000 Skopje, Dame Gruev 6, Former Yugoslav Republic of Macedonia (office).

DŽUNOV, Todor, DSc; Macedonian professor of law and jurist; *President of Constitutional Court;* b. 11 Oct. 1931, Vatasha, Kavadarci; m. Granka Džunov 1958. *Education:* Univ. of Cyril and Methodius, Skopje. *Career:* Asst, Faculty of Law, Skopje 1956, Reader 1964, Assoc. Prof. 1969, Prof. 1974–94, Dean, Faculty of Law 1981–83; Rector, Univ. of 'Cyril and Metodius', Skopje 1985–88; Justice of the Constitutional Court 1994, Pres. 2000–; Pres. Research Council of Macedonia 1973–80; mem. and Chief of dels of interstate bodies for scientific and tech. co-operation with Greece, USA and UK; mem. del. on succession issues on Fmr Repub. of Yugoslavia; 11th of October Award 1980, Gold Award, Faculty of Law, Skopje 2001, Gold Award, Faculty of Philosophy, Univ. of Cyril and Methodius, Skopje, State Medal for Labour, State Medal for People Merit. *Publications:* more than 100 titles including Private International Law (textbook), International Legal Regulation of the Use of Rivers and Lakes of Common Interest Out of Navigation 1964, International Regulation of the Use of Waters 1979, Collection of Laws on the Private International Law 1984, Foreign Policy of SFRY and Non-Alignment 1989.
Address: Constitutional Court, 12 Udarka brig. 2, 1000 Skopje (office); Partizanski odredi No. 8/25, 1000 Skopje, Republic of Macedonia (home). *Telephone:* (2) 163063 (office); (2) 130163 (home). *Fax:* (2) 119355 (office). *E-mail:* tdzunov@usud.gov.mk (office).

E

EASTHAM, Alan W., BA, JD; American lawyer and diplomatist; *Ambassador to Malawi;* b. Dumas, Ark.; m. Carolyn Eastham; two s. *Education:* Hendrix Coll., Conway, Ark. and Georgetown Univ., Washington, DC. *Career:* career mem. Sr Foreign Service since 1975, Vice-Consul, Embassy in Kathmandu 1975–78, Washington assignments have been in Public Affairs 1978–80, Counter-terrorism Office 1980–82, Desk Officer for Sri Lanka and the Maldives 1982–83, for India 1983–84, Prin. Officer, Consulate in Peshawar, Pakistan 1984–87, Special Asst for Near East and S Asia, Office of Under-Sec. for Political Affairs, Washington, DC 1987–89, Political Counselor, Embassy in Nairobi 1989–92, Embassy in Kinshasa 1992–94, Consul Gen. in Bordeaux 1994–95, Political Counselor in New Delhi 1995–97, Deputy Chief of Mission in Islamabad 1997–99, Prin. Deputy Asst Sec. for S Asian Affairs, Dept of State 1999–2001, Acting Asst Sec. Jan.–May 2001, Special Negotiator for Conflict Diamonds, Econs and Business Bureau 2001–02, Dir Office of Cen. African Affairs 2002–05, Amb. to Malawi 2005–; mem. Bar of DC. *Address:* US Embassy, PO Box 30016, 16 Jomo Kenyatta Road, Lilongwe 3, Malawi (office). *Telephone:* 1773166 (office). *Fax:* 1770471 (office). *Website:* lilongwe.usembassy.gov (office).

EASTMAN, Ernest, MIA; Liberian politician and diplomatist; b. 27 March 1930, Monrovia; m. Salma Mohammedali; four s. five d. *Education:* Coll. of West Africa, Oberlin Coll., Ohio, Columbia Univ., New York. *Career:* Dir Bureau of Afro-Asian Affairs (Dept of State) 1957–64; Under-Sec. of State for Admin. 1964–67; Under-Sec. of State 1968–72; Amb. to East Africa (Kenya, Lesotho, Madagascar, Tanzania, Uganda, Zambia) 1972–74; Amb. to the Far East (Japan, Repub. of Korea, Democratic People's Repub. of Korea, Philippines, Indonesia, India) 1974–77; Sec.-Gen. Mano River Union (Economic and Customs Union for the Repubs of Liberia, Sierra Leone and Guinea) 1977–83; Minister of Foreign Affairs 1983–85; mem. special missions to the Presidents of Dahomey, Niger, Guinea, Ivory Coast, Gambia and USA; mem. official del. to several int. confs of the OAU, UN and Non-Aligned Movt; several decorations including Kt Great Band, Humane Order of African Redemption, several European and African decorations. *Publications:* A History of the State of Maryland in Liberia 1957; many newspaper articles on int affairs. *Address:* c/o Ministry of Foreign Affairs, POB 9002, Monrovia, Liberia.

EATON, William Alan, BA; American diplomatist; *Ambassador to Panama;* b. Winchester, Va. *Education:* Univ. of Virginia. *Career:* served in US Army in S Korea and elsewhere; career mem. Sr Foreign Service with rank of Minister-Counselor, has served overseas in Moscow, Istanbul, Milan and Ankara, Political Officer, Georgetown, Guyana, State Dept appointments have been in Office of Deputy Sec., as Under-Sec. for Man. and Asst Secs for Admin and Diplomatic Security, Amb. to Panama 2005–; fmr Exec. Dir and Dir of Int. Operations, Young Presidents' Org.; Virginia Press Asscn Award for journalistic excellence 1978, State Dept's Arnold Raphel Award for Mentoring, Presidential Meritorious Service Award 2001, Presidential Distinguished Service Award 2004, Hon. Nat. Distinguished Prin. Award for leadership in int. educ. 2004, State Dept's Leamon R. Hunt Award for Admin. Excellence. *Address:* Embassy of the USA, Avenida Balboa y Calle 38, Apdo 6959, Panamá 5, Panama (office). *Telephone:* 207-7000 (office). *Fax:* 207-7352 (office). *E-mail:* panamaweb@state.gov (office). *Website:* panama.usembassy.gov (office).

EATWELL, Baron (Life Peer), cr. 1992, of Stratton St Margaret in the County of Wiltshire; **John Leonard Eatwell,** PhD; British academic; *President, Queen's College, Cambridge;* b. 2 Feb. 1945; m. 1st Hélène Seppain 1970 (divorced); two s. one d.; m. 2nd Elizabeth Digby 2006. *Education:* Headlands Grammar School, Swindon, Queens' Coll. Cambridge, Harvard Univ., USA. *Career:* Teaching Fellow, Grad. School of Arts and Sciences, Harvard Univ. 1968–69; Research Fellow, Queens' Coll. Cambridge 1969–70; Fellow, Trinity Coll. Cambridge 1970–96, Asst Lecturer, Faculty of Econs and Politics, Cambridge Univ. 1975–77, Lecturer 1977, currently Prof. of Financial Policy, Pres. Queens' Coll. 1997–; Visiting Prof. of Econs, New School for Social Research, New York 1982–96; Econ. Adviser to Neil Kinnock, Leader of Labour Party 1985–92; Opposition Spokesman on Treasury Affairs and on Trade and Industry, House of Lords 1992–93, Prin. Opposition Spokesman on Treasury and

Econ. Affairs 1993–97; Trustee Inst. for Public Policy Research 1988–95, Sec. 1988–97, Chair. 1997–; Dir (non-exec.) Anglia TV Group 1994–2001, Cambridge Econometrics Ltd 1996–2007; Chair. Extemporary Dance Theatre 1990, Crusaid 1993–98, British Screen Finance Ltd 1997–2000 and assoc. cos; Gov. Contemporary Dance Trust 1991–95; Dir Arts Theatre Trust, Cambridge 1991–98, Bd, Securities and Futures Authority 1997–2001; mem. Bd Royal Opera House 1998–2006; Chair. Royal Ballet 1998–2001, Commercial Radio Cos Asscn 2000–04, British Library Bd 2001–06; mem. Regulatory Decisions Cttee, FSA 2001–05; Dir Cambridge Endowment for Research in Finance 2002–; Gov. Royal Ballet School 2003–06; Dir (non-exec.) Rontech Ltd 2003–. *Publications:* An Introduction to Modern Economics (with Joan Robinson) 1973, Whatever Happened to Britain? 1982, Keynes's Economics and the Theory of Value and Distribution (ed. with Murray Milgate) 1983, The New Palgrave: A Dictionary of Economics, 4 Vols 1987, The New Palgrave Dictionary of Money and Finance, 3 Vols 1992 (both with Murray Milgate and Peter Newman), Transformation and Integration: Shaping the Future of Central and Eastern Europe (jtly) 1995, Global Unemployment: Loss of Jobs in the '90s (ed.) 1996, Not "Just Another Accession": The Political Economy of EU Enlargement to the East (jtly) 1997, Global Finance at Risk: Case for International Regulation (with L. Taylor) 2000, Hard Budgets, Soft States 2000, Social Policy Choices in Central and Eastern Europe 2002, International Capital Markets (with L. Taylor) 2002; articles in scientific journals. *Address:* The President's Lodge, Queens' College, Cambridge, CB3 9ET, England (home). *Telephone:* (1223) 335556 (home). *Fax:* (1223) 335555 (home). *E-mail:* president@queens.cam.ac.uk (office).

EBIHARA, Shin; Japanese diplomatist; *Ambassador to UK;* b. Tokyo; m. Haruko Ebihara. *Career:* joined Ministry of Foreign Affairs 1971, Dir-Gen. N American Affairs Bureau 2006; Exec. Sec. to Prime Minister Keizo Obuchi 1998–2000, Asst Deputy Chief Cabinet Sec. 2005; Amb. to Indonesia 2006–08, to UK 2008–; Fellow, Weatherhead Center for Int. Affairs, Harvard Univ. 2000–01. *Address:* Embassy of Japan, 101–104 Piccadilly, London W1J 7JT, England (office). *Telephone:* (20) 7465-6500 (office). *E-mail:* info@jpembassy.org.uk (office). *Website:* www.uk.emb-japan.go.jp (office).

EBOUTOU, Martin Belinga, LLD; Cameroonian diplomatist; *Permanent Representative, United Nations;* b. 17 Feb. 1940. *Education:* Catholic Univ. Lovanium-Kinshasa, Univ. of Paris and Ecole Nat. d'Admin., Paris, France. *Career:* joined Cameroon Foreign Service 1968; served as Chief of Regional Orgs Unit, Ministry of Foreign Affairs, Nat. Corresp. for Agency for Cultural and Tech. Cooperation; del. to Lomè Convention, Int. Conf. on Namibia and Human Rights, UN Gen. Ass., Ministerial Meetings and Summits of Movt of Non-Aligned Countries, Group 77; Head of Econ. Mission in Paris, Rome, Tunis and Rabat 1985–89; Dir Civil Cabinet, Office of Pres. of the Repub. 1989–97; Perm. Rep. to UN, NY 1997–; Pres. Econ. and Social Council, UN 2001–. *Address:* Permanent Mission of Cameroon to the UN, 22 East 73rd Street, New York, NY 10021, USA (office). *Telephone:* (212) 794-2296 (office). *Fax:* (212) 249-0533 (office). *E-mail:* ambassadeur@cameroonmission.org (office). *Website:* www.cameroonmission.org (office).

ECHÁVARRI, Luis Enrique, MSc; Spanish business executive and international organization official; *Director-General of Nuclear Energy Agency, Organisation for Economic Co-operation and Development;* b. 1950; m.; two c. *Education:* Univ. of Madrid. *Career:* Project and Nuclear Plants Man., Westinghouse Electric, Madrid; Man. Lemóniz, Sayago and Almaraz nuclear power plants; Tech. Dir Consejo de Seguridad Nuclear (Spanish nuclear regulatory comm.), Commr, Man. Dir; Dir-Gen. OECD Nuclear Energy Agency 1997–; rep. of Spain at int. fora on nuclear energy, including Int. Atomic Energy Agency and EU. *Address:* OECD Nuclear Energy Agency, Le Seine Saint-Germain, 12 boulevard des Iles, 92130 Issy-les-Moulineux, France (office). *Telephone:* 1-45-24-10-00 (office). *Fax:* 1-45-24-11-10 (office). *E-mail:* nea@nea.fr (office). *Website:* www.nea.fr (office).

ECONOMY, Elizabeth C., BA, MA, PhD; American academic; *C.V. Starr Senior Fellow and Director, Asia Studies, Council on Foreign Relations;*

Education: Swarthmore Coll., Stanford Univ., Univ. of Mich. *Career:* taught Chinese foreign policy and int. environmental politics at Univ. of Washington 1993–94, Johns Hopkins Univ. 1997; Research Fellow, Columbia Univ. 1994; currently C.V. Starr Sr Fellow and Dir of Asia Studies, Council on Foreign Relations; consultant US Govt agencies; SSRC-MacArthur Dissertation Fellowship in Int. Peace and Security Studies 1990–93; mem. Selection Cttee, MacArthur Foundation Research Writing Competition 1996–98, Woodrow Wilson Center Int. Scholars Program 1999–2000; Co-Chair. Woodrow Wilson Center Working Group on China and the Environment 1997–99; mem. Advisory Bd, Issues and Studies, Woodrow Wilson Center Environmental Change and Security Project; mem. Bd of Councilors China-US Center for Sustainable Devt; mem. Exec. Cttee Program on Int. Studies in Asia, George Washington Univ.; Dr hc (Univ. of Vermont) 2008; Outstanding Teaching Award, Univ. of Mich. 1990. *Publications:* The Internationalization of Environmental Protection (co-ed.) 1997, China Joins the World: Progress and Prospects (co-ed.) 1999, The River Runs Black: The Environmental Challenge to China's Future (Best Social Sciences Book on Asia, Int. Convention on Asia Scholars) 2004; various articles in scholarly and policy journals.
Address: Council on Foreign Relations, The Harold Pratt House, 58 East 68th Street, New York, NY 10065, USA (office). *Telephone:* (212) 434-9641 (office). *Fax:* (212) 434-9800 (office). *E-mail:* eeconomy@cfr.org (office). *Website:* www.cfr.org (office).

EDELMAN, Eric S., PhD; American diplomatist; *Under-Secretary of Defense for Policy;* m. Patricia Davis; two s. two d. *Education:* Cornell Univ., Yale Univ. *Career:* mem. US Del. to West Bank/Gaza Autonomy Talks 1980–81; Watch Officer, State Dept Operations Center 1981–82; Staff Officer, Secr. Staff 1982; Special Asst to Sec. of State 1982–84; with Office of Soviet Affairs, Dept of State 1984–86; Head, External Political Section, Embassy in Moscow 1987–89; Special Asst (European Affairs) to Under-Sec. of State for Political Affairs 1989–90; Asst Deputy Under-Sec. of Defense for Soviet and East European Affairs, Office of Sec. of Defense 1990–93; Deputy Chief of Mission, Prague 1994–96; Exec. Asst to Deputy Sec. of State; Amb. to Finland 1998–2001, to Turkey 2003–05; Under-Sec. of Defense for Policy 2005–; Prin. Deputy Asst to Vice-Pres. for Nat. Security Affairs 2001–03; Award for Distinguished Civilian Service 1993, Superior Honor Award 1989, 1990, 1995.
Address: Office of the Under-Secretary of Defense for Policy, 2000 Defense Pentagon, Washington, DC 20301-2000, USA (office). *Telephone:* (703) 428-0711 (office). *Fax:* (703) 428-1982 (office). *Website:* www.defenselink .mil/policy (office).

EDGAR, James; American fmr politician; *Distinguished Fellow, Institute of Government and Public Affairs, University of Illinois;* b. 22 July 1946, Vinita, Okla; m. Brenda Smith; one s. one d. *Education:* Eastern Ill. Univ., Univ. of Ill. and Sangamon State Univ. *Career:* key Asst to Speaker, Ill. House of Reps. 1972–73; aide to Pres. Ill. Senate 1974, to House Minority Leader 1976; mem. Ill. House of Reps. 1977–91; Dir Legis. Affairs, Gov. of Ill. 1979–80; Sec. of State of Ill. 1981–91; Gov. of Illinois 1991–99; Chair. Nat. Govt's Asscn Comm. Econ. Devt and Tech. Innovation 1991, Strategic Planning Review Task Force 1991; Distinguished Fellow, Inst. of Govt and Public Affairs, Univ. of Ill. 1999–; Republican.
Address: University of Illinois Institute of Government and Public Affairs, 1007 W Nevada Street, Apartment MC-037, Urbana, IL 61801, USA (office). *Telephone:* (217) 333-3340 (office). *Website:* www.igpa.uiuc.edu (office).

EDINBURGH, HRH The Duke of; (Prince Philip), (Prince of the United Kingdom of Great Britain and Northern Ireland, Earl of Merioneth, Baron Greenwich), KG, KT, OM, GBE; b. 10 June 1921, Corfu, Greece; m. 20 Nov. 1947 HRH Princess Elizabeth (HM Queen Elizabeth II q.v.); children: Prince Charles Philip Arthur George, Prince of Wales (q.v.), b. 14 Nov. 1948, Princess Anne Elizabeth Alice Louise, The Princess Royal, b. 15 Aug. 1950, Prince Andrew Albert Christian Edward, Duke of York (q.v.), b. 19 Feb. 1960, Prince Edward Antony Richard Louis, Earl of Wessex , b. 10 March 1964. *Education:* Cheam, Salem and Gordonstoun Schools, Royal Naval Coll., Dartmouth. *Career:* renounced right of succession to thrones of Greece and Denmark, naturalized British subject 1947, adopting surname Mountbatten; served Royal Navy 1939–51, served in Indian Ocean, Mediterranean, North Sea, Pacific Ocean during Second World War; Personal ADC to King George VI 1948–52; PC 1951–; ranks of Adm. of the Fleet, Field Marshal, Marshal of the Royal Air Force, Captain-Gen. Royal Marines 1953–; Chancellor, Univs. of Wales 1948–76, Edinburgh 1952–, Salford 1967–91, Cambridge 1977–; Pres., Patron or Trustee numerous orgs including: Nat. Playing Fields Asscn 1948–, Nat. Maritime Museum 1948–, London Fed. of Clubs for Young People (now called London Youth) 1948–, City & Guilds of London Inst. 1951–, Cen. Council of Physical Recreation 1951–, Design Council 1952–, RSA 1952–, English-Speaking Union of the Commonwealth 1952–, Outward Bound Trust 1952–, Trinity House 1952–, Guild of Air Pilots and Air Navigators 1952–, RCA 1955–, Commonwealth Games Fed. 1955–90, Duke of Edinburgh's Award Scheme 1956–, Duke of Edinburgh's Commonwealth Study Confs 1956–, Royal Agric. Soc. of the Commonwealth 1958–, Voluntary Service Overseas 1961–, World Wildlife Fund UK 1961–82, Int. Equestrian Fed. 1964–86, Maritime Trust 1969–, Royal Commonwealth Ex-Services League 1974–, Royal Acad. of Eng 1976–, British Trust for Ornithology 1987–; Pres. World Wide Fund for Nature 1981–96, Pres. Emer. 1997–; numerous awards, decorations and hon. degrees worldwide. *Publications:* 14 publications 1957–2004.
Address: Buckingham Palace, London, SW1A 1AA, England. *Website:* www.royal.gov.uk.

EDMONDS, Martin, BA, MA (Econ), PhD, FRSA; American defence analyst, research institute director, editor and academic; *Honorary Professorial Fellow and Director of Studies, Centre for Defence and International Security Studies, University of Lancaster; Career:* previous academic positions include Sr McArthur Fellow, Center for Int. and Security Studies, Univ. of Maryland, Prof., Univ. of Southern California, Research Assoc., Columbia Univ., New York; Founding Ed.-in-Chief Defence Analysis (journal); fmr Ministry of Defence Lecturer in Higher Defence Studies, Univ. of Lancaster, UK, later Reader in Defence and Political Studies, Dept of Politics and Int. Relations, Dir Centre for Defence and Int. Security Studies, Henley, Oxon. –2005, Hon. Professorial Fellow, mem. Centre Bd and Dir of Studies 2005–; consultant, UK Defence Acad.'s future doctoral programme 2007–; organized int. conf. on European security, the Black Sea and the Eastern Mediterranean, Burg Schlaining, Austria, a conf. on future of sea-based air power at Fleet Air Arm Museum, Yeovilton; organized two 'conclaves', one on global health issues and role of WHO, and the other on Britain's New Aircraft Carriers 2006; mem. Eurodéfense, Royal United Services Inst.; founding Ed.-in-Chief int. journal Defense and Security Analysis; Fellow, S African Inst. of Int. Affairs. *Publications:* Taiwanese Defence Reform (co-author) 2006, Business and Security (co-ed.), Taiwan's Security and Air Power (co-author) 2004, Future NATO Security (co-author) 2004; numerous articles in professional journals.
Address: Centre for Defence and International Security Studies (CDISS), PO Box 801, Lancaster, LA1 9DX, England (office). *Telephone:* (1524) 221585 (office); 7813-900072 (mobile). *Fax:* (1524) 221585 (office). *E-mail:* m.edmonds@lancaster.ac.uk (office); Martin@haedmonds.freeserve.co .uk. *Website:* www.lancs.ac.uk/fss/politics (office); www.cdiss.org (office); www.tandf.co.uk/journals/titles/14751798.asp.

EDWARD, Sir David Alexander Ogilvy, Kt, KCMG, QC, MA, FRSE; British judge; b. 14 Nov. 1934, Perth; m. Elizabeth Young McSherry 1962; two s. two d. *Education:* Sedbergh School, Univ. Coll., Oxford and Univ. of Edinburgh. *Career:* advocate 1962–, Clerk Faculty of Advocates 1967–70, Treas. 1970–77; Pres. Consultative Cttee, Bars and Law Socs of the EEC 1978–80; Salvesen Prof. of European Insts and Dir Europa Inst., Univ. of Edin. 1985–89, Hon. Prof. 1990, now Chair.; Judge of the Court of First Instance of the European Communities 1989–92, Judge, Court of Justice of the EC 1992–2003; Pres. Scottish Council for Int. Arbitration; fmr Specialist Adviser to House of Lords Select Cttee on the EEC; fmr Chair. Continental Assets Trust PLC; fmr Dir Adam & Co. PLC, Harris Tweed Asscn Ltd; fmr mem. Law Advisory Cttee British Council, Panel of Arbitrators, Int. Centre for Settlement of Investment Disputes; fmr mem. Gründungssenat, Europa-Univ. Viadrina, Frankfurt/Oder; fmr Trustee, Nat. Library of Scotland; Trustee Trier Acad. of European Law, Industry and Parl. Trust, Hopetoun House Trust, Carnegie Trust for the Univs of Scotland; Hon. Bencher, Gray's Inn; Hon. Fellow Univ. Coll. Oxford; Hon. LLD (Univ. of Edin.) 1993, (Aberdeen) 1997, (Napier) 1998; Hon. DIur (Saarland) 2001, (Münster) 2001. *Publications:* The Professional Secret: Confidentiality and Legal Professional Privilege in the EEC 1976, European Community Law: an introduction (with R. C. Lane) 1995; articles in legal journals.
Address: 32 Heriot Row, Edinburgh EH3 6ES, Scotland (home).

EFFAH-APENTENG, Nana, M.A.; Ghanaian diplomatist; b. Bompata, Ashanti; m.; three s. *Education:* Ghana Inst. of Man. and Public Admin., Univ. of Ghana and Univ. of Oxford, U.K. *Career:* joined Ministry of Foreign Affairs 1970; Counsellor, then Minister-Counsellor in Moscow, U.S.S.R. 1986–88; Charge d'affaires then Deputy Chief of Mission in Rome, Italy 1988–90; Deputy Chief of Mission in Washington, D.C., U.S.A. 1993–97; Deputy Dir. Non-Aligned Movt. Secr. 1990–91; Asst. Dir. Int. Conf. Centre, Accra 1991–93; Dir. of Estates and Gen. Services Bureau, Ministry of Foreign Affairs 1992–93, Supervising Dir. of Admin. 1997–2000; Perm. Rep. to UN, New York May 2000–07.
Address: c/o Ministry of Foreign Affairs, Treasury Road, POB M53, Accra, Ghana (office).

EFFENDI, Arizal; Indonesian diplomatist; *Ambassador to France;* m. Ida Effendi. *Career:* overseas postings include missions in Washington, DC and London, Geneva and New York; Deputy Perm. Rep. to UN, New York 1998; fmr Head Int. Org. Directorate, Legal and Int. Treaty Affairs Directorate, Dept of Foreign Affairs; Amb. to Australia –2000; fmr Dir-Gen. America and Europe, Ministry of Foreign Affairs; currently Amb. to France (also accred. to Andorra); Sr Indonesian Official, ASEM (Asia-Europe Meeting) 2005. *Address:* Embassy of Indonesia, 47–49 rue Cortambert, 75116 Paris, France (office). *Telephone:* 1-45-03-07-60 (office). *Fax:* 1-45-04-50-32 (office). *E-mail:* kasubpen@amb-indonesie.fr (office). *Website:* www.amb-indonesie.fr (office).

EFIRD, Cynthia Grissom, BS, MS; American diplomatist; b. Detroit, Mich.; m. Neil Efird; one d. *Education:* Kingswood School, Cranbrook, School of Foreign Service, Georgetown Univ., Duke Univ., War Coll. of the Nat. Defense Univ. *Career:* joined US Foreign Service 1977, posted to embassies in Yugoslavia 1978–82, GDR 1983–85, Mozambique 1988–89, Press Officer, US Embassy and US Del. to CSCE, Vienna 1989–93, volunteered and served on US Liaison Mission to UN Peacekeeping Force (UNOSOM) in Somalia, Deputy Counselor for Public Affairs, Moscow 1997–2000, posted to OSCE to oversee reconstruction of media sector in Kosovo under UN Mission, Special Adviser to Assoc. US Trade Rep. –2004, Dir Public Diplomacy and Public Affairs, Bureau of African Affairs, Dept of State 2004–06, Amb. to Angola 2006–07; "Distinguished Graduate", War Coll. of the Nat. Defense Univ., several Meritorious Honor Awards and a Superior Honor Award. *Address:* US Department of State, 2201 C Street NW, Washington, DC 20520, USA (office). *Telephone:* (202) 647-4000 (office). *Fax:* (202) 647-6738 (office). *Website:* www.state.gov (office).

EFREMOVA, Marija; Macedonian diplomatist; *Ambassador to UK;* m. Dimitar Efremov. *Education:* Master's Programme in Int. Environmental Law, Italian Soc. of Int. Orgs. *Career:* attended Sr Exec. Seminar as Under-Sec. for Ministry of Defence 1995–99; State Counsellor and Head of Int. Legal and Consular Affairs Dept, Ministry of Foreign Affairs 2000–02; Minister Counsellor, Embassy in Rome 2002–07, returned briefly to Macedonia; Amb. to UK (also accred to Ireland) 2008–; named Grad. of the Month by The Marshall Center for April 2008. *Address:* Embassy of the Republic of Macedonia, Suites 2.1 and 2.2, Buckingham Court, 75–83 Buckingham Gate, London, SW1E 6PE, England (office). *Telephone:* (20) 7976-0535 (office). *Fax:* (20) 7976-0539 (office). *E-mail:* info@macedonianembassy.org.uk (office). *Website:* www.macedonianembassy.org.uk (office).

EFTYCHIOU, Petros, BA; Cypriot diplomatist; *High Commissioner to Egypt;* b. 25 Oct. 1950; m.; two d. *Education:* The English School, Nicosia, American Univ., Beirut, Lebanon. *Career:* Admin. Officer, Ministry of Finance 1977–79; joined Ministry of Foreign Affairs as Second Sec. 1979, Deputy Head EEC Dept 1987–89, Chief of Cabinet 1993–94, apptd Dir EU Affairs and Acting Perm. Sec. 2003; served as Sec., Embassy in Damascus, Syria 1980–84, Sec., Perm. Mission to EEC, Brussels 1984–87, Acting High Commr to Australia 1989, Deputy Perm. Rep. to UN, New York 1989–93, Amb. to Israel 1994–97, 2000–03, Perm. Rep. to UN and WTO, Geneva 1997–2000, High Commr to UK 2003–06, to Egypt 2006–; Vice-Pres. Econ. Comm. for Europe 1998. *Address:* Embassy of Cyprus, 23A Ismail Mohammed Street, 1st Floor, Zamalek, Cairo, Egypt (office). *Telephone:* (2) 3411288 (office). *Fax:* (2) 3415299 (office).

EGAN, Christopher F., BS, MPA; American business executive and diplomatist; *Permanent Representative, Organisation for Economic Cooperation and Development;* b. Boston, Mass; m. Jean Egan; three c. *Education:* Univ. of Massachusetts, Amherst, Kennedy School of Govt at Harvard Univ. *Career:* Pres. and Founding mem. Carruth Capital, LLC (commercial real estate investment and devt firm); Co-founder and Dir 'Break the Cycle of Poverty'; Trustee, Egan Family Foundation; fmr mem. Bd of Dirs Fallon Community Health Plan (Chair. Finance Cttee), MassDevelopment; fmr mem. Cen. Mass Regional Competitiveness Council; fmr Dir Corridor Nine Chamber of Commerce; Co-founder and mem. Bd Arc of Innovation/I-495 Initiative; TV commentator for numerous networks; op-ed. contrib. and documentary maker; Amb. to OECD 2007–; fmr Trustee, Univ. of Massachusetts Memorial Health Care. *Television:* Eclipsed by the Sun (documentary) 2004. *Address:* US Mission to the OECD, 12 avenue Raphael, 75016 Paris, France (office). *Telephone:* 1-45-24-74-77 (office). *Fax:* 1-45-24-74-80 (office). *E-mail:* usoecdpao@usoecd.org (office). *Website:* www.usoecd.org (office).

EGELUND, Niels; Danish diplomatist; *Ambassador to France;* b. 4 July 1946, Copenhagen. *Education:* Coll. of Europe, Bruges, Belgium, Univ. of Århus. *Career:* joined Foreign Service 1972, First Sec., Embassy in Washington, DC 1976–80, Deputy Chief of Mission, Bonn 1985–87; Amb., Under-Sec. of State, Political Dir 1992–93; Diplomatic Counsellor to Prime Minister 1993–99; Perm. Rep. to NATO 1999–2003; Amb. to France 2003–; Commdr, Order of Dannebrog and various other decorations. *Address:* Embassy of Denmark, 77 avenue Marceau, 75116 Paris, France (office). *Telephone:* 1-44-31-21-21 (office). *Fax:* 1-44-31-21-88 (office). *E-mail:* paramb@um.dk (office). *Website:* www.amb-danemark.fr (office).

EGILSSON, Jón Egill, MA; Icelandic diplomatist; *Director, Department of Natural Resources and Environmental Affairs, Ministry of Foreign Affairs;* b. 19 Nov. 1945, Glendale, Calif., USA; m. Inga Östrup Hauksdóttir, four c. *Education:* Teacher Training Coll. of Iceland, Univ. of Edin., UK. *Career:* early career as teacher and headmaster; First Sec., Ministry of Foreign Affairs 1984–89, Counsellor 1989; Counsellor, Embassy in Washington, DC 1990–94, Minister, Counsellor, Security Policy Officer 1994–95, Political Dir 1995–96; Amb. to Russia 1998–2001, to Germany 2001–04; Deputy to Perm. Sec. of State, Ministry of Foreign Affairs 2004–05, Dir Defence Dept, Ministry of Foreign Affairs 2005, currently Dir Dept of Natural Resources and Environmental Affairs. *Address:* Department of Natural Resources and Environmental Affairs, Ministry of Foreign Affairs, IS-150, Raudarárstig 25, Reykjavík 150, Iceland (office). *Telephone:* 5459957 (office). *Fax:* 5622373 (office). *E-mail:* jon.egill.egilsson@utn.stjr.is (office). *Website:* utanrikisraduneyti.is (office).

EGILSSON, Ólafur; Icelandic diplomatist and lawyer; *Ambassador to Cambodia, Indonesia, Malaysia, Thailand and Singapore;* b. 20 Aug. 1936, Reykjavik; m. Ragna Sverrisdóttir Ragnars 1960; one s. one d. *Education:* Commercial Coll. of Iceland and Iceland Univ. *Career:* journalist with newspapers Vísir 1956–58, Morgunbladid 1959–62; Publishing Exec. 1963–64; Head, NATO Regional Information Office, Reykjavik 1964–66; Gen.-Sec. Icelandic Asscn for Western Co-operation 1964–66; Political Div., Icelandic Foreign Ministry 1966–69; First Sec., then Counsellor, Icelandic Embassy, Paris 1969–71; Deputy Perm. Rep. OECD, UNESCO and Council of Europe 1969–71; Deputy Perm. Rep. N Atlantic Council, Deputy Head, Icelandic Del. to EEC, Counsellor, Embassy in Brussels 1971–74; Counsellor, then Minister Counsellor, Political Div. of Foreign Ministry 1974–80; Chief of Protocol (with rank of Amb.) 1980–83; Acting Prin. Pvt. Sec. to Pres. of Iceland 1981–82; Deputy Perm. Under-Sec. and Dir-Gen. for Political Affairs, Foreign Ministry 1983–87; Amb. to UK (also accred to Ireland, Netherlands and Nigeria) 1986–89; Amb. to USSR, later Russia 1990–94; Amb. to Denmark (also accred to Japan, Italy, Israel, Lithuania and Turkey) 1994–96; in charge of Arctic co-operation 1996–98 (also accred to Holy See, Turkey, Australia and NZ); Amb. to China (also accred to Australia, Japan, Repub. of Korea, NZ and Viet Nam) 1998–2002, to Cambodia, Indonesia, Malaysia, Thailand and Singapore (non-resident) 2002–; Chair. Bd of Govs Icelandic Int. Devt Agency 1982–87; Exec. mem. Bible Soc. of Iceland 1977–87, History Soc. 1982–88; Commdr Icelandic Order of the Falcon 1981 and decorations from Finland, France, Norway, Spain, Sweden and Luxembourg. *Publications:* Co-author: Iceland and Jan Mayen 1980, NATO's Anxious Birth – The Prophetic Vision of the 1940s 1985; Ed. Bjarni Benediktsson 1983. *Address:* c/o Ministry of Foreign Affairs, Raudararstigur 25, PO Box 1000, Reykjavik 150 (office); Valhúsabraut 35, 170 Saltjarnarnes, Iceland (home). *Telephone:* (354) 545-9900 (office); (354) 551 5411 (home). *Fax:* (354) 562-2373 (office); (354) 551 5411 (home). *E-mail:* olafur.egilsson@utn.stjr.is (office); olegice@simnet.is (home). *Website:* www.mfa.is (office).

EGLIN, Colin Wells, BSc; South African fmr politician and quantity surveyor; b. 14 April 1925, Cape Town; m. 1st Joyce Eglin 1949 (died 1997); three d.; m. 2nd Raili Eglin 2000. *Education:* De Villiers Graaff High School and Univ. of Cape Town. *Career:* army service in Egypt and Italy 1943–45; mem. Pinelands Municipal Council 1951–54, Cape Prov. Council 1954–58; mem. Parl. 1958–61, 1974–2004; Leader Progressive Party 1970–75, Progressive Reform Party 1975–77, Progressive Fed. Party 1977–79, 1986–88; Official Opposition Leader 1977–79, 1986–87; Chief DP Constitutional Negotiator 1991–96; Co-Chair. Transitional Exec. Council 1993–94; mem. Man. Cttee Constitutional Ass. 1994–96; Vice-Pres. Liberal Int. 1990–2003; Sec.-Gen. Org. of African Liberal Parties 1995–99; Democratic Party Spokesman on Foreign Affairs 1989–2004; Pnr, Bernard James and Pnrs (Quantity Surveyors) 1952–2004; consultant on parl. and constitutional matters 2004–; Officer of the Order of the Disa (Prov. of Western Cape) 2005; Hon. LLD (Cape Town) 1997; Parliamentarian of the Century, Leadership Magazine Jan. 2000, Ramon Trias Fargas Memorial Award 2002, St Dunstans Achievers Award 2003, Asscn of SA Quantity Surveyors Achievers Award 2004. *Publications:* Betrayal of Coloured Rights, Forging Links in Africa, Priorities for the Seventies, New

Deal for the Cities, Africa – A Prospect of Reconciliation, Pacesetter for Political Change, Security Through Negotiation, Crossing the Borders of Power (memoirs) 2007.
Address: 4th Floor, 183 Sir Lowry Road, Cape Town 8001, South Africa (office). *Telephone:* (21) 4618707 (office); (21) 7940584 (home). *Fax:* (21) 4618717 (office); (21) 7940584 (home). *E-mail:* coleglin@netactive.co.za (home).

EGUIAGARAY UCELAY, Juan Manuel, BA, PhD; Spanish politician; b. 25 Dec. 1945, Bilbao; m.; one s. *Education:* Univ. of Deusto, Univ. of Nancy, France. *Career:* mem. PSE-PSOE (Workers' Socialist Party of Spain) 1977–; councillor, Town Council, Bilbao 1979, Prov. Deputy, Vizcaya 1979–81, mem. Juntas Generales Vizcaya 1979–83, Deputy and Spokesman for Socialist Party of Basque Parl. 1980–88, mem. Exec. Cttee PSE-PSOE 1979–, Vice-Sec. Gen. Basque Socialists 1985–88, Govt Del. for Autonomous Community of Murcia, then for Autonomous Community of the Basque Country 1988–89; Exec. Sec. PSOE Fed. Exec. Comm. 1990; Minister for Public Admin 1991–93, of Industry and Energy 1993–96; Nat. Deputy for Murcia 1996–; Fed. Sec. for the Economy (34th Fed. Congress of PSOE), fmrly PSOE Nat. Parl. Spokesman and PSOE Nat. Parl. Spokesman for Econ. Affairs; Vice-Chair. Cttee on Econ., Trade and Tax Affairs; Prof. of Econs, Univ. de Deusto.
Address: Congreso de los Diputados, Plaza de las Cortes 9, 28014 Madrid, Spain. *Telephone:* (1) 3907639. *Fax:* (1) 4201648 (office). *E-mail:* juan .eguiagaray@diputado.congreso.es (office).

EHLERS ZURITA, Freddy; Ecuadorean journalist, politician and international organization official; *Secretary-General, Andean Community of Nations;* b. 1945, Quito. *Education:* Cen. Univ. of Ecuador. *Career:* fmr host, TV programme La Televisión; Dir Bd of Cartagena Agreement's Andean TV Program 1980–88; unsuccessful cand. for Pres. of Ecuador 1996, 1998; mem. Andean Parl. for Ecuador 2002–06, Vice-Pres. 2003–04, mem. Cttee on Educ., Culture, Science, Tech. and Communication; Sec.-Gen. Andean Community of Nations (Comunidad Andina de Naciones) 2007–.
Address: Comunidad Andina de Naciones, Paseo de la República 3895, San Isidro, Lima 27, Peru (office). *Telephone:* (1) 4111400 (office). *Fax:* (1) 2213329 (office). *E-mail:* contacto@comunidadandina.org (office). *Website:* www.comunidadandina.org (office).

EHOUZOU, Jean-Marie, MA; Benin diplomatist; *Permanent Representative, United Nations;* b. Sept. 1950; three c. *Education:* Inst. for Public Admin, Paris, Univ. of Benin. *Career:* Deputy Dir for Africa and Middle East Affairs and Deputy Dir for the Communities, Ministry of Foreign Affairs 1993–96; Dir for Co-ordination of External Resources, Ministry of Planning, Econ. Restructuring and Promotion of Employment 1996–2000; Dir Int. Orgs 2000–03; Amb. to Ethiopia (also accred to Kenya, Sudan and Djibouti) 2003–06; Perm. Rep. to African Union and UN Econ. Comm. for Africa 2003–06; Perm. Rep. to UN, New York 2006–.
Address: Permanent Mission of Benin to the United Nations, 4 East 73rd Street, New York, NY 10021, USA (office). *Telephone:* (212) 249-6014 (office). *Fax:* (212) 988-3714 (office). *E-mail:* benin@un.int (office). *Website:* www.un.int/benin (office).

EICHEL, Hans; German politician; b. 24 Dec. 1941, Kassel; m.; two c. *Education:* Univs of Marburg and Berlin. *Career:* fmr schoolmaster; mem. Kassel City Council 1968–75, Chair. Social Democratic Party (SDP) Group 1970–75; mem. Nat. Exec. of Young Socialists 1969–72; Chief Mayor of Kassel 1975–91; mem. SDP Nat. Exec. and Spokesman on Local Govt 1984; Chair. SDP Asscn Hesse 1989; Minister-Pres. of Hesse 1991–99; Federal Minister of Finance 1999–2005.
Address: c/o Sozialdemokratische Partei Deutschlands (SPD), Wilhelmstr. 141, 10963 Berlin, Germany (office).

EICHELBAUM, Rt Hon. Sir (Johann) Thomas, GBE, PC; New Zealand judge; *Judge of Appeal, Fiji;* b. 17 May 1931, Koenigsberg, Germany; m. Vida Beryl Franz 1956; three s. *Education:* Hutt Valley High School and Victoria Univ. Coll. *Career:* admitted solicitor 1953, barrister 1954; Partner, Chapman Tripp & Co. 1958–78; QC 1978; barrister 1978–82; Pres. NZ Law Soc. 1980–82; Judge, High Court of NZ 1982; Chief Justice of NZ 1989–99; Judge of Appeal, Fiji 1999–; Non-Perm. Judge, Court of Final Appeal Hong Kong 2000–; Privy Councillor 1989–; Chair. Royal Comm. on Genetic Modification 2000–01; Hon. LLD (Vic. Univ. of Wellington) 1998. *Publications:* Mauet's Fundamentals of Trial Techniques (Ed.-in-Chief) 1989, Introduction to Advocacy (Consulting Ed.) 2000.
Address: Raumati Beach, New Zealand. *E-mail:* thoseich@actrix.gen.nz (home).

EICHMANIS, Jānis, BA, MA, MPhil; Latvian government official and diplomatist; *Permanent Representative, NATO;* b. 15 Aug. 1942, Riga. *Education:* Univ. of Toronto and Univ. of Guelph, Canada, London School of Econs, UK. *Career:* Researcher, Comm. on Freedom of Information and Individual Privacy, Ont., Canada 1978–80; Analyst, Cttee on Procedural Affairs, Ont. Legislature 1980–83, Analyst, Legis. Research Service 1983–88; Sr Advisor, Office of Information and Privacy Commr, Ont. 1988–90; Man. Dept of Strategic Planning and Policy Devt, Office of the Information and Privacy Commr, Ont. 1990–93, 1995–99; Dir Dept of the Americas, Latvia Ministry of Foreign Affairs 1992–93; Chief of Staff, Chancery, Office of the Pres. and Foreign Policy Advisor, Repub. of Latvia 1993–94; Counsellor, Embassy in Washington, DC 1999–2003, Deputy Chief of Mission 2002–03; Amb. to Greece 2003–06 (also accred. to Cyprus and Bosnia and Herzogovina 2004–06); Vice-Pres. (Political Affairs) Latvian Nat. Fed. of Canada; Adjunct Prof., Dept of Political Science, Univ. of Toronto; Canada Council Fellowship 1970–72; Order of Viesturs, 2nd class (Latvia) 2004; Nat. Business Writing Award for Non-journalists (Canada) 1978, American Latvian Asscn Certificate of Recogntion 2003, Latvia Ministry of Defence Certificate of Recognition 2003, Pres.'s Certificate of Recognition (Latvia) 1999, Certificate of Recognition (Latvia) 2005.
Address: North Atlantic Treaty Organization, blvd Léopold III, 1110 Brussels, Belgium (office). *Telephone:* (2) 707-41-11 (office). *Fax:* (2) 707-45-79 (office). *E-mail:* natodoc@hq.nato.int (office). *Website:* www.nato .int (office).

EIDE, Kai, BA; Norwegian diplomatist; *Special Envoy of the Secretary-General to Afghanistan, United Nations;* b. 28 Feb. 1949, Sarpsborg; m. Gro Holm; two d. *Education:* Univ. of Oslo. *Career:* entered Norwegian Foreign Service 1975, mem. Del. to CSCE Follow-up Meeting in Belgrade 1977–78, Madrid 1980–82, Sec., Embassy in Prague 1977–78, First Sec. 1979–82, First Sec. Del. to Conf. on Disarmament in Europe, Stockholm 1983–84, First Sec. Del. to NATO, Brussels 1984–87; Deputy Dir Pvt. Office of NATO Sec.-Gen. 1987–89; State Sec., Office of the Prime Minister, Oslo 1989–90; Minister Counsellor and Deputy Perm. Rep. to NATO 1991–93, Amb. to Int. Conf. on the Fmr Yugoslavia (ICFY) 1993–95, Amb. and Special Adviser on Balkan Area, Ministry of Foreign Affairs 1996, Special Rep. of UN Sec.-Gen. and Head of UN Mission in Bosnia and Herzegovina, Sarajevo 1997–98, Amb. and Del. to OSCE, Vienna 1998–2002, Chair. OSCE Perm. Council 1999, mem. Mitchell Cttee Staff (Sharm el Sheikh Fact Finding Mission) 2000–01, Perm. Rep. to NATO, Brussels 2002–06, Special Envoy of UN Sec.-Gen. to Kosovo 2005, to Afghanistan 2008–; Political Dir, Ministry of Foreign Affairs 2006–08; Special Adviser, Planning Div., STATOIL 1991. *Publications:* several publs on foreign and security matters.
Address: United Nations Assistance Mission in Afghanistan (UNAMA), PO Box 5858, Grand Central Station, New York, NY 10163-5858, USA (office); UNAMA, PO Box 1428, Islamabad, Pakistan (office); UNAMA, Peace Street, Kabul, Afghanistan. *Telephone:* (0831) 246000 (Brindisi, Italy) (office). *Fax:* (212) 963-2669 (New York) (office); (0831) 246069 (Brindisi, Italy) (office). *E-mail:* spokesperson-unama@un.org (office). *Website:* www.unama-afg.org (office).

EIKENBERRY, Lt-Gen. Karl W., BS, MS, PhD; American army officer and international organization official; *Deputy Chairman of the Military Committee, NATO;* b. 1951. *Education:* US Mil. Acad., West Point, Harvard Univ., Stanford Univ. *Career:* mil. operational assignments included service as commdr and staff officer with mechanized, light, airborne and ranger infantry units in US, South Korea and Europe; has served in numerous admin.-political positions, including Dir. for Strategic Planning and Policy for US Pacific Command, US Security Coordinator and Chief of Office of Mil. Cooperation, Kabul, Afghanistan, Asst Army Attaché and later Defense Attaché, Embassy in Beijing, Sr Country Dir for China, Taiwan, Hong Kong and Mongolia in Office of the US Sec. of Defense, and Deputy Dir. for Strategy, Plans, and Policy on Army Staff; Commdr Combined Forces Command–Afghanistan 2005–07; Deputy Chair.Mil. Cttee, NATO, Brussels 2007–; Defense Superior Service Medal, Legion of Merit, Bronze Star, Ranger Tab, Combat and Expert Infantryman badges, and master parachutist wings, US Dept of State Superior Honor Award, Dir of Cen. Intelligence Award, Akbar Khan Award (Afghanistan) presented by Pres. Hamid Karzai.
Address: North Atlantic Treaty Organization, blvd Léopold III, 1110 Brussels, Belgium (office). *Telephone:* (2) 707-41-11 (office). *Fax:* (2) 707-45-79 (office). *E-mail:* natodoc@hq.nato.int (office). *Website:* www.nato .int (office).

EINAUDI, Luigi R., BA, PhD; American international organization official, diplomatist and academic. *Education:* Harvard Univ. *Career:* researcher RAND Corpn, Santa Monica, Calif. 1964–74; staff mem. Policy Planning Staff, Office of Sec. of State 1974–77, 1993–97; Dir of Policy Planning,

Bureau of Inter-American Affairs, Dept of State 1977–89; Amb. to OAS 1989–93; US Special Envoy to Ecuador–Peru Peace Talks 1995–98; worked on multilateral governance and conflict resolution at Inter-American Dialogue, Washington, DC 1998–2000; Special Rep. of OAS Sec.-Gen. in Honduras–Nicaragua boundary dispute 1999; Asst Sec.-Gen. OAS 2000–04, Sec.-Gen. 2004–05; teacher at UCLA, Harvard, Wesleyan and Georgetown Univs; lecturer in numerous univs in USA, Latin American and Europe; mem. Council on Foreign Relations; recipient of decorations from Presidents of Ecuador and Peru; recipient of awards from Presidents Jimmy Carter, Ronald Reagan, George Bush and Secretaries of State Henry Kissinger, Madeleine Albright, Frasure Award for Peace-keeping 1997, seven other medal citations from Depts of State and Defense; Terry Woods Memorial Award, OAS 2005. *Publications include:* Beyond Cuba, Latin America Takes Charge of Its Future 1974; numerous articles and monographs.
Address: c/o Organization of American States, 17th and Constitution Avenue, NW, Washington, DC 20006, USA (office).

EINHORN, Jessica P., MA, PhD; American academic and fmr government official; *Dean, Paul H. Nitze School of Advanced International Studies (SAIS), Johns Hopkins University;* b. 1948. *Education:* Barnard Coll., Columbia Univ., Paul H. Nitze School of Advanced Int. Studies (SAIS), Princeton Univ. LSE, London, Brookings Inst., Harvard Univ. *Career:* various roles with US Treasury, US State Dept and Int. Devt Cooperation Agency of USA –1992; Vice-Pres. and Treasurer, World Bank 1992–96, Man. Dir 1996-98; Visiting Fellow, IMF 1998–99; Consultant, Clark & Weinstock, Washington 1999–2002; Dean, Paul H. Nitze School of Advanced Int. Studies (SAIS), Johns Hopkins Univ. 2002–; Trustee Rockefeller Brothers Fund; Dir Council on Foreign Relations, Inst. for Int. Econs, Center for Global Devt; Dir Pitney Bowes Inc. 1999–; Chair. Global Advisory Bd J.E. Robert Cos; mem. Exec. Cttee Trilateral Comm.; fmr Trustee German Marshall Fund. *Publications:* Expropriation Politics 1974; various articles.
Address: Paul H. Nitze School of Advanced International Studies, 1740 Massachusetts Avenue, NW, Washington, DC 20036, USA (office). *Telephone:* (202) 663-5624 (office). *Fax:* (202) 663-5621 (office). *E-mail:* jeinhorn@jhu.edu. *Website:* www.sais-jhu.edu.

EINIK, Michael, MBA; American diplomatist; *Executive Director, Project on Ethnic Relations Regional Center for Central, Eastern and Southeastern Europe;* b. 1949, New York. *Education:* Univ. of Miami, George Washington Univ., Washington, DC. *Career:* joined Dept of State 1972; Econ./Commercial Officer Brasilia, then San Salvador; with Bureau of Econ. and Business Affairs, Dept of State; staff Asst to Asst Sec. of State; worked in Office of Fuels and Energy during 1970s oil crisis; Petroleum Officer, Embassy, Nigeria 1981; served in Econ. Section, Moscow; Prin. Officer, Consulate-Gen., Zagreb representing US in both Croatia and Slovenia 1988–92; Chief of Personnel, European Bureau 1992–94; Deputy Chief of Mission, Bucharest; Amb. to Macedonia 1999–2002; Pres. Netcare Healthcare Central Europe (Netcare CE) 2004; Exec. Dir Project on Ethnic Relations (PER) Regional Center for Cen., Eastern and Southeastern Europe, Bucharest, Romania 2006–.
Address: c/o Project on Ethnic Relations, 15 Chambers Street, Princeton, NJ 08542-3707 USA (office). *Telephone:* (609) 683-5666 (office). *Fax:* (609) 683-5888 (office). *E-mail:* per@per-usa.org (office). *Website:* www.per-usa .org/romania.htm (home).

EIRÍKSSON, Gudmundur, BS, AB, LLB, LLM; Icelandic diplomatist, judge and academic; *Professor and Director, Department of International Law and Human Rights, United Nations University for Peace;* b. 26 Oct. 1947, Winnipeg, Canada; m. Thorey Vigdis Ólafsdóttir 1973; one s. three d. *Education:* Rutgers Univ., USA, King's Coll., Univ. of London, UK, Columbia Univ., USA. *Career:* Law of the Sea Officer and Consultant, UN, New York 1974–77; Asst Legal Adviser, Legal Adviser, Ministry of Foreign Affairs, Iceland 1977–96, Amb. 1988–; Rep. of Iceland to Third UN Conf. on Law of the Sea 1978–82; mem. UN Int. Law Comm. 1987–96; Judge, Int. Tribunal for the Law of the Sea 1996–2002 (Pres. Chamber of Fisheries Disputes 1999–2002); Dean for Cooperative Programmes, Sec. of Council, Prof. and Dir of Int. Law and Human Rights Studies, Univ. for Peace, Costa Rica (UPEACE) 2001–; Amb. to Canada (also accred to Colombia, Costa Rica, Ecuador, Nicaragua, Panama, Peru and Venezuela) 2003–05; Visiting Scholar Univ. of Va Law School, USA 1984–85; Lecturer, Univ. of Iceland 1987–96; Visiting Prof. of Law, Univ. of New Mexico School of Law 1994–95; Pres. Council of N Atlantic Salmon Conservation Org. 1984–88; mem. Panel of Conciliators and Arbitrators, Center for Arbitrations, Mediation and Conciliation, Dakar, Panel of Conciliators and Panel of Arbitrators, Int. Centre for the Settlement of Investment Disputes, Washington, DC; Grand Kt, Order of the Icelandic Falcon; Jelf Memorial Medal, King's Coll., Univ. of London 1973. *Publications:* The International Tribunal for the Law of the Sea 2000;

numerous articles on the law of the sea, legal educ., int. criminal law, int. orgs, disarmament and human rights.
Address: University for Peace, Apartado 138-6100, San Jose, Costa Rica (office). *Telephone:* (506) 205-9000 (office); (506) 205-9056 (office). *Fax:* (506) 249-1929 (office). *E-mail:* eiriks@racsa.co.cr (office). *Website:* www .upeace.org/faculty/gericksson.cfm (office).

EK, Sereywath, MA; Cambodian diplomatist; *Ambassador to USA;* m.; two c. *Education:* Inst. of Political Studies Diplomatic Section, Paris. *Career:* journalist, Le Figaro, Paris 1978–80; Ed. Cambodia Center newsletter, Paris 1983–85; Deputy Dir Funcipec 1985–91, Dir of Information 1991–93; Vice-Minister of Information, provisional Govt of Cambodia and mem. Parl. for Phnom Penh constituency 1993; Sec. of State (Vice-Minister), Ministry of Nat. Defence 1993–98; mem. Parl. for Takeo Prov. constituency 1998–99; Amb. to the Philippines 1999–2003; Senator 2004–05; Amb. to USA 2005–.
Address: Embassy of Cambodia, 4530 16th Street, NW, Washington, DC 20011, USA (office). *Telephone:* (202) 726-7742 (office). *Fax:* (202) 726-8381 (office). *E-mail:* mail@embassyofcambodia.org (office). *Website:* www.embassyofcambodia.org (office).

EKEUS, Carl Rolf; Swedish diplomatist; *High Commissioner on National Minorities, Organization for Security and Co-operation in Europe;* b. 7 July 1935, Kristinehamn; m. Christina C. Oldfelt 1970; three s. three d. *Education:* Univ. of Stockholm. *Career:* law practice, Karlstad 1959–62; Legal Div. Ministry of Foreign Affairs 1962–63; Sec. Swedish Embassy, Bonn 1963–65; First Sec. Nairobi 1965–67; Special Asst to Minister of Foreign Affairs 1967–73; First Sec., Counsellor, Perm. Mission to UN, New York 1974–78; Counsellor, The Hague 1978–83; Amb. and Perm. Rep. to Conf. on Disarmament, Geneva 1983–89, Chair. Cttee on Chemical Weapons 1984, 1987; Amb. and Head of Swedish Del. to CSCE, Vienna 1989–93; Chair. Cttee on Principles Chapter of Charter of Paris 1991; Exec. Chair. UN Special Comm. on Iraq 1991–97; Amb. to USA 1997–2000; Chair. Stockholm Int. Peace Research Inst. 2000–; OSCE High Commr on Nat. Minorities 2001–; mem. Canberra Comm. on the Elimination of Nuclear Weapons, advisory Bd Center for Non-Proliferation, Monetary Inst., Tokyo Forum on Non-Proliferation and Disarmament; mem. advisory Bd of UN Sec.-Gen. on Disarmament Matters 1999–2004, Bd Dirs Nuclear Threat Initiative 2001, Bd Axel and Margaret Ax:son Johnson Foundation 2001–; mem. Royal Acad. of War Science, Stockholm 2001; Hon. LLD (California Lutheran Univ.) 1999; Wateler Peace Prize, Carnegie Foundation 1997. *Publications:* reports as Special Investigator on the submarine question 1980–2001, Sweden's security policy 1969–89 2002; several articles on foreign policy, int. economy, nuclear non-proliferation, disarmament and arms control, chemical weapons, European security, Iraq and weapons of mass destruction.
Address: High Commission on National Minorities, Prinsessegracht 22, 2514 AP The Hague, Netherlands (office); Stockholm International Peace Research Institute, Signalistgatan 9, 169 70 Solna (office); Rådmansgatan 57, 11360 Stockholm, Sweden (home). *Telephone:* (70) 3125500 (The Hague) (office); (8) 312653 (home). *Fax:* (70) 3635910 (The Hague) (office). *E-mail:* rekeus@hcnm.org (office). *Website:* www.sipri.se (office); www .osce.org/hcnm (office).

EKREN, Nazim, PhD; Turkish politician; *Deputy Prime Minister and State Minister for Economy;* b. 1956, Istanbul; m.; two c. *Education:* Uludağ and Marmara univs, Manchester Business School, UK. *Career:* fmr Dir Türkiye Vakiflar Bankasi; fmr Dir Banking and Insurance Inst., Univ. of Marmara; mem. of Grand Nat. Ass., representing Istanbul 2002–; Deputy Prime Minister and State Minister for Economy 2007–; Co-founder, Bd Mem. and Deputy Chair. (Econ. Affairs), AKP (Adalet ve Kalkinma Partisi/Justice and Devt Party).
Address: Deputy Prime Ministers' Office, Başbakan Yard, ve Devlet Bakani, Bakanliklar, Ankara, Turkey (office). *Telephone:* (312) 4191621 (office). *Fax:* (312) 4191547 (office). *Website:* www.akparti.org.tr (office).

EL-BADRI, Abdalla Salem, BS; Libyan oil industry executive and international organization official; *Secretary-General, Organization of the Petroleum Exporting Countries (OPEC);* b. 1940, Ghemmines. *Education:* Univ. of Florida, USA. *Career:* began career at Esso-Libya 1965; seconded by state-owned Nat. Oil Corpn (NOC) to become mem. Umm Al-Jawaby Man. Bd 1977; Chair. Waha Oil Co. 1980–83; Chair. NOC 1983–90, 2000–02, Sec. Man. Cttee 2004–06; Sec., Gen. People's Cttee of Petroleum 1990–93, Gen. People's Cttee of Energy 1993–2002, Under-Sec., Gen. People's Cttee 2002–04; Sec.-Gen. OPEC 2007–.
Address: Organization of the Petroleum Exporting Countries (OPEC), Obere Donaustrasse 93, 1020 Vienna, Austria (office). *Telephone:* (1) 21-11-20 (office). *Fax:* (1) 216-43-20 (office). *Website:* www.opec.org (office).

EL-REEDY, Abdel Raouf, BA, MA; Egyptian lawyer and diplomatist; *Chairman, Egyptian Council for Foreign Affairs;* b. July 1932, Ezbet El Borg (Damietta). *Education:* Cairo Univ., Columbia Univ., USA. *Career:* mem. Research Dept, Ministry of Foreign Affairs 1960–61, mem. Foreign Minister's Cabinet 1964–68, Deputy Dir Dept of Int. Orgs 1972–74, Dir Dept of Policy Planning 1977–79, Dir Dept of Int. Orgs 1983–84; with Arab League Secr. 1974–77; Amb. to Pakistan 1979–80; Perm. Rep. toe UN, Geneva 1980–83; Amb. to USA 1984–92; currently Sr Pnr, Ibrachy & Dermarkar (law firm), Cairo; currently Chair. Mubarak Public Library, Giza; Co-founder and Chair. Egyptian Council for Foreign Affairs, Cairo; mem. Bd of Trustees, Egyptian Int. Econ. Forum; mem. L'Institut d'Egypte.
Address: Egyptian Council for Foreign Affairs, Tower No. 2 Osman Buildings, Kornish El Nile, Maadi, Cairo, Egypt (office). *Telephone:* (2) 2528-1091 (office). *Fax:* (2) 2528-1093 (office). *E-mail:* info@ecfa-egypt.org (office). *Website:* www.ecfa-egypt.org (office); www.mpl.org (office).

ELBEGDORJ, Tsakhiagiin, MA; Mongolian politician; b. 30 March 1963, Zereg Som, Hovd Prov.; m.; two c. *Education:* Harvard Univ., USA. *Career:* machinist, Erdenet copper mine 1981–82; army service 1982; mil. reporter, Mil. School, Lvov, Ukraine 1983–88; journalist, Ulaan-Od (Ministry of Defence newspaper) 1988–90; mem. Co-ordinating Council of Mongolian Democratic Union (MDU) 1989, Leader 1990; Deputy to People's Great Hural 1990–92, also mem. State Little Hural; mem. State Great Hural 1992–94, 1996, Vice-Chair. 1996–; mem. Gen. Council Mongolian Nat. Democratic Party 1994, Leader 1996–, also Leader Democratic Union coalition in State Great Hural; Prime Minister of Mongolia April–Dec. 1998, 2004–06.
Address: c/o Prime Minister's Office, State Palace, Sükhbaataryn Talbai 1, Ulan Bator 12 (office); Mongolian National Democratic Party, Chingisiyn Örgön Chölöö 1, Ulan Bator, Mongolia (office).

ELDON, Stewart Graham, CMG, OBE, MSc; British diplomatist; *Permanent Representative, NATO;* b. 18 Sept. 1953, Accra, Ghana; m. Christine Mason 1978; one s. one d. *Education:* Pocklington School, Yorks. and Christ's Coll., Cambridge. *Career:* entered FCO 1976, UK Mission New York 1976, Asst Desk Officer, UN Dept, FCO 1977–78, Third (later Second) Sec., British Embassy, Bonn 1978–82, Head of Section, Repub. of Ireland Dept, FCO 1982–83, Minister of State, FCO 1983–86, First Sec., Chancery, UK Mission, New York 1986–90, Deputy Head, Middle East Dept, FCO 1990–91, seconded to Cabinet Office 1991–93, Centre for Int. Affairs, Harvard Univ. 1993–94, Political Counsellor, UK Del. to NATO/ WEU 1994–97, Dir of Confs, FCO 1997–98, Deputy Perm. Rep. UK Mission, New York 1998–2002; Visiting Fellow, Yale Univ. 2002; Amb. to Ireland 2003–06; Perm. Rep., NATO 2006–.
Address: North Atlantic Treaty Organization (NATO), blvd Léopold III, 1110 Brussels, Belgium (office). *Telephone:* (2) 707-41-11 (office). *Fax:* (2) 707-45-79 (office). *E-mail:* natodoc@hq.nato.int (office). *Website:* www .nato.int (office).

ELENOVSKI, Lazar, BA; Macedonian politician; b. 19 March 1971, Skopje; m.; one s. *Education:* Faculty of Econs, Skopje. *Career:* fmr Deputy CEO JSP (public transport co.); joined Social Democratic Alliance of Macedonia, f. Social Democratic Youth of Macedonia 1992, Sec.-Gen. 1996–99, Pres. 1999–2001; f. Young Europeans for Security (YES Macedonia) 1995; mem. Presidency, Social-Democratic Union of Macedonia 1997–2003; Sec.-Gen. Euro-Atlantic Club of Macedonia 2001–05; Pres. Euro-Atlantic Council of Macedonia 2005–06; Co-founder Cen. and South Eastern European Security Forum (Balkan Mosaic); Minister of Defence 2006–08; mem. New Social Democratic Party 2006–; mem. Atlantic Treaty Asscn. *Publications:* numerous articles on the Euro-Atlantic integration process, the Balkan region, and security sector reforms.
Address: New Social Democratic Party (NSDP), Dame Gruev 5, 1000 Skopje, Former Yugoslav Republic of Macedonia (office). *Telephone:* (2) 3238775 (office). *Fax:* (2) 3290465 (office). *E-mail:* nsdp@nsdp.org.mk (office). *Website:* www.nsdp.org.mk (office).

ELIASSON, Jan, MA; Swedish diplomatist and UN official; b. 17 Sept. 1940, Göteborg; m. Kerstin Englesson 1967; one s. two d. *Education:* School of Econs, Göteborg. *Career:* entered Swedish Foreign Service 1965; Swedish OECD Del., Paris 1967; at Swedish Embassy, Bonn 1967–70; First Sec. Swedish Embassy, Washington 1970–74; Head of Section, Political Dept, Ministry for Foreign Affairs, Stockholm 1974–75; Personal Asst to the Under-Sec. of State for Foreign Affairs 1975–77; Dir Press and Information Div., Ministry for Foreign Affairs 1977–80, Asst Under-Sec., Head of Div. for Asian and African Affairs, Political Dept 1980–82; Foreign Policy Adviser, Prime Minister's Office 1982–83; Under-Sec. for Political Affairs, Stockholm 1983–87; Perm. Rep. of Sweden to UN, New York 1988–92; Chair. UN Trust Fund for SA 1988–92; Personal Rep. to UN Sec.-Gen. on Iran-Iraq 1988–92; Vice-Pres. ECOSOC 1991–92; Under-Sec.-Gen. for

Humanitarian Affairs, UN 1992–94; Chair. Minsk Conf. on Nagornyi Karabakh 1994; State Sec. for Foreign Affairs 1994–2000; Amb. to USA 2000–05; Pres. UN General Ass. 2005–06; Minister of Foreign Affairs 2006; Special Envoy of the UN Sec.-Gen. for Darfur 2006–08; Sec. to Swedish Foreign Policy Advisory Bd 1983–87; Expert, Royal Swedish Defence Comm. 1984–86; Dir Inst. for East–West Security Studies, New York 1989–93, Int. Peace Acad. 1989–2001; Dr hc (American Univ. Washington, DC) 1994, (Gothenburg) 2001, (Bethany Coll., Kansas) 2005, (Uppsala) 2006.
Address: c/o Ministry for Foreign Affairs, Gustav Adolfs torg 1, 103 39 Stockholm, Sweden (office).

ELISAIA, Ali'ioaiga Feturi, BA; Samoan diplomatist; *Ambassador to USA and Permanent Representative, United Nations;* b. 1954; m. Maria Lei Sam-Elisaia. *Education:* Univ. of the South Pacific, Fiji, Univ. of Oxford, UK. *Career:* served in Samoan Mission to UN, New York June–Oct. 1979, Acting Div. Head, later Div. Head, Econ. and Aid Div., Ministry of Foreign Affairs 1979–81, First Sec., High Comm. in New Zealand 1981–84, Deputy Sec. for Foreign Affairs December 1984–88; Co-Dir Hanns Seidel Foundation, Samoa 1988–2001; Asst CEO, Corp. and Support Services, Ministry of Foreign Affairs and Trade 2001–03, Perm. Rep. to UN, New York and Amb. to USA 2003– (also accred to Canada 2004–).
Address: Permanent Mission of Samoa to the United Nations, 800 Second Avenue, Suite 400J, New York, NY 10017, USA (office). *Telephone:* (212) 599-6196 (office). *Fax:* (212) 599-0797 (office). *E-mail:* samoa@un.int (office).

ELIZABETH II, HM Queen (Elizabeth Alexandra Mary), (Queen of Great Britain and Northern Ireland and of Her other Realms and Territories), (see Reigning Royal Families section for full titles); b. 21 April 1926, London. *Career:* succeeded to The Throne following Her father's death 6 Feb. 1952; married 20 Nov. 1947, HRH The Prince Philip, The Duke of Edinburgh (q.v.), b. 10 June 1921; children: Prince Charles Philip Arthur George, Prince of Wales (q.v.) (heir apparent), b. 14 Nov. 1948; Princess Anne Elizabeth Alice Louise, The Princess Royal, b. 15 Aug. 1950; Prince Andrew Albert Christian Edward, Duke of York (q.v.), b. 19 Feb. 1960; Prince Edward Antony Richard Louis, Earl of Wessex, b. 10 March 1964.
Address: Buckingham Palace, London, SW1A 1AA; Windsor Castle, Berkshire, SL4 1NJ, England; Balmoral Castle, Aberdeenshire, AB35 5TB, Scotland; Sandringham House, Norfolk, PE35 6EN, England; Palace of Holyroodhouse, Edinburgh, Scotland. *Website:* www.royal.gov.uk.

ELLIS, Alexander Wykeham; British diplomatist; *Ambassador to Portugal;* m. Maria Teresa Adegas. *Career:* with Southern Africa Dept, FCO 1990–92, Third, later Second Sec., Lisbon 1992–96, First Sec. (Econ., later Insts), Perm. Rep., Brussels 1996–2001, Head of Enlargement Team, EU Directorate, FCO 2001–03, Counsellor and Head of EU and Global Issues Team, Madrid 2003–05, seconded as Adviser to Pres. of EC 2005–07, Amb. to Portugal 2007–.
Address: British Embassy, Rua de São Bernardo 33, 1249-082 Lisbon, Portugal (office). *Telephone:* (21) 3924000 (office). *Fax:* (21) 3924021 (office). *E-mail:* ppa@fco.gov.uk (office). *Website:* www.uk-embassy.pt (office).

ELMANDJRA, Mahdi, PhD; Moroccan academic; *Professor, University Mohamed V;* b. 13 March 1933, Rabat; m. Amina Elmrini 1956; two d. *Education:* Lycée Lyautey, Casablanca, Putney School, Vermont, USA, Cornell Univ., London School of Econs and Faculté de Droit, Univ. de Paris. *Career:* Head of Confs, Law Faculty, Univ. of Rabat 1957–58; Adviser, Ministry of Foreign Affairs and to Moroccan Del. to UN 1958–59; Dir-Gen. Radiodiffusion Télévision Marocaine 1959–60; Chief of African Div., Office of Relations with Mem. States, UNESCO 1961–63; Dir Exec. Office of Dir-Gen. of UNESCO 1963–66; Asst Dir-Gen. of UNESCO for Social Sciences, Human Sciences and Culture 1966–69; Visiting Fellow, Centre of Int. Studies, LSE 1970; Asst Dir-Gen. of UNESCO for Pre-Programming 1971–74; Special Adviser to Dir-Gen. of UNESCO 1975–76; Prof., Univ. Mohamed V, Rabat 1977–; Co-ordinator, Conf. on Tech. Co-operation between Developing Countries (UNDP) 1979–80; Sr Adviser, UN Int. Year of Disabled Persons 1980–81; mem. Consultative Cultural Council of the Inst. of the Arab World (Paris); fmr Pres. World Future Studies Fed. (WFSF), Futuribles Int.; mem. Club of Rome, Acad. of the Kingdom of Morocco; Vice-Pres. Asscn Maroc-Japon; mem. World Acad. of Art and Science, Exec. Cttee, Soc. for Int. Devt, Exec. Cttee, African Acad. of Sciences, Pugwash Confs, Founding Pres. Moroccan Asscn of Human Rights, Acad. of the Kingdom of Morocco; Officier des Arts et des Lettres (France), Order of the Rising Sun (Japan) and numerous other decorations; Master Jury Aga Khan Award for Architecture 1986, Albert Einstein Int. Foundation Medal for Peace 1990. *Television:* various programmes for French, Moroccan, Spanish, Japanese and Arab channels. *Publications:* Africa 2000 1980, The New Age of Culture and Communica-

tion 1981, The Future of Humor 1982, Maghreb 2000 1982, L'Interpellation du Tiers Monde 1982, Les Aspects économiques du dialogue Euro-Arabe 1982, Information and Sovereignty 1983, The Conquest of Space: Political, Economic and Socio-Cultural Implications 1984, Casablanca 2000 1984, Development and Automation 1985, Communications, Information and Development 1985, Tomorrow's Habitat 1985, Learning Needs in a Changing Society 1986, Media and Communications in Africa 1986, The Future of International Cooperation 1986, The Financing of Research and Development in the Third World 1986, Maghreb et Francophonie 1988, Three Scenarios for The Future of International Cooperation 1988, The Place of Arab Culture in the World of Tomorrow 1988, Social Change and Law 1988, China in the 21st Century 1989, Fusion of Science and Culture: Key to the 21st Century 1989, Human Rights and Development 1989, How to Construct a Positive Vision of the Future 1990, Gulf Crisis: Prelude to the North-South Confrontation 1990, Western Discrimination in the Field of Human Rights 1990, Africa: The Coming Upheaval 1990, La Première Guerre Civilisationnelle 1991, Retrospective des Futurs 1992, Nord-Sud: Prélude à l'Ere Post-coloniale 1992, The Agreements Concerning Gaza and Jericho 1993, Biodiversity: Cultural and Ethical Aspects 1994, Cultural Diversity: Key to Survival in the 21st Century 1994, The New Challenges Facing the United Nations 1995, Dialogue de la Communication 1996, Al Quds (Jerusalem): Symbole et mémoire 1996, La décolonisation culturelle: défi majeur du 21ᵉ siècle 1996, Immigration as a Cultural Phenomenon 1997, The Path of a Mind 1997, Communication Dialogue 2000, Reglobalization of Globalization 2000, Intifadate 2000, Humiliation 2003.
Address: BP 53, Rabat, Morocco (office). *Telephone:* (37) 774-258 (office). *Fax:* (37) 757-151 (office). *E-mail:* elmandjra@elmandjra.org (home). *Website:* www.elmandjra.org (home).

ELMER, Michael B.; Danish lawyer; *Vice-President, Danish Maritime and Commercial Court;* b. 26 Feb. 1949, Copenhagen; pnr Annette Andersen; one d. *Education:* Univ. of Copenhagen. *Career:* civil servant, Ministry of Justice 1973–76, 1977–82, Head of Div. 1982–87, 1988–91, Deputy Perm. Sec., Head of Community Law and Human Rights Dept 1991–94; Assoc. Prof., Univ. of Copenhagen 1975–85; Deputy Judge, Hillerød 1976–77; Asst Public Prosecutor 1980–81; Judge, Court of Ballerup 1981–82; external examiner Danish law schools 1985–; High Court Judge (a.i.), Eastern High Court, Copenhagen 1987–88; Vice-Pres. (a.i.) Danish Maritime and Commercial Court, Copenhagen 1988, Vice Pres. 1997–; Rep. EC Court of Justice, Luxembourg 1991–94; Advocate-Gen. EC Court of Justice 1994–97; mem. governing council UNIDROIT, Rome 1999–; int. commercial arbitrator; Chair. and mem. numerous govt and int. orgs and cttees; Kt, Order of Dannebrog, Grand Cross, Order of Merit (Luxembourg). *Publications:* several books and articles on civil law (especially property law), penal law and community law.
Address: Sø-og Handelsretten, Bredgade 70, 1260, Copenhagen (office); Skovallëen 16, 2880 Bagsvaerd, Denmark (home). *Telephone:* 33-47-92-22 (office); 35-55-49-63 (home). *Fax:* 33-47-92-82 (office). *E-mail:* elmer@shret.dk (office); michael.elmer@tdcadsl.dk (home).

ELORZA CAVENGT, Francisco Javier; Spanish diplomatist; *Ambassador to Russia;* b. 17 Oct. 1945, Madrid. *Career:* fmr Asst Dir of Economy and Planning, Directorate of Marine Fishing; fmr Asst Dir for European Integration, Directorate of Int. Econ. Relations; fmr Asst Dir of Bilateral Econ. Relations; Perm. Rep. to EC, Brussels 1986, Sec.-Gen. for EC 1991, Perm. Rep. to EU 1994; Amb. to France 2000–04, to Russia 2004–.
Address: Embassy of Spain, 121069 Moscow, ul. B. Nikitskaya 50/8, Russia (office). *Telephone:* (495) 202-21-61 (office). *Fax:* (495) 291-91-71 (office). *E-mail:* embespru@mail.mae.es. *Website:* www.ispania.aha.ru (office).

ELRINGTON, Wilfred, SC; Belizean lawyer and politician; *Attorney-General and Minister of Foreign Affairs and Foreign Trade; Career:* mem. United Democratic Party; contested Pickstock constituency as an ind. 2002; Attorney-Gen. and Minister of Foreign Affairs and Foreign Trade 2008–.
Address: Ministry of the Attorney-General, General Office, Belmopan (office); Ministry of Foreign Affairs and Foreign Trade and of Tourism, Information and NEMO, New Administration Building, PO Box 174, Belmopan, Belize (office). *Telephone:* 822-2504 (Ministry of the Attorney-Gen.) (office); 822-2167 (Ministry of Foreign Affairs) (office). *Fax:* 822-3390 (Ministry of the Attorney-Gen.) (office); 822-2854 (Ministry of Foreign Affairs) (office). *E-mail:* scregistry@btl.net (office); belizemfa@btl.net (office). *Website:* www.belizelaw.org (office); www.mfa.gov.bz (office).

EMAN, Jan Hendrik Albert (Henny); Aruban politician and lawyer; *Leader, Arubaanse Volkspartij; Career:* Leader Arubaanse Volkspartij (AVP); Prime Minister of Aruba and Minister of Gen. Affairs 1986–89, 1993–2001.
Address: Arubaanse Volkspartij, Oranjestad, Aruba (office). *Telephone:* (8) 33500 (office). *Fax:* (8) 37870 (office).

EMERSON, David L., PhD; Canadian politician; *Minister of Foreign Affairs;* b. 1944, Montreal; m. Theresa Emerson. *Education:* Univ. of Alberta, Queen's Univ. *Career:* Researcher, Econ. Council of Canada, Ottawa 1972; Deputy Minister of Finance, BC 1984, 1990, later Deputy Minister to Premier and Pres. BC Trade Devt Corpn; Pres. and CEO Western and Pacific Bank of Canada, Vancouver 1986–90; Head, Vancouver Int. Airport Authority 1992; Pres. and CEO Canfor Corpn 1998; MP (Vancouver Kingsway) 2004–, Minister of Industry 2004, of Int. Trade and Minister for the Pacific Gateway and the Vancouver-Whistler Olympics 2006–2008, acting Minister for Foreign Affairs May–June 2008, Minister of Foreign Affairs June 2008–.
Address: Foreign Affairs and International Trade Canada, Lester B. Pearson Building, 125 Sussex Drive, Ottawa, ON K1A 0G2, Canada (office). *Telephone:* (613) 944-4000 (office). *Fax:* (613) 996-9709 (office). *E-mail:* enqserv@dfait-maeci.gc.ca (office). *Website:* www.international.gc.ca (office).

EMIÉ, Bernard; French diplomatist; *Ambassador to Turkey;* b. 6 Sept. 1958; m. Isabelle Chabannes La Palice Tournon; three c. *Education:* Institut d'études politiques de Paris, Ecole nationale d'administration. *Career:* joined Ministry of Foreign Affairs 1983, Tech. Adviser to Minister for Foreign Affairs 1986–88, N Africa and Middle East Div. 1992–93, Head, Cabinet of Minister of Foreign Affairs Alain Juppe 1993–95, Tech. and Diplomatic Adviser, Office of the Pres. 1995–98, Dir for N Africa and Middle East 2002–04; overseas positings include Second, then First Sec., Embassy in New Delhi 1984–86, First Sec., then Second Counsellor, Embassy in Washington, DC 1988–92; Amb. to Jordan 1998–2002, to Lebanon 2004–07, to Turkey 2007–; Chevalier, Légion d'Honneur 2005, Chevalier, Ordre national du mérite 2000.
Address: Embassy of France, Paris Caddesi 70, 06540 Kavaklıdere, Ankara, Turkey (office). *Telephone:* (312) 4554545 (office). *Fax:* (312) 4554527 (office). *E-mail:* ambafr@ada.net.tr (office). *Website:* www.ambafrance-tr.org (office).

EMILIO GAY, Lt-Gen. Giuseppe, BSc, MSc; Italian army officer; *Commander, Rapid Deployable Corps, NATO;* m.; two c. *Education:* Univ. of Turin, Univ. of Trieste, Lateran Univ. of Rome, Mil. Acad., Modena. *Career:* commissioned as Second Lt 1971, early assignments include First Lt in 182nd Garibaldi Armoured Regt, Capt. 13th M.O. Pascucci Tank Battalion; Staff Officer, N Eastern Dist. Estate and Facilities Office, Italian Army Gen. Staff Coll.; Army Gen. Staff Personnel Div., Chief, G3 Fifth Army Corps' HQ, Chief, G4 Army Gen. Staff Logistic Div. and First Command Force of Defence; Commdr Seventh Tank Battalion M.O. Di Dio, Vivaro, First Armoured Regt, Teulada; Deputy Commdr then Commdr 132nd Ariete Armoured Brigade, Pordenone, Commdr Multi-national Brigade West, Pec, Kosovo 1999–2000; Deputy Commdr Kosovo Force, Pristina 2003–2004, Deputy Commdr Allied Rapid Reaction Corps 2004–2007, Deputy Commdr (Stability) ISAF IX in Kabul 2006, Commdr Land Forces Support HQ; Commdr NATO Rapid Deployable Corps, Italy 2007–; Kt, Italian Mil. Order, Commdr, Italian Repub. Order of Merit; Italian Army Bronze Medal for Gallantry, First Class Medal Don Alfonso Henriques (Portugal), Gold Cross for Honour (Germany), Meritorious Officer Cross with Swords (Malta).
Address: North Atlantic Treaty Organization (NATO), boulevard Léopold III, 1110 Brussels, Belgium (office). *Telephone:* (2) 707-41-11 (office). *Fax:* (2) 707-45-79 (office). *E-mail:* natodoc@hq.nato.int (office). *Website:* www.nato.int (office).

EMILIOU, Nicholas, BA, LLM, PhD; Cypriot diplomatist and academic; *Permanent Representative, European Union; Education:* Univ. of Athens, Univ. of London. *Career:* early career as teacher of EC Law, Univ. Coll. London 1990–91, Univ. of Southampton 1991–93, Queen Mary and Westfield Coll. 1993–95, Univ. of Durham, UK 1995–97; Special Legal Adviser to Minister for Foreign Affairs 1994–97; apptd to diplomatic service 1997, Deputy Perm. Del., EU 1998–99, Amb. to Ireland 1999–2002, Perm. Rep., EU 2002–; fmr panel mem., Int. Court of Arbitration, The Hague. *Publications:* Principles of Proportionality in European Law: A Comparative Study.
Address: Permanent Mission of Cyprus, Council of the European Union, Square Ambiorix 2, Brussels 1000, Belgium (office). *Telephone:* (2) 735-35-10 (office). *Fax:* (2) 735-45-52 (office). *E-mail:* cy.perm.rep@mfa.gov.cy (office).

EMMANUEL, Ahipeaud Guebo Noël; Côte d'Ivoirian diplomatist. *Career:* fmr Chargé d'Affaires, Perm. Mission to UN, New York; currently Amb. to Mali.
Address: Embassy of Côte d'Ivoire, Square Patrice Lumumba, Immeuble CNAR, BP E 3644, Bamako, Mali (office). *Telephone:* 222-03-89 (office). *Fax:* 222-13-76 (office).

EMMANUELLI, Henri Joseph; French politician; *Chairman, Conseil général des Landes;* b. 31 May 1945, Eaux-Bonnes, Pyrénées-Atlantiques; m. Antonia Gonzalez 1967; one s. one d. *Education:* Lycée Louis-Barthou, Pau, Institut d'études politiques de Paris. *Career:* mem. staff Banque de l'Union Parisienne, then Compagnie financière de banque 1969–78; Deputy for Landes 1978–82, 1986–93, 1993–97, 2000–; Chair. Conseil général, Landes 1982–98, 2000–; Sec. of State for Overseas Territories and Depts 1981–83, for Budget 1983–86; Chair. Finance Comm. of Nat. Ass. 1991–93, Pres. Nat. Ass. 1992–93, Pres. Comm. for Finances, Gen. Econs and Planning 1997, 2000–; mem. Nat. Secr. Parti Socialiste 1987–, Leader 1994–95. *Publications:* Plaidoyer pour l'Europe 1992, Citadelles interdites 2000.
Address: Assemblée nationale, 75355 Paris; Parti Socialiste, 10 rue de Solférino, 75333 Paris Cedex, France; 22–24 rue Victor Hugo, 40000 Mont-de-Marsan (office). *E-mail:* presidence@cg40.fr (office); hemmanuelli@assemblee-nationale.fr (office).

ENDICOTT, John, BA, MA, PhD; American academic and fmr air force officer; *Co-President Woosong University; Vice Chancellor, SolBridge International School of Business;* m. Mitsuyo Kobayashi; one s. one d. *Education:* Ohio State Univ., Univ. of Omaha, Fletcher School of Law and Diplomacy. *Career:* 28 years with USAF; roles included Deputy Head, Political Science Dept, USAF Acad., Dir Int. Affairs, Planning Directorate, Air Force HQ, Pentagon, Assoc. Dean, Nat. War Coll., retd. (rank of Col) 1986; mem Sr Exec. Service, Dept of Defense 1986–89, Dir Inst. for Nat. Strategic Studies 1986–89; Founding Dir Center for Int. Strategy, Tech. and Policy (CISTP), Sam Nunn School of Int. Affairs, Georgia Inst. of Tech. 1989–2007, also Prof. of Int. Affairs 1989–2007; Co-Pres. Woosong Univ., Daejeon, South Korea 2007–, also Vice Chancellor, SolBridge Int. School of Business; Co-Chair. Council for US-Japan Security Relations; fmr Chair. Interim Secr. of Limited Nuclear Weapons-Free Zone for NE Asia; Exec. Vice-Chair. Southeast US-Korean Friendship Soc. 2000–; mem. Exec. Bd Japan-America Soc. of GA; Mike Mansfield Award, Japan—America Soc. of GA 1996. *Publications:* Japan's Nuclear Option, The Politics of East Asia, American Defense Policy, Regional Security Issues.
Address: SolBridge International School of Business, 151-13 SamSeong 1 Dong, Dong-gu, Daejeon 300-814, Republic of Korea (office). *Telephone:* (42) 630-8841 (office). *Fax:* (42) 630-8840 (office). *Website:* www.solbridge.ac.kr (office).

ENESTAM, Jan-Erik, MPolSci; Finnish politician; *Secretary-General, Nordic Council;* b. 12 March 1947, Västanfjäïd; m. Solveig V. Dahlqvist 1970; three c. *Career:* tourism researcher, Åland Provincial Govt 1972–74; researcher, Finnish Tourist Bd 1974; Head of Office, Åland Provincial Govt 1974–78; Municipal Man. Västanfjärd 1978–83; Project Man. Nordic Council of Ministers 1983–91; mem. Regional Policy Advisory Bd 1987–91; mem. Parl. 1991–; Chair. Västanfjärd Municipal Council 1989–96; Special Adviser to Minister of Defence 1990–91; Minister of Defence and Minister at Ministry of Social Affairs (Equality) and Health Jan.–April 1995; Minister of the Interior 1995–99, Minister of Defence, Nordic Co-operation and Foreign Affairs (Adjacent Areas) 1999–2003, of the Environment and Foreign Affairs (Nordic Co-operation) April 2003–07; Deputy Chair. Cen. Fed. of Fishing Industry 1986–94; Vice-Pres. Svenska Folkpartiet – SFP (Swedish People's Party) Parl. Group 1991–94, Chair. SFP 1998–2006; Sec.-Gen. Nordic Council 2007–; Commdr, Order of the White Rose of Finland 1996, Kt (Third Class), Order of Grand Duke Gediminas (Lithuania) 1997, Cross of Merit with Clasp, Armour Guild; Medal for Mil. Merit 1995, Medal of Merit, Cen. Chamber of Commerce of Finland.
Address: Nordic Council, Store Strandstræde 18, 1255 Copenhagen K, Denmark (office). *Telephone:* 33-96-04-00 (office). *Fax:* 33-11-18-70 (office). *E-mail:* jee@norden.org (office). *Website:* www.norden.org (office).

ENGLISH, Charles L., BA; American economist and diplomatist; *Ambassador to Bosnia and Herzegovina;* m. Patricia Espey-English; one s. one d. *Education:* Princeton Univ., New York Univ. *Career:* Vice-Consul/Econ. Officer, Panama City 1978–80, int. financial economist, Bureau for Econ. and Business Affairs, Dept of State 1982–85, Econ. Officer, Athens 1986–88, Special Asst to Deputy Sec., Dept of State 1988–89, Special Asst for Security Assistance and Arms Sales, later Exec. Asst to Under-Sec. for Int. Security Affairs 1989–92, Counselor for Econ. Affairs, Budapest 1992–95, Dir for Policy Coordination, Bureau for Int. Narcotics and Law Enforcement Affairs, Dept of State 1995–98, Deputy Chief of Mission, Zagreb 1998–2001, Dir Office of EU and Regional Affairs, Bureau for European and Eurasian Affairs, Dept of State 2002–03, Dir Office of S Cen. European Affairs 2003–06, Deputy Dir Office of Career Devt and Assignments, Bureau of Human Resources 2006–07, Amb. to Bosnia and Herzegovina 2007–.
Address: US Embassy, Alipašina 43, 71000 Sarajevo, Bosnia and Herzegovina (office). *Telephone:* (33) 445700 (office). *Fax:* (33) 659722

(office). *E-mail:* bhopa@state.gov (office). *Website:* sarajevo.usembassy.gov (office).

ENKHBAYAR, Nambaryn; Mongolian politician, writer and head of state; *President;* b. 1 June 1958, Ulan Bator; m. Onon Tsolmon 1986; four c. *Education:* High School No. 23, Ulan Bator, Literature Inst., Moscow, Leeds Univ., UK. *Career:* Ed. and Interpreter, Exec. Sec. and Head of Dept, Asscn of Mongolian Writers' 1980–90; Vice-Pres. and Ed., Mongolian Interpreters' Union 1990–92; First Vice-Chair. Culture and Art Devt Cttee 1990–92; Minister of Culture 1992–96; Leader of the Opposition 1997–2000; mem. Great Hural (Parl.) 1992–, Speaker 2004–05; President 2005–; Leader, Mongolian People's Revolutionary Party (MPRP) 1997–; Prime Minister of Mongolia 2000–04; World Bank Adviser on Asian Culture and Buddhist Religion 1998–; Chair. Mongolia-India Friendship Asscn; Head Nat. Council of Museums 1995–; Int. Pres. Alliance of Religions and Conservation 2003–; Govt of Mongolia Polar Star 1996; MPRP Politician of the Year 1997; Govt of Mongolia Star of the Flag for Work Achievements 2001. *Publications:* translated several classic Russian novels; About Mongolian Arts, Literature and Emptiness 1989, On the Indicators of Development from the Buddhist Point of View 1998, Some Thoughts on the Relationship between Buddhist Philosophy and Economics 1998, To Develop or Not to Develop 1998.
Address: State Palace, Ulan Bator 12 (office); Ikh Tenger, Suite 50-3, Ulan Bator, Mongolia (home). *Telephone:* (1) 323252 (office). *Fax:* (1) 329281 (office). *E-mail:* president@pmis.gov.mn (office). *Website:* www.pmis.gov.mn/president (office).

ENKHTSETSEG, Ochir; Mongolian diplomatist; *Permanent Representative, United Nations;* b. 26 Nov. 1961, Ulan Bator. *Education:* Moscow State Inst. of Int. Relations, Stanford Univ. *Career:* First Sec., then Counsellor, Perm. Mission to UN, New York 1992–97; Dir-Gen. Multilateral Co-operation Dept, Ministry of Foreign Affairs 2000–07, Sec.-Gen. Fifth Int. Conf. of New or Restored Democracies 2003, Int. Follow-up Conf. 2006; Perm. Rep. to UN, New York 2007–; fmr mem. Govt Advisory Bd, Int. Centre for Democratic Transition, Budapest, Mongol Cultural Heritage Int. Asscn.
Address: Permanent Mission of Mongolia to the United Nations, 6 East 77th Street, New York, NY 10021, USA (office). *Telephone:* (212) 737-3874 (office). *Fax:* (212) 861-9460 (office). *E-mail:* mongolia@un.int (office). *Website:* www.un.int/mongolia (office).

ENOKSEN, Hans; Greenlandic politician; *Prime Minister, Greenland Home Rule Government;* b. 1956. *Career:* mem. Siumut Party, Chair. 2001; mem. Parl. 1995–; Minister for Fisheries, Hunting and Settlements 2001–; Prime Minister, Greenland Home Rule Govt Dec. 2002–; Greenland Home Rule Nersonaat in Gold 2003.
Address: Greenland Home Rule Government, POB 1015, 3900 Nuuk, Greenland (office). *Telephone:* 345000 (office). *Fax:* 325002 (office). *E-mail:* info@gh.gl (office). *Website:* www.nanoq.gl (office).

ENOSAKHARE EDOBOR, Edwin; Nigerian diplomatist; *High Commissioner to Cameroon;* b. 10 May 1947, Benin City; m.; four c. *Career:* postings at Embassies in Moscow, Washington, DC, Cairo and Dublin; Consul in New York 2003–04; High Commr to Cameroon 2004–.
Address: High Commission of Nigeria, Quartier Bastos, BP 448, Yaoundé, Cameroon (office). *Telephone:* 2223-5551 (office).

EÖRSI, Mátyás, PhD; Hungarian lawyer and politician; *Chairman, European Affairs Committee, Hungarian National Assembly;* b. 24 Nov. 1954, Budapest; m.; three c. *Education:* Eötvös Loránd Univ., Budapest. *Career:* founding mem. Alliance of Free Democrats (SZDSZ) and mem. Nat. Cttee, also Legal Rep. 1988, mem. Nat. Governing Cttee 1991, 2003–, Chair. SZDSZ Goodwill and Ethics Cttee 1993–98, Foreign Affairs Spokesman 1994–, Deputy Leader Parl. Group 2002–06, Leader Parl. Group 2007–; mem. Exec. Office Liberal Int. 1997–, Vice-Pres. 2002–; foreign trade lawyer 1981 and worked as legal advisor at int. trading co.; est. Eörsi and Pnrs 1987; following regime change became regular mem. Council of Europe Parl. Ass.; Head, Hungarian del. with observer status Ass. of WEU and Head, del. to Parl. Ass. of Cen. European Initiative; mem. Parl. 1990–; Chair. Foreign Affairs Cttee, Nat. Ass. 1994–97; State Sec. for Policy, Ministry of Foreign Affairs 1997–98; mem. Hungarian Parl. del. to Council of Europe 1998–; Leader, Liberal faction, Council of Europe Parl. Ass. 2001–; Vice-Chair. Nat. Ass. Foreign Affairs Cttee 2002–06; mem. OSCE Parl. Ass. 2002–; Chair. Nat. Ass. European Affairs Cttee 2004–, Foreign Affairs and Hungarian Minorities Abroad Cttee, Nat. Ass., 2006–.
Address: Hungarian National Assemby, 1357 Budapest, Kossuth tér 1–3, Hungary (office). *Telephone:* (1) 441-5000 (office); (1) 441-5765 (office). *Fax:* (1) 441-5952 (office). *Website:* www.parlament.hu (office).

EPHREM, Gen. Sebhat; Eritrean politician and army officer; *Minister of Defence; Career:* served in Eritrean Armed Forces, rank of Gen.; currently Minister of Defence.
Address: Ministry of Defence, POB 629, Asmara, Eritrea (office). *Telephone:* (1) 165952 (office). *Fax:* (1) 124990 (office).

ERAKAT, Saeb, BA, MA, PhD; Palestinian politician and journalist; b. 1955, East Jerusalem; m. two s. two d. *Education:* San Francisco State Univ., USA and Bradford Univ., UK. *Career:* fmr journalist Al Quds daily; Lecturer in Political Science An-Najah Univ. 1983, fmr Sec.-Gen. Arab Studies Soc.; mem. negotiating team Oslo Peace Process 1995; Head Palestinian Negotiation Steering and Monitoring Cttee 1996, currently Chief Palestinian Peace Negotiator; elected mem. Palestinian Legis. Council, Jericho 1996; Minister of Negotiation Affairs, Palestinian Nat. Authority (PNA) 2004–06; Hon. PhD (Peru) 2004. *Publications include:* eight books and numerous articles on foreign policy.
Address: c/o Fatah, Ramallah, Palestinian Autonomous Areas (office). *E-mail:* fateh@fateh.org. *Website:* www.fateh.net.

ERÇEL, Gazi; Turkish banker; b. 20 Feb. 1945, Gelibolu; m. Zeynel Erçel; one d. *Education:* Ankara Univ., Vanderbilt Univ., Tenn. *Career:* bank examiner, Ministry of Finance 1967–77; Deputy Dir-Gen. of Treasury 1977–82; Asst to Exec. Dir IMF, Washington DC 1982–86; Dir-Gen. of Treasury and Foreign Trade 1987–89; Gov. Cen. Bank of Turkey 1996–2001; Cen. Banker of the Year Award, Global Finance, Prague 2000. *Address:* c/o Türkiye Cumhuriyet Merkez Bankasi AS, Istiklal Cad. 10, 06100 Ulus, Ankara, Turkey. *Website:* www.tcmb.gov.tr (office).

ERDENECHULUUN, Luvsangiin; Mongolian diplomatist and politician; b. 10 Oct. 1948, Ulan Bator; m. Sukh-Ochiryn Solongo 1969; two s. one d. *Education:* State Inst. of Int. Relations, Moscow and Diplomatic Acad. Moscow. *Career:* officer, Dept of Int. Relations, Ministry of Foreign Affairs 1972–80; First Sec. Perm. Mission of Mongolia at UN 1980–84; Head, Press and Information Dept Ministry of Foreign Affairs 1985–86; Head, Dept of Int. Orgs 1988–90; Deputy Perm. Rep. to UN 1990, Perm. Rep. 1992–96; Adviser to Pres. of Mongolia 1996–97; Minister of Foreign Affairs 2000–04; Distinguished Service Medal, Order of Polar Star.
Address: c/o Ministry of Foreign Affairs, Peace Avenue Building 7A, Ulan Bator, Mongolia (office).

ERDMAN, Richard W., MA; American diplomatist; b. 1945, Oak Park, Ill.; m. Sibyl Brundage Nye; two c. *Education:* Princeton Univ. and Johns Hopkins School for Advanced Int. Studies. *Career:* Peace Corps volunteer in Turkey 1967–69, Consular Officer, Izmir 1971–73, Cyprus Desk Officer 1973–75, Political Officer, Nicosia 1975–77, Political Officer, Belgrade 1978–81, Spain Desk Officer 1983–85, Sr Watch Officer, State Dept Operations Center 1982–83, Political Counselor and Political-Mil. Affairs Officer, Lisbon 1985–89, Sr Area Advisor to US Del. to UN Gen. Ass. 1989, Deputy Dir for Northern Europe 1991–93, Deputy Head, Int. Border Monitoring Mission in Serbia and Deputy Dir for Eastern Europe 1993–94, Political Counselor, Tel-Aviv 1995–98, Dir for Jordan, Lebanon and Syria, Bureau of Near Eastern Affairs and Special Envoy and Head of US Del. to Israel-Lebanon Monitoring Group 2000–02, Sr Area Advisor for Middle East to US Del. to UN Gen. Ass. 2002, Amb. to Algeria 2003–06; Superior Honor Awards 1998, 2000, Sr Performance Pay Awards 2000, 2001, 2002, 2004, 2005, Presidential Meritorious Service Award 2001.
Address: US Department of State, 2201 C Street NW, Washington, DC 20520, USA (office). *Telephone:* (202) 647-4000 (office). *Fax:* (202) 647-6738 (office). *Website:* www.state.gov (office).

ERDOGAN, Recep Tayyip, BA; Turkish politician; *Prime Minister;* b. 1954, Rize; m.; four c. *Education:* Marmara Univ., Istanbul. *Career:* professional footballer 1969–80; elected Chair. Nat. Salvation Party Youth Org. early 1970s; Chair. Istanbul Br. Welfare Party 1985; Mayor of Metropolitan Istanbul 1994–98, tenure of office ended by court decree 1998, convicted of having read a provocative poem in public, imprisoned for four months and banned for life from holding public office; mem. Virtue Party 1998–2001; Founder and Chair. AK Partisi – AKP (Justice and Development Party), ruling party in Turkey following 2002 elections, constitutional ban preventing him from holding public office overturned Jan. 2003; Prime Minister of Turkey March 2003–; Founder Democratization and Action Movt; European of the Year 2004, Agricola Medal, UN Food and Agric. Org. 2007.
Address: Office of the Prime Minister, Başbakanlik, Bakanliklar, Ankara (office); AK Partisi, Genel Merkezi Ceyhun Atif Kansu Cad., No. 202 Balgat, Ankara, Turkey (office). *Telephone:* (312) 4189056 (office). *Fax:* (312) 4180476 (office). *E-mail:* info@basbakanlik.gov.tr (office). *Website:* www.basbakanlik.gov.tr (office); www.akparti.org.tr (office).

ERDOS, André; Hungarian diplomatist; *Senior Adviser, International Centre for Democratic Transition (ICDT), Budapest;* b. 1941, Algiers, Algeria; m. Katalin Pintér 1965; one d. *Education:* Moscow State Inst. for Int. Relations, Budapest School of Political Sciences. *Career:* joined Hungarian Ministry of Foreign Affairs 1965; attaché, Morocco 1968–72; staff mem., CSCE Dept Ministry of Foreign Affairs 1972–78; assigned to Perm. Mission of Hungary at UN, New York 1978–83; del. to UN Gen. Ass. 1984, 1985, 1989; Adviser to Minister of Foreign Affairs of Hungary 1984–86; Head of Hungary's del. to Vienna CSCE follow-up meeting 1986–89; Perm. Rep. to UN 1990–94, 1997–2001; Pres. UN Disarmament and Int. Security Comm. 2001–02; Hungarian Rep., UN Security Council 1992–93; Deputy State Sec. for Multilateral Affairs, Ministry of Foreign Affairs 1994–97; Amb. to France 2002–06; currently Sr Adviser Int. Centre for Democratic Transition, Budapest; Prof., Corvinus Univ., Budapest; mem. Prime Minister's Council on Foreign and Security Policy; Hon. Prof., Budapest Inst. for Grad. Int. and Diplomatic Studies 1999; Middle Cross of Order of Merit, Hungary, Commdr, Légion d'honneur, Grand Croix, Ordre nat. du Mérite. *Publications:* Co-operation in the United Nations between Socialist and Developing Countries 1981, Soviet-German Relations 1939–41 1984, The Circumstances of the Birth of the 1941 Soviet-German Non-Aggression Pact 1987, Geography vs. Political Reality at the United Nations 2001, Sorsfordító Esztendök (Crucial Years) 2004; numerous articles on int. affairs.
Address: International Centre for Democratic Transition, Arvacska u.12, Budapest 1022, Hungary (office). *Telephone:* (1) 438-0820 (office). *Fax:* (1) 438-0821 (office). *E-mail:* andreerdos@yahoo.com (office). *Website:* www.icdt.hu (office).

ERELI, J(oseph) Adam, BA, MA; American diplomatist; *Ambassador to Bahrain; Education:* Yale Univ., Fletcher School of Law and Diplomacy, Tufts Univ. *Career:* worked as journalist and human rights activist in Paris, France; joined Foreign Service in 1989, served abroad as Jr Officer in Cairo, Program Officer in Damascus, Cultural Affairs Officer in Addis Ababa, and Public Affairs Officer in San'a, served in Washington, DC as Dir Office of Press and Public Affairs, Bureau of Near Eastern Affairs and as Dir Office of Press Relations, Bureau of Public Affairs, Deputy Chief of Mission, Doha, Qatar 2000–03, Deputy Spokesman, Dept of State 2003–06 (oversaw Office of Press Relations, Office of Regional Media Outreach, Office of Broadcast Services, Foreign Press Centers and Press Office at USAID), Sr Advisor to Under-Sec. for Public Diplomacy for Overseas Communications, London 2006–07, Amb. to Bahrain 2007–.
Address: US Embassy, PO Box 26431, Building 979, Road 3119, Block 331, Zinj, Manama, Bahrain (office). *Telephone:* 17242700 (office). *Fax:* 17272594 (office). *E-mail:* consularmanama@state.gov (office). *Website:* bahrain.usembassy.gov (office).

ERJAVEC, Karl Viktor; Slovenian government official; *Minister of Defence;* b. 21 June 1960, Aiseau, Belgium; m.; two d. *Education:* Univ. of Ljubljana. *Career:* mem. Kranj Urban Municipality Ass. Exec. Council 1990–95, apptd Sec. for Gen. Admin and other Legal Affairs 1990; fmr Head, Office of Human Rights Ombudsman, Repub. of Slovenia 1995–2000, fmr Dir Expert Service; State Sec. for Judicial Admin, Ministry of Justice 2001–04; Minister of Defence 2004–. *Publications:* numerous articles on human rights and judicial system functions.
Address: Ministry of Defence, Vojkova 55, 1000 Ljubljana, Slovenia (office). *Telephone:* (1) 4712373 (office). *Fax:* (1) 4319145 (office). *E-mail:* karl.erjavec@mors.si (office). *Website:* www.mors.si (office).

EROĞLU, Derviş, PhD; Turkish-Cypriot politician; *Chairman, Ulusal Bırlık Partisi (National Unity Party);* b. 1938, Ergazi Magosa Dist; m.; four c. *Education:* Univ. of Istanbul. *Career:* fmr urologist, Ankara; mem. Parl. 1976–; Chair. Ulusal Bırlık Partisi (Nat. Unity Party) 1981–; Prime Minister 'Turkish Repub. of Northern Cyprus' 1985–93, 1996–2003.
Address: National Unity Party, 9 Atatürk Meydanı, Lefkoşa (Nicosia), Mersin 10, 'Turkish Republic of Northern Cyprus' (office). *Telephone:* (22) 73972.

ERRERA, Gérard, CVO; French diplomat; *Secretary General, Ministry of Foreign Affairs;* b. 30 Oct. 1943, Brive; m. Virginie Bedoya; three c. *Education:* Inst. d'Etudes Politiques and Ecole Nat. d'Admin. Paris. *Career:* First Sec. Washington, DC 1971–75; Special Adviser to Minister of Foreign Affairs 1975–77, 1980–81; Political Counsellor, Madrid 1977–80; Special Adviser to the Minister of Foreign Affairs 1980–81; Consul-Gen. San Francisco 1982–85; Dir of Int. Relations, French Atomic Energy Comm. and Gov. for France, IAEA 1985–90; Amb. to Conf. on Disarmament, Geneva 1991–95; Amb. and Perm. Rep. to NATO, Brussels 1995–98; Deputy Sec.-Gen. and Dir-Gen. of Political Affairs, Ministry of Foreign Affairs 1998–2002; Amb. to UK 2002–07; Sec.-Gen. Ministry of Foreign Affairs 2007–; Chevalier, Légion d'honneur; Officier de l'Ordre nat. du Mérite.

Address: Ministry of Foreign Affairs, 37 quai d'Orsay, 75351 Paris 07, France (office). *Telephone:* 1-43-17-53-53 (office). *Fax:* 1-43-17-52-03 (office). *E-mail:* gerard.errera@diplomatie.gouv.fr (office). *Website:* www .diplomatie.gouv.fr (office).

ERWA, Lt-Gen. Elfatih Mohamed; Sudanese diplomatist; b. 11 May 1950, Khartoum; m. Kawther Amin Mohamed 1973; seven c. *Education:* Sudan Military Coll. *Career:* fmr pilot; Adviser to Pres. of Repub. 1989–90; State Minister in the Presidency for Nat. Security 1990–95, for Nat. Defence 1995–96; Perm. Rep. to UN 1996–2006; Order of Bravery. *Address:* c/o Ministry of Foreign Affairs, POB 873, Khartoum, Sudan (office). *Website:* www.sudanmfa.com (office).

ERWIN, Alexander (Alec), BEcons; South African politician, academic and trade union official; *Minister of Public Enterprises;* b. 17 Jan. 1948; m. *Education:* Durban High School, Univ. of Natal. *Career:* Lecturer, Dept of Econs, Univ. of Natal 1971–78; visiting lecturer Centre of Southern African Studies, Univ. of York 1974–75; Gen. Sec. Trade Union Advisory and Co-ordinating Council 1977–79; Gen. Sec. Fed. of SA Trade Unions 1979–81; Br. Sec. Nat. Union of Textile Workers 1981–83; Educ. Sec. Fed. of SA Trade Unions 1983–85; Educ. Sec. Congress of SA Trade Unions 1986–88; Nat. Educ. Officer Nat. Union of Metalworkers 1988–93; Interim Exec. mem. ANC S Natal Region 1989; Exec. mem. ANC Western Areas Br. 1990–91; fmr mem. Devt and Reconstruction Cttee, Natal Peace Accord; fmr Congress of SA Trade Unions rep. at Nat. Econ. Forum; fmr Ed. ANC Reconstruction and Devt Programme; Deputy Minister of Finance 1994; Minister of Trade and Industry 1996–99, 1999–2004, of Public Enterprises 2004–; Dr hc 1997. *Address:* Ministry of Public Enterprises, Private Bag X15, Hatfield 0023, South Africa. *Telephone:* (12) 4311000 (office); (12) 4311098 (office). *Fax:* (12) 4302853 (office); (12) 4311039 (office). *E-mail:* info@dpe.gov.za (office). *Website:* www.dpe.gov.za (office).

ESCOBAR CERDA, Luis, MPA; Chilean economist and academic; *Professor of Economics, University of Chile;* b. 10 Feb. 1927; m. 2nd Helga Koch 1973; five c. *Education:* Univ. de Chile and Harvard Univ. *Career:* Dir School of Econs, Univ. de Chile 1951–55, Dean of Faculty of Econs 1955–64; Minister of Econ. Devt and Reconstruction 1961–63; mem. Inter-American Cttee for Alliance for Progress 1964–66; Exec. Dir IMF 1964–66, 1968–70, IBRD 1966–68; Special Rep. for Inter-American Orgs IBRD 1970–75; Trustee of Population Reference Bureau 1968–73; mem. Advisory Cttee on Population and Devt OAS 1968–73, Council Soc. for Int. Devt 1969–72; Deputy Exec. Sec. Jt Bank/Fund Devt Cttee 1975–79; Prof., Georgetown Univ. 1975–79, George Washington Univ. 1977, Dept of Econs, American Univ. 1978–79; CEO private banks 1979–84; Minister of Finance 1984–85; Amb. to UN and Int. Orgs in Geneva 1986–90; Consultant on econ. and financial matters 1990–; Prof., Univ. of Chile 1990–, Dean, Faculty of Business Admin., Iberoamerican Univ. for Sciences and Tech. 1997–2001; Prof. Univ. del Pacifico 2002–, Acad. Mem. for Life and Extraordinary Prof., Univ. of Chile; Vice-Pres. Partido Radical Social Demócrata 1994–95; Gold Medal for Best Graduate in Econs and Honor Medal, Univ. of Chile; recognition for contribution to teaching and research in econs 1996. *Publications:* The Stock Market 1959, Organization for Economic Development 1961, A Stage of the National Economic Development 1962, Considerations on the Tasks of the University 1963, Organizational Requirements for Growth and Stability 1964, The Role of the Social Sciences in Latin America 1965, The Organization of Latin American Government 1968, Multinational Corporations in Latin America 1973, International Control of Investments 1974, External Financing in Latin America 1976, 1978, Mi Testimonio 1991, Financial Problems of Latin American Economic Integration 1992, Globalization and Challenges of Globalization 2000–01; articles in newspapers. *Address:* 1724 Sánchez Fontecilla, Santiago 10, Chile (home). *Telephone:* (2) 2080227 (home). *Fax:* (2) 2286367 (home). *E-mail:* escobarcerda@ yahoo.com (home).

ESCUDERO DURÁN, Lorena, PhD; Ecuadorean academic and politician; *Secretary for Migration;* b. 1965. *Education:* Univ. of Cuenca, Nat. Autonomous Univ. of Mexico and Univ. of Alicante, Spain. *Career:* Dir Centre for Latinamerican Social and Political Studies, Univ. of Cuenca 2002–07, Coordinator of Postgraduate Studies 2003–07; Minister of National Defence Feb.–Aug. 2007; Sec. for Migration 2007–. *Publications:* numerous articles in professional journals. *Address:* Secretariat for Migration, Palacio Nacional, García Moreno 1043, Quito, Ecuador (office). *Telephone:* (2) 221-6300 (office). *Website:* www .presidencia.gov.ec (office).

ESPINAL, Flavio Dario, BL, MA, PhD; Dominican Republic lawyer and diplomatist; *Ambassador to USA;* m. Minerva Del Risco de Espinal; two d. *Education:* Pontificia Universidad Católica Madre y Maestra, Univ. of

Essex, UK, Univ. of Virginia, USA. *Career:* fmr Co-ordinator Civil Society Agenda during the Summits of the Americas; fmr Prof. of Law, Dir Univ. Center of Political and Social Studies and Center for the Study, Prevention and Resolution of Conflicts, and Dean of the Law School, Pontificia Universidad Católica Madre y Maestra, Recinto Santo Tomás de Aquino, Santo Domingo; practised law in Santiago and Santo Domingo; consultant for both pvt. sector and various int. orgs; published weekly op-ed. column in El Caribe newspaper and co-produced En Contexto TV programme; Amb. to OAS 1996–2000, Chair. Perm. Council, Cttee on Legal and Political Issues, Cttee on Hemispheric Security, Amb. to USA 2005–. *Publications:* Constitutionalism and Political Processes in the Dominican Republic; numerous articles and essays on political and constitutional issues in various academic journals. *Address:* Embassy of the Dominican Republic, 1715 22nd Street, NW, Washington, DC 20008, USA (office). *Telephone:* (202) 332-6280 (office). *Fax:* (202) 265-8057 (office). *E-mail:* embassy@us.serex.gov.do (office). *Website:* www.domrep.org (office).

ESPINOSA CANTELLANO, Patricia, MA; Mexican government official, politician and diplomatist; *Secretary of Foreign Affairs; Education:* Ibero-American Univ. *Career:* mem. Nat. Action Party (PAN) 1987–, Head Secr. of Political Promotion of Women, mem. Nat. Exec. Cttee, Head of Sub-coordination for Culture, Educ. and Information, PAN Parl. Group; mem. 57th Legislature, Chamber of Deputies 1997–2000, mem. Equity and Gender Cttee; Chair. Querétaro Municipal Directive Cttee, Head State Secr. of Political Promotion of Women, Head Secr. of Social Devt, Municipality of Querétaro 2000–01; Pres. Nat. Women's Inst. of Mexico (Inmujeres) 2001–06; Sec. of Foreign Affairs 2006–; participated in Non-Governmental Org. (NGO) Forums, Fourth World Conf. on Women, Beijing; Chair. Bd, Regional Conf. on Women of Latin America and the Caribbean; mem. Mexican Asscn for the Integral Advancement of the Family. *Address:* Secretariat of State for Foreign Affairs, Avda Ricardo Flores Magón 2, Col. Guerrero, Del. Cuauhtémoc, 06995 México, DF, Mexico (office). *Telephone:* (55) 5063-3000 (office). *Fax:* (55) 5063-3195 (home). *E-mail:* comentario@sre.gob.mx (office). *Website:* www.sre.gob.mx (office).

ESPIRITU, Edgardo B.; Philippine diplomatist; *Ambassador to UK;* m. Lydia Baskinas Espiritu. *Education:* Univ. of Philippines. *Career:* fmr Owner Westmont Bank; Finance Sec. 1998–2000; Co-Chair. ASEAN Special Jt Ministerial Meeting, Manila 1999; Amb. to UK and Perm. Rep. to IMO 2003–. *Address:* Embassy of the Philippines, 6–8 Suffolk Street, London, SW1Y 4HG, England (office). *Telephone:* (20) 7451-1800 (office). *Fax:* (20) 7930-9787 (office). *E-mail:* embassy@philemb.co.uk (office). *Website:* philembassy-uk.org (office).

ESPOSITO, John L., PhD; American academic; *University Professor and Founding Director, Prince Alwaleed Bin Talal Center for Muslim-Christian Understanding, Georgetown University;* b. 19 May 1940, Brooklyn, NY; m. Jeanette P. Esposito 1965. *Education:* Temple Univ., Univ. of PA, Middle East Centre for Arab Studies, Lebanon. *Career:* Assoc. Prof. and Chair. Dept of Religious Studies, Coll. of the Holy Cross 1975–84, Prof. 1984–95, Loyola Prof. of Middle East Studies and Prof. of Islamic Studies 1991–95; Adjunct Prof. of Diplomacy, Fletcher School of Law and Diplomacy, Tufts Univ. 1986–93, Prof. and Dir Centre for Int. Studies 1987–91; Founding Dir Prince Alwaleed Bin Talal Center for Muslim-Christian Under-standing, Georgetown Univ., also Prof. of Religion and Int. Affairs 1993–, Univ. Prof. 2000–; Pres.-Elect, Pres. and Past-Pres. Middle East Studies Asscn of N America 1988–91; Pres. American Council for Study of Islamic Societies 1989–92; mem. numerous editorial bds, including Middle East Policy, Journal of Islamic Studies, American Journal of Islamic Social Sciences, Journal of Church and State; Visiting Scholar, Center for Study of World Religions, Harvard Univ. 1979–80; Sr Assoc. St Anthony's Coll., Oxford, UK 1982–83; mem. American Soc. for the Study of Religion 1988; Hon. DHumLitt Letters (Immaculata Univ.) 2006; World Book Prize (Iran) 1996, Award for Outstanding Teaching, School of Foreign Service, Georgetown Univ. 2003, Quaid-i-Azzam Award for Outstanding Contribs in Literature and Islamic Studies (Pakistan) 2005, Martin E. Marty Award for the Public Understanding of Religion, American Acad. of Religion 2005. *Publications:* Oxford Encyclopedia of the Modern Islamic World (Ed.-in-Chief) 1995, Oxford History of Islam (Ed.-in-Chief) 2000, Oxford Dictionary of Islam (Ed.-in-Chief); author of more than 25 books including Islam: Women in Muslim Family Law 1982, Islam: The Straight Path 1992, What Everyone Should Know about Islam, Questions and Answers, Islam and Democracy and Makers of Contemporary Islam (with J. Voll) 1996, The Islamic Threat: Myth or Reality? 1999, Islam and Politics 1999, What Everyone Needs to Know About Islam 2002, Unholy War: Terror in the Name of Islam 2002, Geography of Religion 2004, The Islamic World Past

and Present 2004; Modernizing Islam (with F. Burgat); Political Islam: Radicalism, Revolution or Reform?, Iran at the Crossroads (with R. K. Ramazani), Islam, Gender and Social Change (with Y. Haddad).
Address: Prince Alwaleed Bin Talal Center for Muslim-Christian Understanding, Georgetown University, 37th and 0 Streets, NW, ICC 260, Washington DC, 20057, USA (office). *Telephone:* (202) 687-8375 (office). *Fax:* (202) 687-8376 (office). *E-mail:* jle2@georgetown.edu (office). *Website:* cmcu.georgetown.edu (office).

ESPOT MIRÓ, Xavier, LLB; Andorran politician and diplomatist; *Ambassador to Spain;* b. 14 Feb. 1953, Escaldes-Endordany; m.; two c. *Education:* Univ. of Barcelona. *Career:* mem. Parl. 1989–92; Minister of Tourism and Sports 1992–93; Amb. to France 1994–95, to Spain (also accred to Monaco) 2007–, also Perm. Rep. to UN, Geneva 2008–.
Address: Embassy of Andorra, Alcalá 73, 28009 Madrid, Spain (office). *Telephone:* (91) 4317453 (office). *Fax:* (91) 5776341 (office). *E-mail:* embajada@embajadaandorra.es (office).

ESSENHIGH, Adm. Sir Nigel, Kt, KCB; British naval officer; b. 1944; m. Susie Essenhigh. *Education:* Royal Coll. of Defence Studies. *Career:* joined Royal Navy 1963, qualified as Prin. Warfare Officer, specializing in navigation 1972, served in variety of ships, Commdr Type 42 Destroyers HMS Nottingham and HMS Exeter; Hydrographer of the Navy, Chief Exec. UK Hydrographic Office, with rank of Rear Adm.; several appointments at Ministry of Defence including Asst Chief of Defence Staff (Programmes); promoted to Adm., C-in-C Fleet; C-in-C E Atlantic (NATO) and Commdr Allied Naval Forces N (NATO); First Sea Lord and Chief of Naval Staff 2001–02; Fellow Nautical Inst., Royal Inst. of Navigation; mem. Hon. Co. of Master Mariners; Younger Brother Trinity House; ADC.
Address: c/o Ministry of Defence, Main Building, Whitehall, London, SW1A 2HB, England (office).

ESSIMI MENYE, Lazare; Cameroonian government official; *Minister of Finance and Economy;* b. Mfomakap; m.; four c. *Education:* Institut des Statistiques et d'Économie Appliquée, Morocco, Institut National des Sciences et Techniques Nucléaires, Saclay, France. *Career:* UNDP adviser for Rwanda 1990–92; adviser to World Bank 1994; fmr govt adviser for IMF, Washington, DC; fmr Minister-Del. in charge of the budget, Ministry of Finance and Economy, Minister of Finance and Economy 2007–.
Address: Ministry of Economy and Finance, BP 13750, Quartier Administratif, Yaoundé, Cameroon (office). *Telephone:* 7723-2099 (office). *Website:* www.camnet.cm/investir/minfi.

ESSY, Amara, LLM; Côte d'Ivoirian diplomatist; b. 20 Dec. 1944, Bouake; m. Lucie Essy 1971; three s. three d. *Career:* Chief of Div. of Econ. Relations 1970; First Counsellor, Ivory Coast Embassy, Brazil 1971–73, Ivory Coast Mission to the UN 1973–75; Perm. Rep. to the UN Office, Geneva 1975–81, to UNIDO, Vienna 1975–81; Amb. to Switzerland 1978–81; Perm. Rep. to the UN (and non-resident Amb. to Argentina and Cuba), New York 1981–91; Pres. UN Security Council 1990–91; Minister of Foreign Affairs 1990–98; Pres. 49th Session UN Gen. Ass. 1994–95; Minister of State, Minister of Foreign Affairs in charge of Int. Co-operation 1998–99; Sec.-Gen. OAU Sept. 2001–02; Chair. (interim) African Union July 2002–03; fmr UN Special Envoy for Countries Affected by the War in the Democratic Repub. of the Congo (DRC); participated in the following UN confs: Law of the Sea (Caracas, Geneva, New York), Int. Women's Year (Mexico City), Econ. Co-operation among Developing Countries, UNCTAD (Nairobi, Manila) and of the codification of int. law; meetings of the Econ. and Social Council and Comm. on Human Rights.
Address: c/o Ministry of Foreign Affairs, Bloc Ministériel, blvd Angoulvand, BP V109, Abidjan, Côte d'Ivoire.

ETEKI MBOUMOUA, William-Aurélien, LicenDroit; Cameroonian politician; *President, Red Cross (Cameroon);* b. 20 Oct. 1933, Douala; m. Naimi Bessy Eyewe; one s. one d. *Education:* Ecole Nat. de la France d'Outre-mer, Paris. *Career:* Prefect for Nkam 1959, for Sanage Maritime 1960–61; Minister of Educ., Youth and Culture 1961–68; mem. Exec. Council, UNESCO 1962–68, Pres. of Conf., UNESCO 1968–70; Special Adviser, with rank of Minister, to Pres. of United Republic of Cameroon 1971–74, 1978–80; Minister charged with Special Functions at the Presidency 1978; Co-Minister in charge of Missions 1980–84, Minister of Foreign Affairs 1984–87; Sec.-Gen. OAU 1974–78; Special Rep. of UN Sec.-Gen. on Small Arms Proliferation in West Africa, mem. Eminent Persons Group on curbing illicit trafficking in Small Arms and Light Weapons 1999; Nat. Pres. Cameroon Red Cross Soc. 1994–; mem. Ind. Comm. for implementation of proposals in UNDP document Proposals for Africa in this Millennium 1999, Jury du Prix UNESCO Ville pour la Paix; Commdr des Palmes académiques, Grand Officier de l'Ordre de la Valeur and many

other decorations. *Publications:* Un certain humanisme 1970, Démocratiser la culture 1974; and many articles on education and African culture.
Address: PO Box 631, Yaoundé (office); PO Box 1155, Yaoundé, Cameroon (home). *Telephone:* 2224177 (office); 2202592 (home). *Fax:* 2224177 (office); 2202592 (home). *E-mail:* crol-Rcam@iccnet_cm (office).

ETIENNE, Lionel; Haitian diplomatist; *Ambassador to France; Career:* fmr Consul Gen. in Martinique, Guadeloupe, French Guyana and New York; fmr Pres. French-Haitian Chamber of Commerce; fmr Vice-Pres. Chamber of Commerce and Industry of Haiti; currently Amb. to France.
Address: Embassy of Haiti, 10 rue Théodule Ribot, BP 275, Paris 75017, France (office). *Telephone:* 1-47-63-47-78 (office). *Fax:* 1-42-27-02-05 (office). *E-mail:* letienne.ambahaiti.paris@noos.fr (office).

ETTALHI, Giadalla Azzuz Belgassem, BSc; Libyan diplomatist; *Permanent Representative, United Nations;* b. 1939; m.; four c. *Education:* Univ. of Liege, Belgium. *Career:* fmr Minister of Communications, Minister of Industry, Minister of Industry and Mineral Resources, Head of Mining and Geology Dept, Ministry of Industry; Sec.-Gen. People's Cttee 1979–84, 1986–87; Sec. of Communications 1984–86; Minister of Foreign Affairs 1986–90; Minister of Strategic Industries 1990–94; Sec., Great Man-Made River Project 1994–98; Minister of Planning and Sec.-Gen. Planning Bd 1998–2000; Perm. Rep. to UN, New York 2007–. *Publications:* Lest We Die From Thirst, I Made Myself Heard (Point of View).
Address: Permanent Mission of Libya to the United Nations, 309–315 East 48th Street, New York, NY 10017, USA (office). *Telephone:* (212) 752-5775 (office). *Fax:* (212) 593-4787 (office). *E-mail:* libya@un.int (office). *Website:* www.libya-un.org (office).

EUSTACE, Arnhim; Saint Vincent and the Grenadines politician and economist; *President, New Democratic Party;* b. 1946. *Career:* economist specializing in fiscal man.; fmr Minister of Finance; Prime Minister of Saint Vincent and the Grenadines 2000–01; Pres. New Democratic Party (NDP) 2000–.
Address: New Democratic Party, Murray Road, PO Box 1300, Kingstown, Saint Vincent and the Grenadines.

EVANS, Hon. Gareth John, AO, QC, LLB, MA; Australian international organization official and fmr politician; *President and Chief Executive, International Crisis Group;* b. 5 Sept. 1944, Melbourne; m. Merran Anderson 1969; one s. one d. *Education:* Univ. of Melbourne, Magdalen Coll., Oxford. *Career:* Lecturer and Sr Lecturer in Law, Univ. of Melbourne 1971–76; mem. Australian Reform Comm. 1975; Barrister-at-Law 1977–; Senator for Victoria 1978–96; Shadow Attorney-Gen. 1980–83; Attorney-Gen. 1983–84; Minister for Resources and Energy, Minister Assisting the Prime Minister and Minister Assisting the Minister for Foreign Affairs 1984–87; Minister for Transport and Communications 1987–88, for Foreign Affairs 1988–96; Deputy Leader of Govt in the Senate 1987–93, Leader 1993–96; MP for Holt, Vic. 1996–99; Deputy Leader of Opposition, Shadow Treas. 1996–98; Pres. and Chief Exec. Int. Crisis Group 2000–; Co-Chair. Int. Comm. on Intervention and State Sovereignty 2000–; mem. UN Sec. –Gen.'s High Level Panel on Threat, Challenges and Change 2003–04, Weapons of Mass Destruction Comm. 2004–06; Hon. LLD (Melbourne Univ.) 2002, (Carleton Univ., Canada) 2005; Hon. Fellow, Magdalen Coll., Oxford 2004–; Australian Humanist of the Year 1990, ANZAC Peace Prize 1994, Grawemeyer Award for Ideas Improving World Order 1995; Chilean Order of Merit (Grand Cross) 1999. *Publications:* Labor and the Constitution 1972–75 (ed.) 1977, Law, Politics and the Labor Movement (ed.) 1980, Labor Essays 1980, 1981, 1982 (co-ed.), Australia's Constitution: Time for Change? (co-author) 1983, Australia's Foreign Relations (co-author) 1991, Co-operating for Peace 1993.
Address: International Crisis Group, 149 avenue Louise, 1050 Brussels, Belgium (office). *Telephone:* (2) 536-00-74 (office). *Fax:* (2) 502-50-38 (office). *E-mail:* gevans@crisisgroup.org (office). *Website:* www.crisisgroup .org (office).

EVANS, Stephen Nicholas, CMG, OBE, BA; British diplomatist; *High Commissioner to Bangladesh;* b. 29 June 1950; m. Sharon Ann Holdcroft 1975; one s. two d. *Education:* King's Coll., Taunton, Bristol Univ. *Career:* Lt in Royal Tank Regt 1971–74; Third Sec., FCO 1974–75, language student (Vietnamese), SOAS, London 1975, Second Sec., FCO 1976–78, First Sec., Hanoi 1978–80, FCO 1980–82, language training (Thai), Bangkok 1982–83, First Sec., Bangkok 1983–86, FCO 1986–90, First Sec. (Political), Ankara 1990, Counsellor (Econ., Commercial, Aid), Islamabad 1993–96, seconded to UN Special Mission to Afghanistan 1996–97, Counsellor and Head of OSCE and Council of Europe Dept, FCO 1997–98, Counsellor and Head of South Asian Dept 1998–2001, Chargé d'affaires, Kabul 2001–02, High Commr in Sri Lanka 2002–06, Amb. to

Afghanistan 2006–07, Dir Afghanistan Information Strategy, FCO 2007–08, High Commr to Bangladesh 2008–.
Address: British High Commission, PO Box 6079, United Nations Road, Baridhara, Dhaka 1212, Bangladesh (office). *Telephone:* (2) 8822705 (office). *Fax:* (2) 8823437 (office). *E-mail:* Dhaka.Chancery@fco.gov.uk (office). *Website:* www.ukinbangladesh.org (office).

EVATT, Elizabeth Andreas, AC, LLM; Australian lawyer and human rights expert; b. 11 Nov. 1933, Sydney; m. Robert Southan 1960; one d. *Education:* Univ. of Sydney and Harvard Univ. *Career:* called to Bar, Inner Temple; Chief Judge Family Court of Australia 1976–88; Deputy Pres. Conciliation and Arbitration Comm. 1973–89, Australian Industrial Relations Comm. 1989–94; Pres. Australian Law Reform Comm. 1988–93, mem. 1993–94; mem. UN Cttee on Elimination of Discrimination Against Women 1984–92, Chair. 1989–91; Chancellor, Univ. of Newcastle 1988–94; reviewed Aboriginal and Torres Strait Islander Heritage Protection Act 1984; Hearing Commr (part-time), Human Rights and Equal Opportunity Comm. 1995–98; mem. UN Human Rights Cttee 1993–2000, World Bank Admin. Tribunal 1998–, Commissioner, Int. Comm. of Jurists 2003–; Australian Human Rights Medal 1995.
Address: Unit 2003, 184 Forbes Street, Darlinghurst, NSW 2010, Australia. *Fax:* (2) 9331-6734 (home). *E-mail:* eevatt@bigpond.net.au (office); eevatt@post.harvard.edu (office).

EVERARD, John Vivian, MA, MBA; British diplomatist; *Ambassador to Democratic People's Republic of Korea;* b. 24 Nov. 1956; m. Heather Starkey. *Career:* joined FCO 1979, Far Eastern Dept 1979–81, Third, later Second Sec., Chancery, Beijing 1981–83, Second Sec., Chancery, Vienna 1983–84, resgnd from FCO 1984, reinstated 1987, Research Dept 1987, S America Dept 1987–90, First Sec. (Commercial), Santiago 1990–93, Chargé d'affaires, Minsk, later Amb. to Belarus 1993–95, Deputy Head of African Dept (Equatorial), FCO 1996–98, Counsellor (Political), Beijing 1998–2000, Amb. to Uruguay 2001–05, to Democratic People's Republic of Korea 2006–.
Address: British Embassy, Munsu-dong Diplomatic Compound, Pyongyang, Democratic People's Republic of Korea (office). *Telephone:* (2) 3817980 (office). *Fax:* (2) 3817985 (office). *E-mail:* postmaster.PYONX@fco.gov.uk (office).

EVERTS, Daan; Dutch international organization official; b. 1941; m.; two c. *Education:* in Netherlands, USA and India. *Career:* joined Foreign Service 1968, postings include to ILO, Thailand 1970–73, First Sec. Netherlands Embassy, Washington, DC 1978–81; fmr Exec. Sec. UN Capital Devt Fund; Asst Admin. UNDP, Dir Office for Project Services (OPS) –1993; Deputy Exec. Dir for Operations World Food Programme (WFP) 1993–95; Head of OSCE Presence in Albania 1997–99; Head European Community Monitor Mission in fmr Yugoslavia 1997; Head OSCE Mission to Kosovo 2001–2002; Deputy Special Rep. for Inst. Building, UN Interim Admin. Mission in Kosovo (UNMIK) 2001–02; Personal Rep. of the Chair-in-Office, OSCE 2003–04; NATO Sr Civilian Rep. in Afghanistan 2006–07.
Address: c/o Ministry of Foreign Affairs, Bezuidenhoutseweg 67, POB 20061, 2500 EB The Hague, Netherlands (office).

EVRIVIADES, Euripides L., BSc; Cypriot diplomatist; b. 6 Aug. 1954, Larnaca; m. Anastasia Iacovidou-Evriviades. *Education:* Harvard Univ., Univ. of New Hampshire, USA. *Career:* joined diplomatic service 1976, Vice-Consul, Consulate-Gen., New York 1976–78, Consul 1978–82, First Sec., Perm. Rep. to UN 1980–82, mem. Cypriot Del. to Third UN Conf. on Law of the Sea 1976–80, sr posts at Embassies in Tripoli, Moscow and Bonn, Amb. to Israel 1997–2000, to the Netherlands 2000–03, to USA (also accred to Brazil, Canada, Guyana, Jamaica, and Perm. Rep. to ICAO, OAS, World Bank and IMF) 2003–06, Dir Political Div., Ministry of Foreign Affairs 2006–; Order of Merit, First Class (Germany) 1989, Great Commdr, Order of Orthodox Kts of the Holy Sepulchre 2000; Amb. of the Year, Stichting Vrienden van Saur (Netherlands) 2003. *Publications:* numerous articles on Cypriot issues.
Address: Political Division, Ministry of Foreign Affairs, Presidential Palace Avenue, 1447 Nicosia, Cyprus (office). *Telephone:* (22) 401146 (office). *Fax:*

(22) 661881 (office). *E-mail:* elevriviades@mfa.gov.cy (office). *Website:* www.mfa.gov.cy (office).

EYAL, Jonathan, MA, PhD; Romanian/British research institute director; *Director, International Security Studies, Royal United Services Institute;* b. Romania. *Education:* Univs of Oxford and London. *Career:* Teacher of Int. Relations and Law, Univ. of Oxford 1987–90; Dir of Int. Security Studies, Royal United Services Inst. for Defence and Security Studies (RUSI), London 1990–, also Ed. RUSI Newsbrief; fmr Del. to Conf. on Security and Co-operation, UN; mem. Expert Team Preparing Peace Plan for fmr Yugoslavia; adviser on fmr Yugoslav Ethnic Relations to UN and EU; expert Foreign Affairs Cttee and adviser to Defence Cttee, House of Commons; numerous contribs to newspapers and journals.
Address: Royal Defence Services Institute for Defence and Security Studies (RUSI), Whitehall, London, SW1A 2ET, England (office). *Telephone:* (20) 7747-2616 (office). *Fax:* (20) 7321-0943 (office). *E-mail:* jonathane@rusi.org (office). *Website:* www.rusi.org (office).

EYSKENS, Viscount Mark, LLD, DEcon; Belgian politician; *Minister of State;* b. 29 April 1933, Louvain; m. Ann Rutsaert 1962; two s. three d. *Education:* Catholic Univ. of Louvain, Columbia Univ. *Career:* Prof. Catholic Univ. of Louvain; Econ. Adviser, Ministry of Finance 1962–65; mem. of Parl. 1977–; Sec. of State for the Budget and Regional Economy and Minister of Co-operation 1976–80; Minister of Finance 1980–81; Prime Minister 1981; Minister for Econ. Affairs 1981–85, for Finance 1985–88, of Foreign Affairs 1989–92, Minister of State 1998–; Chair. Council of EC Ministers of Finance 1987; Gov. IMF, IBRD 1980–81, 1985–88; mem. Council of Europe 1995–; Pres. Royal Acad. of Sciences, Letters and Fine Arts, Centre for European Culture, Inst. for European Policy; Vice-Pres. Royal Inst. for Int. Relations, Ass. of WEU 1995–; Observer European Convention 2002–, Pres. of Francqui Foundation; mem. of bd, Int. Crisis Group (ICG); numerous Belgian and foreign awards including Benelux-Europe Prize, J.M/ Huyghe Prize, Scriptores Christiani Prize. *Publications:* author of 38 books including Algemene economie 1970, Economie van nu en straks 1975, Ambrunise 1976, Une planète livrée à deux mondes 1980, La source et l'horizon, Le redressement de la société européenne 1985, Economie voor iedereen 1987, Vie et mort du Professeur Mortal 1989, Buitenlandse zaken 1992, Affaires étrangères 1992, Le Fleuve et l'océan 1994, De Reis naar Dabar 1996, De lust van de verbeelding 1996, L'Affaire Titus 1998, Democratie tussen Spin en Web 1999, Het verdriet van het werelddorp 2000, Leven in tijden van Godsverduistering 2001, Het hijgen van de geschiedenis 2003, Omdat wij van de avond nooit genzen 2004, De oude prof en de zee 2005, Le vieux prof et la mer 2006; has written more than 1000 articles, columns and contribs.
Address: Royal Academy of Sciences and Arts, Hertogsstraat 1, 1000 Brussels, Belgium (office). *Telephone:* (2) 550-23-23 (office). *Fax:* (1) 640-60-18 (home). *E-mail:* m.eyskens@skynet.be (office). *Website:* www.eyskens.com (home).

EZEKWESILI, Obiageli K., BSc, MPA, LLM; Nigerian government official, management consultant, chartered accountant and international organization official; *Vice President for the Africa Region, International Bank for Reconstruction and Development (World Bank);* b. 28 April 1963; m. Chinedu Ezekwesili; three c. *Education:* Univ. of Nigeria, Univ. of Lagos, John F. Kennedy School of Government, Harvard Univ. *Career:* has held auditing and consulting positions in numerous finance cos including Katryn Benjamin Assocs and Akintola Williams & Co. (Deloitte & Touche); Founding Mem. and fmr Dir for Africa, Tranparency Int., also served as Sr Special Asst to the Pres. and Head, Budget Monitoring and Price Intelligence Unit; fmr Minister of Solid Minerals Devt, Minister of Educ. 2006; Vice President for the Africa Region, Int. Bank for Reconstruction and Development (World Bank) 2006–; Chair. Nigeria Extractive Industries Transparency Initiative 2004–06; mem. Bd of Dirs New Nigeria Foundation, World Computer Exchange, Global Devt Resources; Head Nigeria Project, Center for Int. Devt, Harvard Univ.
Address: International Bank for Reconstruction and Development, 1818 H Street, NW, Washington, DC 20433, USA (office). *Telephone:* (202) 473-4467 (office). *E-mail:* africainfo@worldbank.org (office). *Website:* web.worldbank.org (office).

F

FABIUS, Laurent; French politician; b. 20 Aug. 1946, Paris. *Education:* Lycées Janson-de-Sailly and Louis-le-Grand, Paris, Ecole normale supérieure, Ecole Nat. d'Admin. *Career:* Auditor, Council of State 1973; First Deputy Mayor of Grand-Quevilly 1977–, Mayor 1995–; Deputy (Seine-Maritime) to Nat. Ass. 1978–81, 1986–, Pres. 1988–92, 1997–2000, 2002–07, 2007–; Nat. Sec. Parti Socialiste, in charge of press 1979–81, 1991–92, First Sec. 1992–93, Pres. Groupe Socialiste in Nat. Ass. 1995–97; Minister-Del. for the Budget, attached to Minister of Econ. and Finance 1981–83; Minister of Industry and Research 1983–84, Minister of Econs, Finance and Industry 2000–02; Prime Minister 1984–86; Pres. Regional Council, Haute Normandie 1981–82; Pres. Syndicat intercommunal à vocations multiples (Sivom) 1989–2000; mem. Gen. Council, Seine-Maritime 2000–; Grand Croix de l'Ordre nat. du Mérite. *Publications:* La France inégale 1975, Le coeur du futur 1985, C'est en allant vers la mer 1990, Les blessures de la vérité (Prize for Best Political Book 1996) 1995, Cela commence par une balade 2003, Une certaine idée de l'Europe 2005.
Address: Assemblée Nationale, Casier de la Poste, Palais Bourbon, 75355 Paris 07 (office); Mairie, Esplanade Tony Larue, 76120 Grand-Quevilly, France (office). *Telephone:* 2-35-68-93-00 (Grand-Quevilly) (office). *Fax:* 2-35-67-27-39 (Grand-Quevilly) (office). *E-mail:* lfabius@assemblee-nationale.fr (office). *Website:* www.laurent-fabius.net (office).

FABRIZI, Pier Luigi, BEcons; Italian banker and professor of finance; *Professor of Financial Markets, Bocconi University;* b. 23 April 1948, Siena; m. Patrizia Vaselli; two c. *Education:* Siena Univ. *Career:* Asst Prof. of Banking Parma Univ. 1974–82, Assoc. Prof. 1982–87, Prof. of Financial Insts 1987–93, Dean Faculty of Econs 1990–97; Prof. of Financial Markets, Bocconi Univ., Milan 1993–; Chair. Banca Monte dei Paschi di Siena SpA 1998–; mem. Bd Dirs S. Paolo IMI, Turin 1998–99, Ing. C. Olivetti SpA, Ivrea 1999, Banca Agricola Mantovana, Mantova 1999, Banco Nazionale del Lavoro SpA, Rome 2001, Unipol Assiarrazioni SpA, Bologna 2001; Grande Ufficiale, Ordine al Merito. *Publications:* L'attività in titoli con clientela nelle banche di deposito 1986, La gestione dei flussi finanziari nelle aziende di credito 1990, La gestione integrata dell'attivo e del passivo nelle aziende di credito 1991, Nuovi modelli di gestione dei flussi finanziari nelle banche 1995, Le banche nell' intermediazione mobiliare e nell'asset management 1996, La formazione nelle banche e nelle assicurazioni-bancaria (ed.) 1998, Il futuro del sistema bancario italiano: Strategie e modelli organizzativi 2000; La gestione del risparmio privato (ed.) 2000.
Address: c/o Banca Monte Paschi Siena SpA, P.za Salimbeni 3, 53100 Siena (office); c/o Università Bocconi, Via Sarfatti 25, 20136 Milan (office); Via Adelaide Coari 11, 20141 Milan, Italy. *Telephone:* (0577) 294211 (Siena) (office); (02) 58365910 (Milan) (office); (02) 55210884 (Milan). *Fax:* (0577) 294017 (Siena) (office); (02) 58365909 (Milan) (office). *E-mail:* pierluigi.fabrizi@banca.mps.it (office); pierluigi.fabrizi@uni.bocconi.it (office).

FACCO BONETTI, Gianfranco, LLB; Italian diplomatist; b. 19 April 1940, Galeata, Forli. *Education:* Univ. of Trieste. *Career:* entered diplomatic corps 1967; Directorate-Gen. for Emigration, later for Personnel 1967–70; First Sec., Embassy in London 1970–74; Sec., Italian–Yugoslav Comm. for Minorities 1974–75; Consul, Capodistria 1975–78; First Counsellor, Embassy in Tehran 1978–81; Dept of Econ. Affairs, Rome 1981–82; Head, Office for Int. Orgs, Dept of Devt and Cooperation 1982–83; Head of Secretariat of First Deputy Minister of Foreign Affairs 1983–86, 1997–99; Consul Gen., Frankfurt 1986–90; Minister, Embassy in Moscow 1990–94; Head of Dept for Italian EU Presidency 1995–96; Head of special unit for reform of Ministry of Foreign Affairs 1997, Head, Cultural Relations Directorate Gen., Ministry of Foreign Affairs 1998–2000, Head of Directorate Gen. for Asia, Oceania and Pacific Region 2001; Amb. to Russian Federation 2001–06.
Address: c/o Ministry of Foreign Affairs, Piazzale della Farnesina 1, 00194 Rome, Italy (office).

FADLALLAH, Sylvie; Lebanese diplomatist; *Permanent Delegate, United Nations Educational, Scientific and Cultural Organization (UNESCO); Career:* First Sec., Embassy in Paris 2001–03, Amb. to France 2003, currently Perm. Del. to UNESCO, Paris.
Address: Délégation du Liban auprès de l'Unesco 1, rue Miollis, 75015 Paris, France.

FAGIOLO, Silvio, LLB; Italian diplomat and academic; *Professor of International Relations, Libera Università Internazionale degli Studi Sociali Guido Carli in Roma;* b. 15 July 1938, Rome; m. Margret Klauth; two c. *Education:* Univ. La Sapienza, Rome. *Career:* joined diplomatic service 1969; foreign missions to Moscow, USSR 1972–76, Detroit, USA 1976–79, Bonn, W Germany 1982–86; Deputy Chief Italian Embassy, Washington, DC 1991–95; Amb. to Germany 2001; Adviser for European and Security Affairs, Ministry of Foreign Affairs, Head of Cabinet 1997–2000; mem. EU Group that organized Intergovernmental Conf. that led to Maastricht Treaty; Personal Rep. of Italian Foreign Minister at Intergovernmental Confs. that led to Treaty of Amsterdam 1996, Treaty of Nice 2002; Perm. Rep. to EU 2001; currently mem. Faculty of Political Science and Prof. of Int. Relations, Libera Università Internazionale degli Studi Sociali Guido Carli in Roma. *Publications:* I gruppi di pressione in URSS 1977, L'operaio americano 1980, La Russia di Gorbaciov 1987, La pace fredda 1998.
Address: Faculty of Political Science, Libera Università Internazionale degli Studi Sociali Guido Carli in Roma, Viale Pola 12, 00198 Rome (office); Via Casolvecchio Sicuro 4, 00133 Rome, Italy (home). *Telephone:* (6) 45472990 (home). *Fax:* (6) 45472990 (home). *E-mail:* silviofagiolo@hotmail.com (home). *Website:* www.luiss.it/scienzepolitiche (office).

FAHEY, Hon. John Joseph, AC; Australian politician and lawyer; b. 10 Jan. 1945, New Zealand; m. Colleen McGurran 1968; one s. two d. *Education:* St Anthony's Convent, Picton and Chevalier Coll. Bowral, Sydney Univ. Law Extension. *Career:* mem. Parl. of NSW 1984–95; Minister for Industrial Relations and Employment and Minister Assisting Premier of NSW 1988–90; Minister for Industrial Relations, Further Educ., Training and Employment, NSW 1990–92; Premier and Treas. of NSW 1992; Premier and Minister for Econ. Devt of NSW 1993–95; Fed. mem. for Macarthur and Minister for Finance 1996–2001, for Admin. 1997–2001; consultant, adviser, dir 2002–; Chair. Sydney 2000 Olympic Bid Co. 1992–93.
Address: c/o J.P. Morgan Australia Ltd, Level 26, Grosvenor Place, 225 George Street, Sydney, NSW (office); Ashford, 39 Hurlingham Avenue, Burradoo, NSW 2576, Australia (home). *Telephone:* (2) 9220-1649 (office). *Fax:* (2) 4861-4113 (office). *E-mail:* faheyj@bigpond.com (home).

FAHEY, Noel; Irish diplomatist; b. 1946, Roscommon; m. Christine O'Rourke; one s. one d. *Education:* Roscommon Christian Brothers' School, Univ. Coll. Dublin, Inst. of Public Admin. *Career:* various roles, Dept of Finance, Dept of Posts and Telegraphs; joined Irish Foreign Service 1974, assignments in New Delhi 1976–80, Brussels 1982–86, mem. EU Div., Ministry of Foreign Affairs 1986–97 (Head of Div. 1991–97), Amb. to Germany 1998–2002, to USA 2002–07.
Address: Department of Foreign Affairs, 80 St Stephen's Green, Dublin 2, Ireland (office). *Telephone:* (1) 4780822 (office). *Fax:* (1) 4781484 (office). *E-mail:* minister@dfa.ie (office). *Website:* www.dfa.ie (office).

FAHIM KHAN, Marshal Mohammad Qassim; Afghan politician and fmr guerrilla leader; b. 1957, Omarz Dist, Panjshir Valley; m.; three c. *Education:* Kabul Islamic Inst., Kabul Univ. *Career:* qualified doctor; joined troops fighting USSR occupation forces 1979–89; joined Northern Alliance (NA), led NA forces into Kabul 1992, Head of Intelligence, Chief of Staff, Leader 2001–02; Vice-Pres. and Minister of Defence, Afghan Interim Authority Dec. 2001–June 2002, Afghan Transitional Authority 2002–04; currently mem. Meshrano Jirga (upper house of parl.) and Sr Adviser to Pres. Karzai.
Address: c/o Office of the President, Gul Khana Palace, Presidential Palace, Kabul, Afghanistan (office).

FAHMY, M. Nabil, BSc, MA; Egyptian diplomatist; *Ambassador to USA;* m. Mrs M. Nabil Fahmy (née Nermin); two d. one s. *Education:* American Univ., Cairo. *Career:* mem. Cabinet of Sec. of Pres. for External Communications 1974; Political Officer Cabinet of Vice-Pres. 1975–76; mem. Cabinet, Ministry of Foreign Affairs 1976–78; Second Sec. Mission to UN for Conf. on Disarmament 1978–82, First Sec. then Counsellor to UN 1986–91; Sr Disarmament Official, Dept for Int. Orgs, Ministry of Foreign Affairs 1991, Counsellor –1995; Amb. to Japan 1997–99, to USA 1999–; mem. UN Sec.-Gen.'s Advisory Bd on Disarmament Matters 1999–. *Publications include:* numerous publs on nuclear proliferation.

Address: Embassy of Egypt, 3521 International Court, NW, Washington, DC 20008, USA (office). *Telephone:* (202) 895-5400 (office). *Fax:* (202) 244-4319 (office). *E-mail:* embassy@egyptembassy.net (office). *Website:* www .egyptembassy.net (office).

FAHSEN, Alfonso Roberto José Matta; Guatemalan diplomatist; *Ambassador to UK;* m. Maria Teresa Maya Mara. *Career:* fmr Amb. to Russia, to the Netherlands; Amb. to UK 2008–.
Address: Embassy of Guatemala, 13 Fawcett Street, London, SW10 9HN, England (office). *Telephone:* (20) 7351-3042 (office). *Fax:* (20) 7376-5708 (office). *E-mail:* ambassador.gtm@btconnect.com (office).

FAINI, Riccardo, PhD; Italian economist and international organization official; *Professor of Political Economy, University of Rome Tor Vergata;* b. 12 April 1957, Lausanne, Switzerland; m. Lauri Faini; three s. *Education:* Laurea Università Bocconi, Massachusetts Inst. of Tech. *Career:* Lecturer, Univ. of Essex, UK 1980–83; Researcher, Univ. of Venezia 1983–85; Assoc. Prof., Bologna Center of Johns Hopkins Univ. 1988–90; Prof. of Econs, Univ. of Brescia 1990–; currently Prof. of Political Economy, Univ. of Rome Tor Vergata; Economist, World Bank Trade Policy Div. 1985–88; Exec. Dir IMF 1998–2001; apptd Dir-Gen. Ministry of the Economy and Finance 2000; Research Fellow Human Resources and Int. Trade Programs, Centre for Econ. and Policy Research; Research Dir Centro Studi Luca d'Agliano; Research Fellow, IZA research inst. 2001–. *Publications:* Non-Traded Inputs and Increasing Returns 1999, Trade and Migration: The Controversies and the Evidence (co-ed.) 1999, Labour Markets, Poverty and Development (co-ed.).
Address: Università di Roma Due Tor Vergata – IZA and CEPR, Centro Studi Luca D'Agliano, via Sarfatti 25, 20136 Milano, Italy. *Telephone:* (02) 58363390 (office). *Fax:* (02) 58363399 (office). *E-mail:* centro.dagliano@ uni-bocconi.it (office).

FAIZULLAEV, Alisher Omonullaevich, PhD; Uzbekistan diplomatist and social scientist; *First Vice-Rector, University of World Economy and Diplomacy;* b. 10 Jan. 1957, Tashkent; m. Shakhnoz Faizullaeva; two s. two d. *Education:* Tashkent State Univ. and Inst. of Psychology, USSR Acad. of Sciences, Moscow. *Career:* Lecturer, Uzbekistan Acad. of Sciences, Tashkent 1979–80, Sr Lecturer 1983–86; Visiting Fellow, Inst. of Psychology, USSR Acad. of Sciences 1986–87; Sr Lecturer, Tashkent State Univ. 1987–88; Head of Dept, Exec. Training Inst., Tashkent 1988–91; Intern, City Council of San Diego, CA 1989; Head of Dept, Inst. of Political Sciences and Man., Tashkent 1991–92; Distinguished Visiting Scholar, Western Washington Univ., Bellingham, USA 1992; Dir Inst. of Man., Univ. of World Economy and Diplomacy, Tashkent 1992–93, currently First Vice-Rector; Consultant on Political Affairs, then Chief Consultant on Int. Affairs and Foreign Econ. Relations, Office of the Pres. of Uzbekistan 1993–94; Deputy Minister of Foreign Affairs 1994–95; Amb. to Belgium and Head of Missions to EU and Euro-Atlantic Partnership Council/NATO 1995–98, concurrently Amb. to the Netherlands and Luxembourg with residence in Brussels 1997–98; State Adviser to Pres. of Uzbekistan on Int. Affairs and Foreign Econ. Relations 1998–99; First Deputy Minister of Foreign Affairs Feb.–Dec. 1999; Amb. to UK 1999–2003; Dir Centre for Political Studies, Tashkent 2003–; Visiting Scholar, Centre of Int. Studies and Visiting Fellow, Jesus Coll., Cambridge 2007; USSR Young Social Scientists Prize 1987. *Publications:* Motivational Self-Regulation of Personality (in Russian) 1987, Human Being, Politics, Management (in Russian and Uzbek) 1995; several papers on behavioural, social and political sciences in learned journals.
Address: University of World Economy and Diplomacy, Buyuk Ipak Yuli 54, Tashkent 100137, Uzbekistan (office). *Telephone:* (71) 2676769 (office). *Fax:* (71) 2670900 (office). *E-mail:* uwed@uwed.freenet.uz (office). *Website:* uwed.freenet.uz (office).

FAIZULLAYEV, Ravshanbek; Uzbekistan politician. *Career:* First Deputy Prime Minister 2004–05.
Address: c/o Office of the Cabinet of Ministers, Government House, 100008 Tashkent, Uzbekistan (office). *Telephone:* (71) 139-82-95 (office). *Fax:* (71) 139-86-01 (office).

FAKI, Moussa Mahamat; Chadian politician; *Minister of Foreign Affairs;* b. 21 June 1960. *Career:* early career as Prof. of Law, Chad Univ.; Dir-Gen. Nat. Sugar Soc. 1996–99; Minister of Transport and Public Works 2002; Prime Minister of Chad 2003–05; Minister of Foreign Affairs 2008–.
Address: Ministry of Foreign Affairs, BP 746, N'Djamena, Chad (office). *Telephone:* 51-80-50 (office). *Fax:* 51-45-85 (office).

FALCAM, Leo A.; Micronesian fmr head of state; b. 20 Nov. 1935. *Career:* fmr Vice-Pres. of Micronesia, Pres. 1999–2003.

Address: c/o Office of the President, PO Box PS-53, Palikir, Pohnpei, Eastern Caroline Islands, FM 96941, Micronesia (office). *Telephone:* 320-2228 (office). *Fax:* 320-2785 (office).

FALCONER OF THOROTON, Baron (Life Peer), cr. 1997, of Thoroton in the County of Nottinghamshire; **Charles Leslie Falconer,** QC; British lawyer and politician; b. 19 Nov. 1951; m. Marianna Hildyard 1985; three s. one d. *Education:* Trinity Coll., Glenalmond, Queen's Coll., Cambridge. *Career:* called to the Bar 1974, took silk 1991; Solicitor-Gen. 1997–98; Minister of State Cabinet Office 1998–2001; Minister with responsibility for Millennium Dome 1998–2001; Minister of State for Housing and Planning 2001, for the Criminal Justice System 2002–03; Lord Chancellor 2003–07; also Sec. of State for Justice May–June 2007; Labour.
Address: House of Lords, London, SW1A 0PW, England (office). *Telephone:* (20) 7219-3000 (office). *Website:* www.parliament.uk (office).

FALK, Richard A., BS, LLB, SJD; American academic; *Professor Emeritus of International Law, Princeton University;* b. 13 Nov. 1930, New York; m. Hilal Elver; three s. one d. *Education:* Wharton School, Univ. of Pennsylvania, Harvard Law School, Yale Law School. *Career:* Asst Prof., later Assoc. Prof., Coll. of Law, Ohio State Univ. 1955–61; Ford Foundation Fellow, Harvard Law School 1958–59; Visiting Assoc. Prof., Princeton Univ. 1961–62, Assoc. Prof. of Int. Law 1962–65, Albert G. Milbank Prof. of Int. Law and Practice 1965–2001, Sr Research Fellow 2002–, later Prof. Emer. of Int. Law; Acting Dir, Center of Int. Studies 1975, 1982; Fellow, Center for Advanced Study in the Behavioral Sciences, Stanford, CA 1968–69; visiting prof. at numerous univs including Stockholm, American Univ. in Cairo, Univ. of Wales, Univ. of Calif., Santa Barbara; Chair. Nuclear Age Peace Foundation; mem. Editorial Bd numerous publs including The Nation, The Progressive, World Politics, Foreign Policy Magazine, Peace Forum; fmr mem. several int. panels of judges; participation in numerous int. and govt comms, including Ind. World Comm. on the Oceans 1995–2000, Ind. Int. Comm. on Kosovo 1999–2001; hon. mem. Bd of Eds American Journal of International Law; hon. degrees from Monmouth Coll. 1987, City Univ. of NY 1999, John Jay Coll., York Univ. 2004. *Publications include:* Law, War and Morality in the Contemporary World 1963, Legal Order in a Violent World 1968, Crimes of War (jt ed.) 1971, A Global Approach to National Policy 1975, Human Rights and State Sovereignty 1981, Reviving the World Court 1986, Revitalizing International Law 1989, International Law and World Order (jt author) 1997, Human Rights Horizons 2001, Religion and Humane Global Governance 2002, The Great Terror War 2003, Unlocking the Middle East 2005; numerous articles in learned journals.
Address: 723 Alston Road, Santa Barbara, CA 93108, USA (home). *Telephone:* (805) 893-7860 (office). *Fax:* (805) 893-8003 (office). *E-mail:* falk@global.ucsb.edu (office).

FALKENRATH, Richard A., BA, PhD; American government security official and academic. *Education:* Occidental Coll., King's Coll. London, UK. *Career:* Research Fellow, Belfer Center for Science and Int. Affairs, Harvard Univ. –1995, Exec. Dir 1995–98; Asst Prof. of Public Policy, John F. Kennedy School of Govt 1998–2000; Dir for Non-Proliferation Strategy, Nat. Security Council 2000–01; mem. Bush-Cheney Transition Team, Nat. Security Council 2000–01; Sr Dir for Policy and Plans and Special Asst to the Pres., Office of Homeland Security, White House 2001–03; Acting Deputy Homeland Security Adviser to the Pres. Jan.–April 2003, Deputy Adviser 2003–04; Visiting Fellow, Foreign Policy Studies Program, The Brooking Inst. 2004–05, Stephen and Barbara Friedman Fellow 2005–06; fmr Man. Dir Civitas Group LLC; currently Deputy Commr for Counter Terrorism, New York Police Department; Visiting Research Fellow, German Soc. of Foreign Affairs (DGAP), Bonn 1995; mem. Aspen Strategy Group; British Marshall Scholarship. *Publications:* Shaping Europe's Military Order 1995, Avoiding Nuclear Anarchy 1996, America's Achilles' Heel: Nuclear, Biological, Chemical Terrorism and Covert Attack 1998; numerous chapters in books and articles in professional journals.
Address: Office of the Deputy Commissioner for Counter Terrorism, New York Police Department, 1 Police Plaza, New York, NY 10038-1403, USA (office). *Telephone:* (212) 374-5000 (office). *Website:* www.nyc.gov/html/ nypd (office).

FALL, David William, MA; British diplomatist (retd); b. 10 March 1948; m. Gwendolyn Fall; three s. *Education:* St Bartholomew's Grammar School, Newbury, New Coll., Oxford. *Career:* teacher, VSO, Bougainville, Papua New Guinea 1970–71; joined FCO 1971, Asst Desk Officer, SW Pacific Dept 1971–72, full-time language training 1972–73, Second, later First Sec., Chancery, Bangkok 1973–77, on loan to Cabinet Office 1977–79, Desk Officer, Defence Dept, FCO 1979–81, First Sec., Chancery, Pretoria 1981–85, Desk Officer, Personnel Operations Dept, FCO 1985–86, Deputy Head of Personnel Policy Dept 1986–88, Head of Narcotics Control and AIDS Dept 1988–90, Deputy Head of Mission/Commercial Counsellor,

Bangkok 1990–93, Deputy High Commr, Canberra 1993–97, Amb. to Viet Nam 1997–2000, Estate Modernisation Man., FCO 2000–02, Amb. to Thailand 2003–07 (retd).
Address: c/o Foreign and Commonwealth Office, King Charles Street, London, SW1A 2AH, England. *Telephone:* (20) 7008-1500.

FALL, François Lonseny, LLM; Guinean politician and diplomatist; *Secretary-General's Special Representative for Somalia and Head, Political Office for Somalia (UNPOS), United Nations;* b. 21 April 1949; m.; four c. *Education:* Conakry Univ. *Career:* First Counsellor, Embassyn in Cairo 1982–85, Abuja 1985–89, Paris 1989–90, Mission to UN, New York 1990–93; Head, Div. of Consular Affairs, Ministry of Foreign Affairs 1993, Deputy Dir of Legal and Consular Affairs 1995–96, Dir 1996–2000; Perm. Rep. to UN, New York 2000–02; Minister at the Presidency, in charge of Foreign Affairs 2002–04; Prime Minister Feb.–April 2004 (resgnd); mem. UN Cttee for the Elimination of Racial Discrimination 2000–02, Econ. Community of W African States (ECOWAS) Ministerial Cttee for Security and Mediation 2002–04; UN Sec.-Gen.'s Special Rep. for Somalia and Head, UN Political Office for Somalia (UNPOS) 2005–.
Address: Political Office for Somalia, United Nations, PO Box 67578, Nairobi, Kenya 00200 (office). *Telephone:* (20) 7621234.

FALL, Ibrahima D., LLM, PhD; Senegalese international organization official, politician and academic; *Resident Coordinator and Resident Representative, Deputy Special Representative of the Secretary-General and Humanitarian Coordinator for Burundi, United Nations Development Programme (UNDP);* b. 1942, Tivaouane, Thies; m. Déguène Fall; five c. *Education:* Univ. of Dakar, Inst. of Political Science, Paris, Faculty of Law, Univ. of Paris, Acad. of Int. Law, The Hague, Netherlands. *Career:* Prof. of Int. Law and Int. Relations, Cheikh Anta Diop Univ., Dakar 1972–81, Dean of Faculty of Law 1975–81; Minister of Higher Educ. 1983–84, of Foreign Affairs 1984–90; Adviser, Supreme Court of Senegal; Asst Sec.-Gen. for Human Rights and Dir UN Centre for Human Rights, Geneva 1992–97; Sec.-Gen. UN World Conf. on Human Rights, Vienna 1993; Asst Gen. Sec. UN Dept of Political Affairs 1997–2000, Special Envoy of UN Sec.-Gen. to Côte d'Ivoire 2000–02, Special Rep. for the Great Lakes Region 2002–08, currently Resident Coordinator and Resident Rep., Deputy Special Rep. of UN Sec.-Gen. and UNDP Humanitarian Coordinator for Burundi, Bujumbura; consultant, UNESCO; Founding-mem. and Hon. Pres. Senegalese Asscn for African Unity; mem. African Council for Higher Educ. *Publications:* articles on int. public law, constitutional law and political science in professional journals.
Address: UNDP Office in Burundi, Bujumbura, Burundi (office); Sicap Fenêtre Mermoz, Dakar, Senegal (home). *Telephone:* 228108 (office). *Fax:* 215213 (office). *E-mail:* ibrahima.fall@undp.org (office); fall5@un.org (office). *Website:* www.undp.org (office).

FAN, Maj.-Gen. Zhilun; Chinese army official; *Deputy Chief of Staff, Beijing Military Region, People's Liberation Army;* b. 1935, Fushun Co., Sichuan Prov.; m. Ding Xin 1966; one s. one d. *Career:* Deputy Commdr and Chief of Staff Chinese People's Armed Police Force 1985–; Deputy Pres. Mil. Educ. Coll. and Mil. Staff Coll. 1991–; Deputy Chief of Staff, Beijing Mil. Region of PLA 1993–.
Address: Headquarters of the Beijing Military Region, No. Jia 1, Badachu, Western Hill, Beijing, People's Republic of China.

FAN HSU, Rita, CBE, JP, BA, MScS; Hong Kong politician; *President of Legislative Council, Hong Kong Special Administrative Region;* b. 20 Sept. 1945, Shanghai, People's Repub. of China; m. Stephen Fan Sheung-tak; two c. *Education:* St Stephen's Girls' Coll., Univ. of Hong Kong. *Career:* mem. Legis. Council 1983–92, Exec. Council 1989–92; Chair. Bd of Educ. 1986–89, Educ. Comm. 1990–92; mem. Preliminary Working Cttee of the Preparatory Cttee for the Hong Kong Special Admin. Region (HKSAR) 1993–95, Preparatory Cttee for the HKSAR 1995–97; Hong Kong Deputy to the 9th NPC, People's Repub. of China 1998–2003, 10th NPC 2003–08; Pres. Provisional Legis. Council 1997–98, First Legis. Council of HKSAR 1998–2000, Second Legis. Council 2000–04, Third Legis. Council 2004–08; Supervising Adviser, Hong Kong Fed. of Women; Hon. Advisor, Jr Chamber Int. Hong Kong; Grand Bauhinia Medal, Gold Bauhinia Star; Hon. LLD (China Univ. of Political Science and Law); Hon. DScS (City Univ. of Hong Kong).
Address: Office of the President of the Legislative Council, Legislative Council Building, 8 Jackson Road, Central, Hong Kong Special Administrative Region, People's Republic of China (office). *Telephone:* 28699461 (office). *Fax:* 28779600 (office). *E-mail:* wlam@legco.gov.hk (office). *Website:* www.ritafan.org (office).

FANNIN, P(aul) Robert, BA, JD; American lawyer, business executive and diplomatist; *Ambassador to the Dominican Republic;* b. Phoenix, Ariz.; m. Dr Elizabeth Wilkinson Fannin; two s. one d. *Education:* Stanford Univ.,

James E. Rogers Coll. of Law, Univ. of Arizona. *Career:* served on active duty for three years as commissioned officer in USAF; lawyer in pvt. practice and business exec. since 1963; has served as an officer and dir of two financial insts; Pnr, Steptoe & Johnson LLP (law firm); mem. Bar, including 14 years as Chair. State Bar legal educ. programmes; apptd by Supreme Court of Ariz. to serve on State Comm. on Salaries of Elected Officials; has served on Bd of Dirs and Exec. Cttee of Ariz. Chamber of Commerce and other Cttees of Greater Phoenix Chamber of Commerce, including Special Events Cttee; has served on numerous cttees under several Govs, including Gov.'s Strategic Partnership for Econ. Devt, Gov.'s Transportation Task Force, Plan B Task Force (stadium financing) and Growing Smarter; Chair. and mem. Gov.'s Motion Picture and TV Advisory Bd; mem. Pres.'s Comm. on White House Fellowships 2005–; mem. Bd Emer. (fmr Chair.) Barrow Neurological Inst. Foundation; Amb. to the Dominican Repub. 2006–; mem. Alexis de Tocqueville Soc. (United Way); Distinguished Service Award, Arizona State Univ. Coll. of Law 1995.
Address: Embassy of the USA, César Nicolás Pensón, esq. Leopoldo Navarro, Santo Domingo, DN, Dominican Republic (office). *Telephone:* 221-2171 (office). *Fax:* 685-6959 (office). *E-mail:* irc@usemb.gov.do (office). *Website:* www.usemb.gov.do (office).

FARAH, Abdikarim; Somali diplomatist. *Career:* Amb. to Ethiopia and Perm. Rep. to African Union 2005–.
Address: Embassy of Somalia, Bole Kifle Ketema, Kebele 20, House No. 588, POB 1643, Addis Ababa, Ethiopia (office). *Telephone:* (11) 6180673 (office). *Fax:* (11) 6180680 (office).

FARAH, Ali Abdi; Djibouti politician; b. 16 Feb. 1947. *Career:* mem. Rassemblement Populaire pour le Progrès (RPP); fmr Minister for Industry, Energy and Minerals and Acting Minister for Public Works and Housing; Minister of Foreign Affairs, Int. Co-operation and Parl. Relations 1999–2005.
Address: c/o Ministry of Foreign Affairs and International Co-operation, BP 1863, Djibouti (office).

FARAH, Col. Hassan Abshir; Somali politician and diplomatist; *Minister of Fishery and Marine Resources;* b. 20 June 1945. *Career:* fmr Mayor of Mogadishu; fmr Gov. of Middle Shabelle and Bakol; fmr Amb. to Austria, Repub. of Korea, Japan, Germany; Minister of Internal Affairs and Security, Puntland State –2000; Minister of Mineral Resources and Water 2000–01; Chair. Somali Peace Conf. 2000; Prime Minister of Somalia 2001–03; Minister of Fishery and Marine Resources 2007–.
Address: Ministry of Fishery and Marine Resources, Mogadishu, Somalia (office).

FARAH, Rachad; Djibouti diplomatist; *Ambassador to France;* m. Tazuko Hala Farah 1996. *Education:* Univ. of Paris (Sorbonne), Int. Public Admin. Inst., Paris. *Career:* joined Ministry of Foreign Affairs in first govt of new Repub. of Djibouti following indepence from France 1977, Head of Bilateral Relations Dept 1977–83, Dir Bilateral Relations Dept and Acting Sec.-Gen. Ministry of Foreign Affairs 1983–89; Amb. to Japan 1989–2004 (also accred to S Korea, Singapore, the Philippines, Malaysia, Indonesia, Thailand and Australia 1990–2004, to China 1990–2001, to India 2001–04); Dean of African Diplomatic Corps 1994–2004, Dean of mem. countries of OIC 1999–2004, later Dean of Diplomatic Corps; Amb. to France (also accred to UK) and Perm. Rep. to UNESCO, Paris 2005–; Grand Officer, Order of Rio Branco (Brazil).
Address: Embassy of Djibouti, 26 rue Emile Ménier, 75116 Paris, France (office). *Telephone:* 1-47-27-49-22 (office). *Fax:* 1-45-53-50-53 (office). *E-mail:* ambassadeur@ambdjibouti.org (office).

FARMER, Bill, AO, BA, MS; Australian diplomatist; *Ambassador to Indonesia;* *Education:* Univ. of Sydney, London School of Econs, UK. *Career:* joined Foreign Service 1969; served in Embassy in Cairo 1969–71, in London 1972–75; Deputy High Commr to Fiji 1979–82; Minister, Perm. Mission to UN, New York 1984–87, Deputy Rep. of Australia on Security Council 1985–86; Amb. to Mexico (also accred to Cen. American countries and Cuba) 1987–89; High Commr to Papua New Guinea 1993–95, to Malaysia 1996–97; Deputy Sec., Dept of Foreign Affairs and Trade 1997–98, Sec., Dept of Immigration and Multicultural Affairs 1998–2001, Sec., Dept of Immigration and Multicultural and Indigenous Affairs 2001–05, also Sec., Dept of Reconciliation and Aboriginal and Torres Strait Islander Affairs; Amb. to Indonesia 2005–; Centenary Medal 2003.
Address: Embassy of Australia, Jalan H. R. Rasuna Said, Kav. C15–16, Kuningan, 12940 Jakarta, Indonesia (office). *Telephone:* (21) 25505555 (office). *Fax:* (21) 25505467 (office). *E-mail:* public-affairs-jakt@dfat.gov.au (office). *Website:* www.austembjak.or.id (office).

FAROOK, M. L. Mohamed Ali; Sri Lankan diplomatist. *Career:* currently High Commr to the Maldives.
Address: High Commission of Sri Lanka, H. Sakeena Manzil, Medhu-ziyaaraiyh Magu, Malé 20-05, The Maldives (office). *Telephone:* 3322845 (office). *Fax:* 3321652 (office). *E-mail:* highcom@dhivehinet.net.mv (office).

FARQUHARSON, Paul H.; Bahamian police officer and diplomatist; *High Commissioner to UK;* m. Sharon Farquharson. *Career:* began career as police corporal 1971, Chief Insp. 1985–94, Chief Supt 1994–2001, Commr of Police 2001–08; ADC to HRH Prince Philip 1993; High Commr to UK (also accred as Amb. to Belgium, France, Germany and Italy and as Amb. and Perm. Rep. to EU) and Perm. Rep. to IMO, London 2008–; associated with Bahamas Div. of Salvation Army; mem. Bahamas Film and TV Comm., Exec. Bd Bahamas Humane Soc.
Address: Bahamas High Commission, 10 Chesterfield Street, London, W1J 5JL, England (office). *Telephone:* (20) 7408-4488 (office). *Fax:* (20) 7499-9937 (office). *E-mail:* information@bahamashclondon.net (office). *Website:* www.bahamashclondon.net/index(1).htm (office).

FARRAR, Jonathan D.; American diplomatist; *Chief of Mission, US Interests Section in Havana;* b. Los Angeles; m.; three c. *Education:* California State Polytechnic Univ., Claremont Graduate School, Industrial Coll. of the Armed Forces. *Career:* econ. officer, US Dept of State 1980, fmr Deputy Dir Office of Andean Affairs; overseas postings to Embassies in Mexico, Belize and Paraguay; fmr Deputy Chief of Mission, Embassy in Uruguay; Chief of Staff to Under-Sec. for Democracy and Global Affairs 2002–04, Deputy Asst Sec. Int. Narcotics and Law Enforcement Bureau 2004–05, Prin. Deputy Asst Sec., Bureau of Democracy, Human Rights, and Labor 2006–07, Acting Asst Sec. 2007–08; Chief of Mission, US Interests Section in Havana 2008–.
Address: US Interests Section, Calzada between L & M Streets, Vedado, Havana, Cuba (office). *Telephone:* (7) 833-3551 (office). *E-mail:* havanaacs@state.gov (office). *Website:* havana.usinterestsection.gov (office).

FASE, Martin M. G., PhD; Dutch banker, economist and academic; *Emeritus Professor of Monetary Economics, University of Amsterdam;* b. 28 Dec. 1937, Boskoop; m. Lida E. M. Franse 1965; two s. *Education:* Univ. of Amsterdam. *Career:* Research Assoc., Inst. of Actuarial Sciences and Econometrics, Amsterdam 1965–69; Ford Foundation Fellow, Dept of Econs, Univ. of Wis., Madison, USA 1969–71; with De Nederlandsche Bank 1971–2001, Deputy Dir 1985–2001; Extraordinary Prof. of Business Statistics, Erasmus Univ., Rotterdam 1978–86; Extraordinary Prof. of Monetary Econs, Univ. of Amsterdam 1986–2003; Fellow Royal Nether-lands Acad. of Arts and Sciences 1987, Hollandsche Maatschappij der Wetenschappen 1989, mem. Maatschappi der Nederlandse Letterhunau 2001; Officier Order of Orange Nassau 1995; N. G. Pierson Medal 1996. *Publications:* An Econometric Model of Age-Income Profiles: a Statistical Analysis of Dutch Income Data 1970, The Monetary Sector of the Netherlands in 50 Equations: a Quarterly Monetary Model for the Netherlands 1970–79, in Analysing the Structure of Econometric Models (ed. J. P. Ancot) 1984, Seasonal Adjustment as a Practical Problem 1991, Demand for Money and Credit in Europe 1999, Tussen behoud en vernieuwing 2000; articles in European Econ. Review, Journal of Int. Econs and other journals; several monographs.
Address: Ruysdaelweg 3B, 2051 EM Overveen, Netherlands (home). *Telephone:* (23) 527 1700 (home). *E-mail:* mmg.fase@wxs.nl (home).

FASSI, Abbas al-; Moroccan politician; *Prime Minister;* b. 18 Sept. 1940, Berkane; m.; four c. *Education:* Univ. Mohammed V, Rabat. *Career:* apptd Sec.-Gen. Moroccan Human Rights League 1972; mem. Exec. Cttee Istiqlal Party 1974–, Gen. Sec. 1998–; Minister of Housing 1977–81, of Handicrafts and Social Affairs 1981–85, of Social Devt, Solidarity, Employment and Professional Training 2000–02, Minister of State 2002–07; Prime Minister of Morocco 2007–; Amb. to Tunisia and Perm. Rep. to League of Arab Nations 1985–90; Amb. to France 1990–94; mem. Bd of Dirs Caisse Nat. de Sécurité Sociale, Entraide Nationale, Social Devt Agency; Grand Officier, Order National de Mérite (France), Commandeur, Ordre de la République (Tunisia).
Address: Office of the Prime Minister, Palais Royal, Touarga, Rabat, Morocco (office). *Telephone:* (3) 7219400 (office). *Fax:* (3) 7769995 (office). *E-mail:* courrier@pm.gov.ma (office). *Website:* www.pm.gov.ma (office).

FASSI-FIHRI, Taïb, PhD; Moroccan government official; *Minister of Foreign Affairs and Co-operation;* b. 9 April 1958, Casablanca; m.; two c. *Education:* Lycée Descartes, Rabat, Institut Nat. de la Statistique et d'Economie Appliquée, Rabat, Université Panthéon-Sorbonne, Paris, Institut d'Etudes Politiques, Paris. *Career:* Lecturer, Univ. of Paris VII, as well as Chargé d'Etudes at Institut Français des Relations Internationales 1983–84;

attached to Dept of Planning, Ministry of Planning 1984, in charge of special duties in Cabinet of Minister in Charge of Relations with the EEC 1985–86; Chief of Div., Ministry of Foreign Affairs and Co-operation in charge of relations with EC 1986–89; Dir Office of the Minister of State in charge of Foreign Affairs and Co-operation 1989–93; Sec. of State for Foreign Affairs and Co-operation 1993–98; Head of Mission at Royal Cabinet 1998–99; Sec. of State for Foreign Affairs 1999–2000, for Foreign Affairs and Co-operation 2000–02, Coordinator, responsible for negotia-tion of free trade agreement with Morocco and USA 2002, Minister Del. for Foreign Affairs and Co-operation 2002–07, Minister of Foreign Affairs and Co-operation 2007–; Officer, Wissam Al Arch Order 2001.
Address: Ministry of Foreign Affairs and Co-operation, avenue Franklin Roosevelt, Rabat, Morocco (office). *Telephone:* (3) 7761583 (office). *Fax:* (3) 7765508 (office). *E-mail:* mail@maec.gov.ma (office). *Website:* www.maec.gov.ma (office).

FASSINO, Piero Franco Rodolfo, BSc; Italian politician; *Shadow Minister for Foreign Affairs;* b. 7 Oct. 1949, Avigliana; m. *Career:* local councillor Turin 1975–80, 1985–90, Prov. Councillor 1980–85; various posts within Turin Fed. of Partito Comunista Italiano (PCI) 1971–83, Prov. Sec. 1983–87, elected to PCI Exec. 1983, Co-ordinator Nat. Secr. 1987, then Head of party org. during transition to Partito Democratico della Sinistra (PDS), mem. Nat. Secr. and Int. Sec. PDS 1991–96, PDS Rep. to Socialist Int. 1992, PDS re-named Democratici di Sinistra (DS) 1998, Leader (Nat. Sec.) DS 2001–07, mem. Partito Democratico (formed after merger between Democratici di Sinistra, Democrazia è Libertà—La Margherita and other left-wing and centrist parties); Pres. Cen. and Western Europe Cttee Socialist Int. 1993, Chair. Cttee for Peace, Democracy and Human Rights 2004–; fmr Vice-Pres. Socialist Group, Council of Europe; mem. Chamber of Deputies from Liguria (PDS) 1994–96, from Piedmont 1996–; Under-Sec. Ministry for Foreign Affairs 1996–98; Minister for Foreign Trade 1998–2000, for Justice 2000–01; Shadow Minister for Foreign Affairs 2008–; mem. Parl. Asscn for Cen. Europe Initiative; Vice-Pres. Italian–Israeli Parl. Friendship Asscn 1995. *Publications:* Per Passione 2003.
Address: Partito Democratico, Piazza Saint'Anastasia 7, 00186 Rome, Italy. *Telephone:* (06) 675471. *Fax:* (06) 67547319. *E-mail:* info@partitodemocratico.it. *Website:* www.partitodemocratico.it.

FAURE, Danny; Seychelles politician; *Minister of Finance and Designated Minister;* b. 1962. *Career:* early career as teacher, Seychelles Polytechnic and Nat. Youth Service; fmr Chair. Seychelles People's Progressive Front; Leader of Govt Business, Nat. Ass. 1993–98; Minister for Educ. and Youth 1998–2006; Minister of Finance and Designated Minister 2006–.
Address: Ministry of Finance, POB 313, Victoria, Mahé, Seychelles (office). *Telephone:* 382000 (office).

FAURE, Philippe René Jean-Paul Yves; French diplomatist; *Ambassador to Japan;* b. 13 June 1950, Toulouse. *Education:* École Nationale d'Admin. *Career:* Sec. of Foreign Affairs, Ministry of Foreign Affairs 1976–77, Asst Dir Cabinet of Sec.-Gen. 1977–79, tech. adviser to Minister of Foreign Affairs Jean François-Poncet 1979–81; served as Second Counsellor and Head of Press, Embassy in Washington, DC 1981–87, First Counsellor, Embassy in Madrid 1987–89; Dir-Gen., then Co-Pres. Cecar (insurance co.) 1990–97; Pres. Marsh McLennan France 1997–2000, Gault et Millau 1997–2000; Sec.-Gen. Ministry of Foreign Affairs 2006–08; Admin. AREVA and EDF (Électricité de France) public energy groups 2006–08; Amb. to Mexico 2000–04, to Morocco 2004–06, to Japan 2008–; Officier de la Légion d'honneur, Officier de l'ordre national du Mérite, Commdr de l'ordre d'Isabelle la Catholique (Spain), Commdr du Mérite de la République fédérale d'Allemagne, Commdr du Wissam Al Alaoui (Morocco), Grand officier de l'Aigle Aztèque (Mexico).
Address: Embassy of France, 4-11-44 Minami-Azabu, Minato-ku, Tokyo 106-8514, Japan (office). *Telephone:* (3) 5420-8800 (office). *Fax:* (3) 5420-8847 (office). *E-mail:* ambafrance.tokyo@diplomatie.fr (office). *Website:* www.ambafrance-jp.org (office).

FAYEZ, Faisal al-, BSc, MA; Jordanian politician; b. 1952. *Education:* Univ. of Cardiff, UK, Boston Univ., USA. *Career:* joined Ministry of Foreign Affairs upon graduation; fmr diplomat, Embassy of Jordan, Brussels; fmr Deputy Dir of Royal Protocol, Royal Court; Chief of Royal Protocol and Minister of the Royal Court 2003; Prime Minister and Minister of Defence 2003–05; Minister of the Royal Court of Jordan –Nov. 2005.
Address: c/o Office of the Prime Minister, POB 80, Amman, Jordan (office).

FAYYAD, Salam, BSc, MBA, PhD; Palestinian politician and economist; *Prime Minister, Minister of Finance and Foreign Affairs;* b. 1952, Tulkarm, West Bank; m.; three c. *Education:* American Univ. of Beirut, Lebanon, Univ. of Texas, USA. *Career:* fmr Lecturer in Econs, Yarmuk Univ., Jordan; fmr official, US Fed. Reserve Bank, St Louis; joined IMF, Washington, DC 1987, various sr positions including Resident Rep. to Palestinian Authority

(PA), Jerusalem 1995–2001; Regional Man. of West Bank–Gaza, Arab Bank 2001–02 (resgnd); Minister of Finance, PA 2002–05 (resgnd), March 2007–, also of Foreign Affairs June 2007–; Prime Minister of Palestinian Autonomous Areas 2007–. *Publications:* numerous research papers on Palestinian economy.
Address: Ministry of Finance, POB 795, Sateh Marhaba, Al-Birah/Ramallah (office); Ministry of Finance, POB 4007, Gaza, Palestinian Autonomous Areas (office). *Telephone:* (2) 2400650 (office); (8) 2826188 (office). *Fax:* (2) 2400595 (office); (8) 2820696 (office). *E-mail:* cbomof@palnet.com (office). *Website:* www.mof.gov.ps (office).

FEAN, Sir (Thomas) Vincent, Kt, KCVO; British diplomatist; *Ambassador to Libya;* b. 20 Nov. 1952; m. Anne Marie Fean; one s. two d. *Career:* Desk Officer, W African Dept, FCO 1975–76, Third Sec., Chancery, Baghdad 1978, Second Sec., Chancery, Gaborone 1978–79, Second, later First Sec., Chancery, Damascus 1979–82, EU Dept (Internal), FCO 1982–84, Western European Dept, Berlin and GDR, FCO 1984–85, Sec., Office of UK Rep. to EU, Brussels 1985–89, Asst Head of Personnel Operations Dept, FCO 1990–91, Head of Unit, Personnel Man. Dept 1991–92, Press and Public Affairs, Paris 1992–96, Head of Counter Terrorism Policy Dept, FCO 1996–99, Dir Trade Pnrs UK (now UKTI), Asia Pacific 1999–2002, High Commr to Malta 2002–06, Amb. to Libya 2006–.
Address: British Embassy, PO Box 4206, Tripoli, Libya (office). *Telephone:* (21) 3403644 (office). *Fax:* (21) 3403648 (office). *Website:* www .britishembassy.gov.uk/libya (office).

FEATHERSTONE, Simon Mark; British diplomatist; b. 24 July 1958; m. Gail Featherstone; one s. two d. *Career:* joined British Diplomatic Service 1980; Asst Desk Officer, S Asian Dept, FCO 1980–81; full-time language training, SOAS and Hong Kong 1981–83; Science and Tech. Officer, Embassy in Beijing 1984–86, Counsellor, Political and Econ. 1996–98; Desk Officer, Falkland Islands Dept, FCO 1987–88; secondment to Cabinet Office 1988–89; First Sec., Environment, UK Rep. to Brussels 1990–94; Consul-Gen., Embassy in Shanghai 1994–96; Head of EU Dept (External), FCO 1998–2003; Amb. to Switzerland (also accred to Liechtenstein) 2004–08.
Address: Foreign and Commonwealth Office, King Charles Street, London, SW1A 2AH, England (office). *Telephone:* (20) 7008-1500 (office). *Website:* www.fco.gov.uk (office).

FEDERSPIEL, Ulrik Andreas, MA; Danish diplomatist; *Permanent Secretary of State for Foreign Affairs;* b. 1943, Copenhagen; m. Birgitte Hartnack Federspiel. *Education:* Univ. of Århus, Univ. of Pennsylvania, USA. *Career:* entered Danish Foreign Service 1971; Expert on EC Affairs, Ministry of Foreign Affairs 1971–77; First Sec. for Political Affairs, Embassy in London 1977–81; Special Asst to Perm. Sec. of State for Foreign Affairs 1981–84; Deputy Chief of Mission, Embassy in Washington, DC 1984–89; Asst to Minister in Reorganising Ministry of Foreign Affairs 1989–90; Perm. Sec. of State for Foreign Affairs 1990–93, 2005–; apptd Chief of Staff (Sec. to Cabinet and Sec. to HM the Queen in Council of Ministers) 1993; Amb. to Ireland 1997–2000, to USA 2000–05; Alt. for Minister for Foreign Affairs in EU Council of Ministers 2005–; Danish Co-Chair. Danish-Russian Intergovernmental Council on Econ. Cooperation 2005–; mem. Advisory Bd Humanity in Action 1997–; Hon. Trustee Crown Prince Frederik Fund, Harvard Univ. 2001–; Commdr, Order of the Danebrog, Grand Cross (Belgium, Finland, Iceland, Italy, Lithuania, Norway, Portugal, Bulgaria, Greece, Sweden, Brazil). *Publications include:* Integration in Theory and Practice 1985.
Address: Ministry of Foreign Affairs, Asiatisk Pl. 2, 1448 Copenhagen K, Denmark (office). *Telephone:* 33-92-00-00 (office). *Fax:* 32-54-05-33 (office). *E-mail:* um@um.dk (office). *Website:* www.um.dk (office).

FEITH, Pieter, LicenPolSci, MA; Dutch diplomatist and international organization official; *Special Representative in Kosovo, European Union;* b. 9 Feb. 1945, Rotterdam; m.; three d. *Education:* Univ. of Lausanne, Switzerland, Fletcher School of Law and Diplomacy, Medford, USA. *Career:* performed mil. military service as reserve officer of Netherlands Marine Corps; with diplomatic service 1970–95, posted to Damascus, Bonn, New York (Mission to UN), Khartoum and Netherlands Mission to NATO and WEU, Brussels, also Chair. first UN Conf. of States Parties to the Chemical Weapons Convention, The Hague 1997; Personal Rep. of NATO Sec.-Gen. Lord Robertson for Yugoslavia, Dir of Crisis Man. and Operations Directorate, Head of NATO Balkans Task Force and Political Advisor to Commdr IFOR Bosnia-Herzegovina 1995–2001; Gen. Secr. of Council of EU, Deputy Dir-Gen. for Politico-Mil. Affairs 2001–; Personal Rep. of EU High Rep., Javier Solana, for Sudan/Darfur 2004; Head of EU Expert Team for Iraq 2005; Head of EU-led Aceh Monitoring Mission (AMM) in Indonesia 2005–06; Civilian Operations Commdr for all civilian ESDP Crisis Man. Operations, Acting Dir of EU Civilian Planning and Conduct

Capability 2007; led team of EU officials and approved the Constitution of the Repub. of Kosovo April 2008, EU Special Rep. in Kosovo 2008–.
Address: Jüri Laas (Press Adviser), Council of the European Union, Rue de la Loi 175, 1048 Brussels, Belgium (office). *Telephone:* 486-79-80-55 (mobile) (office). *Fax:* (2) 281-69-34 (office). *E-mail:* juri.laas@consilium .europa.eu (office). *Website:* www.consilium.europa.eu (office).

FELDMAN, Shai, PhD; Israeli academic; *Judith and Sidney Swartz Director, Crown Center for Middle East Studies, Brandeis University; Education:* Hebrew Univ., Jerusalem, Univ. of California, Berkeley. *Career:* Sr Research Assoc., Jaffee Center for Strategic Studies, Tel-Aviv Univ. 1977–97, Head 1997–2005; Judith and Sidney Swartz Dir Crown Center for Middle East Studies, Brandies Univ. 2005–; Visiting Fellow, Washington Inst. for Near East Policy 1994; Sr Research Fellow, Belfer Center for Science and Int. Affairs (BCSIA), Harvard Univ. John F. Kennedy School of Govt 1995–97, now mem. Bd of Dirs; Assoc. Fellow, Royal United Services Inst. (RUSI), London; mem. UN Sec.-Gen's Advisory Bd on Disarmament Matters 2001–03; mem. Scientific Advisory Cttee, Stockholm Int. Peace Research Inst. (SIPRI), Int. Inst. of Strategic Studies (IISS), London. *Publications:* Israeli Nuclear Deterrence: A Strategy for the 1980s 1982, The Future of US-Israel Strategic Cooperation 1996, Nuclear Weapons and Arms Control in the Middle East 1997, Bridging the Gap: A Future Security Architecture for the Middle East (jt author) 1997, Track-II Diplomacy: Lessons from the Middle East 2003.
Address: Crown Center for Middle East Studies, Heller, Third Floor, 415 South Street, Waltham, MA 02453, USA (office). *Telephone:* (781) 736-5320 (office). *Website:* www.brandeis.edu/crown (office).

FELDSTEIN, Martin Stuart, MA, DPhil; American economist and academic; *President and CEO, National Bureau of Economic Research;* b. 25 Nov. 1939, New York; m. Kathleen Foley 1965; two d. *Education:* Harvard Univ. and Univ. of Oxford, UK. *Career:* Research Fellow, Nuffield Coll., Oxford 1964–65, Official Fellow 1965–67, Lecturer in Public Finance 1965–67; Asst Prof. of Econs, Harvard Univ. 1967–68, Assoc. Prof. 1968–69, Prof. 1969–, George F. Baker Prof. of Econs 1984–; Pres. and CEO Nat. Bureau of Econ. Research 1977–82, 1984–2008; Chair. Pres.'s Council of Econ. Advisers 1982–84; mem. Pres.'s Foreign Intelligence Advisory Bd 2006–; mem. Advisory Bd Congressional Budget Office, New York Fed. Reserve Bank, Boston Fed. Reserve Bank; mem. J.P. Morgan Int. Council; mem. Bd of Contribs, Wall Street Journal; Fellow, American Philosophical Soc., American Acad. of Arts and Sciences, Econometric Soc., Nat. Asscn of Business Economists; mem. American Econ. Asscn, Vice-Pres. 1988, Pres. 2004; mem. Inst. of Medicine, NAS, Council on Foreign Relations (Dir 1998–, Trustee 1999–, (mem. Exec. Cttee 2002–), Trilateral Comm. 1984– (Exec. Cttee 1990–), Nat Cttee on US-China Relations (Dir) 2001–, Group of 30 2002–; Foreign mem. Austrian Acad. of Sciences; Corresp. Fellow, British Acad.; mem. Bd Dirs American Int. 1988–, Eli Lilly 2001–; Hon. Fellow, Nuffield Coll. Oxford 1998; Hon. LLD (Univ. of Rochester) 1984, (Marquette) 1985; Bernhard Harms Prize, Weltwirtschafts Institut, Distinguished Service Award, The Tax Foundation, John Bates Clark Medal, American Econ. Asscn 1977.
Address: National Bureau of Economic Research, 1050 Massachusetts Avenue, Cambridge, MA 02138 (office); 147 Clifton Street, Belmont, MA 02478, USA (home). *Telephone:* (617) 868-3905 (office). *Fax:* (617) 868-7194 (office). *E-mail:* msfeldst@nber.org (office); mfeldstein@harvard.edu (office). *Website:* www.nber.org/feldstein (office).

FELL, Richard Taylor, CVO; British diplomatist (retd); b. 11 Nov. 1948; m. Claire Fell; three s. *Career:* joined British Diplomatic Service 1971, with S Asian Dept, FCO 1971–72; Third Sec., Ottawa 1972–74, Counsellor (Econ. and Commercial) 1989–93, Second Sec., Saigon 1974–75, temporary duty, Vientiane 1975, with Southern European Dept, FCO 1975–76, Cen. and S African Dept 1977–78, Chargé d'Affaires a.i., Hanoi 1979, First Sec., UK Del. to NATO, Brussels 1979–83, Head of Chancery, Kuala Lumpur 1983–86, Asst, SE Asian Dept 1986–88, on loan to industry 1988–89, Deputy Head of Mission, Bangkok 1993–96, with Whitehall Scrutiny Review of Commercial Services, FCO 1996–97, Head of Personnel Services Dept 1997–2000, Consul-Gen., Toronto 2000, Royal Coll. of Defence Studies, London 2000–01, High Commr to NZ (non-resident High Commr to Samoa and concurrent Gov. of Pitcairn, Henderson, Ducie and Oeno Islands) 2001–06.
Address: c/o Foreign & Commonwealth Office, King Charles Street, London, SW1A 2AH, England. *Telephone:* (20) 7008-1500.

FELTMAN, Jeffrey D., BA, MA; American diplomatist; *Acting Deputy Assistant Secretary of State for Near Eastern Affairs;* m. Mary Dale Draper. *Education:* Ball State Univ., Fletcher School of Law and Diplomacy at Tufts Univ., Univ. of Jordan, Amman. *Career:* career mem. Sr Foreign Service since 1986, Consular Officer, Embassy in Port-au-Prince, Haiti 1986–88, Econ. Officer, Embassy in Budapest 1988–91, Special Asst to

Deputy Asst Sec. concentrating on coordination of US assistance to fmr Communist countries of Eastern and Cen. Europe 1991–93, joined Bureau of Near Eastern Affairs 1993, served in Embassy in Tel-Aviv 1995–98, responsible for econ. issues in the Gaza Strip 1998–2000, Chief of Political and Econ. Section, Embassy in Tunisia 2000, Special Asst on Peace Process issues, Embassy in Tel-Aviv 2000–01, Deputy Prin. Officer, US Consulate-Gen. in Jerusalem 2001–02, Acting Prin. Officer 2002–03, Head of Coalition Provisional Authority (CPA) office in Irbil Prov., Iraq and also served as Deputy Regional Coordinator for CPA northern area Jan.–April 2004, Amb. to Lebanon 2004–08, Acting Deputy Asst Sec. of State for Near Eastern Affairs, Dept of State 2008–.
Address: US Department of State, 2201 C Street NW, Washington, DC 20520, USA (office). *Telephone:* (202) 647-4000 (office). *Fax:* (202) 647-6738 (office). *Website:* www.state.gov (office).

FENBY, Jonathan Theodore Starmer, CBE; British writer and journalist; *Editor-in-Chief and China Editor, Trusted Sources;* b. 11 Nov. 1942, London; m. Renée Wartski 1967; one s. one d. *Education:* King Edward's School, Birmingham, Westminster School and New Coll. Oxford. *Career:* corresp. and ed. Reuters World Service, Reuters Ltd 1963–77; corresp. (France and Germany), The Economist 1982–86; Home Ed. and Asst Ed. The Independent 1986–88; Deputy Ed. The Guardian 1988–93; Ed. The Observer 1993–95; Dir Guardian Newspapers 1990–95; Ed. South China Morning Post 1995–99; Ed. Netmedia Group; Assoc. Ed. Sunday Business 2000–01; Ed. Business Europe 2000–01; Ed. www.earlywarning.com 2004–06; currently Ed.-in-Chief and China Ed., Trusted Sources; mem. Bd European Journalism Centre, Belgian–British Colloquium; Chevalier, Ordre du Mérite (France) 1992. *Radio:* broadcasts on BBC, CBC and French and Swiss radio. *Television:* broadcasts on BBC, CNN, CNBC, Channel Four and FR2. *Publications:* The Fall of the House of Beaverbrook 1979, Piracy and the Public 1983, The International News Services 1986, On the Brink: The Trouble with France 1998 (new edn 2002), Comment peut-on être Français? 1999, Dealing With the Dragon: A Year in the New Hong Kong 2000, Generalissimo: Chiang Kai-shek and the China He Lost 2003, The Sinking of the Lancastria 2005, Alliance: The Inside Story of How Roosevelt, Stalin and Churchill Won One War and Began Another 2007; contrib. to newspapers and magazines in Europe, USA, Asia.
Address: Trusted Sources, 48 Charlotte Street, London, W1T 2NS (office); 101 Ridgmount Gardens, Torrington Place, London, WC1E 7AZ, England (home). *Telephone:* (20) 3008-5764 (office). *E-mail:* jtfenby@hotmail.com (home). *Website:* www.trustedsources.co.uk (office).

FENECH, Tonio, BCom, BA (Hons); Maltese accountant, auditor and politician; *Minister of Finance, Economy and Investment;* b. 5 May 1969; m. Claudine Ellul 1998; one s. one d. *Education:* St Aloysius' Coll., Birkirkara, Manoel Theatre Acad. of Dramatic Arts, Univ. of Malta. *Career:* gained early work experience during school summer holidays at Multi Packaging Ltd; mem. Youth Fellowship 1987–96; with Price Waterhouse (later Pricewaterhou-seCoopers) 1993–2004, later became man. in audit practice, subsequently Sr Consultant in man. consultancy practice, several int. work experiences in Italy and Libya, including Instituto per le Opere Religiose (IOR) Vatican Bank; mem. Partit Nazzjonalista (Nationalist Party), mem. Exec. Cttee Nationalist Party Coll. of Councillors 1998–99, Sec.-Gen. Nationalist Party Coll. of Councillors 1999–2003, mem. Nationalist Party Exec. Cttee 1999–; elected as local councillor for Birkirkara 1996–98, Mayor of Birkirkara 1998–2003; mem. Parl. from 8th Dist 2003–, apptd observer to European Parl. 2003–04; Parl. Sec., Ministry of Finance 2004–, participated in Malta's accession to EuroZone; Minister of Finance, Economy and Investment 2008–; mem. Housing Authority Bd 1998–2003, e-Malta Comm. 2001–03.
Address: Ministry of Finance, Economy and Investment, Maison Demandols, 30 South Street, Valletta CMR 02, Malta (office). *Telephone:* 21249640 (office); 25998285 (office); 27327302; 79927302. *Fax:* 21233605 (office); 21251712 (office). *E-mail:* info.mfin@gov.mt (office); fenechtonio@gmail.com. *Website:* www.mfin.gov.mt (office); www.toniofenech.com.

FENECH-ADAMI, Edward, KUOM, BA, LLD; Maltese politician, lawyer and head of state; *President;* b. 7 Feb. 1934, Birkirkara; m. Mary Sciberras 1965; four s. one d. *Education:* St Aloysius Coll., Univ. of Malta. *Career:* entered legal practice 1959; Ed. Il-Poplu (weekly) 1962–69; mem. Nat. Exec. Nationalist Party 1961, Asst Gen. Sec. 1962–75, Pres. Gen. and Admin. Councils 1975–77, Leader 1977–2004; mem. Parl. 1969–2004; Leader of Opposition 1977–82, 1983–87, 1996–98; Prime Minister 1987–96, 1998–2004; Pres. of Malta 2004–; Vice-Pres. European Union of Christian Democrat Parties 1979–99; Nat. Order of Merit.
Address: President's Office, The Palace, Valletta CMR02, Malta (office). *Telephone:* (21) 221221 (office). *Fax:* (21) 241241 (office). *E-mail:* president@gov.mt (office). *Website:* president.gov.mt (office).

FERGUSON, Roy Neil, MA; New Zealand diplomatist; *Ambassador to USA;* m. Dawn Ferguson; two s. *Education:* Univ. of Canterbury, Univ. of Pennsylvania and Harvard Business School, USA. *Career:* postings to Manila and Canberra, worked in Information, UN, Asian and Australian Divs, Ministry of Foreign Affairs, Dir Man. Audit Unit, UN and Commonwealth Div., Environment Div. and Personnel Div., Deputy Chief of Mission, Washington, DC 1991–95, Amb. to S Korea 1999–2002, Dir Americas Div., Ministry of Foreign Affairs and Trade 2002–05, Amb. to USA 2006–; mem. Bds NZ-US Council, Fulbright New Zealand, Ian Axford Fellowships and NZ Centre for Latin American Studies.
Address: Embassy of New Zealand, 37 Observatory Circle, NW, Washington, DC 20008, USA (office). *Telephone:* (202) 328-4800 (office). *Fax:* (202) 667-5227 (office). *E-mail:* nz@nzemb.org (office). *Website:* www.nzembassy.com/home.cfm?c=31 (office).

FERGUSSON, George Duncan Raukawa; British diplomatist; *High Commissioner to New Zealand;* b. 30 Sept. 1955; m. Margaret Wookey; three d. (and one s. deceased). *Career:* NI Office 1978–88; First Sec. (Political), Dublin 1988–91, Soviet, then Eastern Dept, FCO 1991–93, First Sec. (Political/Information), Seoul 1994–96, Deputy Head of Southern African Dept, FCO 1996–97, Head of Repub. of Ireland Dept 1997–99, Consul-Gen., Boston 1999–2003, on loan to Cabinet Office as Head of Foreign Policy Team 2003–06, High Commr to NZ (non-resident High Commr to Ind. State of Samoa and non-resident Gov. of Pitcairn, Henderson, Ducie and Oeno Islands) 2006–.
Address: British High Commission, PO Box 1812, 44 Hill Street, Thorndon, Wellington, New Zealand (office). *Telephone:* (4) 924-2888 (office). *Fax:* (4) 924-2831 (office). *E-mail:* ppa.mailbox@fco.gov.uk (office). *Website:* www.britain.org.nz (office).

FERNALD, Ivan; Suriname government official. *Career:* Minister of Defence 2005–.
Address: Ministry of Defence, Kwattaweg 29, Paramaribo, Suriname (office). *Telephone:* 474244 (office). *Fax:* 420055 (office). *E-mail:* defensie@sr.net.

FERNANDES, George; Indian trade unionist and politician; *Leader, Janata Dal—United;* b. 3 June 1930, Bangalore, Karnataka; m. Leila Kabir 1971; one s. *Education:* St Peter's Seminary, Bangalore. *Career:* joined Socialist Party of India 1949, mem. Nat. Cttee 1955–77, Treas. 1964, Chair. 1971–77; Ed. Konkani Yuvak (Konkani Youth) monthly in Konkani language 1949, Raithavani weekly in Kannada language 1949, Dockman weekly in English 1952–53, also New Society; fmr Chief Ed. Pratipaksha weekly in Hindi; trade union work in S Kanara 1949, 1950, in Bombay (now Mumbai) and Maharashtra 1950–58; Founding Pres. All-India Radio Broadcasters and Telecasters Guild, Khadi Comm. Karmachari Union, All-India Univ. Employees' Confed.; Pres. All-India Railwaymen's Fed. 1973–77; organized nat. railways strike 1974; Treas. All-India Hind Mazdoor Sabha 1958; formed Hind Mazdoor Panchayat 1958, Gen. Sec. for over 10 years; Convenor, United Council of Trade Unions; fmr mem. Gen. Council of Public Services Int., Int. Transport Workers' Fed.; Founder-Chair. New India Co-operative Bank Ltd (fmrly Bombay Labour Co-operative Bank Ltd); Gen. Sec. Samyukta Socialist Party of India 1969–70; mem. Bombay Municipal Corpn 1961–68; mem. for Bombay City, Lok Sabha 1967–77; went underground on declaration of emergency 1975; mem. Janata Party 1977, Gen. Sec. 1985–86; mem. for Muzzafarpur, Bihar, Lok Sabha 1977–79, also elected to Lok Sabha 1980, 1989, 1991, 1996, 1998; Minister of Communications March–July 1977, of Industry 1977–79 (resgnd from Govt 1979), for Railways 1989–90, for Kashmir Affairs 1990–91, of Defence 1998–2001, 2001–04; Deputy Leader Lok Dal 1980–; mem. Standing Parl. Cttee on Finance 1993–96, also Consultative Cttee on Home Affairs, mem. Standing Parl. Cttee on External Affairs 1996, also Consultative Cttee on Human Resources Devt; Pres. Samata Party 1994–2000, 2002–04; fmr Pres. Janata Dal—United, currently Sr Leader; Chair. Editorial Bd Pratipaksh (Hindi monthly); Ed. The Other Side (English language monthly); Pres. Hind Mazdoor Kisan Panchayat; Chair. India Devt Group, London 1979, Schumacher Foundation 1979; fmr mem. Press Council of India; mem. Amnesty International, People's Union for Civil Liberties; involved in anti-nuclear and environmental campaigns. *Publications:* What Ails the Socialists: The Kashmir Problem, The Railway Strike of 1974, George Fernandes Speaks.
Address: Janata Dal—United (People's Party—United), 7 Jantar Mantar Road, New Delhi 110 001 (office); 3 Krishna Menon Marg, New Delhi 110011 (home); 30 Leonard Road, Richmond Town, Bangalore, Karnataka 560025, India. *Telephone:* (11) 23368833 (office); (80) 22214143 (Bangalore); (11) 23793397 (New Delhi) (home); (11) 23015403 (New Delhi) (home). *Fax:* (11) 23368138 (office).

FERNANDES PEREIRA, Manuel Tomás; Portuguese diplomatist; *Permanent Representative, NATO;* b. 2 April 1947, Lisbon; m. Maria José Morais

Pires. *Education:* Lisbon Faculty of Law. *Career:* joined diplomatic service 1972; Second Sec., Embassy in Brasilia 1974–78; with Perm. Del. to NATO, Brussels 1978; Chief of Cabinet of Sec. of State of Foreign Affairs 1982–84, Head, Office of Sec.-Gen. 1984–86, Dir Dept of Defence, Security and Disarmament 1986–90, European Corresp. and Advisor to Minister of Foreign Affairs 1990–94, Deputy Dir-Gen. for Bilateral Affairs 1994–95, Dir-Gen. for EC Affairs 1995–97; Amb. to South Africa (also accred. to Gabon and Maseru) 1997–2003; Dir-Gen. for Political Affairs 2003–06; Perm. Rep. to NATO, Brussels 2006–.
Address: North Atlantic Treaty Organization, blvd Léopold III, 1110 Brussels, Belgium (office). *Telephone:* (2) 707-41-11 (office). *Fax:* (2) 707-45-79 (office). *E-mail:* natodoc@hq.nato.int (office). *Website:* www.nato .int (office).

FERNÁNDES PUENTES, Liliana; Panamanian diplomatist. *Education:* London School of Econs, UK. *Career:* Consul-Gen. and Perm. Rep. to IMO 2000–, Amb. to UK 2005–.
Address: Embassy of Panama, 40 Hertford Street, London, W1J 7SH, England (office). *Telephone:* (20) 7493-4646 (office). *Fax:* (20) 7493-4333 (office). *E-mail:* panama1@btconnect.com (office).

FERNÁNDEZ, Alberto Angel; Argentine politician; b. 2 April 1959, Buenos Aires; m.; one s. *Education:* Universidad de Buenos Aires. *Career:* Prof., Dept of Penal Rights, Universidad de Buenos Aires; Pres. Asociacíon de Superintendentes de Seguros de América Latina 1989–92; Exec. Vice-Pres. Grupo Banco Provincia 1997; mem. Parl. for Buenos Aires 2000; Cabinet Chief 2003–08 (resgnd); Industrialist of the Year in Insurance 1997, Millennium Prize for Industrialist of the Century 2000.
Address: c/o Avenida Pte Julio A. Roca 782, 1067 Buenos Aires, Argentina (office).

FERNÁNDEZ, Carlos Rafael, BEcons; Argentine economist and politician; *Minister of the Economy;* b. 1954, Ciudad de la Plata. *Education:* La Plata Nat. Univ. *Career:* Nat. Dir of tax coordination for provs 1989–97; Sub-Sec., tax coordination and policy for Buenos Aires prov. govt 1997, Under-Sec. for Fiscal Policy, Buenos Aires Prov. 2002–03, becoming Prov. Minister of Economy; Under-Sec. for Relations with the Provinces, Ministry of Economy 2007; Sub-Sec of the Budget, Dec. 2007–March 2008; Dir Administración Fed. de Ingresos Públicos (tax agency) March–April 2008; Minister of Economy 2008–.
Address: Ministry of Economy, Hipólito Yrigoyen 250, C1086AAB Buenos Aires, Argentina (office). *Telephone:* (11) 4349-5000 (office). *E-mail:* sagpya@mecon.gov.ar (office). *Website:* www.mecon.gov.ar (office).

FERNÁNDEZ, Gonzalo; Uruguayan lawyer and politician; *Minister of Foreign Affairs; Career:* Sec. of Presidency 2005–08; Minister of Foreign Affairs 2008–; mem. Partido Socialista del Uruguay.
Address: Ministry of Foreign Affairs, Avda 18 de Julio 1205, 11100 Montevideo, Uruguay (office). *Telephone:* (2) 9022132 (office). *Fax:* (2) 9021349 (office). *E-mail:* webmaster@mrree.gub.uy (office). *Website:* www .mrree.gub.uy (office).

FERNÁNDEZ, Rafael Ludovino; Dominican Republic diplomatist. *Career:* Amb. to UK 2000–.
Address: Embassy of the Dominican Republic, 139 Inverness Terrace, London, W2 6JF, England (office). *Telephone:* (20) 7727-6285 (office). *Fax:* (20) 7727-3693 (office). *Website:* www.serex.gov.do (office).

FERNÁNDEZ DE KIRCHNER, Cristina Elisabeth; Argentine politician, lawyer and head of state; *President;* b. 19 Feb. 1953, La Plata, Buenos Aires; m. Néstor Carlos Kirchner; one s. one d. *Education:* Universidad Nacional de La Plata. *Career:* began political career in Tendencia Revolucionaria faction of Partido Justicialista 1970s; elected prov. rep. in Patagonian prov. of Santa Cruz 1989–95, Chair. Constitutional Affairs, Authorities and Regulations Cttee, Santa Cruz House of Reps 1989–95, First Vice-Chair. 1990; elected to represent Santa Cruz in Senate 1995–97, 2001–05, in Chamber of Deputies 1997, Senator representing prov. of Buenos Aires (Front for Victory faction of party) 2005–07, Pres. of Argentina 2007–; mem. Congress Partido Justicialista 1985, mem. Nat. Congress 1995, Pres. Congress Partido Justicialista 2004.
Address: General Secretariat to the Presidency, Balcarce 50, C1064AAB Buenos Aires, Argentina (home). *Telephone:* (11) 4344-3674 (office). *Fax:* (11) 4344-2647 (office). *E-mail:* dgi@presidencia.gov.ar (office). *Website:* www.secretariageneral.gov.ar (home).

FERNÁNDEZ-FAINGOLD, Hugo; Uruguayan diplomatist and fmr politician; b. 1 March 1947, Montevideo; m.; seven c. *Education:* Columbia Univ., Georgetown Univ. *Career:* fmr Prof. Univ. of the Repub., Montevideo; Dean, School of Social Sciences, Nat. Univ. Costa Rica 1974–76; fmr consultant to several int. orgs including UNDP, ILO, Inter-

American Inst. for Cooperation in Agriculture, Inter-American Devt Bank; mem. Nat. Convention and Montevideo Convention, Colorado Party 1985–, Sec. Gen. Colorado Party Nat. Exec. Cttee 1995–2000; Minister of Labor and Social Security 1985–89; mem. Senate 1995–2000; Dir El Dia (daily newspaper) 1997–98; Vice-Pres. of Uruguay and Pres. of Gen. Ass. 1998–2000; Amb. to USA 2000–05. *Publications:* more than 70 articles and papers.
Address: c/o Ministry of Foreign Affairs, Avda 18 de Julio 1205, 11100 Montevideo, Uruguay (office).

FERNÁNDEZ REYNA, Leonel, DIur; Dominican Republic politician and head of state; *President;* b. 26 Dec. 1953, Santo Domingo; m. Margarita Cedeño; one c. (two c. from previous m.). *Education:* Universidad Autónoma de Santo Domingo. *Career:* joined Partido de la Liberación Dominicana 1973, Pres. 2002–; cand. for Vice-Pres. 1994; Pres. 1996–2000, 2004–.
Address: Administrative Secretariat of the Presidency, Palacio Nacional, Avda México, esq. Dr Delgado, Santo Domingo, DN, Dominican Republic. *Telephone:* 686-4771 (office). *Fax:* 688-2100 (office). *E-mail:* prensa@presidencia.gov.do (office). *Website:* www.presidencia.gov.do (office); www.leonelfernandez.com.

FERRARI, Margaret Hughes, BL; Saint Vincent and the Grenadines United Nations official and lawyer; b. 1 Jan. 1948; m.; three c. *Education:* Univ. of London, UK. *Career:* Sec. and Legal Exec. Hughes and Cummings law firm 1967–90, Partner 1990–; called to Bar, Lincoln's Inn, London, UK 1990; Pres. Bar Asscn of Saint Vincent and the Grenadines 1998–; Deputy Chair. Bd Saint Vincent Co-operative Bank Ltd; Dir Bottlers Ltd. (bottling co.); Perm. Rep. to UN, New York 2000–07.
Address: c/o Ministry of Foreign Affairs, Commerce and Trade, Administrative Building, 3rd Floor, Bay Steet, Kingstown, Saint Vincent and the Grenadines (office). *Telephone:* 456-2060 (office). *Fax:* 456-2610 (office). *E-mail:* office.foreignaffairs@mail.gov.vc (office).

FERREIRA, Domingos Augusto; São Tomé and Príncipe diplomatist. *Career:* fmr Chargé d'Affaires a.i., Perm. Mission to UN, NY.
Address: c/o Ministry of Foreign Affairs, Co-operation and Communities, Av. 12 de Julho, CP 111, São Tomé, São Tomé and Príncipe (office). *Website:* www.mnecc.gov.st (office).

FERREIRA, Fernando Jorge Wahnon; Cape Verde diplomatist; *Ambassador to Belgium; Career:* Amb. to Belgium (also accred to UK) and Perm. Rep. to EU 2007–.
Address: Embassy of Cape Verde, 29 avenue Jeanne, 1050 Brussels, Belgium (office). *Telephone:* (2) 646-62-70 (office). *Fax:* (2) 646-33-85 (office). *E-mail:* emb.caboverde@skynet.be (office).

FERRERO COSTA, Eduardo, LLD, PhD; Peruvian lawyer, academic, diplomatist and fmr politician; b. 1946, Lima; m. Verónica Diaz de Ferrero; four c. *Education:* Pontificia Universidad Católica del Perú, Univ. of Wisconsin, Univ. of California, San Diego. *Career:* Sr Prof. of Int. Public Law, Pontificia Universidad Católica del Perú 1972–; Prof. of Int. Law, Diplomatic Acad. of Peru 1974–88; Visiting Prof., Law School, Univ. of California, Berkeley 1989; Prof. of Int. Law, Universidad de Lima 2001–07; currently Dir of new Program in Law, Universidad del Pacifico; Gen. Legal Counsel, Ministry of Industry, Tourism, Foreign Trade and Integration 1975–78; Sr Partner, Eduardo Ferrero Costa Law Firm 1980–95; Legal Adviser, Peruvian Del. to UN Conf. on Law of the Sea 1978–82; Sr Legal Counsel, Ministry of Foreign Affairs 1980–82, mem. Advisory Cttee 1985–92, Minister of Foreign Affairs 1997–98; Vice-Pres. UN Cttee against Racial Discrimination (CERD) 1988–2000; Pres. Peruvian Comm. for the Pacific Basin and mem. Bd Pacific Econ. Cooperation Council 1992–95; Adviser to Peruvian Del. for Border Negotiation with Ecuador 1996–97; Partner, Estudio Echecopar Law Firm 1999–2001, Partner and Head of Int. Area 2006–; Adviser, Andean Community 1999–2000; Amb. and Perm. Rep. to OAS, Washington, DC 2001–06, Amb. to USA 2004–06; mem. for Peru of Perm. Court of Arbitration, The Hague, Int. Chamber of Commerce, Paris 2000–02; Arbitrator registered in Centre of Arbitration of Peruvian American Chamber of Commerce; Conciliator registered in Ministry of Justice; mem. Bd Dirs Petroleos del Perú 1975–77, Servicio Nacional de Aprendizaje Industrial 1975–77, Banco Financiero 1995–96, Compañia Minera San Ignacio de Morococha 2000–01; mem. Lima Bar Asscn, Peruvian Asscn for Int. Law, Peruvian Asscn for Peace Studies (APEP), Peruvian Center for Int. Studies (CEPEI), Peruvian Center for Prevention and Solution of Conflicts (CEPSCON), Peruvian Asscn for Maritime Law, American Soc. of Int. Law; nat. decorations from Bolivia, Brazil, Colombia, Guatemala, Mexico, Paraguay and Peru. *Publications:* 19 books and more than 50 articles on int. law, int. relations, law of the sea, Peruvian foreign policy.

Address: Estudio Echecopar, Edificio Parque Las Lomas, Avenida de la Floresta 497, Piso 5, San Borja, Lima, Peru (office). *Telephone:* (1) 618-8500 (office). *Fax:* (1) 372-7374 (office). *E-mail:* eduardo.ferrero@echecopar .com.pe (office). *Website:* www.echecopar.com.pe (office).

FERRERO-WALDNER, Benita Maria, DIur; Austrian politician and diplomatist; *Commissioner for External Relations and European Neighbourhood Policy, European Commission;* b. 5 Sept. 1948, Oberndorf, Salzburg. *Education:* Univ. of Salzburg. *Career:* export and sales managerial roles in German and US cos, Germany 1978–83; joined Diplomatic Service 1984, several posts Ministry of Foreign Affairs, Vienna 1984–86, First Sec., Dakar, Devt Aid Dept, Vienna; Counsellor for Econ. Affairs, Deputy Head of Mission, Chargé d'affaires, Paris 1986–93; Deputy Chief of Protocol, Ministry of Foreign Affairs 1993; UN Chief of Protocol, Exec. Office of Sec.-Gen., New York 1994–95; State Sec., Ministry of Foreign Affairs 1995–2000, Minister of Foreign Affairs 2000–04; EU Commr for External Relations and European Neighbourhood Policy 2004–; Mérite Européen Gold Medal. *Publication:* The Future of Development Co-operation, Setting Course in a Changing World.
Address: European Commission, 200 rue de la Loi, 1049 Brussels, Belgium (office). *Telephone:* (2) 2994900 (office). *Fax:* (2) 2981299 (office). *Website:* europa.eu (office).

FEULNER, Edwin J., PhD, MBA; American research institute administrator; *President, Heritage Foundation;* m. Linda Claire Leventhal; one s. one d. *Education:* Regis Univ., Georgetown Univ., Univ. of Edinburgh, LSE. *Career:* Pres. The Heritage Foundation; Treasurer and Trustee, Mont Pelerin Soc. (also fmr Pres.); Trustee and fmr Chair. Intercollegiate Studies Inst.; Dir Nat. Chamber Foundation; adviser to several US govt depts and agencies; fmr Consultant for Domestic Policy to US Pres. Ronald Reagan; US Rep. to UN Special Session on Disarmament 1982; mem. numerous govt comms including Carlucci Comm. on Foreign Aid 1983, Pres.'s Comm. on White House Fellows 1981–83, Meltzer Comm. 1999–2000; mem. Bd of Visitors George Mason Univ.; Trustee Acton Inst., Int. Republican Inst.; fmr Pres. Philadelphia Soc.; fmr Dir Sequoia Bank, Regis Univ., Council for Nat. Policy; regular contrib. to several publs including Chicago Sun Times, Chicago Tribune, New York Times, Washington Post; Dr hc (Nichols Coll.) 1981, (Univ. Francisco Marroquin, Guatemala) 1982, (Bellevue Coll.) 1987, (Gonzaga Univ.) 1992, (Grove City Coll.) 1994, (Pepperdine Univ.) 2000, (St Norbert Coll.) 2002, (Hillsdale Coll.) 2004, (Thomas More Univ.) 2005, (Edin.) 2006, (Hanyang Univ., Korea); Presidential Citizen's Medal 1989. *Publications:* US–Japan Mutual Security: The Next Twenty Years (Ed.), China: The Turning Point (ed.), Looking Back 1981, Conservatives Stalk the House 1983, The March of Freedom 1998, Intellectual Pilgrims 1999, Leadership for America 2000, Getting America Right 2006.
Address: The Heritage Foundation, 214 Massachusetts Avenue, NE, Washington, DC 20002, USA (office). *Telephone:* (202) 546-4400 (office). *Fax:* (202) 544-0904 (office). *E-mail:* president@heritage.org (office). *Website:* www.heritage.org (office).

FEYDER, Jean, DIur; Luxembourg diplomatist; *Director of Co-operation and Humanitarian Action, Ministry of Foreign Affairs;* b. 24 Nov. 1947; m.; two c. *Career:* joined Ministry of Foreign Affairs 1974, Head, UN Dept 1974–76, Deputy Perm. Rep. to UN, New York July–Dec. 1975, currently Dir Co-operation and Humanitarian Action (with title of Amb.); assigned to Luxembourg mission to EC, Brussels (with responsibility for accession negotiations) 1977; Deputy Perm. Rep. to EEC 1983; Perm. Rep. to UN, New York 1987–93; mem. Bd Dirs ATTF (Financial Technology Tech. Agency).
Address: Direction de la Coopération et de l'Aide Humanitaire, 6 rue de la Congregation, 1352 Luxembourg, Luxembourg.

FFRENCH-DAVIS MUÑOZ, Ricardo, PhD; Chilean economist; *Principal Regional Adviser, Economic Commission for Latin America and the Caribbean;* b. 27 June 1936, Santiago; m. Marcela Yampaglia 1966. *Education:* Catholic Univ. of Chile, Univ. of Chicago. *Career:* Researcher and Prof. of Econs, Econ. Research Cen., Catholic Univ. 1962–64; Prof. of Econs, Univ. of Chile 1962–73, 1984–; Deputy Man. Research Dept, Cen. Bank of Chile 1964–70; Research Dir Cen. on Planning Studies, Catholic Univ. 1970–75; Vice-Pres. and Dir Centre for Latin American Econ. Research (CIEPLAN), Santiago 1976–90; Research Dir Cen. Bank of Chile 1990; mem. Acad. Council, Latin American Program, The Woodrow Wilson Center, Washington, DC 1977–80; mem. UN Cttee on Econ. Planning 1990–92; mem. Exec. Cttee Latin American Studies Asscn 1992–94; Visiting Fellow, Univ. of Oxford 1974, 1979; Visiting Prof., Boston Univ. 1976; Pres. Acad. Circle, Acad. de Humanismo Cristiano, Chile 1978–81; Co-ordinator Working Group on Econ. Issues of Inter-American Dialogue 1985–86; Prin. Regional Adviser, Econ. Comm. for Latin America and the Caribbean (ECLAC) 2000–; mem. Editorial Bds

Latin American Research Review, El Trimestre Economico and Colección Estudios Cieplan; Ford Foundation Grants 1971, 1975, 2001, Social Science Research Council Grant 1976, Inter-American Dialogue Grant 1985–86. *Publications:* Políticas Económicas en Chile: 1952–70 1973, El cobre en el desarrollo nacional (co-ed.) 1974, Economía internacional: teorías y políticas para el desarrollo 1979, 1985, Latin America and a New International Economic Order (co-ed.) 1981, 1985, The Monetarist Experiment in Chile 1982, Relaciones financieras externas y la economía latinoamericana (ed.) 1983, Development and External Debt in Latin America (co-ed.) 1988, Debt-equity swaps in Chile 1990, Latin America and the Caribbean: Policies to Improve Linkages with the World Economy (ed.) 1998, Macroeconomics, Trade and Finance 2000, Financial Crisis in 'Successful' Emerging Economies (ed.) 2001, Economic Reforms in Chile: From Dictatorship to Democracy 2002; over 100 articles on int. econs, Latin-American econ. devt and Chilean econ. policies in 8 languages.
Address: Economic Commission for Latin America and the Caribbean, Santiago, Chile (office); Casilla 179-D, Santiago, Chile (home). *Telephone:* (562) 210-2555 (office). *Fax:* (562) 208-1801 (office). *E-mail:* ricardo .ffrenchdavis@cepal.org (office). *Website:* www.eclac.cl (office).

FICO, Robert, DIur; Slovak politician and lawyer; *Prime Minister;* b. 15 Sept. 1964, Topolčany; m.; one c. *Education:* Comenius Univ., Bratislava. *Career:* mem. staff Inst. of Laws, Ministry of Justice 1986–91; mem. Parl. 1992–; Head of Slovak del. to Parl. Meeting of European Council, Rep. to European Cttee for Human Rights and European Court for Human Rights 1994–2000; mem. Party of Democratic Left—SDL 1994–99, Vice-Chair. 1998–99; Founder and Chair. Direction Party—Smĕr 1999– (absorbed Party of Civic Understanding 2003, Social Democratic Alternative, Social Democratic Party of Slovakia and Party of Democratic Left 2004, renamed Direction-Social Democracy 2004), Pres. Parl. Mems Club 2002–; Observer on behalf of European Socialists' faction at European Parl. 2002–04; Prime Minister of Slovakia 2006–. *Publication:* Trest smrti (Punishment of Death).
Address: Office of the Government, nám. Slobody 1, 813 70 Bratislava, Slovakia (office). *Telephone:* (2) 5729-5111 (office). *Fax:* (2) 5249-7595 (office). *E-mail:* urad@vlada.gov.sk (office). *Website:* www.vlada.gov.sk (office); www.strana-smer.sk (office).

FIESCHI, Pascal; French diplomatist; *Ambassador to Latvia;* b. 20 March 1945. *Education:* Inst. d'Etudes Politiques, Ecole Nat. des Langues Orientales. *Career:* joined French Diplomatic Service 1969; Desk Officer for Soviet-Chinese Conflict, Dept for Eastern Europe, Ministry of Foreign Affairs 1969–72; Second Sec., Embassy in Athens 1972–74; First Sec., Embassy in Prague 1974–77; Desk Officer for Greece, Turkey and Cyprus, Dept for Eastern Europe 1977–80; Consul-Gen. in Leningrad 1980–83; Deputy Head of Mission, then Chargé d'Affaires, Embassy in Canberra 1983–85; Head of Political Section, Embassy in Moscow 1985–89; Asst Head of Dept, Gen. Secr. for Nat. Defence, Paris 1989–91; Deputy Head of European Dept, Ministry of Foreign Affairs 1991–93; Head, Dept of French Overseas Citizens, Dept of French Overseas Citizens and Foreigners in France 1993–97; Amb. to Ukraine 1997–2001; Head, OSCE Mission in Kosovo and Deputy Special Rep. of UN Sec.-Gen. responsible for UN Interim Admin. Mission in Kosovo (UNMIK) 2002–05; Inspector, Ministry of Foreign Affairs 2005–08; Amb. to Latvia 2008–.
Address: Embassy of France, Raiņa bulv. 9, Rīga 1050, Latvia (office). *Telephone:* 6703-6600 (office). *Fax:* 6703-6615 (office). *E-mail:* webmastre .ambafrance-lv@diplomatie.gouv.fr (office). *Website:* www.ambafrance-lv .org (office).

FIGEĽ, Ján, MSc; Slovak politician and research scientist; *Commissioner for Education, Training, Culture and Multilingualism, European Commission;* b. 20 Jan. 1960, Vranov nad Topl'ou; m.; four c. *Education:* Košice Technical Univ., Georgetown Univ., USA, UFSIA, Antwerp, Belgium. *Career:* Research and Devt Scientist, ZPA Prešov 1983–1992; mem. Parl. 1992–98, 2002–, mem. Foreign Affairs Cttee, Cttee for European Integration 1992–98, Chair. Foreign Affairs Cttee 2002–; mem. Party Presidium, Christian Democratic Movt 1992–98, Deputy Chair. for Foreign Policy 1994–98, 2000–; State Sec., Ministry of Foreign Affairs 1998–2002; Chief Negotiator for Slovakia's accession to EU 1998–2003; mem. Bd Slovak Democratic Coalition 1998–2000; Vice-Chair. European People's Party 1998; mem. Convention on the Future of Europe 2002–03; Head, Standing Del. of Observers of European Parl. 2003–; mem. European Parl. Cttee on Econ. Affairs and Devt 2003–, Vice-Chair. 2004–; EU Commr without Portfolio 2004, for Educ., Training, Culture and Multilingualism 2004–; mem. Cen. European Forum, Int. Cttee for Support of Democracy in Cuba; Pres. Pan-European Union Slovakia; mem. Bd Dirs Slovak Soc. for Foreign Policy, Anton Tunega Foundation, Foundation for the Support of Social Change; mem. Council Cen. European Inst. for Econ. and Social Reforms; Hon. Pres. Centre for European Policy, Kolping Work Slovakia. *Publications:* Slovakia on the Road to EU Membership (co-author) 2002.

Address: European Commission, rue de la Loi 200, 1049 Brussels, Belgium (office). *Telephone:* (2) 298-87-16 (office). *Fax:* (2) 298-80-88 (office). *E-mail:* CAB-FIGEL@ec.europa.eu (office). *Website:* ec.europa.eu/ commission_barroso/figel (office).

FIGUEROA, Adolfo, PhD; Peruvian economist, academic and international consultant; *Professor of Economics, Catholic University of Lima;* b. 14 April 1941, Carhuaz; m. Yolanda Vásquez 1965; one s. one d. *Education:* Colegio Guadalupe (High School), Lima, San Marcos Univ., Lima, Vanderbilt Univ., Nashville, Tenn., USA. *Career:* Prof. of Econs, Catholic Univ. of Lima 1970–, Head, Dept of Econs 1976–79, 1987–90, 1996–98, Dean Faculty of Social Sciences 2002–05; Dir Research Project on Productivity and Educ. in Agric. in Latin America, ECIEL Program 1983-85; Consultant to ILO, FAO, Inter-American Foundation, Ford Foundation, IFAD, IDB, World Bank; Visiting Prof., Univ. of Pernambuco, Brazil 1973, St Antony's Coll., Oxford 1976, Univ. of Ill., USA 1980, Econs Dept, Univ. of Nicaragua 1985, Univ. of Notre Dame, USA 1992, Univ. of Tex. 1997, Univ. of Wis. 2001; mem. Exec. Council Latin American Studies Asscn 1988–91, Editorial Advisory Bd, Journal of Int. Devt 1988–92, World Devt 1997–, European Review of Latin American Studies 1997–; mem. Int. Network for Econ. Method; Award of Excellence in Grad. Teaching Univ. of Ill., USA 1980, Winner, Collaborative Research Grant Competition, MacArthur Foundation 1999, Winner, Tinker Professorship Competition, Univ. of Wis. 2001. *Publications:* Estructura del Consumo y Distribución de Ingresos en Lima 1968–1969 1974, Distribución del Ingreso en el Perú (co-author) 1975, La Economía Campesina de la Sierra del Perú 1981, Capitalist Development and the Peasant Economy in Peru 1984, Educación y Productividad en la Agricultura Campesina de América Latina 1986, Teorías Económicas del Capitalismo 1992, Crisis Distributiva en el Perú 1993, Social Exclusion and Inequality in Peru 1996, Reformas en sociedades desiguales 2001, La sociedad sigma: una teoría del desarrollo económico 2003; articles in econ. journals on inequality and poverty, econ. growth, econ. devt, agric., labour markets, and econs of educ. *Address:* CENTRUM, Universidad Católica del Perú, Apartado 1761, Lima 1 (office); Robert Kennedy 129, Lima 21, Peru (home). *Telephone:* (1) 313-3400 (office); (1) 261-6241 (home). *Fax:* (1) 626-2874. *E-mail:* afiguer@ pucp.edu.pe (office). *Website:* macareo.pucp.edu.pe/~afiguer/afiguer.htm (office).

FIGUEROA, Salvador Amín; Belizean diplomatist; *Ambassador to Mexico; Career:* fmr Acting Amb. to Guatemala; Amb. to Mexico 1998–. *Address:* Embassy of Belize, Bernardo de Gálvez 215, Col. Lomas de Chapultepec, 11000 México, DF, Mexico (office). *Telephone:* (55) 5520-1274 (office). *Fax:* (55) 5520-6089 (office). *E-mail:* embelize@prodigy.net .mx (office).

FILARDO, Leonor, MS; Venezuelan banker and international finance official; b. 1944; m. (divorced); three d. *Education:* Caracas Catholic Univ., Surrey Univ. *Career:* worked for Cen. Bank of Venezuela 1970–75, Sr Vice-Pres. Int. Operations 1979–84; Sr Vice-Pres. of Int. Finance, Venezuelan Investment Fund 1975–79; Exec. Dir, World Bank Exec. Bd 1984–86; Alt. Exec. Dir IMF 1986–88, Exec. Dir 1988–90; Rep. Office, Washington DC 1990; Vice-Pres. Cen. Bank of Venezuela 1993–94; Minister Counsellor, Embassy in USA 1994; fmr Adviser to Cen. American and Venezuelan govts on stabilization and structural adjustment programmes, participant in negotiations with IMF for External Fund Facility for Venezuela; mem. Exec. Cttee Youth Orchestra of the Americas; Francisco de Miranda Medal, (1st Class) Venezuela 1990.

FILIPOVIĆ, Karlo; Bosnia and Herzegovina politician; *Executive Board President, Social Democratic Party of Bosnia and Herzegovina;* b. 1954, Solakovicima; m.; one d. *Education:* Univ. of Sarajevo. *Career:* Pres. Council of Municipalities, Sarajevo City Ass. 1987–89; mem. Cen. Cttee Communist League of Bosnia and Herzegovina 1988–91, elected mem. of presidency 1989; mem. of presidency Socialist Party of Bosnia and Herzegovina 1991–92; mem. of presidency of Social Democratic Party of Bosnia and Herzegovina (SDP BiH) 1992–95, Sec. 1995–97, Sec.-Gen. 1997–2001, Pres. Exec. Bd 2001–; mem. House of Reps (Parl.) 1998–2001; Pres. Fed. of Bosnia and Herzegovina 2001–02, Vice-Pres. 2002–04. *Address:* Social Democratic Party of Bosnia and Herzegovina, Alipašina 41, 71000 Sarajevo, Bosnia and Herzegovina (office). *Telephone:* (33) 664044 (office). *Fax:* (33) 644042 (office). *E-mail:* predssednik-glavnog -odbora@sdp-bih.org.ba (office). *Website:* www.sdp-bih.org.ba (office).

FILLON, François-Charles Amand; French politician; *Prime Minister;* b. 4 March 1954, Mans; m. Penelope Clarke 1980; three s. one d. *Education:* Univ. of Maine, Univ. René-Descartes, Paris and Fondation Nationale des Sciences Politiques. *Career:* Parl. Asst to Joël Le Theule 1976–77; served in Office of Minister of Transport 1978–80, Office of Minister of Defence 1980–81; Head of Legis. and Parl. Work, Ministry of Industry 1981; Town Councillor, Sablé-sur-Sarthe, Mayor 1983–2001; Pres. Conseil Général, Sarthe 1992–98, of Sablé-sur-Sarthe Dist 2001–; RPR Deputy to Nat. Ass. 1981–93; Pres. Comm. for Nat. Defence and Armed Forces 1986–88; Minister for Higher Educ. and Research 1993–95; Minister of Information Tech. and Posts May–Nov. 1995, Minister del. 1995–97; Spokesman, Exec. Comm. RPR 1998–, Political Adviser 1999–; Chair. Conseil Régional des Pays de la Loire 1998–; Municipal Councillor, Solesmes 2001–; Minister of Social Affairs, Labour and Solidarity 2002–04, Minister of Youth, National Education and Research 2004–05; Senator for Sarthe 2004–07; Prime Minister 2007–. *Address:* Office of the Prime Minister, Hôtel de Matignon, 57 rue de Varenne, 75007 Paris (office); Beaucé, 72300 Solesmes, France (home). *Telephone:* 1-42-75-80-00 (office). *Fax:* 1-42-75-78-31 (office). *E-mail:* premier-ministre@premier-ministre.gouv.fr (office). *Website:* www .premier-ministre.gouv.fr (office); www.blog-fillon.com (home).

FINLEY, Julie; American diplomatist; *Permanent Representative, Organization for Security and Co-operation in Europe;* m. (deceased); two s. *Education:* Vassar Coll. *Career:* worked for NBC, ABC News and Washington Post newspaper; Founder and Bd mem. US Cttee on NATO 1996–2004; mem. Nat. Finance Advisory Council, George and Barbara Bush Endowment for Innovative Cancer Research, M.D. Anderson 1999–2004; fmr Chair. Host Cttee for Prague NATO Summit Nov. 2002; mem. Advisory Council, Brookings Inst. 2003–05, Advisory Council, US Inst. of Peace 2003–05; has served in several capacities on Republican Nat. Cttee, including Chair. DC Republican Cttee 1992–2000; Nat. Finance Co-Chair. for Bush-Cheney '04 for DC and Co-Chair. Team 100 for Republican Nat. Cttee 1997–2004; DC Nat. Committeewoman, Republican Nat. Cttee 2000–04; Trustee, American Acad. in Berlin 2000–05, Nat. Endowment for Democracy 2001–05 (also Treas.); Chair. Project on Transitional Democracies –2005; Amb. and Perm. Rep. to OSCE, Paris 2005–; Trustee, The Washington Opera 1996–2001, Library of Congress Trust Fund Bd 1996–2002, and several school bds. *Address:* US Mission to the OSCE, Obersteinergasse 11/1, 1190 Vienna, Austria (office). *Telephone:* (1) 313390 (office). *Fax:* (1) 368-63-85 (office). *E-mail:* pa-usosce@state.gov (office). *Website:* osce.usmission.gov (office).

FINNEMORE, Martha, MA, PhD; American academic; *Professor of Political Science and International Affairs, Elliott School of International Affairs, George Washington University; Education:* Univ. of Sydney, Australia, Harvard and Stanford Univs, USA. *Career:* Fellow, Social Science Research Council/MacArthur Foundation 1994–96; Guest Scholar, Brookings Inst., Washington, DC 1994–96; currently Prof. of Political Science and Int. Affairs, Elliott School of Int. Affairs, George Washington Univ.; Woodrow Wilson Prize, American Political Science Asscn 2004, Best Book Award, Int. Studies Asscn 2006. *Publications include:* National Interests in International Society 1996, The Purpose of Intervention 2003, Rules for the World 2004. *Address:* Elliott School of International Affairs, George Washington University, Washington, DC 20052, USA (office). *Telephone:* (202) 994-8617 (office). *Fax:* (202) 994-7743 (office). *E-mail:* finnemor@gwu.edu (office). *Website:* www.gwu.edu/~psc (office); www.gwu.edu/~elliott.

FISCHEL VOLIO, Astrid, PhD; Costa Rican politician and university professor; b. 26 March 1954, San José. *Education:* Univ. of Costa Rica, Cen. American Inst. of Business Admin, Southampton Univ., UK. *Career:* Prof., History and Geography School, Univ. of Costa Rica 1984–98, Dir Doctorate Programme in Educ. 1994–95, Researcher, Inst. of Research for the Improvement of Costa Rican Educ. 1986–98; Pres. Fischel Corpn 1991–97; Vice-Pres. Bd of Dirs Chamber of Commerce of Costa Rica 1994–95; Co-ordinator Govt Platform, Unidad Social Cristiana political party 1995–97; Minister of Culture, Youth and Sports 1998–99; First Vice-Pres. of Costa Rica and Minister of Culture 1998–2002; Minister of Public Educ. 2002–03; Aquileo J. Echeverría Nat. Award for History 1987, 1992, Enterprising Woman of the Year 1992. *Publications:* The National Theatre of Costa Rica: Its History 1992, The Magic Box. A Hundred Years of History of the National Theatre 1997, Consensus and Repression, a Socio-Political Interpretation of Costa Rican Education 1987. *Address:* c/o Ministry of Public Education, Apdo 10.087, 1000 San José, Costa Rica (office). *Telephone:* 233-9050 (office). *Fax:* 233-0390 (office).

FISCHER, Heinz, DIur; Austrian politician; *President;* b. 9 Oct. 1938, Graz; m. Margit Fischer; two c. *Education:* Univ. of Vienna. *Career:* Assoc. Prof. of Political Science, Univ. of Innsbruck 1978–94, Prof. 1994–; Sec. Socialist Parl. Party 1963–75, Exec., Floor Leader 1975–83, 1987–90, Deputy Chair. Socialist Party 1979–2004; mem. Nationalrat (Parl.) for Vienna 1971–2004, Pres. Nationalrat 1990–2002, Second Pres. 2002–04; Fed. Minister for Science and Research 1983–87; Deputy Chair. European Socialist Party 1992–2004; Pres. of Austria 2004–; Co-Ed. Europäische Rundschau; fmr mem. Nat. Security Council and Foreign Affairs Council; Pres. Nat. Fund

of the Repub. of Austria for Victims of Nat. Socialism 1995–2002; Vice-Pres. Inst. for Advanced Studies –2004; Pres. Austrian Friends of Nature –2005; Pres. Austrian Univ. Extension Asscn. *Publications:* Positions and Outlook 1977, The Kreisky Era 1993, Reflexionen 1999, Times of Change: An Austrian Interim Report 2003; numerous books and articles on law and political science.
Address: Office of the Federal President, Hofburg, 1014 Vienna, Austria (office). *Telephone:* (1) 534-22-0 (office). *Fax:* (1) 535-65-12 (office). *Website:* www.hofburg.at (office).

FISCHER, Joseph (Joschka); German academic and fmr politician; b. 12 April 1948, Gerabronn; m. 1st 1967 (divorced 1984); m. 2nd (divorced); m. 3rd Claudia Bohm 1987 (divorced 1999); m. 4th Nicola Leske 1999 (divorced 2003); m. 5th Minu Barati 2005. *Career:* joined Green Party 1982, fmr Leader; mem. German Bundestag 1983–85; Minister of the Environment and Energy, Hesse 1985–87, of the Environment, Energy and Fed. Affairs 1991–94; Deputy Bundesrat 1985–87, Chair. Green Parl. Group, Hesse Parl. 1987–91; Deputy Minister-Pres. of Hesse 1991–98; Speaker Parl. Group Alliance 90/Greens, Bundestag 1994–98; Vice-Chancellor and Minister of Foreign Affairs, Fed. Govt 1998–2005; Sr Fellow, Liechtenstein Inst. on Self-Determination, Princeton Univ. 2006–07, also Frederick H. Schultz Class of 1951 Prof. of Int. Econ. Policy, Woodrow Wilson School of Public and Int. Affairs and Fellow, European Union Program;. *Publication:* The Red-Green Years: German Foreign Policy from Kosovo to Sept. 11 2007.
Address: c/o Bündnis 90/Die Grünen (Alliance 90/Greens), Pl. vor dem Neuen Tor 1, 10115 Berlin, Germany (office).

FISHER, Nigel; Canadian UN official; *President and CEO, UNICEF Canada; Career:* with UNICEF early 1980s–, fmr Rep. in Rwanda, Yemen, Jordan, Syria, Occupied Territories of the W Bank and Gaza, later Deputy Regional Dir for the Middle East and N Africa, Special Rep. for Rwanda 1994–95, Dir Office of Emergency Programmes 1995–98, Regional Dir in S Asia 1999–2002, Special Rep. for Special Sub-Regional Programme for Afghanistan and Neighbouring Countries 2001; UN Deputy Special Rep. for Relief, Recovery and Reconstruction in Afghanistan 2002–03; UN Exec. Dir Office for Project Services (UNOPS) 2003–05; Pres. and CEO UNICEF Canada 2005–; Deputy Exec. Sec. World Conf. on Educ. for All 1988–90; Chair. UN Inter-Agency Working Group of Sec.-Gen.'s Exec. Cttee on Humanitarian Affairs 1997; UN Visiting Fellow, Dept of Foreign Affairs and Int. Trade, Canada 1998–2001; Meritorious Service Cross 1998.
Address: UNICEF Canada, 2200 Yonge Street, Suite 1100, Toronto, ON M4S 2C6, Canada (office). *Telephone:* (416) 482-4444 (office). *Fax:* (416) 482-8035 (office). *E-mail:* secretary@unicef.ca (office). *Website:* www.unicef.ca (office).

FISHER, William (Bill) Norman, BEcons; Australian diplomatist; *High Commissioner to Canada;* b. 1946, Canberra; m.; one d. *Education:* Australian Nat. Univ. *Career:* numerous positions at Dept of Foreign Affairs and Trade including Consul, Embassy in Noumea 1975–78, in Port Vila 1978–80, Chargé d'affaires Embassy in Tehran 1982–83, Consul-Gen. in Honolulu 1983–87; Asst Sec., Defence Br, Dept of the Prime Minister and Cabinet 1987–88; Asst Sec., Exec. Secr. 1988–89; Prin. Adviser, Americas and Europe Div. 1989–90; Amb. to Israel 1990–93; First Asst. Sec., Int. Orgs and Legal Div. 1994–95, Consular Programs and Security Div. 1995–96, Public Affairs Div. 1996–97; Amb. to Thailand 1997–2000, to France 2000–05; High Commr to Canada 2005–; Grand Officier de l'Ordre Nat. de Mérite (France).
Address: Australian High Commission, 50 O'Connor Street, Suite 710, Ottawa, ON K1P 6L2, Canada (office). *Telephone:* (613) 236-0841 (office). *Fax:* (613) 236-4376 (office). *Website:* www.ahc-ottawa.org (office).

FISHLOW, Albert, PhD; American economist, academic and fmr government official; *Professor of International and Public Affairs, Director of the Columbia Institute of Latin American Studies, and Director of the Center for the Study of Brazil, Columbia University;* b. 21 Nov. 1935, Philadelphia; m. Harriet Fishlow 1957; one s. two d. *Education:* Univ. of Pennsylvania, Harvard Univ. *Career:* Acting Asst Prof., Assoc. Prof., then Prof., Univ. of Calif., Berkeley 1961–77, Prof. of Econs 1983, Chair. Dept of Econs 1973–75, 1985–89, Dean Int. and Area Studies 1990, Dir Int. House 1990, now Prof. Emer.; currently Prof. of Int. and Public Affairs, Dir of Columbia Inst. of Latin American Studies, and Dir of Center for Study of Brazil, Columbia Univ., New York; mem. Berkeley Foundation Trustees Int. Cttee 1990–; Prof. of Econs, Yale Univ. 1978–83; Visiting Fellow, All Souls Coll. Oxford, UK (Guggenheim Fellow) 1972–73; Co-Ed. Journal of Devt Econs 1986–; Dir-at-Large, Bd of Social Science Research Council 1990–; Deputy Asst Sec. of State for Inter-American Affairs 1975–76; mem. Council on Foreign Relations 1975–; Paul A. Volcker Sr Fellow for Int. Econ. –1999; Consultant to Rockefeller, Ford and other foundations, fmr Consultant to World Bank, IDB, UNDP; Nat. Order of the Southern

Cross (Brazil) 1999; David Wells Prize, Harvard 1963, Arthur H. Cole Prize, Econ. History Asscn 1966, Joseph Schumpeter Prize, Harvard 1971, Outstanding Service Award, Dept of State 1976. *Publications include:* American Railroads and the Transformation of the Ante Bellum Economy 1965, International Trade, Investment, Macro Policies and History: Essays in Memory of Carlos F. Diaz-Alejandro (co-ed.) 1987; numerous articles.
Address: 834 International Affairs Building, Columbia University, Mail Code 3323, New York, NY 10027, USA (office). *Telephone:* (212) 854-1555 (office). *Fax:* (212) 864-4847 (office). *E-mail:* af594@columbia.edu (office). *Website:* www.sipa.columbia.edu (office).

FITOUSSI, Jean-Paul Samuel, DèsScEcon; French economist and academic; *President, Observatoire Français des Conjonctures Economiques (OFCE);* b. 19 Aug. 1942, La Goulette; m. Anne Krief 1964; one s. one d. *Education:* Acad. Commerciale, Paris and Univs of Paris and Strasbourg. *Career:* Asst Lecturer 1968–71; Dir of Studies 1971–73; Maître de Conférence Agrégé 1974–75; Prof. 1975–78; Titular Prof. 1978–82; Dean. Faculty of Econ. Science and Dir Dept of Econ. Science, Strasbourg 1980–81; Prof. in charge of research prog. on foundation of macroeconomic policy, Inst. Universitaire Européen, Florence 1979–83; Prof. Inst. d'Etudes Politiques, Paris 1982–; Dir Dept of Studies Observatoire Français des Conjonctures Economiques (OFCE) 1982–89, Pres. 1990–; Chair. Scientific Council of Inst. d'Etudes Politiques, Paris 1997–; Sec.-Gen. Int. Econ. Asscn 1984–; consultant to EC Comm. 1978–; mem. Bd Ecole Normale Supérieure, Paris 1998–; External Prof. Univ. Européenne, Florence 1984–93, mem. Research Council, Universitaire Européen, Florence 2003–; mem. Econ. Comm. of the Nation 1996–, Council of Econ. Analysis of the Prime Minister 1997–; Expert, Comm. of the European Parl. 2000–; mem. UN Research Inst. for Social Devt 2001–; mem. Exec. Cttee Aspen Inst. Italia 2001–, Comité nationale d'évaluation de la politique de la ville 2002–, Comité national d'initiative et de proposition pour la recherche 2004–, Scientific Bd Austrian Inst. of Economic Research 2004–, Bd of Dirs École Normale Supérieure 2004–, Advisory Bd Centre on Capitalism and Soc., Columbia Univ. 2004–, Cttee for Evaluation of Research 2005–; columnist for Le Monde and La Repubblica; Hon. Prof., Univ. of Trento, Italy; Officier Ordre nat. du Mérite, Chevalier Légion d'honneur, Grand Officier de l'Ordre de l'Infant Henri (Portugal); Dr hc (Buenos Aires); Prix Asscn Française de Sciences Economiques, Prix Acad. des Sciences Morales et Politiques. *Publications:* Inflation, équilibre et chômage 1973, Le fondement macroéconomique de la théorie Keynesienne 1974, Modern Macroeconomic Theory 1983, Monetary Theory and Economic Institutions (with N. de Cecco) 1985, The Slump in Europe (with E. Phelps) 1988, Competitive Disinflation (with others) 1993, Pour l'emploi et la cohésion sociale 1994, Le débat interdit: monnaie, Europe, pauvreté 1995, Economic Growth, Capital and Labour Markets 1995, Le nouvel âge des inégalités (with Pierre Rosanvallon) 1996, Rapport sur l'état de l'Union européenne 1999, 2000, 2002, Réformes structurelles et politiques macroéconomique: les enseignements des modèles de pays (with O. Posset) 2000, contrib. to collected publs, L'enseignement supérieur de l'économie en question, Rapport au ministre de l'éducation nationale 2001, Rapport sur l'état de l'union européenne 2002; La Règle et le choix 2002, How to Reform the European Central Bank (with J. Creel) 2002, Il dilatore benevolo 2003, Rapport sur l'état de l'union européene 2004, Les inégalités 2003, La démocratie et le marché 2004, L'ideologie du monde 2004, Ségrégation urbaine et intégration sociale (jtly) 2004, Macroeconomic Theory and Economic Policy 2004, La politique de l'impuissance 2005, Report on the State of the European Union 2005.
Address: Observatoire Français des Conjonctures Economiques, 69 quai d'Orsay, 75340 Paris Cedex 07 (office); 47 rue de boulainvilliers, 75016 Paris, France (home). *Telephone:* 1-44-18-54-01. *Fax:* 1-44-18-54-71. *E-mail:* presidence@ofce.sciences-po.fr (office). *Website:* www.ofce.sciences-po.fr (office).

FITTS, Robert Wendell, BEng; American diplomatist; b. NH. *Education:* Tufts Univ. *Career:* served in Peace Corps in Malaysia; worked for New York City govt; entered Foreign Service in 1975, first assignment to Embassy in Papua New Guinea, later Chargé d'affaires a.i. and Deputy Chief of Mission, Embassy in Manila, spent nine years in Indonesia and tours in Thailand and the Philippines, Washington appointments have included Legis. Asst for Defense and Foreign Affairs for US Senator George Mitchell, Special Asst to E Asia and Pacific Asst Sec. Winston Lord, Dir for Philippines, Indonesia, Malaysia, Brunei and Singapore, Political Advisor to Commdr of Special Operations Command (SOCOM) –2003, Amb. to Papua New Guinea (also accred to Solomon Islands and Vanuatu) 2003–06; four Superior Honor Awards, State Dept.
Address: US Department of State, 2201 C Street NW, Washington, DC 20520, USA (office). *Telephone:* (202) 647-4000 (office). *Fax:* (202) 647-6738 (office). *Website:* www.state.gov (office).

FITZGERALD, Garret; Irish politician and economist; b. 9 Feb. 1926, Dublin; m. Joan O'Farrell 1947; two s. one d. *Education:* Belvedere Coll., Univ. Coll. and King's Inns, Dublin. *Career:* called to the Bar 1946; Research and Schedules Man., Aer Lingus 1947–58; Rockefeller Research Asst, Trinity Coll., Dublin 1958–59; Lecturer in Political Economy, Univ. Coll., Dublin 1959–73; fmr Chair. and Hon. Sec. Irish Br., Inst. of Transport; mem. Seanad Éireann 1965–69; mem. Dáil Éireann for Dublin SE 1969–92; Leader and Pres. Fine Gael 1977–87; Minister for Foreign Affairs 1973–77; Taoiseach (Prime Minister) of Repub. of Ireland 1981–82, 1982–87; Pres. Council of Ministers of EEC Jan.–June 1975, European Council July–Dec. 1984, fmr Pres. Irish Council of European Movt; fmr Vice-Pres. European People's Party, European Parl.; mem. Senate Nat. Univ. of Ireland 1973–, Chancellor 1997–; fmr Man. Dir Economist Intelligence Unit of Ireland; mem. Trilateral Comm. 1987–; Dir GPA Group 1987–93, Int. Inst. for Econ. Devt, London 1987–95, Trade Devt Inst. 1987–, Comer Int. 1989–94, Point Systems Int. 1996–, Election Commr 1999–; mem. Radio Telefís Éireann Authority; fmr Irish Corresp. BBC, Financial Times, Economist, Columnist Irish Times; Order of Christ (Portugal) 1986, Order of Merit (Germany) 1987, Grand Cordon, Order of the Rising Sun (Japan) 1989, Commdr Légion d'honneur 1995; Hon. LLD (New York, St Louis, Keele, Boston Coll., Westfield Coll., Mass, Nat. Univ. of Ireland, Univ. of Dublin); Hon. DCL (St Mary's Univ., Halifax, Nova Scotia) 1985, (Oxford) 1987; Dr hc (Queen's Belfast) 2000. *Publications:* State-sponsored Bodies 1959, Planning in Ireland 1968, Towards a New Ireland 1972, Unequal Partners (UNCTAD) 1979, Estimates for Baronies of Minimum Level of Irish Speaking Amongst Successive Decennial Cohorts 1771–1781 to 1861–1871 1984, The Israeli/Palestinian Issue 1990, All in a Life (autobiog.) 1991. *Address:* 37 Annavilla, Dublin 6, Ireland. *Telephone:* (1) 496-2600. *Fax:* (1) 496-2126. *E-mail:* Garretfg@iol.ie (home).

FITZGIBBON, Joel; Australian politician; *Minister for Defence;* b. 16 Jan. 1962, Bellingen, NSW; m. Dianne Fitzgibbon; one s. two d. *Education:* Univ. of New England, NSW, Univ. of Newcastle. *Career:* automotive electrician 1978–90; Dir Hunter-Manning Tourist Authority 1987–89; Deputy Mayor of Cessnock 1989–90; part-time Lecturer, Tech. and Further Educ. (TAFE); Del. Hunter Region Assen of Councils 1994–95; MP (Australian Labor Party) for Hunter 1996–, various portfolios including Small Business, Tourism, Banking and Financial Services, Forestry, Mining and Energy, Asst Treas., Shadow Minister for Defence; Minister for Defence 2007–. *Address:* Department of Defence, Russell Offices, Russell Drive, Campbell, Canberra, ACT 2600, Australia (office). *Telephone:* (2) 6265-9111 (office). *E-mail:* J.Fitzgibbon.MP@aph.gov.au (office). *Website:* www.defence.gov.au (office); www.joelfitzgibbon.com.

FITZPATRICK, Cathy; American international organization executive and editor; *Representative to the United Nations, International League for Human Rights; Education:* Univ. of Toronto, St. Michael's Coll., Canada and Leningrad (now St. Petersburg) State Univ., Russia. *Career:* Assoc. Ed. Freedom Appeals 1979–81; Dir Helsinki Watch (now European and Cen. Asia Div. of Human Rights Watch) 1981–90; Human Rights Consultant for Soros Foundation, Mott Foundation, Ford Foundation 1990s; Dir Cen./East European and FSU Cttee to Protect Journalists, New York 1996–97; Exec. Dir Int. League for Human Rights (ILHR), currently ILHR Rep. to UN 1997–. *Publications include:* 15 translations into English by Soviet and Russian political figures including Yeltsin, Shevardnadze and Putin; several studies on growth of civil society in fmr Soviet Union. *Address:* International League for Human Rights, 432 Park Avenue South, 11th Floor, New York, NY 10016, USA (office). *Telephone:* (212) 684-1221 (office). *Fax:* (212) 684-1696 (office). *E-mail:* cfitz@ilhr.org (office). *Website:* www.ilhr.org (office).

FLAHAUT, André, MA; Belgian politician; *Minister for Defence;* b. 18 Aug. 1955, Walhain. *Education:* Université Libre de Bruxelles. *Career:* Asst to Emile Vandervelde Inst. 1979, Man. 1989; Councillor of Walhain 1982–94; Chair. Parti Socialiste Fed. of Wallon Brabant 1983–95; Prov. Councillor of Brabant 1987–91; Chair. Office de la Naissance et de l'Enfance 1989–95; Vice-Chair. of Intercommunale des Oeuvres Sociales du Brabant Wallon 1993–95; Chair. Mutualité Socialiste du Brabant Wallon 1993; Parl. Rep. 1994; Minister for Civil Service 1995–99, for Defence 1999–. *Address:* Ministry of Defence, 8 rue Mont Lambert, 1000 Brussels, Belgium (office). *Telephone:* (2) 550-28-11 (office). *Fax:* (2) 550-29-19 (office). *E-mail:* cabinet@mod.mil.be (office). *Website:* www.mil.be (office).

FLAHERTY, Jim, LLB; Canadian politician; *Minister of Finance;* b. 30 Dec. 1949; m. Christine Flaherty; three s. *Education:* Princeton Univ., Osgoode Hall Law School. *Career:* called to the bar, Ont. 1975; mem. Prov. Parl. for Whitby-Ajax 1995–2005; Attorney Gen. 1995; fmr Solicitor Gen.; fmr Critic for Public Infrastructure Renewal for the Official Opposition; fmr

Minister Responsible for Native Affairs, Minister of Labour, of Enterprise, Opportunity and Innovation, of Finance, of Correctional Services, Deputy Premier; Co-Chair. Task Force on Safe Streets and Healthy Communities 2005; mem. Parl. 2006–; Minister of Finance 2006–. *Address:* Finance Canada, East Tower, 19th Floor, 140 O'Connor Street, Ottawa, ON K1A 0G5, Canada (office). *Telephone:* (613) 992-1573 (office). *Fax:* (613) 996-2690 (office). *E-mail:* jflaherty@fin.gc.ca (office); consltcomm@fin.gc.ca (office). *Website:* www.fin.gc.ca (office).

FLAKE, L. Gordon, MA; American research institute director; *Executive Director, Maureen and Mike Mansfield Foundation;* b. Rehoboth, NM; m. Pakayvanh Sisoutham; six c. *Education:* Brigham Young Univ., Provo, Utah. *Career:* fmr Dir for Research and Academic Affairs, Korea Econ. Inst. of America; Sr Fellow and Assoc. Dir, Program on Conflict Resolution, The Atlantic Council of USA –1999; Exec. Dir Maureen and Mike Mansfield Foundation 1999–; regular contrib. on Korea issues in US and Asian press. *Publications:* Paved with Good Intentions: The NGO Experience in North Korea. *Address:* Maureen and Mike Mansfield Foundation, 1401 New York Avenue, NW, Suite 740, Washington, DC 20005–2102, USA USA (office). *Telephone:* (202) 347-1994 (office). *Fax:* (202) 347-3941 (office). *E-mail:* lgflake@mansfieldfdn.org (office). *Website:* www.mansfieldfdn.org (office).

FLEMING, Osbourne Berrington; Anguillan/British politician and business executive; *Chief Minister and Minister of Home Affairs, Tourism, Agriculture, Fisheries and Environment;* b. 18 Feb. 1940, East End. *Education:* Valley Secondary School. *Career:* Customs Officer, St Kitts 1959–64; lived in St Thomas, US Virgin Islands 1964–68, St Kitts 1968–81; f. Fleming's Transport (transport and shipping co.), St Croix 1974; People's Progressive Party (PPP) MP, Minister of Tourism, Agric. and Fisheries 1981–85; Anguilla Nat. Alliance (ANA) MP, Minister of Finance 1985–89; ind. MP, Minister of Finance and Econ. Devt 1989–94; rejoined ANA, apptd Leader Opposition in House of Ass. 1994–2000; mem. ANA/Anguilla Democratic Party United Front; Chief Minister and Minister of Home Affairs, Tourism, Agric., Fisheries and Environment 2000–. *Address:* Office of the Chief Minister, The Secretariat, The Valley, Anguilla, West Indies (office); Sea Feather's, East End, Anguilla, West Indies (home). *Telephone:* 497-2518 (office); 497-4783 (home). *Fax:* 497-3389 (office). *E-mail:* chief-minister@gov.ai (office). *Website:* www.gov.ai (office).

FLESCH, Colette, MA; Luxembourg politician and European Union official; *Director-General of Information, Communication and Culture, European Commission;* b. 6 April 1937. *Education:* Wellesley Coll. and Fletcher School of Law and Diplomacy, USA. *Career:* Admin. Gen. Secr. EC Council, Brussels 1964–69; nominated MEP 1969–79, elected 1979–80, 1984–85, 1989–90, Vice-Chair. Cttee on Budgets and LDR group 1989–90, mem. (fmr Chair.) Cttee on Devt and Co-operation; mem. Luxembourg Chamber of Deputies 1969–80, 1984–89; fmr Minister of Foreign Affairs, of Trade and Co-operation, of Justice; Mayor of Luxembourg 1970–80; Dir-Gen. Directorate-Gen. X (Information, Communication and Culture), European Comm. *Address:* Directorate-General X, Commission of the EU, 200 rue de la Loi, 1049 Brussels, Belgium (office). *Telephone:* (2) 235-11-11 (office). *Fax:* (2) 235-01-22 (office).

FLOOD, Philip James, AO, BEcons; Australian diplomatist; b. 2 July 1935, Sydney; m. 2nd Carole Henderson 1990; two s. one d. from previous m. *Education:* North Sydney High School, Univ. of Sydney. *Career:* mem. staff Mission to EEC and Embassy, Brussels 1959–62, Rep. to OECD Devt Assistance Cttee, Paris 1966–69, Asst Sec. Dept of Foreign Affairs 1971–73, High Commr in Bangladesh 1974–76, Minister, Embassy, Washington, DC 1976–77, CEO Dept Special Trade Representations 1977–80; First Asst Sec. Dept of Trade 1980–84, Deputy Sec. Dept of Foreign Affairs 1985–89, Amb. to Indonesia 1989–93, Dir-Gen. Australian Int. Devt Assistance Bureau (AUSAID) 1993–95, Dir-Gen. Office of Nat. Assessments 1995–96, Sec. Dept of Foreign Affairs and Trade 1996–98; High Commr in London 1998–2000; Head Inquiry into Immigration Detention 2000–01; Chair. Australia-Indonesia Inst. 2001–05; Head Inquiry into Australian Intelligence Agencies 2004; Chair. Inquiry into Plasma Fractionation 2006; Fellow, Royal Australian Inst. Public Admin.; Bintang Jasa Utama (Indonesian Order of Merit) 1993.

FLORES BERMÚDEZ, Roberto, LLB; Honduran politician and diplomatist; *Ambassador to USA;* b. 15 Aug. 1949; m. Laura Flores; two c. *Education:* Univ. of Honduras. *Career:* Dir-Gen. Diplomatic Protocol, Ministry of Foreign Affairs 1984–86, Dir-Gen. Foreign Politics 1986–87, Head of Cabinet 1988–89, Dir-Gen. Int. Orgs 1990, Minister of Foreign Affairs 2000–02, Amb. to UN, New York 1990–92, to USA 1994–98, to UK 1998–99, Minister of Foreign Affairs 2000–06, Amb. to USA 2006–; fmr

mem. Honduran Del. to Cen. American Parl.; fmr Head of Tech. Del., Cen. American Peace Negotiation Process.
Address: Embassy of Honduras, 3007 Tilden Street, NW, Suite 4M, Washington, DC 20008, USA (office). *Telephone:* (202) 966-7702 (office). *Fax:* (202) 966-9751 (office). *E-mail:* embassy@hondurasemb.org (office). *Website:* www.hondurasemb.org (office).

FLORES FACUSSÉ, Carlos Roberto, BEng, MIntEcon, PhD; Honduran fmr head of state; *President, Partido Liberal;* b. 1 March 1950, Tegucigalpa; m. Mary Carol Flake; one s. one d. *Education:* American School, Tegucigalpa and Louisiana State Univ. *Career:* Rep. for Francisco Morazan to Liberal Convention, Pres. Departmental Liberal Council, Francisco Morazan; Finance Sec. Nat. Directorate Movimiento Liberal Rodista; Congressman Nat. Ass. for Francisco Morazan 1980–97; Presidential Sec. 1982–83; Gen. Co-ordinator Movimiento Liberal Florista; Pres. Cen. Exec. Council Partido Liberal de Honduras; Pres. of Honduras 1998–2002; Co-owner, Man. and mem. editorial Bd La Tribuna, Co-owner and Man. Lithopress Industrial; fmr Man. CONPACASA; fmr Prof. School of Business Admin, Nat. Univ. of Honduras, Cen. American Higher School of Banking; fmr mem. Bd of Dirs Honduran Inst. of Social Security, Cen. Bank of Honduras, Inst. Nacional de Formación Profesional; mem. Industrial Eng Asscn of Honduras, Nat. Asscn of Industries, Consejo Hondureño de la Empresa Privada (COHEP), Honduran Inst. of Inter-American Culture. *Publication:* Forjemos Unidos el Destino de Honduras.
Address: Partido Liberal, Col. Miramonte, No. 1, Tegucigalpa, Honduras.

FLORES PEREZ, Francisco; Salvadorean fmr head of state; b. 17 Oct. 1959; m. Lourdes Rodríguez de Flores; one s. one d. *Education:* Amherst Coll. *Career:* fmr lecturer; fmr Deputy and Pres. Legislative Ass.; fmr Vice-Minister of Planning, then Vice-Pres. and Adviser to Pres. Cristiani; Information Sec. to Pres. Armando Calderón Sol; Pres. of El Salvador 1999–2004; mem. Nat. Republican Alliance (ARENA).
Address: c/o Ministry for the Presidency, Avda Cuba, Calle Darió González 806, Barrio San Jacinto, San Salvador, El Salvador (office).

FLOSSE, Gaston; French Polynesian politician; b. 24 June 1931, Rikitea (Gambier archipelago); m. Marie-Jeanne Mao 1994. *Career:* Pres. City Council Pirae 1963–65, Mayor 1965–2000; Govt Councillor in charge of Agric. 1965–67; mem. French Polynesian Territorial Ass. for Windward Islands 1967–, Pres. 1972–77; Pres. Tahoeraa Huiraatira Party 1971–; Vice-Pres. Govt Council 1982–84, Pres. Governing Council 1984–87, 1991–2004, Pres. of French Polynesia Feb.–June 2004, Oct. 2004–05, 2008; mem. Cen. Cttee Union des Democrates pour la République (UDR), France, then Founding mem. RPR; Deputy for French Polynesia, Nat. Ass., France 1978–97; Sec. of State in charge of S Pacific Affairs, France 1986–88; Senator of French Repub. 1998–; Chevalier, Légion d'honneur, Ordre nat. du Mérite, First 'Grand Maître', Order of Tahiti Nui; Dr hc (Kyung Hee Univ., Korea) 1985.
Address: Tahoera'a Huiraatira, rue du Commandant Destremeau, BP 471, Papeete, French Polynesia. *Telephone:* 429898 (office). *Fax:* 450004 (office). *E-mail:* courrier@tahoeraahuiraatira.pf (office). *Website:* tahoeraahuiraatira.pf (office).

FODOR, Gen. Lajos; Hungarian army officer; b. 29 July 1947, Debrecen; m. Éva Kovács; one s. one d. *Education:* Lajos Kossuth Land Forces Military Acad., Szentendre, Frunze Military Acad., Moscow, Defence Language Inst., San Antonio, American Nat. Defence Univ. *Career:* infantry officer 1970; platoon leader 14th Mechanized Infantry Regt Nagykaniza 1971; Bn Commdr 63rd Mechanized Infantry Regt Nagyatád 1971–79, Deputy Commdr 1981–83, Regt Commdr 1983–85; Brig. 26th Mechanized Infantry Regt Lenti 1985–87; Deputy Chief and Chief of Mechanized Infantry and Armored Service, Gen. Dir of Training 1989; Deputy Commdr 5th Army, Székesfehérvár; Deputy Commdr and Maj.-Gen. of Hungarian Army 1992; Dir of Mil. Intelligence Office 1993; Deputy Chief of Defence Staff 1996–99, Chief 1999–; Under-Sec. for Policy, Ministry of Defence 1999–; Gen. and Commdr of Defence Forces 1999–2005.
Address: c/o Honvédelmi Minisztérium, V. ker., Balaton u. 7–11, 1055 Budapest, Hungary (office). *Telephone:* (1) 236-5111 (office). *Fax:* (1) 447-1111 (office). *E-mail:* honvedelem@armedia.hu (office).

FOKIN, Vitold Pavlovych; Ukrainian politician; b. 25 Oct. 1932, Novomi-kolaivka, Zaporozhye region; m.; one s. one d. *Education:* m. Dnepropetrovsk Mining Inst. *Career:* fmr mem. CP; mining engineer 1954–71; Deputy Chair. Council of Ministers of Ukraine 1987–90; Chair. State Cttee for Econs Aug.–Nov. 1990; Chair. Council of Ministers (Prime Minister) of Ukraine 1990–92; Sr Researcher Inst. of World Econ. and Int. Relations 1993–, Pres. Int. Fund for Humanitarian and Econ. Relations with Russian Fed. 1993–; mem. Higher Econ. Council of Pres. of Ukraine 1997–; People's Deputy 1998–; Prof. Nat. Acad. of Mines; Chair. Supervisory Bd DEWON Inc. 2000–; Miner's Glory Order 1st, 2nd, 3rd class 1961–1963, Decoration of Honour 1967, 2 Orders of Working Red Banner 1970, 1975, Order of St Prince Volodymyr 2002, Order of Yaroslav the Wise 2002, Order of Honour 2004; Laureate of State Prize of Ukraine 1983, Medal for Services 2004, seven medals. *Publications:* about 30 published works and articles in social, political and technical journals and books.
Address: International Fund for Humanitarian and Economic Relations with Russian Federation, 19 Panasa Myrnogo Street, 01011 Kiev (office); Verkhovna Rada, M. Hrushevskoho rul 5, 252019 Kiev; Flat 266, 13 Suvorova Street, 01010 Kiev, Ukraine (home). *Telephone:* (44) 290-75-85 (office); (44) 290-52-55 (home). *Fax:* (44) 290-05-92 (office). *E-mail:* vitold .fokin@dewon.com.ua.

FOKIN, Yuri Yevgenyevich; Russian diplomatist; b. 2 Sept. 1936, Gorky (now Nizhny Novgorod); m.; one s.; one d. *Education:* Moscow Inst. of Int. Relations. *Career:* on staff, USSR Ministry of Foreign Affairs 1960–; with USSR Mission in UN 1960–65, Secr. of Minister of Foreign Affairs 1966–73, Sr Adviser, Dept of Planning of Int. Events 1973–76; Deputy Perm. Rep. of USSR to UN 1976–79; Deputy Dir-Gen. Ministry of Foreign Affairs 1979–80, Dir-Gen. 1980–86; Amb. to Cyprus 1986–90, to Norway 1995–97, to UK 1997–2000; Head, Second European Dept, Russian Ministry of Foreign Affairs 1990–92, Dir Second European Dept 1991–95; on staff, Ministry of Foreign Affairs 1995–, Rector, Diplomatic Acad. of Ministry of Foreign Affairs –2006; decorations from Russia, Austria, Norway. *Publications:* Diplomatic Yearbook 2000, 2001, 2002, State & Diaspora: A Record of Interaction.
Address: c/o Diplomatic Academy of the Ministry of Foreign Affairs, 53/2 Ostozhenka, 119992 Moscow, Russia. *Telephone:* (495) 245-33-86. *E-mail:* Yuri.Fokine@dipacademy.ru.

FOLEY, April H., BA, MBA; American business executive and diplomatist; *Ambassador to Hungary;* b. Avon Lake, OH. *Education:* Smith Coll. and Harvard Univ. *Career:* fmr Dir Business Planning for Corp. Strategy, PEPSICO, Inc.; fmr Dir of Strategy, Reader's Digest Asscn; fmr Chair. Alexis de Tocqueville Soc., Westchester and Putnam Cos, NY; fmr mem. Bd of Dirs and Pres. United Way of Northern Westchester, NY; mem. Bd of Dirs, First Vice-Pres. and Vice-Chair. Export-Import Bank of the US (Ex-Im Bank) 2003–05; Amb. to Hungary 2006–.
Address: Embassy of the USA, Szabadság tér 12, 1054 Budapest, Hungary (office). *Telephone:* (1) 475-4400 (office). *Fax:* (1) 475-4764 (office). *E-mail:* postmaster@usembassy.hu (office). *Website:* budapest.usembassy.gov (office).

FOLEY, James B., MA; American diplomatist; *Senior Co-ordinator for Iraqi Refugee Issues;* b. 4 April 1957, Buffalo, NY; m. Kate Suryan. *Education:* State Univ. of NY (SUNY) at Fredonia, Inst. d'Etudes Politiques, Paris, France, Fletcher School of Law and Diplomacy. *Career:* Research Asst, Inst. for Foreign Policy, Cambridge, Mass. –1983; joined US Foreign Service 1983; Consular Officer, then Political Officer, Embassy in Manila 1984–86; Political Officer, Embassy in Algiers 1986–88; Special Asst, then Political Adviser and Speechwriter to Deputy Sec. of State Eagleburger 1989–93; Deputy Dir, Pvt. Office of NATO Sec.-Gen., Brussels 1993–96; Special Asst to US Senator from Ga Coverdell 1996–97; Deputy Spokes-man, Dept of State and Prin. Deputy Asst Sec. for Public Affairs 1997–2000; Chargé d'Affaires, Perm. Mission to UN, Geneva 2001; Deputy Perm. Rep. to UN and Int. Orgs in Geneva, Switzerland 2002–03; Amb. to Haiti 2003–05; Sr Co-ordinator for Iraqi Refugee Issues 2007–; Int. Affairs Fellow, Council on Foreign Relations, NY 1988–89; Diplomat-in-Residence, SUNY at Fredonia 2005–06; Deputy Comman-dant and Adviser on Int. Affairs, Nat. War Coll. 2006–07.
Address: Department of State, 2201 C St, NW, Washington, DC 20520, USA (office). *Telephone:* (202) 647-4000 (office). *Fax:* (202) 647-6738 (office). *Website:* www.state.gov (office).

FOLEY, Thomas C., BA, MBA; American business executive and diplomatist; *Ambassador to Ireland;* one s. *Education:* Harvard Univ., Harvard Business School. *Career:* worked for McKinsey & Co., New York, later for Citicorp Venture Capital, New York; f. NTC Group (pvt. equity investment business) 1985; Dir of Pvt. Sector Devt for Coalition Provisional Authority, Iraq 2003–04; Amb. to Ireland 2006–; recently served as Trustee Kennedy Center for the Performing Arts, Washington, DC and two Connecticut State Comms involving educ. and children's rights; Dept of Defense Distinguished Public Service Award for service in Iraq 2004.
Address: Embassy of the US, 42 Elgin Road, Ballsbridge, Dublin 4, Ireland (office). *Telephone:* (1) 6688777 (office). *Fax:* (1) 6689946 (office). *E-mail:* webmasterireland@state.gov (office). *Website:* dublin.usembassy.gov (office).

FONG WONG KUT MAN, Nellie; Hong Kong accountant and government official; *Member of Executive Council, Hong Kong Special Administrative Region;* b. 7 Feb. 1949, Hong Kong; m. Eddy C. Fong; one c. *Career:*

practises as chartered accountant; mem. Hong Kong Urban Council 1983–89, Legis. Council 1988–91, People's Repub. of China Hong Kong Special Admin. Region Preliminary and Preparatory Cttees 1993–97 (Leader Econ. Sub-Group), Exec. Council of Hong Kong Special Admin. Region 1997–; Chair. Exec. Cttee The Better Hong Kong Foundation 1995, China Operations, Arthur Andersen, Exec. Cttee Lifeline Express 1997–; Pres. Business Br. PricewaterhouseCoopers in China; mem. Standing Comm. on Civil Service Salaries and Conditions of Service 1989–93, Hong Kong Baptist Univ. Council 1990–92, CPPCC, numerous other cttees and bds; Gold Bauhenia Star 1999.
Address: c/o Executive Council Secretariat, 1st Floor, Main Wing, Central Government Offices, Central, Hong Kong Special Administrative Region, People's Republic of China. *Telephone:* 28520294 (office). *Fax:* 28504092 (office). *E-mail:* nellie.k.fong@hk.arthurandersen.com (office).

FONSECA, Ralph H.; Belizean politician; *Minister of Home Affairs, Public Utilities and Housing;* b. 9 Aug. 1949; m.; three c. *Education:* St John's Coll. *Career:* fmr Asst Gen. Man. Texaco, Belize; fmr Area Gen. Man. Cardinal Distributors, Canada; fmr Research Engineer, Control Data; fmr Systems Analyst, Prescribe Data System; fmr gen. man. brewing co.; fmr Man. Dir Hillbank Agroindustry; fmr Chair. Belize Electricity Co.; fmr Chair. Belize Telecommunications Authority Ltd; fmr Pres. Consolidated Electricity Services; mem. Parl. 1993–; Minister of Budget Man., Investment and Home Affairs 1999–2003, Minister of Finance and Home Affairs 2003–05; Minister of Home Affairs and Public Utilities 2005–, of Housing 2007–.
Address: Ministry of Home Affairs and Public Utilities, Curl Thompson Building, Belmopan, Belize (office). *Telephone:* 822-2218 (office). *Fax:* 822-2195 (office). *E-mail:* investment@btl.net (office).

FONT-ROSSELL, Carles, BBA; Andorran diplomatist; *Permanent Representative, United Nations;* b. 26 Dec. 1967, Canillo. *Education:* European Univ. of Barcelona, Spain. *Career:* hotel owner in Andorra; mem. Parish Council of Canillo 1996–99; Chair. Andorra Rugby Fed. 2003–05; Minister of Youth and Sports 2005–07; Perm. Rep. to UN, New York 2007–, also Amb. to USA; mem. Partit Liberal Andorra.
Address: Permanent Mission of Andorra to the United Nations, 2 United Nations Plaza, 25th Floor, New York, NY 10017, USA (office). *Telephone:* (212) 750-8064 (office). *Fax:* (212) 750-6630 (office). *E-mail:* andorra@un.int (office).

FONTAGNÉ, Lionel Gérard; French economist and academic; *Professor of Economics, Université Paris 1 Panthéon-Sorbonne; Career:* fmr Supply Prof., Free Univ. of Brussels; Prof. of Econs, Univ. of Nantes 1990–94, Univ. of Paris I Panthéon-Sorbonne 1994–; Dir Center for Int. Prospective Studies (CEPII), Paris 2000–06, Research Assoc. 2006–; adviser Int. Trade Center (UNCTAD-WTO), Geneva; Sr Adviser, Int. Trade Centre (UNCTAD-WTO), Geneva; mem. Conseil d'Analyse Econ., Paris School of Econs; fmr consultant to OECD Devt Centre, OECD Directorate for Science, Tech. and Industry, Ministry of Finance of Luxembourg, French Ministry of Finance; Ed. Telos (online think tank); Reseach Fellowship, Global Trade Analysis Project, Purdue Univ. 2007. *Publications:* numerous studies on int. trade and integration issues.
Address: Université Paris 1, Maison des Sciences Economiques, Office 308, 106-112 Bd de l'Hôpital, 75647 Paris Cedex 13, France (office). *Telephone:* 1-44-07-83-37 (home). *Fax:* 1-53-68-55-01 (office). *E-mail:* lionel.fontagne@univ-paris1.fr (office). *Website:* team.univ-paris1.fr/teamperso/fontagne/lionel.htm (office).

FONTAINE, Nicole; French politician and lawyer; b. 1942, Normandy. *Education:* Inst. d'Etudes Politiques, Paris. *Career:* admitted to Bar, Hauts-de-Seine; Legal Adviser Secrétariat général de l'Enseignement catholique, Deputy Sec.-Gen. 1972–81, Chief Rep. 1981–84; mem. Conseil supérieur de l'Educ. nationale 1975–81; mem. Standing Cttee 1978–81; mem. Conseil économique et social 1980–84; mem. European People's Party; MEP 1984–, Vice-Pres. 1989–94, First Vice-Pres. 1994–99, Pres. 1999–2002, mem. Parl. Cttee on Legal Affairs and Citizens' Rights, on Culture, Youth, Educ. and the Media, on Women's Rights 1984–89, apptd by European People's Party as perm. mem. Conciliation Cttee 1994–2002; Vice-Pres. Union pour la Démocratie Française (UDF); Minister for Industry 2003–04. *Publications:* Les députés européens: Qui sont-ils? Que font-ils? 1994, l'Europe de vos initiatives 1997, Le traité d'Amsterdam 1998, My Battles at the Presidency of the European Parliament 2002.
Address: c/o Office of the Minister for Industry, Ministry of Economy, Finance and Industry, 139 rue de Bercy, 75572 Paris Cédex 12, France (office).

FONTES LIMA, Maria Cristina Lopes; Cape Verde politician; *Minister of the Presidency of the Council of Ministers, State Reform and National Defence;* b. 1958. *Career:* Minister of Local Admin 2001–02, Minister of Justice 2001–06, Minister of Interior 2002–04, Minister Adjunct to Prime

Minister and Govt Spokesperson 2004–06, Minister of the Presidency of Council of Ministers, State Reform and Nat. Defence 2006–; fmr Chair. Network of African Women Ministerial and Parliamentarian Bureau.
Address: Ministry of the Presidency of the Council of Ministers, State Reform and National Defence, Praia, Santiago, Cape Verde.

FORD, Charles A., BA, MA; American diplomatist; *Ambassador to Honduras;* b. Dayton, OH; m. Lillian Ford; one s. one d. *Education:* Coll. of William and Mary, Williamsburg, Va, George Washington Univ. *Career:* mem. Foreign Service since 1982, overseas assigments have included Commercial Minister, US Mission to EU, Brussels, Commercial Counselor, Embassy in Caracas, Commercial Minister, Embassy in London, Commercial Attaché, Embassy in Guatemala, Commercial Consul, Barcelona, Commercial Attaché, Embassy in Buenos Aires, Washington assignments have included Deputy Asst Sec. for Int. Operations and Sr Advisor to Deputy Asst Sec. for Int. Operations, US and Foreign Commercial Service, Regional Dir in Europe, US and Foreign Commercial Service, Dept of Commerce, Dir Office of Latin American Trade Policy, Int. Trade Admin, Dept of Commerce; Vice-Pres. American Foreign Service Asscn; Amb. to Honduras 2005–; US Dept of Commerce Silver Medal, US Dept of Commerce Gold Medal for Distinguished Achievement in Fed. Service, US Dept of Commerce/Int. Trade Admin Bronze Medal.
Address: Embassy of the USA, Avenida La Paz, Apdo 3453, Tegucigalpa, Honduras (office). *Telephone:* 236-9320 (office). *Fax:* 236-9037 (office). *Website:* honduras.usembassy.gov (office).

FORD, Peter; British diplomatist (retd). *Career:* career with British Diplomatic Service; overseas assignments in Riyadh, Paris, Cairo and Beirut; positions have included Sr Adviser to Foreign Sec. on Middle East Peace Process, Head of Near East and N Africa Dept, FCO; Amb. to Bahrain 2001–03, to Syria 2003–06 (retd).
Address: c/o Foreign and Commonwealth Office, King Charles Street, London, SW1A 2AH, England (office).

FORD, Robert Stephen, MA; American diplomatist; *Ambassador to Algeria;* b. Md; m. Clare Alison Barkley. *Education:* Johns Hopkins School of Advanced Int. Studies. *Career:* Peace Corps volunteer in Morocco 1980–82; career mem. Sr Foreign Service, joined Foreign Service in 1985, served in Izmir, Cairo, Algiers and Yaounde, Political Counselor, Baghdad 2004–06, Deputy Chief of Mission to Bahrain 2001–04, Amb. to Algeria 2006–; James Clement Dunn Award for outstanding work at mid-level in Foreign Service 2005, numerous other Dept of State awards.
Address: Embassy of the US, BP 549, 4 chemin Cheikh Bachir Ibrahimi, El-Biar 16030, Algiers, Algeria (office). *Telephone:* (21) 69-12-55 (office). *Fax:* (21) 69-39-79 (office). *E-mail:* algiers_webmaster@state.gov (office). *Website:* algiers.usembassy.gov (office).

FORDE, Sir Henry de Boulay, Kt, PC, QC, LLM; Barbadian politician and lawyer; b. 20 March 1933, Christ Church, Barbados; adopted s. of the late Courtley Ifill and of Elise Ifill; m. Cheryl Wendy Forde; four s. *Education:* Harrison Coll., Barbados, Christ's Coll., Cambridge, Middle Temple, London. *Career:* Research Asst, Dept of Criminology, Univ. of Cambridge 1958, Research Student, Int. Law, worked on British Digest of Int. Law, Univ. of Cambridge 1958–59, Supervisor and Tutor in Int. Law, Emmanuel Coll., Cambridge 1958–59; called to English Bar 1959, to Barbadian Bar 1959; Lecturer, Extra-Mural Programme, Univ. of West Indies 1961–68, Part-time Lecturer, Caribbean Studies, 1964–69; mem. House of Ass. for Christ Church West 1971–2003; Minister of External Affairs and Attorney-Gen. 1976–81; Minister of State 1993; Leader of the Opposition 1986–89, 1991–93; mem. Privy Council 1976–92, 1996–; Chair. and Political Leader, Barbados Labour Party 1986–93; Chair. Commonwealth Observer Group to the Seychelles 1991, to Fiji Islands 2001; mem. Commonwealth Cttee on Vulnerability of Small States 1985, Commonwealth Parl. Asscn, Editorial Bds of The Round Table, Int. Comm. of Jurists 1987–92, Barbados Bar Asscn, Hon. Soc. of Middle Temple, Int. Tax Planning Asscn, Interparl. Human Rights Network, Barbados Nat. Trust, Int. Acad. of Estate and Trust Law, Int. Inst. for Democracy and Electoral Assistance, Inter-American Comm. on Human Rights; Kt of St Andrew, Order of Barbados.
Address: Juris Chambers, Fidelity House, Wildey Business Park, Wildey Road, St Michael, Barbados (office); Codrington Court, Society, St John, Barbados, West Indies (home). *Telephone:* (246) 429-5320 (office); (246) 429-2203 (office); (246) 423-3881 (home). *Fax:* (246) 429-2206 (office); (246) 423-3949 (home). *E-mail:* shf@jurischambers.com (office).

FORNÉ MOLNÉ, Marc; Andorran politician and lawyer; *Leader, Partit Liberal d'Andorra;* b. 1946. *Education:* Univ. of Barcelona. *Career:* lawyer; fmr Ed. Andorra 7 magazine; currently Leader Partit Liberal d'Andorra; Head of Govt of Andorra 1994–2004.
Address: Partit Liberal d'Andorra (PLA), Carrer Babot Camp 13, 2°, Andorra la Vella, AD500, Andorra (office). *Telephone:* 807715 (office).

Fax: 869728 (office). *E-mail:* pla@pla.ad (office). *Website:* www .partitliberal.ad (office).

FORST, Michel; French human rights activist and UN official; *Special Rapporteur for Haiti, United Nations, Geneva; Education:* Univ. of Nanterre Paris X. *Career:* Dir-Gen. Amnesty Int., France 1989–99; Chief of Exec. Office, UNESCO 2001–04; Sec.-Gen. CIMADE (Comité intermouvements auprès des évacués) 2003–05, CNCDH (Comm. Nat. Consultative des Droits de l'Homme de la Republique Francaise) 2005–08; Special Rapporteur for Haiti, UN, Geneva 2008–.
Address: Office of the Special Rapporteur for Haiti, United Nations Commission for Human Rights, Palais des Nations, 1211 Geneva, Switzerland (office). *Telephone:* 229179000 (office). *Fax:* 229179022 (office). *E-mail:* infodesk@ohchr.org (office). *Website:* www.ohchr.org (office).

FORSYTHE, David P., MA, PhD; American academic; *Charles J. Mach Distinguished Professor, Department of Political Science, University of Nebraska;* b. Nov. 1941, North Carolina. *Education:* Wake Forest Univ., Princeton Univ. *Career:* Research Asst, Carnegie Endowment for Int. Peace, New York 1966; Research Assoc., Center of Int. Studies, Princeton Univ. 1968; Asst Prof. of Political Science, Agnes Scott Coll., Atlanta 1967–69; Dir Foreign Area Studies and Asst Prof. of Political Science, Georgia State Univ. 1969–73; Consultant, Henry Dunant Inst., Geneva 1972–73; Assoc. Prof., Univ. of Nebraska-Lincoln 1973–77, Prof. 1977–, Chair. Dept of Political Science 1993–98, Charles J. Mach Distinguished Prof. 1997–; Consultant, Int. Red Cross 1974–75; James P. Warburg Visiting Fellow, Princeton Univ. 1975–76; Visiting Prof., Odense Univ., Denmark 1978–79; Visiting Research Scholar, Inst. for Social and Policy Studies, Yale Univ. 1979–80; Visiting Fellow, Human Rights Center, Utrecht Univ., Netherlands 1984–85; Visiting Prof., Grad Inst. of Int. Studies, Geneva 1999–2000; Consultant, UNHCR 2000, 2003; Visiting Scholar, Irish Centre for Human Rights, Univ. of Galway 2002; mem. Int. Studies Asscn (Pres. 1995–96), American Soc. of Int. Law, Academic Council on the UN; mem. Editorial Review Bd Human Rights Quarterly, International Studies Quarterly; fmr Pres. Human Rights Cttee, Int. Political Science Asscn; fmr Vice-Pres. Int. Studies Asscn; fmr mem. Cttee on Scientific Freedom and Responsibility, AAAS; Outstanding Research Award, Univ. of Nebraska 1982, Quincy Wright Distinguished Scholar Award 2003, named Distinguished Scholar, American Political Science Asscn 2007. *Publications include:* Human Rights in International Relations 2000, Human Rights and Comparative Foreign Policy (ed.) 2000, The United States and Human Rights (ed.) 2000, Human Rights and Diversity 2003, The Humanitarians: The International Committee of the Red Cross 2005,; numerous articles in academic journals.
Address: Department of Political Science, University of Nebraska, 511 Oldfather Hall, Lincoln, NE 68588-0328, USA (office). *Telephone:* (402) 472-1690 (office). *Fax:* (402) 472-8192 (office). *E-mail:* dforsythe1@unl.edu (office).

FOSS, Per-Kristian; Norwegian politician; b. 19 July 1950, Oslo. *Education:* Univ. of Oslo. *Career:* journalist 1971–73; mem. Høyre (Conservative Party), Chair. Høyre Municipal Council 1973–77, Chair. Unge Høyre (Young Conservatives) 1973–77, Chair. Høyre Cttee on Party Program 1981–85, Chair. Høyre Cttee on Cultural Objectives and Strategies 1983–85, Deputy Chair. Høyre Party Parl. Mems' Group 1993–2001, Leader of Høyre 2002–; mem. Storting (Parl.) for Oslo 1977–, mem. Cttee on Energy and Industry 1981–89 (Second Vice-Chair. 1985–89), mem. Standing Cttee on Finance 1989–2001 (Chair. 1989–93, Vice-Chair. 1993–97), mem. Enlarged Foreign Affairs Cttee 1997–2001; Minister of Finance 2001–2005; Ed. of Kontur (periodical) 1979–80; Consultant Norges Rederforbund (Norwegian Shipowners' Asscn) 1980–81; mem. Lillehammer Olympic Organizing Cttee 1994.

FOSSEIDBRÅTEN, Odd Lauritz, BA; Norwegian diplomatist; *Ambassador to Sweden;* b. 19 July 1946; m. Ingrid Susanne Farner; three c. *Education:* Univ. of Oslo, Univ. of Lund. *Career:* joined Ministry of Foreign Affairs 1973; overseas assignments with Embassy in Budapest and Perm. Del. to NATO, Brussels; various positions in trade areas including Special Adviser to Minister of Trade, Oslo 1979–85; with Embassy in Bonn 1985–88; Head, Div. of Bilateral Trade Policy and Export Promotion, Ministry of Foreign Affairs 1992–96; Dir Ministry of Industry and Trade 1996–99; fmr Amb. to Singapore; Amb. to Japan 1999–2004, to Sweden 2004–.
Address: Embassy of Norway, Skarpögt. 4, POB 27829, 115 27 Stockholm, Sweden (office). *Telephone:* (8) 665-63-40 (office). *Fax:* (8) 782-98-99 (office). *E-mail:* emb.stockholm@mfa.no (office). *Website:* www.norge.se (office).

FOWLER, Robert R., BA; Canadian diplomatist; b. 18 Aug. 1944, Ottawa; m. Mary Fowler; four d. *Education:* Queen's Univ., Kingston, Ont. *Career:* joined Canadian Int. Devt Agency (CIDA) 1968, Dept of External Affairs 1969; with Embassy in Paris 1971–74; Head of Trade Policy, Commercial Policy Div. 1974–76; First Sec., then Counsellor, Perm. Mission to UN, NY 1976–78, Perm. Rep. 1995–2000; Exec. Asst to Under-Sec. of State for External Affairs 1978–80; secondment to Privy Council, Asst Sec. to Cabinet, Foreign and Defence Policy 1980–82; mem. Perm. Staff, Privy Council 1982–86; Asst Deputy Minister, Policy, Dept of Nat. Defence 1986–89, Deputy Minister 1989–93; Chair. Cttee regarding Resolution 864 on situation in Angola, UN Security Council 1993; Amb. to Italy 2000–06; Senior Fellow, Graduate School of Public and Int. Affairs, Univ. of Ottawa 2007–.
Address: Graduate School of Public and International Affairs, University of Ottawa, 55 Laurier Avenue East, Desmarais Building, Room 11130a, Ottoawa, Ontario, K1N 6N5, Canada (office). *Telephone:* (613) 562-5800 ext. 4772 (office). *Fax:* (613) 562-5241 (office). *E-mail:* Robert.Fowler@ uOttawa.ca (office). *Website:* www.sciencepolitique.uottawa.ca (office).

FOX, Sam; American business executive and diplomatist; *Ambassador to Belgium;* b. 1929, Desloge, Missouri; m. Marilyn Rae Widman 1954; five c. *Education:* public schools in Desloge, Washington Univ., St Louis, Mo. *Career:* Founder, Chair. and CEO Harbour Group; active in civic affairs in St Louis; Lifetime Trustee of Washington Univ., served as Chair. of capital campaign; served as Chair. and Pres. Greater St Louis Area Council, Boy Scouts of America, St Louis Art Museum; Campaign Chair. United Way of Greater St Louis 2003; fmr mem. Bd Dirs St Louis Symphony, Saint Louis Science Center, Arts and Educ. Council of Greater St Louis, Barnes-Jewish Hosp.; f. Fox Family Foundation; Amb. to Belgium (recess appointment) 2007–; Hon. Doctorate of Public Service (St Louis Univ.), Hon. LLD (Washington Univ.); numerous awards and honours, including St Louis Citizen of the Year 2003, Marco Polo Award (People's Repub. of China), Woodrow Wilson Award for Corp. Citizenship, Horatio Alger Award, Washington Univ. dedicated the Sam Fox School of Design and Visual Arts in honour of his service 2006.
Address: Embassy of the USA, 27 Blvd du Régent, 1000 Brussels, Belgium (office). *Telephone:* (2) 508-21-11 (office). *Fax:* (2) 511-21-60 (office). *Website:* brussels.usembassy.gov (office).

FOX QUESADA, Vicente; Mexican fmr head of state and business executive; b. 2 July 1942, Mexico City; m. 1st (divorced); two s. two d.; m. 2nd Marta Sahagún 2001. *Education:* Universidad Iberoamericana, Mexico City, Harvard Univ. *Career:* worked for Coca Cola Group, first as route supervisor, becoming Regional Pres. for Mexico and Latin America; also worked as farmer and shoemaker; joined Partido Acción Nacional (Nat. Action Party—PAN); Fed. Deputy 1988–; Gov. of Guanajuato 1995–; Pres. of Mexico 2000–Dec. 2006.
Address: Partido Acción Nacional (PAN), Avda Coyoacán 1546, Col. del Valle, Del. Benito Juárez, 03100 México, DF, Mexico (office). *Telephone:* (55) 5200-4000 (office). *E-mail:* correo@cen.pan.org.mx (office). *Website:* www.pan.org.mx (office).

FOXLEY RIOSECO, Alejandro, MSc, PhD; Chilean politician and economist; *Minister of Foreign Affairs;* b. 26 May 1939, Viña del Mar; m. Gisela Tapia 1963; two c. *Education:* Univ. of Wisconsin, Harvard Univ. and Catholic Univ., Valparaíso. *Career:* Dir Global Planning Div., Nat. Planning Office, Govt of Chile 1967–70; Dir Center for Nat. Planning Studies, Catholic Univ. of Chile 1970–76; mem. Exec. Council, Latin-American Social Science Council (CLACSO) 1975–81; mem. Jt Cttee Latin-American Studies, Social Science Research Council, New York 1975–78; founder and Pres. Corpn for Latin-American Econ. Research (CIEPLAN), Santiago 1976–90; Minister of Finance 1990–94, also Gov. World Bank and Inter-American Devt Bank; Pres. Christian Democratic Party (PDC) 1994–96; Senator 1998–2006; Minister of Foreign Affairs 2006–; Helen Kellogg Prof. of Econs (part-time) and Int. Devt, Univ. of Notre Dame 1982–; Assoc. Ed. Journal of Development Economics 1977–; Visiting Fellow, Univ. of Sussex 1973, Oxford 1975, MIT 1978; Ford Int. Fellow 1963–64, Daugherty Foundation Fellow 1965–66; Ford Foundation Fellow 1970; Co-Pres. Inter-American Dialogue, Wash. 1994–99, now mem. Exec. Cttee; mem. Int. Advisory Bd Journal Latin American Studies; Dr hc (Univ. of Notre Dame) 1991, (Univ. of Wis.) 1993; Orden al Mérito Civil, Rey de Espana 1991, Gran Cruz Orden Nacional Cruzeiro do Sul (Brazil) 1993, Gran Insignia de Honor (Austria) 1994. *Publications:* Income Distribution in Latin-America 1976, Redistributive Effects of Government Programmes 1979, Estrategia de Desarrollo y Modelos de Planificación, Legados del Monetarismo: Argentina y Chile, Para una Democracia Estable 1985, Chile y su futuro: Un país posible 1989, Chile puede más 1989, numerous articles and working papers.
Address: Ministry of Foreign Affairs Catedral 1158, Santiago (office); Golfo de Darién 10236, Santiago (Las Condes), Chile (home). *Telephone:* (2) 679-4200 (office); 20-7924 (home). *Fax:* (2) 699-4202 (office). *E-mail:*

info@minrel.cl (office); afoxley@congreso.cl (office). *Website:* www.minrel
.cl (office).

FRADKOV, Mikhail Yefimovich; Russian politician; *Director, Federal
Foreign Intelligence Service;* b. 1 Sept. 1950, Kuybyshev (now Samara)
Oblast; m. Yelena; two c. *Education:* Moscow Inst. of Machines and Tools,
USSR Acad. of Foreign Trade. *Career:* on staff, office of Counsellor on
econ. affairs USSR Embassy to India 1973–75; on staff Foreign Trade
Agency Tyazhpromeksport, USSR State Cttee on Econ. Relations
1975–84; Deputy, First Deputy Dir of Dept USSR State Cttee on Econ.
Relations 1985–91; Deputy Perm. Rep. of Russian Fed. to GATT 1991–92;
Sr Adviser Perm. Mission of Russian Fed. to UN; Deputy, First Deputy
Minister of External Econ. Relations 1993; Interim Acting Minister of
External Econ. Relations 1997; Minister of External Econ. Relations and
Trade 1997–98; Chair. Bd of Dirs Ingosstrakh 1998–99, Dir-Gen. 1999;
Minister of Trade 1999–2000; First Deputy Sec. Security Council of Russia
2000–01; Head Fed. Service of Tax Police 2001–03; Plenipotentary Rep. to
EU 2003–04; apptd Special Rep. of the Pres. of the Russian Fed. on the
Devt of Relations with the EU June 2003; Chair. of the Govt (Prime
Minister) of the Russian Fed. 2004–07 (resgnd); Dir Fed. Foreign
Intelligence Service Russian Fed. 2007–.
Address: Federal Foreign Intelligence Service, 119034 Moscow, Ostoz-
henka str. 51/10, Russia (office). *Telephone:* (495) 429-30-09 (office).

FRAKER, Ford M., BA; American business executive and diplomatist;
Ambassador to Saudi Arabia; Education: Harvard Coll. *Career:* Asst Rep.,
Chemical Bank, Beirut 1974, then Vice Pres. and Regional Man., Bahrain;
Div. Head Middle East, Saudi Int. Bank (JP Morgan affiliate), London
1979, then Div. Head of Gen. Banking, Credit, and Client Devt and
Marketing, also Chair. Credit Policy Cttee and mem. Man. Cttee; f. Fraker
& Co., London 1991; Man. Dir MeesPierson Investment Finance Ltd (UK
1993–96; Co-Founder and Chair. Trinity Group Ltd (pvt. investment
banking firm), London 1996–2007; consultant to Intercontinental Real
Estate Corpn, Boston –2007; Amb. to Saudi Arabia 2007–.
Address: American Embassy, POB 94309, Riyadh 11693, Saudi Arabia
(office). *Telephone:* (1) 488-3800 (office). *Fax:* (1) 488-7360 (office). *E-mail:*
usisriyadh@yahoo.com (office). *Website:* riyadh.usembassy.gov (office).

FRANCHET, Yves Georges; French international public servant; b. 4 March
1939, Paris; m. Marie Bernard Robillard; two s. *Education:* Ecole
polytechnique, Paris, Université Paris I, Ecole nationale de la statistique
et de l'admin économique de Paris. *Career:* Dir Statistics Office, UDEAC,
Brazzaville, Congo 1964–68; mem. Govt econ. planning staff 1968–69;
economist, World Bank, Washington, DC 1969–74; Head of Planning, Co-
operation Div., Inst. Nat. de la Statistique et des Etudes Economiques
(INSEE) 1974–77; Dir Ecole Nat. de la statistique et de l'admin
économique (ENSAE) 1977–80; Deputy Dir European Office of World
Bank, Paris 1980–83; Vice-Pres. IDB, Washington, DC 1983–87; Dir-Gen.
Statistical Office of the European Communities (EUROSTAT) 1987–2003;
Chevalier Légion d'honneur, Commdr Order of Merit (Niger); Dr hc
(Bucharest).
Address: c/o Statistical Office of the European Communities (Eurostat),
Bâtiment Jean Monnet, rue Alcide de Gasperi, 2920 Luxembourg,
Luxembourg (office); 7 rue J. P. Brasseur, 1258 Luxembourg, Luxembourg
(home). *Telephone:* 43-01-33-10-7 (office). *Fax:* 43-01-33-01-5 (office).

FRANCK, Edouard; Central African Republic politician; *President, Supreme
Court; Career:* fmrly Minister in charge of Cabinet Secr.; Prime Minister of
the Cen. African Repub. 1991–93; Pres. Supreme Court 1995–.
Address: Cour Suprême, BP 926, Bangui, Central African Republic (office).
Telephone: 61-41-33 (office).

FRANCO GOMEZ, Julio César, PhD; Paraguayan politician and doctor; b.
1952. *Education:* Nat. Univ. of Cordoba, Argentina, Asunción Univ.
Career: Senator 1998; Pres. of the Comm. for Public Health, Social Security
and Drug Control 1999; Vice-Pres. of Paraguay 2000–03.
Address: Congreso Nacional, Asunción, Paraguay (office).

FRANGIALLI, Francesco; French international organization official;
Secretary-General, World Tourism Organization; b. 23 Jan. 1947, Paris;
m. Leila Niiranen; two s. one d. *Education:* Université de Paris, Institut
d'Études Politiques de Paris, École Nationale d'Admin (ENA). *Career:*
Lecturer, Institut d'Études Politiques de Paris 1972–89; extensive background in public admin; Dir Tourism Industry, Govt ministry responsible
for tourism 1986–90; Perm. Rep. to World Tourism Org. 1986–89, Deputy
Sec.-Gen. 1990–96, Sec.-Gen. ad interim 1996–97, Sec.-Gen. 1998–, led the
org.'s conversion to a specialized agency of the UN 2003. *Publications:* La
France dans le tourisme mondial 1991, Tourisme et loisirs – Une question
sociale (co-author), published in Observations on International Tourism

1997–2000, and in International Tourism: The Great Turning Point
2001–2003; numerous articles, speeches and papers.
Address: World Tourism Organization, Capitán Haya 42, 28020 Madrid,
Spain (office). *Telephone:* (91) 567-81-00 (office). *Fax:* (91) 571-37-33
(office). *E-mail:* omt@unwto.org (office). *Website:* www.unwto.org
(office).

FRANK, Ralph; American diplomatist; b. Wash.; m. Susan Gundersen; two
c. *Career:* joined US Foreign Service 1975, overseas assignments in
Belgrade 1975–77, Medan, Indonesia 1977–79, Warsaw 1983–86, Kath-
mandu, Nepal 1986–88, Deputy Asst Sec. of State, Bureau of Diplomatic
Security 1990–92, Bureau of Admin 1996, Bureau of Personnel 1996–97,
Exec. Dir Bureau of Near Eastern and S Asian Affairs, Dept of State
1993–95, Exec. Asst to Under-Sec. of Man. 1995–96, Office Dir Bureau of
Human Resources, Office of Career Devt and Assignments 2001–03, Amb.
to Nepal 1997–2001, to Croatia 2003–06; Superior Honor Award and
Meritorious Honour Awards, Dept of State.
Address: US Department of State, 2201 C Street NW, Washington, DC
20520, USA (office). *Telephone:* (202) 647-4000 (office). *Fax:* (202) 647-
6738 (office). *Website:* www.state.gov (office).

FRANK, Sergey Ottovich; Russian politician; *General Director, Sovkomflot;*
b. 13 Aug. 1960, Novosibirsk; m.; one s. *Education:* Far East Higher
Marine School of Eng, Far East State Univ., Higher School of Commerce,
Ministry of Foreign Econ. Relations of Russian Fed. *Career:* Sec.,
Comsomol Cttee, later Deputy Head, Far East Higher Marine School;
on staff, Far East Marine Navigation Agency 1989–93, Deputy Dir-Gen.
1993–95; Deputy Head, Dept of Marine Transport, Ministry of Transport
of Russian Fed. 1995–96; First Deputy Minister of Transport of Russian
Fed. 1997–98, Minister 1998–2004, First Deputy Minister of Transport and
Communications 2004; Chair. Aeroflot 1999–; Gen. Dir Sovkomflot 2004–.
Address: Sovcomflot, 6 Gasheka str., 125047 Moscow, Russia (office).
Telephone: (495) 626-1434 (office). *Fax:* (495) 626-1850 (office). *E-mail:*
moscow@sovcomflot.ru (office). *Website:* www.sovcomflot.ru (office).

FRASYNIUK, Władysław; Polish politician and union leader; *Chairman,
Freedom Union;* b. 25 Nov. 1954, Wrocław; m. 1978; one s. three d. *Career:*
driver, mechanic Municipal Transport, Wrocław, organizer of strike in bus
depot, Wrocław Aug. 1980; press spokesman Founding Cttee of Ind. Self-
Governing Trade Union; Chair. Solidarity Trade Union, Lower Silesia
1981–90 (resgnd); mem. Nat. Consultative Comm. of Solidarity; active
underground under martial law, Jt Founder Provisional Exec. Cttee of
Solidarity; arrested 1982, amnestied 1984; arrested again Feb. 1985,
sentenced to over 4 years, amnestied 1986; mem. Provisional Council of
Solidarity 1986–87, Nat. Exec. Comm. of Solidarity 1987–90; mem.
Citizens' Cttee of Solidarity, Chair. 1988–90; took part in Round Table
talks, Comm. for Trade Union Pluralism Feb.–April 1989; one of founders
and leaders of Citizens' Movt for Democratic Action (ROAD) 1990–91;
mem. Social-Liberal faction of Democratic Union 1991–94; Vice-Chair.
Democratic Union 1991–94; mem. Freedom Union 1994–, Chair. Silesia
Region 1999–, Chair. 2001–; Deputy to Sejm (Parl.) 1991–2001.
Address: Biuro Krajowe Unii Wolności, ul. Marszałkowska 77–79, 00-683
Warsaw; Biuro Dolnośłaskiej Unii Wolności, ul. Zelwerowicza 16, 53-676
Wrocław, Poland (office). *Telephone:* (22) 827-50-47; (71) 3548390 (office).
Fax: (71) 3548399 (office). *E-mail:* frasyniuk@unia-wolnosci.pl (office).
Website: www.uw.org.pl (office).

FRATTINI, Franco, LLB; Italian attorney and politician; *Minister for Foreign
Affairs;* b. 14 March 1957, Rome. *Education:* La Sapienza Univ., Rome.
Career: State Attorney 1981, Attorney, State Attorney-Gen.'s Office 1984;
Magistrate, Regional Admin. Tribunal, Piedmont 1984–86, Council of
State Judge 1986–; Legal Adviser to Minister of the Treasury 1986, to
Deputy Prime Minister 1990–91, to Prime Minister 1992; Deputy Sec.-Gen.
Office of Prime Minister 1993, Sec.-Gen. 1994; Minister for Civil Service
and Regional Affairs 1995–96; mem. Camera dei Deputati (Parl.) (Forza
Italia) 1995–96, 2001–04; Pres. Parl. Cttee for Intelligence and Security
Services and State Secrets 1996–2004; Minister for Civil Service and for
Coordination of Intelligence and Security Services 2001–02, for Foreign
Affairs 2002–04, 2008–; Vice-Pres. European Comm., Commr for Justice,
Freedom and Security 2004–08; City Councillor, Rome 1997–2000; mem.
Exec. Cttee Forza Italia 1998–. *Publications include:* numerous specialist
articles on law and public works.
Address: Ministry of Foreign Affairs, Piazzale della Farnesina 1, 00194
Rome, Italy (office). *Telephone:* (06) 36911 (office). *Fax:* (06) 36918899
(office). *E-mail:* relazioni.pubblico@esteri.it (office). *Website:* www.esteri.it
(office).

FRAZER, Jendayi E., BA, MA, PhD; American diplomatist and academic;
Assistant Secretary of State for African Affairs; Education: Stanford Univ.
Career: early career as political-mil. planner, US Jt Chiefs of Staff,

Washington, DC; fmr positions on White House staff include Dir for African Affairs, Nat. Security Council, Special Asst to Pres. and Sr Dir of African Affairs 2001–04; Asst Prof. of Public Policy, John F. Kennedy School of Govt, Harvard Univ. 1995–2003; Amb. to S Africa 2004–05; Asst Sec. of State for African Affairs, US State Dept 2005–; fmr Fellow on Foreign Relations Int. Affairs Council.
Address: Bureau of African Affairs, Office 6234A, US State Department, 2201 C Street, NW, Washington DC, 20520, USA (office). *Telephone:* (202) 647-4440 (office). *Website:* www.state.gov (office).

FRCKOVSKY, Ljubomir; Macedonian politician and academic; *Professor of International Law, Skopje University;* b. 2 Dec. 1957. *Education:* Skopje Univ., Ljubljana Univ. *Career:* mem. Inst. Francais des Relations Int., Paris; mem. Int. Law Asscn Skopje, Forum for Human Rights Macedonia; Prof. of Int. Law and Theory of Int. Relations Skopje Univ.; co-author of new Constitution of Repub. of Macedonia 1991; Minister without Portfolio 1990; Minister of Interior 1994; Minister of Foreign Relations 1996–97; Prof., Skopje Univ. 1996–98, currently Prof. of Int. Law; adviser to Pres. Boris Trajkovski 2002–04; Fellow, Schloss Leopoldskron, Salzburg, 21st Century Trust, London.
Address: SS Cyril and Methodius University of Skopje, PO Box 576, Krste Misirkov bb, 91000 Skopje, Macedonia. *Telephone:* (91) 116323 (office).

FRÉCHETTE, Louise, OC, BA; Canadian diplomatist, public servant and international organization official; *Distinguished Fellow, Center for International Governance Innovation;* b. 16 July 1946, Montreal. *Education:* College Basile Moreau, Univ. of Montreal, College of Europe, Bruges, Belgium. *Career:* with Dept of External Affairs, Govt of Canada from 1970s, mem. del. to UN Gen. Ass. 1972, Second Sec., Embassy in Athens 1972–75, worked in European Affairs Div., Dept of External Affairs 1975–77, First Sec., Canadian Mission to UN in Geneva 1978–82, participated in session of CSCE (now OSCE) in Madrid 1980–81, Amb. to Argentina (also accred to Uruguay and Paraguay) 1985–90; Asst Deputy Minister for Latin America and the Caribbean, Ministry of Foreign Affairs, for Int. Econ. and Trade Policy 1990–92; Perm. Rep. to UN 1992–94; Assoc. Deputy Minister, Dept of Finance 1994–95; Deputy Minister of Nat. Defence 1995–98; Deputy Sec.-Gen. UN 1998–2006; Distinguished Fellow, Center for Int. Governance Innovation, Waterloo, Ont. 2006–; Dr hc (Saint Mary's Univ., Kyung Hee Univ., Univ. of Ottawa, Univ. of Toronto, Laval Univ.); ranked by Forbes magazine amongst 100 Most Powerful Women (87th) 2004, (65th) 2005.
Address: The Centre for International Governance Innovation, 57 Erb Street West, Waterloo, ON N2L 6C2, Canada (office). *Telephone:* (519) 885-2444 (office). *Fax:* (519) 885-5450 (office). *E-mail:* cigi@cigionline.org (office). *Website:* www.cigionline.org (office).

FREDERIK ANDRÉ HENRIK CHRISTIAN, HRH Crown Prince, MSc; Danish; b. 26 May 1968, Copenhagen; m. HRH Crown Princess Mary Elizabeth (née Donaldson) 2004; one s. one d. *Education:* Krebs' Skole, École des Roches, France, Øregaard Gymnasium, Univ. of Åarhus and Harvard Univ., USA. *Career:* heir to the throne of Denmark; began mil. service with the Royal Life Guard 1986, apptd Lt Reserve Army 1988, Reconnaissance Platoon Commdr Royal Guard Hussars' Regt 1988, First Lt Reserve Army 1989, completed training with the Royal Danish Navy Frogman Corps 1995, First Lt Reserve Navy 1995, Capt., Reserve Army 1997, Lt Commdr, Reserve Navy 1997, Royal Danish Air Force Flying School 2000, Capt., Reserve Air Force 2000, Command and General Staff Course Royal Danish Defence Coll. 2001–02, Maj., Reserve Army and Air Force 2002, Commdr, Reserve Navy 2002, Staff Officer, Defence Command Denmark 2002–03, Sr Lecturer, Inst. of Strategy, Royal Danish Defence Coll. 2003–, Commdr Sr Grade in the Navy, Lt-Col in the Army and Air Force 2004–; served at the Danish UN Mission, New York 1994, First Sec. Embassy in Paris 1998–99; participated in expedition to Mongolia 1986, Expedition Sirius 2000 to Greenland 2000; Pres. The Royal Danish Geographical Soc.; patronages include Danish Red Cross, Deaf Asscn, Royal Acad. of Music, Åarhus, Save the Children Fund, Assn of Fine Arts, Comm. for Scientific Research in Greenland, Dyslexia Org., Foreign Policy Soc., Georg Jensen Prize, Greenlandic Soc.; mem. Int. Sailing Fed. Events Cttee, Young Global Leaders; hon. memberships include Assn of Cavalry Officers, Mongolian Soc., Naval Assn, Ancient Guild of Christian IV, Aalborg, Guards' Assn, Copenhagen, Royal Danish Yacht Club, Sailors' Soc. of 1856; Knight of the Order of the Elephant, Grand Commdr of the Order of Dannebrog, Silver Cross of the Order of Dannebrog, Commemorative Medal 50th Anniversary of HM Queen Ingrid's arrival in Denmark, Badge of Honour, Officers of the Reserve, Commemorative Medal of HM Queen Margrethe II and HRH Prince Consort Henrik's Silver Wedding, Silver Jubilee Medal of HM Queen Margrethe II, Danish Mil. Athletic Assn Medal, King Frederik IX Centenary Medal, Royal Medal of Recompense with Crown, Commemorative Medal of Queen Ingrid, Greenland Home Rule Medal, Grand Cross

of the Order of Honourable Service, Italy, Adolph of Nassau Civilian and Mil. Service Order, Grand Cross, Luxembourg, Orders of Ojaswi Rajanya, Grand Cross, Nepal, Seraphim, Sweden, Saint Olav Grand Cross, Norway, White Roses Grand Cross, Finland, Terra Mariana Grand Cross, Estonia, Three Stars Grand Cross, Latvia, Leopold Grand Cross, Belgium, Icelandic Falcon Grand Cross, Iceland, Jordanian Renaissance Grand Cross, Jordan, Chrysanthemum, Japan, Southern Cross, Brazil, Rio Branco Grand Cross, Brazil, Chula Chom Klao Grand Cross, Thailand, Stara Planina First Class, Bulgaria, Order of Service for the FRG, Grand Cross, Order of the Star of Romania, Grand Cross.
Address: Court of TRH The Crown Prince and Crown Princess of Denmark, Christian VIII Palace, Amalienborg Slotsplads 7, 1257 Copenhagen K; POB 2143, 1015 Copenhagen K, Denmark. *Telephone:* 33-40-10-10. *Fax:* 33-40-11-15. *Website:* www.crownprincecouple.dk.

FREEDMAN, Sir Lawrence David, Kt, KCMG, CBE, DPhil, FRSA, FRHistS, FBA, FKC; British academic; *Professor of War Studies and Vice-Principal (Research), King's College London;* b. 7 Dec. 1948, Tynemouth; m. Judith Hill 1974; one s. one d. *Education:* Whitley Bay Grammar School and Univs of Manchester, Oxford and York. *Career:* Research Assoc., IISS 1975–76; Research Fellow, Royal Inst. of Int. Affairs 1976–78, Head of Policy Studies 1978–82; Fellow, Head Dept of War Studies, King's Coll. London 1978–, Prof. 1982–, Head School of Social Science and Public Policy 2001–, Vice-Principal (Research); mem. Council, IISS 1984–92, 1993–, School of Slavonic and E European Studies 1993–97; Chair. Cttee on Int. Peace and Security, Social Science Research Council (USA) 1993–98; occasional newspaper columnist; Trustee Imperial War Museum 2001–; Hon. Dir Centre for Defence Studies 1990–; Silver Medallist, Arthur Ross Prize, Council on Foreign Relations (USA) 2002, RUSI Chesney Gold Medal 2006. *Publications:* US Intelligence and Soviet Strategic Threat 1978, Britain and Nuclear Weapons 1980, The Evolution of Nuclear Strategy 1981, 1989, Nuclear War and Nuclear Peace (co-author) 1983, The Troubled Alliance (ed.) 1983, The Atlas of Global Strategy 1985, The Price of Peace 1986, Britain and the Falklands War 1988, US Nuclear Strategy (co-ed.) 1989, Signals of War (with V. Gamba) 1989, Europe Transformed (ed.) 1990, Military Power in Europe (essays, ed.) 1990, Britain in the World (co-ed.) 1991, Population Change and European Security (co-ed.) 1991, War, Strategy and International Politics (essays, co-ed.) 1992, The Gulf Conflict 1990–91, Diplomacy and War in the New World Order (with E. Karsh) 1993, War: A Reader 1994, Military Intervention in Europe (ed.) 1994, Strategic Coercion (ed.) 1998, The Revolution in Strategic Affairs 1998, The Politics of British Defence Policy 1979–1998 1999, Kennedy's Wars 2000, The Cold War 2001, Superterrorism (ed.) 2002, Deterrence 2004, The Official History of the Falklands Campaign 2005; articles etc.
Address: King's College London, Office of the Principal, James Clerk Maxwell Building, 57 Waterloo Road, London, SE1 8WA, England (office). *Telephone:* (20) 7848-3984 (office); (20) 7848-3985 (office). *Fax:* (20) 7848-3668 (office). *E-mail:* lawrence.freedman@kcl.ac.uk (office); LFREED0712@aol.com (home).

FREEMAN, Charles (Chas) Wellman, Jr, BA, JD; American diplomatist; *President, Middle East Policy Council;* b. 2 March 1943, Washington, DC; m. 1st Patricia Trenery 1962 (divorced 1993); three s. (one deceased) one d.; m. 2nd Margaret Van Wagenen Carpenter 1993. *Education:* Milton Acad., Milton, Mass., Nat. Autonomous Univ. of Mexico, México, Yale Univ., Harvard Law School, Harvard Univ., Foreign Service Inst. School of Chinese Language and Area Studies. *Career:* entered US Foreign Service 1965, Vice-Consul, Madras, India 1966–68, Taiwan 1969–71, State Dept, China Desk 1971–74, Visiting Fellow, E Asian Legal Research, Harvard Univ. 1974–75, Deputy Dir, Taiwan Affairs, Dept of State 1975–76, Dir Public Programs, Dept of State 1976–77, Plans and Man. 1977–78, Dir US Information Agency programs 1978–79, Acting US Co-ordinator for Refugee Programs 1979, Dir, Chinese Affairs, Dept of State 1979–81, Minister, US Embassy, Beijing 1981–84, US Embassy, Bangkok 1984–86, Prin. Deputy Asst Sec. of State for African Affairs 1986–89, Amb. to Saudi Arabia 1989–92; Asst Sec. of Defense (Int. Security Affairs) 1993–94; Chair. Bd Projects Int. Inc. 1995–; Vice-Chair. Atlantic Council of USA 1996; Co-Chair. US-China Policy Foundation 1996; Pres. Middle East Policy Council 1997–; Distinguished Fellow, Inst. for Nat. Strategic Studies, Nat. Defense Univ. 1992–93; US Inst. of Peace, Wash. 1994–95; mem. American Acad. of Diplomacy 1995, mem. Bd 2001; mem. Bd Wash. World Affairs Council 1998–, Pacific Pension Inst. 2001–, Assn for Diplomatic Studies and Training 2001–, Inst. for Defense Analyses, Washington World Affairs Council; Overseer Roger Williams Univ.; Order of King Abd Al-Aziz (First Class) 1992; Forrest Prize, Yale Univ., Superior Honor Awards 1978, 1982, Presidential Meritorious Service Awards 1984, 1987, 1989, Group Distinguished Honor Award 1988, Sec. of Defense Award for Meritorious Civilian Service 1991, Distinguished Honor Award 1991, Sec. of Defense Awards for Distinguished Public Service 1994.

Publications: Cooking Western in China 1987, The Diplomat's Dictionary 1994, Arts of Power: Statecraft and Diplomacy 1997.
Address: Projects International Inc., 1800 K Street, NW, Suite 1018, Washington, DC 20006 (office); Middle East Policy Council, 17390 M Street, NW, Washington, DC 20036; 2500 Massachusetts Avenue, NW, Washington, DC 20008, USA (home). *Telephone:* (202) 333-1277 (office); (202) 296-6767 (Middle East Policy Council). *Fax:* (202) 333-3128 (office); (202) 296-5791 (Middle East Policy Council). *E-mail:* info@mepc.org. *Website:* www.mepc.org/about/freeman.asp.

FREI RUIZ-TAGLE, Eduardo; Chilean fmr head of state; b. 24 June 1942, Santiago; m. María Larraechea. *Education:* Univ. of Chile. *Career:* joined Christian Democrat (CD) Party 1958, fmr Pres.; CD presidential cand., Dec. 1993, Pres. of Chile 1994–2000; C-in-C of Armed Forces 1998–2000; elected to Senate 1989; Pres. Fundación Eduardo Frei Montalva 1982–93. *Address:* c/o Partido Demócrata Cristiano, Almeda B. O'Higgins 1460, 2°, Santiago, Chile.

FREIVALDS, Laila, LLB; Swedish lawyer and politician; b. 22 June 1942, Riga, Latvia; m. Johan Hedström; one d. *Education:* Uppsala Univ. *Career:* service in Dist court 1970–72, Svea Court of Appeal 1973–74; Reporting Clerk, Court of Appeal 1974; Counsel, Västerås rent tribunal 1974–75; served in Riksdag Information Office 1975–76; Sr Admin. Officer, Head. of Div. Nat. Bd for Consumer Policies 1976–79, Dir-Gen. and Consumer Ombudsman 1983–88; Minister for Justice 1988–91, 1994–2001; Minister of Foreign Affairs 2003–06 (resgnd); legal consultant, Baltic states 1991–94. *Address:* c/o Ministry of Foreign Affairs, Gustav Adolfs torg 1, 103 39 Stockholm, Sweden.

FRETWELL, Sir John Emsley, Kt, GCMG, MA; British diplomatist (retd); b. 15 June 1930, Chesterfield; m. Mary Ellen Eugenie Dubois 1959; one s. one d. *Education:* Chesterfield Grammar School, Lausanne Univ., King's Coll., Cambridge. *Career:* HM Forces 1948–50; entered diplomatic service 1953, Third Sec., Hong Kong 1954–55, Second Sec., Embassy in Beijing 1955–57, Foreign Office 1957–59, 1962–67, First Sec., Moscow 1959–62, First Sec. (Commercial), Washington, DC 1967–70, Commercial Counsellor, Warsaw 1971–73, Head of European Integration Dept (Internal), FCO 1973–76, Asst Under-Sec. of State 1976–79, Minister, Washington, DC 1980–81; Amb. to France 1982–87; Political Dir and Deputy to Perm. Under-Sec. of State, FCO 1987–90; mem. Council of Lloyd's 1991–92; Specialist Adviser, House of Lords 1992–93; Chair. Franco-British Soc. 1995–2005, mem. Council 2005–; currently freelance adviser in int. affairs; Commdr Legion d'honneur, Grand Officier, Ordre nat. du Mérite. *Address:* c/o Brooks's, St James's Street, London, SW1A 1LN, England.

FREY, Bruno S., FRSE; Swiss economist and academic; *Professor of Economics, University of Zürich;* b. 4 May 1941, Basel. *Education:* Univs of Basel and Cambridge. *Career:* Assoc. Prof., Univ. of Basel 1969–; Prof. of Econs, Univ. of Konstanz 1970–77, Univ. of Zürich 1977–; Visiting Fellow, All Souls Coll., Oxford 1983; Fellow, Coll. of Science, Berlin 1984–85; Visiting Research Prof., Univ. of Chicago, Ill. 1990; Visiting Prof., Univ. of Rome 1996–97, Antwerp Univ. 1999, Univs of Gothenburg, Stockholm, Linz, Klagenfurt, Siena, Kiel, Valencia, Groningen, Research School of Social Sciences, ANU, Queensland Univ. of Tech., ETH-Zurich 2007–; Research Dir Centre for Research in Econs, Man. and the Arts, Zürich 2000–; Fellow, Collegium Budapest 2002, European Econ. Asscn 2004, Public Choice Soc.; First Jelle Zijlstra Professorial Fellow, Inst. of Advanced Study, Wassenaar 2003; Distinguished Fellow, CESifo Research Network 2005; Man. Ed. Kyklos 1969–; Hon. DUniv (St Gallen) 1998, (Gothenburg) 1998; Vernon Prize, Asscn for Public Policy and Man., Stolper Prize of Verein für Socialpolitik. *Publications include:* Economics as a Science of Human Behaviour 1992, Not Just for the Money: An Economic Theory of Personal Motivation 1997, The New Democratic Federalism for Europe 1999, Arts and Economics: Analysis and Cultural Policy 2000, Managing Motivation: Wie Sie die neue Motivationsforschung für Ihr Unternehmen nutzen können (co-author) 2000, Inspiring Economics: Human Motivation in Political Economy 2001, Successful Management by Motivation – Balancing Intrinsic and Extrinsic Incentives 2002, Happiness and Economics: How the Economy and Institutions Affect Human Well-Being 2002, Dealing with Terrorism: Stick or Carrot? 2004, Economics and Psychology 2007, Happiness: A Revolution in Economics 2008. *Address:* Institut für Empirische Wirtschaftsforschung, University of Zürich, Winterthurerstrasse 30, 8006 Zürich (office); Niederdorfstr. 29, 8001 Zürich, Switzerland (home). *Telephone:* (1) 6343731 (office). *Fax:* (1) 6343599 (office). *E-mail:* bsfrey@iew.uzh.ch (office). *Website:* chairs/frey/team/frey.html (office); www.bsfrey.ch (home).

FRIDAY, Angus, MBA, DMedSc; Grenadian physician, business executive and diplomatist; *Permanent Representative, United Nations;* b. 6 Feb. 1965. *Education:* St George's Univ. School of Medicine, Strathclyde Grad.

Business School, Scotland. *Career:* Jr Medical Doctor, Grenada Gen. Hospital 1991–92; Healthcare Relations Physician, Merck & Co., UK 1993–95; Co-founder and Man. Dir Health Systems Integrated Ltd (medical tech. co.) 1995–97; Founder and CEO IntegriSys Ltd (medical informatics co.) 1997–2001; Man. Dir Glenelg Spring Water Inc. 1997–2007; Founder and CEO Atlantean Inc. (econ. devt consultancy) 2001–07; Perm. Rep. to UN, New York 2007–. *Address:* Permanent Mission of Grenada to the United Nations, 800 Second Avenue, Suite 400k, New York, NY 10017, USA (office). *Telephone:* (212) 599-0301 (office). *Fax:* (212) 599-1540 (office). *E-mail:* grenada@un.int (office).

FRIED, Daniel; American diplomatist; *Assistant Secretary of State for European and Eurasian Affairs;* b. Washington, DC; m.; two d. *Career:* joined Foreign Service 1977, served in Econ. Bureau 1977–79, US Consulate Gen., Leningrad 1980–81; Political Officer, Embassy in Yugoslavia 1982–85; Office of Soviet Affairs 1985–87, Poland Desk Officer 1987–89; Political Counsellor, Embassy in Poland 1990–93; Dir Nat. Security Council 1993, Special Asst to Pres. and Sr Dir for Cen. and Eastern Europe –1997; Amb. to Poland 1997–2000; Prin. Deputy Special Advisor to Sec. of State for New Ind. States 2000–01; Special Asst to Pres. and Sr Dir for European and Eurasian Affairs, Nat. Security Council 2001–05; Asst Sec. of State for European and Eurasian Affairs 2005–, Under-Sec. of State for Political Affairs (acting) 2008. *Address:* Bureau of European and Eurasian Affairs, Office 6226, Department of State, 2201 C Street, NW, Washington DC, 20520, USA (office). *Telephone:* (202) 647-9626 (office). *Website:* www.state.gov (office).

FRIEDBERG, Aaron L., PhD; American academic; *Professor of Politics and International Affairs, Woodrow Wilson School, Princeton University;* b. Pittsburgh. *Education:* Harvard Univ. *Career:* currently Prof. of Politics and Int. Affairs, Woodrow Wilson School, Princeton Univ.; Henry A. Kissinger Chair in Foreign Policy and Int. Relations, John W. Kluge Center, Library of Congress 2001–02; fmr Fellow Woodrow Wilson Int. Center for Scholars, Smithsonian Inst., Norwegian Nobel Inst. 1998, Harvard Univ. Center for Int. Affairs; consultant to several agencies in US Govt; Deputy Asst for Nat. Security Affairs, Office of the Vice-Pres. 2003–05; Helen Dwight Reid Award 1986, Edgar S. Furniss National Security Book Award 1988. *Publications include:* The Weary Titan: Britain and the Experience of Relative Decline 1895–1905 (Edgar Furniss Nat. Security Book Award), In the Shadow of the Garrison State: America's Anti-Statism and Its Cold War Grand Strategy 2000, Strategic Asia 2001–02: Power and Purpose (co-editor) 2001. *Address:* Woodrow Wilson School, Bendheim 013, Princeton University, Princeton, NJ 08544-1013, USA (office). *Telephone:* (609) 258-9891 (office). *E-mail:* alf@princeton.edu (office). *Website:* www.princeton.edu (office).

FRIEDEN, Luc; Luxembourg politician; *Minister of Justice and of the Treasury and Budget;* b. 16 Sept. 1963, Esch-sur-Alzette; m.; two c. *Education:* Lycée de garçons, Esch-sur-Alzette, Athénée de Luxembourg, Centre universitaire de Luxembourg, Université de Paris I (Panthéon Sorbonne), France, Univ. of Cambridge, UK, Harvard Law School, USA. *Career:* commentator RTL, Luxembourg Radio 1981–94; attorney-at-law 1989–98; fmr teacher Centre Universitaire de Luxembourg; mem. Parl. 1994–, Chair. Finance and Budget Cttee, Cttee on Constitutional Affairs 1994–98; Minister of Justice, of the Budget and for Relations with Parl. 1998–99; Minister of Justice and of the Treasury and Budget 1999–, also Minister of Defence 2004–05; Gov. World Bank 1998–, Asian Devt Bank 2003–04; mem. moral sciences and politics section, Institut Grand-Ducal. *Address:* Ministry of Justice, 13 rue Erasme, centre administratif Pierre Werner, 1468 Luxembourg (office). *Telephone:* 478-27-01 (office). *Fax:* 22-19-80 (office). *Website:* www.gouvernement.lu (office).

FRIEDMAN, Thomas L., MPhil; American journalist; *Foreign Affairs Columnist, New York Times;* b. 20 July 1953, Minneapolis; m. Ann Friedman; two d. *Education:* Brandeis Univ., St Antony's Coll. Oxford, UK. *Career:* joined The New York Times 1981, Beirut Bureau Chief 1982–84, Israel Bureau Chief 1984–88, Washington Chief Diplomatic Corresp., Chief White House Corresp., Chief Econs Corresp., Foreign Affairs Columnist 1995–; Pulitzer Prize for Int. Reporting 1983, 1988, for Distinguished Commentary 2002. *Television:* documentaries: The Roots of 9/11 (New York Times TV), Straddling the Fence (Discovery Channel). *Publications include:* From Beirut to Jerusalem (Nat. Book Award for Non-Fiction, Overseas Press Club Award) 1989, The Lexus and the Olive Tree (Overseas Press Club Award for Best Non-Fiction Book on Foreign Policy) 2000, Longitudes and Latitudes: America in the Age of Terrorism 2002, The World is Flat (Financial Times/Goldman Sachs Business Book Award) 2005. *Address:* The New York Times, 1627 Eye Street, NW, Suite 700, Washington, DC 20006, USA (office). *Telephone:* (202) 862-0300 (office). *Fax:* (202) 862-0340 (office). *Website:* www.nytimes.com (office).

FRITSCHE, Claudia; Liechtenstein diplomatist; *Ambassador to USA;* b. 26 July 1952; m. Manfred Fritsche 1980. *Education:* business and language schools in Schaan and St Gall. *Career:* personal sec. to Prime Minister 1970–74, to Deputy Prime Minister March–Aug. 1974; joined Office for Foreign Affairs 1978, Diplomatic Officer 1980–87, Sec. to Liechtenstein Parl. del. to Council of Europe and EFTA, First Sec., Embassy in Berne 1987–90, Vienna 1989–90, mem. Liechtenstein Organizing Cttee for the Council of Europe's North-South Campaign 1988, Rep. in EFTA/EC Working Group on Flanking Policies 1989–90, Perm. Rep. of Liechtenstein to UN 1990–2002, Vice-Pres. and mem. Gen. Cttee of UN Gen. Ass. during its 48th Session, Amb. to USA (non-resident) 2000–02 (resident) 2002–; Pres. Int. Asscn of Perm. Reps to the UN 1999–2002; Certificate and Medal of Recognition Foreign Policy Asscn 2002.
Address: 888 17th Street, NW, Suite 1250, Washington, DC 20006, USA (office). *Telephone:* (202) 331-0590 (office). *Fax:* (202) 331-3221 (office). *E-mail:* tamara.brunhart@was.rep.llv.li (office). *Website:* www.washington.liechtenstein.li (office).

FROGIER, Pierre Edouard Nahéa; New Caledonian politician; b. 16 Nov. 1950, Nouméa; m. Annick Morault; three c. *Education:* Lycée Lapérouse, Nouméa and Faculty of Law, Dijon, France. *Career:* elected mem. Ass. Territoriale 1977–, Congress 1977–; Mayor of Mont-Dore 1987–2001; Sec.-Gen. Rassemblement pour la Calédonie dans la République (RPCR) 1989–; Territorial Sec. Rassemblement pour la République (RPR) 1995–; Deputy for New Caledonia in French Nat. Ass. 1996–; Pres. of New Caledonia 2001–04; Chevalier, Ordre nat. du Mérite.
Address: c/o Présidence du Gouvernement, 19 avenue Maréchal Foch, B.P. M2, 98849 Nouméa Cédex, New Caledonia (office).

FROST, David George Hamilton; British diplomatist; *Ambassador to Denmark;* b. 21 Feb. 1965; m. Jacqueline Elizabeth Dias; one s. one d. *Career:* Desk Officer for Afghanistan, S Asia Dept, FCO 1987–88, Third Sec. (Political), Nicosia 1988–90, Desk Officer for NATO and WEU, Security Policy Dept 1992–93, First Sec. (Econ.), UK Representation to EU 1993–96, First Sec. (Third Cttee), UK Mission to UN, New York 1996–98, Pvt. Sec. to Perm. Under-Sec., FCO 1998–99, Deputy Head of EU (External) Dept 1999–2001, Econ. and EU Counsellor, Paris 2001–03, Head of EU (Internal) Dept, FCO 2003–04, Dir EU (Internal) 2004–06, Amb. to Denmark 2006–; tax consultant, KPMG, London 1990–92.
Address: British Embassy, Kastelsvej 36–40, 2100 Copenhagen Ø, Denmark (office). *Telephone:* 35-44-52-00 (office). *Fax:* 35-44-52-93 (office). *E-mail:* info.copenhagen@fco.gov.uk (office). *Website:* www.britishembassy.dk (office).

FROST, Mervyn Lowne, MA, DPhil; South African academic; *Head, Department of War Studies, King's College London; Education:* Stellenbosch Univ., Oxford Univ., UK. *Career:* Grad. Asst, Dept of Political Philosophy, Univ. of Stellenbosch 1971–75; Lecturer, Dept of Political Science, Univ. of Natal 1975–76, Prof. and Head of Dept of Politics 1986–92, Prof. (Level 7) 1992–95; Lecturer, Dept of Political Science, Univ. of Cape Town 1976–77; Lecturer, Dept of Political Studies, Rhodes Univ. 1977–84, Sr Lecturer 1984–85; Prof. of Int. Relations, Univ. of Kent, England 1996–2003; Prof. of Int. Relations, Centre for Int. Relations, King's College London 2003–07, Head, Dept of War Studies 2007–; Visiting Research Fellow, Univ. of Oxford 1990, LSE 1993–94; Chair. Border Branch, S African Inst. of Int Affairs 1977–85, Vice-Chair. Durban Branch 1989–91; Pres. S African Political Studies Asscn 1991–93; mem. British Int. Studies Asscn 1980–, Philosophical Soc. of S Africa 1975–, Int. Political Science Asscn 1995–, Int. Studies Asscn 1995–; Trustee and Founding mem Inst. for Multi-Party Democracy 1990; Trustee Maurice Webb Memorial Trust 1990–; mem. Editorial Bd Review of International Studies 1999–, South African Journal of International Affairs 1996–, Politics and Ethics Review 2004–. *Publications:* Towards a Nominative Theory of International Relations (Univ. of Natal Book Prize, S African Political Studies Asscn Book Prize) 1986, International Relations: A Debate on Methodology (jt ed.) 1989, Ethics in International Relations: A Constitutive Theory 1996, Constituting Human Rights: Global Civil Society and the Society of Democratic States 2002; numerous chapters in books and journal articles.
Address: Department of War Studies, King's College, Strand, London, WC2R 2LS, England (office). *Telephone:* (20) 7848-1873 (office). *Fax:* (20) 7848-2026 (office). *E-mail:* mervyn.frost@kcl.ac.uk (office). *Website:* www.kcl.ac.uk/schools/sspp/ws/index.html (office).

FRY, Sir Graham Holbrook, Kt, KCMG; British diplomatist; b. 20 Dec. 1949, Shrewsbury, Shropshire; m. Toyoko Fry; two s. *Education:* Brasenose College, Oxford. *Career:* joined FCO 1972, Rhodesia Dept 1972–73, full-time language training, UK 1973–74, Kamakura 1974–75, Second Sec., Information, Tokyo 1975–76, Second Sec., Commercial, Tokyo 1976–79, Invest in Britain Bureau, Dept of Trade and Industry 1979–81, EC Dept

(Internal), FCO 1981–83, First Sec. (Political), Paris 1983–87, Western European Dept, FCO 1987–89, Political Counsellor, Tokyo 1989–93, Head of Far Eastern and Pacific Dept, FCO 1993–95, Dir Northern Asia and Pacific 1995–98, High Commr to Malaysia 1998–2001, Dir-Gen. (Econ.), FCO 2001–04, Amb. to Japan 2004–07.
Address: c/o Foreign and Commonwealth Office, King Charles Street, London SW1A 2AH, England (office). *Website:* www.fco.gov.uk (office).

FU, Ying; Chinese diplomatist; *Ambassador to UK;* b. 1953, Inner Mongolian Autonomous Region; m., one d. *Education:* Foreign Languages Inst., Beijing, Univ. of Kent, UK. *Career:* Attaché, Embassy in Romania 1978–82; Attaché, Dept of Translation and Interpretation, Ministry of Foreign Affairs 1982–85, Deputy Dir 1986–90, Deputy Dir, Dept of Asian Affairs 1990–92, Dir and Counsellor 1993–97, Dir-Gen. 2000–04; staff mem. UN Transitional Authority, Cambodia 1992–93; Minister Counsellor, Embassy in Jakarta 1997–98, Amb. to the Philippines 1998–2000, to Australia 2004–07, to UK 2007–.
Address: Embassy of the People's Republic of China, 49–51 Portland Place, London W1B 4JL, England (office). *Telephone:* (20) 7299-4049 (office). *Fax:* (20) 7636-5578 (office). *E-mail:* press@chinese-embassy.org.uk (office). *Website:* www.chinese-embassy.org.uk (office).

FU, Zhihuan; Chinese politician; *Chairman, Financial and Economic Committee, National People's Congress;* b. March 1938, Haicheng Co., Liaoning Prov. *Education:* Moscow Railways Inst., USSR. *Career:* technician, later Deputy Chief, later Chief, later Deputy Dir Zhuzhou Electric Eng Research Inst., Ministry of Railways 1961; joined CCP 1966; Chief Engineer, Science and Tech. Bureau, Ministry of Railways 1983, Dir 1985; Dir Harbin Railway Bureau 1989; Vice-Minister of Railways 1991–98, Minister 1998–2003; Chair. Financial and Econ. Cttee, NPC 2003–; mem. CCP Cen. Comm. for Discipline Inspection 1992–; mem. 15th CCP Cen. Cttee 1997–2002.
Address: c/o Zhongguo Gongchan Dang (Chinese Communist Party), Beijing, People's Republic of China (office).

FUENTES KNIGHT, Juan Alberto, MA, PhD; Guatemalan economist and politician; *Minister of Public Finance; Education:* McGill Univ. and Univ. of Toronto, Canada, Univ. of Geneva, Switzerland, Univ. of Sussex, UK. *Career:* served for 20 years as economist with UN, becoming Co-ordinator Guatemalan Human Devt Report, UNDP; Exec. Dir and Research Co-ordinator Instituto Centroamericano de Estudios Fiscales (Cen. American Inst. for Fiscal Studies) –2007; Minister of Public Finance 2007–. *Publications:* numerous articles in econ. journals.
Address: Ministry of Public Finance, Centro Cívico, 8a Avda y 21 Calle, Zona 1, Guatemala City, Guatemala (office). *Telephone:* 2248-5005 (office). *Fax:* 2248-5054 (office). *E-mail:* info@minfin.gob.gt (office). *Website:* www.minfin.gob.gt (office).

FUKUDA, Yasuo; Japanese politician; *Prime Minister;* b. 16 July 1936, Tokyo; m. Kiyoko Fukuda; two s. one d. *Education:* Waseda Univ. *Career:* with Maruzen Oil (now Cosmo Oil) petroleum refining and marketing co. 1959–76; Chief Sec. to Prime Minister Takeo Fukuda (father) 1977–78, Pvt. Sec. 1979–89; Dir Kinzai Inst. for Financial Affairs 1978–89; mem. Liberal-Democratic Party (LDP), Pres. 2007–; mem. House of Reps for Gunma 4th Dist 1990–; Parl. Vice-Minister of Foreign Affairs 1995–96; Minister of State, Chief Cabinet Sec., Dir-Gen. Okinawa Devt Agency 2000–01; Chief Cabinet Sec. (Gender Equality) and Minister of State 2001–04 (resgnd); Deputy Sec.-Gen. LDP 1997–98, Chair. Finance Cttee 1998, Dir-Gen. Treasury Bureau 1999–2000, Deputy Chair. Policy Research Council 2000–, Prime Minister 2007–.
Address: Prime Minister's Office, 1-6-1, Nagata-cho, Chiyoda-ku, Tokyo 100-8968 (office); Liberal-Democratic Party—LDP (Jiyu-Minshuto), 1-11-23, Nagata-cho, Chiyoda-ku, Tokyo 100-8910, Japan (office). *Telephone:* (3) 3581-2361 (office); (3) 3581-6211 (LDP) (office). *Fax:* (3) 3581-1910 (office). *E-mail:* koho@ldp.jimin.or.jp (office). *Website:* www.kantei.go.jp (office); www.jimin.jp (office).

FUKUYAMA, Francis, PhD; American writer and academic; *Bernard L. Schwartz Professor of International Political Economy, Paul H. Nitze School of Advanced International Studies, Johns Hopkins University;* b. New York. *Education:* Cornell and Harvard Univs. *Career:* fmrly a sr social scientist, RAND Corpn, Washington, DC and Deputy Dir State Dept's Policy Planning Staff; Hirst Prof. of Public Policy, George Mason Univ., Fairfax, Va; Dean of Faculty, Paul H. Nitze School of Advanced Int. Studies, Johns Hopkins Univ. 2002–04, now Bernard L. Schwartz Prof. of Int. Political Economy; mem. Pres.'s Council on Bioethics; mem. advisory Bd National Endowment for Democracy, The National Interest, Journal of Democracy, The New America Foundation; fmr mem. US delegation Egyptian-Israeli talks on Palestinian autonomy. *Publications:* The End of History and the Last Man 1992, Trust: The Social Virtues And the Creation of Prosperity 1996, The Great Disruption: Human Nature and the Reconstitution of the

Social Order 1999, Our Posthuman Future 2002, State-Building: Governance and World Order in the 21st Century 2004, After the Neocons 2006, America at the Crossroads: Democracy, Power, and the Neoconservative Legacy 2006.
Address: Paul H. Nitze School of Advanced International Studies, The Rome Building, Room 507, 1619 Massachusetts Avenue, NW, Washington, DC 20036, USA (office). *Telephone:* (202) 663-5765 (office). *Fax:* (202) 663-5769 (office). *E-mail:* fukuyama@jhu.edu (office). *Website:* www.francisfukuyama.com (office).

FULCI, Francesco Paolo, LLD, MCL; Italian diplomatist; b. 19 March 1931, Messina; m. Claris Glathar 1965; three c. *Education:* Messina Univ., Columbia Univ., New York, Coll. of Europe, Bruges and Acad. Int. Law, The Hague. *Career:* entered Italian Foreign Service 1956; First Vice-Consul of Italy, New York 1958–61; Second Sec. Italian Embassy, Moscow 1961–63; Foreign Ministry, Rome 1963–68; Counsellor Italian Embassy, Paris 1968–74, Minister Italian Embassy, Tokyo 1974–76; Chief of Cabinet Pres. of Senate, Rome 1976–80; Amb. to Canada 1980–85; Amb. and Perm. Rep. to NATO, Brussels 1985–91; Sec.-Gen. Exec. Comm. of Information and Security Services, Rome 1991–93; Amb. and Perm. Rep. to UN, New York 1993–99; Vice-Pres. Ferrero International, Rome 2000–; First Vice-Pres. ECOSOC 1998–99, Pres. 1999–2000; Ed. La Stampa, Turin 2000; Cross of Merit (FRG); Officier, Légion d'honneur (France); Commdr Imperial Order of the Sun (Japan), Great Cross, Order of Merit (Italy), Kt Order of Malta; Hon. LLD (Windsor Univ., Ont.).
Address: c/o La Stampa, Via Marenco 32, 10126 Turin, Italy (office). *Telephone:* (011) 656811 (office). *Fax:* (011) 655306 (office). *E-mail:* lettere@lastampa.it (office). *Website:* www.lastampa.it (office).

FÜLE, Štefan; Czech diplomatist; *Permanent Representative, NATO;* b. 24 May 1962, Sokolov; m. Hana Füleová; two d. one s. *Education:* Charles Univ., Prague, Moscow State Inst. of Int. Relations, Russian Fed. *Career:* Desk Officer, UN Dept, Fed. Ministry of Foreign Affairs, Czechoslovakia 1987–90; First Sec., Mission of Czech Repub. to UN, New York 1990–95, Alt. Rep. to Security Council 1994–95; Dir UN Dept, Ministry of Foreign Affairs, Czech Repub. 1995–96, Security Policy Dept 1996–98; Amb. to Lithuania 1998–2001; First Deputy Minister, Ministry of Defence 2001–02; Amb. to UK 2003–05; Perm. Rep. to NATO 2005–; UN Disarmament Fellow 1988; Cross of Merit of Minister of Defence, Grade I 2001, Order of Grand Duke Gediminas, 3rd Class (Lithuania) 2002.
Address: Delegation of the Czech Republic, NATO Headquarters, Blvd Léopold III, Brussels 1110, Belgium (office). *Telephone:* (2) 707-17-85 (office). *Fax:* (2) 707-17-03 (office). *E-mail:* nato.brussels@embassy.mzv.cz (office). *Website:* www.nato.int/cv/permrep/cz/cz-e.htm (office).

FULFORD, Sir Adrian; British judge; *Judge, International Criminal Court;* b. 8 Jan. 1948. *Career:* called to the Bar, Middle Temple, London 1978; apptd QC 1994; Recorder (Judge in Crown Court) 1996–; Judge, Int. Criminal Court (ICC) 2003–; Lecturer in Advocacy, Middle Temple 1994–; Lecturer to the Bar and Judiciary 1999–2001; mem. Cttee of Criminal Bar Asscn 1997–99, 2001–; Chair. Disciplinary Procedures for Bar Council 1997–; Housing Adviser, Shelter Housing Aid Centre 1975–77; Legal Adviser N Lambeth Law Centre 1979–80; fmr Contrib. Ed. Archbold Criminal Pleading, Practice and Evidence, Atkins Court Forms. *Publications:* A Criminal Practitioners Guide to Judicial Review and Case Stated (co-author) 1999, United Kingdom Human Rights Reports (jt ed.) 2000–, Judicial Review: A Practical Guide (co-author) 2004; articles in professional journals and papers for Criminal Bar Asscn.
Address: International Criminal Court, Maanweg 174, 2516 AB The Hague, The Netherlands. *Telephone:* (70) 5158515. *Fax:* (70) 5158555. *E-mail:* pio@icc-cpi.int. *Website:* www.icc-cpi.int.

FULLERTON, William Hugh, CMG, MA; British diplomatist and consultant; b. 11 Feb. 1939, Wolverhampton; m. Arlene Jacobowitz 1968; one d. *Education:* Cheltenham Coll. and Queens' Coll., Cambridge. *Career:* Shell Int. Petroleum Co., Uganda 1963–65; Foreign Office 1965; MECAS, Shemlan, Lebanon 1965–66; Information Officer, Jeddah 1966–67; UK Perm. Mission to UN, New York 1967; FCO 1968–70; Head of Chancery, High Comm., Jamaica (also accred to Haiti) 1970–73, Head of Chancery, Embassy, Ankara 1973–77; FCO 1977–80; Counsellor, Islamabad 1980–83; Consul Gen. 1981–83; Amb. to Somalia 1983–87; on loan to Ministry of Defence 1987–88; Gov. Falkland Islands, Commr for South Georgia and South Sandwich Islands 1988–92, concurrently High Commr, British Antarctic Territory 1988–89; Amb. to Kuwait 1992–96, to Morocco and Mauritania 1996–99; Trustee, Arab-British Centre, London 2002–, Soc. for the Protection of Animals Abroad, Lord Caradon Lecture Trust; mem. Nat. Trust, Campaign for the Protection of Rural England; Kuwait Medallion (First Class) 1995, Alaouite Decoration (Morocco) 1999.
Address: c/o Travellers' Club, 106 Pall Mall, London, SW1Y 5EP, England. *Telephone:* (20) 7832-1310 (office).

FULTON, Lt-Gen. Sir Robert, KBE; British Royal Marines officer and diplomatist; *Governor and Commander-in-Chief of Gibraltar;* b. 1948; m.; two s. *Education:* Eton Coll. and Univ. of East Anglia. *Career:* joined Royal Marines 1972, has occupied several sr positions within the force, including Commdt-Gen. 1998–2001; moved to Ministry of Defence 2001, promoted to Lt-Gen. on appointment as Deputy Chief of Defence Staff (for Equipment Capability) 2003–06; Gov. and C-in-C of Gibraltar 2006–.
Address: Office of the Governor, The Convent, Main Street, Gibraltar (office). *Telephone:* 45440 (office). *E-mail:* robert.fulton@fco.gov.uk (office).

FURET, Marie Françoise Thérèse, DenD; French academic; *Professor Emerita of International Law, University of Montpellier;* b. 9 March 1928; m. Robert Furet 1954; three d. one s. *Education:* Inst. Ste-Odile, Univ. of Montpellier, Inst. d'Etudes Politiques, Paris and Univ. of Paris. *Career:* Barrister Court of Appeal, Montpellier 1952–57; Asst Faculty of Law, Univ. of Paris 1966–69; Prof. Faculty of Law, Univ. of Poitiers 1969–70; Prof. Faculty of Law, Univ. of Montpellier I 1970–98, Prof. Emer. 1998–; Chevalier, Légion d'Honneur 1998, Officier Ordre nat. du Mérite 1980. *Publications include:* Le désarmement nucléaire 1973, La guerre et le droit 1979, Le droit international et les armes (jtly) 1983, Commentaire de la Charte des Nations Unies (jtly) 1991, Paul et Alfred Coste-Floret: deux jumeaux et trois républiques 2001, ONU: la Charte (jtly) 2004, L'avenement d'une justice pénale internationale 2007; numerous publs in professional journals.
Address: 16 rue du Cardinal de Cabrières, 34000 Montpellier, France (office). *Telephone:* (4) 67-60-65-21 (office).

FURLAN, Luiz Fernando, BEng; Brazilian business executive and government official; b. 1945; m. Ana Maria Gonçalves Furlan 1973; one s. one d. *Education:* São Paulo Univ., INSEAD, France, Georgetown Univ., USA. *Career:* joined Sadia SA 1976, mem. Bd 1978–2002, Exec. Vice-Pres. and Dir, Investor Relations 1978–83, Chair. 1993–2002; Minister of Devt, Industry and Trade 2002–07; Second Vice-Pres. and Dir of Foreign Trade, Industries Fed. of São Paulo State (FIESP/CIESP); Vice-Pres. Brazilian Foreign Trade Asscn; Pres. Entrepreneurial Leaders Forum 2000–02; Pres., Brazilian Asscn of Open Cos (ABRASCA) 1991–94, Brazilian Asscn of Producers and Exporters of Chicken (ABEF) 1997–2001; fmr Pres. Mercosul European Business Forum (MEBF); fmr mem. Bd Pan American Beverages Inc. (PANAMCO) (USA), Telefónica SA (Spain); mem. Advisory Bd Brasmotor SA, ABN-Amro Bank Brazil; mem. Global Corporate Governance Forum; mem. Nat. Council of Human Rights, Int. Council INSEAD, France; fmr mem. Brazil–USA Business Devt Council.
Address: c/o Ministry of Development, Industry and Trade, Esplanada dos Ministérios, Bloco J, 7 andar, Sala 700, 70053–900 Brasília, DF, Brazil (office).

FUTRAKUL, Virasakdi, BA, MA; Thai diplomatist; b. 23 Dec. 1951; m. Aumaporn Futrakul. *Education:* Univ. of Washington, Univ. of Virginia, Nat. Defence Coll., Thailand. *Career:* joined Ministry of Foreign Affairs in 1974, First Sec., Perm. Mission to UN, New York 1984–86, Counselor, Office of Sec. to Minister of Foreign Affairs 1986–87, Dir Americas Div., Dept of Political Affairs 1987–89, Deputy Dir-Gen. Dept of Political Affairs 1989–90, Asst Perm. Sec., Office of Perm. Sec. 1990–91, Amb. to Myanmar 1991–94, to Canada 1994–97, Dir-Gen. Dept of E Asian Affairs, Ministry of Foreign Affairs 1997–2000, Perm. Rep. to UN Office and Int. Orgs, Geneva 2000–02, Deputy Perm. Sec. 2002–04, Amb. to France, Perm. Rep. to UNESCO and mem. Governing Bd Devt Centre, OECD 2004–06, Amb. to USA 2006–07, Perm. Sec. for Foreign Affairs, Ministry of Foreign Affairs 2007–.
Address: Ministry of Foreign Affairs, Thanon Sri Ayudhya, Bangkok 10400, Thailand (office). *Telephone:* (2) 643-5000 (office). *Fax:* (2) 225-6155 (office). *E-mail:* information@mfa.go.th (office). *Website:* www.mfa.go.th (office).

FYODOROV, Nikolai Vasilievich, DrSci; Russian/Chuvash politician and lawyer; *President of Chuvash Republic;* b. 9 May 1958, Chuvash Repub.; m.; one s. one d. *Education:* Kazan State Univ., Inst. of State and Law, USSR Acad. of Sciences. *Career:* worked in legal bodies since 1983; teacher Chuvash State Univ. 1980–82, 1985–89; USSR People's Deputy 1989–91; Deputy Chair. Legis. Comm. Supreme Soviet 1989–90; Minister of Justice of RSFSR (later Russia) 1990–93; Pres. Chuvash Repub. 1994–; mem. Council of Fed. 1996–2002; Order for Merits to Fatherland 1998, 2003; State Prize of Russia 1999. *Publications:* more than 100 articles and several books on problems of democratic and federative structure of the state, freedom of mass media, independent judicial power and economic policy.
Address: Office of the President, Republic Square 1, 428004 Cheboxary, Chuvash Republic, Russia (office). *Telephone:* (8352) 62-46-87 (Cheboxary) (office). *Fax:* (8352) 62-17-99 (office). *E-mail:* president@chuvashia.com (office). *Website:* www.cap.ru (office).

G

GAA, Willy Calaud, AB, LLM; Philippine lawyer and diplomatist; *Ambassador to USA;* m. Erlinda Conception; two s. *Education:* Manuel L. Quezon Univ., Univ. of the Philippines, New York Univ., USA. *Career:* called to the Bar, Philippines 1970, State Bar of Calif. 1990; trial attorney, Office of the Solicitor-Gen. 1971–74; tax and compliance attorney, Petrophil Corpn 1974–75; joined Philippine Foreign Service 1975, Prin. Asst, Office of Admin, Dept of Foreign Affairs, Manila 1975, Vice-Consul, then Consul in San Francisco 1975–80, Consul in New York 1981–85, Sec. Bd of Foreign Service Admin and Bd of Foreign Service Examiners 1985, Acting Chief Coordinator, Office of Acting Minister of Foreign Affairs 1985–86, Dir Office of Middle East and African Affairs 1986, Exec. Dir Office of Consular Services 1986–87, Deputy Consul-Gen. in Los Angeles 1987–90, Amb. to Libya (also accred to Tunisia, Malta and Niger) 1992–97, Consul-Gen. in New York 1997–99, Asst Sec., Office of Asian and Pacific Affairs 1999–2002, Amb. to Australia (also accred to Nauru, Tuvalu and Vanuatu) 1997–2002, to People's Repub. of China 2002–06, Consul-Gen., Los Angeles 2006, Amb to USA Nov. 2006–; Gawad Sentenaryo (Centennial Award), Nat. Centennial Comm. 1999, Distinguished Service Award, Dept of Foreign Affairs 2000.
Address: Embassy of the Philippines, 1600 Massachusetts Avenue, NW, Washington, DC 20036-2274, USA (office). *Telephone:* (202) 467-9300 (office). *Fax:* (202) 467-9417 (office). *E-mail:* info@philippineembassy-usa.org (office). *Website:* www.philippineembassy-usa.org (office).

GABRIEL, Edward M., BS; American diplomatist and business executive; *Visiting Fellow, Middle East Program, Center for Strategic and International Studies; Education:* Gannon Univ., Pa. *Career:* fmr owner and Pres. Gabriel Group; fmr Sr Vice-Pres. in charge of Corp. Public Affairs, CONCORD Corpn; fmr Pres. and CEO Madison Public Affairs Group; Amb. to Morocco 1997–2001; Advisor on Middle East policy for General Wesley Clark's presidential campaign 2004; currently Visiting Fellow, Middle East Program, Center for Strategic and Int. Studies (CSIS); Sr Counsellor, Middle Eastern and Russian Issues, Center for Democracy; Founding mem. Exec. Cttee and Bd of Dirs, American Task Force on Lebanon; Dir Keystone Center.
Address: Middle East Program, Center for Strategic and International Studies (CSIS), 1800 K Street, NW, Washington, DC 20006, USA (office). *Telephone:* (202) 775-3213 (office). *Fax:* (202) 775-3199 (office). *Website:* www.csis.org/mideast (office).

GABRIEL, Sigmar; German politician; *Minister of the Environment, Nature Conservation and Nuclear Safety;* b. 12 Sept. 1959, Goslar; m.; one d. *Education:* Göttingen Univ. *Career:* joined SPD 1977; adult educ. lecturer 1983–88; teacher, Saxony Adult Educ. Inst. 1989–90; Dist Councillor for Goslar 1987–98, City Councillor 1991–, Chair. Environmental Cttee 1991–96, Econ. Affairs and Tourism Cttee 1996; mem. Lower Saxony Parl. 1990–, Leader SPD Group; SPD Speaker for Home Affairs 1994–97; Deputy Chair. SPD 1997–98, Chair. 1998–99; Prime Minister of Lower Saxony 1999–2003; Fed. Minister of the Environment, Nature Conservation and Nuclear Safety 2005–.
Address: Ministry of the Environment, Nature Conservation and Nuclear Safety, Alexanderstr. 3, 10178 Berlin, Germany (office). *Telephone:* (30) 18305-0 (office). *Fax:* (30) 183052046 (office). *Website:* www.bmu.de (office); www.sigmargabriel.de (office).

GABRIELYAN, Vahe, PhD; Armenian diplomatist and professor of linguistics; *Ambassador to UK;* b. 16 May 1965, Yerevan; m. Hasmik Hovhannisyan 1989; two s. *Education:* Yerevan State Univ., Diplomatic Acad., Vienna, Austria, Davidson Coll., USA. *Career:* fmr Prof. of Linguistics; interpreter for Pres. Ter-Petrossian 1993–94, 1997–98, for Pres. Kocharyan 1998–2003; Press Sec. for Pres. Kocharyan 1999–2003; Amb. to UK 2003– (also accred to Ireland 2005–). *Publications:* numerous articles on grammatical aspects of the Armenian and English languages, art, educ. and politics.
Address: Embassy of Armenia, 25A Cheniston Gardens, London, W8 6TG, England (office). *Telephone:* (20) 7938-5435 (office). *Fax:* (20) 7938-2595 (office). *E-mail:* armemb@armenianembassyuk.com (office). *Website:* www.armenianembassyuk.com (office).

GACHECHILADZE, Revaz; Georgian academic and diplomatist; *Ambassador to Armenia; Career:* Prof. and Head of Dept of Human Geography, Tbilisi State Univ.; Visiting Prof., Mount Holyoke Coll., USA 1996–97; apptd Amb. to Israel 1998, currently Amb. to Armenia. *Publication:* The New Georgia: Space, Society, Politics 1995.
Address: Embassy of Georgia, Arami Street 42, Yerevan, Armenia (office). *Telephone:* (10) 56-43-57 (office). *Fax:* (10) 56-41-83 (office). *E-mail:* georgia@arminco.com (office).

GADDAFI, Col Mu'ammar Muhammad al-; Libyan head of state and army officer; *Revolutionary Leader/Chairman of the Revolutionary Command Council;* b. 1942, Serte; m. 1970; four s. one d. *Education:* Univ. of Libya, Benghazi. *Career:* served with Libyan Army 1965–; Chair. Revolutionary Command Council 1969– (Head of State); C-in-C of Armed Forces Sept. 1969; Prime Minister 1970–72; Minister of Defence 1970–72; Sec.-Gen. of Gen. Secr. of Gen. People's Congress 1977–79; Chair. OAU 1982–83; mem. Presidential Council, Fed. of Arab Republics 1972; rank of Maj.-Gen. Jan. 1976, retaining title of Col. *Publications:* The Green Book (3 vols), Military Strategy and Mobilization, The Story of the Revolution.
Address: Office of the President, Tripoli, Libya (office).

GADDAFI, Seif al-Islam, BSc; Libyan charity organization official; *President, Gaddafi Development Foundation;* b. 25 June 1972, Tripoli. *Education:* Al-Fateh Univ., Tripoli, IMADEC Univ., Vienna, Austria, London School of Econs, UK. *Career:* involved in assisting Muslims in Mindanao, southern Philippines 1999, later helped negotiate release of western hostages held by Islamic rebels there; mediated with US and British intelligence in negotiations that led to Libya's abandonment of its weapons programmes 2004; co-owner Nat. Eng Service and Supplies Co.; Pres. Gaddafi Devt Foundation which paid $2.7 billion compensation to families of the 270 victims of Lockerbie bombing; Pres. Libyan Nat. Asscn for Drugs and Narcotics Control.
Address: Gaddafi Development Foundation, El Fatah Tower, 5th Floor, No. 57, PO Box 1101, Tripoli, Libya (office). *Telephone:* (21) 3351370 (office). *Fax:* (21) 3351373 (office). *E-mail:* info@gaddaficharity.org (office). *Website:* www.gdf.org.ly (office).

GADDIS, John Lewis, PhD; American historian and academic; *Robert A. Lovett Professor of History, Yale University;* b. 1942; m. (divorced); two s.; m. 2nd Toni Dorfman 1997. *Education:* Univ. of Texas, Austin. *Career:* Lecturer and later Prof., Dept of History, Ohio Univ. 1969–94, f. Contemporary History Inst., Ohio 1987; Sr Fellow, Hoover Inst. 2000–02; Robert A. Lovett Professor of History, Yale Univ. 1997–; fmr Lecturer, US Naval War Coll., Univ. of Helsinki, Finland, Princeton Univ., Univ. of Oxford, UK; George Eastman Visiting Prof., Balliol Coll., Oxford 2000–01; mem. Editorial Bd Foreign Affairs; mem. Advisory Bd Cold War Int. History Project; Fellow, American Acad. of Arts and Sciences 1995. *Publications:* The United States and the Origins of the Cold War 1941–47 1972, Russia, The Soviet Union and the United States: An Interpretive History 1978, Strategies of Containment: A Critical Appraisal of Postwar American National Security Policy 1982, The Long Peace: Inquiries into the History of the Cold War 1987, The United States and the End of the Cold War: Reconsiderations, Implications, Provocations 1992, We Now Know: Rethinking Cold War History 1997, The Landscape of History: How Historians Map the Past 2002, Surprise, Security, and the American Experience 2004, The Cold War 2006.
Address: Department of History, Yale University, PO Box 208324, New Haven, CT 06520-8353, USA (office). *Telephone:* (203) 432-1374 (office). *Fax:* (203) 432-6520 (office). *E-mail:* john.gaddis@yale.edu (office). *Website:* www.yale.edu/history/faculty/gaddis.html (office).

GADE JENSEN, Søren, MSc, CandEcon; Danish politician; *Minister of Defence;* b. 27 Jan. 1963, Holstebro. *Education:* Århus Univ. *Career:* served as Officer, Jutland Regiment of Dragoons 1983–85, Reserve Officer, rank of Maj. 1985–; UN Observer in Middle East, UNTSO 1990–01; Int. Market Analyst, Cheminova Agro A/S 1991–93; Man., Bilka 1993–95; teacher, Holstebro Business Coll. 1997–98; Chief Operating Finance Officer, Færch Plast A/S 1995–2001; Head of Centre, RAR Regnskabs-center 2001–03; cand. for Holstebro Constituency (Liberal Party) 1995; mem. (temp.) Folketing for Ringkøbing County Constituency Oct.–Nov.

1999, mem. 2001–, Deputy Chair. Defence Cttee 2001; Minister of Defence 2004–; Commdr of the Order of Danneborg.
Address: Ministry of Defence, Holmens Kanal 42, 1060 Copenhagen K, Denmark (office). *Telephone:* 33-92-33-20 (office). *Fax:* 33-32-06-55 (office). *E-mail:* fmn@fmn.dk (office). *Website:* www.fmn.dk (office).

GADIO, Cheikh Tidiane, BA, PhD; Senegalese politician; *Minister of State, Minister of Foreign Affairs, African Unity and Senegalese Abroad;* b. 16 Sept. 1956, Saint-Louis. *Education:* Ohio State Univ., USA, Univ. of Montreal, Canada, Univ. of Paris, France. *Career:* Ed.-in-Chief, Tribune Africaine, Paris 1980–84; Head of Audiovisual section, Festival Panafricain des Arts et de la Culture (FESPAC) 1987–88; various econ. and telecommunications devt advisory posts, World Bank Inst.; Advisor, UN Office for Project Services 1998–; Regional Dir for Africa, School for International Training, Vt, USA 1998–99; Co-ordinator for Africa, World Bank Institute Jan.–April 2000; Minister of State, of Foreign Affairs, African Unity and Senegalese Abroad 2000–.
Address: Ministry of Foreign Affairs, African Unity and Senegalese Abroad, 1 Place de l'Indépendance, BP 4044, Dakar, Senegal (office). *Telephone:* 889-13-00 (office). *E-mail:* cheikhgadio@senegal.diplomatie.sn (office). *Website:* www.diplomatie.gouv.sn (office).

GAFFNEY, Frank J., Jr, BSc, MA; American defence analyst; *President and CEO, Center for Security Policy;* b. 1953. *Education:* Johns Hopkins Univ., Georgetown Univ. *Career:* Aide to Sen. Henry M. Jackson late 1970s; Professional Staff Mem., Senate Armed Forces Cttee 1981–83; Deputy Asst Sec. of Defense for Nuclear Forces and Arms Control Policy 1983–87; Asst Sec. of Defense for Int. Security Policy 1987; Founder, Pres. and CEO Center for Security Policy 1988–; columnist Washington Times, Jewish World Review, TownHall.com; contributing Ed. National Review Online; mem. Bd of Dirs Victory Caucus 2007–. *Publications:* numerous articles in journals and newspapers.
Address: The Center for Security Policy, 1920 L Street, NW, Suite 210, Washington, DC 20036, USA (office). *Telephone:* (202) 835-9077 (office). *Fax:* (202) 835-9066 (office). *E-mail:* info@centerforsecuritypolicy.org (office). *Website:* www.centerforsecuritypolicy.org (office).

GAGOR, Lt-Gen. Franciszek, PhD; Polish army officer; *Chief of General Staff;* b. 8 Sept. 1951, Koniuszowa, Nowy Sącz; m.; one s. one d. *Education:* Adam Mickiewicz Univ., Poznań, Univ. of Wrocław, Acad. of Nat. Defence, Warsaw, NATO Defence Coll., Rome, Italy, Nat. War Coll., Washington, DC, USA. *Career:* began career in Polish Armed Forces 1973; various command and staff posts in mil. units 1973–78; Operations Officer, UNEF II, Egypt 1976–77; Chief of Staff of Pollog to UN Disengagement Observer Force (UNDOF) 1977; Sr Lecturer, Higher Office School of Mechanized Infantry 1978–88; Chief Operations Officer of Polish Battalion, UNDOF, Syria 1980, 1985–86; Sr Staff Officer, Combat Training Inspectorate 1988–90; Deputy Chief Logistics Officer, UNDOF, Syria 1989–90; Head, Peacekeeping Operations Div., Ministry of Defence 1991–92, 1992–94; Deputy Commdr Polish Contingent of Multinational Forces in the Gulf 1991; Deputy Sector Commdr UN Iraq Kuwait Observer Mission (UNIKOM), Kuwait 1991–92; Deputy Dir Mil. Foreign Affairs Dept, Ministry of Defence 1994–96, Dir 1996–99; Chief of Operations Directorate J-3, Gen. Staff 1999–2002; Force Commdr, UNIKOM, Kuwait 2003, UNDOF, Camp Faour 2003–04; Mil. Rep. to NATO and EU, Brussels 2004–05; promoted to Lt-Gen. 2006, Chief of Gen. Staff, Polish Armed Forces 2006–; Officer's and Cavalier's Cross, Order of Polonia Restituta, Golden Cross of Merit.
Address: Ministry of National Defence, 00-909 Warsaw, ul. Klonowa 1, Poland (office). *Telephone:* (22) 6280031 (office). *Fax:* (22) 8455378 (office). *E-mail:* bpimon@wp.mil.pl (office). *Website:* www.wp.mil.pl (office).

GAICIUC, Brig.-Gen. Victor; Moldovan politician and army officer; *Ambassador to Belgium and Permanent Representative, NATO; Career:* served in Moldovan Armed Forces, rank of Brig.-Gen.; Minister of Defence –2004; Amb. to Belgium 2004–; Perm. Rep. to NATO 2004–.
Address: Embassy of Moldova, Tenboschstraat 54, 1050 Brussels, Belgium (office). *Telephone:* (2) 732-96-59 (office). *Fax:* (2) 732-96-60 (office). *E-mail:* bruxelles@mfa.md (office).

GAIDAR, Yegor (see Gaydar, Yegor).

GALAL, Mohamed Noman, BA, MA, PhD; Egyptian diplomatist and academic; *Advisor for Strategic International Studies and the Dialogue of Civilizations, Bahrain Center for Studies and Research;* b. 10 April 1943, Assiut; m. Kawther Elsherif 1969; two s. *Education:* Univ. of Cairo. *Career:* joined Ministry of Foreign Affairs 1965; Third Sec., Embassy in Amman 1969–72; Vice-Consul, Kuwait 1972; Consul, Abu Dhabi 1972–73; Second Sec. Oslo 1975–79; Lecturer, Diplomatic Inst. 1979–80; First Sec. New Delhi 1980, Counsellor 1981–85; Counsellor, Cabinet of Deputy Prime Minister and

Minister of Foreign Affairs 1985–87; Counsellor, Egyptian Mission at UN 1987–90, Minister and Deputy Perm. Rep. 1990–92; Perm. Rep. to League of Arab States, Cairo 1992–95; Amb. to Pakistan 1995–98, to People's Repub. of China 1998–2001; Visiting Lecturer, Farleigh Dickinson Univ., NJ, USA 1989–91, Univ. of Cairo 1994–95; fmr Deputy Dir Centre for Int. Studies, Univ. of Bahrain; currently Adviser for Strategic Int. Studies and Dialogue of Civilizations, Bahrain Center for Studies and Research; mem. Nat. Council on Human Rights, Egypt 2004–(10); St Olav Medal (Norway) 1972, Nat. Medal for Merit (Egypt) 1982. *Publications:* more than 40 publs in Arabic and English on Arab and int. affairs, foreign policy, human rights, Egypt, Middle East, Pakistan, China, non-alignment, Islam in a changing world, human rights and Islam, etc.
Address: Bahrain Centre for Studies and Research, POB 496, Manama, Bahrain (office). *Telephone:* (17) 756270 (office); (17) 625072 (home). *Fax:* (17) 754835 (office); (17) 623492 (home). *E-mail:* mjalal@bcsr.gov.bh (office); galal_m@hotmail.com (home). *Website:* www.bcsr.gov.bh (office); mohamed-n-galal.com (home).

GALLEGOS CHIRIBOGA, Luis Benigno, MA, JD; Ecuadorean diplomatist; *Ambassador to USA;* b. 13 Dec. 1946, Quito; m. Fabiola Jaramillo Almeida de Gallegos; one s. one d. *Education:* Fletcher School of Law and Diplomacy, Tufts Univ., USA, Inst. of Advanced Nat. Studies, Universidad Cen. *Career:* joined Ecuadorian Diplomatic Service 1969; served as Gen. Asst, OAS Dept, Ministry of Foreign Affairs, Consul-Gen. in Chicago 1975–78, Alt. Rep. to OAS 1978–79, Counsellor, Washington, DC 1979–80, Dir-Gen. Int. Projects, Eastern Europe, Information and Press, Tech. Co-operation, then External Credit, Ministry of Foreign Affairs 1984–94, Minister, Embassy in Sofia 1985–89, Amb. to El Salvador 1995–97, Perm. Rep. to UN, Geneva 1997–2002, Amb. Desig. and Perm. Rep. to UN, New York 2002–04, Perm. Rep. 2004–05, Amb. to Australia 2005, to USA Oct. 2005–; Chair. Berne Union 1999–2001; Vice-Chair. Gen. Ass. of Parties to WIPO 1997–99, Human Rights Comm., Geneva 1998, Group of 77 Meeting, Morocco 1999; Hon. Prof., Technological Univ., San Salvador 1997; Gentleman of Madara (Bulgaria) 1989, Ordre nat. du Mérite 1990, Order of Rio Branco (Brazil) 1991, Order José Matías Delgado (El Salvador) 1997, Order Antonio José de Irisarri (Guatemala) 1999, Nat. Order of Merit (Spain) 2001, Order of Quetzal (Guatemala) 2002, Nat. Order of Merit (Ecuador) 2002, Order of Rio Branco (Brazil) 2002, Order of Peruvian Sun 2002, Decoration of the Nat. Congress 'Order Vicente Rocafuerte' 2006, Nat. Order 'Honorato Vasquez' (Ecuador) 2007; Plaque of the Ecuadorian Board of Aviation 1978, Plaque of the Cttee Pres., Chicago 1978, Plaque, Ecuadorian, Chicago 1978, Plaque, Int. AIDS Econs Network 1981, Diploma, Fulbright Comm. 1985, Plaque, Centro Internacional de Estudios Superiores de Comunicación para América Latina (CIESPAL) 1990, Diploma of Honor, Bolivariana Soc. of El Salvador 1995, Letter of Honor, Salvadorean Cultural Center 1997, Humanitarian Plaque, Nat. Congress of Ecuador 1998, Plaque from Ecuadorean Colony in Geneva 2000, Mention of Honor, Human Rights Defender of the Prov. of Guayas 2001, Plaque from Ecuadorian Soc. of New York 2005, Plaque from Ecuadorian Soc. of New Jersey 2005, Resolution, New York City Council 2005, Resolution, New York House of Reps 2005, Resolution, New York Senate 2005, Certificate of Honor, City of San Francisco 2005, Certificate of Honor, City of Los Angeles 2006, Medal of Honor, Ecuadorean News 2006. *Publications:* numerous essays and other publs.
Address: Embassy of Ecuador, 2535 15th Street, NW, Washington, DC 20009, USA (office). *Telephone:* (202) 234-7200 (office). *Fax:* (202) 667-3482 (office). *E-mail:* embassy@ecuador.org (office). *Website:* www.ecuador.org (office).

GALOFRE CANO, Mario, MA, BSc; Colombian diplomatist; *Ambassador to Brazil;* b. 26 Aug. 1939, Bogotá; m.; two s. one d. *Career:* Rector, Gimnasio Moderno, Bogotá 1981–84, 1986–94; Amb. to Brazil 1997–2003, 2005–; Augustin Nieto Caballero Medal, Jose Maria Cordova Medal, and honours from govts of Brazil and Venezuela.
Address: Embassy of Colombia, SES, Av. das Nações, Quadra 803, Lote 10, 70444-900, Brasilia, DF, Brazil (office); Carrera 9, #87–65, Bogotá, Colombia (home). *Telephone:* (61) 3226-8997 (office); (61) 32240919 (home). *Fax:* (61) 3224-4732 (office); (61) 33226972 (home). *E-mail:* embcol@embcol.org.br (office); mario@embcol.org.br (office). *Website:* www.embcol.org.br (office).

GALSWORTHY, Sir Anthony Charles, KCMG, MA; British organization official and fmr diplomatist; b. 20 Dec. 1944, London; m. Jan Dawson-Grove 1970; one s. one d. *Education:* St Paul's School, Corpus Christi Coll., Cambridge. *Career:* Foreign Office, London 1966, Third Sec., Hong Kong 1967, Third, later Second Sec., Beijing 1970, Second, later First Sec., FCO, London 1972, First Sec., Rome 1977, First Sec., later Counsellor, Beijing 1981, Counsellor and Head Hong Kong Dept, FCO 1984, Prin. Pvt. Sec. to Sec. of State for Foreign and Commonwealth Affairs 1986, with Royal Inst.

of Int. Affairs, London 1988, British Sr Rep., Jt Liaison Group, Hong Kong 1989, Cabinet Office 1993, Deputy Under-Sec. of State, FCO 1995, Amb. to People's Repub. of China 1997–2002; Adviser on China, Standard Chartered Bank 2002–; Dir Earthwatch, Europe 2002–06; Dir Bekaert SA 2004–; Scientific Assoc. Nat. History Museum, London 2001–; Hon. Fellow, Royal Botanic Gardens, Edin. 2002; Trustee, Wildfowl and Wetland Trust 2002–, British Trust for Ornithology 2002–06.
Address: c/o Standard Chartered Bank, 1 Aldermanbury Square, London, EC2V 7SB, England (office).

GALTUNG, Johan, PhD; Norwegian academic; *Professor of Peace Studies, University of Alicante;* b. 24 Oct. 1930, Oslo; m. 1st Ingrid Eide 1956 (divorced 1968); two s.; m. 2nd Fumiko Nishimura 1969; one s. one d. *Education:* Univ. of Oslo. *Career:* Prof. of Sociology, Columbia Univ., New York, USA 1957–60; Founder and Dir Int. Peace Research Inst., Oslo 1959–69; Prof. of Peace Research, Univ. of Oslo 1969–77; Prof., Princeton Univ., USA 1985–89; Prof. of Peace Studies, Univ. of Hawaii 1985–2004; Prof. of Peace and Co-operation Studies, Univ. of Witten-Herdecke, Germany; Olof Palme Prof. of Peace, Stockholm, Sweden 1990–91; Prof. of Peace Studies, Univ. of Alicante 2005–; Founder and Dir TRANSCEND (peace and devt network) 1993–; Rector Transcend Peace Univ.; Hon. Prof., Berlin, Alicante, Sichuan, Witten/Herdecke; Dr hc (Finland, Romania, Uppsala, Tokyo, Hagen, Alicante, Osnabrück, Turin and others); Alternative Nobel Peace Prize (Right Livelihood Award), Bajaj Int. Gandhi Prize. *Publications:* Theory and Methods of Social Research (four vols) 1967, 1977, 1980, 1988, There are Alternatives 1983, Hitlerism, Stalinism, Reaganism 1984; Essays in Peace Research Vols I–VI 1974–88, Human Rights in Another Key, Peace by Peaceful Means: Peace, Conflict, Development, Civilization, Conflict Transformation by Peaceful Means 2000, Johan uten land: På fredsveien gjennom verden (Norwegian Literary Prize) 2000.
Address: Casa 227, Urb. Escandinavia, ALFAZ Del Pi, Alicante, Spain; 11009 Kinship Court, Apt 302, Manassas, VA 20109, USA; APA, Garden Court, Apt 912, Kawaramachi/Shomen, Kyoto 600, Japan; 51 Bois Chatton, 01210 Versonnex, France. *Telephone:* (4) 50-42-73-06 (France); (96) 5889919 (Spain). *Fax:* (4) 50-42-75-06 (France); (96) 5889919 (Spain). *E-mail:* galtung@transcend.org (office). *Website:* www.transcend.org (office).

GALUŠKA, Vladimír, JD; Czech diplomatist and lawyer; *Ambassador to Slovakia;* b. 2 Oct. 1952, Prague; m. Marcela Wintrová 1975; two s. *Education:* Charles Univ., Prague. *Career:* corp. lawyer, Škoda Co., Prague 1975–90; Consul, Deputy Chief of Mission, Czech Embassy, Washington, DC 1990–94; Dir Personnel Dept, Ministry of Foreign Affairs 1994–97, Head of Int. Relations 2002–04; Perm. Rep. of Czech Repub. to UN 1997–2001; Amb. to Slovakia 2004–; Pres. ECOSOC 1997, Exec. Bd UNDP/UNFPA 2000; Chair. 3rd Cttee 54th UN Gen. Ass. 1999.
Address: Embassy of the Czech Republic, Hviezdoslavovo nám. 8, PO Box 208, 810 00 Bratislava, Slovakia (office). *Telephone:* (2) 59203303 (office). *Fax:* (2) 59203330 (office). *E-mail:* bratislava@embassy.mzv.cz (office). *Website:* www.mzv.cz/bratislava (office).

GALVÁN GALVÁN, Gen. Guillermo; Mexican military officer and government official; *Secretary of National Defense;* b. 19 Jan. 1943, Mexico City. *Education:* Colegio Militar, Colegio de Defensa. *Career:* has been Commdr in numerous mil. zones; fmr Mil. Attaché Embassy in Madrid; fmr Rector Universidad del Ejército y Fuerza Aérea Mexicanos; Under-Sec. of Nat. Defence 2004–06, Sec. of Nat. Defence 2006–.
Address: Secretariat of State for National Defence, Blvd Manuel Avila Camacho, esq. Avda Industria Militar, 3°, Col. Lomas de Sotelo, Del. Miguel Hidalgo, 11640 México, DF, Mexico (office). *Telephone:* (55) 5557-5571 (office). *Fax:* (55) 5395-2935 (office). *E-mail:* ggalvang@mail.sedena .gob.mx (office). *Website:* www.sedena.gob.mx (office).

GAMA, Jaime José Matos Da; Portuguese politician; *President, Assembleia da República;* b. 8 June 1947, Azores. *Career:* Founding mem. Partido Socialista 1977, unsuccessful cand. for leadership 1986, 1988; Pres. Parl. Comm. for Int. Business 1976–78, of Parl. Comm. for Nat. Defence 1985–91, of Parl. Comm. for European Affairs and Foreign Politics 2002–05; Minister of Home Affairs 1978, Minister of Foreign Affairs 1983–85, 1995–2002; Minister of Nat. Defence 1999; Minister of State 1999–2002; Pres. Assembleia da República (Parl.) 2005–.
Address: Assembleia da República, Palácio de San Bento, 1249-068 Lisbon, Portugal (office). *Telephone:* (213) 919000 (office). *Fax:* (213) 917440 (office). *E-mail:* gabpar@ar.parlament.pt (office). *Website:* www .parlamento.pt (office).

GAMBLE, Christine Elizabeth, PhD; British consultant on culture and sport and fmr cultural administrator; *Consultant to the Commission for Racial Equality;* b. 1 March 1950, Rotherham; m. Edward Barry Antony Craxton.

Education: Royal Holloway Coll., Univ. of London. *Career:* worked in Anglo-French cultural org. 1974–75; Office of the Cultural Attaché, British Embassy, Moscow 1975–76; joined British Council, New Delhi 1977, UK 1979, then Harare 1980–82, Regional Officer for the Soviet Union and Mongolia 1982–85, Deputy Dir Athens 1985–87, Corp. Planning Dept 1988–90, Head, Project Pursuit Dept and Dir Chancellor's Financial Sector Scheme 1990–92, Dir Visitor's Dept 1992–93, Gen. Man. Country Services Group and Head European Services 1993–96; Cultural Councillor, British Embassy, Paris and Dir British Council, France 1996–98; Dir Royal Inst. of Int. Affairs, London 1998–2002; Co. Sec., Ind. Football Comm. 2002–05; Consultant to Comm. for Racial Equality 2005–; Order of Rio Branco, Brazil 2000.
Address: Syke Fold House, Dent, Sedbergh, LA10 5RE, England (home). *E-mail:* cgamble@cre.gov.uk (office). *Website:* www.cre.gov.uk (office).

GAN, Ziyu; Chinese government official and engineer; b. 15 Oct. 1929, Xinyi, Guangdong Prov.; two s. *Education:* Zhongshan Univ. *Career:* engineer and Div. Chief, First Ministry of Machine-Building Industry 1952–56, Ministry of Heavy Industry 1952–56; joined CCP 1953; Sec. Chair.'s Office, State Science and Tech. Comm. 1956–58; apptd Deputy Chief of Planning Group, State Devt and Reform Comm. 1975, Vice-Minister 1978; Deputy Dir State Planning Comm. 1978–, State Admin. Comm. on Import and Export Affairs 1981–82, State Foreign Investment Comm. 1981–82; Vice-Chair. Drafting Cttee for Nat. Defence Law of People's Repub. of China 1993–; Deputy Chair. Nat. Leading Group for Work Concerning Foreign Capital 1994–; mem. Cen. Comm. for Discipline Inspection, CCP Cen. Committee 1992; mem. Preliminary Working Cttee of the Preparatory Cttee of the Hong Kong Special Admin. Region 1993–97, Chinese Govt Del., Hong Kong Handover Ceremony 1997; Chair. Overseas Chinese Affairs Cttee, 9th NPC 1998–2003; Pres. China Asscn for the Peaceful Use of Mil. Industrial Tech.; Prof., Man. Science Centre, Beijing Univ.
Address: c/o Standing Committee of the National People's Congress, Beijing, People's Republic of China.

GANBAATAR, Adiya; Mongolian politician and academic; *Chairman, Standing Committee on the Budget;* b. 8 Feb. 1959, Ulan Bator; m.; three d. *Education:* Łódź Univ., Poland. *Career:* Lecturer, Mongolian State Univ. 1983–90; Chair. Democratic Socialist Movt 1990; mem. State Great Hural (Parl.) 1992–2000, Chair. Standing Cttee on the Budget 1997–; Vice-Chair. Cen. Asia Devt Foundation 1992–; Pres. Mongolian Tennis Asscn 1997–; Distinguished Officer, Banking and Finance 1999, Distinguished Officer, Educ. 2000. *Publications:* three books on mathematics.
Address: Parliament, State House, Ulan Bator 12, Mongolia. *Telephone:* (1) 372980 (office); (1) 321648 (home). *Fax:* (1) 372980. *E-mail:* ganbaatar@ mail.parl.gov.mn (office).

GANDHI, Maneka; Indian politician; b. 26 Aug. 1956, New Delhi; m. Sanjay Gandhi 1974 (died 1980); one s. *Education:* Jawaharlal Nehru Univ., New Delhi. *Career:* Ed. Surya (Sun) magazine 1977–80; Founder and Leader of political party Rashtriya Sanjay Manch (merged with Janata Party 1988) 1983; Minister of State for the Environment and Forests 1989–91; MP 1996–; Minister for Social Justice and Empowerment 1999–2001; Minister of State for Statistics and Programme Implementation 2002–04; Chair. People for Animals Trust, Cttee on Control and Supervision of Experiments on Animals, Soc. for Prevention of Cruelty to Animals; Founder Greenline Trees; Special Adviser to Voice (consumer action forum); cr. environmental film series New Horizons; writer and anchorwoman nat. TV programmes on animals, Heads and Tails, Maneka's Ark, Jeene ki Raah; Pres. Ruth Cowell Trust, Sanjay Gandhi Animal Care Centre; Lord Erskine Award, Royal Soc. for the Prevention of Cruelty to Animals 1991, Vegetarian of the Year, Vegetarian Soc. 1995, Prani Mitra Award, Nat. Animal Welfare Bd 1997, Marchig Prize, Marchig Animal Welfare Trust (GB) 1997, Venu Menon Lifetime Achievement Award 1999, Bhagwan Mahavir Award 1999, Diwaliben Award 1999, Aadishakti Puruskar 2001, Woman of the Year 2001. *Publications:* Sanjay Gandhi 1980, Mythology of Indian Plants, Animal Quiz, Penguin Book of Hindu Names, The Complete Book of Muslim and Parsi Names, First Aid for Animals, Animal Laws of India, Rainbow and Other Stories, Natural Health for Your Dog, Heads and Tails, Wise and Wonderful Animal Alphabet Quiz Book.
Address: 14, Ashoka Road New Delhi 110 001, India. *Telephone:* (11) 23357088. *Fax:* (11) 23354321. *E-mail:* gandhim@nic.in.

GANDHI, Sonia; Indian (b. Italian) politician; *President, Indian National Congress;* b. 9 Dec. 1946, Italy; m. Rajiv Gandhi 1968 (fmr Prime Minister of India) (died 1991); one s. one d. *Education:* Univ. of Cambridge, UK, Nat. Gallery of Modern Art, Delhi. *Career:* Pres. Rajiv Gandhi Foundation; mem. Indian Nat. Congress Cttee, Pres. 1998–2006 (resgnd), reappointed 2007–; mem. Nat. Advisory Council –2006 (resgnd); Leader of Opposition in Parl. (Lok Sabha) –2004; ranked by Forbes magazine

amongst 100 Most Powerful Women (third) 2004, (13th) 2006, (sixth) 2007.
Publications: Rajiv 1992, Rajiv's World 1994.
Address: Indian National Congress, 24 Akbar Road, New Delhi 110011
(office); Rajiv Gandhi Foundation, Jawahar Bhawan, Dr Rajendra Prasad
Road, New Delhi 110001; 10 Janpath, New Delhi 110011, India (home).
Telephone: (11) 23019080 (office); (11) 23014161 (home); (11) 23755117.
Fax: (11) 23017047 (office). *E-mail:* aicc@congress.org.in (office). *Website:*
www.congress.org.in (office); www.soniagandhi.org (home).

GANIĆ, Ejup, DSc; Bosnia and Herzegovina politician and scientist;
Professor, University of Sarajevo; b. 3 March 1946, Novi Pazar; m. Fahrija
Ganić; one s. one d. *Education:* Univ. of Belgrade, Massachusetts Inst. of
Tech. *Career:* researcher, consultant, Prof. of Mechanical Eng, Univ. of
Illinois, Chicago 1975–82; returned to Bosnia and Herzegovina 1982; Prof.,
Univ. of Sarajevo 1982–; worked as Exec. Dir UNIS Co.; mem. Presidency
of Bosnia and Herzegovina 1990–96, Vice-Pres. 1992–96; Vice-Pres. Fed. of
Bosnia and Herzegovina 1994–96, Co-Pres. 1996–2002; Pres. MET
Foundation. *Publications:* Handbook of Heat Transfer Applications
1985, Handbook of Heat Transfer Fundamentals 1985, Handbook of
Essential Engineering Information and Data 1991, Engineering Compa-
nion 2003; more than 100 scientific papers.
Address: Faculty of Mechanical Engineering, Chair for Process Technique,
University of Sarajevo, West Building, Floor IV, Room 407, Vilsonovo
šetalište 9, 71000 Sarajevo, Bosnia and Herzegovina (office). *Telephone:*
(33) 617205 (office). *Fax:* (33) 617205 (office). *E-mail:* ejup_ganic@hotmail
.com; ganic@mef.unsa.ba.

GAOLATHE, Baledzi, MSc; Botswana politician; *Minister of Finance and
Development Planning; Education:* UBLS, Univ. of London, UK. *Career:*
fmr Perm. Sec., Ministries of Finance and Devt Planning, of Mineral
Resource and Water Affairs; fmr Man. Dir Debswana Diamond Co.; fmr
Gov. Bank of Botswana; fmr Chair. Barclays Bank of Botswana Ltd;
currently Minister of Finance and Devt Planning; mem. Bd Bank of
Botswana, Sefelana Holding Co., Botswana Inst. for Devt Policy Analysis;
mem. Bd of Dirs, Botswana Devt Corpn, Botswana Vaccine Inst., Southern
Africa Enterprise Devt Fund; mem. Council, Univ. of Botswana.
Address: Ministry of Finance and Development Planning, Private Bag 008,
Gaborone, Botswana (office). *Telephone:* 3950201 (office). *Fax:* 3956086
(office). *E-mail:* kbaleseng@gov.bw (office); gsethebe@gov.bw (office).
Website: www.finance.gov.bw (office).

GAOMBALET, Célestin-Leroy; Central African Republic politician; b. 1942.
Career: Prime Minister of Central African Repub. 2003–05.
Address: c/o Office of the Prime Minister, Bangui, Central African
Republic (office).

GARCÍA, Amalia; Mexican politician; *Governor, Zacatecas State;* b.
Zacatecas; one d. *Education:* Universidad Autónoma de Puebla. *Career:*
Fed. Deputy 1988–91; mem. Rep. Ass. for Fed. Dist 1991–94; Senator
1997–2002; Gov. Zacatecas State 2004–; Nat. Pres. Partido de la
Revolución Democrática; mem. Consultative Council of Women, Human
Rights Comm.
Address: Office of the President, Partido de la Revolución Democrática,
Monterrey 50, Col Roma, CP 06700, México, DF, Mexico (office).
Telephone: 207-1212 (office). *Website:* www.cen-prd.org.mx (office).

GARCÍA BELAÚNDE, José Antonio; Peruvian diplomatist and academic;
Minister for Foreign Affairs; b. 1948, Lima. *Education:* Pontificia
Universidad Católica de Perú, Academia Diplomática, Univ. of Oxford,
UK. *Career:* joined foreign service 1973, posts included First Sec.,
embassies in Washington, DC, Madrid, Paris, Mexico City, First Sec.,
Perm. Mission to UN, New York; fmr Dir Econ. Affairs, Ministry of
Foreign Affairs; Amb. to Asociación Latinoamericana de Libre Comercio
1986–88; Dir-Sec. Bd Cartegena Agreement 1990–97; Adviser to Sec.-Gen.,
CAN 1997–2001, Dir-Gen. 2002–06; convenor and tutor Int. Relations
Masters Programme, San Martín de Porres Univ.; Minister for Foreign
Affairs 2006–.
Address: Ministry of Foreign Affairs, Jirón Lampa 535, Lima 1, Peru
(office). *Telephone:* (1) 3112402 (office). *Fax:* (1) 3112406 (office). *Website:*
www.rree.gob.pe (office).

GARCÍA DE ALBA ZEPEDA, Sergio Alejandro, BA, MA; Mexican
government official and business executive. *Education:* Instituto Tecnoló-
gico y de Estudios Superiores de Occidente (ITESO), Guadalajara, IPADE,
Mexico City. *Career:* Prof. of Finance ITESO 1980–84; Pres. Regional
Chamber of Manufacturing Industry of Jalisco (CAREINTRA) 1993–94;
Vice-Pres. Confed. of Industrial Chambers of Mexico (CONCAMIN)
1993–95; founding mem. and Dir-Gen. Fibrart –1995; Sec. of Econ.
Promotion, Jalisco state 1995–2001; Regional Vice-Pres. Axtel 2001;
Under-Sec. for Small and Medium-Sized Businesses, Secr. of the Economy

2003–05, Sec. of the Economy 2005–06; CAREINTRA Outstanding
Businessman Award 1989, Asscn of Sales and Marketing Execs of
Guadalajara Exec. of 1993, Ocho Columnas newspaper Columna de Oro
1999, COPARMEX Jalisco Efraín González Luna Prize for Political Merit
2005.
Address: c/o Secretariat of State for the Economy, Alfonso Reyes 30, Col.
Hipódromo Condesa, 06170 México, Mexico (office).

GARCÍA FRANCO, Marco Tulio; Guatemalan politician. *Career:* Minister
of Nat. Defence 2008–.
Address: Ministry of National Defence, Antigua Escuela Politécnica, Avda
La Reforma 1–45, Zona 10, Guatemala City, Guatemala (office).
Telephone: 2360-9890 (office). *Fax:* 2360-9909 (office). *Website:* www
.mindef.mil.gt (office).

GARCÍA LINERA, Álvaro Marcelo; Bolivian politician, mathematician and
sociologist; *Vice-President;* b. 19 Oct. 1962, Cochabamba. *Education:*
Colegio San Agustin, Nat. Autonomous Univ. of Mexico. *Career:* fmr
Prof. of Sociology, Universidad Mayor de San Andrés, La Paz; mem. Tupaj
Katari guerilla group, served five years in prison 1992–97; fmr political
commentator; mem. Movt Toward Socialism party; Vice-Pres. of Bolivia
2006–. *Publications:* several books and articles.
Address: Ministry of the Presidency, Palacio de Gobierno, Plaza Murillo,
La Paz, Bolivia (office). *Telephone:* (2) 237-1082 (office). *Fax:* (2) 237-1388
(office). *E-mail:* webmaster@presidencia.gov.bo (office). *Website:* www
.presidencia.gov.bo (office).

GARCÍA MACAL, José Carlos; Guatemalan economist and politician;
Minister of the Economy; Career: fmr Adviser, Secr. for Cen. American
Econ. Integration (SIECA); fmr Vice-Minister of the Economy; Minister of
the Economy 2008–.
Address: Ministry of the Economy, 8a Avda 10-43, Zona 1, Guatemala
City, Guatemala (office). *Telephone:* 2238-3330 (office). *Fax:* 2238-2413
(office). *E-mail:* einteriano@mineco.gob.gt (office). *Website:* www.mineco
.gob.gt (office).

GARCÍA MONTOYA, Julio José; Venezuelan military officer and diplomatist; *Ambassador to Brazil;* m. Ana Josefina Cumare de García. *Career:*
apptd army Commdt 2002; currently Amb. to Brazil; Commdr Order
General Abreu e Lima, Great Collar 2005.
Address: Embassy of Venezuela, SES, Av. das Nações, Quadra 803, Lote
13, 70451-900 Brasília, DF, Brazil (office). *Telephone:* (61) 3322-1011
(office). *Fax:* (61) 3226-5633 (office). *E-mail:* emb@embvenezuela.org.br
(office).

GARCÍA PÉREZ, Alan Gabriel Ludwig; Peruvian politician and head of
state; *President;* b. 23 May 1949, Lima; m. Pilar Nores; four d. *Education:*
José María Eguren Nat. Coll., Universidad Católica, Lima, Universidad
Nacional Mayor de San Marcos (graduated as lawyer), Universidad
Complutense, Madrid, Spain, Sorbonne and Inst. of Higher Latin
American Studies, Paris, France. *Career:* mem. of Partido Aprista Peruano
since his teens; returned to Peru and elected mem. of Constituent Ass. 1978;
subsequently apptd Org. Sec. and Chair. Ideology of Aprista Party (now
Alianza Popular Revolucionaria Americana), Parl. Deputy 1980–85, Sec.-
Gen. of Party 1982, later Pres.; Senator for Life 1990–; nominated
Presidential cand. 1984, obtained largest number of votes, nat. presidential
elections April 1985; on withdrawal of Izquierda Unida cand., Alfonso
Barrantes Lingán, proclaimed Pres.-elect June 1985, assuming powers
1985–89; granted political asylum in Colombia June 1992; returned from
exile Jan. 2001; Pres. of Peru 2006–.
Address: c/o Ministry of the Presidency, Avda Paseo de la República 4297,
Lima 1 (office); Alianza Popular Revolucionaria Americana, Avda Alfonso
Ugarte 1012, Lima 5, Peru. *Telephone:* (1) 4465886 (office). *Fax:* (1)
4470379 (office). *Website:* www.peru.gob.pe (office).

GARCÍA RAMÍREZ, Sergio, PhD; Mexican politician, lawyer and judge; b. 1
Feb. 1938, Guadalajara. *Education:* Nat. Univ. of Mexico. *Career:*
Research Fellow and teacher of penal law, Inst. of Juridical Research,
Nat. Univ. of Mexico 1966–76; Dir Correction Centre, State of Mexico and
Judge, Juvenile Courts; Asst Dir of Govt Ministry of Interior; Attorney-
Gen. of Fed. Dist; Under-Sec. Ministries of Nat. Resources, Interior,
Educ., Industrial Devt; Dir Prevention Centre of Mexico City; fmr Minister
of Labour; Attorney-Gen. 1982–88; Pres. Inter-American Court of Human
Rights (IACHR) (Corte Interamericana de Derechos Humanos), OAS, San
José, Costa Rica 2004–07; mem. Mexican Acad. of Penal Sciences, Mexican
Inst. of Penal Law, Nat. Inst. of Public Admin., Ibero-American Inst. of
Penal Law etc. *Publications:* Teseo Alucinado 1966, Asistencia a Reos
Liberados 1966, El Artículo 18 Constitucional 1967, La Imputabilidad en el
Derecho Penal Mexicano, El Código Tutelar para Menores del Estado
Michoacán 1969, La Ciudadanía de la Juventud 1970, La Prisión 1975, Los

Derechos Humanos y el Derecho Penal 1976, Legislación Penitenciaria y Correccional Comentada 1978, Otros Minotauros 1979, Cuestiones Criminológicas y Penales Contemporáneas 1981, Justicia Penal 1982.
Address: Circuito Maestro Mario de la Cueva s/n, Cd. Universitaria, CP 04510, Mexico City, Mexico (office). *Telephone:* (55) 5622-7474 (office). *Fax:* (55) 5665-2193 (office). *E-mail:* sgr@servidor.unam.mx (office). *Website:* www.juridicas.unam.mx (office).

GARCÍA SAYAN LARABURRE, Diego, LLB; Peruvian politician and lawyer; b. 1950. *Education:* Univ. of Lima, Univ. of Texas, USA. *Career:* constitutional lawyer; Head Andean Comm. of Jurists; Rep. of Peru Inter-American Comm. on Human Rights; fmr Minister of Justice; Minister of Foreign Affairs 2001–02; Chair. UN Working Group on Enforced or Involuntary Disappearances 2002.
Address: c/o Ministry of Foreign Affairs, Palacio de Torre Tagle, Jirón Ucayali 363, Lima 1, Peru (office).

GARCÍA SEGOVIA DE MADERO, María Teresa, BA; Mexican politician and diplomatist. *Education:* Universidad Labastida, Monterrey, Inst. of Public Admin, Nuevo León, Univs of Oxford and Cambridge, UK. *Career:* joined Nat. Action Party (PAN) 1984, mem. Exec. Cttee, Nuevo León Br. 1984–; Founding mem. Democratic Electoral Ass. for Elective Suffrage 1985; Deputy of State Congress for Nuevo León 1985–88; Municipal Councillor of Monterrey 1991–94; Sec. of Municipal Council, San Pedro Garza García, Nuevo León 1994–97; Mayor of San Pedro Garza García 1997–2000; Amb. to Canada 2001–06; Pres. Cttee of Wives of Industrial Relations Execs (ERIAC); mem. Women's Nat. Asscn 1978–; mem. Bd of Dirs, Univ. of Monterrey, Forum of Feds 2002–; Hon. Mention for Civic Courage, Civilización y Libertad.
Address: c/o Secretariat of State for Foreign Affairs, Avenida Ricardo Flores Magón 2, Col. Guerrero, Del. Cuauhtémoc 06995, Mexico (office). *Website:* www.sre.gob.mx (office).

GARCÍA-VALDECASAS Y FERNÁNDEZ, Rafael, DJur; Spanish judge; *Judge, Court of First Instance of the European Communities;* b. 9 Jan. 1946, Granada; m. Rosario Castaño Parraga 1975. *Education:* Univ. of Granada. *Career:* lawyer, Office of Attorney-Gen. 1976; mem. Office of Attorney-Gen. Tax and Judicial Affairs Office, Jaén 1976–85; mem. Office of Attorney-Gen. Econ. and Admin. Court of Jaén 1979–85; mem. Jaén Bar 1979–89, Granada Bar 1981–89; mem. Office of Attorney-Gen. Econ. and Admin. Court of Córdoba 1983–85, Tax and Judicial Affairs Office of Granada 1986–87; Head, Spanish State Legal Service for cases before EC Court of Justice (Ministry of Foreign Affairs) 1987–89; Judge, Court of First Instance of the European Communities 1989–; Encomienda de la Orden Civil del Mérito Agrícola 1982, Encomienda de la Orden de Isabel la Católica 1990, Gran Cruz de la Orden del Mérito Civil 1999. *Publications:* Comentarios al Tratado de Adhesión de España a la C.E.: La Agricultura 1985, El 'acquis' comunitario 1986, El medio ambiente: conservación de espacios protegidos en la legislación de la CE 1992, La Jurisprudencia del Tribunal de Justicia CE sobre la libertad de establecimiento y libre prestación de servicios por los abogados 1993, El Tribunal de Primera Instancia de las Comunidades Europeas 1993, El respeto del derecho de defensa en materia de competencia 1997, El desarollo normativo de los reglamentos comunitarios 1999; also papers in books and learned journals.
Address: European Court of First Instance of the European Communities, Erasmus 2036, Rue du Fort Niedergrünewald, 2925 Luxembourg, Luxembourg (office).

GARDNER, Richard Newton, DPhil; American diplomatist, lawyer and academic; *Professor of Law and International Organization, Columbia University;* b. 9 July 1927, New York; m. Danielle Almeida Luzzatto 1956; one s. one d. *Education:* Harvard Univ., Yale Law School, Univ. of Oxford, UK. *Career:* Rhodes Scholar to Oxford Univ. 1951–54; Prof. of Law and Int. Org., Columbia Univ. 1957–61, 1965–76, 1981–; Deputy Asst Sec. of State for Int. Org. Affairs, US State Dept 1961–65; Amb. to Italy 1977–81; Lawyer, Coudert Bros 1981–93; Consultant to Sec.-Gen., UN Conf. on Environment and Devt 1992; Amb. to Spain 1993–97; Counsel, Morgan, Lewis and Bockius 1997–; mem. US Advisory Cttee on Law of the Sea 1971–76, Vice-Pres.'s Advisory Cttee for Foreign Trade Policy and Negotiations 1998–; Del. to UN Gen. Ass. 2000; mem. Trilateral Comm., Council on Foreign Relations; mem. American Philosophical Soc.; Arthur S. Flemming Award 1963, Thomas Jefferson Award 1998. *Publications:* Sterling-Dollar Diplomacy 1956, In Pursuit of World Order 1964, Blueprint for Peace 1966, The Global Partnership: International Agencies and Economic Development 1968, Negotiating Survival: Four Priorities after Rio 1992.
Address: Columbia University School of Law, 435 West 116th Street, New York, NY 10027, USA. *Telephone:* (212) 854-4635 (office). *Fax:* (212) 854-7946 (office). *E-mail:* rgardn@law.columbia.edu (office). *Website:* www.law.columbia.edu (office).

GAREYEV, Gen. Makhmud Akhmedovich; Russian army officer and historian; *President, Russian Academy of Military Science;* b. 23 July 1923; m.; two c. *Education:* Tashkent Infantry School, M. Frunze Mil. Acad., Gen. Staff Acad. *Career:* involved in mil. operations on Western Front, officer Operative Div., Gen. Staff of Far E Army at end of Second World War; Commdr of Regt, Tank Div. Belarus Mil. Command, Head of Gen. Staff Urals Mil. Command, then officer Gen. Staff; Head Mil. Scientific Dept, then Deputy Head of Chief Operative Dept, apptd Deputy Head of Gen. Staff 1974; Chief Mil. Counsellor, Afghanistan, then Commdr 1989–; mem. Russian Acad. of Mil. Sciences (later Pres.), Council on Interaction with Orgs of War Veterans; Order of Lenin and numerous other decorations and medals. *Publications:* Frunze – Military Theoretician, General Army Exercises, Marshal G. Zhukov and more than 60 scientific works.
Address: Academy of Military Sciences, Myasnitskaya str. 37, 103175 Moscow, Russia (office). *Telephone:* (495) 293-33-55 (office).

GARNAUT, Ross Gregory, AO, BA, PhD; Australian economist, government official and fmr diplomatist; b. 28 July 1946, Perth, WA; m. Jayne Potter 1974; two s. *Education:* Perth Modern School, WA and Australian Nat. Univ., Canberra. *Career:* Research Fellow, Sr Research Fellow and Sr Fellow, Econs Dept, Research School of Pacific Studies, ANU 1972–75, 1977–83; First Asst Sec.-Gen., Financial and Econ. Policy, Papua New Guinea Dept of Finance 1975, 1976; Research Dir ASEAN-Australia Econ. Relations Research Project 1980–83; Sr Econ. Adviser to Prime Minister Bob Hawke 1983–85; Amb. to People's Repub. of China 1985–88; Prof. of Econs, Head of Dept, Research School of Pacific Studies, ANU 1989–, Dir Asia Pacific School of Econs and Man. 1998–; econs adviser to Prime Minister Kevin Rudd 2007–; Chair. Aluminium Smelters of Victoria 1988–89, Rural and Industries Bank of Western Australia 1988–95, Primary Industry Bank of Australia 1988–94, Lihir Gold 1995–, Australian Centre for Int. Agric. Research 1994–. *Publications:* Irian Jaya: The Transformation of a Melanesian Economy 1974, ASEAN in a Changing Pacific and World Economy 1980, Indonesia: Australian Perspectives 1980, Taxation and Mineral Rents 1983, Exchange Range and Macro-Economic Policy in Independent Papua New Guinea 1984, The Political Economy of Manufacturing Protection: Experiences of ASEAN and Australia 1986, Australian Protectionism: Extent, Causes and Effects 1987, Australia and the Northeast Asian Ascendancy (report to Prime Minister) 1989, Economic Reform and Internationalization 1992, Grain in China 1992, Structuring for Global Realities (report on Wool Industry to Common-wealth Governments) 1993, The Third Revolution in the Chinese Countryside 1996, Open Regionalism: An Asian Pacific Contribution to the World Trading System 1996, East Asia in Crisis 1998, Private Enterprise in China (co-author) 2001, Social Democracy in Australia's Asian Future (co-author) 2001, Resource Management in Asia Pacific Developing Countries (ed.) 2002, China 2002: WTO Entry and World Recession (co-ed.) 2002, China: New Engine of World Growth (co-ed.) 2003, China: Is Rapid Growth Sustainable? (co-ed.) 2004, China's Third Economic Transformation (co-ed.) 2004, China's Ownership Transforma-tion (co-author) 2005, The China Boom and its Discontents (co-ed.) 2005, The Turning Point in China's Economic Development (co-ed.) 2006, China: Linking Markets for Growth (co-ed.) 2007.
Address: Department of Economics, Research School of Pacific and Asian Studies, Australian National University, Canberra, ACT 0200, Australia (office). *Telephone:* (2) 6125-3100 (office). *Fax:* (2) 6249-8057 (home). *E-mail:* Ross.Garnaut@anu.edu.au (office). *Website:* www.dpmc.gov.au (office); rspas.anu.edu.au (office).

GARNJANA-GOONCHORN, Krit, PhD; Thai diplomatist; *Ambassador to USA;* b. 14 Oct. 1948; m. Ravewan Garnjana-Goonchorn. *Education:* Queen's Coll., Oxford and Univ. of Manchester, UK, Nat. Defence Coll. of Thailand. *Career:* Third Sec., Treaty Div., Dept of Treaties and Legal Affairs, Ministry of Foreign Affairs 1978–80, Second Sec., Legal Affairs Div. 1980–83, First Sec. 1983–84, Counsellor, East Asia Div., Dept of Political Affairs 1984–87, Dir Div. of Econ. Relations and Co-operation, Dept of Econ. Affairs 1987–88, Deputy Dir-Gen. Dept of Treaties and Legal Affairs 1988–89; Minister, Embassy in Washington, DC 1989–92; Amb. attached to the Ministry, Office of the Perm. Sec. 1992–93, Dir-Gen. Dept of Treaties and Legal Affairs 1993–95; Amb. and Perm. Rep. to UN and other Int. Orgs, Geneva 1995–2000; Dir-Gen. Dept of Treaties and Legal Affairs and Dir-Gen. Dept of East Asian Affairs 2000–01, Deputy Perm. Sec., Office of the Perm. Sec. 2001–02; Amb. to France 2002–04; Perm. Sec., Ministry of Foreign Affairs 2004–07; Amb. to USA 2007–; Companion (Fourth Class), Most Exalted Order of the White Elephant 1980, Commdr (Third Class), Most Noble Order of the Crown of Thailand 1983, Kt Commdr (Second Class), Most Noble Order of the Crown of Thailand 1985, Kt Commdr (Second Class), Most Exalted Order of the White Elephant 1988, Kt Grand Cross (First Class), Most Noble Order of the Crown of Thailand 1991, Kt Grand Cross (First Class), Most Exalted

Order of the White Elephant 1994, Kt Grand Cordon (Special Class), Most Noble Order of the Crown of Thailand 1997, Kt Grand Cordon (Special Class), Most Exalted Order of the White Elephant 2002, Grand Officier, Ordre nat. du Mérite 2004, Grand Companion (Third Class, Higher Grade), Most Illustrious Order of Chula Chom Klao 2004.
Address: Embassy of Thailand, 1024 Wisconsin Avenue, NW, Washington, DC 20007-3620, USA (office). *Telephone:* (202) 944-3600 (office). *Fax:* (202) 944-3611 (office). *E-mail:* info@thaiembdc.org (office). *Website:* www.thaiembdc.org (office).

GARRÉ, Nilda, BA; Argentine lawyer and politician; *Minister of Defence;* b. 3 Nov. 1945, Buenos Aires; m. Juan Manuel (divorced); three c. *Education:* Universidad del Salvador. *Career:* active in Juventud Peronista in 1970s; elected to prov. ass. Buenos Aires as rep. of Frente Justicialista de Liberación 1973–76; lawyer and human rights activist 1976–82; participated in Renovación Peronista of Partido Justicialista 1983; joined Frente del País Solidario; elected to Cámara de Diputados 1995–2000; Deputy Interior Minister 2000–01; elected to Senado 2001–05; Amb. to Venezuela June 2005; Minister of Defence Nov. 2005–; Rep. of Nat. Chamber of Deputies to UN on Penal Legislation 1997; Vice-Pres. Fundación Carlos Auyero 1997–2002, Pres. 2004–05; mem. Advisory Cttee on Penal Reform 2003–04; Gen. Coordinator Centre for Research and Public Policy Advice (CEAPP).
Address: Ministry of Defence, Azopardo 250, 1328 Buenos Aires, Argentina (office). *Telephone:* (11) 4346–8800 (office). *E-mail:* nildagarre@mindef.gov.ar (office); mindef@mindef.gov.ar (office). *Website:* www.mindef.gov.ar (office).

GARVELINK, William John, BA, MA; American diplomatist; *Ambassador to the Democratic Republic of the Congo;* b. Mich.; m. Linda A. Garvelink. *Education:* Calvin Coll., Univ. of Minnesota, Univ. of N Carolina. *Career:* professional staff mem. Sub-cttee on Int. Orgs, Cttee on Foreign Affairs, US House of Reps, Washington, DC; joined Agency for Int. Devt 1979, served as Man. Auditor in Office of Insp. Gen., as Asst Co-ordinator for African Assistance, as Asst Program Officer and Deputy Program Officer in Bolivia, as Deputy Dir Office of African Refugee Affairs, as Asst Dir for Disaster Response, as Deputy Dir Office of Foreign Disaster Assistance, as Mission Dir of USAID/Eritrea, Sr Deputy Asst Admin, Bureau of Democracy, Conflict and Humanitarian Assistance, Amb. to the Democratic Repub. of the Congo 2007–; six Performance Awards, two Meritorious Honor Awards, Superior Honor Award, Sr Foreign Service Presidential Meritorious Service Award. *Publications include:* several book chapters on int. affairs.
Address: US Embassy, 310 avenue des Aviateurs, BP 697, Kinshasa, Democratic Republic of the Congo (office). *Telephone:* (88) 43608 (office). *Fax:* (88) 43467 (office). *E-mail:* USEmbassyKinshasa@state.gov (office). *Website:* kinshasa.usembassy.gov (office).

GARVEY, Janet E., BA, JD; American diplomatist; *Ambassador to Cameroon;* b. Mass. *Education:* Northeastern Univ., Georgetown Univ. School of Law. *Career:* served as intern at Nat. Endowment for the Arts, Washington, DC; career mem. Sr Foreign Service, served as Deputy Chief of Mission, Budapest, also served at US Consulate Gen., Cape Town, Leipzig, and at Embassies in Yugoslavia, Finland, and fmr East Germany, as well as in various positions at US Information Agency and Dept of State, Washington, DC, has served as Dir Office of N Cen. European Affairs, Bureau of European and Eurasian Affairs and Deputy Coordinator, Bureau of Int. Information Programs; Amb. to Cameroon 2007–; mem. Metropolitan Museum of Art, New York, Museum of Fine Arts, Boston, DC Bar Asscn; Dept of State's or US Information Agency's Superior Honor Award and Meritorious Honor Award (three times each).
Address: Embassy of the USA, Avenue Rosa Parks, BP 817, Yaoundé, Cameroon (office). *Telephone:* 220-15-00 (office). *Fax:* 220-15-00 ext. 4531 (office). *Website:* yaounde.usembassy.gov (office).

GARZA, Antonio O., Jr, BA, JD; American diplomatist, politician and lawyer; *Ambassador to Mexico;* m. María Aramburuzabala Larregui 2005. *Education:* Univ. of Texas at Austin, Southern Methodist Univ. (SMU) School of Law. *Career:* elected to US House of Reps for S Texas 1988; apptd Sec. of State and Sr Adviser to Gov. of Texas George W. Bush 1994, later Chief Elections Officer, State of TX; served on Presidential Dels to observe Fed. Elections in Nicaragua and El Salvador; Cameron Co. Judge –1995; Pnr, Bracewell & Patterson LLP (law firm), Austin –1998; Railroad Commr for TX 1998–2002; Amb. to Mexico 2002–; fmr mem. Advisory Bd George W. Bush School of Govt and Public Service, Texas A&M Univ.; mem. Bd Dirs Texas Exes, Univ. of Texas at Austin; SMU Distinguished Alumnus Award 2001, named Top 100 Most Influential Hispanics by Hispanic Business Magazine.
Address: Embassy of the USA, Paseo de la Reforma 305, Col. Cuauhtémoc, 06500 México, DF, Mexico (office). *Telephone:* (55) 5080-2000 (office).

Fax: (55) 5511-9980 (office). *E-mail:* embeuamx@state.gov (office). *Website:* mexico.usembassy.gov (office).

GARZÓN, Baltasar; Spanish judge; *Investigating Judge, Audiencia Nacional;* b. 1955, Villa de Torres (Jaen); m. Jaen; three c. *Career:* prov. judge 1978–87, Audiencia Nacional (Nat. Court) 1987–; mem. Parl. 1993–94; has investigated numerous high profile cases involving drug trafficking, Basque terrorism, govt corruption, Spain's security forces and human rights abuses and Islamic fundamentalism; issued arrest warrant for Gen. Augusto Pinochet Ugarte to face charges of genocide, terrorism and torture 1998; banned Basque politicial party Batasuna Aug. 2002; Hon. DJur (New York Univ.) 2007.
Address: Audiencia Nacional, García Gutiérrez 1, 28004 Madrid, Spain (office). *Telephone:* (91) 3973339 (office). *Fax:* (91) 3973306 (office).

GASPAR MARTINS, Ismael Abraão, B.A.; Angolan diplomatist; *Permanent Representative, United Nations;* b. 12 Jan. 1940, Luanda; m.; four c. *Education:* Lycoming Coll., Penn., USA, Univ. of Manheim, Germany, Univ. of Oxford, UK. *Career:* Research Officer (Agricultural Devt), UN Research Inst. for Social Devt, Geneva 1971–72; Econ. Affairs Officer, UN Conf. on Trade and Devt (UNCTAD) 1972–75; External and Econ. Affairs Adviser to Pres. of Angola 1975; Gov. Cen. Bank of Angola 1976–77; Minister of Finance 1977–82, of External Trade 1982–87; Exec. Dir African Devt Bank, Abidjan, Côte d'Ivoire 1989–95; Founding-mem. and Co-Pres. Angola–South Africa Chamber of Commerce and Industry 1996–2001; Man. Dir Gaspar Martins and Assocs Int. Business Consultants 1996–2001; Perm. Rep. to UN, New York 2001–; mem. Southern African Devt Community Task Force, World Econ. Forum Summit 1996–2000.
Address: Permanent Mission of Angola to the UN, 125 East 73rd Street, New York, NY 10021, USA (office). *Telephone:* (212) 861-5656 (office). *Fax:* (212) 861-9295 (office). *E-mail:* angola@un.int (office).

GAŠPAROVIČ, Ivan, LLD; Slovak politician, lawyer and head of state; *President;* b. 27 March 1941, Poltár, Lučenec Dist; m. Silvia Gašparovičová 1964; one s. one d. *Education:* Komenský Univ., Bratislava. *Career:* clerk, Prosecutor's Office, Martin Trenčín 1965–66; Municipal Public Prosecutor, Bratislava 1966–68; teacher, Faculty of Law, Komenský Univ., Bratislava 1968–90, Vice-Rector 1990–; Gen. Prosecutor of CSFR 1990–92; mem. Movt for Democratic Slovakia 1992–2002 (movt became a political party 2000); Deputy to Slovak Nat. Council, mem. of Presidium; Chair. of Slovak Nat. Council 1992–98; Chair. Special Body of Nat. Council of Slovakia for Control of Slovak Intelligence Services 1993–98; Founder and Leader Movt for Democracy 2002–; Pres. of Slovakia 2004–. *Publications:* author and co-author of many univ. textbooks, numerous articles and reviews on criminal law.
Address: Office of the President, Hodžovo nám. 1, PO Box 128, 810 00 Bratislava, Slovakia (office). *Telephone:* (2) 5249-8945 (office). *Fax:* (2) 5441-7028 (office). *E-mail:* informacie@prezident.sk (office). *Website:* www.prezident.sk (office).

GASS, Simon, CMG, CVO; British diplomatist; *Ambassador to Greece; Career:* Second, later First Sec., Athens 1984–87, Acting British High Commr to South Africa 1999, Dir of Resources, FCO –2004, Amb. to Greece 2004–.
Address: British Embassy, Odos Ploutarchou 1, 106 75 Athens, Greece (office). *Telephone:* (210) 7272600 (office). *Fax:* (210) 7272734 (office). *E-mail:* britania@hol.gr (office). *Website:* www.british-embassy.gr (office).

GATES, Robert M., PhD; American government official and fmr academic administrator; *Secretary of Defense;* b. 25 Sept. 1943, Wichita, Kansas; m. Becky Gates; two c. *Education:* Coll. of William and Mary, Indiana Univ., Georgetown Univ. *Career:* service with USAF 1966–68; career training program CIA 1968, intelligence analyst 1969–72, staff of Special Asst to the Dir of Central Intelligence for Strategic Arms Limitations 1972–73, Asst Nat. Intelligence Officer for Strategic Programs 1973–74, staff Nat. Security Council The White House 1974–76, staff Center for Policy Support 1976–77, Special Asst to Asst to the Pres. for Nat. Security Affairs 1977–79, Dir Strategic Evaluation Center 1979–80, Exec. Asst to Dir of Cen. Intelligence and Dir of the Exec. Staff, Dir of Office of Policy and Planning and Nat. Intelligence Officer for the Soviet Union and Eastern Europe 1980–81, Deputy Dir for Intelligence 1982–86, Chair. Nat. Intelligence Council 1982–86, Acting Dir of Central Intelligence 1986–87, Deputy Dir of Central Intelligence 1986–89, Asst to the Pres. and Deputy for Nat. Security Affairs The White House 1989–91, Dir CIA 1991–93; Interim Dean, George Bush School of Govt and Public Service, 1999-2001, Pres. Texas A&M Univ. 2002–06; US Sec. of Defense 2006–; fmr mem. Bd of Dirs NACCO Industries Inc., Brinker International Inc., Parker Drilling Company Inc.; fmr mem. Bd of Trustees The Fidelity Funds; mem. Iraq Study Group, US Inst. for Peace 2006; Nat. Intelligence Distinguished Service Medal, Distinguished Intelligence Medal (twice), Intelligence Medal of Merit, Arthur S. Fleming Award, Nat. Security Medal,

Presidential Citizen's Medal. *Publication:* From the Shadows: The Ultimate Insider's Story of Five Presidents and How They Won the Cold War 1996. *Address:* Department of Defense, 1000 Defense Pentagon, Washington, DC 20301, USA (office). *Website:* www.defenselink.mil (office).

GATETE, Claver; Rwandan economist and diplomatist; *Ambassador to UK;* m. Jeanne Gatete. *Career:* fmr Sr Adviser and Personal Rep. of Pres. Paul Kagame to NEPAD (New Partnership for Africa's Devt) Steering Cttee; Sec.-Gen. Ministry of Finance and Econ. Planning and Sec. to the Treasury –2005; Amb. to UK (also accred to Ireland, Denmark, Norway and Sweden) 2005–.
Address: Embassy of Rwanda, 120–122 Seymour Street, London, W1H 1NR, England (office). *Telephone:* (20) 7224-9832 (office). *Fax:* (20) 7224-8642 (office). *E-mail:* uk@ambarwanda.org.uk (office). *Website:* www .ambarwanda.org.uk (office).

GATSINZI, Gen. Marcel; Rwandan politician and army officer; *Minister of Defence;* b. 9 Jan. 1948. *Education:* Ecole de Guerre, Brussels, Belgium, Inst. of World Politics, Washington, DC, USA. *Career:* served in Rwandan Armed Forces, rank of Gen.; fmr Deputy Chief of Staff, then Chief of Staff, Nat. Gendarmerie; mem. Neutral Mil. Observer Group of fmr OAU (now the African Union) 1992–93; Sec.-Gen., Nat. Security Council 2002; currently Minister of Defence; rep. to numerous int. negotiations and meetings including African Union, Easbrig, Golden Spear.
Address: Ministry of Defence, PO Box 23, Kigali, Rwanda (office). *Telephone:* 576032 (office). *Fax:* 573411 (office). *E-mail:* marcel_gatsinzi@ gov.rw (office).

GAVAI, S. M., BA; Indian diplomatist; *Consul General, Houston;* m. Rina Gavai; two s. *Education:* Fergusson College, Pune. *Career:* fmr Head, SAARC Div., Northern Div and Admin. Div., Ministry of Foreign Affairs; fmr Chief of Protocol; served in Embassies in Yugoslavia, Hungary, Zimbabwe, Indonesia, Germany; fmr Consul Gen. in Scotland; fmr High Commr to Maldives; currently Consul Gen., Houston, Tex., USA.
Address: Consulate General of India, 1990 Post Oak Blvd., #600 3 Post Oak, Houston, TX 77056, USA (office). *Telephone:* (713) 626-2148 (office). *Fax:* (713) 626-2450 (office). *E-mail:* cgi-hou@swbell.net (office). *Website:* www.cgihouston.org (office).

GAVIRIA TRUJILLO, César; Colombian politician, international organization official and economist; b. 31 March 1947, Pereira; m. Ana Milena Muñoz de Gaviria. *Education:* Univ. of the Andes. *Career:* mem. town council of Pereira, later Mayor; mem. Chamber of Deputies (Partido Liberal Colombiano—PLC) and Dir Comm. for Econ. Affairs 1974; Vice-Minister for Econ. Devt 1978; Speaker of Parl. 1983; journalist in early 1980s; Minister of Finance and Public Credit 1986–87, of the Interior 1987–89; Pres. of Colombia 1990–94; Sec.-Gen. OAS 1994–2004; mem. Inter-American Dialogue, Club de Madrid, La Conférence de Montréal; Hon. Prof., Universidad ICESI, Colombia, Univ. of Miami, USA, Universidad Libre Colombia 1990, Universidade Estácio de Sá, Rio de Janeiro 1991, Northeastern Univ., USA 2002; Hon. LLB (Univ. Libre de Colombia); Hon. DCL (Northeastern Univ.) 2002; W. Averell Harriman Democracy Award 2002, Nat. Democratic Inst. Democracy Award 2002, Washington Times Int. Courage in Leadership Award 2002. *Publications include:* La Deuda Latinoamericana 1982, Reflexiones para una nueva Constitución 1990, La Revolución Pacífica 1990, Las Bases de la Nueva Colombia: El Revolcón Institucional 1990–1994 1994, Reformas Económicas 1990–1994 1994, Plan de Desarrollo Económico y Social 1990–1994 1994, A New Vision of the OAS 1995, Toward the New Millennium: The Road Travelled 1994–1999 1999; book chapters and articles in journals.
Address: c/o Organization of American States, 17th Street and Constitution Avenue, NW, Washington, DC 20006, USA (office).

GAVRIN, Alexander Sergeyevich; Russian politician and engineer; b. 22 July 1953, Orlovo, Zaporozhye Region, Ukraine. *Education:* Tumen Industrial Inst., Tumen State Inst. of Oil and Gas. *Career:* army service 1972–74; controller, master Zaporozhye plant Radiopribor 1974–79; controlling master Manuylsky Research Inst., Kiev 1979–80; engineer constructor Kiev plant generator 1980–81; technician Kiev production co. 1981–83; electrician Povkhneft Kogalym, Tumen Region 1983–88; engineer head of group Kogalymneftegas Co., Tumen Region 1988–89; Chair. Trade Union LUKOil-Kogalymneftegas 1989–93; Head of Admin. Kogalym. Tumen Region 1993–96; Mayor of Kogalym 1996–2000; Minister of Energy of Russian Fed. 2000–01; fmr Rep. of Tumen Region to Council of Fed., Russian Fed. Ass.
Address: c/o Council of Federation, B. Dmitrovka Str. 26, 103426 Moscow, Russia (office).

GAYAN, Anil Kumarsingh, LLM; Mauritian politician and lawyer; b. 22 Oct. 1948; m. Sooryakanti Nirsimloo; three c. *Education:* Royal Coll., Port Louis, London School of Econs, UK. *Career:* called to the Bar, Inner Temple, London 1972; mem. Mauritius Bar and Seychelles Bar 1972–73, pvt. practice 1973–74, 1982, 1986–90, 1995–2000; Chair. Bar Council 1989–90; joined Chambers of Mauritius Attorney Gen. as Crown Counsel 1974, Sr Counsel 1995; Del. to UN Conf. on the Law of the Sea 1974–82; mem. Parl. 1982–86, Minister of External Affairs, Tourism and Emigration 1983–86, Foreign Affairs and Regional Co-operation 2000–03; Chair. Council of Univ. of Mauritius 1983; Consultant for Geneva-based Centre for Human Rights, consultancy work in Bhutan, Mongolia, Armenia and Togo 1991; Hon. Minister.
Address: c/o Ministry of Foreign Affairs and Regional Co-operation, New Government Centre, Level 5, Port Louis, Mauritius (office).

GAYDAR, Yegor Timurovich, DSc (Econ); Russian politician; b. 19 March 1956, Moscow; m. 2nd Maria Strugatskaya 1986; three s. *Education:* Moscow State Univ. *Career:* journalist, Kommunist and Pravda 1987–90; Dir Inst. of Econ. Policy, USSR (now Russian) Acad. of Sciences 1990–91; Deputy Chair. Russian Govt (and co-ordinator of the 13 ministries responsible for econ. affairs) 1991–92; Acting Chair. Russian Govt June–Dec. 1992; Dir Inst. for the Economy in Transition 1992–93, 1994–; Adviser to Pres. Yeltsin on Econ. Reform 1992–93; First Deputy Chair. Russian Govt 1993–94, Minister of the Economy 1993–94; Head of Political Bloc, Russian Choice (Vibor Rossii) 1993–94; Founder and Leader Democratic Choice of Russia Party 1994–; mem. State Duma (Parl.) 1993–95, 1999–; joined right-wing coalition Pravoye Delo 1999; mem. faction Union of Right-Wing Forces; Cttee mem. for Co-operation in the Baltic Region (attached to Prime Minister of Sweden); mem. Editorial Bd Vestnik Evropy; mem. Consultative Cttee Acta Oeconomica (Budapest); Hon. Prof., Univ. of California, Berkeley. *Publications:* State and Evolution 1996, Anomalies of Economic Growth 1997, Days of Defeats and Victories 1998, A Long Time. Russia in the World: Notes on Economic History 2005, The Death of Empire: Lessons for Contemporary Russia 2006; more than 100 articles in Russian and foreign scientific journals and newspapers.
Address: Institute for the Economy in Transition, Gazetny per. 5, 111024 Moscow, Russia (office). *Telephone:* (495) 229-64-13 (office). *Fax:* (495) 229-64-48 (office).

GAYER, Yevdokiya Alexandrovna, CandHistSc; Russian/Nanai ethnographer and public servant; *Secretary-General, International League of Small Nations and Ethnic Groups;* b. 8 March 1934, Podali, Khabarovsk Territory; m. (deceased); two s. *Education:* in Vladivostok. *Career:* researcher Inst. of History, Archaeology and Ethnography Far E br. of USSR Acad. of Sciences in Vladivostok 1969–89; USSR People's Deputy, mem. Soviet of Nationalities, mem. Comm. on Problems of Int. Relations and Nat. Policy 1989–92; adviser to Pres. 1992–; Deputy Chair. State Cttee on Social-Econ. Devt of the North 1993–; mem. Council of Fed. of Russia 1993–96; Deputy Chair. Comm. of the North and Indigenous Peoples 1996–2000; Sec.-Gen. Int. League of Small Nations and Ethnic Groups 1996–; Chief Adviser State Cttee on Problems of Devt of North Territories (later Cttee on Northern, Siberian and Far Eastern Affairs, Council of Fed.) 1997–98; Prof., Int. Acad. of Marketing and Man. (Mamarmen); mem. Presidium Russian Acad. of Natural Sciences; mem. Acad. of Information Science, Acad. of Polar Medicine.
Address: Rublyovskoye Sh. 3, korp. 2, Apt 388, 121609 Moscow, Russia. *Telephone:* (095) 413-76-95.

GAYOOM, Maumoon Abdul, MA; Maldivian politician and head of state; *President;* b. 29 Dec. 1937, Malé; m. Nasreena Ibrahim 1969; two s. two d. *Education:* Al-Azhar Univ., Cairo, Egypt. *Career:* Research Asst in Islamic History, American Univ. of Cairo 1967–69; Lecturer in Islamic Studies and Philosophy, Abdullahi Bayero Coll., Ahmadu Bello Univ., Nigeria 1969–71; teacher, Aminiya School 1971–72; Man. Govt Shipping Dept 1972–73; writer and trans., Press Office 1972–73, 1974; Under-Sec. Telecommunications Dept 1974; Dir Telephone Dept 1974; Special Under-Sec. Office of the Prime Minister 1974–75; Deputy Amb. to Sri Lanka 1975–76; Under-Sec. Dept of External Affairs 1976; Perm. Rep. to UN 1976–77; Deputy Minister of Transport 1976, Minister 1977–78; Pres. of Repub. of Maldives and C-in-C of the Armed Forces and of the Police 1978–; Gov. Maldives Monetary Authority 1981–2004; Minister of Defence and Nat. Security 1982–2004, of Finance 1989–93, of Finance and Treasury 1993–2004; mem. Constituent Council of Rabitat Al-Alam Al-Islami; Grand Order of Mugunghawa 1984, Hon. GCMG 1997; Hon. DLitt (Aligarh Muslim Univ. of India) 1983, Hon. DrLit (Jamia Millia Islamia Univ., India) 1990, Hon. DLit (Pondicherry Univ.) 1994; Global 500 Honour Roll (UNEP) 1988, Man of the Sea Award (Lega Navale Italiana) 1991, WHO Health-for-All Gold Medal 1998, DRV Int. Environment Award 1998, Al-Azhar Univ. Shield 2002. *Publication:* The Maldives: A Nation in Peril.

Address: The President's Office, Boduthakurufaanu Magu, Malé (office); Ma. Ki'nbigasdhoshuge, Malé, 20229 (home); The Presidential Palace (Theemuge), Orchid Magu, Malé, 20208, Maldives (Official Residence). *Telephone:* 3323701. *Fax:* 3325500. *E-mail:* info@presidencymaldives.gov.mv (office). *Website:* presidencymaldives.gov.mv (office).

GAZIT, Maj.-Gen. Shlomo; Israeli army officer and administrator; *Chairman, Galili Centre for Defence-Hagana Studies;* b. 1926, Turkey; m. Avigayil-Gala Gazit; one s. two d. *Education:* Tel-Aviv Univ. *Career:* joined Palmach 1944, Co. Commdr Harel Brigade 1948; Dir Office of Chief of Staff 1953; Liaison Officer with French Army Del., Sinai Campaign 1956; Instructor Israel Defence Forces (IDF) Staff and Command Coll. 1958–59; Gen. Staff 1960–61; Deputy Commdr Golani Brigade 1961–62; Instructor Nat. Defence Coll. 1962–64; Head IDF Intelligence assessment div. 1964–67; Co-ordinator of Govt Activities in Administered Territories, Ministry of Defence 1967–74; rank of Maj.-Gen. 1973; Head of Mil. Intelligence 1974–79; Fellow at Center for Int. Affairs, Harvard Univ. 1979–80; Pres. Ben Gurion Univ. of the Negev 1981–85; Dir-Gen. Jewish Agency, Jerusalem 1985–88; Sr Research Fellow Jaffee Centre for Strategic Studies, Tel-Aviv Univ. 1988–94; Fellow Woodrow Wilson Center, Washington, DC 1989–90; Distinguished Fellow US Inst. of Peace, Washington, DC 1994–95; Adviser to Israeli Prime Minister on Palestinian Peace Process 1995–96; Chair. Galili Centre for Defence-Hagana Studies 1996–. *Publications:* Estimates and Fortune-Telling in Intelligence Work 1980, Early Attempts at Establishing West Bank Autonomy 1980, Insurgency, Terrorism and Intelligence 1980, On Hostages' Rescue Operations 1981, The Carrot and the Stick – Israel's Military Govt in Judea and Samaria 1985, The Third Way – The Way of No Solution 1987, Policies in the Administered Territories 1988, Intelligence Estimates and the Decision Maker 1988, (ed.) The Middle East Military Balance 1988–89, 1990–91, 1993–94, Trapped Fools: 30 Years of Israeli Policy in Judea, Samaria and Gaza Strip, 2003, The Arab-Israeli Wars: War and Peace in the Middle East 1948–2005 2005.
Address: 58 Enzo Sireni Street, Kfar-Saba 44285, Israel (home). *Telephone:* (3) 6407719 (office); (9) 7466554 (home). *Fax:* (3) 6422404 (office); (9) 7477322 (home). *E-mail:* jcsssg@post.tau.ac.il (office).

GBAGBO, Laurent, MA, PhD; Côte d'Ivoirian head of state; *President;* b. 31 May 1945, Central-Western Prov.; m.; four c. *Education:* Univ. of Abidjan, Univ. of Lyon, Sorbonne, Paris VII Univ. *Career:* taught history and geography at Lycée Classique d'Abidjan 1970–71; imprisoned for unauthorized political activities 1971–73; worked in Dept of Educ. 1973–79; exile in France 1982–88; f. Front populaire Ivoirien (FPI) in secret 1982, FPI Sec.-Gen. 1988–1996; mem. Parl. for Ouragahio 1990–2000; arrested Feb. 1992, sentenced to three years' imprisonment under anti-riot law, granted presidential pardon Aug. 1992; Pres. of Côte d'Ivoire Oct. 2000–.
Address: Office of the President, 01 BP 1354 Abidjan 01, Côte d'Ivoire (office). *Telephone:* 20-22-02-22 (office). *Fax:* 20-21-14-25 (office). *Website:* www.presidence.ci (office).

GBIKPI-BENISSAN, Jean-Pierre; Togolese diplomatist. *Career:* Amb. to Ghana 2003–.
Address: Embassy of Togo, Togo House, near Cantonments Circle, POB C120, Accra, Ghana (office). *Telephone:* (21) 777950 (office). *Fax:* (21) 765659 (office). *E-mail:* togamba@ighmail.com (office).

GEIGER, Helmut; German banker and lawyer; b. 12 June 1928, Nuremberg; m.; one s. one d. *Education:* Univs of Erlangen and Berlin. *Career:* legal asst, Deutsche Bundestag and asst lawyer, Bonn 1957–59; lawyer in Bonn and man. of office of Öffentliche Bausparkassen 1959–66; Man. Dir Deutsche Sparkassen-und Giroverband 1966–72, Pres. 1972–93; Pres. Int. Inst. der Sparkassen (Int. Savings Bank Inst.), Geneva 1978–84; Pres. EEC Savings Banks Group, Brussels 1985–88; Chair. Sparkassenstiftung für Int. Kooperation 1992–98; mem. Bundestag 1965; mem. Admin. Bd Deutsche Girozentrale Int., Luxembourg, Kreditanstalt für Wiederaufbau, Frankfurt, Landwirtschaftliche Rentenbank, Frankfurt, Rhineland-Westphalian Inst. of Econ. Research, Essen; mem. Cen. Cttee, German Group, ICC; mem. Presidium, German Red Cross; Chair. and mem. of various charitable and professional bodies; Grand Fed. Cross of Merit; Dr hc (Cologne). *Publications:* Herausforderungen für Stabilität und Fortschritt 1974, Bankpolitik 1975, Gespräche über Geld 1986, Die deutsche Sparkassenorganisation 1992 and numerous pubs on banking matters.
Address: Simrockstr. 4, 53113 Bonn, Germany. *Telephone:* (228) 9703610.

GEINGOB, Hage Gottfried, MA; Namibian politician; *Executive Secretary, Global Coalition for Africa;* b. 3 Aug. 1941, Grootfontein Dist; m. Loine Kandume 1993; one s. three d. from previous marriage. *Education:* Augustineum Coll. Okahandja and studies in int. relations in USA. *Career:* joined South-West Africa People's Org. (SWAPO) 1962; teacher, Tsumeb 1962; exiled for political activities Dec. 1962; became SWAPO Asst Rep. Botswana 1963–64; subsequently moved to USA, studied at Fordham Univ. and New School for Social Research, New York and became SWAPO Rep. at UN –1971; mem. SWAPO Politburo 1975; Dir UN Inst. for Namibia, Lusaka, Zambia 1975–89; returned to Namibia as Election Dir 1989; Chair. Constituent Ass. and Namibia Independence Celebrations Cttee 1989; Prime Minister of Namibia 1990–2003; Exec. Sec. Global Coalition for Africa 2003–; Officier Palmes Académiques 1980, Ongulumbashe Medal for bravery and long service 1987; Hon. LLD (Col Coll., Chicago) 1994.
Address: Global Coalition for Africa, 1919 Pennsylvania Avenue, NW, Suite 550, Washington, DC 20006, USA. *Telephone:* (202) 458-4338 (office). *Fax:* (202) 522-3259 (office). *Website:* www.gca-cma.org (office).

GELB, Leslie; American defence and foreign affairs specialist; *President Emeritus, Council on Foreign Relations; Career:* Dir of Policy Planning and Arms Control, Dept of Defense 1967–69; Visiting Prof., Georgetown Univ. 1969–73; Sr Fellow, Brookings Inst. 1969–73; Asst Sec. of State for Political/Military Affairs 1977–79; Sr Assoc. Carnegie Endowment 1980–81; corresp., New York Times 1981–93; currently Pres. Emer. Council on Foreign Relations; Fellow, American Acad. of Arts and Sciences; APSA Woodrow Wilson book award, Pulitzer Prize in Explanatory Journalism 1985. *Publications include:* The Irony of Vietnam: the System Worked (jtly) 1980, Our Own Worst Enemy: The Unmaking of American Foreign Policy (jtly) 1984, Claiming the Heavens (jtly) 1988, Anglo-American Relations 1945–1950: Toward a Theory of Alliances 1988.
Address: Council on Foreign Relations, 58 East 68th Street, New York, NY 10021, USA (office). *Telephone:* (212) 434-9536 (office). *Fax:* (212) 434-9800 (office). *E-mail:* mstrauss@cfr.org (office). *Website:* www.cfr.org (office).

GELBARD, Robert Sidney, MPA; American diplomatist and consultant; *Chairman, Washington Global Partners LLC;* b. 6 March 1944, New York; m. Alene Marie Hanola 1968; one d. *Education:* Colby Coll., Harvard Univ. *Career:* volunteer Peace Corps, Bolivia 1964–66, Assoc. Dir, Philippines 1968–70; joined Foreign Service 1967, Staff Asst Sr Seminar in Foreign Policy 1967–68; Vice-Consul Porto Alegre, Brazil 1970–71, Prin. Officer 1971–72; int. economist Office of Devt Finance 1973–75, Office of Regional Political and Econ. Affairs 1976–78; First Sec. Embassy, Paris 1978–82; Deputy Dir Office of Western European Affairs, Washington, DC 1982–84; Dir Office of S African Affairs, Washington, DC 1984–85; Deputy Asst Sec. Bureau of Inter-American Affairs, Washington, DC 1985–88; Amb. to Bolivia 1988–91; Prin. Deputy Asst Sec. of State for Bureau of Inter-American Affairs 1991–93, Asst Sec. of State for Int. Narcotics and Law Enforcement Affairs 1993–97; Special Rep. for Implementation of the Dayton Peace Accords 1997–99; Amb. to Indonesia 1999–2001; Sr Vice-Pres. for Int. Affairs and Govt Relations, ICN Pharmaceuticals 2002; self-employed consultant 2002–05; Chair. Washington Global Pnrs LLC (business consulting firm) 2005–; mem. Bd of Dirs Viisage Tech. Inc.; mem. Museum of American Folk Art int. advisory council, NY, American Foreign Service Asscn, World Affairs Council of Washington, DC; mem. Bd of Trustees Colby Coll.; Hon. LLD; Distinguished Service Award, US State Dept 2002.
Address: c/o Board of Directors, Viisage Technology Inc., 1215 South Clark Street, Suite 1105, Arlington, VA 22202 (office); 371 Huntington Street NW, Washington, DC 20015, USA. *Telephone:* (21) 344-2211. *Fax:* (21) 380-5583 (office).

GELDYMYRADOV, Khojamyrat; Turkmenistan politician; *Deputy Prime Minister, responsible for Economic Affairs; Career:* Deputy Minister of Economy and Finance 2005–07, Co-ordinator of Int. Tech. aid to Turkmenistan 2005–07, Deputy Prime Minister responsible for Econ. Affairs 2007–.
Address: Ministry of Finance, 744000 Aşgabat, ul. 2008 4, Turkmenistan (office). *Telephone:* (12) 51-05-63 (office). *Fax:* (12) 51-18-23 (office).

GELETA, Bekele, BA, MEconSc; Ethiopian international organisation official; *Secretary-General, International Federation of Red Cross and Red Crescent Societies;* b. 1 July 1944; m. Tsehay Mulugeta; four s. *Education:* Addis Abba Univ., Univ. of Leeds, UK. *Career:* fmr Gen.-Man. Franco-Ethiopian Railway Co.; fmr Urban Devt Officer, Irish Concern Int.; fmr programme man. for Kenya and Somalia, Care Canada; fmr Amb. to Japan; fmr Vice-Minister of Transport and Communications; Sec.-Gen. Ethiopian Red Cross 1984–88; various positions within Int. Fed. of Red Cross and Red Crescent Socs (IFRC) 1996–2007 including Head of Africa Dept, Secr., Geneva, Deputy Head, IFRC del. to UN, New York, Head of regional del. in Bangkok, Gen.-Man. Int. Operations, Canadian Red Cross, Sec.-Gen. IFRC 2008–.

Address: International Federation of Red Cross and Red Crescent Societies, PO Box 372, 1211 Geneva, Switzerland (office). *Telephone:* 22734222 (office). *Fax:* 227330395 (office). *Website:* www.ifrc.org (office).

GELLEH, Ismael Omar; Djibouti head of state; *President and Commander-in-Chief of the Armed Forces;* b. 1947, Dire Dawa, Ethiopia. *Career:* joined gen. security dept, French police force 1968, rank of Police Insp. 1970; fmr Chief of Staff of Pres. Hassan Gouled Aptidon; mem. Rassemblement populaire pour le progrès (RPP), currently Pres.; Pres. of Djibouti and Commdr-in-Chief of the Armed Forces May 1999–.
Address: Office of the President, Djibouti, Republic of Djibouti.

GEMEDA, Gen. Abedula; Ethiopian army officer and politician; *Minister of Defence; Career:* career in Ethiopian Armed Forces, rank of Gen.; currently Minister of Defence.
Address: Minister of Defence, POB 125, Addis Ababa, Ethiopia (office). *Telephone:* (1) 445555 (office).

GENG, Huichang; Chinese government official; *Minister of State Security;* b. 1951, Hebei Prov. *Career:* Deputy Dir Univ. of Int. Relations, American Research Dept, Beijing Municipality 1985–90, Dir 1990–92; Head, China Inst. of Contemporary Int. Relations 1992–98; Vice-Minister of State Security 1998–2007, Minister of State Security 2007–; mem. 17th CPC, Cen. Cttee 2007–.
Address: Ministry of State Security, 14 Dongchangan Jie, Dongcheng Qu, Beijing 100741, People's Republic of China. *Telephone:* (10) 65244702.

GENSCHER, Hans-Dietrich; German politician; b. 21 March 1927, Reideburg, Saalkreis; m. 1st Luise Schweitzer 1958; m. 2nd Barbara Schmidt 1969; one d. *Education:* Leipzig and Hamburg Univs. *Career:* Scientific Asst, Parl. Free Democratic Party (FDP) 1956, later Sec., Hon. Chair. 1992–; Fed. Party Man. 1962–64, Vice-Chair. 1968–74, Chair. 1974–85; Deputy in Bundestag 1965–98; Fed. Minister of the Interior 1969–74; Vice-Chancellor, Minister of Foreign Affairs 1974–92; Chair. Bd of Dirs WMP Eurocom AG, Berlin 1998–; Counsel Büsing, Müffelmann & Theye, Berlin 1999–; Man. Partner Hans-Dietrich Genscher Consult GmbH 2000–; Pres. German Council on Foreign Relations 2001–03; Asscn Friends and Patrons State Opera, Berlin; Hon. Prof. Free Univ. of Berlin 1994, Peking 1999; Hon. Citizen of Costa Rica 1988; Freeman of Halle 1993, of Berlin 1997; Bundesverdienstkreuz 1973 and other medals; numerous Dr hc 1977–2002; Onassis Foundation Award 1991. *Publications:* Bundestagsreden 1972, Deutsche Aussenpolitik, Reden und Aufsätze aus 10 Jahren, 1974–84, Nach vorn gedacht... Perspektiven deutscher Aussenpolitik 1986, Erinnerungen (memoirs) 1995.
Address: Hans-Dietrich Genscher's Personal Office, Postfach 200 655, 53136 Bonn, Germany (office). *Fax:* (228) 264652 (office). *E-mail:* buero@genscher.de (office). *Website:* www.genscher.de (office).

GENTILINI, Fernando, LLB; Italian diplomatist; *Senior Civilian Representative in Afghanistan, NATO;* b. 2 March 1962, Subiaco, Rome. *Education:* Univ. of Rome. *Career:* Second Lt, Italian Army (Artillery) 1987; joined diplomatic service 1990, Second Sec. (Econs and Trade), Embassy in Addis Ababa 1992–95, First Sec. 1995–96; First Sec., Perm. Mission to EU, Brussels 1996–99, Rep. Policy Planning and Early Warning Unit, EU Council Secr. 1999–2000; Head of Unit for Western Balkans, Ministry of Foreign Affairs 2002–04; EU High Rep.'s Personal Rep. to Kosovo 2004; seconded to Policy Unit, Office of Sec.-Gen. and High Rep. for Common Foreign and Security Policy, Brussels 2004–06; Deputy Diplomatic Adviser to Prime Minister 2006–08; Sr Civilian Rep. in Afghanistan, NATO 2008–; Cavaliere Ufficiale dell'Ordine al Merito della Repubblica 2006.
Address: North Atlantic Treaty Organization (NATO), boulevard Léopold III, 1110 Brussels, Belgium (office). *Telephone:* (02) 707-50-41 (office). *Fax:* (02) 707-50-57 (office). *E-mail:* natodoc@hq.nato.int (office). *Website:* www.nato.int (office).

GEOGHEGAN-QUINN, Máire; Irish European Union official, politician and fmr business consultant; *Official, Court of Auditors of the European Communities;* b. 5 Sept. 1950, Carna, Co. Galway; m. John V. Quinn 1973; two s. *Education:* Carysfort Teacher Training Coll. Blackrock, Co. Dublin. *Career:* fmr primary school teacher; mem. Galway City Council 1985–92; mem. Dáil (Parl.) 1975–97; Parl. Sec. to Minister of Industry, Commerce and Energy 1977–78; Minister of State with responsibility for Consumer Affairs, Ministry of Industry, Commerce and Energy 1977–78; Minister for the Gaeltacht 1979–81; Minister of State with responsibility for Youth and Sport, Dept of Educ. March–Dec. 1982; Minister of State for European Affairs 1987, 1991; Minister for Tourism, Transport and Communications 1992, of Justice 1993; columnist Irish Times 1997–2000; consultant to several cos; mem. Audit Devt and Reports Group, Court of Auditors of the EC 2000–; fmr Chair. The Saffron Initiative; fmr Vice-Pres., Fianna Fáil;

fmr Dir (non-exec.) The Ryan Hotel Group, Aer Lingus; fmr TV broadcaster. *Publication:* The Green Diamond (novel) 1996.
Address: European Court of Auditors, 12 Rue Alcide de Gasperi, 1615 Luxembourg, Luxembourg (office). *Telephone:* 4398-45303 (office). *Fax:* 4398-46493 (office). *Website:* www.eca.eu.int (office).

GEORGE, Andrew Neil; British diplomatist; *Governor and Commander-in-Chief of Anguilla;* b. 9 Oct. 1952, Scotland; m. Watanalak George; one s. one d. *Career:* Desk Officer, S American Dept, FCO 1980–81, Second Sec., Chancery, Bangkok 1976–80, Desk Officer, West African Dept 1981–82, 1974–75, Under-Sec./Dir Gen. 1982–84, First Sec., Chancery, Canberra 1984–88, First Sec. and Head of Chancery, Bangkok 1988–92, Asst Head, Repub. of Ireland Dept 1993–94, Asst Head, Eastern Dept 1994–95, Head of Section, Counter Proliferation Dept 1995–98, Amb., Asencion 1998–2001, Commercial Counsellor, Jakarta 2002, Asst Dir with Human Resources Directorate 2003–05, Gov. and C-in-C of Anguilla 2006–.
Address: Government House, Old Ta, Anguilla (office). *Telephone:* 497-2621 (office). *Fax:* 497-3314 (office). *E-mail:* governorsoffice@gov.ai (office).

GEORGE, Rt Hon. Sir Edward Alan John, Kt, GBE, PC, MA; British banker; b. 11 Sept. 1938; m. Clarice Vanessa Williams 1962; one s. two d. *Education:* Dulwich Coll., Emmanuel Coll., Cambridge. *Career:* joined Bank of England 1962, seconded to BIS 1966–69, to IMF as Asst to Chair. of Deputies of Cttee of Twenty on Int. Monetary Reform 1972–74, Adviser on Int. Monetary Questions 1974–77, Deputy Chief Cashier 1977–80, Asst Dir Gilt-Edged Div. 1980–82, Exec. Dir 1982–90, Deputy Gov. 1990–93, Gov. 1993–2003; Chair. G10 Govs 1999–2003; Dir (non-exec.) Grosvenor Group 2003–, NM Rothschild, Rothschild Continuation Holdings 2003–; Hon. DSc (Econs) (Hull) 1993, (City) 1995, (Cranfield) 1997, (Manchester) 1998, (Buckingham) 2000; Hon. DLitt (Loughborough) 1994, (Sheffield) 1999; Hon. PhD (Guildhall, London) 1996; Hon. LLD (Exeter) 1997, (Bristol) 1999, (Hertfordshire) 1999, (Cambridge) 2000.
Address: c/o Grosvenor Group Holdings Limited, 70 Grosvenor Street, London, W1K 3JP, England.

GEORGE, Yosiwo P.; Micronesian diplomatist; *Ambassador to USA;* m. Antilise George; one s. one d. *Career:* held various positions in Govt of Trust Territory of the Pacific Islands (TTPI), Federated States of Micronesia (FSM) Nat. Govt as well as in State of Kosrae, including TTPI Social Security Admin., FSM Sec. of Social Services, Lt Gov., later Gov. of Kosrae, FSM Amb. to UN, Senator-at-Large in FSM Congress representing Kosrae, Chief Justice of Kosrae State Supreme Court, Exec. Dir FSM Health Insurance; Amb. to USA 2008–.
Address: Embassy of Micronesia, 1725 N Street, NW, Washington, DC 20036, USA (office). *Telephone:* (202) 223-4383 (office). *Fax:* (202) 223-4391 (office). *E-mail:* fsm@fsmembassy.org (office). *Website:* www.fsmembassy.org (office).

GEORGE TUPOU V, HM The King of Tonga; b. (Siaosi Taufa'ahau Manumataongo Tuku'aho Tupou), 4 May 1948. *Career:* proclaimed Crown Prince Tupouto'a 1966; Minister of Foreign Affairs 1979–98; co-founder and Dir Tonfon/Shoreline Group Ltd and Peau Vavau Airlines; succeeded to throne 10 September 2006 on the death of his father, crowned 23rd King of Tonga 1 Aug. 2008.
Address: The Palace, PO Box 6, Nuku'alofa, Tonga (office). *Website:* www.pmo.gov.to.

GEORGELIN, Gen. Jean-Louis; French military officer; *Chief of Defence Staff;* b. 30 Aug. 1948. *Education:* Mil. Acad. of St Cyr, Command and Gen. Staff Coll., Fort Leavenworth, Kan., Centre for Advanced Mil. Studies, Paris. *Career:* First Lt, Platoon Leader, 9th Airborne Infantry Battalion 1970–73; Instructor, Infantry School, Montpellier 1973–76; Capt. Co. Cadre, 153rd Infantry Battalion 1976–79; Dept of Mil. Intelligence 1979–80; Aide-de-camp to Army Chief of Staff 1980–82; promoted to Maj. 1982, to Lt Col 1985, to Col 1988; Chief of Financial Planning Office, Army Staff 1988–91; Commdr 153rd Infantry Battalion 1991–93; Army Asst to Chief of Mil. Cabinet of the Prime Minister 1994–97; promoted to Brig. Gen. 1997; Second-in-Command 11th Airborne Div., then Chief J5, Stabilisation Force (SFOR) in fmr Yugoslavia 1997–98; Chief of Plans and Programmes Div., Jt Defense HQ 1998–2001; promoted to Maj. Gen. 2000, to Lt Gen. 2002; Chief of Mil. Staff 2002–06; promoted to Gen. 2003; Chief of Defence Staff 2006–; Officier, Légion d'honneur, Ordre Nat. du Mérite.
Address: Ministry of Defence, 14 rue Saint Dominique, 75007 Paris, France (office). *Telephone:* 1-42-19-30-11 (office). *Fax:* 1-47-05-40-91 (office). *E-mail:* courrier-ministre@sdbc.defense.gouv.fr (office). *Website:* www.defense.gouv.fr (office).

GEORGESCU, Florin, PhD; Romanian politician and economist; b. 25 Nov. 1953, Bucharest. *Education:* Acad. of Econ. Studies, Bucharest. *Career:*

Fulbright Scholar, Kansas City Univ., USA 1991–92; Assoc. Prof., Acad. of Econ. Studies; Sec. of State, Ministry of Finance 1992, Minister of State 1992–96; mem. Chamber of Deputies (Social Democratic Party) for Olt Electoral Constituency 1996–, Pres. Chamber of Deputies Comm. for Budget, Finance and Banks 2000–, mem. Del. to Parl. Ass. of Black Sea Econ. Cooperation, Parl. Group of Friendship with Repub. of Slovenia 2000–, Pres. Parl. Group of Friendship with Repub. of Bulgaria 2000–; First Deputy Gov. and Vice-Chair. Nat. Bank of Romania. *Publications:* author of more than 200 studies and papers.
Address: Chamber of Deputies, Parliament Buildings, September 13 Avenue 1, Sector 5, 76117 Bucharest, Romania (office).

GERDTS, Michael H.; German diplomatist; *Ambassador to Poland;* b. 18 Aug. 1947, Bochum; m.; two c. *Education:* Univ. of Cologne, Pennsylvania State Univ., USA. *Career:* joined Ministry of Foreign Affairs 1980; mem. Del. to UN Disarmament Conf., New York and Geneva 1982–86; mem. Planning Staff, Ministry of Foreign Affairs 1986–88, Pvt. Sec. to Minister of Foreign Affairs 1988–93, Ministry Spokesman 1993–95; Amb. to Kenya 1995–99; Deputy Head of Dept of Global Affairs, UN, Human Rights and Humanitarian Aid, Ministry of Foreign Affairs 1999–2002, Head of Communications Dept 2002–04; Amb. to Italy and San Marino 2004–07, to Poland 2007–.
Address: Embassy of Germany, ul. Jazdów 12, 00-467 Warsaw, Poland (office). *Telephone:* (22) 5841700 (office). *Fax:* (22) 5841739 (office). *E-mail:* warszawa@wars.diplo.de (office). *Website:* www.ambasadaniemiec.pl (office).

GESTSSON, Svavar; Icelandic diplomatist; *Ambassador to Denmark;* b. 26 June 1944; m. Gurún Ágústsdóttir. *Career:* Ed.-in-Chief Thjodviljinn (daily newspaper) 1971–78; mem. Parl. 1978–99; Minister of Commerce and Int. Trade 1978–79, of Health and Social Affairs 1980–83, of Culture and Educ. 1988–91; Chair. People's Alliance Party 1980–87, Parl. Group of People's Alliance Party 1995–99; Chair. EFTA Ministers Jan.–June 1979; attended UN Gen. Ass. 1976, 1987, 1988, 1995; mem. Bd of Dirs Nat. Power Co. 1995–97, State Univ. Hosp. of Iceland 1991–94; Pres. Nordic Cultural Fund 1996–97; mem. IPU Icelandic Del. in Togo 1985, India 1993; mem. Parliamentarian Council of Iceland, Greenland and the Faroë Islands 1995–99, Pres. 1997–98; apptd Amb. in Icelandic Foreign Service 1999, Consul Gen. of Iceland and Special Envoy for Millennium Affairs, Winnipeg, Canada 1999–2001, Amb. to Sweden 2001–05 (also accred to Bulgaria, Serbia and Montenegro, and Albania 2002–05, to Bangladesh and Sri Lanka 2003–05), Amb. to Denmark 2005–. *Publications:* Sjónarrönd (Horizon), A Book of Political Affairs 1995; articles in all Icelandic and many Nordic papers.
Address: Embassy of Iceland, Strandgade 89, 1401 Copenhagen K, Denmark (office). *Telephone:* 33-18-10-50 (office). *Fax:* 33-18-10-59 (office). *E-mail:* icemb.coph@utn.stjr.is (office).

GETUGI, Japheth Ratemo, BA, MA; Kenyan diplomatist; *Ambassador to Uganda;* b. 17 April 1952; m.; four c. *Education:* Univ. of Delhi, India, Univ. of Nairobi. *Career:* Supervisor, Accounts Dept, Central Bank of Kenya, Nairobi 1974–80; Asst Sec., Ministry of Foreign Affairs 1984–86; Head of Chancery and First Sec., Embassy in Addis Ababa 1988–93; Acting Head, Africa Div. Ministry of Foreign Affairs 1993–94; Deputy Head of Mission and Counsellor, Embassy in Tel-Aviv 1997-2000; Deputy Head of Mission and Counsellor, High Commission to UK 2001; Amb to Rwanda (also accred to Burundi) 2002–05, to Uganda 2005–.
Address: Embassy of Kenya, 41 Nakasero Road, POB 5220, Kampala, Uganda (office); POB 43537, Nairobi, Kenya (home). *Telephone:* (41) 2258235 (office). *Fax:* (41) 2258239 (office). *E-mail:* kenhicom@africaonline.co.ug (office).

GEVORGIAN, Armen; Armenian politician; *Deputy Prime Minister and Minister of Territorial Administration;* b. 8 July 1973, Yerevan; m.; two sons. *Education:* Orenburg State Pedagogical Inst., St Petersburg Inst. of State Service, Tventey Univ., Netherlands, St Petersburg Gertsen Russian Pedagogical Inst. *Career:* Asst to Prime Minister 1997–98; Asst to Pres. of Armenia and First Deputy Head of Admin.1998–2000, First Asst to Pres. 2000–06; Head Pres.'s Admin. 2006–08; Sec., Nat. Security Council.2007–08; Deputy Prime Minister and Minister of Territorial Admin. 2008–; mem. CIS Econ.Council 2008–.
Address: Ministry of Territorial Administration, 0010 Yerevan, Republic Sq., Government House 2, Armenia (office). *Telephone:* (10) 51-13-02 (office). *Fax:* (10) 51-13-31 (home). *E-mail:* mta@mta.gov.am (office). *Website:* www.region.am (office).

GHADHBANE, Abd al-Moula el-; Libyan diplomatist. *Career:* currently Amb. to Algeria.

Address: Embassy of Libya, 15 chemin Cheikh Bachir Ibrahimi, Algiers, Algeria (office). *Telephone:* (21) 92-15-02 (office). *Fax:* (21) 92-46-87 (office).

GHAFARI, Yousif Boutrous, BA, MA, MS, MBA; American engineer, business executive and diplomatist; *Ambassador to Slovenia;* b. 27 Sept. 1952, southern Lebanon; m. Dr Mara Kalnins-Ghafari; three c. *Education:* Wayne State Univ., Michigan State Univ. Advanced Man. Program. *Career:* emigrated to USA early 1970s, US citizen 1978; licensed professional engineer 1984; Founder and Chair. GHAFARI (firm of architects, engineers, consultants and staffing specialists); Public Del. Designate, US Mission to UN for 59th UN Gen. Ass. 2004–05; apptd by Pres. George W. Bush to J. William Fulbright Foreign Scholarship Bd 2005; Founding mem. 'Partnership for Lebanon'; Amb. to Slovenia 2008–; named as one of the Top 100 Exec. Heroes in Southeastern Michigan 1995, mem. Int. Inst. of Metropolitan Detroit's Hall of Fame, residence bldg renamed Yousif B. Ghafari Hall by Wayne State Univ. 2005.
Address: Embassy of the US, Prešernova cesta 31, 1000 Ljubljana, Slovenia (office). *Telephone:* (1) 2005500 (office). *Fax:* (1) 2005555 (office). *E-mail:* usembassyljubljana@state.gov (office). *Website:* slovenia.usembassy.gov (office).

GHAI, Dharam Pal, PhD; Kenyan international civil servant and economist; b. 29 June 1936, Nairobi; m. Neela Korde 1963; one s. two d. *Education:* Queen's Coll., Oxford, UK and Yale Univ., USA. *Career:* Lecturer in Econs, Makerere Univ., Uganda 1961–65; Visiting Fellow, Econ. Growth Centre, Yale Univ. 1966–67; Research Prof. and Dir of Econs Research, Inst. of Devt Studies, Univ. of Nairobi 1967–71, Dir Inst. of Devt Studies 1971–74; Sr Economist, Comm. on Int. Devt (Pearson Comm.), Washington, DC 1968–69; Chief, World Employment Programme Research Br., Employment and Devt Dept, ILO, Geneva 1973–74, Chief, Tech. Secr., World Employment Conf. 1975–76, Chief, Rural Employment Policies Br., Employment and Devt Dept 1977–87; Dir UN Research Inst. for Social Devt (UNRISD) 1987–97; Coordinator ILO Transition Team 1998–99; Adviser Int. Inst. of Labour Studies; Fellow, African Acad. of Sciences. *Publications:* Collective Agriculture and Rural Development in Soviet Central Asia (with A. R. Khan) 1979, Planning for Basic Needs in Kenya (co-author) 1979, Agricultural Prices, Policy and Equity in Sub-Saharan Africa (with Lawrence Smith) 1987, Labour and Development in Rural Cuba (co-author) 1987, Social Development and Public Policy (ed.), Renewing Social and Economic Progress in Africa (ed.); co-ed. and contrib. to several other books.
Address: 32 chemin des Voirons, 1296 Coppet, Vaud, Switzerland (home). *Telephone:* (22) 7765281 (home). *Fax:* (22) 7765282 (home). *E-mail:* ghai@bluewin.ch (home).

GHAI, Yash P., BA, LLM, DCL; Kenyan constitutional lawyer, legal scholar and UN official; *Secretary-General's Special Representative for Human Rights in Cambodia, United Nations;* b. 1938. *Education:* Univ. of Oxford, UK, Harvard Univ., USA. *Career:* barrister, Middle Temple, London, UK 1962; Lecturer, Univ. of Dar-es-Salaam 1963–66, Sr Lecturer 1966–69, Prof. and Dean 1969–70; Sr Fellow and Lecturer, Yale Univ., USA 1971–73; Prof., Univ. of Warwick, UK 1974–89; Sir Y. K. Pau Prof. of Public Law, Univ. of Hong Kong 1989–; involved in drafting constitutions for Papua New Guinea, Fiji, Solomon Islands and others; Chair. Constitution of Kenya Review Comm. 2000–03; UN Sec.-Gen.'s Special Rep. for Human Rights in Cambodia 2005–; Distinguished Researcher Award, Univ. of Hong Kong 2001. *Publications include:* Hong Kong's New Constitutional Order: The Resumption of Chinese Sovereignty and Basic Law 1997, Hong Kong's Constitutional Debate: Conflict over Interpretation (co-author) 1999, Autonomy and Ethnicity: Negotiating Competing Claims in Multi-Ethnic States (ed. and contrib.) 2000, Public Participation and Minorities 2001.
Address: Department of Law, University of Hong Kong, Pokfulam Road, Hong Kong Special Administrative Region, People's Republic of China (office). *Telephone:* (852) 28592111 (office). *Fax:* (852) 28582549 (office). *E-mail:* hrllgyp@hkucc.hku.hk (office). *Website:* www.hku.hk (office).

GHANEM, Shokri Mohammed, MSc, PhD; Libyan politician and government official; *Chairman, National Oil Corporation (Libya);* b. 9 Oct. 1942, Tripoli; m.; one s. three d. *Education:* Univ. of Benghazi, Fletcher School of Econs, Boston, USA. *Career:* Head of American and European Affairs, Ministry of Econs 1963–65; Deputy Man. Translation Dept, Jamahiriya News Agency (JANA) 1966–68; Dir of Marketing and mem. Man. Council, Nat. Oil Corpn (NOC) 1968–70, Chair. 2006–; Gen. Man. of Econ. Man., Ministry of Oil 1970–75, Acting Minister of Oil 1975, Adviser 1975–77; Head of Econs, Arab Devt Inst. 1977–82; Visitor, SOAS, London 1982–84; Dir Econ. Studies Centre, Tripoli 1984–87; Lecturer, Dept of Econs, al-Jabel al-Gharbi Univ., Gharayan 1987–93; Research Man. OPEC, Vienna 1993–98, Acting Deputy to OPEC Sec. Gen. 1998–2001; Minister of Econs

and Trade 2001–03, Sec. of the Gen. People's Cttee (Prime Minister) 2003–06; Petroleum Exec. of the Year, International Herald Tribune and Oil and Money 2006. *Publications:* The Pricing of Libyan Crude Oil 1975, The Petrochemical Industry in the Arab World 1984, The Rise and Fall of an Exclusive Club 1985.
Address: National Oil Corporation (NOC), Bashir Saadawi Street, POB 2655, Tripoli, Libya (office). *Telephone:* (21) 3342900 (office). *Fax:* (21) 3339539 (office). *E-mail:* Info@noclibya.com (office). *Website:* www .noclibya.com (office).

GHANNOUCHI, Muhammad; Tunisian politician; *Prime Minister;* b. 1941. *Career:* fmr Minister of Finance and the Economy, of Int. Co-operation and Foreign Investment; Prime Minister of Tunisia 1999–.
Address: Bureau du Premier Ministre, La Kasbah, 1008 Tunis, Tunisia (office). *Telephone:* (71) 565-400 (office). *E-mail:* prm@ministeres.tn (office). *Website:* www.ministeres.tn (office).

GHAREKHAN, Shri Chinmaya R.; Indian diplomatist; *Special Envoy for West Asia and Middle East Peace Process, Ministry of External Affairs; Career:* Perm. Rep. to UN, New York 1986–92; Special Rep. of UN Sec. Gen. to Security Council 1992–96; UN Special Coordinator in Occupied Territories 1997–99; Special Envoy for W Asia and Middle E Peace Process, Ministry of External Affairs 2005–; Pres. Indira Gandhi Nat. Centre for the Arts 2007–; fmr Additional Sec., Office of Prime Minister; fmr mem. UN Expert Budget Cttee.
Address: Indira Gandhi National Centre for the Arts, 1, C. V. Mess, Janpath, New Delhi 110 001; C 362, Defence Colony, New Delhi 110 024, India. *Website:* ignca.nic.in.

GHARIANI, Muhammad; Tunisian diplomatist; m. Olfa Ghariani. *Career:* activist in youth wing of Democratic Constitutional Rally (RCD) 1980s, Sec.-Gen. RCD Students' party 1987, Deputy Sec.-Gen. for Youth, Educ. and Culture 1995–96; mem. Econ. and Social Council 1992–96; Gov. southern Tunisian prov. of Sidi Bouzid 1996–2001; Deputy Sec.-Gen. for Relations with Orgs and Asscns 2001–05; Amb. to UK (also accred to Ireland) 2005–07.
Address: Ministry of Foreign Affairs, avenue de la Ligue des états arabes, Tunis, Tunisia (office). *Telephone:* (71) 847-500 (office). *E-mail:* mae@ ministeres.tn (office). *Website:* www.diplomatie.gov.tn (office).

GHARIBJANIAN, Gegham; Armenian diplomatist; *Deputy Foreign Minister;* b. 1951, Yerevan. *Education:* Yerevan State Univ., Univ. of Calif., USA. *Career:* joined Ministry of Foreign Affairs, worked in Cttee on Cultural Links with Diaspora 1973–91; translator in Iran 1978–81; Deputy Minister of Labor and Social Security 1991–95; Deputy Nat. Ass. 1995–99, Deputy Chair. Standing Cttee on Social, Health and Environmental Issues 1995–97, Chair. 1997–1999, Chair.–Founder Social State deputy group; Amb. to Iran 1999–2005; Deputy Foreign Minister 2005–.
Address: Ministry of Foreign Affairs, 375010 Yerevan, Republic Square, Government House 2, Armenia (office). *Telephone:* (10) 52-35-31 (office). *Fax:* (10) 54-39-25 (office). *E-mail:* info@armeniaforeignministry.com (office). *Website:* www.armeniaforeignministry.am (office).

GHASIMI, Mohammad Reza, PhD; Iranian banker; *Economist, Poverty Reduction Economic Management Unit, International Bank for Reconstruction and Development, World Bank Group;* b. 5 June 1947, Tehran; m. Shahrbanoo Nawabi 1980; one d. *Education:* Univ. of Cambridge, London School of Econs, Univ. of Lancaster, UK. *Career:* Deputy Dir Econ. Research Dept, Cen. Bank of Iran 1976–78, Dir 1979–86; Dir-Gen. Econ. Policy Dept, Ministry of Econ. Affairs and Finance 1978–79; Asst to Exec. Dir, World Bank 1986–88, Advisor to Exec. Dir 1988, currently Economist, Poverty Reduction and Econ. Man. Unit; Exec. Dir IMF 1988–90. *Publications:* Boosting Non-Oil Exports 1975, A Marketing Strategy for Exports 1975, An Investigation of the Instruments of Monetary Policy 1985, A Textbook on Macroeconomics 1986, numerous articles.
Address: Poverty Reduction and Economic Management Unit, International Bank for Reconstruction and Development, 1818 H Street, NW, Washington, DC 20433, USA. *Website:* www.worldbank.org.

GHAZZALI, Dato' Sheikh Abdul Khalid, BEcons; Malaysian diplomatist; *Ambassador-at-Large, Ministry of Foreign Affairs;* b. 20 March 1946; m. Datin Faridah Ghazzali. *Education:* Univ. of La Trobe, Australia. *Career:* fmr Deputy Perm. Rep. to UN and Security Council, New York, fmr Deputy High Commr to UK, fmr High Commr to Zimbabwe, fmr Dir-Gen. Inst. of Diplomacy and Foreign Relations, Malaysia, fmr Deputy Sec.-Gen., Ministry of Foreign Affairs, Amb. to USA 1999–2006, Amb.-at-Large, Ministry of Foreign Affairs 2006–.
Address: Ministry of Foreign Affairs (Kementerian Luar Negeri), Wisma Putra, 1 Jalan Wisma Putra, Presint 2, 62602 Putrajaya, Malaysia (office).

Telephone: (3) 88874000 (office). *Fax:* (3) 88891717 (office). *E-mail:* webmaster@kln.gov.my (office). *Website:* www.kln.gov.my (office).

GHEBREMARIAM, Ghirmai; Eritrean diplomatist; *Ambassador to USA. Career:* Chair. Del. at High-Level Plenary Meeting of 60th Session of UN Gen. Ass., New York 2005, Amb. (non-resident) to Ireland 2002–03, to USA (also accred to Canada) 2006–.
Address: Embassy of Eritrea, 1708 New Hampshire Avenue, NW, Washington, DC 20009, USA (office). *Telephone:* (202) 319-1991 (office). *Fax:* (202) 319-1304 (office). *E-mail:* embassyeritrea@embassyeritrea.org (office). *Website:* www.embassyeritrea.org (office).

GHEBREZGHI, Negassi Sengal; Eritrean diplomatist; m. Saba Asefaw Gebrehiwet. *Career:* Amb. to UK 2003–07, also accred to Ireland 2004–07.
Address: Ministry of Foreign Affairs, PO Box 190, Asmara, Eritrea (office). *Telephone:* (1) 127838 (office). *Fax:* (1) 123788 (office). *E-mail:* tesfai@wg .eol (office).

GHEIT, Ahmed Aboul, BSc; Egyptian diplomatist; *Minister of Foreign Affairs;* b. 12 June 1942, Heliopolis; m.; two c. *Education:* Ainshams Univ., Cairo. *Career:* joined Ministry of Foreign Affairs 1965; Attaché-Third Sec., Embassy in Cyprus 1968–72; staff mem. of Adviser to Pres. on Nat. Security Affairs 1972–74; Second-First Sec., Perm. Mission to UN, New York 1974–77; Counsellor, Special Aide, Cabinet of Minister of Foreign Affairs 1977–79; Political Counsellor, Embassy in Moscow 1979–82; Political Adviser to Minister of Foreign Affairs 1982–84, 1989–90, to Prime Minister 1984–85; Counsellor, Perm. Mission to UN 1985–87, Deputy Perm. Rep. 1987–89; Chef de Cabinet, Minister of Foreign Affairs 1990–92, Asst Foreign Minister for Cabinet Affairs 1996–99; Amb. to Italy, Macedonia, San Marino and Rep. to FAO, Rome 1992–96; Perm. Rep. to UN 1999–2004; Minister of Foreign Affairs 2004–.
Address: Ministry of Foreign Affairs, Corniche en-Nil, Cairo (Maspiro), Egypt (office). *Telephone:* (2) 5746871 (office). *Fax:* (2) 5747839 (office). *E-mail:* info@mfa.gov.eg (office). *Website:* www.mfa.gov.eg (office).

GHIBERNEA, Dan; Romanian politician and diplomatist; b. 15 Sept. 1954; m. Tania Filip. *Education:* Univ. of Paris (Sorbonne), France and Univ. of Bucharest. *Career:* trans. for CONECT 1977–80; on staff, Academia de Ştiinţe Sociale 1980–90, Academia Română 1990–93; fmr Gen. Man. media group Lagardiere; mem. Parl. (Parl. group of the Social Democracy Party of Romania) 1993–2000 (resgnd), fmr Head of Foreign Relations Dept, Chamber of Deputies, mem. Standing Cttee for Foreign Policy –2000, mem. Exec. Bd of Romanian Group to the Inter-Parl. Union –2000; fmr Rep. of American Foundation IREX (Int. Research and Exchanges Bd); Amb. to UK 2002–08.
Address: Ministry of Foreign Affairs, Al. Alexandru 31, 011822 Bucharest, Romania (office). *Telephone:* (21) 3192108 (office). *Fax:* (21) 3196862 (office). *E-mail:* mae@mae.ro (office). *Website:* www.mae.ro (office).

GHOBASH, Saqr Ghobash Saeed; United Arab Emirates diplomatist and politician; *Minister of Labour; Education:* UAE Univ., participated in leadership courses at Harvard Univ., USA. *Career:* served in Ministry of the Interior for over 25 years, first beginning as a police officer 1973, f. Police Coll., Abu Dhabi 1985; Deputy Chief UAE Football Asscn –1990; Under-Sec., Ministry of Information and Culture 1998–2006; Amb. to USA 2006–08; Minister of Labour 2008–; fmr mem. Bd of Dirs CODIFY Systems Inc.
Address: Ministry of Labour, PO Box 809, Abu Dhabi, United Arab Emirates (office). *Telephone:* (2) 6931100 (office). *Fax:* (2) 6665889 (office). *E-mail:* minister@mol.gov.ae (office). *Website:* www.mol.gov.ae (office).

GHOZALI, Sid Ahmed; Algerian politician and petroleum executive; *Chairman, Front Démocratique;* b. 31 March 1937, Marnia. *Education:* Ecole des Ponts et Chaussées, Paris. *Career:* fmr Dir of Energy, Ministry of Industry and Energy; Adviser, Ministry of the Economy 1964; Under-Sec., Ministry of Public Works 1964–65; Pres., Dir-Gen. Soc. nationale pour la recherche, la production, le transport, la transformation et la commercialisation des hydrocarbures (SONATRACH) 1966–84, Chair., Man. Dir; Minister of Hydraulics March–Oct. 1979, of Foreign Affairs 1989–91; Prime Minister of Algeria 1991–92; Amb. to Belgium 1987–89, to France 1992–93; mem. Cen. Cttee Front de Libération Nat.; Chair. Front Démocratique 2000–; mem. Org. technique de mise en valeur des richesses du sous-sol saharien 1962.
Address: Front Démocratique, Algiers, Algeria (office).

GIAMBASTIANI, Adm. Edmund P. Jr; American naval officer; b. Canastota, New York. *Education:* US Naval Acad. *Career:* career in US Armed Forces; assignments included Program Man. Navy Recruiting Command HQ, Washington, DC, Special Asst to Deputy Dir of

Intelligence, CIA, Deputy Chief of Staff for Resources, Warfare Requirements and Assessments, US Pacific Fleet, Dir Submarine Warfare Div., Naval Operations, Deputy Chief of Naval Operations for Resources, Requirements and Assessments; fmr Commdr Submarine NR-1 (nuclear-powered deep diving submarine), USS Richard B. Russell (nuclear-powered attack submarine); fmr Leader Submarine Devt Squadron Twelve; fmr First Dir Strategy and Concepts, Naval Doctrine Command; fmr Commdr Atlantic Fleet Submarine Force, Anti-Submarine and Reconnaissance Forces Atlantic; Sr Mil. Asst to Sec. of Defense Donald Rumsfeld (q.v.) –2003; Commdr US Jt Forces Command and Supreme Allied Commdr Transformation (SACT), NATO 2003–05; Vice Chair. Jt Chiefs of Staff, Washington DC 2005–07, also served as Chair. Joint Requirements Oversight Council, Vice Chair. Defense Acquisition Bd, mem. Nat. Security Council Deputies Cttee, Nuclear Weapons Council; numerous awards including Defense Distinguished Service Medal, Joint Meritorious Unit Award, eight Battle Efficiency E's, five Navy Unit Commendations, five Navy Meritorious Unit Commendations.
Address: c/o Office of the Vice Chairman of the Joint Chiefs of Staff, 9999 Joint Staff, Pentagon, Washington, DC 20318-9999, USA (office).

GIANELLI DEROIS, Carlos Alberto, MA, LLD; Uruguayan diplomatist; *Ambassador to USA;* b. 7 March 1948; m.; three c. *Education:* Crandon Inst., Montevideo, Law and Social Studies School, Universidad de la República, Montevideo, Bariloche Foundation, Argentina, Artigas Inst. of Foreign Service of Uruguay. *Career:* held posts in Econ. Integration Dept, Ministry of Foreign Affairs 1979–81, Int. Tech. Cooperation Dept, Pres. of the Repub. 1981–82, IDB, Washington, DC 1983–84; Head of Cabinet for Sec.-Gen. of Org. of Latin American Econ. Integration 1984–87; Alt. Rep. to UN, New York 1987–91, Amb. to Saudi Arabia (also accred to UAE, Kuwait and Oman) 1991–93, Dir-Gen. for Political Affairs, Ministry of Foreign Affairs 1993–95, Amb. to Mexico (also accred to the Bahamas) 1995–2000, Dir-Gen. Int. Econ. Affairs, Ministry of Foreign Affairs and Coordinator of the Free Trade Agreement Negotiations with Mexico 2000–03, Amb. to the Netherlands and Perm. Rep. to OPCW and Int. Criminal Court 2003–05, to USA 2005–; Order of the Aztec Eagle (Mexico), Grand' Ufficiale (Italy), Order of Baron of Rio Branco (Brazil), Order Bernardo O'Higgins (Chile).
Address: Embassy of Uruguay, 1913 I Street, NW, Washington, DC 20006, USA (office). *Telephone:* (202) 331-1313 (office). *Fax:* (202) 331-8142 (office). *E-mail:* uruwashi@uruwashi.org (office). *Website:* www.uruwashi.org (office).

GIBSON, Phillip, BA; New Zealand diplomatist; *Ambassador to Indonesia;* b. 25 Aug. 1949; m.; two s. *Education:* Otago Univ. *Career:* career with NZ Diplomatic Service; overseas assignments in Manila, New York and Rome; fmr Amb. to Thailand (also accred to Viet Nam, Cambodia, Laos and Myanmar); Exec. Dir of Asia 2000 –1999; Amb. to Japan 1999–2004; NZ Commr Gen. for Aicho Expo 2005; Amb. to Indonesia 2006–.
Address: Embassy of New Zealand, Bri II Building, 23rd Floor, Jl. Jend. Sudirman Kav. 44–46, Jakarta 10210, Indonesia (office). *Telephone:* (21) 5709460 (office). *Fax:* (21) 5709457 (office); (3) 3467-2278 (home). *E-mail:* nzembjak@cbn.net.id (office). *Website:* www.nzembassy.com/home.cfm?c=41 (office).

GIDADA, Negaso, MA, PhD; Ethiopian fmr head of state and politician; b. 8 Sept. 1943, Dembi Dollo, Wollega; m. Regina Abelt; one s. two d. *Education:* Addis Ababa Univ., Johann Wolfgang Goethe-Universität, Frankfurt. *Career:* Minister of Labour and Social Affairs 1991–92, Minister of Information 1992–95, Pres. of Ethiopia 1995–2001; mem. House of Reps 2005–; Interreligious and Int. Fed. for World Peace Amb. for Peace, Int. Lions Club Melvin Jones Fellow. *Publications:* History of the Sayo Oromo of Southwestern Wollega, Ethiopia 2001.
Address: House Number 695, Qabele 22, Bole Kifle Ketama, Addis Ababa (home); House Number 1031, Nefas Silk-Lafto Kifle Ketama, Addis Ababa (home); PO Box 26749, C-1000, Addis Ababa, Ethiopia (office). *Telephone:* (1) 231213 (office); (1) 247625 (office). *E-mail:* nereta2003@yahoo.com (home).

GIESBERT, Franz-Olivier; French journalist and writer; *Editor, Le Point;* b. 18 Jan. 1949, Wilmington, Del., USA; m. 1st Christine Fontaine (divorced); two s. one d.; m. 2nd Natalie Freund 2000; one s., one d. *Education:* Centre de Formation des Journalistes. *Career:* journalist at Le Nouvel Observateur 1971, Sr Corresp. in Washington, DC 1980, Political Ed. 1981, Ed.-in-Chief 1985–88; Ed.-in-Chief Le Figaro 1988–2000, Figaro Magazine 1997–2000, mem. Editorial Bd Le Figaro 1993–2000, Figaro Magazine 1997–2000; Ed. Le Point 2000–; Dir/presenter 'le Gai savoir' TV programme, Paris Première cable channel 1997–2001, Dir Culture et Dépendances France 3 TV channel 2001–; mem. jury Prix Théophraste Renaudot 1998–, Prix Louis Hachette, Prix Aujourd'hui; mem. Conseil Admin Musée du Louvre Paris 2000; Aujourd'hui Best Essay Prize 1975, Prix Gutenberg 1987, Prix

Pierre de Monaco 1997, Prix Richelieu 1999, Prix Itheme for Best Talk Show 1999. *Publications:* François Mitterrand ou la tentation de l'Histoire (essay) 1977, Monsieur Adrien (novel) 1982, Jacques Chirac (biog.) 1987, Le Président 1990, L'Affreux (Grand Prix du Roman de l'Acad. Française) 1992, La Fin d'une Époque 1993, La Souille (William the Conqueror and Interallie Prize), Le Vieil homme et la Mort 1996, François Mitterrand, une vie 1996, Le Sieur Dieu (Prix Jean d'Heurs de Nice Baie des Anges) 1998, Mort d'un berger 2002, L'Abatteur 2003, La Tragédie du président: scènes de la vie politique 2006.
Address: Le Point, 74 avenue du Maine, 75682 Paris Cedex, France. *Telephone:* 1-44-10-10-10 (office). *Fax:* 1-44-10-12-49 (office). *E-mail:* fogiesbert@lepoint.tm.fr (office).

GIFFORD, Michael (Mike); British diplomatist; b. 2 April 1961; m. Patricia Gifford; one s. one d. *Career:* joined FCO 1981, S Asian Dept 1982–83, Third Sec. (Commercial), Abu Dhabi 1983–87, full-time language training 1987–88, Second Sec., Chancery, Oslo 1988–90, on secondment to EC 1990–91, EC Dept (External), FCO 1991–93, First Sec. (Econ.), Riyadh 1993–96, Middle East Dept, FCO 1996–99, Counter-Terrorism Policy Dept 1999–2000, Deputy Head of Mission, Cairo 2001–04, Amb. to Yemen 2005–07.
Address: Foreign and Commonwealth Office, King Charles Street, London, SW1A 2AH, England (office). *Telephone:* (20) 7008-1500 (office). *Website:* www.fco.gov.uk (office).

GILLANI, Makhdoom Syed Yousaf Raza, BA, MA; Pakistani politician; *Prime Minister;* b. 9 June 1952, Karachi; m. Elahi Gilani; four s. one d. *Education:* La Salle High School, Multan, Univ. of the Punjab, Lahore. *Career:* mem. Pakistan People's Party 1988–, Sr Vice-Chair. 1998–; mem. Cen. Leadership Muslim League, Pakistan 1978; cabinet mem. in three-year govt of Prime Minister Muhammad Khan Junejo, Minister of Housing and Works 1985–86, of Railways Jan.–Dec. 1986; Chair. Dist Council, Multan; mem. Nat. Ass. from Multan 1985–, Speaker 1993–97; served in cabinet of fmr Prime Minister, the late Benazir Bhutto, as Minister of Tourism 1989–90, of Housing and Works Jan.–Jan. 1990; tried on charges of abusing his authority by govt anti-corruption agency 1997, accused of putting more than 500 unqualified people from his constituency on govt payroll when he was House Speaker, imprisoned 2001–06; Prime Minister of Pakistan 2008–. *Publication:* Reflections of Yusuf's Well.
Address: Office the Prime Minister's Secretariat, Constitution Avenue, F-6/5, Cabinet Division, Cabinet Block, Islamabad, Pakistan (office). *Telephone:* (51) 9206111 (office); (51) 925190512 (office). *E-mail:* contact@cabinet.gov.pk (office). *Website:* www.cabinet.gov.pk (office).

GILAURI, Nikoloz (Nika), BA, MA; Georgian economist and politician; *Minister of Finance;* b. 1975, Tbilisi. *Education:* Ivane Javakhishvili Tbilisi State Univ., Bournemouth Coll., UK, Limerick Univ., Ireland, Temple Univ., Philadelphia, USA, Univs of Paris and Tokyo. *Career:* worked at Dublin Int. Finance Centre as an Admin./Man. Invesco assets man. corpn 1999; financial consultant for energy conservation projects at Philadelphia Small Business Devt Center 2000; financial consultant, Georgia Telecom 2001; financial consultant, Spanish corpn Iberdrola (Georgian energy market man. contractor) 2002; worked for SBE (Ireland) as man. contractor and financial controller of Georgian state electricity 2003–04; Minister of Energy 2004–07, of Finance 2007–.
Address: Ministry of Finance, Irakli Abashidze 70, 0162 Tbilisi, Georgia (office). *Telephone:* (32) 22-68-05 (office). *Fax:* (32) 93-19-22 (office). *E-mail:* minister@mof.ge (office). *Website:* www.mof.ge (office).

GILIOMEE, Hermann Buhr, MA, DPhil; South African university professor and political columnist; *Extraordinary Professor of History, University of Stellenbosch;* b. 4 April 1938, Sterkstroom; m. Annette van Coller 1965; two d. *Education:* Porterville High School and Univ. of Stellenbosch. *Career:* diplomatic service 1963–64; Lecturer in History, Univ. of Stellenbosch 1967–83, Extraordinary Prof. of History 2002–; Prof. of Political Studies, Univ. of Cape Town 1983–2002; recipient of Fellowships to Yale Univ., USA 1977–78, Univ. of Cambridge, UK 1982–83, Woodrow Wilson Center for Int. Scholars, Washington, DC 1992–93; Pres. South African Inst. of Race Relations 1995–97; f. Die Suid-Afrikaan journal 1984; political columnist for Cape Times, Rand Daily Mail, and other periodicals 1980–97, presently writing political column for Die Burger, Beeld and Volksblad morning newspapers; Stals Prize for Political Sciences 2001, Stals Prize for History 2004. *Publications:* The Shaping of South African Society 1652–1820 1979, Ethnic Power Mobilized: Can South Africa Change? 1979, Afrikaner Political Thought 1750–1850 1983, Up Against the Fences: Poverty, Passes and Privilege 1985, From Apartheid to Nation-building 1990, The Bold Experiment: South Africa's New Democracy 1994, Liberal and Populist Democracy in South Africa 1996, Surrender Without Defeat 1997, The Awkward Embrace: Dominant-Party Rule and Democracy in Semi-Industrialized Countries 1999, Kruispad 2001, The Afrikaners – Biography of a People 2003, Die Afrikaners: in Biografie 2004. *Address:* 5 Dennerandweg, Stellenbosch 7600, South Africa (home). *Telephone:* (21) 8832964 (home). *Fax:* (21) 8878026 (home). *E-mail:* hgiliome@mweb.co.za (home).

GILLERMAN, Dan; Israeli economist and diplomatist; *Permanent Representative, United Nations;* b. 26 March 1944; m. Janice Gillerman; two c. *Education:* Tel-Aviv Univ., Hebrew Univ. of Jerusalem. *Career:* Chair. Fed. of Israeli Chambers of Commerce 1985–; fmr mem. Prime Minister's Nat. Econ. and Social Council, Pres.'s Cttee of Coordinating Council of Israel's Econ. Orgs; Chair. Israel-British Business Council; mem. Exec. Cttee ICC; mem. Bd of Dirs First Int. Bank of Israel, Bank Leumi, Central Bank of Israel; CEO Nagum Ltd, Agrotechnology Ltd –2003; Perm. Rep. to UN 2003–; Dr hc Netanya Academic Coll., Bar-Ilan Univ.; Int. Friendship Award, Fed. Law Enforcement Foundation, Golden Eagle Diplomat Wings of Law Award, Respect for Law Alliance. *Address:* Permanent Representative of Israel to the United Nations, 800 Second Avenue, New York, NY 10017, USA (office). *Telephone:* (212) 499-5510 (office). *Fax:* (212) 499-5516 (office). *E-mail:* info-un@newyork.mfa .gov.il (office). *Website:* www.israel-un.org (office).

GILLIES, Rowan, MBBS; Australian physician and international organization official; *President, Médecins Sans Frontières;* b. 1971, Longueville. *Career:* fmr Surgical Registrar, Mona Vale Hosp., Sydney; with Médecins Sans Frontières (MSF) 1998–, postings included Liberia, Sudan, Sierra Leone, Afghanistan, Pres. Feb. 2004–. *Address:* Médecins Sans Frontières, Rue de Lausanne 78, CP 116, 1211 Geneva 21, Switzerland (office). *Telephone:* (22) 8498400 (office). *Fax:* (22) 8498404 (office). *Website:* www.msf.org (office).

GILPIN, Robert G., BA, MS. PhD; American economist and academic; *Eisenhower Professor of Public and International Affairs Emeritus, Woodrow Wilson School of Public and International Affairs, Princeton University;* m.; three c. *Education:* Univ. of Vermont, Cornell Univ., Univ. of Calif., Berkeley. *Career:* Faculty mem., Princeton Univ. 1962–, now Eisenhower Prof. of Public and Int. Affairs Emer., Woodrow Wilson School of Public and Int. Affairs; fmr Congressional Fellow, American Political Science Asscn, also Vice-Pres.; fmr Fellow, Guggenheim Foundation, Rockefeller Foundation (twice), Abe Foundation, Lehrman Foundation, Science and Public Policy Program, Harvard Univ.; fmr Vice-Pres. American Acad. of Arts and Sciences. *Publications include:* Global Political Economy: The Challenge of Global Capitalism, American Scientists and Nuclear Weapons Policy, France in the Age of the Scientific State, US Power and the Multinational Corporation, War and Change in World Politics, The Political Economy of International Relations (Best New Professional and Scholarly Book in Business, Man. and Econ, Woodrow Wilson Foundation Book Award for best book in political science 1988) 1987. *Address:* c/o Woodrow Wilson School of Public and International Affairs, Princeton University, Princeton, NJ 08544-1013, USA (office). *E-mail:* rggilpin@princeton.edu (office). *Website:* www.wws.princeton.edu (office).

GIRARD, Jean-François, MD, MSc; French civil servant and professor of medicine; *President, Institut de recherche pour le développement;* b. 20 Nov. 1944, Luçon (Vendée); one s. two d. *Education:* Univ. of Paris. *Career:* Prof. of Medicine 1979–97; Dir-Gen. Ministry of Health 1986–97; Chair. Exec. Council WHO 1992, 1993; Conseiller d'Etat 1997–; Pres. Inst. de recherche pour le développement 2001–; Chevalier, Légion d'honneur, Commdr, Ordre nat. du Mérite. *Publications:* Quand la santé devient publique 1998, La maladie d'Alzheimer 2000. *Address:* Institut de recherche pour le développement, 213 rue La Fayette, 75010 Paris, France (office). *Telephone:* 1-48-03-77-48 (office). *Fax:* 1-48-03-77-42 (office). *E-mail:* president@ird.fr (office). *Website:* www.ird.fr (office).

GIRARD-diCARLO, David F., BA, JD; American diplomatist; *Ambassador to Austria; Education:* St Joseph's Univ., Villanova Univ. School of Law. *Career:* fmr Chair. Bd and Chair. Exec. Cttee Greater Phila. Chamber of Commerce; fmr Man. Pnr, later Chair. Blank Rome, LLP (law firm); Amb. to Austria 2008–. *Address:* US Embassy, Boltzmanngasse 16, 1090 Vienna, Austria (office). *Telephone:* (1) 31339-0 (office). *Fax:* (1) 310-06-82 (office). *E-mail:* embassy@usembassy.at (office). *Website:* vienna.usembassy.gov (office).

GIRARDET, Herbert, BSc (Econs); German ecologist, consultant, writer and television producer; *Director of Programmes, World Future Council;* b. 25 May 1943, Essen; m. Barbara Hallifax 1967; two s. *Education:* Tübingen and Berlin Univs, London School of Econs, UK. *Career:* consultant to Town and Country Planning Asscn, London 1976–86, Channel 4 TV, London 1987–89, UN Habitat II Conf., Istanbul 1995–96; Visiting Prof. of

Environmental Planning, Middx Univ. 1995–; Visiting Prof. of Sustainable Urban Devt, Univ. of Northumbria 2003–; Visiting Prof. of Cities and the Environment, Univ. of the W of England 2004–; Thinker-in-Residence, Adelaide 2003; Dir Under the Sky Urban Regeneration Co., Bristol 2004–; Dir of Programmes World Future Council 2004–; mem. Balaton Group of int. environment experts 1993–; Chair. The Schumacher Soc., UK 1994–; Trustee, The Sustainable London Trust 1996–; Patron The Soil Asscn, UK 1990–; Hon. FRIBA 2000; UN Global Award for Outstanding Environmental Achievements, prizes for TV documentaries. *Television:* initiator and researcher: Far from Paradise (series) 1983–86; writer and producer: Jungle Pharmacy 1988, Halting the Fires 1989, Metropolis 1994, Urban Best Practices 1996, Deadline (28 three-minute films) 1997–99; series consultant: The People's Planet 1999–2000. *Publications:* Far From Paradise: The Story of Human Impact on the Environment (co-author) 1986, Blueprint for a Green Planet (co-author) 1987, Earthrise 1992, The Gaia Atlas of Cities 1992, Making Cities Work (co-author) 1996, Getting London in Shape for 2000 1997, Creating a Sustainable London (co-author) 1998, Creating Sustainable Cities 1999, Tall Buildings and Sustainable Development (co-author) 2001, Creating a Sustainable Adelaide 2003, Cities, People, Planet 2004, Shanghai Dongtan: An Ecocity (co-author) 2006, Surviving the Century (ed.) 2007. *Address:* Trafalgar House, 11 Waterloo Place, London, SW1Y 4AU, England (office); Forest Cottage, Trelleck Road, Tintern, Chepstow, Monmouthshire, NP16 6SN, Wales (home). *Telephone:* (20) 7863-8833 (office); (1291) 689392 (home). *Fax:* (20) 7389-5162 (office); (1291) 689392 (home). *E-mail:* herbie@worldfuturecouncil.org (office). *Website:* www .worldfuturecouncil.org (office).

GISCARD D'ESTAING, Valéry, KCB; French politician and civil servant; *Chairman, Convention on the Future of Europe, European Union;* b. 2 Feb. 1926, Koblenz, Germany; m. Anne-Aymone de Brantes 1952; two s. two d. *Education:* Ecole Polytechnique, Ecole Nat. d'Admin. *Career:* Official, Inspection des Finances 1952, Insp. 1954; Deputy Dir du Cabinet de Prés. du Conseil June–Dec. 1954; Deputy for Puy de Dôme 1956–58, re-elected for Clermont 1958, for Puy de Dôme 1962, 1967, 1984, 1986, 1988, resgnd 1989; Sec. of State for Finance 1959, Minister for Finance and Econ. Affairs 1962–66, 1969–74; Pres. Comm. des Finances, de l'Economie général et du plan 1967–68; Pres. Cttee des Affaires Etrangères 1987–89; Pres. of the French Repub. 1974–81; Founder-Pres. Fed. Nat. des Républicains Indépendants (from May 1977 Parti Républicain) 1965; Del. to UN Gen. Ass. 1956, 1957, 1958; Chair. OECD Ministerial Council 1960; mem. (ex officio) Conseil Constitutionnel 1981–; Conseiller gen., Puy-de-Dôme 1982–88; Pres. Regional Council of Auvergne 1986–2004; Pres. Union pour la democratie française (UDF) 1988–96; Deputy to European Parl. 1989–93; Pres. European Movt Int. 1989–97; Pres. Council of European Municipalities and Regions 1997–2004; Deputy for Puy-de-Dôme 1993–2002; Pres. Comm. of Foreign Affairs, Nat. Ass. 1993–97; Chair. EU Convention on the Future of Europe 2001–; mem. Royal Acad. of Econ. Science and Finance, Spain 1995–; Académie française 2003–; Grand Croix, Ordre de la Légion d'honneur, Grand Croix, Ordre national du Mérite, Croix de guerre, Bailli Grand-Croix, Chevalier, Ordre de Malte, Gran Cruce, Ordén de Isabel la Católica; Nansen Medal 1979, Onassis Foundation Prize 2000, Trombinoscope Prize for Political Personality of the Year 2000, Jean Monnet Foundation Medal 2001, Trombinoscope European of the Year 2002, Charlemagne Prize 2002. *Publications:* Démocratie française 1976, Deux français sur trois 1984, Le Pouvoir et la vie, Vol. I 1988, Vol. II: L'Affrontement 1991, Vol. III: Choisir 2006, Le Passage 1994, Dans cinq ans, l'an 2000 (essay) 1995, Les Français 2000. *Address:* 199 blvd Saint-Germain, 75007 Paris, France (office). *Telephone:* 1-45-44-30-30 (office). *Fax:* 1-45-49-11-16 (office). *E-mail:* vge-cab -international@servpm.org (office).

GÍSLADÓTTIR, Ingibjörg Sólrún, BA; Icelandic politician; *Minister for Foreign Affairs and External Trade;* b. 31 Dec. 1954, Reykjavík; m. Hjörleifur Sveinbjörnsson; two s. *Education:* Univ. of Iceland, Univ. of Copenhagen, Denmark. *Career:* began political career in Samtök um kvennalista (Women's Alliance), which she represented in Reykjavík's City Council 1982–88; mem. Althing (Parl.) for Reykjavík 1991–94, for Reykjavík N 2005–, mem. Cttee on Foreign Affairs 1991–93, Cttee on Health and Social Security 1991–94, Cttee on Social Affairs 1991–94 (Vice-Chair. 1993–94), Cttee on Economy and Trade 2005–06, Icelandic Del. to EFTA and European Econ. Area Parl. Cttees 2005–; Founding mem. Samfylkingin (Social Democratic Alliance) 2000, Deputy Leader 1994–2003, Leader 2003–05, Chair. 2005–; Mayor of Reykjavík 1994–2003 (resgnd); Minister for Foreign Affairs and External Trade 2007–; fmr Ed. Vera (feminist journal); mem. Exec. Bd Cen. Bank of Iceland 2003–05. *Publication:* egar sálin fer á kreik. *Address:* Ministry for Foreign Affairs and External Trade, Raudarárstigur 25, 150 Reykjavík, Iceland (office). *Telephone:* 5459900 (office). *Fax:*

5622373 (office); 5622386 (office). *E-mail:* external@utn.stjr.is (office). *Website:* www.mfa.is (office).

GIZENGA, Antoine; Democratic Republic of the Congo politician; *Prime Minister;* b. 5 Oct. 1925; m.; one d. *Career:* Deputy Prime Minister 1960, 1961–62, Prime Minister 1960–61, 2006–; Pres. and Head of State, in rebellion, at Stanleyville after death of Patrice Lumumba March–Aug. 1961; imprisoned 1962–July 1964, Oct. 1964–1965; exiled in the former USSR, France, Angola, Congo-Brazzaville (now Republic of the Congo) 1965–1992; Leader, Parti Lumumbiste Unifié 1992–; unsuccessful cand. in presidential elections 2006.
Address: Parti Lumumbiste Unifié, 9 rue Cannas, C/Limete, Kinshasa, Democratic Republic of the Congo.

GJEDREM, Svein, MA; Norwegian banker; *Governor, Norges Bank;* b. 25 Jan. 1950. *Education:* Univ. of Oslo. *Career:* Exec. Officer, Norges Bank (Cen. Bank of Norway) 1975–79, Gov. 1999–; Head, Div. for Banking and Monetary Affairs, Ministry of Finance and Customs 1979–82, Deputy Dir 1982–86, Dir.-Gen. Head of Econ. Policy Dept 1986–95, Sec.-Gen. 1996–98; visiting engagement, EU Comm., Brussels 1994–95.
Address: Office of the Governor, Norges Bank, Bankplassen 2, P.O. Box 1179, Sentrum, 0107 Oslo, Norway (office). *Telephone:* (22) 31-60-67 (office). *Fax:* (22) 33-20-35 (office). *E-mail:* svein.gjedrem@norges-bank.no (office). *Website:* www.norges-bank.no (office).

GLAZER, Charles L., BS; American business executive, politician and diplomatist; *Ambassador to El Salvador; Education:* Univ. of Virginia. *Career:* officer in US Army 1965–67, attached to 502nd Mil. Intelligence Bn while stationed in Seoul, S Korea; fmr Sr Vice-Pres. and Dir Jefferies & Co. (institutional brokerage firm), New York City; fmr Sr Vice-Pres. Blyth Eastman Dillion & Co., Inc. (investment bank and institutional brokerage firm), New York City; Pres. and CEO C. L. Glazer & Co., Inc. (institutional brokerage and investment banking firm), Greenwich, Conn. –2007; Amb. to El Salvador 2007–; fmr mem. Bd of Visitors, Univ. of Virginia, served on Exec. Cttee and chaired Audit and Compliance Cttee, also served on Bd of Univ. of Virginia Investment Man. Co.; fmrly Republican Nat. Committeeman for Conn., served on Exec. Cttee of Republican Nat. Cttee, was Sergeant-at-Arms at Republican Nat. Convention 2004; apptd by Pres. George W. Bush as public mem. Bd of Trustees of Woodrow Wilson Int. Center for Scholars 2004; mem. Bd Dirs Nat. Org. of Investment Professionals, and many civic and charitable orgs, including the Teen Center of Greenwich, Conn. (Founding Chair.).
Address: US Embassy, Blvd Santa Elena Sur, Antiguo Cuscatlán, San Salvador, El Salvador (office). *Telephone:* 2278-4444 (office). *Fax:* 2278-1815 (office). *Website:* www.usinfo.org.sv (office); sansalvador.usembassy .gov (office).

GLAZ'IEV, Sergey Yurievich, DrEcSc; Russian economist and politician; b. 1 Jan. 1961, Zaporozhye; m.; three c. *Education:* Moscow State Univ. *Career:* Head of Lab., Cen. Econ. Math. Inst. 1986–91; First Deputy Chair. Cttee on External Econ. Relations Ministry of Foreign Affairs 1991–92; First Deputy Minister of External Econ. Relations of Russia 1992, Minister 1992–93; mem. State Duma (Parl.) 1993–95 (CP of Russian Fed. faction) 1999–; Chair. Cttee for Econ. Policy of State Duma 1994–95, 2000–; Chair. Nat. Cttee of Democratic Party of Russia 1994–97; Head of Econ. Dept, Security Council 1996; Head, Information-Analytical Bd, Council of Fed. (Parl.) 1996–; Co-Chair. Party of the Russian Regions (Partiya Rossiiskikh Regionov—PRR) –2004; Head of Motherland election bloc, then For a Worthy Life Org.; author of econ. programme for CP of Russian Fed. for Parl. Elections 1999; Corresp. mem. Russian Acad. of Sciences 2000. *Publications:* Economic Theory of Technical Development 1993, Economy and Politics 1994, One and a Half Years in the Duma 1995, Under the Critical Level 1996, Genocide 1997 1998, I'm Just Paying My Debt 2007. *Address:* State Duma, Okhotny Ryad 1, 103265 Moscow, Russia (office). *Telephone:* (495) 292-42-60 (office). *Fax:* (495) 292-43-22 (office). *E-mail:* mailbox@glazev.ru (home). *Website:* www.glazev.ru (home).

GLENDON, Mary Ann, BA, MCompL, JD; American academic, lawyer, writer and diplomatist; *Ambassador to the Holy See (Vatican);* b. 7 Oct. 1938, Pittsfield, Berkshire Co., Mass; m. Edward R. Lev; three d. *Education:* Univ. of Chicago, Université Libre, Brussels, Belgium. *Career:* early career included period as volunteer civil rights attorney; practised law with Mayer, Brown and Platt, Chicago 1963–68; teacher, Boston Coll. Law School 1968–86; Prof. of Law, Harvard Law School 1986–93, Learned Hand Prof. of Law 1993–2007; Amb. to the Holy See (Vatican) 2008–; fmr Visiting Prof., Univ. of Chicago Law School 1974, Gregorian Univ., Rome; fmr Pres. UNESCO-sponsored Int. Asscn of Legal Science 1991; mem. Pontifical Acad. of Social Sciences 1994–, Pres. 2004– (first woman head of a major pontifical acad.); Head of Del. of Holy See to UN Women's Conf., Beijing 1995; mem. Bd of Advisors, Notre Dame Center for Ethics and Culture, Harvard Univ. Human Rights Initiative, Harvard Law School Human Rights Program; mem. Bd of Trustees, Catholic Univ. of America, St John's Seminary; mem. Pres. George W. Bush's Council on Bioethics; hon. doctorates from Univ. of Chicago, Univ. of Louvain and others; Scribes Book Award, American Soc. of Writers on Legal Subjects 1988, Order of the Coif Triennial Book, Legal Acad. 1993. *Publications:* as author: The New Family and the New Property 1981, Abortion and Divorce in Western Law 1987, The Transformation of Family Law 1989, Rights Talk: The Impoverishment of Political Discourse 1991, Law of Decedent's Estates (co-author) 1991, A Nation Under Lawyers 1994, Seedbeds of Virtue (co-author) 1995, Comparative Legal Traditions (co-author) 1999, A World Made New: Eleanor Roosevelt and the Universal Declaration of Human Rights 2001.
Address: US Embassy to the Holy See, Villa Domiziana, Via delle Terme Deciane 26, 00153 Rome, Italy (office); Harvard Law School, Hauser 504, Cambridge MA 02138, USA; Pontifical Academy of Social Sciences, Casina Pio IV, 00120 Vatican City. *Telephone:* (06) 46743428 (US Embassy) (office); (617) 495-4769 (Harvard); (06) 69881441 (Pontifical Acad.). *Fax:* (06) 5758346 (US Embassy) (office); (617) 496-4913 (Harvard); (06) 69885218 (Pontifical Acad.). *E-mail:* vaticaninfo@mail .usembassy.it (office); social.sciences@acdscience.va. *Website:* vatican .usembassy.gov (office); www.law.harvard.edu; glendonbooks.com.

GLITMAN, Maynard Wayne, BA, MA; American diplomatist; *Lecturer in Political Science, University of Vermont;* b. 8 Dec. 1933, Chicago; m. G. Christine Amundsen 1956; three s. two d. *Education:* Univ. of Ill., Fletcher School of Law and Diplomacy, Univ. of California. *Career:* with US army 1957; with Foreign Service Dept of State 1956, 1966–67, Dir Office of Int. Trade 1973–74, Deputy Asst Sec. of State for Internal Trade policy 1974–76; economist 1956–59; Vice-Consul Bahamas 1959–61; Econ. Officer Embassy, Ottawa 1961–65; mem. Del. to UN Gen. Ass. 1967, Nat. Security Council Staff 1968; Political Officer, First Sec. Embassy in Paris 1968–73; Deputy Asst Sec. of Defense for Europe and NATO 1976–77, Deputy Perm. Rep. to NATO 1977–81; Amb. and Deputy Chief US Del. to Intermediate Nuclear Forces Negotiations, Arms Control and Disarmament Agency, Switzerland 1981–84; Amb. and US Rep. Mutual and Balanced Forces Negotiation, Vienna 1985; Amb. and Chief US Negotiator Intermediate Nuclear Forces Negotiation, Geneva 1985–88; Amb. to Belgium 1988–91; Diplomat in Residence, Univ. of Vt 1991–94, Adjunct Prof., now also Lecturer in Political Science, Univ. of Vt 1995–; Public Service Medal (USA Dept of Defense) 1977, 1981, Presidential Distinguished Service Award 1984, 1987.
Address: Department of Political Science, University of Vermont, PO Box 54110, Burlington, VT 05405-0001 (office); PO Box 438, Jeffersonville, VT 05464-0438, USA (home). *E-mail:* mwglitman@pwshift.com (office). *Website:* www.uvm.edu (office).

GNAEDINGER, Angelo; Swiss international organization official; *Director-General, International Committee of the Red Cross;* b. 1951. *Career:* trained as lawyer; examining magistrate, Schaffhausen –1984; joined ICRC 1984, followed field assignments in Middle East and Africa, held various positions in Dept of Operations, Geneva, Head of Detention Div. 1992–94, Del.-Gen. for W Cen. Europe and the Balkans 1994–98, Del.-Gen. for Europe, the Middle East and N. Africa 1998–, Dir-Gen. ICRC 2002–.
Address: International Committee of the Red Cross, 19 avenue de la Paix, 1202 Geneva, Switzerland (office). *Telephone:* (22) 7346001 (office). *Fax:* (22) 7332057 (office). *E-mail:* press.gva@icrc.org (office). *Website:* www .icrc.org (office).

GNASSINGBÉ, Faure Essozimna, MBA; Togolese politician and head of state; *President;* b. 1966. *Education:* Paris-Dauphine, France, Georgetown Univ., USA. *Career:* fmr Deputy, Nat. Ass.; Minister of Public Works, Mines and Telecommunications 2003–05; Pres. of Togo 2005–.
Address: Office of the President, Palais Présidentiel, ave de la Marina, Lomé, Togo (office). *Telephone:* 221-27-01 (office). *Fax:* 221-18-97 (office). *E-mail:* presidence@republicoftogo.com (office). *Website:* www .republicoftogo.com (office).

GNEHM, Edward William, Jr, MA; American diplomatist; *J.B. and Maurice C. Shapiro Visiting Professor of International Affairs and Co-Director, Undergraduate Program in International Affairs, Elliott School of International Affairs, George Washington University;* b. 10 Nov. 1944, Ga; m. Margaret Scott 1970; one s. one d. *Education:* George Washington Univ. and American Univ. Cairo. *Career:* Head, Liaison Office, Riyadh 1976–78; Deputy Chief of Mission, Embassy, Sanaa 1978–81; Dir Jr Officer Div. of Personnel, Washington, DC 1982–83, Dir Secr. Staff 1983–84; Deputy Chief of Mission, Amman 1984–87; Deputy Asst Sec. of Defense for Near East and S Asia 1987–89; Deputy Asst Sec. of State, Bureau of Near East and S Asian Affairs 1989–90; Amb. to Kuwait 1990–94, to Australia

2000–01, to Jordan 2001–04; J.B. and Maurice C. Shapiro Visiting Prof. of Int. Affairs, Co-Dir, Undergraduate Program in Int. Affairs, and Elliott School Kuwait Chair for Gulf and Arabian and Peninsula Affairs, Elliott School of Int. Affairs, George Washington Univ. 2004–; Deputy Perm. Rep. to UN 1994–97; Dir-Gen. of Foreign Service, Dir of Personnel US Dept of State, Washington DC 1997–2000; mem. American Acad. of Diplomacy, Washington Inst. of Foreign Affairs, American Foreign Service Asscn, Diplomatic and Consular Officers Retired; Presidential Distinguished Service Award 2000, Dept of Defense Meritorious Service Award 1989 and 1994, Dept of State Superior Honor Award 1991.
Address: Elliott School of International Affairs, George Washington University, 1957 E Street, NW, Suite 501, Washington, DC 20052, USA (office). *Telephone:* (202) 994-0155 (office). *Fax:* (202) 994-5477 (office). *E-mail:* ambgnehm@gwu.edu (office); www.gwu.edu/~elliott (office).

GNESOTTO, Nicole; French defence analyst; *Director, European Union Institute for Security Studies;* one d. *Education:* Ecole Normale Supérieure. *Career:* Deputy Head, French Foreign Ministry Centre d'Analyse et de Prévision (policy planning staff) 1986–90; Researcher, Institut Français des Relations Internationales 1990–93, also Head of Dir's Dept 1994–99; Prof., Institut d'Etudes Politiques, Paris 1994–99; Dir WEU Inst. for Security Studies 1999–2001; Dir EU Inst. for Security Studies 2001–; Chevalier, Légion d'Honneur. *Publications:* numerous publications on strategic issues and European security, including La puissance et l'Europe 1998, Le partage du fardeau dans l'OTAN : la nouvelle donne (ed.) 1999, La sécurité internationale au début du XXIe siècle 1999.
Address: EU Institute for Security Studies, 43 Avenue du Président Wilson, 75775 Paris Cedex 16, France (office). *Telephone:* 1-56-89-19-41 (office). *Fax:* 1-56-89-19-39 (office). *E-mail:* nicole.gnesotto@iss.europa.eu (office). *Website:* www.iss.europa.eu (office).

GNININVI, Léopold Messan Kokou, DSc; Togolese physicist and politician; *Minister of State for Foreign Affairs and Regional Integration;* b. 19 Dec. 1942, Aného. *Education:* Univ. of Dijon, France. *Career:* Head of Solar Energy Lab., Univ. of Lomé 1978–93, Prof. 1981–97; Dir Nat. Inst. of Educational Science 1979–88, Nat. Dir of Scientific Research 1987–93; three years in exile 1995–98; Sec.-Gen. Convention Démocratique des Peuples Africains, unsuccessful cand. in 1998 presidential election; Minister of State for Mines and Energy 2006–07, for Foreign Affairs and Regional Integration 2007–.
Address: Ministry of Foreign Affairs and Regional Integration, Place du Monument aux Morts, BP 900, Lomé, Togo (office). *Telephone:* 221-36-01 (office). *Fax:* 221-39-74 (office). *E-mail:* diplo@republicoftogo.com (office). *Website:* diplo@republicoftogo.com (office).

GOBURDHUN, Mohunlall, BA; Mauritian diplomatist; m. Mooktabye Goburdhun. *Education:* Punjab Univ., Univ. of Oxford, UK. *Career:* entered Foreign Service 1976, Chief of Protocol with rank of Amb. 1993–94, Amb. to India (also accred to Sri Lanka and Bangladesh) 1994–96; Sec. of State 1997–98; Amb. to Egypt 1999–2001, High Commr to UK 2001–05 (also accred to Denmark and Sweden 2002–05).
Address: c/o Ministry of Foreign Affairs, International Trade and Co-operation New Government Centre, 5th Floor, Port Louis, Mauritius. *Telephone:* 201-1648. *E-mail:* mfa@mail.gov.mu.

GODAL, Bjørn Tore; Norwegian diplomatist and politician; *Ambassador to Germany;* b. 20 Jan. 1945, Skien; m. Gro Balas 1988; one c. *Education:* Oslo Univ. *Career:* office clerk, Skien 1964–65; Pres. Labour League of Youth 1971–73 (Sec. for org. 1970–71), Fritt Forum (Labour Party's Student Org.) 1967–68; research officer, Labour Party 1973–80, Sec.-Gen. Oslo Labour Party 1980–82, Leader 1982–90 (mem. Cen. Cttee Labour Party 1983–90); Pres. Council of European Nat. Youth Cttees 1973–75; Head of Secr. Labour Party Group of the Oslo Municipal Council 1986; Deputy Rep. Storting (Parl.), then elected Rep.; Minister of Trade and Shipping 1991–94, of Foreign Affairs 1994–97, of Defence 2000–01; Amb. to Germany 2003–; mem. Council for the Study of Power Distribution in Norway 1972–80, Standing Cttee on Finance 1986–89, on Foreign and Constitutional Affairs 1989–91, on Defence 1997–2000, Storting; Chair. Middle East Cttee 1997–2000, Socialist Int.; mem. North Atlantic Ass. 1997–2000.
Address: Embassy of Norway, Rauchstr. 1, 10787 Berlin, Germany (office). *Telephone:* (30) 505050 (office). *Fax:* (30) 505055 (office). *E-mail:* emb .berlin@mfa.no (home). *Website:* www.norwegen.org (office).

GODDERIJ, Lt-Gen. P. J. M.; Dutch military officer; *Director, International Military Staff, NATO;* b. 4 April 1950, Brunssum; m. Conny Godderij-Gommans, one s. two d. *Education:* Royal Mil. Acad. *Career:* entered mil. service 1969, posted with 316 Squadron, Gilze-Rijen Air Base 1976, attended Advanced Staff Course 1983–85, Commdr 315 Squadron, Twenthe Air Base 1986–89, promoted to temporary Lt-Col 1989, Col

1991, Commdr Twenthe Air Base 1994–95, promoted to Air Commodore 1995, Maj.-Gen. 1997, Deputy Commdr ICAOC 2 Kalkar 1997–99, Deputy C-in-C Royal Netherlands Air Force 1999–2001, promoted to Lt-Gen. 2001; posted to Defence Staff Plans Div., Ministry of Defence 1989, Head of Operations and Training Section, Air Staff Directorate of Operations 1990–91, Chief, Air Operations Br. 1991–94, Asst Chief of Staff, Integrated Plans and Policy 1995–97, Deputy Chief Defence Staff 2001–04; Mil. Rep. to NATO and EU, Brussels 2004–07; Dir Int. Military Staff, NATO HQ 2007–.
Address: International Military Staff, NATO Headquarters, Bld Léopold III, Brussels 1110, Belgium (office). *Telephone:* (2) 707-41-11 (office). *Fax:* (2) 707-45-79 (office). *E-mail:* natodoc@hq.nato.int (office). *Website:* www .nato.int (office).

GODEC, Robert F., BA, MA; American diplomatist; *Ambassador to Tunisia;* m. Lori G. Magnusson. *Education:* Univ. of Virginia, Yale Univ. *Career:* career mem. Sr Foreign Service, joining Foreign Service 1985, attended State Dept's Sr Seminar, served as Acting Deputy Chief of Mission and Minister Counselor for Econ. Affairs, Pretoria, as Econ. Counselor, Nairobi, as Asst Office Dir for Thailand and Burma, Bureau of East Asian and Pacific Affairs, as Dir for SE Asian Affairs, Office of US Trade Rep., as Deputy Coordinator for Transition in Iraq, Deputy Asst Sec., Bureau of Near Eastern Affairs –2006, Amb. to Tunisia 2006–; numerous Superior and Meritorious Honor Awards and Commendations.
Address: US Embassy, Les Berges du Lac, 1053 Tunis, Tunisia (office). *Telephone:* (71) 107-000 (office). *Fax:* (71) 107-090 (office). *E-mail:* tuniswebsitecontact@state.gov (office). *Website:* tunis.usembassy.gov (office).

GODMANIS, Ivars, DrSci; Latvian scientist and politician; *Prime Minister;* b. 27 Nov. 1951, Rīga; m. Ramona Godmanė 1978; two s. one d. *Education:* Latvian State Univ. *Career:* scientific work since 1973, staff-mem. of the Physical Inst. of Latvian Acad. of Sciences 1973–86; teacher at Univ. of Latvia 1986–90; active involvement in the Movt for Independence of Latvia, Deputy Chair. of the People's Front; Chair. Council of Ministers of the Latvian Repub. (Prime Minister) 1990–93; with commercial co. Software House 1994–95; Vice-Chair. Asscn of Commercial Banks of Latvia 1995–96; Pres. Latvia Savings Bank (jt stock co.) 1996–97; mem. Saeima (Parl.) 1998–; Minister of Finance 1998–99, of the Interior 2006–07, Prime Minister 2007–; Programme Man. JSC Radio SWH 2003–; Chair. Latvijas ceļš (Latvian Way) 2004–07; Co-chair. Latvijas Pirmā Partija/ Latvijas ceļš (Latvian First Party/Latvian Way) 2007; mem. Bd JSC Latvian Shipping Co. 1997–98, JSC Saliena Real 2002–04; Order of the Three Stars (Second Class); Commemorative medal for participation in the barricades of 1991.
Address: Office of the Prime Minister, Brīvības bulv. 36, Rīga 1520 (office); Latvian First Party/Latvian Way (Latvijas Pirmā Partija/Latvijas ceļš), Kungu iela 8, Rīga 1050, Latvia (office). *Telephone:* 6708-2934 (Ministry) (office); 6722-6070 (office). *Fax:* 6728-0469 (Ministry) (office); 6722-6831 (office). *E-mail:* vk@mk.gov.lv (office); lc@lc.lv (office). *Website:* www.mk .gov.lv (office); www.lc.lv (office).

GODSON, Anthony; British diplomatist; b. 1 Feb. 1948; m. Margaret Godson. *Career:* joined FCO 1966, Personnel Operations Dept 1966–70, Attaché, Bucharest 1970–71, Kuala Lumpur 1972–73, Third Sec. (Commercial), Jakarta 1973–76, Pvt. Sec. to British High Commr, Canberra 1976–79, Rhodesia Commr, FCO 1980, Cen. African Dept 1980–82, Second, later First Sec., New York 1983–86, First Sec., Kinshasa 1987–88, Head of Indo-China Section, later Deputy Head, SE Asian Dept, FCO 1988–89, Deputy Head of Mission, Bucharest 1989–91, First Sec., UK Mission, Geneva 1992–95, Deputy Head of Eastern European and Cen. Asia Dept, FCO 1996–98, Counsellor, Later Deputy Head of Mission, Jakarta 1998–2002, FCO 2003–04, High Commr to Mauritius 2004–07.
Address: Foreign and Commonwealth Office, King Charles Street, London, SW1A 2AH, England (office). *Telephone:* (20) 7008-1500 (office). *Website:* www.fco.gov.uk (office).

GOERENS, Charles; Luxembourg politician; *Minister for Co-operation, Humanitarian Action and Defence and for the Environment;* b. 6 Feb. 1952, Ettelbruck; m.; three c. *Education:* Lycée Technique Agricole. *Career:* mem. Parl. for Parti Démocratique 1979; mem. European Parl. 1982–84; Pres. Ass. of EU 1987–90, 1999–; Parti Démocratique 1989–94; Minister for Co-operation, Humanitarian Action and Defence and for the Environment 1999–.
Address: Ministry of Co-operation, Humanitarian Action and Defence, 5 rue Notre Dame, 2240 Luxembourg, Luxembourg (office). *Telephone:* 478-1 (office). *Fax:* 22-31-44 (office).

GOFF, Philip Bruce, MA, MP; New Zealand politician; *Minister of Defence, of Trade, of Pacific Island Affairs, for Disarmament and Arms Control and*

Corrections; b. 22 June 1953, Auckland; m. Mary Ellen Moriarty 1979; two s. one d. *Education:* Papatoetoe High School, Univ. of Auckland, Nuffield Coll., Univ. of Oxford. *Career:* Lecturer in Political Science, Auckland Univ.; field officer in Insurance Workers' Union; fmr Chair. Labour Youth Council; MP for Roskill 1981–90, 1993–96, for New Lynn 1996–99, for Mt Roskill 1999–; Minister of Housing, for the Environment, responsible for Government Life Insurance Corpn, in charge of the Public Trust Office 1986–87, of Employment, of Youth Affairs and Assoc. Minister of Educ. 1987–89, Minister of Tourism 1987–88, of Educ. 1989–90, of Foreign Affairs and Trade and of Justice 1999–2005, Minister of Defence 2005–; Minister of Trade, of Pacific Island Affairs and for Disarmament and Arms Control Oct. 2005–, of Corrections 2007–; British Council Scholarship to Nuffield Coll. 1992; Labour.
Address: Executive Wing, Parliament Buildings, Wellington (office); Creightons Road RD 2, Papakura, Auckland, New Zealand (home). *Telephone:* (4) 496-0999 (office); (9) 292-8377 (home). *Fax:* (4) 496-0859 (office).

GOGOBERIDZE, Lana, DLitt; Georgian film director, translator, politician and diplomatist; *Deputy Permanent Delegate, United Nations Educational, Scientific and Cultural Organization (UNESCO);* b. 13 Oct. 1928, Tbilisi; m. Lado Aleksi-Meskhishvili 1958 (died 1978); two d. *Education:* Georgia State Univ., Tbilisi, State Inst. of Cinematography (VGIK), Moscow. *Career:* Lecturer, Tbilisi Univ. 1953–54; mem. CPSU 1965–89; Sec. Georgian Cineasts Union 1968–99; Artistic Dir Kartuli Filmi (Georgian Film) 1972–99; Dir of studio at Rustaveli Theatre School 1975–; mem. Georgian Parl. 1992–99, Chair. Liberal Democratic Faction 1992–95, Leader of Majority 1995–99, Head, Georgia–France Friendship Group 1997–; mem. Citizens' Union party 1997–99; Head, Perm. Nat. Del. to Council of Europe 1996–99; Amb., Perm. Rep. to Council of Europe 1999–2004, Deputy Perm. Del. to UNESCO 2004–; Minister Plenipotentiary, Georgian Embassy, Paris 2007–; Pres. Int. Asscn of Women Film-Makers 1988; mem. Bd of Union of Georgian Film-Makers; Chevalier, Ordre nat. du Mérite 1997; People's Artist of Georgian SSR 1979. *Films include:* documentary: Gelathi 1957, Tbilisi – 1500 1958, Letters to the Children 1981; fiction: Under the Same Sky 1961, I See the Sun 1965, Boundaries 1970, When the Almond Blossomed (Best Dir Alma Ata Festival) 1973, Turmoil 1974, Interviews on Personal Problems (Grand Prix, San Remo Film Festival 1979, Int. Critics' Prize, Locarno, USSR State Prize 1980, Best Film, Dushanbe Festival) 1978, A Day Longer than Night (Georgia State Prize) 1983, Turnover (Best Dir, Tokyo Film Festival Prize 1987) 1986, Waltz on the Pechora River (Italian Critics' Prize, Navicella Prize, Venice Film Festival Prize 1992, Ecumenical Jury Prize, Berlin Film Festival Prize 1993) 1991. *Publications:* Walt Whitman 1955, Walt Whitman: Leaves of Grass (trans.) 1956, Rabindranath Tagore (trans.) 1957, Foreign Poetry in Georgian (trans.) 1995, What I Remember and How I Remember 2003; also trans of Baudelaire, Verlaine, Eluard, Pasternak.
Address: Embassy of Georgia, 104 avenue Raymond Poincare, 75016 Paris, France (office); UNESCO, 7 Place de Fontenoy, 75352 Paris 07 SP (office); Kazbegi Str. 17, Apt 26, Tbilisi, Georgia (home). *Telephone:* 1-45-68-10-00 (office); (32) 22-76-79 (home). *Fax:* 1-45-67-16-90 (office). *E-mail:* l.gogoberidze@mfa.gov.ge (office). *Website:* www.unesco.org (office).

GOH, Chok Tong, MA; Singaporean politician, lawyer and banker; *Senior Minister and Chairman, Monetary Authority of Singapore;* b. 20 May 1941, Pasir Panjang, Singapore; m. Tan Choo Leng 1965; one s. one d. (twins). *Education:* Raffles Inst., Univ. of Singapore and Williams Coll., USA. *Career:* with Singapore Admin. Service 1964–69, Neptune Orient Lines Ltd 1969–77; MP 1976–; Sr Minister of State, Ministry of Finance 1977–79, Minister for Trade and Industry 1979–81, Minister for Health and Second Minister for Defence 1981–82, Minister for Defence 1982–91, First Deputy Prime Minister 1985–90; Prime Minister of Singapore 1990–2004; Sr Minister 2004–; Chair. Monetary Authority of Singapore 2004–; mem. Central Exec. Cttee People's Action Party 1979–, Second Asst Sec.-Gen. 1979–84, Asst Sec.-Gen. 1984–89, First Asst Sec.-Gen. 1989–92, Sec.-Gen. 1992–2004; Perm. mem. Pres.'s Council for Minority Rights; Grand Knight Cordon (Special Class) of the Most Exalted Order of the White Elephant (Thailand) 1997; Hon. Companion of the Order of Australia 2005; Medal of Honour, Nat. Trade Union Congress (NTUC) 1987, Distinguished Comrade of Labour Award 2001, Jawaharla Nehru Award for Int. Understanding (India) 2004.
Address: Monetary Authority of Singapore (MAS), 10 Shenton Way, MAS Bldg, Singapore 079117; Prime Minister's Office, Orchard Road, Istana, Singapore 238823 (office). *Telephone:* 62255577 (MAS); 62358577 (office). *Fax:* 62299491 (MAS); 67324627 (office). *E-mail:* Goh_Chok_Tong@pmo .gov.sg (office); webmaster@mas.gov.sg. *Website:* www.pmo.gov.sg (office); www.mas.gov.sg.

GOICOECHEA LUNA, Emilio Rafael José; Mexican business executive, politician and diplomatist; *Ambassador to Canada;* b. 22 Oct. 1948, Mazatlan, Sinaloa. *Education:* Instituto Tecnológico y de Estudios Superiores de Monterrey. *Career:* served as Pres. Confederación Nacional de Cámaras de Comercio (Confed. of Nat. Chambers of Commerce), Instituto Mexicano de Mercadotecnia A.C. (Mexican Marketing Inst.) and mem. Consejo Coordinador Empresarial (Entrepreneurial Coordinating Council), Confederación Patronal de la República Mexicana (Employers' Confed. of Mexico); fmr adviser/consultant to nat. orgs including Centro de Estudios Económicos del Sector Privado, Instituto Mexicano de Comercio Exterior, Instituto Mexicano del Seguro Social, Instituto del Fondo Nacional de la Vivienda para los Trabajadores, Fondo Nacional de Fomento al Turismo, Ferrocarriles Nacionales de México, Asociación Nacional de Importadores y Exportadores, Confederación Nacional de Cámaras Industriales; began political career as Senator 1994–2000, mem. Fed. Chamber of Deputies 2000–03, Under-Sec. of Tourism 2003, Chief of Staff to Pres. Vicente Fox 2004–06; Amb. to Canada 2007–; mem. Partido Acción Nacional (mem. Nat. Exec. 1996–); Pres. Asscn of Scouts of Mexico; Acapulco Chamber of Commerce's Exec. of the Year, Key to the City of Miami, Inst. for Promotion of Free Enterprise Golden Eagle award.
Address: Embassy of Mexico, 45 O'Connor Street, Suite 1000, Ottawa, ON K1P 1A4, Canada (office). *Telephone:* (613) 233-8988 (office). *Fax:* (613) 235-9123 (office). *E-mail:* info@embamexcan.com (office). *Website:* www .sre.gob.mx/canada (office).

GOLDBERG, Philip S.; American diplomatist; *Ambassador to Bolivia;* b. Boston, Mass. *Education:* Boston Univ. *Career:* worked for several years as liaison officer between City of New York and UN and consular community; career mem. Sr Foreign Service, served overseas as a Consular and Political Officer in Bogotá and as Political-Econ. Officer in Pretoria, Special Asst 1996–98, Exec. Asst to Deputy Sec. of State, Strobe Talbott 1998–2000, Sr mem. Dept of State team handling transition from Clinton to Bush Admins, served as Acting Deputy Asst Sec. of State for Legis. Affairs Jan.–June 2001, Desk Officer for Bosnia and a Special Asst to Amb. Richard Holbrooke 1994–96 (mem. American negotiating team in lead-up to Dayton Peace Conf. and Chief of Staff for US Del. at Dayton), Deputy Chief of Mission, Santiago 2001–04, Chief of Mission, Pristina 2004–06, Amb. to Bolivia 2006–.
Address: US Embassy, Avenida Arce 2780, Casilla 425, La Paz, Bolivia (office). *Telephone:* (2) 216-8000 (office). *Fax:* (2) 216-8111 (office). *E-mail:* consularlapaz@state.gov (office). *Website:* lapaz.usembassy.gov (office).

GOLDING, (Orrett) Bruce, BSc; Jamaican politician; *Prime Minister;* b. 5 Dec. 1947; m. Lorna Golding; three c. *Education:* Jamaica Coll., Univ. of the W Indies. *Career:* as a student served as Vice-Chair. Jamaica Labour Party (JLP) Constituency Exec. for West St Catherine and mem. Bd of Dirs, Nat. Lotteries Comm.; selected as JLP parl. cand. for West St Catherine 1969, elected to JLP Cen. Exec. 1969, Co-founder Young Jamaica group 1970, elected as youngest-ever MP 1972, defeated in elections 1976; JLP Gen. Sec. 1974–84, Chair. 1984–95; apptd to Senate 1977, re-apptd 1980, Minister of Construction 1980–83; elected MP for South Central St Catherine 1983, re-elected 1989, 1993; left JLP and f. Nat. Democratic Movt (NDM) 1995, Pres. 1995–2002, left NDM and rejoined JLP 2002, Chair. JLP 2003–05, Leader 2005–; Prime Minister 2007–, also Minister of Planning and Devt and of Defence. *Radio:* host, Disclosure 2002.
Address: Office of the Prime Minister, Jamaica House, 1 Devon Road, POB 272, Kingston 10, Jamaica (office). *Telephone:* 927-9941 (office). *Fax:* 927-4101 (office). *E-mail:* pmo@opm.gov.jm (office). *Website:* www .jamaicalabourparty.com (office).

GOLDSMITH, Baron (Life Peer), cr. 1999, of Allerton in the County of Merseyside; **Peter Henry Goldsmith,** PC, MA, LLM, QC; British barrister; b. 5 Jan. 1950, Liverpool. *Education:* Quarry Bank High School, Caius Coll. Cambridge, Univ. Coll. London. *Career:* called to Bar, Gray's Inn, began practising as barrister 1972; a Jr Counsel to Crown (Common Law) 1985–87, QC 1987, Chair. Bar of England and Wales 1995, Financial Reporting Review Panel 1997–2000; called to Paris Bar 1997; Personal Rep. of Prime Minister to EU Charter of Fundamental Rights 1999–2000; Attorney-Gen. 2001–07; Privy Councillor 2002–; European Chair of Litigation, Debevoise & Plimpton LLP, London 2007–; Fellow, American Law Inst. 1997–, Univ. Coll. London 2002–.
Address: House of Lords, London, SW1A 0PW; Debevoise & Plimpton LLP, Tower 42, Old Broad Street, London, EC2N 1HQ, England. *Telephone:* (20) 7219-8614 (Lords); (20) 7786-9000. *Fax:* (20) 75880-4180. *E-mail:* arunacres@debevoise.com. *Website:* www.parliament.uk; www .debevoise.com.

GOLDSTEIN, Joshua, BA, PhD; American academic; *Professor Emeritus of International Relations, American University;* b. 27 Dec. 1952, Boston,

Mass. *Education:* Stanford Univ., Calif., Massachusetts Inst. of Tech. *Career:* Asst Prof., School of Int. Relations, Univ. of Southern California 1986–89, Assoc. Prof. 1989–93; Assoc. Prof., Harvard Univ. Center for Int. Affairs 1991–93; Fellow, Yale Univ. Int. Security Programs 1991–93; Assoc. Prof. of Int. Relations, American Univ., Washington, DC 1993–95, Prof. 1995–2003, Prof. Emer. 2003–; Adjunct Prof. (Research), Watson Inst. for Int. Studies, Brown Univ. 2002–06; Research Scholar, Univ. of Massachussets; Karl Deutsch Award, Int. Studies Asscn, Victoria Schuck Award, American Political Science Asscn, Scholar/Teacher of the Year, School of Int. Service, American Univ. 2002. *Publications:* Long Cycles: Prosperity and War in the Modern Age 1988, Three-Way Street: Strategic Reciprocity in World Politics (co-author) 1990, War and Gender: How Gender Shapes the War System and Vice Versa 2001, The Real Price of War 2004, International Relations (8th edn) 2008; contrib. to The American Political Science Review, Journal of Conflict Resolution, International Studies Quarterly, The New York Times, The Los Angeles Times, The Christian Science Monitor; numerous book chapters and articles in learned journals. *Address:* PO Box 3068, Amherst, MA 01004-3068, USA (home). *Telephone:* (413) 256-6363 (office). *E-mail:* jg@joshuagoldstein.com (home). *Website:* www.joshuagoldstein.com (home).

GOLDSTEIN, Judith L., BA, MIA, PhD; American political scientist and academic; *Professor of Political Science, Stanford University; Education:* Univ. of Calif., Berkeley, Columbia Univ., Univ. of Calif., LA. *Career:* Acting Asst Prof., Stanford Univ. 1981–83, Asst Prof. 1983–90, Assoc. Prof. 1991–98, Prof. 1998–, also currently Sakurako and William Fisher Family Dir of Int., Comparative and Area Studies and Kaye Univ. Fellow in Undergrad. Educ., Dir Grad. Program in Int. Policy Studies 1995–2001, Dir Undergrad. Program in Int. Relations 1998–2001, Sr Assoc. Dean for Grad. and Undergrad. Studies, School of Humanities and Sciences 2002–05, Dir Div of Int., Comparative and Area Studies 2004–07; mem. Editorial Bd International Organization, International Studies Quarterly, World Politics, World Trade Review; mem. Bd of Dirs Social Science History Inst. 1998–; mem. American Political Science Asscn (Sec. 2003–04). *Publications:* Ideas and Foreign Policy (co–ed.) 1993, Ideas, Interests and American Trade Policy 1994, Legalization and World Politics (co-ed.) 2001, Evolution of the Trade Regime 2005; numerous articles. *Address:* School of Humanities and Sciences, Building 1, Main Quad, Stanford University, Stanford, CA 94305-2070, USA (office). *Telephone:* (650) 723-0671 (office). *E-mail:* judy@stanford.edu (office). *Website:* politicalscience.stanford.edu/faculty/goldstein.html (office).

GOLDSTONE, Richard J., LLB; South African judge; b. 26 Oct. 1938, Boksburg; m. Noleen Behrman 1962; two d. *Education:* King Edward VII School, Johannesburg and Univ. of Witwatersrand. *Career:* admitted to Johannesburg Bar 1963, Sr Counsel 1976; Judge, Transvaal Supreme Court 1980–89; Judge, Appellate Div. Supreme Court of SA 1989–94; Justice, S African Constitutional Court 1994–2003; Chair. Comm. of Inquiry regarding Public Violence and Intimidation 1991–94; Prosecutor, Int. Criminal Tribunal for the Fmr Yugoslavia and Int. Criminal Tribunal for Rwanda 1994–96; Nat. Pres. Nat. Inst. for Crime Prevention and Rehabilitation of Offenders 1982–99; Chair. Cttee which drafted Valencia Declaration of Human Duties and Responsibilities 1998; Ind. Int. Comm. on Kosovo 1999–2001, Int. Bar Asscn Task Force on Int. Terrorism 2001–; mem. Council, Univ. of Witwatersrand 1988–94, Chancellor 1996–; Chair. Standing Advisory Cttee on Co. Law (Chair. 1991–), Exec. Cttee World ORT (Pres. 1997–); Chair. Bd Human Rights Inst. of SA; Gov. Hebrew Univ. of Jerusalem 1982–; Chair. Bradlow Foundation 1989–; other professional appts; Faculty mem. Salzburg Seminar 1996, 1998, 2001; Foreign mem. American Acad. of Arts and Sciences; Fellow Centre for Int. Affairs, Harvard Univ. 1989; Hon. mem. Bar Asscn of New York; Hon. Bencher Inner Temple, London; Hon. Fellow, St John's Coll. Cambridge; Hon. LLD (Cape Town) 1993, (Natal, Hebrew Univ. of Jerusalem, Witwatersrand) 1994, (Wilfred Laurier Univ., Waterloo, Canada) 1995, (Maryland Univ. Coll.) 1995, (Tilbury Univ.) 1996, (Univ. of Glasgow, Notre Dame Univ.) 1997, (Univ. of Calgary) 1998, (Emory Univ.) 2001; several awards including Toastmasters Int. Communication and Leadership Award 1994, Int. Human Rights Award (American Bar Asscn) 1994. *Publication:* For Humanity – Reflections of a War Crimes Investigator. *Address:* PO Box 396, Morningside 2057; 22 West Road South, Morningside, South Africa (home). *Fax:* (11) 8035472. *E-mail:* rjgoldstone@iafrica .com.

GOLYSHEV, Vyacheslav Arkadevich, PhD; Uzbekistan government official. *Career:* First Deputy Presidential Adviser for Econ. Affairs –2005; Deputy Prime Minister, Head of the Econ. Sector and Foreign Econ. Relations Sector, Minister of the Economy 2005. *Address:* c/o Ministry of the Economy, pr. Uzbekistanii 45a, 100003 Tashkent, Uzbekistan (office). *Telephone:* (71) 139-63-20 (office). *Fax:* (71)

132-63-72 (office). *E-mail:* mineconomy@mmes.gov.uz (office). *Website:* www.mineconomy.cc.uz (office).

GOMAN, Vladimir Vladimirovich; Russian politician; *Deputy Representative of the President, Siberian Okrug;* b. 29 Jan. 1952, Baku, Azerbaijan. *Education:* Troitsk Higher School of Civil Aviation, Tumen Industrial Inst., Tumen State Univ. *Career:* technician first civil aviation team 1972–74; fmr mechanic Severgazstroi, Nadym, then head of sector, head of dept 1974–89; Chair. Nadym Municipal Exec. Cttee 1989; Head of Admin, Nadym and Autonomous Territory of Yamal 1991–93; mem. State Duma, Chair. State Duma Cttee on Peoples of the N 1993–98, Cttee on Devt of the N 1998–, Cttee on Problems of the N 1999–; Deputy Minister of Regional Policy State Sec. 1999–2000, Deputy Rep. of the Pres. in Siberian Fed. Dist, Novosibirsk 2000–. *Address:* Office of the Plenipotentiary Representative of the President, Derzhavina str. 18, 630091 Novosibirsk, Russia (office). *Telephone:* (3832) 21-56-22 (office).

GOMES, Daniel; Guinea-Bissau politician; *Minister of Fisheries and the Maritime Economy; Career:* fmr Spokesman, Partido Africano da Independência da Guiné e Cabo Verde (PAIGC); Minister of Defence 2004–05, Minister of the Presidency of the Council of Ministers, Social Communication and Parliamentary Affairs 2005–07, of Fisheries and the Maritime Economy 2007–. *Address:* Ministry of Fisheries and the Maritime Economy, Avenida Amílcar Cabral, CP 102, Bissau, Guinea-Bissau (office). *Telephone:* 201699 (office). *Fax:* 202580 (office).

GOMES DOS SANTOS, Júlio Cesar; Brazilian diplomatist; *Ambassador to Colombia;* b. 24 Jan. 1940, Florianópolis. *Education:* Instituto Rio Branco. *Career:* Auxillary to Adjunct Sec.-Gen. for Political Planning 1968–69; Temp. Third Sec., Bogotá 1969; Auxillary to Head of Admin. Dept 1969–70; Asst to Head of African Div. 1970–71; Vice-Consul, New York 1972, Adjunct-Consul 1972–76; Temp. Second Sec., Brussels 1973; Temp. Second Sec., Argel 1975; Second Sec., Montevideo 1976–78, First Sec. 1978–80; Advising Minister, London 1990–92; Special Assessor to Sec. of Treasury 1993–94; Perm. Rep. to UN, Rome 1997–2002; Gen. Consul, New York 2002–05; Amb. to Colombia 2005–. *Address:* Embassy of Brazil, Calle 93, No. 14–20, 8°, Bogotá, DC, Colombia (office). *Telephone:* (1) 218-0800 (office). *Fax:* (1) 218-8393 (office). *Website:* www.brasil.org.co (office).

GOMES JÚNIOR, Carlos; Guinea-Bissau politician; b. 1949. *Career:* banker and businessman; elected to Parl. 1994–; Leader of African Party for the Ind. of Guinea-Bissau; Prime Minister of Guinea-Bissau May 2004–05. *Address:* c/o Office of the Prime Minister, Avda Unidade Africana, CP 137, Bissau, Guinea-Bissau (office).

GOMUŁKA, Stanisław, DEcon; Polish economist and academic; *Reader in Economics, London School of Economics;* b. 11 Sept. 1940, Krężoły; m.; one s. *Education:* Warsaw Univ. *Career:* Researcher, Dept of Econs, Warsaw Univ. 1962–65; Reader in Econs, LSE 1970–; Researcher, Dept of Econs, Netherlands Inst. for Advanced Studies 1980–81, Pennsylvania Univ. 1985–86, Stanford Univ. 1986, Columbia Univ. 1987, Harvard Univ. 1989–90; econ. adviser to Polish govts 1989–, to Chair. Nat. Bank of Poland 1996–97; consultant, IMF, OECD, EU. *Publications:* Inventive Activity, Diffusion and the Stages of Economic Growth 1971, Growth, Innovation and Reform in Eastern Europe 1986, The Theory of Technological Change and Economic Growth 1990, Emerging from Communism – Lessons from Russia, China, and Eastern Europe (co-ed.) 1998, The Theory of Technological Change and Economic Growth (ebook) 2002. *Address:* London School of Economics, Houghton Street, Room S.576, London, WC2A 2AE (office); 4 Woodfield Way, London, N11 2PH, England (home). *Telephone:* (20) 7955-7510 (office). *E-mail:* s.gomulka@ lse.ac.uk (office); gomulka@chrzan.demon.co.uk (office). *Website:* www .lse.ac.uk (office); econ.lse.ac.uk/staff/sgomulka/index_own.html (office).

GONCHIGDORJ, Radnaasümberelyn, PhD, DSc; Mongolian politician and mathematician; *Chairman, Mongolian Social Democratic Party;* b. 1954, Tsakhir Dist, Arkhangai Prov.; m. Damdinsurengiin Hishigt 1977; two s. two d. *Education:* Mongolian State Univ. *Career:* Lecturer in Math., Mongolian State Univ. 1975–88; Dir Inst. of Math., Mongolian Acad. of Sciences 1988–90; Chair. Exec. Cttee Mongolian Social Democratic Movt 1990; Chair. Mongolian Social Democratic Party 1994–; Deputy to Great People's Hural 1990–92; Vice-Pres. of Mongolia and Chair. State Little Hural 1990–92; mem. State Great Hural 1992–96, Chair. 1996–2000; presidential cand. 2001. *Address:* c/o State Great Hural, Government House, Ulan Bator 12, Mongolian People's Republic. *Telephone:* (1) 326877. *Fax:* (1) 322866.

GÖNCZ, Árpád, LLD; Hungarian fmr head of state and writer; b. 10 Feb. 1922, Budapest; m. Mária Zsuzsanna Göntér 1946; two s. two d. *Education:* Pázmány Péter University of Arts and Sciences, Budapest. *Career:* employed as banking clerk with Nat. Land Credit Inst.; joined Ind. Smallholders, Landworkers and Bourgeois Party; leading positions in Ind. Youth Org.; Ed.-in-Chief *Generation* (weekly); sentenced in 1957 to life imprisonment as defendant in political Bibó trial; released under amnesty 1963; then freelance writer and literary translator, especially of English works; Pres. Hungarian Writers Federation 1989–90, Hon. Pres. 1990–; founding mem. Free Initiatives Network, Free Democratic Fed., Historic Justice Cttee; mem. of Parl. 1990; Acting Pres. of Hungary May–Aug. 1990, Pres. of Hungary 1990–2000; Hon. KCMG 1991; Dr hc (Butler) 1990, (Connecticut) 1991, (Oxford) 1995, (Sorbonne) 1996, (Bologna) 1997; Attila József Prize 1983, Wheatland Prize 1989, Premio Meditteraneo 1991, George Washington Prize 2000, Pro Humanitate Award 2001, Polish Business Oscar Award 2002. *Publications include:* Men of God (novel) 1974, Encounters (short stories) 1980, Homecoming and Other Stories (short stories) 1991, Hungarian Medea (play), Balance (play), Iron Bars (play), A Pessimistic Comedy (play), Persephone (play), political essays; translated more than 100 works, mostly by British and American authors, including James Baldwin, Edgar Lawrence Doctorow, William Faulkner, William Golding, Ernest Hemingway, William Styron, Susan Sontag, John Updike, Edith Wharton and others. *Address:* Office of the Former President, 1055 Budapest, Kossuth tér 4, Hungary (office). *Telephone:* (1) 441-3550 (office). *Fax:* (1) 441-3552 (office).

GÖNCZ, Kinga, MD; Hungarian physician and politician; *Minister of Foreign Affairs;* b. 8 Nov. 1947, Budapest; m.; two c. *Education:* Semmelweis Univ., Budapest. *Career:* psychiatrist 1978–86; Sr Asst Prof., Nat. Inst. of Medical Rehabilitation, Budapest 1982–89; Asst Prof., Dept of Social Policy, Inst. of Sociology, Eötvös Loránd Univ., Budapest 1989–2002; Dir, Pnrs Hungary Foundation 1994–2002; teaching appointment at Dept of Human Rights, Cen. European Univ. 1998–2003; Political Sec. of State, Ministry of Health, Social and Family Affairs 2002–04; Minister of Equal Opportunities 2004; Minister of Youth, Family, Social Affairs and Equal Opportunities 2004–06; Minister of Foreign Affairs 2006–; Visiting Scholar, Univ. of Michigan; Lecturer, Mandel School of Applied Social Sciences, Case Western Univ., Cleveland, Ohio, USA. *Publications:* several publications on social work, supervision and training. *Address:* Ministry of Foreign Affairs, 1027 Budapest, Bem rkp. 47, Hungary (office). *Telephone:* (1) 458-1178 (office). *Fax:* (1) 375-3766 (office). *Website:* www.mfa.gov.hu (office).

GONDJOUT, Laure Olga, MA; Gabonese politician; *Minister of Foreign Affairs, Co-operation, Francophonie and Regional Integration;* b. 18 Dec. 1953, Paris, France. *Education:* Catholic Univ. of Paris, Polytechnic of Central London, UK. *Career:* began career as translator; worked at African Devt Bank, Abidjan, mem. Bd of Dirs for Gabon, African Devt Bank, Libreville 1995–2001 returned to Gabon and served as adviser to Pres. 1984–2002, Secrétaire particulière to Pres. 2003; Minister Del. to Minister of State for Foreign Affairs 2006–07; Minister of Communication, Posts, Telecommunications, and New Information Technologies Dec. 2007–Feb. 2008, of Foreign Affairs, Co-operation, Francophonie and Regional Integration Feb. 2008–; Gen. Sec. Children of Africa Foundation, Libreville. *Address:* Ministry of Foreign Affairs, Co-operation, Francophonie and Regional Integration, BP 2245, Libreville, Gabon (office). *Telephone:* 72-95-21 (office). *Fax:* 72-91-73 (office).

GONDWE, Goodall; Malawi politician and economist; *Minister of Finance;* *Career:* Dir of African Div., IMF 1998; fmr Econ. Adviser to Pres. of Malawi; Minister of Finance 2004–. *Address:* Ministry of Finance, POB 30049, Capital City, Lilongwe 3, Malawi (office). *Telephone:* 1789355 (office). *Fax:* 1789173 (office). *Website:* www.finance.malawi.gov.mw.

GOÑI CARRASCO, José; Chilean government official and diplomatist; *Minister of National Defence; Career:* fmr Dir European Section, Dept of Int. Econ. Relations, Ministry of Foreign Affairs; Amb. to Sweden 1997–2000, to Italy 2000–04, to Mexico 2006–07; Head Chilean Trade Office for Sweden, Norway, Finland, Iceland and Baltic Nations, Estocolmo 1997–2000; Rep. to WFP and FAO, Rome 2000–04; Researcher and Prof. of Latin American Econs, Estocolmo Univ. 2000–04; Adviser, Ministry of Foreign Affairs 2005–06; Dir-Gen. Nat. Environment Comm. 2005–06; Minister of Nat. Defence 2007–; mem. Partido por la Democracia (PPD). *Publications include:* various books and articles on econs. *Address:* Ministry of National Defence, Villavicencio No. 364, 22° Edif. Diego Portales, Central, Santiago, Chile (office). *Telephone:* (2) 222-1202

(office). *Fax:* (2) 633-0568 (office). *E-mail:* correo@defensa.cl (office). *Website:* www.defensa.cl (office).

GONSALVES, Camillo M., BA, DIur; Saint Vincent and the Grenadines editor, lawyer and diplomatist; *Permanent Representative, United Nations;* b. 12 June 1972, Philadelphia, Pa, USA. *Education:* Norman Manley Law School, Jamaica, Temple Univ., Philadelphia, George Washington Univ., Washington, DC. *Career:* art dir, writer and copy ed. for Philadelphia Tribune newspaper 1995–96; Founder and Ed.-in-Chief Reggaematic Magazine 1997–; lawyer, Weiner Brodsky Sidman Kider PC 1999–2001, Weiner Brodsky Kider PC 2001–03; Legal Adviser to Govt 2002–05; Assoc. Mehri & Skalet Law Firm 2004; attorney, DunnCox (law firm) 2004–05; Sr Crown Counsel, Attorney Gen.'s Chambers 2005–07, mem. Govt Del. to Ethiopia 2005; Perm. Rep. to UN, New York 2007–. *Address:* Permanent Mission of Saint Vincent and the Grenadines to the United Nations, 801 Second Avenue, 21st Floor, New York, NY 10017, USA (office). *Telephone:* (212) 687-4490 (office). *Fax:* (212) 949-5946 (office). *E-mail:* stvg@un.int (office).

GONSALVES, Ralph, PhD; Saint Vincent and the Grenadines politician and lawyer; *Prime Minister and Minister of Finance, Planning, Economic Development, Labour and Information, National Security;* b. 1946. *Education:* Univ. of West Indies, Victoria Univ. of Manchester, UK. *Career:* called to Bar, Gray's Inn, London; practised law at Eastern Caribbean Supreme Court; fmr Lecturer, Depts of Govt, Political Science and Sociology, Univ. of W Indies; Leader United People's Movt (UPM) 1979–82, Movt for Nat. Unity (MNU) 1994–98; Leader United Labour Party (ULP); Prime Minister of Saint Vincent and the Grenadines and Minister of Finance, Planning, Economic Development, Labour and Information 2001–, Minister of Nat. Security 2005–. *Address:* Office of the Prime Minister, Administrative Building, 4th Floor, Bay Street, Kingstown, Saint Vincent and the Grenadines (office). *Telephone:* 451-2939 (office). *Fax:* 457-2152 (office). *Website:* pmosvg@caribsurf.com (office).

GONUL, Mehmet Vecdi; Turkish politician; *Minister of National Defence;* b. 1939, Erzincan; m.; three c. *Education:* Faculty of Political Science, Ankara Univ. *Career:* participated in state training programme for recruiting dist govs 1967; Dist Gov. in several areas of Turkey 1967–76; Gov. of Kocaeli 1976–77, later of Izmir; Dir-Gen. of Nat. Security (Police) Directorate 1977–79; Gov. of Ankara 1979–88; Under-Sec. Ministry of the Interior 1988–91; apptd Head of State Court of Accounts 1991; elected MP for Kocaeli 1999–2001, Deputy Speaker of Parl. 1999–2001; joined AK Party 2001; currently Minister of Nat. Defence; Del. to EU Parl. Ass. *Address:* Ministry of National Defence, Milli Savunma Bakanlığı, 06100 Ankara, Turkey (office). *Telephone:* (312) 4254596 (office). *Fax:* (312) 4184737 (office). *E-mail:* meb@meb.gov.tr (office). *Website:* www.msb.gov.tr (office).

GONZÁLEZ ARIAS, Luis; Paraguayan diplomatist; *Ambassador to Brazil;* m. Mary Beatriz Ayala de González. *Career:* fmr Minister Counsellor, Embassy in Washington, DC; fmr Perm. Rep. to UN, Geneva; currently Amb. to Brazil. *Address:* Embassy of Paraguay, SES, Av. das Nações, Quadra 811, Lote 42, 70427-900 Brasília DF, Brazil. *Telephone:* (61) 242-3742 (office). *Fax:* (61) 242-4605 (office). *E-mail:* embapar-sec1@yawl.com.br (office).

GONZÁLEZ SEGOVIA, Roberto Eudez; Paraguayan politician; *Minister of National Defence;* b. 1959, Piribebuy; m. Miriam Benítez de González; four c. *Education:* Universidad Nacional de Asunción. *Career:* practised as lawyer from 1986; Legal Adviser, various nat. pvt. enterprises; participant, various congresses, seminars; mem. Students' Rights Centre UNA; Students' Rep. of Hon. Council Bd Law and Social Sciences UNA; apptd Minister of Home Affairs 2002; Minister of Nat. Defence –2007; Minister for Public Works and Communications 2008–. *Address:* Ministry of Public Works and Communications, Oliva y Alberdi, Asunción, Paraguay (office). *Telephone:* (21) 44-4411 (office). *Fax:* (21) 44-4421 (office). *Website:* www.mopc.gov.py (office).

GONZI, Lawrence, LLD; Maltese politician and lawyer; *Prime Minister;* b. 1 July 1953; m. Catherine Gonzi (née Callus); two s. one d. *Education:* Malta Univ. *Career:* practised law 1975–88; Speaker House of Reps. 1988–92, 1992–96; MP (Nationalist Party) 1996–, Whip Parl. Group 1997–99, Sec. Gen. 1997–98; Shadow Minister and Opposition Spokesman for Social Policy 1996–98; Leader of the House and Minister for Social Policy 1998–99, Deputy Prime Minister and Minister for Social Policy 1999–2004, Prime Minister 2004–, Minister of Finance 2004–08; Gen. Pres. Malta Catholic Action 1976–86; Chair. Pharmacy Bd 1987–88, Nat. Comm. for Persons with Disabilities 1987–94 (Pres. 1994–96), Nat. Comm. for Mental

Health Reform 1987–96, Electoral System (Revision) Comm. 1994–95, Mizzi Org. Bd of Dirs 1989–97; mem. Prisons Bd 1987–88.
Address: Office of the Prime Minister, Auberge de Castille, Valletta, CMR 02, Malta (office). *Telephone:* 21242560 (office). *Fax:* 21249888 (office). *E-mail:* lawrence.gonzi@gov.mt (office). *Website:* www.opm.gov.mt (office).

GOODERHAM, Peter, BA, PhD; British diplomatist; *Permanent Representative, United Nations, Geneva; Education:* Univs of Bristol and Newcastle. *Career:* man. trainee, Industrial Facts and Forecasting (market research firm) 1975–76; Research Fellow, Univ. of Essex 1979–81, Univ. of Birmingham 1981–83; joined FCO 1983, Asst Desk Officer, Falkland Islands Dept 1983–85, First Sec., Arms Control, UK Del. to NATO, Brussels 1985–87, Head of Nigeria Section, West Africa Dept, FCO 1987–90, First Sec. (Econ.), Riyadh 1990–93, Deputy Head, Security Policy Dept (NATO and arms control issues), FCO 1993–96, ECOSOC Counsellor, Perm. Mission to UN, New York (econ., environmental, human rights and social issues) 1996–99, Political Counsellor, Embassy in Washington, DC 1999–2003; Rep. to EU Political and Security Cttee, UK Representation, Brussels 2003–04, Dir Middle East and N Africa Directorate, FCO 2004–07, Perm. Rep. to UN and other Int. Orgs, Geneva 2008–.
Address: UK Government Offices, Avenue Louis Casaï 58, 1216 Cointrin GE, Geneva, Switzerland (office). *Telephone:* (22) 918-23-00 (office). *Fax:* (22) 918-23-33 (office). *E-mail:* geneva_un@fco.gov.uk (office).

GOODHART, Charles Albert Eric, CBE, PhD, FBA; British economist and academic; *Norman Sosnow Professor Emeritus of Banking and Finance, London School of Economics;* b. 23 Oct. 1936, London; m. Margaret (Miffy) Smith 1960; one s. three d. *Education:* Eton Coll., Trinity Coll., Cambridge, Harvard Univ. *Career:* Asst Lecturer, Dept of Econs, Univ. of Cambridge and Prize Fellow, Trinity Coll.; Economist, Dept of Econ. Affairs, London 1965–66; Lecturer, LSE 1966–68, Norman Sosnow Prof. of Banking and Finance 1985–2002, Prof. Emer. 2002–, mem. Financial Markets Group 1987– (Deputy Dir 2002–04), Hon. Fellow 2006; Adviser on Monetary Affairs, Bank of England 1968–85, External mem. Monetary Policy Cttee 1997–2000; Adviser to Gov. of Bank of England on Financial Regulation 2002–04; mem. Exchange Fund Advisory Council, Hong Kong 1988–97. *Publications:* Money, Information and Uncertainty 1989, The Evolution of Central Banks 1985, The Central Bank and the Financial System 1995, The Emerging Framework of Financial Regulation (ed.) 1998, The Foreign Exchange Market (with R. Payne) 2000, Financial Crises, Contagion and the Lender of Last Resort (co-ed with G. Illing) 2002, Intervention to Save Hong Kong (with Lu Dai) 2003, Financial Development and Economic Growth (ed) 2004, House Prices and the Macroeconomy (with B. Hofmann) 2006.
Address: Financial Markets Group, Room R414, London School of Economics, Houghton Street, London, WC2A 2AE (office); 27 Abbotsbury Road, London, W14 8EL, England (home). *Telephone:* (20) 7955-7555 (office); (20) 7603-5817 (home). *Fax:* (20) 7371-3664 (home). *E-mail:* c.a.goodhart@lse.ac.uk (office). *Website:* fmg.lse.ac.uk (office).

GOODLAD, Baron (Life Peer), cr. 2005; **Sir Alastair,** KCMG, PC; British diplomatist and fmr politician; b. 1948; m. Cecilia Hurst 1968; two s. *Career:* elected MP for Norwich 1974, for Eddisbury 1983–99; Lord Commr of the Treasury 1981–84; Parl. Under-Sec. of State for Energy 1984–87; Comptroller of HM Household 1989–90; Treasurer of HM Household and Deputy Chief Whip 1990–92; Minister of State for FCO 1992–95; Govt. Chief Whip 1995–97; Shadow Sec. of State for Int. Devt 1997–98; High Commr to Australia 2000–05; Chair. Asia House 2006–; mem. Conservative Party.
Address: House of Lords, London, SW1A 0PW, England (office). *Telephone:* (20) 7219-3000 (office).

GOODMAN, Seymour, BS, MS, PhD; American academic and research institute director; *Co-Director, Center for International Strategy, Technology and Policy, Georgia Institute of Technology;* b. 1943, Chicago; m.; two c. *Education:* Columbia Univ., California Inst. of Tech. *Career:* Asst Prof. of Applied Math., Univ. of Virginia 1970–75, Assoc. Prof. of Applied Math. and Computer Science 1975–81, mem. Center for Russian and East European Studies 1977–81; Visiting Fellow, Princeton Univ. 1977–78, Visiting Prof. of Math. 1977–79; Visiting Assoc. Prof. of Econs, Univ. of Chicago 1979; Prof. of Man. Information Systems, Univ. of Arizona 1981–2000, mem. Steering Cttee, Russian and Soviet Studies Program 1986–91, Dir Int. Business Programs, Coll. of Business and Public Admin 1991–1993, mem. Center for Middle Eastern Studies 1991–2001; Carnegie Science Fellow, Stanford Univ. 1994–97, Dir Project on the Information Techs and Int. Security 1996–98, Visiting Prof., Inst. for Int. Studies 1997–2000, Dir Consortium for Research on Information Security and Policy, Center for Int. Security and Cooperation 1998–2000; Prof. of Int.

Affairs and Computing, Sam Nunn School of Int. Affairs and Coll. of Computing, Georgia Inst. of Tech. 2000–, Co-Dir Center for Int. Strategy, Tech. and Policy and Assoc. Dir for Policy, Georgia Tech Information Security Center 2000–; Contributing Ed. Int. Perspectives for Communications, Asscn for Computing Machinery; fmr advisor to Pres.'s Comm. on Critical Infrastructure Protection; fmr Chair. Nat. Research Council Meeting on Tech. Responses to Cyber-attack and their Legal Implications.
Address: Center for International Strategy, Technology and Policy, Georgia Institute of Technology, 781 Marietta Street NW, Atlanta, GA 30332-0610, USA (office). *Telephone:* (404) 894-3195 (office). *Fax:* (404) 894-1900 (office). *E-mail:* Seymour.Goodman@cc.gatech.edu (office). *Website:* www.cistp.gatech.edu (office).

GOODWIN-GILL, Guy S., MA, DPhil; British/Canadian academic and barrister; *Senior Research Fellow, All Souls College, University of Oxford;* b. 25 Dec. 1946, Ealing, Middx; m. Sharon Rusu. *Education:* Mill Hill School, Wadham Coll., Oxford. *Career:* called to the Bar 1971; barrister, Blackstone Chambers, Temple, London; Lecturer, later Sr Lecturer, Coll. of Law 1971–76; Visiting Lecturer and Examiner in Public Int. Law, Kingston Polytechnic 1973–76; Legal Adviser, UNHCR Br. Office, London 1976–78; Legal Adviser and sometime Officer-in-Charge UNHCR/UNIC/UNICEF Jt Office for Australia, NZ and the South Pacific, Sydney 1978–83; Sr Legal Research Officer, UNHCR, Geneva, Switzerland 1983–88; Visiting Prof., Osgoode Hall Law School, York Univ., N York, Ont., Canada 1988; Visiting Social Sciences Prof., Carleton Univ., Ottawa, Canada 1988–89; Prof. of Law 1989–97; Prof. of Asylum Law, Univ. of Amsterdam, Netherlands 1994–99; Rubin Dir of Research, Inst. of European Studies, Univ. of Oxford 1997–2002; Prof. of Int. Refugee Law, Univ. of Oxford 1998; Sr Research Fellow, All Souls Coll., Oxford 2002–; Adviser, WHO, Geneva 1995; consultant and adviser to Govts of Canada, Australia, USA and numerous int. orgs; Pres. Refugee Legal Centre, London 1997–; Founding Ed. and Ed.-in-Chief International Journal of Refugee Law 1998–2001, mem. Editorial Bd 2001–; Pres. Media Appeals Bd of Kosovo 2000–03; mem. Council Overseas Devt Inst. (ODI); Grand Officer of the Order of Al Istiqlal (Independence), Royal Hashemite Kingdom of Jordan 2004. *Publications:* International Law and the Movement of Persons Between States 1978, The Refugee in International Law 1983, Child Soldiers (co-author) 1994, Free and Fair Elections 1994, Codes of Conduct for Elections 1998, The Reality of International Law (co-ed.) 1999, Basic Documents on Human Rights (co-ed.) 2002, Tolerance in an Age of Uncertainty 2002; numerous chapters in books and journal articles.
Address: All Souls College, Oxford, OX1 4AL (office); Blackstone Chambers, Blackstone House, Temple, London, EC4Y 9BW, England (office). *Telephone:* (1865) 279357 (office); (20) 7583-1770 (office). *Fax:* (1865) 279299 (office); (20) 7822-7350 (office). *E-mail:* guy.goodwin-gill@law.ox.ac.uk (office); guygoodwin-gill@blackstonechambers.com (office). *Website:* www.blackstonechambers.com (office).

GOOLD, (John) Douglas, PhD; Canadian academic, journalist and organization executive; *President and CEO, Canadian Institute of International Affairs;* b. 20 Jan. 1946, Peterborough, Ont.; m. Libby Znaimer 1990. *Education:* McMaster Univ., Univ. of Alberta, Univ. of Cambridge, UK. *Career:* Lecturer, Univ. of Alberta 1975–76, Univ. of Victoria, BC 1976–77; Killam Postdoctoral Fellow, Univ. of BC 1977–79; mem. Editorial Bd Edmonton Journal 1979–81, News Ed. 1981–84, Ottawa Bureau Chief 1984–87; Reporter, Financial Post 1988; Ed. Investment Executive 1988–89; Producer and Commentator, CBC Business World 1989–91; Personal Affairs Ed. The Globe and Mail 1991–93, Columnist 1991–98, Investment Ed. 1997; Ed. Report on Business (ROB) 1997–2000, ROB magazine 2000–02; Pres. and CEO Canadian Inst. of Int. Affairs 2004–. *Publications:* Peace Without Promise (co-author) 1981, How to Get What You Want from Your Bank 1994, The Bre-X Fraud (co-author) 1997; numerous articles.
Address: Canadian Institute of International Affairs, 205 Richmond Street West, Suite 302, Toronto, Ont., M5V 1V3 (office); 42 Wychwood Park, Toronto, Ont., M6G 2V5, Canada (home). *Telephone:* (416) 977-9000 (ext. 33) (office); (416) 653-1233 (home). *Fax:* (416) 977-7521 (office). *E-mail:* dgoold@ciia.org (office). *Website:* www.ciia.org (office).

GOONETILLEKE, Bernard Anton Bandara; Sri Lankan diplomatist (retd); m. Maria Goonetilleke. *Career:* career diplomat, has served as Sec., Ministry of Foreign Affairs, as Acting Perm. Rep. to UN, New York, as Amb. to China and Holy See and Perm. Rep. to UN, Geneva and Vienna, as Amb. to Conf. on Disarmament, Dir-Gen. Secr. for coordinating peace process, Colombo 2001–04, served in Embassy in Washington, DC 2004–05, Amb. to USA (also accred to Mexico) 2005–08 (retd).
Address: c/o Ministry of Foreign Affairs, Republic Building, Colombo 1, Sri Lanka. *Telephone:* (11) 2325371.

GOPEE-SCOON, Paula, BSc, LLB (Hons); Trinidad and Tobago politician and business executive; *Minister of Foreign Affairs;* b. 18 April 1958, Point Fortin; m.; three c. *Education:* St Joseph's Convent, San Fernando, Univ. of the West Indies, Cave Hill, Barbados, Univ. of London, UK. *Career:* professional experience includes teaching (Point Fortin Intermediate Roman Catholic School), banking and finance (Republic Bank and Royal Bank of Trinidad and Tobago), along with sales, marketing and customer service (BioChem Trinidad and Tobago Ltd and Sunspots Plastics Ltd); MP (People's Nat. Movt —PNM) for Point Fortin 2007–; Minister of Foreign Affairs 2007–; mem. Dyslexia Asscn Bursary Fund Cttee, St Joseph's Convent (Port of Spain) Support Group.
Address: Ministry of Foreign Affairs, Knowsley Bldg, 10–14 Queen's Park West, Port of Spain, Trinidad and Tobago (office). *Telephone:* 623-4116 (office). *Fax:* 624-4220 (office). *E-mail:* press@foreign.gov.tt (office). *Website:* www.foreign.gov.tt (office); www.pnm.org.tt.

GORBACHEV, Mikhail Sergeyevich; Russian organization official and politician; *Head, International Foundation for Socio-Economic and Political Studies;* b. 2 March 1931, Privolnoye, Krasnogvardeisky Dist, Stavropol Krai; m. Raisa Titarenko 1953 (died 1999); one d. *Education:* Faculty of Law, Moscow State Univ. and Stavropol Agricultural Inst. *Career:* began work as machine operator 1946; joined CPSU 1952; Deputy Head, Dept of Propaganda, Stavropol Komsomol (V. I. Lenin Young Communist League) Territorial Cttee 1955–56, Second, then First Sec. 1958–62; First Sec., Stavropol Komsomol City Cttee 1956–58; del. to CPSU Congress 1961, 1971, 1976, 1981, 1986, 1990; Party Organizer, Stavropol Territorial Production Bd of Collective and State Farms 1962; Head, Dept of Party Bodies of CPSU Territorial Cttee 1963–66; First Sec., Stavropol City Party Cttee 1966–68; Second Sec., Stavropol Territorial CPSU Cttee 1968–70, First Sec. 1970–78; mem. CPSU Cen. Cttee 1971–91, Sec. for Agric. 1978–85, alt. mem. Political Bureau CPSU, Cen. Cttee 1979–80, mem. 1980–91, Gen. Sec., CPSU Cen. Cttee 1985–91; Deputy Supreme Soviet of USSR 1970–89 (Chair. Foreign Affairs Comm. of Soviet Union 1984–85), mem. Presidium 1985–88, Chair. 1988–89, Supreme Soviet of RSFSR 1980–90, elected to Congress of People's Deputies of USSR 1989, Chair. 1989–90; Pres. of USSR 1990–91; Head, Int. Foundation for Socio-Economic and Political Studies (Gorbachev Foundation) 1992–; Head Int. Green Cross/Green Crescent 1993–; presidential candidate 1996; Co-founder and Co-Chair. Social Democratic Party of Russia 2000–04 (resgnd); syndicated columnist for numerous newspapers worldwide 1992–; Hon. Citizen of Berlin 1992, Freeman of Aberdeen 1993; Nobel Peace Prize 1990, Albert Schweitzer Leadership Award (jt recipient) 1992, Ronald Reagan Freedom Award 1992, Urania-Medaille (Berlin) 1996; Augsburg Peace Prize 2005; Order of Lenin (three times), Orders of Red Banner of Labour, Badge of Honour. *Recording:* Peter and the Wolf: Wolf Tracks (Grammy Award, Best Spoken Word Album for Children (jtly) 2004) 2003. *Publications:* A Time for Peace 1985, The Coming Century of Peace 1986, Speeches and Writings 1986–90, Peace Has No Alternative 1986, Moratorium 1986, Perestroika: New Thinking for Our Country and the World 1987, The August Coup (Its Cause and Results) 1991, December 1991: My Stand 1992, The Years of Hard Decisions 1993, Life and Reforms 1995.
Address: International Foundation for Socio-Economic and Political Studies, 125167 Moscow, Leningradskii pr. 39/14, Russia (office). *Telephone:* (495) 945-74-01 (office). *Fax:* (495) 945-74-01 (office). *E-mail:* gf@gorby.ru (office). *Website:* www.gorby.ru (office); www.mikhailgorbachev.org (office).

GORBULIN, Volodomir Pavlovich, DTech; Ukrainian politician and space scientist; *Head, Supreme Economic Council;* b. 17 Jan. 1939, Zaporozhya. *Education:* Dniepropetrovsk State Univ. *Career:* fmr engineer and mechanic Pivdenne construction co., then jr researcher 1962–76; took part in devt of Cosmos space rockets; mem. Cen. Cttee CP 1977–; Head Rocket, Space and Aviation Tech. Sector 1980–; Head of Defence Complex Section, Cabinet of Ministers 1990–92; Dir-Gen. Ukrainian Nat. Space Agency 1992–94; Sec. Council on Nat. Security 1994–96, Council on Nat. Security and Defence 1996–; Head Supreme Econ. Council 1997–; Deputy Chair. Council on Problems of Science and Tech. Policy 1999–; Chair. State Cttee of Defence-Industrial Complex 1999–; Pres. Ukrainian Basketball Fed.; mem. Ukrainian Nat. Acad. of Sciences 1997–; USSR State Prize 1990, Ukrainian Nat. Acad. of Sciences Prize.
Address: Office of the President, Bankovskaya str. 11, 252011 Kiev, Ukraine (office). *Telephone:* (44) 291-5152 (office).

GORBUNOVS, Anatolijs; Latvian fmr head of state; *Chairman, Latvian–Russian Intergovernmental Commission;* b. 10 Feb. 1942, Pilda, Riga Co.; m. Lidija Klavina; one s. *Education:* Riga Polytech. Inst., Moscow Acad. of Social Sciences. *Career:* constructor on a state farm; Sr Mechanic Riga Polytech. Inst. 1959–62; served Red Army 1962–65; various posts in the structure of the Latvian CP 1974–88; Chair. Supreme Council of Latvia 1988–93 (Pres. of Latvia); Chair. of Saeima (Parl.) 1993–95; mem. Parl. for Latvijas ceļš (Latvian Way); Chair. Saeima Cttee on European Affairs Feb.–Aug. 1996; Minister of Environmental Protection and Regional Devt and Deputy Prime Minister 1996–98; Minister of Communications 1998, of Transport 1999–2004; Chair. Latvian–Russian Intergovernmental Comm. 1996–.
Address: c/o Ministry of Transport, 3 Gogola Street, 1743 Rīga, Latvia (office). *Telephone:* 6722-69-22 (office).

GORDAULT-MONTAGNE, Maurice, BA, MA; French diplomatist; *Ambassador to UK;* b. 16 Nov. 1953, Paris. *Education:* Univ. of Paris Sorbonne IV. *Career:* joined Ministry of Foreign Affairs 1978, Desk Officer for Asian Affairs 1979–81, Pvt. Sec. to Sec.-Gen. 1984–86, tech. adviser to minister, responsible for press and parl. relations 1986–88, Deputy Spokesman 1991–92, Acting Spokesman 1992–93, Deputy Prin. Sec. to Minister 1993–95, Head of Prime Minister's office, Prin. Sec. 1995–97, Personal Rep. of Pres. of France 1997–98, Sr Diplomatic Adviser to Pres. Chirac and G8 Sherpa 2002–07; First Sec., Embassy in New Delhi 1981–83, Counsellor (political affairs) Embassy in Bonn 1988–90, Amb. to Japan 1998–2002, to UK 2007–; Hon. LVO 1992, Hon. CMG 2004; Chevalier de l'Ordre national du Mérite 1998, de la Légion d'Honneur 2001.
Address: Embassy of France, 58 Knightsbridge, London, SW1X 7JT, England (office). *Telephone:* (20) 7073-1000 (office). *Fax:* (20) 7073-1004 (office). *E-mail:* presse.londres-amba@diplomatie.fr (office). *Website:* www.ambafrance-uk.org (office).

GORDEYEV, Aleksey Vassilyevich, CandEconSci; Russian politician and economist; *Minister of Agriculture;* b. 28 Feb. 1955, Frankfurt an der Oder, Germany. *Education:* Acad. of Nat. Econs, USSR Council of Ministers. *Career:* Sr Supervisor SU-4 Govt Glavmosstroi 1980–81, Chief Expert, Head of Div., then Deputy Head Dept of Glavagrostroi 1981–86; Deputy Dir-Gen. Moskva (agro-industrial co.), Moscow region 1986–92; Deputy Head Admin. Lyubertsy Dist, Moscow region 1992–97; Head Dept of Econ., mem. Exec. Bd Ministry of Agric. and Food 1997–98, First Deputy Minister of Agric. and Food 1998–99, Minister of Agric. 1999–, concurrently Deputy Chair. Govt of Russian Fed. 2000–04; Merited Econ. of Russian Fed.
Address: Ministry of Agriculture, Orlikov per. 1/11, 107139 Moscow, Russia (office). *Telephone:* (495) 207-83-86 (office). *Fax:* (495) 207-95-80 (office). *E-mail:* info@mcx.ru (office). *Website:* www.mcx.ru (office).

GORDON, Robert Anthony Eagleson, CMG, OBE; British diplomatist (retd); b. 9 Feb. 1952, Trieste, Italy; m. Pamela Gordon; two s. two d. *Education:* King's School, Canterbury, Magdalen Coll., Oxford. *Career:* entered British Diplomatic Service 1973, Desk Officer, Cen. and Southern Africa Dept 1973–74, Third, then Second Sec., Embassy in Warsaw 1975–77, Second, then First Sec., Embassy in Santiago 1978–83, Desk Officer, S America Dept, FCO 1983–85, EC Dept 1985–87, First Sec., Del. to OECD, Paris 1987–92, Counsellor and Deputy Head of Mission 1992–95, Amb. to Myanmar 1995–99, Head of SE Asia Dept, FCO 1999–2003, Amb. to Viet Nam 2003–07 (retd).
Address: c/o Foreign and Commonwealth Office, King Charles Street, London, SW1A 2AH, England. *Telephone:* (20) 7008-1500.

GORDON, Robert James, PhD; American economist and academic; *Stanley G. Harris Professor in the Social Sciences, Northwestern University;* b. 3 Sept. 1940, Boston, Mass; m. Julie S. Peyton 1963. *Education:* Harvard Univ., Univ. of Oxford, UK, Massachusetts Inst. of Tech. *Career:* Assoc. Prof. of Econs, Harvard Univ. 1967–68, Univ. of Chicago 1968–73; Prof. of Econs, Northwestern Univ. 1973–87, Stanley G. Harris Prof. in the Social Sciences 1987–, Chair. Dept of Econs 1992–96; Fellow, Econometric Soc. 1977, American Acad. of Arts and Sciences 1997; John Simon Guggenheim Memorial Fellowship 1980–81, Lustrum Award, Erasmus Univ., Rotterdam 1999. *Publications:* The American Business Cycle: Continuity and Change 1986, The Measurement of Durable Goods Prices 1990, The Economics of New Goods 1997, Macroeconomics (ninth edn) 2003.
Address: Department of Economics, 349 Andersen Hall, Northwestern University, Evanston, IL 60208-0001 (office); 202 Greenwood Street, Evanston, IL 60201, USA (home). *Telephone:* (847) 491-3616 (office); (847) 869-3544 (home). *Fax:* (847) 491-7001 (office). *E-mail:* rjg@northwestern.edu (office). *Website:* faculty-web.at.northwestern.edu/economics/gordon/indexmsie.html (office).

GORDON-MACLEOD, David; British diplomatist; b. 4 May 1948, Kimberley, S Africa; m. Adrienne Gordon-Macleod; two s. two d. *Career:* joined FCO 1978, Second Sec. (Aid), Mbabane 1978–83, Nuclear Energy Dept, FCO 1983–84, Arms Control and Disarmament Dept 1984–85, S America Dept 1985–87, Deputy Head of Mission, Maputo 1987–91, W Africa Dept, FCO 1991–92, African Dept (External) 1992–93, Non-Proliferation Dept 1993–94, Deputy Head of Mission, Bogota 1995–97, Dir

EU and Econ. Affairs, Athens 1998–2003, High Commr to Papua New Guinea 2003–07.
Address: c/o Foreign and Commonwealth Office, King Charles Street, London, SW1A 2AH, England (office). *Telephone:* (20) 7008-1500 (office). *Website:* www.fco.gov.uk (office).

GORE, Albert (Al), Jr.; American financial executive, academic and fmr politician; *Chairman, Generation Investment Management LLP;* b. 31 March 1948; m. Mary E. Aitcheson 1970; one s. three d. *Education:* Harvard and Vanderbilt Univs. *Career:* served with US Army during Vietnam war; investigative reporter, editorial writer, The Tennessean 1971–76; home-builder and land developer, Tanglewood Home Builders Co. 1971–76; livestock and tobacco farmer 1973–; Head Community Enterprise Bd 1993–; mem. House of Reps 1977–79; Senator from Tennessee 1985–93; Vice-Pres. of USA 1993–2001; Democrat cand. in Presidential Elections 2000; lecturer Middle Tennessee State Univ, Columbia Univ 2001–, Visiting Prof. UCLA, Fisk Univ 2001–; Vice-Chair. Metropolitan West Financial LLC 2001–; Sr Advisor Google Inc. 2001–; co-founder and Chair. Current TV (youth cable TV network) 2004–; co-founder and Chair. Generation Investment Management LLP (fund man. firm) Washington, DC and London, UK 2004–; Partner Kleiner, Perkins, Caulfield and Byers 2007–; mem. Bd of Dirs Apple Computer Inc.; Dr hc (Harvard) 1994, (New York) 1998; UNEP Champion of the Earth Laureate 2007, Prince of Asturias Award for Int. Co-operation 2007, Nobel Peace Prize (shared with UN Intergovernmental Panel on Climate Change) 2007, Dan David Prize 2008. *Film:* An Inconvenient Truth (Best Documentary Los Angeles Film Critics Asscn 2006, Nat. Soc. of Film Critics 2007, Acad. Award for Best Documentary Feature 2007) 2006. *Publication:* Earth in the Balance 1992, An Inconvenient Truth (Quill Award for History, Current Affairs or Politics) 2006, The Assault on Reason: How the Politics of Blind Faith Subvert Wise Decision-Making (Quill Award for History/Current Affairs/Politics 2007) 2007.
Address: Generation Investment Management US LLP, 750 17th Street, 11th Floor, Washington, DC 20006, USA (office). *Telephone:* (202) 785-7400 (office). *Fax:* (202) 785-7401 (office). *Website:* www.generationim.com (office); www.current.tv.

GOTCHEV, Dimitar Bonev; Bulgarian judge; b. 27 Feb. 1936, Sofia; m. Jova Gotcheva-Cholakova 1976; one d. *Education:* Univ. of Sofia St Kliment Ochridsky. *Career:* legal adviser 1959–66; Arbiter, State Court of Arbitration 1966–89; Judge, Supreme Court 1990, Judge, Head of Commercial Div. 1990–, Deputy Chief Justice, Supreme Court 1993; Judge, Constitutional Court 1994–2004; Judge, European Court of Human Rights, Strasbourg 1992–98.
Address: c/o Constitutional Court of Republic of Bulgaria, Bul. Dondoukov 1, 1202 Sofia; Koslodui Str. N34, 1202 Sofia, Bulgaria (home). *Telephone:* (2) 940-23-31; (2) 31-54-25 (home).

GOULDEN, Sir (Peter) John, Kt, GCMG, BA; British diplomatist (retd) and civil servant; b. 21 Feb. 1941; m. Diana Waite 1962; one s. one d. *Education:* Queen's Coll., Oxford. *Career:* joined FCO 1962, Ankara 1963–67, Manila 1969–70, Dublin 1976–79, Head Personnel Services Dept 1980–82, News Dept 1982–84, Asst Under-Sec. of State 1988–92; Counsellor, Head Chancery Office of UK Perm. Rep. to EC 1984–87; Amb. to Turkey 1992–95; Amb., Perm. Rep. to North Atlantic Council and WEU 1995–2001; consultant, Home Office 2001–.
Address: c/o Home Office, 2 Marsham Street, London, SW1P 4DF, England. *Telephone:* (20) 7035-4848.

GOULONGANA, Jean-Robert; Gabonese politician and diplomatist; b. 30 April 1953, Lambarene; m.; three c. *Education:* Dakar Univ., Senegal, Aix-Marseille III Univ., France. *Career:* Minister of Waters, Forests and the Environment 1990–91; Amb. to Italy 1992, to Belgium 1996; Head, Gabonese Mission to EU; Sec.-Gen. African, Caribbean and Pacific States (ACP) 2000–05; Officier, Ordre du Mérite Maritime Gabonais.
Address: c/o African, Caribbean and Pacific States Secretariat, ACP House, 451 avenue Georges Henri, Brussels, Belgium (office).

GOULTY, Alan Fletcher, CMG, BA, MA; British diplomatist; *Ambassador to Tunisia;* m. Dr Lillian Craig Harris; one s. by previous m. *Education:* Corpus Christi Coll., Oxford. *Career:* Third Sec., Arabian Dept, FCO 1968–69, language student, Middle East Centre for Arab Studies, Shemlan, Lebanon 1969–71, Third, later Second Sec., Beirut 1971–72, Second Sec., Khartoum 1972–75, Second, later First Sec., Repub. of Ireland Dept, FCO 1975–77, on loan to Cabinet Office, London 1977–80, First Sec., Washington, DC 1981–85, Deputy Head, later Head of Near East and N Africa Dept, FCO 1985–90, Deputy Head of Mission, Cairo 1990–95, Amb. to Sudan 1995–99, Dir Middle East and N Africa Dept, FCO 2000–02, UK Special Rep. for Sudan 2002–04, Amb. to Tunisia 2004–;

Fellow, Weatherhead Center for Int. Affairs, Harvard Univ., USA 1999–2000.
Address: British Embassy, Rue du Lac Windermere, Les Berges du Lac, Tunis 1053, Tunisia (office). *Telephone:* (71) 108-700 (office). *Fax:* (71) 108-749 (office). *E-mail:* TunisConsular@tunis.mail.fco.gov.uk (office). *Website:* www.britishembassy.gov.uk/tunisia (office).

GOUMBA, Abel, DenM; Central African Republic politician and professor of medicine; *Vice-President;* b. 18 Sept. 1926, Grimari; m.; 15 c. *Education:* Univ. of Bordeaux. *Career:* doctor in People's Repub. of Congo 1950–56; Vice-Pres. Gov. Council of Oubangui-Chari, Minister of Finance and Planning and Deputy to Regional Ass. 1957–58, Pres. Gov. Council July–Nov. 1958; Minister of Finance and Econ. Affairs, Central African Repub. 1958–59; Minister of State April–Oct. 1959; Deputy to Nat. Ass. 1959; Senator 1960; under house arrest 1960; political prisoner 1960–64; in exile abroad 1964–81; lecturer, Ecole Nat. de Santé Publique, Rennes 1971–73; Prof. of Public Health, Faculty of Medicine, Butaré, Rwanda 1973–77; Prof. of Public Health, Centre Régional de Développement Sanitaire, Cotonou, Benin 1977–81; Prof. of Public Health, Univ. of Bangui 1981–82, 1988–, Rector Feb.–Aug. 1982; political prisoner 1982–84; unemployed 1985–88; fmr leader of Consultative Group of Democratic Forces (CFD), alliance of 14 opposition groups; presidential cand. 1993; Deputy for Kouango, Nat. Ass. 1988–; presidential cand. 1999; currently Leader Front Patriotique pour le Progrès (FPP); Prime Minister and Minister of the Economy, Finance, the Budget, Planning and International Co-operation Cen. African Repub. March–Dec. 2003; Vice-Pres. Dec. 2003–.
Address: c/o Office of the President, Palais de la Renaissance, Bangui, Central African Republic (office). *Telephone:* 61-46-63.

GOUNARIS, Elias, LLM; Greek diplomatist; *Chairman, Committee for the Environment and Sustainable Development, Ministry of Foreign Affairs;* b. 7 Sept. 1941, Athens; one s. *Education:* Univ. of Athens. *Career:* Consul, New York 1969; Ministry of Foreign Affairs 1973; Sec. Perm. Mission of Greece to int. orgs, Geneva 1975; Counsellor 1976; Embassy, Belgrade 1979; Ministry of Foreign Affairs 1983; Minister-Counsellor, then Minister, Embassy, Bonn 1987, Minister Plenipotentiary 1988; Amb. to USSR (also accred to Mongolia) 1989; Amb. to UK 1993–96; Dir Gen. for Political Affairs, Ministry of Foreign Affairs 1997–99; Perm. Rep. to the UN, New York 1999–2002; Chair. Cttee for the Environment and Sustainable Devt, Ministry of Foreign Affairs 2002–; mem. Bd of Dirs OTE S.A.; decorations from Austria, Finland, Germany, Greece, Italy, Spain, Ukraine and the Russian Orthodox Church.
Address: Committee for the Environment and Sustainable Development, Ministry of Foreign Affairs, Odos Akadimias 1, 106 71 Athens (office); Akadimias Street 1, 106 71 Athens, Greece. *Telephone:* (21) 03681000 (office). *Fax:* (21) 03624195 (office). *E-mail:* mfa@mfa.gr (office). *Website:* www.mfa.gr (office).

GOURAD HAMADOU, Barkad; Djibouti politician. *Career:* fmr mem. of French Senate; fmr Minister of Health; Prime Minister of Djibouti Sept. 1978–2001, Minister of Ports 1978–87, Minister of Planning and Land Devt 1987, Prime Minister, Minister of Nat. and Regional Devt –2001; mem. Rassemblement Populaire pour le Progrès (RPP).
Address: c/o Office du Premier Ministre, PO Box 2086, Djibouti, Republic of Djibouti (office).

GOUREVITCH, Peter, BA, PhD; American political scientist and academic; *Professor of Political Science, University of California, San Diego;* *Education:* Oberlin Coll., Harvard Univ. *Career:* Asst Prof. of Govt, Harvard Univ. 1969–73, Assoc. Prof. 1973–74; Assoc. Prof. of Political Science, McGill Univ., Montréal 1974–79; Assoc. Prof. of Political Science, Univ. of Calif., San Diego 1979–81, Prof. of Political Science 1981–, Chair. Political Science Dept 1980–83, Founding Dean Grad. School of Int. Relations and Pacific Studies 1986–96, Prof. 1986–; Acting Dir Center for European Studies, Harvard Univ. 1972–73, 1976–77, Visiting Research Fellow 2001–02; Visiting Fellow, Center for Advanced Study in the Behavioral Sciences, Palo Alto 2002–03; Visiting Scholar, Russell Sage Foundation, New York 2005–06, also Guggenheim Fellow; Co-Ed. International Organization 1997–2001, mem. Bd of Eds 1980–86, 1988–93, 1995–2001; mem. American Acad. of Arts and Sciences 1996–; mem. American Political Science Asscn, Asscn of Professional Schools of Int. Affairs (Pres. 1991), Council on Foreign Relations 1991–. *Publications:* France and the Troubled World Economy (jt ed.) 1982, Politics in Hard Times: Comparative Responses to International Crisis 1986, New Challenges to International Cooperation 1993, United States–Japan Relations and International Institutions: After the Cold War (jt ed.) 1995, How Shareholder Reforms Can Pay Foreign Policy Dividends (jt author) 2002; numerous journal articles and book reviews.
Address: Graduate School of International Relations and Pacific Studies, Office 1421, University of California, San Diego, 9500 Gilman Drive, La

Jolla, CA 92093-0519, USA (office). *Telephone:* (858) 534-7085 (office). *Fax:* (858) 534-3939 (office). *E-mail:* pgourevitch@ucsd.edu (office). *Website:* www-irps.ucsd.edu (office).

GOUVEIA, Maria Teresa Pinto Basto Patricio; Portuguese politician; *Executive Director and Member, Board of Trustees, Fundação Calouste Gulbenkian;* b. 18 July 1946, Lisbon; m. Alexandre Manuel Vahia de Castro O'Neill de Bulhões (died 1986); one s. *Education:* Univ. of Lisbon. *Career:* Sec. of State for Culture 1985–1990; elected mem. Parl. 1987, 1991, 1995, 2002; Sec. of State for Environment 1991–93, Minister for Environment 1993–95; mem. Bd of Govs and Exec. Cttee, European Cultural Foundation, Amsterdam 1996–2002; Vice-Pres. Foreign Affairs Parl. Cttee 2002–03; Minister of Foreign Affairs and Portuguese Communities Abroad 2003–04; fmr Pres. Cttee for Cultural Cooperation, Council of Europe, Strasbourg; mem. Gen. Council O Público newspaper 1990–91; Pres. Bd of Trustees Serralves Foundation, Oporto 2001–03; Exec. Dir and mem. Bd of Trustees Calouste Gulbenkian Foundation 2004–; Great Cross, Ordem de Cristo, Great Cross, Ordem Infante D. Henrique. *Address:* c/o Board of Trustees, Fundação Calouste Gulbenkian, Avenida da Berna, 45A, 1067-001 Lisbon, Portugal (office). *Telephone:* (217) 823306 (office). *Fax:* (217) 823088 (office). *E-mail:* tpgouveia@gulbenkian.pt (office). *Website:* www.gulbenkian.org.

GOVORIN, Boris Aleksandrovich; Russian politician and diplomatist; *Ambassador to Mongolia;* b. 27 June 1947. *Career:* Chair. Irkutsk city Exec. Cttee 1990–92; Mayor of Irkutsk city 1992-97; Gov. Irkutsk 1997–2005; Amb. to Mongolia 2006–. *Address:* Embassy of the Russian Federation, Enkh Taivny Gudamj A-6, CPO Box 661, Ulan Bator, Mongolia (office). *Telephone:* (11) 327191 (office). *Fax:* (11) 327018 (office).

GOW, James; British academic; *Professor of International Peace and Security, Department of War Studies, King's College London; Career:* joined King's Coll. 1991, responsible for EC-funded projects on Security and Democracy in Central and Eastern Europe 1991–97, currently Prof. of Int. Peace and Security and Dir Int. Peace and Security Program; served as expert adviser and witness for UN Int. Criminal Tribunal for fmr Yugoslavia 1994–98, first person to give evidence at an int. criminal tribunal; on expert panel advising UK Sec. of State for Defence during Strategic Defence Review 1997–98, 1999–2000; visiting positions at Woodrow Wilson Int. Center for Scholars, Washington DC, Inst. of War and Peace Studies at Columbia Univ., Center of Int. Studies, Princeton Univ.; Reviews Ed. International Peacekeeping 1994–97; mem. Ed. Bd journal of Genocide Research; contributes to numerous collaborative research projects on peace and security issues. *Publications:* Triumph of the Lack of Will: International Diplomacy and the Yugoslav War 1997, The Serbian Project and its Adversaries: a Strategy of War Crimes 2003, Defending the West 2005, War, Image and Legitimacy: Viewing Contemporary Conflict (co-author) 2007. *Address:* Department of War Studies, King's College London, Strand, London, WC2R 2LS, England (office). *Telephone:* (20) 7848 2085 (office). *Fax:* (20) 7848 2026 (office). *E-mail:* james.gow@kcl.ac.uk (office). *Website:* www.kcl.ac.uk (office).

GOWEILI, Ahmed, PhD; Egyptian international organization official; *Secretary-General, Council of Arab Economic Unity; Career:* fmrly Minister of Trade and Supply in Egyptian Govt; Sec.-Gen. Council of Arab Econ. Unity 2000–. *Address:* Council of Arab Economic Unity, 1191 Corniche en-Nil, 4th Floor, PO Box 1, Mohammed Fareed, 11518 Cairo, Egypt (office). *Telephone:* (2) 5755321 (office). *Fax:* (2) 5754090 (office). *E-mail:* caeu@idsc.net.eg (office). *Website:* www.caeu.org.eg (office).

GOZNEY, Sir Richard Hugh Turton, KCMG, BA (Hons); British diplomatist; *Governor and Commander in Chief of Bermuda;* b. 21 July 1951; m. Diana Gozney; two s. *Education:* Magdalen Coll. School, Oxford, St Edmund Hall, Oxford. *Career:* taught briefly at a school in Kenya 1970; joined FCO 1973, E African Dept 1973–74, Third, later Second Sec., Jakarta 1974–78, Second, later First Sec., Buenos Aires 1978–81, Defence Dept, FCO 1981–84, Head of Chancery, Madrid 1984–89, Asst Pvt. Sec., later Pvt. Sec., Sec. of State's Office, FCO 1989–93, High Commr to Swaziland 1993–96, Head of Security Policy Dept, FCO 1996-98, on loan to Cabinet Office (Chief of Assessments) 1998–2000, Amb. to Indonesia 2002–04, High Commr to Nigeria 2004–07, Gov. and C-in-C of Bermuda 2007–. *Publication:* Gibraltar and the EC: Aspects of the Relationship (Royal Inst. of Int. Affairs Discussion Paper) 1993. *Address:* Government House, Hamilton, Bermuda (office). *Telephone:* 292-3600 (office). *Fax:* 295-3823 (office). *E-mail:* rhgozney@gov.bm (office); depgov@ibl.bm (office). *Website:* www.fco.gov.uk (office).

GRABER, Richard W., BA, BL; American lawyer, politician and diplomatist; *Ambassador to Czech Republic;* m. Alexandria Graber; two s. *Education:* Duke Univ., Boston Univ. *Career:* attorney, Reinhart Boerner Van Deuren s.c., Wis. 1981–2006, Pres. and CEO 2004–06; elected Chair. Republican Party of Wis. 1999, re-elected 2001, 2003, 2005, served as Chair. Wis. Del. at Republican nat. convention in New York 2004, del. at 2000 convention, alt. del. at 1992 and 1996 conventions, Finance Chair. Republican Party of Wis. 1993–99 (Sec. 1991–99), served as Wis.'s rep. on Republican Nat. Cttee's Rules Cttee 2002–06; Amb. to Czech Republic 2006–; mem. Greater Milwaukee Cttee; mem. Bd of Dirs Boys & Girls Club of Greater Milwaukee; Co-Chair. Alexis de Tocqueville Soc. for United Way; fmr mem. Bd of Dirs Fed. Home Loan Bank of Chicago; fmr mem. Bd of Trustees Medical Coll. of Wis.; Past Pres. Milwaukee North Shore Rotary Club. *Address:* US Embassy, Tržiště 15, 118 01 Prague 1, Czech Republic (office). *Telephone:* 257022000 (office). *Fax:* 257022809 (office). *E-mail:* webmaster@usembassy.cz (office). *Website:* prague.usembassy.gov (office).

GRADIN, Anita; Swedish politician; b. 12 Aug. 1933, Hörnefors, Väster-botten Co.; m. Lt-Col Bertil Kersfelt; one d. *Education:* Coll. of Social Work and Public Admin., Stockholm and in USA. *Career:* journalist 1950, 1956–58, 1960–63; with Swedish Union of Forest Workers and Log Drivers 1952; with Social Welfare Planning Cttee and Municipal Exec. Bd Cttee on Women's Issues, Stockholm 1963–67; mem. Exec. Cttee, Nat. Fed. of Social Democratic Women 1964–93, Vice-Chair. 1975–93; mem. Stockholm City Council 1966–68; First Sec. Cabinet Office 1967–82; mem. SDP Exec. Cttee of Stockholm 1968–82; mem. Parl. 1968–92; Chair. Dist Br., Fed. of Social Democratic Women, Stockholm 1968–82; Chair. Swedish Union of Social Workers and Public Admin. 1970–81; Chair. Nat. Bd for Intercountry Adoptions 1973–80; del. Council of Europe 1973–82, Chair. Cttee on Migration, Refugees and Democracy 1978–82; Minister with responsibility for Migration and Equality Affairs 1982–86; Vice-Chair. Socialist Int. Women's Council 1983–86, Chair. Socialist Int. Women 1986–92, Vice-Chair. Socialist Int. 1986–92; Minister with responsibility for Foreign Trade and European Affairs 1986–91; Amb. to Austria, Slovenia and to UN insts including IAEA, UNIDO and UNRWA 1992–94; EC Commr for Migration, Home and Judicial Affairs 1995–99; Chair. Research Council of Social Science and Working Life 2001; Chair. of Stockholm Conf. on Vietnam 1974–76, of Swedish Cttee for Vietnam, Laos and Cambodia 1977–82, Sr Club, Foreign Office 2002; mem. Exec. Cttee of RFSU (Nat. Asscn for Sexual Enlightenment) and Otterfonden 1969–92; mem. EFTA del. 1991–92; mem. Bd Stockholm School of Econs, Women's Forum 2001, Comm. on Gene Medicine 2002; Cavalieri di Gran Croce (Italy) 1991, Das Grosse Goldene Ehrenzeichen am Bande (Austria) 1994, The King's Medal in the 12th Dimension with ribbon of the Royal Order of the Seraphim 1998; Dr hc Umeå Univ. 2002; Marisa Bellizario European Prize (Italy) 1998; Pro Merito Medal, Council of Europe 1982, Wizo Woman of the Year 1986. *Address:* Fleminggatan 85, 11245 Stockholm, Sweden (home). *Telephone:* (8) 269872 (home). *Fax:* (8) 269872 (home). *E-mail:* gradin.kersfelt@telia.com (home).

GRAHAM, Benjamin, MBA; Marshall Islands management consultant and diplomatist; *Ambassador-designate to USA. Education:* Georgetown Univ., USA. *Career:* first Gen. Man. Marshall Islands Visitors Authority; pvt. consultant working with both govt and non-profit orgs on strategic planning; Amb.-designate to USA 2008–. *Address:* Embassy of the Marshall Islands, 2433 Massachusetts Avenue, NW, Washington, DC 20008, USA (office). *Telephone:* (202) 234-5414 (office). *Fax:* (202) 232-3236 (office). *E-mail:* info@rmiembassyus.org (office). *Website:* www.rmiembassyus.org (office).

GRAHAM, Rt Hon. Sir Douglas Arthur Montrose 'Doug', KNZM, PC, LLB, JP; New Zealand lawyer and fmr politician and company director; b. 12 Jan. 1942, Auckland; m. Beverley Virginia Graham 1966; two s. one d. *Education:* Southwell School, Auckland Grammar School and Univ. of Auckland. *Career:* practising lawyer since 1965; est. own practice 1968; barrister and solicitor of High Court of NZ; Lecturer in Legal Ethics, Univ. of Auckland 1973–83; MP (Nat. Party) for Remuera 1984–96 (seat abolished), list MP 1996–99; Minister of Justice 1990–99, of Cultural Affairs and Minister for Disarmament and Arms Control 1990–99, Minister in Charge of Treaty of Waitangi Negotiations on behalf of the Crown 1991–99, Minister of Justice and of Courts 1995–99; Attorney Gen. 1997–99; co. dir and consultant 1999–; Dr hc (Waikato) 1999. *Publication:* Trick or Treaty? 1997. *Address:* 3A Martin Avenue, Remuera, Auckland, New Zealand (home). *Telephone:* (9) 524-2921 (home). *Fax:* (9) 524-2923 (home). *E-mail:* douglas.graham@xtra.co.nz (home).

GRANATSTEIN, Jack Lawrence, OC, BA, MA, PhD, FRSC; Canadian historian, academic and author; *Distinguished Research Professor of History Emeritus, York University;* b. 21 May 1939, Toronto; m. *Education:* Le College Militaire Royal de St-Jean, Royal Mil. Coll., Kingston, Univ. of Toronto, Duke Univ., USA. *Career:* served in Canadian Army 1956–66; joined History Dept, York Univ., Toronto 1966, Distinguished Research Prof. Emer. 1995–; Killiam Sr Fellow, Canada Council 1982–84, 1991–93; served on Special Comm. on Restructuring of Canadian Forces Reserves 1995; adviser to Minister of Nat. Defence on future of the Canadian Forces 1997; Rowell Jackman Fellow, Canadian Inst. of Int. Affairs 1996–2000; Adjunct Fellow, Centre for Mil. and Strategic Studies, Univ. of Calgary 1997–; CEO and mem. Bd of Dirs Canadian War Museum, Ottawa 1998–2000, Special Adviser to the museum's Dir 2000–01, Chair. Advisory Council 2001–; Sr Fellow, Massey Coll. 2000–; Chair. Council for Canadian Security in the 21st Century 2001–04; Chair. Advisory Council, Canadian Defence and Foreign Affairs Inst. 2001–, mem. Bd of Dirs 2004–; mem. Bd of Govs Royal Mil. Coll. of Canada 1997–; mem. Advisory Cttee, Dominion Inst.; Founder Org. for the History of Canada; Ed. Canadian Historical Review 1981–84; Dr hc (Memorial Univ. of Newfoundland) 1993, (Univ. of Calgary) 1994, (Ryerson Polytechnic Univ.) 1999, (Univ. of Western Ont., McMaster Univ.) 2000, (Niagara Univ.) 2004; J. B. Tyrrell Historical Gold Medal, Royal Soc. of Canada 1992, Conf. of Defence Asscns Inst. Vimy Award 1996, Pierre Berton Award for popular history 2004, Org. for the History of Canada's Nat. History Award 2006. *Publications:* The Politics of Survival: The Conservative Party of Canada 1939–45 1967, Peacekeeping: International Challenge and Canadian Response 1968, Canada's War: The Politics of the Mackenzie King Government, 1939–45 1975, Ties that Bind: Canadian–American Relations in Wartime 1975, Broken Promises: A History of Conscription in Canada 1977, American Dollars/Canadian Prosperity 1978, A Man of Influence: Norman Robertson and Canadian Statecraft 1981, The Ottawa Men: The Civil Service Mandarins, 1935–57 1982, Bloody Victory: Canadians and the D-Day Campaign 1984, The Great Brain Robbery: Canada's Universities on the Road to Ruin 1984, Sacred Trust: Brian Mulroney and the Conservative Party in Power 1985, Canada 1957–1967: The Years of Uncertainty and Innovation 1986, The Collins Dictionary of Canadian History 1986, How Britain's Weakness Forced Canada into the Arms of the United States 1989, Marching to Armageddon: Canadians and the Great War 1989, A Nation Forged in Fire: Canadians and the Second World War 1989, Pirouette: Pierre Trudeau and Canadian Foreign Policy 1990, Spy Wars: Canada and Espionage from Gouzenko to Glasnost 1990, Mutual Hostages: Canadians and Japanese in World War II 1990, For Better or For Worse: Canada and the United States to the 1990s 1991, expanded edn 2006, War and Peacekeeping: From South Africa to the Gulf – Canada's Limited Wars 1991, Dictionary of Canadian Military History 1992, The Generals: The Canadian Army's Senior Commanders in the Second World War (J. W. Dafoe Prize, UBC Medal for Canadian Biography) 1993, Empire to Umpire: Canadian Foreign Policy to the 1990s 1994, Victory 1945: Canadians from War to Peace 1995, The Good Fight: Canadians and World War II 1995, Yankee Go Home? Canadians and Anti-Americanism 1996, Petrified Campus: Canada's Universities in Crisis 1997, The Canadian 100: The Hundred Most Influential Canadians of the Twentieth Century 1997, The Veterans Charter and Post-World War II Canada 1998, Who Killed Canadian History? 1998, Trudeau's Shadow: The Life and Legacy of Pierre Trudeau 1998, Prime Ministers: Rating the Prime Ministers 1999, Our Century: The Canadian Journey 2000, Canada's Army: Waging War and Keeping the Peace 2002, First Drafts: Eyewitness Accounts from Canada's Past 2003, Canada and the Two World Wars 2003, The Importance of Being Less Earnest: Promoting Canada's National Interests through Tighter Ties with the US 2003, Who Killed the Canadian Military? 2004, Hell's Corner: An Illustrated History of Canada's Great War 2004, Battle Lines: First Person Military Accounts from Our Past 2004, The Last Good War: An Illustrated History of Canada's Second World War (Canadian Authors Asscn's Lela Common Award for Canadian History) 2005. *Address:* Canadian Defence and Foreign Affairs Institute, PO Box 2204, Station M, Calgary, Alb. T2P 2M4, Canada (office). *Telephone:* (403) 231-7624 (office). *Fax:* (403) 231-7647 (office). *E-mail:* contact@cdfai.org (office). *Website:* www.cdfai.org (office).

GRANBERG, Alexander Grigoryevich, DEconSc; Russian economist; *Chairman, Council for the Study of Productive Forces;* b. 25 June 1936, Moscow; m. Tatyana Baranova 1962; one s. *Education:* Moscow State Econ. Inst. *Career:* Sr Economist, USSR State Planning Cttee 1960–63; Prof., Univ. of Novosibirsk 1965–91; Dir Inst. of Econ. and Org. of Production, Siberian Dept, USSR (now Russian) Acad. of Sciences (IEOPP) 1985–91; Corresp. mem. Acad. of Sciences 1984, mem. 1990; Ed.-in-Chief Journal Economics and Organization of Industrial Production 1987–90, Regional Development and Cooperation 1997–; People's Deputy of Russia 1990–93; Chair. Cttee of the Supreme Soviet for Interrepublican Relations and Regional

Policy 1990–92; Counsellor to Russian Pres. 1991–93; Chair. Council for the Study of Productive Forces 1992–; Chair. Nat. Cttee on Pacific Econ. Co-operation 1992–99; Prof., Acad. of Nat. Econ. 1993–; Pres. Int. Acad. of Regional Devt and Co-operation 1996–; mem. Comm. for State Prizes under Pres. of Russian Fed.; mem. Expert Council under Govt of Russian Fed.; mem. Econ. Council under Chair. of Goskomsport of Russia; mem. Presidium Russian Acad. of Sciences 2002–; mem. New York Acad. of Sciences 1993; Order 'The Honour Symbol' 1986, Order 'Friendship' 1999, Rank IV Order For Service to the Fatherland 2006; Dr hc (Oscar Lange Acad. of Econs, Poland) 1990; Hon. Prof. (Acad. of Social Sciences, Heilongjiang Prov., China) 2001, (St Petersburg Acad. of Man. and Economy) 2006, V.S. Nemchinov Prize 1990, 'To Free Russia Defender' Medal 1994, State Prize of Russian Fed. 1997, Russian Govt Prize 1999, Hon. Polar Explorer 2001, Hon. Railwayman 2003, Gold Medal, N.D. Kondrapeva, Int. Fund Kondtrapeva, Nat. Ecological Prize, V.I. Vernadski Fund 2004; L.V. Kantorovich Prize 2008. *Publications:* The Optimization of Territorial Proportions of National Economy 1973, The Russian Federation in the All–Union Economy 1981, Modeling The Socialist Economy 1988, Optimization of Interregional Intersectoral Models 1989, A Way to the 21st Century 1999, Fundamentals of Regional Economics 2000, Regional Development in Russia: Past Policies and Future Prospects (co-ed.) 2000, Strategy of Macro-regions of Russia: Methodological Approaches, Priorities and Ways of Realization 2004, Multiregional Systems: Economic-Mathematical Research 2007; more than 550 monographs and articles. *Address:* Council for the Study of Productive Forces, Vavilova Street 7, 117997 Moscow (office); Koroleva str. 8–2, 491, 129515 Moscow, Russia (home). *Telephone:* (495) 135-61-08 (office); (495) 216-41-71 (home). *Fax:* (495) 135-63-39 (office). *E-mail:* council@sops.ru (office); granberg@ online.ru (home); a-granberg@narod.ru (home). *Website:* www.sops.ru (office); www.a-granberg.narod.ru (home).

GRANCHAROVA, Gergana Hristova, LLM, PhD; Bulgarian politician; *Minister for European Affairs;* b. 14 June 1973, Plovdiv. *Education:* Univ. of Sofia, Asser Coll. of Europe, Belgium. *Career:* legal asst, Djingov, Gouginsky, Kiuchukov and Velichkov law firm 1995–97; legal consultant, Arthur Andersen Bulgaria 1998–99, Fides Interconsult 1999–2001; mem. Nat. Movt Simeon II (Nationalno dvizheniye Simeon Vtori); mem. Narodno Sobraniye (Parl.) 2001–, Chair. Pan-European Union, Bulgaria, USA-Bulgaria Relations Cttee 2001–04, Vice-Chair. Nat. Anti-trafficking Cttee 2005–07, mem. Foreign Policy, Defence and Security Cttee, European Integration Cttee, Jt Parl. Cttee Bulgaria-EU 2001–04, mem. Council for Border Control 2005–07; Spokesperson, Ministry of Foreign Affairs 2004–05; Deputy Minister of Foreign Affairs 2004–07; Minister for European Affairs 2007–. *Address:* Ministry for European Affairs, 1040 Sofia, ul. Al. Zhendov 2, Bulgaria (office). *Telephone:* (2) 948-21-06 (office). *Fax:* (2) 973-36-98 (office). *E-mail:* ggrancharova@mfa.government.bg (office). *Website:* www .evroportal.bg (office).

GRANDMONT, Jean-Michel, LèsL, PhD; French economist and researcher; *Director of Research, Centre de Recherche en Économie et Statistique;* b. 22 Dec. 1939, Toulouse; m. 1st Annick Duriez 1967 (divorced 1978); m. 2nd Josselyne Bitan 1979; two d. *Education:* Ecole Polytechnique, Paris, Ecole Nationale des Ponts et Chaussées, Paris, Université de Paris, Univ. of California at Berkeley, USA. *Career:* Research Assoc., CNRS, Centre d'Etudes Prospectives d'Economie Mathématique Appliquées à la Planification (CEPREMAP) 1970–75, then Dir various research units, Dir of Research, CNRS and CEPREMAP 1987–96, Dir Research Unit, CNRS 928, 'Recherches Fondamentales en Economie Mathématiques' 1991–96, Dir of Research, CNRS and Centre de Recherche en Économie et Statistique (CREST) 1996–; Assoc. Prof., Ecole Polytechnique, Palaiseau 1977–92, Prof. 1992–2004, Chair. Dept of Econs 1997–2000, 2003–04; Prof. (part-time), Yale Univ., USA 1987, 1989–91, 1994; Pres. Econometric Soc. 1990; mem. Academia Europaea 1989–; Hon. mem. American Econ. Asscn; Foreign Hon. mem. American Acad. of Arts and Sciences 1992–; Chevalier, Légion d'honneur 2000; Officier, Palmes académiques 2004; Dr hc (Lausanne) 1990; Alexander von Humboldt Award 1992. *Publications:* Money and Value 1983, Nonlinear Economic Dynamics (ed.) 1987, Temporary Equilibrium (ed.) 1988; articles in scientific econ. journals. *Address:* CREST-CNRS, 15 blvd Gabriel Péri, 92245 Malakoff Cedex (office); 55 boulevard de Charonne, Les Doukas 23, 75011 Paris, France (home). *Telephone:* 1-41-17-78-04 (office); 1-43-70-37-28 (home). *Fax:* 1-41-17-60-46 (office). *E-mail:* grandmon@ensae.fr (office). *Website:* www.crest .fr/pageperso/grandmont/grandmont.htm (office).

GRANT, Charles, BA; British political analyst; *Director, Centre for European Reform;* b. 1958. *Education:* Cambridge Univ., Grenoble Univ., France. *Career:* began career with Euromoney magazine; writer, The Economist 1986–98, Defence Ed. 1994–98; Co-Founder Centre for European Reform

1996, Dir 1998–; Chair. Council of Experts, Moscow School of Political Studies; mem. Bd British Council 2002–; mem. Cttee for Russia in a United Europe; Chevalier, Ordre National du Merite 2003; Adelphi Foundation Prix Stendhal 1992. *Publications:* Delors: Inside the House that Jacques Built 1994, European Choices for Gordon Brown 2007, Preparing for the Multipolar World: European Foreign and Security Policy in 2020 2008; numerous pamphlets on European issues.
Address: Centre for European Reform, 14 Great Colleage Street, London, SW1P 3RX, England (office). *Telephone:* (20) 7233-1199 (office). *Fax:* (20) 7233-1117 (office). *E-mail:* charles@cer.org.uk (office). *Website:* www.cer .org.uk (office).

GRANT, Sir John Douglas Kelso, Kt, KCMG, BA; British diplomatist; *Permanent Representative, European Union;* b. 17 Oct. 1954; m. Anna Maria Lindvall; one s. two d. *Education:* Edinburgh Acad., St Catharine's Coll., Cambridge. *Career:* joined FCO 1976, W African Dept 1976–77, Third Sec. (later Second Sec.), Chancery, British Embassy, Stockholm 1977–80, Russian Language Training 1980–81, First Sec., Commercial, British Embassy, Moscow 1982–84, Desk Officer, Soviet Dept, FCO, London 1984–85, Press Office, FCO 1986–89, Press Spokesman (later First Sec. External Relations, UK Rep. Office, Brussels 1989–93, European Secr., Cabinet Office 1993–94, Counsellor, External Relations, UK Rep. Office, Brussels 1994–97, Prin. Pvt. Sec., Sec. of State's Office, London 1997–99, Amb. to Sweden 1999–2003, Perm. Rep. to EU 2003–; Morgan Grenfell and Co. Ltd 1985–86.
Address: UK Permanent Representation to the EU, 10 ave D'Auderghem, Brussels 1040, Belgium (office). *Telephone:* (2) 287-82-71 (office). *Fax:* (2) 287-83-83 (office). *Website:* ukrep.be (office).

GRAPPO, Gary A., BS, MS, MBA; American diplomatist; *Ambassador to Oman;* m. Rebecca Grappo; one s. two d. *Education:* US Air Force Acad., Purdue Univ., Stanford Univ. Grad. School of Business. *Career:* served as commissioned officer in USAF; worked with Bank of America and Castle & Cook (Dole Co.); career mem. Sr Foreign Service, joined State Dept in 1985, first assignment as Consular and Political Officer in Managua, Nicaragua, subsequently posted to Lisbon as Econ. Officer, then served in Washington, DC as Econ. and Commercial Office, Office of Soviet Union Affairs and Office of Newly Ind. States, as Special Asst to Counselor of Dept and Under-Sec. for Global Affairs, Arabic language training for two years, then Counselor for Econ. and Commercial Affairs, Amman, then served for three years as Deputy Chief of Mission in Muscat, Dir Office of Regional and Econ. Affairs, Bureau of Near East Affairs –2003, Deputy Chief of Mission and Minister Counselor, Embassy in Riyadh 2003–05, Amb. to Oman 2006–; three Superior Honor Awards, several group and individual Meritorious Honor Awards.
Address: US Embassy, Madinate Sultan Qaboos, PO Box 202, Muscat 115, Oman (office). *Telephone:* 24643400 (office). *Fax:* 24699771 (office). *E-mail:* webmastermuscat@state.gov (office). *Website:* muscat.usembassy.gov (office).

GRAPSAS, Gen. Dimitrios; Greek military officer; *Chief of Defence Staff;* b. 1948, Ypati; m.; two c. *Education:* Hellenic Army War Coll., Hellenic Nat. Defense Coll. *Career:* fmr Commdr Armored Reconnaissance Battalion, Chief of Staff of 96th Mil. Command, Asst Chief of Staff of Higher Mil. Command of Interior and Islands, Commdr XXV Armored Brigade, Army Corps Chief of Staff; Dir Training Div., then Training and Doctrine Directorate, Hellenic Army Gen. Staff 2002–03; Commdr XX Mechanized Infantry Div. 2003–04; promoted to Lt Gen. 2004 Commdr Higher Mil. Command of Interior and Islands 2005–06; Chief of Hellenic Army Gen. Staff 2006–07; Chief of Defence Staff 2007–; Golden Cross, Order of Phoenix, Order of Merit, Kt Commdr, Order of Phoenix, Order of Merit, High Cross of the Order of Phoenix, High Cross of the Order of Merit; Medal for Mil. Valor, C Class, Medal for Mil. Valor, B Class, Outstanding Command Commendation Medal, B Class, Staff Officer Service Commendation Medal, B Class, Medal for Mil. Valor, A Class, Formation/Maj. Unit Commendation Medal, C Class, Outstanding Command Commendation Medal, A Class, Staff Officer Service Commendation Medal, A Class, Commendation Medal for Merit and Valor.
Address: Ministry of National Defence, Odos Mesogeion 227–231, 154 51 Athens, Greece (office). *Telephone:* (210) 6598607 (office). *Fax:* (210) 6443832 (office). *E-mail:* minister@mod.mil.gr (office). *Website:* www.mod .gr (office).

GRAUBE, Brig. Raimonds; Latvian military officer; *Military Representative, NATO;* b. 28 Feb. 1957; m. Baiba Graube, two s. *Education:* Infantry Training Centre, Jt Service Command and Staff Coll., UK, Royal Coll. of Defence Studies, UK, Nat. Defense Univ., USA. *Career:* Co. Commdr, Staff Bn, Nat. Guard 1991–92, Training Chief, Special Forces' Special Operations Unit 1992, Deputy Commdr, Special Operations Unit 1992–93, Commdr First Brigade 1993–95, Chief of Staff 1995–98, Commdr 1998–99;

Commdr Nat. Armed Forces 1999–2003; NATO Integration Exec. Sec., Ministry of Defence 2003–; Mil. Rep. to NATO, Brussels 2005–.
Address: Delegation of Latvia, NATO Headquarters, Bld Léopold III, Brussels 1110, Belgium (office). *Telephone:* (2) 707-41-11 (office). *Fax:* (2) 707-45-79 (office). *E-mail:* natodoc@hq.nato.int (office). *Website:* www .nato.int (office).

GRAULS, Jan, LLB; Belgian diplomatist; *Permanent Representative, United Nations;* b. 12 Feb. 1948; m. one s. three d. *Education:* St Berchmans Jesuit Coll., Univ. of Antwerp, Catholic Univ. of Louvain. *Career:* diplomatic assignments at Embassies in Bonn, Tunis, at Perm. Mission to EU, Brussels, London and Washington, DC; diplomatic adviser to Prime Minister 1988–91; Deputy Chef de Cabinet and diplomatic adviser to the King of the Belgians 1994–97; Dir Gen. for Bilateral and Econ. Relations, Ministry of Foreign Affairs 1997–2001, Sec. Gen. 2001–08; Perm. Rep. to UN, New York 2008–.
Address: Permanent Mission of Belgium to the United Nations, 823 United Nations Plaza, 4th Floor, New York, NY 10017, USA (office). *Telephone:* (212) 378-6300 (office). *Fax:* (212) 681-7618 (office). *E-mail:* belgium@un .int (office). *Website:* www.un.int/belgium (office).

GRAY, C. Boyden, BA, JD; American lawyer; *Special Envoy for European Union Affairs and Special Envoy for Eurasian Energy;* b. Winston-Salem, N Carolina. *Education:* Harvard Univ., Univ. of N Carolina, Chapel Hill. *Career:* Ed.-in-Chief the Law Review, Univ. of N Carolina, Chapel Hill; service in US Marine Corps; clerk for Earl Warren, Chief Justice of US Supreme Court 1968–69; Partner, Wilmer, Cutler, Pickering, Hale and Dorr (law firm), Washington, DC 1969–81, 1993–2005; Legal Counsel to US Vice-Pres. George Bush 1981–89, Legal Counsel to Pres. George H. W. Bush 1989–93; Chair. Admin. Law and Regulatory Practice, ABA 2000–02; Amb. to EU, Brussels 2006–07, Special Envoy for EU Affairs Jan. 2008–, Special Envoy for Eurasian Energy March 2008–; fmr mem. Cttee to Visit the Coll. and Cttee on Univ. Devt, Harvard Univ.; has served on bds of numerous charitable, educational and professional orgs; Presidential Citizen's Medal, Univ., Distinguished Alumnus Award, Univ. of N Carolina Law School.
Address: US Mission to the European Union, Zinnerstraat 13 Rue Zinner, 1000 Brussels, Belgium (office). *Telephone:* (2) 508-22-22 (office). *Fax:* (2) 511-32-35 (office). *E-mail:* useupa@state.gov (office). *Website:* useu .usmission.gov (office).

GRAY, Rt Hon. Herb E., CC, PC, QC, BComm, LLD; Canadian politician; *Chairman, Canadian Section, International Joint Commission of Canada and the United States;* b. 25 May 1931, Windsor, Ont.; m. Sharon Sholzberg 1967; one s. one d. *Education:* Victoria Public School, Kennedy Coll. Inst. Windsor, McGill Univ., Montreal and Osgoode Hall Law School, Toronto. *Career:* MP 1962–2002; Chair. of House of Commons Standing Cttee on Finance, Trade and Econ. Affairs 1966–68; Parl. Sec. to Minister of Finance 1968–69; Minister without Portfolio (Finance) 1969–70, Minister of Nat. Revenue 1970–72, of Consumer and Corp. Affairs 1972–74, of Industry, Trade and Commerce 1980–82, of Regional Econ. Expansion Jan.–Oct. 1982; Pres. of Treasury Bd 1982–84; Opposition House Leader 1984–90, Deputy Opposition Leader 1989–90, Leader of the Opposition 1990, Opposition Finance Critic 1991–93; Solicitor Gen. and Leader of the Govt in House of Commons 1993–97; Deputy Prime Minister 1997–2002; given responsibility for co-ordinating Govt of Canada's activities to mark new Millennium 1998–2000; Chair. Canadian section Int. Jt Comm. of Canada and the United States 2002–; Govt Observer Inter-American Conf. of Ministers of Labour, Bogotá 1963; Vice-Chair. Del. to NATO Parl. Conf., Paris 1963; mem. Del. to Canada–France Interparliamentary Conf. 1966; mem. Canadian Del. to IMF and IBRD meeting 1967, Canada–US Interparliamentary Conf. 1967–68; Dr hc (Univ. of Windsor), (Assumption Univ., Windsor), (Catholic Univ. of Lublin, Poland), (McGill Univ.), (Univ. of Ottawa); B'nai Brith Award of Merit, Centennial Medal Queen's Silver Jubilee Medal, Canada 125 Medal, Queen's Golden Jubilee Medal, John Fraser Award for Environmental Achievement, Sierra Club of Canada; Ordre de la Pléiade (Officier).
Address: International Joint Commission of Canada and the United States, 234 Laurier Avenue West, 22nd Floor, Ottawa, Ont., K1P 6K6 (office); 1504–75 Riverside Drive East, Windsor, Ont., N9A 7C4, Canada (home). *Telephone:* (613) 992-2417 (office). *Fax:* (613) 947-9386 (office). *Website:* www.ijc.org (office).

GRAY, (John) Charles (Rodger), CMG; British diplomatist; *Marshal of the Diplomatic Corps;* b. 12 March 1953; m. Anne-Marie Gray; three s. *Career:* W African Dept, FCO 1974–76, Third, later Second Sec., Warsaw 1976–79, Eastern European and Soviet Dept, FCO 1979–83, UK Del. to OECD, Paris 1983–87, seconded to the Cabinet Office 1987–89, Deputy Head, Cen. African Dept, FCO 1989, Deputy Head, Cen. European Dept 1989–92, Head, Eastern Adriatic Dept 1992–93, Counsellor and Head of Chancery,

Jakarta 1993–96, Counsellor, Washington, DC 1997–2001, attached to Counter Terrorism Policy Dept, FCO 2001, Head, Middle East Dept, FCO 2002–04, Iran Coordinator 2004–05, Amb. to Morocco (also accred to Mauritania) 2005–08, Marshal of the Diplomatic Corps 2008–; Fellow, Center for Int. Affairs, Harvard Univ., USA 1996–97.
Address: Foreign and Commonwealth Office, King Charles Street, London, SW1A 2AH, England (office). *Telephone:* (20) 7008-1500 (office). *Website:* www.fco.gov.uk (office).

GRDEŠIĆ, Ivan, PhD; Croatian diplomatist, political scientist and academic; *Professor of Political Science, University of Zagreb;* b. 1952; m.; two c. *Education:* Univ. of Zagreb. *Career:* Fulbright Visiting Prof., Indiana Univ. 1992–93; Vice-Dean, Faculty of Political Science, Univ. of Zagreb 1996–99, Assoc. Prof. of Political Science 1999–2001, 2004–; Pres. Croatian Political Science Asscn 1996–99; Visiting Prof., Virginia Tech. Univ. 1999–2000; Amb. to USA 2000–04. *Publications include:* Political Decision-Making 1995; (as co-author): Croatia in the 1990 Election 1992, The 1990 and 1992–93 Sabor Elections in Croatia 1997, The Radical Right in Central and Eastern Europe 1999; numerous scientific and scholarly articles on democratic transition, political systems and public policies.
Address: Department of Political Science, University of Zagreb, Trg maršala Tita 14, 10000 Zagreb, Croatia (office). *Telephone:* (1) 4564111 (office). *Fax:* (1) 4830602 (office). *E-mail:* office@rektorat.unizg.hr (office). *Website:* ww.unizg.hr (office).

GRECEANÎI, Zinaida, MA; Moldovan economist and politician; *Prime Minister;* b. 7 Feb. 1956. *Education:* Moldova State Univ. *Career:* various roles within finance and budget inspectorate 1974–91; Economist, then Prin. Economist, Dept of Int. Finance, Ministry of Finance 1995–97, various sr positions including Dir of World Bank Section 1997–2001; Vice-Minister of Finance 2001–02, Minister of Finance 2002–05; First Deputy Prime Minister 2006–08, Prime Minister 2008–; fmr Gov. for Moldova to IMF.
Address: Government of Moldova, Piaţa Marii Adunări Naţionale 1, 2033 Chişinău, Moldova (office). *Telephone:* (22) 25-01-41 (office). *Fax:* (22) 23-84-44 (office). *E-mail:* zinaida.greceanii@gov.md (office). *Website:* www .gov.md (office).

GREEN, Jerrold D., BA, MA, PhD; American academic, author and research institute director; *President and CEO, Pacific Council on International Policy; Education:* Univ. of Chicago, Univ. of Mass, Boston. *Career:* fmr Dir Center for Middle Eastern Studies and Prof. of Political Science and Sociology, Univ. of Arizona; served in several leadership positions at RAND Grad. School, Calif., including Dir of Int. Programs and Devt, Dir Center for Middle East Public Policy, Assoc. Chair. of Research Staff Man. Dept, Sr Advisor for Middle East and S Asia; Pnr, Best Assocs (merchant banking firm) 2004–06; Pres. and CEO Pacific Council on Int. Policy 2008–; Visiting Prof., Univ. of Southern Calif., UCLA; mem. Council on Foreign Relations. *Publications:* Revolution in Iran: The Politics of Counter-mobilization 1982, Towards NAFTA: A North African Free Trade Agreement? 1995, NATO's Mediterranean Initiative: Policy Issues and Dilemmas (jtly) 1998, Political Violence and Stability in the States of the Northern Persian Gulf (with D. L. Byman) 1999, The Future of NATO's Mediterranean Initiative 2000, Iran's Security Policy in the Post-Revolutionary Era (jtly) 2001, Terrorism and Asymmetric Conflict in Southwest Asia (with Shahram Chubin) 2002; contrib. to: Democracy and Islam in the New Constitution of Afghanistan 2003; numerous articles in journals.
Address: Pacific Council on International Policy, 3520 Trousdale Parkway, SOS B-15, Los Angeles, CA 90089, USA (office). *Telephone:* (213) 740-4296 (office). *Fax:* (213) 740-9993 (office). *E-mail:* info@pacificcouncil.org (office). *Website:* www.pacificcouncil.org (office).

GREEN, Mark A.; American diplomatist; *Ambassador to Tanzania;* b. Wis.; m. *Education:* Univ. of Wisconsin-Eau-Claire, Univ. of Wisconsin-Madison. *Career:* served (with wife) as secondary school teachers in Kenya through WorldTeach Project (devt org. based at Phillips Brooks House of Harvard Univ.) 1987–88; served four terms in US House of Reps 1999–2007, mem. House Judiciary Cttee and Int. Relations Cttee, served as an Asst Majority Whip; Amb. to Tanzania 2007–.
Address: US Embassy, PO Box 9123, 686 Old Bagamoyo Road, Msasani, Dar es Salaam, Tanzania (office). *Telephone:* (22) 2668001 (office). *Fax:* (22) 2668238 (office). *E-mail:* embassyd@state.gov (office). *Website:* tanzania.usembassy.gov (office).

GREENE, Owen; British academic; *Research Director and Senior Lecturer in International Relations, Department of Peace Studies, University of Bradford; Career:* currently Research Dir and Sr Lecturer in Int. Relations and Security Studies, Dept of Peace Studies, Univ. of Bradford, UK, also Dir Centre for Int. Cooperation and Security (CICS); co-f. Int. Action Network on Small Arms (IANSA); Co-Dir Register of Conventional Arms Project 1992–, EU Tacis Democracy Programme Project 1996–2000; consultant UN Group of Govt Experts on Small Arms, IBRD, EU; Leader EU Council Mission to Cambodia 1999; Chair. Verification Research, Training and Information Centre (VERTIC); mem. Bd Saferworld, Int. Security Information Service (ISIS); mem. Advisory Bd, Centre for Democratic Control of Armed Forces (DCAF), Int. Alert; mem. Exec. Cttee British Int. Studies Asscn. *Publications include:* numerous books and edited vols, chapters, articles and reports on research and policy.
Address: Department of Peace Studies, University of Bradford, Bradford, BD7 1DP, England (office). *Telephone:* (01274) 235172 (office). *Fax:* (01274) 235296 (office). *E-mail:* o.j.greene@bradford.ac.uk (office). *Website:* www.brad.ac.uk (office).

GREENLEE, David N., BA; American diplomatist; b. 3 June 1943, White Plains, NY; m. Clara Jeanet Murillo; four c. *Education:* Yale Univ., Nat. War Coll. and Instituto Internacional, Madrid, Spain. *Career:* Peace Corps volunteer in Bolivia 1965–67; served in US Army 1968–71, honourable discharge with rank of First Lt; entered Foreign Service in 1974, served as Rotational Officer, Embassy in Lima, as Watch Officer, US State Dept Operations Center, as Political Officer, Embassy in La Paz, as Political Officer, Embassy in Tel-Aviv, as Int. Relations Officer, Office of Israel and Arab-Israeli Affairs, as Deputy Dir, Office of Egyptian Affairs, Deputy Chief of Mission, US Embassies in La Paz 1987–89, Santiago 1989–92, Madrid 1992–95, Political Advisor to Army Chief of Staff 1995–96, US Del. (rank of Amb.) and Chair. Israel-Lebanon Monitoring Group 1996–97, Special Coordinator for Haiti, US State Dept 1997–99, Amb. to Paraguay 2000–03, to Bolivia 2003–06; Bronze Star with Oak Leaf Cluster, Vietnam Service Medal; several Superior Honor and other Dept of State awards.
Address: US Department of State, 2201 C Street NW, Washington, DC 20520, USA (office). *Telephone:* (202) 647-4000 (office). *Fax:* (202) 647-6738 (office). *Website:* www.state.gov (office).

GREENSPAN, Alan, KBE, MA, PhD; American economist and central banker (retd) and business consultant; *President, Greenspan Associates LLC;* b. 6 March 1926, New York; m. Andrea Mitchell 1997. *Education:* New York and Columbia Univs. *Career:* Pres., CEO Townsend-Greenspan & Co. Inc. 1954–74, 1977–87; mem. Nixon for Pres. Cttee 1968–69; mem. Task Force for Econ. Growth 1969, Comm. on an All-Volunteer Armed Force 1969–70, Comm. on Financial Structure and Regulation 1970–71; Consultant to Council of Econ. Advisers 1970–74, to US Treasury 1971–74, to Fed. Reserve Bd 1971–74; Chair. Council of Econ. Advisers 1974–77, Nat. Comm. on Social Security Reform 1981–83; Chair. Bd of Govs Fed. Reserve System 1987–2006; Founder and Pres. Greenspan Assocs (consulting firm), Washington, DC 2006–, advisor to Pimco (for fund man.) 2007–, to Deutsche Bank (for investment banking) 2007–; Adviser Paulson and Co., New York 2008–; mem. Sec. of Commerce's Econ. Comm.'s Cen. Market System Cttee 1972, GNP Review Cttee of Office of Man. and Budget, Time Magazine's Bd of Economists 1971–74, 1977–87, Pres.'s Econ. Policy Advisory Bd 1981–87, Pres.'s Foreign Intelligence Advisory Bd 1983–85, Exec. Cttee Trilateral Comm.; Sr Adviser, Brookings Inst. Panel on Econ. Activity 1970–74, 1977–87; Adjunct Prof., Grad. School of Business Man., New York 1977–87; mem. Bd of Dirs Council on Foreign Relations; Past Pres. and Fellow, Nat. Asscn of Business Economists; mem. Bd of Dirs Trans World Financial Co. 1962–74, Dreyfus Fund 1970–74, Gen. Cable Corpn 1973–74, 1977–78, Sun Chemical Corpn 1973–74, Gen. Foods Corpn 1977–86, J.P. Morgan & Co. 1977–87, Mobil Corpn 1977–87, Aluminum Co. of America (ALCOA) 1978–87; Hon. KBE 2002, Commdr Légion d'honneur; Jefferson Award 1976, William Butler Memorial Award 1977, Presidential Medal of Freedom 2005. *Publication:* The Age of Turbulence: Adventures in a New World (memoirs) 2007.
Address: Greenspan Associates LLC, 1133 Connecticut Avenue, Suite 810, NW, Washington, DC 20036, USA (office). *Telephone:* (202) 457-8250 (office).

GREF, German Oskarovich; Russian politician and jurist; b. 8 Feb. 1964, Panfilovo, Pavlodar Region, Kazakh SSR; m. 1st; one s.; m. 2nd 2004. *Education:* Omsk State Univ. *Career:* legal adviser Pavlodar regional agric. co. 1981–82; army service 1982–84; Lecturer in Law, Omsk State Univ. 1990; legal adviser, Cttee on Econ. Devt and Property, Petrodvorets Dist Admin., St Petersburg 1991–92; Chair. Cttee on Property Man., concurrently Deputy Head Petrodvorets Dist Admin. 1992–94; Deputy Chair., Dir Dept of Real Estate, First Deputy Chair. Cttee on Man. of Municipal Property St Petersburg Admin. 1994–97; Vice-Gov., Chair. Cttee on Man. of Municipal Property, St Petersburg Admin. 1997–98; mem. Exec. Bd Ministry of State Property, Russian Fed. 1998; First Deputy Minister 1998–2000; mem. Exec. Bd Fed. Comm. on Market of Securities 1999–; head of team working on econ. reform plan for Pres. Putin 1999–2000; Minister of Econ. Devt and Trade of Russian Fed. 2000–07.

Address: c/o Ministry of Economic Development and Trade, 125993 Moscow, ul. 1-ya Tverskaya-Yamskaya 1/3, Russia (office).

GREGOIRE, Crispin, BA, EdM; Dominican television producer, international organisation official and diplomatist; *Permanent Representative, United Nations;* b. 1956. *Education:* Columbia Univ., New York, Howard Univ., Washington, DC. *Career:* Adjunct Instructor, Brooklyn Coll., New York 1979–1980; Program Assoc., Appropriate Tech. Int., Washington, DC 1982–1983; Assoc. Producer CBS News, New York 1984; Field Office Dir, Save the Children Fed., Conn. 1984–89; Acting Dir New York City Dept of Health 1989–92; Program Adviser to TechnoServe Inc., Conn. 1992–93; Program Consultant, Ford Foundation, New York 1993–98; Dir Consulting and Training for Africa and Latin America, BoardSource, Washington, DC 1998–2002; Perm. Rep. to UN, New York 2002–.
Address: Permanent Mission of Dominica to the United Nations, 800 Second Avenue, Suite 400h, New York, NY 10017, USA (office). *Telephone:* (212) 949-0853 (office). *Fax:* (212) 808-4975 (office). *E-mail:* dominica@un.int (office).

GREGURIĆ, Franjo, DSc; Croatian politician; b. 12 Oct. 1939, Lobor, Zlata Bistrica; m. Jozefina Gregurić (née Abramović); one s. one d. *Education:* Univ. of Zagreb. *Career:* worked in chemical factories; tech. Dir Radonia at Sisak; Dir-Gen. Chromos factory, Zagreb; rep. of Foreign Trade Co. Astra in Moscow, Gen. Dir Astra-Int. Trade, Zagreb –1990; Vice-Dir, then Dir Chamber of Econs, Zagreb; mem. Christian Democratic Union (CDU); Deputy Premier of Croatia 1990; Prime Minister 1991–92; mem. Sabor (Croatian Parl.) 1990–; Adviser to Pres. of Croatia 1992–, apptd Special Del. (with rank of Amb.) to Croat-Bosnian Fed. and Bosnia and Herzegovina 1997; Dir INA Co., Zagreb 1992–; fmr Pres. Croatian Firefighting Asscn; numerous nat. and int. awards for econs.
Address: Ilica 49, 41000 Zagreb, Croatia. *Telephone:* (41) 517-230 (office). *Fax:* (41) 650-110.

GREILSAMER, Laurent, LèsL; French journalist; *Editor, Le Monde;* b. 2 Feb. 1953, Neuilly; m. Claire Méheut 1979; three s. *Education:* Ecole Supérieure de Journalisme, Lille. *Career:* Le Figaro 1974–76, Quotidien de Paris 1976; ed., Le Monde 1977–84, Sr Reporter 1984–94, 1994–2005, Ed. 2005–; Prix des lectrices d'Elle 1999, Grand Prix de la Critique 2004. *Publications:* Interpol, le siège de soupçon 1986, Un certain Monsieur Paul, L'affaire Touvier 1989, Hubert Beuve-Méry 1990, Enquête sur l'affaire du sang contaminé 1990, Les juges parlent 1992, Interpol, Policiers sans frontières 1997, Le Prince foudroyé, la vie de Nicholas de Staël 1998, Où vont les juges? 2002, L'Eclair au front, la vie de René Char 2004.
Address: Le Monde, 80 Boulevard Blanqui, 75013 Paris, France (office). *Telephone:* 1-57-28-26-05 (office). *Fax:* 1-57-28-21-22 (office). *E-mail:* greilsamer@lemonde.fr (office). *Website:* www.lemonde.fr (office).

GRELA, Marek, PhD; Polish diplomatist; *Permanent Representative, European Union;* b. 1949, Kraków; m. Anna Grela; two c. *Education:* Warsaw School of Economics. *Career:* worked in Policy Planning Div., Ministry of Foreign Affairs 1972; mem. del. to CSCE, Geneva and Helsinki 1973–75; based at Embassy in Madrid, Spain 1977–81; Research Fellow, Polish Inst. of Int. Affairs 1981–89, Sr Research Fellow, Inst. of East–West Studies, New York 1983–84; del. CSCE and CFE Mandate talks, Vienna 1986–88; Adviser to Minister of Foreign Affairs 1989; Deputy Dir, Dept of European Institutions, Ministry of Foreign Affairs 1990; based at Embassy in Dublin, Ireland 1991–96; Dir-Gen., Ministry of Foreign Affairs 1996, Deputy Minister of Foreign Affairs 1997; Perm. Rep., FAO, Rome 1998–2002, EU, Brussels 2002–.
Address: Permanent Representation of Poland to the European Union, 282–284 avenue de Tervueren, Brussels 1150, Belgium (office). *Telephone:* (2) 777-72-00 (office). *Fax:* (2) 777-72-97 (office). *E-mail:* mail@polrepeu.be (office).

GRENFELL, 3rd Baron, cr. 1902, of Kilvey; **Julian Pascoe Francis St Leger Grenfell;** British politician; b. 23 May 1935, London; m. 1st Loretta Reali 1961 (divorced 1970); one d.; m. 2nd Gabrielle Raab 1970 (divorced 1987); two d.; m. 3rd Elizabeth Porter Scott 1987 (divorced 1992); m. 4th Dagmar Langbehn Debreil 1993. *Education:* Eton Coll., King's Coll., Cambridge. *Career:* Second Lt, Kings Royal Rifle Corps 1954–56; Pres. Cambridge Union 1959; Capt. Queen's Royal Rifles (Territorial Army) 1963; television journalist 1960–64; with World Bank 1965–95, Chief of Information and Public Affairs in Europe 1969–72, Deputy Dir European Office 1973–74, Special Rep. to the UN Orgs 1974–81, Adviser HQ 1983–90, Head External Affairs, European Office 1990–95; mem. UK del. to Council of Europe 1997–99; sat in the House of Lords as Lord Grenfell of Kilvey 1976–99, cr. Life Peer 2000; Chair. House of Lords Sub-Cttee on Econ. and Financial Affairs 1998–, mem. Select Cttee on EU 1999–, Chair. 2002–; Prin. Deputy Chair. of Committees 2002–; A Deputy Speaker; non-affiliated; Chevalier

Légion d'honneur 2005. *Publications:* novels: Margot 1984, The Gazelle 2004.
Address: 24 rue Chaptal, 75009 Paris, France (home); c/o House of Lords, Westminster, London, SW1A 0PW, England. *Telephone:* (20) 7219-3601. *Fax:* (20) 7219-6715. *E-mail:* grenfellj@parliament.uk (office).

GRIFFITH, Gavan, AO, QC, LLM, DPhil; Australian barrister and international arbitrator; b. 11 Oct. 1941, Melbourne; one s. three d. *Education:* Melbourne Univ. and Magdalen Coll. Oxford. *Career:* barrister 1963; Lincoln's Inn 1969; QC 1981; Solicitor-Gen. of Australia 1984–97; del. to UN Int. Trade Law Comm. (UNCITRAL) 1984–, Vice-Chair. 1987–88, 1994–95; Agent and Counsel for Australia at Int. Court of Justice 1989–95; mem. Perm. Court of Arbitration, The Hague 1987–99; mem. Intelsat Panel of Legal Experts 1988–97, Chair. 1993–94; del. Hague Conf. of Pvt. Int. Law 1992–97; Arbitrator, Int. Comm. for Settlement of Int. Disputes (ISCID) 1994–; Consultant, Office of Legal Counsel, UN, New York 1994–95; Dir Australian Centre for Int. Commercial Arbitration 1997–; mem. Council, Nat. Gallery of Australia 1986–92; Visiting Fellow, Magdalen Coll. Oxford 1973–74, 1976, 1980, 1995; Order of the Repub. of Austria 1997. *Publications:* contribs to various legal journals and books.
Address: Essex Court Chambers, Lincolns Inn Fields, London WC2A 3EG, England (office); 205 William Street, Melbourne 3000, Australia (office). *Telephone:* (3) 9225-7658 (Australia) (office); (20) 7813-8000 (London) (office); (4) 1925-0666 (Australia) (home). *Fax:* (3) 9225-8974 (Australia) (office). *E-mail:* Griffithqc@aol.com (office). *Website:* www.listd.com.au (office); www.essxcourt.net (office).

GRIGORE, Vsevolod, PhD; Moldovan diplomatist; b. 1958, Jora de Jos; m.; one s. *Career:* Head Dept of Modern Languages, Moldovan Ind. Int. Univ. 1994–96; Counsellor, Deputy Dir, Dir-Gen. Dept of Europe and N America, Ministry of Foreign Affairs 1996–99; Minister-Counsellor, Embassy of Moldova, USA 1999–2002; Perm. Rep. to UN 2003–06.
Address: c/o Ministry of Foreign Affairs and European Integration, 2012 Chişinău, str. 31 August 80, Moldova (office). *Website:* www.mfa.md (office).

GRIGORYANTS, Sergey Ivanovich; Russian human rights activist and journalist; *Head, Glasnost-Caucasus Information Agency;* b. 12 May 1941, Kiev; m. Tamara Vsevolodovna Grigoryants; one s. (died 1995) one d. *Career:* studied Moscow Univ., was expelled by KGB 1968; f. and ed. Information Bulletin on violation of human rights in USSR 1982–83; imprisonment for political activities 1975–80, 1983–87; Founder, Ed. and Publr Glasnost magazine 1987–91, Glasnost Information Agency 1991–; Founder, Chair. Public Fund Glasnost 1990–; organized regular conf. KGB Yesterday, Today, Tomorrow; Head Centre on Information and Analysis, Russian Special Service 1993, Initiator of Int. Non-Governmental Tribunal on the War Crimes and Crimes Against Humanity in Chechnya; Co-Chair. Coalition for Support for Int. Criminal Court; Head Glasnost-Caucasus Information Agency 2000–; Gold Pen of Freedom Award, Medal of Bayern Lantague. *Publications:* contribs to New York Times and Washington Post.
Address: Tsvetnoi Boulevard, Building 2215, Apt 40, 103051 Moscow (office); 1st Naprudnaya str. 3, Apt 121, 129346 Moscow, Russia. *Telephone:* (495) 208-28-53 (office); (495) 474-45-90 (home). *Fax:* (495) 299-85-38 (office); (530) 326-88-17. *E-mail:* fondglas@online.ru. *Website:* www.glasnostonline.org (office).

GRIGORYEV, Vladimir Viktorovich; Belarusian politician and diplomatist; b. 5 April 1941, Mogilev; m.; one s. *Education:* Belarus Agricultural Acad., Acad. of Social Sciences. *Career:* began career with local newspaper 1957–58; Second Sec., Komsomol (All-Union Lenin Communist Union of Youth/VLKSM) Dist Cttee, Mogilev Br. 1958–62, 1966–68, First Sec. 1968–70, Instructor, Political Dept, Mogilev 1962–65, Head of Div., Mogilev Regional VLKSM Cttee 1965–66, Sec. VLKSM 1970–72, First Sec. Minsk Regional Cttee 1974, Moscow Regional Cttee 1974–80, Second Sec. Brest Regional Cttee 1980–83; Chair. Exec. Cttee, Brest Prov. Soviet of People's Deputies (Ass.) 1983–85; First Sec. Vitebsk Regional Cttee, Communist Party of Belarus (KPB) 1986–90; Chair. Vitebsk Prov. Soviet of People's Deputies 1990–91; Dir Gen. Dolomite Production Asscn, Vitebsk 1992–96; fmr mem. Supreme Soviet of BSSR (Parl.); Amb. to Russia and Perm. Rep.to Eurasian Econ. Community 1997–2006; Order of the Red Banner of Labour, Order of the Fatherland.
Address: c/o Ministry of Foreign Affairs, 220030 Minsk, vul. Lenina 19, Belarus.

GRILLI, Enzo, PhD; Italian banker and economist; *Professor of International Economics, Paul H. Nitze School of Advanced International Studies, Johns Hopkins University;* b. 7 Oct. 1943, Casarza Ligure; m. Mary A. Jacobs; two d. *Education:* Univ. of Genoa and Johns Hopkins Univ. USA. *Career:* Dir Econ. Research, Confed. of Italian Industries, Rome 1978–80; Dir-Gen.

Ministry of Budget and Planning 1982–84; Dir Econ. Advisory Staff, IBRD, Washington, DC 1989–92; Exec. Dir for Italy, Greece, Portugal, Albania and Malta, IBRD 1993–95; Exec. Dir for Italy, Greece, Portugal, Albania, Malta and San Marino, IMF, Washington, DC 1995–98; Prof. of Int. Econs, Paul H. Nitze School of Advanced Int. Studies, Johns Hopkins Univ. 1998–; Fulbright Fellow; Editorialist of Corriere della Sera; TV Commentator; Grand Officer of Italian Repub. 1981; St Vincent Prize for Econs 1995. *Publications:* The World Rubber Economy: Structure, Changes, and Prospects (co-author) 1980, Sustaining World Economic Recovery: The Challenges Ahead 1985, The New Protectionist Wave (co-ed.) 1990, The European Community and the Developing Countries 1993, Sustaining Export-oriented Development: Ideas from East Asia (co-ed.) 1995, Interdipendenze Macroeconomiche Nord–Sud 1995, Multilateralism and Regionalism after the Uruguay Round (co-ed.) 1997, Prospettive sullo Sviluppo dei Paesi Emergenti 1999. *Address:* The Paul H. Nitze School of Advanced International Studies, Johns Hopkins University, The Nitze Building, 1740 Massachusetts Avenue, NW, Room 408, Washington, DC 20036 (office); 3917 Oliver Street, Chevy Chase, MD 20815, USA (home). *Telephone:* (202) 663-5686 (office). *Fax:* (202) 663-5656 (office). *Website:* apps.sais-jhu.edu (office).

GRÍMSSON, Ólafur Ragnar, PhD; Icelandic head of state; *President;* b. 14 May 1943, Isafjörur; m. 1st Gurún Katrín Thorbergsdóttir 1974 (died 1999); two d. (twins); m. 2nd Dorrit Moussaieff 2003. *Education:* Reykjavik Higher Secondary Grammar School, Univ. of Manchester, UK. *Career:* Lecturer in Political Science, Univ. of Iceland 1970–, Prof. 1973; involved in production of political TV and radio programmes 1966–70; mem. Bd Progressive Party Youth Fed. 1966–73, Exec. Bd Progressive Party 1971-73, Alt. mem. Althing representing East Iceland (Liberal and Left Alliance) 1974–75; Chair. Exec. Bd Liberal and Left Alliance 1974–75; mem. Althing for Reykjavik 1978–83, for Reykjanes (People's Alliance) 1991–; mem. People's Alliance, Chair. Parl. Group 1980–83, Leader 1987–95; Minister of Finance 1988–91; Pres. of Iceland 1996–; Chair. Cttee on Relocation of Public Insts 1972–75, Icelandic Social Sciences Asscn 1975, Organizing Cttee Parl. Conf. of Council of Europe: 'North-South: Europe's Role' 1982-84, Parliamentarians for Global Action 1984–90 (also fmr Pres., mem. Bd 1990–); Vice-Chair. Icelandic Security Comm. 1979–90; mem. Bd Icelandic Broadcasting Service 1971–75, Nat. Power Co. 1983–88; mem. Parl. Ass. Council of Europe 1980–84, 1995; fmr adviser to several Icelandic cos. *Address:* Office of the President, Staðastaður, Sóleyjargata 1, 150 Reykjavik, Iceland (office). *Telephone:* 540-4400 (office). *Fax:* 562-4802 (office). *E-mail:* president@president.is (office). *Website:* www.president.is (office).

GRININ, Vladimir Mikhailovich; Russian diplomatist; *Ambassador to Poland;* b. 15 Nov. 1947; m.; one d. *Education:* Moscow State Univ. for Int. Relations, Diplomatic Acad., USSR Ministry of Foreign Affairs. *Career:* mem. staff Ministry of Foreign Affairs 1971–, took part in Soviet-American disarmament and arms control negotiations, Geneva 1982–86, Embassy of USSR in GDR 1986–1990, in FRG 1990–1992, Dir 4th European Dept 1994–96, Dir Gen. Secr. (mem. Collegium) 2000–03; Amb. to Austria 1996–2000, to Finland 2003–06, to Poland 2006–. *Address:* Embassy of the Russian Federation, 00-761 Warsaw, ul. Belwederska 49, Poland. *Telephone:* (22) 6213453. *Fax:* (22) 6253016. *E-mail:* ambrus@poczta.fm. *Website:* www.poland.mid.ru.

GRIZOLD, Anton, BA, MA, PhD; Slovenian academic and fmr government official; b. 7 Jan. 1956, Radje ob Dravi; m.; two c. *Education:* Univ. of Ljubljana, Univ. of Maryland, USA. *Career:* fmr Guest Researcher, Fletcher School of Law and Diplomacy, Tufts Univ., USA; Lecturer, Faculty of Social Studies, Univ. of Ljubljana 1980–89, Head of Defence Science Courses, 1989–94, Vice-Dean for Financial Affairs 1991–95, Head of Defence Science Research Centre 1992–2000, Prof. of Defense Sciences and Security in Int. Relations 1999–; Pres. Strategic Council, Ministry of Defence 1999–2000; Minister of Defence 2000–04; mem. Slovenian Asscn of Defence Scientists, Slovenian Int. Relations Asscn, Slovenian Political Science Asscn, Int. Political Science Asscn, Int. Sociological Asscn, European Group on Mil. and Soc. *Publications:* Militarisation and the Military-Industrial Complex 1990, International Security 1998, European Security 1999, The Defence System of the Republic of Slovenia 1999, Contemporary Systems of National Security (co-author) 1999, Security Policies of the Superpowers (co-author) 2000, Man, the State and War (co-author) 2001; over 100 academic, professional and popular articles on issues of defence, security, war and peace. *Address:* Faculty of Social Sciences, University of Ljubljana, Kardeljeva ploščad 5, PO Box 2547, 1001 Ljubljana, Slovenia (home). *Telephone:* (1) 5805110 (office). *Fax:* (1) 5805102 (office). *E-mail:* anton.grizold@fdv.uni -lj.si (office). *Website:* www.uni-lj.si (office).

GROMOV, Col-Gen. Boris Vsevolodovich; Russian army officer and politician; *Governor of Moscow Region;* b. 7 Nov. 1943, Saratov; m. 2nd Faina Gromov; two s. two adopted d. *Education:* Leningrad Gen. Troops School, Frunze Mil. Acad., Gen. Staff Acad. *Career:* mem. CPSU 1966–91; Commdr of platoon, co., Bn, Regt, div. 1965–87, Commdr 40 Army in Afghanistan 1987–89, Commdr of troops Kiev Command 1989–90, First Deputy Minister of Internal Affairs of USSR 1990–91, First Deputy Commdr of Armed Forces of CIS 1991–92, First Deputy Minister of Defence of Russia 1992–95; Chief Mil. Expert and Deputy Minister of Foreign Affairs 1995–97; mem. State Duma 1996–99, Chair. Sub-Cttee on Arms Control and Int. Security; Gov. of Moscow Region 2000– (re-elected 2003); f. war veterans' movt, Fighting Fraternity (later Honour and Homeland) 1997–; Hero of Soviet Union and other decorations; Order in the Name of Russia 2004. *Publication:* Memoirs of the Afghan War 1994. *Address:* Administration of Moscow Region, Staraya Pl. 6, 103070 Moscow, Russia (office). *Telephone:* (495) 206-68-62 (office); (495) 206-60-42 (office). *Fax:* (495) 928-98-12 (office). *E-mail:* expo@mvesmo.ru (office).

GRØNDAHL, Kirsti Kolle; Norwegian politician; *President of Storting (Parliament);* b. 1 Sept. 1943, Røyken; m. Svein Erik Groendahl 1967; two c. *Career:* mem. Røyken Municipal Council and Municipal Exec. Bd 1972–77, Chair. Røyken Labour Party 1980–82, Spikkestad Labour Party 1990–, mem. Labour Party's Cttee for Environment 1983–; mem. Storting (Parl.) 1977–; mem. Standing Cttee on Church and Educ. 1977–85, on Foreign and Constitutional Affairs 1989–; Minister of Church and Educ. 1986–88, of Devt Co-operation 1988–89; Vice-Pres. Storting 1990–93, Pres. 1993–; mem. Norwegian del. to Parl. Ass. of Council of Europe 1989–90; Leader del. to CSCE Parl. Ass. 1991–; mem. Nordic Council and of Council's Presidium 1990–93, Leader Norwegian del. to Nordic Council 1992–93. *Address:* Stortinget, Karl Johansgt. 22, 0026 Oslo, Norway (office). *Telephone:* 22-31-30-50 (office). *Fax:* 22-31-38-50 (office). *E-mail:* stortinget.postmottak@st.dep.telemax.no (office). *Website:* www .stortinget.no (office).

GRONKIEWICZ-WALTZ, Hanna, LLD, PhD; Polish banker and lawyer; *Mayor of Warsaw;* b. 4 Nov. 1952, Warsaw; m.; one d. *Education:* Warsaw Univ. *Career:* mem. of academic staff, Warsaw Univ. 1975–; expert on public and econ. law. Polish Parl. 1989; mem. of academic staff, Univ. of Cardinal Wyszy 1990–; Pres. Nat. Bank of Poland 1992–2000; mem. Solidarity Trade Union 1980; Chair. Faculty, Solidarity Br. 1989–92; ind. cand. in presidential election 1995; Vice-Pres. EBRD 2001–05; mem. of Parl., Platforma Obywatelska Party 2005–; first female Mayor of Warsaw 2006–; Dr hc (Marie Curie-Skłodowska Univ., Lublin) 1999; Global Finance magazine award for Best Chair. of a Cen. Bank 1994, 1997, 1998, 1999, The Central European Award 1995, 1998, Życie Gospodarcze Award 1995, The Warsaw Voice Award 1995. *Publications:* Central Bank from Centrally Controlled Economy to Market Oriented Economy: Legal Aspects 1993, Economic Law (co-author) 1996; over 50 works and articles in econ. and financial journals. *Address:* Office of the Mayor, pl. Defilad 1, 00-142 Warsaw, Poland (office). *Telephone:* (22) 6567830. *Fax:* (22) 8270635. *E-mail:* biuroprezydenta@ warszawa.um.gov.pl.

GROS, Francisco Roberto André, BA; Brazilian banker and economist; *President and CEO, Fosfertil;* b. 21 April 1942, Rio de Janeiro; m. 1st Sandra Mattmann 1968; m. 2nd Isabel Teixeira Mendes; two s. one d. *Education:* Woodrow Wilson School of Public and Int. Affairs, Princeton Univ., USA. *Career:* Founding mem. Brazilian Securities and Exchange Comm. 1977–81; Exec. Dir in charge of investment banking activities, Unibanco–Banco de Investimento do Brasil 1981–85; Exec. Dir Nat. Devt Bank (BNDES) 1985–87; Pres. Cen. Bank of Brazil Feb.–May 1987, 1991–92; Pres. and CEO Aracruz SA (eucalyptus pulp exporter) 1987–89; Founding Partner and CEO BFC Banco SA, Rio de Janeiro 1989–91, 1993; Man. Dir Morgan, Stanley and Co., New York 1994–2000; Pres. and CEO Nat. Devt Bank (BNDES) 2000–01; Pres. and CEO Petrobras 2002; Pres. and CEO Fosfertil 2003–; several Brazilian decorations; Officier, Légion d'honneur (France). *Address:* Avenida Luiz Carlos Berrini 1681, 9th Floor, São Paolo, SP 04571-011 (office). *Telephone:* (11) 5501-1156 (office). *Fax:* (11) 5501-1188 (office). *E-mail:* fgros@fosfertil.com.br (office). *Website:* www.fosfertil .com.br (office).

GROSS, Mgr Stanislav, LLM; Czech fmr politician; b. 30 Oct. 1969, Prague; m. 2nd Šárka Gross; two d. *Education:* secondary vocational transport coll., Prague, Charles Univ., Prague. *Career:* worked briefly as electrician, then as engine driver trainee at Prague-Vršovice locomotive depot 1988; mil. service in Olomouc 1988–90; mem. Czech Social Democratic Party (Česká strana sociálně demokratická—ČSSD), Chair. Young Social

Democrats 1990–94, Presidium Cen. Exec. Cttee ČSSD, Vice-Chair. ČSSD 2001–04, Acting Chair. 2004–05; mem. Parl. in Czech Nat. Council, subsequently in Chamber of Deputies 1992–2004, Chair. ČSSD Parl. Club 1995–96, 1996–2000, Deputy Chair. Chamber of Deputies 1998–2000, Spokesman for Security 1996–2005, Vice-Chair. Cttee for Defence and Security 1994–2005, Vice-Chair. of Parl. 1998–2000; Minister of the Interior 2000–04; Deputy Prime Minister 2002–04; Prime Minister of Czech Repub. 2004–05 (resgnd); Cross of Honour First Class 2002.
Address: c/o Česká strana sociálně demokratická, Lidovy dum, Hybernska 7, 110 00 Prague 1, Czech Republic.

GROSSER, Alfred, DèsSc; French academic, writer and journalist; b. 1 Feb. 1925, Frankfurt; m. Anne-Marie Jourcin 1959; four s. *Education:* Univs of Aix en Provence and Paris. *Career:* Asst Dir UNESCO Office in Germany 1950–51; Asst Prof., Univ. of Paris 1951–55; Lecturer, later Prof., Inst. d'études politiques 1954, Prof. Emer. 1992–; Dir Studies and Research, Fondation nat. des Sciences politiques 1956–92; with Ecole des hautes études commerciales 1961–66, 1986–88, with Ecole Polytechnique 1974–95; Visiting Prof., Bologna Center, Johns Hopkins Univ. 1955–69, Stanford Univ. 1964–67; political columnist La Croix 1955–65, 1984–, Le Monde 1965–94, Ouest-France 1973–, L'Expansion 1979–89; Pres. Centre d'information et de recherche sur l'Allemagne contemporaine 1982–, Eurocréation 1986–92 (Hon. Pres. 1992–); Vice-Pres. Int. Political Science Asscn 1970–73; mem. Bd L'Express 1998–2003; Grosses Verdienstkreuz mit Stern 1995 und Schulterband 2003; Grand Officier Légion d'honneur 2001; Dr hc (Aston, Birmingham, UK) 2001, (European Univ. of Humanities, Minsk, Belarus) 2001; Peace Prize, Union of German Publrs 1975, Grand Prix, Acad. des Sciences Morales et Politiques 1998. *Publications:* L'Allemagne de l'Occident 1953, La démocratie de Bonn 1958, Hitler, la presse et la naissance d'une dictature 1959, La Quatrième Republique et sa politique extérieure 1961, La politique extérieure de la Ve République 1965, Au nom de quoi? Fondements d'une morale politique 1969, L'Allemagne de notre temps 1970, L'explication politique 1972, les Occidentaux: Les pays d'Europe et les Etats Unis depuis la guerre 1978, Le sel de la terre. Pour l'engagement moral 1981, Affaires extérieures: la politique de la France 1944–84, 1984 (updated 1989), L'Allemagne en Occident 1985, Mit Deutschen streiten 1987, Vernunft und Gewalt. Die französische Revolution und das deutsche Grundgesetz heute 1989, Le crime et la mémoire 1989 (revised 1991), Mein Deutschland 1993, Was ich denke 1995, Les identités difficiles 1996, Une Vie de Français (memoirs) 1997, Deutschland in Europa 1998, Les fruits de leur arbre: regard athée sur les Chrétiens 2001, L'Allemagne de Berlin 2002, La France, semblable et differente 2005, Die Früchte ihres Baumes 2005.
Address: 8 rue Dupleix, 75015 Paris, France (home). *Telephone:* 1-43-06-41-82 (home). *Fax:* 1-40-65-00-76 (home). *E-mail:* grosser.alfred@wanadoo.fr (home).

GROSSMAN, Gene M., PhD; American academic; *Professor of Economics and International Affairs, Princeton University;* b. 11 Dec. 1955, New York. *Education:* Yale Univ., MIT. *Career:* Asst Prof. of Econs and Int. Affairs, Princeton Univ. 1980–85, Assoc. Prof. 1985–88, Prof. 1988–, Jacob Viner Prof. of Int. Econs 1992–, Dir (Acting) Int. Finance Section 1999–2000, Dir Int. Econs Section 2000–; Visiting Lecturer, Tel-Aviv Univ. 1982–83; Visiting Fellow, Univ. of Stockholm 1983, 1986, 1993, Hebrew Univ. of Israel 1989, Incenzo Gasparini Inst. of Econ. Research, Milan 1994; Visiting Scholar, Inst. for Monetary and Econ. Studies, Bank of Japan 1989; Visiting Prof., Univ. of California, Berkeley 1990, Univ. of Pennsylvania 1992, Univ. d'Aix-Marseille 1994, LSE 1997, 2001, Univ. des Sciences Sociales de Toulouse 1998, City Univ. of Hong Kong 2000; consultant, US Dept of Labour 1977–87, US Office of Int. Econ. Research 1979–80, Fed. Trade Comm. 1983–84, World Bank 1984–1992, OECD 1989, 1992–93; Assoc. Ed. Quarterly Journal of Economics 1984–, Review of International Economics 1992–, German Economic Review 1999–; mem. Editorial Bd, Journal of International Trade and Economic Development 1991–95, European Journal of Political Economy 1994–99, American Economic Review 1995–98, Journal of Economic Growth 1994–; Research Assoc. Nat. Bureau of Econ. Research 1981–; Research Fellow, Centre for Econ. Policy Research, UK; Alfred P. Sloan Research Fellow 1984–88; Richard A. Lestor Preceptorship 1984–87; Fellow, Econometric Soc. 1992, American Acad. of Arts and Sciences 1997; Harry G. Johnson Prize, Canadian Econ. Asscn 1985, Daeyang Prize in Econs, King Sejong Univ. 1987, Yavor Prize, Horowitz Inst. for Developing Countries 1989, John S. Guggenheim Memorial Foundation Fellow 1993–94, Best Book Award, American Political Science Asscn 2002. *Publications include:* (as co-author): Innovation and Growth in the Global Economy 1991, Reflections on Regionalism 1997, Special Interest Politics 2001, Interest Groups and Trade Policy 2002; (as editor): Essays in Development Economics Vols I and II 1985, Imperfect Competition and International Trade 1992, The Handbook of International Economics Vol. 3 1995, Economic Growth: Theory and Evidence Vols I and II 1996, The Political Economy of Trade Policy 1996; numerous journal articles and chapters in books.
Address: Department of Economics, 300 Fisher Hall, Princeton University, Princeton, NJ 08544, USA (office). *Telephone:* (609) 258-4823 (office). *Fax:* (609) 258-1374 (office). *E-mail:* grossman@princeton.edu (office). *Website:* www.princeton.edu/~grossman (office).

GROSSMAN, Marc, BA, MSc; American diplomatist and fmr government official; *Vice-Chairman, Cohen Group;* b. Los Angeles. *Education:* Univ. of Calif., Santa Barbara, London School of Econs, UK. *Career:* joined US Foreign Service 1976; overseas assignments include Political Officer, Mission to NATO, Brussels, Embassy in Budapest, Hungary; various positions at Bureau of Nr Eastern and S Asian Affairs, US Dept of State; fmr Deputy Special Adviser to Pres. Carter; Deputy Dir of Pvt. Office of Sec.-Gen. of NATO Lord Carrington 1984–86; Exec. Asst to Deputy Sec. of State John C. Whitehead 1986–89; Prin. Deputy Asst Sec. of State for Political Mil. Affairs 1989–93; Special Asst to Sec. of State and Exec. Sec. Dept of State 1993–94; Amb. to Turkey 1994–87; Asst Sec. of State for European Affairs 1997–2000; Dir-Gen. of Foreign Service and Dir of Human Resources 2000–01; Under-Sec. of State for Political Affairs 2001–05 (retd); Vice-Chair The Cohen Group, Washington, DC 2005–.
Address: The Cohen Group, 1200 19th Street, NW, Suite 400, Washington, DC 20036, USA (office). *Telephone:* (202) 689-7900 (office). *Fax:* (202) 689-7910 (office). *E-mail:* mgrossman@cohengroup.net (office). *Website:* www.cohengroup.net (office).

GRUBE, Claus, LLM; Danish diplomatist; *Permanent Representative, European Union;* b. 14 Dec. 1950, Copenhagen; m. Susanne Fournais Grube; three c. *Education:* Univ. of Copenhagen. *Career:* Deputy Judge, Ministry of Justice 1976; entered Foreign Service 1977; Embassy Sec., Perm. Mission to EU 1979–83; Head of Section, Ministry of Foreign Affairs 1983; personal asst to State Sec. Foreign Econ. Affairs 1984–88; Counsellor, Econ. Affairs, Embassy in Paris 1988–93; Deputy Head of Dept, Ministry of Foreign Affairs 1993, Head, North Group Third Dept 1994, Under-Sec. North Group 1994; Deputy Perm. Rep. to EU 2000–03, Amb. and Perm. Rep. 2003–; Chevalier Ordre nat. du Mérite (France) 1994, Commdr Ordre de la Couronne (Belgium) 1995, Order of the Dannebrog 2005.
Address: Permanent Mission of Denmark to the European Union, 73 rue d'Arlon, 1040 Brussels (office); 37 avenue Franklin Roosevelt, 1050 Brussels, Belgium (home). *Telephone:* (2) 233-08-11 (office). *Fax:* (2) 230-93-84 (office). *E-mail:* brurep@um.dk (office). *Website:* www.danerep.be (office).

GRUDZINSKI, Przemyslaw, PhD; Polish diplomatist and academic; *Professor, College of International and Security Studies, George C. Marshall Center;* b. 30 Oct. 1950, Torun; m.; two d. *Education:* Univ. of Nicolaus Copernicus, Torun, Inst. of History, Polish Acad. of Sciences, Warsaw. *Career:* Prof., Inst. of History, Polish Acad. of Sciences 1976–96; Adviser to Deputy Minister of Nat. Defence 1990; Dir Bureau of Research and Dir-Gen. Sejm (Parl.) 1991; Deputy Minister of Nat. Defence 1992–93; Prof., Marshall European Centre for Security Studies, Germany 1994–97, Coll. of Int. and Security Studies 2005–; Under-Sec. of State, Ministry of Foreign Affairs 1997–2000; Amb. to USA 2000–05; mem. Solidarity Movt 1980s; Founder-mem. Euro-Atlantic Asscn 1994, Council on Foreign Policy, Warsaw 1996; Fellow, American Council of Learned Socs 1978–80; Fulbright Fellow, Princeton Univ. 1988, Visiting Fellow 1978–80, 1988; Visiting Fellow, Univ. of Southern California, UCLA 1989. *Publications include:* The Future of Europe in the Ideas of Franklin D. Roosevelt 1933–1945 1987, Scientists and Barbarians: The Nuclear Policy of the United States 1939–45 1987, Theology of the Bomb: The Origins of Nuclear Deterrence Vols 1–3 1988, A Critical Approach to European Security: Identity and Institutions 1999; numerous articles in professional journals.
Address: College of International and Security Studies, George C. Marshall Center, Gernackerstrasse 2 82467 Garmisch-Partenkirchen, Germany (office). *Telephone:* (8821) 750-2680 (office). *Fax:* (8821) 750-2688 (office). *E-mail:* cisscontact@marshallcenter.org (office). *Website:* www.marshallcenter.org (office).

GRUEVSKI, Nikola, BEcons, MSc; Macedonian lawyer, economist and politician; *Prime Minister;* b. 31 Aug. 1970, Skopje; m. Borkica Gruevska; one d. *Education:* SS Cyril and Methodius Univ., Skopje, St Clement Ohrid Univ., Bitola. *Career:* with Credit Dept, Foreign Dept, then Currency Dealing, Balkanska Banka Skopje 1994–98, Liquidity, Plan, Analyses and Securities Dept 1995–96; with Metal Bank, Frankfurt 1996–97, MG Finance PLC, London 1997, Flemings Pvt. Asset Man. Ltd, London 1997–98; Minister without Portfolio, then Minister of Trade 1998–99; Minister of Finance 1999–2002; Pres. Econ. Council 2000–02; mem. Macedonian Parl. 2002–06; Adviser, Ministry of Finance, Serbia 2003; Pres., Internal Macedonian Revolutionary Org.-Democratic Party for

Macedonian Nat. Unity (IMRO-DPMNU) 2003–; Prime Minister 2006–; Vice-Pres. Euro-Atlantic Council of the Repub. of Macedonia 2005–06; Pres. Broker's Asscn of Macedonia 1998, State Securities and Exchange Comm. 2000–02, Parl. Cttee for Co-operation with European Parl. 2002–04; financial affairs commentator, MTM TV, Skopje 1998–. *Publications:* The Macedonian Economy at a Crossroad: On the Way to a Healthier Economy 1998, The Way Out: Foreign Direct Investment, Economic Development and Employment 2007; numerous articles on econ. and political issues.
Address: Office of the Prime Minister, 1000 Skopje, Ilindenska bb, Former Yugoslav Republic of Macedonia (office). *Telephone:* (2) 3115389 (office). *Fax:* (2) 3112561 (office). *E-mail:* primeminister@primeminister.gov.mk (office). *Website:* www.gov.mk (office).

GRUSHKO, Alexander; Russian diplomatist and politician; *Deputy Minister of Foreign Affairs;* b. 25 April 1955, Oslo, Norway. *Education:* Moscow State Inst. of Int. Relations (MGIMO). *Career:* father served in Oslo as trainee in Soviet embassy, family lived in Oslo 1954–58, returned to Oslo where his father was Second Sec. 1962–72, returned with his family to Moscow 1972; adviser, Soviet embassy in Brussels 1980–90s; Head of Russian del. at disarmament negotiations between USSR and NATO within framework of jt consultative group under Treaty on Conventional Armed Forces in Europe (CFE Treaty); Chief Adviser to Dept of Security and Disarmament Affairs, Ministry of Foreign Affairs mid-1990s, Deputy Dir Dept of European Cooperation 2002–03, Dir 2003–05, mem. Bd Ministry of Foreign Affairs 2003, rank of Amb. 2004, Deputy Minister of Foreign Affairs with responsibility for pan-European and Euro-Atlantic orgs 2005–; Lecturer, MGIMO; Order of Friendship 2004.
Address: Ministry of Foreign Affairs, Smolenskaya-Sennaya pl. 32/34, 119200 Moscow, Russia (office). *Telephone:* (495) 244-16-06 (office). *Fax:* (495) 230-21-30 (office). *E-mail:* ministry@mid.ru (office). *Website:* www.mid.ru (office).

GRYBAUSKAITĖ, Dalia, PhD; Lithuanian politician and diplomatist; *Commissioner for Financial Programming and Budget, European Commission;* b. 1 March 1956, Vilnius. *Education:* Leningrad (now St Petersburg) Univ., Moscow Acad. of Public Sciences, USSR, School of Foreign Service, Georgetown Univ., Washington, DC, USA. *Career:* Head, Dept for Science, Inst. of Econs 1990–91; Programme Dir, Govt of Repub. of Lithuania, Prime Minister's Office 1991; Dir European Dept, Ministry of Int. Econ. Relations 1991–93; Dir Econ. Relations Dept, Ministry of Foreign Affairs 1993–94; Chair. Comm. for Aid Coordination (PHARE and G-24) 1993–94; Chief of Negotiations with EU on Free Trade Agreement 1993–94; Envoy Extraordinary and Minister Plenipotentiary, Mission of Lithuania to EU, Brussels 1994–95, Deputy Chief Negotiator on Europe Agreement with EU; Rep. of Nat. Aid Coordinator, Brussels 1994–95; Minister Plenipotentiary, Embassy in USA 1996–99; Deputy Minister of Finance 1999–2000, Chief Negotiator in Negotiations with IMF and World Bank; Deputy Minister of Foreign Affairs 2000–01; Deputy Head of Negotiations, Del. to EU; Minister of Finance 2001–04: Nat. Aid Co-ordinator; EU Commr for Financial Programming and Budget 2004–; Commdr's Cross, Order of Grand Duke Gediminas 2003.
Address: European Commission, Rue de la Loi 200, 1040 Brussels, Belgium (office). *Telephone:* (2) 2980191 (office); (2) 2988734 (office). *Fax:* (2) 2988490 (office). *E-mail:* cab-grybauskaite-commissaire@ec.europa.eu (office). *Website:* ec.europa.eu/commission_barroso/grybauskaite/index_en.htm (office).

GRYZLOV, Boris Vyacheslavovich, PhD; Russian engineer and politician; *Chairman, Gosudarstvennaya Duma (State Duma);* b. 15 Dec. 1950, Vladivostok; m. Ada; one s. one d. *Education:* Leningrad Inst. of Electro-Tech. Communications. *Career:* radio engineer, Heavy Duty Radio Industry Scientific Research Inst. (Comintern), took part in devt of communications systems –1977; Head of construction, later Dept Dir, Electronpribor Production Co. 1977–96; Dir New Training Tech. Centre, Baltic State Tech. Univ. 1996–99; cand. in St Petersburg city elections; Pres. Interregional Business Co-operation Fund Devt of Regions 1999–; Chief of Staff for Viktor Zubkov 1999; Founder mem. Unity (Yedinstvo) Movt 1999–, Head of St Petersburg Regional Unit 1999, Chair. Unity Political Council 2000, Chair. United Russia (Yedinaya Rossiya) 2004–; mem. Gosudarstvennaya Duma (State Duma) 1999–2001, 2003–, Leader, Unity faction 2000–01, Chair. State Duma Dec. 2003–; Minister of Internal Affairs 2001–03; Chair. Inter-Parl. Ass., Eurasian Econ. Community (Eurasec IPA); Perm. mem., Security Council of Russian Fed.
Address: Office of the Chairman, Gosudarstvennaya Duma, 103265 Moscow, Okhotnyi ryad 1, Russia (office). *Telephone:* (495) 292-83-10 (office). *Fax:* (495) 292-94-64 (office). *E-mail:* stateduma@duma.ru (office). *Website:* www.duma.ru (office); www.gryzlov.ru.

GRZEŚKOWIAK, Alicja, PhD; Polish politician and academic; *Professor of Criminal Law, Catholic University of Lublin;* b. 10 June 1941, Świrz, Lvov Prov., Ukraine; m. (husband deceased); one d. *Education:* Nicolaus Copernicus Univ., Toruń. *Career:* research worker, Faculty of Law and Admin of Nicolaus Copernicus Univ., Toruń 1966–96, Prof. 1990; on staff, Catholic Univ. of Lublin (KUL) 1990, Prof. of Criminal Law 1991–, mem. Scientific Council of John Paul II Inst.; Lecturer in Religious Law, Higher Ecclesiastic Seminary, Toruń 1994–2002; mem. Solidarity Trade Union 1980; Senator 1989–2001, Vice-Marshal of Senate 1991–93, Marshal 1997–2001, del. Parl. Ass. of the Council of Europe 1989–97, mem. 1991–97, Vice-Chair. Group of Christian Democrats 1992–97; mem. Social Movt of Solidarity Election Action (RSAWS) 1998–2001; mem. Admin. Council of John Paul II Foundation, Vatican 1992–2002; consultant of Pontifical Council for the Family 1993; mem. Pontificia Academia Pro Vita; Founder Foundation of Assistance to Single Mothers, Toruń; Hon. mem. Asscn of Catholic Families; Dr hc (Acad. of Catholic Theology, Warsaw) 1995, (Holy Family Coll., Phila) 1998, (Int. Ind. Univ. of Moldova) 1999; Pro Ecclesia et Pontifice Medal 1991, Medal of 13th Jan. of Lithuanian Repub.; Dame of the Holy Sepulchre Friars of Jerusalem, Great Cross, Order of Crown (Belgium) 1999, Great Cross, Orden del Merito Civil (Spain). *Publications:* numerous scientific publs on penal law, human rights and family rights.
Address: Katolicki Uniwersytet Lubelski, al. Racławickie 14, 20-950 Lublin, Poland (office). *E-mail:* alicja.grzeskowiak@wp.pl (home). *Website:* www.kul.lublin.pl (office).

GU, Xiulian; Chinese economist, politician and party and government official; *President, All-China Women's Federation;* b. 1935, Nantong, Jiangsu Prov. *Education:* public security cadre's school, Shenyang, Liaoning Prov., Public Security Bureau of Benxi City, Liaoning, Secondary Metallurgical School of Shenyang. *Career:* joined CCP 1956; technician and cadre, Communist Youth League of China Metallurgical Corpn 1961–64; technician, Ministry of Textile Industry 1969; cadre, State Council 1970; Vice-Minister, State Planning Comm., State Council 1973–83; Alt. mem. Cen. Cttee, CCP 1977; Vice-Chair. Cen. Patriotic Sanitation Campaign Cttee, Cen. Cttee 1981–89; mem. 12th Cen. Cttee, CCP 1982–87, 13th Cen. Cttee CCP 1987–92, 14th Cen. Cttee CCP 1992–97, 15th Cen. Cttee CCP 1997–2002; Deputy Sec. CCP Prov. Cttee, Jiangsu 1982–89; Gov. of Jiangsu 1983–89; Minister of Chemical Industry 1989–98 (also Party Cttee Sec. at the Ministry); Deputy, 9th NPC 1998–2003, Vice-Chair. 10th NPC Standing Cttee 2003–; Vice-Pres. 7th, 8th and 9th Exec. Cttee, All-China Women's Fed. 1998–2003, Pres. 9th All-China Women's Fed. 2003–; Vice-Pres. 3rd Council, China Women's Devt Fund 1999, Vice-Pres. China Women's Devt Fund 2001–; fmr standing mem. Nat. Fed. of Women.
Address: The All-China Women's Federation, 15 Jian Guo Men Nei Street, Beijing 100730, People's Republic of China (office). *Telephone:* (10) 65211639-222. *Fax:* (10) 65211156. *E-mail:* yzhch@women.org.cn; acwf@women.org.cn. *Website:* www.women.org.cn/english.

GUAJARDO GONZÁLEZ, Jorge Eugenio, BA, MA; Mexican diplomatist; *Ambassador to People's Republic of China;* b. 12 Oct. 1969, Monterrey; m. Paola Sada; one s. one d. *Education:* Georgetown and Harvard Univs, USA. *Career:* worked at Hill and Knowlton and Burson-Marsteller public relations cos, USA 1994–97; Dir-Gen. of Press and Communications, Gov. of Nuevo León 1997–2000; Consul-Gen. in Austin, Tex., USA 2005; Amb. to People's Repub. of China 2007–.
Address: Embassy of Mexico, 5 Dong Wu Jie, San Li Tun, Beijing 100600, People's Republic of China (office). *Telephone:* (10) 65321717 (office). *Fax:* (10) 65323744 (office). *E-mail:* embmxchn@public.bta.net.cn (office). *Website:* www.sre.gob.mx/china (office).

GUAN, Chengyuan; Chinese diplomatist; *Head of Mission, European Union;* b. Sept. 1945, Liaoning Prov.; m. Hu Zuzhen; one d. *Education:* Beijing Foreign Languages Inst. (now Beijing Foreign Studies Univ.). *Career:* with Dept of Translation and Interpretation, Ministry of Foreign Affairs 1974–78; several positions at Embassy in Switzerland 1978–84, including Attaché, Third Sec., Second Sec.; several positions at Dept of West European Affairs, Ministry of Foreign Affairs 1984–92, including Second Sec., First Sec., Deputy Dir, Dir; Counsellor, Embassy in France 1992–96; Counsellor, Deputy Dir-Gen. Dept of West European Affairs 1996–99, Dir-Gen. 1999–2001; Head of Mission to EU, Brussels 2001–0.
Address: Mission of the People's Republic of China to the European Union, 443–445 avenue de Tervuren, 1150 Brussels, Belgium (office). *Telephone:* (2) 771-5857 (office). *Fax:* (2) 772-3745 (office). *Website:* www.chinaembassy-org.be (office).

GUBBAY, Hon. Mr Justice Anthony Roy, MA, LLM; Zimbabwean judge; b. 26 April 1932, Manchester, England; m. Wilma Sanger 1962 (died 2002); two s. *Education:* Univ. of Witwatersrand, S Africa, Univ. of Cambridge.

Career: admitted to practice 1957; advocate Bulawayo, S Rhodesia 1958, Sr Counsel 1974; Pres. Matabeleland and Midlands Valuations Boards; Nat. Pres. Special Court for Income Tax Appeals, Fiscal Court and Patents Tribunal; Vice-Chair. Bar Asscn; Judge of the High Court, Bulawayo 1977–83, Judge of the Supreme Court 1983; Chair. Legal Practitioners' Disciplinary Tribunal 1981–87, Law Devt Comm., Judicial Service Comm.; Chief Justice of Zimbabwe 1990–2001, retd 2001; mem. Perm. Court of Arbitration; Pres. Oxford and Cambridge Soc. of Zimbabwe; Patron Commonwealth Magistrates and Judges Asscn; mem. Advisory Bd of Commonwealth Judicial Educ. Inst., Commonwealth Reference Group on the Promotion of the Human Rights of Women and the Girl Child through the Judiciary; Hon. Fellow Jesus Coll. Cambridge; Hon. Bencher of Lincoln's Inn (UK); Hon. mem. The Soc. of Legal Scholars (UK) 2004; Great Cross, Rio Branco Order (Brazil) 1999; Dr hc (Essex) 1994; Hon. LLD (London) 2002, (Witwatersrand) 2005; Peter Gruber Foundation Justice Award 2001.
Address: 26 Dacomb Drive, Chisipite, Harare, Zimbabwe (home). *Telephone:* (4) 496882 (home). *E-mail:* supreme-court@gta.gov.zw (office); gubbay@zol.co.zw (home).

GUCKIAN, Noel Joseph, OBE; British diplomatist; *Ambassador to Oman;* b. 6 March 1955; m. Lorna Ruth Guckian; one s. three d. *Career:* joined FCO 1980, studied Arabic at School of Oriental and African Studies, London 1982–83, Second Sec. (Commercial), Jedda 1984–87, Embassy, Paris 1987–88, Middle East Section, Research Dept, FCO 1988–90, 1990–91, 1992–93, Head of Section, Tripoli 1990, Kuwait 1991–92, Deputy Head of Mission, Muscat 1993–94, Head of Scott Inquiry Unit, Middle East Dept 1994–97, Head of Section, Near East N African Dept 1998, Deputy Head of Mission, Tripoli 1998–2002, Damascus 2002–04, Head of Post, Consul-Gen. for Northern Iraq, Kirkuk 2004–05, Amb. to Oman 2005–.
Address: British Embassy, PO 185, Mina Al Fahal 116, Sultanate of Oman (office). *Telephone:* 24609000 (office). *Fax:* 24609010 (office). *E-mail:* enquiries.muscat@fco.gov.uk (office). *Website:* www.britishembassy.gov.uk/oman (office).

GUDEV, Vladimir Victorovich; Russian diplomatist (retd); b. 17 Sept. 1940, Moscow; m. Valentina Goudeva 1960; one d. *Education:* Moscow Inst. of Int. Relations. *Career:* sr posts in Ministry of Foreign Affairs at home and abroad 1963–75; Embassy First Sec. in Iraq 1975–79; Chief of Section, Deputy Chief of Near East Dept of Ministry of Foreign Affairs 1979–86; Deputy Dir, Chief of Dept in Directorate of Near East and North Africa 1986–87; Amb. to Iran 1987–93; Head of Africa and Near East Dept, Russian Ministry of Foreign Affairs 1993–95; Amb. to Egypt 1995–2000, to Georgia 2001–02; Dir Fourth Dept of CIS countries, Ministry of Foreign Affairs 2002–05 (retd); Medal for Devt of Virgin Lands 1958, 850th Anniversary of Moscow Jubilee Medal 1998.
Address: c/o Ministry of Foreign Affairs, Smolenskaya-Sennaya 32/34, 119200 Moscow, Russia (office). *Telephone:* (495) 244-4765 (office). *Fax:* (495) 244-3817 (office).

GUDMUNDSSON, Thórdur Ingvi, BA, MA; Icelandic diplomatist; b. 1954, Reykjavík; m. Gudrún Salóme Jónsdóttir, three c. *Education:* Univ. of Iceland, Queen's Univ., Kingston, Ont., Canada. *Career:* with Ministry of Social Affairs 1980–82; Dept Head, Budget Man. Office, Ministry of Finance 1982–84; Financial Dir Marel Electronics 1984–86; Man. Dir Samvinn Investment Fund 1984–86, Lind Finance Company 1986–94; independent consultant 1994–95; joined Defence Dept, Ministry of Foreign Affairs 1995, Deputy Dir 1996–97, Desk Officer, External Trade Dept 1997–98; Deputy Perm. Rep. to WTO, Geneva 1998–2000, OECD, Paris 2000–04; Mil. Rep. to NATO 2004–07.
Address: c/o Ministry for Foreign Affairs, Rauarárstíg 25, 150 Reykjavík, Iceland (office). *Website:* www.utanrikisraduneyti.is (office).

GUEBUZA, Armando Emílio; Mozambican politician and head of state; *President;* b. 20 Jan. 1943, Murrupula, Nampula Prov. *Career:* joined Frente de Libertação de Moçambique (Frelimo) 1963; elected to Cen. Cttee 1966–, to Politburo 1977–; guerrilla commdr during war with Portugal, rising to rank of Lt-Gen.; Political Commissar 1970–; Minister of Home Affairs 1974–78, 1983–84, Deputy Minister of Defence 1978–81, Resident Minister 1981–84, Minister in the Office of the Pres. 1984–86, Minister of Transport and Communication 1986–94; Head of Frente de Libertação de Moçambique (Frelimo) Parl. Bench 1994–2002, Frelimo Sec.-Gen. June 2002–; Pres. of Mozambique 2005–; Head of Govt Del. to Rome peace talks 1992; Chair. two Comms for Burundi peace process under Julius Nyerere and Nelson Mandela.
Address: Office of the President, Avda Julius Nyerere 1780, Maputo (office); Frente de Libertação de Moçambique (Frelimo), Rua Pereira do Lago 229, Maputo, Mozambique (office). *Telephone:* (1) 491121 (office). *Fax:* (1) 492065 (office). *E-mail:* gabimprensa@teldata.mz (office); sg@ frelimo.org.mz (office). *Website:* www.presidencia.gov.mz (office); www.frelimo.org.mz (office).

GUÉGUINOU, Jean, GCVO; French diplomatist; *Ambassador, United Nations Educational, Scientific and Cultural Organization (UNESCO);* b. 17 Oct. 1941. *Education:* Ecole Nat. d'Admin. *Career:* with Press and Information Dept, Ministry of Foreign Affairs 1967–69; Second Sec., London 1969–71; Head of Mission, Ministry of State/Ministry of Defence 1971–73; Head of Cabinet and Counsellor 1973–76; Dir of Cabinet of Sec. of State reporting to Prime Minister 1976–77; Asst Dir for Southern Africa and Indian Ocean 1977–82; Consul-Gen., Jerusalem 1982–86; Dir Press and Information Service 1986–90; Amb. to Czechoslovakia 1990–92, to Czech Repub. 1993, to UK 1993–98, to the Holy See 1998–2000, Ambassadeur de France 2000, Amb. to UNESCO 2003–; Chair., Cttee de patronage, Franco-Scottish Asscn 2001–; mem. Admin Council, Agence France-Presse 1986–90, Soc. of Friends of the Louvre 2000–, Arts florissants 2001–; Chevalier, Légion d'honneur, Ordre Nat. du Mérite; Commdr Order of St Gregory the Great.
Address: Délégation permanente de la République française auprès de l'UNESCO, Maison de l'UNESCO, Bureau M8.14 1, rue Miollis, 75732 Paris Cedex 15 (office); 5 avenue Montespan, 75116 Paris, France (office). *Telephone:* 1-45-68-35-47 (office). *Fax:* 1-53-69-99-49 (office). *E-mail:* dl.france@unesco.org (office). *Website:* erc.unesco.org (office).

GUÉHENNO, Jean-Marie; French diplomatist and fmr UN official; b. 30 Oct. 1949, Boulogne sur Seine; m. 1981; one d. *Education:* Ecole Normale Supérieure, Inst. d'Etudes Politiques, Ecole Nat. d'Admin, Paris. *Career:* mem. Court of Auditors 1976–2000, Sr Auditor 1993–2000; Dir Cultural Affairs, French Embassy in Washington, DC 1982–86; Dir Policy Planning Staff, Ministry of Foreign Affairs 1989–93; Amb. to WEU 1993–95; Under-Sec.-Gen. for Peace-keeping Operations, UN, New York 2000–08; Chair. Bd, Inst. for Higher Defence Studies, Paris 1998–2000; Chevalier, Légion d'honneur; Commdr, Order of Merit (Germany). *Publications:* La fin de la démocratie (English trans. The End of the Nation-State) 1993, L'avenir de la liberté – la démocratie dans la mondialisation 1999.
Address: c/o Ministry of Foreign and European Affairs, 37 quai d'Orsay, 75351 Paris Cedex 07, France. *Telephone:* 1-43-17-53-53. *Fax:* 1-43-17-52-03. *Website:* www.diplomatie.gouv.fr.

GUELAR, Diego Ramiro; Argentine diplomatist and lawyer; b. 24 Feb. 1950; m. Magdalena D. Custodio; three c. *Career:* Prof. Sociology of Law, Univ. of Buenos Aires 1971; outlawed by military for political activities (nat. leader, Peronist Youth) 1972–73; attorney, Justicialist Party of Buenos Aires Province 1973–76; Prof. Faculties of Architecture and Law, Univ. of Buenos Aires 1973–76; outlawed for political activities 1976–78; nat. adviser of coordinator for Justicialist activities 1978–83; Vice-Pres. Comm. for Budget and Finance, Nat. Chamber of Deputies 1984; Sec.-Gen. bloc of Nat. Justicialist Deputies 1985; Ed. and Dir La Razón (newspaper) 1987; Head, Foundation for Growth Arrangement (FUNCRE); Amb. to EC (now EU) 1989–96, to USA 2002–03. *Publications include:* Chronicles of Transition (collection), political and econ. works etc.
Address: c/o Ministry of Foreign Affairs, International Trade and Worship, Esmeralda 1212, Buenos Aires 1007, Argentina.

GUELLUY, Philippe, BA; French diplomatist; b. 30 Nov. 1941, Lille; m.; two c. *Education:* Nat. School of Eastern Languages. *Career:* Sec. French Embassy in Japan, Tokyo 1971–75; Perm. Rep. to NATO, Brussels, Belgium 1975–78, Perm. Rep. and Amb. 1998–2001; Dir of Strategic Affairs, Ministry of Foreign Affairs 1978–79, Deputy Dir, then Head of Strategic Affairs 1983–91, Official Rep. 1997–98; Counsellor, Embassy in Madrid, Spain 1979–83; Amb. to Norway 1992–95, to Canada 2002–04, to People's Repub. of China 2004–06; Diplomatic Counsellor, Ministry of Defence 1995–97; Officier Legion d'Honneur, Nat. Order of Merit, German Commdr of Merit. *Publications include:* various works on disarmament and strategic issues.
Address: c/o Ministry of Foreign and European Affairs, 37 quai d'Orsay, 75351 Paris Cedex 07, France (office).

GUERRA SALGUEIRO, João Manuel; Portuguese diplomatist; *Permanent Representative, United Nations;* b. 21 July 1946; m.; three c. *Education:* Univ. of Lisbon. *Career:* Attaché, Sec. of Embassy, Foreign Ministry 1969–72; served as Embassy Sec. in several locations including Sofia 1974, London 1975–78, Pretoria, S Africa 1981; Chargé d'affaires, Embassy in Guinea-Bissau 1979–80, in S Africa 1983–84; served in sr diplomatic positions including Diplomatic Rep. in Cape Verde 1990–92, in Japan 1993–95; Chief of EU Monitoring Mission, fmr Yugoslavia 1992; Amb. to Netherlands 2002–04; Perm. Rep. to UN, New York 2005–.
Address: Office of the Permanent Representative of Portugal to the United Nations, 866 Second Avenue, 9th Floor, New York, NY 10017, USA

(office). *Telephone:* (212) 759-9444 (office). *Fax:* (212) 355-1124 (office). *E-mail:* portugal@un.int (office). *Website:* www.un.int/portugal (office).

GUESNERIE, Roger Sylvain Maxime Auguste, DèsSc (Econs); French economist; *Professor of Economics, Collège de France;* b. 17 Feb. 1943, Ste Gemmes Le Rt.. *Education:* Lycée de Rennes, Ecole Polytechnique and Ecole Nat. des Ponts et Chaussées, Univ. of Toulouse. *Career:* Research Assoc., Centre d'Études Prospectives et de Recherches en Economie Mathématique Appliquée à la Planification (CEPREMAP) 1967–81; Research Assoc., CNRS 1976, Research Dir 1978; Dir of Studies, Ecole des Hautes Etudes en Sciences Sociales (EHESS) 1979–; Dir Centre d'Études Quantitatives Comparatives (CEQC) 1981–82, Centre d'Études et de Recherches en Analyse Socio-économiques (CERAS) 1982–84, Asscn pour le Développement de la Recherche en Economie et Statistique (ADRES) 1989–94, Dir Delta (mixed research unit of CNRS-EHESS-ENS) 1988–2000, Fédération Paris Jourdan 2001–; Lecturer, l'École Nationale des Ponts et Chaussées 1970–83, Paris X Nanterre 1972–3, École Polytechnique 1974–86, l'Institut d'Études Politiques de Paris 1975–78, Paris IX-Dauphine 1974–76; Prof., École Nationale de la Statistique et de l'Administration Economique 1978–84, Prof., LSE 1990–94, Prof. of Econs, Coll. de France 2000–; Vice-Pres. European Econ. Asscn 1992, Pres. 1994; Pres. Scientific Cttee CEPREMAP 1992–95, Select Cttee on Econ. and Social Sciences, Brussels 1992–95, Asoc. of Applied Econometrics 1997–2001, Asoc. Française de Science Economique 2002–03; mem. Scientific Council EHESS 1985–91, Nat. Cttee CNRS 1987–91, European Ass. of Science and Tech. 1994–97, Research Council of L'École Polytechnique 2000–02, Nat. Cttee on Social and Scientific Coordination 2001–02, Scientific Cttee Ecole Normale Supérieure 2001–05;; Foreign Fellow, Churchill Coll., Univ. of Cambridge 1978; Fellow, Econometric Soc., Pres. 1996; Foreign mem. American Acad. of Arts and Sciences 2000–; Hon. Foreign mem. American Econ. Asscn 1997; Chevalier, Ordre du Mérite, Legion d'Honneur; Dr hc (Ecole des Hautes Etudes Commerciales) 2001; Silver Medal, CNRS 1994. *Publications:* La documentation Française, 2 vols (co-author), Modèles de l'economie publique 1980, A Contribution to the Pure Theory of Taxation 1995, L'Economie de marché 1996, Assessing Rational Expectations 1 2001, Assessing Rational Expectations 2 2005, L'économie de marché 2006; about 100 articles in econ. journals. *Address:* DELTA, 48 boulevard Jourdan, ENS, 75014 Paris, France (office). *Telephone:* 1-43-13-63-15 (office). *Fax:* 1-43-13-63-10 (office). *E-mail:* guesnerie@delta.ens.fr (office); guesnerie@pse.ens.fr (office). *Website:* www.delta.ens.fr (office); www.pse.ens.fr/guesnerie.

GUEVARA OBREGÓN, Alberto José, MSc; Nicaraguan politician and economist; *Minister of Finance and Public Credit;* b. 1963; m.; three c. *Education:* Carlos Fonseca Amador Univ., Catholic Univ. of Chile and Nat. Univ. of Nicaragua. *Career:* various positions at Cen. Bank of Nicaragua 1999–2006; Minister of Finance and Public Credit 2007–. *Address:* Ministry of Finance and Public Credit, Frente a la Asamblea Nacional, Apartado 2170, Managua, Nicaragua (office). *Telephone:* (2) 22-6530 (office). *Fax:* (2) 222-6430 (office). *E-mail:* webmaster@mhcp.gob.ni (office). *Website:* www.hacienda.gob.ni (office).

GUIGOU, Elisabeth Alexandrine Marie, LèsL; French politician; b. 6 Aug. 1946, Marrakesh, Morocco; m. Jean-Louis Guigou 1966; one s. *Education:* Lycée Victor Hugo, Marrakesh, Lycée Descartes, Rabat, Facultés des Lettres, Rabat and Montpellier, Faculté des Sciences Economiques, Montpellier and Ecole Nat. d'Admin. *Career:* civil servant, Ministry of Finance 1974, Office of the Treasury 1974–75, Office of Banks 1976–78, Office of Financial Markets 1978–79; Deputy Chair. Finance Cttee VIIth Plan 1975–78; Maître de Conférences, Inst. d'Etudes Politiques, Paris 1976; Financial Attaché, Embassy, London 1979–81; Head, Office for Europe, America and Asia, Treasury 1981; Tech. Counsellor, Office of Minister of Economy and Finance 1982; Tech. Counsellor 1982–88; Office of Pres. of Repub. 1988–90; Sec.-Gen. Interministerial Cttee on European Econ. Cooperation 1985–90; Minister Delegate for European Affairs 1990–93; mem. Regional Council of Provence Alpes Côte-d'Azur 1992–2002, European Parl. 1994–97; elected Deputy to Nat. Ass. for Vaucluse (Socialist Party) 1997; Minister of Justice 1997–2000, of Employment and Solidarity 2000–02. *Publications:* Pour les Européens 1994, Etre femme en politique 1997. *Address:* c/o Conseil Régional de Provence Alpes Côte d'Azur, 27 place Jules Guesde, 13481 Marseille Cedex, France.

GUILIANI CURY, Hugo, BEcons; Dominican Republic journalist, banker, politician and diplomatist. *Education:* Univ. of Miami, USA, Latin America Econ. Planning Inst., Chile, Man. Research Inst. of Admin. Science, Netherlands. *Career:* fmr Minister of Industry and Commerce, and of Finance; fmr mem. Pres.'s Council of Econ. Advisers; Pnr, Giuliani Cury and Assocs; fmr Dir Banco de Reservas de la Republica; fmr Gov. Banco

Central de la República Dominicana; chief negotiator for Dominican Repub. agreements with IMF and World Bank 1985; fmr Tech. Dir Corpn of Enterprises; Prof. of Business and Econs, Univ. of Santo Domingo for 12 years; fmr producer of weekly TV programme; fmr columnist, Hoy (daily newspaper); Amb. to USA 2002–04. *Publications:* nine books on econ. subjects. *Address:* Secretariat of State for External Relations, Avenida Independencia 752, Santo Domingo, DN, Dominican Republic (office). *Telephone:* 987-7001 (office). *Fax:* 985-7526 (office). *E-mail:* postmaster@serex.gov.do (office). *Website:* www.serex.gov.do (office).

GUILLAUME, Gilbert, LenD; French judge; *Judge ad hoc, International Court of Justice;* b. 4 Dec. 1930, Bois-Colombes; m. Marie-Anne Hidden 1961; one s. two d. *Education:* Univ. of Paris, Paris Inst. of Political Studies and Ecole Nat. Admin. *Career:* mem. Council of State 1957; Legal Adviser, State Secr. for Civil Aviation 1968–79; French Rep. Legal Cttee of ICAO 1968–69, Chair. of Cttee 1971–75; Chair. Conciliation Comm. OECD 1973–78; Dir of Legal Affairs, OECD 1979; French Rep. Cen.l Comm. for Navigation of the Rhine 1979–87, Chair. 1981–82; Dir of Legal Affairs, Ministry of Foreign Affairs 1979–87; Conseiller d'Etat 1981–96; Judge, Int. Court of Justice 1987–2005, Pres. 2000–03, Judge ad hoc 2006–; First Vice-Pres. Institut de droit int.; Counsel/agent for France in int. arbitration proceedings, numerous cases before European Courts etc.; mem. Perm. Court of Arbitration 1980–; Arbitrator, OSCE, ICSID etc.; del. to numerous int. legal and diplomatic confs; Prof. Inst. of Political Studies, Univ. of Paris and other lecturing appointments; mem. Bd Hon. Eds Chinese Journal of International Law; mem. various legal asscns, insts etc.; Commdr, Légion d'honneur, des Arts et des Lettres; Chevalier, Ordre nat. du Mérite, du Mérite agricole, du Mérite maritime. *Publications:* numerous books and articles on admin. and int. law, including Terrorisme et droit international 1989, Les grandes crises internationales et le droit 1994, La Cour Internationale de Justice à l'aube du XXIème siècle 2003. *Address:* International Court of Justice, Peace Palace, 2517 KJ, The Hague, Netherlands (office); 36 rue Perronet, 92200 Neuilly-sur-Seine, France (home). *Telephone:* (70) 302-24-50 (office); 1-46-24-25-67 (home). *Fax:* (70) 302-24-09 (office); 1-47-45-67-84 (home). *E-mail:* g.guillaume@icj-cij.org (office); g.ma.guillaume@wanadoo.fr (home).

GUILLAUME JEAN JOSEPH MARIE, HRH Prince; Luxembourg; b. 11 Nov. 1981. *Education:* Lycée Robert Schuman, RMA Sandhurst, England, Univ. of Durham, England. *Career:* proclaimed Hereditary Grand Duke 18 Dec. 2000; apptd army Lt by Grand-Ducal Decree 2002, apptd First Lt 2003; Chair. Bd of Dirs Kräizberg Foundation 2000–; Hon. Pres. Bd of Econ. Devt 2001–. *Address:* Grand Ducal Palace, 2013 Luxembourg, Luxembourg (office). *Website:* www.gouvernement.lu.

GUINGONA, Teofisto T., Jr; Philippine politician, lawyer and writer; b. 4 July 1928, San Juan, Rizal; m. Ruthie de Lara; two s. one d. *Education:* Ateneo de Manila Univ. *Career:* fmr Gov. Devt Bank of the Philippines and Pres. Chamber of Commerce of the Philippines; served as human rights lawyer 1970s; Founder SANDATA and Hon. Chair. of BANDILA; jailed in 1972 and 1978 for his opposition to marital law; fmr Chair. Comm. on Audit; Senator 1980s, Senate Pres. Pro-tempore and Majority Leader, Chair. Blue Ribbon Cttee, Senator 1998, Minority Leader; fmr Dir Mindanao Devt Authority; fmr Chair. Mindanao Labor Man. Advisory Council; fmr Exec. Sec. to Pres.; fmr Justice Sec.; Vice-Pres. of the Philippines 2001–04; Sec. of Foreign Affairs 2001–02; Pres. Lakas-Christian Muslim Democrats (Lakas—CMD) –2003 (resgnd); adviser to Fernando Poe, Jr. *Address:* c/o Office of the Vice-President, PICC, 2nd Floor, CCP Complex, Roxas Boulevard, Pasay City, Metro Manila, The Philippines (office). *Telephone:* (2) 8312658 (office). *Fax:* (2) 8312614 (office). *E-mail:* gma@easy.net.ph (office). *Website:* www.teofistoguingonajr.ph.

GUINHUT, Jean-Pierre, MA; French diplomatist; b. 26 Feb. 1946, Cholet, Maine-et-Loire. *Education:* Univ. of Paris IV, Inst. d'études islamiques, Inst. nat. de langues et civilisations orientales (Inalco). *Career:* co-founder Sindbad Publishing Co. 1973–74; Attaché, Embassy in Qatar 1975–76; with Dept of Cultural, Scientific and Tech. Relations, Ministry of Foreign Affairs 1976–79; Second Sec., Embassy in Tehran 1980–81, First Sec. and interim Chargé d'affaires 1981–82; First Sec., Embassy in Tripoli 1982–84, Second Counsellor 1984–85; First Sec., Perm. Mission to UN, New York 1985–88, Second Counsellor 1988; First Counsellor, Embassy in Tehran 1988–92; Asst to Deputy Dir in charge of Middle East, Ministry of Foreign Affairs 1993–95, Deputy Dir 1995–96; Amb. to Azerbaijan 1997–2001, to Afghanistan 2002–05; Head of Inter-Ministerial Mission for the Reconstruction of Iraq, Office of the Prime Minister 2005–07; Chevalier, Légion d'honneur, ordre national du Mérite; Médaille d'honneur, Ministry of

Foreign Affairs. *Publication:* The Man Who Loved Too Much: The Legend of Leyli and Majnun (poetry).
Address: c/o Ministry of Foreign and European Affairs, 37 quai d'Orsay, 75351 Paris Cedex 07, France (office).

GÜL, Abdullah, BA, PhD; Turkish politician and head of state; *President;* b. 1950, Qaisari Prov.; m.; three c. *Education:* Istanbul Univ., Univ. of London, UK. *Career:* participated in the foundation of the Dept of Engineering, Sakarya Univ., Lecturer in Econs 1980–83, Assoc. Prof. of Econs 1991–; economist with Islamic Development Bank, Jeddah 1983–91; mem. Parl. representing Al-Rafah Party (now outlawed) 1991, later Al-Rafah Deputy Head of Foreign Affairs; held numerous ministerial posts including Minister of State for Foreign Affairs 1996–97, Spokesman for Al-Rafah Govt, also mem. European Council; Founder-mem. and Deputy Chair. AK Partisi (Justice and Devt Party) 2001–; Prime Minister of Turkey Nov. 2002–March 2003; Deputy Prime Minister and Minister of Foreign Affairs 2003–07; President of Turkey 2007–; Affairs mem. NATO Parl. Ass. 2001–; Pro-Merito Medal of the Council of Europe 2001.
Address: President's Office, Cumhurbaşkanlığı Köşkü, Çankaya, Ankara (office). *Telephone:* (312) 4685030 (office). *Fax:* (312) 4271330 (office). *E-mail:* cumhurbaskanligi@tccb.gov.tr (office). *Website:* www.cankaya .gov.tr (office); www.abdullahgul.gen.tr (home).

GUMENDE, António, MBA; Mozambican journalist and diplomatist; *High Commissioner to UK;* m. Simangalisso Gumende. *Education:* Nottingham Trent Univ. *Career:* reporter, Mozambique News Agency, Maputo 1984–90; Business Ed. SADC Press Trust, Harare, Zimbabwe 1990–96; Econs Ed. SAPEM, Harare 1996–97; Exec. Ed. SARDC, Maputo 1997–2002; Chair. Media Coop, Maputo 1997–2002; High Commr to UK 2002–; Best Investigative Report, Nat. Asscn of Journalists of Mozambique 1988. *Publications:* Ed.: Mozambique National Human Development Report (UNDP) 1998, 1999, 2000, 2001.
Address: High Commission of Mozambique, 21 Fitzroy Square, London, W1T 6EL, England (office). *Telephone:* (20) 7383-3800 (office). *Fax:* (20) 7383-3801 (office). *E-mail:* agumende@mozambiquehc.co.uk (office). *Website:* www.mozambiquehc.org.uk (office).

GUMMER, Rt Hon. John Selwyn, PC, MA; British politician; *Chairman, Quality of Life Commission;* b. 26 Nov. 1939, Stockport; brother of Peter Selwyn Gummer, now Lord Chadlington; m. Penelope J. Gardner 1977; two s. two d. *Education:* King's School, Rochester and Selwyn Coll., Cambridge. *Career:* Ed., Business Publs 1962–64; Ed.-in-Chief, Max Parrish and Oldbourne Press 1964–66; Special Asst to Chair. BPC Publishing 1967; Dir Shandwick Publishing Co. 1966–81; Dir Siemssen Hunter Ltd 1973–80, Chair. 1979–80; Man. Dir EP Group of Cos 1975–81; Chair. Selwyn Sancroft Int. 1976–81; MP for Lewisham W 1970–74, Eye, Suffolk (now Suffolk Coastal) 1979–; Parl. Pvt. Sec. to Minister of Agric. 1972; Vice-Chair. Conservative Party 1972–74, Chair. 1983–85; Asst Govt Whip 1981, Lord Commr Treasury (Whip) 1982; Under-Sec. of State for Employment Jan.–Oct. 1983, Minister of State for Employment 1983–84, Paymaster-Gen. 1984–85; Minister of State at Ministry of Agric., Fisheries and Food 1985–88; Minister for Local Govt, Dept of Environment 1988–89; Minister of Agric. 1989–93; Sec. of State for the Environment 1993–97; Chair. Conservative Group for Europe 1997–2000, Marine Stewardship Council 1998–2005, Sancroft Int. Ltd 1997–, Valpak Ltd 1998–, Quality of Life Comm. 2006–; mem. Gen. Synod of Church of England 1979–92 (resgnd); joined Roman Catholic Church 1994; Medal of Honour, Royal Soc. for the Protection of Birds 1998. *Publications:* When the Coloured People Come 1966, To Church with Enthusiasm 1969, The Permissive Society 1970, The Christian Calendar (with L. W. Cowie) 1971, Faith in Politics (with Alan Beith and Eric Heffer) 1987, Christianity and Conservatism 1990.
Address: House of Commons, Westminster, London, SW1A 0AA, England (office).

GUNA-KASEM, Pracha, PhD; Thai diplomatist; *Adviser to the Minister of Foreign Affairs;* b. 29 Dec. 1934, Bangkok; m. Sumanee Chongcharoen 1962; one s. *Education:* Dhebsirinda School, Bangkok, Marlborough Coll. and Hertford Coll., Oxford, UK and Yale Univ., USA. *Career:* joined Ministry of Foreign Affairs 1959, Chief of Section, Political Div. of Dept of Int. Org. 1960–61, Second Sec., SEATO Div. 1962–63, Alt. mem. for Thailand, SEATO Perm. Working Group 1962–63, Embassy in Egypt 1964–65, Chief of Foreign News Analysis Div. of Information Dept and concurrently in charge of Press Affairs 1966–69, Chief of Press Div. 1970–71, Consul-Gen. in Hong Kong 1971–73, Dir-Gen. of Information Dept 1973–75; Perm. Rep. to UN 1975–80, UN (Geneva) 1980–82; Dir-Gen. ASEAN-Thailand 1982; Dir-Gen. Dept of Econ. Affairs, Foreign Ministry 1984–85; Amb. to France and Algeria 1985–87; Perm. Del. to UNESCO 1985; Dir-Gen. Dept of Econ. Affairs, Bangkok 1988; Perm. Sec. Ministry of Foreign Affairs 1992–1995, Deputy Minister of Foreign Affairs

1996; elected mem. of parliament from Bangkok 1996; Foreign Affairs Adviser to the Prime Minister 1996–98; Adviser to the Minister of Foreign Affairs 2001–; Special Lecturer, Thammasat Univ., Thai Nat. Defence Coll.; mem. del. to UN Gen. Ass. 1962, 1968, 1970, 1974, to 2nd Afro-Asian Conf., Algeria 1965, to SEATO Council 1966; Chair. Oxford Soc. of Bangkok; Grand Cordon of Order of White Elephant, Grand Cordon (Highest Class) of the Order of the Crown of Thailand, Commdr, Order of Chula Chomklao. *Achievements:* elected Vice-Pres. of the UN Gen. Ass. 1978; elected Chair. of the UN Sixth (Legal) Committee.
Address: Ministry of Foreign Affairs, Thanon Sri Ayudhya, Bangkok, Thailand. *Telephone:* (2) 6435000; (2) 6435313 (office); (2) 2514565 (home). *Fax:* (2) 6435320 (office); (2) 2551179 (home). *Website:* www.mfa.go.th (office).

GUNNARSSON, Gunnar Snorri, MA; Icelandic diplomatist; *Ambassador to People's Republic of China;* b. 13 July 1953, Reykjavík. *Education:* Univ. of St Andrews and Univ. of Edinburgh, Scotland, Universidad Complutense, Madrid. *Career:* teacher, Ísafjörur Jr Coll. 1977–78; First Sec., Ministry for Foreign Affairs 1979–81, Deputy Perm. Under-Sec. for External Trade 1991–94, Perm. Sec. of State 2002–06; First Sec., Embassy in Paris 1981–84, Counsellor 1984–87, Deputy Perm. Rep. to OECD and UNESCO 1981–87; Deputy Perm. Rep. to N Atlantic Council, Brussels 1987–88, Minister-Counsellor, Embassy in Brussels 1988–91; Perm. Rep. to UN and other Int. Orgs (including WTO and EFTA), Geneva 1994–97; Amb. to EC, Belgium, Luxembourg and Liechtenstein 1997–2002, to People's Repub. of China (also accred to Australia, Mongolia, New Zealand, Democratic People's Repub. of Korea, Repub. of Korea, Vietnam) 2006–; Kt Order of the Falcon (Iceland), Oficial Ordem do Infante Dom Henrique (Portugal), Officier Ordre du Mérite, Encomienda Orden Isabel la Católica (Spain), Commdr Ordre Grand Ducal de la Couronne de Chêne (Luxembourg), Grand Officier Order of Oranje Nassau (Netherlands), Grande Croix de l'Ordre de la Couronne (Belgium).
Address: Embassy of Iceland, Landmark Tower 1, 802, 8 North Dongsanhuan Lu, Beijing 100004, People's Republic of China (office). *Telephone:* (10) 65907795 (office). *Fax:* (10) 65907801 (office). *E-mail:* Icemb.beijing@utn.stjr.is (office). *Website:* www.iceland.org/cn (office).

GUNNARSSON, Gunnar; Icelandic diplomatist; b. 16 March 1948, Reykjavík; m. Unnur Ulfarsdottir; two d. *Education:* Free Univ., Berlin, Germany. *Career:* Dir Icelandic Comm. on Security and Int. Affairs 1979–87; Lecturer in Int. Politics, Univ. of Iceland 1978–87, Asst. Prof. 1987–91; Adviser to Minister for Foreign Affairs 1989–91; Minister Counsellor, Political Dept, Ministry of Foreign Affairs 1991, Political Dir 1991–92, Amb. 1998–2001, Dir Defence Dept 2001–02; Amb. to CSCE 1992–93; Amb. to Russian Fed. (also accred to Ukraine, Georgia, Moldova, Bulgaria, Romania and Mongolia) 1994–98; Perm. Rep. to NATO and WEU, Brussels, and OPCW, The Hague 2002–08. *Publications:* several publs on foreign and security affairs.
Address: c/o Ministry for Foreign Affairs, Rauarárstíg 25, 150 Reykjavík, Iceland. *Telephone:* 5459900. *Fax:* 5622373. *E-mail:* postur@utn.stjr.is. *Website:* www.utanrikisraduneyti.is.

GUNNLAUGSSON, Sverrir Haukur, LLB; Icelandic diplomatist; *Ambassador to UK;* b. 20 Oct. 1942, Copenhagen, Denmark; m. Gudny Adalsteinsdottir; three c. *Education:* Univ. of Iceland. *Career:* joined Ministry for Foreign Affairs as First Sec., Int. Div. 1970, First Sec., Paris 1971–74, Deputy Perm. Sec. to OECD, UNESCO 1971–74, Chief of Admin. and Consular Affairs 1974–78, Counsellor, Washington, DC 1978–80, Minister-Counsellor 1980–83, Head of Defence Dept, Reykjavík 1983–85, Rep. to NATO 1984–87, Amb. in Foreign Service 1985–87, Perm. Rep. to EFTA, UN, Geneva, Amb. to Egypt (also accred to Ethiopia, Kenya, Tanzania) 1987–89, Head, Dept for Foreign Trade, Reykjavík 1989–90, Perm. Rep. to N Atlantic Council, Brussels, WEU 1990–94, Amb. to France (also accred to Spain, Portugal, Cape Verde, Italy, Andorra), Perm. Rep. to Council of Europe, OECD, UNESCO, FAO 1994–99, Perm. Sec. of State, Reykjavík 1999–2003, Amb. to UK (also accred to Ireland, Netherlands, Greece, Lebanon) 2003–, Perm. Rep. to IMO 2003–.
Address: Embassy of Iceland, 2A Hans Street, London, SW1X 0JE, England (office). *Telephone:* (20) 7245-3999 (office). *Fax:* (20) 7245-9649 (office). *E-mail:* icemb.london@utn.stjr.is (office). *Website:* www.iceland .org/uk (office).

GUO, Lt-Gen. Boxiong; Chinese army officer; *Executive Deputy Chief, Headquarters of the General Staff, People's Liberation Army;* b. 1942, Liquan Co., Shaanxi Prov. *Education:* Mil. Acad. of the Chinese PLA. *Career:* worker, No. 408 Factory, Xingping Co., Shaanxi Prov. 1958–61; joined PLA 1961, CCP 1963; Squad Leader 164th Regt, 55th Div., Army (or Ground Force), PLA Services and Arms 1961–66, Platoon Commdr 8th Co. 1964–65, mem. staff Propaganda Group 1965–66, mem. staff HQ 164th Regt, 55th Div., Combat Training Section 1966–70, Leader HQ 164th Regt,

55th Div., Combat Training Section 1970–71, Staff Officer, Deputy Head, later Head, later Divisional Chief-of-Staff 1971–81; Deputy Dir Combat Dept (HQ), Lanzhou Mil. Area Command 1982–83; Army Chief-of-Staff 1983–85; Deputy Chief-of-Staff Lanzhou Mil. Area Command 1985–90; Army Group Commdr 1990–93; Deputy Commdr Beijing Mil. Area Command 1993–97; Commdr Lanzhou Mil. Area Command 1997–99; Exec. Deputy Gen., PLA 1999–2001, Chief of Staff 1999–2002, Exec. Deputy Chief, HQ of Gen. Staff 2002–; mem. 15th CCP Cen. Cttee 1997–2002 (mem. Cen. Mil. Comm.), Politburo 16th CCP Cen. Cttee 2002– (Vice-Chair. Cen. Mil. Comm. 2002–); Deputy Sec. PLA HQ of Gen. Staff, CCP Party Cttee 1999–.
Address: Ministry of National Defence, Beijing, People's Republic of China (office).

GUO, Dongpo; Chinese politician; *Chairman, Sub-committee for Hong Kong, Macao and Taiwan Compatriots and Overseas Chinese,Chinese People's Political Consultative Conference;* b. Aug. 1937, Jiangdu Co., Jiangsu Prov. *Education:* Beijing Inst. of Foreign Trade. *Career:* joined CCP 1960; Deputy Div. Chief, China Council for the Promotion of Int. Trade 1972 (Sec. CCP Party Br.), Deputy Dir Printing House, Vice-Pres. China Council for the Promotion of Int. Trade (Sec. CCP Party Cttee) 1982, Pres. 1992; fmr Vice-Pres. China Chamber of Int. Commerce, Pres. 1995; Dir Macau Bureau of Xinhua News Agency 1990–95; Vice-Dir Drafting Cttee of the Basic Law of Macau Special Admin. Zone 1990; Pres. Econ. and Trade Coordination Cttee for the Two Sides of the Straits 1996; Dir Foreign Econ. and Trade Arbitration Comm. 1996; Dir Office of Overseas Chinese Affairs of the State Council 1997–2003; Vice-Pres. China Overseas Exchanges Asscn 1998–; mem. 7th CPPCC Nat. Cttee 1988–93, Standing Cttee 8th CPPCC Nat. Cttee 1993–98, Chair. Sub-cttee for Hong Kong, Macao and Taiwan Compatriots and Overseas Chinese 2003–; Alt. mem. 14th CCP Cen. Cttee 1992–97; mem. 15th CCP Cen. Cttee 1997–2002.
Address: Chinese People's Political Consultative Conference, State Council, Beijing, People's Republic of China (office). *Website:* www .cppcc.gov.cn (office).

GUO, Jinlong; Chinese politician; *Secretary, Tibetan Autonomous Region Committee, Chinese Communist Party;* b. July 1947, Nanjing, Jiangsu Prov. *Education:* Nanjing Univ. *Career:* technician, Hydropower Bureau, Zhongxian Co., Sichuan Prov., 1969–73; coach, Physical Culture and Sports Cttee, Zhongxian Co., Sichuan Prov. 1973–79; joined CCP 1979; teacher, Publicity Dept, CCP Co. Cttee 1979–80; Deputy Sec. then Sec. Cultural Bureau of Zhongxian Co., Sichuan Prov. 1980–83; Deputy Sec. CCP Zhongxian Co. Cttee then Magistrate of Zhongxian 1983–85; Deputy Dir Rural Policy Research Office, CCP Sichuan Prov. Cttee, Deputy Dir Sichuan Prov. Rural Econ. Comm. 1985–87; Deputy Sec. then Sec. CCP Leshan City Cttee 1987–92; Deputy Sec. CCP Sichuan Prov. Cttee 1992–93; Deputy Sec. then Exec. Deputy Sec. CCP Tibetan Autonomous Region Cttee 1993–2000, Sec. 2000–; First Sec., Tibet Regional Mil. Command 2000–; Alt. mem. CCP 15th Cen. Cttee 1997–2002, mem. CCP 16th Cen. Cttee 2002–.
Address: Chinese Communist Party Tibetan Autonomous Region Committee, Lhasa, Tibet, People's Republic of China (office).

GURBANMYRADOV, Yolly; Turkmenistan politician and economist; b. 1960, Ashgabat. *Education:* Turkmen State Inst. of Nat. Econ. *Career:* worker in construction co. 1977–82; Sr Econ., Deputy Head Ashgabat br. USSR State Bank 1982–87; Head Div. of Banking Automation State Bank (Ashgabat) 1988; Deputy Head Regional Dept USSR Zhilsotsbank 1988–89; man. of div. Agroprombank 1989–90; Br. Man. USSR Vnesheconombank 1990–92; First Deputy Chair., then Chair. Bd of Dirs State Bank of Foreign Trade of Turkmenistan 1992–96; Dir Turkmenistan State Agency on Foreign Investments 1996–97; Deputy Chair. Turkmen Cabinet of Ministers, concurrently Chair. Interbanking Council 1997–99; Deputy Prime Minister of Turkmenistan 1999–2004.
Address: c/o Cabinet of Ministers, Ashgabat, Turkmenistan (office).

GURBANOV, Fakhraddin; Azerbaijani diplomatist; *Ambassador to UK. Career:* Amb.-at-large for the Repub. of Azerbaijan; Azerbaijan Initiative Fellow, Sr Mans in Govt Program, Kennedy School of Govt, USA Aug. 2002; Amb. to Canada 2004–07, to UK (also accred to Ireland and Norway) 2007–.
Address: Embassy of Azerbaijan, 4 Kensington Court, London, W8 5DL, England (office). *Telephone:* (20) 7938-5482 (office); (20) 7938-3412 (office). *Fax:* (20) 7937-1783 (office). *E-mail:* london@mission.mfa.gov.az (office); azeconsular@btconnect.com (office); sefir@btinternet.com (office). *Website:* www.azembassy.org.uk (office).

GURG, Easa Saleh al-, CBE; United Arab Emirates diplomatist, banker, business executive and politician; *Ambassador to UK;* b. Dubai; m. Soraya Al Gurg. *Career:* Co-founder and Chair. Al Gurg Fosroc LLC 1975–; Dir Emirates Bank Group 1983–; Chair. Easa Saleh Al Gurg Group, Al Gurg Leigh's Pants LLC, Gulf Metal Foundry LLC, Arabian E-Lever LLC; Deputy Chair. Nat. Bank of Fujairah Bank; Dir Investcorp Bank EC, Emirates Merchant Bank Ltd, Emirates Bank International; Amb. to UK (also accred to Ireland) 1991–; sponsorship for grad. students, Oxford Centre for Islamic Studies. *Publications:* The Wells of Memory: An Autobiography 1999.
Address: Embassy of the United Arab Emirates, 30 Prince's Gate, London, SW7 1PT, England (office). *Telephone:* (20) 7581-1281 (office). *Fax:* (20) 7581-9616 (office). *E-mail:* information@uaeembassyuk.net (office). *Website:* www.uaeembassyuk.net (office).

GURGENIDZE, Vladimer (Lado), MBA; Georgian/British banker and politician; *Prime Minister;* b. 7 Dec. 1970, Tbilisi; m. Larissa Gurgenidze; three c. *Education:* Tbilisi State Univ., Middlebury Coll., VT, USA, Goizueta School of Business of Emory Univ. *Career:* began his investment banking career with CEE corp. finance arm of MeesPierson; Dir ABN AMRO Corp. Finance in Russia and CIS 1997–98, served in various sr capacities at ABN AMRO Corp. Finance, London, including as a Dir and Head of Mergers and Acquisitions in the Emerging European Markets 1998–2000 and as a Man. Dir and Head of Tech. Corp. Finance 2001–03; Man. Dir and Regional Man. for Europe, Putnam Lovell NBF (boutique investment banking firm) 2003–04; CEO Bank of Georgia 2004–06, Chair. Supervisory Bd 2006–; Chair. Supervisory Bd Galt & Taggart Securities, Galt & Taggart Capital; mem. Supervisory Bd Georgian Stock Exchange; Prime Minister of Georgia 2007–. *Television:* hosted a reality TV show The Candidate on Rustavi 2 (Georgian version of Donald Trump's franchise The Apprentice) 2006.
Address: Chancellery of the Government, P. Ingorovka 7, 0105 Tbilisi, Georgia (office). *Telephone:* (32) 92-22-43 (office). *Fax:* (32) 92-10-69 (office). *E-mail:* primeminister@geo.gov.ge (office). *Website:* www .government.gov.ge (office).

GURIRAB, Theo-Ben, PhD; Namibian politician; *Speaker, National Assembly;* b. 23 Jan. 1939, Usakos; m. Joan W. Guriras; two s. *Education:* Augustineum Training Coll., Okahandja, Temple Univ. *Career:* in exile 1962; Chief Rep. in N America for South West Africa People's Org. (SWAPO) 1971; Head of SWAPO's Mission, UN 1972–86; mem. of Senate, UN Inst. for Namibia, Lusaka; Sr Adviser to SWAPO Pres. during Resolution 435 negotiations; Minister of Foreign Affairs 1990–2000, Minister of Foreign Affairs, Information and Broadcasting 2000–02, Prime Minister 2002–05; Speaker, Nat. Ass. 2005–.
Address: National Assembly, Windhoek, Namibia (office). *Telephone:* (61) 2882504 (office). *Fax:* (61) 231626 (office). *E-mail:* w.hanse@parliament .gov.na (office). *Website:* www.parliament.gov.na (office).

GUROV, Maj.-Gen. Aleksander Ivanovich, DJur; Russian civil servant and politician; *Chairman, Parliamentary Committee on Security;* b. 17 Nov. 1945, Shushkan-Olshanka, Tambov Dist; m. Yelena Nikolayevna Gurova; one s. *Education:* Moscow State Univ. *Career:* inspector Div. of Criminal Investigation, Vnukovo Airport 1970–74; mem. of staff Dept of Criminal Investigation, USSR Ministry of Internal Affairs 1974–78, Head Dept for Struggle Against Organized Crime, Corruption and Drug Business; USSR People's Deputy 1990–93; First Deputy Head Centre of Public Relations, Ministry of Security; Vice-Pres. Inform-Service; Head Tepko-Bank (security service) 1994–98; Head All-Russian Inst., Ministry of Internal Affairs 1998–99; Co-Founder and Co.-Leader Yedinstvo 1999; mem. State Duma 1999–; Chair. Cttee on Security 2000–. *Publications:* Red Mafia; over 150 scientific articles on struggle against original crime.
Address: State Duma, Okhotny Ryad 1, 103265 Moscow, Russia (office). *Telephone:* (495) 292-89-32 (office). *Fax:* (495) 292-95-75 (office).

GURR, Ted Robert; American academic; *Distinguished Professor Emeritus, University of Maryland;* b. 21 Feb. 1936, Spokane, Wash.; two d. *Education:* Reed Coll., Princeton Univ., New York Univ. *Career:* Prof. Princeton Univ. 1967–69, Northwestern Univ. 1970–84 (Chair. of Dept 1977–80), Univ. of Colo 1984–89; joined Dept of Govt and Politics, Univ. of Md 1989, Distinguished Prof. 1995–, also Founding Dir Minorities at Risk Project; Pres. Int. Studies Asscn 1993–94; Sr Consultant, State Failure Task Force 1994–2005; Olof Palme Visiting Prof., Univ. of Uppsala, Sweden 1996–97; Peace Fellow, US Inst. of Peace 1988–89; Dr hc (Univ. of Sofia) 2002; Woodrow Wilson Prize 1980. *Publications:* Violence in America: Historical and Comparative Perspectives (co-author) 1969, Why Men Rebel 1970, The Politics of Crime and Conflict 1977, Handbook of Political Conflict: Theory and Research 1980, The State and the City (co-author) 1987, Minorities at Risk: A Global View of Ethnopolitical Conflict 1993, Ethnic Conflict in World Politics (co-author) 1994, Preventive Measures: Building Risk Assessment and Crisis Early Warning Systems (co-author) 1998, Peoples Versus States: Minorities at Risk in the New Century 2000, Peace and Conflict: A Global Survey of Armed Conflicts,

Self-Determination Movements and Democracy (co-author) 2001, Journeys Through Conflict: Narratives and Lessons (co-author) 2003.
Address: 11473 Snow Creek Avenue, Las Vegas, NV 89135, USA (office).
Telephone: (702) 255-4702 (home). *E-mail:* trgurr@aol.com (home).
Website: www.minoritiesatrisk.com (office).

GÜRRAGCHAA, Maj.-Gen. Jügderdemidiin; Mongolian politician and army officer. *Career:* served in Mongolian Armed Forces, rank of Maj.-Gen.; Minister of Defence –2004.
Address: c/o Ministry of Defence, Government Building 7, Dandaryn Gudamj, Bayanzürkh District, Ulan Bator 61, Mongolia (office).

GURRÍA TREVIÑO, José Ángel, BA, MA; Mexican economist, diplomatist and international organization official; *Secretary-General, Organisation for Economic Co-operation and Development;* b. 8 May 1950, Tampico, Tamaulipas; Dr Lulu Quintana; three c. *Education:* Universidad Nacional Autónoma de México, Univ. of Leeds, UK, Harvard Univ., USA. *Career:* Perm. Rep. of Mexico to Int. Coffee Org., London 1976–78; held various financial positions in Fed. Electricity Comm., Nat. Devt Bank (Nafinsa), Rural Devt Fund and the Office of the Mayor of Mexico City; position at Finance Ministry 1978–92; Pres. and CEO Bancomext (export-import bank) 1992–93, Nacional Financiera (nat. devt bank) 1993–94; Minister of Foreign Affairs 1994–98, of Finance and Public Credit 1998–2000; Sec.-Gen. OECD 2006–; Chair. mem. External Advisory Group, IDB.
Address: OECD, 2 rue André Pascal, 75775 Paris Cedex 16, France (office).
Telephone: 1-45-24-82-00 (office). *Fax:* 1-45-24-85-00 (office). *E-mail:* secretary.general@oecd.org (office). *Website:* www.oecd.org (office).

GURRY, Francis, LLB, LLM, PhD; Australian lawyer and international organization official; *Director General, World Intellectual Property Organization (WIPO);* m.; b. 17 May 1951; m.; three c. *Education:* Univ. of Melbourne, Gonville and Caius Coll., Cambridge, UK (Tapp Studentship). *Career:* articled clerk, then attorney-at-law, Arthur Robinson & Co., Melbourne 1974–76; admitted barrister and solicitor, Supreme Court of Vic. 1975; Sr Lecturer in Law, Univ. of Melbourne 1979–84, Professorial Fellow 2001–; Visiting Prof. of Law, Univ. of Dijon, France 1982–83; attorney-at-law, Freehills, Sydney 1984; joined WIPO as consultant in Devt Cooperation and External Relations Bureau for Asia and the Pacific, Geneva, Switzerland 1985, held various posts, including Head of Industrial Property Law Section 1988–90, Special Asst to Dir Gen. and Dir-Counselor in Office of the Dir Gen. 1990–93, Dir WIPO Arbitration and Mediation Center and Acting Legal Counsel 1993–97, Legal Counsel 1997–99, also in charge of WIPO Arbitration and Mediation Center and electronic commerce, Asst Dir Gen. and Legal Counsel 1999–2003, Deputy Dir Gen. 2003–08, Dir Gen. WIPO 2008–; Vice-Pres. Int. Fed. of Commercial Arbitration 1996–2004; mem. Governing Bd Int. School of Geneva 1996–99; mem. Advisory Bd Centre for Intellectual Property and Information Law, Univ. of Cambridge, Intellectual Property Research Inst. of Australia, Univ. of Melbourne, Indian Journal of Intellectual Property, International Review of Industrial Property and Copyright Law, Munich, SCRIPT-ed – A Journal of Law, Technology & Society, Edinburgh; Yorke Prize, Univ. of Cambridge. *Publications:* Breach of Confidence 1984, International Intellectual Property System: Commentary and Materials (with Frederick Abbott and Thomas Cottier) 1999, Intellectual Property in an Integrated World Economy (with Frederick Abbot and Thomas Cottier) 2007; several book chapters and articles in professional journals.
Address: WIPO, PO Box 18, 34 chemin des Colombettes, 1211 Geneva 20, Switzerland (office). *Telephone:* (22) 338-91-11 (office). *Fax:* (22) 733-54-28 (office). *E-mail:* info@wipo.int (office). *Website:* www.wipo.int (office).

GUSAROV, Yevgeny Petrovich; Russian diplomatist; b. 30 July 1950, Moscow; m.; one s. *Education:* Moscow State Inst. of Int. Relations. *Career:* on staff Ministry of Foreign Affairs 1972–; reviewer USSR Gen. Consulate, Montreal 1972–77; attaché, Third, Second Sec. Second European Dept Ministry of Foreign Affairs 1977–81; Second, First Sec., Counsellor USSR Embassy to Canada 1981–86; Head of Sector, Deputy Head Second European Dept 1986–88; Deputy Head Div. (then Dept) of USA and Canada 1988–90, Deputy Head Dept of Security and Co-operation in Europe, USSR Ministry of Foreign Affairs 1990–92; Head Dept of Europe, Russian Ministry of Foreign Affairs 1992; Amb. to Repub. of S Africa (also accred to Lesotho) 1992–98; Dir Dept of All-European Co-operation, Ministry of Foreign Affairs 1998–99; Deputy Foreign Minister 1999–2002.
Address: c/o Ministry of Foreign Affairs, Smolenskaya-Sennaya 32/34, 119200 Moscow, Russia (office).

GUSENBAUER, Alfred, PhD; Austrian politician; *Federal Chancellor;* b. 8 Feb. 1960, Sankt Pölten, Lower Austria. *Education:* High School in Wieselburg, Univ. of Vienna. *Career:* Fed. Leader Sozialdemokratische Partei Österreichs (Social Democratic Party of Austria—SPÖ) Youth Wing, Socialist Youth (SJ) 1984–90, Chair. SPÖ in Ybbs an der Donau and mem. Lower Austria Party Exec. 1991, Chair. SPÖ 2000–; Vice-Pres. Socialist Youth Int. (IUSY) 1985–89, Socialist Int. 1989; elected Deputy for Lower Austria to Bundesrat 1991, Chair. Cttee for Devt Co-operation 1996–99, Leader of SPÖ Group in Bundesrat 2000–07; Fed. Chancellor 2007–; mem. Austrian del. to parl. meeting of Council of Europe 1991, Chair. Social Cttee of Council of Europe 1995–98; Sr Research Fellow, Econ. Policy Dept, Lower Austria Chamber of Labour 1990–99.
Address: Office of the Chancellor, Federal Chancellery, Bundeskanzleramt, Ballhausplatz 2, 1014 Vienna, Austria (office). *Telephone:* (1) 53-1150 (office). *E-mail:* Alfred.Gusenbauer@spoe.at (office). *Website:* www.alfred-gusenbauer.at (office); www.austria.gv.at (office).

GUSEV, Pavel Nikolayevich; Russian journalist; *Editor-in-Chief, Moskovsky Komsomolets;* b. 4 April 1949, Moscow; m. Eugenia Efimova; two d. *Education:* Moscow Inst. of Geological Survey, Maxim Gorky Inst. of Literature. *Career:* Komsomol work 1975–; First Sec. Komsomol Cttee of Krasnaya Presnya Region of Moscow 1975–80; Exec. Cen. Komsomol Cttee 1980–83; Ed.-in-Chief Moskovsky Komsomolets (newspaper) 1983–; Minister, Govt of Moscow, Head of Dept of Information and Mass Media Jan.–Oct. 1992; press adviser to Mayor of Moscow 1992–95; Chair. Comm. for the Politics of Information and Freedom of the Word of the Public Chamber, Public Council of Fed. Agency of Culture and Cinematography 2007–. *Plays:* I Love You, Constance (Moscow Gogol Theatre) 1993, Cardinal's Coat (Maly Theatre) 2002.
Address: Moskovsky Komsomolets, 1905 Goda str. 7, 123995 Moscow, Russia (office). *Telephone:* (495) 259-50-36 (office). *Fax:* (495) 259-46-39 (office). *E-mail:* letters@mk.ru (office). *Website:* www.mk.ru (office).

GUS'KOVA, Yelena Yuryevna, DHist; Russian historian and political scientist; *Head, Contemporary Studies, Institute of Slavic and Balkan Studies, Russian Academy of Sciences;* b. 23 Sept. 1949, Moscow; m.; two d. *Education:* Moscow State Univ. *Career:* Head Centre of Contemporary Studies, Inst. of Slavic and Balkan Studies, Russian Acad. of Sciences; leading researcher INION, Russian Acad. of Sciences; mem. Presidium Russian Asscn of Co-operation with the UN; Political and Policy Analyst UN Headquarters of Peace-keeping Operations in fmr Yugoslavia; Outstanding Scientist of Russia, Njegosha Award (Bosnia & Herzegovina) 1997, 850th Anniversary Medal, Moscow 1997, NATO Medal for peace-making operations in Kosovo 2002. *Publications:* over 280 works on the history of Yugoslavia and problems of today's crises in the Balkans, including History of Yugoslavian Crisis (1990–2000) 2001 (Moscow), 2003 (Belgrade).
Address: Institute of Slavic and Balkan Studies, Russian Academy of Sciences, Leninsky prosp. 32A, 112334 Moscow, Russia (office). *Telephone:* (495) 938-58-61 (office). *Fax:* (495) 938-00-96 (office); (495) 420-94-20 (home). *E-mail:* centar@guskova.ru (office); eguskova@com2com.ru (home). *Website:* www.inslav.ru (home).

GUSMAN, Mikhail Solomonovich; Russian journalist; *First Deputy Director-General, ITAR-TASS Agency;* b. 23 Jan. 1950, Baku, Azerbaijan; m.; one s. *Education:* Baku Higher CPSU School, Azerbaijan Inst. of Foreign Languages. *Career:* Deputy Chair. Cttee of Youth Orgs, Azerbaijan 1973–86; Head of Information Dept, then Head of Press Centre, USSR Cttee of Youth Orgs 1986–91; Head of Gen. Admin. of Information Co-operation INFOMOL 1991–95; Vice-Pres. Int. Analytic Press Agency ANKOM-TASS 1995–98; Head of Chief Dept of Int. Co-operation, Public Contacts and Special Projects ITAR-TASS 1998–99, Deputy Dir-Gen., First Deputy Dir-Gen. 1999–; Co-founder World Congress of Russian Press 1999; Exec. Dir World Asscn of Russian Press; Diploma of the USSR Supreme Soviet, numerous medals; Gold Medal for contrib. to devt of TV and radio, Int. Acad. of Radio and Television (Russia) 2007.
Address: ITAR-TASS Agency, Tverskoy Blvd 10-12, 103009 Moscow, Russia (office). *Telephone:* (495) 290-59-89 (office). *E-mail:* info@itar-tass.com (office). *Website:* www.itar-tass.com (office).

GUSMÃO, José Alexandre (Xanana); Timor-Leste politician and fmr head of state; *Prime Minister;* b. (José Alexandre Guzmão), 20 June 1946, Laleia, Manatuto; m. 1st Emilia Batista 1969; one s.; m. 2nd Kirsty Sword 2000. *Education:* Nossa Senhora de Fatima seminary, Dare. *Career:* fmr poet, teacher and chartered surveyor; joined pro-independence Fretilin (Revolutionary Front of the Independence of Timor Leste) 1974, Commdr 1978, now retd; C-in-C FALINTIL (Nat. Liberation Armed Forces of Timor Leste) 1981; arrested by Indonesian troops and sentenced to life imprisonment (later commuted to 20 years) 1992; released August 1999; Pres. Nat. Council of Timorese Resistance 1999–2001; Chair. Timor Leste Nat. Council 2000–01; Pres. of Timor Leste 2002–07; Founder and Pres. Conselho Nacional de Reconstrução do Timor (Nat. Congress for Timorese Reconstruction, CNRT) 2007–; Prime Minister 2007–, also

responsible for defence portfolio; Sakharov Prize for Freedom of Expression 1999.
Address: Office of the Prime Minister, Palácio do Governo, Av. Presidente Nicolau Lobato, Dili, Timor Leste (office). *Telephone:* 7243559 (office). *Fax:* 3339503 (office). *E-mail:* mail@primeministerandcabinet.gov.tp (home). *Website:* www.pm.gov.tp (office).

GUSTOV, Vadim Anatolyevich; Russian politician; *Representative of Vladimir Region, Federation Council;* b. 26 Dec. 1948, Kalinino, Vladimir Region; m.; two c. *Education:* Moscow State Inst. of Geological Prospecting, Leningrad Inst. of Politology. *Career:* Head of uranium mines, Navoi Metallurgy Factory, Uzbekistan 1971–77; Head of mine, Phosphorite Kingisepp, Leningrad Region 1977–78; instructor, Head of Div., Kingisepp City CP Cttee 1978–86; First Deputy Chair. Kingisepp City Exec. Cttee 1986–87; Second Sec. Kingisepp City CP Cttee 1987–90; Chair. Kingisepp City Soviet 1990–91; Chair. Soviet of People's Deputies Leningrad Region 1991–93; mem. Council of Feds of Russia, Chair. Cttee on CIS Cos 1993–98; Gov. Leningrad Region 1996–98; First Deputy Chair., Govt of Russian Fed. 1998–99; Rep. of Vladimir Region to Federation Council 2001–; Chair. Cttee on CIS 2001–; Order of Honour 1998. *Publications:* Russia-CIS: The Path of Integration is Thorny but Tempting (co-author) 2002, Russia-CIS: Co-operation for Development and Progress 2007.
Address: Federation Council, ul B. Dmitrovka 26, 103426 Moscow, Russia (office). *Telephone:* (495) 203-90-74 (office); (495) 692-07-18 (office). *Fax:* (495) 203-46-17 (office). *E-mail:* post_sf@gov.ru (office). *Website:* www .council.gov.ru (office).

GUTERRES, António Manuel de Oliveira; Portuguese politician and UN official; *High Commissioner, United Nations High Commissioner for Refugees;* b. 30 April 1949, Lisbon; m. (wife died 1998); one s. one d. *Education:* Inst. Superior Técnico. *Career:* trained as electrical engineer; joined Socialist Party 1974; Chief of Staff to Sec. of State for Industry 1974–75; fmr asst to several cabinet ministers; Pres. Municipal Ass. of Fundão 1979–95; Deputy to Ass. of the Repub. 1976–83, 1985–, Pres. several parl. comms, Pres. Socialist Parl. Group 1988–91; Strategic Devt Dir IPE (State Investment and Participation Agency) 1984–85; mem. Council of State 1991–; Leader of Socialist Party 1992–; Vice-Pres. Socialist Int. 1992–99, Pres. 1999–; Prime Minister of Portugal 1995–2001; High Commr, UN High Comm. for Refugees 2005–; Coordinator Tech. Electoral Comm. 1980–87; Founder and Vice-Pres. Portuguese Asscn for the Defence of the Consumer 1973–74; mem. Asscn for Econ. and Social Devt 1970–96. *Publications:* various books and articles for newspapers and magazines.
Address: United Nations High Commissioner for Refugees, CP 2500, 1211 Geneva 2 dépôt, Switzerland (office). *Telephone:* (22) 7398254 (office). *Fax:* (22) 7397346 (office). *Website:* www.unhcr.ch (office).

GUTERRES, Jose Luis; Timor-Leste politician and diplomatist; m.; two c. *Education:* Univ. of Cambridge, UK, Univ. of the Western Cape, S Africa, Malaysia Inst. of Diplomacy and Foreign Relations, Inst. of Strategic and Int. Studies, Portugal. *Career:* Founding mem. Frente Revolucionária do Timor Leste Independente (FRETILIN—Revolutionary Front for an Independent East Timor), mem. FRETILIN external del. 1974–, Rep. to Angola, also Perm. Rep. to Mozambique and FRETILIN Rep. to UN; Vice-Minister for Foreign Affairs and Co-operation 2002–03, Head of Timor-Leste del., Council of Ministers meeting, Comunidade dos Países de Língua Portuguesa, Brazil and ACP/EU meeting, Dominican Repub. July 2002, Timor-Leste Rep. to Sustainable Devt Summit, S Africa Aug. 2002; Amb. to USA and Perm. Rep. to UN, New York 2003–06; Minister of Foreign Affairs and Co-operation 2006–07.
Address: c/o Frente Revolucionária do Timor Leste Independente (FRETILIN) (Revolutionary Front for an Independent East Timor), Rua dos Mártires da Pátria, Dili, Timor-Leste (office). *Telephone:* 3321409 (office).

GUTHRIE OF CRAIGIEBANK, Baron (Life Peer), cr. 2001, of Craigiebank in the City of Dundee; **Charles (Ronald Llewelyn) Guthrie,** GCB, LVO, OBE; British army officer and business executive; b. 17 Nov. 1938, London; m. Catherine Worrall 1971; two s. *Education:* Harrow School and Royal Mil. Acad. Sandhurst. *Career:* commissioned Welsh Guards 1959; served in BAOR, Aden; 22 Special Air Service (SAS) Regt 1965–69; Staff Coll. 1972; Mil. Asst (GSO2) to Chief of Gen. Staff, Ministry of Defence 1973–74; Brigade Maj., Household Div. 1976–77; CO, 1st Bn Welsh Guards, Berlin and NI 1977–80; Col, Gen. Staff, Mil. Operations, Ministry of Defence 1980–82; Commdr British Forces, New Hebrides 1980; 4th Armoured Brigade 1982–84; Chief of Staff 1st (British) Corps 1984–86; Gen. Officer Commdg NE Dist and Commdr 2nd Infantry Div. 1986–87; Asst Chief of Gen. Staff, Ministry of Defence 1987–89; Commdr 1st (British) Corps 1989–91; Commdr Northern Army Group 1992–93 and C-in-C BAOR

1992–94; Col Commdt, Intelligence Corps 1986–96; ADC Gen. to HM the Queen 1993–, Gold Stick to HM the Queen 1999–; Chief of Gen. Staff 1994–97, of the Defence Staff 1997–2001; Special Envoy to Pakistan 2001; Dir (non-exec.) N. M. Rothschild & Sons 2001–; Col of the Life Guards 1999–; Col Commdt, SAS 1999–2002; Pres. Army Benevolent Fund, Action Research, London Fed. of Youth Clubs; Freeman, City of London; Kt, Sovereign Mil. Order of Malta 1999; Commdr, Legion of Merit (USA) 2001.
Address: PO Box 25439, London, SW1P 1AG, England.

GUTIERREZ, Lino, MA; American diplomatist; b. Havana, Cuba; m. Miriam Gutierrez (née Messina); three d. *Education:* Univs of Miami and Alabama. *Career:* Social Studies teacher, Dade County School System and Urban League, Miami 1973–75; joined US Foreign Service 1977; overseas assignments Embassies in Lisbon, Port-au-Prince, Grenada, Paris and Nassau; served as Officer-in-Charge of Nicaraguan Affairs, of Portuguese Affairs, Dir Office of Policy Planning, Coordination and Press, Bureau of Inter-American Affairs; Amb. to Nicaragua 1996–99; Prin. Deputy Asst Sec. for Western Hemisphere Affairs, Dept of State 1999–2001, Acting Asst. Sec. 2001–02; Int. Affairs Adviser, Nat. War Coll. 2002–03; Amb. to Argentina 2003–06; founder and currently CEO Gutierrez Global LLC; Dept of State Distinguished Honor Award, Meritorious Honor Award. *Telephone:* (703) 909-0290 (office). *E-mail:* info@gutierrezglobal.com (office). *Website:* www.gutierrezglobal.com (office).

GUTMAN, Lt-Gen. Albin; Slovenian military officer; *Chief of General Staff;* b. 17 Dec. 1947, Novo Mesto; m.; one s. one d. *Education:* Univ. of Ljubljana. *Career:* previous posts include Territorial-Defence Municipal Staff, Novo Mesto, Defence Secr., Novo Mesto, Territorial-Defence Regional Staff, Dolenjska, Ministry of Defence; Chief of Armed Forces Gen. Staff 1993–98, 2007–; Chief Defence Insp. 1998–2003; mil. advisor to Minister of Defence 2003–06; Silver Order of Freedom of Repub. of Slovenia, Order of Gen. Maister with Swords, Légion d'honneur; Manoeuvre Structure of Nat. Defence (MSNZ) Badge 1990, Defended Slovenia Badge, Slovenian Armed Forces Gold Medal, Slovenian Armed Forces Gold Plaque.
Address: Ministry of Defence, 1000 Ljubljana, Vojkova 55, Slovenia (office). *Telephone:* (1) 4712211 (office). *Fax:* (1) 4712978 (office). *E-mail:* info@mors.si (office). *Website:* www.mors.si (office).

GUTMANN, Francis Louis Alphonse Myrtil; French diplomatist; *President of Scientific Council for Defence, Ministry of Defence;* b. 4 Oct. 1930, Paris; m. Chantal de Gaulle 1964; two s. one d. *Education:* Lycée Pasteur, Neuilly-sur-Seine. *Career:* Head of Dept, Ministry of Foreign Affairs 1951–57; Asst Head Office of Sec. of State for Econ. Affairs 1955, mem. French Del. to Econ. and Social Council and to UN Gen. Ass. 1952–55, to Common Market Conf., Brussels 1956–57; Adviser Pechiney Co. 1957–59, Sec.-Gen. 1963, Dir 1970–71; Sec.-Gen. Fria 1960–62; mem. Governing Bd Pechiney-Ugine-Kuhlmann group 1962–78, Pres.-Dir-Gen. Ugine-Kuhlmann 1971–76, in charge of social affairs 1975–78; Pres. Alucam 1968–72; Pres. Frialco and Vice-Pres. Friguia 1977–81; Dir-Gen. French Red Cross 1980–81; Sec.-Gen. Ministry for External Relations 1981–85; Admin. representing the State, Paribas 1982–84, Gaz de France 1984–85, St Gobain 1982–85; Amb. to Spain 1985–88; Pres. Admin. Council Gaz de France 1988–93, Hon. Pres. 1993–; Pres. Fondation Méditerranéenne d'Etudes Stratégiques 1989–2000, Assoc. Eurogas-Union 1990–94, (Admin. Council) Institut Français du Pétrole (IFP) 1993–96; Vice-Pres. Mémoire et espoirs de la Résistance 1994–2000; attached to Ministry of Foreign Affairs 1996–; Pres. Scientific Council for Defence, Ministry of Defence 1998–; Dir French Red Cross 1992–2000; Officier, Légion d'honneur; Commdr, Ordre nat. du Mérite; Grand croix de l'ordre du Merité (Spain); numerous foreign awards. *Publications:* Les chemins de l'effort 1975, Le nouveau décor international 1994.
Address: c/o Institut Français du Pétrole, 1–4 ave. de Bois-Préau, BP 311, 92506 Rueil-Malmaison Cedex, France (office). *Telephone:* 1-47-52-68-84 (office). *Fax:* 1-47-52-67-54 (office).

GUTTMAN, Robert, BA, MA; American journalist; *Director, Center on Politics and Foreign Relations, Johns Hopkins University; Education:* Indiana Univ., American Univ., Washington, DC. *Career:* fmr int. economist, US Dept of Commerce; fmr press sec., White House; writer/researcher for presidential cands 1968, 1972 and 1976; Ed.-in-Chief, Pres. and Publr Political Profiles Inc. 1979–89; fmr Adjunct Prof. of Political Communications, George Washington Univ.; fmr Adjunct Prof. of American Politics and Communications, American Univ.; Head of Publs, EC Office, Washington DC and Ed.-in-Chief, Europe magazine 1989–2003; founder and Ed.-in-Chief Transatlantic magazine 2003–05, currently Ed.; Sr Fellow, Center for Transatlantic Relations, Johns Hopkins Univ. 2004–, currently Dir, Center on Politics and Foreign Relations, School of Advanced Int. Studies; fmr presenter, radio current affairs programme.

Address: Center on Politics and Foreign Relations, The Paul H. Nitze School of Advances International Studies, The Johns Hopkins University, The Nitze Building, 1740 Massachusetts Avenue, N.W., Washington, DC 20036, USA (office). *Telephone:* (202) 663-5600 (office). *Fax:* (202) 663-5656 (office). *E-mail:* rguttman@jhu.edu (office). *Website:* www.sais-jhu.edu/centers/cpfr (office).

GUY, Frances Mary; British diplomatist; *Ambassador to Lebanon;* b. 1 Feb. 1959; m. G. Hugo Raybaudo; one s. two d. *Career:* with British Council, Damascus 1984–85, Researcher, European Parl. 1985, Middle East Dept, FCO 1986–88, Second Sec., Khartoum 1988–91, Finance Dept, FCO 1991–93, Middle East Dept 1993–95, First Sec., Bangkok 1995–96, Deputy Head of Mission, Addis Ababa 1997–2001, Amb. to Yemen 2001–04, Head of Engaging with the Islamic World Group 2004–06, Amb. to Lebanon 2006–.
Address: British Embassy, PO Box 11-471, Serail Hill, Beirut Central District, Beirut, Lebanon (office). *Telephone:* (1) 990400 (office). *Fax:* (1) 990420 (office). *E-mail:* chancery@cyberia.net.lb (office). *Website:* www.britishembassy.gov.uk/lebanon (office).

GUZMÁN SALDAÑA, Mario Gustavo; Bolivian journalist and diplomatist; *Ambassador to USA;* b. 9 Jan. 1957, La Paz; m. Adriana Amparo Guzmán Arroyo. *Education:* Instituto Americano, Universidad Mayor de San Andrés. *Career:* fmr Press Sec. Casa de Municipal de Cultura de La Paz; fmr Ed. Internacional del Diario La Razón; fmr Ed.-in-Chief La Prensa (newspaper) and Pulso (weekly magazine); Amb. to USA 2006–.
Address: Embassy of Bolivia, 3014 Massachusetts Avenue, NW, Washington, DC 20008, USA (office). *Telephone:* (202) 483-4410 (office). *Fax:* (202) 328-3712 (office). *E-mail:* webmaster@bolivia-usa.org (office). *Website:* www.bolivia-usa.org (office).

GYNGELL, Alan; Australian research institute director; *Executive Director, Lowy Institute for International Policy; Career:* joined Ministry of Foreign Affairs 1969, overseas postings include Embassies in Rangoon, Singapore and Washington, DC; fmr First Asst Sec., Int. Div., Dept of Prime Minister and Cabinet; worked on Southeast Asian issues and Maj. Power relations, Office of Nat. Assessments; foreign policy adviser, Office of Prime Minister Paul Keating 1993–96; consultant to numerous pvt. cos 1997–; Founding Exec. Dir Lowy Inst. for Int. Policy 2003–; mem. Australian Foreign Affairs Council. *Publications:* Making Australian Foreign Policy (with Michael Wesley) 2003.
Address: Lowy Institute for International Policy, PO Box H-159, Australia Square, Sydney, NSW 1215, Australia (office). *Telephone:* (2) 8238-9000 (office). *Fax:* (2) 8238-9005 (office). *E-mail:* director@lowyinstitute.org (office). *Website:* www.lowyinstitute.org (office).

GYOHTEN, Toyoo; Japanese economist; *President, Institute for International Monetary Affairs;* b. 1931, Yokohama; m.; one s. one d. *Education:* Univ. of Tokyo, Princeton Univ., USA. *Career:* joined Ministry of Finance 1955; Japan Desk, Asian Dept IMF 1964–66; Special Asst to Pres. of Asian Devt Bank, Manila, Philippines 1966–69; Dir-Gen. Int. Finance Bureau 1984–86, Vice-Minister of Finance for Int. Affairs 1986–89; Visiting Prof., Business School, Harvard Univ., USA 1990, Woodrow Wilson School, Princeton Univ. 1990–91, Univ. of St Gallen, Switzerland 1991; joined Bank of Tokyo Ltd (merged with Mitsubishi Bank Ltd 1996) 1991, Chair. Bd 1992–96, Sr Adviser The Bank of Tokyo-Mitsubishi Ltd 1996–; Pres. Inst. for Int. Monetary Affairs 1995–; Chair. Working Party III, OECD, Paris 1988–90, Inst. of Int. Finance Inc., USA 1994–97; mem. Bd of Trustees, Princeton in Asia, USA 1989–, Advisory Panel, E African Devt Bank, Kampala, Uganda 1990–, Asia Pacific Advisory Cttee, New York Stock Exchange 1990–, Int. Council, The Asia Soc., New York 1991–, Exec. Cttee of Trilateral Comm., New York, Paris and Tokyo 1991–, Group of Thirty, Washington, DC 1992–, Council of Inst. Aspen France, Banking Advisory Group of IFC, Washington, DC 1992–; Founding mem. Int. Advisory Bd of Council on Foreign Relations, New York 1995–; Fulbright Scholar 1956–58. *Publication:* Changing Fortunes (with Paul Volcker) 1992.
Address: 3-2, Nihombashi Hongokucho 1-chome, Chuo-ku, Tokyo 103-0021, Japan.

GYURCSÁNY, Ferenc; Hungarian politician and business executive; *Prime Minister;* b. 4 June 1961, Pápa; m. 2nd Klára Dobrev; three s. one d. *Education:* Faculty of Economy, Janus Pannonius Univ. of Sciences, Pécs. *Career:* Sec. Pécs City Cttee, Communist Youth Alliance (KISZ) 1984–88, Pres. Univ. and Coll. Council, Cen. Cttee 1988–89, Vice-Pres. Democratic Youth Alliance (DEMISZ) 1989; Consultant, CREDITUM Financial Consultant Ltd 1990–92; Dir EUROCORP Int. Financial Inc. 1992; CEO ALTUS Investment and Assets Man. Inc. 1992–2002, Chair. 2002–03; Sr Adviser to Prime Minister Medgyessy 2002–03; mem. Nat. Exec. Cttee Hungarian Socialist Party (MSZP) 2003–, Chair. Gyor-Moson-Sopron Co. Org. Feb.–Sept. 2004; Minister of Children, Youth and Sports 2003–04 (resgnd); Prime Minister of Hungary 2004–. *Publication:* Útközben (On the Way; political essay) 2005.
Address: Office of the Prime Minister, 1055 Budapest, Kossuth Lajos tér 4, Hungary (office). *Telephone:* (1) 441-3000 (office). *E-mail:* Ferenc.Gyurcsany@meh.hu (office). *Website:* www.miniszterelnok.hu (office); www.meh.hu (office).

H

HAAK, Willem E. (Pim), LLM; Dutch fmr chief justice; *President, Court of Appeals for the Central Commission for the Navigation of the Rhine;* b. 19 April 1934, Haarlem; m. Cornelia Jacoba van Heek 1968; two s. *Education:* Univ. of Amsterdam. *Career:* worked as advocate in Amsterdam until 1972; Dist Court Judge 1972–76; Justice, Amsterdam Court of Appeal 1976–79; Advocate Gen. to the Supreme Court 1979–81, Justice, Supreme Court 1981–92, Deputy Pres. 1992–99, Chief Justice 1999–2004; Appointing Authority of the Iran-United States Claims Tribunal 2004–; Chair. Advisory Bd Foundation of the Old Church Amsterdam 2004–; Pres. Court of Appeals for the Gen. Comm. for the Navigation of the Rhine, Strasbourg 2004–; mem. Advisory Bd Resolution Group (Effective Negotiation and Dispute Resolution), The Hague 2005–; fmr Sec. Asscn of Dutch Lawyers; fmr Deputy Chair. Int. Law Inst.; fmr Pres. Appeals Tribunal, Dutch Inst. of Psychologists; fmr mem. Insurance Cos Supervisory Bd; Pres. Bd Frits Lugt art collection; fmr Deputy Chair. Supervisory Bd, Institut Néerlandais, Paris; mem. Advisory Cttee on Endowed Chairs, Univ. of Amsterdam; mem. Perm. Appeals Tribunal of the Gen. Meeting of the Remonstrant Church; Kt, Order of the Dutch Lion, Commdr, Order Oranje-Nassau, Officier, Légion d'honneur. *Publications:* several articles and monographs on pvt. int. law, transport law, comparative law and criminal law. *Address:* Joh. Vermeerstraat 75, 1071 DN Amsterdam, The Netherlands (home). *Telephone:* (20) 6796935 (home). *Fax:* (20) 6701821 (home). *E-mail:* pimhaak@xs4all.nl (home).

HAAKON, HRH Crown Prince (Haakon Magnus), BSc; Norwegian; b. 20 July 1973; m. Mette-Marit Tjessem Høiby 2001; one d. one s. one step-s. *Education:* Kristelig Gymnasium, Officers' Cand. School/Navy, Horten, Royal Norwegian Naval Acad., Bergen, Univ. of California at Berkeley, USA, LSE, UK. *Career:* second-in-command, missile torpedo boat 1995–96; numerous official functions. *Address:* Royal Palace, 0010 Oslo, Norway (home). *Telephone:* (47) 2204-8700 (home). *Fax:* (47) 2204-8790 (home). *Website:* www.kongehuset.no (office).

HAARDE, Geir H., MA; Icelandic politician and economist; *Prime Minister;* b. 8 April 1951; m. Inga Jona Thordardottir; five c. *Education:* Brandeis Univ., Johns Hopkins Univ., Univ. of Minnesota, USA. *Career:* teaching Asst Univ. of Minn. 1976–77; economist Int. Dept, Cen. Bank of Iceland 1977–83; lecturer Econs Dept, Univ. of Iceland 1979–83; Special Asst to Minister of Finance 1983–87; mem. Althing (Parl.) 1987–; mem. Foreign Affairs Cttee 1991–98, Chair. 1995–98; Minister of Finance 1998–2005; Minister of Foreign Affairs 2005–06; Prime Minister 2006–; Chair. Youth Org. of Independence Party 1981–85, Chair. Parl. Group 1991–98, Vice-Chair. 1999–; Pres. Icelandic Group Inter-Parl. Union 1988–98, mem. Exec. Cttee 1994–98, Vice-Pres. 1995–97; mem. Control Cttee Nordic Investment Bank 1991–95; mem. Presidium Nordic Council 1997–98, Pres. 1995, Chair. Conservative Party Group 1995–97; Chair. Standing Cttee of Parliamentarians of Arctic Region 1995–98. *Address:* Office of the Prime Minister, Stjornarradshusid, 150 Reykjavik, Iceland (office). *Telephone:* 5458400 (office). *Fax:* 5624014 (office). *E-mail:* postur@for.stjr.is (office). *Website:* forsaetisraduneyti.is (office).

HAAS, Peter M., PhD; American political scientist and academic; *Professor of Political Science, University of Massachusetts;* b. 23 Jan. 1955, Oakland, Calif.; m. Julize Zuckman; one s. *Education:* Univ. of Mich., Massachusetts Inst. of Tech. *Career:* Visiting Asst Prof., Yale Univ. 1986; Marine Policy Research Fellow, Woods Hole Oceanographic Inst. 1986–87; Asst Prof. of Political Science, Univ. of Mass at Amherst 1986–92, Assoc. Prof. 1992–98, Prof. 1998–; visiting positions Oxford Univ. 2002, Brown Univ. 2002–03. *Publications include:* Saving the Mediterranean 1990, Institutions for the Earth 1993, Knowledge, Power and International Policy Co-ordination (ed.) 1997, The International Environment in the New Global Economy 2003, Emerging Forces in Environmental Governance 2004, Global Environmental Governance 2006; articles and chapters on int. environmental politics and int. relations. *Address:* Department of Political Science, University of Massachusetts, Amherst, MA 01003, USA (office). *Telephone:* (413) 545-6174 (office). *Fax:* (413) 545-3349 (office). *E-mail:* haas@polsci.umass.edu (office). *Website:* www.umass.edu/polsci (office).

HAASS, Richard N., BA, DPhil; American fmr government official and fmr diplomatist; *President, Council on Foreign Relations;* m.; two c. *Education:* Oberlin Coll., Ohio and Univ. of Oxford. *Career:* fmr legis. aide, US Senate; various posts in Dept of Defense 1979–80, Dept of State 1981–85, Special Asst to Pres. and Sr Dir for Near East and S Asian Affairs, Nat. Security Council 1989–93; Vice-Pres. and Dir of Foreign Policy Studies, Sydney Stein Jr Chair in Int. Security, Brookings Inst. –2001; Dir of Policy Planning, Dept of State 2001–03, US Co-ordinator for Afghanistan policy; leading US Govt Official in support of NI peace process, fmr Special Envoy of Pres. George W. Bush to NI Peace Process; fmr Sr Fellow and Dir of Nat. Security Programs, Council on Foreign Relations, Pres. Council on Foreign Relations 2003–; mem. IISS (fmr Research Assoc.), Trilateral Comm.; Sr Assoc. Carnegie Endowment for Int. Peace; fmr Sol. M. Linowitz Visiting Prof. of Int. Studies, Hamilton Coll.; fmr Lecturer in Public Policy, Harvard Univ. Kennedy School of Govt; fmr consultant, NBC News; Presidential Citizen's Medal 1991, Dept of State Distinguished Honor Award 2003. *Publications:* The Reluctant Sheriff: The United States after the Cold War 1998, Economic Sanctions and American Diplomacy 1998, The Bureaucratic Entrepreneur: How to Be Effective in Any Unruly Organization 1998, Intervention: The Use of American Military Force in the Post-Cold War World 1999, The Opportunity: America's Moment to Alter History's Course 2005; frequent contribs to foreign affairs journals. *Address:* Council on Foreign Relations, 58 East 68th Street, New York, NY 10021, USA (office). *Telephone:* (212) 434-9543 (office). *Fax:* (212) 434-9880 (office). *E-mail:* president@cfr.org (office). *Website:* www.cfr.org (office).

HAAVISTO, Heikki Johannes, MSc, LLM; Finnish politician; b. 20 Aug. 1935, Turku; m. Maija Rihko 1964; three s. *Career:* Head of Dept Oy Vehnä Ab 1963–66; Sec.-Gen. Cen. Union of Agricultural Producers and Forest Owners in Finland (MTK) 1966–75, Pres. 1976–94; Vice-Pres. Int. Fed. of Agricultural Producers (IFAP) 1977–80, 1986–90, mem. Bd of Dirs 1984–86; mem. Cen. Council of Nordic Farmer Orgs (NBC), Pres. 1977, 1985–87; Chair. Del. of Finn Cooperative Pellervo (Confed. of Finnish Cooperatives) 1979–2000; mem. Admin. Council, Osuuskunta Metsäliitto, Vice-Chair. 1976–82, Pres. 1982–93; Vice-Chair. Admin. Council, OKO (Cen. Union of Cooperative Credit Banks) 1985–93; mem. Bd of Dirs Metsä-Serla Oy 1986–93; Pres. Admin. Council, Raisio Group 1987–96, Pres. Bd of Dirs 1997–2000; mem. Int. Policy Council on Agric. and Trade 1988–2000; Minister for Foreign Affairs 1993–95, for Devt Co-operation 1994–95; three hon. doctorates. *Address:* Hintsantie 2, 21200 Raisio, Finland. *Telephone:* (2) 4383020. *Fax:* (2) 4383499.

HABIB, Randa, MA; Lebanese/French journalist; *Director and Head, Agence France Presse, Jordan;* b. 16 Jan. 1952, Beirut, Lebanon; m. Adnan Gharaybeh 1973; one s. one d. *Education:* French Lycée, Rio de Janeiro and Univ. of Beirut. *Career:* corresp., Agence France Presse (AFP) 1980, Dir and Head of AFP Office, Amman 1987–; corresp., Radio Monte Carlo 1988–2006, columnist in local Jordanian papers, corresp. also for several int. publs and TV; Chair. Foreign Press Club, Jordan; mem. Bd Dirs Jordan Media Inst.; Gov., Agence France Presse Foundation; Chevalier, Ordre nat. du Mérite 2001; Médaille du Travail (France) 2000. *Publication:* Hussein père et fils, 30 années qui ont changé le Moyen-Orient 2007. *Address:* Agence France Presse, Jebel Amman, 2nd Circle, PO Box 3340, Amman 11181, Jordan (office). *Telephone:* (6) 4642976 (office). *Fax:* (6) 4654680 (office). *E-mail:* randa.habib@afp.com (office).

HABIBIE, Bacharuddin Jusuf, DEng; Indonesian politician and aviation engineer; b. 25 June 1936, Pare-Pare, South Sulawesi; m. H. Hasri Ainun Besari 1962; two s. *Education:* Bandung Inst. of Tech., Technische Hochschule, Aachen. *Career:* Head of Research at Messerschmitt-Boelkow-Blohm, Hamburg 1966; Govt Adviser 1976; Chair., CEO, Pres. Indonesian State Aircraft Industry 1976–98; Minister of State for Research and Tech. 1978–98; Head of Agency for Tech. Evaluation and Application 1978–98; Chair., CEO, Pres. Indonesian Shipbuilding Industry 1978–98; Chair. Batam Industrial Devt 1978–98; Chair. Team for Defence Security Industrial Devt 1980–99; mem. Indonesian Parl. 1982–99; Chair., CEO, Pres. Small Arms and Munitions Industry 1983–98; Chair. Nat. Research Council 1984–; Vice-Chair. Bd of Patrons, Indonesian Strategic Industries

1988–; Chair. Agency for Strategic Industries 1989–98; Head of Indonesian Muslim Intellectuals Asscn 1990–; Vice-Pres. of Indonesia March–May 1998, Pres. 1998–99; Founder and Chair. Indonesian Aeronautics and Astronautics Inst.; mem. Royal Swedish Acad. of Eng Sciences, Acad. Nat. de l'Air et de l'Espace, France; Fellow Royal Aeronautical Soc.; Gran Cruz del Mérito Aeronáutico con Distintivo Blanco (Spain) 1980, Grosses Bundesverdienstkreuz 1980, Dwidya Sistha Medal 1982, Grand Cross of the Order of Orange Nassau 1983, Grand Officier Ordre nat. du Mérite and numerous other awards and decorations. *Publications:* numerous scientific and technical papers.
Address: c/o House of Representatives, Jakarta, Indonesia (office).

HACHANA, Mohamed Nejib, BEcons; Tunisian diplomatist; *Ambassador to USA;* m.; two c. *Education:* Univ. of Law and Econs, Tunisia, Nat. School of Admin, Tunisia, Univ. of Boulder, Colo, Nat. Inst. of Defence for Strategic Studies, Tunisia. *Career:* Deputy Dir of Cooperation with N American countries and the UN and its specialized agencies 1980–83, Deputy Dir in charge of bilateral cooperation with N American and European countries 1986–88, Deputy Chief of Mission, Embassy in Washington, DC 1988–92, Amb. to Kuwait 1992–95, Dir Arab Countries Dept, Ministry of Foreign Affairs 1995–96, Amb. to Lebanon 1996–98, Dir Maghreb (N African) Countries Dept 1998–2000, Cabinet mem. Office of the Pres., Dept of Diplomat Affairs 2000–03, Amb. to UAE 2003–04, to USA 2005–.
Address: Embassy of Tunisia, 1515 Massachusetts Avenue, NW, Washington, DC 20005, USA (office). *Telephone:* (202) 862-1850 (office). *Fax:* (202) 862-1858 (office). *Website:* www.embassy.org/embassies/tn.html (office).

HACHANI, Ali; Tunisian diplomatist; b. 19 Sept. 1946; m.; four c. *Education:* Tunis Univ., Columbia Univ., NY, USA. *Career:* entered Tunisian Foreign Service 1968; with Dept of Int. Cooperation 1968–72; Counsellor, Perm. Mission to UN, NY 1972–79; with Office of the Prime Minister, Tunis 1979–80; Deputy Dir for Multilateral Cooperation and Cooperation among Developing Countries 1980–85; Amb. to UAE 1985–90; Dir of Bilateral and Regional Cooperation with Arab, African and Asian Countries 1990–92; Amb. to Senegal (non-resident Amb. to Cape Verde, Gambia, Guinea, and Guinea-Bissau), Dakar 1992–95; Dir for Research Analysis and Planning, Dir for Relations with EU mems, then Dir-Gen. for Europe 1995–97; Perm. Rep. to UN, NY 1997–2000, 2003–07, Pres. ECOSOC 2006–07; Amb. to Greece 2000–01; Dir Gen. UN and int. confs 2001–03; Ordre de la Repub. Tunisienne.
Address: c/o Ministry of Foreign Affairs, avenue de la Ligue des états arabes, Tunis (office); 6 Impasse 2 des Etoiles, El Menzah 8, Ariana, Tunisia (home). *Telephone:* (71) 713910 (home). *E-mail:* ali_hachani@hotmail.com (home). *Website:* www.diplomatie.gov.tn (office).

HACKETT, Christopher F., BSc, MA, PhD; Barbadian international organization official and diplomatist; *Permanent Representative, United Nations; Education:* UWI, Mona, Jamaica and St Augustine, Trinidad and Tobago, Carlton Univ., Ottawa, Canada, New York Univ., USA. *Career:* began career with Ministry of External Affairs; Second Sec. Perm. Mission to UN, New York 1969–70; various positions with UN in Secr. and UNDP 1970s; Chief Admin. Officer UN Truce Supervision Org. (UNTSO), Jerusalem 1988–89; Chief Jt Planning Section, UN Dept of Econ. and Social Affairs 1991–92; Regional Electoral Coordinator, Cen. Region, UN Angola Verification Mission (UNAVEM II) 1992–93; Deputy Coordinator, Secr. of UN Conf. Sustainable Devt of Small Island Developing States 1993–94; Chief UN Inter-Agency Affairs Section 1995–98; Officer-in-Charge then Chief of Econ. and Social Council (ECOSOC) and Inter-Org. Cooperation Br, UNDP 1999; Chief of Caribbean Div., Regional Bureau for Latin America and the Caribbean, UNDP 1999–2004; Perm. Rep. to UN 2004–.
Address: Permanent Mission of Barbados, 800 Second Avenue, 2nd Floor, New York, NY 10017, USA (office). *Telephone:* (212) 867-8431 (office). *Fax:* (212) 986-1030 (office). *E-mail:* barbados@un.int (office). *Website:* www.un.int (office).

HADDOCK, Michael Kenneth; British diplomatist; *Ambassador to Belarus;* m. Irene Haddock; one s. one d. *Career:* Research Asst, Research Dept, FCO 1973–78, Third Sec. (Comprehensive Test Ban Del.), Geneva 1978–80, Third Sec. (Commercial), Moscow 1981–83, Third Sec. (Chancery), Kuwait 1983–84, language training (Arabic), SOAS 1984–86, Second Sec. and Vice-Consul (Head of Commercial Section), Damascus 1986–88, Second Sec. (Commercial), Prague 1988–91, First Sec. (Head of Commercial Section), Abu Dhabi 1991–94, S Asian Dept, FCO 1994–97, First Sec. (Head of Press and Public Affairs), Moscow 1997–2001, Whitehall Liaison Dept, FCO 2001–03, Deputy Head of WMD (Weapons of Mass Destruction) Review Unit 2004, Head of Int. Orgs Bill Unit 2004–05, Amb. to Belarus 2007–.
Address: British Embassy, vul. K. Marksa 37, 220030 Minsk, Belarus (office). *Telephone:* (17) 210-59-20 (office). *Fax:* (17) 229-23-06 (office).

E-mail: britinfo@nsys.by (office). *Website:* www.britishembassy.gov.uk/belarus (office).

HADI, Maj.-Gen. Abd ar-Rabbuh Mansur al-; Yemeni politician and army officer; *Vice-President;* b. 1944, Al-Wadhee'a Region, Governorate of Abyan; m.; three s. two d. *Education:* Supreme Acad. of Nasser, Egypt, Sandhurst Mil. Acad., UK, Frunze Acad., fmr USSR. *Career:* mem. staff Armoured Brigades, Mil. Acad.; Dir of Combat Training, of Supply and Provisions; Deputy Chief of Staff, Supply and Provisions; Adviser to Presidential Council 1990–; Minister of Defence 1994; Vice-Pres. of Repub. of Yemen 1994–; rank of Gen. 1994, Lt-Gen. 1997, currently Maj.-Gen.; many decorations and awards including Medal of Honour of Mil. Service 1980, Order of the First Grade Badge 1995.
Address: c/o Office of the President, San'a, Yemen (office). *Telephone:* (1) 272283. *Fax:* (1) 252803.

HADRAMI, Abderrahim Ould; Mauritanian diplomatist; *Permanent Representative, United Nations;* b. 31 Dec. 1953, Chinguetti; m.; four c. *Education:* Ecole Nat. d'Admin de Nouakchott, Univ. of Orléans, France. *Career:* Second Counsellor, Embassy in Paris 1977–79; First Counsellor, Perm. Mission to UN, New York 1982, to Embassy in Senegal 1985; Dir for Africa, Asia and Int. Orgs, Ministry of Foreign Affairs and Cooperation 1987–99; Amb. to Canada 1999–2002, to Côte d'Ivoire 2002–07; Perm. Rep. to UN, New York 2007–.
Address: Permanent Mission of Mauritania to the United Nations, 116 East 38th Street, New York, NY 10017, USA (office). *Telephone:* (212) 986-7963 (office). *Fax:* (212) 986-8419 (office). *E-mail:* mauritania@un.int (office). *Website:* www2.un.int/public/mauritania (office).

HAEKKERUP, Hans; Danish politician; *Research Director of China Studies, Royal Danish Defence College;* b. 3 Dec. 1945, Copenhagen; m. Susanne Rumohr Haekkerup; five s. *Education:* Copenhagen Univ. *Career:* with Ministry of Social Affairs 1973–76, of Educ. 1976–77, of Labour 1977–79; Prof. Danish School of Admin. 1977–80; mem. Folketing (Parl.) 1979–2000, served on several cttees including Cttee on Danish Security Policy, Cttee on Greenlandic Affairs, Cttee on Foreign Policy; economist with Civil Servants Org. 1981–85; Chair. Defence Cttee 1991–93; Minister of Defence 1993–2000; Special Rep. of UN Sec.-Gen. for Kosovo Jan.–Dec. 2001; Advisor on Security Policy 2002–07; Research Dir of China Studies, Royal Danish Defence Coll. 2007–.
Address: Groennegade 27, 1107 Copenhagen K, Denmark (office).

HAFSTRÖM, (Sven) Jonas; Swedish diplomatist; *Ambassador to USA;* m. Eva Hafström; three c. *Education:* Lund Univ. *Career:* non-commissioned reserve capt. in Swedish Army; held numerous public sector postings throughout 1980s, including Head of Section, Ministry of Foreign Affairs; First Sec., Embassies in Washington, DC and Tehran; Press Sec. to Minister of Justice; held various positions under fmr Prime Minister and Chair. Moderate Party, Carl Bildt, including Foreign Policy Advisor 1987–2000, Press Sec. 1987–91, Asst Under-Sec. 1991–94, Head of party's Int. Bureau 1994–2000; mem. Swedish Defence Cttee 1998–99; Deputy Dir-Gen. and Head of Dept for Consular Affairs and Civil Law, Ministry of Foreign Affairs 2000–04; Amb. to Thailand (also accred to Laos, Cambodia and Myanmar) 2004–07, to USA 2007–.
Address: Embassy of Sweden, 2900 K Street, NW, Washington, DC 20007, USA (office). *Telephone:* (202) 467-2600 (office). *Fax:* (202) 467-2699 (office). *E-mail:* ambassaden.washington@foreign.ministry.se (office). *Website:* www.swedenabroad.com/washington (office).

HÄGGLUND, Gen. Gustav; Finnish army officer; b. 6 Sept. 1938, Wyborg; m. Ritva Ekström; one s. two d. *Education:* Finnish Mil. Acad., Univ. of Helsinki, Finnish War Coll. *Career:* nat. mil. service 1957–58; commanded Finnish Bn UNEF II, Sinai 1978–79, Nyland Brigade, Finland 1984–85, UNDOF, Golan Heights 1985–86, UN Interim Force in Lebanon (UNIFIL), Lebanon 1986–88, South East Mil. Area Finland 1988–90; Chief of Defence Staff 1990–94, Chief of Defence 1994–2001; Chair. EU Mil. Cttee, Brussels 2001–04; US Army Command and Gen. Staff Coll. 1972–73; Fellow Harvard Univ. Center for Int. Affairs 1981–82. *Publications:* Peace-making in the Finnish Winter War 1969, Northern Europe in Strategic Perspective 1974, US Strategy for Europe 1974, Parliamentary Defence Committees in Finland 1981, Modern US Cruise Missiles, an Evaluation 1982, Peace-keeping in a Modern War Zone 1990, Defence of Finland 2001.
Address: c/o rue de la Loi 175, 1048 Brussels, Belgium (office).

HAGHIGHIAN, Alireza; Iranian diplomatist; *Ambassador to Armenia;* b. 31 Aug. 1958, Isfahan; m.; three c. *Career:* joined Foreign Service 1981; Political Attache 1981–83; 3rd Sec., Embassy in Ottawa, Canada 1983–87, 2nd Sec. 1987–88; 1st Sec., Bonn, Germany 1988–93; Political Counsellor,

Ministry of Foreign Affairs 1993–98, Gen. Dir. Report Analysis Dept 1998–2001; Chargé d'Affaires a.i. to Iraq 2001–03; Amb. to Armenia 2004–. *Address:* Embassy of Iran, Yerevan, Budaghian Street 1, Iran (office). *Telephone:* (10) 28-04-57 (office). *Fax:* (10) 23-00-52 (office). *E-mail:* info@ iranembassy.am (office). *Website:* www.iranembassy.am (office).

HAHN, Lorna, MA, PhD; American national organization executive and academic; *Executive Director, Association on Third World Affairs; Education:* Temple Univ., Univ. of Penn. *Career:* fmr History Lecturer, Temple Univ.; fmr Lecturer on Int. Relations, American, Catholic, Georgetown and Howard Univs; Founding Exec. Dir and Chief Researcher, Asscn on Third World Affairs (ATWA), Washington, DC 1967–; adviser to US and foreign political leaders; mem. Advisory Bd Center for Global Educ., George Mason Univ., Hannibal Club USA, Croatian–American Friendship Asscn, Inst. of Human Rights, UP Law Center, Philippines; guest lecturer at numerous nat. and int. institutions including US Nat. War Coll. (first female), US Naval War Coll., Eglin Air Force Base, US Air Force Staff Coll., CIA, Dept of Int. Affairs, US Foreign Service Inst., Claremont Inst., Asia and World Inst., Taiwan, Croatian Diplomatic Acad. *Publications:* North Africa: Nationalism to Nationhood, Undergrounds in Insurgent, Revolutionary and Resistance Warfare (co-author), Morocco: Old Land, New Nation (co-author), An Historical Dictionary of Libya, Look Again: Better Policies are Possible; numerous articles in scholarly and popular publs including Foreign Affairs, Middle Eastern Affairs, The New York Times; ed. and contrib. to over 40 reports of Capitol Hill Confs organised by ATWA. *Address:* Association on Third World Affairs, Suite 600, 1717 K Street, NW, Washington, DC 20036, USA (office). *Telephone:* (202) 973-0157 (office). *Fax:* (202) 775-7465 (office). *E-mail:* info@atwa.org (office). *Website:* www.atwa.org (office).

HAIN, Rt Hon. Peter Gerald, BSc, MPhil, PC; British politician; b. 16 Feb. 1950, Nairobi, Kenya; m. 1st Patricia Western 1975; two s.; m. 2nd Elizabeth Haywood 2003. *Education:* Queen Mary Coll., Univs of London and Sussex. *Career:* Head of Research, Communication Workers' Union 1976–91; MP (Labour) for Neath 1991–; Labour Party Foreign Affairs Whip 1995–96; Shadow Employment Minister 1996–97; Parl. Under-Sec. of State, Welsh Office 1997–99; Minister of State, FCO 1999–2001; Minister for Energy and Competitiveness in Europe 2001; Minister of State for Europe, FCO June 2001–02; Sec. of State for Wales 2002–08 (resgnd); Leader of the House of Commons 2003–05; Sec. of State for NI Ireland 2005–07, for Work and Pensions 2007–08 (resgnd); Founding mem. Anti-Nazi League 1970s; Chair. Tribune magazine 1993–97; mem. CND, GMB Union, Friends of the Earth, Fabian Soc. *Publications include:* 13 books including Ayes to the Left: A Future for Socialism, Sing the Beloved Country. *Address:* Neath Constituency Office, 39 Windsor Road, Neath SA11 1NB (office); House of Commons London, , England (office). *Telephone:* (20) 7210-3000 (House of Commons) (office); (1639) 630152 (constituency office) (office). *Fax:* (1639) 641196 (constituency office) (office). *E-mail:* hainp@parliament.uk (office). *Website:* www.peterhain.org.

HAJ, Muhammad Hassan al-; Sudanese diplomatist; *Ambassador to Egypt; Career:* Amb. and Perm. Rep. to UN and Int. Orgs, Geneva –2005, Amb. to Egypt 2005–. *Address:* Embassy of Sudan, 4 Sharia el-Ibrahimi, Garden City, Cairo, Egypt (office). *Telephone:* (2) 3545043 (office). *Fax:* (2) 3542693 (office).

HAJJAJI, Najat al-, BA, MA; Libyan international organization official, diplomatist and journalist; *Ambassador and Permanent Representative, United Nations, Geneva;* b. 26 July 1952, Tripoli; one d. *Education:* Cairo Univ., Egypt. *Career:* Ed. Gen. Inst. for Journalism, Tripoli 1973–75; corresp., Alfajer Al-Jadid (daily newspaper) 1975–77; Dir of Foreign Relations and Training, Jamahiriya News Agency 1978–91; Minister Plenipotentiary, Perm. Mission to UN, Geneva 1992–98, Chargé d'affaires 1998–2000, Amb. and Perm. Rep. to UN, Geneva 2000–; Vice-Pres. UN Human Rights Comm., Geneva 2001, Pres. 2003–05; Head Del. to UN Human Rights Comm. and Sub-Comm. on Promotion and Protection of Human Rights 1993–2001; Leader Dels to Human Rights Treaty bodies 1993–2001; rapporteur Main Cttee, World Conf. Against Racism, Racial Discrimination, Xenophobia and Related Intolerance, Durban 2001; Vice-Chair. Preparatory Cttee, World Summit on the Information Soc. 2002, Diplomatic Conf. on the Third Protocol Additional to the Geneva Conventions; mem. UN Special Committee to select winners of UN prize in field of human rights, Working Group on Mercenaries 2005; Pres. Council of Int. Org. for Migration (IOM) 2006–07; Hon. Rep. Int. Org. for Peace, Care and Relief Geneva 2003; Kuala Lumpur World Peace Conf. Award Malaysia 2003, Geneva Inst. for Human Rights 2004, Hon. Distinction, Arab Labour Org. 2004, Medal, Gen. Head of Dubai Police 2004, Medal, Int. Criminal Court on Rwanda, Arab Women Studies Centre

Award, Dubai 2006. *Publications include:* wide range of articles on the promotion and protection of human rights and African affairs. *Address:* Permanent Mission of Libyan Arab Jamahiriya, 25 rue Richemond, 1202 Geneva (office); 10 chemin du Vent Blanc, 1223 Cologny/Geneva, Switzerland (home). *Telephone:* (22) 9598900 (office); (22) 7521862 (home); (22) 9598922. *Fax:* (22) 9598910 (office); (22) 7521458 (home). *E-mail:* mission.libye@bluewin.ch (office); n.alhajjaji@bluewin.ch (home). *Website:* www.unog.ch (office).

HAJJRI, Abdulwahab Abdulla al-, LLM; Yemeni diplomatist; *Ambassador to USA;* b. 1958; m.; three c. *Education:* Sana'a Univ., American Univ., Washington DC, USA, Al Azhar Univ., Cairo, Egypt. *Career:* joined Ministry of Foreign Affairs 1980, Diplomatic Attaché, Political Dept, Sana'a 1980–82, Cultural Attaché, Cairo 1982–87, Washington, DC 1987–92, Counsellor, Cairo 1992–95, Minister Plenipotentiary, Embassy in Washington, DC 1995–97, Amb. to USA (also accred to Mexico and Venezuela) and Perm. Observer of Yemen to OAS 1997–. *Address:* Embassy of Yemen, 2319 Wyoming Avenue, NW, Washington, DC 20008, USA (office). *Telephone:* (202) 965-4760 (office). *Fax:* (202) 337-2017 (office). *E-mail:* ambassador@yemenembassy.org (office). *Website:* www.yemenembassy.org (office).

HAJRI, Ali Bin Fahad Falil Al-Shawany al-, BA; Qatari diplomatist; *Ambassador to USA;* b. 3 March 1960, Doha; m.; six c. *Education:* Univ. of Southern Colorado, USA. *Career:* Third Sec., Ministry of Foreign Affairs 1983, represented Qatar at several regional and int. confs, including 39th, 52nd, 53rd, 54th and 55th sessions of UN Gen. Ass., New York 1983–85, served at Gen. Consulate in Dubai 1985–93, at Embassy in Rabat 1995–97, mem. Perm. Del. to UN, New York 1997–2000, Amb. to Italy (also accred to Greece, Albania, Macedonia, Bosnia and Herzegovina, Croatia, Slovenia and San Marino) and Perm. Rep. to FAO, IFAD, UN World Food Program, Rome 2000–05, Dir European and American Affairs Dept, Ministry of Foreign Affairs 2006–08, Amb. to USA 2008–; Grand Kt of the Cross (Italy). *Address:* Embassy of Qatar, 2555 M Street, NW, Suite 200, Washington, DC 20037-1305, USA (office). *Telephone:* (202) 274-1600 (office). *Fax:* (202) 237-0061 (office). *E-mail:* info@qatarembassy.net (office). *Website:* www.qatarembassy.net (office).

HÄKÄMIES, Jyri, MScS; Finnish business executive and politician; *Minister of Defence and Minister at the Prime Minister's Office;* b. 30 Aug. 1961, Karhula; m. Tuija Arhosola; two s. *Career:* Communications Man. Kymen Viestintä Oy (newspaper publr) 1989–91; Sales Man. Kymen Sanomat (newspaper) 1991–94; Man. Dir Kymenlaakso Chamber of Commerce 1994–99; mem. Suomen Eduskunta (Parl.) (Nat. Coalition Party—NCP) 1999–, mem. NCP Communications Sec., Parl. Group 1987–89, Vice-Chair. (Parl. Group) 2003–06, Chair. 2006–; Minister of Defence 2007–, also Minister at the Prime Minister's Office (ownership steering) 2007–; mem. Kotka City Council 2005–, Regional Council of Kymenlaakso Ass. (Chair. 2005–); mem. Supervisory Bd Port of Kotka Ltd (Chair. 2005–07), Sitra, The Finnish Innovation Fund 2006–07, Kymen Puhelin Oy 1998–2007; Vice-Pres. European People's Party 2003–06; mem. Council, Finland-Russia Soc. 2006–. *Address:* Ministry of Defence, Eteläinen Makasiinikatu 8, PO Box 31, 00131 Helsinki, Finland (office). *Telephone:* (9) 16088103 (office). *Fax:* (9) 16088284 (office). *E-mail:* jyri.hakamies@defmin.fi (office). *Website:* www .defmin.fi (office); www.vnk.fi (office).

HAKIM, Peter, MS, MA; American international organization executive; *President, Inter-American Dialogue; Education:* Cornell Univ., Univ. of Penn., Princeton Univ. Woodrow Wilson School. *Career:* fmr Lecturer, MIT and Columbia Univ.; fmr staff mem. Ford Foundation, New York and Latin America; fmr Vice-Pres. Inter-American Foundation; currently Pres. Inter-American Dialogue, Washington, DC; mem. Bd or Advisory Cttee, Foundation of the Americas, World Bank (IBRD), Inter-American Development Bank (IADB), Foreign Affairs en Español, Intellibridge Corpn, Human Rights Watch; mem. Council of Foreign Relations. *Publications:* articles in Foreign Affairs, Foreign Policy, The New York Times, The Washington Post, Financial Times, Christian Science Monitor. *Address:* Inter-American Dialogue (IAD), 1211 Connecticut Avenue, NW, Suite 510, Washington, DC 20036, USA (office). *Telephone:* (202) 822-9002 (office). *Fax:* (202) 822-9553 (office). *E-mail:* phakim@thedialogue.org (office); iad@thedialogue.org (office). *Website:* www.thedialogue.org (office).

HÄKKÄNEN, Matti Klaus Juhani, LLM; Finnish diplomatist (retd); b. 21 July 1936, Helsinki; m. Pirkko Hentola 1962; two s. *Education:* Univ. of Helsinki. *Career:* served in Finnish Foreign Service Helsinki, Paris, New York, Moscow and Peking 1960–76; Amb. to Romania (also accred to Albania) 1976–80; Under-Sec. of State 1980–83; Amb. to Netherlands (also accred to Ireland) 1983–87, to Argentina (also accred to Chile and Uruguay) 1987–88, to France 1988–93, to Italy (also accred to Malta and San Marino) 1993–97, to Portugal (also accred to Morocco) 1997–2001; mem. Selection and Training Bd Finnish Foreign Ministry 2004–07; mem. Bd French-Finnish Chamber of Commerce, Heinola Del.; First Lt, Finnish Naval Forces; Kt Commdr, Order of Lion of Finland, Grand Cross, Orange Nassau of the Netherlands, Officer, Black Star of France, Grand Cross, Nat. Merit of Italy, Kt Commdr, Ordre nat. du mérite, Mil. Medal of Finland, Grand Cross, Order of Infante Dom Henrique (Portugal). *Address:* Töölönkatu 9, 00100 Helsinki, Finland (home). *Telephone:* (9) 497515 (home); 50-5497895 (mobile). *E-mail:* matti.hakkanen@welho.com (home).

HALE, David; American diplomatist; *Ambassador to Jordan; Education:* Georgetown Univ.'s School of Foreign Service; studied Arabic at Foreign Service Inst.'s Field School, Tunisia. *Career:* joined Foreign Service in 1984, postings to US Mission to UN, to Embassies in Lebanon, Jordan and Bahrain, to Consulate-Gen. in Dhahran, Saudi Arabia, has held several staff positions at US State Dept including Dir Office of Israel and Palestinian Affairs, Deputy Chief of Mission, Embassy in Beirut, Exec. Asst to Sec. of State; Deputy Chief of Mission, Amman 2003–04, Chargé d'affaires a.i. 2004–05, Amb. to Jordan 2005–; several Honor Awards. *Address:* Embassy of the USA, PO Box 354, Amman 11118, Jordan (office). *Telephone:* (6) 5906000 (office). *Fax:* (6) 5920121 (office). *E-mail:* WebmasterJordan@state.gov (office). *Website:* amman.usembassy.gov (office).

HALE, Suzanne K., BA, MA; American diplomatist; b. 21 April 1948, New York; m. Hunter Daniel Hale; one s. one d. *Education:* Beloit Coll., Wis., Int. Christian Univ., Tokyo, Japan, Columbia Univ.'s School of Int. and Public Affairs. *Career:* rank of Career Minister; worked with US Dept of Agric. int. trade policy staff, Washington, DC 1978–81, served at Embassy in Tokyo, first as Agricultural Attaché then as Agricultural Trade Officer 1981–88, Dir Foreign Agricultural Service's AgExport Services Div. 1990–96, Minister-Counselor for Agricultural Affairs, Embassy in Beijing 1997–2000, Embassy in Tokyo 2000–04, Amb. to Federated States of Micronesia 2004–07; Sec. of Agric.'s Distinguished Service Award. *Address:* US Department of State, 2201 C Street NW, Washington, DC 20520, USA (office). *Telephone:* (202) 647-4000 (office). *Fax:* (202) 647-6738 (office). *Website:* www.state.gov (office).

HALILOVIĆ, Safet; Bosnia and Herzegovina politician; *Minister of Human Rights and Refugees; Career:* Chair. Municipal Bd, Party of Democratic Action (Stranka Demokratske Akcije – SDA), Sarajevo 1994–; Pres. of Fed. of Bosnia and Herzegovina 2002–03, Minister of Civil Affairs 2003–07, of Human Rights and Refugees 2007–. *Address:* Ministry of Human Rights and Refugees, 71000 Sarajevo, trg Bosne i Hercegovine 1, Bosnia and Herzegovina (office). *Telephone:* (33) 206673 (office). *Fax:* (33) 206140 (office). *E-mail:* kabmin@mhrr.gov.ba (office). *Website:* www.mhrr.gov.ba (office).

HALL, Andrew Rotely; British diplomatist; *Ambassador to Nepal;* b. 3 May 1950; m. Kathleen Hall; two d. *Career:* Sr Research Officer (S Asia), Research Dept, FCO 1980–84; First Sec. (Political), New Delhi 1984–87; Prin. Research Officer, Research and Analysis Dept, FCO 1987–91; First Sec. and Consul and Deputy Head of Mission, Kathmandu 1991–94; Sr Prin. Research Officer, later Research Counsellor, S and SE Asia Research Group, FCO 1995–2003; Deputy High Commr (Eastern India), Kolkata 2003–06; Amb. to Nepal 2006–. *Address:* British Embassy, PO Box 106, Lainchaur, Kathmandu, Nepal (office). *Telephone:* (1) 4410583 (office); (1) 4411281 (office); (1) 4414588 (office). *Fax:* (1) 4411789 (office). *E-mail:* britemb@wlink.com.np (office). *Website:* www.britishembassy.gov.uk/nepal (office).

HALL, Most Hon. Sir Kenneth O., Kt, GCMG, OJ, BA, MA, PhD; Jamaican academic, university administrator and government official; *Governor-General;* b. 24 April 1941, Hanover, Jamaica; m. Rheima Holding; one d. *Education:* Univ. of the West Indies, Mona, Jamaica, Inst. of Int. Relations, Univ. of the West Indies, St Augustine, Trinidad, Queen's Univ., Canada. *Career:* Prof. of History, State Univ. of NY (SUNY), Oswego, then Adjunct Prof. of Caribbean Studies, SUNY, Albany, then Prof. of American Studies, SUNY, Old Wesbury; Deputy Sec.-Gen. Caribbean Community (CARICOM) Secr. 1994–96; Pro-Vice-Chancellor and Prin. Univ. of the West Indies, Mona campus 1996–2006; Gov.-Gen. of Jamaica 2006–; mem. Univ. Council of Jamaica; mem. Bd Dirs Bank of Jamaica; Chair. Caribbean Examinations Council 2003–07; Order of the Nation. *Address:* King's House, Hope Road, Kingston 10, Jamaica (office). *Telephone:* 927-6424 (office). *Fax:* 978-6025 (office). *E-mail:* kingshouse@cwjamaica.com (office). *Website:* www.kingshousejamaica .gov.jm (office).

HALLER, Bruno, MA, LLM; French international organization official; b. 15 Dec. 1938, Majunga, Madagascar; m.; two c. *Education:* Strasbourg Univ. *Career:* deputy dir of a hospital 1962–63; Dir Training Centre for Devt, Strasbourg 1964–72; Asst Sociologist, Strasbourg Faculty of Social Sciences, then Lecturer, Strasbourg Univ. Inst. of Tech. 1968–72; Deputy Dir European Youth Centre, Council of Europe 1972, Dir 1983–84, Head of Planning and Programme Div. 1980–83, Dir Office of the Sec.-Gen. 1984–88, Dir and Deputy Clerk, Parl. Ass. of Council of Europe (PACE) 1989–95, Sec.-Gen. PACE 1995–2002; Chevalier, Ordre nat. du Mérite, Chevalier, Légion d'Honneur, Commdr Order of Isabella the Catholic (Spain), Commdr of Nat. Order of Merit (Italy), Order of Prince Yaroslav the Wise, Fourth degree (Ukraine); Gold Medal 'Naim Frasheri' (Albania), Gold Medal of Youth and Sports (France). *Publications include:* Law in Greater Europe (co-ed.) 1999; articles on Council of Europe in specialised magazines. *Address:* c/o Office of the Secretary-General, Parliamentary Assembly, The Council of Europe, 67075 Strasbourg Cédex, France (office).

HALLIDAY, Frederick, PhD; Irish academic and journalist; *Professor of International Relations, London School of Economics;* b. 1946, Dublin. *Education:* Queen's Coll., Oxford, SOAS, LSE, UK. *Career:* Prof. of Int. Relations, LSE 1983–; columnist for Prospect magazine, Middle East Research and Information Project (MERIP); broadcaster with ABC, BBC, CNN and CBC; Editorial Assoc. New Left Review; Fellow Transnational Inst. 1976–, also adviser on Middle Eastern and Cen. Asian matters; fmr Chair. Research Cttee, Royal Inst. of Int. Affairs; mem. Advisory Council, Foreign Policy Inst. *Publications include:* 14 books on int. politics including Dictatorship and Development 1978, Rethinking International Relations 1994, Islam and the Myth of Confrontation 1995, Revolution and World Politics 1999, Two Hours that Shook the World 2002. *Address:* Department of International Relations, London School of Economics, Houghton Street, London, WC2A 2AE, England (office). *Telephone:* (20) 7955-7389 (office). *Fax:* (20) 7242-0392 (office). *E-mail:* f.halliday@lse.ac.uk. *Website:* www.lse.ac.uk (office).

HALONEN, Tarja Kaarina, LLM; Finnish politician, lawyer and head of state; *President;* b. 24 Dec. 1943, Helsinki; m. Dr Pentti Arajärvi 2000; one d. from previous relationship with Kari Pekkonen. *Education:* Univ. of Helsinki and Univ. of Kent at Canterbury, UK. *Career:* lawyer, Lainvalvonta Oy 1967–68; social welfare officer, organizing Sec. Nat. Union of Finnish Students 1969–70; lawyer, Cen. Org. of Finnish Trade Unions 1970–2000; Parl. Sec. to Prime Minister Sorsa 1974–75; mem. Helsinki City Council 1977–96; mem. Parl. 1979–2000; Chair. Parl. Social Affairs Cttee 1984–87; Second Minister, Ministry of Social Affairs and Health 1987–90, for Nordic Co-operation 1989–91, of Justice 1990–91, for Foreign Affairs 1995–2000; Pres. of Finland (first woman) 2000– (re-elected 2006); Chair. Int. Solidarity Foundation 1991–2000 (mem. Bd Dirs), TNL Theatre Org.; mem. Social Democratic Party 1971–2000; Co-Chair. World Comm. on the Social Dimension of Globalization, ILO 2002–04; mem. Rep. Body of the Cooperative Retail Co. Elanto 1975–, mem. Supervisory Bd 1980–96; mem. UNCTAD Panel of Eminent Persons 2005–06; mem. Bd Oslo Centre for Peace and Human Rights 2006–; hon. degrees (Univ. of Helsinki) 2000, (Helsinki School of Econs) 2001, (Ewha Womens Univ., Republic of Korea) 2002, (Univ. of Kent) 2002, (Eötvös Loránd Univ., Budapest) 2002, Chinese Acad. of Forestry 2002, (Finlandia Univ., USA) 2003, (Univ. of Turku) 2003, (Univ. of Bluefiels, Nicaragua) 2004, (Univ. of Tartu, Estonia) 2004, (State Univ. of Yerevan, Armenia) 2005; ranked by Forbes magazine amongst 100 Most Powerful Women (31st) 2004, (31st) 2005, (44th) 2006, (50th) 2007. *Address:* Office of the President, Mariankatu 2, 00170 Helsinki, Finland (office). *Telephone:* (9) 661133 (office). *Fax:* (9) 638247 (office). *E-mail:* presidentti@tpk.fi (office); kirjaamo@tpk.fi (office). *Website:* www .presidentti.fi (office).

HALVORSEN, Kristin; Norwegian politician; *Minister of Finance;* b. 2 Sept. 1960; m.; two c. *Career:* mem. Stortinget (Parl.) for Oslo 1989–, mem. Standing Cttee on Finance 1989–97, on Scrutiny and Constitutional Affairs 1997–2001, on Foreign Affairs 2001–05, mem. Parl. Del. in Connection with European Parl. 2001–05; Leader Socialist Left Party of Norway 1997–; Minister of Finance 2005–; Observer UN Gen. Meeting 1985; deputy mem. Cttee on Ex-Gratia Payment of Compensation 1996; mem. Consulting Agency Regarding EEC Matters 1997–2001. *Address:* Ministry of Finance, Akersgt. 40, POB 8008 Dep., 0030 Oslo, Norway (office). *Telephone:* 22-24-90-90 (office). *Fax:* 22-24-95-10 (office). *E-mail:* postmottak@finans.dep.no (office). *Website:* odin.dep.no/fin (office).

HAMAD, Abdul-Latif Yousef al-, BA; Kuwaiti international organization official, banker and politician; *Chairman, Board of Directors, Arab Fund for Economic and Social Development;* b. 1936; m.; four c. *Education:*

Claremont Coll., Calif., Harvard Univ. *Career:* mem. del. to UN 1962; Dir-Gen. Kuwait Fund for Arab Econ. Devt 1963–81; Dir, then Man. Dir Kuwait Investment Co. 1963–71; Man. Dir Kuwait Investment Co. 1965–74; Chair. Kuwait Prefabricated Bldg Co. 1965–78, United Bank of Kuwait Ltd, London 1966–84; Exec. Dir Arab Fund for Econ. and Social Devt 1972–81, Dir-Gen. and Chair. Bd of Dirs 1985–; Chair. Compagnie Arabe et Internationale d'Investissements, Luxembourg 1973–81; mem. Bd of Trustees, Corporate Property Investors, New York 1975–; mem. Governing Body Inst. of Devt Studies, Sussex, UK 1975–87; mem. Ind. Comm. on Int. Devt Issues (Brandt Comm.) 1976–79; mem. Bd Int. Inst. for Environment and Devt, London 1976–80; Minister of Finance and Planning 1981–83; Gov. for Kuwait, World Bank and IMF 1981–83; mem. UN Cttee for Devt Planning 1982–91, Chair. 1987; mem. IFC Banking Advisory Bd Group 1987–, Advisory Group on Financial Flows for Africa (UN) 1987–88, South Comm. 1987–89, Group of Ten (African Devt Bank) 1987–, World Bank's Pvt. Sector Devt Review Group 1988–, UN Panel for Public Hearings on Activities of Transnat. Corpns in S Africa and Namibia 1989–92, Bd Trustees of Stockholm Environment Inst. 1989–92, Comm. on Global Governance 1992–.
Address: Arab Fund for Economic and Social Development, POB 21923, Safat 13080, Kuwait (office). *Telephone:* 4844500 (office). *Fax:* 4815760 (office). *E-mail:* hq@arabfund.org (office). *Website:* www.arabfund.org (office).

HAMAD, Seif Sharif, BA; Tanzanian politician and political scientist; *Secretary-General, Civic United Front;* b. 22 Oct. 1943, Pemba; m. 1st Furtunah Saleh Mbamba 1971; m. 2nd Aweinah Sanani Massoud 1977; one s. four d. *Education:* King George VI Secondary School, Zanzibar, Univ. of Dar es Salaam. *Career:* teacher, Lumumba Coll., Fidel Castro Coll. 1964–72; Asst to Pres. of Zanzibar 1975–77, Minister of Educ., Zanzibar 1977–80; mem. Tanzanian Parl. 1977–80; mem. Zanzibar House of Reps 1980–99; mem. Cen. Cttee Chama Cha Mapinduzi (CCM) Party 1977–88, Head Econ. and Planning Dept of CCM 1982–88; Chief Minister of Zanzibar 1984–88; political prisoner in Zanzibar 1989–91; Nat. Vice-Chair. Civic United Front 1992–, now Sec.-Gen.; presidential cand. Zanzibar elections 2000; Chair. Gen. Ass. Unrepresented Nations and Peoples' Org. (UNPO) 1997–.
Address: Civic United Front, Mtendeni Street, Urban District, PO Box 3637, Zanzibar (office); PO Box 10976, Dar es Salaam, Tanzania. *Telephone:* (54) 237446 (office); (51) 861009; (812) 787790; (811) 324886. *Fax:* (54) 237445 (office); (51) 861010. *E-mail:* headquarters@cuftz.org (office). *Website:* www.cuftz.org (office).

HAMADI, Hassani; Comoran economist and politician. *Career:* Minister of Finance and the Economy 2006–07, of the Economy, Planning, Employment and Female Enterprise 2007–.
Address: Ministry of the Economy, BP 324, Moroni, The Comoros (office). *Telephone:* (74) 4140 (office). *Fax:* (74) 4141 (office).

HAMADOU, Jidda; Niger politician. *Career:* Minister of Nat. Defence 2007–.
Address: Ministry of National Defence, BP 626, Niamey, Niger (office). *Telephone:* 20-72-20-76 (office). *Fax:* 20-72-40-78 (office).

HÄMÄLÄINEN, Sirkka Aune-Marjatta, DSc (Econs); Finnish banker and economist; b. 8 May 1939, Riihimäki; d. of Martti Hinkkala and Aune Hinkkala; m. Arvo Hämäläinen 1961; one s. one d. *Education:* Helsinki School of Econs and Business Admin. *Career:* Economist, Econs Dept, Bank of Finland 1961–72, Head of Office, Econs Dept 1972–79, Acting Head of Dept 1979–81, Dir 1982–91, mem. Bd 1991–92, Gov. and Chair. Bd 1992–98; Dir Econs Dept, Ministry of Finance 1981–82; Chair. Bd of Dirs Financial Supervision Authority 1996–97; mem. Exec. Bd European Cen. Bank, Frankfurt 1998–2003; Docent, Adjunct Prof. of Econs Helsinki School of Econs and Business Admin 1991–; mem. of numerous orgs including Trilateral Comm. 1995–, Supervisory Bd Finnish Cultural Foundation 1996–, Cen. Bank Governance Steering Cttee, Bank of Int. Settlements 1996–, Finnish Public Research and Devt Financing Evaluation Group 1998–; Dir Investor AB March 2004–, HKKK Holding, Sanoma WSOY; Chair. Finnish Nat. Opera; Vice-Chair. KONE Corpn; Commdr First Class of Order of the White Rose, Merit Medal, First Class of Order of the White Star (Estonia); Dr hc (Turku School of Econs and Business Admin.) 1995.
Address: Investor AB, Arsenalsgatan 8C, PO Box 1210, 103 32 Stockholm, Sweden (office).

HAMED FRANCO, Alejandro; Paraguayan diplomatist and politician. *Career:* Amb. to Lebanon –2008; Minister of Foreign Affairs 2008–.
Address: Ministry of Foreign Affairs, Juan E. O'Leary y Presidente Franco, Asunción, Paraguay (office). *Telephone:* (21) 49-4593 (office). *Fax:* (21) 49-3910 (office). *Website:* www.mre.gov.py (office).

HAMID, Ahmed Munaysi Abd al-; Libyan banker and government official; *Secretary of the General People's Committee for Finance; Career:* Gov. Cen. Bank of Libya –2006; Sec. of the Gen. People's Cttee for Finance 2006–.
Address: General People's Committee, Tripoli, Libya.

HAMIDON, Datuk Bin Ali, MA; Malaysian diplomatist; *Permanent Representative, United Nations;* b. 22 Jan. 1950, Tangkak, Johor; m. Datin Amy Low Abdullah; two c. *Education:* Harvard Univ., USA. *Career:* early career with Wisma Putra 1974, overseas postings include Minister Counsellor, Embassy in Tokyo, First Sec., Embassy in Beijing, Second Sec., Embassy in Paris, held several high-ranking positions in Ministry of Foreign Affairs including Under-Sec. for Econs, Prin. Asst Sec. for Maritime and Environment, Prin. Asst Sec. for the Inspectorate; High Commr to Singapore –2003; Amb. to Indonesia 2003–05; Perm. Rep. to UN, New York 2005–.
Address: Office of the Permanent Representative of Malaysia, 313 East 43rd Street, New York, NY 10017, USA (office). *Telephone:* (212) 986-6310 (office). *Fax:* (212) 490-8576 (office). *E-mail:* malaysia@un.int (office). *Website:* www.un.int/malaysia (office).

HAMILTON, Clive, BA, BEcons, DPhil; Australian economist, academic and writer; *Professor of Public Ethics, Centre for Applied Philosophy and Public Ethics, Charles Sturt University;* b. 12 March 1953. *Education:* Australian Nat. Univ., Univ. of Sydney, Inst. of Devt Studies, Univ. of Sussex, UK. *Career:* Research Officer, Shadow Cabinet Minister 1979–90; consultant, Nepal-Australia Forestry Project 1984–87; Research Fellow and Post-Doctoral Fellow, Research School of Pacific Studies, ANU 1984–88, Dir Grad. Program in Econs of Devt, Nat. Centre for Devt Studies 1986–88, Sr Lecturer (part-time) on Public Policy 1994–97, Visiting Fellow, Grad. Program in Public Policy 1997–; Sr Research Economist, Bureau of Industry Econs, Dept of Industry, Tech. and Commerce 1988–90; mem. UN Group of Experts on Least Developed Countries (Bangkok) 1989; Head of Research Br., Resource Assessment Comm. 1990–92; Sr Econ. Adviser to Govt of Indonesia, Natural Resources Man. Project 1992–93; Adjunct Prof., Inst. for Sustainable Future, Univ. of Tech., Sydney 1997–2000; Founder and Exec. Dir The Australia Inst. 1993–2008; Vice-Chancellor's Chair, Charles Sturt Univ. 2008–, also Prof. of Public Ethics, Centre for Applied Philosophy and Public Ethics; Founder Climate Inst. 2005, Chair. 2005–06; Visiting Fellow, Dept of Economy, Univ. of Sydney 2003; Visiting Fellow, Clare Hall and Visiting Scholar, Dept of Land Economy, Univ. of Cambridge, UK 2003; Chair. Climate Inst. (Australia) 2005–; mem. Policy Cttee Sustainable Energy Industries Council of Australia 1995–98, ABS Environmental Statistics Advisory Group 1996–2002, ACT Govt Advisory Panel on Competition Policy 1997–98, Strategic Planning Panel on Competition Policy in NSW Agric. 1997, Governing Council Mulanggarri Foundation 2000–01, Australian Bureau of Statistics Expert Reference Group 2000–, Scientific Cttee Conf. on Int. Soc. for Ecological Economies 2001–02; mem. Bd and Deputy Chair. Padma Mennon Dance Theatre 1995–97; mem. Editorial Bd Journal of Environmental Taxation and Accounting, Ecological Economies 2002–; Arthur Oakes Memorial Prize for the History of Econ. Thought, Univ. of Sydney, 1978. *Publications:* Capitalist Industrialization in Korea 1986, The Economic Dynamics of Australian Industry (ed.) 1991, The Mystic Economist 1994, Human Ecology, Human Nature (co-ed.) 1997, The ESD Process: Evaluating a Policy Experiment (co-ed.) 1998, Running From the Storm: The development of climate change policy in Australia 2001, Growth Fetish 2003, Affluenza 2005, Silencing Dissent 2007, Scorcher 2007, The Freedom Paradox 2008; numerous chapters in books; more than 70 articles in professional and popular journals.
Address: Centre for Applied Philosophy and Public Ethics, LPO Box 8260, Canberra ACT 2601, Australia (office). *Telephone:* (2) 6125-8467 (office). *Fax:* (2) 6125-6579 (office). *E-mail:* mail@clivehamilton.net.au (office). *Website:* www.cappe.edu.au (office).

HAMILTON, Daniel, MA, PhD; American research institute director and professor of international relations; *Director, Center for Transatlantic Relations;* m. Heidi Hamilton; two c. *Education:* Georgetown Univ. School of Foreign Service, Paul H. Nitze School of Advanced Int. Studies (SAIS), Johns Hopkins Univ., Univ. of Konstanz, Germany, St Olaf Coll. *Career:* Program Officer, Chicago Council on Foreign Relations 1979–82; Deputy Dir Aspen Inst., Berlin 1982–90; Sr Assoc. on European–American Relations, Carnegie Endowment for Int. Peace 1990–93; Assoc. Dir of Policy Planning Staff for Secs of State Madeleine Albright and Warren Christopher; Sr Policy Adviser to Asst Sec. of State for European Affairs Richard Holbrooke, to US Embassy in Germany; DaimlerChrysler Fellow, American Inst. for Contemporary German Studies 2001; fmr US Coordinator for SE European Stabilization; fmr Deputy Asst Sec. of State for European Affairs and US Special Coordinator for Northern Europe; currently Dir Center for Transatlantic Relations, Exec. Dir American Consortium on EU Studies (ACES) and Richard von Weizsäcker Prof.,

SAIS, Johns Hopkins Univ.; Dean of Waldsee, Concordia Coll.; Guest Prof., Hertie School of Governance, Berlin; Visiting Fellow, German Council on Foreign Relations; fmr Lecturer, Univ. of Innsbruck, Free Univ. of Berlin; fmr consultant, ABC News/Newsline, Koppel Communications, RAND Corpn, Nat. Geographic Soc., Chicago Council on Foreign Relations; Bundesverdienstkreutz (Germany), Royal Order of the Polar Star (Sweden), Ordre des Palmes Académiques; Dr hc (Concordia Coll.); Dept of State Superior Honor Award, Transatlantic Business Award, American Chamber of Commerce to the EU 2006, Transatlantic Leadership Award, European-American Business Council 2007. *Publications:* After the Revolution 1990, Beyond Bonn: America and the Berlin Republic 1994, Die Zukunft ist nicht mehr was sie war: Europa, Amerika und die neue weltpolitische Lage 2001, Transatlantic Transformations: Equipping NATO for the 21st Century 2004, Partners in Prosperity: The Changing Geography of the Transatlantic Economy 2004, Deep Integration: How Transatlantic Markets are Leading Globalization 2005; Conflict and Cooperation in Transatlantic Relations 2005, Transatlantic Homeland Security 2005, Societal Security 2005, The New Frontiers of Europe 2006, Terrorism and Int. Relations 2006, The Transatlantic Economy (annual editions 2005-2008), The New Eastern Europe 2007, Sleeping Giant: Awakening the Transatlantic Services Market 2007, Globalization and Europe 2008, The Black Sea Region 2008, Networked Foreign Policy 2008; numerous articles in professional journals and newspapers. *Address:* Center for Transatlantic Relations, 1717 Massachusetts Avenue, NW, Washington, DC 20036 (office); Paul. H. Nitze School of Advanced International Studies, Johns Hopkins University, Washington, DC 20036, USA (office). *Telephone:* (202) 663-5880 (office). *Fax:* (202) 663-5879 (office). *E-mail:* transatlantic@jhu.edu (office). *Website:* transatlantic.sais-jhu.edu (office); www.sais-jhu.edu (office).

HAMILTON, Lee H., BA, JD; American research institute director and fmr politician; *Director, Woodrow Wilson International Center for Scholars;* b. Daytona Beach, Fla; m. Nancy Ann Hamilton (née Nelson); two d. one s. *Education:* DePauw Univ., Goethe Inst., Frankfurt, Germany, Indiana Univ. School of Law. *Career:* practised law in Chicago and Columbus, Ind. –1965; mem. US House of Reps from Ind. 9th Dist 1965–99, served as Chair., ranking mem. Cttee on Int. Relations, Chair. and Vice-Chair. Jt Econ. Cttee, Chair. Perm. Select Cttee on Intelligence, Chair. Jt Cttee on Org. of Congress, Chair. Oct. Surprise Task Force, Chair. Select Cttee to Investigate Covert Arms Transactions with Iran, Chair. Sub-Cttee on Europe and Middle E 1970–93, mem. House Standards of Official Conduct Cttee; Dir Woodrow Wilson Int. Center for Scholars (WWIC) 1999–; has served on numerous panels and comms including Commr US Comm. on Nat. Security in the 21st Century (Hart-Rudman Comm.), Co-Chair. Baker-Hamilton Comm. to Investigate Certain Security Issues at Los Alamos, Commr Carter-Baker Comm. on Fed. Election Reform, Vice-Chair. Nat. Comm. on Terrorist Attacks Upon the US (9-11 Comm.); He is currently a member of the advisory council for the U.S. Department of Homeland Security; currently mem. US Dept of Homeland Security Advisory Council, Co-Chair. Ind. Task Force on Immigration and America's Future, Pres.'s Foreign Intelligence Advisory Bd; Co-Chair. Iraq Study Group, US Inst. of Peace 2006–07; Dir Center on Congress, Indiana Univ.; Grand Cross Order of Merit (FRG) 1985, Chevalier Légion d'Honneur (France) 1984, Bundesverdienstkreutz (Germany) 1999; Dr hc (DePauw Univ.), (Hanover Coll.), (Detroit Coll. of Law), (Ball State Univ.), (Univ. of Southern Ind.), (Wabash Coll.) (Union Coll.), (Marian Coll.), (American Univ.), (Ind. Univ.), (Suffolk Univ.), (Ind. State Univ.), (Anderson Univ.), (Franklin Coll.), (Shenandoah Univ.); Defense Intelligence Agency Medallion 1987, CIA Medallion 1988, Indiana Univ. Inst. for Advanced Study Distinguished Citizen Fellow 1994, Indiana Univ. Pres.'s Medal for Excellence 1996, Center for Nat. Policy Edmund S. Muskie Distinguished Public Service Award 1997, Paul H. Nitze Award for Distinguished Authority on Nat. Security Affairs 1999, American Political Science Asscn Hubert H. Humphrey Award 1998, American Bar Asscn CEELI Award 1998, Center for Civic Educ. Civitas Award 1998, Dept of Defense Medal for Distinguished Public Service 1998. *Publication:* Without Precedent: The Inside Story of the 9/11 Commission (with Thomas H. Kean) 2006. *Address:* Woodrow Wilson International Center for Scholars (WWIC), One Woodrow Wilson Plaza, 1300 Pennsylvania Avenue, NW, Washington, DC 20004-3027, USA (office). *Telephone:* (202) 691-4000 (office). *Fax:* (202) 691-4001 (office). *E-mail:* director@wwic.si.edu (office). *Website:* www.wilsoncenter.org (office).

HAMM, Taik-young, MA, PhD; South Korean research institute director and academic; *Director of International Affairs, Institute for Far Eastern Studies, Kyungnam University;* b. 9 June 1950, Seoul; m.; one s. *Education:* Seoul Nat. Univ., Univ. of Mich., USA. *Career:* Dir of Int. Affairs, Inst. for Far Eastern Studies, Kyungnam Univ. 1988–, Prof., Grad. School of N Korean Studies 1988–; Sec.-Gen. Korean Council of Area Studies 1998–99; Assoc

Ed. Korea and World Affairs 1988–98, Ed. 1999–2001; Ed. Asian Perspective 2001–; Exec. Sec. Korean Asscn of Int. Studies 1975–78, mem. Research Cttee 1989–90, mem. Bd and Dir of Research 1997, Vice-Pres. 2002–; mem. Bd Korean Council for the Study of Socialist Systems 1990–92, Korean Political Science Asscn 2000–; Fulbright-Hayes Grant 1979–84, Academic Award for Best Publ., Korean Asscn of Int. Studies 1998. *Publications:* The Political Economy of National Security 1998, Arming the Two Koreas: State, Capital and Military Power 1999; articles in scholarly journals. *Address:* Institute for Far Eastern Studies, Kyungnam University, 28–42 Samchung-dong, Chongro-ku, Seoul 110-230, Republic of Korea (office). *Telephone:* (2) 3700-0700 (office). *Fax:* (2) 3700-0707 (office). *E-mail:* hammty@kyungnam.ac.kr (office). *Website:* ifes.kyungnam.ac.kr (office).

HAMMARBERG, Thomas; Swedish journalist and international organisation official; *Commissioner for Human Rights, Council of Europe;* b. 1942, Örnsköldsvik; m. Alfhild Petrén; one c. *Education:* Stockholm School of Econs. *Career:* Foreign Ed. Expressen (daily newspaper) 1973–76; Foreign Corresp., Swedish Broadcasting 1976–79; Chair. Int. Exec. Cttee, Amnesty Int. 1976–79, Sec.-Gen. 1980–86; Sec.-Gen. Save the Children, Sweden 1986–92; Special Adviser to Swedish Int. Devt Agency (SIDA) 1993–94; Amb. and Special Adviser to Swedish Govt on Humanitarian Affairs 1994–2002; UN Sec.-Gen.'s Special Rep. for Human Rights in Cambodia 1996–2000; Regional Adviser for Europe, Cen. Asia and the Caucasus to UN High Commr for Human Rights 2001–03; Sec.-Gen. Olof Palme Int. Centre 2002–05; Commr for Human Rights, Council of Europe 2006–; Chair. Tech. Advisory Cttee, UN Cttee on the Impact on Children of Armed Conflict 1994–96; mem. Swedish UNESCO Nat. Cttee 1977–80, Swedish UNICEF Cttee 1986–90, Swedish Comm. on Int. Law 1988–92, Children's Rights Advisory Council, UNICEF Innocenti Centre 1992–95; mem. UN Cttee on the Rights of the Child 1992–97, Vice-Chair. 1994–97. *Address:* Office of the Commissioner for Human Rights, Council of Europe, 67075 Strasbourg Cedex, France (office). *Telephone:* (3) 88-41-34-21 (office). *Fax:* (3) 90-21-50-53 (office). *E-mail:* commissioner@coe.int (office). *Website:* www.coe.int (office).

HAMMOND, Aleqa; Greenlandic politician; *Minister for Finance and Foreign Affairs;* b. 23 Sept. 1965, Narsaq. *Education:* in Ellekilde, Denmark, Arctic Coll., Iqaluit. *Career:* Regional Co-ordinator for Greenland Tourism, Diskobugten 1993–95; Information Officer, Landsstyre Secr. 1995–96; worked for Nuuk Tourism 1996–99; Commr Inuit Circumpolar Conf. 1999–2003; Culture Co-ordinator Arctic Winter Games 2002; worked in Tourism and Culture, Sulisartut Høsjkoliat, Qaqortoq 2002–03; Head of Tourism, Qaqortoq 2004–05; mem. Parl. for the Social Democratic Siumut (Forward) party 2005–; Minister for Family Affairs and Justice 2005–07, for Finance and Foreign Affairs 2007–. *Address:* Grønlands Hjemmestyre (Greenland Home Rule Government), POB 1015, 3900 Nuuk, Greenland (office). *Telephone:* 345000 (office). *Fax:* 325002 (office). *E-mail:* homerule@gh.gl (office). *Website:* www.nanoq.gl (office).

HAMMOUD, Mahmoud, BA, LLB; Lebanese politician and diplomatist; b. 1935. *Education:* Lebanese Univ. *Career:* fmr secondary school teacher; fmr Amb. to UAE, FRG, Russia and Finland; Amb. to UK 1990–99; Dir-Gen. State Econ. and Social Council 2000–; Minister of Foreign Affairs and Emigrants 2001–03, 2004–05, of Defence 2003–04. *Address:* c/o Ministry of Foreign Affairs and Emigrants, rue Sursock, Achrafieh, Beirut, Lebanon (office).

HAMRE, John J., BA, PhD; American research institute director; *President and CEO, Center for Strategic and International Studies; Education:* Augustana Coll., Harvard Divinity School, Johns Hopkins Univ. *Career:* served in Congressional Budget Office then Deputy Asst Dir for nat. security and int. affairs 1978–84; staff mem. Senate Armed Services Cttee 1984–93; Under-Sec. of Defense/Comptroller 1993–97, Deputy Sec. of Defense 1997–1999; Pres. and CEO Center for Strategic and Int. Studies 2000–. *Address:* Center for Strategic and International Studies, 1800 K Street, NW, Washington, DC 20006, USA (office). *Telephone:* (202) 775-3227 (office). *Fax:* (202) 775-3199 (office). *E-mail:* jhamre@csis.org (office). *Website:* www.csis.org (office).

HAMUD, Muhammad Ali; Somali politician; *Minister of Finance and Planning; Career:* Minister for Foreign Affairs and Int. Co-operation 2007–08, of Finance and Planning 2008–. *Address:* Ministry of Finance and Planning, Mogadishu, Somalia (office).

HAMŽÍK, Pavol, JUDr; Slovak politician, diplomatist and university lecturer; b. 20 Aug. 1954, Trenčín; m. Dagmar Hamžíková (née Kiššová) 1976; two d. *Education:* Komensky Univ., Bratislava, Diplomatic Acad., Moscow.

Career: lawyer 1978–84; joined Czechoslovak Foreign Ministry 1984; Consul in Copenhagen 1985–89; studied at Diplomatic Acad., Moscow 1989–91; Vice-Chair. del. to int. disarmament negotiations, Vienna 1991; mem. del. to CSCE 1991–92, Pres. CSCE Steering Group on crisis in Yugoslavia 1992, head Slovak del. to CSCE 1993, head Slovak Perm. Mission to CSCE 1993–94; Slovak Amb. to Germany 1994–96; Foreign Minister 1996–97; f. Party of Civic Understanding (SOP) 1998, Chair. 1999–2003; MP 1998–2002, mem. Defence and Security Cttee 2001–02; Vice Prime Minister 1998–2001; Deputy of Slovakia in European Convention; Lecturer, mem. Scientific Bd, Faculty of Political Sciences and Int. Relations, Matej Bell Univ. 1997–; Golden Biatec, Informal Economic Forum 2000.
Address: Svätoplukova 1, 82109 Bratislava (office); Žilinská 1, 81105 Bratislava, Slovak Republic (home). *Telephone:* (2) 5564-5893 (office); (2) 9079-09011 (home). *Fax:* (2) 5556-6990 (office). *E-mail:* intercons@stonline .sk (office).

HAN, Myong-sook, BA, MA; South Korean politician; b. 24 March 1944. *Education:* Ewha Womans Univ., Seoul. *Career:* mem. staff, Korea Christian Acad. 1974–79; jailed as a prisoner of conscience, Christian Acad. Case 1979–81; Lecturer, Dept of Women's Studies, Ewha Womans University 1986–97, Visiting Researcher, Asian Center for Women's Studies 1996–2003; Lecturer, Dept of Women's Studies, Sungsim Womans Univ. 1988–94; Chair. of Special Cttee on Revision of Family Law, Korea Women's Asscns United Jan.–Dec. 1989, Co-rep. 1993–96; Pres. Korean Womenlink 1990–94; Chief Dir Korea Inst. for Environmental and Social Policies 1992; fmr Head, Presidential Comm. on Women's Affairs; mem. Nat. Ass. 2000–01, 2004–, mem. Unification, Foreign Affairs and Trade Cttee; Minister of Gender Equality 2001–03, of the Environment 2003–04; Prime Minister (first woman) 2006–07 (resgnd); Pres. Korean Parliamentary League on Children, Population and Environment 2004–06, Korea-Singapore Parliamentarians' Friendship Asscn June 2004; Pres. Exec. Cttee Asia-Pacific Parliamentarians' Conf. on Environment and Devt 2004–06; Vice-Pres. Korea–Japan Parl. League 2006–; mem. Exec. Cttee Seoul and Pyungyang Symposium Peace of Asian and Women's Role 1992–96; Co-rep., Viewers Alliance for Fair Broadcasting Policy Advisor 1993–94, Cttee for Interchange and Cooperation, Ministry of Unification 1993–94, Citizens' Asscn for Broadcasting Reform 1994–95; mem. Environmental Reservation Cttee, Ministry of Environment 1993–95, Anti-Corruption Cttee, Bd of Audit and Inspection 1993–95; mem. Uri Party, mem. Cen. Standing Cttee April–Nov. 2005, Nat. Ass. Environment and Labour Cttee 2006–; presidential cand. 2007; Civil Merit Medal 1998; Order of Service Merit Medal (Blue Stripes) 2005; ranked 68th by Forbes magazine amongst 100 Most Powerful Women 2006.
Address: c/o Office of the Prime Minister, 77, Sejong-no, Jongno-gu, Seoul, Republic of Korea (office).

HAN, Seung-soo, PhD; South Korean politician, economist, diplomatist and international organization official; *Prime Minister;* b. 28 Dec. 1936, Chunchon, Kangwon Prov.; m. Hong Soja; two c. *Education:* Yonsei Univ., Seoul Nat. Univ. and Univ. of York, UK. *Career:* taught econs at Univ. of York, UK 1965–68, Univ. of Cambridge 1968–70; Prof. of Econs, Seoul Nat. Univ. 1970–88; Sr Fulbright Scholar, Dept of Econs, Harvard Univ. 1985–86; Visiting Prof., Univ. of Tokyo 1986–87; fmr Distinguished Visiting Prof., Yonsei Univ.; served as advisor to Bank of Korea, Korea Export–Import Bank, Korea Industrial Bank, Korea Chamber of Commerce and Industry, Fed. of Korea Industries and Korea Int. Trade Asscn; consultant to World Bank and UN Econ. Comm. for Asia and the Pacific (ESCAP), seconded by World Bank as Financial Adviser to Govt of Jordan 1974–76; Pres. Korea Int. Econ. Asscn 1983–84; first Chair. Korea Trade Commr 1987–88; elected mem. of Nat. Ass., Repub. of Korea 1988–2004; Minister of Trade and Industry 1988–90; Amb. to USA 1993–94; Chair. Council of the Repub. of Korea Group of the Inter-Parl. Union (IPU); Chief of Staff to Pres. of Repub. of Korea 1994–95; Deputy Prime Minister and Minister of Finance and Economy 1996–97; Minister of Foreign Affairs and Trade 2001–02; Pres. 56th Session of UN Gen. Ass. 2001–02; Pres. Korean Water Forum 2004; UN Special Envoy for Climate Change 2007–08; Prime Minister of Repub. of Korea 2008–; f. Korean Acad. of Industrial Tech. (KAITEC) 1989; Pres. Korea–Britain Soc., Korea–UK Forum for the Future, Alumni Asscn of the Grad. School of Public Admin of Seoul Nat. Univ.; mem. Royal Econ. Soc., Korean Econ. Asscn, Int. Inst. of Public Finance, Seoul Forum for Int. Affairs, Korean Council on Foreign Relations, Korean Soc. for Future Studies, Korean Asscn of Public Admin, Bretton Woods Club; Hon. Prof., Univ. of York, Hon. DUniv (York) 1997; Order of Public Service Merit (First Class, Blue Stripes), Order of Industrial Merit (Bronze Tower), Order of Nat. Security Merit (Cheonsu Medal); Sixth European Communities Prize 1971, Columbia Law School/Parker School Award for Distinguished Int. Service 1997. *Publications include:* Taxes in Britain and the EEC: The Problem of Harmonization (jtly) 1968, Britain and the Common Market (jtly) 1971,

The Growth and Function of the European Budget 1971, The Health of Nations 1985; numerous articles in learned journals and press commentaries in both Korean and English.
Address: Office of the Prime Minister, 77, Sejong-no, Jongno-gu, Seoul, South Korea (office). *Telephone:* (2) 737-0094 (office). *Fax:* (2) 739-5830 (office). *E-mail:* m-opm@opm.go.kr (office). *Website:* www.opm.go.kr (office).

HAN, Sung-joo, PhD; South Korean academic and fmr politician; *President, Seoul Forum for International Affairs;* b. 1940. *Education:* Seoul Nat. Univ. and Univ. of California, Berkeley. *Career:* taught at CUNY, New York 1970–78, Columbia Univ., New York 1986–87, Stanford Univ., Calif. 1992; Distinguished Fellow, Rockefeller Brothers Fund 1986–87; fmr Vice-Chair. Int. Political Science Asscn; int. columnist, Newsweek 1984–93; Adviser to Govt on foreign affairs, nat. defence and unification since late 1970s; Minister of Foreign Affairs 1993–95; Prof. of Political Science and Pres. Ilmin Int. Relations Inst., Korea Univ. 1995–, fmr Acting Pres. Korea Univ.; UN Sec.-Gen.'s Special Rep. for Cyprus 1996–97; mem. UN Inquiry Comm. on the 1994 Genocide in Rwanda 1999; Amb. to USA 2003–05; Freeman Foundation Visiting Prof. in Asian Affairs, Claremont McKenna Coll., USA 2006; Pres. Seoul Forum for Int. Affairs; Deputy Chair. for Asia Pacific, Trilateral Comm.; Chair. East Asia Vision Group 2000–01; Co-Chair. Council for Security Co-operation in the Asia-Pacific; mem. Int. Panel on Democracy and Devt, Int. Bd of Govs The Peres Center for Peace; fmr mem. Bd Asia Pacific Foundation of Canada, Hon. Advisers of New Zealand's Asia 2000. *Publications include:* The Failure of Democracy in South Korea 1974, The US-South Korean Alliance 1983, The Division and Unification of Korea 1992, Choice for Korea in a World in Transition 1992, Korean Diplomacy in an Era of Globalization 1995, Korea in a Changing World 1995, Changing Values in Asia: Their Impact on Governance and Development (ed.).
Address: Ilmin International Research Institute, Korea University, 5th Floor, Inchon Memorial Building, 5-1 Anam-dong, Seongbuk-Gu, Seoul 136-701, Korea (office). *Telephone:* (2) 923-2416/7 (office). *Fax:* (2) 927-5265 (office). *E-mail:* irikor@unitel.co.kr (office). *Website:* www.korea.ac .kr/~ilmin (office).

HANFARE, Kadafo Mohammed; Ethiopian diplomatist; *Ambassador to Sudan;* m. *Career:* worked with UNDP, Lagos, Nigeria, fmr Dean of Africa Group in Nigeria, Amb. to Sudan 2002–.
Address: Embassy of Ethiopia, nr Farouq Cemetary, Plot No. 04, Block 384BC PO Box 844, Khartoum South, Sudan (office). *Telephone:* (1) 83471379 (office). *Fax:* (1) 83471141 (office). *E-mail:* eekrt@hotmail.com (office).

HANIYA, Ismail Abd as-Salam Ahmad, BA; Palestinian politician; b. 1962, Gaza. *Education:* Islamic Univ. of Gaza. *Career:* jailed by Israelis for three years, released 1992 and deported to Lebanon; returned to Gaza 1993; Dean, Islamic Univ. of Gaza 1993–97; Head, Office of Sheikh Ahmed Yassin (Hamas spiritual leader) 1997–2004; Prime Minister, Palestinian Nat. Authority (Hamas) 2006–07 (resgnd), March–June 2007 (under unity govt), also Minister of the Interior May–June 2007.
Address: c/o Islamic Resistance Movement (Hamas: Harakat al-Muqawama al-Islamiyya), Gaza Palestinian Autonomous Areas.

HANNAY OF CHISWICK, Baron (Life Peer), cr. 2001, of Chiswick, of Bedford Park in the London Borough of Ealing; **David Hugh Alexander Hannay,** GCMG, CH, MA; British diplomatist; b. 28 Sept. 1935, London; m. Gillian Rosemary Rex 1961; four s. *Education:* Craigflower School, Torryburn, Fife, Scotland, Winchester Coll. and New Coll. Oxford. *Career:* Second Lt, King's Royal Irish Hussars 1954–56; Persian language student, Foreign Office and British Embassy, Tehran 1959–61; Oriental Sec., British Embassy, Kabul 1961–63; Second Sec., Eastern Dept, Foreign Office, London 1963–65; Second, then First Sec., UK Del. to EC, Brussels 1965–70, First Sec. UK Negotiating Team 1970–72; Chef de Cabinet to Sir Christopher Soames, Vice-Pres. of the EC Comm. 1973–77; Counsellor, Head of Energy, Science and Space Dept, FCO, London 1977–79, Counsellor, Head of Middle East Dept 1979, Asst Under-Sec. of State (EC) 1979–84; Minister, Embassy in Washington, DC 1984–85; UK Perm. Rep. to EC 1985–90, to UN 1990–95; British Govt Special Rep. for Cyprus 1996–2003; Prime Minister's Personal Envoy to Turkey and EU Special Rep. for Cyprus 1998; Life Peer (Ind.), House of Lords 2001–; mem. UN Sec. Gen.'s High Level Panel on Threats, Challenges and Change 2003–04, House of Lords EU Select Cttee 2002–06, House of Lords Local Governmental Orgs Cttee 2007–; Chair. Int. Advisory Bd EDHEC 2003–, UN Asscn of the UK 2006–; Vice-Chair. All Party Parl. Group on UN 2005–, on Europe 2006–; Dir (non-exec.) Chime Communications 1996–2006, Aegis 2000–03; mem. Court and Council, Univ. of Birmingham 1998–2006, Pro-Chancellor 2001–06; mem. Council of Britain in Europe 1999–2005, Bd Salzburg Seminar 2002–05, TANGGUH Int. Advisory

Panel 2002–, Advisory Bd Judge Business Schools 2004; Gov. Ditchley Foundation 2005–; Hon. Fellow, New Coll. Oxford; Hon. DLitt (Birmingham). *Publication:* Britain's Entry into the European Community: Report on the Negotiations (ed.) 1970–72, Cyprus: The Search for a Solution 2004, A More Secure World: Our Shared Responsibility (UN Panel Report) 2004, New World Disorder: The UN After the Cold War 2008.
Address: 3 The Orchard, London, W4 1JZ, England (home). *Telephone:* (20) 8987-9012 (home). *Fax:* (20) 8987-9012 (home).

HANNESSON, Hjalmar W.; Icelandic diplomatist; *Permanent Representative, United Nations;* m. Anna Hannesson. *Career:* Dir of Political Affairs, Ministry of Foreign Affairs, Reykjavik 1999; Amb. to Canada –2003; currently Perm. Rep. to UN, New York.
Address: Permanent Mission of Iceland to the UN, 800 Third Avenue, 36th Floor, New York, NY 10022, USA (office). *Telephone:* (212) 593-2700 (office). *Fax:* (212) 593-6269 (office). *E-mail:* icecon.ny@utn.stjr.is (office). *Website:* brunnur.stjr.is/embassy/newyork.nsf/pages/index.html (office).

HANNUM, Hurst, AB, JD; American lawyer and academic; *Professor of International Law, The Fletcher School, Tufts University; Education:* Univ. of California, Berkeley. *Career:* mem. DC and Calif. Bars; legal adviser, Northern Ireland Civil Rights Asscn, Belfast 1972–75; in pvt. civil practice, Calif. 1975–77; attorney, Inst. of Int. Law and Econ. Devt, Washington, DC 1977–79; Exec. Dir Procedural Aspects of Int. Law Inst., Washington, DC 1979–89; Jennings Randolph Peace Fellow, US Inst. of Peace, Washington, DC 1989–90; Prof. of Int. Law, The Fletcher School of Law and Diplomacy, Tufts Univ. 1990–, Assoc. Prof. 1990–96, Academic Dean 1995–96; Co-Dir Center for Human Rights and Conflict Resolution 2000–; Sir YK Pao Prof. of Public Law, Univ. of Hong Kong 2006–; fmr Adjunct Prof., Harvard Law School, American Univ. Coll. of Law, Univ. of Virginia Law School; Visiting Sr Scholar, Woodruff Chair in Int. Law, Univ. of Georgia School of Law 1997; consultant, UN Office of the High Commr for Human Rights, Int. Center on Alcohol Policies 1996–, UN Dept of Political Affairs on East Timor 1998–99, on Westeran Sahara 2002–04, Brcko Law Review Comm. 1999, Govt of Faroe Islands 1999, Henry Dunant Centre for Humanitarian Dialogue; fmr Pres. Survival International USA; mem. Advisory Bd UN Asscn of Greater Boston, Physicians for Human Rights, Boston, Int. Service for Human Rights, Geneva; mem. Editorial Bd Human Rights Quarterly, Human Rights Law Review; Allan MacLeod Cormack Award, Tufts Univ. 1995, Outstanding Faculty Achievement, Tufts Univ. 2001. *Publications:* The Fine Wines of California (co-author) 1971, Brandies and Liqueurs of the World (co-author) 1976, The Right to Leave and Return in International Law and Practice 1987, New Directions in Human Rights (co-ed.) 1989, Documents on Autonomy and Minority Rights 1993, US Ratification of the International Covenants on Human Rights (co-ed.) 1993, International Human Rights: Problems of Law, Policy and Practice (co-author) 1995, (fourth edn) 2006, Autonomy, Sovereignty and Self-Determination: The Accommodation of Conflicting Rights (revised edn) 1996, Guide to International Human Rights Practice (ed., fourth edn) 2001, Negotiating Self-Determination (co-ed.) 2006; Gen. Ed. multi-volume series of books on Universal Declaration of Human Rights 1999–; numerous articles in professional publs.
Address: The Fletcher School of Law and Diplomacy, Tufts University, Medford, MA 02155, USA (office). *Telephone:* (617) 627-2244 (office). *Fax:* (617) 627-3712 (office). *E-mail:* hurst.hannum@tufts.edu (office). *Website:* fletcher.tufts.edu (office).

HANS-ADAM II, HSH Prince of Liechtenstein (Duke of Troppau and Jägerndorf, Count of Rietberg); b. 14 Feb. 1945, Zürich, Switzerland; m. Countess Marie Aglaë Kinsky von Wchinitz und Tettau 1967; three s. (including Hereditary Prince Alois Philipp Maria) one d. *Education:* Schottengymnasium, Vienna, School of Econs and Social Sciences, St Gallen, Switzerland. *Career:* Chief Exec. of Prince of Liechtenstein Foundation 1970–84; took over exec. authority of Liechtenstein Aug. 1984; transferred exec. power to Hereditary Prince Alois Aug. 2004.
Address: Schloss Vaduz, 9490 Vaduz, Principality of Liechtenstein. *E-mail:* office@fuerstenhaus.li (office). *Website:* www.fuerstenhaus.li.

HANSEN, Peter, Cand.Scient.pol; Danish diplomatist and international organization official; *Diplomat-in-Residence, Institute of International Humanitarian Affairs, Fordham University;* b. 2 June 1941, Åalborg; m.; one s. two d. *Education:* Århus Univ. *Career:* Assoc. Prof. Aarhus Univ. 1966–68, Chair. Dept of Political Science 1968–70, Sr Research Fellow 1970–74; Prof. of Int. Relations, Odense Univ.; Adviser, Ministry of Foreign Affairs; Chair. UN Consultative Cttee on Substantive Questions of the Admin. Cttee on Co-ordination and of the Appointment and Promotion Bd, mem. UN Programme Budgeting Bd, Asst Sec.-Gen. Programme Planning and Co-ordination 1978–85; Asst Sec.-Gen. and

Exec. Dir UN Centre on Transnational Corpns 1985–92; Rep. of UN Sec.-Gen. to Food Aid and Policies Cttee, World Food Programme; Team Leader, UN Operation in Somalia 1992; Exec. Dir Comm. on Global Governance, Geneva, Switzerland 1992–94; Special Rep. of Sec.-Gen. ad hoc Liaison Cttee in support of Middle East peace process 1993–; currently Diplomat-in-Residence, Fordham Univ., New York; Under-Sec.-Gen. for Humanitarian Affairs and UN Emergency Relief Co-ordinator, New York, USA 1994–96; Commr-Gen. UNRWA 1996–2005; King Hussein Humanitarian Leadership Prize, King Hussein Foundation 2001, Order of Independence of First Degree (UAE) 2004, Star of Bethlehem Order (Palestine) 2004. *Publications:* World Politics 1969, International Organization 1975.
Address: Institute of International Humanitarian Affairs, Fordham University, Lincoln Center, 113 West 60th Street, LL1120A, NY 10023, USA (office). *Telephone:* (212) 636-6294 (office). *Fax:* (212) 636-7060 (office). *E-mail:* peter_hansen1941@hotmail.com (home). *Website:* www.fordham.edu/iiha (office).

HANSFORD, Dorsey; Liberian diplomatist; *Chargé d'affaires in UK;* m. Beatrice Hansford. *Career:* fmr local chair. for Charles Taylor's Nat. Patriotic Front of Liberia in USA; apptd Consul-Gen., New York 2001; Chargé d'affaires a.i. in UK 2005–.
Address: Embassy of Liberia, 23 Fitzroy Square, London, W1T 6EW, England (office). *Telephone:* (20) 7388-5489 (office). *Fax:* (20) 7380-1593 (office). *E-mail:* info@embassyofliberia.org.uk (office). *Website:* www.embassyofliberia.org.uk (office).

HANSON, Margus, PhD; Estonian politician and university professor; b. 6 Jan. 1958, Tartu; m.; two s. one d. *Education:* Tartu Secondary School No. 2, Leningrad Inst. of Financial Economy, Tartu State Univ. *Career:* Engineer, Lab. of Educational Sociology, Tartu Univ. 1981–84, Asst to Chair of Finance and Credit 1984–87, Sr Lecturer 1990–91, Lecturer and Assoc. Prof. of Public Finance, Inst. of Econ. Policy and Public Economy 1992–94; Chair. Bd Estonian Commercial Bank of Industry and Construction 1995–96; Head of Tartu Br., Tallinn Bank 1996–97; mem. Tartu City Council 1996, 1999, 2002; Deputy Mayor of Tartu 1997–2003; mem. Riigikogu (Parl.) 2003–, mem. Nat. Defence Cttee; Minister of Defence 2003–04 (resgnd after admitting that confidential documents had been stolen from his home); professional training courses with Bank of Finland 1990–91, World Bank and Soros Foundation 1992, Austrian Bankers Club 1995, Estonian Banking Asscn, Barcelona 1996; mem. Eesti Reformierakond (Estonian Reform Party), Tartu Rotary Club.
Address: Riigikogu, Lossi plats 1A, 15165 Tallinn, Estonia (office). *Telephone:* 631-6572 (office). *Fax:* 631-6334 (office). *E-mail:* margus.hanson@riigikogu.ee (office). *Website:* www.riigikogu.ee (office).

HAOMAE, William Ni'i; Solomon Islands politician; *Minister of Foreign Affairs, External Trade and Immigration;* b. 26 Nov. 1960, Mou Village, Small Malaita; m. Filistas T. Haomae; two s. two d. *Education:* East-West Centre, Honolulu. *Career:* early govt posts include Information Officer, Prime Minister's Office, Press Sec. to the Prime Minister, Foreign Affairs Information Officer, Ministry of Foreign Affairs, Dir of Information Dept, Prime Minister's Office; mem. Parl. from Small Malaita, Malaita Prov. 1993–, mem. Parl. House Cttee July–Dec. 2007, Foreign Relations Cttee 2006–07; Minister for Culture, Tourism and Aviation 1994–97; Minister for Police and Justice 2000–01; Deputy Prime Minister and Caretaker Minister for Nat. Unity, Reconciliation and Peace Aug.–Dec. 2001; Minister for Police and National Security April–May 2006; Minister of Foreign Affairs, External Trade and Immigration 2007–.
Address: Ministry of Foreign Affairs, External Trade and Tourism, PO Box G26, Honiara, Solomon Islands (office). *Telephone:* 28612 (office). *Fax:* 20352 (office). *E-mail:* psforeign@pmc.gov.sb (office). *Website:* www.parliament.gov.sb (office).

HAQ, Ameerah, MA, MBA; Bangladeshi international organization official; *Deputy Special Representative of the Secretary-General for Sudan, United Nations; Education:* Western Coll., Oxford, Ohio, Columbia Univ., New York Univ., USA. *Career:* Jr Professional Officer, Jakarta 1976; UNDP Asst Resident Rep., Afghanistan 1978, Coordinator of Round Table Meetings and Area Officer, Regional Bureau for Asia and the Pacific, Chief UNIFEM Asia and the Pacific Unit 1987–88, UN Resident Coordinator and UNDP Resident Rep., Laos 1991–94, Malaysia 1994–97, Assoc. Dir UN Devt Group Office –2002, Deputy Asst Admin. and Deputy Dir, UNDP Bureau for Crisis Prevention and Recovery 2002–04, Deputy Special Rep. of the UN Sec.-Gen. in Afghanistan, responsible for Recovery and Reconstruction, UN Assistance Mission for Afghanistan (UNAMA), also UN Resident Coordinator, Humanitarian Coordinator, UNDP Resident Rep. 2004–07; Deputy Special Rep. of the UN Sec.-Gen. for Sudan, also UN Resident Co-ordinator and Humanitarian Co-ordinator 2007–.

Address: United Nations Assistance Mission for Sudan (UNMIS), Ebeid Khatim Street, PO Box 69, Khartoum, 11111, Sudan (office). *Telephone:* (187) 086000 (office). *Fax:* (917) 3673523 (office). *Website:* www.unmis.org (office).

HAQQANI, Husain, BA, MA; Pakistani journalist and diplomatist; *Ambassador to USA;* b. 1 July 1956, Karachi. *Education:* Univ. of Karachi. *Career:* started career as a journalist, wrote numerous articles on nat. and int. politics published by Pakistan's leading newspapers Jang (Urdu) and Dawn (English); worked in Hong Kong as East Asian Corresp. for London-based Arabia – the Islamic World Review 1980–84; wrote extensively on Muslims in China and East Asia and Islamic political movts in aftermath of Iranian Revolution of 1979; Pakistan and Afghanistan Corresp. for Far Eastern Economic Review 1984–88; covered Pakistani politics, India-Pakistan relations and war in Afghanistan; contributed to Voice of America radio 1984–86; syndicated columnist for The Indian Express, Gulf News, Oman Tribune, Daily Star (Bangladesh) and The Nation (Pakistani newspaper); Special Asst to Chief Minister, Punjab 1988–90; served as main Opposition Spokesman, represented Opposition at int. forums, including in negotiations with US Govt; organized parl. election campaign for IJI alliance led by Nawaz Sharif 1988; Special Asst to Prime Minister Ghulam Mustafa Jatoi 1990, Special Asst and Prin. Spokesman of Prime Minister Nawaz Sharif 1990–92, represented Prime Minister in talks with US Govt over imposition of sanctions in retaliation for Pakistan's nuclear programme; Amb. to Sri Lanka 1992–93; worked in parl. election campaign for Peoples Democratic Front led by Mohtarma Benazir Bhutto 1993, Spokesman for Prime Minister Benazir Bhutto with rank of Minister of State, and Fed. Sec. for Information and Broadcasting 1993–95; Chair. House Building Finance Corpn 1995–96; Assoc. Prof. for Int. Relations, Boston Univ. 2004–; Co-Chair. Project on Islam and Democracy, Hudson Inst., Washington, DC 2004–; Ed. Current Trends in Islamists Ideology (journal) 2004–; Visiting Scholar, Carnegie Endowment for Int. Peace, Washington DC 2002–05; Professional Lecturer, School of Advanced Int. Studies, Johns Hopkins Univ., Washington, DC 2003–04; Amb. to USA 2008–; mem. South Asia Council, Asscn of Asian Studies 2007. *Publications:* Pakistan Between Mosque and Military 2005; numerous book chapters and articles and more than 390 op-ed articles in newspapers and magazines 2000–; articles have been published in The Wall Street Journal, The New York Times, Boston Globe, Financial Times, International Herald Tribune, South China Morning Port, Indian Express, The Hindu, Toronto Globe and Mail, The Ottawa Citizen, Arab News, The New Republic, Gulf News and Le Monde. *Address:* Embassy of Pakistan, 3517 International Court, NW, Washington, DC 20008, USA (office). *Telephone:* (202) 243-6500 (exts 2000/2001) (office). *Fax:* (202) 387-0484 (office). *E-mail:* ambassador@ embassyofpakistanusa.org (office). *Website:* www.embassyofpakistanusa .org (office).

HARABIN, Štefan, DJur; Slovak judge and politician; *Deputy Prime Minister and Minister of Justice;* b. 4 May 1957, Ľubica; m.; four c. *Education:* Univ. of Pavel Jozef Šafárik, Košice. *Career:* Judge, Dist Court, Poprad 1983–90, Regional Court, Košice 1990–91; Judge of the Supreme Court 1991–98, Pres. 1998–2003, Chair. Criminal Panel 2003–06; Head of Penal Dept, Section of Justice Admin., Ministry of Justice, Slovak Repub. 1991–92; Pres. of Senate and Penal Bd 1996–98; Pres. Judicial Council 2002–03; Deputy Prime Minister and Minister of Justice 2006–. *Address:* Ministry of Justice, Župné nám. 13, 813 11 Bratislava, Slovakia (office). *Telephone:* (2) 5935-3504 (office). *Fax:* (2) 5935-3601 (office). *E-mail:* minister@justice.sk (office). *Website:* www.justice.gov.sk (office).

HARALD V, HM The King of Norway; b. 21 Feb. 1937, Skaugum; m. Sonja Haraldsen 1968 (now HM Queen Sonja); one s. (HRH Crown Prince Haakon) one d. *Education:* Oslo Katedralskole, Cavalry Officers' Cand. School, Mil. Acad. and Balliol Coll. Oxford. *Career:* lived in Washington, DC 1940–45; has participated in many int. sailing competitions representing Norway at Olympic Games several times; undertook frequent official visits abroad while Crown Prince; succeeded his father, King Olav V 17 Jan. 1991. *Address:* Royal Palace, 0010 Oslo, Norway. *Telephone:* 22-04-87-00. *Website:* www.kongehuset.no.

HARASZTI, Miklós; Hungarian writer, journalist, human rights advocate, international organization executive and academic; *Representative on Freedom of the Media, Organization for Security and Co-operation in Europe;* b. 1945, Jerusalem, Israel. *Education:* Budapest Univ. *Career:* co-f. Hungarian Democratic Opposition Movt 1976; Ed. samizdat periodical Beszélo 1980; participated in roundtable negotiations on transition to free elections 1989; mem. Hungarian Parl. 1990–94; lectured on democratization and media politics at numerous univs 1990s; Rep. on Freedom of the Media, OSCE 2004–; Dr hc (Northwestern Univ., USA) 1996. *Publications:*

A Worker in a Worker's State, The Velvet Prison (both translated into several languages); several essays have been published in The New York Times and The Washington Post. *Address:* Office of the OSCE Representative on Freedom of the Media, Kärntner Ring 5–7, Top 14, 2. DG, 1010 Vienna, Austria (office). *Telephone:* (1) 512-21-450 (office). *Fax:* (1) 512-21-459 (office). *E-mail:* pm-fom@osce.org (office). *Website:* www.osce.org/fom (office).

HARBINSON, Stuart; Hong Kong international organization official; *Director, Office of the Director General, World Trade Organization; Career:* Perm. Rep. to WTO, Chair. Gen. Council 2001–02, Chair. Special Sessions of WTO Cttee on Agric. 2002-03; currently Dir, Office of the Dir-Gen 2002–; Chair. Working Party on Tonga accession. *Address:* World Trade Organization, Centre William Rappard, rue de Lausanne 154, 1211 Geneva 21, Switzerland (office). *Telephone:* (22) 7395111 (office). *Fax:* (22) 7314206 (office). *E-mail:* enquiries@wto.org (office). *Website:* www.wto.org (office).

HARCOURT, Geoffrey Colin, AO, PhD, LittD, FASSA; Australian academic; *Emeritus Fellow, Jesus College and Reader Emeritus in the History of Economic Theory, University of Cambridge;* b. 27 June 1931, Melbourne; m. Joan Bartrop 1955; two s. two d. *Education:* Univ. of Melbourne and Univ. of Cambridge, UK. *Career:* Lecturer in Econs, Univ. of Adelaide 1958–62, Sr Lecturer 1962–65, Reader 1965–67, Prof. (Personal Chair) 1967–85, Prof. Emer. 1988–; Lecturer in Econs and Politics, Univ. of Cambridge 1964–66, 1982–90, Reader in the History of Econ. Theory 1990–98, Reader Emer. 1998–, Dir of Studies in Econs and Fellow, Trinity Hall, Cambridge 1964–66, Fellow and Lecturer in Econs, Jesus Coll., Cambridge 1982–98, Fellow Emer. 1998–, Pres. 1988–92; Leverhulme Exchange Fellow, Keio Univ., Tokyo 1969–70; Visiting Fellow, Clare Hall, Cambridge 1972–73; Visiting Prof., Univ. of Toronto, Canada 1977, 1980, Univ. of Melbourne 2002; Visiting Fellow, ANU 1997; Pres. Econ. Soc. of Australia and New Zealand 1974–77; mem. Council Royal Econ. Soc. 1990–95, Life mem. 1998–; Distinguished Fellow, Econ. Soc. of Australia 1996, History of Econs Soc., USA 2004; Academician Acad. of Learned Socs for the Social Sciences (AcSS) 2003; Fellow, Acad. of the Social Sciences in Australia 1971 (exec. cttee mem. 1974–77); Hon. Fellow, Queen's Coll., Melbourne 1998, Sugden Fellow 2002; Hon. Prof., Univ. of NSW 1997, 1999; Hon. mem. European Soc. for the History of Economic Thought 2004; Hon. LittD (De Montfort Univ.) 1997; Hon. DCom (Melbourne) 2003; Hon. Dr rer. pol (Fribourg) 2003; Wellington Burnham Lecturer, Tufts Univ., Medford, Mass 1975, Edward Shann Memorial Lecturer, Univ. of Western Australia 1975, Newcastle Lecturer in Political Economy, Univ. of Newcastle 1977, Acad. Lecturer, Acad. of the Social Sciences in Australia 1978, G. L. Wood Memorial Lecturer, Univ. of Melbourne 1982, John Curtin Memorial Lecturer, ANU 1982, Special Lecturer in Econs, Univ. of Manchester 1984, Lecturer, Nobel Conf. XXII, Gustavus Adolphus Coll., Minn. 1986, Laws Lecturer, Univ. of Tennessee at Knoxville 1991, Donald Horne Lecturer 1992, Sir Halford Cook Lecturer, Queen's Coll., Univ. of Melbourne, Kingsley Martin Memorial Lecturer, Cambridge 1996, Colin Clark Memorial Lecturer, Brisbane 1997, Bernard Hesketh Lecturer, Univ. of Minn., Kansas City 2006. *Publications:* Economic Activity (with P. H. Karmel and R. H. Wallace) 1967, Readings in the Concept and Measurement of Income (ed., with R. H. Parker) 1969 (2nd edn with R. H. Parker and G. Whittington) 1986, Capital and Growth, Selected Readings (ed., with N. F. Laing) 1971, Some Cambridge Controversies in the Theory of Capital 1972, The Microeconomic Foundations of Macroeconomics (ed.) 1977, The Social Science Imperialists, Selected Essays (edited by Prue Kerr) 1982, Keynes and his Contemporaries (ed.) 1985, Controversies in Political Economy, Selected Essays of G. C. Harcourt (edited by Omar Hamouda) 1986, International Monetary Problems and Supply-Side Economics: Essays in Honour of Lorie Tarshis (edited with Jon S. Cohen) 1986, On Political Economists and Modern Political Economy, Selected Essays of G. C. Harcourt (ed. by Claudio Sardoni) 1992, Post-Keynesian Essays in Biography: Portraits of Twentieth Century Political Economists 1993, The Dynamics of the Wealth of Nations. Growth, Distribution and Structural Change: Essays in Honour of Luigi Pasinetti (edited with Mauro Baranzini) 1993, Income and Employment in Theory and Practice. Essays in Memory of Athanasios Asimakopulos (ed. with Alessandro Roncaglia and Robin Rowley) 1994, Capitalism, Socialism and Post-Keynesianism. Selected Essays of G. C. Harcourt 1995, A 'Second Edition' of The General Theory (two vols, co-ed. with P. A. Riach) 1997, 50 Years a Keynesian and Other Essays 2001, Selected Essays on Economic Policy 2001, L'Economie rebelle de Joan Robinson (ed.) 2001, Joan Robinson: Critical Assessments of Leading Economists (five vols, ed. with Prue Kerr) 2002, Editing Economics: Essays in Honour of Mark Perlman (co-ed.) 2002, Capital Theory (3 Vols, ed. with Christopher Bliss and Avi Cohen) 2005, The Structure of Post-Keynesian Economics: The Core Contributions of the Pioneers 2006.

Address: 43 New Square, Cambridge, CB1 1EZ (home); Jesus College, Cambridge, CB5 8BL, England (office). *Telephone:* (1223) 760353 (office). *E-mail:* fellows-secretary@jesus.cam.ac.uk (office); GCH3@cam.ac.uk (home).

HARDIE BOYS, Rt Hon. Sir Michael, GNZM, GCMG, QSO, PC; New Zealand fmr Governor-General and fmr judge; b. 6 Oct. 1931, Wellington; m. Edith Mary Zohrab 1957; two s. two d. *Education:* Wellington Coll., Victoria Univ. of Wellington. *Career:* barrister, solicitor with pvt. practice 1950–80; Councillor then Pres. Wellington Dist Law Soc. 1974–79; Judge High Court 1980–89, Court of Appeal 1989–95; Gov.-Gen. of NZ 1996–2001; mem. Legal Aid Bd (Chair.); Hon. Bencher of Gray's Inn; Hon. Fellow, Wolfson Coll., Cambridge; Hon. LLD (Victoria Univ., Wellington) 1997.
Address: 340A Ngarara Road, Waikanae, Kapiti Coast, Wellington, New Zealand (home).

HARDING, Elizabeth Ya Eli; Gambian civil servant and diplomatist; *High Commissioner to UK. Career:* Sec. Gen. Office of the Pres. and Head of the Civil Service 2006–07; High Commr to UK 2007– (also accred as Amb. to the Holy See 2007–, to Ireland 2008–); Mem. of the Nat. Order of the Repub. of The Gambia (MRG) 2006.
Address: Embassy of The Gambia, 57 Kensington Court, London, W8 5DG, England (office). *Telephone:* (20) 7937-6316 (office). *Fax:* (20) (20) 7937-9095 (office). *E-mail:* gambia@gamhighcom.wanadoo.co.uk (office).

HARDING, Harry, MA, PhD; American academic and consultant; b. Boston; m. Roca Lau Harding; one s. *Education:* Princeton and Stanford Univs. *Career:* mem. Faculty of Political Science, Swarthmore Coll. 1970–71, Stanford Univ. 1971–83; Sr Fellow, Foreign Policy Studies Program, Brookings Inst. 1983–94; Dean, Elliott School of Int. Affairs, George Washington Univ 1995–2005, now Prof. of Int. Affairs and Political Science; fmr Visiting or Adjunct Prof. Univ. of Calif., Berkeley, Univ. of Wash. at Seattle, Georgetown Univ., United Coll. of Chinese Univ. of Hong Kong; Dir Research and Analysis, Eurasia Group 2005–07; Visiting Fellow, Asia Soc. 2007; fmr Pres. Asscn of Professional School of Int. Affairs; fmr Nat. Fellow, Hoover Inst.; fmr Dir E Asia Program, Woodrow Wilson Int. Center for Scholars; Dir Nat. Cttee on US–China Relations, US Cttee of Council for Security Cooperation in Asia Pacific, Atlantic Council of US; mem. Cttee for Int. Security Studies, American Acad. of Arts and Sciences; mem. Council on Foreign Relations, Int. Inst. for Strategic Studies (IISS); fmr Fellow, World Econ. Forum; Trustee Asia Foundation; consultant to numerous multinat. corpns; Walter J. Gores Award for Excellence in Teaching, Stanford Univ. 1975, Masayoshi Ohira Memorial Prize 1986, US Dept of State Distinguished Public Service Award 2002. *Publications:* Organizing China: The Problem of Bureaucracy 1949–1976 (Masayoshi Ohira Memorial Prize 1986) 1981, China's Foreign Relations in the 1980s (Ed.) 1984, China's Second Revolution: Reform after Mao 1987, China and Northeast Asia: The Political Dimension 1988, Sino–American Relations 1945–55: A Joint Reassessment of a Critical Debate (Ed.) 1989, A Fragile Relationship: The United States and China since 1972 1992 (Hon. Mention Best Govt and Political Science Books Asscn of American Publishers 1992), The India–China Relationship: What the United States Needs to Know (Ed.) 2004; articles in policy and scholarly journals.
Address: Elliott School of International Affairs, George Washington University, 1957 E Street, NW, Suite 401, Washington, DC 20052, USA (office). *Telephone:* (202) 994-6241 (office). *Fax:* (202) 994-0335 (office). *E-mail:* hharding@gwu.edu (office). *Website:* www.gwu.edu/~elliott (office).

HARDMAN, John B., MD; American research institute executive and psychiatrist; *Executive Director, Carter Center; Education:* Medical Coll. of Georgia. *Career:* resident, Mayo Clinic 1969–71; Fellow, Child Psychiatry, Emory Univ. Medical School 1971–73, various positions in psychiatry and paediatrics; fmr Medical Dir Peachford Hosp.; Head of Initiative to Reduce Global Tobacco Use, The Carter Center (affiliated to Emory Univ.) 1989–90, Rep. to Tobacco and Health Program, WHO 1990–91, Dir Mental Health Program 1991–93, Assoc. Dir Feb.–Dec. 1992, Exec. Dir Dec. 1992–; currently Chair. Bd Ships of the Sea Museum, Beehive Foundation; fmr Pres. Georgia Psychiatric Physicians Asscn, Georgia Council on Child and Adolescent Psychiatry, Leadership Georgia (also Chair.); fmr Chair. Atlanta Historical Soc.; fmr Dir Nat. Asscn of Pvt. Psychiatric Hosps; currently mem. Mayo Medical Alumni Asscn Bd; fmr mem. Bd The High Museum of Art, Exec. Bd Atlanta Area Council of Boy Scouts of America.
Address: The Carter Center, One Copenhill, 453 Freeway Parkway, Atlanta, GA 30307, USA (office). *Telephone:* (404) 420-5100 (office). *Fax:* (404) 420-5196 (office). *E-mail:* carterbweb@emory.edu (office). *Website:* www.cartercenter.org (office).

HARDONO, Djoko; Indonesian diplomatist; *Ambassador to Canada;* b. 1 Aug. 1949, Malang; m. Ulfah Hanif Hardono; three c. *Education:* Airlangga Univ. *Career:* various positions at Dept of Foreign Affairs including Head, Section of Asian Data, Directorate Gen. of Social Cultural Relations and Information 1978–81, Head, Sub Directorate of Bldg and Infrastructure, Directorate of Diplomatic Facility 1986–89, Head, Sub Directorate of Passport, Directorate Gen. of Protocol and Consular Affairs 1993–95, Dir Diplomatic Facility 1997–2000, Dir-Gen. for Protocol and Consular Affairs 2002–06; has served abroad as Head,Sub Section of Protocol and Consular Affairs, Embassy in Ankara 1981–85, Head, Consular Section, Embassy in London 1989–93, Head, Political Section, Embassy in Singapore 1995–97, Deputy Chief of Mission, Embassy in Tokyo 2000–02, Amb. to Canada 2006–.
Address: Embassy of Indonesia, 55 Parkdale Avenue, Ottawa, ON K1Y 1E5, Canada (office). *Telephone:* (613) 724-1100 (office). *Fax:* (613) 724-1105 (office). *E-mail:* info@indonesia-ottawa.org (office). *Website:* www.indonesia-ottawa.org (office).

HARE, Paul, LVO; British diplomatist; b. 20 July 1951; m. Lynda Carol Henderson; three s. three d. *Career:* joined Diplomatic Service 1978, Second Sec., Embassy in Brussels 1979–81, First Sec., Embassy in Lisbon 1981–83, Head of Political Section 1983–85, with FCO 1985–88, Consul and Dir Commercial Section, New York 1988–94, Chief of Mission and Counsellor, Embassy in Caracas 1994–97, with FCO 1997–2001, Amb. to Cuba 2001–04.
Address: c/o Foreign and Commonwealth Office, King Charles Street, London, SW1A 2AH, England.

HARMOKO, Haji; Indonesian politician and journalist; *Co-ordinator of Advisors, Partai Golongan Karya;* b. 7 Feb. 1939, Kertosono, E Java. *Education:* Sr High School, Kediri, E Java and Inst. of Nat. Defence (LEMHANAS), Jakarta. *Career:* journalist, Merdeka (magazine and daily) 1960–65; Ed. Api (daily); Man. Ed. Merdeka and Chief Ed. Merdiko 1966–68; Chief Ed. Mimbar Kita 1968–69; Gen. Man., Chief Ed. Pos Kota (daily); mem. Bd of Film Censors 1974; mem. Press Council 1975; Chief Ed. Warna Sari 1976–83; mem. House of Reps and People's Consultative Ass. and Head of Information and Mass Media Div. of Functional Group (GOLKAR) 1978, Pres. and Chair., then Co-ordinator of Advisors Partai Golongan Karya 1993–; Head of Advisory Bd of Newspaper Publrs Asscn 1979–84; mem. Exec. Bd Press and Graphics Asscn 1980–84; Minister of Information 1983–97; Speaker People's Consultative Ass. and House of Reps 1997–2001.
Address: c/o People's Consultative Assembly, Jalan Gatot Subroto 6, Jakarta, Indonesia.

HARNEY, Mary, BA; Irish politician; *Minister for Health and Children;* b. 1953, Ballinasloe, Co. Galway. *Education:* Presentation Convent (Clondalkin, Co. Dublin) and Trinity Coll. (Dublin). *Career:* mem. Seanad Éireann (youngest ever Senator) 1977–81; TD 1981–, Co-Founder Progressive Democrats 1985, Minister for Environmental Protection 1989–92, Deputy Leader Progressive Democrats 1993, then Leader and Spokesperson on Justice, Equality and Law Reform; Minister for Enterprise and Employment 1997; Tánaiste (Deputy Prime Minister) and Minister for Enterprise, Trade and Employment 1997–2004; Tánaiste (Deputy Prime Minister) 2004–07, Minister for Health and Children 2004–; mem. Dublin Co. Council 1979–91.
Address: Department of Health and Children, Hawkins House, Hawkins Street, Dublin 2; Constituency Office, Clondalkin, Dublin 22, Ireland. *Telephone:* (1) 6354000. *Fax:* (1) 6354001. *E-mail:* info@health.irlgov.ie. *Website:* www.doh.ie; www.maryharney.ie.

HARNISH, Reno L., III, MA; American diplomatist; *Principal Deputy Assistant Secretary of State, Bureau of Oceans and International Environmental and Scientific Affairs;* m. Leslie Harnish; one s. one d. *Education:* San Diego State Univ., American Univ., Massachusetts Inst. of Tech. *Career:* worked as research asst at American Enterprise Inst., as int. economist at US Dept of Treasury and as clerk for US Congressman Dave Martin of Neb.; served as Environment, Science and Tech. Counselor, Embassy in Rome, Econ. and Commercial Counselor, Embassy to GDR, in Office of Developed Country Trade, US State Dept, as Econ. Officer, Embassy in Vienna, as Political Officer, Status Liaison Office, Saipan and as Econ. Commercial Officer, Embassy in Lagos; led US policy on Cen. Asian politics and scientific cooperation with New Independent States, US State Dept 1992–95; fmr Deputy Chief of Mission, Stockholm, then Cairo, fmr Chief of Mission, US Office, Pristina, Amb. to Azerbaijan 2004–06, Gen. Chair. WIREC 2008 Interagency Leadership Group 2006, Prin. Deputy Asst Sec. of State, Bureau of Oceans and Int. Environmental and Scientific Affairs 2006–; honoured for Presidential Meritorious Service, two Sr Performance Pay Awards, Meritorious Honor Award, two Superior Honor Awards.

Address: Bureau of Oceans and International Environmental and Scientific Affairs, US Department of State, 2201 C Street NW, Washington, DC 20520, USA (office). *Telephone:* (202) 647-4000 (office). *Fax:* (202) 647-6738 (office). *Website:* www.state.gov (office).

HAROUTUNIAN, Gagik G., DL; Armenian politician and lawyer; *Chairman, Constitutional Court;* b. 1948, Gekhashen; three c. *Education:* Yerevan State Univ. *Career:* Lecturer, Yerevan Inst. of Industry 1975–77; in Yugoslavia 1977–78; on staff Cen. Cttee Armenian CP 1982–88; Head of Dept 1988–90; joined nationalist opposition 1990; Deputy Chair. Armenian Parliament 1990–91; Vice-Pres. of Armenia 1991–95; Acting Chair. Council of Ministers (Prime Minister) 1991–92; Chair. Constitutional Court 1996–; Pres. Int. Conf. of Constitutional Control Organs of Young Democracy States; Council Pres. Centre of Constitutional Law; mem. Int. Asscn of Constitutional Law, Comm. for Democracy through Law, Council of Europe. *Publications:* 16 books including Constitutional Review (with A. Mavčič) 1999, 2002; contrib. over 100 articles to journals and newspapers. *Address:* Constitutional Court, Marshal Baghramian Street 10, 375019 Yerevan (office); Avan, Quchak Quart., Apt 11, Yerevan, Armenia (home). *Telephone:* (10) 58-81-40. *Fax:* (10) 52-99-91 (office). *E-mail:* armlaw@concourt.am (office). *Website:* www.concourt.am (office).

HAROUTUNIAN, Michael; Armenian army officer and government official; *Minister of Defence;* b. 10 Feb. 1946, Sagiyan village, Shemakhin; m.; three c. *Education:* Frunze Mil. Acad. and Mil. Acad. of the Soviet Armed Forces. *Career:* early career in Soviet Army, posts included CO of reconnaissance unit, Deputy Chief of Staff, Head of Reconnaissance Dept; Sr Instructor of Reconnaissance Unit, Military Acad. of the Soviet Armed Forces 1988–92; enlisted in Armed Forces of Armenia 1992; Head of Operations Dept and Deputy Head, Chief of Staff 1992–93; First Deputy Head, Chief of Staff of Armed Forces 1993–94, Chief of Staff of Armed Forces and First Deputy Minister of Defence 1994–2007, Minister of Defence 2007–; 'Service to the Motherland', Second Degree (USSR), Combat Cross, Second Degree (Armenia), Vardan Mamikonyan (Armenia), Combat Cross, Second Degree (NKR), Legion of Honor (USA), Combat Service, First Degree (Armenia), 'For the Service to the Motherland', First Degree (Armenia), Marshal Baghramyan decoration, Ministry of Defence, 'For Perfect Service', First and Second Degrees, Ministry of Defence, Andranik Ozanyan decoration, Ministry of Defence, 'Coat of Arms', Ministry of Defence, Nominal Weapon, Ministry of Defence, 'For Strengthening Combat Collaboration', Ministry of Defence, Russian Fed. *Address:* Ministry of Defence, G. Shaush Street 60, Yerevan 0088, Armenia (office). *Telephone:* (10) 28-39-22 (office). *Fax:* (10) 28-26-30 (office). *E-mail:* press@mil.am (office). *Website:* www.mil.am (office).

HARRIES, Owen; British editor, fmr government official and academic; *Senior Fellow, Centre for Independent Studies;* b. 1930, Wales. *Education:* Univs of Wales and Oxford. *Career:* taught for 20 years Univ. of Sydney, NSW; apptd Sr Adviser to shadow Foreign Affairs Minister, Australia 1974, subsequently Dir of Policy Planning, Dept of Foreign Affairs; Sr Adviser to Prime Minister; Amb. to UNESCO 1982–83; Visiting Fellow, Heritage Foundation USA 1983–85; founder and Ed.-in-Chief The National Interest (journal) Washington DC 1985–2001; currently Sr Fellow Centre for Independent Studies, Australia, Visiting Fellow, Lowy Inst. for Independent Studies; Sr Assoc. Center for Strategic and Int. Studies USA. *Publications include:* Liberty and Politics (ed.) 1976, Australia and the Third World (ed.) 1979, America's Purpose (ed.) 1991, China in the National Interest (ed.) 2003, Morality and Foreign Policy 2004. *Address:* Centre for Independent Studies, POB 92, St Leonards, NSW 1590, Australia (office). *Telephone:* (2) 9438-4377 (office). *Fax:* (2) 9439-7310 (office). *E-mail:* oharries@lowyinstitute.org (office); cis@cis.org.au (office). *Website:* www.cis.org.au (office).

HARRIS, Timothy Sylvester, BSc, MSc, PhD; Saint Christopher and Nevis politician; *Minister of Foreign Affairs, International Trade, Industry, Commerce and Consumer Affairs;* b. 1964, Tabernacle. *Education:* Cayon High School, Basseterre Sr High School, Univ. of the West Indies, Cave Hill and Sr Augustine, Concordia Univ., Montreal, Canada. *Career:* worked at Social Security Office, Wellington Ltd and S. L. Horsford & Co. Ltd; mem. Labour Party, Constituency Sec. and Constituency Rep. on Nat. Exec. Bd, mem. Young Labour Advisory Cttee, and Youth Co-ordinator, currently Chair. St Kitts-Nevis Labour Party; mem. Parl. 1993–; Minister of Agric., Lands and Housing 1995–2000, of Foreign Affairs and Educ. 2000–04, of Foreign Affairs, Int. Trade, Industry, Commerce and Consumer Affairs 2004–; Victor Cooke Prize, Univ. of W Indies, Post Graduate Award, Cen. Bank of Trinidad and Tobago, Concordia/UWI Post Graduate Award. *Publications:* several articles in journals. *Address:* Church Street, Basseterre (office); Tabernacle, St Kitts (home). *Telephone:* (869) 465-9085 (office); (869) 465-7768 (home). *Fax:* (869) 465-2556 (office). *E-mail:* tonskb@yahoo.co.uk (home).

HARRISON, (William) Alistair, CVO, MA, DipEcon; British diplomatist; *High Commissioner to Zambia;* b. 14 Nov. 1954, Guisborough; m. Sarah Wood; one s. two d. *Education:* Newcastle Grammar School, Univ. Coll., Oxford and Univ. of London. *Career:* joined FCO 1977, served in Warsaw twice, most recently as Deputy Head of Mission; served in British Perm. Mission to UN, New York, twice, most recently as Counsellor (Political), as Foreign Policy Adviser to EC, Brussels, and in FCO in London in several posts, including Pvt. Sec. to Parl. Under-Sec. of State and Head of Int. Orgs Dept; High Commr to Zambia 2005–. *Address:* British High Commission, 210 Independence Avenue, PO Box 50050, 15101 Ridgeway, Lusaka, Zambia (office). *Telephone:* (1) 251133 (office). *Fax:* (1) 253798 (office). *E-mail:* BHC-Lusaka@fco.gov.uk (office). *Website:* www.britishhighcommission.gov.uk/zambia (office).

HART, Oliver D'Arcy, PhD; British economist and academic; *Andrew E. Furer Professor of Economics, Harvard University;* b. 9 Oct. 1948, London; m. Rita B. Goldberg 1974; two s. *Education:* Univs of Cambridge and Warwick and Princeton Univ., USA. *Career:* Lecturer in Econs, Univ. of Essex 1974–75; Asst Lecturer, then Lecturer in Econs, Univ. of Cambridge 1975–81; Prof. of Econs, LSE 1981–85, BP Centennial Visiting Prof. 1992–93, 1997–; Prof. of Econs, MIT 1984–93; Prof. of Econs, Harvard Univ. 1993–97, Andrew E. Furer Prof. of Econs 1997–; Fellow, American Acad. of Arts and Sciences; Corresp. Fellow, British Acad. 2000; Dr hc (Free Univ. of Brussels) 1992; Hon. DPhil (Basle) 1994. *Publications:* Firms, Contracts and Financial Structure 1995; numerous articles in professional journals. *Address:* Department of Economics, Littauer 220, Harvard University, Cambridge, MA 02138, USA (office). *Telephone:* (617) 496-3461 (office). *Fax:* (617) 495-1879 (office). *Website:* economics.harvard.edu/faculty/hart/hart.html (office).

HASAN, Abdulkasim Salad; Somali former head of state; b. 1942. *Career:* Minister of Industry, of Trade, of Labour, of Information and of the Interior 1973–1990; Pres. of Somalia 2000–04. *Address:* c/o Office of the President, People's Palace, Mogadishu, Somalia (office).

HASAN, Wajid Shamsul, BA LLB, MA; Pakistani journalist, writer and diplomatist; *High Commissioner to UK;* m.; one s. *Education:* course for sr journalists in UK, short academic courses at Elizabeth Hall, Oxford and Thomson Media Foundation, Cardiff. *Career:* joined Jang Group of Newspapers 1962, Ed. The Daily News 1969–89, also edited The Weekly Mag from Karachi; received practical training in journalism at the Bristol Evening Post and London Evening Standard; Chair. Nat. Press Trust (conglomerate of more than 14 newspapers and magazines) 1989–92; pvt. media consultant 1992–94, 1996–; adviser to fmr Prime Minister Benazir Bhutto 1992–94, 1996–2007; High Commr to UK 1994–96, 2008–; mem. dels and media teams on official visits of Pres and Prime Ministers, including presidential entourage at Simla Peace Summit with India 1972, visits to USA and China, UN Gen. Ass. Sessions and Jt Session of US Congress, official tour of Prime Minister Zulfikar Ali Bhutto to USA and Canada 1976, lecture tour of Benazir Bhutto to Vancouver 1991; commentator on S Asia and world affairs, contrib. to BBC TV, BBC Radio, Sky, CNN, Zee TV, Middle Eastern TV channels, Ptv Prime, Ary Digital and other electronic and print media; Commonwealth Press Union Scholarship (UK) 1968. *Address:* Pakistan High Commission, 35–36 Lowndes Square, London, SW1X 9JN, England (office). *Telephone:* (20) 7664-9200 (office). *Fax:* (20) 7664-9224 (office). *E-mail:* info@phclondon.org (office). *Website:* www.phclondon.org (office).

HASANOV, Abbasali K.; Azerbaijani diplomatist; *Ambassador to Iran;* b. 1953. *Education:* Baku Univ. *Career:* joined Ministry of Foreign Affairs 1984; fmr Dir Dept for mem. states of Org. of Islamic Conf.; Amb. to Iran 1998–. *Address:* Embassy of Azerbaijan, 10 Akdsihi Street, Tehran, Iran (office). *Telephone:* (21) 22215191 (office). *Fax:* (21) 22217504 (office). *E-mail:* info@azembassy.ir (office). *Website:* www.azembassy.ir (office).

HASEEB, Khair ad-Din, BA, MSc, PhD; Iraqi economist and statistician; *Director-General, Centre for Arab Unity Studies;* b. 1 Aug. 1929, Mosul; m. 1955; one s. two d. *Education:* Univ. of Baghdad, London School of Econs and Univ. of Cambridge, UK. *Career:* civil servant, Ministry of Interior 1947–54; Head of Research and Statistics Dept, Iraqi Oil Co. 1959–60; Full-time Lecturer, Univ. of Baghdad 1960–61, Part-time 1961–63; Dir-Gen. Iraqi Fed. of Industries 1960–63; Gov. and Chair. of Bd, Cen. Bank of Iraq 1963–65; Pres. Gen. Org. for Banks 1964–65; Acting Pres. Econ. Org., Iraq 1964–65; Assoc. Prof., Dept of Econs Univ. of Baghdad 1965–71, Prof. of Econs 1971–74; mem. Bd Dirs Iraq Nat. Oil Co. 1967–68; Chief, Programme and Co-ordination Unit and Natural Resources, Science and

Tech. Div. UN Econ. Comm. for Western Asia, then Lebanon and Iraq 1974–76 and 1976–83; Acting Dir-Gen. Centre for Arab Unity Studies, Lebanon 1978–83, Dir-Gen. 1983–; Chair. Bd of Trustees and Dirs Arab Cultural Foundation, London 1987; Chair. Bd of Trustees Arab Org. for Translation, Lebanon 1999–. *Publications:* The National Income of Iraq 1953–1961, 1964, Workers' Participation in Management in Arab Countries (in Arabic) 1971, Sources of Arab Economic Thought in Iraq 1900–71 (in Arabic) 1972, Arab Monetary Integration (co-ed.) 1982, Arabs and Africa (ed.) 1985, The Future of the Arab Nation 1991, Arab-Iranian Relations (ed.) 2002, The Future of Iraq: Occupation, Resistance, Liberation and Democracy 2004, Planning Iraq's Future: A Detailed Project to Rebuild Post-Liberation Iraq (ed.) 2006; numerous articles.
Address: Centre for Arab Unity Studies, Beit Al-Nahda Bldg- Basra Str., PO Box 113-6001, Hamra, Beirut 2034 2407, Lebanon (office). *Telephone:* (1) 750084 (office); (1) 740631 (home). *Fax:* (1) 750088 (office). *E-mail:* info@caus.org.lb (office). *Website:* www.caus.org.lb (office).

HASHIM, Lt-Col Ahmed S., BA, MA, PhD; American defence and foreign affairs specialist and academic; *Associate Professor of Strategic Studies, US Naval War College; Education:* Univ. of Warwick, UK, Massachusetts Inst. of Tech. *Career:* Research Assoc., IISS, London 1993–94; Fellow, Center for Strategic and Int. Studies, Washington, DC 1994–96; Research Analyst, Center for Naval Analyses, Alexandria, Va 1996–2000; served as advisor to US authorities in Iraq following the fall of Saddam 2003–05; currently Assoc. Prof. of Strategic Studies, US Naval War Coll.; Lecturer in Public Policy, John F. Kennedy School of Govt, Harvard Univ. *Publications:* The Crisis of the Iranian State 1995, Insurgency and Counter-Insurgency in Iraq 2005; contrib. to books and journals.
Address: Center for Naval Warfare Studies, Naval War College, Newport, RI 02841, USA (office). *Telephone:* (401) 841-6981 (office). *E-mail:* hashima@nwc.navy.mil (office). *Website:* www.nwc.navy.mil (office).

HASHIM, Pengiran Dato Maidin, MA; Brunei diplomatist; *High Commissioner to UK;* b. 13 March 1951; m. Datin Hajah Sunah Abdul Hamid; five c. *Education:* Fletcher School of Law and Diplomacy, Tufts Univ., USA and Univs of Oxford and Hull, UK. *Career:* Admin. Officer, Govt Econ. Planning Unit 1976; Asst Dist Officer, Tutong Dist 1977–79; Acting Deputy Controller Royal Customs and Excise Dept 1979–82, Deputy Controller 1982; Admin. Officer (Special Grade) 1982–84; Deputy Dir Econ. Dept 1984–85; Acting Dir Admin Dept 1985–86; Dir-Gen. Dept of ASEAN 1986–89; Dir Political Dept 1990–92; Pvt. Sec. to Minister of Foreign Affairs 1992–94, Amb. to Germany 1994–96 (also accred to Russian Fed. 1996–97), apptd Perm. Rep. UN 1997, High Commr to UK (also accred as Amb. to Ireland) 2006–.
Address: High Commission of Brunei, 19–20 Belgrave Square, London, SW1X 8PG, England (office). *Telephone:* (20) 7581-0521 (office). *Fax:* (20) 7235-9717 (office). *E-mail:* bhcl@brunei-high-commission.co.uk (office).

HASHIMI, Tariq al-, MA; Iraqi politician; *Vice-President of Iraq and Secretary-General, Iraqi Islamic Party;* b. 1942, Baghdad. *Education:* Al-Mustansiriyah Univ. *Career:* attended Mil. Acad. 1959–62, pursued mil. career –1975; instructor, Leadership Acad. 1975; Iraq Br. Man., Arab Shipping Co. 1979–81, moved to Kuwait, served as Dir-Gen., Arab Shipping Co. –1990; returned to Iraq 1990; mem. Iraqi Islamic Party, fmr mem. Planning Cttee and Shura Council, currently Sec.-Gen.; Vice-Pres. of Iraq 2005–.
E-mail: info@alhashimi.org (office); info@iraqigovernment.org (office). *Website:* alhashimi.org (office); www.iraqigovernment.org (office).

HASLACH, Patricia M., BA, MA; American diplomatist; *Senior Official for Asia-Pacific Economic Cooperation (APEC);* b. Lake Oswego, Ore.; m. David Herbert; two d. *Education:* Gonzaga Univ., Spokane, Wash., Columbia Univ., New York. *Career:* economist, Dept of State Intern Program, Embassy in Rome 1980; Admin. Asst, Inst. on Western Europe, Columbia Univ. 1980–81, economist, Dept of Ports and Terminals, New York 1981–83, Int. Economist, Econ. Research Service, Dept of Agric., Washington, DC 1983–84; held various positions in Foreign Agricultural Service (FAS) that included work on food assistance programmes and int. trade policy issues with EU 1984–87; career mem. Sr Foreign Service since 1986, foreign assignments have included service as Agricultural Attaché in New Delhi 1987–90, Area Man. for Latin America, FAS, Dept of Agric. 1990–92, Foreign Service training 1992–93, French language training 1993, Political Officer in US Mission to EU, Brussels 1993–94, Deputy Econ. Counselor, Lagos 1994–96, Indonesian language training, Dept of State 1996–97, Deputy Econ. Counselor, Jakarta 1997–2000, Econ. Counselor in Islamabad 2000–02, Dir Office for Afghanistan, Dept of State 2002–04, Amb. to Laos 2004–07, Sr Official for APEC, Dept of State 2007–; served on bds of American schools in Lagos, Jakarta and Islamabad; Sinclaire Award for the study of a hard language 1997, Herbert Salzman Award for

Excellence in Int. Econ. Performance 1999, Dir Gen.'s Award for Impact and Originality in Reporting 2002.
Address: US Department of State, 2201 C Street NW, Washington, DC 20520, USA (office). *Telephone:* (202) 647-4000 (office). *Fax:* (202) 647-6738 (office). *Website:* www.state.gov (office).

HASLER, Otmar; Liechtenstein politician; *Prime Minister;* b. 28 Sept. 1953; m. Traudi Hasler-Hilti; two s. two d. *Education:* secondary school-teaching diploma from Fribourg Univ. *Career:* teacher, Realschule, Eschen 1979–2001; Pres. Progressive Citizens' Party of Liechtenstein (FBP) 1993–95, mem. Exec. Cttee 1993–; mem. Parl. 1989–2001, Vice-Pres. 1993–94, 1996–2001, Pres. 1995; Prime Minister of Liechtenstein, also responsible for Govt Affairs, Finance, Construction and Public Works 2001–; Pres. newly founded Liechtenstein Sr Citizens' Org. 1999–; mem. Historical Soc., Liechtenstein Art Soc., Liechtenstein Senior Educational Asscn.
Address: Office of the Prime Minister, Regierungsgebäude, 9490 Vaduz, Liechtenstein (office). *Telephone:* 2366007 (office). *Fax:* 2366022 (office). *E-mail:* regierung@liechtenstein.li (office). *Website:* www.liechtenstein.li (office).

HASQUIN, Hervé, PhD; Belgian politician and academic; *Minister-President of French-speaking Community of Belgium;* b. 31 Dec. 1942, Charleroi; m. Michèle Nahum 1986; one s. *Career:* Dean Faculty of Arts and Philosophy, Université Libre de Bruxelles 1979–82, Rector 1982–86, Chair. Bd of Dirs 1986–95, Pres. Inst. for Religious and Secular Studies 1987–; Head French-speaking network Scientific Information and Technological Devt 1986–87; Vice-Pres. Parti Réformateur Libéral (PRL) 1986–89, Gen. Sec. 1990–92, Head PRL Group, Council of Brussels, Capital Region 1991–; Senator 1988–95; Regional Councillor, Brussels 1989–99; Minister of Environmental Planning, Town Planning and Transport, Brussels Capital Region 1995–99; Minister-Pres. of French-speaking Community of Belgium responsible for Int. Relations 1999–; Prés. de la Fédération MR du Hainaut 2000–; Royal Acad. of Belgium Prize 1990, Literary Prize of French-speaking Community Council 1981 and other prizes; Chevalier, Légion d'honneur 1989, Commdr, Order of Leopold II 1984, Order of the Lion (Senegal) 1987; Grand Officer, Order of Leopold 1999;sociétaire hc Acad. des Sciences et des Arts 2000, mem. Acad. Royale de Belgique 2002. *Publications:* La Wallonie: Le Pays et les Hommes, Histoire de la Laïcité principalement en Belgique et en France, La Wallonie, son histoire 1999, Dictionnaire d'histoire de Belgique: Vingt siècles d'institutions. Les hommes. Les faits 1988, Dictionnaire d'histoire de Belgique: Les Hommes, les institutions, les faits, le Congo Belge et le Ruanda–Urundi 2000; Les séparatistes wallons et le gouvernement de Vichy (1940–43), Acad. royale de Belgique lecture 2003; about 150 articles and papers in Belgian and foreign learned journals.
Address: Université Libre de Bruxelles, Ave. F. Roosevelt 50, 1050 Brussels ; Cabinet du Ministre-Président de la Communauté Wallonie-Bruxelles, Place Surlet de Chokier 15-17, 1000 Brussels (office); Rue du Long Bois 1, 7830 Graty Silly, Belgium (home). *Telephone:* (2) 227-32-11 (office). *Fax:* (2) 227-33-53 (office). *E-mail:* contact@hasquin.be (office). *Website:* www .hasquin.be (office).

HASSAN, Adam; Maldivian diplomatist; *Deputy High Commissioner to UK;* m. Aishath Hassan. *Career:* Acting High Commr to UK –2004, Deputy High Commr 2004–.
Address: High Commission of the Maldives, 22 Nottingham Place, London, W1U 5NJ, England (office). *Telephone:* (20) 7224-2135 (office). *Fax:* (20) 7224-2157 (office). *E-mail:* maldives.high.commission@virgin.net (office). *Website:* www.maldiveshighcommission.org (office).

HASSAN, Jafar Abed A., MSc; Jordanian diplomatist; *Deputy Chief of Mission in USA; Education:* Univ. of Geneva, Switzerland, Boston Univ., Harvard Business School, USA, American Coll., Paris, France. *Career:* fmr Head of Human Rights Issues and Humanitarian Affairs, Mission of Jordan to UN European HQ, Geneva, Switzerland; fmr Personal Asst to Dir of Nat. Security, Royal Palace, Jordan; Dir Israel Section, Ministry of Foreign Affairs –2001; Deputy Chief of Mission to Jordanian Embassy, USA 2001–; Doctorate in Political Science. *Telephone:* (202) 966-2664 ext. 120 (office); (202) 966-2664 (office). *Fax:* (202) 966-4527 (office); (202) 966-3110 (office). *E-mail:* djanbek@aol.com (office); Hkjembassydc@aol.com (office).
Address: Embassy of Jordan, 3504 International Drive, NW, Washington, DC 20008, USA (office). *Website:* www.jordanembassyus.org (office).

HASSAN, Jean-Claude Gaston; French banker and public servant; b. 11 Nov. 1954, Tunis, Tunisia; m. Françoise Benhamou 1981; two s. one d. *Education:* Lycée de Mutuelleville, Tunis, Lycée Louis-le-Grand, Paris, Ecole normale supérieure, Ecole nat. d'admin. *Career:* mem. Conseil d'Etat, Auditeur 1981, Counsel 1985; Tech. Adviser to Office of Minister of

Social Affairs and Nat. Solidarity 1984–85; Deputy Dir-Gen. Banque Stern 1986–89, Dir-Gen. 1989–92; Dir-Gen. Banque Worms 1992–94; rejoined Conseil d'Etat 1994–2000, 2002; Conseiller pour l'euro de Laurent Fabins, Ministry of the Econ., Finance and Industry 2000–02; Conseiller d'État 2005–; mem. Cttee de règlement des différends de la CRE, Comm. de Régulation de l'Energie 2006–.
Address: Commission de Régulation de l'Energie, 2 rue du Quatre-Septembre, 75084 Paris Cedex 02 (office); Conseil d'Etat, Palais-Royal, 75100 Paris 01 SP, France (office). *E-mail:* wemmestre@cre.fr (office). *Website:* www.cre.fr (office).

HASSAN, Mohamed Hag Ali, PhD; Sudanese professor of mathematics; *Secretary-General, Third World Network of Scientific Organizations;* b. 21 Nov. 1947. *Education:* Oxford Univ. *Career:* Sr Lecturer Dept of Mathematical Sciences, Khartoum Univ. 1977, Assoc. Prof. 1979, Prof. 1986, Dean of Mathematical Sciences 1985; Fulbright Research Fellow 1984; Exec. Dir Third World Acad. of Sciences 1983–; Sec.-Gen. Third World Network of Scientific Orgs 1988–; Fellow African Acad. of Sciences, Pres. 1999–; Fellow Islamic Acad. of Sciences, mem. Council 1999–; Hon. mem. Colombian Acad. of Exact Sciences. *Publications:* over 40 articles on applied mathematics.
Address: African Academy of Sciences, PO Box 24916, Nairobi, Kenya (office). *Telephone:* (2) 884401 (office). *Fax:* (2) 884406 (office). *E-mail:* aas@africaonline.co.ke (office).

HASSANI, Hajim al-, PhD; Iraqi politician; *Speaker, Transitional National Assembly;* b. 1954, Kirkuk. *Education:* Mosul Univ., Univs of Nebraska and Conn., USA. *Career:* moved to USA 1979; Researcher, Dept of Agricultural and Resource Econs, Univ. of Conn. 1990; Head of American Investment and Trading Co., Claremont, LA 1991–2003; active mem. of Iraqi Islamic Party (IIP) in exile; returned to Iraq following invasion 2003; worked for Iraqi Interim Governing Council 2003; Leader IIP 2003–04; involved in negotiating unsuccessful cease-fire between US forces and insurgents in Fallujah April 2004; Minister of Industry and Minerals 2004; Speaker Transitional Nat. Ass. 2005–.
Address: Office of the Speaker, Transitional National Assembly, Green Zone, Baghad, Iraq.

HAUFF, Volker, Dr rer. pol; German politician and business consultant; *Chairman, German Council for Sustainable Development;* b. 9 Aug. 1940, Backnang; m. Ursula Irion 1967; two s. *Education:* Free Univ. of Berlin. *Career:* with IBM Deutschland, Stuttgart 1971–72; Sec. of State to Fed. Minister for Research and Tech. 1972–78; Fed. Minister for Research and Tech. 1978–80, of Transport 1980–82; mem. Bundestag 1969; mem. Social Democratic Party (SPD) 1959, Vice-Pres. of Parl. Group 1983; Mayor of Frankfurt 1989–91; Generalbevollmächtigte KPMG Germany 1995–2000, mem. Bd Bearing Point GmbH 2002–, Sr Vice Pres. 2003–; Chair. German Council for Sustainable Devt 2001–; fmr mem. UN World Comm. on Environment and Devt; Bundesverdienstkreuz mit Stern und Schulterband. *Publications:* Programmierfibes—Eine verständliche Einführung in das Programmieren digitaler Automaten 1969, Wörterbuch der Datenverarbeitung 1966, Für ein soziales Bodenrecht 1973, Modernisierung der Volkswirtschaft 1975, Politik als Zukunftsgestaltung 1976, Damit der Fortschritt nicht zum Risiko wird 1978, Sprachlose Politik 1979, Global Denken – Lokal Handeln 1992.
Address: Hitzeierstrasse 68, 50968 Köln, Germany (home). *Telephone:* (30) 34703841 (office); (172) 2902902. *E-mail:* volker.hauff@bearingpoint.com. *Website:* www.bearingpoint.de.

HAUGER-JOHANNESSEN, Vice-Adm. Eivind, MSc; Norwegian naval officer (retd); b. 11 Dec. 1946, Oslo. *Career:* career in Norwegian Navy, rank of Vice-Adm.; fmr Deputy Chief of Defence; Mil. Rep. to NATO, Brussels, Belgium 2005–06; Nat. Service Medal 1982, Defence Service Medal 1992; Commdr Kungliga Nordstjärnordenen (Sweden) 1993, Danebrogs Ordenen (Denmark) 1993, Falkeordenen (Iceland) 1993, Lejons Orden (Finland) 1994, Das Grosse Goldene Ehrenzeichen (Austria) 1995, Order del Mèrito Civil (Spain) 1995, St. Olavs Orden (Norway) 1998, Grand Cross of the Order of Al-Istiqlal (Jordan) 2002, Order of the White Rose of Finland 2002.
Address: Ministry of Defence, Myntgt. 1, PO Box 8126 Dep., 0032 Oslo, Norway. *Telephone:* (2) 707-63-50 (office). *Fax:* (2) 707-63-59 (office). *E-mail:* nomilrep@mil.no (office).

HAUSER, Heinz, PhD; Swiss economist, academic and research institute director; *Professor of International Economics and Managing Director, Swiss Institute for International Economics and Applied Economic Research, University of St Gallen;* b. 1943, nr St Gallen. *Education:* Univ. of St Gallen. *Career:* Researcher, Inst. for Public Finance and Tax Law, Univ. of St Gallen 1971–81, Prof. of Int. Econs 1981–, also Man. Dir Swiss Inst. for Int. Econs and Applied Econ. Research (SIAW) 1981–, Vice-Rector of Univ.

1986–90, Pres. Research Cttee 1992–96, Assoc. Dean for Int. Academic Relations 1990–99, Dean of Econs Dept 1997–99; Visiting Scholar in Münster, Germany 1967–68, Phila., USA 1976–77, Berkeley, Calif. 1977–78, Vancouver, Canada 1999–2000; Man. Ed. The Swiss Review of International Economic Relations 1982–; Chair. Community of European Man. Schools 1995–99; Venia Docendi, Univ. of St Gallen 1980. *Publications:* Zur Bindung des Wirtschaftsgesetzgebers durch Grundrechte 1989, Schweizerische Wirtschaftspolitik im internationalen Wettbewerb 1991, EWR-Vertraf, EG-Beitritt, Alleingang: Wirtschaftliche Konsequenzen für die Schweiz 1992, Mut Zum Aufbruch: Eine wirtschaftspolitische Agenda für die Schweiz 1995, Das neue GATT: Die Welthandelsordnung nach Abschluss der Uruguayrunde 1995; numerous articles in scientific journals.
Address: Swiss Institute for International Economics and Applied Economic Research, Bodanstrasse 8, St Gallen 9000, Switzerland (office). *Telephone:* 712242350 (office). *Fax:* 712242298 (office). *E-mail:* Heinz .Hauser@unisg.ch (office). *Website:* www.siaw.unisg.ch (office).

HAUSIKU, Marco Mukoso; Namibian politician; *Minister of Foreign Affairs;* b. 25 Nov. 1953, Kapako; m. *Education:* Bunya Roman Catholic Mission School, Rundu Secondary School, Dobra Training Coll., Augustineum Training Coll. *Career:* teacher Katutura Secondary School 1977–89; mem. SWAPO Windhoek Br. Exec. Cttee 1977–89, mem. Cen. Cttee and Polit-Bureau 1991; Election Dir Kavango and Tsumkwe Area 1989; Minister of Lands, Resettlement and Rehabilitation 1990, of Works, Transport and Communication 1992, of Prisons and Correctional Services 1995, of Labour 2002, of Foreign Affairs 2004–; founding mem. and Pres. Namibia Nat. Teachers Union 1988.
Address: Ministry of Foreign Affairs, Government Buildings, Robert Mugabe Avenue, PMB 13347, Windhoek, Namibia (office). *Telephone:* (61) 2829111 (office). *Fax:* (61) 223937 (office). *E-mail:* headquarters@mfa.gov .na (office). *Website:* www.mfa.gov.na (office).

HAVEL, Václav; Czech playwright, writer and fmr head of state; b. 5 Oct. 1936, Prague; m. 1st Olga Šplíchalová 1964 (died 1996); m. 2nd Dagmar Veškrnová 1997. *Education:* Acad. of Arts, Drama Dept, Prague. *Career:* worked as freelance; fmr spokesman for Charter 77 human rights movement, received a sentence of 14 months in 1977, suspended for three years, for "subversive" and "antistate" activities, under house arrest 1978–79; mem. Cttee for the Defence of the Unjustly Prosecuted (VONS), convicted and sentenced to 4½ years' imprisonment for sedition 1979, released March 1983, arrested Jan. 1989 and sentenced to nine months' imprisonment for incitement and obstruction Feb. 1989; sentence reduced to eight months and charge changed to misdemeanour March 1989; released May 1989; f. Civic Forum 1989; Pres. of Czechoslovakia 1989–92, Pres. of Czech Repub. 1993–2003; C-in-C of Armed Forces 1989–92; Chair. Prague Heritage Fund 1993–; mem. jury Int. Prize Awarding Body for Human Rights 1994–; mem. Acad. des Sciences Morales et Politiques; Hon. mem. Acad. of Sciences and Arts, Salzburg; Hon. Citizen of Vrtislav 2001; Grand Cross, Order of the Legion of Honour 1990, Order of White Eagle, Poland 1993, Golden Hon. Order of Freedom, Slovenia 1993, Chain of Order of Isabel of Castille, Spain 1995, Hon. KCB, UK 1996, Grand Cross Order with Chain (Lithuania) 1999, Federal Cross for Merit, Berlin 2000; numerous hon. degrees including Dr hc (York Univ., Toronto, Le Mirail Univ., Toulouse) 1982, (Columbia Univ., New York, Hebrew Univ., Jerusalem, Frantisek Palacky Univ., Olomouc, Charles Univ., Prague, Comenius Univ., Bratislava) 1990, (Free Univ. of Brussels, St Gallen Univ.) 1991, (Bar Ilan Univ., Israel, Kiev Univ., Ukraine, Jordan Univ., Oxford) 1997, (Glasgow) 1998, (Manitoba, St Thomas Univ., USA) 1999, (Bilkent Univ., Turkey) 2000; Austrian State Prize for European Literature 1968, Jan Palach Prize 1982, (JAMU, Brno) 2001, Erasmus Prize 1986, Olof Palme Prize 1989, German Book Trade Peace Prize 1989, Simón Bolívar Prize 1990, Malaparte Prize 1990, UNESCO Prize for the Teaching of Human Rights 1990, Chalemagne Prize 1991, Sonning Cultural Prize 1991, Athinai Prize (Onassis Foundation) 1993, Theodor Heuss Prize 1993, Indira Gandhi Prize 1994, European Cultural Soc. Award 1993, Philadelphia Liberty Medal 1994, Premi Internacional Catalunya 1995, TGM Prize (Canada) 1997, Medal of Danish Acad. 1997, European Statesman Prize (USA), 1997, Husajn bin Ali Distinction (Jordan) 1997, J. W. Fulbright Prize for Int. Understanding (USA) 1997, Le Prix Spécial Europe, European Theatre Council 1997, Cino del Duca Prize (France), Prince of Asturias Prize (Spain) 1997, Charles Univ. Medal 1998, Open Soc. Prize, Budapest Univ., Gazeta Wyborcza Prize (Poland), St Vojtěch Prize (Slovakia) 1999, Citizen Prize, Berlin 2000, Evelyn Burkey's Prize, Author's Guild of America 2000, Elie Wiesel Prize 2000. *Plays include:* Garden Party 1963, Memorandum 1965, The Increased Difficulty of Concentration 1968, The Conspirators 1971, The Beggar's Opera 1972, Audience 1975, Vernissage 1975, The Mountain Resort 1976, Protest 1978, The Mistake 1983, Largo Desolato 1984, Temptation 1985, Redevelopment 1987, Tomorrow! 1988, Leaving 2007. *Publications include:* Letters to Olga (in

Czech, as Dopisy Olge) 1983, Disturbing the Peace (in Czech, as Dálkový výslech) 1986, (English) 1990, Václav Havel or Living in Truth (essays, in English) 1986, Open Letters: Selected Writings 1965–1990 (in English) 1991, Selected Plays by Václav Havel (in English) 1992, Summer Meditations (in Czech, as Ledric piemidánt) 1991, (English) 1992, Plays (in Czech, as Hry) 1991, Toward a Civil Society 1994, The Art of the Impossible (speeches) 1997, In Various Directions (in Czech, as Do různých stran) 1999, Spisy (seven vols) 1999, The Pizh'duks (in Czech, as Pižd'uchové) 2003, To the Castle and Back (memoir; in Czech as Prosím stručně) 2007.
Address: Voršilská 10, 110 00 Prague 1, Czech Republic (office). *Telephone:* (2) 3409-7830 (office). *Fax:* (2) 3409-7831 (office). *E-mail:* vaclav.havel@volny.cz (office). *Website:* www.vaclavhavel.cz.

HAVRIL, Gen. András; Hungarian military officer; *Chief of Defence Staff;* b. 15 June 1951; m. Mária Havril, one c. *Education:* Lajos Kossuth Mil. Acad., Miklós Zrínyi Staff Coll. *Career:* Second Lt 1973, Lt 1976, served as infantry platoon leader, infantry co. commdr and chief of bn staff 1973–77, Operations Officer, Mechanized Div. Staff 1980–84, Deputy Commdr, Mechanized Regiment 1984–87, Mechanized Brigade Commdr 1987–91, Deputy Commdr First Mil. Dist 1991–93, Chief of Staff Third Mil. Dist 1993–94, promoted to Brig. 1994, Deputy Commdr Third Mil. Dist 1995–96, Commdr Land Forces 1996–2000; Deputy Chief Defence Staff, Ministry of Defence 2001–05, Chief of Defence Staff 2005–; Maj.-Gen. 1997, Lt-Gen. 2001, Gen. 2005.
Address: Ministry of Defence, Balaton u. 7–11, 1055 Budapest, Hungary (office). *Telephone:* (1) 236-5111 (office). *Fax:* (1) 311-0182 (office). *Website:* www.honvedelem.hu (office).

HAWKINS, John Mark; British diplomatist; *Ambassador to Qatar;* m. Rosemarie Hawkins; two s. *Career:* Asst Desk Officer, Econ. Relations Dept, FCO 1982–83, Asst Desk Officer (Iran), Middle East Dept 1983–84; Third, later Second Sec., Chancery, Pretoria/Capetown 1984–88; First Sec., Econ. Relations Dept, FCO 1988–90, Press Officer, News Dept 1990–93; First Sec. (Commercial), New Delhi 1993–96; Int. Dir, Invest UK 1997–99; Counsellor (Commercial) and Dir of Trade and Investment for Spain, Madrid 2000–04; Consul Gen., Dubai 2004–08; Amb. to Qatar 2008–.
Address: British Embassy, PO Box 3, Doha, Qatar (office). *Telephone:* 4421991 (office). *Fax:* 4438692 (office). *E-mail:* consular_qatar@fco.gov.uk (office); bembcomm@qatar.net.qa (office). *Website:* www.britishembassy.gov.uk/qatar (office).

HAY, Barbara Logan, CMG, MBE, FRSA; British diplomatist; *Consul-General in Istanbul;* b. 20 Jan. 1953. *Education:* Boroughmuir Sr Secondary School, Edin. *Career:* joined Diplomatic Service 1971, served in Moscow 1975–78 as third sec. science dept, vice-consul Johannesburg 1978–80, returned to Foreign Office London 1980–85 including Asst Pvt. Sec. to Perm. Under-Sec. and Head of Diplomatic Service 1981–83; vice-consul Montreal, Canada 1985-88; First Sec., Moscow 1988–91; Consul-Gen., St Petersburg (Russian Fed.) 1991–92, 2000–04, Consul-Gen. Istanbul 2004–; with Jt Assistance Unit (Cen. Europe), FCO 1992–94; Amb. to Uzbekistan (also accred. to Tajikistan) 1995–99; Counsellor, FCO 1999–2000.
Address: Consulate-General of the United Kingdom, Istanbul, Turkey (office). *Telephone:* (212) 3346400. *Fax:* (212) 3346403. *E-mail:* britembinf@turk.net. *Website:* www.britishembassy.org.tr.

HAYAMI, Masaru; Japanese banker and economist; b. 24 March 1925. *Education:* Hitotsubashi Univ. *Career:* joined Bank of Japan 1947, Man. Ooita Br. 1967, Chief Rep. Europe 1971, Dir Foreign Dept 1975, Man. Nagoya Br. 1976, Exec. Dir 1978, Gov. Bank of Japan 1998–2003, Alt. Gov. IMF and World Bank for Japan 1998–2003; Sr Man. Dir Nissho Iwai Corpn 1981, Exec. Vice-Pres. 1982, Pres. 1984, Pres. and Chair. 1987, Chair. 1990–94; Chair. Keizai Doyukai (Japan Asscn of Corp. Execs) 1991–95; Chair. Bd of Trustees, Tokyo Woman's Christian Univ. 1992–98. *Publication:* The Day the Yen will be Respected, Integrity of Money, Navigation through Uncharted Water, Honesty (Calling).
Address: c/o Bank of Japan, 2-1-1, Nihonbashi-Hongokucho, Chuo-ku, Tokyo 103-8660, Japan (office).

HAYAMI, Yujiro, PhD; Japanese economist and academic; *Chairman, Graduate Faculty, Foundation for Advanced Studies in International Development;* b. 26 Nov. 1932, Tokyo; m. Takako Suzuki 1962; one s. two d. *Education:* Univ. of Tokyo and Iowa State Univ. *Career:* economist, Japan Nat. Research Inst. of Agricultural Econs 1956–66; Assoc. Prof. of Econs Tokyo Metropolitan Univ. 1966–72, Prof. 1972–86; economist, Int. Rice Research Inst. 1974–76; Prof. of Int. Econs Aoyama-Gakuin Univ. 1986–2000; Dir Grad. Program, Foundation for Advanced Studies in Int. Devt 2000–04, Chair. 2004–; Purple Ribbon and Medal for Contribs to Arts and Sciences (Japan). *Publications:* Development Economics: From

the Poverty to the Wealth of Nations 1997, 3rd edn 2005, A Rice Village Saga: Three Decades of Green Revolution in the Philippines 2000.
Address: GRIPS/FASID Joint Graduate Programme, 7-22-1, Roppongi, Minato-ku, Tokyo 106-8677 (office); 6-8-14 Okusawa, Setagaya-ku, Tokyo 158, Japan (home). *Telephone:* (3) 5413-6033 (office); (3) 3701-1345 (home). *Fax:* (3) 5413-0016 (office); (3) 3701-1345 (home). *E-mail:* hayami@grip.ac.jp (office).

HAYASHI, Yoshimasa, LLB, MPA; Japanese lawyer and politician; *Minister of Defence;* b. 19 Jan. 1961; m.; one d. *Education:* Univ. of Tokyo, Kennedy School of Govt, Harvard Univ., USA. *Career:* Asst to US Congressman Steve Neal,. Washington, DC 1991, also Int. Affairs Intern at Office of US Senator William Roth; worked in pvt. for Mitui & Co Ltd., Tokyo, Sanden Koutsu Co., Yamaguchi, Yamaguchi Godo Gas Co., Keefe Co., Washington, DC; mem. House of Councillors (LDP) for Yamaguchi Prefecture 1995–, Leader Pro-Whaling League; Sec., Ministry of Finance 1999–2000; Deputy Minister, Cabinet Office 2006–07; Minister of Defence 2008–.
Address: Ministry of Defence, 5-1, Ichigaya, Honmura-cho, Shinjuku-ku, Tokyo 162-8801, Japan (office). *Telephone:* (3) 3268-3111. *E-mail:* infomod@mod.go.jp (office). *Website:* www.mod.go.jp (office).

HAYDEN, Gen. Michael Vincent, BA, MA; American air force officer and government official; *Director, Central Intelligence Agency;* b. 17 March 1945, Pittsburgh. *Education:* N Catholic High School, Duquesne Univ., Pittsburgh, Academic Instructor School, Squadron Officer School, Air Command and Staff Coll., Air War Coll., Maxwell AF Base, Ala, Defense Intelligence Agency, Bolling AF Base, Washington DC, Armed Forces Staff Coll., Norfolk, Va. *Career:* rank of Second Lt 1967–70; Analyst and Briefer, Strategic Air Command HQ, Offnut AF Base, Neb. 1970–72; promoted to First Lt 1970, to Capt. 1971; Chief Current Intelligence Div., 8th AF HQ, Andersen AF Base, Guam 1972–75; Academic Instructor and Commdt of Cadets, ROTC Program, St Michael's Coll., Winooski, Vt 1975–79; promoted to Maj. 1980; Chief of Intelligence, 51st Tactical Fighter Wing, Osan Air Base, S Korea 1980–82; Air Attaché, US Embassy, Sofia, Bulgaria 1984–86; promoted to Lt –Col 1985; Politico-Mil. Affairs Officer, Strategy Div., USAF HQ, Washington DC 1986–89, Chief, Sec. of AF Staff Group 1991–93; Dir for Defense Policy and Arms Control, Nat. Security Council 1989–91; promoted to Col 1990; Dir Intelligence Directorate, US European Command HQ, Stuttgart, Germany 1993–95; promoted to Brig. Gen. 1993; Special Asst to Commdr, Air Intelligence Agency HQ, Kelly AF Base Oct.–Dec. 1995, Commdr 1996–97, Dir Jt Command and Control Warfare Center 1996–97; Deputy Chief of Staff, UN Command and US Forces Korea, Yongsan Army Garrison, S Korea 1997–99; promoted to Lt Gen. 1999; Dir Nat. Security Agency 1999–2005, Chief, Cen. Security Service, Fort George G. Meade, Md 1999–2005; promoted to Gen. 2005; Prin. Deputy Dir, Nat. Intelligence, Washington DC 2005–06; Dir CIA 2006–; Defense Distinguished Service Medal, Defense Superior Service Medal with oak leaf cluster, Legion of Merit, Bronze Star Medal, Meritorious Service Medal with two oak leaf clusters, AF Commendation Medal, AF Achievement Medal.
Address: Central Intelligence Agency, Office of Public Affairs, Washington, DC 20505, USA (office). *Telephone:* (703) 482-0623 (office). *Fax:* (703) 482-1739 (office). *Website:* www.cia.gov (office).

HAYWOOD, Nigel; British diplomatist; *Consul-General in Southern Iraq;* m. Louise Haywood; three s. *Career:* joined FCO 1983; served with Embassy in Budapest, Hungary; Deputy Consul-Gen., Johannesburg 1992–96; Deputy Head of Del. to OSCE, Vienna 1996–2000; Deputy Dir for Personnel, FCO 2000–03; Amb. to Estonia 2003–07; Consul-Gen. in Southern Iraq 2007–.
Address: Office of the British Embassy, Al Sarraji, Basra, Iraq (office). *Telephone:* (40) 831000 (office). *Fax:* (40) 832344 (office). *E-mail:* britishconsulbasra@fco.gov.uk (office).

HE, Chunlin; Chinese politician; *Chairman, Internal and Judicial Affairs Committee, 10th National People's Congress;* b. Aug. 1933, Wuxi City, Jiangsu Prov. *Education:* Northeast China Agricultural Coll. *Career:* joined CCP 1951; technician, engineer, then Deputy Section Chief and Section Chief, Chinese Acad. of Agricultural Mechanization Sciences 1962–66; clerk, Org. Dept, CCP Hebei Prov. Cttee 1966–67; Deputy Chief, Science and Tech. Div., Agricultural Machinery Research Inst., First Ministry of Machine-Building Industry 1972–78; Chief, Comprehensive Div., Survey and Research Section, Ministry of Agricultural Machinery 1979–80, Dir, Gen. Office and of Survey and Research Section 1980–82; Dir Special Econ. Zones Office of State Council 1984–93; Deputy Sec.-Gen. State Council 1988–98 (Deputy Sec. CCP Leading Party Group 1988–91); Head, Nat. Leading Group for Suppressing Smuggling 1993; mem. State Leading Group for Science and Tech. 1996; mem. Hong Kong Special Admin. Region Preparatory Cttee, Govt Del. at Hong Kong Hand-Over Ceremony

1997; Sec.-Gen. 9th Standing Cttee of NPC 1998–2003, Chair. Internal and Judicial Affairs Cttee of 10th NPC 2003–, Chair. Credentials Cttee 2003–; mem. 14th CCP Cen. Cttee 1992–97, 15th CCP Cen. Cttee 1997–2002.
Address: State Council, Beijing, People's Republic of China.

HE, Luli; Chinese politician and paediatrician; *Vice-Chairman 10th Standing Committee, National People's Congress;* b. 7 June 1934, Jinan, Shandong Prov.; m. Rong Guohuang 1958 (died 1989); two s. *Education:* Beijing Coll. of Medicine. *Career:* paediatrician, Beijing Children's Hosp. 1957–, Beijing No. 2 Hosp. 1988–96; Deputy Head, People's Govt, Xicheng Dist, Beijing 1984–88; Vice-Mayor Beijing Municipality 1988–96; Vice-Chair. Cen. Cttee, 7th Revolutionary Cttee of the Chinese Kuomintang (RCCK) 1988–92, Vice-Chair. Women and Youth Cttee, RCCK 1988–96, Chair. Beijing Municipal Cttee 1988–93, Chair. Cen. Cttee of 8th RCCK 1992–97, Chair. Cen. Cttee of 9th RCCK 1997–2002; Pres. Cen. Acad. of Socialism 1999–; mem. CPPCC 8th Nat. Cttee 1993–98, Vice-Chair. 1996–98; Vice-Chair. Standing Cttee of 9th NPC 1998–2003, of 10th NPC 2003–; Vice-Pres. Exec. Cttee of All China Women's Fed. 1993–; Pres. China Population Welfare Foundation 2000–; mem. Govt Del. at Macao Hand-Over Ceremony, Macao Special Admin. Region Preparatory Cttee 1999; Hon. Vice-Pres. Red Cross Soc. of China 1999; honoured as Nat. March 8 Red-Banner Bearer 1994.
Address: Central Academy of Socialism, Beijing 100081, People's Republic of China.

HE, Yong; Chinese politician; *Deputy Secretary, Standing Committee, Central Commission for Discipline Inspection, 16th Chinese Communist Party Central Committee;* b. Oct. 1940, Qianxi Co., Hebei Prov. *Education:* Tianjin Univ. *Career:* joined CCP 1958; technician, Metering Office, No. 238 Factory 1968–70, Production Sec., Head Office 1970–75, Dir Political Dept 1975–78 (mem. Standing Cttee of CCP Party Cttee 1975–78), Dir No. 238 Factory 1978–83 (Deputy Sec. CCP Party Cttee 1978–83); Deputy Dir Office of Science, Tech. and Industry for Nat. Defence, Hubei Prov. 1983–85; Dir-Gen. Personnel Dept, Ministry of Ordinance Industry 1985–86; Deputy Head, Org. Dept of CCP Cen. Cttee 1986–87, Dir Bureau of Party and Govt Personnel Engaged in Foreign Affairs 1986–87; Vice-Minister of Supervision 1987–98, Minister 1998–2002; mem. Standing Cttee of 14th CCP Cen. Comm. for Discipline Inspection 1992–97, 15th CCP Cen. Cttee 1997–2002 (Deputy Sec. Cen. Comm. for Discipline Inspection 1997–2002), 16th CCP Cen. Cttee 2002– (mem. Politburo Secr. 2002–, Deputy Sec. Standing Cttee of Cen. Comm. for Discipline Inspection 2002–).
Address: c/o Zhongguo Gongchan Dang (Chinese Communist Party), Beijing, People's Republic of China.

HECKMAN, James Joseph, PhD; American economist and academic; *Henry Schultz Distinguished Service Professor of Economics, University of Chicago;* b. 19 April 1944, Chicago, IL; m. Lynne Pettler Heckman; one s. one d. *Education:* Colorado Coll. and Princeton Univ. *Career:* systems engineer, Martin-Marietta Aerospace 1965; Junior Economist, Council of Economic Advisors 1967; Adjunct Assistant Professor, New York Univ 1972; Assistant Professor, Columbia Univ. 1970–73, Assoc. Prof. 1973–74; Assoc. Prof. of Econs, Univ. of Chicago 1973–77, Prof. of Econs 1977–, Henry Schultz Prof. of Econs 1985–95, Henry Schultz Distinguished Service Prof. of Econs 1995–, Prof., Irving Harris School of Public Policy 1990–, Dir Center For Evaluation of Social Programs 1991–; A. Whitney Griswold Prof. of Econs, Yale Univ. 1988–90, Irving Fisher Prof. 1984, Prof. of Statistics 1990–; Lecturer, Yale Law School 1989–90; Research Assoc., Nat. Bureau of Econ. Research 1971–85, 1987–, Harry Scherman Fellow 1972–73; consultant, RAND Corpn 1975–76; Social Science Research Council Training Fellow 1977–78; Guggenheim Fellow 1978–79; Fellow, Center for Advanced Study in the Behavioral Sciences, Stanford Univ. 1978–79; Research Assoc., Nat. Opinion Research Center: Econs Research Center 1979–; Sr Research Fellow, American Bar Foundation 1991–; Pres.-elect Midwest Econs Asscn 1996–97, Pres. 1998; Fellow, Econometric Soc. 1980, American Acad. of Arts and Sciences 1985, American Statistical Asscn 2001; mem. NAS 1992–; Co-Ed. Journal of Political Economy 1981–87; Assoc. Ed. Journal of Econometrics 1977–83, Journal of Labor Economics 1982–, Review of Economic Studies 1982–85, Econometric Reviews 1987–, Journal of Economic Perspectives 1989–96; mem. Editorial Bd Review of Economics and Statistics 1994–; Hon. Prof., Univ. of Tucuman 1998, Huazhong Univ., China 2001; Hon. mem. Latin and Caribbean Econ. Asscn 1999; Hon. MA (Yale) 1989; Hon. PhD (Colo Coll.) 2001; Hon. DUniv (Chile) 2002, (UAEM, Mexico) 2003; John Bates Clark Medal, American Econs Asscn 1983, First Annual Louis T. Benezet Distinguished Alumnus Award, Colo Coll. 1985, Nobel Prize in Econs 2000, Statistician of the Year, Chicago Chapter, American Statistical Asscn 2002. *Publications include:* Longitudinal Analysis of Labor Market Data (co-ed.) 1985, Performance Standards in A Government Bureaucracy (ed collection), Lecture Notes on Longitudinal Data Analysis (co-author) 1997,

Inequality in America: What Role for Human Capital Policy? (co-ed.) 2003, Law and Employment: Lessons From Latin America and the Caribbean (co-author) 2003, Evaluating Human Capital Policy (The Gorman Lectures) 2004, Incentives in Government Bureaucracies: Can Incentives in Bureaucracies Emulate Market Efficiency? 2004; more than 200 articles in journals.
Address: Department of Economics, University of Chicago, 1126 East 59th Street, Chicago, IL 60637 (office); 4807 S Greenwood, Chicago, IL 60615, USA (home). *Telephone:* (773) 702-0634 (office); (773) 268-4547 (home). *Fax:* (773) 702-8490 (office); (773) 268-6844 (home). *E-mail:* j-heckman@ uchicago.edu (office). *Website:* lily.src.uchicago.edu (office).

HEIFETZ, Zvi; Israeli lawyer and diplomatist; b. USSR; m. Sigalia Heifetz; seven c. *Career:* family exiled from Latvia to Siberia during World War II; following high school, served in army for seven years in Intelligence, now a Maj. in the Reserves, instructor in cadet school; graduated with a law degree, qualified for Israeli Bar, est. practice in Tel-Aviv; went to USSR in 1989; fmr legal advisor to Prime Minister's Office on Soviet matters; fmr Chair. Tower Records; fmr Vice-Chair. Ma'ariv (Israel's second largest publishing group); Hon. Consul of Latvia to Israel –2004, Amb. to UK 2004–07.
Address: Ministry of Foreign Affairs, 9 Yitzhak Rabin Blvd, Kiryat Ben-Gurion, Jerusalem 91035, Israel (office). *Telephone:* 2-5303111 (office). *Fax:* 2-5303367 (office). *E-mail:* feedback@mfa.gov.il (office). *Website:* www.mfa.gov.il (office).

HEIMISSON, Hannes; Icelandic diplomatist; *Ambassador to Finland;* b. 25 March 1960, Reykjavík; m. Gurún Margrét Sólonsdóttir. *Education:* Reykjavík Jr Coll., US Int. Univ., San Diego, Calif., USA. *Career:* journalist, Dagbladid-Visir newspaper 1984–86; First Sec., Ministry for Foreign Affairs 1986, First Sec., Defense Dept 1986–87, First Sec., Dept of Admin. 1987–88; First Sec., Embassy in Paris 1988–92; First Sec., Embassy in Stockholm 1992–95, Counsellor 1995; Deputy Dir Defense Dept 1995–96; Counsellor, Political Dept, responsible for Nordic co-operation 1996–97, also rep. to Council of Baltic Sea States; Minister-Counsellor 1997; Chargé dAffaires ad interim, Embassy in Helsinki 1997–99; Dir Dept of Information, Cultural Affairs and Consular Liaison, Ministry for Foreign Affairs 1999–2003; Consul Gen., New York 2003–05; Amb. to Finland also accred to Estonia, Latvia, Lithuania and the Ukraine) 2005–.
Address: Embassy of Iceland, Pohjoisesplanadi 27C, 00100 Helsinki, Finland (office). *Telephone:* (9) 6122460 (office). *Fax:* (9) 61224620 (office). *E-mail:* hannes.heimisson@utn.stjr.is (office). *Website:* www.iceland.org/fi (office).

HEINBECKER, Paul, BA; Canadian diplomatist, research institute admin-istrator and commentator; *Director, Centre for Global Relations, Govern-ance and Policy and Director, International Relations and Communications Centre for International Governance Innovation, Wilfred Laurier University;* m. Ayse Köymen; two d. *Education:* Waterloo Lutheran Univ. (now Wilfred Laurier Univ.). *Career:* joined Dept of External Affairs 1965; Third/Second Sec., Embassy in Ankara, Turkey 1966–70; First Sec. in Stockholm, Sweden 1972–75; Counsellor (OECD) in Paris 1975–79; Dir US Gen. Relations Div., Dept of External Affairs 1979–83, Chair. Policy Devt Secr. 1983–85; Minister, Embassy in Washington, DC 1985–89; Sr Policy Adviser and Speech Writer for the Prime Minister 1989–91, Chief Foreign Policy Adviser and Asst Sec. to Cabinet (Foreign and Defence Policy), Privy Council Office 1991–92; Amb. to Germany 1992–96; Asst Deputy Minister, Global and Security Policy and Political Dir Dept of Foreign Affairs and Int. Trade 1996–2000; Perm. Rep. to UN, New York 2000–03; led interdepartmental task force on Kosovo; head, Canadian del. for negotiation of Climate Change Convention, Kyoto; Dir Centre for Global Relations, Governance and Policy, Wilfred Laurier Univ. and Dir Int. Relations and Communications Centre for Int. Governance Innovation 2003–; Trudeau Mentor 2005; Hon. DrIur (Wilfred Laurier Univ.) 1993.
Address: Centre for Global Relations, Governance and Policy, Wilfred Laurier University, 75 University Avenue, Waterloo, ON N2L 3C5 (office); Centre for International Governance Innovation, 57 Erb Street West, Waterloo, ON, N2L 6C2, Canada (office). *Telephone:* (519) 885-2444 (office). *Fax:* (519) 885-5450 (office). *E-mail:* pheinbecker@wlu.ca (office); pheinbecker@cigionline.ca (home). *Website:* www.wlu.ca (office).

HEISBOURG, François, FRSA; French academic and business executive; *Special Adviser, Fondation pour la Recherche Stratégique;* b. 24 June 1949, London, England; m. Elyette Levy 1989; two s. *Education:* Coll. Stanislas, Paris, Inst. d'Etudes Politiques, Cycle Supérieur d'Aménagement et d'Urbanisme, Ecole Nat. d'Admin. *Career:* Asst to Dir of Econ. Affairs, Ministry of Foreign Affairs 1977–78; policy planning staff, Ministry of Foreign Affairs 1978–79; First Sec. Perm. Mission of France to UN 1979–81; Int. Security Adviser to Minister of Defence 1981–84; Vice-Pres. Thomson Int. 1984–87; Dir IISS, London 1987–92, Chair. 2001–; Sr Vice-

Pres. Matra Défense Espace 1992–98; Head French Interministerial Group on teaching of and research in, strategic and int. affairs; Chair. Geneva Centre for Security Policy 1998–; Dir Fondation pour la Recherche Stratégique, Paris 2001–05, Special Adviser 2005–; mem. Royal Soc. for Encouragement of Arts, Manufacture and Commerce; Chevalier, Légion d'honneur, Ordre nat. du Mérite, Grosses Verdienstkreuz (Germany), Commdr, Ordre de la Couronne de Chêne (Luxembourg), Merito Militar (Spain). *Publications:* La Puce, les Hommes et la Bombe (with P. Boniface) 1986, Les Volontaires de l'an 2000 1995, The Future of Warfare 1997, European Defence: Making it Work 2000, Hyperterrorisme: La Nouvelle Guerre 2001, Le fin d'Occident? – Les Etats Unis, l'Europe et le Moyen Orient 2005; numerous articles in int. media and scholarly journals. *Address:* Fondation pour la Recherche Stratégique, 27 rue Damesme, 75013 Paris, France (office). *Telephone:* 1-43-13-77-80 (office). *Fax:* 1-43-13-77-78. *E-mail:* f.heisbourg@frstrategie.org (office); heisbour@noos.fr (home). *Website:* www.frstrategie.org (office).

HEKMATYAR, Gulbuddin; Afghan politician and fmr guerrilla leader; *Leader, Gulbuddin Islamic Party;* b. 1947, Imam Saheb, Kunduz Prov. *Education:* Kabul Univ. *Career:* mem. Muslim Youth 1970; imprisoned 1972–73; fled to Pakistan 1973; Leader Hizb-i Islami Mujahidin Movt against Soviet-backed regime; Prime Minister of Afghanistan 1993–94, 1996–97; returned from exile in Iran 1998; currently Leader Hizb-i Islami Gulbuddin (Gulbuddin Islamic Party).

HELENIUS, Harry Gustaf, PhD; Finnish diplomatist; *Ambassador to Russian Federation;* b. 2 June 1946, Oulu; m.; two c. *Career:* worked in Ministry of Foreign Affairs and in diplomatic missions abroad, including in France, Spain, Austria and in Consulate in Moscow, apptd Consul Gen. in St Petersburg 1999, Deputy Dir-Gen. and Head of Div. for Eastern Affairs, Ministry of Foreign Affairs 2003–04, Amb. to Russian Fed. 2004–. *Address:* Embassy of Finland, Kropotkinskii per. 15/17, 119034 Moscow G-34, Russian Federation (office). *Telephone:* (495) 787-41-74 (office). *Fax:* (495) 247-33-80 (office). *E-mail:* harry.helenius@formin.fi (home). *Website:* www.finemb-moscow.fi (office).

HELLER, Claude; Mexican diplomatist; *Permanent Representative, United Nations;* b. 1949, Mexico City; m. Adela Fuchs de Heller. *Education:* Colegio de Mexico, Inst. of High Int. Studies, Geneva. *Career:* Dir-Gen. for UN Orgs, Ministry for Foreign Affairs 1983–87, Asst Sec. for Multilateral Affairs 1988; Political Counsellor, Embassy in Washington, DC 1982–83; Amb. to Switzerland 1989–91, to Austria (also accred to Slovenia) 1992–95, to Cuba 1995–98; Perm. Rep. to OAS 1998–2001; Amb. to France 2001–07; Perm. Rep. to OECD 2002–03; Perm. Rep. to UN, New York 2007–. *Publications:* several books and articles on foreign policy. *Address:* Permanent Mission of Mexico to the United Nations, 2 United Nations Plaza, 28th Floor, New York, NY 10017, USA (office). *Telephone:* (212) 752-0220 (office). *Fax:* (212) 688-8862 (office). *E-mail:* mexico@un.int (office). *Website:* www.un.int/mexico (office).

HELSØ, Gen. Hans Jesper; Danish army officer; *Chief of Defence;* b. 9 July 1948, Copenhagen; m. Pernille Vibeke Helsø; four c. *Career:* nat. service 1968, rank of Sergeant 1969, 2nd Lt 1970, 1st Lt 1974; Gun Position Officer, Fire Direction Officer, Battery Exec. Officer, Battery Commdr, Kings Artillery 1974–78; Co. Exec. Officer UNFICYP 1979; Capt. 1979; Staff Officer, Logistic Br. LANDZEALAND 1979–82, Procurement Br. CHODDEN 1983–87, NATO Office, Ministry of Defence 1987–90; rank of Maj. 1986, Lt-Col 1990; Bn Commdr, 1st and 2nd ARTY-Bn, Kings Artillery 1990–92; DCOS Plans and Policy, Army Operational Command 1992–94; rank of Col 1994; CO Kings Artillery 1994–96; Commdr Bihac Area, UNPROFOR 1995; CO 1st Zealand Brigade 1996–98; rank of Maj.-Gen. 1998; Commdr Army Operational Command 1998–2000; rank of Lt-Gen. 2000; Deputy Chief of Defence 2000–02, Chief of Defence 2002–08; rank of Gen. 2002; Grand Cross, Order of Dannebrog, Badge of Honour for Good Service in the Army, Badge of Honour, Danish Reserve Officers' Org., Grand Officier, Ordre nat. du Mérite, Order of the Cross of the Eagle, Commdr, Légion d'honneur; UN Medals, UNFICYP and UNPROFOR, Medal for Support to Latvia's membership of NATO. *Address:* Defence Command, PO Box 2153, 1016 Copenhagen K, Denmark (office). *Telephone:* 45-67-30-00 (office). *Fax:* 45-89-07-48 (office). *E-mail:* fko-fc@mil.dk (office). *Website:* www.forsvaret.dk (office).

HEMINGFORD, Baron of Watford in the County of Hertford; **(Dennis) Nicholas Hemingford,** MA, FRSA; British journalist; b. (Dennis Nicholas Herbert), 25 July 1934, Watford, Herts.; m. Jennifer Mary Toresen Bailey 1958; one s. three d. *Education:* Oundle School, Clare Coll., Cambridge. *Career:* Sports Desk, Reuters 1956–57, Diplomatic Desk 1957–60, Washington Bureau 1960–61; Asst Washington Corresp., The Times 1961–65, Middle East Corresp. 1965–69, Deputy Features Ed. 1969–70; Ed. Cambridge Evening News 1970–74; Editorial Dir Westminster Press

1974–91, Deputy Chief Exec. 1991–95; Pres. Guild of British Newspaper Eds 1980–81, Media Soc. 1982–84; Hon. Sec. Asscn of British Eds 1985–95; mem. E Anglian Regional Cttee, Nat. Trust 1983–2000, Chair. 1990–2000; Gov. Bell Educational Trust 1985–90; mem. Council Europa Nostra 1999–2005, Culture Cttee, UK Comm., UNESCO 1999–2003; Pres. Huntingdonshire Family History Soc.; mem. Council Friends of the British Library 2005–; Hon. mem. Soc. of Eds 1999; Hon. Sr mem. Wolfson Coll., Cambridge; Liveryman, Grocers' Co. *Publications:* Jews and Arabs in Conflict 1969, Press Freedom in Britain (with David Flintham) 1991. *Address:* The Old Rectory, Hemingford Abbots, Huntingdon, Cambs., PE28 9AN, England (home). *Telephone:* (1480) 466234 (home). *Fax:* (1480) 380275 (home).

HENAULT, Gen. Raymond (Ray), CMM, CD, BA; Canadian armed forces officer; b. 1949, Winnipeg, Man. *Education:* Univ. of Man., Nat. Defence Coll., Kingston, Ont., Ecole Supérieure de Guerre Aérienne, Paris, France. *Career:* began career in Canadian Armed Forces 1968; training at Canadian Force Base (CFB) Borden, Ont. and Gimili, Man.; CF-101 Voodoo Pilot, 425 Squadron, CFB Bagotville, Québec 1971; Flying Instructor, Musketeer, CFB Portage la Prairie 1972–74; Air Traffic Controller, CFB Bagotville 1974–76; Twin Huey Helicopter Pilot, 408 Squadron, CFB Edmonton, Alberta 1976–80; Staff Officer Aviation, 5 Canadian Brigade Group HQ, CFB Valcartier 1980–81; Twin Huey Flight Commdr, 430e Escardon, CFB Valcartier 1981–85; Head of Doctrine and Int. Programs, Directorate of Land Aviation, Nat. Defence HQ, Ottawa 1985; Project Dir Canadian Forces Light Helicopter Project, Ottawa 1985–87; Commdg Officer 444(CA) Tactical Helicopter Squadron, CFB Lahr, Germany 1987–89; Sr Staff Officer Requirements, Air Command HQ, Winnipeg 1989–90; Base Commdr, CFB Portage la Prairie 1990–92; Deputy Commdr 10 Tactical Air Group, CFB Montreal 1992–93, Commdr 1994–95; Chief of Staff Operations, Air Command HQ 1995–96; Chief of Staff J3 and Dir-Gen. Mil. Plans and Operations, Nat. Defence HQ 1996–97; Acting Deputy Chief of Defence Staff 1997, Asst Chief of Air Staff 1997–98, Deputy Chief 1998–2001, Chief 2001–05; Chair. Mil. Cttee NATO 2005–08; promoted to Brigadier-Gen. 1994, Maj.-Gen. 1997, Lt-Gen. 1998, Gen. 2001; Commdr Order of Mil. Merit, Commdr Légion d'honneur, Most Venerable Order of St John of Jerusalem, US Legion of Merit; Hon. LLD (Univ. of Man.), Hon. PhD (Royal Military Coll. of Canada) 2005. *Address:* c/o Department of National Defence, National Defence Headquarters, Maj.-Gen. George R. Pearkes Bldg, 15 NT, 101 Colonel By Dr., Ottawa, ON K1A 0K2, Canada. *Telephone:* (613) 995-2534. *Fax:* (613) 996-8330. *E-mail:* information@forces.gc.ca. *Website:* www.forces.gc.ca.

HENDERSON, Andrew; British diplomatist; *Ambassador to Algeria;* b. 12 July 1952; m. Julia Henderson; two d. *Career:* Desk Officer, West Africa Dept, FCO 1971–72, Defence Dept 1972–75, Latin American Floater 1976–76, Vice-Consul, Rio de Janeiro 1977–80, Second Sec., Embassy in Oslo 1980–84, Asst Pvt. Sec. to Minister of State for Foreign and Commonwealth Affairs 1985–87, Consul, New York 1987–89, First Sec., Embassy in Washington, DC 1988–91, Deputy Head of Mission, Angola 1992–93, First Sec. and Head of Commercial Aid Section, Embassy in Cairo 1994–98, Head of Parl. Relations 1998–99, Consul-Gen., Jeddah 2000–03, São Paulo, Brazil 2003–07, Amb. to Algeria 2007–. *Address:* British Embassy, 12 Rue Slimane Amirat Hydra, Algiers, Algeria (office). *Telephone:* (21) 23-00-68 (office). *Fax:* (21) 23-00-67 (office). *E-mail:* BritishEmbassy.Algiers@fco.gov.uk (office). *Website:* www.britishembassy.gov.uk/algeria (office).

HENKIN, Louis, LLD, LHD; American professor of law; *Chairman, Institute for Human Rights, School of Law, Columbia University;* b. 11 Nov. 1917, Russia; m. Alice Hartman 1960; three s. *Education:* Yeshiva Coll. and Harvard Univ. *Career:* admitted New York Bar 1941, US Supreme Court Bar 1947; law clerk 1940–41, 1946–47; mil. service 1941–45; with State Dept 1945–46, 1948–57; UN Legal Dept 1947–48; Lecturer in Law, Columbia Univ. 1956–57; Visiting Prof. Univ. of Pa 1957–58, Prof. of Law 1958–62; Prof. Columbia Univ. 1962, mem. Inst. for War and Peace Studies 1962–, Hamilton Fish Prof. of Int. Law and Diplomacy 1963–78, Harlan Fiske Stone Prof. of Constitutional Law 1978–79, Univ. Prof. 1979–88, Univ. Prof. Emer. and Special Service Prof. 1988–; Chair. Directorate, Columbia Univ. Center for Study of Human Rights 1986–, Chair. Human Rights Inst., Columbia Univ. Law School 1999–; Pres. US Inst. of Human Rights 1970–93; mem. Lawyers' Cttee on Human Rights, Immigration and Refugee Services 1994–; mem. Human Rights Cttee (UN) under ICCPR 1999–; numerous professional and public appointments, affiliations and distinctions etc. –2002; Fellow, American Acad. of Arts and Sciences; mem. American Philosophical Soc., Council on Foreign Relations, American Soc. of Int. Law, Int. Law Asscn, Inst. de Droit Int., US Asscn of Constitutional Law etc.; Guggenheim Fellow 1979–80; Hon. JD (Brooklyn Law School) 1997. *Publications:* numerous books and articles on

constitutional law, constitutionalism, int. law, Law of the Sea and human rights including: How Nations Behave (2nd edn) 1979, Constitutionalism and Rights: The Influence of the United States Abroad 1989, Foreign Affairs and the US Constitution 1990, International Law: Politics and Values 1995, Foreign Affairs and the US Constitution (2nd edn) 1996, The Age of Rights 1996, Human Rights (with others) 1999, International Law (with others) (4th edn) 2001.
Address: 460 Riverside Drive, New York, NY 10027, USA (home). *Telephone:* 212-854-2634 (office). *Fax:* (212) 854-7946. *E-mail:* lh8@ columbia.edu (office).

HENNEKINNE, Loïc; French diplomatist; b. 20 Sept. 1940, Caudéran, Gironde; m. 2nd Marie Bozelle 1987; one d.; two s. (by first m.). *Education:* Ecole Nat. d'Admin. *Career:* First Sec. French embassies in Viet Nam 1969–71, Chile 1971–73; Minister-Counsellor, Japan 1979–81; Del. for External Action, Ministry of Industry 1981–82; Dir of Cabinet of Minister of Research and Industry 1982; Dir of Personnel and Admin Ministry of Foreign Affairs 1983–86; Amb. to Indonesia 1986–88; Gen. Sec. summit conf. of Western industrialized nations, Paris 1989; Diplomatic Adviser to Pres. Mitterrand 1989–91; Amb. to Japan 1991–93; Inspector-Gen. of Foreign Affairs 1993–96; Amb. to Canada 1997–98; Sec.-Gen. Ministry of Foreign Affairs (with rank of Amb. of France) 1998–2002; Amb. to Italy 2002–05; numerous int. decorations including Officier, Ordre nat. du Mérite, Officier, Légion d'honneur, Grand' Ufficiale Ordine Naz. al Merito della Repub. Italiana.
Address: c/o Ministry of Foreign Affairs, 37 quai d'Orsay, 75351 Paris Cedex 07, France. *Telephone:* 1-43-17-53-53. *Fax:* 1-43-17-52-03. *Website:* www.diplomatie.gouv.fr.

HENRI ALBERT FÉLIX MARIE GUILLAUME, HRH Grand Duke of Luxembourg, LèsScPol; b. 16 April 1955, Château de Betzdorf; m. Maria Teresa Mestre 1981; four s. (including Prince Guillaume Jean Joseph Marie) one d. *Education:* Royal Mil. Acad. Sandhurst, Univ. of Geneva. *Career:* mem. State Council 1980–98; apptd Lt Rep. of Grand Duke March 1988; succeeded father as Grand Duke of Luxembourg Oct. 2000; Chair. Bd of Econ. Devt, Galapagos Darwin Trust Luxembourg; Pres. Organizing Cttee, Int. Trade Fairs of Luxembourg; mem. Mentor Foundation, Int. Olympic Cttee; Hon. Maj. Parachute Regt; Hon. Dr rer. pol (Trier); Hon. DHumLitt (Sacred Heart); Hon. LLD (Miami), Hon. DEcon (Khon Kaen).
Address: Grand Ducal Palace, 2013 Luxembourg, Luxembourg (office). *Website:* www.gouvernement.lu.

HEPTULLA, Najma, MSc, PhD; Indian politician and international organization executive; *Honorary President, Inter-Parliamentary Union;* b. 13 April 1940; m.; three d. *Career:* Deputy Chair. Rajya Sabha (Upper House of Parl.) 1985–86, 1988–; Gen.-Sec. All India Congress Cttee (I) 1986–87, Spokesperson 1986–87, 1998; Special Envoy of the Prime Minister on numerous missions abroad; mem. Exec. Cttee Inter-Parliamentary Union (IPU) 1995–2002, Vice-Pres. 1999, Acting Pres. IPU Council July–Oct. 1999, Pres. 1999–2002, Hon. Pres. 2002–; Chair. Meeting of Women Parliamentarians 1993, mem. Co-ordinating Cttee 1993–; Founder-Pres. Parliamentarians' Forum for Human Devt 1993; Head. Indian Del. to UN Comm. on the Status of Women 1997; Pres. Indian Housewives Fed. 1985–, Azad Foundation for Research and Devt, Indo–Arab Soc.; mem. Nat. Integration Council, Exec. Cttee Indian Council for Cultural Relations (ICCR); Distinguished Human Devt Amb. for UNDP. *Publications include:* Indo–West Asian Relations: The Nehru Era 1992, Reforms for Women: Future Options 1992, Environmental Protection in Developing Countries 1993, Human Social Security and Sustainable Development 1995, AIDS: Approaches to Prevention 1996.
Address: c/o Inter-Parliamentary Union, CP 438, 1211 Geneva 19, Switzerland (office).

HERBISH, Suleiman Jasir al-, MEconSc; Saudi Arabian international organization official; *Director General, OPEC Fund for International Development;* b. 6 Nov. 1942, Ar-Rass; m.; four c. *Education:* Trinity Univ., San Antonio, Tex., USA. *Career:* fmr Dir Saline Water Conversion Corpn, Saudi Co. for Precious Metals; fmr Asst Deputy Minister; fmr Chair. Nat. Shipping Co. of Saudi Arabia, Saudi Arabian Texaco Inc., Arabian Drilling Co.; Saudi Arabian Gov. at OPEC, Vienna 1992–2003; Dir-Gen. Organization of Petroleum Exporting Countries (OPEC) Fund for Int. Devt, Nov. 2003–; Head Saudi Arabian dels to int. confs and negotiations on energy-related issues.
Address: OPEC Fund for International Development, PO Box 995, 1011 Vienna, Austria (office). *Telephone:* (1) 51564 (office); (1) 51166 (office). *Fax:* (1) 513-92-38 (office). *E-mail:* info@ofid.org. *Website:* www.opecfund .org (office).

HERBOLD, Patricia Louise, BA, JD; American diplomatist; *Ambassador to Singapore;* b. (Patricia Louise Kruse), Cincinnati, Ohio; m. Robert J. Herbold; three c. *Education:* Edgecliff Coll., Cincinnati and Salmon P. Chase Coll. of Law, Northern Kentucky Univ. *Career:* began professional career as analytical chemist at Fed. Water Pollution Control Admin, Cincinnati, later served as Chief of Data Processing Unit in its Lake Erie Program Office; Assoc. Regional Counsel for Cincinnati Real Estate Investment Office of Prudential Insurance of America 1979–88; Vice-Pres. and Gen. Counsel, Bank One, Dayton, OH 1988–90; attorney, Taft, Stettinius & Hollister, Cincinnati 1990–94; mem. Council and Mayor of Montgomery, Ohio 1983–87; Commr, Wash. State Gambling Comm. 1997–2000; Chair. King Co. (Wash.) Republican Party 2002–04; Amb. to Singapore 2005–; fmr mem. Pres.'s 21st Century Workforce Council, Bd St Joseph Orphanage, Cincinnati, Bd Salmon P. Chase Coll. of Law, Bd Seattle Art Museum, Bd Performing Arts Center Eastside, Bellevue, Bd Washington Policy Center, Bd Long Live the Kings.
Address: Embassy of the USA, 27 Napier Road, Singapore 258508, Singapore (office). *Telephone:* 64769100 (office). *Fax:* 64769340 (office). *E-mail:* singaporeusembassy@state.gov (office). *Website:* singapore .usembassy.gov (office).

HERBST, John Edward; American diplomatist; *Coordinator, Office for Reconstruction and Stabilization, State Department; Education:* School of Foreign Service, Georgetown Univ., Fletcher School of Law and Diplomacy. *Career:* worked in embassies in Moscow and Saudi Arabia; Dir Office of Ind. States and Commonwealth Affairs; Dir Office of Regional Affairs, Near East Asia Bureau; Political Counsellor, Embassy, Tel-Aviv; Deputy Dir for Econs, Office of Soviet Union Affairs; Dir for Policy, Nat. Security Council; Prin. Deputy to Amb.-at-Large for the New Ind. States; Consul-Gen. Jerusalem 1997–2000; Amb. to Uzbekistan 2000–03, to Ukraine 2003–06; Coordinator, Office for Reconstruction and Stabilization, US State Dept, Washington, DC 2006–.
Address: Office of the Coordinator for Reconstruction and Stabilization, US State Department, 2201 C Street, NW, Washington, DC 20520; 8355 Thompson Road, Annandale, VA 22003, USA (home). *Telephone:* (202) 663-0323 (office). *Fax:* (202) 663-0327 (office). *E-mail:* scrs_info@state.gov (office). *Website:* www.state.gov/s/crs (office).

HERCZEGH, Géza Gábor, PhD; Hungarian judge; b. 17 Oct. 1928, Nagykapos; m. Melinda Petnehazy 1961; one s. one d. *Education:* French Grammar School, Gödöllö, Univ. of Szeged. *Career:* Research Fellow in Public Int. Law Inst. of Political Science, Budapest 1951–67; Prof. of Law, Head Int. Law Dept, Univ. of Pécs 1967–90; Judge, Vice-Pres. Constitutional Court 1990–93; Judge Int. Court of Justice, The Hague 1993–2003; mem. Hungarian Acad. of Sciences 1985; Dr hc (Marburg) 1990, (Pécs) 2000. *Publications:* The Colonial Question and International Law 1962, General Principles of Law and the International Legal Order 1969, Development of International Humanitarian Law 1984, Foreign Policy of Hungary 1896–1919 1987, From Sarajevo to the Potsdam Conference 1999.
Address: Ipoly u.1a III, 1133 Budapest, Hungary. *Telephone:* (1) 339-4581 (home). *Fax:* (1) 412-1009 (home).

HERFKENS, Eveline L.; Dutch diplomat, politician and UN official; *Executive Coordinator of Millennium Development Goals Campaign, United Nations;* b. 1952, The Hague. *Education:* Leiden Univ. *Career:* Policy Officer for Devt Cooperation, Ministry of Foreign Affairs 1976–81; mem. Lower House of Parl. 1981–90; Treasurer and mem. Cttee Parliamentarians for Global Action 1985–96; mem. Econ. Cttee, Parliamentary Ass. of Council of Europe 1986–89, also Jt Organiser North-South Campaign; Exec. Dir World Bank, Washington, DC 1990–96; Amb. and Perm. Rep. to UN, Geneva 1996–98; Minister for Devt Cooperation 1998–2002; Exec. Coordinator Millennium Devt Goals Campaign, UN, NY Oct. 2002–; fmr Chair. Evert Vermeer Foundation, Dutch Fair Trade Org.; fmr mem. Council of the Labour Party (PvdA), Devt Cttee of Netherlands Council of Churches.
Address: UN Millennium Development Goals Campaign, United Nations, New York, NY 10017, USA. *Telephone:* (212) 963-1234. *Fax:* (212) 963-4879. *E-mail:* inquiries@un.org. *Website:* www.un.org.

HERMANN, Jacques; Danish judge (retd); b. 10 Nov. 1934. *Education:* Univ. of Copenhagen. *Career:* civil servant, Ministry of Justice 1959–77, section chief from 1972; Public Prosecutor 1977–80; High Court Judge 1981–83; Permanent Under-Sec. Ministry of Defence 1984–88; Justice, Supreme Court 1988–2004, Chief Justice and Pres. Supreme Court 2001–04.
Address: c/o Supreme Court, Prins Jørgens Gård 13, 1218 Copenhagen K, Denmark (office).

HERNÁNDEZ, Carmen Maria Gallardo; Salvadorean diplomatist; *Permanent Representative, United Nations;* b. 28 Nov. 1949, San Salvador; m.; two

c. *Education:* Univ. of Geneva, Switzerland, Ibero-American Univ., Mexico City. *Career:* parl. interpreter at numerous UN confs 1973–87, including First World Conf. on Women 1975, World Conf. on Human Rights 1993; Interpreter for Pres. of Mexico 1975–79; Amb. to France 1994, to Portugal 1994; Exec. Dir Foundation for Peace (FUNDAPAZ) 1995–96; Coordinator for Int. Cooperation, Supreme Court of Justice 2002–04; Perm. Rep. to UN, New York 2004–; columnist, La Prensa Grafica 1994–97, El Diario de Hoy 1999–2002; Dr hc (Technological Univ.) 1998; Professional of the Year, El Salvador Bar Asscn 1997.
Address: Office of the Permanent Representative of El Salvador to the United Nations, 46 Park Avenue, New York, NY 10016, USA (office). *Telephone:* (212) 679-1616 (office). *Fax:* (212) 725-7831 (office). *E-mail:* elsalvador@un.int (office).

HERTELEER, Vice-Adm. Willy Maurits; Belgian military officer; b. 1 Oct. 1941, Assenede; m. Jacqueline Liekens 1962; one s. three d. *Education:* Royal Cadet School, Brussels, Merchant Navy Acad., Belgian Staff Coll., Brussels, Ecole Supérieure de Guerre Navale, Paris. *Career:* commissioned Belgian Navy 1962, as ensign served on minesweepers and a supply/command ship 1963-68, became mine warfare specialist 1969–70, Staff Officer Mine Countermeasures, Operational Command 1970–72; Commdr coastal minesweeper 1975, ocean minesweeper/hunter 1978, (instructor Belgian-Dutch School for Mine Warfare, Ostend between these postings); rank of Lt-Commdr 1979; apptd to Planning section, Belgian Naval Staff, also mem. Naval Bd, NATO Mil. Standardization Agency 1979–82; Second-in-Command frigate Westdiep 1982–84, Commdg Officer 1984–85; Asst Chief of Staff Operations, Naval Operations Command 1986, Chief of Staff 1986–87; Head Belgian-Dutch School for Mine Warfare 1987–89; mem. Audit Team, Belgian Naval Staff, Brussels 1989, Staff Officer, Operations 1990, Commdr Naval Operations 1990–92; rank of Rear-Adm. 1992; joined Gen. Staff Headquarters, Brussels 1992, Chief of Naval Staff 1993–95; rank of Vice-Adm. 1995; Chief of the Gen. Staff 1995–2002; Aide to King Albert II; Grand Cross, Order of the Crown.
Address: Rue d'Evère, 1140 Brussels, Belgium. *Telephone:* (2) 701-31-50. *Fax:* (2) 701-66-25.

HERTELL, Hans Helmut, BA, JD; American lawyer, business executive and diplomatist; b. San Juan, Puerto Rico; m. Marie Hertell; three c. *Education:* Fordham Univ., NY and Univ. of Puerto Rico. *Career:* political and legal advisor to Gov. of Puerto Rico, Attorney Gen., Sec. of Agric. and Sec. of the Treasury of the Commonwealth of Puerto Rico 1982–84; mem. Republican Party; del. to American Center for Int. Leadership Conf., Moscow 1986; Founding Partner, Goldman, Antonetti, Ferraiuoli, Axtmayer & Hertell, Puerto Rico; Man. Dir for the Caribbean and Latin America, Black, Kelly, Scruggs & Healey, Washington, DC 1992–96; Chair. American Builders Corpn 1999–2001; fmr mem. Bd Dirs OCASO Insurance Officers of Puert Rico, Federal Home Loan Bank of New York, El Comandante Operating Co.; fmr Trustee Interstate Waste Technologies, Inc., Univ. of Puerto Rico Law School 1989–91; mem. Comm. to Review US Magistrates for Reappointment, US Court for the Dist of Puerto Rico 1989; Amb. to the Dominican Repub. 2001–06.
Address: US Department of State, 2201 C Street NW, Washington, DC 20520, USA (office). *Telephone:* (202) 647-4000 (office). *Fax:* (202) 647-6738 (office). *Website:* www.state.gov (office).

HESELTINE, Colin S., BEcons; Australian diplomatist and international organization official; b. 1947; m.; two d. *Education:* Monash Univ. *Career:* joined Dept of External Affairs, Canberra 1969, served in Embassy in Santiago, Chile 1970–75, in Madrid 1975–80, Chinese language training 1981–82, Minister and Deputy Head of Mission, Embassy in Beijing 1982–85, Dir, China Investment Project, Dept of Industry, Tech. and Resources, Victorian Govt 1985–87, Minister and Deputy Head of Mission, Embassy in Beijing 1988–92, Rep. (Head of Mission), Australian Commerce and Industry Office, Taipei 1992–97; Asst Sec., Maritime South East Asia Br. (covering Indonesia, Malaysia, Singapore, Philippines), Dept of Foreign Affairs and Trade 1997–98, First Asst Sec., North Asia Div. 1998–2001; Amb. to South Korea 2001–05; Deputy Exec. Dir APEC Secr. 2006, Exec. Dir 2007–08.
Address: c/o Department of Foreign Affairs and Trade, R. G. Casey Bldg, John McEwen Cres., Barton, ACT 0221, Australia. *Telephone:* (2) 6261-1111. *Fax:* (2) 6261-3111. *Website:* www.dfat.gov.au.

HEYMANN, Daniel, PhD; Argentine economist; *Senior Economist, ECLAC Buenos Aires, and Professor of Economics, University of Buenos Aires;* b. 30 Dec. 1949, Buenos Aires; m. Cristina Bramuglia 1976; two s. *Education:* Coll. Français de Buenos Aires, Univ. of Buenos Aires and Univ. of Calif. Los Angeles. *Career:* Asst Prof. Univ. of Buenos Aires 1973–75, Prof. of Econs 1987–; Research Asst ECLAC, Buenos Aires 1974–78, Sr Economist 1982–; Prof. of Econs, Instituto Torcuato Di Tella, Buenos Aires 1982–2003; Prof. of Econs, Univ. of La Plata 2004–. *Publications:*

Fluctuations of the Argentine Manufacturing Industry 1980, Three Essays on Inflation and Stabilization 1986, The Austral Plan 1987, Distributive Conflict and the Fiscal Deficit: Some Inflationary Games (jtly) 1991, Fiscal Inconsistencies and High Inflation (jtly) 1994, On the Interpretation of the Current Account 1994, High Inflation (jtly) 1995, Business Cycles from Misperceived Trends (jtly) 1998, Price Setting in a Schematic Model of Inductive Learning (jtly) 1999, Learning about Trends: Spending and Business Fluctuations in Open Economies (jtly) 2001, Inconsistent Behavior and Macroeconomic Disturbances 2002, Great Expectations and Hard Times: the Argentine Convertibility (jtly) 2003, Land-Rich Economies, Education and Economic Development (jtly) 2006.
Address: ECLAC Buenos Aires: Paraguay 1178, Piso 2, 1057 Buenos Aires, Argentina (office). *Telephone:* (11) 4815-7810 (office). *Fax:* (11) 4815-2534 (office).

HEYZER, Noeleen, PhD; Singaporean international organization official; *Executive Secretary, Economic and Social Commission for Asia and the Pacific (ESCAP);* m.; two d. *Education:* Univ. of Singapore, Univ. of Cambridge, UK. *Career:* Fellow and Research Officer, Inst. of Devt Studies, Univ. of Sussex, UK 1979–81; with Social Devt Div., ESCAP, Bangkok, Thailand early 1980s; Dir Gender and Devt Programme, Asian and Pacific Devt Centre, Kuala Lumpur, Malaysia 1984–94; Co-ordinator for the Asia-Pacific NGO Working Group for the UN Fourth World Conf. on Women, Beijing, People's Repub. of China; Exec. Dir UN Devt Fund for Women (UNIFEM) 1994–2007; Exec. Sec. ESCAP 2007–; Convener Int. Women's Comm. for a Just and Sustainable Palestinian-Israeli Peace; mem. Bd Pres. Ahtisaari's Crisis Man. Initiative; mem. High-Level Commonwealth Comm. on Respect and Understanding; New Millennium Distinguished Visiting Scholar, Columbia Univ.; Chair. Consortium Advisory Group, Research Programme on Women's Empowerment in Muslim Contexts; has served on bds of several humanitarian orgs including Devt Alternatives with Women for a New Era, the Global South, ISIS, Oxfam, Panos and Soc. for Int. Devt; Global Tolerance Award for Humanitarian Service, Friends of the UN 2000, Lifetime Achievement Award, Inst. for Leadership Devt 2000, Woman of Distinction Award, UN NGO Cttee 2003, Leadership Award, Mount Sinai Hosp., New York 2004, Leadership Award, UN Asscn Greater Boston 2004, Dag Hammarskjöld Medal 2004, NCRW Women Who Make a Difference Award 2005. *Publications include:* Gender, Economic Growth and Poverty, The Trade in Domestic Workers, Working Women in South-East Asia.
Address: Economic and Social Commission for Asia and the Pacific (ESCAP), United Nations Building, Rajadamnern Nok Avenue, Bangkok 10200, Thailand (office). *Telephone:* (2) 288-1234 (office). *Fax:* (2) 288-1000 (office). *E-mail:* unisbkk.unescap@un.org (office). *Website:* www.unescap.org (office).

HIGGINS, Dame Rosalyn, DBE, JSD, QC, FBA; British judge and fmr professor of international law; *President, International Court of Justice;* b. 2 June 1937; m. Rt Hon. Sir Terence L. (now Lord) Higgins 1961; one s. one d. *Education:* Burlington Grammar School, London, Girton Coll. Cambridge and Yale Law School, USA. *Career:* UK Intern, Office of Legal Affairs, UN 1958; Commonwealth Fund Fellow 1959; Visiting Fellow, Brookings Inst. Washington, DC 1960; Jr Fellow in Int. Studies, LSE 1961–63; staff specialist in int. law, Royal Inst. of Int. Affairs 1963–74; Visiting Fellow, LSE 1974–78; Prof. of Int. Law, Univ. of Kent at Canterbury 1978–81; Prof. of Int. Law, LSE 1981–95; Judge, Int. Court of Justice 1995–, Pres. 2006–; mem. UN Cttee on Human Rights 1985–95; Visiting Prof., Stanford Univ. 1975, Yale Univ. 1977; Vice-Pres. American Soc. of Int. Law 1972–74, British Inst. of Int. and Comparative Law 2002–; Ordre des Palmes académiques 1988; Dr hc (Paris XI); Hon. DCL (Dundee) 1992, (Durham, LSE) 1995, (Cambridge, Sussex, Kent, City Univ., Greenwich, Essex) 1996, (Birmingham, Leicester, Glasgow) 1997, (Nottingham) 1999, (Bath, Paris II, Sorbonne) 2001, (Oxford) 2002, (Reading) 2003; Yale Law School Medal of Merit 1997, Manley Hudson Medal (ASIC) 1998, Harold Weig Medal, New York Univ. 1995, Prize of Int. Balzan Foundation 2007. *Publications include:* The Development of International Law Through the Political Organs of the United Nations 1963, Conflict of Interests 1965, The Administration of the United Kingdom Foreign Policy Through the United Nations 1966, Law in Movement – Essays in Memory of John McMahon (co-ed., with James Fawcett) 1974, UN Peacekeeping: Documents and Commentary – (Vol. I) Middle East 1969, (Vol. II) Asia 1971, (Vol. III) Africa 1980, (Vol. IV) Europe 1981, Problems and Process – International Law and How We Use It 1994; articles in law journals and journals of int. relations.
Address: International Court of Justice, Peace Palace, 2517 KJ The Hague, Netherlands (office). *Telephone:* (70) 302-2415 (office). *Fax:* (70) 302-2409 (office). *E-mail:* r.higgins@icj-cij.org (office). *Website:* www.icj-cij.org (office).

HILDEBRAND, Clive, BE, MA; Australian business executive and organization official; *President, Australian Institute of International Affairs;* b. 1937, Gladstone, Queensland. *Education:* Univ. of Queensland, Univ. of Oxford, UK. *Career:* fmr miner; Man. Dir QCT Resources Ltd –1994; fmr Chair. AUSTA Electric; Chair. Sugar R & D Corpn 1995–2002; fmr Chair. Rural R & D Corpn; mem. Canberra's Coordinating Cttee on Science and Tech. 2001–02; Dir Oil Search 2002–07; currently Dir Australian Univs Quality Agency; Pres. Australian Inst. of Int. Affairs, Queensland 2000–04, Nat. Pres. 2005–; mem. Queensland Resource Council; Fellow, Australasian Inst. of Mining and Metallurgy; Hon. DUniv (Griffith) 1999.
Address: Australian Institute of International Affairs, Stephen House, 32 Thesiger Court, Deakin, ACT 2600, Australia (office). *Telephone:* (2) 6282-2133 (office). *Fax:* (2) 6285-2334 (office). *E-mail:* ceo@aiia.asn.au (office). *Website:* www.aiia.asn.au (office).

HILDENBERG, Humphrey; Suriname economist and government official; *Minister of Finance; Education:* Univ. of Groningen, The Netherlands. *Career:* with Nationale Ontwikkelings Bank (NOB) 1981–92, 1996–2000; Minister of Finance 1992–96, 2000–.
Address: Ministry of Finance, Tamarindelaan 3, Paramaribo, Suriname (office). *Telephone:* 472610 (office). *Fax:* 476314 (office). *E-mail:* financien@sr.net (office). *Website:* www.minfin.sr (office).

HILDENBRAND, Werner; German economist and academic; *Professor of Economics, University of Bonn;* b. 25 May 1936, Göttingen. *Career:* lecturer Univ. of Heidelberg 1964–66; Visiting Asst Prof. Univ. of Calif., Berkeley 1966–67, Visiting Assoc. Prof. 1967–68; Research Prof. Univ. of Louvain, Belgium 1968–76; Prof. of Econs Univ. of Bonn 1969–; Visiting Prof. of Econs, Berkeley and Stanford 1970, Berkeley 1973–74, Visiting Ford Prof. Berkeley 1985–86, European Univ. Inst., Florence 1989–, Univ. of California, San Diego 1986–91; Chaire Européenne Coll. de France 1993–94; Fellow, Econometric Soc. 1972; mem. Rhein-West Akad. der Wissenschaften 1981–, Academia Europaea 1985–, Berlin-Brandenburgischen Akad. der Wissenschaften 1993–; Foreign Hon. mem. American Acad. of Arts and Sciences 2005–; Dr hc (Univ. Louis Pasteur Strasbourg) 1988, (Bern) 2002; Leibniz-Preis Deutsche Forschungsgemeinschaft 1987, Max-Planck-Forsch-Preis 1995, Alexander-von-Humboldt-Preis 1997, Gay-Lussac-Preis 1997. *Publications:* Core and Equilibria of a Large Economy 1974, Lineare ökonomische Modelle (with K. Hildenbrand) 1975, Introduction to Equilibrium Analysis (with A. Kirman) 1976, Equilibrium Analysis (with A. Kirman) 1988, Market Demand: Theory and Empirical Evidence 1994; numerous papers.
Address: University of Bonn, Wirtschaftstheorie II, Lennestr. 37, 53113 Bonn (office); Buchbitze 21, 53797 Lohmar, Germany (home). *Telephone:* (228) 739242 (office); (2246) 4339 (home). *Fax:* (228) 737940 (office); (2246) 16610 (home). *E-mail:* with2@uni-bonn.de (office). *Website:* www.wiwi.uni-bonn.de/fgh/ (office).

HILL, Christopher R., MA; American diplomatist; *Assistant Secretary, Bureau of East Asian and Pacific Affairs;* b. Little Compton, RI; m.; three c. *Education:* Bowdoin Coll., Maine, Naval War Coll. *Career:* with Peace Corps in Cameroon; joined Foreign Service, overseas assignments in Yugoslavia, Albania, S Korea and Poland; Sr Country Officer for Polish Affairs, Dept of State; Amb. to Macedonia 1996–99, to Poland 2000–04, to S Korea 2004–05; Asst Sec. Bureau of E Asian and Pacific Affairs 2005–; Head US del. to Six-Party Talks on N Korean nuclear issue 2005; Special Envoy to Kosovo 1998–99; fmr Sr Dir Southeast European Affairs, Nat. Security Council; several State Dept awards including Robert S. Frasure Award and Distinguished Service Award.
Address: Bureau of East Asian and Pacific Affairs, US Department of State, 2201 C Street, NW, Washington, DC 20520, USA (office). *Telephone:* (202) 647-9596 (office). *Website:* www.state.gov/p/eap (office).

HILL, (Peter) Jeremy (Oldham); British lawyer and diplomatist; b. 17 April 1954; m.; one s. one d. *Career:* worked as lawyer; Asst Legal Adviser, FCO 1982–87; Legal Adviser, British Embassy, Bonn 1987–90; Legal Counsellor, Attorney Gen.'s Office, London 1991–95; Counsellor for Legal, Justice and Home Affairs, Brussels 1995–98; Head, Southern European Dept, FCO 1999–2001; Amb. to Lithuania 2001–04, to Bulgaria 2004–07.
Address: Foreign and Commonwealth Office, King Charles Street, London, SW1A 2AH, England (office). *Telephone:* (20) 7008-1500 (office). *Website:* www.fco.gov.uk (office).

HILL, Robert Murray, BA, BLL, LLM; Australian politician and diplomatist; *Permanent Representative, United Nations;* b. 1946, Adelaide, S Australia; m.; four c. *Education:* Scotch Coll., Univ. of Adelaide, Univ. of London. *Career:* barrister and solicitor 1970–; Liberal Party Campaign Chair. 1975–77, Chair., Constitutional Cttee 1977–81; Vice-Pres. Liberal Party, S. Australian Div. 1977–79, State Pres. of S Australia Div. 1985–87; mem. Fed. Exec. of Liberal Party 1985–87, 1990–2006; Senator for S Australia

1981–2006; shadow portfolios in opposition include Foreign Affairs –1993, Defence 1993–94, Public Admin 1993–94, Educ., Science, Tech. 1994–96, Leader of Opposition in Senate 1993–96, Leader of Govt in Senate 1996–2006; Fed. Minister for Environment 1996–98, for Environment and Heritage 1998–2001, of Defence 2001–06; Perm. Rep. to UN, New York 2006–; mem. Law Soc. of S Australia.
Address: Office of the Permanent Representative of Australia to the United Nations, 150 East 42nd Street, 33rd Floor, New York, NY 10017, USA (office). *Telephone:* (212) 351-6600 (office). *Fax:* (212) 351-6610 (office). *E-mail:* australia@un.int (office). *Website:* www.australiaun.org (office).

HILLEN, John, BA, MA, MBA, PhD; American consultant, fmr diplomatist and army officer (retd); *President, Global Strategies Group (USA) LLC; Education:* Duke Univ., King's Coll. London, Univ. of Oxford, UK, Cornell Univ. *Career:* served 12 years as US Army officer; fmr Pres. American Man. Systems; fmr COO Island ECN; mem. US Comm. on Nat. Security/21st Century 1999; Defense Policy Advisor and Speechwriter for Pres. George W. Bush 2000; Asst Sec. of State for Political-Mil. Affairs, US State Dept 2005–07; Pres. Global Strategies Group (USA) LLC 2007–; mem. Chief of Naval Operations Exec. Panel (fed. advisory comm. for head of USN): fmr Contributing Ed., Nat. Review magazine; fmr Consultant, ABC News; mem. Young Pres.s' Org. (YPO); Life Mem. Council of Foreign Relations, Veterans of Foreign Wars; Founding mem. Henry Crown Fellows, Aspen Inst. 1997; Trustee IISS, Cttee on Econ. Devt in the US; fmr mem. Bd, Foreign Policy Research Inst., Univ. of Philadelphia; Bronze Star, Operation Desert Storm 1991. *Publications:* Blue Helmets: The Strategy of UN Military Operations 1998, Future Visions for US Defense Policy (ed.) 2001; numerous articles in leading journals and newspapers.
Address: Global Strategies Group (USA) LLC, 1667 K Street, NW, Washington, DC 20006, USA. *Telephone:* (202) 223-4399 (office). *Website:* www.globalgroup.com (office).

HILLIER, Gen. Rick J., BSc; Canadian army officer; *Chief of Defence Staff;* b. Newfoundland and Labrador; m.; two s. *Education:* Memorial Univ. of Newfoundland. *Career:* posted to 8th Canadian Hussars 1976, Royal Canadian Dragoons 1979; staff officer, Army Headquarters, Montreal, Nat. Defence Headquarters, Ottawa; Canadian Deputy Commdg Gen. 1998–2000; Commdr Multinational Div. (Southwest), Bosnia-Herzegovina; Asst Chief of the Land Staff –2003, Chief of the Land Staff 2003–05, Chief of Defence Staff 2005–; Commdr Int. Security Assistance Force, Kabul, Afghanistan Feb.–Aug. 2004.
Address: National Defence Headquarters, Major-General George R. Pearkes Building, 101 Colonel By Drive, Ottawa, ON K1A 0K2, Canada (office). *Telephone:* (613) 996-3100 (office). *Fax:* (613) 995-8189 (office). *Website:* www.forces.gc.ca (office).

HIMELFARB, Alexander, PhD; Canadian diplomatist; *Ambassador to Italy;* b. 1947; m. Frum Himelfarb. *Education:* Univ. of Toronto. *Career:* Prof. of Sociology, Univ. of New Brunswick 1972–81; Head, Unified Family Court Project, Dept of Justice 1979–81; joined Dept of Solicitor-Gen. 1981, held several positions including Dir-Gen. Planning and Systems Group; other public service posts have included Exec. Dir Nat. Parole Bd, Asst Sec. to Cabinet for Social Policy Devt, Privy Council Office, Assoc. Sec. Treasury Bd, Head, Fed. Task Force on Social Union; Deputy Minister of Canadian Heritage 1999–2002; Clerk of Privy Council and Sec. to Cabinet 2002–06; Amb. to Italy 2006–, (also accred to Albania and San Marino and High Commr to Malta).
Address: Embassy of Canada, Via Salaria 243, 00199 Rome, Italy (office). *Telephone:* (06) 854441 (office). *Fax:* (06) 854443915 (office). *E-mail:* rome@international.gc.ca (office). *Website:* www.canada.it (office).

HINAI, Fuad Mubarak al-, BA; Omani diplomatist and UN official; *Permanent Representative, United Nations;* b. 1951; m.; two c. *Education:* Univ. of Kuwait. *Career:* Second Sec., then First Sec. Perm. Mission of Oman to UN, New York 1974–78, elected Rapporteur Third Cttee (Social, Humanitarian and Cultural), UN Gen. Ass. 1977; fmr Second Sec. and Deputy Chief, Training Dept, Ministry of Foreign Affairs, then Deputy Chief, Int. Confs and Orgs Dept 1982, 1984–86, 1998; First Sec. Embassy in Egypt 1979–82; First Sec. Perm. Mission to UN, Geneva, Switzerland 1983–84; Perm. Rep. to UN, New York August 1998–; Chair. Third Cttee UN Gen. Ass. Sept. 2001–.
Address: Permanent Mission of Oman to the UN, 866 United Nations Plaza, Suite 540, New York, NY 10017, USA (office). *Telephone:* (212) 355-3505 (office). *Fax:* (212) 644-0070 (office). *E-mail:* oman@un.int (office).

HINDS, Samuel Archibald Anthony, BSc; Guyanese politician; *Prime Minister;* b. 27 Dec. 1943, Mahaicony, E Coast, Demerara; m. Yvonne Zereder Burnett 1967; three c. *Education:* Queen's Coll. Georgetown and Univ. of New Brunswick. *Career:* various positions with Bauxite Co.,

Linden, Guyana 1967–92; mem. Science and Industry Cttee Nat. Science Research Council 1973–76; fmr Chair. Guyanese Action for Reform and Democracy (GUARD); Prime Minister of Guyana 1992–97, 1997–99, 2001–; also Minister of Public Works and Communication; leader CIVIC (special political movt of business people and execs).
Address: Office of the Prime Minister, Oranapai Towers, Wights Lane, Georgetown (office); CIVIC, New Garden Street, Georgetown, Guyana. *Telephone:* 227-3101 (office). *Fax:* 226-7573 (office). *E-mail:* pmoffice@ sdnp.org.gov.gy (office).

HIRA, Radjendrakumar Nihalchand Sonny; Suriname diplomatist; m. Letitia Remola Kamladev Hira-Bhikharie. *Career:* Amb. to Brazil 2002–07.
Address: c/o Ministry of Foreign Affairs, Lim A Postraat 25, POB 25, Paramaribo, Suriname. *Telephone:* 71209. *Fax:* 410411. *E-mail:* buza@sr .net.

HIRABAYASHI, Hiroshi; Japanese diplomatist; b. 1940, Tokyo; m.; two c. *Education:* Univ. of Tokyo and Univ. of Poitiers, Aix-en-Provence, France. *Career:* joined Ministry of Foreign Affairs 1963, various overseas posts including Embassy in Italy 1965–67, Embassy in France 1972–74, China 1975–76, Belgium 1982–85, USA 1990–93; apptd Pvt. Sec. to Minister of Foreign Affairs, Dir ASEAN Div., Gen. Affairs and Policy Coordination and Ast Dir Gen. for Econ. Affairs, Ministry of Foreign Affairs 1979; Fellow, Harvard Univ. Center for Int. Affairs, USA 1981–82; Dir-Gen. Econ. Cooperation, Ministry of Foreign Affairs 1993–95; Principal Adviser to Cabinet on Foreign Affairs 1995–98; Amb. to India 1998–2002, to France 2002–06, also accred to Andorra and Djibouti; Amb. in charge of Inspection, Ministry of Foreign Affairs 2006–07; mem. Bd of Dirs Toshiba Corpn 2007–; Chevalier, Order of Merit (Italy) 1967, Officier de l'Ordre nat. de Mérite (France) 1978, Grand Officier de l'Ordre de Léopold II (Belgium); Dr hc (Univ. de Lyon II, France).
Address: Investor Relations Group, Corporate Communications Office, Toshiba Corporation, 1-1, Shibaura 1-chome, Minato-ku, Tokyo 105-8001, Japan (office). *Telephone:* (3) 3457-2096 (office). *Fax:* (3) 5444-9202 (office). *E-mail:* ir@toshiba.co.jp (office). *Website:* www.toshiba.co.jp (office).

HIRCHSON, Abraham; Israeli politician; b. 11 Feb. 1941, Tel Mond; m. (deceased); three c. *Career:* Staff Sergeant, Israeli Army; mem. Knesset 1981–, Deputy Speaker 16th Knesset, also Chair. Finance Cttee; Minister of Tourism 2005–06, of Communications Jan.–May 2006, of Finance 2006–07; fmr mem. Likud, joined Kadima 2005; Sec. Gen., Hanoar Haleumi Haoved Vehalomed 1970–92; Gen. Sec. Nat. Labourers' Youth Org. Israel 1981–84; Founder Jewish Heroism Quiz Project 1987; Founder and Pres. March of the Living Project 1988–; Chair., Nat. Labour Union 1995–, Nat. Health Fund 1996–; mem. Bd Special Swiss Cttee for Needy Holocaust Survivors.
Address: The Knesset, HaKiryah, Jerusalem, 91950, Israel (office). *Telephone:* 2-6753382 (office). *Fax:* 2-6753764 (office). *E-mail:* ahirshson@knesset.gov.il (office). *Website:* www.knesset.gov.il (office).

HIRSCH BALLIN, Ernst, LLD; Dutch lawyer and judge; *Minister of Justice;* b. 15 Dec. 1950, Amsterdam; m. Pauline van de Grift 1974; two c. *Education:* Univ. of Amsterdam. *Career:* mem. Faculty of Law, Amsterdam Univ. 1974–77; Legal Expert, Ministry of Justice 1977–81; Prof. of Constitutional and Admin. Law, Tilburg Univ. 1981–89, Prof. of Int. Law 1994–; Minister of Justice and Netherlands Antillean and Aruban Affairs 1989–94, Minister of Justice 2006–; mem. Parl. (Christian Democrat; Lower House) 1994–95, (Upper House) 1995–2000; Councillor of State 2000–; Pres. Admin. Jurisdiction Div. Council of State 2003–06; mem. Royal Netherlands Acad. of Science 2005; Kt, Order of the Dutch Lion; Grand Cross, Order of the Chest Crown (Luxembourg); Grand Cross, Orden del Libertador (Venezuela); Chevalier de la Légion d'honneur; Kt Order of Holy Sepulchre of Jerusalem; G. A. van Poelje Prize 1980. *Publications:* Publiekrecht en beleid 1979, Rechtsstaat en beleid 1992; 300 other publs on int. and comparative law, legal theory, constitutional and admin. law.
Address: Ministry of Justice, Schedelhoekshaven 100, POB 20301, 2500 EH, The Hague, Netherlands (office); Council of State, PO Box 20019, 2500 EA The Hague (office); Bruggenrijt 12, 5032 BH Tilburg, Netherlands (home). *Telephone:* (70) 3707911 (office); (70) 4264657 (office). *Fax:* (70) 3707900 (office); (13) 5920687 (home). *E-mail:* voorlichting@minjus.nl (office); ballin@uvt.nl (office). *Website:* www.justie.nl (office).

HITAM, Tan Sri Dato' Musa bin; Malaysian politician (retd); b. 18 April 1934, Johor. *Education:* English Coll., Johor Baharu Univ. of Malaya and Univ. of Sussex, UK. *Career:* Assoc. Sec. Int. Student Conf. Secr. (COSEC), Leiden 1957–59; civil servant 1959–64; political sec. to Minister of Transport 1964; mem. Parl. 1968–90; Asst Minister to Deputy Prime Minister 1969; studied in UK 1970, subsequently lectured at Univ. of Malaya; Chair. Fed. Land Devt Authority 1971; Deputy Minister of Trade and Industry 1972–74; Minister of Primary Industries 1974–78, of Educ.

1978–81; Deputy Prime Minister and Minister of Home Affairs 1981–86; Deputy Pres. UMNO 1981–86; Special Envoy to UN 1990–91; Malaysia's Chief Rep. to UN Comm. on Human Rights 1994–; Special Envoy of the Prime Minister to Commonwealth Ministerial Action Group.
Address: No. 12, Selekoh Tunku, Bukit Tunku, 50480 Kuala Lumpur, Malaysia.

HJELDE, Haakon B., LLB; Norwegian diplomatist; *Ambassador and Chief Negotiator, Ministry of Foreign Affairs;* b. 7 Dec. 1941. *Education:* Univ. of Oslo. *Career:* joined Legal Dept, Ministry of Foreign Affairs 1965–68; Attaché and First Sec., Perm. Mission to UN, New York 1968–71; Dir of Int. Div., Ministry of Environment 1971–74; Counsellor, Embassy in New Delhi 1979–81; Head of Div., Political Dept, Ministry of Foreign Affairs 1981–87; Minister Counsellor and Deputy Head of Mission, Embassy in London 1988–90; Amb. and Special Adviser on Human Rights, Ministry of Foreign Affairs 1990–94; Dir Gen. Dept for Bilateral Affairs (Asia, Africa, Latin American and Middle East) 1994–99; Amb. to China 1999–2003, to Finland 2003–07; Amb. and Chief Negotiator, Ministry of Foreign Affairs 2007–; Hon. KCMG. *Publications:* several articles on human rights and devt 1971–94.
Address: Ministry of Foreign Affairs, 7 juni-plassen/Victoria Terrasse, PB 8114 Dep., 0032 Oslo, Norway (office). *Telephone:* 22242649 (office). *Fax:* 22246776 (office). *E-mail:* hbh@mfa.no (home). *Website:* www.mfa.no (office).

HJELM-WALLÉN, Lena, MA; Swedish politician; *Chairman, International Institute for Democracy and Electoral Assistance;* b. 14 Jan. 1943, Sala; m. Ingvar Wallén 1965; one d. *Education:* Univ. of Uppsala. *Career:* teacher in Sala 1966–69; active in Social Democratic Youth League; elected to 2nd Chamber of Parl. 1968; mem. Exec. Cttee Västmanland br. of Socialdemokratiska Arbetarepartiet (Social Democratic Labour Party—SDLP) 1968, mem. SDLP Parl. Exec. 1976–82, SDLP Spokeswoman on Schools, mem. Bd SDLP 1978–87, SDLP Spokeswoman on Educ. 1991–94; Minister without Portfolio, with responsibility for schools 1974–76; Minister of Educ. and Cultural Affairs 1982–85, of Int. Devt Co-operation 1985–91, for Foreign Affairs 1994–98; Deputy Prime Minister of Sweden 1998–2002; Govt Rep. to the EU Convention on the Future of Europe; Chair. Bd Int. Inst. for Democracy and Electoral Assistance (IDEA) 2003–.
Address: International IDEA, Strömsborg, 103 34 Stockholm, Sweden (office). *Telephone:* (8) 698-37-00 (office). *Fax:* (8) 20-24-22 (office). *E-mail:* info@idea.int (office). *Website:* www.idea.int (office).

HLOPHE, Ephraim Mandlenkosi M.; Swazi government official and diplomatist; *Ambassador to USA;* m. Martha Ngakanani Hlophe. *Education:* Eastern and Southern Man. Inst., Arusha, Tanzania, Inst. of Man. Services, London, UK, Univ. of Pittsburgh, USA. *Career:* served in various tech. positions 1965–73; Postmaster, Mbabane 1972–74, Personnel Officer, Posts and Telecommunications 1974–76, Head of Personnel Services, Dept of Posts and Telecommunications 1976–78; Asst Man. Services Officer, Ministry of Labour and Public Service 1978–80, Man. Services Officer 1980–83, Sr Man. Services Officer (Sr Govt Man. Analyst) 1983–84; Under-Sec. and Acting Prin. Sec., Directorate of Personnel Man. 1984–86; Under-Sec. and Dir Man. Services Div., Ministry of Health 1987–91; Prin. Sec., Ministry of Public Works and Construction 1991–94, Ministry of Econ. Planning and Devt 1994–2005; Amb. to USA 2005–; mem. Inst. of Personnel Man. (Swaziland and SA); Fellow, Inst. of Man. Services (UK); Counsellor of the Royal Order of Sobhuza II 1998.
Address: Embassy of Swaziland, 1712 New Hampshire Avenue, NW, Washington, DC 20009, USA (office). *Telephone:* (202) 234-5002 (office). *Fax:* (202) 234-8254 (office). *E-mail:* swaziland@compuserve.com (office).

HLOPHE, Mpumelelo J. N.; Swazi diplomatist; *High Commissioner to Malaysia;* m. Xolisile Phyllis Hlophe. *Career:* fmr High Commr to S Africa; High Commr to Malaysia (non-resident to Thailand, South Korea, Brunei, Australia, Philippines, India) 2006–.
Address: High Commission of Swaziland, Suite 22-03 and 03 (A), Menara Citibank, 165 Jalan Ampang, 50450 Kuala Lumpur, Malaysia (office). *Telephone:* (3) 21632511 (office). *Fax:* (3) 21633326 (office). *E-mail:* swdkl_2@streamyx.com (office).

HO, Edmund H. W., BA; Chinese business executive and politician; *Chief Executive of Macao Special Administrative Region;* b. 1955; m.; one s. one d. *Education:* York Univ., Canada. *Career:* chartered accountant and certified auditor 1981–; worked for accounting firm in Toronto, Ont. 1981–82; Gen. Man. Tai Fung Bank 1983, CEO 1999–; mem. CPPCC 1986–; elected Deputy to NPC 1988, elected to 8th and 9th Standing Cttees; mem. Legis. Ass. of Macao 1988–, Vice-Pres. 1988–99; Macao Chamber of Commerce; Chair. Macao Asscn of Banks 1985–; Chief Exec. Macao Special Admin. Region (MSAR) May 1999–; Vice-Chair. All-China Fed. of Industry and Commerce, Econ. Council of the Macao Govt, Kiang Wu

Hosp. Bd of Charity, Tung Sin Tong Charitable Inst.; Vice-Pres. Drafting Cttee of the Basic Law of the MSAR 1988, Consultative Cttee of the Basic Law of the MSAR 1989, Preparatory Cttee of the MSAR 1998; Convenor of Land Fund Investment Comm. of the MSAR; Chair. Bd of Dirs Univ. of Macao; Vice-Chair. Bd of Dirs Jinan Univ., Guangzhou; Pres. Exec. Cttee Macao Olympic Cttee; Pres. Macao Golf Asscn.
Address: Headquarters of the Government of the Macao Special Administrative Region, Av. da Praia Grande, Macao Special Administrative Region, People's Republic of China (office). *Telephone:* 726886 (office). *Fax:* 726665 (office). *Website:* www.gov.mo (office).

HO, Szu-yin, MA, PhD; Taiwanese political scientist, academic and government official; *Deputy Secretary-General, National Security Council; Education:* Nat. Taiwan Univ., Univ. of Calif., Santa Barbara, Univ. of Michigan, USA. *Career:* Chief, Section of Co-operation and Exchange, Inst. of Int. Relations, Nat. Chengchi Univ., Taipei 1988–90, Research Fellow 1989–99, Deputy Dir 1994–98 then Dir, Adjunct Research Fellow, Election Study Center 1990–, Adjunct Prof., Dept of Political Science 1997–99, Prof. of Political Science 1999–; with Inst. of Euro–America, Academia Sinica 1994–; Ed.-in-Chief, Issues and Studies 1994–99, (Chinese version); Dir Overseas Dept and Vice-Convener, Nat. Security Div., National Policy Foundation, Kuomintang (KMT) –2008; Deputy Sec.-Gen. Nat. Security Council 2008–. *Publications:* America (in Chinese) 1992, Nomination Systems and Party Discipline in America, Britain and Japan (in Chinese) 1992, American Trade Politics (in Chinese) 1994; over 30 articles in professional journals.
Address: National Security Council, c/o Office of the President, 122 Chungking South Rd, Sec. 1, Taipei 10048 (office); Institute of International Relations (IIR), 64, Wan Shou Road, Wen Shan, Taipei 116, Taiwan (office). *Telephone:* (2) 2939-4914 (office). *Fax:* (2) 2938-2133 (office). *E-mail:* sho@nccu.edu.tw (office); iir@nccu.edu.tw (office). *Website:* iir.nccu.edu.tw (office); www.nsb.gov.tw (office).

HOAN, Tran Quang; Vietnamese diplomatist; *Ambassador to UK;* m. Le Thu Son. *Career:* fmr Sec. to Vietnamese Amb. to Cuba, fmr Amb. to Argentina (also accred to Brazil 1998); Asst to Minister of Foreign Affairs and Deputy Chair. Cttee for Overseas Vietnamese –2007; Amb. to UK 2007– (also accred to Ireland 2008–).
Address: Embassy of Viet Nam, 12–14 Victoria Road, London, W8 5RD, England (office). *Telephone:* (20) 7937-1912 (office). *Fax:* (20) 7937-6108 (office); (20) 7565-3853 (office). *E-mail:* embassy@vietnamembassy.org.uk (office). *Website:* www.vietnamembassy.org.uk (office).

HODGE, Sir James William, KCVO, CMG, MA; British diplomatist; b. 24 Dec. 1943; m. Frances Margaret Coyne 1970; three d. *Education:* Holy Cross Acad., Edin., Univ. of Edin. *Career:* entered FCO 1966, Rhodesia Political Dept 1966–67, Second Sec. (Information), Tokyo 1967–72, FCO Marine and Transport Dept 1972–73, UN Dept 1973–75, First Sec. (Devt and later Chancery), Lagos 1975–78, FCO Personnel Operations Dept 1978–81, First Sec. (Econ.) and later Counsellor (Commercial), Tokyo 1981–86, Head of Chancery, Copenhagen 1986–90, FCO Security Dept 1990–93, attached to Royal Coll. of Defence Studies 1994; Minister Consular Gen. and Deputy Head of Mission, Beijing 1995–96; Amb. to Thailand 1996–2000; Consul-Gen. to Hong Kong Special Admin. Region, People's Repub. of China (concurrently non-resident Consul-Gen. to Macao) Aug. 2000–03.
Address: c/o British Consulate-General, 1 Supreme Court Road, Hong Kong, People's Republic of China (office). *Telephone:* (852) 2901-3000. *Fax:* (852) 2901-3066. *E-mail:* information@britishconsulate.org.hk. *Website:* www.britishconsulate.org.hk.

HODGES, Heather M., BA, MA; American diplomatist; *Ambassador to Ecuador;* b. Cleveland, Ohio. *Education:* Coll. of St Catherine, New York Univ. *Career:* lived and worked in Madrid, Spain throughout the 1970s; career mem. Sr Foreign Service with rank of Minister Counselor, joined Foreign Service 1980, Chief of Non-Immigrant Visa Section, Caracas, Deputy Chief of Consular Section, Guatemala 1983–85, Peru Desk Officer, Dept of State 1985–87, Pearson Fellowship to work in US Congress, where she was counsel to Senate Sub-cttee on Immigration and Refugee Affairs 1987–89, Prin. Officer, Consulate in Bilbao 1989–91, Deputy Dir Office of Cuban Affairs, Dept of State 1991–93, Deputy Chief of Mission, Managua 1993–94, promoted to Sr Foreign Service 1994, participated in Dept of State's Sr Seminar 1996–97, Deputy Chief of Mission, Lima 1997–2000, Deputy Chief of Mission, 2000–03, promoted to rank of Minister-Counselor 2000, Amb. to Moldova 2003–06, Prin. Deputy Asst Sec., Bureau of Human Resources, Dept of State 2006–08, Amb. to Ecuador 2008–; Isabel la Catolica – Encomienda de Numero 2000.
Address: US Embassy, Avenida 12 de Octubre 1942 y Patria 120, Quito, Ecuador (office). *Telephone:* (2) 256-2890 (office). *Fax:* (2) 250-2052 (office). *Website:* www.usembassy.org.ec (office).

HOFFMAN, Alfred, Jr, MBA; American diplomatist; m. Dawn Hoffman; five c. *Education:* US Mil. Acad., West Point and Harvard Business School. *Career:* served as fighter pilot in USAF; Founder and Chair. WCI Communities, Inc.; Nat. Co-Chair. and Fla State Finance Chair. for George W. Bush presidential campaign; Co-Chair. Finance for Presidential Inaugural Cttee and Nat. Finance Chair. Republican Nat. Cttee 2001, 2003–04; Chair. Fla Victory 2002, Fla Inaugural Cttee 2003; Finance Chair. Fla Gov. Jeb Bush's campaign 1998, 2002; Chair. Fla Educ. Foundation, Fla Council on Econ. Educ., Fla Council of 100 2001–03; Founding Chair. Clearwater's Ruth Eckerd Performing Arts Center; Vice-Chair. Tampa Bay Performing Arts Hall; Founding Dir Council for Educational Change, Bd Fla Chamber of Commerce; Amb. to Portugal 2005–07; f. Tampa Bay Polo Club, Chair. for 15 years; Trustee The Fla Arts Council.
Address: US Department of State, 2201 C Street NW, Washington, DC 20520, USA (office). *Telephone:* (202) 647-4000 (office). *Fax:* (202) 647-6738 (office). *Website:* www.state.gov (office).

HOFFMAN, Mark, BA, MSc; American academic; *Lecturer, Department of International Relations, London School of Economics;* b. 20 June 1957. *Education:* Univ. of Massachusetts, Amherst, Univ. of Kent, Canterbury, London School of Econs, London, UK. *Career:* Temp. Lecturer in Int. Relations, Dept of Politics, Univ. of Southampton 1985–87; Lecturer, LSE 1987–, Dir Conflict and Devt Unit (CADU) 1997–, Dean of Undergraduate Studies 2000–06, Gen. Course Tutor, Study Year Abroad at LSE Programme 2001–03; Peace Fellow, Randolph Jennings Programme, US Inst. of Peace, Washington, DC 1990–91; mem. Bd Trustees, Conciliation Resources 1994–, Chair. 1998–2006; consultant to various governmental, inter-governmental and non-governmental orgs on conflict resolution and peace-building; media appearances on TV and radio programmes. *Publications:* UK Arms Control Policy in the 1990s (ed.) 1990, Political Theory, International Relations and the Ethics of Intervention (co-E ed.) 1993, International Political Theory 1998, Thinking about Conflict and Peace 2000; chapters in books; reports for int. orgs and govt agencies; numerous articles in professional journals.
Address: Department of International Relations, London School of Economics, Houghton Street, London, WC2A 2AE, England (office). *Telephone:* (20) 7955-7393 (office). *E-mail:* m.hoffman@lse.ac.uk (office). *Website:* www.lse.ac.uk (office).

HOFHEINZ, Paul, MA; American research institute director and journalist; *President, Lisbon Council; Education:* Yale Univ., London School of Econs, UK. *Career:* began journalistic career as reporter, Time magazine, London 1980s; fmr Assoc. Ed. and Moscow Bureau Chief, Fortune magazine; f. Russia Review (news magazine); fmr Man. Ed. Central European Economic Review; Emerging Europe Ed. and weekly columnist, The Wall Street Journal –2000, EU Corresp., Brussels 2000–03; Pres. The Lisbon Council, Brussels 2003–; commentator on East European Affairs, CNBC; Olive Branch Award, Center for War, Peace and the Media, New York Univ. 1992.
Address: The Lisbon Council asbl, International Press Centre, Residence Palace, Block C, 155 rue de la Loi, 1040 Brussels, Belgium (office). *Fax:* (2) 647-95-75 (office); (2) 640-98-28 (office). *E-mail:* info@lisboncouncil.net (office). *Website:* www.lisboncouncil.net (office).

HOGE, James F., Jr, BA, MA; American academic and editor; *Peter G. Peterson Chair and Editor, Foreign Affairs, Council on Foreign Relations; Education:* Yale Univ., Univ. of Chicago, Harvard Univ. *Career:* fmr Ed.-in-Chief Chicago Sun-Times newspaper, then Publr and Pres. NY Daily News; fmr Dir Council on Foreign Relations, now Peter G. Peterson Chair and Ed., Foreign Affairs (journal) 1992–; Congressional Fellow, American Political Science Asscn 1962; Fellow John F. Kennedy School of Govt Harvard Univ. 1991; Sr Fellow Freedom Forum Media Studies Columbia Univ. 1992; Dir Foundation for Civil Society, Human Rights Watch; mem. Bd of Dirs Int. Center for Journalists (ICFJ) 1992–; mem. American Council on Germany; Chair. Program Cttee American Ditchley Foundation; Hon. degree (Columbia Coll.) 1985; Public Service Award, Univ. of Chicago 1973, Award for Contributions to Journalism The Better Govt Asscn of Chicago 1975, Public Service Award The Citizens Cttee for NY City 1985, 6 Pulitzer Prizes (to Chicago Sun Times while Ed. and Publr), Pulitzer Prize (to New York Daily News while Publr). *Television:* The Threat of Terrorism (documentary writer and narrator). *Publications include:* The American Encounter: The United States and the Making of the Modern World (co-ed.) 1997, How Did This Happen? Terrorism and the New War (co-ed.) 2001; numerous articles, reviews and chapters in journals, newspapers and books.
Address: Foreign Affairs, 58 East 68th Street, New York, NY 10021-5987, USA (office). *Telephone:* (212) 434-9504 (office). *Fax:* (212) 434-9849 (office). *E-mail:* jhoge@cfr.org (office). *Website:* www.foreignaffairs.org (office).

HOLBROOKE, Richard C.; American business executive and fmr diplomatist; *Vice Chairman, Persius LLC;* b. 24 April 1941, New York; two s.; m. 2nd Kati Marton 1995. *Education:* Brown Univ. and Woodrow Wilson School, Princeton Univ. *Career:* Foreign Service Officer in Viet Nam and related posts 1962–66; White House Viet Nam staff 1966–67; Special Asst to Under-Secs of State Katzenbach and Richardson and mem. US del. to Paris peace talks on Viet Nam 1967–69; Fellow Woodrow Wilson School, Princeton Univ. 1969–70; Dir Peace Corps, Morocco 1970–72; Man. Ed. Foreign Policy (quarterly magazine) 1972–76; consultant, Pres.'s Comm. on Org. of Govt for Conduct of Foreign Policy and contributing Ed. Newsweek 1974–75; coordinator of nat. security affairs, Carter-Mondale campaign 1976; Asst Sec. of State for E Asian and Pacific Affairs 1977–81; Vice-Pres. Public Strategies (consulting firm) 1981–85; Man. Dir Lehman Brothers 1985–93; Amb. to Germany 1993–94; Asst Sec. of State for European and Canadian Affairs 1994–96; Chief Negotiator for Dayton Peace Accord in Bosnia 1995; Vice-Chair. Credit Suisse First Boston Corpn 1996–99; Adviser Baltic Sea Council 1996–98; Special Presidential Envoy for Cyprus 1997–98, to Yugoslavia; Perm. Rep. to UN 1999–2000, Amb. to UN 1999–2001; currently Vice-Chair. Persius LLC (pvt. equity fund man. co.); mem. Bd of Dirs Council on Foreign Relations, American Int. Group, Quebecor World, American Museum of Natural History, Nat. Endowment for Democracy, The Africa-America Inst., Citizens Cttee for New York City, Refugees Int.; Chair. Bipartisan Comm. on Reorganizing Govt for Foreign Policy 1992; Chair. Refugees Int., American Acad. in Berlin, Nat. Advisory Council of Harriman Inst., Asia Soc. 2002–; mem. Bd of Dirs of numerous orgs; recipient of 12 hon. degrees; numerous awards including Distinguished Public Service Award, Dept of Defense 1994, 1996, Humanitarian of the Year Award, American Jewish Congress 1998, Dr Bernard Heller Prize, Hebrew Union Coll. 1999. *Publications:* Counsel to the President (co-author) 1991, To End a War 1998; articles and essays on foreign policy.
Address: Perseus LLC, 2099 Pennsylvania Avenue, NW, 9th Floor, Washington, DC 20006, USA (office). *Telephone:* (202) 452-0101 (office). *Fax:* (202) 429-0588 (office). *Website:* www.perseusllc.com (office).

HOLGUÍN, Maria Angela, BSc; Colombian diplomatist. *Education:* Gimnasio Femenino, Bogotá, George Brown Coll., Toronto, Canada, Université de la Sorbonne, Paris, Univ. of Los Andes, Bogotá, Harvard Univ., USA, Centre d'Études Diplomatiques et Strategiques (CEDS), Paris, France. *Career:* Dir, Program for Strengthening Democracy, Faculty of Humanities and Social Studies, Univ. of Los Andes 1988; Pvt. Sec. and Acting Sec.-Gen., Office of Gen. Prosecutor 1991; First Sec. in charge of trade and commercial affairs, Embassy in France 1992; Advisor to Deputy Minister, Chief of Staff and Sec.-Gen., Ministry of Foreign Affairs 1994; Coordinator, Tech. Secr., XI Summit of Heads of State and Heads of Govt of Movement of Non-Aligned Countries 1995, 1996, 1997; Deputy Dir, Admin. Dept, Exec. Office of Pres. 1996; Exec. Dir, Regional Conf. on Children of Caribbean and Latin America, Cartagena 1997; Colombian Coordinator, XXXIX Ass. of IDB and Inter-American Investment Corpn 1997; Deputy Minister of Foreign Affairs and Acting Minister of Foreign Affairs 1998; Regional Dir for Latin America, Worldview Int. Foundation 1999–2002; Coordinator, Int. Affairs Cttee, Alvaro Uribe Campaign 2001–02; Amb. to Venezuela 2002–04; Perm. Rep. to UN, New York 2004–06.
Address: c/o Ministry of Foreign Affairs, Palacio de San Carlos, Calle 10a, No 5-51, Bogotá, DC, Colombia. *Telephone:* (1) 282-7811. *Fax:* (1) 341-6777. *Website:* www.minrelext.gov.co.

HOLKERI, Harri Hermanni, KBE, MPolSc; Finnish politician and UN official; b. 6 Jan. 1937, Oripää; m. Marja-Liisa Lepisto 1960; one s. one d. *Career:* Sec. Nat. Coalition Party Youth League 1959–60, Information Sec. 1960–62; Information Sec. Nat. Coalition Party 1962–64, Research Sec. 1964–65, Party Sec. 1965–71, Chair. 1971–79; mem. Helsinki City Council 1969–88, Chair. 1981–87; mem. Parl. 1970–78; mem. Bd Bank of Finland 1978–97; Chair. of Standing Finnish-Soviet Intergovernmental Comm. for Econ. Co-operation 1989–91; Prime Minister of Finland 1987–91; mem. Int. Body addressing the decommissioning of illegal weapons in NI 1995–98; Pres. 55th Session of the UN Gen. Ass. (Millennium Ass.) 2000–01; Head of UN Interim Admin. Mission in Kosovo (UNMIK) 2003–04.
Address: c/o United Nations, United Nations Plaza, New York, NY 10017, USA (office).

HOLLAMBY, David James; British diplomatist; *Governor and Commander-in-Chief, St Helena and Dependencies;* b. 19 May 1945; m. Maria Helena Guzmán 1971; two step-s. *Education:* Albury Manor School, Surrey. *Career:* joined Foreign Office 1964; Beirut 1967–69; Latin American Floater 1970–72; Third Sec. and Vice Consul Asunción 1972–75; Second Sec. FCO 1975–78; Vice Consul (Commercial) New York 1978–82; Consul (Commercial) Dallas 1982–86; First Sec. FCO 1986–90, Rome 1990–94; Asst Head, Western European Dept, FCO 1994–96, Deputy Head, W Indian and Atlantic Dept 1996–98, Dept Head, Overseas Territories Dept 1998–99; Gov. and C-in-C, St Helena and Dependencies 1999–.
Address: c/o Foreign and Commonwealth Office, King Charles Street, London, SW1A 2AH, England (office).

HOLLANDER, Samuel, OC, PhD, FRSC; British/Canadian/Israeli economist and academic; *Professor of Economics, Ben Gurion University;* b. 6 April 1937, London, England; m. Perlette Kéroub 1959; one s. one d. *Education:* Gateshead Talmudical Acad., Hendon Tech. Coll., Kilburn Polytechnic, London School of Econs, Princeton Univ., NJ. *Career:* emigrated to Canada 1963; Asst Prof., Univ. of Toronto 1963–67, Assoc. Prof. 1967–70, Prof. 1970–84, Univ. Prof. 1984–98, Univ. Prof. Emer. 1998–; Research Dir, Univ. of Nice (CNRS) 1999–2000; Visiting Prof., Florence Univ., Italy 1973–74, Univ. of London 1974–75, Hebrew Univ., Jerusalem 1979–80, 1988, La Trobe Univ., Melbourne, Australia 1985, Auckland Univ., NZ 1985, 1988, Sorbonne, Paris 1997, Nice Univ. 2001; several guest lectureships; emigrated to Israel 2000; currently Prof. of Econs, Ben Gurion Univ.; Hon. LLD (McMaster) 1999; Fulbright Fellowship 1959; Guggenheim Fellowship 1968–69; Social Science Fed. of Canada 50th Anniversary Book Award 1990. *Publications:* The Sources of Increased Efficiency 1965, The Economics of Adam Smith 1973, The Economics of David Ricardo 1979, The Economics of J. S. Mill 1985, Classical Economics 1987, Ricardo – The New View: Collected Essays I 1995, The Economics of T. R. Malthus 1997, The Literature of Political Economy: Collected Essays II 1998, John Stuart Mill on Economic Theory and Method: Collected Essays III 2000, Jean-Baptiste Say and the Classical Canon in Economics 2005.
Address: Department of Economics, Ben Gurion University of the Negev, 84105, Beer Sheva (office); 2 Rehov Sapir, 89066 Arad, Israel (home). *Telephone:* (8) 6472305 (office); (8) 9771664 (home). *Fax:* (7) 6472941 (office). *E-mail:* sholland@bgumail.bgu.ac.il (office). *Website:* econ.bgu.ac.il (office).

HOLLIS, Rosemary, MA, PhD; British research institute director and academic; *Director of Research, Chatham House;* b. 1952, England. *Education:* King's Coll., London and George Washington Univ., Washington, DC, USA. *Career:* research posts with print media, TV, advertising agency 1975–80; Lecturer on Int. Relations and Political Science, George Washington Univ., Washington, DC, USA 1980–89; conducted research in Middle East 1989; Head of Middle East Programme, Royal United Services Inst. for Defence Studies 1990–95; Head of Middle East Programme, Royal Inst. of Int. Affairs (now Chatham House) 1995–2005, Dir of Research 2005–. *Publications:* Jordanian–Palestinian Relations: Where to? Four Scenarios for the Future (co-author) 1997, Oil and Regional Developments in the Gulf (ed.) 1998, Managing New Developments in the Gulf (ed.) 2000; chapters in books and articles in professional journals, including Chatham House's monthly magazine The World Today.
Address: Chatham House, 10 St James's Square, London, SW1Y 4LE, England (office). *Telephone:* (20) 7314-3667 (office). *Fax:* (20) 7957-5758 (office). *E-mail:* rhollis@chathamhouse.org.uk (office). *Website:* www.chathamhouse.org.uk (office).

HOLM, Erik, PhD; Danish foundation director and political economist; *Director, Eleni Nakou Foundation;* b. 6 Dec. 1933, Hobro; m. Annie Jacoba Kortleven 1960 (died 1984); two s. two d. *Education:* Univ. of Copenhagen. *Career:* Economist, Cen. Statistical Office, Copenhagen 1961–65; Lecturer in Econs, Univ. of Copenhagen 1962–65, in Political Science 1971–81; Economist, IMF, Washington, DC 1965–69; Sr Economist, Ministry of Econ. Affairs, Copenhagen 1969–72; Adviser on European Affairs to Prime Minister 1972–82; Prin. Adviser (econ. and financial affairs), EC Comm., Brussels 1982–87; Visiting Scholar, Inst. of Int. Studies, Univ. of Calif., Berkeley 1987–89; Dir Eleni Nakou Foundation, London 1989–; Kt of the Dannebrog. *Publications:* Stabilitet og Uligevagt 1986, Money and International Politics 1991, Union eller Nation 1992, Europe, a Political Culture? Fundamental Issues for the 1996 IGC 1994, The European Anarchy: Europe's Hard Road into High Politics 2001; articles in Danish and int. publs on European econ. and political affairs.
Address: Wiedeweltsgade 27, 2100 Copenhagen (home); Xylografensvej 4, 3220 Tisvildeleje, Denmark (Summer) (home). *Telephone:* 48-70-97-15 (Tisvildeleje) (home); 35-42-03-62 (Copenhagen) (home). *E-mail:* erik-holm@mail.dk (home).

HOLMES, Sir John Eaton, Kt, GCVO, KBE, CMG; British diplomatist and UN official; *Under-Secretary-General for Humanitarian Affairs and Emergency Relief Coordinator, United Nations Office for the Coordination of Humanitarian Affairs;* b. 29 April 1951, Preston; m. Penelope Morris 1976; three d. *Education:* Preston Grammar School, Balliol Coll., Oxford. *Career:* joined FCO 1973; with Embassy, Moscow 1976–78; First Sec. FCO

1978–82; Asst Pvt. Sec. to Foreign Sec. 1982–84; First Sec. Embassy, Paris 1984–87; Asst Head Soviet Dept, FCO 1988–89; seconded to Thomas De La Rue & Co. 1989–91; Counsellor, British High Comm., India 1991–95; Prin. Pvt. Sec. to Prime Minister 1996–99; Amb. to Portugal 1999–2001, to France 2001–07; Under-Sec.-Gen. for Humanitarian Affairs and Emergency Relief Coordinator, UN Office for Coordination of Humanitarian Affairs, New York 2007–.
Address: Office for the Coordination of Humanitarian Affairs, United Nations Plaza, New York, NY 10017, USA (office). *Telephone:* (212) 963-2738 (office). *Fax:* (212) 963-0116 (office). *E-mail:* holmes@un.org (office). *Website:* ochaonline.un.org (office).

HOLMES, John T., BA, LLB; Canadian diplomatist; *Ambassador to Indonesia;* m. Carol Bujeau; two c. *Education:* McGill Univ. *Career:* joined Dept of External Affairs 1982, positions in Bridgetown, Accra and Perm. Mission to UN, New York, fmr Dir Legal Advisory Div.; Dir UN Human Rights and Econ. Law Div. 2002–03; Amb. to Jordan 2003–06, concurrently non-resident Amb. to Iraq 2005–06; Amb. to Indonesia, also accred to Timor Leste 2006–.
Address: Canadian Embassy, World Trade Centre, 6th Floor, Jalan Jenderal Sudirman, Kav. 29–31, POB 8324/JKS.MP, Jakarta 12920, Indonesia (office). *Telephone:* (21) 25507800 (office). *Fax:* (21) 25507811 (office). *E-mail:* canadianembassy.jkrta@international.gc.ca (office). *Website:* www.international.gc.ca/asia/jakarta (office).

HOLOMISA, Maj.-Gen. Bantubonke Harrington, (Bantu); South African politician and army officer; *President, United Democratic Movement;* b. 25 July 1955, Mqandull, Transkei; m. Tunyelwa Dube 1981; one s. one d. *Education:* Army Coll. of South Africa. *Career:* joined Transkei Defence Force 1976, Lt Platoon Commdr 1978–79, Capt. Training Wing Commdr 1979–81, Lt-Col Bn Command 1981–83, Col SS01 Operations and Training 1984–85, rank of Brig., Chief of Staff, Transkei Defence Force 1985–87, Commdr 1987–94; Leader of Transkei 1987–94; mem. African Nat. Congress Nat. Exec. Cttee 1994; Deputy Minister of Environmental Affairs, Govt of Nat. Unity 1994–96; Pres. United Democratic Movt 1997–; several mil. medals. *Publications:* Future Plan for South Africa, Comrades in Corruption (booklet).
Address: PO Box 15, Parliament, Cape Town 8000 (office); PO Box 26290, Arcadia 0007, South Africa (home). *Telephone:* (21) 4033921 (Cape Town) (office); (12) 3210010 (Pretoria) (office); (82) 5524156 (Pretoria) (home). *Fax:* (21) 4032525 (Cape Town) (office); (12) 3210014 (Pretoria) (home). *E-mail:* holomisa@udm.org.za (home); bholomisa@holomisa.org.za (office). *Website:* www.udm.org.za (office).

HOLT, Denise Mary, CMG, BA; British diplomatist; *Ambassador to Spain;* b. 1 Oct. 1949, Vienna, Austria; m. David Holt 1987; one s. *Education:* Univ. of Bristol. *Career:* joined British Diplomatic Service 1970; Desk Officer for Spain, Portugal and Gibraltar, FCO; First Sec., Embassy in Dublin 1984–88; Head of Section, Dept of Cen. America and Mexico 1988–90; First Sec., Embassy in Brasilia 1990–93; Deputy Dir Dept of Cen. Asia 1993–94; Deputy Dir of Personnel 1996–98, Dir 2001–02; Counsellor, Embassy in Dublin 1998–2001; Amb. to Mexico 2002–05, to Spain (also accred to Andorra) 2007–; Dir Migration and Overseas Territories 2005–07.
Address: British Embassy, Fernando el Santo 16, 28010 Madrid, Spain (office). *Telephone:* (91) 7008200 (office). *Fax:* (91) 7008210 (office). *E-mail:* enquiries.madrid@fco.gov.uk (office); ddpholt@aol.com (home). *Website:* www.ukinspain.com (office).

HOLUM, John D., BS, JD; American fmr government official; b. 4 Dec. 1940, Highmore, S Dak; m. Barbara P. Pedersen; one d. *Education:* Northern State Teachers' Coll. and George Washington Univ. *Career:* professional staff mem. Foreign Relations Cttee US Senate (on staff of Senator George McGovern) 1965–79; mem. Policy and Planning Staff, US State Dept 1979–81; attorney O'Melveny & Myers 1981–93; defence and foreign policy adviser to Gov. Bill Clinton during 1992 Presidential Campaign; Exec. Dir 1992 Democratic Nat. Convention; Dir Arms Control and Disarmament Agency (ACDA) 1993–98, Sr Advisor for Arms Control and Int. Security Affairs 1998–2000; Undersecretary of State for Arms Control and Int. Security 2000; Vice Pres., Int. and Govt Affairs, Atlas Air Inc. 2000–03; mem. Center for Nonproliferation Studies Int. Advisory Bd.
Address: c/o International Advisory Board, Center for Nonproliferation Studies, Monterey Institute of International Studies, 460 Pierce Street, Monterey, CA 93940, USA.

HOMER-DIXON, Thomas, BA, PhD; Canadian political scientist, academic and author; b. 1956, Victoria, BC; m. Sarah Wolfe; one s. *Education:* Carleton Univ., Ottawa, Massachusetts Inst. of Tech., USA. *Career:* Asst Prof. of Political Science, Univ. of Toronto 1993–98, Assoc. Prof. 1998–2006, Prof. 2006–, also George Ignatieff Chair of Peace and Conflict Studies 2007–08, Dir Trudeau Centre for Peace and Conflict Studies 2001–07; Dir Centre for Int. Governance Innovation (think tank), Waterloo, Ont.; Prof., Balsillie School of Int. Affairs, Waterloo, Ont. 2008–; Assoc. Fellow, Canadian Inst. for Advanced Research 1995–. *Publications:* Environment, Scarcity, and Violence (American Political Science Asscn Caldwell Prize) 1999, The Ingenuity Gap (Gov.-Gen.'s Non-fiction Award 2001) 2000, The Upside of Down: Catastrophe, Creativity, and the Renewal of Civilization (Nat. Business Book Award 2006) 2006; numerous articles in learned journals and newspapers.
Address: Trudeau Centre for Peace and Conflict Studies, University College, 15 King's College Circle, University of Toronto, Toronto, ON M5S 3H7, Canada (office). *Telephone:* (416) 978-2486 (office). *Fax:* (416) 978-8416 (office). *E-mail:* tad@homerdixon.com. *Website:* www.balsillieschool.ca; www.trudeaucentre.ca/faculty-profthomerdixon.html (office); www.homerdixon.com.

HONG, Hu; Chinese politician; *Governor of Jilin Province;* b. June 1940, Jinzhai Co., Anhui Prov. *Education:* Beijing Engineering Inst. *Career:* joined CCP 1965; fmr technician, later Deputy Chief, Dye Plant, Jilin Chemical Industry Co.; fmr Workshop Chief, Liming Chemical Industry Factory, Qinghai Prov. (Vice-Chair. CCP Revolutionary Cttee); fmr Head, Comprehensive Planning Div., 2nd Bureau, Ministry of Chemical Industry; fmr Div. Chief, Planning Bureau, State Machine-Building Industry Comm.; Deputy Sec.-Gen., Sec.-Gen. State Comm. for Econ. Restructuring 1982–91; Vice-Minister, State Comm. for Econ. Restructuring 1991–98; Vice-Gov. Jilin Prov. (also Acting Gov. 1998–99, Gov. 1999–; mem. Comm. of Securities of the State Council 1992–98; mem. CCP Cen. Cttee for Discipline Inspection 1992; mem. 15th CCP Cen. Cttee 1997–2002, 16th CCP Cen. Cttee 2002–; Del., 10th NPC 2002–; holds title of Outstanding CCP Mem. at State Organs Level 2002–.
Address: Office of the Governor, Jilin Provincial People's Government, Changchun, Jilin Province, People's Republic of China.

HONKAPOHJA, Seppo Mikko Sakari, DSocSc; Finnish economist and academic; *Professor of International Macroeconomics, University of Cambridge;* b. 7 March 1951, Helsinki; m. Sirkku Anna-Maija Honkapohja 1973; one s. one d. *Education:* United World Coll. of the Atlantic, UK, Univ. of Helsinki. *Career:* Scientific Dir Yrjö Jahnsson Foundation 1975–87; Prof. of Econs, Turku School of Econs and Business Admin 1987–91, Prof.-at-Large (Docent) 1992–; Prof.-at-Large (Docent) of Econs, Univ. of Helsinki 1981–91, Acting Prof. of Econs (Econometrics) 1985–87, Prof. of Econs 1992–; Visiting Lecturer and Scholar, Harvard Univ., USA 1978–79; Visiting Assoc. Prof. of Econs, Stanford Univ., USA 1982–83; Sr Fellow Acad. of Finland 1982–83, Acad. Prof. 1989–95, 2000–04; Prof. of Int. Macroeconomics, Univ. of Cambridge, UK 2004–, Professorial Fellow, Clare Coll. 2004–; Man. Ed. Scandinavian Journal of Econs 1984–88; Ed. European Econ. Review 1993–; mem. Bd Finnish Econ. Asscn 1989–91, Finnish Soc. for European Studies 1994–; mem. Council, European Econ. Asscn 1985–86, 1999–2003; Vice-Chair. Kansallis Foundation for Financial Research 1989–96; mem. Governing Body The Finnish Cultural Foundation 1994–, Chair. 1997–2001; mem. Advisory Bd Journal of Econ. Surveys 1994–; mem. Supervisory Bd, Okopankki Ltd 1996–, Chair 1997–; mem. Finnish Acad. of Science and Letters, Academia Europaea; Fellow of the Econometric Soc.; Jaakko Honko Medal (Helsinki School of Economics and Business Administration) 1998, Yrjo Jahnsson Foundation Anniversary Prize 2004. *Publications:* Limits and Problems of Taxation 1985; Ed. several books including The State of Macroeconomics 1990, Macroeconomic Modelling and Policy Implications 1993, Learning and Expectations in Macroeconomics 2001; numerous articles in journals.
Address: Faculty of Economics, University of Cambridge, Cambridge, CB3 9DD, England (office). *Telephone:* (1223) 335251 (office). *Fax:* (1223) 335299 (office). *Website:* www.econ.cam.ac.uk (office).

HOOKS, Aubrey, BA, MA; American diplomatist; b. Mullins, S Carolina; m.; three s. three d. *Education:* Univ. of S Carolina, George Washington Univ., Univ. of Michigan, NATO Defence Coll., Rome, Italy. *Career:* joined the Foreign Service 1971, jr officer, Embassy in Tel-Aviv 1971–73, Polish language training 1973, Vice-Consul, Warsaw 1974–76, Cultural Affairs Officer for Poland, Czechoslovakia and Hungary, Dept of State 1974–76, Econ. Officer, Ankara 1979–83, univ. training in econs 1983–84, Head of Econ. Section, Embassy in Port-au-Prince, Haiti 1984–87, Hebrew language training 1987, Econ. Officer, Embassy in Tel-Aviv 1988, mem. US Del. to CSCE, Helsinki 1992, Econ. Counselor, Embassy in Warsaw 1992–95, mem. Senior Seminar 1995–96, Amb. to the Repub. of Congo 1996–99, Coordinator for African Crisis Response Initiative 1999–2001, Amb. to Democratic Repub. of the Congo 2001–04, to Côte d'Ivoire 2004–07.
Address: US Department of State, 2201 C Street NW, Washington, DC 20520, USA (office). *Telephone:* (202) 647-4000 (office). *Fax:* (202) 647-6738 (office). *Website:* www.state.gov (office).

HOON, Rt Hon. Geoffrey William, PC, MA; British politician and lawyer; *Parliamentary Secretary to the Treasury and Chief Whip;* b. 6 Dec. 1953; m. Elaine Ann Dumelow 1981; one s. two d. *Education:* Jesus Coll., Cambridge. *Career:* labourer at furniture factory 1972–73; Lecturer in Law, Leeds Univ. 1976–82; Visiting Prof. of Law, Univ. of Louisville 1979–80; called to the Bar, Gray's Inn 1978; in practice in Nottingham 1982–84; MEP for Derbyshire 1984–94, mem. Legal Affairs Cttee 1984–94; MP for Ashfield 1992–; Opposition Whip 1994–95; Opposition Spokesman on Information Tech. 1995–97; Parl. Sec., Lord Chancellor's Dept 1997–98, Minister of State 1998–99, Sec. of State for Defence 1999–2005; Leader of the House of Commons 2005–06; Minister for Europe, FCO 2006–07; Parl. Sec. to the Treasury and Chief Whip 2007–; Vice-Chair. and Gov. Westminster Foundation 1994–97; mem. Labour Party; US Dept of Defense Distinguished Public Service Award 2004. *Address:* Chief Whip's Office, 9 Downing Street, London, SW1A 2AG (office); 8 Station Street, Kirby-in-Ashfield, Notts., NG17 7AR, England (home). *Telephone:* (20) 7276-2020 (office); (1623) 720399 (home). *Fax:* (20) 7276-2015 (office); (1623) 720398 (home). *E-mail:* ministers@hm-treasury.gov.uk (office); contact@geoffhoonmp.co.uk (office). *Website:* www.hm-treasury.gov.uk (office); www.geoffhoonmp.co.uk (office).

HÖPFNER, Matthias Martin; German diplomatist; *Ambassador to Canada;* b. 18 Dec. 1953, Potsdam; m.; two c. *Education:* Diplomatic School, Bonn. *Career:* Scientific Asst, Max-Planck-Inst. for Comparative Public Law and Int. Law, Heidelberg 1979–81; practicing barrister 1981–87; served at Foreign Office, Bonn 1988–89, 1992–95, Head of Div., Foreign Office, Bonn and Berlin 1997–2002, Deputy Dir-Gen., Dept for Econ. Affairs and Sustainable Devt; at Embassy in Jakarta 1989–92; Deputy Head of Mission, Embassy in Tripoli 1995–97; Amb. to Canada 2006–. *Address:* Embassy of Germany, 1 Waverley Street, Ottawa, ON K2P 0T8, Canada (office). *Telephone:* (613) 232-1101 (office). *Fax:* (613) 594-9330 (office). *E-mail:* germanembassyottawa@on.aibn.com (office). *Website:* www.ottawa.diplo.de (office).

HOR, Nambora; Cambodian diplomatist; *Ambassador to UK;* b. 28 July 1957, Siemreap-Angkor, Watt Prov.; m. Hor Khemtan (née Ouch); one s. two d. *Education:* Paris High School and Univ. of Paris, France, Inst. of Int. Relations and Political Studies, Univ. of Economics of Budapest, Hungary. *Career:* UN Scholarship and Fellowship to UN HQ, Geneva, Switzerland; research and archivist staff, Genocidal Museum of Toul Sleng, Phnom Penh 1980–85; Dir Humanitarian Relief Cttee, Kompong Som Port 1986–87; Desk Officer for Soviet Union and Eastern European Countries Affairs, Ministry of Foreign Affairs 1988–89, Bureau Chief, Ministry of Foreign Affairs 1990–91, Deputy Dir Ministry of Foreign Affairs 1991–93, Dir Bureau of Representation of Cambodia, Bangkok 1993–94, Counsellor, Bangkok 1994–96, Deputy Perm. Rep. to UN Econ. and Social Dept. for Asia and the Pacific, Bangkok 1995–96, Under-Sec. of State and Foreign Affairs Adviser to the Head of State a.i., HE Samdech Chea Sim 1996–98, Amb. to Australia (also accred to NZ) 1999–2004, to UK (also accred to Sweden, Finland, Denmark and Norway) 2004– (also accred to Ireland 2005–); Commdr, Royal Order of Cambodia 2007; honoured as a "Citizen of Humanity" by Australian Cttee on Human Rights Educ. 2002. *Address:* Embassy of Cambodia, 64 Brondesbury Park, Willesden Green, London, NW6 7AT, England (office). *Telephone:* (20) 8451-7850 (office). *Fax:* (20) 8451-7594 (office). *E-mail:* cambodianembassy@btconnect.com (office). *Website:* www.cambodianembassy.org.uk (office).

HORNBY, Ross, BA, LLB, MA; Canadian lawyer and diplomatist; *Permanent Representative, European Union; Education:* Univ. of British Columbia, Univ. of Toronto, Osgoode Hall Law School. *Career:* Counsel, Legal Bureau, Dept of External Affairs 1981–83; Second Sec., Perm. Mission to UN, Geneva 1983–86; Sr Counsel, Public Law Sector, Justice Canada 1986–93; Gen. Counsel, Gen. Legal Services, Dept of Finance 1993–96; Sr Gen. Counsel, Head of Legal Services, Treasury Bd Secr. of Canada 1996–2000, Asst Sec., Govt Operations 2000–03; Asst Deputy Minister, Strategic Policy and Public Diplomacy, Dept of Foreign Affairs and Int. Trade 2003–06; Perm. Rep. to EU, Brussels 2006–. *Address:* Permanent Mission of Canada, 2 ave de Tervueren, 1040 Brussels, Belgium (office). *Telephone:* (2) 741-06-60 (office). *Fax:* (2) 741-06-29 (office). *E-mail:* breu@international.gc.ca (office). *Website:* www.international.gc.ca (office).

HORNHUES, Karl-Heinz, Dr rer. pol; German politician; *Chairman of German Delegation to Assembly, Western European Union;* b. 10 June 1939, Stadtlohn; m. Ellen Buss 1965; two s. *Education:* Univ. of Münster. *Career:* adviser, Catholic Adult Educ. Center, Ludwig-Windthorst-Hause, Holthausen 1966–71, Dir 1970–71; Educ. and Teaching Dir Hofmann-La Roche AG, Grenzbach 1971; Assoc. Prof. of Social Econs and Political Science 1974, Prof. 1977; mem. Bundestag 1972–; Deputy Chair. of CDU/CSU Parl. Party in Bundestag in charge of foreign policy, defence policy

and European affairs 1989–94; Chair. Foreign Affairs Cttee 1994–98; Chair. German Del., Ass. of WEU 2000–; Chair. German African Foundation; mem. Ass., Council of Europe; Kommendeurkreuz 1999. *Address:* Friedrichstr. 83, 10117 Berlin (office); Pius-str. 19, 49134 Wallenhorst, Germany. *Telephone:* (30) 22794348. *Fax:* (30) 22796888 (office).

HOROI, Rex Stephen, BEd, MA; Solomon Islands diplomatist and academic; *Executive Director, Foundation for the Peoples of the South Pacific International;* b. 8 Sept. 1952, Makira; m. Kate Watson; three s. one d. *Education:* Univ. of South Pacific, Univ. of Papua New Guinea, Univ. of Sydney, Australia, Univ. of London and Huddersfield Tech. Educ. Centre, UK. *Career:* teacher, St Joseph Catholic Secondary School 1978–79, Deputy Prin. 1983–84; consultant, Univ. of Hawaii 1979; Perm. Rep. to UN 1992–2001; Amb. to USA and High Commr to Canada 1992–2000; Exec. Dir Foundation for the Peoples of the South Pacific Int. 2000–. *Publications:* Peace Corps Language Handbook (co-author); handbooks on grammar, communications and culture; articles and papers. *Address:* Foundation for the Peoples of the South Pacific International, Victoria Corner, Level 2, Office 2, GPO Box 18006, Suva, Fiji (office). *Telephone:* 3312250 (office). *Fax:* 3312298 (office). *E-mail:* admin@fspi.org.fj (office). *Website:* www.fspi.org.fj (office).

HORTON, Scott, JD; American lawyer, academic and writer; *Lecturer in Law, School of Law, Columbia University; Education:* Univ. of Texas at Austin, Univs of Mainz and Munich, Germany. *Career:* Pnr, Petterson, Belknap, Webb & Tyler (law firm), New York and Moscow –2007; fmr adviser to Cen. Asian Repubs on legal reform issues; currently Lecturer in Law, School of Law, Columbia Univ., New York; legal affairs and nat. security contrib., Harper's magazine 2007–; fmr Pres. Int. League for Human Rights (ILHR); Dir Andrei Sakharov Foundation, Moscow; Dir Int. Center for Not-for-Profit Law, Council on Foreign Relations' Center for Preventive Action and other NGOs;; mem. Lawyers Cttee for Human Rights; Co-founder American Univ. in Cen. Asia. *Publications include:* over 200 articles and monographs on legal issues. *Address:* Columbia Law School, 435 West 116th Street, New York, NY 10027-7297, USA (office). *Telephone:* (917) 216-2319 (office). *E-mail:* shorto@law.columbia.edu (office). *Website:* www.law.columbia.edu (office).

HORVÁTH, István; Hungarian economist and diplomatist; *Ambassador to Austria;* b. 1 Feb. 1943; m.; one d. *Education:* Univ. of Econ. Sciences, Budapest. *Career:* business exec., Belgrade 1973–78; Counsellor for Foreign Econ. Policy of Govt 1978–83; Amb. to the Netherlands 1983–84, to Germany 1984–91; served as adviser to several German cos 1991–2003; Personal Adviser to the Prime Minister 1994–95; Consul of the Grand Duchy of Luxembourg, Budapest 1997–2003; Amb. to Austria 2003–; Great Cross of Merit with Star and Band (Germany) 1990, Medal of Merit of Baden-Wuerttemberg (Germany) 1990, Great Order of Merit (Hungary) 1991. *Publications include:* Die Versuchung Europas 1994, ... und die Mauern fallen 1999, Die Sonne ging in Ungarn auf 2000. *Address:* Embassy of Hungary, Bankgasse 4–6, 1010 Vienna, Austria (office). *Telephone:* (1) 537-80-300 (office). *Fax:* (1) 535-99-40 (office). *E-mail:* vie.missions@kum.hu (office). *Website:* www.mfa.gov.hu/emb/vienna (office).

HOSCHEIT, Jean-Marc, LLM, MA; Luxembourg diplomatist; *Permanent Representative, United Nations;* b. 11 Oct. 1958; m.; two c. *Education:* Univ. of Strasbourg, France. *Career:* Researcher, Lecturer, then Sr Lecturer, European Inst. of Public Admin, Maastricht, The Netherlands 1982–85; European Corresp. to European Political Cooperation 1980s; Chargé d'Affaires, Ministry of Foreign Affairs 1985–86, Dir of Political Affairs 1986–89; in charge of working groups, Perm. Mission to EU, Brussels 1989–98, Deputy Perm. Rep. 1993–98; Amb. to France (also Perm. Rep. to OECD and UNESCO), Paris 1998–2003; Perm. Rep. to UN, NY 2003–. *Publications:* several articles on European political and institutional affairs. *Address:* Permanent Mission of Luxembourg to the UN, 17 Beekman Place, New York, NY 10022, USA (office). *Telephone:* (212) 935-3589 (office). *Fax:* (212) 935-5896 (office). *E-mail:* luxun@undp.org (office). *Website:* www.un.int/luxembourg (office).

HOSKING, Geoffrey Alan, PhD, FBA, FRHistS; British historian and academic; *Professor Emeritus of Russian History, School of Slavonic and East European Studies, University College London;* b. 28 April 1942, Troon, Ayrshire, Scotland; m. Anne Lloyd Hirst 1970; two d. *Education:* Maidstone Grammar School, Moscow State Univ., Kings Coll., Cambridge, St Antony's Coll., Oxford. *Career:* Lecturer in Govt, Univ. of Essex 1966–71, Lecturer in History 1972–76, Sr Lecturer and Reader in History 1976–84; Prof. of Russian History, School of Slavonic and East European Studies, Univ. Coll. London 1984–99, 2004–07, Prof. Emer. of Russian

History 2007–, Leverhulme Research Prof. 1999–2004, Deputy Dir School of Slavonic and East European Studies 1996–98; Visiting Prof. in Political Science, Univ. of Wisconsin-Madison, USA 1971–72, Slavisches Institut, Univ. of Cologne, Germany 1980–81; mem. Inst. for Advanced Studies, Princeton, USA 2006–07; mem. Booker Prize Jury for Russian Fiction 1993; Dr hc (Russian Acad. of Sciences) 2000; LA Times History Book Prize 1986, BBC Reith Lecturer 1988, US Ind. Publrs History Book Prize 2001. *Publications:* The Russian Constitutional Experiment 1973, Beyond Socialist Realism 1980, The First Socialist Society: A History of the Soviet Union from Within 1985, The Awakening of the Soviet Union 1990, The Road to Post-Communism: Independent Political Movements in the Soviet Union 1985–91 (with J. Aves and P. Duncan) 1992, Russia: People and Empire (1552–1917) 1997, Myths and Nationhood (co-ed. with George Schöpflin) 1997, Russian Nationalism Past and Present (co-ed. with Robert Service) 1998, Reinterpreting Russia (co-ed. with Robert Service) 1999, Russia and the Russians: A History from Rus to Russian Federation 2001, Rulers and Victims: The Russians in the Soviet Union 2006.
Address: School of Slavonic and East European Studies, University College London, Gower Street, London, WC1E 6BT (office); 18 Camden Mews, London, NW1 9DA, England (home). *Telephone:* (20) 7267-5543 (office). *E-mail:* geoffreyhosking@mac.com (office).

HOSS, Selim al-, MBA, PhD; Lebanese fmr politician and professor of economics; b. 20 Dec. 1929; m. Leila Hoss (died 1990); one d. *Education:* American Univ. of Beirut, Indiana Univ., USA. *Career:* teacher, later Prof. of Business, American Univ. of Beirut 1955–69; Financial Adviser, Kuwait Fund for Arab Econ. Devt, Kuwait 1964–66; Pres. Banking Supervision Comm. 1967–73; Chair. of Bd and Gen. Man. Nat. Bank for Industrial Devt 1973–76; Prime Minister 1976–80, remaining as Prime Minister in caretaker capacity July–Oct. 1980, Minister of the Econ. and Trade and Information 1976–79, of Industry and Petroleum 1976–77, of Labour, Fine Arts and Educ. 1984–85 (resgnd); Adviser to Arab Monetary Fund, Abu Dhabi, UAE 1983; Chair. of Bd Banque Arabe et Int. d'Investissement, Paris 1982–85; Head, Arab Dinar Study Group, Arab Monetary Fund 1984–85; Minister of Educ. 1985–87; Head, Arab Experts Team commissioned by Arab League 1986–87; Prime Minister 1987–90, also Minister of Foreign and Expatriate Affairs; elected Deputy to Parl. 1992–2000; Pres. of Council of Ministers (Prime Minister of Lebanon) 1976–80, 1987–90, 1998–2000; mem. Bd of Trustees, American Univ. of Beirut 1991–; mem. Consultative Council, Int. Bank for the Middle East and North Africa 1992–. *Publications:* The Development of Lebanon's Financial Markets 1974, Lebanon: Agony and Peace 1982 and 13 books in Arabic; numerous articles on economics and politics.
Address: Aisha Bakkar, Beirut, Lebanon. *Telephone:* 736000. *Fax:* 354929.

HOSSAIN, Mohammed Shahadat; Bangladeshi diplomatist; *High Commissioner to Sri Lanka; Career:* fmr Dir-Gen. Directorate-Gen. of Health Services, Ministry of Health and Family Welfare; High Commr to Sri Lanka 2006–.
Address: Bangladeshi High Commission, 85 Dharmapala Mawatha, Colombo 7, Sri Lanka (office). *Telephone:* (11) 2303943 (office). *Fax:* (11) 2303942 (office). *E-mail:* bdootlanka@eureka.lk (office).

HOSSEINI, Seyed Safdar, BA, PhD; Iranian politician; b. 1954, Khuzestan. *Education:* Shiraz Univ. *Career:* Minister of Labour and Social Affairs 2001–04; Minister of Econ. Affairs and Finance 2004–05.

HOSSEINI, Shamseddin; Iranian politician; *Minister of Economic Affairs and Finance; Career:* fmr Dir-Gen. for Econ. Studies, Ministry of Commerce; fmr Deputy Minister of Welfare and Social Security; Sec., Working Group on Econ. Transformation –2008; Minister of Econ. Affairs and Finance 2008–.
Address: Ministry of Economic Affairs and Finance, Sour Esrafil Avenue, Nasser Khosrou Street, Tehran 11149-43661, Iran (office). *Telephone:* (21) 22553401 (office). *Fax:* (21) 22581933 (office). *E-mail:* info@mefa.gov.ir (office). *Website:* mefa.gov.ir (office).

HOUEIZ, Muhammad Ali al-; Libyan economist and politician; *Deputy Prime Minister; Career:* fmr oil economist, responsible for man. overseas investments; Sec. of Finance, Govt of Libya 2004–06; Deputy Prime Minister 2006–.
Address: General People's Committee, Tripoli, Libya (office).

HOUGH, Michael, MA, PhD; South African political scientist and academic; *Director, Institute for Strategic Studies, University of Pretoria;* b. 8 July 1944, Johannesburg. *Education:* Univ. of Pretoria, Univ. of South Africa (UNISA). *Career:* Student Asst, Dept of Information, Univ. of Pretoria 1967–68, Lecturer, then Sr Lecturer 1968–81, Prof., Dept of Political Sciences 1982–, Dir Inst. for Strategic Studies (affiliated to Univ. of Pretoria) 1979–. *Publications:* 15 book chapters; more than 120 articles in

popular and professional journals; monographs, conf. papers and contribs to research projects.
Address: Institute for Strategic Studies, University of Pretoria, Pretoria 0002, South Africa (office). *Telephone:* (12) 420-2407 (office); (12) 420-2034 (office). *Fax:* (12) 420-2693 (office). *E-mail:* wilma.martin@up.ac.za (office). *Website:* www.up.ac.za/academic/libarts/polsci/home.htm (office).

HOUNGBÉDJI, Adrien; Benin politician and lawyer; *Leader, Parti du renouveau démocratique; Career:* sentenced to death in absentia March 1975 after alleged involvement in attempted coup; Speaker of Nat. Ass. 1991–96; Prime Minister 1996–98; Leader Parti du renouveau démocratique (PRD).
Address: Parti du renouveau démocratique, BP 281, Cotonou, Benin (office). *Telephone:* 33-94-88 (office). *Fax:* 33-94-89 (office). *Website:* www .prd-by.net (office).

HOUNGBO, Gilbert Fossoun, Maîtrise en Gestion d'Entreprises, BA, DESS (Diplôme d' Etudes Supérieures Specialisées); Togolese UN official; *Assistant Secretary-General, Assistant Administrator and Director, Regional Bureau for Africa, United Nations Development Programme (UNDP); Education:* Université de Lomé. *Career:* worked at Price Waterhouse Canada; mem. UNDP Strategic Man. Team and Dir of Finance and Admin then Chief of Staff UNDP, New York 2003–05; Asst Sec.-Gen., Asst Admin. of UNDP and Dir of UNDP's Regional Bureau for Africa 2005–; mem. Canadian Inst. of Chartered Accountants.
Address: United Nations Development Programme, One United Nations Plaza, New York, NY 10017, USA (office). *Telephone:* (212) 906-5000 (office). *Fax:* (212) 906-5364 (office). *Website:* www.undp.org/regions/africa (office).

HOWELL OF GUILDFORD, Baron (Life Peer), cr. 1997, of Penton Mewsey in the County of Hampshire; **David Arthur Russell Howell,** PC, BA; British politician, journalist and economist; *Opposition Spokesman on Foreign and Commonwealth Affairs and Deputy Leader of the Opposition, House of Lords;* b. 18 Jan. 1936, London; m. Davina Wallace 1967; one s. two d. *Education:* Eton Coll., King's Coll., Cambridge. *Career:* Lt Coldstream Guards 1954–56; Econ. Section, HM Treasury 1959, resgnd 1960; Leader-writer The Daily Telegraph 1960; Chair. Bow Group 1961–62; fmr Crossbow; MP for Guildford 1966–97; a Lord Commr of Treasury 1970–71; with Civil Service Dept 1970–72; Parl. Under-Sec. Dept of Employment 1971–72; Minister of State, Northern Ireland Office 1972–74, Dept of Energy Jan.–Feb. 1974; Sec. of State for Energy 1979–81, for Transport 1981–83; Chair. House of Commons Foreign Affairs Cttee 1987–97, One Nation Group of Conservative MPs 1987–97, European Cttee on Common Foreign and Security Policy 1999–2000; Opposition Spokesman on Foreign and Commonwealth Affairs 2000–; Chair. UK–Japan 2000 Group 1989–2001; Dir Conservative Political Centre 1964–66; Dir Monks Investment Trust 1992–2005, John Laing Investments PLC 1997–2002; Advisory Dir UBS-Warburg 1996–2000; Sr Adviser, Japan Cen. Railway Co. 2001–; European Adviser, Mitsubishi Electric BV; Adviser to Kuwait Investment Office; Pres. British Inst. of Energy Economists; mem. Governing Bd Centre for Global Energy Studies; Visiting Fellow, Nuffield Coll., Oxford 1993–2001; Gov. Sadler's Wells Trust 1995–98; Trustee Shakespeare's Globe Theatre 2000–; Foundation Scholar, King's Coll. Cambridge, Richmond Prize 1959; Grand Cordon of the Order of the Sacred Treasure (Japan) 2001. *Publications:* Principle in Practice (co-author) 1960, The Conservative Opportunity 1965, Freedom and Capital 1981, Blind Victory 1986, The Edge of Now 2000.
Address: House of Lords, Westminster, London, SW1A 0PW (office). *Telephone:* (20) 7219-5415 (office). *Fax:* (20) 7219-0304 (office). *E-mail:* howelld@parliament.uk (office). *Website:* www.lordhowell.com (office).

HOWELLS, Kim, BA, PhD; British politician; *Minister of State for the Middle East and South Asia;* b. 27 Nov. 1946, Merthyr Tydfil, Wales; m. Eirlys Howells; three c. *Education:* Mountain Ash Grammar School, Hornsey Coll. of Art, Cambridge Coll. of Art and Tech., Univ. of Warwick. *Career:* lecturer 1975–79; Official Research Officer, Coalfield History Project, Nat. Union of Miners (NUM) 1979–82, research officer and journal ed., NUM S Wales Area 1982–89; writer and broadcaster 1986–89; Labour MP for Pontypridd 1989–, Opposition Spokesman on Devt and Co-operation 1993–94, for Home Affairs 1994–95, for Foreign and Commonwealth Affairs 1994–95, for Trade and Industry 1995; Parl. Under-Sec. of State for Lifelong Learning, Dept for Educ. and Employment 1997–98; Minister for Consumers and Corp. Affairs, Dept for Trade and Industry 1998–2001; Minister for Tourism, Broadcasting and Media, Dept of Culture, Media and Sport 2001–03; Minister of State for Transport 2003–04, for Further and Higher Educ. and Lifelong Learning 2004–05, for the Middle East and South Asia, FCO 2005–; mem. Welsh Affairs Select Cttee 1989–90, mem. Environmental Select Cttee 1990–92, mem. Public Accounts Cttee 1992–93, 1993–94; Dr hc (Anglia Polytechnic Univ.).

Address: Foreign and Commonwealth Office, King Charles Street, London, SW1A 2AH, England (office); 16 Tyfica Road, Pontypridd, Wales (home). *Telephone:* (20) 7008-2090 (office); (1443) 402551 (home). *Fax:* (20) 7008-2988 (office). *E-mail:* helen.perry@fco.gov.uk (office). *Website:* www.fco.gov.uk (office).

HRYSHCHENKO, Kostyantyn I.; Ukrainian politician and diplomatist; *Ambassador to Russia;* b. 28 Oct. 1953, Kyiv. *Education:* Moscow State Institute of Int. Relations, USSR. *Career:* staff mem., UN Secr., NY, USA 1976–80; various positions in Ministry of Foreign Affairs, USSR 1981–91; various positions in Arms Control and Disarmament Directorate, Ministry of Foreign Affairs of Ukraine, Kiev 1992–95; Deputy Foreign Minister 1995–98; Amb. to Belgium, Netherlands and Luxembourg, Head of Mission to NATO and Perm. Rep. to Org. for Prohibition of Chemical Weapons, The Hague, Netherlands 1998–2000; Amb. to USA 2000–03; Minister of Foreign Affairs 2003–05; Counselor of Prime Minister 2006–07; First Deputy, Nat. Security and Defence Council (RNBO) 2008; Amb. to Russia June 2008–; Chair. UN Advisory Bd on Disarmament Matters 2003; mem. Foundation Council, Geneva Centre for Security Policy 1995–98, Coll. of Commrs of UN Monitoring, Verification and Inspection Comm. (UNMOVIC); Order of Merit 1998.
Address: Embassy of Ukraine, 103009 Moscow, Leontiyevskii per. 18, Russia (office). *Telephone:* (495) 629-35-42 (office). *Fax:* (495) 629-46-81 (office). *E-mail:* emb_ru@mfa.gov.ua (office). *Website:* www.mfa.gov.ua/russia (office).

HSIEH, Frank Chang-ting, LLM; Taiwanese politician; b. 18 May 1946, Taipei. *Education:* Nat. Taiwan Univ., Kyoto Univ., Japan. *Career:* practised as attorney 1969–81; Defence Counsel in Kaohsiung Incident 1990; mem. Taipei City Council 1981–88; mem. Cen. Standing Cttee, Democratic Progressive Party (DPP) 1986–96, Legislator 1989–96, Chair. Cen. Review Cttee 1996–98, DPP Vice-Presidential cand. 1996, Chair. DPP 2000–02, Jan.–March 2008; Mayor of Kaohsiung 1998–2005; Premier of Taiwan 2005–06; cand. for Mayor of Taipei 2006; DPP Presidential cand. 2008 elections.
Address: Democratic Progressive Party (DPP), 10/F, 30 Beiping East Road, Taipei 10051, Taiwan (office). *Telephone:* (2) 23929989 (home). *Fax:* (2) 23929989 (office). *E-mail:* foreign@dpp.org.tw (office). *Website:* www.dpp.org.tw (office).

HU, Jason Chih-chiang, DPhil; Taiwanese politician and academic; *Mayor of Taichung City;* b. 15 May 1948, Yungchi Co., Kirin Prov., China; m. Shirley S. Hu; one s. one d. *Education:* Nat. Chengchi Univ., Univ. of Southampton, Univ. of Oxford. *Career:* Exec. Sec. Nat. Union of Students 1966–68; led del. to UN World Youth Asscn 1970; fmr instructor Inst. of Int. Studies, Univ. of SC, USA; taught Oxford Overseas Studies Programme 1982–83, Research Fellow, St Antony's Coll., Oxford 1985; Assoc. Prof. Nat. Sun Yat-sen Univ. 1986–90; Deputy Dir Sun Yat-sen Center for Policy Studies 1986–90; Deputy Dir First Bureau, Office of the Pres. concurrently Presidential Press Sec. 1991; Dir-Gen. Govt Information Office and Govt Spokesman 1991–96; Rep. of Taipei Econ. and Cultural Office, Washington, DC; Minister of Foreign Affairs 1997–99; Presidential Campaign Man., Kuomintang 1999–2000, Dir Cultural and Communication Affairs Central Comm. 2000–01, Deputy Sec.-Gen. 2001; Mayor of Taichung City 2001–; Dr hc (Southampton) 1997; Best Govt Spokesman Award 1993, Top Ten Chinese Award 1994, Outstanding Professional Achievement Award 1996. *Publications include:* Say Yes to Taiwan! 1997, Quiet Revolution (in Chinese) 1996; many other books in Chinese.
Address: No. 99, Ming Chuan Road, Taichung, Taiwan (office). *Telephone:* (2) 2228-8211 (office). *Fax:* (2) 2229-1136 (office). *E-mail:* 10001@tccg.gov.tw (office). *Website:* www.tccg.gov.tw (office).

HU, Jintao; Chinese head of state; *President;* b. 21 Dec. 1942, Jixi, Anhui Prov.; m. Liu Yongqing. *Education:* Tsinghua Univ., Beijing. *Career:* joined CCP 1964; postgraduate and political instructor, Water Conservancy Eng Dept, Tsinghua Univ. 1964–65, researcher 1965–68; Sec. Gansu Prov. Construction Cttee, Deputy Dir 1974–75, Vice-Chair. 1980–82; Chair. All-China Youth Fed. 1982–84; Sec. Gansu Prov. Br. Communist Youth League 1982; Sec. Communist Youth League 1982–84, First Sec. 1984–85; mem. Standing Cttee, 6th NPC, mem. Presidium and mem. Standing Cttee, CPPCC 6th Nat. Cttee 1983–98; Sec. CCP Prov. Cttee, Guizhou 1985–88, Tibet 1988–92; Vice-Pres. of People's Repub. of China (PRC) 1998–2003, Pres. 2003–; Vice-Chair. Cen. Mil. Comm. of PRC 1999–2002; mem. 12th CCP Cen. Cttee 1982–87, mem. 13th CCP Cen. Cttee 1987–92, 14th CCP Cen. Cttee 1992–97 (mem. Secr. and Standing Cttee of Politburo 1992–97), mem. 15th CCP Cen. Cttee 1997–2002 (mem. Secr. and Standing Cttee of Politburo 1992–97, Vice-Chair. Cen. Mil. Comm. 1997–2002), 16th CCP Cen. Cttee 2002–07 (Gen. Sec. 2002–, Vice-Chair. Cen. Mil. Comm. 2002–05, Chair. 2005–07, mem. Standing Cttee of Politburo 2002–07); Gen. Sec. 17th CCP Cen. Cttee 2007– (mem. Standing

Cttee of the Politboro 2007–, Chair. Cen.Mil. Comm.2007–); Pres. Cen. Party School 1993–; Head, Cen. Leading Group for Party Bldg Work.
Address: Office of the President, Great Hall of the People, West Edge, Tiananmen Square, Beijing, People's Republic of China (office). *Website:* www.gov.cn (office).

HUANG, Fanzhang; Chinese economist; *Senior Researcher, Economic Research Centre, State Development and Reform Commission;* b. 8 Feb. 1931, Jiang-Xi; m. Yue-Fen Xue 1959; two s. *Education:* Peking Univ. *Career:* Researcher, Inst. of Econs Chinese Acad. of Social Science (CASS) 1954–, Sr Researcher and Prof. 1979–, Deputy Dir 1982–85; Visiting Scholar, Harvard Univ. 1980–82, Stockholm Univ. 1982; Exec. Dir for China, IMF 1985–86; Visiting Research Assoc. Center for Chinese Studies, Univ. of Mich. 1986–87; Consultant to World Bank 1987–88; Dir Dept of Int. Econ. Studies, State Planning Comm. 1988–90; Vice-Pres. Economic Research Centre, State Planning Comm. 1990–97; Sr Researcher, Econ. Research Centre, State Devt and Reform Comm. 1997–; Consultant for a series of 100 books on current Chinese Economy 1994; CASS Prize 1985. *Publications:* Modern Economics in Western Countries (with others) 1963, The Evolution of Socialist Theories of Income Distribution 1979, Swedish Welfare State in Practice and its Theories 1987, The Reform in Banking System and The Role of Monetary Policy in China 1989, Joint Stock System – An Appropriate Form to China's Socialist Public Ownership 1989, The Characteristics of the World Economy in the 1980s, its Prospects for the 1990s and China's Counter-measures 1990, China's Exploration of the Theories of Economic Reform in the Last Ten Years (1979–89) 1991, Stock Ownership, Privatization, Socialization and Other Topics 1992, Foreign Direct Investment in China Since 1979 1992, On the Trend and Pattern of Economic Growth in East Asia and the Asia-Pacific Region 1993, East Asian Economics: Development, Prospects for Co-operation and China's Strategy 1993, China's Transitional Inflation 1994, China's Use of Foreign Direct Investment and Economic Reform 1995, Selected Works of Huang Fan-Zhang (1980–93) 1995, White Paper on East Asian Economies 1996, Economic Globalization and Financial Supervision In Internationalization 1998, Whither Will the East Asian Economies Go? 1999, To Establish the Social Security Fund and the Fund's Ownership 2000, China's Reform: Opening to the Outside and Its International Environment 2002, China's New Road of Industrialization and its Peaceful Rise 2004, The Blue Book on East Asian Economies 2000–05 2006.
Address: Apartment 801, Building 13, Mu-Xi-Di, Bei-Li, Beijing 100038, People's Republic of China. *Telephone:* (10) 63261950. *Fax:* (10) 63908071. *E-mail:* Huangfz@hotmail.com (home).

HUANG, Zhendong; Chinese politician; *Secretary, Chongqing Municipal Committee, Chinese Communist Party;* b. 1941, Dafeng Co., Jiangsu Prov. *Education:* Nanjing Navigation Eng School, Shanghai Shipping Inst. *Career:* Sr Engineer at Research Fellow level, Nanjing Navigation Eng School 1962; entered workforce, Admin. Bureau, Qinhuangdao Harbour, Hebei Prov. 1963, Deputy Chief of Planning Div. and Deputy Dir Admin. Bureau 1963–82, Dir 1982; joined CCP 1981; Vice-Minister of Communications 1985–88, Minister 1991–2003 (Sec. CCP Leading Party Group, Ministry of Communications 1991); Gen. Man. State Communications Investment Co. 1988–91; Chair. China Merchants' Steam Navigation Group Ltd 1991; mem. 14th CCP Cen. Cttee 1992–97, 15th Cen. Cttee 1997–2002, 16th CCP Cen. Cttee 2002–; Sec. Chongqing CCP Municipal Cttee 2002–; Chair. Standing Cttee Chongqing Municipal People's Congress 2003–.
Address: c/o Zhongguo Gongchan Dang (Chinese Communist Party), 1 Zhong Nan, Beijing, People's Republic of China.

HUANG, Zhiquan; Chinese politician; *Governor of Jiangxi Province;* b. Feb. 1942, Tongxiang, Zhejiang Prov. *Education:* Zhejiang Agricultural Univ. *Career:* joined CCP 1979; Div. Head and Deputy Dir Jiangxi Prov. Planning Comm. 1984–91, Dir 1991–93; Asst Gov. Jiangxi Prov. 1991–93, Vice-Gov. 1993–2001, Gov. 2001–; Deputy Sec. CCP Jiangxi Prov. Cttee 1995–; mem. 15th CCP Cen. Cttee 1997–2002, 16th CCP Cen. Cttee 2002–.
Address: Jiangxi Provincial People's Government, 5 Beijing West Road, Nanchang 330046, People's Republic of China (office).

HUBBARD, Thomas C.; American business executive and fmr diplomatist; *Senior Advisor, Akin Gump Strauss Hauer & Feld LLP;* b. 1943, Ky; m. Joan Magnusson Hubbard; two c. *Education:* Univ. of Ala. *Career:* joined Foreign Service 1965; Political/Econ. Officer, US Embassy, Santo Domingo 1966; Econ./Commercial Officer, Fukuoka, Japan; with Political Section, Tokyo 1971; Econ. Officer, Japan Desk, Dept of State 1973–75; Exec. sec. to Del., then Energy Adviser, US Mission to OECD, Paris 1975–78; with Political Section, Tokyo 1978–81; Dir Training and Liaison Staff, Bureau of Personnel, State Dept, Deputy Dir, Philippine Desk 1984–85, Country Dir 1985–87; Deputy Chief of Mission, Kuala Lumpur 1987; Minister-Counsellor, Sr Foreign Service 1989; Minister and Deputy

Chief of Mission, Manila 1990–93; Deputy Asst Sec., East Asian and Pacific Affairs, Dept of State 1993–96; Amb. to Philippines 1996–2000; Prin. Deputy Asst Sec. of State for E Asian and Pacific Affairs 2000–01; Amb. to Repub. of Korea 2001–04; Sr Advisor, Akin Gump Strauss Hauer & Feld LLP 2004–; Dr hc (Univ. of Maryland), (Univ. of Ala). *Address:* Akin Gump Strauss Hauer & Feld LLP, Robert S. Strauss Building, 1333 New Hampshire Avenue, NW, Washington, DC 20036-1564, USA (office). *Telephone:* (202) 887-4305 (office). *Fax:* (202) 887-4288 (office). *E-mail:* thubbard@akingump.com (office). *Website:* www.akingump.com (office).

HUBERT, Jean-Paul, BA, BCL, MIA, DPolSci, PhD; Canadian lawyer, diplomatist, international organization executive and academic; *President, Inter-American Juridical Committee;* b. 16 Dec. 1941, Grand-Mère, QC; m. 1st Mireya Melgar 1967 (divorced 1995); two s. one d.; m. 2nd Florence Fournier 1995. *Education:* Laval Univ., McGill Univ., Columbia Univ., New York, Univ. of the Sorbonne, Paris, Moncton (New Brunswick) Univ. *Career:* with Dept of Foreign Relations and Int. Trade, Canadian Diplomatic Service, Ottawa 1971–72, Second Sec., Vice-Consul for Spain and Morocco, Madrid 1972–74, Legal Affairs Div., Ottawa 1974–76, Personnel Div. 1976–78, First Sec. and Consul, Havana 1978–81, Political Counsellor and Rep., Agency for Cultural and Tech. Co-operation, Paris 1991–95, Econ. and Treaty Law Div., Ottawa 1985–86, Fed. Co-ordinator for La Francophonie 1986–88, Amb. to Senegal, Mauritania, Guinea, Guinea-Bissau, Cape Verde and Senegal 1988–90, High Commr to the Gambia 1988–90, Prime Minister's Personal Rep. for La Francophonie 1988–90, Embassy in Dakar 1988–90, first Amb. and Perm. Rep. of Canada to OAS, Washington, DC 1990–93, Sr Advisor, Commonwealth La Francophonie/Hemispheric Affairs, Ottawa 1993–94, Prime Minister's Personal Rep. for La Francophonie, Ottawa, Brussels 1994–98, Amb. to Belgium and Luxembourg 1994–98, to Argentina and Paraguay 1998–2005; Pres. Inter-American Juridical Cttee, OAS 2005–; Interim Pres. Int. Centre for Human Rights and Democratic Devt (Rights & Democracy) 2007–; currently Visiting Prof., Dept of History and Political Sciences, Univ. of Sherbrooke, QC; Designated Order of la Pleiade, Int. Asscn of French-Speaking Parliamentarians 1989. *Address:* Comissão Jurídica Interamericana, Avenida Marechal Floriano 196, 3° andar, Palácio de Itamaraty, Centro 20080-002, Rio de Janeiro, RJ, Brazil (office). *Telephone:* (21) 2206-9903 (office). *Fax:* (21) 2203-2090 (office). *E-mail:* cjioea.trp@terra.com.br (office). *Website:* www.oas.org/cji (office).

HÜBNER, Danuta; Polish politician and economist; *Commissioner for Regional Policy, European Commission;* b. 8 March 1948, Nisko; two d. *Education:* Warsaw School of Econs. *Career:* researcher, Main School of Planning and Statistics, Warsaw (now Warsaw School of Econs) 1971–, Deputy Dir Research Inst. for Developing Countries, Warsaw School of Econs 1981–87, Deputy Dir Inst. for Devt and Strategic Studies 1991–94; Deputy Ed.-in-Chief Ekonomista (bi-monthly) 1991–97; Ed.-in-Chief Gospodarka Narodowa (monthly) 1994–97; Under-Sec. of State Ministry of Industry and Trade 1994–96; Sec. Cttee for European Integration 1996–97, 2001–04; Sec. of State for European Integration 1996–97; Head, Chancellery of the Pres. of Poland 1997–98; Econ. Adviser to Pres. of Poland 1998–2001; Deputy Exec. Sec. UN Econ. Comm. for Europe 1998–2000, Exec. Sec. 2000–01, UN Under-Sec.-Gen. 2000–01; Sec. of State, Ministry of Foreign Affairs 2001–04; Minister for European Affairs 2003–04; EU Commr without Portfolio 2004, for Regional Policy 2004–; Chair. Council for Social Planning 1996–98; mem. Exec. Cttee European Asscn of Devt Research and Training Insts 1987–96, Nat. Statistics Council 1995–97, Scientific Bd Econ. Sciences Inst., Polish Acad. of Science 1996–98; Hon. LLB (Sussex Univ.) 2005; Dr hc (Univ. of Nat. and World Economy, Sofia) 2007. *Address:* European Commission, Rue de la Loi 200, 1049 Brussels, Belgium (office). *Telephone:* (2) 298-86-26 (office). *Fax:* (2) 298-86-34 (office). *E-mail:* Cabinet-Huebner@ec.europa.eu (office). *Website:* ec.europa.eu/commission_barroso/hubner (office).

HUCKLE, Alan Edden, MA; British diplomatist; *Governor of Falkland Islands and Commissioner of South Georgia and South Sandwich Islands;* b. 15 June 1948, Penang, Malaya; m. Helen Myra Gibson 1973; one s. one d. *Education:* Rugby School, Univ. of Warwick. *Career:* Personnel Man. Div., Civil Service Dept (CSD) 1971–74; Asst Pvt. Sec. to Sec. of State for Belfast 1974–75, Machinery of Govt Div., CSD 1975–78; Political Affairs Div., NI Office 1978–80; with FCO 1980–83; Exec. Dir British Information Services, New York, USA 1983–87; Head of Chancery, Manila 1987–90; Head, Dept of Arms Control and Disarmament, FCO 1990–92; Counsellor and Head of Del. to CSCE, Vienna 1992–96; Head, Dept Territories Regional Secr., Bridgetown 1996–98; Head, OSCE/Council of Europe Dept, FCO 1998–2001; Head, Overseas Territories Dept, FCO and Commr (non-resident) British Antarctic Territory and British Indian Ocean Territory

2001–04; Gov. of Anguilla 2004–06; Gov. of Falkland Islands and Commr S Georgia and S Sandwich Islands 2006–; Leverhulme Trust Scholar, British School at Rome 1971. *Address:* Office of the Governor, Government House, Stanley, FIQQ 1ZZ, Falkland Islands (office). *Telephone:* 27433 (office). *Fax:* 27434 (office). *E-mail:* gov.house@horizon.co.fk (office).

HUDDLESTON, Vicki, BA, MA; American diplomatist; *Chargé d'affaires in Ethiopia;* b. Ariz. *Education:* Univ. of Colorado and Johns Hopkins School of Advanced Int. Studies. *Career:* Peace Corps volunteer in Peru, later worked for American Inst. for Free Labor Devt in both Peru and Brazil; fmr career mem. Sr Foreign Service with rank of Career Minister, Deputy, then Coordinator Office of the Coordinator for Cuban Affairs 1989–93, Deputy Chief of Mission, Port-au-Prince, Haiti 1993–95, Amb. to Madagascar 1995–97, Deputy Asst Sec. of State for Africa 1997–99, Chief of Mission, US Interests Section, Havana 1999–2002, Amb. to Mali 2002–05, Chargé d'affaires a.i. to Ethiopia 2005–; American Political Science Asscn Congressional Fellow on staff of Senator Jeff Bingaman 1988–89; Fellow, Kennedy School of Govt, Harvard Univ. 2005; Distinguished Alumni Plenary Lecturer, Univ. of Colorado, Distinguished Honor Award, two Presidential Meritorious Service Awards, Lifetime Achievement Award. *Address:* Embassy of the USA, Entoto Street, PO Box 1014, Addis Ababa, Ethiopia (office). *Telephone:* (11) 517-40-00 (office). *Fax:* (11) 517-40-01 (office). *E-mail:* pasaddis@state.gov (office). *Website:* addisababa.usembassy.gov (office).

HUDSON, William J., BA, MA; American diplomatist; m.; three c. *Education:* Univ. of California, Los Angeles. *Career:* entered Foreign Service in 1972, career mem. Sr Foreign Service, overseas assignments have included Admin. Officer, Belgrade, Deputy Chief of Mission in Lomé, Togo, Gen. Services Officer, Tehran and Admin. Officer in Lubumbashi, Democratic Repub. of the Congo, Dir Office of Overseas Employment, Bureau of Human Resources 1989–91, Exec. Dir Bureau of African Affairs 1993–96, Minister-Counselor for Admin. Affairs, Paris 1996–2000, has served as Exec. Dir Bureaus of Near Eastern Affairs and S Asian Affairs 2000–03, Amb. to Tunisia 2003–06; shared Group Meritorious Honor Awards 1975, 1999, Meritorious Honor Award 1988, individual Superior Honor Awards 1991, 2002, Sr Foreign Service Performance Pay Awards 1992, 2000, 2002, Presidential Meritorious Service Award 1993. *Address:* US Department of State, 2201 C Street NW, Washington, DC 20520, USA (office). *Telephone:* (202) 647-4000 (office). *Fax:* (202) 647-6738 (office). *Website:* www.state.gov (office).

HUDSON-PHILLIPS, Karl Terrence, QC, MA, LLM; Trinidad and Tobago judge; b. 20 April 1933. *Education:* Selwyn Coll., Univ. of Cambridge, UK. *Career:* called to the Bar, Gray's Inn, London 1959, Trinidad and Tobago 1959, Jamaica 1974, Antigua and Barbuda 1977, Grenada 1983, St Vincent and the Grenadines 1985, St Kitts and Nevis 1985, Anguilla 1985, Bahamas 1985, St Lucia 1985, Barbados 1985, British Virgin Islands 1985; apptd QC, Bar of Trinidad and Tobago 1970, Sr Counsel of Bar, Cooperative Repub. of Guyana 1971; pvt. practice in Trinidad and Tobago and Commonwealth Caribbean 1959–; mem. Parl. 1966–76; Attorney-Gen. and Minister for Legal Affairs 1969–73; Judge, Int. Criminal Court (ICC), The Hague 2003–08; Founder Nat. Land Tenants and Ratepayers Asscn of Trinidad and Tobago 1974, Org. for Nat. Reconstruction 1980; Chair. Comm. of Inquiry into Operations of St Lucia Police Force 1987; Pres. Law Asscn of Trinidad and Tobago 1999–; mem. Council Commonwealth Law Asscn 1992–, Bd of Dirs Justice Studies Center of the Americas, Santiago, Chile 1999–. *Publications:* articles in professional journals. *Address:* c/o International Criminal Court, Maanweg 174, 2516 AB The Hague, The Netherlands. *Telephone:* (70) 5158515.

HUE, Robert; French politician and nurse; b. 19 Oct. 1946, Cormeilles-en-Parisis; m. Marie-Edith Solard 1973; one s. one d. *Education:* Coll. d'Enseignement Technique and Ecole d'Infirmier. *Career:* mem. Young Communists 1962; mem. French CP 1963–, mem. Secr. Fed. of Val d'Oise 1970–77, mem. Cen. Cttee 1987, mem. Politburo 1990, Nat. Sec. 1994–2001, Pres. 2001, Chair. 2001–03, Senator 2004; cand. of CP in French presidential election 1995, 2002; Mayor of Montigny-les-Cormeilles 1977–; Conseiller-Général Val d'Oise 1988–97; Deputy for Argenteuil-Bezons 1997–; mem. European Parl. 1999–2000; Pres. Nat. Asscn of Communist and Republican elected mems 1991–94, Fondation Gabriel Péri 2003–. *Publications:* Histoire d'un village du Parisis des origines à la Révolution 1981, Du village à la ville 1986, Montigny pendant la Révolution 1989, Communisme: la mutation 1995, Il faut qu'on se parle 1997, Communisme: un nouveau projet 1999, Qui êtes-vous? 2001. *Address:* SENAT, 15 rue de Vauginand, 75291 Paris Cedex 06, France (office). *E-mail:* fondation@gabrielperi.fr (office).

HUGHES, Anthony Vernon, MA; Solomon Islands banking executive and civil servant; b. 29 Dec. 1936, England; m. 1st Carole Frances Robson 1961 (divorced 1970); one s.; m. 2nd Kuria Vaze Paia 1971; one s. one d. two adopted d. *Education:* Queen Mary's Grammar School, Walsall, England, Pembroke Coll., Oxford and Bradford Univ. *Career:* Commr of Lands, Registrar of Titles, Solomon Islands 1969–70, Head of Planning 1974–76, Perm. Sec. Ministry of Finance 1976–81, Gov. Cen. Bank 1982–93; Devt Sec., Gilbert and Ellice Islands 1971–73; Regional Econ. Adviser UN Econ. and Social Comm. for Asia and the Pacific 1994–99; currently freelance consultant in econ. man.; Cross of Solomon Islands 1981. *Publications:* numerous articles on land tenure, econ. planning, devt admin, foreign investment, expecially jt ventures, with special emphasis on small countries. *Address:* PO Box 486, Honiara, Solomon Islands (home).

HUGHES, Ian Noel; British diplomatist; *Ambassador to Guatemala;* b. 5 Dec. 1951, Watchfield, England; m. Teresa Hughes; two s. one d. *Career:* Vice-Consul/Admin. Officer, Kabul 1978–81; Vice-Consul, Warsaw 1981–83; Desk Officer, South Pacific Dept, FCO 1983–85; Second Sec., Aid/Commercial, Tegucigalpa 1985–88; First Sec., Chancery, Berne 1988–91; Desk Officer, Middle Eastern Dept, FCO 1991, Press Office 1991–93; First Sec., Press and Information, New Delhi 1993–97; Deputy Head of Near East and N African Dept, FCO 1997–99; Deputy Head of Mission, Mexico City 2000–03; Deputy High Commr, Mumbai 2003–05; Amb. to Guatemala 2006–. *Address:* British Embassy, Edificio Torre Internacional, 11°, Avda de la Reforma, 16 Calle, Zona 10, Guatemala City, Guatemala (office). *Telephone:* 2367-5425 (office). *Fax:* 2367-5430 (office). *E-mail:* embassy@intelnett.com (office).

HUGHES, John, PhD; British diplomatist; *Ambassador to Argentina;* b. 1947, Wales; m. Lynne Hughes; two s. *Education:* London School of Econs, Lehigh Univ., Pa, USA, Pembroke Coll., Cambridge. *Career:* joined FCO as a Research Analyst on USA and Canada 1973, subsequent assignments in London have included working on the Middle East, Aviation, Maritime and Environmental Affairs, and leading change within FCO; postings abroad included Head of Political Section post in Santiago, Chile, press job in Washington, DC, Deputy Head of Mission, Norway; Amb. to Venezuela 2000–03, to Argentina 2004–, also accred to Paraguay 2005–; has also worked in the Cabinet Office; secondments to British Aerospace 1999, Shell 2003–04. *Address:* British Embassy, Dr Luis Agote 2412, C1425EOF, Buenos Aires, Argentina (office). *Telephone:* (11) 4808-2200 (office). *Fax:* (11) 4808-2274 (office). *E-mail:* askinformation.baires@fco.gov.uk (office). *Website:* www.britain.org.ar (office).

HUGHES, Miriam (Mimi) K., BA; American diplomatist; *Ambassador to the Federated States of Micronesia;* b. New York, NY; one d. *Education:* Barnard Coll., Columbia Univ. *Career:* worked for United Press International; career mem. Sr Foreign Service with rank of Minister Counselor, served as Consul Gen., Mexico City, as Prin. Officer, Consulate Gen., Thessaloniki, other diplomatic postings have included Santo Domingo, Quito, Bangkok and London, Dir Office of Policy, Public and Congressional Affairs, Bureau of Int. Org. Affairs –2005, Deputy US Rep. to Econ. and Social Council of US Mission to UN 2005–07, Amb. to the Federated States of Micronesia 2007–. *Address:* US Embassy, PO Box 1286, Kolonia, Pohnpei, Federated States of Micronesia 96941 (office). *Telephone:* 320-2187 (office). *Fax:* 320-2186 (office). *E-mail:* usembassy@mail.fm (office). *Website:* kolonia.usembassy.gov (office).

HUJYLAN, Saleh bin Abdul-Aziz al-; Saudi Arabian diplomatist. *Career:* Amb. to People's Repub. of China 2006–. *Address:* Embassy of Saudi Arabia, 1 Beixiao Jie, San Li Tun, Bejing 100600, People's Republic of China (office). *Telephone:* (10) 65324825 (office). *Fax:* (10) 65325324 (office). *Website:* www.mofa.gov.sa (office).

HULL, Thomas Neil, BA, MA; American diplomatist; b. 1945, Niskayuna, NY; m. Jill Hull; one d. *Education:* Hebron Acad., Me, Dickinson Coll., Pa, Columbia Univ., New York. *Career:* worked as Peace Corps volunteer in Sierra Leone 1969; joined State Dept in 1976, career mem. Sr Foreign Service, overseas assignments in Pretoria (twice), Lagos, Mogadishu, Ouagadougou and Kinshasa, later Dir African Affairs, US Information Agency, Washington, DC prior to its merger with State Dept, has served at Embassy in Prague, Deputy Chief of Mission, Embassy in Addis Ababa –2004, Amb. to Sierra Leone 2004–07; Int. Fellow, Columbia Univ.; Presidential Meritorious Service Award, Paul Harris Award, Rotary International 2004. *Address:* US Department of State, 2201 C Street NW, Washington, DC 20520, USA (office). *Telephone:* (202) 647-4000 (office). *Fax:* (202) 647-6738 (office). *Website:* www.state.gov (office).

HULTQVIST, Bengt Karl Gustaf, DrSci; Swedish space physicist; *Secretary-General, International Association of Geomagnetism and Aeronomy;* b. 21 Aug. 1927, Hemmesjö; m. Gurli Gustafsson 1953; two s. one d. *Education:* Univ. of Stockholm. *Career:* Dir Kiruna Geophysical Observatory 1956–73, Kiruna Geophysical Inst. 1973–87, Swedish Inst. of Space Physics 1987–94, Int. Space Science Inst. (ISSI), Berne, Switzerland 1995–99; Sec.-Gen. Int. Asscn of Geomagnetism and Aeronomy 2001–; Chair. Swedish Space Science Cttee 1972–97, Swedish Nat. Cttee for Geodesy and Geophysics 1980–94, EISCAT Council 1987–88, Nordic Soc. for Space Research 1989–92, Space Science Advisory Cttee, European Space Agency 1998–2000, and others; Kt of the Northern Star Award 1965; Royal Swedish Acad. of Science Prize 1968, 1972, Gold Medal, Royal Swedish Acad. of Eng Sciences 1988, King's Medal 1991, Berzelius Medal, Royal Swedish Acad. of Science 1994, Julius Bartels Medal, European Geophysical Soc. 1996, Haunes Alfvén Medal, European Geophysical Soc. 2002, and other awards. *Publications include:* Introduction to Geocosmophysics 1967, High Latitude Space Plasma Physics (ed.) 1983, Space, Science and I 1997, Magnetospheric Plasma Sources and Losses (ed.) 1999; more than 200 scientific papers on radiation and space physics. *Address:* Swedish Institute of Space Physics, Box 812, 981 28 Kiruna (office); Grönstensv. 2, 981 40 Kiruna, Sweden (home). *Telephone:* (980) 790-60 (office); (980) 843-40 (home). *Fax:* (980) 790-50 (office); (980) 843-40 (home). *E-mail:* hultqv@irf.se (office); hultqv@irf.se (home).

HUMBERT ARIAS, Federico A., BSc, BBA; Panamanian diplomatist; *Ambassador to USA;* m. Daphne R. de Humbert; three s. one d. *Education:* Colegio de La Salle, Panama City, Univ. of Notre Dame, USA. *Career:* Pres. and CEO Cía. de Mariscos Islas de las Perlas (Pearl Island Seafood Corpn) 1982–2004, Cía. de Materiales Islas de las Perlas 1982–2004, Panama Trucking Corpn 1990–2004; Pres. Corporación Industrial Pesquera 1984–2004, Corporación La Prensa 1996–2004; fmr mem. Bd of Dirs Grupo Banco Gen., Astillero Nacional, Servicios Vacamonte; Amb. to USA 2004–. *Address:* Embassy of Panama, 2862 McGill Terrace, NW, Washington, DC 20008, USA (office). *Telephone:* (202) 483-1407 (office). *Fax:* (202) 483-8413 (office). *E-mail:* info@embassyofpanama.org (office). *Website:* www.embassyofpanama.org (office).

HUME, Cameron R.; American diplomatist; *Ambassador to Indonesia;* m.; four d. *Education:* Princeton Univ., American Univ. School of Law. *Career:* joined Foreign Service 1970, early assignments included Vice-Consul in Palermo, Adviser on Human Rights, US Mission to UN, mem. planning staff, Sec. of State, Desk Officer for South Africa; Political Counsellor in Damascas and Beirut; Dir Foreign Service Inst. field school, Tunis –1986; Advisor on Middle East, Mission to UN 1986–90, Sr Advisor 1990–91; Deputy Chief of Mission, Holy See and US Rep. to Mozambique Peace Talks 1991–94; Minister Counsellor for Political Affairs, Mission to UN 1994–97; Amb. to Algeria 1997–2000; Special Advisor to Perm. Rep. to UN 2000–01; Amb. to South Africa 2001–05, to Sudan 2005–07, to Indonesia 2007–; Fellow, Council on Foreign Relations 1975–76, Harvard Univ. Center for Int. Affairs 1989–90; Guest Scholar, US Inst. of Peace 1994. *Publications include:* The United Nations, Iran and Iraq: How Peacemaking Changed 1994, Ending Mozambique's War 1994, Mission to Algiers: Diplomacy by Engagement 2001; numerous articles on diplomacy. *Address:* Embassy of USA, Jalan Merdeka Selatan 4–5, Jakarta, Indonesia (office). *Telephone:* (21) 34359000 (office). *Fax:* (21) 34359922 (office). *E-mail:* jakconsul@state.gov (office). *Website:* jakarta.usembassy.gov (office).

HUMFREY, Charles Thomas William, CMG; British diplomatist; *Ambassador to Indonesia;* b. 1 Dec. 1947; m. Enid Wyn Thomas; two s. one d. *Education:* Univs of Oxford and Sheffield. *Career:* joined British Diplomatic Service 1969; Third Sec., FCO 1969–70; with Embassy in Tokyo 1971–76, Counsellor 1990–94, Minister and Deputy Head of Mission 1995–2000; Head of Section, SE Asian Dept 1976–79; Pvt. Sec. to Minister of State 1979–81; Perm. Mission to UN, New York 1981–85; Asst Head of Southern African Dept 1985–88, Head 1994–95; Counsellor and Deputy Head of Mission, Embassy in Ankara 1988–90; apptd Amb. to Repub. of Korea 2000; currently Amb. to Indonesia. *Address:* British Embassy, Jalan M H Thamrin 75, Jakarta 10310, Indonesia (office). *Telephone:* (21) 315-6264 (office). *Fax:* (21) 390-7493 (office). *Website:* www.britain-in-indonesia.or.id (office).

HUN SEN, BA, PhD; Cambodian politician; *Prime Minister;* b. 5 Aug. 1952, Stoeung Trang District, Kompang-Cham Prov.; m. Bun Rany 1975; three s. three d. *Education:* Lycée Indra Devi, Phnom Penh, Univ. of Phnom Penh, Nat. Political Acad., Hanoi. *Career:* joined Khmer Rouges 1970, rising to Commdt; in Viet Nam with pro-Vietnamese Kampucheans 1977, returned to Kampuchea (now Cambodia) after Vietnamese-backed take-over; Founding mem. United Front for the Nat. Salvation of Kampuchea

1978; Minister for Foreign Affairs 1979–85; Deputy Prime Minister 1981–85; Chair. Council of Ministers of Cambodia (Prime Minister) 1985–91, Second Prime Minister Royal Govt of Cambodia 1993–98, Prime Minister of Cambodia 1998–; Vice-Pres. Cambodian People's Party (CPP); mem. Russian Acad. of Sciences 2002–, Bar Asscn of Cambodia 2004–; Hon. mem. ASEAN Eng Fed. 2002; Hon. PhD (Southern Calif. Univ.) 1995, (Iowa Wesleyan Coll.) 1996; Dr hc (Dankook Univ., S Korea) 2001, (Ramkhamhaeng, Thailand) 2001, (Irish Int. Univ.) 2004, (Univ. of Cambodia) 2004, (Soon Chun Hyang Univ., S Korea) 2006, (Rajabhat Univ., Thailand) 2006, (Hanoi Nat. Univ. of Educ.) 2007; awarded title Samdech by the King of Cambodia, World Peace Award, Int. Peace Center 'Lifting Up the World with a Oneness-Heart' Award 2001, Irish Int. Univ. Medal of Excellence 2004, U Thant Peace Award 2005.
Address: Council of Ministers, Russian Federation Blvd, Phnom Penh, Cambodia (office). *Telephone:* (12) 804442 (office). *Fax:* (23) 880624 (office). *E-mail:* ocm@cambodia.gov.kh (office). *Website:* www.ocm.gov .kh (office).

HUNAIDI, Rima Khalaf, MA, PhD; Jordanian politician and international organization official; *Assistant Secretary-General and Director of Regional Bureau for the Arab States, United Nations Development Programme (UNDP); Education:* American Univ. of Beirut, Lebanon and Portland State Univ., Ohio, USA. *Career:* fmr Minister of Industry and Trade, of Planning; fmr Deputy Prime Minister; Senator Jordanian Upper House; mem. Jordanian Econ. Consultative Council; Asst Sec.-Gen. and Dir UNDP Regional Bureau for the Arab States (RBAS) June 2000–; speaker at numerous int. confs.
Address: UNDP, Regional Bureau for Arab States, One United Nations Plaza, DC1–22nd Floor, New York, NY 10017, USA (office). *Telephone:* (212) 906-5324 (office). *Fax:* (212) 906-5364 (office). *E-mail:* hq@undp.org (office). *Website:* www.undp.org (office).

HUNG, Nguyen Sinh, PhD; Vietnamese economist and government official; b. 18 Jan. 1946, Nam Dan, Nghe An. *Career:* previous posts include accountant in Finance Ministry, econ. researcher in Bulgaria, Deputy Dir, then Dir Treasury, Vice Minister of Finance; Minister of Finance –2006; mem. Central Standing Cttee Communist Party.
Address: c/o Ministry of Finance, 8 Phan Huy Chu, Hoan Kiem District, Hanoi, Viet Nam (office).

HUNT, Rt Hon. Jonathan Lucas, ONZ, PC, MA; New Zealand politician and diplomatist; b. 2 Dec. 1938, Lower Hutt. *Education:* Auckland Grammar School, Auckland Univ. *Career:* teacher, Kelston Boys' High School 1961–66; tutor, Univ. of Auckland 1964–66; MP for New Lynn 1966–2005; Jr Govt Whip 1972, Chair. of Cttees and Deputy Speaker of House of Reps 1974–75, Acting Speaker 1975; Labour Opposition Spokesman on Health 1976–79, Constitution and Parl. Affairs 1978–81; Sr Opposition Whip 1980–84; Shadow Minister of Broadcasting 1982; Minister of Broadcasting and Postmaster-Gen. 1984–87, Minister of State 1987–89, Leader of the House 1987–90, Minister of Broadcasting 1988–90, for Tourism 1988–89, of Housing 1989, of Communications Jan.–Oct. 1990; Sr Opposition Whip 1990–96, Shadow Leader of the House 1996–99; Speaker, House of Reps 1999–2005; High Commr to UK and Nigeria and Amb. to Ireland 2005–08.
Address: Ministry of Foreign Affairs and Trade, Private Bag 18901, Wellington, New Zealand (office). *Telephone:* (4) 439-8000 (office). *Fax:* (4) 472-9596 (office). *E-mail:* enquiries@mfat.govt.nz (office). *Website:* www .mfat.govt.nz (office).

HUNTINGTON, Samuel Phillips, MA, PhD; American academic and writer; *Albert J. Weatherhead III University Professor, Harvard University;* b. 18 April 1927, New York, NY; m. Nancy Alice Arkelyan 1957; two s. *Education:* Harvard and Yale Univs and Univ. of Chicago. *Career:* Instructor in Govt, Harvard Univ. 1950–53, Asst Prof. 1953–58; Asst Dir Inst. of War and Peace Studies, Columbia Univ. 1958–59, Assoc. Dir 1959–62, Assoc. Prof. of Govt 1959–62; Prof. of Govt, Harvard Univ. 1962–67, Frank G. Thomson Prof. of Govt 1967–81, Clarence Dillon Prof. of Int. Affairs 1981–82, Eaton Prof. of Science of Govt 1982–95, Albert J. Weatherhead III Univ. Prof. 1995–, Chair. Harvard Acad. for Int. and Area Studies 1996–2004; Co-Ed. Foreign Policy Quarterly 1970–77; Dir John M. Olin Inst. for Strategic Studies 1989–99; Co-ordinator of Security Planning for Nat. Security Council, White House, Washington, DC 1977–78; Fellow, Center for Advanced Study of Behavioral Sciences, Stanford Univ. 1969–70; Visiting Fellow, All Souls Coll. Oxford, UK 1973; Fellow, Woodrow Wilson Int. Center for Scholars, Washington, DC 1983–84; Fellow, American Acad. of Arts and Sciences; Sr Research Assoc. IISS, London 1990; mem. American Political Science Asscn (Pres. 1986–87), Council on Foreign Relations, Int. Political Science Asscn; many other academic and professional appointments; Silver Pen Award 1960, Guggenheim Fellow 1972–73, Grawemayer World Order Award 1992. *Publications:* The Soldier and the State: The Theory and Politics of

Civil-Military Relations 1957, The Common Defense: Strategic Programs in National Politics 1961, Changing Patterns of Military Politics (co-ed.) 1962, Political Power: USA/USSR (co-author) 1964, Political Order in Changing Societies 1968, Authoritarian Politics in Modern Society: The Dynamics of Established One-Party Systems (co-ed.) 1970, The Crisis of Democracy (co-author) 1975, No Easy Choice: Political Participation in Developing Countries (with J. M. Nelson) 1976, American Politics: The Promise of Disharmony 1981, The Strategic Imperative: New Policies for American Security 1982, Living with Nuclear Weapons (co-author) 1983, Global Dilemmas (co-ed.) 1985, Reorganizing America's Defense (co-ed.) 1985, Understanding Political Development (co-ed.) 1987, The Third Wave: Democratization in the Late Twentieth Century 1991, The Clash of Civilizations and the Remaking of the World Order 1996, Culture Matters: How Values Shape Human Progress 2000, Who Are We?: The Challenges to America's National Identity 2004; contrib. scholarly articles to books, monographs.
Address: WCFIA, Harvard University, Room 112, 1727 Cambridge Street, Cambridge, MA 02138, USA (office). *Telephone:* (617) 495-4432 (office). *Fax:* (617) 384-9259 (office). *E-mail:* bbaiter@wcfia.harvard.edu (office). *Website:* www.wcfia.harvard.edu (office).

HUOT, Phal; Cambodian diplomatist. *Career:* mem. Cambodian People's Party; fmr Amb. to Laos; currently Dir Middle East and Africa Dept, Ministry of Foreign Affairs and Int. Co-operation.
Address: Middle East and Africa Department, Ministry of Foreign Affairs and International Co-operation, 3 rue Samdech Hun Sen, Khan Chamkarmon, Phnom-Penh, Cambodia (office). *Telephone:* (23) 214441 (office). *Fax:* (23) 216144 (office). *E-mail:* mfaicinfo@mfaic.gov.kh (office). *Website:* www.mfaic.gov.kh (office).

HURAIMIL, Issa Khalfan al-; United Arab Emirates diplomatist. *Career:* currently Amb. to Saudi Arabia.
Address: Embassy of the United Arab Emirates, POB 94385, Riyadh 11693, Saudi Arabia (office). *Telephone:* (1) 482-9652 (office). *Fax:* (1) 482-7504 (office).

HURTADO LARREA, Osvaldo, BrerPol, DIur; Ecuadorean fmr head of state; *President, Corporation for Development Studies (CORDES);* b. 26 June 1939, Chambo, Chimborazo Prov.; m. Margarita Pérez Pallares; three s. two d. *Education:* Catholic Univ. of Quito. *Career:* f. Ecuadorian Christian Democratic Party 1964; Pres. of Congress 1966; Prof. of Political Sociology, Catholic Univ., Quito; Dir Instituto Ecuatoriano de Desarrollo Social (INEDES) 1966; Under-Sec. of Labour 1969; Sub-Dean, Faculty of Econs and Dir Inst. of Econ. Research, Catholic Univ., Quito 1973; invited to form part of World Political Council of Christian Democracy 1975; joined with other political groups to form Popular Democracy 1978; Pres. Org. of Christian Democrats of America, Vice-Pres. Int. Christian Democrats; Pres. Comm. to prepare Law of Referendum of Elections and Political Parties 1977; Vice-Pres. of Ecuador and Pres. Consejo Nacional de Desarrollo (Nat. Devt Council) 1979–81; Pres. of Ecuador 1981–84; Pres. Nat. Ass. 1998; Pres. CORDES (org. for study of Latin American Devt problems), Quito; fmr Vice-Pres. Inst. for European Latin-American Relations, Madrid; mem. Council of ex-Pres, Atlanta, Inter-american Dialogue, Washington, DC (Co-Pres Bd of Dirs), The Carter Center, Atlanta, Club de Madrid, Foro de Biarritz, Emerging Markets Forum, Washington, DC, Foro Iberoamericano; mem. comm. that prepared the environmental reports Nuestra Propia Agenda 1990, Amazonía Sin Mitos 1992 and Amanecer en los Andes 1997 at request of IDB and UNDP; Dr hc (Georgetown); various foreign decorations. *Publications:* numerous essays and several books about Ecuadorian politics, sociology and economy, including El Poder Político en el Ecuador (Political Power in Ecudor) 1977, Las Costumbres de los Ecuatorianos 2005, Los Costos del Populismo 2006; academic work about Latin America gathered in several books published in collaboration with other authors in many countries.
Address: Suecia 277 y Av. Los Shyris Edificio cia Piso 2, PO Box 5087, Quito, Ecuador (office); Tomás Chariove 405 y Agustín Zambrano (home). *Telephone:* (5932) 2455701 (office). *Fax:* (5932) 2446414 (office). *E-mail:* cordes2@cordes.org.ec (office). *Website:* www.cordes.org.ec (office).

HUSBANDS, Sir Clifford (Straughn), Kt, GCMG, CHB, GCM, QC; Barbadian barrister and fmr judge; *Governor-General;* b. 5 Aug. 1926; m. Ruby Parris 1959; one s. two d. *Education:* Parry School, Harrison Coll., Middle Temple, Inns of Court, London, UK. *Career:* called to Bar, Middle Temple 1952; in pvt. practice, Barbados 1952–54; Acting Deputy Registrar, Barbados 1954; Legal Asst to Attorney-Gen., Grenada 1954–56; magistrate, Grenada 1956–57, Antigua 1957–58; Crown Attorney, Magistrate and Registrar, Montserrat 1958–60; Acting Crown Attorney, St Kitts-Nevis-Anguilla 1959, Acting Attorney-Gen. 1960; Asst to Attorney-Gen., Barbados 1960–67 (legal draftsman 1960–63); Dir Public Prosecutions,

Barbados 1967–76; QC Barbados 1968; Judge, Supreme Court, Barbados 1976–91; Justice of Appeal 1991–96; Gov.-Gen. of Barbados 1996–; Pres. Privy Council for Barbados 1996–; Kt of St Andrew, Order of Barbados 1995; Kt of Grace, Order of St John 2204; Queen's Silver Jubilee Medal 1977, Paul Harris Fellowship Award 2001.
Address: c/o Private Secretary to the Governor-General, Government House, St Michael, Barbados (office). *Telephone:* 4292646 (office). *Fax:* 4365910 (office). *E-mail:* ruthnita@sunbeach.net (office). *Website:* www .barbados.gov.bb/gg.htm (office).

HUSO, Ravic Rolf, BA, MA; American diplomatist; *Ambassador to Laos; Education:* Coll. of Idaho, Univ. of Virginia, US Army War Coll., Carlisle, Pa. *Career:* served as Peace Corps volunteer in southern Senegal 1976–78; subsequently worked for USAID Mission in Senegal; joined Foreign Service 1980; Gen. Services Officer, Burkina Faso 1981–82; Political and Econ. Reporting Officer, Burundi 1982–85; Office of Philippine Affairs, Dept of State 1985–87, Office of Australia and NZ Affairs 1987–88, language training 1988–89; Deputy Political Counselor, Kuala Lumpur 1989–93; Deputy Chief of Mission, Niamey, Niger 1993–96; Deputy Dir, later Dir for Burma, Cambodia, Laos, Thailand, and Vietnam Affairs 1996–99, Dir for Asian Affairs, Nat. Security Council 1999–2000; Deputy Chief of Mission, Bangkok 2001–04; Foreign Policy Advisor to Commdr US Pacific Command, Honolulu, Hawaii 2004–07; Amb. to Laos 2007–; Order of the White Elephant conferred by King of Thailand for contribs to US-Thailand defence relations; Dept of State's Superior Honor Award, Jt Distinguished Civilian Service Medal from Chair. Jt Chiefs of Staff for contribs to regional security as Foreign Policy Advisor to US Pacific Command 2007.
Address: US Embassy, BP 114, 19 rue Bartholonie, That Dam, Vientiane, Laos (office). *Telephone:* (21) 267000 (office). *Fax:* (21) 267190 (office). *E-mail:* webmastervientiane@state.gov (office). *Website:* laos.usembassy .gov (office).

HUSSAIN, Chaudhry Shujaat; Pakistani politician; *President, Pakistan Muslim League;* b. 27 Jan. 1946; m.; two s. one d. *Education:* Forman Christian Coll., Lahore and Univ. of London, UK. *Career:* mem. Majlis-e-Shoora 1982–85; mem. Nat. Ass. 1985–, Leader of Opposition 1988–90; Fed. Minister for Infomationa and Broadcasting 1986, for Industries and Production 1987–88, of the Interior 1990–93, 1997–99, of Narcotics Control 1997–99; Pres. Pakistan Muslim League 2004–; Prime Minister of Pakistan June–Aug. 2004; Hon. Consul-Gen. to Repub. of Korea 1982–; Order of Diplomatic Service Merit Ueung-in-Metal.
Address: Pakistan Muslim League, PML House, F-7/3, Islamabad, Pakistan (office). *Telephone:* (11) 1001947 (office). *E-mail:* shujaat_hussain@pakistanmuslimleague.info (office). *Website:* www .pakistanmuslimleague.info (office).

HUSSAIN, Ishrat, MA, PhD; Pakistani economist and central banker (retd); *Chairman, National Commission for Government Reforms;* b. 17 June 1941, Allahabad, India; m. Shahnaz Husain; two d. *Education:* Williams Coll., Boston Univ. and Grad. Exec. Devt Programme (Harvard, Stanford and INSEAD). *Career:* mem. Staff Sr Managerial, Planning and Devt Dept and Finance Dept, Govt of Sindh; Additional Deputy Commr for Devt, Chittagong, Bangladesh; mem. Govt of Pakistan's Panel of Economists; Adjunct Prof. of Econs, Karachi Univ., Dir Poverty and Social Policy Dept; IBRD Resident Rep. for Nigeria 1986, Chief Economist for Africa, IBRD 1991–94, Chief Economist for E Asia and Pacific Region 1995, also Chief Debt and Int. Finance Div., Dir for Cen. Asian Repubs; Gov. State Bank of Pakistan 1999–2005; Chair. Nat. Comm. for Govt Reforms with rank of Fed. Minister 2005–; Hilal-e-Imtiaz; Central Bank Gov. of the Year in Asia Award, The Banker magazine (first Pakistani Gov. to receive award) 2005. *Publications:* Dollars, Debts, and Deficits, Pakistan: The Economy of an Elitist State, The Political Economy of Reforms: Case Study of Pakistan, Adjustment in Africa: Lessons from Case Studies: Dealing with Debt Crisis, African External Finance in the 1990s, The Economy of Modern Sindh; numerous articles and papers on debt, external finance and adjustment issues.
Address: National Commission for Government Reforms, Prime Minister's Secretariat, Block B, Second Floor, Benevolent Fund Building, Zero Point, Islamabad, Pakistan (office). *Telephone:* (51) 9203932 (office). *E-mail:* webmaster@ncgr.gov.pk (office). *Website:* www.ncgr.gov.pk (office).

HUSSAIN, Datin Paduka Rajmah, BSc, MSc, PhD; Malaysian diplomatist; *Ambassador to USA;* b. 21 June 1951, Kuala Lumpur. *Education:* London School of Econs, Univ. of London, UK, Alliance Française, Paris, France. *Career:* career diplomat, apptd to Admin. and Diplomatic Service of Malaysian Civil Service and served as Asst Sec. (ASEAN Div.), Ministry of Foreign Affairs 1976–80; Second Sec., Embassy in Brussels 1980–82; trained as UN Disarmament Fellow 1982, Prin. Asst Sec. (Int. Orgs), Ministry of Foreign Affairs 1982–85; postgraduate studies LSE 1985–88;

Prin. Asst Sec. (Security Council), Ministry of Foreign Affairs 1988–91, Special Officer to Sec.-Gen. 1991–94; Minister Counsellor/Deputy Chief of Mission, Embassy in Washington, DC 1994–98; Amb. to France (also accred to Portugal) 1998–2001, Amb. and Perm. Rep. to UN and other Int. Orgs, Geneva 2001–05; Amb. to Austria (also accred to Slovakia) 2005–06, Resident Rep. of Malaysia to IAEA 2005–06, Perm. Rep. to UN, Vienna, UNIDO and Preparatory Comm. to Comprehensive Nuclear-Test-Ban Treaty (CTBTO) 2005–06; Amb. to USA 2006–; trained as UN Disarmament Fellow, served as Amb. to Conf. on Disarmament, elected Pres. Conf. on Disarmament, Geneva; fmr Chair. OIC Group, NAM Chapter and Asian Group at UN, Geneva, and NAM Chapter, Vienna; title of Datin Paduka Ahli Mangku Negara (AMN) 1992, Darjah Sultan Salahuddin Abdul Aziz Shah (DSSA) 1999.
Address: Embassy of Malaysia, 3516 International Court, NW, Washington, DC 20008, USA (office). *Telephone:* (202) 572-9700 (office). *Fax:* (202) 572-9882 (office). *E-mail:* malwashdc@kln.gov.my (office).

HUSSEIN, Maj.-Gen. Abd ar-Rahim Muhammad; Sudanese politician; *Minister of National Defence; Career:* career in Armed Forces; attained rank of Maj.-Gen.; Minister of Interior 1998; Minister of Presidential Affairs –2001; Minister of Internal Affairs 2001–04; Minister of Nat. Defence 2005–.
Address: Ministry of National Defence, POB 371, Khartoum, Sudan (office). *Telephone:* (183) 774910.

HUSSEIN, Muhammad al-, PhD; Syrian politician; *Minister of Finance; Career:* fmr Chair. Econ. Bureau, Govt Exec.; Minister of Finance 2003–.
Address: Ministry of Finance, BP 13136, rue Jule Jammal, Damascus, Syria (office). *Telephone:* (11) 2239624 (office). *Fax:* (11) 2224701 (office). *E-mail:* mof@net.sy (office). *Website:* www.syriafinance.org (office).

HUSSEIN, Col Nur Hassan, (Nur Adde); Somali lawyer, police officer and politician; *Prime Minister;* b. 1938, Mogadishu; from Abgal sub-clan of Hawiye clan. *Education:* Mogadishu Nat. Univ., Fiscal Law School, Rome. *Career:* started his career as customs officer in 1958, rose through ranks to become Interpol Liaison Officer in Somalia and finally Chief Police Officer in charge of planning and training under fmr regime of Mohamed Siad Barre until the latter's ousting in 1991, served as Attorney Gen. –1991; Sec.-Gen. Somali Red Crescent Soc. 1991–2007; Prime Minister 2007–.
Address: Office of the Prime Minister, Mogadishu, Somalia (office).

HUSSEIN, HRH Prince; Zeid Ra'ad Zeid al-, BA, PhD; Jordanian diplomatist; *Ambassador to USA;* b. 26 Jan. 1964, Amman; m. Sarah Butler 2000; one s. one d. *Education:* Reed's School, Surrey, UK, Johns Hopkins Univ., USA, Christ's Coll. Cambridge, UK. *Career:* commissioned as officer in Jordanian desert police, served with them until 1994; Political Affairs Officer, UN Protection Force (UNPROFOR), Bosnia and Herzegovina 1994–96; Deputy Perm. Rep. to UN, New York 1996–2000, Perm. Rep. 2000–07, Rep. at Treaty-Signing Conf. Banning Landmines, Ottawa, Canada 1997, mem. Rome Conf. (est. Int. Criminal Court) 1998, Deputy Del. Head and Vice-Pres. Maputo Conf. 1999; Chair. Consultative Cttee for UNIFEM 2004–07, chair. or mem. numerous UN cttees on peacekeeping, war crimes and crimes against humanity; Amb. to USA (also accred to Mexico) 2007–. *Publications:* articles in Cambridge Review of International Affairs, Spring 1989, Israel Affairs, Winter 1994.
Address: Embassy of Jordan, 3504 International Drive, NW, Washington, DC 20008, USA (office). *Telephone:* (202) 966-2664 (office). *Fax:* (202) 966-3110 (office). *E-mail:* hkjembassydc@jordanembassyus.org (office). *Website:* www.jordanembassyus.org (office).

HUTCHINGS, Robert L., MA, PhD; American academic and diplomatist; *Diplomat-in-Residence, Princeton University; Education:* US Naval Acad., Coll. of William and Mary, Univ. of Virginia. *Career:* fmr Deputy Dir Radio Free Europe; fmr faculty mem., Univ. of Virginia; fmr Dir Analytic Group and Deputy Nat. Intelligence Officer for Europe, Nat. Intelligence Council; Dir for European Affairs, Nat. Security Council 1989–92; Special Adviser to Sec. of State 1992–93; Fellow and Dir of Int. Studies, Woodrow Wilson Int. Center for Scholars, Washington, DC 1993–97; Prof. of Int. Politics and Asst Dean Woodrow Wilson School of Public and Int. Affairs, Princeton Univ. 1997–2002; Chair. Nat. Intelligence Council (analysis centre reporting to Dir of Cen. Intelligence) 2002–; also currently Diplomat-in-Residence, Princeton Univ.; adjunct posts at Johns Hopkins School School of Advanced Int. Studies and Georgetown Univ. School of Foreign Service; Dir Atlantic Council of USA, Foundation for a Civil Soc.; mem. British-North American Cttee, Council on Foreign Relations; Order of Merit (Poland) 1998.
Address: Woodrow Wilson School of Public and International Affairs, Princeton University, Princeton, NJ 08544-1013, USA (office). *Telephone:* (609) 258-5306 (office). *Fax:* (609) 258-0482 (office). *E-mail:* hutchings@ princeton.edu (office). *Website:* www.wws.princeton.edu (office).

HUXLEY, Tim, BA, MA, MSc (Econ), PhD; British research analyst and academic; *Executive Director, International Institute for Strategic Studies (IISS)-Asia;* b. 22 May 1956, Cirencester, England; one s. one d. *Education:* Oriel Coll., Oxford, Univ. of Wales Aberystwyth, Australian Nat. Univ. *Career:* research and teaching posts at univs in UK and Australia; fmr Fellow, Inst. of SE Asian Studies, Singapore; Reader in SE Asian Politics and Dir Centre for SE Asian Studies, Univ. of Hull –2003; Sr Fellow for Asia-Pacific Security, IISS and Ed. Adelphi Papers 2003–07, Exec. Dir IISS Asia, Singapore 2007–. *Publications:* Defending the Lion City – The Armed Forces of Singapore 2000; monographs, research reports and articles in scholarly and professional journals.
Address: International Institute for Strategic Studies (Asia) Ltd, 9 Raffles Place, #53-02 Republic Plaza, Singapore 048619, Singapore (office). *Telephone:* 64990055 (office). *Fax:* 64990059 (office). *E-mail:* Huxley@iiss .org (office). *Website:* www.iiss.org (office).

HVIDT, Gen. Christian, DFC; Danish air force officer; b. 15 July 1942, Copenhagen; m. 1st; three c.; m. 2nd Jane Hvidt; two step-c. *Career:* flying service (F-100 Super Sabre) 1962–69; test pilot on F-35 Draken at SAAB factories, Linköping, Sweden 1969–72; Deputy Squadron Commdr (F-35 Draken) 1972–74; Br. Chief Tactical Air Command, Denmark 1975–79; Squadron Commdr First Danish F-16 Squadron, Air Station Skrydstrup 1979–83; staff officer and Br. Chief Plans and Policy Div., HQ Chodden 1983–87; Commdg Officer Air Station Karup 1987–88; Chief of Staff Tactical Air Command, Denmark 1989–90; Deputy Chief of Staff Plans and Policy, Operations, Budget and Finance HQ Chodden 1991–93; Perm. Danish Rep., NATO Mil. Cttee 1994–96; Chief of Staff, HQ Chodden 1996; Chief of Defence 1996–2002; Grand Cross of the Order of Dannebrog, Danish Air Force Badge of Honour, Badge of Honour of the Danish Reserve Officers Asscn., Medal of Merit of the Home Guard, Commdr, Grand Cross, Royal Swedish Order of the Northern Star, Jordanian Military Order of Merit of the First Degree, Commdr, Cross with the Star of Merit of the Repub. of Poland, Commdr, Légion d'honneur, de l'Ordre Nat. du Mérite.
Address: c/o Defence Command, PO Box 202, 2950 Vedbaek, Denmark (office).

HYLTON, G. Anthony, BA, JD, LLM; Jamaican lawyer and politician; b. 27 April 1957, Yallahs, St Thomas. *Education:* Kingston Coll., Morgan State Univ. and Georgetown Univ., USA, Univ. of London, UK. *Career:* lawyer with Melnicove, Kaufman, Weiner and Smouse, Baltimore, 1983–85, with Curtis, Mallet-Prevost, Colt and Mosle, New York 1986–88, with Dickstein, Shapiro and Morin, Washington DC 1988–89; fmr legal asst to Gen. Counsel Inter-American Foundation; fmr Dir Jamaica Public Service Co.; mem. Parl. for Western St Thomas 1993–2002; Exec. Dir of Legal and Foreign Affairs, Policy Review Unit, Ministry of Foreign Affairs and Trade 1990–93, Minister of State 1993–2001; Minister of Mining and Energy 2001–02; Amb. and Special Prime Ministerial Envoy 2002–06; Minister of Foreign Affairs and Foreign Trade 2006–07, also mem. of Senate; negotiator at WTO, Contonou Agreement, Free Trade Area of the Americas and CARICOM; Chair. Inst. of Law and Econs, People's Nat. Party Policy Comm.; Chair. Commercial Div., Coffee Industry Bd; mem. Md and Jamaica Bar Asscns; Nat. Honours from Govt of Benin.
Address: People's National Party, 89 Old Hope Road, Kingston 5, Jamaica (office). *Telephone:* 978-1337 (office). *Fax:* 927-4389 (office). *E-mail:* information@pnpjamaica.com (office). *Website:* www.pnpjamaica.com (office).

HYSENI, Skënder; Kosovo politician; *Minister of Foreign Affairs;* b. 17 Feb. 1955, Dobratin; m. Drita Hyseni; two s. two d. *Education:* Dept of English Language and Literature, Univ. of Priština, Bloomberg State Coll., USA, Aberdeen Univ., UK. *Career:* early political career with newly est. Democratic League of Kosava 1989, began working with Kosovo Information Center 1992 as journalist and interpreter; Co-founder and Ed. Kosava Daily Report; Adviser to Pres. Ibrahim Rugova 1992–2006, to Pres. Fatmir Sejdiu 2006–; Spokesperson Kosovo negotiating team that took part in UN-sponsored talks with Serbia, launched in 2006; mem. Kuvendi i Kosovës/Skupština Kosova (Kosovo Ass.) (Parl.), Minister of Culture, Youth and Sports Jan.–April 2008, of Foreign Affairs April 2008–; mem. Kosovo Democratic League, mem. of Presidency and Chair. Ctte for External Relations; mem. Constitutional Comm. charged with compiling first draft of Constitution of Kosovo.
Address: Office of the Government of Kosovo, 10000 Priština; Kuvendi i Kosovës/Skupština Kosova (Kosovo Assembly), 10000 Priština, Rruga Nënë Terezë, Kosovo. *Telephone:* (38) 211186 (Ass.). *Fax:* (38) 211188 (Ass.). *Website:* www.ks-gov.net; www.assembly-kosova.org.

I

IACOVOU, Georgios Kyriakou, MA, MSc; Cypriot politician and diplomatist; b. 19 July 1938, Peristeronopigi, Famagusta Dist; m. Jennifer Bradley 1963; one s. three d. *Education:* Greek Gymnasium for Boys, Famagusta and Univ. of London. *Career:* Eng, Cyprus Building and Road Construction Corpn Ltd 1960–61; Man. Electron Ltd, Nicosia 1961–63; with Operations Research and Finance Depts, British Railways Bd, London 1964–68; Sr Consultant (Man.), Price Waterhouse Assocs, London 1968–72; Dir Cyprus Productivity Centre, Nicosia 1972–76; Dir Special Service for Care and Rehabilitation of Displaced Persons 1974–76; Chief, E African Region, UNHCR, Geneva 1976–79; Amb. to FRG (also accred to Austria and Switzerland) 1979–83; Dir-Gen. Ministry of Foreign Affairs Jan.–Sept. 1983; Minister of Foreign Affairs 1983–93, 2003–06; High Commr to UK 2006–07; Pres. and CEO Nat. Foundation of Overseas and Repatriated Greeks 1993–97; presidential cand., Cyprus presidential elections 1998; Pres. Cttee of Ministers, Council of Europe 1983; participated in Commonwealth Heads of State and Govt Confs in Delhi 1983, Bahamas 1985, Vancouver 1987, Kuala Lumpur 1989 and non-Aligned Summit, Harare 1986, Belgrade 1989; Chair. Ministerial Conf. of Non-Aligned Movt, Nicosia 1988; Hon. Citizen, Tsalka, Georgia and City of Sappes, Thrace, Greece; Hon. Prof. (Donetsk State Univ. Ukraine); Grosses Verdienstkreuz mit Stern und Schulterband (FRG), Grosses Goldenes Ehrenzeichen (Austria), Grand Cross, Order of Phoenix (Greece), Grand Cross of the Order of Isabella the Catholic (Spain), Grand Cross of the Order of Honour (Greece), Order of the Flag with Sash (Yugoslavia), Order of the Repub. First Class (Egypt), Grand Cross of Infante D. Henrique (Portugal), Decoration of the Cross of St Mark of the First Order of the Patriarchate of Alexandria and All Africa, Decoration of St Catherine's Monastery of Sinai; Dr hc (State Univ. of Tblisi, Georgia), (Panteion Univ. Athens); Meritorious Service Award, Municipality of Peristeri, Athens. *Address:* c/o Ministry of Foreign Affairs, Presidential Palace Avenue, 1447 Nicosia, Cyprus. *Telephone:* (22) 401000. *E-mail:* minforeign1@mfa.gov .cy.

IBARRETXE MARKUARTU, Juan José, BEcons; Spanish politician; *President of Basque Government;* b. 15 May 1957, Llodio, Alava. *Education:* Llodio Secondary School, Univ. of the Basque Country. *Career:* mem. Partido Nacionalista Vaso (PNV); Mayor of Llodio 1983–87; Pres. Alava Prov. Parl. 1986–91; mem. Basque Parl., Chair. Econ. and Budgetary Comm. 1986–90, 1991–94; Vice-Pres. Basque Govt and Minister for Inland Revenue and Public Admin 1995–98, Pres. 1999–; fmr mem. Univ. of the Basque Country Social Council. *Address:* Palacio de Ajuria-Enea, Paseo Fray Francisco 5, 01007 Vitoria-Gasteiz (office); Euzko Alderdi Jeltzalea-Partido Nacionalista Vasco, Sabin Etxea, Ibáñez de Bilbao 16, 48001 Bilbao, Spain. *Telephone:* (94) 4039400 (office). *Fax:* (94) 4039413 (office). *E-mail:* prentsa@eaj-pnv.com (office). *Website:* www.eaj.pnv.com (office).

IBRAHIM, Mohamed Asim; Egyptian diplomatist; *Ambassador to Israel; Career:* fmr Amb. to Sudan, Ethiopia, Kenya; Amb. to Israel 2005–. *Address:* Embassy of Egypt, 54 Rehov Bazel, Tel-Aviv 62744, Israel (office). *Telephone:* 3-5464151 (office). *Fax:* 3-5441615 (office). *E-mail:* egypem.ta@ zahav.net.il (office).

IBRAHIM, Moussa Elhadji; Niger diplomatist. *Career:* Amb. to Nigeria 2002–. *Address:* Embassy of Niger, 15 Adeola Odeku Street, Victoria Island, PMB 2736, Lagos, Nigeria (office). *Telephone:* (1) 2612300 (office).

IBRAHIM, Muhyadin Muhammad Haji; Somali politician. *Career:* mem. Parl. 2000–05; Minister of Defence 2008 (resgnd). *Address:* c/o Ministry of Defence, Mogadishu, Somalia (office).

IBRAHIM, Qasim, (Buruma Qasim); Maldivian politician and business executive; *President of People's Special Majlis;* b. 10 Feb. 1952, Malé; m.; four s. four d. *Career:* began career as clerk at Govt Hosp., Malé 1969, accountant 1972–73; Man. M/S Alia Furniture Mart 1973; subsequently worked for Crescent (trading org.) 1973; joined outlet of Maldivian Govt Bodu Store (now known as State Trading Org.) 1974; set up own trading business in 1976, registered business as Villa Shipping and Trading Co. Ltd 1986, Villa Shipping (Singapore) Pte Ltd was incorporated in Singapore 1991, opened offices in Frankfurt, Germany 1996, est. Villa Hotels, Tokyo 2001, Villa Hotels, Hong Kong 2002, currently Chair. and Man. Dir Villa Group of Cos; mem. Parl. 1989; Founding mem. Maldivian Democratic Party 2001; Minister of Finance and Treasury 2005–08; Gov. Maldives Monetary Authority –2008; Pres. People's Special Majlis; Pres. South Asian Asscn for Regional Cooperation Chamber of Commerce and Industry; Founder-mem. and Pres. Maldives Nat. Chamber of Commerce and Industry; Founder-mem., Vice-Pres. and mem. Bd Maldives Asscn of Tourism Industry; mem. Bd Maldives Ports Authority; fmr mem. Bd Bank of Maldives. *Address:* Ministry of Finance and Treasury, Block 379, Ameenee Magu, Malé, 20-379 (office); M-Maafannu Villa, Malé, Maldives (home). *Telephone:* 3317590 (office). *Fax:* 3324432 (office). *E-mail:* admin@ finance.gov.mv (office); qasim@villa.com.mv (home). *Website:* www .finance.gov.mv (office); www.villahotels.com (home).

IBRAHIMI, Bedredin, LLB; Macedonian politician and legal administrator; b. 25 Oct. 1952, Mala Recica, nr Tetovo. *Education:* Pristina Univ. *Career:* fmr doctor; Sr Officer for Legal Affairs and Sec. of Poloska Kotlina Co., Tetovo Agric. Complex, Belgrade 1976–81; Officer in charge of Gen. Legal Affairs and Sec. Jelak Tetovo Co., Interpromet Complex 1981–89; with Tekom-Tetovo Trade Co. 1990–96; Sec. of Council, Municipality of Tetovo 1997–98; fmr Gen. Sec. Democratic Party of Albanians (DPA); Deputy Prime Minister of Macedonia 1998–2002, apptd Minister of Labour and Social Welfare 1998. *Address:* c/o Democratic Party of Albanians (DPA) (Partia Demokratike Shqiptare) (PDSh), Maršal Tito 2, Tetovo, Macedonia (office).

IBRAHIMOV, Rafael; Azerbaijani diplomatist; *Ambassador to Sweden;* m. Dinara Ibrahimov. *Career:* Amb. to UK (also accred to Ireland, Norway and Sweden) 2001–07, Amb. to Sweden 2007–. *Address:* c/o Ministry of Foreign Affairs, 1009 Baku, S. Qurbanov küç. 4, Azerbaijan (office). *Telephone:* (12) 492-96-92. *Fax:* (12) 498-84-80. *E-mail:* secretariat@mfa.gov.az. *Website:* www.mfa.gov.az.

IBROW, Salim Aliyow; Somali politician. *Career:* fmr Sec. of State; Deputy Prime Minister 2004, Minister of Finance 2004–05, of Livestock 2005–07, of Higher Educ. and Culture 2007, and Deputy Prime Minister 2007, Acting Prime Minister Oct.–Nov. 2007; mem. Transitional Fed. Parl. 2004–. *Address:* Transitional Parliament, Mogadishu, Somalia (office).

IBSEN, Thórir, BA, MA; Icelandic diplomatist; *Director of Defence Department and Chief of Defence;* m.; one s. *Education:* Univ. of Iceland, York Univ. *Career:* Policy Counsellor, Ministry for the Environment 1991–93, Head of Int. Affairs Div. 1993–95; Counsellor for Environment, Industry and Commerce, Perm. Mission to EU, Brussels 1995–98; Minister-Counsellor, Dept of Natural Resources and Environmental Affairs, Ministry for Foreign Affairs 1998–2001, Acting Dir 2001–02; Deputy Head of Mission to EU, Brussels 2002–04; Deputy Perm. Rep. to NATO, Brussels 2004–06; Dir Dept of Natural Resources and Environmental Affairs, Ministry for Foreign Affairs 2007, Dir Defence Dept and Chief of Defence 2007–. *Address:* Ministry for Foreign Affairs, Rauarárstíg 25, 150 Reykjavík, Iceland (office). *Telephone:* 5459900 (office). *Fax:* 5622373 (office). *E-mail:* postur@utn.stjr.is (office). *Website:* www.utanrikisraduneyti.is (office).

IDOHOU, Bodéhoussè Simon; Benin diplomatist; b. 23 May 1950, Porto-Novo; m.; four c. *Education:* Univ. of Dakar, Senegal, Armed Forces Training Hospital, Marseilles, Univ. of Clermont-Ferrand. *Career:* Dir Armed Forces Teaching Hospital, Cotonou 1996–98; Dir of Electroradiology Service, Armed Forces Health Service 1991–99, Deputy Dir 1999–2000, Dir 2000–02; Dir BEN/99/PO2 Project, UN Population Fund 2000–02; Dir Centre d'imagerie medicale du littoral (Centre for Medical Imaging), Cotonou 2002–05; Perm. Rep. to UN, New York 2005–06. *Address:* c/o Ministry of Foreign Affairs, African Integration, Francophone Affairs and Beninois Abroad, Zone Résidentielle, route de l'Aéroport, 06 BP 318, Cotonou, Benin (office). *Website:* www.etranger .gouv.bj (office).

IDRISOV, Yerlan Abilfaizovich; Kazakhstani politician and diplomatist; b. 28 April 1959, Karkalinsk, Karaganda Oblast; m. Nurilla Anarbekovna Idrisova; two s. one d. *Education:* Moscow Inst. of Int. Relations, Diplomatic Acad., USSR Ministry of Foreign Affairs. *Career:* rep. for Tyzahpromexport, Pakistan 1981–85; mem. of staff, Ministry of Foreign Affairs, Kazakh SSR 1985–90, trainee USSR Embassy, New Delhi 1991–92, First Sec., Perm. Mission of Kazakhstan to UN, New York 1992–95, Head of American Dept and Amb.-at-Large, Ministry of Foreign Affairs 1995–96, Asst to Pres. on Int. Issues 1996–97, First Deputy Minister of Foreign Affairs 1997–99, 1999–2002, Minister Feb.–Oct. 1999, Amb. to UK (also accred to Ireland, Norway and Sweden) 2002–07, to USA 2007–. *Address:* Embassy of Kazakhstan, 1401 16th Street, NW, Washington, DC 20036, USA (office). *Telephone:* 202-232-5488 (office). *Fax:* 202-232-5845 (office). *E-mail:* kazakh.embusa@verizon.net (office). *Website:* www .kazakhembus.com (office).

IELEMIA, Apisai, BA; Tuvaluan politician; *Prime Minister and Minister of Foreign Affairs and Labor;* b. 19 Aug. 1955; m.; one d. one s. *Education:* USP Suva, Fiji. *Career:* fmr civil servant; Prime Minister and Minister of Foreign Affairs and Labor 2006–. *Address:* Ministry of Foreign Affairs and Labour, Vaiaku, Funafuti, Tuvalu (office). *Telephone:* 20100 (office). *Fax:* 20820 (office). *E-mail:* primeminister@tuvalu.tv (office).

IGLESIAS, Enrique V.; Uruguayan international official; *General Secretary, Iberoamerican General Secretariat;* b. 26 July 1931, Asturias, Spain. *Education:* Univ. de la República, Montevideo. *Career:* held several positions, including Prof. Agregado, Faculty of Political Economy, Prof. of Econ. Policy and Dir Inst. of Econs, Univ. de la República, Montevideo 1952–67; Man. Dir Unión de Bancos del Uruguay 1954; Tech. Dir Nat. Planning Office of Uruguay 1962–66; Pres. (Gov.) Banco Cent. del Uruguay 1966–68; Chair. Council, Latin American Inst. for Econ. and Social Planning, UN 1967–72, Interim Dir-Gen. 1977–78; Head, Advisory Mission on Planning, Govt of Venezuela 1970; Adviser UN Conf. on Human Environment 1971–72; Exec. Sec. Econ. Comm. for Latin America and the Caribbean 1972–85; Minister of External Affairs 1985–88; Pres. IDB 1988–2005; Gen. Sec. Iberoamerican Gen. Secr., Madrid, Spain 2005–; Pres. Soc. for Int. Devt; Acting Dir-Gen. Latin American Inst. for Econ. and Social Planning 1973–78; Pres. Third World Forum 1973–76; mem. Steering Cttee, Soc. for Int. Devt 1973–92, Pres. 1989, Selection Cttee, Third World Prize 1979–82; Sec.-Gen. UN Conf. on New and Renewable Sources of Energy Feb.–Aug. 1981; Chair. UN Inter-Agency Group on Devt of Renewable Sources of Energy, Energy Advisory Panel, Brundtland Comm. 1984–86; mem. North-South Round Table on Energy, Club of Rome; Order of Rio Branco; Grand Cross (Brazil); Grand Cross Silver Plaque, Nat. Order of Juan Mora Fernandez (Costa Rica); Commdr Légion d'honneur; Commdr des Arts et des Lettres 1999; Grand Cross of Isabel the Catholic (Spain); numerous other foreign decorations; Hon. LLD (Liverpool) 1987; Hon. PhD (Univ. de Guadalajara, Mexico) 1994, (Candido Mendes Univ., Rio de Janeiro) 1994; Prince of Asturias Award 1982, UNESCO Pablo Picasso Award 1997. *Address:* Iberoamerican General Secretariat, Paseo de Recoletos 8, 28001 Madrid, Spain (office). *Telephone:* (91) 590-19-80 (office). *E-mail:* info@ segib.org (office). *Website:* www.segib.org (office).

IGNATIEFF, Michael, BA, MA, PhD; Canadian writer, historian, academic and politician; b. 12 May 1947, Toronto, Ont.; m. 1st Susan Barrowclough 1977; one s. one d.; m. 2nd Zsuzsanna Zsohar. *Education:* Univ. of Toronto, Harvard Univ., Univ. of Cambridge. *Career:* reporter, Globe and Mail, Toronto 1966–67; teaching Fellow, Harvard Univ. 1971–74; Asst Prof., Univ. of British Columbia, Vancouver 1976–78; Sr Research Fellow, King's Coll., Cambridge 1978–84; Visiting Prof., École des Hautes Études, Paris 1985; editorial columnist, The Observer, London 1990–93; correspondent for BBC, Observer, New Yorker 1984–2000; mem., Int. Comm. on Sovereignty and Intervention; Carr Prof. of Human Rights Practice Harvard Univ. 2000–05, Dir Carr Center for Human Rights Policy, John F. Kennedy School of Govt 2001–05; Chancellor Jackman Visiting Prof. in Human Rights Policy, Univ. of Toronto 2005; MP (Liberal) for Etobicoke-Lakeshore 2006–, assoc. critic for Human Resources and Skills Devt in Official Opposition Shadow Cabinet 2006; unsuccessful campaign for leadership of Liberal party 2006, currently Deputy Leader; Dr hc (Bishop's Univ.) 1995; Lionel Gelber Award 1994. *Television:* host Thinking Aloud (BBC) 1986–, Voices (Channel Four) 1986, The Late Show (BBC 2) 1989–. *Publications:* A Just Measure of Pain: The Penitentiary in the Industrial Revolution 1978, Wealth and Virtue: The Shaping of Classical Political Economy in the Scottish Enlightenment (ed. with Istvan Hont) 1983, The Needs of Strangers: An Essay on the Philosophy of Human Needs 1984, The Russian Album: A Family Memoir (RSL W. H. Heinemann Award, UK, Governor-General Award, Canada 1988) 1987, Asya 1991, Scar Tissue (novel) 1993, Blood and Belonging: Journeys into the New

Nationalism 1993, Isaiah Berlin: A Life 1998, The Warrior's Honor: Ethnic War and the Modern Conscience 1998, Virtual War: Kosovo and Beyond 2000, The Rights Revolution (Massey Lectures 2000) 2001, Human Rights as Politics and Idolatry (Tanner Lectures) 2001, Charlie Johnson in the Flames 2003, The Lesser Evil: Political Ethics in an Age of Terror 2004, After Paradise 2005; contrib. to New York Times, New Yorker, New York Review of Books. *Address:* Room 435-S, Centre Block, House of Commons, Ottawa ON K1A 0A6 (office); Etobicoke Constituency Office, 656 The Queensway, Toronto, ON M8Y 1K7, Canada (office). *Telephone:* (613) 995-9364 (Ottawa) (office); (416) 251-5510 (office). *Fax:* (613) 992-5880 (Ottawa) (office); (416) 251-2845 (office). *E-mail:* ignatm@parl.gc.ca (office). *Website:* www.michaelignatieffmp.ca (office).

IGRUNOV, Vyacheslav Vladimirovich; Russian politician; *Director, International Institute of Humanitarian and Political Studies;* b. 28 Oct. 1948, Cheznitsky, Zhytomer region, Ukraine; m.; four c. *Education:* Odessa State Inst. of Nat. Econs. *Career:* detained by KGB due to his protest against invasion of Soviet army into Czechoslovakia 1968, participated in dissident movt 1960s, arrested 1975; released after campaign by Andrei Sakharov and Aleksandr Solzhenitsyn in his defence 1977; f. Samizdat Library; mem. staff 20th Century and World (bulletin) 1987; f. ideological Movt Memorial July 1987; f. Moscow Public Information Exchange Bureau M-BIO, newspaper Panorama 1988; Head of Programme Civil Soc. Foundation of Cultural Initiative 1990–92; Head of Analytical Centre in Goscomnats; Dir Int. Inst. of Humanitarian and Political Studies; mem. State Duma (Parl.) 1993–; Deputy Chair. public movt Yabloko 1996–2000, mem. faction Yabloko 1993–2003; mem. Expert Bd of Fed. Council (Parl.) 2005–. *Publications:* Problematics of Social Movements, Informal Political Clubs in Moscow 1989, Economic Reform as One of the Sources of National Clashes 1993, Phantoms of Freedom, Equalilty, and Fraternity 2005. *Address:* International Institute of Humanitarian and Political Studies, Gazetny per. 5, 103918 Moscow, Russia (office). *Telephone:* (495) 232-26-43 (office); (495) 940-83-31 (home). *Fax:* (495) 232-26-43 (office). *E-mail:* igrunov@igpi.ru (office). *Website:* www.igrunov.ru (office).

IHSANOĞLU, Ekmeleddin, MSc, PhD; Turkish academic and international organization official; *Secretary-General, Organization of the Islamic Conference;* b. 1943, Cairo, Egypt; m. Füsun Bilgiç 1971; three s. *Education:* Ankara Univ. *Career:* cataloger of printed and manuscript books, Dept of Oriental Studies, Cairo Nat. Library, 1962–66; Lecturer in Turkish Literature and Language, Ain Shams Univ., Cairo 1966–70, Ankara Univ., Turkey 1971–75; Research Fellow, Univ. of Exeter, UK 1975–77; Lecturer and Assoc. Prof., Faculty of Science, Ankara Univ. 1970–80; Assoc. Prof., İnönü Univ., Malatya, Turkey 1978–80; Dir-Gen. Islamic Conf. Research Centre for Islamic History, Art and Culture, Org. of the Islamic Conf. (OIC), Istanbul 1980–2004, Sec.-Gen. OIC, Jeddah, Saudi Arabia 2005–; Sec. Islamic Conf. Org. Int. Comm. for Preservation of Islamic Cultural Heritage, Istanbul 1983–2000 (now defunct); Founder and Chair. first Dept of History of Science in Turkey, Univ. of Istanbul 1984–2000; Chair. Turkish Soc. for History of Science, Istanbul 1989–; Vice-Chair. Al Furqan Islamic Heritage Foundation, London, UK 1998–; Pres. Int. Union of History and Philosophy of Science/Div. of History of Science 2001–; mem. numerous orgs concerned with study of history of science and Islamic civilization, including Acad. Int. d'Histoire des Sciences, Paris, Cultural Centre of the Atatürk Supreme Council for Culture, Language and History, Ankara, Int. Soc. for History of Arabic and Islamic Sciences and Philosophy, Paris, Royal Acad. of Islamic Civilization Research, Jordan, Middle East and the Balkans, Research Foundation, Istanbul, Acad. of Arabic Language (Jordan, Egypt, Syria), Egyptian History Soc., Cairo, Tunisian Acad. of Sciences, Letters and Arts 'Bait al Hikma', Tunis, Int. Soc. for History of Medicine, Paris; apptd Amb.-at-Large by Govt of Bosnia-Herzegovina 1997; Visiting Prof., Ludwig Maximilians Univ., Munich, Germany 2003; Hon. Consul, The Gambia 1990–; Commdr de l'Ordre Nat. du Mérit (Senegal) 2002, Commdr de l'Ordre Nat. du Lion (Senegal) 2006; Dr hc (Mimar Sinan Univ., Istanbul) 1994, (Dowling Coll., New York) 1996, (Azerbaijan Acad. of Sciences) 2000, (Univ. of Sofia) 2001, (Univ. of Sarajevo) 2001, (Univ. of Padova) 2006, (Islamic Univ. of Islamabad) 2007, (Univ. of Exeter) 2007, (Islamic Univ., Uganda) 2008; Distinction of the First Order Medal (Egypt) 1990, Certificate of Honour and Distinction, Org. of the Islamic Conf. 1995, Independence Medal of the First Order (Jordan) 1996, Medal of Distinguished State Service (Turkey) 2000, World Prize for Book of the Year (Iran) 2000, UNESCO Avicenna Medal 2004, Medal of Glory (Russia) 2006, Medal of Glory (Azerbaijan) 2006,. *Publications:* has written, edited and translated several books on Islamic culture and science; over 70 articles and papers. *Address:* Organization of the Islamic Conference, POB 178, Jeddah 21411, Saudi Arabia (office); Türk Bostani Sokak, Dostlar Sitesi 35, Yenikoy 34464 Istanbul, Turkey (home). *Telephone:* 6900001 (office). *Fax:* 2751953

(office). *E-mail:* cabinet@oic-oci.org (office). *Website:* www.oic-oci.org (office).

IIPUMBU, Leonard Nangolo; Namibian diplomatist; m.; four c. *Career:* Deputy Rep. of Namibia to Zambia 1980–83; Chief Rep. to Botswana 1984–87, People's Repub. of Congo 1988–89; mem. protocol sub-Cttee for Namibian independence celebrations 1990; Special Envoy to the Congo 1991; Amb. to France (also accred to Italy, Portugal and Spain) 1992–99, to USA 1999–2007.
Address: c/o Ministry of Foreign Affairs, Govt Buildings, Robert Mugabe Avenue, PMB 13347, Windhoek, Namibia (office).

IKEDA, Daisaku; Japanese Buddhist philosopher and author; *President, Soka Gakkai International;* b. 2 Jan. 1928, Tokyo; m. Kaneko Shiraki 1952; two s. *Education:* Fuji Coll. *Career:* Pres. Soka Gakkai 1960–79, Hon. Pres. 1979–, Pres. Soka Gakkai Int. 1975–; Founder Soka Univ., Soka Univ. of America, Soka Women's Coll., Tokyo, Kansai Soka Schools, Soka Kindergartens (Japan, Hong Kong, Singapore, Malaysia, Brazil, South Korea), Makiguchi Foundation for Educ., Inst. of Oriental Philosophy, Boston Research Center for the 21st Century, Toda Inst. for Global Peace and Policy Research, Tokyo, Shizuoka Fuji Art Museum, Min-On Concert Asscn, Victor Hugo House of Literature and Komeito Party; mem. Advisory Bd World Centers of Compassion for Children Int., Ireland 2004–; Poet Laureate, World Acad. of Arts and Culture, USA 1981–; World People's Poet, World Poetry Soc., India 2007–; Foreign mem. Brazilian Acad. of Letters 1993–; Hon. Prof., Nat. Univ. of San Marcos 1981, Peking Univ. 1984 and others; Hon. Senator, European Acad. of Sciences and Arts 1997–; Hon. Adviser World Fed. of UN Asscns (WFUNA) 1999–; Hon. mem., The Club of Rome 1996–, Inst. of Oriental Studies of Russian Acad. of Sciences 1996–, Russian Acad. of Arts 2007–, and others; Order of the Sun of Peru with Grand Cross 1984, Grand Cross, Order of Merit of May (Argentina) 1990, Nat. Order of Southern Cross (Brazil) 1990, Kt Grand Cross of the Most Noble Order of the Crown (Thailand) 1991, Hon. Cross of Science and the Arts (Austria) 1992, Kt Grand Cross of Rizal (Philippines) 1996, Grande Officiale, Ordine al Merito (Italy) 2006, Order of Friendship (Russia) 2008, and others; Dr hc (Moscow State Univ.) 1975, (Sofia) 1981, (Buenos Aires) 1990, (Univ. of the Philippines) 1991, (Ankara) 1992, (Fed. Univ. of Rio de Janeiro) 1993, (Glasgow) 1994, (Hong Kong) 1996, (Havana) 1996, (Univ. of Ghana) 1996, (Cheju Nat. Univ.) 1999, (Delhi) 1999, (Queens Coll. City Univ. of NY) 2000, (Univ. of Sydney) 2000, (Morehouse Coll.) 2002, (Univ. of Guadalajara) 2004, (Tagore Int. Univ.) 2006, (Palermo) 2007, and others; UN Peace Award 1983, Kenya Oral Literature Award 1986, UNHCR Humanitarian Award 1989, Rosa Parks Humanitarian Award (USA) 1993, Simon Wiesenthal Center Int. Tolerance Award (USA) 1993, Tagore Peace Award, The Asiatic Soc. (India) 1997 and others. *Exhibition:* Dialogue with Nature (photographic exhbn shown in over 30 countries 1988–). *Publications:* The Human Revolution Vols I–VI 1972–99, The Living Buddha 1976, Choose Life (with A. Toynbee) 1976, Buddhism: The First Millennium 1977, Songs From My Heart 1978, Glass Children and Other Essays 1979, La Nuit Appelle L'Aurore (with R. Huyghe) 1980, A Lasting Peace Vols I–II 1981, 1987, Life: An Enigma, a Precious Jewel 1982, Before It Is Too Late (with A. Peccei) 1984, Buddhism and Cosmos 1985, The Flower of Chinese Buddhism 1986, Human Values in a Changing World (with B. Wilson) 1987, Unlocking the Mysteries of Birth and Death 1988, 2003, The Snow Country Prince 1990, A Lifelong Quest for Peace (with L. Pauling) 1992, Choose Peace (with J. Galtung) 1995, A New Humanism: The University Addresses of Daisaku Ikeda 1996, The Wisdom of the Lotus Sutra, Vols I–VI (in Japanese) 1996–2000, Ikeda-Jin Yong Dialogue (in Japanese) 1998, The New Human Revolution, Vols I–XIX (in Japanese) 1998–2008, The Way of Youth 2000, For the Sake of Peace 2001, Soka Education 2001, Diálogo sobre José Martí (with C. Vitier) 2001, The World is Yours to Change 2002, Choose Hope (with D. Krieger) 2002, Alborada del Pacífico (with P. Aylwin) 2002, On Being Human (with R. Simard and G. Bourgeault) 2002, Global Civilization: A Buddhist–Islamic Dialogue (with M. Tehranian) 2003, Fighting for Peace 2004, Planetary Citizenship (with H. Henderson) 2004, One by One 2004, Moral Lessons of the Twentieth Century (with M. Gorbachev) 2005, Revolutions: To Green the Environment, To Grow the Human Heart (with M. S. Swaminathan) 2005, A Quest for Global Peace (with J. Rothblat) 2006, A Dialogue between East and West (with R. Díez-Hochleitner) 2007 and other writings on Buddhism, civilization, life and peace.
Address: 32 Shinano-machi, Shinjuku-ku, Tokyo 160-8583, Japan (office). *Telephone:* (3) 5360-9831 (office). *Fax:* (3) 5360-9885 (office). *E-mail:* sgipr@sgi.gr.jp (office). *Website:* www.sgi.org (office); www.daisakuikeda .org.

IKLÉ, Fred Charles, PhD; American social scientist and fmr government official; *Distinguished Scholar, Center for Strategic and International Studies;* b. 21 Aug. 1924, Fex, Switzerland; m. Doris Eisemann 1959; two d. *Education:* Univ. of Chicago. *Career:* research scholar, Bureau of Applied Social Research, Columbia Univ. 1950–54; mem. Social Science Dept, Rand Corpn 1955–61, Head of Dept 1968–73; Research Assoc. in Int. Relations, Centre for Int. Affairs, Harvard Univ. 1962–63; Assoc. Prof., then Prof. of Political Science, MIT 1963–67; Dir US Arms Control and Disarmament Agency 1973–77; Under-Sec. of Defense for Policy 1981–88; Distinguished Scholar, Center for Strategic and Int. Studies 1988–; Dir Defense Forum Foundation 1988–; Dir Nat. Endowment for Democracy 1992–2001; Co-Chair. US Comm. on Integrated Long Term Strategy 1987–88; mem. Bd Int. Peace Acad. 1977–81; Chair. Council on Nat. Security of Republican Nat. Cttee 1977–79; Chair. CMC Energy Services 1978–81, mem. Bd 1988–, Chair. Telos Corpn 1995–2002, mem. Bd 2003–; Gov. Smith Richardson Foundation 1996–; Chair. US Cttee for Human Rights in N Korea 2001–04, mem. Bd 2004–; US Defense Dept Distinguished Public Service Awards 1975, 1987, 1988. *Publications:* The Social Impact of Bomb Destruction 1958, After Detection...What? 1961, How Nations Negotiate 1964, Every War Must End 1971, Can Nuclear Deterrence Last Out The Century? 1973, Annihilation From Within 2006; numerous contribs to books and articles in journals on int. affairs.
Address: Center for Strategic and International Studies, 1800 K Street, NW, Washington, DC 20006 (office); 7010 Glenbrook Road, Bethesda, MD 20814, USA (home). *Telephone:* (202) 775-3155 (office). *Fax:* (202) 775-3199 (office). *E-mail:* aditus9@verizon.net (office). *Website:* www.csis .org (office).

IKOUEBE, Basile; Republic of the Congo diplomatist; *Minister of Foreign Affairs;* b. 1 July 1946; m.; six c. *Education:* Int. Inst. of Public Admin, Paris, Inst. for Political Studies, Bordeaux. *Career:* apptd Chief Int. Orgs Div., Minister of Foreign Affairs 1974, Prin. Pvt. Sec. to Minister 1975–77, Sec. to Ministry 1977–79; training assignment in France 1980–82; Diplomatic Adviser to Head of State 1982–92; Minister and Prin. Pvt. Sec. to Head of State 1987–94; Amb.-at-Large 1994–95; Sec. to Ministry of Foreign Affairs and Co-operation 1996–98; Perm. Rep. to UN 1998–2007, Pres. UN Security Council 2006; Minister of Foreign Affairs 2007–.
Address: Ministry of Foreign Affairs, BP 2070, Brazzaville, Republic of the Congo (office). *Telephone:* 81-10-89 (office). *Fax:* 81-41-61 (office).

ILBOUDO, Emile; Burkinabè diplomatist. *Career:* currently Amb. to Côte d'Ivoire.
Address: Embassy of Burkina Faso, Immeuble SIDAM, 5e étage, 34 avenue Houdaille, 01 BP 908, Abidjan 01, Côte d'Ivoire (office). *Telephone:* 20-21-15-01 (office). *Fax:* 20-21-66-41 (office). *E-mail:* amba.bf@africaonline.ci (office).

ILDEM, Tacan; Turkish diplomatist; *Permanent Representative, NATO;* b. 1956, Ankara; m. Arzu Etensel Ildem; two c. *Education:* Univ. of Ankara. *Career:* joined Ministry of Foreign Affairs 1978, Second Sec., NATO Dept; Deputy Special Advisor for Foreign Policy to Sec.-Gen. of Nat. Security Council and the Presidency 1980–81; Second, then First Sec., Turkish Del. to NATO 1981–84; First Sec., Embassy in New Delhi 1984–86; Special Advisor to Under-Sec., Ministry of Foreign Affairs 1986–89; Political Counsellor, Embassy in Washington, DC 1989–93; Head, NATO Mil. Affairs Dept, Ministry of Foreign Affairs 1993–95; Minister Counsellor, Embassy in Athens 1995–99; Head, NATO and WEU Dept, Ministry of Foreign Affairs 1999–2000; Chief of Cabinet and Prin. Foreign Policy Advisor to Pres. 2000–03; Amb. to the Netherlands 2003–06; Perm. Rep. to NATO, Brussels 2006–.
Address: North Atlantic Treaty Organization (NATO), boulevard Léopold III, 1110 Brussels, Belgium (office). *Telephone:* (2) 707-41-11 (office). *Fax:* (2) 707-45-79 (office). *E-mail:* natodoc@hq.nato.int (office). *Website:* www .nato.int (office).

ILIĆ, Venceslav; Bosnia and Herzegovina judge; *President of Appellate Division, Supreme Court of the Federation of Bosnia and Herzegovina;* b. 10 Sept. 1937, Sarajevo; m. Bogdanka Ilić (née Mioković); two d. *Career:* Dist Court Judge 1972–78; Public Prosecutor 1978–84; Supreme Court Judge 1984–87, 1992–96; Pres. Dist Court 1987–92; apptd Pres. Supreme Court, Fed. of Bosnia and Herzegovina 1996, currently Pres. Appellate Div.; Medallion of the City of Sarajevo. *Publications:* work on educ. of juridical personnel.
Address: Appellate Division, Supreme Court of the Federation of Bosnia and Herzegovina, 71000 Sarajevo, Valtera Perića 15, Federation of Bosnia and Herzegovina (office). *Telephone:* (33) 664754 (office).

ILIESCU, Ion; Romanian fmr head of state and engineer; *Senator;* b. 3 March 1930, Olteniţa, Ilfov Dist; m. Elena (Nina) Şerbănescu 1951. *Education:* Bucharest Polytechnic Inst. and Energy Inst., Moscow, USSR. *Career:* researcher, Energy Eng. Inst., Bucharest 1955; Pres. Union of Student Asscns 1957–60; Alt. mem. Cen. Cttee of RCP 1965–68, mem. 1968–84; First Sec. Cen. Cttee of Union of Communist Youth and Minister

for Youth 1967–71; Sec. RCP Cen. Cttee 1971; Vice-Chair. Timiş Co. Council 1971–74; Chair Iaşi Co. Council 1974–79; accused of "intellectual deviationism" and kept under surveillance; Chair. Nat. Water Council 1979–84; Dir Tech. Publishing House, Bucharest 1984–89; Pres. Nat. Salvation Front 1989–90, Provisional Council for Nat. Unity Feb.–May 1990; Pres. of Romania 1990–96, 2000–04; Senator 1996–2000, 2004–; fmr Pres. Party of Social Democracy of Romania (merged with SDP to become Social Democratic Party 2001); Chevalier de la Légion d'honneur and other state decorations; hon. doctorates from numerous univs. *Publications:* Global Problems and Creativity, Revolution and Reform, Romania in Europe and in the World, Where is Romanian Society Going?, Romanian Revolution, Hope Reborn, Integration and Globalisation – A Romanian Vision, Romanian Culture and European Identity, For Sustainable Development, The Great Shock at the End of a Short Century; studies on water man. and ecology, political power and social relations.
Address: c/o Office of the Former President, Athena str. 11, Bucharest; Senate of Romania, Bucharest, Romania.

ILIOPOULOS, Dimitris, BA, Master Dip.; Greek diplomatist; *Deputy Permanent Representative, European Union;* b. 26 Feb. 1953, Athens; m. Julia Iliopoulos; one s. *Education:* Athens Univ., Panteion Athens Univ., Int. Inst. for Human Rights, Strasbourg, France. *Career:* various positions at Embassies in Belgrade, Ankara and Perm. Mission to the UN, Geneva; fmr Amb. to Albania; Political Adviser, NATO, Tirana 2004–06; Deputy Perm. Rep. to EU, Brussels 2006–; Kt, Order of the Phoenix (Greece) 2004, Kt of Honour (Norway) 2005. *Publications:* four collections of poetry 1976, 1979–80; two trans. of Turkish poet Ilyas Halil 2000, 2006; two trans. of Albanian novelist Ismail Kadare 2003, 2006.
Address: Permanent Mission of Greece to the EU, Rue Montoyer 25, 1000 Brussels, Belgium (office). *Telephone:* (2) 551-56-01 (office). *Fax:* (2) 551-56-02 (office). *E-mail:* rp-adj@rp-grece.be (office).

ILKIN, Baki; Turkish diplomatist; *Permanent Representative, United Nations;* b. 3 Oct. 1943, Ankara; m.; two c. *Education:* Univ. of Ankara. *Career:* Third Sec., Dept of Cypriot-Greek Affairs, Ministry of Foreign Affairs 1969–70; Third and First Sec., Embassy in Greece 1970–74; First Sec., Embassy in USSR 1974–75; Chief of Section for Greece, Dept of Political Affairs 1975–77; Counsellor, Embassy in UK 1977–81; Special Adviser to Minister of Foreign Affairs 1981–83; Chief of Cabinet for Pres. 1983–87; Amb. to Pakistan 1987–90, to Denmark 1990–93, to Netherlands 1996–98, to USA 1998–2001; Special Advisor to Minister of Foreign Affairs 1993–96; Deputy Under-Sec. for Bilateral Political Affairs, Ministry of Foreign Affairs 2001–04; Perm. Rep. to UN, New York 2004–.
Address: Office of the Permanent Representative of Turkey to the United Nations, 821 United Nations Plaza, 10th Floor, New York, NY 10017, USA (office). *Telephone:* (212) 949-0150 (office). *Fax:* (212) 949-0086 (office). *E-mail:* turkey@un.int (office). *Website:* www.un.int/turkey (office).

ILLARIONOV, Andrei (Nikolayevich), PhD; Russian economist; *Senior Fellow, Center for Global Liberty and Prosperity, Cato Institute;* b. 16 Sept. 1961, Leningrad (now St Petersburg). *Education:* Leningrad Univ., Univ. of Birmingham, UK, Georgetown Univ., USA. *Career:* Asst Researcher, Leningrad State Univ. 1983–90; Head of Sector, St Petersburg Financial and Econ. Inst. 1990–92; Deputy Dir Centre for Econ. Reforms, Russian Govt 1992–93; Adviser to the Prime Minister 1993–94; Dir Inst. of Econ. Analysis 1994–2000, Pres. 2000–; Adviser to Pres. Putin on Econ. Problems 2000–05 (resgnd); Russian Sherpa to G8 2000–05 (resgnd); Sr Fellow, Center for Global Liberty and Prosperity, Cato Inst., Washington, DC 2006–. *Publications:* Russian Economic Reforms: Lost Year 1994, Financial Stabilization in Russia 1995, Russia in a Changing World 1997, Economic Freedom of the World (co-author and co-ed.) 2000; more than 300 articles on Russian econ. and social policy.
Address: Cato Institute, 1000 Massachusetts Avenue, NW, Washington, DC 20001-5403, USA (office). *Telephone:* (202) 842-0200 (office). *Fax:* (202) 842-3490 (office). *E-mail:* aIllarionov@cato.org (office). *Website:* (office).

ILLES, Henry Lothar; Suriname diplomatist; m.; four c. *Career:* Man. Dir Foundation for the Man. of Railway Properties in Western Suriname 1981–83; Deputy Dir Nat. Planning Office 1983–94; Amb. to Guyana 1994–97, Amb.-at-Large, Ministry of Foreign Affairs 1997–2001, Sr Policy Adviser 2000–01, Amb. to USA and Perm. Rep. to OAS 2001–07.
Address: Ministry of Foreign Affairs, Lim A Postraat 25, PO Box 25, Paramaribo, Suriname (office). *Telephone:* 471209 (office). *Fax:* 410411 (office). *E-mail:* buza@sr.net (office).

ILOILOVATU ULUIVUDA, Ratu Josefa, CF, MBE, JP; Fijian head of state; *President;* b. 29 Dec. 1920, Vuda, Ba Prov.; m. Adi Salaseini Kavunono. *Career:* fmr teacher, civil admin., prov. admin.; Vice-Pres. Methodist

Church of Fiji and Rotuma 1997–98; fmr MP and Pres. of Senate; Vice-Pres. –2000, Acting Pres. Dec. 2000–01, Pres. of Fiji 2001– (presidential powers seized by Cdre Frank Bainimarama Dec. 2006, reinstated to interim govt Jan. 2007); Pres. Bd Trustees Native Land Trust Bd 2001–.
Address: Office of the President, Government House, Berkley Crescent, PO Box 2513, Government Buildings, Suva, Fiji (office). *Telephone:* 3314244 (office). *Fax:* 3301645 (office). *Website:* www.fiji.gov.fj/publish/president .shtml.

ILVES, Toomas Hendrik, MA; Estonian politician, diplomatist, scientist and head of state; *President;* b. 26 Dec. 1953, Stockholm, Sweden; m. 1st Merry Bullock (divorced); one s. one d.; m. 2nd Evelin Ilves; one d. *Education:* Columbia Univ., New York, Univ. of Pennsylvania, USA. *Career:* Research Asst, Dept of Psychology, Columbia Univ. 1974–76, 1979; Asst to Dir and English Teacher, Center for Open Educ., Englewood, NJ 1979–81; Arts Admin. and Dir Vancouver Literary Centre, Canada 1981–82; Lecturer in Estonian Literature and Linguistics, Dept of Interdisciplinary Studies, Simon Fraser Univ., Vancouver 1983–84; Research Analyst, Radio Free Europe, Munich, Germany 1984–88, Dir Estonian Service 1988–93; Amb. to USA (also accred to Canada and Mexico) 1993–96; Minister of Foreign Affairs 1996–98, 1999–2002; Chair. Bd Estonian N Atlantic Trust 1998; mem. Riigikogu (Estonian State Ass.) 1999–; Deputy Chair. Moodukad Party, apptd Chair. 1999; mem. European Parl. (Sotsiaaldemokraatlik Erakond) 1999–2006, Vice-Chair. Cttee on Foreign Affairs, mem. Del. for Relations with the USA, Substitute mem. Cttee on Budgets, Sub-cttee on Security and Defence, Del. to EU–Russia Parl. Cooperation Cttee; Pres. of Estonia 2006–; Pres. Estonian Special Olympics 1997–2004; Bd mem. Tartu Univ. 1996–2003, European Movt Estonia (EME) 1999–2004, Estonian Acad. of Arts 2004–06, Trilateral Comm. 2004–06, Friends of Europe (think-tank) 2005, Viljandi Co. Municipal Fund; Grand Commdr, Légion d'honneur 2001, Third Class, Order of the Seal (Estonia) 2004, Three Star Order of the Repub. (Latvia) 2004, Collar of the Order of the Cross of Terra Mariana (Estonia) 2006, Hon. Kt Grand Cross, Order of the Bath (UK) 2006.
Address: Office of the President, A. Weizenbergi 39, Tallinn 15050, Estonia (office). *Telephone:* 631-6202 (office). *Fax:* 631-6250 (office). *E-mail:* vpinfo@vpk.ee (office). *Website:* www.president.ee (office).

IMAM, Sabah Abdul Wahab al-; Iraqi diplomatist. *Career:* currently Amb. to Syria.
Address: Embassy of the Republic of Iraq, Damascus, Syria (office). *Telephone:* (11) 3341290 (office). *Fax:* (11) 3341291 (office). *E-mail:* dmkemb@iraqmofamail.net (office).

IMANALIEV, Muratbek Sansyzbayevich; Kyrgyzstani diplomatist; *President, Institute for Public Policy;* b. 25 Feb. 1956, Frunze (now Bishkek); m.; one s. one d. *Education:* Moscow State Univ., Leningrad Inst. of Oriental Studies. *Career:* Second, then First Sec., then Head, Consular Dept, Acting Minister of Foreign Affairs of the Kirghiz SSR 1982–91, Minister for Foreign Affairs 1991–92, 1997–2002; Amb. to China 1993–96; Chair. Public Comm. on Foreign Policy 1996–97; co-founder and Pres. Inst. for Public Policy; mem. Justice and Progress Party.
Address: Institute for Public Policy, 42/1 Isanov Str., Bishkek 720040, Kyrgyzstan (office). *Telephone:* (312) 906240 (office). *E-mail:* office@ipp .kg (office). *Website:* ipp.kg (office).

INDRAWATI, HE Sri Mulyani, PhD; Indonesian economist, academic and government official; *Minister of Finance;* b. 26 Aug. 1962, Tanjungkarang, Lampung. *Education:* Univ. of Indonesia, Jakarta, Univ. of Illinois Urbana-Champaign, USA. *Career:* several positions at Inst. for Econ. and Social Research, Faculty of Econs, Univ. Indonesia (LPEM-FEUI) 1992–2004 including Assoc. Dir Research 1992–93, Assoc. Dir Educ. and Training 1993–95, Dir Program Magister, Planning and Public Policy, Grad. Program Econs 1996–99, Dir 1998–2004; Staff Expert in Policy Analysis, Overseas Training Office (OTO) 1994–95; Adviser Nat. Econ. Council 1999–2001; consultant to USAID 2001; Visiting Faculty mem. Andrew Young School of Policy Studies, Ga State Univ. 2001–02; Exec. Dir IMF 2002–; Minister of State, Nat. Devt Planning 2004–05; Minister of Finance 2005–. *Publications include:* Potential and Student Savings in DKI Jakarta 1995, Domestic Industry Preparedness for the Free Trade Era 1997, Forget CBS, Get Serious About Reform 1998.
Address: Ministry of Finance and State Enterprises Development, Jalan Lapangan Banteng Timur 2–4, Jakarta, 10710, Indonesia. *Telephone:* (21) 3814324. *Fax:* (21) 353710. *Website:* www.depkeu.go.id.

INDYK, Martin S., BEcons, PhD; American diplomatist and academic; *Senior Fellow, Foreign Policy Studies and Director, Saban Center for Middle East Policy, Brookings Institution;* b. 1 July 1951, London, England; m. Jill Indyk; two c. *Education:* Sydney Univ., Australian Nat. Univ. *Career:* worked as Deputy Dir of current intelligence for Middle East, Austalia

intelligence service 1978; Adjunct Prof. Johns Hopkins School of Advanced Int. Studies; Exec. Dir Washington Inst. for Near East Policy 1985; sworn in as US citizen 1993; Special Asst to the Pres. and Sr Dir for Near East and S Asian Affairs, Nat. Security Council; Prin. Adviser to the Pres. and Nat. Security Adviser on Arab–Israeli Issues, Iraq, Iran and S Asia; Sr mem. Warren Christopher's Middle East peace team; Amb. to Israel 1995–97, 2000–01; Asst Sec. for Near Eastern Affairs 1997–2000; Sr Fellow and Dir Saban Center for Middle East Policy, The Brookings Institution 2002–; mem. Int. Inst. for Strategic Studies, Middle East Inst. *Publications:* numerous articles and contribs to foreign policy journals.
Address: Saban Center for Middle East Policy, The Brookings Institution, 1775 Massachusetts Avenue, NW, Washington, DC 20036, USA (office). *Telephone:* (202) 797-6462 (office). *Fax:* (202) 797-2481 (office). *E-mail:* SabanCenter@brookings.edu (office). *Website:* www.brookings.edu (office).

INGÓLFSSON, Hermann, BSc, MSc; Icelandic diplomatist; *Military Representative, NATO;* b. 23 July 1966, Akureyri; m. Hildur Blöndal Sveinsdóttir; two s. *Education:* Tech. Coll. of Iceland, Aalborg Univ., Denmark. *Career:* early career as engineer, Borgarverk Contractors, Borgarnes 1991; consulting engineer, FORM-Architects, Akureyri 1992–95; Tech. Adviser, Minor Roads Programme, Mombasa, Kenya 1995; Adviser, Political Dept, Ministry of Foreign Affairs 1997–98; Adviser to Exec. Dir, Nordic and Baltic Countries, World Bank Group, Washington, DC 1998–2001, Sr Adviser 2001–03; Counsellor, Deputy Dir Multilateral Devt Cooperation, Political Dept, Ministry of Foreign Affairs 2003–04, Minister-Counsellor 2004–07; Mil. Rep. to NATO, Brussels 2007–.
Address: NATO HQ, blvd Léopold III, 1110 Brussels, Belgium (office). *Telephone:* (2) 707-41-11 (office). *Fax:* (2) 707-45-79 (office). *E-mail:* natodoc@hq.nato.int (office). *Website:* www.nato.int (office).

INGÓLFSSON, Thorsteinn; Icelandic diplomatist and banker; *Permanent Representative, NATO;* b. 9 Dec. 1944, Reykjavik; m. 1st Gudrún Valdís Ragnarsdóttir (divorced 1986); one s. one d.; m. 2nd Hólmfrídur Kofoed-Hansen 1994. *Education:* Commercial Coll. of Iceland, Univ. of Iceland. *Career:* First Sec. and Deputy Chief of Mission, Washington, DC 1973–78; Chief of Div., Ministry of Foreign Affairs 1978–85; Minister Counsellor 1981; Deputy Perm. Rep. to Int. Orgs, Geneva 1985–87, Acting Perm. Rep. Feb.–June 1987; rank of Amb. 1987; Dir Defence Dept Ministry for Foreign Affairs, 1987–90; Chair. Icelandic-American Defence Council 1987–90; Perm. Under-Sec. for Foreign Affairs 1990–94; Perm. Rep. to N Atlantic Council and WEU 1994–99; Perm. Rep. to UN 1999–2003; Amb. to Cuba 2001, to Barbados 2002, to Jamaica 2003 with residence in New York; Exec. Dir for Nordic and Baltic Countries, World Bank Group, New York 2003–06; Special Envoy of Foreign Minister 2006–08; Perm. Rep. to NATO, Brussels 2008–; Grande Croix, Légion d'honneur, Hon. GCMG, numerous decorations.
Address: Office of the Permanent Representative of Iceland, blvd Léopold III, 1110 Brussels, Belgium (office). *Telephone:* (2) 707-41-11 (office). *Fax:* (2) 707-45-79 (office). *E-mail:* natodoc@hq.nato.int (office). *Website:* www .nato.int (office).

INGRAHAM, Rt Hon Hubert Alexander, PC; Bahamian lawyer and politician; *Prime Minister and Minister of Finance;* b. 4 Aug. 1947, Pine Ridge, Grand Bahama; m. Delores Velma Miller; five c. *Education:* Cooper's Town Public School, Southern Sr School and Govt High School Evening Inst. Nassau. *Career:* called to the Bar, Bahamas 1972; Sr Pnr, Christie, Ingraham & Co. (law firm); fmr mem. Air Transport Licensing Authority; fmr Chair. Real Property Tax Tribunal; mem. Nat. Gen. Council Progressive Liberal Party (PLP) 1975; Nat. Chair. and mem. Nat. Exec. Cttee PLP 1976; elected to House of Ass. as PLP mem. 1977, 1982, fmr Speaker; Minister of Housing, Nat. Insurance and Social Services 1982–84; Chair. Bahamas Mortgage Corpn 1982; Alt. Del. Conf. of IDB, Uruguay 1983, IMF/IBRD 1979–84; expelled from PLP 1986; elected to Nat. Ass. as ind. 1987; Parl. Leader, Official Opposition 1990–92; Leader, Opposition Free Nat. Movt and of Official Opposition 1990–92, 2002–07; Prime Minister of the Bahamas 1992–2002, 2007–, also Minister of Finance and Planning 1992–97, of Housing and Local Govt 1995–97 and Trade and Industry 1995–97, of Housing and Social Devt 2001–02, of Finance 2007–; mem. Privy Council; Dr hc (Buckingham) 2000.
Address: Office of the Prime Minister, Sir Cecil Wallace-Whitfield Centre, West Bay St, PO Box N 3217, Nassau, N.P. Bahamas (office). *Telephone:* 327-1530 (office). *Fax:* 327-1618 (office). *E-mail:* primeminister@bahamas .gov.bs (office); hai@coralwave.com (home). *Website:* www.bahamas.gov .bs (office).

INGRAM, James Charles, AO, BA (Econs); Australian diplomatist and international civil servant; b. 27 Feb. 1928, Warragul, Vic.; m. Odette Koven 1950; one s. two d. *Education:* De la Salle Coll., Melbourne Univ.

Career: joined Dept of External Affairs 1946; Third Sec., Tel-Aviv 1950; First Sec., Washington, DC 1956; Chargé d'Affaires, Brussels 1959; Counsellor, Djakarta 1962, Australian Mission to UN 1964; Asst Sec. External Affairs, Canberra 1967; Amb. to Philippines 1970–73; High Commr in Canada, Jamaica, Barbados, Guyana, Trinidad and Tobago 1973–74; First Asst Sec. Australian Devt Assistance Agency 1975–76; Dir-Gen. Australian Devt Assistance Bureau, Dept of Foreign Affairs 1977–82; Exec. Dir UN World Food Programme 1982–92; Dir Australian Inst. of Int. Affairs 1992–93; Visiting Fellow, Centre for Int. and Public Law, ANU, Canberra 1993–94; Chair., Australian Govt Advisory Cttee on Non-Govt Devt Orgs 1995; mem. Bd of Trustees, Int. Food Policy Research Inst. 1991–98, Crawford Fund for Int. Agric. Research, Melbourne 1994–99 (Chair. 1996–99), Int. Crisis Group, Brussels 1995–99; mem. Governing Council Soc. for Int. Devt 1988–94, Commonwealth Intergovernmental Group on the Emergence of a Global Humanitarian Order, London 1994–95; Chair. UN Asscn of Australia (ACT Div.) 1998–99; mem. Bd Trustees Asia-Pacific Coll. of Diplomacy, ANU 2005–; Alan Shawn Feinstein World Hunger Award, Brown Univ. 1991, Inaugural Food for Life Award UN World Food Programme, Rome (Italy) 2000. *Publication:* Bread and Stones: Leadership and the Struggle to Reform the United Nations World Food Programme 2006; contrib. numerous articles to journals and chapters to books.
Address: 4 Stokes Street, Manuka, ACT 2603, Australia (home). *Telephone:* (2) 6295-0446 (home). *E-mail:* jingram@homemail.com.au (home).

INKELES, Alex, PhD; American sociologist and academic; *Professor Emeritus, Stanford University;* b. 4 March 1920, Brooklyn, New York; m. Bernadette Mary Kane 1942; one d. *Education:* Cornell and Columbia Univs, Washington School of Psychiatry. *Career:* Social Science Research Analyst, Dept of State 1942–46, Int. Broadcasting Div. 1949–51; Instructor in Social Relations, Harvard Univ. 1948–49, Lecturer in Sociology 1948–57, Prof. 1957–71, Dir Russian Research Center Studies in Social Relations 1963–71, Dir Center of Int. Affairs Studies on Social Aspects of Econ. Devt 1963–71; Margaret Jacks Prof. of Educ., Stanford Univ. 1971–78, Prof. of Sociology and, by courtesy, Educ. 1978–90, Prof. Emer. of Sociology 1995–; Sr Fellow, Hoover Inst. on War, Revolution and Peace 1978–, Prof. Emer. 1990–; numerous fellowships including Inst. for Advanced Study, Princeton, Guggenheim, Fulbright, Rockefeller Foundation, Bellagio, Italy, NAS Exchange Program with People's Repub. of China, Nankai Univ. 1983; mem. American Acad. of Arts and Sciences, NAS, AAAS, American Philosophical Soc., American Psychology Asscn; Hon. PhD (Faculdade Candido Mendes, Brazil); numerous awards. *Publications:* Public Opinion in Soviet Russia 1950, How the Soviet System Works 1956, The Soviet Citizen: Daily Life in a Totalitarian Society 1959, What is Sociology? 1964, Social Change in Soviet Russia 1968, Becoming Modern: Individual Change in Six Developing Countries 1974, Exploring Individual Modernity 1983, On Measuring Democracy: Its Consequences and Concomitants 1991, National Character: A Psycho-Social Perspective 1996, One World Emerging? Convergence and Divergence in Industrial Societies 1998, Social Capital as a Policy Resource.
Address: Hoover Institution, LHH-239, Stanford University, Stanford, CA 94305 (office); 1001 Hamilton Avenue, Palo Alto, CA 94301, USA (home). *Telephone:* (415) 723-4856 (office); (415) 327-4197 (home). *Fax:* (415) 723-0576 (office). *E-mail:* inkeles@hoover.stanford.edu (office). *Website:* (office).

INNES-BROWN, Marc, BEcons, MA; Australian diplomatist; *Ambassador to Iraq;* b. 1966, Goulburn. *Education:* Univ. of Sydney, Univ. of Hawaii, USA. *Career:* held numerous positions in Dept of Foreign Affairs and Trade including Third Sec., Embassy in Bangkok 1995–98, First Sec., Embassy in Washington, DC 2000–01; seconded to Int. Div., Dept of the Prime Minister and Cabinet 2001–03; Dir E Timor Section 2003–05, also Dir Indonesia Section 2005; Head, Iraq Task Force 2005–06; Amb to Iraq 2006–; headed govt's temporary tsunami response office in Phuket, Thailand Jan.–Feb. 2005; Humanitarian Overseas Service Medal 2005.
Address: Australian Embassy, House 5, Street 5, Sector 923, Babylon District, Jadriyah, Baghdad, Iraq (office). *Telephone:* (1) 778-2210 (office). *E-mail:* austemb.baghdad@dfat.gov.au (office). *Website:* www.dfat.gov .au/iraq (office).

INONI, Ephraim, MBA; Cameroonian politician; *Prime Minister;* b. 16 Aug. 1947, Bakingili; m.; five c. *Education:* Catholic Teachers' Training Coll., Bonjongo, Higher Elementary Teachers' Training Coll., Mutengene, South Eastern Univ., USA. *Career:* Head Teacher, Catholic Primary School, Mabanda, Kumba, then Teacher, Sasse Coll.; Asst Prov. Chief of Accounts in the NW, then Asst Prov. Treas., Financial Controller, Douala; Financial Attaché, Embassy in Washington, DC, USA; Dir, Gen. Admin, Ministry of Finance, then Sec. of State; Asst Sec.-Gen. to the Presidency 1992–2004; Prime Minister of Cameroon 2004–; mem. Bakweri ethnic group.

Address: Office of the Prime Minister, Yaoundé, Cameroon. *Telephone:* 2223-8005 (office). *Fax:* 2223-5735 (office). *E-mail:* spm@spm.gov.cm (office). *Website:* www.spm.gov.cm (office).

INOTAI, Andras, MS, PhD, DEcon; Hungarian academic and research institute director; *President, Economic Policy Institute;* b. 18 April 1943. *Education:* Eötvös Univ. *Career:* Research Fellow, Inst. for World Economy, Hungarian Acad. of Sciences 1967–79, Sr Research Fellow 1979–80, Head of Dept 1981–89, Deputy Dir 1986–89, Gen. Dir 1991–; Visiting Prof., San Marcos Univ., Peru 1972–73; Staff mem. World Bank 1989–91; Chair. Bd of Dirs Foundation on European Studies 2002; Pres. Econ. Policy Inst., Sofia 2002–; mem. Bd of Dirs Hungarian Devt Bank; mem. Editorial Bd Journal of International Relations and Development, Global Perspectives. *Publications:* The European Communities at the Crossroads 1985, Regional Integrations in the New World Environment 1986, The Hungarian Enterprise in the CMEA Context 1986, The West German Economy and Its Adjustment to the World Economy 1986, International Direct Capital Flows 1989; contribs to journals. *Address:* Economic Policy Institute, 2 Khan Asparouh Street, floor.4, 1463 Sofia, Bulgaria (office). *Telephone:* (2) 9522693 (office). *Fax:* (2) 9520847 (office). *E-mail:* epi@epi-bg.org (office). *Website:* epi-bg.org (office).

INOUE, Yutaka, DMedSc; Japanese politician; b. 17 Nov. 1927, Chiba; m.; three d. *Education:* Tokyo Dental Coll. *Career:* mem. Chiba Prefectural Ass. 1963–72; mem. House of Reps. 1976–79; mem. House of Councillors 1980–, Pres. 2000–02; State Sec. for Finance 1983–84; Minister of Educ. 1990–91; Chair. Cttee on the Budget 1995–96; Chair. Research Cttee on Int. Affairs 1999–2000; Grand Cordon, Order of the Rising Sun. *Publication:* Major Airports in the World. *Address:* c/o Secretariat of the House of Councillors, Kokkai, Nagata-cho, Chiyoda-ku, Tokyo, Japan (office).

INSANALLY, Samuel R. (Rudy), BA; Guyanese diplomatist; *Permanent Representative, United Nations;* b. 23 June 1936, Georgetown. *Education:* Univ. of London, UK and Univ. of Paris, France. *Career:* teacher of modern languages, Kingston Coll., Jamaica, Queen's Coll., Guyana and Univ. of Guyana 1959–66; Counsellor, Embassy in Washington, DC 1966–69; Chargé d'affaires, Embassy in Venezuela 1970, Amb. 1972–78; Deputy Perm. Rep. to UN, New York 1970–72, Perm. Rep. 1987–; Perm. Rep. to EEC 1978–81; Amb. to Belgium (also accred to Sweden, Norway and Austria) 1978–81, to Colombia 1982–86; Head of Political Div. Ministry of Foreign Affairs 1982–86; High Commr to Barbados, Trinidad and Tobago and the Eastern Caribbean 1982–86; Minister of Foreign Affairs 2001–08; mem. Bd of Govs Inst. of Int. Relations, Trinidad and Tobago 1982–86; Gran Cordon, Order of the Liberator (Venezuela) 1973, Cacuque Crown of Hon.1980; Golden Arrow of Achievement 1986. *Publications include:* several articles and works on int. relations and diplomacy. *Address:* Permanent Mission to the United Nations, 866 United Nations Plaza, Suite 555, New York, NY 10017, USA (office). *Telephone:* (212) 527-3232 (office). *Fax:* (212) 935-7548 (office). *E-mail:* guyana@un.int (office).

INSULZA SALINAS, José Miguel, MA; Chilean politician, lawyer and international organization official; *Secretary-General, Organization of American States;* b. 2 June 1943; m. Georgina Núñez Reyes; three c. *Education:* St George's Coll., Santiago, Law School, Universidad de Chile, Facultad Latinoamericana de Ciencias Sociales and Univ. of Michigan, USA. *Career:* Prof. of Political Theory, Universidad de Chile, of Political Sciences, Pontificia Universidad Católica de Chile –1973; Political Adviser to Ministry of Foreign Relations, Dir Diplomatic Acad. –1973; researcher, then Dir Instituto de Estudios de Estados Unidos, Centro de Investigación y Docencia Económicas, Mexico 1981–88; Prof., Universidad Autónoma de México 1981–88; Head, Multilateral Econ. Affairs Dept, Ministry of Foreign Relations, Deputy Chair. Int. Co-operation Agency 1990–94; Under-Sec. for Foreign Affairs 1994, Minister 1994–99, Minister Sec.-Gen. Office of the Pres. 1999; Minister of the Interior (Vice-Pres. of the Repub.) 2000–; Sec.-Gen. OAS 2005–; mem. Bd of Dirs Instituto de Fomento de Desarrollo Científico y Tecnológico; mem. Consejo Chileno de Relaciones Internacionales, Consejo de Redacción, Nexos Magazine, Mexico, Corporación de Desarrollo Tecnológico Empresarial, Chilean Asscn of Political Science, Bar Asscn. *Address:* Organization of American States, 17th Street and Constitution Avenue, NW, Washington, DC 20006, USA (office); Ministry of the Interior, Palacio de la Moneda, Santiago, Chile (office). *Telephone:* (2) 690-4000 (Santiago) (office); (202) 458-3000 (Washington) (office). *Fax:* (2) 699-2165 (Santiago) (office). *E-mail:* pi@oas.org (office). *Website:* www.oas.org (office).

INTELMANN, Tina, BA, MA; Estonian diplomatist; *Permanent Representative, United Nations;* b. 1963; one s. *Education:* Leningrad State Univ.

Career: worked as teacher and translator 1987–90; Asst to Deputy Chair., Supreme Council 1990–92; Desk Officer responsible for relations with Southern European countries and EU, Ministry of Foreign Affairs 1991; Political Officer, Estonian embassies in Paris and Brussels 1992–95; Counsellor, Perm. Mission of Estonia to UN, New York 1995–98; Dir Div. of N and Cen. Europe, countries of Western Balkans, Political Dept, Ministry of Foreign Affairs 1998–99; Perm. Rep. to OSCE, Vienna 1999–2002; Under-Sec. for Political Affairs and Relations with Press, Ministry of Foreign Affairs 2002–05; Perm. Rep. to UN, New York 2005–. *Address:* Office of the Permanent Representative of Estonia to the United Nations, 600 Third Avenue, 26th Floor, New York, NY 10016, USA (office). *Telephone:* (212) 883-0640 (office). *Fax:* (212) 883-0648 (office). *E-mail:* mission.newyork@mfa.ee (office).

INTRILIGATOR, Michael David, SB, MA, PhD; American economist and academic; *Professor Emeritus of Economics, University of California, Los Angeles;* b. 5 Feb. 1938, New York, NY; m. Devrie Shapiro 1963; four s. *Education:* Massachusetts Inst. of Tech., Yale Univ. *Career:* Asst Prof., Dept of Econs, UCLA 1963–66, Assoc. Prof. 1966–72, Prof. 1972–, now Prof. Emer., Dir UCLA Inst. of Contemporary Econs (summer inst. for coll. teachers of econs sponsored by General Electric Foundation) 1967, 1969, Dir The Jacob Marschak Interdisciplinary Colloquium on Math. in the Behavioral Sciences 1977– (Chair. Advisory Cttee), Co-Dir (with Mark Kleiman) 1999–, Prof., Dept of Political Science, UCLA 1981–, mem. Steering Cttee Center for Arms Control and Int. Security 1975–78, Steering Cttee Center for Int. and Strategic Affairs 1978–92, Steering Cttee Summer Inst. for the Study of Conflict Theory and Int. Security 1980–84, Assoc. Dir Center for Int. and Strategic Affairs 1979–82, Prin. Investigator, Ford Foundation Grant to establish Center for Int. and Strategic Affairs 1982–83, Prin. Investigator, Hewlett Foundation grant to establish Center for Int. and Strategic Affairs 1985–92, Dir Center for Int. and Strategic Affairs (predecessor of the Burkle Center for Int. Relations) 1982–92, Vice-Chair. 1991–94, Dir Burkle Center for Int. Relations 2000–02, Prof., Dept of Policy Studies, School of Public Policy and Social Research 1994–, Vice-Chair. 1995–99, Prof., Dept of Public Policy, School of Public Affairs 2004–, Consultant Research Assoc., UCLA Security Studies Project 1967–68; Research Assoc., Human Resources Research Center, Univ. of Southern California 1969–81; Lecturer, Div. of Humanities and Social Sciences, California Inst. of Tech. 1969–71; Sr Economist and Consultant, Analytical Assessments Corpn, Marina del Rey, Calif. 1977–81; Prin. Investigator, NSF Grant on 'Collaborative Research on Economic Models of Arms Races' 1974–77, NSF Grant on 'Collaborative Research on Behavioral and Economic Foundations of Arms Races' 1978–84; Co-Dir Center for Int. Studies: Int. Security at UCLA and Univ. of Southern California 1985–86, Dir 1986–91; Chair. Econs Panel, Cttee for the Undergraduate Program in Math., Math. Social Science Bd project on developing sourcebooks on applications of math. in the social sciences 1973; Vice-Chair. Research Cttee on Quantitative and Math. Approaches to Politics, Int. Political Science Asscn 1985–90; Co-Dir (with Anatoly A. Gromyko), Project on 'Soviet-US Cooperation for Africa' sponsored by IREX 1987–; mem. Organizing Cttee NSF Conf. on 'The Role of Information in Economics and in the Economy', Northwestern Univ. 1980, Working Group on the Current Status of the Interface between information Science and Econs, Advisory Cttee for Information Science and Tech., NSF 1980–82, Nominating Cttee American Econ. Asscn 1991, Nat. Advisory Bd Community Health Funds Flow Project, Arthur Young & Co., Washington, DC 1973–75, Science Advisory Bd Lake Tahoe Research Group, Univ. of California, Davis 1974–76, Sub-cttee on Econ. Information of the City Econ. Advisory Council, City of Los Angeles 1976–78 (Chair. Modeling and Analysis Task Force 1976–77), PSRO Evaluation Tech. Advisory Panel, Office of Research/Office of Policy, Planning and Research/Health Care Financing Admin 1977–81, Prospective Payment Tech. Advisory Panel, Health Care Financing Admin, US Dept of Health and Human Services 1983–86, Econ. Transition Group 1996–, Int. Council of The World of Transformations (in Russian), Moscow 2004–; mem. Bd Dirs California-Russia Trade Asscn, Los Angeles 1989–93, California-Russia Trade Asscn 1992–, Los Angeles-St Petersburg Sister City Cttee 1999–2000; mem. Bd of Advisors, California Council on Europe, San Francisco 1991–94; mem. Panel of Experts, Study on Economic Aspects of Disarmament, UN Inst. for Disarmament Research (UNIDIR), Geneva 1990–92; mem. Int. Advisory Bd Russian Science Foundation, Moscow 1994–; mem. Center for Econ. Design, Bogazici Univ., Istanbul 1997–2003; consultant, Rand Corpn, Santa Monica, Calif. 1962–65, Human Resources Research Center, Univ. of Southern California 1967–69, US Arms Control and Disarmament Agency 1968, on Nat. Models project, Rockwell Int. Corpn, El Segundo 1969–74, Veterans Admin Hosp., Brentwood, Calif. 1973–76, Inst. for Defense Analysis, Arlington 1974–77, CACI, Inc., Arlington, Va 1975–77, Orkand Corpn, Silver Spring, Md, on 'Operational Measures of Health' 1976–77 and on 'Design and Evaluation of PSRO Long Term Care Review' 1980–81,

SysteMetrics, Inc., Bethesda, on 'Evaluation of the Oklahoma Utilization Review System' and on 'Measures of Inappropriate Hospital Utilization' 1979–82, Center for Nat. Security Studies, Los Alamos Nat. Lab. 1988–; reviewer (math. econs) for Mathematical Reviews 1975–79; Assoc. Ed. International Journal of Applied Analysis 1977–80, Journal of Interdisciplinary Modeling and Simulation 1977–82, Journal of Economic Dynamics and Control 1978–83, Journal of Optimization Theory and Applications 1979–92, Journal of Business and Economic Statistics 1981–87, Conflict Management and Peace Science (fmrly Journal of Peace Science) 1980–; Area Ed. Policy Analysis and Information Systems 1979–83; mem. Editorial Bd Information Economics and Policy 1982–88, Economic Directions 1992–; mem. Advisory Editorial Bd Mathematical Social Sciences 1983–97; mem. Bd of Eds Journal of Statistical Physics 1969–75, Defence and Peace Economics 1988–, Comparative Strategy 1980–86; expert witness before admin. agencies and courts, testifying for govt agencies, corpns and asscns 1976–; Pres. Peace Science Soc. (International) 1993; Vice-Chair. Economists Allied for Arms Reduction (ECAAR) 1998–2005 (mem. Bd Dirs 1989–2005), Economists for Peace and Security 2005–; Vice-Pres. Western Econ. Asscn Int. 2006–07, Pres. Elect 2007–08, Pres. 2008–09; mem. American Econ. Asscn, American Political Science Asscn, Council on Foreign Relations, New York 1984 (mem. Int. Affairs Fellowship Selection Cttee 1986–89, Study Group 'The Premises of the Alliance' 1989–90), Econometric Soc., Economists Allied for Arms Reduction, IISS, London 1983, Int. Political Science Asscn, Int. Studies Asscn, Peace Science Soc. (Int.), Western Econ. Asscn Int.; Founding mem. Pacific Council on Int. Policy 1995–; Foreign mem. Russian Acad. of Sciences 1999, inducted 2000; Fellow, Econometric Soc. 1982; Sr Fellow, The Gorbachev Foundation of N America, Boston 1998–, The Milken Inst., Santa Monica 1999–; Fellow, AAAS 2001; Woodrow Wilson Fellow, Yale Univ. 1959–60; MIT Fellow 1960–61; Ford Faculty Research Fellow, Stanford Univ. and LSE 1967–68; Distinguished Teaching Award, Grad. Student Asscn, UCLA 1966, Warren C. Scoville Distinguished Teaching Award, Dept of Econs, UCLA 1976, 1979, 1982, 1984, invited by Swedish Econ. Asscn and Stockholm Int. Peace Research Inst. to present lecture on 'Non-Armageddon Solutions to the Arms Race' to dels to the Conf. on Confidence- and Security-Building Measures and Disarmament in Europe, Stockholm 1984. *Publications:* Strategy in a Missile War: Targets and Rates of Fire, Security Studies Paper No. 10, Los Angeles: Security Studies Project, UCLA (monograph) 1967, Mathematical Optimization and Economic Theory 1971 (translated into several languages), Co-Ed. (with Christopher Bliss) book series Advanced Textbooks in Economics 1972–78, A Forecasting and Policy Simulation Model of the Health Care Sector: The HRRC Prototype Microeconometric Model (with Donald E. Yett, Leonard J. Drabek, and Larry J. Kimbell) 1979, Co-Ed. (with Kenneth J. Arrow) book series Handbooks in Economics 1980, Co-Ed. (with Zvi Griliches) Handbook of Econometrics, Vol. I 1983, Vol. II 1984, Vol. III 1986, Co-Ed. (with Kenneth J. Arrow) Handbook of Mathematical Economics Vol. I 1981, Vol. II 1982, Vol. III 1985, National Security and International Stability (co-ed., with Bernard Brodie and Roman Kolkowicz) 1983, Strategies for Managing Nuclear Proliferation – Economic and Political Issues (co-ed., with Dagobert L. Brito and Adele E. Wick) 1983, Non-Armageddon Solutions to the Arms Race (with Dagobert L. Brito), Lecture presented to the Conference on Confidence- and Security-Building Measures and Disarmament in Europe, Stockholm, Jan 1984 (monograph; reprinted as Center for Int. and Strategic Affairs Reprint No. 1 1985), Ed. Frontiers of Quantitative Economics, Vols IIIA and IIIB, Vols 105 and 106, Arms Control: Problems and Prospects (with Dagobert L. Brito), Univ. of California Inst. on Global Conflict and Cooperation Research Paper No. 2 (monograph) 1987, East-West Conflict: Elite Perceptions and Political Options (co-ed., with Hans-Adolf Jacobsen) 1988, Arms Control: The Changing Strategic Environment and the Long-Term Future (with Andrew S. Bair and Richard Latter), A Report on the CISA-Wilton Park Joint Conference, 2–4 April 1989 (monograph), Accidental Nuclear War (co-ed., with Derek Paul and Paul Smoker) 1990, Economic Aspects of Disarmament: Disarmament as an Investment Process (with Keith Hartley and others), UNIDIR Research Report, Geneva: UN Inst. for Disarmament Research (monograph) 1992, Implications of the Dissolution of the Soviet Union for Accidental/Inadvertent Use of Weapons of Mass Destruction (co-ed., with Carin Atterling Wedar and Peeter Vares) 1992, Cooperative Models in International Relations Research (co-ed., with Urs Luterbacher) 1994, Statistical Sampling in the Medicare Program: Challenging its Use (with Lester J. Perling) 2001, Eurasia: A New Peace Agenda (co-ed., with Alexander Nikitin and Majid Tehranian) 2005, Countering Terrorism and WMD: Creating a Global Anti-Terrorism Network (co-ed., with Peter Katona and John P. Sullivan) 2006. *Address:* 140 Foxtail Drive, Santa Monica, CA 90402 (home); Department of Economics, University of California, Los Angeles, CA 90095-1477, USA (office). *Telephone:* (310) 825-4144 (office); (310) 395-7909 (home). *Fax:* (310) 825-9528 (office); (310) 394-8007 (home). *E-mail:* intriligator@econ.ucla.edu (office). *Website:* econweb.sscnet.ucla.edu (office).

IOAN, Lt-Gen. Sorin, PhD; Romanian military officer; *Military Representative, NATO;* b. 22 June 1954, Bucharest; m. Gabriela Ioan; two d. *Education:* Artillery Mil. School of Active Officers, Sibiu, High Mil. Studies Acad., Bucharest, George C. Marshall Coll. of Strategic Studies and Defence Econs, Germany, Royal Coll. of Defence Studies, UK, NATO Defence Coll., Rome. *Career:* served as Platoon Leader, Battery Commdr and Artillery Bn Chief of Staff 1976–83, Artillery Chief in a Mechanized Regt 1985–86, Artillery Regt Chief of Staff 1986–88, Artillery Regt Commdr 1988–93, Div. Deputy Commdr 1993–94, Army Corps Deputy Commdr 1994–96, Saint George Tactical Detachment Commdr, deployed in Albania as part of ALBA Multinational Force 1997–98, Army Corps Commdr 1999–2000, Deputy Commdr of 2nd Jt Operational Command 2000–01; staff posts have included Chief of Artillery, Directorate of Army Staff 1996–97, Deputy Chief of Strategic Planning and Arms Control Directorate (J5), Gen. Staff 1998–99, Chief of Operations Directorate (J3), Gen. Staff 2001–04, Chief of Land Forces Staff 2004–06, Deputy Chief Gen. Staff 2006–07; Mil. Rep., NATO, Brussels 2007– also to EU; Prof., Nat. Defence Univ.; Hon. Ordine Militare d'Italia 1997, Hon. Citizen Oklahoma City 1998; Mil. Merit Medals (1st, 2nd and 3rd class), Mil. Merit Orders (1st, 2nd and 3rd class), Order of Santa Barbara (USA) 1994, Legion of Merit (USA) 2006. *Publications:* numerous articles on mil. history and affairs. *Address:* NATO HQ, blvd Léopold III, 1110 Brussels, Belgium (office). *Telephone:* (2) 707-41-11 (office). *Fax:* (2) 707-45-79 (office). *E-mail:* natodoc@hq.nato.int (office). *Website:* www.nato.int (office).

IOVV, Vasile, PhD; Moldovan economist and politician; b. 29 Dec. 1942, Corjova, Dubasari dist. *Education:* Technologic Inst. of Kiev, Social Science Acad., Moscow. *Career:* Vice-Pres. then Pres. Balti town exec., fmr inspector, CP of Moldova, First Sec. of Balti Party Cttee then Sec.; fmr Sr Counsellor CP of USSR; fmr Dir Scientific Research and Production, Sugar Industrial Asscn of Moldova; fmr Chief Commercial-Econ. Office, Embassy of Moldova in Moscow; fmr Minister of Transport and Roads, then First Deputy Prime Minister of Moldova 2002–05, 2005–. *Address:* Office of the Council of Ministers, Piaţa Marii Adunări Naţionale 1, 2033 Chişinău, Moldova. *Telephone:* (2) 23-30-92. *E-mail:* info@parlament.md. *Website:* parlament.moldova.md.

IPINGE, Hopelong Uushona, BBA, MBA, MA; Namibian diplomatist; *Ambassador to Brazil;* m.; three c. *Education:* Washington Int. Univ., Pa, Keele Univ., UK. *Career:* Sr Staff Officer, Directorate of Policy and Operations, Ministry of Defence 1990–92; CEO Omusati Regional Counsel 1993–95; mem. Panel of Govt Experts on Small Arms Proliferation 1996–98; Deputy Sec., Ministry of Defence 1995–99; Amb. to China (also accred to S Korea and Viet Nam) 1999–2005, to USA 2005–06, to Brazil 2006–. *Address:* Embassy of Namibia, SHIS QI 09, Conj. 08, Casa 11, Lago Sul, 71625-080 Brasília, DF, Brazil (office). *Telephone:* (61) 3248-6274 (office). *Fax:* (61) 3248-7135 (office). *E-mail:* info@embassyofnamibia.org.br (office). *Website:* www.embassyofnamibia.org.br (office).

IRELAND, S. Leslie, BA, MA; American government official and diplomatist; *Mission Manager for Iran, Office of the Director of National Intelligence; Education:* Franklin and Marshall Coll., Georgetown Univ. *Career:* career intelligence officer and Middle East specialist; has travelled extensively in Middle East; held a variety of positions in analytical, collection, interagency and policy communities; fmr Special Advisor for Iran Collection Issues and fmr Country Dir for Iran and Kuwait, Office of Sec. of Defense; fmr Exec. Asst to Deputy Dir of Cen. Intelligence, fmr Deputy Chief for Arab-Israeli Issues at CIA, Exec. Asst to Dir CIA –2005; Mission Man. for Iran, Office of Dir of Nat. Intelligence 2005–; CIA Intelligence Commendation Medal. *Address:* Office of the Mission Manager for Iran, c/o Office of the Director of National Intelligence, Washington, DC 20511, USA (office). *Telephone:* (202) 201-1111 (office). *Website:* www.dni.gov (office).

IRSAN, Abdul; Indonesian diplomatist; b. 14 Oct. 1939, Sampang, Madura; m.; four c. *Education:* Indonesia Univ. *Career:* joined Dept of Foreign Affairs 1964, positions included Head Bureau of Planning 1985, Dir Asia Pacific 1986–88, Dir-Gen. Protocol, Consular Head of State Protocol 1993–95, Sec.-Gen. 1998–2002; overseas positions in Bangkok, Singapore, Hong Kong, Consul-Gen. LA, USA 1988–89, Deputy Chief Embassy in Australia 1989–91, Amb. to New Zealand 1991–93, to Netherlands 1998–2002, to Japan and Micronesia 2003–06; medals of honour from govts of Thailand, Germany, Netherlands.

Address: c/o Ministry of Foreign Affairs, Jalan Taman Pejambon 6, 10th Floor, Jakarta Pusat, 10110, Indonesia (office). *Website:* www.deplu.go.id (office).

IRTEMÇELIK, Mehmet Ali; Turkish diplomatist; b. 17 March 1950, Istanbul. *Career:* Amb. to Bulgaria 1995; resgnd from Ministry of Foreign Affairs 1999, returned as adviser 2003; fmr Minister of State responsible for Human Rights, for EU Affairs; fmr Deputy in Parl. (Motherland Party); Amb. to Germany 2003–08.
Address: c/o Ministry of Foreign Affairs, Dişişleri Bakanlığı, Dr Sadık Ahmet Cad. 12, 06100 Balgat, Ankara, Turkey.

IRYANI, Abd al-Karim al-, PhD; Yemeni politician and economist; *Secretary-General, General People's Congress Party;* b. 12 Oct. 1934, Eryan; m.; three s. three d. *Education:* Univ. of Georgia, Yale Univ., USA. *Career:* worked in an agricultural project in Yemen 1968–72; Chair. Cen. Planning Org. 1972–76; Minister of Devt 1974–76, of Educ. and Rector San'a Univ. 1976–78; Adviser, Kuwait Fund for Arab Econ. Devt 1978–80; Prime Minister 1980–83; Deputy Prime Minister and Minister of Foreign Affairs 1984–90, 1994–98; Minister of Foreign Affairs 1990–93, of Planning and Devt 1993–94; Prime Minister of Yemen 1998–2001; Sec.-Gen. Gen. People's Congress Party; Chair. Council for the Reconstruction of Earthquake Areas 1983–84.
Address: General People's Congress, San'a, Republic of Yemen (office). *E-mail:* gpc@y.net.ye (office). *Website:* www.gpc.org.ye.

ISA, Tan Sri Rastam Mohammad; Malaysian diplomatist; *Secretary-General, Ministry of Foreign Affairs; Career:* Amb. to Indonesia 2000; Perm. Rep. to UN, New York –2005, also Chair. Arab Group of UN Mems; Chair. Non-Aligned Movt 2003; currently Sec.-Gen. Ministry of Foreign Affairs.
Address: Ministry of Foreign Affairs (Kementerian Luar Negeri), Wisma Putra, 1 Jalan Wisma Putra, Presint 2, 62602 Putrajaya, Malaysia (office). *Telephone:* (3) 88874000 (office). *Fax:* (3) 88891717 (office). *E-mail:* webmaster@kln.gov.my (office). *Website:* www.kln.gov.my (office).

ISAACSON, Walter Seff, MA; American journalist and international organization official; *President and CEO, Aspen Institute;* b. 20 May 1952, New Orleans, La; m. Cathy Wright 1984; one d. *Education:* Harvard Univ., Pembroke Coll., Univ. of Oxford. *Career:* reporter Sunday Times, London 1976–77, States-Item, New Orleans 1977–78; staff writer Time magazine, New York 1978–79, political corresp. 1979–81, Assoc. Ed. 1981–84, Sr Ed. 1985–91, Asst Man. Ed. 1991–93, Man. Ed. 1995–2000; Editorial Dir Time Inc. 2000–01; Chair. and CEO CNN Newsgroup 2001–03; Ed. New Media Time, Inc. 1993–96; Pres. and CEO Aspen Inst. 2003–; mem. Council on Foreign Relations, Century Asscn; Overseas Press Club Award, New York 1981, 1984, 1987, Harry Truman Book Prize 1987. *Publications:* Pro and Con 1983, Kissinger: A Biography 1992, The Wise Men (jtly) 1986, Benjamin Franklin: An American Life 2003, Einstein: His Life and Universe (Quill Award for Biography 2007) 2007.
Address: The Aspen Institute, Suite 700, One Dupont Circle, NW, Washington, DC 20036-1133, USA (office). *Telephone:* (202) 736-5800 (office). *Fax:* (202) 467-0790 (office). *Website:* www.aspeninstitute.org (office).

ISAKOV, Gen. Ismail Isakovich; Kyrgyzstani army officer and government official; *Minister of Defence;* b. 1950, Spou-Korgon, Alai Dist., Osh Duban. *Education:* Tashkent Higher Mil. Acad., Frunze Mil. Acad., Moscow, Gen. Staff Mil. Acad., Moscow. *Career:* Platoon Commdr, then Co. Commdr in southern group of troops, Hungary 1973–78; Deputy Bn Commdr, then Bn Commdr in Ukraine 1978–81; Regimental Chief of Staff, Regimental Commdr, Div. Chief of Staff, Combat Training Deputy Chief of the State Cttee for Defence 1984–94; Chief of the Main Staff 1994–95; First Deputy Minister of Defence 1994–99; Deputy in Legis. Ass. of the Jogorku Kenesh (Parl.) from Alai Dist 2000–05, Chair. Cttee on Nat. Security Issues 2000–05, Dir of Coordinating Cttee For the Resignation of Askar Akaev and For Reforms for the People (political movt) 2003–04; Acting Minister of Defence March–Sept. 2005, Minister of Defence 2005–06 (resgnd), reappointed 2007–; rank of Gen. (two stars); Medal of 3 Degrees For Irreproachable Service, Medal for Combat Merits, Medal For Strengthening of Mil. Cooperation.
Address: Ministry of Defence, 720001 Bishkek, Logvinenko 26, Kyrgyzstan (office). *Telephone:* (312) 66-38-28 (office). *Fax:* (312) 66-16-02 (office). *E-mail:* ud@bishkek.gov.kg (office). *Website:* www.mil.kg (office).

ISAKOV, Army-Gen. Vladimir Ilyich; Russian military officer; *Chief of Logistics and Deputy Minister of Defence;* b. 21 July 1950, Voskresenskoye, Kaluga region. *Education:* Moscow Mil. School of Civil Defence, Mil. Acad. of Home Front Transport, Mil. Acad. of Gen. Staff. *Career:* Platoon Commdr of Civil Defence Forces; served in Group of Soviet Armed Forces in Germany; Deputy Regt Commdr, then Deputy Army Commdr of Home Front.; Deputy Commdr Div. of Home Front, Siberian Mil. Command 1982–84, 40th Army in Afghanistan 1984–86; Deputy Army Commdr, then Head of Home Front, Kiev Mil. Command 1988–89; Head of Gen. Staff of Home Front, W Group of Armed Forces 1989–94; Head of Chair. Mil. Acad. of Gen. Staff 1994; Head of Gen. Staff Armed Forces of Russian Fed. 1996, First Deputy Head of Home Front 1996–97, Head 1997; Chief of Logistics and Deputy Minister of Defence 1997–.
Address: Ministry of Defence, ul. Myasnitskaya 37, 105175 Moscow, Russia (office). *Telephone:* (495) 293-38-54 (office). *Fax:* (495) 296-84-36 (office). *Website:* www.mil.ru (office).

ISARD, Walter, PhD, FAAS, FRSA; American economist and academic; *Professor Emeritus of Economics, Cornell University;* b. 19 April 1919, Philadelphia, Pa; m. Caroline Berliner 1943; four s. four d. *Education:* Temple, Harvard and Chicago Univs. *Career:* Instructor, Wesleyan Univ. 1945, MIT 1947; Visiting Lecturer, Tufts Coll. 1947; Assoc. Prof. of Econs, Assoc. Dir of Teaching, Inst. of Econs, American Univ. 1948–49; Research Fellow and Lecturer, Harvard Univ. 1949–53; Assoc. Prof. of Regional Econs, Dir Urban and Regional Studies, MIT 1953–56; Prof. of Econs, Chair. Dept of Regional Science, Univ. of Pa 1956–75, Head Dept of Peace Science 1975–77; Visiting Prof. of Regional Science, Yale Univ. 1960–61, of Landscape Architecture and Regional Science, Harvard Univ. 1966–71; Chair. Graduate Group in Peace Research and Peace Science Unit 1970–78; Sr Research Assoc., Visiting Prof. of Econs, Regional Science and Policy Planning, Cornell Univ. 1971–79, Prof. 1979, now Prof. Emer.; Distinguished Visiting Prof., Inst. für Regionalwissenschaft, Karlsruhe 1972; Consultant, Tenn. Valley Authority 1951–52, Resources for the Future Inc. 1954–58, Ford Foundation 1955–56; Founder Regional Science Asscn 1954, Ed., Co-Ed. Papers 1954–58, Pres. 1959, Hon. Chair. 1960–; Ford Foundation Fellow in Econs and Business Admin 1959–60; Ed., Co-Ed., Journal of Regional Science 1960–; Chair. OEEC Econ. Productivity Agency Conf. on Regional Econs and Planning, Bellagio, Italy 1960; Co-Chair. AIXPS Forum; Founder Peace Science Soc. (Int.) 1963, Co-Ed. Papers 1963–, Exec. Sec. 1964–, Pres. 1968; Pres. World Acad. of Art and Science 1977–81; Dir ECAAR 1989–, (Trustee 2001); Assoc. Ed. Quarterly Journal of Econs 1968–71, Peace Economics, Peace Science and Public Policy 1994–; mem. Editorial Bd Journal of Conflict Resolution 1972–; mem. NAS; Hon. Prof. (Peking Univ., Northwest Univ.) 1993; Dr hc (Poznan Acad. of Econ.) 1976, (Erasmus Univ.) 1978, (Karlsruhe) 1979, (Umeå) 1980, (Univ. of Ill.) 1982, (Binghamton Univ.) 1997, (Geneva) 2002; August Lösch Ring 1988. *Publications:* Atomic Power: An Economic and Social Analysis 1952, Location Factors in the Petrochemical Industry 1955, Location and Space Economy 1956, Municipal Costs and Revenues Resulting from Community Growth 1957, Industrial Complex Analysis and Regional Development 1959, Methods of Regional Analysis 1960, Regional Economic Development 1961, General Theory: Social, Political, Economic and Regional 1969, Regional Input-Output Study 1971, Ecologic-Economic Analysis for Regional Planning 1971, Spatial Dynamics and Optimal Space-Time Development 1979, Conflict Analysis and Practical Conflict Management Procedures 1982, Arms Races, Arms Control and Conflict Analysis 1988, Practical Methods of Regional Science and Empirical Applications 1990, Location Analysis and General Theory 1990, Economics of Arms Production and the Peace Process 1992, The Science of Peace 1992, Commonalities in Art, Science and Religion 1997, Methods of Interregional and Regional Analysis 1998.
Address: Department of Economics, 476 Uris Hall, Cornell University, Ithaca, NY 14853 (office); 3218 Garrett Road, Drexel Hill, PA 19026, USA (home). *Telephone:* (607) 255-3306 (office); (610) 259-6080 (home). *Fax:* (607) 255-2818 (office). *E-mail:* will@cornell.edu (office). *Website:* www.arts.cornell.edu/econ/mainwindow.shtml (office).

ISCHINGER, Wolfgang Friedrich; German diplomatist; *Ambassador to UK;* b. 6 April 1946, Beuren, Stuttgart; m. Jutta Falke-Ischinger; three c. *Education:* Univs of Bonn and Geneva, Fletcher School of Law and Diplomacy, Harvard Univ. Law School, USA. *Career:* mem. cabinet staff of UN Sec.-Gen., New York 1973–75; joined Foreign Service 1975, mem. Policy Planning Staff 1977–79; posted to Washington, DC 1979–82; mem. cabinet staff, Minister of Foreign Affairs, Bonn 1982–90, Pvt. Sec. to Minister 1985–87, Dir Cabinet and Parl. Affairs 1987–90; Minister-Counsellor, Head Political Section, German Embassy, Paris 1990–93; Dir Policy Planning Staff, Bonn 1993–95, Dir-Gen. for Political Affairs 1995–98, State Sec. 1998–2001, 2000–01; Amb. to USA 2001–06, to UK 2006–; apptd to represent EU in negotiations on status of Kosovo 2007; mem. High Level German-Russian Strategy Group; mem. Bd of Overseers, Fletcher School of Law and Diplomacy, Alfred Herrhausen Gesellschaft, Frankfurt, Council on Public Policy, AFS Germany (American Field Service), Bd East-West Inst., New York; fmr Chair. Ambs' Advisory Bd, Exec. Council on Diplomacy, Washington, DC. *Publications:* numerous articles on foreign policy, security and arms control policy, European policy issues.

Address: German Embassy, 23 Belgrave Square, London, SW1X 8PZ, England (office). *Telephone:* (20) 7824-1300 (office). *Fax:* (20) 7824-1435 (office). *E-mail:* mail@german-embassy.org.uk (office). *Website:* www.german-embassy.org.uk (office).

ISHIBA, Shigeru; Japanese politician; b. 4 Feb. 1957. *Education:* Keio Univ. *Career:* began career with Bank of Mitsui 1979; mem. Liberal Democratic Party; first elected to House of Reps 1986, Parl. Vice-Minister for Agric., Forestry and Fisheries 1992, Chair. Special Cttee on Deregulation 1996, Cttee on Transport 1998; Sr State Sec. for Minister of Agric., Forestry and Fisheries 2000; Sr State Sec. of Defence 2000–01, Sr Vice-Minister for Defence 2001–02, Minister of Defence 2002–04, 2007–08.
Address: Liberal-Democratic Party, 1-11-23, Nagata-cho, Chiyoda-ku, Tokyo 100-8910, Japan (office). *Telephone:* (3) 3581-6211 (office). *E-mail:* koho@ldp.jimin.or.jp (office). *Website:* www.jimin.jp (office).

ISHMAEL, Mohammed Ali Odeen; Guyanese diplomatist; *Ambassador to Venezuela;* m.; two c. *Career:* fmr teacher; served in Ministry of Foreign Affairs 1970s; Amb. to USA 1993–2003, to Venezuela 2003–; Perm. Rep. to OAS 1993–2003, Vice-Chair. Perm. Council 1993, Chair. 1994, 2003; mem. Del. of Guyana to UN Gen. Ass. 1993–; Chief Negotiator Summit of the Americas 1994, 1998; Head Del. of Guyana to CARICOM 1997–, to Org. of Islamic Conf., Tehran 1999; mem. Cen. Cttee Progressive Youth Org., People's Progressive Party; Cacique Crown of Honour 1997; Gandhi Centenary Medal, Univ. of Guyana 1974, King Legacy Award for Int. Service 2002. *Publications include:* Problems of Transition of Education in the Third World, Towards Education Reform in Guyana, Amerindian Legends of Guyana, The Trail of Diplomacy; numerous articles on educ., Guyanese history and int. political issues.
Address: Embassy of Guyana, Quinta 'Roraima', Avenida El Paseo, Prados del Este, Apdo 51054, Caracas 1050, Venezuela (office). *Telephone:* (212) 977-1158 (office). *Fax:* (212) 976-3765 (office). *E-mail:* embaguy@caracas.org.ve (office).

ISLAM, A. B. Mirza Azizul, BA, MA, PhD; Bangladeshi economist and politician; *Adviser (Minister) in charge of Ministry of Finance and Ministry of Planning;* b. 23 Feb. 1941, Sujanagar, Pabna; m. Nilufar Aziz; one s. *Education:* Dhaka Univ., Williams Coll. and Boston Univ., USA. *Career:* Lecturer, Dhaka Univ. 1962–64; joined Civil Service of Pakistan 1964; worked in different capacities in admin. service 1967–82; Econ. Affairs/Sr Econ. Affairs Officer, UN-ESCAP, Bangkok 1982–86, Dir Research and Policy Analysis Div. 1993–2001; Chief of Developing Econs Section, UN Centre on Transnational Corpns, New York 1987–92; consultant to UNCTAD, World Bank and Centre for Policy Dialogue 2002–03; Chair. Bangladesh Securities & Exchange Comm. 2003–06; Chair. Sonali Bank April–Nov. 2006; Hon. Adviser to Caretaker Govt, in charge of Ministry of Finance, of Planning, of Commerce and of Posts and Telecommunications 2007–08, in charge of Ministry of Finance, Ministry of Planning 2008–.
Address: Ministry of Finance, Bangladesh Secretariat, Building 7, 3rd Floor, Dhaka 1000, Bangladesh (office). *Telephone:* (2) 7164444 (office). *Fax:* (2) 7166200 (office). *E-mail:* hfmoff@bdmail.net (office). *Website:* www.mof.gov.bd (office).

ISLAMI, Kastriot, MA, DSc; Albanian politician and physicist; b. 18 Feb. 1952, Tirana; m.; one s. one d. *Education:* Univ. of Tirana, Univ. of Paris XI, Orsay, France. *Career:* Vice-Dean, Faculty of Natural Sciences, Univ. of Tirana 1987–91; Minister of Educ. 1991; Deputy Speaker (Chair.) of Albanian Parl. 1991–92, Head, Parl. Comm. for Preparation of Draft of Albanian Constitution 1991–96; Minister of State to Prime Minister of Albania 1997–98; Deputy Prime Minister 1998–2002; Minister of Finance 2002–03; Minister of Foreign Affairs 2003–05; Deputy Kuvendi Popullor (People's Ass.) 2006–; mem. Parl. Ass., Council of Europe, mem. Cttee on Legal Affairs and Human Rights, Cttee on the Honouring of Obligations and Commitments by Member States of the Council of Europe (Monitoring Cttee) 2006–. *Publications include:* The Basis of Quantum Mechanics Vol. I 1989, Vol. II 1990; publs in nat. and int. media.
Address: Kuvendi Popullor (People's Assembly), Bulevardi Deshmoret e Kombit nr. 4, Tirana (office); Rruga: Dora D'Istria, Pallati R 8-Katesh, Tirana, Albania (home). *Telephone:* (5) 4237413 (office); (5) 4240669 (home). *Fax:* (5) 4227949 (office). *E-mail:* marlind@parlament.al (office); dshtypi@abissnet.com.al; kislami@icc-al.org. *Website:* www.parlament.al (home).

ISLAMOV, Bakhtiyor Anvarovich, DEcon; Uzbekistan diplomatist; *Ambassador to Russia;* b. 6 Jan. 1954, Tashkent; m. Islamova Shahida; one s. two d. *Education:* Moscow State Inst. of Int. Affairs. *Career:* Advisor to Perm. Rep. of UN in Uzbekistan 1994–96; Prof., Hitotsubashi Univ., Tokyo, Japan 1996–2001; Vice-Rector, Banking and Finance Acad. (BFA) 2001–02; Adviser to Minister of Foreign Affairs 2002–03; Amb. to Russia 2003–. *Publications:* Central Asia-Center-Republic Relations 1991, Central

Asian Independent States: Ten Years after How to Avoid Traps of Development, Transformation and Globalization 2001.
Address: Embassy of Uzbekistan, Pogorelskii per. 12, 109017 Moscow, Russia (office). *Telephone:* (095) 230-00-76 (office). *Fax:* (095) 238-89-18 (office). *E-mail:* info@uzembassy.ru (office). *Website:* (office).

ISMAIL, Abdullahi Sheikh; Somali politician. *Career:* Minister of Foreign Affairs 2004–07, of Constitutional and Federal Affairs 2007–; fmr Chair. Southern Somali Nat. Movt (SSNM).
Address: Ministry of Constitutional and Federal Affairs, Mogadishu, Somalia (office).

ISMAIL, Amat; Chinese politician; *Vice-Chairman, 10th Standing Committee, National People's Congress;* b. 1935, Qira, Xinjiang Uygur Autonomous Region. *Education:* CCP Cen. Cttee Cen. Party School (Xinjiang Class). *Career:* joined CCP 1953; active in People's Commune Movt –1960; Magistrate, Qira Co. (Dist) People's Court 1954–62; Deputy Sec. CCP Cttee, a country admin., Xinjiang 1960; Deputy Head, Publicity Dept, CCP Autonomous Prefectural Cttee, Hotan, Xinjiang Uygur Autonomous Region 1963–65; Deputy Dir Cultural, Educ. and Political Work Dept, CCP Xinjiang Uygur Autonomous Regional Cttee 1966–67, mem. Standing Cttee, CCP Revolutionary Cttee and Head, Group for Regional Cultural, Educational and Health Work 1969–72; Sec. and Head, Org. Dept, CCP Xinjiang Uygur Autonomous Regional Cttee 1972–85; Vice-Chair. CCP Revolutionary Cttee, Xinjiang Uygur Autonomous Region 1972–85; Chair. Xinjiang Uygur Autonomous Regional People's Govt 1972–85; Sec. CCP Cttee, Xinjiang 1974–79; Vice-Chair. Aubnavan Regional Revolutionary Cttee, Xinjiang 1974–79; Political Commissar, Xinjiang Mil. Region 1976–85; First Deputy Dir Party School, Xinjiang 1977–85; Chair. People's Govt, Xinjiang 1979–85; Minister of State Nationalities Affairs Comm. 1985–98; Minister in Charge of State Nat. Ethnic Affairs Comm. 1993–98; State Councillor 1993–2003; Dir China Comm. of Int. Decade for Disaster Reduction 1998–2000, China Comm. for Int. Disaster Reduction 2000–; mem. 10th CCP Cen. Cttee 1972–77, 11th CCP Cen. Cttee 1977–82, 12th CCP Cen. Cttee 1982–87, 13th CCP Cen. Cttee 1987–92, 14th CCP Cen. Cttee 1992–97, 15th CCP Cen. Cttee 1997–2002, 16th CCP Cen. Cttee 2002–; Vice-Chair. 7th CPPCC Nat. Cttee 1988–93; mem. Standing Cttee of NPC 1978–83, Vice-Chair. 10th Standing Cttee of NPC 2003–; Pres. China-Turkey Friendship Asscn; Hon. Pres. Chinese Asscn of Ethnic Minorities for External Exchanges.
Address: The State Council, Zhongnanhai, Beijing, People's Republic of China (office).

ISMAIL, Mustafa Osman, PhD; Sudanese politician; b. 1955, Dongola. *Career:* Minister of External Relations 1998–2005; currently Presidential Adviser; mem. Nat. Congress Party.
Address: c/o National Congress Party, Khartoum, Sudan (office).

ISMAIL, Tan Sri Razali, BA; Malaysian diplomatist and foundation executive; *Chairman, Force of Nature Aid Foundation;* b. 1939, Kedah; m.; three c. *Career:* joined Ministry of Foreign Affairs 1962; served in Delhi 1963–64; Asst High. Commr in Madras 1964–66; Second Sec. Paris 1966–68; Prin. Asst Sec. Ministry of Foreign Affairs 1968–70; Counsellor, London 1970–72; various posts at Ministry of Foreign Affairs and Chargé d'affaires, Vientiane 1972–78; Amb. to Poland 1978–82; High Commr in India 1982; Deputy Sec.-Gen. Ministry of Foreign Affairs 1985–88; Perm. Rep. to UN 1988, Pres. UN Gen. Ass. 1996–97; apptd Special Adviser to Prime Minister 1998; UN Special Envoy to Myanmar 1998–2006; currently Chair. Force of Nature Aid Foundation.
Address: Force of Nature Aid Foundation, 23, Lorong Tanjung 5/4D, 46000 Petaling Jaya, Selangor Darul Ehsan, Malaysia (office). *Telephone:* (3) 79600366 (office). *Fax:* (3) 79601366 (office). *E-mail:* contact@forceofnature.org (office). *Website:* www.forceofnature.org (office).

ISSING, Otmar, PhDr; German economist and central banker; *President, Centre for Financial Studies;* b. 27 March 1936, Würzburg. *Education:* Humanistisches Gymnasium, Würzburg, Univ. of Würzburg. *Career:* Prof. of Econs, Univ. of Erlangen-Nuremberg 1967–73, Univ. of Würzburg 1973–90; mem. Council of Experts for Assessment of Overall Econ. Trends at Fed. Ministry of Econs 1988–90; mem. Directorate Deutsche Bundesbank 1990–98; mem. Exec. Bd European Cen. Bank 1998–2006; Pres. Centre for Financial Studies 2006–; mem. Acad. of Sciences and Literature, Mainz, Acad. Europaea, Salzburg; Co-founder and Co-ed. of the scientific journal WiSt; mem. Verein für Socialpolitik, American Econ. Asscn, List Gesellschaft, Arbeitskreis Europäische Integration, European Acad. of Arts and Sciences, Acad. of Sciences and Literature, Walter Eucken Inst.; Hon. Prof., Univ. of Würzburg 1991–, Univ. of Frankfurt 2007–; Grosses Verdienstkreuz des Verdienstordens der Bundesrepublik Deutschland; Dr hc (Bayreuth) 1996, (Konstanz) 1998, (Frankfurt am Main) 1999; Int. Prize, Friedrich-August-Hayek Foundation 2003. *Publications:* Introduction to

Monetary Policy (sixth edn) 1996, Introduction to Monetary Theory 1998 (14th edn 2007), Monetary Policy in the Euro Arena (co-author) 2001, Imperfect Knowledge and Monetary Policy (co-author) 2005, The Euro 2008.
Address: Georg-Sittig-Str. 8, 97074 Würzburg, Germany (office).

ISSOIBEKA, Pacifique; Republic of the Congo politician; *Minister of Finance, the Economy and the Budget; Career:* Vice-Gov. Banque des États de l'Afrique Centrale (BEAC) 2003–; Minister of Finance, the Economy and the Budget 2005–; Alt. Gov. of Repub. of the Congo to World Bank 2005–.
Address: Ministry of Finance, the Economy and the Budget, ave de l'Indépendance, croisement ave Foch, BP 2083, Brazzaville, Republic of the Congo (office). *Telephone:* 81-45-24 (office). *Fax:* 81-43-69 (office). *Website:* www.mefb-cg.or (office).

ISSOUFOU, Mahamadou; Niger mining engineer and politician; *Secretary-General, Parti nigérien pour la démocratie et le socialisme—Tarayya (PNDS);* b. 1952, Illéla. *Career:* Nat. Dir of Mines 1980–85; Sec.-Gen. Mining Co. of Niger (SOMAIR) 1985; Sec.-Gen. Parti nigérien pour la démocratie et le socialisme—Tarayya (PNDS); Prime Minister of Niger 1993–94 (resgnd); Chief Economist 1999; presidential cand. 1993, 1996, 1999, 2004.
Address: Parti nigérien pour la démocratie et le socialisme—Tarayya (PNDS), pl. Toumo, Niamey, Niger. *Telephone:* 20-74-48-78.

ITZIK, Dalia, BA; Israeli politician and teacher; *Speaker of the Knesset;* b. 1952, Jerusalem; m.; three c. *Education:* Hebrew Univ. of Jerusalem, Interdisciplinary Centre, Herzliya, Efrata Teachers Seminary, Jerusalem. *Career:* fmr Deputy Mayor of Jerusalem in charge of Educ.; fmr mem. Bd of Govs of Israel Broadcasting Authority, Bd of Jerusalem Theatre, Gerard Behar Centre; mem. Knesset 1992–; served in Finance Cttee 1992–96, Educ. and Culture Cttee 1992–99 (Chair. 1995–96), Cttee on Status of Women 1992–99; Chair. Special Cttee for Research and Scientific Technological Devt 1997–99; Minister of the Environment 1999–2001, of Industry and Trade 2001–02, of Communications 2005; Speaker of the Knesset 2006–, Acting Pres. (while Israeli prosecutors decide whether to bring charges of rape and sexual assaults against Pres. Mishe Katsav) Jan. 2007–; fmr mem. Labour Party, mem. Kadima party 2006–; fmr Chair. Legis. Panel, Labour Party, fmr mem. Cen. Cttee, fmr Head of Knesset Group.
Address: The Knesset, HaKiryah, Jerusalem, 91950, Israel (office). *Telephone:* 2-6753333 (office). *E-mail:* IzikD@knesset.gov.il (office). *Website:* www.knesset.gov.il (office).

IVANENKO, Sergei Victorovich, CandEcon; Russian politician and economist; *Deputy Chairman, Yabloko Russian Democratic Party (Rossiisskaya demokraticheskaya partiya 'Yabloko');* b. 12 Jan. 1959, Zestafoni, Georgia. *Education:* Lomonosov Moscow State Univ. *Career:* researcher and Asst Prof., Moscow State Univ. 1985–90; Chief Expert State Comm. on Econ. Reform RSFSR Council of Ministers 1994–96; Researcher, Cen. of Econ. and Political Studies 1991–92; mem. State Duma 1993–, Chair. Cttee on Property, Privatisation and Econs 1993–95, mem. Cttee on Ecology 1995–99; currently Deputy Chair. Yabloko Russian Democratic Party (Rossiisskaya demokraticheskaya partiya 'Yabloko'), Chair. Moscow Yabloko; Vice-Pres. Russian Chess Fed. 2003–.
Address: Yabloko Russian Democratic Party (Rossiisskaya demokraticheskaya partiya 'Yabloko'), 119034 Moscow, per. M. Levshinskii 7/3, Russia (office). *Telephone:* (495) 201-43-79 (office). *Fax:* (495) 292-34-50 (office). *E-mail:* admin@yabloko.ru (office). *Website:* www.yabloko.ru (office).

IVANOV, Igor Sergeyevich; Russian diplomatist and politician; b. 23 Sept. 1945, Moscow; m.; one d. *Education:* Moscow Pedagogical Inst. of Foreign Languages. *Career:* Jr researcher Inst. of World Econs and Int. Relations, USSR Acad. of Sciences 1969–73; diplomatic service 1973–; Second, then First Sec., Counsellor, Counsellor-Envoy USSR Embassy, Spain 1973–83; expert First European Dept, Ministry of Foreign Affairs 1983–84; Counsellor of Minister 1984–85; Asst Minister 1985–86; Deputy Chief, then Chief of Dept 1987–92; Chief Gen. Sec., mem. of Bd 1989–91; Russian Amb. to Spain 1991–93; First Deputy Minister of Foreign Affairs 1994–98, Minister of Foreign Affairs 1998–2004; Perm. mem. Security Council of Russia 1998–, Sec. 2004–07; Lecturer, Moscow State Inst. of Int. Relations 2007–; Co-Chair. EU-Russia Co-operation Council 1998–; Orders For Services to the Fatherland (2nd, 3rd and 4th Degrees); Order of Honour; Hon. Dr of Historical Science. *Publications:* New Russian Diplomacy 2001, External Russian Policy in the Epoch of Globalization 2002, Global Security in the Epoch of Globalization: Russia in Global Policy 2003, Russia in the Contemporary World: Responses for the Challenges of the 21st Century 2004; numerous papers and articles.

Address: Moscow State Institute of International Relations, 119454 Moscow, pr. Vernadskogo, 76, Russia (office). *Telephone:* (495) 434-00-89 (office). *Fax:* (495) 434-90-66 (office). *E-mail:* inf@mgimo.ru (office). *Website:* www.mgimo.ru (office).

IVANOV, Ivan Dmitriyevich, DEcon; Russian diplomatist, politician and economist; *Deputy Director, Institute of Europe, Russian Academy of Sciences;* b. 1934, Moscow; m.; two c. *Education:* Moscow Inst. of Foreign Trade. *Career:* Head of Div., Inst. of USA and Canada, USSR (now Russian) Acad. of Sciences 1971–76, Deputy Dir, Prof., Inst. of World Econs and Int. Relations 1977–86, Deputy Dir Inst. of Europe, Russian Acad. of Sciences 2001–; Deputy Chair. State Cttee for Foreign Econ. Relations, USSR Ministry of Foreign Affairs, also Chair. USSR State Comm. on Foreign Econ. Orgs 1986–91; Deputy Dir Inst. of Foreign Econ. Research 1991–94; Russian Trade Rep. to Belgium 1994–96, Deputy Perm. Rep. to EU, Brussels 1996–99; Deputy Minister of Foreign Affairs 1999–2001.
Address: Institute of Europe, Russian Academy of Sciences, 11-3B, Mokhovaya Street, 125993 Moscow, Russia (office). *Telephone:* (495) 203-41-87 (home). *Fax:* (495) 609-92-98 (office). *E-mail:* europe@ieras.ru (office). *Website:* www.ieras.ru (office).

IVANOV, Lubomir, MSc; Bulgarian diplomatist; *Permanent Representative, NATO;* b. 21 Oct. 1956, Sofia; m.; one c. *Education:* Sofia English Language School, Moscow State Univ. *Career:* joined Ministry of Foreign Affairs 1983, Attaché, Asian Dept 1983–86, Third, later Second Sec. 1990–92, First Sec. and Counsellor Int. Orgs Dept 1993–95, Deputy Dir NATO, WEU and Security Issues Directorate and Head, NATO and Euroatlantic Co-operation Dept 1998–2001, Dir Int. Security Directorate 2001–02, Deputy Minister of Foreign Affairs 2002–04; Third Sec. Embassy in Beijing, China 1986–90; Foreign Policy Advisor to Deputy Minister of Defence 1992–93; Deputy to Amb. to Belgium and Luxembourg and Deputy Head Mission to NATO and WEU, Brussels 1995–98; Perm. Rep. to NATO 2004–.
Address: Delegation of Bulgaria, NATO Headquarters, Bld Léopold III, Brussels 1110, Belgium (office). *Telephone:* (2) 707-41-11 (office). *Fax:* (2) 707-45-79 (office). *E-mail:* natodoc@hq.nato.int (office). *Website:* www.nato.int (office).

IVANOV, Col Viktor Petrovich; Russian administrator; *Adviser to the President;* b. 12 May 1950, Novgorod; m.; one s. one d. *Education:* Leningrad Bonch-Bruyevich Electrical Inst. of Communications. *Career:* engineer, Scientific-Production co. Vektor 1971–77; employee in nat. security orgs rising to Head of Div., Dept of Fed. Service of Security of St Petersburg and Leningrad region 1977–94, Head of Dept 1998, Deputy Dir, concurrently Head of Dept of Econ. Security 1999–2000; Head of Admin, Office of Mayor of St Petersburg 1994–98; Deputy Head of Admin, Office of the Pres. 2000–04; Adviser to the Pres. 2004–; participated in mil. operations in Afghanistan 1987–94; Medal for Mil. Service.
Address: Administration of President of Russian Federation, Staraya pl. 4, 103132 Moscow, Russia (office). *Telephone:* (495) 206-34-17 (office).

IVANOVSKII, Vladimir Evgenyevich; Russian diplomatist; *Ambassador to Turkey;* b. 1948; m.; one s. *Education:* Moscow State Inst. of Int. Relations. *Career:* joined Foreign Service 1977, served in Embassy in Yugoslavia 1979–84, 1986–91, Consul-Gen. in Istanbul 1997–98, Amb. to Macedonia 2000–02, to Yugoslavia 2002–04, Amb.-at-Large 2004–07, Amb. to Turkey 2007–.
Address: Embassy of Russia, Karyağdı sok. 5, 06692, Çankaya, Ankara, Turkey (office). *E-mail:* rus-ankara@yandex.ru (office). *Website:* www.turkey.mid.ru (office).

IVANYAN, Eduard Aleksandrovich, DHist; Russian journalist and political scientist; *Editor-in-Chief, USA and Canada: Economics, Politics and Culture, Institute for USA and Canadian Studies, Russian Academy of Sciences;* b. 14 June 1931, Tbilisi, Georgia; m.; two d. *Education:* Moscow State Inst. of Int. Relations. *Career:* mem. staff, Ministry of Culture 1955–60, UN Secr., Geneva and New York 1961–71; Head of Sector, Prof., Inst. for USA and Canadian Studies, USSR (now Russian) Acad. of Sciences 1971–, Ed.-in-Chief USA and Canada: Economics, Politics and Culture (monthly journal) 1998–; Prof., State Univ. for Humanitarian Sciences 2000–; Order of the Friendship of Nations; Distinguished Scholar of the Russian Fed. 1999. *Publications:* more than 100 scientific publs, including 25 books on the history of USA, presidential power in USA, Russian (Soviet)-American relations, Russian-American cultural relations, including 'Istoriya SShA.' Uchebnoye posobiye. 2 e izdaniye, pererabotannoye (The History of the USA: A Study Aid, 2nd edn, revised) 2006, U istokov sovetsko-amerikanskikh otnoshenii, fevral 1917 g.-yanvar 1924 g. (Among the Sources of Soviet-American Relations, February 1917 to January 1924) 2006, Reader on US History (ed.) 2005, Inaugural Speeches of US Presidents (ed.) 2001), John F. Kennedy's 'Profiles in Courage'

(trans. and ed.) 2005, David Rockefeller's 'Memoirs' (ed. of Russian trans.) 2003, When Muses Speak – History of Russian-American Cultural Relations 2007.
Address: USA–Canada Journal, Khlebny per. 2/3, 123995 Moscow, Russia (office). *Telephone:* (495) 202-14-77 (office). *Fax:* (495) 200-12-07 (office). *E-mail:* edivanian@yahoo.com (office). *Website:* www.iskran.ru (office).

IVASHENTSOV, Gleb A.; Russian diplomatist; *Ambassador to South Korea;* b. 7 June 1945, St Petersburg; m.; one d. *Education:* Moscow State Inst. of Int. Relations. *Career:* served at Ministry of Foreign Affairs and USSR Acad. of Sciences 1967–75; First Sec. USSR Embassy in India 1975–81, Consul Gen., Mumbai 1991–95, Amb. of Russia to Myanmar 1997–2001, to Repub. of Korea 2005–; Counsellor, Head of Section, S Asia Dept, USSR Ministry of Foreign Affairs 1981–83, Head of Section 1985–91, First Deputy Dir Third Asia Dept, Russian Ministry of Foreign Affairs 1995–97, Dir-Gen. Third, Second Asia Dept 2001–05; Order of Friendship 2003.
Address: Embassy of Russia, 34–16 Jeong-dong, Jung-gu, Seoul 100–120, Republic of Korea (office). *Telephone:* (2) 318-2116 (office). *Fax:* (2) 754-0417 (office). *E-mail:* rusemb@uriel.net (office). *Website:* www.russian -embassy.org (office).

IVASHOV, Col-Gen. Leonid Grigoryevich, CandHistSc; Russian business executive and security officer; b. 1943, m. *Education:* Tashkent Commdr School, M. Frunze Mil. Acad. *Career:* army service 1964, various positions 1964–76; with cen. staff, Ministry of Defence 1976–, Head Admin. Dept 1987–92; Sec. Council of Defence Ministers, CIS Countries 1992–96; Head of Dept, Int. Mil. Co-operation 1996–2001, Head of Staff, Co-ordination of Mil. Co-operation, CIS Countries 1999–2001; Adviser to Minister of Defence 2001–03; mem. Leadership, Great Russia–Eurasian Union electoral bloc, State Duma elections 2003; Chair. Soyuz russkogo naroda (Russian People's Union) 2006–; Vice-Pres. Acad. of Geopolitics 2002–; Order Red Star; six medals.
Address: Ministry of Defence, ul. Myasnitskaya 37, 105175 Moscow, Russia (office). *Telephone:* (495) 293-38-54 (office). *Fax:* (495) 296-84-36 (office). *Website:* www.mil.ru (office); www.ivashov.ru.

IZRAEL, Yury Antonievich, DPhys-MathSc; Russian geophysicist, ecologist and meteorologist; *Director, Institute of Global Climate and Ecology;* b. 15 May 1930, Tashkent; m. Elena Sidorova 1958; one s. one d. *Education:* Tashkent State Univ. *Career:* engineer, Research Assoc., Geophysics Inst. of USSR Acad. of Sciences 1953–63; Deputy Dir, Dir of Inst. of Applied Geophysics 1963–70; First Deputy Head of Main Admin. of Hydrometeorological Service of USSR 1970–74, Head 1974–78; Corresp. mem. USSR (now Russian) Acad. of Sciences 1974, mem. 1994, Acad.-Sec., Dept of Oceanography, Atmospheric Physics and Geography 1996–2002; mem. Russian Acad. of Ecology 1994–, Pres. 2000–; Chair. USSR State Cttee for Hydrometeorology and Environmental Control 1978–88; Chair. USSR State Cttee for Hydrometeorology 1988–91, Dir Research Inst. of Global Climate and Ecology 1990–; Deputy to Supreme Soviet 1979–89; Sec. and First Vice-Pres. World Meteorological Org. 1975–87; Vice-Chair. Inter-governmental Panel on Climate Change 1992–; mem. Int. Acad. of Astronautics 1990; Hon. mem. Int. Radiological Union 1999; State Prize in the field of Environment 1981, Gold Medal of USSR Acad. of Sciences in the field of Ecology 1983, Fedorov's Environmental Prizes 1984, 1991, 1997, Gold Medal (per Chernobyl) of Int. Centre 'Ettore Majorana' (Italy) 1990, Gold Medal of Soviet State Exhbn 1991, UN-UNEP Sasakawa Environmental Prize 1992, Gold Medal and Prize of Int. Meteorological Org. 1992, Renowned Scientist of the Russian Fed. 1996, mem. of team sharing Nobel Peace Prize with Al Gore 2007; seven state orders. *Publications:* Peaceful Nuclear Explosions and Environment 1974, Ecology and Control of Environment 1979, Global Climatic Catastrophes 1986, Anthropogenic Climate Change 1987, Anthropogenic Ecology of the Ocean 1989, Chernobyl: Radioactive Contamination of the Environment 1990, Earth's Ozone Shield and its Changes (co-author) 1992, Radioactive Fallout after Nuclear Explosions and Accidents 1996; and numerous other scientific books and articles.
Address: Institute of Global Climate and Ecology (IGCE), Glebovskaya str. 20B, 107258 Moscow (office); Department of Earth Sciences, Russian Academy of Sciences, Leninsky pr. 32A, 117993 Moscow (office); Apt 84, Romanov per. 3, 84, Moscow, Russia (home). *Telephone:* (495) 169-24-30 (IGCE) (office); (495) 938-14-63 (office). *Fax:* (495) 160-08-31 (IGCE) (office); (495) 938-18-59 (office). *E-mail:* yu.izrael@g23.relcom.ru (office). *Website:* www.igce.comcor.ru.

J

JA, Song-nam; North Korean diplomatist; *Ambassador to UK;* m. Jang Hye Gyong. *Career:* career diplomat with expertise in arms reduction and US affairs; fmr mem. Perm. Mission to UN, New York; Amb. to UK 2007– (also accred to Ireland and Luxembourg 2007–, to Belgium 2008–).
Address: Embassy of the Democratic People's Republic of Korea, 73 Gunnersbury Avenue, London, W5 4LP, England (office). *Telephone:* (20) 8992-4965 (office). *Fax:* (20) 8992-2053 (office).

JAAFAR ALBAR, Datuk Seri Syed Hamid bin Syed; Malaysian lawyer and politician; *Minister of Home Affairs and Internal Security;* b. 15 Jan. 1944, Kampong Melayu Air Hitam, Penang; m. Datin Seri Sharifah Aziah bte Syed Zainal Abidin; three s. three d. *Education:* Monash Univ., Melbourne, Australia. *Career:* Magistrate and Pres. of Sessions Court, Kuala Lumpur 1970–72; Head of Legal Dept, Bank Bumiputra Malaysia Bhd (BBMB) 1972, Legal Adviser and later Sr Man. 1972–78, Asst Sec. and Sec. to Man. 1974–79, first Gen. Man. of Bahrain Br. 1979–80, Gen. Man. of London Br., transferred to Kuala Lumpur as Head of Int. Banking Div. (Credit Supervision) 1980–82, Chief Gen. Man. and Sec. of the Bank 1985–86; Sec. Kewangan Bumiputra and Bank Pembangunan Malaysia Bhd 1976–79, Inst. of Bankers 1978–79; Dir and CEO Bumiputra Merchant Bankers 1982–85; Dir Koperasi Usaha Bersatu 1983–88, Kewangan Bumiputra Malaysia Bhd, Bumiputra Lloyds Leasing Bhd, Bumiputra Merchant Bankers, Syarikat Nominee Sdn Bhd, BBMB Properties 1985–86; Advocate and Solicitor-Gen. Pnr, Albar Zulkifly and Yap 1986–90; Chair. Shamelin Holdings 1989–90, Koperasi Shamelin Bhd 1989–90; MP for Kota Tinggi (Johor) 1990; Minister of Justice in Prime Minister's Dept (in charge of oil and gas affairs) 1990–92; Minister of Law and Minister in Prime Minister's Dept 1992–95; Minister of Defence 1995–99, of Foreign Affairs 1999–2008, of Home Affairs and Internal Security 2008–.
Address: Ministry of Home Affairs (Kementerian Hal Ehwal Dalam Negeri), Blok D2, Parcel D, Pusat Pentadbiran Kerajaan Persekutuan, 62546 Putrajaya, Malaysia (office). *Telephone:* (3) 88863000 (office). *Fax:* (3) 88891613 (office). *E-mail:* azmi@mofa.gov.my (office). *Website:* www .moha.gov.my (office).

JA'AFARI, Bashar, BA, PhD; Syrian diplomatist; *Permanent Representative, United Nations;* b. 14 April 1956; m.; three c. *Education:* Damascus Univ., Univ. of Paris V-La Sorbonne, Univ. of Sharif Hedayatuallah, Jakarta. *Career:* joined Ministry of Foreign Affairs 1980, Attaché and Third Sec., Embassy in Paris 1983–88; First Sec. and Counsellor, Perm. Mission to UN, New York 1991–94; Charge d'Affaires, Embassy in Jakarta 1998–2002; Dir Dept of Int. Orgs and Conferences 2002–04; Perm. Rep. to UN, Geneva 2004–06, to UN, New York 2006–.
Address: Permanent Mission of Syria, 820 Second Avenue, 15th Floor, New York, NY 10017, USA (office). *Telephone:* (212) 661-1313 (office). *Fax:* (212) 867-3985 (office). *E-mail:* syria@un.int (office). *Website:* www.syria -un.org (office).

JAAFARI, Ibrahim al-, MD; Iraqi politician and physician; b. 1947, Karbala. *Education:* Mosul Univ. *Career:* after medical school joined Islamic Dawa Party (Hizb ad-Da'wa al-Islamiya), Chief Spokesman 1966, remains leader; moved to Iran when Dawa party in Iraq was outlawed 1980, then to London 1989; fmr mem. Iraq Governing Council; Interim Vice-Pres. of Iraq 2004–05; Prime Minister of Iraq 2005–April 2006.
Address: Islamic Dawa Party (Hizb ad-Da'wa al-Islamiya), Baghdad, Iraq (office). *E-mail:* info@islamicdawaparty.org (office). *Website:* www .islamicdawaparty.org (office).

JAANI, Karin, BA; Estonian diplomatist and politician; *Director General, Second Political Department, Ministry of Foreign Affairs;* b. 27 Aug. 1952, Tartu; m.; one d. *Education:* Univ. of Tartu. *Career:* Sec. Council of Churches of Estonia 1989–92; elected Mem. of Riigikogu (Parl.) 1992–95, 1995–; mem. Del. to Council of Europe Parl. Ass. (PACE) 1993–95, Vice-Chair. Group on European People's Party 1994; Amb. and Perm. Rep. to Council of Europe 1995–99; Head of Foreign Relations Dept, Riigikogu and Counsellor, Ministry of Foreign Affairs 1999–2001; Amb. to Russian Fed. 2001–05; currently Dir-Gen. Second Political Dept, Ministry of Foreign Affairs and non-resident Amb. to Repub. of Montenegro; White Cross, Third Class (Estonia).

Address: Ministry of Foreign Affairs, Islandi Väljak 1, Tallinn 15049, Estonia (office). *Telephone:* 637-7000 (office). *Fax:* 637-7099 (office). *E-mail:* vminfo@vm.ee (office). *Website:* www.vm.ee (office).

JACKSON, Jeanine, BA, MBA; American diplomatist; *Ambassador to Burkina Faso;* b. (Jeanine Mathew), Wyo.; m. Mark Jackson. *Career:* Col in US Army Reserve (retd); worked in Saigon as a civil service employee, Defense Attaché Office; later served ten years as active duty army officer, primarily in Germany and Korea; career mem. Sr Foreign Service, overseas appointments have included postings to Switzerland, Nigeria, Saudi Arabia, Hong Kong, Kenya and Afghanistan, as Post Man. Officer for the Soviet Union 1990, then managed from Washington, DC establishment of embassies in 14 new CIS, est. programs in Hong Kong to protect interests of US Govt civilian, mil. and local employees upon colony's reverting to Chinese sovereignty 1997, served as Supervisory Gen. Services Officer of Embassy in Nairobi following Al Qaeda bombing 1998, led team that reopened US Embassy in Kabul 2001, then served as Deputy Chief of Mission, later Man. Counselor, Man. Coordinator responsible for reestablishing US Embassy in Baghdad, Amb. to Burkina Faso 2006–; Presidential Rank Award 2006.
Address: Embassy of the USA, 622 avenue Raoul Follereau, Koulouba, Sector 4, 01 BP 35, Ouagadougou 01, Burkina Faso (office). *Telephone:* 50-30-67-23 (office). *Fax:* 50-31-23-68 (office). *E-mail:* amembouaga@state .gov (office). *Website:* ouagadougou.usembassy.gov (office).

JACKSON, Rev. Jesse Louis; American clergyman and civic leader; *President, Rainbow PUSH Coalition;* b. 8 Oct. 1941, Greenville, N Carolina; m. Jacqueline Lavinia Brown 1964; three s. two d. one d. by Karin Stanford. *Education:* Univ. of Illinois, Illinois Agricultural and Tech. Coll., Chicago Theological Seminary. *Career:* ordained to Ministry Baptist Church 1968; active Black Coalition for United Community Action 1969; Co-Founder Operation Breadbasket S Christian Leadership Conf.; Co-ordinating Council Community Orgs, Chicago 1966, Nat. Dir 1966–77; Founder and Exec. Dir Operation PUSH (People United to Save Humanity), Chicago 1971–96, Pres. Rainbow PUSH Coalition (formed with merger with Rainbow Coalition) 1996–; unsuccessful cand. for Democratic nomination for US Presidency 1983–84, 1987–88; TV Host, Voices of America 1990–; Pres. Award Nat. Medical Asscn 1969; Humanitarian Father of the Year Award Nat. Father's Day Cttee 1971.
Address: Rainbow PUSH Coalition, 930 East 50th Street, Chicago, IL 60615, USA (office). *Telephone:* (773) 373-3366 (office). *Fax:* (773) 373-3571 (office). *E-mail:* jjackson@rainbowpush.org (office). *Website:* www .rainbowpush.org (office).

JACOBOVITS DE SZEGED, Adriaan; Dutch diplomatist; *EU Special Representative for Moldova;* b. 27 Dec. 1935, Vienna, Austria; m. Françoise S. Montant 1968; two s. *Education:* Univ. of Leiden. *Career:* Master of Netherlands Law; Ministry of Finance 1963; joined Foreign Service 1964; postings at Embassy, Moscow, Perm. Mission to UN and other int. orgs, Geneva, Embassy, London, Embassy, Nairobi, Perm. Del. to EC, Brussels; Dir Econ. Co-operation, Ministry of Foreign Affairs 1978–82; Dir-Gen. Political Affairs 1982–86; Perm. Rep. to UN, New York 1986–89; Perm. Rep. to NATO, Brussels 1989–93; Amb. to USA 1993–97; Pres. Int. Comm. for the Protection of the River Rhine 1999–2001; Personal Rep. of the OSCE Chair.-in-Office for Moldova 2002–03; EU Special Rep. for Moldova 2005–; Kt, Order of the Netherlands Lion; Grosses Verdienstkreuz (Germany); Commdr Légion d'honneur.
Address: European Commission's Delegation to the Republic of Moldova, Kogalniceanu Street nr 12, MD 2001 Chisinau, Moldova (office); Riouwstraat 76, 2585 HD The Hague, Netherlands. *Telephone:* (2) 50-52-10 (office). *Fax:* (2) 27-26-22 (home). *E-mail:* Delegation-Moldova@cec.eu .int (office). *Website:* www.delmda.cec.eu.int/en (office).

JACOBS, Rt Hon. Sir Francis Geoffrey, DPhil, KCMG, QC; British lawyer; *Professor of Law, King's College, London;* b. 8 June 1939, Cliftonville; m. 1st Ruth Freeman 1964; m. 2nd Susan Felicity Gordon Cox 1975; two s. three d. *Education:* City of London School, Christ Church, Oxford and Nuffield Coll., Oxford. *Career:* lecturer in Jurisprudence, Univ. of Glasgow 1963–65; lecturer in Law, LSE 1965–69; Prof. of European Law, King's Coll., London 1974–88, Prof. of Law 2006–, Fellow, King's Coll. 1990;

Secr. European Comm. of Human Rights and Legal Directorate, Council of Europe 1969–72; Legal Sec. Court of Justice of the EC 1972–74, Advocate Gen. 1988–2006; Barrister, Middle Temple 1964, QC 1984, Bencher 1990; Gov. Inns of Court School of Law 1996–2001; apptd to Privy Council 2005; Commdr, Ordre de Mérite 1983; Hon. LLD (Birmingham) 1996, (Glasgow) 2006; Hon. DCL (City Univ., London) 1997. *Publications include:* several books on European law and Yearbook of European Law (founding ed.) 1981–88.
Address: School of Law, King's College, Strand, London, WC2R 2LS (office); Fountain Court Chambers, Temple, London, EC4Y 9DH (office); Wayside, 15 St Alban's Gardens, Teddington, Middx, TW11 8AE, England (home). *E-mail:* francis.jacobs@kcl.ac.uk (office).

JACOBS, Janice L., BA, MA; American diplomatist; *Principal Deputy Assistant Secretary of State for Consular Affairs;* b. Va. *Education:* Southern Illinois Univ., Nat. War Coll., Washington, DC. *Career:* career mem. Sr Foreign Service, overseas assignments to Mexico, France, Ethiopia and Nigeria, Washington assignments in State Dept Visa Office, Operations Center and Office of Cuban Affairs, Deputy Chief of Mission, Embassy in Santo Domingo 2000–02, Deputy Asst Sec. of State for Visa Services 2002–06, Amb. to Senegal 2006–07, Prin. Deputy Asst Sec. of State for Consular Affairs, Dept of State 2007–.
Address: US Department of State, 2201 C Street NW, Washington, DC 20520, USA (office). *Telephone:* (202) 647-4000 (office). *Fax:* (202) 647-6738 (office). *Website:* www.state.gov (office).

JACOBSON, Tracey Ann, BA, MA; American diplomatist; *Ambassador to Tajikistan; Education:* John Hopkins Univ., Baltimore, Md and John Hopkins Univ. Nitze School of Advanced Int. Studies. *Career:* career mem. Sr Foreign Service, overseas assignments have included Seoul, Nassau and Moscow, domestic assignments have included Bureau of Intelligence and Research, Bureau of Western Hemisphere Affairs, Office of Under-Sec. for Man., Deputy Exec. Sec. Nat. Security Council at White House, Deputy Chief of Mission, Embassy in Riga 2001–04, Amb. to Turkmenistan 2004–06, to Tajikistan 2006–; several Superior and Meritorious Honor Awards, Dept of State.
Address: US Embassy, 109-A Ismoili Somoni Avenue, 734019 Dushanbe, Tajikistan (office). *Telephone:* (37) 229-20-00 (office). *Fax:* (37) 229-20-50 (office). *E-mail:* usembassydushanbe@state.gov (office). *Website:* dushanbe.usembassy.gov (office).

JACOBY, Ruth; Swedish diplomatist, international civil servant and organization official; *Ambassador to Germany;* b. 13 Jan. 1949, New York, USA; m. Bjorn Meidal 1976; two s. *Education:* Univ. of Uppsala. *Career:* First Sec., Ministry for Foreign Affairs, Stockholm 1972, Deputy Asst Under-Sec. 1984–88, Asst Under-Sec. and Head of Dept 1990–94, Dir-Gen. for Devt Co-operation 2002–; mem. Swedish del. to OECD, Paris 1980–84; Deputy Asst Under-Sec., Ministry of Finance 1988–90; Exec. Dir World Bank 1994–97; Amb. for Econ. and Social Affairs, Perm. Mission of Sweden to the UN 1997–2002; Co-Chair. Preparatory Cttee of the Int. Conf. on Financing for Devt (FfD) 2001–02; Amb. to Germany 2006–.
Address: Embassy of Sweden, Rauchstrasse 1, 10787 Berlin, Germany (office). *Telephone:* (30) 50506610 (office). *E-mail:* ruth.jacoby@foreign.ministry.se (home). *Website:* www.ud.se (office).

JAFFEER, Musthafa Mohamed, BComm, MA; Sri Lankan diplomatist; *Permanent Representative, United Nations;* m.; two c. *Education:* Univ. of Jaffna, Monash Univ., Australia. *Career:* Asst Dir Econ. Affairs Div., Ministry of Foreign Affairs 1988–90; Third Sec., High Comm. in New Delhi 1990–91; Second Sec., High Comm. in London 1991–94; Deputy Dir, West Div., Ministry of Foreign Affairs 1995–96, Deputy Dir East Div. 1996–97; Minister Councillor, Embassy in Beijing 1997–2001; Dir UN and Multilateral Affairs, Human Rights and Conf. Div., Ministry of Foreign Affairs 2001–02; Amb. to Viet Nam 2003–06; Chief of Protocol, Ministry of Foreign Affairs 2006–08; Perm. Rep. to UN, New York 2008–; Fellow, Monash Univ. 1995–96.
Address: Permanent Mission of Sri Lanka to the United Nations, 630 Third Avenue, 20th Floor, New York, NY 10017, USA (office). *Telephone:* (212) 986-7040 (office). *Fax:* (212) 986-1838 (office). *E-mail:* srilanka@un.int (office).

JAFFRELOT, Christophe, PhD; French political scientist and academic; *Director, Centre d'Études et de Recherches Internationales (CERI); Education:* Institut d'études politiques, Univ. Paris I – Sorbonne, Institut nat. des langues et civilisations orientales. *Career:* Lecturer in South Asian Politics, Institut d'études politiques, Univ. Paris I – Sorbonne and Institut nat. des langues et civilisations orientales; Dir Centre d'études et de recherches internationales (CERI); Ed. Critique internationale. *Publications:* The Hindu Nationalist Movement and Indian Politics 1996, L'Inde contemporaine de 1950 à nos jours (ed.) 1997, La démocratie en Inde –

Religion, caste et politique 1998, BJP – The Compulsions of Politics (co-ed.) 1998, Le Pakistan, carrefour de tensions régionales (ed.) 1999, Démocraties d'ailleurs: démocraties et démocratisations hors d'Occident (ed.) 2000, Le Pakistan (ed.) 2000, Dr Ambedkar 2000, Inde: La Démocratie par la caste 2005.
Address: CERI, 56 rue Jacob, 75006 Paris, France (office). *Telephone:* 1-58-71-70-00 (office). *Fax:* 1-58-71-70-91 (office). *E-mail:* info@ceri-sciences-po.org (office). *Website:* www.ceri-sciences-po.org (office).

JAGAN, Janet, OE; Guyanese politician and author; b. 20 Oct. 1920, Chicago, Ill., USA; m. Cheddi Jagan 1943 (died 1997); one s. one d. *Career:* Gen. Sec. People's Progressive Party (PPP) 1950–70; Ed. Thunder 1950–56, 2005–; Deputy Speaker House of Assembly 1953; six months' political imprisonment 1954; Minister of Labour, Health and Housing 1957–61; Minister of Home Affairs 1963–64; mem. Elections Comm. 1967–68; Ed. Mirror 1969–72, 1973–97; Int. Sec. PPP 1970–84, Exec. Sec. 1984–90; mem. Nat. Ass. 1953, 1957–61, 1976–97, Senate 1963–64; Amb. at Large and acting Amb. to the UN Oct.–Dec. 1993; First Lady of Guyana 1992–97; Prime Minister of Guyana March–Dec. 1997; Pres. of Guyana 1997–99; Pres. Women's Progressive Org., Union of Guyanese Journalists; fmr Chair. Comm. on Rights of the Child; Chair. Man. Cttee Castellani House (nat. art collection); Trustee and Chair. Cheddi Jagan Research Centre; mem. Council of Women Leaders; Order of Excellence 1993; Order of the Liberator (Venezuela) 1998; Outstanding Woman Award, Univ. of Guyana 1989, Mahatma Gandhi Award, UNESCO, for contrib. to democracy, peace and women's rights. *Publications:* History of the People's Progressive Party 1971, Army Intervention in the 1973 Elections in Guyana 1973, An Examination of National Service 1976, When Grandpa Cheddi Was a Boy and other stories (children's) 1993; children's books: Patricia the Baby Manatee and other stories 1995, Children's Stories of Guyana's Freedom Struggles 1995, Anastasia, the Ant Eater and other stories 1997, The Dog Who Loved Flowers 2000, The Alligator Ferry Service and other stories 2000, Anthology of Children's Stories by Guyanese Writers 2002.
Address: Freedom House, 41 Robb Street, Georgetown (office); Place Bel Air, Georgetown, Guyana (home). *Telephone:* 72095 (office). *Fax:* 72096 (office). *E-mail:* ppp@guyana.net.gy (office).

JAGDEO, Bharrat, MEconSc; Guyanese politician and head of state; *President;* b. 23 Jan. 1964, Unity Village, East Coast Demerara. *Education:* Moscow State Univ. *Career:* mem. People's Progressive Party (PPP); fmrly Dir Guyana Water Authority; Dir Caribbean Devt Bank, Nat. Bank of Industry and Commerce, Gov. for Guyana, World Bank; Sr Finance Minister; Pres. of Guyana 2000–.
Address: Office of the President, New Garden Street, Bourda, Georgetown, Guyana (office). *Telephone:* 225-1330 (office). *Fax:* 227-3050 (office). *E-mail:* opmed@op.gov.gy (office). *Website:* www.op.gov.gy (office).

JAGLAND, Thorbjørn; Norwegian politician; *Chairman, Parliamentary Standing Committee on Foreign Affairs;* b. 5 Nov. 1950; m. Hanne Grotjord 1975; two c. *Education:* Univ. of Oslo. *Career:* Exec. Sec. Norwegian Labour League of Youth (AUF) 1977–81; Project and Planning Officer, Norwegian Labour Party 1981–86, Acting Gen. Sec. 1986, Gen. Sec. 1987, Chair. 1992–; mem. Storting; Chair. Labour Party Parl. Group; Prime Minister of Norway 1996–97; Minister of Foreign Affairs 2000–01; Chair. Parl. Standing Cttee on Foreign Affairs 2001–. *Publications include:* Min europeiske drøm 1990, Ny solidaritet 1993, Brev 1995, Vår sårbare verden 2002, For det blir for sent (co-author) 1982, Ti tescr om EU og Norge 2003; articles on defence, nat. security and disarmament.
Address: Stortinget, 0026 Oslo, Norway (office). *Telephone:* 23313055 (office). *Fax:* 23313818 (office). *E-mail:* thorbjorn.jagland@stortinget.no (office).

JAGNE, Baboucarr-Blaise Ismaila, MA; Gambian diplomatist; *Head, United Nations Political Affairs Division, African Union;* b. 11 Feb. 1955, Banjul; m.; four c. *Education:* Univ. of Dakar and Univs of Grenoble and Paris, France. *Career:* Asst Sec., Foreign Ministry 1980–84, Sec. to Pres. of Gambia, Chair. Islamic Peace Cttee on Iran–Iraq War 1984–88, Sr Asst Sec. for Political Legal Affairs 1986–89, Prin. Asst Sec. 1989–92; Deputy Perm. Sec. for Educ. 1992–93, for Political Affairs 1993–95; Minister of External Affairs 1995–97; Amb. to Saudi Arabia 1997–98; Perm. Rep. to UN 1998–2001; Sec. of State for Foreign Affairs 2001–05; Head, UN Political Affairs Div., African Union HQ, Addis Abba.
Address: UN Political Affairs Division, African Union, POB 3243, Addis Ababa, Ethiopia (office). *Telephone:* (1) 51-7700 (office). *Fax:* (1) 51-7844 (office). *E-mail:* webmaster@africa-union.org (office). *Website:* www.africa-union.org (office).

JAHAN, Ismat, BA, MA; Bangladeshi lawyer and diplomatist; *Permanent Representative, United Nations; Education:* Dhaka Univ., Fletcher School, Tufts Univ., with cross-registered course works at Harvard Univ., USA.

Career: career diplomat 1982–; fmr Fellow, School of Foreign Service, Georgetown Univ., Washington, DC; served in various capacities at Ministry of Foreign Affairs as well as missions abroad including Perm. Missions to UN in New York and Geneva, and High Comm. in New Delhi; Dir-Gen. Int. Orgs, UN and Multilateral Econ. Affairs, Ministry of Foreign Affairs –2005; Amb. to the Netherlands 2005–07; Amb. and Perm. Rep. to UN, New York 2007–.
Address: Permanent Mission of Bangladesh, 227 East, 14th Floor, 45th Street, New York, NY 10017, USA (office). *Telephone:* (212) 867-3434 (office). *Fax:* (212) 972-4038 (office). *E-mail:* bangladesh@un.int (office). *Website:* www.un.int/bangladesh (office).

JAIME, Aguinaldo; Angolan politician; *Deputy Prime Minister; Career:* fmr Pres. Banco Africano de Investimentos; Gov. Nat. Bank of Angola 1999–2002; Deputy Prime Minister of Angola 2002–.
Address: c/o Ministry of Information, Avenida Comandante Valódia, Luanda, Angola.

JAKOBSEN, Mimi; Danish politician; *Leader, Centre Democrats Party;* b. 19 Nov. 1948, Copenhagen. *Career:* Lecturer in German Philology and Phonetics, Univ. of Copenhagen; MP 1977–; Minister for Cultural Affairs 1982–86, for Social Affairs 1986–88, of Business Affairs 1993–96, of Industry 1994–96; Leader Centre Democrats party 1989–.
Address: Centrum-Demokraterne, Folketinget, Christiansborg, 1240 Copenhagen K, Denmark. *Telephone:* 33-37-48-77. *Fax:* 33-37-48-56. *E-mail:* cd@ft.dk (office). *Website:* www.centrumdemokraterne. dk (office).

JALAN, Bimal, PhD; Indian economist; *Chairman, Public Interest Foundation; Education:* Univ. of Calcutta, Univs of Cambridge and Oxford, UK. *Career:* various positions at IMF, World Bank, Pearson Comm. 1964–70; Chief Economist, Industrial Credit and Investment Corpn of India 1970–73; Econ. Adviser, Ministry of Finance and of Industry, India 1973–79; Chief Econ. Adviser, Ministry of Finance 1981–88, Sec. for Banking 1985–88; Dir Econ. Affairs, Commonwealth Secr., London 1979–81; Exec. Dir IMF 1988–90; fmr Exec. Dir IBRD (India); Gov. Reserve Bank 1997–2003; MP for Rajya Sabha 2003–; Chair. Public Interest Foundation, New Delhi 2008–. *Publications include:* India's Economic Crisis: The Way Ahead 1991; The Future of India: Politics, Economics and Governance 2005.
Address: 4 Babar Road, New Delhi 110001, India (office). *Telephone:* (11) 2378-2037 (office). *Fax:* (11) 2378-2037 (office). *E-mail:* bjalan@nic.in (home). *Website:* www.bimaljalan.com (office).

JALILI, Saeed, PhD; Iranian government official; *Secretary, Shura-ye Ali-ye Amniyyat-e Melli (Supreme National Security Council);* b. 1965, Mashhad. *Education:* Univ. of Science and Industry, Tehran. *Career:* veteran of the 1980–88 Iran-Iraq war; Dir-Gen. Office of Supreme Leader Ayatollah Ali Khamenei 2001–05; adviser to Pres. Mahmoud Ahmadinejad 2005–; Deputy Foreign Minister for European and American Affairs 2005–07; Sec., Shura-ye Ali-ye Amniyyat-e Melli (Supreme Nat. Security Council) 2007–, role includes being Iran's chief nuclear negotiator.
Address: Office of the Secretary, Shura-ye Ali-ye Amniyyat-e Melli, Tehran, Iran.

JALLOUD, Maj. Abd as-Salam; Libyan politician and army officer; *Second-in-Command to Revolutionary Leader;* b. 15 Dec. 1944. *Education:* Secondary School, Sebha, Mil. Acad., Benghazi. *Career:* mem. of Revolutionary Command Council 1969–77, Gen. Secr. of Gen. People's Congress 1977–79; Minister of Industry and the Econ., Acting Minister of the Treas. 1970–72; Prime Minister 1972–77; Second-in-Command to Revolutionary Leader Col Gaddafi 1997–.
Address: c/o General Secretariat of the General People's Congress, Tripoli, Libya.

JALLOW, Tamsir; Gambian diplomatist; *Ambassador to USA;* m. Mariama Jallow; one s. one d. *Education:* St Augustine's and Swedru Secondary School in Ghana, Univ. of Cape Coast, Ghana, Univ. of Birmingham, UK, Univ. of Kenya. *Career:* fmr Head, Gambia Teacher's Union; fmr Publicity Sec. for ruling Alliance for Patriotic Reorientation and Construction party; fmr Deputy and House Majority Leader, Nat. Ass.; fmr Dir-Gen. Immigration Dept; Acting High Commr to UK 2005–07 (also Chargé d'affaires a.i., Stockholm 2006–07), Perm. Rep. to UN, New York 2007, Amb. to USA 2007–.
Address: Embassy of Gambia, 1424 K Street, NW, Suite 600, Washington, DC 20005, USA (office). *Telephone:* (202) 785-1399 (office). *Fax:* (202) 785-1430 (office). *E-mail:* www.gambiaembassy.us (office).

JAMALI, Mir Zafarullah Khan, MA; Pakistani politician; b. 1 Jan. 1944, Rowjhan, Balochistan; m.; four s. one d. *Education:* Murree Royal Coll.,

Aitchison Coll., Lahore, Punjab Univ. *Career:* tribal elder from SW Prov. of Balochistan; joined Pakistan People's Party1970s; elected mem. Prov. Ass., Balochistan 1977; fmr Minister for Food and Information; Minister for Food and Agric. 1982, for Local Govt, for Water and Power 1985, for Railways 1986; mem. Nat. Ass. 1985–89; Chief Minister for Balochistan 1988–89; Rep. to UN 1991; elected ind. mem. Nat. Ass. 1993–, mem. Cabinet 1997–2004; Senator for Balochistan 1997–2006; Sr mem. Pakistan Muslim League –1999; mem. Pakistan Muslim League—Quaid-e-Azam; Prime Minister of Pakistan 2002–04 (resgnd); fmr mem. Nat. Security Council.
Address: c/o Office of the Prime Minister, Constitution Avenue, Islamabad, Pakistan (office).

JAMBREK, Peter, MA, PhD; Slovenian judge, legal consultant and author; b. 14 Jan. 1940, Ljubljana. *Education:* Grammar School, Ljubljana, Ljubljana Univ. and Univ. of Chicago, USA. *Career:* Prof., Dept of Theory of Law and State, Ljubljana; Judge, Constitutional Court of Repub. of Slovenia 1990, Pres. 1991–95; Judge, European Court of Human Rights 1993–99; Dean, Grad. School of Govt and European Affairs, Univ. of Ljubljana 2003; mem. Venice Comm. 2003; currently ind. consultant and author. *Publications:* Development and Social Change in Yugoslavia: Crises and Perspectives of Building a Nation 1975, Participation as a Human Right and as a Means for the Exercise of Human Rights 1982, Contributions for the Slovenian Constitution 1988, Constitutional Democracy 1992.
Address: c/o University of Ljubljana, Kongresni trg 12, 1000 Ljubljana; Ceste v Megre 4, 64260 Bled, Slovenia (home). *Telephone:* (64) 77449 (home).

JAMEEL, Yusuf M.; Bahraini diplomatist; m. Asma Jameel. *Career:* Counsellor and Chargé d'affaires a.i. to UK and Perm. Rep. to OPCW –2007, 2008–.
Address: Embassy of Bahrain, 30 Belgrave Square, London, SW1X 8QB, England (office). *Telephone:* (20) 7201-9170 (office). *Fax:* (20) 7201-9183 (office). *E-mail:* information@bahrainembassy.co.uk (office). *Website:* www.bahrainembassy.co.uk (office).

JAMES, Edison Chenfil, MSc; Dominican politician and agronomist; *Leader, Dominica United Workers Party (UWP);* b. 18 Oct. 1943, Marigot; m.; one s. two d. *Education:* North East London Polytechnic, Univ. of Reading, Imperial Coll., Univ. of London. *Career:* teacher, St Mary's Acad. Sept.–Dec. 1973; agronomist Ministry of Agric. 1974–76; Farm Improvement Officer, Caribbean Devt Bank (attached to Dominica Agricultural and Industrial Devt Bank) 1976–80, Loans Officer 1976–80; Co-ordinator Coconut Rehabilitation and Devt Project; Chief Exec. (Gen. Man.) Dominica Banana Marketing Corpn 1980–87; Adviser to Dirs Bd of Windward Islands Banana Growers Asscn (WINBAN) 1980–87; Man. Dir Agricultural Man. Corpn Ltd (AMCROP) 1987–95; Leader Dominica United Workers Party (UWP) and Parl. Leader of the Opposition 1990–95, 2000–; Prime Minister of Dominica 1995–2000, also Minister of Legal and Foreign Affairs and Labour; leading negotiator with several int. aid agencies; served on numerous public service cttees.
Address: Dominica United Workers Party, 37 Cork Street, Roseau, Dominica (office).

JAMES, Harold, PhD; British academic; *Professor of History and International Affairs, Princeton University;* b. 19 Jan. 1956, Bedford; m. Marzenna Kowalik 1991; two s., one d. *Education:* Perse School, Cambridge and Gonville & Caius Coll. Cambridge. *Career:* Fellow of Peterhouse, Cambridge 1978–86; Fellow, Inst. for European History, Mainz, Germany 1981; Asst Prof. of History and Int. Affairs, Princeton Univ. 1986–91, Assoc. Prof. 1991–95, Prof. 1995–; Prof. of History, Grad. Inst. of Int. Studies, Geneva, Switzerland 1996; Prof., European Univ. Inst., Florence, Italy 2006–; Ellen Macarthur Prize for Econ. History 1982, Helmut Schmidt Prize for Econ. History 2004, Ludwig Erhard Prize for Econs 2005. *Publications:* The Reichsbank and Public Finance in Germany 1985, The German Slump: Politics and Economics 1924–36 1986, A German Identity 1770–1990 1989, Vom Historikerstreit zum Historikerschweigen 1993, The Deutsche Bank 1870–1890 1995, International Monetary Co-operation Since Bretton Woods 1995, The Deutsche Bank and the Nazi Economic War Against Jews 2001, The End of Globalization 2001, Europe Reborn 2003, Family Capitalism 2005, The Roman Predicament 2005.
Address: Department of History, 218 Dickinson Hall, Princeton University, Princeton, NJ 08544 (office); 10 Dickinson Street, Princeton, NJ 08540, USA (home). *Telephone:* (609) 258-4160 (office). *Fax:* (609) 258-5326 (office). *E-mail:* hjames@princeton.edu (office). *Website:* his.princeton.edu (office).

JAMIR, S. C., BA, LLB; Indian politician; *Governor of Maharashtra;* b. 17 Oct. 1931, Ungma, Nagaland; m. Alemia Jamir 1959; three s. two d. *Education:* Univ. of Allahabad. *Career:* mem. Interim Body of Nagaland, then Jt Sec.

Naga People's Convention; Vice-Chair. Mokokchung Town Cttee 1959–60; MP 1961–70, MP Rajya Sabha 1987–89; Parl. Sec., Ministry of External Affairs, Govt of India 1961–67; Union Deputy Minister of Railways, of Labour and Rehabilitation, of Community Devt and Co-operation, Food and Agric. 1968–70; elected mem. to Nagaland Legis. Ass. 1971–73, re-elected mem. from Aonglenden Constituency 1974; subsequently apptd Minister of Finance, Revenue and Border Affairs; re-elected 1977 and apptd Deputy Chief Minister in UDF Ministry; Chief Minister of ULP Ministry April 1980; resgnd when NNDP Ministry came to power June 1980; Leader of Opposition Congress (I) in State Legis. Ass. 1980–82; elected from 26 Aonglenden Constituency, Gen. Elections 1982; unanimously elected Leader Congress (I) Legislature Party, Chief Minister Nagaland 1982–86, 1989–92, 1993–2003; Gov. of Goa 2004–08, of Maharashtra 2008–.
Address: The Raj Bhavan, Maharashtra State Government, Malabar Hill, Mumbai 400 035, Maharashtra, India (office). *Telephone:* (22) 23630635 ext 231 (office). *Fax:* (22) 2363 3272 (office). *E-mail:* rajbhavan@maharashtra.gov.in (office). *Website:* www.maharashtra.gov.in (office).

JAMMEH, Col Yahya A. J. J.; Gambian head of state and fmr army officer; *President;* b. 25 May 1965, Kanilai Village, Foni Kansala Dist, Western Div.; m. Zineb Yahya-Jammeh (née Soumah); one d. *Education:* Gambia High School. *Career:* joined fmr Gambia Nat. Gendarmerie as pvt. 1984; with Special Intervention Unit, Gambia Nat. Army 1984–86, Sergeant 1986, Escort Training Instructor, Gendarmerie Training School 1986–89, Cadet Officer 1987, commissioned 1989, Second Lt 1989, in charge of Presidential Escort, Presidential Guards 1989–90, CO Mobile Gendarmerie Jan.–June 1991, Mil. Police Unit June–Aug. 1991, Lt 1992, Commdr Gambia Nat. Army Mil. Police Aug.–Nov. 1992, Capt. 1994, Col 1996; became Chair. Armed Forces Provisional Ruling Council, Head of State 1994–; retd from army 1996; elected Pres. of The Gambia 1996–; Chair., Pres. Alliance for Patriotic Reorientation and Construction (APRC) 1996–; Chair. Inter-states Cttee for Control of Drought in the Sahel 1997–2000; 1st Vice-Chair. Org. of the Islamic Conf. 2000–; Grand Commdr, Order of Al-Fatah (Libya) 1995; Order of Distinction (Liberia) 2000; Grand Master of the Repub. of The Gambia 2001; Pan-African Humanitarian Award 1997 and numerous other awards.
Address: Office of the President, State House, Banjul, The Gambia (office); Alliance for Patriotic Reorientation and Construction, GAMSTAR Building, Banjul. *Telephone:* 4223811 (office). *Fax:* 4227034 (office). *E-mail:* info@statehouse.gm (office). *Website:* www.statehouse.gm (office); www.jammeh2001.org (office).

JANDROKOVIĆ, Gordan; Croatian politician and diplomatist; *Minister of Foreign Affairs and European Integration;* b. 2 Aug. 1967, Bjelovar; m.; three c. *Education:* Faculties of Civil Eng and Political Science, Univ. of Zagreb, Diplomatic School, Ministry of Foreign Affairs, The Netherlands Inst. of Int. Relations, Clingendael, Erasmus Universiteit, Rotterdam. *Career:* pvt. construction co. 1989–94; with Ministry of Foreign Affairs 1994–2000; Man. Stanić Co., Zagreb 2000–02; Gen. Man. Beming Co., Bjelovar 2002–03; mem. Croatian Democratic Union (HDZ) 1992–, Chair. HDZ Cttee for Small and Medium-Size Enterprises 2002–, HDZ Cttee for Bjelovar-Bilogora Co. 2003–, mem. HDZ Presidency 2004–; mem. Parl. 2003–, Chair. Parl. Cttee for the Economy, Devt and Reconstruction 2003–04, Parl. Foreign Policy Cttee 2004–07, Head of Parl. Del. to Croatia-EU Jt Parl. Cttee 2004–07; Minister of Foreign Affairs and European Integration 2008–; Man. Ed. The Witnesses to History series 1997–2002.
Address: Ministry of Foreign Affairs and European Integration, trg Nikole Šubića Zrinskog 7–8, 10000 Zagreb, Croatia (office). *Telephone:* (1) 4569964 (office). *Fax:* (1) 4569977 (office). *E-mail:* mvpei@mvpei.hr (office). *Website:* www.mvpei.hr (office).

JANKOWITSCH, Peter, DDL; Austrian diplomatist and politician; *Secretary-General, Franco-Austrian Centre for East–West Encounters;* b. 10 July 1933, Vienna; m. 1st Odette Prevor 1962 (divorced); one s.; m. 2nd Silvia Lahner 2001. *Education:* Vienna Univ. and The Hague Acad. of Int. Law. *Career:* fmr lawyer; joined foreign service 1957, worked in Int. Law Dept; Pvt. Sec., Cabinet of Minister of Foreign Affairs 1959–62; posted to London 1962–64; Chargé d'affaires, Dakar, Senegal 1964–66; Head of Office of Bruno Kreisky, Chair. Austrian Socialist Party 1967; Chief of Cabinet of Fed. Chancellor (Kreisky) 1970–72; Perm. Rep. to UN 1972–78; Chair. UN Cttee on Peaceful Uses of Outer Space 1972–91; Vice-Chair. of Bd, Int. Energy Agency 1979–83; Rep. for Austria to UN Security Council 1973–75, Pres. Security Council 1973, Vice-Pres. 29th Gen. Assembly; Vice-Pres. 7th Special Session of Gen. Assembly 1975; mem. UN Security Council Mission to Zambia 1973; Perm. Rep. to OECD 1978–82; Deputy Perm. Under-Sec., Chief of Cabinet, Fed. Ministry of Foreign Affairs 1982–83; Fed. Minister for Foreign Affairs 1986–87; mem. Austrian Nat. Ass. (Nationalrat) 1983–90 (Chair. Foreign Relations Cttee 1987–90), 1992–93; Minister of State for Integration and Devt Co-operation 1990–92;

Perm. Rep. to OECD and ESA 1993–98; Chair. OECD Devt Centre 1994–98; Chair. Jt Cttee European Parl.–Austrian Parl.; Sec.-Gen. Franco-Austrian Centre for East–West Encounters 1998–; Int. Sec. Soc. Dem. Party of Austria 1983–90; Chair. Human Rights Cttee Socialist Int. 1987–97, Vice-Chair. Socialist Int. Cttee on Econ. Affairs 1997–99; Pres. Cttee of Parliamentarians of EFTA 1989–90; Hon. Pres., Austrian Soc. for European Policy 1996–; mem. Bd Austrian Foreign Policy Soc, Austrian Inst. for Int. Politics, Vienna Inst. for Devt, Austrian UN League (fmrly Vice-Pres.), Int. Acad. of Astronautics 1998; Pres. Austrian Nat. Cttee for Unispace 1999; Chair. Austrian Space Agency 1998–; Pres. Austria-Viet Nam Soc. 1999–, Jerusalem Foundation, Austria 2002–; Assoc. Ed. Acta Astronomica 2003–; Hon. mem. Bd Int. Inst. of Space Law; Commdr Légion d'honneur; Allan D. Emil Memorial Award for Int. Co-operation in Astronautics 1981, Social Sciences Award, Int. Acad. of Astronautics 2001, and many other awards. *Publications:* Kreisky's Era in Austrian Foreign Policy (co-ed. with E. Bielka and H. Thalberg) 1982, Red Markings–International (co-ed. with H. Fischer) 1984, The European Integration Process and Neutral Austria 1994, Austria and the Non-Aligned 2002; and papers and articles on Austria and on econ. and political devt of the Third World; contrib. to Wörterbuch des Völkerrechts 1960.
Address: Franco-Austrian Centre for East–West Encounters, Salzgries 19, 1010 Vienna, Austria (office). *Telephone:* (1) 5352335 (home); (1) 5338927 (office). *Fax:* (1) 5338927 (office). *E-mail:* jankowitsch@nextra.at (office). *Website:* www.peter-jankowitsch.net (home); www.oefz.at (office).

JANNEH, Abdoulie, MA; Gambian international organization executive; *Under-Secretary-General and Executive Secretary, United Nations Economic Commission for Africa; Education:* Fourah Bay Coll., Sierra Leone, Univs of Nottingham and Bradford, UK, Econ. Devt Inst., World Bank (Project Man.). *Career:* joined UNDP from Govt of Gambia as Programme Adviser 1979, Adviser, Office to Combat Desertification and Drought (UNSO), Burkina Faso 1979–80, Programme Officer, UNSO, New York 1981–83, Deputy Resident Rep. in Guinea 1984–86, Sierra Leone 1987–89, Deputy Exec. Sec. UN Capital Devt Fund 1990–93, Resident Coordinator and Resident Rep., Niger 1993–96, Ghana 1996–99, reassigned to New York to lead Transition Team 1999, Asst Sec.-Gen. and UNDP Regional Dir for Africa 2000–05, Under-Sec.-Gen. and Exec. Sec. UN Econ. Comm. for Africa, Addis Ababa, Ethiopia 2005–.
Address: United Nations Economic Commission for Africa, Africa Hall, PO Box 3001, Addis Ababa, Ethiopia (office). *Telephone:* (1) 517200 (office). *Fax:* (1) 514416 (office). *E-mail:* ecainfo@uneca.org (office). *Website:* www.uneca.org (office).

JANŠA, Janez; Slovenian politician; *Prime Minister;* b. 17 Sept. 1958, Ljubljana. *Education:* Univ. of Ljubljana. *Career:* after graduation became intern at Republican Secr. for Defence; apptd Pres. Cttee for Basic People's Defence and Social Self Protection, Alliance of Socialist Youth of Slovenia 1982; wrote a paper critical of conditions within Yugoslav People's Army which was labelled counter-revolutionary 1983, indicted by mil. prosecutor 1985; served as Defence Minister in newly formed Repub. of Slovenia early 1990s; Leader Slovenian Democratic Party; Prime Minister 2004–. *Publications:* several books including On My Own Side 1988, Premiki (Movements) 1992, Okopi (The Barricades) 1994, Seven Years Later 1995, Eight Years Later 1996; hundreds of articles, commentaries, essays and scientific discussions; also several poems and literary compositions.
Address: Office of the Prime Minister, 1000 Ljubljana, Gregorčičeva 20, Slovenia (office). *Telephone:* (1) 4781000 (office). *Fax:* (1) 4781721 (office). *E-mail:* gp.kpv@gov.si (office). *Website:* www.kpv-rs.si (office).

JANVIER, Gen. Bernard Louis Antonin; French army officer; b. 16 July 1939, La Voulte-sur-Rhône, Ardèche; m. Denise Diaz 1963; two s. one d. *Education:* Lycée de Nice, Coll. d'Orange, Lycée Bugeaud, Algiers, Univ. of Rennes and Ecole Spéciale Militaire de Saint-Cyr. *Career:* commissioned 2nd Lt 1960; served in Algeria 1962–64, Madagascar and Comoros 1964–67; Co. Commdt 9th Parachute Regt 1968–70; Commdt in charge of trainee officers, Ecole Spéciale Militaire de Saint-Cyr 1970–72; Bn Chief 1974; training course, Ecole Supérieure de Guerre 1974–76; Lt-Col 1978; Second-in-Command, Bureau of Operations-Instruction 1981; Col 1982; Chef de Corps, 2nd Overseas Parachute Regt 1982–84; Head, Office of Personnel, Chief of Ground Forces 1984–87; Deputy to Gen. Commdt 6th Armoured Div. 1987–89; Brig.-Gen. 1988; Chief. Org.-Logistic Div. of Army Chief of Staff 1989–91; Commdt Operation Requin, Port Gentil, Gabon 1991; Commdt Daguet Div. Saudi Arabia and Iraq 1991; Div. Gen. 1991; Commdt 6th Armoured Div. Nîmes 1991–93; Army Chief of Staff, Operational Planning (Emia) 1993–95; Gen. Army Corps 1994; apptd Army Chief of Staff 1995; Dir Centre des hautes études militaires, Inst. des hautes études de la défense nat. 1996–98; Commdt UN Peace Forces in Fmr Yugoslavia 1995–96; Commdr Légion d'honneur, Ordre nat. du Mérite, Legion of Merit (USA); numerous other decorations including medals from Kuwait and Saudi Arabia.

Address: 6 place de l'Eglise, 83310 Grimaud, France (home).

JAPAN, H.M. Emperor of (see Akihito).

JAPARIDZE, Tedo, PhD; Georgian politician and diplomatist; b. 18 Sept. 1946, Tbilisi; m. Tamar Japaridze; one s. *Education:* Tbilisi State Univ., Inst. of USA and Canadian Studies, Moscow, Russia. *Career:* fmr teacher, Dept of Int. Relations and Int. Law, Tbilisi State Univ.; with Ministry of Foreign Affairs 1989–92, positions include Head of Political Dept, Deputy Foreign Minister, First Deputy Foreign Minister, Vice-Chair. Council for UNESCO Affairs 1989–92, Nat. Security Adviser to Head of State 1992–94; Amb. to USA, Canada and Mexico 1995–2002; Sec. Nat. Security Council 2002–03; Minister of Foreign Affairs 2003–04; Hon. Chair. Transcaucasus Foundation and Special Advisor to Washington Strategic Advisors, LLC –2004; Sec.-Gen. Org. of the Black Sea Econ. Cooperation (BSEC), Perm. Int. Secr. (PERMIS) 2004–06. *Publications include:* White House: Mechanism of Decision-Making 1985, American Political Institutions: History and Currrent State (co-author) 1987; numerous articles on US domestic and foreign policy.
Address: c/o Organization of the Black Sea Economic Cooperation Permanent International Secretariat, İstinye Caddesi, Müşir Fuad Paşa Yalısı, Eski Tersane, 80860 İstinye- İstanbul, Turkey (office).

JARA, Alejandro; Chilean diplomatist and international organization executive; *Deputy Director-General, World Trade Organization;* b. 1949, Santiago; m. Daniela Benavente; one s. two d. *Education:* high schools in Rio de Janeiro, Brazil and Santiago, Chile, Universidad de Chile, Law School, Univ. of California, Berkeley, USA (Fulbright Scholarship). *Career:* joined Chilean Foreign Service 1976, specialized in int. econ. relations, served in Del. to GATT, Geneva 1979–84, seconded as Coordinator for Trade Policy Affairs to Econ. System for Latin America (SELA), Caracas, Venezuela, Dir for Bilateral Econ. Affairs 1993–94, Dir for Multilateral Econ. Affairs 1994–99, Sr Official to APEC and Deputy Chief Negotiator for the Chile–Canada Free Trade Agreement 1996–97, Chief Negotiator for the Chile–Mexico Free Trade Agreement 1997–98, Dir-Gen. for Int. Econ. 1999–2000, Amb. and Perm. Rep. to WTO, Geneva 2000–05, Chair. WTO Cttee on Trade and Environment 2001, Chair. Special Session of the Council for Trade in Services 2002; Deputy Dir-Gen. WTO 2005–. *Publications:* numerous articles and papers on int. trade.
Address: World Trade Organization, Centre William Rappard, rue de Lausanne 154, 1211 Geneva, Switzerland (office). *Telephone:* (22) 7395111 (office). *Fax:* (22) 7314206 (office). *E-mail:* enquiries@wto.org (office). *Website:* www.wto.org (office).

JARALLAH, Muhammad Ibrahim al-; Saudi Arabian diplomatist; *Ambassador to Italy;* b. 1944, Al-Methnab City. *Education:* Univ. of Riyadh, Stanford Univ. and Univ. of Mich., USA. *Career:* Asst Prof. of Civil Eng, King Saud Univ. 1978–82, Assoc. Prof. 1982–87, Prof. 1987; Dir-Gen. Saudi Real Estate Soc. 1992–95; mem. Majlis Al-Shoura (Consultative Council) 1992–95; Minister for Urban and Rural Affairs 1995–2003; currently Amb. to Italy.
Address: Embassy of Saudi Arabia, Via G. B. Pergolesi 9, 00198 Rome, Italy (office). *Telephone:* (06) 844851 (office). *Fax:* (06) 8551781 (office). *E-mail:* ambasciata.saudita@arabia-saudita.it (office). *Website:* www .arabia-saudita.it (office).

JARRIN, Gen. (retd) Oswaldo; Ecuadorean government official, academic and fmr army officer; *Minister of National Defence; Career:* Chair. Jt Chiefs of Staff –2003; fmr Sec. Nat. Security Council; Minister of Nat. Defence 2005–; Prof. Latin American Faculty of Social Sciences.
Address: Ministry of National Defence, Exposición 208, Quito, Ecuador (office). *Telephone:* (2) 221-6150 (office). *Fax:* (2) 256-9386 (office). *E-mail:* paginaweb@fuerzasarmadasecuador.org (office). *Website:* www .fuerzasarmadasecuador.ec-gov.net (office).

JASKIERNIA, Jerzy Andrzej, DJur; Polish diplomatist, politician and professor of law; b. 21 March 1950, Kudowa Zdrój; m. Alicja Słowińska 1980; one s. one d. *Education:* Jagiellonian Univ., Kraków. *Career:* teacher, Law and Admin. Faculty of Jagiellonian Univ., Kraków 1972–81; mem. Main Bd Socialist Youth Union 1973–76; mem. Polish Socialist Youth Union (ZSMP) 1976–85; mem. Main Arbitration Bd 1976–80, Chair. 1980–81, Chair. ZSMP Gen. Bd 1981–84; mem. Polish United Workers' Party (PZPR) 1970–90, deputy mem. PZPR Cen. Cttee 1982–86, Vice-Chair., Youth Comm. of PZPR Cen. Cttee 1981–86; mem. Inter-party Problems Comm. of PZPR Cen. Cttee 1986–88, Nat. Council of Patriotic Movt for Nat. Rebirth 1983–89, Sec.-Gen. 1984–87; Adviser to Minister of Foreign Affairs 1987–88; Counsellor, Embassy in Washington 1988–90; mem. Scientific Bd, Research Inst. of Youth Problems (Warsaw) 1984–89; mem. Social Democracy of the Repub. of Poland (SdRP) 1990–99, SdRP Cen. Exec. Cttee 1991–92 (Head Parl. and Self-Govt Affairs Dept 1990–91),

SdRP Presidium of the Main Council 1993–97, Chair. Cttee on Int. Cooperation 1998–99; Deputy to Sejm (Parl.) 1985–89, 1991–; mem. Nat. Ass. Constitutional Cttee 1992–95; Chair. Legis. Cttee of the Sejm 1993–95, 1996–97, Foreign Affairs Cttee 2001–; Minister of Justice and Attorney-Gen. 1995–96; Prof. Świętokrzyska Acad., Kielce 1995–; Deputy Chair. Democratic Left Alliance (SLD), Parl. Caucus 1996–2001, Chair. 2001–04; mem. Parl. Ass. of Council of Europe 1994–, Chair. Subcttee on Human Rights 1998–2001, Chair. Subcttee on Criminal Law and Criminology 2001–03, Deputy Chair. Cttee on Legal Affairs and Human Rights 2003–; Chair. Polish-British Parl. Group 1993–, Deputy Chair. Cttee on European Integration 1997–2001; mem. SLD Nat. Cttee 1999–, SLD Nat. Exec. Bd 2000–04; mem European Parl (Group of the Party of European Socialists) 2004–, mem. Cttee on Foreign Affairs, Human Rights, Common Security and Defence Policy 2004–; Corresp. mem. European Acad. of Science, Arts and Literature, Paris 2002–; Chair. Inst. for Strategic Issues (IPS) 2002–.
Publications: Pozycja stanów w systemie federalnym USA 1979, Dylematy młodych 1984, Dialog naszą szansą 1985, (co-author) System polityczny PRL w procesie przemian 1988, Problemy pluralizmu, porozumienia narodowego i consensusu w systemie politycznym PRL 1989, Stany Zjednoczone a współczesne procesy i koncepcje integracji europejskiej 1992, Zasada równości w prawie wyborczym USA 1992, Wizja parlamentu w nowej Konstytucji Rzeczypospolitej Polskiej 1994, Zasady demokratycznego państwa prawnego w sejmowym postepowaniu ustawodawczym 1999, Zgromadzenie Parlamentarne Rady Europy (English trans.: The Parliamentary Assembly of the Council of Europe 2003) 2000, Członkostwo Polski w Unii Europejskiej a Problem Nowelizagi Konstytagi RP 2004.
Address: European Parliament, Rue Wiertz, 1047 Brussels, Belgium (office). *Telephone:* (2) 284-21-11 (office). *Fax:* (2) 284-69-74 (office); (2) 230-69-33 (office).

JASROTIA, K.S.; Indian diplomatist. *Career:* High Commr to Maldives –2000; Amb. to Bhutan 2000–05.
Address: Ministry of External Affairs, South Block, New Delhi 110 011, India (office). *Telephone:* (11) 23011127 (office). *Fax:* (11) 23011463 (office). *Website:* meaindia.nic.in (office).

JASUDASEN, T., LLB; Singaporean diplomatist; *High Commissioner to Malaysia;* b. June 1952, Malaysia; m.; one s. two d. *Education:* Univ. of Singapore, Ecole Nat. d'Admin, Paris. *Career:* joined Ministry of Foreign Affairs 1979; mem. of staff, Perm. Mission to UN, New York 1979–81; Counsellor and Chargé d'Affaires, Embassy in Manilla 1988–90; Minister-Counsellor and Deputy High Commr, High Comm. in Kuala Lumpur 1991–94; Dir Asean Directorate, then Policy, Planning and Analysis Directorate IV, Ministry of Foreign Affairs 1994–97; Amb. to France 1997–2004, to Myanmar 2004–06; High Commr to Malaysia 2006–; Commdr, Palmes Académiques 2002, Officier, Légion d'Honneur 2004; Public Admin Medal 1990, Long Service Award Medal 2000.
Address: High Commission of Singapore, 209 Jalan Tun Razak, 50400 Kuala Lumpur, Malaysia (office). *Telephone:* (3) 21616277 (office). *Fax:* (3) 21616343 (office). *E-mail:* singhc_kul@sgmfa.gov.sg (office). *Website:* www.mfa.gov.sg/kl (office).

JAVORČIK, Radovan; Slovak diplomatist; m. Michelle Joanne Javorcik. *Career:* fmrly with Security Policy Dept, Ministry of Foreign Affairs; Chargé d'affaires a.i. in UK –2007, Counsellor, London 2007–.
Address: Embassy of Slovakia, 25 Kensington Palace Gardens, London, W8 4QY, England (office). *Telephone:* (20) 7313-6470 (office). *Fax:* (20) 7313-6481 (office). *E-mail:* mail@slovakembassy.co.uk (office). *Website:* www.slovakembassy.co.uk (office).

JAWAD, Said Tayeb, LLB, MBA; Afghan diplomatist; *Ambassador to USA;* m. Shamim Jawad; one s. *Education:* Lycée Istiglal, Kabul Univ., Westfaelishe Wilhelms Univ., Germany, Golden Gate Univ., USA. *Career:* left Afghanistan after Soviet Union invasion 1980, exiled in Germany –1986, moved to USA, worked on Wall Street –1989, moved to San Francisco; Chief of Staff for Afghan Pres. Hamid Karzai, also Pres.'s spokesman, Press Sec. and Dir of Int. Relations 2001–03; Amb. to USA (also accred to Argentina, Bolivia, Brazil, Chile, Colombia, Ecuador, Mexico, Nicaragua, Panama, Uruguay, Venezuela) 2003–; has worked as writer and commentator on Afghan and int. affairs.
Address: Embassy of Afghanistan, 2341 Wyoming Avenue, NW, Washington, DC 20008, USA (office). *Telephone:* (202) 483-6410 (office); (202) 483-6414 (office). *Fax:* (202) 483-6488 (office); (202) 483-9523 (office). *E-mail:* info@embassyofafghanistan.org (office). *Website:* www .embassyofafghanistan.org (office).

JAYAKUMAR, Shanmugam, LLM; Singaporean diplomatist; *Deputy Prime Minister, Minister of Law and Co-ordinating Minister for National Security;* b. 12 Aug. 1939, Singapore; m. Dr Lalitha Rajahram 1969; two s. one d.

Education: Univ. of Singapore and Yale Univ., USA. *Career:* Dean, Law Faculty, Univ. of Singapore 1974–80, Prof. of Law; Perm. Rep. of Singapore to UN 1971–74, High Commr to Canada 1971–74; MP 1980–; Minister of State for Law and Home Affairs 1981–83, Minister of Labour 1983–85, of Home Affairs 1985–94, of Foreign Affairs 1994–2004, of Law 1988–, Deputy Prime Minister and Co-ordinating Minister for Nat. Security 2004–. *Publications:* Constitutional Law Cases from Malaysia and Singapore 1971, Public International Law Cases from Malaysia and Singapore 1974, Constitutional Law (with documentary material) 1976 and articles in journals.
Address: c/o Ministry of Law, 100 High Street, 08-02 The Treasury, Singapore 179434 (office). *Telephone:* 63328840 (office). *Fax:* 63328842 (office). *E-mail:* mlaw_enquiry@minlaw.gov.sg (office). *Website:* www .minlaw.gov.sg (office).

JAYASINGHE, Chandra Nihal; Sri Lankan attorney, judge and diplomatist; *High Commissioner to UK. Education:* Univ. of Colombo, Univ. of Illinois, USA, Univ. of Lund, Sweden. *Career:* began legal career as State Counsel in Attorney Gen.'s Dept 1971, rose to become Deputy Solicitor Gen.; fmr Judge, Court of Appeal, Judge, Supreme Court of Sri Lanka –2008; High Commr to UK (also accred as Amb. to Ireland) 2008–; served on UN War Crimes Tribunal and represented Sri Lanka in many int. legal fora.
Address: High Commission of Sri Lanka, 13 Hyde Park Gardens, London, W2 2LU, England (office). *Telephone:* (20) 7262-1841 (office). *Fax:* (20) 7262-7970 (office). *E-mail:* mail@slhc-london.co.uk (office). *Website:* www .slhclondon.org (office).

JAYASINGHE, Chrysantha Romesh; Sri Lankan diplomatist; *High Commissioner to India;* b. 1955. *Career:* joined Foreign Service as Asst Dir UN Div. 1981, apptd Amb. to Belgium and EU 2000, High Commr to India 2005–, also accred as Amb. to Bhutan 2006–; Adviser, Sri Lankan Del. to Bd of Govs, Asian Devt Bank 2006.
Address: Sri Lankan High Commission, 27 Kautilya Marg, Chanakyapuri, New Delhi 110 021, India (office). *Telephone:* (11) 23010201 (office). *Fax:* (11) 23793604 (office). *E-mail:* lankacom@del2.vsnl.net.in (office).

JAZ, Awad Ahmad al-; Sudanese politician; *Minister of Finance and National Economy; Career:* Minister of Energy and Mining –2008, of Finance and Nat. Economy 2008–; mem. Nat. Congress.
Address: Ministry of Finance and National Economy, PO Box 735, Khartoum, Sudan (office). *Telephone:* (183) 777563 (office). *Fax:* (183) 775630 (office). *E-mail:* info@mof-sudan.net (office). *Website:* mof-sudan .com (office).

JAZAIRY, Idriss, MA, MEcons, MPA; Algerian international administrator and diplomatist; *Special Delegate of the President;* b. 29 May 1936, Neuilly-sur-Seine, France; four s. one d. *Education:* Univ. of Oxford, UK, Ecole Nat. d'Admin, Paris, France, Harvard Univ., USA. *Career:* Chief Econ. and Social Dept Algiers 1963–71; Dir Int. Co-operation, Ministry of Foreign Affairs 1963–71; Adviser to Pres. of Repub. 1971–77; Under-Sec.-Gen. Ministry of Foreign Affairs 1977–79; Amb. to Belgium, Luxembourg and EEC 1979–82; Amb.-at-large specializing in int. econ. affairs, Ministry of Foreign Affairs 1982–84; Pres IFAD Rome 1984–93; Exec. Dir Agency for Co-operation and Research in Devt (ACORD), London 1993–99; Sr Consultant to UNDP 1994–98; Amb. to USA 1999–2004; currently Special Del. of Pres. of Algeria; mem. Bd of Dirs South Centre, Geneva 2002–; Pres. Bd of Govs African Devt Bank 1971–72; Chair. UN Gen. Ass. Cttee of the Whole on North–South Dialogue 1978–79; organized first World Summit on the Econ. Advancement of Rural Women, Geneva 1992; Grand Officer Order of Merit (Italy), Officer of the Wissam Alaouite (Morocco), Officer of the Order of Merit (Mauritania); Medal of Independence (Jordan); numerous other foreign decorations and awards. *Publication:* The State of World Rural Poverty 1992.
Address: Office of the President, Présidence de la République, el-Mouradia, Algiers, Algeria. *Telephone:* (21) 69-15-15. *Fax:* (21) 69-15-95. *Website:* www.el-mouradia.dz.

JEENBAEV, Nurbek, MSc, PhD; Kyrgyzstani diplomatist; *Permanent Representative, United Nations;* b. 5 Feb. 1962, Bishkek; m.; one s. two d. *Education:* Kyrgyz State Univ. *Career:* Lab. Asst and Jr Science Researcher, Kyrgyz State Univ. 1984–90; Researcher, Inst. of Physics, Nat. Acad. of Sciences of Kyrgyz Repub. 1990–95; First Sec., Ministry of Foreign Affairs 1995; fmr Deputy Head then Head, Int. Orgs Dept, Ministry of Foreign Affairs; Minister-Counsellor, Kyrgyz Embassies in USA and Canada 1998–2001; Head, Int. Security Dept, Ministry of Foreign Affairs 2002; Referent, External Policy Dept, Office of Pres. 2002–03, Expert 2003–04; Perm. Rep. to UN, New York 2004–. *Publications:* 19 scientific articles; three publs on diplomacy.
Address: Office of the Permanent Representative of Kyrgyzstan to the United Nations, 866 United Nations Plaza, Suite 477, New York, NY

10017, USA (office). *Telephone:* (212) 486-4214 (office). *Fax:* (212) 486-5259 (office). *E-mail:* kyrgyzstan@un.int (office).

JEETAH, Usha, PhD; Mauritian diplomatist and educator; m.; four c. *Education:* Delhi Univ. *Career:* secondary school teacher 1971–91; creator of educational TV and radio programmes 1971–; social worker and politician 1991–; lecturer on philosophy and culture; Pres. Women's Wing, Movt Socialiste Militant; Amb. to USA 2001–05.
Address: c/o Ministry of Foreign Affairs, International Trade and Co-operation, New Government Centre, 5th Floor, Port Louis, Mauritius. *Telephone:* 201-1648.

JEEWOOLALL, Sir Ramesh, Kt, LLB; Mauritian politician and lawyer; b. 20 Dec. 1940; m.; two c. *Education:* Middle Temple, London, UK. *Career:* lawyer 1969–71; magistrate 1971–72; Chair. Tea Devt Authority 1976; elected to Legis. Ass. (Labour Party) 1976, Deputy Speaker 1976–79, Speaker 1979–82, 1996–2001; elected to Legis. Ass. (Alliance Party) 1987; Minister of Housing, Lands and Environment 1987–90.
Address: c/o National Assembly, Port Louis; 92 Belle Rose Avenue, Quatre Bornes, Mauritius.

JEFFERY, Maj.-Gen. (Philip) Michael, AC, CVO, MC; Australian government official and army officer (retd); b. 12 Dec. 1937, Wiluna, WA; m. Marlena Kerr 1967; three s. one d. *Education:* Cannington School, E Victoria Park State School, Kent Street High School, Royal Mil. Coll., Duntroon, Canberra. *Career:* comm. as Lt in Royal Australian Infantry Corps 1958; Platoon Commdr, 17 Nat. Service Training Co., Swanbourne, WA, Reconnaissance Officer, 1 Special Air Service (SAS) Co., Swanbourne 1959; promoted Temporary Capt., 1 SAS Co., Swanbourne 1962; Signal Platoon Commdr, Second Bn, Royal Australian Regt (2 RAR), Malaya 1962; promoted Capt., 2 RAR, Malaya 1962; Signal Platoon Commdr, 3 RAR, Malaya 1963; ADC to Chief of Gen. Staff, Lt-Gen. Sir John Wilton, Army HQ, Canberra, ACT 1964; SAS Regt, Swanbourne 1965; Operations Officer, SAS HQ, Labuan, Borneo 1965; Adjutant, SAS Regt, Swanbourne 1966; promoted Temporary Maj. 1966; Co. Commdr, First Bn, Pacific Islands Regt (1 PIR), Papua New Guinea (PNG); promoted Maj. 1968; Co. Commdr, 8 RAR, Enoggera, Viet Nam (Phuoc Tuy Prov.) and Enoggera 1969–70; Instructor, Battle Wing, Jungle Training Centre, Canungra, Queensland 1971; Student, Royal Mil. Coll. of Science, Schrivenham and British Army Staff Coll., Camberley, UK 1971; Staff Officer, Grade 2 Operations, Directorate of Operations, Army HQ, Canberra 1973; promoted Temporary Lt-Col 1973; Staff Officer Grade 1, Jt Warfare, Directorate of Operations, Army HQ, Canberra; Staff Officer Grade 1, Land Operations, HQ, PNG Defence Force, Port Moresby 1974; promoted Lt-Col 1974; CO Second Bn, Pacific Islands Regt (2 P1R), Wewak, PNG 1975; CO Special Air Service Regt, Swanbourne 1976; Student, Jt Services Staff Coll., Canberra 1978; Mil. Sec.'s Pool of Lt-Cols, Office of the CGS, Canberra 1978; Staff Officer Grade 1, Special Warfare, Operations Br., Army HQ, Canberra 1978; promoted Col and Dir Special Action Forces, Operations Br., Army Office, Canberra 1979; promoted Brig. and Head of Protective Services Co-ordination Centre, Dept of Admin. Services, Canberra 1981; Commdr 1 Brigade, Holsworthy, NSW 1983; Student, Royal Coll. of Defence Studies, UK 1984; promoted Maj. Gen. and Commdr 1 Div., Paddington, NSW 1985; Asst Chief of Gen. Staff, Logistics, Army Office, Canberra 1989; Deputy Chief of Gen. Staff, Army Office, Canberra 1990 Asst Chief of Gen. Staff, Material, Army Office, Canberra, 1991; transferred to Inactive Australian Army Reserve 1993; Gov. of Western Australia 1993–2000; Gov.-Gen. of Commonwealth of Australia 2003–08; Founder and Chair. Future Directions International, Perth, WA 2000–03; Citizen of Western Australia; Hon. Life mem. Returned and Services League; AO (Mil.) 1988; KStJ; Grand Companion of the Order of Logohu (Papua New Guinea) 2005; AASM with Bars, Malaysia, Thai/Malay, Borneo and Viet Nam 1945–75, GSM with Bars Borneo and Malay Peninsula 1962, Viet Nam Service Medal, ASM with Bars, Papua New Guinea and South East Asia 1945–75, Australian Centenary Medal, Defence Force Service Medal with four Bars, Nat. Medal with Bar, Papua New Guinea Independence Medal, Mil. Cross and S Vietnamese Cross of Gallantry with Gold Star, S Viet Nam Campaign Medal, Vietnamese Cross of Gallantry Unit Citation, Pingat Jasa Medal Malaysia 2006; Hon. DTech (Curtin Univ.) 2000; Paul Harris Fellow, The Rotary Foundation 1996, Citizen of Western Australia (CitWA) 2000.
Address: c/o Government House, Dunrossil Drive, Yarralumla, ACT 2600, Australia (office).

JEFFREY, Henry Benfield; Guyanese government official; *Minister of Foreign Trade and International Co-operation; Career:* fmr Minister of Health and Labor, Minister of Educ. –2006, of Foreign Trade and Int. Co-operation 2006–.
Address: Ministry of Foreign Trade and International Co-operation 254 South Road, Bourda, Georgetown, Guyana (office). *Telephone:* 226-5064

(office). *Fax:* 226-8426 (office). *E-mail:* minister@moftic.gov.gy (office). *Website:* www.moftic.gov.gy (office).

JEGERMANIS, Gints; Latvian diplomatist; b. 5 April 1964; m.; two c. *Education:* Univ. of Latvia, Int. Relations Inst., Geneva, Switzerland. *Career:* Sr Technician and Jr Science Assoc., Inst. of Language and Literature, Latvian Science Acad. 1987–90; Chief of Analysis Div. and Vice-Ed.-in-Chief Diena newspaper 1990–93; Head of Policy Planning Div., Ministry of Foreign Affairs 1994–95; Counsellor Embassy in Russia 1995–98; Amb. to Estonia 1998–2001; Perm. Rep. to UN, New York 2001–05; currently Head of Policy Planning Unit, Ministry of Foreign Affairs; Marjamaa Rist Order (Estonia), Cross of Recognition (Latvia). *Publications:* articles in Latvian papers. *Address:* Ministry of Foreign Affairs, Valdemara 3, Rīga 1010, Latvia (office). *Telephone:* 701-6201 (office). *Fax:* 782-8121 (office). *E-mail:* mfa.cha@mfa.gov.lv (office). *Website:* www.mfa.gov.lv (office).

JEICHANDE, Mussagy; Mozambican lawyer and diplomatist. *Career:* staff mem., Ministry of Foreign Affairs; fmr Amb. to South Africa (Mozambique's first); Rep. of the Sec.-Gen. and Head of UN Office in Angola (UNOA) 2000–01. *Address:* c/o Department of Peace-keeping Operations, Room S-3727-B, United Nations, New York, NY 10017, U.S.A. (office).

JENIE, Rezlan Ishar; Indonesian diplomatist; b. 6 Jan. 1952; m.; two c. *Education:* Univ. of Indonesia. *Career:* joined Dept of Foreign Affairs 1980, served Office of Minister 1988–91, Deputy Dir Int. Orgs, 1996–98, Dir American Affairs 2002–03, Sr Official 2003, Dir Gen. for Multilateral Affairs 2007–; served Perm. Mission to UN, Geneva 1984–88; First Sec. for Political Affairs Perm. Mission to UN, NY 1991–96; Head Indonesian Interest Section Lisbon, Portugal 1999, Chargé d'Affaires Embassy in Lisbon 1999–2000; Deputy Perm. Rep. to UN 2003–04; Perm. Rep. 2004–07. *Address:* Ministry of Foreign Affairs, Jalan Taman Pejambon 6, 10th Floor, Jakarta, Pusat, 10110, Indonesia (office). *Telephone:* (21) 3813453 (office). *Fax:* (21) 3857316 (office). *E-mail:* infomed@deplu.go.id (office). *Website:* www.deplu.go.id (office).

JENKINS, John, CMG, LVO; British diplomatist; b. 26 Jan. 1955; m. Nancy Jenkins. *Career:* joined FCO 1980, full-time language training 1981–83, Desk Officer, Southern European Dept 1980–81, E Africa Dept 1986–89, Deputy Head Jt Assessment Unit 1992–95; studies at SOAS, Univ. of London 1998–99; Second, later First Sec., Abu Dhabi 1983–86; Head of Chancery, Kuala Lumpur 1989–92; Deputy Head of Mission, Kuwait 1995–98; Amb. to Myanmar 1999–2002; Consul Gen. to Palestinian Nat. Authority, East Jerusalem 2003–06; Amb. to Syria 2006–07. *Address:* Foreign and Commonwealth Office, King Charles Street, London, SW1A 2AH, England (office). *Telephone:* (20) 7008-1500 (office). *Website:* www.fco.gov.uk (office).

JENKINSON, Eric, OBE; British diplomatist; *High Commissioner to Trinidad and Tobago;* m. Marie Theresa Jenkinson; two s. *Career:* Protocol Div., FCO 1967–70, Immigration/Entry Clearance Officer, Islamabad 1973–76, full-time language training 1976–77, temporary duty, then Third Sec. (Commercial), Jeddah 1978–80, Second Sec. (Commercial), Riyadh 1980–82, Science, Energy and Nuclear Dept 1982–84, Asst Pvt. Sec., Perm. Under-Sec.'s Office, FCO 1984–86, First Sec. (Econ.), Bonn 1986–90, Deputy Consul Gen., Frankfurt 1990–91, Deputy Head of Mission/Consul, Bahrain 1992–95, Head of Parl. Relations Dept, FCO 1995–99, First Sec. (Econ./Commercial), later Acting Deputy Head of Mission, Tehran 1999–2002, High Commr to The Gambia 2002–07, to Trinidad and Tobago 2007–. *Address:* British High Commission, PO Box 778, 19 St Clair Circle, St Clair, Port of Spain, Trinidad and Tobago (office). *Telephone:* 622-2748 (office). *Fax:* 622-4555 (office). *E-mail:* csbhc@tstt.net.tt (office). *Website:* www.britishhighcommission.gov.uk/trinidadandtobago (office).

JENNART, Lt-Gen. Hendrik; Belgian military officer; *Assistant Chief of Staff for Strategic Affairs;* b. 21 Sept. 1948, Uccle; m. Carine Jennart, one s. one d. *Education:* Royal Cadet School, Royal Mil. Acad., Royal Inst. of Defence, Brussels. *Career:* platoon leader C-Squadron, Second Regt Gidsen 1971–75, Commdr C-Squadron 1978–81, Tank Bn Commdr 1989–92; asst officer/mechanics engineer, Experimental Detachment Tank Units 1975, asst officer/electromechanics engineer, Mil. Construction Service 1975–78; asst ACOS Programming and Budgeting Div., Army Staff 1983–86; tutor, Royal Inst. of Defence 1987–89, promoted to Lt-Col 1989, Head of Man. and Communication Chair, Sr Staff Course 1992–93, promoted to Col 1994; Chief Logistic Br., First Corps in Germany 1993–97; Army Staff inspector, tank and infantry units 1997–2001; Chief Infrastructure Div., Directorate Gen. of Material Resources 2001–04; Mil. Rep. to NATO, Brussels 2004–07; Asst Chief of Staff for Strategic Affairs 2007–; promoted to Maj.-Gen. 2000, Lt-Gen. 2002. *Address:* Staff Department of Strategy, Quartier Reine Elisabeth, Rue d'Evere 1, 1140 Brussels, Belgium (office). *Telephone:* (2) 701-30-26 (office). *Fax:* (2) 701-65-16 (office). *E-mail:* infogate.strat@mil.be (office).

JEREMIĆ, Vuk, PhD, MPA; Serbian politician; *Minister of Foreign Affairs;* b. 3 July 1975, Belgrade; m. *Education:* Univ. of Cambridge, Imperial Coll., London, UK and Harvard Univ., USA. *Career:* fmr Financial Analyst, Deutsche Bank, Dresdner Kleinwort Benson Bank and AstraZeneca Pharmaceuticals, London; Adviser to Minister of Telecommunications 2000–03; Adviser to Minister of Defence of Serbia and Montenegro 2003–04; Adviser on Int. Relations and Head, Office of the Pres. of Serbia 2004–07; Minister of Foreign Affairs 2007–; f. Org. of Serbian Students Abroad (OSSI); mem. Demokratska Stranka (Democratic Party), Pres. Bd of Int. Relations 2004–06, mem. Exec. Bd 2006–. *Address:* Ministry of Foreign Affairs, 11000 Belgrade, Kneza Miloša 24–26, Serbia (office). *Telephone:* (11) 3616333 (office). *Fax:* (11) 3618366 (office). *E-mail:* msp@smip.sv.gov.yu (office). *Website:* www.mfa.gov.yu (office).

JERMAN, Ahmed Abdulrahman Al-, LLB; United Arab Emirates diplomatist; *Permanent Representative, United Nations;* b. 1950, Ajman; m.; two c. *Education:* Cairo Univ. *Career:* joined Ministry of Foreign Affairs 1975, Dir Dept of Legal Affairs and Studies 1994–99; Head, Standing Cttee for Legal Affairs, League of Arab States 2001–03; Asst Under-Sec. for Specialized Affairs, Ministry of Foreign Affairs 2004–07; Perm. Rep. to UN, New York 2007–. *Address:* Permanent Mission of United Arab Emirates to the United Nations, 747 Third Avenue, 36th Floor, New York, NY 10017, USA (office). *Telephone:* (212) 371-0480 (office). *Fax:* (212) 371-4923 (office). *E-mail:* uae@un.int (office).

JERVIS, Robert, BA, PhD; American political scientist and academic; *Adlai E. Stevenson Professor of International Affairs, Columbia University; Education:* Oberlin Coll., Univ. of Calif. at Berkeley. *Career:* Asst Prof. of Govt, Harvard Univ. 1968–74, Assoc. Prof. 1972–74; Prof. of Political Science, Univ. of Calif. at LA 1974–80; fmr Prof. Yale Univ., Hebrew Univ.; currently Adlai E. Stevenson Professor of Int. Affairs, Columbia Univ.; Vice-Pres. American Political Science Asscn (APSA) 1988–89, Pres. 1999–2000; Co-Ed. Security Studies Series, Cornell Univ. Press; Fellow AAAS, American Acad. of Arts and Sciences; mem. bd of eight scholarly journals; Career Achievement Award, Security Studies Section, Int. Studies Asscn 1996, Nevitt Sanford Award for Distinguished Professional Contrib. to Political Psychology 1998, Lionel Trilling Award for Best Book by Columbia Faculty Mem. 1998; NAS Award for Behavioral Science Research Relevant to the Prevention of Nuclear War 2006. *Publications:* The Logic of Images in International Relations 1970, Perception and Misperception in International Politics 1976, The Illogic of American Nuclear Strategy 1984, Psychology and Deterrence (co-author) 1985, The Meaning of the Nuclear Revolution (Grawemeyer Award for Ideas Improving World Order 1990) 1989, Systems Effects: Complexity in Political and Social Life 1997, International Politics; Enduring Concepts and Contemporary Issues (co-ed.) 1999, The Origins of Major War (co-ed.) 2000, American Foreign Policy in a New Era 2005; numerous articles in professional journals and chapters in books. *Address:* Department of Political Science, International Affairs Building, Floor 7, 420 West 118th Street, New York, NY 10027, USA (office). *Telephone:* (212) 854-4616 (office). *Fax:* (212) 864-1686 (office). *E-mail:* rlj1@columbia.edu (office). *Website:* www.columbia.edu/cu/polisci (office).

JESSEN-PETERSEN, Søren; Danish United Nations official; m.; four c. *Career:* trained as lawyer and journalist; served in Africa UNHCR 1972–77, Chief of Secr. UNHCR Exec. Cttee 1981–82, Exec. Sec. Second Int. Conf. on Assistance to Refugees in Africa 1983–84, Exec. Sec. Intergovernmental Conf. on Asylum Seekers and Refugees in Europe 1985, opened UNHCR Regional Office for Nordic Countries, Stockholm 1986, served as High Commr's Regional Rep. 1986–89; Special Adviser to UN Under-Sec.-Gen. for Political Affairs 1989; mem. UN Sec.-Gen.'s Task Force on Namibia 1989; Chef de Cabinet of High Commr UNHCR 1990–93, Dir External Relations 1992–94, Dir UNHCR Liaison Office at UN HQ, NY 1994–98, UN Special Envoy to fmr Yugoslavia 1995–96, Asst High Commr UNHCR, Geneva 1998–2001; Chair. EU Stability Pact's Migration, Asylum, Refugees Regional Initiative (MARRI), Chair. MARRI Steering Cttee 2002–04; EU Special Rep. in Skopje 2004; Special Rep. of UN Sec.-Gen. and Head, UN Interim Admin Mission in Kosovo (UNMIK) 2004–06. *Address:* c/o Ministry of Foreign Affairs, Asiatisk Pl. 2, 1448 Copenhagen K, Denmark.

JESZENSZKY, Géza, PhD; Hungarian historian and politician; b. 10 Nov. 1941, Budapest; m. Edit Héjj; one s. one d. *Education:* Eötvös Loránd Univ., Budapest. *Career:* banned from higher educ. for two years 1956–57; subject specialist with Nat. Széchényi Library 1968–76; Sr Lecturer, Budapest Univ. of Econs (now Corvinus Univ. of Budapest) 1976–81, Reader 1981–, Dean of the School of Political and Social Sciences 1989–90, Head, Faculty of Int. Relations 1990–91; Guest Scholar, Woodrow Wilson Center, USA 1985; Visiting Fulbright Prof., Univ. of Santa Barbara, Calif. 1984–86 and UCLA, USA 1986; Helen De Roy Visiting Prof., Univ. of Michigan, Ann Arbor, USA 1996; Visiting Prof., Coll. of Europe, Warsaw-Natolin, Babes-Bolyai Univ., Cluj-Napoca/Kolozsvár, Romania; Founding mem. Hungarian Democratic Forum 1988–96, Head Foreign Affairs Cttee 1988–90, mem. Presidency 1990–94; Minister of Foreign Affairs 1990–94; mem. Parl. 1994–98; Pres. Hungarian Atlantic Council 1995–98; Amb. to USA 1998–2002; Pres. Hungarian Carpathian Asscn; numerous decorations; C.I.E.S. Fulbright Grant 1984–86. *Publications:* Prestige Lost, The Changing Image of Hungary in Great Britain 1894–1918 1986, The Hungarian Question in British Politics 1848–1914 1986, István Tisza: Villain or Tragic Hero? 1987, Lessons of Appeasement 1994, More Bosnias? National and Ethnic Tensions in the Post-Communist World 1997; other studies in Hungarian and English. *Address:* c/o Ministry of Foreign Affairs, Bem rkp. 47, 1027 Budapest, Hungary (office).

JETTOU, Driss; Moroccan politician; b. 24 May 1945, El Jadida; m.; four c. *Education:* Lycée El Khawarizmi de Casablanca, Univ. of Rabat, Cordwainers Coll., London, UK. *Career:* fmr Pres. Moroccan Fed. of Leather Industries (FEDIC); fmr Vice-Pres. Moroccan Asscn of Exporters (ASMEX); Minister of Trade and Industry 1994–95, of Culture and Foreign Trade 1995–97, of Trade, Industry and Culture 1997–98, of the Interior 1998–2002; Prime Minister of Morocco 2002–07; apptd Pres. Office Cherifien des Phosphates (OCP) 2002; fmr mem. Gen. Confed. of Moroccan Enterprises (CGEM); Grande Chevalier, Wissam du Trône. *Address:* c/o Office of the Prime Minister, Palais Royal, Le Méchouar, Rabat, Morocco (office).

JEVREMOVIĆ, Pavle, LLB, PhD; Serbian diplomatist; *Permanent Representative, United Nations;* b. 1940, Užice; m.; three s. *Education:* Univ. of Belgrade, Univ. of Delhi, India. *Career:* Counsellor, Embassy in New Delhi 1973–77; Counsellor, Policy Planning Dept, Ministry of Foreign Affairs 1977–80; Counsellor, Embassy in Washington, DC 1980–84; Dir Dept for S and SE Asia, Ministry of Foreign Affairs 1984–87; Dir Foreign Policy Dept 1987–92; Minister-Counsellor, Directorate for Non-Aligned Movt, Ministry of Foreign Affairs 1992–2000; Foreign Policy Adviser to Pres. 2000; Amb. of Fed. Repub. of Yugoslavia to EU, Brussels 2002–03, of Serbia and Montenegro 2003–05; Asst Minister for EU Affairs, Ministry of Foreign Affairs 2005–06; Perm. Rep. to UN, New York 2006–. *Address:* Permanent Mission of Serbia to the United Nations, 854 Fifth Avenue, New York, NY 10021, USA (office). *Telephone:* (212) 879-8700 (office). *Fax:* (212) 879-8705 (office). *E-mail:* serbia-montenegro@un.int (office). *Website:* www.un.int/serbia (office).

JEWELL, Linda L., MA; American diplomatist; b. Little Rock, Ark.; m. John Walsh; two c. *Education:* Yale Univ. and Johns Hopkins School of Advanced Int. Studies. *Career:* began her professional career in publishing at Prentice-Hall, Inc.; career mem. Sr Foreign Service since 1976, rank of Minister-Counselor, Educational Exchanges Officer, Jakarta 1976, other overseas postings have included Econs Program Officer, Mexico City, Press Attaché, New Delhi and Warsaw, Washington assignments have included Mexico/Cen. America Desk, Deputy Dir Office of Western Hemisphere Affairs, US Information Agency 1996–97, Dir 1997–99, Deputy Chief of Mission, San José, Costa Rica 1999–2002, Dir Office of Policy Planning and Coordination, Bureau of Western Hemisphere Affairs 2002, Deputy Asst Sec. of State, Bureau of Western Hemisphere Affairs –2005, Amb. to Ecuador 2005–08. *Address:* US Department of State, 2201 C Street NW, Washington, DC 20520, USA (office). *Telephone:* (202) 647-4000 (office). *Fax:* (202) 647-6738 (office). *Website:* www.state.gov (office).

JI, Yunshi; Chinese politician; b. 26 Sept. 1945, Haimen, Jiangsu Prov.; m. Lu Guohong; one d. *Education:* Shandong Univ. *Career:* sent to do manual labour in Xishan Coal Mine, Suzhou City, Jiangsu Prov. 1970; worker, man. clerk and workshop dir Suzhou Light Industrial Electrical Machinery Plant 1971, Deputy Dir then Dir 1978–80; joined CCP 1975; Deputy Dir then Dir No. 2 Light Industry Bureau, Suzhou City 1980–82 (Deputy Sec. CCP Party Cttee 1980–82); Deputy Sec. then Sec. Jiangsu Prov. Cttee CCP Communist Youth League 1980–82; Sec. CCP Jiangsu City Cttee, Jiangsu Prov. 1984; apptd Vice-Gov. Jiangsu Prov. 1989–93, elected Vice-Gov. 1993–98, Acting Gov. 1998–2002; Gov. Hebei Prov. 2002–06; Alt. mem.

15th CCP Cen. Cttee 1997–2002, mem. 16th CCP Cen. Cttee 2002–; Deputy Sec. CCP Jiangsu Prov. Cttee 2001, mem. Standing Cttee 2001. *Address:* c/o Zhongguo Gongchan Dang (Chinese Communist Party) (CCP), Beijing, People's Republic of China.

JIANG, Zemin; Chinese fmr head of state; *Chairman, Central Military Commission of the People's Republic of China;* b. 17 Aug. 1926, Yangzhou City, Jiangsu Prov. *Education:* Jiaotong Univ., Shanghai. *Career:* joined CCP 1946; worked in Shanghai Yimin No. 1 Foodstuffs Factory, Shanghai Soap Factory, First Ministry of Machine-Bldg Industry; trainee, Stalin Automobile Plant, Moscow, USSR 1955–56; Deputy Chief Power Div., Deputy Chief Power-Engineer, Dir, Power Plant, Changchun No. 1 Auto Works 1957–62; Deputy Dir Shanghai Electric Equipment Research Inst., Dir and Acting Party Sec. Wuhan Thermo-Tech. Machinery Research Inst., Deputy Dir, Dir Foreign Affairs Bureau of First Ministry of Machine-Bldg Industry 1962–80; Vice-Chair. and Sec.-Gen. State Comm. on Admin of Imports and Exports, State Comm. on admin of Foreign Investment 1980–82; First Vice-Minister Electronics Industry 1982–83, Minister 1983–85; Mayor of Shanghai 1985–88; Deputy Sec., Sec. Shanghai Municipal Party Cttee 1985–89; mem. 12th Nat. Congress CCP Cen. Cttee 1982, Politburo 1st Plenary Session of 13th Cen. Cttee 1987, Gen. Sec. 4th Plenary Session 1989, Chair. Mil. Cttee 5th Plenary Session 1989; mem. Standing Cttee Politburo, Gen. Sec. and Chair. Mil. Cttee 14th and 15th CCP Cen. Cttees 1992–2002; Chair. Cen. Mil. Comm. of CCP Cen. Cttee 1990–2004, Cen. Mil. Comm. of People's Repub. of China 2003–; Pres. People's Repub. of China 1993–2003; Hon. Chair. Red Cross Soc. of China; Hon. Pres. Software Industry Asscn. *Address:* Chinese Communist Party, Zhongguo Gongchan Dang, 1 Zhongnanhai, Beijing, People's Republic of China.

JIANG, Zhenghua; Chinese politician; *Vice-Chairman, Standing Committee, National People's Congress;* b. Oct. 1937, Hangzhou City, Zhejiang Prov. *Education:* Xi'an Jiaotong Univ., Int. Demography Acad., Bombay, India. *Career:* Lecturer, Auto Control Dept and Dir Population Research Centre, Inst. of Systematic Eng 1958–78; Dir Population and Econs Inst. 1958–78; Prof., Xi'an Jiaotong Univ. 1978–91; Visiting Prof., Univ. of Paris, France, Stanford Univ., USA; Specialist, India Int. Devt Centre 1986; fmr Tech. Advisor, State Census Office; Vice-Minister, State Family Planning Comm. 1991–99; joined Chinese Peasants' and Workers' Democratic Party 1992; Vice-Chair. Cen. Cttee 11th Chinese Peasants' and Workers' Democratic Party (CPWDP) 1992–97, Chair. Cen. Cttee 12th CPWDP 1997–2002; mem. 7th CPPCC Nat. Cttee 1988–93, Standing Cttee 8th CPPCC Nat. Cttee 1993–98 (mem. Sub-cttee of Educ., Science, Culture, Health and Sports 1993–98); Vice-Chair. Standing Cttee of 9th NPC 1998–2003, of 10th NPC 2003–; mem. Macao Hand-Over Ceremony Govt Del., Macao Special Admin. Region Preparatory Cttee 1999; now Prof. of Systems Eng, Econometrics and Demography; fmr Pres. China Soc. of Tech. and Demography; fmr Vice-Pres. Demographic Inst., Shaanxi Prov.; fmr adviser to and mem. Exec. Council Demography Soc. of China; mem. Council Int. Demography Soc. 1993–; Gold Medal, Bombay Int. Demography Acad., India 1981, Outstanding Expert at Nat. Level of China 1985, Nat. Advanced Worker of China 1989, First Class Nat. Science and Tech. Progress Prize 1987. *Publications:* Economic Development Planning Models 1981, Country Report on Population of China 1997, Sustainable Development of China 1999, Population – Systematic and Quantitative Study and its Application (First Class Award, State Scientific and Technological Advancement), Analysis and Planning of Population, Programming Regional Population and Coordination Development of Economy. *Address:* Standing Committee of National People's Congress, Beijing 100805 (office); 11 Min Zu Yuan Road, Room 601, Beijing 100029, People's Republic of China (home). *Telephone:* (10) 63091615 (office); (10) 62357120 (home). *Fax:* (10) 63091614 (office). *E-mail:* jenjenny@sina.com (office).

JIHAD, Abdullah; Maldivian economist, central banker and politician; *Minister of Finance and Treasury; Career:* held several positions in Ministry of Finance, including Minister of State; Gov. Maldives Monetary Authority (first ind. gov.) 2007–08; Minister of Finance and Treasury 2008–. *Address:* Ministry of Finance and Treasury, Block 379, Ameenee Magu, Malé 20-379, Maldives (office). *Telephone:* 3328790 (office); 3349200 (office). *Fax:* 3324432 (office). *E-mail:* admin@finance.gov.mv (office). *Website:* www.finance.gov.mv (office).

JIMÉNEZ REMUS, Gabriel; Mexican lawyer, politician and diplomatist; *Ambassador to Cuba; Career:* fmr Senator and Leader, Partido Acción Nacional; Amb. to Spain –2007; Amb. to Cuba 2007–.

Address: Embassy of Mexico, Calle 12, No 518, Miramar, Playa, Havana, Cuba (office). *Telephone:* (7) 204-2553 (office). *Fax:* (7) 204-2717 (office). *E-mail:* embamex@ip.etecsa.cu (office).

JIN, Renqing; Chinese politician; b. July 1944, Suzhou, Jiangsu Prov. *Education:* Cen. Inst. of Finance and Banking. *Career:* staff mem. Grain Bureau, Yongsheng Co., Yunnan Prov. 1968–97, Deputy Dir 1977–80; joined CCP 1972; Deputy Dir Financial Office, Yongsheng Co. 1977–80; mem. Standing Cttee CCP Yongsheng Co. Cttee 1980–82 (Vice-Chair. CCP Revolutionary Cttee 1980–82), Deputy Sec. CCP Yongsheng Co. Cttee 1982–83; Deputy Magistrate, Yongsheng Co. (Dist) People's Court 1980–82, Acting Magistrate and Magistrate 1982–83; mem. CCP Lijiang Prefectural Cttee, Yunnan Prov. 1985–91; Deputy Commr Lijiang Prefectural Admin. Office 1985–91; Vice-Gov. Lijiang 1985–91; Vice-Minister of Finance 1991–95; Deputy Sec.-Gen. State Council 1995; apptd Vice-Mayor of Beijing 1995, elected Vice-Mayor 1998; mem. Standing Cttee CCP Beijing Municipal Cttee 1995; Deputy Sec. CCP Beijing Municipal Cttee 1997, Deputy Dir Planning and Construction Cttee 1997; Dir State Tax Bureau 1998–2003; Alt. mem. CCP 15th Cen. Cttee 1997–2002, mem. CCP 16th Cen. Cttee 2002–; Minister of Finance 2003–07; Hon. Chair. Exec. Cttee All-China Fed. of Industry and Commerce 1996–97.
Address: c/o Zhongguo Gongchan Dang (Chinese Communist Party), Beijing, People's Republic of China (office).

JIN, Yongjian; Chinese diplomatist and national organization official; *President, United Nations Association of China;* b. 15 Sept. 1934; m. Wang Youping 1955; two s. *Education:* Beijing Univ. of Foreign Studies. *Career:* officer People's Inst. of Foreign Affairs of China 1954–63; Attaché Embassy, Nairobi 1964–67; officer African Dept Ministry of Foreign Affairs, Beijing 1967–71, Deputy Dir-Gen., Dir-Gen. 1984–88, Dir-Gen. Dept of Int. Orgs and Conferences 1988–90; Third Sec., Second Sec. Embassy, Lagos 1971–76; Second Sec., First Sec., Counsellor Perm. Mission to UN, NY, Alt. Rep. to UN Security Council, Rep. to Security Council Special Cttee on Decolonization, UN Council for Namibia 1977–84, Deputy Perm. Rep., Amb. to UN, Deputy Rep. to Security Council 1990–92; Amb., Perm. Rep. to UN, Geneva, also accred to other int. orgs in Switzerland 1992–96; Under-Sec.-Gen. for Devt Support and Man. Services, UN 1996–97, for Gen. Ass. Affairs and Conf. Services 1997–2001; Pres. UN Asscn of China 2001–; Adjunct Prof., Nankai Univ. 2005–.
Address: United Nations Association of China, 71 Nanchizi, Beijing 100 006, People's Republic of China (office). *Telephone:* (10) 65120585 (office). *Fax:* (10) 65131831 (office). *E-mail:* secretariat@unachina.org (office). *Website:* www.unachina.org (office).

JINDRÁK, Rudolf, DIur; Czech diplomatist; *Ambassador to Germany;* b. 25 Jan. 1964, Prague; m.; two d. *Education:* Charles Univ., Prague. *Career:* Head of Western and Cen. Europe Unit, Ministry of Foreign Affairs 1990–91; Consul, Consulate Gen. in Munich 1991–93, Consul Gen. 1993–95; Head of First Countries Unit, Ministry of Foreign Affairs 1995–97, Head of Legal and Consular Affairs Section 1997–98, Deputy Minister for Foreign Affairs 2001–04; Amb. to Hungary 1998–2001, to Austria 2004–06, to Germany 2006–.
Address: Embassy of the Czech Republic, Wilhelmstrasse 44, 10117 Berlin, Germany (office). *Telephone:* (30) 226380 (office). *Fax:* (30) 2294033 (office). *E-mail:* berlin@embassy.mzv.cz (office). *Website:* www.mfa.cz/ berlin (office).

JINGA, Ion, BSc, MA, PhD; Romanian physicist, academic and diplomatist; *Ambassador to UK;* b. 1 Sept. 1961, ; m. Daniela Doina Jinga; one d. *Education:* Dinicu Golescu High School, Câmpulung-Muscel, Faculties of Physics and Law, Univ. of Bucharest, Nat. School for Political and Admin. Studies, Bucharest, Inst. for Int. Studies, Univ. of Leeds, UK, Coll. of Europe, Bruges, Belgium, Al. I. Cuza Acad., Bucharest. *Career:* mil. service 1980–81; teacher, Economic High School No. 4, Bucharest 1984–85, Secondary School No. 127, Bucharest 1985–86; physicist-engineer, Nuclear Energy Reactors Inst., Pitesti 1986–91; Head of Protocol, Mass Media and External Relations Office, Arges Co. Govt, Pitesti 1991–92; Third Sec., Directorate for EU Affairs, Ministry of Foreign Affairs 1992–94, Second Sec., Minister's Office 1994–95;, First Sec., Perm. Mission to EU, Brussels 1995–98, Deputy Head of Mission 1998–99; Counsellor, Directorate for EU Affairs, Ministry of Foreign Affairs 1999–2000; Deputy Head of Mission, later Chargé d'affaires a.i., Perm. Mission to EU, Brussels 2000–01, mem. Del. to Convention on the Future of Europe (Alt. to Govt Rep.) and Co-ordinator Nat. Secr. of Del. 2002; Dir Gen. for EU Affairs, Ministry of Foreign Affairs 2002–03; Amb. to Belgium 2003–08, to UK 2008–; Assoc. Prof., Nat. School for Political and Admin. Studies, Bucharest 1992–95, 1999–2000, 2002–03, Diplomatic Acad., Bucharest 2002–03; guest speaker at confs and seminars on Romania's European

integration, Univ. of Valladolid, Spain 2002, College of Europe, Bruges 2003, Free Univ. of Brussels 2004, 2007, LSE 2004, European Parl. 2004, 2005, 2006, European Inst. for Int. Relations, Brussels 2007, 2008; mem. Scientific Council of Romanian Magazine for Community Law, Bucharest 2003–, European Group for Evaluation and Prospective, European Inst. for Int. 2005–; NATO Research Fellowship 1997–99; Hon. Citizen of Câmpulung-Muscel 2007; Officer of the Nat. Order for Merit (Romania) 2000, Officier, Ordre nat. du Mérite 2003, Patriarchal Cross of Romanian Orthodox Church 2003, Great Cross of the Crown's Order (Belgium) 2008; Diploma of Excellence and the title 'Son of the Arges County' (Romania) 2007, awarded title 'The Ambassador of the Year 2007 in Belgium' 2008. *Publications:* author or co-author of five books and numerous studies and articles on EU policies, European integration, reform of EU insts, Romania's accession to the EU, and the Constitutional Treaty 1994–2008.
Address: Embassy of Romania, Arundel House, 4 Palace Green, London, W8 4QD, England (office). *Telephone:* (20) 7937-9666 (office). *Fax:* (20) 7937-8069 (office). *E-mail:* roemb@roemb.co.uk (office). *Website:* londra .mae.ro (office).

JINGILI, Ali Ahmad Jama; Somali politician. *Career:* Minister for Information 2007–08, of Foreign Affairs and Int. Co-operation 2008 (resgnd).
Address: c/o Ministry of Foreign Affairs and International Co-operation, Mogadishu, Somalia (office).

JOB, Brian, PhD; Canadian academic and research institute director; *Director, Centre of International Relations, University of British Columbia;* *Education:* Indiana Univ. *Career:* Prof., Univ. of British Columbia 1989–, Dir Centre of Int. Relations 1992–; mem. Foreign Minister's Advisory Bd 1995–97; Co-founder Canadian Consortium on Asia Pacific Security, Canadian Consortium on Human Security; fmr Ed. Int. Studies Quarterly; fmr Treas. and Vice-Pres. Int. Studies Asscn; Co-Chair. Council for Security Cooperation in the Asian Pacific.
Address: Office of the Director, Centre of International Relations, Liu Institute of Global Issues, University of British Columbia, 6476 NW Marine Drive, Vancouver, BC V6T 1Z2, Canada (office). *Telephone:* (604) 822-0237 (office). *Fax:* (604) 822-6966 (office). *E-mail:* bjob@interchange .ubc.ca (office). *Website:* www.iir.ubc.ca (office).

JOBIM, Nelson Azevedo; Brazilian lawyer and politician; *Minister of Defence;* b. 12 April 1946, Santa Maria. *Education:* Universidade Federal do Rio Grande do Sul. *Career:* practised as lawyer 1969–94; Assoc. Prof. of Law, Universidade Federal de Santa Maria, Universidade de Brasília 1973–87; Pres. Santa Maria section, Bar Asscn 1977–78, Vice-Pres. Rio Grande Do Sul section 1984–86; mem. Partido do Movimento Democrá-tico Brasileiro (PMDB), Leader PMDB in Nat. Ass. 1988; elected mem. of Parl. for Rio Grande do Sul 1987–91, re-elected 1991; Minister of Justice 1995–97, Minister of Defence 2007–; served as judge and Pres. Supreme Fed. Court.
Address: Ministry of Defence, Esplanada dos Ministérios, Bloco Q, 70049-900 Brasília, DF, Brazil (office). *Telephone:* (61) 3312-4000 (office). *Fax:* (61) 3225-4151 (office). *E-mail:* faleconosco@defesa.gov.br (office). *Website:* www.defesa.gov.br (office).

JOCKIN, Lt-Gen. Jean-Marie; Belgian military officer; *Military Representative, NATO;* b. 1949, Lanaye; m. Betty Jockin; three c. *Education:* Royal Mil. School, Royal Defence Coll. *Career:* began mil. career with 2nd Cycle Riflemen Bn, served as Armoured Infantry Platoon Commdr, Reconnais-sance Platoon Commdr, Co. Second in Command; completed officer training in Montpellier, France and Fort Benning, Ga USA; served successively as Deputy Operations Officer, Intelligence Officer and Operations Officer, 17th Armoured Brigade Staff 1983–88; Commdr 2nd Cycle Riflemen Bn 1990–92, 1st Belgo-Luxembourg Bn, UN Protection Force Yugoslavia 1992; teacher, Army Div., Royal Defence Coll. 1992; Dir for Mil. and Sports Training, Royal Mil. School 1995; Chief of Staff, UN Transitional Admin of Eastern Slavonia (Croatia) 1996; Aide to the King 1997; Chief of Staff, Army Operational Command 1997–99; Commdr 7th Mechanized Brigade 1999–2000; Deputy-Gen. Interservice Territorial Command 2000; Vice-Chief of Defence 2002–07; Mil. Rep., NATO, Brussels 2007–.
Address: NATO HQ, blvd Léopold III, 1110 Brussels, Belgium (office). *Telephone:* (2) 707-41-11 (office). *Fax:* (2) 707-45-79 (office). *E-mail:* natodoc@hq.nato.int (office). *Website:* www.nato.int (office).

JOELLA-SEWNUNDUN, Urmila; Suriname politician and diplomatist; *Ambassador to the Netherlands; Career:* mem. Progressive Reform Party (VHP) 1990; mem. VHP Admin 1998; Minister of Trade and Industry 2000–01, of the Interior 2000–05; Amb. to the Netherlands (also accred to UK) 2006–.

Address: Embassy of Suriname, Alexander Gogelweg 2, 2517 JH The Hague, Netherlands (office); Honorary Consulate of Suriname, 89 Pier House, 31 Cheyne Walk, London, SW3 5HN, England (office). *Telephone:* (70) 365-08-44 (office). *Fax:* (70) 361-74-45 (office). *E-mail:* ambassade.suriname@wxs.nl (office).

JÕERÜÜT, Jaak; Estonian politician and diplomatist; *Ambassador to Latvia;* b. 9 Dec. 1947, Tallinn; m. *Education:* Faculty of Econs, Tallinn Technical Inst. *Career:* Ed. Eesti Raamat publishing house 1976–77; Sec. and Deputy Chair. Estonian Writers' Union 1977–89; Deputy Minister, Ministry of Culture 1989–90; mem. Parl. 1990–92, Chair. Standing Cttee on Research, Educ. and Culture; Amb. to Finland 1993–97; Dir-Gen. Protocol Dept, Ministry of Foreign Affairs 1997–98; Amb. to Italy 1998–2002, to Malta 1999–2002, to Cyprus 1999–2004; Inspector-Gen., Ministry of Foreign Affairs 2002–04; Special Adviser to the Govt 2002–03; Perm. Rep. to UN, New York July–Nov. 2004; Minister of Defence 2004–05; Amb. to Latvia 2006–; mem. Estonian Writers' Union, Estonian PEN.
Address: Embassy of Estonia, Skolas iela 13, Rīga 1010, Latvia (office). *Telephone:* 6781-2020 (office). *Fax:* 6781-2029 (office). *E-mail:* embassy.riga@mfa.ee (office). *Website:* www.estemb.lv (office).

JOFFE, Josef, PhD; German journalist, editor and international relations scholar; *Publisher-Editor, Die Zeit;* b. 15 March 1944; m. Dr Christine Joffe; two d. *Education:* Harvard Univ., USA. *Career:* Foreign and Editorial Page Dir Suddeutsche Zeitung 1985–2000; Publr-Ed. Die Zeit newspaper 2000–; Professorial Lecturer, Johns Hopkins Univ. 1982–84; Adjunct Prof. of Political Science, Stanford Univ. 2004–, Fellow, Inst. for Int. Studies and Hoover Inst., Stanford 2004–; Visiting Prof. of Govt, Harvard Univ. 1999–2000, Assoc., Olin Inst. for Strategic Studies; Visiting Lecturer, Princeton Univ., Dartmouth Univ.; Founding Bd mem. The National Interest 1995–2005; mem. Editorial Bd International Security, Prospect; Order of Merit, Germany 1998; hon. degree (Swarthmore) 2002, (Lewis and Clark Coll.) 2005; Theodor-Wolff-Prize in Journalism (Germany), Ludwig Börne Prize in Essays/Literature (Germany). *Publications include:* The Limited Partnership: Europe, the United States and the Burdens of Alliance 1987, The Great Powers 1998, Überpower: The Imperial Temptation of America 2006; numerous articles in scholarly journals and chapters in books.
Address: Die Zeit, Speersort 1, 20095 Hamburg, Germany (office). *Telephone:* (40) 328-00 (office). *Fax:* (40) 3280-596 (office). *E-mail:* gentsch@zeit.de (office). *Website:* www.zeit.de (office).

JÓHANNESSON, Stefán Haukur; Icelandic diplomatist; *Ambassador to the European Communities, Belgium, Liechtenstein, Luxembourg and Morocco;* b. 4 Jan. 1959, Westman Islands; m.; three c. *Education:* Univ. of Iceland. *Career:* Deputy, Civil and Criminal Court Dist of the Westman Islands 1985–86; First Sec., Ministry for Foreign Affairs 1986–87, First Sec., Perm. Del. to NATO 1987–90, First Sec., and from 1992, Counsellor and Deputy Perm. Rep. to GATT, Perm. Mission of Iceland, Geneva 1990–93, Counsellor, External Trade Dept, Ministry for Foreign Affairs 1993–96, Minister Counsellor and Dir Dept of Admin and Personnel 1996–98, Amb. and Dir External Trade Dept 1999–2001, Amb. and Perm. Rep. to UN and Int. Orgs, Geneva, including EFTA and WTO 2001–05, also accred to Slovenia 2002–05, Amb. to EC, Belgium, Liechtenstein, Luxembourg and Morocco, Brussels 2005–; Lecturer on Int. Trade Law, Int. Marketing, Tech. Coll. of Iceland 1995–96; Chair. WTO/Working Group on Trade and Transfer of Tech. 2002–04, WTO/Dispute Settlement Panel –US Steel Safeguards 2002–03, Man. Bd of WTO Pension Plan 2003–04, Working Party on the Accession of the Russian Fed. to WTO 2003–, WTO/Negotiating Group on Market Access for Non-Agricultural Products (NAMA) 2004–06; EFTA Chief Negotiator and Spokesman in free trade negotiations with Lebanon 2003–04.
Address: Embassy of Iceland, Rond Point Schuman 11, 1040 Brussels, Belgium (office). *Telephone:* (2) 238-50-00 (office). *Fax:* (2) 230-69-38 (office). *E-mail:* emb.brussels@mfa.is (office). *Website:* www.iceland.org/be (office).

JÓHANNSSON, Kjartan, CE, PhD; Icelandic politician and diplomatist; b. 19 Dec. 1939, Reykjavik; m. Irma Karlsdóttir 1964; one d. *Education:* Reykjavik Coll., Tech. Univ. of Stockholm, Sweden, Univ. of Stockholm, Illinois Inst. of Tech., Chicago. *Career:* Consulting Eng in Reykjavik 1966–78; Teacher in Faculty of Eng and Science, later Prof. in Faculty for Econs and Business Admin, Univ. of Iceland 1966–78, 1980–89; Chair. Org. for Support of the Elderly, Hafnarfjördur; mem. Bd of Dir Icelandic Aluminium Co. Ltd 1970–75; Chair. Fisheries Bd of Municipal Trawler Co., Hafnarfjördur 1970–74; mem. Municipal Council, Hafnarfjördur 1974–78; mem. Party Council and Exec. Council, Social Democratic Party 1972–89, Vice-Chair. of Social Democratic Party 1974–80, Chair. 1980–84; mem. Althing (Parl.) 1978–89, Speaker of the Lower House 1988–89; Minister of Fisheries 1978–80, also Minister of Commerce 1979–80; Amb.

and Perm. Rep. to UN and other int. orgs Geneva 1989–94; Sec.-Gen. EFTA 1994–2001; mem. staff External Trade Department, Ministry of Foreign Affairs 2002; Amb. to Belgium, Liechtenstein, Luxembourg and Chief of Mission to the EU 2002–05.
Address: c/o Ministry of Foreign Affairs, Raudarárstíg 25, 150 Reykjavík (office); Vatusstig 21, 101 Reykjavík, Iceland (home). *Telephone:* 5459900 (office); 5342597 (home). *Fax:* 5622373 (office). *E-mail:* postur@utn.stjr.is (office); kjartan.johannsson@gmail.com (home). *Website:* utanrikisraduneyti.is.

JOHN, Ellsworth I. A., BBA, MSc; Saint Vincent and the Grenadines trade unionist and diplomatist. *Education:* Baruch Coll., City Univ. of New York, Strayer Univ., USA. *Career:* fmr Gen.-Sec. Org. in Defence of Democracy; Gen.-Sec. Saint Vincent and Grenadines Public Service Union 1980s; Counsellor, Washington, DC and Alt. Rep. to OAS 1992–96, Regional Co-ordinator for the Caribbean, OAS 1996–2002, Amb. to USA 2002–08.
Address: Ministry of Foreign Affairs, Commerce and Trade, Administrative Building, 3rd Floor, Bay Street, Kingstown, Saint Vincent and the Grenadines (office). *Telephone:* 456-2060 (office). *Fax:* 456-2610 (office). *E-mail:* office.foreignaffairs@mail.gov.vc (office).

JOHN, Eric G.; American diplomatist; *Ambassador to Thailand;* b. Ind.; m. Sophia John; one s. one d. *Career:* joined Foreign Service 1983, has served as Deputy Consul Gen. in Ho Chi Minh City, and in Bangkok 1989–92, has served extensively throughout East Asia, served 13 years in Seoul, Busan and Washington, DC working on relations with the Korean Peninsula, served as Minister Counselor for Political Affairs, Seoul, Deputy Asst Sec. of State for SE Asia 2005–07, lead negotiator in US-ASEAN Enhanced Partnership 2006, Amb. to Thailand 2007–.
Address: US Embassy, 120/22 Wireless Road, Bangkok, 10330, Thailand (office). *Telephone:* (2) 205-4000 (office). *Fax:* (2) 254-2990 (office). *E-mail:* acsbkk@state.gov (office). *Website:* bangkok.usembassy.gov (office).

JOHNNY, Sonia Merlyn, MA, DrJur; Saint Lucia diplomatist and lawyer; m.; one s. *Education:* Univ. of the West Indies, Port-of-Spain, Trinidad, Johns Hopkins School of Advanced Int. Studies and Georgetown Univ. Law School, USA. *Career:* political and econ. attaché, Ministry of Foreign Affairs 1979, Head of Div. 1980–84, sent to USA to establish new mission in Washington, DC 1984, First Sec. and Counsellor Desig. 1984–87; pursued legal career 1991–97; served in Office of the Corpn Counsel, Washington, DC 1993–97, Amb. to USA and Perm. Rep. to OAS (Saint Lucia's first female Amb.) 1997–2007.
Address: Ministry of External Affairs, International Financial Services, Information and Broadcasting, Conway Business Centre, Waterfront, Castries, Saint Lucia (office). *Telephone:* 468-4501 (office). *Fax:* 452-7427 (office). *E-mail:* foreign@candw.lc (office).

JOHNSON, Anthony Smith Rowe, BA, MA; Jamaican business executive, politician and diplomatist; *Ambassador to USA;* m. Pamela Rosalee Johnson; four c. *Education:* Univ. of California, Los Angeles, USA. *Career:* fmr news reporter and producer, Jamaica Broadcasting Corpn; Gen. Man. and Dir for Jamaica Frozen Foods 1970–74; Man. Dir and Manufacturer with Jampro Ltd 1975–76; Exec. Dir Pvt. Sector Org. of Jamaica 1976–80; Senator 1980–83, 1993–2007, Minority Leader of the Senate 2002, Opposition Spokesman on Agric. 2002–07; Minister of State, Ministry of Industry and Commerce 1980–83, Ministry of Agric. 1983–89, Spokesman on Mining, Energy and Tech. 1983–87, on Educ. 1987–2002; MP 1983–93; Lecturer, Dept of Man. Studies, Univ. of the West Indies 1992–2006, Sr Lecturer 2006–08; Amb. to USA and Perm. Rep. to OAS 2008–.
Address: Embassy of Jamaica, 1520 New Hampshire Avenue, NW, Washington, DC 20006, USA (office). *Telephone:* (202) 452-0660 (office). *Fax:* (202) 452-0081 (office). *E-mail:* info@emjamusa.org (office). *Website:* www.embassyofjamaica.org (office).

JOHNSON, Brenda LaGrange; American business executive, diplomatist and philanthropist; *Ambassador to Jamaica;* m. J. Howard Johnson; four c. *Career:* Pnr, BrenMer Industries 1977–2005; Amb. to Jamaica 2005–; Founding mem. and Pres. and Chair. Women's Bd of Madison Square Boys and Girls Club, now a Trustee; apptd to Pres.'s Advisory Council to the Arts, John F. Kennedy Center for the Performing Arts, Washington, DC 2002–, mem. Bd Trustees 2004–; mem. Woodrow Wilson Council 1999–; fmr mem. Duke Univ. Advisory Bd of Nasher Art Museum; fmr mem. Bd Dirs American Cancer Soc., NIH Nat. Cancer Advisory Bd; mem. Nat. Finance Advisory Council for the George and Barbara Bush Endowment at M.D. Anderson Cancer Center, Houston, Tex.
Address: US Embassy, 142 Old Hope Road, Kingston 6, Jamaica (office). *Telephone:* 702-6000 (office). *E-mail:* opakgn@state.gov (office). *Website:* kingston.usembassy.gov (office).

JOHNSON, David T., BEcons; American diplomatist; *Minister and Deputy Chief of Mission, US Embassy in London;* b. Georgia; m. Scarlett M. Swan; two d. one s. *Education:* Emory Univ., Canadian National Defence Coll. *Career:* Asst Nat. Trust Examiner, Treasury Dept; joined US Foreign Service 1977; Vice-Consul, Consulate-Gen., Ciudad Juárez, Mexico 1978–79; Econ. Officer, US Embassy, Berlin 1981–83; Deputy Dir, State Dept Operations Center 1987–89; Consul.-Gen., Vancouver 1990–93; Deputy Spokesman, State Dept; Dir State Dept Press Office 1993–95; Deputy Press Sec. for Foreign Affairs at the White House and Spokesman for Nat. Sec. Council 1995–97; Chief (with rank of Amb.), US Mission to OSCE 1998, Minister and Deputy Chief of Mission, US Embassy, London 2003–. *Address:* Embassy of the USA, 24–32 Grosvenor Square, London, W1A 1AE, England (office). *Telephone:* (20) 7499-9000 (office). *Fax:* (20) 7629-9124 (office). *Website:* www.usembassy.org.uk (office).

JOHNSON, Donald C., BA, MPA, JD; American lawyer and diplomatist; *Ambassador to Equatorial Guinea;* m. *Education:* Lewis and Clark Coll., Univ. of Oklahoma, George Washington Univ. *Career:* grew up in Mexico; draftee in US Army 1971–73; mem. DC Bar, State Bar of Tex., US Supreme Court Bar; career mem. Sr Foreign Service since 1989, entered Foreign Service 1974, Third Sec. in Guatemala, other overseas postings have been in Moscow, Taipei, Beijing, Madrid and Tegucigalpa; Washington, DC assignments have included Desk Officer at Dept of State and service on Nat. Security Council at White House; Amb. to Mongolia 1993–96, Head of Mission in Moldova for OSCE 1996–97; in Irish peace process as one of three mems of Ind. Int. Comm.; Amb. to Cape Verde 2002–05, worked in US Mission to OAS, led US team in negotiations for a Social Charter of the Americas 2005–06; Amb. to Equatorial Guinea 2006–; decorated by Pres. of Mongolia and Pres. of Cape Verde in recognition of service as Amb.; Superior Honor Award and several performance pay awards. *Address:* US Embassy, K-3, Carretera de Aeropuerto, Al lado de Restaurante El Paraíso, Malabo, Equatorial Guinea (office). *Telephone:* (9) 88-95 (office). *Fax:* (9) 88-94 (office). *E-mail:* usembassymalabo@yahoo.com (office). *Website:* malabo.usembassy.gov (office).

JOHNSON, Susan Rockwell, MA; American diplomatist. *Education:* Principia Coll., Elsah Ill., Johns Hopkins School of Advanced Int. Studies, Washington DC. *Career:* early career includes positions with Giovanni Angelli Foundation, Torino Italy and Valmont Industries, Omaha, Neb.; joined US State Dept 1979, positions included Vice-Consul to US interest Section, Havana, Cuba 1979–80, Political Officer to US Mission to UN 1980–84, Special Asst to Undersec. for Political Affairs (responsible for Near E and S Asian Affairs) 1984–86; Pearson Fellow Legis. Asst to Senator Bill Bradley 1986–87; Advisor to Office of Under-Sec. 1988; Acting Refugee Counsellor, Embassy in Pakistan 1988; Detail to Nat. Endowment for Democracy 1988–89; Deputy Chief of Mission, Mauritius 1989–91; Dir for Cen. Asia, Int. Exec. Service Corps (IESC) 1992–94; Dir Amb.'s Assistance Unit (AAU), Dir G7 Support Implementation Group, Embassy in Moscow 1994–98; Office of Sec. of Resources, Plans and Policy 1998–99; Deputy Chief of Mission, Embassy in Bucharest 1999–2002; Sr Advisor to Iraqi Ministry of Foreign Affairs, Coalition Provisional Authority, Baghdad 2002–04; Acting Dir Civil Affairs Ministries 2002–04; Dist Supervisor and Deputy High Rep., Brcko, Bosnia and Herzegovina 2004–06; fmr Chair. Bd American Int. School of Bucharest. *Address:* c/o Office of the High Representative, 76100 Brcko, Bosnia and Herzegovina. *Website:* www.ohr.int.

JOHNSON, Wesley Momo, MBA, CPA; Liberian politician and diplomatist; *Ambassador to UK;* b. 27 May 1944, Monrovia; m.; eight c. *Education:* Monrovia Coll., St Francis Coll., Brooklyn, NY, Long Island Univ., NY, USA. *Career:* Baptist Licentiate and Deacon, Zion Grove Baptist Church, Brewerville; fmr Auditor, Old Colony Newport Nat. Bank, Providence, RI, USA; Auditor, Treasury Dept of Liberia (now Ministry of Finance) 1968–72; Sr Bookkeeper (Class-I) and Brokerage Man., Skyline Shipping Co. 1972–77; Founding mem. and Vice-Chair. Progressive Alliance of Liberia 1973, Progressive People's Party 1980; Founding mem. United People's Party 1984, Chair. 1999–; fmr Amb. to Egypt, Consul Gen. to New York 1981; mem. Interim Legis. Ass. 1990–94, Chair. House Standing Cttee on Banking and Currency, Cttee on Ways, Means, Finance and Maritime Affairs, Co-Chair. Cttee on Rules, Cttee on Order and Executive, Sec.-Gen. Liberian Parl. Union; Vice-Chair. Nat. Transitional Govt 2003–07; Amb. to UK 2007–; led Liberian del. to several int. confs including 36th Gen. Ass. of UN (Chair. Cttee on Disarmament) 1981, African Pacific Caribbean Comm., Rosenberg 1992, mem. del. to Inter-Parl. Union, New Delhi, India; Partner, Nimley & Assocs, CPA Inc.; Lecturer, Univ. of Liberia, United Methodist Univ., AME Zion Univ. Coll.; mem. numerous accounting firms and financial insts, including Liberian Certified Public Accountants, Inst. of Certified Internal Auditors, Inc., Atlanta, Ga, American Banking Asscn, RI, MBA Executive, NY USA. *Address:* Embassy of Liberia, 23 Fitzroy Square, London, W1 6EW, England (office). *Telephone:* (20) 7388-5489 (office). *Fax:* (20) 7380-1593 (office). *E-mail:* liberianembassy@yahoo.co.uk (office). *Website:* www.embassyofliberia.org.uk (office).

JOHNSON-SIRLEAF, Ellen, BBA, MPA; Liberian politician and head of state; *President;* b. 29 Oct. 1938; four s. *Education:* Coll. of West Africa, Monrovia, Madison Business Coll., Madison, Wis., Univ. of Colorado and Harvard Univ., USA. *Career:* Asst Minister of Finance 1972–78, Deputy Minister of Finance 1979–80; Sr Loan Officer, IBRD, Washington, DC 1973–77, 1980–81; sentenced to ten years' imprisonment for speech that was critical of mil. ruler Samuel Doe; briefly detained twice in prison before fleeing country; fmr Pres. Liberian Bank for Devt Investment; Vice-Pres. Citibank Regional Office for Africa, Nairobi 1982–85; Vice-Pres. and mem. Bd Dirs Equator Holders, Hong Kong Equator Bank Ltd, Washington, DC –1992; Asst Admin. UNDP and Dir Regional Bureau for Africa 1992–97; Chair. and CEO Kormah Investment and Devt Corpn; Leader Unity Party (UP), Presidential Cand. 1997; charged with treason by Taylor regime and forced into political exile; Chair. Open Soc. Inst. West Africa (part of Soros Foundation Network); External Adviser, UN Econ. Comm. for Africa; mem. Advisory Bd Modern Africa Growth and Investment Co.; Sr Adviser and W/Cen. Africa Rep. of Modern Africa Fund Mans; Founder Measuagoon (Liberian NGO); rep. Liberia on bds of IMF, IBRD and African Devt Bank; selected by OAU to investigate Rwanda genocide 1999; elected Pres. of Liberia (world's first elected black female pres. and Africa's first elected female head of state) 2005–; Chair. Comm. on Good Governance (Liberia) 2004–05; Founding mem. Int. Inst. for Women in Political Leadership; mem. Bd Dirs Synergos Inst. 1988–99; Distinguished Fellow, Claus M. Halle Inst. for Global Learning, Emory Univ. 2006; Grand Commdr, Star of Africa Redemption of Liberia; Commdr de l'Ordre du Togo; Franklin Delano Roosevelt Freedom of Speech Award 1988, Ralph Bunche Int. Leadership Award, Common Ground Award 2006, Laureate of the Africa Prize for Leadership for the Sustainable End of Hunger 2006, ranked by Forbes magazine amongst the 100 Most Powerful Women (51st) 2006, (100th) 2007, Bishop John T. Walker Distinguished Humanitarian Service Award, Africare 2007. *Publications:* From Disaster to Development 1991, The Outlook for Commercial Bank Lending to Sub-Saharan Africa 1992, Women, War and Peace: The Independent Experts' Assessment on the Impact of Armed Conflict on Women and Women's Role in Peace-building (co-author) (project of UNIFEM) 2002. *Address:* Executive Mansion, PO Box 10-9001, Capitol Hill, 1000 Monrovia 10, Liberia (office).

JOHNSSON, Anders B., LLM; Swedish international organization official; *Secretary-General, Inter-Parliamentary Union;* b. 1948, Lund; m.; three c. *Education:* Univs of Lund and New York. *Career:* mem. staff UNHCR, posts in Honduras, Pakistan, Sudan and Viet Nam, then Prin. Legal Adviser to High Commr, Geneva 1976–91; Under-Sec.-Gen. IPU 1991–94, Deputy Sec.-Gen. and Legal Adviser 1994–98, Sec.-Gen. 1998–. *Address:* Inter-Parliamentary Union, CP 330, 1218 Le Grand-Saconnex/Geneva, Switzerland (office). *Telephone:* (22) 9194150 (office). *Fax:* (22) 9194160 (office). *E-mail:* postbox@mail.ipu.org (office). *Website:* www.ipu.org (office).

JOHNSTONE, L. Craig, BA; American diplomatist and UN official; *Deputy High Commissioner, United Nations High Commissioner for Refugees;* b. 1 Sept. 1942, Seattle, Wash.; m. Janet Gail Buechel; three c. *Education:* Univ. of Maryland, Harvard Univ. *Career:* worked in Viet Nam for USAID and as US Foreign Service Officer 1965–70; also held positions embassy in Ottawa, on the staff of Sec. of State Henry Kissinger; coordinator with UN Gen. Ass.; fmr Deputy Asst Sec. of State for Latin America; Amb. to Algeria 1985–88; held several sr man. positions at Cabot Corpn, Brussels 1989–94; Dir for Resources, Plans and Policy, Office of the Sec. of State 1994–99; fmr Sr Vice-Pres. US Chamber of Commerce; European Vice-Pres. and Gen. Man. The Boeing Co. –2007; Deputy High Commr, UNHCR 2007–; mem. Bd of Dirs Vital Voices Global Partnership; mem. Bd of Trustees Humanitarian Aid Foundation; fmr Fellow, Council on Foreign Relations, New York, Inst. of Politics, Harvard. *Address:* United Nations High Commissioner for Refugees, Case Postale 2500, 1211 Geneva 2 Dépôt, Switzerland (office). *Telephone:* (22) 7398111 (office). *Website:* www.unhcr.org (office).

JOHNSTONE, Peter; British diplomatist and administrator; b. 30 July 1944; m. Diane Claxton 1969; one s. one d. *Career:* joined Foreign Office 1962, postings abroad include Berne 1965–66, Benin City 1966–68, Budapest 1968–69, Maseru 1969–72, Dhaka 1977–79; First Sec. Dublin 1979–82, Harare 1986–89; Consul-Gen. Edmonton 1989–91; Counsellor for Com-

mercial Devt, Jakarta 1995–2000; Gov. of Anguilla and Chair. Exec. Council 2000–04.
Address: c/o Foreign and Commonwealth Office, King Charles Street, London, SW1A 2AH, England. *Telephone:* (20) 7008-1500. *Website:* www .fco.gov.uk.

JOHOR, HRH The Sultan of; Tuanku Mahmood Iskandar ibni al-Marhum Sultan Ismail; Malaysian; b. 8 April 1932, Johore Bahru, Johore; m. 1st Josephine Trevorrow 1956; m. 2nd Tengku Zanariah Ahmad Zanariah Ahmad 1961. *Education:* Sultan Abu Bakar English Coll., Johore Bahru, Trinity Grammar School, Sydney, Australia, Devon Tech. Coll., Torquay, UK. *Career:* Tengku Makota (Crown Prince) 1959–61, 1981; Raja Muda (second-in-line to the throne) 1966–81; fifth Sultan of Johore 1981–; Col-in-Chief, Johore Mil. Forces 1981–; Yang di-Pertuan Agung (Supreme Head of State) 1984–89; f. Mado's Enterprises and Mados-Citoh-Daiken (timber cos).

JOKIĆ, Ljubiša; Montenegrin military officer; b. 24 Sept. 1958, Plav; m.; two s. *Career:* fmr pilot and flight instructor; positions held include Commdr Golubovci Airfield, Podgorica, Sec. Supreme Defense Council, head of military cabinet of Pres. of Serbia and Montenegro, head personnel department Defense Ministry; Chief of Staff Army of Serbia and Montenegro 2005–06.
Address: c/o Ministry of Defence, Birčaninova 5, 11000 Belgrade, Serbia (office). *Fax:* (11) 3651430 (home).

JOLEVSKI, Zoran, BEcons, MSc, PhD; Macedonian diplomatist; *Ambassador to USA;* b. 16 July 1959, Skopje; m. Suzana Jolevska; two s. *Education:* Faculties of Law and Economy, Univ. of Sts Cyril and Methodius, Skopje, Inst. of Social Studies, The Hague, Netherlands. *Career:* freelance dir 1983–88; officer responsible for preparing all necessary documents for observer status of Repub. of Macedonia in GATT as well as Desk Officer for UK and Germany 1988–92; Sec. to Coordination Group on Fmr Yugoslavia Succession Issues 1992–94; Sec., Perm. Mission of Macedonia to WTO and UN, Geneva 1994–98; Chief Adviser to Minister of Economy on WTO accession, Ministry of Foreign Affairs, Deputy Nat. Coordinator on Humanitarian Issues for Kosovo refugee crises, WTO accession and other int. trade and financial affairs 1998–99; Sec.-Gen. Cabinet of Pres. of Macedonia 2000–04; Pres. European Univ. 2003; Chief of Party 'WTO Compliance Activity', USAID Funded Project, Booz Allen & Hamilton 2004–06, 'Macedonian Business Environment Activity', USAID Funded Project 2006; adviser to presidential cand. Boris Trajkovski 1999; Econ. and Foreign Policy Advisor to Nikola Gruevski, Leader of VMRO-DPMNE party and Prime Minister; Special Adviser to Antonio Milososki, Minister of Foreign Affairs; Amb. to USA 2007–; Pres. Man. Bd Prilep 2006–; Sec. to Macedonian del. to Int. Conf. on Succession of the Fmr Yugoslavia 1992–94; Deputy Negotiator and Chief Advisor to Govt of Macedonia for accession to WTO 1999–2004; Chief Negotiator on re-establishment of diplomatic relations between Macedonia and People's Repub. of China 2000–01; mem. negotiation team for Ohrid Framework Agreement and rep. of Pres. of Macedonia to session of Ass. of Repub. of Macedonia for constitutional changes required by Ohird Framework Agreement 2001; Vice-Chair. UNCTAD Expert Meeting on Existing Regional and Multilateral Investment Treaties and their Devt Dimensions 1998; Chair. Workshop: IPR and Trade Facilitation: 'Identifying Opportunities and Roadblocks', Second Int. Forum on Trade Facilitation, UN ECE May 2003; mem. Bureau of Comm. of UNCTAD on Investment, Tech. and Related Financial Issues 1998–99, Team of Specialists on Internet Enterprise Devt, UN/ECE, Geneva 1999–2005, Vice-Chair. Cttee on Trade 2005–; mem. Bd Center for Strategic Research, Macedonian Acad. of Sciences and Art; mem. Man. Bd Alumina 2001–02, Skopje Fair 2000–01, SEVUS 2005–, Airports Makedonija 2006–; mem. Presidency of Swimming Club Vardar, of Tourist Asscn of Skopje 1989–92, of Macedonian-Japanese Friendship Asscn 1990–94, of Macedonian Euro-Atlantic Club 2006–; mem. Cttee 'E-Macedonia for All' under auspices of Pres. of Macedonia 2000–04; Pres. Int. Foundation Boris Trajkovski 2004–05; mem. Lions Centar, Skopje 2005–; Founder and Pres. Inst. for Econ. Strategies and Int. Affairs – Ohrid 2006–. *Publications:* Succession of States: The Case of Ex-Yugoslavia 1993, Multinational Corporations: Challenge of the Contemporary Economy 1997, The World Trading System 2006; Chief Ed.: Report on the Foreign Trade of Macedonia 2005, Report on the Foreign Trade of Macedonia 2006, Mandate for Leadership: Principles for Governing Macedonia 2006–2010 2006; several published articles.
Address: Embassy of Macedonia, 2129 Wyoming Avenue, NW, Washington, DC 20008, USA (office). *Telephone:* (202) 667-0501 (office). *Fax:* (202) 667-2131 (office). *E-mail:* usoffice@macedonianembassy.org (office). *Website:* www.macedonianembassy.org (office).

JONES, Alan; British diplomatist (retd); *High Commissioner to Belize;* b. 26 Oct. 1953; m. Daphne Jones; one d. *Career:* joined FCO 1971, worked in Information Dept 1971–75; Third Sec. Aid, Tehran, Iran 1975–78; Entry Clearance Officer, Islamabad, Pakistan 1978–81; with Ministry of Defence 1981–83; with Maritime, Aviation and Environment Dept, FCO 1983, Security Coordination Dept 1983–86; First Sec. Commercial, Cairo 1986–89; posts in UN and Estates Depts, 1989–93; Deputy High Commr in Angola 1993–96, Tanzania 1996–99; High Commr in Sierra Leone 2000–03, in Belize 2003–07.
Address: c/o Foreign and Commonwealth Office, King Charles Street, London, SW1A 2AH, England. *Telephone:* (20) 7008-1500.

JONES, Deborah K., BS, MS; American diplomatist; *Ambassador to Kuwait;* m. Richard G. Olson; two d. *Education:* Brigham Young Univ., Nat. War Coll., Nat. Defense Univ. *Career:* career mem. Sr Foreign Service, joined Foreign Service 1982, overseas assignments have included Abu Dhabi, Addis Ababa, Baghdad, Buenos Aires, Damascus; Washington, DC appointments have included two years as Country Dir Office of Arabian Peninsula and Iran Affairs, in addition to assignments as Staff Asst to Asst Sec. for Near East and S Asia Affairs, Acting Public Affairs Advisor to Asst Sec. for Near East Affairs, Desk Officer for Jordan, and duty in Dept of State's Operations Center, has also served on Bd of Examiners for the Foreign Service; Prin. Officer, Consulate Gen., Istanbul –2008; Amb. to Kuwait 2008–.
Address: US Embassy, PO Box 77, Bayan, Al-Masjed al-Aqsa Street, Plot 14, Block 14, 13001 Safat, Kuwait City, Kuwait (office). *Telephone:* 2591001 (office). *Fax:* 5380282 (office). *E-mail:* paskuwaitm@state.gov (office). *Website:* kuwait.usembassy.gov (office).

JONES, Gen. James L., BSc; American diplomatist and army officer (retd); *President and CEO, US Chamber of Commerce Institute for 21st Century Energy;* b. 19 Dec. 1943, Kansas City, Mo.; m. Diane Jones (née Johnson); four c. *Education:* Georgetown Univ. School of Foreign Service, Basic and Amphibious Warfare Schools, Quantico, Virginia, Nat. War Coll., Washington, DC. *Career:* Second Lt, Marine Corps 1967; Platoon Commdr and Co. Commdr Co. G, 2nd Bn, 3rd Marines, Viet Nam 1967–68; rank of First Lt 1968; Co. Commdr Camp Pendleton, Calif. 1968–70, Marine Barracks, Washington, DC 1970–73, Co. H, 2nd Bn, 9th Marines, 3rd Marine Div., Okinawa 1974–75; served in Officer Assignments Section, HQ Marine Corps, Washington, DC 1976–79; rank of Maj. 1977; Marine Corps Liaison Officer to US Senate 1979–84; rank of Lt-Col 1982; Commdr 3rd Bn, 9th Marines, 1st Marine Div., Camp Pendleton 1985–87; Sr Aide to Commdr of Marine Corps 1987–89; rank of Col 1988; Mil. Sec. to Commdt 1989–90; CO 24th Marine Expeditionary Unit, Camp Lejeune, NC 1990–92; rank of Brig.-Gen. 1992; Deputy Dir J-3, US European Command, Stuttgart, Germany 1992–94; Chief of Staff Jt Task Force Provide Promise, Operations in Bosnia and Herzegovina and Macedonia 1992–94; rank of Maj.-Gen. 1994; Commanding Gen. 2nd Marine Div., Marine Forces Atlantic, Camp Lejeune 1994–96; Dir Expeditionary Warfare Div., Office of the Chief of Naval Operations 1996; Deputy Chief of Staff for Plans, Policies and Operations, HQ Marine Corps 1996; rank of Lt-Gen. 1996; Mil. Asst to Sec. of Defense 1997–99; rank of Gen. 1999; 32nd Commdt Marine Corps 1999–2003; Commdr US European Command and 14th Supreme Allied Commdr Europe, NATO 2003–06; Chair. US Ind. Comm. on the Security Forces of Iraq 2007; Pres. and CEO US Chamber of Commerce Inst. for 21st Century Energy 2007–; apptd by US State Dept to act as Special Envoy for Middle East Security 2007–; mem. Bd of Dirs Invacare Corp.; numerous decorations; Dr hc (Georgetown Univ.) 2002; Defense Distinguished Service Medal, Silver Star Medal, Legion of Merit with 4 Gold Stars, Bronze Star Medal with Combat V, Combat Action Ribbon and numerous other awards.
Address: Institute for 21st Century Energy, US Chamber of Commerce, 1615 H Street, NW, Washington, DC 20062, USA (office). *Telephone:* (202) 659-6000 (office). *Website:* www.uschamber.com/about/management/jones .htm (office).

JONES, Mervyn Thomas, BA; British diplomatist; b. 23 Nov. 1942; m. Julia Mary Newcombe 1965; two s. *Education:* Univ. Coll., Swansea. *Career:* entered Diplomatic Service 1964; FCO 1964–66; Calcutta 1966, Bonn 1966–70, Warsaw 1970–73, FCO 1973–77, Oslo 1977–80; First Sec. (Man.), then Head of Chancery, Bangkok 1981–85; on secondment to Commonwealth Secr. as Asst Dir Int. Affairs Div. 1985–90; Deputy Consul Gen. and Consul (Commercial), LA 1990–94; Asst Head, Migration and Visa Dept, FCO 1994–96; Counsellor (Commercial and Econ.), Brussels (also accred to Luxembourg) 1996–99; Consul Gen. and Deputy Head of Mission, Brussels 1999; Gov. Turks and Caicos Islands 2000–02.
Address: c/o Foreign and Commonwealth Office, King Charles Street, London, SW1A 2AH, England (office).

JONES, Richard; British diplomatist. *Career:* served in British Embassy, Abu Dhabi; fmr UK Rep. to EU, Brussels; held several positions in London, including in the then Conf. on Security and Co-operation Unit, Near East and N Africa Dept, Common Foreign and Security Policy Dept and EU Dept (Internal); Amb. to Albania 2003–06.
Address: c/o Foreign and Commonwealth Office, King Charles Street, London, SW1A 2AH, England.

JONES, Richard H., BS, MA, PhD; American diplomatist; *Ambassador to Israel;* b. 26 Aug. 1950, Barksdale Air Force Base, nr Shreveport, La; m. Joan Jones; four c. *Education:* Harvey Mudd Coll., Claremont, Calif., Univ. of Wisconsin. *Career:* career mem. Sr Foreign Service with rank of Minister-Counselor, twice posted to Embassy in Riyadh, has served in Paris and Tunis, Dir Div. of Developed Country Trade 1987–89, Dir Office of Egyptian Affairs 1993–95, Amb. to Lebanon 1996–98, to Kazakhstan 1998–2001, Amb. to Kuwait 2001–04, Chief Policy Officer and Deputy Admin. for Coalition Provisional Authority, Baghdad 2003–04, Sec. of State's Sr Advisor and Coordinator for Iraq Policy Feb.–Sept. 2005, Amb. to Israel 2005–; Sr Fellow, Belfer Center, John F. Kennedy School of Govt, Harvard Univ. 2004–05; served two terms on Bd of Saudi Arabian Int. School, Riyadh; State Dept awards, US Govt for his work as Amb. to Kazakhstan and to Lebanon, for performance during the Gulf War and for contribs to commercial and trade negotiations; two US patents.
Address: Embassy of the USA, 71 Hayarkon Street, Tel-Aviv 63903, Israel (office). *Telephone:* 3-5197575 (office). *E-mail:* ac5@bezeqint.net (office). *Website:* telaviv.usembassy.gov (office).

JONES PARRY, Sir Emyr, KCMG, PhD; British diplomatist; *President, University of Aberystwyth;* b. 21 Sept. 1947, Carmarthen, Wales; m. Lynn Jones Parry; two s. *Education:* Gwendraeth Grammar School, Univ. Coll., Cardiff, St Catharine's Coll., Cambridge. *Career:* joined FCO 1973; Deputy Chef du Cabinet and Pres. of the European Council 1987–89; Head EC Dept (External) FCO 1989–93; Minister, Embassy in Madrid 1993–96; Deputy Political Dir FCO 1996–97; Dir EU, FCO 1997–98; Political Dir FCO 1998–2001; Perm. Rep. to N Atlantic Council, NATO 2001–03, to UN 2003–07; Pres., Univ. of Aberystwyth 2007–.
Address: Aberystwyth University, Old College, King Street, Aberystwyth, Ceredigion, SY23 2AX, Wales (office). *Telephone:* (1970) 623111 (office). *Website:* www.aber.ac.uk (office).

JÓNSSON, Albert, BA, MSc; Icelandic journalist, academic and diplomatist; *Ambassador to USA;* m. Ása Baldvinsdóttir; two c. *Education:* Univ. of Iceland, London School of Econs, Univ. of London, UK. *Career:* researcher, Icelandic Comm. on Security and Int. Affairs 1980–82, Exec. Dir 1988–91; External Lecturer in Int. Politics, Faculty of Political Science, Univ. of Iceland 1983–2006; radio journalist, Iceland Broadcasting Service 1984–87, TV journalist 1987–88; Foreign Policy Adviser to Prime Minister 1991–2004, June–Nov. 2006, Amb. and Special Adviser to Minister of Foreign Affairs 2004–06, Amb. to USA (also accred to Argentina, Brazil, Chile, El Salvador, Guatemala, Mexico and Uruguay) 2006–. *Publications:* books and articles on int. security issues and on Icelandic foreign and security policy, including Iceland, NATO and the Keflavik Base 1989.
Address: Embassy of Iceland, 1156 15th Street, NW, Suite 1200, Washington, DC 20005-1704, USA (office). *Telephone:* (202) 265-6653 (office). *Fax:* (202) 265-6656 (office). *E-mail:* icemb.wash@utn.stjr.is (office). *Website:* www.iceland.org/us (office).

JOPLING, Baron (Life Peer), cr. 1997, of Ainderby Quernhow in the County of North Yorkshire; **(Thomas) Michael Jopling,** PC, BSc; British politician and farmer; *Member of Parliamentary Assembly, NATO;* b. 10 Dec. 1930, Ripon, Yorks.; m. Gail Dickinson 1958; two s. *Education:* Cheltenham Coll. and King's Coll., Newcastle-upon-Tyne. *Career:* mem. Thirsk Rural Dist Council 1958–64; Conservative MP for Westmorland 1964–83, Westmorland and Lonsdale 1983–97; Jt Sec. Conservative Parl. Agric. Cttee 1966–70; Parl. Pvt. Sec. to Minister of Agric. 1970–71; an Asst Govt Whip 1971–73; Lord Commr of the Treasury 1973–74; an Opposition Spokesman on Agric. 1974–75, 1976–79; Shadow Minister of Agric. 1975–76; Parl. Sec. to HM Treasury and Chief Whip 1979–83; Minister of Agric., Fisheries and Food 1983–87; mem. Nat. Council, Nat. Farmers' Union 1962–64, UK Exec., Commonwealth Parl. Assn 1974–79, 1987–97, Vice-Chair. 1977–79, Int. Exec. 1988–89; Chair. Select Cttee on Sittings of the House 1991–92; mem. Select Cttee on Agric. 1967–69, on Foreign Affairs 1987–97; mem. NATO Parl. Ass. 1987–97, 2001–; Leader UK Del. to Parl. Ass., OSCE 1990–97, mem. 2000–01; mem. Lords Sub-Cttee 'C' European Defence and Security 1999–2003 (Chair. 2000–03); Pres. Auto-Cycle Union 1989–2003, Pres. Emer. 2003–; DL Cumbria 1991–97, N Yorks. 1998–2006; Hon. Sec. British American Parl. Group 1987–2001; Hon. DCL (Newcastle) 1992.
Address: Ainderby Hall, Thirsk, North Yorks., YO7 4HZ, England. *Telephone:* (1845) 567224.

JORDA, Claude Jean Charles; French judge and international official; *Judge, International Criminal Court;* b. 16 Feb. 1938, Bône, Algeria. *Education:* Institut d'Etudes Politiques and School of Law, Univ. of Toulouse, Ecole Nat. de la Magistrature (ENM). *Career:* called to Bar, Toulouse 1961; Auditeur de Justice (magistrate in training) 1963–66; Magistrate, Cen. Admin. Services Dept, Ministry of Justice 1966–70, Deputy Dir for Legal Org. and Regulations 1976–78, Dir Legal Services 1982–85; Sec.-Gen. ENM 1970–76; Vice-Pres. Tribunal de Grande Instance, Paris 1978–82; Prosecutor-Gen. Court of Appeals, Bordeaux 1985–92, Paris 1992–94; Judge at Int. Criminal Tribunal for Fmr Yugoslavia (ICTY) 1994–96, Pres. Trial Chamber I 1995–99, Pres. ICTY 1999–2003; Judge, Int. Criminal Court 2003–Aug. 2007 (resgnd); Officier, Légion d'honneur 1993, Commdr, Ordre nat. du Mérite 2000, Commdr des Palmes académiques, Commdr du Mérite agricole; Médaille de l'Educ. Surveillée (for services to young people in difficulty and in prison). *Publications include:* Un nouveau statut pour l'accusé dans la procédure du Tribunal pénal international pour l'ex-Yougoslavie (essays) 2000; academic contribs, book chapters and conf. proc., articles on ICTY .
Address: International Criminal Court, Maanweg 174, 2516 AB, The Hague, The Netherlands (office). *Telephone:* (70) 5158065 (office). *Fax:* (70) 5158789 (office). *E-mail:* claude.jorda@icc-cpi.int (office). *Website:* www .icc-cpi.int/php/index.php (office).

JORDANOVSKI, Ljupco, PhD; Macedonian fmr head of state, politician and diplomatist; b. 13 Feb. 1953, Štip. *Career:* Pres. Sobranie (Ass.); Acting Pres., Fmr Yugoslav Repub. of Macedonia Feb.–May 2004; Amb. to USA July–Dec. 2006 (recalled); mem. Social Democratic Alliance of Macedonia (Socijaldemokratski Sojuz na Makedonije–SDSM).
Address: c/o Office of the President, 11 Oktomvri bb, 1000 Skopje, Republic of Macedonia (office).

JORGENSON, Dale W., PhD; American economist and academic; *Director, Programme on Technology and Economic Policy, Harvard University;* b. 7 May 1933, Bozeman, Mont.; m. Linda Ann Mabus 1971; one s. one d. *Education:* Reed Coll., Portland, Ore. and Harvard Univ. *Career:* Asst Prof. of Econs, Univ. of Calif., Berkeley 1959–61, Assoc. Prof. 1961–63, Prof. 1963–69; Ford Foundation Research Prof. of Econs, Univ. of Chicago 1962–63; Prof. of Econs, Harvard Univ. 1969–80, Frederic Eaton Abbe Prof. of Econs 1980–2002, Samuel W. Morris Univ. Prof. 2002–, Frank William Taussig Research Prof. of Econs 1992–94, Chair. Dept of Econs 1994–97; Dir Program on Tech. and Econ. Policy, Kennedy School of Govt, Harvard Univ. 1984–; mem. Science Advisory Cttee, Gen. Motors Corpn 1996–2002; Visiting Prof. of Econs, Hebrew Univ., Jerusalem, Israel 1967, Stanford Univ. 1973; Visiting Prof. of Statistics, Univ. of Oxford, UK 1968; Chair. Section 54, Econ. Sciences, Nat. Acad. of Sciences 2000–03; Founding mem. Bd on Science, Tech. and Econ. Policy, Nat. Research Council 1991–98, Chair. 1998–; Consulting Ed., North-Holland Publishing Co., Amsterdam, Netherlands 1970–2002; Fellow, American Statistical Asscn 1965, AAAS 1982, Econometric Soc. 1984 (Pres. 1987); mem. American Acad. of Arts and Sciences 1969, NAS 1978, American Econ. Asscn (Pres. 2000, Distinguished Fellow 2001), Royal Econ. Soc., Econ. Study Soc., Conf. on Research in Income and Wealth, Int. Asscn for Research in Income and Wealth, American Philosophical Soc. 1998; Foreign mem. Royal Swedish Acad. of Sciences 1989; several fellowships including NSF Sr Postdoctoral Fellowship, Netherlands School of Econs, Rotterdam 1967–68; lectures include Shinzo Koizumi, Keio Univ., Tokyo, Japan 1972, Fisher-Schultz, 3rd World Congress, Econometric Soc. 1975, Frank Paish, Asscn of Univ. Teachers of Econs Conf., UK 1980, Erik Lindahl Lectures, Uppsala Univ. 1987, Inst. Lecture, Inst. of Industrial Econs, Univ. of Toulouse 2001, Astra Zeneca/Ericsson Lecture, Research Inst. of Industrial Econs, Stockholm 2002; Hon. DPhil (Oslo) 1991, (Uppsala) 1991, (Mannheim) 2004; Dr hc (Keio) 2003; John Bates Clark Medal, American Econ. Asscn 1971, Outstanding Contrib. Award, Int. Asscn of Energy Economists 1994. *Publications:* Optimal Replacement Policy (co-author) 1967, Measuring Performance in the Private Economy of the Federal Republic of Germany 1950–1973 (co-author) 1975, Economentric Studies of U.S. Energy Policy (ed.) 1976, Technology and Economic Policy (co-ed. with R. Landau) 1986, Productivity and U.S. Economic Growth (co-author) 1987, Technology and Capital Formation (co-ed. with R. Landau) 1989, General Equilibrium Modeling and Economic Policy Analysis (co-ed.) 1990, Technology and Agricultural Policy (co-ed.) 1990, Tax Reform and the Cost of Capital (with Kun-Young Yun) 1991, Tax Reform and the Cost of Capital: An International Comparison (co-ed. with R. Landau) 1993, Postwar U.S. Economic Growth (Productivity, Vol. 1) 1995, International Comparisons of Economic Growth (Productivity, Vol. 2) 1995, Capital Theory and Investment Behavior (Investment, Vol. 1) 1996, Tax Policy and the Cost of Capital (Investment, Vol. 2) 1996, Improving the Performance of America's Schools: The Role of Incentives (co-author) 1996, Aggregate Consumer Behavior (Welfare, Vol. 1) 1997, Measuring Social Welfare

(Welfare, Vol. 2) 1997, Econometric General Equilibrium Modeling (Growth, Vol. 1) 1998, Energy, the Environmental and Economic Growth (Growth, Vol. 2) 1998, Economic Modeling of Producer Behavior (Econometrics, Vol. 1) 2000, Lifting the Burden: Tax Reform, the Cost of Capital and U.S. Economic Growth (Investment, Vol. 3) (with Kun-Young Yun) 2001, Industry-Level Productivity and International Competitiveness Between Canada and the United States (co-ed. with Franck C. Lee) 2001, Economic Growth in the Information Age (Econometrics, Vol. 3) 2002, Measuring and Sustaining the New Economy (co-ed. with C. Wessner) 2002; over 232 papers and contribs to learned journals and collections of essays.
Address: Department of Economics, 122 Littauer Center, Harvard University, Cambridge, MA 02138-3001 (office); 1010 Memorial Drive, Cambridge, MA 02138, USA (home). *Telephone:* (617) 495-4661 (office); (617) 491-4069 (home). *Fax:* (617) 495-4660 (office); (617) 491-4105 (home). *E-mail:* djorgenson@harvard.edu (office). *Website:* post.economics .harvard.edu/faculty/jorgenson (office).

JOSEPH, Cedric Luckie, MA; Guyanese diplomatist (retd) and historian; b. 14 May 1933, Georgetown; m. Dona Avril Barrett 1973; two s. *Education:* London School of Econs, Univ. Coll. of Wales, Aberystwyth. *Career:* taught history at a London comprehensive school 1962–66; Lecturer in History, Univ. of the W Indies, Kingston, Jamaica 1966–71; Prin. Asst Sec., Ministry of Foreign Affairs, Guyana 1971–74; Deputy High Commr to Jamaica 1974–76; Counsellor, Embassy in Washington, DC 1976; Deputy Perm. Rep., Perm. Mission of Guyana to the UN, New York 1976–77; High Commr to Zambia (also accred to Angola, Botswana, Mozambique, Tanzania and Zimbabwe) 1977–82, to UK (also accred as Amb. to France, the Netherlands, Yugoslavia and UNESCO) 1982–86; Chair. Common-wealth Cttee on Southern Africa 1983–86; Head of the Presidential Secr. 1986–91; Sec. to Cabinet 1987–91; Sr Amb., Ministry of Foreign Affairs 1991–94; foreign policy analyst/consultant with reference to Guyana's frontiers 1995–; Cacique's Crown of Honour 1983. *Publications include:* Reconstruction of the Caribbean Community 1994, Dependency and Mendicancy 1995, Transition and Guyana 1995, Caribbean Community – Security and Survival 1997, Intervention, Border and Maritime Issues in CARICOM (tech. ed.) 2007, Anglo-American Diplomacy and the Reopening of the Guyana/Venezuela Boundary Controversy 1961–1966 1998 (revised edn 2008); several articles in professional journals.
Address: 332 Republic Park, Peter's Hall, East Bank Demerara, Guyana (home). *Telephone:* 233-5751 (home). *Fax:* 233-5782 (home). *E-mail:* clmdj@networksgy.com (home).

JOSEPH, Raymond Alcide, BA, MA; Haitian journalist and diplomatist; *Ambassador to USA. Education:* Wheaton Coll., Ill., Univ. of Chicago, graduate pastor from Moody Bible Institute, Chicago. *Career:* est. print shop and f. Reyon Limy (Rays of Light) (monthly Christian newspaper), Cayes; went on to become a radio personality 1960s, having founded first radio broadcast in New York beamed against the Duvalier dictatorship (Radio Vonvon or Radio Bug nicknamed the 'Six O'Clock Mass'); translated New Testament and Psalms into Haitian Creole under auspices of American Bible Soc. 1960; financial writer, Wall Street Journal, New York 1970s–1980s; co-f., with his brother Leo Joseph, Haiti Observateur (weekly); Chargé d'affaires a.i. and Perm. Rep. to OAS 1990; helped with first democratic elections Dec. 1990; returned to Haiti Observateur 1990–2004; fmr Contributing Ed., New York Sun (newspaper); Chargé d'affaires a.i. in USA 2004–05, Amb. to USA 2005–.
Address: Embassy of Haiti, 2311 Massachusetts Avenue, NW, Washington, DC 20008, USA (office). *Telephone:* (202) 332-4090 (office). *Fax:* (202) 745-7215 (office). *E-mail:* embassy@haiti.org (office). *Website:* www.haiti.org (office).

JOSEPH, Robert G., MA, PhD; American academic and diplomatist; *Senior Scholar, National Institute for Public Policy;* b. 1949, Williston, North Dakota. *Education:* US Naval Acad., St. Louis Univ., Univ. of Chicago, Columbia Univ. *Career:* several positions in US State Dept including Commr to Standing Consultative Comm., Amb. to US-Russian Consultative Comm. on Nuclear Testing, Prin. Deputy Asst, Sec. of Defense for Int. Security Policy, Deputy Asst, Sec. for Nuclear Forces and Arms Control Policy; Prof. of Nat. Security Studies and Founder/Dir, Center for Counterproliferation Research, Nat. Defense Univ. 1992–2001; Special Asst to Pres. and Sr Dir for Proliferation Strategy, Counterproliferation and Homeland Defense, Nat. Security Council –2005; UnderSec. for Arms Control and Int. Security 2005–07 (resgnd); Dir of Studies, Nat. Inst. for Public Policy 2004–05, Sr Scholar 2004–; mem. Nat. Security Advisory Council, Center for Security Policy; fmr Research Consultant, Inst. for Foreign Policy Analysis.
Address: National Institute for Public Policy, 9302 Lee Highway, Suite 750, Fairfax, VA 22031, USA (office). *E-mail:* Amy.joseph@nipp.org (office). *Website:* www.nipp.org (office).

JOSPIN, Lionel Robert; French politician; b. 12 July 1937, Meudon, Hauts-de-Seine; m. 2nd Sylviane Agacinski 1994; one s. one d. (from previous m.), one step-s. *Education:* Institut d'études politiques de Paris, École nat. d'admin. *Career:* Sec. Ministry of Foreign Affairs 1965–70; Prof., Econ. Inst. universitaire de tech. de Paris-Sceaux, also attached to Univ. de Paris XI 1970–81; Nat. Sec. Socialist Party, mem. Steering Cttee 1973–75, spokesman on Third World Affairs 1975–79, Int. Relations 1979–81, First Sec. 1981–88, Head 1995–97; Councillor for Paris (18E arrondissement) 1977–86; Socialist Deputy to Nat. Ass. for Paris (27E circ.) 1981–86, for Haute-Garonne 1986–88; mem. Gen. Council Haute-Garonne 1988–; Conseiller régional, Midi-Pyrénées 1992–98; Minister of State, Nat. Educ., Research and Sport May–June 1988; Minister of State, Nat. Educ., of Youth and Sport 1988–91, Minister of Nat. Educ. 1991–92; presidential cand. 1995, 2002; Prime Minister of France 1997–2002; Trombinoscope Politician of the Year 1997. *Publications:* L'Invention du Possible 1991, 1995–2000: Propositions pour la France 1995, Le Temps de répondre 2002, Le Monde comme je le vois 2005.
Address: c/o Parti Socialiste, 10 rue de Solférino, 75333 Paris, Cédex 07, France.

JOSSELIN, Charles, LenD; French economist and politician; b. 31 March 1938, Pleslin-Trigavou; m. 2nd Evelyne Besnard 1987; four c. *Career:* fmr attaché, financial secr., Banque de l'Union Parisienne, economist, Soc. centrale pour l'équipement du territoire; Parti Socialiste (PS) Nat. Ass. Deputy for 2nd Côtes d'Armor Constituency (Dinan) 1973–78, 1981–97 1; Minister of State for Transport 1985–86, for the Sea 1992–93; Sec. of State attached to Minister of Foreign Affairs, with responsibility for Co-operation 1997, for Co-operation and Francophonie 1997–98, Deputy Minister for Co-operation and Francophonie 1998–2002, Minister of State 1998–2002; Mayor of Pleslin-Trigavou 1977–97; mem. European Parl. 1979–81; Chair. Nat. Council for Regional Economies and Productivity 1982–86, Nat. Ass.'s EC Select Cttee 1981–85, 1988–92, Vice-Chair. EU Select Cttee 1993–; Chair. Parl. Study Group on int. aid orgs; mem. Côtes d'Armor Gen. Council for Ploubalay canton 1973–, Chair. 1976–97, Vice-Chair. 1997–; mem. Nat. Council for Town and Country Planning, Local Finance Cttee, EU Cttee of the Regions; Vice-Pres. High Comm. Int. Co-operation 2003–; Chair. Cités Unies France (twin city org.) 2004–; Senator representing, Côtes d'Armor 2006–.
Address: 12 Bis Rue de Brest, 22100 Dinan (office); c/o Le Sénat, Casier de la Poste, 15 Rue de Vaugirard, 75291 Paris Cedex 06, France (office). *Telephone:* 2-96-85-43-52 (office). *E-mail:* c.josselin@senat.fr (office); charles-josselin@orange.fr (home). *Website:* www.senat.fr (office); www .cites-unies-france.org (office).

JOUANNEAU, Daniel, LLM; French diplomatist; *Ambassador to Canada;* b. 15 Sept. 1946, Vendôme; m.; one d. *Education:* French Inst. of Political Studies, École nationale d'admin (French Nat. School of Public Admin. *Career:* worked in Legal Adviser's Office, Ministry of Foreign Affairs 1971–74; First Sec. in Egypt 1974–76; Office of Econ. and Financial Affairs (multilateral commercial matters) 1976–80; Consul Gen., Salisbury, Rhodesia 1980; Chargé d'affaires, Zimbabwe 1980–81; Asst-Dir for Western Europe, then European Correspondent 1981–85, Ministry of Foreign Affairs; Chief of Mission (ODA), Guinea 1985–87; Consul Gen., Québec, Canada 1987–89; Chief of European-Union Dept 1989–90; Amb. to Mozambique, non-resident Amb. in Lesotho and Swaziland 1990–93; Chief of Protocol 1993–97; Amb. to Lebanon 1997–2000; Inspector Gen. of Foreign Affairs 2000–04; Amb. to Canada 2004–.
Address: Embassy of France, 42 Sussex Drive, Ottawa, ON K1M 2C9, Canada (office). *Telephone:* (613) 789-1795 (office). *Fax:* (613) 562-3735 (office). *E-mail:* politique@ambafrance-ca.org (office). *Website:* www .ambafrance-ca.org (office).

JOUBLANC MONTAÑO, Luciano Eduardo; Mexican diplomatist; *Ambassador to Switzerland;* b. 16 Aug. 1949, México. *Education:* Colegio de México. *Career:* joined Foreign Service 1973, Coordinator of Advisers to Asst Sec. for Int. Co-operation 1988, Dir-Gen. for Europe 1988–90; overseas postings include at Perm. Mission to UN, New York and Embassies in Nicaragua, Soviet Union, Germany; Amb. to Hungary (also accred to Bulgaria 1993–95) 1990–95; Deputy Perm. Rep. to Int. Orgs, Geneva 1995–99, Rep. to meetings of Group of Fifteen 1997–99; Amb. to Russia (also accred to Armenia, Georgia and Belarus) 2000–07, to Switzerland (also accred to Liechtenstein) 2007–; has taught at Instituto Tecnológico Autónomo de México.
Address: Embassy of Mexico, Welpoststrasse 20, Piso 5, 3015 Bern, Switzerland (office). *Telephone:* (31) 3574747 (office). *Fax:* (31) 3574748 (office). *E-mail:* embamex1@swissonline.ch (office). *Website:* www.sre.gob .mx/suiza (office).

JOVANOVIĆ, Vladislav, LLB; Serbian diplomatist; b. 9 June 1933, Prokuplje; m. Mirjana Jovanović (née Borić) 1985; one s. *Education:*

Belgrade Univ. *Career:* joined Foreign Service 1957; served in Belgium, Turkey and UK 1960–79, Amb. to Turkey 1985–89; various sr posts in Fed. Ministry for Foreign Affairs 1990–91; Head, Yugoslav Dels to Disarmament and Human Dimension confs of CSCE 1990–91; Minister of Foreign Affairs, Repub. of Serbia 1991–92; Fed. Minister for Foreign Affairs of Yugoslavia 1992, 1993–95; Amb. and Perm. Rep. of Yugoslavia to UN 1995–2000; Chevalier de la Légion d'honneur and other decorations. *Publications:* two books of poetry In Search for Searches 1991, Butterfly and Light 1994.
Address: c/o Ministry of Foreign Affairs, 11000 Belgrade, Kneza Milosa 24, Serbia (office).

JOXE, Pierre Daniel, LenD; French politician; *Member, Conseil Constitutionnel;* b. 28 Nov. 1934, Paris; m. 3rd Valérie Cayeux 1981; two s. two d. from previous m. *Education:* Lycée Henri IV, Faculté de droit and Ecole Nat. d'Admin. *Career:* mil. service 1958–60; auditor, later Counsellor Cour des Comptes; mem. Exec. Bureau and Exec. Cttee, Socialist Party 1971–93; Deputy for Saône and Loire 1973, 1978, 1981, 1986, 1988; Minister of Industry and Admin May–June 1981, of the Interior, Decentralization and Admin July 1984 and March 1986, of the Interior 1988–91, of Defence 1991–93; First Pres. Cour des Comptes (audit court) 1993–2001; mem. Conseil Constitutionnel 2001–; mem. European Parl. 1977–79; Pres. Regional Council, Burgundy 1979–82, Socialist Parl. Group 1981–84, 1986–88; Hon. KBE; Commdr, Ordre nat. du Mérite. *Publications:* Parti socialiste 1973, Atlas du Socialisme 1973, L'édit de Nantes (Literary Prize, Droits de l'homme) 1998, A propos de la France 1998, Pourquoi Mitterrand 2006.
Address: Conseil Constitutionnel, 2 rue de Montpensier, 75100 Paris, France (office). *Telephone:* 1-40-15-30-00 (office). *Fax:* 1-40-20-93-27 (office). *E-mail:* relations-exterieures@conseil-constitutionnel.fr (office). *Website:* www.conseil-constitutionnel.fr (office).

JOYCE, Mark, BA, MPhil; British international affairs scholar; *Americas Fellow, Royal United Services Institute; Education:* Univ. Coll., St Antony's, Oxford Univ. *Career:* previously business and political journalist; fmr Head, Trans-Atlantic Programme, Royal United Services Inst. (RUSI), currently Americas Fellow, Fellow, Grupo de Estudios Estratégicos, Madrid; Americas Ed. Jane's Country Risk.
Address: Royal United Services Institute, Whitehall, London, SW1A 2ET, England (office). *Telephone:* (20) 7747-2633 (office). *Fax:* (20) 7321-0943 (office). *E-mail:* markj@rusi.org (office). *Website:* www.rusi.org (office).

JU, Gen. Sang-song; North Korean army officer and politician; *Minister of People's Security; Career:* career in Korean People's Armed Forces; attained rank of Gen. 1997; commdr of army unit stationed on border with S Korea 2000; cand. mem. Korean Worker's Party 1970–90, full mem. 1990–; mem. Supreme People's Parl. 1990–98; Minister of People's Security and mem. Nat. Defence Comm. 2004–.
Address: Ministry of Defence, Pyongyang, Democratic People's Republic of Korea (office).

JUAN CARLOS I, HM The King of Spain; b. 5 Jan. 1938, Rome, Italy; m. Princess Sophia, d. of the late King Paul of the Hellenes and of Queen Frederica, 1962; one s., HRH Prince Felipe, The Prince of Asturias, b. Jan. 1968; two daughters, Princess Elena, Princess Cristina. *Education:* privately in Fribourg, Switzerland, Madrid, San Sebastián, Inst. of San Isidro, Madrid, Colegio del Carmen, Gen. Mil. Acad., Zaragoza and Univ. of Madrid. *Career:* spent childhood in Rome, Lausanne, Estoril and Madrid; commissioned into the three armed forces and undertook training in each of them 1957–59; studied the org. and activities of various govt ministries; named by Gen. Franco as future King of Spain 1969, inaugurated as King of Spain 22 Nov. 1975, named as Capt.-Gen. of the Armed Forces Nov. 1975; Foreign mem. Acad. des sciences morales et politiques, Assoc. mem. 1988; Dr hc (Strasbourg) 1979, (Madrid), (Harvard) 1984, (Sorbonne) 1985, (Oxford) 1986, (Trinity Coll., Dublin) 1986, (Bologna) 1988, (Cambridge) 1988, (Coimbra) 1989, (Tokyo, Bogotá, Limerick, Tufts, Chile) 1990, (Toronto) 1991, (Jerusalem) 1993; Charlemagne Prize 1982, Bolívar Prize (UNESCO) 1983, Gold Medal Order 1985, Candenhove Kalergi Prize, Switzerland 1986, Nansen Medal 1987, Humanitarian Award Elie Wiesel, USA 1991, shared Houphouët Boigny Peace Prize (UNESCO) 1995, Franklin D. Roosevelt Four Freedoms Award 1995.
Address: Palacio de la Zarzuela, 28071 Madrid, Spain. *Website:* www.casareal.es.

JUBEIR, Adel bin Ahmed al-, BA, MA; Saudi Arabian diplomatist; *Ambassador to USA;* b. 1 Feb. 1962, Riyadh. *Education:* Univ. of N Texas and Georgetown Univ., USA. *Career:* fmr Special Asst to Amb., Embassy in Washington, DC; fmr Dir Saudi Arabian Information and Congressional Affairs Office; Foreign Affairs Advisor, Crown Prince's Court 2000–05; Custodian of the Two Holy Mosques, Advisor, Royal Court 2005–07; Amb. to USA 2007–; served in Jt Information Bureau in Dhahran during Operation Desert Shield/Desert Storm 1990–91; Visiting Diplomatic Fellow, Council of Foreign Relations, New York 1994–95; Hon. DHumLitt (N Texas) 2006.
Address: Embassy of Saudi Arabia, 601 New Hampshire Avenue, NW, Washington, DC 20037, USA (office). *Telephone:* (202) 342-3800 (office). *Fax:* (202) 944-6750 (office). *E-mail:* info@saudiembassy.net (office). *Website:* www.saudiembassy.net (office).

JUGNAUTH, Rt Hon. Sir Anerood, KCMG, PC, QC; Mauritian politician, lawyer and head of state; *President;* b. 29 March 1930, Palma; m. Sarojni Devi Ballah; one s. one d. *Education:* Church of England School, Palma, Regent Coll., Quakre, Borneo, Lincoln's Inn, London. *Career:* called to Bar 1954; won seat on Legis. Ass., Mauritius 1963; Minister of State and Devt 1965–67, of Labour 1967; Dist Magistrate 1967; Crown Counsel and Sr Crown Counsel 1971; co-founder and Pres. Mouvement Militant Mauricien with Paul Bérenger Dec. 1971–; Leader of Opposition 1976; Prime Minister of Mauritius 1982–95, other portfolios include Minister of Finance 1983–84, of Defence and Internal Security and Reform Insts, of Information, Internal and External Communications and the Outer Islands, of Justice; Prime Minister and Minister of Defence and Home Affairs and of External Communications Sept. 2000–03; Pres. 2003–; Order of the Rising Sun (Japan) 1988, Grand Officier, Légion d'honneur 1990; Hon. DCL (Mauritius) 1985; Hon. LLD (Madras) 2001; Dr hc (Aix-en-Provence) 1985.
Address: President's Office, Clarisse House, Vacoas, Port Louis; La Caverne No. 1, Vacoas, Mauritius (home). *Telephone:* 697-0077 (office). *Fax:* 697-2347 (office). *E-mail:* statepas@intnet.mu (office). *Website:* ncb .intnet.mu/president.htm (office).

JUGNAUTH, Pravind Kumar, LLB; Mauritian politician and barrister; *Leader, Mouvement Socialiste Militant;* b. 25 Dec. 1961; m.; three c. *Education:* Univ. of Buckingham, UK. *Career:* joined Mouvement Socialiste Militant 1987, Deputy Leader 1999–2003, Leader 2003–; Councillor, Municipality of Vacoas/Phoenix 1996; mem. Parl. for Constituency No. 11 (Vieux Grand Port and Rose Belle); Minister of Agric., Food, Trade and Natural Resources 2000–03, Deputy Prime Minister and Minister of Finance Sept.–Dec. 2003, Deputy Prime Minister and Minister of Finance and Econ. Devt Dec. 2003–05.
Address: Mouvement Socialiste Militant, Sun Trust Building, 31 Edith Cavell Street, Port Louis (office); La Caverne No. 1, Vacoas, Mauritius (home). *Telephone:* 212-8787 (office). *Fax:* 208-9517 (office). *E-mail:* request@msmsun.com (office). *Website:* www.msmparty.org (office).

JUHÁSZ, Ferenc; Hungarian politician; b. 6 Jan. 1960, Nyíregyháza; m.; two c. *Education:* Lajos Kossuth Vocational School, György Bessenyei Teachers' Training Coll., Nyíregyháza, Coll. of Finance and Public Accountancy, Univ. of Pécs. *Career:* Head of Co. Office, HSP (Magyar Szocialista Párt—MSZP) 1991–94; elected mem. of Parl. 1994, mem. Defence Cttee 1994–96, Vice-Chair. 1996–98; apptd Vice-Chair. Defence Cttee on Legislation, Chair. Control Comm. 1998; Head, Working Group of HSP faction for Defence and Nat. Security 1998–2002, Deputy Head of faction for Parl. 1999–2000; Deputy Chair. HSP 2000–; Minister of Defence 2002–.
Address: Hungarian Socialist Party, Köztársaság tér 26, 1081 Budapest, Hungary (office). *Telephone:* (1) 210-0046 (office). *Fax:* (1) 210-0081 (office). *E-mail:* info@mszp.hu (office); ferenc.juhasz@mszp.hu. *Website:* www.mszp.hu (office).

JULIUS, DeAnne, CBE, PhD; American/British economist; *Chairman, Chatham House;* b. 14 April 1949; m. Ian A. Harvey 1976; one s. one d. *Education:* Iowa State Univ. and Univ. of Calif., Davis. *Career:* Econ. Adviser for Energy, IBRD 1975–82; Man. Dir Logan Assocs, Inc. 1983–86; Dir of Econs Royal Inst. of Int. Affairs (RIIA), London 1986–89; Chief Economist Shell Int. Petroleum Co., London 1989–93, British Airways 1993–97; mem. Monetary Policy Cttee, Bank of England 1997–2001, Dir Bank of England Court 2001–04; Chair. British Airways Pension Investment Man. Ltd 1995–97; Dir (non-exec.) Lloyds TSB 2001–07, BP (British Petroleum) 2001–, Serco Group 2001–, Roche 2002–; Chair. Royal Inst. of Int. Affairs (now Chatham House) 2003–; Dr hc (Warwick) 2000, (South Bank) 2001, (Bath) 2002, (Birmingham) 2006. *Publications:* The Economics of Natural Gas 1990, Global Companies and Public Policy: The Growing Challenge of Foreign Direct Investment 1990, Is Manufacturing Still Special in the New World Order? (jtly) 1993 (Amex Bank Prize); and articles on int. econs.
Address: Chatham House, 10 St James's Square, London, SW1Y 4LE, England (office). *Telephone:* (137) 245-1878 (office). *Fax:* (137) 245-4770 (office). *E-mail:* chairman@chathamhouse.org.uk (office). *Website:* www .chathamhouse.org.uk (office).

JULY, Serge; French journalist; b. 27 Dec. 1942, Paris; one s. *Career:* journalist Clarté 1961–63; Vice-Pres. Nat. Union of Students 1965–66; French teacher Coll. Sainte-Barbe, Paris 1966–68; Asst Leader Gauche prolétarienne 1969–72 (disbanded by the Govt); co-f. newspaper, Libération 1973, Chief Ed. 1973–2006, Publishing Dir 1974–75, Jt Dir 1981, Man. Dir 1987–2006; Reporter Europe 1983; mem. Club de la presse Europe 1976–. *Publications:* Vers la guerre civile (with Alain Geismar and Erlyne Morane) 1969, Dis maman, c'est quoi l'avant-guerre? 1980, Les Années Mitterrand 1986, La Drôle d'Année 1987, Le Salon des artistes 1989, La Diagonale du Golfe 1991, Entre quatre z'yeux (with Alain Juppé).

JUMAGULOV, Apas; Kyrgyzstani diplomatist, politician and business executive; b. Sept. 1934, Arashan. *Education:* Moscow Inst. of the Petrochemical and Gas Industry. *Career:* began working as geologist in state oil industry; actively participated in activities of local CP br.; Chief Engineer, Kyrgyzneft (state oil and gas co.) –1973; apptd Head of Industry and Transportation Dept, Cen. Cttee of CP of Kyrgyz SSR 1973; later took on several other admin. posts at regional and nat. levels; Head of Govt of Kyrgyzia 1986–91; nominated himself as a cand. in presidential elections 1990; Admin. Head of his native region of Chu 1990–93; Prime Minister 1993–98 (retd); Amb. to Germany 1998–2003, also accred to Holy See and Scandinavian countries 1999–2003; withdrew from politics and became intermediary and consultant; Chair. Moscow br. of Postnoff co. 2003–; entered leadership ranks of Eurasian Movt 2004–; Amb. to Russian Fed. 2005–07; Order of Merit (Germany) 2003.
Address: c/o Ministry of Foreign Affairs, 720040 Bishkek, bul. Erkindik 57, Kyrgyzstan.

JUMEAU, Ronald Jean; Seychelles journalist, politician and diplomatist; *Permanent Representative, United Nations;* b. 24 Jan. 1957, Dar es Salaam, Tanzania. *Education:* Seychelles Coll. *Career:* reporter, Govt Information Services 1978–80; Seychelles stringer, Reuters Int. News Agency 1980–83; First Ed. Seychelles Agence Presse 1980–82; fmr Chief Ed. Seychelles Nations; instructor in journalism, Seychelles Polytechnic 1986–89; mem. Seychelles People's Progressive Front; adviser to Ministry of Educ. 1991–93; Sec. to Cabinet and Dir of Research, Office of Pres. 1993–98, also Sec. of bipartisan Nat. Econ. Consultative Cttee; Sec. to four Cabinet inter-ministerial cttees 1994–98; Minister for Agric. and Marine Resources 1998–99, for Culture and Information 2000–01, for Environment 2001–03, for Environment and Natural Resources 2004–07; Perm. Rep. to UN, New York 2007–, also Amb. to USA.
Address: Permanent Mission of the Seychelles to the United Nations, 800 Second Avenue, Room 400c, New York, NY 10017, USA (office). *Telephone:* (212) 972-1785 (office). *Fax:* (212) 972-1786 (office). *E-mail:* seychelles@un.int (office).

JUNCKER, Jean-Claude, LLM; Luxembourg politician; *Prime Minister and Minister of State and of Finance;* b. 9 Dec. 1954, Redange-sur-Attert; m. Christiane Frising 1979. *Education:* Univ. of Strasbourg. *Career:* Parl. Sec. to Christian Social Party 1979–82; Sec. of State for Labour and Social Affairs 1982–84, Minister of Labour, Minister in charge of Budget 1984–89, Minister of Labour, of Finance 1989–94; Prime Minister of Luxembourg 1995–, also Minister of State, of Finance and the Treasury, of Labour and Employment 1995–99, of State and of Finance 1999–; Chair. Christian Social Party 1990–95; Chair. Social Affairs and Budget Councils 1985; Gov. IBRD 1989–95, fmr Gov. IMF, EBRD; elected first Perm. Pres. Eurogroup 2005; Int. Karlspreis, Aachen 2006.
Address: Hôtel de Bourgogne, 4 rue de la Congrégation, 1352 Luxembourg, Luxembourg (office). *Telephone:* 478-21-00 (office). *Fax:* 46-17-20 (office). *E-mail:* ministere.etat@me.etat.lu (office).

JUNEAU, Jean-Pierre, MA; Canadian diplomatist; *Ambassador to Cuba;* b. 24 April 1945, Quebec City; m. Emitza Escobar-Jurado; one s. one d. *Education:* Coll. des Jésuites, Quebec City, Laval Univ., Banff School of Advanced Man. *Career:* joined Dept of External Affairs 1969; served in various positions in NY, Havana and Paris 1969–91; Counsellor, Embassy in Washington, DC 1981–85; Minister-Counsellor, Embassy in Paris 1985–88; Dir-Gen. Western Europe Bureau, HQ, Ottawa 1988–91; Amb. to Spain 1991–94; Asst Deputy Minister for Europe 1994–96; Amb. to EU 1996–2000, to Brazil 2000–03; Amb. and Perm. Rep. to NATO, Brussels 2003–07; Amb. to Cuba 2007–.
Address: Embassy of Canada, Calle 30 No. 518 esquina 7ma, Miramar, Havana 11300, Cuba (office). *Telephone:* (7) 204-2516 (office). *Fax:* (7) 204-2044 (office). *E-mail:* havan-gr@international.gc.ca (office). *Website:* www.international.gc.ca/cuba (office).

JUNG, Franz Josef, DJur; German lawyer and politician; *Minister of Defence;* b. 5 March 1949, Erbach, Rheingau-Taunus Dist, Hesse; m.; three c. *Education:* Rheingau School, Geisenheim, Univ. of Mainz. *Career:* legal training at Wiesbaden Dist Court 1974–76; solicitor in Eltville 1976–, public notary 1983–; mem. Dist Ass. of Rheingau-Taunus 1972–87; mem. Nat. Exec., CDU German Youth Union 1973–93, Vice-Chair. 1981–83; elected to Hessen State Parl. (Landtag), Wiesbaden 1983–2005; Hessian State Minister for Fed. and European Affairs and Head of Hessian State Chancellory 1999–2000; Gen. Sec. of CDU in Hessen 1987–91, CDU Parl. Sec., Hessen Landtag 1987–99; CDU Parl. Whip in Hessen Landtag 2003–05; mem. CDU Nat. Exec. Cttee 1998–; elected to Fed. Parl. (Bundestag), Berlin 2005–; Minister of Defence 2005–; Chair. Producers' Asscn Research Inst. of Geisenheim 1999, Friends of ZDF TV 2002; mem. Rheingau Music Festival Cttee 1989–, ZDF TV Advisory Bd 1999, Eintracht Frankfurt e.V. Man. Bd 1999, Eintracht Frankfurt AG Supervisory Bd 2003–05.
Address: Ministry of Defence, Arbeitsbereich 2, Stauffenbergstrasse 18, 10785 Berlin, Germany (office). *Telephone:* (18) 8820048000 (office). *Fax:* (18) 8820048004 (office). *E-mail:* sabrinakluemper@bmvg.bund400.de (office). *Website:* www.bundeswehr.de (office); www.franz-josef-jung.de (office).

JUNZ, Helen B., PhD; American economist and consultant; *President, HBJ International; Education:* Univ. of Amsterdam, Netherlands and New School of Social Research. *Career:* Acting Chief, Consumer Price Section, Nat. Industrial Conf. Bd, New York 1953–58; Research Officer, Nat. Inst. of Social and Economic Research, London 1958–60; Economist, Bureau of Economic Analysis, Dept of Commerce, Washington 1960–62; Adviser, Div. of Int. Finance, Bd of Govs, Fed. Reserve System 1962–77; Adviser, OECD, Paris 1967–69; Sr int. economist, Council of Econ. Advisers, The White House, Washington 1975–77; Deputy Asst Sec., Office of Asst Sec. for Int. Affairs, Dept of the Treasury, Washington, 1977–79; Vice-Pres. and Sr Adviser, First National Bank of Chicago 1979–80; Vice-Pres. Townsend Greenspan and Co. Inc., New York 1980–82; Sr Adviser, European Dept, IMF, Washington 1982–87, Deputy Dir Exchange and Trade Relations Dept 1987–89, Special Trade Rep. and Dir, Geneva Office 1989–94, Dir Gold Econ. Service, World Gold Council, Geneva and London 1994–96; Pres. HBJ Int., London 1996–. *Publications:* Where Did All the Money Go? 2002; numerous articles in professional journals.
Address: HBJ International, 39 Chalcot Square, London, NW1 8YP, England (office). *E-mail:* hbjunz@planet.nl (office).

JUPPÉ, Alain Marie; French politician and fmr government official; *Mayor of Bordeaux;* b. 15 Aug. 1945, Mont-de-Marsan, Landes; m. 1st Christine Leblond 1965; one s. one d.; m. 2nd Isabelle Legrand-Bodin 1993; one d. *Education:* Lycée Louis-le-Grand, Paris, Ecole normale supérieure, Inst. d'études politiques, Paris and Ecole Nat. d'Admin. *Career:* Insp. of Finance 1972; Office of Prime Minister Jacques Chirac (q.v.) June–Aug. 1976; tech. adviser, Office of Minister of Cooperation 1976–78; Nat. del. of RPR 1976–78, Nat. Sec. of RPR with responsibility for econ. and social recovery 1984–88, Sec.-Gen. 1988–95, Acting Pres. 1994–95, Pres. 1995–97; tech. adviser, Office of Mayor of Paris (Jacques Chirac) 1978; Dir-Gen. with responsibility for finance and econ. affairs, Commune de Paris 1980; Councillor, 18th arrondissement, Paris 1983–95; Second Asst to Mayor of Paris in charge of budget and financial affairs 1983–95; Deputy to Nat. Ass. from Paris 1988–97, from Gironde 1997–; Mayor of Bordeaux 1995–2001, 2001–04, 2006–; mem. European Parl. 1984–86, 1989–93; Deputy to Minister of Economy, Finance and Privatization with responsibility for budget 1986–88; Minister of Foreign Affairs 1993–95; Prime Minister of France 1995–97; cleared of embezzlement charges 1999; Pres. Union pour la majorité presidentielle (UMP) 2002–04 (resgnd); Minister of State for Ecology and Sustainable Devt May–June 2007; Grand Cross of Merit, Sovereign Order of Malta. *Publications:* La Tentation de Venise 1993, Entre Nous 1996, Montesquieu, Le moderne 1999, Entre quatre z'yeux (with Serge July q.v.) France mon pays – Lettres d'un voyageur 2006.
Address: Mairie, place Pey-Berland, 33077 Bordeaux, France (office). *Website:* www.bordeaux.fr (office).

JÜRGENSON, Sven, BSc; Estonian diplomatist; *Foreign Policy Adviser to the President of Estonia;* b. 2 April 1962; m.; three c. *Education:* Tallinn Tech. Univ., Institut Internationale d'Admin Publique, Paris, Ingenieurhochschule, Dresden. *Career:* Jr Research Assoc. and Lecturer in Data Processing, Tallinn Tech. Univ. 1987–90; Sr Assoc., Estonian Inst. 1990–91; Counsellor, Chargé d'affaires, Helsinki, Counsellor, Office for Estonian Culture, Helsinki 1991–93; Minister-Counsellor, Chargé d'affaires, Embassy, Vienna 1993–95; Deputy Political Dir, Ministry of Foreign Affairs, then Dir Div. for Int. Orgs and Security Policy 1995–96, Dir-Gen. Political Dept 1996–98; Amb. to Turkey 1996–98; Perm. Rep. to UN 1998–2000; Amb. to USA 2000–03; Under-Sec. for Political Affairs and for EU Affairs, Ministry of Foreign Affairs 2004–06; Foreign Policy Adviser to the Pres. of Estonia 2006–.
Address: Office of the President, A. Weizenbergi 39, 15050 Tallinn, Estonia (office). *Telephone:* 6316202 (office). *Fax:* 6316250 (office). *E-mail:* vpinfo@vpk.ee (office). *Website:* www.kadriorg.ee (office).

JURICA, Neven, BA, MA; Croatian politician and diplomatist; *Permanent Representative, United Nations;* m.; two c. *Education:* Univ. of Zagreb. *Career:* Founding mem. Croatian Democratic Union, Political Sec. 1989–92, 2000–04; mem. Parl. and Chair. Human Rights Cttee 1990–92, 2003–04; mem. Parl. and Chair. Parl. Foreign Affairs Cttee –2004; Amb. to Australia and NZ 1992–95, to Bulgaria 1996–97; Govt Spokesman 1997–98; Amb. to Norway 1998–2000, to USA 2004–08, Perm. Rep. to UN 2008–; fmr Dir Literary Friday forum; mem. Croatian Writers' Asscn, PEN. *Publications:* more than 16 books on literary theory, criticism, and anthologies of essays and poems.
Address: Permanent Mission of Croatia to the United Nations, 820 Second Avenue, 19th Floor, New York, NY 10017, USA (office). *Telephone:* (212) 986-1585 (office). *Fax:* (212) 986-2011 (office). *E-mail:* croatia@un.int (office). *Website:* www.un.int/croatia (office).

JURKOVIĆ, Pero, PhD; Croatian economist; b. 4 June 1936, Brštanica, Neum, Bosnia and Herzegovina. *Education:* Univs of Sarajevo, Skopje and Zagreb. *Career:* chief accountant, construction materials industry Neretva, Čapljina 1956–57; Officer for Planning, Municipality of Čapljina 1960–61, Chief Officer for Agric. 1961–63; Dir Inst. of Economy, Mostar 1963–67; Assoc. to Adviser, Econ. Inst., Zagreb (also Assoc. Prof., Foreign Trade School and Faculties of Econs Zagreb and Mostar) 1967–80; Prof., Faculty of Econs, Zagreb 1980–92; currently lectures at Univ. of Zagreb Grad. School of Econs and Business; Gov. Nat. Bank of Croatia 1992–96; apptd Chief Econ. Adviser to Pres. of Croatia 1997; mem. Int. Inst. for Financing, Saarbrücken, Int. Asscn of Economists; Guest Lecturer, Univs of Rotterdam, London, Lexington and Florida; B. Adžija and M. Mirkovic awards. *Publications:* more than 150 publs including System of Public Financing (with Ksente Bogoev) 1977, Introduction to the Theory of Economic Policy 1984, Fundamentals of the Economics of Public Services 1987, Commercial Finances 1987, Fiscal Policy 1989.
Address: University of Zagreb Graduate School of Economics and Business, Room 101, Trg. J. F. Kennedy 6, 10000 Zagreb, Croatia (office). *Telephone:* (1) 238-3199 (office). *Fax:* (1) 233-5633 (office). *E-mail:* pero.jurkovic@efzg.hr (office). *Website:* www.efzg.hr (office).

JUSYS, Oskaras; Lithuanian diplomatist; *Undersecretary, Ministry of Foreign Affairs;* b. 13 Jan. 1954, Anyksciai Region; m.; one s. *Education:* Vilnius Univ., V. Lomonosov Univ., Moscow. *Career:* Sr Lecturer, Faculty of Law, Vilnius Univ. 1981–1985, Assoc. Prof. 1986–90; Scientific Scholarship, IREX Exchange Programme, Law School, Columbia Univ., New York, USA 1985–86; Dir Legal Dept, Ministry of Foreign Affairs 1990–92, Counsellor to Minister of Foreign Affairs 1993–94; Amb., Perm. Rep. of Lithuania to UN 1994–2000; Deputy Minister of Foreign Affairs 2000–01, currently Undersec.; fmr Perm. Rep. to EU; Dir Lithuanian Br. of US law firm McDermott, Will & Emery 1993–94.
Address: Ministry of Foreign Affairs, J. Tumo-Vaižganto 2, Vilnius 01511, Lithuania (office). *Telephone:* (5) 236-2444 (office). *Fax:* (5) 231-3090 (office). *E-mail:* urm@urm.lt (office). *Website:* www.urm.lt (office).

K

KA, Ibra Deguène; Senegalese diplomatist; b. 4 Jan. 1939, Koul-Mecke, Thies Region. *Education:* Ecole Nationale d'Admin et de Magistrature. *Career:* Chief Div. of UN Affairs, Ministry of Foreign Affairs 1969–72, Chef de Cabinet 1972–73, Exec. Sec. Senegalo-Gambian Interministerial Cttee 1973–78; Amb. to several countries, including Algeria, Tunisia, Liberia, USA, Argentina, Mexico and Switzerland 1978–96; Perm. Rep. to UN, New York 1996–2001; Chair. UN Group of Experts to monitor Security Council arms embargo against Democratic Republic of the Congo 2005; mem. UN Special Cttee investigating Israeli activities in the Occupied Territories 1994; Founding mem. UN Asscn Senegal; Commdr Nat. Order of Merit and other decorations.
Address: c/o Ministry of Foreign Affairs, place de l'Indépendance, BP 4044, Dakar, Senegal.

KABA, Mory Karamoko; Guinean diplomatist; *Ambassador to USA. Career:* fmr Counsellor, Perm. Mission of Guinea to UN, New York; fmr Minister for Co-operation; Consul Gen. in Jeddah –2007, Amb. to USA 2007–.
Address: Embassy of Guinea, 2112 Leroy Place, NW, Washington, DC 20008, USA (office). *Telephone:* (202) 483-9420 (office). *Fax:* (202) 483-8688 (office).

KABA, Sidiki; Senegalese human rights organization executive and lawyer; *President, International Federation for Human Rights; Career:* human rights lawyer assoc. with cases in Senegal, Chad, Côte d'Ivoire, Guinea; Pres. Nat. Org. for Human Rights, Senegal; Vice-Pres. Int. Fed. of the League for Human Rights, Paris, Pres. 2001–.
Address: Fédération Internationale des Droits de l'Homme, 17 Passage de la Main d'Or, 75011 Paris, France (office). *Telephone:* 1-43-55-25-18 (office). *Fax:* 1-43-55-18-80 (office). *E-mail:* fidh@fidh.org (office). *Website:* www.fidh.org (office).

KABBAH, Alhaji Ahmed Tejan, BEcons; Sierra Leonean fmr head of state; b. 16 Feb. 1932, Pendembu, Kailahun Dist, Eastern Prov.; m. Patricia Tucker (deceased); four c. *Education:* St Edward's School, Freetown, Cardiff Coll. of Tech., Univ. Coll. Aberystwyth, Wales. *Career:* called to the Bar (Gray's Inn), London; fmr Dist Commr Moyamba, Kono, Bombali and Kambia Dists., Deputy Sec., Ministry of Social Welfare and Perm. Sec., Ministries of Educ. and of Trade and Industry; joined staff of UN, served as UNDP Rep. Lesotho 1973, Tanzania and Uganda 1976, temporarily assigned to Zimbabwe 1980, apptd head of Eastern and Southern Africa Div. 1979, Deputy Personnel Dir, then Dir, Div. of Admin. and Man. 1981–92; mem. Sierra Leone People's Party (SLPP) 1954–; Chair. Nat. Advisory Council 1992–96; Pres. of Sierra Leone 1996–97, March 1998–2007, also Minister of Defence and C-in-C of Armed Forces; fmr Chancellor Univ. of Sierra Leone; Grand Commdr Order of the Repub. of Sierra Leone; Hon. LLD (Univ. of Sierra Leone), (Southern Connecticut State Univ.) 2001.
Address: Sierra Leone People's Party, 29 Rawdon Street, Freetown, Sierra Leone (office). *Telephone:* (22) 228222 (office). *Fax:* (22) 228222 (office). *E-mail:* sq-slpp@hotmail.com (office). *Website:* www.slpp.ws (office).

KABBAJ, Omar; Moroccan international organization official; b. 15 Aug. 1942, Rabat; m. Saida Lebbar; four s. *Education:* Ecole Supérieure de Commerce et d'Administration des Entreprises de Toulouse, France. *Career:* mem. Exec. Bd IMF and World Bank; fmr Minister of Econ. Affairs Minister; Exec. Pres. and Chair. Bd of Dirs African Devt Bank (ADB) and African Devt Fund (ADF) 1995–2005, now Hon. Pres.; fmr mem. UN Comm. on HIV/AIDS and Governance in Africa (CHGA); Kt of the Order of the Throne of Morocco, Grand Officer of the Nat. Order of Tunisia, Officer of the Nat. Order of Burkina Faso. *Publications:* The Challenge of African Development 2003.
Address: c/o African Development Bank, rue Joseph Anoma, 01 BP 1387, Abidjan 01, Côte d'Ivoire (office).

KABERUKA, Donald, MPhil, PhD; Rwandan economist, politician and international organization official; *Executive President and Chairman, African Development Bank; Education:* Tanzania, Glasgow Univ., LSE. *Career:* early career in banking industry; fmr State Minister for Budget and Planning; Minister of Finance and Econ. Planning 1997–2005; Exec. Pres. and Chair. African Devt Bank 2005–; Chair. Bd of Govs Africa Trade Insurance Agency (ATI) 2003–; Chair. Nat. Africa Peer Review Comm.

2004–; Chair. PTA Bank (East, Central and Southern Africa devt bank) 2001–02; Vice-Chair. Nat. AIDS Comm. 2002–03.
Address: African Development Bank, rue Joseph Anoma, 01 BP 1387, Abidjan 01, Côte d'Ivoire (office). *Telephone:* 20-20-44-44 (office). *Fax:* 20-20-49-59 (office). *E-mail:* afdb@afdb.org (office). *Website:* www.afdb.org (office).

KABILA KABANGE, Maj.-Gen. Joseph, BA; Democratic Republic of the Congo army officer and head of state; *President;* b. 4 June 1970, Sud-Kivu Prov.; m. Olive Lembe; one d. *Education:* Nat. Defence Univ., People's Repub. of China. *Career:* Deputy Chair. Jt Chiefs of Staff, Congolese Armed Forces 1998–2000, Army Chief of Staff 2000–01; Pres. Democratic Repub. of the Congo 2001–, fmrly Minister of Defence; Dr hc (Hankuk Univ., S Korea).
Address: Office of the President, Hôtel du Conseil Exécutif, ave de Lemera, Kinshasa-Gombé, Democratic Republic of the Congo (office). *Telephone:* (12) 30892 (office). *E-mail:* pr@presidentrdc.cd (office). *Website:* www .presidentrdc.cd (office).

KABIR, M. Humayun, BL, MA; Bangladeshi diplomatist; *Ambassador to USA;* m.; two s. *Education:* Univ. of Dhaka, Acad. of Int. Law, The Hague, Netherlands, Univ. of Paris XI, France. *Career:* fought during Liberation War of Bangladesh 1971; Lecturer, Univ. of Dhaka 1977–80; career diplomat with rank of Deputy Perm. Sec., Pvt. Sec. to Advisor for Foreign Affairs and Section Officer, Ministry of Foreign Affairs 1984–87; Second, later First Sec., Embassy in Washington, DC 1987–91, First Sec. and Counsellor, New Delhi 1991–94; Dir UN and Foreign Sec.'s Office, Ministry of Foreign Affairs 1994–96; Counsellor, Perm. Mission to UN, New York 1996–99, Deputy High Commr, New Delhi 1999–2001; Dir-Gen. for the UN, Ministry of Foreign Affairs 2001, for Europe 2002, for S Asia and the S Asian Asscn for Regional Co-operation 2003; Amb. to Nepal 2003–06, High Commr to Australia (also accred to New Zealand and Fiji) 2006–07, Amb. to USA 2007–. *Publications:* has written extensively on diplomacy with a focus on multilateral and public diplomacy and UN peacekeeping.
Address: Embassy of Bangladesh, 3510 International Drive, NW, Washington, DC 20007, USA (office). *Telephone:* (202) 244-0183 (office). *Fax:* (202) 244-5366 (office). *E-mail:* bdootwash@bangladoot.org (office). *Website:* www.bangladoot.org (office).

KABORÉ, Roch Marc-Christian; Burkinabè politician; *President, Congrès pour la démocratie et le progrès; Career:* Minister of State in charge of Relations with Insts 1990–94; Prime Minister of Burkina Faso 1994–96; mem. Organisation pour la démocratie populaire/Mouvement du travail (ODP/MT), First Vice-Pres., then Pres. Congrès pour la démocratie et le progrès (CDP) (f. 1996 as successor to ODP/MT) 1996–.
Address: Congrès pour la démocratie et le progrès, 1146 ave Dr Kwamé N'Krumah, 01 BP 1605, Ouagadougou 01, Burkina Faso (office). *Telephone:* 50-31-50-18 (office). *Fax:* 50-31-43-93 (office). *E-mail:* contact@cdp-burkina.org (office). *Website:* www.cdp-burkina.org (office).

KABULOV, Zamir N.; Russian diplomatist; *Ambassador to Afghanistan; Career:* jr officer, Embassy in Kabul 1980s, Deputy Dir Third Dept, Ministry of Foreign Affairs –2001, Acting Head of Mission, Kabul 2001, Dir for Asia, Ministry of Foreign Affairs –2004, Amb. to Afghanistan 2004–. *Publications:* articles on politics, diplomacy and int. relations.
Address: Embassy of the Russian Federation, House 63, Lane 5, St 15, Wazir Akbar Khan, Kabul, Afghanistan (office). *Telephone:* (20) 2300500 (office). *E-mail:* rusembafg@neda.af (office).

KACER, Rastislav, MSc; Slovak diplomatist; *Ambassador to USA;* b. 9 July 1965, Nova Bana; m. Otilia Kacerova 1966; one d. one s. *Education:* Slovak Tech. Univ., Commenius Univ., Bratislava, Research Centre TNO Delft, The Netherlands, Univ. of Leeds, UK. *Career:* staff mem. Autobrzdy Vrable 1983–84; Research Fellow, Research Centre for Animal Production 1989–91; joined Ministry of Foreign Affairs 1992, Head of Analytical Unit, Dept of Planning and Analysis 1994, Liaison Officer to NATO HQ, Brussels 1994–98, Dir Dept of Analysis and Planning 1998–99, Dir-Gen. Div. of Int. Orgs and Security Policy 1999–2001; State Sec. (Deputy Minister), Ministry of Defence 2001–03; Amb. to USA 2003–.

Address: Embassy of the Slovak Republic, 3523 International Court, NW, Washington, DC 20008, USA (office). *Telephone:* (202) 237-1054 (office). *Fax:* (202) 237-6438 (office). *E-mail:* information@slovakembassy-us.org (office). *Website:* www.slovakembassy-us.org (office).

KACHORNPRASART, Maj.-Gen. Sanan; Thai politician; *Leader, Mahachon Party;* b. 7 Sept. 1944, Phichit. *Education:* Chulachomklao Royal Mil. Acad. *Career:* aide-de-camp to Gen. Chalard Hiranyasiri; involved in attempted coup 1981; mem. Parl. (Democrat Party) for Phichit 1983, 1986, 1988; Deputy Communications Minister 1986; Minister of Agric. and Co-operatives 1989, of the Interior 1998–2000; Deputy Prime Minister 1990–91; Sec.-Gen. Democrat Party –2004; Leader, Mahachon Party 2004–.
Address: Mahachon, Bangkok, Thailand.

KACZMAREK, Wiesław; Polish politician; b. 1 Jan. 1958, Wrocław; m.; two d. *Education:* Warsaw Univ. of Technology. *Career:* Sr Asst, Mechanics and Tech. Dept, Warsaw Univ. of Tech. 1984–89; Deputy Dir Industrial & Commercial Chamber of Foreign Investors 1989–91; Co-founder and mem. Social Democracy of the Repub. of Poland (SdRP) 1990–99; Deputy in Sejm (Parl.) 1989–; Man. Warsaw Br., First Commercial Bank SA, Lublin 1991–93; Minister of Privatization 1993–96, of the Economy 1997, of the Treasury 2001–03; mem. Nat. Bd Democratic Left Alliance (SLD) 1999–2004; mem. Polish Social Democracy (Socjaldemokracja Polski—SDPL, splinter group of SLD) 2004–.
Address: c/o Polish Social Democracy (Socjaldemokracja Polski—SDPL), 02-904 Warsaw, ul. Bernardyńska 14a, Poland (office). *Telephone:* (22) 8406008 (office). *E-mail:* sdpl.wybory@onet.pl (office). *Website:* www.sdpl .pl (office); www.kaczmarek.pl.

KACZYŃSKI, Jarosław Aleksander, DJur; Polish politician and lawyer; *Leader, Law and Justice (PiS) (Prawo i Sprawiedliwość);* b. 18 June 1949, Warsaw; brother of Lech Kaczyński (q.v.). *Education:* Warsaw Univ. *Career:* Asst, Sr Asst in Inst. of Science and Higher Educ. 1971–76; collaborator, Workers' Defence Cttee (KOR) 1976–80; scientific worker, Białystok br. of Warsaw Univ. 1977–81; ed. Głos (independent magazine) 1980–82; warehouseman 1982; mem. Solidarity Trade Union 1980–90; Sec. Nat. Exec. Comm. of Solidarity 1986–87; took part in Round Table talks in Comm. for Political Reforms Feb.–April 1989; Ed.-in-Chief Tygodnik Solidarność (weekly) 1989–90; Deputy to Senate 1989–91; Dir Office of Pres. and Minister of State 1990–92; Deputy to Sejm (Parl.) 1991–93, 1997–, mem. Ethics Comm. 2001–; Founder and Chair. Centre Alliance 1990–98; Co-Founder with his brother and mem. Main Bd Law and Justice (Prawo i Sprawiedliwość—PiS) 2001–, Pres. Law and Justice Parl. Club 2001–03, Pres. PiS and Chair. Main Bd 2003–, Prime Minister of Poland 2006–07; mem. Helsinki Comm. in Poland 1982–89.
Address: Law and Justice (PiS) (Prawo i Sprawiedliwość), 02-018 Warsaw, ul. Nowogrodzka 84/86 (office); Sejm RP, 00-902 Warsaw, ul. Wiejska 4/6/8, Poland. *Telephone:* (22) 6215035 (office). *Fax:* (22) 6216767 (office). *E-mail:* biuro.organizacyjne@pis.org.pl (office). *Website:* www.pis.org.pl (office).

KACZYŃSKI, Lech Aleksander, PhD; Polish politician, civic trade union leader, lawyer and head of state; *President;* b. 18 June 1949, Warsaw; brother of Jarosław Kaczyński (q.v.); m. Maria Mackiewicz 1978; one d. *Education:* Warsaw, Gdańsk Univ. *Career:* Asst, Sr Asst in Labour Law Dept, Gdańsk Univ. 1971–97; adviser to striking workers in Gdańsk Aug. 1980; mem. Solidarity Ind. Self-governing Trade Union 1980–; head Group for Current Analysis and Intervention Bureau of Founding Cttee of Solidarity Trade Union, then head regional Centre for Social and Professional Work, Gdańsk 1980–81; mem. Regional Bd of Solidarity, Gdańsk 1981; interned 1981–82; assoc. of Lech Wałęsa (q.v.) 1982–91 and Provisional Co-ordinating Comm. of Solidarity 1983–84, its rep. in Gdańsk Jan.–July 1986, Sec. 1986–87; sec. Nat. Exec. Comm. of Solidarity 1988–90; took part in Round Table talks in Comm. for Trade Union Pluralism Feb.–April 1989; mem. Presidium Nat. Exec. Comm. of Solidarity 1989–90, First Deputy Chair. Nat. Comm. May 1990–91, Assoc. Workers' Defence Cttee (KOR) 1977–78, Free Trade Unions on the Seacoast 1978–80; Citizens' Cttee of Solidarity Chair. 1988–91; Senator 1989–91, Minister of State for Nat. Security Affairs in Chancellery of Pres. of Poland March–Nov. 1991; Pres. Cen. Audit Comm. 1992–95; Deputy to Sejm (Parl.) 1991–93, 2001–, Chair. Comm. of Admin. and Interior Affairs 1991–93; Vice-Leader Programme Bd of Public Affairs Inst., Warsaw 1996–; mem. EUROSAI Governing Bd 1993–95, Admin. Bd of ILO; Prof., Acad. of Catholic Theology (now Cardinal S. Wyszyński Univ.), Warsaw 1998–; Minister of Justice and Prosecutor-Gen. 2000–01; Co-Founder and Chair. Nat. Cttee Law and Justice (Prawo i Sprawiedliwość—PiS) Party 2001–03, Chair. Political Bd 2003–; Mayor of Warsaw 2002–05; Pres. of Poland 2005–. *Publications:* Social Pension 1989 and some 15 works on labour law and social insurance.

Address: Chancellery of the President, 00-902 Warsaw, ul. Wiejska 10, Poland (office). *Telephone:* (22) 6952900 (office). *Fax:* (22) 6952238l (office). *E-mail:* listy@prezydent.pl (office). *Website:* www.prezydent.pl (office).

KADAKIN, Alexander Mikhailovich; Russian diplomatist; *Ambassador to Sweden;* b. 22 July 1949, Kishinev, Moldova. *Education:* Moscow Inst. of Int. Relations. *Career:* translator Special Construction Bureau Vibpribor, Kishinev 1966–67; joined diplomatic service 1972; with USSR Embassy, India 1972, Attaché 1972–75, Third Sec. 1975–78; Second Sec. Secr., First Deputy to USSR Minister of Foreign Affairs 1978–80, First Sec., Secr. 1980–83, Asst 1983–86, Asst to Deputy Minister 1986–88, Asst First Deputy Minister 1988–89; Minister-Counsellor USSR Embassy, India 1989–91; First Deputy Head of Dept USSR Ministry of Foreign Affairs 1991; Counsellor Embassy, India 1991–93; Amb. to Nepal 1993–97; mem. Collegium, Dir of Linguistic Support Dept, Ministry of Foreign Affairs 1997–99; Amb. to India 1999–2004, to Sweden 2004–; Asst Prof., Dept of Indian Studies, Moscow State Inst. of Int. Relations 1979–85.
Address: Embassy of the Russian Federation, Gjörwellsgt. 31, 112 60 Stockholm, Sweden (office). *Telephone:* (8) 13-04-41 (office). *Fax:* (8) 618-27-03 (office). *E-mail:* rusembassy@telia.com (office). *Website:* www .ryssland.se (office).

KÁDÁR, Béla, PhD, DSc; Hungarian politician, economist and academic; b. 21 March 1934, Pécs; m. Patricia Derzso; one s. *Education:* Budapest Univ. of Economy. *Career:* worked for Int. Econ. Dept, Nat. Bank of Hungary, Elektro-impex Foreign Trading Co.; fmr dept head and research man., Business and Market Research Inst.; with Hungarian Acad. of Sciences Research Inst. of World Economy 1965–88; Lecturer, Eötvös Loránd Univ. of Budapest; Visiting Prof., Santiago de Chile and San Marcos Univ. of Lima; Dir Econ. Planning Inst. 1988–90; Minister of Int. Econ. Relations 1990–94; mem. Parl. 1994–98, Chair. Cttee on Budget and Finances; Vice-Chair. Hungarian Asscn of Economists 1990–2000, Chair. 2002–; Univ. Prof. 1998–; Pres. Hungarian Export-Import Bank 1998–99; Vice-Pres. Hungarian Soc. of Foreign Affairs 1998–; Amb. to OECD 1999–2003; mem. Monetary Council of Hungarian Nat. Bank 1999–; Chair. Hungarian Group in Trilateral Comm. 1999–; Academician, Hungarian Acad. of Sciences; Dr hc (San Marcos Univ., Lima) 1970, (Budapest) 1999; Grand Prix, Hungarian Acad. of Sciences 1984, Econ. Policy Club (Bonn) Prize for Social Market Econs 1993. *Publications:* author of eight books and more than 400 papers.
Address: Mártonhegyi u. 38/B, Budapest 1124, Hungary. *Telephone:* (1) 355-7987. *Fax:* (1) 355-7987.

KADEGE, Alphonse Marie; Burundian politician. *Career:* Vice-Pres. of Burundi 2003–04; acquitted on charges of coup plot 2007; mem. Union pour le progrès national (UPRONA).
Address: c/o Union pour le progrès national (UPRONA), BP 1810, Bujumbura, Burundi (office).

KADHAFI, Col Mu'ammar Muhammed al- (see GADDAFI, Col Mu'ammar Muhammed al-).

KADYROV, Ramzan Akhmadovich; Russian (Chechen) government official; *President, Chechen (Nokchi) Republic;* b. 5 Oct. 1976, Tsenteroi, Checheno-Ingush ASSR (now Chechen—Nokchi Repub.); m.; seven c. *Career:* fmr Commdr of 'Kadyrovtsy' militia (Presidential security service); fmr Head of Security, Chechen (Nokchi) Repub.; First Deputy Chair. of Govt, Chechen (Nokchi) Repub. 2004–05, Acting Chair. of Govt 2005–06, Chair. of Govt 2006–07, Pres. 2007–; Chair. Ramzan boxing club, Terek Grozny football club; Hero of Russia Medal, Order of Courage, Order of Akhmad Kadyrov, Caucasus Service Medal, Defender of the Chechen Repub. Medal.
Address: Office of the President, 364000 Chechen (Nokchi) Republic, Groznyi, ul. Garazhnaya 10a, Russian Federation (office). *Telephone:* (8712) 22-20-01 (office); (8712) 22-20-09 (office). *Fax:* (8712) 22-20-14 (office). *E-mail:* secretariat_chr@mail.ru (office). *Website:* www.chechnya .gov.ru (office).

KAFANDO, Michel, LLB, PhD; Burkinabè diplomatist; *Permanent Representative, United Nations;* b. 1942, Ouagadougou; m.; one c. *Education:* Univ. of Bordeaux, Inst. of Political Studies, Sorbonne Univ., Paris, France, Carnegie Endowment for Int. Peace and Diplomatic Training, Geneva, Switzerland. *Career:* Minister of Foreign Affairs 1982–83; fmr Amb. to Cuba; Vice-Pres. UN Gen. Ass. 1982; Head Del. to numerous OAS confs; Perm. Rep. of Burkina Faso to UN, New York April (second time) 1998–; fmr Chair. Nat. Remote Sensing Comm., Comm. on External Assistance.
Address: Permanent Mission of Burkina Faso to the UN, 115 East 73rd Street, New York, NY 10021, USA (office). *Telephone:* (212) 288-7515 (office). *Fax:* (212) 772-3562 (office). *E-mail:* burkinafaso@un.int (office).

KAFKA, Alexandre; Brazilian economist, academic and international finance consultant; b. 25 Jan. 1917; m. Rita Petschek 1947 (died 2006); two d. *Education:* Law School German Univ., Prague, Grad. School of Int. Studies, Geneva, Balliol Coll. Oxford, England. *Career:* Prof. of Econs, Univ. de São Paulo 1941–46; Adviser to Brazilian Del. to Preparatory Cttee and Conf. of Int. Trade Org. 1946–48; Asst Div. Chief, Int. Monetary Fund (IMF) 1949–51, Exec. Dir 1966–98, Vice-Chair. Deputies of Cttee on Reform of Int. Monetary System and Related Matters 1972–74; Adviser, Superintendency of Money and Credit (now Banco Central do Brasil); Dir of Research, Brazilian Inst. of Econs 1951–56, Dir 1961–63; Chief Financial Inst. and Policies Section, UN 1956–59; Prof. of Econs, Univ. of Va, US 1959–60, 1963–75, lecturer Law School 1977–87; Lecturer, George Washington Univ. 1989, Visiting Prof. of Econs, Boston Univ. 1975–79; Adviser to Minister of Finance 1964; Comendador Ordem do Rio Branco (Brazil) 1973, Grand Cross (Colombia), Order de Boyaca (Colombia), Grand Officer (Peru), Order del sol (Peru). *Publication:* IMF Governance, in G-24: commemorating 50th year after Bretton Woods Conf. 1994. *Address:* 4201 Cathedral Avenue, NW, Apt. 805E, Washington, DC 20016, USA. *Telephone:* (202) 623-7870 (office); (202) 362-1737 (home).

KAGAME, Maj.-Gen. Paul; Rwandan politician, army officer and head of state; *President;* b. 1957; m.; four c. *Education:* Fort Leavenworth, USA. *Career:* escaped to Uganda with family from anti-Tutsi persecution 1960; joined Ugandan Rebel Army 1982, Chief of Intelligence Ugandan Army 1986; formed rebel army of Rwandan exiles 1990, Leader campaign in Rwanda 1990–94, helped broker cease-fire 1993; Vice-Pres. and Minister of Nat. Defence 1994–2000, Pres. of Rwanda April 2000–; Head Rwandan Patriotic Front Party (FPR) 2000; Young Presidents' Org. 2003, Africa Gender Award 2007. *Address:* Office of the President, BP 15, Kigali, Rwanda (office). *Telephone:* (590) 62007 (office). *Fax:* 752431 (office). *E-mail:* pkagame@gov.rw (office). *Website:* www.gov.rw (office).

KAGARLITSKY, Boris Yuliyevich, PhD; Russian journalist and writer; *Director, Institute of Globalization Studies and Social Movements;* b. 1958, Moscow. *Education:* State Inst. of Theatrical Art. *Career:* Ed. Leviy povorot (samizdat journal) 1978–82; Co-ordinator Moscow People's Front 1988; Deputy, Moscow city Soviet (prov. Parl.) 1990–93; Founding mem. Party of Labour 1992; fmr adviser to Chair., Fed. of Ind. Trade Unions of Russia; Sr Research Fellow, Inst. of Comparative Political Studies, Russian Acad. of Sciences 1994–2002; Dir Inst. of Globalization Studies 2003–07, Inst. of Globalization Studies and Social Movts 2007–; columnist, The Moscow Times, ZNet. *Publications:* The Thinking Reed (Deutscher Memorial Prize) 1988, The Dialectic of Hope 1989, Farewell Perestroika: A Soviet Chronicle 1990, Disintegration of the Monolith 1993, Square Wheels: How Russian Democracy Got Derailed 1994, The Mirage of Modernisation 1995, Restoration in Russia 1995, New Realism, New Barbarism: Socialist Theory in the Era of Globalization 1999, The Twilight of Globalization: Property, State and Capitalism 1999, The Return of Radicalism: Reshaping the Left Institutions 2000, Russia under Yeltsin and Putin: Neo-liberal Autocracy 2002, The Politics of Empire: Globalisation in Crisis (co–ed.) 2004; contribs Novaya Gazeta, The Progressive, Red Pepper, Green Left Weekly. *Address:* Institute of Globalization Studies and Social Movements, Gazetny per. 5, Moscow, Russia (office). *E-mail:* kagarlitsky@narod.ru. *Website:* kagarlitsky.narod.ru (office); www.iprog.ru (office).

KAHIN, Dahir Riyale; Somali politician; *President of "Republic of Somaliland";* *Career:* Vice-Pres. self-proclaimed Repub. of Somaliland (NW Somalia) –2002, Pres. May 2002–. *Address:* Office of the President of the Republic of Somaliland, Hargeysa, Somalia (office). *Website:* www.somalilandgov.com.

KAHN, Alfred Edward, PhD; American economist and fmr government official; *Robert Julius Thorne Professor Emeritus of Political Economy, Cornell University;* b. 17 Oct. 1917, Paterson, NJ; m. Mary Simmons 1943; one s. two d. *Education:* New York Univ. and Graduate School, Univ. of Missouri, Yale Univ. *Career:* Research Staff of Brookings Inst. 1940, 1951–52; joined US Govt Service with Antitrust Div., Dept of Justice, Dept of Commerce, War Production Bd 1941–43; Research Staff, 20th Century Fund 1944–45; Asst Prof. Dept of Econs, Ripon Coll., Wis. 1945–47; joined Dept of Econs, Cornell Univ., Ithaca, NY, as Asst Prof. 1947, Chair. Econs Dept 1958–63, Robert Julius Thorne Prof. of Political Economy 1966–89, Prof. Emer. 1989–, mem. Bd of Trustees 1964–69, Dean Coll. of Arts and Sciences 1969–74; Chair. New York Public Service Comm. 1974–77, Civil Aeronautics Bd 1977–78; Adviser to the Pres. on Inflation and Chair. Council on Wage and Price Stability 1978–80; Special Consultant, Nat. Econ. Research Associates 1980–; Chair. Int. Inst. for Applied Systems Analysis Advisory Cttee on Price Reform and Competition in the USSR 1990–91, Blue Ribbon Panel to Study Pricing in the Calif. Electricity

Market 2000; Vice-Pres. American Econ. Asscn 1981–82; mem. Advisory Cttee The Digital Age Communications Act Project 2005–; mem. American Acad. of Arts and Sciences, Fellow 1977; Hon. LLD (Colby Univ., Ripon Coll., Univ. of Mass., Northwestern Univ., Colgate Univ.); Hon. DHL (State Univ. of New York) 1985; Distinguished Alumni Award, Univ. of New York 1976, L. Welch Pogue Award for Lifetime Contribs to Aviation 1997, Sovereign Fund Award 1997, J. Rhoads Foster Award for achievements in econ. regulation 1999, Wilbur Cross Medal, Yale Univ. 1995, AEI-Brookings Jt Center for Regulatory Studies First Distinguished Lecturer 1999, American Antitrust Inst. Award for Lifetime Achievement in Antitrust 2003. *Publications:* Great Britain in the World Economy 1946, (co-author) Fair Competition, the Law and Economics of Antitrust Policy 1954, (co-author) Integration and Competition in the Petroleum Industry 1959, The Economics of Regulation (two vols) 1970, 1971, 1988, Letting Go: Deregulating the Process of Deregulation 1998, Whom the Gods Would Destroy, or How Not to Deregulate 2001, Lessons from Deregulation: Telecommunications and Airlines After the Crunch 2004. *Address:* 308 N Cayuga Street, Ithaca, NY 14850, USA (office). *Telephone:* (607) 277-3007 (office). *Fax:* (607) 277-1581 (office). *E-mail:* alfred.kahn@nera.com (office).

KAI-BANYA, Melrose; Sierra Leonean diplomatist; *Ambassador to Russia;* b. Freetown. *Career:* fmr staff mem., Human Resources Man., Cen. Bank of Sierra Leone; fmr teacher, Milton Margai Teacher's Coll., Freetown; Amb. to Russia (also accred to Albania, Armenia, Serbia and Montenegro, Croatia, Kosovo, Azerbaijan, Belarus, Estonia, Georgia, Kazakhstan, Kyrgyzstan, Latvia, Lithuania, Moldova, Tajikistan, Ukraine, Uzbekistan, Czech Repub., Slovakia, Poland, Hungary and Bulgaria) 1996–. *Address:* Embassy of Sierra Leone, 26 Rublyovskoye shosse 26/1/58–59, POB 141, 121615 Moscow, Russia (office). *Telephone:* (495) 415-41-66 (office). *Fax:* (495) 415-29-85 (office).

KAISER, Karl, PhD; German professor of political science; *Ralph I. Straus Visiting Professor, John F. Kennedy School of Government, Harvard University;* b. 8 Dec. 1934, Siegen; m. Deborah Strong 1967; two s. one d. *Education:* Univs of Cologne, Bonn and Grenoble and Nuffield Coll., Oxford, UK. *Career:* Lecturer, Harvard Univ. 1963–67, Univ. of Bonn 1968–69, Johns Hopkins Univ. Bologna Center 1968–69; Prof. of Political Science, Univ. of the Saarland 1969–74, Univ. of Cologne 1974–91, Univ. of Bonn 1991–; Otto-Wolf Dir Research Inst. of German Soc. for Foreign Affairs, Bonn and Berlin 1973–2003; currently Ralph I. Straus Visiting Prof., John F. Kennedy School of Govt., Harvard Univ.; mem. German Council of Environmental Advisors; mem. Bd of Dirs Foreign Policy, Internationale Politik, Asian-Pacific Review; mem. Advisory Bd American-Jewish Cottee, Berlin; mem. Bd Fed. Acad. of Security Policy, Berlin; Hon. CBE 1989; Officier, Légion d'honneur, Bundesverdienstkreuz Erster Klasse 1999; Prix Adolphe Bentinck 1973; NATO Atlantic Award 1986. *Publications:* EEC and Free Trade Area 1963, German Foreign Policy in Transition 1968, Europe and the USA 1973, New Tasks for Security Policy 1977, Reconciling Energy Needs and Proliferation 1978, Western Security: What Has Changed, What Can be Done? 1981, Atomic Energy Without Nuclear Weapons 1982, German–French Security Policy 1986, British–German Co-operation 1987, Space and International Politics 1987, Germany's Unification, The International Aspects 1991, Germany and the Iraq Conflict 1992, Foreign Policies of the New Republics in Eastern Europe 1994, Germany's New Foreign Policy, Vol. 1 1994, Vol. 2 1995, Vol. 3 1996, The Foreign Policies of the New Democracies in Central and Eastern Europe 1994, Acting for Europe, German-French Co-operation in a Changing World 1995, World Politics in a New Era 1996, Interests and Strategies 1996, Institutions and Resources 1998, The Future of German Foreign Policy 1999. *Address:* Kennedy School of Government, Belfer-G-3, Mailbox 40, 79 JFK Street, Cambridge, MA 02138-5801, USA. *Telephone:* (617) 495-1899 (office). *Fax:* 617) 495-8292 (office). *E-mail:* karl_kaiser@ksg.harvard.edu (office). *Website:* ksgfaculty.harvard.edu/karl_kaiser (office).

KAKABADSE NAVARRO, Yolanda; Ecuadorean politician, environmentalist and international organization executive; *President, World Conservation Union; Education:* Catholic Univ. of Quito. *Career:* Exec. Dir Fundación Natura, Quito 1979–90; Civil Society Org. Co-ordinator, UN Conf. for Environment and Devt (Earth Summit), Geneva, Switzerland 1990–92; f. Fundación Futuro Latinamericano 1993, Exec. Pres. 1993–; Pres. World Conservation Union (Int. Union for Conservation of Nature and Natural Resources—IUCN) 1996–; Minister of the Environment 1998–2000; mem. Bd Dirs World Wide Fund for Nature (WWF) 1995–97, World Resources Inst. 1996–, Ford Foundation 1998–98, 2000–, Millennium Ecosystem Assessment 2000–; mem. Int. Advisory Bd INBio 2000–; Adviser to Pres. Global Environment Facility (GEF) 1993–98, 2000–; Nat. Order of Merit (Ecuador) 1990, Order of the Golden Ark (The Netherlands) 1991; UNEP Global 500 Award 1991, Zayed Prize 2001.

Address: World Conservation Union, 28 rue Mauverney, 1196 Gland, Switzerland (office). *Telephone:* (22) 9990001 (office). *Fax:* (22) 9990002 (office). *E-mail:* president@iucn.org (office). *Website:* www.iucn.org (office).

KAKLAMANIS, Apostolos; Greek politician and lawyer; b. 7 Sept. 1936, Lefkas; m. Athina-Anna Gavera 1972; one s. one d. *Education:* Univ. of Athens. *Career:* Gen. Sec. Ministry of Welfare 1964–65; political prisoner during colonels' dictatorship; Founding mem. Pasok and mem. Cen. Cttee and Exec. Cttee; mem. Vouli (Parl.) for Athens B 1974–; Minister of Labour 1981–82, of Educ. and Religious Affairs 1982–86, of Justice 1986–87, Minister in charge of the Prime Minister's Office 1987–88, Minister of Health, Welfare and Social Services 1988–89, of Labour 1989–90; Speaker of Parl. 1993–2004.
Address: Vouli, Parliament Bldg, Syntagma Square, 101 80 Athens (office); Solomou 58, 106 82 Athens, Greece (office). *Telephone:* (210) 3608640 (office); (210) 3288434 (office). *Fax:* (210) 3708210 (office). *E-mail:* apkaklamanis@parliament.gr (office); ak@apkaklamanis.gr (office). *Website:* www.parliament.gr (office); www.apkaklamanis.gr (office).

KAKOURIS, Andreas S., BA, MA; Cypriot diplomatist; *Ambassador to USA;* b. 1960, England; m. Kareen Farrell Kakouris; one s. one d. *Education:* Univ. of Lancaster, UK, Norman Paterson School Int. Affairs, Carleton Univ., Canada. *Career:* del. to successive UN Gen. Ass. sessions 1984–92, covered First Cttee (Disarmament), Second Cttee (Econ.), Fourth Cttee (Decolonization) issues, served in Cypriot Consulate-Gen. and Perm. Mission to UN, New York 1984–88; in Political Div., Ministry of Foreign Affairs 1989–92; in Cypriot Perm. Del. to EU, Brussels (Assoc. Countries Political Dirs Meetings and Sr Official for Euro-Mediterranean Partnership) 1992–96; Deputy Chief of Mission, Embassy in Washington, DC 1996–2000; Dir Political Affairs Div. (Multilateral Affairs), Ministry of Foreign Affairs 2000–02; Amb. to Ireland 2002–06, to USA 2006– (also accred to Canada 2007–).
Address: Embassy of Cyprus, 2211 R Street, NW, Washington, DC 20008, USA (office). *Telephone:* (202) 462-5772 (office). *Fax:* (202) 483-6710 (office). *E-mail:* cypembwash@earthlink.net (office). *Website:* www .cyprusembassy.net (office).

KALAM, Aavul Pakkiri Jainulabidin Abdul, PhD; Indian fmr head of state and nuclear scientist; b. 15 Oct. 1931, Dhanushkodi, Rameswaram Dist. *Education:* Madras Inst. of Tech. *Career:* mem. staff Space Dept 1960s and 1970s, later Defence Lab., Hyderabad; launched India's first satellite 1980, masterminded integrated guided missile devt and nuclear programmes, developed Agni, Trishul and Prithvi missiles, responsible for carrying out underground nuclear tests 1998; fmr Cabinet Minister and Prin. Scientific Adviser to Govt 1999–2001; Chair. Tech. Information, Forecasting and Assessment Council; head of an agricultural devt agency; Pres. of India 2002–07; Padma Bhusan 1981, Padma Vibhushan 1990, Bharat Ratna 1997. *Publications include:* Yenudaya Prayana (Tamil poems), Wings of Fire (bestselling autobiog.) 1999, Eternal Quest (children's novel), Ignited Minds: Unleashing the Power Within India 2001.
Address: c/o President's Office, Rashtrapati Bhavan, New Delhi 110 004 (office); 10 Rajaji Marg, New Delhi, India (home).

KALAMANOV, Vladimir Avdashevich, DrHist; Russian politician; *Representative of Russian Federation, United Nations Educational, Scientific and Cultural Organization (UNESCO);* b. 1951, Moscow. *Education:* Moscow State Inst. of Int. Relations. *Career:* Head of Dept Ministry of Problems with Nationalities; Plenipotentiary Rep. of Pres. in Repubs. of N Ossetia and of Ingushetia 1997–99; Dir Fed. Migration Service of Russian Fed. 1999–2002; Special Rep. of Pres. to supervise observance of human rights and freedom in Chechen Repub. 2000; Rep. of Russian Fed. at UNESCO 2002–.
Address: 1 rue Miollis, 75732, Paris, Cedex 15, France. *Telephone:* 1-45-68-26-82; 1-45-04-37-52. *Fax:* 1-42-67-51-99. *E-mail:* unerus@club-internet.fr.

KALASHNIKOV, Sergey Vyacheslavovich, DPsych; Russian politician; b. 3 July 1951, Akmolinsk, Kazakh SSR; m. Natalia Kalashnikova; three c. *Education:* Leningrad State Univ., Inst. of Psychology, USSR (now Russian) Acad. of Sciences, Acad. of Nat. Econs USSR Council of Ministers, Russian Diplomatic Acad. *Career:* Head, Social-Psychological service of the Research Inst., USSR Ministry of Defence Industry, concurrently Chair. Inst. of Advanced Studies, USSR Ministry of Oil and Chemical Industry, Dir Intermanager State Enterprise 1979–91; Chair. European-Asian Bank; concurrently Dir-Gen. Asscn of Defence against Unemployment and Poverty, Chair. Cttee on Labour and Social Policy in the State Duma, Deputy of the Duma, Chair. Perm. Cttee on Social Policy, Interparliamentary Ass. of CIS 1993–98; Minister of Labour and Social Devt 1998–2000; Deputy Sec.-Gen. Union of Russia and Belarus 2000–03; Head, Dept of Social Devt, Office of the Govt 2003–; Pres. Russian Fed. of

the Sports Lover, Russian Asscn of Professional Golf; Chair. Nat. Council for Political and Social Reform; Co-Chair. Int. Forum 'World Experience and the Russian Economy'; mem. Bd Moscow English Club, Jury All-Russian Competition 'Best Russian Firms'; mem. Int. Acad. of Informatics, Russian Acad. of Science; Order of Friendship; Badge of Excellence for Border Services, Distinguished Worker of the Russian Ministry of Labour, Laureate, Nat. Peter the Great Prize. *Publications:* more than 50 works including two monographs and textbook Social Psychology of Management.
Address: Office of the Government, Krasnopresnenskaya nab. 2, 103274 Moscow, Russia (office). *Telephone:* (495) 205-57-35 (office). *Fax:* (495) 205-42-19 (office). *Website:* www.government.ru (office).

KALEEBA, Noerine; Ugandan physiotherapist and international organization official; *Chairperson, Board of International Trustees, Action Aid International; Education:* Makerere Univ. *Career:* physiotherapist, Mulago Hosp. –1987; Prin., Mulago School of Physiotherapy –1987; Founder and Exec. Dir AIDS Support Org. Uganda 1987–95, Patron 1995–; Adviser UN Programme on HIV/AIDS 1996–; community mobilisation adviser for jt UN programme on HIV/AIDS (UNAIDS), Geneva 1995–2003; fmr Vice-Chair. Action Aid UK, Chair. Bd of Int. Trustees Action Aid Int. 2003–, manages Africa HIV/AIDS portfolio for Children Investments Fund Foundation, Kampala; served on WHO Global Comm. on HIV/AIDS, Uganda AIDS Comm., Global AIDS Policy Coalition; King Baudouin Prize for Devt, Belgium 1995.
Address: c/o Action Aid, Hamlyn House, Macdonald Road, Archway, London, N19 5PG, England (office). *Telephone:* (20) 7561-7561 (office). *Fax:* (20) 7272-0899 (office). *E-mail:* mail@actionaid.org.uk (office). *Website:* www.actionaid.org (office).

KALFIN, Ivailo Georgiev, MSc; Bulgarian politician; *Deputy Prime Minister and Minister of Foreign Affairs;* b. 30 May 1964, Sofia; m.; one d. *Education:* French Language School, Sofia, Univ. of Nat. and World Economy, Sofia, Business Univ., Vienna, Austria, Univ. of Loughborough, UK, Coll. of Europe, Bruges, Belgium. *Career:* scholarship student under Chevening program, UK and German Marshall Fund, USA; taught Finance at Int. Univ., Sofia; worked for Machinoexport as well as in pvt. sector in the field of foreign trade, finance and consulting; mem. Municipal Council of Bulgarian Socialist Party (BSP), Supreme Council of BSP, Political Council of the Bulgarian Euroleft; Spokesperson for pre-election coalition 'Together for Bulgaria' 1996; mem. Parl. for Sofia (Parl. Group of the Democratic Left) 1994–97, 2000–01, 2005–, mem. Foreign Policy Cttee, Budgeting and Finance Cttee, Deputy Chair. Bulgarian-EU Jt Parl. Cttee; Sec. for Econ. Affairs to the Pres. 2002–05; Deputy Prime Minister and Minister of Foreign Affairs 2005–; Founder Social Democrats Political Movt; Man. and Sr Partner in consulting cos 1990–94, 1997–2000; Sr Prof., Univ., Sofia 2000–; observer of elections in Kosovo as mem. OSCE Missions 2001, 2003; mem. Advisory Bd Bulgarian Nat. Bank 2004–, Bulgaria Beyond the Facts Early Warning System implemented by UNDP and USAID; Founding mem. Bulgarian Macroeconomics Asscn; mem. Asscn of British Alumni in Bulgaria, Bd Dirs Inst. for Econs and Int. Relations, Fellows Network of the German Marshall Fund of the USA, Asscn of Scholarship Fellows of the Chevening programme, UK. *Publications:* Bulgaria 2010: Economic Challenges (report to Pres. of Bulgaria) (co-author) 2005, Factors of Economic Growth in Bulgaria (co-author) 2000; numerous articles in Bulgaria and in int. trade journals on EU and macroeconomic issues.
Address: Ministry of Foreign Affairs, 1040 Sofia, ul. Al. Zhendov 2, Bulgaria (office). *Telephone:* (2) 971-14-08 (office). *Fax:* (2) 870-30-41 (office). *E-mail:* iprd@mfa.government.bg (office). *Website:* www.mfa .government.bg (office); www.kalfin.eu (home).

KALIMBETOVA, Tajikan B.; Kyrgyzstani politician; *Minister of Finance;* b. 1964. *Career:* Deputy Minister of Finance –2007, also head financial intelligence service 2005–07, Minister of Finance 2007–, Chair. Iran-Kyrgyzstan Jt Econ. Comm.; Deputy Chair. EurAsian Group 2006–07; Chair. Social Fund 2007–.
Address: Ministry of Finance, pr. Erkindik 58, 720040 Bishkek, Kyrgyzstan (office). *Telephone:* (312) 66-13-50 (office). *Fax:* (312) 66-16-45 (office). *E-mail:* t.kalimbetova@mf.gov.kg (office). *Website:* www.mf.gov.kg (office).

KALJURAND, Marina, LLB, MA; Estonian diplomatist; *Ambassador to Russian Federation;* b. 6 Sept. 1962, Tallinn; m. Kalle Kaljurand; two c. *Education:* Tartu Univ., Estonian School of Diplomacy, Fletcher School of Law and Diplomacy, Tufts Univ., USA, Univ. of Lapland, Finland, Univ. of Pittsburgh, USA, Univ. of Durham, UK. *Career:* Lecturer in Law, Tallinn Econ. Tech. School 1986–91; Dir Int. Treaties Div., Ministry of Foreign Affairs 1991–96, Counsellor, Embassy in Helsinki 1996–99, Dir-Gen. Legal Dept, Ministry of Foreign Affairs 1999–2001, Deputy Under-

Sec. of Legal and Consular Affairs 2002–05, Amb. to Russian Fed. 2005–; fmr Lecturer in Public Int. Law, Estonian School of Diplomacy; fmr Lecturer in Int. Treaties Law, Estonian Law Center; Founding mem. Estonian Br. of Int. Law Asscn 1996–; Order of the White Star (3rd Class) 2004.
Address: Embassy of Estonia, M. Kislovskii per. 5, 125009 Moscow (office); Pärnu str. 245, 11622, Tallinn, Estonia (home). *Telephone:* (495) 737-36-40 (office). *Fax:* (495) 737-36-46 (office). *E-mail:* embassy.moskva@mfa.ee (office); Marina.Kaljurand@mfa.ee (office). *Website:* www.estemb.ru (office).

KALLAS, Siim; Estonian politician and banker; *Vice-President for Administrative Affairs, Audit and Anti-Fraud, European Commission;* b. 2 Oct. 1948, Tallinn; m. Kristi Kallas (née Kartus) 1972; one s. one d. *Education:* Tartu State Univ. *Career:* Chief Specialist Ministry of Finance Estonian SSR 1975–79; Gen. Man. Estonian Savings Banks 1979–86; Deputy Ed. Rahva Hääl 1986–89; Chair. Asscn of Estonian Trade Unions 1989–91; Pres. Eesti Pank (Bank of Estonia) 1991–95; Founder and Chair. Estonian Reform Party (Eesti Reformierakond) 1994–2004: elected to Riigikogu (Parl.) 1995–99, also mem. Parl. Nat. Defence Cttee and Parl. Foreign Affairs Cttee 2003–04; Minister of Foreign Affairs 1995–96; Minister of Finance 1999–2002; Prime Minister of the Repub. of Estonia 2002–03; Visiting Prof., Tartu State Univ.; EU Commr without Portfolio 2004, Vice-Pres. for Admin. Affairs, Audit and Anti-Fraud 2004–; Cross of the Order of Merit (Germany) 2000, Grand Officier, Légion d'honneur 2001, Order of the Nat. Coat of Arms 2003.
Address: European Commission, 200 Rue de la Loi, Berlaymont, 1040 Brussels, Belgium (office). *Telephone:* (2) 298-87-62 (direct line) (office); (2) 298-87-63 (office). *Fax:* (2) 298-84-92 (office). *E-mail:* siim.kallas@ec .europa.eu (office). *Website:* ec.europa.eu/commission_barroso/kallas (office).

KALLIOMÄKI, Antti Tapana; Finnish politician; b. 8 Jan. 1947, Siikainen; m. Helena Marjatta Kalliomäki 1969; two s. *Career:* physical training teacher, Hämeenkylä Upper Comprehensive School 1973–91; Project Man. Finnish Sports Asscn 1981–83; mem. Vantaa City Council 1984–2000; Chair. Vantaa Municipal Org. 1988–92; mem. Parl. 1983–, Chair. SDP Parl. Group 1991–95, 1999–2003, Vice-Chair. Cttee for the Future 1993–95, mem. Parl. Cttee on Defence Policy 1986–87, Cttee on Sports 1988–90, Parl. Advisory Bd on Defence Policy 1989–91; Chair. Parl. Security Policy Monitoring Group 2002–03; mem. SDP Party Cttee/Party Exec. 1990–2002; Vice-Chair. European SDP 2001–; Sec. to Prime Minister 1986–87; Minister of Trade and Industry 1995–99; Deputy Prime Minister and Minister of Finance 2003–05; Minister of Educ. 2005–07; mem. Parl. Supervisory Council, Bank of Finland 1987–91, Admin. Council, Finnish Broadcasting Co. (YLE) 2002–03 (Vice-Chair. 2002–03); Chair. Supervisory Bd Neste 1994–95.
Address: c/o Suomen Sosialidemokraattinen Puolue (SDP) (Finnish Social Democratic Party), Saariniemenkatu 6, 00530 Helsinki, Finland (office).

KALLSBERG, Anfinn; Faroe Islands politician; b. 19 Nov. 1947. *Career:* with J. F. Kjølbro 1964–74; self-employed bookkeeper, Vidareidi 1974–96; Mayor of Vidareidi 1974–80; mem. Faroese Rep. Council 1980–, Chair. 1991–93, Chair. Finance Cttee 1989–91, 2004–, mem. Foreign Affairs Cttee 2004; Prime Minister and Minister of Constitutional Affairs, Foreign Affairs and Municipal Affairs 1998–2004; one of two reps of Faroe Islands in Danish Folketing (Parl.) 2005–; mem. Nordic Council 1991, 1994–98; mem. Man. Cttee Klaksvik Hosp. 1991–96; mem. Fólkaflokkurin (People's Party).
Address: FO-750, Vidareidi; c/o Fólkaflokkurin (People's Party), Jónas Broncksgøta 29, 100 Tórshavn, Faroe Islands. *Telephone:* 451032. *Fax:* 451032. *E-mail:* anfinn.kallsberg@ft.dk; folkaflokkurin@logting.fo. *Website:* www.kallsberg.fo; folkaflokkurin.fo.

KALNIETE, Sandra, MA; Latvian politician and diplomatist; b. 22 Dec. 1952, Togur, Tomsk Region, Russia; m. (divorced). *Education:* Latvian Acad. of Art, Univ. of Leeds, UK and Univ. of Geneva, Switzerland. *Career:* Sec.-Gen. Latvian Artists' Union 1987–88; f. Latvian Popular Front 1988, Sec.-Gen., Deputy Chair. Co-ordinating Council 1988–90; Chief of Protocol Dept, Deputy Foreign Minister, Ministry of Foreign Affairs 1990–93, Minister of Foreign Affairs 2002–04; Amb. to UN, Geneva, Switzerland 1993–97, to France 1997–2000, to UNESCO 2000–02; EU Commr without Portfolio May–Nov. 2004; mem. Saeima (Parl.) (New Era—Jaunais laiks) 2006–; Patron, Prix Europa 2005; Commdr, Order of the Three Stars 1995, Commdr, Légion d'honneur 2001, Commdr des Palmes académiques 2002, Cross of Commdr of the Order of the Grand Duke Gediminas 2005; Latvian Cabinet Ministers' Award. *Publications:* Latviesu tekstilmaksla (Latvian Textile Art) 1989, Es lauzu, tu lauzi, mes lauzam. Vini luza (I Broke, You Broke, We Broke. They Fell Apart) 2000,

Ar balles kurpem Sibirijas sniegos (With Dancing Shoes in Siberian Snows) 2001.
Address: Saeima (Parliament), Jekaba iela 11, Rīga 1811, Latvia (office). *Telephone:* 6708-7111 (office). *Fax:* 6708-7100 (office). *E-mail:* Sandra .Kalniete@saeima.lv (office). *Website:* www.saeima.lv (office).

KALOSIL, Moana Carcasses; Ni-Vanuatu politician. *Career:* mem. Parl. (Green Party), currently Deputy Leader of Opposition; Minister of Foreign Affairs 2003–04, for Finance and Econ. Devt 2004–05; Leader, Green Party 2001–.
Address: Parliament House, Port Vila, Vanuatu (office).

KALOUSEK, Miroslav; Czech politician; *Minister of Finance;* b. 17 Dec. 1960, Tábor; m.; two c. *Education:* Inst. of Chemical Tech., Prague. *Career:* Head of Investment, Mitas Praha (tyre mfrs) 1985–90; Econ. Adviser to Vice-Chair. of Czech Govt 1990–92, Dir Dept of Advisors 1992–93, Govt Rep. on Advisory Cttee, South-Bohemian Brewery 1991–92; mem. Parl. (Christian Democratic Party, KDU-ČSL) 1993–, Deputy Minister of Defence 1993–98, Chair. Parl. Budget Cttee 2002–05, Vice-Chair. 2006–, Minister of Finance 2007–; Chair. Christian Democratic Party (KDU-ČSL) 2003–06; mem. Bd of Dirs West-Bohemian Brewery 1992–94, Land Fund of the Czech Republic 1994–96.
Address: Ministry of Finance, Letenská 15, 118 00 Prague 1, Czech Republic (office). *Telephone:* 257042719 (office). *Fax:* 257049272 (office). *E-mail:* informace@mfcr.cz (office). *Website:* www.mfcr.cz (office).

KALPOKAS, Donald; Ni-Vanuatu politician and diplomatist; *Permanent Representative, United Nations; Education:* Univ. of South Pacific. *Career:* fmr Minister of Educ. and Judicial Services; Pres. Vanuaaku Pati (VP), now Hon. Pres.; Prime Minister of Vanuatu Sept.–Dec. 1991, 1998–99, also Minister of Comprehensive Reform Programme 1998–99, the Public Service, of Foreign Affairs and acting Minister of Agric., Forestry and Fisheries, Deputy Prime Minister and Minister of Educ. 1996–97, –2004; unsuccessful cand. for Pres. 2004; Perm. Rep. to UN, New York 2007–.
Address: Permanent Mission of Vanuatu to the United Nations, 866 United Nations Plaza, 3rd Floor, New York, NY 10017, USA (office). *Telephone:* (212) 425-9600 (office). *Fax:* (212) 425-9653 (office). *E-mail:* vanuatu@un .int (office).

KALUGIN, Aleksander; Russian diplomatist; *Ambassador to Jordan;* b. 20 Sept. 1945, Moscow; m.; one s. one d. *Career:* joined Foreign Ministry 1968, held various overseas posts including service at Embassy in Egypt 1970–74, Embassy in Iraq 1980–85, 1989–94; Chief of Section, Deputy Dir of Middle East and N Africa Dept, Ministry of Foreign Affairs 1994–98; Amb. to Yemen 1998–2002; Amb.-at-Large for Iraq and Gulf region issues 2002–03; Special Middle East Envoy of Foreign Minister for peace process issues 2003-06; Amb. to Jordan 2006–.
Address: Embassy of Russia, POB 2187, 22 Zahran St, Amman 11181, Jordan (home). *Telephone:* (6) 4641158 (home). *Fax:* (6) 4647448 (office). *E-mail:* rusembjo@mail.ru (office). *Website:* www.jordan.mid.ru (office).

KALYUZHNY, Victor Ivanovich; Russian diplomat and politician; *Ambassador to Latvia;* b. 18 April 1947, Birsk, Bashkiria. *Education:* Ufa Inst. of Oil. *Career:* Mgr, then Deputy Head Tomskneft Co. 1970–78, First Deputy Dir.-Gen. 1993–97; Chief Engineer Dept of Oil and Gas Vasyuganneft Co., Strezhevoy; Sec. CP Cttee Strezhevoyneft Co. 1980–84, later Deputy Dir; Second Sec. Strezhevoy Town CP Exec. Cttee 1984–86; Deputy Dir USSR Ministry of Oil Industry 1986; Chief Engineer, then Dir Priobneft Co., Nizhevartovsk Tumen 1986–90; Dir Vietsovpetro, Vu Tan, Viet Nam 1990–93; First Vice-Pres. Vostochnaya Neftyanaya Komapniya, Tomsk 1997–98; First Deputy Minister of Fuel and Power Industry 1998–99, Minister 1999–2000; Special Rep. of Pres. for Caspian Sea with rank of Deputy Minister of Foreign Affairs 2000–; Amb. to Latvia 2004–.
Address: Embassy of the Russian Federation, Antonijas iela 2, Rīga, 1010, Latvia (office). *Telephone:* 733-2151 (office). *Fax:* 783-0209 (office). *E-mail:* rusembas@delfi.lv (office). *Website:* www.latvia.mid.ru (office).

KAMAL, Yousuf bin Hussein, BBA; Qatari government official; *Minister of Finance, and of Economy and Trade;* b. 1948. *Education:* Cairo Univ. *Career:* previous positions in Ministry of Finance include Asst Deputy Dir, Deputy Dir, Gen. Dir, Deputy Minister, Minister of Finance 1998–, also Acting Minister of Economy and Trade 2006–; fmr Deputy Head, Bd of Dirs Qatar Petroleum; fmr mem. Bd of Dirs Qatar Cen. Bank, Q-Tel; fmr Head, Bd of Dirs Ras Laffan LNG.
Address: Ministry of Finance, POB 3322 Doha, Qatar (office). *Telephone:* 4461444 (office). *Fax:* 4431177 (office). *E-mail:* webmaster@mec.gov.qa (office). *Website:* www.mec.gov.qa (office).

KAMANZI, Stanislas; Rwandan diplomatist. *Career:* Perm. Rep. to UN, New York 2003–06; Minister of Infrastructure 2006–08, of Natural Resources 2008–.
Address: Ministry of Lands, Environment, Forestry, Water and Natural Resources, Kigali, Rwanda (office). *Telephone:* 582628 (office). *Fax:* 582629 (office). *Website:* www.minitere.gov.rw (office).

KAMARA, Ibrahim M'Baba, BSc; Sierra Leonean diplomatist; b. 1948; m.; four c. *Education:* Univ. of East London, UK. *Career:* Parl. Special Asst –1978; MP for Kambia 1985–92; Minister of Lands 1978–79, of Lands, Housing and Country Planning 1979–85, of Social Welfare and Rural Devt 1985; Gen. Man. OSTENACO Mining and Trading Co. 1992–95; Nat. Chair. People's Democratic Party of Sierra Leone 1994–96; Amb. to Ethiopia and Perm. Rep. to OAU and Econ. Comm. for Africa (ECA) 1996–99, Leader Sierra Leone del. to OAU 1998, OAU Mission to Angola and Zambia 1998, Perm. Rep. to UN, New York 1999–2003, High Commr to Trinidad and Tobago and Amb. to Cuba and Repub. of Korea 1999–2003, Amb. to USA 2003–06.
Address: Ministry of Foreign Affairs, Gloucester Street, Freetown, Sierra Leone (office). *Telephone:* (22) 223260 (office). *Fax:* (22) 225615 (office). *E-mail:* mfaicsl@yahoo.com (office).

KAMARCK, Andrew Martin, BS, MA, PhD; American international bank official, economist and writer; b. 10 Nov. 1914, Newton Falls, New York; m. Margaret Goldenweiser Burgess 1941; one s. two d. *Education:* Harvard Univ. *Career:* Int. Section, Fed. Reserve Bd 1939–40; US Treasury 1940–42; US Army 1942–44; Allied Control Comm., Italy 1943–44; Allied Control Council, Germany 1945; Office of Int. Finance, US Treasury, Chief of Nat. Advisory Council on Int. Monetary and Financial Problems (NAC) Div., Financial Policy Cttee preparing Marshall Plan 1945–48; US Treasury Rep., Rome 1948–50; Chief of Africa section, Econ. Dept, World Bank 1950–52; Econ. Adviser, Dept of Operations, Europe, Africa and Australasia, World Bank, Chief of Econ. Missions to 14 countries, 1952–64; Dir Econ. Dept, World Bank 1965–71; Dir Econ. Devt Inst. 1972–77, Sr Fellow 1977–78; mem. American Econ. Asscn, Council on Foreign Relations; Dir African Studies Asscn 1961–64; Visiting Fellow, Harvard Inst. Int. Devt 1977–86; Regents Prof., Univ. of Calif. 1964–65; mem. Council, Soc. for Int. Devt 1967–70, 1973–76; Pres. Housing Assistance Corpn of Cape Cod 1980–83; US War Dept Certificate of Merit 1945. *Publications:* The Economics of African Development 1967, Capital Movements and Economic Development (co-author) 1967, The Tropics and Economic Development 1976, La Politica Finanziaria degli Alleati in Italia 1977, Economics and the Real World 1983, Health, Nutrition and Economic Crises (co-author) 1988, The Role of the Economist in Government (co-author) 1989, The Bretton Woods-GATT System (co-author) 1995, Economics for the Twenty-First Century 2001, Economics as a Social Science 2002.
Address: 118 Pine Ridge Road, Brewster, MA 02631, USA (home). *Telephone:* (508) 385-8221 (home). *E-mail:* kamarck@post.harvard.edu (home).

KAMBA, Walter Joseph, BA, LLB, LLM; Zimbabwean administrator and academic; *Professor Emeritus of Law, University of Namibia;* b. 6 Sept. 1931, Marondera; m. Angeline Saziso Dube 1960; three s. (one deceased). *Education:* Univ. of Cape Town, Yale Law School. *Career:* attorney, High Court of Rhodesia (now Zimbabwe) 1963–66; Research Fellow, Inst. of Advanced Legal Studies, London Univ. 1967–68; Lecturer then Sr Lecturer in Comparative Law and Jurisprudence, Univ. of Dundee 1969–80, Dean Faculty of Law 1977–80; Legal Adviser ZANU (PF) 1977–80; Prof of Law, Univ. of Zimbabwe 1980–, Vice-Prin. 1980–81, Vice-Chancellor 1981–91; Vice-Chair. Zimbabwe Broadcasting Corpn 1980–87, Chair. 1987; Inaugural UNESCO Africa Prof., Univ. of Utrecht 1992–96; Founding Dean and UNESCO Prof. of Human Rights, Democracy and Law, Univ. of Namibia 1994–2000, legal adviser, Prof. 1995, now Prof. Emer.; Trustee, Zimbabwe Mass Media Trust 1981–, Conservation Trust of Zimbabwe 1981–87, Zimbabwe Cambridge Trust 1987–; mem. Bd Gov.'s Rauche House Coll. Harare 1980–; mem. Working Party on Future Policy of Asscn of Commonwealth Univs 1981; mem. Council, Exec. Cttee and Budget Review Cttee Asscn of Commonwealth Univs 1981–83; mem. Council UN Univ. for Peace, Costa Rica 1982–86, Univ. of Zambia 1982–86, Commonwealth Standing Cttee on Student Affairs 1982–88, UN Univ., Tokyo 1983–89, Zimbabwe Nat. Comm. for UNESCO 1987–, Bd of Govs Zimbabwe Inst. of Devt Studies 1982–, Chair. 1986–, Exec. Bd Asscn African Univs 1984–; Chair. Electoral Supervisory Comm. 1984, Kingston's (Booksellers and Distributors) 1984–, Asscn of Eastern and Southern African Univs 1984–87; Chair. Council UN Univ., Tokyo 1985–87; Vice-Pres. Int. Asscn of Univs 1985–90, Pres. 1990–; Trustee, African-American Inst. (New York) 1985–; mem. Int. Bd, United World Colls 1985–87, Bd of Govs, Int. Devt Research Centre, Canada 1986–, Nat. Cttee Law and Population Studies Project 1986–, Swaziland Univ. Planning Comm. 1986,

Bd, Commonwealth of Learning 1988, Int. Cttee for Study of Educ. Exchange 1988–; Patron, Commonwealth Legal Education Asscn 1986–; Hon. LLD (Dundee) 1982, (Natal) 1995, (Zimbabwe) 1998; Officer, Ordre des palmes académiques. *Publications:* articles in law journals.
Address: Faculty of Law, University of Zimbabwe, PO Box MP 167, Mount Pleasant, Harare, Zimbabwe (office); International Association of Universities, 1 rue Miollis, 75732 Paris, cedex 15, France (office).

KAMBALA, Philemon; Namibian diplomatist; *High Commissioner to South Africa; Career:* High Commr to Nigeria –2006, High Commr to South Africa 2006– (also accred to Seychelles 2007–).
Address: High Commission of Namibia, 197 Blackwood Street, Arcadia, Pretoria 0083, South Africa (office). *Telephone:* (12) 4819100 (office). *Fax:* (12) 3445998 (office). *E-mail:* secretary@namibia.org.za (office).

KAMILOV, Abdulaziz H., PhD; Uzbekistan diplomatist; *Ambassador to USA;* b. 16 Nov. 1947, Yangiyul; m.; one s. *Education:* Moscow Inst. of Oriental Languages. *Career:* served at Diplomatic Acad., USSR Ministry of Foreign Affairs; joined USSR diplomatic service 1972, Attaché, USSR Embassy in Beirut 1973–76, Second Sec., Damascus 1980–84, mem. Div. of Near East, USSR Ministry of Foreign Affairs 1984–88; Sr Researcher, Inst. of World Econs and Int. Affairs, USSR Acad. of Sciences 1988–91; Counsellor, Uzbekistan Embassy in Moscow 1991–92; Deputy Chair. Security Service of Uzbekistan Repub. 1992–94; First Deputy Minister of Foreign Affairs Jan.–Aug. 1994, Minister of Foreign Affairs 1994–2003, Amb. to USA 2003–.
Address: Embassy of Uzbekistan, 1746 Massachusetts Avenue, NW, Washington, DC 20036-1903, USA (office). *Telephone:* (202) 887-5300 (office). *Fax:* (202) 293-6804 (office). *E-mail:* root@relay.tiv.uz (office). *Website:* www.uzbekistan.org (office).

KAMOUGUÉ, Gen. Wadal Abdelkader; Chadian politician and army officer; *Minister of National Defence;* b. 20 May 1939, Bitam, Gabon; m. 1st Eve-Marie Baba 1967; m. 2nd Martine Rondoh 1983; nine c. *Career:* Minister of Foreign Affairs and Co-operation, mem. of Supreme Mil. Council in Govt of Brig.-Gen. Félix Malloum 1975–78; Commdr of Gendarmerie 1978–79; mem. Provisional State Council following Kano peace agreement March–May 1979, in charge of Agric. and Animal Resources; Leader, Front Uni du Sud (later Forces Armées Tchadiennes, Forces Unifiées) 1979; Vice-Pres. Transitional Gov. of Nat. Unity (GUNT) 1979–82; Pres. State Council 1980–82; fled to Cameroon, then Gabon Sept.–Oct. 1982, after defeat by forces of FAN; Leader, Mouvement révolutionnaire du peuple, Brazzaville, Congo 1983–87; returned to N'Djamena Feb. 1987; Minister of Agric. 1987–89, of Justice 1989–90, of Trade and Industry 1990, of Civil Service and Labour 1993–94, of Nat. Defence 2008–; Pres. Assemblée Nat. (Parl.) 1997; Pres. Union pour le renouveau et la démocratie (URD) 1992–; Général de Brigade 1992–; mem. Conseil Provisoire de la République (CPR) 1991–92; Commdr Ordre nat. avec Palme d'Or Chevalier du Mérite Civique, Commdr Ordre nat. du Tchad, Chevalier Ordre nat. du Mérite (France), Commdr Ordre nat. Centrafricain (Central African Repub.), Commdr Ordre Coréen (Repub. of Korea).
Address: Ministry of National Defence, BP 916, N'Djamena (office); Union pour le renouveau et la démocratie, BP 92, N'Djamena, Chad. *Telephone:* 52-35-13 (Ministry) (office); 51-44-23. *Fax:* 52-65-44 (Ministry) (office); 51-41-87.

KAMPFNER, John; British writer and journalist; *Editor, New Statesman; Career:* fmr foreign corresp. with Reuters and Daily Telegraph; Chief Political Corresp., Financial Times mid-1990s; fmr political commentator, Today programme (BBC Radio 4); Political Ed. New Statesman 2002–05, Ed. 2005–; regular appearances on radio and TV; British Soc. of Magazine Eds. Ed. of the Year Award for Current Affairs Magazines 2006. *Television documentary films:* (all for BBC) Israel Undercover 2002, The Ugly War: Children of Vengeance (Foreign Press Asscn Award for Film of the Year and Journalist of the Year) 2002, War Spin 2003, Robin Cook: The Lost Leader (profile) 2003, Clare Short: The Conscientious Objector (profile) 2003, Who Runs Britain (series) 2004. *Publications:* Inside Yeltsin's Russia: Corruption, Conflict, Capitalism 1995, Robin Cook: The Life and Times of Tony Blair's Most Awkward Minister 1999, Blair's Wars 2003, Dangerous Liaisons: Blair, Britain and the Failure of Europe 2007; contrib. to The Herald, The Observer, The Independent, The Guardian, Daily Express, The Times, Sunday Times, Daily Mail, Financial Times, Los Angeles Times, Daily Telegraph, Evening Standard,.
Address: Knight Ayton Management, 114 St Martin's Lane, London, WC2N 4BE, England (office); New Statesman, Third Floor, 52 Grosvenor Gardens, London, SW1W 0AU, England (office). *Telephone:* (20) 7836-5333 (office). (20) 7881-5676 (office). *Fax:* (20) 7836-8333 (office); (20) 7259-0181 (office). *E-mail:* info@knightayton.co.uk (office); info@newstatesman.co.uk (office); john@jkampfner.net (home). *Website:* www

.knightayton.co.uk (office); www.newstatesman.com (office); www .jkampfner.net (home).

KAMYNIN, Mikhail Leonidovich; Russian diplomatist; *Director of the Information and Press Department, Ministry of Foreign Affairs;* b. 13 Aug. 1956, Moscow; m.; one d. one s. *Education:* Moscow Inst. of Int. Relations, Diplomatic Acad. of Ministry of Foreign Affairs. *Career:* various positions, Embassy in Mexico 1978–82, 1987–91; Press Sec., Ministry of Foreign Affairs 1991–92; Counsellor, Embassy in Spain 1992–97; Asst Dir of Press and Information, Ministry of Foreign Affairs 1997–99; Minister Counsellor, Embassy in Cuba 1999–2002; Asst Dir European Affairs, Ministry of Foreign Affairs 2002; Amb. to Spain 2002–05; Dir of Information and Press Dept, Ministry of Foreign Affairs 2005–; del. to numerous int. meetings; mem. Russian Union of Journalists. *Address:* Ministry of Foreign Affairs, 119200 Moscow, Smolenskaya-Sennaya pl. 32/34, Russia (office). *Telephone:* (495) 244-41-19 (office). *Fax:* (495) 230-41-12 (office). *E-mail:* dip@mid.ru (office); pressdept@mid.ru (office). *Website:* www.mid.ru (office).

KAN-DAPAAH, Albert; Ghanaian politician and chartered accountant; *Minister of Defence;* b. 14 March 1953, Maase-Boaman, Ashanti Region. *Education:* Acherensua Secondary School, Inst. of Professional Studies, North East London Polytechnic and Emile Woolf Coll. of Accountancy, UK. *Career:* Audit Sr with Pannel Kerr Forster, transferred to Monrovia, Liberia and London, UK offices 1978–86; Head of Audit, Social Security and Nat. Insurance Trust Jan.–Sept. 1987; Dir of Audit, Electricity Co. of Ghana 1987, later Dir of Finance for six years; Pnr, Kwesie, Kan-Dapaah & Baah Co., Accra; Man. Consultant Kan-Dapaah and Assocs; fmr part-time Lecturer in Auditing, School of Admin, Univ. of Ghana, Inst. of Professional Studies; Pres. Inst. of Chartered Accountants (Ghana) 1996; Vice-Pres. Asscn of Accountancy Bodies in West Africa 1996; mem. Bd of Dirs SSB Consumer Credit Ltd 1987–95; Alt. Bd mem. Kabel Metal Ghana Ltd 1987–95, New Times Corpn 1987–95; Ashanti Regional Rep. on Nat. Council of the New Patriotic Party, mem. Finance and Econ. Affairs Cttee 1992–96; mem. Parl. for Afigya Sekyere West 1997–; Minister for Energy 2000–03, for Communications and Tech. 2003–07, for Interior 2006–07, of Defence 2007–; mem. Ghana Inst. of Chartered Accountants; Fellow, Chartered Asscn of Certified Accountants (UK). *Address:* Ministry of Defence, Burma Camp, Accra, Ghana (office). *Telephone:* (21) 777611 (office). *Fax:* (21) 778549 (office). *E-mail:* kaddok@ internetghana.com (office). *Website:* www.ghana.gov.gh/ ministry_of_defence (office).

KANBUR, Ravi, MA, DPhil; British economist and academic; *T. H. Lee Professor of World Affairs, International Professor of Applied Economics and Management and Professor of Economics, Cornell University;* b. 28 Aug. 1954, Dharwar, India; m. Margaret S. Grieco 1979. *Education:* King Edward VII Camp Hill School, Birmingham, Gonville & Caius Coll. Cambridge and Merton and Worcester Colls. Oxford. *Career:* Prize Fellow, Nuffield Coll. Oxford 1978–79; Fellow in Econs, Clare Coll. Cambridge 1979–83; Prof. of Econs, Univ. of Essex 1983–85; Visiting Prof., Princeton Univ. 1985–87; Prof. of Econs and Dir Devt Econs Research Centre, Univ. of Warwick 1987–89, Hon. Prof. 1994; Sr Adviser and Ed. World Bank Economic Review and World Bank Research Observer, IBRD, Washington, DC 1989–92; World Bank Resident Rep. in Ghana 1992–94, World Bank Chief Economist for Africa 1994–96, Prin. Adviser to Sr Vice-Pres. and Chief Economist 1996–97; T. H. Lee Prof. of World Affairs, Int. Prof. of Applied Econs and Man. and Prof. of Econs, Cornell Univ., Ithaca, NY 1997–; American Agricultural Econs Asscn Research Award (jtly with L. Haddad) 1991. *Publications:* articles in learned journals. *Address:* 309 Warren Hall, Cornell University, Ithaca, NY 14853-7801, USA (office). *Telephone:* (607) 255-7966 (office). *Fax:* (607) 255-9984 (office). *E-mail:* sk145@cornell.edu (office). *Website:* people.cornell.edu/ pages/sk145 (office).

KANDBORG, Lt-Gen. Ole Larson; Danish army officer (retd) and consultant; *Military Adviser, DCS Group;* b. 16 May 1941, nr Skanderborg; m. Lis Kandborg; two c. *Education:* Viborg, Army Officers' Acad., Copenhagen, Canadian Forces' Staff Coll., Toronto, Canada, NATO Defence Coll., Rome, Italy. *Career:* nat. service with Prince's Life Regt, Viborg, Sergeant, Lt; First Lt, Capt. of mechanized infantry Bn 1966–72; Instructor, Danish Combat Arms School 1974–77; Staff Officer, HQ of the UN Peace-keeping Force in Cyprus 1977–78; Co. Commdr, Skive, G3 of Mechanized Brigade 1978–82; at Faculty of Danish Defence Coll. 1982–84; Instructor, annual Nordic UN Staff Officers' Course (Sweden), Chief Instructor; Lt-Col, Commdr of 1st Tank Bn, Jutland Dragoon Regt, Holstebro 1984–85; Public Information Adviser and Deputy to Chief of Defence, Defence HQ, Copenhagen 1986–89, Deputy Chief of Staff for Plans and Policy 1992; Col, Commdr 2nd New Zealand Brigade, Vordingborg 1989–90; Maj.-Gen., Commdr Jutland Div., Fredericia

1990–92; Commdr of Danish Operational Command based in Århus and Kamp 1993–96; Danish Mil. Rep. to NATO Mil. Cttee April–Sept. 1996, Dir Int. Mil. Staff, NATO 1996–2001 (retd); currently Mil. Adviser on strategic and NATO matters, DCS Group; Commdr, Order of Dannebrog, Mil. Good Service Medal, Reserve Officers' Asscn's Good Service Medal, Commdr 1st Degree, Order of the Swedish North Star, Legion of Merit (Degree of Commdr); UN Medal 7. *Address:* c/o DCS Group, Virkelyst 10, 9400 Noerresundby, Denmark (office). *Telephone:* 70-23-13-70. *Fax:* 98-19-07-00. *Website:* www.dcsgroup .dk.

KANG, Man-soo; South Korean civil servant and politician; *Minister of Strategy and Finance;* b. 1945, Hapcheon, S Gyeongsang Prov. *Career:* began career at Ministry of Finance 1970, Vice-Minister of Finance 1997–98 (resgnd over Asian financial crisis); econ. affairs adviser to Pres. Lee for several years, Head of Econ. Affairs Sub-cttee on Lee's Transition Cttee –2008; Pres. Seoul Devt Inst. during Lee's tenure as Mayor of Seoul; co-ordinated Lee's economy-related pledges during presidential campaign; Minister of Strategy and Finance 2008–. *Address:* Ministry of Strategy and Finance, Government Complex II, 88 Gwanmunro, Gwacheon City, Gyeonggi Province, 427-725, South Korea (office). *Telephone:* (2) 2150-2975 (office). *Fax:* (2) 504-1335 (office). *E-mail:* fppr@mofe.go.kr (office). *Website:* www.mofe.go.kr (office).

KANG, Sok-ju; North Korean politician; *Vice-Minister of Foreign Affairs;* b. 4 Aug. 1939, Pyongwan, S Pyongan Prov. *Career:* First Vice-Minister, Admin. Council, Ministry of Foreign Affairs 1986–87, First Vice-Minister of Foreign Affairs 1987–, del. to UN following N Korean accession to UN 1991, Head of Del. to negotiations with USA 1993, attended meeting of Kim Il Sung and US Pres. Jimmy Carter 1994, signed nuclear agreement with USA, Geneva 1994, accompanied Kim Jong Il to Russia 2001, to summit with Japanese Prime Minister Junichiro Koizumi 2002; mem. Cen. Cttee Korean Workers' Party 1991–. *Address:* Ministry of Foreign Affairs, Pyongyang, Democratic People's Republic of Korea (office).

KANYA, Mary Madzandza; Swazi diplomatist; *High Commissioner to UK;* m. Leo Kanya. *Education:* Zombodze Nat. School. *Career:* fmr teacher, Swaziland Teacher Training Coll., Univ. of Swaziland; tutored children of King Sobhuza II; f. royal school; fmr Sr Insp. of Schools; became Swaziland's first female Amb. 1990, High Commr to Canada 1990–94, Amb. to USA 1994–2005, High Commr to UK 2005–. *Address:* Swaziland High Commission, 20 Buckingham Gate, London, SW1E 6LB, England (office). *Telephone:* (20) 7630-6611 (office). *Fax:* (20) 7630-6564 (office). *E-mail:* enquiries@swaziland.org.uk (office); swaziland@swaziland.btinternet.com (office).

KAPAMBWE, Lazarous, BSc; Zambian diplomatist; *Permanent Representative, United Nations;* b. 31 Dec. 1959. *Education:* Univ. of Zambia, Nairobi Univ., Kenya, New York Univ. *Career:* Exec. Officer, Directorate of Int. Orgs and Research Dept, Ministry for Foreign Affairs 1981–85, Prin. in Research Dept 1985–87; Prin. in Cabinet Office and speech writer for Prime Minister of Zambia 1987; Counsellor for Political Affairs, Perm. Mission to UN, New York 1987–88; Counsellor and Deputy Chief of Mission, Embassy in Washington, DC 1988–93, Embassy in Bonn 1993–96; Dir for European Affairs, Ministry for Foreign Affairs, 1996, Dir for Africa and OAU Affairs 1996–2000, Deputy Perm. Sec. responsible for Asia, Africa and the Middle East 2000–02, Perm. Sec. 2002–03; Amb. to Ethiopia and African Union 2003–07; Perm. Rep. to UN, New York 2007–. *Address:* Permanent Mission of Zambia to the United Nations, 237 East 52nd Street, New York, NY 10022, USA (office). *Telephone:* (212) 888-5770 (office). *Fax:* (212) 888-5213 (office). *E-mail:* zambia@un.int (office). *Website:* www.un.int/zambia (office).

KAPOMA, Tens C.; Zambian diplomatist; b. 26 June 1946; m.; three c. *Education:* UNITAR, Georgetown Univ., Washington DC, USA. *Career:* joined civil service as Immigration Officer, Ministry of Home Affairs 1967; Second Sec., Mission to UN, New York 1973–79; First Sec. Embassy in Washington, DC 1979–85; Dir of Africa, Ministry of Foreign Affairs 1985–86, 1990–93; Deputy Dir of Cabinet, Office of OAU Sec.-Gen., Addis Ababa 1986–90; Deputy Perm. Sec. in charge of Asia, Africa, Middle E Directorates, Ministry of Foreign Affairs 1993–2000, Foreign Affairs Perm. Sec. 2007–; Deputy Head of Mission, Addis Ababa 2000–03; Amb. to Democratic Repub. of Congo 2003–05; Perm. Rep. to UN, New York 2005–07; mem. Fourth and Third Cttees, UN Gen. Ass. 1973–84; Special Asst (Liaison) to Pres. of 39th UN Gen. Ass. 1984; mem. team that negotiated Lusaka Protocol 1993–94. *Address:* Ministry of Foreign Affairs, POB RW50069, Lusaka, Zambia (office). *Telephone:* (1) 213822 (office). *Fax:* (1) 222440 (office).

KAPOOR, Gen. Deepak, MA, MBA; Indian army officer; *Chief of Army Staff;* b. 1948; m. Kirti Kapoor; one s. one d. *Education:* Sainik School, Kunjpara, Defence Services Staff Coll., Wellington, Nat. Defence Coll., New Delhi, Indira Gandhi Nat. Open Univ., New Delhi. *Career:* commissioned into Regt of Artillery 1967, veteran of Indo-Pak War in eastern theatre (Bangladesh) 1971, Chief Operations Officer for UNOSOM II (UN Operation in Somalia – Phase 2) 1994–95, commanded 161 Infantry Brigade in Uri, Jammu and Kashmir, 22nd Mountain Div. (as part of a Strike Corps during Operation Parakram) 2001–02, Chief of Staff of 4 Corps in Tezpur (involved in counter-insurgency operations in Assam), promoted to Lt-Gen., commanded 33 Corps at Siliguri, West Bengal, commanded Army Training Command (ARTRAC) in Shimla, Commdr Northern Army, apptd Hon. ADC to Pres. of India, Sr Col Commdt Regt of Artillery, Vice-Chief of Army –2007, Chief of Army Staff 2007–, Hon. Col of Brigade of the Guards 2008–; Vishisht Seva Medal 1996, Sena Medal 1998, Ati Vishisht Seva Medal 2006, Param Vishisht Seva Medal 2007. *Address:* Additional Directorate General of Public Information B 30, South Block, Integrated HQ of MoD (Army), DHQ PO, New Delhi 110 011, India (office). *Telephone:* (11) 23018531 (office). *Fax:* (11) 23015403 (office). *E-mail:* a_l_c@vsnl.com (office). *Website:* indianarmy.nic.in (office).

KAPPES, Stephen R., BS, MS; American government official; *Deputy Director of Operations, Central Intelligence Agency;* b. 22 Aug. 1951, Cincinnati; m. Kathleen Kappes (née Morgan); two c. *Education:* Athens High School, Ohio Univ., Ohio State Univ. *Career:* served as Officer in US Marine Corps 1976–81; worked at CIA 1981–2004, 2006–, various positions including Chief of Counterintelligence Center, Assoc. Deputy Dir for Operations for Counterintelligence, Asst Deputy Dir of Operations 2002–04, Deputy Dir of Operations 2004, 2006–; Exec. Vice-Pres. for Global Strategy, ArmorGroup Int. 2005–06, COO 2006. *Address:* Central Intelligence Agency, Office of Public Affairs, Washington, DC 20505, USA (office). *Telephone:* (703) 482-0623 (office). *Fax:* (703) 482-1739 (office). *Website:* www.cia.gov (office).

KARABAYEV, Ednan Oskonovich., PhD; Kyrgyzstani academic and government official; *Minister of Foreign Affairs;* b. 17 Jan. 1953, Talas. *Education:* Kyrgyz State Univ., Inst. of History of Kyrgyz SSR Acad. of Sciences. *Career:* early career as history teacher, Frunze (now Bishkek); Minister of Foreign Affairs 1992–93, 2007–; Head Int. Relations Dept, Kyrgyz-Russian Slavic Univ. 1994–2007, also fmr Dean; Advisor to Pres. 2000; Pres., UNA of Kyrgyzstan; mem. Cyril-Mefody Acad. of Slavic Enlightenment; Honored Worker of Educ. in Kyrgyz Republic. *Publications include:* more than 200 scientific and other articles and contribs to monographs. *Address:* Ministry of Foreign Affairs, 720040 Bishkek, bul. Erkindik 57, Kyrgyzstan (office). *Telephone:* (312) 62-05-45 (office). *Fax:* (312) 66-05-01 (office). *E-mail:* gendep@mfa.gov.kg (office). *Website:* www.mfa.kg (office).

KARAGANOV, Sergei Aleksandrovich, DHist; Russian defence and foreign affairs specialist; *Chairman of the Presidium, Council of Foreign and Defence Policy, Russian Academy of Sciences;* b. 12 Sept. 1952, Moscow; m.; one d. *Education:* Moscow State Univ., postgraduate study in USA. *Career:* Jr Fellow, Sr Fellow, Head of Section, USA and Canada Studies Inst. 1978–88; Research Fellow, Perm. Mission of USSR at UN 1976–77; Head of Dept, Deputy Dir Inst. of Europe of Russian Acad. of Sciences 1988–; mem. Foreign Policy Council, Ministry of Foreign Affairs of Russia 1991; Founder and Chair. of the Presidium, Council of Foreign and Defence Policy, Russian Acad. of Sciences 1991–; mem. Presidential Council of Russia 1992–99; Adviser to Presidential Admin.; mem. Consulting Council to Security Council of Russia 1993–; mem. Consultative Council of Fed. 1996–; Chair. Dept on World Politics, State Univ. Higher School of Econs 2002–, Dean, School of Int. Econs and Foreign Affairs 2006–; Chair. Editorial Bd Russia in Global Affairs magazine 2002–; mem. Pres.'s Public Council for Assisting the Devt of Civil Society and Human Rights 2004–, Ministry of Defence Public Council 2006–; mem. IISS, London. *Publications:* 18 books and brochures, including Russia: State of Reforms 1993, Security of the Future Europe (ed.; in Russian) 1993, Harmonization the Evolution of U.S. and Russian Defense Policies (co-ed. with F. Ikle; also published in Russian) 1993, Where Russia Goes? Foreign and Defense Policy in the New Era 1994, Damage Limitation or Crisis? Russia and the World (co-ed. with Robert D. Blackwill) 1994, Wither Western Aid to Russia" (ed. and dir of the study; also published in Russian) 1994, Russia's Economic Role in Europe. Report of the Commission for the Greater Europe, Vol. II (co-authored with O. Lambsdorf; also published in Russian) 1995, Geopolitics Change in Europe, Policies of the West and Russia's Alternatives (ed. and head of the study) 1995, Towards a New Democratic Commonwealth (co-authored with Graham Allison and Karl Kaiser) 1996, Russian-American Relations on the Threshold of Two Centuries (co-author) 2000, Strategy for Russia: Agenda for the President-

2000 (ed.; in Russian) 2000, Strategy for Russia: Ten Years of CFDP (ed.) 2002; more than 350 articles in Russian on econs of foreign policy, arms control, nat. security strategy, Russian foreign and defence policies. *Address:* Mokhovaya Street 11-3B, 125993 Moscow (office); Chernyahovskogo, 9/5 Apt 387, 125139 Moscow, Russia (home). *Telephone:* (495) 692-84-72 (office); (495) 152-99-82 (home). *Fax:* (495) 609-92-98 (office). *E-mail:* cfdp@online.ru (office); cfdp@mail.ru (home). *Website:* www.svop.ru.

KARAMANLIS, Konstantinos (Kostas), PhD; Greek politician and lawyer; *Prime Minister;* b. Sept. 1956; m. Natasha Pazaitis 1998; one d. one s. *Education:* Athens Univ. Law School, Deree Coll., Fletcher School of Law and Diplomacy, Tufts Univ. *Career:* served in Greek Navy 1977–79; Lecturer in Political Science, Diplomatic History and Corp. Law, Deree Coll.; mem. Parl. 1989, 1990, 1993, 1996, 2000; Pres. Nea Demokratia (New Democratic Party) 1997; Vice-Pres. European People's Party 1999–; Prime Minister of Greece 2004–; Vice-Pres. Int. Democratic Union 2002–; Chair. European Democrat Union Party Leaders Conf. 2003. *Publications:* Eleftherios Venizelos and Greek Foreign Relations 1928–32 1986, Spirit and Era of Gorbachev 1987. *Address:* Office of the Prime Minister, Maximos Mansion, Herodou Atticou 19, 106 74 Athens, Greece (office). *Telephone:* (210) 3385491 (office). *Fax:* (210) 3238129 (office). *E-mail:* primeminister@primeminister.gr (office). *Website:* www.primeminister.gr (office).

KARAMAT, Gen. Jehangir, MA; Pakistani army officer (retd) and diplomatist. *Education:* Nat. Defence Coll., Command and Staff Coll., Quetta, US Army Command and Gen. Staff Coll., Fort Leavenworth, Kan. *Career:* joined Pakistan Army in 13th Lancers Cavalry Div. of the Armoured Corps in 24th PMA Long Course 1961, served in Indo-Pakistan Wars of 1965 and 1971, Chair. Jt Chiefs of Staff and Chief of Army Staff 1997–98 (retd), sr-level assignments have included Dir-Gen. Mil. Operations, Chief of Gen. Staff 1996–98, has also commanded troops in Saudi Arabia as Commdr Ind. Armored Brigade Group 1985–88, remains Col Commdt and Col-in-Chief (ceremonial posts) of Pakistan Armoured Corps; Amb. to USA 2004–06; Founder, Dir Spearhead Research (socio-political policy and analysis inst., to which he is a regular contrib.); Visiting Fellow, Int. Confed. of Socs of Authors and Composers (CISAC), Stanford Univ. and Brookings Inst., Washington, DC; fmr mem. UN Study on Afghanistan; fmr Chair. Bd of Govs Islamabad Policy Research Inst.; President of the Pakistan Polo Associatio. *Address:* c/o Ministry of Foreign Affairs, Constitution Avenue, Islamabad, Pakistan. *Telephone:* (51) 9210335.

KARAOSMANOGLU, Attila, PhD; Turkish economist; b. 20 Sept. 1932, Manisa; m. Sukriye Ozyet 1960; one s. *Education:* Univs of Ankara and Istanbul, Harvard and New York Univs, USA. *Career:* mem. Faculty, Middle East Tech. Univ. and Ankara Univ. 1954–63; Head, Econ. Planning Dept, State Planning Org. of Turkey 1960–62; Adviser, Fed. of Turkish Trade Unions and consultant to Turkish Scientific and Tech. Research Council 1963–65; Consultant, Directorate for Scientific Affairs, OECD 1965–66; Economist, then Sr Economist, World Bank 1966–71, Chief Economist 1973–75, Dir of Devt Policy 1975–79, Dir of Europe, Middle East and N Africa Region Country Programmes 1979–82, Vice-Pres. E Asia and Pacific Region 1983–87, Asia Region 1987–91 Man. Dir World Bank 1991–95 (retd); Deputy Prime Minister in Charge of Econ. Affairs and Chair. High Planning Council, Turkish Govt 1971; mem. Exec. Bd Is Bank, Turkey 1972; Chief Adviser, Istanbul Chamber of Industry 1995–; mem. Bd Scientific and Technological Research Council of Turkey 1995–; Alt., Bank of Turkey 1996–; Chair. Bd Nat. Inst. of Metrology 1997–. *Publications:* Towards Full Employment and Price Stability (OECD publ., co-author) 1977, Poverty and Prosperity – The Two Realities of Asian Development 1989, Diversity and Consensus – The Emergence of an Asian Development Paradigm 1991. *Address:* c/o Istanbul Chamber of Industry, Meşrutiyet Cad. No:62, Istanbul; Dr. Faruk Ayanoglu Cad. 37 D.5, 81030 Fenerbahce, Istanbul, Turkey.

KARASIN, Grigory Borisovich; Russian diplomatist; *Deputy Minister of Foreign Affairs;* b. 23 Aug. 1949, Moscow; m.; two d. *Education:* Moscow Inst. of Oriental Languages, Moscow State Univ. *Career:* diplomatic service since 1972; translator, attaché USSR Embassy, Senegal 1972–76; attaché First African Div., USSR Ministry of Foreign Affairs 1976–77; sec. to Deputy Minister of Foreign Affairs 1977–79; Second, First Sec. Embassy, Australia 1979–85; First Sec., Counsellor Second European Div. Ministry of Foreign Affairs 1985–88; Counsellor USSR Embassy, UK 1988–92; Head of Dept of Africa, Ministry of Foreign Affairs of Russia 1992–93, Head. Dept of Information and Press 1993–96; Deputy Minister of Foreign Affairs 1996–2000; Amb. to UK 2000–05; Deputy Minister of Foreign Affairs 2005–.

Address: Ministry of Foreign Affairs, 119200 Moscow, Smolenskaya-Sennaya pl. 32/34, Russia (office). *Telephone:* (495) 244-16-06 (office). *Fax:* (495) 230-21-30 (office). *E-mail:* ministry@mid.ru (office). *Website:* www.mid.ru (office).

KARIM, Iftikharul; Bangladeshi diplomatist. *Career:* career diplomat; overseas assignments in Stockholm, Ankara and with Perm. Mission to UN, Geneva; fmr Political Minister and Deputy Chief of Mission, Embassy in Washington, DC; Amb. to Repub. of Korea –2002, to People's Repub. of China 2002–04; Order of Diplomatic Service Merit Gwanghwa Medal (Repub. of Korea) 2002.
Address: c/o Ministry of Foreign Affairs, Segunbagicha, Dhaka 1000, Bangladesh (office). *Telephone:* (2) 9556020 (office). *Fax:* (2) 9555283 (office). *E-mail:* info@mofabd.org (office). *Website:* www.mofabd.org.

KARIMOV, Dzhamshed Khilolovich, DEcon; Tajikistan politician; b. 4 Aug. 1940, Dushanbe; m.; two c. *Education:* Moscow Technological Inst. of Light Industry. *Career:* researcher Cen. Research Inst. of Econs and Math., USSR Acad. of Sciences; Asst Chair of Econ. of Industry Tajik State Univ., Jr researcher, Head of Div. of Optimal Planning Inst. of Econ., Tajik Acad. of Sciences 1962–72, Deputy Dir, Dir Research Inst. of Econ. and Econ.-Mathematical Methods of Planning, State Planning Cttee, Tajik SSR 1972–81; Corresp. mem. Tajik Acad. of Sciences; Deputy Chair. State Planning Cttee 1981–88; Deputy Chair. Council of Ministers, Chair. State Planning Cttee 1988–89; First Sec. Dushanbe City Cttee of CP Tajikistan 1989–91; USSR People's Deputy 1989–92; Deputy, First Deputy Chair. Council of Ministers Tajik Repub. 1991–92; represented Repub. of Tajikistan in Russia 1992–93; Chief Adviser on Econ. to Pres. Sept.–Nov. 1994; Prime Minister of Tajikistan 1994–96 (forced to resign after bloodless coup); Adviser to Pres. Rakhmonov 1996–97; apptd Amb. to People's Repub. China 1997.
Address: c/o Ministry of Foreign Affairs, Rudaki prosp. 42, 734051 Dushanbe, Tajikistan.

KARIMOV, Islam Abduganiyevich, CandEconSc; Uzbekistan politician and head of state; *President;* b. 30 Jan. 1938, Samarqand; m. Tatyana Karimova; two d. *Education:* Cen. Asian Polytechnic Inst. and Tashkent Econs Inst. *Career:* mem. CPSU 1964–91; Engineer, then Leading Engineer-Constructor in Tashkent aviation construction factory 1960–66; Chief Specialist, Head of Dept, First Deputy Chair. State Planning Cttee 1966–83, Chair. 1986; Minister of Finance, Deputy Chair. of Council of Ministers, Uzbek SSR 1983–86; First Sec., Qashqadaryo Viloyat Party Cttee 1986–89; First Sec., Uzbek SSR CP Cen. Cttee 1989–91; USSR People's Deputy 1989–91; mem. Cen. Cttee CPSU and Politburo 1990–91; Pres. of Uzbek SSR 1990; Chair. People's Democratic Party of Uzbekistan 1991–96; Pres. of Uzbekistan 1991– (elected by Supreme Soviet 24 March 1990; term of office extended by popular referendum 27 March 1995; re-elected 9 Jan. 2000 and 23 Dec. 2007); concurrently Chair. Cabinet of Ministers; mem. Acad. of Sciences of Uzbekistan; Hon. Chair. Fund of Friendship of Cen. Asia and Kazakhstan; Hon. DEcon; Dr hc and from nine foreign univs and acads; Mustakillik (Independence) Award, Amir Temur Award, Borobudur Gold Medal, UNESCO 2006. *Publications:* Uzbekistan: Its Own Model of Renovation and Progress 1992, Uzbekistan—A State with a Great Future 1992, On the Priorities of the Economic Policy of Uzbekistan 1993, Uzbek Model of Deepening Economic Reforms 1995, Uzbekistan's Way of Restoration and Progress, To Complete the Noble Cause, Stability and Reforms 1996, Uzbekistan on the Threshold of the Twenty-First Century 1997, Uzbekistan Striving Towards the 21st Century 1999, The Spiritual Path of Renewal 2000.
Address: Office of the President, 100163 Tashkent, O'zbekiston shox ko'ch. 43, Uzbekistan (office). *Telephone:* (71) 139-53-25 (office). *Fax:* (71) 139-54-04 (office). *E-mail:* presidents_office@press-service.uz (office). *Website:* www.press-service.uz.

KARIMULLAH, Adm. Shahid; Pakistani naval officer (retd); *Ambassador to Saudi Arabia; Education:* Nat. Defence Coll., US War Coll. *Career:* joined navy operations br. 1965, Pakistan Fleet Commdr, apptd Admiral 2002, Chief of Naval Staff 2002–05; currently Amb. to Saudi Arabia; mem. Nat. Security Council; Sitara-i-Jurrat, Sitara-i-Imtiaz (mil.), Hilal-i-Imtiaz (mil.), Medal of Merit of the Turkish Armed Forces 2003.
Address: Embassy of Pakistan, POB 94007, Riyadh 11693, Saudi Arabia (office). *Telephone:* (1) 488-7272 (office). *Fax:* (1) 488-7953 (office).

KARIYAWASAM, Prasad, BS; Sri Lankan diplomatist; b. 21 March 1954, Galle; m.; one s. one d. *Education:* Univ. of Peradeniya. *Career:* joined Foreign Service 1981; positions include assignments in UN and Non-Aligned Div., Political Affairs (West) Div., Admin Div.; Special Asst to Foreign Sec. 1987–89; diplomatic assignments include missions in Geneva, Riyadh, Washington, DC, New Delhi; fmr Deputy High Commr in India, then Amb. 1998–2001; Perm. Rep. to UN, Geneva 2001–03, Consul Gen. to

Switzerland 2001; Perm. Rep. to UN, New York 2005–08, Perm. Rep. to Conf. on Disarmament, Personal Rep. to Head of State to Group of 15; fmr mem. UN Panel of Experts on Small Arms, Group of Governmental Experts on Relationship between Disarmament and Devt; Vice-Chair. Main Cttee, World Conf. on Racism, UN Comm. on Human Rights, Durban, S Africa 2001; Special Coordinator for Improved Functioning, Conf. on Disarmament 2001, 2002; Del. to Ad Hoc Cttee on Int. Terrorism 2001–03; Leader, Sri Lanka Del. to Conf. on Disarmament, Geneva 2001–03; Chair. Global System of Trade Preferences Cttee of Participants, UNCTAD, UNCTAD Expert Group on Market Access Issues in Mode 4 (Movement of Natural Persons to Supply Services) 2002–03; mem. UN Cttee on Protection of Rights of All Migrant Workers and Members of Their Families 2003–, currently Chair.; Chair. Chairpersons of Human Rights, Treaty Bodies and Inter-Cttee Meetings 2004.
Address: c/o Ministry of Foreign Affairs, Republic Bldg, Colombo 1, Sri Lanka (office). *Telephone:* (11) 2325371 (office). *Fax:* (11) 2446091 (office). *E-mail:* publicity@formin.gov.lk (office). *Website:* www.slmfa.gov.lk (office).

KARKI, Tanka, MA; Nepalese academic and diplomatist; *Ambassador to the People's Republic of China;* b. 29 June 1955, Hangedewa-7, Taplejung; m.; two c. *Education:* Tribhuvan Univ. *Career:* joined Communist Party of Nepal 1981, Cen. Cttee mem. 1997–2001, mem. Cen. Dept of Planning and Research 2003–; Asst Lecturer, Tribhuvan Univ. 1987–93, Sec., Nepal Teachers' Asscn 1989–91; Gen.-Sec. Prajatantrik Lok Dal 1992–95; Observer, Gen. Elections in Pakistan 2002; Amb. to People's Repub. of China 2007–. *Publications:* numerous articles in newspapers and journals.
Address: Embassy of Nepal, 1 Xi Liu Jie, San Li Tun Lu, Beijing 100600, People's Republic of China (office). *Telephone:* (10) 65322739 (office). *Fax:* (10) 65323251 (office). *E-mail:* beijing@nepalembassy.org.cn (office). *Website:* www.nepalembassy.org.cn (office).

KARLSSON, Jan O., BA; Swedish politician, international organization official and fmr civil servant; b. 1 June 1939, Stockholm. *Education:* Univ. of Stockholm. *Career:* Admin. Officer, Head of Section, Ministry of Agric. 1962–68; Political Adviser, Cabinet Office 1968–73, Co-ordinating Adviser 1990–91; Sec. to City Commr, Stockholm City Council 1973–77; Deputy Sec. to Presidium, Nordic Council 1977–82; Under-Sec. of State to Minister for Nordic Co-operation 1982–85; Under-Sec. of State, Ministry of Finance 1985–88; Chair. Comm. on Metropolitan Problems 1988–90; Prime Minister's Personal Rep. on Nordic Co-operation in connection with membership of European Environment Agency and EU 1991–92; Negotiator and Adviser, SDP 1992–94; Dir-Gen. Ministry for Foreign Affairs 1994; Minister for Devt Co-operation, Migration and Asylum Policy 2002–03; Acting Minister for Foreign Affairs and Minister (Devt Co-operation, Migration and Asylum Policy), Ministry of Foreign Affairs 2003; mem. European Court of Auditors 1995, Pres. 1999–; mem. editorial staff, TIDEN periodical 1974–82, Ed.-in-Chief 1978–82; mem. Bd Nordic Investment Bank 1983–89, Nat. Pharmacy Corpn 1986–91; Chair. Bd Swedish Nat. Housing Finance Corpn 1986–89; Chair. OECD Project Group on Housing, Social Integration and Liveable Environments in Cities 1991–93; fmr mem. Bd Stockholm Philharmonic.
Address: c/o Ministry for Foreign Affairs, 10339 Stockholm, Sweden (office).

KAROUI, Hamed, PhD; Tunisian physician and politician; *First Vice-Chairman, Rassemblement constitutionnel démocratique;* b. 30 Dec. 1927, Sousse; m.; four c. *Education:* Faculté de Médecine de Paris, France. *Career:* worked as physician at Sousse Regional Hosp. 1957–; active in Destour Movt 1942–, including responsibility for Al Kifah journal; Pres. Féd. Destourienne de France; Municipal Councillor, Sousse 1957–72; elected Mayor 1985; Deputy to the Nat. Ass. 1964, re-elected 1981 and 1989; Vice-Pres. Chamber of Deputies 1983–86; Minister for Youth and Sports 1986–87; Dir Parti Socialiste Destourien (renamed Rassemblement constitutionnel démocratique 1988) 1987, First Vice-Chair. 1999–; Minister for Justice 1988–89; Prime Minister 1989–99; Grand Cordon Ordre de l'Indépendance, Ordre de la République (Tunisia), Ordre du 7 Novembre. *Address:* Rassemblement constitutionnel démocratique, blvd 9 avril 1938, Tunis, Tunisia. *E-mail:* info@rcd.tn (office); maherkar@hexabyte.tn (home). *Website:* www.rcd.tn (office).

KARRAN, Bayney Ram; Guyanese diplomatist and lawyer; *Ambassador to USA;* m. Donna Karran; three c. *Career:* worked in broadcasting as announcer, operator and programme producer; est. pvt. law firm, Guyana 1984–91; Partner, De Caires & Fitzpatrick (law firm) 1992–97; Dir Georgetown Legal Aid Clinic (non-profit clinic) 1993–96; Chair. Guyana Nat. Service Scheme Appeals Tribunal 1994–95; Sec. Guyana Bar Asscn 1994–95; Amb. to Venezuela 1997–2003 (also accred to Chile and Colombia 1998–2003, to Ecuador 1999–2003), Amb. to USA and Perm. Rep. to OAS 2003–, del. to ministerial and multilateral meetings of the Rio Group, OAS,

Assen of Caribbean States, Latin American Econ. System 1997–; mem. advisory group of lawyers to Attorney-Gen. and Minister of Legal Affairs 1993–96; fmr Chair. Guyana Broadcasting Corpn; Order of the Great Liberator First Class (Venezuela).
Address: Embassy of Guyana, 2490 Tracy Place, NW, Washington, DC 20008, USA (office). *Telephone:* (202) 265-6900 (office). *Fax:* (202) 232-1297 (office). *E-mail:* amb.karran@verizon.net (office).

KARRUBI, Mahdi; Iranian cleric and politician; *Secretary-General, Hezb-e Etemad-e Melli (National Confidence Party—NCP);* b. 1937, Aligoudarz, Lorestan. *Career:* mem. Majles (Parl.) and Speaker 1989–92, 2000–04; unsuccessful cand. for Pres. 2005; Founder and Sec.-Gen. Hezb-e Etemad-e Melli (Nat. Confidence Party—NCP) 2005–; mem. Assen of Militant Clerics –2005 (fmr Sec.-Gen.), Expediency Discernment Council of the System –2005 (resgnd); f.. Etemad-e Melli (daily newspaper) 2006.
Address: Hezb-e Etemad-e Melli (National Confidence Party—NCP), Tehran, Iran (office). *Telephone:* (21) 88373306 (office). *E-mail:* Ravabet_Omomi@Etemademelli.ir (office). *Website:* www.etemademelli.ir (office).

KARSENTI, René, MS, MBA, PhD; French international finance official; *Executive President, International Capital Market Association;* b. 27 Jan. 1950, Tlemcen, Algeria; m. Hélène Dayan 1978; two d. *Education:* ESCIL, Lyons; Paris Business School and Sorbonne, Paris. *Career:* researcher in finance and econs, Univ. of Calif. Berkeley 1973; investment analyst/portfolio man. Caisse des Dépôts, Paris 1975–79; Finance Officer, World Bank (IBRD), Washington, DC 1979–83, Financial Adviser 1983–85, Div. Chief 1985–87, Sr Man. Finance Dept, Treasury 1987–89; Treas., Dir Financial Policy Dept, Int. Finance Corp, World Bank Group, Washington, DC 1989–91; Treas. EBRD 1991–95; Dir-Gen. Finance, European Investment Bank 1995–2006; Exec. Pres. and mem. Bd of Dirs Int. Capital Market Assen, Zürich and London 2006–; Chair. Euro Debt Market Assen 2004–; mem. Man. Selection Cttee, French Pensions Reserve Fund (FRR) and Strategic Cttee, Agence France Trésor (French Ministry of Finance); mem. Investment Advisory Cttee, FAO, Rome; Chevalier Légion d'honneur. *Publications:* Research in Pharmaceutical Industry 1977; various financial lectures and articles on int. finance, capital markets and European Monetary Union.
Address: International Capital Market Association, Talacker 29, 8001 Zurich, Switzerland (office). *Telephone:* 443634222 (office). *Fax:* 443637772 (office). *E-mail:* rene.karsenti@icmagroup.org (office). *Website:* www.icmagroup.org (office).

KARTASHKIN, Vladimir Alekseevich, DJur; Russian politician; *Editor-in-Chief, International Lawyer Magazine;* b. 4 March 1934; m. Elena Kovanova 1991; one s. one d. *Education:* Moscow State Univ. *Career:* Chief Scientific Researcher, Inst. of State and Law 1957–63, Chief Researcher, Prof. 1985–; with Div. of Human Rights UN 1969–73; consultant, UN Dir-Gen. on Juridical Problems 1979–85; Chair. Comm. on Human Rights, Russian Presidency 1996–2002; Prof., Int. Inst. of Human Rights, Strasbourg, Cornell Univ., Santa-Clair Univ., Univ. of Peoples' Friendship, Moscow; Ed.-in-Chief International Lawyer Magazine 2003–; Meritorious Lawyer of Russia. *Publications:* over 200 books and articles including Human Rights in International and State Law.
Address: Institute of State and Law, Russian Academy of Sciences, Znemaenka str. 10, 119841, Moscow, Russia (office). *Telephone:* (495) 291-34-90 (office); (495) 242-37-63 (home). *E-mail:* kartashkin@comtv.ru (office).

KARUKUBIRO-KAMUNANWIRE, Perezi, PhD; Ugandan diplomatist and academic; *Ambassador to USA;* b. 25 July 1937, Mbarara; m.; two c. *Education:* Columbia Univ., New York, USA. *Career:* Chair. Uganda People's Congress Youth League 1958–63; Pres. and Chair. Pan-African Students' Org. in the Americas 1965–70; Prof., CUNY, USA 1974–86, fmr Prof., Black Studies Program; Amb. to Austria (also accred to FRG and the Holy See) and Perm. Rep. to Int. Orgs in Vienna 1986–88, Perm. Rep. to UN, New York 1988–95, Chair. UN Gen. Ass. Special Political Cttee 1990–95; Adjunct Prof., Center for Conflict Man. and Organizational Research, Sophia Univ., Bulgaria 2003–06; Amb. to USA 2006–. *Publications:* A Study Guide to Uganda (co-ed.) 1970; numerous articles in the field of int. relations.
Address: Embassy of Uganda, 5911 16th Street, NW, Washington, DC 20011, USA (office). *Telephone:* (202) 726-4758 (office). *Fax:* (202) 726-1727 (office). *E-mail:* pkamunanwire@ugandaembassyus.org (office). *Website:* www.ugandaembassy.com (office).

KARUME, Amani Abeid; Tanzanian accountant and politician; *President and Chairman, Supreme Revolutionary Council of Zanzibar;* b. 1 Nov. 1948, Zanzibar; m. Shadya Amani Karume; six c. *Education:* Lumumba Coll. Zanzibar. *Career:* accountant, Zanzibar Treasury 1969–70, Chief Accoun-

tant 1970–71, Prin. Sec., Ministery of Finance 1971–74, Prin. Sec., Ministry of Planning 1974–78, Prin. Sec., Ministry of Communications and Transport 1978–80, Zanzibar; Pvt Business Consultant Rep., G.E.C. of UK, Zanzibar 1980–90; mem. House of Reps 1990–2000, served as Minister of Trade and Industries and Minister of Communications and Transport; Chair. and Pres. Supreme Revolutionary Council of Zanzibar 2000–, also Minister of Finance and Econ.Planning; mem. Chama Cha Mapunduzi (CCM – Revolutionary Party of Tanzania); mem. Bd of Dirs East African Harbours Corpn –1973.
Address: State House, PO Box 776, Zanzibar, Tanzania (office). *Telephone:* (24) 2230814 (office). *Fax:* (24) 2233722 (office).

KARUME, Hon. (James) Njenga; Kenyan politician and business executive; *Minister of State for Defence in the Officer of the President;* b. 1929, Nakuru district. *Career:* farmer and businessman; fmrly Chair. Gikuyu, Embu and Meru Assen (GEMA); mem. Parl. for Kiambaa 1979–; Asst Minister, Ministry of Lands, Local Govt, Energy and Co-operative Devt and Marketing 1979–91; Special Programmes Minister 2004–05; Minister of State for Defence, Office of the Pres. 2005–; mem. Democratic Party of Kenya –1992, mem. Kanu party 1992–; Elder of the Order of the Golden Heart of Kenya.
Address: c/o Defence Administration, Office of the President, Haranbee House, Harambee Avenue, POB 30510, Nairobi (office); PO Box 30594-00100, Nairobi, Kenya (home). *Telephone:* (20) 227411 (office). *Website:* www.officeofthepresident.go.ke (office).

KARZAI, Hamid, MA; Afghan politician and head of state; *President;* b. 24 Dec. 1954, Karz, Qandahar; m. Zeenat Karzai 1999; one s. *Education:* Habibia High School, Simla Univ., India. *Career:* Dir of Information, Nat. Liberation Front 1985–86, Deputy Dir, Political Office 1986–89; Dir Foreign Relations Dept, Office of Interim Pres. 1989–91; fmr official rep. of deposed Afghan king, Zahir Shah; Deputy Foreign Minister 1992–96; went into exile 1996–2001; Chief of Popolzai tribe, S Afghanistan 1999–; served as consultant to Union Oil Co. of Calif. (UNOCAL), USA; mem. Del. to Future of Afghanistan Govt Talks, Bonn Nov. 2001; Chair. Afghan Interim Authority Dec. 2001–June 2002; Pres. of Transitional Authority (elected by Loya Jirga) June 2002–Nov. 2004, elected Pres. of Afghanistan Nov. 2004–; Hon. KCMG 2003; Hon. DLitt (Himachal Univ.) 2003, Hon. DLit (Nebraska Univ.) 2005, Hon. DJur (Georgetown Univ.) 2006; Int. Rescue Cttee Freedom Award 2002, American Bar Assen Asia Rule of Law Award 2003, Int. Republican Inst. Freedom Award 2003, Philadelphia Liberty Medal 2004, Int. Der Steiger Award 2007.
Address: Office of the President, Gul Khana Palace, Presidential Palace, Kabul, Afghanistan (office). *E-mail:* president@afghanistangov.org (office). *Website:* www.president.gov.af (office).

KASASBEH, Hamad al-, PhD; Jordanian economist and politician; *Minister of Finance;* b. 1956, Karak. *Education:* Columbia Univ., USA. *Career:* Econ. Researcher and Adviser, Cen. Bank of Jordan –1996; Gen. Man. Cities and Villages Devt Bank 1996–99; Sec.-Gen. Accounting Bureau 1999–2003, Sec.-Gen., Ministry of Finance 2003–07, Minister of Finance 2007–; fmr Lecturer, Univ. of Jordan; Chair. Jordanian Free Zones Corpn; Dir Royal Jordanian Airline. *Publications:* 14 publs in the field of finance.
Address: Ministry of Finance, POB 85, Amman 11118, Jordan (office). *Telephone:* (6) 4636321 (office). *Fax:* (6) 4618528 (office). *E-mail:* info@mof.gov.jo (office). *Website:* www.mof.gov.jo (office).

KASEL, Jean-Jacques, DenD; Luxembourg diplomatist; *Maréchal and Chef de Cabinet at the Court of the Grand Duke of Luxembourg;* b. 17 Jan. 1946, Luxembourg; m. Jacqueline Vandervorst; one s., two d. *Education:* Inst. d'Etudes Politiques, Paris. *Career:* joined Foreign Ministry 1973, Embassy in Paris (also Deputy Perm. Rep. to OECD) 1976–79; Pvt. Sec. to Gaston Thorn 1979–81; Dir for Budget and Staff Regulation, Gen. Secr. EC Council 1981–84; Chargé, Special Missions, Perm. Mission of Luxembourg to EC 1984–86; Dir Political and Cultural Affairs, Foreign Ministry 1986–89; Amb. to Greece (resident in Luxembourg) 1989; Perm. Rep. to EU 1991–98, Chair. Perm. Reps Cttee of Council of Ministers of EU 1997–98; Perm. Rep. to NATO 1998–2003; Amb. to Belgium 1998; Maréchal at the Court of Grand Duke of Luxembourg and Chef de Cabinet 2002–; Grand-Croix Ordre Civil et Militaire d'Adolphe de Nassau, Grand Officier Ordre de la Couronne de Chêne, Officier Ordre de Mérite, Grand Croix Ordre de la Couronne (Belgium), Grand Croix Ordre de Léopold II (Belgium), Grand Croix Ordre du Phoenix (Greece), Grand Croix Ordre de Mérite (Italy), Grand Croix Ordre de Danebrog (Denmark), Grand Croix Ordre Infant Henrique (Portugal),Grand Croix Ordre Nat. (Romania), Grand Officier Mérite (Austria), Grand Officier Mérite (Sweden), Grand Officier Mérite (Norway), Grand Officier Faucon (Iceland), Grand Officier Mérite (Germany), Commdr Ordre de Mérite (France), Commdr Ordre de Mérite (Spain).
Address: Palais Grand-Ducal, Luxembourg, Luxembourg (office).

KASER, Michael Charles, MA, DLitt; British economist; b. 2 May 1926, London; m. Elizabeth Anne Mary Piggford 1954; four s. one d. *Education:* King's Coll., Cambridge. *Career:* with Econs Section Ministry of Works, London 1946–47; HM Foreign Service 1947–51, Second Sec., Moscow 1949; UN Econ. Comm. for Europe, Geneva 1951–63; Lecturer in Soviet Econs, Univ. of Oxford 1963–72, Chair. Faculty Bd 1974–76, mem. Gen. Bd of Faculties 1972–78, Chair. Advisory Council of Adult Educ. 1972–78, Univ. Latin Preacher 1982; Gov. Plater Coll., Oxford 1968–95, Emer. Gov. 1995–; Visiting Prof. of Econs, Univ. of Mich., USA 1966; Visiting Lecturer, European Inst. of Business Admin, Fontainebleau 1959–82, 1988–92, Univ. of Cambridge 1967–68, 1977–78, 1978–79; Reader in Econs and Professorial Fellow, St Antony's Coll., Oxford 1972–93, Sub-Warden 1986–87, Reader Emer. 1993–; Dir, Inst. of Russian, Soviet and E European Studies, Univ. of Oxford 1988–93; Assoc. Fellow Templeton Coll., Oxford 1983–; Visiting Faculty mem. Henley Man. Coll. 1987–2002; mem. Centre for Euro-Asian Studies, Univ. of Reading 1997–; Vice-Chair. Social Science Research Council Int. Activities Cttee 1980–84; Special Adviser House of Commons Foreign Affairs Cttee 1985–87; Chair. Co-ordinating Council, Area Studies Asscns 1986–88 (mem. 1980–93, 1995), Wilton Park Academic Council (FCO) 1986–92 (mem. 1985–2001); Pres. British Asscn of Slavonic and E European Studies 1988–91, Vice-Pres. 1991–93; Prin. Charlemagne Inst., Edin. 1993–94, Hon. Fellow Divinity Faculty, Univ. of Edin. 1993–96; mem. Int. Social Science Council (UNESCO) 1980–91, Council Royal Inst. of Int. Affairs 1979–85, 1986–92 (mem. Meetings Cttee 1976-88, Chair. Central Asian and Caucasus Advisory Bd 1993–), Royal Econ. Soc. 1975–86, 1987–90, Council School of Slavonic and East European Studies 1981–87, Cttee Nat. Asscn for Soviet and East European Studies 1965–88, Steering Cttee Königswinter Anglo-German Confs 1969–90, Exec. Cttee Int. Econ. Asscn 1974–83, 1986– (Gen. Ed.), also various editorial bds, Anglo-Soviet, British-Mongolian, Anglo-Polish, British-Bulgarian, British-Yugoslav (Chair.), Canada-UK, British-Romanian and UK-Uzbek Round Tables, British-Polish Mixed Comm.; Sec. British Nat. Cttee of AIESEE 1988–93; Pres. British Asscn of Fmr UN Civil Servants 1994–2001 (Hon. Vice-Pres. 2001–), Albania Soc. of Britain 1992–95; Chair. Council, the Keston Inst., Oxford 1994–2002; Trustee Foundation of King George VI and Queen Elizabeth, St Catharine's 1987–2006 (Chair. Academic Consultative Cttee 1987–2002), Sir Heinz Koeppler Trust 1987–2001 (Chair. 1992–2001); mem. Higher Educ. Funding Council for England Advisory Bd on Eastern European Studies 1995–2000, CAFOD East Europe Cttee 2001–; Hon. Prof., Inst. for German Studies, Univ. of Birmingham 1994–; Kt Order of St Gregory the Great 1990, Order of Naim Frashëri (Albania) 1995, Kt Order of Merit (Poland) 1999; Hon. DSocSc (Birmingham) 1996. *Publications:* Comecon: Integration Problems of the Planned Economies 1965, Planning in East Europe (with J. Zielinski) 1970, Soviet Economics 1970, Health Care in the Soviet Union and Eastern Europe 1976, Economic Development for Eastern Europe 1968, Planning and Market Relations (with R. Portes) 1971, The New Economic Systems of Eastern Europe (jointly) 1975, The Soviet Union since the Fall of Khrushchev (with A. H. Brown) 1975, Soviet Policy for the 1980s (with A. H. Brown) 1982, Economic History of Eastern Europe, Vols I–III (with E. A. Radice) 1985–86, Early Steps in Comparing East-West Economies (with E. A. G. Robinson) 1991, Reforms in Foreign Economic Relations of Eastern Europe and the Soviet Union 1991, The Macroeconomics of Transition in Eastern Europe (with D. Morris) 1992, The Central Asian Economies after Independence (with S. Mehrotra) 1992, 1996, Education and Economic Change in Eastern Europe and the Former Soviet Union (with D. Phillips) 1992, Cambridge Encyclopedia of Russia and the Former Soviet Union (jtly) 1994, Privatization in the CIS 1996, The Economies of Kazakstan and Uzbekistan 1997, The Prudential Management of Hydrocarbon Revenues in Resource-Rich Transition Economies (co-author) 2006; articles in econ. and Slavic journals. *Address:* 31 Capel Close, Oxford, OX2 7LA, England (home). *Telephone:* (1865) 515581 (home). *Fax:* (1865) 515581 (home). *E-mail:* michael.kaser@ economics.ox.ac.uk (office).

KASHLEV, Yuriy Borisovich, DHist; Russian diplomatist; *First Vice-Rector, Diplomatic Academy of the Ministry of Foreign Affairs;* b. 13 April 1934, Tejen; m. 1957; one s. one d. *Education:* Moscow Inst. of Int. Relations. *Career:* fmr mem. CPSU; worked for Soviet Cttee for Youth Orgs. 1961–65; CPSU Cen. Cttee 1965–68; Counsellor, USSR Ministry of Foreign Affairs 1968–70; served in Embassy, UK 1970–71, Counsellor, Head of Sector, Deputy Head, Dept of Information, Ministry of Foreign Affairs 1971–78, Head Dept 1982–86; Sec.-Gen. USSR Comm. for UNESCO 1978–82; Head Dept of Humanitarian and Cultural Relations 1986–89, Deputy First Vice-Minister, USSR Ministry of Foreign Affairs 1986–90; mem. or head of Soviet dels to CSCE confs Geneva, Berne, Vienna, Paris; Russian Amb. to Poland 1990–96; Rector and Prof., Diplomatic Acad. of the Ministry of Foreign Affairs 1996–2000, First Vice-Rector 2001–; 11 state awards (orders and medals), from USSR, Mongolia,

Poland and Bulgaria. *Publications:* Détente in Europe: from Helsinki to Madrid, International Information Exchange, After Fourteen Thousand Wars, Mass Media and International Relations, Ideological Struggle or Psychological War, Information and PR in International Relations, Manfaced Diplomacy: Confessions of an Ambassador, The Helsinki Process 1975–2005: Lights and Shadows through the Eyes of a Participant 2005, Information, Mass Communication and international Relations 2005; other books on int. affairs. *Address:* Diplomatic Academy of the Ministry of Foreign Affairs, Ostozhenka str. 53/2, 119021 Moscow, Russia (office); Dolgorukowskaya Str. 22, App. 38, Moscow (home). *Telephone:* (495) 973-07-74 (also fax) (home); (495) 245-39-43 (office). *Fax:* (495) 244-18-78 (office). *E-mail:* yuri .kashlev@dipacademy.ru (office). *Website:* www.dipacademy.ru/english (office).

KAŠICKÝ, František; Slovak government official and diplomatist; *Permanent Representative, NATO;* b. 18 Nov. 1968, Gelnica; m.; two c. *Education:* Mil. Pedagogical Acad., Bratislava, Akademie der Bundeswehr fur Information und Kommunikation, Strausberg, Germany. *Career:* Sr Officer for Social Man., Ministry of Defence 1991–93; Ed. Specialist, OBRANA (mil. newspaper) 1993–98, also Press Sec. for Minister of Defence; Asst Sec. of State, Ministry of Defence 1998–2000; Defence Ministry Spokesman, Office Dir and Dir of Communications Dept 2001–03; Dir Mil. Defence Intelligence 2003–04; Sec. Parl. Cttee of Nat. Council for Defence and Security, Special Control Cttee of Nat. Council for Control of Activities of Nat. Security Authority, Cttee of Nat. Council for Control of Information Tech. 2004–06; Minister of Defence 2006–08 (resgnd); Perm. Rep. to NATO, Brussels May 2008–; mem. Direction-Social Democracy (Smer-Sociálna demokracia). *Address:* Office of the Permanent Representative of Slovakia, blvd Léopold III, 1110 Brussels, Belgium (office). *Telephone:* (2) 707-41-11 (office). *Fax:* (2) 707-45-79 (office). *E-mail:* natodoc@hq.nato.int (office). *Website:* www .nato.int (office).

KASIMOV, Erkin Sadriddinovich, MA; Tajikistan diplomatist; *Ambassador to UK;* b. 19 May 1951, Dushanbe; m. Eleonora Kasimov; two d. *Education:* Tajik State Univ. *Career:* joined Ministry of Foreign Affairs 1974, Acting Sr Advisor 1980–81, First Sec. 1981–82, Head of Protocol, Consular section 1982–89; various positions at USSR Gen. Consulate, Basra, Iraq 1989–90, Second Sec., Russian Fed., Embassy in Baghdad 1990–92; Head of Dept of Int. Orgs, Ministry of Foreign Affairs of Tajikistan 1993–2001; participated frequently in UN Gen. Ass., First Deputy Minister of Foreign Affairs and Chair. Co-ordinating Group for the Provisioning of Humanitarian Assistance to Afghanistan 2001–03, Perm. Rep. of Tajikistan to OSCE and other Int. Orgs, Vienna 2003–08, Amb. to Austria (also accred to Hungary and Switzerland) 2003–08; Deputy Foreign Minister 2008; Amb. to UK 2008–. *Publication:* Tajikistan UN: History of Relationship (with R. Alimov and M. Lebedev) 1995. *Address:* Consulate of Tajikstan, 33 Ovington Square, London, SW3 1LJ, England (office). *Telephone:* (20) 7584-5111 (office). *Fax:* (20) 7581-2669 (office).

KASKARELIS, Vassilis, BSc, LLB; Greek diplomatist; *Permanent Representative, European Union;* b. 26 Nov. 1948, Athens; m. Anna Kaskarelis; two s. *Education:* Univ. of Thessalonoki, Univ. of Athens. *Career:* Embassy Attaché, Ministry of Foreign Affairs 1974; Third Sec. in Ankara, Turkey 1976; Consul in Venice, Italy 1979; First. Sec. in Nicosia, Cyprus 1984; Head of Mil. Mission in Berlin, Germany 1987, Consul-Gen. in Greece 1990; Deputy Dir. Turkish Desk, Ministry of Foreign Affairs 1991, Minister Plenipotentiary, Head of Cabinet of Sec.-Gen. 1993; Deputy Perm. Rep. to UN, New York 1995; Perm. Rep. to NATO, Brussels 2000–04; currently Perm. Rep. to EU, Brussels; Grand Commdr, Order of the Phoenix (Greece), Chevalier, Ordre nat. du Mérute. *Address:* Office of the Permanent Representative, rue Montoyer 25, 1000 Brussels, Belgium (office). *Telephone:* (2) 551-56-37 (office). *Fax:* (2) 512-79-12 (office). *E-mail:* brp.kaskarelis@rp-grece.be (office). *Website:* www .greekembassy-press.be (office).

KASSEM, Muhammad Abd al-Hamid; Egyptian diplomatist; *Ambassador to Saudi Arabia;* m. Amal El Desouki. *Career:* fmr Counsellor, Embassy in Washington, DC, currently Amb. to Saudi Arabia. *Address:* Embassy of Egypt, PO Box 94333, Riyadh 11693, Saudi Arabia (office). *Telephone:* (1) 481-0464 (office). *Fax:* (1) 481-0463 (office).

KASYANOV, Mikhail Mikhailovich; Russian politician; *Leader, Russian People's Democratic Union;* b. 8 Dec. 1957, Solntsevo, Moscow Oblast. *Education:* Moscow Inst. of Automobile Transport. *Career:* held sr positions at RSFSR State Planning Comm., then Ministry of Econs 1981–90; Chief of Section for Foreign Econ. Relations, Russian State Cttee for Econs 1990–91; Head, Dept for Foreign Econ. Relations, Ministry of

Finance 1991–93, Head, Dept of Overseas Credits 1993–95, Deputy Minister of Finance 1995–99, First Deputy Minister, then Minister 1999–2000; main negotiator with Western financial orgs on questions of Russian liabilities; Deputy Man. for Russian Fed., EBRD 1999; First Deputy Prime Minister Jan. 2000, Acting Chair. of Govt, then Chair. of Govt 2000–04; mem. Presidium of Russian Govt 1999–2004, Security Council 1999–2004; f. MK-Analytics (consultancy) 2005; currently Leader, Russian People's Democratic Union.
Address: Russian People's Democratic Union (Rossiiskii narodno–demok-raticheski soyuz), 117279 Moscow, ul. Profsoyuznaya 93, korp. 4, Russia (office). *Telephone:* (495) 429-61-70 (office). *Fax:* (495) 429-63-10 (office). *E-mail:* newtypeparty@mail.ru (office). *Website:* nardemsoyuz.ru (office); kasyanov.ru.

KATAINEN, Jyrki, MScS; Finnish politician; *Deputy Prime Minister and Minister of Finance;* b. 14 Oct. 1971, Siilinjärvi; m. Mervi Katainen. *Career:* mem. Siilinjärvi Municipal Council 1993–; Vice-Chair. Regional Council of Pohjois-Savo 1994–95; mem. Parl. (Finnish Nat. Coalition Party—Kokoomus) 1999–, Vice-Chair. Kokoomus Youth League 1994–95, Vice-Chair. Kokoomus 2001–04, Chair. 2004–; Chair. Cttee for the Future 2003–; mem. Finnish Del. to W European Union Parl. Ass. 2004–; Deputy mem. Finnish Del. to OSCE Parl. Ass. 2003–; mem. Admin. Bd Finnish Broadcasting Corpn 2003–; Deputy Prime Minister and Minister of Finance 2007–; named among World Econ. Forum's Global Leaders for Tomorrow 2003.
Address: Ministry of Finance, Snellmaninkatu 1, PO Box 28, 00023 Helsinki, Finland (office). *Telephone:* (9) 16033004 (office). *Fax:* (9) 16034712 (office). *E-mail:* jyrki.katainen@vm.fi (office). *Website:* www .vm.fi (office); www.jyrkikatainen.fi (office).

KATANANDOV, Sergey Leonidovich; Russian politician; *Head of the Republic of Karelia;* b. 21 April 1955, Petrozavodsk; m.; two s. *Education:* Petrozavodsk State Univ., NW Acad. of State and Municipal Service. *Career:* worked as Head of Sector, Sr Engineer, Petrozavodskstroi 1977–91; mem. Petrozavodsk City Exec. Cttee, Chair. City Soviet 1991–98, Mayor of Petrozavodsk 1994–98; elected Chair. Karelian Govt 1998–2002; Head of the Repub. of Karelia 2002–; Merited Worker of Nat. Economy of Repub. of Karelia 1995, Order of Honour of Russian Fed. 2000, Medal of Merits 2004. *Publications include:* articles in Russian and Finnish journals and newspapers.
Address: Government of Karelia, Lenina prosp. 19, Petrozavodsk 185020, Karelia (office); Andropova av. 30, Petrozavodsk, Karelia, Russia. *Telephone:* (8142) 79-93-00 (office). *Fax:* (8142) 79-93-91 (office). *E-mail:* government@karelia.ru (office). *Website:* www.gov.karelia.ru.

KATENDE, Mull Sebujja; Ugandan diplomatist; *Ambassador to Sudan;* b. Masaka. *Career:* Second Sec. Embassy in Sudan 1986–90; Special Asst to Foreign Minister, Kampala 1990–94; First Sec. and Counselor, Embassy in Ethiopia 1994–97; 1997, Head, Department of E Africa and ring states with special responsibility for peace and security in Great Lakes Region 1997; Amb. to Sudan 2003–.
Address: Embassy of Uganda, POB 2676, Khartoum, Sudan (office). *Telephone:* (183) 158571 (office). *Fax:* (183) 797868 (office). *E-mail:* ugembkht@hotmail.com (office).

KATILI, John (Younis) Ario, DSc; Indonesian geologist, academic and politician; b. 9 June 1929, Gorontalo, Sulawesi; m. Iliana Syarifa Uno; one s. one d. *Education:* Univ. of Indonesia, Inst. of Tech., Bandung, Univ. of Innsbruck, Austria. *Career:* fmr Prof. of Structural and Tectonic Geology, Head Dept of Geology and Dean Faculty of Mineral Tech., Inst. of Tech. Bandung (ITB); Vice-Pres. of ITB 1961; Deputy Chair. Indonesian Inst. of Sciences –1973; Dir-Gen. of Mines 1973-84, of Geology and Mineral Resources 1984–89; fmr Sr Adviser to State Minister of Research and Tech. and to Minister of Mines and Energy; fmr Vice-Chair. Indonesian Nat. Research Council; Vice-Speaker House of Reps (Parl.) and Vice-Chair. People's Consultative Ass. 1992–97; Amb. to Russian Fed., Turkmenistan, Kazakhstan and Mongolia 1999–2004; First Pres. Southeast Asia Union of Geological Sciences 1984; Vice-Pres. Indonesian Acad. of Sciences 1998; mem. Nat. Geographic Soc.; Foreign mem. Russian Acad. of Natural Sciences 2000; Fellow, Islamic Acad. of Sciences; Hon. mem. RGS, Indonesian Asscn of Geologists, Geological Soc. of Sweden, Royal Geological Soc. and Mining Soc. of the Netherlands; Commdr Ordre Nat. du Mérite 1988, Order of Orange Nassau 1995; Dr hc (Stockholm) 1988; Van Waterschoot van der Gracht Medal 1995. *Publications:* 12 books; over 150 scientific and policy papers in English and Indonesian.
Address: c/o IAGI Secretariat, Mineral and Batubara Building, 6th Floor, No.10, Jakarta 12870, Indonesia (office).

KATJU, Shri Vivek; Indian diplomatist; *Additional Secretary, Ministry of External Affairs; Career:* batch IFS officer 1975; fmr Jt Sec., Ministry of External Affairs in charge of Iran, Pakistan and Afghanistan; headed team of Indian officials who went to Kandahar to negotiate release of passengers of hijacked Indian Airlines plane 1999; Amb. to Myanmar –2002, to Afghanistan 2002–04, to Thailand 2004–06; currently Additional Sec., Ministry of External Affairs; fmr mem. Bd of Trustees Asian Inst. of Tech., Pathumthani.
Address: Ministry of External Affairs, South Block, Room 144c, New Delhi 110 011, India (office). *Telephone:* (11) 23011849 (office). *Fax:* (11) 23013387 (office). *E-mail:* asppr@mea.gov.in (office). *Website:* meaindia .nic.in (office).

KATO, Ryozo; Japanese diplomatist; b. 1941, Saitama Pref.; m. Hanayo Kato; three c. *Education:* Univ. of Tokyo. *Career:* joined Ministry of Foreign Affairs 1965, Dir Security Affairs Div. 1981–84, Dir Treaties Div. 1984–87, Dir-Gen. Affairs Div. 1990–92, Deputy Dir N American Affairs Bureau 1992–94, Dir-Gen. Asian Affairs Bureau 1995–97, Dir-Gen. Foreign Policy Bureau 1997–99, Minister, Washington, DC 1987, Consul-Gen., San Francisco 1994, Deputy Minister for Foreign Affairs 1999–2001, Amb. to USA 2001–08.
Address: Ministry of Foreign Affairs, 2-11-1, Shiba-Koen, Minato-ku, Tokyo 105-8519, Japan (office). *Telephone:* (3) 3580-3311 (office). *Fax:* (3) 3581-2667 (office). *E-mail:* webmaster@mofa.go.jp (office). *Website:* www .mofa.go.jp (office).

KATONA, Tamás; Hungarian diplomat, politician and historian; *Chairman, Manfred Wörner Foundation;* b. 2 Feb. 1932, Budapest; m. Klára Barta; one s. two d. *Education:* Archiepiscopal High School (Rákóczianum), Budapest, Eötvös Loránd Univ., Budapest. *Career:* head of public libraries 1954–61; Ed. Magyar Helikon Publishing House and Európa Publishing House 1961–86; Lecturer in 19th-century Hungarian History, Eötvös Coll. 1980–85, József Attila Univ. of Szeged 1986–90; mem. Parl. 1990–98; Sec. of State for Foreign Affairs 1990–92; Sec. of State, Prime Minister's Office 1992–94; First Vice-Pres. IPU, Hungary; Mayor, Castle Dist, Budapest 1994–98; Prof., Károli Gáspár Protestant Univ. 1998–2000; Amb. to Poland 2000–03; Chair. Hungarian Scout Asscn 1994–98, Manfred Wörner Foundation 1998–; Scientific Advisor, Inst. of History, Hungarian Acad. of Sciences 2003–; Ed. serial publs Bibliotheca Historica and Pro Memoria (pocket library of history and cultural history); Grand Officer, Order of Merit (Poland), Grand Officer, Order of Merit of the Sovereign Order of St John, Hungarian Defence Cross (First Class). *Publications:* Az aradi vértanúk (The Martyrs of Arad) 1979, 1983, 1991, 2003, A korona kilenc évszázada (Nine Centuries of the Crown) 1979, A tatárjárás emlékezete (The Mongol Invasion) 1981, 1987, Budavár bevételének emlékezete, 1849 (Capture of Fort Buda in 1849) 1991, Csány László erdélyi fokor-mánybiztos (László Csány High Commissioner of Transylvania) 1991.
Address: Fortuna-utca 13, 1014 Budapest, Hungary (home). *Telephone:* (1) 201-13-65 (home). *Fax:* (1) 225-32-93 (home). *E-mail:* fortunau13@hotmail .com (home).

KATSAV, Moshe; Israeli politician; b. 5 Dec. 1945, Iran; m. Gila Katsav; four s. one d. *Education:* Hebrew Univ. of Jerusalem. *Career:* reporter for Yediot Aharonot (newspaper) 1966–68; Mayor of Kiryat Malachi 1969, 1974–81; mem. Knesset 1977–99; mem. Interior and Educ. Cttees 1977–81; Deputy Minister of Housing and Construction 1981–84; Minister of Labour and Social Affairs 1984–88, of Transportation 1988–92; mem. Cttee on Defence 1988–92, 1996–99; Chair. Likud faction in the Knesset, Parl. Cttee of Chinese–Israeli Friendship League 1992–96; Deputy Prime Minister 1996–99, also Minister of Tourism, for Israeli Arab Affairs; Pres. of Israel 2000–07 (resgnd); Chair. Cttee for Nat. Events 1996–99; mem. Foreign Affairs and Defence Cttee 1999–2000; mem. Bd of Trustees Ben-Gurion Univ. 1978–; Dr hc (Univ. of Nebraska) 1998, (George Washington Univ.) 2001, (Hartford Univ., Conn.) 2001, (Yeshivah Univ., NY) 2002, (Bar Ilan Univ., Israel) 2003, (China Agricultural Univ., Beijing) 2003, (Sorbonne, Paris) 2004, (ELTE Univ. of Budapest) 2004; Bene Merito Medal of the Acad. of Science of Austria 2004.
Address: c/o Office of the President, Beit Hanassi, 3 Hanassi Street, Jerusalem 92188, Israel (office).

KATSONGA, Davies Chester, BA, MBA; Malawi politician; *Minister of Labour and Vocational Training;* b. 6 Aug. 1955, Mwanza; m.; two s. *Education:* Schiller Int. Univ., Inst. of Marketing, South-Bank Univ., London, UK. *Career:* MP for Mwanza Cen. Constituency 1999–; Minister of Mines, Natural Resources and Environmental Affairs, then Speaker of Parl. 1999–2004; Minister of Natural Resources 2004–05, of Foreign Affairs 2005–06, of Defence 2006–07, for Presidential and Parl. Affairs 2007–08, of Labour and Vocational Training 2008–; mem. Democratic Progressive Party 2005–.
Address: Ministry of Labour, Private Bag 344, Capital City, Lilongwe 3, Malawi (office). *Telephone:* 1772080 (office). *Fax:* 1773803 (office). *E-mail:*

labour@malawi.net (office); dkatsonga@yahoo.co.uk (home). *Website:* www.malawi.gov.mw/Labour/Home%20%20Labour.htm (office).

KATZENSTEIN, Peter Joachim, PhD; American academic; *Walter S. Carpenter Jr Professor of International Studies, Cornell University;* b. 17 Feb. 1945; m.; two c. *Education:* Swarthmore Coll., LSE (UK), Harvard Univ. *Career:* Teaching Fellow, Dept of Govt, Harvard Univ. 1971–72; Instructor (part-time), Politics Dept, Univ. of Mass., Boston 1972–73; Asst Prof. of Govt, Cornell Univ. 1973–77, Assoc. Prof. 1977–80, Prof. of Govt 1980–87, Walter S. Carpenter, Jr Prof. of Int. Studies 1988–; Fellow, Wissenschaftskolleg Berlin 1995–96, Woodrow Wilson Int. Center, Washington, DC 1997–98; Visiting Karl Deutsch Research Prof., Wissenschaftszentrum Berlin 1998–99, Chair. Acad. Advisory Cttee 2007–; Ed. Cornell Studies in Political Economy 1982–; mem. Exec. Cttee Int. Org. 1976–99, Ed. 1980–86, Chair. Bd of Eds 1990–91; mem. Ed. Advisory Bd Int. Studies Quarterly 1990–, Ed Bd Japanese Journal of Political Science 1999–; mem. Academic Advisory Bd Inst. of Fiscal and Monetary Policy, Japanese Ministry of Finance 1985–, German–European Inst. for Civic Rights and Public Security, Berlin 1990–, Hessische Stiftung für Friedens- und Konfliktforschung 1997–, Inst. for Advanced Study Berlin 1998–2001; mem. Int. Advisory Cttee, Max-Planck Inst., Cologne 1987–; mem. Advisory Council, Dept of Politics, Princeton Univ. 1993–2000; mem. American Acad. of Arts and Sciences 1987–, Soc. for Comparative Research 1998–, American Political Science Asscn (Pres–elect 2008–09); fellowships from Andrew W. Mellon Foundation/Aspen Inst. for Humanistic Studies 1976–77, Rockefeller Foundation 1977–79, Council on Foreign Relations 1979–81, German Marshall Fund 1979–81, 1990–91, American Council of Learned Socs 1988–89, John Simon Guggenheim Memorial Foundation 1988–89, Social Science Research Council 1998–2000, Russell Sage Foundation 2001–02, Stanford Center for Advanced Study in the Behavioral Sciences 2004–05, Stephen H. Weiss Presidential Fellow, Cornell Univ. 2004; Sumner Dissertation Prize, Harvard Univ. 1973, Helen Dwight Reid Award, American Political Science Asscn 1974, Woodrow Wilson Foundation Book Award 1986, Stephen and Margery Russell Distinguished Teaching Award, Cornell Univ. 1993. *Publications:* Bibliography of Comparative Public Policy in Britain, West Germany, Japan and France (co-author) 1976, Disjoined Partners: Austria and Germany since 1815 1976, Comparative Public Policy: A Cross-National Bibliography (co-author) 1978, Territorial Politics in Industrial Nations (co-ed.) 1978, Between Power and Plenty: Foreign Economic Policies of Advanced Industrial States 1978, Corporatism and Change: Austria, Switzerland and the Politics of Industry 1984, Small States in World Markets: Industrial Policy in Europe 1985, Policy and Politics in West Germany: The Growth of a Semisovereign State 1987, Industry and Politics in West Germany: Toward the Third Republic (ed.) 1989, Comparative Theory and Political Experience: Mario Einaudi and the Liberal Tradition (co-ed.) 1990, Defending the Japanese State (co-author) 1991, Japan's National Security: Structures, Norms and Policy Responses in a Changing World (Masayoshi Ohira Memorial Prize, co-author) 1993, Norms and National Security: Police and Military in Postwar Japan 1996, The Culture of National Security: Norms and Identity in World Politics (ed.) 1996, Tamed Power: Germany in Europe (ed.) 1997, Network Power: Japan and Asia (co-ed.) 1997, Mitteleuropa: Between Europe and Germany (ed.) 1998, International Organization: Exploration and Contestation in the Study of World Politics (co-ed.) 1999, Asian Regionalism (co-author) 2000, Rethinking Security in East Asia: Identity, Power and Efficiency (co-ed) 2004, A World of Regions: Asia and Europe in the American Imperium 2005, Beyond Japan: The Dynamics of East Asian Regionalism (co-ed) 2006, Religion in an Expanding Europe (co-ed) 2006, Anti-Americanisms in World Politics (co-ed) 2006; numerous articles, essays, chapters in books, monographs. *Address:* Government Department, Cornell University, Ithaca, NY 14853, USA. *Telephone:* (607) 255-6257 (office). *Fax:* (607) 255-4530 (office). *E-mail:* pjk2@cornell.edu (office). *Website:* falcon.arts.cornell.edu/Govt (office); www.economyandsociety.org (office).

KAUL, Hans-Peter, JD; German , judge and diplomatist; *Judge and President, Pre-Trial Division, International Criminal Court;* b. 25 July 1943; m.; four c. *Education:* Int. Peace Acad., Vienna, Austria, Max Planck Inst., Heidelberg, Acad. of Int. Law, The Hague, The Netherlands, Ecole Nat. d'Admin, Paris, France, Univs of Heidelberg and Lausanne. *Career:* mil. service in German army 1963–67, attained rank Capt.; Consul and Press Attaché, Embassy in Oslo, Norway 1977–80; with Office for UN Affairs, Fed. Foreign Office, Bonn 1980–84; Press Counsellor and Spokesman, Embassy in Tel-Aviv, Israel 1984–86; Political Counsellor, Embassy in Washington, USA 1986–90; Deputy Dir, Office of Nr Eastern Affairs, Fed. Foreign Office, Bonn 1990–93; First Counsellor, Perm. Mission to UN, NY 1993–96; Dir Office for Public Int. Law, Fed. Foreign Office, Bonn and Berlin 1996–2002; Amb. and Commr of Fed. Foreign Office for Int. Criminal Court (ICC) 2002–03; Judge, ICC 2003–, Pres. Pre-Trial Div.

2004–; Head of German Dels to Preparatory Cttee for ICC 1996–98, 1999–2002; mem. Nat. Advisory Cttee of German Red Cross Soc. on Int. Humanitarian Law 1996–; mem. German Soc. for Int. Law, German Soc. for the UN, German Soc. for Foreign Policy, Int. Criminal Law Network. *Publications:* chapters in books, country reports, articles in professional journals in German, English, Spanish, Portuguese and Arabic languages. *Address:* International Criminal Court, Maanweg 174, 2516 AB The Hague, The Netherlands (office); Buchsweildrstr. 16, 14195, Berlin, Germany (office). *Telephone:* (70) 5158237 (office); 84418040 (home). *Fax:* (70) 5158789 (office). *E-mail:* hanspeter.kaul@icc-cpi.int (office). *Website:* www.icc-cpi.int.

KAUNDA, Kenneth David; Zambian fmr politician; *Chairman, Kenneth Kaunda Children of Africa Foundation;* b. (Buchizya), 28 April 1924, Lubwa; m. Betty Banda 1946; six s. (two s. deceased) two d. one adopted s. *Education:* Lubwa Training School and Munali Secondary School. *Career:* schoolteacher at Lubwa Training School 1943, Headmaster 1944–47; Sec. Chinsali Young Men's Farming Asscn 1947; welfare officer, Chingola Copper Mine 1948; school teaching 1948–49; Founder-Sec. Lubwa branch, African Nat. Congress (ANC) 1950, district organizer 1951, prov. organizer 1952, Sec.-Gen. for N Rhodesia 1953; imprisoned for possession of prohibited literature Jan.–Feb. 1954; broke away from ANC to form Zambia African Nat. Congress 1958; imprisoned for political offences May 1959–Jan. 1960; Pres. United Nat. Independence Party 1960–92, 1995–2000; Minister of Local Govt and Social Welfare, N Rhodesia 1962–64; Prime Minister of N Rhodesia Jan.–Oct. 1964; Pres. Pan-African Freedom Movt for East, Central and South Africa (PAFMECSA) 1963; First Pres. of Zambia 1964–91 and Minister of Defence 1964–70, 1973–78; Head of Sub-Cttee for Defence and Security 1978–91; Minister of Foreign Affairs 1969–70, also of Trade, Industry, Mines and State Participation 1969–73; Chair. Mining and Industrial Devt Corpn of Zambia 1970; Chair. Org. of African Unity (OAU) 1970–71, 1987–88, Non-Aligned Nations Conf. 1970–73, fmr Chair. ZIMCO; Chancellor, Univ. of Zambia 1966–91, Copperbelt Univ. 1988; f. Peace Foundation 1992; charged with 'misprison of treason' over alleged involvement in attempted coup d'état 1997; freed after six months of house arrest after charges dropped June 1998; deprived of citizenship March 1999; citizenship restored by Supreme Court 2000; Founder and Chair. Kenneth Kaunda Children of Africa Foundation 2000–; Freeman of the Municipality of Chipata 1994; Order of the Collar of the Nile, Kt of the Collar of the Order of Pius XII, Order of the Queen of Sheba; Hon. LLD (Fordham, Dublin, Windsor (Canada), Wales, Sussex, York and Chile Univs); Dr hc (Humboldt State Univ., Calif.) 1980; Jawaharlal Nehru Award for Int. Understanding, Quaide Azam Human Rights Inst. Prize (Pakistan) 1976; honoured for his Keynote Address on Conflict Resolution in Africa and for Distinguished Leadership of African People for Over Half A Century, African Studies Coalition, Calif. State Univ., Sacramento 1995, WANGO Universal Peace Award 2004. *Publications:* Black Government 1961, Zambia Shall Be Free 1962, A Humanist in Africa (with Colin Morris) 1966, Humanism in Zambia and a Guide to its Implementation 1967, Humanism Part II 1977, Letter to my Children 1977, Kaunda On Violence 1980. *Address:* Office of the First President of the Republic of Zambia, 21 A Serval Road, PO E 501, Lusaka, Zambia. *Telephone:* (1) 260327 (office); (1) 260323 (home). *Fax:* (1) 220805 (office); (1) 220805 (home). *Website:* www .kkcaf.org.

KAVADZE, Amiran, PhD; Georgian engineer, biochemist and diplomatist; *Ambassador to Sweden;* b. 21 April 1951, Tblisi; m. Ia Kavadze; two d. *Education:* Tblisi Agricultural Univ., Moscow Bakh Biochemistry Inst., Baku Inst. of Political Studies. *Career:* Amb. to Switzerland and Perm. Rep. to UN and Int. Orgs, Geneva and Dir Int. Econ. Relations Dept, Ministry of Foreign Affairs 1993, 1997; Amb. to Holy See 2001; Deputy Minister of Foreign Affairs 2003; Amb. to UK and Amb. to Ireland (non-resident) 2004–06, to Sweden (also accred. to Finland) 2007–. *Publications:* Georgia's Path to the Multilateral Trading System 2003. *Address:* Embassy of Georgia, Humlegårdsgt. 19, 1st Floor, 114 46 Stockholm, Sweden (office). *Telephone:* (8) 678-02-60 (office). *Fax:* (8) 678-02-64 (office). *E-mail:* geoemb.sweden@telia.com (office). *Website:* www .sweden.mfa.gov.ge (office).

KAVAKURE, Laurent; Burundian diplomatist; *Ambassador to Belgium; Career:* Amb. to Belgium (also accred to Luxembourg, the Netherlands and UK and as Amb. and Perm. Rep. to EU) 2006–, also Perm. Rep. to OPCW, to European Atomic Energy Cttee 2007–. *Address:* Embassy of Burundi, 46 square Marie-Louise, 1000 Brussels, Belgium (office). *Telephone:* (2) 230-45-35 (office). *Fax:* (2) 230-78-83 (office). *E-mail:* ambassade.burundi@skynet.be (office).

KAVAN, Jan Michael, CH, BSc; Czech politician and journalist; *Foreign Policy Adviser to the President of the Chamber of Deputies;* b. 17 Oct. 1946,

London; m. Lenka Mázlová 1991 (divorced 2005); one s. three d. *Education:* Charles Univ., Prague, London School of Econs, Univ. of Reading and St Antony's Coll., Oxford, UK. *Career:* journalist, Univerzita Karlova, Prague 1966–68; Ed. East European Reporter, London 1985–90; Dir Palach Press Ltd, London 1974–90, Deputy Dir Jan Palach Information and Research Trust 1982–90; Vice-Pres. East European Cultural Foundation, London 1985–90; mem. Parl. Fed. Ass. of Czech Repub. 1990–92, 2002–, mem. Foreign Affairs Cttee; mem. Czech Social Democratic (CSSD) Party 1993–, mem. Foreign Affairs Comm. 1994–98, Spokesman on Foreign Affairs 1996–98, elected to Presidium of Cen. Exec. Cttee 1997; Chair. Helsinki Citizens' Ass. in Czech Rep. 1990–95, Policy Centre for the Promotion of Democracy, Prague 1992–98; Senator, Parl. of Czech Repub. 1996–2000; Minister of Foreign Affairs 1998–2002, Deputy Prime Minister 1999–2002; Deputy Chair. Cen. and East European Cttee of the Socialist International 1997, State Security Council 1999–2002; Chair. Council for Intelligence Activities 1999–2002; Pres. UN Gen. Ass. 2002–03; mem. Parl. 2002–06, Deputy Chair. Foreign Affairs Cttee 2004–06, Deputy Leader of Parl. Group of Soc. Democratic Party (CSSD), mem. Presidium of Party of European Socialists (PES) 2006–; foreign policy advisor to Pres. of Chamber of Deputies, Czech Repub.; foreign policy adviser to Prime Minister of Slovakia; Visiting Prof. of Politics and History, Adelphi Univ., New York 1993–94; Karl Loewenstein Fellow in Politics and Jurisprudence, Amherst Coll., Mass 1994; lectured at Columbia and Stanford Univs, Wellesley Coll., Harvard Center for European Studies; taught at London Adult Educ. Inst. for 15 years; Pres. 57th Session UN Gen. Ass. 2002–03; Hon. Prof., Faculty of Int. Relations, Mongolia State Univ. 1999; Hon. Fellow LSE 2001; Companion of Honour 2003, Int. Order of Merit 2003; Hon. DHumLitt (Adelphi) 2001; TGM Medal of Honour 2001. *Publications:* Czechoslovak Socialist Opposition 1976, Voices of Czechoslovak Socialists 1977, Voices from Prague 1983, Justice with a Muzzle 1996, McCarthyism Has a New Name: Lustration, Transition to Democracy in Eastern Europe and Russia 2002; more than 100 articles. *Address:* Parliament of the Czech Republic, Snemovni 4, 118 26 Prague 1 (office); Klausova 13c, Prague 5, 155 00, Czech Republic (home). *Telephone:* (257) 173013 (office). *Fax:* (257) 534403 (office). *E-mail:* kavanjm@seznam.cz (home).

KAVANAGH, Paul, BA; Irish diplomatist and UN official; *Permanent Representative, United Nations;* b. 12 March 1956; m.; two c. *Education:* Univ. Coll. Dublin. *Career:* served in Embassy in Beijing 1979–82; Exec. Officer, Dept of Defence 1977–78; Special Asst to UN Sec.-Gen.'s Personal Rep. for the fmr Yugoslavia 1991–92; with Sec.-Gen.'s Cabinet, UN, New York 1983–92; political advisor to UN Operation in Cyprus 1992–96; Dir UN Office, Tokyo 1996–98; deputy coordinator of Ireland's campaign for election to UN Security Council, Dept of Foreign Affairs 1998–2000; political coordinator, Irish Del. to UN Security Council 2001–02; Deputy Political Dir, Dept of Foreign Affairs 2003–04; Amb. to EU Political and Security Cttee, Brussels 2004–06; Perm. Rep. to UN, Geneva 2006–07, to UN, New York 2007–. *Address:* Permanent Mission of Ireland to the United Nations, 1 Dag Hammarskjöld Plaza, 885 Second Avenue, 19th Floor, New York, NY 10017, USA (office). *Telephone:* (212) 421-6934 (office). *Fax:* (212) 752-4726 (office). *E-mail:* ireland@un.int (office). *Website:* www.un.int/ireland (office).

KAVINDELE, Enoch Percy; Zambian politician. *Career:* Vice-Pres. Movt for Multi-Party Democracy; Minister of Health –2001; Vice-Pres. of Zambia 2001–03; mem. Nat. Assembly for Kabompo West. *Address:* c/o National Assembly, Lusaka, Zambia (office).

KAWAGUCHI, Yoriko, BA, MPh; Japanese economist and politician; b. 14 Jan. 1941, Tokyo; m.; two c. *Education:* Univ. of Tokyo, Yale Univ., USA. *Career:* at Ministry of Int. Trade and Industry 1965–76, 1979–90, Dir-Gen. Global Environmental Affairs 1992–93; economist, World Bank (IBRD) 1976–78; Minister, Embassy in Washington, DC 1991–92; Man. Dir Suntory Ltd 1993–2000; Minister of the Environment 2000–02, of Foreign Affairs 2002–04; Special Advisor to the Prime Minister responsible for Foreign Affairs 2004–05; mem. House of Councillors (Liberal Democratic Party) 2005–, mem. Cttee on the Environment, Cttee on House Affairs, Dir Special Cttee on Political Ethics and the Electoral System, Dir Research Cttee on Int. Issues and Climate Change; Chair. Research Comm. on Environment, Policy Research Council, Liberal Democratic Party, Vice-Chair. Econ. and Industry Cttee, Vice-Chair. Special Cttee on Regional Vitalization, Vice-Chair. Special Cttee on Women, Advisor Research Comm. on Int. Competitiveness, Advisor Special Cttee on Water Resource Security, Chair. Environment Orgs Cttee, Org HQ; fmr mem. Regulatory Reform Cttee, Cen. Council for Educ., Univ. Council; mem. jury Zayed Int. Prize for the Environment, UNEP; Chair. Asia-Pacific Forum for Environment and Devt 2; mem. Foundation Bd of Forum of Young Global Leaders, World Econ. Forum; Councillor Int. Cttee, Parliamentar-

ians for Global Action; mem. Hon. Advisory Cttee, UN Univ.; Vice-Chair. GLOBE Japan, GLOBE Int; Band, Order of the Aztec Eagle (Mexico) 2003, Extraordinary Grand Cross, Nat. Order of Merit (Paraguay) 2004; Dr hc (Nat. Univ. of Mongolia) 2004. *Address:* Room 418, Saingiin-kaikan, 2-1-1 Nagata-cho, Chiyoda-ku, Tokyo 100-8962, Japan (office). *Telephone:* (3) 3508-8418 (office). *Fax:* (3) 35512-2418 (office). *E-mail:* yoriko_kawaguchi@sangiin.go.jp (office). *Website:* www.yoriko-kawaguchi.jp (office).

KAWAH, Lami, BS, MALD; Liberian politician, economist and international organization official; b. 14 May 1936, Robertsport; m.; two c. *Education:* Cuttington Coll. and Tufts Univ., USA. *Career:* economist Ministry of Planning and Econ. Affairs, Asst Sec. for Econ. Affairs 1968, Deputy Minister for Planning and Econ. Affairs 1975–77, Minister 1999–2001; man. and consultant positions Lamco Jt Venture Co. (iron-ore mining operation) 1997–89, African Mining Corpn 1990–97; Minister of Transport 1998–99; Perm. Rep. to UN, New York 2001–06. *Address:* c/o Ministry of Foreign Affairs, Mamba Point, POB 10-9002, 1000 Monrovia 10, Liberia (office). *Telephone:* 226763 (office). *Website:* www.mofa.gov.lr (office).

KAWAMURA, Takekazu; Japanese diplomatist; *Permanent Representative, European Union;* b. 1943, Tokyo; m.; three c. *Career:* joined Foreign Service 1965, overseas postings include Embassy in Paris, Deputy Chief of Mission, Embassy in Brussels 1985–88, Consul-Gen. in New York 1999; Amb. to Iran 2002–04; in charge of arms control and scientific affairs, Ministry of Foreign Affairs, Tokyo 1995–97, Chief of Protocol 1997–99, Amb. in charge of Inspection 2004–05; Perm. Rep. to EU, Brussels 2005–. *Address:* Permanent Mission of Japan, 5–6 square de Meeûs, 1000 Brussels, Belgium (office). *Telephone:* (2) 500-77-11 (office). *Fax:* (2) 513-32-41 (office). *E-mail:* infomationdesk@scarlet.be (office). *Website:* www.eu.emb -japan.go.jp (office).

KAWARA, Tsutomu; Japanese politician. *Career:* mem. House of Reps; fmr Deputy Chief Cabinet Sec.; fmr Dir.-Gen. Defence Agency; fmr Construction Minister; Dir.-Gen. Defence Agency 1999–2000. *Address:* c/o Defence Agency, 9-7-45, Akasaka, Minato-ku, Tokyo 107-8513, Japan (office).

KAY, Nicholas Peter, CMG; British diplomatist; *Ambassador to Democratic Republic of the Congo;* m. Susan Wallace; one s. two d. *Career:* First Sec., FCO 1994–95, Head of Pakistan and Afghanistan Section 1995–97, Deputy Head of Mission, Havana 1997–2000, Deputy Head of Policy Planning Staff, FCO 2000–02, Deputy Head of Mission, Madrid 2002–06, Sr FCO Rep., S Afghanistan UK Regional Co-ordinator Southern Afghanistan, Kabul 2006–07, Amb. to Democratic Repub. of the Congo 2007–. *Address:* British Embassy, 83 Avenue du Roi Baudouin, BP 8049, Kinshasa, Democratic Republic of the Congo (office). *Telephone:* (81) 715-0761 (office); (98) 169100 (office). *Fax:* (81) 346-4291 (office); (88) 46102 (office). *E-mail:* ambrit@ic.cd (office).

KAYE, Harvey Jordan, PhD; American academic and writer; *Ben and Joyce Rosenberg Professor of Social Change and Development and Director, Center for History and Social Change, University of Wisconsin-Green Bay;* b. 9 Oct. 1949, Englewood, NJ; m. Lorna Stewart 1973; two d. *Education:* Paramus High School, Rutgers Univ., Univ. of Mexico, Univ. of London, UK and Louisiana State Univ. *Career:* Asst Prof. of Interdisciplinary Studies, St Cloud Univ., Minn. 1977–78; Asst Prof. of Social Change and Devt, Univ. of Wis., Green Bay 1978–83, Assoc. Prof. 1983–86, Head of Dept 1985–88, Prof. 1986–, Ben and Joyce Rosenberg Prof. of Social Change and Devt 1990–, Dir Center for History and Social Change 1991–; Visiting Fellow, Univ. of Birmingham, UK 1987; mem. Editorial Bd Marxist Perspectives 1978–80, The Wisconsin Sociologist, Wis. Sociological Asscn 1985–87, Rethinking History 1996–; Consulting Ed., Verso Publishers, London 1988–94, NYU Press 1996–; Series Ed., American Radicals (Routledge) 1992–98; columnist, Times Higher Educational Supplement 1994–2001, Tikkun magazine 1996–97, Index on Censorship 1996–, The Guardian Unlimited 2007–; mem. Exec. Bd, Center for Democratic Values 1996–2000, Scholars, Artists and Writers for Social Justice 1997–2000; mem. American Historical Asscn, American Sociological Asscn, Org. of American Historians, PEN; Nat. Endowment for the Humanities Fellowship 2002–03; Founders' Award for Scholarship 1985, Isaac Deutscher Memorial Prize 1993, Best Book for the Teen Age, New York Public Library 2001, Best Book 2006, Wisconsin Library Asscn. *Publications:* The British Marxist Historians 1984, The Powers of the Past 1991, The Education of Desire 1992, Why do Ruling Classes Fear History? 1996, Thomas Paine 2000, Are We Good Citizens? 2001, Thomas Paine and the Promise of America 2005; (Ed.) History, Classes and Nation-States 1988, The Face of the Crowd: Studies in Revolution, Ideology and Popular Protest 1988, Poets, Politics and the People 1989, E. P. Thompson: Critical

Perspectives (with K. McClelland) 1990, The American Radical (with M. Buhle and P. Buhle) 1994, Imperialism and its Contradictions 1995, Ideology and Popular Protest 1995; numerous articles on history and historians.
Address: Social Change and Development Department, University of Wisconsin–Green Bay, 2420 Nicolet Drive, Green Bay, WI 54311, USA (office). *Telephone:* (920) 465-2355 (office); (920) 465-2755 (office). *Fax:* (920) 465-2791 (office). *E-mail:* kayeh@uwgb.edu (office). *Website:* www.uwgb.edu/centerhsc (office).

KAYSEN, Carl, AB, MA, PhD; American economist and academic; *Professor Emeritus, Massachusetts Institute of Technology;* b. 5 March 1920, Philadelphia; m. 1st Annette Neutra 1940 (died 1990); two d.; m. 2nd Ruth A. Butler 1994. *Education:* Overbrook High School, Philadelphia, Univ. of Pennsylvania and Harvard Univ. *Career:* Nat. Bureau of Econ. Research 1940–42; Office of Strategic Services, Washington, DC 1942–43; US Army (Intelligence) 1943–45; Teaching Fellow in Econs, Harvard Univ. 1947, Jr Fellow, Soc. of Fellows 1947–50, Asst Prof. in Econs 1950–55, Assoc. Prof. 1955–57, Prof. 1957–66, Assoc. Dean, Grad. School of Public Admin 1960–66, Lucius N. Littauer Prof. of Political Economy 1964–66; Dir Inst. of Advanced Study, Princeton 1966–76, Dir Emer. 1976–, Prof. of Social Science 1976–77; David W. Skinner Prof. of Political Econ., MIT 1976–90, Prof. Emer. 1990–, Sr Research Scientist 1992–, Dir Program in Science, Tech. and Soc. 1981–86, now Faculty Emer.; Vice-Chair. and Dir Research, Sloan Comm. on Govt and Higher Educ. 1977–79; Sr Fulbright Research Scholar, LSE 1955–56; Econ. Consultant to Judge Wyzanski, Fed. Dist. Court of Mass 1950–52; Deputy Special Asst to Pres. for Nat. Security Affairs 1961–63. *Publications:* United States v. United Shoe Machinery Corporation, an Economic Analysis of an Anti-Trust Case 1956, The American Business Creed (with others) 1956, Anti-Trust Policy (with D. F. Turner) 1959, The Demand for Electricity in the United States (with Franklin M. Fisher) 1962, The Higher Learning, the Universities and the Public 1969, Nuclear Power, Issues and Choice, Nuclear Energy Policy Study Group Report (with others) 1977, A Program for Renewed Partnership, Report of the Sloan Commission on Government and Higher Education (with others) 1980, Emerging Norms of Justified Intervention 1993, Peace Operations by the United Nations (with George Rathjens) 1996, The American Corporation Now (ed.) 1996, The United States and the International Criminal Court (co-ed. with S. Sewall) 2000, War in Iraq (co-author) 2002, Alternatives, Costs, and Consequences.
Address: Massachusetts Institute of Technology Program in Security Studies, 292 Main Street, E38-614 Cambridge, MA 02139, USA (office). *Telephone:* (617) 253-4054 (office). *Fax:* (617) 253-9330 (office).

KAZANTSEV, Col-Gen. Victor Germanovich; Russian army officer; b. 22 Feb. 1946, Kokhanovo, Vitebsk Region, Belarus; m. Tamara Valentinovna Kazantseva. *Education:* Leningrad Higher School of Gen. Army, M. Frunze Mil. Acad., Mil. Acad. of Gen. Staff. *Career:* officer in Caucasian, Middle-Asian, Turkestan, Baikal Mil. Commands, Cen. Army Group in Czechoslovakia, First Deputy Commdr of Army N Caucasian Mil. Command; Chief of Staff to Commdr of troops N Caucasian Mil. Command 1996–97; Commdr 1997–99; Commdr group of Fed. forces in N Caucasus 1999–2000; Rep. of Pres. to S Fed. Dist 2000–04; Hero of Russia for operations in Dagestan and Chechnya 1999.
Address: c/o Office of the Representative of the President to Southern Federal District, Bolshaya Sadovaya str. 73, 344006 Rostov-on-Don, Russia (office).

KAZHEGELDIN, Akezhan Magzhan-Uly; Kazakhstani politician and economist; b. 27 March 1952, Georgiyevka, Semipalatinsk Region; m. Bykova Natalia Kazhegeldina; one s. one d. *Education:* Kazakh State Univ., Moscow Inst. of Oriental Studies. *Career:* Chair. Regional Exec. Cttee of Semipalatinsk 1983; Dir Ore-enriching Factory, Deputy Gov. Admin. of Semipalatinsk Region 1991–94; Pres. Kazakhstan Union of Industrialists and Entrepreneurs 1992–; apptd First Deputy Prime Minister of Kazakhstan 1994, Prime Minister 1994–97; Adviser to Pres. Nazarbayev May–Oct. 1998; disbarred from presidential election in 1998; f. Republican People's Party of Kazakhstan 1998, Chair. Bd 1998–2001; mem. Politburo Bd United Democratic Party 2001; in opposition to Pres. Nazarbayev 1999–, now lives abroad, sentenced to 10 years imprisonment in absentia 1999. *Publications include:* six books including Kazakhstan in the Conditions of Reforms, Problems of State Regulation in the Conditions of Socio-Economic Transformation, Socio-Economic Problems of Development of Kazakhstan in the Conditions of Reforms 1999, Opposition to Middle Ages 2000.
Address: c/o Republican Independent Political Club Association (Assotsiatsiya Respublianskogo Nezavisimogo Politicheskogo Kluba– RNPK), ul. Zhestoksan 12/514–515, 480050, Almaty, Kazakhstan. *Telephone:* (7172) 32-59-58. *Fax:* (7172) 32-39-85. *E-mail:* akkz@inbox.ru.

KAZIBWE, Speciosa Wandira, MD, ChB; Ugandan politician; b. 1 July 1955, Iganga Dist. *Education:* Makerere Univ., Kampala. *Career:* mem. Nat. Resistance Movt (NRM); MP for Kigulu S Iganga Dist; Deputy Minister for Industry 1989–91; fmr Minister for Gender and Community Devt; fmr Minister of Agric., Animal Industry and Fisheries; Vice-Pres. of Uganda 1994–2003; Chair. Sr Women's Advisory Group (SWAG) on the environment; mem. Uganda Women Entrepreneurs Asscn, Uganda Women Doctors Asscn, UN Commission on the Status of Women 2006; fmr Co-Chair Study Panel on Agricultural Productivity in Africa, InterAcademy Council; mem. Global Bd, Hunger Project.
Address: c/o Office of the Vice-President, PO Box 7359, Kampala, Uganda (office).

KAZYKHANOV, Yerzhan; Kazakhstani diplomatist; *Deputy Minister for Foreign Affairs;* b. 21 Aug. 1964; m.; two c. *Education:* St Petersburg State Univ., Moscow Diplomatic Acad., Foreign Service Training Inst., New Delhi, Foreign Service Inst. Washington, DC. *Career:* served as Second then First Sec. Ministry of Foreign Affairs 1989–93, Chief of Protocol 1993–95, Counsellor Perm. Mission to UN 1995–2000, Sec.-Gen. Nat. Comm. for UNESCO and Dir Dept of Multilateral Cooperation 2000–03; Perm. Rep. to UN 2003–07; Deputy Minister for Foreign Affairs 2007–.
Address: Ministry of Foreign Affairs, 010000 Astana, Kazakhstan (office). *Telephone:* (7172) 32-76-69 (office). *Fax:* (7172) 32-76-67 (office). *E-mail:* midrk@mid.kz (office). *Website:* www.mfa.kz (office).

KEANEY, Thomas, BSc, MA, PhD; American research institute director and defence analyst; *Executive Director and Senior Adjunct Professor of Strategic Studies, Foreign Policy Institute; Education:* USAF Acad., Colo, Univ. of Mich. *Career:* fmr Prof. of Mil. Strategy, Nat. War Coll.; several positions with USAF including Air Staff planner, Forward Air Controller, B-52 Squadron Commdr; Assoc. Prof. of History, USAF Acad.; Exec. Dir and Sr Adjunct Prof. of Strategic Studies, Foreign Policy Inst. 1998–, Merrill Center for Strategic Studies 2004–, Paul H. Nitze School of Advanced Int. Studies, Johns Hopkins Univ. *Publications:* Revolution in Warfare? Air Power in the Persian Gulf 1995, US Allies in a Changing World 2000, The Armed Forces in the Contemporary Middle East (co-ed.) 2001, War in Iraq, Planning and Execution (co-ed.) 2007.
Address: Foreign Policy Institute and Merrill Center for Strategic Studies, Paul H. Nitze School of Advanced International Studies, Johns Hopkins University, The Rome Building, 1619 Massachusetts Avenue, NW, Washington, DC 20036, USA (office). *Telephone:* (202) 663-5886 (office). *Fax:* (202) 663-5769 (office). *E-mail:* tkeaney@jhu.edu (office). *Website:* www.sais-jhu.edu/centers/fpi (office).

KEAT CHHON, PhD; Cambodian politician; *Senior Minister and Minister of the Economy and Finance;* b. 11 Aug. 1934, Kratie Prov.; m. Lay Neari; one s. one d. *Education:* Charles Stuart Univ., Australia. *Career:* naval architect, marine engineer and nuclear engineer; fmr Gov. Bank of Cambodia; elected mem. of Parl.; currently Sr Minister, Minister of the Economy and Finance and Sr Minister in charge of Rehabilitation and Devt; Coordinator Working Group for Govt Pvt. Sector Forum; Vice Chair. Council for the Devt of Cambodia; Vice-Chair. Cambodian Inst. for Cooperation and Peace, Phnom-Penh; Commdr Légion d'honneur, Grand Cross Order of Sowathara (Cambodia), Grand Cross Order of Kingdom of Cambodia. *Publications:* Cambodia's Economic Development: Policies, Strategies and Implementation 1999.
Address: Ministry of the Economy and Finance, 60 rue 92, Phnom-Penh, Cambodia (office). *Telephone:* (23) 723164 (office). *Fax:* (23) 723164 (office). *E-mail:* mef@mef.gov.kh (office). *Website:* www.mef.gov.kh (office).

KEBEDE, Berhanu, MA; Ethiopian diplomatist; *Ambassador to UK;* b. 11 April 1956, Addis Ababa; m. Senait Zeleke; three c. *Education:* Haileselassie I Secondary School, Addis Ababa Univ., Free Univ. of Brussels, Belgium. *Career:* joined Ministry of Foreign Affairs as Ethiopia/EEC Relations Desk Officer 1978–83, Economist, Diplomatic Mission in Brussels 1983–92, Counsellor and Head of Western European Div., Ministry of Foreign Affairs 1992–93, Acting Dir-Gen. for Int. Org. and Econ. Cooperation 1993, Dir-Gen. 1993–2000, Chargé d'affaires a.i., Embassy in Moscow with rank of Amb. 2000–02, Amb. to Sweden (also accred to Norway, Denmark, Finland and Iceland) 2002–06, to UK 2006–; fmr mem. EU/Ethiopia Relations Ministerial Conf., Nat. Cttee on WTO Membership of Ethiopia Cttee Established to Study the Impact of the Free Trade Area Under COMESA on the Ethiopian Economy.
Address: Embassy of Ethiopia, 17 Prince's Gate, London, SW7 1PZ, England (office). *Telephone:* (20) 7838-3887 (office). *Fax:* (20) 7584-7054 (office). *E-mail:* ambassador@ethioembassy.org.uk (office). *Website:* www.ethioembassy.org.uk (office).

KECHICHE, Muhammad Rachid; Tunisian politician; *Minister of Finance; Career:* fmr Sec.-Gen. of the Govt; Minister of Finance 2004–.
Address: Ministry of Finance, place du Gouvernement, 1008 Tunis, Tunisia (office). *Telephone:* (71) 571-888 (office). *Fax:* (71) 963-959 (office). *E-mail:* mfi@ministeres.tn (office).

KEDAH, HRH The Sultan of; Tuanku Haji Abdul Halim Mu'adzam Shah ibni al-Marhum Sultan Badlishah, DK, DKH, DKM, DMN, DUK, DK (Kelantan), DK (Pahang), DK (Selangor), DK (Perlis), DK (Johore), DK (Trengganu), DP (Sarawak), SPMK, SSDK, DHMS; Malaysian; *Timbalan Yang di-Pertuan Agong (Deputy Supreme Head of State)*b. 28 Nov. 1927, Alor Setar; m. Tuanku Bahiyah binti Al-Marhum Tuanku Abdul Rahman, d. of 1st Yang di Pertuan Agong of Malaya, 1956; three d. *Education:* Sultan Abdul Hamid Coll., Alor Setar and Wadham Coll., Oxford. *Career:* Raja Muda (Heir to Throne of Kedah) 1949, Regent of Kedah 1957, Sultan 1958–; Timbalan Yang di Pertuan Agong (Deputy Head of State of Malaysia) 1965–70, Yang di Pertuan Agong (Head of State) 1970–75; Col Commdt Malaysian Reconnaissance Corps 1966; Col-in-Chief of Royal Malay Regiment 1975; Timbalan Yang di-Pertuan Agong (Deputy Supreme Head of State) 2006–; Kt St J. First Class Order of the Rising Sun (Japan) 1970, Bintang Maha Putera, Klas Satu (Indonesia) 1970, Kt Grand Cross of the Bath (UK) 1972, Most Auspicious Order of the Rajamithrathorn (Thailand) 1973.
Address: Istana Anak Bukit, Alor Setar, Kedah, Darul Aman, Malaysia.

KEDDAFI, Col Mu'ammar al- (see Gaddafi, Col Mu'ammar al-).

KEEFE, Denis Edward Peter Paul; British diplomatist; *Ambassador to Georgia;* m. Kate Keefe; three s. three d. *Career:* with Southern European Dept, FCO 1982–83, Second Sec., Prague 1984–88, First Sec., EC Dept, FCO 1988–90, Desk Officer (Germany), Western European Dept 1990–91, European Corresp., Common Foreign and Security Policy Dept 1991–92, Head of Political Section, Nairobi 1992–95, Deputy Head of S Asia Dept, FCO 1996–97, Counsellor and Head of Asia-Europe Meeting Unit 1997–98, Deputy Head of Mission, Prague 1998–2002, Team Leader, Counter-Terrorism Strategy, Cabinet Office 2002–03, Head of China Hong Kong Dept, FCO 2003–04, Head of Far East Group 2004–06, Amb. to Georgia 2007–.
Address: British Embassy, Sheraton Metechi Palace Hotel, 380003 Tbilisi, Georgia (office). *Telephone:* (32) 955-497 (office). *Fax:* (32) 001-065 (office). *E-mail:* british.embassy@caucasus.net (office). *Website:* www.britishembassy.gov.uk/georgia (office).

KEELY, Charles, PhD; American demographer and academic; *Donald G. Hertzberg Professor Emeritus of International Migration, Georgetown University;* b. 17 April 1942, Brooklyn, NY; m. 1967; one s. one d. *Education:* Fordham Univ. *Career:* Sr Assoc., Center for Policy Studies, Population Council, New York 1977–87, directed two research programs on fertility and health status in developing world funded by USAID; Donald G. Hertzberg Prof. of Int. Migration and Prof. of Demography, Walsh School of Foreign Service, Georgetown Univ. 1987–2005, Prof. Emer. 2005–; Fellow, Inst. of the Study of Int., Migration; Ed. International Migration (policy journal); fmr Sr Visiting Fellow and Lecturer, Queen Elizabeth House, Univ. of Oxford; fmr Visiting Researcher, Econs Dept, Royal Scientific Soc. of Jordan; served on Cttee on Population and Jt Cttee on Contraceptive Devt, NAS, working groups of Council on Foreign Relations; consultant to agencies of US Govt, UN, Center for Strategic and Int. Studies (CSIS); Fulbright Scholar, Philippines 1962; Nat. Assoc., NAS 2001. *Publications:* nine books including Global Refugee Policy: The Case for a Development Approach 1982, Forced Migration and Mortality (co-Ed.) 1999; over 50 research articles on migration, int. refugee policy, US immigration policy and security.
Address: Edmund A. Walsh School of Foreign Service, Georgetown University, 301 InterCultural Center, 37th and O Streets, NW, Washington, DC 20057, USA (office); 7706 San Gabriel Street, Raleigh NC 27613-1493 (home). *Telephone:* (919) 792-0276 (office). *E-mail:* keelyc@georgetown.edu (office). *Website:* www.georgetown.edu (office).

KEITA, Ibrahima Boubacar; Malian politician; *President, National Assembly; Career:* Minister of Foreign Affairs 1993–94; Prime Minister of Mali 1994–2000; fmr Chair. of External Relations, Alliance pour la démocratie au Mali (ADEMA); Leader, Rassemblement pour le Mali 2001–, presidential cand. 2002; currently Pres. Nat. Ass.
Address: Assemblée nationale, BP 284, Bamako, Mali (office). *Telephone:* 221-57-24 (office). *Fax:* 221-03-74 (office). *E-mail:* mamou@blonba.malinet.ml (office). *Website:* www.animali.org (office).

KEÏTA, Lansana; Guinean philosopher, academic and diplomatist; *Ambassador to UK;* m. Aminata Keïta. *Career:* fmr Assoc. Prof. of Africana Studies; taught philosophy at Fourah Bay Coll., Sierra Leone; Amb. to UK 2005–; editorial consultant, Quest (journal). *Publications:* Science, Ration-

ality, and Neoclassical Economics, The Human Project and the Temptations of Science; numerous articles in int. philosophy journals, including Philosophy of the Social Sciences, The British Journal for the Philosophy of Science, Metaphilosophy, Quest, and Praxis International, on philosophy of science, philosophy of econs, contemporary African thought, and the sociology of knowledge.
Address: Embassy of Guinea, 48 Onslow Gardens, London, SW7 3PY, England (office). *Telephone:* (20) 7594-4819 (office). *Fax:* (20) 7594-4819 (office). *E-mail:* ambaguineeuk@yahoo.co.uk (office).

KEITA, Modibo, DScS; Malian academic, psychologist and adviser on development issues; *Managing Director, Cabinet d'Etudes Keita-Kala Saba;* b. 13 Jan. 1953, Bamako; m.; three s. *Education:* Tübingen Univ., Germany. *Career:* Prof. of Higher Educ., École normale supérieure de Bamako 1984–86; f. Cabinet d'Etudes pour l'Education et le Développement (CED) 1987 (renamed Cabinet d'Etudes Keita-Kala Saba—CEK-Kala Saba 1997–); Dir Boutique de Gestion, d'Echanges et de Conseils – Promotion de l'Artisanat 1993–94; Co-ordinator of Urban Waste Expertise Programme in W Africa 1996–, Making Decentralization Work/Mali 2001. *Publications:* numerous articles in magazines.
Address: Cek-Kala Saba, BP 9014, Bamako (office); 868 Rue Faladié Sema, Porte 66, Bamako, Mali (home). *Telephone:* 220-94-12 (office); 220-12-60 (home). *Fax:* 220-94-13 (office). *E-mail:* cek@afribone.net.ml (office); mokesn@yahoo.fr (home). *Website:* www.cek.com.ml (office).

KEITH, James R., BA; American diplomatist; *Ambassador to Malaysia;* b. Roanoke, Va; m. Jan Carter; six c. *Education:* Coll. of William and Mary, Williamsburg, Va. *Career:* grew up in Tokyo, Jakarta, Hong Kong and Taipei; career mem. Sr Foreign Service, joined Foreign Service 1980, numerous tours of duty in Washington, DC working on Asian Affairs, has also served at Embassies in Beijing, Jakarta and Seoul; mem. Nat. Security Council under Pres. Bush, Sr in early 1990s and Pres. Clinton in late 1990s, Dir Office of Chinese Affairs, Dept of State –2002, Consul Gen. Hong Kong 2002–05, Deputy Asst Sec. of State for China, Mongolia, Taiwan, Hong Kong and Macau, Dept of State 2005–06, Deputy Coordinator Avian Influenza Action Group 2006–07; Amb. to Malaysia 2007–.
Address: US Embassy, PO Box 10035, 376 Jalan Tun Razak, 50400 Kuala Lumpur, Malaysia (office). *Telephone:* (3) 21685000 (office). *Fax:* (3) 21422207 (office). *E-mail:* lrckl@po.jaring.my (office); klconsular@state.gov (office). *Website:* malaysia.usembassy.gov (office).

KEITH, Rt Hon. Sir Kenneth James, KBE, PC, LLB, LLM, QC; New Zealand judge; *Judge, International Court of Justice;* b. 19 Nov. 1937; m. Jocelyn Margaret Buckett 1961; two s. two d. *Education:* Auckland Grammar School, Univ. of Auckland, Victoria Univ. of Wellington, Harvard Law School. *Career:* with Dept of External Affairs, Wellington 1960–62; with Law Faculty, Vic. Univ. 1962–64, 1966–91, Prof. 1973–91, Dean 1977–81; UN Secr. Office of Legal Affairs 1968–70; with NZ Inst. of Int. Affairs 1971–73; Judge, Courts of Appeal of Samoa 1982–, Cook Islands 1982–, Niue 1995–, NZ 1996–2003; Judge, Supreme Court of Fiji 2003–05, Supreme Court of NZ 2004–05, Int. Court of Justice 2006–; mem. NZ Law Comm. 1986–91, Pres. 1991–96; mem. NZ Nat. Group of Perm. Court of Arbitration 1985–, panel of arbitrators, Int. Centre for Settlement of Investment Disputes 1994–, Inst. of Int. Law 2003–; Pres. NZ Inst. of Int. Affairs 2000–; Commemoration Medal 1990; Hon. LLD (Auckland) 2001, (Victoria) 2004. *Publications:* Advisory Jurisdiction of the International Court 1971, Essays on Human Rights (ed.) 1968; numerous Law Comm. publs and papers on constitutional and int. law in legal journals.
Address: International Court of Justice, Peace Palace, 2517 KJ, The Hague, Netherlands (office); 11 Salamanca Road, Kelburn, Wellington, New Zealand (home). *Telephone:* (70) 3022323 (office); (4) 472-6664 (home). *Fax:* (70) 3649928 (office); (4) 472-6664 (home). *E-mail:* k.keith@icj-cij.org (office). *Website:* www.icj-cij.org (office).

KEKE, Kieren Aedogan, MD; Nauruan physician and politician; *Minister of Foreign Affairs and Trade, Transport and Telecommunications;* b. 1971, Yaren. *Career:* fmr Parl. Speaker; mem. Naoero Amo (Nauru First) party; Minister of Health and Transport –2007 (resgnd), led breakaway opposition faction following vote of no-confidence in Prime Minister Nov. 2007, Minister of Foreign Affairs and Trade, Transport and Telecommunications Nov. 2007–; fmr Pres. Nat. Youth Council for Nauru.
Address: Ministry of Foreign Affairs and Trade, Yaren, Nauru (office). *Website:* www.naoeroamo.com (office).

KEKEDO, Jean Lucilla, OBE; Papua New Guinea diplomatist; *High Commissioner to UK. Education:* Univ. of South Australia. *Career:* Man. Dir Nat. Forest Authority 1992–95; High Commr to UK (also accred to Israel, Egypt and Zimbabwe) 2002–.
Address: 3rd Floor, 14 Waterloo Place, London, SW1R 4AR, England (office). *Telephone:* (20) 7930-0922 (office). *Fax:* (20) 7930-0828 (office).

E-mail: info@png.org.uk (office); kunduldnhc@btconnect.com (office). *Website:* www.pnghighcomm.org.uk (office).

KELANTAN, HRH The Sultan of; Tuanku Ismail Petra ibni al-Marhum Sultan Yahaya Petra; Malaysian. *Career:* mem. The Conf. of Rulers, Malaysia; Sultan of Kelantan 1979–. *Website:* www.kelantan.gov.my.

KELCHE, Gen. Jean-Pierre; French army officer; *Le Grand Chancelier de la Légion d'honneur;* b. 19 Jan. 1942, Macon; m.; two c. *Education:* Mil. Acad., Saint Cyr. *Career:* served in Côte d'Ivoire, then Djibouti 1971–73, Jr Staff Course, Staff Coll., then with French Caribbean and Guiana Territorial Command 1979–81; Commdr 5th Combined Bn, Djibouti 1985–87; Staff Officer, Doctrine and Devt Div., rank of Brig.-Gen. 1991; Deputy Commdr 5th Armoured Div., Landau, Germany 1991; Chief Plans, Programmes and Evaluation Div., Gen. Staff 1992–95; Chief of Prime Minister's Mil. Cabinet 1995–96; Vice-Chief of Defence Staff 1996–98, Chief of Defence Staff, rank of Gen. 1998–2002; Le Grand Chancelier de la Légion d'honneur 2004–; Commdr, Légion d'honneur, Officier, Ordre nat. du Mérite.
Address: c/o Le Musée national de la Légion d'honneur, 2, rue de la Légion d'honneur, 75007 Paris; Palais de Salm, 64 rue de Lille, Paris, France (office). *Website:* www.legiondhonneur.fr.

KELLENBERGER, Jakob, DPhil; Swiss diplomatist and international organization official; *President, International Committee of the Red Cross;* b. 19 Oct. 1944, Heiden; m. Elisabeth Kellenberger-Jossi 1973; two d. *Education:* Univ. of Zürich, with stays at Univs of Tours, Granada. *Career:* joined Swiss diplomatic service 1974, diplomatic postings in Madrid, Brussels and London; Head of Office in Charge of European Integration, Berne 1984–92, Minister 1984, Amb. 1988, State Sec. Fed. Dept of Foreign Affairs 1992–99; Pres. Int. Cttee of the Red Cross and Red Crescent (ICRC) 2000–; Dr hc (Basle Univ.) 2003.
Address: International Committee of the Red Cross and Red Crescent, 19 avenue de la Paix, 1202 Geneva, Switzerland (office). *Telephone:* (22) 7302246 (office). *Fax:* (22) 7349057 (office). *Website:* www.icrc.org (office).

KELLY, Craig A., PhD; American diplomatist; *Principal Deputy Assistant Secretary, Bureau of Western Hemisphere Affairs;* m. Kimberly Fitzgerald Kelly; one s. one d. *Education:* UCLA, Ecole Nationale d'Admin, Paris, Nat. War Coll., Washington, DC. *Career:* career mem. Sr Foreign Service, with rank of Minister-Counselor, overseas postings include Bogotá, Rome and Paris, Washington postings include Western Hemisphere and European Bureaus and Nat. Security Council, served as Exec. Asst to Under-Sec. of State for Political Affairs 1999–2001, to Sec. of State Colin Powell 2001–04, Amb. to Chile 2004–07, Prin. Deputy Asst Sec., Bureau of Western Hemisphere Affairs, State Dept 2007–; Fulbright Scholar in Italy.
Address: US Department of State, 2201 C Street NW, Washington, DC 20520, USA (office). *Telephone:* (202) 647-4000 (office). *Fax:* (202) 647-6738 (office). *Website:* www.state.gov (office).

KELLY, Iain Charles MacDonald; British diplomatist; *Ambassador to Uzbekistan;* m. Linda Kelly; two s. *Career:* Desk Officer, Caribbean Dept, FCO 1974–76, Third Sec., Moscow 1976–79, Third Sec., Kuala Lumpur 1979–82, Desk Officer, East European and Soviet Dept, FCO 1982–85, Consul, Istanbul 1986–88, Desk Officer, N and S Korea, FCO 1988–90, Consul, Los Angeles 1990–92, Head of Commercial Dept, Moscow 1992–95, Head of Post, Consulate Gen., Amsterdam 1996–98; Amb. to Belarus 1999–2003; Deputy Head of Whitehall Liaison Dept, FCO 2003–07; Amb. to Uzbekistan 2007–.
Address: British Embassy, ul. Ya. G'ulomov ko'ch. 67, Tashkent 700000, Uzbekistan (office). *Telephone:* (71) 120-78-52 (office). *Fax:* (71) 120-65-49 (office). *E-mail:* brit@emb.uz (office). *Website:* www.britain.uz (office).

KELLY, John Hubert, BA; American diplomatist; *Ambassador-in-Residence, Center for International Strategy, Technology and Policy, Sam Nunn School of International Affairs, Georgia Institute of Technology;* b. 20 July 1939, Fond du Lac, Wis.; m. Helena Marita Ajo; one s. one d. *Education:* Emory Univ., Atlanta. *Career:* Second Sec. US Embassy, Ankara 1966–67; American Consul, Songkhla, Thailand 1969–71; First Sec. US Embassy, Paris 1976–80; Deputy Exec. Sec., Dept of State, Washington DC 1980–81, Sr Deputy Asst Sec. of State for Public Affairs 1982–83, Prin. Deputy Asst Sec. of State for European Affairs 1983–85; Amb. to Lebanon 1986–88, to Finland 1991–94; Prin. Deputy Dir of Policy Planning Staff 1988–89; Asst Sec. for Near Eastern and SE Asian Affairs 1989–93; Man. Dir Int. Equity Partners, Atlanta 1995–98; Pres. John Kelly Consulting Inc. 1999–; Dir Finnish-American Chamber of Commerce 1998, American Int. Petroleum Co. 1999; Trustee, Lebanese American Univ. 1997; Amb.-in-Residence, Sam Nunn School for Int. Affairs, Georgia Inst. of Tech. 1999–; mem. Council on Foreign Relations, American-Turkish Council, Middle East Inst., Southern Center for Int. Studies.
Address: Sam Nunn School of International Affairs, Georgia Tech, 781 Marietta Street, NW, Atlanta, GA 30332-1610; John Kelly Consulting, Inc., 1808 Over Lake Drive SE, Suite D, Conyers, GA 30013, USA (office). *Telephone:* (770) 918-9957 (office). *Fax:* (770) 483-3090 (office). *Website:* www.cistp.gatech.edu.

KEMAKEZA, Sir Allan; Solomon Islands politician; b. 1951, Panueli village, Central Prov. *Career:* joined Royal Solomon Islands Police Force 1972, apptd Asst Superintendent 1988; Minister for Housing and Govt Service, Solomon Islands 1989–1993; Minister for Forests, Environment and Conservation 1995–96; Deputy Prime Minister for Peace and Nat. Reconciliation; Prime Minister 2001–06 (resgnd).
Address: c/o Office of the Prime Minister, POB G1, Honiara, Solomon Islands (office).

KEMISH, Ian Ferguson, AM, BA; Australian diplomatist; *Ambassador to Germany;* b. Pearce, ACT; m.; two d. *Education:* Univ. of Queensland. *Career:* served in various positions at Dept of Foreign Affairs and Trade including Exec. Officer, Philippines, Thailand and Burma Section 1992–94, Exec. Officer, UN Political and Commonwealth Section 1994–95, Dir ASEAN, Regional Issues and Burma Section 1998–99, Dir Corp. Planning Section 1999–2000, Asst Sec., Consular Branch 2000–02, First Asst Sec., Public Diplomacy, Consular and Passports Div. 2002–04, First Asst Sec., South and South-East Asia Div. 2004; served abroad as Third Sec. (later First Sec.), High Comm. in Bandar Seri Begawan 1990–92, Counsellor and Deputy Head of Mission, Embassy in Vienna 1995–98; First Asst Sec., Int. Div., Dept of Prime Minister and Cabinet 2004–06; Amb. to Germany (also accred to Switzerland and Liechtenstein) 2006–.
Address: Embassy of Australia, Wallstraße 76-79, 10179 Berlin, Germany (office). *Telephone:* (30) 8800880 (office). *Fax:* (30) 880088210 (office). *E-mail:* Info.berlin@dfat.gov.au (office). *Website:* www.germany.embassy .gov.au (office).

KENDECK MANDENG, André E.; Cameroonian diplomatist; m. Esther Olga Kendeck Mandeng. *Career:* fmr Tech. Adviser to Presidency; fmr Deputy High Commr to Nigeria, currently High Commr.
Address: High Commission of Cameroon, 5 Elsie Femi Pearse Street, Victoria Island, PMB 2476, Lagos, Nigeria (office). *Telephone:* (1) 2612226 (office). *Fax:* (1) 7747510 (office).

KENNEDY, Rt Hon. Sir Paul (Joseph Morrow), PC, MA, LLB; British judge (retd); b. 12 June 1935, Sheffield; m. Virginia Devlin 1965; two s. two d. *Education:* Ampleforth Coll., York, Gonville & Caius Coll., Cambridge. *Career:* called to Bar Gray's Inn 1960, Bencher 1982, Treas. 2002; Recorder of Crown Court 1972–83; QC 1973; Judge, High Court of Justice, Queen's Bench Div. (QBD) 1983–92, Vice-Pres. QBD 1997–2002; Presiding Judge, NE Circuit 1985–89; Lord Justice of Appeal 1992–2005 (retd); Chair. Criminal Cttee Judicial Studies Bd 1993–96; mem. Sentencing Guidelines Council –2005, Court of Appeal of Gibraltar 2006–, Interception of Communications Comm. 2006–; Hon. Fellow, Gonville & Caius Coll. Cambridge 1998; Hon. LLD (Sheffield) 2000.
Address: c/o Court of Appeal Civil Division, The Royal Courts of Justice, Strand, London, WC2A 2LL, England.

KENNEDY, Paul Michael, CBE, MA, DPhil, FRHistS, FBA; British historian and academic; *J. Richardson Dilworth Professor of History and Director, International Security Studies, Yale University;* b. 17 June 1945, Wallsend; m. 1st Catherine Urwin 1967 (died 1998); three s.; m. 2nd Cynthia Farrar 2001. *Education:* St Cuthbert's Grammar School, Newcastle-upon-Tyne, Univ. of Newcastle and Oxford Univ. *Career:* Research Asst to Sir Basil Liddell Hart 1966–70; Lecturer, Reader and Prof., Univ. of E Anglia 1970–83; J. Richardson Dilworth Prof. of History, Yale Univ. 1983–, Dir Int. Security Studies 1988–; Visiting Fellow, Inst. for Advanced Study, Princeton 1978–79; Fellow, Alexander von Humboldt Foundation, American Philosophical Soc., American Acad. of Arts and Sciences; Hon. DHL (New Haven, Alfred, Long Island, Connecticut); Hon. DLitt (Newcastle, East Anglia); Hon. LLD (Ohio); Hon. MA (Yale, Union, Quinnipiac); Dr hc (Leuven). *Publications:* The Samoan Tangle 1974, The Rise and Fall of British Naval Mastery 1976, The Rise of the Anglo-German Antagonism 1980, The Realities Behind Diplomacy 1981, Strategy and Diplomacy 1983, The Rise and Fall of the Great Powers 1988, Grand Strategy in War and Peace 1991, Preparing for the Twenty-First Century 1993, Pivotal States: A New Framework for US Policy in the Developing World (ed.) 1998, The Parliament of Man: The United Nations and the Quest for World Government 2006.
Address: Department of History, Yale Univ., PO Box 208353, New Haven, CT 06520-8353, USA (office). *Telephone:* (203) 432-6242 (office). *Fax:* (203) 432-6250 (office). *E-mail:* paul.kennedy@yale.edu (office). *Website:* www .yale.edu/iss (office).

KENNEDY, Thomas John; British diplomatist; *Ambassador to Costa Rica;* b. 3 Feb. 1957; m. Clare Marie Kennedy; one s. *Career:* Marketing and Training Man., Bata Shoe Co., UK and E Africa 1982–91; Desk Officer, Southern European Dept, FCO 1992–93, Second Sec. (Press and Public Diplomacy), Buenos Aires 1994–97, Head of Levant Section, Near East and N Africa Dept, FCO 1997–99, Head of WMD (Weapons of Mass Destruction) Export Controls Section, Non-Proliferation Dept 1999–2001, Consul-Gen., Bordeaux 2002–06, Amb. to Costa Rica 2006–.
Address: British Embassy, Edif. Centro Colón, 11°, Apdo 815, 1007 San José, Costa Rica (office). *Telephone:* 2258-2025 (office). *Fax:* 2233-9938 (office). *E-mail:* britemb@racsa.co.cr (office). *Website:* www .britishembassycr.com (office).

KENNEY, Kristie A., BA, MA; American diplomatist; *Ambassador to the Philippines;* b. Washington, DC; m. William R. Brownfield. *Education:* Clemson Univ., Tulane Univ., Nat. War Coll., Washington, DC. *Career:* worked as page in US Senate, as tour guide in Capitol Bldg and as intern in US House of Reps; staff mem. Senate Human Resources Cttee; now career mem. Sr Foreign Service, overseas postings have included Econ. Counselor, US Mission to Int. Orgs, Geneva, Econ. Officer, Embassy in Buenos Aires, Consular Officer, Embassy in Kingston, Jamaica, Washington assignments have included Dir State Dept Operations Center, mem. Nat. Security Council staff, White House, and Political-Mil. Officer, Office of NATO Affairs, Exec. Sec. of State Dept (first woman) 1998–2001, Sr Advisor to Asst Sec. for Int. Narcotics and Law Enforcement 2001–02, Amb. to Ecuador 2002–05, to the Philippines 2006–; State Dept's Distinguished Honor Award, Arnold Raphel Award for leadership, motivation, and mentoring, several Superior Honor Awards.
Address: Embassy of the USA, 1201 Roxas Boulevard, 1000 Metro Manila, The Philippines (office). *Telephone:* (2) 5286300 (office). *Fax:* (2) 5223242 (office). *E-mail:* manila1@pd.state.gov (office). *Website:* manila.usembassy .gov (office).

KENT, Mark Andrew Geoffrey; British diplomatist; *Ambassador to Viet Nam;* m. Martine Delogne; one s. one d. *Career:* with Near East and N Africa Dept, FCO 1987–89, Third, later Second Sec., Brasilia 1989–93, First Sec. (External Relations), UK Perm. Representation to EU, Brussels 1993–98, News Dept, FCO 1998–2000, First Sec., later Consul Gen. and Commercial Counsellor, Mexico City 2000–04, secondment as Int. Affairs Advisor to Supreme Allied Commdr Europe, SHAPE, Brussels 2004–05, Head of Migration Group, FCO 2005–; Amb. to Viet Nam 2007–.
Address: British Embassy, Central Building, 4th–5th Floor, 31 Hai Ba Trung, Hanoi, Viet Nam (office). *Telephone:* (4) 936-0500 (office). *Fax:* (4) 936-0561 (office). *E-mail:* behanoi@hn.vnn.vn (office). *Website:* www.uk -vietnam.org (office).

KEOHANE, Robert Owen, BA, MA, PhD; American political scientist and academic; *Professor of International Affairs, Woodrow Wilson School, Princeton University;* b. 3 Oct. 1941, Chicago, Ill.; m. Nannerl Overholser 1970; three s. one d. *Education:* Shimer Coll., Illinois, Harvard Univ. *Career:* Fellow, Harvard Univ., Woodrow Wilson School of Public and Int. Affairs, Princeton Univ. 1961–62; mem. Woodrow Wilson Award Cttee 1982, Chair. Nominating Cttee 1990–91, Chair. Minority Identification Project 1990–92; Instructor, then Assoc. Prof., Swathmore Coll. 1965–73; Assoc. Prof., then Prof., Stanford Univ. 1973–81; Ed. Int. Org. 1974–80, mem. Bd Eds 1968–77, 1982–88, 1992–97, 1998–, Chair. 1986–87; Prof., Brandeis Univ. 1981–85; Pres. Int. Studies Asscn 1988–89, Chair. Nominations Cttee 1985; Prof., then Stanfield Prof. of Int. Peace, Harvard Univ. 1985–96, Chair. Dept of Govt 1988–92; James B. Duke Prof. of Political Science, Duke Univ. –2004; Prof. of Int. Affairs, Woodrow Wilson School, Princeton Univ. 2004–; Sherill Lecturer, Yale Univ. Law School 1996; Pres. American Political Science Asscn 1999–2000; mem. NAS 2005; Fellow, American Acad. of Arts and Sciences 1983–, Center for Advanced Study in Behavioral Sciences 1977–78, 1987–88, 2004–05; Frank Kenan Fellow, Nat. Endowment for the Humanities 1995–96; Bell Research Fellow, German Marshall Fund 1977–78; Fellow, Council on Foreign Relations 1967–69, Guggenheim Foundation 1992–93, Sr Foreign Policy Fellow, Social Science Research Council 1986–88; Bellagio Resident Fellow 1993; Hon. PhD (Univ. of Århus, Denmark) 1988; Grawemeyer Award for Ideas Improving World Order 1989, First Mentorship Award, Soc. for Women in Int. Political Economy 1997, Skytte Prize, Johan Skytte Foundation, Uppsala, Sweden 2005. *Publications include:* After Hegemony: Cooperation and Discord in the World Political Economy 1984, Neorealism and Its Critics 1986, International Institutions and State Power: Essays in International Relations Theory 1989; (as co-author): Power and Interdependence: World Politics in Transition 1977, Institutions for the Earth: Sources of Effective International Environmental Protection 1993, After the Cold War: State Strategies and International Institutions in Europe, 1989–91 1993, Designing Social Inquiry: Scientific Inference in Qualitative Research 1994; (as co-ed.): Transnational Relations and World

Politics 1972, The New European Community: Decision-Making and Institutional Change 1991, Ideas and Foreign Policy 1993, From Local Commons to Global Interdependence 1994, Institutions for Environmental Aid: Pitfalls and Promises 1996, Internationalization and Domestic Politics 1996, Imperfect Unions: Security Institutions Across Time and Space 1999, Exploration and Contestation in the Study of World Politics 1998, Legalization and World Politics 2000.
Address: Woodrow Wilson School, 408 Robertson Hall, Princeton University, Princeton, NJ 08544-1013, USAUSA (office). *Telephone:* (609) 258-1856 (office). *Fax:* (609) 258-0019 (office). *E-mail:* rkeohane@ princeton.edu (office). *Website:* www.wws.princeton.edu/rkeohane (office).

KÉRÉKOU, Brig.-Gen. Mathieu (Ahmed); Benin politician and army officer; b. 2 Sept. 1933, Natitingou. *Education:* Saint-Raphael Mil. School, France. *Career:* served French Army until 1961; joined Dahomey Army 1961; Aide-de-camp to Pres. Maga 1961–63; took part in mil. coup d'état which removed Pres. Christophe Soglo 1967; Chair. Mil. Revolutionary Council 1967–68; continued studies at French mil. schools 1968–70; Commdr Ouidah Paratroop Unit and Deputy Chief of Staff 1970–72; leader of the mil. coup d'état which ousted Pres. Ahomadegbe Oct. 1972; Pres. and Head of Mil. Revolutionary Govt, Minister of Nat. Defence 1972–91, fmr Minister of Planning, of Co-ordination of Foreign Aid, Information and Nat. Orientation; Pres. of Benin 1996–2006; Chair. Cen. Cttee Parti de la révolution populaire du Bénin.
Address: c/o Présidence de la république, PO Box 1288, Cotonou, Benin.

KERGIN, Michael Frederick, BA, MA (Econs); Canadian government official, academic and fmr diplomatist; *Premier of Ontario's Special Advisor on Border Issues;* b. Canadian Mil. Hosp., Bramshott, England; m. Margarita Fuentes Kergin; three s. *Education:* Univ. of Toronto, Magdalen Coll. Oxford, UK. *Career:* joined Dept of Foreign Affairs and Int. Trade (fmrly Dept. of External Affairs) as Foreign Services Officer 1967, positions include Sr Dept Asst to Sec. of State for External Affairs 1984–86, Asst Deputy Minister responsible for Political and Int. Security Affairs 1994–96, and for the Americas and Security and Intelligence Affairs 1996–98; Amb. to Cuba 1986–89, to USA 2000–05; Premier of Ont. Special Advisor on Border Issues 2005–; currently Adjunct Prof., Faculty of Political Studies, Univ. of Ottawa, also Sr Fellow, Grad. School of Public and Int. Affairs; Visiting Scholar, Western Michigan Univ., Kalamazoo 2006–07; Foreign Policy Adviser to the Prime Minister and Asst Sec. to the Cabinet for Foreign and Defence Policy 1998–2000; mem. Del. to Inter-American Devt Bank; fmr Embassy Minister, Washington, DC, USA, Santiago, Chile and Yaoundé, Cameroon; fmr Deputy Head of Mission to UN, New York.
Address: 55, Laurier Avenue East, Desmarais Building, Room 11129a, University of Ottawa, Ottawa, ON K1N 6N5; c/o Office of the Premier, Legislative Building, Queen's Park, Toronto, ON M7A 1A1, Canada (office). *Telephone:* (613) 562-5800, ext. 4691 (Ottawa) (office). *Fax:* (613) 562-5241 (Ottawa). *E-mail:* Michael.Kergin@uOttawa.ca. *Website:* www .premier.gov.on.ca (office); www.governance.uottawa.ca/api/eng/ word_director.asp.

KERIM, Tijani Ould Mohamed El-, MA; Mauritanian diplomatist; b. 31 Dec. 1951, Mederdra; m.; five c. *Education:* Univ. Pantheon-Sorbonne (Paris III), Nat. Conservatory of Arts and Crafts in Paris. *Career:* teacher, Nouakchott High School 1976–77; Dir of Studies, Atar High School 1978–79; teacher, Aïoun High School 1979–80, Nat. Pedagogy Inst. 1984–85; Chief of Project of School Printing-IPN 1985–88; Consul-Gen., Dakar, Senegal 1988–89; Insp.-Gen. of High Schools 1990–92; mem. Nat. Parl. 1992–96; Consul-Gen., Banjul, The Gambia 1996–99, Amb. to Côte d'Ivoire 1999–2002, to Canada 2002–04, to USA 2004–07 (also accred to Australia 2005–07).
Address: Ministry of Foreign Affairs and Co-operation, BP 230, Nouakchott, Mauritania (office). *Telephone:* 525-26-82 (office). *Fax:* 525-28-60 (office).

KERKAVOV, Rovshen Bairamnazarovich; Turkmenistan politician and economist; b. 1961, Ashgabat. *Education:* Novosibirsk Inst. of Electro-technology. *Career:* engineer, Turkmenpromsvyazstroi Co. 1983–84; engineer, Ashgabat GPO 1986; economist and Head of Div., Ashgabat Glavpochtamt Co. 1991–93; First Deputy Dir-Gen., then Dir-Gen. State Co. of Post Communications, Turkmenpochta 1995–97; Minister of Telecommunications Repub. of Turkmenistan 1997–2001; Deputy Chair. Cabinet of Ministers 2001; Order of Galkynysh.
Address: c/o Cabinet of Ministers, Ashgabat, Turkmenistan (office).

KERT, Lt-Gen. Johannes; Estonian army officer; b. 3 Dec. 1959, Petseri; m.; two d. *Education:* Tartu Univ., War Coll. of Penn., USA, George C. Marshall Centre, Garmish, Germany. *Career:* fmr professional photo-grapher; coach of Greco-Roman wrestling for Estonian sporting orgs 1981–83; called to service Soviet Army 1983–85; active in est. of Estonian

Defence League (Kaitseliit) 1990; Chief of Staff, then Commdr Defence League Tartu Regional Unit (Malev) 1991; Operational Commdr Defence League 1991–92, Commdr 1992–96; Commdr Kuperjanov Single Infantry Battalion 1992; Commdr Estonian Defence Forces 1996–2000; Commdr Land Forces 2001–02; Mil. Rep. to NATO, Brussels 2002–08; Advisor to Ministry of Defence 2008–; apptd Lt-Gen. 1998; Order of the Cross of the Eagle, Order of Merit of Estonian Defence Forces, Officers Union Golden Medal of Merit (Finland), Order of Merit (Latvia), Order of Merit of Kuperjanov Battalion, Order of Merit of Defence League Units.
Address: Ministry of Defence, Sakala 1, Tallinn 10141, Estonia (office). *Telephone:* 717-0022 (office). *Fax:* 717-0001 (office). *E-mail:* info@kmin.ee (office). *Website:* www.mod.gov.ee (office).

KESAVAPANY, K., BA, MA; Singaporean research institute director and diplomatist; *Director, Institute of Southeast Asian Studies;* b. Kuala Lumpur, Malaysia; m. Padmini Kesavapany; two s. *Education:* Univ. of Malaya, London Univ., UK. *Career:* joined Singaporean Foreign Service 1972, sr positions include Dir of ASEAN, Dir of Directorate II (N America and Europe), Dir of Directorate IV (Int. Orgs and Third World); Perm. Rep. to UN, Geneva 1991–97; High Commr to Malaysia 1997–2002; Dir Inst. of Southeast Asian Studies (ISEAS) 2002–; Chair. Gen. Council WTO 1995; del. to multilateral meetings of UN; Order of Independence-First Class, Govt of Jordan; Singapore Govt Public Admin medal (Gold).
Address: Institute of Southeast Asian Studies, 30 Heng Mui Keng Terrace, off Pasir Panjang Road, 119614, Singapore (office). *Telephone:* 67780955 (office). *Fax:* 67781735 (office). *E-mail:* admin@iseas.edu.sg (office). *Website:* www.iseas.edu.sg (home).

KESTERIS, Andris, MA,PhD; Latvian diplomatist; *Head of Cabinet, Commissioner, responsible for Energy, European Commission;* b. 1960. *Education:* Univ. of Latvia, Wales Univ. *Career:* fmr Amb. to Germany; fmr Head, Latvian Del. to OSCE, Vienna; fmr Under-Sec. of State for Foreign Affairs and Chief Negotiator to Latvia's Accession to EU; Perm. Rep. to EU 2003–04; Head of Cabinet of Energy Commr Piebalgs, EC 2004–; Three Star Order of Latvia, Grand Order of Merit (Germany).
Address: Office of Commissioner Andris Piebalgs, 200 rue de la Loi, 1049 Brussels, Belgium (office). *Telephone:* (2) 299-11-11 (office). *Fax:* (2) 295-01-38 (office). *E-mail:* Andris.Kesteris@ec.europa.eu (office). *Website:* ec .europa.eu/commission_barroso/piebalgs (office).

KEY, Andrew Jonathan Thomas; British diplomatist; *Ambassador to Former Yugoslav Republic of Macedonia;* m. Joanna Key; two d. *Career:* Desk Officer, Eastern Adriatic Dept and later Security Policy Dept, FCO 1992–93, full-time Mandarin language training 1993–95, Second Sec. (Econ.), Beijing 1995–99, Head of Climate Change Team, FCO 1999–2001, Bd Sec., Directorate for Strategy and Innovation 2000–03, Head of EU External Relations Group and later Head of Unit for Special Rep. for Climate Change 2003–06, full-time language training 2006, Amb. to Fmr Yugoslav Repub. of Macedonia 2007–.
Address: British Embassy, Salvador Aljende 73, 1000 Skopje, Macedonia (office). *Telephone:* (2) 3299299 (office). *Fax:* (2) 3179726 (office). *E-mail:* britishembassyskopje@fco.gov.uk (office). *Website:* www.britishembassy .gov.uk/macedonia (office).

KEZERASHVILI, Davit; Georgian politician and government official; *Minister of Defence;* b. 22 Sept. 1978, Tbilisi; m.; two s. *Education:* Ivane Javakhishvili Tbilisi State Univ. *Career:* Sr Inspector, Penitentiary Dept, Ministry of Justice April–Sept. 2001; Head, Information and Analysis Div., Dept of Informatics, Ministry of Justice 2001–02; Asst to Chair. Tbilisi City Council 2002–04; Head, Finance Police, Ministry of Finance 2004–06; Minister of Defence 2006–.
Address: Ministry of Defence, 0112 Tbilisi, Gen. Kvinitadze 20, Georgia (office). *Telephone:* (32) 91-19-63 (office). *Fax:* (32) 91-06-45 (office). *E-mail:* pr@mod.gov.ge (office). *Website:* www.mod.gov.ge (office).

KHACHATRIAN, Vardan; Armenian politician; *Minister of Finance and the Economy;* b. 6 April 1959, Jermuk City; m.; two c. *Education:* Yerevan Polytech. Inst., Moscow Supreme Tech. Univ. *Career:* engineer Mineral Waters of Armenia Industrial Union 1980–83, Yerevan Polytech. Inst. 1983–85; Sr Engineer in Tech. Div., Div. Head, then Head of Production Tech. Div., Industrial Bakery Union of Armenia 1985–90; Workshop Head in Zovk Production Unit, then Dir Zovk Factory, Food Ministry of ASSR 1990–92; mem. Privatization Cttee, Repub. of Armenia 1992–95; mem. Nat. Ass. and Deputy Head Standing Cttee for Finance, Credit, Fiscal and Econ. Affairs 1995–98, Head Standing Cttee 1999–2000; Head of Finance, Budgetary Dept, Ministry of Defence 1998–99; Minister of Finance and the Economy 2000–.
Address: Ministry of Finance and the Economy, Melik-Adamian St 1, 375010 Yerevan, Armenia (office). *Telephone:* (10) 52-70-82 (office). *Fax:* (10) 52-37-45 (office). *Website:* mfe.gov.am (office).

KHACHATRYAN, Armen; Armenian politician and philologist; b. 13 Aug. 1957, Yerevan; m. Larisa Khachatryan; one s. two d. *Education:* Yerevan State Pedagogical Inst. *Career:* Instructor, Shaumyan Regional CP Cttee and Yerevan City Comsomol Cttee 1981–87; Dir Yerevan School 191 1987–90; Founder and Vice-Pres. for Science and Educ. Yerevan Univ. of Hrachya Asharyan, Prof. 1991–99; elected Deputy and apptd Speaker, Nat. Ass. 1999–2002, also fmr Chair. Standing Cttee on Foreign Relations; Prof. and Academican, New York Acad. of Sciences; est. Barcelona restaurant 2004; Sodruzhestvo Award, Council Inter-Parl. Ass. of CIS 2001; Saint Andreas Order, Patriarch of Constantinople.
Address: c/o National Assembly, 19 M. Baghramyan Avenue, 375095 Yerevan, Armenia (office).

KHADAM, Abdul Karim; Afghan diplomatist. *Career:* currently Amb. to Turkmenistan.
Address: Embassy of Afghanistan, 744000 Aşgabat, Gerogly 14, Turkmenistan (office). *Telephone:* (12) 39-58-21 (office). *Fax:* (12) 39-58-20 (office).

KHADDAM, Abd al-Halim; Syrian lawyer and politician; *Leader, National Salvation Front in Syria;* b. 15 Sept. 1932, Baniyas. *Career:* early career as lawyer in Damascus 1954–64; Gov. of Damascus 1967–69; Minister of the Economy and Foreign Trade 1969–70; Deputy Prime Minister and Minister of Foreign Affairs 1970–84; mem. Regional Command, Baath Party 1971–84; Vice-Pres. for Political and Foreign Affairs 1984–2005 (resgnd); moved to Paris 2005; charged with treason by Syrian Parl. and expelled from Baath Party, announced govt-in-exile 2006; Founding Assembly Mem. and Leader, Nat. Salvation Front in Syria, opposition group based in Washington, DC.
E-mail: info@SaveSyria.org. *Website:* www.savesyria.org.

KHAIRUZZAMAN, Mohammad; Bangladeshi diplomatist; *High Commissioner to Malaysia;* b. 5 July 1952. *Career:* Second Lt in Armoured Corps, Pakistan 1971, promoted to rank of Maj. 1976; joined Ministry of Foreign Affairs 1976, served in various capacities in Ministry and diplomatic missions in Cairo, Abu Dhabi, London and Manila, Additional Sec. for China, Ministry of Foreign Affairs –2005, Amb. to Myanmar 2005–06, Sec., Ministry of Foreign Affairs 2006; High Commr to Malaysia 2007–.
Address: Embassy of Bangladesh, Block 1, Lorong Damai 7, Jalan Damai, 55000 Kuala Lumpur, Malaysia (office). *Telephone:* (3) 21487940 (office). *Fax:* (3) 21413381 (office). *E-mail:* bddoot@streamyx.com (office). *Website:* www.bangladesh-highcomkl.com (office).

KHAJI, Ali Asghar; Iranian diplomatist; *Special Representative to Iraq and Director, Special Office for Iraqi Affairs, Ministry of Foreign Affairs;* *Career:* Dir-Gen., Persian Gulf Dept, Ministry of Foreign Affairs –2000; Amb. to Saudi Arabia 2000–04; Special Rep. to Iraq and Dir, Special Office for Iraqi Affairs, Ministry of Foreign Affairs 2004–.
Address: Special Office for Iraqi Affairs, Ministry of Foreign Affairs, Shahid Abd al-Hamid Mesri Street, Ferdowsi Avenue, Tehran, Iran (office). *Telephone:* (21) 61151 (office). *Fax:* (21) 33212763 (office). *E-mail:* matbuat@mfa.gov.ir (office). *Website:* www.mfa.gov.ir (office).

KHALED, Mohamed Sidiya Ould Mohamed; Mauritanian politician; *Minister of Finance; Career:* Dir-Gen. of the Treasury –2004; Minister of Finance 2004–07.
Address: c/o Ministry of Finance, BP 181, Nouakchott, Mauritania (office).

KHALEEL, Ahmed; Maldivian diplomatist; *Permanent Representative, United Nations;* b. 17 March 1962; m.; one d. *Career:* Third Sec., High Comm. in Colombo, Sri Lanka 1981–83; Third Sec., Perm. Mission to UN, New York 1984–88; Sr Sec., Dept of External Resources, Ministry of Foreign Affairs 1988–90; Second Sec., Perm. Mission to UN, New York 1990–91; Deputy Dir Protocol Div., Ministry of Foreign Affairs 1992–93; First Sec., Perm. Mission to UN, New York 1994–2002, Counsellor, 2002–06, Deputy Perm. Rep. 2005–06; Minister-Counsellor, Embassy in Tokyo 2006–07; Perm. Rep. to UN, New York 2008–.
Address: Permanent Mission of the Maldives to the United Nations, 820 Second Avenue, Suite 800c, New York, NY 10017, USA (office). *Telephone:* (212) 599-6195 (office). *Fax:* (212) 661-6405 (office). *E-mail:* mdv@undp.org (office). *Website:* www.un.int/maldives (office).

KHALIFA, Sheikh Ahmad bin Khalifa al-; Bahraini diplomatist. *Career:* currently Amb. to United Arab Emirates.
Address: Embassy of Bahrain, POB 3367, Abu Dhabi, United Arab Emirates (office). *Telephone:* (2) 6657500 (office). *Fax:* (2) 6674141 (office).

KHALIFA, Sheikh Ahmed bin Mohammed al-, MBA; Bahraini economist and government official; *Minister of Finance and National Economy;* b. 1961; m.; three c. *Education:* Univ. of Texas, USA. *Career:* Sr Financial Analyst, Ministry of Commerce 1986–89; Head of Operations, Bahrain Stock

Exchange 1989–96; Dir of Econ. Planning, Ministry of Finance and Nat. Economy 1996–2001; Dir Bahrain Stock Exchange 1997–2001; Gov. Bahrain Monetary Agency 2001–05; Minister of Finance and Nat. Economy 2005–.
Address: Ministry of Finance and National Economy, POB 33, Diplomatic Area, Manama, Bahrain (office). *Telephone:* 17575777 (office). *Fax:* 17533324 (office). *E-mail:* Minister@mof.gov.bh (office). *Website:* www .mofne.gov.bh (office).

KHALIFA, HM Sheikh Hamad bin Isa al-, (King of Bahrain); b. 28 Jan. 1950, Bahrain; m. Sheikha Sabeeka bint Ibrahim al-Khalifa 1968; six s. (including HH Sheikh Salman bin Hamad al-Khalifa) four d. *Education:* Secondary School, Manama, Bahrain, Leys School, Cambridge Univ., Mons Officer Cadet School, Aldershot, England and US Army Command and Gen. Staff Coll., Fort Leavenworth, Kan., USA. *Career:* formed Bahrain Defence Force 1968, Commdr-in-Chief 1968–, also C-in-C Nat. Guard, raised Defence Air Wing 1978; mem. State Admin. Council 1970–71; Minister of Defence 1971–88; Deputy Pres. Family Council of Al-Khalifa 1974–; succeeded as Ruler on the death of his father March 1999; introduced constitutional monarchical system and assumed title of King Feb. 2002; created Historical Documents Centre 1976; Founder mem. and Pres. Bahrain High Council for Youth and Sports 1975–; initiated Al-Areen Wildlife Parks Reserve 1976; f. Salman Falcon Centre 1977, Amiri Stud, Bahrain 1977; f. Bahrain Equestrian and Horse Racing Asscn, Pres. 1977–; f. Bahrain Centre for Studies and Research 1989; hon. mem. Helicopter Club of GB; Orders of the Star of Jordan (1st Class) 1967, Al-Rafidain of Iraq (1st Class) 1968, National Defence of Kuwait (1st Class) 1970, Al-Muhammedi of Morocco (1st Class) 1970, Al-Nahdha of Jordan (1st Class) 1972, Qiladat Gumhooreeya of Egypt (1st Class) 1974, The Taj of Iran (1st Class) 1973, King Abdul-Aziz of Saudi Arabia (1st Class) 1976, Repub. of Indonesia (1st Class) 1977, Repub. of Mauritania (1st Class) 1969, El-Fateh Al-Adheem of Libya (1st Class) 1979, Kuwait Liberation 1994, Hon. KCMG (UK), Ordre nat. du Mérite de la République française (1st Class) 1980, Grand Cross of Isabel la Católica of Spain (1st Class) 1981; Freedom of the City of Kansas 1971, US Army Certificate of Honour 1972.
Address: PO Box 555, Ritala Palace, Manama, Bahrain. *Website:* www .bahrainembassy.org/rulingfam (office).

KHALIFA, Sheikh Khalid bin Ahmad al-, BSc; Bahraini diplomatist; *Minister of Foreign Affairs;* b. 4 April 1960; m. Shaikha Wesal bint Mohamed Al Khalifa. *Education:* Islamic Scientific Coll., Amman, Jordan, Univ. of Texas, USA. *Career:* served at Embassy in Washington, DC 1985–94; Chief Liaison Officer, Office of Deputy Prime Minister of Foreign Affairs 1995–2000; Amb. to UK 2001–05 (also accred to Netherlands 2002–05, to Ireland 2002–05, to Norway 2002–05, to Sweden 2003–05); Minister of Foreign Affairs 2005–; Bahrain Medal 2001.
Address: Ministry of Foreign Affairs, POB 547, Government House, Government Road, Manama, Bahrain (office). *Telephone:* 17227555 (office). *Fax:* 17212603 (office). *Website:* www.mofa.gov.bh.

KHALIFA, Sheikh Khalifa bin Sulman al-; Bahraini politician; *Prime Minister;* b. 1935. *Career:* Dir of Finance and Pres. of Electricity Bd 1961; Pres. Council of Admin 1966–70; Pres. State Council 1970–73, Prime Minister 1973–; fmr Chair. Bahrain Monetary Agency; UN Special Citation of the Habitat Scroll of Honour Award 2006.
Address: Office of the Prime Minister, PO Box 1000, Government House, Government Road, Manama, Bahrain. *Telephone:* 17253361. *Fax:* 17533033.

KHALIFA, Sheikh Mohammed bin Abdulla al-; Bahraini politician. *Career:* Minister of State for Defence Affairs 2006–.
Address: c/o Office of the Prime Minister, PO Box 1000, Government House, Government Road, Manama, Bahrain.

KHALIFA, Sheikh Muhammad bin Mubarak bin Hamad al-, BA; Bahraini government official; *Deputy Prime Minister;* b. 1935; m.; two c. *Education:* American Univ. of Beirut, Lebanon, Univ. of Oxford and Univ. of London, UK. *Career:* attended Bahrain Courts as cand. for the bench, Dir of Information 1962; Head of Political Bureau 1968 (now Dept of Foreign Affairs); State Council 1970; Minister of Foreign Affairs 1971–2005; currently Deputy Prime Minister with additional responsibilities for ministerial cttees.
Address: c/o Office of the Prime Minister, POB 1000, Government House, Government Road, Manama, Bahrain.

KHALIFA, Nasser bin Hamad bin Mubarak al-, MA; Qatari fmr diplomatist. *Education:* Western Michigan Univ., Johns Hopkins Univ., USA, City Univ., London and London School of Econs, UK. *Career:* served as Information Attaché, Embassy in Washington, DC 1977–78, First Sec., Perm. Mission to UN, New York 1978–81, Deputy Chief of Mission,

Embassy in Washington, DC 1981–86, Deputy Chief of Mission, Embassy in Paris 1986–87, Counsellor 1988–90, Head of European and American Affairs Dept, Ministry of Foreign Affairs 1990–92, Amb. to Repub. of Korea 1992–93, to Italy (also accred to Bosnia and Herzegovina and Malta) 1994–96, Head of Qatari Del. to Canada and Norway 1995–97, Perm. Rep. to UN (also accred to Canada, Cuba, Colombia, Nicaragua and Argentina) 1996–98, Amb.-at-Large, Ministry of Foreign Affairs 1998–2000, Amb. to UK (also accred to Ireland, the Netherlands, Denmark, Sweden, Norway and Iceland) –2005, Perm. Rep. to Org. for the Prohibition of Chemical Weapons and IMO 2000–05, Amb. to USA (also accred to Mexico) 2005–07 (left diplomatic service); mem. Advisory Bd Next Century Foundation; administers the $100 million Hurricane Katrina relief fund est. by the State of Qatar; fmr Fellow, Princeton Univ.; fmr Visiting Fellow, Centre for Islamic Studies, Oxford, UK.
Address: Next Century Foundation, 4 Vincent Square, Westminster, London, SW1P 2LX, England (office). *Telephone:* (20) 7821-6566 (office). *E-mail:* ncfpeace@aol.com (office). *Website:* www.ncfpeace.org (office).

KHALIFA, HH Sheikh Salman bin Hamad al-, BPA, MA; Bahraini government official; *Crown Prince and Deputy Commander in Chief, Bahrain Army;* *Education:* American Univ., Washington, DC, USA, Univ. of Cambridge, UK. *Career:* Chair. Bahrain Centre for Studies and Research 1992–95; Under-Sec. for Defence 1995–99, Crown Prince and C-in-C Bahrain Defence Force 1999–2008; Deputy C-in-C Bahrain Army 2008–; Chair. Bd of Trustees Bahrain Centre for Studies and Research 1995–99; Chair. Supreme Council of Youth and Sport; CEO Econ. Development Bd.
Address: Ministry of Defence, PO Box 245, West Rifa'a (office); Crown Prince Court, POB 29091, Bahrain (office). *Telephone:* 17662100. *Fax:* 17661200. *Website:* www.bahrainembassy.org/rulingfam (office).

KHALIFAH, Hani Mustafa; Jordanian diplomatist. *Career:* currently Amb. to Saudi Arabia.
Address: Embassy of Jordan, POB 94316, Riyadh 11693, Saudi Arabia (office). *Telephone:* (1) 488-0051 (office). *Fax:* (1) 488-0072 (office). *E-mail:* jordan.embassy@nesma.net.sa (office).

KHALIL, Muhammad el-Fadhal; Tunisian diplomatist; *Ambassador to Algeria;* b. 11 Nov. 1944, Gafsa; m.; one s., three d. *Education:* Inst. Supérieur des Etudes Agronomiques. *Career:* fmrly Minister of Social Affairs; fmr Amb. to Syria, to Austria; currently Amb. to Algeria.
Address: Embassy of Tunisia, 5 rue du Bois, Hydra, 16405 Algiers (office); 35 rue des vertes feuilles Saïd Hamdine Hydra, Algiers, Algeria (home). *Telephone:* (21) 60-13-88 (office); (21) 54-79-62 (home). *Fax:* (21) 69-23-16 (office); (21) 54-81-57 (home). *E-mail:* ambassade@ambtunisie-dz (office).

KHALILI, Abdul Karim; Afghan politician; *Second Vice-President;* *Career:* Leader Hizb-i Wahadat i Islami (Unity Party), an alliance of anti-Taliban fighters from Hazara ethnic minority, located in Bamian prov.; driven out of Cen. Afghanistan by Taliban 1998; Leader Bamian prov. 2001–; apptd Vice-Pres. Transitional Authority 2002, elected Second Vice-Pres. 2004–.
Address: c/o Office of the President, Gul Khana Palace, Presidential Palace, Kabul, Afghanistan (office). *Website:* www.president.gov.af (office).

KHALILI, Masood; Afghan diplomatist; *Ambassador to Turkey; Career:* mem. Jamiat-i-Islami, staff mem. Political Office 1980s; various positions in govt admin 1992–95; Amb. to Pakistan 1995–96, to India 1996–2005, to Turkey 2005–.
Address: Embassy of Afghanistan, Cinnah Cad. 88, 06551 Çankaya, Ankara, Turkey (office). *Telephone:* (312) 4422523 (office). *Fax:* (312) 4422269 (office).

KHALILOV, Erkin Khamdamovich, DJur, CandJur; Uzbekistan politician; b. 1955, Buxoro; m.; three s. *Education:* Tashkent State Univ. *Career:* engineer, Research-Production Unit Cybernetics 1977–79; Jr, then Sr Researcher, Head of Div. Inst. of Philosophy and Law Uzbek Acad. of Sciences, 1979–90; Deputy, then Chair. Cttee on Law, Deputy Chair. (Speaker) Supreme Soviet (Oliy Majlis) 1990–93, Acting Chair. 1993–95, Chair. 1995–1999, re-elected 2000, Speaker Qoqunchilik palatasi Kengashi (Legis. Chamber) 2005–08; Order Mehnat Shuhrati 1999. *Publications:* about 100 articles on law and politics.
Address: c/o Qoqunchilik palatasi Kengashi, Oliy Majlis, 100008 Tashkent, Xalqlar Do'stligi shoh ko'ch. 1, Uzbekistan (office). *Telephone:* (71) 139-87-07 (office); (71) 139-41-51 (office). *Website:* www.parliament.gov.uz (office).

KHALILZAD, Zalmay; American (b. Afghan) diplomatist; *Permanent Representative, United Nations;* b. 22 March 1951, Mazar-i-Sharif, Afghanistan; m. Cheryl Benard; two s. *Education:* American Univ. of Beirut, Lebanon, Univ. of Chicago. *Career:* Asst Prof. of Political Science, School of Int. and Public Affairs, Columbia Univ. 1979–85; received

Council on Foreign Relations fellowship to join US State Dept 1984, Special Advisor on Afghanistan to Undersecretary of State 1985–89, Under-Sec. of Defence for Policy Planning 1990–92; Defence Analyst Rand Corpn 1993–2000; headed Bush-Cheney transition team for Dept of Defense, also served as Counselor to Sec. of Defense, also Special Asst to Pres. and Sr Dir for Southwest Asia, Near East, and North African Affairs, Nat. Security Council 2001; Special Envoy to Kabul, Afghanistan 2002, to Iraqi Nat. Congress, Iraqi Opposition 2003; Amb. to Afghanistan 2003–05, to Iraq 2005–07; Perm. Rep. to UN, New York 2007–; King Ghazi Ammanullah Medal, Afghanistan, Defense Dept Medal for Outstanding Public Service (twice). *Publications include:* The Government of God: Iran's Islamic Republic (with Cheryl Benard) 1984, Sources of Conflict in the 21st Century: Strategic Flashpoints and US Strategy 1998, Strategic Appraisal: United States Air and Space Power in the 21st Century (with Jeremy Shapiro) 2002; numerous articles in journals and books.
Address: Permanent Mission of the United States to the UN, 799 United Nations Plaza, New York, NY USA (office). *Telephone:* (212) 415-5000 (office). *Fax:* (212) 415-4443 (office). *E-mail:* usa@un.int (office). *Website:* www.un.org/usa (office).

KHALLAF, Hany; Egyptian diplomatist. *Career:* fmr Amb. to Libya; currently serving at Ministry of Foreign Affairs, Cairo.
Address: Ministry of Foreign Affairs, Corniche en-Nil, Cairo (Maspiro), Egypt. *Telephone:* (2) 5749820. *Fax:* (2) 5748822. *E-mail:* info@mfa.gov.eg. *Website:* www.mfa.gov.eg.

KHAMA, Lt-Gen. (Seretse) Ian; Botswana politician and head of state; *President; Career:* fmr Commdr Botswana Defence Force; Minister of Presidential Affairs and Public Admin March–July 1998; elected mem. Nat. Ass. 1998; Vice-Pres. of Botswana 1998–2008, Pres. 2008–.
Address: Office of the President, Private Bag 001, Gaborone, Botswana (office). *Telephone:* 3950825 (office). *Fax:* 3950858 (office). *E-mail:* op .registry@gov.bw (office). *Website:* www.gov.bw/government/ ministry_of_state_president.html#office_of_the_president (office).

KHAMENEI, Ayatollah Sayyed Ali; Iranian politician and religious leader; *Wali Faqih (Supreme Religious Leader);* b. 17 July 1939, Mashad, Khorassan; m. 1964; four s. one d. *Education:* Qom. *Career:* studied in Islamic seminary of Najaf 1957, in Islamic seminary of Qom 1958–64, returned to Mashad 1964; joined Revolutionary Movt of Imam Khomeini 1962; imprisoned six times 1964–78, once exiled in 1978; Co-founder Islamic Republican Party 1979, Sec.-Gen. and Pres. Cen. Cttee 1980–87; Sec. of Defense, Supervisor of Islamic Revolutionary Guards, Leader of the Friday Congregational Prayer, Tehran Rep. in Consultative Ass. 1980; Imam Khomeini's Rep. in High Security Council 1981; Pres. of Iran 1981–89; mem. Revolutionary Council until its dissolution Nov. 1979; survived assassination attempt June 1981; Pres. Expedience Council 1988; Wali Faqih (Supreme Religious Leader) 1990–.
Address: Office of the Wali Faqih, Shoahada Street, Qom, Iran. *E-mail:* info@leader.ir; istiftaa@wilayah.org. *Website:* www.leader.ir.

KHAN, Aziz Ahmed; Pakistani diplomatist. *Career:* various diplomatic assignments including postings in New Delhi, Vienna, Los Angeles, Brasilia, Buenos Aires, Lisbon, Maputo; fmr Dir-Gen. Foreign Service Acad.; spokesman Foreign Ministry –2003; High Commr to India 2003–06.
Address: c/o Ministry of Foreign Affairs, Constitution Ave, Islamabad, Pakistan (office).

KHAN, Irene Zubaida; Bangladeshi international organization executive; *Secretary-General, Amnesty International;* b. 24 Dec. 1956, Dhaka; one d. *Education:* Victoria Univ. of Manchester, UK and Harvard Law School, USA. *Career:* joined Office of UNHCR 1980, adviser to local project offices, worked in Pakistan, SE Asia, UK, Ireland and numerous crisis deployments 1980–90, Sr Exec. Officer to Sadako Ogata 1991–95, Chief of Comm. in India 1995, Head of Documentation and Research Centre 1998–99, Head of Comm. in Fmr Yugoslav Repub. of Macedonia 1999, Deputy Dir Dept for Int. Legal Protection; Sec.-Gen. Amnesty Int. 2001–; Dr hc (Ferris State Univ.) 2005, (Ghent Univ.) 2007; Pilkington Woman of the Year 2002, Sydney Peace Prize 2006; Ford Foundation Fellowship.
Address: Amnesty International, 1 Easton Street, London, WC1X 0DN, England (office). *Telephone:* (20) 7413-5500 (office). *Fax:* (20) 7956-1157 (office). *E-mail:* secgen@amnesty.org (office). *Website:* www.amnesty.org (office).

KHAN, M. Morshed, BEng; Bangladeshi politician; b. 8 Aug. 1940, Chittagong; m.; one s. four d. *Education:* Tokyo Univ. of Tech. and Agric. and Sofia Univ., Japan. *Career:* fmr Alt. Gov. ILO; Founder-Chair. Arab Bangladesh Bank Ltd; Chair. Pacific Group of Industries, Pacific Bangladesh Telecom Ltd, Bangladesh Asscn of Banks; co-f. Global Foundation for Christian–Muslim Partnership; elected mem. Standing

Cttee, Int. Conf. of Asian Political Parties; Pres. Metropolitan Chamber of Commerce and Industries, Bangladesh Employers' Fed.; elected mem. of Parl. several times; Chair. Special Cttee on Foreign Affairs 1991–96; apptd Special Envoy of the Prime Minister 1996, subsequently mem. Advisory Council, Vice-Chair. Bangladesh Nationalist Party; Minister of Foreign Affairs 2001–06.
Address: c/o Ministry of Foreign Affairs, Segunbagicha, Dhaka 1000, Bangladesh (office).

KHAN, Gen. Mohammed Ismail; Afghan politician; *Minister of Water and Energy;* b. 1954, Herat. *Education:* Kabul Mil. Coll. *Career:* served as officer in Afghan army; fmr Mujahidin Commdr during Soviet occupation; joined Jamiat-i Islami (Islamic Soc.) 1979; led uprising and liberated Herat from Soviet control; Gov. of Herat 1993–97, 2001–04; taken prisoner by Taliban following re-occupation of Herat 1997, escaped in 2000; Mil. Commdr Herat –2003; Minister of Water and Energy 2004–; mem. Northern Alliance.
Address: Ministry of Water and Energy, Kabul, Afghanistan (office).

KHAN, Riaz Mohammad, BA, MA; Pakistani diplomatist; b. 1 Oct. 1945. *Education:* Punjab Univ. *Career:* Asst Prof., Math. Dept., Punjab Univ., Lahore 1965–69; joined foreign service 1969, held various posts including Beijing 1970–73 and New York 1979–86; served in Ministry of Foreign Affairs as Section Officer/Dir 1973–79, Dir Gen. 1986–88, 1990–92; Amb. to Kazakhstan and Kyrgyzstan 1992–95, to Belgium, Luxemburg and EU 1995–98; Additional Foreign Sec. responsible for multilateral affairs, disarmaments control issues and econ. coordinations 1998–2002; Amb. to People's Repub. of China 2002–05; Foreign Sec. 2005–08, currently working in Establishment Div., Ministry of Foreign Affairs.
Address: c/o Ministry of Foreign Affairs, Constitution Avenue, Islamabad, Pakistan (office). *Telephone:* (51) 9210335 (office). *Fax:* (51) 9207600 (office). *E-mail:* sadiq@mofa.gov.pk (office). *Website:* www.mofa.gov.pk (office).

KHAN, Tariq Aziz-ud-din; Pakistani diplomatist; *Ambassador to Afghanistan;* b. Peshawar. *Career:* fmr Consul Gen., Los Angeles; served twice in Kabul in sr diplomatic positions; Chief of Protocol, Ministry of Foreign Affairs –2005; Amb. to Afghanistan 2005–.
Address: Embassy of Pakistan, 10 Nijat Watt Rd, Wazir Akbar Khan, Kabul, Afghanistan (office). *Telephone:* (20) 2300911 (office). *Fax:* (20) 2300912 (office). *E-mail:* embassy@pakembassykbl.com (office). *Website:* www.pakembkbl.com (office).

KHAN WILLIAMS, Mehr, MA; Pakistani international organization official; *Deputy High Commissioner for Human Rights, United Nations;* b. 1945, India; m.; one c. *Education:* Univ. of Karachi. *Career:* fmrly with Univ. of Karachi, United Press Int., Associated Press of Pakistan, World Bank, Washington, DC; joined UN 1976, Deputy Dir UNICEF Programme Funding Office, Dir UNICEF Div. of Communication 1989–96, Acting Dir UN Information Centre, Sydney, Dir UNICEF Innocenti Research Centre, Florence 1998–2000, Regional Dir East Asia and the Pacific, UNICEF Bangkok –2004, Special Adviser to Exec. Dir of UNICEF 2004, Deputy High Commr for Human Rights, UN 2004–, fmr Chair. Jt UN Information Cttee; fmr Trustee TV Trust for the Environment, London.
Address: Office of the United Nations High Commissioner for Human Rights (OHCHR), Palais de Nations, 1211 Geneva 10, Switzerland (office). *Telephone:* (22) 9179000 (office). *Fax:* (22) 9179022 (office). *E-mail:* infodesk@ohchr.org (office). *Website:* www.ohchr.org (office).

KHANFAR, Wadah; Jordanian journalist; *Director-General, Al-Jazeera Satellite Network; Education:* Univ. of Jordan. *Career:* joined Al-Jazeera 1999, fmr corresp. Africa Bureau, New Delhi corresp. on war in Afghanistan 2002, Baghdad Bureau Chief 2003, Man. Dir Al-Jazeera 2003–06, Dir-Gen. Al-Jazeera Satellite Network 2006–.
Address: Al-Jazeera Satellite Network, POB 23123, Doha, Qatar (office). *Telephone:* 4890881 (office). *Fax:* 4885333 (office). *Website:* english .aljazeera.net (office).

KHARCHENKO, Ihor, PhD; Ukrainian diplomatist; *Ambassador to UK;* b. 15 May 1962, Kiev; m. Mariia Kharchenko; two d. *Education:* Taras Shevchenko Kyiv State Univ. *Career:* Lecturer, Chair of Humanitarian Disciplines, Shevchenko Kyiv State Univ. 1985, post-graduate student, Chair of Int. Relations' History and Foreign Policy, 1985–88, Lecturer, Chair of Int. Relations' History and Foreign Policy, Inst. of Int. Relations 1988–92; First Sec. and Head of European Policy Sector, Div. of Political Analysis and Planning, Ministry of Foreign Affairs of Ukraine 1992–93, Acting Head of Div. and Acting Dir Dept of Political Analysis and Planning 1993, Dir 1993–97; Deputy Perm. Rep. to UN (Head of Secr. of Pres. of 52nd UN Gen. Ass. Meeting) and Amb. at Large 1997–98, Amb. to Romania 1998–2000, Deputy Minister for Foreign Affairs 2000–03, Special

Rep. of Pres. of Ukraine to the Balkan States 2001–, Amb. to Poland 2003–05, to UK 2005–, Perm. Rep. to IMO 2006–.
Address: Embassy of Ukraine, 60 Holland Park, London, W11 3SJ, England (office). *Telephone:* (20) 7727-6312 (office). *Fax:* (20) 7792-1708 (office). *E-mail:* emb_gb@mfa.gov.ua (office). *Website:* www.ukremb.org .uk (office).

KHARRAZI, Kamal, PhD; Iranian diplomatist and fmr academic; *Chairman, Strategic Council on Foreign Relations;* b. 1 Dec. 1944, Tehran; m. Mansoureh Kharrazi; two c. *Education:* Tehran Univ., Univ. of Houston, USA. *Career:* Teaching Fellow, Univ. of Houston 1975–76; Man. of Planning and Programming, Nat. Iranian TV 1979; Man. Dir Centre for Intellectual Devt of Children and Young Adults 1979–81; Deputy Foreign Minister for Political Affairs 1979–80, Minister of Foreign Affairs 1997–2005; Chair., Strategic Council on Foreign Relations 2006–; Man. Dir Islamic Repub. News Agency 1980–89; mem. Supreme Defence Council, Head War Information HQ 1980–89; Prof. of Man. and Psychology, Tehran Univ. 1983–89; Perm. Rep. to UN, New York 1989–97; Founding mem. Islamic Research Inst., London; mem. American Asscn of Univ. Profs. *Publications:* numerous textbooks and journal articles on psychology and foreign affairs.
Address: Kashani Alley 1, Keshvardust Street, Jomhuri Avenue, Tehran, Iran (office). *Telephone:* (21) 64413131 (office); (21) 64413178 (office). *Fax:* (21) 66466270 (office). *E-mail:* kharrazi@imam-khamenei.ir (office). *Website:* www.leader.ir.

KHASAWNEH, Awn Shawkat al-, MA, LLM; Jordanian judge; *Vice-President, International Court of Justice;* b. 22 Feb. 1950, Amman. *Education:* Islamic Educational Coll. of Amman, Queens' Coll. Cambridge, England. *Career:* entered diplomatic service 1975; with Perm. Mission to UN 1976–80, later as First Sec.; with Ministry of Foreign Affairs 1980–90, Head of Legal Dept 1985–90; Legal Adviser to Crown Prince 1990–95, Adviser to the King 1995, Chief of the Royal Hashemite Court 1996–98; mem. (Judge) Int. Court of Justice Feb. 2000–, Vice-Pres. 2006–; mem. Arab Int. Law Comm. 1982–89; mem. Subcomm. on Prevention of Discrimination and Protection of Minorities (Chair. 1993), Comm. on Human Rights 1984–93, Special Rapporteur of Comm. on Human Rights on the human rights dimensions of forcible population transfer; mem. Int. Law Comm. 1986–; mem. Royal Jordanian Comm. on Legislative and Admin. Reform 1994–96; mem. Bd of Eds Palestine Yearbook of Int. Law; mem. Int. Law Asscn, Chair. Cttee on Islamic Law and Int. Law 2003–; mem. Council of the Centre of Islamic and Middle Eastern Law, SOAS; Istiqlal Order 1st Class 1993, Kawkab Order 1st Class 1996, Nahda Order 1st Class 1996, Grand Officier Légion d'honneur 1997.
Address: International Court of Justice, Peace Palace, Carnegieplein 2, 2517 KJ The Hague, Netherlands (office). *Telephone:* (70) 302-23-23 (office). *Fax:* (70) 364-99-28 (office). *E-mail:* information@icj-cij.org (office). *Website:* www.icj-cij.org (office).

KHASBULATOV, Ruslan Imranovich, DEconSc; Chechen politician, economist and academic; *Chair of International Economic Relations Department, Plekhanov Academy of Economics;* b. 22 Nov. 1942, Grozny; m.; one s. one d. *Education:* Kazakh State Univ., Moscow State Univ. *Career:* instructor, Cen. Cttee of Comsomol 1970–72, Head of Information Sector Inst. of Social Sciences, USSR Acad. of Sciences 1972–74, Head of Sector, Research Inst. of Higher Educ. 1974–79, Lecturer, Prof., Head, Chair of Int. Econ. Relations, Int. Economy Plekhanov Inst. (now Acad.) of Econs 1979–90, 1995–; Deputy of Supreme Soviet in Russia 1990–93, First Vice-Chair., then Acting Chair. Supreme Soviet 1990–91, Chair. 1991–93; Chair. Interparl. Ass. of CIS 1992–93; charged with fraud and imprisoned Sept.–Oct. 1993, released by State Duma Feb. 1994; one of the leaders of opposition to Pres. Dudaev-Mashadof in Chechen crisis 1991–96 and to mil. policy of Kremlin; Corresp. mem. Russian Acad. of Sciences 1991. *Achievement:* Il Golpe di Agosto 1992. *Publications:* Bureaucracy and Socialism 1989, Russia: Time of Change 1991, International Economic Relations (two vols) 1991, Power 1992, The Struggle for Russia 1993, Les Ombres au-dessus de la Maison Blanche (France) 1993, Great Russian Tragedy (two vols) 1994, World Economy 1994, World Economy (two vols) 2001, Crisis of Commonwealth of Independent States and Positive Experience of European Union 2002, The Great American Tragedy and What Should the World Do to Prevent Terrorism? 2001–02, The Kremlin and Russian–Chechen War (five vols): Vol. 1 Exploded Life 2002, Vol. 2 Power: Sword and Guile 2002, Vol. 3 Thoughts of War and Peace 2002, Vol. 4 A Big Strategic Game 2003, Vol. 5 Aliens 2003, Which Policy is Needed for Russia from the Point of View of the World Scientific Community? 2004, Fairy Tales About Reforms 2004, The Principle of Optimum in the Economic System and Social Functions of the State 2005, States and Revolutions 2005, The World Economy and International Economic Relations, Vols 1 and 2 2006.

Address: Russian G. Plekhanov Academy of Economics, Stremyanny per. 36, 113054 Moscow (office); Granatnay per. 10/35, Moscow, Russia (home). *Telephone:* (495) 958-50-15 (office); (495) 203-53-92 (home). *Fax:* (495) 958-46-22 (office); (495) 202-84-84 (home). *E-mail:* hasbulatov@rea .ru (home).

KHATAMI, Hojatoleslam Sayed Muhammad, BPhil; Iranian cleric, politician and fmr head of state; b. 1943, Ardkan, Yazd; m. 1974; one s. two d. *Education:* Qom and Isfahan seminaries and Univ. of Tehran. *Career:* Man. Islamic Centre, Hamburg; mem. for Ardakan and Meibod, first Islamic Consultative Ass. (Parl.); rep. of Imam Khomeini and Dir Kayhan newspaper; fmr Minister of Culture and Islamic Guidance; Cultural Deputy HQ of C-in-C and Head Defence Publicity Cttee; fmr Minister of Culture and Islamic Guidance; fmr Adviser to Pres. Rafsanjani and Pres. Nat. Library of Iran; fmr mem. High Council of Cultural Revolution; Pres. of Iran 1997–2006; apptd mem. UN group Alliance of Civilizations 2005–; Head, Int. Center of Dialogue Among Civilizations; numerous hon. degrees. *Publications:* Fear of Wave, From World of City to World City, Faith and Thought Trapped by Selfishness; and numerous articles and speeches.
Address: c/o Office of the President, Pastor Avenue, Tehran, Iran. *Website:* www.khatami.ir.

KHATIWADA, Pradeep; Nepalese diplomatist; *Ambassador to Bangladesh; Career:* career diplomat, Counsellor and Chargé d'affaires a.i., later Amb. to USA, Washington, DC 1990s, First Sec. and Deputy Chief of Mission, Embassy in New Delhi –2006; Jt Sec., Ministry of Foreign Affairs 2006–07; Amb. to Bangladesh 2007–.
Address: Embassy of Nepal, United Nations Road, Road 2, Diplomatic Enclave, Baridhara, Dhaka, Bangladesh (office). *Telephone:* (2) 601790 (office). *Fax:* (2) 8826401 (office). *E-mail:* rnedhaka@bdmail.net (office).

KHAYRULLOYEV, Maj.-Gen. Sherali; Tajikistan government official and fmr army officer; *Minister of Defence;* b. 8 Nov. 1949, Dangarin Dist, Kulob Region; m.; c. *Education:* Tajikistan State Univ. *Career:* conscripted to serve in USSR Ministry of Internal Affairs 1970, served various positions including Platoon Commdr 1970–77, subsequently served in various Ministry depts; Deputy Internal Affairs Minister 1988–95; Minister of Defence 1995–.
Address: Ministry of Defence, 734025 Dushanbe, ul. Bokhtar 59, Tajikistan (office). *Telephone:* (372) 23-18-97 (office). *Fax:* (372) 23-19-37 (office).

KHAYYAT, Abdulrahman bin Muhammad Amin al-; Saudi Arabian diplomatist. *Career:* career diplomat; Amb. to Indonesia 2006–.
Address: Embassy of Saudi Arabia, Jalan M. T. Haryono Kav 27, Cawang Atas, Jakarta Timur, Indonesia (office). *Telephone:* (21) 8011533 (office). *Fax:* (21) 3905864 (office). *E-mail:* idemb@mofa.gov.sa (office). *Website:* www.mofa.gov.sa (office).

KHAZAEE, Mohammad, BA, MA; Iranian academic, government official and diplomatist; *Permanent Representative, United Nations;* b. 12 April 1953; m.; three c. *Education:* Gilan Univ. George Mason Univ., USA. *Career:* mem. Parl. 1981–88, rapporteur, Econ. Cttee, Banking Reform Cttee; Lecturer and Instructor in Econs and Philosophy, Allameh Univ., Tehran 1981–88; Rep. to World Bank 1988–2002, Sr Advisor to Bd of Dirs, mem. Planning, Devt and Personnel Cttees; Chair. Bd of Dirs Iran Foreign Investment Co. 2003–07; Vice Minister for Int. Affairs and Pres. Org. for Econ. and Tech. Assistance, Ministry of Econ. Affairs and Finance 2002–07; Gov. OPEC Fund 2002–07, Vice Chair. Investment Cttee; Alt. Gov. Islamic Devt Bank 2002–07; mem. Bd of Dirs Iran-Misr Devt Bank 2002–07; Perm. Rep. to United Nations, New York 2007–.
Address: Permanent Mission of Iran to the United Nations, 622 Third Avenue, 34th Floor, New York, NY USA (office). *Telephone:* (212) 687-2020 (office). *Fax:* (212) 867-7086 (office). *E-mail:* iran@un.int (office). *Website:* www.un.int/iran (office).

KHEK, Caimealy; Cambodian diplomatist. *Career:* Amb. to People's Repub. of China 2007–.
Address: Embassy of Cambodia, 9 Dong Zhi Men Wai Dajie, Beijing 100600, People's Republic of China (office). *Telephone:* (10) 65321889 (office). *Fax:* (10) 65323507 (office). *E-mail:* cambassybeijing@sohu.com (office).

KHERBI, Amine, MA, PhD; Algerian diplomatist; *Ambassador to USA;* m.; three c. *Education:* Uppsala Univ., Sweden, Algiers Univ. *Career:* career diplomat; Asst in charge of Econ. Affairs and Int. Relations, Office of Pres. 1967–68; Adviser to Minister of Agric. and Perm. Sec. on Cttee of Coordination 1968–70; Head of Regional Planning, Governorate of Algiers 1970–72; Counsellor for Econ. Affairs and Deputy Perm. Rep., Algerian Perm. Mission to UN 1973–77; Counsellor, Econ. and Finance Dept 1972;

Dir Political Affairs for Western Europe and Northern America 1977–80, Amb. to Brazil, Colombia, Spain, Indonesia and Austria and Perm. Rep. to Int. Orgs, Vienna 1980–91, served in various posts in Ministry of Foreign Affairs, including Dir-Gen. Multilateral Relations 1992–96, Amb. to China 1996–2001, Minister-Delegate for Foreign Affairs June 2001, Adviser on Int. Security Issues to Pres. of Algeria June 2002, Amb. to USA 2005–.
Address: Embassy of Algeria, 2118 Kalorama Road NW, Washington, DC 20008, USA (office). *Telephone:* (202) 265-2800 (office). *Fax:* (202) 667-2174 (office). *E-mail:* ambassadoroffice@yahoo.com (office). *Website:* www.algeria-us.org (office).

KHIEM, Pham Gia, DSc; Vietnamese politician and government official; *Minister of Foreign Affairs;* b. 6 Aug. 1944, Hanoi. *Education:* Hanoi Univ. of Tech. and postgraduate studies in Czechoslovakia. *Career:* Lecturer, Bac Thai Univ. of Mechanical Eng and Electronics 1967–70; worked at Ministry of Investment and Planning 1976–96, positions included Head, Industrial Div. and Dir Dept of Science, Educ. and Environment, then Deputy Minister of Investment and Planning, Minister of Science, Tech. and Planning 1996–97; Deputy Prime Minister 1997–2006; Minister of Foreign Affairs 2006–; Deputy Nat. Ass.; mem. CP of Viet Nam Central Cttee (CPVCC), Politburo.
Address: Ministry of Foreign Affairs, 1 Ton That Dam, Ba Dinh District, Hanoi, Viet Nam (office). *Telephone:* (4) 1992000 (office). *Fax:* (4) 8445905 (office). *E-mail:* banbientap@mofa.gov.vn (office). *Website:* www.mofa.gov.vn (office).

KHIYAMI, Sami M., PhD; Syrian computer engineer, diplomatist and academic; *Ambassador to UK;* b. 28 Aug. 1948, Damascus; m. Amina Khiyami; three c. *Education:* American Univ. of Beirut, Lebanon and Univ. of Claude Bernard, Lyon, France. *Career:* Head of Electronics Dept, Higher Inst. of Applied Science and Tech. (HIAST), Damascus, Chief Researcher and then Dir of Research, HIAST 1986–95, Vice-Dir then Acting Dir HIAST at Nat. Research Centre 1993–95; Project Coordinator for design and implementation of large software projects in Syria including Transport Directorate 1995, Cen. Bank 1995, Investment Certificate Lottery 1995, Damascus Univ. Admin 1996–98, Popular Credit Bank 1995–96, Agriculture Bank 1998–2000, Nat. Civil Registration Pilot Project 1998–99, Ministry of Tourism 1998–99, Civil Registration Nat. Project 2000–; Nat. Telecom and Tech. Consultant; consultant, Systems International "SI" (software group); worked for Siemens-Karlsruhe, Germany; mem. Bd and Consultant, Spacetel/Syrian GSM Operator 2004–; mem. Bd Syrian Arab Airlines 2004; Prof. of Computer Eng and Electronic Measurements, Faculty of Mechanical and Electrical Eng, Damascus Univ.; Visiting Prof., Institut Nat. Polytechnique de Grenoble, France 1993; Co-founder and mem. Bd Syrian Computer Soc. 1989–; Amb. to UK 2004–. *Publications:* contribs and papers in many scientific reviews, seminars and computer confs.
Address: Embassy of Syria, 8 Belgrave Square, London, SW1X 8PH, England (office). *Telephone:* (20) 7245-9012 (office). *Fax:* (20) 7235-4621 (office). *E-mail:* info@syrianembassy.co.uk (office). *Website:* www.syrianembassy.co.uk (office).

KHODAKOV, Aleksander Georgyevich; Russian diplomatist; b. 8 March 1952, Moscow; m.; two s. *Education:* Moscow State Inst. of Int. Relations, Algiers Univ., Algeria. *Career:* worked in USSR Embassy, Gabon 1974–79; Legal and Treaty Dept, Ministry of Foreign Affairs 1980–85, Deputy Dir Legal Dept 1992–94, Dir 1994–97; First Sec., then Second Sec. Perm. Mission of USSR to UN, New York 1985–91; Perm. Rep. to Org. for banning Chemical Armaments, The Hague; Amb. to the Netherlands 1997–2003; mem. of staff Ministry of Foreign Affairs 2003–.
Address: Ministry of Foreign Affairs, Smolenskaya-Sennaya pl. 32/34, 121200 Moscow, Russia (office). *Telephone:* (095) 244-16-06 (office). *Fax:* (095) 230-21-30 (office). *E-mail:* ministry@mid.ru (office). *Website:* www.mid.ru (office).

KHOUNA, Cheikh el Avia Ould Mohamed; Mauritanian politician; b. 1956. *Career:* mem. Democratic and Social Republican Party (replaced by Republican Party for Democracy and Renewal—RPDR 2005); fmr Minister of Fisheries and Marine Economy; Minister of Foreign Affairs 1998, 2008; Prime Minister of Mauritania 1996–97, 1998–2003.
Address: Republican Party for Democracy and Renewal (RPDR), ZRB, Tevragh Zeina, Nouakchott, Mauritania (office). *Telephone:* 529-18-36 (office). *Fax:* 529-18-00 (office). *E-mail:* info@prdr.mr (office). *Website:* www.prdr.mr (office).

KHRUSHCHEV, Sergei, MA, PhD; Russian scholar; *Senior Fellow, Watson Institute for International Studies, Brown University;* b. 2 July 1935, Moscow; m. Valentina Golenko 1985; three s. *Education:* Ukrainian Acad. of Science, Moscow Technical Univ., Moscow Electric Power Inst. *Career:* participated as engineer and admin. in Soviet missile and space programme

1958–68; Section Head then First Deputy Dir Control Computer Inst. Moscow 1968–91; Fellow, Inst. of Politics, Harvard Univ. 1990; Visiting Scholar, Watson Inst. for Int. Studies, Brown Univ. 1991–96, Senior Fellow 1996–; mem. Int. Acad. of Information, Russian Space Acad., Russian Soc. of Informatics, Russian Eng Soc., Vladimir Chelomey Scientific and Eng Soc.; has lectured extensively on Soviet history, the Cold War, Russian political and econ. reforms 1989–; Lenin Prize, Prize of the Council of Ministers, Hammer and Sickle Golden State Medal of the Hero of Socialist Labour, Order of Lenin. *Publications include:* as Ed.: Four Vols of Nikita Khrushchev's memoirs in Russian, three vol. English and Chinese trans.; as Author: Khrushchev on Khrushchev, Nikita Khrushchev: Crisis and Missiles, The Political Economy of Russian Fragmentation, Three Circles of Russian Market Reforms, Nikita Khrushchev and Creation of a Superpower 2000; author of 145 books and articles on eng and computer science.
Address: The Watson Institute for International Studies, Brown University, 111 Thayer Street, POB 1970, Providence, RI 02912-1970, USA (office). *Telephone:* (401) 863-7442 (office); (401) 943-3165 (home). *Fax:* (401) 863-1270 (office). *E-mail:* Sergei_Khrushchev@brown.edu (office). *Website:* www.watsoninstitute.org (office).

KHVOSTOV, Mikhail Mikhaylovich; Belarusian diplomatist; *Ambassador to USA;* b. 27 June 1949, Vytebsk Region; m.; two c. *Education:* Minsk Inst. of Foreign Languages, Belarussian State Univ. *Career:* with Ministry of Foreign Affairs 1982–91; Sr Diplomatic Officer, Perm. Mission of Belarus to UN, New York 1991–92, at Embassy in Washington, DC 1992–93; Head, State Protocol Dept, Legal Dept, Ministry of Foreign Affairs 1993–94, Deputy Minister of Foreign Affairs 1994–97; Amb. to Canada 1997–2000; Asst to Pres. for Foreign Policy Issues Aug.–Nov. 2000; Deputy Prime Minister and Minister of Foreign Affairs 2000–01, Minister of Foreign Affairs 2001–03; Amb. to USA 2003–.
Address: Embassy of Belarus, 1619 New Hampshire Avenue, NW, Washington, DC 20009, USA (office). *Telephone:* (202) 986-1604 (office). *Fax:* (202) 986-1805 (office). *E-mail:* usa@belarusembassy.org (office). *Website:* www.belarusembassy.org (office).

KIAMAKOSA, Mutombo; Democratic Republic of the Congo politician. *Career:* Minister of Finance –2004; currently Pres. Autorité de Régulation de la Poste et des Télécommunications du Congo.
Address: Autorité de Régulation de la Poste et des Télécommunications du Congo, Immeuble GECAMINES Boulevard du 30 juin, Kinshasa, Democratic Republic of the Congo (office). *Telephone:* (13) 92491 (office). *Fax:* (13) 92492 (office). *E-mail:* info.arptc@arptc.cd (office). *Website:* www.arptc.cd (office).

KIBAKI, Mwai, BA, BSc (Econs); Kenyan politician and head of state; *President and Commander-in-Chief of the Armed Forces;* b. 15 Nov. 1931, Gatuyaini, Othaya Div., Nyeri Dist., Cen. Prov.; m. M. Lucy Muthoni; three s. one d. *Education:* Mang'u High School, Makerere Univ., London School of Econs, UK. *Career:* Lecturer in Econs, Makerere Univ. Coll. 1959–60; Nat. Exec. Officer, Kenya African Nat. Union (KANU) 1960–64; elected by Legis. Council as one of Kenya's nine reps in E African Legis. Ass. of E African Common Services Org. 1962; mem. House of Reps for Nairobi Doonholm 1963–78; Parl. Sec. to Treasury 1963–65; Asst Minister of Econ. Planning and Devt 1964–66; Minister for Commerce and Industry 1965–69, of Finance 1969–70, of Finance and Econ. Planning 1970–78, of Finance 1978–82, of Home Affairs 1978–88, of Health 1988–91; Vice-Pres. of Kenya 1978–88; Vice-Pres. KANU 1978–88; Pres. Democratic Party 1991–2002; Leader of the Official Opposition 1998–2002; Pres. of Kenya and C-in-C of the Armed Forces Dec. 2002–; mem. Party of Nat. Unity—PNU (coalition of several parties); Chief, Order of the Golden Heart; Hon. DrIng (Nairobi), Hon. DLitt (Jomo Kenyatta Univ. of Science and Tech.; Gandhi-King Award for Non-Violence 2003, FDI Personality of the Year Award 2004.
Address: State House, PO Box 40530, 00100 Nairobi, GPO, Kenya (office). *Telephone:* (20) 227436 (office). *Fax:* (20) 2720572 (office). *E-mail:* pps@statehousekenya.go.ke (office). *Website:* www.statehousekenya.go.ke (office).

KIBELLOH, Hassan Omar Gumbo, BEd, MScS; Tanzanian diplomatist; *Ambassador to France;* b. 23 Sept. 1947; m. Amina Kibelloh; four c. *Education:* Univ. of Dar-es-Salaam, Inst. of Applied Linguistics, Univ. of Madagascar, Tokyo Int. Centre, Japan, postgraduate man. studies in Eindhoven, Netherlands, Univ. of Stockholm, Sweden. *Career:* Educ. Officer, Ministry of Nat. Educ. 1971–72; Second Sec. and Desk Officer, Rwanda, Burundi and East Africa Community, Africa and Middle East Dept, Ministry of Foreign Affairs 1974–75; First Sec. and Head of Section, East and Cen. Africa Bureau 1975–78; Counsellor and Head of Chancery, Lagos, Nigeria 1978–80, Tokyo, Japan 1980–83; Dir of Marketing and Confs, Arusha Int. Conf. Centre, Tanzania 1983–87; Councillor, Arusha

Municipality 1983–87; Minister-Counsellor, Stockholm, Sweden 1987–92; Dir of Tourism 1992–95; Amb. and Dir of Africa and Middle East, Ministry of Foreign Affairs and Int. Co-operation 1995–2000, Amb. and Perm. Sec. 2000–02, High Commr to UK (also accred as Amb. to Ireland) 2002–06, Amb. to France (also accred to Spain, Portugal, Algeria, Morocco and Tunisia) 2006–; Chair. SADC Group Envoys, London 2003–04; mem. Bd Govs Commonwealth Foundation 2002–; Trustee, Tanzania Tourism Council 2000–, Commonwealth Inst., London; Hon. Citizen of Abeline City, Tex., USA.
Address: Embassy of Tanzania, 13 avenue Raymond Poincaré, 75116 Paris, France (office). *Telephone:* 1-53-70-63-66 (office). *Fax:* 1-47-55-05-46 (office). *E-mail:* ambtanzanie@wanadoo.fr (office). *Website:* (office).

KIDWA, Nasser al-; Palestinian diplomatist. *Education:* Cairo Univ. *Career:* mem. Fatah 1969–, mem. PLO Cen. Council 1981–86, 1999–; mem. Palestine National Council 1975–; Amb. and Perm. Observer to UN, New York 1991–2005; Minister of Foreign Affairs, Palestinian Authority (PA) 2005.
Address: c/o Ministry of Foreign Affairs, POB 4017, Ramallah, Gaza, Palestinian Autonomous Areas (office).

KIDWAI, Akhlaq R., BA, MS, PhD; Indian politician, academic, scientist and administrator; *Governor of Haryana and Rajasthan;* b. 1 July 1920, Baragaon, Barabanki Dist, UP; m. Shrimati Jadmila Kidwai (deceased); two s. four d. *Education:* Jamia Millia Islamia, New Delhi, Univ. of Illinois and Cornell Univ., USA. *Career:* research and devt chemist, Cipla Labs, Bombay 1941–45; Prof. and Head of Dept of Chem., Dean Faculty of Science, Aligarh Muslim Univ. 1951–67, Dir, Dept of Research Plant Products, Chancellor 1983–92; Chair. Union Public Service Comm. 1967–79; Gov. of Bihar 1979–85, 1993–98, of W Bengal 1998–99; Chair. Dr Ambedkar Centre for Biomedical Research, Univ. of Delhi 1998–2003; Nat. Chair. Inst. of Marketing and Devt 2000–; Chair. Bombay Mercantile Cooperative Bank 1999–2003; mem. Rajya Sabha (Upper House of Parl.) 2000–04, mem. Consultative Cttee for Ministries of Science and Tech., Environment and Forest 2000–04, mem. Standing Cttee on Agric., Water Resources and Food Processing Industries 2000–04; Gov. of Haryana 2004–, also of Rajasthan 2007–; mem. Nat. Cttee on Science and Tech. 1968–75, Perspective Science and Tech. Plan Cttee, Dept of Science and Tech. and the Planning Comm., Council and Governing Body of Indian Council of Agricultural Research 1970–73, Bd of Council of Scientific and Industrial Research, Regional Imbalances Enquiry Comm., Jammu and Kashmir State 1979, State Planning Bd and Heavy Industries Plan Cttee, Govt of Uttar Pradesh, Univ. Grants Comm. and Chair. Sub-cttee on Non-Formal Methods of Educ., mem. and Patron Delhi Public School Soc. 1968–, Chair. Review Cttee on Unani Medicine, Ministry of Health, Govt of India, Chair. Selection Bd of Scientists Pool 1968–79, Chair. Bd of Assessment of Educational and Tech. Qualification for Employment, Ministry of Educ., Govt of India 1967–79; Pres. Vocational Educ. Soc. for Women 1985–; mem. AAAS; Hon. Fellow, Inst. of Engineers, India; Dr hc (Vidhya Vajaspati, Inst. of Tibetan Studies, Sarnath) 1997. *Publications:* more than 40 research papers in organic chem. and biochemistry.
Address: 196 Zakir Bagh, Okhla Road, New Delhi 110 025 (home); Haryana Raj Bhavan, Chandigarh 160 019, India (office). *Telephone:* (172) 2740643 (home); (172) 2740654 (office). *Fax:* (172) 2740557 (office). *E-mail:* arkidwai@sansad.nic.in (office); governor@hry.nic.in (office).

KIEBER-BECK, Rita; Liechtenstein politician; *Minister of Foreign Affairs, Culture and of Family and Equal Opportunity;* b. 27 Dec. 1958, Nenzing, Austria; m. Manfred Kieber. *Education:* Oberstufenrealgymnasium, Feldkirch, Univ. of Fribourg, Switzerland, Univ. of Innsbruck, Austria, Chulalongkorn Univ. of Bangkok and Chiang Mai, Thailand. *Career:* Instructor in German, Business, Political Science and Econs, Commercial Business School, Buchs, Switzerland 1979–81; full-time instructor, Realschule (Upper School) Balzers 1982–90; with Liechtenstein Inst., Bendern 1990–94, Man. Dir 1991–94; Man. Dir Adiuvaris Treuunternehmen reg. (Fiducary), Triesen 1993, 2001; Consulting mem. Parl. Group of Progressive Citizens' Party (Fortschritte Bürgerpartei, FBP) 1997–2000, mem. Presidency 1997–, Chair. Educ. Working Group 1997–, mem. Man. Presidency and Financial Adviser 2000–01; Deputy Prime Minister with responsibility for Educ., Justice, Transport and Telecommunications 2001–05; Minister of Foreign Affairs, Cultural Affairs and Family and Equal Opportunity 2005–; Pres. Liechtenstein Upper School Teachers' Asscn 1988–90; mem. Educational Comm., Upper Schools, Liechtenstein 1984–88, Adult Educ. Comm. 1992–98.
Address: Regierungsgebäude, 9490 Vaduz, Liechtenstein (office). *Telephone:* 2366008 (office). *Fax:* 2366022 (office). *E-mail:* office@liechtenstein.li (office). *Website:* www.liechtenstein.li (office).

KIIR MAYARDIT, Salva; Sudanese politician and fmr mil. leader; *President of Southern Sudan and Vice-President of Sudan;* b. 1951. *Career:* joined Anyanya separatist movt. during First Sudanese Civil War, early 1960s, later becoming an officer, joined regular army after peace settlement 1972; with Army of Sudan 1972–83, attaining rank of Capt.; Founding mem. Sudan People's Liberation Movt (SPLM) 1983, later Deputy Party Leader, Chief of Staff Sudan Peoples Liberation Army (mil. wing of SPLM) 1999, Chair. SPLM after death of John Garang) 2005, C-in-C SPLA 2005–; Vice-Pres. of Southern Sudan 2005, Pres. 2005–, Pres. of Southern Sudan 2005–.
E-mail: webmaster@splmtoday.com (office). *Website:* www.splmtoday.com (office).

KIKWETE, Lt-Col Jakaya Mrisho; Tanzanian politician and head of state; *President;* b. 7 Oct. 1950, Msoga village. *Career:* after graduation joined Tanzania African Nat. Union (now Chama Cha Mapinduzi (CCM) party); seconded to Tanzania People's Defence Forces as Chief Political Instructor at Monduli Cen. Mil. Acad.; commissioned as Lt and retd Col 1992; Deputy Minister, Ministries of Finance, of Water and Livestock Devt, of Energy and Minerals 1987–90, Minister 1990–94; Chair. Council of Ministers of the E African Community; Minister of Foreign Affairs and Int. Co-operation 1995–2005; Pres. 2005–; Chair. African Union Ass. 2008–; Patron Tanzania Nat. Basketball Asscn.
Address: Office of the President, State House, PO Box 9120, Dar es Salaam, Tanzania (office). *Telephone:* (22) 2116679 (office). *Fax:* (22) 2113425 (office). *Website:* www.tanzania.go.tz/poffice (office).

KILLION, Redley (Rere), MA (Econs); Micronesian politician and economist; b. 23 Oct. 1951, Weno, Chuuk State; m. Jacinta Killion; nine c. *Education:* Mizpah High School, Weno, Marist High School, Eugene, Oregon, Univ. of Hawaii, Vanderbilt Univ., Nashville, Tenn., USA. *Career:* economist, Dept of Resources and Devt, Trust Territory Govt 1974–79; Dir Dept of Resources and Devt, Chuuk State Govt 1979–86; Nat. Senator 1987–99, Vice-Pres. Federated States of Micronesia 1999–2007; Congress of Micronesia Scholarship Awards 1969–70; UN Fellowship for Graduate Studies at Vanderbilt Univ. 1977–78.
Address: c/o PO Box PS-53, Palikir, Pohnpei State, FSM 96941 (office); PO Box PS 237, Palikir, Pohnpei State, FSM 96942, Micronesia (home). *Telephone:* (691) 320-2833 (home). *Fax:* (691) 320-2930 (home).

KIM, Dae-jung, MA, PhD; South Korean politician; b. 3 Dec. 1925, Hugwang-ri, S Jeolla Prov.; m. Lee Lee Ho. *Education:* Mokpo Commercial High School, Korea and Kyunghee Univs, Diplomatic Acad. of Foreign Ministry of Russia. *Career:* Pres. Mokpo Merchant Ship Co. 1948; arrested by N Korean Communists, escaped from jail 1950; Pres. Mokpo Daily News 1950; Deputy Commdr S Jeolla Region, Maritime Defence Force 1950; Pres. Heungkuk Merchant Shipping Co. 1951; Pres Dae-yang Shipbldg. Co. 1951; mem. Cen. Cttee Democratic Party 1957, Spokesman 1960, Spokesman, Nat. Alliance to Protect Human Rights 1958; elected to 5th Nat. Ass. 1961, 6th Nat. Ass. 1963; Spokesman, People's Party 1965, Chair. Policy Planning Council and mem. Cen. Exec. Bd 1966; Spokesman, New Democratic Party and mem. of Party Cen. Exec. Bd 1967; elected to 7th Nat. Ass. 1967, 8th Nat. Ass. 1971; injured in assassination attempt 1971; in exile, organized anti-dictatorship movts in Japan and USA 1972; abducted from Japan by Korean CIA agents, survived two assassination attempts, forcibly returned to Seoul, placed under house arrest 1973; arrested for criticizing Constitution 1976; sentenced to five years' imprisonment 1977; sentence suspended; released from jail, placed under house arrest 1978; house arrest lifted 1979; amnesty granted, civil rights restored; rearrested, charged with treason, sentenced to death 1980; sentence commuted to life imprisonment 1981; sentence reduced to 20 years, later suspended 1982; went into exile in USA 1982; f. Korean Inst. for Human Rights, Va 1983; returned to Korea 1985; under intermittent house arrest 1985–87; Co-Chair. Council for Promotion of Democracy 1985; Standing Adviser, Reunification Democratic Party 1987; f. Party for Peace and Democracy, Pres. 1987–91; reappointed to 13th Nat. Ass. 1988; f., Pres. New Democratic Party April–Sept. 1991; f. Democratic Party, Co.-Chair. 1991–92; reappointed to 14th Nat. Ass., later retd from politics 1992; f. Kim Dae-Jung Peace Foundation for Asia-Pacific Region, Chair. Bd of Dirs 1994; ended retirement from politics 1995; f. Nat. Congress for New Politics 1995; Pres. of Repub. of Korea 1997–2003; Pres. Millennium Democratic Party 2000–01; Co-Pres. Forum of Democratic Leaders in Asia-Pacific 1994; Visiting Fellow, Clare Hall Coll., Univ. of Cambridge, UK 1993, Life Fellow 1993; mem. Int. Ecological Acad. Moscow 1994–; Adviser, Int. Cttee for Relief of Victims of Torture, USA 1984–, Union Theological Seminary, USA 1984–; Visiting Fellow, Centre for Int. Affairs, Harvard Univ., USA 1983–84; Trustee, Fed. of Unions of Korean Shipbldg Agents 1951; Ed.-in-Chief, Centre for Study of Korean Labour 1995; Hon. Prof. (Moscow Univ.) 1992, (Chinese Acad. of Social Sciences, Nankai Univ., Fudan Univ., People's Repub. of China) 1994; Hon. LLD (Emory Univ., USA) 1983, (Catholic Univ. of America) 1992; Hon. Dr of Political Science (Wonkwang Univ.) 1994; numerous honours and awards including Bruno Kreisky Human Rights Award, Austria 1981, Union Medal, Union Theol.

Seminary, USA 1994; awarded Nobel Peace Prize 2000. *Publications include:* Conscience in Action 1985, Prison Writings 1987, Building Peace and Democracy 1987, Kim Dae-jung's Views on International Affairs 1990, In the Name of Justice and Peace 1991, Korea and Asia 1994, The Korean Problem: Nuclear Crisis, Democracy and Reunification 1994, Unification, Democracy and Peace 1994, Mass Participatory Economy: Korea's Road to World Economic Power 1996.
Address: c/o Office of the President, Chong Wa Dae, 1 Sejongno, Jongno-gu, Seoul, Republic of Korea (office).

KIM, Gen. Dong-shin, BA, MS; South Korean politician and army general (retd); b. 13 March 1941, Kwangju City. *Education:* Seoul Nat. Univ., Korean Mil. Acad. and Hannam Univ. *Career:* Regimental Commdr, Army of Repub. of Korea 1983; apptd Chief, Foreign Policy Div., Ministry of Nat. Defence 1984; Deputy Dir of Strategic Planning, Jt Chief of Staff 1989–90; Commanding Gen. 51st Infantry Div. 1990–92; Dir of Force Planning 1992–93; Commanding Gen. Capital Corps, 3rd Army 1993–94; Chief Dir of Operations, Jt Chiefs of Staff 1995–96; Deputy C-in-C, Repub. of Korea–US Combined Forces Command 1996–98; Army Chief of Staff 1998–99; Adviser, Nat. Security Cttee 2000; Minister of Nat. Defence 2001–02; Visiting Scholar, RAND Center for Asia Pacific Policy 2002–03; Silver Star Medal 1972, Order of Nat. Security Merit (Samil Medal 1983, Gukson Medal 1993, Tangil Medal 1997), Order of Mil. Merit 1991, US Army Meritorious Service Medal 1999, Legion of Merit 2001.
Address: c/o Ministry of National Defence 1, 3-ga, Yonsan-don, Yongsan-gu, Seoul, Republic of Korea (office).

KIM, Gye-kwan; North Korean politician and diplomatist; *Deputy Minister of Foreign Affairs;* b. 1943. *Career:* participated in Pyongyang-Washington negotiations and Geneva talks as working-level rep. of N Korea; close confidante of Pres. Kim Jong-il; one of N Korea's most experienced negotiators; travelled widely in Europe before 1993; served as Amb.-at-Large and maintained ties with socialist parties in Western Europe; designated Deputy Negotiator in first nuclear talks with USA, later Chief Negotiator; head of del. to four-party talks between N and S Korea, China and USA to address Korean peninsula issues; currently Deputy Minister of Foreign Affairs.
Address: Ministry of Foreign Affairs, Pyongyang, Democratic People's Republic of Korea (office).

KIM, Hak-su, BA, MA, PhD; South Korean international civil servant, economist and academic; *Distinguished Visiting Professor, Graduate School of International Studies, Yonsei University;* b. 27 Feb. 1938, Wonju, Kangwon. *Education:* Yonsei Univ., Univ. of Edinburgh, UK, Univ. of S Carolina, USA. *Career:* economist, Cen. Bank 1960; Sec. to Minister of Commerce and Industry 1969; London Rep., Bank of Korea 1971–73; Exec. Dir Daewoo Corpn 1977, later Pres.; Chief Planning Officer, Chief Tech. Advisor UN Dept for Tech. Co-operation and Devt 1980s; Sr Research Fellow, Korea Inst. for Int. Econ. Policy 1989–93; Pres. Hanil Banking Inst. 1993–95; Sec.-Gen. of the Colombo Plan, Sri Lanka 1995–99; Korean Amb. for Int. Econ. Affairs 1999; UN Under-Sec.-Gen. and Exec. Sec. UN ESCAP 2000–07 (appointment renewed 2005); Distinguished Visiting Prof., Grad. School of Int. Studies, Yonsei Univ., Seoul 2007–.
Address: Graduate School of International Studies, Yonsei University, 134 Sinchon-dong Seodamun-gu, Seoul 120-749 (office); 319-1601 Hanyong Apt, Bundang, Kyunggi, South Korea (home). *Telephone:* (2) 2123-6297 (office); (2) 656-7556 (home). *E-mail:* magkim16@hotmail.com (office). *Website:* gsis.yonsei.ac.kr (office).

KIM, Vice-Marshal Il-chol; North Korean politician; *Minister of People's Armed Forces;* b. 1928, Pyongyang. *Education:* Mangyongdae Revolutionary School, Navy Acad., USSR. *Career:* apptd Commdr East Sea Fleet 1970; mem. Party Cen. Cttee 1980–; Deputy in Supreme People's Ass. 1982; apptd Commdr of Navy 1982; rank of Lt-Gen. 1982, Col-Gen. 1985, Gen. 1992, Vice-Marshal 1997; First Minister of the People's Armed Forces 1997–98, Minister 1998–; Vice-Chair. Nat. Defence Comm. 1998–; Kim Il Sung medal 1982, Nat. Flag Order, Nat. Hero title 1995.
Address: Office of the Minister, Ministry of the People's Armed Forces, Pyongyang, Democratic People's Republic of Korea (office).

KIM, Jae-sup; South Korean diplomatist; b. 1945. *Education:* Nat. Univ. of Seoul. *Career:* joined Ministry of Foreign Affairs 1969, Counsellor to Pres. 1990–92, apptd Deputy Minister of Foreign Affairs and Trade 2003; overseas posts include Counsellor, Embassy in India 1981–84, Amb. to Czech Repub. 1995–98, fmr Amb. to Indonesia, Amb. to Russian Federation 2004–07.
Address: c/o Ministry of Foreign Affairs and Trade, 95-1, Doryeom-dong, Jongno-gu, Seoul 110-787, Republic of Korea (office). *Website:* www.mofat.go.kr (office).

KIM, Marshal Jong-il; North Korean supreme head of state; *General Secretary, Workers' Party of Korea, Chairman, National Defence Commission, Supreme Commander of Korean People's Army and Marshal of the Democratic Republic of Korea;* b. 16 Feb. 1942, secret camp on Mt Paekdu. *Education:* Kim Il-sung Univ., Pyongyang. *Career:* Officer, then Section Chief, then Deputy Dir, then Dir a Dept of Cen. Cttee Workers' Party of Korea 1964–73, mem. Cen. Cttee 1972, Sec. 1973; mem. Political Comm. Cen. Cttee 1974, mem. Presidium of Politburo of Cen. Cttee of Workers' Party of Korea 1980–, Gen. Sec. 1997–; First Vice-Chair., Nat. Defence Comm. 1990–93, Chair. (Head of State) Sept. 1993–; mem. Mil. Comm. Cen. Cttee at Sixth Party Congress 1980; Deputy to Supreme People's Assembly 1982–; Supreme Commdr Korean People's Army 1991–; Marshal of the Democratic People's Repub. of Korea 1992–; Hon. Dr (Inca Garsilaso, Vega Univ., Peru) 1986, (Chiclayo Univ., Peru) 1986; Kim Il Sung Order (three times), title of Marshal; Orden de Solidaridad, Cuba, Grand Croix de l'Ordre Nat. des Mille Collines, Rwanda, Necklace Order of Egypt; Kim Il Sung Prize; Hero of Democratic People's Repub. of Korea (three times), and many other foreign and domestic awards and honours. *Publications include:* Kim Jong Il Selected Works (15 Vols), For the Completion of the Revolutionary Cause of Juche (10 Vols).
Address: Central Committee of the Workers' Party of Korea, Pyongyang, Democratic People's Republic of Korea.

KIM, Joong-jae; South Korean diplomatist; *Ambassador to Italy;* b. May 1952; m.; two s. *Education:* Yonsei Univ. *Career:* joined Ministry of Foreign Affairs 1975, held several sr posts including Dir of Computer System and Dir of Admin. Man., Office of Planning and Man., Dir East Europe Div. II, Dir-Gen. European Affairs Bureau 2002; overseas postings include Third Sec., Embassy in Rome 1979, Vice-Consul in Cairo 1981, First Sec., Embassy in the Philippines 1985, Counsellor, Perm. Mission to UN, New York 1991, Counsellor, Embassy in Prague 1994, Minister and Consul-Gen., Embassy in UK 1999; Amb. to Libya 2003, to Italy (also accred to Malta) 2007–, also Perm. Rep. to FAO, Rome 2007–; Sec.-Gen. 2011 Daegu IAAF World Championships Bidding Cttee 2006.
Address: Embassy of The Republic of Korea, Via Barnaba Oriani 30, 00197 Rome, Italy (office). *Telephone:* (06) 802461 (office). *Fax:* (06) 802462259 (office). *Website:* ita.mofat.go.kr/index.jsp (office).

KIM, Joong-keun; South Korean diplomatist; *Ambassador to Singapore;* b. 6 May 1952; m.; one s. one d. *Education:* Seoul Nat. Univ. *Career:* joined Ministry of Foreign Affairs 1978; Third Sec., Embassy in Cote d'Ivoire 1980–85, Consul, Consulate-Gen. in Los Angeles 1985–90, First Sec., Embassy in Washington, DC 1990–93, Counsellor, Embassy in Czech Repub. 1993–95; Dir Int. Trade Div. II, Int. Trade Bureau, Ministry of Foreign Affairs 1996; Counsellor, Perm. Mission to UN and other Int. Orgs, Geneva 1997–2000; Deputy Dir-Gen. Bilateral Trade Bureau, Ministry of Foreign Affairs and Trade 2000–01; Sr Researcher, Georgetown Univ., Washington, DC 2003–05; Head of Office of Foreign Disaster Relief and Reconstruction, Korea Int. Cooperation Agency 2005; Deputy Minister for Trade, Ministry of Foreign Affairs and Trade 2005–07; Amb. to Singapore 2007–.
Address: Embassy of the Republic of Korea, 47 Scotts Road, 08-00 Goldbell Towers, Singapore City 228233, Singapore (office). *Telephone:* 68362263 (office). *Fax:* 62352581 (office). *E-mail:* info@koreaembassy.org.sg (office). *Website:* www.koreaembassy.org.sg (office).

KIM, Sam-hoon; South Korean diplomatist; b. 12 Jan. 1944; m.; one s. one d. *Education:* Seoul Nat. Univ. *Career:* joined Ministry of Foreign Affairs 1968; Consul in Chicago, USA 1971–75, First Sec., Embassy in USA 1979–81, Political Counsellor 1984–87, Counsellor, Embassy in Saudi Arabia 1981–83; Dir-Gen. Int. Affairs Seoul Olympic Organizing Cttee 1987–88; mem. delegation South-North Korean dialogue 1989–90; Dir-Gen. for Information and Cultural Affairs, Ministry of Foreign Affairs 1989, for American Affairs 1989–90, for Int. Trade 1990–91; Deputy Perm. Rep. to UN and Int. Orgs, Geneva 1991–93; apptd Special Asst to Minister for Foreign Affairs 1993, Amb. for Nuclear Issues 1993–94; Deputy Minister for Int. Orgs and Policy Planning 1998–99; Amb. to Brazil 1996–98, to Canada 1999–2002, Perm. Rep. to UN, New York 2003–05; Gov. for Korea, Asia-Europe Foundation, Singapore 2006–; Order of Civil Service Merit (Green Stripes), Sport Merit Medal of Honour, Ordem Nacional do Cruzeiro do Sul, Brazil.
Address: Asia-Europe Foundation, 31 Heng Mui Keng Terrace, Singapore 119595, Singapore. *Telephone:* 68749700. *Fax:* 86721135. *E-mail:* info@asef.org. *Website:* www.asef.org.

KIM, Soo-dong; South Korean diplomatist; *Ambassador to Canada;* b. 24 April 1948; m.; one d. *Education:* Seoul Nat. Univ. *Career:* joined Foreign Service 1977, overseas postings include Second Sec., Embassy in Copenhagen 1980, Second Sec., Embassy in Tokyo 1986, First Sec., Embassy in Mogadishu 1987, Counsellor, Embassy in Ottawa 1992, Minister-

Counsellor, Embassy in Tokyo 1997; Amb. to Serbia and Montenegro 2003–05, to Canada 2007–; Dir for Planning and Budget, Office of Planning and Man., Ministry of Foreign Affairs 1990–92, Dir West Europe Div., European Affairs Bureau 1992; Dir, Office of Prime Minister 1995; Sr Coordinator for Planning and Man., Ministry of Foreign Affairs and Trade 2001–02, Dir-Gen., Middle East and African Affairs Bureau 2002–03, Amb. for Inspection 2005, Deputy Minister for Planning and Man. 2005–07.
Address: Embassy of the Republic of Korea, 150 Boteler Street, Ottawa, ON K1N 5A6, Canada (office). *Telephone:* (613) 244-5010 (office). *Fax:* (613) 244-5043 (office). *E-mail:* can-ottawa.mofat.go.kr (office).

KIM, Suk-soo; South Korean lawyer, politician and judge; b. 20 Nov. 1932. *Education:* Yonsei Univ., Seoul. *Career:* admitted to Korean Bar 1958; Judge Advocate, Repub. of Korea Army HQ 1960–63; judge, Masan Br., Court of Pusan Dist Court 1963–67, Pusan Dist Court 1967–69, Incheon Br., Court of Seoul Civil and Criminal Dist Court 1969–70, Seoul Criminal Dist Court 1970–71, Seoul High Court 1971–73; Research Judge, Supreme Court 1973–74; Presiding Judge, Pusan Dist Court 1974–77, Sungbook Br., Court of Seoul Dist Court 1977–79, Seoul Civil Dist Court 1979–80; Chief Judge, Incheon Br., Court of Suwon Dist Court 1980–81; Presiding Judge, Seoul High Court and Chief Judge Nambu Br., Seoul Dist Court 1981–83; Sr Presiding Judge, Seoul High Court 1983–86; Chief Judge, Pusan Dist Court 1986–88; Vice-Minister of Court Admin 1988–91; Supreme Court Justice 1991–97; Chair. Nat. Election Comm. 1993–97; Chair. Judicial Officers' Ethics Cttee of Supreme Court 1997–2001; Chair. Korea Press Ethics Comm. 2000–02; Chair. Govt Public Service Ethics Cttee 2002; Prime Minister of Repub. of Korea 2002–03; Auditor Bd of Dirs Yonsei Univ. Foundation 1997–2002; Dir Samsung Electronics Co. 1999–2001, Yonsei Law Promotion Foundation 2002; Order of Service Merit (Blue Stripes) 1997; Hon. PhD (Yonsei Univ.) 1997.
Address: c/o Office of the Prime Minister, 77 Sejong-no, Jongno-gu, Seoul, Republic of Korea (office).

KIM, Woo-sang; South Korean diplomatist. *Career:* Ambassador to Australia 2008–.
Address: Embassy of the Republic of Korea, 113 Empire Circuit, Yarralumla, ACT 2600, Australia (office). *Telephone:* (2) 6270-4100 (office). *Fax:* (2) 6273-4839 (office). *E-mail:* info@korea.org.au (office). *Website:* www.korea.org.au (office).

KIM, Gen. Yong-chun; North Korean army official; *Vice-Chairman, National Defence Commission;* b. 1922. *Career:* Assoc. mem. Workers' Party Cen. Cttee (WPCC) –1980, Deputy Chief of Dept, WPCC 1980–83; rank of Gen. 1992, Vice Marshall 1995; Chief of Staff, North Korean People's Party 1995–07; Vice-Chair. Nat. Defence Comm. 2007–; mem. Nat. Defence Comm. 1998–.
Address: National Defence Commission, Pyongyang, People's Republic of Korea (office).

KIM, Yong-il; North Korean politician; *Prime Minister;* b. 2 May 1944. *Education:* Rajin Univ. of Marine Transport. *Career:* served in army 1961–70; various positions in Ministry of Land and Marine Transport 1980–94, including Instructor and Deputy Dir, Minister for Marine and Land Transport 1994–2007; Prime Minister 2007–.
Address: Office of the Premier, Pyonyang, Democratic People's Republic of Korea (office).

KIM, Yong-nam; North Korean politician; *President, Presidium of the Supreme People's Assembly;* b. 1925, North Hamgyong prov. *Education:* Kim Il Sung Univ., Moscow Univ. *Career:* mem. Cen. Cttee Workers' Party of Korea (WPK) 1970, Political Commissar 1977, mem. Political Bureau 1980–; Vice-Premier and Minister of Foreign Affairs 1983–98; Del. to Supreme People's Ass.; Pres. Presidium of the Supreme People's Ass. 1998–.
Address: Choe ko in min hoe ui (Supreme People's Assembly), Pyongyang, Democratic People's Republic of Korea (office).

KIMONYO, James, BSc, MEng; Rwandan diplomatist; *Ambassador to USA.* *Career:* fmr Gov. of Eastern and Southern provs (Kibungo and Butare, respectively); apptd Head of Dept of Rehabilitation and Reconstruction under several ministries, including Rehabilitation and Social Integration, Home Affairs, Communal Devt and Resettlement, as well as Ministry of Lands, Resettlement and Environmental Protection after 1994; also played key role in repatriation, resettlement and re-integration programmes of fmr Rwandan refugees; served as a nat. dir and co-ordinator of several projects funded by UNHCR, UNDP and UN-HABITAT; Amb. to South Africa (also accred to Zambia, Mozambique, Zimbabwe, Angola, Namibia, Botswana, Swaziland and Lesotho) 2005–07, to USA (also accred to Mexico, Brazil, Argentina and Chile) 2007–.

Address: Embassy of Rwanda, 1714 New Hampshire Avenue, NW, Washington, DC 20009, USA (office). *Telephone:* (202) 232-2882 (office). *Fax:* (202) 232-4544 (office). *E-mail:* rwandaembassy@rwandaembassy.org (office). *Website:* www.rwandaembassy.org (office).

KIMUNYA, Amos Muhinga, BA, CPA,; Kenyan accountant and politician; b. 6 March 1962, Embu. *Education:* Univ. of Nairobi. *Career:* early career as accountant; mem. Parl. for Kipipiri, Minister for Lands and Settlement 2003–06, of Finance 2006–08 (resgnd); Chair. Inst. of Certified Accountants of Kenya 1999–2001; mem. Nat. Rainbow Coalition.
Address: National Rainbow Coalition (NARC), Mwenge House, Ole Odume Road, Nairobi, Kenya (office). *Telephone:* (20) 571506 (office).

KINCHEN, Richard, MVO; British diplomatist (retd); b. 12 Feb. 1948; m. Cheryl Kinchen; one s. three d. *Career:* joined British Diplomatic Service 1970, with N Africa Dept, FCO 1970–72; Third, then Second Sec., Embassy in Kuwait 1973–74; with Middle East Dept 1974–75; Second, then First Sec., Embassy in Luxembourg 1975–77; First Sec., Embassy in Paris 1977–80; with EC Dept 1989–82; Pvt. Sec., Office of Parl. Under-Sec. of State 1982–84; Head of Chancery and First Sec., Embassy in Rabat 1984–88; Financial Counsellor, Mission to New York 1988–93; Head of Dependent Territories Secr., Embassy in Bridgetown, Barbados 1993–97; with Resource Planning Dept, FCO 1997–2000; Amb. to Lebanon 2000–03, to Belgium 2003–07.
Address: c/o Foreign and Commonwealth Office, King Charles Street, London, SW1A 2AH, England. *Telephone:* (20) 7008-1500.

KINELEV, Vladimir Georgiyevich, DTechSc; Russian politician; *Director, Institute for Information Technologies in Education, United Nations Educational, Scientific and Cultural Organization (UNESCO);* b. 28 Jan. 1945, Ust-Kalmanka, Altay Region; m.; one d. *Education:* Bauman Higher Tech. School. *Career:* worked Cen. Bureau of Experimental Machine-Construction, Asst, Prof., Pro-rector Bauman Higher Tech. School; First Deputy Chair. State Cttee on Science and Higher School 1990–91; Chair. Cttee on Higher School Ministry of Science, Higher School and Tech. Policy of Russian Fed., concurrently First Deputy Minister 1992–93; Chair. State Cttee on Higher Educ. 1993–96; Deputy Chair. Russian Govt 1996; Minister of Gen. and Professional Educ. 1996–98; Dir UNESCO Inst. for Information Technologies in Educ. (IITE) 1998–; Academician Russian Acad. of Educ., Russian Eng Acad.; Prize of USSR Govt 1990, State Prize of Russia 1997; Order of Honour, Russian Fed. 1995. *Publications:* The Objective Necessity 1995, Education and Culture in the History of Civilization 1998.
Address: UNESCO Institute for Information Technologies in Education, Kedrova str. 8, 117292 Moscow, Russia (office). *Telephone:* (495) 129-19-98 (office). *Fax:* (495) 718-07-66 (office). *E-mail:* kinelev@iite.ru (office). *Website:* www.iite.ru.

KING, Anthony Stephen, DPhil; Canadian political scientist and academic; *Professor of Government, University of Essex;* b. 7 Nov. 1934; m. 1st Vera Korte 1965 (died 1971); m. 2nd Jan Reece 1980. *Education:* Queen's Univ., Kingston, Ont., Magdalen and Nuffield Colls, Oxford. *Career:* Fellow, Magdalen Coll., Oxford 1961–65; Sr Lecturer, Univ. of Essex 1966–68, Reader 1968–69, Prof. of Govt 1969–; Visiting Prof., Univ. of Wis. 1967, Princeton Univ. 1984; Fellow, Center for Advanced Study in Behavioral Sciences, Stanford Univ., Calif. 1977–78; elections commentator for BBC, Daily Telegraph (UK); mem. Cttee on Standards in Public Life 1994–98, Royal Comm. on House of Lords Reform 1999; mem. Academia Europaea 1998; Hon. Foreign mem. American Acad. of Arts and Sciences 1993. *Publications:* The British General Election of 1964 (co-author) 1965, The British General Election of 1966 (co-author) 1966, British Politics: People, Parties and Parliament (ed.) 1966, The British Prime Minister (ed.) 1969, Westminster and Beyond (co-author) 1973, British Members of Parliament: A Self-portrait 1974, Why is Britain Becoming Harder to Govern? (ed.) 1976, Britain Says Yes: The 1975 Referendum on the Common Market 1977, The New American Political System (ed.) 1978, Both Ends of the Avenue: the Presidency of the Executive Branch and Congress in the 1980s (ed.) 1983, Britain at the Polls 1992 (ed.) 1992, SDP: The Birth, Life and Death of the Social Democratic Party (co-author) 1995, Running Scared: Why America's Politicians Campaign Too Much and Govern Too Little 1997, New Labour Triumphs: Britain at the Polls (ed.) 1997, British Political Opinion 1937–2000 (ed.) 2001, Does the United Kingdom Still Have a Constitution? 2001, Britain at the Polls 2001 (ed.) 2001, Leaders' Personalities and the Outcomes of Democratic Elections (ed.) 2002; numerous papers in British and American journals.
Address: Room 5.022, Department of Government, University of Essex, Wivenhoe Park, Colchester, Essex, CO4 3SQ (office); The Mill House, Lane Road, Wakes Colne, Colchester, Essex, CO6 2BP, England (home). *Telephone:* (1206) 873393 (office); (1787) 222497 (home). *Fax:* (1787) 224221 (home). *Website:* www.essex.ac.uk/government (office).

KING, Mervyn Allister, BA, FBA; British economist, academic and central banker; *Governor, Bank of England;* b. 30 March 1948. *Education:* Wolverhampton Grammar School, King's Coll., Cambridge. *Career:* Jr Research Officer, Dept of Applied Econs, Cambridge Univ., mem. Cambridge Growth Project 1969–73, Research Officer 1972–76, Lecturer, Faculty of Econs 1976–77; Esmée Fairbairn Prof. of Investment, Univ. of Birmingham 1977–84; Prof. of Econs, LSE 1984–95; Exec. Dir Bank of England 1991–98, Chief Economist 1991–98, Deputy Gov. (Monetary Policy) 1998–2003, Gov. 2003–; Pres. Inst. of Fiscal Studies 1999–2003; Research Officer, Kennedy School at Harvard Univ., USA 1971–72, Visiting Prof. of Econs 1982–; Visiting Prof. of Econs MIT 1983–84, LSE 1996–; Co-Dir LSE Financial Markets Group 1987–91; Man. Ed. Review of Economic Studies 1978–83; founder mem. Monetary Policy Cttee 1997; mem. City Capital Markets Cttee 1989–91; Bd mem. The Securities Asscn 1987–89; mem. Council and Exec. Cttee Royal Econ. Soc. 1981–86, 1992–97; Fellow, Econometric Soc. 1982–; mem. Acad. Europaea 1992; mem. Council, European Econ. Asscn (Pres. 1993); Research Assoc. Nat. Bureau of Econ. Research; Assoc. mem. Inst. of Fiscal and Monetary Policy, Ministry of Finance, Japan 1986–91; mem. The Group of Thirty 1997, Advisory Council of the London Symphony Orchestra 2001; Chair. of OECD's Working Party 3 (WP3) Cttee 2001–03; Visiting Fellow, Nuffield Coll. Oxford 2002–03; mem. Cttee All England Lawn Tennis and Croquet Club; Patron, Worcester Co. Cricket Club; Trustee Nat. Gallery; Hon. Sr Scholarship and Richards Prize, King's Coll. Cambridge 1969; Hon. Fellow, St John's Coll., Cambridge 1997, King's Coll. Cambridge 2004; Foreign Hon. Mem. American Acad. of Arts and Sciences 2000; Hon. Life Mem. Inst. for Fiscal Studies 2006; Dr hc (London Guildhall Univ.) 2001, (Birmingham) 2002, (City Univ., London) 2002, (LSE) 2003, (Wolverhampton) 2003, (Edin.) 2005, (Helsinki) 2006, (Cambridge) 2006; Wrenbury Scholarship, Univ. of Cambridge 1969, Stevenson Prize, Univ. of Cambridge 1970, Kennedy Scholarship and Harkness Fellowship 1971, Medal of Univ. of Helsinki 1982. *Publications:* Public Policy and the Corporation 1977, The British Tax System (with J. A. Kay), Indexing for Inflation (co-ed. with T. Liesner) 1975, The Taxation of Income from Capital Growth (co-author) 1984; numerous articles in various journals. *Address:* Bank of England, Threadneedle Street, London, EC2R 8AH, England. *Telephone:* (20) 7601-4444 (office). *Fax:* (20) 7601-4953 (office). *E-mail:* nicole.morey@bankofengland.co.uk (office). *Website:* www.bankofengland.co.uk (office).

KING, Michael Ian; Barbadian diplomatist; *Ambassador to USA;* m.; two s. *Education:* Harrison Coll., Barbados, City Univ. of New York (CUNY), USA, Univ. of Oxford, UK. *Career:* mem. Foreign Service 1979–, secondments as Exec. Dir Caribbean Conservation Asscn and Dir OAS Nat. Office, Bahamas; fmr Amb. (non-resident) and Perm. Rep. to UN and WTO, Geneva; fmr Perm. Del. to UNESCO, Paris; fmr Amb. to France, Germany, Austria, Benelux countries and EU; Amb. to USA and Perm. Rep. to OAS Oct. 2000–. *Address:* Embassy of Barbados, 2144 Wyoming Avenue, NW, Washington, DC 20008, USA (office). *Telephone:* (202) 939-9200 (office). *Fax:* (202) 332-7467 (office). *E-mail:* washington@foreign.gov.bb (office).

KING, Stephenson; Saint Lucia politician; *Prime Minister and Minister of Finance (including International Financial Services), External Affairs, Home Affairs and National Security; Career:* MP for Castries North 2006–; Minister for Health and Labour Relations 2006–07, of Finance (including Int. Financial Services), External Affairs, Home Affairs and Nat. Security 2007–, Prime Minister 2007–; mem. United Workers Party. *Address:* Office of the Prime Minister, Greaham Louisy Administrative Bldg, 5th Floor, Waterfront, Castries, Saint Lucia (office). *Telephone:* 468-2111 (office). *Fax:* 453-7352 (office). *E-mail:* admin@pm.gov.lc (office). *Website:* www.pm.gov.lc (office).

KING AKERELE, Olu Banke (Bankie), BA, MA; Liberian politician; *Minister of Foreign Affairs;* b. 11 May 1946, granddaughter of fmr Liberian Pres. Charles D. B. King. *Education:* Univ. of Ibadan, Nigeria, Brandeis Univ., Northeastern Univ., Colombia Univ., USA. *Career:* Sr Planning Officer, Ministry of Planning and Econ. Affairs 1968–69, Deputy Dir Nat. Social Security and Welfare Corpn 1975–1980; Deputy Dir UNIFEM 1982–89, Deputy Resident Rep. of UN in Senegal 1989–91, UNDP Rep. in Mauritius and the Seychelles 1991–94, Man. Dir Country Strategy and Program Devt Div., UNIDO 1994–1996, Chief, E and Cen. Africa Div. Regional Bureau for Africa, UNDP 1996–1997, Country Programme Advisor UNDP Africa 1998, UNDP Resident Rep. and Resident Co-ordinator UN System Operational activities for Devt in Zambia 1998–2003, Programme Co-ordinator UNDP-UNESCO Project Foundations for Africa's Future Leadership, UNESCO's Regional Officer for Educ. in Africa, 2006; Minister of Commerce and Industry 2006–07, of Foreign Affairs 2007–; Order Distinguished Services, Second Div. (Zambia); Liberian Business Asscn Award.

Address: Ministry of Foreign Affairs, Mamba Point, PO Box 10-9002, 1000 Monrovia 10, Liberia (office). *Telephone:* 226763 (office). *Website:* www.mofa.gov.lr (office).

KINSMAN, Jeremy K. B.; Canadian diplomatist and academic; *Diplomat in Residence, Woodrow Wilson School of Public and International Affairs, Princeton University;* b. 28 Jan. 1942, Montreal; m. Hana Kinsman; two d. *Education:* Princeton Univ., USA and Institut d'études politiques, Paris, France. *Career:* joined diplomatic service 1966; officer Mission to EC 1968–70; with Mission to UN, New York 1975–80, Minister and Deputy Perm. Rep. 1979–80; Minister of Political Affairs, Embassy in Washington DC 1981–85; Asst Deputy Minister of Cultural Affairs and Broadcasting, Dept of Communications 1985–89; Asst Deputy Minister of Political and Int. Security Affairs, Dept of External Affairs 1990–92; Amb. to Russia 1992–96, to Italy 1996–2000; High Commr to UK 2000–02; Amb. to EU 2002–06 (retd); currently Diplomat in Residence, Woodrow Wilson School of Public and Int. Affairs, Princeton Univ. *Address:* Woodrow Wilson School of Public and International Affairs, Princeton University, 304 Robertson Hall, Princeton, NJ 08544-1013, USA (office). *Telephone:* (609) 258-5125 (office). *Fax:* (609) 258-2809 (office). *E-mail:* jkinsman@princeton.edu (office). *Website:* wws.princeton.edu (office).

KIOA, Sione Ngongo, PhD; Tongan diplomatist; *High Commissioner to UK;* m. Victorina Kioa. *Education:* Tonga High School, Univ. of the South Pacific, Fiji, Australian Nat. Univ., Canberra. *Career:* Deputy Dir Cen. Planning 1992–96; Deputy Sec. Ministry of Finance 1996–99; Asst Exec. Dir IMF, Washington, DC 1999–2001; Dir Fiscal and Econ. Policies, Ministry of Finance 2001–02; Project Man. Reconstruction and Rehabilitation Operation of Cyclone Waqa 2002; CEO and Gen. Man. Leiola Duty Free Shops 2002–05; Pres. Tonga Chamber of Commerce and Industries, Nuku'alofa 2002–05; High Commr to UK 2006– (also accred to the Netherlands and other mem. countries of the EU 2007–). *Address:* High Commission of Tonga, 36 Molyneux Street, London, W1H 5BQ, England (office). *Telephone:* (20) 7724-5828 (office). *Fax:* (20) 7723-9074 (office). *E-mail:* snkioa@tongahighcom.co.uk (office).

KIPPER, Judith, BA; American foreign policy analyst; *Director for Middle East Programs, Institute of World Affairs; Education:* UCLA. *Career:* Resident Fellow, American Enterprise Inst. 1980–86; Guest Scholar, Brookings Inst. 1987–95; Co-Dir Middle East Studies Program, Center for Strategic and Int. Studies (CSIS) 1995–97; Dir of Energy Security Group, Council on Foreign Relations (CFR) 1985–2007; currently Dir for Middle East Programs, Inst. of World Affairs, Arlington, Va; co-ed. Middle East in Global Perspective journal; consultant to ABC News, interviews with Saddam Hussein, Baghdad 1990, Mikhail Gorbachev, Moscow, 1991; fmr consultant on int. affairs, RAND Corpn; participant Middle East and N Africa Econ. Summits, Casablanca 1994, Amman 1995; contrib. to The Washington Post, The Los Angeles Times, The New York Times; consultant to private sector on Middle East issues. *Publications:* The Arab–Israeli Military Balance and the Art of Operations 1987, The Middle East in Global Perspective (co-Ed.) 1991. *Address:* PO Box 21805, Washington, DC 20009, USA (office). *Telephone:* (202) 387-0456 (office). *E-mail:* jkipper@iwa.org (office). *Website:* www.iwa.org (office).

KIRAKOSSIAN, Arman J., DHist; Armenian diplomatist, civil servant and academic; *Deputy Foreign Minister;* b. 10 Sept. 1956, Yerevan; m. Susanna Nazarian; one s. *Education:* Armenian State Pedagogical Univ. *Career:* Fellow, then Head of Dept and Project Dir Centre for Social Sciences, Nat. Acad. of Sciences 1980–86, Assoc. Dir Armenian Diaspora Studies Dept 1990–91; consultant CP Cen. Cttee and mem. Govt Advisory Panel on Science and Int. Relations 1986–90; First Deputy Foreign Minister 1991–94, Acting Minister 1992–93; Amb. to Greece (also accred to Cyprus, Slovenia, Croatia, Albania and fmr Fed. Repub. of Yugoslavia) 1994–99; apptd Dean of Diplomatic Corps in Athens 1999; Amb. to USA 1999–2005; Deputy Foreign Minister 2005–. *Publications include:* numerous books and more than 100 scientific publs. *Address:* Ministry of Foreign Affairs, 375010 Yerevan, Republic Square, Government House 2, Armenia (office). *Telephone:* (10) 52-35-31 (office). *Fax:* (10) 54-39-25 (office). *E-mail:* mail@armankirakossian.com; info@armeniaforeignministry.com (office). *Website:* www.armeniaforeignministry.am (office); www.armankirakossian.com.

KIRBY, Hon. Justice Michael Donald, AC, CMG, BA, BEcons, LLM; Australian judge; *Justice, High Court;* b. 18 March 1939, Sydney; partner Johan van Vloten 1969. *Education:* Fort Street Boys' High School and Univ. of Sydney. *Career:* Fellow, Senate, Univ. of Sydney 1964–69; mem. NSW Bar Council 1974; Deputy Pres., Australian Conciliation & Arbitration Comm. 1975–83; Chair. Australian Law Reform Comm. 1975–84, OECD Expert

Group on Privacy and Int. Data Flows 1978–80, Cttee of Counsellors, Human and People's Rights UNESCO 1985, UNESCO Expert Group on the Rights of Peoples 1989; mem. Admin. Review Council of Australia 1976–84; mem. Council, Univ. of Newcastle, NSW 1977–83, Deputy Chancellor 1978–83; mem. Australian Nat. Comm. for UNESCO 1980–84, 1997– (Hon. mem. 1997–2007), Australian Inst. of Multicultural Affairs 1979–83; Judge, Fed. Court of Australia 1983–84; mem. Exec. CSIRO 1983–86; Chancellor, Macquarie Univ., Sydney 1984–93; Pres. Court of Appeal, Supreme Court of NSW 1984–96; Acting Chief Justice of NSW 1988, 1990, 1993, 1995, 2007, 2008; Admin. (Acting Gov.) NSW 1991; Justice, High Court of Australia 1996–; Acting Chief Justice of Australia 2007–08; Commr WHO Global Comm. on AIDS 1989–91; mem. Int. Comm. of Jurists, Geneva 1985–99, mem. Exec. Cttee 1989–95, Chair. 1992–95, Pres. 1995–98, Pres. Australian Section 1989–96; Special Rep. of Sec.-Gen. of UN on Human Rights for Cambodia 1993–96; Pres. Court of Appeal of Solomon Islands 1995–96; Pres. Australian Acad. of Forensic Sciences 1987–89; mem. Ethics Cttee of Human Genome Org. 1995–2003; mem. Council of the Australian Opera; mem. ILO Fact-Finding and Conciliation Comm. on Freedom of Asscn Inquiry on South Africa 1991–92; mem. Perm. Tribunal of Peoples' Session on Tibet 1992; Trustee, AIDS Trust of Australia 1987–93; Gov. Int. Council for Computer Communications, Washington 1984–; mem. UNESCO Jury for Prize for Teaching of Human Rights 1994–96, UNESCO Int. Bioethics Cttee 1996–2006; Rapporteur Int. Group on Judicial Integrity (UNHCR) 2001–, UNAIDS Global Panel on HIV/AIDS and Human Rights 2003–; Co-Chair. Expert Group on Bioethics and Human Rights, High Commr of Human Rights 2002–; Chair. UNAIDS Expert Group on HIV Testing in UN Peacekeeping Operations 2001–02, Jt UNAIDS/High Commr for Human Rights Expert Group on Revision of UN Guidelines on HIV/AIDS and Human Rights 2002–; Chair. Group of Experts, UNESCO IBC drafting of Declaration of Universal Norms in Bioethics 2004–05; mem. Judicial Reference Group, High Commr for Human Rights 2007–; mem. Advisory Bd Int. Human Rights Inst., De Paul Univ., Chicago, USA; Hon. Fellow, NZ Research Foundation, Australian Acad. of Social Sciences 1996, Acad. of Social Sciences in Australia 2004, Australian Acad. of Humanities 2006; Hon. Bencher, Inner Temple (London) 2006; Hon. mem. American Law Inst. 2000, Soc. of Legal Scholars (UK) 2007; Hon. DLitt (Newcastle, NSW) 1987, (Ulster) 1998, (James Cook Univ.) 2003, Hon. LLD (Macquarie Univ.) 1995, (Sydney Univ.) 1996, (Buckingham Univ.) 2000, (ANU) 2004, Hon. DUniv (S Australia) 2001, (Southern Cross Univ.) 2007; Loewenthal Medal, Sydney Univ., Australian Human Rights Medal 1991, Laureate, UNESCO Prize for Human Rights Educ. 1998. *Publications:* Industrial Index to Australian Labour Law 1978, 1984, Reform the Law 1983, The Judges 1984, A Touch of Healing 1986 (co-ed.), Through the World's Eye 2000, Judicial Activism (Hamlyn Lectures 2003) 2004. *Address:* Judge's Chambers, High Court of Australia, Level 19, Law Court's Building, 184 Phillip Street, Sydney, NSW 2000 (office); 2C Dumaresq Road, Rose Bay, NSW 2029, Australia (home). *Telephone:* (2) 6270-6969 (office). *Fax:* (2) 6270-6970 (office). *E-mail:* kirbyj@hcourt.gov .au (office).

KIRBY, Michael D., BA; American diplomatist; *Ambassador to Moldova;* m. Sara Powelson Kirby; two d. *Education:* Univ. of Pennsylvania, Univ. of N Carolina, Chapel Hill. *Career:* career mem. Sr Foreign Service, joined Foreign Service 1979, served in Embassies in Copenhagen, Dar es Salaam and Georgetown, Consul, Consulate Gen., Kraków 1988–91, Regional Consular Officer, Consulate Gen., Frankfurt 1996–98; served as Dir Office of Intelligence Coordination, Bureau of Intelligence and Research, Dept of State and as Desk Officer, Office of Caribbean Affairs; Consul Gen., Warsaw 2001–04, Seoul 2004–06; Amb. to Moldova 2006–. *Address:* US Embassy, str. Mateevici 103, 2009 Chisinau, Moldova (office). *Telephone:* (22) 40-83-00 (office). *Fax:* (22) 23-30-44 (office). *E-mail:* IRCChisinau@state.gov (office). *Website:* moldova.usembassy.gov (office).

KIRCHNER, Néstor Carlos; Argentine lawyer, politician and fmr head of state; *President, Partido Justicialista (PJ);* b. 25 Feb. 1950, Río Gallegos, Santa Cruz; m. Cristina Fernandez de Kirchner; one s. one d. *Education:* La Plata Nat. Univ. *Career:* fmr lawyer; jailed briefly during 1976–83 mil. dictatorship; Pres. Fund for Social Provision 1983–84; Mayor of Río Gallegos 1987–91; Gov. Prov. of Santa Cruz 1991–2003; mem. Partido Justicialista (Peronist party), Pres. 2008–; Pres. of Argentina 2003–07; Pres. Pres. Fed. Org. for Producers of Hydrocarbons 1992–. *Address:* Partido Justicialista (PJ), Domingo Matheu 130, 1082ABD Buenos Aires, Argentina (office). *Telephone:* (11) 4954-2450 (office). *Fax:* (11) 4954-2421 (office). *E-mail:* contacto@pj.org.ar (office). *Website:* www .pj.org.ar (office).

KIRKILAS, Gediminas; Lithuanian politician; *Prime Minister;* b. 30 Aug. 1951, Vilnius; m. Liudmila Kirkilienė; one s. one d. *Education:* Vilnius

Teachers' Training Coll., Vilnius Higher School of Politics, Vilnius Univ. *Career:* interior restorer, Monument Restoration Trust 1972–78; worked within CP 1982–90; Asst to First Sec. of Cen. Cttee of Lithuanian CP, later to Deputy of Supreme Council–Reconstituted Seimas (Parl.), Repub. of Lithuania 1989–92; Ed. and Publr Golos Litvy (The Voice of Lithuania) daily newspaper 1991–95; mem. Seimas 1992–; fmr Chair. Cttee on Nat. Security and Defence, Cttee on Foreign Affairs, Deputy Chair. Cttee on European Affairs, Head of Seimas Del. to NATO Parl. Ass.; Elder Group of Lithuanian Social Democratic Labour Party 1993–96; head, Presidential working group to develop nat. security strategy 1993–96; Special Rep. of Pres. for matters related to transportation between Lithuania and Kaliningrad region of Russian Fed. 2002; given rank of Amb. 2003; Minister of Nat. Defence and mem. Cttee on Nat. Security and Defence 2004–06; Prime Minister of Lithuania 2006–; acting Sec. of Ind. Cen. Cttee of Lithuanian CP 1990; elected Deputy Chair. Constitutive Ass. of Lithuanian Democratic Labour Party (LDLP) 1990, first Asst to the Sec. 1991–96, temporary Chair. 1993, mem. Presidium 1996–2001; following absorption of LLDP in 2001, Deputy Chair. Lithuanian Social Democratic Party 2001–; Cross of Officer of the Lithuanian Grand Duke Vytautas, Order of the Cross of Vytis, Commdr Cross of the Repub. of Poland, Grand Cross of Portugal. *Publications:* Political Commentary for the Period 1995, numerous articles on policy and public life. *Address:* Office of the Prime Minister, Gedimino pr. 11, Vilnius 01103, Lithuania (office). *Telephone:* (5) 266-3848 (office). *Fax:* (5) 216-3877 (office). *E-mail:* kanceliarija@lrvk.lt (office). *Website:* www.lrv.lt (office); www.ministraspirmininkas.lt (office).

KIRN, Roman, BA; Slovenian diplomatist; b. 23 Feb. 1952, Trbovlje; m.; two c. *Education:* Univ. of Ljubljana. *Career:* joined Fed. Ministry of Foreign Affairs of SFR Yugoslavia 1977; served on Cttee on Foreign Relations of Slovenia 1978–80, 1984–86; First Sec. Yugoslav Embassy in Burma 1980–84; Head Multilateral Relations Dept Ministry of Foreign Affairs 1991–92, 1996–2000; Minister Counsellor Embassy in Czech Repub. 1992–96; Perm. Rep. to OSCE Vienna 2000–02; Perm. Rep. to UN 2002–07. *Address:* c/o Ministry of Foreign Affairs, 1001 Ljubljana, Prešernova 25, Slovenia (office). *Website:* www.mzz.gov.si (office).

KIRSCH, Philippe, QC, LLM; Canadian judge and fmr diplomatist; *President, International Criminal Court;* b. 1 April 1947, Quebec. *Education:* Stanislas Coll., Montreal, Univ. of Montreal, Acad. of Int. Law, The Hague, The Netherlands, Int. Peace Acad., Vienna, Austria. *Career:* called to the Bar, Quebec 1970; apptd QC 1988; joined diplomatic service, assignments with Bureau of Legal Affairs and US Div., Dept of Foreign Affairs and Int. Trade, Ottawa, with Embassy in Peru, Perm. Mission to the UN, New York –1985; Dir Legal Operations Div., Dept of External Affairs, Ottawa 1983–88; Amb. and Deputy Perm. Rep. to UN, New York 1988–92; Deputy Legal Adviser and Dir-Gen., Bureau of Legal Affairs, Dept of Foreign Affairs and Int. Trade 1992–94, Asst Deputy Minister for Legal and Consular Affairs 1994–96, Legal Adviser 1994–99; Amb. to Sweden 1999–2003; Judge, Int. Criminal Court (ICC), The Hague 2003–, Pres. 2006–; Amb. and Agent of Canada in legal disputes 1985–86, 1995–98, 1999–2003; Chair. Preparatory Comm. for ICC 1999–2002; Rep. of Canada to various int. orgs and confs; Chair. UN Legal Ad Hoc Cttees 1993–94, 1997–99; mem. Perm. Court of Arbitration 1995–99; Robert S. Litvack Human Rights Memorial Award 1999, Minister of Foreign Affairs Award for Foreign Policy Excellence 1999, William J. Butler Human Rights Medal 2001. *Publications:* chapters in books, articles in professional journals. *Address:* International Criminal Court, Maanweg 174, 2516 AB The Hague, The Netherlands (office). *Telephone:* (70) 5158515 (office). *Fax:* (70) 5158555 (office). *E-mail:* pio@icc-cpi.int (office). *Website:* www.icc-cpi.int/ presidency/president.html (office).

KIRTCHEVA, Elena Petkova, DJur; Bulgarian diplomatist, politician and lawyer; *Secretary General, Vienna Economic Forum;* b. 18 Sept. 1949, Lom; m. 1980; one s. *Education:* Univ. of Sofia. *Career:* Legal Adviser industrial plant 1973–76; Lecturer in Nat. and World Econ. 1976–90; Legal Expert Nat. Round Table 1990; Opposition mem. Grand Nat. Ass. 1990, Vice-Chair. New Constitution Comm. 1990, mem. Bd of Dirs Parl. Agrarian Party 1990, mem. Bulgarian Parl. Del. to Ass. of Council of Europe 1990; mem. Bulgarian Del. to CSCE 1990–91; Amb. to Switzerland 1991–96, to Liechtenstein 1994–96, to Finland 1999–2001, to Austria 2001–05; Sec. Gen. Vienna Econ. Forum 2005–; Adviser to United Bank of Switzerland (UBS), Direktion Zürich 1997–99. *Publications include:* various scientific articles and studies and manuals and handbooks for univ. students. *Address:* Vienna Economic Forum, Hotel Hilton, Office Centre, Level M2, 1030 Vienna, Am Stadtpark, Austria (office); Bresa Street 2, 1421 Sofia, Bulgaria (home). *Telephone:* (1) 714-10-14 (office); (2) 865-91-88 (home). *Fax:* (1) 714-10-14 (office). *E-mail:* office@vienna-economic-forum.com (office); elena.kirtcheva@bigfoot.com (home). *Website:* www.vienna -economic-forum.com (office).

KISLOV, Aleksander Konstantinovich, DHist; Russian political scientist; *Head, Peace Research Centre, Institute of World Economy and International Relations (IMEMO), Russian Academy of Sciences;* b. 11 Sept. 1929, Moscow; m.; one s. two d. *Education:* Moscow Inst. of Int. Relations. *Career:* corresp., Head of Div., Head of Sector, Deputy Ed.-in-Chief Foreign Information Dept, TASS News Agency 1956–71; Head of Sector, Inst. for USA and Canadian Studies, USSR Acad. of Sciences 1971–86, Deputy-Dir Inst. of World Econs and Int. Relations 1986–96; Dir Peace Research Inst., Inst. of World Economy and Int. Relations (IMEMO), Russian Acad. of Sciences 1990–96, Head Peace Research Centre 1996–; fmr consultant Dept of Planning Int. Events, USSR Ministry of Foreign Affairs; mem. editorial bd numerous journals; mem. Russian Acad. of Nat. Sciences 1992–. *Publications:* USA and the Islamic World, Contemporary Foreign Policy of the USA (two vols, ed. and co-author). *Address:* Institute of World Economy and International Relations (IMEMO), Profsoyuznaya str. 23, 117997 Moscow (office); Apt 374, prospekt Vernadskogo 127, 117571 Moscow, Russia (home). *Telephone:* (495) 128-93-89 (office); (495) 438-61-59 (home). *Fax:* (495) 120-65-75 (office). *E-mail:* imemoran@online.ru (office). *Website:* www.imemo.ru (office).

KISLYAK, Sergey I.; Russian diplomatist; *Deputy Minister of Foreign Affairs;* b. 1950. *Education:* Moscow State Inst. of Eng and Tech.; Acad. of Foreign Trade. *Career:* joined Ministry of Foreign Affairs 1977 serving in numerous positions; Dir Dept of Security and Disarmament 1995–98; Amb. to Belgium, concurrently Perm. Rep. to NATO, Brussels 1998–2003, Deputy Minister of Foreign Affairs 2003–; fmr mem. Coll. of the Ministry of Foreign Affairs. *Address:* Ministry of Foreign Affairs, Smolenskaya–Sennaya pl. 32/34, 119200 Moscow, Russia (office). *Telephone:* (495) 244-16-06 (office). *Fax:* (495) 230-21-30 (office). *E-mail:* ministry@mid.ru (office). *Website:* www .mid.ru (office).

KISS, Tibor; Hungarian diplomatist; *Permanent Representative, European Union;* b. 9 Oct. 1954, Budapest; m.; two c. *Education:* Univ. of Econ. Sciences, Budapest. *Career:* various posts at Ministry of Foreign Affairs including Desk Officer, Directorate-Gen. for Econ. Policy 1977, Head USA Desk (Second Sec.), Directorate-Gen. for N Atlantic region 1985, Dir-Gen. Directorate-Gen. for European Integration 1992, Deputy Dir-Gen. Directorate-Gen. One (Western and Northern Europe) 2000; overseas postings include Third Sec., Embassy in The Hague 1980, Deputy Chief of Mission (First Counsellor), Embassy in Brussels 1989; Amb. to Belgium (also accred to Luxembourg) 1995, to Netherlands 2002; currently Perm. Rep. to EU, Brussels; Founding mem. and fmr Vice-Pres. Hungarian Atlantic Council; mem. Advisory Bd Hungarian European Studies Foundation (Europe 2000); Grand Officier de l'Ordre de Léopold II (Belgium). *Address:* Permanent Representation of Hungary to the EU, 92–98 Rue de Trèves, 1040 Brussels, Belgium (office). *Telephone:* (2) 234-12-00 (office). *Fax:* (2) 372-07-84 (office). *E-mail:* sec.beu@kum.hu (office). *Website:* www.hunrep.be (office).

KISSINGER, Henry Alfred, MA, PhD; American academic, international consultant and fmr government official; *Chairman, Kissinger McLarty Associates;* b. 27 May 1923, Fuerth, Germany; m. 1st Anne Fleisher 1949 (divorced 1964); one s. one d.; m. 2nd Nancy Maginnes 1974. *Education:* George Washington High School, Harvard Coll., Harvard Univ. *Career:* went to USA 1938; naturalized US Citizen 1943; US Army 1943–46; Dir Study Group on Nuclear Weapons and Foreign Policy, Council of Foreign Relations 1955–56; Dir Special Studies Project, Rockefeller Brothers Fund 1956–58; Consultant, Weapons System Evaluation Group, Joint Chiefs of Staff 1956–60, Nat. Security Council 1961–63, US Arms Control and Disarmament Agency 1961–69, Dept of State 1965–68 and to various other bodies; Faculty mem. Harvard Univ. 1954–69; Dept of Govt and Center for Int. Affairs; faculty Harvard Univ. Center for Int. Affairs 1960–69; Dir Harvard Int. Seminar 1951–69, Harvard Defense Studies Program 1958–69, Asst to Pres. of USA for Nat. Security Affairs 1969–75; Sec. of State 1973–77; prominent in American negotiations for the Viet Nam settlement of Jan. 1973 and in the negotiations for a Middle East ceasefire 1973, 1974; Trustee, Center for Strategic and Int. Studies 1977–; Chair. Kissinger Assocs Inc. (since 1999 Kissinger McLarty Assocs Inc.) 1982–; mem. Pres.'s Foreign Intelligence Advisory Bd 1984–90; Chair. Nat. Bipartisan Comm. on Cen. America 1983–84; fmr Chair. US Comm. investigating Sept. 11 attacks; Counsellor to J. P. Morgan Chase Bank and mem. of its Int. Advisory Council; Hon. Gov. Foreign Policy Asscn; Sr Fellow, Aspen Inst., syndicated columnist LA Times 1984–; Adviser to Bd of Dirs American Express, Forstmann Little & Co., Dir Emer. Freeport

McMoran Copper and Gold Inc., Conti Group Cos Ltd, The TCW Group, US Olympic Cttee, Int. Rescue Cttee; Chair. American Int. Group, Int. Advisory Bd; mem. Exec. Cttee Trilateral Comm.; Chair. Eisenhower Exchange Fellowships; Chancellor The Coll. of William and Mary; Hon. Chair. World Cup USA 1994; Woodrow Wilson Book Prize 1958, American Inst. for Public Service Award 1973, Nobel Peace Prize 1973, American Legion Distinguished Service Medal 1974, Wateler Peace Prize 1974, Presidential Medal of Freedom 1977, Medal of Liberty 1986, Hon. KCMG 1995, and many other awards and prizes. *Publications:* Nuclear Weapons and Foreign Policy 1956, A World Restored: Castlereagh, Metternich and the Restoration of Peace 1812–22 1957, The Necessity for Choice: Prospects of American Foreign Policy 1961, The Troubled Partnership: A Reappraisal of the Atlantic Alliance 1965, American Foreign Policy (3 essays) 1969, White House Years 1979, For the Record 1981, Years of Upheaval 1982, Observations: Selected Speeches and Essays 1982–84 1985, Diplomacy 1994, Years of Renewal 1999, Does America Need a Foreign Policy? 2001, Ending the Vietnam War 2003, Crisis 2003; and numerous articles on US foreign policy, international affairs and diplomatic history. *Address:* 350 Park Avenue, New York, NY 10022; Suite 400, 1800 K Street, NW, Washington, DC 20006, USA. *Telephone:* (212) 759-7919 (NY); (202) 822-8182 (DC). *Website:* www.kmaglobal.com.

KITAMURA, Hiroshi, KBE; Japanese diplomatist and university president; b. 20 Jan. 1929, Osaka; m. Sachiko Kitamura 1953; two d. *Education:* Tokyo Univ., Fletcher School of Law and Diplomacy, Tufts Univ., Mass., USA. *Career:* joined Foreign Affairs Ministry 1953, served in Washington, DC, New York, Delhi; First Sec., Embassy in London 1963–66; with Mission to OECD, Paris 1971–74; Exec. Asst to Prime Minister 1974–76; Deputy Dir-Gen. American Affairs Bureau 1977–79, Dir-Gen. 1982–84, Deputy Vice-Minister of Foreign Affairs 1984–87, Deputy Minister 1987–88; Consul-Gen. San Francisco 1979–82, Amb. to Canada 1988–90, to the UK 1991–94; Corp. Adviser, Mitsubishi Corpn 1994–99; Pres. Shumei Univ. 1998–2001; Prime Minister's Personal Rep. to Venice Summit 1987, Toronto Summit 1988; Fellow, Center for Int. Affairs, Harvard Univ. 1970; Chair. Japan–British Soc. 1994–2003; Gold and Silver Star, Order of the Rising Sun 1999; Hon. LLD (Northumbria) 1993. *Publications include:* Psychological Dimensions of US–Japanese Relations 1971, Between Friends (co-author) 1985, The UK Seen through an Ambassador's Eyes (in Japanese), Diplomacy and Food (in Japanese), An Ambassador and his Lhasa Apso (in Japanese). *Address:* 1-15-6 Jingumae, Shibuya-ku, Tokyo, Japan. *Telephone:* (3) 3470-4630. *Fax:* (3) 3470-4830.

KITTIKHOUN, Alounkèo; Laotian diplomatist; *Assistant Minister of Foreign Affairs;* b. 10 Oct. 1951, Pakse, Champasark; m. Dr Kongpadith Kittikhoun; two s. *Education:* Royal Inst. of Law and Admin, Vientiane, Univ. of Paris I (Panthéon-Sorbonne), Int. Inst. of Public Admin, Paris, France. *Career:* joined Foreign Ministry 1977; Second Sec., then First Sec. and Counsellor, Perm. Mission to UN 1980–90, Perm. Rep. 1993–2007; Chair. Landlocked Developing Countries Group at the UN 1999–2003 and of numerous other UN bodies and cttees; Deputy Dir Dept of Int. Orgs, Foreign Ministry 1990–92, Dir 1992–93; Assistant Minister of Foreign Affairs 2007–. *Address:* Ministry of Foreign Affairs, rue That Luang 01004, Ban Phonxay, Vientiane, Laos (office). *Telephone:* (21) 413148 (office). *Fax:* (21) 414009 (office). *E-mail:* cabinet@mofa.gov.la (office); alkktk@hotmail.com (home). *Website:* www.mofa.gov.la (office).

KIVRIKOGLU, Gen. Huseyin; Turkish army officer; b. Dec. 1934, Bozuyuk, Bilecik; m.; one s. *Education:* Isiklar Mil. School, Army Acad., Army War Coll., Armed Forces Coll., NATO Defence Coll., Rome, Italy. *Career:* served as platoon and battery commdr in various artillery units 1957–65, Staff Officer 9th Infantry Div. in Sarikamis 1967–70; Planning Officer, Allied Forces S Europe Operations Div., Italy 1979–72; Instructor, Army War Coll. 1972–73; Section Chief of Gen. Staff and Br. Chief of Land Forces Command; Commdr of Cadet Regt, Army Acad., Ankara 1978–80; rank of Brig.-Gen. 1980; Chief of Operations Centre, Supreme HQ Allied Powers in Europe (SHAPE), Belgium 1980–83; Commanding Officer 3rd and 11th Brigades 1983–84; rank of Maj. Gen. 1984; Chief of Staff NATO Allied Land Forces SE Europe (CLSE), Izmir 1984–86; Commanding Officer 9th Infantry Div. 1986–88; rank of Lt-Gen. 1988; Asst Chief of Staff, Gen. Staff HQ; Commanding Officer 5th Corps and Under-Sec. Ministry of Nat. Defence 1990–93; promoted to Four Star 1993; Commdr CLSE 1993–96, First Army, Istanbul 1996–97, Land Forces 1997–98; C-in-C Armed Forces and Chief of Gen. Staff 1998–2002; Armed Forces Distinguished Service Medal, Grand Cross and Golden Honour Medal (Turkey), Star of Romania, Order of Merit (USA), Order of Distinction Medal (Pakistan); numerous Army Acad. Badges, NATO Service Badge, Commdr Armed Forces Identification Badge.

Address: c/o Ministry of National Defence, Milli Savunma Bakanligi, 06100 Ankara, Turkey (office).

KIYANI, Gen. Ashfaq Pervez; Pakistani army officer; *Chief of Army Staff;* b. April 1952, Jehlum; m.; one s. one d. *Education:* Mil. Coll., Jhelum, Command and Staff Coll., Quetta, Command and Gen. Staff Coll., Fort Leavenworth, USA, Nat. Defence Coll., Islamabad. *Career:* commissioned in Baloch Regt 1971 and participated in war; commanded infantry bn, infantry brigade, infantry div. and corps; Deputy Mil. Sec. for Benazir Bhutto 1988–89; fmr Dir-Gen. of Mil. Operations; Corps Commdr of Rawalpindi 2003–04; Dir-Gen. Inter-Services Intelligence 2004–07; chosen to carry out investigations of two assassination attempts on Gen. Pervaiz Musharraf; Vice-Chief of Army Staff (also promoted to four-star Gen.) Oct.–Nov. 2007, Chief of Army Staff Nov. 2007–; Pres. Pakistan Golf Fed. 2004–.
Address: Ministry of Defence, Pakistan Secretariat, No. II, Rawalpindi 46000, Pakistan (office). *Telephone:* (51) 9271107 (office). *Fax:* (51) 9271113 (office).

KIYONGA, Crispus, MD; Ugandan physician and politician; *Minister of Defence;* b. Kasese. *Education:* Johns Hopkins Univ., USA. *Career:* mem. Parl. for Bukonzo West; posts have included Minister for Cooperatives and Marketing 1986, Minister of Finance 1986–92, Minister of Health –2001, Minister without Portfolio Nat. Political Commissar, Nat. Resistance Movt 2001–06, Minister of Defence 2006–; apptd Chair Transitional Working Group for Establishment of Global AIDS and Health Fund by UN Sec.-Gen. 2001.
Address: Ministry of Defence, Bombo, POB 7069, Kampala, Uganda (office). *Telephone:* (41) 2270331 (office). *Fax:* (41) 2245911 (office). *E-mail:* spokesman@defenceuganda.mil.ug (office). *Website:* www.defenceuganda.mil.ug (office).

KJELLÉN, Bo, MPolSc; Swedish diplomatist; *Senior Research Fellow, Stockholm Environment Institute;* b. 8 Feb. 1933, Stockholm; m. 1st Margareta Lindblom 1959 (died 1978); m. 2nd Gia Boyd 1980; four c. *Education:* Univ. of Stockholm. *Career:* entered Foreign Service 1957, posted to Rio de Janeiro, Brussels, Stockholm 1959–69; Prin. Pvt. Sec. to Sec.-Gen., OECD 1969–72; Deputy Head of Mission Del. to EEC, Brussels 1972–74; Amb. to Viet Nam 1974–77; Head Multilateral Dept for Devt Co-operation, Ministry of Foreign Affairs 1977–81; Under-Sec. Admin. and Personnel 1981–85; Amb. to OECD and UNESCO 1985–91; Chief Negotiator, Ministry of Environment 1991–98; Negotiator Climate Convention 1991–2001; Chair. Swedish Research Council for Environment, Agricultural Sciences and Spatial Planning 2001–04; Visiting Fellow, Tyndall Centre, Univ. of E Anglia 2003, 2005; Sr Research Fellow, Stockholm Environment Inst. 2005–; Hon. DSc (Cranfield, UK) 1997; Hon. PhD (Gothenburg) 1999; Hon. DTech (Mälardalen Univ., Sweden) 2005; Elizabeth Haub Prize for Environmental Diplomacy 1999, GEF Award for Environmental Leadership 1999. *Publications:* several articles in academic publs and in the press on environment and sustainable devt.
Address: Stockholm Environment Institute, Kräftriket 2 B, 10691 Stockholm, Sweden (office). *Telephone:* (8) 674-74-00 (office); (18) 71-03-07 (home). *E-mail:* bo.kjellen@sei.se (office). *Website:* www.sei.se (office).

KLAIBER, Klaus Peter, DrJur; German diplomatist and civil servant (retd); *Chairman, Australasia Global Panel Foundation;* b. 21 June 1940, Stuttgart. *Education:* Tübingen Univ., Univ. of Mainz and Univ. Inst. of Int. Studies, Geneva, Switzerland. *Career:* joined Fed. Ministry of Foreign Affairs 1968, Deputy Head of Trainee Dept 1973–77, Deputy Head of European Political Co-operation Dept 1982–85, Deputy Dir of Pvt. Office of Minister of Foreign Affairs 1985–87, Deputy Political Dir 1992–95, Head of Security Policy Sub-Div. 1992–96, Head of Policy Planning 1995–97; Third Sec. Embassy in Kinshasa, Zaïre 1971–73; First Sec., Political Affairs, Embassy in Washington, DC, USA 1977–80; Deputy Head of Mission, Embassy in Nairobi, Kenya 1980–82; Minister-Counsellor, Political Affairs, Embassy in London, UK 1988–91; Asst Sec.-Gen. for Political Affairs, NATO, Brussels, Belgium 1997–2001, apptd. EU Special Envoy to Afghanistan 2001–02; Amb. to Australia 2002–05; Chair. Australasia Global Panel Foundation 2005–; Hon. KCMG 1992; Bundesverdienstkreuz Erste Klasse 20022.
Address: Furtbachstrasse 12A, 70178 Stuttgart, Germany (office). *Telephone:* (711) 220-7786 (office). *E-mail:* klaiber139@netspace.net.au (office).

KLAUS, Václav, PhD; Czech politician, economist and head of state; *President;* b. 19 June 1941, Prague; m. Livia Klausová 1968; two s. *Education:* Prague School of Econs, Cornell Univ., Czech Acad. of Sciences. *Career:* researcher, Inst. of Econs Czechoslovak Acad. of Sciences –1970; various positions Czechoslovak State Bank 1971–86; head Dept of Macroeconomic Policy, Inst. of Forecasting, Acad. of Sciences 1987–; f. Civic Forum Movt (Chair. 1990–91); Minister of Finance 1989–92; Chair.

Civic Democratic Party 1991–2002; Deputy Prime Minister 1991–92; Prime Minister of the Czech Republic 1992–97; Chair. State Defence Council 1993–97; Chair. Govt Cttee for Integration of Czech Repub. in NATO 1997; Chair. Chamber of Deputies 1998–2002; Pres. of Czech Republic 2003–; serves as a Nat. Centre for Policy Analysis Distinguished Leader; mem. Scientific Council, Palacký Univ. 1997–; Hon. Prof. Univ. Guadalajara 1993; Hon. Chair. ODS (Civic Democratic Party) 2002–; Hon. DHumLitt (Suffolk Univ.) 1991, Dr hc (Rochester Inst. of Tech.) 1991, (Univ. Francisco Marroquín, Guatemala) 1993, (Jacksonville, USA) 1995, (Buckingham, UK) 1996, (Prague School of Econs) 1994, (Belgrano Univ., Argentina) 1994, (Tufts Univ., USA) 1994, (Univ. of Aix-Marseilles) 1994, (Tech. Univ. of Ostrava) 1997, (Toronto, Canada) 1997, (Arizona) 1997, (Dallas) 1999, (Chicago) 1999; Schumpeter Prize for Econs, Freedom Award (New York) 1990, Max Schmidheiny Freedom Prize, St Gallen 1992, Ludwig Erhard Prize, Germany 1993, Poeutinger Collegium Prize 1993, Hermann Lindrath Prize (Hanover) 1993, Konrad Adenauer Prize (Prague) 1993, Club of Europe Award 1994, Prix Transition (Fondation du Forum Universal) 1994, Adam Smith Award (Libertas, Copenhagen) 1995, Int. Democracy Medal (Center for Democracy, Washington, DC) 1995, Transatlantic Leadership Award (European Inst., Washington, DC) 1995, Prognos Award (Prognos Forum, Basel) 1995, James Madison Award (James Madison Inst., Jacksonville, USA) 1995, Karel Engliš Prize (Universitas Masarykiana Foundation, Brno) 1995, European Prize for Craftsmanship, Germany 1996, Goldwater Medal for Econ. Freedom, Phoenix, USA 1997, Bernhard Harms Medal (Kiel Inst. of World Econs) 1999. *Publications:* A Road to Market Economy 1991, Tomorrow's Challenge 1991, Economic Theory and Economic Reform 1991, Why am I a Conservative? 1992, Dismantling Socialism: A Road to Market Economy II 1993, The Year–How much is it in the History of the Country? 1993, The Czech Way 1994, Rebirth of a Country: Five Years After 1994, Counting Down to One 1995, Between the Past and the Future: Philosophical Reflections and Essays 1996, The Defence of Forgotten Ideas 1997, Tak pravil Václav Klaus (So Said Václav Klaus, conversations with J. Klusáková), Why I Am Not a Social Democrat 1998, Země, kde se již dva roky nevládne (The Land that has not been Governed for 2 years) 1999, Cesta z pasti (The Way Out of the Trap) 1999 From the Opposition Treaty to the Tolerance Patent 2000, Evropa pohledem politika a pohledem ekonoma (Europe, The View of the Politician and the View of the Economist) 2001, Conversations with Václav Klaus 2001, Klaus v Bruselu (Klaus in Brussels) 2001, On the Road to Democracy–The Czech Republic From Communism to Free Society 2005; numerous articles.
Address: Office of the President, Pražský hrad, 119 08 Prague 1, Czech Republic (office). *Telephone:* 224371111 (office). *Fax:* 224373300 (office). *E-mail:* ladislav.jakl@hrad.cz (office). *Website:* www.hrad.cz (office); www.klaus.cz (home).

KLEIN, Maj.-Gen. Jacques Paul; American air force officer (retd) and international organization official; m. Dr Margrete Siebert Klein; two c. *Career:* fmr Air Force Officer (retd as Maj.-Gen.); joined Foreign Service in Operations Center of Exec. Secr. of Sec. of State 1971; Consular Officer, Consulate-Gen., Bremen; Political Officer, Office of Southern European Affairs, Dept of State; Counsellor Officer, Berlin; Political Officer, Embassy in Bonn; Man. Analysis Officer, Office of Dir-Gen. of Foreign Service; seconded to Dept of Defense as Adviser on Int. Affairs to Sec. of Air Force with rank of Deputy Asst Sec.; Dir Office of Strategic Tech. Matters, Bureau of Politico-Mil. Affairs, Dept of State; Asst Deputy Under-Sec. of Air Force for Int. Affairs, Dept of Defense 1989–90; Prin. Adviser to Dir-Gen. Foreign Service 1990–93; Political Adviser to C-in-C, US European Command, Stuttgart 1993–96; Prin. Deputy High Rep., Bosnia and Herzegovina 1997–99; UN Transitional Admin. for Eastern Slavonia, Baranja and Western Sirmium, rank of Under-Sec.-Gen. 1996–97; Special Rep. of Sec.-Gen. to Bosnia and Herzegovina, rank of Under-Sec.-Gen. 1999–2003; UN Special Rep. for Liberia 2003–05; Visiting Lecturer in Int. Affairs and Frederick Schultz Visiting Prof. of Public and Int. Affairs, Woodrow Wilson School, Princeton Univ. 2005–06 (retd); mem. Cosmos Club and Army and Navy Clubs of Washington, DC, Acad. d'Alsace, Council on Foreign Relations; Grand Officer, Order of the Crown (Belgium), Grand Cross of Merit (Germany), Order of King Dmitar Zvonimir with Sash and Morning Star (Croatia), Commdr, Aeronautical Order of Merit (Brazil), Commdr, Order of the Lion (Senegal), Officier, Légion d'honneur, Kt Great Band of the Humane Order of African Redemption (Nat. Transitional Govt of Liberia); Air Force Distinguished Service Medal, Legion of Merit (with oak leaf cluster), Bronze Star, Distinguished Honor Award, Dept of State, Defense Medal for Outstanding Public Service, Dept of the Air Force Award for Exceptional and Meritorious Civilian Service.
Address: c/o Cosmos Club, 2121 Massachusetts Avenue, NW, Washington, DC 20008, USA.

KLEMM, Hans G., BA, MA; American diplomatist; *Ambassador to Timor-Leste; Education:* Indiana Univ., Stanford Univ. *Career:* career mem. Sr Foreign Service 2001–, joined Foreign Service 1981, overseas assignments at embassies in Bonn, Seoul and Port of Spain; grad. of Sr Seminar; served as Dir Office of Career Devt and Assignments, Bureau of Human Resources, Dept of State, also served as Dir Office of Agric., Biotechnology and Textile Trade Affairs, Bureau of Econ. and Business Affairs; Minister Counselor for Econ. Affairs, Embassy in Tokyo –2007; Amb. to Timor-Leste 2007–; Superior Honor Award 1993, 2000.
Address: US Embassy, Avenida de Portugal, Praia dos Coqueiros, Dili, Timor-Leste (office). *Telephone:* 3324684 (office). *Fax:* 3313206 (office). *E-mail:* larsonta@state.gov (office).

KLEMPERER, Paul David, BA, MBA, PhD, FBA; British economist and academic; *Edgeworth Professor of Economics, University of Oxford;* b. 15 Aug. 1956; m. Margaret Meyer 1989; two s. one d. *Education:* King Edward's School, Birmingham, Peterhouse, Cambridge, Stanford Univ., USA. *Career:* Consultant, Andersen Consulting (now Accenture) 1978–80; Harkness Fellow of Commonwealth Fund 1980–82; Lecturer in Operations Research and Math. Econs, Univ. of Oxford 1985–90, Reader in Econs 1990–95, Edgeworth Prof. of Econs 1995–, John Thomson Fellow and Tutor, St Catherine's Coll. 1985–95, Fellow, Nuffield Coll. 1995–; Visiting Lecturer, MIT 1987, Univ. of Calif., Berkeley 1991, 1993, Stanford Univ. 1991, 1993, Yale Univ. 1994, Princeton Univ. 1998; consultant to Dept of Trade and Industry 1997–2000, US Fed. Trade Comm. 1999–2001, Dept for Energy, Transport and the Regions 2000–01, Dept for the Environment, Food and Rural Affairs 2001–02 and pvt. cos; mem. UK Competition Comm. 2001–05; Ed. RAND Journal of Economics 1993–99; assoc. or mem. editorial Bd Oxford Economic Papers 1986–, Review of Economic Studies 1989–97, Journal of Industrial Economics 1989–96, International Journal of Industrial Organization 1993–2000, European Economic Review 1997–2001, Review of Economic Design 1997–2000, Economic Policy 1998–99, Economic Journal 2000–04, Frontiers in Economics 2000–, Journal of Economic Analysis and Policy 2001–, Journal of Competition Law and Economics 2004–; mem. of Council, Royal Econ. Soc. 2001–, Econometric Soc. 2001– (Fellow 1994), European Econ. Asscn 2002–; Hon. Fellow, ELSE 2001–, Foreign Hon. mem. American Acad. of Arts and Sciences 2005–. *Publications:* The Economic Theory of Auctions 1999, Auctions: Theory and Practice 2004; articles in econs journals.
Address: Nuffield College, Oxford, OX1 1NF, England (office). *Telephone:* (1865) 278588 (office). *E-mail:* paul.klemperer@economics.ox.ac.uk (office). *Website:* www.economics.ox.ac.uk/index.php/staff/klemperer (office); www.paulklemperer.org.

KLESTIL-LÖFFLER, Margot; Austrian diplomatist; *Ambassador to the Czech Republic;* m. Thomas Klestil (fmr Pres. of Austria) 1999 (died 2004). *Career:* cultural attachée, Embassy in Moscow 1978–82, Deputy Head of Mission, Embassy in Bangkok 1985–88, Office of Sec.-Gen. for Foreign Affairs, Fed. Ministry for Foreign Affairs 1988–92; campaign man. for Thomas Klestil in presidential elections 1992, Office of Fed. Pres. 1992–94, Head of Office of Sec.-Gen. for Foreign Affairs 1994–2002, Head of Dept for the Americas 2003–05, Amb. to Czech Repub. 2005–.
Address: Embassy of Austria, Viktora Huga 10, 151 15 Prague 5, Czech Republic (office). *Telephone:* 257090511 (office). *Fax:* 257316045 (office). *E-mail:* austrianembassy@vol.cz (office); prag-ob@bmaa.gv.at (office). *Website:* www.austria.cz (office).

KLICH, Bogdan, MA; Polish physician, politician and academic; *Minister of National Defence;* b. 8 May 1960, Kraków. *Education:* Kraków Medical Acad., Jagiellonian Univ. *Career:* Adviser to Chief Negotiator of Poland with EU 1989–99; doctoral studies, Dept of Historical Philosophy 1991–95; mem. Parl. 2001–04, Vice-Chair. Cttee on Foreign Affairs, mem. Cttee on Nat. Defence; Deputy Minister of Nat. Defence 1999–2000; Observer to European Parl. 2003–04; Polish Rep. and mem. Policy Cttee of Parl. Ass. of Council of Europe 2001–04; mem. European Parl. (Group of European People's Party (Christian Democrats) and European Democrats) 2004–07, Chair. Del. for Relations with Belarus 2004–07, mem. Cttee on Foreign Affairs, Human Rights, Common Security and Defence Policy 2004–07, Conf. of Del. Chairmen 2004–07; Minister of Nat. Defence 2007–; Pres. Inst. of Strategic Studies 1997–; mem. IISS, London; Lecturer, Centre for European Studies, Jagiellonian Univ.; Order of Merit for Defence of Lithuania, Gold Medal of Merit, Ministry of Foreign Affairs, Slovakia.
Address: Ministry of National Defence, ul. Klonowa 1, 00-909 Warsaw, Poland (office). *Telephone:* (22) 6280031 (office). *Fax:* (22) 8455378 (office). *E-mail:* bpimon@wp.mil.pl (office). *Website:* www.wp.mil.pl (office).

KLOSSON, Michael, MA, MPA; American diplomatist and academic; b. 22 Aug. 1949, Washington; m. Boni Klosson; two d. *Education:* Hamilton Coll. and Princeton Univ. *Career:* teacher of English and modern Chinese History, Hong Kong Baptist Coll. 1971–72; joined Foreign Service 1972, served with Bureau of E Asian and Pacific Affairs, State Dept, Washington and Taipei and with Office of Japanese Affairs 1975–81; Special Asst to Secs of State Alexander Haig and George Schultz 1981–83; Deputy Dir Office of European Security and Political Affairs, Dir Secr. Staff, Office of Sec. of State 1984–90; Deputy Chief of Mission and Chargé d'Affaires, US Embassy, Stockholm and The Hague 1990–96; Prin. Deputy Asst Sec. of State for Legis. Affairs 1996–99; Consul-Gen. for Hong Kong and Macao 1999–2002; Amb. to Cyprus 2002–05; State Dept Chair, Industrial Coll. of the Armed Forces 2005–06; Visiting Lecturer, Hamilton Coll., 2006–07; Herbert H. Lehman Fellowship, Winston Churchill Fellowship; six Superior Honor Awards, US Dept of State. *Music:* Behold the Word 1968.
Address: c/o Government Department, Hamilton College, 198 College Hill Road, Clinton, NY 13323, USA.

KMONICEK, Hynek, EdD; Czech diplomatist, civil servant, musician and educationalist; *Ambassador to India;* b. 22 Oct. 1962, Pardubice; m.; one s. two d. *Education:* South Bohemian Univ., Charles Univ., Prague, Hebrew Univ., Israel. *Career:* music teacher and concert player 1986–91; Lecturer Univ. of Pardubice 1991–94; Fellow Hebrew Univ., Jerusalem (on Rothberg Overseas Programme) 1994–95; joined Ministry of Foreign Affairs 1995, served in Dept of Middle East and N Africa 1995–96, Dir of Dept 1997, Dir-Gen. for Asia, Africa and the Americas 1999, Deputy Minister of Foreign Affairs 1999–2001; Amb. and Perm. Rep. to UN, New York Oct. 2001–06; Amb. to India 2006–.
Address: Embassy of the Czech Republic, 50m Niti Marg, Chanakyapuri, New Delhi 110 021, India (office). *Telephone:* (11) 26110205 (office). *Fax:* (11) 26886221 (office). *E-mail:* newdelhi@embassy.mzv.cz (office). *Website:* www.mfa.cz/newdelhi (office).

KNAPP, Oscar, PhD; Swiss economist and diplomatist; *Ambassador to Austria;* m. *Education:* Univ. of St Gall. *Career:* fmr Head of Financial, Econ. and Trade Div., Embassy in Washington, DC; Amb. to Brazil 1996–2000; Exec. mem., State Secr. of Econ. Affairs, mem. Bd of Dirs and Head, Econ. Devt Co-operation Office 2003–06; Amb. to Austria 2006–.
Address: Embassy of Switzerland, Prinz-Eugen-Str. 7, 1030 Vienna, Austria (office). *Telephone:* (1) 795-05-0 (office). *Fax:* (1) 795-05-21 (office). *E-mail:* vie.vertretung@eda.admin.ch (office). *Website:* www.eda.admin.ch/wien (office).

KNIGHT, Keith Desmond St. Aubyn, BA, QC; Jamaican lawyer and politician; b. Brompton, St Elizabeth; m.; two c. *Education:* Howard Univ. and Univ. of Pittsburgh, USA. *Career:* admitted to Bar, Grays Inn, London, UK 1973, admitted to Inner Bar as QC 1995; entered elective politics 1989; MP for E Cen. St Catherine, Minister of Nat. Security and Justice 1989–2001, of Foreign Affairs and Foreign Trade 2001–06; Council Pres., UN Security Council Meeting concerning Afghanistan 2001; Co-founder and Sr Pnr, Knight, Junor & Samuels, Kingston (law firm) 2006–; Exec. mem. People's Nat. Party; mem. Advocate Asscn, Jamaican Bar Asscn; Founder-Pres. Jamaica Nat. Asscn; fmr Pres. Caribbean Asscn of Students.
Address: Upstairs Bog Walk Post Office, St. Catherine, Jamaica (office). *Telephone:* 985-1192 (office). *Fax:* 985-1192 (home).

KNIGHT, Malcolm D., MSc, PhD; Canadian economist; *General Manager, Bank for International Settlements;* b. Windsor, Ont.; m.; three d. *Education:* Univ. of Toronto and London School of Econs, UK. *Career:* teacher of econs, Univ. of Toronto and LSE 1971–75; joined Research Dept, IMF 1975, served successively as economist in Financial Studies Div., Chief of External Adjustment Issues, Asst Dir of Research Dept for Developing Country Studies, Deputy Dir of Middle East Dept, Monetary and Exchange Affairs Dept, European Dept; fmrly COO Bank of Canada, Sr Deputy Gov. 1999–2003, mem. Bd of Dirs; Gen. Man. BIS 2003–; fmrly Adjunct Prof., Centre for Canadian Studies, Johns Hopkins Univ. School of Advanced Int. Studies, Virginia Polytechnic and State Univ.; Academic Visitor, Centre for Labour Econs, LSE 1985–86; mem. Editorial Bd IMF Staff Papers 1987–97; Trustee, Int. Accounting Standards Cttee Foundation, Per Jacobsson Foundation; mem. Bd of Patrons of the European Asscn for Banking and Financial History, Johns Hopkins Univ. Soc. of Scholars. *Publications include:* numerous publs in fields of macroeconomics, int. finance and banking.
Address: Bank for International Settlements, Centralbahnplatz 2, 4052 Basel, Switzerland (office). *Telephone:* (61) 2808080 (office). *Fax:* (61) 2809100 (office). *E-mail:* emailmaster@bis.org (office). *Website:* www.bis.org (office).

KNIGHT, Terry; British diplomatist; *High Commissioner to Antigua and Barbuda; Career:* previously served in St Vincent and the Grenadines, High Commr to Antigua and Barbuda (also accred to St Kitts and Nevis) 2005–.
Address: British High Commission, Price Waterhouse Coopers Centre, PO Box 483, 11 Old Parham Road, St John's, Antigua and Barbuda (office).

Telephone: 462-0008 (office). *Fax:* 562-2124 (office). *E-mail:* britishc@candw.ag (office).

KNIPPING VICTORIA, Eladio, LLB; Dominican Republic diplomatist; b. 28 June 1933, Santiago de los Caballeros; m. Soledad Knipping 1963; one s. one d. *Education:* Autonomous University of Santo Domingo, Diplomatic School of Spain, School of Int. Affairs, Madrid. *Career:* Asst to Madrid Consulate 1963–65, Econ. Attaché, Netherlands 1966–68; Sec. Consultative Comm. Ministry of Foreign Affairs; Minister-Counsellor and Deputy Chief of Div. of UN Affairs, OAS and Int. Orgs 1966–68, 1969–74; Minister-Counsellor Perm. Mission to UN, New York 1968–69, Amb. to Honduras 1974–78; Perm. Rep. to OAS 1979–83, 1987–95; Amb. (non-resident) to Barbados, Jamaica, St Lucia and Trinidad and Tobago 1990–, to Haiti 1995–97, to Panama 1997–2001, to Honduras 2001; Perm. Rep. to UN, New York 1983–87; Pres. Juridical and Political Comm., OAS Perm. Council 1981–82, 1992–93; Dominican mem. Int. Court of Arbitration, The Hague; Del. UN III Conf. of Law of the Sea; Lecturer in Int. Law Pedro Henríquez Ureña Univ. 1969; f. Inst. Comparative Law; mem. Spanish-Portuguese-American and Philippine Inst. of Int. Law (Pres. 1990–92); UN Adlai Stevenson Fellow.
Address: c/o Secretariat of State for External Relations, Avda Independencia 752, Santo Domingo, DN, Dominican Republic (office).

KNUDSEN, Olav Fagelund, PhD; Norwegian research director and professor of political science; b. Stockholm, Sweden; m. Inga Lena Welander Knudsen. *Education:* Univ. of Oslo, Norway, Univ. of Denver, USA. *Career:* Dean of Social Sciences, Univ. of Oslo 1981–83, Prof. of Political Science 1985–90; Dir of Research, Norwegian Inst. of Int. Affairs 1988–90, Dir 1990–95; Head of Research, Södertörns högskola (Univ. Coll.) 1998–2000, Prof. of Political Science 2001–06; Chair. European Standing Group on Int. Relations (ECPR) 1998–2004; Dir of Research, Swedish Inst. of Int. Affairs (SIIA) 2003–06; consultant to research councils and govt ministries of Norway and Sweden, Home Rule Govt of Greenland, Nordic Council of Ministers, Council of Europe; Chair. Norwegian Asscn for Int. Studies 1989–91; Pres. Nordic Int. Studies Asscn 1993–96; Vice-Pres. Int. Studies Asscn 2005–06; Woodrow Wilson Dissertation Fellow. *Publications:* The Politics of International Shipping 1973, Multinational Corporations in the Nordic Economies 1980, Anarchy and Community 1994, Stability and Security in the Baltic Sea Region 1999, Security Strategies, Power Disparity and Identity 2007; articles in professional journals. *Address:* Swedish Institute of International Affairs, Drottning Kristinas väg 37, POB 27035, 10251 Stockholm, Sweden (office). *Fax:* (8) 51176899 (office). *E-mail:* info@ui.se (office). *Website:* www.ui.se (office); www.oilspillregimes.com.

KOBEH GONZÁLEZ, Roberto; Mexican engineer, public servant and international organization official; *President, Council, International Civil Aviation Organization; Education:* Nat. Polytechnic Inst. of Mexico. *Career:* fmr Prof. of Aeronautical Electronics, Nat. Polytechnic Inst.; 40 years of experience as public servant in Mexican Govt, occupying various posts in Civil Aeronautics Directorate, including Deputy Dir-Gen. for Admin and Air Transport, Dir-Gen. Air Navigation Services of Mexico (SENEAM) 1978–97; Rep. of Mexico on Council of ICAO, serving as First Vice-Pres., Chair. Finance Cttee, and as mem. Air Transport and Unlawful Interference Cttees 1998–2006, Pres. Council 2006–; Emilio Carranza Medal, Award for Extraordinary Service, Fed. Aviation Admin (USA), honoured by Cen. American Corpn of Aerial Navigation Services for his contrib. to devt of aviation in Cen. America. *Address:* International Civil Aviation Organization, External Relations and Public Information Office, 999 University Street, Montréal, PQ H3C 5H7, Canada (office). *Telephone:* (514) 954-8220 (office); (514) 954-8221 (office). *Fax:* (514) 954-6376 (office). *E-mail:* icaohq@icao.int (office). *Website:* www.icao.int (office).

KODJO, Edem; Togolese politician and administrator; *Chairman, Coalition des forces démocrates (CFD);* b. 23 May 1938, Sokodé; m. 1962; two s. two d. *Education:* Coll. St Joseph, Univ. of Admin, Paris, France. *Career:* worked as admin. for Office de Radiodiffusion-Télévision Française (ORTF) 1964–67; returned to Togo 1967; Sec.-Gen., Ministry of Finance, Economy and Planning 1967–72; Admin., Banque Centrale des Etats de l'Afrique de l'Ouest 1967–76, Pres. of Admin. Council 1973–76; Dir-Gen. Soc. Nat. d'Investissement 1972–73; Minister of Finance and Economy 1973–76, of Foreign Affairs 1976–77, of Foreign Affairs and Co-operation 1977–78; Sec.-Gen. of the OAU 1978–84; Assoc. Prof. Sorbonne, Paris 1985–90; Prime Minister of Togo 1994–96, 2005–06; Founder and Chair. Pan-African Inst. of Int. Relations (IPRI); Ed. Afrique 2000; mem. Rassemblement du Peuple Togolaise (RPT), RPT Political Bureau (Sec.-Gen. 1967–71); Leader Togolese Union for Democracy (UTD) –1999, Pres. Convergence patriotique panafricaine 1999–2003, then merger with several other parties to form Coalition des forces démocrates (CFD), currently

acting Chair; mem. Club of Rome; Gov. for Togo, IMF 1973–76; fmr Chair. OAU Council of Ministers, Afro-Arab Perm. Comm. on Co-operation, OAU Cttee of Ten; Commdr, Ordre du Mono, Togo, Officier, Légion d'honneur; Dr hc (Univ. of Bordeaux I); Univ. of Sorbonne Medal. *Address:* Coalition des forces démocrates (CFD), Lomé, Togo (office).

KODJO, Messan Abgéyomé; Togolese politician; b. 12 Oct. 1954, Tokpli, Yoto Pref.; m. *Education:* Higher School of Sciences and Tech., Univ. of Benin, Univ. of Poitiers, France. *Career:* fmr Sales Man. SONACOM; Minister for Youth, Sports and Culture 1988–91, for Territorial Admin and Security 1992; organized Constitutional Referendum; Gen. Man. Port Authority of Lomé 1993–99; elected Deputy 1999; Prime Minister of Togo 2000–02. *Address:* c/o Bureau du Premier Ministre, BP 5618, Lomé, Togo (office).

KOENIGS, Tom, MBA; German UN official; *Special Representative of the Secretary-General for Afghanistan and Head, Assistance Mission in Afghanistan (UNAMA), United Nations;* b. 25 Jan. 1944, Frankfurt am Main; m.; three c. *Education:* Univ. of Berlin. *Career:* co-f. (with Joschka Fischer) first Ministry for Environmental Protection of Hessen Fed. Region 1985; Head of Environmental Protection Dept, City of Frankfurt 1989–, Treas. for Frankfurt 1993–97; Co-Founder and Deputy Pres. Alliance for the Climate (int. NGO) 1990–99; Deputy Special Rep. for Civil Admin, UN Interim Admin Mission in Kosovo (UNMIK) 1999–2002; Special Rep. of the Sec.-Gen. and Head, UN Verification Mission in Guatemala (MINUGUA) 2002–05; Commr for Human Rights Policy and Humanitarian Aid, Ministry of Foreign Affairs 2005; Special Rep. of the Sec.-Gen. for Afghanistan and Head, UN Assistance Mission in Afghanistan (UNAMA) 2006–. *Address:* United Nations Assistance Mission in Afghanistan (UNAMA), POB 5858, Grand Central Station, New York, NY 10163-5858, USA (office); UNAMA, POB 1428, Islambad, Pakistan; UNAMA, Peace Street, Kabul, Afghanistan. *Telephone:* (0831) 246000 (Italy) (office); (212) 963-2669 (NY) (office). *Fax:* (0831) 24 6069 (office). *E-mail:* spokesperson-unama@un.org (office). *Website:* www.unama-afg.org (office).

KOETSCHET, Régis, LLB, LLM, MA; French diplomatist; *Ambassador to Afghanistan;* b. 4 May 1949, Boulogne-Billancourt; m. Perrine Koetschet 1972; four c. *Education:* Coll. Saint-Martin de France, Univ. of Paris X-Nanterre. *Career:* Second Sec., Embassy in Tripoli 1977–79, First Sec., Embassy in Baghdad 1979–81; at Strategical Affairs and Disarmament Dept, Ministry of Foreign Affairs 1981–84; Second Counsellor, Embassy in Islamabad 1984–86, Embassy in The Hague 1987–90; Acting Deputy for Middle East Affairs, Ministry of Foreign Affairs 1990–92; Amb. to Oman 1992–95, to Togo 1995–99; Deputy Dir for N Africa and Middle East, Ministry of Foreign Affairs 1999–2002; Consul-Gen. in Jerusalem 2002–05; Amb. to Afghanistan 2005–; Chevalier, Ordre Nat. du Mérite 1993, Légion d'Honneur 2001, Officer, Order of Orange-Nassau (The Netherlands), Commdr, Order of Mono (Togo). *Address:* Embassy of France, Cherpour Avenue, Shar-i-Nau, POB 62, Kabul, Afghanistan (office). *Telephone:* (70) 284032 (office). *E-mail:* chancellerie.kaboul-amba@diplomatie.gouv.fr (office). *Website:* www.ambafrance-af.org (office).

KOFFI, Yao Charles; Côte d'Ivoirian diplomatist. *Career:* Amb. to USA 2007–. *Address:* Embassy of Cote d'Ivoire (temporary address), 3421 Massachusetts Avenue, NW, Washington, DC 20007, USA (office). *Telephone:* (202) 797-0300 (office). *Fax:* (202) 462-9444 (office).

KOFFIGOH, Joseph Kokou; Togolese politician; *President, Coordination nationale des forces nouvelles;* b. 1948, Kpele Dafo; m.; three s. one d. *Education:* Univs of Abidjan and Poitiers, France. *Career:* called to the Bar, Poitiers, France; joined Viale Chambers, Togo; f. Togo Bar Asscn 1980, Pres. 1990; founder mem. Observatoire panafricain de la démocratie (OPAD) 1991, Ligue togolaise des droits de l'homme 1990; founder mem. and Vice-Pres. FAR (Asscn for reform); Vice-Pres. Nat. Sovereign Conf.; Prime Minister of Togo 1991–94, also Minister of Defence, Minister of Foreign Affairs and Co-operation 1999–2001; apptd Minister of Regional Integration responsible for relations with Parl. 2001; Pres. Coordination nat. des forces nouvelles. *Address:* Coordination nationale des forces nouvelles, Lomé, Togo (office).

KOH, Tommy Thong Bee, LLD; Singaporean diplomatist and law professor; b. 12 Nov. 1937, Singapore; m. Siew Aing 1967; two s. *Education:* Univ. of Singapore, Harvard Univ., USA and Univ. of Cambridge, UK. *Career:* Asst Lecturer, Univ. of Singapore 1962–64, Lecturer 1964–71, Sub-Dean, Faculty of Law, Univ. of Singapore 1965–67, Vice-Dean 1967–68, Assoc. Prof. of Law and Dean, Faculty of Law 1971–74, currently Prof. of Law; Perm. Rep. of Singapore to UN 1968–71, concurrently High Commr to

Canada 1969–71; Perm. Rep. to UN, (also accred to Canada and Mexico) 1974–84; Amb. to USA 1984–90; Amb.-at-Large, Ministry of Foreign Affairs 1990–; Dir Inst. of Policy Studies 1990–97; Exec. Dir Asia–Europe Foundation 1997–; Pres. Third UN Law of the Sea Conf. (Chair. Singapore Del. to Conf.) 1981–82; Chair. Preparatory Cttee, Chair. Main Cttee UN Conf. on Environment and Devt 1990–92; UN Sec.-Gen.'s Special Envoy to Russian Fed., Latvia, Lithuania and Estonia Aug.–Sept. 1993; Chair. Nat. Arts Council 1991–96; Chair. Nat. Heritage Bd 2002–; Commdr Order of the Golden Ark, The Netherlands 1993, Grand Cross of Order of Bernardo O'Higgins, Chile 1997; Hon. LLD (Yale) 1984; Adrian Clarke Memorial Medal 1961, Leow Chia Heng Prize 1961, Public Service Star 1971, Meritorious Service Medal 1979, Wolfgang Friedman Award 1984, Jackson H. Ralston Prize 1985, Annual Award of the Asia Soc., New York, 1985, Int. Service Award, Fletcher School of Law and Diplomacy, Tufts Univ., USA 1987, Jit Trainor Award for Distinction in Diplomacy, Georgetown Univ., USA 1987, Distinguished Service Order Award 1990, Elizabeth Haub Prize, Univ. of Brussels and Int. Council on Environmental Law 1997, Fok Ying Tung Southeast Asia Prize, Hong Kong 1998. *Publications:* United States and East Asia: Conflict and Cooperation 1995, The Quest for World Order: Perspectives of a Pragmatic Idealist 1998. *Address:* c/o Faculty of Law, National University of Singapore, Eu Tong Sen Building, 469G Bukit Timah Road, Singapore 259776, Singapore (office). *Telephone:* 65161305 (office). *Fax:* 67790979 (office). *E-mail:* lawkohtb@nus.edu.sg (office). *Website:* law.nus.edu.sg (office).

KOHL, Helmut, DPhil; German fmr politician; b. 3 April 1930, Ludwigshafen; m. 1st Hannelore Renner 1960 (died 2001); two s.; m. 2nd Maike Richter 2008. *Education:* Univs of Frankfurt and Heidelberg. *Career:* mem. of man. of industrial union 1959; Chair. Christian Democrat Party (CDU), Rhineland-Palatinate 1966–73, Deputy Chair. CDU Deutschlands 1969–73, Chair. 1973–98, Hon. Chair. 1998–2000; Minister-Pres. Rhineland-Palatinate 1969–76; Leader of the Opposition in the Bundestag 1976–82; Fed. Chancellor, FRG 1982–98; Adviser on Foreign Policy 2000–; mem. Bundestag 1976–2002; Dr hc (Cambridge) 1998, Prof. hc (Tongji Univ., China) 1993, Karlspreis (Aachen) 1988, 1991, Jawaharlal Nehru Award 1990, Konrad Adenauer Prize 1994, Leo Baeck Prize 1996, Int. Leadership Award, Chicago Council on Foreign Relations; Grosses Bundesverdienstkreuz 1979, Bundesverdienstkreuz 1998, Grand Cross of Dutch Lion 1999Grand Cross, Order of Merit. *Publication:* Mein Tagebuch 1998–2000, Recollections 1930–1982, 2004. *Address:* Marbacher Strasse 11, 67071 Ludwigshafen Rhein-Oggersheim, Germany (home).

KÖHLER, Horst, Dr rer. pol; German banker, politician and head of state; *Federal President;* b. 22 Feb. 1943, Skierbieszow, Poland; m.; two c. *Education:* Univ. of Tübingen. *Career:* began career as scientific research asst, Inst. for Applied Econ. Research, Univ. of Tübingen, 1969–76; held various positions in Germany's Ministries of Econs and Finance 1976–89; Sec. of State, Ministry of Finance, Bonn 1990–93; Pres. Deutsche Sparkassen- und Giroverband, Bonn 1993–98; Deputy German Gov. IBRD and EBRD, Pres. EBRD 1998–2000; Pres. European Asscn of Savings Banks 1994–97; Man. Dir IMF 2000–04; Fed. Pres. of Germany 2004–; Hon. Prof., Univ. of Tübingen 2003; Grosses Verdienstkreuz der Bundesrepublik Deutschland 1992; Commdr de l'Ordre Grand-ducal de la Couronne de Chêne 1994; Officier, Légion d'honneur 1995; Verdienstmedaille des Landes Baden-Württemberg 2002. *Address:* Office of the Federal President, 11010 Berlin, Germany (office). *Telephone:* (30) 20000 (office). *E-mail:* poststelle@bpra.bund.de (office). *Website:* www.bundespraesident.de (office).

KOHOUT, Jan; Czech diplomatist; b. 29 March 1961, Pilsen; m. (divorced); one s. *Education:* Charles Univ. Prague. *Career:* military service 1984–85; research work Inst. of Int. Relations, Prague 1985–90; Desk Officer Int. Orgs Dept, Ministry of Foreign Affairs 1990–92, Dir UN Dept 1993–95; Deputy Head Perm. Mission to UN, OSCE and other orgs, Vienna 1995–2000; Deputy Dir EU and Western Europe Dept, Ministry of Foreign Affairs 2000–01, apptd Political Dir 2001, apptd Deputy Minister 2002; Perm. Rep. to EU 2004–08. *Address:* c/o Ministry of Foreign Affairs, Loretánské nám. 5, 118 00 Prague, Czech Republic (office).

KOIZUMI, Junichiro; Japanese fmr politician; b. 8 Jan. 1942, s. of Junya Koizumi; m. Kayoko Miyamoto 1978 (divorced 1982); three s. *Career:* mem. House of Reps from Kanagawa 1972–2006; fmr Parl. Vice-Minister of Finance and of Health and Welfare; Minister of Posts and Telecommunications 1992–93; Chair. House of Reps Finance Cttee; mem. Mitsuzuka Faction of LDP; Minister of Health and Welfare 1996–98; Prime Minister of Japan 2001–06; Pres. Jiyu Minshuto (Liberal-Democratic Party) 2001–06.

Address: c/o Jiya Minshuto, 1-11-23, Nogata-che, Chiyoda-ku, Tokyo 100-8910, Japan (office).

KOJIMA, Kiyoshi, PhD; Japanese economist and academic; *Professor Emeritus of Economics, Hitotsubashi University;* b. 22 May 1920, Nagoya; m. Keiko Kojima 1947. *Education:* Tokyo Univ. of Commerce and Econs, Leeds Univ., UK and Princeton Univ., USA. *Career:* Asst Prof. of Int. Econs, Hitotsubashi Univ. 1945–60, Prof. 1960–84, Prof. Emer. 1984–; Secr. (Dir) for UN Conf. on Trade and Devt 1963; Prof. Int. Christian Univ. 1984–91, Surugadai Univ. 1991–97; mem. Science Council of Japan 1985; British Council Scholarship 1952–53, Rockefeller Foundation Fellowship 1953–55; Second Order of the Sacred Treasure 1996. *Publications:* (in Japanese): Theory of Foreign Trade 1950, Japan's Economic Development and Trade 1958, Japan in Trade Expansion for Developing Countries 1964 (in English), Japan and a Pacific Free Trade Area 1971, Japan and a New World Economic Order 1977, Direct Foreign Investment 1978, Japanese Direct Investment Abroad 1990, Trade, Investment and Pacific Economic Integration 1996, The Flying-Geese Theory of Economic Development 2003; Ed. Papers and Proceedings of a Conference on Pacific Trade and Development 1968, 1969, 1973; also articles in English on int. trade. *Address:* 3-24-10 Maehara-cho, Koganei-shi, Tokyo 184-0013, Japan. *Telephone:* (3) 381-1041.

KOJIMA, Seiji; Japanese diplomatist; *Ambassador to Pakistan; Education:* Tokyo Univ. *Career:* joined Ministry of Foreign Affairs 1972, Dir Devt Co-operation Div., Econ. Co-operation Bureau 1989–90, Dir Research and Programming Div. 1990–93, Dir Regional Policy Div., Asian Affairs Bureau 1993–94, Deputy Dir-Gen. Econ. Co-operation Bureau 1999–2001, Dir-Gen. Abandoned Chemical Weapons Office 2001–02; overseas posts include Counsellor Embassy in India 1994–96, Minister 1996–97, Minister, Embassy in USA 1997–99, Minister Plenipotentiary Embassy in UK 2002–04, Amb. to Pakistan 2006–; Vice-Pres. Japan Int. Co-operation Agency 2004–06. *Address:* Embassy of Japan, Plot No. 53–70, Ramna 5/4, Diplomatic Enclave 1, Islamabad 44000, Pakistan (office). *Telephone:* (51) 2279320 (office). *Fax:* (51) 2279340 (office). *E-mail:* japanemb@comsats.net.pk (office). *Website:* www.pk.emb-japan.go.jp (office).

KOJIMA, Takaaki, BA, LLB; Japanese diplomatist; *Ambassador to Australia;* b. 19 Feb. 1947. *Education:* Tokyo Univ., Univ. of Cambridge, UK. *Career:* joined Ministry of Foreign Affairs 1971, Dir Int. Agreements Div. 1987–89, Deputy Dir Consular and Migration Affairs Dept 1995–97, Deputy Sec.-Gen. for Int. Affairs, Fair Trade Comm. 1997–99, Dir-Gen. Intelligence and Analysis Bureau 2002–04; overseas posts include Counsellor Embassy in China 1989–92, Counsellor Embassy in UK 1992–95, Minister 1995, Consul-Gen. in São Paulo, Brazil 1999–2001, Minister Embassy in USA, Amb. to Singapore 2004–07, to Australia 2007–; Fellow, Weatherhead Center for Int. Affairs, Harvard Univ. 2001–02. *Address:* Embassy of Japan, 112 Empire Circuit, Yarralumla, ACT, 2600, Australia (office). *Telephone:* (2) 6273-3244 (office). *Fax:* (2) 6273-1848 (office). *E-mail:* cultural@japan.org.au (office). *Website:* www.au.emb-japan.go.jp (office).

KOKOSHIN, Andrei Afanasievich, DHisSc; Russian political scientist, politician and academic; *Professor and Dean of School of World Politics, Lomonosov Moscow State University;* b. 26 Oct. 1945, Moscow; m.; two d. *Education:* Bauman Moscow Higher Tech. Univ. *Career:* scientific researcher, Head of Dept, Deputy Dir Inst. of USA and Canada Acad. of Sciences 1974–92; First Deputy Minister of Defence of the Russian Fed. 1992–97; Chair. Interagency Cttee on Defence Security, Security Council of the Russian Fed. 1993–97; mem. Govt Council on Industrial Policy 1993–97; Sec. Council of Defence of Russian Fed. 1993–97; Chief Military Inspector of Russian Fed.; Sec. Security Council of Russian Fed. 1997–98; mem. State Duma 1999– (mem. Otechestvo–All Russia faction –2003, United Russia faction 2003–), Vice-Chair. Cttee on Industry, Construction and High Technologies 1999–2003, Chair. Cttee on Nat. Security, CIS and Compatriot Affairs 2003–; mem. Russian Acad. of Sciences 1987 (Acting Vice-Pres. 1998–99, Dir Inst. of Int. Security 2000–), Russian Acad. of Social Sciences 1993, Russian Acad. of Artillery and Rocket Science and Eng 1993–, Russian Acad. of Natural Sciences; Chair. Bd High Tech. Foundation/Gorbachev Project 2001, Russian Public Bd for Educ. Devt 2001; mem. Scientific Advisory Council, Inst. for Int. Studies, Stanford Univ. 2000, Gen. Council United Russia Party 2001–, Bd Dirs Nuclear Threat Initiative 2001–, Bd of Trustees Russian–American Business Council 2002, Nat. Anticorruption Comm. 2002; Dean School of World Politics, Prof., Lomonosov's Moscow State Univ. (MGU) 2003–; Hon. Chair. Russian Rugby Football League 1992–; Services for the Fatherland, Mark of Honour, Military Comradeship 1987, 1997, 2000. *Publications:* 20 books (including six as co-author) on nat. security, int. affairs, Russian nat.

industrial policy and econs including Forecasting and Foreign Policy 1975, The USA in the System of International Relations in the 1980s 1984, Weapons in Space: Security Dilemma 1986, National Industrial Policy of Russia 1992, Soviet Strategic Thought 1918–1991 1999, The National Industrial Policy and the National Security of Russia (jtly) 2001, Deterrence in the Second Nuclear Age (jtly) 2001, Types and Categories of Nuclear Conflicts in the XXI Century 2003, Strategic Governance 2003; more than 150 articles and papers.
Address: State Duma, Okhotny Ryad 1, 103265 Moscow, Russia. *Telephone:* (495) 292-52-18 (office); (495) 938-18-92 (office). *Fax:* (495) 292-99-91 (office); (495) 938-18-93 (office).

KOLA, Llesh; Albanian diplomatist; *Ambassador to Italy;* b. 27 Dec. 1960, Lezha. *Education:* Univ. of Tirana. *Career:* joined Ministry of Foreign Affairs 1986; First Sec. Embassy in Algiers 1988–91, Counsellor and chargé d'affaires for Communications, Embassy in Madrid 1995–97; Diplomatic Adviser to Pres. 2002–05, Dir Cabinet of Minister of Foreign Affairs 2005–06; Amb. to Italy (also accred to Malta, San Marino) 2006–, also Perm. Rep. to FAO.
Address: Embassy of Albania, Via Asmara 5, 00199 Rome, Italy (office). *Telephone:* (06) 86224114 (office). *Fax:* (06) 86224120 (office). *E-mail:* llkola@mfa.gov.al (office). *Website:* www.ambalbania.it (office).

KOLADE, Christopher Olusola, CON; Nigerian diplomatist and business executive; *Chairman, Convention on Business Integrity;* b. 1932, Erin – Oke, Osun State; m. Beatrice Kolade. *Education:* Govt Coll., Ibadan, Fourah Bay Coll., Freetown, Sierra Leone. *Career:* varied career includes posts as Lecturer in Corp. Governance and Human Resources Man., Lagos Business School, CEO and Chair. Cadbury Nigeria PLC, Dir-Gen. Nigerian Broadcasting Corpn; High Commr to UK 2002–08; Chair. The Convention on Business Integrity, Lagos 2008–; Pres. Int. Inst. for Communications 1973–75, World Asscn for Christian Communication 1975–82, Nigerian Inst. of Man. 1985–88, Inst. of Personnel Man. of Nigeria 1988–93; mem. Bd Dirs New Nigeria Foundation, Africa Centre, Lagos Business School; Chair. Governing Bd, Convention on Business Integrity; Lay Canon, Cathedral of the Holy Spirit, Guildford, UK; Order of Saint Augustine 1981.
Address: The Convention on Business Integrity, 5th Floor, SIO Towers, 25 Boyle Street, Onikan, Lagos, Nigeria (office). *Telephone:* (1) 4738689 (office). *Fax:* (1) 2707092 (office). *E-mail:* info@theconvention.org (office). *Website:* www.theconvention.org (office).

KOLAR, Petr; Czech diplomatist; *Ambassador to USA;* m. Jaroslava Kolarova; two s. *Education:* Charles Univ., Prague, Woodrow Wilson Int. Center, Washington, DC, Univ. of London Inst. of Historical Research. *Career:* researcher at various insts, including Inst. for Int. Relations, Prague, Norwegian Nobel Inst., Inst. for Strategic Studies, Prague, Inst. for Contemporary History, Czechoslovak Acad. of Science; foreign policy ed., commentator and corresp. for several Czech dailies and magazines; various postings in Ministry of Foreign Affairs 1993–96; Dir Dept for Czechs Living Abroad and Nongovernmental Relations 1993–95; Dir Eastern and Southern Europe Territorial Dept and Foreign Policy Adviser to Foreign Minister 1995–96; Amb. to Sweden 1996–98; Adviser for European Integration and Balkans to Czech Pres. 1998–99; Amb. to Ireland 1999–2003; Deputy Minister of Foreign Affairs for Bilateral Relations 2003–05; Amb. to USA 2005–.
Address: Embassy of the Czech Republic, 3900 Spring of Freedom Street, NW, Washington, DC 20008, USA (office). *Telephone:* (202) 274-9100 (office). *Fax:* (202) 966-8540 (office). *E-mail:* washington@embassy.mzv.cz (office). *Website:* www.mzv.cz/washington (office).

KOLBY, Ole Peter, LLM; Norwegian diplomatist; b. 1939, Oslo; m.; two c. *Education:* Univ. of Oslo. *Career:* joined Ministry of Foreign Affairs 1965, served as Jr Officer 1965–67, Sr Exec. Officer (UN Bureau) 1973–77, Deputy Dir-Gen. for Political Affairs 1984–87, Political Dir 1989–82; Vice-Consul in New York 1967–70; Deputy Perm. Rep. to UN Industrial Devt Org. (UNIDO) and Int. Atomic Energy Agency (IAEA); First Sec. Embassy in Vienna, Austria 1970–73; Counsellor for Political Affairs, Perm. Mission to UN, New York 1977–80, Deputy Perm. Rep. to UN 1981–84, Vice-Chair. UN Cttee on Decolonization 1982–83, Head of Del. UN Comm. on Human Rights 1985–87, Vice-Chair. 1986, Perm. Rep. to UN 1998–2003; Amb. for Human Rights 1988; Chair. Advisory Council on Disarmament Affairs 1989–92; Perm. Rep. to Org. for Security and Co-operation in Europe (OSCE) 1992–97; Amb. to Austria 1995–98, to Denmark 2004–07.
Address: c/o Ministry of Foreign Affairs, 7 juni pl. 1, POB 8114 Dep., 0032 Oslo, Norway (office).

KOLEV, Gen. Nikola Ivanov; Bulgarian government official and fmr air force commander; *Head of the Office to the President of the Republic;* b. 9 Aug.

1951, Karadzhalovo, Plovdiv Region; m. Velichka Asenova Koleva; two d. *Education:* Electrical Eng Tech. School, Plovdiv, Air Force Acad., G. S. Rakovski Nat. War Coll., Gen. Staff Coll., Moscow, Russia, Defence Language Inst., San Antonio, USA. *Career:* Asst Chief of Staff for Plans, 19th Fighter Air Regiment HQ 1975–76; Asst Chief Operations Dept, 10th Mixed Air Corps HQ 1976–78; Chief of Staff, 19th Fighter Air Regt 1982–85; Sr Asst Chief of Operations Dept, Air Defence and Air Force HQ 1985–88; Chief of Staff, 1st Air Defence Div. 1990–92; Mil. Adviser for Air Force and Air Defence to Pres. of Bulgaria 1992–96; First Deputy Chief of Air Force HQ 1996–98; Deputy Chief of Gen. Staff for Resources 1998–2000, for Operations 2000–02; Chief of Gen. Staff, Bulgarian Armed Forces 2002–06; Head of Office to Pres. of Repub. 2006–; mem. NATO Mil. Cttee 2002–06; apptd Maj.-Gen. 1996, Lt-Gen. 1997, Gen. 2002; eight medals and awards presented by Ministry of Defence.
Address: Office of the President, 1123 Sofia, bul. Dondukov 2, Bulgaria (office). *Telephone:* (2) 923-93-33 (office). *E-mail:* press@president.bg (office). *Website:* www.president.bg (office).

KOLODKIN, Anatoliy Lazarevich, DCL; Russian judge, maritime law scholar and academic; *Professor of Law of Sea, Institute of State and Law, Russian Academy of Sciences;* b. 27 Feb. 1928, Leningrad; m.; one s. *Education:* Leningrad Univ. *Career:* mem. numerous USSR dels to int. confs on maritime affairs; headed USSR dels at confs of Int. Maritime Satellite Org. (INMARSAT) 1981; participated in creation of Russian maritime satellite org. 'Morsvyassputnik'; Deputy Dir Gen., Prof., Scientific Research Inst. of Maritime Transport 1981–; Spokesman and Co-ordinator Group D, Eastern European states, at UN Conf. for elaboration, UN Convention on conditions of registration of ships 1982–86; co-author draft Convention on legal status of Ocean Data Acquisition Systems; Prof. of Law of Sea, Inst. of State and Law, Russian Acad. of Sciences 1994–, Head of Int. Law Div.; mem. Perm. Court of Arbitration, The Hague 1990–; mem. (Judge) UN Int. Tribunal for Law of Sea 1996–; has lectured extensively on law of sea in Russia and abroad; Pres. Maritime Law Asscn of USSR (now CIS) 1981–, Russian Int. Law Asscn 1994–; Chair. Nat. Cttee of Russian Fed. on UN Decade of Int. Law 1996–2001; Co-Chair. Scientific Expert Council of State Duma (Parl.) for Int. Law 1996–; Chair. Asscn of Lawyers of Russia Int. Law Comm. 2007–; Hon. Vice-Pres. Int. Maritime Cttee 1994–; mem. Council, Int. Oceanic Inst. 'Pacem in Maribus', Malta 1971–; mem. Acad. Councils, Inst. of State and Law, Russian Acad. of Sciences 1993–; mem. Higher Degree Cttee, Expert Council on Legal Sciences of Russian Fed. 1985–2001; mem. World Acad. of Science and Art 1989–; mem. Council, Law of the Sea Inst. (USA) 1989–95; mem. group of experts of State Duma for elaboration of new Russian marine legislation, internal waters, the State Frontier, Territorial Sea and Contiguous Zone, Continental Shelf, Exclusive Econ. Zone, Merchant Shipping Code, UNESCO Underwater Cultural Heritage Conversion 1993–; mem. Scientific Expert Council of the Council of Russian Fed. (Parl.) 2003, Scientific Council of the Marine Bd of the Govt, Russia; several decorations of Russia; Hon. Medal, Free Univ. of Brussels 1993–2002. *Publications:* 270 scientific articles, books and manuals (co-authorship) in Russia, USA, UK, FRG, Belgium, Italy, Poland and other countries.
Address: Bolshoi Koptevsky per. 3a, 125319 Moscow; Leningradsky prospect 66,60a, 125167 Moscow, Russia (home). *Telephone:* (495) 151-75-88 (office); (495) 151-54-54 (home). *Fax:* (495) 152-09-16. *E-mail:* kolodkin@smniip.ru.

KOŁODKO, Grzegorz Witold, PhD; Polish politician, economist, academic and author; *Founding Director and Professor, Transformation, Integration and Globalization Economic Research;* b. 28 Jan. 1949, Tczew; m.; two d. *Education:* Warsaw School of Econs. *Career:* Prof., Warsaw School of Econs 1972–2001, Dir Inst. of Finance 1989–94; Prof. of Econs, Leon Kozminski Acad. of Entrepreneurship and Man. (WSPiZ), Warsaw 2000–; fmr consultant, World Inst. for Devt Econs Research of UN, Helsinki; IMF and World Bank expert 1991–92, 1999–2000; First Deputy Prime Minister 1994–97, 2002–03; Minister of Finance 1994–97, 2002–03; Founding Dir and Prof., Transformation, Integration and Globalization Econ. Research (TIGER) 2000–; Visiting Prof., Yale Univ., UCLA; John C. Evans Prof. in European Studies, Univ. of Rochester, NY 1998–; Hon. Prof., Indian Inst. of Finance 2004, Tianjin Univ., China 2005, Moscow Acad. of Econs and Law 2005; Commdr's Medal, Order of Polonia Restituta 1997; Dr hc (Univ. of Lvov) 2003, (Univ. of Chengdu) 2004; numerous prizes and awards including Polish Broadcasting Award 1985, Man of the Year Award 1994, Polish TV Best Politician Award 1997, Award of Minister for Science 2002. *Publications:* more than 400 publs in 23 languages on econ. theory and policy, including books in English: Strategy for Poland 1994, The Polish Alternative: Old Myths, Hard Facts and New Strategies in Successful Transformation of the Polish Economy 1997, From Shock to Therapy: The Political Economy of Postsocialist Transformations 2000, Post-Communist Transition: The Thorny Road 2000, Globalization and Transformation: Illusions and Reality 2001, Globalization and Catching-

up in Transition Economies 2001, Emerging Market Economies: Globalization and Development 2003, Globalization and Social Stress 2005, The Polish Miracle: Lessons for Emerging Markets 2005, The World Economy and Great Post-Communist Change 2006.
Address: Transformation, Integration and Globalization Economic Research (TIGER), 59 Jagiellonska Street, 03-301 Warsaw, Poland (office). *Telephone:* (22) 5192108 (office). *Fax:* (22) 5192265 (office). *E-mail:* kolodko@tiger.edu.pl (office). *Website:* www.tiger.edu.pl (office); www.kolodko.net (home).

KOMBO YAYA, Dieudonné; Central African Republic politician. *Career:* fmr Deputy Dir Org. for African Unity, fmr Sr Political Officer, Africa Union Comm.; Minister of Foreign and Francophone Affairs and Regional Integration 2008–.
Address: Ministry of Foreign and Francophone Affairs and Regional Integration, Bangui, The Central African Republic (office). *Telephone:* 61-54-67 (office). *Fax:* 61-26-06 (office).

KOMOROWSKI, Stanislaw, DSc; Polish diplomatist; *Under Secretary of State, Ministry of Foreign Affairs;* b. 18 Dec. 1953, Warsaw; m. Ewa Komorowska; three s. *Education:* Warsaw Univ. *Career:* researcher, Inst. of Physical Chem., Polish Acad. of Sciences 1978–90, lecturer 1987–89; lecturer, Univ. of Utah, USA 1989; Dir Dept of Western Europe, Ministry of Foreign Affairs 1991–94; Amb. to The Netherlands 1994–98, to UK 1999–2004; Dir Secr. of Minister of Foreign Affairs 1998–99; Dir Asia Pacific Dept, Ministry of Foreign Affairs 2004–05, UnderSec. of State 2005–; Grand Cross of the Order of Orange Nassau 1988, Hon. KCVO.
Address: Ministry of Foreign Affairs, Al. 7 ch. Szucha 23, 00580 Warsaw, Poland (office). *Telephone:* (22) 5239302 (office). *Fax:* (22) 5239599 (office). *E-mail:* stanislaw.komorowski@msz.gov.pl (office). *Website:* www.msz.gov.pl (office).

KOMŠIĆ, Željko; Bosnia and Herzegovina lawyer and politician; *Member of the Tripartite State Presidency;* b. 20 Jan. 1964, Sarajevo; m.; one d. *Education:* Univ. of Sarajevo, Edmund A. Walsh School of Foreign Service at Georgetown Univ., Washington, DC, USA. *Career:* served in Army of Repub. of Bosnia and Herzegovina during Bosnian War; embarked on political career during which he served as Deputy Mayor of Sarajevo, twice as Head of Municipal Govt of Novo Sarajevo 2000–06, and Amb. to Fed. Repub. of Yugoslavia 2001–02; Vice-Pres Social Democratic Party of Bosnia and Herzegovina (SDP BiH) (Socijaldemokratska Partija BiH) 2006–; Croat mem. Tripaprtite State Presidency 2006–; Golden Lily, Bosnian Govt.
Address: Office of the State Presidency, 71000 Sarajevo, Musala 5, Bosnia and Herzegovina (office). *Telephone:* (33) 664941 (office). *Fax:* (33) 472491 (office). *Website:* www.predsjednistvobih.ba (office).

KONDIĆ, Novak, MBA, PhD; Bosnia and Herzegovina economist, academic and fmr government official; *Professor of Economics, University of Banja Luka;* b. 20 July 1952, Stratinska, Banja Luka; m. Nevenka Predragović 1980; two s. *Education:* Univ. of Banja Luka. *Career:* Prof., Univ. of Banja Luka; Head Co. Accountancy Dept, Serbian Devt Bank, Banja Luka 1977–86, Head of Inspectorate Control and Information Analysis 1986–90, Dir Municipal Admin. of Public Revenues 1990–92, mem. Municipal Exec. Bd 1990–92; Deputy Dir-Gen. Payment Transaction Services for Repub. of Srpska 1992–95, for Banja Luka 1997; Minister of Finance, Repub. of Srpska 1995–97, 1998–2000; Rep. of Bosnia and Herzegovina to IMF 1998; Exec. Dir Razvojna Banka, Gen. Dir 2004–06; currently Prof. of Econs, Univ. of Banja Luka; Medal for Mil. Valour.
Address: Faculty of Economics, University of Banja Luka, Trg srpskih vladara 2, 78000 Banja Luka, Bosnia and Herzegovina. *Telephone:* (51) 218-997. *Fax:* (51) 315-694. *E-mail:* uni-bl@blic.net. *Website:* unibl.org.

KONDO, Seiichi, BA; Japanese government official and diplomatist; *Permanent Representative, United Nations Educational, Scientific and Cultural Organization (UNESCO);* m.; one d. *Education:* Univ. of Tokyo, St Catherine's Coll., Oxford, UK. *Career:* seconded by Foreign Ministry to Ministry of Int. Trade and Industry 1977–80, to Int. Energy Agency, OECD 1980–83; Deputy Dir OECD Desk, Foreign Ministry 1983–86, Deputy Head Korea Desk 1986–87, Chef de Cabinet, Vice-Minister of Foreign Affairs 1987–88, Dir Int. Press Div. 1988–90; Head of Chancery, Manila 1990–92; Counsellor for Public Affairs, Washington, DC 1992–95, Minister 1996; Head Co-ordination and Logistics Office for G8 Summits, Asia-Pacific Econ. Co-operation and Asia-Europe Meeting 1996–97; Deputy Dir-Gen. Econ. Affairs Bureau 1998–99; Deputy Sec.-Gen. OECD 1999–2003; Dir-Gen. for Public Diplomacy, Ministry of Foreign Affairs 2003–06; Perm. Rep. to UNESCO, Paris 2006–; Chevalier, Légion d'honneur. *Publications:* Image of Japan in the American Media 1994, The Distorted Image of Japan – The Perception Game Inside The Beltway 1997; many articles in Japanese and English-language magazines.

Address: Permanent Delegation of Japan to UNESCO, 148, rue de l'Université, 75007 Paris, France (office); 1-11-16 Kamiosaki, Shinagawa-ku, Tokyo 141-0021, Japan (home). *Telephone:* 1-53-59-27-00 (office); (3) 5501-8136 (office). *Fax:* 1-53-59-27-27 (office). *E-mail:* deljpn.ambr@unesco.org (office). *Website:* www.unesco.emb-japan.go.jp (office).

KONDRATYEV, Col-Gen. Georgy Grigorievich; Russian army officer; *Chief Military Expert, Ministry of Emergencies and Natural Disasters;* b. 17 Nov. 1944, Klintsy, Bryansk Region; m.; two c. *Education:* Kharkov Guards Tank School, Mil. Acad. of Armoured Forces, USSR Gen. Staff Acad. *Career:* served as Commdr of tank platoon, Bn, Commdr Regt, Gen. Staff 1973–74; Regt Commdr 1974–76; Deputy Commdr, Div. Commdr 1976–85; Deputy C-in-C Turkestan Army Mil. Command 1985–87, Commdr 1987–89; First Deputy C-in-C Turkestan Mil. Command 1989–91, Commdr 1991–92; Deputy Minister of Defence of Russian Fed. 1992–95; Deputy Minister Ministry of Emergencies and Natural Disasters 1995–99, Chief. Mil. Expert 1999–.
Address: Ministry of Emergencies and Natural Disasters, Teatralny per. 4, 103012 Moscow, Russia. *Telephone:* (495) 926-38-57 (office).

KONG, Quan; Chinese diplomatist; *Ambassador to France;* b. 1955, Beijing; m.; one d. *Career:* served at Embassy in Brussels 1977–82; Attaché, Western Europe Dept, Ministry of Foreign Affairs 1982–84, Third, then Second Sec. 1985–95, Counsellor 1995–96, Asst Dir-Gen. 1999–2000; Dir-Gen. of Communications 2001–06, Dir-Gen. Western Europe Dept 2006, Vice-Minister for Foreign Affairs 2006–08; Counsellor, then Minister-Counsellor, Embassy in Paris 1996–99; Amb. to France 2008–; mem. Perm. Cttee CCP, Tanggu Dist, Tianjin 2000–01.
Address: Embassy of the People's Republic of China, 11 Ave George V, 75008 Paris, France (office). *Telephone:* 1-49-52-19-50 (office). *Fax:* 1-47-20-24-22 (office). *E-mail:* chinaemb_fr@mfa.gov.cn (office). *Website:* www.amb-chine.fr (office).

KONI, Gen. Allafouza; Chadian army officer and politician. *Career:* career in Chadian Armed Forces; fmr presidential adviser; Minister of Nat. Defence, Veterans and Victims of War 2004.
Address: c/o Ministry of National Defence, Veterans and Victims of War, BP 916, N'Djamena, Chad (office).

KONJANOVSKI, Zoran; Macedonian engineer and politician; *Minister of Defence;* b. 3 March 1967, Bitola. *Education:* St Kliment Ohridski Univ. *Career:* engineer, Strezevo Public Enterprise 1999–; mem. Vnatrešno-Makedonska Revolucionerna Organizacija—Demokratska Partija za Makedonsko Nacionalno Edinstvo (VMRO—DPMNE) 1993–, mem. Exec. Cttee 2005–; Pres. Municipal Council of Bitola 2005–; Minister for Local Self-Govt 2006–08, for Defence 2008–.
Address: Ministry of Defence, Orce Nikolov bb, Skopje 1000, former Yugoslav Republic of Macedonia (office). *Telephone:* (2) 3282042 (office). *Fax:* (2) 3282042 (office). *E-mail:* info@morm.gov.mk (office). *Website:* www.morm.gov.mk (office).

KONO, Yohei; Japanese politician; *Speaker, House of Representatives;* b. 15 Jan. 1937. *Education:* Waseda Univ., Stanford Univ. *Career:* mem. House of Reps from Kanagawa; fmr Parl. Vice-Minister of Educ., Dir-Gen. Science and Tech. Agency; Chief Cabinet Sec. (State Minister) 1992–93; Chair. LDP Research Comm. on Foreign Affairs, Pres. 1993–99; Deputy Prime Minister and Minister of Foreign Affairs 1994–96, Minister of Foreign Affairs 1999–2001; Speaker, House of Reps 2003–; left LDP to co-found New Liberal Club (now defunct) 1976–86; mem. Miyazawa faction of LDP.
Address: Office of the Speaker of the House of Representatives, National Diet Building, Chiyoda-ku, Tokyo, Japan (office); Liberal Democratic Party (Jiyu-Minshuto), 1-11-23, Nagata-cho, Chiyoda-ku, Tokyo 100-8910, Japan. *Telephone:* (3) 3581-6211. *E-mail:* koho@ldp.jimin.or.jp (office). *Website:* www.jimin.jp (office).

KONTRA, Ferenc, PhD; Hungarian diplomatist; *Ambassador to Belarus;* b. 1954, Budapest. *Education:* Univ. of Kiev. *Career:* joined Ministry of Foreign Affairs 1978; Head of Secr., Ministry of Foreign Affairs 1998; Amb. to Ukraine 2001–05 (also accred. to Georgia, Moldova, Belarus, and Russian Fed. 2002–05, to Armenia 2004–05); Amb. to Belarus 2008–.
Address: c/o Ministry of Foreign Affairs, 1027 Budapest, Bem rkp. 47, Hungary. *Telephone:* (1) 458-1000. *Fax:* (1) 212-5981. *Website:* www.mfa.gov.hu.

KOOIJMANS, Pieter Hendrik, DJur; Dutch politician and lawyer; b. 6 July 1933, Heemstede; m. A. Kooijmans-Verhage; four c. *Education:* Free Univ. Amsterdam. *Career:* mem. Faculty of Law, Free Univ. of Amsterdam 1960–65, Prof. of European Law and Public Int. Law 1965–73; State Sec. for Foreign Affairs 1973–77; Prof. of Public Int. Law, Univ. of Leiden

1978–92, 1995–97; Minister for Foreign Affairs 1993–94; mem. (Judge) Int. Court of Justice 1997–2006; Minister of State 2007–; Chair. or mem. numerous orgs including Chair. Bd Carnegie Foundation; Head Netherlands del. to UN Comm. on Human Rights 1982–85, 1992, Chair. Comm. 1984–85, Special Rapporteur on questions relevant to torture 1985–92; mem. Inst. of Int. Law; mem. various UN and CSCE missions to fmr Yugoslavia 1991–92. *Publications:* various textbooks and articles on int. law and human rights.
Address: Prinsenweg 111, 2242 ED Wassenaar, Netherlands (home). *Telephone:* (70) 5141738 (home). *E-mail:* kooijmansverhage@planet.nl.

KOOLMAN, Olindo; Aruban politician; b. 1942. *Career:* Gov. Gen. of Aruba 1992–2004.
Address: c/o Office of the Governor, Plaza Henny Eman 3, Oranjestad, Aruba (office).

KOOMPIROCHANA, Vikrom, BA, MA, PhD; Thai diplomatist (retd) and business executive; m. Sasin Monvoisin. *Education:* Chulalongkorn Univ., Michigan State Univ., USA. *Career:* Lecturer in History, Faculty of Arts, Chulalongkorn Univ. –1973; joined Ministry of Foreign Affairs in 1973, Amb. to Singapore 1991–95, to Malaysia 1996, to New Zealand 1997–99, Deputy Perm. Sec., Ministry of Foreign Affairs 2000–01, Amb. to Italy 2002, to UK 2003–06 (retd); Chair. Dragon One PLC 2006–; Chair. Audit Cttee, Oishi Group of Cos; Adviser to TCC Holding Co. Ltd, TCC Land Co. Ltd.
Address: c/o Ministry of Foreign Affairs, Thanon Sri Ayudhya, Bangkok 10400, Thailand. *Telephone:* (2) 643-5000.

KOONJUL, Jagdish; Mauritian diplomatist; b. 14 April 1952; m.; four c. *Education:* Univ. of Mumbai, India. *Career:* Educ. Officer, Presidency Coll., Mauritius 1974; Second Sec. Ministry of External Affairs, Tourism and Emigration 1976–78; with Perm. Mission to UN, New York 1978; staff mem. Embassies in Brussels, Paris and Washington, DC 1980–94; apptd. Deputy High Commr in New Delhi, India Oct. 1994; Head of Multilateral Political Directorate, Ministry of Foreign Affairs and Int. Trade 1997–98; apptd Amb. Extraordinary and Plenipotentiary Jan. 1999; Perm. Rep. to UN 2001–06; rep. at numerous int. confs including UN Industrial Devt Org. (UNIDO) and Conf. of Labour Ministers of Non-Aligned Countries. *Publications include:* Mauritius and the Lomé Convention, Ethnic Conflict in Sri Lanka.
Address: c/o Ministry of Foreign Affairs, International Trade and Co-operation, New Government Centre, 5th Floor, Port Louis, Mauritius (office). *Website:* foreign.gov.mu (office).

KORMILTSEV, Col-Gen. Nikolai Viktorovich; Russian army officer; b. 14 March 1946, Omsk. *Education:* Omsk Higher Military General Army School, Moscow M.V. Frunze Military Acad., Moscow Military Acad. of General Staff. *Career:* Commdr of Army corpus, Turkestan Mil. Command –1994; Deputy Commdr, then Commdr of Armed Forces, Baikal Mil. Command 1994–98; Commdr of Armed Forces, Siberian Mil. Command 1998–2001; C-in-C Land Armed Forces 2001–04; Deputy Minister of Defence 2001–04.
Address: c/o Ministry of Defence, Znamenka str. 19, 103160 Moscow, Russia (office).

KORNUKOV, Col-Gen. Anatoly Mikhailovich; Russian army officer (retd); *Officer, Ministry of Defence;* b. 10 Jan. 1942, Stakhanovo, Lugansk Region; m.; one s. one d. *Education:* Chernigov Higher Mil. Aviation School, Zhukov Mil. Acad., Mil. Gen. Staff Acad. *Career:* Commdr of fighter squadron, Aviation Regt of Fighter Div. in Far E; qualified as Mil. Pilot-Sniper; Commdr Anti-Aircraft Defence Forces of Moscow Command 1991–97; C-in-C Mil. Aircraft Forces of Russian Fed. 1998–2002 (resgnd); on staff of Ministry of Defence 2002–.
Address: c/o General Air Force Staff, B. Pirogorskaya str. 23, K-160 Moscow, Russia (office). *Telephone:* (495) 296-18-00 (office).

KOROMA, Abdul G.; Sierra Leonean diplomatist and lawyer; *Judge, International Court of Justice; Education:* King's Coll., London, UK, Kiev State Univ., USSR (now Ukraine). *Career:* barrister and Hon. Bencher (Lincoln's Inn) and legal practitioner, High Court of Sierra Leone; joined Sierra Leone Govt service 1964, Int. Div., Ministry of External Affairs 1969; del. to UN Gen. Ass.; mem. Int. Law Comm. (Chair. 43rd Session; mem. of dels to 3rd UN Conf. on the Law of the Sea, UN Conf. on Succession of States in Respect of Treaties, UN Comm. on Int. Trade Law, Special Cttee on the Review of the UN Charter and on the Strengthening of the Role of the Org. Cttee on the Peaceful Uses of Outer Space; Vice-Chair. UN Charter Cttee 1978; Chair. UN Special Cttee of 24; Deputy Perm. Rep. of Sierra Leone to the UN 1978–81, Perm. Rep. 1981–85; fmr Amb. to S Korea, to Cuba and to EEC and Perm. Del. to UNESCO; Amb. to France, Belgium, Netherlands, Luxembourg and to Ethiopia and OAU 1988; Perm.

Rep. to UN –1994; Judge, Int. Court of Justice 1994–; fmr High Commr in Zambia, Tanzania and Kenya; Chair. UN 6th Cttee (Legal); Vice-Pres. African Soc. of Int. and Comparative Law, African Soc. of Int. Law; Pres. Henry Dunant Centre for Humanitarian Dialogue, Geneva; mem. Int. Planning Council of Int. Ocean Inst., Cttee of Experts on the Application of Conventions and Recommendations, ILO, Geneva; del. to numerous int. confs; Visiting Prof., Univ. of Bangalore, India; lecturer at numerous univs; mem. American Soc. of Int. Law, Inst. of Int. Law; Insignia of Commdr of Rokel 1991, Order of Grand Officer of Repub. of Sierra Leone; Hon. LLD. *Publications:* numerous articles on int. law.
Address: International Court of Justice, Peace Palace, Carnegieplein, 2517 KJ The Hague, Netherlands (office). *Telephone:* (70) 3022323 (office). *Fax:* (70) 3022409 (office). *E-mail:* information@icj-cij.org (office). *Website:* www.icj-cij.org (office).

KOROMA, Ernest Bai; Sierra Leonean politician and head of state; *President;* b. 23 Oct. 1953, Makeni, Bombali Dist; m. Sia Koroma; two c. *Education:* Univ. of Sierra Leone. *Career:* began career as teacher, St Francis Secondary School, Makeni; joined Sierra Leone Nat. Insurance Co. 1978; joined Reliance Insurance Trust Corpn 1985, Man. Dir 1988–2002; represented All People's Congress (APC) in presidential and parl. elections 2002, lost presidential vote but elected to parl. representing Bombali Dist; Leader APC 2002–, temporarily stripped of leadership due to internal party dispute 2005; Pres. of Sierra Leone 2007–; Fellow, West African Insurance Inst.; Assoc. Inst. of Risk Man., UK; mem. Inst. of Dirs, UK.
Address: All-People's Congress, 137h Fourah Bay Road, Freetown, Sierra Leone (office). *E-mail:* info@new-apc.org (office). *Website:* apcparty.org (office).

KOROMA, Momodu, MSc; Sierra Leonean politician; b. 12 Sept. 1956; m.; five c. *Education:* Njala Univ. Coll., Univ. of Nairobi, Kenya, Univ. of Reading, UK, Int. Centre for Theoretical Physics, Trieste, Italy. *Career:* govt minister 1996–, fmr Minister of Presidential Affairs; Minister of Foreign Affairs and Int. Cooperation 2002–07; mem. Sierra Leone Peoples Party (SLPP).
Address: MQ8 Spur Road, Wilberforce, Freetown, Sierra Leone (home). *Telephone:* 232873 (home). *E-mail:* graceful@sierratel.se (home).

KORTHALS ALTES, Frederik; Dutch lawyer and politician; *Chairman, Advisory Council on International Affairs;* b. 15 May 1931, Amsterdam; m. Henny Matthijssen. *Education:* Leiden Univ. *Career:* practised as solicitor 1958–82; mem. First Chamber, States-Gen. 1981–82, 1991–2001; Minister of Justice 1982–89; Chair. Volkspartij voor Vrijheid en Democratie (VVD) 1975–81, Floor Leader in First Chamber, States-Gen. 1995–97, Pres. 1997–2001; currently Chair. Advisory Council on Int. Affairs; Pnr, Nauta Dutilh (law firm) 1990–96; Hon. Minister of State 2001–; Grand Officier, Légion d'honneur 1984, Grosses Verdienskreuz des Verdienstordens 1985, Commdr, Order of Orange-Nassau, Grand Cross Ordem do Mérito 1989, Grand Cross Ordre nat. du Mérite, Grand Cross of Sacred Treasure (Japan) 2000; Prof. E.M. Meijers Medal of Law Faculty (Leiden) 1988, Nat. Police Award 1990.
Address: Oudorpweg 9, 3062 RB, Rotterdam (home); Advisory Council on International Affairs, Bezuidenhoutseweg 67, Room 9E19, PO Box 20061, 2500 EB, The Hague, Netherlands (office). *Telephone:* (70) 3485325 (office); (10) 4526163 (home); 653-301424 (mobile) (home). *Fax:* (70) 3486256 (office); (10) 4529491 (home). *E-mail:* aiv@minbuza.nl (office); fka@planet .nl (home). *Website:* www.aiv-advies.nl (office).

KORUTÜRK, Osman Taney; Turkish diplomatist; *Ambassador to France;* m. Suzan Korutürk. *Career:* fmr Amb. to Iran; Amb. to Germany –2003; Special Envoy to Iraq 2003–04; fmr Special Envoy to Cyprus; currently Amb. to France.
Address: Embassy of Turkey, 16 ave de Lamballe, 75016 Paris, France (office). *Telephone:* 1-53-92-71-12 (office). *Fax:* 1-45-20-41-91 (office). *E-mail:* paris.be@mfa.gov.tr (office).

KOSACHEV, Konstantin, PhD; Russian diplomatist and politician; *Chairman, State Duma International Affairs Committee;* b. 17 Sept. 1962, Moscow region. *Education:* Moscow State Inst. of Int. Relations. *Career:* Deputy Dir Ministry of Foreign Affairs, Moscow 1984; fmr Counsellor, Embassy in Stockholm; mem. State Int. Affairs Council 1998; Deputy, State Duma (Parl.) 1999–, First Vice Chair., Fatherland All Russia Party, State Duma 2001–, Chair. State Duma Int. Affairs Cttee 2003–; Chair. Russian Del., Parl. Ass. of Council of Europe (PACE) 2004–, Vice-Pres. PACE 2005–; Order of Friendship (Russia), Royal Order of the N Star (Sweden).
Address: International Affairs Committee, 103265 Moscow, Gosudarstvennaya Duma, Okhotnyi ryad 1, Russia (office). *Telephone:* (495) 292-83-10 (office). *Website:* www.duma.ru (office).

KOSCHNICK, Hans Karl-Heinrich; German politician; *Chairman of Steering Committee on Refugee Matters, Stability Pact for South Eastern Europe;* b. 2 April 1929, Bremen; m. Christel Risse. *Education:* Mittelschule. *Career:* Local Govt Official, Bremen 1945–51, 1954–63; Trade Union Sec. of the Union of Public Employees, Transport and Communications (ÖTV) 1951–54; mem. Social Democratic Party (SPD) 1950–, Fed. Exec. Council 1970–, Party Bd 1975–, Deputy Chair. SPD 1975–79; mem. Provincial Diet of Land Bremen (Landtag) and City Admin. 1955–63; Senator for the Interior 1963–67; Mayor of Bremen 1967–85; Pres. of the Senate, Bremen 1967–85; mem. Fed. Council (Bundesrat) 1965–, Pres. 1970–71, 1981–82; Nat. Vice-Chair. SPD 1975–79; Chair., German Union of Local Authorities (Deutscher Städtetag) 1971–77; mem. Bd Städtetag (Assoc. of German Municipalities) 1970–, Pres. 1971–77; mem. Exec. Cttee Int. Union of Local Authorities (IULA) 1972–77, 1980–85, Pres. 1981–85; mem. Parl. 1987–94; EU Admin. in Mostar 1994–95; Govt Rep. for Bosnia 1998–; currently Chair. Steering Cttee on Refugee Matters, Stability Pact for SE Europe; Hon. Citizen of Gdansk 1985, of Bremen 1999; Dr hc (Haifa Univ.) 1997. *Address:* Rudolstädterweg 9, 28329 Bremen, Germany. *Telephone:* 4673733.

KOSKENNIEMI, Martti, LLD; Finnish professor of international law and fmr diplomatist; *Professor of International Law and Director, Erik Castrén Institute of International Law and Human Rights, University of Helsinki;* b. 18 March 1953, Turku; m.; two c. *Career:* served with Finnish Diplomatic Service 1978–96, positions include Rep. to UN Gen. Ass. and Security Council, Co-Agent Int. Court of Justice 1991–92, Dir Div. of Int. Law –1996; Judge, Asian Devt Bank, Admin. Tribunal 1997–2003; currently Prof. of Int. Law and Dir Erik Castrén Inst. of Int. Law and Human Rights, Univ. of Helsinki; Global Prof. of Law, New York Univ., USA; mem. UN Int. Law Comm. 2002–; Acad. Prof., Acad. of Finland 2005–; mem. Institut de droit international. *Publications:* From Apology to Utopia: The Structure of International Legal Argument 1989, International Law (ed.) 1991, International Sanctions and Finland (in Finnish) 1994, International Law Aspects of the European Union (ed.) 1998, State Succession: Codification Tested against the Facts 2000, The Sources of International Law 2000, The Gentle Civilizer of Nations: The Rise and Fall of International Law 1870–1960 2001; numerous articles in professional journals. *Address:* The Erik Castrén Institute of International Law and Human Rights, PO Box 4 (Yliopistokatu 3), University of Helsinki, 00014 Helsinki, Finland (office). *Telephone:* (9) 1912-2469 (office). *Fax:* (9) 1912-3076 (office). *E-mail:* martti.koskenniemi@helsinki.fi (office); intlaw-institute@helsinki.fi (office). *Website:* www.helsinki.fi (office).

KOSONEN, (Pentti) Eikka, MSc; Finnish diplomatist; *Permanent Representative, European Union;* b. 16 Sept. 1947; m. Raija Kosonen; three c. *Education:* Univ. of Helsinki. *Career:* joined Ministry of Foreign Affairs 1973; Attaché, Embassy in Algeria 1975–79, First Sec. 1979–80; First Sec., Dept for External Econ. Relations 1980–83, Dir West European Integration 1988–93, Deputy Dir-Gen. 1993–94, Dir-Gen. 2000–01; Counsellor, Perm. Mission to EU 1987–88; Dir-Gen. Secr. for EU Affairs 1994–2000; Perm. Rep. to EU 2001–. *Address:* Permanent Mission of Finland to the EU, 100 rue de Trèves, 1040 Brussels, Belgium (office). *Telephone:* (2) 287-84-11 (office). *Fax:* (2) 287-84-00 (office). *E-mail:* press.eue@formin.fi (office). *Website:* www.uunet.be/finland (office).

KOSOVAN, Col-Gen. Alexander Davydovich; Russian army officer and construction engineer; b. 26 Oct. 1941, Akhtyrskaya, Krasnodar Territory, Russia; m.; one s. one d. *Education:* Novosibirsk Inst. of Eng and Construction. *Career:* head of construction group, chief engineer, Deputy Head Dept of Eng Construction, Ministry of Defence 1966–84; Chief Eng, Deputy Head Construction Dept Volga Mil. Command 1984–88; Deputy Commdr Caucasus Mil. Command on construction and quartering of forces 1988–92; First Deputy Head of Dept on Construction and Quartering of Forces, Russian Ministry of Defence 1992–97, Deputy Minister of Defence in charge of military construction and housing 1997; currently First Deputy Head Dept of City Construction Policy Making, Devt and Reconstruction of Moscow; Order for Service to Motherland in Armed Forces 1989, Order of Labour Red Banner 1990, other Govt decorations. *Publications:* numerous articles on problems of mil. construction, text-books and methodical manuals for univ. and mil. schools. *Address:* Department of City Construction Policy Making, Development and Reconstruction of Moscow, 5, Nikitsky Lane, Moscow, 103864, Russia (office). *Telephone:* (495) 202-09-11 (office). *Fax:* (495) 956-64-84 (office). *Website:* www.dgp.stroi.ru (office).

KOSTELKA, Lt-Gen. Miroslav; Czech politician, diplomatist and army officer (retd); *Ambassador to Russia;* b. 31 Jan. 1951, Františkovy Lázně;

m.; one s. two d. *Education:* Mil. Acad. of Brno, NATO Defence Coll., Rome, Italy. *Career:* began mil. career as bn commdr; Deputy Chief of Nat. Rear Anti-Aircraft Defences 1987–92; Chief of Staff of Main Rear Service 1992–93; Inspector, Czech Repub. Army Logistics 1994–98; Mil. Attaché, Embassy in Ottawa, Canada 1998–2002; Deputy Chief of Gen. Staff 2002–03; Minister of Defence 2003–04; Dir Prime Minister Section 2004–05; Amb. to Russia 2005–; Ordre nat. du Mérite; Hon. Memorial Badge for services in IFOR, UN Peace Service Medal, Medal of Army of Czech Repub., Přemysl Otakar II Hon. Memorial Badge. *Address:* Velryslanectví ČR v Ruské federaci, J. Fučíka 12/14, 123056 Moscow 1, Russia (office). *Telephone:* (495) 251-05-44 (office). *Fax:* (045) 250-15-23 (office). *E-mail:* moscow@embassy.mzv.cz (office). *Website:* www.mfa.cz/moscow (office).

KOSTOV, Ivan Yordanov; Bulgarian politician; b. 23 Dec. 1949; m.; two d. *Education:* Karl Marx Higher Inst. of Econs, Sofia and Kliment Ohridski Univ., Sofia. *Career:* fmr economist; Asst Prof., Karl Marx Higher Inst. of Econs 1974; Sr Asst Prof., Scientific Communism Dept, V. Iyich Lenin Higher Inst. of Mechanical and Electrical Eng, Sofia (now Tech. Univ.) 1979, Asst Prof. 1991; elected Deputy (Union of Democratic Forces—UDF) to 7th Grand Nat. Ass., Chair. Econ. Affairs Cttee 1990, Deputy to 36th Nat. Ass. 1991, 37th Ass. 1993, Deputy Floor Leader of UDF Parl. Group 1993, Deputy to 38th Ass. 1997, 39th Ass. 2001; Minister of Finance 1990–92; Chair. and Pres. Union of Democratic Forces (SDS) 1993; Prime Minister of Bulgaria 1997–2001; led group of deputies who split from UDF to form new parl. group (United Democratic Forces) and, later, found a new political party, Democrats for a Strong Bulgaria (Demokrati za silna Balgarija—DSB), Chair. 2004–07 resgnd). *Address:* Demokrati za silna Balgariya, ul. G. Ignatiyev 10A, 1000 Sofia, Bulgaria (office). *Telephone:* (2) 980-53-34 (office). *Fax:* (2) 987-17-51 (office). *E-mail:* mediacentre@dsb.bg (office). *Website:* www.dsb.bg (office).

KOSUMI, Bajram; Kosovo politician; b. 20 March 1960, Tuxhec, Kamenicë; m.; four c. *Education:* Univ. of Priština. *Career:* student movement leader, Priština 1981; sentenced to 10 years for opposing communist govt of Yugoslavia; journalist 1991–93; mem. Alliance for Future of Kosova (AAK), Vice-Pres.; mem. Ass. of Kosovo; Pres. Parl. Party 1994–96, 2000–02; Minister of Public Information, Interim Govt of Kosovo 1999; Deputy-Pres. Alliance for Future of Kosovo (AAK); Minister for Environment and Spatial Planning of Kosovo 2004–05; Prime Minister of Kosovo 2005–06 (resgnd). *Publications:* A Concept on Sub-Policy 1995, Vocabulary of Barbarians 2000, A Concept on the New Political Thought 2001, Lyric of Fishta 2004, Literature from Prison 2006, A Decisive Year 2006. *Address:* c/o Government Building, Nene Tereze N.N., Priština, Kosovo (office); c/o Alliance for the Future of Kosovo (Aleanca për Ardhmërinë e Kosovës—AAK), Priština, Kodra e Trimave, Serbia. *E-mail:* bajram .kosumi@ks-gov.net (office); lamippk@yahoo.com (home).

KOTAITE, Assad, LLD; Lebanese lawyer and international aviation official (retd); b. 6 Nov. 1924, Hasbaya; m. Monique Ayoub 1983. *Education:* French Univ., Beirut, Univ. of Paris and Acad. of Int. Law, The Hague. *Career:* Head of Legal and Int. Affairs, Directorate of Civil Aviation, Lebanon 1953–56; Rep. of Lebanon, Council of ICAO 1956–70; Sec.-Gen. ICAO 1970–76, Pres. Council 1976–2006 (retd); Pres. Int. Court of Aviation and Space Arbitration, Paris 1995–; many decorations from academic insts and foreign states. *Address:* 5955 Wilderton Avenue, Apt O4A, Montreal, PQ, H3S 2V1 (home); c/o International Civil Aviation Organization, 999 University Street, Suite 12.20, Montreal, PQ H3C 5H7, Canada.

KOTENEV, Vladimir V.; Russian diplomatist; *Ambassador to Germany;* b. 1957, Moscow; m. Maria S. Koteneva; two c. *Education:* Moscow State Univ. *Career:* joined diplomatic corps 1979, various positions including Cen. Apparatus, Ministry of Foreign Affairs, becoming Adviser and Deputy Dir, Secretariat of Minister of Foreign Affairs, various postings abroad including Cultural Attaché, Russian Embassy, Vienna, Amb. to Switzerland, Chargé d'Affaires, Russian Embassy, Berne 1999–2001; Dir, Dept for Consular Services, Ministry of Foreign Affairs 2001–04; Amb. to Germany 2004–. *Address:* Russian Embassy, Unter den Linden 63–65, 10117 Berlin, Germany (office). *Telephone:* (30) 2291110 (office). *Fax:* (30) 2299397 (office). *E-mail:* info@russische-botschaft.de (office). *Website:* www .russische-botschaft.de (office).

KÖTSCHAU, Gabriele, Drlur; German barrister, politician and international organization official; *Director of the Secretariat, Council of the Baltic Sea States;* b. (Gabriele Bögelsack), 1950, Berlin; m.; two c. *Education:* Free Univ. of Berlin, Univ. of Kiel. *Career:* mem. Schleswig-Holstein Parl.

1988–2005, fmr Vice-Pres.; Dir Secr. Council of Baltic Sea States 2005–; Bundesverdienstkreuz. *Publications:* numerous lectures and articles on Baltic Sea cooperation and Eastern Europe.
Address: Council of the Baltic Sea States, Strömsborg, PO Box 2010, Stockholm 103 11, Sweden (office). *Telephone:* (8) 440-19-20 (office). *Fax:* (8) 440-19-44 (office). *E-mail:* gabriele.koetschau@cbss.org (office). *Website:* www.cbss.org (office).

KOTZEV, Boyko Vassilev; Bulgarian diplomatist; *Permanent Representative, European Union;* b. 18 June 1956, Sofia; m.; two c. *Education:* Moscow State Univ., further studies at Int. Court of Justice, The Hague, Int. Law Comm., Geneva, Inst. of Int. and Comparative Law, London. *Career:* held numerous posts at Ministry of Foreign Affairs including Head, EU Relations Unit, Deputy Dir, European Integration Directorate; overseas postings include Deputy Head, Mission in Zimbabwe 1989–93, Deputy Head, Mission to EU, Brussels 1995–98; fmr mem. del. to UN Diplomatic Conf. on adoption of Vienna Convention; Deputy Minister of Internal Affairs 2001, 2005; currently Perm. Rep. to EU, Brussels.
Address: Permanent Representation of Bulgaria to the EU, 49 place Marie-Louise, 1000 Brussels, Belgium. *Telephone:* (2) 235-83-00 (office). *Fax:* (2) 374-91-88 (office). *E-mail:* info@bg-permrep.eu (office). *Website:* www.bgpermrep.eu (office).

KOUASSI, Edmond Kwam, Dr rer. pol; Togolese academic and fmr diplomatist; *First Vice-Dean of the Faculty of Law, Catholic University of West Africa; Education:* Caen Univ. and Univ. of the Sorbonne, Paris, France. *Career:* Asst in Public Law, Univ. of Benin 1975, Lecturer, École Supérieure d'Admin et des Carrières Juridiques, later Asst Dir of Univ. and Chair. of Univ.'s Comité de Lectures des Annales; served as Togo's Amb. to Cuba and to Costa Rica; Vice-Pres. UN Conf. for the Announcement of Contributions to Int. Year of Peace, Pres. of same to World Disarmament Campaign; Perm. Rep. to UN, New York 1985–88, Vice-Chair. UN Special Political Cttee 1985, Chair. 1986–88; currently First Vice-Dean of Faculty of Law, Catholic Univ. of West Africa, Abidjan.
Address: Faculty of Law, Catholic University of West Africa, Abidjan, Côte d'Ivoire.

KOUASSI, Hyacinthe Marcel; Côte d'Ivoirian diplomatist; *Ambassador to France;* m.; four c. *Career:* career diplomat; overseas assignments include First Sec. in Copenhagen, First Sec. in Tokyo, First Sec. with Perm. Mission to UN, Geneva; Amb. to Japan (non-resident to Singapore, Indonesia and the Philippines), Tokyo –2002, Amb. to France, Paris 2002–.
Address: Embassy of Côte d'Ivoire, 102 avenue Raymond Poincaré, 75116 Paris, France (office). *Telephone:* 1-53-64-62-62 (office). *Fax:* 1-45-00-47-97 (office). *E-mail:* bureco-fr@cotedivoire.com (office).

KOUASSI, René Aphing; Côte d'Ivoirian government official. *Career:* fmr magistrate; Minister of Defence 2006–07.
Address: c/o Ministry of Defence, Camp Galliéni, côté Bibliothèque nationale, BP V241, Abidjan, Côte d'Ivoire (office).

KOUCHNER, Bernard, (Bernard Gridaine), KBE, DenM; French politician, physician and screenwriter; *Minister of Foreign and European Affairs;* b. 1 Nov. 1939, Avignon; two s. one d. by Evelyne Pisier; one s. by Christine Ockrent. *Career:* gastro-enterologist, Hôpital Cochin, Paris; Co-founder and Pres. Médecins sans Frontières 1971–79; Founder, Médecins du Monde 1980; has organized and undertaken numerous humanitarian missions world-wide since 1968; Sec. of State, Ministry of Social Affairs and Employment May 1988; Sec. of State responsible for Humanitarian Action, Office of Prime Minister 1988–91, Ministry of Foreign Affairs 1991–92; Minister of Health and Humanitarian Action 1992–93, 1997–99, Minister Del., Ministry of Health 2001–02; mem. European Parl. 1994–97; UN Chief Admin., Kosovo 1999–2001; Founder, Foundation for Humanitarian Action 1993–; radio broadcaster RTL 2 1995; Founder, Malades sans Frontières 2003; currently Prof. of Public Health and Devt, CNAM; Minister of Foreign and European Affairs 2007–; Dr hc (Durham, Pristina, Sarajevo, Ben Gurion, Erasmus Rotterdam); Dag Hammarskjöld Prize 1979, Louis Weiss Prize (European Parl.) 1979, Athinai Prize (Alexander Onassis Foundation) 1981, Prix Europa 1984, Nobel Peace Prize (with Médecin sans Frontières) 1999, Prix de la Tolerance 2003. *Television:* as Bernard Gridaine has written scripts for series including Médecins de Nuit, Hotel de Police, Bonjour Maitre. *Publications:* La France Sauvage, Les Voraces, L'Ile de Lumière, Charité Business, Le Devoir d'Ingérence (jtly) 1988, Les Nouvelles Solidarités 1989, Le Malheur des Autres 1991, Dieu et les Hommes (jtly) 1993, Vingt idées pour l'an 2000 1995, Ce que je crois 1995, La dictature médicale 1995, le Premier qui dit la Verité 2002, Les Guerres de la Paix 2004, Quand tu sera Président (jtly) 2004.

Address: Ministry of Foreign Affairs, 37 quai d'Orsay, 75351 Paris Cedex 07, France (office). *Telephone:* 1-43-17-53-53 (office). *Fax:* 1-43-17-52-03 (office). *Website:* www.diplomatie.gouv.fr (office).

KOUMURA, Masahiko, LLB; Japanese politician; *Minister of Foreign Affairs;* b. Ehime; m.; two s. one d. *Education:* Chuo Univ. *Career:* Parl. Vice-Minister Defence Agency 1987, for Finance 1989, for Foreign Affairs 1996; Minister of State, Dir-Gen. Econ. Planning Agency 1994–95; mem. House of Reps for Yamaguchi 1980–, Chair. Special Cttee on Disasters 1991, on Agric., Forestry and Fisheries 1991, on Prevention of Int. Terrorism and Japan's Cooperation and Support 2003, on Humanitarian Assistance for Reconstruction in Iraq 2003; Deputy Sec.-Gen. LDP, Dir Nat. Defence Div. 1991, Chair. Special Cttee on External Econ. Cooperation 2002; Minister of Foreign Affairs 1999, 2007–, of Justice 2000–01, of Defence 2007.
Address: Ministry of Foreign Affairs, 2-11-1, Shiba-Koen, Minato-ku, Tokyo 105-8519, Japan (office). *Telephone:* (3) 3580-3311 (office). *Fax:* (3) 3581-2667 (office). *E-mail:* webmaster@mofa.go.jp (office). *Website:* www.mofa.go.jp (office).

KOURULA, Erkki, LLL, LLM, PhD; Finnish lawyer, diplomatist and judge; *Judge, International Criminal Court;* b. 12 June 1948; m. Pirkko Kourula; two c. *Education:* Univ. of Helsinki, Univ. of Oxford, UK. *Career:* research posts at Univs of Oxford and Helsinki, Acad. of Finland, UN, Geneva 1972–82, 1984–85; Dist Judge 1979; Prof. of Int. Law, Univ. of Lapland, Rovaniemi 1982–83; Counsellor and Legal Adviser, Ministry of Foreign Affairs 1986–89, Dir Int. Law Div. 1989–91; Minister Counsellor and Legal Adviser, Perm. Mission to UN, NY 1991–95; Amb., Deputy Dir Gen. for Legal Affairs, Ministry of Foreign Affairs 1995–98, Dir Gen. for Legal Affairs 2002–03; Amb., Perm. Rep. to Council of Europe, Strasbourg 1998–2002; Judge, Int. Criminal Court (ICC), The Hague 2003–; Head Del. to Preparatory Cttee for ICC 1994–98; Agent of Finland to European Courts of Justice and Human Rights; mem. Del. to UN Gen. Ass. 1986–90, 1995–97; mem., chair. or del. to numerous int. orgs, cttees and confs. *Publications:* The Identification and Characteristics of Regional Arrangements for the Purpose of the United Nations Charter (doctoral thesis); contribs to publs and articles on activities of UN and ICC.
Address: International Criminal Court, Maanweg 174, 2516 AB The Hague, Netherlands (office). *Telephone:* (70) 5158515 (office). *Fax:* (70) 5158555 (office). *E-mail:* pio@icc-cpi.int (home). *Website:* www.icc-cpi.int (office).

KOUYATÉ, Lansana; Guinean international organization official, diplomatist and politician; b. 1950, Koba; m.; three c. *Career:* joined diplomatic service 1983, Counsellor, Embassy in Cote d'Ivoire 1983–85; Head, Africa and OAU Dept, Ministry of Foreign Affairs 1985–87; Amb. to Egypt, Sudan, Turkey, Jordan, Syria and Lebanon 1987–92; Perm. Rep. to UN, New York 1992–97, Vice-Pres. ECOSOC 1992–93, Sec. Gen's Special Rep. to Somalia 1993–94, Under-Sec. Gen. in charge of Political Affairs for Africa, Western Asia and Middle East, UN Security Council 1994–97; Exec. Sec. Econ. Community of W African States (ECOWAS) 1997–2002; Perm. Rep. to Int. Org. of Francophone Countries 2002–07; Prime Minister of Guinea 2007–08; Commdr, Légion d'honneur, Commdr of the Mono Order (Togo), African Star (Liberia). *Publications include:* International Funding of State-owned Companies in Guinea: Problems and Prospects, The End of the Cold War and its Impact on Third-World Countries.
Address: c/o Office of the Prime Miinister, National Assembly, Palais du Peuple, BP 414, Conakry, Guinea (office).

KOVAČEVIĆ, Božo; Croatian politician and diplomatist; *Ambassador to Russian Federation; Career:* mem. Liberal Party (LS); Minister of Regional Planning, Building and Housing 2000; Minister of Environmental Protection and Spatial Planning 2001–03; currently Amb. to Russian Fed.
Address: Embassy of Croatia, 119034 Moscow, per. Korobeinikov 16/10, Russian Federation (office). *Telephone:* (095) 201-38-68 (office). *Fax:* (095) 201-46-24 (office). *E-mail:* croemb.russia@mvpei.hr (office). *Website:* ru.mvp.hr (office).

KOVÁCS, László; Hungarian politician; *Commissioner for Taxation and Customs Union, European Commission;* b. 3 July 1939; m.; one d. *Education:* Coll. of Politics, Univ. of Econ. Sciences, Petrik Lajos Tech. School. *Career:* chemical technician, Medicolor, Kobánya Pharmaceutical Works 1957–66; youth and student movt 1966–75; consultant and Deputy Head, Dept for Int. Relations, Hungarian Socialist Workers' Party 1975–86; mem. Parl. 1990–2004, mem. Foreign Affairs Cttee 1990–93 (Chair. 1993–94); mem. Presidium Hungarian Socialist Party (MSZP) 1990–2004, Head of Parl. Faction 1998–2000, Chair. 1998–2004; Deputy Minister of Foreign Affairs 1986–89, State Sec. 1989–90, Minister of Foreign Affairs 1994–98, 2002–04; EU Commr for Taxation and Customs Union 2004–; Chair.-in-Office OSCE 1995; Vice-Chair. Socialist International 2003–05; Co-Chair.

Cen. and East European Cttee 1996–2003; mem. Council of Wise Men of Council of Europe 1997–99.
Address: European Commission, 200 Rue de la Loi, 1049 Brussels, Belgium (office). *Telephone:* (2) 299-11-11 (office). *Fax:* (2) 295-01-38 (office). *E-mail:* Laszlo.Kovacs@ec.europa.eu (office). *Website:* ec.europa.eu/commission_barroso/kovacs (office).

KOVALENKO, Vyacheslav; Russian diplomatist; *Ambassador to Georgia; Career:* joined Ministry of Foreign Affairs 1972; posting in Embassy in Belarus 1992–97, 1999–2003; Dir Second Dept of CIS Countries, Ministry of Foreign Affairs 2003-06; Amb. to Georgia 2006–.
Address: Embassy of Russia, 0162 Tbilisi, Chavchavadze 51, Georgia (office). *Telephone:* (32) 91-24-06 (office). *Fax:* (32) 91-27-38 (office). *E-mail:* russianembassy@caucasus.net (office). *Website:* www.georgia.mid.ru (office).

KOVANDA, Karel, MBA, PhD; Czech diplomatist; *Deputy Director General of External Relations, European Commission;* b. 5 Oct. 1944, Gilsland, UK; m. Noemi Berová 1993; one s. two d. *Education:* Prague School of Agric., Massachusetts Inst. of Tech. and Pepperdine Univ., USA. *Career:* leadership, Czech Nat. Student Union 1968–69; emigrated to USA 1970; lecturer in political science and freelance journalist 1975–80; man. positions in US pvt. sector 1980–90; returned to Czechoslovakia 1990; Czech Ministry of Foreign Affairs 1991–93, Political Dir 1993, Deputy Minister 1997–98; Perm. Rep. of Czech Repub. to UN 1993–97, to UN Security Council 1994–95, to NATO 1998–2005; Deputy Dir Gen. of External Relations, EC 2005–; Pres. ECOSOC 1997; Czech Order of Merit, First Class 2003.
Address: Directorate-General External Relations, European Commission, 1049 Brussels, Belgium (office). *Telephone:* (2) 298-07-65 (office). *E-mail:* Karel.Kovanda@ec.europa.eu (office). *Website:* (office).

KOWLESSAR, Saisnarine; Guyanese politician and banking executive. *Career:* fmr Gov. of Bank for Guyana, IMF; Minister of Finance –2006.
Address: c/o Ministry of Finance, Main and Urquhart Streets, Georgetown, Guyana (office).

KOZHOKIN, Mikhail Mikhailovich, CandHist; Russian journalist; b. 23 Feb. 1962, Moscow. *Education:* Moscow State Univ. *Career:* Jr researcher, researcher, Sr researcher Inst. of USA and Canada, USSR (now Russian) Acad. of Sciences 1988–92, Sr researcher Cen. of Econ. and Political Studies, worked with G. Yavlinsky 1992–93; Head Information Dept ONEXIM bank 1993–96; Deputy Chair. Exec. Cttee 1996–; Asst to First Deputy Chair. of Russian Govt, mem. Govt Comm. on Econ. Reform 1997–; Dir Holding Co. Interros on work with mass media and public relations; Chair. Bd of Dirs Izvestia (newspaper) 1997–98, Ed.-in-Chief 1998–2003 (resgnd).
Address: c/o Izvestia, Tverskaya str. 18, korp. 1, 127994 Moscow, Russia (office).

KOZLÍK, Sergej; Slovak politician; b. 27 July 1950, Bratislava. *Education:* Univ. of Econs. *Career:* clerk with Price Authority 1974–88; Head Dept of Industrial Prices, Ministry of Finance 1988–90; Dir Exec. Dept of Antimonopoly Office 1990–92; Sec. Movt for a Democratic Slovakia (became political party 2000) 1992–; Vice-Premier, Govt of Slovakia 1993–94; Minister of Finance of Slovak Repub. 1994–97; Deputy to Nat. Council 1994–2004; mem. European Parl. (Non-attached Mems) 2004–, mem. Cttee on Budgets, Substitute mem. Cttee on Econ. and Monetary Affairs, mem. Del. to ACP-EU Jt Parl. Ass.; Gov. World Bank 1994–98 Alt. Gov. IMF 1994–98.
Address: European Parliament, Bâtiment Altiero Spinelli, 01E252, 60 rue Wiertz, 1047 Brussels, Belgium (office). *Fax:* (2) 284-92-57 (office). *E-mail:* sergej_kozlik@nrsr.sk (office). *Website:* www.europa.eu (office).

KPOTSRA, Roland Yao; Togolese politician, diplomatist and civil servant; *Permanent Representative, United Nations;* b. 20 Feb. 1947, Lom; m.; two c. *Career:* joined Foreign Ministry as Desk Officer in Admin. Affairs Div. 1974, Dir Treaties and Legal Affairs Div. 1982–88, Dir Admin and Personnel 1987–90; Sec. Perm. Mission to UN, New York 1976–79, Counsellor 1979–, Chargé d'affaires April–Aug. 1980, Perm. Rep. to UN 1996–2002 and currently; Chargé de Mission, Ministry of Foreign Affairs and Co-operation 1992–93, Sec.-Gen. 1993–96, Minister of Foreign Affairs and Co-operation 2002–03; First Counsellor Embassy in Brazil 1980–82; Chargé d'affaires in Zimbabwe 1990–91; Leader of Del. to 63rd session of OAU Council of Ministers, 10th Ministerial Conf. of Movt of Non-Aligned Countries 1995; Deputy Head of Del. to OAU 50th Ass.; headed team at int. French-speaking conf. on conflict resolution from African perspective 1995; Lecturer in Diplomatic History, École Nat. d'Admin, Togo; Chevalier, Nat. Order of Merit 1984; Officer, Order of Mono 1996.

Address: Permanent Mission of Togo to the UN, 112 East 40th Street, New York, NY 10016, USA (office). *Telephone:* (212) 490-3455 (office). *Fax:* (212) 983-6684 (office). *E-mail:* onu@republicoftogo.com (office); togo@un.int (home).

KRAAG-KETELDIJK, Lygia; Suriname politician; *Minister of Foreign Affairs;* b. 1941. *Career:* Dir of Political Affairs, Cabinet of the Pres. 2000–05; Minister of Foreign Affairs 2005–.
Address: Ministry of Foreign Affairs, 25 Lim A Po Street, POB 25, Paramaribo, Suriname (office). *Telephone:* 471209 (office). *Fax:* 410411 (office). *E-mail:* buza@sr.net (office).

KRAČUN, Davorin, MA, PhD; Slovenian economist, academic and fmr diplomatist; b. 31 Oct. 1950, Maribor; m.; two c. *Education:* Univ. of Maribor, Univ. of Zagreb, Croatia. *Career:* teacher and researcher, School of Business and Econs, Univ. of Maribor 1974–, Vice-Dean 1983–87, Prof. 1995–, Co-f. Inst. for Econ. Diagnosis and Prognosis; Minister of Planning 1992–93; Deputy Prime Minister and Minister of Econ. Relations and Devt 1993–95; Chair. Econ. Council of Govt 1995–97; Minister of Foreign Affairs 1996–97; Amb. to USA 2000–04; fmr Chair. Supervisory Bd, Nova Kreditna Banka Maribor, Terme Maribor Corpn; mem. Council Slovenian Nat. Bank 1986–91; mem. Bd of Dirs Slovenian Econ. Chamber 1988–92; fmr mem. Supervisory Bd Pharos Foundation Ljubljana; fmr host of TV educational series. *Publications:* over 300 scientific and professional papers, books, univ. textbooks and research reports.
Address: University of Maribor, Faculty of Economics and Business, Razlagova 14, Maribor 2000, Slovenia.

KRAEHENBUEHL, Pierre, BA; Swiss international organization executive; *Director of Operations, International Committee of the Red Cross;* b. 1966; m.; three c. *Education:* Univ. of Geneva. *Career:* began a career in journalism and photography, but then began work at Lutheran World Fed.; joined Int. Cttee of Red Cross (ICRC) 1991, first served in field operations as del. in El Salvador and Peru, given managerial responsibilities in Afghanistan 1993–95, and subsequently in Bosnia and Herzegovina, served as Head of Operations for Cen. and South-Eastern Europe in Geneva, personal adviser to Jakob Kellenberger (Pres. ICRC) 2000–02, Dir of Operations 2002–.
Address: International Committee of the Red Cross, 19 avenue de la Paix, 1202 Geneva, Switzerland (office). *Telephone:* (22) 734-60-01 (office). *Fax:* (22) 733-20-57 (office). *E-mail:* press.gva@icrc.org (office). *Website:* www.icrc.org (office).

KRAJESKI, Thomas Charles, BA, MA; American diplomatist; b. Groveland, Mass; m.; one s. two d. *Education:* Univ. of Massachusetts and Univ. of N Carolina. *Career:* entered Foreign Service in 1979, served in Embassy in Kathmandu 1980–82, Chief of Consular Section in Madras 1982–84, in State Dept Press Office 1985, Deputy Chief of Consular Section in Warsaw 1985–88, Political Desk Officer, India Desk, State Dept, Sr Watch Officer, Operations Center during first Gulf War, completed two years of Arabic language studies at Foreign Service Inst., assigned to Political Section, Embassy in Cairo –1997, Prin. Officer and Consul Gen., Dubai –2003, Political Advisor on Amb. Bremer's staff, Baghdad July–Oct. 2003, Dir Office of Northern Gulf Affairs (Iran and Iraq), Bureau of Near Eastern Affairs, Dept of State 2003–04, Amb. to Yemen 2004–07.
Address: US Department of State, 2201 C Street NW, Washington, DC 20520, USA (office). *Telephone:* (202) 647-4000 (office). *Fax:* (202) 647-6738 (office). *Website:* www.state.gov (office).

KRAMER, Martin, PhD; American academic; *Wexler-Fromer Research Fellow, Washington Institute for Near East Policy;* b. 9 Sept. 1954, Washington, DC. *Education:* Princeton Univ., Columbia Univ. *Career:* fmr Dir Moshe Dayan Center for Middle Eastern and African Studies, Tel-Aviv Univ., Israel; Wexler-Fromer Research Fellow, Washington Inst. for Near East Policy 2004–; Sr Fellow, Shalem Center, Jerusalem 2006–; fmr Visiting Prof., Brandeis Univ., Univ. of Chicago, Cornell Univ., Georgetown Univ.; fmr Ed. Middle East Quarterly, Phila; fmr Fellow, Woodrow Wilson Int. Center for Scholars, Washington, DC. *Publications:* Islam Assembled, Shi'ism, Resistance and Revolution, Middle Eastern Lives, Arab Reawakening and Islamic Revival, The Islamism Debate: The Jewish Discovery of Islam, Ivory Towers on Sand: The Failure of Middle Eastern Studies in America.
Address: Washington Institute for Near East Policy, Suite 1050, 1828 L Street NW, Washington, DC 20036, USA (office). *Telephone:* (202) 452-0650 (office). *Fax:* (202) 223-5364 (office). *E-mail:* martink@washingtoninstitute.org (office). *Website:* www.washingtoninstitute.org (office); www.martinkramer.org (office).

KRAMER, Mary Elizabeth, BA, MA; American politician and diplomatist; m. Kay Kramer; two c. *Education:* Univ. of Iowa. *Career:* fmr teacher and

admin., Iowa Public School Systems; fmr Vice-Pres. Community Investments, Wellmark Blue Cross, Blue Shield; fmr Corp. Personnel Dir of Younkers, Inc.; State Senator for Iowa 1991–2004, Pres. Iowa Senate 1997–2004; Commr White House Comm. on Presidential Scholars 2001–, Chair. 2002–04; Amb. to Barbados (also accred to Antigua and Barbuda, Dominica, Grenada, Saint Christopher and Nevis, Saint Lucia and Saint Vincent and the Grenadines) 2004–06; mem. Bd of Dirs State Legislative Leaders Foundation; Chair. Bd Senate Pres.'s Forum; mem. Reforming States Group (Health Care Issues), facilitated the Milbank Memorial Fund; fmr mem. Bd of Dirs numerous Iowa public and pvt. insts; mem. Rotary Club; several civic awards, including annual awards of Best Elected Official, the Humanitarian Award and Senator of the Year, as well as the Nat. Award for Professional Excellence, Soc. for Human Resource Man.
Address: US Department of State, 2201 C Street NW, Washington, DC 20520, USA (office). *Telephone:* (202) 647-4000 (office). *Fax:* (202) 647-6738 (office). *Website:* www.state.gov (office).

KRASNER, Stephen David, BA, MIA, PhD; American political scientist and academic; *Graham H. Stuart Professor of International Relations, Department of Political Science, Stanford University;* b. 15 Feb. 1942, New York City. *Education:* Cornell, Columbia, and Harvard Univs. *Career:* Asst Prof., Harvard Univ. 1970–75; Asst, then Assoc. Prof., UCLA 1976–81; Prof. of Political Science, Stanford Univ. 1981–91, Graham H. Stuart Prof. of Int. Relations 1991–, Sr Fellow, Inst. for Int. Studies 1991–; Dir Policy Planning, State Dept, Washington, DC 2005–07; Ed. International Organization (journal) 1986–91, mem. Bd of Eds 1978–83, 1992–98, 2000–02 (mem. Exec. Cttee 1995–97, Chair. 1996–98); mem. Bd of Eds Review of International Studies 1981–, International Relations of the Asia Pacific 2000–; mem. Editorial Advisory Bd Studies in American Political Development 1985–, Studies in International Trade Policy 1990–; Gen. Ed. Studies in International Political Economy (book series) 1979–; mem. American Political Science Asscn, American Econs Asscn, Council on Foreign Relations, Int. Studies Asscn; Fellow, American Acad. of Arts and Sciences. *Publications include:* Sovereignty: Organized Hypocrisy 1999, Exploration and Contestation in the Study of World Politics (co-ed.) 1999, Problematic Sovereignty: Contested Rules and Political Possibilities 2000. *Address:* Department of Political Science, 616 Serra Street, Encina West, Room 405, Stanford University, Stanford, CA 94305, USA (office). *Telephone:* (650) 723-0676 (office). *Fax:* (650) 723-1808 (office). *E-mail:* skrasner@stanford.edu (office). *Website:* polisci.stanford.edu (office).

KRASNOHORSKÁ, Mária, PhD; Slovak academic and diplomatist; *General Director, Ministry of Foreign Affairs;* b. 15 Aug. 1949, Topolčany; m. Juraj Krasnohorský 1974; one d. one s. *Education:* Comenius Univ. (Bratislava). *Career:* Researcher, Acad. of Dramatic Arts, Bratislava, Head of Language Dept and teacher of Modern French Drama 1972–91; mem. staff Ministry of Foreign Affairs 1991–93; Counsellor, Perm. Mission to UN, Geneva 1993–94, Perm. Rep. 1994, Pres. UN Conference on Disarmament 1997; Amb. to France –2007; Gen. Dir Ministry of Foreign Affairs 2007–; has translated several plays from French and Russian 1970–91.
Address: Ministry of Foreign Affairs, Hlboká cesta 2, 833 36 Bratislava, Slovakia (office). *Telephone:* (2) 5978-1111 (office). *Fax:* (2) 5978-2213 (office). *E-mail:* informacie@foreign.gov.sk (office). *Website:* www.mzv.sk (office).

KRASTS, Guntars; Latvian politician and economist; b. 16 Oct. 1957, Riga, Latvia; m.; three s. *Education:* Latvian State Univ. *Career:* researcher Inst. of Agric. Econ. 1983–91; Chair. Exec. Bd RANG Ltd 1991–95; Minister of Econs 1995–97; Prime Minister of Latvia 1997–98; Vice-Prime Minister for EU Affairs 1998–99; Chair Saeima (Parl.) Foreign Affairs Cttee 1998–2002, European Affairs Cttee 2002–04; MEP 2004–, Vice-Chair. Cttee on Economic and Monetary Affairs. *Publications:* numerous publs in Latvia and abroad on econ. and foreign policy issues.
Address: European Parliament, rue Wiertz ASP A4F370. 1047 Brussels, Belgium. *Telephone:* (2) 284-59-09 (office). *Fax:* (2) 284-99-09 (office). *E-mail:* g.krasts@europarl.eu.int (office).

KRATOCHWIL, Friedrich Viktor, MA, PhD; German academic; *Chair of International Politics, European University Institute;* b. Lundenburg. *Education:* Maximiliansgymnasium, Munich, Univ. of Munich, Georgetown Univ., Washington, DC and Princeton Univ., NJ, USA. *Career:* Researcher, Christian Democratic Party (CDU) 1965–67; Asst, Technische Hochschule München 1969–70; Teaching Fellow, Georgetown Univ. 1979–71, Princeton Univ. 1973–74; Instructor and Asst Prof., Univ. of Maryland, Baltimore 1975–79; Visiting Asst Prof., Princeton Univ. 1979–80; Asst Prof. of Political Science, Columbia Univ. 1981–87, Assoc. Prof. 1987–88; Assoc. Prof. of Political Science, Univ. of Penn. 1988, apptd Lawrence B. Simon Prof. in Social Sciences 1990; Andrew Mellon Prof., Grad. School of Int. Studies, Univ. of Denver 1990; Chair. of Int. Politics, European Univ. Inst. (EUI), Florence, Italy 2003–; Ed. European Journal

of Int. Relations 2000–04; mem. Editorial Bd, Millennium 1989–91, World Politics 1989–92, 1992–95, Int. Org. 1990–93, 1993–96, Int. Studies Quarterly 1998–2001, Journal of Int. Relations of the Asia-Pacific 2000–; Co-Founder and Trustee, Baltimore Council on Foreign Relations; Consultant, US Dept of Defense 1978; mem. American Political Science Asscn, American Soc. of Int. Law, Int. Soc. of Political Psychology. *Publications:* International Order and Foreign Policy 1978, The Human Conception of International Relations 1981, International Law: A Contemporary Perspective (co-ed.) 1985, Peace and Disputed Sovereignty: Reflections on Conflict over Territory (co-author) 1985, Rules, Norms and Decisions: On the Conditions of Practical and Legal Reasoning in International Relations and Domestic Society 1989, International Organisation: A Reader (co-ed.) 1993, The Return of Culture and Identity in IR Theory (co-ed.) 1996, Transformative Change and Global Order (co-ed.) 2002; numerous articles in professional journals.
Address: Department of Political and Social Sciences, European University Institute, Badia Fiesolana, Via dei Roccettini, 9, 50016 San Domenico di Fiesole (FI), Italy (office). *Telephone:* (055) 4685220 (office). *Fax:* (055) 4685201 (office). *E-mail:* friedrich.kratochwil@eui.eu (office). *Website:* www.iue.it/SPS (office).

KRAUSS RUSQUE, Enrique, LLB; Chilean lawyer, politician and diplomatist; *Ambassador to Ecuador;* b. 8 Jan. 1932, Valdivia; m. Gabriela Krauss Rusque; four c. *Education:* Univ. of Chile. *Career:* solicitor, Luis Alemparte, Francisco Pinto & Mario Creek (law firm) 1953–60; f. Krauss & Donoso (law firm) 1961; lawyer, Sofofa Insurance Agency; columnist, Mercury 1953–58, Sopesur 1971–80, various newspapers 1979–97; Asst of Comm., Nat. Congress 1955–64; Legal Adviser, Dept of the Interior 1965–66, Under-Sec. 1966–68; Minister of the Economy, Commerce and Reconstruction 1968–69; Minister of Housing 1968, 1969; Minister of External Relations 1969; various sr positions in Christian Democratic Party 1969–, elected Pres. 1997; elected Deputy for Dist of Santiago 1973–77, 1998–2002; Minister of the Interior 1990–93; Vice-Pres. of Chile 1993; Amb. to Spain (also accred. to Cyprus) –2006, Amb. to Ecuador 2006–; mem. Nat. Council of TV 1971–73; fmr Dir Viviec SA, Soc. of Savings and Loans.
Address: Embassy of Chile, Edif. Xerox, 4°, Juan Pablo Sanz 3617 y Amazonas, Quito, Ecuador (office). *Telephone:* (2) 224-9403 (office). *Fax:* (2) 244-4470 (office). *E-mail:* embachileecu@trans-telco.net (office).

KRAVCHUK, Leonid Makarovych, Cand. Econ. Sc; Ukrainian politician; b. 10 Jan. 1934, Velykyi Zhytyn; m. Antonina Mikhailivna 1957; one s. *Education:* Kyiv State Univ. and Acad. of Social Sciences, Moscow. *Career:* teacher of Political Economy, Chernovitsky Tech. School; party work since 1960, on staff Ukrainian CP Cen. Cttee 1970–; Head, Propaganda Dept 1980–88, Ideology Dept 1988–89, Sec., Cen. Cttee, mem. Politburo 1990; Chair. Ukrainian Supreme Soviet 1990–91; Pres. of Ukraine 1991–94; C-in-C Armed Forces of Ukraine 1991–94; mem. Verkhovna Rada (Parl.) 1994–; f. Mutual Understanding Movt 1994; mem. Social Democratic Party; Head, All-Ukrainian Union of Democratic Forces Zlagoda 1999–; Chair. State Cttee for Admin. Reforms 1997–99; Protector Mohyla Acad. –Nat. Univ. of Kyiv 1991; Head, Trusteeship Council, Children and Youth Activity Cen. of Ukraine 1992; Hon. Pres. East European Asscn of Businessmen; Dr hc (La Salle Univ., Phila., USA) 1992. *Publications include:* State and Authorities: Experience of Administrative Reforms 2001, We Have What We Have 2002.
Address: Verkhovna Rada, 01008 Kyiv, vul. M. Hrushevskoho 5, Ukraine (office). *Telephone:* (44) 255-21-15 (office). *Fax:* (44) 253-32-17 (office). *E-mail:* umz@rada.gov.ua (office). *Website:* www.rada.gov.ua (office).

KREMP, Herbert, DPhil; German journalist; b. 12 Aug. 1928, Munich; m. Brigitte Steffal 1956; two d. (one deceased). *Education:* Munich Univ. *Career:* reporter, Frankfurter Neue Presse 1956–57; Political Ed. Rheinische Post 1957–59; Dir Political Dept, Der Tag, Berlin 1959–61; Bonn Corresp. Rheinische Post 1961–63; Ed.-in-Chief Rheinische Post 1963–68; Ed.-in-Chief Die Welt 1969–77, Co-Ed. 1981, Co-Publr 1984–87, Chief Corresp. in Beijing 1977–81, Ed.-in-Chief 1981–85, apptd Chief Corresp. in Brussels 1987, Co-Ed., Springer Group newspapers 1984–87, commentator, Die Welt, Berliner Morgenpost, Welt am Sonntag, Bild, B.Z. Berlin, Hamburger Abendblatt; currently associated with Axel Springer publishing house; Bundesverdienstkreuz 1988; Konrad Adenauer Prize 1984, Theodor-Wolff Prize 1978, 2003. *Publications:* Am Ufer der Rubikon: Eine politische Anthropologie, Die Bambusbrücke: Ein asiatisches Tagebuch 1979, Wir brauchen unsere Geschichte 1988.
Address: c/o Axel Springer Verlag AG, Axel-Springer-Str. 65, 10888 Berlin, Germany.

KRISHNAMOORTHY, V.; Sri Lankan diplomatist; *High Commissioner to Bangladesh; Career:* fmr First Sec. and Head of Chancery, Perm. Rep. of Sri Lanka to Org. for Prohibition of Chemical Weapons, The Hague,

Netherlands; currently High Commr to Bangladesh; Patron Sri Lanka-Bangladesh Chamber of Commerce and Industry.
Address: High Commission of Sri Lanka, House 4A, Road 113, Gulshan Model Town, Dhaka 1212, Bangladesh (office). *Telephone:* (2) 9896353 (office). *Fax:* (2) 8823971 (office). *E-mail:* slhc@citechco.net (office).

KRIŠTO, Borjana; Bosnia and Herzegovina politician; *President, Federation of Bosnia and Herzegovina;* b. 13 Aug. 1961, Livno; m. *Career:* fmr Vice-Pres. of Parl.; fmr Vice-Pres., Fed. of Bosnia and Herzegovina; Minister of Justice 2003–07; Rep. to Council of Europe 2007–; Pres. Fed. of Bosnia and Herzegovina 2007–; mem. Croatian Democratic Union of Bosnia and Herzegovina.
Address: Office of the President of the Federation of Bosnia and Herzegovina, 71000 Sarajevo, Alipašina 41, Bosnia and Herzegovina (office). *Telephone:* (33) 472618 (office). *Fax:* (33) 472618 (office). *E-mail:* info@fbihvlada.gov.ba (office). *Website:* www.fbihvlada.gov.ba (office).

KRIVINE, Alain; French journalist and politician; b. 10 July 1941, Paris; m. Michèle Martinet 1960; two d. *Education:* Lycée Condorcet and Faculté des Lettres de Paris. *Career:* mem. Jeunesses communistes 1956, French CP 1958; Leader Union of Student Communists, Paris-Sorbonne Univ. 1964–65; f. Revolutionary Communist Youth 1966 (disbanded by the Govt 1968), Communist League 1969 (dissolved 1973); cand. presidential elections 1969, 1974; journalist, Rouge 1969–; mem. Political Bureau of Ligue Communiste Révolutionnaire 1974–2006; mem. European Parl. 1999–2004; mem. Secretariat UNIFI de la IVe Internationale. *Publications:* La Farce électorale 1969, Questions sur la révolution 1973, Mais si, rebelles et repentis (with Daniel Bensaïd) 1988.
Address: Ligue Communiste Révolutionnaire (LCR), 2 rue Richard-Lenoir, 93100 Montreuil, France. *Telephone:* 1-48-70-42-30. *Fax:* 1-48-59-23-28. *E-mail:* lcr@les-rouge.org. *Website:* www.lcr-rouge.org.

KRLIU, Oliver; Macedonian diplomatist; *Deputy Chief of Mission in USA;* m. Sonja Gievska. *Career:* apptd First Sec. (Political and Econ.), later Minister Counselor and Deputy Chief of Mission, Embassy in Washington, DC 1998–, Chargé d'affaires a.i. 2006.
Address: Embassy of former Yugoslav republic of Macedonia, 2129 Wyoming Avenue, NW, Washington, DC 20008, USA (office). *Telephone:* (202) 667-0501 (office). *Fax:* (202) 667-2131 (office). *E-mail:* usoffice@macedonianembassy.org (office). *Website:* www.macedonianembassy.org (office).

KROES, Neelie, MSc (Econs); Dutch politician and economist; *Commissioner for Competition, European Commission;* b. 19 July 1941, Rotterdam. *Education:* Erasmus Univ., Rotterdam. *Career:* Asst Prof. of Transport Econs, Erasmus Univ. 1965–1971; mem. Rotterdam Municipal Council, Rotterdam Chamber of Commerce 1969–71; mem. Parl. 1971–77; Vice-Minister of Transport, Public Works and Telecommunication 1977–81, Minister of Transport, Public Works and Telecommunication 1982–89; Advisor to EU Commr for Transport 1989–91; EU Commr for Competition 2004–; Pres. Nijenrode Univ. 1991–2000; Chair. Supervisory Bd MeyerMonitor –2004, Nederlands Luchtvaart Overleg (Dutch Aviation Platform) –2004; mem. Supervisory Bd Cório, Royal P&O Nedlloyd NV, Ballast Nedam, New Skies Satellites, Lucent Technologies BV (Netherlands), Nederlandse Spoorwegen NV (Dutch Railways), Volvo Group, Thales Group –2004; Dir (non-exec.) MM02 plc –2004; mem. Bd of Trustees ProLogis International –2004; Chair. Governing Bd Delta Psychiatrical Hosp., Het Rembrandthuis Foundation, Poets of All Nations, Overlegorgaan Waterbeheer en Noordzee-aangelegenheden; fmr Chair. Nyenrode Fund, Supervisory Bd Port Support International BV, Governing Bd TBS Mental Hosp. De Kijvelanden, Governing Bd Bezinnings Groep Water, Supervisory Bd NIB Capital NV, Supervisory Bd Intis BV, Governing Bd Kunsthal; mem. Governing Bd Nelson Mandela Children Fund Member, Bd Dirs World Cancer Research Fund; fmr mem. Governing Bd Royal Trade Fair (Koninklijke Jaarbeurs), Governing Bd Stichting International Human Resources, Development VNO/NCW, Advisory Bd International Problems (AIV), Supervisory Bd Dirs Prologis European Properties, Advisory Bd PriceWaterhouseCooper, Supervisory Bd NCM Holding NV, Bd of Dirs Brambles Industries Ltd (Australia), Supervisory Bd McDonald's, Bd of Dirs SC Johnson Wax Euro Bd, Supervisory Bd Digital Equipment BV, Supervisory Bd Groeneveld Transport Efficiency, Raad van Toezicht Veerstichting, Competitiveness Group to Chair. EC, Governing Bd Insurance Authority, Governing Bd Conservation of Nature, High Level Group on the trans-European Network; fmr adviser, Monitor Group, Arcadis (Heidemij/Grabowsky); Kt, Order of the Dutch Lion 1981, Grand Officier, Légion d'honneur 1984, Bundesverdienstkreuz 1985, Grand Officer, Order of Orange Nassau 1989, Bintang Mahaputra Adiprana Order (Indonesia) 1993; Dr hc (Hull) 1989; Woman of the Year in Infrastructure, Int. Road Fed. 1993, ranked by Forbes magazine amongst 100 Most Powerful Women (44th) 2005, (38th) 2006, (59th) 2007.
Address: European Commission, 200 rue de la Loi, 1049 Brussels, Belgium (office). *Telephone:* (2) 299-11-11 (office). *Fax:* (2) 295-01-38 (office). *E-mail:* Neelie.Kroes@cec.eu.int (office). *Website:* ec.europa.eu/comm/commission_barroso/kroes/index_en.html (office).

KROHN DEVOLD, Kristin, MSc; Norwegian politician; b. 12 Aug. 1961, Ålesund; m.; two c. *Education:* Univ. of Bergen, Norwegian School of Econs, Univ. of Oslo, Norwegian Nat. Defence Coll. *Career:* mem. Parl. (Stortinget) for Oslo 1993–97, 1997–2001, 2001–05; Sec. of the Lagting (Presidium, Stortinget) 1993–97; mem. Standing Cttee on Business and Industry 1993–97, Election Cttee 1997–2001, 2001–05, Working Procedures Cttee 1997–2001, Extended Foreign Affairs Cttee 1997–2001; Chair. Standing Cttee on Justice 1997–2001; Minister of Defence 2001–05; Substitute mem. Del. to Consultation Organ for European Econ. Area Affairs, Brussels 1993–97; Group Sec. Parl. Group, Conservative Party 1987–92, mem. Bd Party 1996–, Parl. Steering Cttee 1997–2001; mem. Oslo City Parl. 1991–93; mem. Bd Statistics Norway 1989–93, St Hanshaugen Residence for the Elderly and Nursing Home 1991–92, Main Cttee of World Handball Championship 1999, Save the Children Norway 1999–.
Address: c/o Ministry of Defence, Myntgt. 1, POB 8126 Dep., 0032 Oslo, Norway (office).

KROL, George Albert, BA, MA; American diplomatist; b. NJ. *Education:* Harvard Univ. and Univ. of Oxford, UK. *Career:* career mem. Sr Foreign Service since 1982, various assignments in Poland, India, USSR, Russia and Ukraine, Deputy Chief of Mission and Chargé d'affaires in Minsk 1993–95, Special Asst to Amb.-at-Large for New Independent States, Dept of State 1995–97, Dir Office of Russian Affairs 1997–99, Minister-Counselor for Political Affairs, Embassy in Moscow 1999–2002, Amb. to Belarus 2003–06; several State Dept Superior and Meritorious Honor Awards.
Address: US Department of State, 2201 C Street NW, Washington, DC 20520, USA (office). *Telephone:* (202) 647-4000 (office). *Fax:* (202) 647-6738 (office). *Website:* www.state.gov (office).

KRÖNER, Christiaan Mark Johan, LLM; Dutch diplomatist; *Ambassador to USA;* b. 8 Oct. 1945, Ibbenbüren; m. Harriët van der Wal. *Education:* Univ. of Leiden. *Career:* entered diplomatic corps 1973, postings to embassies in Vienna, Accra, New Delhi, Belgrade, Deputy Dir Dept of Atlantic Co-operation and Security Affairs, The Hague 1987–88, Consul-Gen., Munich 1988–90, Amb.-at-Large and Jt Dir-Gen. of Political Affairs 1990–93, Amb. to Israel 1993–97, to Italy 1997–2001, to France 2001–06, to USA 2006–.
Address: Embassy of the Netherlands, 4200 Linnean Avenue, NW, Washington, DC 20008, USA (office). *Telephone:* (1-877) 388-2443 (office); (202) 244-5300 (office). *Fax:* (202) 362-3430 (office). *E-mail:* webmaster@netherlands-embassy.org (office). *Website:* www.netherlands-embassy.org (office).

KRONKAITIS, Maj.-Gen. Jonas A., BS, MBA; Lithuanian army officer; m. Rūta Kronkaitis; one s. one d. *Education:* Univ. of Connecticut, Syracuse Univ., US Army War Coll., US Army Command and Gen. Staff Coll., USA. *Career:* 27 years mil. service in US Armed Forces; held positions successively as infantry platoon leader, battalion commdr, G-4 of 1st Armoured Div., Instructor in Man. Studies Ordnance School and Centre, served with 4th Armoured Corps, 2nd Armoured Cavalry Regiment and 1st Armoured Div., Germany, with 1st Cavalry Div., Viet Nam, Insp.-Gen. US Army, Jt Project Man. (Army and Navy) Guided Projectiles and Cannon Artillery Weapons Systems; Man.-Gen. Rock Island Arsenal (state-owned armament mfg co.); Dir Dept of Defence Programs, Atlantic Research Corpn (co. mfg rocket motors), USA –1997; Vice-Minister of Defence, Repub. of Lithuania 1997–99; Commdr Lithuanian Armed Forces 1999–2004; apptd Brig.-Gen. 1999, Maj.-Gen. 2001; fmr mem. AIAA, Assoc. of US Army, Lithuanian–American Community, Nat. Security Industrial Asscn, Navy League; fmr Chair. Bd Trustees Baltic Inst.; Legion of Merit; Viet Nam Cross of Gallantry, three Bronze Stars, three Meritorious Service Medals, Army Commendation Medal, Air Medal.
Address: c/o Ministry of National Defence, Šv. Ignoto 8/29, 2001 Vilnius, Lithuania.

KROON, Lt-Adm. Luuk; Dutch naval officer (retd); b. Dec. 1942, Ridderkerk; m. Annie Kroon. *Career:* joined Royal Netherlands Navy 1961; apptd to destroyer HNLMS Amsterdam 1964, USS Zellars (naval exchange programme) 1967; commdr inshore and coastal minesweepers 1968–72; served in Directorate Material, Ministry of Defence, The Hague 1972–75; Commdg Officer HNLMS Staphorst 1975–77; Staff Officer Minewarfare, Naval HQ, The Hague 1978–81; Commdg Officer HNLMS Jaguar 1981–82, HNLMS Callenburgh 1982–84; Naval Staff Planner to

Chief of Defence Staff 1984–89; Deputy Chief of the Naval Staff (Plans) 1989–92; Commdr Netherlands Task Group 1992–93; Admiral Netherlands Fleet, Commdr Maritime Forces BeneNorthWest and Admiral Benelux 1993–95; C-in-C of Royal Netherlands Navy 1995–98; Chief of Netherlands Defence Staff 1998–2004 (retd); apptd Rear Admiral 1992, Vice-Admiral 1993, Admiral 1998, now Lt-Adm.
Address: c/o Ministry of Defence, Library, POB 20701 ES The Hague, The Netherlands (office).

KROPIWNICKI, Jerzy Janusz, DEcon; Polish politician and economist; *Mayor of Łódź;* b. 5 July 1945, Częstochowa; m.; one s. *Education:* Warsaw School of Econs. *Career:* scientific worker, Łódź Univ. 1968–81 (dismissed); mem. Solidarity Ind. Self-governing Trade Union 1980–, Deputy Chair. Solidarity Łódź Region Br., mem. Solidarity Nat. Comm., co-organizer demonstration against martial law, arrested 13 Dec. 1981, sentenced to 6 years' imprisonment, released under amnesty July 1984; illegal activity 1984–90, co-organizer, Solidarity Regional Exec. Comm., Łódź 1984–86, co-organizer and activist, Working Group of Solidarity Nat. Comm. 1986–90; co-organizer and activist of Pastoral Care of Working People 1985–; lay worker, St Teresa's Roman Catholic Parish Church, Łódź 1986–89; scientific worker, Econ.-Sociological Faculty of Łódź Univ. 1989–; mem. Christian-Nat. Union (ZChN) 1989–; mem. Presidium of ZChN Gen. Bd 1989–93, Vice-Pres. 1991–93, 2000–; Deputy to Sejm (Parl.) 1991–93 and 1997–2001; Minister of Labour and Social Policy 1991–92; Minister-Head of Cen. Office of Planning 1992–93; Minister and Head of Governmental Centre for Strategic Studies 1997–2001; Minister of Regional Devt and Construction 2000–01; Mayor of Łódź 2004–. *Publications:* numerous articles on econs and four books.
Address: The City of Lodz Office, 104 Piotrkowska St., 90-926 Łódź (office); Christian National Union, ul. Twarda 28, 00-853 Warsaw, Poland. *Telephone:* (42) 638-41-15 (office); (42) 638-41-24 (office). *Fax:* (22) 6280804. *E-mail:* tombush@polbox.com. *Website:* www.uml.lodz.pl (office).

KROSS, Jacques Ruben Constantijn, LLM; Suriname diplomatist; *Ambassador to USA. Education:* Anton de Kom Univ. *Career:* fmr Minister of Labour, of Social Affairs and Public Housing; fmr mem. Nat. Election Bureau; fmr Chair. Surinamese team of Jt Surinamese-Dutch Anti-Narcotics Steering Cttee; chaired Surinamese team during negotiations with Brazil on treaties for extradition and mutual assistance in criminal matters 2003; Dir Ministry of Justice and Police –2007; Amb. to USA and Perm. Rep. to OAS, Washington, DC 2007–.
Address: Embassy of Suriname, 4301 Connecticut Avenue, Suite 460, NW, Washington, DC 20008, USA (office). *Telephone:* (202) 244-7488 (office). *Fax:* (202) 244-5878 (office). *E-mail:* esuriname@covad.net (office). *Website:* www.surinameembassy.org (office).

KRUGMAN, Paul Robin, PhD; American economist and academic; *Professor of Economics and International Affairs, Princeton University;* b. 28 Feb. 1953, Albany, New York; m. Robin Leslie Bergman 1983. *Education:* Yale Univ., Massachusetts Inst. of Tech. *Career:* Asst Prof., Yale Univ. 1977–79; Asst Prof., MIT 1979–80, Assoc. Prof. 1980–82, Prof. 1983–2000; Sr Staff Economist, Council of Econ. Advisers 1982–83; Columnist, New York Times 1999–; Prof. of Econs and Int. Affairs, Princeton Univ. 2000–; John Bates Clark Medal 1991. *Publications:* Market Structure and Foreign Trade (with E. Helpman) 1985, International Economics, Theory and Policy (with M. Obsfeld) 1988, The Age of Diminished Expectations 1990, Rethinking International Trade 1990, Geography and Trade 1991, Currencies and Crises 1992, Peddling Prosperity 1994, The Great Unravelling: From Boom to Bust in Three Short Years 2003, The Conscience of a Liberal 2007.
Address: Department of Economics, 414 Robertson Hall, Princeton University, Princeton, NJ 08544, USA (office). *E-mail:* pkrugman@ princeton.edu (office). *Website:* www.princeton.edu/~pkrugman (office); www.econ.princeton.edu (office); topics.nytimes.com/top/opinion/ editorialsandoped/oped/columnists/paulkrugman.

KUBIŠ, Ján; Slovak diplomatist and government official; *Minister of Foreign Affairs;* b. 12 Nov. 1952, Bratslavia; m.; one d. *Education:* Moscow State Inst. for Int. Affairs. *Career:* served in Dept of Int. Econ. Orgs, Ministry of Foreign Affairs (Czechoslovakia) 1976–80, Head of Security and Arms Control Section 1985–88, Dir-Gen. Euro-Atlantic Section 1991–92; served in Embassy in Addis Ababa 1980–85; First Sec. Embassy in Moscow 1989–90, Deputy Head and Head of Political Dept 1990–91; Chair. CSCE Cttee of Sr Officials and Amb.-at-Large 1992; Perm. Rep. (for Slovakia), UN Office, GATT and other Int. Orgs, Geneva 1993–94; Chief Negotiator (for Slovakia) for Pact for Stability in Europe 1994; Dir OSCE Conflict Prevention Centre 1994–98; Special Rep. of UN Sec.-Gen. for Tajikistan and Head, UN Mission of Mil. Observers 1998–99; Sec.-Gen. OSCE 1999–2005, Personal Rep. of Chair.-in-Office for Cen. Asia 2000; EU

Special Rep. for Cen. Asia 2005–06; Minister of Foreign Affairs 2006–; OSCE Medal 1998.
Address: Ministry of Foreign Affairs, Hlboká cesta 2, 833 36 Bratislava, Slovakia (office). *Telephone:* (2) 5978-1111 (office). *Fax:* (2) 5978-2213 (office). *E-mail:* informacie@foreign.gov.sk (office). *Website:* www.mzv.sk (office).

KUČA, Brig.-Gen. Jaroslav; Slovak army officer; *Military Representative, NATO;* b. 8 May 1961; m. Slávka Kuča; one s. *Education:* Mil. Acad. Vyskov, Czech Repub., Acad. of Nat. Defence, Warsaw, Poland, US Army War Coll. *Career:* Tank Platoon Leader, 14th Tank Div. 1981–82, CO Tank Cov 1982–83, Battalion G3 1987–88, CO 1988–91, DCO of Tank Regt 1993; academic duty, Mil. Acad. 1993–96; Dir Mil. Strategic Studies Group, Center for Strategic Studies, Ministry of Defence 1997–99, Deputy Dir Defence Planning Div., Defence Policy and Defense Planning Dept 2000–01; Mil. Asst to Minister of Defence 2001–02; Dir Minister of Defence Office 2002; Chief of Staff of Personnel Man., Gen. Staff of the Armed Forces 2002–06; Mil. Rep., NATO, Brussels 2006–.
Address: North Atlantic Treaty Organization (NATO), blvd Léopold III, 1110 Brussels, Belgium (office). *Telephone:* (2) 707-41-11 (office). *Fax:* (2) 707-45-79 (office). *E-mail:* natodoc@hq.nato.int (office). *Website:* www .nato.int (office).

KUCHINS, Andrew C., MA, PhD; American academic; *Senior Fellow and Director, Russia and Eurasia Program, Center for Strategic and International Studies; Education:* Amherst Coll., Paul H. Nitze School of Advanced Int. Studies, Johns Hopkins Univ. *Career:* Exec. Dir Berkeley-Stanford Program on Soviet and Post–Soviet Studies 1989–93; Sr Program Officer, John D. and Catherine T. MacArthur Foundation 1993–97; Assoc. Dir Center for Int. Security and Cooperation, Stanford Univ. 1997–2000; Dir Carnegie Endowment for Int. Peace, Moscow, Russia 2000–06; Sr Fellow and Dir Russia and Eurasia Program, Center for Strategic and Int. Studies, Washington, DC 2006–; mem. Governing Council, Program on Basic Research and Higher Educ. in Russia, Advisory Cttee Washington Profile; mem. Editorial Bd Democratizatsiya. *Publications:* Russia and Japan: An Unresolved Dilemma Between Distant Neighbours (co-ed.) 1993, Russia after the Fall (ed.) 2002; research reports and articles.
Address: Center for Strategic and International Studies, 1800 K Street, NW, Washington, DC 20006, USA (office). *Telephone:* (202) 775-3233 (office). *Website:* www.csis.org (office).

KUCHINSKY, Valeriy P.; Ukrainian diplomatist and civil servant; b. 25 Oct. 1944, Kiev; m.; one s. one d. *Career:* with Ministry of Foreign Affairs 1971–, served as Ministry Bd mem., Exec. Sec. Nat. Comm. for UNESCO, Dir Dept of Arms Control and Disarmament 1990–92; Deputy Chief of Mission to USA 1992–97; Dir-Gen. Dept of Int. Orgs. 1997–98, Dept of the Americas 1998–99; First Deputy Perm. Rep. to UN, New York 1999, Acting Perm. Rep. 2000–07; mem. UN Secr. 1975–80; Visiting Prof., Univ. of Columbia 2007.
Address: c/o Ministry of Foreign Affairs, 01018 Kiev, pl. Mykhailivska 1, Ukraine (office). *Website:* www.mfa.gov.ua (office).

KUCHMA, Leonid Maksimovych, CTechSc; Ukrainian politician and manager; b. 1938, Chatikine, Chernihiv Oblast; m. Ludmyla Mykolayovna Kuchma; one d. *Education:* Dnipropetrovsk Nat. Univ. *Career:* mem. CPSU 1960–91; eng., constructor, Chief Constructor Research-Production Yuzmash eng. plant 1960–75, Sec., Party Cttee 1975–82, Deputy Dir-Gen. 1982–86, Dir-Gen. 1986–92; mem. Cen. Cttee CP Ukrainian SSR 1981–91; People's Deputy of Ukraine 1991–94; Prime Minister of Ukraine 1992–93 (resgnd); Chair. Ukrainian Union of Industrialists and Entrepreneurs 1993–94; Pres. of Ukraine 1994–2005; Lenin Prize 1981, State Prize 1993; Order of St Volodymyr (Gold) 1999.
Address: Ukrainian Presidential Fund of Leonid Kuchma Charity Organisation, 01024 Kyiv, vul. P. Orlyka 1/15, Ukraine (office). *Telephone:* (44) 465-93-77 (office). *Fax:* (44) 465-93-78 (office). *E-mail:* press@ldk -fund.org.ua (office). *Website:* www.kuchma.org.ua (office).

KUCZYNSKI, Pedro Pablo, BA, MA, MPA; Peruvian economist and politician; b. 1939, Lima. *Education:* Oxford Univ., UK, Princeton Univ., USA. *Career:* Loan Officer and Economist Latin America and New Zealand, World Bank 1961–66; Deputy Dir Peruvian Central Bank 1967–69; Sr Economist IMF 1973–75; Chief Economist Northern Latin America, World Bank 1971–72, Head Planning Div. 1972–73; Vice-Pres. Kuhn, Loeb & Co. Int. 1973–75; Chief Economist Int. Finance Corpn 1975–77; Pres. Halco Mining Co. 1977–80; Minister of Energy and Mines 1980–82; Man. Dir First Boston Corpn then Pres. First Boston Int. 1982–92; Pres. Westfield Capital 1992–94; Pres. and CEO Latin America Enterprise Fund 1994–; Minister of Economy and Finance 2001–02, 2004–2005; Prime Minister 2005–06; fmr mem. Bd Tenaris SA, Southern Peru Copper Corpn,

current mem. Comm. on Growth and Devt. *Publications:* Peruvian Democracy under Economic Stress 1977.
Address: c/o Secretariat of the Commission on Growth and Development, c/o Dorota A. Nowak, 1818 H Street NW, MSN- MC-4-401, Washington, DC 20433, USA (office).

KUDERJAVÝ, Jan; Slovak diplomatist; *Ambassador to France; Education:* Econ. Univ., Bratislava. *Career:* Commercial Dir Dunavia Ltd 1979–85; Trade Rep., Embassy in the Netherlands 1985–90; Second Sec., Perm. Mission of Czechoslovakia to EU, Brussels 1991–92, Perm. Mission of Slovakia 1993–96; Dir European Integration Dept, Ministry of Foreign Affairs 1996–98, Dir-Gen. European Affairs 1998–2000, 2005–07; Amb. to Netherlands 2000–05, to France 2007–.
Address: Embassy of Slovakia, 125 rue du Ranelagh, 75016 Paris, France (office). *Telephone:* 1-44-14-56-00 (office). *Fax:* 1-42-88-76-53 (office). *E-mail:* paris@amb-slovaquie.fr (office). *Website:* www.amb-slovaquie.fr (office).

KUDRIN, Aleksei Leonidovich, Cand Econ; Russian politician; *Deputy Chairman and Minister of Finance;* b. 12 Oct. 1960, Dobele, Latvian SSR; m. Irina; one d. *Education:* Leningrad (now St Petersburg) State Univ., Inst. of Econs USSR Acad. of Sciences. *Career:* on staff Inst. of Social-Econ. Problems Acad. of Sciences 1983–90; Deputy Chair. Cttee on Econ. Reform Leningrad City Exec. Bd 1990–91; Chair. Cttee on Finance St Petersburg Mayor's Office 1992–94; First Deputy Mayor of St Petersburg, Head Dept of Finance Mayor's Office, St Petersburg 1994–96; Deputy Head of Admin., Head Controlling Dept at Russian Presidency 1996–97; First Deputy Minister of Finance Russian Fed. 1997–99, concurrently Deputy Man. BRD 1997–99; First Deputy Chair. Unified Power Grids of Russia (state co.) 1999–2000; Deputy Chair. of the Govt 2000–04, 2007–, Minister of Finance 2000–.
Address: Ministry of Finance, 109097 Moscow, ul. Ilyinka 9, Russia (office). *Telephone:* (495) 298-91-01 (office). *Fax:* (495) 925-08-89 (office). *Website:* www.minfin.ru (office).

KUFUOR, John Kofi Agyekum, MA; Ghanaian lawyer, business executive and head of state; *President;* b. 8 Dec. 1938, Kumasi, Ashanti Region; m. Theresa Kufuor; five c. *Education:* Osei Tutu Boarding School, Prempeh Coll., Kumasi, Lincoln's Inn, London and Exeter Coll., Oxford, UK. *Career:* called to Bar, Lincoln's Inn 1961; Clerk of Kumasi City Council; Council Rep., Constituent Ass. 1968–69; mem. Parl.; mem. of Progress Party; a Deputy Foreign Minister; arrested after mil. coup and imprisoned for 15 months 1972–73; returned to law practice; presidential cand. for New Patriotic Party 1996; Pres. of Ghana and C-in-C of Armed Forces 2001– (re-elected 2004); Chair. African Union Ass. 2007–08.
Address: Office of the President, PO Box 1627, Osu, Accra, Ghana (office). *Telephone:* (21) 665415 (office). *Website:* www.ghanacastle.gov.gh (office).

KUJAT, Gen. Harald; German air force officer (retd); b. 1 March 1942, Mielke; m. Sabine Kujat (née Becker); three c. *Education:* Armed Forces and Command College Hamburg, NATO Defence Coll. Rome, Italy. *Career:* Instructor in Non-commissioned Officer Training, Fed. Armed Forces, then Platoon Leader, Co. Exec. Officer and Personnel Officer 1959–72; with Fed. Ministry of Defence, positions included ADC to Minister 1972–75, Mil. Asst 1977–78, Armed Forces Staff Asst Br. Chief (Operational Doctrines, AF) 1978–80, Br. Chief (Nuclear and Global Arms Control) 1990–92, Deputy Chief of Staff (Mil. Policy and Strategy) 1995, Dir Policy and Advisory Staff to Minister 1998–2000; 20th Gen. Staff Course (AF), Bundeswehr Command and Staff Coll. 1975–77; Section Chief (A3a), AF Support Command N 1977; Commdr Second Bn AF Training Regt 1985–88; Section Chief, Staff German Mil. Rep., NATO Mil. Cttee, Brussels 1988–90, Dir of Staff and Deputy Mil. Rep. 1992–95, Asst Dir Int. Mil. Staff (Plans and Policy) and Deputy Dir IMS, NATO 1996–98, Chair. NATO Mil. Cttee 2002–05; Dir IFOR Co-ordination Centre (ICC), Supreme HQ Allied Powers in Europe (SHAPE), Belgium 1996; Chief of Staff, Fed. Armed Forces 2000–02; rank of Lt 1968, First Lt 1968, Capt. 1971, Maj. 1974, Lt-Col 1979, Col 1988, Brig.-Gen. 1992, Maj.-Gen. 1995, Lt-Gen. 1998, Gen. 2000; Gold Cross of Honour of the Bundeswehr, Commdr's Cross of the Order of Merit of the FRG, Commdr Ordre Nat. de la Légion d'honneur France, Commdr's Cross of Merit Poland, Order of the Cross of the Eagle 1st class Estonia; Tidal Flood Memorial Medal 1962. *Publications:* numerous works on int. security and military policy.
Address: c/o Federal Ministry of Defence, Stauffenbergstr. 18, 10785 Berlin, Germany.

KULIYEV, Vilayat Mukhtar oglu; Azerbaijani politician; b. 1952. *Career:* mem. New Azerbaijan Party (NAP) 1992–; Minister of Foreign Affairs 1999–2004.

Address: c/o Ministry of Foreign Affairs, Ghanjlar meydani 3, 370004 Baku, Azerbaijan (office).

KULL, Steven; American research institute director; *Director, Program on International Policy Attitudes, University of Maryland; Career:* Fellow, Center for Int. Security and Arms Control and teacher, Stanford Univ. 1980s; fmr MacArthur Fellow, Social Sciences Research Council (SSRC); f. Center for Policy Attitudes (COPA), School of Public Affairs, Univ. of Maryland 1992, currently Dir Program on Int. Policy Attitudes (PIPA) and Dir WorldPublicOpinion.org, co-Dir Project on Foreign Policy, Center for Int. and Security Studies at Maryland (CISSM); briefings to Congress, Dept of State, NATO, UN and EU; mem. Council on Foreign Relations, American Asscn for Public Opinion Research. *Publications:* Minds at War: Nuclear Reality and the Inner Conflicts of Defense Policy Makers 1988, Burying Lenin: The Revolution in Soviet Ideology and Foreign Policy 1992, Misreading the Public: The Myth of a New Isolationism (co-author) 1999; articles in Foreign Policy, Public Opinion Quarterly, The Washington Post.
Address: Program on International Policy Attitudes (PIPA), 1779 Massachusetts Avenue, NW, Suite 510, Washington, DC 20036, USA (office). *Telephone:* (202) 232-7500 (office). *Fax:* (202) 232-1159 (office). *E-mail:* skull@pipa.org (office). *Website:* www.worldpublicopinion.org (office).

KUMALO, Dumisana Shadrack, MA; South African diplomatist and journalist; *Permanent Representative, United Nations;* b. 16 Sept. 1947; m. (divorced); one s. *Education:* Univ. of South Africa, Indiana Univ., USA. *Career:* reporter for Golden City Post 1967–79; feature writer Drum magazine 1969–70; political reporter Sunday Times, Johannesburg 1970–76; Marketing Exec. Officer, Total Oil Co. 1976–77; in exile 1977; Int. Educ. Program Co-ordinator, Phelps Stokes Fund, New York 1978–80; Projects Dir Africa Fund and American Cttee on Africa 1980–97; Dir of US Desk, Dept of Foreign Affairs 1997–99; Perm. Rep. to UN, New York 1999–.
Address: Permanent Mission of South Africa to the United Nations, 333 East 38th Street, 9th Floor, New York, NY 10016, USA (office). *Telephone:* (212) 213-5583 (office). *Fax:* (212) 692-2498 (office). *E-mail:* soafun@worldnet.att.net (office). *Website:* www.southafrica-newyork.net/pmun (office).

KUMARATUNGA, Chandrika Bandaranaike, PhD; Sri Lankan politician and fmr head of state; b. 29 June 1945, Colombo; m. Vijaya Kumaratunga 1978 (assassinated 1988); one s. one d. *Education:* St Bridget's Convent, Colombo, Univ. of Paris, France. *Career:* mem. Exec. Cttee Women's League of SLFP 1974, Exec. Cttee and Working Cttee 1980, Cen. Cttee 1992, Deputy Leader of SLFP; Chair., Man. Dir Dinakara Sinhala (daily newspaper) 1977–85; Vice-Pres. Sri Lanka Mahajana (People's) Party (SLMP) 1984, Pres. 1986; Leader SLMP and People's Alliance; Chief Minister, Minister of Law and Order, Finance and Planning, Educ., Employment and Cultural Affairs of the Western Prov. Council 1993–94; Prime Minister Aug.–Nov. 1994, also held posts of Minister of Finance and Planning, Ethnic Affairs and Nat. Integration, of Defence, of Buddha Sasana; Pres. of Sri Lanka 1994–2005; fmrly also Minister of Defence, of Constitutional Affairs, of Educ. and of Public Security, Law and Order; Pres. Sri Lanka Freedom Party –2006; Additional Prin. Dir Land Reform Comm. 1972–75; Chair. Janawasa Comm. 1975–77; Expert Consultant, FAO 1977–80; Research Fellow, Univ. of London, UK 1988–91; Guest Univ. Lecturer, Univ. of Bradford, UK 1989, Jawaharlal Nehru Univ., India 1991; ranked by Forbes magazine amongst 100 Most Powerful Women (44th) 2004, (25th) 2005. *Publications:* several research papers on land reform and food policies.
Address: c/o Sri Lanka Freedom Party, 301 T.B. Jayah Mawatha, Colombo 10, Sri Lanka (office).

KUNADZE, Georgy Fridrikhovich, CHisSc; Russian diplomatist and academic; *Ambassador-at-Large and Chief Scientific Researcher, Institute of World Economy and International Relations (IMEMO), Russian Academy of Sciences;* b. 21 Dec. 1948, Moscow; m.; one s. *Education:* Moscow Inst. of Oriental Languages. *Career:* researcher Inst. of Oriental Studies USSR Acad. of Sciences 1971–83; diplomatic service 1983–, scientific attaché Embassy in Japan 1982–87, head of sector, Chief of Div. Inst. of World Econs and Int. Relations 1987–91; Deputy Minister of Foreign Affairs of Russia 1991–93; Amb. to Repub. of Korea 1993–96, Amb.-at-Large 1996–; Deputy Dir Inst. of USA and Canada, Russian Acad. of Sciences 1997–99, Chief Scientific Researcher Inst. of Int. Econ. and Int. Relations (IMEMO), Russian Acad. of Sciences 1999–. *Publications:* numerous articles.
Address: IMEMO, Profsoyuznaya str. 23, 117859 Moscow, Russia (office). *Telephone:* (495) 128-81-09 (office). *Fax:* (495) 128-25-18 (office). *Fax:* (495) 310-70-27 (office). *E-mail:* imemoran@imemo.ru (office). *Website:* www.imemo.ru/eng (office).

KUNDASAMY, Abhimanu Mahendra, MBA; Mauritian diplomatist; *High Commissioner to UK;* m. Mahalutchmee Kundasamy. *Career:* Marketing Planning Manager 1990, then Group Brand Manager, British American Tobacco (Mauritius) –1996; High Commr to S Africa 1996–2001, also accredited to Secr. Southern African Devt Community (SADC) States, Common Market for Eastern and Southern Africa (COMESA), and UN Regional Office, Nairobi, Kenya; High Commr to UK 2005–; mem. Mauritius Labour Party.
Address: High Commission of Mauritius, 32–33 Elvaston Place, London, SW7 5NW, England (office). *Telephone:* (20) 7581-0294 (office). *Fax:* (20) 7823-8437 (office). *E-mail:* londonmhc@btinternet.com (office).

KUNEVA, Meglena Shtilianova, LLM; Bulgarian politician and lawyer; *EU Commissioner for Consumer Protection;* b. 22 June 1957, Sofia; m. Andrey Pramov; one s. *Education:* St Kliment Ohridski Univ. of Sofia. *Career:* Ed. and presenter Bulgarian Nat. Radio 1987–91; Asst Prof., Faculty of Law St Kliment Ohridski Univ. of Sofia 1988–89; Sr Legal Advisor Council of Ministers 1990–2001; lecturer Free Univ. of Burgas and New Bulgarian Univ. 1992–94; legal specialist Human Rights Inst. Turku, Finland 1993 and in Int. Relations and Environmental Law, Georgetown Univ. 1995, 1999–2000, and Environmental Law at Oxford Univ. 1996; mem. Bulgarian Del. to 4th session of UN Comm. on Sustainable Devt 1995; elected MP in 39th Nat. Ass. 2001; Deputy Minister, Ministry of Foreign Affairs and chief negotiator with EU 2001–02; Minister of European Affairs 2002–07; Special Rep. at Convention for Future of Europe 2002; Commr for Consumer Protection, EC 2006–; mem. Berlin Conference on European Cultural Policy; mem. Nat. Movement Simeon II, Atlantic Club, Union of Bulgarian Jurists, UN Int. Council of Environmental Law, Advisory Bd Time Eco-projects Foundation; Order for Civil Merit, Spain 2002, Légion d'honneur 2003, Order Prince Enrique, Portugal 2004, Order of the Star of Italian Solidarity 2005, Gold Distinction of the Atlantic Club, Bulgaria 2005; Face of Bulgaria Award, Politika (newspaper) 2006.
Address: Health and Consumer Protection Directorate-General, 232 rue Belliard, 1040 Brussels, Belgium (office). *Telephone:* (2) 299-11-11 (office). *Fax:* (2) 296-62-98 (office). *E-mail:* sanco-mailbox@cec.eu.int (office). *Website:* ec.europa.eu/dgs/health_consumer/index_en.htm (office).

KUPA, Miles; Australian diplomatist; *High Commissioner to Singapore;* b. 1946, Czechoslovakia; m. Zulaikha Chudori; one s. *Education:* Univ. of Melbourne. *Career:* early overseas service in Egypt and France; Amb. to Iraq 1983–86; Deputy Head of Mission, Embassy in Indonesia 1986–88; Asst Sec., Foreign Affairs Br., Dept of Prime Minister and Cabinet 1991; Head, Office of the Minister for Foreign Affairs and Trade 1991–93; First Asst Sec., South and South East Asia Div. 1993–95; Amb. to Philippines 1996–99; Deputy Sec., Dept of Foreign Affairs and Trade 1999–2000; Amb. to Thailand 2000–04; High Commr to Singapore 2005–.
Address: Australian High Commission, 25 Napier Road, Singapore 258507, Singapore (office). *Telephone:* 68364223 (office). *Fax:* 67337134 (office). *E-mail:* public-affairs-sing@dfat.gov.au (office). *Website:* www.australia .org.sg (office).

KUPCHAN, Charles A., MA, DPhil; American foreign policy analyst and academic; *Senior Fellow and Director of European Studies, Council on Foreign Relations; Education:* Harvard Univ., Mass., Univ. of Oxford, UK. *Career:* Instructor in Int. Relations, Univ. of Oxford, UK 1983–84; Instructor in East Asian Studies, Harvard Univ. 1984–86; Asst Prof. of Politics, Princeton Univ. 1986–93; mem. Council on Foreign Relations 1988–, currently Sr Fellow and Dir of European Studies; mem. Policy Planning Staff, US Dept of State 1992, Dir for European Affairs, Nat. Security Council, White House 1993–94; Assoc. Prof., School of Foreign Service and Dept of Govt, Georgetown Univ. 1994–, currently Prof. of Int. Affairs, Dir Mortara Center for Int. Studies 2004–05; Research Affiliate, Center for Science and Int. Affairs, Kennedy School of Govt, Harvard Univ. 1985–86; Visiting Fellow, Int. Inst. for Strategic Studies, London 1987, Centre d'Etudes et de Recherches Internationales, Paris 1988; Visiting Scholar, Inst. for War and Peace Studies, Columbia Univ. 1989–90; several fellowships from nat. and int. orgs including NATO 1985, German Marshall Fund 1989, UN Univ. 1998, Japan Soc. 2001. *Publications:* The Persian Gulf and the West: The Dilemmas of Security 1987, The Vulnerability of Empire 1994, Nationalism and Nationalities in the New Europe (ed.) 1995, Atlantic Security: Contending Visions (ed.) 1998, Civic Engagement in the Atlantic Community (co-ed.) 1999, Power in Transition: The Peaceful Change of International Order (co-author) 2001, The End of the America Era: US Foreign Policy and the Geopolitics of the Twenty-first Century 2002; numerous scholarly articles on int. and strategic affairs.
Address: Council on Foreign Relations, 1779 Massachusetts Avenue, NW, Washington, DC 20036 (office); School of Foreign Service, ICC 807, Georgetown University, Washington, DC 20057, USA (office). *Telephone:* (202) 518-3402 (office); (202) 687-3998 (office). *Fax:* (202) 986-2984 (office); (202) 687-5116 (office). *E-mail:* ckupchan@cfr.org (office); kupchanc@

georgetown.edu (office). *Website:* www.cfr.org (office); www.georgetown .edu (office).

KUPIECKI, Robert, PhD; Polish diplomatist; *Ambassador to USA;* m.; two c. *Education:* Warsaw Univ., Nat. School of Public Admin, USA, Geneva Centre for Security Policy, Switzerland. *Career:* interned at Texas Dept of Commerce affiliated with LBJ School of Public Affairs, Austin, Tex., USA; fmr Jr Lecturer, Historical Inst. of Polish Acad. of Science; expert in field of security policy, played key role in Poland's accession to NATO 1990s, has led Polish dels working with NATO, OSCE, UN and other forums dealing with disarmament, armament control and nonproliferation issues; joined Ministry of Foreign Affairs 1994, served in various positions, including Deputy Amb., Perm. Representation to NATO and WEU, Brussels 1999–2004, Dir Security Policy Dept, Ministry of Foreign Affairs 2004–08, Amb. to USA 2008–. *Publications:* author or co-author of several books and numerous articles on modern history and int. relations.
Address: Embassy of Poland, 2640 16th Street, NW, Washington, DC 20009, USA (office). *Telephone:* (202) 234-3800 (office). *Fax:* (202) 328-6271 (office). *E-mail:* polemb.info@earthlink.net (office). *Website:* www .polandembassy.org (office).

KURBI, Abu Bakr al-; Yemeni politician. *Career:* currently Minister of Foreign Affairs.
Address: Ministry of Foreign Affairs, PO Box 1994, San'a, Yemen (office). *Telephone:* (1) 276612 (office). *Fax:* (1) 286618 (office). *E-mail:* mofa1@ mofa.gov.ye (office). *Website:* www.mofa.gov.ye (office).

KURODA, Haruhiko, BA, MPhil; Japanese international banking official; *Chairman and President, Asian Development Bank;* b. 25 Oct. 1944; m. Kumiko Kuroda; two s. *Education:* Univ. of Tokyo, Univ. of Oxford, UK. *Career:* joined Ministry of Finance 1967; secondment to IMF, Washington, DC 1975–78; Dir Int. Orgs Div., Int. Finance Bureau 1987–88; Sec. to Minister of Finance 1988–89; Dir of several divs, Tax Bureau 1989–92; Deputy Vice Minister of Finance for Int. Affairs 1992–93; Commr Osaka Regional Taxation Bureau 1993–94; Deputy Dir-Gen., Int. Finance Bureau 1994–96, Dir-Gen. 1997–99; Pres. Inst. of Fiscal and Monetary Policy 1996–97; Vice Minister of Finance for Int. Affairs 1999–2003; Special Adviser to Cabinet 2003–05; Chair. Bd of Dirs and Pres. Asian Devt Bank 2005–; Prof., Grad. School of Econs, Hitotsubashi Univ. 2003–05. *Publications:* several books on monetary policy, exchange rates, int. finance policy, int. taxation and int. negotiations.
Address: Asian Development Bank, 6 ADB Avenue, Mandaluyong City 0401 Metro Manila (office); PO Box 789, 0980 Manila Philippines. *Telephone:* (632) 632-4444 (office). *Fax:* (632) 6362444 (office). *E-mail:* information@adb.org (office). *Website:* www.adb.org (office).

KURTZER, Daniel C., BA, PhD; American diplomatist and academic; *Lecturer and S. Daniel Abraham Visiting Professor in Middle East Policy Studies, Woodrow Wilson School of Public and International Affairs, Princeton University;* m. Sheila Kurtzer; three s. *Education:* Yeshiva Univ., Columbia Univ. *Career:* joined Foreign Service 1976; Dean, Yeshiva Coll. 1977–79; political officer, Bureau of Int. Organizational Affairs, embassies in Cairo and Tel-Aviv; Deputy Dir Office of Egyptian Affairs 1996; on Policy Planning Staff 1987; Deputy Asst Sec. for Near Eastern Affairs 1989; Prin. Deputy Asst Sec. for Intelligence and Research 1994, then Acting Asst Sec.; Amb. to Egypt 1997–2001, to Israel 2001–05; Lecturer and S. Daniel Abraham Visiting Prof. in Middle East Policy Studies, Woodrow Wilson School of Public and Int. Affairs, Princeton Univ. 2005–; Commr Israel Baseball League; Pres.'s Distinguished Service Award, Henrietta Szold Award by Hadassah 2005, Dir-Gen. of Foreign Service Award for Reporting.
Address: 418 Robertson Hall, Woodrow Wilson School, Princeton University, Princeton, NJ 08544-1013, USA (office). *Telephone:* (609) 258-9859 (office). *E-mail:* dkurtzer@princeton.edu (office). *Website:* www .wws.princeton.edu (office); www.israelbaseballleague.com.

KUSHAKOV, Andrei Anatolyevich; Russian diplomatist; b. 1952. *Education:* Moscow State Inst. of Int. Relations. *Career:* mem. staff, Ministry of Foreign Affairs 1974–93; Adviser to Counsellor, Russian Embassy, South Africa 1993–97; Deputy Dir-Gen. Secr. of Ministry of Foreign Affairs, then Deputy Sec.-Gen. 1998–2000; Amb. to South Africa and Kingdom of Lesotho 2001–06.
Address: c/o Ministry of Foreign Affairs, 119200 Moscow, Smolenskaya-Sennaya pl. 32/34, Russian Federation (office). *Website:* www.mid.ru (office).

KUSSBACH, Erich, LLM, Dr. rer. pol, DrIur; Austrian academic and fmr diplomat; *Honorary Professor of International Humanitarian Law, Johannes Kepler University;* b. 5 May 1931. *Education:* Eötvös Lóránd Univ., Budapest, Hungary, Univ. of Vienna, Yale Univ., USA. *Career:* served in

Austrian Diplomatic Service 1963–96, sr positions included Head of Dept of Legal and Consular Affairs; served as legal advisor of Austrian Del. negotiating Free-Trade-Agreements with EEC; Deputy Rep. to Council of Europe and Consul Gen. in Strasbourg 1981–85; Amb. to Hungary 1993–96, also Perm. Rep. to Int. Danube Comm.; fmr Prof. of Int. Humanitarian Law, Faculty of Law, Johannes Kepler Univ., Linz, now Hon. Prof.; Prof. of Public Int. Law and Int. Criminal Law, Catholic Pázmány Péter Univ., Budapest 1999–; Founding Pro-rector and fmr Prof. of Diplomacy, Faculty of Int. Relations, Andrássy Gyula German Speaking Univ., Budapest; mem. Arbitration Panel, Nat. Fund for Victims of Nat. Socialism 2001–; Dr hc (Eoetvoes Lorand Univ.).
Address: c/o National Fund of the Republic of Austria for Victims of National Socialism, Kirchberggasse 33, 1070 Vienna, Austria.

KUTESA, Sam; Ugandan lawyer and politician; *Minister of Foreign Affairs;* b. 1 Feb. 1949. *Career:* in pvt law practice with Kutesa and Co. Advocates 1973–2001; Attorney Gen. 1985–86; mem. Parl. representing Mawogola Co 1996–; fmr Minister of State for Investment, Ministry of Finance, Planning and Econ. Devt 2001–05; Minister of Foreign Affairs 2005–.
Address: Ministry of Foreign Affairs, Embassy House, POB 7048, Kampala, Uganda (office). *Telephone:* (41) 2345661 (office). *Fax:* (41) 2258722 (office). *E-mail:* info@mofa.go.ug (office). *Website:* www.mofa.go.ug (home).

KUUGONGELWA-AMADHILA, Saara, MSc; Namibian politician; *Minister of Finance; Education:* Univ. of London, UK, Univ. of Namibia. *Career:* Dir-Gen. Nat. Planning Comm. 1997–2003; fmr Gov. African Devt Bank; Minister of Finance 2003–.
Address: Ministry of Finance, Fiscus Building, John Meinert Street, PMB 13295, Windhoek, Namibia (office). *Telephone:* (61) 2099111 (office). *Fax:* (61) 230179 (office). *E-mail:* skuugongelwa-amadhila@mof.gov.na (office).

KUWAIZ, Abdullah Ibrahim el-, MA, MBA, PhD; Saudi Arabian banker, politician and diplomatist; *Ambassador to Bahrain;* b. 21 Aug. 1939, Dawadmi; two s. two d. *Education:* King Saud Univ. Saudi Arabia, Pacific Lutheran Univ. and St Louis Univ., USA. *Career:* accountant, Pensions Dept, Ministry of Finance and Nat. Economy 1959–67, economist, 1967–81 (adviser 1977–81); Exec. Dir Arab Monetary Fund, Abu Dhabi 1977–80; Co-Chair. Financial Co-operation Cttee, Euro-Arab Dialogue 1978–83; Asst Under-Sec. for Econ. Affairs 1981–87; Deputy Minister of Finance and Nat. Economy, Saudi Arabia 1987–2001; Dir-Gen. and Chair. of Bd Arab Monetary Fund, Abu Dhabi 1987–89; Chair. of Bd, Saudi-Kuwait Cement Co., Saudi Arabia 1991–93; Asst Sec.-Gen. for Econ. Affairs, Co-operation Council for the Arab States of the Gulf 1981–95; mem. of Bd and mem. Exec. Cttee, Gulf Int. Bank, Bahrain 1977–90; mem. of Bd Gulf Co-operation Council's Org. for Measures and Standards 1984–95, Oxford Energy Inst., Oxford, UK 1985–, Int. Maritime Bureau, London 1985–88, Econ. Forum, Cairo 1994–2001, Islamic Devt Bank, Jeddah 1997–2003, Arab Fund for Econ. Devt, Kuwait 1998–2000; Gen. Man. Gulf Int. Bank, Bahrain 1997–2001; Chair. of Bd Bosna Bank Int. Sarajevo 2000; Amb. to Bahrain 2002–; Medal of Merit for Accomplishment in Global Climate Coalition (GCC) from King Fahd Ibn Abdulaziz 1989, Lifetime Accomplishment Award Arab Bankers Association of North America (ABANA) 2003. *Publications:* numerous papers relating to banking, oil, finance and econ. devt and integration delivered at symposia in N America, Europe and the Middle East.
Address: Royal Embassy of Saudi Arabia, PO Box 1085, Bldg 82, Rd 1702, Block 317, Diplomatic Area, Manama, Bahrain (office); PO Box 10866, Riyadh 11443, Saudi Arabia (home). *Telephone:* (1) 753-7722 (office); (1) 488-0882 (home). *Fax:* (1) 753-3261 (office); (1) 480-2190 (home). *E-mail:* kuwaiz@hotmail.com (home).

KVASHNIN, Col-Gen. Anatoly Vassilyevich; Russian politician; *Representative of Russian President to Siberian Federal District;* b. 15 Aug. 1946, Ufa. *Education:* Kurgan Machine Construction Inst., Acad. of Armoured Units, Acad. of Gen. Staff. *Career:* army service, Commdr of regiment, div., army 1969–; Deputy, First Deputy Head Main Operation Dept 1993–95; Commdr Allied Group of armed forces in Chechnya 1994–95; Commdr Armed Forces of N Caucasian Command 1995–97; Acting Head, Head Gen. Staff of Armed Forces of Russian Fed. 1997–2004; First Deputy Minister of Defence, Russian Fed. 1997–2004; Rep. of Russian Pres. to Siberian Fed. Dist 2004–; Legion d'honneur 2004, Order of Honour 2006. *Address:* Krasnyi pr. 62, 630091 Novosibirsk, Russia (office). *Telephone:* (383) 217-35-17 (office); (383) 220-17-80 (office). *E-mail:* sibokrug@atlas-nsk.ru (office). *Website:* www.sfo.nsk.su (office).

KVITSINSKY, Yuliy Aleksandrovich, CandJur; Russian politician and diplomatist; b. 28 Sept. 1936, Rzev; m. Inga Kuznetsova 1955; two d. *Education:* Moscow Inst. of Int. Relations. *Career:* served in Embassy in GDR 1959–65, in FRG 1978–81; head of Soviet del., negotiations on

medium-range nuclear weapons until latter broken off 1983; subsequently responsible for negotiations on Strategic Defence Initiative (SDI) Geneva talks 1985; Amb. to FRG 1986–90; Deputy Foreign Minister 1990–91, First Deputy Foreign Minister May–Sept. 1991; Chief Adviser, Dept of Planning 1991–92; Vice-Pres. Foreign Policy Asscn 1992–; Adviser to Pres., Council of Russian Fed. (Upper Chamber) 1996–97; Amb. to Norway 1997–2003; cand. mem. CPSU Cen. Cttee 1986–89, mem. 1989–91; elected State Duma (Parl.) (Communist Party) 2003–; Honoured Diplomat of Russian Fed. 2002; Order of Red Banner 1971, Order of Friendship Among People 1981, Order of October Revolution 1986. *Publications:* Vor dem Sturm 1993, Judas Ischariot 1996, General Vlassov 1997, Apostate 2002.
Address: State Duma, Okhotnyi ryad 1, 103265 Moscow, Russia (office). *Telephone:* (495) 982-24-12 (office). *Fax:* (495) 692-98-25 (office). *E-mail:* www@duma.ru (office). *Website:* www.duma.ru (office).

KWARI, Yakubu, PhD; Nigerian diplomatist. *Career:* currently Amb. to Niger.
Address: Embassy of Nigeria, rue Goudel, BP 11130, Niamey, Niger (office). *Telephone:* 73-24-10 (office). *Fax:* 73-35-00 (office). *E-mail:* embnig@intnet.ne (office).

KWON, Chul-hyun, PhD; South Korean politician and diplomatist; *Ambassador to Japan;* b. 1947, Geoje, S Gyeongsang Prov. *Education:* Yonsei Univ. *Career:* fmr mem. Nat. Ass.; fmr Spokesman Grand Nat. Party; fmr Vice-Chair. Korea-Japan Parl. Friendship Asscn; Amb. to Japan 2008–.
Address: Embassy of the Republic of Korea, 1-2-5, Minami Azabu, Minato-ku, Tokyo 106-0047, Japan (office). *Telephone:* (3) 3452-7611 (office). *Fax:* (3) 5232-6911 (office). *Website:* jpn-tokyo.mofat.go.kr (office).

KYALIGONZA, Brig. Matayo, (Abwoli Bitamazire), MBA; Ugandan diplomatist and army officer (retd); *High Commissioner to Kenya;* b. 18 Sept. 1945, Kakooge Hoima; five s. four d. *Education:* Univ. of Knightsbridge, UK. *Career:* fmr Leader of Nat. Resistance Army (NRA), involvement in Ugandan rebellion 1985; mem. Nat. Ass. NRC 1986–96, Constituent Ass. 1994–95; mem. Parl. 1997–2001; High Commr to Kenya 2003–; Luwero Triangle Medal, Katonga Medal. *Publications:* The Agony of Power 2001, From Businessman to Freedom Fighting, One Shilling Tea.
Address: High Commission of Uganda and Permanent Mission to UNCHS (Habitat) and UNEP, PO Box 60853, Riverside Paddocks, off Riverside Drive, Nairobi, Kenya (office); PO Box 5689, Golf Course Road, Kampala, Uganda (home). *Telephone:* (20) 4445420 (office); (721) 632323 (Mobile) (office); (77) 470086 (Mobile) (home). *Fax:* (20) 4443772 (office); (41) 345555 (home). *E-mail:* ugahicom@todays.co.ke (office); ugacomnbr@todays.co.ke (office); matayok@parl.co.ug (home). *Website:* www.ugandahighcommission.co.ke.

KYMLICKA, Will, BA, DPhil; Canadian academic; *Canada Research Chair in Political Philosophy, Queen's University; Education:* Queen's Univ., Kingston, Ont., Univ. of Oxford, UK. *Career:* Lecturer, Dept of Philosophy, Queen's Univ. 1986–87, Queen's Nat. Scholar 1998–2003, Canada Research Chair in Political Philosophy 2003–; Lecturer, Dept of Philosophy, Princeton Univ., NJ 1987–88; Lecturer, Dept of Philosophy, Univ. of Toronto 1988–89, Asst Prof. 1989–90; Sr Policy Analyst, Royal Comm. on New Reproductive Technologies 1990–91; Research Dir Canadian Centre for Philosophy and Public Policy, Univ. of Ottawa 1994–98; Visiting Prof., Univ. of Ottawa 1991–93, Carleton Univ. 1994–98, Inst. for Advanced Studies, Vienna, Austria 1997, Nationalism Studies Program, Cen. European Univ., Budapest, Hungary 1998–, Univ. Pompeu Fabra, Barcelona, Spain 1998, 2003, Sciences-Po, Paris 2007; Visiting Fellow, European Forum, European Univ. Inst., Florence, Italy 1996; Pres. American Soc. for Political and Legal Philosophy 2004–06; mem. several editorial and advisory bds; Guiseppe Acerbi Prize 2001, Excellence in Research Prize, Queen's Univ. 2002, RSC Award 2003, Killam Prize in Social Sciences, Canada Council 2004; several fellowships. *Publications:* Liberalism, Community and Culture 1989, Contemporary Political Philosophy 1990, Justice in Political Philosophy (ed.) 1992, Multicultural Citizenship: A Liberal Theory of Minority Rights (Macpherson Prize, Canadian Political Science Asscn 1996, Bunche Award, American Political Science Asscn 1996) 1995, The Rights of Minority Cultures 1995, Ethnicity and Group Rights (co-ed.) 1997, States, Nations and Cultures: Spinoza Lectures 1997, Finding Our Way: Rethinking Ethnocultural Relations in Canada 1998, Citizenship in Diverse Societies (co-ed.) 2000, Politics in the Vernacular: Nationalism, Multiculturalism and Citizenship 2001, Alternative Conceptions of Civil Society (co-ed.) 2001, Can Liberal Pluralism be Exported? (co-ed.) 2001, Language Rights and Political Theory (co-ed.) 2003, Ethnicity and Democracy in Africa (co-ed.) 2004, Multiculturalism in Asia (co-ed.) 2005, Multiculturalism and the Welfare State (co-ed.) 2006, The Globalization of Ethics (co-ed.) 2007, Multicultural Odysseys: The

New International Politics of Diversity 2007; numerous book chapters and articles in professional journals.
Address: Department of Philosophy, Watson Hall 313, Queen's University, Kingston, ON K7L 3N6, Canada (office). *Telephone:* (613) 533-2182 (office); (613) 533-6000 (ext. 77043) (office). *Fax:* (613) 533-6545 (office). *E-mail:* kymlicka@post.queensu.ca (office). *Website:* post.queensu.ca/~kymlicka (office).

KYOTA, Hersey, MA; Palauan diplomatist and politician; *Ambassador to USA;* m.; five c. *Education:* US Int. Univ., San Diego, Calif., USA. *Career:* served in Palau Nat. Congress, Legal Researcher, House of Dels 1981–84, Chief Clerk 1985–88, Dir of House Legal Counsel's Office 1989–90, Senator in Palau Nat. Congress 1990–96; Amb. to USA 1997–; mem. Bd of Dirs Asscn of Pacific Island Legislatures 1992–96.
Address: Embassy of Palau, 1700 Pennsylvania Avenue, NW, Suite 400, Washington, DC 20006, USA (office). *Telephone:* (202) 452-6814 (office). *Fax:* (202) 452-6281 (office). *E-mail:* info@palauembassy.com (office). *Website:* www.palauembassy.com (office).

KYPRIANOU, Markos, MA; Cypriot politician; *Minister of Foreign Affairs;* b. 22 Jan. 1960, Limassol. *Education:* Univ. of Athens, Greece, Univ. of Cambridge, UK, Harvard Law School, USA. *Career:* Assoc., Antis Triantafyllides & Sons 1985–91; Partner, Kyprianou & Boyiadjis 1991–95, George L. Savvides & Co. (following merger) 1995–2003; Municipal Councillor, Nicosia 1986–91; Mem. Parl. for Nicosia 1991–2003, fmr Deputy Chair. Cttee on Foreign and European Affairs, fmr mem. Cttee on Legal Affairs, Chair. House Cttee on Financial and Budgetary Affairs 1999–2003; mem. and Chair. House of Reps Del. to Parl. Ass. of OSCE; fmr Parl. Leader Democratic Party; Minister of Finance 2003–04; EU Commr without Portfolio 2004, for Health and Consumer Protection 2004–06, for Health 2006–08; Minister of Foreign Affairs 2008–; Assoc. mem. ABA.
Address: Ministry of Foreign Affairs, Presidential Palace Avenue, 1447 Nicosia, Cyprus (office). *Telephone:* 22401000 (office). *Fax:* 22661881 (office). *E-mail:* minforeign1@mfa.gov.cy (office). *Website:* www.mfa.gov.cy (office).

KYUMA, Fumio; Japanese politician; b. 4 Dec. 1940. *Education:* Tokyo Univ. *Career:* mem. Nagasaki Prefectural Ass. 1971–80; mem. House of Reps 1980–, Parl. Vice-Minister of Transport 1987, Minister of State for Defence 1996–98, Dir-Gen. Defence Agency (State Minister) 1996–99; Chair. LDP Panel on Security Issues 2000, Chair. (acting) LDP Policy Research Council 2001, Acting LDP Sec.-Gen. 2002, Chair. LDP Gen. Council 2004, Minister of State for Defence 2006–07, Minister of Defence Jan.–July 2007.
Address: c/o Ministry of Defence, 5-1 Ichigaya, Honmura-cho, Shinjuku-ku, Tokyo 162-8801, Japan (office).

L

LA LIME, Helen R. Meagher, BS, MS; American diplomatist; *Consul General in Cape Town;* m. Robert La Lime; one s. one d. *Education:* Georgetown Univ. and Nat. War Coll., Washington, DC. *Career:* worked as teacher in France, Portugal and Holland; joined Foreign Service in 1980, career mem. Sr Foreign Service, held a range of consular and admin. positions at US missions in Warsaw, Bern and Stuttgart, Consul Gen. in Zurich, assignment in Bureau of Int. Org. Affairs, State Dept 1993–95, Deputy Chief of Mission, Embassy in N'Djamena, Chad 1996–99, Dir Office of Cen. African Affairs 2000–01, Deputy Chief of Mission, Embassy in Rabat 2001–03, Amb. to Mozambique 2003–06, Consul Gen., Cape Town 2006–. *Address:* US Consulate General, PostNet Suite 50, Private Bag x26, Tokai 7966 (office); US Consulate General, 2 Reddam Avenue, Westlake 7945, South Africa (office). *Telephone:* (21) 702-7300 (office). *Fax:* (21) 702-7493 (office). *Website:* southafrica.usembassy.gov (office).

LA RUSSA, Ignazio; Italian lawyer and politician; *Minister of Defence;* b. 18 July 1947, Paternò; three s. *Education:* St Gallen, Switzerland, Univ. of Pavia. *Career:* served in Italian mil.; early career in pvt. law practice; Regional Councillor, Lombardy 1985; mem. Camera dei Deputati (Parl.) for Liguria 1992–, Deputy Speaker 1994, Chair. Cttee on Parl. Immunity 1996–2001; Minister of Defence 2008–; mem. Italian Socialist Movt 1992–95, Alleanza Nazionale 1995–2008, Chair. AN Parl. Group in Chamber of Deputies 2001, 2004–05, AN – The People of Liberty 2008–. *Address:* Ministry of Defence, Palazzo Baracchini, Via XX Settembre 8, 00187 Rome, Italy (office). *Telephone:* (06) 46911 (office). *E-mail:* pi@smd .difesa.it (office); larussa_i@camera.it (office). *Website:* www.difesa.it (home); www.ignaziolarussa.it (office).

LAAJAVA, Jaakko, BA, MA; Finnish diplomatist; *Ambassador to UK;* b. 23 June 1947, Joensuu; m. Pirjoriitta Laajava; three c. *Education:* Stockholm Univ., Sweden, Univ. of Helsinki. *Career:* entered Finnish Foreign Service 1971, attaché, Ministry for Foreign Affairs 1972–73, attaché, CSCE Mission of Finland, Geneva 1972–75, Second Sec., Warsaw 1975–77, Second Sec., Belgrade 1977–78, First Sec., Ministry for Foreign Affairs 1978–80, Counsellor, Madrid 1980–82, Head of Arms Control Section, Ministry for Foreign Affairs 1982–85, Minister-Counsellor and Deputy Chief of Mission, Washington, DC 1986–90, Amb. and Deputy Dir-Gen. for Political Affairs, Ministry for Foreign Affairs 1993–96, Amb. to USA 1996–2001, Under-Sec. of State for Political Affairs 2001–04, Amb. to UK 2005–; Fellow, Centre for Int. Affairs, Harvard Univ., USA 1985–86. *Address:* Embassy of Finland, 38 Chesham Place, London, SW1X 8HW, England (office). *Telephone:* (20) 7838-6200 (office). *Fax:* (20 7235-3680 (office). *E-mail:* sanomat.lon@formin.fi (office). *Website:* www.finemb.org .uk (office).

LAANEOTS, Lt-Gen. Ants; Estonian military officer; *Chief of Defence;* b. 16 Jan. 1948, Kilingi-Nõmme; m.; two c. *Education:* Higher Mil. School, Ukraine, Malinovsky Armoured and Mechanized Forces Acad., Moscow, NATO Defence Coll., Rome, Finnish Nat. Defence Coll. *Career:* Platoon Leader, then Co. Commdr, then Battalion Commdr, 300th Tank Regt for Soviet Army in Ukraine 1970–78; posted to Soviet-Chinese border in Eastern Kazakhstan 1981–87, Exec. Officer, 96th Tank Regt 1981–83, Commdr 180th Tank Regt 1983–85, Deputy Commdr Chief of Staff, 78th Armoured Div. 1985–87; deployment to Ethiopia 1987–89, mil. advisor to infantry div. Commdr 1987, mil. advisor to Army Corps Gen. 1988–89; Chief of Regional Dept of Defence, Tartu, Estonia 1989–91; Chief of Gen. Staff 1991–94, 1997–99; Insp. Gen. of Defence Forces 1997–2000; promoted to Maj. Gen. 1998; Head of Baltic Defence Research Centre 2000–01; Commdt, Estonian Nat. Defence Coll. 2001–06; Chief of Defence 2006–; promoted to Lt Gen. 2008; Order of the Cross of the Eagle. *Address:* Ministry of Defence, Sakala 1, Tallinn 15094, Estonia (office). *Telephone:* 717-0022 (office). *Fax:* 717-0001 (office). *E-mail:* info@kmin.ee (office). *Website:* www.mod.gov.ee (office).

LAAR, Mart, MA; Estonian politician and historian; b. 22 April 1960, Viljandi; m. Katrin Kask 1982; one s. one d. *Education:* Tartu State Univ. *Career:* history teacher, schools of Tallinn 1983–85; Head of Dept, Ministry of Culture of Estonia 1987–90; Deputy of Christian Democratic Party, Supreme Soviet of Estonia 1989–92; mem. Constitutional Ass. 1991–92; mem. Riigikogu (Estonian Parl.) 1992–; Founder and Chair. Pro Patria

Union (Isamaaliit) Party 1992–95; Prime Minister of Estonia 1992–94, 1999–2002; apptd mem. ISTAL by European Comm.; mem. Advisory Bd Springfellow 2003–; fmr Pres. Council of Historians of the Foundation of the Estonia Inheritance, Soc. for the Preservation of Estonia History, Soc. of Univ. Students of Estonia; Estonian Order of the Nat. Coat of Arms (Second Class); Cavaliere di Gran Groce dei Santi Maurizio e Lazzaro; Das Grosskreuz des Verdienstorderns des Bundesrepublic Deutschland; Nat. Order of Merit, Malta; Grand Cross, Ordre nat. du Mérite, France; Young Politician of the World (Jr Chamber Int.) 1993; European Tax Payer Asscn Year Prize 2001, European Bull, Davastoeconomic Forum, Global Link Award 2001, Adam Smith Award 2002. *Publications:* June 14 1941, Estonian History, War in the Woods, Little Country That Could, Back to the Future, Ten Years of Freedom in the CEE, and a number of scientific papers. *Address:* Estonian Parliament Riigikogu, Lossi plats 1A, 15161 Tallinn, Estonia (office). *Telephone:* 631-6612 (office). *Fax:* 631-6604 (office). *E-mail:* mart.laar@riigikogu.ee (office). *Website:* www.riigikogu.ee (office).

LABIDI, Hamida M'rabet; Tunisian lawyer and diplomatist; *Ambassador to UK;* m. Kamel Azzem Labidi. *Career:* early career as business attorney; served in Embassy in Buenos Aires, Amb. to the Netherlands –2007, to UK (also accred to Ireland) 2007–. *Address:* Embassy of Tunisia, 29 Prince's Gate, London, SW7 1QG, England (office). *Telephone:* (20) 7584-8117 (office). *Fax:* (20) 7584-3205 (office). *E-mail:* gorgi_h_2000@yahoo.fr (office).

LABUS, Miroljub, MSc, PhD; Serbian politician, lawyer and economist; b. 27 Feb. 1947, Mala Krsna; m. Olivera Labus (née Grabic); two d. *Education:* Belgrade Univ. *Career:* attorney-at-law, Belgrade 1970–71; Lecturer in Law, Belgrade Univ. 1971, Prof. of Econs 1971–; Fulbright Lecturer, Cornell Univ., USA 1983, Visiting Asst Prof. 1984; Sr Adviser, Fed. Statistics Office 1986–94; mem. Bd Ekonomska Misl i Ekonomske Analize journals; Fellow, Econ. Inst. 1993–99; Deputy Prime Minister and Minister of Foreign Econ. Relations, Fed. Repub. of Yugoslavia 1987–91, Deputy Prime Minister, with responsibility for econ. relations with the int. community 2001–03; presidential cand. 2002; Deputy Prime Minister in charge of European Integration, Repub. of Serbia 2004–06; mem. Fed. Parl. and Cttee on Monetary Policy; Vice-Pres. Democratic Party 1994–97; mem. Standing Cttee on Econ. Affairs, UNDPM Sarajevo 1996; with UNDP 1996–97; joined IBRD 1997; Ed. The Economic Trends, Fed. Statistics Office, Belgrade, The Economic Barometer, Econ. Inst., Belgrade 2000–; Pres. Admin. Bd G17 Plus movt (later G17 Plus party) 1999–2000, Pres. G17 Plus 2003–. *Publications:* Social and Collective Property Rights 1987, General Equilibrium Modelling (co-author) 1990, Contemporary Political Economy 1991, Foundations of Political Economy 1992, Foundations of Economics 1995, other books and numerous articles on econ. problems. *Address:* c/o Office of the Prime Minister, Nemanjina 11, 11000 Belgrade (office); Gospodar Jevremova str. 13, Belgrade, Serbia (home).

LACKEY, Kathleen (Kate) J.; New Zealand diplomatist; *High Commissioner to Canada;* m.; two c. *Career:* posts have included Deputy High Commr to Canada, Consul Gen. in Los Angeles, Dir Foreign Ministry's Americas Div., Acting CEO Pacific Island Affairs; Deputy Sec. of Foreign Affairs and Trade (first woman) 1997; High Commr to Australia (first woman) 2002–06, to Canada 2006–. *Address:* New Zealand High Commission, Clarica Centre, 99 Bank Street, Suite 727, Ottawa, ON K1P 6G3 (office). *Telephone:* (613) 238-5991 (office). *Fax:* (613) 238-5707 (office). *E-mail:* info@nzhcottawa.org (office). *Website:* www.nzembassy.com/canad (office).

LACOTTE, Urs; Swiss international organization executive; *Director-General, International Olympic Committee; Education:* Univ. of Berne, Univ. of Bayreuth, Germany. *Career:* fmr tech. official for ski competitions in Switzerland; worked with Electrowatt Eng Co. in Asia and with forerunner to Swiss Sports Asscn; fmr planner, Ministry of Defence; Dir-Gen. IOC 2003–.

Address: International Olympic Committee, Château de Vidy, 1007 Lausanne, Switzerland (office). *Telephone:* (21) 621 6111 (office). *Fax:* (21) 621 6216 (office). *Website:* www.olympic.org (office).

LADSOUS, Hervé; French diplomatist; *Ambassador to People's Republic of China;* b. 12 April 1950. *Education:* École nationale des langues orientales. *Career:* Vice-Consul in Hong Kong 1973–75; with Econ. Affairs Div., Ministry of Foreign Affairs 1976–81; Second Counsellor, Embassy in Canberra 1981–83, Beijing 1983–86; Second Counsellor, Perm. Mission to UN, Geneva 1986–88, First Counsellor 1988–90; Asst Dir for the Americas, Ministry of Foreign Affairs 1990–92; Acting Chargé d'affaires, Embassy in Port-au-Prince 1991–92; First Counsellor, Perm. Mission to UN, New York 1992–94, Minister Counsellor 1994–97; Perm. Rep. to OSCE, Vienna 1997–2001; Amb. to Indonesia 2001–03 (also accred to E Timor 2002–03); Communications Dir Ministry of Foreign Affairs 2003–05, Dir for Asia and Oceania 2005; Amb. to People's Repub. of China 2006–; Chevalier de la Légion d'honneur, Officier de l'ordre national du Mérite. *Address:* Embassy of France, 3 Dong San Jie, San Li Tun, Chao Yang Qu, Beijing 100600, People's Republic of China (office). *Telephone:* (10) 65321331 (office). *Fax:* (10) 65324841 (office). *E-mail:* secretariat@ambafrance-cn.org (office). *Website:* www.ambafrance-cn.org (office).

LAFER, Celso; Brazilian politician and professor of law; b. 7 Aug. 1941, São Paulo. *Career:* Prof. of Law, Univ. of São Paulo; Minister of Foreign Affairs 1992, 2001–03; Amb. to WTO and Head WTO Gen. Council and Dispute Settlement Comm. 1995–98; Minister of Industry and Commerce 1999; Pres. Fiesp 2000; mem. Brazilian Acad. of Letters 2006; Grand Cross (Brazil) 2002, Grand Officer, Légion d'honneur 2002; Dr hc (Buenos Aires Univ.) 2001, (Cordoba Univ.) 2002. *Address:* Avenida Brigadeiro Faria Lima 1306, Jardim Paulistano, 01451-914 São Paulo, Brazil (office). *E-mail:* c_lafer@uol.com.br (home).

LAFFAN, Brigid, PhD, MRIA; Irish political scientist and academic; *Principal, College of Human Sciences, University College Dublin;* b. 6 Jan. 1955, Co. Kerry; m. Michael Laffan 1979; one s. two d. *Education:* Univ. of Limerick, Coll. of Europe, Bruges, Trinity Coll. Dublin. *Career:* researcher, European Cultural Foundation 1977–78; Lecturer, Coll. of Humanities, Univ. of Limerick 1979–86; Lecturer, Inst. of Public Admin 1986–89; Newman Scholar, Univ. Coll. Dublin 1989–90, Lecturer, Dept of Politics 1990–91, Jean Monnet Prof. of European Politics 1991–, Research Dir Dublin European Inst.; Visiting Prof., Coll. of Europe, Bruges 1992–; adviser on EU enlargement, Oireachtas (Parl.) Foreign Affairs Cttee; mem. Council, Inst. of European Affairs, Dublin. *Publications:* Ireland and South Africa 1988, Integration and Co-operation in Europe 1992, Constitution Building in the European Union (ed.) 1996, The Finances of the European Union 1997, Europe's Experimental Union: Re-thinking Integration (co-author) 1999, Renovation or Revolution: New Territorial Politics in Ireland and the United Kingdom (contributing co-ed. with J. Coakley and J. Todd) 2005, Ireland in the European Union (with Jane O'Mahoney) 2008; numerous articles on Irish foreign policy, EC budgetary policy, insts, governance and political union. *Address:* College of Human Sciences, University College, Belfield, Dublin 4 (office); 4 Willowbank, The Slopes, Monkstown, Co. Dublin, Ireland (home). *Telephone:* (1) 7168344 (office); (1) 2862617 (home). *Fax:* (1) 7161171 (office); (1) 2845331 (home). *E-mail:* brigid.laffan@ucd.ie (office). *Website:* www.ucd.ie/humansciences (office).

LaFLEUR, Christopher J., BA, MA; American diplomatist; m. Keiko Miyazawa; two d. *Education:* Oberlin Coll. *Career:* career mem. Sr Foreign Service since 1973, served as Political Officer, Embassies in Tokyo and Paris, as Consul in Sapporo, Japan, as Political Advisor, US Mission to UN, later served as Chief of Offices of Political-Mil. Affairs and of External Affairs, Embassy in Tokyo, as Staff Officer, Exec. Secr., as Special Asst to Asst Sec. for E Asia and Pacific Affairs, as Dir Office of Vietnam, Laos and Cambodia, Deputy Dir American Inst., Taiwan 1993–97, Deputy Chief of Mission, Embassy in Tokyo 1997–2001, Prin. Deputy Asst Sec. for E Asian and Pacific Affairs 2001–03, represented State Dept in consultations on future of US alliances with Japan and with Repub. of Korea 2003–04, Cyrus Vance Fellow in Diplomatic Studies, Council on Foreign Relations, New York 2003–04, Amb. to Malaysia 2004–07. *Address:* US Department of State, 2201 C Street NW, Washington, DC 20520, USA (office). *Telephone:* (202) 647-4000 (office). *Fax:* (202) 647-6738 (office). *Website:* www.state.gov (office).

LAGARDE, Christine; French lawyer and government official; *Minister of Economy, Finance and Industry;* b. 1956; m. (divorced); two s. *Education:* Univ. of Aix-en-Provence, Political Science Inst., Paris Law School, Paris Univ. *Career:* started career as lecturer at Paris X Univ.; joined Baker & McKenzie LLP (law firm) 1981, Partner 1987–, Man. Partner 1991–95, elected to Global Exec. Cttee 1995, Chair. European Regional Council and

Professional Devt Cttee 1995–98, Chair. Exec. Cttee 1999–2004, Chair. Global Policy Cttee 2004–05; Minister for Foreign Trade 2005–07, of Agric. 2007, of Economy, Finance and Industry 2007–; mem. Supervisory Bd ING Group 2005–; mem. Int. Advisory Bd Escuela Superior de Administración y Dirección de Empresas; mem. Int. Bd of Overseers, Ill. Inst. of Tech.; mem. Bd and Sec., Execs Club of Chicago; mem. Strategic Council on Attractivity of France; co-Chair. US-Europe-Poland Action Comm., Center for Strategic and Int. Studies; mem. Int. Business Advisory Bd, Mayor of Beijing; Chevalier de la Légion d'honneur; Jaume Cordelles Award from ESADE 2004, ranked by Forbes magazine amongst 100 Most Powerful Women (76th) 2004, (88th) 2005, (30th) 2006, (12th) 2007. *Address:* Ministry of the Economy, Finance and Industry, 139 rue de Bercy, 75572 Paris Cedex 12, France (office). *Telephone:* 1-40-04-04-04 (office). *Fax:* 1-43-43-75-97 (office). *Website:* www.minefi.gouv.fr (office).

LAGOS ESCOBAR, Ricardo, PhD; Chilean politician; *President, Club de Madrid;* b. 2 March 1938, Santiago; m. Luisa Durán; five c. *Education:* Univ. of Chile, Duke Univ., N Carolina. *Career:* Prof. Univ. of Chile 1963–72, fmr Head School of Political and Admin. Sciences, fmr Dir Inst. of Econs, Gen. Sec. 1971; Visiting Prof. Univ. of N Carolina, Chapel Hill 1974–75; Chair. Alianza Democrática (AD) 1983–84; Chair. Partido por la Democracia (PPD) 1987–90; Minister of Educ. 1990–92, of Public Works 1994; Pres. of Chile 2000–06; Founder and Pres. Fundación Democracia y Desarrollo (Foundation for Democracy and Development) 2006–; Pres. Club de Madrid 2006–; UN Special Envoy on Climate Change 2007–. *Publications:* Población, Pobreza y Mercado de Trabajo en América Latina 1997, numerous books and articles on econs and politics. *Address:* Club de Madrid, Casa Goya 5-7, Pasaje 2ª, 28001 Madrid, Spain (office). *Telephone:* (91) 1548230 (office). *Fax:* (91) 1548240 (office). *E-mail:* clubmadrid@clubmadrid.org (office). *Website:* www.clubmadrid.org (office).

LAGUMDŽIJA, Zlatko, MSc, PhD; Bosnia and Herzegovina politician; b. 26 Dec. 1955, Sarajevo; m.; two c. *Education:* Univ. of Sarajevo, Harvard Univ., USA. *Career:* Visiting Prof., Arizona Univ. 1988–89; Prof. of Econ. and Electrical Eng, Univ. of Sarajevo 1989–, Dir Centre for Man. and Computer Tech. 1995; co-f. Social and Democratic Party of Bosnia and Herzegovina (Socijaldemokratska Partija —SDP BiH) 1990, Chair. 1997–; mem. House of Reps of Parl. Ass. 1996–; Prime Minister, Minister of Foreign Affairs and Treasurer of the Insts of Bosnia and Herzegovina 2001; Minister of Foreign Affairs 2001–03. *Address:* Socijaldemokratska Partija BiH, Alipašina 41, 71000 Sarajevo, Bosnia and Herzegovina (office). *Telephone:* (33) 664044 (office). *Fax:* (33) 644042 (office). *E-mail:* generalni.sekretar@sdp-bih.org.ba (office). *Website:* www.sdp-bih.org.ba (office).

LAHOUD, Gen. Emile; Lebanese politician, naval officer and fmr head of state; b. 1936, Baabdat; m. Andrée Amadouni; two s. one d. *Education:* Brumana High School, also attended various courses at Naval Acads in UK and USA 1958–80. *Career:* joined Mil. Acad. as cadet officer 1956, promoted to Sub.-Lt 1959, Lt 1962, Lt-Commdr 1969, Commdr 1974, Cap. 1980, Rear-Adm. 1985, Vice-Adm. 1989; Commdr of Second Fleet 1966–68, of First Fleet 1968–70; Staff of Army Fourth Bureau 1970–72; Chief of Personal Staff of Gen. Commdr of Armed Forces 1973–79; Dir of Personnel, Army HQ 1980–83; Head of Mil. Office, Ministry of Defence 1983–89; Commdr-in-Chief of Armed Forces 1989; Pres. of the Repub. of the Lebanon 1998–2007; Lebanese Medal of Merit Gen. Officer 1989; Medal of Merit and Honour, Haiti 1974; War Medals 1991, 1992; Dawn of the South Medal 1993; Nat. Unity Medal 1993; Medal of Esteem 1994; Grand Cordon Order of the Cedar 1993; Commdr Légion d'Honneur 1993; Grand Cross (Argentina) 1998; Order of Merit Sr Officer Level (Italy) 1997; Order of Hussein ibn Ali (Jordan) 1999, Order of St Misrope Mashtos (Armenia) 2000, King Abdul-Aziz Collar (Saudi Arabia) 2000, Great Collar of the Union (UAE) 2000, Great Collar of Mubarak (Kuwait) 2000, Great Collar of the Nile (Egypt) 2000, Great Collar of Independence (Qatar) 2000, Great Collar of the Khalifah Order (Bahrein) 2000, Order of the White Double Cross 1st Class (Slovakia) 2001, Star of Romania Collar 1999, 2001, Great Cross Légion d'honneur (France) 2001, Al Muhammadi Decoration Extraordinary Grade (Morocco) 2001, Order of November 7th (Tunisia) 2001, Great Cross Order of the Grimaldis (Monaco) 2001, Great Cross Order of the Redeemer (Greece) 2001, Grand Cordon Nat. Order of Oumaya (Syria) 2002, Badge Order of Prince Yaroslav the Wise 1st class (Ukraine) 2002, Grand Collar Order of Makarios III (Cyprus) 2002, Nat. Order of Merit Al-Athir (Algeria) 2002, Order of the Repub. (Yemen) 2002, Order Stara Planina (Bulgaria) 2003, Nat. Order of the South Cross (Brazil) 2004, Grand Cross of the Ipiranga Order (Brazil) 2004, Grand Cross with Chain of Order of Merit (Hungary) 2004, Knight Grand Cross of Merit with Gold Star of the Sacred Military Constantinian Order of St George 2004, Grand Cross of Order of Merit (Poland) 2004, Knight Grand Cross of

Merit with Gold Plate of the Sacred Military Constantinian Order of St George 2005. *Publication:* Method and Style, Promise and Fulfilment. *Address:* c/o Presidential Palace, Baabda, Lebanon (office).

LAIDLER, David Ernest William, PhD, FRSC; Canadian/British economist and academic; *Fellow-in-Residence, C. D. Howe Institute;* b. 12 Aug. 1938, Tynemouth, UK; m. Antje Charlotte Breitwisch 1965; one d. *Education:* Tynemouth School, London School of Econs, Univs of Syracuse and Chicago, USA. *Career:* Asst Lecturer, LSE 1961–62; Asst Prof., Univ. of Calif., Berkeley 1963–66; Lecturer, Univ. of Essex 1966–69; Prof., Univ. of Manchester 1969–75; Prof. of Econs, Univ. of Western Ont. 1975–2004, Bank of Montreal Prof. 2000–05, now Prof. Emer., Dept Chair. 1981–84; Special Adviser, Bank of Canada 1998–99; Fellow-in-Residence, CD Howe Inst., Toronto 1990–; Visiting Economist, Reserve Bank of Australia 1977; Assoc. Ed. Journal of Money, Credit and Banking 1979–; mem. Editorial Bd Pakistan Devt Review 1987–, European Journal of the History of Econ. Thought 1993–; fmr mem. editorial Bd several other journals; Co-Founder and mem. Exec. Cttee Money Study Group 1970–75; mem. Econs Cttee, CNAA, GB 1971–75, Econs Cttee, SSRC, GB 1972–75, Consortium on Macroeconomic Modelling and Forecasting, ESRC, GB 1981–88, Econ. Advisory Panel to Minister of Finance, Canada 1982–84; Co-ordinator Research Advisory Group on Econ. Ideas and Social Issues, Royal Comm. on the Econ. Union and Devt Prospects for Canada (Macdonald Comm.) 1984–85; Dir Philip Allan Publrs Ltd 1972–99; Pres. Canadian Econs Asscn 1987–88; BAAS Lister Lecturer 1972; Canadian Econs Asscn Douglas Purvis Prize 1994, Hellmuth Prize, Univ. of Western Ontario 1999, Donner Prize 2004. *Publications:* The Demand for Money 1969, Essays on Money and Inflation 1975, Monetarist Perspectives 1982, Taking Money Seriously 1990, The Golden Age of the Quantity Theory 1991, The Great Canadian Disinflation (with W. P. B. Robson) 1993, Money and Macroeconomics: Selected Essays 1998, Fabricating the Keynesian Revolution 1999, Two Percent Target (with W. P. B. Robson) 2004, Macroeconomics in Retrospect: Selected Essays 2004. *Address:* C.D. Howe Institute, 67 Yonge Street, Suite 300, Toronto, Ont. M5E 1J8 (office); Department of Economics, Room 4024, SSC, University of Western Ontario, London, Ont., N6A 5C2 (office); 45–124 North Centre Road, London, Ont., N5X 4R3, Canada (home). *Telephone:* (416) 865-1904 (C.D. Howe) (office); (519) 661-3400 (office); (519) 673-3014 (home). *Fax:* (416) 865-1866 (C.D. Howe) (office); (519) 661-3666 (office). *E-mail:* laidler@uwo.ca (office); cdhowe@cdhowe.org (office). *Website:* www.ssc .uwo.ca/economics/faculty/Laidler (office); www.cdhowe.org (office).

LAIDRE, Margus, PhD; Estonian diplomatist and academic; *Ambassador to UK;* m. Eva Laidre. *Education:* Tartu Univ. *Career:* fmr Amb. to the Holy See, to Germany, to Sweden; Gen. Dir Foreign Ministry Political Dept –2005, Amb. to UK 2006–. *Publications include:* Lõpu võidukas algus: Karl XII Eesti- ja Liivimaal 1700–1701 1995, Narva – The Victorious Beginning of the End 2002, Messenger or Spy? The Origins of Present-day Diplomacy 1454–1725 2003. *Address:* Embassy of Estonia, 16 Hyde Park Gate, London, SW7 5DG, England (office). *Telephone:* (20) 7589-3428 (office). *Fax:* (20) 7589-3430 (office). *E-mail:* embassy.london@estonia.gov.uk (office). *Website:* www .estonia.gov.uk (office).

LAING, (John) Stuart, MA; British diplomatist; *Ambassador to Kuwait;* b. 22 July 1948, Limpsfield, Surrey; m. Sibella Dorman 1971; one s. two d. *Education:* Rugby School, Corpus Christi Coll., Cambridge. *Career:* joined HM Diplomatic Service in 1970, served in Jedda 1973–75, 1992–95, Brussels 1975–78, Cairo 1983–87, Prague 1989–92 and Riyadh, High Commr in Brunei 1999–2002, Amb. to Oman 2002–05, to Kuwait 2005–. *Address:* British Embassy, PO Box 2, Safat, 13001, Kuwait (office). *Telephone:* 2403334 (office). *Fax:* 2426799 (office). *E-mail:* stuart.laing@ fco.gov.uk (office); britemb@qualitynet.net (office). *Website:* www .britishembassy.gov.uk/kuwait (office).

LAJČÁK, Miroslav; Slovak diplomatist; *High Representative of the International Community and Special Representative of the European Union in Bosnia and Herzegovina;* b. 20 March 1963, Poprad; m.; two d. *Education:* Comenius Univ., Bratislava, State Inst. of Int. Relations, Moscow, Russia and George C. Marshall European Center for Security Studies, Germany. *Career:* joined Ministry of Foreign Affairs in 1988; served in Embassy in Moscow 1991–93; Dir Cabinet of Minister of Foreign Affairs 1993–94, 1998–2001; Dir Cabinet of Prime Minister of Slovakia 1993–94; Amb. to Japan 1994–98, to Fed. Repub. of Yugoslavia (also accred to Albania and FYR Macedonia) 2001–05; Special Asst to UN Sec.-Gen.'s Special Envoy to the Balkans 1999–2001; Dir-Gen. of Political Affairs, Ministry of Foreign Affairs 2005–07; Special Rep. of EU for Common Foreign and Security Policy, Montenegro 2005–; High Rep. of Int. Community Mission in Bosnia and Herzegovina 2007–.

Address: Office of the High Representative of the International Community and the Special Representative of the European Union in Bosnia and Herzegovina, Emerika Bluma 1, 71000 Sarajevo, Bosnia and Herzegovina (office). *Telephone:* (33) 283500 (office). *Fax:* (33) 283501 (office). *Website:* www.ohr.int (office).

LAJOLO, HE Cardinal Giovanni, BCL; Italian ecclesiastic and diplomatist; *President, Governatorate of Vatican City State;* b. 3 Jan. 1935, Novara. *Career:* ordained priest of Novara 1960; entered Vatican diplomatic service 1970, served at Vatican Nunciature in Germany and in Secr. of State; Titular Archbishop of Caesariana and Sec. of Admin of Patrimony of the Apostolic See 1988–95; Apostolic Nuncio to Germany 1995–2003; Sec. for Relations with States 2003–06; Pres. Governatorate of Vatican City State 2006–, Pontifical Comm. for Vatican City State 2006–; cr. Cardinal 2007, apptd Cardinal-Deacon of S. Maria Liberatrice a Monte Testaccio 2007. *Address:* Governatorate of Vatican City State, Palazzo Apostolico Vaticano, Città del Vaticano 00120, Italy (office). *E-mail:* info@vatican .va (office). *Website:* www.vatican.va/vatican_city_state (office).

LAKATANI, Sani; Niuean politician. *Career:* Prime Minister of Niue March 1999–2001; Minister for External Affairs, Finance, Customs and Revenue, Econ. and Planning Devt and Statistics, Business and Pvt. Sector Devt, Civil Aviation, Tourism, Int. Business Co. and Offshore Banking, Niue Devt Bank March 1999–2001; fmr Leader Niue People's Party (NPP); Chancellor Univ. of the South Pacific, Fiji 2000–03; Deputy Premier and Minister for Planning, Econ. Devt and Statistics, the Niue Devt Bank, Post, Telecommunications and Information Computer Tech. Devt, Philatelic Bureau and Numismatics, Shipping, Investment and Trade, Civil Aviation and Police, Immigration and Disaster Man. 2002. *Address:* c/o Office of the Prime Minister, Alofi, Niue (office).

LAKE, Anthony, PhD; American fmr government official and academic; *Distinguished Professor in Practice of Diplomacy, Edmund A. Walsh School of Foreign Service, Georgetown University;* b. 1939, New York; m.; three c. *Education:* Harvard Univ., Cambridge Univ., UK, Woodrow Wilson School of Public and Int. Affairs, Princeton Univ. *Career:* joined Foreign Service 1962, Special Asst to Amb. Henry Cabot Lodge, Viet Nam; aide to Nat. Security Adviser Henry Kissinger 1969–70; Head State Dept's policy planning operation –1981; Prof., Amherst Coll., Mass. 1981–84, Mount Holyoke Coll. 1984–92; currently Distinguished Prof. in Practice of Diplomacy, Edmund A. Walsh School of Foreign Service, Georgetown Univ.; co-f. journal Foreign Policy; foreign policy adviser to fmr Pres. Clinton during presidential campaign 1992; Nat. Security Adviser 1993–96. *Publications:* The 'Tar Baby' Option: American Policy Toward Southern Rhodesia 1976, Third World Radical Regimes: US Policy under Carter and Reagan 1985, Somoza Falling: A Case Study of Washington at Work 1990, Six Nightmares 2001. *Address:* Edmund A. Walsh School of Foreign Service, Georgetown University, 37th and O Street, NW, Washington, DC 20057, USA. *Telephone:* (202) 687-6083. *Fax:* (202) 687-1427. *E-mail:* lakea@ georgetown.edu. *Website:* www.georgetown.edu/sfs (office).

LAKE-TACK, Louise Agnetha; Antigua and Barbuda nurse, magistrate and government official; *Governor-General;* b. 26 July 1944, Long Lake Estate, Parish of St Phillips, Antigua. *Education:* Antigua Girls High School, Charing Cross Hosp., UK. *Career:* worked as nurse at Nat. Heart Hosp. and Harley Street Clinic, UK; magistrate Marylebone and Horseferry Magistrate Courts 1995, also sat at Pocock Street Crown Court; Gov.-Gen. of Antigua and Barbuda (first woman) 2007–; mem. Antigua and Barbuda Nat. Asscn. *Address:* Office of the Governor-General, St John's, Antigua and Barbuda (office). *Website:* www.antigua.gov.ag (office).

LAL, Deepak Kumar, MA, BPhil; British academic; *James S. Coleman Professor of International Development Studies, Department of Economics, University of California, Los Angeles;* b. 3 Jan. 1940, Lahore, India; m. Barbara Ballis 1971; one s. one d. *Education:* Doon School, Dehra Dun, St Stephen's Coll., Delhi, India, Jesus Coll., Oxford. *Career:* Indian Foreign Service 1963–65; Lecturer, Christ Church, Oxford 1966–68; Research Fellow, Nuffield Coll., Oxford 1968–70; Lecturer, Univ. Coll. London 1970–79, Reader 1979–84, Prof. of Political Economy, Univ. of London 1984–93, Prof. Emer. 1993–; James S. Coleman Prof. of Int. Devt Studies, UCLA 1991–; Consultant, Indian Planning Comm. 1973–74; Research Admin., World Bank, Washington, DC 1983–87; Dir Trade Policy Unit, Centre for Policy Studies 1993–96, Trade and Devt Unit, Inst. of Econ. Affairs 1997–2002; consultancy assignments ILO, UNCTAD, OECD, IBRD Ministry of Planning, Sri Lanka, Repub. of Korea 1970–; Int. Freedom Award for Econs, Società Liberia (Italy) 2007. *Publications:* Wells and Welfare 1972, Methods of Project Analysis 1974, Appraising Foreign Investment in Developing Countries 1975, Unemployment and Wage

Inflation in Industrial Economies 1977, Men or Machines 1978, Prices for Planning 1980, The Poverty of "Development Eonomics" 1983, Labour and Poverty in Kenya (with P. Collier) 1986, Stagflation, Savings and the State (co-ed. with M. Wolf) 1986, The Hindu Equilibrium (two vols) 1988, 1989, Public Policy and Economic Development (co-ed. with M. Scott) 1990, Development Economics (four vols) (ed.) 1991, The Repressed Economy 1993, Against Dirigisme 1994, The Political Economy of Poverty, Equity and Growth (with H. Myint) 1996, Unintended Consequences 1998, Unfinished Business 1999, Trade, Development and Political Economy (co-ed. with R. Snape) 2001, In Praise of Emires 2004, The Hindu Equilibrium 2005, Reviving the Invisible Hand: The Case for Classical Liberalism in the 21st Century 2006.
Address: Department of Economics, 8369 Bunche Hall, UCLA, Box 951477, Los Angeles, CA 90095-1477, USA (office); A30 Nizamuddin West, New Delhi 110013, India; 2 Erskine Hill, London, NW11 6HB, England. *Telephone:* (310) 825-4521 (office); (310) 206-2382 (office); (20) 8458-3713 (London); (11) 462-9465 (New Delhi). *Fax:* (310) 825-9528 (office). *Website:* econweb.sscnet.ucla.edu (office).

LALONDE, Brice; French politician and environmental consultant; *Chairman, Round Table on Sustainable Development, Organisation for Economic Co-operation and Development;* b. 10 Feb. 1946, Neuilly; m. Patricia Raynaud 1986; two s. (one deceased) two d.; one s. one d. from previous marriage. *Career:* student leader 1968; Chair. Friends of the Earth 1972, French Br. 1978; Candidate for the Green Party, French Presidential Election 1981; Admin. European Environment Bureau 1983; Dir Paris Office Inst. for European Environmental Policy 1987; Sec. of State for the Environment 1988–89, for the Environment and the Prevention of Tech. and Natural Disasters 1989–90, Minister Del. 1990–91, Minister of the Environment 1991–92; Pres. Génération Ecologie (political movt) 1990–2002, Hon. Pres. 2002–; Mayor of Saint-Briac-sur-Mer 1995–; Chair. Cttee to Free Alexandr Nikitin 1996–; mem. Conseil Régional, Brittany 1998, Comité nat. de l'eau 1998–; Chair. Round Table on Sustainable Development, OECD 2007–. *Publication:* L'écologie en bleu.
Address: Round Table on Sustainable Development, 2 rue André Pascal, 75016 Paris (office); 65 boulevard Arago, 75013 Paris (home); Mairie, 18 rue de la Mairie, 35800 Saint-Briac-sur-Mer, France. *Telephone:* 1-45-24-90-82 (office). *Fax:* 1-45-24-84-08 (office). *E-mail:* webmaster@oecd.org (office). *Website:* www.oecd.org (office).

LAMB, Robin David; British diplomatist and business executive; *Head of Business Development, Arab-British Chamber of Commerce;* m. Sue Lamb; two s. one d. *Education:* Brasenose Coll., Oxford, Middle East Centre for Arabic Studies, Lebanon. *Career:* joined FCO 1971, served at British embassies in Khartoum, Tripoli, Jeddah, Muscat, Riyadh, Kuwait and Cairo, held several London-based positions including Dir at Trade Partners UK (now called UK Trade and Investment), Deputy Head of Middle East Dept (MED), FCO, Deputy Head, Information Dept, Head, Scott Inquiry Unit, several other appointments in MED and FCO's Research and Analysis Dept; fmr Deputy Head of Mission, Kuwait –2003; Amb. to Bahrain 2003–06; Head of Business Devt, Arab-British Chamber of Commerce 2007–.
Address: Arab-British Chamber of Commerce, 43 Upper Grosvenor Street, London, W1K 2NJ, England (office). *Telephone:* (20) 7659-4854 (office). *Fax:* (20) 7245-6688 (office). *E-mail:* robin.lamb@abcc.org.uk (office). *Website:* www.abcc.org.uk (office).

LAMBA, Isaac Chikwekwere; Malawi academic and diplomatist; *Ambassador to Germany;* b. 10 Nov. 1945, Nasoni Chembe, Lilongwe Dist.; m.; three c. *Education:* Dalhousie Univ., Halifax, Nova Scotia, Canada and Univ. of Edinburgh, UK. *Career:* part-time Lecturer in History, Univ. of Malawi 1970–72, Assoc. Prof. of History 1972–75, Teaching Practice Organizer, Faculty of Educ. 1977–80, Dean of Faculty of Social Sciences 1984–85; Deputy Prin. Malawi Inst. of Educ. 1985–88; Prin. Sec., Ministry of Educ. and Culture 1988–91; Diplomatic Minister to France, and Deputy Perm. Del. to UNESCO, Paris 1991–93; Pres. Southern African Univs Social Science Conf. 1997–99; Consul Gen. to South Africa 2000–01; Perm. Rep. to UN, New York 2001–03; Amb. to Germany 2007–; Chair. Bd of Dirs Air Malawi 1999–2000; Regional Gov. United Democratic Party 1999.
Address: Embassy of Malawi, Westfälische Str. 86, 10709 Berlin, Germany (office). *Telephone:* (30) 8431540 (office). *Fax:* (30) 84315430 (office). *E-mail:* malawibonn@aol.com (office). *Website:* www.malawi-botschaft.de (office).

LAMBERT, Yves Maurice; French international organization official and engineer; b. 4 June 1936, Nancy, Meurthe-et-Moselle; m. Odile Revillon 1959; three s. two d. *Education:* Ecole Polytechnique, Paris, Nat. Civil Aviation School, Centre de Préparation à l'Admin des Entreprises. *Career:* Dir Org. de Gestion et de Sécurité de l'Algérie (OGSA), Algeria 1965–68; Tech. Adviser to Minister of Transport, France 1969–72; Rep. of France to

ICAO Council 1972–76; Sec.-Gen. ICAO Aug. 1976–88, Dir of Air Navigation, Ministry of Equipment and Housing, Transport and the Sea 1989–93; Dir-Gen. Eurocontrol 1994–2001; Fellow Royal Aeronautical Soc. (UK); mem. Acad. Nat. de l'Air et de l'Espace; Officier, Légion d'honneur, Ordre nat. du Mérite; Médaille de l'Aéronautique, Glen Gilbert Award, Air Traffic Control Asscn 1997.
Address: c/o Eurocontrol, 96 rue de la Fusée, 1130 Brussels, Belgium.

LAMEDA, Guaicaipuro, MA; Venezuelan business executive, army officer and engineer; b. 6 Aug. 1954, Barquisimeto, Estada Lara. *Education:* Mil. Acad. of Venezuela, Pacific Univ., USA, Inst. of Advanced Studies of Nat. Defense, Gen. Staff and Command School, USA. *Career:* numerous managerial and educational posts in Venezuelan army and govt, including Chief Planning Officer, Venezuelan Co. of Mil. Industries (CAVIM) 1992, Dir of Budget Office, Ministry of Defence 1996, Dir Govt Cen. Budget Office 1998; Chair. Petróleos de Venezuela SA (PDVSA) 2000–02; Pres. of the Repub. Award, Nat. School for Advanced Defense Studies; 15 nat. and foreign distinctions; 3 mil. merit badges, 23 mil. honour awards.
Address: c/o Edif. Petróleos de Venezuela, Torre Est, Avda Libertador, La Campina, Apdo 169, Caracas 1010-A, Venezuela.

LAMM, Vanda Éva, PhD, DSc; Hungarian professor of international law and international legal official; *Director, Institute for Legal Studies, Hungarian Academy of Sciences;* b. 26 March 1945, Budapest. *Education:* Univ. of Budapest, Faculté int. pour l'enseignement du droit comparé, Strasbourg, France, Hague Acad. of Int. Law, Netherlands, Columbia Univ., USA. *Career:* Research Fellow, Inst. for Legal Studies, Hungarian Acad. of Sciences, Dir 1991–; Prof. of Int. Law Univ. of Miskolc 1998, Univ. of Budapest-Gyor; Head, Dept of Int. Law, Széchenyi István Univ.; mem. Perm. Court of Arbitration 1999–; Deputy mem. Court of Arbitration of OSCE; mem. UN CEDAW Cttee monitoring implementation of 1979 Convention on Elimination of Discrimination against Women; Pres. Int. Nuclear Law Asscn 2000–01; Hon. Pres. and mem. Bd of Man. 2004–05; Sec.-Gen. Hungarian Br., Int. Law Asscn; Vice-Chair. Group of Governmental Experts on Third Party Liability, OECD-NEA; Assoc. mem. Inst. of Int. Law 2001–; Ed.-in-Chief Állam-és Jogtudomány; Ed. Acta Juridica Hungarica. *Publications:* numerous publs on nuclear law and int. law.
Address: Institute for Legal Studies, Hungarian Academy of Sciences, PO Box 25, I. Országház u. 30, 1250 Budapest (office); Department of International Law, Széchenyi István University, Egyetem tér 1, 9026 Gyor, Hungary. *Telephone:* (1) 355-7384 (office); (96) 503-478. *Fax:* (1) 375-7858 (office); (96) 503-400/3535. *E-mail:* lamm@jog.mta.hu (office); lammv@mail.sze.hu.

LAMONT, Donald Alexander, MA; British diplomatist; *CEO, Wilton Park;* b. 13 Jan. 1947; m. Lynda Margaret Campbell 1981; one s. one d. *Education:* Univ. of Aberdeen. *Career:* with British Leyland Motor Corpn 1970; Second Sec., then First Sec. FCO 1974; First Sec. UNIDO/IAEA, Vienna 1977; First Sec. (Commercial) Moscow 1980; First Sec. FCO 1982; Counsellor on secondment to IISS 1988; Political Adviser and Head of Chancery, British Mil. Govt, Berlin 1988–91; Amb. to Uruguay 1991–94; Head of Repub. of Ireland Dept, FCO 1994–97; Chief of Staff and Deputy High Rep., Sarajevo 1997–99; Gov. of Falkland Islands and Commr for S Georgia and S Sandwich Islands 1999–2002; Amb. to Venezuela 2003–07; CEO Wilton Park (FCO conference unit) 2007–.
Address: Wilton Park Conferences, Wiston House, Steyning, West Sussex, BN44 3DZ, England (office). *Telephone:* (1903) 817766 (office). *Fax:* (1903) 879647 (office). *E-mail:* admin@wiltonpark.org.uk (office). *Website:* www.wiltonpark.org.uk (office).

LAMY, Pascal Lucien Fernand, MBA; French civil servant and international organization official; *Director-General, World Trade Organization;* b. 8 April 1947, Levallois-Perret (Seine); m. Geneviève Luchaire 1972; three s. *Education:* Lycée Carnot, Paris, Ecole des Hautes Etudes Commerciales, Paris, Inst. d'Etudes Politiques, Ecole Nationale d'Admin. Paris. *Career:* Lt-Commdr (navy); served in Inspection Générale des Finances 1975–79; Sec.-Gen. Mayoux Cttee 1979; Deputy Sec.-Gen., then Sec.-Gen. Interministerial Cttee for the Remodelling of Industrial Structures (CIASI) Treasury Dept 1979–81; Tech. Adviser, then Deputy Dir Office of the Minister for Econ. and Financial Affairs 1981–82; Deputy Dir Office of the Prime Minister (Pierre Mauroy) 1983–84; Chef de Cabinet to Pres. of Comm. of EC (Jacques Delors) 1984–94; Dir Gen. and mem. Exec. Cttee Crédit Lyonnais 1994–99; Commr for Trade, European Comm. 1999–2004; Pres. Asscn 'Notre Europe' 2004–; Assoc. Prof. Institut d'Etudes Politiques, Paris 2004–; Dir Gen. WTO 2005–; Officier, Légion d'honneur 1990, Kt Commdr's Cross (Badge and Star) of the Order of Merit (Germany) 1991, Commdr Order of Merit (Luxembourg) 1995, Officer of the Order of Merit (Gabon) 2000, Order of the Aztek Eagle (Mexico) 2003, Order of Merit (Chile) 2004; Dr hc (Louvain) 2003. *Publications:* Report on Welfare Assistance for Children (co-author) 1979, Report on "Monde-

Europe" (XI Plan of the Commissariat Général au Plan) 1993, L'Europe en première ligne 2002, L'Europe de nos volontés (co-author) 2002, La démocratie monde 2004.
Address: Office of the Director-General, World Trade Organization, Centre William Rappard, rue de Lausanne 154, 1211 Geneva, Switzerland (office); Les Annonciades, le Boisgeloup, 27140 Gisors, Belgium (home). *Telephone:* (22) 7395111 (office). *Fax:* (22) 7314206 (office). *E-mail:* enquiries@wto .org (office). *Website:* www.wto.org (office).

LANC, Erwin, LLB; Austrian politician and banker; *President, International Institute for Peace;* b. 17 May 1930, Vienna; m. 1st Melitta Fröhlich (died 1983); m. 2nd Christiane Karen Maria Krammer 1990; one s. one d. *Career:* mem. Socialist Party 1948–; with Fed. Ministry of Social Admin. 1949–55; Nat. Sec. Austrian Youth Hostels Asscn 1955–59; mem. Diet and Municipal Council of Vienna 1960–66; mem. Special Cttee for Examination of Vienna Public Transport Co. 1961, Chair. 1964; Man. Information Bureau for Communal Financing 1965; mem. Parl. 1966–83; Pres. Viennese Workers' Asscn for Sport and Physical Culture (ASKO) 1968–82; Minister of Transport 1973–77, of Interior 1977–83, of Foreign Affairs 1983–84; Man. Bank Austria, Vienna; Man. Handelsbank AG, Vienna 1985–93; Chair. Bd of Advisers ICD-Austria 1985–96; mem. Exec. Cttee Austrian Socialist Party 1977–91; Pres. Int. Handball Fed. 1984–2000; Pres. Int. Inst. for Peace 1988–; Grosse Goldene Ehrenzeichen (Austria), Grosse Verdienstkreuz (Germany), Grand Officier, Légion d'honneur and numerous other decorations. *Publications:* Volksaktie ohne make-up 1960, Gemeinden und Kapitalmarkt 1967, Sozialdemokratie i.d. Krise 1996.
Address: International Institute for Peace, Möllwaldplatz 5/2, 1040 Vienna (office); Feldkellergasse 70, 1130 Vienna, Austria (home). *Telephone:* (1) 5046437 (office); (1) 8049965 (home). *Fax:* (1) 5053236 (office); (1) 8049965 (home). *E-mail:* secretariat@iip.at (office). *Website:* www.iip.at (office).

LANCASTER, Carol J., PhD; American academic and fmr diplomatist; *Associate Professor and Director, Mortara Center for International Studies, Georgetown University;* b. 23 Aug. 1942, Washington, DC; m. Curtis Farrar 1980; one s. *Education:* Georgetown Univ., Washington, DC and London School of Econs, UK. *Career:* Budget Examiner, Office of Man. and Budget 1972–76; mem. Policy Planning Staff, Dept of State 1977–89, Deputy Asst Sec. of State for Africa 1980–81; Dir of African Studies, Georgetown Univ. 1981–89, Asst Prof. 1989–93; Deputy Admin. USAID 1993–96; Asst Prof., School of Foreign Service, Georgetown Univ. 1996–98, Assoc. Prof. and Dir MSc in Foreign Service 1999-2002, Dir African Studies Program and Assoc Prof., School of Foreign Service 2004–05, Dir Mortara Center for Int. Studies and Assoc Prof. 2005–; Visiting Fellow, Center for Global Devt 2002–03; Visiting Fellow, Inst. for Int. Econs 1987–91; IREX Exchanges with USSR Acad. of Sciences 1986, 1988; Fulbright Fellowship, Bolivia 1964–65, Montegu Burton Fellowship, LSE 1966–68, Congressional Fellowship 1976–77, Davidson Sommers Fellowship, Overseas Devt Council 1992–93. *Publications include:* African Debt and Financing 1986, US Aid to Africa 1988, Economic Reform in Africa 1989.
Address: Mortara Center for Interntional Studies, Georgetown University, 3600 N Street, NW, Washington, DC 20057 (office); 1727 S Street, NW, Washington, DC 20009, USA. *Telephone:* (202) 687-8171 (office); (202) 234-2915. *Fax:* (202) 687-5116 (office); (202) 234-2915. *E-mail:* lancastc@ georgetown.edu (office). *Website:* mortara.georgetown.edu (office).

LANCRY, Yehuda; Israeli diplomatist; b. 25 Sept. 1947, Bujad, Morocco; m.; two s. *Education:* Univ. of Haifa, Univ. of Nice, France. *Career:* served in Israel Defense Forces 1966–70, airplane mechanic in Israel Air Force; Head, Documentary and Film Publs Dept, Authority for Defence Tech. 1980–83; Mayor of Shlomi 1983–92; Guest Lecturer in French Literature, Haifa Univ. 1988–92; Head, Public Council, Israel TV and Radio (Channel Two) 1991; Amb. to France 1992–95; mem. Knesset (Parl.) 1996–99; Perm. Rep. to UN, New York 1999–2002; Co-Chair. High-level France-Israel Group, Ministry of Foreign Affairs 2003–; Commdr, Légion d'honneur. *Publications:* Michel Butor ou la résistance 1994, Trêves et rêves (with Michel Butor and Henri Maccheroni) 1996.
Address: c/o Ministry of Foreign Affairs, Hakirya, Romema, Jerusalem 91950, Israel. *Telephone:* 2-5303111. *Fax:* 2-5303367. *E-mail:* feedback@ mfa.gov.il. *Website:* www.mfa.gov.il.

LANDABURU ILLARRAMENDI, Eneko; Spanish international organiza-tion official; *Director-General for External Relations, European Commis-sion;* b. 11 March 1948, Paris; m. Dominique Rambaud 1971; two s. one d. *Education:* Univ. of Paris, France. *Career:* mem. staff Admin. and Financial Man. Dept, Société Labaz, Paris 1971–73, Asst to Man. Belgian subsidiary SA Labaz NV, Brussels 1973–75; Head of Study and Lecture Programmes, Centre Européen d'Etudes et d'Information sur les Sociétés Multinationales (CEEIM), Brussels 1975–79; PSOE Deputy, Spanish

Basque Regional Parl. 1980–81; Adviser to Latin American Dept, Nestlé, Vevey, Switzerland 1981–82; Dir Institut de Recherche sur les Multi-nationales (IRM), Geneva, Switzerland 1983–86; Dir-Gen. for Regional Politics, EC Comm., Brussels 1986–2000, for Enlargement (later External Relations) 2000–; Lecturer, Institut d'Etudes Européennes, Free Univ. of Brussels 1990–94; Alt. mem. Bd of Dirs of EIB 1993–; mem. Supervisory Bd European Investment Fund FEI-EIF 1994–; mem. Bd of Dirs Fondation 'Notre Europe' 1996–.
Address: Office Char 15/119, 1049 Brussels (office); Avenue Brugmann 125, 1190 Brussels, Belgium (home). *Telephone:* (2) 295-19-68 (office). *Fax:* (2) 299–32–19 (office). *E-mail:* eneko.landaburu@cec.eu.int (office).

LANDAU, Uzi, PhD; Israeli politician and systems analyst; b. 1943, Haifa; m.; three c. *Education:* Haifa Technion, Mass. Inst. of Tech., USA. *Career:* served as a paratrooper officer during mil. service; mem. Knesset (Likud Party) 1984–, Chair. Foreign Affairs and Defense Cttee, State Control Cttee; Knesset Observer at the European Council; mem. Israeli Del. to Madrid Peace Conf.; Observer at the European Council; Minister of Public Security 2001–03; fmr Minister in charge of overseeing the intelligence services and the US–Israel strategic dialogue in the Prime Minister's Office; Dir-Gen. Ministry of Transport; Lecturer, Technion, Israel Inst. of Tech., Haifa; mem. Bd El-Al Airlines, Israel Port Authority, Israel Airport Authority, Soc. for the Protection of Nature, Si'ah Vasig (Israel Debating Soc.). *Publications:* articles in professional journals on transport planning, articles in the press on foreign policy, strategic and security affairs.
Address: The Knesset, Jerusalem 91181, Israel (office). *Telephone:* (2) 6753868 (office). *E-mail:* klandau@knesset.gov.il (office). *Website:* www .knesset.gov.il (office).

LANDSBERGIS, Vytautas, (Jonas Zemkalnis); Lithuanian politician, musicologist, pianist and fmr head of state; b. 18 Oct. 1932, Kaunas; m. Grazina Ručyte; one s. two d. *Education:* J. Gruodis School of Music, Kaunas, Aušra Gymnasium, Kaunas, Lithuanian Acad. of Music, Vilnius. *Career:* Teacher of Piano and Prof. of Musicology, Vilnius Conservatoire, Vilnius Pedagogical Inst.; fmr mem. Exec. Council and Secr. Composers' Union; Pres. M.K. Čiurlionis Soc.; mem. various arts and science bodies; elected to Initiative Group, Sajūdis Reform Movt, then to Sajūdis Seimas (Ass.) and Council 1988, Pres. Sajūdis Seimas Council 1988–90, Hon. Pres. Sajūdis Dec. 1991–; f. Lithuanian Conservative Party, Chair. 1993–2003; elected Deputy to USSR Congress of People's Deputies 1989–90; elected to Supreme Council of Lithuania Feb. 1990, Pres. Supreme Council (Head of State) 1990–91; mem. Seimas (Parl.) 1992–2004, Leader of Parl. Opposition 1992–96, Pres. Seimas 1996–2000; cand. for presidential elections 1997; mem. European Parl. 2004–; Paul Harris Fellow (Rotary) 1991; Academi-cian, Lithuanian Catholic Acad. 1997; gave concert at Moscow Con-servatoire with Russian Nat. Acad. Symphonic Orchestra 1999; piano recitals in Calw, Hanover, Helsinki, Kwangjou, Moscow, New York, Paris, Tokyo, Trieste, Usedom, Vilnius, Warsaw, etc.; Hon. Fellow, Univ. of Cardiff, UK 2000; Hon. Citizen of Turin, Italy 2007; Grand Officer, European St Sebastian's Order of Kts 1995, Chevalier, Légion d'Honneur 1997, Order of Grand Duke Vytautas, First Class (Lithuania) 1998, Grand Cross, Royal Norwegian Order of Merit 1998, Grand Cross Order of the Repub. (Poland) 1999, Order of Merit (Grand Cross), Order of Malta 1999, Grand-Croix Ordre Honneur (Greece) 1999, Pléiade Ordre de la Francophonie (France) 2000, Three Stars Order (Second Class) (Latvia) 2001, Order of the Cross of St Mary's Land (First Class) (Estonia) 2002, Constitutional Medallion of Saxonian Parl. (Germany) 2003, Robert Schuman Medal, European Parl. 2005, Mérite Européen Medal (Luxem-bourg) 2006; Hon. LLD (Loyola Univ., Chicago) 1991; Hon. PhD (Vytautas the Great Univ., Kaunas) 1992, (Klaipėda Univ., Lithuania) 1997; Hon. HD (Weber Univ., USA) 1992; Hon. DIur (Lithuanian Acad. of Law) 2000; Dr hc (Helsinki) 2000, (Sorbonne) 2001, (Lithuanian Acad. of Art) 2003, (St Lucas Acad., Netherlands-Germany) 2004; Lithuanian State Award (for monograph on M. K. Čiurlionis) 1975; Norwegian People's Peace Prize (for role in restoration of Lithuanian independence; has used prize to establish Landsbergis Foundation to help disabled children and young musicians) 1991, Award of France Fund of Future 1991, Hermann-Ehlers Prize 1992, Catalan Ramon Llull IX Int. Prize 1994, Vibo Valentia Testimony Prize (Italy) 1998, Truman-Reagan Freedom Award (USA) 1999, Lithuanian Foundation Award 2004, Aschaffenburger Mutig-Preis, Germany 2004. *Recording:* Čiurlionis, Born of the Human Soul (works for solo piano) 1998. *Publications:* 23 books on musicology, art and music history (especially on artist and composer M. K. Čiurlionis) and politics, including M. K. Čiurlionis – Time and Content 1992, Lithuania Independent Again 2000; numerous edns of scores (mostly of works by M. K. Čiurlionis); M. K. Čiurlionis – Thoughts, Pictures, Music (film script) 1965; poetry collections: Intermezzo 1991, Intermezzo non finito 2004, Who Are We? (under pseudonym Jonas Zemkalnis) 2004, Glimmers of History 2006, It's Serious, Children (poems) 2006, memoirs, essays, Un peuple sort de prison 2007.

Address: Traidenio Street 34–15, Vilnius 08116, Lithuania (office); European Parliament, Bâtiment Altiero Spinelli, 11E157, 60 rue Wiertz, 1047 Brussels, Belgium. *Telephone:* (52) 663676 (office); (52) 724466 (home); (2) 284-55-50 (Brussels). *Fax:* (52) 663675 (office); (52) 790505 (home); (2) 284-95-50 (Brussels). *E-mail:* vyland@lrs.lt (office); vytautas .landsbergis@europarl.europa.eu (office). *Website:* www.landsbergis.lt (office); europarl.europa.eu (office).

LANDYMORE, Peter; British diplomatist; *Permanent Representative, United Nations Educational, Scientific and Cultural Organization (UNESCO); Career:* Counsellor (Devt), Perm. Mission to EU, Brussels –2006, Amb. and Perm. Rep. to UNESCO, Paris 2007–.
Address: UK Permanent Delegation to UNESCO, Maison de l'UNESCO, Bureau M3.06, 1 rue Miollis, 75732 Paris Cedex 15, France (office). *Telephone:* 1-45-68-27-84 (office). *Fax:* 1-47-83-27-77 (office). *E-mail:* peter .landymore@fco.gov.uk (office); dl.united-kingdom@unesco.org (office). *Website:* erc.unesco.org (office).

LANG, Rein, LLM; Estonian politician; *Minister of Justice;* b. 4 July 1957, Tartu; one d. *Education:* Tartu State Univ. *Career:* previous positions include Deputy Man. Linnahall arena, Deputy Dir Muusik club, Chair., then Head Supervisory Council, Trio media co.; apptd Deputy Mayor of Tallinn 2001; mem. Tallinn City Council 2002; founding mem. Reform Party; mem. Parl. 2003–, First Deputy Speaker –2005; Minister of Foreign Affairs 2005, of Justice 2005–; mem. Rotary Club of Tallinn; Commdr Ordre Nat. (France) 2004, Order of the White Star (2nd class) 2006; Estonian Police Award (2nd class) 2003.
Address: Ministry of Justice, Tõnismägi 5a, Tallinn 15191, Estonia (office). *Telephone:* 620-8100 (office). *Fax:* 620-8109 (office). *E-mail:* rein.lan@just .ee (office); rein@kuku.ee (home). *Website:* www.just.ee (office); www.lang .ee (home).

LANGA, Bheki Winston Joshua; South African diplomatist; *Ambassador to Russia;* b. Stengo. *Education:* Pie- khan ov State Inst. of Agric., Moscow. *Career:* joined ANC 1974; worked at Dept of Econ. Devt and Tourism; fmr Dir Nat. Inst. for Econ. Policy; Amb. to Russia 2006–.
Address: Embassy of South Africa, 123001 Moscow, Granatny per. 1/9, Russia (office). *Telephone:* (495) 540-11-77 (office). *Fax:* (495) 540-11-78 (office). *E-mail:* southafrica@embassy-moscow.ru (office). *Website:* saembassy.ru (office).

LANGDALE, Mark, BBA, LLB; American diplomatist and business executive; b. 1954; m.; two c. *Education:* Univ. of Texas and Univ. of Houston School of Law. *Career:* practised law in Houston, Tex. for ten years; Pres. Posadas USA, Inc. (US subsidiary of Grupo Posadas) 1989–2005, mem. Bd Dirs Grupo Posadas 1992–2004; Co-founder CapRock Communications Corpn; Chair. Texas Dept of Econ. Devt 1997; Amb. to Costa Rica 2005–08; mem. Young Presidents Org. (YPO) 1992–2004; YPO Legacy Award 2004.
Address: US Department of State, 2201 C Street NW, Washington, DC 20520, USA (office). *Telephone:* (202) 647-4000 (office). *Fax:* (202) 647-6738 (office). *Website:* www.state.gov (office).

LANGER, Ivan, MD, MCL; Czech politician; *Minister of the Interior;* b. 1 Jan. 1967, Olomouc; m. Markéta Vobořilová; one s. one d. *Education:* Univ. of Palacký, Charles Univ., Prague. *Career:* Secr. Ministry for Justice of Czech Repub. 1993–96; mem. Council Olomouc 1994; mem. of Civic Democratic Party (ODS), Vice-Chair. 1998–2002, 2004–; mem. Parl. 1996–; Shadow Minister of the Interior 1999–2002; Vice-Chair. Chamber of Deputies (Parl.) 1998–2006; Minister of the Interior June–Oct. 2006 (resgnd), reinstated Jan. 2007–, of Information 2007; Hon. mem. Maltese Order of Help 1994–. *Publications:* Rational Anti-drug Policy, After the Velvet Revolution.
Address: Ministry of the Interior, Nad štolou 3, Prague 7, 170 34 Czech Republic (office). *Telephone:* 974811111 (office). *Fax:* 261433552 (office). *E-mail:* langer@psp.cz (office); posta@mvcr.cz (office). *Website:* www .langer.cz; www.mvcr.cz (office).

LANGTON, Col Christopher, OBE; British defence specialist and fmr army officer; *Senior Fellow for Conflict and Defence Diplomacy, International Institute for Strategic Studies (IISS); Career:* served in British Army for 32 years, posts in Northern Ireland, Russia, CIS; held attaché posts Russia, South Caucasus, Central Asia; fmr Deputy Chief UN Observer Mission in Georgia; mem. IISS staff 2001–, fmr Head of Defence Analysis Dept, currently Sr Fellow for Conflict and Defence Diplomacy. *Publications:* The Military Balance (ed.), four edns 2001–05.
Address: International Institute for Strategic Studies (IISS), Arundel House, 13–15 Arundel Street, Temple Place, London, WC2R 3DX, England (office). *Telephone:* (20) 7379-7676 (office). *Fax:* (20) 7836-3108 (office). *E-mail:* langton@iiss.org (office). *Website:* www.iiss.org (office).

LAOHAPHAN, Khunying Laxanachantorn; Thai diplomatist. *Career:* joined Foreign Ministry 1972, serving in several positions including in Dept of Econ. Affairs, Embassy in Rome as Alternate Rep. to FAO and IFAA, Dept of Int. Orgs, UN in NY as Alternate Rep. to Security Council, and Dept of ASEAN Affairs; Amb. to Australia 1994–2000; Dir-Gen. Dept of Int. Orgs, Geneva 2000, then Deputy Perm. Sec. of Ministry –2003, Perm. Rep. to UN, Geneva 2003–04, Perm. Rep. to UN, New York 2004–07; mem. Bd of Dirs Int. Inst. for Sustainable Devt (IISD) 2003–; Chair. G-77 Chapter, Geneva 2003.
Address: c/o Ministry of Foreign Affairs Thanon Sri Ayudhya, Bangkok 10400, Thailand. *Telephone:* (2) 643-5000. *Fax:* (2) 225-6155. *E-mail:* information@mfa.go.th. *Website:* www.mfa.go.th.

LAOUROU, Grégoire; Benin politician. *Career:* Pres. Council of Ministers, W African Econ. and Monetary Union (UEMOA); Minister of Finance and the Economy 2003–05.
Address: c/o Ministry of Finance and the Economy, BP 302, Cotonou, Benin (office).

LAPIDOTH, Ruth, PhD; Israeli professor of international law; *Fellow, Jerusalem Center for Public Affairs;* b. 1930, Eschelbacher, Germany. *Education:* Hebrew Univ. of Jerusalem, Institut des Hautes Etudes Int., Paris, France. *Career:* immigrated to Palestine 1938; Lecturer on Int. Law, Law of the Sea and Arab–Israeli conflict, Hebrew Univ. of Jerusalem 1956–2001, Dir Inst. of European Studies 1994–96, Bessie and Michael Greenblatt Prof. of Int. Law –2001, now Prof. Emer.; Sr Research Fellow, Jerusalem Inst. for Israel Studies; Prof. of Int. Law, School of Law, Coll. of Man. Academic Studies 2001–, fmr Chair. Concord Research Center; fmr Visiting Prof. or Fellow, Univ. of Paris, Woodrow Wilson Center, Washington, DC, New York Univ. School of Law, Center for the Study of Marine Policy, Univ. of Delaware, Univ. of Geneva, Bellagio Study and Conf. Centre, Univ. of Southern California, Tulane and Northwestern Univs, Duke Univ. School of Law, US Inst. of Peace, Georgetown Univ. Law Center, St Antony's Coll., Oxford, Inst. of Public Law and Int. Relations of Thessaloniki, Ludwig-Maxmilians Univ., Munich, Univ. of Melbourne; Chair. Editorial Bd Israel Law Review 1984–86, Univs Study Group of Middle Eastern Affairs 1985–89; mem. Israeli Del. to UN 1976, Humanitarian Law Conf. 1977, Red Cross Conf. 1981; participated in negotiations for Peace Treaty between Israel and Egypt 1979; Legal Adviser to Israeli Ministry of Foreign Affairs 1979–81; mem. Arbitration Panel, boundary dispute in Taba area 1986–88; mem. Perm. Court of Arbitration 1989–, Expert Group, High Commr on Nat. Minorities, OSCE 1999; Fellow, Jerusalem Center for Public Affairs; Prominent Woman in Int. Law Award, WILIG Group, American Soc. of Int. Law 2000, Gass Award 2001, Excellence in Research Award, Israel Bar Asscn 2004. *Publications:* nine books and more than 90 articles on int. law, the law of the sea, human rights, the Arab–Israeli conflict and its resolution, and Jerusalem.
Address: c/o Jerusalem Center for Public Affairs, Beit Milken, 13 Tel Hai Street, Jerusalem 92107, Israel. *Telephone:* 2-5619281. *Fax:* 2-5619112. *Website:* www.jcpa.org.

LAPLI, Father Sir John Ini, Kt, DipLicTheol; Solomon Islands government official and Anglican priest; b. June 1955; m. Helen Lapli 1985; three s. one d. *Education:* Selwyn Coll., Guadalcanal, St John's Theological Coll., Auckland, New Zealand. *Career:* tutor Theological Coll., Auckland 1982–83; teacher Catechist School, Rural Training Centre 1985; Parish Priest 1986; Bible Translator 1987–88; Premier of Temotu Prov. 1988–99; Gov.-Gen. of Solomon Is July 1999–2004; Order of St Michael and St George; Order of Propitious Clouds with Special Grand Cordon (ROC).
Address: Luepe Village, Graciosa Bay, c/o Lata Post Office, Temotu Province, Solomon Islands (home). *Telephone:* 53111 (home).

LARA-PEÑA, Erasmo, MA; Dominican Republic diplomatist and academic; *Permanent Representative, United Nations;* b. 26 Nov. 1947; m.; three c. *Education:* Columbia Univ., Catholic Univ. of America, Universidad Autonoma de Santo Domingo. *Career:* Lecturer, Dept of Educ., State Univ. of Dominican Repub. 1974–80; worked in UN Secr. 1981–2005, served in Kenya, Israel, Lebanon, Jordan; fmr positions include Regional Dir, UN Electoral Observation Mission in Nicaragua, Chief of Training Mission, Angola, Deputy Chief, UN Training Services; Perm. Rep. to UN, New York 2005–; Dir Dominican Center for Peace. *Publications:* several books; articles for newspapers.
Address: Office of the Permanent Representative of Dominican Republic to the United Nations, 144 East 44th Street, 4th Floor, New York, NY 10017, USA (office). *Telephone:* (212) 867-0833 (office). *Fax:* (212) 986-4694 (office). *E-mail:* drun@un.int (office). *Website:* www.un.int/dr (office).

LARIJANI, Ali Ardashir, BSc, MS, PhD; Iranian politician; *Speaker, Majlis-e-Shura-e Islami (Parliament);* b. 1958, Najaf, Iraq. *Education:* Sharif Univ., Tehran Univ. *Career:* began career after 1979 revolution as dir of state TV;

served in sr positions at Ministry of Revolutionary Guards, including Deputy Minister; Minister of Culture and Islamic Guidance 1992–94; Head Islamic Repub. of Iran Broadcasting 1994–2004; Sec. Shura-ye Ali-ye Amniyyat-e Melli (Supreme Nat. Security Council) (one of two reps of Supreme Leader of Iran, Ayatollah Khamenei) 2005–07 (resgnd), roles included chief nuclear negotiator; Speaker Majilis-e-Shura-e Islami (Parliament) 2008–; presidential cand. 2005.
Address: Office of the Speaker, Majlis-e-Shura-e Islami (Parliament), Tehran, Iran. *E-mail:* info@abadgaran.ir (office). *Website:* www.abadgaran.ir (office).

LAROCCO, James A., MA; American diplomatist; *Director General, Sinai Multinational Force and Observers;* b. Chicago, Ill.; m. Janet Larocco; three c. *Education:* Univ. of Portland, Johns Hopkins School of Advanced Int. Studies. *Career:* entered Foreign Service 1973; staff Asst Office of Congressional Relations, State Dept; Commercial Attaché, Jeddah 1975–77; Econ. Officer, Cairo 1978–81; Econ. Section Chief Kuwait 1981–83; Deputy Dir, Office of Pakistan, Afghanistan and Bangladesh Affairs, Near East Asia Bureau 1984; Minister-Counsellor for Econ. Affairs, Beijing; Kuwait Task Force Co-ordinator, State Operations Center, Operation Desert Storm 1990; Deputy Dir American Inst. in Taiwan 1991; Deputy Chief of Mission, Tel-Aviv 1993; Amb. to Kuwait 1996–2001; Prin. Deputy Asst Sec. Bureau of Near Eastern Affairs, Dept of State 2001–; Dir Gen. Sinai Multinational Force and Observers (ind. (non-UN) peacekeeping mission) 2004–; Congressional Fellowship 1983.
Fax: (2) 4156796. *E-mail:* Email@mfo.org. *Website:* www.mfo.org.

LARRAIN, Juan, BA; Chilean diplomatist; *Expert Adviser, United Nations Security Council Counter Terrorism Committee Executive Directorate;* b. 29 Aug. 1941, Santiago; m. Mariel Cruchaga Belaunde; four c. *Education:* German School and Mil. Acad., Chile, Univ. of Chile, Diplomatic Acad., Ministry of Foreign Affairs. *Career:* Asst Prof. School of Journalism, Catholic Univ. of Chile 1964–65; Prof. of Contemporary History Diplomatic Acad., Ministry of Foreign Affairs and Ed. Diplomacia (publ. of Acad.) 1978–79; Deputy Chief of Mission, OAS 1983–87, London 1988–90, Head First Commercial Mission to Ireland 1991, Deputy Dir Multilateral Econ. Affairs 1991–92, Consul-Gen. New York 1992–94, Deputy Perm. Rep. to UN 1994–99, Perm. Rep. 1999–2001, also Deputy Perm. Rep. to UN Security Council 1996–97; fmr Head Monitoring Mechanism for Angola; Expert Adviser UN Security Council Counter Terrorism Cttee Exec. Directorate 2003–.
Address: United Nations, 405 Lexington Avenue, Room 5075, New York, NY 10174 (office); 66 Mallard Drive, Greenwich, CT 06830, USA (home). *Telephone:* (212) 457-1078 (office); (203) 629-6075 (home). *Fax:* (212) 457-4041 (office); (203) 629-2855 (home). *E-mail:* larrain@un.org (office); december79@aol.com (home).

LARSON, Charles W., Jr, BA, JD; American lawyer, politician and diplomatist; *Ambassador to Latvia;* m.; two s. *Education:* Univ. of Iowa, Univ. Coll. of Law. *Career:* asst co. attorney, Jones Co., Ia 1997–99; Gen. Counsel, ESCO Group, Marion, Ia (tech. services firm) 1999–2006; mem. Iowa House of Reps 1993–2001, Chair. Judiciary Cttee, Econ. Devt Cttee; Chair. Iowa Republican Party 2001–05; Iowa State Senator 2003–07; Amb. to Latvia 2008–; Founding Pnr, Lincoln Strategies Group, West Des Moines, Ia; apptd by Pres. George W. Bush to Pres.'s Advisory Comm. for Drug Free Communities 2003; Maj. in US Army Reserves, served for one year in Iraq during Operation Iraqi Freedom, stationed in LSA Anaconda, in charge of command's legal affairs and humanitarian missions, flew more than 50 combat missions as a CH-47 'Chinook' helicopter door gunner; Bronze Star for meritorious service in combat, Combat Action Badge. *Publication:* Heroes Among Us (ed.) 2008.
Address: US Embassy, Raiņa bulv. 7, Rīga 1510, Latvia (office). *Telephone:* 703-6200 (office). *Fax:* 782-0047 (office). *E-mail:* ambassador-riga@state.gov (office); pas@usembassy.lv (office). *Website:* riga.usembassy.gov (office).

LATHA REDDY, Vijaya, BA, MA; Indian diplomatist; *Ambassador to Thailand;* b. 5 April 1951, Madras. *Education:* Women's Christian Coll., Bangalore Univ. *Career:* joined Ministry of External Affairs 1975, overseas postings include Embassies in Lisbon, Washington, DC, Kathmandu and Brasilia, Consul Gen. in Durban 1994–97, Deputy Chief of Mission, Embassy in Vienna 1997–2000; Head of Admin. Div., Ministry of External Affairs 2000–03; Amb. to Portugal 2003–06, to Thailand 2007–.
Address: Embassy of India, 46 Soi Prasarnmitr, 23 Thanon Sukhumvit, Bangkok 10110, Thailand (office). *Telephone:* (2) 258-0300 (office). *Fax:* (2) 258-4627 (office). *E-mail:* indiaemb@mozart.inet.co.th (office). *Website:* indianembassy.gov.in/bangkok (office).

LATHEEF, Mohamed, MA, PhD; Maldivian diplomatist, politician and civil servant; m.; three c. *Education:* Univ. of Wales, UK, postgraduate studies in Cardiff Univ., Wales. *Career:* mem. and Deputy Speaker People's Special Majlis (Ass.) 1979–97; Dir-Gen. Maldives Centre for Man. and Admin 1992–93; Nat. Dir Project for Public Admin. Reform 1992–93; Deputy Minister, Ministry of Atolls Admin 1993; Minister of Educ. 1993–2002; Vice-Chair. Nat. Educ. Council 1993–2002; mem. Parl. 2000–02; held posts at Ministry of Foreign Affairs and Embassy in Sri Lanka; Amb. to USA Feb. 2002–; Chargé d'affaires a.i., Perm. Mission of Maldives to UN Sept.–Nov. 2002, Perm. Rep. to UN Nov. 2002–08.
Address: c/o Ministry of Foreign Affairs, Boduthakurufaanu Magu, Malé 20-307, Maldives (office).

LATUSHKA, Pavel P., LLB; Belarusian diplomatist; *Ambassador to Poland;* b. 1973, Minsk. *Education:* Belarus State Univ. *Career:* fmr legal Adviser to Govt; Attaché, Ministry of Foreign Affairs 1995–96, Vice-Consul, Poland 1996–2000, Press Sec. and Chief of Information Office, Ministry of Foreign Affairs 2000–02, Amb. to Poland 2002–.
Address: Embassy of Belarus, 022-952 Warsaw, ul. Wiertnicza 58, Poland (office). *Telephone:* (22) 7420990 (office). *Fax:* (22) 7420980 (office). *E-mail:* poland@belembassy.org (office). *Website:* www.belembassy.org/poland (office).

LATYPAW, Ural Ramdrakovich, LLD; Belarusian (b. Bashkir) politician; *Head of Presidential Administration;* b. 28 Feb. 1951, Katayevo, Bashkir ASSR; m.; one s. one d. *Education:* Kazan State Univ., State and Law Inst., USSR Acad. of Sciences, Higher KGB courses in Minsk. *Career:* researcher for KGB, involvement in anti-terrorist measures, latterly Deputy Chief, Educational and Research Centre, Minsk 1974–98; retd from mil. (rank of Col) 1993; Jt Founder, Head, Deputy Head for Research and Science, Research Inst. for Devt and Security, Repub. of Belarus 1993–94; Asst on int. affairs to Belarus Pres. 1994–95, Chief Asst to Pres. 1995–98; Minister of Foreign Affairs 1998–99; Deputy Prime Minister and Minister of Foreign Affairs 1999–2000; State Sec. Feb.–Sept. 2001; Head of Presidential Admin Sept. 2001–; mem. Belarus and Russian Asscns of Int. Law. *Publications:* Legislative Problems in Combating Terrorism; articles on legislative, nat. and int. security issues.
Address: Office of the President, vul. K. Marksa 38, Dom Urada, 220016 Minsk, Belarus. *Telephone:* (17) 222-60-06.

LATYSHEV, Col-Gen. Pyotr Mikhailovich; Russian politician and security officer; *Representative of President to Urals Federal District;* b. 30 Aug. 1948, Khmelnitsky, Ukraine; m.; two s. *Education:* Omsk Higher School of Ministry of Internal Affairs, Acad. of Ministry of Internal Affairs. *Career:* inspector, then Head Perm Div. for Fight against Econ. Crime 1970–86; Head Dept of Internal Affairs Perm Oblast 1986–91; Head Dept of Internal Affairs, Krasnodar Territory 1991–94; Deputy Minister of Internal Affairs, Russian Fed. 1994–2000; Rep. of Pres. to Urals Fed. Dist 2000–; People's Deputy of Russian Fed. 1990–93; mem. Cttee of Supreme Soviet on Law and Fight against Crime 1993; State orders.
Address: Office of the Plenipotentiary Representative of the President, Oktyabrskaya pl. 3, 620031 Yekaterinburg, Russia (office). *Telephone:* (3432) 77-18-96 (Yekaterinburg) (office); (495) 206-09-66 (Moscow).

LAUTENBERG, Alexei P., LicPolSc; Swiss diplomatist; *Ambassador to UK;* b. 1945, Zurich; m. Gabrielle Lautenberg. *Education:* Univs of Berne and Lausanne. *Career:* entered Ministry of Foreign Affairs 1974, service in Berne, Geneva and Stockholm, Deputy Head of Mission, Warsaw 1976–77, mem. Swiss Del. to EFTA and GATT, Geneva 1977–81, Econ. Counsellor, Bonn 1981–85, Deputy Dir Dept of Int. Orgs, Ministry of Foreign Affairs 1985–86, Head, Finance and Econ. Dept 1986–93, Head, Perm. Mission to EU, Brussels 1993–99, Amb. to Italy 2000–04, to UK 2004–.
Address: Embassy of Switzerland, 16–18 Montagu Place, London W1H 2BQ, England (office). *Telephone:* (20) 7616-6000 (office). *Fax:* (20) 7724-7001 (office). *E-mail:* vertretung@lon.rep.admin.ch (office). *Website:* www.swissembassy.org.uk (office).

LAVERDURE, Claude; Canadian diplomatist; m. Suzanne Bisson; three c. *Education:* Coll. André-Grasset, Montreal, Univ. of Montreal. *Career:* joined Dept of External Affairs 1965; overseas assignments in Brussels, Paris and Tunis; Amb. to Haiti 1986–88, to Zaire (concurrent accred. to Burundi, Rwanda and the Congo) 1989–92, to Belgium 1998–2000, to France 2003–07; sr positions with Dept of External Affairs include Fed. Coordinator for La Francophonie, Dir-Gen. of Human Resources, Asst Deputy Minister for Africa and Middle E, Asst Deputy Minister for Europe, Middle E and N Africa; Prime Minister's Personal Rep. to La Francophonie 1998–2000, to G-8 Summit 2002–03; Foreign Policy Adviser to Prime Minister, Privy Council Office 2000–02; Senior Fellow, Graduate School of Public and Int. Affairs, Univ. of Ottawa 2007–.
Address: Graduate School of Public and International Affairs, University of Ottawa, 55 Laurier Avenue East, Desmarais Building, Room 11101, Ottawa, Ontario, K1N 6N5, Canada (office). *Telephone:* (613) 562-5689

(office). *Fax:* (613) 562-5241 (office). *E-mail:* api@uOttawa.ca (office). *Website:* www.socialsciences.uottawa.ca (office).

LAVERTU, Gaëtan, BA, BSc, MA, MBA; Canadian diplomatist; b. 25 Jan. 1944, Saint-Hyacinthe, Quebec; m., two c. *Education:* Laval Univ., Univ. of Western Ont., Univ. of Quebec, École nationale d'administration publique. *Career:* served as Naval Reserve Officer; taught political science and econs in Quebec City; joined foreign service 1969, overseas posts include Third Sec. and Vice-Consul, Madrid 1971–72, Second Sec. and Vice-Consul, Rabat 1972–73, First Sec. and Consul, Caracas 1976–79, Counsellor, Mission to EC, Brussels 1979–82, Amb. to Colombia 1987–89, Deputy High Commr, London 1989–92, Amb. to FRG 1996–2000, to Mexico 2003–07; positions at Dept of Foreign Affairs and Int. Trade, Ottawa include UN Div. 1969, NATO and NORAD Div. 1970, Personnel Div. 1970–71, Fed. –Prov. Relations Div. 1975–76, Exec. Asst to Deputy Minister 1982–83, Dir of Intelligence Analysis 1983–85, Dir-Gen. Foreign Intelligence Bureau 1985–87, Asst Deputy Minister, Political and Security Affairs 1992–94, Assoc. Deputy Minister of Foreign Affairs 1994–96, Deputy Minister of Foreign Affairs 2000–03; Senior Fellow, Graduate School of Public and Int. Affairs, Univ. of Ottawa 2008–. *Address:* Graduate School of Public and International Affairs, University of Ottawa, 55 Laurier Avenue East, Desmarais Building, Room 11101, Ottawa, Ont., K1N 6N5, Canada (office). *Telephone:* (613) 562-5689 (office). *Fax:* (613) 562-5241 (office). *E-mail:* api@uOttawa.ca (office). *Website:* www.socialsciences.uottawa.ca (office).

LAVÍN, Joaquín; Chilean politician and economist; *Mayor of Santiago;* b. (Joaquín José Lavín Infante), 23 Oct. 1953, Santiago; m. María Estela León Ruiz; seven c. *Education:* Pontificia Univ. Católica de Chile, Univ. of Chicago. *Career:* econ. adviser, ODEPLAN (Ministry for Planning) 1975–77, Dean Faculty of Econ. and Admin. Sciences, Concepción Univ. 1979–81; Econ. Ed. El Mercurio 1986–88; fmr Sec.-Gen. UDI (Ind. Democratic Union); Dean Faculty of Econs and Business, Univ. del Desarrollo 1996–98; Mayor Las Condes 1992–96, 1996–2000; presidential cand. 1999, 2005; Mayor of Santiago 2000–; Founder La Vaca (NGO); mem. Opus Dei. *Publications:* Miguel Kast: Pasión de Vivir 1986, Chile Revolución Silenciosa 1987. *Address:* Partido Unión Demócrata Independiente, Suecia 286, Santiago, Chile (office). *E-mail:* joaquin@joaquinlavin.cl (office). *Website:* www.joaquinlavin.cl (office).

LAVROV, Sergei Viktorovich; Russian diplomatist and politician; *Minister of Foreign Affairs;* b. 21 March 1950, Moscow; m. Maria Lavrova; one d. *Education:* Moscow State Inst. of Int. Relations. *Career:* has served in diplomatic service since 1972; attaché, USSR Embassy in Sri Lanka 1972–76, Sec., Dept of Int. Econ. Orgs, Ministry of Foreign Affairs 1976–81, Sec. and Counsellor, Perm. Mission of USSR to UN, New York 1981–88; Deputy Chair., then Chair. Dept of Int. Econ. Relations, Ministry of Foreign Affairs 1988–90; Dir Dept of Int. Orgs and Global Problems, Ministry of Foreign Affairs of Russia 1990–92, Deputy Minister 1992–94, Perm. Rep. to UN, New York 1994–2004, Minister of Foreign Affairs 2004–; Order of Honour 1996; Order of Service to the Nation 1997. *Address:* Ministry of Foreign Affairs, 119200 Moscow, Smolenskaya-Sennaya pl. 32/34, Russia (office). *Telephone:* (095) 244-16-06 (office). *Fax:* (095) 230-21-30 (office). *E-mail:* ministry@mid.ru (office). *Website:* www.mid.ru (office).

LAYDEN, Anthony Michael; British diplomatist (retd); b. 27 July 1946; m. Josephine Layden; three s. one d. *Career:* joined British Diplomatic Service 1968, Desk Officer, Atomic Energy and Disarmament Dept, FCO 1968–69, Second Sec., Jedda 1971–73, Head of Chancery 1982–85, First Sec. and Head of Chancery, Rome 1973–77, Desk Officer, Middle East Dept 1977–79, Rhodesia Dept 1979–80, Personnel Operations Dept 1980–82, Deputy Head of Hong Kong Dept 1985–87, Deputy Head of Mission, Muscat 1987–91, Deputy Head of Mission and Counsellor, Copenhagen 1991–95, Head of W European Dept, FCO 1995–98, Amb. to Morocco 1999–2002, to Libya 2002–06. *Address:* c/o Foreign & Commonwealth Office, King Charles Street, London, SW1A 2AH, England. *Telephone:* (20) 7008-1500.

LAZAR, Boris, PhDr; Czech diplomatist; *Ambassador to Switzerland;* b. 29 Jan. 1946, Bratislava; m.; two s. *Education:* Univ. of Bratislava. *Career:* scientific researcher, Slovak Acad. of Sciences, Bratislava 1980–86; in exile, Munich 1986–90; Adviser to Ministry of the Interior, Czechoslovakia 1990–92, to Ministry of Foreign Affairs 1993–95; Envoy, Head of Mission in Berlin 1995–99; Adviser to Sec. of State and Head of EU Relations on accession of Czech Repub. 1999–2001; Amb. to Germany 2001–06, to Switzerland 2006–. *Address:* Embassy of the Czech Republic, Muristr. 53, Postfach 537, 3000 Bern 31, Switzerland (office). *Telephone:* 313504070 (office). *Fax:*

313504098 (office). *E-mail:* bern@embassy.mzv.cz (office). *Website:* www.mfa.cz/bern (office).

LAZARENKO, Pavlo Ivanovych, DEconSc; Ukrainian politician; b. 23 Jan. 1953, Karpivka, Dniepropetrovsk Region; m. Tamara Ivanivna Lazarenko; one s. two d. *Education:* Dniepropetrovsk Inst. of Agric. *Career:* worked as agronomist 1972–79, Chair. of Kolkhoz 1979–84, Head Dist Dept of Agric. Man.; First Deputy Chair. Dist Exec. Cttee; Chair. Council of Agro-Industrial Complex Dniepropetrovsk Region, First Deputy Chair. Regional Exec. Cttee; People's Deputy 1990–; Rep. of Pres. of Ukraine in Dniepropetrovsk Region 1992–95, concurrently Chair. Dniepropetrovsk Regional State Admin.; elected deputy of Verkhivna Rada (Ukrainian legislature) 1994; First Vice-Prime Minister of Ukraine 1995–96, Prime Minister of Ukraine 1996–97; elected to lead Unity faction in legislature 1997; Head Hromada (political movt); charged with corruption 1999, arrested in USA 2000, charges lifted by Parl. of Ukraine 2002, convicted by US jury of money-laundering and extortion June 2004. *Address:* c/o Hromada, Laboratornyi provylok 1, 01133, Kyiv, Ukraine (office).

LAZOVIĆ, Vujica, PhD; Montenegrin economist, academic and politician; *Deputy Prime Minister, responsible for Economic Policy;* b. 10 March 1963. *Education:* Univ. of Podgorica. *Career:* fmr mem. Faculty of Econs, Univ. of Montenegro; currently Prof. of Econs and Dean of Faculty of Econs, Univ. of Podgorica; Deputy Prime Minister, responsible for Econ. Policy 2007–. *Publications:* numerous books and articles on economics. *Address:* Ministry of Economic Development, 81000 Podgorica, Rimski trg 46, Montenegro (office). *Telephone:* (81) 234156 (office). *Fax:* (81) 234131 (office). *E-mail:* vujicalazovic@mn.yu (office). *Website:* www.gom.cg.yu (office).

LE BERNARD, Sissa; Central African Republic diplomatist. *Career:* currently Amb. to Democratic Repub. of Congo. *Address:* Embassy of the Central African Republic, 11 avenue Pumbu, BP 7769, Kinshasa, Democratic Republic of Congo (office). *Telephone:* (12) 30417 (office).

LE BLANC, Bart, PhD; Dutch banker; *Professor of Political Economy, University of Tilburg;* b. 4 Nov. 1946, Bois-le-Duc; m. Gérardine van Lanschot; one s. two d. *Education:* Leiden and Tilburg Univs. *Career:* Special Adviser, Prime Minister's Office, Deputy Sec. to Cabinet 1973–79; Deputy Dir-Gen. for Civil Service at Home Office 1979–80; Dir-Gen. for Budget at Treasury 1980–83; Deputy Chair. Man. Bd F. van Lanschot Bankiers NV, 's-Hertogenbosch 1983–91; Sec.-Gen. EBRD, London 1991–94, Vice-Pres., Finance 1994–98; Dir Int. Finance, Caisse des Dépôts et Consignations, Paris 1998–; Prof. of Political Economy Univ. of Tilburg 1991–; Hon. Prof. Tilburg Univ. 1991–; Kt, Order of Netherlands Lion. *Publications:* books and contribs on econ. and fiscal policy to nat. and int. journals. *Address:* University of Tilburg, Warandelaan 2, PO Box 90153, 5000 LE Tilburg, Netherlands.

LE PEN, Jean-Marie, LenD; French politician; *President, Front National;* b. 20 June 1928, La Trinité-sur-Mer, Morbihan; m. 1st Pierrette Lalanne, 1960 (divorced); three d.; m. 2nd Jeanne-Marie Paschos 1991. *Education:* Coll. des Jésuites Saint-François-Xavier, Vannes, Lycée de Lorient, Univ. de Paris. *Career:* Pres. Corpn des étudiants en droit de Paris 1949–51; Sub-Lt 1st foreign Bn of paratroopers, Indochina 1954–55; Political Ed. Caravelle 1955, Nat. Del. for Union de défense de la jeunesse française, then Deputy 1st Sector, La Seine; mem. Groupe d'union et de fraternité at Nat. Ass., independent Deputy for la Seine 1958–62; Gen. Sec. Front Nat. Combattant 1956, of Tixier Vignancour Cttee 1964–65; Dir Soc. d'études et de relations publiques 1963–; Pres. Front Nat. 1972–, Front Nat. Provence-Alpes-Côte d'Azur 1992–2000; mem. Nat. Ass. 1986–88; mem. European Parl. 1984–2000, Pres. groupe des droites européennes 1984–2000; presidential cand. 1988, 2002, 2007; guilty of physical assault and banned from holding or seeking public office for two years, given three-month suspended prison sentence April 1998; sentence on appeal: immunity removed by European Parl. Oct. 1998; Croix de la Valeur militaire. *Publications:* Les Français d'abord 1984, La France est de retour 1985, L'Espoir 1986, J'ai vu juste 1998. *Address:* Serp, 6 rue de Beaune, 75007 Paris (office); 8 parc de Montretout, 92210 St-Cloud, France (home).

LE PENSEC, Louis; French politician; *Senator;* b. 8 Jan. 1937, Mellac; m. Colette Le Guilcher 1963; one s. *Career:* Personnel Officer, Soc. nationale d'étude et de construction de moteurs d'aviation 1963–66, Soc. anonyme de véhicules industriels et d'équipements mécaniques 1966–69; Teacher of Personnel Man., Legal Sciences Teaching and Research Unit, Univ. of Rennes 1970–73; Mayor of Mellac 1971–97; Deputy (Finistère) to Nat. Ass.

1973–81, 1983–88, 1993; Councillor for Finistère 1976–, Senator 1998–; mem. Steering Cttee, Parti Socialiste 1977, Exec. Bureau 1979; Minister for the Sea 1981–83, 1988, of Overseas Depts and Territories 1988–93; Govt Spokesperson 1989–91; Vice-Pres. for Europe, Council of European Communities 1983–; Minister of Agric. and Fisheries 1997–98; Vice-Pres. County Council (Finistère) 1998–; Head ASEAN Mission for External Trade; mem. Senate Del. for EU 1999–; Vice-Pres. Council of European Municipalities and Regions 2007–; Commdr du Mérite maritime, du Mérite agricole; Order du Mérite (Côte d'Ivoire); Grand-croix du Royaume (Thailand). *Publication:* Ministre à Babord 1997.
Address: Hôtel du département, 32 quai Dupleix, 29196 Quimper Cedex (office); Sénat, 75291 Paris (office); Kerviguennou, 29300 Mellac, France (home). *Telephone:* (2) 98-76-20-24 (office); (2) 98-35-08-00 (home). *Fax:* (2) 98-76-21-96 (office); (2) 98-35-08-09 (home). *E-mail:* louis.le-pensec@wanadoo.fr (office).

LE ROY, Alain; French diplomatist and UN official; *Under-Secretary-General for Peacekeeping Operations, United Nations;* b. 5 Feb. 1953; m.; one s. *Education:* Ecole nationale supérieure des Mines, Paris, Paris 1 (Sorbonne) Univ. *Career:* early career as petroleum engineer for Total; with Sous-préfet d'Avallon 1991–92; Cabinet Chief, Ministry of Agric. 1992–93; Counsellor Cour des comptes 1993–95, 1995–99; Deputy to UN Special Co-ordinator for Sarajevo and Dir of Operations for restoration of essential public services March-Sept. 1995; UN Regional Admin. in Kosovo (W Region) 1999–2000; Nat. Co-ordinator for Stability Pact for South-East Europe, Ministry of Foreign Affairs 2000; fmr EU Special Rep. in the Fmr Yugoslav Repub. of Macedonia; fmr Asst Sec. for Econ. and Financial Affairs, Ministry for Foreign Affairs; fmr Amb. to Madagascar; Conseiller Maître, Cour des comptes and Amb. in charge of Union for Mediterranean Initiative 2007–08; UN Under-Sec.-Gen. for Peacekeeping Operations 2008–.
Address: Department of Peacekeeping Operations, United Nations, New York, NY 10017, USA (office). *Telephone:* (212) 963-1234 (office). *Fax:* (212) 963-4879 (office). *Website:* www.un.org/Depts/dpko/dpko (office).

LEAHY, Anne Suzanne Lucette, MA; Canadian diplomatist; *Special Advisor on Business Continuity to the Associate Deputy Minister of Foreign Affairs;* b. 18 Nov. 1952, Québec. *Education:* Ursulines de Québec, Queen's Univ., Kingston, Ont. and Univ. of Toronto. *Career:* joined diplomatic service 1973, mem. Mission to the EC 1974–76, mem. staff Embassy, Moscow 1980–82, Rep. to the Devt Assistance Cttee, Paris 1982–86, Dir of Personnel, External Affairs 1987–89, Amb. to Cameroon, Chad and Cen. African Repub. 1989–92, Dir-Gen. Policy and Planning Staff, External Affairs and Int. Trade Canada 1992; Amb. to Poland 1993–96, to Russian Fed. (also accred to Uzbekistan, Armenia and Belarus) 1996–99; Diplomat-in-Residence Centre for Int. and Security Studies, York Univ., Toronto 1999; Fed. Coordinator for World Youth Day 2002 2000–02; first Dir Institut d'études internationales de Montréal à l'UQAM 2002–04; Amb. to the Great Lakes Region of Africa 2004–07; Special Advisor on Business Continuity to the Assoc. Deputy Minister 2007–; mem. State Hermitage Foundation of Canada 1999–; Trustee Queen's Univ. 2000–; Order of Merit (Poland) 1996; Fondation Y des Femmes de Montréal Grand Prix Avancement de la Femme 2004. *Publications include:* L'éthique de l'intervention dans la politique étrangère canadienne: la responsabilité de protéger (contrib. to L'intervention armée peut-elle être juste?) 2007.
Address: Foreign Affairs and International Trade Canada, Lester B. Pearson Bldg, 125 Sussex Drive, Ottawa, ON K1A 0G2, Canada (office). *Telephone:* (613) 944-1692 (office). *E-mail:* anne.leahy@international.gc.ca (office). *Website:* www.international.gc.ca (office).

LEASK, Derek William, BCA, MComm (Hons); New Zealand diplomatist; *High Commissioner to UK;* b. 1948, Waiki, Wellington; m. Annabel Esme Murray 1972; pnr, Patricia (Trish) Stevenson. *Education:* Victoria Univ., Canterbury Univ. *Career:* joined Ministry of Foreign Affairs 1969, served initially in Econ. Div.; overseas postings include Suva, Ottawa and London 1985–89, Amb. to European Communities, Brussels 1994–99; Deputy Sec., Ministry of Foreign Affairs and Trade, responsible for trade and econ. matters –2008; High Commr to UK (also accred to Nigeria and as Amb. to Ireland) 2008–.
Address: New Zealand High Commission, New Zealand House, 80 Haymarket, London, SW1Y 4TQ, England (office). *Telephone:* (20) 7930-8422 (office). *Fax:* (20) 7839-4580 (office). *E-mail:* email@newzealandhc.org.uk (office). *Website:* www.nzembassy.com/uk (office).

LeBARON, Joseph Evan, BS, PhD; American diplomatist; *Ambassador to Qatar;* b. Ore.; m. Elinor Drake; one d. *Education:* Portland State Univ., American Univ. of Beirut, Princeton Univ., Seminar XXI on Int. Relations, Massachusetts Inst. of Tech. *Career:* served in USAF during Vietnam War as TV newscaster and radio broadcaster in Thailand and Turkey for American Forces Radio and TV Service (AFRTS), helped produce 'Air

Force Now' while at AFRTS HQ, Calif.; Doctoral Research Fellow, Univ. of Khartoum, Sudan 1978–79; career mem. Foreign Service since 1980, Vice-Consul, Embassy in Doha, Qatar 1980–82, later assignments included rotational assignment (political and econ.-commercial officer), Embassy in Amman 1982–84, Staff Asst to Amb., Embassy in Ankara 1984–85, Political Officer, Consulate Gen. in Istanbul 1985–87, Desk Officer for Lebanon, Bureau of Near Eastern Affairs, State Dept 1987–89, detailed to US Senate to serve on nat. security and foreign affairs staff of Majority Leader, George J. Mitchell 1989–90, Persian language studies at Foreign Service Inst., Consul Gen., Dubai, UAE 1990–91, Deputy Chief of Mission, Embassy in Manama, Bahrain 1994–96, Deputy Dir Office of Iran and Iraq, Bureau of Near Eastern Affairs 1996–98, Deputy Asst Sec., Bureau of Intelligence and Research –2003, Amb. to Mauritania 2003–06, to Qatar 2008–; part-time mem. grad. faculty, Elliott School for Int. Affairs, George Washington Univ., Washington, DC 2001–03; numerous State Dept Sr Performance, Superior and Meritorious Honor Awards, Sinclaire Language Award for the distinguished study of Persian, Presidential Meritorious Service Award 2003.
Address: US Embassy, PO Box 2399, 22nd February Street, Al Luqta Dist, Doha, Qatar (office). *Telephone:* 488-4101 (office). *Fax:* 488-4298 (office). *E-mail:* pasdoha@state.gov (office). *Website:* qatar.usembassy.gov (office).

LeBARON, Richard, BA, MA; American diplomatist; *Deputy Chief of Mission, Embassy in London;* m. Jean Foshee LeBaron. *Education:* Univ. of Colorado and George Washington Univ. *Career:* consultancy in Brazil 1977–79; career mem. Sr Foreign Service since 1979, postings have included Managua 1980–82, New Delhi 1982–84, Tunis 1986–89, Lisbon 1989–91; Political Officer, Office of EC Affairs 1989–91; Dir for Near East and S Asian Affairs, Nat. Security Council, then Dir Peace Process and Regional Affairs Office, Bureau of Near Eastern Affairs, later Public Affairs Adviser for Near Eastern Bureau 1991–98; Minister-Counselor for Econ. and Political Affairs, Embassy in Cairo 1998–2001; Deputy Chief of Mission, Tel-Aviv 2001–04, Amb. to Kuwait 2004–07; Deputy Chief of Mission Embassy in London 2007–; six State Dept Sr Performance Awards, Presidential Rank Award 2003.
Address: Embassy of the USA, 24 Grosvenor Square, London W1A 1AE, England (office). *Telephone:* (20) 7894-0225 (office). *Fax:* (20) 7493-3425 (office). *Website:* london.usembassy.gov (office).

LEBED, Aleksey Ivanovich; Russian politician; *Head of Government, Republic of Khakassia;* b. 14 April 1955, Novocherkassk, Rostov Region; m.; one s. one d. *Education:* Ryazan Higher School of Airborne Troops, Frunze Mil. Acad., St Petersburg State Univ. *Career:* mil. service in Afghanistan 1982; participated in mil. operations in different parts of USSR 1980–92; Regt Commdr, 14th Army in Chişinău 1992, resgnd 1995; mem. State Duma 1995–96; Head of Govt Repub. of Khakassia 1996–; mem. Council of Fed. 1996–2001; mem. Congress of Russian Communities; Order of the Red Star; Dr hc (Khakassia Katanov State Univ.); Hon. Diploma (Supreme Council, Repub. of Khakassia); Medal for Courage, Peter the Great Prize 2001. *Publication:* article on regional econ. devt.
Address: House of Government, prosp. Lenina 67, 655019 Abakan, Republic of Khakassia, Russia. *Telephone:* (39022) 9-91-02 (office). *Fax:* (39022) 6-50-96 (office). *E-mail:* pressa@khakasnet.ru (office). *Website:* www.gov.khakassia.ru.

LEBEDEV, Col-Gen. Sergey Nikolayevich; Russian international organization official and fmr intelligence officer; *Executive Secretary, Commonwealth of Independent States;* b. 9 April 1948, Djizak, Syrdaryinsky region, Uzbekistan; m. Vera Mikhailovna; two s. *Education:* Kiev Polytechnic Inst., Diplomatic Acad. of USSR. *Career:* staff mem., Chernigov br., Kiev Polytechnic Inst. 1970; army service 1971–72; with state security bodies 1973–75, Foreign Intelligence Service 1975–78; Rep. of Foreign Intelligence Service to USA 1998–2000; Dir Fed. Foreign Intelligence Service, Russian Fed. 2000–07; Exec. Sec. CIS 2007–; numerous state awards.
Address: Office of the Executive Secretary, Commonwealth of Independent States, 220000 Minsk, Kirava 17, Belarus (office). *Telephone:* (17) 222-35-17 (office). *Fax:* (17) 227-23-39 (office). *E-mail:* anna@cis.minsk.by (office). *Website:* www.cis.minsk.by (office).

LEBOUDER, Jean-Pierre; Central African Republic politician; b. 1944. *Education:* Ecole nationale supérieure agronomique, Toulouse, France. *Career:* Dir Research Centre, Union cotonnière centrafricaine 1971–72, Dir-Gen. 1974–76; Minister of Rural Devt 1976, of Planning, Statistics and Int. Co-operation 1978–80; Prime Minister 1980–81; Minister of State, responsible for Planning, the Economy, Finance, the Budget and Int. Co-operation Dec. 2003–05.

LEBRANCHU, Marylise; French politician and university lecturer; b. 25 April 1947, Loudéac (Côtes-d'Armor); m. Jean Lebranchu 1970; three c. *Career:* responsible for research, Nord-Finistère Semi-public Co. 1973–78;

joined Parti Socialiste Unifié (PSU) 1972, Parti Socialiste (PS) 1977; Parl. Asst to Marie Jacq 1978–93; municipal councillor, Morlaix (Finistère) 1983, Mayor 1995–97; regional councillor 1986–; Nat. Ass. Deputy for Morlaix Constituency 1997–; Minister of State attached to Minister for the Economy, Finance and Industry, with responsibility for small and medium-sized enterprises, trade and artisan activities 1997–2000, Minister of Justice and Keeper of the Seals 2000–02; Jr Lecturer in Econs applied to town and country planning, Univ. of Brest 1990–; Trombinoscope Politician of the Year Award 2000. *Publication:* Etre Juste, Justement.
Address: 6 Place Emile Souvestu (office); Assemblée nationale, 126 rue de l'Université, 75355 Paris 07 SP, France. *Fax:* 1-40-63-77-65 (office). *E-mail:* mlebranchu@assemblee-nationale.fr.

LECLERCQ, Patrick; French diplomatist; b. 2 Aug. 1938, Lille; m. 2nd Marie-Alice Berard; two s.; one s. from previous m. *Education:* Institut d'Etudes Politiques, Paris, Ecole Nat. d'Admin. *Career:* joined Diplomatic Service 1966; Consul-Gen. Montréal, Canada 1982–85; Amb. to Jordan 1985–89, to Egypt 1991–96, to Spain 1996–99; Minister of State and Dir of External Relations for Monaco 2000–05; Officier, Légion d'honneur, Ordre nat. du Mérite; several foreign decorations including Orden del Merito and Isabel la Católica, Spain, Ordre de Saint-Charles, Monaco.
Address: c/o Office of the Minister of State, Ministry of State, Place de la Visitation, 98000 Monaco (office).

LEE, David Tawei, PhD; Taiwanese government official; b. 15 Oct. 1949, Taipei; m.; one s. one d. *Education:* Nat. Taiwan Univ., Univ. of Virginia, USA. *Career:* Man. Ed. Asia and the World Forum 1976–77; staff consultant, Co-ordination Council for North American Affairs, Washington, DC 1982–88; Prin. Asst to Minister of Foreign Affairs 1988–89; Adjunct Assoc. Prof. of Int. Politics, Grad. School of Social Science, Nat. Taiwan Normal Univ. 1988–93; Deputy Dir Dept of Int. Information Services, Govt Information Office 1989–90; Deputy Dir Dept of N American Affairs, Ministry of Foreign Affairs 1990–93, Dir 1996, Deputy Minister 1998–2001; Assoc. in Research, Fairbank Center for E Asian Research, Harvard Univ. 1993–96; Dir-Gen. Taipei Econ. and Cultural Office, Boston 1993–96; Deputy Dir-Gen. Govt Information Office, Exec. Yuan 1996–97; Dir-Gen. Govt Information Office, Exec. Yuan and Govt Spokesman 1997–2000; Rep. to Belgium, Luxembourg and EU 2001, currently Rep. to USA, Taipei Econ. and Cultural Rep. Office.
Address: Taipei Economic and Cultural Representative Office, 4201 Wisconsin Avenue, NW, Washington, DC 20016, USA. *Telephone:* (202) 895-1800 (office).

LEE, Hoi-chang, BA; South Korean politician; b. 2 June 1935, Sohung, Hwanghae Prov.; m.; two s. one d. *Education:* Kyonggi High School, Seoul Nat. Univ., Harvard Univ., USA. *Career:* service in AF, attained rank of Capt.; Judge, Incheon and Seoul Dist Court 1960–65; apptd Judge, Seoul High Court 1965, Sr Judge 1977; Prof., Judicial Research and Training Inst. 1971; Dir Planning and Co-ordination Office, Ministry of Court Admin 1980; Justice, Supreme Court 1981–86, 1988–93; practised law 1986–88, 1994–; Head of Nat. Election Comm. 1988–93; Head of Bd of Audit and Inspection 1993; Prime Minister of Repub. of Korea 1993; cand. of ruling New Korea Party in presidential elections 1997; Pres. Grand Nat. Party (GNP) 2000–02; cand. of GNP in presidential elections 2002, ind. cand. 2007.
Address: 10-1401 Asia Seonsuchon Apt, Jamsil-7-dong, Songpa-gu, Seoul, Republic of Korea (home). *Telephone:* (2) 3432-2030 (home).

LEE, Hong-koo, PhD; South Korean politician and political scientist; *President, Seoul Forum for International Affairs;* b. 9 May 1934, Seoul; m.; one s. two d. *Education:* Seoul Nat. Univ., Emory and Yale Univs, USA. *Career:* Asst Prof., Emory Univ. 1963–64, Case Western Reserve Univ. 1964–67; Asst Prof., Assoc. Prof., Prof. of Political Science, Seoul Nat. Univ. 1968–88, Dir Inst. of Social Sciences 1979–82; Fellow Woodrow Wilson Int. Center for Scholars, Smithsonian Inst. 1973–74, Harvard Law School 1974–75; Minister of Nat. Unification 1988–90; Special Asst to Pres. 1990–91; Amb. to UK 1991–93; Sr Vice-Chair. Advisory Council for Unification; Chair. Seoul 21st Century Cttee, The World Cup 2002 Bidding Cttee 1993–94; Deputy Prime Minister and Minister of Nat. Unification April–Dec. 1994, Prime Minister 1994–95; mem. Comm. on Global Governance 1991–95; Chair. New Korea Party May 1996; Amb. to USA 1998–2001; currently Pres. Seoul Forum for Int. Affairs; Sheth Distinguished Int. Alumni Award from Emory Univ. 2002. *Publications:* An Introduction to Political Science, One Hundred Years of Marxism, Modernization.
Address: c/o Ministry of Foreign Affairs and Trade, 77 1-ga, Sejong-no, Jongno-gu, Seoul, Republic of Korea (office).

LEE, Brig.-Gen. Hsien Loong, (BG Lee); Singaporean politician and fmr military officer; *Prime Minister;* b. 10 Feb. 1952; m. 1st (deceased 1982), one s. one d.; m. 2nd Ho Ching 1985; two s. *Education:* Catholic High School, Nat. Jr Coll., Cambridge Univ., UK, Kennedy School of Govt Harvard Univ., USA. *Career:* nat. service 1971; Sr Army course at Fort Leavenworth, USA; Asst Chief of Gen. Staff (Operations) 1981–82, Chief of Staff (Gen. Staff) Singapore Army 1982–84; resgnd as Brig.-Gen. Aug. 1984, Nat. Reserves –2002; Political Sec. to Minister of Defence; MP for Teck Ghee 1984–; Chair. Comm. for Restructuring of the Economy 1985; Minister of State for Defence and for Trade and Industry 1985–86, for Trade and Industry 1986–93; Deputy Prime Minister 1990–2004, also Minister of Finance, Minister of Defence 1993–95, Second Minister of Defence (Services), Head Monetary Authority of Singapore; Prime Minister of Singapore and Minister of Finance 2004–07, Prime Minister 2007–; Second Asst Sec.-Gen. People's Action Party 1989–.
Address: Office of the Prime Minister, Orchard Road, Istana Annexe, Istana, Singapore 238823 (office). *Telephone:* 2358577 (office). *Fax:* 7324627 (office). *Website:* www.pmo.gov.sg (office).

LEE, Hun-jai, MA; South Korean government official and financial analyst; b. 17 April 1944, Shanghai, China. *Education:* Seoul Nat. Univ., IMF Inst., Boston Univ. and Harvard Business School, Mass, USA. *Career:* Dir Financial Policy Div., Ministry of Finance 1974–78, Deputy Dir-Gen. Office of Public Finance and Monetary Policy 1978–79; Exec. Man. Dir and CEO Daewoo Semiconductor Co. Ltd 1984–85; Pres. and CEO Korea Investors Service Co., Ltd 1985–1991; Head of Secr. to Jt Presidential Cttee for Econ. Policy 1997–98; Chair. Financial Supervisory Comm. 1998–2000; Minister of Finance and Economy 2000; Chair. Korean Inst. of Dirs 2002–04; Deputy Prime Minister and Minister of Finance and the Economy 2004–05 (resgnd); Chair. Bd of Govs, Asian Devt Bank; mem. Advisory Bd, Cen. Cttee of Agric. Cooperative Union 1993–97; mem. Citizens Advisory Cttee, City of Seoul 1995–97. *Publications:* Development of the Credit Rating System in Korea 1988.
Address: c/o Ministry of Finance and the Economy, 1 Jungang-dong, Gwacheon City, Gyeonggi Province, Republic of Korea (office).

LEE, Jye; Taiwanese naval officer; b. 6 June 1940, Tianjin City; m.; three d. *Education:* ROC Naval Acad., Navy Command and Staff Coll., Naval War Coll., USA. *Career:* served as Submarine Commdg Officer, Submarine Squadron Commdr, Antisubmarine Warfare Commdr, Taiwan Navy 1992–94, Chief of Staff Navy Gen. HQ 1994–95, Commdg Gen. of Fleet Command 1995–96, Deputy Commdr-in-Chief Navy Gen. HQ 1996–97, Commdr-in-Chief Navy Gen. HQ 1999–2002; Vice Chief of Gen. Staff, Ministry of Nat. Defence Taiwan 1997–99, Chief of Gen. Staff 2002–04, Minister of Nat. Defence 2004–05, 2006–07; mem. Kuomintang (KMT, Nationalist Party of China) –2007.
Address: c/o Ministry of National Defence, 2/F, 164 Po Ai Road, Taipei, Taiwan (office).

LEE, Kuan Yew, MA; Singaporean politician and barrister; *Minister Mentor;* b. 16 Sept. 1923, Singapore; m. Kwa Geok Choo 1950; two s. one d. *Education:* Raffles Coll., Singapore, Fitzwilliam Coll. Cambridge, UK. *Career:* called to Bar, Middle Temple, London 1950, Hon. Bencher 1969; Advocate and Solicitor, Singapore 1951; a founder of People's Action Party 1954, Sec.-Gen. 1954–92; mem. Legis. Ass. 1955–; first Prime Minister Repub. of Singapore 1959, re-elected 1963, 1968, 1972, 1976, 1980, 1984, 1988; resgnd as Prime Minister Nov. 1990; Sr Minister in the Prime Minister's Office 1990–2004; Minister Mentor 2004–; mem. Singapore Internal Security Council 1959–; MP Fed. Parl. of Malaysia 1963–65; Chair. Singapore Investment Corpn 1981–; Fellow, Inst. of Politics, Harvard Univ. 1968; Hoyt Fellow, Berkeley Coll., Yale Univ. 1970; Hon. Fellow, Fitzwilliam Coll. Cambridge 1969, Royal Australasian Coll. of Surgeons 1973, RACP 1974; Hon. LLD (Royal Univ. of Cambodia) 1965, (Hong Kong) 1970, (Liverpool) 1971, (Sheffield) 1971; (Hon. CH 1970); Hon. GCMG 1972; Bintang Republik Indonesia Adi Pradana 1973, Order of Sikatuna (Philippines) 1974, Most Hon. Order of Crown of Johore (First Class), 1984, Hon. Freeman, City of London 1982, numerous other distinctions. *Publications:* The Singapore Story – Memoirs of Lee Kuan Yew (Vol. 1), From Third World to First: The Singapore Story 1965–2000 (Vol. 2).
Address: c/o Prime Minister's Office, Istana Annexe, 238823 Singapore.

LEE, Kyu-hyung; South Korean diplomatist; *Ambassador to Russia;* b. 24 Oct. 1951; m.; one s. one d. *Education:* Seoul Nat. Univ. *Career:* joined Ministry of Foreign Affairs 1974, Asst Sec., Political Section, Office of Pres. 1983–85, Dir UN Affairs Div. 1989–91, Dir UN Affairs Div. I 1991–93, Sr Research Officer, Inst. of Foreign Affairs and Nat. Security (IFANS) 1996–97, Public Information Officer 1997–98, Dir-Gen. for Int. Orgs, Office of Policy Planning and Int. Orgs 1998–99, Dir-Gen. for Asian and Pacific Studies, IFANS 2002, Spokesman 2004, Vice-Minister of Foreign Affairs and Trade 2005–07; overseas postings include Third Sec., Perm. Mission to UN, New York 1980–81, Second Sec., Embassy in Cen. African

Repub. 1981–83, First Sec., Embassy in Tokyo 1985, Counsellor, Perm. Mission to the UN, New York 1993–96, Minister, Embassy in Beijing 1999–2002; Amb. to Bangladesh 2002–04, to Russia 2007–; Order of Service Merit (Red Stripes) 1992.
Address: Embassy of the Republic of Korea, 131000 Moscow, ul. Plyushchikha 56/1, Russia (office). *Telephone:* (495) 783-27-27 (office). *Fax:* (495) 783-27-77 (office). *E-mail:* info@koreaemb.ru (office). *Website:* rus-moscow.mofat.go.kr/eng/index.jsp (office).

LEE, Martin Chu Ming, QC, JP, BA; Hong Kong politician and barrister; *Legislative Councillor;* b. 8 June 1938, Hong Kong; m. Amelia Lee 1969; one s. *Education:* Univ. of Hong Kong. *Career:* Chair. Hong Kong Bar Asscn 1980–83; mem. Hong Kong Legis. Council 1985–, Hong Kong Law Reform Comm. 1985–91, Basic Law Drafting Cttee 1985–90 (expelled for criticism of People's Repub. of China); Chair. Hong Kong Consumer Council 1988–91; formed United Democrats of Hong Kong, party opposed to Chinese mil. suppression of Tiananmen Square demonstrators in 1989, Leader 1990–94 (merged with Meeting Point party to become Democratic Party of Hong Kong), Chair. 1994–2002; Goodman Fellow, Univ. of Toronto 2000; Bencher, Hon. Soc. of Lincoln's Inn 2000; Hon. LLD (Holy Cross Coll.) 1997, (Amherst Coll., USA) 1997; Prize for Freedom, Liberal Int. 1996, Int. Human Rights Award (American Bar Asscn) 1995, Democracy Award, Nat. Endowment for Democracy, USA 1997, Statesmanship Award, Claremont Inst., USA 1998, Schuman Medal, European Parl. 2000. *Publication:* The Basic Law: some basic flaws (with Szeto Wah) 1988.
Address: Admiralty Centre, Room 704A, Tower I, 18 Harcourt Road, Hong Kong Special Administrative Region, People's Republic of China (office); c/o Central Government Offices, Rooms 401–409, West Wing, 11 Ice House Street, Central, Hong Kong Special Administrative Region (office). *Telephone:* 25290864 (office). *Fax:* 28612829 (office). *E-mail:* oml@martinlee.org.hk (office). *Website:* www.martinlee.org.hk (office).

LEE, Myung-bak, BA; South Korean business executive, politician and head of state; *President;* b. 19 Dec. 1941, Yeongil-gun Gyeongsangbuk-do; m. Kim Yun-ok; one s. three d. *Education:* Korea Univ., Seoul Nat. Univ., Yonsei Univ. *Career:* worked for Hyundai Group 1977–92, fmr Pres. Hyundai Construction; Assemblyman, 16th Nat. Ass. 1996–2001; Mayor of Seoul City 2002–06; Pres. of South Korea 2008–; Chair., Korea Atomic Industry Forum Inc. 1980; Chair. Int. Contractors Asscn of Korea 1980; Pres. Korea Amateur Swimming Fed. 1981; Exec. mem. Korean Olympic Cttee 1982; Chief, Construction Div., Econ. Cooperation Cttee in SE Asian Countries 1982; Deputy Chair. Korea Chamber of Commerce 1982; Vice Pres., Korea Man. Asscn 1983; Bureau Mem. FINA 1984; Deputy Chair., Korea-USSR Econ. Asscn 1989; Exec. Dir, Korea Electric Asscn 1990; mem. NE Asia Econ. Cttee 1991; Vice Chair., World Fed. of Korean Asscn of Commerce 1993; Founder E Asia Foundation, Chair. 1994–2002; Pres. Asian Pacific Foundation, Korea 2000–02; Commr, Sub-Cttee on Future Competitiveness, Nat. Cttee, Grand Nat. Party 2001–02; Advisor, Overseas Korean Traders Asscn 2001–; advisor to Hun Sen, Prime Minister of the Kingdom of Cambodia 2002; Hon. Consul General of the Kingdom of Bhutan to Korea 1986–99; Hon. Amb. of AR State 1992–; Hon. Instructor, Undergraduate School of Business Admin, Korea Univ. 1993–; Hon. Instructor, Grad. School of Political Science, Kookmin Univ. 1995–, Hon. Instructor, Grad. School of Business Admin, Korea Univ. 1997–; Dr hc (Korea Nat. Univ. of Physical Educ.) 1998; Excellent Enterprise Award by Pres. 1979, Excellent Enterprise Award, Business Admin Center, Korea Univ. 1983, Order of Industrial Service Merit, Gold Tower 1985; selected as one of the top 50 business leaders contributing to Nat. Devt, Daily Chosun 1998, selected as one of the top 30 business leaders in Korea in 20th century, Daily Maekyung and Fed. of Korean Industries 1999. *Publications:* History of June 3rd Student Movement 1994, Nothing is Impossible 1995, I See the Hope Rather than Despair 2002.
Address: Office of the President, Chong Wa Dae (The Blue House), 1, Sejong-no, Jongno-gu, Seoul, South Korea (office). *Telephone:* (2) 770-0055 (office). *Fax:* (2) 770-0344 (office). *E-mail:* president@cwd.go.kr (office). *Website:* www.bluehouse.go.kr (office).

LEE, Gen. Sang-hee; South Korean army officer (retd) and politician; *Minister of National Defense;* b. 12 Aug. 1945, Wonju, Gangwon Prov.; m. Kim Sun Young; one s. one d. *Education:* Kyung-Gi High School, Seoul, Repub. of Korea (ROK) Mil. Acad., Coll. of Liberal Arts and Science, Seoul Nat. Univ., Center for Int. Security Studies, Univ. of Maryland, USA. *Career:* Commdr 29th Regt, 9th Infantry Div. 1989–91, Chief of Mil. Strategy, J-5 Directorate, Jt Chiefs of Staff 1991–92, Advisor to the Pres. for Nat. Defense Policy, Office of the Presidential Secr. 1992–94, Chief of Force Planning, G-5 Directorate, ROK Army HQ 1995–96, Commanding Gen., 30th Infantry Div. (Mechanized) 1996–98, Dir Policy Planning Bureau, Ministry of Nat. Defense 1998–99, Commanding Gen. 5th Corps 1999–2001, Chief Dir, Strategy and Plans (J5), Jt Chiefs of Staff 2001–02,

Chief Dir, Operations (J3), Jt Chiefs of Staff 2002–03, promoted to four-star Gen. and Commanding Gen., Third ROK Army 2003, 32nd Chair. Jt Chiefs of Staff 2005–06 (retd); Minister of Nat. Defense 2008–; Visiting Fellow, Brookings Inst., Washington, DC 2007; Presidential Citation, Order of Nat. Security 'Samil' Medal, Order of Nat. Security 'Chonsu' Medal, Order of Nat. Security 'Gukson' Medal, Armed Forces Merit Award (Turkey), Legion of Merit, Commdr and Officer Grade, (USA).
Address: Ministry of National Defense, 1, 3-ga, Yeongsan-dong, Yeong-san-gu, Seoul 140-701, South Korea (office). *Telephone:* (2) 795-0071 (office). *Fax:* (2) 703-3109 (office). *E-mail:* cyber@mnd.go.kr (office). *Website:* www.mnd.go.kr (office).

LEE, Sun-jin; South Korean diplomatist; *Ambassador to Indonesia;* m.; one s. one d. *Education:* Seoul Nat. Univ. *Career:* joined Ministry of Foreign Affairs 1975, overseas postings include Second Sec., Embassy in Beirut 1980, First Sec., Embassy in Washington, DC 1985, Counsellor, Embassy in Beijing 1992, Minister-Counsellor, Embassy in Tokyo; fmr Vice-Consul in Seattle, Wash., USA; Deputy Dir-Gen., Int. Trade Bureau, Ministry of Foreign Affairs and Trade 1996, Dir-Gen. for Policy Planning, Office of Policy Planning and Int. Orgs 2001, Deputy Minister for Policy Planning and Int. Orgs 2003; Amb. to Indonesia 2005–.
Address: Embassy of the Republic of Korea, Jalan Jenderal Gatot Subroto 57, Jakarta Selatan, Indonesia (office). *Telephone:* (21) 5201915 (office). *Fax:* (21) 5254159 (office). *E-mail:* koremb_in@mofat.go.kr (office); koemb@indo.net.id (office). *Website:* idn.mofat.go.kr (office).

LEE, Tae-sik; South Korean diplomatist; *Ambassador to USA;* m.; three s. *Education:* Seoul Nat. Univ., School of Advanced Int. Studies at Johns Hopkins Univ., USA. *Career:* career diplomat for more than four decades, representing Repub. of Korea in Liberia, the Philippines, Austria, Yugoslavia, Israel, UK and Belgium; First Sec., Embassy in Washington, DC 1981–84; fmr Dir-Gen. Trade Bureau, Ministry of Foreign Affairs; fmr Deputy Exec. Dir Korea Peninsula Energy Devt Org.; fmr Asst Sec. to Korean Pres.; Amb. to Israel 2000–02; Deputy Minister of Foreign Affairs and Trade 2002–03, Jan.–Nov. 2005; Amb. to UK 2003–05, to USA 2005–.
Address: Embassy of the Republic of Korea, 2370 Massachusetts Avenue, NW, Washington, DC 20008, USA (office). *Telephone:* (202) 939-5600 (office). *Fax:* (202) 797-0595 (office). *E-mail:* webmaster@dynamic-korea.com (office). *Website:* www.koreaembassyusa.org (office).

LEE, Yock Suan, BSc; Singaporean politician; b. 30 Sept. 1946, Singapore; m.; one s. one d. *Education:* Queenstown Secondary Technical School, Raffles Institution, Imperial Coll., Univ. of London, UK, Univ. of Singapore. *Career:* Div. Dir (Projects), Econ. Devt Bd 1969–80; MP 1980–; Deputy Man. Dir Petrochemical Corpn of Singapore (Pte.) Ltd Jan.–Sept. 1981; Minister of State (Nat. Devt) 1981–83, (Finance) 1983–84, Sr Minister of State and Acting Minister for Labour 1985–86, Minister for Labour 1987–91, Second Minister of Educ. 1991–92, Minister of Educ. 1992–97, of Trade and Industry 1998–99, for Information and the Arts 1999–2001, of Environment 1999–2000, Minister in Prime Minister's Office and Second Minister of Foreign Affairs 2001–04; Deputy Chair. People's Asscn 1984–91.
Address: 9 Bishopsgate, Singapore249988. *Telephone:* 62381600. *E-mail:* leeyocksuan2004@yahoo.com.sg. *Website:* www.parliament.gov.sg.

LEE HANG, Niko; Samoan accountant and politician; *Minister of Finance;* *Career:* fmr Public Trustee; elected to one of the two parl. seats reserved for Individual Voters March 2006; nominated to cabinet post by the Prime Minister; Minister of Finance 2007–.
Address: Ministry of Finance, Private Bag, 2–4th Floors, Central Bank Building, Matafele, Apia, Samoa (office). *Telephone:* 34333 (office). *Fax:* 21312 (office). *E-mail:* treasury@samoa.ws (office); information@mof.gov.ws (office). *Website:* www.mof.gov.ws (office).

LEES, Martin, BMechEng; British engineer, international official and university administrator; *Rector Emeritus, United Nations University for Peace;* b. 1941; m.; four c. *Education:* Fettes Coll., Edinburgh, Univ. of Cambridge, Coll. of Europe, Belgium. *Career:* joined OECD 1971; Special Adviser to Bradford Morse, Admin. UNDP 1978, Exec. Dir UN Financing System for Science and Tech. for Devt 1979–84, Asst Sec.-Gen. UN 1984; Exec. Dir InterAction Council of Former Heads of State and Govt 1983; Founder mem. Toyota Int. Advisory Bd 1996; Rector and CEO UN Univ. for Peace 2001–05, Rector Emer. 2005–.
Address: United Nations University for Peace, Apartado 138, 6100 San José, Costa Rica (office). *Telephone:* 205-9000 (office). *Fax:* 249-1929 (office). *E-mail:* info@upeace.org (office). *Website:* www.upeace.org (office).

LEGHARI, Farooq Ahmed Khan; Pakistani politician and fmr head of state; *Chairman, Millat Party;* b. 29 May 1940, Dera Ghazi Khan; m. 1965; two s.

two d. *Education:* Punjab Univ. and Univ. of Oxford, UK. *Career:* joined Pakistan People's Party 1973; Chief Baluchi Leghari Tribe; Pakistan Civil Service 1964–73; elected to Senate 1975, to Nat. Ass. 1977; Minister for Production 1977; periods of imprisonment for opposition to Govt 1977–88; Sec.-Gen. Pakistan People's Party and mem. Exec. Cttee 1978; elected mem. Nat. Ass. and Prov. Ass. 1988–, Leader of Opposition, Prov. Ass. 1988; Minister for Water and Power 1988–90; Deputy Leader of Opposition 1990–93; Minister of Finance 1993, of Foreign Affairs Oct.–Nov. 1993; Pres. of Pakistan 1993–97; dismissed Govt of Benazir Bhutto 1996; Organizer and Founder Millat Party 1998, currently Chair. *Address:* Millat Party, 21-E/3, Gulberg, Lahore (office); Village Choti, District Dera Ghazikhan, Punjab, Pakistan (home). *Telephone:* (42) 5757805 (office); (42) 5756718 (home). *E-mail:* millat@lhr.comsats.net.pk (office).

LEGQOG; Chinese politician; *Chairman, Standing Committee, Tibet Autonomous Regional People's Congress;* b. Oct. 1944, Gyangze Co., Tibet. *Education:* CCP Cen. Cttee Cen. Party School. *Career:* teacher, Gyangze Co., Tibet Autonomous Region 1964–71; Political Cadre, Gyangze Co., Tibet Autonomous Region 1971–73; joined CCP 1972; Sec. Gyangze Co. Autonomous Co. Cttee, CCP Communist Youth League 1973–75; mem. Standing Cttee CCP Communist Youth League Autonomous Prefectural Cttee, Xigaze Prefecture, Tibet Autonomous Region 1973–75; Sec. Org. Dept (Supervisory and Org. Divs) CCP Tibet Autonomous Regional Cttee 1975–80, Deputy Head Org. Dept and Deputy Chief Org. Div. 1980–86, Exec. Deputy Head Org. Dept 1986–91, mem. Standing Cttee CCP Tibet Autonomous Regional Cttee 1991–, Deputy Sec. CCP Tibet Autonomous Regional Cttee 1994–; Sec. CCP Lhasa City Cttee 1991–94; Vice-Chair. Tibet Autonomous Region People's Govt 1995–98, Chair. 1998–2004; Chair. Standing Cttee Tibet Autonomous Regional People's Congress 2003–; Alt. mem. CCP 15th Cen. Cttee 1997–2002, mem. CCP 16th Cen. Cttee 2002–07, mem. CCP 17th Cen. Cttee 2007–. *Address:* c/o People's Government of Tibetan Autonomous Region, Lhasa, Tibet, People's Republic of China.

LEGWAILA, Legwaila Joseph, MA; Botswana diplomatist; *Secretary General's Special Adviser on Africa, United Nations;* b. 2 Feb. 1937, Mathathane; m. Pholile Matsebula 1975; three d. *Education:* Bobonong School, Brussels School, SA, Serowe Teacher Training Coll., Univs of Calgary and Alberta, Canada. *Career:* Asst Prin. External Affairs, Govt of Botswana 1973–74, Sr Pvt. Sec. to Pres. of Botswana 1974–80; apptd Perm. Rep. to UN 1980, High Commr in Guyana 1981, in Jamaica 1982, Amb. to Cuba 1983; Deputy Special Rep. of the UN Sec.-Gen. for Namibia 1989–90, Head of UN Mission in Ethiopia and Eritrea (UNMEE) 2000–06, Sec.-Gen.'s Special Adviser on Africa 2006–. *Publication:* Safari to Serowe (co-author) 1970. *Address:* Office of Special Adviser on Africa, c/o Office of the Secretary General, United Nations, New York, NY 10017, USA (office). *Telephone:* (212) 963-1858 (office). *Fax:* (212) 963-4879 (office). *E-mail:* wrightd@un .org (office). *Website:* www.un.org/africa/osaa (office).

LEHMAN, Ronald Frank, II, PhD; American security expert and government official; *Director, Center for Global Security Research, Lawrence Livermore National Laboratory;* b. 25 March 1946, Napa, Calif.; m. Susan Young 1979. *Education:* Claremont Men's Coll. and Claremont Grad. School. *Career:* army service, Viet Nam 1969–71; Legis. Asst US Senate 1976–78; mem. professional staff, US Senate Armed Services Cttee 1978–82; Deputy Asst Sec. of Defense, Office of Int. Security Policy 1982–83; Sr Dir Defense Programs and Arms Control, Nat. Security Council 1983–86; Deputy US Negotiator for Strategic Nuclear Arms, Dept of State, Washington, DC 1985–86, Chief US Negotiator Geneva 1986–88; Deputy Asst to Pres. for Nat. Security Affairs 1986; Asst Sec. of Defense 1988–89; Dir Arms Control and Disarmament Agency, Washington, DC 1989–93; Asst to Dir Lawrence Livermore Nat. Lab. 1993–, Dir Center for Global Security Research 1996–; mem. Presidential Advisory Bd on Arms Proliferation Policy 1995–96; Adjunct Prof. Georgetown Univ. 1982–89; mem. Bd Dirs US Inst. of Peace 1988–93, Keck Center for Int. and Strategic Studies (now Chair.), Claremont McKenna Coll.; mem. Int. Advisory Bd Inst. of Global Conflict and Cooperation, Univ. of Calif. San Diego 1994–; mem. IISS, Council on Foreign Relations, Atlantic Council. *Address:* Center for Global Security Research, Lawrence Livermore National Laboratory, PO Box 808, L-1, Livermore, CA 94551 (office); 693 Encina Grande Drive, Palo Alto, CA 94306, USA (home). *Telephone:* (925) 422-6141. *Fax:* (925) 422-5252. *E-mail:* lehman3@llnl.gov. *Website:* cgsr.llnl.gov.

LEHMANNOVA, Zuzana, PhD, CSc; Czech academic and research institute director; *Director, Jan Masaryk Centre of International Studies, University of Economics, Prague;* b. 25 April 1951. *Education:* Charles Univ., Prague. *Career:* fmr Assoc. Prof., Charles Univ. and Univ. of Econs Prague;

Visiting Prof., Columbia Univ., USA 1995; external advisor to Minister of Foreign Affairs of Czech Repub.; currently Dir Jan Masaryk Centre of Int. Studies, Univ. of Econs Prague; Pres. Central and East European Int. Studies Asscn; mem. Editorial Bd Journal of International Relations and Development International Relations. *Publications:* Globalni Problema-tika z Pohledu Ved o Kulture 1995; numerous chapters and articles in books and journals. *Address:* Jan Masaryk Centre of International Studies, Faculty of International Relations, University of Economics, nám. W. Churchilla 4, 130 67 Prague 3, Czech Republic (office). *Telephone:* (2) 24095660 (office). *Fax:* (2) 24095289 (office). *E-mail:* lehmann@vse.cz (office). *Website:* www .vse.cz (office).

LEHNER, Ulrich, BEcons; Swiss diplomatist; *Ambassador to France;* b. 1954, Sion. *Education:* Univ. of Geneva. *Career:* joined Fed. Dept of Foreign Affairs 1981; Sec., Embassy in Brasilia 1983–85, First Asst to Head of Mission, Embassy in Oslo 1985–86; Diplomatic Asst, Political Affairs Secr., Fed. Dept of Foreign Affairs 1986–90, Dir Political Affairs Div. III 1990–91; Counsellor, Embassy in Rome 1991–95; First Asst to Head of Mission, Embassy in Cairo 1995–98; Dir Geneva Centre for Security Policy 1998–2002; Head of Political Affairs Div. III, Fed. Dept of Foreign Affairs 2004–07; Amb. to France (also accred to Monaco) 2007–. *Address:* Embassy of Switzerland, 142 rue de Grenelle, 75007 Paris, France (office). *Telephone:* 1-49-55-67-00 (office). *Fax:* 1-49-55-67-67 (office). *E-mail:* par.vertretung@eda.admin.ch (office). *Website:* www.eda.admin .ch/paris (office).

LEHOHLA, Archibald Lesao, BSc, BA, MA; Lesotho politician; *Deputy Prime Minister and Minister of Home Affairs, Public Safety and of Parliamentary Affairs;* b. 28 July 1946, Mafeteng; m.; two s. one d. *Education:* Mafeteng Secondary School, Basutoland High School, Univ. of Botswana, Lesotho and Swaziland, Roma, Univ. of Oxford, UK. *Career:* Teaching Asst in Math., Univ. of Botswana, Lesotho and Swaziland 1971–72; Asst Teacher, Bereng High School 1975–76, Headmaster 1977–93; mem. Parl. for Mafeteng 1993–; Minister of Home Affairs (Local Govt, Rural and Urban Devt) 1993–95, of Transport, Posts and Telecommunications 1995–96, of Educ. and Manpower Devt 1996–2004, of Home Affairs and Public Safety 2004–, and of Parl. Affairs 2007–; Deputy Prime Minister 2003–; Chair. Scott Hosp. Comm. of Inquiry 1990; fmr Chair. Mafeteng Tractor Owners' Cooperative; Church Elder and mem. Mafeteng LEC consistory; fmr mem. Lesotho Headmasters' and Headmistresses' Asscn, Lesotho Evangelical Church Law Review Comm., LEC Educational Sec.'s Advisory Cttee on Educ.; rep. Lesotho at Commonwealth Seminar on Educational Admin and Supervision, Univ. of Nairobi, Kenya 1977; UNESCO Fellowship to Univ. of Oxford 1975. *Address:* Ministry of Home Affairs and Public Safety, POB 174 Maseru 100, Lesotho (office). *Telephone:* 323771 (office). *Website:* www.lesotho .gov.ls (office).

LEHTOMÄKI, Paula Ilona, MSc; Finnish politician; *Minister of the Environment;* b. 29 Nov. 1972, Kuhmo; m.; one c. *Career:* acting sr teacher 1995; research asst 1996; mem. Kuhmo Town Council 1997; mem. Parl. (Centre Party) 1999–; mem. Finnish Del. to Nordic Council 1999–2003, to Council of Europe 2003; Minister for Foreign Trade and Devt and Minister at the Prime Minister's Office 2003–07, of the Environment 2007–; mem. Supervisory Bd VR-Group Ltd 2000–03, Bd Audiator Oy 2000–03, Exec. Cttee Lasten Keskus Publishing House 2000–01, Cttee Finnish 4H Fed. 2001–03, Bd Finland-Russia Soc. 2000–03. *Address:* Ministry of the Environment, Kasarmikatu 25, POB 35, 00023 Helsinki, Finland (office). *Telephone:* (20) 4907001 (office). *Fax:* (9) 16039307 (office). *E-mail:* paula.lehtomaki@ymparisto.fi (office). *Website:* www.environment.fi (office).

LEIFLAND, Leif, LLB; Swedish diplomatist; b. 30 Dec. 1925, Stockholm; m. Karin Abard 1954 (died 1999); one s. two d. *Education:* Univ. of Lund. *Career:* joined Ministry of Foreign Affairs 1952; served Athens 1953, Bonn 1955, Washington 1961, 1970; Sec. Foreign Relations Cttee, Swedish Parl. 1966–70; Under-Sec. for Political Affairs 1975–77; Perm. Under-Sec. of State for Foreign Affairs 1977–82; Amb. to UK 1982–91; Chair. Bd, Swedish Inst. of Int. Affairs 1991–2002; Hon. GCVO. *Publications:* The Blacklisting of Axel Wenner-Gren 1989, General Böhme's Choice 1992, The Year of the Frost 1997; various articles on foreign policy and national security questions. *Address:* Nybrogatan 77, 114 40 Stockholm, Sweden. *Telephone:* 86-61-46-12.

LEIJONHUFVUD, Baron Axel Stig Bengt, PhD; Swedish professor of economics; *Professor of Monetary Economics, University of Trento;* b. 9 June 1933, Stockholm; m. 1st Marta E. Ising 1955 (divorced 1977), 2nd Earlene J. Craver 1977; one s. two d. *Education:* Univs of Lund, Pittsburgh and Northwestern Univ. *Career:* Acting Asst Prof. of Econs, UCLA 1964–67, Assoc. Prof. 1967–71, Prof. of Econs 1971–94, Chair. Dept of Econs 1980–83, 1990–92, Dir Center for Computable Econs 1991–97; Prof. of Monetary Econs, Univ. of Trento 1995–; Dir Computable and Experimental Econs Lab. 1996–; Visiting Prof., Stockholm School of Econ. and Commerce 1979–80, 1986, 1987, 1996, Inst. for Advanced Studies, Vienna 1976, 1987, Inst. for Advanced Studies, Jerusalem 1987, Nihon Univ. Tokyo 1980, European Univ. Inst., Florence 1982, 1986–87, 1989, Istituto Torcuato di Tella, Buenos Aires 1989, 1995; Ständiger Gastprofessor Univ. of Konstanz 1982–85; mem. Econ. Export Cttee of Pres. of Kazakhstan 1991; other professional appointments, Cttee memberships etc.; Brookings Inst. Fellow 1963–64; Marshall Lecturer, Univ. of Cambridge 1974; Overseas Fellow, Churchill Coll. Cambridge 1974; Inst. for Advanced Study Fellow 1983–84; Dr hc (Lund) 1983, (Nice, Sophia Antipolis) 1995. *Publications:* On Keynesian Economics and the Economics of Keynes: A Study in Monetary Theory 1968, Keynes and the Classics: Two Lectures 1969, Information and Coordination: Essays in Macroeconomic Theory 1981, High Inflation (jtly) 1995, Macroeconomic Instability and Coordination 2000, Monetary Theory as a Basis for Monetary Policy (ed.) 2001, Monetary Theory and Policy Experience (ed.) 2001; contribs to professional journals. *Address:* Department of Economics, University of Trento, Via Inama 5, 38100 Trento, Italy. *Telephone:* (0461) 882279. *E-mail:* axel@ucla.edu (office). *Website:* www.ceel.economia.unitn.it.

LEIPOLD, Gerd, PhD; German environmentalist; *Executive Director, Greenpeace International;* b. 1 Jan. 1951, Rot an der Rot; two c. *Education:* Max-Planck Inst. for Meteorology, Hamburg. *Career:* trained as scientist; joined Greenpeace Germany as volunteer 1980, joined full-time 1983, later mem. Exec. Cttee and Trustee, Int. Co-ordinator Nuclear Free Seas Campaign 1987, fmr Chair. Bd Green Peace Nordic, mem. Bd Greenpeace USSR, Dir Greenpeace Nuclear Disarmament Campaign, London, Acting Int. Exec. Dir Greenpeace Int. Feb.–June 2001, Int. Exec. Dir June 2001–; set up own consultancy to advise NGOs on strategy and communications 1993. *Address:* Greenpeace International, Ottho Heldringstraat 5, Amsterdam 1066 AZ, Netherlands (office); c/o Im Hebsack 4, 88430 Rot, Germany (home). *Telephone:* (20) 718-2081 (office). *Fax:* (20) 718-2578 (office). *E-mail:* gerd.leipold@int.greenpeace.org (office). *Website:* www .greenpeace.org (office).

LEIR, Michael, BA, LLB, LLM; Canadian lawyer and diplomatist; *High Commissioner to Australia;* b. 1949. *Education:* Dalhousie Univ., Halifax, Univ. of London. *Career:* fmr lecturer in law, Univ. of Ottawa; Asst Gen. Counsel, Trade Negotiations Office (lead lawyer on implementation of N American Free Trade Agreement—NAFTA) 1987–90; Dir Legal Advisory Div., Dept of Foreign Affairs and Int. Trade 1990–91, Dir-Gen. USA Bureau 1996–99, Legal Adviser 1999–2002; Minister-Counsellor for Congressional and Legal Affairs, Embassy in Washington, DC 1991–96; Amb. to Turkey (also accred to Azerbaijan, Georgia and Turkmenistan) 2002–05; High Commr to Australia (also accred to Federated States of Micronesia, Marshall Islands, Nauru, Palau, Papua New Guinea, Solomon Islands, Vanuatu) 2005–. *Address:* Canadian High Commission, Commonwealth Avenue, Canberra ACT 2600, Australia (office). *Telephone:* (2) 6270-4000 (office). *Fax:* (2) 6273-3285 (office). *E-mail:* cnbra@international.gc.ca (office). *Website:* www.canada.org.au (office).

LEITER, Michael E., BA, JD; American naval officer, lawyer and government official; *Director, National Counterterrorism Center; Education:* Columbia Univ., Harvard Law School. *Career:* Naval Flight Officer, USN 1991–97, served on US, NATO and UN missions in fmr Yugoslavia and Iraq; fmr Harvard Law School Human Rights Fellow, Int. Criminal Tribunal for the Fmr Yugoslavia, The Hague; fmr law clerk to Assoc. Justice Stephen G. Breyer of US Supreme Court and to Chief Judge Michael Boudin of US Court of Appeals for the First Circuit; Asst US Attorney, Eastern Dist of Va, US Dept of Justice 2002–05; Deputy Gen. Counsel and Asst Dir, Pres.'s Comm. on Intelligence Capabilities of US Regarding Weapons of Mass Destruction (Robb-Silberman Comm.) 2005; Deputy Chief of Staff, Office of Dir of Nat. Intelligence 2005–07; Prin. Deputy Dir Nat. Counter-terrorism Center Feb.–Nov. 2007, Acting Dir 2007–08, Dir 2008–. *Address:* United States National Counterterrorism Center, c/o Director of National Intelligence, Washington, DC 20511, USA (office). *Telephone:* (703) 733-8600 (office). *Website:* www.nctc.gov (office).

LEKO, Tomislav; Bosnia and Herzegovina diplomatist; b. 1961, Zagreb, Croatia. *Career:* Amb. to Serbia 2003–. *Address:* Embassy of Bosnia and Herzegovina, Milana Tankosića 8, Belgrade 11000, Serbia (office).

LEKOA, Lapologang Caesar, BA; Botswana diplomatist; *Ambassador to USA;* m.; two c. *Education:* Univ. of Botswana, Lesotho and Swaziland. *Career:* Third Sec., Ministry of Foreign Affairs 1977–80, Second Sec. 1980–84, First Sec., Embassy in, and Mission to EU, Brussels, Belgium 1984–85, First Sec., High Comm., London 1985–87, Counsellor and Head of Chancery 1987–91, Dir of Int. Relations, Dept of Foreign Affairs 1992–95, High Commr to Zambia, Tanzania, Kenya and Uganda 1996–2002, Amb. to USA 2002–. *Address:* Embassy of Botswana, 1531–1533 New Hampshire Avenue, NW, Washington, DC 20036, USA (office). *Telephone:* (202) 244-4990 (office). *Fax:* (202) 244-4164 (office). *E-mail:* llekoa@gov.bw (office). *Website:* www.botswanaembassy.org (office).

LEKOTA, Mosiuoa Patrick (Terror); South African politician; *Minister of Defence;* b. 13 Aug. 1948, Senekal, Orange Free State; m. Cynthia Lekota 1975; two s. two d. (deceased). *Education:* Univ. of the North (Turfloop). *Career:* perm. organizer, South African Students' Org. (SASO) 1972–74; charged under Terrorism Act 1974; tried and imprisoned on Robben Island 1976–82; Nat. Publicity Sec. United Democratic Front (UDF) 1983–91; fmrly with ANC org. in Natal; organizer for ANC in Northern Free States 1990; mem. ANC Working Cttee 1991–, Nat. Chair. ANC Nat. Exec. Cttee 1991–, Chair. Southern OFS of Nat. Exec. Comm. 1991, Sec. Elections Comm. 1992–94; Nat. Chair. ANC 1997–, detained 1983, 1984, 1985; on trial with 21 others charged with treason and murder in Delmas case 1986, convicted 1988, sentenced to 12 years' imprisonment after being held in custody for 4 years; conviction overturned by Appeal Court 1989; in exile, returned to S Africa 1990; Premier Free State Prov. Legislature 1994; Chair. Nat. Council of Provinces 1997–; Minister of Defence 1999–. *Address:* Ministry of Defence, Armscor Building, Block 5, Nossob Street, Erasmusrand 0001, South Africa (office). *Telephone:* (12) 3556321 (office). *Fax:* (12) 3556398 (office). *E-mail:* info@mil.za (office). *Website:* www.mil .za (office).

LELONG, Pierre Alexandre; French administrative official; *President, Commission des Marchés Publics de l'Etat;* b. 22 May 1931, Paris; m. Catherine Demargne 1958; four s. one d. *Education:* Coll. Stanislas, Paris, Univ. of Paris and Ecole Nat. d'Admin. *Career:* Ministry of Finance and Econ. Affairs 1958–62; Econ. Adviser to Prime Minister Pompidou 1962–67; Gen. Man. Fonds d'Orientation et de Régularisation des Marchés Agricoles (FORMA) 1967–68; MP for Finistère 1968–74; Sec. of State for Posts and Telecommunications 1974–75; Judge, Court of Accounts 1975–77; mem. European Court of Auditors 1977–84, Pres. 1981–84; Pres. of Section (Defence) at Court of Accounts 1990–94, Pres. of Chamber (European Affairs) 1994–97; Pres. Interministerial Cttee for Mil., Aero-nautic and Mechanical State Procurements 1997–2004; Pres. Consultative Cttee on Secret Defence Affairs 1999–2005; Pres. Commission des Marchés Publics de l'Etat 2005–; Commdr, Légion d'Honneur, Officier, Ordre du Mérite; Grand Cross, Ordre de la Couronne de Chêne (Luxembourg). *Address:* Ministere de l'Economie et des Finances, 6 rue Louise Wein, 75013 Paris (office); 130 rue de Rennes, 75006 Paris, France (home). *Telephone:* 1-42-75-75-00 (office); 1-45-44-12-49 (home). *Fax:* 1-42-75-75-97 (office); 1-45-44-12-49 (home). *E-mail:* pierre.lelong@pm.gouv.fr (office); lelongdemargne@noos.fr (home).

LEMIERRE, Jean; French international civil servant; b. 6 June 1950, Sainte Adresse; m.; three c. *Education:* Institut d'Etudes Politiques de Paris, Ecole Nationale d'Admin. *Career:* Inspection Générale des Finances 1976; various positions, Tax Policy Admin 1980–87, Head 1987–89; Directeur Général des Impôts 1989–95; Directeur de Cabinet, French Pvt. Office, Minister of Economy and Finance, Paris 1995; Head of Treasury 1995–2000; mem. European Monetary Cttee 1995–98; Chair. European Econ. and Finance Cttee 1999–2000, Paris Club 1999–2000; Pres. EBRD 2000–08. *Address:* c/o European Bank for Reconstruction and Development, One Exchange Square, 175 Bishopgate, London, EC2A 2JN, England (office).

LEMINE, Mohamed Mahmoud Ould Mohamed, DEcon; Mauritanian politician; *Minister of National Defence;* b. 1952, Hodh El Gharbi; m. *Education:* studied in Cairo, Egypt. *Career:* fmr Prof. of Econs, Univ. of Nouakchott –1996; Dir-Gen. Ecole Nationale de l'Administration (ENA), Nouakchott 1996–2007; Minister of Nat. Defence 2007–. *Address:* Ministry of National Defence, Nouakchott, Mauritania (office). *Telephone:* 525-41-42 (office).

LENAERTS, Baron; Koen, Lic.iuris, LLM, MPA, PhD; Belgian judge; *Judge, Court of Justice of the European Communities;* b. (Koenraad Lenaerts), 20 Dec. 1954, Mortsel; m. Kris Grimonprez; six d. *Education:* Univs of Namur and Leuven, Belgium and Harvard Univ., USA. *Career:* Asst Prof., Leuven Univ. 1979–82, Assoc. Prof. 1982–83, Prof. of EC Law 1983–; Prof. of European Insts, Coll. of Europe, Bruges 1984–89; law clerk to Judge R.

Joliet, Court of Justice of the European Communities 1984–85; mem. Brussels Bar 1986–89; Judge, Court of First Instance of the European Communities, Luxembourg 1989–2003, Court of Justice of the European Communities 2003–; Visiting Prof. of Law, Univ. of Burundi 1983, 1986, Univ. of Strasbourg 1986–89, Harvard Univ. 1988–89; numerous academic distinctions, fellowships and prizes. *Publications:* 'The Negative Implications' of the Commerce Clause and 'Preemption' Doctrines as Federalism Related Limitations on State Power: a Historical Review 1978, Constitutie en rechter 1983, International privaatrecht (with G. Van Hecke) 1986, Le juge et la constitution aux Etats-Unis d'Amérique et dans l'ordre juridique européen 1988, Two Hundred Years of U.S. Constitution and Thirty Years of EEC Treaty: Outlook for a Comparison 1988, Constitutional Law of the European Union (with P. Van Nuffel) 1999 (revised second edn 2005), Procedural Law of the European Union (with D. Arts and I. Maselis) 1999 (revised second edn 2006), articles and contribs to reviews etc. *Address:* Court of Justice of the European Communities, blvd Konrad Adenauer, 2925 Luxembourg (office). *Telephone:* 4303-3553 (office). *Fax:* 4303-3541 (office). *E-mail:* koen.lenaerts@curia.europa.eu (office). *Website:* www.curia.europa.eu (office).

LENIHAN, Brian Joseph, BA, LLB; Irish lawyer and politician; *Minister for Finance;* b. 21 May 1959, Dublin; m. Patricia Ryan; one s. one d. *Education:* Belvedere Coll., Trinity Coll. Dublin, Univ. of Cambridge, King's Inns Dublin. *Career:* Lecturer in Law, Trinity Coll. Dublin 1984; called to the Bar, Dublin 1984; mem. Criminal Injuries Compensation Tribunal and Garda Síochána Complaints Appeal Bd 1992–95; elected TD (mem. Parl.) for Dublin West in by-election 1996, re-elected in gen. election 1997, Chair. All-Party Oireachtas Cttee on Constitution 1997–2002, mem. Cttee on Procedure and Privileges 1997–2002, Minister of State (with special responsibility for children) 2002–07, Minister for Justice 2007–08, Minister for Finance 2008–; mem. Fianna Fail; mem. Inc. Council of Law Reporting. *Address:* Department of Finance, Government Buildings, Upper Merrion Street, Dublin 2 (office); Laurel Lodge Shopping Centre, Dublin 15, Ireland. *Telephone:* (1) 6767571 (office); (1) 8220970 (constituency) (office). *Fax:* (1) 6789936 (office); (1) 8220972 (constituency) (office). *E-mail:* webmaster@finance.irlgov.ie (office); brianlenihantd@gmail.com (office). *Website:* www.finance.gov.ie (office); www.brianlenihan.ie (office).

LENNKH, Georg, LLD; Austrian diplomatist; *Special Envoy for Africa for the Austrian Presidency, European Union;* b. 8 Dec. 1939, Graz; m. Annie Lechevalier 1966; one s. one d. *Education:* Univ. of Graz, Johns Hopkins School of Advanced Informational Studies, Bologna and Univ. of Chapel Hill, NC, USA. *Career:* entered Fed. Ministry for Foreign Affairs 1965; served Tokyo 1968–72, Austrian Mission to UN, New York 1972–76, Dept for Int. Orgs, Ministry of Foreign Affairs 1976–78; served Cabinet Office of Fed. Chancellor Kreisky, with responsibility for foreign relations 1978–82; Perm. Rep. to OECD 1982–93; Dir Gen. Dept for Devt Cooperation, Fed. Ministry of Foreign Affairs 1993, currently Special Envoy for Africa for the Austrian Presidency, EU; Pres. Global Forum on Sustainable Energy. *Address:* Ministry for Foreign Affairs, Ballhausplatz 2, 1014 Vienna, Austria. *Telephone:* (1) 531-15-0. *Fax:* (1) 535-45-30. *E-mail:* georg .lennkh@aon.at; georg.lennkh@bmaa.gv.at (office). *Website:* www.bmaa .gv.at (office).

LEÓN RODRÍGUEZ, René Antonio; Salvadorean diplomatist, economist and civil servant; *Ambassador to USA. Career:* Prof. of Econs, Cen. American Univ. (UCA) 1985–86, Univ. of Dr. Jose Matías Delgado 1990–92; currently Guest Prof. in Econs, Univ. of Georgetown, Washington, DC, USA; Tech. Man. El Salvador Chamber of Commerce and Industry 1989–91; Adviser to Nat. Asscn of Pvt. Enterprises (ANEP) and Coffee Processors and Exporters of El Salvador (ABECAFE) 1989–91; Dir Int. Trade Negotiations and Econ. Integration, Ministry of Economy 1992–94, Vice-Minister responsible for Trade Policy, Int. Negotiations and Promotion of Investment 1994–97, also Rep. to WTO; Amb. to USA 1997–; mem. working group on Access to Markets of Free Trade Area of the Americas, on Design and Implementation of Nat. Programme of Competitiveness; del. to confs and seminars on trade, integration and econ. devt; Great Latin American Chamber of Commerce of Washington, DC Amb. Award 2000, American Chamber of Commerce of El Salvador Eagle Award 2000. *Address:* Embassy of El Salvador, 1400 16th Street, NW, Suite 100, Washington, DC 20036, USA (office). *Telephone:* (202) 265-9671 (office). *Fax:* (202) 232-3763 (office). *E-mail:* correo@elsalvador.org (office). *Website:* www.elsalvador.org (office).

LEONARD, David K., MA, PhD; American political scientist and academic; *Professor Emeritus of Political Science, University of California, Berkeley;* b. 11 Nov. 1941, Orange, NJ; m. Leslie Leonard; four c. *Education:* Haverford Coll., Univ. of Chicago. *Career:* Jr Research Fellow, Inst. for Devt Studies, Univ. of Nairobi, Kenya 1969–71, Lecturer, Dept of Govt 1971–73, Fulbright Research Fellow 1986; Visiting Lecturer, Dept of Political Science, Univ. of Calif., Berkeley 1973–74, Asst Prof. 1975–79, Assoc. Prof. 1979–90, Prof. 1990, now Prof. Emer., Chair. Center for African Studies 1986–92, Co-Chair. Berkeley–Stanford Jt Center for African Studies 1986–92, Chair. Peace and Conflict Studies 1996–98, Dean of Int. and Area Studies 1999–2004; Sr Lecturer, Dept of Political Science, Univ. of Dar es Salaam, Tanzania 1974–76; Programme Sec., YMCA, Salisbury, Rhodesia (now Harare, Zimbabwe) 1963–64, Acting Dist Sec., Kitwe, Zambia 1965; Man. Adviser, Ministries of Agric. and Livestock Devt 1980–82; Prin. Investigator for projects for Nat. Science Foundation 1985–87, Int. Livestock Center for Africa 1990, Dutch Ministry of Foreign Affairs 1993–96; consultant to USAID 1980–81, Govt of Kenya 1983, World Bank, UNDP 1984–; mem. Editorial Bd Kumarian Press 1986–, Public Admin. and Devt 1995–; Fellow, Danforth Foundation 1965–68; First Prize, Research Essay Contest, Dutch Govt Advisory Council for Scientific Research (RAWOO), 1992. *Publications:* Rural Administration in Kenya: A Critical Appraisal (ed.) 1973, Reaching the Peasant Farmer: Organization Theory and Practice in Kenya 1977, Institutions of Rural Development for the Poor: Decentralization and Organizational Linkages (co-ed.) 1982, African Successes: Four Public Managers of Kenyan Rural Development 1991, Africa's Changing Markets for Health and Veterinary Services: The New Institutional Issues (ed.) 2000; numerous articles in professional journals. *Address:* c/o Department of Political Science, 210 Barrows Hall, University of California, Berkeley, CA 94720-1950, USA (office). *E-mail:* leonard@ berkeley.edu.

LEONARD, Mark; British research institute director; *Senior Research Associate, Foreign Policy Centre; Career:* worked on policy and strategy devt for several nat. govts, int. governmental assocs and cos; Dir of European Programme, Demos –1998; Founding Dir. Foreign Policy Centre 1998, now Sr Research Assoc.; currently Dir of Foreign Policy Centre for European Reform. *Publications include:* research reports: Rebranding Britain, Network Europe 1998, The Future Shape of Europe 2000, Public Diplomacy (co-author) 2000, Public Diplomacy in the Middle East, Re-Ordering the World: The Long-Term Implications of September 11 (collection of essays), What Does China Think? 2007; 24 articles, including Rebranding Europe; Why Europe Will Run the 21st Century 2004. *Address:* Foreign Policy Centre, Suite 14, 2nd Floor, 23-28 Penn Street, Hoxton, London, N1 5DL, England (office). *Telephone:* (20) 7729-7566 (office). *Fax:* (20) 7729-7668 (office). *E-mail:* info@fpc.org.uk (office). *Website:* www.fpc.org.uk (office).

LEPAGE, Corinne Dominique Marguerite; French politician and lawyer; *Leader, CAP 21-Citoyenneté Action Participation pour le 21è siècle;* b. 11 May 1951, Boulogne-Billancourt; m. 1st Christian Jessua, one d.; m. 2nd Christian Huglo, one s. *Education:* Lycée Molière, Univ. of Paris II and Inst. d'Etudes Politiques, Paris. *Career:* in legal partnership 1971–76; barrister, Paris 1978–; Dir of Studies, Univ. of Paris II 1974–77; Dir of Educ. Univ. of Metz 1978–80; Mayor adjoint of Cabourg 1989–2001; Maître de conférences, Inst. d'Etudes Politiques, Paris 1979–87 / 1989–1994; Course Dir Univ. of Paris II 1982–86, Univ. of Paris XII 1987–92; mem. Bar Council 1987–89; Vice-Pres., Pres. Asscn of Admin. Law Advocates 1989–95; Minister of the Environment 1995–97; Pres. Asscn nationale des docteurs en droit 1998–2003; Vice-Pres. Environnement sans frontières 1998–, Asscn européenne des Générations emploi mondialisation 1999–; Pres. Comité de Recherche Indépendante et d'Information sur le Génie Génétique (CRII-GEN); Leader CAP 21-Citoyenneté Action Participation pour le 21è siècle, presidential cand. 2002; Prof., Inst. d'Etudes Politiques de Paris 1994–; Pres., Observatoire do Vigilance at d'Alerte Ecologique; Chevalier de la Légion d'Honneur. *Publications:* Code annoté des procédures administratives contentieuses 1990, Les audits de l'environnement 1992, On ne peut rien faire, Madame le ministre 1998, Bien gérer l'environnement, une chance pour l'entreprise 1999, La Politique de Précaution 2001, Oser l'Espérance, Robert Jauze 2002, De l'Écologie, Hors de l'Imposture et l'Opportunisme 2003; numerous articles in La Gazette du Palais. *Address:* CAP 21, 40 rue de Monceau, 75008 Paris, France (office). *Telephone:* 1-56-59-29-59 (office). *Fax:* 1-56-59-29-39 (office). *E-mail:* corinne.lepage@huglo-lepage.com. *Website:* www.huglo-lepage.com.

LEPANI, Charles W.; Papua New Guinea economist, diplomatist and fmr civil servant; *High Commissioner to Australia;* b. Trobiand Islands; m.; four c. *Education:* Charters Towers High School, Queensland, univ. educ. in Australia, Kennedy School of Govt, Harvard Univ., USA. *Career:* fmr sr civil servant in Port Moresby, Dir Nat. Planning Office 1976–80, fmr Dir Bureau of Industrial Orgs; fmr Man. Dir Lepani Consultants and Lepani Investments; fmr Dir Pacific Islands Devt Program, East West Center; fmr Rep. to UN Working Group on Indigenous Populations, High Commr to

Australia 2005–; mem. and fmr Leader Nat. Alliance Party; mem. Bd Lihir Gold Ltd –1998. *Publications:* Development Issues in Papua New Guinea; articles in professional journals.
Address: Embassy of Papua New Guinea, PO Box E6317, Kingston, ACT 2604, Australia (office). *Telephone:* (2) 6273-3322 (office). *Fax:* (2) 6273-3732 (office). *Website:* www.pngcanberra.org (office).

LEPPING, Sir George, GCMG, MBE; Solomon Islands politician and government official; *President, People's Alliance Party;* b. 22 Nov. 1947; m. Margaret Kwalea Teioli 1972; two s. five d. *Education:* King George VI Secondary School, Agric. Coll., Vudal, Univ. of Reading, UK. *Career:* field officer, Dept of Agric. and Rural Econ. 1968, Pres. Solomon Is. Amateur Athletics Union 1970–73, 1981–82; Sr Field Officer then Under-Sec. (Agric.), Ministry of Agric. 1979–80; Perm. Sec. Ministry of Home Affairs and Nat. Devt 1981–84; Project Dir Rural Services Project 1984–87; Minister of Finance 1988; Gov.-Gen. 1988–94; Leader, then Pres. People's Alliance Party 1996–; Perm. Sec., Policy Evaluation Unit 2002–; fmr mem., Dir or Chair. various govt bodies.
Address: PO Box 1431, Honiara; People's Alliance Party, PO Box 722, Honiara, Solomon Islands.

LERANG, Khek; Cambodian diplomatist; b. 11 Nov. 1939, Kampot Province; m.; two c. *Career:* served in Ministry of Trade 1966–70; Sec. Gen. then Dir Gen. French Nat. Soc. of Imported Products; Sec. Gen. Prince Norodom Sihanouk's Cabinet's Magazine 1968–70; CEO Soc (Paris) France 1971–78; Chief of Secr. of Prince Sihanouk 1979–81, Chief of Cabinet 1982–90, Counsellor of Cabinet 1991; Amb. to Gabon 1991, to Laos 1994–96; fmr Acting Dean of Diplomatic Corps; Amb. to China –2006.
Address: c/o Ministry of Foreign Affairs and International Co-operation, 3 rue Samdech Hun Sen, Khan Chamkarmon, Phnom-Penh, Cambodia. *Telephone:* (23) 214441. *Fax:* (23) 216144. *E-mail:* mfaicinfo@mfaic.gov.kh. *Website:* www.mfaic.gov.kh.

LESIN, Mikhail Yuryevich; Russian politician and journalist; b. 11 July 1958; m.; one s. *Education:* Moscow Inst. of Eng and Construction. *Career:* fmr eng constructor; f. Igrotechnika (later Intelleks) Co-operative 1989–91; Founder and Chair. Bd of Dirs Videoint. (advertising co.) 1991–94; mem. of staff RIA Novosti, Dir-Gen. Novosti-TV Co. 1993–96; Head of Dept of Public Relations, Russian Presidency 1996–97 (resgnd); First Deputy Chair. All-Russian State TV Co. 1997–99; Minister of Press, TV, Broadcasting and Telecommunications (subsequently the Press, Broadcasting and Mass Media) 1999–2004; Adviser to the Pres. 2004–08; mem. Bd of Dirs Pervyi Kanal 2004–.
Address: c/o Office of the President, Kremlin, 103073 Moscow, Russia (office).

LESLIE, Stuart Warren, BSc; Belizean diplomatist and educationalist; b. 30 Sept. 1964. *Education:* Loyola Univ., New Orleans, USA. *Career:* with St John's Coll. Belize 1985–92, positions included Pastoral Dir, Dir of Activities, Head Councillor and Special Asst to the Pres.; Lecturer on Political Science and Communications 1994–98; radio and TV talk show host 1998; Foreign Services Officer, Ministry of Foreign Affairs then Deputy Perm. Mission to UN, New York 1998–2000; Perm. Rep. to UN July 2000–05; Chief Election Officer 2005–06; Amb. for Trade, Ministry of Foreign Affairs and Foreign Trade 2006–; St John's Coll. Berchman's Award for Outstanding Service 1997.
Address: Ministry of Foreign Affairs and Foreign Trade, New Administration Building, POB 174, Belmopan Belize (office). *Telephone:* 822-2167 (office). *Fax:* 822-2854 (office). *E-mail:* belizemfa@btl.net (office). *Website:* www.mfa.gov.bz (office).

L'ESTRANGE, Michael, MA; Australian diplomatist and civil servant; *Secretary, Department of Foreign Affairs and Trade;* b. 12 Oct. 1952, Sydney; m. Jane Allen 1982; five s. *Education:* St Aloysius Coll. (Milson's Point), Sydney Univ., Univ. of Oxford, UK. *Career:* mem. staff Dept of Prime Minister and Cabinet 1981–87; Visiting Fellow, Georgetown Univ., Washington, DC 1987–88, Univ. of California at Berkeley, USA 1988–89; Sr Policy Adviser Office of Fed. Leader of Opposition 1989–94; Exec. Dir Menzies Research Centre 1995–96; Sec. to Cabinet and Head of Cabinet Policy Unit, Canberra 1996–2000; High Commr in UK 2000–05; Sec. Dept of Foreign Affairs and Trade 2005–; Hon. Fellow, Worcester Coll. Oxford; Harkness Fellowship 1986, Rhodes Scholar, Univ. of Oxford 1975.
Address: Department of Foreign Affairs and Trade, John McEwen Crescent, Barton, ACT 0221, Australia (office). *Telephone:* (2) 6261-2214 (office). *Fax:* (2) 6273-2081 (office). *Website:* www.dfat.gov.au (office).

LETERME, Yves Camille Désiré, LLB, BSc, LLM, MPA; Belgian politician; *Prime Minister;* b. 6 Oct. 1960, Wervik, West Flanders; m. Sofie Haesen. *Education:* Catholic Univ. of Leuven, Ghent Univ. *Career:* served as

auditor at Court of Audit (Rekenhof/Cour des Comptes); Adjunct, then Nat. Sec. CVP, resigned to become civil servant with EU, indefinite leave 1997, apptd mem. Belgian Parl. (House of Reps) 1997–, elected 1999, 2003; mem. City Council of Ypres 1995–2001, Alderman of Ypres 1995–2001; Chair. Christen-Democratisch en Vlaams (Christian Democratic and Flemish party—CD&V) 2003–04; Minister-Pres. of Flanders 2004–07; fmr Flemish Minister of Agric. and Fisheries; fmr Deputy Prime Minister and Minister of Budget, Institutional Reforms, Transport and the North Sea in Belgian Fed. Govt; Prime Minister of Belgium 2008–.
Address: Federal Public Service Office of the Prime Minister, 16 rue de la Loi, 1000 Brussels (office); Diksmuidsestraat 58, 8900 Iepre, Belgium. *Telephone:* (2) 210-19-11 (office); (2) 501-02-11 (office); (57) 20-63-61. *Fax:* (2) 217-33-28 (office); (2) 512-69-53 (office); (57) 20-08-14. *E-mail:* info@premier.be (office); info@leterme.fed.be. *Website:* www.premier.be (office); leterme.cdenv.be.

LETSIE III, King of Lesotho, BLL; b. 17 July 1963, Morija; m. Anna Karabo Mots'oeneng (now Queen 'Masenate Mohato Seeiso) 2000; two d. *Education:* Nat. Univ. of Lesotho, Univs of Bristol, Cambridge and London. *Career:* Prin. Chief of Matsieng 1989; installed as King Nov. 1990, abdicated Jan. 1995, reinstated following his father's death Feb. 1996–; Patron of Prince Mohato Award (Khau Ea Khosana Mohato).
Address: Royal Palace, Maseru, Lesotho.

LEUELU, Tine; Tuvaluan diplomatist; *High Commissioner to Fiji;* m. *Career:* fmr Perm. Sec. for Foreign Affairs and Labour; High Commr to Fiji 2006–.
Address: High Commission of Tuvalu, 16 Gorrie Street, POB 14449, Suva, Fiji (office). *Telephone:* 3301355 (office). *Fax:* 3308479 (office).

LEUENBERGER, Moritz; Swiss politician and lawyer; *Head, Federal Department of Transport, Energy and Communications;* b. 21 Sept. 1946, Biel/Bienne; two s. *Education:* Univ. of Zürich. *Career:* pvt. practice as lawyer 1972–91; joined Social Democratic Party (SP) 1969, Leader Zürich SP 1972–80; mem. Zürich City Council 1974–83; Pres. Swiss Tenants' Asscn 1986–91; elected to Nat. Council 1979; elected to Zürich Cantonal Council 1991, Dir of Justice and Internal Affairs 1991–95; Fed. Councillor 1995–; Minister Fed. Dept of Transport, Communications and Energy 1995–, Head Fed. Dept of Environment, Transport, Energy and Communications (subsequently Transport, Energy and Communications) 2001–; Vice-Pres. of the Swiss Confed. 2000, 2005, Pres. 2001, 2006.
Address: Federal Department of Transport, Energy and Communications, Bundeshaus-Nord, 3003 Berne, Switzerland (office). *Telephone:* (31) 3225511 (office). *Fax:* (31) 3225976 (office). *E-mail:* webmaster@gs-uvek.admin.ch (office). *Website:* www.uvek.admin.ch (office).

LEUNG, Oi Sie (Elsie), LLM, JP; Chinese politician and legal official; *Secretary for Justice, Hong Kong Special Administrative Region;* b. 24 April 1939, Hong Kong. *Education:* Univ. of Hong Kong. *Career:* admitted as solicitor of Hong Kong 1968, as overseas solicitor, UK Supreme Court 1976; Notary Public 1978; admitted as solicitor and barrister of Victoria, Australia 1982; founding mem. Hong Kong Fed. of Women Lawyers 1975, Hong Kong Fed. of Women 1993; Pres. Int. Fed. of Women Lawyers 1994; del. 7th People's Congress of Guangdong Prov. 1989–93, 8th Nat. People's Congress 1993–97, People's Repub. of China; Sec. for Justice of Hong Kong Special Admin. Region 1997–; Fellow Int. Acad. of Matrimonial Lawyers 1994; Hon. LLD (China Univ. of Political Science and Law) 2004, (Warwick) 2005; Grand Bauhinia Medal (Hong Kong) 2002.
Address: Department of Justice, Secretary for Justice's Office, 4th Floor, High Block, Queensway Government Offices, 66 Queensway, Hong Kong Special Administrative Region, People's Republic of China (office). *Telephone:* (852) 28692001 (office). *Fax:* (852) 28773978 (office). *E-mail:* sjo@doj.gov.hk (office). *Website:* www.info.gov.hk/justice (office).

LEUNG KAM CHUNG, Antony, BSc; Hong Kong banker and government official; b. 29 Jan. 1952, Hong Kong; m. 1st Sophie Leung; m. 2nd Fu Mingxia (q.v.) 2002; one d. *Education:* Univ. of Hong Kong, Harvard Business School, USA. *Career:* Man. Dir and Regional Man. for Greater China and the Philippines, Chase Manhattan Bank; Chair. Univ. Grants Cttee 1993–98; Dir Hong Kong Futures Exchange 1987–90, Hong Kong Policy Research Inst. 1996–; Trustee Queen Mary Hosp. Charitable Trust 1993–, Hong Kong Centre for Econ. Research 1995–98; Hong Kong Affairs Adviser 1994–97; Arbitrator China Int. Econ. and Trade Arbitration Comm. 1994–; mem. Industrial Devt Bd 1985, Univ. and Polytechnic Grants Cttee 1990–93, Bd Provisional Airport Authority 1990–95, Bd Airport Authority 1995–99, Cen. Policy Unit 1992–93, Bd Hong Kong Community Chest 1992–94, Educ. Comm. 1993–98 (Chair. 1998), Standing Council Chinese Soc. of Macroeconomics, State Planning Comm. 1994–, Exchange Fund Advisory Cttee 1993–, Prep. Cttee of Hong Kong Special

Admin. Region 1996–97, Exec. Council Hong Kong Special Admin. Region 1997–; Financial Sec. Exec. Council 2001–03 (resgnd).

LEUTHARD, Doris; Swiss politican; *Head, Federal Department of Economic Affairs;* b. 10 April 1963; m. Roland Hausin. *Education:* Zürich Univ. *Career:* mem. Swiss Nat. Council 1999–2006; Grossrätin, Aragau Canton 1997–2000; Vice-Pres. Christian Democratic Party 2001–04, Pres. 2004–06; mem. Fed. Council and Head, Fed. Dept of Econ. Affairs 2006–, also responsible for Agric., Veterinary Affairs, Consumer Affairs, Housing, Vocational Training, European Integration.
Address: Federal Department of Economic Affairs, Bundeshaus Ost, 3003 Bern, Switzerland (office). *Telephone:* 313222007 (office). *Fax:* 313222194 (office). *E-mail:* info@gs-evd.admin.ch (office). *Website:* www.evd.admin.ch (office); www.doris-leuthard.ch.

LEVENS, Marie E.; Suriname politician and international organization official; *Director, Human Development Fund Committee, Organization of American States;* b. 1950. *Career:* fmr Sr Policy Adviser, Higher Educ. Devt Scholarship and Exchange Programs, Ministry of Educ. and Community Devt; Consultant Inter-American Devt Bank 1998; Minister of Foreign Affairs 2000–05; mem. Suriname Nat. Party (NPS-Nationale Partij Suriname); currently Dir Human Devt Fund Cttee, OAS.
Address: Organization of American States, General Secretariat Building (GSB), Office 760, 1889 F Street, NW, Washington, DC 20006, USA (office). *Telephone:* (202) 458-6166 (office). *Website:* www.oas.org (office).

LEVI, Noel, CBE, BA; Papua New Guinea politician and diplomatist; b. (Wasangula Noel Levi), 6 Feb. 1942, Nonopai, Kavieng; m. Josepha Muna Levi; two s. two d. *Education:* Scots Coll., Queensland, Papua New Guinea Admin. Coll., Cromwell Coll. Univ. of Queensland and Univ. of Papua New Guinea. *Career:* patrol officer Dept of Dist Admin., Papua New Guinea 1967, later Asst Dist Commr; Asst Sec. Dept of Chief Minister 1973; Sec. Dept of Defence 1974; Minister of Foreign Affairs 1980; Amb. to People's Repub. of China 1987; High Commr to UK (also accred to Israel, Zimbabwe and Egypt) 1991; Sec. Dept of the Prime Minister and Nat. Exec. Council 1995; Sec.-Gen. Pacific Islands Forum Secr. 1998–2003.
Address: c/o Pacific Islands Forum Secretariat, Private Mail Bag, Suva (office); House No. 4, Forum Secretariat Compound, Ratu Sukuna Road, Suva, Fiji (home). *Telephone:* (679) 3306535 (home).

LEVITTE, Jean-David, LLB; French diplomatist and civil servant; b. 14 June 1946, Moissac; m. Marie-Cécile Levitte 1970; two d. *Education:* Inst. of Political Science, Nat. School of Oriental Languages. *Career:* joined Ministry of Foreign Affairs 1970, positions included Man. Econ. Affairs 1974–75, Asst Dir Dept for W Africa 1984–86, Adjunct Dir of Cabinet 1986–88, Dir Dept for Asia and Oceania 1990–93, Dir-Gen. of Cultural, Scientific and Tech. Relations 1993–95; Vice-Consul in Hong Kong 1971; Third Sec., Embassy in Beijing, People's Repub. of China 1972–74; Counsellor, Perm. Mission to UN, New York 1981–84, Perm. Rep. to UN, Geneva 1988–90, New York 2000–02; Amb. to USA 2002–07; Diplomatic Adviser to Pres. 1995–2000, 2007–; Chargé de Mission, Secr.-Gen. of Presidency 1975–81; Officier, Légion d'honneur.
Address: c/o Office of the President, Palais de l'Elysée, 55–57 rue du Faubourg Saint Honoré, 75008 Paris, France. *Telephone:* 1-42-92-81-00. *Fax:* 1-47-42-24-65. *Website:* www.elysee.fr.

LEVY, Itzhak; politician and rabbi; b. 1947, Morocco; m.; five c. *Education:* Kerem B'Yavne and Yeshivat Hakotel. *Career:* emigrated to Israel in 1957; ordained rabbi; served in Israeli Defence Forces, to rank of Maj.; Nat. Religious Party mem. Knesset (Parl.) 1988–, mem. Knesset House Cttee, Cttees on Finance, on Constitution, Law and Justice, on Labour and Social Welfare 1988–92, on Knesset House Cttee and Cttee on Constitution, Law and Justice 1992–96; Minister of Transport 1996–98, later of Housing, Minister without Portfolio; mem. Bnei Akiva Exec. and World Secr.; Leader Nat. Religious Party; Chair. Israel–Argentina Parl. Friendship League.
Address: National Religious Party, Jerusalem, Israel. *Telephone:* 2-377277. *Fax:* 2-377757.

LEVY, Baron (Life Peer), cr. 1997, of Mill Hill in the London Borough of Barnet; **Michael Abraham Levy,** FCA, CA; British consultant; b. 11 July 1944, London; m. Gilda Levy (née Altbach) 1967; one s. one d. *Education:* Hackney Downs Grammar School. *Career:* chartered accountant Lubbock Fine 1961–66; Prin. M. Levy & Co. 1966–69; Pnr Wagner, Prager, Levy & Partners 1969–73; Chair. Magnet Group of Cos 1973–88, D & J Securities Ltd 1988–92, M & G Records 1992–97; Vice-Chair. Phonographic Performance Ltd 1979–84, British Phonographic Industry Ltd 1984–87; Chair. British Music Industry Awards Cttee 1992–95, Patron 1995–; Nat. Campaign Chair. United Jt Israel Appeal 1982–85, Hon. Vice-Pres. 1994–2000, Hon. Pres. 2000–; Special Envoy of Prime Minister and

Adviser on Middle East, South America and Kazakhstan 1997–2007; Chair. Jewish Care 1992–97, Pres. 1998–; fmr Chair. Jewish Care Community Foundation, Foundation for Educ.; Vice-Chair. Cen. Council for Jewish Community Services 1994–, Chief Rabbinate Awards for Excellence 1992–2007; mem. Jewish Agency World Bd of Govs 1990–95, World Chair. Youth Aliyah Cttee 1991–95; mem. Keren Hayesod World Bd of Govs 1991–95, World Comm. on Israel–Diaspora Relations 1995–, Int. Bd Govs Peres Centre for Peace 1997–, Advisory Council Foreign Policy Centre 1997–, Nat. Council Voluntary Orgs Advisory Cttee 1998–, Community Legal Service Champions Panel 1999–, Hon. Cttee Israel, Britain and the Commonwealth Asscn 2000–; Pres. CSV (Community Service Volunteers) 1998–; Trustee Holocaust Educ. Trust 1998–2007; Patron Save a Child's Heart Foundation 2000–; Gov. Jewish Free School 1990–95, Hon. Pres. 2001–; Chair. Wireart Ltd and Chase Music Ltd (fmrly M & G Music Ltd) 1992–; mem. Exec. Cttee Chai-Lifeline 2001–02; Patron, Prostate Cancer Charitable Trust 1997–, Friends of Israel Educ. Trust 1998–, Simon Mark's Jewish Primary School Trust 2002–; Hon. Patron, Cambridge Univ. Jewish Soc. 2002–; Hon. PhD (Middlesex Univ.) 1999; B'nai B'rith First Lodge Award 1994, Scopus Award Hebrew Univ. of Jerusalem 1998, Israel Policy Forum Special Recognition Award (USA) 2003. *Publication:* A Question of Honour (memoir) 2008.
Address: House of Lords, Westminster, London, SW1A 0PW, England (office). *Telephone:* (20) 7487-5174 (office). *Fax:* (20) 7486-7919 (office). *E-mail:* ml@lmalvy.demon.co.uk (office).

LEWIS, Bernard, PhD, FBA, FRHistS; American writer and academic; *Cleveland E. Dodge Professor Emeritus of Near Eastern Studies, Princeton University;* b. 31 May 1916, London, England; m. Ruth Hélène Oppenhejm 1947 (divorced 1974); one s. one d. *Education:* Univs of London and Paris. *Career:* Lecturer in Islamic History, School of Oriental Studies, Univ. of London 1938; served in RAC and Intelligence Corps 1940–41; attached to Foreign Office 1941–45; Prof. of History of the Near and Middle East, Univ. of London 1949–74; Cleveland E. Dodge Prof. of Near Eastern Studies, Princeton Univ. 1974–86, Prof. Emer. 1986–; Dir Annenberg Research Inst., Philadelphia 1986–90; Visiting Prof. of History, Univ. of Calif. at LA 1955–56, Columbia Univ. 1960, Ind. Univ. 1963, Princeton Univ. 1964, Univ. of Calif. at Berkeley 1965, Coll. de France 1980, École des Hautes Études en Sciences Sociales, Paris 1983, 1988, Univ. of Chicago 1985; Visiting mem. Inst. for Advanced Study, Princeton Univ. 1969, mem. 1974–86; A. D. White Prof.-at-Large, Cornell Univ. 1984–90; mem. Bd of Dirs Institut für die Wissenschaften von Menschen, Vienna 1988; Jefferson Lecturer in the Humanities, US Nat. Endowment for the Humanities 1990; Tanner Lecturer, Brasenose Coll., Oxford 1990; Henry M. Jackson Memorial Lecturer (Seattle) 1992; mem. British Acad., American Philosophical Soc. 1973, American Acad. of Arts and Sciences 1983; American Oriental Soc., Corresp. mem. Inst. d'Egypte, Cairo 1969–, Inst. de France 1994–; Fellow, Univ. Coll., London 1976; Hon. mem. Turkish Historical Soc., Société Asiatique, Paris, Atatürk Acad. of History, Language and Culture, Ankara, Turkish Acad. of Sciences; Hon. Fellow SOAS, London 1986; 15 hon. doctorates including (Hebrew Univ., Jerusalem) 1974, (Tel-Aviv) 1979, (State Univ. of NY Binghamton, Univ. of Penn., Hebrew Union Coll., Cincinnati) 1987, (Univ. of Haifa, Yeshiva Univ., New York) 1991, (Bar-Ilan Univ.) 1992, (Brandeis) 1993, (Ben-Gurion, Ankara) 1996, (Princeton Univ.) 2002; Citation of Honour, Turkish Ministry of Culture 1973, Harvey Prize, Technion-Israel Inst. of Tech. 1978, Educ. Award for Outstanding Achievement in Promotion of American-Turkish Studies 1985, Atatürk Peace Prize 1998, Golden Plate Award, Acad. of Achievement, Washington DC 2004, Nat. Endowment for the Humanities 2007, Irving Kristol Award 2007. *Publications:* The Origins of Ismā'ilism: A Study of the Historical Background of the Fatimid Caliphate 1940, Turkey Today 1940, British Contributions to Arabic Studies 1941, Handbook of Diplomatic and Political Arabic 1947, Land of Enchanters (ed.) 1948, The Arabs in History 1950, Notes and Documents from the Turkish Archives: A Contribution to the History of the Jews in the Ottoman Empire 1952, Encyclopedia of Islam (co-ed.) 1956–86, The Emergence of Modern Turkey 1961, The Kingly Crown 1961, Historians of the Middle East (co-ed. with P. M. Holt) 1962, Istanbul and the Civilization of the Ottoman Empire 1963, The Middle East and the West 1964, The Assassins: A Radical Sect in Islam 1967, The Cambridge History of Islam (ed. with P. M. Holt and Ann K. S. Lambton, two vols) 1970, Race and Colour in Islam 1971, Islam in History: Ideas, Men and Events in the Middle East 1973, Islamic Civilization (ed.) 1974, Islam from the Prophet Muhammad to the Capture of Constantinople (ed. and trans., two vols) 1974, History: Remembered, Recovered, Invented 1975, Studies in Classical and Ottoman Islam: Seventh to Sixteenth Centuries 1976, The World of Islam: Faith, People, Culture (ed.) 1976, Population and Revenue in the Towns of Palestine in the Sixteenth Century (with Amnon Cohen) 1978, The Muslim Discovery of Europe 1982, Christians and Jews in the Ottoman Empire (two vols) 1982, The Jews of Islam 1984, Semites and Anti-Semites: An Inquiry into Conflict and Prejudice 1986, As Others See

Us (co-ed.) 1986, The Political Language of Islam 1988, Race and Slavery in the Middle East: A Historical Enquiry 1990, Islam and the West 1993, The Shaping of the Modern Middle East 1994, Cultures in Conflict: Christians, Muslims and Jews in the Age of Discovery 1995, The Middle East: Two Thousand Years of History from the Rise of Christianity to the Present Day 1995, The Future of the Middle East 1997, The Multiple Identities of the Middle East 1998, A Middle East Mosaic: Fragments of Life, Letters and History 2000, Music of a Distant Drum, Classical Arabic, Persian, Turkish and Hebrew Poems 2001, What Went Wrong? Western Impact and Middle Eastern Response 2002, The Crisis of Islam: Holy War and Unholy Terror 2003, From Babel to Dragomans: Interpreting the Middle East 2004; numerous contribs to professional journals.
Address: c/o Department of Near Eastern Studies, 110 Jones Hall, Princeton University, Princeton, NJ 08544, USA. *Telephone:* (609) 258-4280.

LEWIS, Cenio Elwin; Saint Vincent and the Grenadines diplomatist; *High Commissioner to UK;* m. Ita Lewis. *Career:* Minister Counsellor, High Comm. in London 1998–2001, High Commr to UK 2001–.
Address: Saint Vincent and the Grenadines High Commission, 10 Kensington Court, London, W8 5DL, England (office). *Telephone:* (20) 7565-2874 (office). *Fax:* (20) 7937-6040 (office). *E-mail:* info@svghighcom.co.uk (office); svghighcom@clara.co.uk (office).

LEWIS, Patricia, BSc, PhD; British international organization executive and nuclear physicist; *Director, United Nations Institute for Disarmament Research;* b. 11 April 1957, Coventry; two c. *Education:* Univ. of Manchester, Univ. of Birmingham. *Career:* Dir Verification Tech. Information Centre (VERTIC) 1989; consultant on Conventional Force Reduction Treaty Negotiations, FCO 1988–90, apptd Govt Expert to UN Study on Role of UN in Verification 1989–90; Visiting Lecturer, Imperial Coll. London 1990–92; Elizabeth Poppleton Fellow, Australian Nat. Univ. 1992–93; Chair. UK Gulf Syndrome Study Group 1994–97; Dir United Nations Institute for Disarmament Research (UNIDIR) 1997–; mem. int. advisory cttee Bonn Int. Conversion Centre (BICC), Germany; mem. IISS; Fellow British–American Project; reviewer Canberra Comm. Report on Elimination of Nuclear Weapons; mem. Scientists for Global Responsibility, Tokyo Forum for Nuclear Non-proliferation and Nuclear Disarmament 1998–99, Weapons of Mass Destruction Comm. (Blix Comm.) 2004–06. *Publications include:* numerous works on all aspects of arms control and disarmament issues.
Address: United Nations Institute for Disarmament Research, Palais des Nations, 1211 Geneva 10, Switzerland (office). *Telephone:* (22) 9173186 (office). *Fax:* (22) 9170176 (office). *E-mail:* unidir@unog.ch (office); plewis@unog.ch (home). *Website:* www.unidir.org (office).

LEWIS, Hon. Samuel Winfield, MA; American diplomatist; *Senior Adviser, Israel Policy Forum;* b. 1 Oct. 1930, Houston; m. Sallie S. Smoot 1953; one s. one d. *Education:* Yale and Johns Hopkins Univs. *Career:* Exec. Asst American Trucking Asscn, Washington 1953–54; entered Foreign Service 1954; with Consulate, Naples 1954–55; Consul, Florence 1955–59; Officer-in-Charge Italian Affairs, Dept of State 1959–61; Special Asst to Under-Sec. of State 1961–63; Deputy Asst Dir US AID Mission to Brazil 1964–66; Deputy Dir Office for Brazil Affairs, Dept of State 1967–68; senior staff mem. for Latin American Affairs, Nat. Security Council, White House 1968–69; Special Asst for Policy Planning, Bureau of Inter-American Affairs 1969, to Dir-Gen. Foreign Service 1969–71; Deputy Chief of Mission and Counsellor, US Embassy, Kabul 1971–74; Deputy Dir Policy Planning Staff, Dept of State 1974–75, Asst Sec. of State for Int. Orgs 1975–77; Amb. to Israel 1977–85; Pres. US Inst. of Peace 1987–93; Dir Policy Planning Staff, Dept of State 1993–94; Visiting Fellow, Princeton Univ. 1963–64; Diplomat-in-Residence, Johns Hopkins Foreign Policy Inst. 1985–87; Guest Scholar, The Brookings Inst., Washington, DC 1987; Visiting Prof., Hamilton Coll. 1995, 1997, 2008; Counselor, Washington Inst. for Near East Policy 1995–98; Adjunct Prof. Georgetown Univ. 1996; mem. Council on Foreign Relations, Vice-Chair. Center for Preventive Action 1995–97; Vice-Chair. American Acad. of Diplomacy 1995–99; mem. The Middle East Inst., Cousteau Soc.; mem. Bd of Dirs Inst. for the Study of Diplomacy, Georgetown Univ. 1994–, Asscn for Diplomatic Studies and Training 1994–2005, Pnrs for Democratic Change 2004–; Sr Adviser Policy Forum 1998–; Chair. Bd of Overseers, Harry S. Truman Inst. for Advancement of Peace, Hebrew Univ. of Jerusalem 1986–91; Sr Int. Fellow, Dayan Centre for Middle Eastern and African Affairs, Tel-Aviv Univ. 1986–87; Professorial Lecturer, School of Advanced Int. Studies, Johns Hopkins Univ. 2005; Chair. Advisory Cttee Search for Common Ground in the Middle East 2005–; Dr hc, Hon. DHumLitt; William A. Jump Award 1967, Meritorious Honor Award (Dept of State, AID) 1967, Presidential Man. Improvement Award 1970, Distinguished Honor Awards 1977, 1985, Wilbur J. Carr Award 1985. *Publications:* Soviet and American Attitudes toward the Arab-Israeli Peace Process, in Super Power

Rivalry in the Middle East 1987, The United States and Israel 1977–1988, in The Middle East: Ten Years after Camp David 1988, Making Peace among Arabs and Israelis 1991, The United States and Israel: Evolution of an Unwritten Alliance 1999; numerous articles.
Address: 6232 Nelway Drive, McLean, VA 22101, USA (home). *Telephone:* (703) 448-1997 (home). *Fax:* (703) 448-1997 (home). *E-mail:* sixtymeter@aol.com (home).

LEWIS, Stephen, CC; Canadian international advocate and academic; *Co-Director, AIDS-Free World;* b. 11 Nov. 1937, Ottawa; m. Michele Landsberg 1963; three c. *Education:* Univ. of Toronto, Univ. of British Columbia. *Career:* spent one year teaching and travelling in Africa; fmr Dir of Org., New Democratic Party (NDP), Prov. Leader 1970–77; MP for Scarborough W, Ont. Legis. 1963–78; Amb. and Perm Rep. of Canadian Mission to UN 1984–88; Special Adviser to UN Sec.-Gen. on African Econ. Recovery 1986–91; Special Rep. to UNICEF 1990–95, Deputy Exec. Dir 1995–99; mem. Int. Panel of Eminent Persons to investigate genocide in Rwanda 1999–2000; UN Special Envoy for HIV/AIDS in Africa 2001–06; Co-Dir AIDS-Free World 2006–; Prof., McMaster Univ. 2007–; Founder and Chair. Stephen Lewis Foundation; Hon. LLD from 27 univs; Gordon Sinclair ACTRA Award 1982, Macleans Magazine Canadian of the Year 2003, listed by TIME magazine as one of 100 most influential people in the world 2005. *Publications:* Art Out of Agony 1983, Race Against Time 2005.
Address: AIDS-Free World, 6 Montclair Avenue, Toronto, Ont. M4V 1W1, Canada. *Telephone:* (416) 533-9292 (office), (416) 657-4458 (home). *Fax:* (416) 850-4910 (office). *E-mail:* info@stephenlewisfoundation.org (office); info@aids-freeworld.org; stephenhlewis@aol.com (home). *Website:* www.stephenlewisfoundation.org (office); www.aids-freeworld.org.

LEWIS, Vaughan Allen, PhD, CBE; Saint Lucia politician and academic; *Professor of International Relations, University of the West Indies;* b. 17 May 1940; m. Shirley May Lewis; two d. *Education:* Univ. of Manchester, UK. *Career:* temporary Asst Lecturer, Dept of Political Theory, Univ. Coll. Swansea, Wales 1963–64; Asst Lecturer, Dept of Politics, Univ. of Liverpool 1964–66; Research Fellow Dept of Govt, Univ. of Manchester 1966–68; Lecturer, Dept of Govt, Univ. of the West Indies, Mona, Jamaica 1968–72; Part-time Lecturer, Inst. of Int. Relations, Univ. of the West Indies, St Augustine, Trinidad 1974–80, Acting Dir Inst. of Social and Econ. Research, Univ. of the West Indies 1974, Dir (rank of Full Prof.) 1977–82; Dir-Gen. Org. of Eastern Caribbean States, Castries, St Lucia 1982–95; Prime Minister of Saint Lucia 1996–97; Prof. of Int. Relations, Inst. of Int. Relations, Univ. of the West Indies 1999–; Visiting Prof. Fla Int. Univ. 1980, Ford Foundation Visiting Fellow Yale Univ. 1981. *Publications:* numerous books, papers and articles on int. relations, particularly concerning the Caribbean.
Address: Institute of International Relations, University of the West Indies, St Augustine Campus, St Augustine, Trinidad and Tobago. *E-mail:* lewisv@diplomacy.edu (office); lewisv@candw.lc (home).

LI, Baodong; Chinese diplomatist; *Permanent Representative, United Nations, Geneva; Career:* Dir-Gen. Dept of Int. Orgs and Confs, Ministry of Foreign Affairs –2005; Amb. to Zambia 2005–07; Perm. Rep. to UN Office at Geneva, Switzerland 2007–.
Address: Permanent Mission of the People's Republic of China to the United Nations Office at Geneva, Chemin de Surville 11, 1213 Petit-Lancy 2, Switzerland (office). *Telephone:* (22) 879-56-78 (office). *Fax:* (22) 793-70-14 (office). *E-mail:* chinamission_gva@mfa.gov.cn (office). *Website:* www.china-un.ch (office).

LI, Bin; Chinese diplomatist; *Ambassador of Korean Peninsula Affairs, Ministry of Foreign Affairs; Career:* Amb. to Repub. of Korea 2001-05; Ambassador of Korean Peninsula Affairs, Ministry of Foreign Affairs 2005–.
Address: Ministry of Foreign Affairs, 225 Chaoyangmen Nan Dajie, Chaoyang Qu, Beijing 100701, People's Republic of China (office). *Telephone:* (10) 65961114 (office). *Fax:* (10) 65962146 (office). *E-mail:* webmaster@mfa.gov.cn (office). *Website:* www.fmprc.gov.cn (office).

LI, Changchun; Chinese party and government official; b. Feb. 1944, Dalian City, Liaoning Prov.; m. Zhang Shurong. *Education:* Harbin Inst. of Tech. *Career:* joined CCP 1965; at Harbin Inst. of Tech. 1966–68; technician, Shenyang Switchgear Plant, Liaoning Prov. 1968–75; Deputy Man. later Man. Shenyang Electrical Equipment Co. 1975–80 (Vice-Chair. CCP Revolutionary Cttee, mem. Standing Cttee and Deputy Sec. CCP Party Cttee 1975–80); Deputy Dir Bureau of Mechanical and Electrical Industry, Shenyang City 1980–81 (Deputy Sec. CCP Party Cttee 1980–81); Deputy Sec.-Gen. CCP Municipal Cttee, Shenyang City 1981–82; Vice-Mayor Shenyang City 1982–83, Mayor 1983–85; Sec. Shenyang Municipal CCP Cttee 1983–86 (Chair. Econ. Cttee 1982–83); Deputy Sec. Liaoning Prov.

CCP Cttee 1985–90; Vice-Gov. (also Acting Gov.) of Liaoning Prov. 1986–87, Gov. 1987–90; Vice-Gov. (also Acting Gov.) of Henan Prov. 1990–91, Gov. 1991–92; Sec. CCP 5th Henan Prov. Cttee 1992–98; Chair. Standing Cttee Henan Prov. People's Congress 1993–98; Alt. mem. 12th CCP Cen. Cttee 1981–82, mem. 13th CCP Cen. Cttee 1987–92, 14th CCP Cen. Cttee 1992–97, 15th CCP Cen. Cttee 1997–2002, Politburo 15th CCP Cen. Cttee 1997–2002, 16th CCP Cen. Cttee 2002–07, Politburo 16th CCP Cen. Cttee 2002–07, Standing Cttee Politburo 16th CCP Cen. Cttee 2002–07, 17th CCP Cen. Cttee 2007–, Standing Cttee Politburo 17th CCP Cen. Cttee 2007–; Sec. CCP Guangdong Prov. Cttee 1998–2002.
Address: Standing Committee of the Politburo, Chinese Communist Party Central Committee, Beijing, People's Republic of China (office).

LI, Daoyu; Chinese diplomatist; *Chairman, Chinese Association of Arms Control and Disarmament;* b. 7 Aug. 1932, Shanghai; m. Ye Zhao Lie 1956; two s. *Education:* Univ. of Shanghai. *Career:* joined Foreign Service 1952; held various posts Dept of Int. Orgs and Confs; Deputy Perm. Rep. to UN at Geneva 1983–84; Dir Dept of Int. Orgs, Foreign Ministry 1984–88; Asst Foreign Minister 1988–90; Perm. Rep. to UN, New York 1990–93, Amb. to USA 1993–98; led Chinese Del. to ESCAP session 1989; fmr Vice-Chair. Chinese Nat. Comm., UNESCO, Nat. Cttee for Pacific Econ. Co-operation, Preparatory Cttee of China for Int. Space Year 1992, Nat. Cttee for Int. Decade for Natural Disaster Reduction; fmr rep. of China on Comm. on Human Rights, ECOSOC and UNCTAD; Vice-Chair. Overseas Chinese Affairs Cttee of 9th NPC 1998; mem. Standing Cttee NPC 1998–2003; Prof. School of Int. Studies, Beijing Univ., Inst. of Int. Studies, Tsinghua Univ., Foreign Affairs Coll., Center for American Studies, Fudan Univ., Pacific Inst., Tongji Univ.; Chair. China Int. Public Relations Asscn 1999–, Chinese Asscn of Arms Control and Disarmament 2001–; Vice-Pres. China Int. Friendship Exchange Asscn, China Women Devt Fund; mem. Council Chinese People's Inst. of Foreign Affairs; Sr Adviser China Inst. of Int. Strategic Studies; Adviser China Int. Law Soc., Centre for Across-the-Straits Relationship Studies, Shanghai WTO Affairs Consulting Centre.
Address: China International Public Relations Association, Room 918, 7 Fuchengmenwai Street, Beijing, 100037, People's Republic of China (office). *Telephone:* (10) 68095777 (office). *Fax:* (10) 68095775 (office). *E-mail:* info@cipra.org.cn (office). *Website:* www.cipra.org.cn (office).

LI, Keqiang, MA, PhD; Chinese politician; *Vice Premier, State Council;* b. 1955, Dingyuan Co., Anhui Prov. *Education:* Beijing Univ. *Career:* sent to do manual labour, Dongling Production Brigade, Damiao Commune early 1970s (Sec. CCP Party Br. 1976–78); joined CCP 1976; Head, Beijing Univ. Students' Fed. 1978–82; Sec. Communist Youth League, Beijing Univ. 1978–82; fmr Deputy Dir Dept of Schools and Colls of Communist Youth League Cen. Cttee; Sec.-Gen. All-China Students' Fed. 1982, Vice-Chair. 1990; Sec. Secr. of Communist Youth League Cen. Cttee 1982–93, First Sec. 1993–98; Pres. China Youth Political Coll. 1993; Deputy Sec. CCP Henan Prov. Cttee 1998–2002 (mem. Standing Cttee 2001–), Sec. 2002–04; Deputy Gov. Henan Prov. 1998, Acting Gov. 1998–99, Gov. 1999–2003; Chair. Standing Cttee Henan Prov. People's Congress 2003–04, Standing Cttee Liaoning Prov. People's Congress 2004–07; Sec. CCP Liaoning Prov. Cttee 2004–07; mem. Standing Cttee of NPC 1993–98, Cttee for Internal and Judicial Affairs of NPC 1993–98, Credentials Cttee of NPC 1993–98; mem. 15th CCP Cen. Cttee 1997–2002, 16th CCP Cen. Cttee 2002–07, Standing Cttee Politburo 17th CCP Cen. Cttee 2007–; Vice-Premier of State Council 2008–.
Address: Office of the Vice-Premier, Great Hall of the People, West Edge, Tiananmen Square, Beijing, People's Republic of China (office). *Website:* english.gov.cn (office).

LI, Kwok Nang Andrew, CBE, MA, LLM, QC; Chinese judge; *Chief Justice, Court of Final Appeal, Hong Kong Special Administrative Region;* b. 12 Dec. 1948, Hong Kong; m. Judy Mo Ying Li; two d. *Education:* St Paul's Co-Educational Coll., Hong Kong, Repton School, Hong Kong, Univ. of Cambridge, UK. *Career:* called to the Bar, Middle Temple 1970, Hong Kong 1973; practised at Hong Kong Bar 1973–97; QC, Hong Kong 1988; Chief Justice, Court of Final Appeal Hong Kong 1997–; JP, Hong Kong 1995; Hon. Bencher Middle Temple 1997; Hon. Fellow, Fitzwilliam Coll. Cambridge 1999; hon. degrees (Hong Kong Univ. of Science and Tech.) 1993, (Baptist Univ.) 1994, (Open Univ. of Hong Kong) 1997, (Univ. of Hong Kong), (The Griffith Univ.) 2001, (Univ. of NSW) 2002, (Univ. of Tech., Sydney) 2005, (Chinese Univ. of Hong Kong) 2006.
Address: Court of Final Appeal, No. 1 Battery Path, Central, Hong Kong Special Administrative Region (office); Chief Justice's House, 18 Gough Hill Road, The Peak, Hong Kong Special Administrative Region, People's Republic of China (home). *Telephone:* 21230011 (office); 28497169 (home). *Fax:* 21210310 (office); 28492191 (home). *E-mail:* andrewknli@judiciary .gov.hk (office). *Website:* www.judiciary.gov.hk (office).

LI, Qiangmin; Chinese diplomatist; *Ambassador to Zambia; Career:* fmr Political Counsellor in Tel-Aviv; Amb. to Uganda 2002–05; Deputy Dir-Gen. Africa Dept, Ministry of Foreign Affairs 2005–07; Del. to UN Gen. Ass., New York 2006; Amb. to Zambia 2007–.
Address: Embassy of People's Republic of China, Plot 7430, United Nations Avenue, Longacres, POB 31975, 10101 Lusaka, Zambia (office). *Telephone:* (1) 251169 (office). *Fax:* (1) 251157 (office). *E-mail:* chinaemb_zm@mfa.gov.cn (office). *Website:* www.fmprc.gov.cn (office).

LI, Rongrong; Chinese economist and state official; *Chairman, State-Owned Assets Supervision and Administration Commission (SASAC);* b. Dec. 1944, Suzhou, Jiangsu Prov. *Education:* Tianjin Univ. *Career:* workshop chief, Wuxi Oil Pump and Oil Throttle Factory, Deputy Dir, then Dir 1968–86; Vice-Chair. Wuxi Municipal Econ. Comm. 1986, later Dir Wuxi Municipal Light Industry Bureau and Chair. Wuxi Municipal Planning Comm.; Vice-Chair. Jiangsu Prov. Planning and Econ. Comm. 1986–91; Production Planning Bureau, State Council Production Office 1992; Deputy Dir-Gen., Foreign Econ. Cooperation Dept, State Council Econ. and Trade Office 1992, later Dir-Gen., Technical Renovation Dept and Sec.-Gen., State Econ. and Trade Comm. (SETC), becoming Vice-Chair. and Deputy Party Sec., Chair. 2001–; Vice-Chair., State Devt and Planning Comm. (SDPC) 1998–; Chair. State-Owned Assets Supervision and Admin Comm. (SASAC) 2003–; joined CCP 1983, mem. 16th CCP Cen. Cttee 2002–.
Address: Office of the Chairman, State-Owned Assets Supervision and Administration Commission (SASAC), 26 Xuanxumen Xidajie, Beijing 100053, People's Republic of China (office). *Telephone:* (10) 63193615 (office). *Fax:* (10) 63193571 (office). *E-mail:* iecc@sasac.gov.cn (office). *Website:* www.sasac.gov.cn (office).

LI, Ruihuan; Chinese party and government official; b. Sept. 1934, Baodi Co., Tianjing. *Education:* part-time studies at an architecture eng inst. *Career:* construction worker, Beijing No. 3 Construction Co. 1951–65; Joined CCP 1959; Deputy Sec. Beijing Building Materials Co. CCP Party Cen. 1965–66; Vice-Chair. Beijing Municipal Trade Union Fed. 1971; Vice-Chair. All-China Youth Fed. 1971–80; Dir-Gen. Work Site for Mao Zedong Memorial Hall, Beijing 1977; Deputy for Beijing, 5th NPC 1978; Sec. Communist Youth League 1979–81; mem. Standing Cttee, 5th NPC 1978–83; Deputy Mayor Tianjin 1981, Acting Mayor 1982, Mayor Tianjin 1982–89; Sec. CCP Municpal Cttee, Tianjin 1982–84; mem. 12th CCP Cen. Cttee 1982–87, 13th CCP Cen. Cttee 1987–92, 14th CCP Cen. Cttee 1992–97, 15th CCP Cen. Cttee 1997–2002; mem. Politburo 1987–2002, Standing Cttee Politburo 1989, Perm. mem. Politburo 1992–2002; Chair. 8th Nat. Cttee CPPCC 1993–98, 9th Nat. Cttee CPPCC 1998–2003; Hon. Pres. Chinese Fed. for the Disabled 1993–; Hon Pres. Chinese Table Tennis Asscn 1990–; named Nat. Model Worker 1979.
Address: c/o National Committee of the Chinese People's Political Consultative Conference, No.23, Taipingqiao Street, Beijing 100811; Zhongguo Gongchan Dang (Chinese Communist Party), Zhongnanhai, Beijing, People's Republic of China (office).

LI, Tieying; Chinese state official; *Vice-Chairman, 10th Standing Committee, National People's Congress;* b. Sept. 1936, Changsha City, Hunan Prov.; m. Qin Xinhua. *Education:* Charles Univ., Czechoslovakia. *Career:* joined CCP 1955; worker, Research Inst., Ministry of Electronics Industry 1961, Chief Engineer and Dir 1976; Deputy Dir Science and Tech. Cttee, Shenyang City, Liaoning Prov. 1976; Sec. CCP Shenyang City Cttee 1981–83, CCP Liaoning Prov. Cttee 1983–86; Minister of Electronics Industry 1985–88; Minister in charge of State Comm. for Econ. Restructuring 1987–88, 1993–98, of State Educ. Comm. 1988–93; Chair. Cen. Patriotic Public Health Campaign Cttee; State Councillor 1988–98; Head Leading Group for the Reform of the Housing System 1991–; Deputy Head Nat. Leading Group for Anti-Disaster and Relief Work 1991–; Dir Nat. Cttee for the Patriotic Public Health Campaign; Vice-Chair. NPC 10th Standing Cttee 2003–; Pres. Chinese Acad. of Social Sciences 1998–; Del., World Conf. on Educ., Bangkok 1990, visited India, Laos 1992; Alt. mem. 12th CCP Cen. Cttee 1982, mem. 1985, mem. 13th CCP Cen. Cttee 1987–92, 14th CCP Cen. Cttee 1992–97, 15th CCP Cen. Cttee 1997–2002, mem. Politburo of CCP 1992–2002; Hon. Pres. Mao Zedong Acad. of the Arts 1997–, Athletics Asscn, Soc. of Nat. Conditions; Nat Nat. ional Science Conf. Prize 1978.
Address: Zhongguo Gongchan Dang, Beijing (office); Chinese Academy of Social Sciences, 5 Jianguomen Nei Da Jie, Beijing 100732, People's Republic of China (office). *Telephone:* 65137744 (office).

LI, Yuanchao, MS, PhD; Chinese politician; *Secretary, Jiangsu Provincial Party Committee, CPC;* b. 1950, Lianshui Co., Jiangsu Prov. *Education:* Shanghai Fudan Univ., Beijing Univ., Central Party School. *Career:* joined CPC 1978; Sec. Shanghai Municipal Cttee Communist Youth League 1983; mem. Sec. Youth League Central Cttee 1983–90; Dir Nat. Cttee for Young Pioneers' work 1984; Vice-Chair. Nat. Youth Fed.

1986–96; Dir First Bureau, Int. Publicity Leading Group 1990–93, Vice-Minister Int. Publicity Office under CCP Central Cttee 1993–96, Vice-Minister of Culture 1996–2000; Deputy Sec. CCP Jiangsu Prov. Party Cttee 2000–02, Sec. 2002–07, Chair. Standing Cttee 2003–07; Sec. CCP Party Cttee Nanjing City 2001–03; Vice-Chair. Women and Youth Sub-Cttee, CPPCC; mem. CPPCC 7th Nat. Cttee 1988–93, 8th Nat. Cttee 1993–98, 9th Nat. Cttee 1998–2003; Alt. mem. 16th CPC Cen. Cttee 2002–07; mem. 17th Cen. Cttee 2007–; mem. Political Bureau and Secr. Cen. Cttee, Ministry of Org. Dept 2007–.
Address: Organization Department, Central Committee of the Communist Party of China, People's Republic of China (office).

LI, Zhaoxing, MA; Chinese politician and diplomatist; b. Oct. 1940, Jiaonan, Shandong Prov.; m.; one s. *Education:* Beijing Univ., Beijing Foreign Languages Inst. *Career:* joined CCP 1965; on staff, Chinese People's Inst. of Foreign Affairs 1967–70; attaché, Embassy, Nairobi, Kenya 1970–77; Third Sec., later Second Sec., later Deputy Div. Chief, Information Dept, Ministry of Foreign Affairs 1977–83, Deputy Dir-Gen., later Dir-Gen. 1985–90 (also Spokesman, Ministry of Foreign Affairs 1985–90), Asst to Vice-Minister of Foreign Affairs 1990–93; First Sec. Embassy, Maseru, Lesotho 1983–85; Chinese Rep. and Amb. to UN 1993–95; Vice-Minister of Foreign Affairs 1995–98; Amb. to USA 1998–2001; Vice-Minister of Foreign Affairs in charge of American and Latin American Affairs 2001–03, Minister of Foreign Affairs 2003–07; Alt. mem. 15th CCP Cen. Cttee 1997–2002, mem. 16th CCP Cen. Cttee 2002–.
Address: c/o Ministry of Foreign Affairs, 225 Chaoyangmen Nan Dajie, Chaoyang Qu, Beijing 100701, People's Republic of China (office).

LI, Zhaozhuo; Chinese politician; *Chairman, People's Government of Guangxi Zhuang Autonomous Region;* b. Sept. 1944, Pingguo, Guangxi Zhuang Autonomous Region. *Education:* Guangxi Univ., Nanning, CCP Guangxi Zhuang Autonomous Regional Cttee Party School, CCP Cen. Cttee Cen. Party School. *Career:* sent to do manual labour, Army Farms, Guangxi Zhuang Autonomous Region and Hunan Prov. 1968–70; technician, Du'an Commune, Debao Co., Guangxi Zhuang Autonomous Region 1970–74; joined CCP 1974; technician, Sec., later Deputy Dir Debao Co. Hydro-electric Power Bureau, Guangxi 1975–80; Deputy Dir Capital Construction Bureau, Debao Co., Guangxi Zhuang Autonomous Region 1980–83, Deputy Dir Planning Cttee 1980–83; Dir Econ. Cttee, CCP Autonomous Co. Cttee, Debao Co., Guangxi Zhuang Autonomous Region 1983–84 (also mem. Standing Cttee), Sec. CCP Autonomous Co. Cttee 1984–85; Deputy Sec. CCP Autonomous Prefectural Cttee, Bose Prefecture, Guangxi Zhuang Autonomous Region 1985–92 (Sec. 1992–93), Commr, Prefectural Admin. Office 1985–93; Sec. CCP Fangchenggang Autonomous City Cttee, Guangxi Zhuang Autonomous Region 1993–95, Chair. Autonomous Regional People's Congress 1993–95; Sec. Nanning Autonomous City Cttee, Guangxi Zhuang Autonomous Region 1994–96; Deputy Sec. Guangxi Zhuang Autonomous Regional Cttee 1996–2002 (mem. Standing Cttee 1996–2002); Chair. People's Govt of Guangxi Zhuang Autonomous Region 1997–; mem. 15th CCP Cen. Cttee 1997–2002, 16th CCP Cen. Cttee 2002–; Vice-Chair. 10th CPPCC Nat. Cttee 2003–.
Address: People's Government of Guangxi Zhuang Autonomous Region, 1 Minle Road, Nanning 530012, Guangxi, People's Republic of China (office). *Telephone:* (771) 284114 (office). *E-mail:* gov@gxi.gov.cn (office). *Website:* www.gxi.gov.cn (office).

LIAN, Hans Jacob Biörn; Norwegian diplomatist; b. 31 March 1942, Oslo. *Education:* Univ. of Neuchâtel, Switzerland. *Career:* Political Dir 1992–94, Amb. and Perm. Rep. to UN, New York 1994–98, to NATO 1998–2002.
Address: c/o North Atlantic Treaty Organization, blvd Léopold III, 1110 Brussels (office); 2, clos Henri Vaes, Brussels, Belgium (home). *Telephone:* (2) 731-86-62 (home).

LIANG, Lt-Gen. Guanglie; Chinese army officer and government official; *Minister of National Defence;* b. Dec. 1940, Santai Co., Sichuan Prov. *Education:* Xinyang Infantry Acad. 1963, PLA Mil. Acad., Nat. Defence Univ. *Career:* joined CCP 1958, PLA 1959; Vice-Div. Commdr and then Div. Commdr 1979–82; Vice-Army Commdr then Army Commdr, Vice-Commdr PLA Beijing Mil. Area Command 1983–97; rank of Lt-Gen. 1995; Commdr PLA Shenyang Mil. Area Command 1997–2000; Commdr PLA Nanjing Mil. Area Command 2000–03; Alt. mem. 13th CCP Cen. Cttee 1982–87, 14th CCP Cen. Cttee 1987–92, mem. 15th CCP Cen. Cttee 1997–2002, 16th CCP Cen. Cttee 2002– (mem. Cen. Mil. Comm. 2002–); Chief, HQ of Gen. Staff, PLA 2002–07; Minister of Nat. Defence 2008–.
Address: Ministry of National Defence, 20 Jingshanqian Jie, Beijing 100009, People's Republic of China (office). *Telephone:* (10) 66730000 (office). *Fax:* (10) 65962146 (office).

LIAO, Gen. Xilong; Chinese army officer; *Director, Logistics Department, People's Liberation Army;* b. June 1940, Sinan Co., Guizhou Prov.

Education: Mil. Acad. of Chinese PLA. *Career:* joined PLA 1959, CCP 1963; served as Platoon Commdr 1966–67, Co. Commdr 1969–71, Deputy Chief of a regimental combat training section 1971–73, Deputy Chief of a div. mil. affairs section 1973–78, Deputy Regt Commdr 1978–79, Regt Commdr 1979–80, Deputy Div. Commdr 1981–83, Div. Commdr 1983, Army Commdr 1984–85, Deputy Commdr Chengdu Mil. Region 1985–95, Commdr 1995–2003; rank of Maj.-Gen. 1988–93, Lt-Gen. 1993–2000, Gen. 2000–; Dir Logistics Dept, PLA 2002–; mem. 15th CCP Cen. Cttee 1997–2002, 16th CCP Cen. Cttee 2002– (mem. Cen. Mil. Comm. 2002–).
Address: People's Liberation Army, c/o Ministry of National Defence, 20 Jingshanqian Jie, Beijing 100009, People's Republic of China.

LIBERADZKI, Bogusław Marian, DEcon; Polish politician and economist; b. 12 Sept. 1948, Sochaczew; m.; two s. *Education:* Main School of Planning and Statistics, Warsaw and Univ. of Illinois, USA. *Career:* Scientist, Main School of Planning and Statistics (now Warsaw School of Econs) Warsaw 1971–75, Asst 1971–75, Tutor 1975–82, Asst Prof. 1982–99, Prof. of Econs 1999–, Head, Dept of Transport; Dir Transport Econs Research Centre, Warsaw 1986–89; Prof., Maritime Univ., Szcecin 1998–; Deputy Minister of Transport 1989–93; mem. Transport Comm., Polish Acad. of Sciences 1988–96, European Rail Congress Council, Brussels; Chair. Supervisory Bd Polish LOT Airways –1993; Minister of Transport and Maritime Economy 1993–97; mem. Democratic Left Alliance (Sojusz Lewicy Demokratycznej-Unia Pracy—SLD-UP) Parl. Club; Deputy to Sejm (Parl.) 1997–2004, Vice-Chair. Infrastructure Cttee 2001–04, European Cttee 2003–04, Polish-Nordic Group 2001–04, Chair. Perm. Sub-cttee on Transport 2001–04, Perm. Sub-cttee for Monitoring the Utilization of EU Funds 2001–04; Observer to European Parl. 2003–04; mem. European Parl. (Socialist Group) 2004–, Cttee on Transport and Tourism 2004–, Substitute mem. Cttee on the Internal Market and Consumer Protection 2004–, mem. Del. to the EU-Russia Parl. Cooperation Cttee 2004–, Substitute mem. Del. for Relations with the United States 2004–; Golden Medal of Merit 1978; Medal of the National Education Committee, Fulbright Scholarship 1986. *Publications:* Economics of Railways 1980, Supply of Railroad Services 1981, Transport: Demand, Supply, Equilibrium 1999.
Address: European Parliament, 07H141, 60 rue Wiertz, 1047 Brussels, Belgium (office); Biuro Poselskie, ul. Garncarska 5, 70-402 Szczecin, Poland. *Telephone:* (91) 4341918. *Fax:* (2) 284-9423 (office). *Website:* www .europarl.eu.int (office).

LIDDELL, Rt Hon. Helen Lawrie, PC; British politician, diplomatist and economist; *High Commissioner to Australia;* b. 6 Dec. 1950; m. Alistair Henderson Liddell 1972; one s. one d. *Education:* St Patrick's High School, Coatbridge, Univ. of Strathclyde. *Career:* Head, Econ. Dept Scottish TUC 1971–75, Asst Sec. 1975–76; Econ. Corresp. BBC Scotland 1976–77; Scottish Sec. Labour Party 1977–88; Dir Personnel and Public Affairs, Scottish Daily Record and Sunday Mail Ltd 1988–92; Chief Exec. Business Venture Programme 1993–94; MP for Monklands E 1994–97, for Airdrie and Shotts 1997–, Opposition spokeswoman on Scotland 1995–97; Econ. Sec. HM Treasury 1997–98, Minister of State Scottish Office 1998–99; Minister of Transport 1999, Minister for Energy and Competitiveness in Europe 1999–2001; Sec. of State for Scotland 2001–03; High Commr to Australia 2005–; Hon. LLD (Strathclyde). *Publication:* Elite (novel) 1990.
Address: British High Commission, Commonwealth Avenue, Canberra, ACT 2600, Australia (office). *Telephone:* (2) 6270-6666 (office). *Fax:* (2) 6273-3236 (office). *E-mail:* bhc.canberra@britaus.net (office). *Website:* bhc .britaus.net (office).

LIDÉN, Anders, PhD; Swedish diplomatist; *Permanent Representative, United Nations;* b. 1949, Oskarshamn; m. Linnéa Lidén Hermance; four c. *Education:* Univ. of Lund. *Career:* Second Sec., Embassy in Lebanon (also acred to Jordan and Syria) 1980–83; First Sec., Political Dept in charge of East, West and Cen. Africa, Ministry for Foreign Affairs 1983–84, Dept in charge of Middle East 1984–87; First Sec., Perm. Mission to UN, New York 1987–91, Special Asst to Personal Rep. of UN Sec.-Gen. in Iran-Iraq peace talks 1988–90; Counsellor, Political Dept in charge of EU Affairs, Ministry for Foreign Affairs 1991–92, Deputy Asst Under-Sec. and Head of Subdivision for Western Europe and N America 1992–93, Asst Under-Sec. and Head of Div. for Int. Orgs 1993–96; Deputy Perm. Rep. to UN, New York 1996–99, Deputy Rep. to UN Security Council 1997–98; Chargé d'Affaires, Embassy in Jordan 1999; Amb. to Israel (also acred to Cyprus) 1999–02, Head of local EU Presidency in Tel Aviv 2001; Dir-Gen. for Political Affairs, Ministry for Foreign Affairs 2002–04; Perm. Rep. to UN, New York 2004–. *Publications:* numerous Publs on Int. Affairs.
Address: Permanent Mission of Sweden to the United Nations, 1 Dag Hammarskjöld Plaza, 885 Second Avenue, 46th Floor, New York, NY 10017, USA (office). *Telephone:* (212) 583-2500 (office). *Fax:* (212) 832-0389 (office). *E-mail:* sweden@un.int (office). *Website:* www.un.int/sweden (office).

LIE, John, AB, AM, PhD; American (b. South Korean) sociologist and academic; *Class of 1959 Professor and Dean, International and Area Studies, University of California, Berkeley;* b. Seoul, South Korea. *Education:* Harvard Univ. *Career:* Foreign Research Scholar, Inst. of Social Science, Univ. of Tokyo 1985–86; Asst Prof., Dept of Sociology, Univ. of Oregon 1989–92; Visiting Asst Prof., Grad. School of Business Admin, Univ. of Hawaii-Manoa 1988, Grad. School of Int. Studies and Grad. School of Business Admin, Yonsei Univ., S Korea 1988–89; Asst Prof. then Full Prof., Dept of Sociology, Univ. of Illinois 1992–2001, Head of Dept 1996–2001, Dir Program in Asian American Studies 1996–97; Visiting Prof., Keio Univ., Japan 1993, Nat. Taiwan Univ. 1997, Univ. of Waikato, New Zealand 1998; Prof., Dept of Sociology, Univ. of Michigan 2001–03, Dir Center for Japanese Studies 2002–03, Korean Studies Program 2002–03; Visiting Prof., Univ. of California, Berkeley 2002–03, Prof., Dept of Sociology 2003–, Class of 1959 Prof. 2004–, Dean, Int. and Area Studies 2004–, Chair. Center for Korean Studies 2003–04. *Publications:* Readings/Study Guide for Introduction to Sociology 1991, Global Sociology 1994, Blue Dreams: Korean Americans and the 1992 Los Angeles Riots (co-author) 1995, Sociological Outlooks (co-author) 1996, Han Unbound: The Political Economy of South Korea 1998, Multiethnic Japan 2001, Sociology (co-author) 2003, Modern Peoplehood 2004. *Address:* 360 Stephens Hall, University of California, Berkeley, CA 94720-2300 USA (office). *Telephone:* (510) 642-9656 (office). *Fax:* (510) 642-9466 (office). *E-mail:* iasone@berkeley.edu (office). *Website:* ias.berkeley.edu (office).

LIEBERMAN, Avigdor, BA; Israeli politician; *Leader, Iisrael Beytenu;* b. 5 June 1958, USSR; m.; three c. *Education:* Hebrew Univ. *Career:* rank of corporal during mil. service; mem. Knesset (Israel Beytenu Party, Ihud Leumi-Israel Beytenu Party) 1999–, Founder and Chair. Iisrael Beytenu Party 1999–, mem. Foreign Affairs and Defence Cttee; Minister of Nat. Infrastructure 2001–02, of Transport 2003–04; Deputy Prime Minister and Minister of Strategic Affairs 2006–08; Sec. Nat. Workers' Union; Chair. Bd of Dirs of Information Industries; Dir of Econ. Corpn of Jerusalem 1983–88; Dir Likud Movt 1993–96; Dir Prime Minister's Office 1996–97; f. Zionist Forum. *Address:* Israel Beytenu (Israel Is Our Home) (Nash dom Izrail), 78 Ermeyahu Street, Jerusalem 94467, Israel. *Telephone:* 2-5012999. *Fax:* 2-5377188. *E-mail:* gdv7191@hotmail.com; info@beytenu.org.il. *Website:* www.beytenu.org.il.

LIEGIS, Imants Viesturs, LLB; Latvian diplomatist; *Representative to the Political and Security Committee, European Union;* b. 30 April 1955, England; m. Ingrida Vija Liege (née Balodis); two d. *Education:* Univ. of Newcastle Upon Tyne, UK. *Career:* trained and practised as solicitor, Supreme Court of England and Wales 1979–91; European Rep. (part-time) to Baltic World Council 1989–91; Desk Officer for EC and Council of Europe, Ministry of Foreign Affairs of Repub. of Latvia 1992; Counsellor, Embassy in London, UK 1992–93; Under Sec. of State for Int. Org. and Foreign Trade 1993; Deputy Head of Mission, Counsellor and Chargé d'Affaires, Embassy in Stockholm, Sweden 1994–97; Amb. to Belgium, the Netherlands, Luxembourg 1997–99; Envoy to NATO and WEU 1997–2003; Perm. Rep. to NATO and WEU, Brussels 2003–04; Under-Sec. of State for Security Policy and Int. Orgs 2004–05; Rep. to Political and Security Cttee, Perm. Rep. to EU 2005–; mem. Brussels Latvian Choir. *Address:* Permanent Representation of Latvia to the European Union, Rue d'Arlon 39-41, 1000 Brussels, Belgium (office). *Telephone:* (2) 282-44-35 (office). *Fax:* (2) 282-03-69 (office). *E-mail:* vineta.jansone@mfa.gov.lv (office). *Website:* www.mfa.gov.lv/en/brussels (office).

LIEN, Chan, MSc, PhD; Taiwanese politician; *Chairman, Kuomintang (KMT);* b. 27 Aug. 1936, Sian, Shansi; m. Yui Fang; two s. two d. *Education:* Nat. Taiwan Univ. and Univ. of Chicago, USA. *Career:* Assoc. Prof. Nat. Taiwan Univ. 1968–69, Prof. and Chair. Dept of Political Science and Dir Graduate Inst. of Political Science 1969–75; Amb. to El Salvador 1975–76; Dir Dept of Youth Affairs, Cen. Cttee Kuomintang 1976–78; Deputy Sec.-Gen. Cen. Cttee Kuomintang 1978, mem. Cen. Standing Cttee 1983–, Chair. 2000–; Chair. Nat. Youth Comm., Exec. Yuan 1978–81; Minister of Communications 1981–87; Vice-Premier 1987–88; Minister of Foreign Affairs 1989–90; Gov. Taiwan Provincial Govt 1990–93; Premier of Taiwan 1993–97; Vice-Pres. of Taiwan 1997–2000; Presidential Cand. 2000; Pres. Chinese Asscn of Political Science 1979–82. *Publications:* The Foundation of Democracy, Taiwan in China's External Relations, Western Political Thought. *Address:* Kuomintang, 11 Chung Shan South Road, Taipei 100, Taiwan (office). *Telephone:* (2) 23121472 (office). *Fax:* (2) 2343524 (office). *Website:* www.kmt.org.tw (office).

LIGHT, Margot, PhD; British political scientist and academic; *Professor Emeritus of International Relations, London School of Economics;* Career:

Prof. Emer. of Int. Relations, LSE, Centre for Study of Human Rights, European Inst.; Chair. Steering Cttee, Centre for Int. Studies; long and short-term political consultancy work for various publs including Europa Publications; regular commentator and featured expert on post-Soviet and S African politics on radio and TV; Co-Ed. Journal of Communist Studies and Transition Politics. *Publications include:* International Relations: A Handbook of Current Theory (co-ed.) 1985, International Relations (co-ed.) 1985, Soviet Theory of International Relations 1988, Troubled Friendships (ed.) 1993, Contemporary International Relations (co-ed.) 1994, Internal Factors in Russian Foreign Policy (co-author) 1996, Ethics and Foreign Policy (co-ed.) 2001; numerous articles in professional journals. *Address:* International Relations Department, London School of Economics, Houghton Street, London, WC2A 2AE, England (office). *Telephone:* (20) 7955-7209 (office); 7803-296948 (mobile). *Fax:* (20) 7242-0392 (office). *E-mail:* m.m.light@lse.ac.uk (office). *Website:* www.lse.ac.uk (office); www.tandf.co.uk/journals/titles/13523279.asp.

LILIĆ, Zoran; Serbian politician; *Vice-President, Socialist Party of Serbia;* b. 27 Aug. 1953, Brza Palanka, Serbia; m. Ljubica Brković-Lilić 1980; one s. *Education:* Belgrade Univ. *Career:* several posts as grad. engineer, then man., with state-owned Rekord enterprise, Belgrade; fmr Pres. Exec. Bd Yugoslav Tyre Makers Business Asscn, mem. Presidency of Belgrade Chamber of Economy, Pres. Man. Bd of Belgrade Airport, mem. Council of Faculty of Tech.; mem. Serbian League of Communists, subsequently Socialist Party of Serbia (SPS); Deputy to Nat. Ass. of Repub. of Serbia 1990, Chair. Cttee on Industry, Energy, Mining and Construction, Chief of Group of SPS Deputies; re-elected Deputy and also Pres. of Nat. Ass. 1992; Pres. of Fed. Repub. of Yugoslavia 1993–97; Vice-Prime Minister of Yugoslavia 1997–2000; Vice-Pres. Socialist Party of Serbia (SPS) 1995–; testified against successor Slobodan Milosevic at Int. Criminal Tribunal for Fmr Yugoslavia, The Hague, Netherlands July 2002. *Address:* Socijalistička partija Srbije, bul. Lenjina 6, 11000 Belgrade, Serbia (office). *Telephone:* (11) 634291 (office). *Fax:* (11) 628642 (office). *Website:* www.sps.org.yu (office).

LILLIKAS, Yiorgos, MA; Cypriot politician; b. 1 June 1960, Pafos; m. Barbara Petropoulou; one s. *Education:* Inst. of Political Science, Lyon, France, Inst. of Political Science, Grenoble, Switzerland. *Career:* mem. Historic Politology Research Team, Nat. Scientific Research Centre of France 1985–87; Special Advisor to Pres. of Repub. of Cyprus 1988–90; Gen.-Sec. Secr. for the New Generation 1990–93; Man. Dir of public relations, strategic marketing and advertising co. 1993–96; mem. House of Reps from Nicosia electoral district 1996–; Minister of Commerce, Industry and Tourism 2003–06, of Foreign Affairs 2006–07; fmr mem. Parl. Cttees on Finance, Foreign and European Affairs, Educ., Trade, fmr Chair. Environment Cttee; fmr Head, Del. to Parl. Ass. of OSCE; Vice-Pres., OSCE Political Affairs and Security Cttee Jan.-June 2006; mem. AKEL party (Progressive Party of the Working People); active in asscns and orgs involved in the anti-drug movement and social integration of children with special needs. *Address:* AKEL Progressive Party of the Working People (Anorthotiko Komma Ergazomenou Laou), POB 21827, 4 E. Papaioannou Street, 1513 Nicosia, Cyprus (office). *Telephone:* 22761121 (office). *Fax:* 22761574 (office). *E-mail:* k.e.akel@cytanet.com.cy (office). *Website:* www.akel.org.cy (office).

LIM, Dong-won; South Korean politician and diplomatist; *Chairman, Sejong Foundation;* b. 25 July 1934. *Education:* Korea Mil. Acad., Seoul Nat. Univ. *Career:* Asst Prof. Korean Mil. Acad. 1964–69; with Armed Forces, attained rank of Maj.-Gen. 1980, now retd; apptd Amb. to Nigeria 1981, to Australia 1984; Chancellor Inst. of Foreign Affairs and Nat. Security, Ministry of Foreign Affairs 1988–92; Chair. Presidential Comm. on Arms Control 1990; Del. South–North High-Level Talks 1990–92; apptd Chair. Asscn for Nat. Unification of Korea 1993; mem. Unification Policy Evaluation Cttee 1993; Sec.-Gen. Kim Dae Jung Peace Foundation for the Asia-Pacific 1995; Sr Sec. for Nat. Security and Foreign Affairs, Pres. Sec. 1998; Minister for Unification (involved in reconciliatory Sunshine Policy towards North Korea) 1999–2001; Dir-Gen. Nat. Intelligence Service 1999–2001; Special Envoy to North Korea April 2002; fmr staff mem. Sejong Inst., Chair. Sejong Foundation 2004–. *Address:* c/o Sejong Institute, Shihung-dong 230, Sujeong-gu, Seongnam-shi, Kyonggi-do, Seoul 461-370, Republic of Korea (office). *E-mail:* public@sejong.org (office). *Website:* www.sejong.org/foundation/eng/main01.htm (office).

LIMA, Antonio Pedro Monteiro; Cape Verde diplomatist; *Permanent Representative, United Nations;* b. 5 Jan. 1948, Dakar, Senegal; m.; five c. *Education:* Univ. of Paris VIII, Univ. of Tours, France. *Career:* Head, Africa, Asia and Oceania Dept, Directorate-Gen. of Political, Econ. and

Cultural Affairs, Ministry of External Affairs 1975–81; Amb. to Guinea-Bissau (non-resident) 1983–1990, to Algeria 1982–90; Diplomatic Adviser to Presidency 1985–87; Dir-Gen. Political, Econ. and Cultural Affairs, Ministry of External Affairs and Emigration 1988–90, Sec. of State 1990–91; Sec.-Gen. Communications, Compensation and Devt Fund, Econ. Community of West African States 1992–98, Dir 1999–2001; Political and Diplomatic Adviser to Pres. 2001–07, concurrently Perm. Rep., Int. Org. of La Francophonie and Chair. Nat. Francophonie Cttee; Perm. Rep. to UN, New York 2007–.
Address: Permanent Mission of Cape Verde to the United Nations, 27 East 69th Street, New York, NY 10021, USA (office). *Telephone:* (212) 472-0333 (home). *Fax:* (212) 794-1398 (office). *E-mail:* capeverde@un.int (office).

LIMBACH, Jutta; German judge and professor of law; *President, Goethe Institut;* b. 27 March 1934, Berlin. *Education:* Freie Universität Berlin and Freiburg Univ. *Career:* Prof. of Civil Law and Legal Sociology, Freie Universität Berlin 1971–; Senator of Justice, Berlin 1989–94; Pres. Fed. Constitutional Court 1994–2002; Pres. Goethe Institut 2002–; Dr hc (Basle) 1999; Justice in the World Award, Madrid 2000; Grosses Goldene Ehrenzeichen der Republik Österreich 1998. *Publications:* Theorie und Wirklichkeit der GmbH 1966, Der verständige Rechtsgenosse 1977, Die gemeinsame Sorge geschiedener Eltern in der Rechtspraxis 1988, "In Namen des Volkes" – Macht und Verantwortung der Richter 1999, Das Bundesverfassungsgericht 2001.
Address: Goethe Institut InterNationes e.V., Helene-Weber-Allee 1, 80637 Munich, Germany (office). *Telephone:* (89) 159210 (office). *Fax:* (89) 15921450 (office). *E-mail:* zv@goethe.de (office). *Website:* www.goethe.de (office).

LIMON, Ewald Wensley; Suriname diplomatist. *Career:* Del. to Caribbean Community (CARICOM) 2003; fmr Perm. Rep. to UN, NY; Vice-Chair. UN Comm. for Social Devt 2004.
Address: c/o Ministry of Foreign Affairs, 25 Lim A Postraat, POB 25, Paramaribo, Suriname (office).

LIMURA, Yutaka; Japanese diplomatist; *Ambassador to France;* b. 16 Oct. 1946. *Career:* joined Ministry of Foreign Affairs 1969, Dir of Tech. Co-operation 1988, Dir of Press 1990, Asst Dir-Gen., Europe Dept 1997, Dir-Gen. of Econ. Co-operation 1999, Deputy Vice Foreign Minister 2001; Second Sec., Embassy in Moscow 1977, First Sec., Embassy in Paris 1979, First Sec., later Counsellor Embassy in Pasay City, Philippines 1985, Counsellor, later Minister Embassy in Washington, DC 1992, Minister Embassy in Paris 1995, Amb. to Indonesia 2002–06, to France 2006–.
Address: Embassy of Japan, 7 ave Hoche, Paris 75008, France. *Telephone:* 1-48-88-62-00 (office). *Fax:* 1-42-27-50-81 (office). *E-mail:* info-fr@amb-japon.fr (office). *Website:* www.fr.emb-japan.go.jp (office).

LIN, Hsin-i, BSc; Taiwanese politician and business executive; b. 2 Dec. 1946; m.; three c. *Education:* Nat. Cheng Kung Univ. *Career:* engineer, China Motor Corpn, later Deputy Man. Eng Div. 1972–76, Deputy Man. Marketing Div. 1976–79, Man. Yangmei Plant 1980–82, Vice-Pres. 1982–87, Exec. Vice-Pres. 1987–90, Pres. 1991–96, Vice-Chair. 1997–2000; Chair. Sino Diamond Motors Ltd 1993–2000, Automotive Research and Testing Centre 1996–2000, Newa Insurance Co. Ltd 1999–2000; Minister of Econ. Affairs 2000–02; Vice-Premier and Chair. Council of Econ. Planning and Devt 2002–04 (resgnd).
Address: c/o Council for Economic Planning and Development, 9th Floor, 87 Nanking East Road, Section 2, Taipei, Taiwan (office).

LINDBECK, Assar, PhD; Swedish economist and academic; *Professor of International Economics, University of Stockholm;* b. 26 Jan. 1930, Umeå; m. Dorothy Nordlund 1953; one s. one d. *Education:* Univs of Uppsala and Stockholm. *Career:* Asst Prof., Univ. of Michigan, USA 1958; with Swedish Treasury 1953–56; Asst Prof. of Econs, Univ. of Stockholm 1962–63, Prof., Stockholm School of Economics 1964–71, Prof. of Int. Econs 1971–, Dir Inst. of Int. Econs 1971–94; Visiting Prof., Columbia Univ., USA 1968–69, Univ. of California, Berkeley 1969, ANU 1970, Yale Univ. 1976, Stanford Univ. 1977; Consultant, World Bank 1986–87; mem. Nobel Prize Cttee on Econs 1969–94 (Chair. 1980–94); Frank Siedman Distinguished Award in Political Economy 1996, Bernard Harms Prize in Int. Econs 1996, Great Gold Medal of the Royal Swedish Acad. of Eng Sciences 2001. *Art exhibitions:* paintings in Gallery Svenska Bilder 1997, 2001, 2005. *Music:* Sonata for Clarinet and piano: Fantasi i folkton 1948, performed in City Hall, Luleå 1948. *Publications:* A Study in Monetary Analysis 1963, The Political Economy of the New Left 1971, Economics of the Agricultural Sector 1973, Swedish Economic Policy 1975, The Insider-Outsider Theory (with Dennis Snower) 1988, Unemployment and Macroeconomics 1993, The Swedish Experiment 1997.
Address: Institute for International Economic Studies, Stockholm University, 106 91 Stockholm (office); Karlavägen 78, 114 59 Stockholm,

Sweden (home). *Telephone:* (8) 16-30-78 (office); (8) 21-23-37 (home). *Fax:* (8) 16-29-46 (office); (8) 21-23-37 (home). *E-mail:* assar@iies.su.se (office). *Website:* www.iies.su.se/~assar (office).

LINDSAY, James M., AB, MA, MPhil, PhD; American academic; *Tom Slick Chair for International Affairs and Director, Robert S. Strauss Center for International Security and Law, University of Texas;* b. Mass; m.; four c. *Education:* Univ. of Michigan, Yale Univ. *Career:* Instructor in Political Science, Univ. of Iowa 1987–88, Asst Prof. 1988–92, Assoc. Prof. 1992–95, Prof. 1995–99; Dir Global Issues and Multilateral Affairs, Nat. Security Council, White House 1996–97; Sr Fellow in Foreign Policy Studies, Brookings Inst. 1999–2003, Deputy Dir 2003; Consultant to US Comm. on Nat. Security/21st Century, Hart-Rudman Comm. 2000–01; Vice-Pres., Maurice R. Greenberg Chair. and Dir of Studies, Council on Foreign Relations 2003–06; Tom Slick Chair for Int. Affairs and Dir Robert S. Strauss Center for Int. Security and Law, Univ. of Texas at Austin 2006–; fmr Fellow, Center for Int. Affairs and Center for Science and Int. Affairs, Harvard Univ.; mem. Editorial Bd PS: Political Science & Politics 1993–96, Exec. Cttee Midwest Consortium for Int. Security 1992–; mem. Acad. of Political Science, American Political Science Asscn, Midwest Political Science Asscn; several fellowships including Pew Faculty Fellow in Int. Affairs 1990, Council on Foreign Relations Int. Affairs Fellow 1995; contribs to The Washington Post, LA Times, The Globe and Mail; William Jennings Bryan Prize, Univ. of Michigan 1981, James N. Murray Teaching Award, Univ. of Iowa 1990, Collegiate Teaching Award, Univ. of Iowa 1991. *Publications:* Congress and Nuclear Weapons 1991, Congress Resurgent: Foreign and Defense Policy on Capitol Hill (co-ed.) 1993, Congress and the Politics of US Foreign Policy 1994, Dynamics of Democracy (co-author) 1995, US Foreign Policy after the Cold War (co-ed.) 1997, Defending America: The Case for Limited Nat. Missile Defense (co-author) 2001, Protecting the American Homeland: One Year On (co-author) 2003, Agenda for the Nation (co-ed.) 2003, America Unbound: The Bush Revolution in Foreign Policy (co-author, Lionel Gelber Prize 2003) 2003; numerous articles in professional journals and chapters in books.
Address: Robert S. Strauss Center for International Security and Law, University of Texas at Austin, 2315 Red River Street, Austin, TX 78712, USA (office). *Telephone:* (512) 471-6267 (office). *Fax:* (512) 471-6961 (office). *E-mail:* info@robertstrausscenter.org (office). *Website:* www.robertstrausscenter.org (office).

LINDSEY, Lawrence B., AB, MA, PhD; American economist and fmr government official; *President and CEO, Lindsey Group;* b. 18 July 1954, Peekskill, NY; m. Susan Lindsey 1982; three c. *Education:* Bowdoin Coll., Harvard Univ. *Career:* on staff of Pres. Reagan's Council of Econ. Advisers; Special Asst for Policy Devt to Pres. Bush; fmr Prof. of Econs, Harvard Univ.; mem. Bd of Govs Fed. Reserve System 1991–97; Man. Dir Econ. Strategies Inc. 1997–2001; Econ. Adviser to Pres. 2001–02; Dir Nat. Econ. Council 2001–02; Pres. and CEO Lindsey Group 2003–; Chair. Bd Neighborhood Reinvestment Corpn 1993–97; Resident Scholar and holder Arthur C. Burns Chair., American Enterprise Inst. 1997–2001, now Visiting Scholar; Hon. JuD (Bowdoin Coll.) 1993; Distinguished Public Service Award, Boston Bar Asscn 1994. *Publications:* The Growth Experiment: How the New Tax Policy is Transforming the US Economy 1990, Econ. Puppetmasters: Lessons From the Halls of Power 1999; numerous articles in professional publs.
Address: The Lindsey Group, 11320 Random Hills Road, Suite 310, Fairfax, VA 22030; American Enterprise Institute, 1150 17th Street, NW, Washington, DC 20036, USA (office). *Telephone:* (703) 621-1170 (office). *Fax:* (703) 218-3956 (office). *E-mail:* info@thelindseygroup.com (office); LLindsey@aei.org (office). *Website:* www.thelindseygroup.com (office).

LINDSTRØM, Bjarne; Norwegian diplomatist; *Ambassador to UK;* m. Berit Lindstrøm. *Career:* Asst, Admin. Affairs Dept, Ministry of Foreign Affairs 1962–66, First Sec. 1966–68, Attaché, Embassy in Lagos 1968–70, Jr Exec. Officer, Trade Policy Dept, Ministry of Foreign Affairs 1970–71, Second Sec., Embassy in Budapest 1973–75, First Sec., Mission to UN, New York 1975–78, Exec. Officer, Dept of Political Affairs, NATO Div., Ministry of Foreign Affairs 1978–80, Sr Exec. Officer, Dept of Political Affairs, UN Div. 1980–83, Head of Div. 1983–86, Consul-Gen., S Africa 1986–90, Deputy Dir-Gen. Admin. Affairs Dept, Ministry of Foreign Affairs 1990–93, Dir-Gen. 1993–96, Sec.-Gen. 1996–2005, Amb. to UK 2005–.
Address: Embassy of Norway, 5 Belgrave Square, London, SW1X 8QD, England (office). *Telephone:* (20) 7591-5500 (office). *Fax:* (20) 7245-6993 (office). *E-mail:* emb.london@mfa.no (office). *Website:* www.norway.org.uk (office).

LING, Norman Arthur; British diplomatist; *Ambassador to Ethiopia;* m. Selma Osman. *Career:* Desk Officer, Hong Kong and Gen. Dept, FCO 1978–79, Persian language training 1979–80, Second Sec., Tripoli 1980–81, Second, later First Sec., Tehran 1981–84, Head of Section, E Africa Dept,

FCO 1984–86, Head of Argentina Section, Falkland Islands Dept 1986–88, Deputy Consul Gen., Johannesburg 1988–92, Turkish language training 1992–93, Deputy Head of Mission, Ankara 1993–97, Head of Aviation, Maritime, Science and Energy Dept, FCO 1997–2000, secondment to Dept for Int. Devt 2001, High Commr to Malawi 2001–04; Dir of Business Change, FCO 2005–07; Amb. to Ethiopia 2008–.
Address: British Embassy, Comoros Street, PO Box 858, Addis Ababa, Ethiopia (office). *Telephone:* (11) 6612354 (office). *Fax:* (11) 6610588 (office). *E-mail:* britishembassy.addisababa@fco.gov.uk (office). *Website:* www.britishembassy.gov.uk/ethiopia (office).

LING LIONG SIK, Dato' Seri, MB, BS; Malaysian politician; b. 18 Sept. 1943, Kuala Kangsar, Perak; m. Datin Ee Nah Ong 1968; two c. *Education:* King Edward VII School, Royal Mil. Coll. and Univ. of Singapore. *Career:* Parl. Sec. Ministry of Local Govt and Fed. Territory 1976–77; Deputy Minister of Information 1978–82, of Finance 1982–84, of Educ. 1985–86; fmr Minister of Transport; Deputy Pres. Malaysian Chinese Asscn 1985–87, Pres. 1987–2003.
Address: c/o Malaysian Chinese Association, 8th Floor, Wisma MCA, 163, Jalan Ampang, 50450 Kuala Lumpur, Malaysia (office).

LINI, Ham; Ni-Vanuatu politician; *Prime Minister; Career:* mem. Nat. United Party (NUP), Pres. 2003; Deputy Prime Minister 2003–04, also Minister of Home Affairs, of Infrastructure and Public Utilities, of Civil Aviation; Prime Minister of Vanuatu 2004–.
Address: Prime Minister's Office, PMB 053, Port Vila, Vanuatu (office). *Telephone:* 22413 (office). *Fax:* 22863 (office). *Website:* www .vanuatugovernment.gov.vu (office).

LINKEVIČIUS, Linas Antanas; Lithuanian politician and diplomatist; *Permanent Representative, NATO;* b. 6 Jan. 1961, Vilnius; m. 1982; two d. *Education:* Kaunas Polytechnical Inst. *Career:* worked in technical insts 1983–92; reviewer, newspaper Tiesa 1992–93; mem. Democratic Labour Party 1990–95; elected to Seimas (Parl.) 1992; Chair. Parl. delegation to N Atlantic Ass. 1992–93; Deputy Chair. Parl. Comm. on Foreign Affairs 1992–93; Minister of Nat. Defence 1993–96, 2000–04; Amb. and Head of Lithuanian Mission to NATO and to WEU 1997–99; Amb. for special missions, Ministry of Foreign Affairs 2004–05; Perm. Rep. of Lithuania to NATO 2005–.
Address: NATO Headquarters, Blvd Leopold III, 1110 Brussels, Belgium (office). *Telephone:* (2) 707-28-49 (office). *Fax:* (2) 707-28-50 (office). *E-mail:* delagation@ltunato.org (office). *Website:* amb.urm.lt/nato (office).

LINKLATER, Andrew, PhD, FBA; British academic; *Woodrow Wilson Professor of International Politics, University of Wales; Education:* Aberdeen Univ., Univ. of Oxford, London School of Econs. *Career:* taught at Univ. of Tasmania 1976–81, Monash Univ., Australia 1982–92; Prof. of Int. Relations, Keele Univ. 1993–99, Dean of Post grad. Affairs 1997–99; Woodrow Wilson Prof. of Int. Politics, Univ. of Wales 2000–; mem. Acad. of Learned Socs in the Social Sciences 2001. *Publications include:* The Idea of Harm in International Relations, The English School on Order and Justice, Critical Theories of International Relations, Men and Citizens in International Relations 1982, Beyond Realism and Marxism: Critical Theory and International Relations 1990, The Transformation of Political Community, Polity 1998, International Relations: Key Concepts in Political Science 2000, The English School of International Relations (with H. Suganami) 2006.
Address: Room S34, Edward Llwyd Building, Department of International Politics, University of Wales, Penglais, Aberystwyth, Ceredigion, SY23 3DA, Wales (office). *Telephone:* (1970) 621596 (office). *Fax:* (1970) 622709 (office). *E-mail:* adl@aber.ac.uk (office). *Website:* www.aber.ac.uk/ ~inpwww (office).

LINNER, Carl Sture, MA, PhD; Swedish international civil servant and writer; b. 15 June 1917, Stockholm; m. Clio Tambakopoulou 1944; two s. *Education:* Stockholm and Uppsala Univs. *Career:* Assoc. Prof. of Greek, Uppsala Univ. 1943; Del. to Int. Red Cross, Greece 1943–45; Dir AB Electrolux, Stockholm 1945–50; Dir Swedish Employers' Confed. 1950–51; Exec. Vice-Pres. AB Bahco, Stockholm 1951–57; Pres. Swedish Lamco Syndicate 1957; Exec. Vice.-Pres. and Gen. Man. Liberian-American-Swedish Minerals Co., Monrovia 1958–60; Chief UN Civilian Operations, later UN Mission, in the Congo 1960–61; Special Rep. of UN Sec.-Gen. in Brussels and London 1962; UN Rep. in Greece, Israel and Cyprus 1962–65, in London 1965–68, in Tunis 1968–71, UNDP, New York 1971–73; Resident Rep. UNDP in Egypt 1973–77; Sr Consultant, FAO 1977–87; mem. Royal Swedish Acad. of Letters, History and Antiquities, Royal Acad. of Arts and Sciences, Uppsala, Societas Litterarum Humaniorum Regiae Upsaliensis; Hon. Prof. (Uppsala) 1992, Amb. of Hellenism (Gov. of Athens); Star of Africa, Commdr Order of Phoenix, Commdr Order of Honour (Greece); Hon. DPhil (Cyprus) 1998; Prince Carl Medal, Royal

Award, Swedish Acad., Letterstedts Award, Royal Acad. of Science, Cultural Award, Natur & Kultur, Bonniers Award, City of Athens Award, Ax:son Johnsons Stiftelse Award. *Publications:* Syntaktische und lexikalische Studien zur Historia Lausiaca des Palladios 1943, Giorgos Seferis 1963, Roms Konungahävder 1964, Fredrika Bremer i Grekland 1965, W. H. Humphreys' First Journal of the Greek War of Independence 1967, Thucydides 1978, Min odyssé 1982, Bysantinska porträtt 1984, Homeros 1985, Bistånd till Afrika 1985, Disaster Relief for Development 1986, Hellenika 1986, En värld utan gränser 1988, Den gyllene lyran: Archilochos, Sapfo, Pindaros 1989, Europas födelse 1991, Lans och bage: Aischylos Perserna 1992, Anna Komnenas värld 1993, Bysantinsk Kulturhistoria 1994, Ensamhet och gemenskap 1995, Mulåsnan på Akropolis 1996, Pol Pot och Kambodja 1997, Ökenfäderna 1998, Hellenskt och romerskt 1998, Sicilien 1999, Tidevarv komma, tidevarv försvinna 2000, Europas ungtid 2002.
Address: 24 Phokylidou, 10673 Athens, Greece. *Telephone:* (1) 3611780.

LINTONEN, Kirsti Eeva Helena; Finnish diplomatist; *Permanent Representative, United Nations;* b. 23 May 1945, Tampere; m.; one s. *Education:* Helsinki Univ. *Career:* joined Ministry of Foreign Affairs 1971, worked in several positions abroad including in Brussels, Berlin, Belgrade, London; Special Adviser to Prime Minister, Foreign Policy and Int. Affairs 1983–87; Deputy Amb., Stockholm, Sweden 1987–90; Amb. to Namibia 1990–94; Deputy Dir Gen. for Political Affairs, Ministry of Foreign Affairs 1994–96, UnderSec. of State 1996–2000; Amb. to S Africa 2000–05, Rep. in Botswana, Lesotho, Mauritius, Namibia, Swaziland 2001–05, fmr Rep. to SADC; Perm. Rep. to UN, New York 2005–; has served on Governing Councils of African Devt Bank, IDB, IFAD, Asian Devt Bank.
Address: Office of the Permanent Representative of Finland to the United Nations, 866 United Nations Plaza, Suite 222, New York, NY 10017, USA (office). *Telephone:* (212) 355-2100 (office). *Fax:* (212) 759-6156 (office). *E-mail:* sanomat.yke@formin.fi (office). *Website:* www.un.int/finland (office).

LINTU, Pekka; Finnish diplomatist; *Ambassador to USA;* b. 1947; m. Laurel Colless; one d. *Education:* Univ. of Helsinki. *Career:* Amb. to Japan 1994–2000; Under-Sec. of State for External Econ. Relations –2005; Amb. to USA 2006–; mem. Bd of Dirs Finnvera plc, Fide Oy 2001.
Address: Embassy of Finland, 3301 Massachusetts Avenue, NW, Washington, DC 20008, USA (office). *Telephone:* (202) 298-5801 (office). *Fax:* (202) 298-6030 (office). *E-mail:* sanomat.was@formin.fi (office). *Website:* www.finland.org (office).

LIPIČ, Maj.-Gen. Ladislav, BSc; Slovenian army officer; b. 30 Nov. 1951, Murska Sobota. *Education:* Univ. of Ljubljana. *Career:* Asst for Organizational and Mobilization Affairs, Murska Sobota Municipal Territorial Defence HQ 1987–90; Chief of Logistics, Territorial Defence Regional Command (Vzhodna Štajerska Region) 1990–94, Commdr 1994–97; Chief of Logistics, Slovenian Armed Forces Gen. Staff 1997–2000, Deputy Chief of Gen. Staff 2000–01, Chief of Gen. Staff 2001–06; Co-Dir CAE 98 Exercise (jt NATO and PfP member countries exercise), Slovenia 1998; apptd Brig. 1998, Maj.-Gen. 2003; guest lecturer, Faculty of Social Sciences, Univ. of Ljubljana.
Address: c/o Ministry of Defence, General Staff, Kardeljeva ploščad 25, 1000 Ljubljana, Slovenia (office).

LIPPONEN, Paavo Tapio; Finnish politician; *Speaker of the Parliament;* b. 23 April 1941, Turtola (now Pello); m. Päivi Lipponen 1998; three d. *Education:* Univ. of Helsinki, Dartmouth Coll., USA. *Career:* journalist 1963–67; Research and Int. Affairs Sec. and Head Political Section Finnish Social Democratic Party (SDP) 1967–79; Pvt. Sec. (Special Political Adviser) to Prime Minister 1979–82; Political Sec. to Minister of Labour 1983; Man. Dir Viestintä Teema Oy 1988–95; Head Finnish Inst. of Int. Affairs 1989–91; Chair. Supervisory Bd Outokumpu Oy 1989–90; mem. Helsinki City Council 1985–95; MP 1983–87, 1991–; mem. SDP Party Cttee 1987–90, Chair. SDP Helsinki Dist 1985–92, Chair. of SDP 1993–2005; Speaker of Parl. March–April 1995, 2003–; Prime Minister of Finland 1995–2003; Dr hc (Dartmouth Coll., USA) 1997, (Finlandia Univ.) 2000. *Publications:* Muutoksen suunta 1986, Kohti Eurooppaa 2001.
Address: Parliament of Finland, 00102, Helsinki, Finland (office). *Telephone:* (9) 4323101 (office). *Fax:* (9) 4322705 (office). *E-mail:* paavo .lipponen@parliament.fi (office). *Website:* www.eduskunta.fi (home).

LIPSKY, John, BA, MA, PhD; American international organization official; *First Deputy Managing Director, International Monetary Fund; Education:* Wesleyan and Stanford Univs. *Career:* spent a decade at IMF, where he helped manage exchange rate surveillance procedure and analysed devts in int. capital market, also participated in negotiations with several mem. countries and served as IMF Resident Rep. in Chile 1978–80, Chair. Financial Sector Review Group 2000, First Deputy Man. Dir IMF 2006–;

joined Saloman Brothers Inc. 1984, directed European Econ. and Market Analysis Group, London, UK 1989–92, Chief Economist 1992–97; Chief Economist and Dir of Research, Chase Manhattan Bank 1997; fmr Chief Economist, JPMorgan, later Vice-Chair. JPMorgan Investment Bank; mem. Bd of Dirs Nat. Bureau of Econ. Research and several corpns and non-profit orgs.
Address: International Monetary Fund, 700 19th Street, NW, Washington, DC 20431, USA (office). *Telephone:* (202) 623-7000 (office). *Fax:* (202) 623-4661 (office). *E-mail:* webmaster@imf.org (office). *Website:* www.imf.org (office).

LISSAKERS, Karin Margareta, MA; American economist and fmr government official; *Director, Revenue Watch Institute;* b. 16 Aug. 1944; m.; two c. *Education:* Ohio State Univ. and Johns Hopkins Univ. *Career:* mem. staff, Cttee on Foreign Relations, US Senate, Washington, DC 1972–78; Deputy Dir Econ. Policy Planning Staff, US Dept of State 1978–80; Sr Assoc. Carnegie Endowment for Int. Peace, New York 1981–83; Lecturer in int. banking, Dir int. business and banking programme, School of Int. Public Affairs, Columbia Univ. 1985–93; US Exec. Dir IMF 1993–2001; mem. Council on Foreign Relations; Chief Adviser to George Soros on globalization issues, Soros Fund Management LLC 2001–06; Dir Revenue Watch Inst. 2006–. *Publications:* Banks, Borrowers and the Establishment 1991; articles in professional journals.
Address: Revenue Watch Institute, 400 West 59th Street, New York, NY 10019, USA (office). *Fax:* (646) 557-2494 (office). *E-mail:* klissakers@revenuewatch.org (office). *Website:* www.revenuewatch.org (office).

LISWANISO, George Mbanga; Namibian diplomatist; *High Commissioner to UK;* b. Katima Mulilo; m. Agnes Manga Liswaniso. *Education:* studied int. law in Moscow. *Career:* left home in 1975 to join SWAPO, travelled to Botswana, then to camp in Zambia, was sent to Sierra Leone to finish his schooling; returned from exile in 1989 to participate in Namibia's first democratic elections; helped build Foreign Service, first posting was to Perm. Mission to UN, New York, served at UN agencies in Vienna, before returning to New York to represent Namibia on Security Council; fmr Chief Foreign Relations Officer, Ministry of Foreign Affairs; posted to Addis Ababa, involved in drafting institutional blueprint transforming OAU into African Union, fmr Perm. Rep., also Amb. to Ethiopia –2006;High Commr to UK (also accred to Ireland and Cyprus) 2006–.
Address: Namibia High Commission, 6 Chandos Street, London, W1G 9LU, England (office). *Telephone:* (20) 7636-6244 (office). *Fax:* (20) 7637-5694 (office). *E-mail:* namibia.hicom@btconnect.com (office); namibia-highcomm@btconnect.com (office).

LITWAK, Robert, BA, PhD; American foreign policy analyst; *Director, International Studies Division, Woodrow Wilson International Center for Scholars; Education:* Haverford Coll., LSE, UK. *Career:* fmr Dir for Nonproliferation and Export Controls, Nat. Security Council; fmr Adjunct Prof., School of Foreign Service, Georgetown Univ.; currently Dir Div. of Int. Studies, Woodrow Wilson Int. Center for Scholars (WWIC); mem. Council on Foreign Relations; Fellow, Center for Int. Affairs and Russian Research Center, Harvard Univ., Exec. Fellow, US Inst. of Peace. *Publications:* Security in the Persian Gulf: Sources of Inter-State Conflict 1981, Détente and the Nixon Doctrine: American Foreign Policy and the Pursuit of Stability 1969–76, Nuclear Proliferation after the Cold War (co-Ed.) 1994, Rogue States and US Foreign Policy: Containment After the Cold War 2000.
Address: Woodrow Wilson International Center for Scholars, One Woodrow Wilson Plaza, 1300 Pennsylvania Avenue, NW, Washington, DC 20004-3027, USA (office). *Telephone:* (202) 691-4179 (office). *Fax:* (202) 691-4001 (office). *E-mail:* litwakro@wwic.si.edu (office). *Website:* www.wilsoncenter.org (office).

LIU, Gen. Dongdong; Chinese army officer; *Political Commissar, Jinan Military Region, People's Liberation Army;* b. Oct. 1945, Wuhan, Hubei Prov. *Education:* PLA Political Acad., Beijing. *Career:* joined PLA 1961, CCP 1963; soldier, later staff mem., later Head of Propaganda Dept, later Deputy Political Commissar Artillery Regt, later Dir Artillery Regt (Political Section), later Section Head Org. Section (Army Political Dept), later Dir Political Dept, later Deputy Political Commissar, later Political Commissar, 139th Div.Div., 47th Group Army, PLA Services and Arms, later Dir Political Dept, 47th Group Army, later Deputy Political Commissar 47th Group Army; Dir Political Dept, PLA Lanzhou Mil. Region, Gansu Prov. –2000, Political Commissar 2000–03; Political Commissar PLA Jinan Mil. Region, Shandong Prov. 2003–; rank of Maj.-Gen. 1992, Lt-Gen. 1999; mem. 16th CCP Cen. Cttee 2002–.
Address: People's Liberation Army Lanzhou Military Area Command, Lanzhou, Gansu Province, People's Republic of China (office).

LIU, Guchang; Chinese diplomatist; *Ambassador to Russian Federation;* b. 1946, Jiangsu Prov. *Career:* entered Foreign Ministry 1973; assigned to Embassy in Bucharest, Romania 1973–80, Third Sec. 1986–90, First Sec. 1986–90; Deputy Chief, Soviet Union and E European Affairs Dept 1980–86, Chief 1990–92; Chief, Europe-Asia Dept, Ministry of Foreign Affairs 1992–95; Amb. to Romania 1996–99; Asst to Minister of Foreign Affairs 1999–2002, Vice-Minister of Foreign Affairs 2002–03; Amb. to Russian Fed. 2003–.
Address: Embassy of the People's Republic of China, 117330 Moscow, ul. Druzhby 6, Russian Federation (office). *Telephone:* (495) 956-11-68 (office). *Fax:* (495) 956-11-69 (office). *E-mail:* chiemb@microdin.ru (office). *Website:* ru.china-embassy.org (office).

LIU, Huaqiu; Chinese diplomatist; *Director of Foreign Affairs Office, State Council;* b. Nov. 1939, Wuchuan Co., Guangdong Prov. *Education:* Foreign Affairs Inst., Beijing. *Career:* joined CCP 1965; Second Sec., Embassy, Accra, Ghana 1973–81; Clerk, Gen. Office of State Council 1981; Counsellor then Minister, Embassy, Sydney, Australia 1984–86; Dir Dept of Affairs of the Americas and Oceania, Ministry of Foreign Affairs 1986–87; Asst Minister of Foreign Affairs 1987–89; Vice-Minister of Foreign Affairs 1989–98; Dir Foreign Affairs Office, State Council 1994–; Alt. mem. 14th CCP Cen. Cttee 1992–97, mem. 15th CCP Cen. Cttee 1997–2002, 16th CCP Cen. Cttee 2002–; Dir Cen. Foreign Affairs Office, CCP Cen. Cttee 1998–; fmr Deputy Dir China Cttee of the Int. Decade for Natural Disaster Reduction; fmr Vice-Chair. Chinese Preparatory Committee, UN World Summit on Social Devt.
Address: c/o Ministry of Foreign Affairs, 225 Chaoyangmen Nan Dajie, Chaoyang Qu, Beijing 100701, People's Republic of China. *Telephone:* (10) 65961114. *Fax:* (10) 65962146. *E-mail:* webmaster@mfa.gov.cn. *Website:* www.fmprc.gov.cn.

LIU, Jianfeng; Chinese politician and provincial administrator; *Minister for General Administration of Civil Aviation of China;* b. 1936, Ninghe Co., Hebei Prov. *Education:* Kiev Eng Coll., USSR. *Career:* joined CCP 1956; Deputy Dir, later Dir No. 1425 Research Inst., 4th Ministry of Machine-Building Industry 1968–84 (Acting Sec. CCP Party Cttee 1968–84); Vice-Minister of Electronics Industry 1984–88; Sec. Work Cttee, CCP Hainan Prov. Cttee 1988; Deputy Sec. CCP Hainan Prov. Cttee 1988–93; Gov. Hainan Prov. 1989–93; Vice-Minister of Electronics Industry 1993–98; Vice-Minister of Information Industry 1998–2003; Minister for Gen. Admin. Civil Aviation Admin of China 1998–; mem. 14th CCP Cen. Cttee 1992–97, 15th CCP Cen. Cttee 1997–2002, 16th CCP Cen. Cttee 2002–; Del., 13th CCP Nat. Congress 1987–92; Pres. Electronics Br., China Council for the Promotion of Int. Trade.
Address: Ministry for The General Administration of Civil Aviation of China, Beijing, People's Republic of China.

LIU, Jiang; Chinese government official; *Vice-Chairman, State Development and Reform Commission;* b. 1940, Beijing; m.; two d. *Education:* Shihezi Agricultural Coll., Xinjiang Uygur Autonomous Region, CCP Cen. Cttee Cen. Party School. *Career:* technician, later Chief, Mil. Farm, Tibet Autonomous Region; Farm Head, later Dir Animal Husbandry Bureau, Beijing 1972–84 (Sec. CCP Party Cttee 1972–84); joined CCP 1978; Vice-Minister of Agric., Animal Husbandry and Fishery 1986–90; Vice-Chair. State Planning Comm. 1990–93; Minister of Agric. 1993–98; Chair. Beijing Greening Cttee 1997; Vice-Chair. State Devt and Reform Comm. 1998–; Deputy Head State Working Group for Comprehensive Agricultural Devt, Leading Group, Aid-the-Poor Projects 1998–; mem. 15th CCP Cen. Cttee 1997–2002.
Address: State Development and Reform Commission, 38 Yuetan Nan Jie, Xicheng Qu, Beijing, People's Republic of China.

LIU, Jibin; Chinese politician; b. Dec. 1938, Longkou, Shandong Prov. *Education:* Beijing Aeronautics Inst. *Career:* joined CCP 1966; engineer, Section Dir then Vice-Man. Shenyang Songling Machinery Factory 1981–85; Deputy Chief Engineer, Ministry of Aeronautics Industry 1985; Minister of Aeronautics Industry 1985–88; Dir State Admin of State Property 1985–88; Vice-Minister of Finance 1988–98; Minister in Charge of Comm. of Science, Tech. and Industry for Nat. Defence 1998–2003; Del., 14th CCP Nat. Congress 1992–97; mem. Cen. Comm. for Discipline Inspection, CCP Cen. Cttee 1992–2002, Nat. Narcotics Control Comm. 1993, State Academic Degrees Cttee 1995–97, Hong Kong Special Admin. Region Preparatory Cttee 1995–97 (mem. Govt Del., Hong Kong Hand-Over Ceremony 1997), State Steering Group of Science, Tech. and Educ. 1998–.
Address: c/o Zhongguo Gongchan Dang (Chinese Communist Party), 1 Zhongnanhai, Beijing, People's Republic of China (office).

LIU, Mingzu; Chinese political official; *Chairman, Agriculture and Rural Affairs Committee, National People's Congress;* b. 1936, Weihai City,

Shandong Prov. *Career:* joined CCP 1959; fmr Deputy Dir Office of CCP Weihai City Cttee, later Deputy Sec. then Sec. Weihai City Cttee; fmr Sec. CCP Rushan Co. Cttee, Shandong Prov.; fmr Deputy Sec. CCP Yantai Prefectural Cttee, Shandong Prov.; fmr Sec. CCP Linyi Prefectural Cttee, Shandong Prov.; Chair. Guangxi Regional People's Congress 1993–94; Deputy Sec., Standing Cttee and mem. CCP Guangxi Regional Cttee 1988–94; mem., Standing Cttee, mem. and Sec. CCP Inner Mongolia Autonomous Region Cttee 1994–2000; Chair. Inner Mongolia Regional People's Congress 1997–99; Alt. mem. 14th CCP Cen. Cttee 1992–97, mem. 15th CCP Cen. Cttee 1997–2002; Deputy, 8th NPC 1993–98, 9th NPC 1998–2003, Vice-Chair. Ethnic Affairs Cttee 2002, Chair. Agric. and Rural Affairs Cttee 2003–; Del., 12th CCP Nat. Congress 1982–87, 13th CCP Nat. Congress 1987–92.
Address: National People's Congress, Beijing, People's Republic of China (office).

LIU, Qi; Chinese government official; *Secretary of Beijing Municipal Committee;* b. 1942, Wujin Co., Jiangsu Prov. *Education:* Beijing Inst. of Iron and Steel Eng. *Career:* joined CCP 1975; gas controller, furnaceman and founder, No. 2 Blast Furnace, Steel Works, Wuhan Iron and Steel Co. 1968–78, technician and Deputy Head, No. 3 Blast Furnace 1978–83, Deputy Dir Steel Works and Head Production Dept 1983–85, First Deputy Man. Wuhan Iron and Steel Co. 1985–90 (mem. Standing Cttee CCP Party Cttee 1985–93), Man. 1990–93; Minister of Metallurgical Industry 1993–98 (Sec. CCP Leading Party Group at Ministry 1993–98); Deputy Sec. CCP Beijing Municipal Cttee 1998–2002, Sec. 2002–; Vice-Mayor of Beijing 1998–99, Mayor of Beijing 1999–2002; Alt. mem. 14th CCP Cen. Cttee 1992–97, mem. 15th CCP Cen. Cttee 1997–2002, 16th CCP Cen. Cttee 2002–, mem. Politburo 2002–; currently also Pres. Beijing Organizing Cttee for 2008 Olympic Games.
Address: Beijing Municipal People's Government, Beijing, People's Republic of China (office).

LIU, Zhenmin, LLM; Chinese diplomatist; *Deputy Permanent Representative, United Nations;* b. 1955, Shanxi Prov.; m. *Education:* Peking Univ. *Career:* joined Foreign Service 1982; Staff Mem. Dept of Treaty and Law 1982–84, Third Sec. then Deputy Div. Dir, 1988–92, First Sec. 1996, Counsellor 1996–98, Deputy Dir-Gen 1998–2003, Dir-Gen 2003–06; Attaché then Third Sec., Perm. Mission to UN, New York 1984–88, Deputy Perm. Rep. 2006–; Second Sec. then First Sec., Perm. Mission to UN, Geneva 1992–95.
Address: Permanent Mission of the People's Republic of China, 350 East 35th Street, New York, NY 10016, USA (office). *Telephone:* (212) 655-6100 (office). *Fax:* (212) 634-7626 (office). *E-mail:* chinamission_un@fmprc.gov .cn (office). *Website:* www.china-un.org (office).

LIU, Zhongli; Chinese state official; *President, National Social Security Fund Council;* b. 1934, Ningbo City, Zhejiang Prov. *Career:* joined CCP 1954; Deputy Div. Chief, Vice-Chair., Chair. Heilongjiang Prov. Planning Comm. 1973–84, Chair. Planning and Econ. Comm. 1984–95; Vice-Gov. Heilongjiang Prov. 1985–88; Vice-Chair. State Cttee for Enterprise Man. 1988; Vice-Minister of Finance 1988–92, Minister 1992–98; Deputy Sec.-Gen. State Council 1990, Dir Econ. System Reform Office of State Council 1998–2000; Dir State Gen. Admin. of Taxation 1994–98; Deputy Head Cen. Financial and Econ. Leading Group; mem. 14th CCP Cen. Cttee 1992–97, 15th CCP Cen. Cttee 1997–2002; Pres. Nat. Social Security Fund Council 2000–; Chair. CPPCC Sub-Cttee of Economy 2003–.
Address: Chinese Communist Party, Beijing, People's Republic of China (office).

LIVERPOOL, Nicholas Joseph Orville, LLD; Dominican head of state; *President;* b. 9 Sept. 1934. *Education:* Sheffield Univ. (UK). *Career:* called to the Bar, Inner Temple, London 1961; lawyer and legal consultant 1970s; prepared new criminal code for Belize 1980; Justice of Appeal for Belize 1990–92; Law Review Commr 1992; Judge, Eastern Caribbean Court of Appeal 1993–95; fmr Judge Court of Appeal, Grenada, Bahamas and High Court of Antigua and Montserrat; Chair. Constitution Review Comm. for Grenada 2002; Pres. of Dominica 2003–; fmr Prof. of Law, Univ. of the West Indies, Barbados; fmr Amb. of Dominica to the UN; fmr Project Dir Caribbean Justice Improvement Project; Dominica Award of Honour (DAH) 2003.
Address: Office of the President, Morne Bruce, Roseau (office); 37 Margaret's Gap, Goodwill, Roseau (home); POB 233, Roseau, Dominica. *Telephone:* 4482054 (office); 4488968 (home). *Fax:* 4498366 (office). *E-mail:* presidentoffice@cwdom.dm (office).

LIVNE, Yosef, BA, MA; Israeli diplomatist; *Ambassador to Mexico; Education:* Univs of Tel-Aviv and Haifa. *Career:* joined Ministry of Foreign Affairs 1977, mem. del. to UN Gen. Ass., New York 1979, Vice-Dir S America Dept 1990–93, Dir of Dept, Latin America and Caribbean Div. 1997–99, Dir Mexico, Cen. America and Caribbean Dept 2004–06;

overseas postings include Second Sec., Embassy in Mèxico 1980–82, First Sec., Embassy in Chile 1985–87, Counsellor, Embassy in Brasília 1987–90; Amb. to El Salvador 1993–97, 2001–04; Consul-Gen. in New York 1999–2001; Amb. to Mexico (also accred to Bahamas) 2006–.
Address: Embassy of Israel, Sierra Madre 215, Lomas de Chapultepec, 11000 Mèxico, DF, Mexico (office). *Telephone:* (55) 5201-1500 (office). *Fax:* (55) 5201-1555 (office). *E-mail:* embisrael@prodigy.net.mx (office). *Website:* mexico-city.mfa.gov.il (office).

LIVNI, Tzipi, LLB; Israeli politician and lawyer; *Vice-Premier and Minister of Foreign Affairs;* b. 5 July 1958; m.; two c. *Education:* Bar-Ilan Univ. *Career:* with Mossad 1980–84; practised law in pvt. firm for ten years before entering public life; Gen. Man. Govt Cos Authority 1996–99; mem. Likud Party –2005, Co-founder and mem. Kadima Party 2005–; mem. Knesset 1999–, served as mem. Constitution, Law and Justice Cttee, Cttee on the Status of Women, Chair. Sub-cttee responsible for legislation of the Prevention of Money Laundering Law; Minister of Regional Co-operation –2001, without Portfolio 2001–02, of Agric. and Rural Devt 2002, of Immigrant Absorption; Acting Minister of Housing and Construction 2004, Minister of Housing and Construction 2004–05; Acting Minister of Justice 2004–05, 2006–07, Minister of Justice 2005–06; Minister of Foreign Affairs 2006–, Vice-Premier May 2006–; Champion of Good Govt Award 2004, ranked by Forbes magazine amongst 100 Most Powerful Women (40th) 2006, (39th) 2007.
Address: Minister of Foreign Affairs, Hakirya, Romema, Jerusalem 91950, Israel (office). *Telephone:* (2) 5303111 (office). *Fax:* (2) 5303367 (office). *E-mail:* zlivni@knesset.gov.il (office). *Website:* www.mfa.gov.il (office).

LIVSHITZ, Aleksander Yakovlevich, DEcon; Russian economist; *Adviser to Prime Minister;* b. 6 Sept. 1946, Berlin, Germany; m. Galina Markina 1966; two d. *Education:* G. Plekhanov Inst. of Nat. Econ. *Career:* teacher, Chair, Prof. Moscow Machine Tool Instrumentation Inst. 1974–; Deputy Chief Analytical Centre, Admin. of Pres. 1992–94; Head of Pres.'s Advisers 1994; Asst to Pres. on problems of economy 1994–96; Deputy Prime Minister and Minister of Finance 1996–97; Deputy Head of Pres. Admin. 1997–98; Head Econ. Policy Fund 1998–; Pres. Rep. for relations with G7 countries 1999; Adviser to Prime Minister 2000–; Deputy Dir-Gen. Russian Aluminium Co. 2001–; mem. UN Comm. on Financing of Devt 2001. *Publications:* Introduction to Market Economy 1991, Economic Reform in Russia and its Price 1994, more than 150 works on econ. problems of Russia, econ. situation in USA in 1980s.
Address: Russkiy Aluminiy, Nikoloyamskaya str. 13, Bldg 1, 109240 Moscow, Russia. *Telephone:* (495) 720-51-70.

LOAYZA MARIACA, Armando; Bolivian government official; b. 8 Dec. 1943, La Paz; m. Teresita Keel de Loaiza; one s. *Education:* Univ. of Montevideo, Uruguay. *Career:* Undersec. of Econ. Integration 1980; Gen. Adviser of the Chancellery 1991; Undersec. of Bilateral Policy 1993; diplomatic postings in Montevideo, Caracas, Geneva, Brussels; Dir Academia Diplomática Boliviana Rafael Bustillo 1991, 1998–2003; Consul-Gen. in Santiago 1993; Amb. to Santa Sede (Vatican) 1994–98; Amb. to Uruguay and Perm. Rep. to ALADI 2003; Minister of Foreign Affairs and Worship –2006.
Address: c/o Ministry of Foreign Affairs and Worship, Calle Ingavi, esq. Junín, La Paz, Bolivia (office).

LOBKOWICZ, Nicholas, DPhil; American academic; *Director, Institute of Central and Eastern European Studies, Catholic University of Eichstätt;* b. 9 July 1931, Prague, Czechoslovakia (now Czech Repub.); m. 1st Countess Josephine Waldburg-Zeil 1953; three s. two d.; m. 2nd Aleksandra N. Cieślińska 1999. *Education:* Collegium Maria Hilf, Switzerland, Univs of Erlangen and Fribourg. *Career:* Assoc. Prof. of Philosophy, Univ. of Notre Dame, Ind. 1960–67; Prof. of Political Theory and Philosophy, Univ. of Munich 1967–90, Dean School of Arts and Letters 1970–71, Rector Magnificus 1971–76, Pres. Univ. of Munich 1976–82; Pres. Catholic Univ. of Eichstätt 1984–96, Dir Inst. of Cen. and Eastern European Studies 1994–; mem. Bd of Dirs Fed. Inst. of Int. and E European Studies, Cologne 1972–75, Senate, West German Rectors' Conf. 1976–82, Perm. Cttee European Rectors' Conf. 1979–84, Council Int. Fed. of Catholic Univs 1984–91; founding mem. Int. Metaphysical Asscn; mem. Cen. Cttee of German Catholics 1980–84; mem. Ukrainian Acad. of Arts and Science (USA) 1979–; mem. W Europe Advisory Cttee to Radio Free Europe/Radio Liberty 1980–2002, Chair. 1994–2002; Founder mem., Vice-Pres. European Acad. of Sciences and Arts 1990–; Pres. Freier Deutscher Autorenverband 1985–91; mem. Pontifical Council for Culture 1982–93; Pres. Czechoslovak Christian Acad. in Rome 1983–90; Administrator of Faculty of Catholic Theology, Charles Univ. Prague 2002–03; ; Hon. Citizen Dallas, Tex.; Hon. DHL (Wayne State Univ.); Hon. DLL (Univ. of Notre Dame); Hon. DrPhil (Seoul and Ukrainian Univ., Munich, Catholic Univ. of America); Hon. DTheol (Charles Univ., Prague). *Publications:*

Theory and Practice 1967, Ende aller Religion? 1976, Marxismus und Machtergreifung 1978, Wortmeldung zu Staat, Kirche, Universität 1981, Irrwege der Angst 1983, Das europäische Erbe 1984, Das Konzil 1986, Zeitwende 1993, Czas przelomu 1996, Rationalität und Innerlichkeit 1997, Duše Evropy 2001.
Address: Oskar-von-Hiller-Strasse 20, 82319 Starnberg (home); Katholische Universität, 85071 Eichstätt, Germany. *Telephone:* (8421) 931717 (office). *Fax:* (8421) 931780 (office). *E-mail:* 05299@ku-eichstaett.de (office); nikolaus.lobkowicz@nexgo.de (home). *Website:* www.zimos/KUE .de (office).

LODDER, Celsius Antônio, MSc; Brazilian international administrator and economist; b. 28 May 1944, Nova Lima, Minas Gerais; three d. *Education:* Fed. Univ. of Minas Gerais, Belo Horizonte, Getúlio Vargas Foundation, Rio de Janeiro and Inst. of Social Studies, The Hague. *Career:* researcher, Applied Econs Research Inst. Ministry of Econ., Finance and Planning 1970–80; subsequently held appointments with State of Minas Gerais and Fed. Govt of Brazil; Sec. for Commercial Policy, Ministry of Finance, later at Ministry of Industry, Commerce and Tourism; Supt Nat. Supply Authority, Ministry of Finance; Chief Adviser, State Bank of Minas Gerais 1983–84; Co-ordinator, Intergovernmental Relations Office, Civil Cabinet of Pres. of Brazil; Lecturer in Econs at various Brazilian univs; Exec. Dir Int. Coffee Org. 1994–2002. *Publications:* books and reports on matters related to regional planning and devt.
Address: c/o International Coffee Organization, 22 Berners Street, London, W1P 4DD, England.

LODGAARD, Sverre, MA; Norwegian research institute director; *Director, Norwegian Institute of International Affairs;* b. 6 April 1945, s. of Emil Andreas Lodgaard and Ingeborg Lodgaard. *Education:* Univ. of Oslo. *Career:* Research Fellow, Norwegian Research Council for Science and the Humanities (NAVF) 1972–73, Dept of Political Science, Univ. of Oslo 1973–77, Int. Peace Research Inst. Oslo (PRIO) 1977–80; Dir European Security and Disarmament Studies, Stockholm Int. Peace Research Inst. 1980–86; Dir PRIO 1987–92; Dir UN Inst. for Disarmament Research (UNIDIR), UN Office at Geneva 1992–96; Dir Norwegian Inst. of Int. Affairs (NUPI), Oslo 1997–; mem. Advisory Council for Arms Control and Disarmament, Norwegian Govt 1972–85, 1989–92, 1998–, UN Sec.-Gen.'s Advisory Bd on Disarmament Matters 1992–96, 1996–99; mem. Editorial Bd Internasjonal Politikk 1973–97, Journal of Peace Research 1979–80; mem. Scientific Council, Hessishce Stiftung Friedens und Konfliktforschung, Frankfurt 1989–, Int. Pugwash Council 1992–2002, Council UN Univ. for Peace 1999–, Int. Advisory Bd Bonn Int. Centre for Conversion 1995–; Soka Univ. Award of Highest Honour, Tokyo 1990.
Address: Norwegian Institute of International Affairs (NUPI), PO Box 8159 Dep., 0033 Oslo, Norway (home). *Telephone:* 22-05-65-50 (office). *Fax:* 22-17-60-44 (office). *E-mail:* sl@nupi.no (office). *Website:* www.nupi .no (office).

LODHI, Maleeha, BSc, PhD; Pakistani diplomatist, journalist and academic; b. Lahore; m. (divorced); one s. *Education:* Univ. of Oxford and London School of Econs, UK. *Career:* Lecturer in Politics and Sociology, LSE 1980–85; fmr Lecturer, Dept of Public Admin, Quaid-i-Azam Univ., Islamabad; Ed. The Muslim; Ed. and Co-founder The News (daily newspaper) 1985–93, 1997–2000; Amb. to USA 1993–97, (with rank of Minister of State) 1999–2002, High Commr to UK 2003–08; mem. UN Sec.-Gen.'s Advisory Bd on Disarmament; Fellow, Pakistan Inst. of Devt Econs; award from All Pakistan Newspaper Soc. 1994, named by Time Magazine as one of 100 global pacesetters and leaders who would define the 21st century 1994, Hilal-e-Imtiaz Presidential Award for public service 2002. *Publications:* Pakistan's Encounter with Democracy, The External Dimension 1994; numerous contribs to int. journals.
Address: Ministry of Foreign Affairs, Constitution Avenue, Islamabad, Pakistan (office). *Telephone:* (51) 9210335 (office). *Fax:* (51) 9207600 (office). *E-mail:* sadiq@mofa.gov.pk (office). *Website:* www.mofa.gov.pk (office).

LOEMAA, Brig.-Gen. Vello; Estonian military officer; *Military Representative, NATO;* b. 18 Jan. 1951; m. Ludmilla Loemaa; one s. one d. *Education:* High Mil. Flight School, Yeisk, Russia, Air Force Acad., Monino, Russia. *Career:* pilot in fighter-bomber regt, Ukraine 1973; resgnd from Soviet Air Forces to join newly ind. Estonian armed forces 1992, Commdr (in the rank of Col) Estonian Air Force 1994–98, Operational Commdr, Estonian Defence Forces 2003; Mil. Rep. to NATO, Brussels 1998–2002, 2008–, has also served as the Mil. Rep. to EU; Defence, Military, Naval and Air Attaché to USA and Canada 2005.
Address: NATO HQ, blvd Léopold III, 1110 Brussels, Belgium (office). *Telephone:* (2) 707-41-11 (office). *Fax:* (2) 707-45-79 (office). *E-mail:* natodoc@hq.nato.int (office). *Website:* www.nato.int (office).

LOESCHER, Gilbert (Gil), PhD; American academic; *Visiting Professor, Refugees Study Centre, University of Oxford; Education:* LSE. *Career:* Prof. of Int. Relations Univ. of Notre Dame, USA 1975–2001; visiting posts Princeton Univ., LSE, Oxford Univ., IISS, US State Dept; fmr Sr Adviser UNHCR; fmr Sr Policy Analyst European Council on Refugees and Exiles; consultant to Ford Foundation, Rand Corpn, UNHCR, UNESCO; fmr Sr. Fellow for Migration, Forced Displacement and Int. Security, IISS; currently Visiting Prof., Refugee Studies Centre, Queen Elizabeth House, Univ. of Oxford. *Publications include:* Human Rights and American Foreign Policy 1979, Calculated Kindness: Refugees and America's Half-Open Door, 1945 to the Present 1986, Refugees and International Relations 1989, Beyond Charity: International Cooperation and the Global Refugee Crisis 1993, UNHCR and World Politics: A Perilous Path 2001.
Address: Refugee Studies Centre, Department of International Development (QEH), University of Oxford, Mansfield Road, Oxford, OX1 3TB, England (office). *Telephone:* (1865) 270729 (office). *Fax:* (1865) 270721 (office). *E-mail:* gilbert.loescher@qeh.ox.ac.uk (office). *Website:* www.rsc .ox.ac.uk (office).

LOGOGLU, Osman Faruk, PhD; Turkish diplomatist; *Chairman, Eurasian Strategic Studies Center; Education:* Brandeis Univ., Princeton Univ., USA. *Career:* Counsellor and Perm. Del. to UN, New York 1980–84; Consul-Gen., Hamburg, Germany 1986–89; held various positions at Ministry of Foreign Affairs, including Deputy Dir-Gen., Dept of Bilateral Political Affairs in Greece 1989–93, Deputy Under-Sec. of Political Affairs 1998–2000, Under-Sec. 2000–01; Amb. to Denmark 1993–96, to Azerbaijan 1996–98, to USA 2001–05; currently Chair. Eurasian Strategic Studies Center, Ankara. *Publication:* Ismet Inonu and the Making of Modern Turkey.
Address: Avrasya Stratejik Araştırmalar Merkezi (Eurasian Strategic Studies Center), Konrad Adenauer Caddesi No: 61, Yıldız, Çankaya 06550 Ankara, Turkey (office). *Telephone:* (312) 4916070 (office). *Fax:* (312) 4916097 (office). *E-mail:* flogoglu@asam.org.tr (office); faruklogoglu@gmail.com (home). *Website:* www.asam.org.tr (office).

LOHANI, Prakash Chandra, PhD; Nepalese politician; b. 1944. *Education:* Univ. of Calif., USA. *Career:* fmr Lecturer, Univ. of Calif.; fmr Minister of Foreign Affairs and of Finance; Minister of Finance, Interim Govt 2003–04; currently Joint Gen.-Sec. Rashtriya Jana Shakti Party (National People's Power Party).
Address: Rashtriya Jana Shakti Party (National People's Power Party), Ramalphokhari, Kathmandu, Nepal (office). *Telephone:* (1) 4437063 (office). *Fax:* (1) 4437064 (office). *E-mail:* rjpnepal@info.com.np (office). *Website:* www.rjpnepal.org (office).

LOHLÉ, Juan Pablo, LLB; Argentine diplomatist and academic; *Ambassador to Brazil;* b. 1 March 1948; m. Delfina Linck; three c. *Education:* San Juan Precursor High School, Univ. Católica Argentina, Univ. de Belgrano. *Career:* Asst Prof. of Int. Relations, Univ. Católica Argentina 1976, Asst Prof. of Int. Public Law 1980; Prof. of Latin American Politics, Univ. del Salvador 1983, Dir Post-Grad Course in Int. Relations 1987, Prof. of Int. Relations 1995; Pres. Centre for Int. and Political Studies, Buenos Aires 1983–89; Prof., Nat. Inst. of Public Admin, Buenos Aires 1991–92; Pnr, Lohlé and Assocs (law firm) 1975–95, Estudios Rossi Camilión and Assocs 2000; Adviser, External Relations Comm., House of Deputies 1973–76, Adviser to Vice-Pres. of Comm. 1983–87; Adviser on Int. Relations to Prov. of Buenos Aires 1987–89; Rep. to OAS Gen. Ass., Washington, DC 1989, Asunción, Paraguay 1990; Amb. to OAS 1989–91, to Spain 1991–93; Adviser on Integration to Ministry of Justice 1994–95; Rep. SEMA Group (Soc. Anónima Española) 1997; Cabinet Adviser, Ministry of Justice 1998; Dir Cámara Española de Comercio 1998; Dir Contelen SA 1999; currently Amb. to Brazil; mem. Bd of Dirs Banco de la Provincia de Buenos Aires 1999; Del. to numerous int. confs; guest lecturer several academic insts; Hon. Prof. of Int. Studies, Madrid, Spain; Gran Cruz de la Orden del Mérito Civil (Spain). *Publications:* La Argentina y sus perspectivas 1989, Relaciones España-Argentina, su proyecto de futuro 1992, La Argentina y el Mercosur 1992, La Argentina y la situación internacional 1992; several articles in professional journals.
Address: Embassy of Argentina, SHIS, QL 02, Conj. 01, Casa 19, Lago Sul, 70442-900 Brasilia DF, Brazil (office). *Telephone:* (61) 3364-7600 (office). *Fax:* (61) 3364-7666 (office). *E-mail:* ebras@mrecic.gov.br (office). *Website:* www.brasil.embajada-argentina.gov.ar (office).

LOIZAGA, Eladio, LLB; Paraguayan diplomatist, civil servant and politician; *Permanent Representative, United Nations;* b. 17 March 1949, Asunción; m.; two c. *Education:* Catholic Univ. and Nat. Univ., Asunción. *Career:* joined Ministry of Foreign Affairs 1967, various posts with Dept of Int. Orgs Treaties and Instruments 1981, Dir of Dept 1983–88, Rep. to Yacyretá Binational Agency 1989–92, Adviser to Minister; elected to Nat. Chamber of Deputies 1989, mem. cttees concerning constitutional and

legis. issues; Pvt. Sec. to Pres. of Paraguay and Minister Exec. Br. 1989–92; mem. Perm. Cttee of Congress 1992–93; Perm. Rep. to UN, WTO and other specialized agencies, Geneva 1995–98; served with Embassy in Washington, DC and Alt. Rep. to OAS; Perm. Rep. to UN, New York 2001–.
Address: Permanent Mission of Paraguay to the UN, 211 East 43rd Street, Suite 400, New York, NY 10017, USA (office). *Telephone:* (212) 687-3490 (office). *Fax:* (212) 818-1282 (office). *E-mail:* paraguay@un.int (office).

LØJ, Ellen Margrethe, CandPol(Econs), MPolSc; Danish diplomatist; *Ambassador to Czech Republic;* b. 17 Oct. 1948, Gedesby. *Education:* Univ. of Copenhagen. *Career:* joined staff of Ministry of Foreign Affairs 1973; Sec. Perm. Mission to UN, New York 1977–80; Counsellor at Perm. Rep. of Denmark to EC, Brussels 1982–85; Head of Dept Ministry of Foreign Affairs 1986–89; Amb. to Israel 1989–92; Under-Sec. South Group (Multilateral, later Bilateral Affairs), Ministry of Foreign Affairs, State Sec. 1996–2001; Perm. Rep. to UN 2001–06; Amb. to Czech Repub. 2007–; mem. Advisory Bds Industrialization Fund for Developing Countries 1994–96, Investment Fund for Cen. and Eastern Europe 1994–96, Supervisory Bd Scandlines AG and Scandlines A/S 1998–.
Address: Embassy of Denmark, Maltézské nám. 5, POB 25, 118 01 Prague 1, Czech Republic (office). *Telephone:* 257531600 (office). *Fax:* 257531609 (office). *E-mail:* prgamb@um.dk (office). *Website:* www.ambprag.um.dk (office).

LONDOÑO PAREDES, Julio; Colombian politician and diplomatist; *Ambassador to Cuba;* b. 10 June 1938, Bogotá; m. *Education:* San Isidro Hermanos Maristas School, El Carmen Inst. and Mil. Cadet School, Bogotá. *Career:* Prof. of Int. Politics, Univ. of Jorge Tadeo Lozano, Bogotá; Prof. of Int. Public Law, Univ. of El Rosario, Bogotá; served in army, retd 1981 with rank of Lt-Col; Head of Frontier Div., Ministry of Foreign Affairs 1968–79, Sec.-Gen. 1979–82, Vice-Minister 1982–83, Minister 1986–90; Amb. to Panama 1983–86; Perm. Rep. to UN 1994–99; currently Amb. to Cuba. *Publications:* History of the Colombo-Peruvian Conflict of 1932, Colombian Territorial Law, Colombian Border Issues.
Address: Embassy of Colombia, Calle 14, No 515, entre 5 y 7, Miramar, Havana, Cuba (office). *Telephone:* (7) 24-1246 (office). *Fax:* (7) 24-1249 (office). *E-mail:* embacub@cancilleria.gov.co (office).

LONG, Marceau, LèsL, LenD; French civil servant; *President, Institut français des relations internationales;* b. 22 April 1926, Aix-en-Provence, Bouches-du-Rhône; m. Josette Niel 1949; two s. three d. *Education:* Lycée Mignet, Univ. of Aix-en-Provence, École nat. d'admin. *Career:* Lecturer, Ecole nat. d'admin 1953–56, Inst. d'Etudes politiques 1953–56; seminars Ecole nat. d'admin 1963–68; at Council of State 1952–57, 1975–, Vice-Pres. 1987–95, apptd auditor 1952, master of petitions 1957, Sec.-Gen. to Govt 1975–82, Counsellor of State on long-term secondment 1976; apptd to Govt Comm. 1957, Tech. Counsellor to Cabinet, Sec. of State on Tunisian and Moroccan Affairs, then Foreign Affairs, then Judicial Counsellor to French Embassy, Morocco 1958, Dir-Gen. Admin. and Public Offices 1961–67, Sec. Gen. Admin, Ministry of Armies 1967–73, mem. Atomic Energy Cttee 1975–82; Chair. Organisation de la radio et de la télévision françaises (ORTF) 1973–74; Chair. Cie Air-Inter 1982–84; Chair. Cie Air France 1984–87; Chair. Cttee Inquiry on Law of Nationality 1987, Council of Admin. Tribunals and Courts of Appeal 1988–95; Lecturer Inst. d'études politiques de Paris, Ecole nat. d'admin 1963–68 (Chair. Bd of Govs 1987); Dir Crédit industriel et banque commericale 1982–87, Soc. de Gestion de participations aéronautiques 1985; Vice-Pres. Conseil d'Etat 1987–95; apptd Pres. Admin. Council, Ecole nat. d'admin, Institut int. d'admin publique 1987, Inst. français des relations int. 1998–; Pres. Franco-American Foundation 1989–92, Hon. Pres. 1993–; Pres. Haut conseil à l'intégration 1989–93, 1994–95, Inst. des hautes études de la justice 1995–97, Inst. de la gestion déléguée 1996–2001; mem. Court of Arbitration, The Hague 1991–; mem. numerous admin. councils and cttees; Grand Officier, Légion d'honneur; Commdr Ordre nat. du Mérite; Officier des Palmes académiques. *Publications:* L'Economie de la Fonction Publique 1967, Les Services de Premier Ministre 1981, Les Grands Arrêts de la Jurisprudence Administrative (co-author) 1984, Etre Français aujourd'hui et demain, Rapport de la Commission de la Nationalité 1988, L'Esprit de justice: Portalis 1997, Les grands arrêts de la jurisprudence administrative (jtly 2005 and numerous contribs to magazines and books on public office and law.
Address: Institut français des relations internationales, 27 rue de la Procession, 75015 Paris (office).

LONG, Yongtu; Chinese economist and diplomatist; *Secretary General, Boao Forum For Asia;* b. June 1943, You Co., Hunan Prov. *Education:* Guizhou Univ. *Career:* joined Ministry of Foreign Trade 1965; Commercial Attaché and Third Sec., Perm. Mission to UN, New York 1978–80; with UNDP 1980–86; Exec. Deputy Dir China Int. Centre for Econ. and Tech.

Exchanges 1986–92; Dir Dept of Int. Econ. Relations, Ministry of Foreign Trade and Econ. Co-operation 1992–94, Asst Minister 1994–97, apptd Vice-Minister 1997; Chief Negotiator of China's accession to WTO 1997; currently Gen. Sec. Boao Forum For Asia.
Address: Secretariat of Boao Forum for Asia, Suite 2410, China World Tower 2, No. 1 Jianguomenwai Avenue, Chaoyang Dist, Beijing 100004 (office); Boao Forum For Asia, 1, Gold Coast Boulevard, Qiong Hai, Hainan Province, 571434, People's Republic of China (office). *Telephone:* (898) 62778703 (office). *Fax:* (898) 62778702 (office). *E-mail:* bfa@boaoforum.org (office). *Website:* www.boaoforum.org (office).

LØNNING, Inge Johan, DTheol; Norwegian politician and theologian; *President, Lagtinget;* b. 20 Feb. 1938, Bergen; m. Kari Andersen 1962; two s. two d. *Education:* Univs of Bergen and Oslo and Pastoral Seminary of Church of Norway. *Career:* Naval Chaplain 1964–65; Asst Prof. Univ. of Oslo 1965–70; Research Fellow, Univ. of Tübingen 1967; Prof. of Systematic Theology, Univ. of Oslo 1971–, Dean, Faculty of Theology 1977–81, Rector, Univ. of Oslo 1985–92; mem. Oslo City Council 1972–76; Chair. Bd Norwegian Research Council for Science and Humanities 1980–84; Pres. Norsemen's Fed. 1989–2000, Nat. Rectors' Conf. 1989–92; Leader, European Movt in Norway 1993–95; mem. Parl. 1997–, Vice-Pres. Stortinget (Parl.) 2001–05, Pres. Lagtinget 2005–; Vice-Pres. Høyre 1997–2002; Pres. Nordic Council 2003; Ed. Kirke og Kultur journal 1968–; mem. Norwegian Acad. of Science and Letters, Royal Norwegian Soc., Royal Soc. of Letters, Sweden; Commdr, Royal Norwegian Order of St Olav; Commdr with Star, Order of Merit of FRG; Hon. DD (Luther Coll. Decorah, USA, Åbo Acad., Finland). *Publications:* Kanon im Kanon. Zum Dogmatischen Grundlagenproblem des Neutestamentlichen Kanons 1972, Martin Luther: Selected Writings (six vols, ed.) 1978–83, Fellesskap og frihet. Tid for idepolitikk 1997.
Address: Stortinget, Karl Johans Gate, 0026 Oslo (office); Skullerudstubben 22, 1188 Oslo, Norway (home). *Telephone:* 23-31-30-04 (office); 22-28-95-12 (home). *Fax:* 23-31-38-38 (office). *E-mail:* inge.lonning@stortinget.no (office). *Website:* www.stortinget.no (office).

LONSDALE, Charles; British diplomatist; *Ambassador to Armenia; Career:* Second Sec., Budapest 1990–93, First Sec., Moscow 1998–2003, Deputy Head of Afghanistan Group, FCO 2003–05, Deputy Head of Human Rights, Democracy and Governance Group 2005–08, Amb. to Armenia 2008–.
Address: British Embassy, 34 Baghramian Avenue, Yerevan 375019, Armenia (office). *Telephone:* (10) 26-43-01 (office). *Fax:* (10) 26-43-18 (office). *E-mail:* enquiries.yerevan@fco.gov.uk (office). *Website:* www.britishembassy.am (office).

LOPES, Carlos, PhD; Guinea-Bissau economist and diplomatist; *Executive Director, United Nations Institute for Training and Research (UNITAR);* b. 7 March 1960. *Education:* Univ. of Geneva, Univ. of Paris 1 Panthéon-Sorbonne. *Career:* taught at univs in Lisbon, Coimbra, Zurich, Uppsala, Mexico, San Paulo and Rio de Janeiro; fmr consultant for UNESCO, Swedish Int. Devt Cooperation Agency, UN Econ. Comm. for Africa, Research and Technological Exchange Group, Ruraltec Switzerland; Devt Economist, UNDP 1988, then Deputy Dir Office of Evaluation and Strategic Planning, Resident Rep. in Zimbabwe, Deputy, then Dir Bureau for Devt Policy, Asst Admin. UNDP, UN Resident Coordinator and UNDP Resident Rep. in Brazil 2003–05; Dir Exec. Office of Sec. Gen. in charge of Political, Peacekeeping and Humanitarian affairs 2005–; Exec. Dir UNITAR 2007–.
Address: United Nations Institute for Training and Research (UNITAR), Palais des Nations, 1211 Geneva 10, Switzerland (office). *Telephone:* 229178455 (office). *Fax:* 229178047 (office). *E-mail:* info@unitar.org (office). *Website:* www.unitar.org (office).

LOPES, Henri Marie Joseph; Republic of the Congo author, politician and diplomatist; *Ambassador to France, Portugal, Spain, UK and Holy See (Vatican);* b. 12 Sept. 1937, Léopoldville, Belgian Congo (now Kinshasa, Democratic Repub. of the Congo); m. Nirva Pasbeau 1961; one s. three d. *Education:* France. *Career:* Minister of Nat. Educ. 1968–71, of Foreign Affairs 1971–73; mem. Political Bureau, Congolese Labour Party 1973; Prime Minister and Minister of Planning 1973–75, of Finance 1977–80; UNESCO Asst Dir-Gen. for Programme Support 1982–86, UNESCO Asst Dir-Gen. for Culture and Communication 1986–90, for Culture 1990–94, for Foreign Affairs 1994–95, Deputy Dir-Gen. 1996–98; Amb. to France (also accred to Portugal, Spain, UK and Holy See (Vatican)) 1998–; mem. Haut Conseil de la Francophonie; Chevalier, Légion d'honneur, Commdr du Mérite Congolais, etc.; Prix littéraire de l'Afrique noire 1972, Prix SIMBA de littérature 1978, Prix de littérature du Président (Congo), Prix de l'Acad. de Bretagne et des Pays de la Loire 1990, Grand Prix de la Francophonie de l'Acad. française 1993. *Publications:* Tribaliques (short stories), La Nouvelle Romance (novel), Learning to be (with others), Sans

tam-tam (novel) 1977, Le Pleurer Rire (novel) 1982, Le Chercheur d'Afriques (novel) 1990, Sur l'autre Rive (novel) 1992, Le Lys et le flamboyant (novel) 1997.
Address: Embassy of the Republic of the Congo, 37 bis rue Paul Valéry, 75116 Paris, France (office). *Telephone:* 1-45-00-60-57 (home). *Fax:* 1-40-67-17-33 (office). *E-mail:* ambacongo_france@yahoo.fr (office). *Website:* www.ambacongo.org (office).

LOPES DA SILVA, Ramiro Armando de Oliveira; Portuguese diplomatist and UN official; b. 16 Jan. 1949; m.; three c. *Career:* with UN 1985–, served in several capacities including UN Humanitarian Co-ordinator in Angola 1996–98, World Food Programme (WFP) Special Envoy in Afghanistan 2001–02; Dir of Transportation and Logistics Div., World Food Program HQ, Rome –2002, 2004–; UN Humanitarian Co-ordinator in Iraq 2002–03; acting UN Special Rep. in Iraq 2003–04.
Address: United Nations Office of the World Food Programme (WFP), Via Cesare Giulio Viola 68, Parco dei Medici, Rome, 00148, Italy (office). *Telephone:* (06) 65131 (office). *E-mail:* ramiro.lopesdasilva@wfp.org. *Website:* www.wfp.org (office).

LÓPEZ CABALLERO, Alfonso, MA, MPhil, MBA, PhD; Colombian diplomatist and politician; grandson of Alfonso López Pumarejo, Pres. of Chile 1934–38, 1942–45; m. Josefina Andreu Lopez-Caballero. *Education:* Georgetown and Columbia Univs, USA, Inst. Européen d'Admin des Affaires (INSEAD), Fontainebleau, France. *Career:* fmr Asst Man., First City Bank of New York; Business Consultant, Arthur Young & Co.; elected mem. Congress and Senate; fmr Amb. to France, to Canada; fmr Minister of Agric., of the Interior, in charge of presidential functions; Govt Negotiator with FARC guerilla faction during Peace Process; Amb. to UK 2002–06; Prof. of Latin American Studies, Univ. de Los Andes; Prof. of Macroecons and Financial Man., Universidad de Bogota Jorge Tadeo Lozano.
Address: Ministry of Foreign Affairs, Palacio de San Carlos, Calle 10A, No 5-51, Bogotá, DC, Colombia (office). *Telephone:* (1) 282-7811 (office). *Fax:* (1) 341-6777 (office). *Website:* www.cancilleria.gov.co (office).

LÓPEZ SUÁREZ, Guillermo; Salvadorean politician and banker; *Secretary for Commercial Affairs and International Finance; Education:* Inst. of Tech. and Higher Studies, Monterrey, Mexico, N Dakota State School of Science, USA. *Career:* Asst to Dir-Gen., Empresa Cocotera and Empresa Cafetalera Sol Mollet 1978–81; Head of Finance, Granjero and Sello de Oro 1983–84; Dir-Gen. Grupo Lotisa, Maquilishuat, and Cumbres de Cuscatlán 1984–97; Financial Dir Grupo Avicola Salvadoreña and Grupo La Sultana 1987–95, Dir-Gen. 1995–; Dir-Gen. Grupo Pollo Campero 1994–2004; Minister of the Treasury 2004–06; Sec. for Commercial Affairs and Int. Finance 2006–; Adviser to Nat. Commerce, Asscn of Poultry Farmers of El Salvador, Fed. of Poultry Farmers of Cen. America and the Caribbean; mem. Bd of Govs World Bank, IBRD, Int. Finance Corpn, IDA.
Address: Office of the Secretary for Commercial Affairs and International Finance, Ministry for the Presidency, Avenida Cuba, Calle Darío González 806, Barrio San Jacinto, San Salvador, El Salvador (office). *Telephone:* 2248-9000 (office). *Fax:* 2248-9370 (office). *E-mail:* casapres@casapres.gob.sv (office). *Website:* www.casapres.gob.sv (office).

LORDKIPANIDZE, Vazha Giorgevich, DEcon; Georgian politician, sociologist and demographer; *Head of Demography Department, Tbilisi State University;* b. 29 Nov. 1949, Tbilisi; m. Irina Khomeriki; two d. *Education:* Tbilisi State Univ., Moscow Acad. of Social Sciences. *Career:* Teacher Tbilisi State Univ. 1975–, Head Demography Dept 2000–; Sec., Second, First Secr. Cen. Comsomol Cttee of Georgia 1980–86; First Sec. Tbilisi Dist CP Cttee 1986–88; Head Dept of Culture and Ideology Cen. Cttee, CP of Georgia 1988–90; Sr Researcher Inst. of Demography and Sociology, Georgian Acad. of Sciences 1991–92; Chief State Counsellor State Council of Georgia 1992; Head of Personnel Eduard Shevardnadze Admin. 1992–95; Amb. to Russia 1995–98; Minister of State 1998–2000; mem. Parl. 2000–; Pres. Demographers' Asscn of Georgia 2000–; Vice-Pres. Int. Research Centre for East–West Relationships 2000–; mem. Georgian Acad. of Econs 1996–, UN Int. Acad. of Informatics; Pres. Special Olympic Cttee 2001; Head Christian Democrat Party of Georgia 2002–. *Publications:* various scientific articles, monographs and books.
Address: Tbilisi State University, 1 Chavchavadze Avenue, 380079 Tbilisi (office); 5 Larsi Street, Flat 9, Tbilisi, Georgia (home). *Telephone:* (32) 25-12-38 (office); (32) 23-20-70 (home). *Fax:* (32) 25-12-39 (office); (32) 233259 (office); (32) 99-05-13 (home). *E-mail:* ikhomeriki@hotmail.com.

LORTIE, Marc, BA; Canadian diplomatist; *Ambassador to France;* b. 1948, Beauport, Québec; m. Patricia Dunn. *Education:* Séminaire de Québec, Laval Univ. *Career:* joined Dept of External Affairs 1971, overseas postings include in Tunisia 1973–75, in USA 1979–83; Head, Int. Media

Relations, Office of Prime Minister, Ottawa 1985–87, Press Sec. 1987–89; Minister-Counsellor for Political Affairs, Embassy in Paris and Personal Rep. of Prime Minister for La Francophonie 1989–93; Sr Coordinator for Fed.-Prov. Relations, Dept of Foreign Affairs and Int. Trade 1998–2000, Asst Deputy Minister of Americas 2001; Personal Rep. of Prime Minister, Third Summit of the Americas 2000; Amb. to Chile 1993–97, to Spain 2004–07, to France 2007–; fmr Fellow, Centre for Int. Affairs, Harvard Univ.
Address: Embassy of Canada, 35 avenue Montaigne, 75008 Paris, France (office). *Telephone:* 1-44-43-29-00 (office). *Fax:* 1-44-43-29-99 (office). *E-mail:* paris_webmaster@international.gc.ca (office). *Website:* www.amb-canada.fr (office).

LOSHCHININ, Valery Vassilyevich; Russian diplomatist; *Permanent Representative, United Nations, Geneva;* b. 11 Sept. 1940, Gomel Region, Byelorussia; m.; two s. two d. *Education:* Belarus State Univ., Diplomatic Acad. of USSR Ministry of Foreign Affairs. *Career:* with Ministry of Foreign Affairs Belarus SSR, then USSR Ministry of Foreign Affairs 1965–77; with Perm. Mission to Russia 1977–89; Deputy Perm. Rep. to int. orgs, Geneva 1989–95, Perm. Rep. 2006–; Dir Second European Dept, Russian Ministry of Foreign Affairs 1995–96; Amb. to Belarus 1996–99; Perm. Rep. to int. orgs, Vienna 1999–2001; Deputy Minister of Foreign Affairs (responsible for relations with CIS countries) 2001–2002, First Deputy Minister of Foreign Affairs 2002–05.
Address: Permanent Mission of the Russian Federation, 15 Avenue de la Paix, 1211 Geneva 20, Switzerland (office). *Telephone:* (22) 7331870 (office). *Fax:* (22) 7344044 (office). *E-mail:* mission.russian@vtxnet.ch (office). *Website:* www.geneva.mid.ru (office).

LOSYUKOV, Alexander Prokhorovich; Russian diplomatist; b. 15 Nov. 1943; m.; two d. *Education:* Moscow State Inst. of Int. Relations. *Career:* Intern, USSR Embassy, Afghanistan 1968–70, Attaché, 1970–72; Attaché, Third Sec., then Second Sec. Secr. of the First Deputy Minister of Foreign Affairs 1972–78; Second Sec., then First Sec. USSR Embassy, USA 1978–81; First Sec., Gen. Secr., Ministry of Foreign Affairs 1981–82; Asst to Deputy Minister of Foreign Affairs 1982–85; Minister-Counsellor, USSR Embassy, The Philippines 1985–90; Head, Directorate of Pacific and SE Asia countries, Ministry of Foreign Affairs 1990, 1992, Head, Directorate of Gen. Problems of Asian-Pacific Ocean region 1990–92; Amb. to New Zealand (concurrently Kingdom of Tonga, Western Samoa) 1992–94, to Australia (concurrently Fiji, Vanuatu and Nauru) 1994–97; Dir Second Dept of Asia 1997–99, Ministry of Foreign Affairs, Sec.-Gen. 1999–2000, Deputy Minister of Foreign Affairs 2000–04; Amb. to Japan 2004–07.
Address: c/o Ministry of Foreign Affairs, 119200 Moscow Smolenskaya-Sennaya pl. 32/34, Russia (office). *Website:* www.mid.ru (office).

LOTEN, Graeme Neil; British diplomatist; *Ambassador to Tajikistan;* b. 10 March 1959, Portsmouth, Hants. *Education:* Portsmouth Grammar School and Univ. of Liverpool. *Career:* joined FCO 1981, Pvt. Sec. to British Amb. to NATO, Brussels 1983–86, Third Sec. (Aid), Khartoum 1986–87, Second Sec. (Econ. and Agricultural Affairs), The Hague 1988–92, Deputy Head of Mission, Almaty (accred to Kazakhstan and Kyrgyzstan) 1992–97, Amb. to Rwanda (also accred to Burundi) 1998–2001, to Mali 2001–03, to Tajikistan 2004–; on leave of absence doing voluntary work with Anglican Church in Cyangugu, Rwanda 2003–04.
Address: British Embassy, 65 MirzoTursunzade Street, Dushanbe 734002, Tajikistan (office). *Telephone:* (37) 224-22-21 (office). *Fax:* (37) 227-17-26 (office). *E-mail:* dushanbe.reception@fco.gov.uk (office). *Website:* www.britishembassy.gov.uk/tajikistan (office).

LOUIS, Jean-Victor, DenD; Belgian lawyer and academic; *Professor Emeritus, Université Libre de Bruxelles;* b. 10 Jan. 1938, Uccle; m. Maria Rosa Moya Benavent 1963; three s. *Education:* Univ. Libre de Bruxelles. *Career:* Sec. Inst. d'Etudes Européennes, Univ. de Bruxelles 1967–71, Dir 1971–72, Dir of Research 1977–80, Pres. 1980–92; Lecturer, Univ. Libre de Bruxelles 1970–73, Prof. 1973–2003, Prof. Emer. 2003–; Prof. European Univ. Inst. 1998–2002; Adviser, Nat. Bank of Belgium 1972–80, Head, Legal Dept 1980–97, Adviser to Bd of Dirs 1990–97; Pres. Belgian Asscn for European Law 1983–85; legal expert, Institutional Cttee European Parl. 1992–94; Pres. Initiative Cttee 96, Int. European Movt 1995–98; mem., Monetary Cttee of Int. Law Asscn; Ed. Cahiers de Droit Européen 1977–; Exec. Dir Philippe Wiener-Maurice Anspach Foundation 1971–2002, Pres. 2002–; Francqui Chair 2007–08; Dr hc (Univ. Paris 2) 2001; Commdr, Order of Belgian Crown; Emile Bernheim Prize 1969, P.H. Spaak Prize 1979. *Publications:* Les règlements de la Communauté économique européenne 1969, Le Droit de la Communauté économique européenne (dir and co-author), 15 vols 1970–, The European Community Legal Order 1979, Implementing the Tokyo Round (with J. Jackson and M. Matsushita) 1984, Vers un Système européen de banques centrales (ed.)

1989, From the EMS to the Monetary Union 1990, Banking Supervision in the EC (ed.) 1995, L'Union européenne et l'avenir de ses institutions 1996, The Euro and European Integration (ed.) 1999, The Euro in the National Context (ed.) 2002, The Euro: Law, Politics, Economics (ed. with A. Komninos), L'Ordre juridique de l'Union européenne (with T. Ronse) 2005; many articles on EC law, especially in field of monetary cooperation and integration.
Address: 524 avenue Louise, Boîte 9, 1050 Brussels, Belgium (home).

LOUISY, Dame Calliopa Pearlette, GCMG, DSU, BA, MA, PhD; Saint Lucia government official and academic; *Governor-General;* b. 8 June 1946, Laborie, Saint Lucia. *Education:* St Joseph's Convent Secondary School, Univ. of the West Indies, Université Laval, Québec, Canada, Univ. of Bristol, UK. *Career:* grad. teacher, St Joseph's Convent 1969–72, 1975–76; tutor, Saint Lucia 'A' Level Coll. 1976–1981, Prin. 1981–86; Dean Sir Arthur Lewis Community Coll. 1986–94, Vice-Prin. 1994–95, Prin. 1996–97; Gov.-Gen. of Saint Lucia 1997–; Commonwealth Scholar 1972; Hon. Distinguished Fellow, Univ. of the West Indies 2003; Grand Cross, Order of St Lucia 1997, Dame of the Equestrian Order of St Gregory the Great 2002; Hon. LLD (Bristol) 1999, (Sheffield) 2003; Int. Woman of the Year 1998, 2001, Paul Harris Fellow, Rotary Int. 2001, Caribbean Luminary 2007. *Publications:* A Guide to the Writing of Creole 1985, The Changing Role of the Small State in Higher Education 1993, Dilemmas of Insider Research in a Small Country Setting 1997, Higher Education in the Caribbean: Issues and Strategies 1999, Expanding the Horizons of Creole Research 1999, Globalisation and Comparative Education: A Caribbean Perspective 2001, Nation Languages and National Development in the Caribbean 2002, Whose Context for What Quality? – Informing Educational Strategies for the Caribbean 2004, Global Trends in Education – The Cultural Dimension 2007.
Address: Government House, Morne Fortune, Castries, Saint Lucia, West Indies (office). *Telephone:* (758) 452-2481 (office). *Fax:* (758) 453-2731 (office). *E-mail:* govgenslu@candw.lc (office). *Website:* stluciagovernmenthouse.com (office).

LØVALD, Johan Judvik, PhD; Norwegian diplomatist; *Permanent Representative, United Nations;* m. Jennifer A. Ehly; three c. *Education:* Northwestern Univ., USA. *Career:* joined Ministry of Foreign Affairs 1970, Exec. Officer 1975–77, 1981–82, Head Disarmament Div. 1982–86, Asst Dir-Gen. Political Div. 1989–91, Deputy Dir-Gen. 1991–94, Political Dir 1994–96, Deputy Sec.-Gen. Foreign Policy 2000–03; overseas posts include Second Sec. Embassy in China 1973–75, First Sec. Perm. Mission to UN, New York 1977–80, Vice Consul, New York 1981, Counsellor Perm. Mission to NATO, Brussels 1986–89, Amb. to Canada 1996–2000, Perm. Rep. to UN 2003–.
Address: Permanent Mission of Norway to the UN, 825 Third Avenue, 39th Floor, New York, NY 10022, USA (office). *Telephone:* (212) 421-0280 (office). *Fax:* (212) 688-0554 (office). *E-mail:* delun@mfa.no (office). *Website:* www.un.norway-un.org (office).

LOVELL, Deborah Mae; Antigua and Barbuda diplomatist; *Ambassador to USA. Career:* career civil servant, joined Antigua and Barbuda Foreign Service 1983, Third Sec., High Comm. for Eastern Caribbean States, London 1983, held several positions, including Acting High Commr, Antigua and Barbuda Office, Ottawa (headed Mission for three years), Minister Counsellor, Embassy in Washington, DC and mem. Perm. Mission of Antigua and Barbuda to UN, New York –2005, Amb. to USA and Perm. Rep. to OAS 2005–.
Address: Embassy of Antigua and Barbuda, 3216 New Mexico Avenue, NW, Washington, DC 20016, USA (office). *Telephone:* (202) 362-5211 (office). *Fax:* (202) 362-5225 (office). *E-mail:* embantbar@aol.com (office).

LOWELL, John; Maltese diplomatist; b. 24 Feb. 1936, Sliema; m. Marie-Therese Lowell (née Zarb); three c. *Education:* St Aloysius Coll. *Career:* employed by Barclays Bank DCO 1952–56; Man. Dir Ells Ltd, Malta 1967–97; Amb. to Bosnia and Herzegovina (also accred to Romania and Bulgaria 1999–2003, to Croatia 2000–03), Amb. to USA 2003–07 (also accred as High Commr to Canada) 2003–07; Chair. Manoel Theatre Cttee 1993–2003; fmr Pres. SKAL Club, Inst. of Dirs, Malta, Chamber of Commerce, Floriana Football Club; mem. Fondazzjoni Patrimonju Malti, United Fed. of Travel Agents, Asscn of Tennis Professionals; Commendatore, Repub. of Italy, Order of Merit, Bulgaria.
Address: Ministry of Foreign Affairs, Palazzo Parisio, Merchants Street, Valletta VLT 1171, Malta (office). *Telephone:* 21242191 (office). *Fax:* 21242853 (office). *E-mail:* john.lowell@gov.mt (office). *Website:* www.mfa.gov.mt (office).

LOWENTHAL, Abraham F., AB, MPA, PhD; American academic; *Robert F. Erburu Professor of Ethics, Globalization and Development, University of Southern California;* b. 4 June 1941; m. 1st Janet Wrzanski 1962 (divorced

1980); one d.; m. 2nd Jane Jaguette 1991; one s. *Education:* Harvard Univ. *Career:* early position with Ford Foundation in Peru, Dominican Repub.; fmr Asst Dir then Dir of Studies, Council on Foreign Relations, New York; Founding Dir Latin American Program, Woodrow Wilson Int. Center for Scholars, Washington, DC 1977–83; currently Robert F. Erburu Prof. of Ethics, Globalization and Devt, Univ. of Southern California, Dir Center for Int. Studies 1992–97, Founding Pres. Pacific Council on Int. Policy, now Pres. Emer., Int. Policy Fellow 2007–, mem. Faculty Advisory Council Center on Public Diplomacy; Founding Dir Inter-American Dialogue; visiting posts include Univ. of Oxford, Princeton Univ., Hebrew Univ., Harvard Univ., UCLA, Brookings Inst., IISS, Woodrow Wilson Center, Public Policy Inst. of Calif.; Vice-Pres. Council on Foreign Relations; mem. Trade Advisory Council; Order of the Southern Cross, Brazil, Order of Duarte, Sanchez, Dominican Repub. 2006. *Publications include:* The Dominican Intervention 1972, Partners in Conflict: the United States and Latin America in the 1990s 1987; as ed. or co-ed.: The California–Mexico Connection 1993, Latin America in a New World 1994, Constructing Democratic Governance: Latin America in the Mid-1990s 1996, Exporting Democracy: The United States and Latin America; numerous articles in journals and newspapers.
Address: School of International Relations, University of Southern California, Social Science Building, SOS B3, Los Angeles, CA 90089-0037, USA (office). *Telephone:* (213) 740-6954 (office). *E-mail:* afl@usc.edu (office). *Website:* www.usc.edu (office).

LU, (Hsiu-lien) Annette; Taiwanese politician; *Vice-President;* b. 7 June 1944, Taoyuan. *Education:* Taiwan Prov. Taipei First Girls' High School, Nat. Taiwan Univ., Univ. of Illinois and Harvard Univ., USA. *Career:* fmr Sr Specialist, Section Chief Exec. Law and Regulations Cttee of Exec. Yuan; participated in street demonstrations; sentenced to twelve years' imprisonment 1979, released after five years and four months on medical parole; f. N American Taiwanese Women's Asscn, Clean Election Coalition 1985–90; organized and led Alliance for the Promotion of UN Membership for Taiwan 1991; Democratic Progressive Party (DPP) mem. Legis. Yuan for Taoyuan, mem. Foreign Affairs Cttee 1992–95; Nat. Policy Adviser to Pres. 1996; Magistrate for Taoyuan Co. 1996–99; Vice-Pres. of Taiwan 2000–; Chair. Third Global Summit of Women, Taiwan 1994; f. Centre for Women's and Children's Safety; World Peace Prize 2001. *Publications:* novels: These Three Women, Empathy; non-fiction: New Feminism, I Love Taiwan, Viewing Taiwan from Abroad, Retrying the Formosa Case.
Address: Office of the President, Chiehshou Hall, 122 Chunking, South Road, Sec. 1, Taipei 100, Taiwan (office). *Telephone:* (2) 23703526 (office). *Fax:* (2) 23703527 (office). *E-mail:* public@mail.oop.gov.tw (office). *Website:* www.oop.gov.tw (office).

LU, Ruihua, MA; Chinese politician; *Governor of Guangdong Province;* b. Nov. 1938, Chaozhou City, Guangdong Prov. *Education:* Zhongshan Univ., Guangdong Prov. *Career:* joined CCP 1972; fmrly engineer, Deputy Dir, Dir Foshan Analytical Instrument Factory; fmrly Mayor of Foshan, Vice-Chair. Foshan City Econ. Cttee, mem. Standing Cttee CCP Guangdong Prov. Cttee, mem. then Deputy Sec. Standing Cttee CCP Foshan City Cttee; Vice-Gov. Guangdong Prov. 1991–96, Gov. 1996–; Deputy Sec. CCP Guangdong Prov. Cttee 1996– (mem. Standing Cttee 2002–); Alt. mem. 14th CCP Cen. Cttee 1992–97, mem. 15th CCP Cen. Cttee 1997–2002; Deputy 7th NPC 1988–93, 8th NPC 1993–98, 9th NPC 1998–2003.
Address: People's Government of Guangdong, Guangzhou, Guangdong Province, People's Republic of China (office).

LU, Shumin; Chinese diplomatist; *Ambassador to Canada;* b. 24 Feb. 1950, Xi'an, Shanxi Province; m. Gao Shuqing; one d. *Career:* staff mem. Dept of N American and Oceanian Affairs, Ministry of Foreign Affairs 1976–77, Embassy in Canada 1977–79, Diplomatic Personnel Services Bureau, Beijing 1979–85; Third Sec., Embassy in Australia 1985; Second Sec. –1989; various staff positions at Ministry of Foreign Affairs including Deputy Div. Chief, Div. Chief, Counsellor –1993, Deputy Dir-Gen 1993–94, Counsellor, Embassy in USA 1994, Minister Counsellor –1998; Dir-Gen 1998–2002; Amb. to Indonesia 2002–05, to Canada 2005–.
Address: Embassy of the People's Republic of China, 515 St Patrick Street, Ottawa, ON K1N 5H3, Canada (office). *Telephone:* (613) 789-3434 (office). *Fax:* (613) 789-1911 (office). *E-mail:* cooffice@buildlink.com (office). *Website:* www.chinaembassycanada.org (office).

LUAT, Tran Van; Vietnamese diplomatist. *Career:* currently Amb. to People's Repub. of China.
Address: Embassy of Viet Nam, 32 Guang Hua Lu, Jian Guo Men Wai, Beijing 100600, People's Republic of China (office). *Telephone:* (10) 65321155 (office). *Fax:* (10) 65325720 (office).

LUBBERS, Ruud (Rudolphus) Frans Marie; Dutch politician and international organization official; b. 7 May 1939, Rotterdam; m. Maria E. J. Hoogeweegen 1962; two s. one d. *Education:* Erasmus Univ., Rotterdam. *Career:* Sec. to Man. Bd, Lubbers Hollandia Eng Works 1963–65, Co-Dir 1965; mem. Bd Netherlands Christian Employers' Fed., Fed. of Mechanical and Electrical Eng Industries; mem. Programmes Advisory Council of Catholic Broadcasting Asscn; Minister of Econ. Affairs 1973–77; mem. Christian Democratic Appeal 1977, Parl. Leader 1978; mem. Second Chamber of States-Gen. (Parl.) 1977–2000; Prime Minister of the Netherlands 1982–94; Hon. Minister of State; taught Globalization Studies at Tilburg Univ. and John F. Kennedy School of Govt, Harvard Univ., USA 1995–2000; Chair. Globus, the Inst. for Globalization and Devt, Tilburg 1995–2000; Vice-Chair. Ind. World Comm. on the Oceans 1995–2000; UN High Commr for Refugees 2000–05 (resgnd); Dr hc (Radboud Univ., Nijmegen) 2004. *Address:* c/o United Nations High Commissioner for Refugees, CP 2500, 1211 Geneva 2 dépôt, Switzerland (office).

LUBRANI, Uri; Israeli diplomatist; *Adviser, Ministry of Defence;* b. 7 Oct. 1926, Haifa; m. Sarah Levi 1953; four d. *Education:* Univ. of London, UK. *Career:* fmr Head of Chancery, Office of Foreign Minister, Office of Prime Minister, Adviser to Prime Minister on Arab Affairs; later Amb. to Uganda, Rwanda, Burundi, Ethiopia and Iran; now Govt Co-ordinator for Lebanese Affairs; in charge of airlift of 18,000 Ethiopian Jews (Falashas) to Israel 1991; head Israeli team, negotiations on release of Israeli hostages in Lebanon and Shia Muslim prisoners in Israel; head Israeli del. to bilateral peace talks with Lebanon, Washington, DC 1992; now Adviser to the Minister of Defence; Hon. DPhil (Ben-Gurion Univ.) 1991, (Beer) 1991; Jabotinsky Annual Award for Services to the Jewish People 1991, David Ben-Gurion Award. *Address:* Office of the Adviser to the Minister of Defence, Ministry of Defence, Hakirya, Tel-Aviv (office); Shamgar Street 34, Tzahala, Tel-Aviv, Israel (home). *Telephone:* (3) 6975157 (office); (3) 6474919 (home). *Fax:* (3) 6977358 (office); (3) 6493084 (home). *E-mail:* liban@mod.gov.il (office).

LUCAS, Robert Emerson, BA, PhD; American economist and academic; *John Dewey Distinguished Service Professor, Department of Economics, University of Chicago;* b. 15 Sept. 1937, Yakima, Wash. *Career:* Asst Prof. of Econs, Carnegie Inst. of Tech. 1963–67; Assoc. Prof. Carnegie-Mellon Univ. 1967–70, Prof. 1970–74; Prof. Univ. of Chicago 1975–80, John Dewey Distinguished Service Prof. 1980–; Assoc. Ed. Journal of Monetary Econs 1977–; Ed. Journal of Political Economy 1988–; Fellow AAAS; mem. NAS; Dr hc (Université Paris-Dauphine) 1992, (Athens Univ. of Econs and Business) 1994, (Univ. of Montreal) 1998; Nobel Prize for Econs 1995. *Publications:* Studies in Business-Cycle Theory 1981, Lectures in Economic Growth 2001. *Address:* Department of Economics, University of Chicago, 1126 E 59th Street, Chicago, IL 60637, USA (office). *E-mail:* relucas@uchicago.edu (office). *Website:* home.uchicago.edu/~sogrodow (office); economics .uchicago.edu.

LUCINSCHI, Petru, CandPhilSc, PhD; Moldovan fmr head of state and politician; *Head, Fund for Strategic Studies and Development of International Relations;* b. 27 Jan. 1940, Floreşti; m. Antonina Georgievna Lucinschi 1965; two s. *Education:* Kishinev (Chişinău) Univ. and CPSU Cen. Cttee Higher Party School. *Career:* served in Soviet Army 1962–63; Komsomol work for Cen. Cttee of Moldavian CP 1963–71; mem. CPSU 1964–91; First Sec. of Bălti City Komsomol Cttee 1964–65; Head of Section, Second Sec., First Sec. of Cen. Cttee of Moldavian Komsomol 1965–71; Sec. of Cen. Cttee of Moldavian CP 1971–76, First Sec. Nov. 1989–91; First Sec. of Kishinev City Cttee 1976–78; Deputy Head, Propaganda Dept of CPSU Cen. Cttee 1978–86; Second Sec. of Cen. Cttee of Tadzhik CP 1986–89; Cand. mem. of CPSU Cen. Cttee 1986–89, mem. 1989–91, Sec. 1990–91; Deputy to USSR Supreme Soviet 1986–89; USSR People's Deputy 1989–91; mem. CPSU Politburo, 1990–91; Moldovan Amb. to Russia 1992–93; fmr Leader Agrarian Democratic Party; Chair. Moldovan Parl. 1993–2001; Pres. of Moldova 1996–2000; Head, Fund for Strategic Studies and Devt of Int. Relations 2001–; mem., Russian Fed. Social Sciences Acad.; Chevalier, Légion d'honneur 1998, Order of Repub. of Moldova; Dr hc (Minsk, Baku); numerous awards, including Int. Pilgrim of Peace Award, Assisi (Italy). *Publications:* The Last Days of the USSR 1998, The Life and Death 2003, Moldova and Moldavians 2007. *Address:* 76 Bucuresti str., Chişinău, Moldova (home). *Telephone:* (22) 237979 (office). *Fax:* (22) 237981 (office). *E-mail:* office@ipa.dnt.md (office).

LUCKE, Lewis W., BA, MBA; American diplomatist; b. Austin, Tex.; m.; three c. *Education:* Univ. of N Carolina, Thunderbird, Garvin School of Int. Man. *Career:* joined Foreign Service in 1978, career mem. Sr Foreign Service with rank of Minister-Counsellor, has served in Mali, Senegal, Costa Rica, Tunisia, Bolivia, Jordan, Haiti and Iraq, served for 25 years with USAID, including as Mission Dir in Bolivia, Jordan and Haiti, as first Mission Dir in Iraq and as Deputy Asst Admin. USAID in charge of Iraq 2002–04, Amb. to Swaziland 2005–07; Presidential Merit Award 2001, Admin. Distinguished Career Award, USAID 2001, Award for Heroism, USAID 2004, named Distinguished Alumnus of the Year, Thunderbird, Garvin School of Int. Man. 2003. *Publication:* Waiting for Rain: Life and Development in Mali, West Africa. *Address:* US Department of State, 2201 C Street NW, Washington, DC 20520, USA (office). *Telephone:* (202) 647-4000 (office). *Fax:* (202) 647-6738 (office). *Website:* www.state.gov (office).

ŁUCZAK, Aleksander Piotr, PhD; Polish politician and historian; *Vice-President, National Broadcasting Council;* b. 10 Sept. 1943, Legionowo; m. Janina Zakrzewska; one d. *Education:* Warsaw Univ. and Adam Mickiewicz Univ., Poznań. *Career:* mem. United Peasants' Party (ZLS) 1966–91; mem. Polish Peasants' Party (PSL) 1991–; lecturer, Dept of History of the Peasant Movt Cen. Cttee ZSL until 1976; mem. Faculty, Univ. of Warsaw 1976–, Asst Prof. 1983–91, Prof. 1991; Adviser to Pres. of Cen. Cttee ZSL 1976–79; Head, Dept of Ideology, Press and Propaganda, Cen. Cttee PSL 1986, Vice-Chair., Head Council PSL 1991–97; Deputy Minister of Nat. Educ. 1986–87; Head, Office of Council of Ministers June–Oct. 1992; Deputy Prime Minister and Minister of Educ. 1993–94; Deputy Prime Minister, Minister and Head of Scientific Research Cttee 1994–96; Minister and Head of Scientific Research Cttee 1996–97; Deputy to Sejm (Parl.) 1989–2001; Chair. Polish Asscn of Adult Educ. 1995–2001; Pres. World Scout Parl. Union 1997–2000; mem. Nat. Broadcasting Council (KRRiT) 2001–, Vice-Pres. 2003–. *Publications:* more than 30 publs on recent history of Poland and the peasant movt. *Address:* National Broadcasting Council, ul. Sobieskiego 101, 00-763 Warsaw, Poland (office). *Telephone:* (22) 8402379 (office). *E-mail:* luczak@ krrit.gov.pl (office).

LUERS, William Henry, MA, FAAS; American diplomatist and museum president; *President and CEO, United Nations Association of the USA;* b. 15 May 1929, Springfield, Ill.; m. Wendy Woods Turnbull 1979; three s. one d. by previous marriage and two step-d. *Education:* Hamilton Coll., Columbia and Northwestern Univs. *Career:* Foreign Service Officer Dept of State 1957; Vice-Consul, Naples, Italy 1957–60; Second Sec. Embassy, Moscow 1963–65; Political Counsellor, Caracas, Venezuela 1969–73; Deputy Exec. Sec., Dept of State 1973–75; Deputy Asst Sec. for Inter-American Affairs, Washington 1975–77, Deputy Asst Sec. for Europe 1977–78; Amb. to Venezuela 1978–82, to Czechoslovakia 1983–86; Pres. Metropolitan Museum of Art, New York 1986–99; Pres. and CEO UN Asscn of USA 1999–; mem. Bd Rockefeller Brothers Fund, AOL-Latin America, Scudder Funds, Wickes Corpn; mem. Council on Foreign Relations, American Acad. of Arts and Sciences, American Acad. of Diplomacy; Hon. LLD (Hamilton Coll.) 1982; American Foreign Service Cup 1988. *Address:* UNA-USA, 801 Second Avenue, New York, NY 10017 (office); 419 East 57th Street, Apt 14A, New York, NY 10022, USA (home). *Telephone:* (212) 907-1313 (office); (212) 593-0586 (home). *Fax:* (212) 972-3585 (office). *E-mail:* wluers@unausa.org (office). *Website:* www.unausa .org (office).

LUGO MÉNDEZ, Fernando Armindo; Paraguayan politician, fmr bishop and head of state; *President;* b. 30 May 1949, San Pedro. *Career:* ordained priest of Society of the Divine Word 1977, RC Bishop of San Pedro 1994–2005 (resgnd), resgnd from priesthood 2006; Leader, Movimiento Popular Tekojoja; Pres. of Paraguay 2008–. *Address:* Palacio de López, Asunción (office); Movimiento Popular Tekojoja, Asunción, Paraguay. *Telephone:* (21) 4140200 (office). *E-mail:* joaquinbonett@gmail. *Website:* www.presidencia.gov.py (office).

LUIK, Jüri; Estonian diplomatist, politician and journalist; *Permanent Representative, NATO;* b. 17 Aug. 1966, Tallinn; m. one s. *Education:* Tallinn 7th High School, Tartu Univ. and postgraduate research, Carnegie, USA. *Career:* Political Ed. Vikerkaar (monthly) 1988–90, Ed. 1990; specialist on Anglo-Saxon Countries, Estonian Inst. 1989–91; mem. Pro Patria (Isamaaliit) Party 1989–; attaché, Embassy of Estonia, UK 1991; Head, Political Dept, Ministry of Foreign Affairs 1991–92; mem. Riigikogu (Parl.) 1992–95; Minister without portfolio responsible for Estonian-Russian Negotiations 1992–93; Minister of Defence 1993–94, 1999–2002, of Foreign Affairs 1994–95; Sr Research Fellow, Carnegie Foundation 1995–96; Amb. to NATO and Benelux States, Brussels 1996–99; head of govt del. for accession talks with NATO 2002–03; Amb. to USA (also accred to Canada) 2003–07, Perm. Rep. to NATO, Brussels 2007–. *Address:* Office of the Permanent Representative of Estonia, Blvd Léopold III, 1110 Brussels, Belgium (office). *Telephone:* (2) 707-41-11 (home). *Fax:* (2) 707-45-79 (office). *E-mail:* natodoc@hq.nato.int (office). *Website:* www .nato.int (office).

LUJABE-RANKOE, Thandi; South African diplomatist; *High Commissioner to Mozambique; Education:* Johannesburg Tech. Coll. *Career:* with ANC 1962–94, various positions abroad in Egypt, Zambia, Nigeria, Botswana, Zimbabwe, Chief Rep. in Norway 1988–94; High Commr in Tanzania 1995–99, in Botswana 1995–2002, currently High Commr to Mozambique. *Address:* High Commission of South Africa, Av. Eduardo Mondlane 41, CP 1120, Maputo, Mozambique (office). *Telephone:* 21493030 (office). *Fax:* 21493029 (office). *E-mail:* sahc@tropical.co.mz (office).

LUKASHENKA, Alyaksandr Rygorovich; Belarusian politician, economist and head of state; *President;* b. 30 Aug. 1954, Kopys; m. Halyna Rodionovna Lukashenko (estranged); two s. *Education:* Mogilev State Univ. and Belarus Agric. Acad. *Career:* served in Soviet Army 1975–77, 1980–82; Sec. Komsomol Cttee, Shklov, instructor Political Div. Komsomol Cttee W Border Dist 1975–77; Sec. Komsomol Cttee Mogilev City Food Dept; instructor regional Exec. Cttee 1977–80; Deputy Commdr of Co. 1980–82; Deputy Chair. Udarnik collective farm 1982–83; Deputy Dir Enterprise of Construction Materials 1983–85; Sec. CP Cttee Collective Farm of V.I. Lenin, Shklov Dist 1985–87; Dir Gorodets state farm 1987–94; elected Deputy of Supreme Council of Belarus SSR 1990–94; Chair. Parl. Comm. on Struggle against Corruption 1993–94; elected Pres. of Belarus 1994–; C-in-C Armed Forces of Belarus 1994–; Chair. Higher Council of Belarus and Russia Union 1997–; Chair. Supreme State Council of the Union State of Belarus and Russia 2000–; Hon. Academician of the Russian Acad. of Sciences 1995; Order of the Holy Cross of the Knights of the Holy Sepulchre 2000, Order of St Vladimir (First Class), Russian Orthodox Church 2007; M. Sholokhov Int. Award 1997. *Address:* Office of the President, 220016 Minsk, vul. K. Marksa 38, Dom Urada, Belarus. *Telephone:* (17) 222-35-03 (office). *Fax:* (17) 222-30-20 (office). *E-mail:* press@president.gov.by (office); www.president.gov.by (office).

LUKIN, Vladimir Petrovich, PhD, DSc; Russian politician and diplomatist; *Commissioner for Human Rights (Federal Ombudsman);* b. 13 June 1937, Omsk; m.; two s. *Education:* Moscow State Pedagogical Inst., USSR Acad. of Sciences. *Career:* researcher, Museum of Revolution, Inst. of World Econs and Int. Relations, USSR Acad. of Sciences 1959–65; on staff of journal World Review, Prague until Aug. 1968 when he was recalled to USSR for protesting against Soviet invasion of Czechoslovakia; Research Fellow, Inst. of US and Canadian Studies, USSR Acad. of Sciences 1969–87; Deputy Dir Dept of Assessment and Planning of the USSR Ministry of Foreign Affairs 1987–90; People's Deputy of RSFSR (now Russia) 1990–93; Chair. Foreign Affairs Cttee of the Russian Supreme Soviet 1990–92; Amb. to USA 1992–93; Co-Founder and Leader, pre-election bloc (later political movt) Yabloko (with G. Javlinsky) 1993, currently Deputy Chair.; mem. State Duma (Parl.) 1993–2003, Chair. Cttee for Foreign Affairs 1994–99; Deputy Chair. State Duma 2000–02; Commr for Human Rights of Russian Fed. (Fed. Ombudsman) 2004–; two decorative orders, one medal. *Publications include:* Centres of Power: Conceptions and Reality, China's Place in US Global Policy, With Concern and Hope: Russia and the West. *Address:* Office of the Commissioner for Human Rights in the Russian Federation, Myasnitskaya str. 47, 103084 Moscow (office); c/o Yabloko Party, Novy Arbat str. 21, 18th Floor, 121019 Moscow, Russia (office). *Telephone:* (495) 207-39-69 (office). *Fax:* (495) 207-39-77 (office). *E-mail:* lukin@rodnet.ru (office). *Website:* www.ombudsman.gov.ru (office).

LUKMAN, Rilwanu, BSc, CEng; Nigerian international civil servant, business executive and engineer; b. 26 Aug. 1938, Zaria, Kaduna State; m. 1966; two s. one d. *Education:* Govt Coll. Zaria (now Barewa), Nigerian Coll. of Arts, Science and Tech. (now Ahmadu Bello Univ.), Royal School of Mines, Imperial Coll. of Science and Tech., Univ. of London, Inst. of Prospecting and Mineral Deposits, Univ. of Mining and Metallurgy, Leoben, Austria, McGill Univ., Montreal, Canada. *Career:* Asst Mining Engineer, A.G. Statagruvor, Sweden 1962–64; Inspector of Mines and Sr Inspector of Mines, Ministry of Mines and Power, Jos 1964–67; Acting Asst Chief Inspector of Mines 1968–70; Gen. Man. Cement Co. of Northern Nigeria Ltd, Sokoto 1970–74; Gen. Man. and Chief Exec. Nigerian Mining Corpn, Jos 1974–84; Fed. Minister of Mines, Power and Steel, Lagos 1984–85, of Petroleum Resources, Lagos 1986–89, of Foreign Affairs 1989–90; Pres. OPEC Conf. 1986–89, Sec.-Gen. OPEC 1995–2000, Head Del. from Nigeria 2001, Alt. Pres. 2001–02; Fellow and Hon. Fellow Inst. of Mining and Metallurgy; Fellow Imperial Coll. London, Nigerian Mining and Geoscience Soc.; Past Vice-Pres. Asscn of Geoscientists for Int. Devt; mem. Soc. of Mining Engineers of AIME; Hon. KBE 1989; Officier Légion d'honneur 1990; Order of Liberator, First Class, Venezuela 1990; Hon. PhD (Bologna) 1988; Hon. DSc (Maiduguri) 1989, (Ahmadu Bello) 1991; Dr hc (Moore House Coll. Atlanta) 1989. *Address:* c/o OPEC, Obere Donaustrasse 93, 1020 Vienna, Austria.

LUKŠIĆ, Igor, MA, PhD; Montenegrin politician; *Minister of Finance;* b. 1976, Bar. *Education:* Univ. of Montenegro, Podgorica. *Career:* twice elected Deputy of Parl. of Repub. of Montenegro; fmr Sec. of Ministry of Foreign Affairs; Deputy Minister of Foreign Affairs of Serbia and Montenegro 2003; adviser to Prime Minister of Montenegro 2003; Minister of Finance 2004–06 (resgnd), Nov. 2006–; mem. Democratic Socialist Party of Montenegro. *Publications include:* several academic works as well as poetry. *Address:* Ministry of Finance, 81000 Podgorica, Stanka Dragojevića 2, Montenegro (office). *Telephone:* (81) 224609 (office). *Fax:* (81) 224450 (office). *E-mail:* mf@mn.yu (office). *Website:* www.vlada.cg.yu/minfin (office).

LULA DA SILVA, Luis Inácio; Brazilian trade unionist and head of state; *President;* b. 27 Oct. 1945, Garanhuns, Pernambuco; m. Marisa Leticia 1974; five c. *Career:* qualified as mechanic; started working at Indústrias Villares steelworks 1966; Assoc. mem. Exec. Cttee, São Bernardo do Campo and Diadema Metalworkers' Union 1969–72, First Sec. (responsible for social security) 1972–75, Pres. 1975–80; led steelworkers' strikes 1978, 1979; Pres. Partido dos Trabalhadores (Labour Party) 1980–87, 1993; a leader of the 'Elections Now' campaign for direct presidential elections 1984; a leader of campaign to impeach Pres. Collor de Mello 1992; Fed. Deputy 1986–; Presidential cand. 1989, 1994, 2002; f. a 'Parallel Govt' (to prepare an alternative set of policies for the country) 1990; Councilor, Citizenship Inst. 1992–; Pres. of Brazil 2003–. *Address:* Office of the President, Palácio do Planalto, Praça dos Três Poderes, 70150-900, Brasília, DF, Brazil (office). *Telephone:* (61) 3411-1225 (office). *E-mail:* protocolo@planalto.gov.br (office). *Website:* www.presidencia.gov.br (office).

LUNA MENDOZA, Ricardo V., AB, MIA; Peruvian diplomatist; *Ambassador to UK;* b. 19 Nov. 1940, Lima; m. Margarita Proaño 1969; one d. *Education:* Princeton Univ., NJ and Columbia Univ., USA, Diplomatic Acad. of Peru. *Career:* joined Diplomatic Service 1967, posts held include Third Sec., Div. of Econ. Affairs, Foreign Ministry 1967, Third Sec., Embassy in UK 1968–70, Second Sec., Embassy in Israel 1970–71, First Sec., Perm. Mission of Peru to UN Office at Geneva, Head, UN Dept, Foreign Ministry 1975–77, Counsellor, Washington, DC 1978, Chef du Cabinet of Minister for Foreign Affairs 1979, Minister Counsellor, Mission of Peru to UNESCO 1980, Quito 1987, Minister, Perm. Mission to UN 1984, Under-Sec. for Multilateral Policy, Ministry of Foreign Affairs 1987–89, Perm. Rep. to UN 1989–92, Amb. to USA 1992–99, to UK 2006–; Fellow, Center for Int. Affairs, Harvard Univ., USA 1980–81; Adjunct Prof. of Latin American Affairs, The Fletcher School, Tufts Univ. 1999–2006; fmr Lecturer, Woodrow Wilson School of Public and Int. Affairs, Princeton Univ.; Founding mem. Peruvian Centre for Int. Studies; mem. Peruvian Soc. of Int. Law. *Address:* Embassy of Peru, 52 Sloane Street, London, SW1X 9SP, England (office). *Telephone:* (20) 7235-1917 (office). *Fax:* (20) 7235-4463 (office). *E-mail:* postmaster@peruembassy-uk.com (office). *Website:* www.peruembassy-uk.com (office).

LUND, (Nils) Gunnar Wiggo; Swedish diplomatist and politician; *Ambassador to France;* b. 26 July 1947, Karlskoga; m. Kari Lotsberg; two s. one d. *Education:* Univs of Uppsala and Stockholm, Columbia Univ., New Yorkm USA. *Career:* postings in Paris and Copenhagen 1974–76, Desk Officer, Ministry of Finance and Ministry for Foreign Affairs 1976–80, Counsellor for Econ. and Financial Affairs, Swedish Del. to OECD, Paris 1980–83, Asst Under-Sec. and Dir for Int. Affairs, Ministry of Finance 1983–88, State Sec., Budget Affairs, Domestic and Int. Econ. Affairs, Ministry of Finance 1988–91, Amb., Ministry for Foreign Affairs 1992–94, Insp. Gen. of Mil. Equipment, Ministry for Foreign Affairs 1994, State Sec. for EU Affairs, Ministry for Foreign Affairs 1994–99, Chief Negotiator for EU Intergovernmental Conf. (Treaty of Amsterdam) 1995–97, Amb. and Perm. Rep. to EU, Chief Negotiator for EU Intergovernmental Conf. 2000 (Treaty of Nice) 1999–2002, Minister of Int. Econ. Affairs and Finance Markets 2002–04, Amb. to USA 2005–07, to France 2007–. *Address:* Embassy of Sweden, 17 rue Barbet-de-Jouy, 75007 Paris, France (office). *Telephone:* 1-44-18-88-00 (office). *Fax:* 1-44-18-88-40 (office). *E-mail:* info@amb-suede.fr (office). *Website:* www.swedenabroad.com/paris (office).

LUNSTEAD, Jeffrey J., BA, PhD; American diplomatist; *Assistant Vice-President of International Affairs, American University;* m. Deborah Sharpe-Lunstead; two d. *Education:* Univ. of Notre Dame and Univ. of Pennsylvania. *Career:* served in USN 1969–70; entered Foreign Service in 1971, career mem. Sr Foreign Service with rank of Minister-Counsellor, has served in Pakistan, India, Bangladesh and Malaysia, Washington appointments have included S Asia Bureau Coordinator for Afghanistan, as Dir for Pakistan, Afghanistan and Bangladesh, as Dir Office for Environmental Policy, Amb. to Sri Lanka (also accred to the Maldives) 2003–06; Asst Vice-

Pres. of Int. Affairs, American Univ. 2006–; two Superior Honor Awards, Meritorious Honor Award, Dept of State. *Publications:* several articles on ancient and modern S Asia.
Address: American University, 4400 Massachusetts Avenue, NW, Washington, DC 20016, USA (office). *Telephone:* (202) 885-1524 (office). *E-mail:* lunstead@american.edu (office). *Website:* www.american.edu (office).

LUO, Gan, DipEng; Chinese state and party official and engineer; b. 14 July 1935, Jinan, Shandong Prov.; m. He Zuozhi 1965; one s. one d. *Education:* Beijing Inst. of Iron and Steel Eng, Karl Marx Univ. and Freiburg Inst. of Mining and Metallurgy, Leipzig, GDR, May 7th Cadre School. *Career:* worker, Leipzig Iron and Steel Plant and Leipzig Metal Casting Plant 1955–56; joined CCP 1960; Project Group Leader and Technician, Mechanical Eng Research Inst., First Ministry of Machine-Building Industry, Zhengzhou City, Henan Prov. 1962–69, Deputy Dir, later Dir Luohe Preparatory Office 1970–80; Chair. Science and Tech. Cttee, Henan Prov. 1980–81; Vice-Gov. Henan Prov. 1981–83; Sec. CCP Henan Prov. Cttee 1981–83; Minister of Labour and Social Services 1988; Sec.-Gen. of State Council 1988–98, State Councillor 1993–, Vice-Premier of State Council 1998–2003; Sec. Work Cttee for Cen. Govt Organs 1989–; Alt. mem. 12th CCP Cen. Cttee 1982–87, mem. 13th Cen. Cttee 1987–92, 14th Cen. Cttee 1992–97, 15th CCP Cen. Cttee 1997–2002, 16th CCP Cen. Cttee 2002–07; mem. CCP Politburo, Sec. Secr. CCP Cen. Cttee 1997–2002; mem. Standing Cttee, CCP Politburo 2002–07; Deputy Sec. Political and Legis. Affairs Cttee, Offices Under Cen. Cttee, 14th CCP Cen. Cttee 1993–98, Sec. 1998–07; mem. Secr. and Vice-Pres. All-China Fed. of Trade Unions 1983–88 (Deputy Sec. CCP Leading Party Group 1983–88).
Address: c/o State Council, Zhong Nan Hai, Beijing, People's Republic of China (office).

LUO, Haocai; Chinese judge and politician; *President, Chinese Society for Human Rights Studies (CSHRS);* b. March 1934, Anxi Co., Fujian Prov. *Education:* Beijing Univ. *Career:* teaching asst, Lecturer, Assoc. Prof., Prof., Dept of Law, Beijing Univ. 1960–86; Vice-Pres. Beijing Univ. 1986–95; joined China Zhi Gong Party (Public Interest Party) 1992, Vice-Chair. Cen. Cttee 1992–97, Chair. Cen. Cttee 1997–2002; mem. Standing Cttee and Deputy Sec.-Gen. CPPCC 8th Nat. Cttee 1993–98, Vice-Chair. 9th Nat. Cttee 1998–2003, 10th Nat. Cttee 2003–; Chair. Beijing Fed. of Returned Overseas Chinese, Vice-Chair. All-China Fed. of Returned Overseas Chinese; adviser, Chinese Asscn for Int. Understanding 1999; fmr Vice-Chair. China Law Soc., Vice-Pres. 1986; Vice-Pres. and mem. Judicial Cttee Supreme People's Court 1995–2000; Pres. Chinese Soc. for Human Rights Studies (CSHRS) 2007–; mem. Exec. Council China Admin. Man. Asscn; mem. Govt Del., Macao Hand-Over Ceremony, Macao Special Admin. Region Preparatory Cttee 1999.
Address: National Committee of Chinese People's Political Consultative Conference, 23 Taipingqiao Street, Beijing, People's Republic of China (office). *E-mail:* zhigong@public2.east.net.cn (office). *Website:* www .humanrights-china.org (office).

LUO, Yuanzheng, PhD; Chinese university professor; b. 14 Feb. 1924, Chengdu, Sichuan Prov.; m. Lida Feng 1947; one s. one d. *Education:* West Union Univ. Chengdu, Univ. of Calif., St Olife Coll., USA and Univ. of Leningrad, Russia. *Career:* Sec. Econ. Dept Scientific Planning Cttee State Council 1956–57; Dir Co-ordination Office for Econ. Affairs, State Planning Comm. 1978–80; Deputy Dir and Research Fellow, Inst. of World Econs and Politics, Chinese Acad. of Social Sciences 1978–83; mem. Econ. Research Centre, State Council 1980–84; Exec. Chair. Sec. and Founder, All-China Union of Asscns for Econ. Studies 1981–84; Visiting Prof. Australian Nat. Univ. 1981; Prof., Beijing Univ. (and a dozen other Chinese univs) 1981–; sr adviser to several provs and municipalities 1981–; Pres. Chinese Correspondence Univ. of Econ. Sciences 1984–88; Prof., European Man. School, Paris 1988; other professional appointments, editorships etc.; Vice-Pres. Int. Econ. Asscn 1989–92; Pres. China Int. Cultural Educ. Inst. 1992–; Chair. Econ. Forum of Hong Kong 1992; mem. Academic Advisory Bd Int. Centre for Econ. Growth 1992–; mem. CPPCC 1986–, mem. Econ. Cttee 1986–; Gen. Adviser to China Chamber of Commerce; Dir Asia Pacific Bd of Lucas; recipient of awards of State Council, Ministry of Higher Educ. etc. *Publications include:* On an Economic Community in the Pacific Region 1981, Impact of Socio-Economic Model on Education, Science and Culture 1983, Internationa-lization of Economic Life and China's Policy of Opening to the Outside World 1984, World Economy and China, On the Developmental Strategy Problems of an Economic Society 1986, Structural Reform and Economic Development in China 1989, Selected Works of Luo Yuangheng, The New Phase of China's Economic Development and Prospects for the New Century; papers on China's economy, world econ. devt etc.

Address: 10-7-41 Xibianmenwai Dajei, 100045 Beijing, People's Republic of China. *Telephone:* 8523152 (office); 8312308 (home). *Fax:* 8534865 (office); 8312308 (home).

LUTON, Jean-Marie; French engineer; *Honourary President, Starsem;* b. 4 Aug. 1942, Chamalières; m. Cécile Robine 1967; three s. *Education:* Lycée Blaise Pascal, Clermont-Ferrand, Lycée St Louis, Paris, Faculté des Sciences, Paris and Ecole Polytechnique. *Career:* with CNRS 1964–71; Ministry of Industrial and Scientific Devt 1971–73; Head of Research, Centre Nat. d'Etudes Spatiales 1974–75, Head of Planning 1975–78, Dir of Programmes and Planning 1978–84, Deputy Dir-Gen. 1984–87, Dir-Gen. 1989–90; Dir of Space Programmes, Aérospatiale 1987–89; Dir-Gen. European Space Agency 1990–97; Pres., Dir-Gen., then Chair. Arianespace 1997–2006; Chair. and CEO Starsem 2002–06, Hon. Pres. 2006–; Chevalier, Légion d'honneur, Officier, Ordre nat. du Mérite; Prix de l'Astronautique; Prix de l'Innovateur industriel, Society of Satellite Professionals (USA) 1998.
Address: Starsem, 2 rue François Truffaut, 91042 EVRY Cedex, France (office). *Telephone:* 1-69-87-01-10 (office). *Fax:* 1-60-78-31-99 (office). *E-mail:* communication@starsem.com (office). *Website:* www.starsem.com (office).

LUTTWAK, Edward Nicolae, PhD; American academic, international consultant and writer; *Senior Fellow, Center for Strategic and International Studies;* b. 4 Nov. 1942, Arad, Romania; m. Dalya Iaari 1970; one s. one d. *Education:* elementary schools in Palermo and Milan, Carmel Coll., Wallingford, UK, London School of Econs and Johns Hopkins Univ. *Career:* Lecturer, Univ. of Bath, UK 1965–67; Consultant, Walter J. Levy SA (London) 1967–68; Visiting Prof., Johns Hopkins Univ. 1974–76; Sr Fellow, Center for Strategic and Int. Studies 1977–87, Burke Chair. of Strategy 1987–92, Sr Fellow 1992–; Consultant to Office of Sec. of Defense 1975, to Policy Planning Council, Dept of State 1981, Nat. Security Council 1987, Dept of Defense 1987, to Govts of Italy, Korea, Spain; Prin., Edward N. Luttwak Inc. Int. Consultants 1981–; Pres. Servicios Agricolas Tupinamba, Bolivia; Int. Assoc. Inst. of Fiscal and Monetary Policy, Japan Ministry of Finance (Okurasho); mem. editorial Bd of The American Scholar, Journal of Strategic Studies, The National Interest, Géopolitique, The Washington Quarterly, Orbis; Nimitz Lectureship, Univ. of Calif. 1987, Tanner Lecturer, Yale Univ. 1989, Rosenstiel Lecturer, Grinner Coll. 1992, Hon. LLD (Bath) 2007. *Publications:* Coup d'Etat 1968, Dictionary of Modern War 1972, The Israeli Army 1975, The Political Uses of Sea Power 1976, The Grand Strategy of the Roman Empire 1978, Strategy and Politics: Collected Essays 1979, The Grand Strategy of the Soviet Union 1983, The Pentagon and the Art of War 1985, Strategy and History: collected essays 1985, International Security Yearbook 1984/85 (with Barry M. Brechman) 1985, On the Meaning of Victory 1986, Strategy: The Logic of War and Peace 1987, The Dictionary of Modern War (with Stuart Koehl) 1991, The Endangered American Dream 1993, Il Fantasma della Povertà (co-author) 1996, Cose è davvero la Democrazia 1996, La Renaissance de la puissance aérienne stratégique 1998, Turbo-Capitalism 1999, Il Libro della Libertà 2000, Strategy: The Logic of War and Peace (ed.) 2002; his books have been translated into 14 languages.
Address: Center for Strategic and International Studies, 1800 K Street, NW, Washington, DC 20006, USA. *Telephone:* (301) 656-1972 (office); (202) 775-3145. *Fax:* (202) 775-3199. *Website:* www.csis.org.

LWIN, Myint; Myanma diplomatist; *Chargé d'affaires in USA. Career:* currently Minister-Counselor, Embassy in Washington, DC, Chargé d'affaires a.i. 2005–.
Address: Embassy of Myanmar, 2300 S Street, NW, Washington, DC 20008, USA (office). *Telephone:* (202) 332-3344 (office). *Fax:* (202) 332-4351 (office). *E-mail:* info@mewashingtondc.com (office). *Website:* www .mewashingtondc.com (office).

LWIN, U Thein; Myanma diplomatist; *Ambassador to People's Republic of China; Career:* Amb. to China (also accred. to Mongolia) 2003–.
Address: Embassy of Myanmar, 6 Dong Zhi Men Wai Dajie, Chao Yang Qu, Beijing 100600, People's Republic of China (office). *Telephone:* (10) 65321425 (office). *Fax:* (10) 65321344 (office). *E-mail:* info@ myanmarembassy.com (office). *Website:* www.myanmarembassy.com (office).

LYALL GRANT, Sir Mark Justin, Kt, KCMG; British diplomatist; *Political Director, Foreign and Commonwealth Office; Career:* worked at FCO, London, also served in Paris and in Islamabad 1982–85, Deputy Head of Mission, Pretoria 1996–98, Head of EU Dept (Internal), FCO 1999, Dir for Africa –2003, High Commr to Pakistan 2003–06, Political Dir, FCO 2006–.
Address: Foreign and Commonwealth Office, King Charles Street, London, SW1A 2AH, England (office). *Telephone:* (20) 7008-1500 (office). *Website:* www.fco.gov.uk (office).

LYKKETOFT, Mogens; Danish politician; *Spokesman on Foreign Affairs, Social Democratic Party;* b. 9 Jan. 1946, Copenhagen; two d. *Education:* Univ. of Copenhagen. *Career:* worked at Econ. Council of the Labour Movt 1966–81, Head of Dept 1975–81; mem. Folketing (Parl.) 1981–, Political Spokesman for Social Democratic Party 1991–93, 2001–02, Leader 2002–05, Spokesman on Foreign Affairs 2005–; Minister for Inland Revenue 1981–82; Minister of Finance 1993–2000, of Foreign Affairs 2000–01. *Publications:* ed. of several books and numerous articles in magazines, periodicals and newspapers.
Address: Folketinget, Christiansberg, 1240 Copenhagen (office); Odensegade 17, 1, 2100 Copenhagen, Denmark (home). *Telephone:* 33-37-40-34 (office). *Fax:* 33-89-40-34 (office). *E-mail:* smoly@ft.dk (office). *Website:* www.socialdemokratiet.dk (office); www.kykketoft.dk.

LYMAN, Princeton, PhD; American diplomatist; *Adjunct Senior Fellow for African Policy, Council on Foreign Relations;* b. 20 Nov. 1935, San Francisco, Calif.; m. Helen Ermann 1957; three d. *Education:* Univ. of Calif. at Berkeley and Harvard Univ. *Career:* joined US Govt service 1961; Agency for Int. Devt 1961–80; Dir USAID, Addis Ababa 1976–78; Dept of State 1980–; Deputy Asst Sec. for Africa 1981–86; Amb. to Nigeria 1986–89, to South Africa 1992–95; Dir Bureau of Refugee Programs 1989–92; Asst Sec. of State for Int. Org. Affairs 1996–98; fmr Exec. Dir Global Interdependence Initiative, Aspen Inst.; fmr Ralph Bunche Sr Fellow for African Policy, Council on Foreign Relations, currently Adjunct Sr Fellow; mem. Bd of Dirs Acad. of Diplomacy; Dept of State Superior Honor Award, Pres.'s Distinguished Service Award. *Publications:* Korean Development: The Interplay of Politics and Economics 1971.
Address: Council on Foreign Relations, 19779 Massachusetts Avenue, NW, Washington, DC 20036, USA (office). *Telephone:* (202) 518-3469 (office). *Fax:* (202) 986-2984 (office). *E-mail:* plyman@cfr.org (office). *Website:* www.cfr.org (office).

LYNE, Kevin Douglas; British diplomatist; *Ambassador to Montenegro;* m. Anne Lyne; two d. *Career:* Research and Analysis Dept, FCO 1988–91, Second Sec., Chancery, Santiago 1991–94, Prin. Research Officer/Head of Americas Research Group, FCO 1994–96, First Sec., Drugs and Int. Crime Dept 1996–98, First Sec., Human Rights, Perm. Mission to UN, Geneva 1998–2003, Deputy Head of Mission, Rabat 2003–07, Amb. to Montenegro 2007–.
Address: British Embassy, bul. Svetog Petra Cetinjskog 149, 81000 Podgorica, Montenegro (office). *Telephone:* (81) 205460 (office). *Fax:* (81) 205441 (office).

LYNE, Richard John; British diplomatist; *High Commissioner to Solomon Islands;* b. 20 Nov. 1948; m. Anne Lyne; one s. one d. *Career:* joined FCO 1970, S Pacific Dept 1970–71, E European Dept 1971–72, Registry Officer, Belgrade 1972–74, Accountant, Algiers 1974–77, Admin Officer, Damascus 1977–80, Policy Planner, FCO 1980–81, on loan to Dept of Trade and Industry 1982–84, Second Sec. (Commercial), New Delhi 1984–87, Second, later First Sec. (Chancery/Information), Stockholm 1988–91, Western European Dept, FCO 1992–94, Personnel Man. Dept 1995–96, Deputy High Commr, Port of Spain 1996–2000, Conf. and Visits Group, FCO Services, FCO 2000–02, Personnel Services, later Human Resources Pay and Benefits Policy Team 2002–04, High Commr to Solomon Islands 2004–.
Address: British High Commission, PO Box 676, Telekom House, Mendana Avenue, Honiara, Solomon Islands (office). *Telephone:* 21705 (office). *Fax:* 21549 (office). *E-mail:* bhc@solomon.com.sb (office).

LYSYSHYN, Ralph James, MA, PhD; Canadian diplomatist; *Ambassador to Russia;* b. Canora, Sask. *Education:* Univ. of Alberta. *Career:* served in various posts at Dept of Foreign Affairs and Int. Trade including Head of Section, Eastern European Div., Dir Arms Control and Disarmament Div.; fmr policy adviser to Prime Minister, Privy Council Office, Dir-Gen. Int. Security and Arms Control Bureau; fmr Pres. Forum of Feds; overseas positings include Third, then Second Sec., Embassy in Moscow 1974–76, Head of Chancery, Embassy in Lagos 1979–82, Counsellor, Embassy in Washington, DC 1982–86, Deputy Perm. Rep., Del. to NATO, Brussels 1990–94; Amb. to Poland 2002–05, to Russia (also accred to Armenia) 2006–.
Address: Embassy of Canada, 119002 Moscow, 23 Starokonyushennyi per. 23, Russia (office). *Telephone:* (495) 105-60-00 (office). *Fax:* (495) 105-60-25 (office). *E-mail:* mosco@international.gc.ca (office). *Website:* www.dfait -maeci.gc.ca/canada-europa/russia (office).

LYUTSKANOV, Vice-Adm. E. I.; Bulgarian military officer; b. 20 July 1951, Levski, Pleven Dist; m., two c. *Education:* N. Y. Vaptsarov Naval Acad., Naval War Coll., St Petersburg, Gen. Staff Acad., Moscow. *Career:* commissioned as Lt, assigned to Naval Strike Forces Brigade 1976, Chief of Staff, later Squadron Commdr 1985–90, assigned to Operational Dept, Navy HQ 1990–96, Deputy Commdr Varna Naval Base 1996–97, Commdr 1997–2001, promoted to Rear-Adm. 2000, Chief, Operational Directorate, Navy HQ 2001, Deputy Chief, Navy Operations 2001–03, Chief of the Navy 2003–04, First Deputy Chief of Gen. Staff, Bulgarian Armed Forces 2006–, promoted to Vice-Adm. 2006; Mil. Rep. to NATO 2004–06;.
Address: Ministry of Defence, 1000 Sofia, ul. Dyakon Ignatiy 3, Bulgaria (office). *Telephone:* (2) 922-09-22 (office). *Fax:* (2) 987-32-28 (office). *E-mail:* pressentr@mod.bg (office). *Website:* www.md.government.bg (office).

M

MA, Chanrong; Chinese diplomatist; *Ambassador to Germany;* b. 1945, Jiangsu Prov. *Education:* Nanjing Univ. *Career:* joined Foreign Service 1972; with W European Affairs Dept, Ministry of Foreign Affairs 1972–73, Deputy Section Chief, then Section Chief 1981–87, Deputy Dir-Gen. 1993–96, Dir-Gen. 1996–99; Attaché, Embassy in Berlin 1973–81, Counsellor 1987–93; Asst Minister, Ministry of Foreign Affairs 1999–2001; Amb. to Germany 2001–.
Address: Embassy of the People's Republic of China, Märkisches Ufer 54, 10179 Berlin, Germany (office). *Telephone:* (30) 275880 (office). *Fax:* (30) 27588221 (office). *E-mail:* chinesischebotschaft@debital.net (office). *Website:* www.china-botschaft.de (office).

MA, Ying-jeou, LLM, SJD; Taiwanese politician, academic and head of state; *President;* b. 13 July 1950, Hong Kong; m. Chow Mei-ching; two d. *Education:* Nat. Taiwan Univ., New York Univ. Law School, Harvard Univ. Law School, USA. *Career:* with Marine Corps, Navy 1972–74; Legal Consultant First Nat. Bank of Boston, USA 1980–81; Research Consultant Univ. of Maryland Law School 1981; Assoc. Cole and Deitz Law School, New York 1981; Deputy Dir First Bureau, Office of the Pres. of Taiwan 1981–88; Adjunct Assoc. Prof., Graduate School of Law, Nat. Chengchi Univ. 1981, Assoc. Prof. of Law, Nat. Chengchi Univ. Law School 1997–98; Deputy Sec.-Gen. Cen. Cttee, Kuomintang (KMT) 1984–88, Chair. 2005–07 (resgnd); Chair. Research, Devt and Evaluation Comm., Exec. Yuan 1988–91, Sr Vice-Chair. Mainland Affairs Council 1991–93; Minister of Justice 1993–96; Minister of State without Portfolio 1996–97; Mayor of Taipei 1998–2006; Kuomintang (KMT); Pres. 2008–. *Publications:* Legal Problems of Seabed Boundary Delimitation in the East China Sea 1984, The Diauyutai (Senkaku) Islets and the Maritime Boundary Problems in the East China Sea (Chinese) 1986, Cross-Straits Relations at a Crossroad: Impasse of Breakthrough 2001; 17 academic papers.
Address: Office of the President, 122 Chungking South Road, Sec. 1, 10048 Taipei (office); Kuomintang, 232 Sec. 2, Bade Rd, Taipei 10492, Taiwan (office). *Telephone:* (2) 23113731 (office); (2) 87711234 (office). *Fax:* (2) 23311604 (office); (2) 23434561 (office). *E-mail:* public@mail.oop.gov.tw (office). *Website:* www.president.gov.tw (office); www.kmt.org.tw (office).

MA, Yuzhen; Chinese diplomatist; b. 26 Sept. 1934, Beijing; m. Zou Jichun 1961; one s. one d. *Education:* Beijing Inst. of Foreign Languages. *Career:* served in Information Dept, Ministry of Foreign Affairs 1954–63, Deputy Div. Chief, then Div. Chief 1969–80, Dir 1984–88; Attaché, Third Sec. Embassy, Burma 1963–69, First Sec., Counsellor Embassy, Ghana 1980–84, Consul-Gen. (ambassadorial rank) LA 1988–91, Amb. to UK 1991–95; Deputy Dir State Council's Information Office 1995–97; Foreign Ministry Commr for China, Hong Kong 1997–2001, Amb., Ministry of Foreign Affairs 2001–04; mem. 9th CPPCC Nat. Cttee 1998–2003.
Address: c/o Ministry of Foreign Affairs, Beijing 100701 (office); Room 501, No. 30, Dongjiaominxiang, Beijing 100006, People's Republic of China (home).

MA, Zhengang; Chinese diplomatist; *President, China Institute of International Studies;* b. 9 Nov. 1940, Shandong; m. Chen Xiaodong; one s. *Education:* Beijing Foreign Languages Univ., Ealing Tech. Coll., London, LSE. *Career:* staff mem., Attaché, Embassy in Yugoslavia 1970–74; Attaché N American and Oceanic Affairs Dept, Ministry of Foreign Affairs, Beijing 1974–81, Deputy Dir, then Dir N American and Oceanic Affairs Dept 1985–90, Deputy Dir-Gen., then Dir-Gen. N American and Oceanic Affairs Dept 1991–95; Vice-Consul, Consul, Consulate-Gen., Vancouver 1981–85; Counsellor, Embassy in Washington, DC 1990–91; Vice-Minister of Foreign Affairs 1995–97; Amb. to UK 1997–2002; Vice-Chair. 10th CPPCC Nat. Cttee 2003–; Amb., Ministry of Foreign Affairs 2002–04; Pres. China Inst. of Int. Studies (CIIS) 2004–, Chair. China Nat. Cttee, Council for Security Cooperation in Asia Pacific (CSCAP), Chair. editorial bd International Studies, Chair. of Academic Cttee.
Address: China Institute of International Studies, No.3, Toutiao, Taijichang, Beijing 100005, People's Republic of China. *Website:* www.ciis.org .cn/english.

MAAFO, Yaw Osafo; Ghanaian politician. *Career:* Minister of Finance and Econ. Planning –2005.

Address: c/o Ministry of Finance and Economic Planning, POB M40, Accra, Ghana (office).

MA'AHANUA, Joseph; Solomon Islands diplomatist; *Permanent Representative; European Union;* m. Noelyn Ma'ahanua. *Career:* Amb. and Perm. Rep. to EU, Brussels, (also accred as High Commr to UK) 2006–.
Address: Embassy of Solomon Islands, Avenue Edouard Lacomble 17, 1040 Brussels, Belgium (office). *Telephone:* (2) 732-70-85 (office). *Fax:* (2) 732-68-85 (office). *E-mail:* siembassy@compuserve.com (office).

MAAJAR, Mwanaidi Sinare; Tanzanian lawyer and diplomatist; *High Commissioner to UK;* m. Shariff Hassan Maajar; three c. (one s. deceased). *Career:* Corp. Legal Advisor, Coopers & Lybrand (now PriceWaterhouseCoopers), promoted to Sr Man. and Head of Legal and Business Devt Dept; fmr advocate of High Court of Tanzania, specializing in corp. and commercial law; fmr Chair. Social Action Trust Fund; Legal Advisor attached to Co. Matters Dept under Directorate of Exchange Control, Cen. Bank of Tanzania 1978–83; f. pvt. law firm M/s Maajar Law Office 1991; helped found Tanzania Women Lawyer's Asscn 1990, Chair. 2001–03; High Commr to UK (also accred to Ireland) 2006–; helped Govt draft new mining law and regulations for Investment Act; mem. Ministerial Advisory Bd Minister for Industry and Trade on performance of Business Registration and Licensing Agency.
Address: Tanzania High Commission, 3 Stratford Place, London, W1C 1AS, England (office). *Telephone:* (20) 7569-1470 (office). *Fax:* (20) 7491-3710 (office). *E-mail:* tanzarep@tanzania-online.gov.uk (office). *Website:* www.tanzania-online.gov.uk (office).

MAATHAI, Wangari, BS, MS, PhD; Kenyan ecologist, organization official and politician; *Presiding Officer, Economic Social and Cultural Council of the African Union (ECOSOCC);* b. 1 April 1940, Ihithe village, Nyeri Dist; m. Mwangi Maathai 1969 (divorced 1980); five c. *Education:* Loreto Convent Secondary School, Limuru, studied biology in USA and Germany, Mount St Scholastica (now Benedictine Coll.), Univ. of Pittsburgh, Univ. of Nairobi. *Career:* Dean of Faculty and Chair. Dept of Veterinary Anatomy, Univ. of Nairobi 1976, apptd Assoc. Prof. of Veterinary Anatomy 1977; f. Maendeleo Ya Wanawake (Nat. Council of Women of Kenya) 1964; Dir Kenya Red Cross 1973–80; Founder and Co-ordinator Kenya Green Belt Movt 1977–2002, Founding Chair. Green Belt Movt Int. 2005–; Founding mem. GROOTS Int. 1985; violently attacked and imprisoned several times during regime of Daniel Arap Moi for demanding multi-party elections and an end to political corruption and tribal politics; fmr mem. Forum for Restoration of Democracy; presidential cand. 1997; mem. Parl. (Nat. Rainbow Coalition) for Tetu Constituency 2002–; Asst Minister for Environment, Natural Resources and Wildlife 2003–05; f. Mazingira Green Party of Kenya 2003; first Presiding Officer Econ., Social and Cultural Council of the African Union (ECOSOCC) 2005–; mem. advisory bd Clinton Global Initiative, UN Sec.-Gen.'s Advisory Bd on Disarmament Matters, UN Comm. on Global Governance, advisory bd Democracy Coalition Project, Earth Charter Comm., Selection Cttee Sasakawa Environmental Prize, UNEP, Kenya; mem. Bd of Dirs Women's and Environment Devt Org., World Learning, Green Cross Int., Environment Liaison Centre Int., Kenya, WorldWIDE Network of Women in Environmental Work, Nat. Council of Women of Kenya; Montgomery Fellow, Dartmouth Coll., USA 2001; Dorothy McCluskey Visiting Fellow for Conservation, Global Inst. for Sustainable Forestry, Yale Univ. 2002; Goodwill Amb., Congo Basin Forest Initiative 2005–; Paul Harris Fellow, Rotary Int; Order of the Golden Ark (The Netherlands) 1994, Elder of the Burning Spear (Kenya) 2003, Chevalier, Légion d'honneur (France) 2006; Hon. LLD (Williams Coll.) 1990, (Yale Univ.) 2004; Hon. DSc (Hobart Coll.) 1994, (William Smith Coll.) 1994, (Aoyama Gakuin Univ.) 2004, (Soka Univ.) 2004, (Univ. of Nairobi) 2005, (Willamette Univ.) 2005, (Morehouse Coll.) 2006; Hon. DAgric (Univ. of Norway) 1997; Hon. DHumLitt (Connecticut Coll.) 2006; Woman of the Year Award 1983, Right Livelihood Award (Sweden) 1984, Better World Society Award 1986, Windstar Foundation Award for the Environment 1988, WomenAid Women of the World Award (UK) 1989, Benedictine Coll. Offeramus Medal 1990, Goldman Foundation Environmental Prize 1991, UN Hunger Project Africa Prize for Leadership (co-recipient) 1991, MRC Edinburgh Medal 1993, Jane Addams Conf. Leadership Award

1993, Endowed Chair in Gender and Women's Studies named 'Fuller-Maathai', Connecticut Coll. 2000, Temple of Understanding Juliet Hollister Award (USA) 2001, Kenyan Community Abroad Excellence Award (USA) 2001, Bridges to Community Outstanding Vision and Commitment Award (USA) 2002, World Asscn of Non-Governmental Orgs (WANGO) Environment Award 2003, Columbia Univ. Center for Environmental Research and Conservation Scientist Award 2004, Arbor Day Foundation J. Sterling Morton Award 2004, Heinrich Boell Foundation Petra Kelly Environment Prize 2004, Sophie Foundation Prize 2004, Nobel Peace Prize (Norway) 2004, New York Women's Foundation Century Award 2005, Disney Wildlife Conservation Fund Award 2006, Int. Asscn for Impact Assessment (IAIA) Global Environment Award 2006. *Achievement:* one of the eight flag bearers at Winter Olympics Opening Ceremony, Turin, Italy 2006. *Publications:* Bottom is Heavy Too: Edinburgh Medal Lecture 1994, The Canopy of Hope: My Life Campaigning for Africa, Women and the Environment 2002, The Greenbelt Movement: Sharing the Approach and the Experience 2003, Unbowed: A Memoir 2007.
Address: Economic Social and Cultural Council of the African Union (ECOSOCC), First Floor, Hughes Building, Kenya Avenue Wing, Muindi Mbingu Street, Nairobi, Kenya (office). *Telephone:* (202) 11842 (office). *Fax:* (202) 21628 (office). *E-mail:* info@ecosocc.org (office); jkaruga@greenbeltmovement.org (office). *Website:* www.ecosocc.org (office); www.greenbeltmovement.org (office).

MABILANGAN, Felipe H., MA; Philippine diplomatist and international organization official; *Senior Foreign Affairs Adviser;* m. Ada Kalaw Ledesma; three c. *Education:* Univs of Oxford, UK and Geneva, Switzerland. *Career:* various positions, Dept of Foreign Affairs 1971–79, Dir-Gen. for European Affairs 1988; Amb. to France (also accred to Portugal) 1979–87, to China (also accred to Mongolia) 1989–95; Perm. Rep. to UN 1995–2001; currently Sr Foreign Affairs Adviser, Dept of Foreign Affairs; mem. UN Advisory Cttee on Admin. and Budgetary Questions 2001–04; del. to numerous int. confs; Chevalier Ordre nat. du Mérit (France), Gawad Mabini (Philippines).
Address: Department of Foreign Affairs, DFA Building, 2330 Pasay City, Metro Manila, Philippines (office). *Telephone:* (2) 8189449 (office).

MABUZA, Lindiwe, BA, MA, PhD; South African diplomatist; *High Commissioner to UK;* b. Newcastle, Kwa-Zulu Natal. *Education:* Univ. of Edinburgh. *Career:* began career teaching English and Zulu Literature, Manzini Cen. School, Swaziland 1962; subsequently Lecturer, Dept of Sociology, Univ. of Minnesota, USA; Asst Prof., Ohio Univ. 1969–76; moved to Zambia as a radio journalist on African Nat. Congress (ANC) Radio Freedom, becoming Ed. Voice of Women, ANC journal; Chair. ANC Cultural Cttee; Rep. of ANC in Scandinavia (based in Sweden) 1979–87; Chief Rep. of ANC to USA 1989–94; mem. Parl. 1994; Amb. to Germany 1995–99, High Commr (non-resident) to Malaysia, Brunei, Amb. (non-resident) to Philippines 1999–2001, High Commr to UK 2001–; Dr hc (Durban Westville), (Edinburgh) 2003; Yari Yari Award, New York Univ. *Publications include:* Malibongwe, One Never Knows (ed.); poetry titles include From ANC to Sweden, Letter to Letta, Africa to Me, Voices That Lead, South African Animals.
Address: High Commission of South Africa, South Africa House, Trafalgar Square, London, WC2N 5DP, England (office). *Telephone:* (20) 7451-7299 (office). *Fax:* (20) 7451-7284 (office). *E-mail:* general@southafricahouse.com (office). *Website:* www.southafricahouse.com (office).

MACADIE, Jeremy James; British diplomatist; b. 10 July 1952; m. Chantal Macadie; one d. *Career:* joined FCO 1972, Commodities Dept 1972–74, Econ. Adviser 1974–75, Registry, Dakar 1975–79, Head of Registry, Addis Adaba 1980–81, Communications Operations Dept, FCO 1981–84, Head of Aid Section, Sana'a 1984–87, Deputy Head of Mission, Antananarivo 1989–91, News Dept, FCO 1991–94, Security Policy Dept 1994–95, Asst Pvt. Sec. to Minister of State for Europe 1995–97, Deputy Head of Mission, Algiers 1997–99, Head of Section, Drugs and Int. Crime Dept, FCO 2000–03, secondment to Quai d'Orsay, Paris 2003–04, Amb. to Rwanda 2004–07.
Address: Foreign and Commonwealth Office, King Charles Street, London, SW1A 2AH, England (office). *Telephone:* (20) 7008-1500 (office). *Website:* www.fco.gov.uk (office).

McALEESE, Mary Patricia, LLB, MA, FRSA, MRIA; Irish academic, journalist and head of state; *President;* b. 27 June 1951, Belfast, Northern Ireland; m. Dr Martin McAleese 1976; one s. two d. *Education:* Queen's Univ. Belfast, Inn of Court of Northern Ireland, King's Inns, Dublin and Trinity Coll., Dublin. *Career:* called to Northern Ireland Bar 1974; Reid Prof. of Criminal Law, Criminology and Penology, Trinity Coll., Dublin 1975–79, 1981–87; current affairs journalist and presenter, Radio Telefis Éireann 1979–85; Dir Inst. of Professional Legal Studies 1987–97; Pro-Vice-

Chancellor, Queen's Univ., Belfast 1994–97; Pres. of Ireland 1997– (re-elected 2004); Dir (non-exec.) Northern Ireland Electricity 1992–97, Channel 4 TV 1993–97, fmr Dir Royal Group of Hosps Trust; Founder mem. Irish Comm. for Prisoners Overseas; mem. Catholic Church Episcopal Del. to the New Ireland Forum 1984, Catholic Church Del. to the North Comm. on Contentious Parades 1996; Del. to White House Conf. on Trade and Investment in Ireland 1995, and to the follow-up Pittsburg Conf. 1996; Hon. Fellow Trinity Coll. Dublin, Inst. of Engineers of Ireland, Royal Coll. of Surgeons, Coll. of Anaesthetists, Liverpool John Moore's Univ., Royal Coll. of Physicians and Surgeons, Glasgow; Hon. Bencher, King's Inns, Inn of Court of Northern Ireland; Hon. LLD (Nat. Univ. of Ireland, Vic. Univ. of Tech., Australia, Saint Mary's Univ., Canada, Loyola Law School, LA, Univ. of Aberdeen, Univ. of Surrey, Queen's, Belfast), (Nottingham) 1998, (Trinity Coll. Dublin, Metropolitan Univ., Manchester, Univ. of Delaware, Univ. of Bristol); Hon. DHumLitt (Rochester Inst. of Tech., NY, USA); Hon. DLitt (Univ. of Ulster); Silver Jubilee Commemoration Medal, Charles Univ., Prague, Great Gold Medal, Comenius Univ., Bratislava, ranked by Forbes magazine amongst 100 Most Powerful Women (33rd) 2004, (21st) 2005, (55th) 2006, (58th) 2007. *Publications:* The Irish Martyrs 1995, Reconciled Being 1997.
Address: Áras an Uachtaráin, Phoenix Park, Dublin 8, Ireland (office). *Telephone:* (1) 617-1000. *Fax:* (1) 617-1001. *E-mail:* webmaster@president.ie (office). *Website:* www.president.ie (office).

MACAN, Tom, BA; British diplomatist; b. 14 Nov. 1946, Manchester; one s. one d. *Education:* Shrewsbury School, Univ. of Sussex. *Career:* joined HM Diplomatic Service 1969, served in Bonn, Brasília and FCO; Press Sec. Embassy at Bonn 1981; Head Commonwealth Co-ordination Dept, FCO 1986–88, Head Training Dept 1988–90; Deputy Head of Mission at Lisbon 1990–95; Amb. to Lithuania 1995–98; seconded to BOC Group 1998–99; Minister at New Delhi 1999–2002; Gov. of the Virgin Islands 2002–06; mem. Inst. of Linguists.
Address: c/o Foreign and Commonwealth Office, King Charles Street, London, SW1A 2AH, England (office).

MACAPAGAL ARROYO, Gloria, PhD; Philippine politician, economist, journalist and head of state; *President;* b. 5 April 1947, San Juan; m. Jose Miguel Tuason Arroyo 1968; two s. one d. *Education:* Assumption Convent, Georgetown Univ., Assumption Coll., Ateneo de Manila Univ., Univ. of the Philippines. *Career:* Asst Prof., Ateneo de Manila Univ. 1977–87; Chair. Econs Dept, Assumption Coll. 1984–87; Prof., Univ. of the Philippines School of Econs 1977–87; Prof., Mary Knoll Coll., St Scholastica's Coll.; Asst Sec., Dept of Trade and Industry 1987–89, Under-Sec. 1989–92; Exec. Dir Garments and Textile Export Bd 1988–90; Senator 1992–98; Sec. Dept of Social Welfare and Devt 1998–2000; Vice-Pres. of Repub. 1998–2001, Pres. of the Philippines 2001– (re-elected 2004); Chair. and Pres. Univ. of the Philippines Health Maintenance Org. 1989–98; Exec. Dir Philippine Center for Econ. Devt 1994–98; Chair. Univ. of the Philippines Econ. Foundation 1994–98; mem. Presidential Task Force on Tax and Tariff Reforms 1994–98, Tech. Working Group of the Philippine Nat. Devt Plan for the 21st Century (Cttee on Nat. Framework for Regional Devt and Macroeconomics Framework for Devt Financing); mem. or fmr mem. Asscn for Philippines-China Understanding, Philippine Econs Soc., Georgetown Club of the Philippines, Concerned Women of the Philippines; Hon. LLD (La Trobe Univ.) 2000, (Waseda Univ.) 2002, (Fordham Univ.) 2003, (Old Dominion Univ.) 2003; Hon. DEcon (Tsinghua Univ.) 2001; Hon. DH (Mapua Inst. of Tech.) 2004; Hon. Community Coll. Assoc. Degree in Int. Relations (City Coll. of San Francisco) 2003; UPSE Fellowship 1970–71, Japan Foundation Grant 1976–77, Rockefeller Foundation Scholarship 1978–83, named Outstanding Senator and One of Asia's Most Powerful Women by Asiaweek, Woman of the Year by Catholic Educ. Asscn of the Philippines, Ulirang Ina, Ulirang Ina Awards Cttee 2001, Most Distinguished Alumna, Univ. of the Philippines Alumni Asscn 2001, Making a Difference for Women – Women of Distinction Award, Soroptimist International of the Philippines Region 2003, ranked by Forbes magazine amongst 100 Most Powerful Women (ninth) 2004, (fourth) 2005, (45th) 2006, (51st) 2007.
Address: Office of the President, New Executive Building, Malacañang Palace Compound, J.P. Laurel Street, San Miguel, Metro Manila, Philippines (office). *Telephone:* (2) 7356047 (office). *Fax:* (2) 7358006 (office). *E-mail:* gma@easy.net.ph (office). *Website:* www.kgma.org (office).

McCAFFREY, Gen. Barry R., MA; American army officer (retd), academic, news analyst and consultant; *President, BR McCaffrey Associates LLC;* b. 17 Nov. 1942, Taunton, Mass.; m. Jill Ann Faulkner 1964; one s. two d. *Education:* Phillips Acad., Mass, US Mil. Acad., American Univ., Harvard Univ., Western Behavioral Science Inst., Nat. Defense Univ., Command and Gen. Staff Coll., Army War Coll. *Career:* commissioned into US Army 1964; served in Viet Nam 1966–67, 1968–69; Asst Prof. of Social Sciences,

Dept of Social Sciences, US Mil. Acad. 1972–75, currently Adjunct Prof. of Int. Affairs; 3rd Infantry Div., Germany 1979–83; Div. Chief of Staff 9th Infantry Div. 1982–86; Asst Commandant US Army Infantry School 1986–88; US Deputy Mil. Rep. to NATO 1988–89; Prin. Staff Asst to Chair. of Jt Chiefs of Staff, Chief of Strategic Planning 1989–90; 24th Infantry Div. 1990–92; led div. into Iraq in Operation Desert Storm 1991; fmr Commdr-in-Chief US Armed Forces Southern Command; at retirement youngest four-star Gen. in Army and most highly decorated combat officer; Dir White House Office of Nat. Drug Control Policy 1996–2001; fmr mem. prin. negotiation team START II Nuclear Arms Control Treaty; mem. Nat. Security Council, Council on Foreign Relations, Nat. Asscn for Advancement of Colored People; Pres. B. R. McCaffrey Assocs; currently NBC News analyst on terrorism; decorations from France, Brazil, Argentina, Colombia, Peru, and Venezuela; Distinguished Service Cross (twice), Silver Star (twice), Distinguished Service Medal, Combat Infantry Badge, US Health and Human Services Lifetime Achievement Award For Extraordinary Achievement in the Field of Substance Abuse Prevention 2004, recognized as one of the 500 Most Influential People in American Foreign Policy by World Affairs Councils of America 2004, US Dept of State Superior Honor Award for the Strategic Arms Limitation Talks, CIA Great Seal Medallion, US Coast Guard Distinguished Public Service Award, NAACP Roy Wilkins Renown Service Award, Norman E. Zinberg Award of the Harvard Medical School, Fed. Law Enforcement Foundation Nat. Service Award, Community Anti-Drug Coalitions of America Lifetime Achievement Award, Nat. Leadership Award by Community Anti-Drug Coalitions of America 2007, Golden Eagle, Soc. of American Mil. Engineers (SAME) 2007, inducted into US Army Ranger Hall of Fame 2007. *Television:* appeared in over 6000 TV interviews; media coverage includes Meet the Press, This Week, Fox Sunday News, Nightline, Today, Good Morning America, John McLaughlin's One on One,numerous feature interviews on CBS Evening News, NBC Nightly News, on World News, on PBS, on CNN, Montel Williams, Charlie Rose, Diane Rehm on NPR, C-Span Washington Journal. *Publications:* Proceedings of the Twenty-Fifth Student Conference on United States Affairs 1973, We Are Soldiers All: An Analysis of Possible Roles for Women in the Army 1973, numerous articles on mil. subjects, drugs law enforcement and money laundering.
Address: BR McCaffrey Associates LLC, 2900 South Quincy Street, Suite 300A, Arlington, VA 22206, USA (office). *Telephone:* (703) 824-5160 (office). *Fax:* (703) 671-6318 (office). *E-mail:* brm@mccaffreyassociates .com (office). *Website:* www.mccaffreyassociates.com (office).

McCALLUM, Robert Davis, Jr, MA; American lawyer and diplomatist; *Ambassador to Australia; Education:* Yale Univ. and Univ. of Oxford, UK (Rhodes Scholar). *Career:* joined Alston & Bird, Atlanta, Ga 1973, Pnr –2001; Asst Attorney Gen. for Civil Div. 2001–03, Assoc. Attorney Gen. 2003–05, Acting Deputy Attorney Gen. 2005–06; Amb. to Australia 2006–. *Address:* Embassy of the USA, Moonah Place, Yarralumla, ACT 2600, Australia (office). *Telephone:* (2) 6214-5600 (office). *Fax:* (2) 6214-5970 (office). *E-mail:* info@usembassy-australia.state.gov (office). *Website:* canberra.usembassy.gov (office).

McCARTHY, John Philip, AO, MA, LLB; Australian lawyer and diplomatist; *High Commissioner to India;* b. 29 Nov. 1942, Washington, DC, USA; two d. *Education:* Cambridge Univ. *Career:* practised as barrister, London 1965–66; with Shearman and Sterling (law firm), New York 1966–67; 1964; joined Dept of Foreign Affairs 1968; Second Sec. Vientiane 1969–72; First Sec. Washington 1973–75; Chargé d'affaires, Damascus 1977–78; Sr Pvt. Sec. to Minister for Foreign Affairs 1979–80; Amb. to Democratic Repub. of Viet Nam 1981–83, to Mexico 1985–87, to Thailand 1992–94, to USA 1995–97, to Indonesia 1997–2000, to Japan 2001–05; High Commr in India and Amb. to Bhutan 2005–; Deputy Sec. Dept of Foreign Affairs and Trade, Canberra 1994–95.
Address: Embassy of Australia, 1/50-g Shanti Path, Chanakyapuri, New Delhi 110 021, India (office). *Telephone:* (11) 51399900 (office). *Fax:* (11) 26885199 (office). *Website:* www.ausgovindia.com (office).

McCAW, Susan Rasinski, BA, MBA; American diplomatist; b. 1962, Orange Co., Calif.; m. Craig McCaw; three c. *Education:* Stanford Univ. and Harvard Business School. *Career:* worked as an Assoc. in Robertson Stephens' Venture Capital Group, fmr Prin. at Robertson Stephens & Co., San Francisco; served as a Business Analyst for McKinsey & Co., New York and Hong Kong; fmr Pres. COM Investments; fmr Man. Pnr, Eagle Creek Capital, Wash.; Amb. to Austria 2006–07; fmr mem. Bd of Trustees Stanford Univ.; served as Co-Chair. Stanford Univ.'s $1 billion Campaign for Undergraduate Educ.; Co-founder and Chair. Bd Team Read, Seattle; fmr mem. Univ. of Washington Investment Cttee, Grameen Technology Advisory Council; fmr Finance Co-Chair. for Bush-Cheney '04, Wash.; fmr mem. Nat. Steering Cttee for W Stands for Women; served on Women's Coalition Advisory Bd, Republican Nat. Cttee.

Address: US Department of State, 2201 C Street NW, Washington, DC 20520, USA (office). *Telephone:* (202) 647-4000 (office). *Fax:* (202) 647-6738 (office). *Website:* www.state.gov (office).

McCLEARY, William Boyd, CVO, BA; British diplomatist; *High Commissioner to Malaysia;* b. 30 March 1949, Belfast, Northern Ireland; m. Jeannette Ann Collier; three d. *Education:* Royal Belfast Academical Inst., Queen's Univ., Belfast. *Career:* Asst Prin., later Deputy Prin., Dept of Agric. for NI 1972–75; First Sec. (Agric.), Bonn 1975–78, First Sec., Chancery, Bonn 1979–80, Western European Dept, FCO 1981–83, EC Dept (External) 1983–85, First Sec. and Head of Chancery, Seoul 1985–88, Asst Head of Far Eastern Dept, FCO 1988–89, Deputy Head of Mission and Dir of Trade Promotion for Turkey, Ankara 1990–93, Counsellor (Econ./ Commercial), Ottawa 1993–97, Head of Overseas Estates Dept, FCO 1997–98, Head of Estates Strategy Unit 1998–2000, Consul Gen. and Dir Gen. of Trade and Industry in Germany, Düsseldorf 2000–05, High Commr to Malaysia 2006–; Hugh Hyndman Scholarship 1967.
Address: British High Commission, 185 Jalan Ampang, 50450 Kuala Lumpur, Malaysia (office). *Telephone:* (3) 2170-2200 (office). *Fax:* (3) 2170-2303 (office). *E-mail:* boyd.mccleary@fco.gov.uk (office). *Website:* www .britain.org.my (office).

McCONNELL, Rt Hon. Jack Wilson, BSc, DipEd; British politician and diplomatist; b. 30 June 1960, Irvine, Ayrshire; m. Bridget Mary McLuckie 1990; one s. one d. *Education:* Arran High School, Isle of Arran, Stirling Univ. *Career:* math. teacher, Alloa 1983–92; Labour mem. Stirling Dist Council 1984–92, Treas. 1988–92, Leader 1990–92; Gen. Sec. Scottish Labour Party (SLP) 1992–98, Leader 2001–07 (resgnd); co-ordinated Labour's Yes Yes Referendum Campaign 1997; mem. Scottish Constitutional Convention 1989–98; currently MSP for Motherwell and Wishaw; Minister for Finance, Scottish Exec. 1999–2000, for Educ. and External Affairs 2000–01; First Minister of Scotland 2001–07; Head, Clinton Hunter Devt Initiative on developing educ. in Malawi and Rwanda; apptd High Commr to Malawi 2007, term to start 2009; mem. Convention of Scottish Local Authorities (COSLA) 1988–92; mem. GMB, Amnesty Int.
Address: Scottish Parliament, Edinburgh, EH99 1SP (office); Constituency Office, 265 Main Street, Wishaw, Lanarkshire, ML2 7NE, Scotland (office). *Telephone:* (131) 348 5831 (Parl.) (office); (1698) 303040 (office). *Fax:* (131) 348 5562 (Parl.) (office); (1698) 303060 (office). *E-mail:* Jack .Mcconnell.msp@scottish.parliament.uk (office). *Website:* www .jackmcconnell.org.uk (office).

McCONNELL, Vice Adm. John Michael (Mike); American naval officer (retd) and government official; *Director of National Intelligence;* b. 26 July 1943, Greenville, South Carolina; m. Terry McConnell; two c. two step-c. *Education:* Furman Univ. *Career:* commissioned as line officer in USN in 1967, served a tour in Vietnam and became intelligence officer, served as intelligence officer for Jt Chiefs Chair. Colin Powell during first Gulf War; Dir Nat. Security Agency 1992–96; Sr Vice Pres. Booz Allen Hamilton 1996–2007, also Dir Infrastructure Assurance Center of Excellence; Dir of Nat. Intelligence 2007–; mem. Bd of Dirs CompuDyne Corpn 2004–07.
Address: Office of the Director of National Intelligence, Washington, DC 20511 (office). *Telephone:* (202) 201-1111 (office). *Website:* www.dni.gov (office).

McCORMICK, William P. (Bill); American business executive, diplomatist and philanthropist; *Ambassador to New Zealand and Samoa;* b. 18 Aug. 1939, Providence, RI; m. Gail McCormick; six c. *Education:* Roger Williams, Jr Coll., Boston Univ., Harvard Grad. School of Business Exec. Man. Program. *Career:* served in Army Reserve Mil. Police, Hon. Discharge 1963; worked in brokerage office of Conn. Gen. Life Insurance Co., San Francisco 1963–65; Partner, Refectory Steak House Restaurant chain 1965–early 1970s; purchased Jake's Famous Crawfish restaurant, Portland, Ore. 1973, Partner with Doug Schmick 1974 (currently there are 56 McCormick & Schmick's Seafood Restaurants in 24 states), co. went public 2004, Chair. Emer. 2005–; Amb. to New Zealand (also accred to Samoa) 2005–; f. Shamrock Run, Portland 1979; fmr Chair. Affairs, Nat. Restaurant Asscn; fmr Finance Chair. for Gordon Smith for US Senate; fmr Finance Co-Chair. Bush for President; fmr Ore. Chair. Republican Nat. Cttee Finance Cttee; fmr Co-Chair. Portland Opera Foundation; fmr mem. Pres.'s Cttee of the Arts & Humanities; fmr mem. Bd Ore. Historical Soc., The Portland Opera, NorthWest Mental Health Services, Ore. Museum of Science and Industry, Portland Police Chief's Forum (Pres.), St Vincent's Hosp. Heart Inst., High Desert Museum, Citizen's Crime Comm. (Vice-Chair.), Ore. Coast Aquarium, Portland State Univ.'s Business School Advisory Cttee, Ore. Health Science Univ., The Ore. Restaurant Asscn's Bd Exec. Cttee (and Political Advisory Cttee); Sec.'s Award, US Dept of Veterans' Affairs.
Address: US Embassy, PO Box 1190, 29 Fitzherbert Terrace, Thorndon, Wellington, New Zealand (office). *Telephone:* (4) 462-6000 (office). *Fax:* (4)

499-0490 (office). *Website:* newzealand.usembassy.gov (office); samoa .usembassy.gov (office).

McCREEVY, Charlie, BComm, FCA; Irish politician; *Commissioner for Internal Market and Services, European Commission;* b. Sept. 1949, Sallins, Co. Kildare; m. (separated); three s. three d. *Education:* Univ. Coll. Dublin. *Career:* partner, Tynan Dillon & Co. (chartered accountants), Dublin, Naas and Ballyhaunis; mem. Kildare Co. Council 1979–85; mem. Dáil 1977–; Minister for Social Welfare 1992–93, for Tourism and Trade 1993–94, for Finance 1997–2004; EU Commr for Internal Market and Services 2004–; fmr Fianna Fáil Spokesperson on Finance. *Address:* European Commission, 200 rue de la Loi, 1049 Brussels, Belgium (office); Hillview House, Kilcullen Ross, Naas, Co. Kildare, Ireland. *Telephone:* (2) 299-11-11 (office). *Fax:* (2) 295-01-38 (office). *E-mail:* charlie .mccreevy@cec.eu.int (office). *Website:* europa.eu (office).

McCULLEY, Terence Patrick, BA; American diplomatist; *Ambassador to Mali;* b. Medford, Ore.; m. Renée McCulley; two s. *Education:* Univ. of Oregon, Université de Haute Bretagne, Rennes, France (Rotary Foundation Grad. Fellow), Fletcher School of Law and Diplomacy at Tufts Univ. *Career:* career mem. Sr Foreign Service since 1985, rank of Counselor, posted to Niger, S Africa and Chad, later Consul, Consulate Gen. in Mumbai, Desk Officer for Zaïre, Office of Cen. African Affairs, Dept of State, Deputy Chief of Mission, Embassies in Togo, Senegal and Tunisia 1995–2004, Deputy Coordinator for Iraq Assistance, Bureau of Near Eastern Affairs 2004–05, Amb. to Mali 2005–; four Dept of State Superior Honor Awards. *Address:* US Embassy, ACI 2000, Rue 243, Porte 297, Bamako, Mali (office). *Telephone:* 270-23-00 (office). *Fax:* 270-24-79 (office). *E-mail:* webmaster@usa.org.ml (office). *Website:* mali.usembassy.gov (office).

MacDERMOTT, Alasdair Tormod; British diplomatist (retd); b. 17 Sept. 1945; m. 2nd Gudrun MacDermott; two d. from first m. *Career:* joined FCO 1966, SE Asian Dept 1966–68, Int. Claims Dept 1968–71, Asst Admin Officer and Accountant, Kabul 1971–73, Consular Dept, FCO 1973, Aid Attaché, Accra 1973–77, Conf. Unit, Int. and EU Confs, FCO 1977–79, full-time Japanese language training, School of Oriental and African Studies, London 1977–78, Kamakura, Tokyo 1978–79, Second Sec., Commercial and Information, Tokyo 1979–82, temporary duty in Togoland, Accra 1982–83, Second Sec. (Political), Colombo 1983–86, Press Officer, Tokyo 1986–91, Acting Resident Rep., Castries 1991, S Asian Dept, FCO 1992–94, temporary duty, Hanoi 1994, Turkish language training, FCO 1995, Commercial Sec., Ankara 1995–98, Head of Section, Southern African Dept, FCO 1998–2001, High Commr to Namibia 2002–07 (retd). *Address:* c/o Foreign and Commonwealth Office, King Charles Street, London, SW1A 2AH, England. *Telephone:* (20) 7008-1500.

McDONAGH, Bobby; Irish diplomatist; *Permanent Representative, European Union;* b. 29 June 1954, Washington, DC, USA. *Education:* Gonzaga Coll., Balliol Coll., Univ. of Oxford. *Career:* joined Dept of Foreign Affairs 1977, has held numerous EU-related posts including mem. Secr. European Parl. 1983–85, based at Perm. Mission to EU 1987–90, joined Cabinet of Farm Commr 1990, served as Deputy Chef de Cabinet to Commr for Social Affairs, fmr Deputy to IGC Rep., Treaty of Amsterdam negotiations, apptd Dir-Gen. EU Div., Dept of Foreign Affairs 2001, fmr Alternate Mem. Convention on Future of Europe, Perm. Rep. to EU 2005–. *Publications:* Original Sin in a Brave New World 1998. *Address:* Permanent Representation of Ireland, Council of the European Union, 89/93 rue Froissart, Brussels 1040, Belgium (office). *Telephone:* (2) 230-85-80 (office). *Fax:* (2) 230-32-03 (office). *E-mail:* irlprb@iveagh.irlgov .ie (office). *Website:* foreignaffairs.gov.ie.

MacDONALD, Hon. Flora Isabel, CC, PC; Canadian politician and consultant; *Secretary, Future Generations Canada;* b. 3 June 1926, North Sydney, NS. *Education:* North Sydney High School, Empire Business Coll. and National Defence Coll., Kingston, Ont. *Career:* Exec. Dir Progressive Conservative HQ 1957–66; admin. officer and tutor, Dept of Political Studies, Queen's Univ. 1966–72; Nat. Sec. Progressive Conservative Asscn of Canada 1966–69; MP for Kingston and the Islands, Ont. 1972–88; Sec. of State for External Affairs 1979–80; Minister of Employment and Immigration 1984–86, of Communications 1986–88; host, weekly TV series North/South 1990–94; Chair. Int. Devt Research Centre 1992–97, Shastri Indo-Canada Advisory Council 1997–2004, HelpAge Int., London, UK 1997–2001; Co-Chair. Canadian Co-ordinating Cttee UN Year of Older Persons 1999; Pres. Future Generations, Franklin, W Va 1998–2007, Sec. Future Generations Canada 2007–, Partnership Africa-Canada 2002–04; mem. Carnegie Comm. on Preventing Deadly Conflict 1994–99; Visiting Fellow, Centre for Canadian Studies, Univ. of Edin. Sept.–Dec. 1989; Pres. Asscn of Canadian Clubs 1999–2003, World Federalist Movt —Canada

(fmrly World Federalists of Canada) 2001–04, UNIFEM Canada; Patron, Commonwealth Human Rights Initiative; Hon. Patron for Canada of Nat. Museums of Scotland; Companion Order of Ont. 1995, Order of NS 2007; Padma Shri (India) 2004; 18 hon. degrees; Pearson Peace Medal, UN Asscn 2000, UNIFEM Canada Award 2002. *Address:* 1103 – 350 Queen Elizabeth Driveway, Ottawa, ON K1S 3N1, Canada (home). *Telephone:* (613) 238-1098 (home). *Fax:* (613) 238-6330 (home). *E-mail:* flora@intranet.ca (home).

McDONALD, Gabrielle Kirk, LLB; American judge; *Judge, Iran–US Claims Tribunal;* b. 12 April 1942, St Paul, Minn.; m. Mark T. McDonald; one s. one d. *Education:* Howard Univ. *Career:* fmr law professor; Fed. Judge, Houston, Tex. 1979–88; Pnr, Matthews Branscomb, Austin, Tex. (law firm) 1988–; Judge UN int. tribunal on war crimes in fmr Yugoslavia, The Hague 1993–99, Pres. 1997–99; Judge Iran–US Claims Tribunal, The Hague 2001–; mem. Bd of Dirs Freeport-McMoran Copper & Gold (mining co.), Special Counsel on Human Rights to Bd Chair.; mem. ABA, Nat. Bar Asscn; hon. degrees from Georgetown Univ., Univ. of Notre Dame, Amherst Coll.; American Bar Asscn Margaret Brent Women Lawyers of Achievement Award, Central E European Law Initiative Leadership Award 2003. *Address:* Iran–United States Claims Tribunal, Parkweg 13, 2585 JH The Hague, Netherlands (office). *Telephone:* (70) 352-0064 (office). *Fax:* (70) 350-2456 (office). *E-mail:* registry@iusct.org (office). *Website:* www.iusct .org (office).

MACDONALD, Henry Leonard, LLM; Suriname diplomatist; *Permanent Representative, United Nations;* b. 3 Aug. 1963, N W Nickerie; m.; five c. *Education:* Anton de Kon Univ., American Univ., Washington, DC. *Career:* Coordinator for Int. Affairs and Human Rights, Ministry of Justice and Police 1989–1998; Deputy Chief of Mission to OAS 1998–2000; Chargé d' Affairs ad Interim, Embassy in Washington, DC 2000, Deputy Chief of Mission, 2001–07, also Alt. Rep. to OAS; Coordinator to Summit of Americas Implementation Process 2004–07; Perm. Rep. to UN, New York 2007–; UNITAR Fellowship 1994, Law Fellowship, Univ. Amsterdam 1998. *Address:* Permanent Mission of Suriname to the United Nations, 866 United Nations Plaza, Suite 320, New York, NY 10017, USA (office). *Telephone:* (212) 826-0660 (office). *Fax:* (212) 980-7029 (office). *E-mail:* suriname@un.int (office). *Website:* www.un.int/suriname (office).

McDONALD, Jackson Chester, BS, MA; American diplomatist; b. Fla; m.; three c. *Education:* School of Foreign Service, Georgetown Univ., Washington, DC, Institut d'Etudes Politiques and Ecole Nationale d'Admin, Paris, France. *Career:* career mem. Sr Foreign Service since 1980, Third Sec. and Vice-Consul, Embassy in Dhaka 1980–82, Country Officer for Bangladesh, Dept of State 1982–84, Second Sec. for Political Affairs, Embassy in Beirut 1984–86, studies at Ecole Nationale d'Admin 1986–87, First Sec. for Political Affairs, Embassy in Paris 1987–89, Russian language training 1989–90, First Sec. for Political Affairs, Embassy in Moscow 1990–91, Chargé d'affaires a.i., then Deputy Chief of Mission, Embassy in Almaty, Kazakhstan 1992–94, Consul-Gen. in Marseille (also accred to Monaco) 1994–97, mem. Senior Seminar exec. devt program 1997–98, Deputy Chief of Mission, Embassy in Abidjan, Côte d'Ivoire 1998–2001, Amb. to The Gambia 2001–04, to Guinea 2004–07; Hon. Officer, Nat. Order of the Repub. of The Gambia; six Superior Honor Awards. *Address:* US Department of State, 2201 C Street NW, Washington, DC 20520, USA (office). *Telephone:* (202) 647-4000 (office). *Fax:* (202) 647-6738 (office). *Website:* www.state.gov (office).

McDONALD, Simon Gerard, CMG; British diplomatist; *Chief Foreign Policy Adviser to the Prime Minister;* b. 9 March 1961; m. Olivia McDonald; two s. two d. *Education:* Univ. of Cambridge. *Career:* joined British Diplomatic Service 1982; Benelux Desk Officer, Western European Dept, FCO 1982–83; Third Sec., Embassy of Jeddah 1985; Second Sec., Embassy in Riyadh 1985–88, Embassy in Bonn 1988–90; speechwriter for Foreign Sec., Policy Planning Staff 1990–93; Pvt. Sec., Office of Perm. Under-Sec., FCO 1993–95; First Sec., Embassy in Washington, DC 1995–98; Deputy Head of Mission and Consul-Gen., Embassy in Riyadh 1998–2001; Prin. Pvt. Sec., Office of Sec. of State, FCO 2001–02; Amb. to Israel 2003–06; Chief Foreign Policy Adviser to Prime Minister 2007–. *Address:* c/o Prime Minister's Office, 10 Downing St, London, SW1A 2AA, England (office). *Telephone:* (20) 7270-3000 (office). *Fax:* (20) 7295-0918 (office). *Website:* www.number10.gov.uk (office).

MACEDO, Horacio Antonio; Argentine diplomatist; *Ambassador to Bolivia;* b. 15 Nov. 1952, San Salvador de Jujuy. *Education:* Universidad Nacional de Cordoba. *Career:* Deputy from Jujay 1993–97; Sec. Pro-tem Conferencia Interparlamentaria Empresarial del Cono Sur de América 1994; Prov.

Minister 1997–98; Minister of Production, Trade and Environment 2000–01; Amb. to Bolivia 2003–; Founding mem. Jt Parl. Comm. of Mercosur 1995.
Address: Embassy of Argentina, Calle Aspiazú 497, esq. Sánchez Lima, Casilla 64, La Paz, Bolivia (office). *Telephone:* (2) 241-7737 (office). *Fax:* (2) 242-2727 (office). *E-mail:* ebolv@mrecic.gov.ar (office).

McELHANEY, Douglas L., BA, MA; American diplomatist. *Education:* Univ. of Michigan, Columbia and Stanford Univs. *Career:* career officer, US Foreign Service since 1973, Vice-Consul, Embassy in Lisbon 1973–75, State Dept Operations Center 1975–77, worked on the Namibia independence negotiations, posting to Embassy in Brussels, Deputy Political Counselor, Embassy in Cairo 1987–89, assignment, Embassy in Rome, returned to Washington, DC to work on European mil. issues, Political Counselor, then Deputy Perm. Rep. at US Mission to NATO 1995–2000, Deputy Chief of Mission and Chargé d'affaires, Embassy in Paris, Consul-Gen. in Milan, Amb. to Bosnia and Herzegovina 2004–07; mem. American Foreign Service Asscn; numerous Meritorious and Superior Honor Awards.
Address: US Department of State, 2201 C Street NW, Washington, DC 20520, USA (office). *Telephone:* (202) 647-4000 (office). *Fax:* (202) 647-6738 (office). *Website:* www.state.gov (office).

McENTEE, Andrew, BA, LLB; British lawyer; b. 2 July 1957, Glasgow, Scotland. *Education:* Univ. of Stirling, Univ. of Wolverhampton, Univ. of N. London. *Career:* case worker, Citizens' Advice Bureau 1982–83, Scottish Council for Civil Liberties (now Scottish Human Rights Centre) 1983–84; community care worker, Strathclyde Social Work Dept 1985–86; Gen. Sec. Chile Cttee for Human Rights/South American Human Rights Coordination 1986–91; Gen. Sec. Cen. America Human Rights Cttee 1993–96; UK-apptd Chair. Amnesty Int. Lawyers Network 1994, Chair. Amnesty Int. UK 1998; Sr Consultant Atlantic Celtic Films Co. 1996–; UK Chair. Coalition for an Int. Criminal Court 1997–; adviser to Spanish and Chilean lawyers and victims and coordinator of Amnesty Int. case during extradition proceedings against Gen. Augusto Pinochet 1998–2000; writer and lecturer on human rights.
Address: c/o Amnesty International, 99 Rosebery Avenue, London, EC1R 4RE, England (office).

McFADDEN, Daniel L., BS, PhD; American economist and academic; *Professor of Economics, University of California, Berkeley;* b. 29 July 1937, Raleigh, NC; m. Beverlee Tito Simboli McFadden; one d. two s. *Education:* Univ. of Minnesota. *Career:* Asst Prof. of Econs Univ. of Pittsburgh 1962–63; Asst Prof. of Econs Univ. of Calif. at Berkeley 1963–66, 1966–68, Prof. of Econs 1968–79, 1990–, E. Morris Cox Chair 1990–, Dir Econometrics Lab. 1991–95, 1996–, Chair. Dept of Econs 1995–96; Visiting Assoc. Prof. Univ. of Chicago 1966–67; Irving Fisher Research Prof. Yale Univ. 1977–78; Prof. of Econs Mass Inst. of Tech. 1978–91, James R. Killian Chair, 1984–91, Dir Statistics Center 1986–88; Sherman Fairchild Distinguished Scholar Calif. Inst. of Tech. 1990; Pres.-Elect American Econ. Asscn 2004–; mem. American Acad. of Arts and Sciences, Nat. Acad. of Science; hon. degree (Univ. Coll. London) 2003; Econometrics Soc. Frisch Medal 1986, Nemmers Prize in Econs 2000, Nobel Prize for Econs (jt recipient) 2000, Richard Stone Prize in Applied Econometrics 2000. *Publications include:* Lectures on Longitudinal Analysis (Underground Classics in Economics) (jt author), Handbook of Econometrics IV (with R. Engle) 1994.
Address: Department of Economics, University of California, 549 Evans Hall #3880, Berkeley, CA 94720-3880, USA (office). *Telephone:* (510) 643-8428 (office). *Fax:* (510) 642-0638 (office). *E-mail:* mcfadden@econ.berkeley.edu (office). *Website:* emlab.berkeley.edu/users/mcfadden (office).

McFAUL, Michael Anthony, BA, MA, PhD; American political scientist, academic and foreign policy analyst; *Professor of Political Science, Stanford University;* b. Mont. *Education:* Stanford Univ., Univ. of Oxford, UK. *Career:* Research Fellow, Center for Int. Security and Arms Control, Stanford Univ. 1988–90, Research Assoc. 1992–94, Visiting Research Fellow, Hoover Inst. 1990–91, Research Fellow 1995–2003, Asst Prof., Dept of Political Science, 1995–2001, Assoc. Prof. 2001–05, Prof. 2007–, Peter and Helen Bing Sr Fellow, Hoover Inst. 2003–, Dir Center on Democracy, Devt and Rule of Law, Freeman Spogli Inst. (FSI) for Int. Studies 2005–, Deputy Dir FSI 2006–, Co-Dir FSI Iran Democracy Project 2003–; Visiting Scholar, Moscow State Univ. 1990–91; Sr Assoc. Moscow Carnegie Center, Carnegie Endowment for Int. Peace 1993–95 (now non-resident); Sr Consultant and Commentator (Russian Parl. Elections), CBS News 1995, CNN 1996, 1999, 2000; Research Assoc. Center for Int. Security and Arms Control; Sr Adviser to Nat. Democratic Inst.; mem. Bd of Dirs Eurasia Foundation, Firebird Fund, Freedom House, Int. Forum for Democratic Studies of Nat. Endowment for Democracy, Int. Research and Exchange Bd; mem. Steering Cttee Europe and Eurasia Div., Human

Rights Watch; mem. Editorial Bd Current History, Journal of Democracy, Demokratizatsiya, Perspectives on European Politics and Society; consultant to several govt agencies and cos; contribs to New York Times, LA Times, Chicago Tribune, Moscow Times, Washington Post. *Publications:* The Troubled Birth of Russian Democracy: Political Parties, Programs and Profiles (co-author) 1993, Post-Communist Politics: Democratic Prospects in Russia and Eastern Europe 1993, Privatization, Conversion and Enterprise Reform in Russia (co-author) 1995, Russia's 1996 Presidential Election: The End of Bi-Polar Politics 1997, Russia's Unfinished Revolution: Political Change from Gorbachev to Putin 2001, Popular Choice and Managed Democracy: The Russian Elections of 1999 and 2000 (co-author) 2003, After the Collapse of Communism: Comparative Lessons of Transitions (co-author) 2004, Between Dictatorship and Democracy: Russian Postcommunist Political Reform (co-author) 2004, Revolution in Orange: The Origins of Ukraine's Democratic Breakthrough (co-author) 2006; articles in professional journals.
Address: Department of Political Science, Encina West, Stanford, CA 94305, USA (office). *Telephone:* (650) 724-6448 (office). *Fax:* (650) 724-2996 (office). *E-mail:* mcfaul@stanford.edu (office). *Website:* www.stanford.edu/~mcfaul (office).

McGEE, James D., BA, MA; American diplomatist; *Ambassador to Zimbabwe;* b. 1949, Chicago, Ill.; one s. one d. *Education:* Indiana Univ., Vietnamese language studies at Defense Language Inst., Monterey, Calif. *Career:* served in USAF 1968–74; career mem. Sr Foreign Service, entered Foreign Service 1981, Third Sec. and Vice-Consul, Lagos 1982–84, Admin. Officer, Consulate General, Lahore 1984–86, Second Sec. and Supervisory Gen. Services Officer, The Hague 1986–89, Admin. Officer, Consulate Gen., Bombay 1989–91, Special Asst, Bureau of Finance and Man. Policy, Dept of State 1991–92, volunteered for duty at Embassy in Bridgetown, Barbados 1992, Admin. Counselor 1992–95, Admin. Counselor, Kingston, Jamaica 1995–98, Admin. Counselor, Abidjan, Côte d'Ivoire 1998–2001, Amb. to Swaziland 2002–04, to Madagascar 2004–07, to Zimbabwe 2007–; three Distinguished Flying Crosses.
Address: US Embassy, PO Box 3340, 172 Herbert Chitepo Avenue, Harare, Zimbabwe (office). *Telephone:* (4) 250593 (office). *Fax:* (4) 796488 (office). *E-mail:* consularharare@state.gov (office); hararepas@state.gov (office). *Website:* harare.usembassy.gov (office).

McGOVERN, George Stanley, PhD; American international organization official and fmr politician; *Global Ambassador on Hunger, United Nations Food and Agriculture Organization;* b. 19 July 1922, Avon, S Dak; m. Eleanor Faye Stegeberg 1943; one s. four d. *Education:* Dakota Wesleyan Univ. and Northwestern Univ. *Career:* served USAF, Second World War; Teacher, Northwestern Univ. 1948–50; Prof. of History and Political Science, Dakota Wesleyan Univ. 1950–53; Exec. Sec. SDak Democratic Party 1953–56; mem. US House of Reps 1957–61, served Agricultural Cttee; Dir 'Food for Peace' Programme 1961–62; Senator from South Dakota 1963–81; Pnr, John Kornmeier Assocs, Washington, DC 1981; Lecturer, Northwestern Univ. 1981; Democratic cand. for US President 1972, 1984; Chair. Americans for Common Sense 1981–82; apptd Perm. Rep., FAO, Rome 1998, UN Global Amb. on Hunger 2001–; fmr Pres. Middle East Policy Council; fmr jt owner roadside inn, Stratford, Conn.; Presidential Medal of Freedom 2000, Food for Life Award, World Food Program 2000. *Publications:* The Colorado Coal Strike 1913–14 1953, War Against Want 1964, Agricultural Thought in the Twentieth Century 1967, A Time of War, a Time of Peace 1968, The Great Coalfield War (with Leonard Guttridge) 1972, An American Journey 1974, Grassroots (autobiog.) 1978, Terry: My Daughter's Life-and-Death Struggle with Alcoholism 1996.
Address: PO Box 5591, Friendship Station, Washington, DC 20016, USA (home).

MacGREGOR, John Malcolm, CVO, BA; British diplomatist (retd); b. 3 Oct. 1946; m. Judith Anne MacGregor; three s. one d. *Education:* Balliol Coll., Oxford, Univ. of Birmingham. *Career:* joined British Diplomatic Service 1973; Second, then First Sec., High Comm. in New Delhi 1975–79; Desk Officer, EU Dept, FCO 1979–81; Pvt. Sec. to Minister of State 1981–82; Speechwriter for Minister of Foreign Affairs 1982–83; Asst Head of Soviet Dept 1983–86; Deputy Head of Mission, Embassy in Prague 1986–90; Head of Chancery, Embassy in Paris 1990–93; Head of External EU Dept 1993–95; Dir-Gen. for Trade Promotion in Germany and Consul-Gen. in Düsseldorf 1995–98; Amb. to Poland 1998–2000; Dir of Wider Europe, FCO 2000–03; Amb. to Austria 2003–07, Perm. Rep. to UNIDO 2006–07.
Address: c/o Foreign and Commonwealth Office, King Charles Street, London, SW1A 2AH, England. *Telephone:* (20) 7008-1500. *E-mail:* john.macgregor@fco.gov.uk. *Website:* www.fco.gov.uk.

MacGREGOR, Judith Anne, MA, LVO; British diplomatist; b. 17 June 1952, London; m. John MacGregor; three s. one d. *Education:* Univ. of Oxford.

Career: joined FCO 1976, First Sec., Belgrade 1978–81, Polish and Hungarian Desk Officer, FCO 1981–83, Head of Recruitment 1983–84, mem. Planning Staff 1985–86, First Sec., Prague 1989, Paris 1992, Deputy Head of Western European Dept 1993–95, Counsellor and Head of Security Strategy Unit 2001–03, FCO Chair. Civil Service Selection Bd 2003–04, Amb. to Slovakia 2004–07.
Address: Foreign and Commonwealth Office, King Charles Street, London, SW1A 2AH, England (office). *Telephone:* (20) 7008-1500 (office). *Website:* www.fco.gov.uk (office).

McGUINNESS, Martin; Irish politician; *Deputy First Minister of Northern Ireland;* b. 23 May 1950, Derry; m.; four c. *Career:* took part in secret London talks between Sec. of State for NI and Irish Republican Army (IRA) July 1972; imprisoned for six months during 1973 in Irish Repub. after conviction for IRA membership; elected to NI Ass., refused seat; stood against John Hume in gen. elections of 1982, 1987, 1992; MP for Mid-Ulster, House of Commons 1997–; mem. Ulster-Mid, NI Ass. 1998–2000 (Ass. suspended Feb. 2000), 2000–02 (Ass. suspended Oct. 2002); Minister of Educ. 1999–2002; spokesman for Sinn Féin, also mem. Nat. Exec.; involved in peace negotiations with British Govt; Deputy First Minister of NI Ass. 2007–.
Address: Office of the Deputy First Minister, Parliament Buildings, Stormont Estate, Belfast, BT4 3XX (office); Sinn Féin, 51–55 Falls Road, Belfast, BT12 4PD, Northern Ireland (office). *Telephone:* (28) 9022-3000. *E-mail:* sinnfein@iol.ie (office). *Website:* www.irlnet.com/sinnfein (office).

MACHADO VENTURA, Jose Ramon; Cuban physician and politician; *First Vice-President, Council of State;* b. 26 Oct. 1930, San Antonio de las Vueltas, Las Villas. *Education:* Universidad de La Habana. *Career:* served as guerrilla in Sierra Maestra mountains and cared for mems of rebel army during Cuban Revolution against Batista govt; Asst to the President and Chief of Medical Services, City of Havana 1959; Minister of Health 1960–67; Politburo Del. to Matanzas Prov. 1968–71; First Sec. Havana Provincial Cttee, Partido Comunista de Cuba 1971–75, mem. Secr. of Cen. Cttee 1975–2008, mem. Politburo 1975–; Deputy, Asamblea Nacional del Poder Popular (Parl.) for Guantánamo 1976–2008; Vice-Pres and Secr. Political Bureau 1976–2008, First Vice-Pres. 2008–.
Address: Oficina del Primer Vice-Presidente, Havana, Cuba.

McHENRY, Donald F., MSc; American diplomatist and academic; *Professor of Diplomacy, Georgetown University;* b. 13 Oct. 1936, St Louis, Mo.; m. Mary Williamson (divorced 1978); one s. two d. *Education:* Illinois State Univ., Southern Illinois and Georgetown Univs. *Career:* taught Howard Univ., Washington 1959–62; joined Dept of State 1963, Head Dependent Areas Section, Office of UN Political Affairs 1965–68; Asst to US Sec. of State 1969; Special Asst to Dept Counselor 1969–71; lecturer, School of Foreign Service, Georgetown Univ., Guest Scholar, The Brookings Inst. and Int. Affairs Fellow, Council on Foreign Relations (on leave from State Dept) 1971–73; resgnd from State Dept 1973; Project Dir Humanitarian Policy Studies, Carnegie Endowment for Int. Peace, Washington 1973–76; served Pres. Carter's transition team 1976–77; Amb. and Deputy Perm. Rep. to UN 1977–79, Perm. Rep. 1979–81; Distinguished Prof. in the Practice of Diplomacy, School of Foreign Service, Georgetown Univ. 1981–; Pres. IRC Group; Dir Int. Paper Co., Coca Cola Co., Inst. for Int. Econs, The American Ditchley Foundation, AT&T, mem. Council on Foreign Relations (fmr Dir); mem. Editorial Bd Foreign Policy Magazine; fmr Trustee The Brookings Inst., fmr Trustee Johnson Foundation, Ford Foundation; fmr Chair. Bd Africare; fmr Gov. Mayo Foundation; American Stock Exchange; Fellow American Acad. of Arts and Sciences; fmr Dir GlaxoSmithKline PLC, Fleet Boston Financial, Fleet Boston Bank; Superior Honor Award, Dept of State 1966. *Publication:* Micronesia: Trust Betrayed 1975.
Address: School of Foreign Service, Georgetown University, ICC 301, Washington, DC 20057, USA (office). *Telephone:* (202) 687-6083 (office). *Fax:* (202) 687-1427 (office). *E-mail:* mchenryd@georgetown.edu. *Website:* www.georgetown.edu/sfs (office).

MACHINEA, José Luis, PhD; Argentine international organization official; *Executive Secretary, United Nations Economic Commission for Latin America and the Caribbean; Education:* Univ. of Minnesota, USA. *Career:* fmr Prof. of Macroeconomics, Catholic Univ. of Argentina; fmr Chief of Public Finance Dept and Chief of Research Dept at Argentine Cen. Bank, later Pres. Argentine Cen. Bank; Under-Sec. of Political Economy and Under-Sec. of Planning 1980s; consultant to World Bank and Inter-American Devt Bank 1990s (currently Special Expert in Integration and Trade, Integration and Regional Dept and mem. External Advisory Group); Dir of Research, Industrial Devt Inst. of the Argentine Industrial Union 1992–97; Pres. consultancy firm 1995–99; Pres. Argentine Founda-tion for Devt with Equity 1998–99; Minister of Economy 1999–2001; Exec.

Sec. ECLAC 2003–. *Publications:* numerous articles in books and journals on macroeconomics, monetary and financial issues.
Address: Economic Commission for Latin America and the Caribbean, Casilla de Correo 179-D, Santiago de Chile, Chile (office). *Telephone:* (2) 471-2000 (office); (2) 210-2000 (office); (2) 208-5051 (office). *Fax:* (2) 208-0252 (office). *E-mail:* eseclac@eclac.cl (office). *Website:* www.eclac.cl (office).

MACHINGA, Gabriel Mharadze; Zimbabwean diplomatist; *Ambassador to UK;* m. Esteri Machinga. *Career:* MP 1985–2000; fmr Minister of Educ., Sport and Culture; fmr Minister of State for Nat. Affairs, Employment Creation and Co-operatives; Amb. to Canada 2001–05, to UK 2005–.
Address: Embassy of Zimbabwe, Zimbabwe House, 429 Strand, London, WC2R 0JR, England (office). *Telephone:* (20) 7836-7755 (office). *Fax:* (20) 7379-1167 (office). *E-mail:* zimlondon@yahoo.co.uk (office). *Website:* zimbabwe.embassyhomepage.com (office).

MACINA, Stefano; San Marino politician; *Secretary of State for Finance, the Budget, Post and Relations with the Azienda Autonoma di Stato Filatelica e Numismatica (AASFN);* b. 23 Jan. 1956; m.; one d. *Career:* Sec. Fed. Industry, San Marino Labour Confed. –1980, Adjunct Gen. Sec. 1981–84, Gen. Sec. 1984–91; Sec. Partito Progressista Democratico Sammarinese (PPDS) 1992–96, mem. Grand and Gen. Council 1993, Pres. Group to advise PPDS-IM 1996; Sec. of State for Econ. Planning, Foreign Trade, Social Security, Labour and Co-operation 2000–01; Pres. Comm. on Foreign Policy, Emigration and Immigration, Information, Transport and Telecommunications, Security and Public Order 2002–03; Dir Centro Commerciale 'Azzurro' 2003–06; Sec. of State for Finance, the Budget, Post and Relations with the Azienda Autonoma di Stato Filatelica e Numismatica (AASFN) 2006–; mem. several orgs and institutional comms, including Inter-parl. Group and Council of the XII; mem. Secr. Partito dei Socialisti e dei Democratici; Pres. San Marino Baseball Club.
Address: Secretariat of State for Finance, the Budget, Post and Relations with the Azienda Autonoma di Stato Filatelica e Numismatica (AASFN), Palazzo Begni, Contrada Omerelli, 47890 San Marino (office). *Telephone:* (0549) 882242 (office). *Fax:* (0549) 882244 (office). *E-mail:* segr.finanze@ omniway.sm (office). *Website:* www.finanze.sm (office).

MacINTOSH, Sarah; British diplomatist; *High Commissioner to Sierra Leone;* b. 7 Aug. 1969. *Career:* Peacekeeping Desk Officer, UN Dept, FCO 1991–93, Third Sec. (Nuclear), Perm. Mission to UN, Vienna 1994–95, Second Sec. (EU and Econ.), Madrid 1996–97, Strategic Planning Unit, FCO 1997–2000; First Sec. (Devt, Macroeconomics, Health), Perm. Mission to UN, New York 2000–02; Deputy Head of UN Dept and later Deputy Head of Conflict Issues Group, FCO 2002–04; Strategy Coordi-nator, UN Interim Admin Mission In Kosovo (UNMIK) 2004–05; High Commr to Sierra Leone 2006–.
Address: British High Commission, 6 Spur Road, Wilberforce, Freetown, Sierra Leone (office). *Telephone:* (22) 232565 (office). *Fax:* (22) 232070 (office). *E-mail:* bhc@sierratel.sl (office). *Website:* www .britishhighcommission.gov.uk/sierraleone (office).

MacKAY, Donald James, BL; New Zealand diplomatist and lawyer; *Permanent Representative and Ambassador for Disarmament, United Nations, Geneva;* b. 1948; m.; two c. *Education:* Victoria Univ. of Wellington. *Career:* solicitor and law clerk to Judges of Court of Appeal and High Court 1971–75; with Ministry of Foreign Affairs 1975–2001, positions include Head of Special Arbitration Unit, Dir of Disarmament and Int. Security Div., Amb. to Fiji and High Commr to Naura and Tuvalu 1991–95; Dir of Legal Div. 1995–96, Deputy Sec. Ministry of Foreign Affairs and Trade 1997–2001; Perm. Rep. to UN, New York 2001–05; Perm. Rep. to UN, Geneva and Amb. for Disarmament 2006–.
Address: New Zealand Permanent Mission to the Office of the United Nations in Geneva, POB 334, 1211, Geneva 19, Switzerland (office). *Telephone:* 229290350 (office). *Fax:* 229290374 (office). *E-mail:* mission .nz@itu.ch (office).

MacKAY, Peter Gordon; Canadian politician; *Minister of National Defence;* b. 27 Sept. 1965, New Glasgow, Nova Scotia. *Education:* Acadia and Dalhousie Univs. *Career:* called to the Bar, Nova Scotia 1991; Crown Attorney for Cen. Region, Nova Scotia 1993; mem. Parl. 1997–; Leader Progressive Conservative Party of Canada 2003–04; Deputy Leader Conservative Party of Canada 2004; fmr Critic for the Prime Minister, for the Solicitor Gen., for Public Security, for the Leader of the Govt in the House of Commons, for Justice, for Public Safety and Emergency Preparedness; fmr mem. Interim Cttee on Nat. Security and Intelligence; Minister of Foreign Affairs 2006–07, of Nat. Defence 2007–.
Address: Department of National Defence, National Defence Head-quarters, Maj.-Gen. George R. Pearkes Building, 101 Colonel By Drive,

Ottawa, ON K1A 0K2, Canada (office). *Telephone:* (613) 995-2534 (office). *Fax:* (613) 992-4739 (office). *Website:* www.forces.gc.ca (office).

MACKI, Ahmad bin Abd an-Nabi; Omani government official. *Career:* fmr Minister of Civil Service; currently Minister of Nat. Economy, Supervisor of Finance Ministry and Deputy Chair. Financial Affairs and Energy Resources Council.
Address: Ministry of National Economy, POB 881, Muscat 100, Oman (office). *Telephone:* 24698900 (office). *Fax:* 24698467 (office). *E-mail:* mone@omantel.net.om (office). *Website:* www.moneoman.gov.om (office).

McKIERNAN, Gen. David D., MPA; American army officer; *Commander, International Security Assistance Force (ISAF), NATO; Education:* The Coll. of William & Mary, Shippensburg Univ., Pa. *Career:* received ROTC comm., entered US Army 1972, gained experience in the Balkans as a staff officer 1990s, joined Allied Command Europe Rapid Reaction Corps (ARRC) serving as Deputy Chief of Staff G-2/G-3 forward deployed in both Sarajevo, Bosnia-Herzegovina and Rheindahlen (Mönchengladbach), Germany 1996–98, Deputy Chief of Staff, Operations, HQ, US Army, Europe and Seventh Army during period of simultaneous operations in Bosnia, Albania and Kosovo 1998–99, assigned as G-3 (Operations), HQ, Dept of the Army 2001–02, assumed command of Third US Army and US Army Forces Cen. Command (ARCENT) 2002, became Coalition Forces Land Component Commdr for US Cen. Command in preparation for Operation Iraqi Freedom, led all coalition and US conventional ground forces that attacked Iraq March 2003, assigned as Deputy Commdg Gen./ Chief of Staff for US Army Forces Command (largest major command in US Army), assumed command of 7th Army/US Army Europe, commands have included: 1st Bn, 35th Armor (Iron Knights), 1st Armored Div. 1988–90, 1st Brigade (Iron Horse), 1st Cavalry Div. 1993–95, 1st Cavalry Div. 1999–2001, 3rd US Army/Combined Forces Land Component Command 2002–04, Commdr CFLCC 2002–04, 7th US Army/US Army Europe 2005–, Commdg Gen. US Army, Europe 2004–08, Commdr Int. Security Assistance Force (ISAF), NATO 2008–; awards and decorations include Ranger Tab, Parachutist Badge, Army Achievement Medal (with Oak Leaf Cluster), Army Commendation Medal (with 3 Oak Leaf Clusters), Meritorious Service Medal (with 3 Oak Leaf Clusters), Defense Meritorious Service Medal, Bronze Star, Legion of Merit (with 2 Oak Leaf Clusters), Defense Superior Service Medal, Army Distinguished Service Medal (with Oak Leaf Cluster), Defense Distinguished Service Medal; hon. doctorate in Public Service (The Coll. of William & Mary).
Address: International Security Assistance Force (ISAF) Headquarters, Kabul, Afghanistan (office); Media Operations Center, NATO Head-quarters, Blvd Leopold III, 1110 Brussels, Belgium. *E-mail:* moc.web@hq.nato.int (office). *Website:* www.nato.int/isaf (office).

McKINLEY, Brunson, BA, MA; American diplomatist and international organization official; b. 8 Feb. 1943, Fla; m. Nancy McKinley (née Padlon); one s. one d. *Education:* Univ. of Chicago, Harvard Univ. *Career:* US Army 1965–70, with service in Viet Nam; joined diplomatic service, overseas postings include Italy, China, Vietnam, UK, Germany; Amb. to Haiti 1986–89, specialized in refugee and migration issues 1990–94, helped defuse Haitian-Cuban boat crisis 1994, developed trans-Atlantic dialogue on migration, successfully directed US participation in comprehensive action plan for Indo-Chinese refugees; US Bosnia Humanitarian Coordinator 1995–98; prin. compiler of refugee annex of Dayton Accords; Dir-Gen. Int. Org. for Migration, Geneva 1998–2008; Bronze Star, Air Medal, Award for Valor. *Publications:* numerous studies on migration subjects.
Address: c/o International Organization for Migration, 17 route des Morillons, CP 71, 1211 Geneva 19 (office); 15 Grande Rue, 1260 Nyon, Switzerland (home).

McKINLEY, P(eter) Michael, DPhil; American diplomatist; *Ambassador to Peru;* b. Venezuela; m. Fatima Salces Arce; three c. *Education:* Univ. of Oxford, UK. *Career:* grew up in Brazil, Mexico, Spain and USA; joined Foreign Service 1982, assignments have included Embassy in La Paz, Bolivia 1983–85; three tours in Dept of State, Washington, DC 1985–90; served in Embassy in London 1990–94, Deputy Chief of Mission and Chargé d'affaires a.i. at Embassies in Mozambique, Uganda and Belgium 1994–2001; Deputy Asst Sec., Bureau of Population, Refugees, and Migration, Department of State 2001–04; Deputy Chief of Mission, Perm. Mission to EU, Brussels 2004–07; Amb. to Peru 2007–. *Publication:* a history of colonial Venezuela published by Cambridge University Press as part of its Latin America series (also in Spanish edn).
Address: US Embassy, Avenida La Encalada cdra. 17 s/n, Surco, Lima 33, Peru (office). *Telephone:* (1) 4343000 (office). *Fax:* (1) 6182397 (office). *Website:* lima.usembassy.gov (office).

McKINNON, Rt Hon. Donald (Don) Charles, PC, ONZ; New Zealand politician and international organization official; b. 27 Feb. 1939; m. 1st Patricia Maude Moore 1964 (divorced 1995); three s. one d.; m. 2nd Clare de Lore 1995; one s. *Career:* fmr estate agent and farm man. consultant; Nat. Party MP for Albany 1978–; fmr Jr and Sr Govt Whip, Opposition Spokesperson for Defence and Health; Sr Opposition Whip 1984–87; Deputy Prime Minister 1990–96; Leader of the House 1993–96; Minister of Foreign Affairs and Trade, of Pacific Island Affairs, 1990–99, for Disarmament and Arms Control 1996–99; Sec.-Gen. of the Commonwealth 2000–08; Hon. DComm (Lincoln, NZ); Dr hc (four Univs of Manchester) 2002, (Heriot-Watt Univ., Edinburgh).
Address: c/o Commonwealth Secretariat, Marlborough House, Pall Mall, London, SW1Y 5HX, England. *Telephone:* (20) 7747-6103.

MacLAREN OF MacLAREN, Donald; British diplomatist; b. 22 Aug. 1954; m. Maida Jane MacLaren; three s. two d. *Career:* joined FCO 1978, with SE Asian Dept 1978–79, Second Sec., Berlin 1980–83, First Sec., Moscow 1984–87, mem. Policy Planning Staff, FCO 1987–89, Head of Section, COMED, FCO 1989–91, Deputy Head of Mission, Havana 1991–94, with Environmental Policy Dept, FCO 1995–97, Counsellor and Deputy Head of Mission, Caracas 1997–99, Deputy Head of Mission and Consul-Gen., Kiev 2000–03, Amb. to Georgia 2004–07.
Address: Foreign and Commonwealth Office, King Charles Street, London, SW1A 2AH, England (office). *Telephone:* (20) 7008-1500 (office). *Website:* www.fco.gov.uk (office).

McLEAN, Alistair Murray, BA; Australian diplomatist; *Ambassador to Japan;* b. 1947; m., two c. *Education:* Univs of Melbourne and Hong Kong. *Career:* joined Dept of Foreign Affairs 1970, Asst Sec. E Asia Br 1992–96, First Asst Sec. N Asia Div. 2001–04, Deputy Sec. 2004; overseas posts in Hong Kong 1971–73, Beijing 1973–76, Counsellor Embassy in Beijing 1979–83, in Washington, DC 1983–86, Consul-Gen. in Shanghai 1987–92, High Commr to Singapore 1997–2001, Amb. to Japan 2004–; Order of Australia Medal 1991.
Address: Embassy of Australia, 2-1-14 Mita, Minato-ku, Tokyo 108-8361, Japan (office). *Telephone:* (3) 5232-4111 (office). *Fax:* (3) 5232-4149 (office). *E-mail:* murray.mclean@dfat.gov.au (office). *Website:* www.australia.or.jp (office).

MACLEAN OF PENNYCROSS, ; Nicolas Maclean, MA, CMG; British economist; *Senior Fellow for International Affairs, International Institute for Strategic Studies (IISS);* b. 3 Jan. 1946, London; m. Qamar Sultan Aziz 22 Aug. 1978; two s. *Education:* Eton Coll., Oriel Coll., Univ. of Oxford. *Career:* fmrly with Samuel Montagu, Midland Bank Group; fmr Group Adviser, Prudential Corpn, and Exec. Dir Prudential Corpn Asia Ltd; Sr Fellow for Int. Affairs, IISS 2000–; mem. Chatham House Council, Chair. of Membership 1988–94; fmr mem. Jt Exec. British-American Project; mem. Bd UK-Korea Forum for the Future; Founder mem. UK–Japan 21st Century Group; mem. UNICE Asia Cttee, Brussels; fmr Chair. Japan Festival Educ. Trust; Founder, British English Teaching Programme, prototype of Japan Exchange and Teaching (JET) Programme; co-ordinator for sponsors, The Great Japan Exhibition, Royal Acad. of Arts; Special Adviser, Treasures from Korea, British Museum; organiser, Visions from Vietnam, Royal Coll. of Art; Special Millennium Award, Japan Soc. 2000 Fellow Emer., British Asscn of Japanese Studies 2003. *Publications:* Trading with China: A Practical Guide (jtly), Journey into Japan 1600–1868 (jtly) 1981, The Eurobond and Eurocurrency Markets (jtly) 1984, Mongolia Today (jtly) 1988; several articles.
Address: International Institute for Strategic Studies, Arundel House, 13–15 Arundel Street, Temple Place, London, WC2R 3DX, England (office). *Telephone:* (20) 7379-7676 (office). *Fax:* (20) 7836-3108 (office). *E-mail:* Maclean@iiss.org (office). *Website:* www.iiss.org (office).

McMANUS, John, BA; British diplomatist; *Ambassador to Guinea;* b. 20 May 1955, Whitehaven, Cumbria. *Education:* Frizington Whitehaven Grammar School, Univ. of Sussex. *Career:* joined FCO 1977, Southern European Dept 1977–78, Policy Planner 1978–80, posting in Paris 1980–82, Personnel Policy, FCO 1982–83, Vice-Consul, Algiers 1983–85, Security Policy, FCO 1985–87, Second Sec. (Commercial), Moscow 1988–91, Rep. to EU, Brussels 1992–93, Second, later First Sec., Information, Berne 1993–97, Head of Section, Korea Section, FCO 1997–2000, Head of Political Section, Brussels 2000–04, Amb. to Guinea 2004–.
Address: British Embassy, BP 6729, Conakry, Guinea (office). *Telephone:* 63-35-53-29 (office). *Fax:* 63-35-90-59 (office). *E-mail:* britembconakry@hotmail.com (office). *Website:* www.fco.gov.uk (office).

McMILLAN, David, BA; British civil servant and international organization executive; *Director General, EUROCONTROL; Education:* Univ. of Edinburgh. *Career:* began his career in FCO 1976, served in Morocco and Zimbabwe, also worked as Transport Sec.-Gen. at British Embassy in

Washington, DC; held several posts in Dept of Transport (DfT), including Head of Information, Leader Div. responsible for air traffic control policy 1998–2001, DfT Dir of Rail Restructuring 2001–02, Dir of Strategy and Delivery, responsible for DfT's delivery agenda and for relations with the EU 2002–04, Dir-Gen. of Civil Aviation 2004–07; Dir Gen. EUROCONTROL (European Org. for the Safety of Air Navigation) 2008–; First Vice-Pres. European Civil Aviation Conf. and spokesman for Europe on aviation and environment at Int. Civil Aviation Org. 2005–07; participated in EU's High Level Group on the future of aviation regulation in Europe 2006, 2007.
Address: c/o Ms Pauline Coady, Assistant to the Director General, EUROCONTROL, Rue de la Fusée 96, 1130 Brussels, Belgium (office). *Telephone:* (2) 729-35-01 (office). *Fax:* (2) 729-91-00 (office). *E-mail:* pauline.coady@eurocontrol.int (office). *Website:* www.eurocontrol.int (office).

McMULLEN, Ronald K., BA, MA, PhD; American diplomatist; *Ambassador to Eritrea;* b. Ia. *Education:* Drake Univ., Univ. of Minnesota, Univ. of Iowa. *Career:* served as State Dept intern in Khartoum, Sudan 1980s; Visiting Prof., US Mil. Acad., West Point 1990–93; career mem. Sr Foreign Service, joined Foreign Service in 1982, overseas assignments have included Deputy Prin. Officer, Cape Town, Econ. Officer, Libreville, Political Officer, Colombo, Vice-Consul, Santo Domingo, Deputy Chief of Mission and Chargé d'affaires a.i. in Fiji 1999–2002, Deputy Chief of Mission, Rangoon 2002–05; Assoc. Dean of Foreign Service Inst.'s School of Leadership and Man. 2005–06; Dir Office of Afghanistan and Pakistan, Bureau of Int. Narcotic and Law Enforcement Affairs 2006–07; Amb. to Eritrea 2007–; three Superior Honor Awards, Dept of State. *Publications:* author of a dozen scholarly works.
Address: US Embassy, PO Box 211, 28 Franklin D. Roosevelt Street, Asmara, Eritrea (office). *Telephone:* (1) 120004 (office). *Fax:* (1) 127584 (office). *Website:* asmara.usembassy.gov (office).

McNEE, John, MA; Canadian diplomatist; *Permanent Representative, United Nations;* m. Susan; two c. *Education:* York and Cambridge Univs. *Career:* joined Dept of External Affairs 1978, positions in Madrid, London, Tel Aviv; Amb. to Syria 1993–97, also accred to Lebanon 1993–95; positions with Policy Devt Secr., Canada–US Transboundary Div., Ottawa, fmr Dir Personnel Div., Dir Gen., Middle East, North Africa and Gulf States Bureau; fmr mem. Prime Minister Trudeau's Task Force on Int. Peace and Security, Privy Council Office; Asst Deputy Minister, Africa and Middle East, Foreign Affairs, Ottawa 2001; Amb. to Belgium, also accred to Luxembourg –2006; Perm. Rep. to UN 2006–.
Address: Office of the Permanent Representative from Canada, 1 Dag Hammarskjöld Plaza, 885 Second Avenue, 14th Floor, New York, NY 10017, USA (office). *Telephone:* (212) 848-1100 (office). *Fax:* (212) 848-1195 (office). *E-mail:* canada@un.int (office). *Website:* www.un.int/canada (office).

McRAE, Robert, BA, MA, PhD; Canadian diplomatist; *Permanent Representative, NATO;* m. Dorise Nina. *Education:* Queen's Univ., Univ. of Toronto, Laval Univ. *Career:* has taught at McGill Univ., Queen's Univ., Laval Univ., Charles Univ., Prague; fmr Dir-Gen. Int. Security Bureau, Dept of Foreign Affairs, Dir Policy Planning Staff 1995–1998, Dir-Gen. Cen., East, and South Europe Bureau 2002–03, Dir-Gen. Policy Planning Bureau 2003–06; served at Embassy in Belgrade 1982–1984, in Prague 1988–1991, in London 1993–1995; Deputy Perm. Rep. to NATO, Brussels 1998–2002, Perm. Rep. 2007–; Foreign Minister's Award for Foreign Policy Excellence 1997, 2000. *Publications:* Resistance and Revolution: Vaclav Havel's Czechoslovakia, Human Security and the New Diplomacy, The Matter with Truth, Philosophy and the Absolute.
Address: North Atlantic Treaty Organization (NATO), boulevard Léopold III, 1110 Brussels, Belgium (office). *Telephone:* (2) 707-41-11 (office). *Fax:* (2) 707-45-79 (office). *E-mail:* natodoc@hq.nato.int (office). *Website:* www.nato.int (office).

MADDEN, Paul Damian; British diplomatist; *High Commissioner to Singapore;* b. 25 April 1959; m. Sarah Madden; two s. one d. *Education:* School of Oriental and African Studies, Univ. of London. *Career:* began career at Dept for Trade and Industry 1980, Pvt. Sec. to Minister for Small Business 1984–85, to Minister for Corp. Affairs 1985–86, Head Japan Desk 1986–87; First Sec., Embassy in Tokyo 1988–92, Desk Officer, Environment, Science and Energy Dept, FCO 1992–94, EU Dept 1994–96, First Sec., Embassy in Washington, DC 1996–2000, Deputy High Commr 2000–03, Head of Public Diplomacy Policy Dept, FCO 2003–04, Man. Dir UK Trade and Investment 2004–07, High Commr to Singapore 2007–.
Address: British High Commission, 100 Tanglin Road, Singapore 247919, Singapore (office). *Telephone:* 64244200 (office). *Fax:* 64244218 (office). *E-mail:* commercial.singapore@fco.gov.uk (office). *Website:* www.britain.org.sg (office).

MADDICOTT, (David) Sydney (Syd); British diplomatist; *High Commissioner to Cameroon;* b. 27 March 1953; m. Elizabeth Maddicott; four s. one d. *Career:* with Sales/Marketing Man., Rank Xerox (UK) Ltd 1976–89; Gen. Sales and Marketing Man., Pitney Bowes (Ireland) Ltd 1989–90; postgraduate studies 1990–93; freelance consultant 1993–94; joined FCO 1994, Head of Section, Econ. Relations and UN Depts 1994–96, on secondment to Canadian Dept of Foreign Affairs and Int. Trade 1996–97, Head of Political and Information Sections, Ottawa 1997–2000, Deputy Head of Latin American and Caribbean Dept and later Head of Caribbean Team, FCO 2000–03, Sr Duty Man., Response Centre 2003–05; Amb. to Cameroon (also accred to Gabon, Chad and Cen. African Repub.) 2006–.
Address: British Embassy, Avenue Winston Churchill, BP 547, Yaoundé, Cameroon (office). *Telephone:* 222-0545 (office). *Fax:* 222-0148 (office). *E-mail:* BHC@yaounde.mail.fco.gov.uk (office). *Website:* www.britcam.org (office).

MADELIN, Alain, LenD; French politician and lawyer; b. 26 March 1946, Paris; three c. *Career:* lawyer, Paris office, Fed. nat. des Républicains indépendants (FNRI) 1968–; mem. Nat. Secr. FNRI 1977; elected Deputy to Nat. Ass. (Union pour la démocratie française— UDF) 1978–86, 1988–93, 1995–2002, 2002–07 (UMP); co-organizer UDF 1989–93; Vice-Pres. UDF 1991–96; Minister of Industry, Posts and Telecommunications and Tourism 1986–88, of Enterprise and Econ. Devt 1993–95, of Econ. and Finance May–Aug. 1995; Sec.-Gen. Republican Party 1988–89, Vice-Pres. 1989–96; Pres. France-Corée Assen 1991–93; Vice-Pres. Regional Council of Brittany 1992–98; Mayor of Redon 1995–2000; mem. European Parl. 1989–2002; Pres. Inst. Euro 92 1988–97, f., Pres. Idées Action 1993–97; Leader Démocratie libérale 1997–2002; mem. UMP 2002–; presidential cand. 2002. *Publications:* Pour libérer l'école 1984, Chers compatriotes 1994, Quand les autruches relèveront la tête 1995, Aux Sources du modèle libéral français 1997, Le Droit du plus faible 1999.
Address: c/o Union pour un Mouvement Populaire, 55 rue La Boétie, 75384 Paris Cedex 08, France (office).

MADI, Gehad Refaat; Egyptian diplomatist; *Ambassador to UK;* m. Mona Madi. *Career:* Counsellor, later Minister Plenipotentiary, Embassy in London 1992–96; Deputy Asst Foreign Minister for Int. Legal Affairs *c.* 1998; Amb. to India *c.* 2002; Deputy Asst to Foreign Minister for Human Rights 2003–04; Amb. to UK 2004–; Trustee, Islamic Cultural Centre and London Cen. Mosque.
Address: Egyptian Consulate, No. 2 Lowndes Street, London, SW1X 9ET, England (office). *E-mail:* info@egyptianconsulate.co.uk (office). *Website:* www.egyptianconsulate.co.uk (office).

MÁDL, Ferenc, PhD; Hungarian fmr head of state and lawyer; b. 29 Jan. 1931, Bánd Co. Veszprém; m. Dalma Némethy 1955; one s. *Education:* Univ. of Pécs, Eötvös Loránd Univ., Budapest and Univ. of Strasbourg, France. *Career:* worked as legal clerk and then as court sec. 1955; political and legal rapporteur, Hungarian Acad. of Sciences Cen. Office 1956–71, later promoted to head of dept and later to controlling supervisor; Docent, Dept of Civil Law, Budapest Univ. of Sciences 1971–73, Univ. Tutor 1973–, Dir Faculty of Pvt. Int. Law 1985–; mem. Inst. for Legal Sciences and State Admin, Hungarian Acad. of Sciences 1972–80; Dir Inst. of Civil Law Disciplines, Eötvös Univ., Budapest 1978–85; head Dept of the Law of Conflicts and Int. Economic Relations 1985; apptd cen. judge on Washington-based Int. Selected Court for States and Foreign Investors 1989; govt commr Bos-Nagymaros hydroelectric power plant project 1991; Minister without Portfolio 1990–93, of Culture and Educ. 1992–94; Chair. Bd Dirs State Property Agency 1990, Science Policy Cttee 1990; Supervisor State Bank Supervisory Authority 1992, Chair. Bank Supervisory Authority Cttee 1992–93; Controlling Supervisor Nat. Scientific Research Fund 1992; Chair. inter-portfolio cttee to research those works of art illegally taken to the fmr Soviet Union from Hungary during and after World War II 1992; Head, Human Resources Policy Cabinet 1992–93; Minister for Culture and Educ. 1993–94; Chair. Council for Higher Educ. and Science February–July 1994, Nat. Cultural Fund 1994; stood as opposition MDF-KDNP-Fidesz's presidential cand. 1995; Chair. Hungarian Civil Cooperation Assen 1996–; mem. Scientific Advisory Body for the Viktor Orbán govt 1999; Pres. of Hungary 2000–05; Corresp. mem. Hungarian Acad. of Sciences 1987–93, mem. 1993–; mem. Int. Acad. of Commercial Law, Harvard 1985–, Governing Council Rome Int. Inst. (UNIDROIT) 1988–; mem. European Acad. of Sciences and Art 1989–, European Acad. of Sciences 1990–, Inst. of Int. Law 1991–; Chevalier de la Légion d'honneur 1999; Széchenyi Prize 1999. *Publications:* author of 20 books on law of int. econ. relations, int. investment law, EEC law, etc. and about 200 law review articles.
Address: Egyetem tér 1-3, 1364 Budapest, Hungary. *Telephone:* (1) 266-6486.

MADUEKWE, Chief Ojo; Nigerian politician; *Minister of Foreign Affairs;* b. 6 May 1945, Abia State. *Education:* Univ. of Nigeria. *Career:* called to Nigerian Bar 1973; mem. House of Reps 1983, Constituent Ass. 1988; Adviser to Minister of Foreign Affairs 1993–95; mem. Nat. Constituent Conf. 1994–95; Tech. Adviser to Vision 2010 Cttee 1997; elected Senator 1998; Minister of Culture and Tourism 1999–2000, of Transport 2000–03; Legal Adviser to the Pres. 2003–05; Minister of Foreign Affairs 2007–; Nat. Sec. People's Democratic Party (PDP).
Address: Ministry of Foreign Affairs, Maputo St, Zone 3, Wuse District, PMB 130, Abuja, Nigeria (office). *Telephone:* (9) 5230570 (office). *Website:* www.mfa.gov.ng (office).

MADUNA, Penuell Mpapa, LLD; South African politician and lawyer; b. 29 Dec. 1952; m. Nompumelelo Cheryl Maduna; three c. *Education:* Univ. of Zimbabwe, Univ. of Witwatersrand. *Career:* worked in underground structures of ANC in 1970s, twice incarcerated and prosecuted; left SA 1980; fmr Regional Admin. Sec. Tanzania, Office of Treasurer-Gen. of ANC; fmr staff mem. and Legal Adviser, ANC HQ Lusaka, est. Dept of Legal and Constitutional Affairs 1985, founder mem. Constitutional Cttee, participated in meetings with South African Govt and officials in 1980s and early 1990s leading to establishment of Convention for a Democratic South Africa, mem. Negotiating Comm., now mem. Nat. Exec. Cttee; MP Nat. Ass.; Minister of Mineral and Energy Affairs 1996–99, of Justice and Constitutional Devt 1999–2004; Bd mem. Faculty of Law, Univ. of Witwatersrand 1996–. *Publication:* Fundamental Rights in the New Constitution 1994 (co-author).
Address: c/o Ministry of Justice and Constitutional Development, Presidia Building, 8th Floor, corner Pretorius and Paul Kruger Streets, Pretoria 0002, South Africa (office).

MADURO MOROS, Nicolás; Venezuelan politician; *Minister of Foreign Affairs;* b. 23 Nov. 1961, Caracas; m. Cilia Flores; two c. *Career:* worker on Caracas metro and founder of trade union for Caracas metro workers 1980s; also mem. Movimiento Bolivariano Revolucionario 200 1980s, mem. Nat. Directorate 1994–97; Founding mem. Movimiento Quinta Republica 200 (MVR) 1997, elected to Asamblea Nacional 1998, Pres. of Citizens' Participation Cttee 1999, Co-ordinator of MVR parl. team 2000–01, Co-ordinator of majority bloc parl. team 2001–05, Pres. Asamblea Nacional 2005–06; Minister of Foreign Affairs 2006–.
Address: Ministry of Foreign Affairs, Torre MRE, esq. Carmelitas, Avda Urdaneta, Caracas 1010, Venezuela (office). *Telephone:* (212) 862-1085 (office). *Fax:* (212) 864-3633 (office). *E-mail:* criptogr@mre.gov.ve (office). *Website:* www.mre.gov.ve (office).

MAEIKIS, Brig.-Gen. Edvardas, MSc; Lithuanian military officer; *Military Representative, NATO;* b. 18 Nov. 1961, Papile; m. Aukse Maeikis; three d. *Education:* Cernigov Mil. Pilot Acad., Ukraine, Bundeswehr Command and Staff Coll., Germany, Nat. Defense Univ., USA. *Career:* served as fighter pilot, flight leader and Deputy Squadron Commdr, Soviet Air Force 22nd Fighter Regt 1983–91; Deputy Chief, Planning Section, Lithuanian Air Force 1992–95, Chief, Operational Dept 1995–97, Commanding Officer, Siauliai Air Base 1997–2000, promoted to Col 2000, Commdr of Air Force 2000–04, promoted to Brig.-Gen. 2004; Mil. Rep. to NATO and EU 2004–; Darius ir Girenas Medal, Armed Forces Medal, Land Forces Medal, Air Force Steel Wings, Latvian Air Force Hon. Medal.
Address: Lithuanian Delegation, NATO Headquarters, Bld Léopold III, Brussels 1110, Belgium (office). *Telephone:* (2) 707-28-49 (office). *Fax:* (2) 707-28-50 (office). *E-mail:* delegation@ltunato.org (office). *Website:* www.nato.int (office).

MAEMA, Lebohang Fine, KC, LLM, LLB, BA; Lesotho diplomatist and lawyer; *Permanent Representative, United Nations;* b. 22 July 1957, Masery; three d. *Education:* Nat. Univ. of Lesotho, Univ. of Cambridge, England. *Career:* fmr mem. of Bd Cen. Bank of Lesotho; fmr Pres. Matlama Football Club; worked at Nat. Univ. of Lesotho; Crown Counsel, Attorney-Gen.'s Chambers 1982–83; Lecturer-in-Law, Nat. Univ. of Lesotho 1984–87; Deputy Pvt. Sec. to King of Lesotho, Royal Palace 1987–89, Pvt. Sec. 1989–90; Prin. Sec., Ministry of Justice and Prisons 1990–93; Attorney-Gen. 1993–2005; Perm. Rep. to UN, New York 2005–; Commdr of the Most Meritorious Order of Mohlomi; Cambridge Livingstone Scholar 1983.
Address: Office of the Permanent Representative of Lesotho to the United Nations, 204 East 39th Street, New York, NY 10016, USA (office). *Telephone:* (212) 661-1690 (office). *Fax:* (212) 682-4388 (office). *E-mail:* prlesotho@un.int (office). *Website:* www.un.int/lesotho (office).

MAGANDE, Ng'andu Peter, BA, MSc; Zambian diplomatist, business executive and farmer; *Minister of Finance and National Planning;* b. 5 July 1947, Namaila, Mazabuka; m.; three d. two s. *Education:* Univ. of Zambia, Makerere Univ., Uganda. *Career:* joined Civil Service 1971; apptd

Dir of Budget, Ministry of Finance 1981; Perm. Sec. various depts 1983–94; Man. Dir Zambia Nat. Commercial Bank, Lima Bank; Exec. Dir Industrial Devt Corpn, Zambia Industrial and Mining Corpn 1986–94; technical assistance consultant to Govt 1994; Sec.-Gen. African, Caribbean and Pacific Secr. 1996–; Minister of Finance and Nat. Planning 2003–; Commdr of the Order of the Repub. of Benin; Best Commercial Tobacco Farmer 1989.
Address: Ministry of Finance and National Planning, Finance Building, POB 50062, Lusaka, Zambia (office). *Telephone:* (1) 253512 (office). *Fax:* (1) 251078 (office). *Website:* www.finance.gov.zm (office).

MAGARIÑOS, Carlos Alfredo, MBA; Argentine international civil servant; b. 16 Aug. 1962, Buenos Aires. *Education:* Nat. Univ. of Buenos Aires, Int. Devt Law Inst., Italy, Wharton School, Univ. of Pennsylvania. *Career:* analyst, Office of Strategic Planning and Foreign Trade, Banco Ciudad de Buenos Aires 1984–86; joined Ministry of Economy 1992, Under-Sec. of State for Industry 1992–93, Sec. of State for Mining and Industry 1993–96; Econ. and Trade Rep. of Argentina, Washington, DC, USA 1996–97; rank of Amb. 1996; Dir-Gen. UNIDO 1997–2005 (re-elected 2001); Order of San Carlos, Colombia 2000, Order of Quetzal, Guatemala 2001, Order of Merit, Gov. of Italy 2003, Order of Industrial Merit, Gov. of Colombia 2004; Dr hc (Lomonosov, Moscow) 1999, (Econ. Sciences and Public Admin., Budapest) 2000, (Social and Business Sciences, Buenos Aires) 2001, Doctor hc, Nat. Tech. University of Ukraine 2002; Trophée des performances de l'année 2000, Inst. Supérieur de Gestion, Paris 2000, Peter the Great Int. Award, Russian Fed. 2002, Prix de la Fondation 2002, Crans Montana Forum, Monte Carlo 2002, Kennedy Cross, John F. Kennedy Univ. Argentina 2004, Priyadarshni Acad. Award, India 2004. *Publications:* El Rol del Estado en la Política Industrial de los 90 1995, China in the WTO: The Birth of a New Catching-Up Strategy 2002; articles on econ. and industrial issues: Gearing Up for a New Development Agenda 2000, Reforming the UN System: UNIDO's Need-Driven Model 2001, Updating and Fleshing Out the Development Agenda 2003, Economic Development and UN Reform: Towards a Common Agenda for Action 2005.
Address: c/o United Nations Industrial Development Organization (UNIDO), Vienna International Centre, PO Box 300, 1400 Vienna, Austria (office).

MAGASSOUBA, Mahamadou; Malian diplomatist and magistrate; *Ambassador to Algeria;* b. 6 June 1954, Nioro du Sahel; m.; four c. *Education:* Lycée bada la bisugou, Ecole Nationale d'Admin, Centre Nat. de Formation des Magistrats, Poko, Ecole Nat. de la Magistrarie. *Career:* fmr Gen. Sec., Deputy Sec.-Gen., Office of Pres.; Legal Counsellor to Pres. of Mali 2001; currently Amb. to Algeria; examining magistrate, Pres., Tribunal Commune I and VI, Bamako; Chevalier, Ordre nat. du Mérite. *Publications:* L'Importance de la Coopération Régionale dans les Efforts de Lutte contre la Corruption (IXeme Conference Internationale, Durban) 1999, Rôle des Gouvernements dans la mise en oeuvre effective des Instruments et Internationaux de Coopération (Xeme Conference Internationale Lutte contre Corruption, Prague) 2001.
Address: Embassy of Mali, Villa 15, Cité DNC/ANP, chemin Ahmed Kara, Hydra, Algiers (office); BP 05, Poir Mourad Raïs, 16300, Algeria (office). *Telephone:* (21) 69-13-51 (office). *Fax:* (21) 69-20-82 (office).

MAGIGWANE SHOPE, Lenin; South African diplomatist; *Ambassador to Italy;* b. March 1962, Johannesburg; m.; three c. *Education:* José Antonio Echeverr'a Sr Polytechnic Inst., Cuba. *Career:* Head, Tech. Unit, ANC Dept of Educ., Zambia 1989–91; Analyst Programmer, South African Airways 1992–93, Engun Petroleum Ltd 1993–95; joined Dept of Foreign Affairs 1995, First Sec., then Counsellor, Embassy in Havana 1996–99, Chargé d'Affaires 1999–2000; Dir Latin America Bureau, Ministry of Foreign Affairs 2000–02; Amb. to Cuba (also accred to Dominican Repub.) 2002–03, to Italy (also accred to Malta) 2003–, also Perm. Rep. to FAO.
Address: Embassy of South Africa, Via Tanaro 14, 00198 Rome, Italy (office). *Telephone:* (06) 852541 (office). *Fax:* (06) 85254301 (office). *E-mail:* sae2@sudafrica.it (office). *Website:* www.sudafrica.it (office).

MAGYAR, Bálint; Hungarian sociologist and politician; *State Secretary for Development Policy, Prime Minister's Office;* b. 1952, Budapest; m. Róza Hodosán; one d. *Education:* Eötvös Loránd Univ. of Budapest. *Career:* Research Fellow, Inst. of World Econ., Hungarian Acad. of Sciences 1977–81, Inst. of Co-operation 1982–88; Financial Research Ltd 1988–90; involved in dissident political activities from 1979; Founding mem. Alliance of Free Democrats (SZDSZ), Pres. 1998–2000, mem. Exec. Bd 2001–; mem. Parl. 1990–; Minister of Culture and Educ. 1996–98, of Educ. 2002–06; State Sec. for Devt Policy, Prime Minister's Office 2007–; János Neumann Prize 1998. *Film:* Dir Hungarian Stories (documentary) (Special Prize, Critics' Prize, Budapest Film Festival 1988). *Publication:* Dunaapáti 1944–1958 (sociography of a Hungarian village, three vols) (Ferenc Erdei Prize 1986).

Address: National Development Agency, Mozsár u. 16, 1066 Budapest (office); SZDSZ, Gizella u. 36, 1143 Budapest, Hungary. *Telephone:* (1) 472-2930 (office). *Fax:* (1) 472-2932 (office). *E-mail:* magyar.balint@meh.hu (office). *Website:* www.meh.hu (office).

MAHA VAJIRALONGKORN, HRH Crown Prince, BA, LLB; Thai; b. 28 July 1952, Bangkok; m. 1st Mom Luang Soamsawali Kitiyakara 1977 (divorced); one d.; fmr pnr Yuvadhida Polpraserth; four s. one d.; m. 2nd Mom Srirasmi Mahidol na Ayudhya (HRH Princess Srirasmi, The Royal Consort) 2001; one s. *Education:* Royal Military Coll. Duntroon and Univ. of New South Wales, Australia, Royal Thai Army Command and Gen. Staff Coll., Sukhothai Thammatirat Univ., Bangkok, Royal Coll. of Defence Studies, UK. *Career:* conferred title Somdech Phra Boroma Orasadhiraj Chao Fah Maha Vajiralongkorn Sayam Makutrajakuman (heir to the throne) 28 Dec. 1972; Staff Officer Directorate of Army Intelligence 1975–78, Exec. Officer King's Own Bodyguard 1978–80, Commdr 1980–84, Commanding Officer 1984–88, Commanding Gen. 1988–92, Commanding Gen. Royalty Security Command, Office of the Supreme Commander 1992–, Instructor Pilot F-5 E/F fighter 1994, holds ranks of Gen. of the Royal Thai Army, Adm. of the Royal Thai Navy, Air Chief Marshal of the Royal Thai Air Force.
Address: c/o The Government Public Relations Department, Rama VI Road, Bangkok, Thailand (office). *Telephone:* 618-2373 (office). *Fax:* 618-2358 (office). *Website:* www.thaimain.org.

MAHAMA, Alhaji Aliu, BSc; Ghanaian politician; *Vice-President;* b. 3 March 1946, Yendi. *Education:* Govt Secondary School, Tamale, Kwame Nkrumah Univ. of Science and Tech., Kumasi, Inst. in Project Planning and Man. and in Leadership. *Career:* construction engineer, Bolgatanga Regional Office, State Construction Corpn 1972–75, Asst Regional Man., Koforidua Regional Office 1975–76, Regional Man. in charge of Northern Region 1976–82; Founder and Man. Dir LIDRA Ltd 1982–; Councillor, Yendi Dist Council 1978; mem. Tamale Municipal Assembly 1990; fmr Minister of Defence; Vice-Pres. of Ghana 2001–; Chair. Northern Regional Contractors' Asscn 1996–2000; fmr Chair. Econ. Devt Cttee, Tamale-Louisville Sister State Cttee; fmr Bd mem. several secondary schools in Northern Region including Tamale Polytechnic; alumnus, Ghana Inst. of Man. and Public Admin; Founding mem. Real Tamale United Football Club; Fellow Inst. of Surveyors, Fellow Inst. of Administrators.
Address: c/o Office of the President, POB 1627, Osu, Accra, Ghana (office). *Telephone:* 665415 (office). *Fax:* 663044 (office).

MAHAT, Ram Sharan, MA, PhD; Nepalese politician; *Interim Minister of Finance;* b. 1 Jan. 1951, Nuwakot; m. Roshana Mahat; one s. one d. *Education:* Tribhuban Univ., Gokhale Inst. of Politics and Econs, Pune, India, School of Int. Service, American Univ. *Career:* Asst Resident Rep. UNDP, Islamabad 1989–90; econ. adviser to Prime Minister of Nepal 1991–92; Vice-Chair. Nat. Planning Comm. 1991–94; MP from Nuwakot Dist 1994–; Minister of Finance 1995–99, 2001, 2006–07, currently Interim Minister of Finance; Minister of Foreign Affairs 1999. *Publications:* Industrial Financing in Nepal, numerous articles on nat. and int. econ. issues.
Address: Ministry of Finance, POB 12845, Kathmandu (office); Bansbari, Kathmandu, Nepal (home). *Telephone:* 4259837 (office); (1) 373132 (home). *Fax:* (1) 372356 (home). *Website:* www.mof.gov.np (office).

MAHATHIR BIN MOHAMAD; Malaysian politician (retd); b. 20 Dec. 1925, Alur Setar, Kedah; m. Dr Siti Hasmah binti Haji Mohd Ali 1956; three s. two d. *Education:* Sultan Abdul Hamid Coll. and Univ. of Malaya in Singapore. *Career:* Medical Officer, Kedah, Langkawi and Perlis 1953–57; private practice 1957–64; mem. UMNO (now Umno Baru) Supreme Council 1965–69, 1972–2008 (Pres. 1981), mem. Supreme Council 1972–2008; mem. House of Reps. for Kota Setar Selatan 1964–69, for Kubang Pasu 1974–; mem. Senate 1973; Chair. Food Industries of Malaysia Sdn. Bhd. 1973; Minister of Educ. 1974–77, of Trade and Industry 1977–81, of Defence 1981–86, of Home Affairs 1986–99, of Justice 1987, of Natural and Rural Devt; Deputy Prime Minister 1976–81, Prime Minister of Malaysia 1981–2003; Advisor, Petronas, Proton 2003–. *Publication:* The Malay Dilemma 1969, The Way Forward 1998.
Address: c/o Petroliam Nasional Berhad (PETRONAS), Tower 1, Petronas Twin Towers, Kuala Lumpur City Centre, 50088 Kuala Lumpur, Malaysia (office). *E-mail:* webmaster@petronas.com.my (office). *Website:* www.petronas.com.my (office).

MAHAYNI, Mohammad Khaled al-, PhD; Syrian politician and economist; b. 30 May 1943, Damascus; m. Falak Sakkal 1966; two s. two d. *Education:* Damascus Univ. *Career:* various public financial and econ. appointments 1961–70; auditor 1970–77; Dir of Debt Fund and Information, Ministry of Finance 1979–80, of Public Enterprises 1981–84; Deputy Minister of Finance 1984–87, Minister 1987–2001; Gov. IBRD 1987–2001, Arab Bank

for Econ. Devt in Africa 1989–; Prof. Damascus Univ. 1992–. *Publications:* Methodology of the General Budget of the State in the Syrian Arab Republic 1984, Supplementary Policies for Financial Planning 1995, Government Accounting 1996, Public Finance and Tax Legislation 1999.
Address: c/o Ministry of Finance, P.O. Box 13136, Jule Jamal Street, Damascus, Syria.

MAHBUBANI, Kishore; Singaporean diplomatist, university administrator and author; *Professor in the Practice of Public Policy and Dean, Lee Kuan School of Public Policy, National University of Singapore;* b. 24 Oct. 1948, Singapore; m. Anne King Markey 1985; two s. one d. *Education:* Univ. of Singapore and Dalhousie Univ., Canada. *Career:* joined Ministry of Foreign Affairs 1971, Deputy Dir 1979–82, Deputy Sec. 1989–93, Perm. Sec. 1993–; Chargé d'affaires to Cambodia 1973–74; Counsellor at Singapore Embassy in Malaysia 1976–79; mem. of Singapore dels to several sessions of UN Gen. Ass. and int. confs 1979–83; Deputy Chief at Washington, DC Embassy 1982–84; Perm. Rep. to UN, New York (concurrently High Commr in Canada and Amb. to Mexico) 1984–89, Perm. Rep. to UN 1998–2004; Dean, Civil Service Coll. 1993–96; Prof. in the Practice of Public Policy and Dean, Lee Kuan Yew School of Public Policy, Nat. Univ. of Singapore 2004–; Public Administration Medal (Gold), Singapore Govt 1998, Foreign Policy Asscn Medal 2004, Dr Jean Mayer Global Citizenship Award, Inst. for Global Leadership, Tufts Univ. 2003–04, ranked by Foreign Policy and Prospect magazines amongst Top 100 Public Intellectuals in the World 2005. *Publications:* Can Asians Think? 2002, Beyond The Age of Innocence: Rebuilding Trust between America and the World 2005; contrib. of articles to journals and newspapers, including Foreign Affairs, Foreign Policy, Washington Quarterly, Survival, American Interest, National Interest, Time, Newsweek and New York Times.
Address: Lee Kuan Yew School of Public Policy, National University of Singapore, Oei Tiong Ham Building, 469C Bukit Timah Road, Singapore 259772 (office). *Telephone:* 65166134 (office). *Fax:* 67781020 (office). *E-mail:* sppdean@nus.edu.sg (office); Kishore.Mahbubani@mahbubani.net (home). *Website:* www.spp.nus.edu.sg (office); www.mahbubani.net (home).

MAHDI, Adil Abd al-, PhD; Iraqi politician and economist; *Vice-President;* b. 1942, Baghhad; m.; four c. *Career:* moved to France 1969, worked for several think tanks; has also lived in Lebanon and Iran; returned to Iraq; interim Minister of Finance –2005; Vice-Pres. of Iraq 2005–; mem. Supreme Council for the Islamic Revolution in Iraq.
Address: c/o Office of the President, Baghdad, Iraq.

MAHER ES-SAYED, Ahmad, LLB; Egyptian politician; b. 14 Sept. 1935, Cairo; m. *Education:* Cairo Univ. *Career:* served in embassies in Cairo, Kinshasa, Paris, Zürich 1959–77; Amb. to Portugal 1980–82, to Belgium 1982–84, to USSR 1988–92, to USA 1992–99; Dir Arab Fund for Tech. Assistance to African States, League of Arab States 2000–01; Minister of Foreign Affairs 2001–04 (resgnd); Order of the Repub. First Class (Egypt), Order of Merit Commdr Class (France), Order of the Great Cross (Portugal).
Address: c/o Ministry of Foreign Affairs, Corniche en-Nil, Cairo, Egypt (office).

MAHIGA, Augustine Philip, BA, MA, PhD; Tanzanian diplomatist; *Permanent Representative, United Nations;* b. 28 Aug. 1945; m. *Education:* Univ. of East Africa, Dar-es-Salaam, Univ. of Toronto, Canada. *Career:* Sr Lecturer in Int. Affairs and Regional Co-operation, Univ. of Dar-es-Salaam 1975–77; Dir of Research and Training, Office of the Pres. of Tanzania 1977–80, Acting Dir Gen. Office of the Pres. 198–83; High Commr to Canada 1983–89; Perm Rep to UN, Geneva 1989–92; on secondment to UNHCR 1993, UNHCR Chief of Mission, Monrovia, Liberia 1992–94, Deputy Dir and Co-ordinator Great Lakes Region of Africa Refugee Emergency Operation, Geneva 1994–98, UNHCR Chief of Mission, New Delhi 1998–2002, UNHCR Rep. to Italy (also accred to Malta and San Marino) 2002–03; Perm. Rep. to UN, New York 2003–, mem. Security Council 2005, also Asst Sec.-Gen. for Peacebuilding Support for UN Peacebuilding Comm.; Lifetime Achievement Award, Miracle Corners of the World 2007.
Address: Permanent Mission of Tanzania to the UN, 201 East 42nd Street, 17th Floor, New York, NY 10017, USA (office). *Telephone:* (212) 972-9160 (office). *Fax:* (212) 682-5232 (office). *E-mail:* tzrepny@aol.com (office).

MAHKAMOV, Farhod; Tajikistan agronomist and diplomatist. *Career:* transferred from USSR mil. to diplomatic service 1981; served at USSR Embassy in Kabul 1981–87, at USSR Gen. Consulate in Mazar-i-Sharif 1987–89; mem. of staff, Tajikstan Embassy in Tashkent –2002; Amb. to Afghanistan 2002–; State Medal of Sayed Jamaluddin Afghan 2008.

Address: Embassy of Tajikistan, House 41, St 10, Wazir Akbar Khan, Kabul, Afghanistan (office). *Telephone:* (20) 2101080 (office). *Fax:* (20) 2300392 (office). *E-mail:* kabultj@tojikistan.com (office).

MAHMOUD, Ali Abdullah al-; Qatari diplomatist. *Career:* currently Amb. to Saudi Arabia.
Address: Embassy of Qatar, POB 94353, Riyadh 11461, Saudi Arabia (office). *Telephone:* (1) 482-5544 (office). *Fax:* (1) 482-5394 (office).

MAHMUDI, Al-Baghdadi Ali al-; Libyan politician; *General Secretary, General People's Committee; Career:* fmr Sec., Gen. People's Cttee for Health and Social Security; Deputy Prime Minister responsible for production –2006, Gen. Sec., Gen. People's Cttee (Prime Minister) 2006–. *Address:* General People's Committee, Tripoli, Libya.

MAIGA, Ousmane Issoufi; Malian politician. *Career:* Minister of Finance 2002–03; Minister of Equipment and Transport 2003–04; Prime Minister of Mali 2004–07.
Address: c/o Office of the Prime Minister, quartier du Fleuve, BP 790, Bamako, Mali (office).

MAJEED, Gen. Tariq, MA; Pakistani army officer; *Chairman, Joint Chiefs of Staff Committee;* b. Aug. 1950, Lahore. *Education:* Command and Staff Coll., Quetta, Malaysian Armed Forces Staff Coll., Kuala Lumpur, Asia-Pacific Center for Security Studies, Honolulu, Hawaii, Nat. Defence Coll., Islamabad. *Career:* commissioned in Pakistan Army (Infantry, Baloch Regt) 1971, has commanded Light Anti-Tank Unit and an Infantry Bn, two Infantry Brigades, Infantry Div., participated in Indo-Pakistan War 1971, took part, as GOC Lahore in absence of Corps Commdr, in counter-coup launched by army high command against then govt of Mian Nawaz Sharif Oct. 1999, also led mil. operation on Jamia Hafsa, Dir Gen. Mil. Intelligence 2001–03, promoted to Lt-Gen. Dec. 2003, Chief of Gen. Staff 2003–06, Commdr 10 Corps, Rawalpindi 2006–07, in charge of armed forces who took down armed militias stationed inside mosque at Lal Masjid Siege 2007, promoted to four-star Gen. Oct. 2007, Chair. Jt Chiefs of Staff Cttee Oct. 2007–; Hilal-e-Imtiaz (Mil.), Nishan-e-Imtiaz (Mil.).
Address: Joint Chiefs of Staff Committee, Joint Staff Headquarters, Chaklala, Rawalpindi, Pakistan (office).

MAJINDA, Naomi Ellen, BA; Botswana diplomatist; *Ambassador to People's Republic of China;* b. 10 June 1957; m.; two c. *Education:* Univ. of Botswana. *Career:* joined Dept of Foreign Affairs 1982; Third Sec., High Comm. in London 1982–85, Second Sec. 1985–86; served on S Africa Desk 1986–90; First Sec., Embassy in Washington, DC 1990–93; Counsellor, High Comm. in Lusaka, Zambia 1993–94; Deputy Chief of Protocol 1994; Counsellor, Embassy in Washington, DC 1998–2000; Amb. to Sweden (also accred to Norway, Finland, Denmark, Iceland, Russian Fed.) 2000–05, to People's Repub. of China (also accred to S Korea, N Korea, Malaysia, Pakistan, Singapore) 2005–.
Address: Embassy of Botswana, Unit 811, IBM Tower, Pacific Century Place, 2A Gong Ti Bei Lu, Beijing 100027, People's Republic of China (office). *Telephone:* (10) 65391616 (office). *Fax:* (10) 65391199 (office).

MAJKO, Pandeli Sotir, LLB; Albanian politician; *Secretary General, Socialist Party of Albania;* b. 15 Nov. 1967; m. Enkeleida Majko; one s., one d. *Education:* Univ. of Tirana. *Career:* Rep. Dec. 1990 Movt; co-f. Democratic Party 1990, left party 1991; Jt Socialist Party of Albania 1991, Sec.-Gen. of Public Relations 1996–97, Sec. 1997–99, also leader of Parl. Group, Head of Del. to OSCE; Prime Minister of Albania 1998–99, Feb.–July 2002; Minister of Defence 2002–05; currently Sec. Gen., Socialist Party of Albania; f. Forum of Euro-Socialist Youth 1991; Chair. Euro-Socialist Forum 1992–95; mem. Parl. 1992–; Torch of Democracy Award 1993. .
Telephone: (4) 227409 (office); (42) 251299 (home). *Fax:* (4) 227417 (office). *E-mail:* pandelimajko@hotmail.com (home). *Website:* www.ps-al.org (office).

MAJOOR, Franciscus (Frank) Antonius Maria, MCL; Dutch diplomatist; *Permanent Representative, United Nations;* b. 1 April 1949; m.; two c. *Education:* Univ. of Leiden, Inst. for Int. Relations, The Hague. *Career:* served in Dutch embassies in Dar es Salaam 1977–79, Bonn 1979–82; Head of Environmental Affairs Section, Econ. Cooperation Dept, Ministry of Foreign Affairs 1982–85; Asst to Dir Gen. of Political Affairs 1985–86; Special Advisor on Political Security Matters, Deputy Dir of Atlantic Cooperation and Security Affairs Dept 1992–93; Dir of Security Policy Dept 1993–97; Amb.-at-Large 1999–2000; Sec. Gen. 2000–05; First Sec. (Political Matters), Perm. Mission to UN, New York 1986–88, Minister Plenipotentiary (Econ. and Financial Matters) 1988–92; Amb. to Conf. on Disarmament, Geneva 1997–99; Perm. Rep. to UN, New York 2005–.

Address: Office of the Permanent Representative of the Netherlands to the United Nations, 235 East 45th Street, 16th Floor, New York, NY 10017, USA (office). *Telephone:* (212) 519-9612 (office). *Fax:* (212) 370-1954 (office). *E-mail:* nyv@minbuza.nl (office). *Website:* www.pvnewyork.org (office).

MAJOR, Air Chief Marshal Fali Homi; Indian air force officer; *Chief of the Air Staff;* b. 29 May 1947, Secunderabad; m. Zareen Major; one s. one d. *Education:* Wesley High School, Secunderabad, Nat. Defence Coll., Army War Coll. *Career:* commissioned in Indian Air Force (IAF) 1967, has flown over 7,000 hours on Sentinel, T-6G, Mi-4, Mi-8 and Mi-17 helicopters, as Wing Commdr, commanded IAF's first Mi-17 Squadron, which operated at Siachen Glacier (world's highest battlefield), as Group Capt., commanded another Mi-17 Squadron, leading it during operations of Indian Peace Keeping Force in Sri Lanka, as Station Commdr of Air Force Station Sarsawa, led rescue of 11 passengers from stranded cable car at resort in Himachal Pradesh, has held several important staff and field appointments, including Jt Dir (Helicopter Operations) and Dir Operations (Transport & Helicopter), Air Officer Commdg Leh (Ladakh) following Kargil conflict 1999, promoted to rank of Air Vice-Marshal 2002, Asst Chief of the Air Staff (Personnel Airmen & Civilians) at Air HQ 2002–04, promoted to rank of Air Marshal 2004, Deputy Chief of Integrated Defence Staff (Operations), HQ Integrated Defence Staff 2004–05, directed relief, rescue and rehabilitation operations of Indian Armed Forces in India and abroad in aftermath of tsunami of Dec. 2004, Air Officer C-in-C Eastern Air Command 2005–07, Chief of the Air Staff 2007–; Vayu Sena Medal (Gallantry), Shaurya Chakra for gallantry, Ati Vishist Seva Medal 2002, Param Vishisht Seva Medal 2006.
Address: Public Relations Officer, Indian Air Force, Directorate of Public Relations, Ministry of Defence, Room No. 91, South Block, New Delhi, 110 011, India (office). *Telephone:* (11) 23019745 (office); (11) 23010231 (ext. 6903) (office). *E-mail:* pro_iaf2006@yahoo.co.in (office). *Website:* indianairforce.nic.in (office).

MAKALIMA, Mlungisi, BA, MA; South African academic and diplomatist; *Ambassador to Zimbabwe;* b. 30 May 1948, Ntabankulu, Eastern Cape. *Education:* Univ. of S Africa, Univ. of Fort Hare, State Univ. of New York, Binghampton, USA, Univ. of York, UK. *Career:* Lecturer, Univ. of Fort Hare 1972–96; Dir Dept of Transport 1996–98; Perm. Sec., Welfare Dept, Eastern Cape 1998–2001; Amb. to Argentina (also accred to Paraguay and Uruguay) 2001–05, to Zimbabwe 2005–; Founding mem. Nat. Inst. for Econ. Policy.
Address: Embassy of South Africa, 7 Elcombe Road, Belgravia, POB A1654, Harare, Zimbabwe (office). *Telephone:* (4) 753147 (office). *Fax:* (4) 749657 (office). *E-mail:* admin@saembassy.co.zw (office).

MAKARCZYK, Jerzy, LLD; Polish judge and professor of law; *Professor of Legal Sciences, Polish Academy of Sciences;* b. 24 July 1938. *Education:* Warsaw Univ. and Inst. of Legal Sciences, Polish Acad. of Sciences. *Career:* Assoc. Prof. of Int. Public Law 1975, Prof. 1988; Deputy Dir Inst. of Legal Sciences, Polish Acad. of Sciences 1981–88, Prof. 1992–; Deputy Minister of Foreign Affairs 1989–90; Sec. of State, Ministry of Foreign Affairs 1990–92; in charge of negotiations with USSR and then Russia on withdrawal of troops from Polish territory 1990–2002; Judge, European Court of Human Rights 1992–; mem. ILO High Level Team to Myanmar 2001–; Adviser to Pres. of Repub. of Poland 2002–; Pres. Int. Law Asscn 1988–90; mem. Inst de Droit Int. 1993, Pres. 2003–; nominated cand.-judge to European Communities Court of Justice 2004; Commdr Légion d'honneur; Manfred Lachs Foundation Award 1998. *Publications:* Financing of Economic Development in the United Nations System 1974, Principles of a New International Economic Order 1988; ed. Collection of Essays in Honour of Judge Manfred Lachs 1984, Theory of International Law at the Threshold of the XXIst Century (ed.) 1996.
Address: Al. Przyjaciol 3 m. 14, 00-565 Warsaw, Poland. *Telephone:* (22) 6769135. *Fax:* (22) 6429540. *E-mail:* jmakarczyk@prezydent.pl.

MAKAROV, Valery Leonidovich, PhD; Russian economist; *Director, Central Economics and Mathematics Institute, Russian Academy of Sciences;* b. 25 May 1937, Novosibirsk; m. Irena Nikolaev 1961; one s. one d. *Education:* Moscow Econ. Inst. *Career:* scientific worker, Inst. of Math., Siberian Div. USSR Acad. of Sciences 1961–67, Lab. Chief 1967–73, Deputy Dir 1973–80, Gen. Sec. Siberian Div. 1980–83; Prof. of Mathematical Econs Novosibirsk Univ. 1970–83; Dir Nat. Inst. of Industrial Man., Moscow 1983–85; Dir Central Econs and Math. Inst. 1985–; Prof. at Moscow Univ.; Founder and Rector, New Econ. School, Moscow 1992–; Ed.-in-Chief, Journal of Math. and Econ. Methods.; mem. Ed. Bd Econs of Planning, Econs of Transition, Econ. Systems Research; mem. Exec. Cttee, Int. Econ. Asscn 1995–; mem. several govt comms; Corresp. mem. USSR (now Russian) Acad. of Science 1979, mem. 1990; Fellow Econometric Soc.; Kantorovich Award (for contrib. to econ. theory) 1995. *Publications:*

Mathematical Theory of Economic Dynamics and Equilibria (with A. Rubinov) 1977, Models and Computers in Economics 1979, Computer Simulation in Analysis of Regional Problems 1987, Mathematical Economic Theory: Pure and Mixed Types of Economic Mechanisms (with A. Rubinov and M. Levin) 1994.
Address: Central Economics and Mathematics Institute, Russian Academy of Sciences, Nakhimouski Prospect 47, 117418 Moscow, Russia. *Telephone:* (495) 129-10-11 (office); (495) 229-01-50 (home). *Fax:* (495) 310-70-15.

MAKEPEACE, Richard Edward; British diplomatist; *Consul General to the Palestinian National Authority;* b. 24 June 1953; m. Rupmani Catherine Pradhan; two s. *Career:* entered FCO 1976, Science, Energy and Nuclear Dept 1976–77, Overseas Language Training 1977–79, Third Sec., Chancery, Muscat, Oman 1979–81, Second, later First Sec., Chancery, Prague 1981–85, Near East and N Africa Dept, FCO 1985–86, Parl. Under-Sec. 1987–89, First Sec., Office of UK Perm. Rep. to EU, Brussels 1989–93, Deputy Head of Personnel Dept, FCO 1993–95, Deputy Head of Mission, Cairo 1995–98, Amb. to Sudan 1999–2002, to UAE 2003–06, Consul Gen. to Palestinian Nat. Authority, East Jerusalem 2006–.
Address: British Consulate General, 19 Nashashibi Street, Sheikh Jarrah Quarter, PO Box 19690, East Jerusalem 97200 (office). *Telephone:* (2) 541-4100 (office). *Fax:* (2) 532-2368 (office). *E-mail:* britain.jerusalem@fco.gov.uk (office).

MAKHMUDOV, Lt-Gen. Eldar Akhmed oğlu; Azerbaijani government official and politician; *Minister of National Security;* b. 1956, Baku; m.; three c. *Education:* D. Bunyatzade Inst. of Economy, Baku State Univ. *Career:* career in mil. service; served Organized Crime and Criminal Investigation Divs, Ministry of Interior 1980–2004, positions included Chief of Br, Drugs Suppression Unit 1993, Chief, Economic Crimes Dept, Chief of Branch, Drugs Suppression Dept 2004; Minister of Nat. Security 2004–; promoted to Maj.-Gen. 2004, to Lt-Gen. 2005.
Address: Ministry of National Security, 1602 Baku, Parliament pr. 2, Azerbaijan (office). *Telephone:* (12) 493-76-22 (office). *Fax:* (12) 495-04-91 (office). *E-mail:* cpr@mns.gov.az (office). *Website:* www.mns.gov.az (office).

MAKKAWI, Khalil, PhD; Lebanese diplomatist; *Officer, Ministry of National Defence;* b. 15 Jan. 1930, Beirut; m. Zahira Sibaei 1958; one s. one d. *Education:* American Univ. of Beirut, Cairo Univ., Egypt, Columbia Univ., New York, USA. *Career:* joined Foreign Ministry 1957, served in UN Section 1957–59, Deputy Perm. Rep. to UN, New York 1961–64, First Sec., Embassy in Washington, DC 1964–67, Chief of Int. Relations Dept, Foreign Ministry, Beirut 1967–70, Counsellor, Embassy in London 1970–71, Minister Plenipotentiary, London 1971–73, Amb. to GDR 1973–78, to UK and Repub. of Ireland 1978–83; Dir Political Dept, Foreign Ministry, Beirut, Chair. Preparatory Cttee of Lebanese Nat. Dialogue, mem. Lebanese Security Arrangement Cttee for South of Lebanon 1983–85, Amb. to Italy and Perm. Rep. to FAO 1985–90, Perm. Rep. to UN, New York 1990–94; Vice-Chair. Exec. Bd UNICEF 1993–95, Pres. 1995; Co-Chair. Int. Support Group for mine clearance in Lebanon (representing Ministry of Nat. Defence) 2002–05; Pres. Lebanese-Palestinian Dialogue Cttee, Presidency of the Council of Ministers; Pres. Worldwide Alumni Asscn of Univ. of Beirut 2007–; Chevalier, Nat. Order of the Cedar (Lebanon), Great Cross of Merit (Italy).
Address: Bldg Al-Nada, 9th Floor, John Kennedy Street, Ein Mareissi, Beirut, Lebanon (home). *Telephone:* (1) 362662 (home). *Fax:* (1) 372550 (home). *E-mail:* khalil30@inco.com.lb (home).

MAKLAKOVS, Brig.-Gen. Juris; Latvian military officer; *Commander, National Armed Forces;* b. 27 Oct. 1964, Ņukšu; m.; one s. *Education:* Mil. Aviation Eng School, US Army War Coll. *Career:* radio technician, Mil. Aviation Eng School 1985–87, Head of Radio Tech. Equipment Service Group 1987–88; Chief Engineer, Computer Centre, Nat. Defence Acad. 1993, Lecturer, Dept of Mil. Weapons and their Usage 1993–94, Dept of Eng 1994–95, Head of Dept of Eng 1995–97, Deputy Commdt in Academics 1997–2001, Commdt Nat. Defence Acad. 2001–04; Air Force Commdr 2004–06; Commdr Nat. Armed Forces 2006–; Button Award 1997, Honour Sign for contribs to devt of Latvian Nat. Armed Forces 2000, Honour Sign of Recognition Award 2001, Memorial Medal 2004.
Address: Ministry of Defence, K. Valdemāra iela 10–12, Rīga 1473, Latvia (office). *Telephone:* 6721-0124 (office). *Fax:* 6721-2307 (office). *E-mail:* kanceleja@mod.gov.lv (office). *Website:* www.mod.gov.lv (office).

MAKRAM-EBEID, Mona, PhD; Egyptian professor of political science and politician; b. Cairo; m.; one s. *Education:* Harvard Univ. (MA, USA), Univ. of Cairo and American Univ. in Cairo. *Career:* Prof. of Political Science and Political Sociology, American Univ. in Cairo; mem. People's Ass. (Parl) 1990–95, mem. Foreign Affairs and Educ. Cttees; Pres. Parliamentarians for Global Action 1990–95; Founder-mem. Arab Org. for Human

Rights; Adviser to World Bank for the Middle East and North Africa Region 1992; Consultant to Search for Common Ground, Initiative for Peace and Co-operation in the Middle East, Washington, DC; Exec. mem. Ibn Khaldum Centre for Developmental Studies, Nat. Centre for Middle Eastern Studies; mem. Int. Consultative Group for the Middle East Center for Strategic and Int. Studies, Washington, DC 1991, UNICEF Women for Devt Cttee, Women for Foreign Policy Group, Washington, DC, The Arab Thought Forum, Amman; several articles on politics in journals and magazines published in English, Arabic and French; Fulbright Scholar 1981, 1983; Chevalier de la Légion d'Honneur 1994; Woman of the Year, Civil Soc. Review 1994; Commdr de la Pléiade, AIPLF (Int Asscn for French-speaking Parliamentarians) 1995.
Address: c/o The American University in Cairo, P.O. Box 2511, 113 Sharia Kasr El Aini, Cairo, Egypt; Apt 16, 4th Floor, 14 Guezira St, Zamalek, Cairo, Egypt (home). *Telephone:* (2) 3407603. *Fax:* (2) 2608288.

MAKTOUM, Hamdan bin Muhammad al-; United Arab Emirates politician; *Crown Prince of Dubai;* b. 14 Nov. 1982. *Education:* Rashid Private School, Sandhurst Mil. Acad., UK, London School of Econs, UK, Dubai School of Govt. *Career:* Chair. Dubai Exec. Council 2006–; named Crown Prince of Dubai 2008–; Head of Sheikh Muhammad bin Rashid Establishment for Young Business Leaders; Pres. Dubai Sports Council. *Achievement:* won gold medal in equestrian event, Asian Games, Doha 2006.
Address: Dubai Executive Council, Emirates Towers Building, 37th Floor, Sheikh Zayed Road, POB 73311, Dubai, United Arab Emirates (office). *Telephone:* (4) 330-2111 (office). *Fax:* (4) 330-3636 (office). *Website:* www.fazza3.com.

MAKTOUM, Sheikh Hamdan bin Rashid al-; United Arab Emirates politician; *Deputy Ruler of Dubai and Minister of Finance and Industry;* b. 1945, brother of the late Sheikh Maktoum Bin Rashid Al Maktoum. *Career:* Deputy Prime Minister UAE 1971–73, Minister of Finance and Industry 1971–, also Jt Deputy Ruler of Dubai 1995–; Pres. Dubai Municipal Council.
Address: Ministry of Finance and Industry, PO Box 433, Abu Dhabi, United Arab Emirates. *Telephone:* (2) 6726000 (office). *Fax:* (2) 66663088 (office). *E-mail:* mofi@uae.gov.ae (office).

MAKTOUM, Maktoum bin Muhammad al-, BSc; United Arab Emirates politician; *Joint Deputy Ruler of Dubai;* b. 24 Nov. 1983. *Education:* Rashid School, American Univ. of Dubai. *Career:* Chair. Dubai Tech. and Media Free Zone Authority (TECOM Investments); Chair. Dubai Media Inc.; Jt Deputy Ruler of Dubai 2008–; Vice-Pres. Al-Ahli Club (football club).
Address: Office of the Chairman, Dubai Media Inc., POB 835, Dubai, United Arab Emirates (office). *Telephone:* (4) 336-9999 (office).

MAKTOUM, HH Sheikh Muhammad bin Rashid al-, (Ruler of Dubai); United Arab Emirates race-horse owner; *Vice-President and Prime Minister;* b. 1948; m. 1st Sheikha Hind bint Maktoum bin Juma al-Maktoum 1979; m. 2nd Princess Haya bint al-Hussein 2004. *Education:* Mons Officer Cadet Training Coll., Sandhurst Coll., Univ. of Cambridge, UK. *Career:* trained in British army and RAF; Dir of Police and Public Security 1971; Minister of Defence 1972; Crown Prince of Dubai 1990–2006, succeeded his brother, Sheikh Maktoum bin Rashid al-Maktoum, as 6th Sheikh 2006, Vice-Pres. of Dubai 2006–, Prime Minister 2006–; with brothers the late Sheikh Maktoum al-Maktoum, Sheikh Hamdan al-Maktoum and Sheikh Ahmed al-Maktoum, has had racing interests in UK 1976–; first winner, Hatta, Goodwood 1977; with brothers owns studs, stables, country houses and sporting estates in Newmarket and elsewhere in UK; worldwide racing interests based at Dalham Hall Stud, Newmarket; horses trained in England, Ireland and France; founder and Dir Godolphin Racing, Dubai 1994; f. Racing Post (daily) 1986; owner, Balanchine, winner, Irish Derby 1994; winner, numerous classic races; leading owner 1985–89, 1991–93. *Publication:* My Vision: Challenges in the Race for Excellence 2006.
Address: Ruler's Palace, Dubai (office); Office of the Prime Minister, POB 12848, Dubai, United Arab Emirates (office); c/o Warren Towers, Newmarket, Suffolk, England (office). *Telephone:* (4) 3534550 (office). *Fax:* (4) 3530111 (office). *Website:* www.sheikhmohammed.co.ae.

MAKUZA, Bernard; Rwandan politician and fmr diplomatist; *Prime Minister;* b. 1961; m. *Career:* fmr mem. Mouvement démocratique républicain; fmr Amb. to Burundi, Amb. to Germany –2000; Prime Minister of Rwanda 2000–.
Address: Office of the Prime Minister, Kigali, Rwanda (office). *Telephone:* 585444 (office). *Fax:* 583714 (office). *E-mail:* primature@gov.rw (office). *Website:* www.primature.gov.rw (office).

MALAJ, Arben; Albanian politician and economist; b. 19 Sept. 1961; m.; one c. *Education:* Univ. of Tirana. *Career:* began career with Nat. Commercial

Bank of Albania, Vlora; Dir Foundation of SME-s, Tirana –1997; Assoc. Prof. of Econ. Sciences, Univ. of Tirana 1997–; Minister of Finance and Gov. of Albania to the World Bank 1997–98; Chief of Parl. Comm. for the Economy and Econ. Table of the Stability Pact 1998–2000; Chief of Parl. Group of the Socialist Party 2000–02; Minister of Economy 2002–04, of Finance 2004–05; currently mem. Parl. for Kelmendi Dist (Socialist Party); lecturer in numerous academic insts including Univ. of Bocconi, Italy, Univ. of Tetova, Macedonia, Univ. of Pristina, Kosova; mem. Int. Acad. of Emerging Markets, New York, USA. *Publications:* author or co-author of several publications and scientific articles.
Address: c/o Ministria e Financave, Kuvendi i Shqiperise, Bulevardi Dëshmorët e Kombit, Nr. 4, Tirana, Albania (office).

MALCORRA, Susana; Argentine engineer and international organization official; *Under-Secretary-General and Head of Department of Field Support, United Nations;* b. 1954; m.; one s. *Education:* Univ. of Rosario. *Career:* grad. trainee with IBM, eventually becoming Dir of Public Sector, later assigned to IBM's corp. HQ in USA where she oversaw relations between HQ and Mexico and the Andean region of Latin America –1993; various admin. positions with Telecom Argentina 1993–2003, COO and Exec. Dir 1995–2001, CEO 2001–02; co-f. Vectis Management 2002; Deputy Exec. Dir (Admin) WFP 2004–07 (led initial phase of operational response to tsunami emergency Dec. 2004), Deputy Exec. Dir and COO Jan.–March 2008, UN Under-Sec.-Gen. and Head of Dept of Field Support 2008–; Founding mem. Argentine chapter, Int. Women's Forum; mem. Advisory Bd of Business School of Univ. of San Andres, Buenos Aires, Advisory Bd of Equidad.
Address: Department of Field Support, United Nations, First Avenue at 46th Street, New York, NY 10017, USA (office). *Website:* www.un.org/Depts/dpko/dpko/dfs.shtml (office).

MALEKI, Fada Hossein; Iranian diplomatist; *Ambassador to Afghanistan; Career:* fmr adviser to Minister of Interior; fmr Deputy Head, Gen. Inspectorate of Iran; Presidential Adviser and Sec.-Gen. Drug Control HQ, Ministry of Foreign Affairs –2007; Amb. to Afghanistan 2007–.
Address: Embassy of Iran, Charahi Shir Pur, Kabul, Afghanistan (office). *Telephone:* (20) 2101393 (office).

MALEWEZI, Rt Hon. Justin Chimera, BA; Malawi teacher, educational administrator and politician; b. 23 Dec. 1944, Ntchisi; m. Felicity Rozina Chizalema 1970; two s. two d. *Education:* Columbia Univ., New York. *Career:* secondary school teacher 1967–69, headmaster 1969–74, educ. admin. 1974–78; Deputy Sec., Ministry of Finance and Prin. Sec. in various ministries 1978–89; Head of Civil Service 1989–91; Vice-Pres. of Malawi 1994–99, 1999–2003; unsuccessful cand. presidential elections 2004.
Address: c/o Office of the Vice-President, PO Box 30399, Capital City, Lilongwe 3; PO Box 30086, Lilongwe 3, Malawi (home).

MALHOUTRA, Manmohan (Moni), MA; Indian international official and consultant; *Trustee, Indira Gandhi Memorial Trust and Jawaharlal Nehru Memorial Fund;* b. 15 Sept. 1937, Izatnagar; m. Leela Nath 1963; two d. *Education:* Delhi Univ., Balliol Coll., Oxford, UK. *Career:* entered Indian Admin. Service 1961; mem. Prime Minister's Secr. 1966–73; joined Commonwealth Secr. 1974; Dir Sec.-Gen.'s Office and Int. Affairs Div. 1977–82, Asst Commonwealth Sec.-Gen. 1982–93; Conf. Sec. to Commonwealth Heads of Govt Meetings, London 1977, Lusaka 1979, Melbourne 1981, also at Asia-Pacific Regional Heads of Govt Meetings; led Commonwealth Secr. team in Observer Group at pre-independence elections in Zimbabwe 1980; elections in Uganda 1980; Sec. Commonwealth Southern Africa Cttee; Head of Secr. of Commonwealth Group of Eminent Persons on South Africa 1986; Chef de Cabinet, Commonwealth Sec.-Gen.'s Office 1982–90, Head Commonwealth Secr. Human Resource Devt Group 1983–93; mem. Bd Dirs Int. Inst. for Democracy and Electoral Assistance, Stockholm 1996–2003; Sec.-Gen. Rajiv Gandhi Foundation, New Delhi 2001–07; Trustee, Indira Gandhi Memorial Trust, Jawaharlal Nehru Memorial Fund; Rhodes Scholar 1958. *Publications:* First Proof (contrib.) 2004, New Century: Whose Century (ed. and publr) 2000, India: The Next Decade (ed. and publr) 2006.
Address: 118 Golf Links, New Delhi 110 003, India (home). *Telephone:* (11) 24643630 (home). *Fax:* (11) 24643630 (home). *E-mail:* moni.malhoutra@airtelbroadband.in (home).

MALIELEGAOI, Tuila'epa Sailele; Samoan politician; *Prime Minister and Minister of Foreign Affairs; Career:* fmr Deputy Prime Minister and Minister of Finance, Trade, Industry and Commerce and Tourism; Prime Minister of Samoa 1998–; concurrently Minister of Foreign Affairs; mem. Human Rights Protection Party.
Address: Prime Minister's Department, PO Box L 1861, Apia, Samoa. *Telephone:* 63122. *Fax:* 21339. *E-mail:* pmdept@ipasifika.net (office).

MALIK, Shahid, MA; Pakistani diplomatist; *High Commissioner to India;* m. Ghazala Malik. *Career:* joined Foreign Service Acad. 1972, worked as section officer, Ministry of Foreign Affairs; fmr directing staff mem. Lahore Civil Services Acad.; Deputy High Commr, New Delhi 1992–95, High Commr to India 2006–; served as Political Affairs Counsellor, Washington, DC, also postings to embassies in Tokyo and Rome; Dir-Gen. and Additional Foreign Sec., Ministry of Foreign Affairs 2001–02; High Commr to Canada 2002–06 (also accred to Guyana 2003–06).
Address: High Commission of Pakistan, 2/50g Shanti Path, Chanakyapuri, New Delhi 110 021, India (office). *Telephone:* (11) 26110601 (office). *Fax:* (11) 26872339 (office). *E-mail:* pakhc@nda.vsnl.net.in (office).

MALIKI, Nuri Kamal (Jawad) al-; Iraqi politician; *Prime Minister;* b. (Nouri Kamel al-Maliki), 1 July 1950, Hindiya; m.; four c. *Education:* Baghdad Univ. *Career:* official of Dawa party, fled Iraq to Syria 1980; returned to Iraq as one of Dawa leaders serving as spokesman and adviser to Dawa leader and Iraq interim Prime Minister Ibrahim al-Jaafari 2003; helped draft new constitution; mem. cttee tasked to purge Iraq Baathist legacy; Prime Minister of Iraq 2006–.
Address: Office of the Prime Minister, Baghdad, Iraq.

MALINOWSKI, Michael E.; American diplomatist; *Chairman, National Defense Intelligence College;* b. 1948, Chicago; m. Karen Gerlach Malinowski 1975. *Career:* social worker and teacher in Chicago –1976; joined foreign service 1976, served in Embassies in Mexico City 1976–78, Kabul 1979–80, Colombo 1980–83; Political Affairs Analyst on S Asia, Dept of State 1983–85; Prin. Officer at Consulates in Peshawar, Pakistan 1987–89 and Maracaibo, Venezuela 1985–87; Deputy to Presidential Envoy to Afghan Resistance 1989; Special Asst. for Nr East, S Asian Affairs and Counterterrorism to Under-Sec. for Political Affairs 1989–91; Deputy Chief of Mission in Kathmandu 1991–94, in Mbabane, Swaziland 1994–97; Office Dir for Pakistan, Afghanistan and Bangladesh, Bureau of S Asian Affairs, Dept of State 1997–98; Deputy Chief of Mission in Manila 1998–99, Chief 2000–01; Amb. to Nepal 2001–2004; currently Chair. Nat. Defense Intelligence Coll., Washington, DC.
Address: National Defense Intelligence College, 200 MacDill Blvd, Bolling Air Force Base, Washington, DC 20340, USA (office). *Telephone:* (202) 231-3299 (office). *Fax:* (703) 866-0832 (office). *Website:* www.dia.mil/college (office).

MÄLK, Raul; Estonian diplomatist, economist and fmr journalist; *Permanent Representative, European Union;* b. 14 May 1952, Parnu, Estonia. *Education:* Tartu Univ., Leningrad Inst. of Political Studies. *Career:* economist and researcher, Inst. of Econs, Estonian Acad. of Sciences 1975–77; Sr Ed., Deputy Ed.-in-Chief, Ed.-in-Chief Estonian Radio 1977–90; Deputy Head Office of Chair. Supreme Soviet of Estonia 1990–92; adviser to Minister of Foreign Affairs 1992–93; Head Office of Minister of Foreign Affairs 1993–94; Deputy Perm. Under-Sec. Ministry of Foreign Affairs 1994–96; Amb. to UK 1996–2001, also accred to Ireland 1996–2003, Amb. to Portugal 2000–03; Minister of Foreign Affairs 1998–99; Head Estonian dels for negotiations with Russia, Finland, Latvia 1994–96; Dir-Gen. Policy Planning Dept, Ministry of Foreign Affairs 2001–07; Perm. Rep. of Estonia to EU 2007–; Order of the White Star, Third Class (Estonia), also decorations from Portugal, Latvia, Malta and Poland; Estonian Journalists' Union Award 1990.
Address: Ministry of Foreign Affairs, Islandi square 1, 15049 Tallinn, Estonia (office). *Telephone:* 3222273925 (office). *Fax:* 3222274333 (office). *E-mail:* vminfo@vm.ee (office). *Website:* www.vm.ee (office).

MALKI, Majdi El-, PhD; Palestinian academic; *Director, Ibrahim Abu-Lughod Institute of International Studies, Birzeit University; Education:* Univ. of Nanterre (Paris X), France. *Career:* has worked in several research insts; currently Dir Ibrahim Abu-Lughod Inst. of Int. Studies, Birzeit Univ. *Publications include:* Singapore-Taiwan – The Cost of Success: A Critical Review, and the Possibilities of Local Implementations, Socio-economic Changes in Three Palestinian Villages: Rural Family Reproduction Under the Israeli Ccupation, The Socio-economic Impacts of the Intifada on Refugees. The Jalazon Refugee Camp Case, Towards a Sociology of Civil Resistance: Palestinian Society During the Second Intifada, MUWATIN-The Palestinian Institute For the Study of Democracy 2004, Social and Economic Characteristics of the Informal Sector in the West Bank and Gaza Strip 2004; numerous articles on socio-economic changes in Palestinian society, patrimonialism, social policy, devt, globalization, democracy and civil society.
Address: The Ibrahim Abu-Lughod Institute of International Studies, Birzeit University, PO Box 14, Birzeit, Palestinian Authority (office). *Telephone:* 2-2-2982939 (office). *Fax:* 2-2-2982946 (office). *E-mail:* mmalki@birzeit.edu (office); mmalki@planet.edu (office). *Website:* home.birzeit.edu/giis (office).

MALLIAS, Alexandros P., BEcons; Greek diplomatist; *Ambassador to USA;* m. Françoise-Anne Mallias; two d. *Education:* Univ. of Athens, Univ. of Geneva, Switzerland, Institut des Hautes Etudes Européennes. *Career:* joined Foreign Service 1976, served as Head of Unit for Council of Europe as attaché and later as Third Sec., Dept for Int. Orgs 1976–78, Deputy to Greek Perm. Rep. to Council of Europe, promoted to Second Sec. 1978–82, posted to Embassy in Tripoli 1982–84, First Sec. 1984, served with Middle East Dept, Gen. Inspection, West Europe Dept and Cabinet of Sec.-Gen. of Ministry of Foreign Affairs 1984–86, involved with Greek Del. to Charter of Paris for a New Europe (CSCE) 1986–90, Head of Del. 1990, Head of EC Monitor Mission Regional Office, Sofia, Deputy Dir Diplomatic Cabinet of Minister of Foreign Affairs, First Counsellor for Political Affairs, Greek Perm. Mission to UN, New York 1989–93, Head of Div. for Bulgaria and Romania, Dept for Balkan Affairs, first Head of Mission, Liaison Office of Hellenic Repub., Skopje 1995–99, Amb. to Albania 1999–2002, Nat. Coordinator at Stability Pact for Southeastern Europe 2002–03, Dir A3 South Eastern Europe (Balkan Affairs) Dept 2000–, Chair. Coordinating Cttee for the Greek EU presidency's program for the Balkans 2002–03, Amb. to USA 2005–. *Address:* Embassy of Greece, 2217 Massachusetts Avenue, NW, Washington, DC 20008, USA (office). *Telephone:* (202) 939-1300 (office). *Fax:* (202) 939-1324 (office). *E-mail:* greece@greekembassy.org (office). *Website:* www.greekembassy.org (office).

MALLOCH BROWN, Baron (Life Peer), cr. 2007, of St Leonard's Forest in the County of West Sussex; **(George) Mark Malloch Brown,** , KCMG, MA; British business executive, academic and fmr international organization official; *Minister for Africa, Asia and the United Nations;* b. 1953; m.; four c. *Education:* Magdalene Coll., Cambridge, Univ. of Michigan, USA. *Career:* Political Corresp., Economist 1977–79; worked for UNHCR first in Thailand in charge of field operations for Cambodian refugees 1979–81, then in Geneva as Deputy Chief of Emergency Unit 1981–83; Founder Economist Devt Report 1983–86; lead int. partner, Sawyer Miller Group (communications management firm), advising govts political leaders and corpns 1986–94; mem. Soros Advisory Cttee on Bosnia and Herzegovina 1993–94; Dir of External Affairs, IBRD 1994–96, Vice-Pres. for External Affairs 1996–99, for UN Affairs 1996–99, Admin. UNDP 1999–2005, Chief of Staff in Exec. Office of UN Sec.-Gen. 2005–06, Deputy Sec.-Gen. April–Dec. 2006; Distinguished Visiting Fellow, Yale Center for the Study of Globalization 2007; Vice-Chair. Quantum Group of Funds (hedge fund group) 2007; Vice-Chair. Open Soc. Inst. 2007; Minister for Africa, Asia and UN 2007–, also attending Cabinet; Chair. UN Devt Group; fmr Vice-Chair. Bd of Refugees Int., Washington, DC, USA; Dr hc (Michigan State) 2003, (Catholic Univ., Lima) 2004, (Pace Law School) 2005; numerous awards including one of Time Magazine's 100 Most Influential People in the World 2005. *Address:* House of Lords, London, SW1A 0PW; Foreign and Commonwealth Office, King Charles Street, London, SW1A 2AH, England. *Telephone:* (20) 7219-5353 (House of Lords); (20) 7008-1500. *Website:* www.fco.gov.uk.

MALLOY, Eileen Anne, BS; American diplomatist; *Senior Inspector, Office of the Inspector General, State Department;* b. 9 July 1954, New Jersey; m. 1st Ilmar Paegle 1975 (divorced); m. 2nd James G. McLachlan 1985; two d. *Education:* Georgetown Univ., Washington, DC. *Career:* Reporter and Div. Man., Dun and Bradstreet, New York 1975–78; joined Foreign Service 1978; worked at US embassies in London, Moscow and Dublin, and Consulate-Gen. in Calgary, Canada; worked at Dept of State as UK Desk Officer, Analyst in Consular Affairs, Head of Secr. staff for Sec. of State, Special Asst to Under-Sec. for Political Affairs, US Deputy Asst Sec. of State for European and Canadian Affairs; Amb. to Kyrgyzstan 1994–97; US Consul-Gen., Sydney 2001–04; Sr Inspector, Office of the Inspector Gen., US Dept of State 2004–; mem. Advisory Bd Women in Int. Security. *Address:* c/o Office of the Inspector General, PO Box 9778, Arlington, VA 22219, USA (office). *Telephone:* (703) 284-1934 (office). *Website:* oig.state.gov (office).

MALLY, Komlan; Togolese politician; *Prime Minister;* b. 12 Dec. 1960, Adiva. *Education:* Ecole Nationale d'Administration, Univ. of Benin, Lomé. *Career:* Prefect, Wawa Pref. 1996–99, Golfe Pref. 2002–06; mem. Parl. 2007–; Minister of Towns and Town Planning 2006–07; Prime Minister 2007–; mem. Rassemblement du peuple togolais (RPT). *Address:* Office of the Prime Minister, Palais de la Primature, BP 1161, Lomé, Togo (office). *Telephone:* 221-15-64 (office). *Fax:* 221-37-53 (office). *Website:* www.gouvernement.tg (office).

MALMIERCA DÍAZ, Rodrigo, BEcons; Cuban diplomatist; *Permanent Representative, United Nations;* b. 14 Oct. 1956; m.; two c. *Education:* Univ. of Havana. *Career:* Project Man. ECIMETAL Enterprise 1981–82; Specialist on Co-operation, Div. of Econ. Int. Insts, State Cttee for Econ.

Co-operation 1982–92; Counsellor, Embassy in Brasilia 1992–97; Dir European and N American Div., Ministry of Foreign Investment and Econ. Cooperation 1997–98, Deputy Minister 1998–2002; Amb. to Belgium, EU and Luxembourg 2002–05; Perm. Rep. to UN, New York 2005–. *Address:* Permanent Mission of Cuba to the United Nations, 315 Lexington Avenue and 38th Street, New York, NY 10016, USA (office). *Telephone:* (212) 689-7215 (office). *Fax:* (212) 779-1697 (office). *E-mail:* cuba@un.int (office). *Website:* www.un.int/cuba (office).

MALMSTRÖM, Cecilia, BA, PhD; Swedish academic and politician; *Minister for EU Affairs;* b. 15 May 1968, Stockholm; m.; two c. *Education:* Gothenburg Univ., Sorbonne, Paris. *Career:* tech. asst and translator, SKF, Paris, Stuttgart, Barcelona 1986–89; psychiatric nurse, Lillhagen Hosp., Gothenburg 1989–92; social studies teacher, Lindholmen 1991–92; lay assessor, Gothenburg City Court 1991–94; Vice-Chair. Gothenburg Municipal Immigration Cttee 1994–98; Research Asst, Dept of Political Science, Gothenburg Univ. 1994–98, Sr Lecturer 1998–99; mem. Västra Götaland Regional Council 1998–2001; MEP 1999–2006, Vice-Chair. Dels to Hungary and Croatia Jt Parl. Cttees, served on Constitutional and Foreign Affairs cttees, Sub-cttee on Human Rights, substitute mem. Sub-cttee on Security and Defence 2004–06, Cttee on Internal Market and Consumer Protection 2004–06; Minister for EU Affairs 2006–; mem. Liberal Party, mem. of Bd 1997–, mem. of Exec. 2001–. *Publications:* books and articles on European regionalism and politics, Spanish politics, terrorism and immigration. *Address:* Office of the Minister for European Affairs, Prime Minister's Office, Rosenbad 4, 103 33 Stockholm, Sweden (office). *Telephone:* (8) 405-10-00 (office). *Fax:* (8) 723-11-71 (office). *E-mail:* registrator@primeminister.ministry.se (office). *Website:* www.sweden.gov.se (office).

MALONE, David M.; Canadian diplomatist and writer; *High Commissioner to India; Career:* joined Dept of External Affairs in 1975, served in numerous sr positions; overseas postings included Cairo, Amman, New York; Perm. Rep. to the UN 1993; High Commr to India (also accred. to Nepal and Bhutan) 2006–; Pres. Int. Devt Research Centre, Ottawa 2008–; Pres. Int. Peace Acad., New York 1998–2004; has taught at Univ. of Toronto, Columbia Univ., New York Univ. School of Law, Institut d'Etudes Politiques, Paris; lectures frequently in India, occasionally in UK, USA, France, Canada. *Publications:* Decision-Making in the UN Security Council: The Case of Haiti 1999, Greed and Grievance: Economic Agendas in Civil Wars (co-ed.) 2000, From Reaction to Conflict Prevention (co-ed.) 2002, Unilateralism and US Foreign Policy (co-ed.) 2002, The UN Security Council from Cold War to Twenty-First Century 2004, The International Struggle Over Iraq: Politics in the UN Security Council, 1980–2005 2006, Preventing a Future Generation of Conflict in Iraq (co-ed.) 2007, The Law and Practice of the United Nations (co-author) 2008. *Address:* High Commission of Canada, 7/8 Shantipath, Chanakyapuri, New Delhi 110 021, India (office). *Telephone:* (11) 41782000 (office). *Fax:* (11) 4178-2020 (office). *E-mail:* delhi@international.gc.ca (office). *Website:* www.india.gc.ca (office); www.idrc.ca (office).

MALTSEV, Col Gen. Leonid Semenovich, MA; Belarusian army general and government official; *Minister of Defence;* b. 29 Aug. 1949, Slonim Dist, Grodno Region. *Education:* Minsk Suvorov Mil. High School, Kiev Higher Combined Arms Command School, Frunze Mil. Acad. *Career:* commdr of platoon, co. and battalions in Grouping of Soviet Forces, Germany 1970s; Motorised Rifle Regiment Deputy Commdr, Commdr, Chief of Staff then Commdr of Motorised Rifle Div. in Far E Dist 1979–92; First Deputy Commdr of Combined Arms and Services of Belarus Mil. Dist, 28th Arms Corps Commdr, Chief of Gen. Staff, First Deputy Minister of Defence then Minister of Defence of Repub. of Belarus 1992–97; First Deputy Chief, CIS Mil. Cooperation Coordination Staff 1997–2000; Deputy State Sec., Security Council of Belarus 2000–01; Minister of Defence 2001–. *Address:* Ministry of Defence, vul. Kamunistychnaya 1, 220034 Minsk, Belarus (office). *Telephone:* (17) 239-23-79 (office). *Fax:* (17) 289-19-74 (office). *Website:* www.mod.mil.by (office).

MAMATGELDIYEV, Maj.-Gen. Agageldy, MD; Turkmenistan army officer and politician; *Minister of Defence; Career:* trained as physician; career in Turkmenistan Armed Forces, rank of Maj.-Gen.; fmr Head of Turkmen Border Guard Service; Minister of Defence 2003–. *Address:* Ministry of Defence, 744000 Aşgabat, ul. 1995 4, Turkmenistan (office). *Telephone:* (12) 35-22-59 (office).

MAMATSASHVILI, Teimuraz; Georgian diplomatist, engineer and economist; b. 10 Nov. 1942, Tbilisi; m. Irina Arkhangelskaya 1967; two d. *Education:* Georgian Ploytech. Inst., Tbilisi, Acad. of Foreign Trade, Moscow. *Career:* Sr Engineer, Inst. of Metrology, Tbilisi 1965–70; Sr Engineer, Trade Representation of USSR in Australia 1973–77; Sr Engineer, Deputy Dir, Dir Licensmash co. (part of Licensintorg Corpn),

Moscow 1977–89; Trade Rep. to Tokyo, Japan 1989–92; Minister of Foreign Econ. Relations 1992–93; Amb. to UK 1995–2004, to Ireland 1998–2004; Perm. Rep. to Int. Maritime Org. 1995–; Gov. EBRD 1996–; two state Orders of USSR 1979, 1989.
Address: c/o Ministry of Foreign Affairs, 9 April 4, 380018 Tbilisi (office); 4 Uznadze St., Appt. 31, Tbilisi, Georgia (home).

MAMBA, Clifford Sibusio, BSc; Swazi diplomatist; *Permanent Secretary for Foreign Affairs and Trade;* b. 5 May 1963, Manzini; m. *Education:* Univ. of Middlesex, UK and Seoul Inst. of Int. Affairs and Strategic Studies, Repub. of Korea. *Career:* Amb. to Repub. of Korea then the EU 1991–96; Amb. to Malaysia 1996–2000; Perm. Rep. to UN 2000; currently Perm. Sec. for Foreign Affairs and Trade; fmr Chair. African, Caribbean and Pacific Group of States Cttee of Ambs, ACP Ambassadorial Sub-cttee for Sugar; Dean, Southern African Devt Community ambs 1996.
Address: c/o Ministry of Foreign Affairs and Trade, POB 518, Mbabane, Swaziland. *Telephone:* 4042661. *Fax:* 4042669.

MAMBERTI, Archbishop Dominique François Joseph; French ecclesiastic and diplomatist; *Secretary for Relations with States, Roman Curia;* b. 7 March 1952, Marrakesh, Morocco. *Career:* ordained priest 1981; traveled to Rome to study diplomacy at Pontifical Ecclesial Acad. 1984, joined Vatican diplomatic service 1986, has held posts in Algeria, Chile, UN, New York, Lebanon, has also worked in Secr. of State Section for Foreign Affairs, Apostolic Del. to Somalia 2002–04, Apostolic Nuncio (Amb.) to Sudan 2002–06, to Eritrea 2004–06, Sec. for Relations with States, Roman Curia 2006–; Titular Archbishop of Sagona 2002–.
Address: Secretariat of State, Roman Curia, Palazzo Apostolico Vaticano, Citta del Vaticano 00120 Rome, Italy (office). *Telephone:* (06) 69883014 (office). *Fax:* (06) 69885364 (office). *E-mail:* vati032@relstat-segstat.va (office). *Website:* www.vatican.va/roman_curia/secretariat_state (office).

MAMBETALIEV, Kuban Ilyasovich, PhD; Kyrgyzstani academic, journalist and diplomatist; *Ambassador to UK;* m. Gulbara Abdurazakova. *Career:* fmr Prof. of Literature, left position to establish ind. newspaper Stolitsa 1995; formed union of journalists and became mem. Int. Fed. of Journalists; asked by Pres. Bakiyev to head comm. to formulate proposals for an ind. public broadcaster; Amb. to UK 2006–.
Address: Embassy of Kyrgyzstan, Ascot House, 119 Crawford Street, London, W1U 6BJ, England (office). *Telephone:* (20) 7935-1462 (office). *Fax:* (20) 7935-7449 (office). *E-mail:* mail@kyrgyz-embassy.org.uk (office). *Website:* www.kyrgyz-embassy.org.uk (office).

MAMEDOV, Georgy Enverovich, PhD, CHisSc; Russian diplomatist; *Ambassador to Canada;* b. 9 Sept. 1947, Moscow; m.; one s. one d. *Education:* Moscow Inst. of Int. Relations. *Career:* researcher Inst. of USA and Canada 1970–77, mem. staff USSR Embassy in USA 1972–73, 1977–81, Sec., Counsellor, Deputy Chief, then Chief Dept of USA and Canada, USSR Ministry of Foreign Affairs 1981–91, Deputy Minister of Foreign Affairs of Russia 1991–2003; Amb. to Canada 2003–; mem. State Cttee on Defence Industry 1996–98.
Address: Embassy of the Russian Federation, 285 Charlotte Street, Ottawa, K1N 8L5, Canada (office). *Telephone:* (613) 235-4341 (home). *Fax:* (613) 236-6342 (office). *E-mail:* rusemb@magma.ca (office).

MAMMEDYAROV, Elmar Maharram oğlu, PhD; Azerbaijani diplomatist; *Minister of Foreign Affairs;* b. 2 July 1960, Baku; m.; two s. *Education:* Kyiv State Univ. School of Int. Relations and Int. Law, Ukrainian SSR, USSR Diplomatic Acad. *Career:* Second Sec. then First Sec., Ministery of Foreign Affairs 1982–88, Dir Div. of State Protocol 1991–92, First Sec. Perm. Mission to UN, New York 1992–95, Deputy Dir Dept of Int. Orgs 1995–98, Counselor, Embassy in Washington, DC 1998–2003; Amb. to Italy 2003–04; Minister of Foreign Affairs 2004–.
Address: Ministry of Foreign Affairs, 1009 Baku, S. Qurbanov küç. 4, Azerbaijan (office). *Telephone:* (12) 596-90-00 (office). *Fax:* (12) 498-84-80 (office). *E-mail:* press-service@mfa.gov.az (office). *Website:* www.mfa.gov .az (office).

MANAEV, Oleg T., MA, PhD; Belarusian research institute director and professor of media and communications studies; *Founding Director, Independent Institute of Socioeconomic and Political Studies;* b. 3 Feb. 1952, Vladivostok. *Education:* Belarusian State Univ. *Career:* Jr Research Fellow, Scientific Centre for Sociological Research, Belarusian State Univ. 1976–78, Sr Research Fellow 1978–84, Head of Div. 1984–88, Prof. Dept of Sociology 1991–, Founder and Prof., Dept of Social Communication; Founding Dir, Ind. Inst. of Socioeconomic and Political Studies 1992–; Founding Chair. Belarusian Asscn of Think-Tanks (BTT), also Ed. BTT Analytical Bulletin; Chair. Bd Belarusian Soros Foundation 1993–95; Visiting Lecturer and Fellow at univs and insts in USA, Canada, Brazil, UK, France, Sweden and Germany; dir several nat. and int. projects for

UNESCO, OSCE, MacArthur Foundation, Westminster Foundation; Corresp. Ed. European Journal of Communication, London, Political Communication, Durham, NC; mem. Int. Assoc. for Media and Communications Research (IAMCR). *Publications include:* Youth and the Democratization of Soviet Society (co-ed.) 1990, Interaction of Media, Public and Power in the Democratization Process (co-ed.) 1991, Media in Transition: From Totalitarianism to Democracy (ed.) 1993, Emerging Civil Society in Independent Belarus. Sociological Experience 1991–2000 2000, Belarus on the Way to the Third Millennium (ed.) 2001, Mass Media in Belarus 2003; over 150 scholarly articles and chapters in books.
Address: Independent Institute of Socioeconomic and Political Studies, 424 Moskovskaya Street, 18, Minsk, Belarus (office). *Telephone:* (17) 222-8049 (office). *Fax:* (17) 222-8049 (office). *E-mail:* iiseps@iiseps.org (office). *Website:* www.iiseps.org (office).

MANATHAT, Rathakit; Thai diplomatist; *Ambassador to the People's Republic of China; Career:* Consul-Gen., Consulate in Hong Kong 1999–2001; Spokesman for Ministry of Foreign Affairs 2001–06; Amb. to Laos 2006–07, to N Korea 2007, to People's Repub. of China 2007–.
Address: Embassy of Thailand, 40 Guang Hua Lu, Jian Guo Men Wai, Beijing 100600, People's Republic of China (office). *Telephone:* (10) 65321903 (office). *Fax:* (10) 65321748 (office). *E-mail:* thaibej@public.bta .net.cn (office). *Website:* www.thaiembbeij.org (office).

MANDELA, Nelson Rolihlahla; South African politician, lawyer, international affairs consultant and fmr head of state; b. 1918, Umtata, Transkei; m. 1st Evelyn Mandela 1944 (divorced 1957, died 2004); four c. (three deceased); m. 2nd Winnie Mandela 1958 (divorced 1996); two d.; m. 3rd Graca Machel (widow of the late Pres. Machel of Mozambique) 1998. *Education:* Univ. Coll. of Fort Hare, Univ. of the Witwatersrand. *Career:* legal practice, Johannesburg 1952; Nat. organizer African Nat. Congress (ANC); on trial for treason 1956–61 (acquitted 1961); arrested 1962, sentenced to five years' imprisonment Nov. 1962; on trial for further charges 1963–64, sentenced to life imprisonment June 1964; released Feb. 1990; Deputy Pres. ANC 1990–91, Pres. 1991–97, mem. Nat. Exec. Cttee 1991–; Pres. of South Africa 1994–99; Chancellor Univ. of the North 1992–; Jt Pres. United World Colls 1995–; Hon. Fellow Magdalene Coll., Cambridge 2001; Hon. Freeman of London; Freedom of City of Glasgow 1981; Hon. Citizen of Rome 1983; Freeman of Dublin 1988; Hon. Bencher Lincoln's Inn 1994; Hon. QC 2000; Order of the Niger 1990; Hon. LLD (Nat. Univ. of Lesotho) 1979, (City Coll. of City Univ. of New York) 1983, (Lancaster) 1984, (Strathclyde) 1985, (Calcutta) 1986, (Harare) 1987, (Kent) 1992, Hon. DLitt (Texas Southern Univ.) 1991; Dr hc (Complutense) 1991; Hon. DCL (Oxford) 1996, Cambridge (1996); Hon. LLD (London) 1996, Bristol (1996), (Nottingham) 1996, (Warwick) 1996, (De Montfort) 1996, (Glasgow Caledonian) 1996; Jawaharlal Nehru Award (India) 1979, Bruno Kreisky Prize for Human Rights 1981, Simon Bolivar Int. Prize (UNESCO) 1983, Third World Prize 1985, Sakharov Prize 1988, Gaddafi Human Rights Prize 1989, Bharat Ratna (India) 1990, Jt winner Houphouët Prize (UNESCO) 1991, Nishan-e-Pakistan 1992, Asturias Prize 1992, Liberty Medal (USA) 1993; shared Nobel Prize for Peace 1993; Mandela-Fulbright Prize 1993, Tun Abdul Razak Award 1994, Anne Frank Medal 1994, Int. Freedom Award 2000, Johannesburg Freedom of the City Award 2004, Amnesty Int. Amb. of Conscience Award 2006. *Publications:* No Easy Walk to Freedom 1965, How Far We Slaves Have Come: South Africa and Cuba in Today's World (with Fidel Castro) 1991, Nelson Mandela Speaks: Forging a Non-Racial Democratic South Africa 1993, Long Walk to Freedom 1994.
Address: c/o ANC, 51 Plein Street, Johannesburg 2001, South Africa (office). *Telephone:* (11) 3307000 (office). *Fax:* (11) 3360302 (office). *E-mail:* info@anc.org.za (office).

MANDELBAUM, Michael, MA, PhD; American academic and writer; *Senior Fellow, Council on Foreign Relations; Education:* Yale Univ., King's Coll. Cambridge, UK, Harvard Univ. *Career:* mem. Faculty, Harvard Univ., MA, Columbia Univ., NY, US Naval Acad., Annapolis 1975–90; Christian A. Herter Prof. of American Foreign Policy, Nitze School of Advanced Int. Studies, Johns Hopkins Univ. 1990–, Dir of American Foreign Policy Program; currently Sr Fellow, Council on Foreign Relations; Assoc. Dir Aspen Inst. Congressional Project on American Relations with the Fmr Communist World; foreign affairs columnist Newsday. *Publications:* The Nuclear Question: The United States and Nuclear Weapons, 1946–1976 1979, The Nuclear Revolution: International Politics Before and After Hiroshima 1981, The Nuclear Future 1983, Reagan and Gorbachev (co-author) 1987, The Fate of Nations: The Search for National Security in the 19th and 20th Centuries 1988, Making Markets: Economic Transformation in Eastern Europe and the Post-Soviet States (co-ed.) 1993, The Global Rivals (co-author) 1988, Western Approaches to the Soviet Union (ed.) 1988, The Rise of Nations in the Soviet Union (ed.) 1991, Central Asia and the World (ed.) 1994, The Strategic Quadrangle: Russia, China, Japan and

the United States in East Asia (ed.) 1995, The Dawn of Peace in Europe 1996, Postcommunism: Four Perspectives (co-ed.) 1996, The Social Safety Net in Postcommunist Europe (co-ed.) 1997, The New Russian Foreign Policy (ed.) 1998, The New European Diasporas (ed.) 2000, The Ideas that Conquered the World: Peace, Democracy and Free Markets in the Twenty-First Century 2002, The Meaning of Sports: Why Americans Watch Baseball, Football and Basketball and What They See When They Do 2004, The Case for Goliath: How America Acts as the World's Government in the Twenty-First Century 2007; numerous articles in professional journals.
Address: Council on Foreign Relations, 1779 Massachusetts Avenue, NW, Washington, DC 20036, USA (office). *Telephone:* (202) 663-5669 (office). *Fax:* (202) 986-2984 (office). *E-mail:* dcmeetings@cfr.org (office). *Website:* www.cfr.org (office).

MANDIL, Claude; French administrative official, engineer and business executive; b. 9 Jan. 1942, Lyon; m. Annick Goubelle 1966; four s. one d. *Education:* Lycée Pasteur de Neuilly and Ecole Polytechnique. *Career:* mining engineer, Metz 1967–71, Rennes 1971–74; Délégation à l'Aménagement du Territoire et à l'Action régionale (DATAR) 1974–77; Inter-Dept Dir and Regional Del. Agence nat. de Valorisation de la Recherche, Anvar 1978–81; Tech. Adviser to Prime Minister 1981–82; Dir-Gen. Inst. of Industrial Devt (IDI) 1983, Pres. 1984–88; Dir-Gen. Bureau des recherches géologiques et minières 1988; Dir-Gen. Energies et Matières Premières, Ministry of Industry and Land Devt 1990–98; Deputy Man. Dir Gaz de France 1998–2000; Pres. Institut français du pétrole 2000–03; Exec. Dir IEA 2003–07 (retd); Officier, Ordre nat. du Mérite, Officier, Légion d'honneur, decorations from Germany and Norway.
Address: 6 rue du Plateau Saint Antoine, 78150 Le Chesnay, France (home).

MANDINGA, Vítor; Guinea-Bissau politician. *Career:* Minister of Finance 2005–07.
Address: c/o Ministry of Finance, Rua Justino lopes 74a, CP 67, Bissau, Guinea Bissau (office).

MANH, Nong Duc; Vietnamese politician; *General Secretary, Dang Cong San Viet Nam (Communist Party of Viet Nam);* b. 11 Sept. 1940, Cuong Loi, Na Ri Dist., Bac Can Prov. *Career:* Deputy Dir. Provincial Forestry Service and Dir. Construction Co. of the Forestry Service, fmr. Bac Thai Prov. 1976–77, Dir. 1977–80; Deputy Chair. Bac Thai Provincial People's Cttee. 1980–83, Chair. 1983–86; elected Deputy Chair. Nat. Ass. Nationalities Council, 8th Nat. Ass., Chair. 9th Nat. Ass. 1992, 1997; mem. Communist Party of Viet Nam 1963, mem. Provincial Party Exec. Cttee. for Bac Thai 1977, mem. Standing Bd., Provincial Party Cttee., Deputy Sec. Party Cttee. for Bac Thai Prov. 1983–86, Sec. 1986, alt. mem. to Cen. Cttee. of Communist Party of Viet Nam, full mem. 1989, Dir. Nationalities Comm. 1989–91, elected mem. Political Bureau 1991, 1996, Gen. Sec. 2001–.
Address: Dang Cong San Viet Nam, 1 Hoang Van Thu, Hanoi, Viet Nam (office). *E-mail:* cpv@hn.vnn.vn (office). *Website:* www.cpv.org.vn (office).

MANIGLIA FERREIRA, Adm. Ramón Orlando; Venezuelan government official and naval officer. *Career:* mem. Navy, fmr Navy Commdr, C-in-C 2003, rank of Vice-Adm., then Three-Sun Adm. 2005; Inspector Gen. Nat. Armed Forces 2004–05; Minister of Nat. Defence 2005–06.
Address: c/o Ministry of National Defence, Edif. 17 de Diciembre, planta baja, Base Aérea Francisco de Miranda, La Carlota, Caracas, Venezuela (office).

MANIKU, Mohamed Hussain, BBA; Maldivian diplomatist; *Ambassador to USA. Education:* American Univ., Beirut, Lebanon. *Career:* began career as public servant after joining govt in 1980, worked for Ministry of Finance, then for Maldives Monetary Authority, has held sr posts including Deputy Dir Fisheries Projects Implementation Dept 1989–90; Deputy Dir State Trading Org. 1990–91, Man. Dir 1991–2008; Amb. to USA 2008–.
Address: Embassy of the Republic of Maldives, 1111 19th Street, NW, Suite 211, Washington, DC 20036, USA (office). *Telephone:* (202) 507-8934 (office). *Fax:* (202) 507-8935 (office). *E-mail:* info@maldivesembassy.us (office). *Website:* www.maldivesembassy.us (office).

MANLEY, Albert Leslie; South African diplomatist; b. 1945, Cape Town; m. Charlene Manley 1988; three s. one d. *Education:* Univ. of Free State. *Career:* entered Dept of Foreign Affairs 1969, Desk Officer for Middle East 1974–76, Planning Section of Ministry, Pretoria and Cape Town 1981–82, other posts 1982–86; Vice-Consul in Lourenço Marques (now Maputo) 1970–74; Counsellor for Political Affairs at Embassy, London 1977–81; Perm. Rep. to UN, New York 1987–88, Geneva 1988–92; Head Int. Econs, Foreign Ministry 1992–94, Head Int. Devt and Econ. Affairs 1995–98; Minister at South African Embassy and Mission to the EU, Brussels 1998;

currently Chief Dir (acting) of Econ. and Social Affairs, Dept of Foreign Affairs; Fellow, Center for Int. Affairs, Harvard Univ., USA 1994–95.
Address: Department of Foreign Affairs, 1234 Church Street, Arcadia, Pretoria 0002, South Africa (office). *Telephone:* (12) 3511360 (office). *Fax:* (12) 3511331 (office). *E-mail:* manleya@foreign.gov.za (office). *Website:* www.dfa.gov.za (office).

MANN, James, BA; American political analyst and journalist; *Author-in-Residence, Paul H. Nitze School of Advanced International Studies, Johns Hopkins University; Education:* Harvard Univ. *Career:* Supreme Court corresp. Los Angeles Times 1978, Chief of Beijing Bureau 1984–87, fmr diplomatic corresp. and foreign affairs columnist –2001; fmr Guest Scholar, Woodrow Wilson Int. Center for Scholars and Sr Writer-in-Residence, Int. Security Program, Center for Strategic and Int. Studies (CSIS); currently Author-in-Residence School of Advanced Int. Studies, Johns Hopkins Univ. and Fellow Foreign Policy Inst.; commentator All Things Considered radio program PBS; contrib. LA Times; mem. Council on Foreign Relations; Edwin M. Hood Award 1993, 1999, Edward Weintal Prize 1999. *Publications:* Beijing Jeep 1989, About Face: A History of America's Curious Relationship with China from Nixon to Clinton (New York Public Library Helen Bernstein Award 2000, Asia-Pacific Prize) 1999, Rise of the Vulcans: The History of Bush's War Cabinet 2004.
Address: Paul H. Nitze School of Advanced International Studies, Foreign Policy Institute, Johns Hopkins University, 1619 Massachusetts Avenue, NW, Washington, DC 20036, USA (office). *Telephone:* (202) 663-5600 (office). *Fax:* (202) 663-5656 (office). *Website:* www.sais-jhu.edu/centers/fpi/index.html (office).

MANN, Michael, BA, DPhil; British/American sociologist and academic; *Professor of Sociology, University of California, Los Angeles;* b. Manchester. *Education:* Univ. of Oxford. *Career:* Research Officer, Dept of Applied Econs, Univ. of Cambridge 1967–71; Lecturer and Sr Lecturer, Univ. of Essex 1971–77; Reader in Sociology, LSE 1977–87; Prof., Dept of Sociology, UCLA 1987–; Visiting Research Prof., Queens Univ. Belfast 2003–07; Visiting Prof., Instituto Juan March, Madrid 1992–93, Birkbeck Coll., Univ. of London 1995–97; Visiting Pitt Prof. of American History and Insts, Univ. of Cambridge 2004–05; mem. Sociological Research Asscn 1989–; Eligible Fellow, Center for Advanced Arts, Palo Alto 1990; Hon. Fellow, Univ. of Leiden, Netherlands 1996; Hon. DLitt (McGill Univ., Montreal) 1998; Gold Medal, Univ. of Helsinki 1993. *Publications include:* Consciousness and Action in the Western Working Class 1973, The Working Class in the Labour Market 1979 (jt ed.), The Sources of Social Power; Vol. I: A History of Power From the Beginning to 1760 AD 1986, States, War and Capitalism 1988, The Sources of Social Power; Vol. II: The Rise of Classes and the Nation-States 1760–1914 1993, Incoherent Empire 2003, Fascists 2004, The Dark-Side of Democracy Explaining Ethnic Cleansing (Barrington Moore Award of the American Sociological Asscn) 2005, and numerous articles in journals.
Address: Department of Sociology, UCLA, 264 Haines Hall, PO Box 951551, Los Angeles, CA 90095-1551, USA (office). *Telephone:* (310) 825-1822 (office). *Fax:* (310) 206-9838 (office). *E-mail:* mmann@soc.ucla.edu (office). *Website:* www.soc.ucla.edu/faculty/mann (office).

MANNAI, Jassim Abdullah al-, PhD; Bahraini business executive and international organization official; *Director-General and Chairman, Arab Monetary Fund;* b. 1948. *Education:* Univ. of the Sorbonne, Paris, France and Harvard Business School. *Career:* Exec. Vice-Pres. Gulf Investment Corpn, Kuwait 1987–94; CEO and Chair. Arab Trade Financing Program, Abu Dhabi 1994–; Dir-Gen. and Chair. Arab Monetary Fund, Abu Dhabi 1994–; Chair. Inter Arab Rating Co. EC (mem. Fitch IBCA Group) 1995–2001. *Publications:* numerous articles on economic and financial issues in various publs.
Address: Office of the Director-General, Arab Monetary Fund Building, Corniche Road, PO Box 2818, Abu Dhabi, United Arab Emirates (office). *Telephone:* (2) 6171400 (office). *Fax:* (2) 6326454 (office). *E-mail:* centralmail@amfad.org.ae (office). *Website:* www.amf.org.ae (office).

MANNING, Sir David Geoffrey, Kt, GCMG, BA; British diplomatist; b. 5 Dec. 1949, Portsmouth, Hants.; m. Catherine Marjory Parkinson 1973. *Education:* Ardingly Coll., Oriel Coll. Oxford, Johns Hopkins Univ., USA. *Career:* Third Sec., FCO (Mexico, Cen. America Dept) 1972; Third, later Second Sec., Warsaw 1974–76; Second, later First Sec., New Delhi 1977–80; E European and Soviet Dept FCO 1980–82; Policy Planning Staff, FCO 1982–84; First Sec. (Political Internal), Paris 1984–88; Counsellor on loan to Cabinet Office 1988–90; Counsellor, Head of Political Section, Moscow 1990–93; Head, Eastern Dept (fmrly Soviet Dept), FCO 1993–94; British mem. of ICFY Contact Group on Bosnia April–Nov. 1994; Head of Planning Staff 1994–95; Amb. to Israel 1995–98; Deputy Under-Sec. of State, FCO 1998–2000; Perm. Rep. to NATO Jan.–Aug. 2001; Foreign Policy Adviser to Prime Minister 2001–03; Head

of Cabinet Office Defence and Overseas Secr. 2001–03; Amb. to USA 2003–07.
Address: c/o Foreign and Commonwealth Office, King Charles Street, London, SW1A 2AH, UK (office).

MANNING, Patrick Augustus Mervyn, BSc; Trinidad and Tobago politician; *Prime Minister and Minister of Tobago Affairs;* b. 17 Aug. 1946, San Fernando, Trinidad; m. Hazel Anne-Marie Kinsale 1972; two s. *Education:* Presentation Coll., San Fernando and Univ. of the West Indies. *Career:* refinery operator Texaco, Trinidad 1965–66; Parl. Sec. 1971–78, Minister 1978–86; Minister of Information and of Industry and Commerce 1981, of Energy 1981–86; Leader of the Opposition 1986–90; Prime Minister 1991–95, 2001–, also Minister of Tobago Affairs; Minister of Finance 2001–07; fmr Minister of Nat. Security; Leader People's Nat. Movt (PNM) 1987–.
Address: Office of the Prime Minister, Whitehall, Maraval Road, Port of Spain; People's National Movement, 1 Tranquillity Street, Port of Spain, Trinidad. *Telephone:* 622-1625 (office); 625-1533. *Fax:* 622-0055 (office). *E-mail:* opm@trinidad.net; opm@ttgov.gov.tt (office). *Website:* www.opm.gov.tt.

MANOLI, Mihail; Moldovan economist and diplomatist; b. 1954. *Career:* Minister of Finance 1999–2002; Amb. to USA (also accred to Canada) 2002–06.
Address: Ministry of Foreign Affairs and European Integration, str. 31 August 80, 2012 Chişinău, Moldova (office). *Telephone:* (22) 57-82-07 (office). *Fax:* (22) 23-23-02 (office). *E-mail:* secdep@mfa.md (office). *Website:* www.mfa.md (office).

MANOLIČ, Josip, (Joža); Croatian politician and lawyer; b. 22 March 1920, Kalinovac; m. Marija Manolić (née Eker); three d. *Education:* Zagreb Univ. *Career:* mem. youth orgs and trade union activist 1938–; mem. anti-fascist movt; Sec. Dist Cttee League of Communist Youth of Croatia; Chief Dept of Nat. Security in Bjelovar 1945–46 (dismissed); worked in Ministry of Internal Affairs of Croatia 1948–60; Interior Affairs Secr. in Zagreb 1960–65; mem. of Parl. Repub. of Croatia, Pres. Legis. Body of Constitutional Comm. 1965–71; mandate suspended because of nationalist activities; Co-founder Croatian Democratic Union (HDZ) first Chair. Exec. Cttee 1989, elected Vice-Pres. 1990; mem. of Croatian Parl. 1990–; Pres. Croatian Govt 1990–91, Vice-Pres. Presidency of Repub. of Croatia –1999; Pres. House of Counties of Croatian Parl. 1992–94; Pres. Emergency Bd of Croatia; Dir Bureau for the Protection of Constitutional Order 1991–93; Founder Croatian Ind. Democrats (HND), Pres. of HND; an organizer of Croatian army; certificate for participation in anti-Fascist struggle 1941–45, certificate for participation in the defence of the homeland 1991–92. *Publication:* Manolić 1989–95 (collection of interviews).
Address: Nazorova Str. 57, 41000 Zagreb, Croatia (office). *Telephone:* (1) 4848476 (office).

MANOROHANTA, Cécile; Malagasy politician and academic; *Minister of National Defence; Career:* fmr Dir of Research and Dean of Universite Nord, Antsiranana Prov.; Nat. Vice-Pres. ruling Tiako i Madagasikara (I Love Madagascar—TIM) party; Minister of Defence (first woman) 2007–.
Publications: A Quantitative Study of Voice in Malagasy (UCLA Working Papers in Linguistics 6: Papers in African Linguistics 1) 2001; numerous papers on linguistics in professional journals.
Address: Ministry of National Defence, BP 08, Ampahibe, 101 Antananarivo, Madagascar (office). *Telephone:* (20) 2222211 (office). *Fax:* (20) 2235420 (office). *E-mail:* mdn@wanadoo.mg (office).

MANSINGH, Lalit, MA; Indian diplomatist; b. 29 April 1941, Cuttack; m. Indira Singh 1976; one s. one d. *Education:* Stewart and C. S. Zila Schools, Utkal Univ., Indian School of Int. Studies, New Delhi. *Career:* lecturer in political science 1961–63; joined diplomatic service 1963, Deputy Chief of Mission to Kabul 1971–74, to Brussels 1976–80, to Washington, DC 1989–92, Amb. to UAE 1980–83; High Commr to Nigeria 1993–95, to London 1998–99; Jt Sec. Dept of Econ. Affairs, Ministry of Finance 1984–85; Dir Gen. Indian Council for Cultural Relations 1985–89; Dean Foreign Service Inst., New Delhi 1995–96; Perm. Sec. Ministry of External Affairs 1997–98; Amb. to USA 2001–04. *Publication:* Indian Foreign Policy: Agenda for the 21st Century (Ed.-in-Chief) 1998.
Address: N-38 Panchsheel Park, New Delhi 110 017, India (home).

MANSOUR, Habib, BA, BEcons; Tunisian diplomatist; *Permanent Representative, United Nations;* b. 23 Feb. 1949, Hammam Sousse; m.; four c. *Education:* Lycee de garcons de Sousse, Univ. of Tunis. *Career:* Head, Industrial Div., Nat. Office of Fisheries 1972–78; Admin. in Int. Co-operation Dept in charge of bilateral co-operation for Arab World, Africa and Europe, Ministry of Foreign Affairs 1979–80; Consul to W Berlin

1981–82; First Sec., then Counselor, Embassy in Doha 1983–1984; First Counselor, Embassy in Prague 1984–88; Consul Gen. to Belgium and Luxemburg 1988–90; Charge de Mission, Cabinet of Minister of Foreign Affairs 1992–94; Amb. to Zaire 1990–92, to Argentina 1994–97, to Chile 1995–97, to Spain 1997–2001; Charge de Mission and Head of Human Rights Unit, Ministry of Foreign Affairs 2001–02; Perm. Rep. to UN, Geneva 2002–04; Amb. to Italy 2005–07, to Cyprus 2006–07; Perm. Rep. to UN, New York 2007–; fmr Researcher, Nat. Center of Industrial Studies, Ministry of Nat. Economy; fmr Head of Studies and Man. Control Section of Studies and Devt, Sousse Nord Co. (Integrated Tourist Project); fmr Head of Studies and Planning Section, Nat. Office of Family Planning and Population; Officer, Order of the Repub. of Tunisia, Grand Cruz, Order of Saint Martin (Argentina), Order of Isabelle the Catholic (Spain), Special Star, Order of the Italian Solidarity.
Address: Permanent Mission of Tunisia to the United Nations, 31 Beekman Place, New York, NY 10022, USA (office). *Telephone:* (212) 751-7503 (office). *Fax:* (212) 751-0569 (office). *E-mail:* tunisia@un.int (office). *Website:* www.tunisiaonline.com/tunisia-un/index.html (office).

MANSOURI, Khalid bin Rashid bin Salim al-Hamoudi al-; Qatari diplomatist; *Ambassador to UK;* m. Mooza Saif S. A. al-Mansouri. *Career:* Amb. to UK 2005–.
Address: Embassy of Qatar, 1 South Audley Street, London, W1K 1NB, England (office). *Telephone:* (20) 7493-2200 (office). *Fax:* (20) 7493-2661 (office).

MANTEGA, Guido, MA, PhD; Brazilian economist, academic and government official; *Minister of Finance;* b. 7 April 1949, Genoa, Italy; m. Eliana Berger Mantega. *Education:* School of Econs and Admin, Universidade de Sao Paulo, Inst. of Devt Countries, Univ. of Sussex, UK. *Career:* Prof. of Econs, School of Business Admin, Fundação Getúlio Vargas 1981–; Budget Dir and Head, Office of Municipal Dept of Planning, São Paulo, 1982–92; Prof. of Econs, Pontificia Universidade Católica de São Paulo-PUC-SP 1984–87; mem. Coordination of Econ. Program for Brazilian Labor Party (PT) in presidential elections 1984, 1989, 1998; Econ. Advisor to President Luiz Inácio Lula da Silva 1993–2002; coordinator PT's Econ. Program 2002; Minister of Planning, Budget, and Admin 2003–04; Pres. Banco Nacional de Desenvolvimento Econômico e Social (BNDES) 2004–06; Minister of Finance 2006–. *Publications:* numerous articles and books including Acumulação Monopolista e Crises no Brasil 1981, A Economia Política Brasileira 1984, Custo Brasil: Mito ou Realidade 1997.
Address: Ministry of Finance, Esplanada dos Ministérios, Bloco P, 5° andar, 70048-900 Brasília, DF, Brazil (office). *Telephone:* (61) 3412-2515 (office). *Fax:* (61) 3412-1721 (office). *E-mail:* gabinete.df.gmf@fazenda.gov.br (office). *Website:* www.fazenda.gov.br (office).

MANUEL, Trevor Andrew; South African politician; *Minister of Finance;* b. 31 Jan. 1956, Cape Town; m. Lynn Matthews; three s. *Education:* Harold Cressy High School. *Career:* mem. Labour Party Youth 1969–71, Policy Man. on Devt 1989–; construction technician 1974–81; Sec. Kensington Civic Asscn 1977–82; Founding mem. Western Cape United Democratic Front (UDF) 1980s, Sec. Regional Exec. UDF 1983–90, mem. UDF Nat. Exec. Cttee 1983–86, 1989–90; Organizer CAHAC 1981–82; field worker Educational Resource and Information Centre 1982–84; in detention 1985, 1987–88, 1989, restricted 1985–86, 1986–90 (when not in detention); Publicity Sec. ANC Western Cape; mem. ANC Nat. Exec. Cttee 1991–; Minister of Trade and Industry, Govt of Nat. Unity 1994–96; Minister of Finance 1996–.
Address: Private Bag X115, Pretoria 0001, South Africa. *Telephone:* (012) 315-5372. *Fax:* (012) 323-3262.

MAOATE, Terepai, PhD; Cook Islands politician; *Deputy Prime Minister and Minister of Finance and Economic Development; Career:* Prime Minister and Minister of Finance 2000–02, Deputy Prime Minister and Minister of Finance 2005, currently Deputy Prime Minister and Minister of Finance and Econ. Devt, Financial Intelligence Unit, Public Expenditure and Review Cttee, Health, Ombudsman, Devt Investment Bd, Small Business Enterprise Centre, Attorney-Gen., Commerce Comm., Nat. Superannuation, Parl. Services and Broadcasting; fmr Gov. Asian Devt Bank; Leader, Democratic Party.
Address: Ministry of Finance and Economic Management, POB 120, Rarotonga, Cook Islands (office). *Telephone:* 22878 (office). *Fax:* 23877 (office). *E-mail:* cifinsec@mfem.gov.ck (office). *Website:* www.mfem.gov.ck (office).

MARCANO, Luis Herrera, DIur; Venezuelan diplomatist and academic; *Professor of Law, Universidad Central de Venezuela;* b. 13 Dec. 1931, Caracas; m. Maria Sardi de Herrera. *Education:* Universidad Cen. de Venezuela. *Career:* staff mem. Ministry of Foreign Affairs 1950–55, adviser 1956–57, Dir Int. Orgs 1958, Dir Office of the Commrs for Guyana

1965–67, Dir Int. Policy 1968, Adviser to the Minister 1969–72, 1978, mem. Foreign Relations Advisory Comm. 1979–84, Amb. and mem. Comm. for Maritime Delimitation with Colombia 1980, mem. Council of Legal Advisers 1984–, legal adviser 1990–91, Co-ordinator of Pro Tempore Secr. of Rio Group 1990, external adviser 1992–99, adviser to Ministers of Interior and Justice 1999; Amb. and Deputy Perm. Rep. to UN, New York 2000; Amb. and Deputy Chief of Mission in Washington, DC 2001, Chargé d'affaires (acting) 2002–03; Prof. of Public Int. Law, Universidad Cen. de Venezuela 1963–, Dir School of Law 1978–81, Dean Faculty of Legal and Political Sciences 1981–84; also currently external adviser in legal matters to Latin American and Caribben Econ. System (SELA); Exec. Sec. Organizing Comm., Universidad Simón Rodríguez 1972–76; mem. Interamerican Juridical Cttee, OAS 1982–, Pres. 1990–92; legal adviser Latin American Econ. System 1986–90; adviser to UN Truth Comm. for El Salvador 1992–93, mem. UN Comm. of Inquiry for Burundi 1995–96; adviser to Petróleos de Venezuela 1985–86.
Address: c/o Faculty of Law and Political Science, Universidad Central de Venezuela, Apdo Postal 1050, Ciudad Universitaria, Los Chaguaramos, Caracas, 1051, Venezuela (office). *Website:* www.ucv.ve (office).

MARCHUK, Gen. Yevgen Kirilovich, CJur; Ukrainian politician; b. 28 Jan. 1941, Dolinivka, Kirovograd Region; m.; two s. *Education:* Kirovograd Pedagogical Inst. *Career:* worked as school teacher of Ukrainian and German Languages; with Ukrainian KGB (State Security Cttee) 1963–91, Deputy Chair. 1990–91; Chair. Nat. Security Service of Ukraine 1991; State Minister of Defence, Nat. Security and Emergencies 1991–94; Deputy Prime Minister July 1994, First Deputy Prime Minister 1994–95; Prime Minister of Ukraine 1995–96; mem. Verkhovna Rada (United Social Democratic Party faction) 1996–; Head Cttee of Social Policy and Labour 1998–; Sec. Ukrainian Nat. Security and Defence Council 2000–03; Minister of Defence 2003–04; Pres. Ukrainian Transport Union 1998; presidential cand. 1999.
Address: c/o National Security and Defence Council of Ukraine, Domandarma Kameneva Str. 8, 01133 Kiev, Ukraine. *Telephone:* (44) 291-60-27.

MAREHALAU, Jesse Bibiano; Micronesian diplomatist; b. 25 Dec. 1948, Ulithi, Yap; m. Martha Lorerang; one s. *Education:* Chaminade Univ., Hawaii. *Career:* served in many elected and apptd positions in Yap State Govt and Federated States of Micronesia (FSM) Nat. Govt; fmr Chief of Marine Resources and Asst Fisheries Officer, Yap State Govt; fmr FSM Rep. to USA, Amb. to USA 1990–2007; charged with bribery, criminal conspiracy, over-obligation of govt funds, tampering with public records and information, and theft against the Govt May 2007.
Address: Department of Foreign Affairs, PO Box PS-123, Palikir, Pohnpei, FM 96941, Federated States of Micronesia (office). *Telephone:* 320-2641 (office). *Fax:* 320-2933 (office). *E-mail:* foreignaffairs@mail.fm (office). *Website:* www.fsmgov.org/ovmis.html (office).

MARES, Petr, PhD; Czech politician and academic; b. 15 Jan. 1953; m.; two d. *Education:* Charles Univ., Prague, Warsaw Univ., Poland. *Career:* engineer, Strojinvestav Eng Co. 1989–81; researcher, Inst. of Czechoslovak History 1981–84; record keeper, Dept of Archives, Gen. Trade Union 1987–88; researcher, Dept of History and Theory of Film-Making, Czechoslovak Films Inst. 1988–90; Sec. Chair. of Political Sciences, Faculty of Social Sciences, Charles Univ. 1990, Vice-Dean for Study Affairs, Head Dept of American Studies Inst. of Int. Studies –1996; Fellow, Univ. of Calgary, Canada 1996; Chair. Cttee for Science, Educ., Culture and Youth, Chamber of Deputies 1998–2002; Deputy Prime Minister for Minorities of Czech Repub. 2002–04; Chair. Freedom Union –2004.
Publications include: History of the Lands of the Czech Crown: Part II (co-author) 1992, United States Presidents 1994, History and NATO (co-author) 1997; many articles in professional journals.
Address: c/o Office of the Government, nábř. Edvarda Beneše 4, 118 01 Prague 1, Czech Republic (office).

MARGRETHE II, HM, Queen of Denmark; b. 16 April 1940; m. Count Henri de Laborde de Monpezat (now Prince Consort Henrik of Denmark) 1967; two s., HRH Crown Prince Frederik and HRH Prince Joachim. *Education:* Univs of Copenhagen, Århus and Cambridge, Sorbonne, Paris and London School of Econs. *Career:* succeeded to the throne 14 Jan. 1972; has undertaken many official visits abroad with her husband, travelling extensively in Europe, the Far East, N and S America; Hon. KG 1979; Hon. Freedom of City of London 2000; Hon. Bencher of the Middle Temple 1992; Hon. Fellow Lucy Cavendish Coll. Cambridge 1989, Girton Coll. Cambridge 1992; Hon. LLD (Cambridge) 1975; Dr hc (London) 1980, (Univ. of Iceland) 1986, (Oxford) 1992, (Edin.) 2000; Medal of the Headmastership, Univ. of Paris 1987. *Achievements (miscellaneous):* illustrated J. R. R. Tolkien's Lord of the Rings (1977), Historierne om Regnar Lodbrog, Norse Legends as told by Jorgen Stegelmann (1979),

Bjarkemaal (1982), Poul Oerum's Comedy in Florens (1990) and Cantabile poems by HRH the Prince Consort (2000), designed costumes for TV Theatre's The Shepherdess and the Chimney-sweep (1987), scenography and costumes for the ballet A Folk Tale, Royal Theatre (1991), découpages for TV film about the Hans Christian Andersen fairy tale Snedronningen (1999–2000), scenography and costumes for Tivoli pantomime ballet Kaerlighed i Skarnkassen (2001), illustrations for Karen Blixen's Seven Gothic Tales (2002). *Art exhibitions include:* exhbn of sketches and finished works at Køge Art Gallery Sketch Collection (1988), The Glass Museum, Ebeltoft (1988), Millesgården, Stockholm (1989), Blåfarveværket, Norway (1991), Baron Boltens Gård, Copenhagen (1991), Gammel Holtegaard (1993), Herning Art Gallery (1993), exhbns of paintings and church textiles in Århus Museum of Art, in Marienlyst Palace and The Danish Library in Flensburg, Germany, of church textiles in Reykjavik, Iceland (1998), of paintings and lithographs in Gallery J.M.S., Oslo (1999), of paintings at Sofiero, Sweden (2002), of découpages used as illustrations in new edn of Seven Gothic Tales at Karen Blixen Museum Rungstedlund (2002), of paintings and ecclesiastical textiles at Didrichsen Art Museum, Helsinki 2002–03, of ecclesiastical textiles and works of embroidery at Yamanashi, Hemslöjd, Tokyo 2003, of paintings at Waldemarsudde, Stockholm 2004.
Publications: (trans.) All Men are Mortal (with HRH the Prince Consort) 1981, The Valley 1988, The Fields 1989, The Forest (trans.) 1989.
Address: Amalienborg, 1257 Copenhagen K; PO Box 2143, 1015 Copenhagen K, Denmark. *E-mail:* hofmarskallatet@kongehuset.dk (office). *Website:* www.kongehuset.dk (office).

MARIN, Vice-Adm. Gheorghe, PhD; Romanian naval officer; *Chief of the General Staff;* b. 1 Jan. 1952, Negru-Vodă, Constanţa dist; m. Elena Marin; one d. *Education:* Mircea cel Bătrân Naval Acad., Constanţa, Faculty of Econ. Planning and Cybernetics, Econ. Studies Acad., Bucharest. *Career:* Navigation and Communication Officer FPB (M) Squadron 1974–78; CO, Fast Patrol Boat 1980–81; Staff Officer, N3 1981–85; Chief Software Programming Section, Naval Informatics Centre 1985–89; Chief Naval Informatics Center 1989–95; CO Electronic Warfare Brigade within Naval Forces 1995–99; Supt, Mircea cel Bătrân Naval Acad. 1999–2003; Dir of Gen. Staff 2003–04, Chief of Naval Forces Staff 2004–06, Chief of Gen. Staff 2006–.
Address: Office of the Chief of the General Staff, Ministry of National Defence, 050561 Bucharest 5, Str. Izvor 13–15, Sector 5, Romania (office). *Telephone:* (21) 4023400 (office). *Fax:* (21) 3195698 (office). *E-mail:* drp@mapn.ro (office). *Website:* www.mapn.ro (office).

MARIN GONZALEZ, Manuel, MA; Spanish international official; *President, Congress of Deputies;* b. 21 Oct. 1949, Ciudad Real; m. Carmen Ortiz; two c. *Education:* Madrid Univ., Coll. of Europe, Bruges and Univ. of Nancy. *Career:* joined Spanish Socialist Party 1974; mem. Parl. for Ciudad Real, La Mancha 1977–86, 2000–; Sec. of State for Relations with the EEC 1982–85; EEC (now EU) Commr for Social Affairs, Employment, Educ. and Training 1986–89, for Co-operation and Devt 1989–94, for External Relations with the Mediterranean (South), Near and Middle East, Latin America and Asia (except Japan, People's Repub. of China, Repub. of Korea, Hong Kong, Macao, Taiwan) 1995–99, Vice-Pres. of Comm. 1993–99, Pres. (Acting) 1999; Spokesman, Foreign Affairs Cttee, Congress of Deputies 2001–04, Pres. Congress of Deputies 2004–; Grand Cross, Order of Isabel la Católica.
Address: Congress of Deputies, Carrera de San Jerónimo s/n, 28071 Madrid, Spain (office). *Telephone:* (91) 3906000 (office). *Fax:* (91) 4298707 (office). *Website:* www.congreso.es (office).

MARINE, Michael W., BA; American diplomatist; b. 1947, New York City; m. Carmella Marine; two adopted d. *Education:* Univ. of California, Santa Barbara. *Career:* enlisted in US Marine Corps 1967, completed his service with rank of Capt. 1971; entered Foreign Service in 1975, now career mem. Sr Foreign Service with rank of Minister Counselor, posted as Consular Officer to Martinique, London and Guangzhou, China 1979–81, Political Officer in Hong Kong 1982–85, served in series of positions at State Dept including Dir Office of Fraud Prevention Programs, Bureau of Consular Affairs, Deputy Dir Bureau of E Asia and the Pacific's Office of Vietnam, Laos and Cambodia Affairs, and Special Asst, Bureau of Consular Affairs 1985–91, Deputy Chief of Mission, Suva 1991–93, Chargé d'affaires a.i. 1993–94, Minister Counselor for Consular Affairs, Bonn 1994–95, Moscow 1995–97, Deputy Chief of Mission, Nairobi 1997–2000 (Chargé d'affaires a.i. May–Sept. 1999), Beijing 2000–04, Amb. to Viet Nam 2004–07; Superior Honor Award 1981, 1990, 1993, 1999, 2001, 2002.
Address: US Department of State, 2201 C Street NW, Washington, DC 20520, USA (office). *Telephone:* (202) 647-4000 (office). *Fax:* (202) 647-6738 (office). *Website:* www.state.gov (office).

MARINOS, Yannis, BA; Greek journalist; b. 20 July 1930, Hermoupolis. *Education:* Univ. of Athens. *Career:* journalist, To Vima (daily) 1953–65;

journalist, Economicos Tachydromos, Ed.-in-Chief 1956, Ed. and Dir 1964–96, consultant/columnist 1996–; political commentator in Ta Nea (daily) 1972–75; columnist, To Vima (daily political journal) 1992–; commentator for many radio and TV stations in Greece; mem. European Parl. 1999–2004; Deputy Nea Democratia and European Popular Party 1999–; mem. Bd Lambrakis Research Foundation, Org. of Music Hall of Athens; Hon. PhD (Aristotelian Univ. Salonika) 1999; more than 30 awards including Best European Journalist of 1989 (EC Comm. and Asscn of European Journalists) and awards from UN and Athens Acad. *Publications:* The Palestinian Problem and Cyprus 1975, For a Change Towards Better 1983, Greece in Crisis 1987, Common Sense 1993. *Address:* 9 Merlin Street, Athens 106 71 (office); 2 Kontziadon Street, Piraeus 185 37, Greece (home). *Telephone:* (210) 3641828 (office); (210) 4526823 (home). *Fax:* (210) 3641839. *E-mail:* jmarinos@dolnet.gr (office).

MARKARIAN, Tatoul, MA, PhD; Armenian diplomatist; *Ambassador to USA;* m.; two s. *Education:* Yerevan Univ. of Nat. Economy, Johns Hopkins Univ. School of Advanced Int. Studies, USA, London School of Econs, UK. *Career:* Asst to Vice-Chair. Armenian Parl. 1990–91; Asst, then adviser to Vice-Pres. of Armenia 1991–94, also served as Acting Chief of Staff to Prime Minister 1991–92; Deputy Chief of Mission and Minister-Counselor, Embassy in Washington, DC 1994–99; Deputy Minister of Foreign Affairs 2000–05, acted as Armenian coordinator for US-Armenia Strategic Dialogue and NATO-Armenia Political-Mil. Dialogue; Special Rep. of Pres. of Armenia for Nagorno-Karabakh negotiations 2002–03; Amb. to USA 2005–. *Address:* Embassy of Armenia, 2225 R Street, NW, Washington, DC, 20008 USA (office). *Telephone:* (202) 319-1976 (office). *Fax:* (202) 319-2982 (office). *E-mail:* armecon@speakeasy.net (office). *Website:* www.armeniaemb.org (office).

MARKOPOULOS, Christos, DSc; Greek politician and nuclear chemist; *President, Federation of Balkan Non-Governmental Organizations for Peace and Co-operation;* b. 25 Dec. 1925, Athens; m. 1st Sapfo Mazaraki 1954 (divorced 1960); one s.; m. 2nd Kleopatra Papadopoulou 1974; two s. *Education:* Varvakios High School, Teachers' Acad., Athens, Univ. of Athens, Leicester Coll. of Tech., UK. *Career:* Nat. State Chem. Lab. 1956–59; Group Leader, Greek Atomic Energy Comm. 1962–69, Dir Radio-immunochem. 1977–81; Asst Prof., Nat. Tech. Univ. of Athens 1965; Sr Researcher, Imperial Coll., London 1968; Visiting Scientist, Tech. Hochschule, Darmstadt, FRG; Visiting Prof., Univ. of Bologna 1973; Pres. Hellenic Nuclear Soc. 1975–81; mem. Steering Cttee, European Nuclear Soc. 1979–81; mem. Cen. Cttee, Panhellenic Socialist Movement (PASOK) 1975–93; mem. European Parl. 1981–84 (mem. Energy, Research and Tech. Comm.); Amb.-at-Large for West European Countries 1984–85; mem. Nat. Parl. of Greece 1985–89 (Pres. Foreign Affairs Cttee 1986–87); Head of Greek Parl. Del. in Council of Europe 1986–88 (Vice-Pres. Parl. Ass. 1987–88); Minister in charge of Int. Orgs 1988–89; Pres. Panhellenic Movt for Nat. Independence, World Peace and Disarmament 1981–90; Founder Int. Peace Olympiad Bureau, Co-ordinator First Peace Olympiad 1989; Founder and Pres. Movt for Peace, Human Rights and Nat. Independence 1991–2001 (Hon. Pres. 2001–), Fed. of Balkan Non-Governmental Orgs for Peace and Co-operation 1993–; Pres. Int. Organizing Cttee, 2nd European Conf. on Peace, Democracy and Co-operation in Balkans 1996; Pro Merito Medal, Parl. Ass. Council of Europe 1986, Model of Council of Europe 1988, Medal of Civilization, UNESCO 1989, Diploma and Medal for Contrib. to Peace and Welfare of Humanity, Int. Peace Bureau 1992, Honour Award for Contrib. to Progress of Science of Chem., Asscn of Greek Chemists 1997, Honour Prize for Participation in Nat. Resistance against German occupation 1999. *Publications:* Organic Chemistry (2 vols) 1963 and 1971, Inorganic Chemistry (2 vols) 1968 and 1971, Introduction to Modern Chemistry 1973, The Dominance of Prota and the Theory of Enforced Randomness 1991, Order and Anarchy 1996, Chance and Order 1997, Alexander and Diogenes 1999, Conjectures and Arpisms 1999; and numerous articles on nuclear disarmament, peace, int. affairs, European relations and human rights. *Address:* 23 Kzitonos, 16121 Athens (office); 34 Eratous Street, 15561 Holargos, Athens, Greece (home). *Telephone:* (1) 7211929 (office); (1) 6524687 (home). *Fax:* (1) 7211035 (office); (1) 6526847. *E-mail:* febang@otenet.gr (office); ch_marko@otenet.gr (home).

MARMOLEJO, Francisco José Ruiz; Colombian international organization official; *Acting Secretary-General and Executive Director, Amazon Cooperation Treaty Organization;* b. Cali. *Education:* Nat. Univ. of Colombia, Fed. Univ. of Pará, Brazil, Univ. of Las Palmas, Gran Canaria. *Career:* previous posts include Environmental Del. Comptroller, Colombia, Chair. Techno-logical Transfer Nat. Program (Pronatta), mem. Panel of Experts on the Amazon, Co-Dir Ecofondo (org. of environmental NGOs); Exec. Dir Amazon Cooperation Treaty Org. (Organización del Tratado de Cooperación Amazónica) 2003–, Acting Sec.-Gen. 2007–.

Address: Amazon Cooperation Treaty Organization, SHIS–QI 05, Conjunto 16, casa 21, Lago Sul, Brasília, DF 71615-160, Brazil (office). *Telephone:* (61) 3248-4119 (office). *Fax:* (61) 3248-4238 (office). *E-mail:* fjruiz@otca.org.br (office). *Website:* www.otca.org.br (office).

MAROUFI, Yahya; Afghan diplomatist; *Ambassador to Iran; Career:* fmr Chief of Foreign Relations, Office of the Pres.; Amb. to Iran 2007–. *Address:* Embassy of Afghanistan, Dr Beheshti Avenue, Corner of 4th Street, Pakistan Street, Tehran, Iran (office). *Telephone:* (21) 88737050 (office). *Fax:* (21) 88735600 (office). *E-mail:* afghaembassytehran@hotmail.com (office).

MARQUARDT, R. Niels; American diplomatist; *Ambassador to Madagascar and the Comoros;* b. San Diego, Calif.; m. Judy Marquardt; four d. *Education:* Lewis and Clark Coll., American Grad. School of Int. Man., Nat. War Coll. *Career:* Peace Corps volunteer, Rwanda 1977–79; career mem. Sr Foreign Service since 1980, class of Minister-Counselor, overseas assignments as an Econ. Officer in Brazzaville, Congo 1983–85, Thailand 1981–83, 1987–90, France 1990–94, Germany 1995–98, Dir State Dept's Entry-level Counseling and Assignments Div., Bureau of Human Resources 1998–2000, Special Coordinator for Diplomatic Readiness 2001–04, also served in Bureau of E Asian and Pacific Affairs and as a Country Risk Analyst at Export-Import Bank of the US, attended the Senior Seminar and the Econ.-Commercial Studies Program, Foreign Service Inst., Amb. to Cameroon 2004–07 (also accred to Equatorial Guinea 2004–06), to Madagascar (also accred to the Comoros) 2007–; several Meritorious and Superior Honor Awards, four Presidential Performance Pay awards. *Address:* US Embassy, BP 620, 14 rue Rainitovo, Antsahavola, Antananarivo 101, Madagascar (office). *Telephone:* (20) 2221257 (office). *Fax:* (20) 2234539 (office). *E-mail:* uswebmaster@wanadoo.mg (office). *Website:* www.usmission.mg (office).

MARQUES AMADO, Luis Filipe; Portuguese government official; *Minister of Foreign Affairs;* b. 17 Sept. 1953; m.; two c. *Education:* Universidade Técnica de Lisboa. *Career:* Sec. of State for Internal Admin –1997, for Foreign Affairs and Co-operation 1997; Minister of Nat. Defence and Maritime Affairs 2005–06, of Foreign Affairs 2006–. *Address:* Ministry of Foreign Affairs, Palácio das Necessidades, Largo do Rilvas, 1399-030 Lisbon, Portugal (office). *Telephone:* (21) 3946000 (office). *Fax:* (21) 3946053 (office). *E-mail:* gii@mne.gov.pt (office). *Website:* www.min-nestrangeiros.pt (office).

MARSDEN, Rosalind Mary, CMG, BA, DPhil; British diplomatist; *Ambassador to Sudan;* b. 27 Oct. 1950. *Education:* Woking Girls' Grammar School, Somerville Coll. and St Antony's Coll., Oxford. *Career:* joined FCO 1974, Near East and North Africa Dept 1974–75, language training, SOAS 1975–76, Second, later First Sec., Chancery in Tokyo 1976–80, Policy Planning Staff, FCO 1980–83, Head of Section, EC Dept (Internal) 1983–85, First Sec. (Econ.), Chancery in Bonn 1985–88, Deputy Head of Hong Kong Dept, FCO 1989–91, Counsellor on secondment to National Westminster Bank 1991–93, Political Counsellor and Head of Chancery, Tokyo 1993–96, Head of UN Dept, FCO 1996–99, Dir Asia-Pacific Affairs 1999–2003, Amb. to Afghanistan 2003–06, Consul-Gen., Basra 2006–07, Amb. to Sudan 2007–. *Address:* British Embassy, PO Box 801, St 10, off Baladia Street, Khartoum, Sudan (office). *Telephone:* (183) 777105 (office). *Fax:* (183) 776457 (office). *E-mail:* Media.Khartoum@fco.gov.uk (office). *Website:* www.britishembassy.gov.uk/sudan (office).

MARSHALL, Ray, PhD; American economist, academic and fmr government official; *Professor Emeritus, Lyndon B. Johnson School of Public Affairs, University of Texas;* b. 22 Aug. 1928, Oak Grove, La.; m. Patricia Williams 1946; one s. three d. *Education:* Millsaps Coll., Miss., Louisiana State Univ., Univ. of Calif. at Berkeley. *Career:* Fulbright Research Scholar, Finland; post-doctoral research, Harvard Univ.; Instructor San Francisco State Coll.; Assoc. Prof. and Prof. Univs of Miss., Ky, La.; Prof. of Econs, Univ. of Texas 1962–67, Prof. of Econs 1969, Chair. Dept 1970–72, Prof. of Econs and Public Affairs, Lyndon B. Johnson School of Public Affairs 1981, Rapoport Prof. Econs and Public Affairs, Prof. Emer. 1998–, fmrly Dir Center for Study of Human Resources; US Sec. of Labor 1977–81; Co-Chair. Comm. on the Skills of the American Workforce; Trustee German Marshall Fund and Carnegie Corpn of NY 1982–90; mem. Comm. on Future of Labor/Man. Relations; Hon. degrees (Maryland, Cleveland State, Millaaps Coll., Bates Coll., Rutgers, Ind., Tulane, Utah State, St Edward's); Lifetime Achievement Award, Industrial Relations Research Asscn 2001. *Publications:* The Negro Worker 1967, The Negro and Apprenticeship 1967, Cooperatives and Rural Poverty in the South 1971, Human Resources and Labor Markets 1972, Anthology of Labor Economics 1972, Human Resources and Labor Markets 1975, Labor

Economics: Wages, Employment and Trade Unionism 1976, The Role of Unions in the American Economy 1976, An Economic Strategy for the 1980s 1981, Work and Women in the Eighties 1983, Unheard Voices: Labor and Economic Policy in a Competitive World 1987, Economics of Education 1988, Losing Direction: Families, Human Resource Development and Economic Performance 1991, Thinking for a Living (with Marc Tucker) 1992, Back to Shared Prosperity (ed.) 2000.
Address: c/o University of Texas, L.B.J. School of Public Affairs, Drawer Y, University Station, Austin, TX 78713, USA. *Telephone:* (512) 471-6242 (office); (512) 345-1828 (home). *Fax:* (512) 345-8491 (home). *E-mail:* ray .marshall@mail.utexas.edu (office). *Website:* www.utexas.edu/lbj (office).

MARŠIĆANIN, Dragan; Serbian politician and diplomatist; *Ambassador to Switzerland; Career:* worked in private sector for several cos including Elektron, Novi Kolektiv, Belgrade Water Utility; Chair. Vracar municipality –1996; fmr Sec. Democratic Party of Serbia, currently Vice-Pres.; fmr Minister of Economy; Speaker, Nat. Assembly –2004; cand. in presidential election 2004 (finished fourth); currently Amb. to Switzerland.
Address: Embassy of Serbia, Seminarstr. 5, 3006 Bern, Switzerland (office). *Telephone:* 313526353 (office). *Fax:* 313514474 (office). *E-mail:* info@ ynamb.ch (office). *Website:* www.ynamb.ch.

MARSILI, Carlo; Italian diplomatist; *Ambassador to Turkey;* b. 26 Nov. 1943, Cupra Montana; m. Selva Marsili. *Education:* Univ. of Padova. *Career:* joined Ministry of Foreign Affairs 1970, with Directorate-Gen. of Personnel 1970–73, Head, Office of Competition, Directorate-Gen. of Personnel 1981–84; served as Asst Diplomatic Adviser to four Prime Ministers De Mita, Andreotti, Amato, Ciampi 1988–93; Dir-Gen. for Italians Abroad and Migration Policies 2000–02, Dir-Gen. for Personnel 2002–04; overseas postings include Consul in Munich 1973–75, First Sec., Embassy in Bangkok 1975–78, Political Adviser, NATO, Ankara 1979–81, Cosul-Gen. for Scotland and NI, Edinburgh 1984–88, Minister Counsellor in Bonn 1993–98, Amb. to Indonesia 1998–2000, to Turkey 2003–.
Address: Embassy of Italy, Atatürk Bulvarı 118, 06680 Kavaklıdere, Ankara, Turkey (office). *Telephone:* (312) 4574200 (office). *Fax:* (312) 4574280 (office). *E-mail:* ambasciata.ankara@esteri.it (office). *Website:* www.italian-embassy.org.ae/ambasciata_ankara (office).

MARTENS, Wilfried A. E., DLaws, Lic. Notary, Bac. Thomistic Phil.; Belgian politician and lawyer; *President, European People's Party;* b. 19 April 1936, Sleidinge. *Education:* Katholieke Universiteit Leuven (Louvain). *Career:* lawyer, Court of Appeal, Ghent 1960; fmr Leader Vlaamse Volksbeweging; Adviser to Harmel Cabinet 1965, to Vanden Boeynants Cabinet 1966; Head of Mission to Tindemans Cabinet (Community Affairs) 1968; Pres. Christelijke Volkspartij-Jongeren (CVP Youth Org. 1967–71), Pres. CVP 1972–79; mem. Parl. for Ghent-Eeklo 1974–91, mem. Senate for Brussels-Halle-Vilvoorde 1991–94; Co-founder European People's Party (EPP) 1976, Pres. Working Cttee on Policy 1976–77, Pres. 1990–, Pres. EPP Group, European Parl. 1994–99; Prime Minister 1979–81, 1981–92; Minister of State 1992–; Pres. European Union of Christian Democrats 1993–96; Pres. Christian Democratic Int. 2000–01; Charles V Prize (for contrib. to EU) 1998; numerous Belgian and int. awards.
Address: European People's Party, 10 rue du Commerce, 1000 Brussels, Belgium (office). *Telephone:* (2) 285-41-59 (office). *Fax:* (2) 285-41-55 (office). *E-mail:* presid@epp.eu (office). *Website:* www.epp.eu (office).

MARTIKONIS, Rytis; Lithuanian diplomatist; *Permanent Representative, European Union;* b. 8 Feb. 1967, Kaunas; m. Agnė Nastopkaitė-Martikonienė; three c. *Education:* Vilnius Univ., Bowdoin Coll., USA, Århus Univ., Denmark, Clingendael Inst., Netherlands. *Career:* posts with Ministry of Foreign Affairs include European Integration, W Europe unit 1992–95, Counsellor, Mission to the EU 1995–99, Dir European Integration Dept 1999–2001, Undersecretary 2001–04, Deputy Head del. for EU accession negotiations 2001–03, fmr Deputy Minister of Foreign Affairs, Amb. Political and Security Cttee 2004–05; Perm. Rep. to EU 2005–; mem. European Convention 2002–03; Cross of Commdr Order for Merits to Lithuania; Commdr, Ordre nat. du Mérite; Encomienda de la Orden de Izabel la Catolica.
Address: Permanent Representation of Lithuania, Council of the European Union, rue Belliard 41–43, Brussels 1040, Belgium (office). *Telephone:* (2) 771-01-40 (office). *Fax:* (2) 771-45-97 (office). *E-mail:* rytis.martikonis@lt -mission-eu.be (office). *Website:* www.lt-mission-eu.be (office).

MARTIN, Claude Pierre Marcel; French diplomatist; b. 14 April 1944, Saint-Germain-en-Laye; m. *Education:* Lycée de Saint-Germain-en-Laye, Institut d'Etudes Politiques de Paris, Ecole Nationale des Langues Orientales. *Career:* joined Ministry of Foreign Affairs 1968; Adviser to Cabinet on European Affairs 1974–78; Minister at Embassy in China 1979–84; Perm. Rep. to EC 1984–86; Dir Asia/Oceania Div. Ministry of Foreign Affairs

1986–90; Amb. to China 1990–93; Assoc. Sec.-Gen. to Dir-Gen. European and Econ. Affairs 1993–98; Amb. to Germany 1999–2007.
Address: c/o Ministry of Foreign and European Affairs, 37 quai d'Orsay, 75351 Paris Cedex 07, France (office).

MARTIN, Dominic David William, CVO; British diplomatist; *Permanent Representative, Organisation for Economic Co-operation and Development;* m. Emily Martin; three d. *Education:* Coll., Univ. *Career:* joined FCO 1987, Asst Desk Officer, Falkland Islands Dept 1987, Third, later Second Sec. (Political), New Delhi 1989–92, First Sec., European Communities Dept (External), FCO 1992–93, First Sec., Policy Planning Staff 1994, First Sec. (Political and Econ.), Buenos Aires 1995–99, Deputy Head, EU Dept (External), FCO 1999–2001, Counsellor (Political), New Delhi 2001–04, Counsellor (Political, Econ. and Public Affairs), Washington, DC 2004–07, Amb. and Perm. Rep. to OECD, Paris 2008–.
Address: UK Delegation to the OECD, 140 Avenue Victor Hugo, 75116 Paris, France (office). *E-mail:* uk-del.oecd@wanadoo.fr (office).

MARTIN, Francis James; British diplomatist; *High Commissioner to Botswana;* b. 3 May 1949; m. Aileen Martin; two s. two d. *Career:* joined FCO 1968, Third Sec. (Commercial), Reykjavik 1971–73, Vice-Consul (Commercial), Stuttgart 1973–76, Desk Officer, Financial Relations Dept, FCO 1976–77, Desk Officer, Protocol Div. 1977–79, Vice-Consul, Cape Town 1979–83, Second, later First Sec., UK Rep.'s Office, Brussels 1983–88, Deputy Head of Mission, Freetown 1988–91, Desk Officer, Near East and N African Dept, FCO 1991–92, on loan to Dept of Trade and Industry 1992–94, Desk Officer, Southern European Dept, FCO 1995, Deputy Head of Mission, Luanda 1996–98, First Sec. (Commercial), Copenhagen 1998–2001; High Commr to Lesotho 2002–05, to Botswana 2005–.
Address: British High Commission, Plot 1079–1084 Main Hall, off Queens Road, Gaborone, Botswana (office). *Telephone:* (267) 395-2841 (office). *Fax:* (267) 395-6105 (office). *E-mail:* bhc@botsnet.bw (office). *Website:* www.britishhighcommission.gov.uk/botswana (office).

MARTIN, Harold; New Caledonian politician and head of state; *President;* b. 6 April 1954, Nouméa. *Career:* Pres. Council on the Regulation and Establishment of Agricultural Prices 1991, 1993, 1994–95; Pres. Territorial Congress 1997–98, 2004–07; Pres. 2007–, also responsible for mining and taxes; Pres. L'Avenir Ensemble (Future Together Party) 2007–; Mayor of Paita.
Address: Office of the President, 8 route des Artifices, BP M2, 98849 Nouméa Cédex (office); L'Avenir Ensemble, 19 blvd Extérieur, Faubourg Blanchot, Nouméa, New Caledonia. *Telephone:* 246565 (office); 870371 (AE) (office). *Fax:* 246580 (office); 870379 (AE) (office). *E-mail:* cellule .communication@gouv.nc (office). *Website:* www.gouv.nc (office); www .avenirensemble.nc (office).

MARTIN, Micheál, MA; Irish politician; *Minister of Foreign Affairs;* b. 16 Aug. 1960, Cork; m. Mary O'Shea; one s. *Education:* Colaiste Chríost Rí, Univ. Coll., Cork. *Career:* fmr secondary school teacher; elected to Cork Corpn 1985, Alderman 1991; fmr Chair. Arts Cttee; Lord Mayor of Cork 1992–93; mem. Dáil Éireann 1989–; fmr Chair. Oireachtas All Party Cttee on the Irish Language; fmr mem. Dail Cttee on Crime, Dail Cttee on Finance and Gen. Affairs; Minister for Educ. 1997–2000, for Health and Children 2000, for Enterprise, Trade and Employment –2008, of Foreign Affairs 2008–; Nat. Chair. Fianna Fail Nat. Exec. 1988–; Nat. Chair. Ogra Fianna Fail; mem. Bd Cork Opera House, Graffiti Theatre Co., Nat. Sculpture Factory, Everyman Palace Theatre, Crawford Gallery, College of Commerce and several school bds; fmr mem. Governing Body Univ. Coll., Cork; won Cork Examiner Political Speaker of the Year Award 1987.
Address: Department of Foreign Affairs, 80 St Stephen's Green, Dublin 2, Ireland (office). *Telephone:* (1) 4780822 (office). *Fax:* (1) 4781484 (office). *E-mail:* minister@dfa.ie (office). *Website:* www.dfa.ie (office).

MARTIN MUÑOZ, Gema, PhD; Spanish academic; *Professor of the Sociology of the Arab and Islamic World, Autonomous University of Madrid;* b. 1955, Madrid. *Education:* Cairo Univ. *Career:* Prof. of the Sociology of the Arab and Islamic World, Autonoma Univ. of Madrid; Dir Gen. Casa Árabe and Int. Inst. of Arab and Islamic Studies, Madrid; fmr Visiting Prof., Harvard Univ., Roma Tre Univ., Colegio de Mejico, La Habana Univ., Institut for Political and Int. Studies of Teherán, Iran; Founding mem. Network on Comparative Research on Islam and Muslims in Europe, Sorbonne Univ., Paris; mem. scientific cttee European Inst. of the Mediterranean, Real Instituto Elcano, L'Annuaire de la Méditerránée, Rabat; mem. Advisory Bd Anna Lindh Euro-Mediterranean Foundation for Dialogue between Cultures; columnist El País. *Publications:* El Estado Arabe: Crisis de legitimidad y contestación islamista 1999, Islam, Modernism and the West (ed.) 1999, Iraq, A Failure of the West 2003.

Address: Universidad Autónoma de Madrid, Ciudad Universitaria de Cantoblanco, Carretera de Colmenar Km. 15, 28049 Madrid, Spain (office). *Telephone:* (91) 3975000 (office). *Fax:* (91) 3974123 (office). *E-mail:* informacion.general@uam.es (office). *Website:* www.uam.es (office).

MARTINEZ, Carmen M., MA, MS; American diplomatist; *Ambassador to Zambia;* m. Victor Reimer; one s. *Career:* career mem. Sr Foreign Service with rank of Minister-Counselor, postings as Consular Officer in Caracas 1983–85, in Bangkok 1986–89, Chief of Consular Section in Quito 1989–93, Prin. Officer, US Consulate in Barranquilla, Colombia 1993–94, Sr Training at Nat. Defense Univ., Washington, DC 1994–95, served in State Dept Bureau of Human Resources 1995–97, Deputy Chief of Mission in Maputo, Mozambique 1997–99, Prin. Officer, US Consulate Gen. in São Paulo 1999–2002, Chief of Mission in Yangon, Myanmar 2002–05, Amb. to Zambia 2005–; Sr Foreign Service Performance Awards 2000, 2001, 2002, 2003, 2005, Presidential Meritorious Service Award 2003.
Address: Embassy of the USA, corner of Independence and United Nations Avenues, PO Box 31617, Lusaka, Zambia (office). *Telephone:* (1) 250955 (office). *Fax:* (1) 252225 (office). *E-mail:* ConsularLusaka@state.gov (office). *Website:* zambia.usembassy.gov (office).

MARTINEZ, Jorge Martí; Cuban diplomatist. *Career:* currently Amb. to Russian Fed. (also accred to Armenia 2003–); Pushkin Medal.
Address: Embassy of Cuba, 103009 Moscow, ul. B. Ordynka 66, Russian Federation (office). *Telephone:* (495) 933-79-57 (office). *E-mail:* embsecret@ecurusia.ru (office). *Website:* www.posolstvo-cuba.ru (office).

MARTINUSZ, Zoltán, BA, MA; Hungarian diplomatist; *Permanent Representative, NATO;* b. 5 July 1964, Budapest; m. Csilla Ferenczy, three c. *Education:* Univ. of Econs, Budapest, US Army War Coll., Carlisle, Pa. *Career:* Desk Officer, Ministry of Foreign Affairs 1988–90; Attaché, Perm. Mission to UN, Geneva 1990–94; Head, NATO Dept, Ministry of Defence 1994–98, Head, Defence Policy Dept 1998–99, Deputy State Sec. for Defence Policy 1999–2001; researcher and guest lecturer, ELTE Univ., Budapest 2001–02; Sr Adviser to Prime Minister 2002–05; Deputy State Sec. for Multilateral Affairs, Ministry of Foreign Affairs 2005; Perm. Rep. to NATO 2005–; mem. Hungarian Atlantic Council, Hungarian Foreign Affairs Asscn, IISS; Small Cross, Order of Merit of the Repub. of Hungary 1998, Knight's Cross, French Legion of Honour 2002.
Address: NATO Headquarters, Bld Léopold III, Brussels 1110, Belgium (office). *Telephone:* (2) 707-41-11 (office). *Fax:* (2) 707-45-79 (office). *E-mail:* natodoc@hq.nato.int (office). *Website:* www.nato.int (office).

MARTIROSIAN, Armen, BS; Armenian business executive and diplomatist; *Permanent Representative, United Nations;* b. 1961, Yerevan; m.; two s. *Education:* Yerevan Polytechnic Univ. *Career:* engineer, Hrazdanmash Factory 1983–92, Deputy Dir 1994–96; CEO Haieconombank 1996–98; mem. Parl. 1990–99, Chair. Standing Cttee on Finance and Budget 1998–99; Int. Relations Adviser to Armenian Prime Minister 1992–93; Deputy Minister of Foreign Affairs 1999–2003; Perm. Rep. to UN, New York 2003–.
Address: Permanent Mission of Armenia to the UN, 119 East 36th Street, New York, NY 10016, USA (office). *Telephone:* (212) 686-9079 (office). *Fax:* (212) 686-3934 (office). *E-mail:* armenia@un.int (office). *Website:* www.un.int/armenia (office).

MARTO, Michel, MA, PhD; Jordanian economist and politician; b. 21 Aug. 1940, Jerusalem; m. Lucy Peridakis 1970; one s. two d. *Education:* Middle East Tech. Univ., Ankara, Univ. of Southern Calif., LA. *Career:* Dir Econ. Research, Central Bank of Jordan 1969–70, Deputy Gov. 1989–97; Dir Econ. Research, Royal Scientific Soc. 1970–75; economist, World Bank, Washington DC 1975–77; Deputy Gen. Man. Jordan Fertilizer Industry 1977–79; Deputy Gen. Man. Bank of Jordan 1979–86, Man. Dir 1986–89; Chair. Jordanian Securities Comm. 1997–98; Minister of Finance 1998–2003; Chevalier, Ordre du mérite national, France; Commdr Légion d'honneur; Al-Hussein Distinguished Service Medal, Jordanian Star Medal (1st Class), Jordanian Independence Medal (1st Class), Omicron Delta Epsilon (Honor Soc. in Econs), USA, Phi Kappa Phi (Top Univ. Grad.), USA. *Publications:* various articles on economic topics in specialist journals.
Address: c/o Ministry of Finance, PO Box 85, Amman 11118 (office); PO Box 2927, Amman 11181, Jordan. *Telephone:* (6) 5926745 (home). *Fax:* (6) 5930718 (home). *E-mail:* michelmarto@hotmail.com.

MARTYNOW, Syarhey M.; Belarusian politician and diplomatist; *Minister of Foreign Affairs;* b. 22 Feb. 1953; m.; two s. *Education:* Moscow State Inst. of Int. Econ. Relations, USSR. *Career:* with Dept of Int. Econ. Orgs, Ministry of Foreign Affairs, USSR 1975–80, Asst to Minister of Foreign Affairs 1980–88, Deputy Head Dept of Int. Orgs 1988–91; Deputy Perm. Rep. of Repub. of Belarus to UN, New York, 1991–92; Chargé d'Affaires,

Washington, DC, 1992–93; Amb. to USA 1993–97; First Deputy Minister of Foreign Affairs 1997–2001; Amb. to Belgium, Head of Mission to European Communities and Head of Mission to NATO 2001–03; Minister of Foreign Affairs 2003–; Vice-Chair. First Cttee (Int. Security and Disarmament) of UN Gen. Ass. 1988–97; fmr Vice-Pres. Amendment Conf. of the State Parties to the (1963) Treaty Banning Nuclear Tests in the Atmosphere in Outer Space and Under Water; three-times Chair. Nuclear Disarmament Group of UN Disarmament Comm., several-times Vice-Chair. and Rapporteur UN Disarmament Comm., Chair. 1998; Pres. Conf. on Disarmament, Geneva 2000; mem. UN Cttee on Econ., Cultural and Social Rights, Geneva 2001–; mem. Minsk Int. Educational Centre.
Address: Ministry of Foreign Affairs, 220030 Minsk, vul. Lenina 19, Belarus (office). *Telephone:* (17) 227-29-22 (office). *Fax:* (17) 227-45-21 (office). *E-mail:* mail@mfabelar.gov.by (office). *Website:* www.mfa.gov.by (office).

MASEKELA, Barbara Joyce Mosima; South African political activist, diplomatist and business executive; b. 18 July 1941, Johannesburg; sister of Hugh Masekela; two c. *Education:* St Michael's Anglican School, Alexandra Township, Inanda Girls' Seminary, Durban, Fordham Univ., New York, USA, Univ. of Zambia. *Career:* in exile from SA for 27 years; moved to New York, USA to enrol as student 1965, moved to Zambia 1967, returned to USA following motor accident 1969; has lived in Ghana, UK and USA; taught literature at Staten Island Community Coll. 1972–73; Asst Prof. of Literature, CUNY, USA 1970s; Asst Prof., Dept of English, Rutgers Univ., NJ 1973–82; Head, African Nat. Congress (ANC) Arts and Culture Dept, Zambia 1983–90; Head of Staff, Office of the Pres. of ANC 1991–95, mem. Nat. Exec. Cttee 1991; mem. Govt of Nat. Unity 1994; first S African Amb. to France 1995–2003, Official Amb. to UNESCO 1995, Amb. to USA 2003–07; ind. Dir (non-exec.) Altron 2008–.
Address: Allied Electronics Corpn Ltd (Altron), Altron House, PO Box 981, Houghton 2041 South Africa (office). *Telephone:* (11) 645-3600 (office). *Fax:* (11) 726-5778 (office). *E-mail:* info@altron.co.za (office). *Website:* www.altron.co.za (office).

MASIMOV, Karim K., DEcon; Kazakhstani economist and politician; *Prime Minister;* b. 15 June 1965, Tselinograd (now Astana). *Education:* Beijing Linguistic Inst., Wuhan Univ., China and Kazakh State Acad. of Man. *Career:* began career as senior economist at Ministry of Labour; fmr senior specialist, Kazakh Ministry of Foreign Econ. Affairs, Urumqi, China; fmr CEO, Kazakh Trading House, Hong Kong; Chair. Almaty Merchant Bank 1995–97, JSC Halyk Bank of Kazakhstan 1997–2000; Minister of Transport and Communications 2001–04; Chief Policy Adviser to Pres. Nazarbayev 2004–06; Deputy Prime Minister 2006–07; Minister of Economy and Budget Planning April–Oct. 2006; Prime Minister 2007–; Dr hc (Peoples' Friendship Univ., Russia) 2007.
Address: Office of the Prime Minister, 010000 Astana, Beibitshilik 11, Kazakhstan (office). *Telephone:* (7172) 32-31-04 (office). *Fax:* (7172) 32-40-89 (office). *Website:* www.government.kz (office).

MASIRE, Quett Ketumile Joni, LLD, JP; Botswana former head of state; *Congo Facilitator, Southern African Development Community;* b. 23 July 1925, Kanye; m. Gladys Olebile Molefi 1957; three s. three d. *Education:* Kanye and Tiger Kloof. *Career:* f. Seepapitso Secondary School 1950; reporter, later Dir, African Echo 1958; mem. Bangwaketse Tribal Council, Legis. Council; fmr mem. Exec. Council; Founder-mem. Botswana Democratic Party; mem. Legis. (now Nat.) Ass. March 1965; Deputy Prime Minister 1965–66; attended Independence Conf., London Feb. 1966; Vice-Pres. and Minister of Finance 1966–80 and of Devt Planning 1967–80, Pres. of Botswana 1980–98; Chair. Southern African Devt Community 1999, Congo Facilitator 1999–; Hon. GCMG; Hon. LLD (Williams Coll.) 1980, (Sussex) 1986, (St John); Naledi Ya Botswana (Star of the Nation) 1986.
Address: PO Box 70, Gaborone, Botswana (home). *Telephone:* 353391 (home).

MASIRE-MWAMBA, Gabaipone Mmasekgoa, BSc, MBA; Botswana business executive and international organization official; *Deputy Secretary-General, Commonwealth Secretariat; Education:* Univ. of London, UK, Univ. of Pittsburgh, USA. *Career:* fmr Chief Exec. Investment Promotion Agency (BEDIA); fmr Group Man. of Corp. Business and Regulatory Affairs, Botswana Telecommunications Corpn; fmr UK Business Devt Man., Commonwealth Telecommunications Org.; Deputy Sec.-Gen. Commonwealth Secr. 2008–.
Address: Commonwealth Secretariat, Marlborough House, Pall Mall, London, SW1Y 5HX, England (office). *Telephone:* (20) 7747-6385 (office). *Fax:* (20) 7839-9081 (office). *E-mail:* info@commonwealth.int (office). *Website:* www.commonwealth.int (office).

MASISI, Motlhware Kgori James; Botswana diplomatist; m. Naledi T. Masisi. *Career:* fmr Charges d'affairs, Embassy in Tokyo; fmr Minister-Counsellor, Embassy in Brussels; fmr High Commr to S Africa.
Address: Ministry of Foreign Affairs and International Co-operation, Private Bag 00368, Gaborone, Botswana. *Telephone:* 3600700. *Fax:* 3913366. *E-mail:* csmaribe@gov.bw. *Website:* www.gov.bw/government/ministry_of_foreign_affairs.html.

MASORIN, Adm. Vladimir; Russian naval officer; *Navy Commander-in-Chief;* b. 24 Aug. 1947, Beloye, Tver region. *Education:* Black Sea Nakhimov Naval School, Naval Acad., Gen. Staff Acad. *Career:* Chief of Staff 1993–96, First Deputy Commdr Kola Flotilla 1993–96, Commdr Caspian Flotilla 1996–2002, Black Sea Fleet 2002–05, Chief of Navy Staff 2005, Navy C-in-C 2005–.
Address: c/o Ministry of Defence, ul. Myasnitskaya 37, 105175 Moscow, Russia (office). *Telephone:* (495) 293-38-54 (office). *Fax:* (495) 296-84-36 (office). *Website:* www.mil.ru (office).

MASOUD, Ahmad Zia; Afghan diplomatist and politician; *First Vice-President;* b. 1 May 1956, brother of the late Ahmad Shah Masoud and Ahmad Wali Masoud. *Education:* Lycée Esteqlal and Kabul Polytechnic Inst. *Career:* mem. Shora-e-Nizar Movt; Amb. to Russian Fed. (non-resident Envoy to Moldova, Armenia, Azerbaijan, Georgia and Belarus), Moscow 2002–04; First Vice-Pres. 2004–.
Address: c/o Office of the President, Gul Khana Palace, Presidential Palace, Kabul, Afghanistan (office). *E-mail:* president@afghanistangov.org (office). *Website:* www.president.gov.af (office).

MASRI, Taher Nashat, BBA; Jordanian politician and diplomatist; *Senator, Jordanian Parliament (Upper House);* b. 5 March 1942, Nablus; m. Samar Bitar 1968; one s. one d. *Education:* Al-Najah Nat. Coll., Nablus and North Texas State Univ., USA. *Career:* with Cen. Bank of Jordan 1965–73; mem. Parl. (Lower House) 1973–74, 1984–88, 1989–97; Minister of State for Occupied Territories Affairs 1973–74; Amb. to Spain 1975–78, to France 1978–83, also accred to Belgium 1979–80, Rep. to EEC 1978–80; Perm. Del. to UNESCO 1978–83; Amb. to UK 1983–84; Minister of Foreign Affairs 1984–88, Jan.–June 1991; Deputy Prime Minister and Minister of State for Econ. Affairs April–Sept. 1989; Chair. Foreign Relations Cttee 1989–91, 1992–93; Prime Minister and Minister of Defence June–Nov. 1991; Speaker Nat. Ass. 1993–94; Senator 1998–2001, 2005–; fmr Rep. to Arab League; mem. and Rapporteur, Royal Comm. for Drafting the Nat. Charter 1990; Chair. Bd Princess Haya Cultural Center for Children 1992–; Pres. Nat. Soc. for the Enhancement of Freedom and Democracy (JUND) 1993–97, Jordanian-Spanish Friendship Asscn 1998–, Bd of Trustees Jordan Univ. for Science and Tech., Irbid 1998–; Commr for Civic Socs with Arab League, Cairo (stationed in Amman) 2002–; mem. and Head, Political Cttee of the Royal Comm. for Drafting the Nat. Agenda 2005–; mem. Alkuods Al-Sharif Defending Asscns 1996–2001, 2003–, Advisory Cttee Anna Lindh Euro-Mediterranean Foundation for the Dialogue between Cultures 2004–; Grand Cordon, Jewelled Al-Nahda (Order of the Renaissance) (Jordan), Order of Al-Nahda (1st Degree) (Jordan), Order of Al-Kawkab (Jordan) 1974, Gran Cruz de Mérito Civil (Spain) 1977, Order of Isabel la Católica (Spain) 1978, Commdr, Légion d'honneur 1981, Grand Officier, Ordre Nat. du Mérite, Order of Merit (Grand Cross, First Class, FRG), Kt Grand Cross (Italy); Hon. GBE; Grand Cordon, Ordre Nat. de Cedre (Lebanon), Grand Decoration of Honour in Gold with Sash for Services (Austria), Order of Diplomatic Service Merit and Gwanghawa Medal (Repub. of Korea); numerous awards.
Address: PO Box 5550, Amman 11183, Jordan. *Telephone:* (6) 4642227 (office); (6) 5920600 (home). *Fax:* (6) 4642226 (office). *E-mail:* t.n.masri@index.com.jo (office).

MASSAD, Carlos, MA, PhD; Chilean banker and economist; b. 29 Aug. 1932, Santiago; m.; five c. *Education:* Univ. of Chile, Chicago Univ. *Career:* Dir of Dept of Econs, Univ. of Chile 1959–64; Vice-Pres. Cen. Bank of Chile 1964–67, Pres. 1967–70, Gov. 1996–2003 (resgnd); Exec. Dir of IMF 1970–74; mem. of Advisory Cttee, World Bank 1978–81; various posts, Econ. Comm. for Latin America (CEPAL) 1970–92; Exec. Pres., Eduardo Frei Montalva Foundation 1993–94; Minister of Health 1994–96; Euromoney Best Cen. Banker of Latin America 1997, The Banker Cen. Bank Gov. For the Americas Region of the Year 2001. *Publications:* Macroeconomics 1979, Rudiments of Economics 1980, Adjustment With Growth 1984; Economic Analysis: An Introduction to Microeconomics 1986, Internal Debt and Financial Stability (Vol. 1) 1987, (Vol. 2) 1988, The Financial System and Resource Distribution: Study based on Latin America and the Caribbean 1990, Elements of Economics: An Introduction to Economic Analysis 1993, On Public Health and Other Topics 1995, Macroeconomia en un mundo interdependiente (with Guillermo Patillo) 2000; and numerous articles.

Address: c/o Central Bank of Chile, Agustinas 1180, Castilla 967, Santiago, Chile (office).

MASSÉ, Hon. Marcel, PC, MP, OC, QC, BA, LLB, BPhilEcon; Canadian banker and civil servant; *Executive Director for Canada, World Bank Group;* b. 23 June 1940, Montreal; m. Josée M'Baye 1965; three s. one d. *Education:* Univ. of Montreal, McGill Univ., Montreal, Univ. of Warsaw, Poland, Oxford Univ., UK. *Career:* called to Bar, Québec 1963; Admin. and Econs Div., World Bank, Washington, DC 1967–71; Econ. Adviser, Privy Council Office, Ottawa 1971–73; Deputy Minister of Finance, Prov. of NB 1973–74, Chair. Cabinet Secr. 1974–77; Deputy Sec. Cabinet for Fed. Prov. Relations, Ottawa 1977–79, Deputy Sec. Cabinet (Operations), Privy Council Office 1979, Sec. to the Cabinet and Clerk of the Privy Council Office 1979–80; Pres. Canadian Int. Devt Agency, Ottawa 1980–82; Under-Sec. of State for External Affairs, Ottawa 1982–85; Canadian Exec. Dir IMF, Washington 1985–89; Pres. Canadian Int. Devt Agency (CIDA) 1989–93; Sec. to Cabinet for Intergovernmental Affairs March–June 1993; MP for Hull-Aylmer 1993–99; Pres. of the Privy Council and Minister of Intergovernmental Affairs and responsible for Public Service Renewal 1993–96; Pres. of Treasury Bd 1996–99, Exec. Dir Inter-American Devt Bank 1999–2002; Exec. Dir for Canada, World Bank Group 2002–; Hon. DCL (Acadia Univ.) 1983; Hon. LLD (New Brunswick) 1984; Dr hc (Univ. du Québec) 1992, (Ottawa Univ.) 1996.
Address: 1818 H Street, NW, Washington, DC 20433, USA (office). *Telephone:* (202) 458-0077 (office). *Fax:* (202) 477-4155 (office). *E-mail:* mmasse@worldbank.org (office). *Website:* www.worldbank.org (office).

MATASKELEKELE, Kalkot; Ni-Vanuatu lawyer, judge and head of state; *President;* *Career:* fmr Judge on Supreme Court; Pres. of Vanuatu 2004–.
Address: Office of the President, Port Vila, Vanuatu (office).

MATENDA KYELU, Athanase; Democratic Republic of the Congo politician; *Minister of Finance; Career:* Admin., Fed. of Businesses of the Democratic Repub. of Congo (FEC) –2003; mem. Parl. 2003–; Minister of Public Works and Infrastructure 2004–06, of Finance 2007–; mem. People's Party for Reconstruction and Democracy (PPRD).
Address: Ministry of Finance, Boulevard du 30 juin, BP 12998, KIN I, Kinshasa–Gombe, Democratic Republic of the Congo (office). *Telephone:* (12) 31197 (office). *Website:* www.minfinrdc.cd (office).

MATENJE, Steve Dick Tennyson, MA LLB; Malawi diplomatist; *Permanent Representative, United Nations;* b. 17 Feb. 1956, Zomba; m.; four c. *Education:* Univ. of Malawi, City of London Polytechnic, Univ. Coll. London. *Career:* Sr State Advocate 1985–89; Parl. Draftsman 1989–92, Chief Parl. Draftsman 1992–95; Solicitor-Gen. and Perm. Sec. of Justice 1995–2006; Perm. Rep. to UN, New York 2006–; mem. Law Comm. on Tech. Review of Constitution 1998, Task Force on Review of Legal and Admin. Instruments 2002, Review of Legal Aid Act Comm. 2003.
Address: Permanent Mission of Malawi to the United Nations, 600 Third Avenue, 21st Floor, New York, NY 10016, USA (office). *Telephone:* (212) 949-0180 (office). *Fax:* (212) 599-5021 (office). *E-mail:* malawiun@aol.com (office).

MATEPARAE, Lt-Gen. Jerry, MA; New Zealand army officer and government official; *Chief, New Zealand Defence Force;* b. Nov. 1954; m. Janine Mateparae; five c. *Education:* Officer Cadet School, Portsea, Australia, Univ. of Waikato. *Career:* enlisted Regular Force of NZ Army 1972; mem. Royal NZ Infantry Regiment (RNZIR) 1976; appointments included command at platoon, co. and battalion level in NZ Infantry Battalions, also served with NZ Special Air Service, commanded First Battalion RNZIR; other appointments included Chief Instructor NZ Army's Tactical School, Staff Officer Operations, NZ Army Training Group, Army Gen. Staff and Dir of Force Devt, HQ NZ Defence Force; apptd NZ Army's Land Commdr 1999; joint command of NZ forces in East Timor 1999–2001; re-apptd Land Component Commdr in HQ of Joint Forces New Zealand 2001; Chief of Army 2002–06; Chief NZ Defence Force (first Maori) 2006–; Assoc. Fellow, NZ Inst. of Man.; Additional Officer NZ Order of Merit 1999.
Address: Chief of Defence Force, Defence House, Wellington, New Zealand (office). *Telephone:* (4) 496-0999 (office). *Fax:* (4) 496-0859 (office). *Website:* www.nzdf.mil.nz (office).

MATEŠA, Zlatko, MA; Croatian politician, judge, academic and organization executive; *Assistant Dean, Zagreb School of Economics and Management;* b. 17 June 1949, Zagreb; m.; two c. *Education:* Zagreb Univ., Henley Man. College, UK, J. F. Kennedy School of Govt, Harvard, USA. *Career:* Asst Judge, Judge Zagreb Municipal Court 1978–; Asst Man., Man. Legal Dept INA-Trade (Industrija Nafte Asscn) 1978–82, Dir Legal and Personnel Dept 1982–85, Dir Joint Admin. Services 1985–89, mem. Man. Bd, Vice-Pres. 1989–90; Asst to Gen.-Man. INA-HQ 1990–92; mem.

Croatian Democratic Union (HDZ); Dir Agency for Reconstruction and Devt of Govt of Croatia 1992–93; Minister without Portfolio 1993–95; Minister of Economy Sept.–Nov. 1995; Prime Minister of Croatia 1995–2000; currently Asst Dean Zagreb School of Econs and Man.; Pres. Croatian Olympic Cttee.
Address: Zagreb School of Economics and Management, Jordanovac 110, 10000 Zagreb, Croatia (office). *Telephone:* (1) 2354242 (office). *Fax:* (1) 2354243 (office). *E-mail:* zlatko.matesa@zsem.hr (office). *Website:* www .zsem.hr (office).

MATEU PI, Meritxell; Andorran diplomatist and politician; *Minister of Foreign Affairs, Culture and Co-operation;* b. 19 Jan. 1966. *Education:* Paul Valéry Univ., Montpellier and Inst. of Int. Relations, Paris, France. *Career:* Amb. to France 1995–99, also Perm. Rep. to Council of Europe and UNESCO; Amb. to EU, Belgium and Luxembourg 1997–98, to Netherlands 1998–99, to Denmark 1999, to Germany 1999–2004, to Slovenia 2001; Minister of Housing, Higher Educ. and Research 2001–07, of Foreign Affairs, Culture and Co-operation 2007–.
Address: Ministry of Foreign Affairs, Carrer Prat de la Creu, 62-64, AD500 Andorra la Vella, Andorra (office). *Telephone:* 875700 (office). *Fax:* 869559 (office). *E-mail:* exteriors.gov@andorra.ad (office). *Website:* www.maecc .ad (office).

MATEU-ZAMORA, Vicenç; Andorran diplomatist. *Career:* fmr Leader, National Democratic Initiative or IDN; fmr Amb. to Spain, Amb. to France 2007–, also Perm. Rep. to UNESCO.
Address: Embassy of Andorra, 51 bis rue de Boulainvilliers, 75016 Paris, France (office). *Telephone:* 1-40-06-03-30 (office). *Fax:* 1-40-06-03-64 (office). *E-mail:* ambaixada@andorra.ad (office). *Website:* www.amb -andorre.fr (office).

MATEV, Lachezar Nikolov, MA, MSc, PhD; Bulgarian diplomatist; *Ambassador to UK;* b. 5 Aug. 1951, Sofia; m. Bisserka Mateva; two c. *Education:* Tech. Univ., Sofia, Sofia Univ., Moscow Diplomatic Acad. *Career:* mem. Bd, Higher Educ. Council, Ministry of Education 1977–82; Eastern European Countries Dept, Ministry of Foreign Affairs 1982; First Sec., Embassy in Prague 1982–89; Foreign Econ. Policy and Econ. Organisations Directorate 1992–93; Co-founder and Man. Dir Int. Business Devt magazine, 1992–93; Man. Dir VECCO Ltd; Head UN Agencies Section, Foreign Econ. Policy Dept 1993–95; mem., then Head, Bulgarian Del. to UNDP Exec. Bd 1994–95; Counsellor, Embassy in Madrid 1995–98; Head of Unit, European Integration Directorate, Ministry of Foreign Affairs, mem. Accession Negotiations Team, mem. Inter-Ministerial Cen. Coordination Unit for Nat. Plan for Econ. Devt, mem. Inter-Ministerial Cttee for Intellectual Rights' Protection, mem. Cttee on Use of Atomic Energy for Peaceful Purposes 1998–2002; Minister Plenipotentiary, Embassy in London 2002–05, Amb. to UK 2005–; Commendatore, Royal Order of Francis I of Sicily (KCFO) 2006.
Address: Bulgarian Embassy, 186–188 Queen's Gate, London, SW7 5HL, England (office). *Telephone:* (20) 7584-9400 (office). *Fax:* (20) 7584-4948 (office). *E-mail:* ambass.office@bulgarianembassy.org.uk (office). *Website:* www.bulgarianembassy-london.org (office).

MATHAI, Ranjan; Indian diplomatist; *Ambassador to France; Career:* fmr Amb. to Israel, Qatar; fmr Deputy High Commr to UK –2007, Amb. to France (also accred to Monaco) 2007–.
Address: The Embassy of India, 15 rue Alfred Dehodecq, 75016 Paris (office). *Telephone:* 1-40-50-70-70 (office). *Fax:* 1-40-50-09-96 (office). *E-mail:* eiparis.admin@wanadoo.fr (office); ambassador2@wanadoo.fr (office). *Website:* www.amb-inde.fr (office).

MATHER, Graham Christopher Spencer, MA; British politician, solicitor and administrator; *President, European Policy Forum;* b. 23 Oct. 1954, Preston, Lancs.; m. 1st Fiona Marion McMillan Bell 1981 (divorced 1995); two s.; m. 2nd Geneviève Elizabeth Fairhurst 1997. *Education:* Hutton Grammar School, New Coll., Oxford (Burnet Law Scholar). *Career:* Asst to Dir-Gen. Inst. of Dirs 1980, est. Policy Unit 1983, Head of Policy Unit 1983–86; Deputy Dir Inst. of Econ. Affairs 1987, Gen. Dir 1987–92; Pres. European Policy Forum 1992–, European Media Forum 1997–, European Financial Forum 1999–; MEP for Hampshire North and Oxford 1994–99; Visiting Fellow, Nuffield Coll. Oxford 1992–99; mem. Competition Appeals Tribunal 2000; mem. Monopolies and Mergers Comm. 1989–94, Westminster City Council 1982–86; Conservative parl. cand. for Blackburn 1983; Vice-Pres. Strategic Planning Soc. 1993–, Asscn of Dist Councils 1994–97; mem. Public Policy Advisory Bd Queen Mary and Westfield Coll. London 1993–; Consultant Tudor Investment Corpn 1992–. *Publications:* Striking out Strikes (with C. G. Hanson) 1988; Europe's Constitutional Future (contrib.) 1990, Making Decisions in Britain 2000; papers and contribs to journals.

Address: 125 Pall Mall, London, SW1Y 5EA, England. *Telephone:* (20) 7839-7557. *Fax:* (20) 7839-7339. *E-mail:* graham.mather@epfltd.org (office). *Website:* www.epfltd.org.

MATHERS, Peter James, LVO; British diplomatist (retd); b. 2 April 1946; m. Elisabeth Mathers; one s. one d. *Education:* Bradfield Coll., Berks., School of Oriental and African Studies, London. *Career:* joined British Diplomatic Service 1971; with Commercial Section, Embassy in Tehran 1973–75, 1986–87; Political Section, Embassy in Bonn 1976–78; West Indian Dept, FCO 1978–81; Political and Information Sections, Embassy in Copenhagen 1981–85; EU Dept, FCO 1987–88; secondment to UN Office, Vienna 1988–91; EU and Royal Matters Depts, FCO 1991–95; Deputy High Commr to Barbados and Eastern Caribbean 1995–98; Counsellor and Dir of Trade and Investment Promotion, Embassy in Stockholm 1998–2002; High Commr to Jamaica 2002–05.
Address: c/o Foreign & Commonwealth Office, King Charles Street, London, SW1A 2AH, England. *Telephone:* (20) 7008-1500.

MATHIESEN, Arni M., MSc; Icelandic politician; *Minister of Finance;* b. 2 Oct. 1958, Reykjavík; m. Steinnun Kristín Fridjónsdóttir 1991; three d. *Education:* Flensborgarskóli, Hafnarfjödur, Univs of Edin. and Stirling, Scotland, UK. *Career:* qualified as veterinarian 1983; worked as veterinary officer for fish diseases 1985–95; Man.-Dir of Acquaculture, Faxalax hf. 1988–89; Chair. Flensborgarskóli Student Asscn 1977–78; Vice-Pres. Icelandic Asscn of Young Conservatives (SUS) 1985–87; Pres. Asscn of Young Conservatives (Stefnir), Hafnarfjödur 1986–88; elected mem. of Parl.; Rep. of Iceland to Nordic Council 1991–95; mem. Parl. Cttee on EFTA and EEC 1995–99; Minister of Fisheries 1999–2005, of Finance 2005–; fmr Chair. Prevention of Cruelty to Animals; mem. Bd Guarantee Div., Acquaculture Loans 1990–94, Bd Icelandic Veterinary Asscn 1986–87, Bd of Búnadarbanki Islands; mem. Salary Council, Confed. of Univ. Grads 1985–87; mem. Flensborgarskóli School Bd 1990–99; fmr mem. Bd of Búnadarbanki Islands, Agricultural Loan Fund.
Address: Ministry of Finance, Arnarhváli, Lindargata 150, Reykjavik, Iceland (office). *Telephone:* 5459200 (office). *Fax:* 5628280 (office). *E-mail:* mail@fjr.stjr.is (office). *Website:* fjarmalaraduneyti.is (office).

MATHIEU, Gail Dennise, BA, JD; American lawyer and diplomatist; *Ambassador to Namibia;* b. New Jersey; m.; one d. *Education:* Antioch Coll., Rutgers Univ. School of Law, Johns Hopkins School of Advanced Int. Studies. *Career:* fmr Asst Prosecutor, City of Newark, NJ; mem. NJ and DC Bars; Deputy Dir Office of Pacific Island Affairs 1995–97, Deputy Dir Office of West African Affairs, Dept of State 1997–99; Deputy Chief of Mission, Accra 1999–2002, has held other key positions in Paris, Geneva, Jeddah, Port of Spain and Santo Domingo; Amb. to Niger 2002–05; Dir Office of Tech. Specialized Agencies, Bureau of Int. Orgs Affairs, Dept of State 2005–07; Amb. to Namibia 2007–; Performance Pay and several Meritorious and Superior Honor Awards.
Address: US Embassy, Private Bag 12029, 14 Lossen Street, Ausspannplatz, Windhoek 9000, Namibia (office). *Telephone:* (61) 2958500 (office). *Fax:* (61) 2958603 (office). *E-mail:* healykc2@state.gov (office). *Website:* windhoek.usembassy.gov (office).

MATHIEU, Michel Pierre Marie, LEnD; French diplomatist; b. 25 July 1944, Montpellier (Hérault); s. of Henri Mathieu and Paulette Mathieu (née Ducand); m. Florence Granier 1973; one s. two d. *Education:* Saint-François-Régis Coll., Montpellier, Institut d'Etudes Politique, Ecole Nat. d'Admin and Faculty of Law, Paris. *Career:* Head Office of Dir of Overseas Territories 1973; Head of Mission of High Commr in the Pacific 1974; Administrator of the Admin. Subdiv. East of New Caledonia 1975–77; Deputy Prefect of Briançon 1977–79, of Cognac 1979–81; Sec.-Gen. of S. Corsica 1981–83; Dir. Office of Dir.-Gen. of Nat. Police 1983; Sec.-Gen. of Prefecture of Isère 1983–85; Prefect and Sec.-Gen. for Admin. of Paris Police 1985–89; Prefect of Eure 1989–92, of Oise 1992–96, without rank 1996, of Val d'Oise 1999–2001; Interministerial Del. to Struggle Against Illegal Work 1997–99; Prefect High Commr of French Polynesia 2001–05, of New Caledonia 2005–07; Auditor, Institut des hautes études de défense nationale 1998–99; Chevalier Légion d'Honneur, Officier l'Ordre nat. du Mérite, Mérite agricole, Chevalier du Mérite de la FDR .
Address: c/o Ministry of the Interior, the Overseas Possessions and Territorial Collectivities, place Beauvau, 75008 Paris, France (office).

MATHURIN, Gail M.; Jamaican diplomatist; *Permanent Representative, United Nations, Geneva; Career:* held various positions in Ministry of Foreign Affairs and Foreign Trade, including Sr Dir Foreign Trade Dept, Minister and Deputy Perm. Rep. to OAS, Washington, DC, Counsellor, Perm. Mission to UN, New York, First Sec., Embassy in Brussels and Mission to EU, Under-sec. for Trade, Amb. for External Negotiations, Ministry of Foreign Affairs and Foreign Trade and non-resident Amb. to Brazil, Argentina and Uruguay –2005, High Commr to UK (also accred to

Denmark, Finland, Norway, Sweden, Spain and Portugal) 2005–06, Perm. Rep. to UN and other Int. Orgs, Geneva 2006–.
Address: Permanent Mission of Jamaica to the United Nations, Rue de Lausanne 36, 1201 Geneva, Switzerland (office). *Telephone:* (22) 908-07-60 (office). *Fax:* (22) 738-44-20 (office). *E-mail:* mission.jamaica@ties.itu.int (office).

MATIN, Abdul, MA, PhD; Pakistani economist; *Member, Higher Education Commission;* b. 1 March 1932, Sawabi; m. Azra Matin 1959; three s. *Education:* Univ. of Peshawar and Univ. of Bonn, FRG. *Career:* Chair. Dept of Econs, Univ. of Peshawar and Dir Bd of Econs, North-West Frontier Prov. (NWFP) 1959–70; Chief Economist, Govt of NWFP 1970–72; Minister and Deputy Perm. Rep., Pakistan Mission at UN, New York 1973–76; Exec. Dir ADBP, Islamabad 1977–85; Vice-Chancellor Univ. of Peshawar 1987–89; Vice-Pres. and mem. of Cen. Cttee, Pakistan Tehrik-i-Insaaf (Movt for Justice) 1996–; Chair. of Task Forces to Regulate Pvt. Educational Insts in NWFP 1999–, to Reform Higher Secondary Govt Schools in NWFP 2000–; mem. Nat. Comm. on Manpower, Govt of Pakistan, Educ. Inquiry Cttee, NWFP, Prov. Finance Comm., NWFP 2002–, Health Regulatory Authority, NWFP 2003–, Higher Educ. Comm. of Pakistan 2003–, Econ. Reform Comm., NWFP 2004, Search Cttee for Vice-Chancellors, NWFP; Chair. Govt Working Group on Transport Policy 1991–92, Universities Services Reforms and Man. Cttee, Govt of NWFP 1998; mem. Bd of Man. Quaid-e-Azam Mazar 2000–, Pakistan Bait-ul-Mal; engaged in research project 'Revival and Reconstruction of Muslim World'; prepared policy draft for Nat. Centre for Rehabilitation of Child Labour 2001; Hamdard Foundation Award for Outstanding Services 1992, Khawaja Farid Sang, Lahore 2004. *Publications:* Industrialization of NWFP 1970; 85 articles on the problems, policies and pattern of econ. devt in professional journals.
Address: House No. 27, Street No. 9, Sector D-3, Phase I, Hayatabad, Peshawar, NWFP, Pakistan (home). *Telephone:* 5817144 (home). *Fax:* 5817144 (home).

MATLOCK, Jack Foust, Jr, MA; American diplomatist; b. 1 Oct. 1929, Greensboro; m. Rebecca Burrum 1949; four s. one d. *Education:* Duke and Columbia Univs and Russian Inst. *Career:* Instructor, Dartmouth 1953–56; joined foreign service, State Dept 1956, Official in Washington 1956–58, Embassy Official, Vienna 1958–60, Consul Gen., Munich 1960–61, Embassy Official, Moscow 1961–63, Accra 1963–66, Zanzibar 1967–69, Dar es Salaam 1969–70, Country Dir for USSR, State Dept 1971–74, Deputy Chief of Mission, Embassy in Moscow 1974–78, Diplomat-in-Residence, Vanderbilt Univ. 1978–79, Deputy Dir, Foreign Service Inst., Washington 1979–80, Amb. to Czechoslovakia 1981–83, to USSR, 1987–91; Special Asst to Pres. and Sr Dir European and Soviet Affairs, Nat. Security Council 1983–87; Sr Research Fellow Columbia Univ. 1991–93, Kathryn and Shelby Collum Davis Prof. 1993–96; George F. Kennan Prof., Inst. for Advanced Study, Princeton, NJ 1996–2001; John L. Weinberg/Goldman Sachs and Co. Visiting Prof. of Public and Int. Affairs, Woodrow Wilson School of Public and Int. Affairs, Princeton Univ. 2001–04; mem. American Acad. of Diplomacy, Council on Foreign Relations, American Philosophical Soc.; Dickey Fellow Dartmouth Coll. 1992; Hon. mem. Latvian Acad. of Sciences 2002 Hon. LLD (Greensboro Coll.) 1989, Albright Coll. (1992), Connecticut Coll. (1993); Superior Honor Award, US State Dept, Presidential Meritorious Service Award, McIver Award for Distinguished Public Service 1994 and many others. *Publications:* Ed. Index to J.V. Stalin's Works 1971, Autopsy on an Empire: The American Ambassador's Account of the Collapse of the Soviet Union 1995, Reagan and Gorbachev: How the Cold War Ended 2004.
Address: 940 Princeton-Kingston Road, Princeton, NJ 08540, USA. *Telephone:* (609) 252-1953 (home). *Fax:* (609) 252-9373 (home). *E-mail:* jfmatlo@attglobal.net (home).

MATOKA, Peter Wilfred, PhD; Zambian politician, international civil servant and diplomatist; b. 8 April 1930, Mwinilunga, NW Prov.; m. Grace J. Mukahlera 1957; two s. one d. *Education:* Rhodes Univ., S Africa, American Univ., Washington, DC, Univ. of Zambia, Univ. of Warwick, UK. *Career:* civil servant, Northern Rhodesia Govt 1954–64; mem. of Parl. of Zambia 1964–78; Minister of Information and Postal Services 1964–65, of Health 1965–66, of Works and Housing 1967, of Power, Transport and Works 1968; mem. Cen. Cttee, United Nat. Independence Party (UNIP) 1967, 1971–78; Minister for Luapula Prov. 1969; High Commr of Zambia in UK 1969–70, concurrently accred to the Holy See (Vatican); Minister for the S Prov. 1970, of Health 1971–72, of Local Govt and Housing 1972–77, of Devt Planning 1977, of Econ. and Tech. Co-operation 1977–78; Chief Whip, Nat. Ass. 1973–78; Sr Regional Adviser, UN Econ. Comm. for Africa, Addis Ababa 1979–83; High Commr in Zimbabwe 1984–88; Chair. Social and Cultural Sub-Cttee of Cen. Cttee of UNIP 1988–90, of Science and Tech. Sub-Cttee 1990–91; Sr Lecturer, Social Devt Studies Dept, Univ. of Zambia 1995–; Chair. WHO Africa Region 1966; Pres. Africa,

Caribbean and Pacific Group of States 1977; Chair. Nat. Inst. of Scientific Research 1977; Chair. Zambia-Kenya and Zambia-Yugoslavia Perm. Comms 1977; Chair. Lusaka MULPOC 1977; Chair. and Man. Dir FilZam Projects and Investments Services Centre Ltd 1992–; Vice-Chair. Nat. Tender Bd 1977; Life mem. CPA; mem. Perm. Human Rights Comm. of Zambia 1997–; Nat. Consultant on Child Labour Issues 1997–; Kt of St Gregory (Vatican) 1964; Kt, Egypt and Ethiopia, Grand Commdr of the Companion Order of Freedom 2006.
Address: University of Zambia, PO Box 32379, Lusaka (office); Ibex Hill, P.O. Box 50101, Lusaka, Zambia (home). *Telephone:* (1) 291777 (office); (1) 260221 (home). *Fax:* (1) 253952 (office). *E-mail:* registra@unza.zm (office).

MATOLCSY, György; Hungarian politician and economist; b. 1955, Budapest; m.; two c. *Education:* Budapest Univ. of Economic Sciences. *Career:* jr official, Industrial Org. Inst. 1977–78; mem. staff Ministry of Finance 1978–81, mem. Secr. 1981–85; Fellow, Finance Research Inst. 1985–90; Political State Sec. Prime Minister's Office 1990–91; Dir Privatization Research Inst. 1991; Dir EBRD, London 1991–94; Dir Property Foundation, Inst. for Privatization Studies 1995–99; Minister of Econ. Affairs 1999–2002; econ. strategist, Hungarian Civic Union (Magyar Polgári Szövetség—Fidesz).
Address: Magyar Polgári Szövetség, Budapest, Hungary (office). *E-mail:* info@hirlap.com (office). *Website:* www.fidesz.hu (office).

MATOTO, 'Otenifi Afu'alo, BA, MA; Tongan civil servant and politician; *Minister for Finance and Information;* m. Lavinia Matoto; two d. *Education:* Univ. of Auckland, New Zealand, Univ. of Durham, UK. *Career:* Asst Teacher, Tonga High School 1968; joined Ministry of Finance as an Asst Sec. in 1971, twice acted as Devt Officer 1971–77, Sec. of Finance 1977–83; Man., Devt and Planning, Bank of Tonga 1983, held various managerial positions 1983–99; Man. Dir Tonga Devt Bank 1999–2006; Minister for Public Enterprises 2006–07, for Public Enterprises and Information 2007–, for Finance and Information 2008–; mem. bds or chair. numerous govt agencies, statutory bodies and cttees; mem. exec. cttees numerous professional and business asscns; Treas. Tonga Rugby Football Union (TRFU) 1975–82; Chair. TRFU Referees' Asscn early 1980s–early 1990s; mem. Nuku'alofa Rotary Club 1974–, served as Pres. for several years; ordained Minister of the Constitutional Free Church of Tonga.
Address: Ministry of Finance, Treasury Building, PO Box 87, Vuna Road, Kolofo'ou, Nuku'alofa, Tonga (office). *Telephone:* 23066 (office). *Fax:* 21010 (office). *E-mail:* minfin@candw.to (office).

MATSUURA, Koichiro; Japanese international organization official and diplomatist; *Director-General, United Nations Educational, Scientific and Cultural Organization (UNESCO);* b. 1937, Tokyo. *Education:* Univ. of Tokyo, Haverford Coll., Pa. *Career:* began diplomatic career 1959; Dir-Gen. Econ. Co-operation Bureau, Ministry of Foreign Affairs 1988, Dir-Gen. N American Affairs Bureau 1990; Deputy Minister for Foreign Affairs; Amb. to France 1994–98; Chair. UNESCO's World Heritage Cttee 1998–99; Dir-Gen. UNESCO 1999–.
Address: Office of the Director-General, UNESCO, 7 place de Fontenoy, 75352 Paris 07 SP, France (office). *Telephone:* 1-45-68-10-00 (office). *Fax:* 1-45-67-16-90 (office). *E-mail:* scg@unesco.org (office). *Website:* www .unesco.org (office).

MATTARELLA, Sergio; Italian politician and lecturer in law; b. 23 July 1941, Palermo; m.; three c. *Education:* Palermo Univ. *Career:* fmr mem. Nat. Council and Cen. Leadership Christian Democrat Party, Deputy Political Sec. 1990–92; now mem. Italian Popular Party; Deputy for Palermo-Trapani-Agrigento-Caltanissetta 1983–, for Sicilia 1 1994–; fmr Minister for Relations with Parl., Minister for Educ. –1990, Deputy Prime Minister 1998–2001, Minister for Defence 1999–2001; fmr Deputy Chair. Bicamerale; fmr Vice-Pres. Parl. Cttee on Terrorism; fmr mem. Parl. Inquiry Cttee on Mafia; mem. Third Standing Comm. on Foreign and EC Affairs; Political Ed. Il Popolo 1992–94; Prof. of Parl. Law Palermo Univ.
Address: c/o Camera dei Deputati, Piazza di Monte Citorio 1, 00186 Rome, Italy (office).

MATTIS, Gen. James N.; American army officer; *Supreme Allied Commander Transformation, NATO; Commander, United States Joint Forces Command; Education:* Cen. Washington State Univ., Amphibious Warfare School, Marine Corps Command and Staff Coll., Nat. War Coll. *Career:* entered US Marine Corps and commissioned as Second Lt 1972; as a Lt, served as rifle and weapons platoon commdr in 3rd Marine Div., as a Capt., commanded rifle co. and weapons co. in 1st Marine Brigade; as Maj., commanded Recruiting Station Portland; as Lt-Col, commanded 1st Bn, 7th Marines, one of Task Force Ripper's assault bns in Operation Desert Shield and Desert Storm; as Col, commanded 7th Marines (Reinforced); as Brig.-Gen., commanded 1st Marine Expeditionary Brigade and then Task Force 58, during Operation Enduring Freedom in southern Afghanistan; as

Maj.-Gen., commanded 1st Marine Div. during initial attack (2003) and subsequent stability operations in Iraq during Operation Iraqi Freedom; in first tour as Lt-Gen., commanded Marine Corps Combat Devt Command and served as Deputy Commdt for combat Devt; commanded I Marine Expeditionary Force, Camp Pendleton, Calif. 2006–07; served as Commdr of US Marine Forces Cen. Command; rank of Gen. 2007; Supreme Allied Commdr Transformation, NATO 2007–; Commdr US Jt Forces Command (USJFCOM), Norfolk, Va 2007–; Kuwait Liberation Medal (Kuwait), Kuwait Liberation Medal (Saudi Arabia), Marine Corps Recruiting Service Ribbon (with Bronze Service Star), Sea Service Deployment Ribbon (with one Silver and two Bronze Service Stars), Humanitarian Service Medal, Global War on Terrorism Service Medal, Global War on Terrorism Expeditionary Medal, Iraq Campaign Medal, Afghanistan Campaign Medal, Southwest Asia Service Medal (with two Bronze Service Stars), Nat. Defense Service Medal (with two Bronze Service Stars), Marine Corps Expeditionary Medal, Navy and Marine Corps Meritorous Unit Commendation, Navy Unit Commendation, Jt Meritorious Unit Award, Presidential Unit Citation, Combat Action Ribbon, Navy and Marine Corps Achievement Medal, Meritorious Service Medal (with two Gold Award Stars), Bronze Star (with Combat Valor Device), Legion of Merit, Defense Superior Service Medal, Navy Distinguished Service Medal, Defense Distinguished Service Medal (with Oak Leaf Cluster).
Address: US Joint Forces Command, 1562 Mitscher Avenue, Suite 200, Norfolk, VA 23551-2488, USA (office). *Telephone:* (757) 836-6555 (office). *E-mail:* info@jfcom.mil (office). *Website:* www.jfcom.mil (office).

MATTOX, Henry Ellis, MA, MPA, PhD; American editor, university lecturer and fmr diplomatist; *Editor, American Diplomacy; Education:* Univ. of Southern Mississippi, Univ. of Mississippi, Harvard Univ., Univ. of N Carolina, Chapel Hill. *Career:* mil. service, US Army 1950–52, Army Nat. Guard 1952–64; economist US Dept of Agric. 1955–57; career diplomat, US Foreign Service 1957–80, assigned in Washington, Paris, Ponta Delgada, Kathmandu, Port-au-Prince, London, Cairo, retd as Embassy Counsellor; Lecturer in Econs, Univ. of Miss. 1955–; Lecturer in US History and Econs, Alamance Community Coll. 1989–90, 1991–94; Adjunct Asst Prof. of US and World History, NC State Univ. 1989–90, 1991–2000; Co-Founder and Ed. American Diplomacy (electronic internet journal) 1996–, Vice-Pres. and Acting Pres. American Diplomacy Publrs 1996–2002; Visiting Prof., St Andrews Presbyterian Coll., Laurinburg, NC 1983, 1985, 1987; Visiting Lecturer, Appalachian State Univ. 1985, Univ. of NC at Chapel Hill 1984–88, 1990, Duke Inst. for Learning in Retirement 2001–; mem. American Foreign Service Asscn, Fulbright Asscn; Meritorious Honour Award, US Dept of State 1965, Fulbright Scholar Award, Nigeria 1990–91, Co-Recipient, Teacher Excellence Initiative Research Grant, NC State Univ. 1994, American Foreign Service Asscn Nat. Alumni Soc. Award 2003. *Publications:* The Twilight of Amateur Diplomacy: America's Foreign Service and its Senior Officers in the 1890s 1989, Army Football in 1945: Anatomy of a Championship Season 1990, World Terrorism 1901–2001: A Digest of Notable Events 2004; numerous articles in professional journals.
Address: American Diplomacy, 110 White Oak Way, PO Box 3114, Chapel Hill, NC 27515, USA (office). *Telephone:* (919) 929-6764 (office). *Fax:* (919) 929-2845 (office). *E-mail:* hmattox@mindspring.com (office). *Website:* www.americandiplomacy.org (office).

MATVIYENKO, Valentina Ivanovna; Russian politician; *Governor of St Petersburg City;* b. 7 April 1949, Shepetovka, Ukrainian SSR; m. Vladimir Vasilyevich Matviyenko; one s. *Education:* Leningrad Inst. of Chem. and Pharmaceuticals, Acad. of Social Sciences at CPSU Cen. Cttee, Acad. of Diplomacy USSR Ministry of Foreign Affairs. *Career:* Komsomol work 1972–84; First Sec. Krasnogvardeisk Dist CP Cttee, Leningrad 1984–86; Deputy Chair. Exec. Cttee Leningrad City Council 1986–89; USSR Peoples' Deputy, mem. Supreme Soviet 1989–92; mem. of Presidium, Chair. Cttee on Family, Motherhood and Childhood Protection Affairs 1989–91; Russian Amb. to Malta 1991–94, to Greece 1997–98; rank of Amb. Extraordinary and Plenipotentiary; Dir Dept on Relations with Federal Subjects, Parl. and Public Orgs Ministry of Foreign Affairs 1995–97, Deputy Prime Minister responsible for social issues 1998–2003, Chair. Comm. on Int. Humanitarian Aid and Religious Orgs; Presidential Rep. in the North-Western Fed. Okrug 2003; mem. Security Council of the Russian Fed. 2003; Gov. of St Petersburg 2003–; Badge of Honour 1976, Order of the Red Banner of Labour 1982, Order for Service to the Homeland (3rd Class) 1999.
Address: Office of the Mayor (Governor and Premier of the City Government of St Petersburg), 191060 St Petersburg, Smolnyi, Russia (office). *Telephone:* (812) 276-45-01 (office); (812) 276-18-27 (office). *E-mail:* gov@gov.spb.ru (office). *Website:* www.gov.spb.ru (office).

MATZNER-HOLZER, Gabriele; Austrian diplomatist; *Ambassador to UK.* *Education:* Newton High School, Mass, USA, Univ. of Vienna, Diplomatic

Acad., Vienna. *Career:* joined Fed. Ministry for Foreign Affairs 1971, various postings in Moscow, New York, Washington, DC 1971–81, Dir Diplomatic Acad., Vienna 1993–97, Amb. to Slovakia 1997–2001, to Tunisia 2002–05, Chargé d'affaires a.i., Embassy in London 2005, Amb. to UK 2005–. *Publications:* two books.
Address: Embassy of Austria, 18 Belgrave Mews West, London, SW1X 8HU, England (office). *Telephone:* (20) 7344-3250 (office). *Fax:* (20) 7344-0292 (office). *E-mail:* london-ob@bmeia.gv.at (office). *Website:* www.bmeia.gv.at/london (office).

MAUNG AYE, Deputy Sr Gen., BSc; Myanma military officer; *Vice-Chairman, State Peace and Development Council;* b. 25 Dec. 1937, Kon Balu; m. *Education:* Defence Services Acad. *Career:* joined Myanma Army 1959, C-in-C 1993–; Deputy C-in-C Defence Services; Vice-Chair. State Law and Order Restoration Council (SLORC) 1994–97, State Peace and Devt Council 1997–.
Address: c/o Office of the Chairman of the State Peace and Development Council, 15–16 Windermere Park, Yangon, Myanmar (office). *Telephone:* (1) 282445 (office).

MAURER, Peter, PhD; Swiss diplomatist; *Permanent Representative, United Nations;* b. 1966, Thun; m.; two c. *Education:* Univ. of Bern. *Career:* joined Fed. Dept of Foreign Affairs 1987, served as Diplomatic Adviser, Political Secr. 1989–91, Pvt. Sec. to State Sec. for Foreign Affairs 1991–96; Deputy Perm. Observer to Observer Mission to UN, New York 1996–2000; Head, Political Affairs Div. IV (Human Security), Political Affairs Govt Directorate 2000–04; Perm. Rep. to UN, New York 2004–.
Address: Office of the Permanent Representative of Switzerland to the United Nations, 633 Third Avenue, 29th Floor, New York, NY 10017, USA (office). *Telephone:* (212) 286-1540 (office). *Fax:* (212) 286-1555 (office). *E-mail:* vertretung-un@nyc.rep.admin.ch (office). *Website:* www.un.int/switzerland (office).

MAURÍCIO, Armindo Cipriano; Cape Verde politician. *Career:* currently Minister of Defence and Parl. Affairs.
Address: Ministry of Defence and Parliamentary Affairs, Palácio do Governo, Várzea, Praia, Santiago, Cape Verde (office). *Telephone:* 61-03-44 (office). *Fax:* 61-20-81 (office). *E-mail:* armindo.mauricio@palgov.cv (office).

MAVRIKOS, George; Greek trade union official and international organization executive; *General Secretary, World Federation of Trade Unions; Career:* Deputy Pres. Gen. Confed. of Workers in Greece; Sec. All Workers Militant Front (PAME) (a CP of Greece-affiliated trade union); Vice-Pres. WFTU and Coordinator of its European Office –2005, Gen. Sec. WFTU 2005–.
Address: World Federation of Trade Unions, 40 Zan Moreas Str., 117 45 Athens, Greece (office). *Telephone:* (21) 09236700 (office). *Fax:* (21) 09214517 (office). *E-mail:* info@wftucentral.org (office). *Website:* www.wftucentral.org (office).

MAVROYIANNIS, Andreas D., DipLaw; Cypriot diplomatist; *Permanent Representative, United Nations;* b. 20 July 1956, Agros; m. Calliopi Efthyvoulou; one s. one d. *Education:* Univ. of Thessalonica, Greece, Université de Droit et de Sciences Economique, Paris, Université de Paris X, Nanterre. *Career:* joined Ministry of Foreign Affairs 1987; served at Embassy in Paris 1989–93, also in Political Div., Cyprus Question Div., EU Div., and as Assoc. European Correspondent; Dir, Office of Minister of Foreign Affairs 1995–97, 2002–03; Amb. to Ireland 1997–99, to France 1999–2002 (non-resident to Andorra, Tunisia, Morocco); Acting Perm. Sec., Ministry of Foreign Affairs 2003; Perm. Rep. to UN, New York 2003–, also High Commr to St Lucia 2003–; Chair. UN Cttee on Relations with Host Country 2003–; Rep. at Cttee of Legal Advisers on Public Int. Law (CAHDI), Council of Europe 1988–92; Rep. Prep. Comm. for High Authority, Law of the Sea 1989; mem. Greek Cypriot negotiating team in bi-communal talks for solution of Cyprus issue 2002–03; Lecturer, Cyprus Mediterranean Inst. of Man., Cyprus Acad. for Public Admin, Law School of Univ. of Athens; Diploma of The Hague Acad. of Int. Law 1984. *Publications:* articles and reviews in scholarly journals and newspapers.
Address: Office of the Permanent Representative of Cyprus to the United Nations, 13 East 40th Street, New York, NY 10016, USA (office). *Telephone:* (212) 481-6023 (office). *Fax:* (212) 685-7316 (office). *E-mail:* cyprus@un.int (office). *Website:* www.un.int/cyprus (office).

MAXWELL, Kenneth R., MA, PhD; American historian and academic; *Professor of History and Senior Fellow, David Rockefeller Center for Latin American Studies, Harvard University; Education:* St John's Coll. Cambridge, Princeton Univ. *Career:* Prof., Univ. of Kansas, Yale Univ., Princeton Univ. and Columbia Univ. 1976–84; Program Dir Tinker Foundation 1979–85; Dir of Latin-American Studies, Council on Foreign

Relations, New York 1989–2004; Nelson and David Rockefeller Sr Fellow for Inter-American Studies 1995–2004, Vice-Pres. and Dir of Studies 1996; Prof. of History, Harvard Univ. 2004–, Sr Fellow, David Rockefeller Center for Latin American Studies 2004–, Dir Brazil Studies Program; mem. Bd Luso–American Foundation, Tinker Foundation, Human Rights Watch (Americas Div.), Princeton Univ. Program of Latin American Studies; columnist, Folha de Sao Paulo, Epoca Magazine; book reviewer for Western Hemisphere 1994–2004, Foreign Affairs; corresp. mem. Inst. Histórico e Geográfico Brasileiro, Rio de Janeiro 1994–; Commdr Order of Rio Branco (Brazil) 1997, Grand Cross of Nat. Order of Scientific Merit (Brazil) 1996, Commdr Order of Infante Dom Henrique (Portugal) 2004; Herodotus Fellow, Inst. for Advanced Study, Princton Univ. 1971–75, Guggenheim Fellow 1976–77. *Publications:* Conflicts and Conspiracies: Brazil and Portugal 1750–1808 1973, The Press and the Rebirth of Iberian Democracy (ed.) 1983, Portugal in the 1980s: Dilemmas of Democratic Consolidation (ed.) 1986, The New Spain: From Isolation to Influence (co-author) 1994, Pombal: Paradox of the Enlightenment 1995, The Making of Portuguese Democracy 1995, Chocolate Piratas e outros Malandros: Ensaios Tropicais 1999, Mais Malandros: Ensaios Tropicais e Outros 2002, Naked Tropics: Essays on Empire and Other Rogues 2003; articles in popular and professional publs.
Address: Harvard University, Robinson Hall, Cambridge, MA 02138, USA (office). *Telephone:* (617) 496-4780 (office). *Fax:* (617) 496-2802 (office). *E-mail:* kmaxwell@fas.harvard.edu (office). *Website:* drclas.fas.harvard.edu (office).

MAXWELL, Simon Jeffrey, CBE, BA (Oxon.), MA; British economist; *Director, Overseas Development Institute;* b. 1 May 1948, Birmingham; m. Catherine Pelly 1973; three c. *Education:* Univs of Oxford and Sussex. *Career:* Jr Professional Officer, UNDP, Nairobi, Kenya 1970–72, Asst Resident Rep., New Delhi, India 1973–77; Temp. Research Officer, Inst. of Devt Studies, Univ. of Sussex 1977–78, Fellow and Head of Food Security Unit 1989–97, Programme Man. Poverty Reduction, Sustainable Devt and the Rural Sector 1991–97; Agricultural Economist, Centro de Investigacion Agricola Tropical, Santa Cruz, Bolivia 1978–81; Dir Overseas Devt Inst. 1997–; Pres. Devt Studies Asscn of UK and Ireland 2001–05; mem. Ind. Group on British Aid 1982–, Program Advisory Panel, Foundation for Devt Co-operation 1997–; Patron One World Broadcasting Trust 1998–; Forum Fellow, World Econ. Forum 2003–; Hon. Fellow, Foreign Policy Asscn, New York 2003–. *Publications:* Real Aid: A Strategy for Britain (co-author) 1982, Aid Is Not Enough: Britain and the World's Poor (co-author) 1984, Missed Opportunities: Britain and the Third World (co-author) 1986, Real Aid: What Europe Can Do (co-author) 1989.
Address: Overseas Development Institute, 111 Westminster Bridge Road, London, SE1 7JD, England (office). *Telephone:* (20) 7922-0300 (office). *Fax:* (20) 7922-0399 (office). *E-mail:* s.maxwell@odi.org.uk (office). *Website:* www.odi.org.uk (office).

MAYANJA, Rachel N., BL, LLM; Ugandan UN official; *Special Adviser to the Secretary-General on Gender Issues and Advancement of Women, United Nations;* three c. *Education:* Makarere Univ., Harvard Univ. Law School, USA. *Career:* early career in UN Div. for Equal Rights for Women, Centre for Social Devt and Humanitarian Affairs; served in UN peacekeeping missions in Namibia (UNTAG) 1989–90 and Iraq/Kuwait (UNIKOM) 1992–94; sr positions in UN Office of Human Resources Man. including Chief of Common System, Specialist Services, Sec. to Sec.-Gen.'s Task Force on reform of Human Resources Man. 1999, Dir of Human Resources Man. Div., UN FAO 2000–04; Special Adviser to Sec.-Gen. on Gender Issues and Advancement of Women 2004–.
Address: Office of the Special Adviser on Gender Issues and Advancement of Women (OSAGI), Department of Economic and Social Affairs, Two United Nations Plaza, 12th Floor, New York, NY 10017, USA (office). *Telephone:* (212) 963-5086 (office). *Fax:* (212) 963-1802 (office). *E-mail:* osagi@un.org (office). *Website:* www.un.org/womenwatch/osagi (office).

MAYORAL, César Fernando, LLB, PhD; Argentine diplomatist and academic; b. 21 Dec. 1947; m. Birginia Mabel Silvestre. *Education:* Univ. of Buenos Aires, Universidad del Salvador, Inst. of Foreign Service. *Career:* Pnr, Silvestre, Mayoral and Assocs (pvt. law firm) 1971–77; Assoc. Prof. of Argentine History, Univ. Nat. de Buenos Aires 1973–76; Assoc. Prof. of Int. Relations, Universidad del Salvador 1976–80; Prof. of Constitutional History, Univ. Argentina de la Empresa 1976–80; Prof. of Int. Relations, Univ. de Lomas de Zamora 1987–89; joined Argentine Diplomatic Service 1976; Third Sec., Sec. of Int. Econ. Relations 1977–80; Second then First Sec., Embassy in Asunción, Paraguay 1981–86; Consul-Gen., Embassy in Paris, France 1986–99; Dir Div. of Int. Orgs, Ministry of External Relations and Culture 1986–89; apptd Counsellor 1988; with Perm. Mission to UN and Int. Orgs, Geneva 1989–92, also Del. to Comm. on Human Rights; Perm. Rep. to ILO 1992–94; with Ministry of External Relations 1994–96; Adviser on Int. Relations to Pres. Fernando de la Rúa

1999–2000; Amb. to Canada 2000–03; Perm. Rep. to UN, NY 2003–07; Expert, Senate Comm. on External Relations 1973–76.
Address: Ministry of Foreign Affairs, International Trade and Worship Esmeralda 1212, C1007ABR Buenos Aires, Argentina (office). *Telephone:* (11) 4819-7000 (office). *E-mail:* webmaster@mrecic.gov.ar (office). *Website:* www.cancilleria.gov.ar (office).

MAYORSKY, Boris Grigoryevich; Russian diplomatist; *Adviser, Ministry of Foreign Affairs;* b. 19 May 1937, Odessa, Ukraine; m.; two d. *Education:* Moscow Inst. of Int. Relations, UNO Translation Courses. *Career:* with Africa Div. USSR Ministry of Foreign Affairs 1961; on staff USSR Embassy, Ghana 1961–64; attaché 1964–65; with UN European Secr., Geneva 1966–69, WHO, Geneva 1969–70; First Sec., Head of Sector Law Div. USSR Ministry of Foreign Affairs 1970–73, adviser, Comm. on Law Problems of Space 1973–89; First Deputy Head, Head Dept on Int. Scientific and Tech. Co-operation 1989–92; Amb. to Kenya 1992–2000, to Spain 2000–02; currently Adviser to Ministry of Foreign Affairs.
Address: Ministry of Foreign Affairs, Smolenskaya-Sennaya 32/34, 119200 Moscow, Russia (office). *Telephone:* (495) 244-16-06 (office). *Fax:* (495) 230-21-30 (office). *E-mail:* ministry@mid.ru (office). *Website:* www.mid.ru (office).

MAYRHOFER-GRÜNBÜHEL, Ferdinand; Austrian diplomatist and fmr UN official; *Ambassador to Hungary;* b. 7 Jan. 1945, Klagenfurt; m.; five c. *Career:* joined Ministry of Foreign Affairs 1968; overseas postings in Madrid, Warsaw and New York; Adviser to UN Sec.-Gen., New York 1975, later Dir UN Disaster Relief Org., Geneva, fmr Dir UN Dept of Humanitarian Affairs, fmr Deputy to Co-ordinator, fmr Chair. UN Comm. on Crime Prevention and Criminal Justice; Perm. Rep. to UN, Vienna 1994–97; Amb. to Slovenia 2001–05, to Hungary 2005–; Pres. Together Foundation 2004. *Publication:* Avstrija–Slovenija: Preteklost in Sedanjost (with Miroslav Polzer) 2002.
Address: Embassy of Austria, Budapest 1068, Benczúr u. 16, Hungary (office). *Telephone:* (1) 479-7010 (office). *Fax:* (1) 352-8795 (office). *E-mail:* budapest-ob@bmeia.gv.at (office). *Website:* www.austrian-embassy.hu (office).

MAYSTADT, Philippe, MA, PhD; Belgian politician and international finance executive; *President, European Investment Bank;* b. 14 March 1948, Verviers; three c. *Education:* Claremont Grad. School, Los Angeles and Catholic Univ. of Louvain. *Career:* Asst Prof., Catholic Univ. of Louvain 1970–77, Prof. 1989–2007; Adviser, Office of Minister for Regional Affairs 1974; Deputy for Charleroi 1977–91; Sec. of State for Regional Economy and Planning 1979–80; Minister of Civil Service and Scientific Policy 1980–81, for the Budget, Scientific Policy and Planning 1981–85, of Econ. Affairs 1985–88; Deputy Prime Minister 1986–88; Minister of Finance 1988–98, of Foreign Trade 1995–98; Deputy Prime Minister 1995–98; Pres. Parti Social Chrétien 1998–99; mem. Senate June–Dec. 1999; Pres. European Investment Bank 2000–; Chair. IMF Interim Cttee 1993–98; Finance Minister of the Year, Euromoney magazine 1990. *Publications:* Listen and then Decide 1988, Market and State in a Globalized Economy 1998, Comprendre l'économie: l'Etat et le marché à l'heure de la mondialisation 1998.
Address: European Investment Bank, 100 Boulevard Konrad Adenauer, 2950 Luxembourg (office). *Telephone:* 4379-94464 (office). *Fax:* 4379-64474 (office). *E-mail:* p.maystadt@eib.org (office). *Website:* www.eib.org (office).

MAZHUKHOU, Alyaksei, DSc; Belarusian scientist and diplomatist; b. 17 Aug. 1952, Minsk; m.; one d. *Education:* Minsk Radio-Eng Inst., Minsk State Pedagogical Inst. for Foreign Languages, All-Union Acad. for Foreign Trade, Moscow, Russia. *Career:* Asst Researcher, Minsk Br., Science and Research Inst. of Automated Equipment 1969–70; engineer, researcher and lecturer, Minsk Radio-Eng Inst. 1970–86; Head of Dept of Scientific Affairs, Cen. Cttee, Nat. Youth League 1978–86; Second Sec., Dept of Int. Econ. Orgs, Ministry of Foreign Affairs 1989–91, Head of Dept of Int. Co-operation 1991–92, Counsellor, Perm. Rep. Mission to UN, New York 1992–94, Deputy Perm. Rep. 1994–96, Consul, Consulate-Gen., New York 1996–97, Counsellor for Asia and Africa, Political Dept, Ministry of Foreign Affairs 1998–99, Deputy Head of Dept of Multilateral Econ. Orgs 1999–2000, Head of Div. of Int. Econ. Orgs 2000–01, Deputy Head of Dept of Int. Orgs and Head of Div. of Int. Econ. Orgs 2001–2, Amb. to UK 2002–06 (also accred to Ireland 2004–06); holds 14 nat. patents. *Publications:* several articles on int. co-operation and environmental issues.
Address: Ministry of Foreign Affairs, vul. Lenina 19, 220030 Minsk, Belarus (office). *Telephone:* (17) 227-29-22 (office). *Fax:* (17) 227-45-21 (office). *E-mail:* mail@mfabelar.gov.by (office). *Website:* www.mfa.gov.by (office).

MAZI, Zef; Albanian diplomatist; *Ambassador to UK;* b. 27 Jan. 1956. *Education:* Univ. of Tirana. *Career:* announcer and trans., Radio Tirana World Service 1975–85; ed. and trans., 8 Nentori Publishing House 1978–86; Lecturer, Univ. of Tirana 1979–88; Head of Int. Relations Dept, Gen. Directorate of PTT 1987–89; with Dept of Multilateral Relations, Ministry of Foreign Affairs 1989–91, Minister Counsellor and Chargé d'affaires a.i., Embassy in Austria and Switzerland 1991–92, Minister Counsellor, Chargé d'affaires a.i., Amb. and Perm. Rep. to UN, IAEA, OSCE and other Int. Orgs 1991–97, Dir UN Dept, Ministry of Foreign Affairs, Tirana 1997–98; Adviser, Conflict Prevention Centre, Dept of Admin and Operations, OSCE Secr. 1998–2000; served in Dept of Tech. Cooperation, IAEA 2000–02; cand. in presidential elections 2002; Perm. Rep. to UN 2003–05, Amb. to UK (also accred to Ireland) 2007–; Grand Officer, Byzantine Order of the Kts of the Holy Grave. *Publications:* several books, trans, articles and political analyses on int. relations. *Address:* Embassy of Albania, 2nd Floor, 24 Buckingham Gate, London SW1E 6LB, England (office). *Telephone:* (20) 7828-8897 (office). *Fax:* (20) 7828-8869 (office). *E-mail:* embassy.london@mfa.gov.al (office). *Website:* www.albanianembassy.co.uk (office).

MAZRUI, Ali A., MA, DPhil; Kenyan political scientist and academic; *Albert Schweitzer Professor in the Humanities and Director, Institute of Global Cultural Studies, State University of New York, Binghamton;* b. 24 Feb. 1933, Mombasa; m. 1st Molly Vickerman 1962 (divorced 1982); three s.; m. 2nd Pauline Ejima Uti-Mazrui 1991; two s. *Education:* Columbia Univ., USA, Univs of Manchester and Oxford, UK. *Career:* Lecturer in Political Science, Makerere Univ., Uganda 1963–65, Prof. of Political Science 1965–72, Dean of Social Sciences 1967–69; Assoc. Ed. Transition Magazine 1964–73, Co-Ed. Mawazo Journal 1967–73; Visiting Prof. Univ. of Chicago 1965; Research Assoc. Harvard Univ. 1965–66; Dir African Section, World Order Models Project 1968–73; Visiting Prof. Northwestern Univ., USA 1969, McGill and Denver Univs 1969, London and Manchester Univs 1971, Dyason Lecture Tour of Australia 1972; Vice-Pres. Int. Political Science Asscn 1970–73, Int. Congress of Africanists 1967–73, Int. Congress of African Studies 1978–85, Int. African Inst. 1987–, World Congress of Black Intellectuals 1988–; Fellow, Center for Advanced Study in the Behavioral Sciences, Stanford 1972–73; Prof. of Political Science, Univ. of Michigan 1973–91; Sr Visiting Fellow, Hoover Inst. on War, Revolution and Peace, Stanford 1973–74; Dir Centre for Afro-American and African Studies 1979–81; Research Prof. Univ. of Jos, Nigeria 1981–86; Andrew D. White Prof.-at-Large, Cornell Univ. 1986–92, currently Sr Scholar in Africana Studies; Albert Schweitzer Prof. in the Humanities, State Univ. of New York, Binghamton 1989–, also Dir Inst. of Global Cultural Studies; Ibn Khaldun Prof.-at-Large School of Islamic and Social Sciences, Leesbury, Va 1997–; Walter Rodney Distinguished Prof. Univ. of Guyana, Georgetown 1997–98; Albert Luthuli Prof.-at-Large in the Humanities and Devt Studies, Univ. of Jos, Nigeria; Reith Lecturer 1979; Presenter BBC TV series The Africans 1986; mem. World Bank's Council of African Advisers; Int. Org. Essay Prize 1964, Northwestern Univ. Book Prize 1969. *Publications:* Towards a Pax Africana 1967, On Heroes and Uhuru-Worship 1967, The Anglo-African Commonwealth 1967, Violence and Thought 1969, Protest and Power in Black Africa (co-ed.) 1970, The Trial of Christopher Okigbo 1971, Cultural Engineering and Nation Building in East Africa 1972, Africa in World Affairs: The Next Thirty Years (co-ed.) 1973, A World Federation of Cultures: An African Perspective 1976, Political Values and the Educated Class in Africa 1978, Africa's International Relations 1978, The African Condition (Reith Lectures) 1980, Nationalism and New States in Africa (co-author) 1984, The Africans: A Triple Heritage 1986, Cultural Forces in World Politics 1989, Africa Since 1935 (Vol. VIII of UNESCO General History of Africa; ed.) 1993, The Power of Babel: Language and Governance in Africa's Experience 1998. *Address:* State University of New York, Institute of Global Culture Studies, Office of Schweitzer Chair, P.O. Box 6000, Binghamton, NY 13902 (office); 313 Murray Hill Road, Vestal, NY 13850, USA (home). *Telephone:* (607) 777-4494 (office). *Website:* www.binghamton.edu/igcs (office).

MAZUREK, Maj.-Gen. Rostislav; Czech military officer; *Military Representative, NATO;* b. 24 Feb. 1955, Havírov; m. Eva Mazurková, one s. one d. *Education:* Orlová High School, Mil. Officers School, Hranice na Moravě, Mil. Artillery Acad., St Petersburg, Command and Gen. Staff Coll., Fort Leavenworth, USA, Nat. Defense Coll., USA. *Career:* began mil. career as Commdr artillery platoon 1975–76, Commdr artillery battery 1979–81, Chief of Staff, artillery bn 1981–84, Commdr artillery bn 1984–87, Chief of Staff, artillery brigade 1987–1992, Chief of Staff, missile technical base 1992–93, Commdr Jt Rocket Launchers Regt 1993–96, Chief of Section, Chief of Artillery of Armed Forces of Czech Repub. 1997–98, Commdr Second Mechanised Brigade, Ground Forces 1998–2000, Chief, Strategic Planning Div. 2001–02, Deputy Chief of Gen. Staff, Chief of Staff 2002–03, commissioned Maj.-Gen. 2003, Deputy Chief of Gen. Staff, Dir

Force Planning Section 2003–; Mil. Rep. to NATO 2006–; Nat. Service Medal 1981, Service Medal for Nat. Defence 1986, Medal of the Army of the Czech Repub., (Third Class) 1998, (Second Class) 2003, NATO 50th Anniversary Commemorative Badge 1999, Cross of Merit, third class 2000, second class 2003, Gen. Staff Badge 2004. *Address:* Permanent Delegation of the Czech Republic to NATO, Bld Léopold III, Brussels 1110, Belgium (office). *Telephone:* (2) 707-17-27 (office). *Fax:* (2) 707-17-03 (office). *E-mail:* nato.brussels@embassy.mzv.cz (office). *Website:* www.nato.int (office).

MAZURU, Bogdan; Romanian diplomatist; *Ambassador to Germany;* b. 26 March 1962, Bucharest; m. Emilia Mazuru. *Education:* Bucharest Polytech. Univ. *Career:* computer engineer, Inst. for Meteorology and Hydrology 1987–89, Inst. for Research in Transportation 1989–90, Romanian Writers Union 1990–91; Third then Second Sec., Policy Planning Staff, Ministry of Foreign Affairs, Bucharest 1991–95; participant in training programme for Cen. and E European Diplomats, Ministry of Foreign Affairs, Berlin and Bonn, Germany 1992; Deputy Dir EU Div., Ministry of Foreign Affairs, Bucharest 1995–96; First Sec. Political, Embassy in Washington, DC 1996–98; Deputy Head of Mission to NATO and WEU, Brussels 1998–99; Dir-Gen. for Europe and N America 1999–2000; Dir-Gen. for Bilateral and Regional Affairs 2000; Deputy Head of Mission and Minister Counsellor, Embassy in Washington, DC Sept.–Dec. 2000, Chargé d'Affaires 2000–01; Amb. and Perm. Rep. to NATO and WEU, Brussels 2001–06; Amb. to Germany 2006–. *Address:* Embassy of Romania, Dorotheenstr. 62–66, 10117 Berlin, Germany (office). *Telephone:* (30) 21239202 (office). *Fax:* (30) 21239399 (office). *E-mail:* office@rumaenische-botschaft.de (office). *Website:* berlin.mae.ro (office).

MBA NGUEMA, Gen. Antonio; Equatorial Guinean military officer. *Career:* Minister of Nat. Defence 2004–. *Address:* Ministry of National Defence, Malabo, Equatorial Guinea. *Telephone:* (09) 27-94.

M'BAREK, Sghair Ould; Mauritanian politician; b. 1954, Néma; m.; four c. *Education:* Univ. of Nouakchott. *Career:* Minister of Nat. Educ. 1992–93, 1997–98, 2000, of Rural Devt and the Environment 1994–95, of Health and Social Affairs 1995, of Commerce and Tourism 1998–99, of Equipment and Transport 1999, of Justice 2001–03; Prime Minister of Mauritania 2003–07. *Address:* c/o Office of the Prime Minister, Nouakchott, Mauritania (office).

MBASOGO, Lt-Col Teodoro Obiang Nguema; Equatorial Guinean politician and army officer; *President and Supreme Commander of the Armed Forces; Education:* in Spain. *Career:* fmr Deputy Minister of Defence; overthrew fmr Pres. Macias Nguema in coup; Pres. of Equatorial Guinea 1979–; Supreme Commdr of the Armed Forces 1979–; Minister of Defence 1986. *Address:* Oficina del Presidente, Malabo, Equatorial Guinea.

M'BAYE, Kéba; Senegalese judge; b. 5 Aug. 1924, Kaolack; m. Mariette Diarra 1951; three s. five d. *Education:* Ecole Nat. de la France d'Outremer. *Career:* Judge of Appeal, Supreme Court of Senegal, First Pres. 1964; fmr Chair. Int. Comm. of Jurists, Chair. Comm. on Codification of Law of Civil and Commercial Liabilities; Vice-Chair. Exec. Cttee, Int. Inst. of Human Rights (René Cassin Foundation); mem. Supreme Council of Magistrature, Int. Penal Law Asscn (and Admin. Council), Int. Criminology Asscn, Société de Législation comparée, Int. Olympic Cttee (mem. Exec. Bd); Judge, Int. Court of Justice, The Hague 1982–91 (Vice-Pres. 1987–91); fmr mem. various UN bodies, fmr mem. or Chair. Comm. on Human Rights and other such cttees and various symposia organized by Int. Asscn of Legal Sciences, Red Cross, Unidroit and UNESCO; fmr Pres. and mem. Int. Cttee on Comparative Law, Int. African Law Asscn, Int. Cttee for Social Science Documentation; Hon. Pres. World Fed. of UN Asscns. *Publications:* numerous publs on Senegalese law, the law of Black Africa and human rights. *Address:* Rue G, angle rue Léon Gontran Damas, BP 5865, Dakar, Senegal. *Telephone:* (221) 25-55-01.

MBEI, Samuel Libock; Cameroonian diplomatist; m. Hermine Libock. *Career:* High Commr to UK 1995–, Dean of African Missions in London. *Address:* Cameroon High Commission, 84 Holland Park, London, W11 3SB, England (office). *Telephone:* (20) 7727-0771 (office). *Fax:* (20) 7792-9353 (office). *Website:* www.cameroonhighcommission.co.uk (office).

MBEKI, Thabo Mvuyelwa, MA; South African politician and head of state; *President;* b. 18 June 1942, Idutywa; m. Zanele Dlamini 1974. *Education:* Lovedale, Alice, St John's Umtata, Univs of London and Sussex. *Career:* Leader African Students Org. 1961; Youth Organizer for African Nat. Congress (ANC), Johannesburg 1961–62; six weeks' detention, Byo 1962;

left SA 1962; official, ANC offices, London, England 1967–70; mil. training, USSR 1970; Asst Sec. ANC Revolutionary Council 1971–72; Acting ANC Rep., Swaziland 1975–76; ANC Rep., Nigeria 1976–78, mem. ANC, Nat. Exec. Cttee 1975, re-elected 1985,; Dir Information and Publicity, ANC 1984–89, Head, Dept of Int. Affairs 1989–93, Del. on Talks about Talks, with SA Govt 1990, Chair. ANC 1993; First Deputy Pres. of SA 1994–99; Pres. ANC 1997–2007; Pres. of South Africa 1999–; mem. Bd IOC 1993–; Pres. African Union 2002–; Hon. KCMG; KStJ.
Address: Office of the President, Private Bag X1000, Pretoria 0001, South Africa (office). *Telephone:* (12) 3191500 (office). *Fax:* (12) 3238246 (office). *E-mail:* president@po.gov.za (office). *Website:* www.gov.za/president (office).

MBIKUSITA-LEWANIKA, Inonge, PhD; Zambian diplomatist, university lecturer and fmr politician; *Ambassador to USA;* two d. *Career:* Prof. of Educ. and Teacher Training, Univ. of Zambia and Lecturer, Evelyn Hone Coll. of Further Educ. and Mongu Teacher Training Coll. 1972–80; Regional Adviser and Sr Programme Officer, West, Cen., E and Southern Africa, UNICEF 1980–90; MP 1991–2001, served on various cttees on foreign affairs, educ., science and tech., youth and women; Amb. and Special Envoy of Pres. of Zambia 2001–02, Amb. to USA 2003–; served as community activist.
Address: Embassy of Zambia, 2419 Massachusetts Avenue, NW, Washington, DC 20008, USA (office). *Telephone:* (202) 265-9717 (office). *Fax:* (202) 265-9718 (office). *E-mail:* embzambia@aol.com (office). *Website:* www .zambiaembassy.org (office).

MBOWENI, Tito, MA; South African politician and banker; *Governor, South African Reserve Bank;* b. 16 March 1959, Tzaneem, Nothern Prov. *Education:* Nat. Univ. of Lesotho and Univ. of E Anglia. *Career:* mem. ANC 1980 (ANC, Zambia 1988), fmr Deputy Head Dept of Econ. Planning, Co-ordinator for Trade and Industry; Minister of Labour, Govt of Nat. Unity 1994–99; Gov. SA Reserve Bank 1999–; Hon. Prof. of Econs (Univ. of S Africa) 2002–03; Hon. DComm (Univ. of Natal) 2001.
Address: South African Reserve Bank, 370 Church Street, PO Box 427, Pretoria 0001, South Africa (office). *Telephone:* (12) 3133911 (office); (12) 3133526 (office). *Fax:* (12) 3134181 (office). *E-mail:* mpho.mtimkulu@ resbank.co.za (office). *Website:* www.resbank.co.za (office).

MBUENDE, Kaire Munionganda, PhD; Namibian academic and diplomatist; *Permanent Representative, United Nations;* b. Nov. 1953; m.; four c. *Education:* Univ. of Lund, Sweden. *Career:* held several academic positions in Sweden and Denmark; Information Officer, SWAPO 1974–75; mem. Parl. 1990–93, 2000–05; Head of Omaheke Regional Election Directorate, SWAPO 1989–1990; Deputy Minister for Agric., Water and Rural Devt 1990–93; Exec. Sec. to SADC 1994–99; Deputy Minister for Foreign Affairs 2002–04; Perm. Rep. to UN, New York 2006–. *Publications:* several books and articles.
Address: Permanent Mission of Namibia to the United Nations, 135 East 36th Street, New York, NY 10016, USA (office). *Telephone:* (212) 685-2003 (office). *Fax:* (212) 685-1561 (office). *E-mail:* namibia@un.int (office). *Website:* www.un.int/namibia (office).

MBULA, Leslie Sainot; Zambian diplomatist; *High Commissioner to South Africa; Career:* fmr Sec. to Cabinet; High Commr to S Africa (also accred to Lesotho) 2005–.
Address: High Commission of Zambia, Zambia House, 570 Ziervogel Street, Arcadia, Pretoria, 0083, South Africa (office). *Telephone:* (12) 3261854 (office). *Fax:* (12) 3262140 (office). *Website:* www.zambiapretoria .net (office).

MBUSA NYAMWISI, Antipas; Democratic Republic of the Congo politician; *Minister of Foreign Affairs and International Co-operation; Career:* fought with Rally for Congolese Democracy (RCD) against Govt 1998–99; Founder and Chair. RCD-Kisangani Party (later Forces for Renewal Party) 1999–; Minister of Regional Co-ordination 2003–07, of Foreign Affairs and Int. Co-operation 2007–; unsuccessful cand. in 2006 presidential election.
Address: Ministry of Foreign Affairs and International Co-operation, place de l'Indépendance, BP 7100, Kinshasa-Gombe, Democratic Republic of the Congo (office). *Telephone:* (12) 32450 (office).

MEAD, Walter Russell, BA; American foreign policy analyst, academic and writer; *Henry A. Kissinger Senior Fellow in US Foreign Policy, Council on Foreign Relations; Education:* Yale Univ. *Career:* Contributing Ed. Harper's Magazine 1986–91; Pres.'s Fellow, World Policy Inst., The New School, New York 1987–97; Henry A. Kissinger Sr Fellow in US Foreign Policy, Council on Foreign Relations 1998–; Project Dir Ind. Task Force on US–Cuban Relations in the 21st Century 1998–, Working Group on Devt, Trade and Int. Finance 1999–, Study Group on History of US

Foreign Policy, Phase II 1999–; Sr Contributing Ed. Worth; contribs to New York Times, Int. Herald Tribune, Wall Street Journal, New Yorker. *Publications:* Mortal Splendor: The American Empire in Transition 1987, Geoeconomics in American Foreign Policy 1999, Special Providence: American Foreign Policy and How It Changed the World (Lionel Gelber Prize 2002, Premio Acqui Storia) 2001, Power, Terror, Peace and War: America's Grand Strategy in a World at Risk 2004.
Address: Council on Foreign Relations, The Harold Pratt House, 58 East 68th Street, New York, NY 10021, USA (office). *Telephone:* (212) 434-9548 (office). *Fax:* (212) 434-9800 (office). *E-mail:* wmead@cfr.org (office). *Website:* www.cfr.org (office).

MEARSHEIMER, John J., BS, MA, PhD; American academic; *R. Wendell Harrison Distinguished Service Professor of Political Science, University of Chicago; Education:* Univ. of Southern Calif., Cornell Univ., West Point Mil. Acad. *Career:* served as officer in USAF 1970–75; Research Fellow, Brookings Institution 1979–80; Research Assoc., Center for Int. Affairs, Harvard Univ. 1980–82; Asst Prof., Political Science Dept, Univ. of Chicago 1982–84, Assoc. Prof. 1984–87, Prof. 1987–96, R. Wendell Harrison Distinguished Service Prof. 1996–, also Co-Dir Program on Int. Security Policy; Visiting Scholar, Olin Inst. for Strategic Studies, Harvard Univ. 1992–93; mem. American Acad. of Arts and Sciences, IISS, Chicago Council on Global Affairs, Council on Foreign Relations; mem. or fmr mem. editorial bds International Security, Security Studies, International History Review, JFQ: Joint Forces Quarterly, Journal of Transatlantic Studies, Asian Security, China Security; Clark Award for Distinguished Teaching, Cornell Univ., Quantrell Award for Distinguished Teaching, Univ. of Chicago 1985, George Kistiakowsky Scholar, American Acad. of Arts and Sciences 1986–87, Distinguished Scholar Award, Int. Studies Asscn 2004. *Publications:* Conventional Deterrence (Edgar S. Furniss, Jr Book Award) 1983, Nuclear Deterrence: Ethics and Strategy (jt ed.) 1985, Liddell Hart and the Weight of History 1988, The Tragedy of Great Power Politics (Joseph Lepgold Book Prize) 2001, The Israel Lobby and US Foreign Policy (with Stephen M. Walt) 2007; contribs to Perspectives on International Relations, London Review of Books, Middle East Policy, Foreign Policy, International Relations, New Republic, International Security, New York Times, Chicago Tribune and numerous chapters in books.
Address: Political Science Department, University of Chicago, 5828 South University Avenue, Chicago, IL 60637, USA (office). *Telephone:* (773) 702-8667 (office). *Fax:* (773) 702-1689 (office). *E-mail:* j-mearsheimer@ uchicago.edu (office). *Website:* www.uchicago.edu (office).

MEDELCI, Mourad, LèsSc, DS; Algerian government official; *Minister of Foreign Affairs;* b. 30 April 1943, Tlemcen; m.; five c. *Education:* Univ. of Algiers. *Career:* began career working in Algerian energy industry 1970–80; Sec.-Gen., Ministry of Commerce 1980–88; Minister of Trade 1988–89, 1999–2001, of Finance 2001–02, 2005–07, of Foreign Affairs 2007–; Minister Delegate of the Budget 1990–91; Adviser to Pres. of Algeria 2002–05; Gov. for Algeria, Islamic Devt Bank; Vice-Pres. Emir Abdelkader Foundation 1996; founding mem. Asscn for Int. Relations 1997; Founder and Pres. Asscn for Promotion of Eco-effectiveness and Quality in Enterprises (APEQUE) 1998; mem. African Peer Review (APR) Panel of Eminent Persons 2004.
Address: Ministry of Foreign Affairs, place Mohamed Seddik Benyahia, el-Mouradia, Algiers, Algeria (office). *Telephone:* (21) 69-23-33 (office). *Fax:* (21) 69-21-61 (office). *Website:* www.mae.dz (office).

MEDGYESSY, Péter, PhD; Hungarian politician, economist and diplomatist; b. 19 Oct. 1942, Budapest; m. 2nd Katalin Csaplár; one s. one d. (from previous marriage). *Education:* Budapest Univ. of Econs (then Karl Marx Univ.). *Career:* held several positions in Ministry of Finance, Dept of Finance, Dept of Prices, Dept of Int. Finances; fmr Dir-Gen. Dept of State Budget; Deputy Minister of Finance 1982–87; Minister of Finance 1987–88; Deputy Prime Minister in interim Govt of Miklós Németh 1988–89; Pres., Chief Exec. Magyar Paribas 1990–94; Pres. and CEO Hungarian Bank for Investment and Devt Ltd 1994–96; Minister of Finance 1996–98; Chair. Bd Dirs Inter-Europa Bank 1998–2001; Vice-Pres. Atlasz Insurance Co. 1998–2001; Prime Minister of Hungary 2002–04 (resgnd), Man. Prime Minister Aug.–Sept. 2004; Amb. at Large 2004–; Prof., Coll. of Finance and Accounting, Budapest; Pres. Hungarian Econ. Soc.; Dir Int. Inst. of Public Finance, Saarbrücken; mem. Presidium Hungarian Bank Asscn 1996–, Council of World Econ. Forum; Commdr's Cross with Star, Order of Merit of Hungarian Repub. 1998, Chevalier de la Légion d'honneur 2000, Officer's Cross 2004, Order of Crown of Belgium 2002, Order of the Rising Sun – Gold and Silver Star (Japan) 2002, Grand Cross, Order of Merit (Chile) 2003, Grand Cross, Order of Merit (Norway) 2003, Grand Cross, Order of Merit (Germany) 2004; Medal of Irish Hungarian Econ. Asscn 2005. *Publications:* several articles on budgetary and exchange rate policies and monetary system in financial and econ. publs.

Address: c/o Office of the Prime Minister, Kossuth Lajos tér 1–3, 1055 Budapest. *Telephone:* (1) 441-4000. *Fax:* (1) 441-4543. *E-mail:* medgyessyp@meh.hu (office). *Website:* www.medgyessy.hu (office).

MEDINA-QUIROGA, Cecilia, Licenciada en Ciencias Jurídicas y Sociale, DIur; Chilean jurist and academic; *President, Inter-American Court of Human Rights (Corte Interamericana de Derechos Humanos);* b. 1935, Concepción. *Education:* Univ. of Chile, Santiago, Univ. of Utrecht, Netherlands. *Career:* Prof. of Int. Law of Human Rights, Faculty of Law, Univ. of Chile, Founder and Co-Dir Human Rights Centre; Visiting Prof., Harvard Law School, USA; has also taught at Lund Univ., Int. Inst. of Human Rights, Univ. of Toronto, UN Univ. for Peace, Univ. of Utrecht and in Sweden; mem. UN Human Rights Cttee 1995–2002, Chair. 1999–2000, author of General Comment 28 on the rights of men and women as set out in Article 3 of the Int. Covenant on Civil and Political Rights; Judge, Inter-American Court of Human Rights (Corte Interamericana de Derechos Humanos) 2004–, Vice-Pres. 2007–08, Pres. 2008–; mem. Int. Comm. of Jurists 2004–; selected by UN Human Rights Council for group of ind. experts assigned to investigate Nov. 2006 Beit Hanoun incident Dec. 2006; Gruber Prize for Women's Rights, Peter Gruber Foundation Int. Awards 2006. *Publications:* Nomenclature and Hierarchy: Basic Latin American Sources (co-author) 1979, Chile: La Nueva Constitución, Democracia y Derechos Humanos, Cuadernos ESIN, No. 18 1981, The Battle of Human Rights: Gross, Systematic Violations and the Inter-American System 1988, Derecho Internacional de los Derechos Humanos. Manual de Enseñanza (ed.) 1990, SIM Special No. 13, Training Course on International Human Rights Law: Selected Lectures, Peace Palace, The Hague, 16 Sept.–4 Oct. 1991 (ed.) 1992, Special Issue on The Americas, NQHR, Vol. 10, No. 2 (ed.) 1992, Constitución, Tratados y Derechos Esenciales Introducción y Selección de textos, Corporación Nacional de Reparación y Reconciliación 1994, Sistema Jurídico y Derechos Humanos. El derecho nacional y las obligaciones internacionales de Chile en materia de Derechos Humanos (co-ed.) 1996; numerous book chapters and articles in professional journals. *Address:* Corte Interamericana de Derechos Humanos, Apdo Postal 6906-1000, San José, Costa Rica (office). *Telephone:* (506) 234-0581 (office). *Fax:* (506) 234-0584 (office). *E-mail:* corteidh@corteidh.or.cr (office). *Website:* www.corteidh.or.cr (office).

MEDVEDEV, Dimitri Anatolyevich, PhD; Russian business executive, government official and head of state; *President;* b. 14 Sept. 1965, Leningrad (now St Petersburg); m. Svetlana Medvedeva; one s. *Education:* Leningrad State Univ. *Career:* Asst Prof., Leningrad State Univ. 1990–99; Adviser to Chair. Leningrad City Council and Expert Consultant, Cttee for External Relations, St. Petersburg Mayor's Office 1990–95; Deputy Chief of Staff, Govt of Russian Fed. 1999–2000; Deputy Head, then First Deputy Head of the Presidential Admin 2000–03, Head 2003–05; mem. Bd of Dirs OAO Gazprom 2000–08, Chair. 2000–01, 2002–08, Deputy Chair. 2001–02; mem. Exec. Cttee on Int. Relations, St Petersburg Mayor's Office 1991–95; First Deputy Prime Minister 2005–08; Pres. 2008–; Order in the Name of Russia 2004. *Address:* Office of the President, 103132 Moscow, Staraya pl. 4 (office). *Telephone:* (495) 925-35-81 (office). *Fax:* (495) 206-07-66 (office). *E-mail:* president@gov.ru (office). *Website:* www.kremlin.ru (office).

MEDVEDEV, Roy Aleksandrovich, PhD; Russian historian and sociologist; b. 14 Nov. 1925, Tbilisi; twin brother of Zhores Medvedev; m. Galina A. Gaidina 1956; one s. *Education:* Leningrad State Univ., Acad. of Pedagogical Sciences of USSR. *Career:* mem. CPSU –1969, 1989–91; worker at mil. factory 1943–46; teacher of history, Ural Secondary School 1951–53; Dir of Secondary School in Leningrad region 1954–56; Deputy to Ed.-in-Chief of Publishing House of Pedagogical Literature, Moscow 1957–59; Head of Dept, Research Inst. of Vocational Educ., Acad. of Pedagogical Sciences of USSR 1960–70, Senior Scientist 1970–71; freelance author 1972–; People's Deputy of USSR, mem. Supreme Soviet of USSR 1989–91; mem. Cen. Cttee CPSU 1990–91; Co-Chair. Socialist Party of Labour 1991–2003. *Publications:* Vocational Education in Secondary School 1960, Faut-il réhabiliter Staline? 1969, A Question of Madness (with Zhores Medvedev) 1971, Let History Judge 1972, On Socialist Democracy 1975, Qui a écrit le 'Don Paisible'? 1975, La Révolution d'octobre était-elle inéluctable? 1975, Solschenizyn und die Sowjetische Linke 1976, Khrushchev–The Years in Power (with Zhores Medvedev) 1976, Political Essays 1976, Problems in the Literary Biography of Mikhail Sholokhov 1977, Samizdat Register 1978, Philip Mironov and the Russian Civil War (with S. Starikov) 1978, The October Revolution 1979, On Stalin and Stalinism 1979, On Soviet Dissent 1980, Nikolai Bukharin–The Last Years 1980, Leninism and Western Socialism 1981, An End to Silence 1982, Khrushchev 1983, All Stalin's Men 1984, China and Superpowers 1986, L'URSS che cambia (with G. Chiesa) 1987, Time of Change (with G. Chiesa) 1990, Brezhnev: A Political Biography 1991, Gensek s Lybianki: A Political Portrait of Andropov 1993, 1917. The Russian Revolution 1997,

Capitalism in Russia? 1998, The Unknown Andropov 1998, Post-Soviet Russia 2000, The Unknown Stalin (with Zhores Medvedev) 2001, Putin 2004, Solzhenitsyn and Sakharov (with Zhores Medvedev) 2004, Moscow Model of Yuri Luzhkov 2005, Putin 2007, Divided Ukraine 2007; and over 400 professional and general articles. *Address:* c/o Z. A. Medvedev, 4 Osborn Gardens, London, NW7 1DY, England; Abonnement Post Box 258, 125475 Moscow A-475; Dybenko str 2 apt 20, 125475 Moscow A-475, Russia (home). *Telephone:* (495) 597-61-20 (home).

MEECE, Roger A., BS; American diplomatist; b. 1949, Indianapolis, Ind. *Education:* Michigan State Univ. *Career:* Peace Corps volunteer, Sierra Leone 1971, several Peace Corps staff assignments, including Assoc. Dir for Peace Corps in Niger and Cameroon, Deputy Dir for Peace Corps, Brazzaville, Repub. of the Congo, Dir Peace Corps in Gabon; joined Foreign Service 1979, served in Embassies in Cameroon and Malawi, worked in Bureau of Int. Narcotics Matters, Washington, DC, assigned to Office of Vice-Pres. of the USA, Deputy Chief of Mission, Brazzaville, Consul-Gen., Halifax, Canada, Deputy Chief of Mission, Kinshasa 1995–98, Dir for Cen. African Affairs, State Dept 1998–2000, Amb. to Malawi 2000–03, Diplomat-in-Residence, Florida Int. Univ. 2003, served as Chargé d'affaires a.i., Embassy in Nigeria 2003, Amb. to Democratic Repub. of the Congo 2004–07. *Address:* US Department of State, 2201 C Street NW, Washington, DC 20520, USA (office). *Telephone:* (202) 647-4000 (office). *Fax:* (202) 647-6738 (office). *Website:* www.state.gov (office).

MEGAWATI, Sukarnoputri; Indonesian fmr head of state and politician; b. 23 Jan. 1947, Jogjakarta; m. 1st Surendro (deceased); m. 2nd Hassan Gamal Ahmad Hassan; m. 3rd Taufik Kiemas; three c. *Career:* mem. House of Reps (Partai Demokrasi Indonesia–PDI) 1987; Leader PDI 1993–96 (deposed); Chair. Partai Demokrasi Indonesia Perjuangan (PDI-P) 1996–; Vice-Pres. of Indonesia 1999–2001, Pres. 2001–04; ranked by Forbes magazine amongst 100 Most Powerful Women (eighth) 2004. *Address:* c/o Partai Demokrasi Indonesia Perjuangan (PDI-P), c/o Dewan Perwakilan Rakyat, Jalan Gatot Subroto 16, Jakarta, Indonesia.

MEHDIYEV, Agshin, PhD; Azerbaijani diplomatist; *Permanent Representative, United Nations;* b. 28 April 1949, Baku; m.; three c. *Education:* Azerbaijan State Univ., Diplomatic Acad., USSR Ministry of Foreign Affairs, Moscow. *Career:* Asst to Counsellor for Econ. Affairs, USSR Embassy in Egypt 1971–75; at Ministry of Foreign Affairs, Azerbaijan 1975–77, 1982–85; served at Embassy in Yemen 1977–82, 1987–92; Chief Dept for Europe, USA and Canada, Ministry of Foreign Affairs 1993–2001; Perm. Rep. to Council of Europe 2001–06, to UN, New York 2006–; Amb. to Cuba 2007–; Hon. Prof. (Baki Avrasiya Univ.) 2007. *Address:* Permanent Mission of Azerbaijan to the United Nations, 866 United Nations Plaza, Suite 560, New York, NY 10017, USA (office). *Telephone:* (212) 371-2559 (office). *Fax:* (212) 371-2784 (office). *E-mail:* azerbaijan@un.int (office).

MEHMET, Alper (Alp), MVO; British diplomatist (retd); b. 28 Aug. 1948, Cyprus; m. Elaine Mehmet; two d. *Career:* Immigration Officer 1970–79, seconded to British High Comm. from the Home Office, Lagos 1979–83, transferred to FCO 1983, Asst Pvt. Sec. to Parl. Under-Sec. of State 1983–85, Second Sec., Chancery/Information, Bucharest 1986–89, Deputy Head of Mission and Consul, Reykjavík 1989–93, Parl. Clerk, FCO 1993–95, FCO Spokesman for Asia, Press Office 1995–98, First Sec. and Head of Press and Public Affairs, Bonn Jan.–Sept. 1999, First Sec. and Head of Press and Public Affairs, Berlin 1999–2003, Amb. to Iceland 2004–08 (retd). *Address:* c/o Foreign and Commonwealth Office, King Charles Street, London, SW1A 2AH, England. *Telephone:* (20) 7008-1500.

MEHTA, Adm. Sureesh; Indian naval officer; *Chief of Naval Staff and Chairman, Joint Chiefs of Staff Committee;* b. 18 Aug. 1947; m. Maria Teresa Mehta; two c. *Education:* Nat. Defence Acad., Defence Services Staff Coll., Wellington, Nat. Defence Coll., New Delhi. *Career:* commissioned in Indian Navy 1967, joined Fleet Air Arm and flew Sea Hawk jet fighters from carrier INS Vikrant 1967, carried out instructional duties as Directing Staff in Defence Services Staff Coll., earlier appointments included command of frigate INS Beas and guided missile frigate INS Godavari, also commanded Naval Air Stations, INS Garuda, C-in-C Eastern Naval Command 2005–06, other operational Flag appointments have included Flag Officer Naval Aviation, Fleet Commdr Western Fleet during Kargil Crisis 1999, has held various staff appointments in Flag rank at New Delhi, including Asst Controller Carrier Projects, Asst Chief of Personnel (Human Resources Devt), Controller of Personnel Services, Chief of Personnel, Dir-Gen. Coast Guard, Deputy Chief of Naval Staff,

Chief of Naval Staff 2006–, currently Chair. Jt Chiefs of Staff Cttee; Ati Vishist Seva Medal 1995, Param Vishist Seva Medal 2005.
Address: Office of the Chief of Naval Staff, Integrated Headquarters of Ministry of Defence (Navy), Sena Bhawan, New Delhi, 110 0111, India (office). *E-mail:* webmasterindiannavy@nic.in (office). *Website:* indiannavy.nic.in (office).

MEI, Ping; Chinese diplomatist; *Chairman, China National Committee for Pacific Economic Cooperation; Career:* Amb. to Canada 1998–2005; Chair. China Nat. Cttee for Pacific Econ. Cooperation 2005–; mem. Foreign Affairs Cttee, CPPCC.
Address: China National Committee for Pacific Economic Cooperation, China Institute of International Studies, 3 Toutiao Taijichang, Beijing 100005, People's Republic of China (office). *Telephone:* (10) 85119648 (office). *Fax:* (10) 85119647 (office). *E-mail:* cncpec@netchina.com.cn (office).

MEIDANI, Rexhep Qemal, DèsSc; Albanian fmr head of state; b. 17 Aug. 1944, Tirana; m.; two c. *Education:* Univs of Caen and Paris XI, France, Univ. of Tirana. *Career:* scientific collaborator, C. E. N., Saclay, France 1974–96; Asst, then Lecturer, then Docent, Univ. of Tirana and Univ. of Pristina, Kosova 1966–96, Prof. of Theoretical Physics 1987–, Dean of Faculty of Natural Sciences 1988–92; Visiting Scientist and Visiting Prof., Italy, France, Germany, UK, USA, Greece etc.; mem. Socialist Party of Albania 1996–97, 2002–, Gen. Sec. 1996–97; mem. Parl. 1997; Pres. of Albania 1997–2002; Chair. Bd Albanian Centre for Human Rights 1994–96, Ed.-in-Chief Human Rights quarterly 1994–96; Co-Founder Citizens of Helsinki, Democratic Albania; mem. Albanian Cttee for Understanding and Cooperation in the Balkans 1986–90; Co-Ed. Bulletin of Natural Sciences 1978–89, Ed.-in-Chief 1989–94; Co-Ed. Balkan Physics Letters 1992–96; mem. Acad. of Sciences 2003, Club of Madrid, Int. Cttee for Democracy in Cuba, Int. Raoul Wallenberg Foundation, Editorial Advisory Bd World Leaders Magazine, European Asscn of Law Students (Elsa), Albania, War Invalids' Asscn against Nazism; Hon. Amb. of Millennium Goals, Amb. for Peace, Int. Hon. Citizen, New Orleans, USA 2002; Order 'Naim Frasheri', Third Class 1981, Nat. Order Golden Star of Romania 1999, Order of King Tomislav (Croatia) 2001, Nat. Order of Merit (Grade of Companion of Honour) (Malta) 2002; Hon. PhD (Istanbul Tech. Univ.) 1998, Dr hc (Aristotle Univ. of Thessaloniki) 1998, (Sofia Univ.) 1998, Hon. DHumLitt (American Univ., Rome) 1999, (Univ. of Bridgeport, Conn.) 2001, Preside d'Onore (Università Mediterranea René Cassin, Bari) 1999, Hon. DSc (Portsmouth, UK) 2002; Prize of the Repub., Second Class 1988, Gold Medal of Merit of the City of Athens 1998, Great Cross of Salvation (Greece) 1998, Médaille du Mérite (U.P. Universelle) 1998, Honorary Medal of the Centre Democritos (Greece) 1998, F. Lux Award, Clark Univ., Worcester, Mass, USA 2000, Golden Key of the City of Worcester 2000, Golden Key of the City of Prague, Czech Repub. 2001, Jan Masaryk Medal, Univ. of Economics, Prague 2001, Medal of the Robert Schumann Foundation, Paris 2001, Chancellor's Int. Medallion of Distinction, New Orleans Univ. 2002, Golden Key of the City of New Orleans 2002. *Publications:* President Meidani and Kosovo 2000, The Balkans – A General Outlook. Montenegro, Bosnia, Kosovo, FYR of Macedonia, Serbia: Near-Term Challenges 2001, Dall'Indipendenza verso L'Interdipendenza dell'Integrazione 2002, Globalization, Integration and the Albanian Nation 2002, Jus Gentium 2003, Politics, Moral and State 2003, Agreement with Myself 2004, The Traps of Nation-State 2005, Politics in Vivo-in Vitro 2006; 31 scientific monographs and books and hundreds of scientific and political articles published in Albania; more than 36 articles in int. scientific publs and numerous others on political and social problems.
Address: Academy of Sciences, Akademia e Shkencave, Tirana (office); Bulevardi Zogu I, Pallati 57, Shkalla 1, Ap. 12, Tirana, Albania (home). *Telephone:* (4) 271844 (office); (4) 271887 (home). *E-mail:* rmeidani@hotmail.com (home); rmeidani@gmail.com (home); rmeidani@rmeidani.info (home).

MEIER ESPINOSA, José Antonio; Peruvian diplomatist; *Ambassador to Colombia;* m. Astrid Kämmerer Mejia. *Education:* Pontifical Catholic Univ. of Peru, Diplomatic Acad. of Peru. *Career:* Third Sec., Secr. for Econ. Affairs, Ministry of Foreign Affairs 1974–75, Third Sec., Secr. for Econ. Affairs and Integrity 1975–76, Third Sec., Head of Dept of Int. Econ. Policy, Bureau of Econ. Affairs 1976–77; Third Sec., Embassy in Tokyo 1977–78, Second Sec. 1978–80; Second Sec., Embassy in FRG 1980–81, First Sec. 1981–84; First Sec., Secr. for Economic Affairs and Integrity 1984–87, Counsellor, Directorate of Econ. Promotion, Secr. for Econ. Affairs and Integrity 1987–88, Counsellor, Head of Dept of Mexico, Cen. America and Caribbean, Bureau of Americas, Under-Sec. of Bilateral Policy 1988, Counsellor, Deputy Director of Americas II, Under-Sec. 1988–89, Counsellor, Directorate Gen. for Coordination 1989–90; Counsellor, Embassy in Bogotá 1990–91, Minister Counsellor 1991–93; Minister

Counsellor, Embassy in FRG 1993–94; Minister 1994; Minister and Dir Gen. of Tech. Office of Trade Promotion, Ministry of Foreign Affairs 1994–96; Amb. to South Africa (also accred to Zimbabwe) 1996–98; Asst Sec. for American Affairs, Ministry of Foreign Affairs 2000–02; Amb. to Chile 2002–06, to Columbia 2006–; Orden del Sol in the degree of Grand Cross (Peru), Order of San Carlos in the degree of Grand Cross (Colombia), Honor of Merit in the degree of Grand Officer (Colombia), Order of Civil Merit, Liberator Simón Bolívar in the degree of Grand Cross (Bolivia), Nat. Order of Merit in the degree of Grand Cross (Ecuador), Order of Merit (Japan). *Publications:* has published several articles on Peruvian foreign policy and int. trade and econ. affairs in journal of the Diplomatic Academy of Peru and other academic journals.
Address: Embassy of Peru, Calle 80a, No 6-50, Bogotá, DC, Colombia (office). *Telephone:* (1) 257-0505 (office). *Fax:* (1) 249-8581 (office). *E-mail:* embajadaperu@supercabletv.net.co (office). *Website:* www.embajadadelperu.org.co (office).

MEILŪNAS, Egidijus; Lithuanian diplomatist; *Ambassador to Poland; Career:* fmr Nat. Security and Foreign Policy Deputy Advisor on Foreign Policy to the Pres., Amb. to Poland 2004–.
Address: Embassy of Lithuania, Al. Jana Chrystiana Szucha 5, 00-580 Warsaw, Poland (office). *Telephone:* (22) 6253368 (office). *Fax:* (22) 6253440 (office). *E-mail:* ambasada@lietuva.pl (office); amb.pl@urm.lt (office). *Website:* www.lietuva.pl (office).

MEIMARAKIS, Evangelos; Greek lawyer and politician; *Minister of National Defence;* b. 14 Dec. 1953, Athens; m. Ioanna Kolokota; two d. *Education:* Athens Univ. Law School, Panteion Univ. *Career:* founding mem. New Democracy youth group ONNED, fmr Pres.; mem. Parl. (New Democracy party) 1989–, New Democracy Political Planning and Programme Sec. 2000–01, Cen. Cttee Sec. 2001–06; Deputy Minister for Culture, responsible for sports 1992–1993; Minister of Nat. Defence 2006–.
Address: Ministry of National Defence, Odos Mesogeion 227–231, 154 51 Athens, Greece (office). *Telephone:* (210) 6598607 (office). *Fax:* (210) 6443832 (office). *E-mail:* minister@mod.mil.gr (office). *Website:* www.mod.gr (office); www.meimarakis.gr.

MEJDOUB, Noureddine, PhD; Tunisian diplomatist; b. 20 Jan. 1935, Tunis; m.; three c. *Education:* Inst. for Political Sciences. *Career:* joined diplomatic service 1960; Spokesman, Ministry of Foreign Affairs 1962–63; Press Officer, Embassy in London 1963–65; Deputy Dir of Political Affairs, Ministry of Foreign Affairs 1970–71, Dir for Europe and America 1977–80; Minister Plenipotentiary and Deputy Chief of Mission, Embassy in Paris 1971–73; Chargé d'affaires and Amb. to Austria (also Rep. to UNIDO and IAEA) 1973–77; Amb. to Italy and Czechoslovakia 1980–89; Diplomatic Counsellor and Chair. Nat. Cttee on Tunisia's Relations with EC 1990–91; Sec. of State to Minister for Foreign Affairs 1991–92; Amb. to Japan 1992–97, to USA 1997–2000; Perm. Rep. to UN, New York 2001; currently Rep. to UN group seeking to establish proposed World Solidarity Fund.
Address: c/o Ministry of Foreign Affairs, ave de la Ligue des états arabes, Tunis, Tunisia (office). *Telephone:* (71) 847-500 (office). *E-mail:* mae@ministeres.tn (office).

MEJIA CARRANZA, Aristides; Honduran government official; *Minister of National Defence; Career:* Pres. Supreme Electoral Tribunal 2005; Minister of Nat. Defence 2006–; mem. Liberal Party.
Address: Ministry of National Defence, 5a Avda, 4a Calle, Tegucigalpa, Honduras (office). *Telephone:* 238-3427 (office). *Fax:* 238-0238 (office).

MEKOUAR, Aziz, BA; Moroccan diplomatist; *Ambassador to USA; Independent President, Council, United Nations Food and Agriculture Organization;* m.; one c. *Education:* French High School Charles Lepierre, Lisbon, Portugal, Grad. Business School, France. *Career:* First Counsellor and Deputy Chief of Mission, Rome 1977–85, Perm. Rep. to Int. Bureau for Information Tech. 1978–85, Minister Plenipotentiary, Ministry of Foreign Affairs and Co-operation 1985–86, Amb. to Angola 1986–93, to Portugal 1993–99, to Italy 1999–2002, to USA 2002–; Ind. Pres. UN FAO Council 2001–; Grand Croix de l'Ordre du Mérite of Portugal, Grand Croix de l'Ordre Militaire du Christ (Portugal), Grand Croix de l'Ordre du Mérite of Italy.
Address: Embassy of Morocco, 1601 21st Street, NW, Washington, DC 20009, USA (office). *Telephone:* (202) 462-7980 (office). *Fax:* (202) 265-0161 (office).

MÉLAÏNINE, Ould Moctar Neche; Mauritanian diplomatist; m. Oumkelthoum Mélaïnine. *Career:* fmr Amb. to Italy, Amb. to UK 2005–07.
Address: Ministry of Foreign Affairs and Co-operation, BP 230, Nouakchott, Mauritania (office). *Telephone:* 525-26-82 (office). *Fax:* 525-28-60 (office).

MELEDJE, Clément Kaul; Côte d'Ivoirian diplomatist. *Career:* fmr Cultural Attaché Perm. Mission to UNESCO, Paris; Sec. of State for External Affairs 1974–76; Minister of Co-operation 1976–77; currently Amb. to Liberia.
Address: Embassy of Côte d'Ivoire, Tubman Blvd, Sinkor, POB 126, Monrovia, Liberia (office). *Telephone:* 261123 (office).

MELÉNDEZ, Florentín, MA, PhD; Salvadorean academic and international organization official; *President, Inter-American Commission on Human Rights (IACHR—Comisión Interamericana de Derechos Humanos); Education:* National Univ. of El Salvador, Complutense Univ. of Madrid, Spain. *Career:* worked at UN and in public and pvt. insts in El Salvador on issues related to human rights; joined Inter-American Comm. on Human Rights (IACHR—Comisión Interamericana de Derechos Humanos), OAS 2004, Special Rapporteur for rights of persons deprived of liberty in Americas, prepared Draft Declaration of Principles on Protection of Persons Deprived of Freedom, has also been Rapporteur for Argentina, Bolivia, Mexico and Dominican Repub., del. on several occasions to Inter-American Court of Human Rights, Pres. IACHR 2004–; visiting lecturer on human rights at several univs; Freedom Award, Marcelino Pan Y Vino/ MAPAVI Foundation 2007. *Publications:* numerous books and compilations on human rights.
Address: Inter-American Commission on Human Rights, 1889 F Street, NW, Washington, DC 20006, USA (office). *Telephone:* (202) 458-6002 (office). *Fax:* (202) 458-3992 (office). *E-mail:* cidhoea@oas.org (office). *Website:* www.cidh.oas.org (office).

MELEŞCANU, Teodor Viorel, PhD; Romanian jurist and politician; *Minister of Defence;* b. 10 March 1941, Brad, Hunedoara Co.; m. Felicia Meleşcanu; one d. *Education:* Moise Nicoara High School, Arad, Bucharest Univ., Univ. Inst. for Higher Int. Studies, Geneva. *Career:* with Ministry of Foreign Affairs 1966; mem. numerous dels to UN confs; First Sec. UN, Geneva; Secretary, Ministry of Foreign Affairs, Minister of Foreign Affairs 1992–96, also Deputy Prime Minister; Senator (for Prahova constituency) 1996–2000, Minister of Defence 2007–; Assoc. Prof. of Int. Law, Univ. of Bucharest 1996–; researcher, Romanian Inst. for Int. Studies 1996–; Founder and Pres. Alliance for Romania (social democratic party) 1997–2001, merged into Nat. Liberal Party (Partidul Naţional Liberal—PNL) 2001, First Vice-Pres. 2001–; presidential cand. 2000; mem. Asscn of Int. Law and Int. Relations (ADIRI), Int. Law Comm. (UN) (First Vice-Chair. 55th Session, Chair. 56th Session). *Publications:* Responsibility of States for the Peaceful Use of Nuclear Energy 1973, International Labour Organization Functioning and Activity, numerous studies and articles.
Address: Ministry of Defence, 050561 Bucharest 5, Str. Izvor 3–5, Romania (office). *Telephone:* (21) 4023400 (office). *Fax:* (21) 3195698 (office). *E-mail:* drp@mapn.ro (office). *Website:* www.mapn.ro (office).

MELKERT, Ad, MA; Dutch politician, banker and United Nations official; *Under-Secretary-General and Associate Administrator, United Nations Development Programme (UNDP);* b. 1956, Gouda; m. Mónica León Borquez; two d. *Education:* Univ. of Amsterdam. *Career:* Pres., Council of European Nat. Youth Cttees 1979–81; Sec.-Gen. Youth Forum of the EC 1981–84; Pres. Nat. Cttee, UN Int. Youth Year 1984–85; Asst to Gen. Sec., Dir Internal Affairs, Netherlands Org. for Int. Devt Co-operation 1984–86; mem. Parl. 1986–; Minister of Social Affairs and Employment 1994–98; Parliamentary Leader Partij van de Arbeid (PvdA – Labour Party) 1998–2002, Party Leader 2001–02 (resgnd after 2002 election defeat); Exec. Dir for Moldova, World Bank (IBRD) 2002–06; Under-Sec.-Gen. and Assoc. Admin. UNDP 2006–.
Address: United Nations Development Programme, One United Nations Plaza, New York, NY 10017, USA (office). *Telephone:* (212) 906-5000 (office). *Fax:* (212) 906-5364 (office). *Website:* www.undp.org (office).

MEMBE, Bernard Kamillius, MA; Tanzanian politician; *Minister of Foreign Affairs and International Relations;* b. 9 Nov. 1953. *Education:* Univ. of Dar es Salaam and John Hopkins Univ., USA. *Career:* Nat. Security Analyst, Office of the Pres. 1977–90; Ambassadorial Adviser, Ministry of Foreign Affairs 1992–2000; mem. Parl. (Chama Cha Mapinduzi Party—CCM) for Mtama 2000–; Deputy Minister of Home Affairs Jan.–Oct. 2006, of Energy and Minerals 2006–07; Minister of Foreign Affairs and Int. Relations 2007–.
Address: Ministry of Foreign Affairs and International Relations, POB 9000, Dar es Salaam, Tanzania (office). *Telephone:* (22) 2111906 (office). *Fax:* (22) 2116600 (office). *E-mail:* bmembe@parliament.go.tz (office).

MENAGIAS, Maj.-Gen. Ioannis; Greek military officer; *Military Representative, NATO;* b. 17 March 1951, Athens; m. Eugenia Gelezi, three c. *Education:* Air Force Acad., Hellenic War Coll. *Career:* commissioned Second Lt in F-5 squadron, served in various squadrons for 14 years with 4000 flying hours; Head, Operational Intelligence Section, Hellenic Air Force Gen. Staff 1990–93; staff officer Mil. Del. to NATO, Brussels 1993–95; staff officer, later Head of Hellenic–NATO relations, Hellenic Nat. Defence Gen. Staff 1995–2000, Defence Policy Dir 2001–04, Dir of Strategies and Policies 2005–; Commdr 130 CG, Limnos Island 2000–01; Chief of Staff Tactical Air Force HQ, Larissa 2004; Mil. Rep. to NATO 2005–; Knight Commdr Order of Honour, Mil. Merit Medal, Commendation Medal of Merit and Honour, Medal of Order of Honour Commdr's Badge, Grand Commdr's Badge Order of Phoenix, Staff Officer Commendation Medal.
Address: Delegation of Greece, NATO Headquarters, Bld Léopold III, Brussels 1110, Belgium (office). *Telephone:* (2) 707-41-11 (office). *Fax:* (2) 707-45-79 (office). *E-mail:* natodoc@hq.nato.int (office). *Website:* www.nato.int (office).

MENCHÚ TUM, Rigoberta; Guatemalan human rights activist; b. 9 Jan. 1959, San Miguel Uspantán; m. Angél Canil 1995; two c. *Career:* began campaigning for rights of Indians as a teenager; fled to Mexico after parents and brother were murdered by security forces 1980; co-ordinated protests in San Marcos against 500th anniversary of arrival of Columbus in Americas 1992; f. Rigoberta Menchú Tum Foundation, Guatemala City; Int. Goodwill Amb. UNESCO 1996–; cand. for Pres. 2007; Pres. UN Indigenous Initiative for Peace 1999; Nobel Peace Prize 1992. *Publications:* I, Rigoberta (trans. into 12 languages) 1983, Rigoberta: Grandchild of the Mayas (co-author) 1998.
Address: Fundacion Rigoberta Menchú Tum, 1 Calle 7-45, zona 1, Ciudad de Guatemala, Guatemala (office). *Telephone:* 254-5860 (office). *Fax:* 254-4477 (office). *E-mail:* rmt@terra.com.gt (office). *Website:* www.frmt.org (office).

MENDES CABEÇADAS, Adm. José Manuel; Portuguese naval officer; b. 1943, Lisbon; m. Sibylle Ninette; two s. one d. *Education:* Naval Acad., Portuguese Naval War Coll. *Career:* began career in Portuguese Navy 1961; several sea duty tours with various ships, Commdr NRP Quanza and NRP Oliveira e Carmo; held positions successively as Dir Communication Centre, Lake Niassa and Ministry of Defence, Dir Naval Radio Station, Metangula, Mozambique, Staff Officer Personnel and Org. Div., Staff Officer Intelligence Div., Naval Command, Head of 1st Section Directorate of Personnel, Teacher of Man. Portuguese Naval War Coll.; assigned to Mil. Rep. to NATO, Brussels 1984, later Exec. Asst Iberian Atlantic Area, NATO HQ; Exec. Asst to Chief of Naval Command 1996–2000; Dir of Portuguese Naval War Coll. 2000–02; Chief of Naval Staff May–Nov. 2000; Chief of Defence 2002–06; apptd Vice Adm. 2000, Adm. 2002; Grand Officier Ordem Militar de Avis Distinguished Service Gold Medal, 2 Distinguished Service Silver Medals, Mil. Merit Medals 1st, 2nd and 3rd Class, 2 Navy Cross Medals 2nd Class.
Address: c/o Ministry of National Defence, Av. Ilha de Madeira, 1400-204 Lisbon, Portugal (office).

MÉNDEZ GUTIÉRREZ, Gonzalo; Bolivian government official and academic; b. Cochabamba. *Education:* Universidad Mayor de San Sımón, Univ. of Amberes, Catholic Univ. of Louvain, Belgium. *Career:* fmr Nat. Dir of Academic Planning, Universidad Católica Boliviana; fmr Prof. Universidad Andina Simón Bolívar; fmr Dir of Finance and Planning, Municipality of Cochabamba; Minister of Nat. Defence 2005–06 (resgnd).
Address: c/o Ministry of National Defence, Plaza Avaroa, esq. Pedro Salazar y 20 de Octubre 2502, La Paz, Bolivia (office).

MÉNDEZ ROMERO, Brig.-Gen. (retd) Arévalo Enrique; Venezuelan diplomatist and fmr army officer; *Ambassador to Argentina; Education:* Mil. Acad. of Venezuela, Inst. of Higher Defense Studies. *Career:* Pvt. Sec. to Pres. and Vice Minister of Foreign Affairs 2000–05; Amb. to Spain 2005–07, to Argentina 2007–; fmr Dir Banco de Desarrollo Económico y Social de Venezuela.
Address: Embassy of Venezuela, Virrey Loreto 2035, C1426DXK Buenos Aires, Argentina (office). *Telephone:* (11) 4788-4944 (office). *Fax:* (11) 4784-4311 (office). *E-mail:* embajador@argentina.gob.ve (office). *Website:* www.argentina.gob.ve (office).

MENDONCA E MOURA, Alvaro; Portuguese politician and diplomatist; *Permanent Representative, European Union;* b. 17 March 1951, Oporto; m.; four c. *Education:* Univ. of Colmbra. *Career:* Embassy Attaché 1975–78; Third Sec. 1978; Second Sec. 1978–82; First Sec. 1982–90; Counsellor 1990–93; Minister 1993–2002; Amb. 2002–; posted to Perm. Del. to EFTA, GATT, Geneva 1979, posted to Embassy, Pretoria, S Africa 1985, Chargé d'affaires a.i. 1988–89; Dir forAfrican Affairs, Ministry of Foreign Affairs 1990–91; Chef de Cabinet, Sec. of State for Foreign Affairs and Co-operation 1991–92; Chef de Cabinet, Minister for Foreign Affairs 1992–95; Amb. in Vienna, Perm. Rep. to UN Office in Vienna 1995; non-resident Amb. in Ljubljana 1996; non-resident Amb. in Bratislava 1996; Amb., Perm. Rep. to UN Office and other Int. Orgs, Geneva 1999; Amb., Perm.

Rep. to EU 2002–; Head of Portuguese Del. to UN Comm. on Crime Prevention and Criminal Justice 1996, 1997, 1998, 1999; Chair. Preparatory Cttee, Cttee of Whole of UN Gen. Ass.'s Special Session on Narcotic Drugs 1997–98; Vice-Chair. UN Human Rights Comm. 2001–02; Chair. Gen. Ass., World Intellectual Property Org. 2001–02; Prof., Dept of Int. Relations, Lusiada Univ., Lisbon; mem. High-Level Group of Experts appointed by UN Sec. Gen. to review Int. Drug Control Programme, to strengthen UN machinery for Int. Drug Control, Vienna, New York 1998. *Address:* Permanent Mission of Portugal, 12/22 Avenue de Cortenbergh, 1040 Brussels, Belgium (office). *Telephone:* (2) 286-42-11 (office). *Fax:* (2) 231-00-26 (office). *E-mail:* reper@reper-portugal.be (office). *Website:* www .reper-portugal.be (office).

MENDOUGA, Jerome, BA; Cameroonian diplomatist; *Ambassador to USA;* b. 15 Aug. 1938, Yaoundé; m.; six c. *Education:* George Washington, American and Johns Hopkins Univs, USA. *Career:* Attaché, Embassy in Ottawa 1961, First Sec. and Acting Chief of Mission 1964, Acting Dir for Tech. and Econ. Affairs, Ministry of Foreign Affairs 1966–67, Div. Chief for Int. Org., Dept of Political Affairs 1967–70, Second Counsellor to Bonn, Moscow and Ethiopia 1970–80, Analyst, Ministry of External Relations 1980, Head of Cameroon Econ. Mission to EEC and Benelux countries, Brussels –1984, Amb. to Senegal, to Zaïre, Burundi and Rwanda 1984, to USA 1994–, Special Envoy to UN, New York 1996; Officier de l'Ordre de la Valeur (Cameroon), Grand Officier de l'Ordre Nat. du Lion (Senegal), Commdr de l'Ordre Nat. du Leopard (Democratic Repub. of the Congo). *Address:* Embassy of Cameroon, 2349 Massachusetts Avenue, NW, Washington, DC 20008, USA (office). *Telephone:* (202) 265-8790 (office). *Fax:* (202) 387-3826 (office). *E-mail:* cdm@ambacam-usa.org (office). *Website:* www.ambacam-usa.org (office).

MENEGATTI, Gabriele, LLB; Italian diplomatist; b. 28 Nov. 1939, Bologna. *Education:* Univ. of Bologna. *Career:* entered diplomatic corps 1965; Personnel Dept, Ministry of Foreign Affairs 1965–68, 1977–79, 1988–90; Vice-Consul, Hong Kong 1968–72; First Sec., Perm. Mission to UN, New York 1972–75; Attaché (Commercial Affairs) Embassy in Hanoi 1975–77; Dir of Research and Planning, Ministry of Foreign Affairs 1979–80, of Travel and Passport Services 1980–84; Consul-Gen., Hong Kong 1984–87; Minister Plenipotentiary (Second Class) 1987–97, (First Class) 1997–; Amb. to India 1990–95; Head of Press and Information Dept, Ministry of Foreign Affairs 1995–96, Dept of Econ. Affairs 1996–99; Amb. to Japan 1999–2001, to People's Repub. of China 2003–06. *Address:* c/o Ministry of Foreign Affairs, Piazzale della Farnesina 1, 00194 Rome, Italy (office).

MENEGHETTI DE CAMILLO, Contessa Marina; San Marino diplomatist; *Ambassador to UK;* m. Count Amelio Meneghetti de Camillo. *Career:* Amb. to UK (non-resident) 2002–. *Address:* c/o Consulate of the Republic of San Marino, Flat 51, 162 Sloane Street, London, SW1X 9BS, England (office). *Telephone:* (20) 7823-4762 (office). *Fax:* (20) 7823-4768 (office).

MENEZES, Fradique Bandeira Melo de; São Tomé and Príncipe head of state and business executive; *President and Commander-in-Chief of the Armed Forces;* b. 1942; m. (deceased). *Education:* Instituto Superior de Psicologia Aplicada, Lisbon, Portugal and Univ. of Brussels, Belgium. *Career:* fmr Minister for Foreign Trade; fmr Amb. to Belgium and Netherlands; mem. Acção Democrática Independente (ADI) Party; Pres. of São Tomé e Príncipe 2001–, also C-in-C of Armed Forces. *Address:* Office of the President, São Tomé, São Tomé e Príncipe (office).

MENG, Jianzhu; Chinese politician; *Minister of Public Security;* b. July 1947, Wuxian Co., Jiangsu Prov. *Career:* joined CCP 1968; Deputy Political Instructor and Deputy Leader of Boat Fleet, Supply Marketing and Transport Station, Qianwei Farm (also Sec. CCP Shanghai Communist Youth League) 1968–73, Sec. CCP Party Br. 1973–76, mem. CCP Qianwei Farm Party Cttee 1976–77 (also Leader, Publicity Dept), Sec. Cork Gen. Plant, Qianwei Farm, CCP Party Br. 1977–81, Dir Political Dept, Qianwei Farm 1977–81, Deputy Sec., later Dir CCP Party Cttee 1981–86; Sec. CCP Chuansha Co. Cttee, Shanghai 1986–90, Jiading Co. Cttee, Shanghai 1990–91; Sec. Rural Work Cttee, CCP Shanghai Municipal Cttee 1991–92; Deputy Sec.-Gen. Shanghai Municipal Govt 1992–93; Vice-Mayor and Chair. Shanghai Econ. Restructuring Comm. 1993–96; Deputy Sec. Shanghai Municipal Cttee 1996; Sec. Jiangxi Prov. Cttee 2001–07, Chair. Standing Cttee Jiangxi People's Congress 2001; Alt. mem. 15th CCP Cen. Cttee 1997–2002, mem. 16th CCP Cen. Cttee 2002–07, mem. 17th CCP Cen. Cttee 2007–; Minister of Public Security 2007–. *Address:* Ministry of Public Security, 14 Dongchangan Jie, Dongcheng Qu, Beijing 100741, People's Republic of China (office). *Telephone:* (10)

65122831 (office). *Fax:* (10) 65136577 (office). *Website:* www.mps.gov.cn (office).

MENKERIOS, Haile, MA; South African (b. Eritrean) diplomat and economist; *Assistant Secretary General for Political Affairs, United Nations;* b. 1 Oct. 1946, Adi Felesti; m. Tesfamariam Ghennet 1979 (divorced); one s. one d. *Education:* Addis Ababa, Brandeis and Harvard Univs, USA. *Career:* teaching asst, Harvard Univ. 1971–73; combatant in Eritrean People's Liberation Army (EPLA) 1973–74; Head of Tigrigna Section, Dept of Information and Propaganda, Eritrean People's Liberation Front (EPLF) 1974–75, mem. Foreign Relations Cttee 1976–77, mem. Cen. Council 1977–2001, Asst to Head of Dept of Foreign Relations 1977–79, Head of African Relations 1977–79, Research Div., Dept of Conscientization, Educ. and Culture 1979–86; Dir Research and Information Centre of Eritrea 1986–87; Head, Research and Policy Div., Dept of Foreign Relations 1987–90; Gov. of East and South Zone of Eritrea 1990–91; mem. Eritrean Nat. Council 1991–2001; Rep. of Provisional Govt of Eritrea to Ethiopia 1991–93; Special Envoy of Pres. to Somalia 1991–96, to the Greater Lakes Region 1996–97; mem. High Level Horn of Africa Cttee on Somalia 1993–95; Amb. of State of Eritrea to Ethiopia and OAU 1993–96; Amb., Perm. Rep. of State of Eritrea to UN 1997–2001; Sr Advisor to Special Envoy of Sec.-Gen. to the Inter-Congolese Dialogue, Moustapha Niasse 2002–03; Dir Africa Div., UN Dept of Political Affairs 2003–05; Sec.-Gen.'s Deputy Special Rep. for UN Mission in the Democratic Repub. of the Congo (MONUC) 2005–07; UN Asst Sec.-Gen. for Political Affairs 2007–. *Publications include:* various articles on African politics. *Address:* UN Secretariat, DPA, S-3570A, New York, NY 10017 (office); 440 East 23rd Street, Apt 12G, New York, NY 10010, USA (home). *Telephone:* (212) 963-4049 (office). *E-mail:* menkerios@un.org (office). *Website:* www.un.org (office).

MENON, Shiv Shankar, MA; Indian diplomatist; *Foreign Secretary;* b. 5 July 1949; m. Mohini Sathe. *Education:* Delhi Univ. *Career:* joined Foreign Service 1972, Second Sec., Embassy in Beijing 1974–77; UnderSec. in charge of Africa and then China 1977–79; First Sec., Embassy in Vienna 1979–83, also Alt. Gov. IAEA Bd and Deputy Perm. Rep. to UN Orgs; Dir Dept of Atomic Energy, Mumbai 1983–86; Counsellor and DCM, Embassy in Beijing 1986–89; Deputy Chief of Mission, Embassy in Tokyo 1989–92; Jt Sec. in charge of N E Div. 1992–95; Amb. to Israel 1995–97; High Commr to Sri Lanka 1997–2000; Amb. to China 2000–03; High Commr to Pakistan 2003–06; Foreign Sec. 2006–; Madhav Award 2000. *Address:* Ministry of External Affairs, South Block, New Delhi 110 011, India (office). *Telephone:* (11) 23011127 (office). *Fax:* (11) 23011463 (office). *Website:* meaindia.nic.in (office).

MENON, Vanu Gopala, BBA, MS; Singaporean diplomatist; *Permanent Representative, United Nations;* b. 8 Sept. 1960; m. Jayanthi Menon; one s. *Education:* Nat. Univ. of Singapore, London School of Econs and Political Science, Univ. of London, UK. *Career:* joined Ministry of Foreign Affairs 1985; First Sec., Perm. Mission to UN 1988–91; Counsellor, later Minister-Counsellor, High Comm. to Malaysia 1994–97; Sr Deputy Dir, Policy, Planning and Analysis Directorate I, Ministry of Foreign Affairs 1997–98, Dir 1998–2001; Perm. Rep. to UN, Geneva 2001–04; Amb. to Turkey 2002–04; Perm. Rep. to UN, New York 2004–; Public Administration (Silver), Singapore. *Address:* Permanent Mission of Singapore to the United Nations, 231 East 51st Street, New York, NY 10022, USA (office). *Telephone:* (212) 826-0840 (ext 104) (office). *Fax:* (212) 826-2964 (office). *E-mail:* singapore@un.int (office). *Website:* www.mfa.gov.sg/newyork (office).

MENSAH-ZOGUELET, Alain; Gabonese diplomatist and politician; *Minister of Public Affairs, Administrative Reform and Modernization of the State;* b. 1 Jan. 1959, Mimongo; m. Florence Mensah-Zoguelet; two d. *Education:* Lycée T.A.B. Bon LBV Gabon, ASE Bucharest, Romania, IAE Caen, France. *Career:* Asst, Ministry of Plan, Tourism and Environment 1997–98; Asst Ministry of Foreign Affairs 1999–2002, Amb. to UK 2003–08; Minister of Public Affairs, Admin. Reform and Modernization of the State 2008–. *Address:* Ministry of Public Affairs, Administrative Reform and Modernization of the State, BP 496, Libreville, Gabon (office). *Telephone:* 76-38-86 (office).

MERAFHE, Lt-Gen. Mompati, LLB; Botswana politician; *Vice-President;* b. 6 June 1936, Serowe; two s. three d. *Education:* Univ. of S Africa. *Career:* police officer, later Deputy Commr of Police 1960–77; Commdr Botswana Defence Force, ranked Maj.-Gen. 1977, Lt-Gen. 1988; MP for Mahalapye; fmr Cabinet Minister for Public Admin; Minister of Foreign Affairs 1994, 1996–2008; Vice-Pres. 2008–.

Address: c/o Office of the President, Private Bag 001, Gaborone, Botswana (office). *Telephone:* 3950825 (office). *Fax:* 3950858 (office). *E-mail:* op .registry@gov.bw (office). *Website:* www.gov.bw/government/ ministry_of_state_president.html#office_of_the_president (office).

MEREDOV, Rashid; Turkmenistan politician; *Deputy Prime Minister and Minister of Foreign Affairs;* b. 1960. *Career:* Deputy Dir Nat. Inst. for Democracy and Human Rights –1999, Dir 2001–05; apptd Speaker in Majlis (Nat. Ass.) 1999, Chair. –2001; Minister of Foreign Affairs 2001–, Deputy Prime Minister 2003–.
Address: Ministry of Foreign Affairs, 744000 Aşgabat, pr. 2076 83, Turkmenistan (office). *Telephone:* (12) 26-62-11 (office). *Fax:* (12) 35-42-41 (office). *E-mail:* mfatm@online.tm (office).

MERIDOR, Dan; Israeli politician and lawyer; b. 1947, Jerusalem; m.; four c. *Education:* Hebrew Univ. *Career:* served in Israel Defence Forces (IDF) as tank commander in 1967 Six Day War, continued to serve as captain in IDF reserves; practised law Jerusalem 1973–82; fmr mem. Likud Party; Cabinet Sec. of Govt 1982–84; mem. Knesset 1984–2003; Minister of Justice 1988–92, of Finance 1996–97; Chair. Foreign Affairs and Defense Cttee 1997–2001; Minister without Portfolio responsible for Nat. Defence and Diplomatic Strategy 2001–03; Leader Centre Party 2001; has been Knesset observer to the Council of Europe.
Address: c/o Office of the Prime Minister, POB 187, 3 Rehov Kaplan, Kiryat Ben-Gurion, Jerusalem 91919, Israel.

MERIDOR, Sallai Moshe, BA; Israeli diplomatist; *Ambassador to USA;* m. No'a Meridor; three d. *Education:* Hebrew Univ. of Jerusalem. *Career:* served as intelligence officer in Israeli Defence Forces; served as adviser to Minister of Defence and Minister of Foreign Affairs, played role in peace process leading to Madrid Peace Conf., participated in subsequent negotiations as rep. of Ministry of Defence, led Israel's Inter-Agency Steering Cttee on Arms Control; Treas. Jewish Agency for Israel and World Zionist Org. (WZO) and Head of WZO Settlement Div. –1999, Chair. Jewish Agency for Israel and WZO 1999–2005; Amb. to USA 2006–.
Address: Embassy of Israel, 3514 International Drive, NW, Washington, DC 20008, USA (office). *Telephone:* (202) 364-5500 (office). *Fax:* (202) 364-5607 (office). *E-mail:* info@washington.mfa.gov.il (office); ask@israelemb .org (office). *Website:* www.israelemb.org (office).

MERIMÉE, Jean-Bernard, LenD; French diplomatist; *Special Adviser to Secretary-General on European Affairs, United Nations;* b. 4 Dec. 1936, Toulouse (Haute-Garonne); m. Anna Mirams 1965; one s. two d. *Education:* Lycées Pasteur, Neuilly-sur-Seine and Louis-le-Grand, Paris, Institut d'Etudes Politiques de Paris, Ecole Nat. d'Admin, Paris. *Career:* with Cen. Admin, Ministry of Foreign Affairs 1965, with Sec.-Gen. 1972–75; Second then First Sec. to UK 1966–72; Chief of Mission of Co-operation, Côte d'Ivoire 1975–78, Chief of Protocol 1978–81; Amb. to Australia 1982–85, to India 1985–87, to Morocco, Rabat 1987–91; Amb. and Perm. Rep. to Security Council and Chief of Perm. Mission to UN, New York 1991–95; Amb. to Italy, Rome 1995–98, to Repub. of San Marino (resident in Rome) 1997–98, to Cen. Admin 1998–99; Perm. Rep. to UN 1999, Special Adviser to Sec.-Gen. on European Affairs with rank of Under-Sec.-Gen. 1999–; Dir Groupe Benjelloun (mobile telephone, banking and insurance cos), Morocco; mem. Advisory Bd BMCE Bank, France; Officier, Légion d'honneur, Officier, Ordre nat. du Mérite, Commdr of the Order of Christ (Portugal), Grand Officer of the Order of the Phoenix (Greece), Kt of the Dannebrog (Denmark), Officer of the Oak Crown (Luxembourg), Merit Commdr of the Supreme Order of Malta.
Address: Office of the Secretary-General, United Nations, New York, NY 10017, USA. *Telephone:* (212) 963-1234. *Fax:* (212) 963-4879. *E-mail:* inquiries@un.org. *Website:* www.un.org.

MERKEL, Angela, Dr rer. nat; German politician; *Chancellor;* b. 17 July 1954, Hamburg; m. 1st Ulrich Merkel (divorced 1982); m. 2nd Joachim Sauer 1998. *Education:* Univ. of Leipzig. *Career:* Research Assoc. in quantum chemistry, Zentralinstitut für physikalische Chemie, East Berlin 1978–90; joined Demokratischer Aufbruch (DA) 1989, Press Spokesperson 1990; Deputy Spokesman for Govt of Lothar de la Maizière, March–Oct. 1990; joined CDU (Christian Democratic Union) 1990, mem. Bundestag 1990–, Deputy Fed. Chair. 1991–98, CDU Chair. Fed. State of Mecklenburg-Vorpommern 1993–2000, Gen. Sec. CDU 1998–2000, Chair. 2000–, also Parl. Leader 2002–05; Fed. Minister for Women and Young People 1991–94, for Environment, Nature Conservation and Nuclear Safety 1994–98; Chancellor 2005–; ranked by Forbes magazine amongst 100 Most Powerful Women (first) 2006, (first) 2007. *Publication:* Der Preis des Überlebens: Gedanken und Gespräche über zukünftige Aufgaben der Umweltpolitik (The Price of Survival: Ideas and Conversations about Future Tasks for Environmental Policy) 1997.

Address: Office of the Federal Chancellery, Willy-Brandt str. 1, 10557 Berlin, Germany (office). *Telephone:* (30) 40000 (office). *Fax:* (30) 40002357 (office). *E-mail:* internetpost@bundeskanzler.de (office). *Website:* www .bundeskanzler.de (office); www.angela-merkel.de.

MERLINI, Cesare; Italian international affairs scholar and fmr professor of nuclear technologies; b. 29 April 1933, Rome; m.; two s. two d. *Career:* lecturer in Nuclear Technologies 1967–76; Prof. of Nuclear Technologies, Turin Polytechnic 1976–85; Dir Istituto Affari Internazionali, Rome 1970–79, Pres. 1979–2000, fmr Chair., currently Pres. Bd of Trustees; Pres. Exec. Cttee Council for USA and Italy 1983–92; mem. Bd of Dirs. and Exec. Cttee Unione Tipografico-Editrice Torinese publrs SpA, Turin, Chair. 1999–; mem. Trilateral Comm. 1973–2001, Council, Int. Inst. for Strategic Studies, London 1993–99, Gen. Council, Aspen Inst. Italia, Rome; mem. Bd of Dirs, Asscn Jean Monnet, Paris, ISPI, Milan. *Publications:* Fine dell'atomo? Passato e futuro delle applicazioni civili e militari dell'energia nucleare 1987, L'Europa degli Anni Novanta; Scenari per un futuro imprevisto (Co-author and Ed.) 1991; co-author and ed. of numerous books on nuclear energy and int. strategy, author of numerous articles on European and int. affairs and of scientific publs on nuclear reactors and related technological and eng problems.
Address: Istituto Affari Internazionali, Via Angelo Brunetti 9, 00186 Rome, Italy (office). *Telephone:* (6) 3224360 (office). *Fax:* (6) 3224363 (office). *E-mail:* iai@iai.it (office).

MERON, Theodor, LLM, MJ, JSD; American judge and academic; *Appeals Judge, United Nations International Criminal Tribunal for the Former Yugoslavia;* b. 28 April 1930, Poland. *Education:* Univ. of Jerusalem, Harvard Univ. Law School, Univ. of Cambridge, UK. *Career:* joined Israeli Foreign Ministry, fmr Amb. of Israel to Canada, later to UN in Geneva, resgnd 1977; US citizen 1984–; Charles L. Denison Prof. of Int. Law, New York Univ. School of Law 1978–; Prof. of Int. Law Grad. Inst. of Int. Studies, Geneva, Switzerland 1991–95; Ed.-in-Chief American Journal of Int. Law 1993–98; elected Judge UN Criminal Tribunal for the Fmr Yugoslavia (ICTY) 2001–05, Pres. 2003–05, Appeals Judge 2005–, also mem. Appeals Chamber (ICTY) and UN Criminal Tribunal for Rwanda (ICTR) 2001–; fmr Counsellor on Int. Law US Dept of State; mem. Council on Foreign Relations; Public mem. US Del. to CSCE Conf. on Human Dimension, Copenhagen; numerous visiting lectureships in univs in Europe and USA. *Publications include:* Investment Insurance in International Law, Henry's Wars and Shakespeare's Laws 1994, Bloody Constraint: War and Chivalry in Shakespeare 1998, War Crimes Law Comes of Age: Essays 1999, International Law in the Age of Human Rights 2003; numerous articles and publs on int. law and human rights.
Address: UN Criminal Tribunal for the Former Yugoslavia, Public Information Unit, PO Box 13888, 2501 The Hague, Netherlands (office); New York University School of Law, Vanderbilt Hall, 40 Washington Square South, Room 304, New York, NY 10012-1099, USA. *Telephone:* (70) 512-5233 (office); (212) 998-6191. *Fax:* (70) 512-5355 (office). *E-mail:* meront@juris.law.nyu.edu. *Website:* www.un.org/icty (office).

MÉRORÈS, Léo, LLB, MA, PhD; Haitian diplomatist and UN official; *President, Economic and Social Council (ECOSOC);* b. 21 April 1943; m. *Education:* State Univ. of Haiti, Ecole de Commerce Maurice Laroche, Port-au-Prince, New York Univ., USA. *Career:* early career as salesman, Enterprises Gerard Theard, Port-au-Prince 1961; worked part-time as accountant and Asst to Head of Credit Dept, Shapiro & Sons Textile Corpn, New York, USA 1969–73; UNDP Deputy Resident Rep. in Togo and Madagascar 1978–84, worked in UNDP office in Rwanda 1974–78, UNDP Deputy Resident Rep. for Liberia, Mali and Cameroon 1984–92, responsible for UNDP offices in Gabon and Burundi 1989–92, a Prin. Counsellor for UNDP working with Econ. Community of West African States (ECOWAS) countries 1992–2001, consultant on man. and econ. co-operation issues for several UN entities, including Dept of Econ. and Social Affairs, UN Office for Project Services (UNOPS) and UNDP 2001–04; Chargé d'affaires, Perm. Mission to UN, New York 2004–05, Perm. Rep. to UN 2005–; Vice-Pres. ECOSOC, representing Group of Latin America and Caribbean 2006–08, Pres. ECOSOC 2008–.
Address: Permanent Mission of Haiti to the United Nations, 801 Second Avenue, Room 600, New York, NY 10017, USA (office). *Telephone:* (212) 370-4840 (Perm. Mission) (office); (212) 963-4640 (ECOSOC) (office). *Fax:* (212) 661-8698 (Perm. Mission) (office); (212) 963-5935 (ECOSOC) (office). *E-mail:* haiti@un.int (office); ecosocinfo@un.org (office). *Website:* www .un.org/ecosoc (office).

MERRY, David Byron, CMG; British diplomatist; b. 16 Sept. 1945; m. Patricia Merry; one s. two d. *Education:* School of Oriental and African Studies, Univ. of London. *Career:* joined British Diplomatic Service 1965; with Defence Dept, FCO 1965–67; Asst Pvt. Sec. to Perm. Under-Sec. of State 1967–68; Attaché, Embassy in Bangkok 1969–73; Second Sec., Embassy in

Budapest 1974–77; with Personnel Operations Dept, FCO 1977–79, Migration and Visa Dept 1979–81, Security Dept 1989–90; First Sec., Embassy in Bonn 1981–85; Head of Chancery in East Berlin 1985–88; Head of Unit, Personnel Operations Dept 1990–91, Desk Officer, Personnel Man. Dept 1991–93; Deputy Head of Mission, Embassy in Manila 1993–97; Deputy High Commr to Pakistan 1997–2000; Head of Local Staff Man. Unit, Personnel Command, FCO 2000–01; High Commr to Botswana 2001–05.
Address: c/o Foreign and Commonwealth Office, King Charles Street, London, SW1A 2AH, England. *Telephone:* (20) 7008-1500.

MERSCH, Yves; Luxembourg central banker; *Governor, Luxembourg Central Bank;* b. 1 Oct. 1949. *Education:* Univ. of Paris. *Career:* called to the Bar, Luxembourg 1974; Public Law Asst, Univ. Paris-XI 1974; Budget Asst, Ministry of Finance 1975; mem. staff IMF, Washington, DC, USA 1976–77; Ministry of Finance, Fiscal Affairs and Structural Policies 1977–80; Adviser, Ministry of Finance, Monetary Affairs and Int. Financial Relations 1981; Govt Commr Luxembourg Stock Exchange 1985; Dir Treasury 1989; Gov. Luxembourg Cen. Bank 1998–; mem. Governing Council, European Cen. Bank.
Address: Banque Centrale du Luxembourg, 2 boulevard Royal, 2983, Luxembourg (office). *Telephone:* 4774-1 (office). *Fax:* 4774-4901 (office). *E-mail:* info@bcl.lu (office). *Website:* www.bcl.lu (office).

MERZ, Hans-Rudolf, Dr rer. pol; Swiss management consultant and politician; *Vice President of Federal Council and Head of Federal Department of Finance;* b. 10 Nov. 1942, Herisau; m.; three s. *Education:* Univ. of St Gallen. *Career:* Asst Lecturer St Gallen Univ. 1967–69; Sec. FDP St Gallen; Man. Appenzell Ausserhoden Industrial Asscn 1969–74; Deputy Dir UBS Wolfsberg training centre 1974–77; pvt. practice as ind. consultant 1977–2003; Chair. Helvetia Patria Insurance Co., AG Cilander Textile Finishing, Anova Holding 1977–2003; elected Rep. Council of States 1997, served as Chair. Finance Cttee, mem. Foreign Affairs and Security Cttee; Vice-Pres. OCSE del.; elected to Fed. Council 2003; Head Fed. Dept of Finance 2004–; Vice-Pres. Federal Council 2008.
Address: Federal Department of Finance, Bernerhof, Bundesgasse 3, 3003 Bern, Switzerland (office). *Telephone:* 313226033 (office). *Fax:* 313233852 (office). *E-mail:* info@gs-efd.admin.ch (office). *Website:* www.efd.admin .ch (office).

MESEZNIKOV, Grigorij, PhDr; Slovak political scientist; *President, Institute for Public Affairs;* b. 25 March 1958, Orel, Russia; m.; five s. two d. *Education:* Moscow State Univ., Russia. *Career:* fmr Lecturer, Dept of Political Science, Trnava Univ.; Expert Assoc. Comenius Univ. 1983–93; Analyst, Political Science Inst., Slovak Acad. of Sciences 1993–97; Co-founder Inst. for Public Affairs (IVO) 1997, Program Dir of Domestic Politics 1997–, Pres. 1999–; External Collaborator Radio Liberty/Radio Free Europe 1993–; Sec. Slovak Asscn for Political Sciences 1994–98; fellowships from Swedish Int. Devt Authority 1992, US Devt Agency Grad. School 1994. *Publications:* co-ed. and co-author various publs including the Global Report on Slovakia; articles in scholarly journals and magazines, chapters in monographs.
Address: Institute for Public Affairs (IVO), Bastova ul. 3, Bratislava 811 03, Slovakia (office). *Telephone:* (2) 5443-4030 (office). *Fax:* (2) 5443-4041 (office). *E-mail:* mesez@ivo.sk (office). *Website:* www.ivo.sk (office).

MESFIN, Seyoum; Ethiopian politician; *Minister of Foreign Affairs;* b. Jan. 1949, Tigray; m.; four c. *Education:* Bahir Dar Polytechnic Inst., Addis Ababa Univ. *Career:* exec. mem. Tigray People's Liberation Front (TPLF); Chair. Foreign Affairs Cttee, Ethiopian People's Revolutionary Democratic Front (EPRDF); Minister of Foreign Affairs 1991–.
Address: Ministry of Foreign Affairs, PO Box 393, Addis Ababa, Ethiopia (office). *Telephone:* (11) 5517345 (office). *Fax:* (11) 5514300 (office). *E-mail:* mfa.addis@telecom.net.et. *Website:* www.mfa.gov.et.

MESHKOV, Aleksey Yuryevich; Russian diplomatist and politician; *Ambassador to Italy;* b. 22 Aug. 1959, Moscow; m. Galina Ivanovna Meshkova; two s. two d. *Education:* Moscow State Inst. of Int. Relations. *Career:* with diplomatic service 1981–; referent, attaché then Third Sec., USSR Embassy, Spain 1981–86, First Sec., Counsellor then Sr Counsellor (Russian Embassy) 1992–97; Third, Second, First Sec. then Head of Div., Dept of Co-operation in Science and Tech., Ministry of Foreign Affairs 1986–92, Deputy Head, Dept of European Co-operation 1997–98, Head, Dept of Foreign Policy Planning 1999–2001, mem. Collegiate Ministry of Foreign Affairs 2000–, Deputy Minister of Foreign Affairs 2001–04; Amb. to Italy 2004–; Order of Friendship.
Address: Embassy of the Russian Federation, Via Gaeta 5, 00144 Rome, Italy (office). *Telephone:* (06) 4941680 (office). *Fax:* (06) 491031 (office). *E-mail:* ambrus@ambrussia.it (office). *Website:* www.ambrussia.it (office).

MESIĆ, Stjepan (Stipe); Croatian lawyer and head of state; *President;* b. 24 Dec. 1934, Orahovica; m. Milka Mesić (née Dudunić); two d. *Education:* gymnasium in Požega and Univ. of Zagreb. *Career:* active in student politics; lawyer in Orahovica and Našice; compulsory mil. service; became a municipal judge after passing judicial exams; ind. cand. in municipal council elections 1966; Mayor of Orahovica 1967; mem. Parl. of Socialist Repub. of Croatia 1967; indicted for 'acts of enemy propaganda', served one-year prison sentence in Stara Gradiška prison for participation in Croatian Spring Movt 1975; Sec. Croatian Democratic Union (Hrvatska demokratska zajednica—HDZ), later Chair. Exec. Council; Prime Minister first govt of Repub. of Croatia 1990; mem. Presidency of Socialist Fed. Repub. of Yugoslavia, subsequently Pres. until resgnd 1991; Speaker Croatian Parl. 1992–94; left HDZ and f. Croatian Ind. Democrats (Hrvatski Nezavisni Demokrati—HND) 1994, merged with Croatian People's Party (Hrvatska narodna stranka—HNS) 1997, later Exec. Vice-Pres.; Pres. Repub. of Croatia 2000– (re-elected 2005); Hon. mem. Int. Foundation of Raoul Wallenberg 2002; Hon. Citizen of Podgorica, Montenegro 2007; State Order of the Star of Romania 2000, Grand Star of the Decoration of Honour for Merit (Austria) 2001, Golden Order Gjergj Kastrioti Skënderbeu (Albania) 2001, Grand Cross of the Order of Saviour (Greece) 2001, Order of St Michael and St George (UK), Kt of the Grand Cross with Grand Sash (Italy) 2001, Grand Order of the Crown of Malaysia 2002, Order of the Grand Cross with Chain (Hungary) 2002, DOSTYK Medal of the First Degree (Kazakhstan) 2002, Medal for Merit (Chile) 2004, Grand Order of King Tomislav with Sash and Grand Star (Croatia) 2005; Charles Univ. Medal (Czech Repub.) 2001, Crans Montana Forum Award 2002, ABA Award 2002, Gold Medal of the Presidency of the Italian Repub. 2004, Raoul Wallenberg Award 2006, Int. League of Humanists Award 2007. *Publications:* The Break-up of Yugoslavia: Political Memoirs 1992, 1994.
Address: Office of the President, 10000 Zagreb, Pantovčak 241, Croatia (office). *Telephone:* (1) 4565191 (office). *Fax:* (1) 4565299 (office). *E-mail:* office@president.hr (office). *Website:* www.predsjednik.hr (office).

MESTRE, Philippe, LLB; French politician and civil servant; b. 23 Aug. 1927, Talmont, Vendee; m. Janine Joseph 1951; one s. two d. *Education:* Paris Univ. *Career:* Admin. Overseas France 1951; Pvt. Sec. to High Commr, Congo 1957–60, to Indre-et-Loir Prefect 1967, to Prime Minister Raymond Barre 1978–81; Tech. Adviser to Pierre Messmer (Minister of Defence) 1964–69, to Prime Minister Jacques Chaban-Delmas 1969–70, 1971–72; Pres. Inter-ministerial Mission of Repatriation from Overseas Territories 1969–70; Prefect of Gers 1970–71, of Calvados 1973–76, of Loire-Atlantique 1976–78, of Mayotte 2001–02; Pres. Serpo 1981–93; Deputy of Vendée 1981–86, 1986–93; Vice-Pres. Nat. Ass. 1986–88; Minister of War Veterans 1993–95; fmr Vice-Pres. Union pour la Démocratie Française (UDF); Commdr Légion d'honneur, Officier Ordre nat. du Mérite, du Mérite agricole, Croix de la Valeur militaire. *Publications:* Quand flambait le bocage 1969, Demain, rue Saint-Nicaise 1990 (Prix Claude Farrère), Devant douze fusils 2000 (Prix des Ecrivains de Vendée).
Address: c/o Union pour la démocratie française, 133 bis, rue de l'Université, 75007 Paris (office); 95 rue de Rennes, 75006 Paris, France (home). *Telephone:* 1-53-59-20-00 (office). *Fax:* 1-53-59-20-59 (office). *Website:* www.udf.org (office).

METIA, Lotoala; Tuvaluan politician; *Minister of Finance, Economic Planning and Industries; Career:* Auditor Gen. 1990–97, 2002; fmr Sec. for Commerce, Tourism and Trade; mem. Parl. 2006–, Minister of Finance, Econ. Planning and Industries 2006–; fmr Chair. Tuvalu Telecommunications Corpn.
Address: Ministry of Finance, Economic Planning and Industries, PMB, Vaiaku, Funafuti, Tuvalu (office). *Telephone:* 20408 (office). *Fax:* 20210 (office).

METTLER, Ann, MA; German/Swedish research institute director and political scientist; *Executive Director, Lisbon Council; Education:* Univ. of New Mexico, USA, Centre for European Integration Studies, Bonn, Germany; American Coll. of Greece, Athens. *Career:* fmrly with Governmental Affairs Cttee, US Senate; fmrly with strategic communications firm, Washington DC; with Foreign Policy Div., EC, Brussels; World Econ. Forum 2000–03, most recently Dir for Europe; Co-founder and Exec. Dir Lisbon Council 2003–. *Publications:* contribs to Wall Street Journal Europe, Financial Times, Newsweek, Handelsblatt, FT Deutschland, European Voice, USA and Europe in Business.
Address: The Lisbon Council for Economic Competitiveness, International Press Center, Residence Palace, Block C, 155 rue de la Loi, 1040 Brussels, Belgium (office). *Fax:* (2) 640-9828 (office). *E-mail:* info@lisboncouncil.net (office). *Website:* www.lisboncouncil.net (office).

MEYER, Karl, BA, PhD; American journalist and academic; *Editor, World Policy Journal, World Policy Institute;* b. Wisconsin; m. Shareen Blair

Brysac. *Education:* Wisconsin State Univ., Princeton Univ. *Career:* fmr editorial writer The New York Times, Washington Post; Ed. World Policy Journal, World Policy Inst. (WIP) 2000–08, Ed. Emer. 2008–; fmr Visiting Prof. Yale, Princeton, Tufts Univs, Bard Coll.; fmr Visiting Fellow, Univ. of Oxford, Inst. for Advanced Study, Berlin; mem. Toynbee Prize Foundation. *Publications include:* The Dust of Empire: The Race for Mastery in the Asian Heartland 2004, Tournaments of Shadows: The Great Game and the Race for Empire in Asia (with Shareen Blair Brysac) 2006, Kingmakers (with Shareen Blair Brysac) 2008; numerous articles. *Address:* World Policy Journal, World Policy Institute, New School University, 66 Fifth Avenue, 9th Floor, New York, NY 100100, USA (office). *Telephone:* (212) 229-5808 (office). *Fax:* (212) 807-1153 (office). *E-mail:* meyer@worldpolicy.org (office). *Website:* www.worldpolicy.org/journal (office).

MEZA-CUADRA VELÁSQUEZ, Gustavo; Peruvian diplomatist; *Director General, Ministry of Foreign Affairs;* m. Sonia Meza-Cuadra. *Education:* Diplomatic Acad. of Peru. *Career:* fmr Econ. Counsellor, Embassy in Washington, DC; fmr Chargé d'Affaires a.i., Embassy in London; currently Dir Gen. responsible for int. econ. negotiations, Ministry of Foreign Affairs. *Address:* Ministry of Foreign Affairs, Jirón Lampa 535, Lima 1, Peru (office). *Telephone:* (1) 3112402 (office). *Fax:* (1) 3112406 (office). *Website:* www.rree.gob.pe (office).

MEZOUAR, Salaheddine, MSc (Econ); Moroccan politician and administrator; *Minister of the Economy and Finance;* b. 11 Dec. 1953, Meknès; m.; two c. *Education:* Institut européen d'admin des affaires (INSEAD), Fontainebleau, France, Institut supérieur de commerce et d'admin des entreprises (ISCAE), Casablanca, Université des sciences sociales, Grenoble, France. *Career:* held admin. and financial posts with Régies d'Eau et d'Électricité de Rabat et de Tanger early 1980s; Chief Financial Officer Franco-Tunisian electrical, plumbing, refrigeration and maintenance co. based in Tunis –1986; Chief of Div. and in charge of mission, Office d'exploitation des Ports (ODEP) 1986–91; joined Spanish co. specializing in manufacture of tissue where he served as Gen. Man. of subsidiary Settat and Commercial Dir of group for Morocco, Africa and Middle East 1991; Pres. Moroccan Asscn of Textile Industries and Clothing (AMITH) 2002; also served as Pres. Textile and Leather Fed. in Gen. Confed. of Moroccan Enterprises (CGEM); Minister of Industry, Trade and Upgrading of the Economy 2004–07, of the Economy and Finance 2007–; mem. Cen. Cttee Rassemblement nat. des Indépendants; fmr Vice-Pres. Raja athletic club; fmr capt. nat. basketball team. *Address:* Ministry of the Economy and Finance, Blvd Muhammad V, Quartier Administratif, Chellah, Rabat, Morocco (office). *Telephone:* (3) 7677501 (office); (3) 7677200 (office). *Fax:* (3) 7677527 (office). *E-mail:* daag@daag.finances.gov.ma (office). *Website:* www.finances.gov.ma (office).

M'HENNI, Hedi; Tunisian politician. *Career:* fmr Minister of Public Health; Minister of Interior and Local Devt 2003–04, of Nat. Defence 2004–05; Sec.-Gen. of the governing Rassemblement constitutionnel démocratique 2005–. *Address:* c/o Ministry of National Defence, blvd Bab Menara, 1030 Tunis, Tunisia (office).

MICELI-FARRUGIA, Mark; Maltese business executive and diplomatist; *Ambassador to USA;* m. Josette Miceli-Farrugia; one s. *Education:* Mediterranean Acad. of Diplomatic Studies, London School of Econs, Univ. of London, UK. *Career:* early career marketing beverages in Malta, Canada and Italy, pioneered Meridiana Wine Estate at Ta' Qali, Malta, in partnership with Marchese Piero Antinori 1994, CEO –2007; Pres. AmCham Malta (Maltese-American Chamber of Commerce) 2002–07; has served on bds of several Maltese public insts, including Malta Chamber of Commerce & Enterprise, Malta Enterprise and Young Enterprise, as well as bds of pvt. initiatives including L. Farrugia & Sons Ltd and Farsons Group of Cos; Amb. (non-resident) to Lithuania, Latvia and Estonia 2002–07, Amb. to USA 2007–. *Address:* Embassy of Malta, 2017 Connecticut Avenue, NW, Washington, DC 20008, USA (office). *Telephone:* (202) 462-3611 (office). *Fax:* (202) 387-5470 (office). *E-mail:* maltaembassy.washington@gov.mt (office).

MICHALAK, Michael W., BS, MS, MPA; American diplomatist; *Ambassador to Viet Nam;* b. Detroit, Mich.; m.; three d. *Education:* Oakland Univ., Catholic Univ. of America, Washington, DC, John F. Kennedy School of Govt, Harvard Univ. *Career:* career mem. Sr Foreign Service, has worked in Tokyo, Sydney, Islamabad, Beijing; State Dept assignments Bureau of East Asian and Pacific Affairs, Office for Japan, and Office of Chinese and Mongolian Affairs; US Sr Official to APEC, Bureau of East Asian and Pacific Affairs –2007, Amb. to Viet Nam 2007–; Group Award for Valor.

Address: US Embassy, 7 Lang Ha Street, Ba Dinh District, Hanoi, Viet Nam (office). *Telephone:* (4) 8314590 (office). *Fax:* (4) 8505010 (office). *E-mail:* irchanoi@state.gov (office); hanoiac@state.gov (office). *Website:* vietnam.usembassy.gov (office).

MICHEL, James Alix; Seychelles politician and head of state; *President;* b. 16 Aug. 1944. *Education:* Teacher Training Coll., Seychelles. *Career:* teacher 1960–61; with Cable & Wireless Telecommunications 1962–71; treas. and sec. staff union 1970–71; Accountant, Asst Man., then Man. Hotel des Seychelles 1971–74; mem. Exec. Cttee Seychelles People's United Party and Co-ordinator of Party Brs, also Ed. of The People 1974–77; Minister of State, Admin and Information 1977–79; mem. Cen. Exec. Cttee Seychelles People's Progressive Front 1978–, also Sec.; Chief of Staff Seychelles People's Defence Forces 1979–93; Minister of Educ., Information, Culture and Telecommunications 1979–86, of Educ., Information, Culture and Sports 1986–89, of Finance 1989–91, of Finance and Information 1991–93, of Finance, Information, Communications and Defence, also First Desig. Minister to discharge the functions of Pres. 1993–96; Vice-Pres. (retaining portfolios for Finance, Information and Communications) 1996; Vice-Pres. (with portfolios of Econ. Planning and Environment and Transport) 1998–2000; Vice-Pres. and Minister of Finance, Econ. Planning, Information Tech. and Communications 2001–04; Pres. of the Seychelles 2004–, and Minister of Finance 2005–06; Patron Seychelles Football Fed.; foreign mem. Russian Acad. of Natural Sciences; Gran Croce dell'Ordine al Merito Melitense, Kt of Malta, Outstanding Civilian Service Medal, US Army Dept 1995. *Address:* Office of the President, State House, POB 55, Victoria, Mahé, Seychelles (office). *Telephone:* 224155 (office). *Fax:* 224985 (office). *Website:* www.virtualseychelles.sc.

MICHEL, Louis; Belgian politician; *Commissioner for Development and Humanitarian Aid, European Commission;* b. 2 Sept. 1947, Tirlemont. *Career:* fmr lecturer at Inst. Supérieur de Commerce Saint-Louis; Prof. of Dutch, English and German Literature, Ecole Normale provinciale de Jodoigne 1968–78; Alderman of Jodoigne 1977–83, Mayor 1983–; Sec.-Gen. Parti Réformateur Libéral (PRL) 1980–82, Pres. 1982–90; Pres. Fed. of Local and Provincial PRL Office Holders 1990–92; Pres., parl. group in Council of Walloon Region 1991–92, in House of Reps 1992–95; MP 1978–99; Pres. PRL 1995–2001; Deputy Pres. of Liberal Int.; Deputy Prime Minister and Minister of Foreign Affairs July 1999–2004; Rep. of Belgium to EU Special Convention on a European Constitution 2001–; EU Commr for Devt and Humanitarian Aid 2004–; mem. Parl. Comms on Finance, Budget, Institutional Reforms and Comm. charged with supervising electoral expenditures; mem. Benelux Inter parl. Consultative Council; Commdr Order of Leopold. *Address:* European Commission, 200 rue de la Loi, 1049 Brussels, Belgium (office). *Telephone:* (2) 299-11-11 (office). *Fax:* (2) 295-01-38 (office). *Website:* europa.eu (office).

MICHNIK, Adam; Polish journalist and historian; *Editor-in-Chief, Gazeta Wyborcza;* b. 17 Oct. 1946, Warsaw; m.; one s. *Education:* Adam Mickiewicz Univ., Poznań. *Career:* active in anti-communist movt 1965–80, spent six years in prison; Co-Founder and mem. Cttee for the Defence of Workers (KOR) 1976–80; Biuletyn Informacyjny, Krytyka, Zapis (ind. periodicals); activist Solidarity Self-governing Ind. Trade Union in the 1980s; imprisoned 1985–86; participant Round Table plenary debates 1989; Deputy to Sejm (Parl.) 1989–91; Ed.-in-Chief Gazeta Wyborcza (daily) 1989–; mem. Int. Advisory Bd, Council on Foreign Relations; Officer's Cross of Merit (Hungary) 1998, Bernardo O'Higgins Commdr's Order (Chile) 1999, Order for Contrib. to Polish-German Reconciliation, European Univ. Viadriana, Frankfurt 2000, Grand Prince Gedymin Order (Lithuania) 2001, Grand Cross of Merit (Germany) 2001; Dr hc (New School for Social Research, New York, Univ. of Minnesota, Univ. of Michigan, Connecticut Coll.); French Pen Club Freedom Award 1982, Robert F. Kennedy Human Rights Award 1986, Alfred Jurzykowski Foundation Award, La Vie Man of the Year 1989, Shofar Award 1991, Brucke-Preis (Germany) 1995, Award of the European Journalists Asscn 1995, Medal of Imre Nagy 1995, OSCE Prize in Journalism and Democracy 1996, The Golden Pen (Bauer Verlag) 1998, The Francisco Cerecedo Journalist Prize 1999, Int. Press Inst. Freedom Hero 2000, Carl Bertelsmann Prize 2001, Erasmus Prize 2001, Dan David Prize 2006. *Publications:* Cienie zapomnianych przodków (The Shadows of the Forgotten Ancestors) 1975, Kościół, Lewica, Dialog (Church, The Left, Dialogue) 1977, Penser la Pologne 1983, Szanse polskiej Demokracji (Chances for Polish Democracy) 1984, Z dziejów honoru w Polsce. Wypisy więzienne (From the History of Honour in Poland. Prison Notes) 1985, Takie czasy: Rzecz o kompromisie (Such Other Times: Concerning Compromise) 1985, Listy z Białołęki (Letters from Białołęka), Polskie pytania (Polish Questions) 1987, Druga faza rewolucji 1990, Między Panem a Plebanem 1995, Diabeł naszego czasu 1995, Letters From Freedom 1998,

Confessions of a Converted Dissident – Essay for the Erasmus Prize 2001; many articles in Gazeta Wyborcza, Der Spiegel, Le Monde, Libération, El País, Lettre Internationale, New York Review of Books, The Washington Post and others.
Address: Gazeta Wyborcza, ul. Czerska 8/10, 00-732 Warsaw, Poland (office). *Telephone:* (22) 5504000 (office); (22) 5554002 (office). *Fax:* (22) 8416920 (office). *E-mail:* contact@agora.pl (office).

MICOSSI, Stefano; Italian economist and international official; *Professor of European Integration, College of Europe, Bruges;* b. 27 Oct. 1946, Bologna; m. Daniela Zanotto; one s. one d. *Education:* Università Statale di Milano, Yale Univ., USA. *Career:* economist, Bank of Italy Research Dept 1974–78, Head 1980–84, Asst Dir 1984–86, Dir Int. Div. 1986–88; seconded to IMF as Asst to Italy's Exec. Dir 1978–80; Dir of Econ. Research Confindustria (Confed. of Italian Industries) 1988–94; Prof. of Macro-economic Policy Int. Free Univ. of Social Sciences 1989–94, Prof. of Monetary Theory and Policy 1993–94; Prof. of Int. Monetary Econs, Coll. of Europe, Bruges 1990–94, Prof. of European Integration 1999–; Dir-Gen. for Industry, EC 1994–99; Dir-Gen. Asscn of Italian Ltd Cos (ASSO-NIME) 1999–. *Publications:* Jt Ed. Adjustment and Integration in the World Economy 1992, The Italian Economy 1993, Inflation in Europe 1997 and books on the European Monetary System 1988, numerous articles in professional journals.
Address: ASSONIME, Piazza Venezia 11, 00187 Rome, Italy.

MICULESCU, Simona Mirela; Romanian diplomatist; *Permanent Representative, United Nations;* m.; two c. *Education:* Mihai Eminescu Coll., Babes-Bolyai Univ., Georgetown Univ., Washington, DC. *Career:* Press Sec., Embassy in Washington, DC 1994–98; Deputy Head N America Dept, Ministry of Foreign Affairs 1998, Ministry Spokesperson 1999; Deputy Head, Press and Public Information Office, OSCE 1999–2000; Minister Counsellor and Sr Foreign Policy Adviser to Pres. of Romania 2000–04; with Western Balkan and Cen. European Co-operation Div., Ministry of Foreign Affairs 2005; Sr Adviser to Govt of Iraq 2006–07; Dir Communication and Public Diplomacy Div., Ministry of Foreign Affairs 2007–08; Perm. Rep. to UN, New York 2008–.
Address: Permanent Mission of Romania to the United Nations, 573–577 Third Avenue, New York, NY 10016, USA (office). *Telephone:* (212) 682-3273 (office). *Fax:* (212) 682-9746 (office). *E-mail:* romania@un.int (office). *Website:* www.un.int/romania (office).

MIFSUD BONNICI, Ugo, BA, LLD; Maltese politician, lawyer and fmr head of state; *Member, Council of Europe Commission for Democracy Through Law (Venice Commission);* b. 8 Nov. 1932, Cospicua; m. Gemma Bianco; two s. one d. *Education:* Royal Univ. of Malta. *Career:* practising lawyer 1955–87; mem. Parl. 1966–94; Opposition Spokesman for Educ. 1972–87; Pres. Gen. Council and Admin. Council of Nationalist Party 1977–87; Minister of Educ. 1987, of Educ. and Interior 1990–92, of Educ. and Human Resources 1992–94, Pres. of Malta 1994–99; currently Lecturer on History of Law and Human Rights, Univ. of Malta, also Lecturer on Comparative Law, Int. Maritime Law Inst.; Chair. Cttee of Guarantee under the Law for the Protection of the Cultural Heritage; mem. Council of Europe Comm. for Democracy Through Law (Venice Comm.) 2002–; Hon. DLitt (Univ. of Malta) 1995, (Univ. of Paris IV) 1999. *Publications:* Biex il-futur jerga' jibda 1976, Il-linja t-tajba 1981, Biex il-futur rega' beda 1992, Il-Manwal tal-President 1997, Kif Sirna Republika 1999, Introduction to Comparative Law 2004; newspaper articles.
Address: c/o Venice Commission, Council of Europe, 67075 Strasbourg Cedex, France; 18 Erin Serracino Inglott Road, Cospicua, Malta (home). *Telephone:* 826975 (home). *E-mail:* ugomb@maltanet.net (home). *Website:* www.venice.coe.int.

MIGIRO, Asha-Rose Mtengeti, LLB, LLM, PhD; Tanzanian lawyer, politician, academic and UN official; *Deputy Secretary-General, United Nations;* b. 9 July 1956, Songea; m. Prof. Cleophas Migiro; two d. *Education:* Univ. of Dar-es-Salaam, Univ. of Konstanz, Germany. *Career:* Head, Dept of Constitutional and Admin. Law, Univ. of Dar-es-Salaam 1992–94, fmr Sr Lecturer, Faculty of Law; mem. Parl. (Chama Cha Mapinduzi party); Minister of Community Devt, Gender and Children's Affairs 2000–06, of Foreign Affairs and Int. Cooperation 2006–07; Deputy Sec.-Gen. UN 2007–.
Address: Office of the Deputy Secretary-General, United Nations, United Nations Plaza, New York, NY 10017 USA (office). *Telephone:* (212) 963-1234 (office). *Fax:* (212) 963-4879 (office). *Website:* www.un.org (home).

MIGRANYAN, Andranik Movsesovich, CandHisSc; Russian/Armenian civil servant; *Professor, Moscow Institute of International Relations;* b. 10 Feb. 1949, Yerevan; m.; one d. *Education:* Moscow State Inst. of Int. Relations, Inst. of Int. Workers' Movt USSR Acad. of Sciences. *Career:* teacher, Prof. Moscow Inst. of Automobile Construction 1976–85; leading researcher

Inst. of Econ. and Political Studies Acad. of Sciences 1985–88; Head Cen. for Studies of Social-Political Problems and Interstate Relations of CIS 1992–93; mem. Pres.'s Council 1993–; Chief Expert Cttee on CIS countries of State Duma 1993–96; Chair. Bd Scientific Council on CIS Countries; Prof. Moscow State Inst. of Int. Relations (MGIMO) 1994–; co-f. Politika Fund; Vice-Pres. Reforma Fund.
Address: Reforma Fund, Staromonetny per.10, 109180 Moscow (office); MGIMO, Vernadskogo prosp. 76, 117454, Moscow, Russia (office). *Telephone:* (095) 433-34-95.

MIHAJLOV, Mihajlo; Serbian author, scholar and human rights administrator; b. 26 Sept. 1934, Pančevo. *Education:* High School, Sarajevo and Zagreb Univ. *Career:* served in armed forces 1961–62; freelance writer and trans., magazines, newspapers and radio 1962–63; Asst Prof. of Modern Russian Literature, Zagreb Univ. 1963–65; freelance writer, western press 1965–66, 1970–74; imprisoned 1966–70, 1974–77; lectures, USA, Europe and Asia 1978–79; Visiting Lecturer, Yale Univ. 1981; Visiting Prof. of Russian Literature and Philosophy, Univ. of Virginia 1982–83; Visiting Prof. Ohio State Univ. 1983–84, Univ. of Siegen 1984, Univ. of Glasgow 1985; Commentator on Ideological Matters, Radio Free Europe/Radio Liberty Inc. 1986; Sr Fellow, Program on Transitions to Democracy, Elliott School of Int. Affairs, George Washington Univ. 1994–99, Adjunct Fellow, Hudson Inst. 1999; Vice-Pres. Democracy Int.; Chair. Democracy Int. Comm. to Aid Democratic Dissidents in Yugoslavia 1990; mem. Editorial Bd int. magazine Kontinent 1975–84, Tribuna Magazine, Paris and Forum Magazine, Munich, Contributing Ed. Religion in Communist Dominated Areas, New York; mem. Int. PEN (French br. 1977, American 1982); mem. Int. Helsinki Group, Cttee for the Free World; mem. Bd Int. Gesellschaft für Menschenrechte 1982–, Bd of Consultants, Centre for Appeals for Freedom 1980, Nat. Cttee of Social Democrats USA 1989, Advisory Bd CAUSA Int. 1986; Special Analyst for Intellectual and Ideological Events in the Soviet Union and Eastern Europe, Research Div. of Radio Free Europe 1985–86; Fellow, Nat. Humanities Cen.; Trustee, World Constitution and Parl. Asscn 1982–; Int. League for Human Rights Award 1978, Council against Communist Aggression Award 1975, 1978, Ford Foundation Award for the Humanities 1980. *Publications:* Moscow Summer 1965, Russian Themes 1968, Underground Notes 1976, 1982, Unscientific Thoughts 1979, 2004, Planetary Consciousness 1982, Djilas versus Marx 1990, Homeland is Freedom 1994; hundreds of articles in newspapers, magazines and scholarly books (weekly column in Belgrade daily Borba (renamed Nasa Borba 1995) 1990–).
Address: Obilićev Venac 6, Stan 5, 11000 Belgrade, Serbia (home). *Telephone:* (11) 303-3218 (home). *E-mail:* mishamih@yahoo.com (home).

MIHÓK, Peter, PhD; Slovak business administrator and fmr diplomatist; *President, Slovak Chamber of Commerce and Industry;* b. 18 Jan. 1948, Topolčianky; m. Elena Škulová 1971; two d. *Education:* Econ. Univ., Bratislava. *Career:* with Czechoslovak Chamber of Commerce 1971–78; Commercial Counsellor, Embassy, Morocco 1978–82; Dir Foreign Relations Dept; INCHEBA (Foreign Trade Co.) 1982–90; Dir Foreign Dept, Office of Govt of Slovak Repub. 1990–91; Vice-Pres. Czechoslovak Chamber of Commerce and Industry (CCI) 1991–92; Dir Int. Politics Dept, Ministry of Foreign Affairs of Slovak Repub. 1991; Plenipotentiary of Govt of Slovak Repub. in EU, Head Negotiator in Brussels 1991–94; Pres. Slovak CCI 1992–; Vice-Chair. Supervisory Bd of Heineken Slovakia 1998–, Globtel Orange Bratislava 2001–; Vice-Chair. World Chamber Fed. Paris 2001–; Pres. Ecosoc Slovakia 2000–; Deputy Pres. Eurochambers 2001–; mem. Supervisory Bd Incheba a.s. Bratislava 1999–, Chair. 2004–; mem. Supervisory Bd OTP Bank Bratislava 2003–; mem. Presidency, European Econ. and Social Cttee, Brussels 2004–; Gold Medal of Hungarian CCI 1999, Officer, Order of Léopold II, Belgium 1995, Officier Ordre du Mérite, France 1996, Prominent of Economy, Slovakia 1997, Great Silver Order, Austria 1998, Commendatore Ordine, Stella della Solidarita Italiana 2003, Gold Medal, House of Europe 2003. *Publication:* Advertising in the Market Economy.
Address: Slovak Chamber of Commerce and Industry, Gorkého 9, 816 03 Bratislava, Slovakia (office). *Telephone:* (2) 5443-3291 (office). *Fax:* (2) 5413-1159 (office). *E-mail:* sopkurad@scci.sk (office). *Website:* www.scci .sk (office).

MIHOV, Gen. Miho, MA; Bulgarian air force officer; *Adviser to the President;* b. 1 Feb. 1949, Sennik; m. 1973; one s. one d. *Education:* Benkovski Air Force Acad., Dolna Mitropolia, Rakovski Nat. War Coll., Sofia, Gen. Staff Coll., Moscow, USAF Special Operations School. *Career:* Training Flight Air Unit Deputy Commdr/Instructor; Air Squadron Deputy Commdr, Commdr, Air Regt, Deputy Commdr, Commdr; Air Corps Deputy Commdr; Air Defence Div. Commdr, Air Force Commdr; Chief of Gen. Staff of the Bulgarian Armed Forces 1997–2002; Adviser to Pres. of Bulgaria 2002–; Order of Merit and Valour; Medal for Service to the Bulgarian Armed Forces; Medal for the 40th Anniversary of the Victory over Hitler and Fascism; Medals and Orders of Distinguished Service; Order of Merit of Aviation (presented by King of Spain); Order presented by King of Sweden; Order presented by Pres. of Repub. of Bulgaria; Legion of Merit (USA). *Address:* 2 Dondoukov blvd, 1123 Sofia, Bulgaria. *Telephone:* (2) 923-91-08 (office). *Fax:* (2) 981-75-79 (office). *E-mail:* mihov@president.bg (office). *Website:* www.president.bg (office).

MIKELADZE, Levan, MA, PhD; Georgian diplomatist; m.; two d. *Education:* Tbilisi State Univ., Inst. of Geography, USSR Acad. of Sciences, Moscow. *Career:* Researcher, Inst. of Geography, Georgian Acad. of Science 1978–89, Scientific Sec., Presidium of Acad. 1989–92; Head of European Dept, Ministry of Foreign Affairs 1992; State Adviser, Staff of Head of State 1992–95; Counsellor, Political Affairs, Embassy in Washington, DC 1995–96; Amb. to Austria 1996–2002, also Head of Perm. Mission to OSCE and Int. Orgs in Vienna, Austria 2001–02; Amb. to USA, Mexico and Canada 2002–06; Amb. to Switzerland and Perm. Rep. to UN and other Int. Orgs, Geneva 2007 (resgnd); Fulbright Scholar, Center for Int. Security and Arms Control, Stanford Univ., USA 1994. *Address:* c/o Ministry of Foreign Affairs, 0118 Tbilisi, Sh. Chitadze 4, Georgia.

MIKEREVIĆ, Dragan, PhD, DSc; Bosnia and Herzegovina politician; *Vice-President, Party of Democratic Progress;* b. 12 Feb. 1955, Doboj; m.; two c. *Education:* Univ. of Novi Sad. *Career:* fmr Chief of Finance Dept, Municipality of Doboj, later Pres. Municipality Ass.; fmr Financial Dir Health Assurance Bureau, Republika Srpska; fmr Prof. of Econs, Univ. of Banja Luka, later Man. and mem. of research teams, Inst. for Economy, Univ. of Banja Luka; mem. Party of Democratic Progress 1999–, currently Vice-Pres.; Chair. Council of Ministers (Prime Minister) of Bosnia and Herzegovina 2002, Minister for European Integration 2001–02; Prime Minister of Serb Repub. (Republika Srpska) of Bosnia and Herzegovina 2003–05. *Address:* c/o Office of the Prime Minister, 78000 Banja Luka, Republika Srpska, Bosnia and Herzegovina. *Telephone:* (51) 331333.

MIKHAILOV, Nikolai Vasilyevich, DPhil; Russian politician; *Co-Chairman, Russian-American Commission on Economic and Technical Co-operation;* b. 14 May 1937, Sevsk, Bryansk Region; m.; one s. *Education:* Moscow Bauman Higher School of Tech. *Career:* with defence industry enterprises 1961–96; Dir-Gen., Vympel Co. 1986–96; Deputy Sec. Security Council of Russian Fed. 1996–97; State Sec., First Deputy Minister of Defence of Russian Fed. 1997–2000; Co-Chair. Russian-American Comm. on Econ. and Tech. Co-operation 1998–, mem. Bd of Dirs AFC Systema Co. 2001–; USSR State Prize, State Prize of Russian Fed. 1997. *Publications:* (titles in trans.) Global World and Global Problems: Science and Labour in a Modern World; Military Defence Complex: Analyses and Challenges; Science and Knowledge: From Modern Times to the Future. *Address:* Systema Financial Corporation, Leont'yevsky per. 10, 103009 Moscow (office); Raspletina str. 39, bied 14, 123060, Moscow, Russia (home). *Telephone:* (495) 730-15-14 (office); (495) 598-04-34 (home); (495) 105-44-21 (home). *Fax:* (495) 730-03-07 (office). *E-mail:* nmikhailov@sistema.ru (office); nmikhailov@mtu-net.ru (home). *Website:* www.sistema .ru (office).

MIKHNEVICH, Aleksandr; Belarusian engineer and diplomatist; *Ambassador to UK;* b. 1953, Minsk; m. Tatiana Mikhnevich; one s. *Education:* Moscow Eng and Physical Inst., All-Union Foreign Commerce Acad., Moscow. *Career:* Engineer, Integral Production and Tech. Amalgamation, Minsk 1977–78, Deputy Sec. Youth League Cttee; Head of Div., Minsk City Cttee of Youth League of Belarus 1980–83; Acting Head of Personnel Div., Belarusian Research Inst. of Scientific and Tech. Information and Tech. and Econ. Research, State Planning Cttee of Belarus SSR 1986–87, Head of Patent and Licence Research Div. 1987–88; Head of Foreign Econ. Relations Div., Ministry of Light Industry 1988–92; Head of Div., later Head of Foreign Econ. Relations Dept, Belarusian State Production and Trade Concern of Light Industries 'Bellegprom' 1992–95, First Vice-Pres. Belarusian State Production and Trade Concern of Light Industries 'Bellegprom' 1995–2000; Deputy Minister for Foreign Affairs 2000–06; Amb. to UK (also accred to Ireland) 2006–; several nat. decorations. *Address:* Embassy of Belarus, 6 Kensington Court, London, W8 5DL, England (office). *Telephone:* (20) 7937-3288 (office). *Fax:* (20) 7361-0005 (office). *E-mail:* uk@belembassy.org (office). *Website:* www.belembassy .org/uk (office).

MILAŠINOVIĆ, Tanja, MSc, DTechSc; Bosnia and Herzegovina scientist, academic, civil servant and diplomatist; b. Prijedor. *Education:* Primary Music School (violin), Mining Geology and Petroleum Faculty, Zagreb, Croatia, Faculty of Mechanical Eng, Ljubljana, Slovenia, Ludwig Maximilians Univ., Inst. for Experimental Physics, Munich, Germany.

Career: Asst, Mining Geology and Petroleum Faculty, Zagreb, Croatia 1986–87, Ludwig Maximilians Univ., Munich, Germany 1989–91; Asst Prof. of Thermodynamics and Thermotechnique 1997; Asst and Asst Prof., Univ. of Belgrade, Serbia, Faculty of Agric. and Faculty of Forestry 1992–98; Asst Minister, Ministry of Foreign Econ. Affairs, Republika Srpska 1998–2001; Minister Counsellor and Chargé d'affaires a.i., Mission of Bosnia and Herzegovina to EU 2001–05, Amb. to UK (also accred to Ireland) 2005–08. *Publications:* about 20 professional publs. *Address:* Ministry of Foreign Affairs, Musala 2, 71000 Sarajevo, Bosnia and Herzegovina (office). *Telephone:* (33) 281100 (office). *Fax:* (33) 472188 (office). *E-mail:* info@mvp.gov.ba (office). *Website:* www.mvp.gov.ba (office).

MILES, Marilyn Cheryl, MA; Guyanese diplomatist; *Ambassador to Brazil;* b. 22 May 1945, Georgetown; m. John Mills 1969; two s. *Education:* Univ. of the W Indies, Jamaica, London Univ. *Career:* Amb. to Venezuela 1985–92, Dir-Gen. (Perm. Sec.), Ministry of Foreign Affairs 1993–99, Amb. to Brazil (also accred. to Argentina, Uruguay, Peru and Bolivia) 1999–; Univ. of Guyana Outstanding Guyanese Woman Award for Diplomacy 1989 Order of San Carlos (Colombia) 1981, Cacique's Cross of Honor (Guyana) 1991, Order of Francisco de Miranda, First Class (Venezuela) 1992. *Address:* Embassy of Guyana, SHIS, QI 05, Conj. 19, Casa 24, 71615-190 Brasília, DF, Brazil (office). *Telephone:* (61) 248-0874 (office). *Fax:* (61) 248-0886 (office). *E-mail:* embguyana@embguyana.org.br (office). *Website:* www.embguyana.org.br (office).

MILINTACHINDA, Piamsak; Thai international organization official; *Director-General, Department of Technical and Economic Cooperation, Ministry of Foreign Affairs;* b. 1950, Bangkok. *Education:* Chulalongkorn Univ. and Wayne State Univ., USA. *Career:* Attaché, Dept of Econ. Affairs, Ministry of Foreign Affairs 1977–80; Second Sec., Royal Thai Embassy, Singapore 1981–84; First Sec. Dept of ASEAN Affairs, Ministry of Foreign Affairs 1985–87, Deputy Dir-Gen. 1999; Counsellor, Perm. Mission to UN, New York 1988–91; Dir North American Div., Dept of American and South Pacific Affairs, Ministry of Foreign Affairs 1992–94; Minister, Deputy Perm. Rep. to WTO, Geneva 1995–99; Deputy Dir-Gen. Dept of European Affairs, Ministry of Foreign Affairs 2000–01; Amb., Deputy Exec. Dir APEC Secr. 2002, Exec. Dir 2003–05; Dir-Gen. Dept of Tech. and Econ. Cooperation (DTEC) 2004–. *Address:* Department of Technical and Economic Cooperation, Ministry of Foreign Affairs, 443 Sri Ayudhya Road, Bangkok, Thailand 10400 (office). *Telephone:* (2) 643-5000 (office). *Fax:* (2) 225-6155 (office). *Website:* www .dtec.thaigov.net (office).

MILLER, Walter Geoffrey Thomas, AO; Australian diplomatist; *Vice-President, Australian Institute of International Affairs;* b. 25 Oct. 1934, Tasmania; m. Rachel C. Webb 1960; three s. one d. *Education:* Launceston High School and Univs of Tasmania and Oxford. *Career:* served in Australian missions in Kuala Lumpur, Djakarta and at UN, New York; Deputy High Commr, India 1973–75; Amb. to Repub. of Korea 1978–80; Head, Int. Div. Dept of the Prime Minister and Cabinet, Canberra 1982; Deputy Sec. Dept of Foreign Affairs 1985–86; Amb. to Japan 1986–89; Dir-Gen. Office of Nat. Assessments Canberra 1989–95; High Commr to NZ 1996–2000; Vice-Pres. Australian Inst. of Int. Affairs 2005–; Rhodes Scholar 1956. *Address:* 124 Kent Street, Sydney, NSW 2000 (office); 85 Union Street, McMahons Point, NSW 2060, Australia (home). *Telephone:* (2) 9247-2709 (office).

MILLERON, Jean-Claude; French economist and international finance official; b. 8 Jan. 1937, Paris; m. Marie-France Dannaud 1966; two s. one d. *Education:* Ecole Polytechnique, Paris, Ecole Supérieure des Sciences Econ., Paris. *Career:* with Nat. Inst. of Statistics and Econ. Studies (INSEE), Paris 1963–70, Dir-Gen. 1987–92; Visiting Research Dept of Econs, Univ. of Calif., Berkeley 1970–71; Deputy Dir Nat. School of Statistics and Econ. Admin. (ENSAE), Paris 1977–78; Head of Dept of Econs, Planning Commissariat-Gen., Paris 1978–81; Dir of Forecasting, Ministry of Econ. and Finance 1982–87; Dir-Gen. INSEE 1986–92; Under-Sec.-Gen. Dept of Econ. and Social Information and Policy Analysis, UN, New York 1992–97; Special Adviser to French Minister of Econ., Finance and Industry 1997–98; apptd Exec. Dir of IMF and IBRD 1998; apptd Financial Minister, Embassy in Washington, DC 1998; Fellow, Econometric Soc. *Publications:* various books and articles on econ. theory and public econs. *Address:* c/o Ministry of the Economy, Finance and Industry, 139 rue de Bercy, 75572 Paris, France.

MILLETT, Peter Joseph; British diplomatist; *High Commissioner to Cyprus;* b. 23 Jan. 1955; m. June Millett; three d. *Career:* joined FCO 1974, Vice-

Consul, Caracas 1978–80, Second Sec., Doha 1981–85, Minister of State's Office, FCO 1986-87, UN Dept 1987–89, UK Rep.'s Office, Brussels 1989–93, Head of Personnel Policy Unit, FCO 1993–96, Deputy Head of Mission, Athens 1997–2001, Head of Security FCO 2002–05, High Commr to Cyprus 2005–.
Address: British High Commission, PO Box 21978, Alexander Pallis Street, 1587 Nicosia, Cyprus (office). *Telephone:* 22861100 (office). *Fax:* 22861125 (office). *E-mail:* infobhc@cylink.com.cy (office). *Website:* www.britain.org .cy (office).

MILLS, Greg, BA, MA, PhD; South African security analyst; *Director, Brenthurst Foundation;* b. 1962, Cape Town; m. Janet Wislon; one s. two d. *Education:* Univ. of Cape Town, Univ. of Lancaster, UK. *Career:* has conducted research in over 60 countries, including Algeria, Morocco, Kenya, 'Somaliland', Nigeria, Senegal, Iraq, Israel and Kuwait; Teacher of Devt and Security Issues, Univs of the Western Cape and Cape Town –1994; Dir of Studies, S African Inst. of Int. Affairs 1994–96, Nat. Dir 1996–2005; Visiting Fellow, Strategic and Defence Studies Centre, ANU 1998; Visiting Fellow, Spanish Ministry of Foreign Affairs 2002; Dir Brenthurst Foundation 2005–; Founding Ed. SA Yearbook of Int. Affairs; Ed. SA Journal of International Affairs; mem. Ed. Bd RUSI Journal, Defense and Security Analysis, Argentine Journal of International Research, Taiwan Defense Review; Sr Research Assoc., Centre for Defence and Int. Securities Studies; Assoc. Fellow, Royal United Services Inst. (RUSI), UK 2005–. *Publications:* more than 20 books including The Wired Model: South Africa Foreign Policy and Globalisation (CNA Business Book of the Month 2000, Recht Malan Prize for Best S African Non-Fiction Work 2001) 2000, Poverty to Prosperity: Globalisation, Good Governance and African Recovery 2002, The Security Intersection: The Paradox of Power in an Age of Terror 2005; numerous articles in local and int. journals.
Address: The Brenthurst Foundation,POB 61631, Marshalltown 2107, South Africa (office). *Telephone:* (11) 274-2092 (office). *Fax:* (11) 643-1882 (office). *E-mail:* millsg@euson.co.za (office). *Website:* www .thebrenthurstfoundation.com (office).

MILLS, John Evans Atta, PhD; Ghanaian politician and academic; b. 21 July 1944, Cape Coast, Cen. Region; m. Ernestina Naadu. *Education:* Univ. of Ghana, London School of Econs, School of Oriental and African Studies, London Univ., Stanford Law School, Calif. *Career:* Lecturer, Faculty of Law, Univ. of Ghana 1971–80, Assoc. Prof. of Law 1992; Visiting Prof., Temple Law School, Phila, USA 1978–79, 1986–87, Leiden Univ., Netherlands 1985–86; Acting Commr Internal Revenue Service 1986–93, Commr 1993–96; Nat. Democratic Congress cand. in presidential election 2000; Vice-Pres. of Ghana 2000; presidential cand. 2004.
Address: c/o National Democratic Congress, 641/4 Ringway Close, Kokomlemle, PO Box 5825, Accra -North, Ghana (office).

MILNER, Henry, MA, PhD; Canadian political scientist, researcher and author; *Research Fellow and Canada Research Chair in Electoral Studies, Department of Political Science, University of Montreal;* b. 17 April 1946; m. Frances Boylston. *Education:* McGill Univ., Montreal, Carleton Univ., Ottawa. *Career:* Teaching Asst, Univ. of Maryland 1968–69; Prof. of Political Science, Vanier Coll., Montreal 1971–; Visiting Researcher, Univ. of Stockholm, Sweden 1985–86, Univ. of Turku, Finland 1991; Assoc. Prof., Laval Univ. 1993–2004; Visiting Prof., School of Policy Studies, Queen's Univ. 1995–99; Visiting Researcher, Victoria Univ., NZ 1996, Univ. of Umeå, Sweden 1998–; Chair in Canadian Studies Univ. of the Sorbonne, Paris, France 2004–05; Visiting Fellow, Inst. for Policy Studies 2004–; Research Fellow, Inst. for Research in Public Policy (IRPP), Montreal; mem. Editorial Bd Quebec Studies 1983–85; Founder and Co-Dir Inroads (policy journal) 1992–; Pres. Soc. québécoise de science politique 2003–04; mem. Exec. Cttee Int. Political Science Asscn 2003–06, Int. Advisory Bd Democracy: A Citizen Perspective: Interdisciplinary Centre of Excellence, Abo Acad. Univ., Finland; Hon. Prin. Fellow, Melbourne Univ., Australia 1999; Fulbright Fellowship, State Univ. of NY 2005–06. *Publications:* Sweden: Social Democracy in Practice 1989, Social Democracy and Rational Choice 1994, Making Every Vote Count: Reappraising Canada's Electoral System (ed.) 1999, Gösta Rehn and the Swedish Model at Home and Abroad 2000, Civic Literacy: How Informed Citizens Make Democracy Work 2002, Steps Toward Making Every Vote Count (ed.) 2004.
Address: C-5069, Pavillon Lionel Groulx, Université de Montréal, Montréal (office); 3777 avenue Kent, Montréal, PQ H3S 1N4, Canada (home). *Telephone:* (514) 343-6111 (ext. 3442) (office); (514) 731-8383 (home). *Fax:* (514) 343-2360 (office). *E-mail:* henry.milner@pol.umu.se (office); Henry.Milner@umontreal.ca (office). *Website:* www.crcee .umontreal.ca/equipe_hm_a.html (office).

MILOŠOSKI, Antonio, MA; Macedonian lawyer, politician, diplomatist and researcher; *Minister of Foreign Affairs;* b. 29 Jan. 1976, Tetovo; m. *Education:* SS. Cyril and Methodius Univ., Skopje, Friedrich Wilhelm Univ. Bonn, Germany, Gerhard Merkator Univ. of Duisburg, Germany. *Career:* mem. Exec. Cttee Youth Force Union of Internal Macedonian Revolutionary Org—Democratic Party for Macedonian Nat. Unity 1995–97, Vice-Pres. 1997–98; Chair. Office of the Deputy Prime Minister of FYR Macedonia 1999–2000; Govt Spokesman 2000–01; Counsellor to the Prime Minister Jan.–May 2001; Research Fellow, Inst. for Political Science, Gerhard Merkator Univ., Duisburg 2005–06; Minister of Foreign Affairs 2006–; Founder Youth Euro-Atlantic Forum (MEAF); columnist, Dnevnik (newspaper) 2000.
Address: Ministry of Foreign Affairs, 1000 Skopje, Dame Gruev 6, Former Yugoslav Republic of Macedonia (office). *Telephone:* (2) 3110333 (office). *Fax:* (2) 3115790 (office). *E-mail:* mailmnr@mfa.gov.mk (office). *Website:* www.mfa.gov.mk (office).

MILOVANOVIĆ, Gillian Arlette, BA, MA; American diplomatist; *Ambassador to Former Yugoslav Republic of Macedonia;* b. NY; m.; two one d. *Education:* Univ. of Pennsylvania, Temple Univ., Ecole Nationale d'Admin, Paris, France. *Career:* career mem. Sr Foreign Service since 1978, early assignments included tour as Int. Relations Officer, Bureau of Oceans and Int. Environmental and Scientific Affairs, Office of Fisheries Affairs, served as Vice-Consul in Sydney, as Staff Asst to Asst Sec. of State for E Asian and Pacific Affairs, as Political Officer in Paris, as Political-Econ. Officer and Deputy Consul Gen. in Cape Town 1987, Political-Mil. Affairs Officer and Deputy Political Counselor, Embassy in Brussels 1990–94, Deputy Chief of Mission, Embassy in Gaborone, Botswana 1994–97, Dir Office of Nordic and Baltic Affairs, State Dept 1997–99, Deputy Chief of Mission, Embassy in Stockholm 1999–2002, Embassy in Pretoria 2002–05, Amb. to Former Yugoslav Repub. of Macedonia 2005–; two Superior Honor Awards, two Meritorious Honor Awards.
Address: Embassy of the USA, Bul. Ilinden bb, 1000 Skopje, Former Yugoslav Republic of Macedonia (office). *Telephone:* (2) 3116180 (office). *Fax:* (2) 3117103 (office). *E-mail:* AmEmbSkopje@mt.net.mk (office). *Website:* skopje.usembassy.gov (office).

MILUTINOVIĆ, Milan, LLM; Serbian politician, diplomatist and lawyer; b. 19 Dec. 1942, Belgrade; m. Olga Branko Spasojević; one s. *Education:* Belgrade Univ. *Career:* mem. Presidency of Socialist Youth Union of Yugoslavia 1969–71; MP 1969–74; Sec. Communal Cttee of League of Communists 1972–74; Sec. for Ideology, City Cttee of League of Communists 1974–77; Minister of Science and Educ. of Serbian Repub. 1977–82; Dir Serbian Nat. Library 1983–87; Head of Sector for Press, Information and Culture, Sec. for Foreign Affairs 1987–89; Amb. to Greece 1989–95; Minister of Foreign Affairs, Fed. Repub. of Yugoslavia 1995–98; Pres. of Serbia 1997–2002; accused of crimes against humanity and violations of the customs of war by UN War Crimes Tribunal 2001, charged with crimes against humanity and war crimes by Int. Court of Justice 2003, provisionally released 2005 pending trial; Order of Merit with Silver Star 1974, Medal for work with Gold Coronet 1980. *Publications include:* University – Eppur si muove! 1985.
Address: c/o Office of the President, Andrićev venac 1, 11000 Belgrade; Koste Glavinica 9, 11000 Belgrade, Serbia (home).

MINDAOUDOU, Aichatou, PhD; Niger politician, lawyer and academic; *Minister of Foreign Affairs, Co-operation and African Integration; Education:* Univ. of the Sorbonne, Paris, France. *Career:* Minister of Social Devt, Population and Women 1996–99, of Foreign Affairs 1999–2000, of Foreign Affairs, Co-operation and African Integration 2001–; Sr Lecturer in Int. Law.
Address: Ministry of Foreign Affairs and Co-operation and African Integration, BP 396, Niamey (office); PO Box 11529, Niamey, Niger (home). *Telephone:* 72-29-07 (office); 72-35-15 (home). *Fax:* 73-52-31 (office). *E-mail:* indo-ai@ifrance.com (home).

MINFORD, (Anthony) Patrick (Leslie), CBE, PhD; British economist and academic; *Professor of Applied Economics, Cardiff Business School;* b. 17 May 1943; m. Rosemary Irene Allcorn 1970; two s. one d. *Education:* Horris Hill, Winchester Coll., Univ. of Oxford, London School of Econs. *Career:* Econ. Asst, Ministry of Overseas Devt 1966; Economist, Ministry of Finance, Malawi 1967–69; Econ. Adviser Courtaulds Ltd 1970–71; HM Treasury 1971–73; HM Treasury Del. Washington, DC 1973–74; Visiting Hallsworth Fellow, Univ. of Manchester 1974–75; Edward Gonner Prof. of Applied Econs, Univ. of Liverpool 1976–97; Visiting Prof., Cardiff Business School 1993–97, Prof. of Applied Econs 1997–; Dir Merseyside Devt Corpn 1988–89; mem. Monopolies and Mergers Comm. 1990–96, Treasury Panel of Independent Econ. Forecasters 1993–96; Ed. Nat. Inst. for Econ. and Social Research Review 1975–76, Liverpool Quarterly Econ. Bulletin 1980–. *Publications:* Substitution Effects, Speculation and

Exchange Rate Stability 1978, Unemployment – Cause and Cure 1983, Rational Expectations and the New Macroeconomics 1983, The Housing Morass 1987, The Supply-Side Revolution in Britain 1991, The Cost of Europe (ed.) 1992, Rational Expectations Macroeconomics 1992, Markets not Stakes 1998, Britain and Europe: Choices for Change (with Bill Jamieson) 1999, Advanced Macroeconomics: A Primer (with David Peel) 2002, Money Matters: Essays in honour of Alan Walters 2004, Should Britain Leave the EU? – An Economic Analysis of a Troubled Relationship (co-author) 2005, An Agenda for Tax Reform 2006; articles in journals. *Address:* Cardiff Business School, University of Wales Cardiff, Cardiff, CF10 3EU, Wales (office). *Telephone:* (29) 2087-5728 (office). *Fax:* (29) 2087-4419 (office). *E-mail:* MinfordP@cardiff.ac.uk (office). *Website:* www.cf.ac.uk/carbs/faculty/minfordp/index.html (office).

MINH, Le Luong, MA; Vietnamese diplomatist; *Permanent Representative, United Nations;* b. 1 Sept. 1952, Thanh Hoa; m.; two d. *Education:* Inst. of Int. Relations, Hanoi, Jawaharlal Nehru Univ., New Delhi. *Career:* joined Ministry of Foreign Affairs 1975, has served in several sr positions including Deputy Dir Gen., Dir-Gen. for Int. Orgs, Dir-Gen. for Multilateral Econ. Co-operation; Perm. Rep. to UN and other Int. Orgs, Geneva 1995–97, Deputy Perm. Rep. to UN, New York 1997–99, Perm. Rep. to UN, New York 2004–. *Address:* Permanent Mission of Viet Nam, 866 United Nations Plaza, Suite 435, New York, NY 10017, USA (office). *Telephone:* (212) 644-0594 (office). *Fax:* (212) 644-5732 (office). *E-mail:* vietnamun@aol.com (office). *Website:* www.un.int/vietnam (office).

MINOR, Charles A.; Liberian diplomatist; *Ambassador to USA;* b. Sinoe; m.; three c. *Education:* Michigan State Univ., USA. *Career:* taught at Univ. of Monrovia; fmr Acting Man. Liberian Produce Marketing Corpn; consultant to Arthur D. Little; joined African Man. Services Co., Amsterdam, Netherlands 1993; Amb. to USA 2004–. *Address:* Embassy of Liberia, 5201 16th Street, NW, Washington, DC 20011, USA (office). *Telephone:* (202) 723-0437 (office). *Fax:* (202) 723-0436 (office). *E-mail:* info@embassyofliberia.org (office). *Website:* www.embassyofliberia.org (office).

MINOVES TRIQUELL, Juli F., MA, MPhil; Andorran politician and diplomatist; b. 15 Aug. 1969, Andorra la Vella. *Education:* Lycée Comte de Foix, Andorra, Music School of the Lyceum of Barcelona, Spain, Fribourg Univ., Switzerland, Yale Univ., USA. *Career:* teacher of Catalan, Migrosklubschule, Bern, Switzerland 1989–91; Special Corresp. of Radio Andorra, Gulf War 1991; Asst Prof. of Constitutional Law and Political Economy, Dept of Political Science, Yale Univ. 1993; Counsellor, first Perm. Mission of Andorra to the UN 1993–94, Deputy Perm. Rep. and Chargé d'affaires 1994–95, Perm. Rep. 1995–2004; Alt. Head Andorran Del. to World Summit on Social Devt, Copenhagen; Special Plenipotentiary Rep. of Andorran Govt in negotiations to establish diplomatic relations with various govts 1994–95; Amb. to USA and Canada 1996; Vice-Pres. UN Gen. Ass. 1997; Head, Andorran del. to UN Special Ass. Rio + 5 1997; Chief of Cabinet a.i. of the Minister of Foreign Affairs 1997–99; mem. special group of UN diplomats for inspections in Iraq 1998; Head, Andorran del. for the establishment of an Int. Criminal Court, Rome, 1998; Amb. to Spain 1998, to Finland and Switzerland 1999, to UK 2000; Minister of Foreign Affairs, Culture and Co-operation 2001–07; Great Cross, Order of Merit of Portugal 1997; Tristaina de periodisme journalism award 1986, Crédit Suisse Award for stock exchange research 1988, El futur de les Valls Research Award 1989, Grad. Fellowship, Foundation Crèdit Andorrà 1991. *Publications:* articles in Andorra 7 weekly magazine 1986–88, Segles de Memòria (novel) (Fiter i Rossell Award) 1989, Les Pedres del Diable (short stories) (Sant Carles Borromeu Award 1992). *Address:* c/o Ministry of Foreign Affairs, Culture and Co-operation, Carrer Prat de la Creu 62–64, Andorra la Vella AD500, Andorra (office).

MINTON, Mark C., BA, MA; American diplomatist; *Ambassador to Mongolia; Education:* Columbia Univ., Yale Univ. *Career:* served for three years in US Army; career mem. Foreign Service, began his career as a Political Officer in Tokyo 1977, served on Policy Planning Staff, Washington, DC, followed by assignment with Office of Soviet Union Affairs, Consul Gen. in Sapporo, Japan 1984, served in subsequent assignments with Dept of State's Exec. Secr., as Pearson Fellow with US Senate and as Deputy Dir (Japanese Affairs) at Dept of State, Minister-Counselor for Political Affairs, Embassy in Seoul 1992, returned to Washington, DC as Dir of Korean Affairs, Minister-Counselor for Political Affairs, US Mission to the UN, New York 1998, Deputy Chief of Mission, Embassy in Seoul –2006, served for over six months as Chargé d'affaires a.i., then Amb. to Mongolia 2006–; fmr Diplomat-in-Residence, CUNY. *Address:* Embassy of the USA, PO Box 1021, Ikh Toiruu 59/1, Ulan Bator 13, Mongolia (office). *Telephone:* (11) 329095 (office). *Fax:* (11) 320776

(office). *E-mail:* pao@usembassy.mn (office); webmaster@us-mongolia.com (office). *Website:* mongolia.usembassy.gov (office).

MINUTO-RIZZO, Alessandro, LLD; Italian diplomatist and international organization official; *Deputy Secretary-General, NATO;* b. 10 Sept. 1940, Rome; m.; two s. *Career:* mem. staff Directorate of Cultural Affairs, Ministry of Foreign Affairs, Rome 1969–72; First Sec. Washington, DC 1972–75; Counsellor, Prague 1975–80; Head Eastern Europe Desk, Directorate for Econ. Affairs 1980–81, Head EEC External Relations Desk 1981–86; Minister Counsellor OECD, Paris 1986–92; Minister Plenipotentiary Jan. 1992; Diplomatic Counsellor of Minister for Budget and Econ. Planning 1992–96, of Minister for Co-ordination of European Policies (a.i.) 1995–96; Deputy Chief of Cabinet, Ministry of Foreign Affairs Jan.–Oct. 1996, Co-ordinator for EU Affairs 1996–97; Diplomatic Counsellor of Minister of Defence 1997–2000; Amb. to Cttee for Policy and Security of EU 2000–01; Deputy Sec.-Gen. NATO 2001–; Del. to Council, ESA 1986–92; Chair. Admin. and Financial Cttee 1993–96; Chair. Ass. of Parties of Eutelsat 1989; mem. Man. Bd Italian Space Agency 1994–95; Chair. EU Cttee for Territorial Devt 1996. *Address:* NATO, blvd Léopold III, 1110 Brussels, Belgium (office). *Telephone:* (2) 707-49-06 (office). *Fax:* (2) 707-46-66 (office). *E-mail:* sgoffice@hq.nato.int (office). *Website:* www.nato.int (office).

MIQDAD, Faisal al-; Syrian diplomatist; *Deputy Foreign Minister; Career:* fmr Deputy, then Acting Amb. to UN New York, Perm. Rep. 2002–05; Deputy Foreign Minister 2006–. *Address:* Ministry of Foreign Affairs, ave Shora, Muhajireen, Damascus, Syria (office). *Telephone:* (11) 3331200 (office). *Fax:* (11) 3320686 (office).

MIRAKHOR, Abbas, PhD; Iranian international banking executive and economist; *Executive Director, International Monetary Fund;* b. 1 July 1941, Tehran; m. Loretta Thomas 1965; two s. *Education:* Kansas State Univ., USA. *Career:* Asst and Assoc. Prof. and Chair. Dept of Econs, Univ. of Alabama 1968–77, Prof. and Chair. Dept 1977–79, Vice-Chancellor 1979–80; Az-Zahra Univ., Tehran; Prof. and Chair. Grad. Study Dept, Alabama A&M Univ. 1980–83; Prof. of Econs Fla Inst. of Tech. 1983–84; Economist, IMF 1984–87, Sr Economist 1987–90, Exec. Dir 1990–; Quaid-e-Azam Star for Service to Pakistan 1999, Order of Companion of Volta for Service to Ghana 2005; IEEE Eng Man. Soc. First Paper Prize 1972, Islamic Development Bank Annual Prize for Research in Islamic Econs (jtly) 2003. *Publications:* numerous articles on econs. *Address:* International Monetary Fund, 700 19th Street, NW, Washington, DC 20431, USA (office). *Telephone:* (202) 623-7370 (office). *Fax:* (202) 623-4966 (office). *E-mail:* amirakhor@imf.org (office). *Website:* www.imf.org (office).

MIRANDA Y ELÍO, Carlos, Count of Casa Miranda; Spanish diplomatist; *Ambassador to UK;* b. 27 Feb. 1943, Cairo, Egypt; m. Señora Doña Elena Meneses, Countess of Casa Miranda, Marchioness of la Rambla; two c. *Education:* secondary schools in Brussels and Madrid. *Career:* Third Sec., Second Sec. and subsequently First Sec., Washington, DC 1970–75, First Sec., Algiers 1975–77, Counsellor-Dir for Political Int. Orgs, Ministry of Foreign Affairs 1977–80, Counsellor, Dept of European and Atlantic Affairs 1980–82, Dir-Gen. Foreign Policy for Latin America 1982–83, Special Advisor on Int. Affairs to Minister of Defence 1983–86, Dir-Gen. for Int. Security and Disarmament Affairs, Ministry of Foreign Affairs 1986–91, Perm. Rep. to NATO 1991–97, fmr Perm. Rep., Mission of Spain to Int. Orgs, Geneva, Amb. to UK 2004–. *Address:* Embassy of Spain, 39 Chesham Place, London, SW1X 8SB, England (office). *Telephone:* (20) 7235-5555 (office). *Fax:* (20) 7259-5392 (office). *E-mail:* embespuk@mail.mae.es (office). *Website:* www.mae.es/embajadas/londres (office).

MIRAPEIX LUCAS, Ferran, LenD, MBA; Andorran politician; *Minister of Finance;* b. 7 Sept. 1957. *Education:* Univ. of Barcelona, Spain, LSE, UK, Northwestern Univ., USA. *Career:* Finance Counselor of Comú de Sant Julià 2000–03, Chief Finance Counselor 2004–05; Minister of Finance 2006–; Vice-Pres. Liberal Party of Andorra. *Address:* Ministry of Finance, Carrer Prat de la Creu 62–64, Andorra la Vella Ad 500, Andorra (office). *Telephone:* 875700 (office). *E-mail:* finances.gov.ad (office). *Website:* www.finances.ad (office).

MIRONOV, Sergei Mikhailovich, CandJur; Russian engineer and politician; *Chairman, Sovet Federatsii (Federation Council);* b. 14 Feb. 1953, Pushkin, Leningrad Oblast; m.; one s. one d. *Education:* Leningrad (now St Petersburg) Plekhanov Mining Inst., St Petersburg State Tech. Univ., North-Western Acad. of Civil Service, St Petersburg State Univ. *Career:* army service 1971–73; engineer, Rusgeophysica (production co.) 1978–86; Sr Geophysicist, USSR Ministry of Geology, Mongolia 1987–91; Exec. Dir Russian Trade Chamber 1991–93, Construction Corpn – Restoration of St

Petersburg 1994–95; mem., First Deputy Chair. then Chair. Legis. Ass. of St Petersburg 1995–2000; Head, Political Council The Will of Petersburg (Volya Peterburga) regional political movt 2000–01; Rep. of St Petersburg Ass. to Fed. Council, June 2001, Chair. Fed. Council Dec. 2001–; Founder and Chair. Russian Leader Party of Life 2003, Chair. A Just Russia (Spravedlivaya Rossiya) (merger of Motherland, Russian Party of Life and Russian Pensioners' Party) 2006–; unsuccessful presidential cand. 2004. *Address:* Sovet Federatsii (Federation Council), 103426 Moscow, ul. B. Dmitrovka 26 (office); A Just Russia (Spravedlivaya Rossiya), 107031 Moscow, ul. B. Dmitrovka 32/1, Russia (office). *Telephone:* (495) 203-90-74 (office); (495) 650-38-80 (A Just Russia) (office). *Fax:* (495) 203-46-17 (office). *E-mail:* VPParfenov@mironov.ru (home); info@spravedlivo.ru (office). *Website:* www.council.gov.ru (office); www.spravedlivo.ru (office); www.mironov.ru; mironov.info.

MIROŠIČ, Iztok, BA; Slovenian diplomatist; *Ambassador to UK;* b. 21 March 1968, Postojna; m. Tina Kokalj. *Education:* Faculty of Social Sciences, Ljubljana. *Career:* Sr Adviser for Relations with Italy, the Vatican and Cooperation, Cen. European Initiative, Dept for Neighbouring States, Ministry of Foreign Affairs 1995–97, Head, Office of State Sec. and Deputy Minister, Head of the Minister's Office, Ministry of Foreign Affairs 1997–2000, Adviser to the Minister, Sec. Comm. for Succession to Fmr Yugoslavia, Main Sec. State Cttee for the Preparation for the Visit of the Pres. of USA to Slovenia 1999, Adviser to Govt, Head of Dept for South-Eastern Europe and Head of Special Working Group for the Establishment of Diplomatic Relations with Fed. Repub. of Yugoslavia 2000, Under-sec. of State and Head of Minister's Office 2000–03, State Sec. and Deputy Foreign Minister Jan.–Oct. 2003, State Sec., Office of the Prime Minister and Foreign Policy Adviser to Prime Minister 2003–04, Ministerial Councillor for Int. Relations and Foreign Policy and EU Adviser to the Prime Minister 2004; Amb. to UK 2004–; mem. Cttee for Cooperation between the Repub. of Slovenia and Autonomous Region of Friuli-Venezia Giulia 2002; Prešeren Award and Award of UNA of Slovenia for graduation thesis, Faculty of Social Sciences, Ljubljana. *Address:* Embassy of Slovenia, 10 Little College Street, London, SW1P 3SH, England (office). *Telephone:* (20) 7222-5700 (office). *Fax:* (20) 7222-5277 (office). *E-mail:* vlo@gov.si (office). *Website:* london.embassy.si (office).

MIROW, Thomas; German economist and banking executive; *President, European Bank for Reconstruction and Development (EBRD);* b. 6 Jan. 1953, Paris, France; m. Barbara Mirow; two d. *Education:* Univ. of Bonn. *Career:* Asst and later Chef de Cabinet to fmr Chancellor Willy Brandt 1975–83; Dir Hamburg City State 1983–87; Political and Man. Consultant 1988–91; State Minister and Head of Chancellery, Hamburg State Admin 1991–93, State Minister for Urban Devt and Head of Chancellery 1993–97, State Minister for Econs 1997–2001; mem. EC High-Level Group on Lisbon Strategy 2004, Personal Rep. of Fed. Chancellor for Lisbon Strategy and Dir-Gen. for Econ. Policy, Fed. Chancellery 2005, State Sec. Fed. Finance Ministry 2005–08; Pres. EBRD 2008–; Chair. Supervisory Bd Hamburger Hafen- und Lagerhaus AG (Hamburg Port) 1997–2001, Flughafen Hamburg GmbH 1997–2001; mem. Supervisory Bd Daimler Chrysler Luft- und Raumfahrtholding (Daimler Chrysler Aerospace Holding) 1997–2001; Man. Dir Alstertor Schienenlogistik Beteiligung GmbH 2002–05; mem. Admin. Council Hamburgische Landesbank 1997–2001; mem. Bd of Supervisory Dirs Kreditanstalt für Wiederaufbau 1997–2001; Sr Adviser Ernst & Young AG 2002–05; Adviser MM Warburg Bank 2002–05. *Address:* European Bank for Reconstruction and Development, One Exchange Square, London, EC2A 2JN, England (office). *Telephone:* (20) 7338-6000 (office). *E-mail:* ukoffice@ebrd.com (office). *Website:* www.ebrd .com (office).

MIRPURI, Ashok Kumar, MA; Singaporean diplomatist; *High Commissioner to Indonesia;* b. 13 Dec. 1959; m. Gouri Uppal; one s. one d. *Education:* Nat. Univ. of Singapore, School of Oriental and African Studies, Univ. of London, UK. *Career:* joined Ministry of Foreign Affairs 1984, First Sec. (Political), Embassy in Jakarta 1987–91; Dir Policy Planning and Analysis Directorate I (Southeast Asia) 1994–97; seconded to Shell Int. Ltd., UK as Corp. Adviser for Asia Pacific 1997–98; Minister-Counsellor and Deputy Chief of Mission, Embassy in Jakarta 1998–2000, High Commr to Australia 2000-02, to Malaysia 2002–06, Amb. to Indonesia 2006–. *Address:* Embassy of Singapore, Jalan H. R. Rasuna Said, Blok X/4, Kav. 2, Kuningan, Jakarta 12950, Indonesia (office). *Telephone:* (21) 5201489 (office). *Fax:* (21) 5201486 (office). *E-mail:* singemb_jkt@sgmfa.gov.sg (office). *Website:* www.mfa.gov.sg/jkt (office).

MIRRÉ, D. Federico; Argentine lawyer and diplomatist; *Ambassador to UK;* b. 1939; m. Cecilia Duhau; two d. *Career:* fmr journalist; jr diplomat, Embassy in London 1970–76, Consul in Frankfurt, Germany 1981–82,

involved in first contact between British Foreign Office and Argentine Foreign Ministry following Falklands conflict 1984, various positions, Embassies in The Vatican and France, fmr Amb. to the Ivory Coast and Norway, Dir Western Europe Desk, Ministry of Foreign Affairs, Buenos Aires –2003, Amb. to UK 2003–. *Address:* Embassy of Argentina, 65 Brook Street, London, W1K 4AH, England (office). *Telephone:* (20) 7318-1300 (office). *Fax:* (20) 7318-1301 (office). *E-mail:* info@argentine-embassy-uk.org (office). *Website:* www .argentine-embassy-uk.org (office).

MIRRLEES, Sir James Alexander, Kt, MA, PhD, FBA; British professor of economics; *Distinguished Professor at Large, Chinese University of Hong Kong;* b. 5 July 1936, Scotland; m. 1st Gillian M. Hughes 1961 (died 1993); two d.; m. 2nd Patricia Wilson 2001. *Education:* Univ. of Edinburgh and Trinity Coll., Cambridge. *Career:* Adviser, MIT Center for Int. Studies, New Delhi 1962–63; Asst Lecturer in Econs and Fellow, Trinity Coll., Univ. of Cambridge 1963, Univ. Lecturer 1965; Research Assoc. Pakistan Inst. of Devt Econs 1966–67; Fellow, Nuffield Coll. and Edgeworth Prof. of Econs, Univ. of Oxford 1968–95; Prof. of Political Economy, Univ. of Cambridge 1995–2003; Distinguished Prof. at Large, Chinese Univ. of Hong Kong 2003–; Adviser to Govt of Swaziland 1963; Visiting Prof., MIT 1968, 1970, 1976, 1987; Ford Visiting Prof., Univ. of California, Berkeley 1986; Visiting Prof., Yale Univ. 1989; Laureate Prof., Univ. of Melbourne, Australia; mem. Treasury Cttee on Policy Optimization 1976–78; Pres. Econometric Soc. 1982, Royal Econ. Soc. 1989–92, European Econ. Asscn 2000; Hon. FRSE, Foreign Hon. mem. American Acad. of Arts and Sciences, NAS, Hon. mem. American Econ. Asscn; Hon. DLitt (Warwick) 1982, (Portsmouth) 1997, (Oxford) 1998, Hon. DScS (Brunel) 1997, Hon. DSc (Social Sciences) (Edin.) 1997, Dr hc (Peking, Chinese Univ. of Hong Kong, Macao, Liège, Helsinki School of Econs); Nobel Prize for Econ. 1996. *Publications:* jt author of three books and articles in academic journals. *Address:* Chinese University of Hong Kong, Shatin, Hong Kong Special Administrative Region, People's Republic of China (office). *Telephone:* 2609-7831 (office); 2603-6670 (home). *Fax:* 2603-6586 (office). *E-mail:* jam28@cam.ac.uk (office).

MIRZAEV, Ruslan Erkinovich; Uzbekistan politician; *Minister of Defence; Career:* Sec. Nat. Security Council –2005; Minister of Defence 2005–. *Address:* Ministry of Defence, 100000 Tashkent, Ak. Abdullayev k'och. 100, Uzbekistan (office). *Telephone:* (71) 169-82-43 (office). *Fax:* (71) 169-82-28 (office).

MIRZIYOYEV, Shavkat Miromonovich; Uzbekistan politician; *Prime Minister;* b. 1957, Samarkand, Dzhizak region. *Education:* Tashkent Inst. of Irrigation, Eng and Agric. Mechanization. *Career:* Pro-rector Tashkent Inst. of Irrigation and Mechanization of Agric. –1996; Hokim (Gov.) Jizzax Viloyat 1996–2001, Samarqand Viloyat 2001–03; mem. Oly Majlis (Parl.) 1999–, Prime Minister 2003–. *Address:* Office of the Cabinet of Ministers, 100078 Tashkent, Mustaqillik maydoni 5, Uzbekistan (office). *Telephone:* (71) 139-82-95 (office). *Fax:* (71) 139-84-63 (office). *Website:* www.gov.uz (office).

MIRZOYEV, Ramason Zarifovich; Tajikistan diplomatist; b. 15 Feb. 1945, Kulyab Region; m.; six c. *Education:* Tadjik Inst. of Agric. *Career:* worked with construction teams Kulyab Region; in Afghanistan 1975–78; worked in CP bodies and orgs 1983–; USSR People's Deputy 1989–92; Deputy Chair. USSR Supreme Soviet 1989–91; Man. Council of Ministers Repub. of Tajikistan 1992–95; Amb. to Russian Fed. 1995–2001, to Iran 2001. *Address:* Ministry of Foreign Affairs, Rudaki Prosp. 42, 73405 Dushanbe, Tajikistan. *Telephone:* (2) 211808.

MISHAAN, Faisal Abdullah Ibrahim al-; Kuwaiti diplomatist. *Career:* fmr Dir Protocol Dept, Ministry of Foreign Affairs; currently Amb. to UAE. *Address:* Embassy of Kuwait, POB 926, Abu Dhabi, United Arab Emirates (office). *Telephone:* (2) 4446888 (office). *Fax:* (2) 4444990 (office).

MITCHELL, Andrew J.; British diplomatist; *Ambassador to Sweden;* b. 7 Feb. 1967; m. Helen Mitchell; two s. one d. *Career:* Desk Officer, Southern European Dept, FCO 1991–93, Second Sec., Embassy in Bonn 1993–96, Head of Section, Human Rights Policy Dept 1996–99, Deputy Head of Mission, Kathmandu 1999–2002, Dir Future Firecrest IT Programme 2002–07; Amb. to Sweden 2007–. *Address:* British Embassy, Skarpögt. 6–8, PO Box 27819, 115 93 Stockholm, Sweden (office). *Telephone:* (8) 671-30-00 (office). *Fax:* (8) 671-310-49 (office). *E-mail:* info@britishembassy.se (office). *Website:* www .britishembassy.se (office).

MITCHELL, Hon. Fred, JR, MPA, BA, LLB; Bahamian politician; b. 5 Oct. 1953, Nassau. *Education:* St. Augustine's Coll., Antioch Univ., OH and

John F. Kennedy School of Govt, Harvard Univ., USA, Univ. of Buckingham, UK. *Career:* elected to Senate; fmr Chair. Senate Select Cttee on Culture; Public Relations Consultant, Al Dillette & Assocs; fmr Opposition Spokesman on Foreign Affairs, Labour and Immigration; Minister of Foreign Affairs and Public Service 2002-7; Founding-mem. Bahamas Cttee on S Africa; mem. Progressive Liberal Party; mem. New Providence Human Rights Asscn.
Address: c/o Ministry of Foreign Affairs, East Hill Street, PO Box N-3746, Nassau, Bahamas (office).

MITCHELL, Rt Hon. Sir James Fitzallen, BSc, C.Biol, KCMG, PC; Saint Vincent and the Grenadines politician, agronomist, biologist and hotelier; b. 15 May 1931, Bequia, Grenadines; m. Patricia Parker 1965 (divorced); four d. *Education:* St Vincent Grammar School, Imperial Coll. of Tropical Agric., Trinidad and Univ. of British Columbia. *Career:* Agricultural Officer, Saint Vincent 1958–61; Ed. Pest Control Articles and News Summaries, Ministry of Overseas Devt, London 1964–65; MP for the Grenadines 1966–2001; Minister of Trade, Agric., Labour and Tourism 1967–72; MP (as an ind.) for the Grenadines 1972–79, re-elected in by-election 1979–2001; Premier of St Vincent 1972–74; Prime Minister of Saint Vincent and the Grenadines 1984–2000, also Minister of Finance and Planning and fmr Minister of Foreign Affairs; Founder New Democratic Party 1975, then Pres.; Chair. Caribbean Democrat Union 1991; Vice-Chair. Int. Democrat Union 1992–; Chair. Hotel Frangipani, Gingerbread, and several other cos; mem. Inst. of Biologists, London 1965–; Order of the Liberator (Venezuela) 1972, Grand Cross Knights of Malta 1998, Order of Propitious Clouds, Grand Cross Don Infanta (Portugal), Chevalier d'Honneur, Chaine de Rotisseur 1995, and other awards. *Publications include:* World Fungicide Usage 1965, Caribbean Crusade 1989, Guiding Change in the Islands 1996, A Season of Light 2001, Beyond the Island (autobiography) 2005.
Address: Hotel Frangipani, Box One, Bequia, Saint Vincent (office). *Telephone:* (458) 3255 (office). *Fax:* (458) 3824 (office). *E-mail:* frangi@caribsurf.com (office).

MITCHELL, Keith Claudius, MS, PhD; Grenadian politician; *Leader, New National Party;* b. 12 Nov. 1946, St George's; m. Marietta Mitchell; one s. *Education:* Presentation Coll., Grenada, Univ. of West Indies, Barbados, Howard Univ. and American Univ., Washington, DC. *Career:* cand. for Grenada Nat. Party in 1972 elections; Gen. Sec. New Nat. Party 1984–89, Leader 1989–; Minister of Communication, Works, Public Utilities, Transportation, of Civil Aviation and Energy 1984–87, of Communications, Works, Public Utilities, Co-operatives, Community Devt, Women's Affairs and Civil Aviation 1988–89; Prime Minister of Grenada and Minister of Finance, External Affairs, Mobilization, Trade and Industry, Information and Nat. Security 1995–99; Prime Minister and Minister of Nat. Security and Information 1999–2008, re-elected 2003, also Minister of Finance 2007–08; Capt. Grenada Nat. Cricket Team 1971–74; Order of the Brilliant Star (Taiwan) 1995.
Address: New National Party (NNP), Upper Lucas Street, St. George's, Grenada (office). *Telephone:* 440-1875 (office). *Fax:* 440-1876 (office). *E-mail:* nnpadmin@spiceisle.com (office). *Website:* nnpnews.com (office).

MITCHINER, John Edward, MA, PhD; British diplomatist; b. 12 Sept. 1951; m. Elizabeth Mary Ford 1983. *Education:* Univs of Bristol and London. *Career:* began diplomatic career 1980, posts have included Istanbul, New Delhi, Berne, Amb. to Armenia 1997–99, Deputy High Commr to India 2000–03, High Commr to Sierra Leone 2003–06; Fellow, Visva-Bharali, Santiniketan 1977–78, Calcutta Univ. 1978–79. *Publications:* Studies in the Indus Valley Inscriptions 1978, Traditions of the Seven Rsis 1982, The Yuga Purana 1986, Guru: The Search for Enlightenment 1992.
Address: Bower Farm, Whitland, SA34 0QX, Dyfed, Wales (home).

MITIFU, Faida, BSc, MA, PhD; Democratic Republic of the Congo diplomatist and academic; *Ambassador to USA;* b. 16 March 1959, Bukavu, Kivu; m.; three c. *Education:* Nat. Univ. of Zaïre, Kinshasa, Auburn Univ., Ala, Univ. of Georgia, USA. *Career:* teacher of French literature, language and culture and African and Caribbean cultural studies, Univ. of Georgia 1994–97, Columbus State Univ., Ga 1997–98; supervised teaching assts and co-ordinated French language program, Dept of Romance Languages, Univ. of Georgia 1995–97; Amb. to USA 1999–.
Address: Embassy of the Democratic Republic of the Congo, 1726 M Street, Suite 601, NW, Washington, DC 20036, USA (office). *Telephone:* (202) 234-7690 (office). *Fax:* (202) 234-2609 (office).

MITRI, Tariq; Lebanese politician and academic; *Minister of Culture;* b. 1950, Tripoli. *Career:* fmr Prof., Balamand Univ.; Dir Faith and Unity Bureau, WCC, Geneva mid-1980s, later Co-ordinator Islamic-Christian Dialogue; Minister of Environment and Admin. Devt 2005–06; Minister of Culture 2006–, Acting Minister of Foreign Affairs and Emigrants 2006–08; Co-founder Centre of Christian-Muslim Studies; active mem. in several groups and orgs concerning Muslim-Christian dialogue in Middle East and world-wide.
Address: Ministry of Culture, Immeuble Hatab, rue Madame Curie, Verdun, Beirut (office); Ministry of Foreign Affairs and Emigrants, rue Sursock, Achrafieh, Beirut, Lebanon. *Telephone:* (1) 744250 (Ministry of Culture) (office); (1) 333100 (Ministry of Foreign Affairs) (office). *Fax:* (1) 756303 (Ministry of Culture) (office). *E-mail:* omarhala_48@hotmail.com (office); info@emigrants.gov.lb (office). *Website:* www.culture.gov.lb (office); www.emigrants.gov.lb (office).

MITROFANOV, Aleksey Valentinovich; Russian politician and writer; b. 16 March 1962, Moscow; m. Marina Lillevyali. *Education:* Moscow Inst. of Int. Relations. *Career:* with Ministry of Foreign Affairs 1985–88; researcher, Inst. of USA and Canada 1988–91; producer TV programmes, Leisure Centre Sokol; mem. Higher Council, Liberal Democratic Party of Russia 1991–93; Minister of Foreign Affairs, Shadow Cabinet of Liberal Democratic Party 1992–96; mem. State Duma 1993–; Deputy Chair. Cttee on Int. Relations 1993–96, Chair. Cttee on Geopolitics 1996–99; joined A Just Russia 2007. *Films:* scriptwriter: Pchiojka (A Little Bee), Yuliya 2006; numerous documentaries including Yury Andropov 1993, Andrey Gromyko 1993. *Publications include:* Steps of New Geopolitics, Secret Visit of Professor Voland, t.A.T.u Come Back 2006.
Address: State Duma, 103265 Moscow, Okhotny ryad 1, Russia. *Telephone:* (495) 292-83-10 (office). *Fax:* (495) 292-94-64 (office). *Website:* www.duma.ru (office); alexeymitrofanov.ru (home).

MITROPOULOS, Efthimios; Greek international organization official; *Secretary-General, International Maritime Organization;* b. 30 May 1939, Piraeus; m.; one s. one d. *Education:* Aspropyrgos Merchant Marine Acad., Hellenic Coast Guard Acad. *Career:* with Greek Merchant Navy 1959–62; Coast Guard Officer, Corfu and Piraeus 1964–65; mem. Greek Del. to IMO 1966–77, becoming Head; Harbour Master, Corfu 1977–79; joined IMO Secr. 1979, Head of Navigation Section 1985–89, Sr Deputy Dir for Navigation and Related Matters 1989–92, Dir Maritime Safety Div. 1992–2003, Asst Sec.-Gen. 2000–03, Sec.-Gen. 2004–07; Chancellor, World Maritime Univ., Malmo, Sweden 2004–; Chair. Int. Maritime Law Inst., Malta 2004–; Gov. Royal Nat. Lifeboat Inst.; mem. Hellenic Inst. of Marine Tech., Shipmasters' Union of Greece, Int. Fed. of Shipmasters' Asscns, Propeller Club, Royal Automobile Club; Fellow, Royal Inst. of Navigation; Hon. Citizen of Galaxidi, Greece; Hon. Mem., Int. Asscn of Marine Aids to Navigation and Lighthouse Authorities; Hon. Fellow, Nautical Inst., Inst. of Marine Eng, Science and Tech.; Officier de l'Orde du Mérite Maritime de la France, Mil. Valour Medal and Phoenix Order (Hellenic Repub.), Commendatore, Order of Merit (Italy), St Marcus Cross, Patriarchate of Alexandria and All Africa; hon. degrees from Nicola Vaptsarov Naval Acad., Bulgaria, Maritime Univ., Constanza, Romania, Schiller Int. Univ., Dalian Maritime Univ., Chung-Ang Univ., Seoul, Repub. of Korea, Univ. of Messina, Italy, City Univ., London, Univ. of the Aegean, Greece, Odessa Nat. Maritime Acad., Ukraine; numerous awards, including Coastguard Award (Grand Cross), Argentina, 15 November Medal, Uruguay, Medal of Naval Merit, Brazil, US Coast Guard Distinguished Public Service Award, Colombian Navy Medal for "Servicios Distinguidos a la Dirección General Marítima, Silver Bell Award, The Seamen's Church Institute, New York, Danish Shipowners' Asscn Maritime Award, Union of Greek Shipowners Environment Award 2006, Interferry Person of Distinction 2006, Int. Hall of Fame Award, New York 2007. *Publications:* Tankers: Evolution and Technical Issues 1969, Studies in Shipping Economics 1970, Safety of Navigation 1971, Categories and Types of Merchant Ships 1973, Collision Avoidance at Sea 1975, Separation of Traffic at Sea 1976, Shipping Economics and Policy 1981.
Address: 7 Cornwall House, Cornwall Gardens, London, SW7 4AE (home); International Maritime Organization, 4 Albert Embankment, London, SE1 7SR, England (office). *Telephone:* (20) 7735-7611 (office). *Fax:* (20) 7587-3210 (office). *E-mail:* secretary-general@imo.org (office). *Website:* www.imo.org (office).

MITSIALIS, Anastassis; Greek diplomatist; b. 1952, Athens; m.; two c. *Education:* Univ. of Athens. *Career:* started diplomatic career as Attaché, Ministry of Foreign Affairs 1975; worked at Embassy in Rome 1978, Second Sec. 1980; worked at Perm. Mission, UN, Geneva 1981; subsequent positions include Consul General, General Consulate in Johannesburg and Consul General, General Consulate in London (also Chief of Protocol); Amb. to Argentina 1995–99, to Israel 1999–2004, to Italy (also accred to Malta) 2004, currently Protocol Dir Ministry of Foreign Affairs.
Address: Ministry of Foreign Affairs, Odos Akadimias 3, 106 71 Athens, Greece (office). *Telephone:* (210) 3682700 (office). *Fax:* (210) 3624195 (office). *E-mail:* mfa@mfa.gr (office). *Website:* www.mfa.gr (office).

MIYAMOTO, Yuji, MA; Japanese diplomatist; *Ambassador to People's Republic of China;* b. 3 July 1946, Fukuoka; m.; one s. one d. *Education:*

Kyoto Univ., Harvard Univ. Grad. School of Arts and Sciences. *Career:* joined Ministry of Foreign Affairs 1969, worked in China and Mongolia Div. 1973–75, Devt Cooperation Div. 1975-78; First Sec., Perm. Mission to UN, New York 1978–81; First Sec., Embassy of Japan, Beijing 1981–83; Deputy Dir Soviet Union Div., Ministry of Foreign Affairs 1983–85, Dir of Arms Control and Disarmament 1985–87, Pvt. Sec. to Minister for Foreign Affairs 1987–89, Dir of Policy Planning Div. 1989–90, Dir of China and Mongolia Div. 1990–91; Research Assoc., IISS, London 1991–92; Sr Supervisor, Foreign Service Training Inst., Ministry of Foreign Affairs 1992, Vice-Pres. –1994; Consul Gen., Consulate Gen. of Japan, Atlanta, Ga, USA 1994–97; Minister to People's Repub. of China 1997, Minister Extraordinary and Plenipotentiary –2001; Dir-Gen. for Arms Control and Scientific Affairs 2001–02; Amb. to Myanmar 2002–04; Amb. in charge of Okinawan Affairs, Rep. of Govt of Japan 2004–06; Amb. to People's Repub. of China 2006–.
Address: Embassy of Japan, 7 Ri Tan Lu, Jian Guo Men Wai, Beijing 100600, People's Republic of China (office). *Telephone:* (10) 65322361 (office). *Fax:* (10) 65324625 (office).

MKAIMA, Miguel da Costa; Mozambican diplomatist; *Ambassador to Portugal; Education:* Univ. of Humboldt, Germany. *Career:* fmr Dir Nat. Art Museum; Minister of Culture 1999–2004; Amb. to Portugal 2005–.
Address: Embassy of Mozambique, Av. de Berna 7, 1050-036 Lisbon, Portugal (office). *Telephone:* (21) 7961672 (office). *Fax:* (21) 7932720 (office). *E-mail:* embamoc.portugal@minec.gov.mz (office).

MKAPA, Benjamin William, BA; Tanzanian politician, journalist and diplomatist; b. 12 Nov. 1938, Masasi; m. Anna Joseph Maro 1966; two s. *Education:* Makerere Univ. Coll. *Career:* Admin. Officer, Dist Officer 1962; Foreign Service Officer 1962; Man. Ed. Tanzania Nationalist and Uhuru 1966, The Daily News and The Sunday News 1972; Press Sec. to Pres. 1974; Founding Dir Tanzania News Agency 1976; High Commr in Nigeria 1976; Minister for Foreign Affairs 1977–80, for Information and Culture 1980–82; High Commr in Canada 1982–83; Amb. to USA 1983–84; Minister for Foreign Affairs 1984–90; MP for Nanyumbu 1985–95; Minister for Information and Broadcasting 1990–92, for Science, Tech. and Higher Educ. 1992–95; Pres. of Tanzania and C-in-C of Armed Forces 1995–2005; Chair. Chama Cha Mapinduzi (CCM) party 1996–2005; Dr hc (Soka Univ., Tokyo) 1998; Hon. DHumLitt (Morehouse Coll., Atlanta, USA) 1999.
Address: c/o Office of the President, PO Box 9120, Dar es Salaam, Tanzania.

MKULO, Mustapha; Tanzanian politician; *Minister of Finance, Planning, Economy and Empowerment; Career:* fmr Dir-Gen. Nat. Social Security Fund; Deputy Minister of Finance –2008, Minister of Finance, Planning, Economy and Empowerment 2008–.
Address: Ministry of Finance, Planning, Economy and Empowerment, PO Box 1154, Zanzibar, Tanzania (office). *Telephone:* (24) 231169 (office).

MLADENOV, Branimir; Bulgarian diplomatist; *Ambassador to Turkey; Career:* numerous postions at Ministry of Foreign Affairs including Third Sec., Turkish Desk, Balkan Dept, Head, Int. Humanitarian Orgs Dept., Consul Gen., Embassy in Istanbul; Amb. to Turkey 2006–.
Address: Embassy of Bulgaria, Atatürk Bul. 124, 06680 Kavaklıdere, Ankara, Turkey (office). *Telephone:* (312) 4672071 (office). *Fax:* (312) 4672574 (office). *E-mail:* bulemb@superonline.com (office).

MLADINEO, Mirjana; Croatian diplomatist; b. 15 Feb. 1946, Zagreb; m.; one d. *Education:* Univ. of Zagreb. *Career:* Counsellor to Repub. Cttee for Educ., Culture, Tech., Culture and Sports 1977–84; Asst Dir and Head of Dept, Repub. Admin for Scientific and Tech. Int. Cooperation 1984–91; Counsellor and Personal Sec. to Chief of Staff, Office of Pres. 1991–92; Minister Counsellor, Perm. Mission to UN, New York 1992–97; Nat. Coordinator for Cen. European Initiative 1997–99; Head, Office for European Integration 1999–2000, Deputy Minister for European Integration 2000–03, Head, Croatian Mission to EU 2003–05, Perm. Rep. to UN, New York 2005–08.
Address: Ministry of Foreign Affairs and European Integration, trg Nikole Šubića Zrinskog 7–8, 10000 Zagreb, Croatia (office). *Telephone:* (1) 4569964 (office). *Fax:* (1) 4551795 (office). *E-mail:* mvpei@mvpei.hr (office). *Website:* www.mvpei.hr (office).

MO'AMARY, Hamad H. al-; Omani diplomatist. *Career:* currently Amb. to Saudi Arabia.
Address: Embassy of Oman, POB 94381, Riyadh 11693, Saudi Arabia (office). *Telephone:* (1) 482-3120 (office). *Fax:* (1) 482-3738 (office).

MOCHAN, Charles Francis; British diplomatist (retd); b. 6 Aug. 1948; m. Ilse Mochan; one s. one d. *Career:* joined FCO 1967, Desk Officer, Econ.

Advisers 1967, Desk Officer, Consular Dept 1967–70, Vice-Consul, Port Elizabeth 1970–72, Entry Clearance Officer, Kingston 1972–74, Desk Officer, Accommodation/Services Dept, FCO 1974–77, Man. Officer, Seoul 1977–80, Desk Officer, Library and Records Dept, FCO 1980, full-time language training 1980–81, 1987, Second, later First Sec. (Commercial), Helsinki 1981–84, Desk Officer, Personnel Operations Dept, FCO 1985–87, Deputy High Commr, Port Louis 1988–91, Cen. European Dept, FCO 1991–93, Deputy Head of Training Wing 1993–95, Consul-Gen., Casablanca 1995–98, Amb. to Madagascar 1999–2002, High Commr to Fiji 2002–06.
Address: c/o Foreign and Commonwealth Office, King Charles Street, London, SW1A 2AH, England. *Telephone:* (20) 7008-1500.

MOCUMBI, Pascoal Manuel, MD; Mozambican medical doctor and fmr politician; *High Commissioner, European-Developing Countries Clinical Trials Programme (EDCTP);* b. 10 April 1941, Maputo; m. Adelina Isabel Bernardino Paindane 1970; two s. two d. *Education:* Lausanne Univ. of Lausanne. *Career:* founding mem. Frente de Libertação de Moçambique 1962, Rep. FRELIMO Algeria –1967, 1967–1974, Head, Information Dept; Dir José Macamo Hosp., Maputo 1976; Provincial Health Dir, Chief Medical Officer, Clinical Doctor Beira Central Hosp., Sofala 1976–80; Clinical Doctor Maputo Hosp. 1980–87; Asst Lecturer, Faculty of Health, Eduardo Mondlane Univ., Maputo 1984–85; mem. National Assembly, FRELIMO Political Cttee 1980–87, Minister of Health 1980–87, Minister of Foreign Affairs 1987–94; Prime Minister of Mozambique 1994–2004; High Commissioner, European-Developing Countries Clinical Trials Programme (EDCTP) 2004–.
Address: 1874 Av. Armando Tivane, Maputo, Mozambique (home). *Telephone:* (1) 495517 (home). *E-mail:* pascoal.mocumbi@tvcabo.co.mz (home).

MOE, Thorvald, PhD; Norwegian economist; *Deputy Secretary General, Ministry of Finance;* b. 4 Oct. 1939, Oslo; m. Nina Kjeldsberg 1968; one s. one d. *Education:* Stanford Univ. *Career:* held various sr posts in Ministry of Finance; Dir-Gen. Econ. Policy Dept Ministry of Finance 1978–86, Chief Econ. Adviser and Deputy Perm. Sec. 1989–97; Amb. to OECD 1986–89; Deputy Sec.-Gen. OECD 1998–2002; Deputy Sec. Gen. Ministry of Finance 2002–; Head Norwegian Del. to Econ. Policy Cttee at OECD 2002–.
Address: Ministry of Finance, Akersgt. 40, POB 8008, Dep., 0030 Oslo, Norway (office). *Telephone:* 22-24-90-90 (office). *Fax:* 22-24-95-10 (office). *E-mail:* arkiv.postmottak@finans.dep.no (office). *Website:* odin.dep.no/fin (office).

MOERMAN, Joséphine Rebecca (Fientje), LLM; Belgian politician and lawyer; *Deputy-Minister-President and Minister of the Economy and of Foreign Trade, Vlaamse Regering (Flemish Government);* b. 19 Oct. 1958, Ghent. *Education:* Univ. of Ghent Law Faculty, Harvard Univ. Law School. *Career:* lawyer, Cleary, Gottlieb, Steen & Hamilton, New York and Brussels 1982–84; Deputy Ed. Econs and Finance, Standaard 1984–85; Municipal Councillor, City of Ghent 1988–95, Alderman for Educ. 1995–99; Adviser to Pres. of France Valéry Giscard d'Estaing 1989–91, Chief Adviser for Institutional Reforms and Relations with Israel and Gulf States 1991–95; mem. Exec. Cttee, Flemish Liberal Party (VLD) 1991–93, 1997–, Sec.-Gen. 1999–2003; mem. Parl. 1999–2003; Minister of Economy, Energy, Foreign Trade and Science Policy 2003–04, of Foreign Trade 2003–04, also Vice-Minister-Pres.; Flemish Minister of Science Policy 2003–04, of the Economy 2004–, of Foreign Trade 2004–, also Deputy-Minister-Pres; mem. Council of European Liberals.
Address: Vlaamse Regering (Flemish Government), Boudewijnlaan 30, 1000 Brussels, Belgium (office). *Telephone:* (2) 553-29-11 (office). *Fax:* (2) 553-29-05 (office). *E-mail:* voorlichtingsambtenaar@vlaanderen.be (office). *Website:* www.vlaamseregering.be (office); www.fientjemoerman.be.

MOERSCH, Karl; German politician and journalist; b. 11 March 1926, Calw/Württemberg; m. Waltraut Schweikle 1947; one s. *Education:* Univ. of Tübingen. *Career:* journalist in Ludwigshafen, Bad Godesberg (Deutscher Forschungsdienst) and Frankfurt (Ed. of Die Gegenwart) 1956–58; Head of Press Dept, Freie Demokratische Partei (FDP) 1961–64; freelance journalist 1964–; fmr mem. Bundestag; Parl. Sec. of State, Minister of State, Ministry of Foreign Affairs 1970–76; mem. Exec. Bd of UNESCO 1980–85; Ludwig-Uhland Prize 1997. *Publications:* Kursrevision–Deutsche Politik nach Adenauer 1978, Europa für Anfänger 1979, Sind wir denn eine Nation? 1982, Bei uns im Staate Beutelsbach 1984, Geschichte der Pfalz 1987, Sueben, Württemberger und Franzosen 1991, Sperrige Landsleute 1996, Es geht seltsam zu – in Württemberg 1998, Immer wieder war's ein Abenteuer–Erinnerungen 2001, Kontrapunkt Baden-Württemberg 2002; and numerous newspaper articles, etc.
Address: Gebhard-Müller-Allee 14, 71638 Ludwigsburg, Germany. *Telephone:* (7141) 905745. *Fax:* (7141) 905643.

MOFAZ, Lt-Gen. Shaul, BA; Israeli politician and army officer; *Deputy Prime Minister and Minister of Transport;* b. 1948, Iran; m. Orit Mofaz; four c. *Education:* Bar-Ilan Univ., US Marine Corps Command and Staff Coll., Va, USA. *Career:* immigrated to Israel 1957; paratrooper, Israel Defense Forces (IDF) 1966, served in Six-Day War 1967; command positions in Paratroop Brigade; Commdr Paratroop Reconnaissance Unit 1973; Deputy Commdr Paratroop Brigade; infantry brigade commdr 1982; Commdr IDF Officers' School 1984; Commdr Paratroop Brigade 1986–88; promoted Brig.-Gen. 1988; Sr Officer Ground Corps Command 1988–90; Commdr Galilee Div. 1990–92; Commdr IDF forces in Judea and Samaria 1993–94; promoted Maj.-Gen. 1994; GOC Southern Command 1994–96; Chief of Planning Directorate Gen. Staff 1996–97; Deputy Chief Gen. Staff 1997; 16th Chief of Gen. Staff 1998–2002; Minister of Defence 2002–06; Deputy Prime Minister and Minister of Transport 2006–; left Likud party to join newly formed Kadima party Dec. 2005.
Address: Ministry of Transport, Government Complex, 5 Bank of Israel Street, Jerusalem, Israel (office). *Telephone:* 2-6663190 (office). *Fax:* 2-6663195 (office). *E-mail:* dover@mot.gov.il (office). *Website:* www.mot.gov.il (office).

MOHAMAD, Abdalmahmood Abdalhaleem, BSc, MSc, PhD; Sudanese diplomatist; *Permanent Representative, United Nations; Education:* Univ. of Khartoum, Ohio Univ., USA. *Career:* joined Ministry of Foreign Affairs 1975; mem. Perm. Mission to UN, New York 1982–86; posted to Embassy in Riyadh 1987–89; Deputy Head of Mission to Ethiopia 1990–95, Presidential envoy to Somalia 1994; Dir Africa Dept, Ministry of Foreign Affairs 1995–97, Dir of Tech. and Econ. Co-operation 1997–1999; Special Envoy to Afghanistan 2003; Amb. to India (also accred to Sri Lanka and Nepal) 2003–06; Perm. Rep. to UN, New York 2006–. *Publications include:* numerous journal articles.
Address: Permanent Mission of Sudan to the United Nations, 655 Third Avenue, Suite 500–510, New York, NY 10017, USA (office). *Telephone:* (212) 573-6033 (office). *Fax:* (212) 573-6160 (office). *E-mail:* sudan@un.int (office).

MOHAMMAD-NAJJAR, Mostafa; Iranian politician; *Minister of Defence and Armed Forces Logistics;* b. 1956. *Education:* Org. of Industrial Man. *Career:* trained as mechanical engineer; participated in suppression of Kurdish insurgency 1978–79; joined Islamic Revolution Guards Corps 1979, various logistical and admin. positions, Head of Expeditionary Force in Lebanon 1980s, Commdr of Guard Operations in Middle E region 1990s; Minister of Defence and Armed Forces Logistics 2005–; mem. Bd of Dirs Defence Industries Org.
Address: Ministry of Defence and Armed Forces Logistics, Shahid Yousuf Kaboli Street, Sayed Khandan Area, Tehran, Iran (office). *Telephone:* (21) 21401 (office). *Fax:* (21) 864008 (office). *E-mail:* info@mod.ir (office). *Website:* www.mod.ir (office).

MOHAMMED, Dato' Abdul Aziz; Malaysian diplomatist; *High Commissioner to UK;* m. Datin Munah Aziz Razak. *Career:* career diplomat with more than 30 years' experience, an expert on SE Asian relations with an ambassadorial posting in the Philippines, fmr Deputy Sec.-Gen., Ministry of Foreign Affairs, High Commr to UK 2003–.
Address: High Commission of Malaysia, 45–46 Belgrave Square, London, SW1X 8QT, England (office). *Telephone:* (20) 7235-8033 (office). *Fax:* (20) 7235-5161 (office). *E-mail:* mwlondon@btinternet.com (office).

MOHSIN, Selina; Bangladeshi educationalist, academic and diplomatist; *High Commissioner to the Maldives; Education:* various degrees and postgraduate diplomas and sr officer training from univs and int. insts in USA, France and UK. *Career:* joined Educ. Service of the then East Pakistan 1970; Chief Educ. Officer, Commonwealth Secr., London, UK 1990s; Sr Educ. Adviser to Programme Support Unit, Canadian Int. Devt Agency –2008; High Commr to the Maldives 2008–.
Address: Bangladesh High Commission, M. Kurinbee Lodge, 5th Floor, Izzudheen Magu, Malé, Maldives (office). *Telephone:* 3315541 (office). *Fax:* 3315543 (office). *E-mail:* bdootmal@dhivehinet.net.mv (office).

MOHTASHAMI, Ali Akbar, DTheol; Iranian politician; *Secretary-General, International Conference on Palestinian Intifada;* b. 30 Aug. 1946, Tehran; m. Fatemeh Mohtashami 1968; two s. five d. *Career:* studied theology in Iran and Iraq; mil. training in Palestinian camps, Lebanon; went to Paris with Ayatollah Khomeini 1978; returned to Iran and took part in overthrow of monarchy 1979; mem. political advisory office of Ayatollah Khomeini; Dir of Ayatollah's representative delegation in Foundation of the Oppressed 1980; mem. IRIB Supervisory Council 1980–81; Amb. to Syria 1981–85; a founder of Hezbollah in Lebanon; Minister of the Interior 1985; mem. Parl. 1989–91; Chair. Parl. Cttee on Defence; Sec.-Gen. IPU Group of Iran (Chair. 1989–91); mem. Cttee to Protect the Islamic Revolution of Palestine, Cen. Council of Combatant Clergy; Sec.-Gen. of

Int. Conf. on Intifada; Deputy Chair. Bd of Trustees Qods Inst.; Social Adviser to Pres. of Iran; Man. Bayan newspaper (banned June 2000). *Publications include:* Plurality, From Iran to Iran (Memoirs) 1965–79. *Address:* General Secretariat of International Conference on Palestinian Intifada, 11 Khorshid Street, Pastor Avenue, Tehran (office); Islamic Consultative Assembly, Tehran (office); 11, Adib-ol-Mamalek Street, Ray Street, Tehran, Iran (home). *Telephone:* (21) 6135672 (office); (21) 361892 (home). *Fax:* (21) 6460046 (office). *E-mail:* info@gods-path.org (office). *Website:* www.gods-path.org (office).

MOÏSI, Dominique; French professor of international relations; *Deputy Director, Institut français des relations internationales;* b. 21 Oct. 1946, Neuilly-sur-Seine; m. Diana Pinto-Moïsi 1977; two s. *Education:* Lycée Buffon, Paris, Institut d'études politiques, Paris, Faculté de droit de Paris, Harvard Univ., USA. *Career:* Visiting Lecturer, Hebrew Univ. of Jerusalem 1973–75; Asst Lecturer, Univ. of Paris X 1975–89; Deputy Dir Inst français des relations internationales 1979–; Lecturer, Ecole Nationale d'Admin 1980–85, Ecole des hautes études en sciences sociales 1988–; Sec.-Gen. Groupe d'étude et de recherche des problèmes internationaux 1975–78; Assoc. Prof., Johns Hopkins Univ. European Centre, Bologna 1983–84; Visiting Prof., Collège d'Europe, Warsaw, Poland; Ed. Politique étrangère 1983–; Prof., Inst. d'études politiques, Paris; mem. Bd of Dirs Salzburg Seminar, Aspen Inst., Berlin; editorial writer for Financial Times and Die Zeit. *Publications include:* Crises et guerres au XXe siècle: analogies et différences 1981, Le nouveau continent: plaidoyer pour une Europe renaissante (with Jacques Rupnik) 1991, Les cartes de la France à l'heure de la mondialisation (jtly) 2000, Politique étrangère (jtly) 2003.
Address: Institut français des relations internationales (IFRI), 27 rue de la Procession, 75015 Paris (office); 4 rue Saint-Florentin, 75001 Paris, France (home). *Telephone:* 1-40-61-60-00 (office). *Fax:* 1-40-61-60-60 (office). *E-mail:* moisi@ifri.org (office). *Website:* www.ifri.org (home).

MOISIU, Alfred; Albanian fmr head of state; b. 1 Dec. 1929, Shkodër; m. (wife deceased); one s. three d. *Education:* High School of Tirana, mil. eng school in Leningrad (now St Petersburg) and Acad. of Mil. Eng, Moscow, USSR, Defence Acad., Tirana, NATO Mil. Coll. Rome, Italy. *Career:* participant in Nat. Liberation War 1943–45; platoon commdr, Jt Officers' School, Tirana 1948–49; Instructor, Skanderbeg Mil. Acad., Tirana 1949–51; assigned to Eng Directory, Ministry of Defence 1958–66; Commdr Pontoon Brigade, Kavaja 1966–71; Head of Eng and Fortification Directory, Ministry of Defence 1971–81; Deputy Minister of Defence 1981–82, Minister 1991–92, Adviser on Defence 1992–94, Vice-Minister of Defence for the Defence Policy 1994–97; Commdr of Eng Co., Burrel 1982–84; Pres. of Albania 2002–07; Pres. Albanian Atlantic Asscn (pro-NATO NGO) 1994; Freeman of Bajram Curri, of Bari, Italy; Order of the Red Star, Order for Mil. Services, Skanderbeg Order (2nd Class), Order of St Michael (UK), Order of St George (UK); Dr of Mil. Sciences 1979; Medal for Mil. Services, Medal of Liberation, Medal of the 10th Army Anniversary. *Publications:* has published many articles and studies in Albania and abroad on mil. affairs, defence and regional security policy, and about events in Kosovo.
Address: c/o Office of the President, Bulevardi Dëshmorët e Kombit, Tirana, Albania (office).

MOLEBOGE, Norman; Botswana diplomatist and fmr police officer; *High Commissioner to Namibia; Career:* joined Botswana Police Force 1967, fmr Commr (retd 2004); High Commr to Namibia 2004–; fmr Chair. Southern African Regional Police Chiefs' Co-operation Org., World Regional Chair. for Sub-Saharan Africa, Int. Asscn for Chiefs of Police –2004.
Address: Botswana High Commission, 101 Nelson Mandela Avenue, POB 20359, Windhoek, Namibia (office). *Telephone:* (61) 221942 (office). *Fax:* (61) 221948 (office).

MOLINA CONTRERAS, Gen. Jorge Alberto; Salvadorean army officer and politician; *Minister of National Defence; Career:* Del. to UN Conf. to Review Progress made in Implementation of Programme of Action to Prevent, Combat and Eradicate the Illicit Trade in Small Arms and Light Weapons in All Its Aspects, New York 2006; fmr Jt Chief of Staff of the Armed Forces; Minister of Nat. Defence 2008–; rank of Brig.-Gen. 2005, Maj.-Gen. 2006, Gen. 2007.
Address: Ministry of National Defence, Alameda Dr Manuel E. Araújo, Km 5, Carretera a Santa Tecla, San Salvador, El Salvador (office). *Telephone:* 2250-0100 (office); 2250-0325 (office). *E-mail:* fuerzaarmada@faes.gob.sv (office). *Website:* www.fuerzaarmada.gob.sv (office).

MØLLER, Michael, BA, MA; Danish UN official and diplomatist. *Education:* Univ. of Sussex, UK, Johns Hopkins Univ., USA. *Career:* joined UN 1979, served as Programme Officer, Legal Officer, Asst to Dir Div. of Int. Protection, and Asst Regional Rep., Office of UNHCR 1979–84, Political Adviser to UN Mil. Inspection Team in Iran 1985, Inter-Agency Affairs

Officer and Special Asst to Asst Sec.-Gen., Office for Secr. Services for Econ. and Social Matters 1985–87, Head of Sub-Office for Southern Mexico, Office of UNHCR 1987–88, Special Asst to Asst Sec.-Gen., Centre Against Apartheid, Dept for Political and Security Council Affairs 1988–92, Special Asst to Asst Sec.-Gen., Dept of Political Affairs (DPA) 1992, Deputy Dir Americas Div., DPA 1992–93, Head of UN Component in Jt UN/OAS Int. Civilian Mission to Haiti (MICIVIH) 1993, Head of Office of Special Adviser to Sec.-Gen. 1994–95, Sr Political Adviser to Dir-Gen. UN Office, Geneva 1995–97, Special Asst to Under-Sec.-Gen. for Political Affairs, UN Secr. 1997–2001, Dir for Political, Peacekeeping and Humanitarian Affairs, Exec. Office of Sec.-Gen. 2001–05, Acting Deputy Chef de Cabinet to Sec.-Gen. March 2005, Special Rep. for Cyprus and Head of UN Peacekeeping Operation in Cyprus (UNFICYP) 2005–08.
Address: c/o Ministry of Foreign Affairs, Asiatisk Pl. 2, 1448 Copenhagen K, Denmark (office).

MOLLER, Patricia N.; American diplomatist; *Ambassador to Burundi;* m. Gilbert Sperling. *Career:* worked for ten years as investment banker and tax shelter specialist with Smith Barney; career mem. Sr Foreign Service, joined State Dept as Foreign Service Officer 1987, assigned to Consular Section in Munich 1987–89, Man. Officer, Consulate Gen., Madras 1989–91, Watch Officer, then Staff Aide to Asst Sec. for Intelligence and Research, Dept of State 1991–96, Vietnam Desk Officer 1997, Serbian language training 1998, Man. Officer, Embassy in Belgrade 1998–99, Deputy Chief of Mission, Yerevan, Armenia 2000–02, Tbilisi, Georgia 2002–05, Amb. to Burundi 2006–; three Superior Honor Awards, Leamon R. Hunt Award for Admin Excellence 2000.
Address: Embassy of the USA, avenue des Etats-Unis, BP 1720, Bujumbura, Burundi (office). *Telephone:* 223454 (office). *Fax:* 222926 (office). *E-mail:* mollerpn@hotmail.com (home). *Website:* bujumbura .usembassy.gov (office).

MØLLER, Per Stig, MA, PhD; Danish politician; *Minister for Foreign Affairs;* b. 1942. *Education:* Univ. of Copenhagen. *Career:* Lecturer, Sorbonne Univ., Paris 1974–76; Cultural Ed. Radio Denmark 1973–74, Deputy Head, Culture and Soc. Dept 1976–79, Chief of Programmes 1979–84; Vice-Chair. Radio Council 1985–86, Chair. 1986–87; Commentator, Berlingske Tidende 1984–2001; Chair. Popular Educ. Asscn (FOF) 1983–89; mem. Parl. (Danish Conservative Party) 1984–, mem. Exec. Cttee 1985–89, 1993–98, Chair. 1997–98, Parl. Leader 1997–98, Foreign Policy Spokesman 1998–2001; mem. Council of Europe 1987–90, 1994–97, 1998–2001; Minister for the Environment 1990–93; Chair. Security Policy Cttee 1994–96, mem. Foreign Policy Cttee 1994–2001; Minister for Foreign Affairs 2001–; Nat. Chair. Union of Conservative Gymnasium Students 1960–61, Vice-Chair. Conservative Students' Asscn 1961–62, Pres. Students' Union; Chevalier, Ordre Nat. du Lion 1975, Chevalier des Arts et des Lettres 1986, Grosskreuz des Verdienstordens der Bundesrepublik Deutschland 2002, Commdr of the first class of the Order of the Dannebrog 2002, Commdr, Ordre Nat. du Benin 2003, Grand-Croix de l'Ordre de la Couronne de Chêne 2003, Order of Stara Planina (1st Class) 2006; Sound and Environment Award 1993, Georg Brandes Award 1996, Einer Hansen Research Fund Award 1997, G-1930s Politician of the Year 1997, Cultural Award of the Popular Educ. Asscn 1998, Raoul Wallenberg Medal 1998, Kaj Munk Award 2001, Rosenkjaer Award 2001, Robert Schumann Medal 2003, Nersornaat Medal of Merit in Gold 2005. *Publications include:* La Critique dramatique et littéraire de Malte-Brun 1971, Erotismen 1973, København-Paris (trans.) 1973, På Sporet af det forsvundne Menneske 1976, Livet I Gøgereden 1978, Fra Tid til Anden 1979, Tro, Håb og Faellesskab 1980, Midt I Redeligheden 1981, Orwells Håb og Frygt 1983, Nat uden Daggry 1985, Mulighedernes Samfund 1985, Stemmer fra Øst 1987, Historien om Estland, Letland og Litauen 1990, Kurs mod Katastrofer? 1993, Miljøproblemer 1995, Den naturlige Orden: Tolv år der flyttede Verden 1996, Spor: Udvalgte Skrifter om det åbne Samfund og dets Vaerdier 1997, Magt og Afmagt 1999, Munk 2000, Mere Munk 2003.
Address: Ministry of Foreign Affairs, Asiatisk Plads 2, 1448 Copenhagen K, Denmark (office). *Telephone:* 33-92-00-00 (office). *Fax:* 32-54-05-33 (office). *E-mail:* um@um.dk (office). *Website:* www.um.dk (office).

MOLOMO, Motlhagodi, BSc; Botswana pharmacist and diplomatist; *High Commissioner to South Africa;* *Education:* Sunderland Polytechnic, UK. *Career:* pharmacist, St George's Hospital, London 1977–78; with Ministry of Health 1978–82; Chair. Kgatleng Dist Council 2000–04; High Commr to S Africa 2007–; mem. Cen. Cttee Botswana Democratic Party –2007 (resgnd); fmr Chair. Agric. Marketing Bd, Confed. of Mill Owners Asscn; mem. Pharmaceutical Soc. of Botswana.
Address: High Commission of Botswana, 24 Amos Street, Colbyn, Pretoria 0083, South Africa (office). *Telephone:* (12) 4309640 (office). *Fax:* (12) 3421845 (office).

MOLTERER, Wilhelm, MSc; Austrian politician; *Vice-Chancellor and Federal Minister of Finance;* b. 14 May 1955, Steyr; m. Brigitte Molterer; two c. *Education:* Fed. Agricultural Coll., St Florian and Johannes Kepler Univ., Linz. *Career:* Research Asst Dept of Agric. Policy, Univ. of Linz 1979–81; Head Econ. Policy Div., Austrian Farmers Fed. 1981–84, Dir 1989–93; Municipal Councillor, Sierning 1985–87; Sec. Office of Fed. Minister Dr. Josef Riegler 1987–89; mem. Nat. Council 1990–94; Sec. –Gen. Austria People's Party (ÖAP) 1993–94, Parl. Group Leader 2003–07; Fed. Minister of Agric. and Forestry 1994–2003 (and Environment and Water Man. 2000–03), of Finance 2007–, Vice-Chancellor of Austria 2007–.
Address: Ministry of Finance, Himmelpfortgasse 8, Vienna 1015, Austria (office). *Telephone:* (1) 514-33 (office). *Fax:* (1) 512-62-00 (office). *E-mail:* wilhelm.molterer@bmf.gv.at (office). *Website:* www.bmf.gv.at (office).

MOLYVIATIS, Petros; Greek diplomatist and politician; b. 12 June 1928, Chios; m. Niovi Christaki; one d. one s. *Education:* Univ. of Athens. *Career:* Gen. Sec. Presidency of the Repub. 1980–85, 1990–95, fmr Diplomatic Adviser to the Pres.; mem. Parl. 1996–, fmr mem. Standing Cttees on Defence, Foreign Affairs, European Affairs; fmr mem. Greek dels to UN, NATO; fmr Amb.; Minister of Foreign Affairs 2004–06.
Address: c/o Ministry of Foreign Affairs, Odos Akadimias 1, 106 71 Athens, Greece (office).

MOMBOULI, Serge; Republic of the Congo business executive and diplomatist; *Ambassador to USA;* b. 1959, Pointe-Noire; m.; six c. *Career:* trained in corp. law and business negotiations; joined Corp. Sales Dept, Air Afrique, Paris; Vice-Pres. A.W.E. Group, Houston, USA; Vice-Pres. Int. Operations and Project Devt, Transworld Consortium Corpn, Houston 1995–97; Spokesman for Repub. of the Congo Pres. Denis Sassou N'Guesso in USA 1997–; Chargé d'affaires a.i. in Washington, DC 1997–2001, Amb. to USA 2001–.
Address: Embassy of the Republic of the Congo, 4891 Colorado Avenue, NW, Washington, DC 20011, USA (office). *Telephone:* (202) 726-5500 (office). *Fax:* (202) 726-1860 (office). *E-mail:* info@embassyofcongo.org (office). *Website:* www.embassyofcongo.org (office).

MONCADA, Samuel, PhD; Venezuelan academic, politician and diplomatist; *Ambassador to UK;* b. 13 June 1959; m. Nelci Marin de Moncada. *Education:* Universidad Cen. de Venezuela, Caracas, Venezuelan Mil. Acad., Caracas, Boston Coll., USA, St Anthony's Coll., Oxford, UK. *Career:* Prof., Faculty of Mil. History, Venezuelan Mil. Acad. 1982–84, Head of Faculty of Polemology 1984–87; Assoc. mem. St Anthony's Coll., Univ. of Oxford 1990; Prof. of MBA Programme in History of America, Faculty of Humanities and Educ., Post-grad. Section, Universidad Cen. de Venezuela 1996, Prof. of PhD Programme in Political Sciences, Faculty of Political and Admin. Sciences, Post-grad. Studies Section 1997, Head of Faculty of History of America, Faculty of Humanities and Educ., School of History 1994, Head of Dept of History Theory and Practice 1998, Dir School of History 1999–2004; Minister of Higher Educ. 2004–07; Amb. to UK (also accred to Ireland) 2007–; Head of Div. of Int. Affairs for electoral campaign of Pres. Hugo Rafael Chavez for the Referendum 2004; lecturer at several nat. and int. univs in Latin America, N America and Europe; mem. Commando Maisanta; Order of the First Class General Francisco de Miranda 2007; Dr hc (Univ. of Yacambu) 2005; Magister Honoris (Inst. of Higher Studies of the Nat. Defence—IAEDEN) 2005. *Radio:* producer of programme Combates por la Historia (Battles for History), Station YVKE 2002–. *Publications:* Partidos Políticos y Sindicatos en Venezuela (1936–1950) (co-author) 1982, Los Huevos de la Serpiente (Fedecámaras por dentro) 1984, Organizaciones Empresariales. Diccionario Histórico de Venezuela 1988, Momentos Decisivos en la Historia de la Asamblea Nacional. Poder Legislativo: Pasado, Presente y Futuro 2000, Vigencia del Pensamiento Bolivariano 2003, Las Relaciones Internacionales de la Revolución Bolivariana 2004, Las inmigraciones en Venezuela durante el siglo XX y la Redefinición de la Identidad Nacional 2005, Historia del Racismo en Venezuela 2005, Los Problemas de la Democracia en el siglo XX Venezolano 2006; numerous articles in Venezuelan and Latin American newspapers and magazines.
Address: Embassy of Venezuela, 1 Cromwell Road, London, SW7 2HW, England (office). *Telephone:* (20) 7584-4206 (office); (20) 7584-5375 (office). *Fax:* (20) 7589-8887 (office). *E-mail:* ambassador@venezlon.co.uk (office). *Website:* www.venezlon.co.uk (office).

MONGELLA, Gertrude; Tanzanian international organization official; *President, Pan African Parliament (PAP);* four c. *Education:* Univ. of Dar Es Salaam. *Career:* fmr teacher and politician; fmr Amb. to India; mem. staff UN, Chair. Fourth UN Conf. on the Status of Women, Beijing 1995; Head of African Union's election monitoring team, Zimbabwe presidential election 2002; first Pres., Pan African Parl. (PAP) 2004–.
Address: c/o African Union Headquarters, PO Box 3243, Roosvelt Street (Old Airport Area), W21K19 Addis Ababa, Ethiopia. *Telephone:* (1) 51 77

00 (office). *Fax:* (1) 51 78 44 (office). *Website:* www.africa-union.org (office).

MONKS, John Stephen, BA; British trade union official; *Secretary-General, European Trade Union Confederation;* b. 5 Oct. 1945, Manchester; m. Francine Jacqueline Schenk 1970; two s. one d. *Education:* Univ. of Nottingham. *Career:* joined TUC Org. Dept 1969, Asst Sec. Employment and Manpower Section 1974, Head Org., Employment Law and Industrial Relations Dept 1977–87, Deputy Gen.-Sec. 1987–93, Gen.-Sec. 1993–2003; Sec.-Gen. European Trade Union Confed. (ETUC) 2003–; mem. Council Advisory, Conciliation and Arbitration Service (ACAS) 1979–95; mem. British Govt and EU Competitiveness Councils 1997; Visiting Prof., School of Man., Manchester Business School 1996–; Trustee People's History Museum 1988–, Chair. 2005–; Dr hc (Nottingham, UMIST, Salford, Cranfield, Cardiff, Kingston, Southampton and Open Univs). *Address:* European Trade Union Confederation, 5 Boulevard Roi Albert II, 1210 Brussels, Belgium. *Telephone:* (2) 224-04-11. *Fax:* (2) 224-04-54. *E-mail:* etuc@etuc.org (office). *Website:* www.etuc.org (office).

MONNOU, Edgar-Yves; Benin diplomatist and politician; *Ambassador to France;* b. 1953; m. Virginie Monnou. *Career:* Minister of Foreign Affairs 1995–96, currently Amb. to France (also accred to UK 2004–). *Address:* Embassy of Benin, 87 avenue Victor Hugo, 75116 Paris, France (office). *Telephone:* 1-45-00-98-82 (office). *Fax:* 1-45-01-82-02 (office). *E-mail:* ambassade@ambassade-benin.org (office). *Website:* www.ambassade-benin.org (office).

MONROE, William T., BA, MA; American diplomatist; m. Benedicte du Cheyron d'Abzac; two s. one d. *Education:* Stanford Univ. and The Fletcher School of Law and Diplomacy. *Career:* joined the Foreign Service in 1978, has served in various positions at US Embassies in Egypt, Iraq, Burma, Oman, China, Singapore, Kuwait and Pakistan, Int. Trade Specialist, Dept of Commerce, worked in Bureau of Political-Mil. Affairs and Bureau of E Asia and Pacific Affairs, Dept of State, Arabic language training in Tunis and Chinese in Taipei, Deputy Chief of Mission, Embassy in Kuwait –2002, Embassy in Islamabad 2002–04, Amb. to Bahrain 2004–07; Cordell Hull Award for Economic Achievement by Sr Officers, State Dept 2008. *Address:* US Department of State, 2201 C Street NW, Washington, DC 20520, USA (office). *Telephone:* (202) 647-4000 (office). *Fax:* (202) 647-6738 (office). *Website:* www.state.gov (office).

MONTEIRO, António Isaac; Guinea-Bissau politician. *Career:* fmr Minister of Rural Devt and Agric.; fmr Del. to FAO; Minister of Foreign Affairs, Int. Co-operation and Communities 2005–07. *Address:* c/o Ministry of Foreign Affairs, International Co-operation and Communities, Rua Gen. Omar Torrijo, Bissau, Guinea-Bissau (office).

MONTEIRO, António Victor Martins; Portuguese diplomatist; *Ambassador to France;* b. 22 Jan. 1944, Angola; m.; two d. *Education:* Univ. of Lisbon. *Career:* Perm. Rep. to FAO 1978; Deputy Chief of Protocol, Ministry of Foreign Affairs 1979; joined Perm. Mission to UN 1981, apptd Deputy Perm. Rep. 1984; Chief of Cabinet, Sec. of State for Foreign Affairs and Co-operation 1987; Head of Temporary Mission for Peace Process Structures in Angola 1991, Rep. to Jt Political and Mil. Comm.; Dir-Gen. for Political and Econ. Affairs 1993, Dir-Gen. for External Policy 1994; apptd Perm. Rep. to UN 1996; Co-ordinator Cttee for Perm. Co-ordination of the Community of Portuguese-Speaking Countries 1996; Amb. to France –2004; Minister of Foreign Affairs and Portuguese Communities Abroad 2004–05; High Rep. of the UN for Elections in Côte d'Ivoire 2005; Amb. to France 2006–. *Address:* Embassy of Portugal, 3 rue de Noisiel, 75116 Paris, France (office); Rua Joao de Deus, No. 15–2E, 1200-694 Lisbon, Portugal (home). *Telephone:* 1-47-27-35-29 (office); (21) 3870313 (home). *Fax:* 1-44-05-94-02 (office). *E-mail:* avmmonteiro@hotmail.com (home); mailto@embaixada-portugal-fr.org (office). *Website:* www.embaixada-portugal-fr.org (office).

MONTGOMERY, William D., BA, MBA; American diplomatist; b. 8 Nov. 1945, Carthage, Mo.; m. Lynne Germain; one s. two d. *Education:* Buckness and George Washington Univs, Nat. War Coll. *Career:* served US Army 1967–70; joined Foreign Service 1974, Econ.-Commercial Officer, Belgrade, Commercial Officer, Moscow, Political Officer, Moscow, Deputy Chief of Mission, Dar es Salaam; several posts in Dept of State; Deputy Chief of Mission, Sofia 1989–91; Amb. to Bulgaria 1993–96; Special Adviser to Pres. and Sec. of State for Bosnian Peace Implementation 1996–97; Amb. to Croatia 1998–2000, to Yugoslavia 2000–01, to Serbia and Montenegro 2001–04 (retd); several Army decorations including Bronze Star; Distinguished Honor Award and other awards from Dept of State; Order of Prince Trpimir, Croatia, Order of Star Planina, First Class, Bulgaria, Order of Madara Horseman, First Class, Bulgaria.

Address: c/o Department of State, 2201 C Street, NW, Washington, DC 20520, USA.

MONTILLA AGUILERA, Jose, LLB; Spanish politician; *President,Government of Catalonia;* b. 15 Jan. 1955, Iznázar, Cordoba; m.; five c. *Education:* Univ. of Barcelona. *Career:* mem. Partit dels Socialistes de Catalunya (PSC) 1978–, mem. Exec. Comm. 1987–, Sec. 1994, First Sec. 2000; mem. City Council, Sant Joan Despí 1979–83; mem. Council and Mayor, Cornellá de Llobregat 1983–2004; Second Vice-Pres., Barcelona Del. 1987–95, First Vice-Pres. 1999; Deputy, Barcelona Congress 2004–; Minister of Industry, Tourism and Trade 2004–06; Pres. Govt of Catalonia 2006–. *Address:* Government of Catalonia, Plaça de Sant Jaume 4, 08002 Barcelona, Spain (office). *Telephone:* (93) 4024600 (office). *Fax:* (93) 3183488 (office). *E-mail:* gbpresident.presidencia@gencat.cat (office). *Website:* http://www.gencat.cat/president (office).

MONYAKE, Lengolo Bureng, MSc, UED; Lesotho government official; b. 1 April 1930, Lesotho; m. Molulela Mapetla 1957; two s. one d. *Education:* Fort Hare Univ. Coll., Univ. of Toronto, Carleton Univ., London School of Econs. *Career:* Headmaster, Jordan High School 1958–61; Dir of Statistics, Govt of Lesotho 1968–74, Perm. Sec. 1974–76, Deputy Sr Perm. Sec. 1976–78; Amb. 1979–83; Man. Dir Lesotho Nat. Devt Corpn 1984–86; Minister for Foreign Affairs 1986–88, for Works 1988; Alt. Exec. Dir IMF 1988–90, Exec. Dir 1990–92; Deputy Exec. Sec. Southern African Devt Community 1993–98; currently with African Peer Review Mechanism (APRM), Lesotho; also currently Pres. Eighteenth Episcopal Dist, Connectional Lay Org., African Methodist Episcopal Church, Lesotho. *Address:* PO Box 526, Maseruloo, Lesotho, South Africa. *E-mail:* lmonyake@amec-connectionallay.org.

MOON, Richard Bartlett (Bart), MA; American diplomatist and publisher; *Publisher, American Diplomacy;* b. 16 Nov. 1930, St Joseph, Mo.; m. Calista Moon; one s. one d. *Education:* Univ. of Missouri, Univ. of California, Berkeley, Columbia Univ., New York, US Naval War Coll. *Career:* USAF Officer, Korean War 1954–56; entered US Foreign Service 1956; overseas assignments in Paris, Antananarivo, Quito, Maracaibo, San Jose, Caracas, Panama 1956–80; Deputy Chief of Mission and Chargé d'Affaires in Caracas 1980–84; Political Adviser to C-in-C Southern Command, Panama 1984–87; served as Political Adviser to US Amb. to OAS, Dir Office of Performance Evaluation, Dept of State, Sr Foreign Service Inspector; retd Minister Counsellor 1992; Pres. Hispanic Liaison (charity) 1996–97; currently Publr American Diplomacy (electronic journal), also mem. Bd of Dirs; mem. American Foreign Service Asscn, Diplomatic and Consular Officers Retd (DACOR), Nat. Alliance for the Mentally Ill, Triangle Inst. for Security Studies; Orden de Francisco de Miranda (Venezuela) 1984; Dept of Defense Outstanding Civilian Service Medal 1987, Dept of State Superior Service Award. *Publication:* contrib to American Diplomacy 2006, 2007. *Address:* 609 Fearrington Post, Fearrington Village, Pittsboro, NC 27312 (home); PO Box 3114, Chapel Hill, NC 27515, USA (office). *Telephone:* (919) 542-6976 (office). *E-mail:* publisher@americandiplomacy.org (office). *Website:* www.americandiplomacy.org (office).

MOON, Richard John; British diplomatist; *Ambassador to Latvia;* m. Sandra Sheila Francis Eddis; one s. one d. *Career:* joined FCO 1983, Second Sec. (Political), Jakarta 1984–88, EU Dept (Internal), FCO 1988–90, Head of Section, Security Policy Dept 1990–92, First Sec. (Political Affairs), Rome 1993–95, First Sec. (Econ./EU Affairs), Rome 1995–97; Deputy Head of EU Directorate (Internal), FCO 1997–99, Finance Counsellor, later mem. UN Advisory Cttee on Admin. and Budgetary Questions; served at Perm. Mission to UN, New York 1999–2004; Deputy Perm. Rep. to OECD, Paris 2005–07; Amb. to Latvia 2007–. *Address:* British Embassy, J. Alunana iela 5, Riga 1010, Latvia (office). *Telephone:* 6777-4700 (office). *Fax:* 6777-4707 (office). *E-mail:* british.embassy@apollo.lv (office). *Website:* www.britain.lv (office).

MOORE, Margaret, PhD; Canadian academic; *Professor of Political Studies, Queen's University;* m. John McGarry; two s. one d. *Education:* London School of Econs, UK. *Career:* Prof. of Political Science, York Univ. 1990–93, Univ. of Waterloo 1993–2002; Prof., Dept of Political Studies, Queen's Univ., Kingston, Ont. 2002–. *Publications:* Foundations of Liberalism 1993, National Self-Determination and Secession (ed.) 1998, Ethics of Nationalism 2001, Nations, States and Borders: Diverse Ethical Theories (co-ed.) 2003; chapters in books and articles in professional journals. *Address:* Mackintosh-Corry Hall, Room C400, Department of Political Studies, Queen's University, 99 University Avenue, Kingston, ON K7L 3N6, Canada (office). *Telephone:* (613) 533-6126 (office). *Fax:* (613) 533-

6848 (office). *E-mail:* margaret.moore@queensu.ca (office). *Website:* www
.queensu.ca (office).

MOORE, Rt Hon. Michael Kenneth, PC, MP; New Zealand politician and
international organization official; b. 28 Jan. 1949, Whakatane; m. Yvonne
Dereaney 1975. *Career:* fmr social worker, printer etc.; MP for Eden
1972–75, Papanui, Christchurch 1978–84, Christchurch N 1984–96,
Waimakariri 1996–99; Minister of Overseas Trade and Marketing, also
Minister of Tourism and Publicity and of Recreation and Sport 1984–87;
Minister of Overseas Trade and Marketing and of Publicity 1987–88,
1989–90, of External Relations and Int. Trade 1988–90; Minister of Foreign
Affairs Jan.–Oct. 1990; Prime Minister Sept.–Oct. 1990; Leader of the
Opposition 1990–93; fmr Assoc. Minister of Finance; Dir-Gen. WTO
1999–2002. *Publications include:* A Pacific Parliament, Hard Labour,
Fighting for New Zealand 1993, Children of the Poor 1996, A Brief History
of the Future 1998.
Address: c/o Privy Council, Government of New Zealand, Parliament
Buildings, Wellington, New Zealand.

MOORE, Roderick W., BA, MA; American diplomatist; *Ambassador to
Montenegro; Education:* Brown Univ. *Career:* career mem. Sr Foreign
Service, diplomatic postings at Embassies in Port-au-Prince 1988–89 and
Sofia 1990–92; worked in State Dept's Operations Center, Washington, DC
1992, Dept of State's Rep. in Skopje 1992–93; Political-Mil. Officer for all
states in Cen. and Eastern Europe, Dept of State 1993–95; Sr Political
Adviser, OSCE Mission in Sarajevo 1996; Political-Econ. Counselor,
Zagreb 1996–99;, State Dept Fellow, Fletcher School of Law and
Diplomacy, Tufts Univ. 1999–2000, taught about US policy towards fmr
Yugoslavia; Deputy Chief of Mission, Sofia 2000–03, Deputy Chief of
Mission, Belgrade 2004–07, Amb. to Montenegro 2007–.
Address: US Embassy, Ljubljanska bb, 81000 Podgorica, Montenegro
(office). *Telephone:* (81) 225417 (office). *Fax:* (81) 241358 (office). *E-mail:*
PodgoricaACS@state.gov (office). *Website:* podgorica.usembassy.gov
(office).

MORA-ANDA, Eduardo; Ecuadorean diplomatist; *Ambassador to Brazil;
Education:* Center for American and Int. Law, Tex., USA. *Career:*
attorney, later Deputy Sec. for Multilateral Political Affairs, Ministry of
Foreign Relations 1990s; Amb. to Brazil 2004–.
Address: Embassy of Ecuador, SHIS, QI 11, Conj. 09, Casa 24, 71625-290
Brasília, DF, Brazil (office). *Telephone:* (61) 3248-5560 (office). *Fax:* (61)
3248-1290 (office). *E-mail:* embeq@solar.com.br (office).

MORA RODAS, Nelson Alcides, Dr en Derecho; Paraguayan lawyer, politician
and academic. *Education:* Nat. Coll. of the Capital, Faculty of Social
Sciences, Nat. Univ. of Asunción, Catholic Univ. of Colombia, Bogotá,
Univ. of Salamanca, Spain, Colegio Mayor de Nuestra Sra. del Rosario,
Bogotá, Nat. War Coll., Asunción. *Career:* Titular Prof. of Criminal
Procedural Law, Catholic Univ., Villarrica; taught classes, courses and held
confs at Nat. Univ. of Asunción, Visiting Prof., Faculty of Law and Social
Sciences; fmr civil employee, Ministry of Justice and Labour; fmr Sec. of
Court; fmr solicitor for Prosecutor Gen.; fmr Judge of First Instance in
Penal and Civil Law; mem. Court of Criminal Appeal; Amb. to Colombia
1995–2003; Solicitor Gen. 2003–04; Minister of the Interior 2004–05, of
Nat. Defence 2007–08; mem. Asoc. Nacional Republicana–Partido Color-
ado (Nat. Republican AssCn–Colorado Party); Degree of Grand Cross
'Academic Excellence', the Hispano-American Acad. of Sciences and
Letters and Univ. Piloto of Colombia, Bogotá 1997, Grand Cross of
Boyacá (Colombia) 2003. *Publications:* Amarras fraternas, Colombia
Paraguay 1999, Delincuencias Internacional Organizada. Drogas. Narco-
tráfico. Espacio Judicial Común 2000, Código Penal Paraguayo, Doctrina,
Comentarios, Concordancias, Leyes Especiales 2000, Cerca del amanecer
2001.
Address: Asociación Nacional Republicana–Partido Colorado, Casa de los
Colorados, 25 de Mayo 842, Asunción, Paraguay (office). *Telephone:* (21)
44-4137 (office). *Fax:* (21) 49-7857 (office). *Website:* www.anr.org.py
(office).

MORAES CABRAL, José Filipe; Portuguese diplomatist; *Ambassador to
Spain; Career:* Counsellor to Pres. –1999; apptd Amb. to Israel 2000; Chief
of Civil Household of Pres. –2005; Amb. to Spain 2005–.
Address: Embassy of Portugal, Calle Pinar 1, 28006 Madrid, Spain (office).
Telephone: (91) 7824960 (office). *Fax:* (91) 7824972 (office). *E-mail:*
embmadrid@emb-portugal.es (office). *Website:* www.embajadaportugal
-madrid.org (office).

MORAIS, José Pedro de; Angolan politician and economist; *Minister of
Finance;* b. 20 Dec. 1955. *Education:* in France. *Career:* fmr Sec. of State for
Construction Materials; Minister of Planning and Econ. Co-ordination
1992; Angola's nominee to Bd of IMF 1990s; Minister of Finance 2002–.

Address: Ministry of Finance, Avda 4 de Fevereiro 127, CP 592, Luanda,
Angola (office). *Telephone:* 222338548 (office). *Fax:* 222338548 (office).
E-mail: cdi@minfin.gv.ao (office). *Website:* www.angola-portal.ao/
MINFIN (office).

MORALES AIMA, Juan Evo; Bolivian politician and head of state;
President; b. 29 Oct. 1959, Orinoca, Oruru. *Career:* fmr llama herder and
trumpet player; farmed piece of land in Chapare for coca production 1980s;
Founder and Leader, Movimiento al Socialismo (MAS) 1987; became
leader of the 'cocaleros' (coca producers) following US attempts to
eradicate cocaine production (Plan Dignity) 1998; expelled from govt after
three policemen were killed in farmers' riots; mem. Congress; ran second in
presidential elections 2002, succeeded in gaining resignation and exile of
Pres. Gonzalo Sanchez de Lozada on issue of Bolivian gas exports 2003;
Pres. of Bolivia 2006–.
Address: Office of the President, Palacio de Gobierno, Plaza Murillo, La
Paz; Movimiento al Socialismo, La Paz, Bolivia (office). *Telephone:* (2) 237-
1082 (office). *Fax:* (2) 237-1388 (office). *E-mail:* despacho@presidencia.gov
.bo (office). *Website:* www.presidencia.gov.bo (office); www.masbolivia
.org (office).

MORALES TRONCOSO, Carlos; Dominican Republic politician; *Secre-
tary of State for External Relations;* b. 29 Sept. 1940; m. Luisa Alba de
Morales; four d. *Education:* Louisiana State Univ. *Career:* several positions
at Gulf & Western Americas Corpn 1976–84; Vice-Pres. of Dominican
Repub. 1990–94; Sec. of State for External Relations 1994–96, 2004–; mem.
Instituto Americano de Ingenieros Quimicos (AICHE); Dr hc (Dominican
Chamber of Commerce of New York) 1984; Gulf & Western Americas
Industrialist of the Year 1982. *Publications:* De Lo Privado a Lo Público
2002.
Address: Secretariat of State for External Relations, Avenida Independencia 752, Santo Domingo, DN, Dominican Republic (office). *Telephone:*
535-6280 (office). *Fax:* 535-5772 (office). *E-mail:* correspondencia@serex
.gov.do (office). *Website:* www.serex.gov.do (office).

MORAN, David John; British diplomatist; b. 22 Aug. 1959; m. Carol Ann
Marquis. *Career:* Exec. Officer, OFTEL, Dept of Trade and Industry 1985;
joined FCO 1985, Higher Exec. Officer, Zimbabwe/Africa Gen. Section,
Overseas Devt Admin (ODA) 1985–86, Higher Exec. Officer, Finance
Dept, ODA 1986–87, Spokesman, ODA News Dept 1987–88, Second Sec.,
ODA Devt Div. in E Africa, Nairobi 1988–91, Head of IMF/Debt Section,
Econ. Relations Dept, FCO 1991–93, First Sec., Know How Fund,
Moscow 1993–96, Head of France and Switzerland Section, Western
European Dept, FCO 1996–98, Head of Justice and Home Affairs Section,
EU Dept (Internal) 1998–99, Head of Charter of Rights Section, EU Dept
(Internal) 1999–2000, Deputy Perm. Rep., UK Del. to OECD, Paris
2001–05, Amb. to Uzbekistan 2005–07.
Address: Foreign and Commonwealth Office, King Charles Street, London,
SW1A 2AH, England (office). *Telephone:* (20) 7008-1500 (office). *Website:*
www.fco.gov.uk (office).

MORATINOS CUYAUBÉ, Miguel Ángel; Spanish diplomatist and politician; *Minister of Foreign Affairs and Co-operation;* b. 8 June 1951, Madrid;
m. Dominique Maunac; three c. *Career:* Dir Eastern Europe Co-ordination
Desk 1974–79; First Sec., Spanish Embassy, Yugoslavia 1979–80, Chargé
d'Affaires 1980–84; political adviser, Spanish Embassy, Rabat 1984–87;
Deputy Dir-Gen. for N Africa 1987–91; Dir-Gen. Inst. for Co-operation
with the Arab World 1991–93; apptd Dir-Gen. of Foreign Policy for Africa
and the Middle East 1993; Amb. to Israel June–Dec. 1996; EU Special Rep.
for the Middle East Peace Process Dec. 1996–2003; Minister of Foreign
Affairs and Co-operation 2004–; Commdr of Civil Merit, Knight of the
Order of Civil Merit, Officer of the Order of Isabel la Cátolica, Commdr of
the Order of the Repub. of Tunisia, Commdr of the Orange-Nassau Order
of the Netherlands; Arab Journalists Asscn Co-operation Prize 1994.
Address: Ministry of Foreign Affairs and Co-operation, Plaza Marqués de
Salamanca 8, 28071 Madrid, 2806 Spain (office). *Telephone:* (91) 3798300
(office). *Fax:* (91) 3667098 (office). *E-mail:* buzonweb@mae.es (office).
Website: www.mae.es (office).

MORAUTA, Sir Mekere, Kt, BEcons; Papua New Guinea politician and
banker; b. 12 June 1946; m. Roslyn Morauta; two s. *Education:* Univ. of
Papua New Guinea, Flinders Univ. of S. Australia. *Career:* research officer,
Dept of Labour 1971; economist, Office of the Econ. Adviser 1972; fmr dir
of numerous cos; Sec. for Finance, Govt of Papua New Guinea 1973–82;
Man. Dir Papua New Guinea Banking Corpn 1983–92; Chair. Nat. Airline
Comm. 1992–96; Gov. Bank of Papua New Guinea 1993–94; Exec. Chair.
Morauta Investments Ltd 1994–97; MP for Moresby NW 1997–; Minister
for Planning and Implementation 1997, for Fisheries 1998–99; Prime
Minister and Treas. of Papua New Guinea 1999–2002; mem. Bd of Dirs

Angco; Hon. DTech (Univ. of Tech., Lae) 1987. *Publications:* numerous econs-related papers.
Address: c/o Prime Minister's Office, PO Box 639, Naigani, NCD, Papua New Guinea (office).

MORAVCSIK, Andrew, BA, MA, PhD; American professor of political science; *Professor of Politics and Director, European Union Program, Princeton University;* m. Anne-Marie Slaughter; two s. *Education:* Stanford Univ., Johns Hopkins School of Advanced Int. Studies (SAIS), Harvard Univ. *Career:* Econ. Ed. and Speechwriter, Office of Deputy Prime Minister, Ministry of Econ. Planning, Seoul, South Korea 1980; Research Asst, Atlantic Council of the US 1982–83; Asst to Dir and Trade Negotiator, US Dept of Commerce, Office of Import Admin. (SIPS) 1982–84; Press Asst, Del. to EC 1985–86; Consultant on European Affairs, Defense Industrial Issues, US Foreign Policy 1989–; Asst Prof. of Govt, Harvard Univ. 1992–96, Assoc. Prof. 1996–99, Prof. 1999–2004, Dir Center for European Studies 2000–02, Dir EU Program 2002–04; Prof., Dept of Politics, Princeton Univ. 2004–, Founding Dir EU Program 2004–; Visiting Sr Research Fellow, Dept of Politics, Princeton Univ. 2003–04; Co-Dir Future of Europe Project, Council on Foreign Relations 1998; Ed.-in-Chief SAIS Review 1982–83; mem. Editorial Bd Int. Encyclopedia of European Integration 1995–, European Journal of International Relations 1995–, Journal of Public Policy 1996–, Cambridge Review of International Affairs 1997–, Journal of EU Politics 1998–, Journal of Cold War History 1998–; mem. Int. Advisory Bd Contemporary Europe Research Centre 2000–; mem. Editorial Advisory Bd International Relations of the Asia-Pacific 2000–, Journal of International Relations and Development 2000–, World Politics 2002–05; mem. Bd of Dirs New Jersey Opera Theater 2006–; Fulbright Fellow, Univs of Hamburg, Bielefeld and Marburg, FRG 1980–82, Distinguished Teaching Fellow Award, Harvard Univ. 1988; numerous fellowships, grants and awards. *Publications:* The Choice for Europe: Social Purpose and State Power from Messina to Maastricht 1998, Centralization or Fragmentation? Europe Facing the Challenges of Deepening, Diversity and Democracy 1998, Europe without Illusions, European Integration and the Liberal Theory of World Politics: Essays 1991–2001, Europe in the New World Economy, A Liberal Theory of Int. Law (co-author), Europe without Illusions 2005; over 100 articles, chapters and working papers.
Address: Department of Politics, Woodrow Wilson School, Robertson Hall, Princeton University, Princeton, NJ 08544, USA (office). *Telephone:* (609) 258-1161 (office). *E-mail:* amoravcs@princeton.edu (office). *Website:* www.princeton.edu/~amoravcs (office).

MOREAN-PHILLIP, Glenda Patricia; Trinidad and Tobago solicitor, diplomatist and government official; *Ambassador to USA;* m. Oscar Adrian Phillip. *Career:* first woman in Trinidad and Tobago to qualify as solicitor, enrolled Solicitor of Supreme Court 1974; Chair. Nursing Comm. 1979; Dir Dunross Co-operative Soc. 1980–81; Commr Public Utilities Comm. 1981–86; Assoc. Tutor, Hugh Wooding Law School 1987–2001; Pres. Law Soc. 1989–91; mem. Disciplinary Cttee of Law Asscn 1992–95, 1998, 1999; Deputy Chair. Airports Authority 1993–96; mem. Legal Aid and Advisory Authority 1994–2001; Acting Judge, High Court of Justice 1999–2000; Govt Senator and Attorney Gen. 2001–03; High Commr to UK 2003–08 (also accred as Amb. to Denmark, Norway, Sweden, Finland and Germany 2005–08), Amb. to USA 2008–; Pres. Tennis Asscn 1991–97; Hon. Pres. Blind Welfare Asscn 1994–97.
Address: Embassy of Trinidad and Tobago, 1708 Massachusetts Avenue, NW, Washington, DC 20036, USA (office). *Telephone:* (202) 467-6490 (office). *Fax:* (202) 785-3130 (office). *E-mail:* embttgo@erols.com (office). *Website:* www.ttembassy.cjb.net (office).

MOREL, Claude Sylvestre Anthony; Seychelles diplomatist; *Ambassador to France;* b. 25 Sept. 1956, Victoria, Mahé; m. Margaret Morel; one s. one d. *Education:* Seychelles Coll., Univ. of Lille, France, Cairo Inst. of Diplomatic Studies, Inst. Int. d'Admin Publique, Paris. *Career:* Chief of Protocol, Ministry of Foreign Affairs 1983–87, Dir Bilateral/Multilateral Affairs 1987–88; Chargé d'affaires, Embassy, Paris 1988–90; Dir-Gen. Ministry of Foreign Affairs 1990–96; Amb. to EU (also accred to Benelux and Germany) 1997–98; Perm. Rep. to UN and Amb. to USA and Canada 1998–2005; Prin. Sec., Ministry of Foreign Affairs 2005–07; Amb. to France (also accred to UK 2007–, to Monaco 2008–) and Perm. Rep. to UNESCO and FAO 2007–.
Address: Seychelles Embassy, 51 avenue Mozart, 75016 Paris, France (office). *Telephone:* 1-42-30-57-47 (office). *Fax:* 1-42-30-57-40 (office). *E-mail:* ambsey@aol.com (office).

MOREL, Pierre Jean Louis Achille; French diplomatist; *Special Representative for Central Asia, European Union;* b. 27 June 1944, Romans (Drôme); m. Olga Bazanoff 1978; three c. *Education:* Lycée du Parc, Lyon, Paris, Ecole nat. d'admin. *Career:* Europe Dept, Ministry of Foreign Affairs 1971–73, Analysis and Forecasting Centre 1973–76, First Sec. then Second Counsellor, Embassy, Moscow 1976–79, Ministerial Rep., Gen. Secr. Interministerial Cttee on European Econ. Co-operation 1979–81, Office of Pres. of Repub., Technical Adviser to Gen. Secr. 1981–85, Dir Political Affairs, Ministry of Foreign Affairs 1985–86, Amb. and France's Rep. Disarmament Conf. Geneva 1989, Head French Del. Preparatory Cttee Conf. on Security and Co-operation in Europe 1990, Diplomatic Adviser, Office of Pres. of Repub. 1991–92, Amb. to Georgia 1992–93, to Russia (also Accred to Moldova, Turkmenistan, Mongolia, Tajikistan and Kyrgyzstan) 1992–96, to China 1996–2002; Amb. to Holy See 2002–05; Advisor to the Policy Planning Centre, Ministry of Foreign Affairs 2005–06; EU Special Rep. for Central Asia 2006–; Officier, Légion d'honneur, Officier Ordre nat. du Mérite. *Publications:* trans. Mantrana 1984, Sauts de Temps 1989, Serpentara 1998 by Ernst Jünger.
Address: c/o Council of the European Union, Rue de la Loi, 175, B-1048 Brussels, Belgium (office). *Telephone:* (2) 281 64 51 (office). *Fax:* (2) 281 51 46 (office). *E-mail:* pierre.morel@consilium.europa.eu (office). *Website:* www.consilium.europa.eu (office).

MORENILLA, José María, DR.IUR; Spanish judge; b. 29 Aug. 1926, Granada; m. Joanne Allard 1962; one s. one d. *Education:* School of Law, Granada, Columbia Univ., Univ. of Granada. *Career:* Judge of First Instance 1952; Legal Adviser (in int. law) Ministry of Justice 1978–87; Supreme Court Judge Criminal Section 1987–90, Admin. Section 1990–; Agent/Rep. of Spanish Govt before European Comm. of Human Rights 1988–90; apptd Judge European Court of Human Rights 1990; Cross of Honour of San Raimundo de Peñafort. *Publications:* Organization of the Courts and Judicial Reform in the United States 1968, Poder Judicial en los Estados Unidos 1979, La Igualdad (Jurídica) de la Mujer en España 1980, Medidas Alternativas de la Prisión 1983, Protección Internacional de los Derechos Humanos 1984, Convenio Europeo de Derechos Humanos – Ámbito, Organos, Procedimientos 1985.
Address: Juan Ramón Jiménez 2, 9°C, 28036 Madrid, Spain. *Telephone:* (91) 4574591.

MORENO, Maurizio, LLB; Italian diplomatist; *President, International Institute of Humanitarian Law;* b. 23 June 1940, Rome; one s. *Education:* Univ. of Rome. *Career:* joined Diplomatic Service 1963; assignments included Vice-Consul in Basel, First Sec. Embassy in Rabat, Consul in Bordeaux 1965–74; Alt. Perm. Rep. to Conf. on Disarmament, Geneva 1976–80; Consul-Gen. in Lyon 1980–84; Deputy Head Del. to CDE-CSCE, Stockholm 1984–85; Dir Policy Planning Office 1985–87; in charge of Africa, Political Affairs Gen. Directorate 1987–88; Amb. to Senegal 1988–92; Deputy Head of Cabinet of the Minister 1992–93; Special Envoy to Somalia 1993–94; Dir Press and Information Dept 1994–95; Dir of Diplomatic Inst. 1995–96; Amb. to Czech Repub. 1996–99; Dir-Gen. for European Countries 1999–2002; Perm. Rep. to NATO, Brussels 2002–07; Pres. Int. Inst. of Humanitarian Law, Sanremo, Italy 2007–; mem. Bd Italian Soc. for Int. Org (SIOI), Inst. of Int. Affairs (IAI), Italian Inst. for Africa and the E (IsIAO); nat. orders from Austria, Germany, Greece, Italy, Morocco, Norway, Portugal, San Marino, Senegal, and UK.
Address: International Institute of Humanitarian Law, Villa Ormond C.so Cavallotti 113, 18038 Sanremo, Italy (office). *Telephone:* (018) 4541848 (office). *Fax:* (018) 4541600 (office). *E-mail:* sanremo@iihl.org (office). *Website:* www.iihl.org (office).

MORENO, Rafael, PhD; Chilean scientist, economist, politician and diplomatist; *Ambassador to UK;* b. 14 Aug. 1936, Santiago; m. Gloria Orb; two s. *Education:* Instituto de Humanidades Luis Campino, Instituto Nacional, Santiago, San Luis Coll., Antofagasta, Catholic Univ., Santiago, Univ. of Illinois, USA. *Career:* economist, Agrarian Econ. Dept, Ministry of Agric. 1960–61; Head of Agricultural Dept, Tech. Co-operation Service of Chile 1961–64; Exec. Vice-Pres. Corpn for Agrarian Reform (Corporación de la Reforma Agraria—CORA) 1964–70; consultant, World Bank and Inter-American Inst. for Cooperation on Agriculture 1974–78; Dir of Human Resources, Insts and Agrarian Reform, FAO, Rome 1978–86, Pres. and Organizer of World Food Day, Rome 1981–89, FAO Asst Dir-Gen., Rome 1986–89, FAO Asst Dir-Gen. for Latin America and the Caribbean 1989–93; Prof. of Econs, Universidad Católica, Valparaiso 1961–64; Prof. of Agrarian Economy, Universidad de Chile, Santiago 1970–74, Prof. of Economics 1973–74; Prof. of Rural Devt, Universidad Católica de Chile, Santiago 1970–78; Prof., Gregorian Univ., Rome 1984–86; Adviser, Instituto de Educación Rural 1994–98; Nat. Adviser for Christian Democratic (CD) Party 1957–64, Chair. CD Youth Party 1962–64, mem. Bd CD Party 1971–78, Nat. Sec. CD Party 1974–76, 1997–98, Nat. Vice-Chair. 1976–79, Rep. of CD Party at int. congresses and meetings 1980–89, Nat. Adviser 1994–97; Senator for O'Higgins and Rancagua 1972–73, for VI region 1997–2006, mem. Cttees for Int. Agreements, Constitutional Matters and Environment; Amb. to UK 2006–; Pres. Instituto de Educación Rural 1996–97, Int. Chapter of Rome, Int. Soc. for Devt

(SID); mem. Agricultural Scientists Coll. of Chile, Geographical Soc. of Mexico, Jacques Maritain Inst., Rome; Grand Cross of Brazil, Chilean Senate Nat. Decoration; Int. Award, Agricultural Scientists Coll. of Chile, Int. Award, Geographical Soc. of Mexico, Peruvian Medal for Agricultural Achievements. *Publications:* author of several publs, articles and interventions in econ., rural and agricultural subjects; author and co-author of several laws related to the farming industry and agrarian reform.
Address: Embassy of Chile, 12 Devonshire Street, London, W1G 7DS, England (office). *Telephone:* (20) 7580-6392 (office). *Fax:* (20) 7436-5204 (office). *E-mail:* embachile@embachile.co.uk (office). *Website:* www.echileuk.demon.co.uk (office).

MORENO BARBERA, Admiral Antonio; Spanish naval officer; *Chief of Defence Staff;* b. 17 April 1940, Madrid; m. Pepa Deckler Andreu; four c. *Education:* Naval War Coll. *Career:* began career in Spanish Navy 1956; apptd Lt JG 1961; served on board destroyer Alava, submarines Almirante García de los Reyes S-31, Delfin S-61, Marsopa S-63, Submarine Flotilla Staff; Commdr submarines Tonina S-62 and Galerna S-71 1975–83; Commdg Officer frigate Asturias F-74 1983–89; Commdr Submarine Flotilla 1988–92; shore assignments include Leading Lecturer on Logistics, Naval Warfare Coll., Lecturer on Tactics, Submarine School, Chief of Tactical Studies, Dept at Naval Staff, Exec. Asst to Chief of Naval Staff; Commdr of Fleet of Amphibious Force (Delta Group) 1992–94; Chief of Rota Naval Base 1994–95; Chief of the Jt Defence Staff 1995–97; Chief of Naval Staff 1997–99; Chief of Defence Staff 1999–; apptd Vice-Admiral 1994, Admiral 1997; Grand Cross of St Hermenegildo, Commdr US Legion of Merit four Naval Merit Crosses, Sahara Medal (Combat Zone), Brazilian Naval Merit Medal, Naval Merit Grand Cross, Mil. Merit Grand Cross, Chilean Great Star Mil. Merit Cross, Brazilian Naval Merit Grand Cross.
Address: Ministry of Defence, Paseo de la Castellana 109, 28071 Madrid, Spain (office). *Telephone:* (91) 3955000 (office). *Fax:* (91) 5563958 (office). *E-mail:* infodefensa@mde.es (office). *Website:* www.mde.es.

MORENO-MEJÍA, Luis Alberto, BA, MBA; Colombian diplomatist and international organization official; *President, Inter-American Development Bank;* b. 3 May 1953, Philadelphia, USA; m. Gabriela Febres-Cordero 1970; one s. one d. *Education:* Florida Int. Univ., Thunderbird Univ., Phoenix, Ariz. and Harvard Univ. *Career:* Div. Man. Praco 1977–82; exec. producer of nationwide nightly news programme and other entertainment and children's programmes 1982–90; Neiman Fellow, Harvard Univ. 1990–91; Pres. Inst. de Foment Industrial 1991–92; Minister of Econ. Devt 1992–94; telecommunications adviser and pvt. consultant, Luis Carlos Sarmiento Org., Bogotá 1994–97; Pnr Westsphere Andean Advisers 1997–98; Campaign Man. of Andrés Pastrana 1994; Amb. to USA 1998–2005; Pres. IDB, Washington, DC 2005–; Orden al Mérito Civil Ciudad de Bogotá, en el Grado de Gran Cruz, awarded by Mayor of Bogotá 1990, Orden al Mérito Industrial – José Gutiérrez Gómez, Colombian Nat. Business Asscn 2002, Orden de Boyacá en el Grado de Gran Cruz awarded by the Pres. of Colombia 2002; King of Spain Prize for journalistic excellence. *Publications include:* articles on Colombian and int. politics and econs for publs in Colombia and USA; writings have appeared in New York Times, Boston Globe, Miami Herald, El Tiempo, Foreign Affairs en Español and Semana.
Address: Inter-American Development Bank (IDB), 1300 New York Avenue, NW, Washington, DC 20577, USA (office). *Telephone:* (202) 623-1000 (office). *Fax:* (202) 623-3096 (office). *E-mail:* pic@iadb.org (office). *Website:* www.iadb.org.

MORENO OCAMPO, Luis; Argentine lawyer; *Chief Prosecutor, International Criminal Court;* b. 1953, Buenos Aires. *Education:* Univ. of Buenos Aires. *Career:* Deputy Public Prosecutor in trials against mil. junta 1985–87; Dist Attorney, Fed. Circuit, City of Buenos Aires 1987–92; in pvt. practice (specializing in corruption control programmes and ethical advice for large cos) 1992–; Chief Prosecutor (first in position), Int. Criminal Court 2003–; Sub-Dir Research Centre, Univ. of Buenos Aires Law School 1984, currently Adjunct Prof. of Penal Law; Visiting Prof. of Law, Harvard Univ., USA; co-f. Poder Ciudadano; mem. Advisory Cttee Transparency Int., Pres. for Latin America and the Caribbean. *Film appearance:* (as himself) The Devil Came on Horseback 2006. *Publications include:* In Self Defense: How to Avoid Corruption 1993, When Power Lost the Trial: How to Explain the Dictatorship to Our Children 1996.
Address: International Criminal Court, Maanweg 174, 2516 AB, The Hague, The Netherlands (office). *Telephone:* (70) 5158515 (office). *Fax:* (70) 5158555 (office). *Website:* www.icc-cpi.int.

MORI, Immanuel (Manny), BA; Micronesian politician and head of state; *President;* b. 25 Dec. 1948, Fefan Island, Chuuk State; m. Elina Ekiek (deceased); four d. *Education:* Xavier High School, Chuuk and Univ. of Guam. *Career:* began career at Citicorp Credit-Guam Bank 1973, Asst

Man., Saipan Branch 1974–76; Asst Admin. Trust Territory Social Security Admin 1976–79; Nat. Revenue Officer, State of Chuuk 1979–81; Controller, Federated States of Micronesia Devt Bank 1981–84, Pres. and CEO 1984–97; Exec. Vice-Pres. Bank of Federated States of Micronesia 1997–99; mem. Micornesian Congress 1999–2003, 2004–, Vice-Chair. Judiciary and Govt Operations Cttee 1999–2003, Health Educ. and Social Affairs Cttee 1999–2003, Chair. Ways and Means Cttee 2001–03, Vice-Chair. External Affairs Cttee 2004–05, Chair. Resources and Devt Cttee 2005–07; Gen.-Man. and CEO Chuuk Public Utility Corpn 2004–07; President of Federated States of Micronesia 2007–.
Address: Office of the President, PO Box PS-53 Palikir, Pohnpei FM 96941, Federated States of Micronesia (office). *Telephone:* 320-2228 (office). *Fax:* 320-2785 (office). *E-mail:* ppetrus@mail.fm (office). *Website:* www.fsmpio.fm (office).

MORIARTY, James F., BA; American diplomatist; *Ambassador to Bangladesh;* b. Ware, Mass; m. Lauren Moriarty; one s. one d. *Education:* Dartmouth Coll. *Career:* career mem. Sr Foreign Service with rank of Minister-Counselor, joined Foreign Service as Political Officer in 1975, first tour as Consular Officer, Embassy in Rabat, subsequently served as Political/Econ. Officer, Embassy in Mbabane, Swaziland, then as Econ. Officer, State Dept Office of Southern African Affairs, then served as Political Officer, Embassy in Islamabad, Deputy Chief of US Embassy's Political Section, Beijing 1989–91, Deputy Dir Office of UN Political Affairs 1991–93, Diplomat-in-Residence, East-West Center, Honolulu 1993–94, Chief of Gen. Affairs (Political) Section, American Inst., Taiwan 1994–98, Minister-Counselor for Political Affairs, Beijing 1998–2001, worked in White House as Nat. Security Council (NSC) Dir for China Affairs 2001–02, Special Asst to Pres. George W. Bush and Sr Dir NSC 2002–04, Amb. to Nepal 2004–07, to Bangladesh 2008–; Group Superior Honor Awards 1985, 1992, Dir Gen.'s Award for Best Reporting Officer 1987, individual Dept of State Superior Honor Awards for his work on Yugoslavia 1993 and in China 2000, Rivkin Award, American Foreign Service Asscn 1994, Presidential Pay Award 2005, numerous State Dept Performance Pay Awards.
Address: US Embassy, Madani Avenue, Baridhara, Dhaka 1212, Bangladesh (office). *Telephone:* (2) 8855500 (office). *Fax:* (2) 8823744 (office). *E-mail:* ustc@bangla.net (office). *Website:* dhaka.usembassy.gov (office).

MORILLON, Gen. Philippe; French army officer and politician; b. 24 Oct. 1935, Casablanca, Morocco; m. 1st Anne Appert 1958 (deceased); three d.; m. 2nd Christine Gaudry 1998. *Education:* Ecole Militaire de Saint-Cyr, Ecole Supérieure, Army Staff Coll. *Career:* platoon leader, French Foreign Legion during Algerian war of independence; fmr Div. Commdr of French units stationed in Germany; mil. expert, Assemblée Nationale 1984–86; Deputy Under-Sec. for Int. Relations, Ministry of Defence 1988–90; Deputy Commdr, then Commdr UN Protection Force (UNPROFOR) in Bosnia-Herzegovina 1992–93; Adviser on Defence to Govt of France 1993; Commdr Force d'Action Rapide 1994–96; mem. European Parl. (Union pour la démocratie française, mem. Group of the Alliance of Liberals and Democrats for Europe) 1999–, Chair. Cttee on Fisheries, mem. Conf. of Cttee Chairmen, Cttee on Foreign Affairs, Sub-cttee on Security and Defence, Del. to ACP-EU Jt Parl. Ass., Del. to Euro-Mediterranean Parl. Ass.; Pres. Asscn L'envol pour les enfants européens; fmr Pres. French Inter-ministerial Coordinating Cttee for the 12th World Youth Day, Paris 1997; Commdr Ordre nat. du Mérit 1988, Grand Officier de la Légion d'honneur 1993; Servitor Pacis Award, Path to Peace Foundation 1999. *Publications:* Croire et Oser 1993, Paroles de Soldat 1996, Mon Credo 1999, Le Testament de Massoud 2005.
Address: European Parliament, Bâtiment Altiero Spinelli, 09G205, 60 rue Wiertz, 1047 Brussels, Belgium (office); Ministère de la Défense, 14 rue Saint-Dominique, 75700 Paris, France. *Telephone:* (2) 284-5506 (office). *Fax:* (2) 284-9506 (office). *E-mail:* philippe.morillon@europarl.europa.eu (office). *Website:* www.europarl.eu.int/members/expert/alphaOrder/view.do?language=EN&id=4332.

MORIN, Hervé; French politician; *Minister of Defence;* b. 17 Aug. 1961, Pont-Audemer; m. Catherine Broussot; one s. one d. *Education:* Deauville Lycée, Ecole Jeanne d'Arc, Caen, Univ. of Caen, Univ. of Paris II, Inst. of Political Studies, Paris. *Career:* Dir of Services, Nat. Ass. 1987–93, 1998; Lecturer, Univ. of Paris V 1989–95; Municipal Councillor 1989–95; mem. Gen. Council of Eure 1992–2004; Tech. Adviser on Nat. Affairs and the Environment, Office of the Minister of Defence 1993–95; Mayor of Epaignes 1995–; Pres. Cormeilles Town Community 1995–; mem. Union pour la Démocratie Française (UDF) 1998–2007, Leader Parl. Group 2002–07; mem. Nouveau Centre 2007–, Leader 2008–; Deputy for Eure 1998–; Spokesperson for François Bayrou during presidential campaign 2002; Regional Councillor for Haute-Normandie 2004–; Minister of Defence 2007–; Pres. France-Niger Group, Nat. Ass.; Pres. Asscn for the Reunification of Normandy 1999–.

Address: Ministry of Defence, 14 rue Saint Dominique, 75007 Paris, France (office). *Telephone:* 1-42-19-30-11 (office). *Fax:* 1-47-05-40-91 (office). *E-mail:* courrier-ministre@sdbc.defense.gouv.fr (office). *Website:* www.defense.gouv.fr (office); www.herve-morin.net.

MORJANE, Kamel; Tunisian international organization official, diplomat and government official; *Minister of National Defence;* b. 1948, Hammam-Sousse; two c. *Education:* Univ. of Tunis, Ecole Nat. d'Admin Tunis, Univ. of Geneva. *Career:* worked as journalist; Asst Prof. Univ. of Geneva; joined staff UNHCR 1977, Asst High Commr 2001–05; Minister of Defence 2005–; apptd Perm. Rep. to UN, Geneva 1996, later UN Sec.-Gen.'s Special Rep. for Democratic Repub. of Congo 1999.
Address: Ministry of National Defence, blvd Bab Menara, 1030 Tunis, Tunisia (office). *Telephone:* (71) 560-240. *Fax:* (71) 561-804. *E-mail:* defnat@defense.tn. *Website:* www.defense.tn.

MORRIS, Greta N., BA, MA; American diplomatist; *Dean of School of Language Studies, Foreign Service Institute, Department of State;* b. Redlands, Calif. *Education:* Univ. of Redlands and UCLA. *Career:* taught English at high school and univ. levels in Calif. and Indonesia; career mem. Sr Foreign Service since 1980, postings as Counselor for Public Affairs, The Philippines, as Public Affairs Officer, Uganda, as Press Attaché, Thailand, as Dir Office of Public Affairs, Bureau of African Affairs, as Dir Information Center, Nairobi, as Cultural and Exchanges Coordinator for Africa, as Deputy Dir Office of Public Diplomacy, Bureau for E Asian and Pacific Affairs, Counselor for Public Affairs, Jakarta –2003, Amb. to the Marshall Islands 2003–06, Dean of School of Language Studies, Foreign Service Inst., Arlington, Va 2006–; two Superior Honor Awards, three Sr Foreign Service Performance Pay Awards.
Address: Foreign Service Institute, George P. Shultz National Foreign Affairs Training Center, 4000 Arlington Blvd, Arlington, VA 22204, FSI/EX/REG SA-42, USA (office). *Telephone:* (703) 302-7144 (Registrar) (office). *Fax:* (703) 302-7152 (office). *E-mail:* fsi@state.gov (office). *Website:* www.fsitraining.state.gov (office).

MORRIS, Timothy Colin; British diplomatist; *Ambassador to Morocco;* m. Patricia Tena; three d. *Career:* with Mexico and Cen. American Dept, FCO 1981–82, Japanese language training 1982–84, Second Sec. (Commercial), Embassy in Tokyo 1984–87; Southern African Dept, FCO 1987–89, Head of Exports to Japan Unit, Dept of Trade and Industry 1989–91; First Sec. and Head of Political Section, Embassy in Madrid 1991–96; Deputy Head of UN Dept, FCO 1996–98; Counsellor (Trade and Investment), Embassy in Tokyo 1998–2002; Deputy Head of Mission, Embassy in Lisbon 2003–05; Head of Int. Orgs Dept, FCO 2005–08; Amb. to Morocco (also accred to Mauritania) 2008–.
Address: British Embassy, 17 Boulevard de la Tour Hassan, PO Box 45, Rabat, Morocco (office). *Telephone:* (37) 238600 (office). *Fax:* (37) 704531 (office). *E-mail:* british@mtds.com (office). *Website:* www.britain.org.ma (office).

MORRIS, Warwick; British fmr diplomatist; b. 10 Aug. 1948; m. Pamela Morris; one s. two d. *Career:* joined FCO 1969, Information Dept 1969–71, Third Sec. (Information) Paris 1972–74, full-time language training, Seoul 1975–76, Second Sec. (Political), Seoul 1977–79, Pvt. Sec. to Deputy Perm. Under-Sec., FCO 1979–80, Personnel Operations Dept 1980–82, Head of Section, Hong Kong Dept 1982–84, First Sec. (Commercial), Mexico City 1984–87, First Sec., Head of Chancery, Seoul 1988–91, Deputy Head, Far Eastern Dept, FCO 1992–93, Counsellor, later Head of Perm. Under-Sec.'s Dept 1993–94, Counsellor (Econ. and Commercial), New Delhi 1995–98, Royal Coll. of Defence Studies, London 1999–, Amb. to Viet Nam 2000–03, to Repub. of Korea 2003–08 (retd).
Address: c/o Foreign and Commonwealth Office, King Charles Street, London SW1A 2AH, England (office). *Website:* www.fco.gov.uk (office).

MORTADA, Jihad; Lebanese diplomatist; m. Rima Mortada. *Career:* apptd Head of Comm. to EU, Brussels 1996; Amb. to UK (also accred to Ireland) 1999–2007.
Address: Ministry of Foreign Affairs and Emigrants, rue Sursock, Achrafieh, Beirut, Lebanon (office). *Telephone:* (1) 333100 (office). *E-mail:* info@emigrants.gov.lb (office). *Website:* www.emigrants.gov.lb (office).

MORTIMER, Hugh Roger, LVO, BSc, MA; British diplomatist; *Deputy Head of Mission, British Embassy, Berlin;* b. 19 Sept. 1949, Salisbury. *Education:* Cheltenham Coll., Univ. of Surrey, King's Coll. London. *Career:* joined FCO 1973, served Rome, Singapore, UN, New York; on secondment to German Ministry of Foreign Affairs 1990; Deputy Head of Mission, Berlin 1991–94, 2005–; FCO 1994–95, Ankara 1997–2000; Amb. to Slovenia 2001–05.

Address: British Embassy, Wilhelmstr. 70–71, 10117 Berlin, Germany (office). *Telephone:* (30) 204570 (office). *Fax:* (30) 20457594 (office). *E-mail:* info@britischebotschaft.de (office). *Website:* www.britischebotschaft.de (office).

MOSCOSO DE GRUBER, Mireya Elisa; Panamanian politician and former head of state; b. 1 July 1946, Panama; m. Arnulfo Arias (died 1988); one s. *Education:* Colegio Comercial María Inmaculada, Miami Dade Community Coll. *Career:* fmr Exec. Sec. Social Security Agency; fmr Sales Man., Deputy Man. and Gen. Man. Arkapal SA (coffee co.); Govt rep. on numerous int. missions; spent ten years in exile in USA; Pres. Partido Arnulfista; Pres. of Panama 1999–2004; fmr Pres. Arias Foundation, Madrid; mem. Asscn of Boquete Coffee Growers, Asscn of Milk Producers, Nat. Asscn of Ranchers.
Address: c/o Office of the President, Palacio Presidencial, Valija 50, Panamá 1, Panama (office).

MOSCOVICI, Pierre; French politician; b. 16 Sept. 1957. *Education:* Univ. of Paris X, I, IV, Ecole nat. d'administration. *Career:* official, Cour des Comptes 1984–88; Adviser, pvt. office of Minister of Nat. Educ., Youth and Sport 1988–89, Special Adviser to Minister 1989–90; Head. Gen. Planning Comm.'s Public Sector Modernization and Finance Dept 1990; mem. Parti Socialiste (PS) Nat. Council and Nat. Bureau 1990, Nat. Sec. responsible for policy research and devt 1990–92, 1995–97, Nat. Treas. 1992–94; mem. Doubs Gen. Council, Sochaux-Grand-Charmont canton 1994–2001; Montbéliard municipal councillor 1995–2001; Regional Councillor Franche Comté 1998–2004 mem. European Parl. 1994–97; Nat. Ass. Deputy for 4th Doubs constituency 1997, 2007–; Minister Del. attached to Minister for Foreign Affairs, with responsibility for European Affairs 1997–2002; Rep. Convention on the Future of Europe 2002; Regional Councillor Franche-Comté. *Publications include:* A la recherche de la gauche perdue 1994, L'urgence, plaidoyer pour une autre politique 1997, Au coeur de l'Europe 1999, L'Europe, une puissance dans la mondialisation 2001, Les 10 questions qui fâchent les Européens 2004, L'Europe est morte, vive l'Europe 2006.
Address: 51 avenue des Allies, 25200 Montbéliard (office); Assemblée Nationale, 126 rue de la Université, 75355 Paris 07 SP, France. *Telephone:* 3-81-32-31-69 (office). *Fax:* 3-81-32-31-67 (office). *E-mail:* pmoscovici@assemblee-national.fr (office). *Website:* www.assemblee-nationale.fr.

MOSES, Marlene Inemwin; Nauruan diplomatist; *Permanent Representative, United Nations; Ambassador to USA;* b. 1961. *Education:* Canberra Coll. of Advanced Univ., Monash Univ., Melbourne, Australia. *Career:* Foreign Affairs Officer 1983–87; Consul in Tokyo, Japan 1988–90; Consul-Gen., Auckland, NZ 1991–95, Melbourne, Australia 1995–96; Asst Dir, Dept of Foreign Affairs 1996–99; Perm. Sec. for Internal Affairs 1999–2000; Perm. Sec. for Health and Medical Services 2000–03; Acting Chief Sec. to Public Service Commr and Sec. to Cabinet 2003; Deputy Perm. Rep. to UN, New York 2003–05, Perm. Rep. 2005–, also Amb. to USA and Amb. Desig. to Cuba; previous positions include Chair. Lands Negotiation Cttee, Coordinator Econ. Strategy Cttee; fmr mem. Nauru Rehabilitation Corpn-Land Use Planning Cttee.
Address: Office of the Permanent Representative of the Republic of Nauru to the United Nations, 800 Second Avenue, Suite 400A, New York, NY 10017, USA (office). *Telephone:* (212) 937-0074 (office). *Fax:* (212) 937-0079 (office). *E-mail:* nauru@un.int (office); nauru@onecommonwealth.org (office). *Website:* www.un.int/nauru (office).

MOSISILI, Bethuel Pakalitha, BA, MEd; Lesotho politician; *Prime Minister and Minister of Defence and Public Service;* b. 14 March 1945, Waterfall; m.; two s. two d. *Education:* Univ. of Botswana, Lesotho and Swaziland, Univ. of Wis., USA, Univ. of SA, Simon Fraser Univ., Canada. *Career:* joined Basutoland Congress Party 1967; Deputy Headmaster Bereng High School 1972–73; Asst Lecturer in African Languages, Univ. of Botswana, Lesotho and Swaziland 1973–76; Lecturer in African Languages, Nat. Univ. of Lesotho 1976–83; Sr Lecturer, Univ. of Fort Hare, SA 1983–84, Univ. of Transkei 1985–88, Univ. of Zululand 1989–92; mem. Parl. 1993–; Minister of Educ. and Training, Sports, Culture and Youth Affairs 1993–95; apptd Deputy Prime Minister 1995; Minister of Home Affairs and Local Govt 1995–98; Prime Minister of Lesotho and Minister of Defence and Public Service 1998–; fmr Deputy Leader Lesotho Congress for Democracy, Leader 1998–; mem. Lesotho Educational Research Asscn, African Languages Asscn of SA, S African Pedagogical Soc.
Address: Office of the Prime Minister, Government Office Complex, Phase 1 Qhobosheaneng, 50, PO Box 527, Maseru 100, Lesotho (office). *Telephone:* 22325043 (office). *Fax:* 22320662 (office). *E-mail:* mmajobo@cabinet.gov.ls (office). *Website:* www.lesotho.gov.ls (office).

MOSKOVSKY, Col-Gen. Aleksey Mikhailovich; Russian army officer; *Deputy Minister of Defence and Head of Armaments;* b. 1947, Smolensk.

Education: Kiev Higher Military Engineering Radio Technical School, Novosibirsk State Univ. *Career:* worked in devt and testing of armaments and mil. tech.; Deputy State Mil. Insp. of Russia, Sec. Council of Defence 1997–98; Deputy Sec. Russian Council of Security 1998–2001, supervised security in defence, tech. and scientific areas; Deputy Minister of Defence, Head of Armaments 2001–; State Prize of Russian Fed., Prize of Council of Ministers for devt of new weapons.
Address: Ministry of Defence, 105175 Moscow, ul. Myasnitskaya 37, Russia (office). *Telephone:* (495) 293-38-54 (office). *Fax:* (495) 296-84-36 (office). *Website:* www.mil.ru (office).

MOTO, Francis, BEd, MA, PhD; Malawi diplomatist and academic; *High Commissioner to UK;* m. Elizabeth Moto. *Career:* Assoc. Prof. and Prin. of Chancellor Coll., Faculty of Educ., Univ. of Malawi; High Commr to UK 2006–. *Publication:* Trends in Malawian Literature 2001.
Address: Malawi High Commission, 70 Winnington Road, London, N2 0TX, England (office). *Telephone:* (20) 8455-5624 (office). *Fax:* (20) 3235-1066 (office). *E-mail:* malawihighcom@btconnect.com (office). *Website:* www.malawihighcom.org.uk (office).

MOTOC, Mihnea Ioan, LLM, JD; Romanian diplomatist; *Permanent Representative, European Union;* m. Iulia Motoc; one s. *Education:* Univ. of Bucharest, Univ. of Nice, George Washington Univ., USA. *Career:* joined Ministry of Foreign affairs 1991, Attaché Legal Treaties Dept 1991–92, Second Sec., Deputy Dir Human Rights Dept 1994–97, First Sec., Dir EU Dept 1996–97, Dir-Gen. Dept for European and Euro-Atlantic Orgs 1997–99; Amb. to Netherlands, Perm. Rep. to Org. for the Prohibition of Chemical Weapons 1999–2001; Sec. of State for European Integration and Multilateral Affairs 2001–03; Perm. Rep. to UN, New York 2003–08; Perm. Rep., EU, Brussels 2008–; Pres. Nat. Security Authority, Inter-Departmental Comm. for accession to NATO; Nat. Coordinator Stability Pact for Southeastern Europe; mem. Int. Humanitarian Fact Finding Comm.; Commdr, Nat. Order of Merit, Romania.
Address: Office of the Permanent Representative of Romania, 12 rue Montoyer, 1000 Brussels, Belgium (office). *Telephone:* (2) 700-06-40 (office). *Fax:* (2) 700-06-41 (office). *E-mail:* bru@roumisue.org (office). *Website:* www.ue.mae.ro (office).

MOTTAKI, Manouchehr, MA; Iranian diplomatist and politician; *Minister of Foreign Affairs;* b. 1953, Bandar Gaz, Golestan. *Education:* Bangalore Univ., India, Tehran Univ. *Career:* joined Islamic Revolutionary Guards Corps (IRGC) 1979, IRGC Liaison Officer to Ministry of Foreign Affairs (MOF) 1979–80; Deputy of Islamic Consultative Ass. (Majlis) 1980–84, 2004–; Head of Political Bureau, MOF 1984–85; Amb. to Turkey 1985–89, to Japan 1994–99; Dir-Gen. of W European Affairs, MOF 1989; Deputy Foreign Minister for Int. Affairs 1989–92, for Consular and Parl. Affairs 1992–4; Adviser to Minister of Foreign Affairs 1999–2001; Vice-Pres. Islamic Culture and Communications Org. 2001–04; Campaign Man. for Presidential Cand. Ali Larijani 2005; Minister of Foreign Affairs 2005–.
Address: Ministry of Foreign Affairs, Shahid Abd al-Hamid Mesri Street, Ferdowsi Avenue, Tehran, Iran (office). *Telephone:* (21) 61151 (office). *Fax:* (21) 33212763 (office). *E-mail:* matbuat@mfa.gov.ir (office). *Website:* www.mfa.gov.ir (office).

MOUALLEM, Walid; Syrian diplomatist; *Minister of Foreign Affairs;* b. 1941. *Education:* Cairo Univ. *Career:* joined diplomatic corps 1964; held positions at missions in Saudi Arabia, Spain; fmr charge d'affaires London, UK; Amb. to Romania 1975–80; Head, Foreign Ministry Bureau, Damascus 1984–90; Amb. to USA 1990–2000; Deputy Minister of Foreign Affairs 2005–06, Minister of Foreign Affairs 2006–.
Address: Ministry of Foreign Affairs, rue ar-Rashid, Damascus, Syria (office). *Telephone:* (11) 3331200 (office). *Fax:* (11) 3327620 (office).

MOUBARAK, Samir, PhD; Lebanese diplomatist; *Ambassador to Spain;* b. 3 March 1943, Beirut. *Education:* Ecole des Hautes Etudes Commerciales, Paris, Sorbonne, Paris. *Career:* Political Section, Ministry of Foreign Affairs, Beirut 1967–69; mem. Lebanese Del., Perm. Mission of Lebanon to UN, New York 1969–73; First Sec., Embassy, Paris 1973–77, Chargé d'affaires a.i., Embassy, Madrid; Special Adviser to Minister of Foreign Affairs, Beirut 1977–82; Amb. to Sweden 1982–88; Amb., Ministry of Foreign Affairs 1988–94; Perm. Rep. of Lebanon to UN, New York 1994–99, Vice-Pres. 50th Session UN Gen. Ass. 1995, Vice-Pres. ECOSOC, New York 1996; Amb. to Spain 1999–.
Address: Lebanese Embassy, Paseo de la Castellana 178, 3° Izqda, 28046 Madrid, Spain (office). *Telephone:* (91) 3451368 (office). *Fax:* (91) 3455631 (office). *E-mail:* leem_e@teleline.es (office).

MOUNTAIN, Ross; New Zealand UN official; *Acting Special Representative for Iraq, United Nations; Career:* Inter-Agency Liaison Officer, Div. of Social Affairs, UN, Geneva 1973–75, Coordinator UN Non-Governmental

Liaison Service 1975–83; Chief of Information Section, UNDP European Office 1976–85; Deputy Resident Rep. in S Pacific, Fiji 1985–88; UNDP Resident Rep. ad interim and Dir UN Information Centre, Kabul, Afghanistan 1988–91; UN Special Coordinator for Emergency Relief Operations, UNDP Resident Rep. to World Food Programme and UN Population Fund (UNFPA) Rep. in Liberia 1991–93; UNDP Rep. and UN Humanitarian Affairs Coordinator, Haiti, on secondment from UN Resident Coordinator and UNDP Resident Coordinator for Eastern Caribbean, Barbados 1993–95; UN Resident Coordinator in Lebanon and Resident Rep. of UNDP and UNFPA 1995–98; Asst Emergency Relief Coordinator and Dir Geneva Office, Office for the Coordination of Humanitarian Relief (OCHA) 1998–2003; UN Acting Special Rep. for Iraq Dec. 2003–; fmr Humanitarian Coordinator ad interim for E Timor Crisis, Special Humanitarian Envoy for floods in Mozambique, Special Humanitarian Coordinator for Liberia, Head OCHA Crisis Task Team for Iraq.
Address: Office of the Special Representative for Iraq, United Nations, New York, NY 10017, USA. *Telephone:* (212) 963-1234. *Fax:* (212) 963-4879. *E-mail:* inquiries@un.org. *Website:* www.un.org/Depts/oip.

MOURIKIS, John; Greek diplomatist; *Permanent Representative, United Nations; Education:* Univ. of Zurich, Univ. of Athens, Univ. of Paris II. *Career:* attaché, Ministry of Foreign Affairs 1976; served in office of Prime Minister 1976–79; mem. Perm. Mission to UN, New York 1979–82; with NATO Dept, Ministry of Foreign Affairs 1982–85, with Cabinet of Minister of Foreign Affairs 1985–90; Minister Counsellor, Embassy in Washington, DC 1991–93; Minister, Embassy in Cyprus 1993–96; Amb. to Syria 1996–2000; Dir North America Dept, Ministry of Foreign Affairs 2000–04; Amb. to Canada 2004–07; Perm. Rep. to UN, New York 2007–.
Address: Permanent Mission of Greece to the United Nations, 866 Second Avenue, 13th Floor, New York, NY 10017, USA (office). *Telephone:* (212) 888-6900 (office). *Fax:* (212) 888-4440 (office). *E-mail:* mission@greeceun.org (office). *Website:* www.greeceun.org (office).

MOUSAWI, Faisal Radhi al-, MB, BCh, FRCSE; Bahraini government official and orthopaedic surgeon; b. 6 April 1944, Bahrain; one s. three d. *Education:* Univ. of Cairo, Egypt. *Career:* fmr Rotary Intern, Cairo Univ. Hosp.; House Officer, Sr House Officer, Dept of Surgery, Govt Hosp., Bahrain; Sr House Officer, Accident and Orthopaedic Surgery, Cen. Middx Hosp., London; Orthopaedic Surgery, St Helier Hosp., Carshalton, Surrey; Gen. Surgery, Nelson Hosp., London, St Bartholomew's Hosp., London; Registrar, Orthopaedic Surgery, Whittington Hosp., London, Gen. and Traumatic Surgery, Wexford Co. Hosp., Ireland; locum consultant, Whittington Hosp. 1983–84; Consultant Orthopaedic Surgeon, Salmaniya Medical Centre, Bahrain 1976–, Chair. Dept of Surgery 1982–84, Chief of Medical Staff June–Aug. 1982, Chair. Dept of Orthopaedic Surgery; Asst Prof. Coll. of Medicine and Medical Sciences, Arabian Gulf Univ.; Asst Under-Sec., Ministry of Health 1982–85, Minister of Health 1995–2002; Chair. Shura Council 2002–06; mem. Scientific Council, Arab Bd for Surgery 1979–; Chair. Arab Bd Cttee for Sub-specialities in Surgery, Arab Bd for Orthopaedic Surgery 1990–, Chair. Training Cttee 1988–; Chair. Nat. Arab Bd Cttee and Co-ordinator, Arab Bd Programme in Surgery, Bahrain; Examiner, Ministry of Health Qualification Examination 1982–, Royal Coll. of Surgeons, Ireland, Part B Fellowship Examination; mem. Editorial Bd Bahrain Medical Bulletin; Founding mem. and Pres. Gulf Orthopaedic Asscn; mem. European Soc. for Sport Medicine, Knee Surgery and Arthroscopy; Fellow, British Orthopaedic Asscn, Royal Coll. of Surgeons, Ireland. *Publications:* numerous papers and articles.
Address: c/o Shura Council, PO Box: 2991, Shaikh Duaij Road, Ghudaibiya, Bahrain (office). *Website:* www.shura.gov.bh (office).

MOUSSA, Amre Mahmoud, LLB; Egyptian politician and diplomatist; *Secretary-General, League of Arab States;* b. 3 Oct. 1936, Cairo. *Education:* Cairo Univ. *Career:* joined Ministry of Foreign Affairs 1957; served in several diplomatic posts abroad, including Amb. to India 1983–86; Perm. Rep. to the UN 1990–91; Minister of Foreign Affairs 1991–2001; Sec.-Gen., League of Arab States (Arab League) 2001–.
Address: League of Arab States, POB 11642, Tahrir Square, Cairo, Egypt (office). *Telephone:* (2) 3934499 (office). *Fax:* (2) 5740331 (office). *E-mail:* secretary-general@las.int (office). *Website:* www.arableagueonline.org (office).

MOUSTAPHA, Imad, PhD; Syrian diplomatist and computer scientist; *Ambassador to USA. Education:* Univ. of Surrey, UK. *Career:* consultant to several int. and regional orgs on science and tech. policies in Middle East; Co-founder Network of Syrian Scientists, Technologists and Innovators Abroad (NOSSTIA); Dean, Faculty of Information Tech., Univ. of Damascus and Sec.-Gen. Arab School of Science and Tech. –2004; Amb. to USA 2004–; fmr mem. Syrian Team responsible for drafting reform strategies for Ministries of Culture, Educ. and Higher Educ.; media

appearances on nat. and int. TV programmes. *Publications:* several books and more than 200 articles in English and Arabic.
Address: Embassy of Syria, 2215 Wyoming Avenue, NW, Washington, DC 20008, USA (office). *Telephone:* (202) 232-6313 (office). *Fax:* (202) 234-9548 (office). *E-mail:* info@syrembassy.net (office). *Website:* www.syrianembassy.us (office).

MOVAHEDIAN ATTAR, Rasoul; Iranian diplomatist; *Ambassador to UK;* m. Azam Kolahdouzan. *Career:* fmr Advisor to Minister of Foreign Affairs, fmr Head of Dept for Soviet Union, Eastern Europe, N America in Ministry of Foreign Affairs, fmr Amb. to Czech Repub. and Slovakia, to Portugal, Amb. to UK 2006–.
Address: Embassy of Iran, 16 Prince's Gate, London, SW7 1PT, England (office). *Telephone:* (20) 7225-3000 (office). *Fax:* (20) 7589-4440 (office). *E-mail:* info@iran-embassy.org.uk (office). *Website:* www.iran-embassy.org.uk (office).

MOYO, S(imon) K(haya); Zimbabwean politician and diplomatist; *Ambassador to South Africa;* b. 1945. *Career:* fmr mem. Parl. (ZANU (PF)) for Bulilima-mangwe South; fmr ZANU (PF) Politburo Deputy-Sec. for Legal Affairs; Minister of Transport and Energy 1996, of Mines, Environment and Tourism 1998; Amb. to South Africa 2000–.
Address: Embassy of Zimbabwe, 798 Merton Street, Arcadia, Pretoria 0083, South Africa (office). *Telephone:* (12) 3425125 (office). *Fax:* (12) 3425126 (office). *E-mail:* zimpret@lantic.net (office).

MOZENA, Dan, MA; American diplomatist; *Ambassador to Angola;* b. Ia; m. Grace Mozena; one s. one d. *Education:* Iowa State Univ., Univ. of Wisconsin, Madison. *Career:* spent 20 years working on family dairy farm; served as Peace Corps Volunteer in Zaïre; began his Foreign Service career in Lusaka, Zambia 1982, later Deputy Chief of Mission, Officer-in-Charge for S Africa and Deputy Dir for Southern African Affairs, Dept of State 1990s, posted to Kinshasa 1990s, Dir Office of Southern African Affairs, Dept of State 2004–07, Amb. to Angola 2008–.
Address: US Embassy, Rua Houari Boumedienne 32, CP 6468, Luanda, Angola (office). *Telephone:* 222641000 (office). *Fax:* 222641232 (office). *E-mail:* econusembassyluanda@yahoo.com (office). *Website:* luanda.usembassy.gov (office).

MPAHLWA, Mandisi B. M.; South African politician; *Minister of Trade and Industry; Career:* fmr Deputy Minister of Finance; Minister of Trade and Industry 2004–.
Address: Ministry of Trade and Industry, House of Trade and Industry, 11th Floor, cnr Prinsloo and Pretorius Streets, Pretoria 0002 (office); Private Bag X84, Pretoria 0001, South Africa (office). *Telephone:* (12) 3109791 (office). *Fax:* (12) 3222701 (office). *E-mail:* alec@dti.pwv.gov.za (office). *Website:* www.dti.gov.za (home).

M'POKO, Bene L., BA, MBA; Democratic Republic of the Congo economist and diplomatist; *Ambassador to South Africa;* m. R. M'Poko. *Career:* worked in int. banking for 15 years with posts in USA, Europe and Africa; has held positions at World Bank, UNDP, USAID; consultant on privatization and pvt. sector devt; Amb. to SA 2001–; mem. Southern African Devt Community Standing Cttee of Officials 2007–.
Address: Embassy of the Democratic Republic of Congo, 791 Schoeman Street, Arcadia, Pretoria 0083, South Africa (office). *Telephone:* (12) 3441478 (office). *Fax:* (12) 3441510 (office). *E-mail:* rdcongo@lantic.net (office).

MPOMBO, George W.; Zambian politician; *Minister of Defence; Career:* mem. Nat. Ass. (Movt for Multi-party Democracy—MMD) 2001–, Minister of Energy and Water Devt 2003-05, Minister for Copperbelt Prov. 2005-06, Minister of Defence 2006–.
Address: Ministry of Defence, PO Box 31931, Lusaka, Zambia (office). *Telephone:* (1) 252366 (office).

MRAMOR, Dušan, DEcon; Slovenian economist and academic; *Professor of Finance, University of Ljubljana;* b. 1 Nov. 1953, Ljubljana. *Education:* Univ. of Ljubljana. *Career:* fmr Visiting Prof., Indiana Univ., USA, Cen. European Univ., Budapest, Wirtschaftuniversität, Vienna, Assoc. Dean, Faculty of Econs, Univ. of Ljubljana, Chair. Man. Board, Univ. of Ljubljana; fmr mem. Prime Minister's Strategic Econ. Council; Minister of Finance 2002–04; Prof. of Finance, Univ. of Ljubljana 2004–; fmr Pres. Expert Council Agency for the Securities Market; fmr Pres. Bd of Dirs Univ. of Ljubljana; mem. Expert Council Slovenian Inst. of Auditing, Coordinating Cttee Slovenian Asscn of Economists, Slovenian Asscn of Accountants.
Address: Faculty of Economics, University of Ljubljana, Kardeljeva ploscad 17, Ljubljana, 1000, Slovenia (office). *Telephone:* (1) 5892400 (office). *Fax:* (1) 5892698 (office). *E-mail:* dusan.mramor@ef.uni-lj.si

(office). *Website:* www.ef.uni-lj.si/pedagogi/pe_pedagog.asp?id=51 (office).

MROUDJAE, Ali; Comoran politician; *Leader, Parti Comorien pour la Démocratie et le Progrès;* b. 2 Aug. 1939, Moroni; m. Nourdine Batouli 1967; three s. five d. *Career:* Minister of Foreign Affairs and Co-operation 1979–82; Prime Minister of the Comoros 1982–85; Minister of State for Internal and Social Affairs Jan.–Sept. 1985; numerous other portfolios; currently Leader Parti Comorien pour la Démocratie et le Progrès (PCDP). *Address:* PCDP, Route Djivani, BP 179, Moroni; BP 58, Rond Point Gobadjou, Moroni, Comoros. *Telephone:* (73) 1733 (PCDP); (73) 1266. *Fax:* (73) 0650 (PCDP).

MROZ, John Edwin, BA, MA; American research institute executive; *President, EastWest Institute;* m. Karen Linehan Mroz; two s. one d. *Education:* Northeastern Univ., Univ. of Notre Dame, Fletcher School of Law and Diplomacy, Tufts Univ. *Career:* Founder, Pres. and CEO EastWest Inst. (EWI), New York 1981–, centres est. in Moscow, Brussels and Prague, centres-turned-ind. non-governmental orgs in Warsaw, Belgrade, Kiev, Budapest, Groningen, Kosice; adviser to more than 20 govts including USA, Germany, Poland, Russia and EU Comm., NATO, Council of Europe and G8; contribs to Foreign Affairs; mem. Council on Foreign Relations; numerous int. awards. *Publications:* Beyond Security: Private Perceptions Among Arabs and Israelis 1980; articles and chapters in books.
Address: EastWest Institute (EWI), 700 Broadway, 2nd Floor, New York, NY 10003, USA (office). *Telephone:* (212) 824-4110 (office). *Fax:* (212) 824-4149 (home). *E-mail:* zormj@ewi.info (office). *Website:* www.iews.org (office).

MROZIEWICZ, Robert; Polish politician and historian; *Professor, Collegium Civitas, Polish Academy of Sciences;* b. 20 Sept. 1942, Warsaw; m. Elżbieta Nowik; two s. *Education:* Univ. of Warsaw. *Career:* Asst, Warsaw Univ. 1965–68, Polish Inst. of Int. Affairs 1968–70; Inst. of History, Polish Acad. of Sciences 1971–89, Asst Prof., Inst. of History 1985, currently Prof., Collegium Civitas; Minister-Adviser, Ministry of Foreign Affairs; Deputy Perm. Rep. to UN, New York, then Perm. Rep. of UN, New York 1990–92; Under-Sec. of State in Ministry of Foreign Affairs; Pres. of UN Social and Economic Council 1992–97, Pres. of Gen. Ass. 1992; Under-Sec. of State for Co-operation with Abroad and Integration with NATO in Ministry of Nat. Defence 1997; mem. Solidarity Trade Union 1980–99; Commdr's Cross of Order Polonia Restituta 1995. *Publications:* author and co-author of six monographs and various scientific articles.
Address: Collegium Civitas, Palace of Culture and Science, Plac Defilad 1, 12 piętro, 00-901 Warsaw, Poland (office). *Telephone:* (22) 625-7187 (office). *Fax:* (22) 656-7175 (office). *Website:* www.collegium.edu.pl (office).

MSIKA, Joseph; Zimbabwean politician; *Vice-President;* m. Maria Msika. *Career:* Co-Vice-Pres. Zimbabwe African Nat. Union (ZANU) Dec. 2000–; Co-Vice-Pres. of Zimbabwe 2001–.
Address: Office of the Vice-Presidents, Munhumutapa Building, Samora Machel Avenue, Private Bag 7700, Harare, Zimbabwe (office). *Telephone:* (4) 707091 (office).

MSWANE, Phillip Nhlanhla Muntu, BA, MBA; Swazi politician and diplomatist; *High Commissioner to South Africa;* b. 25 June 1955, Ludzeludze; m. *Career:* Gen. Man. Swaziland Trade Fairs Ltd 1990–93; Minister for Commerce and Industry 1993–95, Minister for Health and Social Welfare 1995–96, Minister for Public Service and Information 1996–98, Senator, Pres. of Senate 1998–2001; Chair. Ludzeludze Devt Cttee 2004–05; mem. Bd of Dirs and Chair. Finance Cttee, Pigg's Peak Hotel and Casino Pty Ltd (parastatal co.) 2004–05; High Commr to S Africa 2005–, also accred to Angola, Botswana, Lesotho, Namibia, Zambia; mem. Econs Asscn of Swaziland, Inst. of Marketing Man.
Address: PO Box 3363, Swaziland, Southern Africa; Embassy of Swaziland, PO Box 14294, Hatfield 0028 (office); Embassy of Swaziland, 715 Government Avenue, Arcadia, Pretoria, 0007, South Africa (office). *Telephone:* 6181842 (Swaziland) (office); (12) 3441910 (SA) (office); 5504748 (Swaziland) (home). *Fax:* (12) 3430455 (SA) (office).

MSWATI III, HM The King of Swaziland; Makhosetive; b. 19 April 1968; m. to 13 wives (Emakhosikati); 24 c. *Education:* Sherborne School, UK. *Career:* crowned King of Swaziland 25 April 1986.
Address: Lozitha Palace, Mbabane, Swaziland.

MTSHALI, G. J., PhD; South African diplomatist; *Permanent Representative, United Nations, Geneva; Career:* fmr Chief Dir Nat. Programmes, Dept of Health; currently Perm. Rep. to UN and Int. Orgs, Geneva; fmr mem. Project Cttee, Nat. Law Comm.

Address: Permanent Mission of South Africa to the United Nations, 65 Rue du Rhône, 1204 Geneva, Switzerland (office). *Telephone:* (22) 849-5454 (office). *Fax:* (22) 849-5432 (office). *E-mail:* mission.south-africa@ties.itu .int (office).

MU'ALLA, HH Sheikh Rashid bin Ahmad al-, (Ruler of Umm al-Qaiwain); United Arab Emirates; b. 1930. *Career:* apptd Deputy Ruler of Umm al-Qaiwain, succeeded as Ruler on the death of his father Feb. 1981–; Chair. Umm al-Qaiwain Municipality 1967; constituted the Emirate's first municipal council 1975.
Address: Ruler's Palace, Umm al-Qaiwain, United Arab Emirates.

MUASHER, Marwan Jamil, MS, PhD; Jordanian politician and diplomatist; *Senior Vice-President for External Affairs, Communications and United Nations Affairs, World Bank Group;* b. 14 June 1956, Amman; two c. *Education:* American Univ. of Beirut, Lebanon, Purdue Univ., USA. *Career:* Asst Research Engineer, Univ. of Petroleum and Minerals, Saudi Arabia 1983–84; Dir Computer Centre, Jordan Electric Power Co. 1984; Sr Consultant Special System Co. 1984–85; Head, Computer Unit and Monitory System, Ministry of Planning 1985–87, Dir Socio-Econ. Information Centre, Nat. Information System 1987–90; Press Adviser to Prime Minister 1990–91; Head, Jordan Information Bureau, USA 1991–94; Amb. to Israel 1995–96, to USA and Mexico 1997–2002; Minister of Information 1996, of Foreign Affairs 2002–04; Deputy Prime Minister and Minister of State for Prime Ministry Affairs and Govt Performance 2004–05; Senator 2006–07; Sr Vice-Pres. for External Affairs, Communications and UN Affairs, World Bank, Washington, DC 2007–; political columnist, Jordan Times 1983–90; Al-Kawkab Medal, First Order (Jordan) 2000, Dr hc (Purdue Univ.) 1999, Independence Medal 2000, Diplomat of the Year Award, LA Int. Affairs Council 2000.
Address: The World Bank, 1818 H Street, NW, Washington, DC 20433, USA (office). *Telephone:* (202) 473-1000 (office). *Fax:* (202) 477-6391 (office). *Website:* www.worldbank.org (office).

MUBARAK, (Muhammad) Hosni, BMilSci, BA; Egyptian air force officer and head of state; *President;* b. 4 May 1928, Kafr El-Moseilha, Minuffya Governorate; m. Suzanne Sabet; two s. *Education:* Mil. Acad., Air Acad. *Career:* joined Air Force 1950, Lecturer Air Force Acad. 1952–59; Commdr Cairo West Air Base 1964; Dir-Gen. Air Acad. 1967–69; Air Force Chief of Staff 1969–72; C-in-C 1972–75; promoted to Lt-Gen. 1974; Vice-Pres. of Egypt 1975–81; Pres. 1981– (cand. of NDP); Vice-Pres. Nat. Democratic Party (NDP) 1979, Pres. 1982; mem. Higher Council for Nuclear Energy 1975–; Sec.-Gen. NDP and Political Bureau 1981–82, Chair. 1982–; Chair. OAU 1989–90, 1993–94, Arab Summit 1996–, GI5 1998, 2000; Pres. Emergency Arab Summit 2000, D-8 Summit 2001, COMESA Summit 2001; Order of Star of Honour 1964, 1974, Medal of the Star of Sinai of the First Order 1983 and numerous other foreign decorations; Dr hc (Bulgaria) 1998, (Beijing) 1999, (St Johns) 1999, (George Washington) 1999; Louise Michel Prize 1990, Prize of Democratic Human Rights, Social and Political Studies Centre, Paris 1990, UN Prize of Population 1994 and numerous other awards and honours.
Address: Presidential Palace, Abdeen, Cairo, Egypt.

MUBURI-MUITA, Zachary Dominic; Kenyan diplomatist; *Permanent Representative, United Nations;* b. June 1957; m.; three c. *Education:* Univ. of Nairobi, Univ. of Khartoum, Univ. of Oxford, UK. *Career:* Asst Sec., Middle East and Americas Divs, Ministry of Foreign Affairs 1982–84; Third Sec., Embassy in Sudan 1984–89; Asst Sec., Protocol Div. and Asia and Australasia Div., Ministry of Foreign Affairs 1989–92, Head, Americas Div. 2002, Head, Middle East Div. 2002–03; seconded to Faculty, Nat. Defense Coll. 1998–2002; Prin. Counsellor, Embassy in Israel 2004; Amb. to Tanzania 2004–06; Perm. Rep. to UN, New York 2006–.
Address: Permanent Mission of Kenya to the United Nations, 866 United Nations Plaza, Rm 486, New York, NY 10017, USA (office). *Telephone:* (212) 421-4740 (office). *Fax:* (212) 486-1985 (office). *E-mail:* kenya@un.int (office). *Website:* www.un.int/kenya (office).

MUCHEMI, Joseph Kirugumi; Kenyan diplomatist; *High Commissioner to UK;* b. Nyeri; m. Cecilia Muchemi; one s. two d. *Education:* Univ. of London, UK, Univ. of Pittsburgh, USA. *Career:* more than 30 years' experience in public service and pvt. sector; began his career working for the East African Community (EAC) from 1967, later Sec.-Gen. EAC –1977, served as Deputy Head to Secr. and the Community Councils, notably Finance, Communication, Trade and Research; joined Govt of Kenya as Perm. Sec. 1977, served in several ministries, including Social Services and Housing, Public Works, and Foreign Affairs; took leave from Govt to gain experience in business sector 1984; headed a financial inst. est. to assist indigenous entrepreneurs to start up businesses; acted as consultant in training for financial and admin. man. of small-scale business, local govt officials and political party activists; High Commr to UK (also accred as

Amb. to Ireland and Switzerland) 2003–, Perm. Rep. to IMO 2005–; Moran of the Order of the Burning Spear (MBS).
Address: High Commission of Kenya, 45 Portland Place, London, W1N 4AS, England (office). *Telephone:* (20) 7636-2371 (office). *Fax:* (20) 7323-6717 (office). *E-mail:* consular@kenyahighcommission.net (office). *Website:* www.kenyahighcommission.net (office).

MUELLER, Robert Swan, III, MA, JD; American lawyer and federal official; *Director, Federal Bureau of Investigation (FBI);* b. 7 Aug. 1944, New York City; m. Ann Standish 1966; two d. *Education:* Princeton Univ., New York Univ. and Univ. of Virginia. *Career:* Capt. US Marine Corps 1967–70; Assoc. Pillsbury, Madison & Sutro, San Francisco 1973–76; Asst US Attorney, US Attorney's Office, Northern Dist Calif., San Francisco 1976–80, Chief, Special Prosecutions Unit 1980–81, Criminal Div. 1981–82; Chief, Criminal Div. Mass. Dist, US Attorney's Office, Boston 1982–85; First Asst US Attorney in Boston 1985, US Attorney for Mass. Dist 1986–87, Deputy US Attorney for Mass. Dist 1987–88; Pnr Hill and Barlow, Boston 1988–89; Asst to Attorney Gen. for criminal matters, US Dept of Justice, Washington, DC 1989–90, Asst Attorney Gen. for criminal div. 1990–93, Interim US Attorney, Northern Dist Calif. 1998–2001; Dir FBI 2001–; lawyer, Hale & Dorr, Washington 1993; Bronze Star, Purple Heart, Vietnamese Cross of Gallantry.
Address: Department of Justice, Federal Bureau of Investigation, J. Edgar Hoover Building, 950 Pennsylvania Avenue, NW, Washington, DC 20530, USA (office). *Telephone:* (202) 324-3000 (office). *Website:* www.fbi.gov (office).

MUFTI, Hania, MSc; Jordanian lawyer and international organization executive; *Director, Middle East and North Africa Division, Human Rights Watch;* b. Amman. *Education:* in Jordan and Lebanon and Univ. of Bath, UK. *Career:* more than 20 years' professional experience in human rights research and advocacy; Researcher, Middle East Research Dept, Amnesty Int.'s Secr., London, UK 1981–97; Dir Middle East and North Africa Div., Human Rights Watch, London 2000–. *Publications:* author of numerous reports for Amnesty International, including Iraq: The World Would Not Listen 1994, Kuwait: Three Years of Unfair Trials 1994, Iraq: Human Rights Abuses in Iraqi Kurdistan Since 1991 1995, Bahrain: A Human Rights Crisis 1995.
Address: Human Rights Watch, 2nd Floor, 2-12 Pentonville Road, London, N1 9HF, England (office). *Telephone:* (20) 7713-1995 (office). *Fax:* (20) 7713-1800 (office). *E-mail:* hrwuk@hrw.org (office). *Website:* www.hrw.org (office).

MUGABE, Robert Gabriel, BA, BAdmin, BEd, MSc (Econ), LLM; Zimbabwean politician, head of state and fmr teacher; *President;* b. 21 Feb. 1924, Kutama; m. 1st Sarah Mugabe (died 1992); one s. (deceased); m. 2nd Grace Marufu 1996. *Education:* Kutama and Empandeni Mission School, Fort Hare Univ. Coll., S Africa, Univs of S Africa and London. *Career:* teacher, at Drifontein Roman Catholic School, Umvuma 1952, Salisbury S Primary School 1953, in Gwelo 1954, Chalimbana Teacher Training Coll. 1955, in Accra, Ghana 1958–60; entered politics 1960; Publicity Sec. of Nat. Dem. Party 1960–61; Publicity Sec. Zimbabwe African People's Union 1961; detained Sept.–Dec. 1962, March–April 1963; escaped to Tanzania April 1963; Co-Founder of Zimbabwe African Nat. Union (ZANU) Aug. 1963; Sec.-Gen. Aug. 1963; in detention in Rhodesia 1964–74; Pres. ZANU; mem. Politburo ZANU 1984–; Jt Leader of Patriotic Front (with Joshua Nkomo) 1976–79; contested Feb. 1980 elections as Leader of ZANU (PF) (name changed to ZANU 1984) Party, Pres. 1988–; Minister of Defence 1980–87, also fmrly of Public Works, Industry and Tech.; Prime Minister of Zimbabwe 1980–87; Pres. of Zimbabwe 1988–; Chancellor Univ. of Zimbabwe; apptd Amb. for southern Africa, African Union 2003; Newsmaker of the Year Award (S African Soc. of Journalists) 1980, Africa Prize 1988; Dr hc (Ahmadu Bello Univ., Nigeria) 1980; Int. Human Rights Award (Howard Univ., Washington) 1981, Jawarhalal Nehru Award 1992.
Address: Office of the President, Munhumutapa Building, Samora Machel Avenue, Private Bag 7700, Causeway, Harare, Zimbabwe. *Telephone:* (4) 707091 (office).

MUGASHA, Florence; Ugandan international organization official and civil servant. *Career:* joined Ugandan Public Service in 1970s; Govt rep. to numerous regional and int. confs and summits; Head of Public Service and Sec. to Cabinet (first woman to head public services in Africa) 1996–2002; Deputy Sec.-Gen. (Political) of Commonwealth (second woman to assume position) 2002–08; mem. Bd Dirs Commonwealth Asscn for Public Admin and Man.
Address: c/o Commonwealth Secretariat, Marlborough House, Pall Mall, London, SW1Y 5HX, England. *Telephone:* (20) 7839-3411. *Fax:* (20) 7930-0827 (office).

MUGHAIRY, Hunaina Sultan Ahmed al-; Omani diplomatist; *Ambassador to USA;* m.; one s. one d. *Education:* Politechnical Inst., Cairo, Egypt, New York Univ., USA. *Career:* Asst to Economical Advisor of His Majesty the Sultan of Oman 1973–74; Dir Loans Admin, Ministry of Commerce and Industry 1979–84; Perm. Mission of the Sultanate of Oman to UN, New York 1984–85; Dir of Industrial Planning and Research, Ministry of Commerce and Industry 1985–91; Advisor for Industrial Affairs, Office of Under-Sec. for Commerce and Industry 1991–96; Dir Gen. for Investment Promotion and Export Devt 1996–98, Rep. of Omani Center for Investment Promotion and Export Devt 1999–2005; Amb. to USA 2005–. *Address:* Embassy of Oman, 2535 Belmont Road, NW, Washington, DC 20008, USA (office). *Telephone:* (202) 387-1980 (office). *Fax:* (202) 745-4933 (office). *Website:* www.omani.info (office).

MUHAMMAD VI, HM The King of Morocco; b. 21 Aug. 1963, Rabat; m. Lalla Salma Bennani 2002; one s. (Crown Prince Moulay Hassan, b. 2003) one d. (b. 2007). *Education:* Collège Royal, Université Mohammed V, Faculté des Sciences Juridiques, Economiques et Sociales de Rabat. *Career:* Head Moroccan del., 7th Summit of Non-Aligned Nations, New Delhi 1983, 10th Franco–African Conf., Vittel 1983; apptd Co-ordinator Admin. and Services, Armed Forces 1985; rank of Gén. de Div. 1994; Hon. Pres. Asscn Socio–Culturelle du Bassin Méditerranéen 1979–; Chair. Org. Cttee 9th Mediterranean Games, Casablanca 1982; succeeded to the throne on the death of his father 23 July 1999. *Address:* Royal Palace, Rabat, Morocco.

MUHTADEE BILLAH, HRH Crown Prince, Haji al-; Brunei; b. 17 Feb. 1974, Istana Darul Hana, Bandar Seri Begawan; m. HRH Pengiran Anak Isteri Pengiran Anak Sarah binti Pengiran Salleh Ab Rahaman 2004. *Education:* Univ. of Brunei Darussalam, Oxford Centre for Islamic Studies, England. *Career:* proclaimed Crown Prince 10 Aug. 1998; attachments to various govt ministries and depts, and to private cos. *Address:* c/o Istana Nurul Iman, Bandar Seri Begawan, BA 1000, Brunei (office). *Website:* www.crownprince.bn.

MUIR, Richard John Sutherland, CMG, BA; British diplomatist; *Ambassador to Kuwait;* b. 25 Aug. 1942, London; m. Caroline Simpson 1965; one s. one d. *Education:* Stationers' Co. School and Univs of Reading and Strasbourg. *Career:* entered HM Diplomatic Service 1966; Second Sec. Jeddah 1967–70, Tunis 1970–72; FCO 1972–75; First Sec. Washington, DC 1975–79; Prin. Dept of Energy 1979–81; Counsellor, Jeddah 1981–85; FCO 1985–91; Under-Sec. and Chief Insp. Diplomatic Service 1991–94; Amb. to Oman 1994–98, to Kuwait 1999–. *Address:* United Kingdom Embassy, PO Box 2, 13001 Safat, Arabian Gulf Street, Kuwait City, Kuwait (office); c/o Foreign and Commonwealth Office, London, SW1A 2AH, England. *Telephone:* 2403336 (office). *Fax:* 2426799 (office). *E-mail:* general@britishembassy-kuwait.org (office). *Website:* www.britishembassy-kuwait.org (office).

MUJAWAR, Ali Muhammad, BA, MA, PhD; Yemeni academic and politician; *Prime Minister;* b. 1953, Shabwa. *Education:* Algiers Univ., Algeria and Grenoble Univ., France. *Career:* mem. Higher Studies Cttee, Business Dept, Univ. of Aden 1990–2000, Head, Business Man. Dept, Faculty of Econs 1994–96, Dean of Faculty of Oil and Minerals 1996–99, Dean, Faculty of Man. Studies 2001–03; Gen. Man. Al-Barah Cement Factory 1999–2000; fmr Deputy Minister of Civil Service and Insurance, Minister of Fisheries 2003–06, of Electricity and Water 2006–07, Prime Minister 2007–. *Address:* Office of the Prime Minister, San'a, Yemen (office). *Telephone:* (1) 274662 (office).

MUJICA CANTELAR, René Juan, Lic.Hist; Cuban diplomatist; *Ambassador to UK;* m. Silvia Blanca Nogales. *Education:* Univ. of Havana. *Career:* fmr Minister-Counsellor, Perm. Mission to UN, New York; Amb. to EU –2002, to UK 2005–. *Publications:* several lectures and articles on Cuban-US relations and Cuban foreign policy. *Address:* Embassy of Cuba, 167 High Holborn, London, WC1 6PA, England (office). *Telephone:* (20) 7240-2488 (office). *Fax:* (20) 7836-2602 (office). *E-mail:* embacuba@cubaldn.com (office). *Website:* www.cubaldn.com (office).

MUJURU, Joyce Teurai-Ropa; Zimbabwean politician; *Vice-President;* b. 15 April 1955, Mount Darwin; m. Tapfumanei Ruzambu Solomon Mujuru (Nhongo) 1977; four d. *Education:* Women's Univ. in Africa, Zimbabwe. *Career:* Minister of Youth, Sport and Recreation 1980–81, of Community Devt and Women's Affairs 1981–88, of Community and Co-operative Devt 1989–92, of Rural Resources and Water Devt 1996–2004; Vice-Pres. of Zimbabwe 2004–; Gov. and Resident Minister of Mashonaland Cen. Prov. 1993–96; Liberation Medal, War Veteran Order of Merit. *Address:* Office of the Vice-President, Munhumutapa Building, Samora Machel Avenue, Private Bag 7700, Causeway, Harare (office); No. 9 Tara Township, Ruwa (home); Box 57, Ruwa, Zimbabwe (home). *Telephone:* (4) 707091 (office).

MUKAMBAYEV, Usup Mukambayevich; Kyrgyzstani politician and lawyer; *President's Representative in Parliament;* b. 28 Jan. 1941, Dzholgolot, Kyrgyzia; m. Prof. Galina Mukumbayeva; two d. *Education:* Kyrgyz State Univ., higher courses at State Security Cttee of USSR. *Career:* shepherd, Kolkhoz Ak-Suy Region; army service; Sec. CP Cttee of State Security Cttee 1974–78; Deputy Head of Admin, State Security Cttee, Osh Region 1978–80, Head of Admin, State Security Cttee, Talass and Osh Regions 1980–86; First Deputy Chair. State Security Cttee, Kyrgyz Repub. 1986–91; Minister of Justice 1991–93; mem. Parl. (Zhogorku Kenesh) of Kyrgyzstan 1987–2000, Chair. Legis. Ass. 1996–2000, Pres.'s Rep. in Parl. 2001–; Academician, Int. Acad. of Turk Nations, Moscow 1997; Honoured Lawyer of the Kyrgyz Repub. 1993; Order of the Red Star 1985; Dank Medal 2000. *Publications:* Constitutional Development of Kyrgyzstan 1999, About the Activity of the Legislative Assembly of Zhogorku Kenesh of the Kyrgyz Republic 2000. *Address:* Office of the President, 720003 Bishkek (office); 176 Kurenkeeva str. Bishkek, Kyrgyzstan (home). *Telephone:* (312) 62-63-95 (office); (312) 66-13-28 (office); (312) 67-00-37 (home). *Fax:* (312) 21-86-27 (office).

MUKHAMETSHIN, Farid Khairullovich, DScS; Russian/Tatar politician; *Chairman, State Council of Tatarstan;* b. 22 May 1947, Almetyevsk, Tatarstan; m.; two c. *Education:* Almetyevak Higher Professional Tech. School, Ufa Inst. of Oil. *Career:* metal turner in factories; CP functionary; Sec. Almetyevsk City CP Cttee; Chair. Exec. Cttee, Almetyevsk City Soviet; Deputy Chair. Council of Ministers, Minister of Trade of Tatar ASSR 1970–91; Chair. Supreme Soviet of Tatarstan Repub. 1991–94; mem. Council of Fed. 1991–94, 1998–; Prime Minister of Tatarstan Repub. 1995–98; Chair. State Council of Tatarstan 1998–; del. to Council of Europe, Chair. Regional Comm.; Leader Tatarstan New Age political movt 1999–. *Address:* Parliament Buildings, Svobody pl. 1, 420060 Kazan, Tatarstan, Russia. *Telephone:* (8432) 67-63-00 (office). *Fax:* (8432) 92-73-59 (office). *E-mail:* first@gossov.tatarstan.ru (office). *Website:* www.gossov.tatarstan.ru (office).

MUKHERJEE, Pranab Kumar, LLB, MA; Indian politician; *Minister of External Affairs;* b. 11 Dec. 1935, Kirnahar, Birbhum Dist, W Bengal; m.; two s. one d. *Education:* Univ. of Calcutta. *Career:* started career as lecturer; Ed. Palli-O-Panchayat Sambad (Bengali monthly); Founder-Ed. Desher Dak (Bengali weekly) 1967–71; mem. Rajya Sabha 1969–, Leader 1980–88; Deputy Minister of Industrial Devt, Govt of India 1973; Deputy Minister for Shipping and Transport Jan.–Oct. 1974; Minister of State, Ministry of Finance 1974–75; Minister for Revenue and Banking 1975–77; Minister of Commerce 1980–82, of Finance Jan.–Sept. 1982, 1982–85, of Commerce 1993–95, of External Affairs 1995–96, of Defence 2004–06, of External Affairs 2006–; Deputy Chair. Planning Comm. with Cabinet rank; f. Rashtriya Samajwadi Congress 1987–; mem. Exec. Cttee Congress (I) Party 1972–73, All India Congress Cttee 1986; Treas. Congress (I) Party, mem. Working Cttee, Deputy Leader in Rajya Sabha; Pres. W Bengal Pradesh Congress Cttee; Hon. DLitt. *Publications:* Bangla Congress: An Aspect of Constitutional Problems in Bengal 1967, Mid-term Election 1969, Off the Track 1987, Challenges Before the Nation 1992. *Address:* Ministry of External Affairs, South Block, New Delhi 110 011 (office); S-22, Greater Kailash-II, New Delhi 110 048 (office); 13 Talkatora Road, New Delhi 110 001, India (home); 2-A, 1st Floor, 602/7 Kabi Bharti Sarni (Lake Road), Kolkata 700 029. *Telephone:* (11) 23011127 (ministry) (office); (11) 3737623 (office); (11) 6474025; (11) 6435656 (home). *Fax:* (11) 23011463 (ministry) (office). *E-mail:* pkm@sansad.nic.in (office). *Website:* meaindia.nic.in (office).

MUKHERJEE, Shiv Shankar; Indian diplomatist; *High Commissioner to UK;* m.; two c. *Education:* Delhi Univ. *Career:* joined Ministry of External Affairs 1971, fmr Amb. to Egypt, High Commr to S Africa –2004, Amb. to Nepal 2004–08, High Commr to UK 2008–; fmr Dir-Gen. Council for Cultural Relations. *Address:* High Commission of India, India House, Aldwych, London, WC2B 4NA, England (office). *Telephone:* (20) 7836-8484 (office). *Fax:* (20) 7836-4331 (office). *E-mail:* communicationwing@hcilondon.net (office). *Website:* www.hcilondon.net (office).

MUKHTAR, Chaudhry Ahmed; Pakistani politician and business executive; *Minister of Defence, with additional charge of Commerce and Textile Industry; Career:* Owner Service Shoe business and several other cos in Pakistan; sr leader of Pakistan People's Party, Gujrat Dist; fmr Minister of Commerce in Govt of Benazir Bhutto 1993–96; mem. Parl. for Guwjrat-II 2008–; Minister of Defence, with additional charge of Commerce and Textile Industry 2008–; Chair. Pakistan International Airlines.

Address: Ministry of Defence, Pakistan Secretariat, No. II, Rawalpindi 46000, Pakistan (office). *Telephone:* (51) 9271107 (office). *Fax:* (51) 9271113 (office). *E-mail:* tahir@mod.gov.pk (office). *Website:* www.mod.gov.pk (office).

MULET, Edmond; Guatemalan lawyer, politician, UN official and diplomatist; *Assistant Secretary-General for Peace-keeping Operations, United Nations;* b. 13 March 1951; m. Karen Lind; two s. *Education:* Universidad Mariano Galvez. *Career:* notary public; elected to Nat. Congress 1982, cand. to Nat. Constituent Ass. 1984, elected to Congress 1986–91, re-elected 1991–96; elected Sec.-Gen. Union del Centro Nacional party 1996; mem. Guatemalan-Belize Comm., first as Rep. of Congress and later as Del. from Exec. Br.; Amb. to USA 1993 (resgnd following coup d'état in Guatemala) resumed duties 1994–96, Amb. to EU, Belgium and Luxembourg 2000–06; Special Rep. of UN Sec.-Gen. in Haiti and Head of UN Stabilization Mission in Haiti (MINUSTAH) 2006–07; Asst Sec.-Gen. for Peace-keeping Operations, UN 2007–.
Address: Department of Peace-keeping Operations, Room S-3727-B, United Nations, New York, NY 10017, USA (office). *Telephone:* (212) 963-8077 (office). *Fax:* (212) 963-9222 (office). *Website:* www.un.org/Depts/dpko/dpko (office).

MULFORD, David Campbell, BA, MA, DPhil; American economist and diplomatist; *Ambassador to India;* m. Jeannie Simmons. *Education:* Lawrence Univ., Boston Univ., Univ. of Oxford, UK. *Career:* served as Special Asst to Sec. of Treasury as White House Fellow 1965–66; Man. Dir and Head of Int. Finance White, Weld and Co. Inc. 1966–74; Sr Investment Advisor Saudi Arabia Monetary Agency 1974–83; Under Sec. and Asst Sec. for Int. Affairs, US Treasury Dept 1984–92; Int. Chair. Credit Suisse First Boston, London 1992–2003; Amb. to India 2004–; mem. Council on Foreign Relations; affiliated with Center for Strategic and Int. Studies, Washington, DC; Chevalier, Légion d'honneur 1990, Order of May for Merit (Argentina) 1993, Officer's Cross Medal for Merit (Poland) 1995; Dr hc (Lawrence Univ.) 1984; Alexander Hamilton Award, US Treasury Dept 1992, Distinguished Alumni Award, Boston Univ. 1992.
Address: Embassy of the USA, Shanti Path, Chanakyapuri, New Delhi 110 021, India (office). *Telephone:* (11) 24198000 (office). *Fax:* (11) 241900170 (office). *E-mail:* ndcentral@state.gov (office). *Website:* newdelhi.usembassy.gov (office).

MULKI, Hani, MSc, PhD; Jordanian diplomatist and politician; b. 1951. *Education:* Rensselaer Polytechnic Inst., New York, USA. *Career:* fmr Sec.-Gen. Higher Council for Science and Tech.; fmr Minister of Industry and Trade, Sully, Water and Irrigation; Amb. to Egypt and the Arab League –2004; Minister of Foreign Affairs 2004–05; Special Adviser to King of Jordan 2005–; fmr Pres. Royal Scientific Soc.
Address: c/o Ministry of Foreign Affairs, PO Box 35217, Amman 11180, Jordan (office).

MULLA, Nabeela Abdulla al-, BA, MA; Kuwaiti diplomatist; *Ambassador to Belgium;* b. Kuwait City. *Education:* American Univ. of Beirut. *Career:* joined Ministry of Foreign Affairs 1968; del. to UN Gen. Ass. 1973–93, with various posts at Perm. Mission to UN including Deputy Perm. Rep. 1977–1994; Amb. to Zimbabwe 1994–95 (also accred to S Africa, Namibia, Mauritius and Botswana 1994–99), to Austria 1999–2003 (also accred Hungary, Slovakia and Slovenia), to Belgium 2006–; mem. Bd Dirs IAEA 2001–02, Chair. 2002–03; Rep. of Kuwait at OPEC 2002, 2003; resident Rep. to UN Office, Vienna, UNIDO, Comprehensive Test Ban Treaty Org., IAEA; fmr Amb. and Perm. Rep. to UN.
Address: Embassy of Kuwait, 43 avenue F. D. Roosevelt, 1050 Brussels, Belgium (office). *Telephone:* (2) 647-79-50 (office). *Fax:* (2) 646-12-98 (office). *E-mail:* embassy.kwt@euronet.be (office).

MULLEE, Patrick; British diplomatist; *Ambassador to Uruguay;* m. Joanna Mullee; two d. *Career:* joined Western European Dept, FCO 1974, Attaché, Prague 1976–77, Attaché, Caracas 1977–80, Latin America and Africa Floater 1980–84, Policy Planning Staff, FCO 1985–88, Vice-Consul, San José 1988–91, Head of Press and Public Affairs, British High Comm., Bridgetown 1991–95, Eastern Caribbean Desk, FCO 1995–97, Deputy Head of Personnel Man. Unit, Personnel Man. Dept 1997–2000, Deputy Head of Mission and HM Consul, Quito 2000–03, Human Resources Man., Directorate Gen. for Defence and Intelligence, FCO 2003–07, Amb. to Uruguay 2008–.
Address: British Embassy, Marco Bruto 1073 (Buceo), 11100 Montevideo, Uruguay (office). *Telephone:* (2) 6223630 (office). *Fax:* (2) 6227815 (office). *E-mail:* ukinuruguay@gmail.com (office). *Website:* www.britishembassy.gov.uk/uruguay (office).

MULLEN, Adm. Michael (Mike) Glenn, MSc; American military officer; *Chairman, Joint Chiefs of Staff;* b. 4 Oct. 1946, Los Angeles, Calif.; m.; two

s. *Education:* Naval Postgraduate School, Monterey, Calif., Harvard Business School. *Career:* served as junior officer aboard USS Collett, USS Blandy, USS Fox, USS Sterrett, held command posts aboard USS Noxubee, USS Goldsborough, USS Yorktown, as Flag Officer commanded Cruiser-Destroyer Group Two and the George Washington Battle Group, fmr Commdr US Second Fleet/NATO Striking Fleet Atlantic; non-operational posts have included Co. Officer and Exec. Asst to Commdt of Midshipmen, US Naval Acad., Annapolis, Dir, Surface Officer Distribution, Bureau of Naval Personnel; posts with Chief of Naval Operations include Deputy Dir and Dir of Surface Warfare, Deputy Chief of Naval Operations for Resources, Requirements and Assessments, 32nd Vice-Chief of Naval Operations 2003–04; served as Commdr Allied Jt Force Command Naples, Chief of Naval Operations 2004–07; Chair. Jt Chiefs of Staff 2007–; Jt Chiefs of Staff Identification Badge, Navy Surface Warfare Badge (Officer), Defense Distinguished Service Medal, Navy Distinguished Service Medal (2), Defense Superior Service Medal, Legion of Merit Decoration (6), Meritorious Service Medal, Navy and Marine Corps Commendation Medal, Navy and Marine Corps Achievement Medal, Navy Unit Commendation Ribbon, Navy Meritorious Unit Commendation Ribbon, Navy 'E' Ribbon, Navy Expeditionary Medal, Nat. Defense Service Medal (3), Armed Forces Expeditionary Medal, Vietnam Service Medal, Global War on Terrorism Service Medal, Humanitarian Service Medal (2), Navy Overseas Service Ribbon (4), Navy Sea Service Deployment Ribbon (2), Republic of Vietnam Gallantry Cross Unit Citation Medal, Republic of Vietnam Civil Actions Unit Citation Ribbon.
Address: Office of the Chairman of the Joint Chiefs of Staff, 400 Joint Staff Pentagon, Washington, DC 20318-0400, USA (office). *Website:* www.jcs.mil (office).

MUMBENGEGWI, Samuel, PhD; Zimbabwean politician; *Minister of Finance; Career:* began career as primary school teacher; Lecturer, Morgenster Teachers Coll.; Civil Servant, Ministry of Educ. 1980–87, Ministry of Higher Educ. and Tech. 1988–94; Deputy Sec. of Planning, Ministry of Higher Educ. and Tech. 1994; Head of Appointments, Promotions and Conditions, Public Service Comm. 1994–2000; mem. Parl. 2000–; Minister of Educ., Sports and Culture 2000–01, of Higher Educ. and Tech. 2001–03, of Industry and Int. Trade 2003–05, of Indigenisation and Empowerment 2005–07, of Finance 2007–.
Address: Ministry of Finance, Blocks B, E and G, Composite Building, Corner Samora Machel Avenuee and Fourth Street, Private Bag 7705, Causeway, Harare, Zimbabwe (office). *Telephone:* (4) 738603 (office). *Fax:* (4) 792750 (office). *Website:* www.mofed.gov.zw (office).

MUMBENGEGWI, Simbarashe Simbanenduku, BA, DipEd; Zimbabwean diplomatist, politician and public servant; *Minister of Foreign Affairs;* b. 20 July 1945, Chivi Dist; m. Emily Charasika 1983; one s. four d. *Education:* Monash Univ., Melbourne, Australia, Univ. of Zimbabwe. *Career:* active in Zimbabwe African Nat. Union (ZANU) Party 1963–, in exile, Australia 1966–72, Deputy Chief Rep. in Australia and Far East 1973–76, Chief Rep. 1976–78, Chief Rep. in Zambia 1978–80, mem. Cen. Cttee 1984–94; elected MP 1980, 1985; Deputy Minister of Foreign Affairs 1981–82, Minister of Water Resources and Devt 1982, of Housing 1982–84, of Public Construction and Nat. Housing 1984–88, of Transport 1988–90; Perm. Rep. to UN 1990–95; Amb. to Belgium, the Netherlands and Luxembourg, Perm. Rep. to EU 1995–99; Perm. Rep. to Org. for the Prohibition of Chemical Weapons (OPCW) 1997–99, Chair. Conf. of the State Parties 1997–98, mem. Exec. Council 1997–99; Amb. to the UK and Ireland 1999–2005; Minister of Foreign Affairs 2005–.
Address: Ministry of Foreign Affairs, Munhumutapa Building, Samora Machel Avenue, POB 4240, Causeway, Harare, Zimbabwe (office). *Telephone:* (4) 727005 (office); (4) 705420 (office). *Fax:* (4) 705161 (office); (4) 727175 (office).

MUN, Il-bong; North Korean politician. *Career:* mem. Supreme People's Ass.; Minister of Finance 2000–.
Address: Ministry of Finance, Pyongyang, Democratic People's Republic of Korea (office).

MUNASINGHE, Gamini Surath; Sri Lankan diplomatist. *Career:* High Commr to South Africa 1998–2001, to Zambia 2001–03, to Bangladesh 2003–06.
Address: c/o Ministry of Foreign Affairs, Republic Building, Colombo 1, Sri Lanka (office). *Telephone:* (11) 2325371 (office). *Fax:* (11) 2446091 (office). *Website:* www.slmfa.gov.lk (office).

MUNDELL, Robert Alexander, PhD; Canadian professor of economics; *Professor of Economics, Columbia University;* b. 24 Oct. 1932, Kingston, Ont.; m. Barbara Sheff 1957 (divorced 1972); two s. one d. *Education:* Univ. of British Columbia, Univ. of Washington, Massachusetts Inst. of Tech., London School of Econs, Univ. of Chicago. *Career:* Instructor, Univ. of

BC 1957–58; economist, Royal Comm. on Price Spreads of Food Products, Ottawa 1958; Asst Prof. of Econs, Stanford Univ., USA 1958–59; Prof. of Econs, Johns Hopkins Univ., School of Advanced Int. Studies, Bologna, Italy 1959–61; Sr Economist, IMF 1961–63; Visiting Prof. of Econs, McGill Univ. 1963–64, 1989–90; Prof. of Int. Econs, Grad. Inst. of Int. Studies, Geneva, Switzerland 1965–75; Prof. of Econs Univ. of Chicago 1966–71; Prof. of Econs and Chair. Dept of Econs, Univ. of Waterloo, Ont. 1972–74; Prof. of Econs Columbia Univ., USA 1974–; Ed. Journal of Political Economy 1966–71; Annenburg Distinguished Scholar in Residence, Univ. of Southern Calif. 1980; Richard Fox Visiting Prof. of Econs, Univ. of Pa 1990–91; First Rockefeller Visiting Research Prof. of Int. Econs, Brookings Inst. 1964–65; Guggenheim Fellow 1971; Marshall Lectures, Cambridge Univ. 1974; Distinguished Lecturer, Ching-Hua Inst., Taipei, Taiwan 1985; Pres. N American Econ. and Financial Asscn 1974–78; Dr hc (Univ. of Paris) 1992, (People's Univ. of China) 1995; Jacques Rueff Prize and Medal 1983, Nobel Prize for Econs 1999. *Publications:* The International Monetary System: Conflict and Reform 1965, Man and Economics 1968, International Economics 1968, Monetary Theory: Interest, Inflation and Growth in the World Economy 1971, Global Disequilibrium in the Lloyd Economy (co-author) 1989, Building the New Europe (co-author) 1991, Inflation and Growth in China (co-author) 1996; numerous papers and articles in journals.
Address: Department of Economics, Columbia University, 420 West 118th Street, New York, NY 10027; 35 Claremont Avenue, New York, NY 10027, USA (home); Palazzo Mundell, Santa Colomba, Siena, Italy (June–Aug.). *Telephone:* (212) 854-3669 (office); (212) 749-0630 (Home, USA); (0577) 57068 (Italy). *Fax:* (212) 854-8059.

MUÑOZ, Heraldo, BA, Dip Int. Relations, PhD; Chilean diplomatist; *Permanent Representative, United Nations;* b. 22 July 1948, Santiago; m. Pamela Quick; one d. *Education:* State Univ. of NY, Oswego, Harvard Univ., Catholic Univ. of Chile, Univ. of Denver. *Career:* Nat. Supervisor, People's Stores (Almacenes del Pueblo) 1973; Co-founder, Party for Democracy (PPD); mem. Political Comm. Sec. of Int. Relations, Socialist Party 1983–85; Chair. Metropolitan Santiago Region of PPD 1988–90; Jt Rep. of Socialist Party and PPD, Exec. Cttee, NO Campaign to defeat Gen. Pinochet 1988; Campaign Chief, Ricardo Lagos' senatorial race 1989; Amb. to OAS 1990–94, Pres. Environment Comm. 1991–92, Pres., Perm. Council 1993; Amb. to Brazil 1994–98; Pres., Economist Confs 1998–99; Int. Coordinator, Presidential Campaign of Ricardo Lagos 1999; Head of Int. and Defense Comm. 1999; Deputy Foreign Minister 2000–02; Minister Sec. Gen. of Govt 2002–03; Perm. Rep. to UN, New York 2003–; Founder and Dir, Programa de Seguimiento de las Politicas Exteriores Latinoamericanas (PROSPEL, foreign policy Inst.), Santiago 1983–90; fmr Pres. Latinanalyst Consultores; currently Prof., Inst. of Int. Studies, Univ. of Chile; Fellowships from Resources for the Future, Ford Foundation, Tinker Foundation, Twentieth Century Fund, MacArthur Foundation; contrib. to newspapers including: El Mercurio, Folha de Sao Paulo, Los Angeles Times, Miami Herald, Página 12; PhD Fellow, Brookings Inst., Washington DC 1977; Dr hc (State Univ. of NY) 1996; Distinguished Alumnus Award, Grad. School of Int. Studies, Univ. of Denver 1991. *Publications:* more than 20 books including Latin American Nations in World Politics (co-editor) 1998, Globalización XXI 2000; numerous essays in published academic journals including: Foreign Policy, Journal of Democracy, Journal of Interamerican and World Affairs, Latin American Research Review.
Address: Office of the Permanent Representative of Chile to the United Nations, 885 Second Avenue, 40th Floor, New York, NY 10017, USA (office). *Telephone:* (917) 322-6800 (office). *Fax:* (917) 322-6891 (office). *E-mail:* chile@un.int (office). *Website:* www.un.int/chile/indexenglish (office).

MUNTER, Cameron, PhD; American diplomatist; *Ambassador to Serbia; Education:* Johns Hopkins Univ., Univs of Freiburg and Marburg, Germany, Cornell Univ. *Career:* career mem. Sr Foreign Service, joined Foreign Service 1985, overseas postings in Warsaw 1986–88, Prague 1992–95, Bonn 1995–97, Staff Asst, European Bureau, Dept of State 1988–89, Country Dir for Czechoslovakia 1989–91, Chief of Staff, NATO Enlargement Ratification Office 1997–98, Dir Northern European Initiative 1998, Exec. Asst to Counselor of Dept of State 1998–99, Dir for Cen. and Eastern Europe, Nat. Security Council 1999–2001, Deputy Chief of Mission, Warsaw 2002–05, Prague 2005–07, volunteered as first team leader of Prov. Reconstruction Team, Mosul, Iraq 2006, Amb. to Serbia 2007–.
Address: US Embassy, Kneza Miloša 50, 11000 Belgrade, Serbia (office). *Telephone:* (11) 3619344 (office). *Fax:* (11) 3615489 (office). *E-mail:* Consularbelgrd@state.gov (office). *Website:* belgrade.usembassy.gov (office).

MURAD, Abdullah Ahmed Mohamed Al-; Kuwaiti diplomatist; *Permanent Representative, United Nations;* b. 3 July 1947; m.; four c. *Education:* Univ.

of Aix-Marseille, France. *Career:* attaché, Ministry of Foreign Affairs 1972, with Political Affairs Dept 1973–74; Third Sec., Embassy in Paris 1974, Second Sec. 1975, First Sec. 1978; Deputy Dir Consular Dept, Ministry of Foreign Affairs 1984; Consul-Gen. in Malaga, Spain 1987; with Political Affairs Dept, Ministry of Foreign Affairs 1987–88, European Affairs Dept 1988–90; Minister, Embassy in Belgrade 1990–91; Dir Int. Orgs, Ministry of Foreign Affairs 1991–92, 2004–06; Amb. to Venezuela 1993–96, to Turkey (also accred to Azerbaijan 1997–99) 1996–99, to India (also accred to Nepal and Bhutan) 1999–2004; Perm. Rep. to UN, New York 2006–.
Address: Permanent Mission of Kuwait to the United Nations, 321 East 44th Street, New York, NY 10017, USA (office). *Telephone:* (212) 973-4300 (office). *Fax:* (212) 370-1733 (office). *E-mail:* kuwait@kuwaitmission.com (office). *Website:* www.kuwaitmission.com (office).

MURERWA, Herbert; Zimbabwean politician; m. *Career:* mem. Zimbabwe African Nat. Union-Patriotic Front (ZANU-PF); High Commr to UK 1984–1990; Minister of Environment and Tourism 1990–95, of Industry and Commerce 1995–96, of Finance and Econ. Devt 1996–2000, 2002, of Higher Educ. and Tech. 2000–01, of Int. Trade and Tech. 2001–02; Minister of Higher Educ. and Tech. and Acting Minister of Finance and Econ. Devt –2005, Minister of Finance and Econ. Devt 2005–07.
Address: c/o Ministry of Finance and Economic Development, Blocks B, E and G, Composite Bldg, cnr Samora Machel Ave and Fourth St, Private Bag 7705, Causeway, Harare, Zimbabwe (office).

MURESAN, Liviu, PhD; Romanian economist and national security expert; *Executive President, European Institute for Risk, Security and Communication Management (EURISC) Foundation;* b. 28 June 1946, Sibiu; m.; two c. *Education:* Acad. of Economic Studies, Bucharest, Nat. Defence Coll., Bucharest, NATO Defence Coll., Italy, Institut des Hautes Etudes de Defense Nationale, France. *Career:* strategic development consultant; journalist, Informatia Bucurestiului newspaper, AgerPress (Nat. Press Agency) 1969–72; researcher Nat. Patent Office 1972–80; Sales Man. FIRO Glass Fibre Plant 1980–90; Sr Adviser to Prime Minister 1990–91, Sr Adviser to Govt 1991–99, Sr Adviser to Minister Interior 1999–2001; first civilian in command position in Romanian MoD after 1989; mem. Parl. 1990–92, Majority Leader 1990–91, mem. Romanian del. to Council of Europe; Deputy Dir Nat. Defence Coll. 1993–94, Founding mem. Nat. Defence Coll. Foundation; Founder and Exec. Pres. European Inst. for Risk, Security and Communication Man. (EURISC) Foundation 1995–; High Rep. of Romanian Govt of Anti-Corruption Initiative of Pact of Stability (SPAI) and of Combating Organized Crime Initiative (SPOC) 2000–01; Chair. in Office, Jt Co-operation Cttee, Interim Rep. of Regional Centre for Combating Trans-Border Organized Crime 2000; Assoc. mem. Club of Rome 1997–; mem. Founding Round Table of Int. Risk Governance Council, Geneva 2002; Founding mem. WSF (World Security Forum), Bern 2004; Founding Pres. Romanian Public Relations Asscn; Pres. Romanian Asscn of Graduates, IHEDN Paris; Founding mem. EURODEFENSE Romania; nat. coordinator/int. expert Bertelsmann Foundation (Germany); mem. Center for European Security Studies, Netherlands, SAFERWORLD, GB; Visiting Prof., Acad. for Econ. Studies, Bucharest 1997–; Nat. Order 'Star of Romania'; MIPRA 2000, Diploma of Merit NATO Integration Award from Pres. of Romania 2002. *Publications include:* Intrarea Europei in Romania 2001; as co-author: The European Security and Defense Policy: A Factor of Influence on the Actions of Romania in the Field of Security and Defense 2004, Elements of a Romanian Strategy in the Post Enlargement EU 2006, coordinator Regional Security Strategy from the Perspective of the Civil Society 2006; numerous articles in newspapers and magazines.
Address: EURISC Foundation, PO Box 2-101, Bucharest 2, Romania (office). *Telephone:* (21) 312-0805 (office). *Fax:* (21) 316-9417 (office). *E-mail:* eurisc@eurisc.org (office); muresan@eurisc.org (home). *Website:* www.eurisc.org (office).

MURR, Elias; Lebanese government official, lawyer and business executive; *Deputy Prime Minister and Minister of National Defence;* b. 1962, Bteghrin; m. Karine Lahoud 1992; three c. *Career:* fmr Ed.-in-Chief Al-Jumhouriyah newspaper; business interests in finance and real estate; Minister of the Interior 2000–04; Deputy Prime Minister and Minister of Defence 2005–.
Address: Ministry of National Defence, Yarze, Beirut, Lebanon (office). *Telephone:* (5) 920400 (office). *Fax:* (5) 951014 (office). *E-mail:* ministry@lebarmy.gov.lb (office). *Website:* www.lebarmy.gov.lb (office).

MURRAY, Michael (Mike) Thomas; British diplomatist; b. 13 Oct. 1945; m. Birgitta Murray; one s. one d. *Career:* joined FCO 1964, Archives Dept/Communications Dept 1964–67, Registry, Prague 1967–71, Office Services, FCO 1971–71, Archivist, Vienna 1971–73, Vice-Consul (Commercial), Frankfurt 1973–77, Second Sec. (Devt), Khartoum 1977–79, Personnel Operations Dept/Perm. Under-Sec.'s Dept, FCO 1980–83, Head of

Chancery, Banjul 1983-86, temporary duty, Stanley 1987, Head of Unit, Personnel Policy Dept, FCO 1988-90, Perm. Under-Sec.'s Dept 1990-95, First Sec. (Devt/Econ.), Lusaka 1995-98, Deputy Consul-Gen., Chicago 1999-2001, Amb. to Eritrea 2002-06.
Address: Foreign and Commonwealth Office, King Charles Street, London, SW1A 2AH, England (office). *Telephone:* (20) 7008-1500 (office). *Website:* www.fco.gov.uk (office).

MURRAY, Rachel, LLM, PhD; British academic; *Professor of International Human Rights Law, University of Bristol; Education:* Univs of Leicester, Bristol and W of England. *Career:* Lecturer (temporary), Univ. of W of England 1995-98, Lecturer in Law 1998-2000; Tutor (part-time), Univ. of Bristol 1996-99, Reader, then Prof. of Int. Human Rights Law 2003-; Asst Dir Centre for Human Rights, Queens Univ., Belfast 2000-01, Lecturer in Law 2000-01; Lecturer in Law, Birkbeck Coll., London 2002-03; Co-Ed. African Journal of International and Comparative Law; mem. Editorial Bd Journal of African Law; consultant to human rights orgs., govt comms; Fellow, Human Rights Centre, Univ. of Essex. *Publications:* The African Commission on Human Rights and Peoples' Rights and International Law 2000, Documents of the African Commission on Human Rights and Peoples' Rights, Vols I and II, (co-author) 2001, The African Human Rights System. The System at Work (co-author) 2002, Human Rights in Africa 2004, An Evaluation of the Effectiveness of the Northern Ireland Human Rights Commission 2004; chapters in books, articles and conf. papers.
Address: School of Law, University of Bristol, Wills Memorial Building, Queens Road, Bristol, BS8 1RJ, England (office). *Telephone:* (117) 954-5374 (office). *Fax:* (117) 925-1870 (office). *E-mail:* Rachel.Murray@bristol.ac.uk (office). *Website:* www.bristol.ac.uk (office).

MURSHED, Yasmeen, BA, MA; Bangladeshi educationalist, business executive and diplomatist; *High Commissioner to Pakistan;* b. 19 May 1945, Calcutta, India; grand-d. of Khawaja Shahabuddin, fmr Prime Minister of Pakistan; m. Syed Tanweer Murshed (died 1988); one s. one d. *Education:* Viqarunnisa Noon School, Dhaka, Univ. of the Punjab, Pakistan. *Career:* began career in educ. as a teacher in various insts, including Karachi Grammar School, Islamabad Model School for Girls, Govt Coll. for Women, Islamabad 1967-71; returned to Bangladesh after Liberation and began teaching small groups of students at home 1971; est. Scholastica Tutorial 1977 (later known as Scholastica), currently Chair. Bd of Man.; Chair. Etcetera Bangladesh (Pvt.) Ltd, Office and Home Solutions (Pvt.) Ltd, Scholastica Transport Services (Pvt.) Ltd, Printcraft Co. Ltd, Services for Professional Educ. and Enterprise Devt; mem. Bd of Dirs United Insurance Co. Ltd, Chittagong Stock Exchange; undertook role in Centre for Analysis and Choice early 1990s; has represented Bangladesh at several int. confs and meetings, participated in Sixth Int. Conf. of the Asscn for Women in Devt, Washington, DC 1993; Founding mem. and first Pres. Asia/Pacific Women in Politics Network; del. to Muslim Women's Conf., Beijing and Beyond: Implementing the Platform for Action in Muslim Societies, Washington, DC 1996, Asscn for Women in Devt Forum, Washington, DC 1996, NDI Conf. on Consolidating the Third Wave Democracies: Trends and Challenges, Taiwan 1995, Global Best Practices with Cambridge, Delhi 2006 and others; writes column on books and writers for The Daily Star; mem. Ascent Educ. Devt Trust (Founder-mem.), Educ., Science, Tech. and Cultural Devt Trust, Standard Chartered-Financial Express Corp. Social Responsibility Trust, Int. Chamber of Commerce (Bangladesh), Commonwealth Soc. of Bangladesh; mem. Jury Bd The Daily Star and DHL Business Awards 2004, DCCI Business Awards 2005. *Publications:* several textbooks on econs and Islamic studies and articles for journals, newspapers and magazines.
Address: Bangladesh High Commission, House No. 1, Street No. 5, F-6/3, Islamabad, Pakistan (office). *Telephone:* (51) 2279267 (office). *Fax:* (51) 2279266 (office). *E-mail:* bdhcisb@dsl.net.pk (office). *Website:* www.bdhcpk.org (office).

MURTON, John Evan; British diplomatist; *High Commissioner to Mauritius;* m. Sarah Elizabeth Murton; two s. one d. *Career:* Desk Officer (Conflict Prevention), UN Dept, FCO 1997-98, language training (Japanese), FCO and Japan 1998-2000, Second Sec. (Trade Policy Global Issues), Tokyo 2000-02, First Sec. (Energy and Environment), Tokyo 2002-04, Deputy Dir of Sec.-Gen.'s Pvt. Office, NATO 2004-07, High Commr to Mauritius 2007-.
Address: British High Commission, Les Cascades Building, Edith Cavell Street, PO Box 1063, Port Louis, Mauritius (office). *Telephone:* 202-9400 (office). *Fax:* 202-9408 (office). *E-mail:* bhc@intnet.mu (office).

MUSEMINALI, Rosemary; Rwandan diplomatist and politician; *Minister of Foreign Affairs and Co-operation;* b. 1962; m.; five c. *Education:* Makerere Univ., Kampala. *Career:* Amb. to UK (also accred Scandinavian countries and Ireland) to 2000-05; Minister of State for Regional Cooperation

2005-08, Minister of Foreign Affairs and Co-operation 2008-; Chair. Foreign Affairs Ministers COMESA 2007-.
Address: Ministry of Foreign Affairs and Co-operation, blvd de la Révolution, BP 179, Kigali, Rwanda (office). *Telephone:* 574522 (office). *Fax:* 572904 (office). *Website:* www.minaffet.gov.rw (office).

MUSEVENI, Gen. Yoweri Kaguta; Ugandan head of state; *President and Commander-in-Chief of Armed Forces;* b. 1944, Ntungamo, Mbarara; m. Janet Kataaha; four c. *Education:* Mbarara High School, Ntare School, Univ. Coll. of Dar es Salaam. *Career:* Research Asst Office of fmr Pres. Milton Obote 1971; in Tanzania planning overthrow of regime of Idi Amin 1971-79; f. Front for Nat. Salvation (FRONASA) 1972; taught at Moshi Co-operative Coll., Tanzania 1972; participated in Tanzanian invasion of Uganda 1979; Defence Minister in interim Govt of Uganda Nat. Liberation Front (UNLF) following overthrow of Amin 1979-80; following election of Dr Obote, amid allegations of ballot-rigging, in 1980, spent five years as leader of Nat. Resistance Army (NRA) waging a guerrilla war 1981-86; Pres. of Uganda (following overthrow of Govt by NRA forces) and Minister of Defence, then Pres. and C-in-C of Armed Forces 1986-; Chair. Preferential Trade Area (PTA) 1987-88, 1992-93, OAU 1990-91. *Publications:* Selected Essays 1985, Selection of Speeches and Writings, Vol. I: What is Africa's Problem? 1992, Vol. II 1997, Sowing the Mustard Seed – The Struggle for Freedom and Democracy 1997.
Address: Office of the President, Parliament Building, P.O. Box 7168, Kampala, Uganda. *Telephone:* (41) 258441. *Fax:* (41) 256143. *E-mail:* info@gouexecutive.net (office). *Website:* www.gouexecutive.net (office).

MUSHARRAF, Gen. (retd) Pervez; Pakistani fmr army officer and fmr head of state; b. 11 Aug. 1943, Delhi, India; m. Sehba Farid 1968; one s. one d. *Education:* St Patrick's High School, Karachi, Forman Christian Coll., Lahore, Command and Staff Coll., Quetta, Nat. Defence Coll., Rawalpindi, Royal Coll. of Defence Studies, UK. *Career:* spent early childhood in Turkey 1949-56; joined Pakistan Mil. Acad. 1961; commd in Artillery Regt 1964; fought in 1965 war with India (Imtiazi Sanad Gallantry Award); spent much of mil. career in Special Services Group; Company Commdr Commando Battalion Indo-Pakistan War 1971; Dir-Gen. Mil. Operations, Gen. HQ 1993-95; apptd C-in-C of Pakistani Army Oct. 1998, Chair. Jt Chiefs of Staff Cttee 1999, led mil. coup 1999, Chief of Staff 1999-2007; Chief Exec. Nat. Security Council of Pakistan 1999-2002; Pres. of Pakistan 2001-08 (resgnd). *Publication:* In the Line of Fire: A Memoir 2006.
Address: c/o Office of the President, Aiwan-e-Sadr, Islamabad, Pakistan (office).

MUSONI, James; Rwandan politician; *Minister of Finance and Economic Planning; Career:* Commr Gen., Rwanda Revenue Authority –2005; Minister for Commerce, Industry, Investment Promotion, Tourism and Cooperatives 2005-06, of Finance and Economic Planning 2006-; mem. Front Patriotique Rwandais.
Address: Ministry of Finance and Economic Planning, BP 158, Kigali, Rwanda. *Telephone:* 575756 (office). *Fax:* 577581 (office). *E-mail:* mfin@rwanda1.com (office). *Website:* www.minecofin.gov.rw (office).

MUSSA, Michael; American economist and academic; *Senior Fellow, Institute for International Economics;* b. 1944. *Education:* Univs of Calif. and Chicago. *Career:* Asst Prof. of Econs Univ. of Rochester; Research Fellow, LSE and Grad. Inst. of Int. Studies; William H. Abbott Prof. of Int. Business, Univ. of Chicago Grad. School of Business 1980-; Research Assoc. Nat. Bureau of Econ. Research 1981-; fmr mem. US Council of Econ. Advisers; fmr Visiting Prof. Asian and Research Depts of IMF; Econ. Counsellor and Dir Research Dept IMF 1991-2001, Special Adviser to Man. Dir 2001-; currently Sr Fellow, Inst. for Int. Econs.
Address: Institute for International Economics, 1750 Massachusetts Avenue, NW, Washington, DC 20036, USA (office). *Telephone:* (202) 328-9000 (office). *Fax:* (202) 695-3225 (office). *Website:* www.iie.com (office).

MUSSOMELI, Joseph A., BA, JD; American lawyer and diplomatist; *Ambassador to Cambodia;* b. 26 May 1952, New York City; m. Sharon Flack Mussomeli; three s. *Education:* Camden Catholic High School, Rutgers Univ., Trenton State Coll., Rutgers Law School. *Career:* law clerk, Appellate Court of NJ 1978-79; Deputy Attorney Gen., NJ Div. of Gaming Enforcement 1979-80; entered Foreign Service 1980, Gen. Officer, Embassy in Cairo; staff asst to Under-Sec. for Security Assistance, Dept of State; Consular Officer, Embassy in Manila 1984-86; N Korea Desk Officer 1986-88, Sr Watch Officer 1989-90; Econ. Counselor, Embassy in Colombo 1990-92; Insp., Office of Insp. Gen. 1992-94; Political Counselor, Embassy in Rabat 1995-98, Deputy Chief of Mission, Embassy in Manama 1998-2001; mem. Sr Seminar 2001-02; Deputy Chief of Mission, Embassy in Manila 2002-05, Amb. to Cambodia 2005-; two Superior Honor

Awards, one Group Superior Honor Award, two Meritorious Honor Awards.
Address: Embassy of the USA, No. 1 rue 96, Sangkat Wat Phnom, Phnom-Penh, Cambodia (office). *Telephone:* (23) 728000 (office). *Fax:* (23) 728600 (office). *Website:* phnompenh.usembassy.gov (office).

MUSTAFA, Muhammad Taha, BA; Yemeni diplomatist; *Ambassador to UK;* b. 15 Jan. 1951, San'a; m. Seena Omar Ambool; three s. one d. *Education:* Cairo Univ., Egypt, George Washington Univ., USA. *Career:* Third Sec., Political Dept, Ministry of Foreign Affairs 1979–81, Second Sec. and Information Officer, Washington, DC 1981–85, First Sec. to Deputy Prime Minister and Minister of Foreign Affairs 1985–88, 1994–98, Counsellor, Political and Information Officer and Deputy Chief of Mission, Washington DC 1988–93, Deputy Dir Ministers' Bureau 1993–94, Amb. to Malaysia 1998–2003, Chief of Protocol 2003–05, Amb. to UK 2005–.
Address: Embassy of Yemen, 57 Cromwell Road, London, SW7 2ED, England (office). *Telephone:* (20) 7584-6607 (office). *Fax:* (20) 7589-3350 (office). *E-mail:* yemen.embassy@btconnect.com (office). *Website:* www .yemenembassy.org.uk (office).

MUSTAFAJ, Besnik; Albanian academic and politician; b. 23 Sept. 1958, Bajram Curri City; m.; two c. *Education:* Tirana Univ. *Career:* Prof. of Foreign Literature, Faculty of History and Philology, Tirana Univ. 1983–91; founding mem. Democratic Party of Albania (DPA) 1990–, Sec. for Int. Relations 1999–2005; elected MP 1991, Deputy Chair. Foreign Relations Comm. 2001–05, Deputy Chair. of Perm. Del. to European Parl. 2001–05; Amb. to France and Perm. Rep. to UNESCO, Paris 1992–97; Minister of Foreign Affairs 2005–07 (resgnd); co-founder Albanian Helsinki Cttee 1990; Founding Chair. Albanian Writers' Pen Club. *Publications:* Vera pa kthim (The Summer of no Return) 1989, Gjinkallat e vapës (The Cicadas of the Heat) 1994, Një sagë e vogël (A Little Saga) 1995, Daullja prej letre (The Paper Drum) 1996, Boshti (The Void) 1998; several books and papers on poetry and aesthetics.
Address: c/o Ministry of Foreign Affairs, Bulevardi Gjergj Fishta 6, Tirana, Albania (office).

MUSYOKA, (Stephen) Kalonzo, LLB; Kenyan lawyer and politician; *Vice President;* b. 24 Dec. 1953, Tseikuru village, Mwingi Dist; m. Pauline Musyoka; four c. *Education:* Univ. of Nairobi. *Career:* lawyer with Kaplan & Stratton Advocates; Sr Partner, Musyoka & Wambua Advocates; mem. Parl. 1985, Deputy Speaker, Nat. Ass. 1988–93; Sec. Kitui branch, Kenya African National Union (KANU) Party 1985–88, fmr Nat. Organizing Sec. 1988, Vice-Chair. 2002; Asst Minister for Work, Housing and Planning 1986–88; Minister of Foreign Affairs 1992–98, 2002–04; fmr Minister of Educ., Tourism and Information; Minister of the Environment and Natural Resources 2004–05; defected from KANU to launch Liberal Democratic Party just before Dec. 2002 presidential elections, currently Leader, Orange Democratic Movement – K; unsuccessful cand. in presidential elections 2007; Vice Pres. of Kenya 2008–.
Address: Kenya National Assembly, Parliament Buildings, PO Box 41842, Nairobi (office); Rehani House, 9th Floor, Koinange Street, PO Box 67121, Nairobi, Kenya (office). *Telephone:* (20) 221291 (Parliament) (office); (20) 213460 (office). *Fax:* (20) 336589 (Parliament) (office); (20) 214787 (office). *Website:* www.bunge.go.ke (office).

MUTAMBA TSHAMPANGA, Jean-Pierre; Democratic Republic of the Congo diplomatist; *Ambassador to Belgium;* b. Lubumbashi, Katanga Prov.; m.; one d. *Career:* specialist in marketing finance; communications adviser, Ministry of the Interior 1998; worked in Bureau des Réserves stratégiques générales 1998; fmr Pres. Comité d'Initiatives pour la Paix et l'Unification de tous les Congolais (CIPUC); fmr Vice-Pres. for Communication and Information, Union des Congolais pour la Paix; Amb. to Belgium 2003–.
Address: Embassy of the Democratic Republic of the Congo, 30 Rue Marie de Bourgogne, 1040 Brussels, Belgium (office). *Telephone:* (2) 213-49-810 (office). *Fax:* (2) 213-49-95 (office). *E-mail:* secretariat.cmd@amba -rdcongo.be (office).

MUTHARIKA, Bingu Wa, BCom, MA, PhD; Malawi politician, economist and head of state; *President;* b. Feb. 1934, Thyolo; m. Ethel Zvauya Nyoni; three d. one s. *Education:* Univ. of Delhi, India, George Washington Univ., USA, Univ. of Nairobi, Kenya, Pacific Western Univ., USA. *Career:* accounts clerk Soche Authority 1957–58; admin. officer Civil Service 1963–64; sr principal Civil Service, Zambia 1965–66; Chief, Africa Trade Centre, UN Econ. Comm. for Africa 1966–75; loan officer World Bank 1975–78; several UN posts 1978–90 including Dir African Trade and Devt Finance; Sec.-Gen. COMESA 1991–97; fmr Minister for Econ. Planning and Devt; Pres. of Malawi May 2004–; fmr mem. United Democratic Front; est. Democratic Progressive Party 2005; founder and Pres. Reach Int.; mem. COMESA, Asscn of African Central Banks, Conf. of African Ministers of Finance, African Fed. of Chambers of Commerce and Industry, Fed. of Nat. Asscns of Women in Business in E and S Africa. *Publications:* Towards Multinational Economic Cooperation in Africa 1972, One Africa, One Destiny 1995, Out of Poverty: The Resumption of Economic Growth in Malawi 2003, Mabizinesi Aphindu 2003; numerous articles in int. journals.
Address: Office of the President and Cabinet, Private bag 301, Lilongwe 3, Malawi (office). *Telephone:* 1789311 (office). *Fax:* 1788456 (office). *E-mail:* opc@malawi.gov.mw (office). *Website:* www.malawi.gov.mw (office).

MATUSSEK, Thomas; German diplomatist; *Permanent Representative, United Nations;* b. 1947, Lauda, Baden-Württemberg; m.; three c. *Education:* Univs of Paris, France and Bonn. *Career:* joined German Foreign Service 1975; overseas assignments to London, New Delhi and Lisbon; seconded to Fed. Chancellory; Pvt. Sec. to Minister of Foreign Affairs 1991, later Head of Office of Ministers Genscher and Kinkel; Deputy Head of Mission, Embassy in Washington, DC 1994–99; Dir-Gen. for Political Affairs, Ministry of Foreign Affairs 1991–2001; responsible for organising UN Talks on Afghanistan 2001; Amb. to UK 2002–06; Perm. Rep., UN, New York 2006–.
Address: Office of the Permanent Representative, 871 United Nations Plaza, New York, NY 10017, USA (office). *Telephone:* (212) 940-0400 (office). *Fax:* (212) 940-0402 (office). *E-mail:* germany@un.int (home). *Website:* www.germany-info.org/un (home).

MÜTZELBURG, Bernd, MA; German diplomatist; *Ambassador to India;* b. 17 Jan. 1944, Mainz; m.; one s. one d. *Education:* law studies in Mainz and Marburg, Fletcher School of Law and Diplomacy, USA. *Career:* joined foreign service 1972; served as personal sec. to Minister of State Karl Moersch 1974–75; Deputy Head Embassy in Kingston, Jamaica 1975–78; Desk Officer, Disarmament and Arms Control, Fed. Foreign Office 1978–81; served with Perm. Mission to UN, New York 1981–85; Deputy Head of Div., Cen. Services 1986–88, Deputy Head Minister's Office 1988–91; Amb. to Kenya and Perm. Rep., UNEP 1991–95, Amb. to Estonia 1995–99; Deputy Dir-Gen. Foreign and Security Policy Directorate, Fed. Chancellery 1999–2001; Dir-Gen. for Global Issues, the UN and Human Rights 2001–02, Dir-Gen. and Foreign and Security Policy Adviser, Fed. Chancellery 2002–05; Amb.-at-Large 2005–06; Amb. to India 2006–.
Address: Embassy of Germany, 6 Block 50g, Shanti Path, Chanakyapuri, New Delhi 110 021, India (office). *Telephone:* (11) 26871831 (office). *Fax:* (11) 26873117 (office). *Website:* www.germanembassy-india.org (office).

MVOUBA, Isidore; Republic of the Congo politician; *Prime Minister, responsible for the Co-ordination of Government Action and Privatization;* b. 1954, Kindamba. *Career:* with Chemin de fer Congo Océan 1977; mem. Parti Congolais du Travail; Countryside Dir for Sassou Nguesso 1992, 2002; Prin. Pvt. Sec. for Head of State 1997–99; fmr Minister for Transport, Civil Aviation and the Merchant Navy; Prime Minister, responsible for the Co-ordination of Govt Action and Privatization 2005–.
Address: Office of the Prime Minister, Brazzaville, Republic of the Congo (office). *Telephone:* 81-10-67 (office). *Website:* www.congo-site.net (office).

MWAKAWAGO, Daudi Ngelautwa; Tanzanian politician; b. Sept. 1939. *Education:* Makerere Univ., Uganda, Victoria Univ. of Manchester, England. *Career:* Tutor at Kivukoni Coll., Dar es Salaam 1965–72, Vice-Prin. 1970, Prin. 1971, 1977; Nat. MP 1970–75; Minister for Information and Broadcasting 1972–77; Constituent MP 1975; mem. Party of Constitution Comm. 1976; mem. Constituent Ass. 1977, Cen. Cttee Chama cha Mapinduzi 1977–; Minister of Information and Culture 1982–84, of Labour and Manpower Devt 1984–86, of Industries and Trade 1986–88; Perm. Rep. to UN, New York 1994–2003; Special Rep. of the UN Sec.-Gen. to Sierra Leone 2003–06; fmr mem. Historical Asscn of Tanzania, Nat. Adult Educ. Asscn of Tanzania, African Adult Educ. Asscn, Income Tax Local Cttee, Bd of Inst. of Adult Educ., Nat. Advisory Council on Educ.; fmr Dir Nat. Devt Corpn, Nat. Museum; Chair. Wildlife Corpn 1979–; Vice-Chair. Co-operative Coll., Moshi; mem. TIRDO.

MWAPE, Augustine Festus Lupando; Zambian politician; *Ambassador to China; Career:* fmr engineer, teacher; mem. Parl. for Lukashya constituency; Minister of Communications and Transport –2003; Deputy Minister of Northern Prov. –2004; Vice-Pres. of Zambia 2004–06; Ambassador to China 2007–; Spontaneous Award, Ngoma Awards.
Address: Zambian Embassy, Dong Si Jie, San Li Tun, Beijing, 100600, People's Republic of China (office). *Telephone:* (10) 65321554 (office). *Fax:* (10) 65321891 (office).

MWEMWENIKARAWA, Nabuti; I-Kiribati politician. *Career:* Minister for Finance and Econ. Devt –2007.

Address: c/o Ministry of Finance and Economic Development, POB 67, Bairiki, Tarawa, Kiribati (office).

MWENCHA, J. E. O. (Erastus), MA, MBS; Kenyan economist and international finance official; *Secretary-General, Common Market for Eastern and Southern Africa;* m.; three c. *Education:* Univ. of Nairobi, York Univ., Canada. *Career:* entered civil service 1974, becoming Prin. Industrial Devt Officer; Dir Kenya Medical Research Inst.; Dir Kenya Industrial Research and Devt Inst.; Sec. Industrial Sciences Advisory Council; Sr Industrial Expert, Econ. Comm. for Africa 1983; Dir of Industry, Energy and Environment, Preferential Trade Area for Eastern and Southern Africa 1987–97; Acting Sec.-Gen. Common Market for Eastern and Southern Africa (COMESA) 1997–98, Sec.-Gen. 1998–; Order of the Moran of the Burning Spear 1998. *Publications:* contrib. to The Free Trade Area of the Common Market for Eastern and Southern Africa (COMESA). *Address:* COMESA Centre, Ben Bella Road, P.O. Box 30051, 10101 Lusaka, Zambia (office). *Telephone:* (1) 229726 (office). *Fax:* (1) 227318 (office). *E-mail:* comesa@comesa.int (office); jmwencha@comesa.int (office). *Website:* www.comesa.int (office).

MWINYI, Hussein Ali, MD; Tanzanian physician and politician; *Minister of Defence and National Service;* b. 23 Dec. 1966. *Education:* Azania Secondary School, Tambaza High School, Marmara Univ., Turkey, Hammersmith Hosp., UK. *Career:* doctor, Ministry of Health 1993–97, specialist doctor 1997–98; Lecturer in Medicine, Hubert Kairuki Memorial Univ. 1998–2000; Deputy Minister of Health 2000–05; MP for Kwahani 2005–; Minister of State for Union Affairs 2006–08; Minister of Defence and Nat. Service 2008–; mem. Chama Cha Mapinduzi (CCM—Revolutionary Party of Tanzania). *Address:* Ministry of Defence and National Service, PO Box 9544, Dar es Salaam, Tanzania (office). *Telephone:* (22) 2117153 (office). *Fax:* (22) 2116719 (office).

MYAING, U Linn, BSc; Myanma diplomatist; b. 15 Oct. 1947, Yangon; m. Daw Thi Thi Ta; two d. *Education:* Defence Studies Acad. *Career:* commissioned as officer in Myanmar Navy 1967–93; Deputy Dir Americas Div., Political Dept, Ministry of Foreign Affairs 1993–94, served first as Counsellor, then as Minister Counsellor, Perm. Mission to UN and other Int. Orgs, Geneva 1994–97, Deputy Dir Gen. Ministry of Foreign Affairs, also attached as Minister, Deputy Perm. Rep. to Perm. Mission of Myanmar, Geneva 1998–99, Amb. to France (also accred to UNESCO) 1999–2001 (also accred to Belgium, the Netherlands, Switzerland and EU) 2000–01, Amb. to USA 2001–07. *Address:* Ministry of Foreign Affairs, Nay Pyi Taw, Myanmar (office). *Website:* www.mofa.gov.mm (office).

N

NABLI, Mustapha K., MEcons, PhD; Tunisian economist; *Chief Economist and Sector Director, Middle East and North Africa, World Bank Group; Education:* Faculté de Droit et des Sciences Politiques et Economiques de Tunis, Univ. of California at Los Angeles, USA. *Career:* int. consultant; Prof. of Econs, Univ. of Tunis 1975–; Visiting Prof. and Research Fellow at univs in USA, Canada, Belgium and France and admin. of insts of econ. man. training; Chair. Tunis Stock Exchange 1988–90; Minister of Planning and Regional Devt then Minister of Econ. Devt 1990–95; Sr Econ. Advisor, Devt Prospects Group, Devt Econs, IBRD, Washington, DC 1997–99, Chief Economist and Sector Dir, Social and Econ. Devt, Middle East and N Africa, World Bank Group 1999–; mem. Bd Trustees Econ. Research Forum of the Arab Countries, Iran and Turkey; Adviser, Exec. Cttee, Int. Econ. Asscn. *Publications include:* numerous books and articles in int. journals on trade, econ. integration, applied econometrics, macro- and monetary econs and econ. devt.
Address: World Bank Group, 1818 H Street, NW, Washington, DC 20433, USA (office). *Telephone:* (202) 473-1784 (office). *Fax:* (202) 477-0432 (office). *E-mail:* MNabli@worldbank.org (office). *Website:* www.worldbank.org (office).

NADINGAR, Emmanuel; Chadian politician; *Minister of Petroleum; Career:* Deputy Chief of Staff, Govt of Chad –2004; Minister of Nat. Defence, Veterans and Victims of War 2004–07, of Petroleum 2007–.
Address: Ministry of Petroleum, BP 816, N'Djamena, Chad (office). *Telephone:* 52-56-03 (office). *Fax:* 52-36-66 (office). *E-mail:* mme@intnet.td (office). *Website:* www.ministere-petrole.td (office).

NAFEH, Ibrahim; Egyptian journalist; *President, Arab Journalists' Union;* b. 1934, Suez; m.; two c. *Career:* diplomatic corresp., Cairo Radio 1956–60; Econ. Ed. Al-Gumhuriya newspaper 1960–62; Econ. Ed. Al-Ahram newspaper 1962–67, Head Econ. Dept 1974–75, Chief Ed. 1975, Chair. and Ed.-in-Chief 1975–82, Chair. and Exec. Ed. 1982–2005; Middle East specialist in IBRD, Information Dept 1971–73; currently Pres. Arab Journalists' Union. *Publication:* Translation into Arabic of Lester Pearson's Report: Partners in Development 1971.
E-mail: info-faj@faj.org.eg (office). *Website:* www.faj.org.eg (office).

NAG, Rajat M.; Canadian engineer, economist and banker; *Managing Director-General, Asian Development Bank; Education:* Indian Inst. of Tech., Delhi, Univ. of Saskatchewan, London School of Econs, UK. *Career:* worked as energy and water resources planning specialist with int. consulting firm, becoming chief economist; worked as economist/financial analyst for five years at Bank of Canada; joined Asian Devt Bank (ADB) as Project Economist in Agric. Dept 1986, assigned to ADB's Nepal Resident Mission 1991–94, held various sr positions in ADB's Programs Dept (West) and in Financial Sector and Industry Div., Infrastructure Dept (West), mem. man. cttee that formulated proposals for re-organization of ADB operations 2001, Deputy Dir Programs Dept (West) 2000–02, Dir Gen. Mekong Dept 2002–06, Special Advisor to ADB Pres. on Regional Econ. Cooperation and Integration 2005–06, Dir Gen. newly amalgamated Southeast Asia Dept 2006, Man. Dir-Gen. ADB 2006–.
Address: Asian Development Bank, 6 ADB Avenue, 1500 Mandaluyong City, Philippines (office). *Telephone:* (2) 632-4444 (office). *Fax:* (2) 636-2444 (office). *E-mail:* mediacenter@adb.org (office). *Website:* www.adb.org (office).

NAGA, Fayza Abu an-; Egyptian diplomatist; b. 1951. *Career:* joined foreign service in early 1970s; aide to Minister of State for Foreign Affairs Boutros Boutros Ghali 1981–91; served at Perm. Mission to UN, New York 1992–96; Asst Foreign Minister for African Affairs 1996–2001; Perm. Rep. to UN, Geneva 1999–2001; Minister of State for Foreign Affairs (first woman) 2001–04; Minister of Int. Co-operation 2004–.
Address: Ministry of International Co-operation, 8 Sharia Adly, Cairo, Egypt (office). *Telephone:* (2) 3901801 (office). *Website:* www.mic.gov.eg (office).

NAGEL, Mónica; Costa Rican politician, lawyer and international organization official; *President of the Board, Justice Studies Center of the Americas;* b. 5 May 1960, Chile; m. Mario Fishman 1981; two d. *Education:* Univ. Autónoma de Centro America, San José. *Career:* law teacher; worked in

law office 1984–90; Vice-Minister of Justice with special responsibility for the rights of children 1990; Rep. of Costa Rica on Inter-American Comm. on Drug Abuse Control (CICAD), OAS 1990–94, Vice-Chair. 1992–93, Chair. 1993–94; mem. Exec. Bd UNICEF 1995; Pres. Chair. Third Conf. of Ministers of Justice or Attorney-Gens of the Americas 2000; Minister of Justice and Grace 1998–2002; currently Pres. of Bd, Justice Studies Center of the Americas. *Publications include:* articles on drugs and rights of children in newspapers and magazines.
Address: Justice Studies Center of the Americas, Northwestern University School of Law, 357 East Chicago Avenue, Chicago, IL 60611, USA (office). *Telephone:* (312) 503-3100 (office). *Website:* www.law.northwestern.edu/depts/clinic/ihr/JSCA/Index.cfm.

NAHYAN, Sheikh Abdullah bin Zayed an-; United Arab Emirates government official and diplomatist; *Minister of Foreign Affairs; Career:* Minister of Information and Culture –2006, Minister of Foreign Affairs 2006–; mem. Council of Ministers; Chair. Emirates Media Inc.
Address: Ministry of Foreign Affairs, POB 1, Abu Dhabi, United Arab Emirates (office). *Telephone:* (2) 4444488 (office). *Fax:* (2) 4449100 (office). *E-mail:* mofa@mofa.gov.ae (office). *Website:* www.mofa.gov.ae (office).

NAHYAN, HH Sheikh Khalifa bin Zayed an-, (Ruler of Abu Dhabi); United Arab Emirates; *President;* b. 1948, al-Ain. *Career:* apptd Ruler of Abu Dhabi's Rep. in Eastern Region of Abu Dhabi and Head of Courts Dept in Al-Ain on his father's accession as Ruler of Abu Dhabi 1966, Crown Prince of Abu Dhabi and Head of Abu Dhabi Defence Force 1969; Prime Minister of Abu Dhabi and Minister of Defence and Finance 1971–74, first Chair. Abu Dhabi Exec. Council 1974; Deputy Prime Minister of UAE 1973; Supreme Commdr UAE Armed Forces 1976; Chair. Supreme Petroleum Council late 1980s–, Abu Dhabi Fund for Devt, Abu Dhabi Investment Authority, Research and Wildlife Devt Agency; Pres. of UAE and Ruler of Emirate of Abu Dhabi 2004–.
Address: Office of the President of the United Arab Emirates and Ruler of Abu Dhabi, Manhal Palace, PO Box 280, Abu Dhabi, United Arab Emirates (office). *Telephone:* 6652000 (office). *Fax:* 6651962 (office).

NAHYAN, Sheikh Sultan bin Zayed an-; United Arab Emirates government official and soldier; *Deputy Prime Minister;* b. 1955. *Education:* in Abu Dhabi, Lebanon, Sandhurst Mil. Acad., UK. *Career:* Commdr Western Mil. Dist 1976; Gen. Commdr UAE Armed Forces 1978; now Deputy Commdr Abu Dhabi Defence Forces; Deputy Prime Minister 1991–.
Address: PO Box 831, Abu Dhabi, United Arab Emirates. *Telephone:* (2) 651881.

NAIDOO, Jayaseelan (Jay); South African trade union leader, banker and business executive; *Chairman, Development Bank of Southern Africa;* b. 20 Dec. 1954, Durban; m. Mrs Lucie Pagé 1992; two s. one d. *Education:* Sastri Coll., Durban and Univ. of Durban-Westville. *Career:* mem. SASO 1977; involved in community orgs, Natal 1976–79; studies interrupted by political events 1978; Organizer Fed. of South African Trade Unions (FOSATU) 1980; Gen. Sec. Sweet Food & Allied Workers Union 1982, Congress of South African Trade Unions (COSATU) 1985–93; Minister, Office of the Pres., Govt of Nat. Unity 1994–96; Minister of Posts and Telecommunications and Broadcasting 1996–99; Chair. Devt Bank of Southern Africa 2000–, Global Alliance for Improved Nutrition 2003–; mem. Bd Dirs J&J Group 2000–, ITU Telecom 2007–; mem. Health Advisory Comm. Clinton Global Initiative 2007–; Chevalier de la Légion d'honneur 2006.
Address: Development Bank of Southern Africa, PO Box 1234, Halfway House, Midrand 1685, South Africa (office). *Telephone:* (11) 447-3215 (office). *Fax:* (11) 447-7621 (office). *E-mail:* jay@jandjgroup.com (office). *Website:* www.dbsa.org (office); www.jandjgroup.com (office); www.gainhealth.org (office).

NAILATIKAU, Ratu Epeli, OBE; Fijian government official, diplomatist and army officer; *Minister of Foreign Affairs, International Co-operation and Civil Aviation;* b. 5 July 1941, Levuka, Ovalau; m. Adi Koila Mara; one s. one d. *Education:* Levuka Public School and Queen Victoria School. *Career:* completed mil. training in New Zealand, seconded to 1st Battalion, Royal New Zealand Infantry Regt in Sarawak, Malaysia 1966, Brig.-Gen. Fiji Infantry Regt 1987–88, Commdr of Armed Forces 1982–88; fmr High

Commr to UK; fmr Amb. to Denmark, Egypt, Germany, Israel and Holy See, to the Pacific 1998–99; Perm. Sec. for Foreign Affairs and External Trade 1999–2000; Deputy Prime Minister 2000–01; Minister for Fijian Affairs 2000–01; Speaker of House of Reps 2001–06, Chair. Parl. Appropriations and House Cttees 2001–06; Minister of Foreign Affairs and Trade 2007– (in Cdre Josaia Bainimarama's interim govt), now Minister of Foreign Affairs, Int. Co-operation and Civil Aviation; LVO, Meritorious Service Decoration, Venerable Order of the Hospital of Saint John of Jerusalem.
Address: Ministry of Foreign Affairs, International Co-operation and Civil Aviation, PO Box 2220, Government Buildings, Suva, Fiji (office). *Telephone:* 9309631 (office). *Fax:* 9301741 (office). *E-mail:* info@ foreignaffairs.gov.fj (office). *Website:* www.foreignaffairs.gov.fj (office).

NA'IM, Abdullahi Ahmed An-, LLB, Dip.Crim., PhD; Sudanese/American academic; *Charles Howard Candler Chaired Professor of Law, Emory University;* b. 19 Nov. 1946, Shendi, Sudan. *Education:* Univ. of Khartoum, Univs of Cambridge and Edin., UK. *Career:* Lecturer and Assoc. Prof. of Law, Univ. of Khartoum 1976–85; Rockefeller Fellow, Columbia Univ. Center for Study of Human Rights 1981–82; Visiting Prof., UCLA 1985–87; Fellow, Woodrow Wilson Int. Center for Scholars 1987–88; Ariel F. Sallows Prof. of Human Rights, Univ. of Sask., Canada 1988–91; Olof Palme Visiting Prof., Uppsala Univ., Sweden 1991–92; Visiting Fellow, Harvard Law School Human Rights Program 1991; Scholar-in-Residence, Ford Foundation Office for Middle East and North Africa, Cairo, Egypt 1992–93; Prof. of Law and Fellow of Law and Religion Program, Emory Univ. 1995–, Charles Howard Candler Chaired Prof. of Law 1999–; Visiting Prof., Utrecht Univ. 1999, Harvard Law School 2003; Wiarda Chair, Faculty of Law, Utrecht Univ. 2005–06; Exec. Dir Human Rights Watch/Africa, Washington DC 1993–95; Vice-Pres. Int. Third World Studies Asscn 1986–; Commr, Int. Comm. of Jurists; mem. Bd Urban Morgan Inst. for Human Rights, Cairo Inst. for Human Rights Studies, Research, Action and Information Network for Bodily Integrity of Women (RAINBOW), Int. Council on Human Rights Policy, Geneva, Inst. for Human Rights, The Gambia, The Population Council, New York; mem. ed. bds Third World Legal Studies, Human Rights Quarterly, Int. Politics, Rawaq Arabi; Dr J.P. van Praag Award of Dutch Humanist Ethical Soc. 1999, Marion Creekmore Award for Internatoinalization, Emory Univ. *Publications:* Sudanese Criminal Law: The General Principles of Criminal Responsibility 1985, The Second Message of Islam by Ustadh Mahmoud Mohamed Taha (English trans.) 1987, Toward an Islamic Reformation: Civil Liberties, Human Rights and International Law 1990, Human Rights in Africa: Cross-Cultural Perspectives (co-ed.) 1990, Cry of the Owl by Francis Deng (Arabic trans.) 1991, Human Rights in Cross Cultural Perspectives: Quest for Consensus (ed.) 1992, Human Rights and Religious Values (co-ed.) 1995, Proselytization and Communal Self-Determination in Africa (ed.) 1999, The Politics of Memory: Truth, Healing and Social Justice (ed.) 2002, Cultural Transformation and Human Rights in Africa (ed.) 2002, Human Rights Under African Constitutions (ed.) 2003, African Constitutionalism and the Role of Islam 2006, Islam and the Secular State 2008; numerous writings since 1974, including 55 articles and 28 short articles and book reviews.
Address: School of Law, Emory University, 1301 Clifton Road, Atlanta, GA 30322, USA (office). *Telephone:* (404) 727-1198 (office). *E-mail:* Abduh46@law.emory.edu (office). *Website:* www.law.emory.edu/aannaim (office).

NAIR, Dileep, BMechEng, MPA; Singaporean international organization official. *Education:* McGill Univ., Montreal, Canada, Kennedy School of Govt, Harvard Univ., USA. *Career:* with Housing and Devt Bd 1974–79; joined Admin. Service 1979, various posts including Dir in charge of expenditure control, Deputy Sec. Ministry of Trade and Industry 1986–89, Ministry of Defence 1989–97; CEO Post Office Savings Bank of Singapore 1997–98, Man. Dir Devt Bank of Singapore (DBS) 1998–2000; Under-Sec.-Gen. for Internal Oversight Services, UN 2000–05; fmr Vice-Pres. Singapore Indian Devt Asscn; mem. Hindu Advisory Bd; mem. Bd of Govs Raffles Inst.; Colombo Plan Scholar 1969–73.
Address: c/o UN Office of Internal Oversight Services, United Nations Plaza, New York, NY 10017, USA (office).

NAIRN, Tom, BA, MA, PhD; British academic and writer; *Professor of Nationalism and Cultural Diversity, Globalism Research Institute, Royal Melbourne Institute of Technology (RMIT);* b. 1932, Freuchie, Fife. *Education:* Univs of Edinburgh, Oxford, and Rome, Italy. *Career:* taught at Univ. of Birmingham and Hornsey Coll. of Art, London 1960s; Sr Research Fellow, Transnational Inst., Amsterdam, Netherlands 1973–79; worked for Scottish TV as writer-producer with Agenda Productions 1980s before returning to acad. life; worked with Ernest Gellner at Cen. European Univ., Prague, Czechoslovakia; f. Nationalism Studies degree at Grad. School, Univ. of Edinburgh 1995–2000; taught at Monash Univ., Australia

2001–02; Prof. of Nationalism and Cultural Diversity, Globalism Research Inst., Royal Melbourne Inst. of Tech. (RMIT Univ.) 2002–. *Publications include:* The Left Against Europe 1973, The Enchanted Glass: Britain and its Monarchy 1988, Faces of Nationalism: Janus Revisited 1997, The Break-Up of Britain: Crisis and Neo-Nationalism 1977, Pariah: Misfortunes of the British Kingdom 2002, After Britain: New Labour and the Return of Scotland 2000, Global Matrix: Nationalism, Socialism and State-Terror (with Paul James) 2005.
Address: Royal Melbourne Institute of Technology, Globalism Research, GPO Box 2476V, 411 Swanston Street, Melbourne, Vic. 3001, Australia (office). *Telephone:* (3) 9925-9586 (office). *E-mail:* tom.nairn@rmit.edu.au (office); tcnairn@ecosse.net (home). *Website:* www.rmit.edu.au (office).

NAJMIDDINOV, Safarali; Tajikistan politician; *Minister of Finance; Education:* Tajik State Univ. *Career:* fmr Chief Accountant and Head Dept of Finance, State Cttee of Statistics; Head Trade Dept, Municipality of Dushanbe 1982–92; Deputy Minister of Trade 1991–2000; Minister of Finance 2000–.
Address: Ministry of Finance, 734025 Dushanbe, ul. Ak. Rajabovykh 3, Tajikistan (office). *Telephone:* (372) 21-62-37 (office). *Fax:* (372) 21-33-29 (office).

NAKAMURA, Yuji; Japanese diplomatist; *Ambassador to Italy;* b. Sept. 1944, Tokyo; m. Kazuko Nakamura. *Education:* Tokyo Univ. *Career:* joined Ministry of the Foreign Affairs 1966, Counsellor, Third Dept, Cabinet Legislation Bureau 1981–83, Dir Cen. and Eastern Europe Div., European and Oceanian Affairs Bureau 1983–85; posted to Germany 1985, Minister, Embassy in Bonn 1990–91, Minister, Embassy in Vienna 1991, fmr Consul-Gen. in Sydney; Amb. to Switzerland 2002–05 (also accred to Liechtenstein 2003–05), Amb. to Italy (also accred to Albania) 2006–.
Address: Embassy of Japan, Via Quintino Sella 60, 00187 Rome, Italy (office). *Telephone:* (06) 487991 (office). *Fax:* (06) 4873316 (office). *E-mail:* fao@embjpn.it (office). *Website:* www.it.emb-japan.go.jp (office).

NAKANDALA, Amaralal Sumith; Sri Lankan diplomatist; *Ambassador to Nepal;* m. Dammika Nakandala. *Education:* Univ. of Peradeniya, Inst. of Social Studies, The Hague, Netherlands. *Career:* spent three years at High Comm. in New Delhi, Deputy High Commr for southern India, Chennai 2001–06, Amb. to Nepal 2006–.
Address: Embassy of Sri Lanka, Chundevi Marg, Maharajung, Kathmandu, Nepal (office). *Telephone:* (1) 4720623 (office); (1) 4721381 (office). *Fax:* (1) 4720128 (office). *E-mail:* embassy@srilanka.info.com.np (office).

NAKAYAMA, Masao; Micronesian diplomatist; *Permanent Representative, United Nations;* b. 24 March 1941. *Education:* Coll. of Guam, Univ. of the Philippines. *Career:* teacher, Truk Dist High School 1966; mem. Congress of Micronesia 1968–69; Asst Chief of Training, Personnel Dept, Office of the Trust Territory of the Pacific Islands 1974–76, Chief of Training 1976–80; Chief of Int. Affairs, Dept of Foreign Affairs 1980–88; Amb. to Japan (also accred to People's Repub. of China, Indonesia, Malaysia, South Korea, Singapore) 1989–92; Perm. Rep. to UN, New York 1998–, also Chair. Asian States; mem. Chunk State Constitutional Convention 1988, Onoun Municipality Constitutional Convention 1992.
Address: Permanent Mission of the Federated States of Micronesia, 820 Second Avenue, Suite 17a, New York, NY 10017, USA (office). *Telephone:* (212) 697-8370 (office). *Fax:* (212) 697-8295 (office). *E-mail:* fsmun@ fsmgov.org (office). *Website:* www.fsmgov.org/fsmun (office).

NALBANDYAN, Edvard, Ph.D; Armenian diplomatist; *Minister of Foreign Affairs;* b. 1956; m.; one d. *Education:* Moscow State Inst. of Int. Relations, Inst of Oriental Studies, USSR Nat. Acad. of Sciences. *Career:* worked at USSR Embassy in Lebanon 1978–83; at USSR Ministry of Foreign Affairs, Moscow 1983–86; Counsellor of USSR Embassy (then Russian Fed. Embassy) in Egypt 1986–92; Chargé d'Affaires in Egypt 1992–93, Amb. to Egypt 1994–98 (also accred Marocco and Oman); Amb. to France 1999–2008 (also accred to Israel, the Vatican, to Andorra) 2004–08; Minister of Foreign Affairs 2008–; Special Rep. of the Pres.of Armenia to Int. Org. of Francophony 2006; Commdr, Légion d'honneur 2001, Grand Cross of St Gregory (Holy See) 2003; Award of Friendship of Nations (USSR) 1982, Mkhitar Gosh Medal 2001.
Address: Ministry of Foreign Affairs, 0010 Yerevan, Republic Square, Government House 2, Armenia (office). *Telephone:* (10) 54-40-41 (office). *Fax:* (10) 54-39-25 (office). *E-mail:* info@armeniaforeignministry.com (office). *Website:* www.armeniaforeignministry.com (office).

NAM HONG, Hor, LLB, ML; Cambodian diplomatist and politician; *Deputy Prime Minister and Minister of Foreign Affairs and International Co-operation;* b. 15 Nov. 1935, Phnom-Penh; m.; five c. *Education:* Univ. of Phnom-Penh, Univ. of Paris, L'Ecole Royale d'Admin., France. *Career:* Amb. to Cuba 1973–75; Khmer Rouge prisoner 1975–79; Vice-Minister of

Foreign Affairs 1980–82; Amb. to fmr USSR 1982–89; Minister of Foreign Affairs 1990–93, 1998–, currently Deputy Prime Minister and Minister of Foreign Affairs and Int. Co-operation; mem. Nat. Ass. 1998–; mem. Supreme Nat. Council of Cambodia 1991–93, Amb. to France 1993–98; mem. Cambodian People's Party (CPP); Grand Officer of Monisaraphon, Ordre Nat. du Mérite, Grand Cross, Royal Order of Cambodia, Order of the White Elephant (Thailand), Grand Collier, Royal Order of Cambodia. *Address:* Ministry of Foreign Affairs and International Co-operation, 3 rue Samdech Hun Sen, Khan Chamkarmon, Phnom-Penh, Cambodia (office). *Telephone:* (23) 214441 (office). *Fax:* (23) 216144 (office). *E-mail:* mfaicinfo@mfaic.gov.kh (office). *Website:* www.mfaic.gov.kh (office).

NAMALIU, Rt Hon. Sir Rabbie Langanai, KCMG, PC, BA, MA; Papua New Guinea politician; b. 3 April 1947, Raluana, E New Britain Prov.; m. 1st Margaret Nakikus 1978 (died 1993); two s. one step-d.; m. 2nd Kelina Tavul 1999; one s. *Education:* Keravat High School, Univ. of Papua New Guinea, Univ. of Victoria, BC, Canada. *Career:* fmrly scholar and Fellow, Univ. of Papua New Guinea; tutor and Lecturer in History, Univ. of Papua New Guinea; Prin. Pvt. Sec. to Chief Minister 1974; fmr Prov. Commr, E New Britain and Chair. Public Services Comm.; held sr positions in the Office of the Prime Minister and Leader of the Opposition under Mr Somare; MP for Kokopo Open 1982–; Minister for Foreign Affairs and Trade 1982–84, for Primary Industry 1984–85; Deputy Leader, Pangu Pati 1985–88, Leader 1988–92; Prime Minister 1988–92; Speaker Nat. Parl. 1994–97; Sr Minister for State 1997–98, for Petroleum and Energy 1998–99; Minister of Foreign Affairs and Immigration 2002–06, of Finance 2006–07, of the Treasury 2007; Pres. African Caribbean Pacific Council of Ministers 1984; Co-Pres. ACP/EEC Jt Council of Ministers 1984; Vacation Scholar, ANU 1968; Visiting Fellow, Univ. of Calif., Center for Pacific Studies, Santa Cruz, Calif., USA 1976; Hon. MA, LLD, (Victoria, BC) 1983; Independence Medal 1975, Queen's Silver Jubilee Medal 1977, Pacific Man of the Year 1988. *Address:* c/o Department of Finance and Treasury, POB 710, Waigani, Vulupindi Haus, NCD, Papua New Guinea; POB 6655, Boroko, National Capital District, Papua New Guinea.

NAMBIAR, Vijay K.; Indian diplomatist; *Chef de Cabinet to the Secretary-General, United Nations;* b. Aug. 1943, Poona; m. Malini Nambiar; two d. *Education:* Bombay Univ. *Career:* joined Foreign Service 1967, early years specializing in Chinese language and serving in Hong Kong and Beijing; subsequent posts included Belgrade, Yugoslavia in mid-1970s; numerous bilateral and multilateral postings in Beijing, Belgrade and New York in 1970s and 1980s, also Jt Sec. (Dir Gen.) for E Asia 1988 and multilateral affairs at New Delhi HQ 1980s; Amb. to Algeria 1985–88, to Afghanistan 1990–92, to Malaysia 1993–96, to China 1996–2000, to Pakistan 2000–01; Perm. Rep. to UN, New York 2002–04; Deputy Nat. Security Adviser (DNSA) and Head, Nat. Security Council Secr. 2005–06; Under-Sec.-Gen. and Special Adviser to UN Sec.-Gen., New York 2006–07, Chef de Cabinet (Chief of Staff), UN Sec.-Gen. 2007–. *Address:* Office of the Secretary-General, United Nations, New York, NY 10017, USA (office). *Telephone:* (212) 963-1234 (office). *Fax:* (212) 963-4879 (office). *Website:* www.un.org (home).

NAMOLOH, Maj.-Gen. (retd) Charles Dickson Ndaxu Phillip; Namibian military officer, government official and politician; *Minister of Defence;* b. 28 Feb. 1950, Odibo. *Education:* St Mary's Mission Anglican School, Indira Gandhi Univ., Delhi. *Career:* graduated from northern centre as guerrilla detachment commdr 1975, from Vystrel Field Acad. as motorised Infantry Brigade Commdr 1982; fmr High Commr to India; currently Minister of Defence; Head, Politics, Security and Defence Cttee, South African Devt Community; Swapo Highest Medal of Ongulumbashe 1989, Order of the Eagle 2004. *Address:* Ministry of Defence, Private Bag 13307, Windhoek, Namibia (office). *Telephone:* (61) 2042005 (office). *Fax:* (61) 232518 (office). *E-mail:* cnamoloh@mod.gov.na (office). *Website:* www.mod.gov.na (office).

NANDA, Biren, MA; Indian diplomatist; *Ambassador to Indonesia;* b. 21 Jan. 1955; m. Rukmani Nanda; one s. *Education:* Delhi School of Econs. *Career:* joined Foreign Service 1978, served as Third Sec., High Comm. in Singapore 1980–82, Second Sec., Embassy in Beijing 1982–85, First Sec. (Political), Embassy in Washington, DC 1988–91, Counsellor (Political), Embassy in Beijing 1993–96, Consul-General in Shanghai 1996–2000, Deputy Chief of Mission, Embassy in Tokyo 2000–04; fmr Under-Sec. (China), Ministry of External Affairs, Jt Sec. (South), responsible for relations with ASEAN countries (excluding Myanmar), Australia, New Zealand, Fiji, Papua New Guinea, Pacific Islands 2004–08; Amb. to Indonesia 2008–. *Address:* Embassy of India, Jalan H. R. Rasuna Said, Kav. S/1, Kuningan, Jakarta 12950, Indonesia (office). *Telephone:* (21) 5204150 (office). *Fax:* (21) 5204160 (office). *E-mail:* eiojakarta@indo.net.id (office). *Website:* www.embassyofindiajakarta.org (office).

NANDAGO, Patrick; Namibian diplomatist; *Ambassador to USA;* m. Elina Nandago. *Career:* Amb. to Brazil 2004–06, to USA 2006– (also accred to Mexico 2007– and as High Commr to Canada 2008–, the Bahamas 2008–). *Address:* Embassy of Namibia, 1605 New Hampshire Avenue, NW, Washington, DC 20009, USA (office). *Telephone:* (202) 986-0540 (office). *Fax:* (202) 986-0443 (office). *E-mail:* info@namibianembassyusa.org (office). *Website:* www.namibianembassyusa.org (office).

NANDAN, Satya Nand, CF, CBE, LLB; Fijian diplomatist and lawyer; *Secretary-General, International Seabed Authority;* b. 10 July 1936, Suva; m. 1st Sreekumari Nandan 1966 (died 1971); m. 2nd Zarine Merchant 1976; one s. *Education:* DAV Coll. Suva, John McGlashan Coll. Dunedin, NZ, Univs of Wellington, NZ and London, UK, and Lincoln's Inn, London. *Career:* called to Bar, Lincoln's Inn 1965; barrister and solicitor, Supreme Court of Fiji 1966–; pvt. law practice, Suva 1965–70; Counsellor then Amb. Perm. Mission of Fiji to UN 1970–76; Leader, Fiji Del. to Third UN Conf. on Law of Sea 1973–82; Amb. to EEC (also accred to Belgium, France, Italy, Luxembourg, Netherlands) 1976–80; Perm. Sec. for Foreign Affairs, Fiji 1981–83; UN Under-Sec.-Gen. for Ocean Affairs and the Law of the Sea and Special Rep. of UN Sec.-Gen. for Law of the Sea 1983–92; mem. Perm. Mission of Fiji to UN 1993–96; Chair. UN Conf. on Straddling Fish Stocks and Highly Migratory Fish Stocks 1993–95; Rep. of Fiji to Int. Seabed Authority 1994–95, Sec.-Gen. 1996–2008; Pres. Meeting of States Parties, 1982 UN Convention on the Law of the Sea 1994–96; Int. Law Adviser to Govt of Fiji 1994–95; Chair. Conf. on Conservation and Man. of Highly Migratory Fish Stocks in Cen. and Western Pacific 1997–2000, UN Int. School 1996–2000, 2005–08; mem. Int. Advisory Group, Maritime and Port Authority of Singapore 1997–2000; del. to numerous int. confs etc.; Visiting Lecturer, Columbia Univ. New York and Univ. of Virginia, Charlottesville; Sr Visiting Fellow, US Inst. of Peace 1992; many other professional appointments; Grand Cross, Order of Merit (FRG) 1996, Companion Order of Fiji 1999; Hon. LLD (Newfoundland) 1995; Dr hc (Univ. of the South Pacific) 1996. *Publications include:* Commentary on 1982 UN Convention on Law of Sea (seven vols) (ed.); numerous articles on UN and aspects of Law of the Sea. *Address:* International Seabed Authority, 14–20 Port Royal Street, Kingston, Jamaica (office); 301 East 48th Street, New York, NY 10017, USA (home). *Telephone:* (876) 922-9105 (office). *Fax:* (876) 967-3011 (office). *E-mail:* snandan@isa.org.jm (office). *Website:* www.isa.org.jm (office).

NAPOLITANO, Giorgio; Italian politician and head of state; *President;* b. 29 June 1925, Naples; m. Clio Maria Bittoni. *Education:* Univ. of Naples Frederico II. *Career:* joined Italian Communist Party (PCI) 1945, mem. Nat. Cttee, subsequently responsible for Comm. for Southern Italy 1956, then Sec. for Naples and Caserta, coordinator of Party Sec.'s Office and Political Office 1966–69, responsible for culture and later econ. policy and int. relations during 1970s and 80s; joined Democratic Party of the Left (later Democrats of the Left) following dissolution of PCI, 1981; elected to Chamber of Deputies 1953, Pres. 1992–94; Minister of the Interior 1996–98; MEP 1999–2004; Senator for Life 2005–; Pres. of Italy 2006–; Dr hc (Università degli Studi di Bari) 2004. *Publications:* Movimento Operaio e Industria di Stato 1962, Intervista sul PCI (jtly) 1975, In Mezzo al Guado 1979, Oltre i Vecchi Confini 1988, Europa e America dopo l'89 1992, Dove va la Repubblica - Una Transizione Incompiuta 1994, Europa Politica 2002, Dal PCI al Socialismo Europeo: Un 'Autobiografia Politica 2005. *Address:* Office of the President, Palazzo del Quirinale, 00187 Rome, Italy (office). *Telephone:* (06) 46991 (office). *Fax:* (06) 46993125 (office). *E-mail:* presidenza.repubblica@quirinale.it (office). *Website:* www.quirinale.it (office).

NARAYAN, Rajamani Lakshmi; Indian diplomatist; *High Commissioner to Canada;* m. Regina Narayan; one s. *Career:* joined Foreign Service 1972; overseas postings include Moscow (twice), Washington, DC, Malé, Belgrade, Bangkok; Amb. to Qatar 1996–2000, fmr Amb. to Poland; fmr High Commr to Malaysia, High Commr to Canada 2007–. *Address:* High Commission of India, 10 Springfield Road, Ottawa, ON K1M 1C9, Canada (office). *Telephone:* (613) 744-3751 (office). *Fax:* (613) 744-0913 (office). *E-mail:* hicomind@hciottawa.ca (office). *Website:* www.hciottawa.ca (office).

NARAYANAN, M. K., BA (Econs); Indian government official; *National Security Adviser to the Prime Minister;* b. 10 March 1934, New Delhi; m. Padmini Narayanan; one s. one d. *Career:* fmr Head, Indian Intelligence Bureau; Special Adviser to Prime Minister Manmohan Singh with rank of Minister of State 2004–; Nat. Security Adviser to the Prime Minister 2005–; Padmashree Award 1992.

Address: c/o Prime Minister's Office, South Block, New Delhi 110 011 (office); 10 Teen Murti Lane, New Delhi 110 011, India (home). *Telephone:* (11) 23019227 (office); (11) 23015890 (office); (11) 23019856 (home). *Fax:* (11) 23017990 (office); (11) 23018788 (home). *E-mail:* mk.narayanan@pmo .nic.in (office). *Website:* www.pmindia.nic.in (office).

NARISOA, Rajaonarivony, MA, PhD; Malagasy diplomatist and politician; *Ambassador to France;* m.; three c. *Education:* Univ. of Madagascar, Auburn Univ., Ala and Univ. of Pittsburgh, USA. *Career:* Lecturer and Research Assoc., Techniques of Planning, Inst. of Madagascar 1981–89; Econ. and Commercial Officer, British Embassy in Madagascar 1989–93; Nat. Coordinator, Program on Governance and Public Policies for Sustainable Human Devt, UNDP 1998–2002; Deputy Prime Minister and Minister of Finance and Budget 2002–03; Amb. to USA 2003–07, to France 2007–; sec.-gen. of a holding co. and dir gen. of a consulting firm, Madagascar 1996–98. *Address:* Embassy of Madagascar, 4 avenue Raphaël, 75016 Paris, France (office). *Telephone:* 1-45-04-62-11 (office). *Fax:* 1-45-03-58-70 (office). *E-mail:* info@ambassade-madagascar.fr (office). *Website:* www.ambassade -madagascar.fr (office).

NARYSHKIN, Sergei Yevgenyevich; Russian engineer and government official; *Head of Presidential Administration;* b. 27 Oct. 1954, Leningrad. *Education:* Leningrad Inst. of Mechanics, Petersburg International Management Institute. *Career:* Head Foreign Investments Dept, Promstroybank 1995–97; with Leningrad Regional Govt, positions including Head Investments Dept, Head Int. Affairs Cttee 1997–98; Chair. Cttee for External Economic and Int. Relations, Leningrad Regional Govt 1998–2004; Deputy Head of the Govt Staff, Russian Fed. 2004, Chief of Staff 2004–07, Deputy Prime Minister responsible for external econ. activity 2007–08; Head, Presidential Admin. 2008–. *Address:* Office of the President, 103132 Moscow, Staraya pl. 4, Russia (office). *Telephone:* (495) 925-35-81 (office). *Fax:* (495) 206-07-66 (office). *E-mail:* president@gov.ru (office). *Website:* www.kremlin.ru (office).

NASH, Ronald Peter, CMG, LVO, BA, MICL; British diplomatist; b. 18 Sept. 1946; m.; three s. *Education:* Univ. of Manchester. *Career:* joined FCO 1970, Personnel Operations Dept 1970, Western Operations Dept 1970–72, full-time Russian language training 1972–73, Second, later First Sec., Chancery, Moscow 1974–76, First Sec., UK Del., Vienna 1976–79, Western European Dept, FCO 1979–81, UN Dept 1981–83, First Sec. (Information), New Delhi 1983–86, Deputy Head of E European Dept, FCO 1986–87, Deputy Head of Mission, Vienna 1988–92, Deputy High Commr, Colombo 1992–95, Coordinator, London Peace Implementation Conf. for Bosnia 1995, Head of Human Rights Policy Dept, FCO 1996–99, Amb. to Nepal 1999–2002, to Afghanistan 2002–03, High Commr to Trinidad and Tobago 2003–07 (retd). *Address:* c/o Foreign and Commonwealth Office, King Charles Street, London, SW1A 2AH UK (office).

NASR, Seyyed Hossein, MS, PhD; Iranian academic; *University Professor of Islamic Studies, George Washington University;* b. 7 April 1933, Tehran; m. Soussan Daneshvari 1958; one s. one d. *Education:* Mass. Inst. of Tech. and Harvard Univ. *Career:* Teaching Asst Harvard Univ. 1955–58, Visiting Prof. 1962, 1965; Assoc. Prof. of History of Science and Philosophy, Tehran Univ. 1958–63, Prof. 1963–79, Dean, Faculty of Letters 1968–72, Vice-Chancellor 1970–71; Chancellor (Pres.) Aryamehr Univ. 1972–75; First Prof. of Islamic Studies, American Univ. of Beirut 1964–65; Prof. of Islamic Studies, Temple Univ. 1979–84; Univ. Prof. of Islamic Studies, George Washington Univ. 1984–; Visiting Prof., Harvard Univ. 1962, 1965, Princeton Univ. 1975, Univ. of Utah 1979; A. D. White Prof.-at-Large, Cornell Univ. 1991–98; Founder and first Pres. Iranian Acad. of Philosophy 1974–79; mem. Inst. Int. de Philosophie, Greek Acad. of Philosophy, Royal Acad. of Jordan; Dr hc (Uppsala) 1977, (Lehigh) 1996. *Publications:* more than 30 books and 300 articles in Persian, Arabic, English and French in leading int. journals. *Address:* 709R Gelman Library, The George Washington University, Washington, DC 20052, USA (office). *Telephone:* (202) 994-5704 (office). *Fax:* (202) 994-4571 (office). *E-mail:* zsirat@gwu.edu (office). *Website:* www.nasrfoundation.org/default.html (office).

NASRALLAH, Sheikh Hasan; Lebanese ecclesiastic and political leader; *Secretary-General, Hezbollah;* b. 31 Aug. 1960, Beirut; m. Fatima Yassin; five c. (one deceased). *Career:* at age 15 joined Amal movt, Bassouriyeh, 1975, then moved to Najaf, Iraq to study at Hawza (Islamic Seminary); forced to leave Iraq and returned to Lebanon to study with Amal leader Sheikh Abbas al-Musawi; elected Amal political del. in Biqaa; resgnd from Amal and joined Hezbollah 1982, chief exec. and mem. Consultative Council, Beirut 1987–89, moved to Qom, Iran to resume studies 1989;

returned briefly to Lebanon then back to Tehran to represent Hezbollah 1989; Sec.-Gen. Hezbollah 1992–. *E-mail:* hizbollahmedia@hizbollah.org. *Website:* www.moqawama.org/ english; www.hizbollah.org.

NASSER, Nassir bin Abdulaziz an-; Qatari diplomatist; *Permanent Representative, United Nations;* b. Doha. *Career:* currently Perm. Rep. to UN, New York; Chair. Group of 77 2004; High Honour Awards from Italian Govt 2005. *Address:* Permanent Mission of Qatar, 809 United Nations Plaza, 4th Floor, New York, NY 10017, USA (office). *Telephone:* (212) 486-9335 (office). *Fax:* (212) 758-4952 (office). *E-mail:* newyork@mofa.gov.qa (office).

NASSER, Siba; Syrian diplomatist. *Career:* fmr Head of Mission to the EC; fmr Deputy Minister of Foreign Affairs; Amb. to France 2002–06, also accred. to Holy See 2003–06. *Address:* c/o Ministry of Foreign Affairs, rue ar-Rashid, Damascus, Syria. *Telephone:* (11) 3331200. *Fax:* (11) 3327620.

NASSOUR, Gen. Mahamat Ali Abdallah; Chadian army officer and politician. *Career:* fmr Minister of Territorial Admin; State Minister and Minister of Mines and Energy 2006–08; Minister of Nat. Defence Feb.– March 2008. *Address:* c/o Ministry of National Defence, BP 916, N'Djamena, Chad (office).

NĂSTASE, Adrian, LLM, PhD; Romanian academic and politician; b. 22 June 1950, Bucharest; m. Daniela Miculescu 1985; two s. *Education:* Bucharest Univ. *Career:* Research Fellow, Inst. of Legal Research, Bucharest 1973–90; Prof. of Public Int. Law, Bucharest Univ. 1990–, Titu Maiorescu, Dimitrie Cantemir and Nicolae Titulescu pvt. univs 1992–; Assoc. Prof. of Public Int. Law, Paris-Panthéon Sorborne I 1994–; Minister of Foreign Affairs 1990–92; Speaker Chamber of Deputies 1992–96, Deputy Speaker 1996–; Exec. Pres. Social Democracy Party of Romania 1992–97, First Vice-Pres. 1997–2000, Pres. 2001–06 (resgnd); Prime Minister of Romania 2000–04; Vice-Chair. Camera Deputaţilor (Chamber of Deputies) 1996–2000, Chair. 2004–06 (resgnd); apptd mem. Romanian Parl. Del. to Parl. Asscn Council of Europe 1996; Vice-Pres. Asscn of Int. Law and Int. Relations, Bucharest 1977–; Dir of Studies, Int. Inst. of Human Rights, Strasbourg 1984; Pres. Titulescu European Foundation 1990–92 (Hon. Pres. 1992–); Exec. Pres. Euro-Atlantic Centre, Bucharest 1991–92; mem. Bd of Dirs Inst. for East-West Studies, New York 1991–97; mem. Human Rights Information and Documentation System; mem. French Soc. of Int. Law 1984–, American Soc. of Int. Law 1995–; lecturer at numerous univs and insts of int. relations and human rights and speaker at many int. confs; Order of Diplomatic Service Merit 1991, Gwanghwa Medal, Repub. of Korea 1991, Grande Croix de Mérite, Sovereign Order of Malta 1992; Nicolae Titulescu Prize, Romanian Acad. 1994, The Political Man of 1995, Turkish Businessmen's Asscn, Global Leader for Tomorrow Prize 1993. *Publications include:* Human Rights: An End-of-the-Century Religion 1992, International Law: Achievements and Prospects (co-author) 1992, Human Rights, Civil Society, Parliamentary Diplomacy 1994, Public International Law (co-author) 1995, Nicolae Titulescu – Our Contemporary 1995, Parliamentary Humour 1996, International Economic Law II 1996, Romania and the New World Architecture 1996, Documenta universales I (with law documents) 1997, 1998, The Treaties of Romania (1990–1997) 1998, Documenta universales II: The Rights of Persons Belonging to National Minorities 1998, Battle for the Future 2000, Contemporary International Law-Essential Texts 2001; more than 240 articles and papers. *Address:* c/o Social Democratic Party (SDP) (Partidul Social Democrat) (PSD), 71271 Bucharest 2, Str. Kiseleff 10, Romania (office). *Website:* www .adriannastase.ro.

NATALEGAWA, Raden Mohammad Marty Muliana, BSc, MPhil, PhD; Indonesian diplomatist; *Permanent Representative, United Nations;* b. 22 March 1963, Bandung; m. Sranya Bamrungphong Natalegawa; three c. *Education:* London School of Econs and Corpus Christi Coll., Cambridge, UK, Australian Nat. Univ. *Career:* with Perm. Mission to UN, New York 1994–99, Deputy Dir, later Dir Int. Org. 1999–2002, Perm. Rep. to UN 2007–; Chief of Staff, Office of Minister for Foreign Affairs 2002–04, Spokesperson, Dept of Foreign Affairs 2002–05; Dir-Gen. for ASEAN Cooperation 2004–05; Amb. to UK (also accred to Ireland) 2005–07; First Public Relations Soc. Award, Public Relations Soc. of Indonesia 2004. *Address:* Permanent Mission of Indonesia to the United Nations, 325 East 38th Street, New York, NY 10016, USA (office). *Telephone:* (212) 972-8333 (office). *Fax:* (212) 972-9780 (office). *E-mail:* ptri@indonesiamission-ny .org (office). *Website:* www.indonesiamission-ny.org (office).

NATBILADZE, Nikoloz, PhD; Georgian business executive, politician and diplomatist; *Ambassador to Azerbaijan;* b. 17 Nov. 1971, Tbilisi; m.; two d. *Education:* Georgian Tech. Univ. *Career:* Sr Expert at Foreign Relations and Investment Dept, Ministry of Industry 1993–95; Regional Dir for CIS countries, Lone Star Corpn 1995–96; Tech. Supervisor, Municipal Infrastructure Devt Project 1996–97; Deputy Dir Tbilisi-London Insurance Co. Ltd 1997–98; Gen.-Dir British-Caucasian Insurance Co. (BCI), Chair. Supervisory Bd and Hon. Pres. 1998–2004; Chair. Supervisory Bd ENERGOTRANS Ltd 2002–04; Dir Econ. Security Dept, Nat. Security Council 2004–05, Deputy Sec. 2005; Deputy Minister of Foreign Affairs 2005–07; Amb. to Azerbaijan 2007–; World Young Entrepreneurs Millennium Award 2000.
Address: Embassy of Georgia, 1073 Baku, Yasamal rayon, section 523, S. Dadashev küç. 29, Azerbaijan (office). *Telephone:* (12) 497-45-60 (office). *Fax:* (12) 497-45-61 (office). *E-mail:* embgeo@azeurotel.com (office). *Website:* www.az.mfa.gov.ge (office).

NATH, Kamal, BCom; Indian politician; *Minister of Commerce and Industry;* b. Nov. 1946, Kanpur; m.; two s. *Education:* Doon School, Dehra Dun, St Xavier's Coll. *Career:* joined Indian Nat. Congress 1968 as youth worker; first elected to Parl. for Chhindwara 1980, re-elected 1985, 1989, 1991, 1998, 1999, 2004; mem. Del. to UN Gen. Ass. 1982–83; apptd Minister of Environment and Forests 1991, later Minister of Textiles; Minister of Commerce and Industry 2004–; Sec.-Gen. Indian Nat. Congress; mem. Congress Working Cttee; Pres. Bd Govs Inst. of Man. Tech.; Chair. Madhya Pradesh Devt Council.
Address: Ministry of Commerce and Industry, Udyog Bhavan, New Delhi 110 011 (office); No. 1 Tughlak Road, New Delhi 110 011, India (home). *Telephone:* (11) 23016664 (office); (11) 23792233 (home). *Fax:* (11) 23014335 (office); (11) 23793396 (home). *E-mail:* cim@ub.nic.in (office); knath@knath.com (home). *Website:* www.commin.nic.in (office).

NATHAN, S(ellapan) R(amanathan); Singaporean head of state; *President;* b. (Sellapan Ramanathan), 3 July 1924; m. Urmila (Umi) Nandey; one s. one d. *Education:* Victoria School and Univ. of Malaya, Singapore. *Career:* almoner Medical Dept, Gen. Hosp. 1955–56; Seaman's Welfare Officer, Ministry of Labour 1956–62; Asst Dir Labour Research Unit 1962–63, Dir 1964–66; Asst Sec. Ministry of Foreign Affairs Feb.–June 1966, Prin. Asst Sec. 1966–67, Deputy Sec. 1967–71; Dir Security and Intelligence Div. Ministry of Defence 1971–79; First Perm. Sec. Ministry of Foreign Affairs 1979–82; Exec. Chair. The Straits Times Press 1982–88; High Commr in Malaysia 1988–90; Amb. to USA 1990–96; Amb.-at-Large, Ministry of Foreign Affairs 1996–99; Dir Inst. of Defence and Strategic Studies, Nanyang Technological Univ. 1996–99; Pres. of Singapore 1999–; Pro-Chancellor Nat. Univ. of Singapore; Chair. Hindu Endowments Bd, Mitsubishi Singapore Heavy Industries (Pte) Ltd; mem. Bd of Trustees NTUC Research Unit, Singapore Indian Devt Asscn; Dir Singapore Nat. Oil Co. (Pte) Ltd, New Nation Publishing Berhad, Times Publishing Berhad, Singapore Press Holdings Ltd, Marshall Cavendish Ltd, Singapore Mint (Pte) Ltd, Singapore Int. Media (Pte) Ltd; mem. Bd of Govs Civil Service Coll.; Friend of Labour Award 1962, Public Service Star 1964, Public Admin Medal (Silver) 1967, Meritorious Service Medal 1974, NTUC May Day Meritorious Service Award 1984.
Address: President's Office, Istana, Orchard Road, Singapore 238823 (office). *Telephone:* 67375522 (office). *Website:* www.istana.gov.sg (office).

NAVARETTE LÓPEZ, Jorge Eduardo; Mexican economist, diplomatist and academic; *Head of Research on International Affairs, National Autonomous University of Mexico;* b. 29 April 1940, Mexico City; m. Martha L. López; one s. *Education:* Nat. Autonomous Univ. of Mexico (UNAM). *Career:* Prof., Nat. School of Econs and Nat. School of Political and Social Sciences, UNAM 1964–71, Head of Research on Int. Affairs, 2004–; various positions with Foreign Trade Nat. Bank 1966–72; Ed. Comercio Exterior; with Secr. of Finance and Public Credit –1972; Amb. to Venezuela 1972–75, to Austria 1975–77, to Yugoslavia 1977–78, to UK 1986–89, to People's Repub. of China 1989–93, to Chile 1993–95, to Brazil 1997–2001, to Germany 2002–04; Rep. of Mexico at Int. Conf. for Co-operation and Devt, Paris 1976–77; Deputy Perm. Rep. to UN and Vice-Pres. Econ. and Social Council 1978–79, Perm. Rep. to UN 2001–02; Under-Sec. for Econ. Affairs, Secr. of Foreign Relations 1979–86; Under-Sec. for Policy and Devt, Secr. of Energy 1995–97; fmr consultant for Inter-American Bank and UNDP; fmr Perm. Rep. to UNIDO; fmr mem. Bd of Govs IAEA; fmr mem. South Comm. *Publications include:* The International Transference of Technology: The Mexican Case (with Gerardo Bueno and Miguel Wionczek) 1969, Mexico: The Economic Policy of the New Government 1971, The Latin American External Debt 1986.
Address: National Autonomous University of Mexico, Ciudad Universitaria, Del. Coyoacán, 04510, Mexico (office). *Telephone:* (55) 5623-0264 (office). *Fax:* (55) 1107-6963 (office). *E-mail:* joredune@servidor.unam.mx (office). *Website:* www.unam.mx (office).

NAVARRO, Samuel Lewis; Panamanian politician; *First Vice-President and Minister of Foreign Affairs;* b. 1958, Panama City; m.; several c. *Education:* Georgetown and American Univs, Washington, DC, USA. *Career:* worked in pvt. sector; Founder Partido de Solidaridad 1993, formed alliance with Partido Revolucionario Democrático 1999, left to serve as running mate to presidential cand. Martín Torrijos 2004; Vice-Pres. of Panama and Minister of Foreign Affairs 2004–; Pres. and Dir Empaques de Colón 1985–2001, Grupo ELE 1985–2001, Northsound Corpn, Inc. 1985–2001; mem. Bd of Dirs Panama Canal Authority 1997–2001; fmr mem. Bd of Dirs Distribuidora de Productos de Papel, Inmobiliaria Costa Azul, Cervecería Nacional, Red Crown Corpn.
Address: Ministry of Foreign Affairs, Altos de Ancón, Complejo Narciso Garay, Panamá 4, Panama (office). *Telephone:* 227-0013 (office). *Fax:* 227-4725 (office). *E-mail:* prensa@mire.gob.pa (office). *Website:* www.mire.gob.pa (office).

NAZARBAYEV, Nursultan Abishevich, DSc; Kazakhstani politician and head of state; *President;* b. 6 July 1940, Chemolgan, Kaskelen raion, Almaty Oblast; m. Sara Alpisovna Kounakayeva 1962; three d. *Education:* Higher Tech. Course at Karaganda Metallurgical Combine, Russian Acad. of Management and Higher Party School of Cen. Cttee CPSU. *Career:* mem. CPSU 1962–91; worked for Karaganda Metallurgical Plant 1960–64, 1965–69; Sec. Temirtau City Cttee of Kazakh CP 1969–84; Sec. party Cttee of Karaganda Metallurgical Combine 1973–77; Second, then First Sec. Karaganda Dist Cttee of Kazakh CP 1977–79; Sec. Cen. Cttee of Kazakh CP 1979–84; Chair. Council of Ministers of Kazakh SSR 1984–89; USSR People's Deputy 1989–91; First Sec. Cen. Cttee of Kazakh CP 1989–91, Socialist Party 1991–; Chair. Kazakh Supreme Soviet 1989–90; Exec. Pres. Kazakh SSR 1990–91; Pres. Repub. of Kazakhstan 1991–; Chair. World Kazakh Union 1992–; mem. Int. Eng Acad. 1993, Acad. of Social Sciences of the Russian Fed. 1994, Nat. Acad. of Sciences of the Repub. of Kazakhstan 1995; Hon. Citizen of Temirtau 1991, Duluth, USA 1991, Almaty 1995; Diploma of Freeman of Municipality of Bucharest 1998; Hon. Prof., Al-Farabi Kazakh State Nat. Univ., M. V. Lomonosov Moscow State Univ. 1996; Hon. mem. Belarusian Acad. of Sciences 1996, Nat. Acad. of Applied Sciences of Russia 1997; Order of the Red Banner of Labour; Badge of Honour 1972; Order of Saint Lord-and-Master Prince Daniil of Moscow, First Class 1996; Order of Yaroslav Mudryi (Ukraine) 1997; Order of Big Cross Holder with Ribbon (Italy) 1998; Order of Holy Apostole Andrei Pervosvannyi 1998; Ismoili Samoni Order (Tajikistan) 2000; Pi Order (Vatican) 2001; Dr hc (Kazakh Inst. of Man., Economy and Forecasting) 1995, (Bilkent Univ., Ankara) 1998; Capri Award (Italy) 1992, Rukhaniyat Man of the Year 1993, Gold Medal of Guild of Econ. Devt and Marketing of the City of Nurnberg (FRG) 1993, Award of Crans-Montana Int. Forum 1996, star No. Perseus RA 3h 23v Osd 40* 43 named after him 1997, Medal No. 1 of Al-Farabi Kazakh State Nat. Univ. 1998, Award for Int. Understanding, Indian Fund Unity International 1998, Award For Service to Turkish World 1998, Gold Medal and Diploma for Special Contrib. to Devt of CIS Aviation, Int. Aviation Comm. 1998, Peace Dove Prize, UNESCO Club of Dodecanese Islands (Greece) 1999, Man of the Century Award, Abylai Khan Int. Fund 2000, Grand Star of Respect for Merits (Austria) 2000. *Publications:* Steel Profile of Kazakhstan, With Neither the Right nor the Left, Strategy of Resource Saving and Market Transition, Strategy of Formation and Development of Kazakhstan as a Sovereign State, Market and Social-and-Economic Development, On the Threshold of the XXIst Century, Eurasian Union: Ideas, Practice, Prospects 1994–1997, In the Flood of History, The Epicenter of Peace, and others; numerous scientific articles and articles on econs.
Address: Office of the President, 010000 Astana, Beibitshilik 11, Kazakhstan (office). *Telephone:* (7172) 32-13-99 (office). *Fax:* (7172) 32-61-72 (office). *Website:* www.akorda.kz (office).

NAZARIAN, Karen; Armenian diplomatist; *Ambassador to Iran;* b. 29 Nov. 1966, Yerevan; m.; two c. *Education:* Faculty of Oriental Studies, Yerevan State Univ. *Career:* worked in Dept on Mil.-Political Problems, Ministry of Foreign Affairs 1991–92, at Embassy of Armenia, Moscow 1992–94; Chief of Secr., Ministry of Foreign Affairs 1994–96; Amb. to UN, Geneva 1996, Resident Rep. to UN, Geneva –2002; Adviser to Minister of Foreign Affairs 2002–05; Amb. to Iran 2005–; fmr mem. Armenian-American Inter-Governmental Comm.
Address: Embassy of Armenia, 1 Ostad Shahriar St., Razi Street, Jomhouri Islami Avenue, Tehran 11337, Iran (office). *Telephone:* (21) 66704833 (office). *Fax:* (21) 66700657 (office). *E-mail:* emarteh@yahoo.com (office).

NAZAROV, Talbak Nazarovich, DEconSc; Tajikistan politician and academic; b. 15 March 1938, Danghara, Kulyab District; m. Tatyana Grigorievna Teodorovich 1959; one s. one d. *Education:* Leningrad (now St Petersburg) Inst. of Finance and Econs. *Career:* Asst, then Deputy Dean Econs Faculty, Tajik State Univ. 1960–62, Head of Dept, Dean 1965–80, Rector

1982–88; Chair Supreme Soviet Tajik SSR 1986–88; Minister of Public Educ. 1988–90; USSR People's Deputy 1989–92; First Deputy Chair. Tajikistan Council of Ministers, Chair. State Planning Cttee 1990–91; Minister of Foreign Affairs 1994–2006; mem. Tajikistan Acad. of Sciences 1980–; Vice-Pres. 1991–94; Merited Worker of Science and many other awards and medals. *Publications:* books and articles on Tajikistan's economy and external policies.
Address: c/o Ministry of Foreign Affairs, 734051 Dushanbe, pr. Rudaki 42, Tajikistan (office).

NAZIF, Ahmad Mahmoud Muhammad, BSc, MA, PhD; Egyptian computer engineer and government official; *Prime Minister;* b. 8 July 1952, Alexandria; m.; two s. *Education:* Cairo Univ., McGill Univ., Canada. *Career:* Prof. of Computer Eng. Cairo Univ. 1994; Exec. Man. IDSC 1989–95; apptd Minister for Communications and Technology 1999; Prime Minister 2004–; First Order Medal of Science and Art.
Address: 2 Magles El Shaab Street, Kasr El Aini St., Cairo; Office of the Prime Minister, Sharia Majlis ash-Sha'ab, Cairo, Egypt (office). *Telephone:* (2) 7935000 (office); (2) 7958014 (office). *Fax:* (2) 7958016 (office); (2) 7958048 (office). *E-mail:* questions@cabinet.gov.eg (office). *Website:* www .cabinet.gov.eg (office).

NDIAYE, Ndioro, MD, PhD; Senegalese politician and international organization official; *Deputy Director-General, International Organization for Migration;* b. 6 Nov. 1946, Bignona; m.; six c. *Education:* Univ. Cheikh Anta Diop of Dakar and Univ. of Paris VII. *Career:* Head Oral Health Section, Bopp Medical Centre 1976–78; Asst Inst. of Odonto-Stomatology, Faculty of Medicine and Pharmacy, Univ. Cheikh Anta Diop of Dakar 1976–77, Lecturer 1982, Head Preventive and Social Odontology Section 1983, Acting Head 1983, Prof., Head of Inst. 1988–1999; Head of Specialized Nursing Training in Odontology 1976–77; Head of Studies Nat. School of Advanced Technicians in Odontology 1977–79, Acting Dir 1979, Head 1980; Technical Adviser Ministry of Public Health 1982–88; Minister of Social Devt 1988, for Women and Children 1990; Chief SEN HMD 001, Int. Oral Fed. Project in co-operation with WHO 1983, apptd Rep. 1985; WHO expert in Oral Health for Africa Region 1985; Gen. Sec. Nat. Asscn of Oral Surgeons 1975–77; Gen. Sec. Secr. of Oral Health for Africa; Pres. Fifth Regional Conf. of African Women 1995; Head Del. from Senegal, Int. Conf. on Population, Cairo 1995; mem. UN Advisory Bd in preparation for int. summit, Copenhagen 1995; Deputy Dir Gen. Int. Org. for Migration (IOM) 1999–; participant at numerous confs; has worked with a number of int. NGOs; numerous papers and contribs to academic journals; Commdr dans l'Ordre des Palmes Académiques 1992, Chevalier dans l'ordre de la Légion d'Honneur, Commandeur de l'Ordre du Lion du Sénégal.
Address: International Organization for Migration (IOM), 17, Route des Morillons, 1211 Geneva 19, Switzerland (office); Villa 7, Cité Fayçal, Cambérène, Dakar, Senegal (home). *Telephone:* 251944. *E-mail:* info@iom .int (office). *Website:* www.iom.int (office).

NDILOWE, Hawa Olga, BA, MA; Malawi civil servant and diplomatist; *Ambassador to USA;* widowed; four c. (one adopted). *Education:* Chancellor's Coll., Univ. of Malawi, London School of Econs, UK. *Career:* entered Malawi Public Service in 1981, served as information systems analyst –1997, served in sr levels of public sector leadership, man., admin and public policy man. in Ministry of Water Devt, of Defence, of Home Affairs and Internal Security, of Housing, of Information and Tourism 1997–2006; Amb. to USA 2006–.
Address: Embassy of Malawi, 1029 Vermont Avenue, NW, Suite 1000, Washington, DC 20005, USA (office). *Telephone:* (202) 721-0270 (office). *Fax:* (202) 721-0288 (office). *E-mail:* malawidc@aol.com (office). *Website:* www.malawiembassy-dc.org (office).

NDOLOU, Brig. Gen. Jacques Yvon; Republic of the Congo army officer. *Career:* Minister-Del. at the Presidency, responsible for Nat. Defence 2002–.
Address: Office of the Minister-Delegate of the Presidency, responsible for National Defence, Brazzaville, Republic of the Congo (office). *Telephone:* 81-22-31 (office).

NDONG, Jean Eyeghe; Gabonese politician; *Prime Minister;* b. 12 Feb. 1946, Libreville. *Education:* Ecole des Hautes Études en Sciences Sociales, Paris, Université de Paris X Nanterre, France. *Career:* elected mem. Nat. Ass. 1996; Sec. of State for Finance 1996, later Minister-Del. to Minister of State, Minister of Economy, Finance, Budget and Privatisation; Prime Minister of Gabon 2006–; mem. Gabonese Democratic Party.
Address: Office of the Prime Minister, BP 546, Libreville, Gabon (office). *Telephone:* 77-89-81 (office).

NDOU, Jeremiah; South African diplomatist. *Career:* Amb. to Zimbabwe 1999–2005, to Libya 2005–.
Address: c/o Ministry of Foreign Affairs, Union Bldgs, East Wing, 1 Government Avenue, Arcadia, Pretoria 0002, South Africa.

N'DOURO, Issifou Kogui, PhD; Benin government official; *Minister of National Defence;* b. Bembereke. *Education:* Université Louis Pasteur, Strasbourg, France. *Career:* consultant to UNSO Tree Planting Project, FAO 1979; fmr Finance Dir Organisation Internationale de la Francophonie; fmr Dir Office of Minister of Rural Devt; Minister of Nat. Defence 2006–.
Address: Ministry of National Defence, BP 2493, Cotonou, Benin (office). *Telephone:* 21-30-08-90 (office). *Fax:* 21-30-18-21 (office). *E-mail:* sgm@ defense.gouv.bj (office). *Website:* www.defense.gouv.bj (office).

NEALON, James D., BA; American diplomatist; b. Va; m. Kristin Nealon; four c. *Education:* Brown Univ. and Boston Coll. *Career:* career mem. Sr Foreign Service since 1984, now with rank of Minister Counselor, has served in public diplomacy positions in Chile, Hungary (twice), the Philippines, Spain and Washington, DC, served previously in Uruguay 1986–90, Deputy Chief of Mission and Chargé d'affaires a.i. in Uruguay 2005–06.
Address: US Department of State, 2201 C Street NW, Washington, DC 20520, USA (office). *Telephone:* (202) 647-4000 (office). *Fax:* (202) 647-6738 (office). *Website:* www.state.gov (office).

NEARY, J. Peter, DPhil; Irish economist and academic; *Professor of Economics and Professorial Fellow, Merton College, University of Oxford;* b. 11 Feb. 1950, Drogheda; m. 1st Frances Ruane 1972 (divorced); two s.; m. 2nd Mairéad Hanrahan 1997; two d. *Education:* Clongowes Wood Coll., Co. Kildare, Univ. Coll. Dublin, Univ. of Oxford. *Career:* Jr Lecturer, Trinity Coll. Dublin 1972–74, Lecturer 1978–80; Heyworth Research Fellow, Nuffield Coll. Oxford 1976–78; Prof. of Political Economy, Univ. Coll. Dublin 1980–2006; Prof. of Econs and Professorial Fellow, Merton Coll. Oxford 2006–; Visiting Prof., Princeton Univ. 1980, Univ. of California, Berkeley 1982, Queen's Univ., Ont. 1986–88, Univ. of Ulster at Jordanstown 1992–93; Research Assoc. Centre for Econ. Performance, LSE 1993–2003; Dir de Recherche, Ecole Polytechnique, Paris 1999–2000; mem. Council Royal Econ. Soc. 1984–89, European Econ. Asscn 1985–92, Econometric Soc. 1994–99; Co-Ed. Journal of International Economics 1980–83; Assoc. Ed. Economic Journal 1981–85, Econometrica 1984–87, Review of Economic Studies 1984–93, Economica 1996–2000; Ed. European Economic Review 1986–90; Pres. Irish Econ. Asscn 1990–92, Int. Trade and Finance Soc. 1999–2000, European Econ. Asscn 2002, Econs Section, BAAS 2005; Fellow, Centre for Econ. Policy Research, London 1983–, Econometric Soc. 1987–, European Econ. Asscn 2004–; mem. Academia Europaea 1989–; Royal Irish Acad. Gold Medal in the Social Sciences 2006. *Publications:* Measuring the Restrictiveness of International Trade Policy (with J. E. Anderson) 2005, three edited books and more than 100 publs on econs, especially int. econs.
Address: Department of Economics, University of Oxford, Manor Road Building, Manor Road, Oxford, OX1 3UQ, England (office). *Telephone:* (1865) 271085 (office). *Fax:* (1865) 271094 (office). *E-mail:* peter.neary@ economics.ox.ac.uk (office). *Website:* www.economics.ox.ac.uk/members/ peter.neary/neary.htm (office).

NEČAS, Petr, DrScNat; Czech politician; *Deputy Prime Minister and Minister for Labour and Social Affairs;* b. 19 Nov. 1964, Uherské Hradiště; m. Radka Nečas; two s. two d. *Education:* Univ. Brno. *Career:* research engineer, Tesla Rožnov 1988–92; mem. Civic Democratic Party 1991–, Jt Vice-Chair. 1999–2004, First Deputy Chair. 2004–; mem. Parl. for Zlin 1992–; mem. Parl. Cttee for Foreign Affairs 1992–96; Deputy Minister of Defence 1995–96; Chair. Parl. Cttee for Defence and Security 1996–2002; Vice-Chair. Parl. Cttee for European Affairs 2002–06; Deputy Prime Minister 2007–, Minister for Labour and Social Affairs 2007–.
Address: Ministry of Labour and Social Affairs, Na poříčním právu 1, 128 01 Prague 2, Czech Republic (office). *Telephone:* 221921111 (office). *Fax:* 221922664 (office). *E-mail:* posta@mpsv.cz (office). *Website:* www.mpsv.cz (office).

NEEP, Daniel, BA, MA; British research coordinator. *Education:* St John's Coll., Univ. of Oxford, School of Oriental and African Studies. *Career:* has taught Middle East politics and history at SOAS and LSE; Head of Middle East and N Africa Programme, Royal United Services Inst. 2002–04, Assoc. Fellow 2004–; regular media contributor on Middle Eastern affairs.
Address: c/o Royal United Services Institute, Whitehall, London, SW1A 2ET, England (office). *Telephone:* (20) 7930-5854 (office). *Website:* www .rusi.org (office).

NEEWOOR, Anund Priyay, BA; Mauritian diplomatist and international organization official; *Secretary for Foreign Affairs;* b. 26 June 1940; m. Chandranee Neewoor 1971; two s. one d. *Education:* Delhi Univ., Makerere Univ., Uganda. *Career:* teacher, Prin. Northern Coll. (secondary school), Mauritius 1964–67; joined Ministry of External Affairs, Tourism and Emigration (in charge of UN affairs and West Asia affairs) 1970; Admin. Asst, Civil Service 1972; Second Sec., High Comm., London 1973–75; First Sec., High Comm., New Delhi 1975–81; Minister-Counsellor, Embassy, Washington, DC 1982; Amb. to Pakistan 1983, to USA 1993–96; High. Commr to India 1983–93; Amb. in Ministry of External Affairs in charge of Multilateral Econ. Affairs 1996; Sec. for Foreign Affairs 1996–99, 2005–; Amb. and Perm. Rep. to UN, New York 1999–2001; Commdr of the Order of the Star and Key of the Indian Ocean — C.S.K. 2003.
Address: c/o Ministry of Foreign Affairs, International Trade and Co-operation, New Government Centre, Level 5, Port Louis; 17 Avenue des Dodos, Sodnac, Quatre Bornes, Mauritius (home). *Telephone:* (230) 2112692 (office). *Fax:* (230) 2088087 (office). *E-mail:* apneewoor@hotmail.com (office). *Website:* foreign.gov.mu (office).

NEGERI SEMBILAN, Yang di-Pertuan Besar; Tuanku Ja'afar ibni al-Marhum Tuanku Adbul Rahman; Malaysian; b. 19 July 1922; m. Tuanku Najihah binti Tuanku Besar Burhanuddin 1943; three s. three d. *Education:* Malay School Sri Menanti, Malay Coll. and Worcester Coll., Oxford. *Career:* entered Malay Admin. Service 1944; Asst Dist Officer, Rembau 1946–47, Parti 1953–55; Chargé d'affaires, Washington, DC 1947; First Perm. Sec., Malayan Perm. Mission to the UN 1957–58; First Sec., Trade Counsellor, rising to Deputy High Commr, London 1962–63; Amb. to UAR 1962; concurrently High Commr to Nigeria and Ghana 1965–66; Timbalan Yang di-Pertuan Agong (Deputy Supreme Head of State) 1979–84, 1989–94, Yang di-Pertuan Agong (Supreme Head of State) 1994–99.

NEGROPONTE, John Dimitri, BA; American diplomatist; *Deputy Secretary of State;* b. 21 July 1939, London, England; m. Diana Mary Villiers 1976; two s. three d. *Education:* Phillips Exeter Acad., NH, Yale Univ., New Haven, Conn. *Career:* entered Foreign Service 1960, Amb. to Honduras 1981–85; Asst Sec. of State for Oceans and Int. Environmental and Scientific Affairs 1985–87; Deputy Asst to Pres. for Nat. Security Affairs 1987–89; Amb. to Mexico 1989–93, to the Philippines 1993–95; Special Co-ordinator for post-1999 US Presence in Panama 1996–97; Exec. Vice-Pres. Global Markets McGraw-Hill 1997–2001; Perm. Rep. to UN 2001–04; Amb. to Iraq 2004–05; Dir of Nat. Intelligence 2005–07; Deputy Sec. of State 2007–; Chair. French-American Foundation 1998–; mem. Council on Foreign Relations, American Acad. of Diplomacy.
Address: Office of the Deputy Secretary, Department of State, 2201 C Street, NW, Washington, DC 20520 (office); 4936 Lowell Street, NW, Washington, DC 20016, USA (home). *Telephone:* (202) 647-4000 (office). *Fax:* (202) 647-6738 (office). *Website:* www.state.gov (office).

NEIL, Stafford Oliver, BA, MSc, JD; Jamaican diplomatist; m.; two c. *Education:* Univ. of West Indies, London School of Econs, UK, St John's Univ., New York, Norman Manley Law School. *Career:* Prin. Asst Sec., Ministry of Foreign Affairs 1976; Counsellor/Minister Counsellor, Perm. Mission to UN 1976–83; Dir Political Div., Ministry of Foreign Affairs 1983–86, Econs Div. 1986–87; Amb. to Venezuela, Colombia, Argentina, Brazil, Ecuador 1987–89; High Commr to Trinidad and Tobago, Antigua and Barbuda, Barbados, St Lucia, St Kitts and Nevis, St Vincent and the Grenadines, Grenada, Dominica, Guyana; Amb. to Suriname 1989–94, to Cuba, Brazil 1995–97; Dir-Gen. Ministry of Foreign Affairs 1995–97, Perm. Sec. 1997–2002; Perm. Rep. to UN 2002–06, mem. UN Advisory Cttee on Administrative and Budgetary Questions 2007–; Order of Distinction, CD.
Address: c/o Ministry of Foreign Affairs and Foreign Trade, 21 Dominica Drive, POB 624, Kingston 5, Jamaica (office). *Website:* www.mfaft.gov.jm (office).

NEILL, Wayne E., BA; American lawyer and diplomatist; b. Nev.; m. Doris Neill; one s. two d. *Education:* Univ. of Southern California, Nat. War Coll., Univ. of California, Los Angeles. *Career:* licensed to practice law in Calif.; career mem. Sr Foreign Service, Class of Counselor, overseas assignments have included postings in Riyadh, Tunis, Budapest and Poznań, State Dept assignments focused on the Balkans and the fmr Soviet Union, US Energy Advisor, OSCE, Paris 1993–96, Political and Econ. Counselor, Cairo 1997–99, Dir African Bureau's Office of Regional Affairs 2000–02, Special Advisor to Asst Sec. of State for African Affairs 2002–03, Amb. to Benin 2003–06; mem. ABA; Superior Honor Award, two Meritorious Honor Awards, two group Superior Honor Awards.
Address: US Department of State, 2201 C Street NW, Washington, DC 20520, USA (office). *Telephone:* (202) 647-4000 (office). *Fax:* (202) 647-6738 (office). *Website:* www.state.gov (office).

NEJAD-HOSSEINIAN, Seyed Mohammad Hadi, MS; Iranian diplomatist and politician; *Deputy Oil Minister;* b. 2 Feb. 1947, Karbala; m. Fatemeh Tadbir; two s. two d. *Education:* Tehran Univ., George Washington Univ., Washington, DC. *Career:* Deputy, Plan and Budget Org. 1980–81; Minister for Road and Transportation 1981–85; Deputy Minister of Oil 1985–89, 1994–97; Minister for Heavy Industry 1989–94; apptd Amb. and Perm. Rep. to UN 1998; currently Deputy Oil Minister, Ministry of Oil.
Address: Ministry of Oil, Hafez St, Taleghani Avenue, Tehran, Iran (office). *Telephone:* (21) 6152738 (office). *Fax:* (21) 6152823 (office). *E-mail:* webmaster@nioc.org (office). *Website:* www.nioc.org (office).

NEKIPELOV, Alexander Dmitriyevich, DrEcon; Russian economist and academic; *Director, Moscow School of Economics, Lomonosov Moscow State University;* b. 16 Nov. 1951, Moscow; m.; one d. *Education:* Moscow State Univ. *Career:* jr researcher, sr researcher, Head of Sector, Deputy Dir, Inst. of. Int. Econ. and Political Studies, Russian Acad. of Sciences 1973–98, Dir 1998–; Dir Moscow School of Econs, Lomonosov Moscow State Univ. 2004–; mem. Russian Acad. of Sciences 1997, currently Vice-Pres.; also currently Co-Chair. Bd of Trustees Nat. Investment Council; Medal of Order for Service to Motherland. *Publications:* numerous scientific publs including monograph Essays on Economics of Postcommunism 1996.
Address: Moscow School of Economics, 1, Building 44, Leninskie Gory, M.V. Lomonosov MSU, 119992 Moscow, Russia (office). *Telephone:* (495) 939-45-00 (office). *Website:* www.mse-msu.ru (office).

NEKVASIL, Lt-Gen. Jiří; Czech army officer and diplomatist; *Ambassador to Mongolia;* b. 24 April 1948, Benešov; m. 1st Jaroslava Papeová; m. 2nd Danuše Kadlečková; two s. two d.; m. 3rd Nanuli Kobaladze; two s. three d. *Education:* Tech. Inst. Liptovský Mikuláš, Mil. Acad., Kalinin, Acad. of Gen. Staff of Mil. Forces, Moscow, NATO Defence Coll., Rome. *Career:* 2nd in Command Czech AF and Anti-Air Defence System 1990–92; Commdr of Gen. Staff 1993–98; Adviser to Ministry of Defence 1998–99; Amb. to Georgia 2000–04, to Mongolia 2004–; Order of Red Star (Czechoslovakia) 1985, Commdr, Legion of Merit 1996, Legion d'honneur 1996, Bundeswehr Gold Cross (Germany) 1998, Gold Cross (Austria) 1998.
Address: Embassy of the Czech Republic, PO Box 665, Olimpiin Gudamj 14, Ulan Bator, Mongolia (office). *Telephone:* (11) 321886 (office); (11) 327969 (home). *Fax:* (11) 323791 (office). *E-mail:* czechemb@magicnet.mn (office); jirinekva@seznam.cz (home). *Website:* www.mzv.cz/ulaanbaatar (office).

NÉMETH, Zsolt; Hungarian politician; *Chairman of the Foreign Affairs and Hungarian Minorities Abroad Committee, Hungarian National Assembly;* b. 14 Oct. 1963, Budapest; m.; three c. *Education:* Radnóti Miklós Grammar School, Budapest, Karl Marx Univ. of Economics (MKKE), Univ. of Oxford, UK. *Career:* trainee, Inst. for Hungarian Studies 1987–90; resident educator, Széchenyi István Coll., MKKE 1987–90; Founding mem. Alliance of Free Democrats (FIDESZ), Party Spokesman 1988–89, mem. Nat. Cttee 1989–93, Vice-Pres. 1993–2003, Deputy Faction Leader 2003–; Pres. Széchenyi Coll. Asscn 1992–95; Chief Trustee, then Hon. Chief Trustee, Transylvanian (Calvinist) Church 1995–; mem. Kts of St John 1999–; mem. Nat. Ass. 1990–; mem. Council of Europe Parl. Ass. 1994–98; State Sec., Ministry of Foreign Affairs 1998–2002; Deputy Leader, Hungarian Delegation to Council of Europe 2002–; Chair. Foreign Affairs Cttee, Nat. Ass. 2002–06, Foreign Affairs and Hungarian Minorities Abroad Committee 2006–.
Address: Hungarian National Assembly, 1357 Budapest, Kossuth tér 1–3, Hungary. *Telephone:* (1) 441-4000 (office); (1) 441-4626 (office). *Fax:* (1) 441-4816 (office). *Website:* www.parlament.hu (office).

NEMYRYA, Hryhoriy, BA, PhD; Ukrainian academic and politician; *Deputy Prime Minister for European and International Integration;* b. 5 April 1960, Donetsk; m.; one s. *Education:* Donetsk State Univ., Kiev Shevchenko Univ. *Career:* began career as Lecturer, Dept of History, Donetsk State Univ., becoming Head Centre for Political Research 1992–96; Nat. Forum Foundation Fellow, Centre for Strategic and Int. Studies, Washington DC, USA 1994; Dean, Mohyla Acad., Kiev 1996–98; fmr Deputy Head European Integration Faculty, Nat. Acad. of Public Admin; fmr Head Centre for European and Int. Studies, Shevchenko Univ.; Chair. George Soros Int. Renaissance Foundation, Kiev 2002; fmr Ed. Noval Bezpeka (New Security); mem. Tymoshenko Bloc, Adviser to Yuliya Tymoshenko 2005–; mem. Verkhovna Rada (Supreme Council, Parl.) 2006–; Deputy Prime Minister for European and Int. Integration 2007–; mem. Socialist Group, Council of Europe 2006–.
Address: Verkhovna Rada, Grushevsky 5, 01008 Kiev, Ukraine (office). *Telephone:* (44) 253-32-17 (office). *Fax:* (44) 253-32-17 (office). *E-mail:* Nemyria.Hrihorii@rada.gov.ua (office). *Website:* www.kmu.gov.ua/control (office).

NERITANI, Adrian, LLB, LLM, MALD; Albanian lawyer and diplomatist; *Permanent Representative, United Nations;* b. 26 Oct. 1967, Lushnja; m.; two c. *Education:* Univ. of Tirana, Univ. of Malta, John Marshall School of Law, Chicago, USA. *Career:* Lecturer, Luigi Gurakuqi Univ. 1989–91; Desk Officer, US Desk, Ministry of Foreign Affairs 1991–93, China and the Far East Desk 1993–97; First Sec. and Chargé d'Affaires, Embassy in Beijing 1997–98; lawyer, Cullison & Cullison, PC, Chicago 2003–; Perm. Rep. to UN, New York 2006–. *Address:* Permanent Mission of Albania to the United Nations, 320 East 79th Street, New York, NY 10075, USA (office). *Telephone:* (212) 249-2059 (office). *Fax:* (212) 535-2917 (office). *E-mail:* albania@un.int (office).

NESBITT, Wanda L., BA, MA; American diplomatist; *Ambassador to Côte d'Ivoire;* b. 7 Dec. 1956, Phila, Pa; m. James Stejskal. *Education:* Univ. of Pennsylvania, Nat. War Coll. *Career:* joined Foreign Service 1981, Consular Officer, Port-au-Prince 1982–83, Paris 1983–85, Kinshasa 1990–92 State Dept assignments have include work in Dept's Exec. Secr. Staff 1989–91, 1994–95, CA's Citizens Emergency Center 1992–93, and Bureau of Legislative Affairs 1994–96; Deputy Chief of Mission, Embassy in Kigali 1997–99, Embassy in Dar es Salaam 1999–2001; Amb. to Madagascar 2002–04; Dir Sr Level Assignments Div., Bureau of Human Resources, State Dept 2004–05, Prin. Deputy Asst Sec., Bureau of Consular Affairs 2005–07; Amb. to Côte d'Ivoire 2007–; numerous Superior Honor Awards. *Address:* US Embassy, Cocody Riviera Golf, 01 BP 1712, Abidjan 01, Côte d'Ivoire (office). *Telephone:* 22-49-40-00 (office). *Fax:* 22-49-43-23 (office). *E-mail:* cca_ci@pd.state.gov (office). *Website:* abidjan.usembassy.gov (office).

NETANYAHU, Benjamin, MSc; Israeli politician and diplomatist; *Leader, Likud Party;* b. 21 Oct. 1949, Tel-Aviv; m.; three c. *Education:* Massachusetts Inst. of Tech., USA. *Career:* Man. Consultant, Boston Consulting Group 1976–78; Exec. Dir Jonathan Inst. Jerusalem 1978–80; Sr Man. Rim Industries, Jerusalem 1980–82; Deputy Chief of Mission, Israeli Embassy, Washington, DC 1982–84; Perm. Rep. to UN 1984–88; Deputy Minister of Foreign Affairs 1988–91; Deputy Minister, Prime Minister's Office 1991–92; Prime Minister of Israel, Minister of Housing and Construction 1996–99; Leader Likud 1993–99, 2005–; Minister of Foreign Affairs 2002–03, of Finance 2003–05; mem. Knesset 1988–. *Publications:* Yoni's Letters (ed.) 1978, Terror: Challenge and Reaction (ed.) 1980, Terrorism: How the West Can Win (ed.) 1986, International Terrorism: Challenge and Response (ed.) 1991, A Place Among the Nations: Israel and the World 1993, Fighting Terrorism: How Democracies Can Defeat Domestic and International Terrorism 1995, A Durable Peace 2000. *Address:* Likud (Consolidation), 38 Rehov King George, Tel-Aviv 61231, Israel (office). *Telephone:* 3-5630666 (office). *Fax:* 3-5282901 (office). *E-mail:* likud@likud.org.il (office). *Website:* www.likud.org.il (office).

NETTLETON, Catherine Elizabeth; British diplomatist; *Ambassador to Peru;* b. 13 March 1960. *Career:* joined FCO 1983, Desk Officer, S America Dept 1983–84, Vice-Consul, Beijing 1987–89, EC Dept (External), FCO 1989–91, First Sec. (Political/Econ.), Mexico City 1991–95, Head of Summit Section and Deputy Head of EU Dept (External), Econ. Relations Dept, FCO 1995–99, War Crimes Coordinator, UN Dept 1999–2000, Counsellor (Political/Econ.), Beijing 2000–04, Counsellor and Head of FCO Services (Presidencies), FCO 2004–06, Amb. to Peru 2006–. *Address:* British Embassy, Torre Parque Mar, 22nd Floor, Av. Jose Larco 1301, Miraflores, Lima, Peru (office). *Telephone:* (1) 6173000 (office). *Fax:* (1) 6173100 (office). *E-mail:* belima@fco.gov.uk (office). *Website:* www.britemb.org.pe (office).

NEUMANN, Ronald E., BA, MA; American diplomatist; b. 30 Sept. 1944, Washington, DC. *Education:* Univ. of Calif., Riverside. *Career:* served as infantry officer, Vietnam 1969–70; entered Foreign Service 1970; tour in Senegal 1971–73; Vice Consul Tabriz, Iran 1973–74, Prin. Officer 1974–76; worked in Office of Southern European Affairs 1976–77; Staff Asst to Asst Sec. for Near Eastern and S Asian Affairs 1977–78; Desk Officer, Jordan 1978–81; Deputy Chief of Mission, Yemen 1981–83; Deputy Dir Bureau of Near Eastern Affairs, Office of Arabian Peninsula Affairs 1983–87; Deputy Chief of Mission in UAE 1987–90; Dir Office of Northern Gulf Affairs (Iran and Iraq) 1991–94; Amb. to Algeria 1994–97; Deputy Asst Sec. of State for Near Eastern Affairs 1997–2000; Amb. to Bahrain 2000–04; political adviser in Iraq 2004; Amb. to Afghanistan 2005–07. *Address:* c/o Department of State, 2201 C Street, NW, Washington, DC 20520, USA (office).

NEVES, José Maria Pereira, BA; Cape Verde politician; *Prime Minister;* b. 28 March 1960, Santa Catarina; three s. *Education:* São Paulo School of Business and Admin. *Career:* consultant in organizational devt and human resources man., Cape Verde 1987–96; Dir Nat. Public Admin Training Centre 1988–89; Coordinator Admin Reform and Modernization Projects 1987–88; mem. Parl. 1996–; Mayor of Santa Catarina 2000–01; Chair. Partido Africano da Independência de Cabo Verde 2000–; Prime Minister of Cape Verde 2001–; Asst Prof. of Man., Higher Educ. Inst.; Marechal Floriana Peixoto Merit Award, Brazil 2005, Patrons of Century Ruby Cross 2006. *Address:* Office of the Prime Minister, Palácio do Governo, Várzea, CP 16, Praia, Santiago, Cape Verde (office). *Telephone:* 2610411 (office). *Fax:* 2613099 (office). *E-mail:* gab.imprensa@gpm.gov.cv (office). *Website:* www.primeirominister.cv (office).

NEWALL, Peter; British diplomatist (retd); b. 20 March 1947; m. Marina Newall; one s. two d. *Career:* joined FCO 1966, Accommodation Dept 1966–69, Attaché, Asst Admin Officer, Tehran 1970–72, Entry Clearance Officer, New Delhi 1972–76, Finance Dept, FCO 1976–79, Second Sec. (Commercial), Belgrade 1979–82, First Sec. (Commercial), Kuwait 1982–86, Nuclear Energy Dept, FCO 1986–89, HM Consul, Marseille 1989–90, First Sec. and Jt Man. Officer, Geneva 1990–95, Counter-Terrorism Policy Dept, FCO 1995–97, Deputy Head of Non-Proliferation Dept 1997–99, Counsellor and Head of Jt Man. Office, Brussels 1999, Amb. to Senegal 1999–2007 (retd). *Address:* c/o Foreign and Commonwealth Office, King Charles Street, London, SW1A 2AH England. *Telephone:* (20) 7008-1500.

NEWBERY, David Michael Garrood, PhD, ScD, FBA; British economist and academic; *Professor of Applied Economics, University of Cambridge;* b. 1 June 1943, Bucks.; m. Terri E. Apter 1975; two d. *Education:* Portsmouth Grammar School, Trinity Coll. Cambridge. *Career:* Economist, Treasury of Tanzanian Govt 1965–66; Asst Lecturer, Faculty of Econs and Politics, Univ. of Cambridge 1966–71, Lecturer 1971–86, Reader in Econs 1986–88, Prof. of Applied Econs 1988–, Dir Dept of Applied Econs 1988–2003, Fellow, Churchill Coll. 1966–; Div. Chief, World Bank 1981–83; Fellow, Econometric Soc. 1989; Vice-Pres. European Econ. Asscn 1994–95, Pres. 1996; hon. degree (Antwerp) 2004; Frisch Medal, Econometric Soc. 1990, Harry Johnson Prize (jtly), Canadian Econ. Asscn 1993, Int. Asscn for Energy Econs 2002 Outstanding Contribs to the Profession Award 2003. *Publications:* Project Appraisal in Practice (co-author) 1976, The Theory of Commodity Price Stabilization: A Study in the Economics of Risk (with J. E. Stiglitz) 1981, The Theory of Taxation for Developing Countries (with N. H. Stern) 1987, Hungary: An Economy in Transition (with I. Székely) 1993, Tax and Benefit Reform in Central and Eastern Europe 1995, A European Market for Electricity? (co-author) 1999, Privatization, Restructuring and Regulation of Network Utilities 2000; numerous articles. *Address:* Faculty of Economics, Sidgwick Avenue, Cambridge, CB3 9DE (office); 9 Huntingdon Road, Cambridge, CB3 0HH, England (home). *Telephone:* (1223) 335248 (office). *Fax:* (1223) 335299 (office). *E-mail:* david.newbery@econ.cam.ac.uk (office). *Website:* www.econ.cam.ac.uk/dae/people/newbery/index.html (office).

NEWMAN, Jocelyn Margaret, LLB; Australian public official and fmr politician; b. 8 July 1937. *Education:* Melbourne Univ. *Career:* Senator (Liberal Party) for Tasmania 1986–2002; Shadow Minister for Defence, Science and Personnel 1988–92, Veterans' Affairs 1990–92; Shadow Minister Assisting Leader on Status of Women 1989–93; Shadow Minister for the Aged and Veterans' Affairs 1992–93; Shadow Minister for Family Health, Shadow Minister Assisting Leader on Family Matters, Chair. Health, Welfare and Veterans' Affairs Group 1993–94; Shadow Minister for Defence 1994–96; Minister for Social Security and Minister Assisting Prime Minister on Status of Women 1996–98, for Family and Community Services and Minister Assisting Prime Minister on Status of Women 1998–2001; mem. Bd Australian Strategic Policy Inst. 2001–; mem. Australian War Memorial Council 2002–. *Address:* Australian Strategic Policy Institute, Level 2, Arts House, 40 Macquarie Street, Barton ACT 2600, Australia (office); POB 146, Red Hill, ACT 2063, Australia. *Website:* www.aspi.otr.au (office).

NFUBEA, Ricardo Mangue Obama; Equatorial Guinean politician. *Career:* mem. Democratic Party of Equatorial Guinea (PDGE); fmr State Minister for Labor and Social Security; Deputy Prime Minister 2004–06, Prime Minister 2006–08 (resgnd). *Address:* Office of the Prime Minister, Malabo, Equatorial Guinea.

NFUMU, Agustin Nze; Equatorial Guinean diplomatist; *Ambassador to UK;* b. 18 May 1949, Anisok; m. Josefina Mifumu. *Education:* Centro Laboral La Salle. *Career:* held various posts in OAU and other orgs 1960s; returned to Equatorial Guinea as trans. in Ministry of Foreign Affairs 1970, Chief of Dept of Protocol and Trans. 1974–79; political exile in Cameroon Feb. 1979, invited to return home Aug. 1979; Tech. Man. of Protocol, Ministry of Foreign Affairs 1980; Council Amb. of the Pres. for the Affairs of

Protocol 1981; Delegated Minister of External Affairs responsible for French-speaking nations 1992–93; Minister of Culture, Tourism and French-speaking nations 1993–96; Gen.-Sec. Partido Democrático de Guinea Ecuatorial (Democratic Party of Equatorial Guinea) 1996, mem. Nat. Council and Exec. Cttee; Diplomatic Counsellor, Personal Rep. of the Pres. and mem. Perm. Council of French-speaking nations to int. French-speaking nations since 1996; Amb. to UK 2005–; Cross of the Ind. Order, Commdr, Guinea Equatorial Ind. Order, Commdr, Order of the Day of Cen. African Repub. *Publications:* Eyom Ndong, de la Tribu Mikanfung 2006, Macias, Verdugo o Victima 2006.
Address: Embassy of Equitorial Guinea, 13 Park Place, St James's, London, SW1A 1LP, England (office). *Telephone:* (20) 7499-6867 (office). *Fax:* (20) 7499-6782 (office). *E-mail:* embarege-londres@embarege-londres.org (office). *Website:* www.embarege-londres.org (office).

NGAITHE, Leonard Njogu; Kenyan diplomatist and civil servant. *Career:* career diplomat since 1981, High Commr to UK 1999–2000, Amb. to the Netherlands (also accred to Czech Repub.) 2000–04, to USA 2004–06; Deputy Sec., Ministry of Trade and Industry 2007–.
Address: Ministry of Trade and Industry, Teleposta Towers, Kenyatta Avenue, PO Box 30430, Nairobi, Kenya (office). *Telephone:* (20) 331030 (office). *Fax:* (20) 248722 (office). *E-mail:* ps@tradeandindustry.go.ke (office). *Website:* www.tradeandindustry.go.ke (office).

NGO, Quang Xuan; Vietnamese diplomatist; *Permanent Representative, United Nations, Geneva;* b. 1 Jan. 1951, Nghe An; m. Le Thi Hoa 1975; two d. *Education:* Inst. of Int. Relations, Hanoi, Inst. des Hautes Etudes Internationales, Geneva, Diplomatic Acad. of Moscow. *Career:* Deputy Gen. Dir Dept for Multilateral Econ. and Cultural Co-operation, Foreign Ministry 1988–91, Deputy Dir Int. Orgs Dept 1992–93, Dir of Ministry 1995–; Nat. Rep. to Francophone Community 1990–93; Acting Perm. Rep. to UN 1993–95, Perm. Rep. 1995–2000; currently Perm. Rep., UN, Geneva; Medal for Diplomatic Service.
Address: Vietnam Mission to United Nations and International Organizations, Chemin des Corbillettes 30, 1218 Grand-Saconnex, Geneva, Switzerland (office). *Telephone:* 227982485 (office). *Fax:* 227980724 (office). *E-mail:* mission.vietnam@ties.itu.int (office). *Website:* www.unog.ch.

NGOUPANDE, Jean-Paul; Central African Republic politician and fmr diplomatist; b. 6 Dec. 1948, Dekoa; m.; three s. three d. *Career:* Dean Faculty of Letters Univ. de Bangui 1982–85; Minister of Educ. 1985–87; fmr Amb. to France and to Côte d'Ivoire; Prime Minister of Cen. African Repub. 1996–97; mem. Parl. 1998–; Leader Parti pour l'union nationale; Minister of Foreign and Francophone Affairs and Regional Integration 2006; Commdr Meritorious Order of Cen. African Rep., Commdr Ordre de Palmes Académiques, Grand Officier Ordre Nat. de Côte d'Ivoire. *Publications include:* Racines historiques et culturelles de la crise africaine 1994, Chronique de la crise centrafricaine 1997.
Address: National Assembly of Central African Republic, Bangui (office); PO Box 179, Bangui, Central African Republic (home). *Telephone:* 61-82-96. *Fax:* 61-78-66 (home).

NGOWENUBUSA, Dieudonné; Burundi politician; *Minister of Finance;* b. 8 Sept. 1964, Ngagara. *Career:* Minister of Finance 2005–; mem. Conseil nat. pour la defense de la democratie–Forces pour la defense de la democratie (CNDD-FDD).
Address: Ministry of Finance, BP 1830, Bujumbura, Burundi (office). *Telephone:* 225142 (office). *Fax:* 223128 (office). *E-mail:* minifin@usan.bu.net (office).

NGUBANE, Baldwin Sipho, MD; South African politician and diplomatist; *Ambassador to Japan;* b. 22 Oct. 1941, Camperdown, KwaZulu-Natal; m. Sheila Buthelezi. *Education:* St Francis Coll., Mariannhill, Univ. of the Witwatersrand, Univ. of Natal, Durban-Westville Medical School. *Career:* fmr Latin teacher, St Francis Coll.; Minister of Health, KwaZulu-Natal Govt. 1991–94; mem. Parl. 1994–2004; mem. Exec. Council KwaZulu-Natal Prov. Govt 1996–97, Premier 1997–99; Minister of Arts, Culture, Science and Tech. 1999–2004; Amb. to Japan 2004–; Chair. Commonwealth Science Council 2002–; mem. SA Red Cross Soc. 1977–, Regional Councillor 1978; mem. Nat. Boxing Bd of Control 1999; Officer in the Order of St John 1999; Dr hc (Natal) 1960, (Zululand) 1998.
Address: Embassy of South Africa, Oriken Hirakawa Bldg, 2-1-1, Hirakawa-cho, Chiyoda-ku, Tokyo 102-0093, Japan (office). *Telephone:* (3) 3265-3366 (office). *Fax:* (3) 3265-1108 (office). *E-mail:* rsatk-info@rsatk.com (office). *Website:* www.rsatk.com (office).

NHLAPO, Welile Witness Augustine; South African diplomatist; *Ambassador to USA;* b. Alexandra Township, Johannesburg; m. Sissy Nhlapo; one s. two d. *Career:* active in SA Students Org.; banning order served 1973,

went into exile to Botswana 1974; joined ANC 1974 and served various positions, including Deputy Ed. Sechaba (official ANC publ.), London 1978–81, Head, ANC Youth Section 1982–87, mem. Regional ANC Political Cttee –1990, ANC Chief Rep. in Botswana 1991–93, Head, Political Section in ANC Sec.-Gen. office in Shell House 1993, then joined ANC Int. Affairs Dept; joined SA Dept of Foreign Affairs 1994, mem. SA del. to UN Gen. Ass., New York when SA was readmitted 1994; Amb. to Ethiopia (also accred. to Djibouti, Eritrea and Sudan), also Perm. Rep. to Org. of African Unity and UN Econ. Comm. for Africa 1995; Special Envoy for Burundi 1996; fmr Deputy Dir. Gen. for Africa, fmr Dir. Gen. Presidential Support Unit, Ministry of Foreign Affairs; fmr Dir. Africa Div., UN Dept of Political Affairs; Amb. to USA 2007–.
Address: Embassy of South Africa, 3051 Massachusetts Avenue, NW, Washington, DC 20008, USA (office). *Telephone:* (202) 232-4400 (office). *Fax:* (202) 265-1607 (office). *E-mail:* ambassador.washington@foreign.gov.za (office); info@saembassy.org (office). *Website:* www.saembassy.org (office).

NIANG, Gen. Mamadou; Senegalese diplomatist and army officer (retd); b. 1938; m. Marie-Charlotte Gueye; seven c. *Education:* Ecole Spéciale Militaire de Saint-Cyr, Ecole Supérieurre de Guerre, Paris. *Career:* briefly a primary schoolteacher; army service 1962–98, various roles including fmr Commdr Dakar Bango Training Co., St Louis; fmr ADC to Gen. Jean Alfred Diallo, fmr Commdr Blindé Bn, fmr Head of Cabinet of Army Chief of Staff, fmr Nat. Dir of Documentation and External Security, fmr Gen. Insp. of Armed Forces; Pres. Observatoire Nat. des Elections 1998–99; Amb. to Guinea-Bissau 1999–2000; Minister of the Interior 2000–03; Amb. to UK 2004–07.
Address: Ministry of Foreign Affairs, pl. de l'Indépendance, BP 4044, Dakar, Senegal (office). *Telephone:* 33-889-1300 (office). *E-mail:* maeuase@senegal.diplomatie.sn (office). *Website:* www.diplomatie.gouv.sn (office).

NIASSE, Cheikh Moustapha; Senegalese politician, United Nations official and company director; *Special Envoy to the Democratic Republic of the Congo, United Nations;* b. 4 Nov. 1939. *Education:* Lycée Faidherbe, St Louis, Univs of Dakar and Paris, Nat. School of Admin, Dakar. *Career:* Dir for Information and Press Affairs, Ministry of Information 1968–69; Dir de Cabinet at Presidency 1970–78; Minister of Town Planning, Housing and Environment March–Sept. 1978, of Foreign Affairs 1978–84; Minister of Foreign Affairs of the Confed. of Senegambia 1982–84; fmr Minister of State, Minister of Foreign Affairs and Senegalese Abroad; Presidential cand. 2000; Prime Minister of Senegal April 2000–01; UN Special Envoy to Peace Process of the Democratic Repub. of the Congo June 2002–; Political Sec. Union Progressiste Sénégalaise until 1984; Founder and Leader Alliance des forces de progrès (AFP) 1999–; mem. Bd Dirs several pvt.-sector cos world-wide.
Address: Alliance des forces de progrès, BP 5825, Dakar, Senegal (office); Special Envoy to the Democratic Republic of the Congo, United Nations, New York, NY 10017, USA (office). *Telephone:* 825-40-21 (office). *Fax:* 825-77-70 (office). *E-mail:* admin@afp-senegal.org (office). *Website:* www.afp-senegal.org (office).

NIBLETT, Robin, MA, PhD; British academic; *Director, Chatham House;* b. 1962. *Education:* Univ. of Oxford. *Career:* Politics Lecturer, Univ. of Oxford 1985–88; Research Assoc., Political-Mil. Studies Program, Center for Strategic and Int. Studies (CSIS) 1988–92, European Rep. 1992–97, Dir Strategic Planning 1997–2001, Exec. Vice-Pres. 2001–07, Dir Europe Program 2004–07; Dir Chatham House 2007–. *Publications:* Rethinking European Order (with William Wallace) 2000; numerous contributions to CSIS publications including The Atlantic Alliance Transformed 1992, From Shadows to Substance: An Action Plan for Transatlantic Defense Cooperation 1995; contrib. to Euro-Focus, Washington Quarterly, International Herald Tribune, NPR, CNN, Fox News, BBC World News.
Address: Office of the Director, Chatham House, 10 St James's Square, London, SW1Y 4LE, England (office). *Telephone:* (20) 7314-2798 (office). *Fax:* (20) 7957-5710 (office). *E-mail:* kburnet@chathamhouse.org.uk (office). *Website:* www.chathamhouse.org.uk (office).

NICHOLS, John Roland, BScc; British diplomatist; *Ambassador to Switzerland;* b. 13 Nov. 1951; m. Suzanne Davies; one s. one d. *Education:* Latymer Upper School, London and Univ. of Surrey. *Career:* qualified solicitor 1977; joined FCO 1977, Desk Officer, S Asian Dept 1977–78, Second, then First Sec., Budapest 1979–82, Desk Officer, Energy, Science and Space Dept, FCO 1982–85, First Sec., Brasilia 1985–89, Deputy Head of Commercial Relations and Exports Dept, FCO 1989–91, Deputy Head of Arms Control and Disarmament Dept 1991–93, Deputy High Commr, Dhaka 1993–95, Consul-Gen., Geneva 1995–97, Deputy Head of Mission and Dir Trade Promotion, Berne 1997–2000, on secondment in City of London, Acting/Deputy CEO British Invisibles and Int. Financial Services

2000–03, Amb. to Hungary 2003–07, to Switzerland (also accred to Liechtenstein) 2008–.
Address: British Embassy, Thunstr. 50, 3000 Bern 15, Switzerland (office). *Telephone:* (31) 3597700 (office). *Fax:* (31) 3597701 (office). *E-mail:* info@ britain-in-switzerland.ch (office). *Website:* www.britishembassy.ch (office).

NICOLL, Alexander G. R., MA; British journalist, editor and research coordinator; *Director of Editorial, International Institute for Strategic Studies (IISS);* b. 24 Aug. 1952; m. Lisa Vaughan; one s. one d. *Education:* Cheltenham Coll. and St John's Coll., Oxford. *Career:* Reuters news agency corresp. in Hong Kong, London, Paris, Tehran, New York 1975–83; fmr Asia Ed., UK News Ed., Int. Edn Ed. Financial Times 1984–1997, Defence Corresp. 1997–2002; on secondment as Consulting Ed. Business Standard, New Delhi, India 1994–97; Asst Dir and Sr Fellow for Defence Industry and Procurement, IISS 2003–04, Dir of Defence Analysis and Publs 2004–07, Dir of Editorial 2007–, Leader of IISS European Capabilities Project; Ed. Strategic Survey 2006–, Strategic Comments 2007–.
Address: International Institute for Strategic Studies, Arundel House, 13–15 Arundel Street, Temple Place, London, WC2R 3DX, England (office). *Telephone:* (20) 7379-7676 (office). *Fax:* (20) 7836-3108 (office). *E-mail:* nicoll@iiss.org (office). *Website:* www.iiss.org (office); www.tandf .co.uk/journals/titles/04597230.asp;   www.tandf.co.uk/journals/titles/ 13567888.asp.

NICULESCU, Alexandru A.; Romanian diplomatist and international organization official; b. 1 Jan. 1941, Bucharest; m.; three c. *Education:* Polytechnical Inst. and Univ. of Law, Bucharest. *Career:* Chargé d'affaires, Perm. Mission to UN, Geneva 1990–91, Deputy Perm. Rep. 1991–95; Dir Div. for UN and Specialized Agencies, Ministry of Foreign Affairs, Bucharest 1995–98; Deputy Perm. Rep. to UN, New York 1999–2000, Perm. Rep. 2000–03. *Publications:* essays and articles on world econ. relations, globalization and UN system's activities.
Address: 13A, Dumbrava Rosie Street, Ap. 6, Sector 2, Bucharest, Romania (home). *Telephone:* (1) 2117877 (home).

NIEHAUS QUESADA, Bernd H., DJur; Costa Rican diplomatist, politician and academic; *Ambassador to Germany;* b. 14 April 1941, San José; m.; two c. *Education:* Univs of Bonn, Hamburg and Cologne, Germany, Univ. of Costa Rica, Univ. of Strasbourg, France. *Career:* lawyer and Prof. of Pvt. and Public Int. Law, Univ. of Costa Rica 1974–; Prof., Nat. Univ. 1975–76; Vice-Minister, Ministry of Foreign Affairs and Worship 1978–80, Minister 1980–82, 1990–94; Sec.-Gen. for Int. Relations, Social Christian Unity Party 1988–90; Cultural Attaché, Embassy in Bonn, FRG 1963–66; Perm. Rep. to UN, New York 1998–2002; Amb. to Germany (also accred to Hungary and Czech Repub.) 2002–.
Address: Embassy of Costa Rica, Dessauer Strasse 28–29, 10963 Berlin, Germany (office). *Telephone:* (30) 26398990 (office). *Fax:* (30) 26557210 (office). *E-mail:* emb@botschaft-costarica.de (office). *Website:* www .botschaft-costarica.de (office).

NIEN, Nguyen Dy; Vietnamese politician; b. 9 Dec. 1935, Thanh Hoa; m.; three d. *Education:* Banaras Hindu Univ., India. *Career:* mem. Nat. Liberation Movt 1951; joined Ministry of Foreign Affairs 1954, Deputy Dir, then Dir 1980–83, Asst Minister 1984–86, Deputy 1987–2000, Minister of Foreign Affairs 2000–06; elected mem. Cen. Cttee Communist Party of Viet Nam 1991–; Pres. Viet Nam Nat. Comm. for UNESCO 1987; Pres. Nat. Cttee for Overseas Vietnamese 1995; retd 2007.
Address: c/o Ministry of Foreign Affairs, 1 Ton That Dam, Ba Dinh District, Hanoi, Viet Nam (office).

NIGRO, Louis J., Jr, PhD; American diplomatist; *Ambassador to Chad; Education:* Vanderbilt Univ. *Career:* fmr Fulbright-Hays Research Fellow in Italy; taught modern European history at Stanford Univ.; has served as officer in Calif. Army Nat. Guard; career mem. Sr Foreign Service, joined Foreign Service 1980, has served overseas at Embassies in Bahamas, Chad, Haiti, Holy See, Guinea and Cuba (was Deputy Chief of Mission in last three postings); State Dept assignments have included Operations Center, Policy Planning Council, Office of Western European Affairs and Office of Canadian Affairs; Amb. to Chad 2007–; Prof. of Int. Relations, US Army War Coll. 2004–06; Diplomat in Residence, Univ. of Houston 2006–07; Superior Honor Award, Dept of State. *Publications:* The New Diplomacy in Italy: American Propaganda and U.S.-Italian Relations, 1917-1919 1999; articles on historical and diplomatic themes.
Address: US Embassy, avenue Félix Eboué, BP 413, N'Djamena, Chad (office). *Telephone:* 51-62-11 (office). *Fax:* 51-56-54 (office). *E-mail:* dyingra@yahoo.fr (office). *Website:* ndjamena.usembassy.gov (office).

NIKOLOZISHVILI, Nikoloz, PhD; Georgian diplomatist; *Ambassador to Slovakia and Slovenia;* b. 9 May 1965, Tbilisi; m. Andrea Adamovičova;

two d. *Education:* Tbilisi State Univ., Tbilisi Theological Acad., Tbilisi Ivane Javakhishvili State Inst. of History and Ethnology. *Career:* trainee, Faculty of Philology, Tbilisi State Univ. 1988–89, Jr Scientific Researcher 1989–93; Chief Ed. Iveria Express (daily newspaper) 1993–95; Head of State Dept of Youth Affairs 1995–98; Amb. to Armenia 1998–2004; State Commr of Pres. in the region of Samtskhe-Javakheti 2004–05; Amb. to Slovakia and Slovenia 2005–; Co-founder Georgian Political Club 1993; mem. Asscn of Friends of Mount Athos 1998.
Address: Embassy of Georgia, Michalska 9, 811 01 Bratslavia 1, Slovakia (office). *Telephone:* (2) 5464-6484 (office). *Fax:* (2) 5464-6484 (office). *E-mail:* bratislava.emb@mfa.gov.ge (office).

NIKONOV, Vyacheslav Alekseyevich, DrHis; Russian politician and academic; *President, Unity for Russia Foundation;* b. 5 June 1956, Moscow; grandson of Vyacheslav Molotov; m. 1st Viktoria Makarovna Kostyuk 1976; m. 2nd Olga Mikhailovna Rozhkova 1987; three s. *Education:* Moscow State Univ. *Career:* researcher, Moscow State Univ.; on staff Admin. Cen. Cttee CPSU 1989–90; on staff of Pres. Gorbachev 1990–91; Asst to Chair. USSR State Security Cttee (KGB) 1991–92; counsellor, Dept of Political Problems, Int. Foundation of Econ. and Social Reforms (Foundation Reforma) 1992–93; mem. State Duma (Parl.); Chair. Sub-cttee on Int. Security and Arms Control 1994–95; Deputy Chair. Cttee to Re-elect the Pres. 1996; Dean of History and Political Science Moscow Int. Univ. 2001; Deputy Chair. Editorial Bd Russia in Global Affairs 2002; Pres. Unity for Russia Foundation 2003–; Head, Int. Cooperation and Public Diplomacy Cttee, Public Council of the Russian Fed. 2006–; Ed.-in-Chief Strategy for Russia Journal 2003–. *Publications:* Republicans: From Eisenhower to Nixon 1984, Iran-Contra Affair 1988, Republicans: From Nixon to Reagan 1989, The Age of Change: Russia in the 90s as Viewed by a Conservative 1999, Contemporary Russian Politics (ed.) 2003, 2005, Agenda for Russia 2004 (ed.), Russia in Contemporary Politics 2005 (ed.), Agenda for Russia 2005 (ed.), Molotov: Youth 2005.
Address: Politika Foundation, Zlatoustinsky per. 8/7, 101000 Moscow, Russia (office). *Telephone:* (495) 206-81-49 (office). *Fax:* (495) 206-86-61 (office). *E-mail:* info@polity.ru (office). *Website:* www.polity.ru (office).

NIKOVSKI, Risto; Macedonian diplomatist. *Career:* fmr Deputy Foreign Minister; Charge d'affaires Embassy in London then Amb. 1994–96; Amb. to Albania 1998–2002; fmr State Sec., Ministry of Foreign Affairs; Amb. to Russian Fed. 2005; Adviser, Macedonian Arts Council; Medal Vite 2005.
Address: c/o Ministry of Foreign Affairs, 1000 Skopje, Dame Gruev 6, Former Yugoslav Republic of Macedonia.

NILES, Thomas Michael Tolliver, MA; American diplomatist; *Vice Chairman, United States Council for International Business;* b. 22 Sept. 1939, Lexington, Ky; m. Carroll C. Ehringhaus 1967; one s. one d. *Education:* Harvard Univ. and Univ. of Kentucky. *Career:* Foreign Service Officer, Dept of State 1962; posts in Moscow, Belgrade and Brussels; Amb. to Canada 1985–89, to Greece 1993–97; Perm. Rep. to the EEC, Brussels 1989; Vice-Pres. Nat. Defense Univ. 1997–98 (retd); Pres. US Council for Int. Business 1998–2005, Vice Chair. 2005–; mem. Bd of Dirs Jacobs Eng Group Inc., Internet Corpn for Assigned Names and Numbers (ICANN) 2003–05; Superior Honor Award, Dept of State 1982, 1985.
Address: United States Council for International Business, 1212 Avenue of the Americas, New York, NY 10036, USA (office). *Telephone:* (212) 354-4480 (office). *Fax:* (212) 575-0327 (office). *E-mail:* info@uscib.org (office). *Website:* www.uscib.org (office).

NIMLEY, Thomas Yaya; Liberian politician. *Career:* Minister of Foreign Affairs 2003–06; Chair. Movt for Democracy in Liberia (MODEL).
Address: Ministry of Foreign Affairs, Mamba Point, POB 10-9002, 1000 Monrovia 10, Liberia (office).

NIMROD, Elvin, MA, DJur; Grenadian politician; b. Carriacou. *Education:* Brooklyn Coll., John Jay Coll. of Criminal Justice, NY, New York Law School, USA, Hugh Wooding Law School, Port-of-Spain, Trinidad and Tobago. *Career:* teacher Mt. Pleasant Govt Primary School, Carriacou; called to the Bar, Grenada 1993; Minister of Labour 1999, of Foreign Affairs and Int. Trade and of Carriacou and Petit Martinique Affairs 1999–2008, and of Legal Affairs 1999–2007; fmr Attorney-Gen. of Grenada; currently Chair. New National Party (NNP).
Address: New National Party (NNP), Upper Lucas Street, St George's, Grenada (office). *Telephone:* 440-1875 (office). *Fax:* 440-1876 (office). *E-mail:* nnpadmin@spiceisle.com (office). *Website:* nnpnews.com (office).

NING, Fukui; Chinese diplomatist; *Ambassador to South Korea; Career:* Deputy Dir-Gen., Dept of Asian Affairs, responsible for N-Eastern Asian affairs 1995–2000; Vice-Head Chinese del., Four-Party talks on Korean Peninsular question 1997–99, Special Envoy on Korean Peninsular Affairs,

involved in Six-Party talks on nuclear arms issues 2003–05; Amb. to Cambodia –2003, Amb. to South Korea 2005–.
Address: Embassy of The People's Republic of China, 54, Hyoja-dong, Jongno-gu, Seoul, Republic of Korea (office). *Telephone:* (2) 738-1038 (office). *Fax:* (2) 738-1059 (office). *E-mail:* chinaemb_kr@mfa.gov.cn (office). *Website:* www.chinaemb.or.kr (office).

NINH, Vu Van, MBA; Vietnamese government official; *Minister of Finance;* b. 23 Feb. 1955, Hai Duong Prov. *Education:* Hanoi Univ. of Finance and Accountancy. *Career:* mem. staff, Ministry of Finance 1977–82, Head of Economy Div. 1982–90, Deputy Dir of State Budget Dept 1990–93, Dir 1993–99; Vice-Minister of Finance 1999–2003, Minister of Finance 2006–; Vice-Chair. Hanoi People's Cttee 2003–06; mem. CP of Viet Nam Central Cttee (CPVCC).
Address: Ministry of Finance, 8 Phan Huy Chu, Hoan Kiem District, Hanoi, Viet Nam (office). *Telephone:* (4) 8264872 (office). *Fax:* (4) 8262266 (office). *E-mail:* support@mof.gov.vn (office). *Website:* www.mof.gov.vn (office).

NISHIDA, Tsuneo; Japanese diplomatist; *Ambassador to Canada;* m. Keiko Nishida. *Career:* joined Foreign Ministry 1970, Dir-Gen. Econ. Co-operation Bureau 2001, fmr Head, Foreign Policy Bureau, Deputy Minister for Foreign Affairs 2006; fmr Consul-Gen. in Los Angeles; Amb. to Canada 2007–.
Address: Embassy of Japan, 255 Sussex Drive, Ottawa, ON K1N 9E6, Canada. *Telephone:* (613) 241-8541 (office). *Fax:* (613) 241-4261 (office). *E-mail:* infocul@embjapan.ca (office). *Website:* www.ca.emb-japan.go.jp (office).

NISKALA, Markku, MPA; Finnish international organization executive; *Secretary General, International Federation of Red Cross and Red Crescent Societies;* b. 5 Dec. 1945; m. *Career:* began career as Dist Sec., Red Cross 1970; various positions in Red Cross Soc. of Finland 1970–78; Rep. of League of Red Cross and Red Crescent Socs, Zambia, Tanzania and Zimbabwe 1978–81, oversaw implementation of S African Programme –1985; Head of Europe Dept, Int. Fed. of Red Cross and Red Crescent Socs (IFRC) Secr., Geneva 1985–87; missions to Tanzania, Zambia, Zimbabwe and Ethiopia IFRC 1987–88; Sec. Gen. Finnish Red Cross 1988–2003; Chair. Comm. of the Financing of Int. Cttee of Red Cross 1992–; Acting Sec. Gen. IFRC July–Nov. 2003, Sec. Gen. Nov. 2003–.
Address: International Federation of Red Cross and Red Crescent Societies, PO Box 372, 1211 Geneva 19, Switzerland. *Telephone:* 227304222. *Fax:* 227330395. *E-mail:* secretariat@ifrc.org. *Website:* www .ifrc.org.

NIWA, Toshiyuki, BA, MALD; Japanese diplomatist and UN official; *Deputy Executive Director, United Nations Children's Fund (UNICEF);* m.; four c. *Education:* Waseda Univ., Fletcher School of Law and Diplomacy, USA. *Career:* worked in pvt. sector; joined UN Devt Programme (UNDP) 1971, served in various positions including UN Resident Co-ordinator and UNDP Resident Rep. in Yemen 1980–83, Nepal 1983–88, Thailand and Dir UN Border Relief Operation (UNBRO) for displaced Cambodians along Thai–Cambodian border 1988–90, Asst Sec.-Gen. and Asst Admin. and Dir Bureau for Finance and Admin. 1990–97, Acting Assoc. Admin. 1994; Exec. Co-ordinator for Common Services at UN Secr. 1977, responsible for common services, Asst Sec.-Gen. for Cen. Support Services, Asst Sec.-Gen. 1998–2003, Exec. Dir. Capital Master Plan 2003–04; Deputy Exec. Dir UNICEF 2004–.
Address: United Nations Children's Fund (UNICEF), 3 United Nations Plaza, New York, NY 10017, USA (office). *Telephone:* (212) 326-7000 (office). *Fax:* (212) 887-7465 (office). *E-mail:* info@unicef.org (office). *Website:* www.unicef.org (office).

NIYONGABO, Celestin; Burundian diplomatist; *Ambassador to USA;* m. *Career:* fmr Dir-Gen. for Africa, Asia, Latin America and Oceania, Ministry of External Relations and Co-operation; Amb. to USA 2006–.
Address: Embassy of Burundi, 2233 Wisconsin Avenue, NW, Suite 212, Washington, DC 20007, USA (office). *Telephone:* (202) 342-2574 (office). *Fax:* (202) 342-2578 (office). *E-mail:* burundiembassy@erols.com (office). *Website:* www.burundiembassy-usa.org (office).

NIYOYANKANA, Lt-Gen. Germain; Burundian politician; *Minister of National Defence and War Veterans; Career:* commdr during civil war; Armed Forces Chief of Staff, Nat. Defence Force 2004–05; Minister of Nat. Defence and War Veterans 2005–; mem. Union pour le progresse nationale (Uprona).
Address: Ministry of National Defence, Bujumbura, Burundi (office). *Telephone:* 2222148 (office).

NIZIGAMA, Clotilde; Burundian politician; *Minister of Finance; Career:* fmr Dir-Gen. Office Nat. Pharmaceutique (ONAPHA); Minister of the Economy, Finance and Co-operation and Devt 2007–; mem. Conseil national pour la défense de la démocratie—Force pour la défense de la démocratie (CNDD—FDD).
Address: Ministry of Finance, BP 1830, Bujumbura, Burundi (office). *Telephone:* 22225142 (office). *Fax:* 22223128 (office).

NKOMO, Abraham Sokhaya, MD; South African physician and diplomatist; *High Commissioner to Canada;* m. *Career:* began career as family physician; fmr High Commr. to Malaysia; High Commr. to Canada 2006–.
Address: South Africa High Commission, 15 Sussex Drive, Ottawa, ON K1M 1M8, Canada (office). *Telephone:* (613) 744-0330 (home). *Fax:* (613) 741-1639 (office). *E-mail:* rsafrica@southafrica-canada.ca (office). *Website:* www.southafrica-canada.ca (office).

NKURUNZIZA, Pierre, BA; Burundi politician and head of state; *President;* b. Dec. 1963, Mwumba, Ngozi Prov.; m.; three s. *Education:* Gitega Secondary School, Univ. of Burundi, Bujumbura. *Career:* began career as sports teacher, Vugizo and Muramvya Secondary Schools 1991; fmr Asst Lecturer, Faculty of Physical Educ. and Sports, Univ. of Burundi and ISCAM Mil. Acad. of Burundi; coached Army Football Team, Muzinga, and Union Sporting (first div. football team); forced into exile following inter-ethnic clashes 1995; joined Hutu rebellion CNDD-FDD (Force for the Defence of Democracy) 1995, elected Leader of CNDD-FDD 2001; signed ceasefire accord with Govt Nov. 2003; Minister of State for Good Governance 2004–05; Pres. of Burundi 2005–.
Address: Office of the President of Burundi, Bujumbura, Burundi. *Telephone:* 22226063. *E-mail:* ikiyago@burundi-gov.bi (office). *Website:* presidence.burundi-gov.bi (office).

NOBILO, Mario, MA, PhD; Croatian diplomatist; *Ambassador to Slovenia;* b. 15 June 1952, Lumbarda, Korcula Island; m. Marijana Kujundzić; two s. one d. *Education:* Univ. of Zagreb. *Career:* Research Assoc. Dept of Political and Strategic Studies, Inst. for Int. Relations, Zagreb 1979–89; Guest Prof. in USA, Germany and Spain 1985–90; Co-Founder and Vice-Pres. Croatian Council of European Movt 1990–92; Spokesman and Foreign Policy Adviser to Pres. of Croatia 1991–92; Perm. Rep. of Croatia to UN 1992–96, to OSCE 1996; currently Amb. to Slovenia; Decoration of Homeland War 1993. *Publications:* Western Sahara 1984, Namibia 1985, South Africa 1986, Atlas 1989, War Against Croatia 1992, Croatian Phoenix 2000.
Address: Croatian Embassy, Gruberjevo nabrežje 6, 1000 Ljubljana, Slovenia (office). *Telephone:* (1) 4256220 (office). *Fax:* (1) 4258106 (office). *E-mail:* croemb.slovenia@siol.net (office).

NOBLE, Ronald Kenneth, BA, JD; American law enforcement executive; *Secretary-General, International Criminal Police Organization (INTER-POL); Education:* Univ. of New Hampshire, Stanford Univ. Law School. *Career:* fmr Asst to US Attorney, then Deputy Asst to Attorney-Gen., Dept of Justice; Pres. Financial Action Task Force (26 mem. multi-nat. org. est. to fight money-laundering by G7) 1989; Chief Law Enforcement Officer, US Treasury Dept 1989–96, responsible for The Secret Service, Customs Service, Bureau of Alcohol, Tobacco and Firearms, Fed. Law Enforcement Training Center, Financial Crimes Enforcement Network, Office of Foreign Assets Control and Criminal Investigation Div. of Internal Revenue Service; Prof. of Law, New York Univ. School of Law; fmr mem. Exec. Cttee INTERPOL, Sec.-Gen. 2000–.
Address: International Criminal Police Organization (INTERPOL), 200 quai Charles de Gaulle, 69006 Lyon, France (office). *Telephone:* 4-72-44-70-00 (office). *Fax:* 4-72-44-71-63 (office). *E-mail:* cp@interpol.int. *Website:* www.interpol.int (office).

NOBRE CABRAL, Maria da Conceição; Guinea-Bissau politician; m. Alfredo Lopes Cabral; three c. *Career:* Minister of Foreign Affairs, Int. Co-operation and Communities 2007–.
Address: Ministry of Foreign Affairs, International Co-operation and Communities, Rua Gen. Omar Torrijo, Bissau, Guinea-Bissau (office). *Telephone:* 204301 (office). *Fax:* 202378 (office).

NOGAMI, Yoshiji; Japanese diplomatist; b. 1942; m. Geraldine Nogami; three s. *Education:* Tokyo Univ. *Career:* joined Ministry of Foreign Affairs 1966, held positions as Dir-Gen. Econ. Affairs Bureau, Deputy Minister, later Vice-Minister for Foreign Affairs 2001, Consul-Gen. to Hong Kong, Amb. to OECD, Paris, to UK 2004–08; Sr Visiting Fellow, Chatham House (fmrly Royal Inst. of Int. Affairs) 2002–.
Address: Ministry of Foreign Affairs, 2-11-1, Shiba-Koen, Minato-ku, Tokyo 105-8519, Japan (office). *Telephone:* (3) 3580-3311 (office). *Fax:* (3) 3581-2667 (office). *E-mail:* webmaster@mofa.go.jp (office). *Website:* www .mofa.go.jp (office).

NOGHÈS, Gilles Alexandre, BEng, MBA; Monegasque diplomatist; *Ambassador to USA;* b. 26 March 1947; m. Ellen Noghès; one s. *Education:* Swiss Fed. Inst. of Tech. (ETH), Zurich, Institut Européen d'Admin des Affaires (INSEAD), Fontainebleau, France. *Career:* joined Admin of Principality of Monaco in 1979, First Sec., Bonn, FRG 1983–85; Dir of Tourism and Conventions, Monaco 1985–93; Minister-Counsellor, Paris and Deputy Perm. Del. to UNESCO 1993–2003; Rep. of Monaco to Bureau Int. des Expositions (BIE), Chair. Exec. Cttee BIE 1999, Pres. BIE 1999–2003; Amb. to Switzerland (also accred to Liechtenstein) and Perm. Rep. to UN, Geneva 2003; Perm. Rep. to UN, New York 2004–, Amb. to USA 2006–; Officer of the Order of Saint-Charles (Monaco), Grand Cross of Merit (Germany); Golden Magnolia Medal, Shanghai, People's Repub. of China. *Address:* Embassy of Monaco, 2314 Wyoming Avenue, NW, Washington, DC 20008, USA (office). *Telephone:* (202) 234-1530 (office). *Fax:* (202) 552-5778 (office). *E-mail:* embassy@monaco-usa.org (office). *Website:* monaco-usa.org/embassy (office).

NOKKEN, Frida; Norwegian international organization official; *Director of the Presidium, Nordic Council; Education:* Univs of Oslo and Bergen. *Career:* fmr Dir of Personnel and Dir of Customs, Norway Post; Dir-Gen. of Customs and Excise 1995–99; Sec.-Gen. Nordic Council 1999–2007, now Dir of the Presidium; mem. Bd Int. Peace Research Inst., Oslo 1990–2000, Chair. 1995–2000. *Address:* Nordic Council, Store Strandstræde 18, Copenhagen 1021, Denmark (office). *Telephone:* 3396-0400 (office). *Fax:* 3311-1870 (office). *E-mail:* fn@norden.org (office); nordisk-rad@nordisk-rad.dk (office). *Website:* www.norden.org (office).

NOLAN, Robert B., BA; American diplomatist; *Ambassador to Lesotho;* m. Nancy Wilson Nolan; one s. two d. *Education:* Villanova Univ., George Washington Univ. *Career:* career mem. Sr Foreign Service with rank of FE-MC, overseas assignments have included Gen. Services Officer, Conakry 1977–78, Antananarivo 1978–81, Havana 1986–88, Admin. Officer, Helsinki 1992–94; Dir Office of Overseas Employment, Bureau of Human Resources, Dept of State 1994–96, Dir of Policy and Planning, Office of the Under-Sec. of State for Man. 1996–97, Exec. Dir Bureau of Western Hemisphere Affairs 1997–2000; Prin. Officer, Consulate in Monterrey, Mexico 2000–01; Dir Office of Performance Evaluation, Bureau of Human Resources, Dept of State 2001–06, Dir Office of Career Devt and Assignments in the Bureau of Human Resources 2006–07; Amb. to Lesotho 2007–. *Address:* US Embassy, PO Box 333, 254 Kingsway Road, Maseru 100, Lesotho (office). *Telephone:* 22312666 (office). *Fax:* 22310116 (office). *E-mail:* infomaseru@state.gov (office). *Website:* maseru.usembassy.gov (office).

NONOO, Houda, (Huda Azra Ibrahim Nunu); Bahraini business executive and diplomatist; *Ambassador to USA;* m.; two s. *Career:* served as legislator in Shura Council for three years; Head of Bahrain Human Rights Watch –2008; Amb. to USA 2008–. *Address:* Embassy of Bahrain, 3502 International Drive, NW, Washington, DC 20008, USA (office). *Telephone:* (202) 342-1111 (office). *Fax:* (202) 362-2192 (office). *E-mail:* ambsecretary@bahrainembassy.org (office). *Website:* www.bahrainembassy.org (office).

NONSRICHAI, Jullapong; Thai diplomatist; *Ambassador to Norway;* m. Siriporn Nonsrichai. *Career:* fmr Deputy Dir-Gen. of American and South Pacific Affairs, Ministry of Foreign Affairs; Amb. to Switzerland –2004, to People's Repub. of China (also accred to North Korea and Mongolia) 2004–06, to Norway (also accred to Latvia) 2006–. *Address:* Embassy of Thailand, Eilert Sundtsgt. 4, 0244 Oslo, Norway (office). *Telephone:* 22-12-86-60 (home). *Fax:* 22-04-99-69 (office). *E-mail:* thaioslo@online.no (office). *Website:* www.thaiembassy.no (office).

NOOR AL-HUSSEIN, HM Queen, BA; Jordanian public servant and international humanitarian activist; *United Nations Expert Adviser;* b. (Lisa Najeeb Halaby), 23 Aug. 1951, USA; m. King Hussein I of Jordan 1978 (died 1999); two s.: HRH Prince Hamzah (b. 29 March 1980), HRH Prince Hashim (b. 10 June 1981) two d.: HRH Princess Iman (b. 24 April 1983), HRH Princess Raiyah (b. 9 February 1986). *Education:* attended schools in Los Angeles, Washington, DC and New York City, Concord Acad., Mass, Princeton Univ., USA. *Career:* architectural and urban planning projects in Australia, Iran and Jordan 1974–78; f. in Jordan: Royal Endowment for Culture and Educ. 1979, annual Arab Children's Congress 1980, annual int. Jerash Festival for Culture and Arts 1981 (also Chair.), Noor Al-Hussein Foundation 1985 (also Chair.), King Hussein Foundation (also Chair.) 1999; Chair. UN Univ. Int. Leadership Inst. (UNU/ILI), Amman; UN Expert Adviser; Founding mem. Int. Comm. on Peace and Food 1992; Pres. United World Colls 1995; mem. Int. Eye Foundation, Int. Council Near East Foundation, Int. Comm. on Missing Persons, The Mentor

Foundation, Hunger Project; Trustee Refugees Int., Conservation Int., WWF Int., Aspen Inst. 2004–; Adviser, Women Waging Peace and Seeds of Peace; Patron Royal Soc. for the Conservation of Nature, World Conservation Union 1988, Int. Campaign to Ban Landmines, Landmine Survivors Network (also Chair.) 1998, Int. Alert's Women and Peace-building Campaign, Council of Women World Leaders' Advisory Group 2004–; many other affiliations; Hon. Pres. Jordan Red Crescent, Birdlife Int. 1996–2004 (Hon. Pres. Emer. 2004–); Hon. Chair. Petra Nat. Trust, SOS Children's Asscn, McGill Middle East Program in Civil Society and Peace Building; numerous hon. doctorates, numerous int. awards and decorations for the promotion educ., culture, women and children's welfare, sustainable community devt, environmental conservation, human rights, conflict resolution, cross-cultural understanding and world peace, ranked 83rd by Forbes magazine amongst 100 Most Powerful Women 2004. *Publication:* Leap of Faith: Memoirs of an Unexpected Life 2002. *Address:* Office of Her Majesty Queen Noor, Bab Al Salam Palace, Amman, Jordan. *Telephone:* (6) 551-5191. *Fax:* (6) 464-7961. *E-mail:* noor@queennoor.jo. *Website:* www.noor.gov.jo.

NORBU, Lyonpo Wangdi, BA; Bhutanese politician and civil servant; *Minister of Finance;* b. 1954, Galing, Trashigang Dist; m. Aum Pem Zangmo; one s. one d. *Education:* Scotch Coll., Australia, Univ. of Western Australia. *Career:* various posts within Ministry of Finance since 1977 including Dir Dept of Budget and Accounts, Auditor Gen. Royal Audit Authority, Finance Sec.; Minister of Finance 2003–07 (resgnd), 2008–; mem. Nat. Ass. from Bartsham-Shongphu constituency, Trashigang; fmr Chair. Royal Monetary Authority. *Address:* Ministry of Finance, Tashichhodzong, PO Box 117, Thimphu, Bhutan (office). *Telephone:* (2) 322223 (office). *Fax:* (2) 323154 (office). *E-mail:* yanki@mof.gov.bt (office).

NORDMANN, François, LLB; Swiss diplomatist; b. 13 May 1942, Fribourg; m. Myriam Nordmann. *Education:* Univs of Fribourg and Geneva. *Career:* joined Dept of Foreign Affairs 1971; mem. Political Secr. and Diplomatic Sec.; Councillor, Observer Mission to UN 1980–84; Amb. to Guatemala (also accred to Costa Rica, Honduras, Nicaragua, El Salvador, Panama) 1984–87; Head, Perm. Del. to UNESCO, Paris 1987–94, Dir Int. Orgs 1992–94; Amb. to UK 1994–99; Perm. Rep. to Int. Orgs, Geneva 1999–2002; Perm. Rep. to UN, New York 2002–04; Amb. to France 2004–07; mem. Advisory Bd Centre for Int. Governance, Geneva. *Address:* c/o Advisory Board, Centre for International Governance, Graduate Institute of International and Development Studies, 132, rue de Lausanne, PO Box 136, 1211 Geneva 21, Switzerland.

NORDSLETTEN, Öyvind; Norwegian diplomatist; *Ambassador to Russian Federation;* b. 1 June 1944; m. Asslaug Undheim; two c. *Education:* Univ. of Oslo. *Career:* Second Sec., Embassy in Ankara 1977–79; First Sec., Embassy in Moscow 1979–82; held various positions in Ministry of Int. Affairs 1982–92, including Head of Div. and Asst Deputy Dir of Section for Soviet and Eastern European Affairs 1988–92; Amb. to Ukraine and Belarus 1992–96; Deputy Dir-Gen, Ministry of Foreign Affairs 1996–97; Dir-Gen. Int. Dept, Prime Minister's Office 1997–2000; Amb. to Russian Fed. 2000–; Order of St Olav. *Address:* Embassy of Norway, ul. Povarskaya 7, 131940 Moscow, Russia (office). *Telephone:* (495) 933-14-10 (office). *Fax:* (495) 933-14-12 (office). *E-mail:* emb.moscow@mfa.no (office). *Website:* www.norvegia.ru (office).

NORDSTRÖM, Anders, MD; Swedish physician and international organization official; m.; two c. *Education:* Karolinska Institut. *Career:* worked with Swedish Red Cross in Cambodia and Int. Cttee of the Red Cross in Iran; worked for Swedish Int. Devt Co-operation Agency (SIDA) for 12 years, including three years as Regional Advisor, Zambia and four years as Head, Health Div., Stockholm; Interim Exec. Dir Global Fund to Fight AIDS, Tuberculosis and Malaria 2002; Asst Dir-Gen. for Gen. Man., WHO 2003-06, Acting Dir-Gen. 2006–07. *Address:* c/o World Health Organization (WHO), Ave Appia 20, 1211 Geneva 27, Switzerland (office).

NORLAND, Richard B., BA, MA; American diplomatist; *Ambassador to Uzbekistan;* m. Mary Hartnett; two c. *Education:* Georgetown Univ. School of Foreign Service, Johns Hopkins Univ. School of Advanced Int. Studies, Nat. War Coll. *Career:* career mem. Sr Foreign Service, joined Foreign Service 1980, first tour to Manama, Bahrain 1981–82, Political Officer, Moscow 1988–90, Chief of US Information Office, Tromsø, Norway, served as a peacekeeping monitor in Repub. of Georgia with CSCE 1993, visited Chechnya in a similar capacity 1995, provided advice on NI Peace Process as Political Counselor in Dublin 1995–98 and as Dir for European Affairs, Nat. Security Council 1999–2001; Sr Arctic Official coordinating US chairmanship of Arctic Council 1998–99; Political Officer, Mazar-e-Sharif, Afghanistan 2002–03; Deputy Chief of Mission, Embassy in Riga

2003–05; Deputy Chief of Mission, Embassy in Kabul 2005–07; Amb. to Uzbekistan 2006–.

Address: US Embassy, Moyqorghon kʻoch. 3, 5th Block, Yunusobod District, 100093 Tashkent, Uzbekistan (office). *Telephone:* (71) 120-54-50 (office). *Fax:* (71) 120-63-35 (office). *E-mail:* consul_tashkent@yahoo.com (office). *Website:* uzbekistan.usembassy.gov (office).

NORODOM SIHAMONI, HM King of Cambodia; b. 14 May 1953, Phnom Penh. *Education:* Norodom School, Descartes High School, Phnom Penh, Prague High School, Nat. Conservatory of Prague, Acad. of Musical Art, Prague, Czechoslovakia (now Czech Repub.). *Career:* studied dance, music, theatre and cinematography; Prof. of Classical Dance and Artistic Pedagogy, Marius Petipa Conservatory, Gabriel Faure Conservatory, W. A. Mozart Conservatory, Paris 1981–2004; Pres. Khmer Dance Asscn, France 1984–2004; Dir-Gen. and Artistic Dir Deva Ballet Group 1984–2004; Dir-Gen. and Artistic Dir Khmer Cinematographic Soc.'Khemara Pictures' 1990–2004; Perm. Rep. to UN 1992–2004; Amb. to UNESCO 1993–2004; elevated to rank of Sdech Krom Khun (Great Prince) 1994; crowned King of Cambodia Oct. 2004; Grand Collier de L'Ordre National de l'Independence, Grand Cross of the Royal Order of Monisaraphon, Grand Cross of the Légion d'honneur, Grand Cross of the Royal Order of Cambodia.

Address: Royal Palace, Phnom Penh, Cambodia. *E-mail:* cabinet@ norodomsihanouk.info.

NORODOM SIHANOUK, fmr King of Cambodia Samdech Preah; b. 31 Oct. 1922, Phnom Penh; m. Queen Norodom Monineath Sihanouk; fourteen c. (six deceased). *Education:* Chasseloup-Labaut High School, Saigon (now Ho Chi Minh City), Viet Nam, School of Instruction, Army Cavalry and Armoured Div., Saumur, France. *Career:* mil. training in Saumur, France; elected King by Council of the Crown April 1941, claimed and obtained independence of Cambodia from France 1952–53, abdicated in favour of his father HM Norodom Suramarit March 1955, granted rank of Samdech and title of Upayuvareach of Cambodia; f. Sangkum Reastr Niyum (People's Socialist Community) 1955, (Leader 1955–70), won 82% of vote at legislative elections 1955; Prime Minister and Minister of Foreign Affairs Oct. 1955, March 1956, Sept. 1956, April 1957; Co-Founder Movt of Non-aligned Countries 1956; Perm. Rep. to UN Feb.–Sept. 1956; elected Head of State after death of his father 1960, took oath of fidelity to vacant throne 1960, deposed while on official visit to Soviet Union by forces of Lon Nol and Siri Matak March 1970; became Pres. Cambodian Resistance (FUNC –Nat. United Front of Cambodia) March 1970; resided in Peking (now Beijing), People's Repub. of China; est. Royal Govt of Nat. Union of Cambodia (GRUNC) May 1970; restored as Head of State (Pres.) of Democratic Kampuchea when FUNC forces overthrew Khmer Repub. April 1975, resgnd April 1976; Special Envoy of Khmer Rouge to UN 1979; f. Nat. United Front for an Ind., Neutral, Peaceful Co-operative Kampuchea 1981–89; Head of State in exile of Govt of Democratic Kampuchea and Head Cambodian Nat. Resistance 1982–88, 1989–90; in exile 13 years, returned to Cambodia Oct. 1991; Chair. Supreme Nat. Council 1991–93; Pres. of Cambodia 1991–93; crowned King of Cambodia Sept. 1993–2004 (abdicated); C-in-C of Armed Forces June 1993–; musician and composer; producer of films including Le Petit Prince. *Publications:* L'Indochine vue de Pékin (with Jean Lacouture) 1972, My War With the C.I.A. (with Wilfred Burchett) 1973, War and Hope: The Case for Cambodia 1980, Souvenirs doux et amers 1981, Prisonnier des Khmers Rouges 1986, Charisme et Leadership 1989.

Address: Khemarindra Palace, Phnom Penh, Cambodia.

NOROV, Vladimir L., PhD; Uzbekistan diplomatist and government official; *Minister of Foreign Affairs;* b. 31 Aug. 1955, Buxoro; m.; three c. *Education:* Buxoro State Pedagogical Inst., Moscow Acad. of Internal Affairs. *Career:* school teacher 1976; mil. service 1976–77; worked in Dept of Internal Affairs, Buxoro 1978–88, Head of Criminal Investigation Dept 1990–93; consultant on admin. and legal issues, Pres.'s Office 1993–95, State Adviser for Foreign Relations 1996–98; Deputy Minister, Ministry of Foreign Affairs 1995–96, First Deputy Minister 2003–04, Minister of Foreign Affairs 2006–; Amb. to Germany 1998–2003 (also accred. to Switzerland and Poland 2002–03); Amb. to Belgium and Chief of Missions to EU and NATO, Brussels 2004–06.

Address: Ministry of Foreign Affairs, 100029 Tashkent, Oʻzbekiston koʻch. 9, Uzbekistan (office). *Telephone:* (71) 133-64-75 (office). *Fax:* (71) 139-15-17 (office). *E-mail:* letter@mfa.uz (office). *Website:* www.mfa.uz (office).

NORRBACK, Johan Ole; Finnish diplomatist and politician; *Ambassador for Baltic Sea Issues, Ministry of Foreign Affairs;* b. 18 March 1941, Övermark; m. Vivi-Anna Lindqvist 1959; two c. *Career:* teacher 1966–67; Dist Sec. Swedish People's Party in Ostrobothnia 1967–71; Exec. Man. Prov. Union of Swedish Ostrobothnia 1971–91; Political Sec. to Minister of Communications 1976–77; mem. Parl. 1979–87, 1991–99; mem. Exec. Cttee

Svenska Folkpartiet (SFP) (Swedish People's Party) 1983–89, Chair. 1990–99; Minister of Defence 1987–90, of Educ. and Science 1990–91, of Transport and Communications 1991–95, for Europe and Foreign Trade 1995–99; Amb. to Norway 1999–2003, to Greece 2003–07; Amb. for Baltic Sea Issues, Ministry for Foreign Affairs 2007–, Special Adviser to the Prime Minister on border obstacles between Nordic countries 2007–.

Address: Ministry for Foreign Affairs, Maringatan 22H, 00161 Helsingfors, Finland (office); c/o Svenska Folkpartiet (SFP), Simonsgatan 8A, 00100 Helsinki, Finland. *Telephone:* (9) 16055438 (office). *Fax:* (9) 16055653 (office). *E-mail:* ole.norrback@formin.fi (office).

NORTH, Douglass Cecil, PhD; American economist and academic; *Spencer T. Olin Professor in Arts and Sciences, Department of Economics, Washington University;* b. 5 Nov. 1920, Cambridge, Mass; m. Elisabeth Willard Case 1972; three s. by previous m. *Education:* Univ. of Calif. at Berkeley. *Career:* Asst Prof., Univ. of Washington 1950–56, Assoc. Prof. 1957–60, Prof. of Econs 1960–63, Prof. Emer. 1983–, Chair. Dept of Econs 1967–79; Dir Inst. of Econ. Research 1960–66, Nat. Bureau of Econ. Research 1967–87; Pitt Prof. of American History and Inst., Univ. of Cambridge, UK 1981–82; Luce Prof. of Law and Liberty, Prof. of Econs, Washington Univ., St Louis 1983–, Spencer T. Olin Prof. in Arts and Sciences 1996–; Bartlett Burnap Sr Fellow, Hoover Inst. 2000–; mem. Bradley Foundation 1986–; Fellow, Center for Advanced Study on Behavioral Sciences 1987–88; Guggenheim Fellow 1972–73; Fellow, American Acad. of Arts and Sciences; mem. American Econ. Asscn, Econ. History Asscn; Hon. Dr rer. pol (Cologne) 1988, (Zürich) 1993, (Stockholm School of Econs) 1994, (Prague School of Econs) 1995; shared Nobel Prize for Econs 1993. *Publications:* The Economic Growth of the US 1790–1860 1961, Growth and Welfare in the American Past 1971, Institutional Change and American Economic Growth (with L. Davis) 1971, The Economics of Public Issues (with R. Miller) 1971, The Rise of the Western World (with R. Thomas) 1973, Structure and Change in Economic History 1981, Institutions, Institutional Change and Economic Performance 1990, Understanding the Process of Economic Change 2004.

Address: Department of Economics, Eliot 305, Washington University, Campus Box 1208, St Louis, MO 63130, USA (office). *Telephone:* (314) 935-5809 (office); (314) 935-5670 (office). *Fax:* (314) 935-4156 (office). *E-mail:* north@economics.wustl.edu (office). *Website:* economics.wustl .edu (office).

NOSSAL, Sir Gustav Joseph Victor, AC, CBE, MB, BS, PhD, FRS, FRCP, FRACP, FRCPA, FRCPath, FRSE, FTSE, FAA; Australian medical research scientist; *Professor Emeritus, University of Melbourne;* b. 4 June 1931, Bad Ischl, Austria; m. Lyn B. Dunnicliff 1955; two s. two d. *Education:* St Aloysius Coll., Sydney, Univs of Sydney and Melbourne. *Career:* Jr and Sr Resident Officer, Royal Prince Alfred Hosp., Sydney 1955–56; Research Fellow, The Walter and Eliza Hall Inst. of Medical Research, Melbourne 1957–59, Deputy Dir (Immunology) 1961–65, Dir 1965–96; Asst Prof., Dept of Genetics, Stanford Univ. School of Medicine, Calif., USA 1959–61; Prof. of Medical Biology, Univ. of Melbourne 1965–96, Prof. Emer. 1996–; Chair. WHO Global Programme for Vaccines and Immunization 1992–2002; Partner, Foursight Assocs Pty Ltd 1996–; Dir, CRA Ltd 1977–97; Pres. Australian Acad. of Science 1994–98; Foreign Assoc. NAS; mem. or hon. mem. many other nat. and foreign acads and learned socs; Hon. FRACOG; Hon. LLD (Monash, Melbourne); Hon. MD (Mainz, Newcastle, Leeds, Univ. of Western Australia); Hon. DSc (Sydney, Queensland, ANU, Univ. of NSW, La Trobe, McMaster, Oxford); Robert Koch Gold Medal, Albert Einstein World Award of Science, Emil von Behring Prize, Rabbi Shai Shacknai Prize, Australian of the Year 2000, Australia Post 6th Annual Australian Legends Award and many other awards and prizes. *Publications:* Antibodies and Immunity 1968, Antigens, Lymphoid Cells and Immune Response 1971, Medical Science and Human Goals 1975, Nature's Defences (1978 Boyer Lectures), Reshaping Life: Key Issues in Genetic Engineering 1984; 500 publs on immunology.

Address: Department of Pathology, University of Melbourne, Melbourne, Vic. 3010 (office); 46 Fellows Street, Kew, Vic. 3101, Australia (home). *Telephone:* (3) 8344-6946 (office). *Fax:* (3) 9347-5242 (office).

NOVOTNÁ, Klára, DPhil; Slovak diplomatist; b. 11 May 1961, Nove Zamky, Czechoslovakia (now Slovakia); m. Lubomir Novotny 1983; one s. *Education:* Comenius Univ. (Bratislava). *Career:* civil servant 1985–91, at Ministry for Int. Relations 1991–92; at Embassy of Czechoslovakia in Germany 1992–94; Amb. to Sweden 1994; fmr Deputy Perm. Rep. of Slovakia to UN, New York.

Address: c/o Ministry of Foreign Affairs, Hlboká cesta 2, 833 36 Bratislava, Slovakia. *Telephone:* (2) 5978-1111. *Fax:* (2) 5978-2213. *E-mail:* informacie@foreign.gov.sk; www.mzv.sk.

NOWAK, Jerzy M., PhD; Polish diplomatist; *Senior Research Fellow, Centrum Stosunków Międzynarodowych;* b. 1937; m. Izabella Janowska-

Nowak; two c. *Education:* Cen. Coll. of Foreign Service, Warsaw, Univ. of Torun. *Career:* joined Foreign Service 1960; served in Dar-es-Salaam 1962–65, Buenos Aires 1967–71; Deputy Rep. to UN, New York 1981–86; Head of Mission to OSCE and Perm. Rep. to UN European Office, IAEA and UNIDO, Vienna 1991–97; apptd. Amb. (ad personam) and Security Policy Gen.-Dir, Ministry of Foreign Affairs, later Personal Rep. of Minister for Polish OSCE Chairmanship 1998, mem. of team negotiating accession to NATO; Amb. to Spain and Principality of Andorra 2000–02, Amb. and Perm. Rep. to NATO, Brussels 2002–07; Sr Research Fellow, Centrum Stosunków Międzynarodowych (Centre for Int. Relations), Warsaw 2007–; Head of Policy Planning Staff and European Insts Dept, Foreign Ministry; mem. and later Head of Dels to various expert and political meetings, involved in Conf. on Security and Co-operation in Europe (CSCE)/OSCE and CFE proc. and negotiated revision of CFE Treaty; mem. Polish Euroatlantic Asscn, Polish Club of Rome Section, American Eisenhower Fellowship; fmr mem. Bd of Dirs East–West Inst., New York; Officer's Cross, Order Polonia Restituta, Order of Isabel La Catolica (Spain), Commdr's Cross, Order For Merit to Lithuania. *Publications include:* more than 40 publs on int. affairs.
Address: Centrum Stosunków Międzynarodowych, Emilii Plater 25, 00-688 Warsaw, Poland (office). *Telephone:* (22) 6465267 (office). *Fax:* (22) 6465258 (office). *Website:* www.csm.org.pl (office).

NOWINA-KONOPKA, Piotr Maria, MSc (Econs), PhD; Polish politician, economist, publicist and scholar; b. 27 May 1949, Chorzów; m. Wanda Nowina-Konopka 1975; two d. *Education:* Higher School of Econs, Sopot and Gdańsk Univ. 1972. *Career:* Asst Gdańsk Tech. Univ. 1972–74; Deputy Head, Centre of Revocatory Maritime Chamber, Gdynia 1977–79; Lecturer, Foreign Trade Econs Inst. of Gdańsk Univ. 1979–; Co-Founder and Sec. Catholic Intelligentsia Club in Gdańsk 1980–81; mem. Solidarity Independent Self-governing Trade Union 1980–1990, Press Spokesman 1988–89, Chief of Press 1989; mem. Civic Cttee attached to Lech Wałęsa (q.v.) 1988–91; Lecturer, Gdańsk Theology Inst. 1988–; Minister of State in Chancellery of Pres. of Poland 1989–90; Sec.-Gen. Democratic Union 1990–94; Union for Freedom Sec. for Foreign Affairs 1994–98; Deputy to Sejm (Parl.) 1991–2001, Vice-Chair. Cttee for the European Treaty 1992–97; Sec. of State Office of the Cttee for European Integration 1998; Sec. of State in Chancellery of Prime Minister 1998–99; Deputy Chair. Jt Parl. Cttee Poland-European Parl. 1993–97; mem. Foreign Affairs Comm. 1991–2001; Pres. Polish Robert Schuman Foundation 1996–; Vice-Rector Coll. of Europe, Bruges/Warsaw 1999–2004; Deputy Chief Negotiator for negotiations with EU 1998–99; Chevalier Ordre du Mérite Verdienstkreuz Erste Klasse des Verdienstordens. *Publicatons:* weekly columnist in Wprost, political articles in different books/periodicals.
Address: c/o College of Europe, Rezydencja Natolin, ul. Nowoursynowska 84, Box 120, 02-797 Warsaw, Poland (office). *Fax:* (22) 750-9000 (home). *E-mail:* pnk@omet.pl (home).

NOWOTNY, Eva, PhD; Austrian diplomatist and academic; *Ambassador to USA;* b. 17 Feb. 1944, Vienna; m. Thomas Nowotny. *Education:* Univ. of Vienna. *Career:* Asst Prof., Faculty of Philosophy, Univ. of Vienna 1969–73; joined Austrian Foreign Service 1973; with Dept of Press and Information, Div. of Legal Affairs, Fed. Ministry for Foreign Affairs 1973–75; First Sec. Cultural Inst., Embassy in Cairo, Egypt 1975–78; Counsellor, Perm. Mission to UN, New York 1978–83, also Vice-Pres. Special Political Cttee of 36th Gen. Ass.; Foreign Policy Adviser to Fed. Chancellor 1983–92; Amb. to France 1992–97, to Court of St James (UK) 1997–99; Dir-Gen. of European Integration and Econ. Affairs, Ministry of Foreign Affairs 1999–2003; Amb. to USA 2003–; mem. Bd of Dirs Inst. for East-West Studies, New York, Salzburg Seminar in American Studies, Vienna Inst. for Int. Econ. Research; Fellow, Aspen Inst. of Humanistic Studies.
Address: Embassy of Austria, 3524 International Court, NW, Washington, DC 20008-3022, USA (office). *Telephone:* (202) 895-6700 (office). *Fax:* (202) 895-6750 (office). *E-mail:* obwas@sysnet.net (office). *Website:* www .austria.org (office).

NSANZE, Augustin, PhD; Burundian academic and diplomatist; *Permanent Representative, United Nations;* b. 1953, Kibumbu, Mbuye; m. *Education:* Univ. of Burundi, Univ. of Paris, France. *Career:* Instructor, Lycee Clarte-Notre Dame, Bujimbura 1978–79; Lecturer, Univ. of Burundi 1979–1990, Prof. 1987–90, Advisor to Dir of Dept of Scientific Research 1989, Chief of Scientific Research Service 1990; First Advisor to Pres. on social and cultural issues 1992–98; Consultant on the history of Burundi, UNESCO 1998; Researcher, Univ. of Lieden 1999; Research Asst, Univ. of Laval, Canada 2001–03; Counsellor, Perm. Mission to UN, New York 2004–06; Amb. to Ethiopia (also accred to Djibouti) and Rep. to African Union and Econ. Comm. for Africa 2006–08; Perm. Rep. to UN, New York 2008–. *Publications:* several books and academic articles.

Address: Permanent Mission of Burundi to the United Nations, 336 East 45th Street, 12th Floor, New York, NY 10017, USA (office). *Telephone:* (212) 499-0001 (office). *Fax:* (212) 499-0006 (office). *E-mail:* burundi@un .int (office).

NSENGA, Zac, MA, MD; Rwandan diplomatist; b. 22 Dec. 1958, Byumba; m.; three c. *Education:* Makerere Univ., Univ. of Westminster, UK. *Career:* career diplomatist, fmr Amb. to Israel, UK, Ireland and Nordic Countries, fmr Sec.-Gen. Ministry of Internal Affairs, Amb. to USA 2003–07.
Address: Ministry of Foreign Affairs and Co-operation, boulevard de la Révolution, BP 179, Kigali, Rwanda (office). *Telephone:* 574522 (office). *Fax:* 572904 (office). *Website:* www.minaffet.gov.rw (office).

NSENGIMANA, Joseph, BA, PhD; Rwandan academic, business executive, politician and diplomatist; *Permanent Representative, United Nations;* b. 11 May 1950; m.; five c. *Education:* Univ. of Zaïre, Univ. of Limoges, France. *Career:* Prof., Nat. Univ. of Rwanda 1978–94; Minister for Higher Educ., Scientific Research and Culture 1994–1997, for Public Service and Labour 1997–1999, for Lands, Human Resettlement and Environmental Protection 1999–2000; Special Adviser to Pres. of Rwanda 2000–06; Perm. Rep. to UN, New York 2006–; Chair. Bd of Dirs COGEAR 2000–05, Rwandan Medical Insurance Co. 2002–04, Copenhague 2005–.
Address: Permanent Mission of Rwanda to the United Nations, 124 East 39th Street, New York, NY 10016, USA (office). *Telephone:* (212) 679-9010 (office). *Fax:* (212) 679-9133 (office). *E-mail:* rwanda@un.int (office).

NSEREKO, Daniel David Ntanda, LLB, MCJ, LLM, JSD; Ugandan judge; *Judge, International Criminal Court;* m. *Education:* Univ. of East Africa, Dar es Salaam, Tanzania, Howard Univ. School of Law, Washington, DC, USA, The Hague Acad., Netherlands, New York Univ. School of Law, USA. *Career:* pupil advocate with Kiwanuka & Co., Advocates, Kampala 1968; Advocate, High Court of Uganda 1972–, included on List of Counsel eligible for appointment to represent accused or victims before Int. Criminal Court 2007; Lecturer in Law, Makerere Univ., Kampala 1971–75, Sr Lecturer in Law 1975–78; full-time pvt. law practice, Kampala 1978–82; expert consultant, Crime Prevention and Criminal Justice Br. of UN Centre for Social Devt and Humanitarian Affairs, New York, USA 1983–84, Social Affairs Officer, UN Centre for Social Devt and Humanitarian Affairs 1983; Sr Lecturer in Law, Univ. of Botswana, Gaborone 1984–92, Head of Dept of Law 1985–93, Assoc. Prof. of Law 1992–96, Prof. of Law 1996–; Walter S. Owen Visiting Prof. of Law, Univ. of British Columbia, Canada 1993–94; Visiting Scholar, Max Planck Inst. for Foreign and Int. Criminal Law, Freiburg, Germany 1995, 2006; Judge (Trial Div.), Int. Criminal Court 2008–; served as Amnesty International Trial Observer to Swaziland 1990, Amnesty International mission to Swaziland to investigate allegations of human rights abuses and to inspect prison conditions 1991, Amnesty International Trial Observer to Ethiopia 1996, Head of an Amnesty International del. to Lesotho to investigate allegations of human rights and humanitarian law violations and inspecting prison conditions following S African and Botswana mil. intervention 1998; mem. Exec. Cttee Uganda Red Cross Soc. 1975–80, Bd Int. Soc. for Reform of Criminal Law, Vancouver, Canada 1988–; Advisory Exec. War Crimes Research Office, American Univ., Washington, DC 2006–; mem. Editorial Council Journal of Church and State 1985–, Editorial Bd Journal Violence, Aggression and Terrorism 1986–90, Criminal Law Forum: An International Journal 1990–, University of Botswana Law Journal 2005–; mem. Int. Advisory Bd Int. Doctorate School of Excellence, Univ. of Cologne, Germany 2006–; mem. Uganda Law Soc. 1972– (mem. Law Council (Exec. Cttee) 1975–80), East African Law Soc. 2004–; Fellow, Inst. of Int. Law and Int. Relations Research, The Hague Acad. of Int. Law 1982; Medal of Int. Soc. for Reform of Criminal Law 1996. *Publications:* Police Powers and the Rights of the Individual in Uganda 1973, The International Protection of Refugees (doctoral dissertation) 1975, Antigone: A Greek Play by Sophocles (trans. into the Luganda language) 1989, English–Luganda Law Dictionary 1993, Eddembe Lyaffe (Our Rights; treatise written in the Luganda language) 1995, Criminal Law and Procedure in Uganda (in, International Encyclopaedia of Laws) 1996, Criminal Procedure in Botswana: Cases and Materials (third edn) 2002, Constitutional Law in Botswana (in, International Encyclopaedia of Laws) 2002, Legal Ethics in Botswana: Cases and Materials (with K. Solo) 2004, Criminal Law and Procedure in Botswana 2007; several book chapters and reviews and numerous articles in professional journals.
Address: International Criminal Court, PO Box 19519, 2500 CM The Hague, The Netherlands (office). *Telephone:* (70) 515-8515 (office). *Fax:* (70) 515-8555 (office). *E-mail:* info@icc-cpi.int (office). *Website:* www.icc -cpi.int (office).

NSIMBAMBI, Apollo; Ugandan politician; *Prime Minister; Career:* fmr Minister of Educ. and Sports; Prime Minister of Uganda 1999–; mem. Nat. Resistance Movt.

Address: Office of the Prime Minister, PO Box 341, Kampala, Uganda (office). *Telephone:* (41) 259518 (office). *Fax:* (41) 242341 (office).

NTAMOBWA, Antoine; Burundian diplomatist; m.; four c. *Education:* Univ. of Burundi, Cheikh Anta Diop de Dakar Univ., Senegal, École Nationale Supérieure and Centre d'Etudes et Débats Internationales, France. *Career:* various positions, Univ. of Burundi 1980s; Amb. to Japan 1989–92, to Germany (also accred to Switzerland, Austria, Poland, Czech Repub. and Saint-Siège (Holy See) 1992–93, to Ethiopia (also accred to Eritrea and Djibouti) 1995–97, Perm. Rep. to OAU and Econ. Comm. for Africa 1995–97, Vice-Pres., Chief of Cabinet and Minister of External Relations and Co-operation 1999–2002, Amb. to USA 2002–06.
Address: Ministry of External Relations, Bujumbura, Burundi (office). *Telephone:* 22222150 (office).

NTETURUYE, Marc; Burundian diplomatist; b. 23 Nov. 1954, Murambi; m.; six c. *Education:* Univ. of Burundi, Inst. Int. d'Admin. Publique, Paris. *Career:* taught history in a Jesuit secondary school 1978–81; Dir of secondary school 1981–82; Adviser to Pres. of Repub. on press and information matters 1982–85; First Counsellor, Embassy in Tanzania 1981–87; Amb. to Kenya 1987–91 (also accred to Somalia and Namibia and to Rwanda 1991–93); Perm. Rep. to UNEP and UN Habitat 1990–91; Diplomatic and Political Adviser to Prime Minister 1994–95; Dir Office of Prime Minister 1995–96; Dir External Intelligence 1997–98; Perm. Rep. to UN (also accred to Cuba) 1999–2008. *Publications:* A Study of the Problem of Energy in the Rural Villages of Burundi 1978, A Study on the Role of Sorghum in the Socio-Culture of Burundi.
Address: c/o Ministry of External Relations, Bujumbura, Burundi (office); 16 Murray Hill Road, Scarsdale, NY 10583, USA (home). *Telephone:* (914) 722-0915 (home).

NTSHINGA, Ndumiso Ndima; South African diplomatist; *Ambassador to China;* m. *Career:* African Nat. Congress Deputy Chief Rep. in Australia 1991, later Chief Rep.; fmr Deputy Chief of Mission, Washington, DC, fmr Deputy Dir-Gen. Ministry of Foreign Affairs, Head of Europe and Americas Br., Ministry of Foreign Affairs –2006, Amb. to People's Repub. of China 2006–.
Address: Embassy of South Africa, 5 Dong Zhi Men Wai Dajie, Chao Yang Qu, Beijing 100600, People's Republic of China (office). *Telephone:* (10) 65320171 (office). *Fax:* (10) 65327319 (office). *E-mail:* safrican@163bj.com (office).

NUAIMI, Ali ibn Ibrahim an-, MS; Saudi Arabian government official and fmr oil industry executive; *Minister of Petroleum and Mineral Resources;* b. 1935, Eastern Prov.; m. 1962; four c. *Education:* Int. Coll. Beirut, American Univ., Beirut and Lehigh Univ., Pennsylvania and Stanford Univ., USA. *Career:* Asst Geologist, Exploration Dept, Aramco 1953, Hydrologist and Geologist 1963–67, worked in Econs and Public Relations Dept 1967–69, Vice-Pres. Aramco 1975, Sr Vice-Pres. 1978, Dir 1980, Exec. Vice-Pres., Operations 1982, Pres. 1984, CEO 1988; Minister of Petroleum and Mineral Resources 1995–.
Address: Ministry of Petroleum and Mineral Resources, PO Box 247, King Abd al-Aziz Road, Riyadh 11191, Saudi Arabia. *Telephone:* (1) 478-1661. *Fax:* (1) 478-1980.

NUAIMI, HH Sheikh Humaid bin Rashid an-, (Ruler of Ajman); United Arab Emirates. *Career:* Ruler of Ajman 1981–; mem. Supreme Council of UAE 1981–; Patron, Sheikh Humaid bin Rashid Prizes for Culture and Science 1983–.
Address: Ruler's Palace, PO Box 1, Ajman, United Arab Emirates.

NUDER, Pär, BL; Swedish politician; b. 1963; m.; two d. *Career:* mem. Österåker Municipal Exec. Cttee 1982–94; Chair. Stockholm co. br. Swedish Social Democratic Youth League 1986–89, mem. Nat. Exec. Cttee 1989–90; Political Adviser to Minister for Justice 1986–87, to Prime Minister's Office 1988–91, to Prime Minister 1994–96, 1996–97; Alt. mem. Riksdag 1988–94, mem. 1994–, mem. Parl. Cttee on Justice 1994–97; Political Sec. Social Democratic Parl. Party Group 1992–94, mem. Exec. Cttee, Stockholm county br. Social Democratic Party 1992–94; Exec. mem. Prime Minister's Advisory Council for Baltic Sea Cooperation 1996–2000; Chair. Task Force on Organized Crime in the Baltic Sea Area 1996–2000; State Sec. Prime Minister's Office 1997–2002, Minister for Policy Coordination 2002–04, for Finance 2004–06; Chair. Vasallen AB 2001–02; mem. Bd Vin & Sprit AB 2001–02; Vice-Pres. Bd Nat. Swedish Art Museums 1995–97.
Address: c/o Sveriges Socialdemokratiska Arbetareparti (SAP) (Swedish Social Democratic Party), Sveavägen 68, 105 60 Stockholm, Sweden.

NUJOMA, Sam; Namibian fmr head of state; *Founding President of the Republic of Namibia and Founding Father of the Namibian Nation;* b.

(Samuel Shafiihuma Nujoma), 12 May 1929, Etunda Village, Ongandjera Dist; m. Kovambo Theopoldine Katjimune 1956; three s. one d. *Education:* Okahaol Finnish Mission School, St Barnabas School, Windhoek. *Career:* with State Railways until 1957; Municipal Clerk, Windhoek 1957; clerk in wholesale store 1957–59; elected Leader of Ovamboland People's Org. (OPO) 1959; arrested Dec. 1959; went into exile 1960; Founder, with Herman Toivo ja Toivo and Pres. SWAPO (SW Africa People's Org.) April 1960–2007; appeared before UN Cttee on SW Africa June 1960; set up SWAPO provisional HQ in Dar es Salaam, Tanzania March 1961; arrested on return to Windhoek and formally ordered out of the country March 1966; turned to armed struggle after rejection by Int. Court of Justice of SWAPO complaint against S Africa Aug. 1966; gave evidence at UN Security Council Oct. 1971; led SWAPO negotiations at numerous int. negotiations culminating in implementation in March 1989 of UN Resolution 435 providing for independence of Namibia; returned to Namibia Sept. 1989; mem. Constituent Ass. 1989–90; Pres. of Namibia 1990–2005, also Minister of Home Affairs 1995–96; Fellow, Inst. of Governance and Social Research – Jos, Plateau State, Nigeria 2003–; Grand Master, Order of Merit Grand Cruz (Brazil), Companion of the Order of Star of Ghana 2004; Hon. LLD (Ahmadu Bello Univ., Nigeria) 1982, (Lincoln Univ., USA) 1990, (Ohio Cen. State Univ., USA) 1993, (State Univ. of NJ, USA) 1997; Hon. DTech (Fed. Univ. of Tech., Minna) 1992, Hon. DEd (Univ. of Namibia) 1993; Hon. DSc (Abubakar Tafawa Balewa Univ., Nigeria) 2003; Dr hc (Academic Council, Russian Econ. Acad.) 1998, (People's Friendship Univ. of Russia); Lenin Peace Prize 1973, Frederic Joliot Curie Gold Medal 1980, Ho Chi Minh Peace Award 1988, Indira Gandhi Peace Prize 1990, Africa Prize for Leadership for Sustainable End to Hunger, New York 1995, Order of Friendship Award (Viet Nam) 2000; numerous honours and awards. *Publications:* To Free Namibia 1994, Where Others Wavered – My Life in SWAPO and My Participation in the Liberation Struggle of Namibia (autobiog.) 2001.
Address: The Sam Nujoma Foundation, Private Bag 13220, Robert Mugabe Avenue, Windhoek, Namibia (office). *Telephone:* (61) 377700 (office). *Fax:* (61) 253098 (office). *E-mail:* jnauta@iway.na (office).

NUKAGA, Fukushiro; Japanese politician and fmr journalist; b. 1944. *Education:* Waseda Univ. *Career:* fmr political and econ. reporter for Sankei Shimbun; fmr mem. Ibaraki Prefectural Ass.; mem. LDP; mem. for Ibaraki, House of Reps; fmr Deputy Chief Cabinet Sec.; Dir-Gen. Defence Agency 1998–2000, of Econ. Planning Agency 2000–01; Minister of State for Defence 2005–06; Minister of Finance 2007–08; fmr Chair. Policy Research Council, Liberal-Democratic Party–LDP (Jiyu-Minshuto).
Address: Liberal-Democratic Party, 1-11-23, Nagata-cho, Chiyoda-ku, Tokyo 100-8910, Japan (office). *Telephone:* (3) 3581-6211 (office). *E-mail:* koho@ldp.jimin.or.jp (office). *Website:* www.jimin.jp (office).

NULAND, Victoria, BA; American diplomatist; *Permanent Representative, NATO;* m. Robert Kagan. *Education:* Brown Univ. *Career:* diplomatic postings in Embassy in Guangzhou, China 1985–86, US State Dept East Asian and Pacific Bureaus 1987, Soviet Desk, Embassy in Mongolia 1988–90, Embassy in Moscow 1991–93; Chief of Staff to US Deputy Sec. of State 1993–96, Deputy Dir for fmr Soviet Union Affairs 1997–99; Deputy Perm. Rep. to NATO, Brussels 2000–03; Prin. Deputy Nat. Security Advisor to Vice Pres. Cheney 2003–05; Perm. Rep. to NATO 2005–; Sec. of Defense's Distinguished Civilian Award.
Address: NATO Headquarters, Bld Léopold III, Brussels 1110, Belgium (office). *Telephone:* (2) 707-41-11 (office). *Fax:* (2) 707-45-79 (office). *E-mail:* usnato@hotmail.com (office). *Website:* nato.usmission.gov (office).

NUMATA, Sadaaki; Japanese diplomatist; b. 1943, Hyogo Prefecture; m. Kyoko Numata; one s. one d. *Education:* Tokyo Univ., Univ. Coll., Oxford, UK. *Career:* served in Embassy in London 1968–70; positions at Ministry of Foreign Affairs, Tokyo dealing with econ. cooperation, then N American affairs 1970–76; served in Embassy in Jakarta, Indonesia 1976–78; Politico-Mil. Officer, Embassy in Washington DC 1978–82; Dir, First Int. Orgs (GATT) Div., Econ. Affairs Bureau, Tokyo 1982–84; Dir Japan-US Security Div., N American Affairs Bureau 1984–85, Dir First N America Div. 1985–87; Deputy Japanese Rep. to Conf. on Disarmament, Geneva 1987–88; Deputy Head of Mission, Embassy in Canberra, Australia 1989–91; Deputy Spokesman of Foreign Ministry, Tokyo 1991–94; Deputy Head of Mission, Embassy in London 1994–98; Foreign Ministry Spokesman and Dir Gen. for Press and Public Information, Tokyo 1998–2000; Amb. to Pakistan 2000–02; Amb. in Charge of Okinawan Affairs 2003–04; Amb. to Canada 2005–07; Exec. Dir Center for Global Partnership, Japan Foundation 2007–.
Address: Center for Global Partnership, 4-4-1 Yotsuya, Shinjuku-ku, Tokyo 160-0004, Japan (office). *Telephone:* (03) 5369-6072 (office). *Fax:* (03) 5369-6042 (office). *Website:* www.cgp.org (office).

NUNEZ-TESHEIRA, Karen, MBA; Trinidad and Tobago lawyer, politician, educator and writer; *Minister of Finance;* m. (deceased); two c. *Education:* St Joseph's Convent, San Fernando and Port of Spain, Univ. of the West Indies. *Career:* fmr Sr Lecturer and Vice-Prin. Hugh Wooding Law School; currently MP (People's Nat. Movt) for D'Abadie/O'Meara; Minister of Finance 2007–. *Publications:* Non-Contentious Probate Practice in the English-Speaking Caribbean 2001, The Legal Profession in the English-Speaking Caribbean 2004, Non-Contentious Probate Cases in the English-Speaking Caribbean 2005.
Address: Ministry of Finance, Eric Williams Finance Bldg, Independence Square, Port of Spain, Trinidad and Tobago (office). *Telephone:* 627-9700 (office). *Fax:* 627-5882 (office). *E-mail:* mofcmu@tstt.net.tt (office). *Website:* www.finance.gov.tt (office).

NYABENDA, Ferdinand; Burundian diplomatist; *Assistant-Secretary General, Dept of Sustainable Economic Development and Trade, Secretariat of the African, Caribbean and Pacific Group of States;* m. Jeanine Inabuntu. *Career:* Chief Counsellor and Chargé d'affaires, Embassy in Rome 1998; fmr adviser to Pres. and Prime Minister on diplomatic affairs; Amb. to Belgium and Perm. Rep. to EU (also accred as Amb. to UK) 2003–05; Asst Sec. Gen., Dept of Sustainable Econ. Devt and Trade, Secr. of the African, Caribbean and Pacific Group of States, Brussels 2005–.
Address: ACP Secretariat, ACP House, 451 ave Georges Henri, 1200 Brussels, Belgium (office). *Telephone:* (2) 743-06-00 (office). *Fax:* (2) 735-55-73 (office). *E-mail:* info@acp.int (home). *Website:* www.acpsec.org (office).

NYAN WIN, Maj.-Gen.; Myanma government official; *Minister of Foreign Affairs; Career:* fmr mem. of staff, Office of Strategic Studies (OSS); Vice-Chief of Defence Services Training –2004; Minister of Foreign Affairs 2004–; mem. Nat. Convention Convening Comm.
Address: Ministry of Foreign Affairs, Pyay Road, Dagon Township, Yangon, Myanmar (office). *Telephone:* (1) 222844 (office). *Fax:* (1) 222950 (office). *E-mail:* mofa.aung@mptmail.net.mm (office). *Website:* www.mofa.gov.mm (office).

NYBERG, Ernst René Anselm; Finnish diplomatist; *Ambassador to Germany;* b. 13 Feb. 1946, Helsinki; m.; three d. *Education:* German School of Helsinki, Univ. of Helsinki. *Career:* employed by Ministry of Educ. 1969–71; joined Ministry of Foreign Affairs (MFA) 1971; Embassy in Moscow 1973–76; Consulate-Gen. in Leningrad 1976–77; Finnish–Soviet Econ. Cooperation Comm., Helsinki 1977–79; Political Dept, MFA 1979–82, 1986–88; Embassy in Brussels 1983–86; Dir of Security Policy 1988–91; Minister, Embassy in Bonn 1991–92; Amb., Head of Del. to CSCE, Vienna 1992–95; Co-Chair. OSCE Minsk Group 1995–96; Deputy Dir-Gen. of Political Affairs 1996–98; Deputy Dir-Gen. and Head of Div. for Eastern Affairs 1998–2000; Amb. to Russian Fed. 2000, currently Amb. to Germany; mem. Royal Acad. of War Sciences, Sweden 1995. *Publications:* Finland and Nordic Security 1983.
Address: Embassy of Finland, Rauchstr. 1, 10787 Berlin, Germany (office). *Telephone:* (30) 505030 (office). *Fax:* (30) 5050333 (office). *E-mail:* sanomat.ber@formin.fi (office). *Website:* www.finnland.de (office).

NYE, Joseph Samuel, Jr, BA, PhD; American political scientist, academic and fmr government official; *University Distinguished Service Professor and Sultan of Oman Professor of International Relations, Harvard University;* b. 19 Jan. 1937; m. Molly Harding 1961; three s. *Education:* Princeton and Harvard Univs, Univ. of Oxford, UK. *Career:* Prof. of Govt, Harvard Univ. 1969–, also Dir Centre for Int. Affairs 1989–93, Dean and Don K. Price Prof. of Public Policy, John F. Kennedy School of Govt 1995–2004,

Univ. Distinguished Service Prof. and Sultan of Oman Prof. of Int. Relations 2004–; Deputy Under-Sec. Dept of State, Washington, DC 1977–79, Chair. Nat. Intelligence Council 1992–; Asst Sec. of Defense for Int. Security Affairs 1994–95; mem. Trilateral Comm.; mem. Council, Int. Inst. of Strategic Studies; mem. Council on Foreign Relations; Fellow, American Acad. of Arts and Sciences, Aspen Inst.; Dept of State Distinguished Honor Award 1979, Intelligence Distinguished Service Award 1994, Dept of Defense Distinguished Service Medal 1995, Charles E. Merriman Award, American Political Science Asscn 2003, Woodrow Wilson Award, Princeton Univ. 2004. *Publications:* Power and Independence (co-author) 1977, The Making of America's Soviet Policy (ed. and co-author) 1984, Hawks, Doves and Owls (co-author and ed.) 1985, Nuclear Ethics 1986, Fateful Visions (co-ed.) 1988, Bound to Lead: The Changing Nature of American Power (co-ed.) 1990, Understanding International Conflicts: An Introduction to Theory and History 1993 (fourth edn) 2002, Governance in a Globalizing World 2000, The Paradox of American Power 2002, Soft Power: The Means to Success in World Politics 2004, Power in a Global Information Age 2004, The Power Game (novel) 2004, The Powers to Lead 2008.
Address: Harvard University, John F. Kennedy School of Government, Mailbox 53, 79 John F. Kennedy Street, Cambridge, MA 02138-5801, USA (office). *Telephone:* (617) 495-1123 (office). *Fax:* (617) 495-8963 (office). *E-mail:* joseph_nye@harvard.edu (office). *Website:* ksgfaculty.harvard.edu/Joseph_Nye (office).

NYRUP RASMUSSEN, Poul; Danish politician; *President, Party of European Socialists (PES);* b. 15 June 1943, Esbjerg, Western Jutland; m. 1st (divorced); m. 2nd (divorced); m. 3rd Lone Dybkjar; one c. (deceased). *Education:* Esbjerg Statsskole and Univ. of Copenhagen. *Career:* worked for Danish Trade Union Council in Brussels for a year; Chief Economist, Danish Trade Union Council 1981; Man. Dir Employees' Capital Pension Fund 1986–88; Deputy Chair. Social Democratic Party 1987–92, Chair. 1992–2002; mem. Folketing (Parl.) 1988–2004; Prime Minister of Denmark 1993–2001; MEP 2004–, Pres. Party of European Socialists (PES) 2004–.
Address: Office 11, G 130, European-Parliament, Rue Wiertz, 1047, Brussels, Belgium (office). *Telephone:* (2) 284-54-63 (office). *Fax:* (2) 284-94-63 (office). *E-mail:* pnrasmussen@europarl.europa.eu (office). *Website:* www.nyrup.dk.

NZIBO, Yusuf Abd ar-Rahman, BA, MPhil, MBA, PhD; Kenyan banking executive, historian and diplomatist; *Ambassador to Saudi Arabia;* b. 27 Nov. 1951, Nairobi; m.; four c. *Education:* Univ. of Nairobi, Strayer Coll., Univ. of Glasgow, UK. *Career:* Lecturer, Univ. of Nairobi 1979–89; Deputy Man. Dir Industrial Devt Bank Ltd, Nairobi 1989–92, Man. Dir 1992–96; Commr-Gen. Kenya Revenue Authority Feb. 1996; Amb. to the Netherlands and Czech and Slovak Repubs 1998–2000, to Mexico, Colombia and USA 2000–04, to Saudi Arabia, Kuwait, Yemen, Oman and Bahrain 2004–; mem. Kenya Inst. of Man., Inst. of Bankers, Asscn of African Devt Finance Insts, World Ass. of Small and Medium Enterprises, Aga Khan Foundation and Giants Int; Order of the Grand Warrior, Moran of the Burning Spear. *Publications:* several articles on Latin American history, diplomacy, History of Swahili-Speaking Community of Nairobi.
Address: Embassy of Kenya, PO Box 94358, Riyadh 11693 (office); Diplomatic Quarters, Riyadh, Saudi Arabia (home). *Telephone:* (1) 488-0871 (office); (1) 488-2530 (home). *Fax:* (1) 488-2629 (office); (1) 482-2351 (home). *E-mail:* kenya@shaheer.net.sa (office); yanzibo@yahoo.com (home). *Website:* www.nzibo.com (home).

O

OAKDEN, Edward Anthony, CMG; British diplomatist; *Ambassador to United Arab Emirates;* b. 93 Nov. 1959; m. Ana Oakden; two d. *Education:* School of Oriental and African Studies, London. *Career:* Repub. of Ireland Dept, FCO 1981–82, Third Sec. (Chancery), Baghdad 1984–85, Second Sec. (Chancery), Khartoum 1985–88, Pvt. Sec. to the British Amb., Washington, DC 1988–92, Asst Head of EC Dept (External), FCO 1992–94, Asst Head of Eastern Adriatic Unit 1994–95, Pvt. Sec. to Prime Minister 1995–97, Deputy Head of EU Union Dept (Internal), FCO 1997–98, Deputy Head of Mission, Madrid 1998–2002, Head of Security Policy Dept, FCO 2002, Dir for Defence and Strategic Threats and Envoy for Counter-Terrorism 2002–06, Amb. to UAE 2006–.
Address: British Embassy, 22 Khalid bin Al Waleed Street, PO Box 248, Abu Dhabi, United Arab Emirates (office). *Telephone:* (2) 6101100 (office). *Fax:* (2) 6101586 (office). *E-mail:* chancery.abudhabi@fco.gov.uk (office). *Website:* www.britishembassy.gov.uk/uae (office).

OBAID, Thoraya Ahmed, BA, MA, PhD; Saudi Arabian UN official; *Executive Director, United Nations Population Fund;* b. 2 March 1945, Baghdad, Iraq; m. Mahmoud Saleh; two d. *Education:* Mills Coll., Oakland, Calif., Wayne State Univ., Detroit, Mich., USA. *Career:* mem. League of Arab States working group for formulating the Arab Strategy for Social Devt 1984–85; mem. Editorial Bd Journal of Arab Women 1984–90; mem. Int. Women's Advisory Panel, Int. Planned Parenthood Fed. 1993; Chair. UN Interagency Task Force on Gender, Amman 1996; mem. UN Inter-agency Gender Mission to Afghanistan Nov. 1997; mem. UN Strategic Framework Mission to Afghanistan 1997; Assoc. Social Affairs Officer (Women and Devt), Econ. and Social Comm. for W Africa (ESCWA) Social Devt and Population Div. (SDPD) 1975–81, Women and Devt Programme Man. ESCWA SDPD 1981–92, Chief ESCWA SDPD 1992–93, Deputy Exec. Sec. ESCWA 1993–98; Dir Div. for Arab States and Europe, UN Population Fund (UNFPA) 1998–2000, Exec. Dir and Under-Sec. Gen. UNFPA 2001–; mem. Middle East Studies Asscn, Al-Nahdha Women's Philanthropic Asscn; Dr hc of Law (Mills Coll.) 2002; George P. Younger Award, UN Cttee of Religious NGOs 2002, Medal and Key to the City of Managua, Nicaragua 2003, Pedro Joaquin Chamorro Award, Nicaragua 2003, Second Century Award for Excellence in Health Care, Columbia Univ. 2003.
Address: UN Population Fund, 220 East 42nd Street, 19th Floor, New York, NY 10017, USA (office). *Telephone:* (212) 297-5020 (office); (212) 297-5111 (office). *Fax:* (212) 297-4911 (office). *E-mail:* obaid@unfpa.org (office). *Website:* www.unfpa.org (office).

OBASANJO, Gen. Olusegun; Nigerian politician and fmr army officer and fmr head of state; b. 5 March 1937, Abeokuta, Ogun State; m. 1st Oluremi Akinbwon; two s. four d.; m. 2nd Stella Abebe (died 2005). *Education:* Abeokuta Baptist High School and Mons Officers' Cadet School, UK. *Career:* joined Nigerian Army 1958, commissioned 1959; served in Congo (now Democratic Repub. of the Congo) 1960; promoted Capt. 1963, Maj. 1965, Lt-Col 1967, Col 1969, Brig. 1972, Lt-Gen. 1976, Gen. 1979; Commdr Eng Corps 1963, later Commdr 2nd Div. (Rear), Ibadan; GOC 3rd Infantry Div. 1969; Commdr 3rd Marine Commando Div. during Nigerian Civil War, accepted surrender of Biafran forces Jan. 1970; Commdr Eng Corps 1970–75; Fed. Commr for Works and Housing Jan.–July 1975; Chief of Staff, Supreme HQ 1975–76; mem. Supreme Mil. Council 1975–79; Head of Fed. Mil. Govt and C-in-C of Armed Forces 1976–79; mem. Advisory Council of State 1979; farmer 1979–; arrested March 1995, interned 1995; Pres. of Nigeria and C-in-C of Armed Forces 1999–2007; Chair. Bd of Trustees, People's Democratic Party (PDP) 2007–; fmr Chair. African Union; Fellow, Univ. of Ibadan 1979–81; mem. Ind. Comm. on Disarmament and Security 1980, mem. Exec. Cttee Inter Action Council of fmr Heads of Govt; Chair. Africa Leadership Forum and Foundation; Co-Chair. Eminent Persons Group on S Africa (EPG) 1985; Grand Commdr Fed. Repub. of Nigeria 1980; Hon. DHumLitt (Howard); Hon. LLD (Maiduguri) 1980, (Ahmadu Bello Univ., Zaria) 1985, (Ibada) 1988. *Publications:* My Command 1980, Africa in Perspective 'Myths and Realities' 1987, Nzeogwu 1987, Africa Embattled 1988, Constitution for National Integration and Development 1989, Not My Will 1990, Elements of Development 1992, Elements of Democracy 1993, Africa: Rise to Challenge 1993, Hope for Africa 1993, This Animal Called Man 1999, Exemplary Youth in a Difficult World 2002, I See Hope 2002.

Address: Olusegun Obasanjo Presidential Library Foundation, Presidential Boulevard, Oke-Mosan Abeokuta, Ogun, Nigeria (office). *Telephone:* (9) 245821 (office); (9) 245690 (office). *E-mail:* info@ooplibrary.org (office). *Website:* www.ooplibrary.org (office).

OBEID, Jean, BA; Lebanese politician; b. 8 May 1939, Alma, Zghorta; m. Loubna Emile El-Boustani; two s. three d. *Education:* Collège de Frères-Pères Carmélites-Lycée Officiel, Tripoli, St Joseph's Univ., Beirut. *Career:* journalist, Magazine and Isbouh El Arabi 1959–62, Lissan Al Hal 1960–63, Al Nahar 1963–66, Assayad 1963–66, Ed. Assayad 1966–72; began political career 1973; adviser to Pres. Elias Sarkis of Lebanon 1973; counsellor and presidential del. to Summit of Non-Aligned States, New Delhi, India 1983; participated in Inter-Lebanese Nat. Reconciliation Conf., Geneva, Switzerland; Deputy of the Chouf 1991; Deputy for Tripoli, N Lebanon 1992; Minister of State 1993; Deputy for N Lebanon 1996–2004; Minister of Nat. Educ., Sports and Youth 1996–2003, of Foreign Affairs and Emigrants 2003–04; unsuccessful cand. for Pres. of Lebanon 2007.
Address: c/o Ministry of Foreign Affairs and Emigrants, rue Sursock, Achrafieh, Beirut, Lebanon (office).

OBENG, Lt-Gen. Seth Kofi, MSc; Ghanaian army officer; *Chief of Defence Staff;* b. 26 Jan. 1945, Lagos, Nigeria. *Education:* London School of Econs, UK. *Career:* commissioned into Ghanaian Army as artillery officer 1965, various sr command and staff appointments including Commdt Mil. Acad. and Training School and Ghana Armed Forces Command and Staff College as well as Chief of Staff/Gen. HQ; Defence Adviser, Ghana High Comm., London 1984–88; Chief Staff Officer, Army HQ 1988–89; Man. Dir State Housing Corpn (now State Housing Co. 1989–92, 1992–93; Deputy Force Commdr Econ. Community of W African States (ECOWAS) Monitoring Group in Liberia 1994–96; Force Commdr UN Observer Mission to Angola 1998–99; Force Commdr UN Interim Force in Lebanon (UNIFIL) 1999–2001; Chief of Defence Staff 2001–Chair. ECOWAS Defence and Security Comm.; Commdr Nat. Legion of Cedars (Lebanon) 2001; Officer Nat. Order of Côte d'Ivoire 2002, Meritorious Service Medal (USA) 2004; ECOWAS Award 1996, Int Officer Hall of Fame (USA) 2004.
Address: Ministry of Defence, Burma Camp, Accra (office); No 1, Drake Avenue Airport Residential Area, Accra, Ghana (home). *Telephone:* (21) 762709 (office); (44) 317360 (home). *Fax:* (21) 776936 (office).

OBIOZOR, George Achulike, BA, MIA, MPhil, PhD; Nigerian diplomatist; b. 15 Aug. 1942, Imo State; m.; several c. *Education:* Awo-Omamma Comprehensive Secondary School, Institute of African Studies, Geneva, Switzerland, Albert Schweitzer College, Corcelles-Sur-Chavonay, Univ. of Puget Sound, Wash. and Columbia Univ., New York, USA. *Career:* teacher and later PRO, Awo-Omamma Comprehensive School 1964–66; Research Asst, African Inst., Columbia Univ., New York 1969–75; Internship with Int. League for Human Rights (under Roger Baldwin), New York 1971–72; part-time Lecturer, Pratt Inst., Brooklyn NY 1971–75; Assoc. Prof. of Political Science, Medgar Evers Coll., CUNY, USA 1975–79, Ralph Bunche Research Fellow in the UN, sponsored by the Grad. Center, CUNY 1977–78; Special Asst (Research), Office of the Political Adviser to the Pres. 1980–83; Sr Research Fellow, Nigerian Inst. of Int. Affairs 1984–87, Dir-Gen. 1991–99, on secondment to Ministry of Foreign Affairs 1988–91, Special Adviser to the Minister 1988; Special Asst to Pres. of Nigeria 1990; Amb. to Israel 1999–2003 (also accred as High Commr to Cyprus 2000–03), to USA 2004–08; Visiting Prof. in Int. Affairs, African Inst., Russian Acad. of Sciences, Moscow, Russian Fed. 1998–; Chimes Cup for Service to Fellow Students 1969, Albert Schweitzer Fellowship 1969–71, Alice Stetten Fellowship, Columbia Univ. School of Int. Affairs 1969–71, Grad. Fellowship, Columbia Univ. 1971–75, Ugwumba 1 of Orlu 1991. *Publications:* Nigerian Participation in United Nations 1985, Basic Issues in Nigerian Foreign Policy: IBB Foreign Policy Pronouncements 1986–1991, Nigerian Foreign Policy in Perspective: Admiral Augustus Akhomu's Foreign Policy Statements from 1987–1992, Uneasy Friendship: Nigeria–United States Relations 1992, The United States and the Nigeria Civil War: An American Dilemma in Africa 1993, The Politics of Precarious Balancing: An Analysis of Contending Issues in Nigerian Domestic and Foreign Policy 1994, Nigeria's Vision 2010: Agenda for the Nation 1997; co-ed.: Nigeria at the United Nations: Partnership for a Better

World 1991, Nigeria and the Organization of African Unity: In Search of an African Reality 1991, Nigeria and ECOWAS: Towards a Dynamic Regional Integration 1991, West African Regional Economic Integration: Nigerian Policy Perspectives for the 1990s 1996, Africa and the UN System: The First Fifty Years 1998, Human Right as a Universal Concern: A Nigerian Case Study 1998; contributed to several other books on Nigerian politics and int. relations.
Address: Ministry of Foreign Affairs, Maputo Street, Zone 3, Wuse District, PMB 130, Abuja, Nigeria (office). *Telephone:* (9) 5230570 (office). *E-mail:* omaduekwe@nigeria.gov.ng (office). *Website:* www.mfa.gov.ng (office).

O'BRIEN, Basil G., CMG; Bahamian diplomatist; m. Marlene O'Brien. *Career:* High Commr to UK, Amb. and Perm. Rep. to Euripean Communities, Brussels and Perm. Rep. to IMO, London 1999–2008.
Address: Ministry of Foreign Affairs, East Hill Street, PO Box N-3746, Nassau, The Bahamas (office). *Telephone:* 322-7624 (office). *E-mail:* bobrien@mfabahamas.org (office). *Website:* www.mfabahamas.org (office).

O'BRIEN, Patricia, BA, MA, LLB; Irish lawyer; *Under-Secretary-General for Legal Affairs and Legal Counsel, United Nations;* b. 8 Feb. 1957; m.; three c. *Education:* Trinity Coll., Dublin, Kings Inns, Dublin, Univ. of Ottawa, Canada. *Career:* lawyer, Irish Bar 1979–88; called to Bar of England and Wales 1986; fmr lawyer, Bar of BC, Canada; Lecturer, Dept of Law, Univ. of British Columbia 1989–92; fmr Sr Legal Adviser to Irish Attorney-Gen.; fmr Legal Counsellor, Irish Perm. Representation to EU, Brussels; Legal Adviser, Dept of Foreign Affairs, Dublin 2003–08; Under-Sec.-Gen. for Legal Affairs and Legal Counsel, UN 2008–; Fellow, Soc. for Advanced Legal Studies, Inst. of Advanced Legal Studies, London.
Address: Office of Legal Affairs, United Nations Headquarters, Room No. 3427A, New York, NY 10017, USA (office). *Fax:* (212) 963-6430 (office). *Website:* untreaty.un.org/ola (office).

OBSITNIK, Vincent, BA, MBA; American business executive and diplomatist; *Ambassador to Slovakia;* b. 1938, Moravany, Slovakia; m. Annemarie Harden; four s. *Education:* Linden High School, NJ, US Naval Acad., American Univ., Washington, DC, IBM Advanced Man. School, Sands Point, Long Island, NY, IBM Int. Man. School, La Hulpe, Belgium, Unisys Exec. Program, Wharton School, Univ. of Pennsylvania, Phila. *Career:* moved to USA with parents prior to occupation of Czechoslovakia by Nazi Germany 1938; served as officer in USN in destroyers and submarines 1959–64; fmr Pres. Systems Devt Div., Unisys Corpn; fmr Vice-Pres., International, Litton Corpn; spent 27 years at IBM Corpn, responsible for Marketing, Sales, Mfg, Eng and Program Man., spent eight years with IBM World Trade Corpn with mfg responsibilities in Europe, Latin America and Asia; Founder and Pres. International Investments, Inc.; apptd by Pres. George W. Bush to US Comm. for Preservation of America's Heritage Abroad 2001–06, to US Presidential Del. for Austrian State Treaty Anniversary 2005, to US Presidential Del. to Commemoration of 65th Anniversary of Tragedy in Babyn Yar in Ukraine 2006; Amb. to Slovakia 2007–.
Address: US Embassy, PO Box 309, 814 99 Bratislava, Slovakia (office). *Telephone:* (2) 5443-3338 (office). *Fax:* (2) 5441-8861 (office). *E-mail:* consulbratislava@state.gov (office). *Website:* slovakia.usembassy.gov (office).

OCAMPO, José Antonio, PhD; Colombian United Nations official; b. 20 Dec. 1952; m. Ana Lucia Ocampo; three c. *Education:* Univ. of Notre Dame, Yale Univ., USA. *Career:* researcher, Centre for Devt Studies, Univ. de los Andes 1976–80, Dir 1980–82; at Foundation for Higher Educ. and Devt 1983–93, Deputy Dir 1983–84, Exec. Dir 1984–88, Sr Researcher and mem. Bd of Dirs; Minister of Agric. 1993–94, of Planning 1994–96, of Finance and Public Credit 1996–97; Exec. Sec. UN Econ. Comm. for Latin America and the Caribbean 1998–2003; UN Under-Sec.-Gen. for Econ. and Social Affairs 2003–07; Nat. Dir Employment Mission 1985–86; Adviser, Colombian Foreign Trade Bd 1990–91; Adviser, Colombian Nat. Council of Entrepreneurial Asscn; mem. Tech. Comm. on Coffee Affairs, Public Expenditure Comm., Advisory Comm. for Fiscal Reform, Mission on Intergovernmental Finance; consultant to IBRD, IDB and UN; mem. Colombian Acad. of Econ. Science 1987; Visiting Fellow, Univ. of Oxford, England, Yale Univ.; Nat. Science Prize 1988.
Address: c/o Office of the Under Secretary-General for Economic and Social Affairs, United Nations, Room DC2–2320, New York, NY 10017, USA.

O'CEALLAIGH, Dáithí; Irish diplomatist; *Permanent Representative, United Nations, Geneva;* b. 24 Feb. 1945; m. Antoinette Reilly 1968; one s. one d. *Career:* Third Sec., Dept of Foreign Affairs 1973, First Sec. 1974, First Sec. Anglo-Irish Div. 1982, Counsellor 1985, Asst Sec., Admin. Div. 1998,

Second Sec.-Gen. Anglo-Irish Div. 2000, First Sec., Moscow 1975, London 1977, Counsellor, Anglo-Irish Secr., Maryfield 1985, Consul-Gen., New York 1987, Amb. to Finland and Estonia 1993, to UK 2001–07, Perm. Rep. to UN, Geneva 2007–.
Address: Permanent Mission of Ireland to the United Nations, Rue de Moillebeau 58, 1209 Geneva, Switzerland (office). *Telephone:* 229191950 (office). *Fax:* 229191951 (office). *E-mail:* genevapmun@dfa.ie (office). *Website:* www.dfa.ie (office).

O'CON-SOLORZANO, Thelma, MA; Nicaraguan United Nations official; *Director, United Nations Information Centre;* b. 24 Feb. 1942. *Education:* Women's Univ., Mexico, Univs of Pittsburgh and New York, USA and Inst. of Political Science, France. *Career:* Third Sec. Perm. Mission to UN, New York 1966–67; Protocol Officer Exec. Office of the Sec.-Gen., UN 1968–74; Information Officer Non-Govt Section, External Relations Div., Dept of Public Information 1974; Dir UN Information Centre, Colombia 1974–76, El Salvador 1976–77, Argentina 1980–87, Australia 1987–92, Mexico 1994–98, Japan 2000–; Political Affairs Officer, Office of the Under-Sec.-Gen. for Special Political Affairs, UN 1977–80; Dir and Rep. UN and UNICEF 1987–88; UN Rep. and Resident UN Co-ordinator in Armenia 1992–94; mem. American Soc. of Int. Law 1968. *Publications include:* The Central American Union Research on the Exploration and Exploitation of the Seabed 1961, El Caso Nicaragua 1983.
Address: UN Information Centre, UNU Building, 8th Floor, 53–70 Jingumae S-chome, Shibuya-ku, Tokyo 150 0001, Japan (office). *Telephone:* (3) 5467-4451 (office). *Fax:* (3) 5467-4455 (office). *E-mail:* inictok@blue.ocn.ne.jp (office). *Website:* www.unic.or.jp (office).

O'CONNOR, Gordon, BSc, BA; Canadian politician and military officer (retd); *Minister of National Revenue;* b. 18 May 1939, Toronto; m.; two c. *Education:* Concordia and York Univs. *Career:* fmr mil. officer, Second Lt Armour Br., later Brig. Gen.; fmr Sr Assoc., Hill and Knowlton Canada; MP 2004–, mem. Standing Cttee on Nat. Defence and Veterans Affairs, Subcttee on Veterans Affairs; fmr Official Opposition Critic for Nat. Defence; Minister of Nat. Defence 2006–07, of Nat. Revenue 2007–.
Address: Canada Revenue Agency, 871 Heron Road, Ottawa, ON K1A 0L8, Canada (office). *Telephone:* (613) 952-0384 (office). *E-mail:* OConnor.G@parl.gc.ca (office). *Website:* www.cra-arc.gc.ca (office); www.gordonoconnor.ca (home).

O'DEA, Willie, LLM, CA; Irish politician; *Minister for Defence;* b. Nov. 1952, Limerick; m. Geraldine Kennedy. *Education:* Patrician Brothers Coll., Ballyfin, Co. Laois, Univ. Coll. Dublin (UCD), Kings Inns, Inst. of Certified Accountants. *Career:* fmr barrister and accountant; fmr Lecturer, UCD and Univ. of Limerick; TD 1982–, Minister of State at Dept of Justice 1992–93, at Depts of Justice and Health 1993–94, at Dept of Educ. 1997–2002, at Dept of Justice, Equality and Law Reform with special responsibility for Equality Issues 2002–04, Minister for Defence 2004–; regular columnist, Sunday Independent and other nat. newspapers.
Address: Department of Defence, Parkgate, Infirmary Road, Dublin 7, Ireland (office). *Telephone:* (1) 8042000 (office). *Fax:* (1) 6703399 (office). *E-mail:* webmaster@defence.irlgov.ie (office). *Website:* www.defence.ie (office); www.willieodea.ie (office).

ODIERNO, Lt-Gen. Raymond T., BSc, MS, MA; American army officer; *Commander, Multi-National Force—Iraq;* b. 1953, Rockaway, NJ; m. Linda Burkarth; two s. one d. *Education:* US Mil. Acad., West Point, NC State Univ., Naval War Coll. *Career:* began army career with US Army Europe and US Seventh Army, Germany, becoming Platoon Leader and Survey Officer, 1st Bn, US 41st Field Artillery Brigade, 56th Field Artillery Brigade, and Aide-de-Camp to Commanding Gen.; Exec. Officer, 2nd Bn, 3rd Field Artillery and later Div. Artillery, 3rd Armored Div., Operation Desert Storm 1990–91; fmr Chief of Staff, US States V Corps, US Army Europe; Commdr, US 4th Infantry Div. (4th ID) 2001–04; Asst to Chair. of Jt Chiefs of Staff and Sr Mil. Adviser to Sec. of State, Washington DC 2004–06; Commanding Gen., US III Corps., Iraq, also Commanding Gen. Multi-National Force – Iraq, Baghdad 2008–; numerous medals including Army Distinguished Service Medal, Defense Superior Service Medal, Legion of Merit, Bronze Star.
Address: Multi-National Force—Iraq, 7115 South Boundary Boulevard, MacDill AFB, Tampa, FL 33621, USA (office). *E-mail:* mnfi.webmaster@iraq.centcom.mil (office). *Website:* www.mnf-iraq.com (office).

ODINGA, Raila Amollo, MSc; Kenyan politician; *Prime Minister;* b. 7 Jan. 1945, Nyanza; m. Ida Anyango Oyoo; four c. *Education:* Herder Inst., Leipzig, Otto von Guericke Tech. Univ., Magdeburg, Germany. *Career:* Asst Lecturer, Dept of Mechanical Eng, Univ. of Nairobi 1971–72; f. Spectre Ltd (later East African Spectre Ltd) eng co. 1971; Group Standards Man. Kenya Bureau of Standards 1974–78, Deputy Dir 1978–82; detained without trial following coup attempt by Kenya Air Force personnel

1982–88, re-arrested and detained 1988, 1990, spent four months in political asylum in Norway 1991; Co-founder Forum for the Restoration of Democracy 1991; elected mem. Parl. for Langata 1992, joined NDP (Nat. Devt Party) 1996; finished third in presidential election 1997; Minister for Energy 2001–02; joined LDP (Liberal Democratic Party) 2002; Minister for Roads and Public Works 2002–05; Co-founder Orange Democratic Movt 2005, Leader 2007–; Prime Minister 2008–.
Address: Orange Democratic Movement–Kenya, Orange House, Vanga Road, POB 2478, 00202 Nairobi, Kenya (office). *E-mail:* odmk2007@yahoo.com (office); contact@raila07.com (office). *Website:* odmk.org (office); www.raila2007.com (office).

ODIO BENITO, Elizabeth; Costa Rican politician, lawyer and international arbitrator; *Judge, International Criminal Court; Education:* Univ. of Costa Rica, Univ. of Buenos Aires. *Career:* Minister of Justice and Attorney-Gen. 1978–82, Minister of Justice 1990–94, Second Vice-Pres. of Costa Rica and Minister of Environment and Energy 1998–2002; Perm. Rep. to UN, Geneva 1993; mem. Sub-Comm. for the Prevention of Discrimination and Minorities Protection, Human Rights Comm., UN 1980–83, Special Rapporteur, Sub-Comm. on Discrimination and Intolerance Based on Religion or Creed 1983–86, Vice-Pres. of the Criminal Tribunal for the Fmr Yugoslavia 1993–95, mem. Admin. Tribunal of the Inter-American Devt Bank 1997–98, mem. and Vice-Pres. Bd of Dirs Univ. para la Paz, UNESCO 1999–, Pres. Working Group on Optional Protocol for the Int. Convention against Torture 1998, Judge, Int. Tribunal for the fmr Yugoslavia 1993–98, mem. Costa Rican Nat. Group to the Perm. Court of Arbitration 2000–03, Judge, Int. Criminal Court 2003–; Visiting Prof. Univs of Strasbourg, France 1986, Utrecht, Netherlands 1995, Zaragoza, Spain 1996, Leiden, The Netherlands 1998, Barcelona, Spain 1998; Prof. Univ. of Costa Rica 1986–94, Vice-Pres. of Academic Affairs 1988–90, Prof. Emer. 1994–; Prof. Inter-American Inst. of Human Rights, Costa Rica 1992–; mem. Costa Rican Law Asscn, Steering Cttee Asser Inst., The Hague, Bd Dirs Inter-American Inst. of Human Rights, Int. Comm. of Jurists.
Address: International Criminal Court (ICC), Maanweg 174, 2516 AB, The Hague, Netherlands (office); PO Box 2292/1000, San José, Costa Rica. *Telephone:* (70) 5158515 (office); (506) 2809654 (home). *Fax:* (70) 5158555 (office); (506) 253-6984 (home). *E-mail:* pio@icc-cpi.int (office); eodio@racsa.co.cr (home). *Website:* www.icc-cpi.int (office).

O'DONNELL, Edward B., BA, MA; American economist and diplomatist; *Special Negotiator, US Mission to the Organization of Ameican States;* b. Memphis, Tenn.; m.; three c. *Education:* Southern Methodist Univ., American Univ., and Univ. of Heidelberg, Germany. *Career:* served with US Army 1968–72; joined Foreign Service 1975, positions included W German and E German Desk Officer, Econ. Counsellor, Embassy in Vienna, Commercial Officer, US Mission in Berlin, Charge d'Affaires and Deputy Chief, Embassy in Panama, Econ. and Commercial Officer, Embassies in Colombia and Paraguay, Prin. Officer and Consul-Gen., Frankfurt, Germany; served as Exec. Asst to three Under-Secs and as Special Asst to two Dirs of Policy Planning Staff, US State Dept; fmr Dir Dept of State Liaison Office to US House of Reps; Special Envoy for Holocaust Issues, US State Dept 2003–06; currently Special Negotiator, US Mission to OAS.
Address: WHA/USOAS Bureau of Inter-American Affairs, Department of State, Room 5914, Washington, DC 20520, USA (office). *Telephone:* (202) 647-9430 (office). *Fax:* (202) 647-0911 (office). *Website:* www.state.gov (office).

O'DONNELL, Guillermo, LLB, PhD; Argentine academic; *Helen Kellogg Professor of Government and Senior Fellow, Kellogg Institute for International Studies, University of Notre Dame;* b. Buenos Aires; m.; three s. two d. *Education:* Nat. Univ. of Buenos Aires, Argentina, Yale Univ., USA. *Career:* Fellow, Inst. for Advanced Study, Princeton 1974–75; Visiting Prof., Univ. of Michigan 1974, Univ. of Calif., Berkeley 1983; Prof. of Political Science, Univ. of El Salvador, Buenos Aires 1971–75; Dir and Sr Researcher, CEDES, Buenos Aires 1975–78; Sr Researcher, IUPERJ, Rio de Janeiro 1978–80, CEBRAP, São Paulo, Brazil 1980–83; Academic Dir Helen Kellogg Inst. for Int. Studies, Univ. of Notre Dame 1983–98, currently Sr Fellow, Helen Kellogg Prof. of Govt 1983–; Chair. World Congress of Political Science Programme Cttee 1980; Vice-Pres. of Int. Political Science Asscn 1982–88, Pres. 1988–91; Vice-Pres. American Political Science Asscn 1999–2000; Fellow, American Acad. of Arts and Sciences 1995–; Kalman Silvert Award for Lifetime Contrib. Latin American Studies Asscn 2001, Award for Lifetime Contrib. Int. Political Science Asscn 2006. *Publications include:* Modernization and Bureaucratic-Authoritarianism 1972, Bureaucratic-Authoritarianism: Argentina 1966–1973 in Comparative Perspective 1988, Counterpoints: Selected Essays on Authoritarianism and Democratization; (co-ed.) Transitions from Authoritarian Rule: Prospects for Democracy 1986, Development,

Democracy and the Art of Trespassing: Essays in Honor of Albert O. Hirschman 1986, A Democracia no Brasil: Dilemas e Perspectivas 1988, Issues in Democratic Consolidation: The New South American Democracies in Comparative Perspective 1992, Poverty and Inequality in Latin America 1998, Counterpoints, Selected Essays on Authoritarianism and Democratization 1999, The (Un)Rule of Law and the Underprivileged in Latin America, The Quality of Democracy – Theory and Experiences 2004; numerous articles in learned journals and chapters in books.
Address: Kellogg Institute for International Studies, Hesburgh Center, University of Notre Dame, Notre Dame, IN 46556-5677, USA (office). *Telephone:* (574) 631-6580 (office). *Fax:* (574) 631-6717 (office). *E-mail:* godonnel@nd.edu (office). *Website:* www.nd.edu/~kellogg (office).

ODUBER, Nelson Orlando; Dutch politician; *Prime Minister of Aruba;* b. 7 Feb. 1947; m. Glenda Oduber; three s. *Education:* St Antonius Coll., Santa Cruz, Administrative Acad. of Brabant, Tilburg, Univ. of Utrecht. *Career:* Teacher, Governmental Org. and mem. Exams Preparatory Cttee 1973–75; mem. Cttee of the Kingdom to prepare the independence of Suriname 1973–75; Deputy in charge of Dept for Legislative and Constitutional Affairs 1975–85; Vice-Pres. Consultative Cttee for Independence of Aruba 1978–85; mem. Kingdom Cttee for political restructuring of Antilles 1978–80; Leader Movimento Electoral di Pueblo (MEP) (People's Electoral Movt); Prime Minister of Aruba 1989–; Minister of Gen. Affairs 1989–94, 2001–; Ordén Francisco de Miranda (Venezuela) 1989, Order of the Liberatador First Class (Venezuela) 1991, Kt in the Order of Orange Nassau 1995; Man of the Year (Diario) 1980, Gold Award for contributing to educ. of Aruba 1983, Politician of the Year by readers of Extra 1990, Man of the Year (MEP) 1993, Man of the Year 2001.
Address: L. G. Smith Boulevard 76, Oranjestad (office); Nayostraat 5, Oranjestad (home); MEP, Nayostraat 5, Oranjestad, Aruba. *Telephone:* (297) 5880300 (office); (297) 5824206 (home). *Fax:* (297) 5880024 (office).

OGATA, Sadako, PhD; Japanese international organization official; *President, Japan International Cooperation Agency;* b. 1927; one s. one d. *Education:* Univ. of Sacred Heart, Tokyo, Georgetown Univ., Univ. of Calif., Berkeley. *Career:* Minister, Japan's Mission to UN 1978–79; UN special emissary investigating problems of Cambodian refugees on Thai-Cambodian border; rep. of Japan on UN Comm. for Human Rights 1982–85; fmr Chair. Exec. Bd UNICEF; fmr Dir Inst. of Int. Relations, Sophia Univ. Tokyo; Dean, Faculty of Foreign Studies, Sophia Univ. until 1990; UN High Commr for Refugees 1991–2000; Co-Chair. Comm. for Human Security 2001–03; Prime Minister's Special Rep. for Afghanistan 2002–04; mem. UN High Level Panel on Threat, Challenges and Change 2003–04, Chair. Advisory Bd on Human Security 2003–; Pres. Japan Int. Cooperation Agency 2003–; Ford Foundation Scholar-in-Residence 2002; Dr hc (Harvard) 1994, Hon. DCL (Oxford) 1998; UNESCO Houphouët-Boigny Peace Prize 1996, Ramon Magsaysay Award for Int. Understanding 1997, Seoul Peace Prize 2000, Delta Prize for Global Understanding 2002, J. William Fulbright Prize for Int. Understanding 2002, Eleanor Roosevelt Val-Kill Medal 2002, Great Negotiator Award, Harvard 2005, Woodrow Wilson Award for Public Service 2007, Malalai Heroine of Maiwand Medal. *Publication:* The Turbulent Decade: Confronting the Refugee Crises of the 1990s 2005.
Address: Shinjuku Maynds Tower, 1-1 Yoyogi 2chome, Shibuya-ku, Tokyo 151-8558, Japan (office).

OGBAGHIORGHIS, Tesfamicael Gerahtu; Eritrean diplomatist; *Ambassador to UK;* m. Dr Alem Teclu Hagos. *Career:* Amb. to UK 2007– (also accred to Ireland 2008–).
Address: Embassy of Eritrea, 96 White Lion Street, London, N1 9PF, England (office). *Telephone:* (20) 7713-0096 (office). *Fax:* (20) 7713-0161 (office). *E-mail:* eriemba@eriembauk.com (office). *Website:* www.eritrean-embassy.org.uk (office).

OGEGO, Peter Nicholas Rateng'Oginga, BA, MA; Kenyan diplomatist; *Ambassador to USA;* m. *Education:* Makerere Univ., Uganda, Inst. of Social Studies, The Hague, Netherlands. *Career:* held several positions in Office of the Pres., including Commr of Special Programs, Vice-Chair. of Nat. Disaster, and mem. Emergency Response Cttee; fmr consultant for various orgs in Nairobi, including donor agencies, Devt Communication Inst., Centre for Institutional Devt, Research and Consultancy Services, Social Devt Network, as well as lead consultant for Strategic Public Relations and Research Ltd; Consulting Dir for Jaramogi Oginga Odinga Foundation; Coordinator Nyanza Professional Caucus; High Commr to Canada (also accred as Amb. to Cuba) –2006, Amb. to USA 2006–.
Address: Embassy of Kenya, 2249 R Street, NW, Washington, DC 20008, USA (office). *Telephone:* (202) 387-6101 (office). *Fax:* (202) 462-3829 (office). *E-mail:* information@kenyaembassy.com (office). *Website:* www.kenyaembassy.com (office).

OGOUEBANDJA, Jules Marius; Gabonese diplomatist and civil servant; m. Blandine Ogouebandja; two c. *Education:* Institut d'Etudes Supérieures en Relations Internationales, Paris, France. *Career:* with Ministry of Foreign Affairs and Co-operation, positions included Head of Studies and Dir N and S America Dept, Amb. and Dir Africa Dept 1979–87; Amb. to Italy 1987–92, to Spain 1992–2001, to USA 2001–07.
Address: Ministry of Foreign Affairs, Co-operation and Francophone Affairs BP 2245, Libreville, Gabon (office). *Telephone:* 72-95-21 (office). *Fax:* 72-91-73 (office).

OGRIS, Werner, DIur; Austrian academic; *Professor Emeritus of Law, University of Vienna;* b. 9 July 1935, Vienna; m. Eva Scolik 1963; two s. *Education:* Univ. of Vienna. *Career:* Asst, Inst. für Deutsches Recht, Vienna 1958–61; Prof., Freie Univ. Berlin 1962, Univ. of Vienna 1966, now Prof. Emer.; Prof. Bratislava School of Law 2004, Dean 2005–07; mem. Austrian Acad. of Sciences; Corresp. mem. Saxon Acad.; Foreign mem. Royal Netherlands Acad.; Großes Silbernes Ehrenzeichen für Verdienste um die Republik Österreich 2003; Hon. DrIur (Prague, Bratislava); Theodor-Körner-Stiftung Prize 1961, Brothers Grimm Prize, Univ. of Marburg 1997. *Publications:* Der mittelalterliche Leibrentenvertrag 1961, Der Entwicklungsgang der österreichischen Privatrechtswissenschaft im 19. Jahrhundert 1968, Die Rechtsentwicklung in Österreich 1848–1918 1975, Personenstandsrecht 1977, Recht und Macht bei Maria Theresia 1980, Goethe—amtlich und politisch 1982, Jacob Grimm. Ein politisches Gelehrtenleben 1986, Friedrich der Grosse und das Recht 1987, Joseph von Sonnenfels als Rechtsreformer 1988, Zur Entwicklung des Versicherungsaufsichtsrechts und des Versicherungsvertragsrechts in Österreich von 1850 bis 1918 1988, Deutsche und österreichische Rechtsgeschichte in Japan 1991, Tatort Rechtsgeschichte 1994, Vom Galgenberg zum Ringtheaterbrand 1997, Tatort Rechtsgeschichte 2 1998, Mozart im Familien und Erbrecht seiner Zeit 1999, Die Universitätsreform des Ministers Leo Graf Thun-Hohenstein 1999, Joseph von Sonnenfels (Grundsätze) 2003, Elemente europäischer Rechskultur 2003, Die Zensur in der Ära Metternich 2006, Ubi sponsa ibi sponsalia 2006, Einige Aspekte der Beziehungen Böhmens zum Reichshofrat (with Eva Ortlieb) 2006.
Address: c/o Österreichische Akademie der Wissenschaften, Dr Ignaz Seipel-Platz 2, 1010 Vienna (office); Mariahilferstrasse 71/21, 1060 Vienna, Austria (home). *Telephone:* (1) 515-81-2446 (office); (1) 586-41-57 (home). *Fax:* (1) 515-81-2400 (office). *E-mail:* werner.ogris@oeaw.ac.at (office). *Website:* www.oeaw.ac.at/krgoe (office).

OGUIN, Cyrille S.; Benin diplomatist and civil servant; *Ambassador to USA;* m.; two c. *Education:* Algiers Nat. School of Admin. (Foreign Service), Geneva Grad. Inst. of Int. Relations, Switzerland. *Career:* Second Sec., Accra 1979–84, Chargé d'affaires a.i. 1981–82, Asst to Minister of Foreign Affairs, then to Chief of Staff of Minister of External Affairs and Co-operation 1995–96; Dir Human Rights, Ministry of Justice, Legislation and Human Rights 1998–2000; Amb. to USA 2001–; mem. Nat. Cttee for Reconciliation and Devt; Chevalier de l'Ordre Nat. du Benin 2000, Officier 2001.
Address: Embassy of Benin, 2124 Kalorama Road, NW, Washington, DC 20008, USA (office). *Telephone:* (202) 232-6656 (office). *Fax:* (202) 265-1996 (office). *E-mail:* csoguin@beninembassy.us (office). *Website:* www.beninembassy.us (office).

OGUZ, Lt-Gen. Yilmaz; Turkish military officer; *Military Representative, NATO;* b. Konya; m. Meral Oguz, two c. *Education:* Air Acad., Air War Coll. *Career:* served as tactical fighter pilot and flight instructor with various squadrons; apptd Training and Operations Officer, 2nd Main Jet Base Flight Training Centre Command 1979, served as Chief of Training and OPS Section 8th Main Jet Base, Diyarbarkir, later apptd Squadron Commdr; posted to Air Command and Staff Coll., USA for further training 1989; faculty instructor, Air War Coll., Turkey 1989–91; NMR Air Planning Officer, SHAPE HQ 1991–93; Operations Commdr, 6th Main Jet Base 1993–95; promoted to Brig.-Gen. 1995; Commdr 4th Main Jet Base 1995–97; Chief of Air Defence Div. 1997, Chief of Plans and OPS Div. 1998; promoted to Maj.-Gen. 1999; Airsouth Deputy Commdr, Naples, Italy 1999–2002; Deputy Commdr, 2nd Tactical Air Force Command 2002, Chief of Operations 2003; promoted to Lt-Gen. 2004; Air Training Commdr 2004–05; Mil. Rep. to NATO 2005–.
Address: Delegation of Turkey, NATO Headquarters, Bld Léopold III, Brussels 1110, Belgium (office). *Telephone:* (2) 707-41-11 (office). *Fax:* (2) 707-45-79 (office). *E-mail:* natodoc@hq.nato.int (office). *Website:* www.nato.int (office).

OGWU, Joy, BA, MA; Nigerian diplomatist and academic; *Permanent Representative, United Nations;* b. 22 Aug. 1946. *Education:* Rutgers Univ., USA. *Career:* began career as Lecturer, Nat. War Coll. and Nat. Inst. for Policy and Strategic Studies; Lecturer, Nigerian Inst. of Int. Affairs 1977, subsequently Head, Research Dept in Int. Politics, then Dir-

Gen. –2006; mem. Presidential Advisory Council on Int. Relations –2006; Minister of Foreign Affairs 2006–07; Perm. Rep. to UN, New York 2008–; Chair. UN Sec.-Gen.'s Advisory Bd on Disarmament Matters, also mem. Chair. Bd of Trustees UN Inst. for Disarmament Research (UNIDIR) 2006.
Address: Permanent Mission of Nigeria to the United Nations, 828 Second Avenue, New York, NY 10017, USA (office). *Telephone:* (212) 953-9130 (office). *Fax:* (212) 697-1970 (office). *E-mail:* nigeria@un.int (office).

OHANIAN, Col-Gen. Seyran; Armenian government official and fmr army officer; *Minister of Defence;* b. 1 July 1962, Shushi, Nagorno Karabakh; m.; three s. *Education:* Baku Higher Jt Command Coll. *Career:* began mil. service serving as Platoon Commdr with USSR motorized rifle platoon, Germany 1987–88, Co. Commdr 1987–88; Co. Commdr, 366th motorized rifle regiment, Stepanakert 1988–89, Battalion Deputy Commdr 1989–90, Battalion Commdr 1990–92; Commander of 366th motorized rifle regiment; Chief of Staff of Self-Defense Forces, Repub. of Nagorno Karabakh 1992–94, First Deputy Commdr of Defense Army 1994–98; Commdr 5th Army Corps of Armenia 1998–99; Minister of Defense, Repub. of Nagorno Karabakh 1999–2000, Minister of Defense and Commdr of Defense Army 2000–07; Chief of Staff, Armenian Armed Forces 2007–08; Minister of Defence of Armenia 2008–; 70th Anniversary of USSR Armed Forces, For Perfect Service, For Excellency, Soviet Union Marshal Zhukov(all from USSR); Hero of Artsakh, Golden Eagle, Combat Cross 1st degree, For the Liberation of Shushi (Nagorno Karabakh); Combat Cross 1st degree, Tigranes the Great, For the Service to the Motherland, For Perfect Service 1st and 2nd Degrees, Drastamat Kanayan, Marshal Baghramyan, For the Strengthening of Cooperation, Maternal Gratitude, Coat of Arms.
Address: Ministry of Defence, 0088 Yerevan, Proshian Settlement, G. Shaush Street 60, Armenia (office). *Telephone:* (10) 28-39-22 (office). *Fax:* (10) 28-26-30 (office). *E-mail:* press@mil.am (office). *Website:* www.mil.am (office).

O'HANLON, Michael E., AB, MSE, PhD; American defence analyst and academic; *Senior Fellow in Foreign Policy Studies, Brookings Institution; Education:* Princeton Univ. *Career:* Peace Corps Volunteer, Kinshasa, Zaire (now Democratic Repub. of the Congo) 1982–84; fmr Research Asst, Inst. for Defense Analyses; fmr Adjunct Prof., Georgetown Univ.; Defense and Foreign Policy Analyst, Congressional Budget Office 1989–94; Sr Fellow in Foreign Policy Studies, Brookings Inst. 1994–, also Sydney Stein, Jr. Chair, Dir Opportunity 08: Ind. Ideas for Our Next Pres., Dir of Research, 21st Century Defense Initiative; Adjunct Asst Prof. of Int. Affairs, School of Int. and Public Policy (SIPA), Columbia Univ. 1996–; Visiting Lecturer Princeton Univ; contrib. to several newpapers including The Washington Post, The New York Times, The Wall Street Journal, The Los Angeles Times; frequent radio and TV appearances; mem. IISS, Council on Foreign Relations. *Publications:* The Art of War in the Age of Peace 1992, Defense Planning for the Late 1990s: Beyond the Desert Storm Framework 1995, Saving Lives with Force: Military Criteria for Humanitarian Intervention 1997, A Half Penny on the Federal Dollar: The Future of Development Aid (co-author) 1997, How To Be a Cheap Hawk: The 1999 and 2000 Defense Budgets 1998, Military Technology and the Future of Warfare 2000, Winning Ugly: NATO's War to Save Kosovo (co-author) 2000, Defending America: The Case for Limited National Missile Defense (co-author) 2001, Protecting the American Homeland: A Preliminary Analysis (co-author) 2002, Defense Policy Choices for the Bush Administration 2001-2005 2002, Expanding Global Military Capacity for Humanitarian Intervention 2003, Protecting the American Homeland: One Year On (co-author) 2003, Crisis on the Korean Peninsula: How to Deal with a Nuclear North Korea (co-author) 2003, Hard Power: The New Politics of National Security 2006, A War Like No Other: The Truth About China's Challenge to America 2007; numerous articles in journals.
Address: Brookings Institution, 1775 Massachusetts Avenue, NW, Washington DC 20036, USA (office). *Telephone:* (202) 797-6000 (office). *Fax:* (202) 797-6004 (office). *E-mail:* communications@brookings.edu (office). *Website:* www.brookings.edu (office).

OHLSSON, Per Evald Torbjörn; Swedish journalist and author; *Senior Columnist, Sydvenska Dagbladet;* b. 3 March 1958, Malmö; m. Maria Rydqvist-Ohlsson 1989; one s. *Education:* Univ. of Lund. *Career:* Ed. Lundagard 1980–81; editorial writer, Expressen, Stockholm 1981–85; New York Corresp., Sydvenska Dagbladet 1985–88, Ed.-in-Chief 1990–2005, Sr Columnist 2005–; Soderberg Foundation Prize for Journalism 1998. *Publications:* Over There – Banden Över Atlanten 1992, Gudarnas Ö 1993, 100 År Av Tillväxt 1994.
Address: Sydvenska Dagbladet, 205 05 Malmö, Sweden (office). *Telephone:* 40-28-12-00 (office). *Fax:* 40-28-13-86 (office). *E-mail:* per.t.ohlsson@sydsvenskan.se (office).

OHRYZKO, Volodymyr S., PhD; Ukrainian diplomatist; *Minister of Foreign Affairs;* b. 1 April 1956, Kyiv; m.; one s. two d. *Education:* Taras Shevchenko Kiev Univ. *Career:* joined Ukrainian SSSR Ministry of Foreign Affairs 1978; Attaché, Press Dept 1978–80, Third Sec. 1980–81, 1983–85 (mil. service 1981–83), Second Sec. 1985–88; First Sec., Prin. Counselor's Dept 1988–91, Counselor June–July 1991; Counselor Political Analysis and Co-ordination Dept July 1991–March 1992; Counselor, Embassy in FRG 1992–93, 1994–96; Minister, Embassy in Vienna 1993–94; Head, Foreign Policy Dept and Head, Main Foreign Policy Dept of the Presidential Admin 1996–99; Chair. External Policy Dept 1996–99; Amb. to Austria and Perm. Rep. to Int. Orgs, Vienna 1999–2004; Amb.-at-Large, Dept of Euro-Atlantic Co-operation 2004–05; First Deputy Minister of Foreign Affairs 2005–07; Acting Minister of Foreign Affairs Jan.–March 2007, Minister of Foreign Affairs Dec. 2007–. *Address:* Ministry of Foreign Affairs, 01018 Kyiv, pl. Mykhailivska 1, Ukraine (office). *Telephone:* (44) 238-15-06 (office). *Fax:* (44) 226-31-69 (office). *Website:* www.mfa.gov.ua (office).

Ó'HUIGINN, Séan, MA; Irish diplomatist; *Ambassador to Italy;* b. 25 Sept. 1944, Castlebar, Co. Mayo; m. Bernadette Ó'Huiginn. *Education:* Univ. Coll. Galway. *Career:* joined Dept of Foreign Affairs as Third Sec. 1969, First Sec., Information Section 1972–73, Information/Political Div. 1973–76, Counsellor Anglo-Irish Div. 1976–80, Asst Sec. 1987, 1991–95, Second Sec. 1995–97, Asst Sec., Anglo-Irish Secr. 1987–90; involved in NI peace process leading to signing of Good Friday Agreement 1998; overseas postings include Third Sec., Embassy in Berne 1971–72, Counsellor, Consulate Gen. in New York 1980–83, Amb. to Saudi Arabia 1983–87, to Denmark 1990–91, to USA 1997–2002, to Germany 2002–06, to Italy 2006–. *Address:* Embassy of Ireland, Piazza di Campitelli 3, 00186 Rome, Italy (office). *Telephone:* (06) 6979121 (office). *Fax:* (06) 6792354 (office). *E-mail:* romeembassy@dfa.ie (office). *Website:* www.ambasciata-irlanda.it (office).

OKANLA, Moussa, PhD; Benin politician; *Minister of Foreign Affairs, African Integration, Francophonie and Beninese Diaspora;* b. 2 Sept. 1950; m. *Education:* Univ. of Michigan, USA. *Career:* Prof. of Law, Univ. of Benin; Minister of Foreign Affairs, African Integration, Francophonie and Beninese Diaspora 2007–; Chair. Group of Least Developed Countries, UNDP. *Address:* Ministry of Foreign Affairs, Zone Résidentielle, route de l'Aéroport, 06 BP 318, Cotonou, Benin (office). *Telephone:* 21-30-09-06 (office). *Fax:* 21-30-19-70 (office). *E-mail:* sgm@etranger.gouv.bj (office). *Website:* www.etranger.gouv.bj (office).

OKETA, Gazmend; Albanian engineer and politician; *Minister of Defence;* b. 14 Dec. 1968, Durrës; m.; two c. *Education:* General High School 'Gjergj Kastrioti', Durrës, Faculty of Civil Eng, Tirana Polytechnic Univ., Siegen Univ., Germany. *Career:* Prof., Faculty of Civil Eng, Tirana 1994–95; Specialist of World Bank project on water supply rehabilitation, Durrës 1995–97; designing engineer and pvt. admin. in pvt. construction enterprises 1997–2003; adviser to Voith Siemens (Austria), project on Bistrica hydroelectric power station rehabilitation 2003–04; mem. Democratic Party of Albania (Partia Demokratike e Shqipërisë), Deputy Head of DPA, Durrës Br. 2004, Head of DPA and Spokesman Nov. 2005; mem. Durrës Municipal Council 2003–05; mem. Parl. for Durrës City, Zone No. 29 2005–, mem. Parl. Comm. for Legal Issues, Public Admin and Human Rights; Successive Pres. Cen. European Initiative Parl. Dimension Jan. 2006; Deputy Prime Minister 2007–08; Minister of Defence 2008–. *Address:* Ministry of Defence, Bulevardi Dëshmorët e Kombit, PO Box 2031, Tirana, Albania (office). *Telephone:* (4) 225726 (office). *E-mail:* kontakt@mod.gov.al (office). *Website:* www.mod.gov.al (office).

OKITUNDO, Léonard She, LLB; Democratic Republic of the Congo politician, diplomatist and lawyer; b. 26 March 1946. *Education:* Congo Univ., Lovanium Univ. of Kinshasa, Univ. of Lausanne, Switzerland. *Career:* lawyer, Amnesty International (Swiss chapter), Offices of Legal Consultation, Caritas–Switzerland, Caritas–GENEVE 1982–97; legal consultant to numerous int. human rights orgs; Amb. (itinerant) of Democratic Repub. of the Congo 1997; Minister of Human Rights 1998, of Foreign Affairs and Int. Co-operation 2001–02; mem. Vaud SOS–Asylum, Swiss League of Human Rights, Swiss Cttee for the Defence of the Right of Asylum (CSDDA), European Network of Lawyers Defending the Right of Asylum (ELENA); fmr Chief of Staff to Pres. Joseph Kabila; currently mem. Sénat. *Address:* c/o Ministry of Foreign Affairs and International Co-operation, Place de l'Indépendance, BP 7100, Kinshasa-Gombé, Democratic Republic of the Congo (office).

OKONJO-IWEALA, Ngozi, AB, PhD; Nigerian economist, politician and international organization official; *Managing Director, World Bank Group;*

b. 13 June 1954; m.; four c. *Education:* Harvard Univ., Massachusetts Inst. of Tech., USA. *Career:* joined World Bank (IBRD) 1982, various positions including Economist, Country Dir in E Asia Region responsible for Malaysia, Cambodia, Laos and Mongolia 1997–99, Dir of Operations Middle East Region 2001–02, Vice-Pres. and Corp. Sec., World Bank Group 2002–03, Man. Dir 2007–; Adviser on Econ. Issues to Pres. of Nigeria 2000; Minister of Finance and Economy (first woman) 2003–06, of Foreign Affairs (first woman) June–Aug. 2006 (resgnd); Distinguished Visiting Fellow in the Global Economy and Devt Program, Brookings Inst., Washington, DC 2007; Founder NOI-Gallup polls; Co-founder African Inst. for Applied Econs, Enugu (currently Chair.), Makeda Fund; mem. bd several NGOs and think-tanks, including DATA, World Resources Inst., Clinton Global Initiative, Nelson Mandela Inst. and African Insts of Science and Tech., Mo Ibrahim Foundation Governance Prize Cttee, Friends of the Global Fund Africa; adviser to World Bank on the Stolen Assets Recovery (STAR) initiative; fmr mem. Malan Cttee on Bank-Fund collaboration; Hon. LLD (Brown Univ.) 2006, (Colby Coll.) 2007; Hon. DHumLitt (Northern Caribbean Univ., Jamaica); Dr hc (Trinity Coll., Dublin); Euromarket Forum Award for Vision and Courage 2003, Time Magazine European Hero 2004, This Day Nigeria Minister of the Year 2004, 2005, Euromoney Magazine Global Finance Minister of the Year 2005, Financial Times/The Banker African Finance Minister of the Year 2005, ranked 62nd by Forbes magazine amongst 100 Most Powerful Women 2006. *Publications include:* The Debt Trap in Nigeria: Towards a Sustainable Debt Strategy (co-ed.); several papers in devt journals. *Address:* World Bank Group, 1818 H Street, NW, Washington, DC 20433, USA (office). *Telephone:* (202) 473-1000 (office). *Fax:* (202) 477-6391 (office). *E-mail:* pic@worldbank.org (office). *Website:* www.worldbank.org (office).

OKOULA, Edouard Roger; Republic of the Congo diplomatist; *Ambassador to Democratic Republic of the Congo; Career:* fmr Amb. to Gabon, currently Amb. to Democratic Repub. of the Congo. *Address:* Embassy of the Republic of the Congo, 179 Blvd du 30 juin, BP 9516, Kinshasa, Democratic Republic of the Congo (office). *Telephone:* (12) 34028 (office).

O'LEARY, Brendan, BA, PhD; Irish academic and constitutional advisor; *Lauder Professor of Political Science, University of Pennsylvania;* b. 19 March 1958, Cork; one d. *Education:* St MacNissi's Coll., Co. Antrim, NI, Keble Coll., Oxford, LSE, UK. *Career:* Lecturer in Public Administration, LSE 1983–88, Lecturer B in Public Administration 1989–90, Sr Lecturer in Political Science 1990–92, Reader 1992–96, Prof. 1996–2002, Convenor of Govt Dept 1998–2001, Academic Gov. (elected) and mem. Governing Council 2000–01, mem. Centre for the Study of Human Rights and LSE Public Policy Group; Visiting Prof. of Political Science, Univ. of Pennsylvania 2001–02, Dir Solomon Asch Center for the Study of Ethnopolitical Conflict 2002–07, Stanley I. Sheerr Endowed Term Chair in the Social Sciences 2002–03, Lauder Prof. of Political Science 2003–, Dir Penn Program on Ethnic Conflict 2007–; Visiting Research Scholar, Univ. of Uppsala, Sweden 1991; Visiting Lecturer, Univs of Western Ontario and Waterloo, Canada 1994; Visiting Prof. of Public Policy, Univ. of Western Ontario 1995–96; Jt Ed. Public Administration 1988–89; Co-Ed. LSE Quarterly 1988–89; Commissioning Ed. and mem. Editorial Bd Politics 1985–88; mem. Editorial or Advisory Bd Ethnic and Racial Studies 1989–97, International Journal of Diversity in Organizations Communities and Nations 2003–, Irish Information Partnership 1989–91, Journal on Ethnopolitics and Minority Issues in Europe 2002–, Journal of Ethnopolitics 2001–, Nations and Nationalism 1994–2003, Peace and Conflict Studies 2002–; regular contrib. to Irish, British and American newspapers, including Financial Times, Guardian, Irish News, Irish Times, Los Angeles Times, Philadelphia Inquirer, Sunday Business Post; contrib. to proposals for policing in N Ireland; Constitutional Advisor to Parl. and Govt of Kurdistan Regional Govt 2004; constitutional advisor for UN, EU and UK, on SA, Somalia, and Nepal, and for the UN Human Devt Report 2004; PhD Examiner at Univs of London, Oxford, Nat. Univ. of Ireland, and Queen's Nat., Belfast; mem. American Political Science Asscn, Asscn for the Study of Ethnicity and Nationalism, Irish Political Studies Asscn, European Consortium for Political Research, Int. Political Science Asscn; Best Individual Speaker, Irish Times/Trinity Coll. Dublin All-Ireland Schools Debating Competition 1975, Jt Asscn of Classical Teachers Prize for First Place in Ancient History 1976, Open Scholarship, 1977-81, Keble Coll. Oxford 1977–81, Robert McKenzie Memorial Prize, LSE 1988, Guardian Newspaper Celebrity Scholar 1996, Rockefeller Foundation Residential Fellowship, Bellagio, Italy, 2002, US Inst. of Peace Award (jtly), US Social Science Research Council Grant (jtly). *Television:* regular broadcaster on British, Irish, American, Canadian, Australian, European, and Japanese networks including BBC, ITN, Channel 4, BSkyB, RTE, ABC, CBS, NBC, CNN, Voice of America, ABC (Australia), CBC, NHK; Investigator and Co-presenter of Northern Ireland, The Big Picture Show,

October Films, Channel 4 1992. *Radio:* regular broadcaster for Analysis BBC Radio 4, 1992–2001; presenter, co-presenter and co-author of eight radio documentaries: Fair Cops, Peace in Our Time?, The Hand of History?, Bringing Rights Back Home, Splitting the State?, Breaking the Logjam, Renewing the Peace Process?, Beyond the Cease-fire, The Fate of Nations, A Place Apart?. *Publications include:* books: Theories of the State (with P. Dunleavy) 1987, The Asiatic Mode of Production 1989, Jack Watson's World History Since 1945 (ed.) 1990, The Future of Northern Ireland (co-ed. with J. McGarry) 1990, The Politics of Ethnic Conflict Regulation (co-ed. with J. McGarry) 1993, Northern Ireland: Sharing Authority (with T. Lyne, J. Marshall, and B. Rowthorn) 1993, State of Truce: Northern Ireland after Twenty-Five Years of War (Special Issue of Ethnic and Racial Studies, co-ed. with J. McGarry) 1995, Explaining Northern Ireland: Broken Images (with J. McGarry) 1995, The Politics of Antagonism: Understanding Northern Ireland (2nd edn, with J. McGarry) 1996, Policing Northern Ireland: Proposals for a New Start (with J. McGarry) 1999, Right-Sizing the State: The Politics of Moving Borders (co-ed. with I. S. Lustick and T. Callaghy) 2001, The Northern Ireland Conflict: Consociational Engagements (with J. McGarry) 2004, The Future of Kurdistan in Iraq (with J. McGarry and K. Salih) 2004, Terror, Insurgency and the State (co-ed with M. Heiberg and J. Tirman) 2007, Investing in a Bright Future: The Kurdistan Regional Govt 2008; other publications: over 200 chapters and articles.
Address: Suite 103, Penn Program on Ethnic Conflict, University of Pennsylvania, 3819-33 Chestnut Street, Philadelphia, PA 19104, USA (office). *Telephone:* (215) 573-0645 (office). *Fax:* (215) 746-0165 (office). *E-mail:* boleary@sas.upenn.edu (office). *Website:* www.polisci.upenn.edu/ppec/PPEC.html (office).

OLECHOWSKI, Andrzej, MA, PhD; Polish politician, economist and writer; *European Deputy Chairman, Trilateral Commission;* b. 9 Sept. 1947, Kraków; m. Irena Olechowska 1971; two s. *Education:* Cen. School of Planning and Statistics, Warsaw. *Career:* Assoc. Econ. Affairs Officer, UNCTAD Multilateral Trade Negotiations Project, Geneva 1973–78; Head, Dept of Analysis and Projections, Foreign Trade Research Inst. Warsaw 1978–82; Econ. Affairs Officer, UNCTAD, Geneva 1982–84; Economist, IBRD, Washington, DC 1985–87; Adviser to Gov. Nat. Bank of Poland 1987; Dir World Bank Cooperation Bureau, Nat. Bank of Poland 1988; Dept Dir Ministry of Foreign Econ. Relations 1988–89; Deputy Gov. Nat. Bank of Poland 1989–91; Sec. of State, Ministry of Foreign Econ. Relations and Chief Negotiator of Asscn Treaty with EU and Cen. European Free Trade Agreement 1991–92; Minister of Finance Feb.–May 1992; Sr Adviser, EBRD 1992–93; Econ. Adviser to Pres. of Repub. 1992–93, 1995; Minister of Foreign Affairs 1993–95; Chair. Bd Dirs Bank Handlowy w Warszawie SA 1991–96, 1998–2000, Cen. Europe Trust 1996–2000; Chair. Civic Platform (Platforma Obywatelska—PO, a centrist political movt) 2001–04, Pres. Program Council; presidential cand. 2000; Commr US–Poland Action Comm.; currently European Deputy Chair. Trilateral Comm.; mem. Advisory Bd Baltic Devt Forum; mem. Bd Globe Theatre Group. *Publications include:* Wygrac przyszlosc; publs on int. trade and foreign policy.
Address: The Trilateral Commission, 5 rue de Téhéran, 75008 Paris, France (office); ul. Emilii Plater 53, (WFC XXI), 00-113 Warsaw, Poland. *Telephone:* 1-45-61-42-80 (office). *Fax:* 1-45-61-42-80 (office). *E-mail:* trilateral.europe@wanadoo.fr (office). *Website:* www.trilateral.org (office).

OLEKAS, Juozas; Lithuanian physician and politician; *Minister of National Defence;* b. 30 Oct. 1955, Krasnojarsk Kraj, Siberia; m. Aurelija Olekas; one s. two d. *Education:* Kaunas Medical Inst., Vilnius Univ. *Career:* worked at hosp. in Vilnius 1980–90; physician and sr researcher, Vilnius Univ. Microsurgery Centre 1982–89; particiated in Sàjûdis activity, elected mem. Sàjûdis Seimas 1988, People's Deputy of USSR 1989; mem. Lithuanian Del., Supreme Council of USSR 1989–91; Minister of Health 1990–92 (resgnd), 2003–04; surgeon, Vilnius Ambulance Univ. Hosp. 1993–94; Chief Physician, Vilnius Univ. Hosp. 1994; staff mem. Stomatology Clinic, Medical Faculty, Vilnius Univ. Hosp. 1994–99; mem. Social Democratic Party 1989–, mem. Seimas 1996–; Minister of Nat. Defence 2006–; mem. Org. Comm., European Regional Bureau of WHO 1992–93; Chair. Lithuanian Trade Union Centre 1997; Medal of Independence 2000; Nat. Award of Lithuania 1998. *Publications:* over 100 scientific articles.
Address: Ministry of National Defence, Totoriu 25/3, Vilnius 01121, Lithuania (office). *Telephone:* (5) 262-4821 (office). *Fax:* (5) 212-6082 (office). *E-mail:* vis@kam.lt (office). *Website:* www.kam.lt (office).

OLHAYE, Roble; Djibouti diplomatist; *Ambassador to USA and Dean of the Diplomatic Corps; Permanent Representative, United Nations;* b. 24 April 1944; m.; five c. *Education:* Commercial School of Addis Ababa. *Career:* worked in area of financial and admin. man. in various orgs in Ethiopia engaged in communication, printing, export trade, insurance and mfg 1964–73; regional accountant, TAW Int. Leasing Corpn Nairobi 1973,

Financial Dir 1975; ind. consultant 1980–82; Hon. Consul of Djibouti to Kenya 1980–85; f. (as jt venture with Middle East Bank of Dubai) Banque de Djibouti et du Moyen Orient, SA 1982; Perm. Rep. to UNEP and UN Centre for Human Settlements (Habitat), Nairobi 1986–88; Amb. to USA 1988– (also accred to Canada 1989–), Perm. Rep. to UN 1988–, Dean of the Diplomatic Corps; Pres. of Council 1994, Chair. of Sanctions Cttee 1994, mem. Security Council Mission to Mozambique 1994, Dean of African Diplomatic Corps 1999, Chair. Second Cttee (Econ. and Social) 1999–; Fellow, Asscn of Int. Accountants, UK; mem. British Inst. of Man.
Address: Embassy of Djibouti, 1156 15th Street, NW, Suite 515, Washington, DC 20005 (office); Permanent Mission of Djibouti to the United Nations, 866 United Nations Plaza, Suite 4011, New York, NY 10017, USA. *Telephone:* (202) 331-0270 (Washington, DC) (office); (212) 753-3163 (New York) (office). *Fax:* (202) 331-0302 (Washington, DC) (office); (212) 223-1276 (New York) (office). *E-mail:* djibouti@nyct.net (office).

OLI, K. P. Sharma; Nepalese politician; b. 22 Feb. 1952; m. *Career:* mem. CP of Nepal 1970–, mem. Area Cttee 1970, Dist Cttee 1971, Head, Jhapa Movt Organizing Cttee 1972; imprisoned 1973–87; mem. CP Cen. Cttee 1987, head of Lumbini zone –1990; mem. Standing Cttee and Head of Foreign Dept 1992–; Founder and Pres. Nat. Democratic Youth Fed. 1990; Head, Dept of Publicity and Propaganda 1993; Head, Parl. Affairs 1995–, Deputy Leader 1999–2002, Head, Party School 2004–; mem. House of Reps for Jhapa Dist 1991–2002, 2006–; Minister for Home Affairs, 1994–95; Deputy Prime Minister and Minister for Foreign Affairs 2006–07; led comm. investigating Dasdhunga jeep accident 1993; mem. Presidium of Afro-Asian Peoples' Solidarity Org. (AAPSO) in Nepal 1994–2000, Pres. 2000–.
Address: Parliament of Nepal, Singha Durbar, Kathmandu, Nepal (office). *Telephone:* 4227480 (office). *Fax:* 4222923 (office). *E-mail:* nparl@ntc.net .np (office). *Website:* www.parliament.gov.np (office).

OLIVER, Louise V.; American diplomatist; *Permanent Representative, United Nations Educational, Scientific and Cultural Organization (UNESCO);* m. Daniel Oliver; five c. *Education:* Smith Coll. *Career:* expert in fields of educ., philanthropy, public policy and org. man., has led nat. orgs in these and related fields, has worked extensively in pvt. sector and with US Dept of Educ.; apptd by Pres. George H. W. Bush as Commr on Nat. Comm. on Children 1989; served on bds of five educational insts, including American Univ. of Bulgaria; fmr mem. Bd John Carter Brown Library, Brown Univ.; fmr Chair. Philanthropy Roundtable; helped found New Atlantic Initiative; Amb. and Perm. Rep. to UNESCO, Paris 2004–.
Address: US Mission to UNESCO, 2 avenue Gabriel, 75382 Paris, Cedex 08, France (office). *Telephone:* 1-45-24-74-56 (office). *Fax:* 1-45-24-74-58 (office). *E-mail:* ParisUNESCO@state.gov (office). *Website:* unesco .usmission.gov (office).

OLMERT, Ehud, BA, LLB; Israeli politician and lawyer; *Prime Minister and Minister for Social Affairs;* b. 1945, Binyamina; m.; four c. *Education:* Hebrew Univ. of Jerusalem. *Career:* served in Israeli Defence Force (IDF) as combat infantry unit officer; mil. corresp. for IDF journal Bamachane; mem. Likud Party; mem. Knesset 1973–98, 2003–, mem. Foreign Affairs and Security Cttee 1981–88; Minister without Portfolio responsible for Minority Affairs 1988–90; Minister of Health 1990–92; Mayor of Jerusalem 1993–2003; Vice-Prime Minister and Minister of Industry, Trade, Labor and Communications 2003–05, Vice-Premier and Minister of Finance 2005–06; left Likud party to join newly formed Kadima party Dec. 2005; Acting Chair. of Kadima Jan.–April 2006, Chair. April 2006–08; Acting Prime Minister Jan.–April 2006, Prime Minister and Minister for Social Affairs April 2006–, Minister of Finance April–July 2007.
Address: Office of The Prime Minister, POB 187, 3 Rehov Kaplan, Kiryat Ben-Gurion, Jerusalem, Israel. *Telephone:* 2-6705511 (office). *Fax:* 2-6512631 (office). *E-mail:* webmaster@pmo.gov.il (office). *Website:* www .pmo.gov.il (office).

OMER, Sahih; Eritrean diplomatist. *Career:* currently Chargé d'affaires in Ethiopia.
Address: Embassy of Eritrea, POB 2571, Addis Ababa, Ethiopia (office). *Telephone:* (1) 512844 (office). *Fax:* (1) 514911 (office).

OMOREGIE, Shola, BSc; Nigerian diplomatist and UN official; *Representative in Guinea Bissau, United Nations;* b. 12 Dec. 1946, Benin City. *Education:* Univ. of Lagos. *Career:* with Ministry of Foreign Affairs 1972–78; First Resident Rep. of UN High Commr for Namibia in Botswana 1978–83, Head of Information and Assistance Unit 1983–88, Rep. of UN High Commr for Namibia in Angola 1988–90, Head of Research and Reports Unit and Head of Task Force for Angola and South Africa 1990–91; Sec., UN Special Cttee on Peacekeeping Operations 1992–94; Sec. subsidiary organs, UN Security Council 1992–95, Sr Political Affairs Officer, Security Council Secr., Security Council Affairs Div., Dept

of Political Affairs 1995–2005; Head of Security Council Practices Br 2005–06, mem. Task Force on Assistance to African Union 2003–2005; UN Rep. in Guinea Bissau and Head of UN Peacebuilding Support Office in Guinea Bissau (UNOGBIS) 2006–.
Address: United Nations Building, 5th Floor, Rua Rui Djassi, 1011 Bissau, Guinea-Bissau (office). *Website:* www.unogbis.org (office).

OMRANA, Abderrahim, PhD; Moroccan economist and banker; *Bank Secretary, Islamic Development Bank;* b. 1947, Quezane; m.; three c. *Career:* with Govt Gen. Inspection Dept 1970; Head of Mission, Treasury Dept, Ministry of Finance 1973; Asst Lecturer, Univ. of Rabat 1974, Sr Lecturer 1975–78; Exec. Attaché, Banque Nationale pour le Développement Economique 1975–78; Lecturer, Univ. of Dakar, Senegal 1978–79; Deputy Dir Gen. African Centre for Monetary Studies and Fed. of African Cen. Banks 1978–87; Dir Gen. ICOMA and NASCOTEX 1989–95; Bank Sec., Islamic Devt Bank 1996–2001, 2003–, Dir Gen. Fund for Municipal Equipments 2001–03. *Publications:* three books on finance, accountancy and modern econs and more than 100 articles on econs and finance.
Address: c/o Islamic Development Bank, PO Box 5925, Jeddah 21432, Saudi Arabia (office). *Telephone:* (2) 644-2432 (office). *Fax:* (2) 644-2432 (office). *E-mail:* aomrana@isdb.org (office). *Website:* www.isdb.org (office).

ONDO, Purificación Angue; Equatorial Guinean diplomatist; *Ambassador to USA. Career:* Amb. to Cameroon 2000–05, to USA 2005–.
Address: Embassy of Equatorial Guinea, 2020 16th Street, NW, Washington, DC 20009, USA (office). *Telephone:* (202) 518-5700 (office). *Fax:* (202) 518-5252 (office).

O'NEAL, Hon. Ralph T., OBE; British Virgin Islands politician and business executive; *Chief Minister and Minister of Finance;* b. 1933; m. Edris O'Neal. *Career:* Leader Virgin Islands Party; fmr civil servant and mem. of govt in various capacities; Deputy Chief Minister –1995; Chief Minister and Minister of Finance 1995–2003, 2007–; fmr Dir British Virgin Islands Red Cross; founding mem. Rotary Club, Tortola.
Address: Office of the Chief Minister, 33 Admin Drive, Wickham's Cay 1, Tortola VG1110, The British Virgin Islands (office). *Telephone:* 468-3701 (office). *Fax:* 468-4435 (office). *E-mail:* cmo@surfbvi.com (office). *Website:* www.bvigazette.org (office).

ONG, Keng Yong, LLB; Singaporean international organization official and diplomatist; b. 6 Jan. 1954; m. Irene Tan Lee Chen. *Education:* Univ. of Singapore, Georgetown Univ., Washington, DC, USA. *Career:* Chargé d'affaires, Embassy in Riyadh 1984–88; Counsellor, High Comm. in Kuala Lumpur 1989–91; Minister Counsellor and Deputy Chief of Mission, Embassy in Washington, DC 1991–94; Press Sec. to Minister of Foreign Affairs and Ministry Spokesperson 1994–95; High Commr to India and Amb. to Nepal 1996–98; Press Sec. to Prime Minister 1998–2002; Deputy Sec. Ministry of Information, Communication and the Arts 1998; Chief Exec. Dir The People's Asscn 1999–2002; Sec.-Gen. ASEAN 2003–08; Amb. at Large, Ministry of Foreign Affairs 2008–; Public Admin Medal, Long Service Medal.
Address: Ministry of Foreign Affairs, MFA Building, Tanglin, off Napier Road, Singapore 248163 (office). *Telephone:* 63798000 (office). *Fax:* 64747885 (office). *E-mail:* ongkengyong@gmail.com. *Website:* www.mfa .gov.sg (office).

ONG, Romualdo Añover, BSc; Philippine diplomatist; *Director, Foreign Service Institute;* b. 25 April 1939, Manila; m. 1st Cecilia Hidalgo 1964 (deceased); m. 2nd Farita Aguilucho 1994; two s. two d. *Education:* Ateneo de Manila and Univ. of the Philippines. *Career:* joined Ministry of Foreign Affairs 1968; served Bonn 1972–75, Geneva 1975–79, Minister Counsellor, Beijing 1979–82; Special Asst to Deputy Minister for Foreign Affairs 1983; Asst Minister for ASEAN Affairs 1984–85; Sr Econ. Consultant, Tech. Secr. for Int. Econ. Relations/Bd. of Overseas Econ. Promotion 1985; Amb. to Australia (also accred to Vanuatu) 1986–89; Asst Sec. for Asian and Pacific Affairs, Dept of Foreign Affairs, Manila 1990–93; Amb. to Russia 1993–94, to People's Repub. of China 1994–2000; Dir Foreign Service Inst. 2000–.
Address: Foreign Service Institute, 5th Floor, DFA Building, 2330 Roxas Blvd, 1300 Pasay City, Metro Manila, The Philippines (office). *E-mail:* afsd@fsi.gov.ph (office). *Website:* www.info.com.ph/~fsi (office).

ONGOUORI NGOUBILI, Félicité; Gabonese diplomatist; *Ambassador to France; Career:* fmr mem. del. to African Union; Deputy Chief of Staff, Office of the Pres. –2008; Amb. to France 2008–.
Address: Embassy of Gabon, 26 bis ave Raphaël, 75016 Paris, France (office). *Telephone:* 1-72-70-01-50 (office). *Fax:* 1-72-81-05-89 (office). *E-mail:* hditsougou@caramail.com (office).

O'NIONS, Sir Robert Keith, Kt, MA, PhD, FRS; British geochemist and academic; *Director General of Research Councils, Office of Science and Technology, Department of Trade and Industry; Chief Scientific Adviser, Ministry of Defence;* b. 26 Sept. 1944, Birmingham; m. Rita Bill 1967; three d. *Education:* Univ. of Nottingham, Univ. of Alberta. *Career:* Postdoctoral Fellow, Univ. of Alberta, Canada 1969–70; Unger Vetlesen Postdoctoral Fellow, Univ. of Oslo, Norway 1970–71; Demonstrator in Petrology, Univ. of Oxford 1971–72, Lecturer in Geochemistry 1972–75; Assoc. Prof. and Prof. of Geology, Columbia Univ., New York, USA 1975–79; Royal Soc. Research Prof., Univ. of Cambridge 1979–95; Fellow Clare Hall Cambridge 1980–95; Prof. of Physics and Chem. of Minerals, Univ. of Oxford 1995–2003; Chief Scientific Adviser, Ministry of Defence 2000–; Dir Gen. Research Councils 2004–; Fellow St Hugh's Coll. Oxford 1995–2003; Fellow American Geophysical Union; Foreign Fellow Indian Nat. Science Acad.; mem. Norwegian Acad. of Sciences; Foreign mem. India Acad. of Sciences; Hon. Fellow, Univ. of Cardiff; J. B. Macelwane Award 1979, Bigsby Medal 1983, Holmes Medal 1995, Lyell Medal 1995, Urey Medal 2001. *Publications:* numerous publs in scientific journals on geochemistry.
Address: Office of Science and Technology, Department of Trade and Industry, Victoria Street, London, SW1H 0ET, England (office). *Telephone:* (20) 7215-3803 (office). *Fax:* (20) 7215-0054 (office). *E-mail:* keith .oonions@dti.gsi.gov.uk (office). *Website:* www.ost.gov.uk (office).

ONYSZKIEWICZ, Janusz, DMath; Polish government official and mathematician; *Senior Fellow, Center for International Relations;* b. 18 Dec. 1937, Lvov; m. 1st Witoslawa Boretti (died 1967); m. 2nd Alison Chadwick (died 1978); m. 3rd Joanna Jaraczewska 1983; two s. three d. *Education:* Warsaw Univ. *Career:* Asst, Math. Engines Inst., Polish Acad. of Sciences, Warsaw 1958–61; Asst, later Sr Asst, Faculty of Math., Informatics and Mechanics, Math. Inst., Warsaw Univ. 1963–67, Lecturer 1967–75, now Sr Lecturer; Lecturer, Univ. of Leeds, UK 1976–79; lectured at many univs abroad; mem. Polish Teachers' Union (ZNP) 1969-80, Ind. Self-governing Trade Union of Science, Tech. and Educ. Workers 1980, Deputy Chair. Br. at Warsaw Univ. Sept.–Oct. 1980; adviser to Interfactory Founding Cttee of Solidarity Ind. Self-governing Trade Union–Mazovia Region, subsequently mem. Presidium of Nat. Comm. of Solidarity Trade Union, Bd and Press Spokesman of Mazovia Region of Solidarity Trade Union; Press Spokesman Nat. Understanding Comm. and First Nat. Congress of Solidarity Trade Union 1980–81; interned 1981–82; arrested April 1983, released under amnesty July 1983; sentenced to six weeks' confinement May 1988; Press Spokesman Nat. Exec. Comm., Solidarity Trade Union; mem. Civic Cttee attached to Lech Wałęsa (q.v.) 1988–91; participant Round Table debates, mem. team for mass media and opposition press spokesman Feb.–April 1989; Deputy to Sejm (Parl.) 1989–2001; Vice-Minister of Nat. Defence 1990–92, Minister 1992–93, 1997–2000; Chair. Defence Cttee, Council of Ministers 1997–99; mem. Democratic Union Parl. 1991–94, Freedom Union Parl. 1994–; Vice-Pres. Polish Asia-Pacific Council 1996–; mem. Nat. Council Freedom Union 1996; mem. Euro-Atlantic Asscn 1994– (Pres. 1994–98); currently Sr Fellow Center for Int. Relations; Pres. Polish Mountaineering Fed. 2001–; mountaineer and speleologist, participant mountaineering expeditions in Himalayas, Hindu Kush, Karakoram, Pamir; Great Cross of Gedymin (Lithuania), Great Cross of King Leopold II (Belgium); Hon. DSc (Leeds) 1991; Gold Medal (For Outstanding Sporting Achievements), Manfred Wörner Medal. *Publications:* 15 works on foundations of math., including Complete Abstract Logics 1979; co-author Zdobycie Gasherbrumów 1977.
Address: Center for International Relations, ul. Emilii Plater, 00-688 Warsaw, Poland (office). *Telephone:* (22) 6465267 (office). *Fax:* (22) 6465258 (office). *E-mail:* onyszkiewicz@csm.org.pl (office); janusz .onyszkiewicz@n17.waw.pl (home). *Website:* www.csm.org.pl (office).

OPERTTI BADDAN, Didier, PhD; Uruguayan lawyer, politician and international organization official; b. 1937, Montevideo; m.; four c. *Education:* Univ. of Uruguay. *Career:* fmr Asst Prof. of Int. Pvt. Law, Univ. of Uruguay, Prof. of Int. Relations 1986; Dir Office of Codification and Devt of Int. Law, Gen. Secr., OAS 1979–81, Perm. Rep. to OAS 1988–93, Pres. OAS Perm. Council's Comm. of Juridical and Political Matters 1989, Pres. OAS Perm. Council 1990; Dir Diplomatic Law Advisory Council, Ministry of Foreign Affairs 1985–88; Prof. of Int. Pvt. Law, Int. Law Acad., The Hague; Prof. of Int. Pvt. Law, Catholic Univ. of Uruguay 1994; Minister of the Interior 1995–98, of Foreign Affairs 1998, 2000–05; Sec.-Gen., Latin-American Integration Asscn (Asociación Latinoamericana de Integración—ALADI) 2005–08; Pres. 53rd Session of UN Gen. Ass. 1998–2000; Special Counsellor for MERCOSUR issues to IDB and Inst. for Integration of Latin America and the Caribbean 1993–94; mem. UN Law Comm.; fmr mem. Uruguayan Nat. Group of Perm. Court of Arbitration; Founder and Bd mem. Int. Law Asscn of Uruguay; mem. and Dir Uruguayan Comparative Law Inst.; mem. Lawyers Asscn of Uruguay, Portuguese-Spanish American Int. Law Inst., Int. Law Asscn of Argentina, Int. and Comparative Law Acad. of Brazil.

Address: c/o Asociación Latinoamericana de Integración, Cebollati 1461, Casilla 577, CP 11200, Montevideo, Uruguay. *Telephone:* (2) 410-1121.

ORANGE, The Prince of; Willem-Alexander Claus George Ferdinand, MA; Dutch; b. 27 April 1967, Utrecht; m. Máxima Zorreguieta 2002; three d. *Education:* Baarns Lyceum, Eerste Vrijzinnig Christelijk Lyceum, The Hague, Atlantic Coll. Llantwit Major, Wales, Leiden Univ. *Career:* mil. service in Royal Netherlands Navy 1985–87, gained Mil. Pilot's Licence 1993, attended Netherlands Defence Coll. 1994, currently holds ranks of Commodore Navy Reserve and Air Force Reserve, Brig.-Gen. Army Reserve and Royal Mil. Constabulary Reserve, Aide-de-Camp Extra-ordinary to HM The Queen; Patron Global Water Partnership 1998; fully-qualified pvt, commercial and airline pilot, volunteer pilot African Medical Research and Educ. Foundation 1989, Kenya Wildlife Service 1991; mem. founding cttee World Water Vision 1999–2000; Chair. Second World Water Forum, The Hague 2000; mem. Panel of Eminent Persons, UN conf. on sustainable devt, Johannesburg 2002; Chair. Integrated Water Man. Comm. 2002–04; Chair. Water Advisory Cttee 2004–; mem. IOC 1998–; Patron Orange Fund; hon. mem. Royal Naval Yacht Club, Royal Dutch Yachting and Rowing Asscn; Officers' Long Service Decoration 2001. *Address:* Noordeinde Palace, Postbus 30412, The Hague 2500 GK, The Netherlands (office). *Website:* www.koninklijkhuis.nl.

ORAZMUKHAMEDOV, Nury Orazovich; Turkmenistan politician and diplomatist; b. 1949, Mary. *Education:* Turkmenistan Polytech. Inst. *Career:* master, engineer, chief engineer Turkmencentrstroi 1971–; head Ashkhabad construction units; Deputy Chair. State Construction Cttee 1990–91; Minister of Construction of Turkmenistan 1991–94; Minister of Construction and Architecture 1994–95; Head of Admin. Khikim Ashkhabad Feb. 1995; Amb. to Russian Fed. 1996–2000, to Moldova 2000. *Address:* c/o Ministry of Foreign Affairs, Ashgabat, Turkmenistan (office).

ORAZOV, Meret Bayramovich, DPhysMathSci, PhD; Turkmenistan diplomatist, politician and academic; *Ambassador to USA;* b. 1951. *Education:* Moscow State Univ., St Petersburg Univ. of Econs and Finance, Russia. *Career:* several academic and govt positions 1983–92, including Asst Prof., Rector and Dean of Int. Relations Dept, Magtymguly Turkmen State Univ. (est. Jt Programme with Texas A&M Univ. Faculty of Business and Man. 1998); fmr Minister for Foreign Econ. Relations and Vice-Prime Minister; Amb. to USA 2001–; est. in-service training for personnel in econ. and man. with EU; est. research collaboration with univs and scientific centres in eight countries; Academician of Acad. of Sciences of Turkmenistan 1993–; numerous prizes and awards for work in science and tech. *Publications include:* more than 120 scientific papers on math. and econs; five treatises on econs. *Address:* Embassy of Turkmenistan, 2207 Massachusetts Avenue, NW, Washington, DC 20008, USA (office). *Telephone:* (202) 588-1500 (office). *Fax:* (202) 588-0697 (office). *Website:* www.turkmenistanembassy.org (office).

ORDWAY, John M., BA, MA; American diplomatist; *Ambassador to Kazakhstan;* b. Calif.; m. Maryjo Ordway; one s. one d. *Education:* Stanford Univ.; studied for nine months in Florence, Italy; Hastings Coll. of Law, Univ. of California, Univ. of California, Berkeley. *Career:* career mem. Sr Foreign Service since 1975, rank of Minister-Counselor, served in Embassies in Prague 1978–81, Moscow 1985–87, US Mission to NATO, Brussels 1993–95, posted to Moscow 1996–2001, Deputy Chief of Mission, Moscow 1999–2001, worked in State Dept's Press Office, Office of Southern African Affairs and twice in Office of Soviet Union Affairs, Washington, DC, twice served as Dir African Affairs for Nat. Security Council, Amb. to Armenia 2001–04, to Kazakhstan 2004–; Chair. Anglo-American School Bd, Moscow 1996–2001. *Address:* US Embassy, Ak Bulak 4, Str. 23-22, Building #3, Astana 010010, Kazakhstan (office). *Telephone:* (7172) 70-21-00 (office). *Fax:* (7172) 34-08-90 (office). *E-mail:* info@usembassy.kz (office). *Website:* kazakhstan .usembassy.gov (office).

ORDZHONIKIDZE, Sergei Alexandrovitch; Russian diplomatist and UN official; *Director-General, United Nations, Geneva;* b. 14 March 1946, Moscow; m.; two s. *Education:* Moscow State Inst. of Int. Relations, Diplomatic Acad., Moscow. *Career:* mem. staff USSR Ministry of Foreign Affairs –1991; Deputy Perm. Rep. to UN, New York 1991–96; Head Dept of Int. Orgs, Ministry of Foreign Affairs 1996–99, Deputy Minister of Foreign Affairs 1999–2002; Under-Sec.-Gen. UN and Dir-Gen. UN Office, Geneva 2002–, Sec. Gen., Conf. on Disarmament and Personal Rep. of Sec.-Gen. to the Conf.; numerous state awards. *Publications:* numerous publs on int. and legal affairs, in particular on UN problems. *Address:* United Nations Office at Geneva, Palais des Nations, 1211 Geneva 10, Switzerland (office). *Telephone:* (22) 9172100 (office). *Fax:* (22) 9170002 (office). *Website:* www.unog.ch (office).

ORELLANA MERCADO, Angel Edmundo, DJur; Honduran diplomatist and legal executive; *Minister of Foreign Affairs;* b. 20 Oct. 1948, Honduras; m. *Education:* Universidad Autónoma de Honduras, Univ. of Bologna, Italy. *Career:* Asst to Legal Counsel of Nat. Housing Inst. 1968; Legal Counsel of Tech. Secr. of Council for Econ. Planning 1976–79; Dir Honduran Pre-Investment Fund 1980–84; Dir-Gen. Admin. Reform of the State Secr. for Planning, Co-ordination and Budget 1985–88; Pty Magistrate of Court of Appeals, Admin. Jurisdiction 1989–94; Attorney-Gen. 1994–99; Perm. Rep. to UN, New York 1999–; mem. Faculty of Law and Social Sciences, Universidad Nacional Autónoma de Honduras 1976–; Hon. Consul in Genoa, Italy 1974–75; mem. Admin. Law Comm., Honduran Bar Asscn 1980–91; Vice-Chair. for Co-ordination, Comm. on Judicial Reform 1988–93; Co-ordinator Cttee on Admin. Oversight of the Judiciary 1988–93; Minister of the Interior 2007–08, for Foreign Affairs 2008–. *Publications include:* numerous articles and books; participated in promulgation of several bills. *Address:* Ministry of Foreign Affairs, Centro Cívico Gubernamental, Antigua Casa Presidencial, Boulevard Kuwait, Contiguo a la Corte Suprema de Justicia, Tegucigalpa, Honduras (office). *Telephone:* 234-1962 (office). *Fax:* 234-1484 (office). *Website:* www.sre.hn (office).

ORESHARSKI, Plamen, PhD; Bulgarian politician; *Minister of Finance;* b. 21 Feb. 1960, Dupnitsa; m. *Education:* Univ. of Nat. and World Economy. *Career:* Vice-Dean Finance Dept, Univ. of Nat. and World Economy 1992–93, Vice-Chancellor and Prof., Teaching on Finance Man., Invest-ments, Investment Analysis 2003–; Dir State Treasury and Debt Directorate, Ministry of Finance 1993–97, Deputy Minister 1997–2001, Minister of Finance 2005–; Pres. Man. Bd Sofiabank 1996–96; mem. Man. Bd Bulgarian Stock Exchange 1995–99, State Saving Bank 1996–97, Bulbank 1997–2000, Bulgarian Consolidation Co. 1997–2000; mem. Union of Democratic Forces (UDF), Deputy Chair. and mem. UDF Nat. Exec. Bd –2003 (resgnd), UDF nominee for Mayor of Sofia at 2003 elections, candidature withdrawn; Emerging Markets magazine Finance Minister of the Year Award 2007. *Publications:* Investment Analysis, Finance; more than 100 articles, reviews and comments. *Address:* Ministry of Finance, 1000 Sofia, ul. G.S. Rakovski 102, Bulgaria (office). *Telephone:* (2) 985-920-00 (office). *Fax:* (2) 987-05-81 (office). *E-mail:* feedback@minfin.bg (office). *Website:* www.minfin.bg (office).

O'RIORDAN, Timothy, MA, PhD, FRSA, FBA; British academic; *Professor of Environmental Sciences, University of East Anglia;* b. 21 Feb. 1942, Edinburgh; m. Ann Philip 1968 (died 1992); two d. *Education:* Univs of Edinburgh and Cambridge, Cornell Univ., USA. *Career:* Asst Prof., Dept of Geography, Simon Fraser Univ. Vancouver, BC 1967–74; Visiting Lecturer, Univ. of Canterbury, New Zealand 1970; Visiting Assoc. Prof., Clark Univ., Worcester, Mass. 1972; Reader, Univ. of East Anglia 1974, Prof. of Environmental Sciences 1980–; Chair. Environment Cttee Broads Authority 1989–, Environment Science and Soc. Programme, European Science Foundation 1989–; Adviser, Environmental Research Directorate 1996–97; Trustee, Soil Asscn 2005–; mem. Environmental Advisory Council, Dow Chemical 1992–, Eastern Group PLC 1995–; Fellow, British Acad. 1999; mem. UK Sustainable Devt Comm. 2000–06; DL, Co. of Norfolk 1998; Gill Memorial Prize, Royal Geographical Soc. *Publications:* Environmentalism 1976, Countryside Conflicts 1986, Sizewell B: An Anatomy of the Inquiry 1987, The Greening of the Machinery of Government 1990; ed. Interpreting the Precautionary Principle 1994, The Politics of Climate Change in Europe 1996, Ecotaxation 1996, The Transition to Sustainability in Europe 1998, Environmental Science for Environmental Management 2000, Globalism, Localism and Identity 2001, Reinterpreting the Precautionary Principle 2001, Biodiversity, Sustain-ability and Human Communities 2002. *Address:* School of Environmental Sciences, University of East Anglia, Norwich, NR4 7TJ, England (office). *Telephone:* (1603) 810534. *Fax:* (1603) 593739. *E-mail:* t.oriordan@uea.ac.uk (office). *Website:* www.uea .ac.uk/env (office).

ORITA, Masaki, LLB; Japanese diplomatist; *Special Envoy (Europe) for United Nations Reform, Ministry of Foreign Affairs;* b. 29 July 1942, Tokyo; m. Masako Orita; one s. *Education:* Univ. of Tokyo, St Catherine's Coll., Oxford, UK. *Career:* diplomatic postings to UK 1967, USSR 1975–77, OECD, Paris 1977–79, Washington, DC 1984–87; Exec. Asst to Prime Minister 1989–1992; Consul-Gen., Hong Kong 1992–94, Dir Gen. Treaties Bureau and N American Affairs Bureau, Ministry of Foreign Affairs 1994–97, Amb. to Denmark 1997–2001, Insp. Gen., Ministry of Foreign Affairs 2001, Amb. to UK 2001–04, Special Envoy (Europe) for UN Reform, Ministry of Foreign Affairs 2005–; Commdr, Order of Orange (Netherlands) 1991; Grand Cross, Order of the Dannebrog (Denmark) 1998.

Address: Ministry of Foreign Affairs, Kasumigaseki 2-2-1, Chiyoda-ku, Tokyo 100-8919, Japan (office). *Telephone:* (3) 3580-3311 (office). *Website:* www.mofa.go.jp (office).

ORLOV, Vladimir A.; Russian defence analyst; *Director, Centre for Policy Studies (PIR), Moscow; Education:* Moscow State Inst. for Int. Relations (MGIMO). *Career:* Vice-Pres., Dir and Head of Dept, Moscow News 1990–96; Visiting Scholar and Sr Research Assoc. Center for Nonproliferation Studies, Monterey Inst. of Int. Studies, Calif. 1994, 2001–02; Consultant, UN 2001–02; Founder and Dir Centre for Policy Studies (PIR), Moscow; Prof., Moscow Eng. Physics Inst. (MEPI); mem. faculty, Geneva Center for Security Policy 2004–; Visiting Lecturer, St Petersburg State Univ., Tomsk Polytechnic Univ., Nizhni Novgorod State Univ., Tehran Univ., Acad. OSCE, Bishkek; Co-ed. Yaderny Kontrol (Nuclear Control); regular contrib. to Russia in Global Affairs, Bulletin of Atomic Scientists, Pro et Contra; mem. Inst. of Nuclear Materials Man., IISS, Russian Pugwash Cttee. *Publications:* Export Controls: Policies and Practices 2000, Nuclear Nonproliferation 2002; numerous journal articles and book chapters.
Address: PIR Center, Moscow 123001, Trekhprudny Pereulok 9, Bldg 1, office 025, Russia (office). *Telephone:* (495) 234-0525 (office). *Fax:* (495) 234-9558 (office). *E-mail:* orlov@pircenter.org (office). *Website:* www.pircenter.org (office).

ORREGO VICUÑA, Francisco, PhD; Chilean lawyer and professor; *Professor of International Law, University of Chile;* b. 12 April 1942, Santiago; m. Soledad Bauza; three c. *Education:* schools in Chile, Argentina, Spain and Egypt, Univ. of Chile and London School of Econs. *Career:* fmr Dir Inst. of Int. Studies Univ. of Chile; fmr Visiting Prof., Stanford Univ., Univ. of Paris II Law School, Univ. of Miami Law School; participated in projects for Acad. of Int. Law, The Hague, UNITAR and various studies and projects undertaken by univs in Europe, USA, Asia and Latin America; fmr legal adviser to OAS; fmr del. to Law of Sea Conf.; fmr int. corresp., El Mercurio (daily newspaper); Amb. to UK 1983–85; Prof. of Int. Law, Inst. of Int. Studies, Law School, Univ. of Chile 1985–; Pres. Chilean Council on Foreign Relations 1989–2000, Chilean Acad. of Social Sciences 1995–2000; mem. Chilean-US Comm. for Settlement of Disputes; mem. Advisory Cttee on Foreign Policy, Ministry of Foreign Affairs; Conciliator and Arbitrator of ICSID 1995–; Judge and Vice-Pres. Admin. Tribunal of IBRD, Pres. 2001–2004; Commr UN Compensation Comm. 1998–2000; Arbitrator Int. Chamber of Commerce, London Court of Int. Arbitration; mem. Inst. of Int. Law; arbitrator, 20 Essex Street Chambers (Barristers), London; Nat. Award for the Humanities and Social Sciences 2001, Medal of Merit, Univ. of Heidelberg. *Publications:* Antarctic Resources Policy 1983, Antarctic Mineral Exploitation 1988, The Exclusive Economic Zone 1989, The Changing International Law of High Seas Fisheries 1999, International Dispute Settlement in a Global 2004, and other books and articles.
Address: Francisco Orrego Vicuña y Cia., Avenida El Golf No. 40, Sixth Floor, Santiago 755-0107, Chile (office). *Telephone:* (2) 4416326 (office). *Fax:* (2) 4416399 (office). *E-mail:* forrego@uchile.cl (office). *Website:* francisco.orrego.googlepages.com.

ORTEGA, Cristina, BS, MA; Philippine diplomatist; *Ambassador to Belgium, Luxembourg and the European Union;* b. 5 Nov. 1948, Quezon City, Metro Manila. *Education:* Univ. of the Philippines, Univ. of Southern Calif., USA. *Career:* joined Dept of Trade and Industry 1972; Commercial Analyst, then Commercial Attaché, Embassy in Paris 1972–78; Foreign Trade Rep., then Special Trade Rep., Consulate-Gen. in LA 1978–84, Embassy in Paris 1984–86, Embassy in Brussels 1988–91; Head Foreign Trade Service Corps, Dept of Trade and Industry 1986–88; joined Dept of Foreign Affairs 1991; Head Econ. Diplomacy Unit and Special Asst to Sec. of Foreign Affairs 1993–94; Minister Counsellor, Consulate-Gen. in NY 1994–97, Embassy in Beijing 1997–99; Minister Counsellor, then Deputy Consul-Gen. in LA 1999–2001; Exec. Dir, then Asst Sec., Office for American Affairs 2001–03; Amb. to Australia (accred. to Nauru, Tuvalu and Vanuatu) 2003–06, to Belgium, Luxembourg and the EU 2006–; Presidential Award for Outstanding Foreign Service (Gawad Mabini Award) 1994.
Address: Embassy and Mission of the Philippines, 297 Avenue Moliere, Brussels 1050, Belgium (office). *Telephone:* (2) 340-33-77 (office). *Fax:* (2) 345-64-25 (office). *E-mail:* brusselspe@philembassy.be (office). *Website:* www.dfa.gov.ph (office).

ORTEGA SAAVEDRA, José Daniel; Nicaraguan politician and fmr resistance leader and head of state; *President;* b. 11 Nov. 1945, La Libertad, Chontales; m. Rosario Murillo; seven c. *Education:* Univ. Centroamericano, Managua. *Career:* joined Frente Sandinista 1963; active in various underground resistance movts against regime of Anastasio Somoza from 1959 and was several times imprisoned and tortured for revolutionary activities; ed. El Estudiante, official publ of Frente Estudiantil Revolucionaria and directed org. of Comités Cívicos Populares in Managua 1965; mem. Nat. Directorate of FSLN (Sandinista Liberation Front) 1966–67; imprisoned 1967–74; resumed position with FSLN and with José Benito Escobar became involved in further revolutionary activities; fought on front in two-year mil. offensive which overthrew Somoza regime 1979; mem. Junta of Nat. Reconstruction Govt 1979, Co-ordinator of Junta 1981–85, Pres. of Nicaragua 1985–90, 2006–; presidential cand. 2001; Gen. Sec. FSLN.
Address: c/o Oficina del Presidente, Managua, Nicaragua. *Telephone:* (2) 28-9090. *E-mail:* Presidente@presidencia.gob.ni (office). *Website:* www.presidencia.gob.ni (office).

ORTIZ DE LA CADENA, Fausto, MBA; Ecuadorean economist and government official. *Education:* Universidad Católica de Guayaquil. *Career:* served as State Treasurer 2005, Sub-Sec. of Public Credit 2005; Deputy Minister of Economy 2005–07, Minister of the Economy and Finance 2007–08 (resgnd); mem. Alianza País.
Address: Alianza País, Of. 501, Edif. Torres Whimper, Diego de Almagro 32-27 y Whimper, Quito, Ecuador (office). *Telephone:* (2) 600-0630 (office). *Fax:* (2) 600-1029 (office). *E-mail:* info@rafaelcorrea.com (office). *Website:* www.rafaelcorrea.com (office).

ORTIZ DE ROZAS, Carlos; Argentine diplomatist, lawyer and academic; *Professor of International Relations, University of Belgrano;* b. 26 April 1926, Buenos Aires; m. Carmen Sarobe 1952. *Education:* Univ. de Buenos Aires School of Diplomacy. *Career:* entered foreign service 1948; Chargé d'Affaires, Bulgaria 1952–54; Sec. Greece 1954–56; mem. Cabinet, Argentine Ministry of Foreign Affairs 1958–59; Counsellor, Argentine Mission at UN 1959–61; subsequently Dir-Gen. Policy Dept, Ministry of Foreign Affairs and later Minister at embassies in UAR and UK; Amb. to Austria 1967–70; Chief Rep. to Conf. of Cttee on Disarmament, Geneva 1969 (Chair. of Cttee 1979); Perm. Rep. to UN 1970–77; Amb. to UK 1980–82, to France 1984–89, to USA 1991–93; Under-Sec. of State for Foreign Relations 1990; Head of Argentine Special Mission to Holy See 1982–83; Pres. UN Security Council 1971, 1972; mem. Advisory Bd to Sec.-Gen. on Disarmament 1978–92; Prof. of Int. Relations, Univ. of Belgrano, Buenos Aires 1995–; Dir and Pres. Del. of Conf. on Law of the Sea 1973; Chair. First (Political and Security) Cttee of the 29th General Ass. 1974; has held several teaching posts including Prof. of Public Law and Int. Relations, Univ. del Salvador, Buenos Aires (now mem. Bd Dirs); Pres. Bunge and Born Foundation 1994–99, Alliance Française de Buenos Aires 1999–2001; mem. Exec. Bd Argentine Council for Int. Relations 1994–; mem. Nat. Acad. of Social and Political Sciences, Buenos Aires 2005; decorations from Italy, Chile, Brazil, Greece, Japan, Peru, Thailand, Egypt, Austria, Nicaragua, the Republic of Korea, Spain, Holy See and France; Personality of the Year in Int. Relations, Rotary Club, Buenos Aires 1995. *Publications:* Paths to Peace – The UN Security Council and its Presidency 1981, La reunion de Palm Beach – J.F. Kennedy – A. Frondizi 1994, Contribuciones Argentinas a las Naciones Unidas 1995.
Address: Avenida Gelly y Obes 2263, 1425 Buenos Aires, Argentina (home). *Telephone:* (11) 4803-3630 (home). *Fax:* (11) 4804-6791 (home). *E-mail:* corzas@yahoo.com (home).

ORTIZ DE ZEVALLOS MADUEÑO, Felipe, BA, MA; Peruvian economist, academic, business executive and diplomatist; *Ambassador to USA;* b. Aug. 1947, Lima. *Education:* Universidad Nacional de Ingeniería, Lima, Univ. of Rochester, New York and Owner-Pres. Man. Program, Harvard Business School, USA. *Career:* worked as consulting engineer in Peru 1970–77; f. APOYO (consultancy and publishing firm) 1977, currently Chair. Grupo APOYO; ind. mem. of Bd of several businesses, educational and cultural insts, including Buenaventura Mining Co., Credicorp; Chair. Eisenhower Fellowship's Nominating Cttee Peru, mem. Eisenhower Fellowship's Advisory Int. Council; Founder and Dir Inst. of Econ. Devt, ESAN (Grad. School of Business Admin), Lima 1979–1982; Chair. Nat. Corpn of Devt (CONADE) and Inversiones Cofide (holding cos of all state-owned enterprises) 1982; Pres. Annual Conf. of Execs 1985; Visiting Scholar, Inst. of Latin American Studies, Univ. of Texas, Austin, USA 1983, 1984; Prof., Econs Dept, Universidad del Pacifico 1978–, Pres. Universidad del Pacífico –2006; guest columnist in magazines; Amb. to USA 2006–; Instituto Peruano de Administracion de Empresas Award 1990, Eisenhower Exchange Fellowship 1996, Jerusalem Award of Journalism 1998. *Publications:* The Peruvian Puzzle 1989, Respuestas para los 90s (Answers to the 90s) (with Pedro Pablo Kuczynski) 1990, In the Shadow of the Debt (co-author) 1992, A Mitad de Camino (Half Way Through) 1992, El Reto 2001: Competir y Crear Empleo (The 2001 Challenge: Compete and Create Employment) (with Pedro Pablo Kuczynski) 2001; numerous articles in nat. and int. journals.
Address: Embassy of Peru, 1700 Massachusetts Avenue, NW, Washington, DC 20036, USA (office). *Telephone:* (202) 261-0271 (office); (202) 463-8125

(office); (202) 833-9860 (office). *Fax:* (202) 659-8124 (office). *E-mail:* ccampana@embassyofperu.us (office). *Website:* www.peruvianembassy.us (office).

ORTMANN, Gunnar, CandPol; Danish diplomatist; *Ambassador to Italy;* b. July 1947, Copenhagen; m. Anne Lise Ortmann; two c. *Education:* Univ. of Copenhagen. *Career:* joined Ministry of Foreign Affairs 1975, Head of Section 1979, Head of Div. 1988, Under-Sec. for EC Questions 1992, State Sec., Amb., Head of the North Group 1997; Sec., Embassy in Saudi Arabia 1976; Counsellor Embassy in W Germany 1984; Amb. to Sweden 1995, to Germany 2001–05, Amb. to Austria (also accred as Perm. Rep. to UN, Vienna, UNIDO and as Amb. to Former Yugoslav Repub. of Macedonia) 2005, to Italy (also accred to Malta) 2006–; Commdr of the Dannebrog Order; Grand Cross of FRG; Swedish North Star Order. *Address:* Embassy of Denmark, Via dei Monti Parioli 50, 00197 Rome, Italy (office). *Telephone:* (06) 9774831 (office). *Fax:* (06) 97748399 (office). *E-mail:* romamb@um.dk (office). *Website:* www.ambrom.um.dk (office).

ORTONA, Ludovico; Italian diplomatist; *Ambassador to France;* b. 11 Feb. 1942, Zara; m., three c. *Education:* Univ. of Rome. *Career:* joined diplomatic service 1967, posted to European Office, Directorate-Gen. of Foreign Affairs, posted to Secr. 1968, apptd Attaché 1968, Sec. 1970, First Sec. 1972, Counsellor 1977, Chief of Press Office 1977–79, posted to Office of Int. Affairs, Chairmanship of Cabinet 1979–82, Chief of Press Service, Secr.-Gen. of Pres. 1985–88, apptd Special Envoy, Second Class 1988, First Class 1992, Minister Plenipotentiary to Directorate-Gen. of Personnel 2000, Dir-Gen. for Americas 2000–04; overseas posts include Second Sec. Embassy in Mexico 1969, Consul in Montreal, Canada 1972, First Sec. Perm. Mission to Int. Orgs, Geneva 1974–77, First Counsellor Embassy in Washington, DC 1982–85, Amb. to Portugal 1992–95, Iran 1995–2000, France 2005–; Grand Officer Order of Merit (Italy), Commandeur de l'Ordre National du Mérite (France). *Address:* Embassy of Italy, 51 rue de Varenne, 75343 Paris Cedex 07, France (office). *Telephone:* 1-49-54-03-00 (office). *Fax:* 1-45-54-04-10 (office). *E-mail:* ambasciata.parigi@esteri.it (office). *Website:* www.ambparigi.esteri.it (office).

OSBORNE, Christopher Wyndham; British diplomatist; *Ambassador to Mongolia;* b. 18 June 1946; pnr Emma Pinnell; three s. *Career:* Attaché, Lusaka 1968–70, Kampala 1970–73, Third Sec. (Consular), Bridgetown 1973–76, Desk Officer for the Falkland Islands, FCO 1976–79, Second Sec. (Political), Dacca 1979–81, Second Sec. (Commercial), Caracas 1982–85, Press Officer, FCO 1986–89, First Sec., Press and Public Affairs, Hong Kong 1989–94, Non-Proliferation Dept, FCO 1994–96, Hong Kong 1996–97, Deputy Head of Mission, Luanda 1998-2000, Deputy Head of Protocol and Asst Marshal of the Diplomatic Corps, FCO 2001–05, Amb. to Mongolia 2006–. *Address:* British Embassy, Enkh Taivny Gudamj 30, CPO Box 703, Ulan Bator 13, Mongolia (office). *Telephone:* (11) 458133 (office). *Fax:* (11) 458036 (office). *E-mail:* britemb@mongol.net (office).

OSEI-ADJEI, Akwasi, MSc; Ghanaian politician; *Minister of Foreign Affairs, Regional Integration and New Partnership for Africa's Development (NEPAD);* b. 29 Dec. 1949, Onwe, Ashanti Region; m.; five c. *Education:* De Montfort Univ., UK. *Career:* trained and qualified as an ccountant, worked at Ozze Ghana Ltd; mem. Parl. for Ejisu/Juabeng constituency; fmr Deputy Minister of Foreign Affairs, Regional Integration and New Partnership for Africa's Devt (NEPAD), Minister of Foreign Affairs, Regional Integration and NEPAD 2007–; mem. New Patriotic Party. *Address:* Ministry of Foreign Affairs, Regional Integration and NEPAD, Treasury Road, POB M53, Accra, Ghana (office). *Telephone:* (21) 664951 (office). *Fax:* (21) 680017 (office). *E-mail:* ghmaf00@ghana.com (office).

OSHIMA, Kenzo; Japanese diplomatist; b. 1943. *Education:* Tokyo Univ. *Career:* served in diplomatic posts in Australia, France, India, USA and at Perm. Mission to UN; Dir-Gen. Econ. Co-operation Bureau, Ministry of Foreign Affairs; Sec.-Gen. Secr. for Int. Peace Co-operation HQ, Office of the Prime Minister –2000; UN Under-Sec.-Gen. for Humanitarian Affairs and Emergency Relief Co-ordinator 2001–03; Amb. to Australia 2003; Perm. Rep. to UN 2004–07; Senior Vice Pres. Japan Int. Cooperation Agency 2007–. *Address:* Japan International Cooperation Agency, 6th–13th floors, Shinjuku Maynds Tower 2-1-1 Yoyogi, Shibuya-ku, Tokyo 151-8558, Japan (office). *Telephone:* (3) 5352-5311 (office). *Website:* www.jica.go.jp (office).

OSHIMA, Shotaro; Japanese diplomatist; *Ambassador to South Korea;* b. 20 Sept. 1943. *Education:* Univ. of Tokyo. *Career:* joined Ministry of Foreign Affairs 1968; fmr positions include Foreign Service Officer, First Sec., Embassy in Washington DC, Counsellor, Embassy in Israel; Dir in charge

of First SE Asia Div., Asian Affairs Bureau, Ministry of Foreign Affairs 1985–87, Dir of Policy Planning Div., Information Analysis-Research-Planning Bureau 1987–89, Dir of Overseas Establishment Div. 1989–91; Minister, Embassy in Moscow 1991–94, Embassy in Washington, DC 1994–97; Dir-Gen., Econ. Affairs Bureau 1997–2000; Amb. to Saudi Arabia 2000–01; Deputy Minister for Foreign Affairs, Ministry of Foreign Affairs 2001–02; Perm. Rep. to UN, Geneva 2002–05; Amb. to South Korea 2005–07; mem. Appellate Body, WTO 2008–. *Address:* World Trade Organization, rue de Lausanne 154, 1211 Geneva, Switzerland (office). *Telephone:* 227395111 (office). *Fax:* 227314206 (office). *E-mail:* enquiries@wto.org (office). *Website:* www.wto.org (office).

OSHO, Pierre, MA; Benin politician; b. 5 May 1945, Porto Novo; m.; six c. *Education:* Acad. of Grenoble, Univ. of Dakar, Univ. of Aix-en-Provence, France. *Career:* Prof. of History and Geography, Coll. Père Aupiais, Cotonou 1968–70, Coll. d'Enseignement Moyen Général de Gbégamey, Cotonou 1970–73; Dir of Information and Propaganda (MISON) 1976–78; mem. Cen. Cttee, Party of Popular Revolution (PRPB) 1979–90; Chief of Dist of Klouékanmey, Prov. of Mono 1978–84; Peoples' Commr, Nat. Ass. 1980–90; Pres. Comm. on Govt and Ass. Relations 1980–84; Dir Nat. Centre of Revolutionary Educ. 1982–84; Sec.-Gen. Perm. Cttee of Nat. Ass. 1984–89; Pres. Comm. on Constitutional Affairs 1989–90; Dir Cabinet of Pres. of Benin 1989–91; with Dept of Research of Human and Social Sciences 1991–96; Minister of Foreign Affairs and Cooperation 1996–98; Minister to Pres. of Benin 1998–2001; Minister of Nat. Defence 2001–06 (resgnd); del. to int. and multilateral confs. *Address:* c/o Ministry of National Defence, BP 2493 Cotonou, Benin (office).

OSKANIAN, Vardan, BS, MSc, MA; Armenian diplomatist; *Minister of Foreign Affairs;* b. 7 Feb. 1955, Syria; m. Dr Nani Oskanian; two s. *Education:* Yerevan Polytechnic Inst., Tufts Univ., Mass, Harvard Univ., Fletcher School of Law and Diplomacy, USA. *Career:* Founder and Ed. Armenian Int. Magazine 1990; on staff, Armenian Ministry of Foreign Affairs 1992–; Deputy Head, Middle East Dept, Head, Dept of N America 1992–94; prin. negotiator in Misk process on Nagorno-Karabakh conflict 1994–97; Visiting Asst Prof. of Int. Relations, American Univ. of Armenia 1994–96; Deputy Foreign Minister 1994–96, First Deputy Foreign Minister 1996–98, Minister of Foreign Affairs 1998–. *Address:* Ministry of Foreign Affairs, 0010 Yerevan, Republic Sq., Govt House 2, Armenia (office). *Telephone:* (10) 52-35-31 (office). *Fax:* (10) 54-39-25 (office). *E-mail:* oskanian@mfa.am (office). *Website:* www.armeniaforeignministry.com (office).

OSORIO ISAZA, Luis Camilo, LLB, PhD; Colombian professor of law, lawyer and diplomatist; *Ambassador to Mexico;* b. 11 Nov. 1943, Medellín; m.; three c. *Education:* Javeriana Univ., Friedrich Wilherm Univ., Germany. *Career:* Under-Sec. for Educ., Dept of Cundinamarca 1969; Tech. Officer Nat. Dept of Planning 1969–70; Econ. Adviser, Embassy in Germany 1970–74; Prof. of Admin Law, Javeriana Univ. 1970, 1975–76, 1995–2000; Prof. of Public Admin Law, Jorge Tadeo Lozano Univ. 1975–77; Dist Attorney, Medellín 1982–86; Vice-Minister for Educ. 1983; Exec. Dir Nat. Asscn of Commercial Consortiums 1986–87; Registrar, Nat. Office of Registration 1991–94; Titular Prof. Universidad Externado de Colombia 1992–2001; Prof. of Constitutional Law, Univ. of the Andes 1995; Visiting Prof. of Law, Univ. Libre Seccional Pereira, Univ. Libre Seccional Barranquilla, Univ. of Sinú, Univ. of Medellín 1996–2000; Attorney Gen. 2001–05; Chair. Ibero-American Asscn of Public and Fiscal Ministries 2002–04; Amb. to Italy (also accred to Greece, Malta, Cyprus and San Marino) 2005–06, to Mexico 2006–; Chair. Bd of Dirs Nat. Univ. of Colombia 1983, Sociedad Electra SA 1991; mem. Bd of Dirs Social Security Inst. (ISS) 1982–87, Univ. Estatal del Sur 1983–86, Supernova SA 1988–91, Ahorramás SA 1989–90, Sociedad Corluz SA 1991. *Address:* Embassy of Colombia, Paseo de la Reforma 379, 1°, 5° y 6°, Col. Cuauhtémoc, Del. Cuauhtémoc, 06500, Mexico (office). *Telephone:* (55) 5525-0277 (office). *Fax:* (55) 5208-2876 (office). *E-mail:* emcolmex@prodigy.net.mx (office). *Website:* www.colombiaenmexico.org (office).

OSPINA BERNAL, Camilo; Colombian government official and lawyer. *Education:* Colegio Mayor de Nuestra Señora del Rosario. *Career:* Vice-Dean Faculty of Law, Colegio Mayor de Nuestra Señora del Rosario 1990–91; Legal Adviser Ministry of Finance and Public Credit 1991–92, Sec.-Gen. Budget Directorate 1992–94; Consultant UNDP 1994–95; Legal Adviser to Pres. 2002–05; Minister of Nat. Defence 2005–06; Founding Pnr and mem. Soc. of Constitutional Rights, Sec. 1997–99. *Address:* c/o Ministry of National Defence, Centro Administrativo Nacional (CAN), 2°, Avda El Dorado, Santafé de Bogotá, Colombia (office).

OSSIO, Pablo; Bolivian diplomatist; m. Patricia Ossio. *Career:* Chargé d'affaires a.i. to UK –2006, Counsellor 2006–.
Address: Embassy of Bolivia, 106 Eaton Square, London, SW1W 9AD, England (office). *Telephone:* (20) 7235-4248 (office). *Fax:* (20) 7235-1286 (office). *E-mail:* possio@embolivia.co.uk (office). *Website:* www .embassyofbolivia.co.uk (office).

ØSTERGAARD-ANDERSEN, Hugo, LLM; Danish diplomatist; *Ambassador to Austria;* b. 1946. *Education:* Univ. of Copenhagen. *Career:* Head of Section, Ministry of Defence 1971–73; Head of Section, Ministry of Finance 1973–76; Head of Section, Danish Research Admin 1976–80; Head of Section, Ministry of Foreign Affairs 1980–82, 1985–88; Counsellor, Embassy in Nairobi 1982–85, Embassy in Vienna 1988–92; Head of Dept, Ministry of Foreign Affairs 1992–96; Amb. to Iran 1996–2001; Insp.-Gen., Ministry of Foreign Affairs 2001–04, Under-Sec. for Admin. Affairs 2004–07; Amb. to Austria 2007, also Perm. Rep. to UN, Vienna 2007–; mem. Bd of Dirs Nordic Devt Fund 1992–96; mem. Govt Council on Information Tech. 2004–.
Address: Embassy of Denmark, Führichgasse 6, 1010 Vienna, Austria (office). *Telephone:* (1) 512-79-04-0 (office). *Fax:* (1) 513-81-20 (office). *E-mail:* vieamb@um.dk (office). *Website:* www.ambwien.um.dk (office).

OSTRY, Sylvia, CC, PhD, FRSC; Canadian economist and academic; *Distinguished Research Fellow in International Studies, University of Toronto;* b. Winnipeg; m. Bernard Ostry; two s. *Education:* McGill Univ. and Univ. of Cambridge, UK. *Career:* Chief Statistician, Statistics Canada 1972–75; Deputy Minister of Consumer and Corp. Affairs and Deputy Registrar Gen. 1975–78; Chair. Econ. Council of Canada 1978–79; Head, Econ. and Statistics Dept, OECD 1979–83; Deputy Minister (Int. Trade) and Co-ordinator for Int. Econ. Relations, Dept of External Affairs 1984–85; Amb., Multilateral Trade Negotiations and Personal Rep. of the Prime Minister, Econ. Summit, Dept of External Affairs 1985–88; Per Jacobsson Foundation Lecture, Washington 1987; Sr Research Fellow, Univ. of Toronto 1989–90; Volvo Distinguished Visiting Fellow, Council on Foreign Relations, New York 1989; Chair. Centre for Int. Studies, Univ. of Toronto 1990–97, Distinguished Research Fellow 1997–; Chancellor, Univ. of Waterloo 1991–97; Western Co-Chair. Blue Ribbon Comm. for Hungary's Econ. Devt 1990–94; Chair. Council Canadian Inst. for Int. Affairs 1990–94; mem. Int. American Dialogue, Advisory Bd Inst. of Int. Econs, Washington, DC, Academic Advisory Council of Deputy Minister for Int. Trade; Founding mem. Pacific Council on Int. Policy; mem. several learned socs and professional orgs; Fellow American Statistical Asscn; Sylvia Ostry Foundation annual lecture series launched 1992; 19 hon. degrees; Outstanding Achievement Award, Govt of Canada 1987, Career Achievement Award, Canadian Policy Research 2000. *Publications include:* International Economic Policy Co-ordination (with Michael Artis) 1986, Governments and Corporations in a Shrinking World: The Search for Stability 1990, The Threat of Managed Trade to Transforming Economies 1993, Technonationalism and Technoglobalism: Conflict and Cooperation (with Richard Nelson) 1995, Rethinking Federalism: Citizens, Markets and Governments in a Changing World (jtly) 1995, The Halifax G7 Summit: Issues on the Table (ed. with Gilbert Winham) 1995, Who's On First? The Post Coldwar Trading System 1997, The Future of the World Trading System 1999, Convergence and Sovereignty: Policy Scope for Compromise 2000, Business, Trade and the Environment 2000, The Changing Scenario in International Governance 2000, The World Trading System: In Dire Need of Reform 2003, The WTO: Post Seattle and Chinese Accession (in China and the Long March to Global Trade) 2003, External Transparency: The Policy Process at the National Level of the Two-level Game (in Doha and Beyond: The Future of the Multilateral Trading System) 2004, Between Feast and Famine: Fixing Global Trade (in Feeding the Future From Fat to Famine: How to Solve the World's Food Crises) 2004, Summitry and Trade: What Could Sea Island Do for Doha? (in New Perspectives on Global Governance) 2005, Global Integration: Currents and Counter Currents (in The World Trade Organization: Legal, Economic and Political Analysis) 2005; articles on labour econs, demography, productivity, competition policy.
Address: Munk Centre for International Studies, University of Toronto, 1 Devonshire Place, Toronto, Ont., M5S 3K7, Canada (office). *Telephone:* (416) 946-8927 (office). *Fax:* (416) 946-8915 (office). *E-mail:* sylvia.ostry@ utoronto.ca (office). *Website:* www.utoronto.ca/cis/ostry (office).

O'SULLIVAN, David, BA; Irish international civil servant; *Director-General for Trade, European Commission;* b. 1 March 1953, Dublin; m. Agnes O'Hare; one s. one d. *Education:* Trinity Coll. Dublin, Collège d'Europe, Bruges. *Career:* Dept of Foreign Affairs, Dublin 1976–79; mem. staff External Relations, EC 1979–81, First Sec. (Econ. and Commercial), Del. of EC in Japan 1981–85; mem. Cabinet of Commr P. Sutherland 1985–89; Head of Unit (Educ. and Youth, Training) 1989–92; mem. Cabinet of Commr P. Flynn 1993–96, Deputy Head 1994–96; Dir Social Affairs,

European Social Fund 1996–98, Social Affairs, Man. of Resources 1998–99; Dir-Gen. DGXXII 1999; Head of Cabinet of Pres. of Comm. 1999–2000; Sec.-Gen. European Comm. 2000–05, Dir-Gen. Trade 2005–; Dr hc (Dublin Inst. of Tech.) 2005; European of the Year, Irish Council of the European Movt 1999.
Address: Directorate General for Trade, European Commission, 1049 Brussels (office); 87 rue Langeveld, 1180 Brussels, Belgium (home). *Telephone:* (2) 295-09-48 (office); (2) 372-32-55 (home). *Fax:* (2) 299-05-87 (office). *E-mail:* david.o'sullivan@ec.europa.eu (office). *Website:* ec .europa.eu/trade/index_en.htm (office).

OTA, Hiroko; Japanese economist, academic and government official; *Minister of State for Economic and Fiscal Policy;* b. 2 Feb. 1954. *Education:* Faculty of Social Sciences, Hitotsubashi Univ. *Career:* with Mikimoto Corpn 1976–81; Research Fellow, Japan Inst. of Life Insurance 1981–93; Guest Lectuer, Econs Dept, Osaka Univ. 1993–96; Assoc. Prof., Grad. School of Political Science, Saitama Univ. 1996–97; Assoc. Prof. Nat. Grad. Inst. for Policy Studies 1997–2001, Prof. of Econs 2001–; Dir of Policy Analysis, Cabinet Office 2002–03, Deputy Dir Gen. for Econ. Research 2003–04, Dir Gen. for Econ. Research 2004–05; Minister of State for Econ. and Fiscal Policy 2006–.
Address: Ministry of Economy, Trade and Industry, 1-3-1, Kasumigaseki, Chiyoda-ku, Tokyo 100-8901, Japan (office). *Telephone:* (3) 3501-1511 (office). *Fax:* (3) 3501-6942 (office). *E-mail:* webmail@meti.go.jp (office). *Website:* www.meti.go.jp (office).

OTAIBA, Yusuf Mana al-; United Arab Emirates diplomatist. *Career:* Amb. to USA 2008–.
Address: Embassy of the United Arab Emirates, 3522 International Court, NW, Suite 400, Washington, DC 20008, USA (office). *Telephone:* (202) 243-2400 (office). *Fax:* (202) 243-2595 (office). *E-mail:* info@uaeembassy -usa.org (office). *Website:* www.uae-embassy.org (office).

OTARI, Muhammad Naji al-; Syrian politician; *Prime Minister;* b. 1944, Aleppo. *Career:* Head of Aleppo City Council 1983–87; fmr Gov. of Hums; mem. Baath Party Central Cttee 2000–, mem. Regional Command 2000–; Deputy Prime Minister for Services Affairs 2000–03; Speaker of the People's Ass. (Parl.) 2003; Prime Minister of Syria 2003–.
Address: Office of the Prime Minister, rue Chahbandar, Damascus, Syria (office). *Telephone:* (11) 2226000 (office).

OTERO LANZAROTTI, Hugo; Peruvian diplomatist; *Ambassador to Chile;* *Career:* fmr publicist for Partido Aprista Peruano; fmr advisor to Pres. of Peru; fmr consultant to Minera Yanacocha (gold mining co.); Amb. to Chile 2006–.
Address: Embassy of Peru, Avda Andrés Bello 1751, Casilla, 16277 Providencia, Santiago, Chile (office). *Telephone:* (2) 235-2356 (office). *Fax:* (2) 235-8139 (office). *E-mail:* embstgo@entelchile.net (office).

OTTHUW, Félix Mumengui; Democratic Republic of the Congo diplomatist; *Ambassador to Republic of the Congo;* b. 18 Oct. 1936; five s. three d. *Education:* Institut des Sciences Economiques et Financières, Moscow, USSR. *Career:* Dir of Personnel, Ministry of the Economy 1985, Councillor 1998; Amb. to Repub. of the Congo (also accred to Gabon) 1999–; Founder and Pres. Asscn Internationale de Lutte Contre la Drogue et les Stupefiants (AICD) 1985–; Gold Medal, Institut des Sciences Economiques et Financières, Moscow. *Publication:* Le voyage de l'alcool dans le corps humain 1992.
Address: Embassy of the Democratic Republic of the Congo, Brazzaville, Republic of the Congo (office); BP 12482, Kin I, Kinshasa, Democratic Republic of the Congo. *Telephone:* 83-29-38 (office).

OTTONE, Ernesto, DPolSci; Chilean sociologist, academic and international organization official; *Deputy Executive Secretary, Economic Commission for Latin America and the Caribbean; Education:* Catholic Univ. of Valparaiso, Sorbonne Nouvelle, Paris III. *Career:* Sr Adviser to Pres. of Chile on Strategic Analysis 2000–06; Deputy Exec. Sec. ECLAC; Prof. of History of Latin America, European School of Advanced Studies; consultant to UNESCO and other int. orgs. *Publications include:* Rethinking Secondary Education (UNESCO) 1997, El gran eslabón: Educacion y desarrollo en el umbral del siglo XXI (with Martin Hopenhayn) 2000, La morernidad problemática 2000, Osadia de la prudencia 2004.
Address: Economic Commission for Latin America and the Caribbean, Edif. Naciones Unidas, Avda Dag Hammarskjöld, Casilla 179B, Santiago, Chile (office). *Telephone:* (2) 2102000 (office). *Fax:* (2) 2080252 (office). *E-mail:* secepal@eclac.cl (office). *Website:* www.eclac.org (office).

OTUNNU, Olara; Ugandan diplomatist and fmr United Nations official; *President, LBL Foundation for Children;* b. Sept. 1950, Mucwini, northern

Uganda; guardian of six c. *Education:* Makerere Univ., Univ. of Oxford, UK, Harvard Law School, USA. *Career:* practised law in USA; Asst Prof. of Law, Albany Law School, USA; participated in resistance activities against regime of Idi Amin; Perm. Rep. to UN 1980–85, Pres. Security Council 1981, Vice-Pres. Gen. Ass. 1982–83; Minister of Foreign Affairs 1985–86; Pres. Int. Peace Acad. 1990–97; Special Rep. of UN Sec.-Gen. for Children and Armed Conflict 1997–2005, UN Under-Sec.-Gen. for Children and Armed Conflict 1998–2005; Founder and Pres. LBL Foundation for Children, New York 2005–; mem. Bd of Dirs Carnegie Endowment for Int. Peace, Aspen Inst., Aspen France, Carnegie Corpn of New York; mem. Int. Selection Comm. of the Phila Liberty Medal, Jury for Hilton Humanitarian Prize; German Africa Prize 2002, Sydney Peace Prize 2005.
Address: c/o Carnegie Corporation of New York, 437 Madison Avenue, New York, NY 10022, USA (office).

OUALALOU, Fathallah, DèsSc; Moroccan economist and politician; b. 1942, Rabat; m.; four c. *Education:* Lycée Moulay Youssef, Univ. of Rabat, Univ. of Paris. *Career:* began career as Research Asst, Centre Universitaire de Recherche Scientifique, also Pres. Union Nationale des Etudiants (UNEM); Lecturer, Law Dept, Univs of Rabat, Casablanca and Ecole Nat. d'Admin 1968; mem. Groupe de Rabat; co-founder Socialist Union of Popular Forces (USFP) 1972, mem. Political Bureau 1989–, Leader Parl. Group 1984–98; Minister of Economy, Finance, Privatization and Tourism 1998–2002, of Finance and Privatization 2002–07; mem. Nat. Bureau, Syndicat Nat. de l'Enseignement Supérieur (SNESUP); co-founder Asscn des économistes marocains 1972, Pres. 1982–; Pres. Union des économistes Arabes; mem. Chambre des Représentants. *Publications:* numerous articles on econ. theory and Maghreb economies.
Address: Union socialiste des forces populaires (USFP), 9 ave al-Araâr, Hay Riad, Rabat, Morocco (office). *Telephone:* (3) 7565511 (office). *Fax:* (3) 7565510 (office). *E-mail:* webmaster@usfp.ma (office). *Website:* www .usfp.ma (office).

OUANE, Moktar, MA; Malian diplomatist; *Minister of Foreign Affairs and International Co-operation;* b. 11 Oct. 1955, Bidi; m.; two c. *Education:* Univ. of Dakar, Senegal. *Career:* with Gen. Secr. of Govt 1982–86, Chief Div. of Int. Agreements and Conventions, Foreign Ministry March–June 1986, Diplomatic Counsellor, Office of the Prime Minister 1986–88, Prin. Pvt. Sec. to Minister Sec.-Gen., Office of the Pres. and Diplomatic Counsellor to the Pres. 1988–91; mem. del. to UN Gen. Ass. 1988–91, 1993, mediation del., Senegal–Mauritania and Liberian conflicts; Diplomatic Counsellor, Office of the Head of State 1991–92, Office of the Prime Minister June–Oct. 1992, Tech. Counsellor, Political and Diplomatic Affairs, Foreign Ministry 1994–95; Perm. Rep. to the UN 1995–2004; Minister of Foreign Affairs May 2004–; Founder and Pres. Democracy and Repub. Club, Mali.
Address: Ministry of Foreign Affairs and International Co-operation, Koulouba, Bamako, Mali (office). *Telephone:* 222-83-14 (office). *Fax:* 222-52-26 (office). *E-mail:* info@maliensdelexterieur.gov.ml. *Website:* www .maliensdelexterieur.gov.ml.

OUCHI, Tsutomu, DEcon; Japanese professor of economics; *Emeritus Professor of Economics, University of Tokyo;* b. 19 June 1918, Tokyo; m. Setsuko Otsuka 1944; one s. one d. *Education:* The Daiichi Kotogakko and Tokyo Imperial Univ. *Career:* researcher Japan Inst. of Agric. 1942–46; Assoc. Prof. Univ. of Tokyo 1947–60, Prof. 1960–79, Prof. Emer. 1979–; Prof. Shinshu Univ. 1979–84, Prof. Emer. 1984–; Prof. Daito Bunka Univ. 1987–91; Dean Faculty of Econs, Univ. of Tokyo 1968–69; Vice-Pres. Univ. of Tokyo 1972–73; Dir Nat. Fed. of Univ. Co-operative Asscns 1988–99; Dir Nat. Fed. of Co-operatives of Aged People of Japan 2001–; Chair. Cen. Cttee for Security of Employment 1976–88, Employment Cttee, Ministry of Labour 1988–96; mem. Japan Acad. 1981–; Mainichi Press Prize, Nasu Prize, Nihon Keizai Press Prize. *Publications:* Agricultural Crisis 1954, American Agriculture 1965, State Monopolistic Capitalism 1970, American Agriculture in the 1960s 1975, Japanese Agriculture 1978, Methodology of Economics 1980, Principles of Economics (2 vols) 1981–82, Imperialism (2 vols) 1984–85, World Economy 1991, Japanese Economy 2000.
Address: 26-19 Hyakunin-cho II, Shinjuku-ku, Tokyo 169 0073, Japan. *Telephone:* (3) 3371-3760.

OUEDRAOGO, Ablassé, DEcon; Burkinabè international organization official; *Regional Adviser for Africa, African Development Bank;* b. 30 June 1953, Burkina Faso. *Education:* Univ. of Nice, France. *Career:* Deputy Resident Rep. of UNDP, Kinshasa 1991–93; Head of Regional Office for E Africa of UN Sudano-Sahélienne Office (also accred to OAU, ECA, UNEP) 1993–94; Minister of Foreign Affairs 1994–99; Special Adviser to Pres. of Burkina Faso 1999; Jt Deputy Dir-Gen. WTO 1999–2000; Regional Adviser for Africa, African Devt Bank 2006–; Officer of Nat. Order of Burkina Faso 1997; Officer of Equatorial Order of Gabon

2000. *Publications:* Réflexions sur la crise industrielle en France 1979, Les firmes multinationales et l'industrialisation des pays en voie de développe-ment 1981.
Address: African Development Bank, Rue Joseph Anoma 1, BP 1387, Abidjan 01, Cote d'Ivoire.

OUEDRAOGO, Kadré Désiré; Burkinabè politician, economist and banker; *Ambassador to the European Union;* m. Solange Ouedraogo. *Education:* Haute Ecole, Paris, Université Paris I (Sorbonne). *Career:* fmr Deputy Exec. Sec. ECOWAS in charge of Econ. Affairs; fmr Gov. of Cen. Bank of West African States; Prime Minister of Burkina Faso 1996–2000; currently Amb. to the EU (also accred to Belgium, Luxembourg, Netherlands and UK); Grand Officier de l'Ordre National du Burkina Faso 1996.
Address: Mission of Burkina Faso to the European Union, 16 place Guy d'Arezzo, 1180 Brussels, Belgium (office); 01 BP 3474, Ouagadougou 01, Burkina Faso (home). *Telephone:* (322) 3459912 (office). *Fax:* (322) 3450612 (office). *E-mail:* ambassade.burkina@skynet.be (office). *Website:* www.ambassadeduburkina.be (office).

OUÉDRAOGO, Youssouf, PhD; Burkinabè politician; b. 25 Dec. 1952, Tikaré, Bam Prov.; m.; two c. *Education:* Univ. of Dijon and Univ. of Clermont-Ferrand, France. *Career:* Head of Business Admin Course, Univ. of Dijon, France 1979–82; Prof. of Admin, Univ. of Ouagadougou 1983–84; Minister of Planning and Population Devt 1984–87, of Planning and Co-operation 1987–89; Pres. Social and Econ. Council 1989–92; Deputy, Nat. Ass. (Parl.) 1992–; Prime Minister 1992–94; Amb. to Belgium, the Netherlands, Luxembourg, the UK and EU 1994–99; Minister of State, Ministry of Foreign Affairs 1999–2002; State Minister and Minister of Foreign Affairs and Regional Co-operation 2002–07; Gov. Islamic Bank for Devt, World Bank and African Bank for Devt 1987–89; Silver Medal of the Torch of the Revolution 1986, Grand Officier of the Nat. Order 1994, Grand Cordon, Order of the Shining Star, Taiwan 2002, Grand Officier, Order of the Crown, Belgium 2005.
Address: c/o Ministry of Foreign Affairs, rue 988, blvd de Faso, 03 BP 7038, Ouagadougou 03, Burkina Faso (office).

OULD-ABDALLAH, Ahmedou, BA; Mauritanian UN official and diplomat-ist; *Special Representative for West Africa, United Nations;* b. 21 Nov. 1940; one s. *Education:* Univ. of Grenoble, Univ. of Paris and Univ. of Paris, Sorbonne, France. *Career:* held several positions in Govt of Mauritania, including Minister for Foreign Affairs and Cooperation, Minister of Commerce and Transportation, Amb. to USA, to Belgium, Luxembourg and the Netherlands and to EEC, Dir-Gen. Mauritanian Industries, and Dir-Gen. Soc. Nationale Industrielle et Minière; Exec. Dir Global Coalition for Africa, Washington, DC –2002; several UN positions including Sec.-Gen.'s Special Rep for Burundi and Special Coordinator for New and Renewable Sources of Energy and Energy Issues, Sec.-Gen.'s Special Rep. for West Africa 2002–.
Address: UN Office for West Africa (UNOWA), 5 Avenue Carde, Immeuble Caisse de Sécurité Sociale, BP 23851, Dakar, Senegal (office). *Telephone:* 849-07-29 (office). *Fax:* 842-50-95 (office). *Website:* www.un .org/unowa (office).

OULD AHMED WAGHF, Yahya; Mauritanian economist and politician. *Career:* fmr Prof. of Econs, Univ. of Nouakchott; fmr Minister Sec.-Gen. of the Presidency; Chair. Nat. Pact for Devt and Democracy (PNDD-ADIL); Prime Minister 2008 (ousted in coup).
Address: c/o Office of the Prime Minister, BP 237, Nouakchott, Mauritania.

OULD BEN HMEIDA, Abdallahi; Mauritanian diplomatist and politician; b. 1954. *Career:* fmr Amb. to Libya; Minister of Foreign Affairs and Co-operation 2008–.
Address: Ministry of Foreign Affairs and Co-operation, BP 230, Nouakchott, Mauritania (office). *Telephone:* 525-26-82 (office). *Fax:* 525-28-60 (office).

OULD TAH, Sidi, PhD; Mauritanian economist and politician. *Career:* fmrly with Islamic Devt Bank; fmr econ. advisor to Prime Minister; Minister of Economy and Finance 2008–.
Address: Ministry of Finance, BP 181, Nouakchott, Mauritania (office). *Telephone:* 525-20-20 (office).

OUMAROU, Seyni; Niger politician; *Prime Minister; Career:* mem. Nat. Movt for a Developing Soc. (Mouvement national pour la société de développement, MNSD), Pres. Tillabéry regional council; Minister of Trade and Industry 1999–2004; Minister of State for Equipment 2004–07; Prime Minister 2007–.
Address: Office of the Prime Minister, BP 893, Niamey, Niger (office). *Telephone:* 20-72-26-99 (office). *Fax:* 20-73-58-59 (office).

OURISMAN, Mary M., BS; American diplomatist; *Ambassador to Barbados and the Eastern Caribbean; Education:* Univ. of Texas, Austin. *Career:* apptd by Pres. George W. Bush to Bd of Trustees of Kennedy Center, Founding mem. Center's Int. Cttee; mem. Bd of Trustees Washington Nat. Opera under Direction of Placido Domingo; mem. Bd of Dirs Blair House (Pres.'s guest house for foreign Heads of State); Trustee Emer. Smithsonian Inst., Washington, DC; Amb. to Barbados (also accred to Antigua and Barbuda, Dominica, Grenada, Saint Kitts and Nevis, Saint Lucia, and Saint Vincent and the Grenadines) 2006–.
Address: US Embassy, Canadian Imperial Bank of Commerce Building, Broad Street, PO Box 302, Bridgetown, Barbados (office). *Telephone:* 436-4950 (office). *Fax:* 429-5246 (office). *E-mail:* consularbridge2@state.gov (office). *Website:* bridgetown.usembassy.gov (office).

OUTLULE, Samuel Otsile, BPA; Botswana diplomatist; *Permanent Representative, United Nations;* b. 8 July 1957; m.; three c. *Education:* Gaborone Campus, Univ. of Botswana and Swaziland, Inst. of Devt Man., Gaborone, Ranche House Coll., Harare, German Foundation for Int. Devt, Berlin. *Career:* Foreign Affairs Officer, Ministry of Foreign Affairs 1982–85; served at High Comm. in Harare 1985–89, in London 1993–95; First Sec. to Perm. Mission to UN, New York 1989, Political Counsellor and Alternate Rep. to Security Council 1995; Deputy Dir for Africa and Middle E, Ministry of Foreign Affairs 1997–99, Dir of Int. Relations 1999–2000; Clerk to Cabinet and Sr Pvt. Sec. to Pres. Mogae 2000–05; Perm. Rep. to UN, New York 2005–.
Address: Office of the Permanent Representative of Botswana to the United Nations, 103 East 37th Street, New York, NY 10016, USA (office). *Telephone:* (212) 889-2277 (office). *Fax:* (212) 725-5061 (office). *E-mail:* botswana@un.int (office).

OWADA, Hisashi, LLB; Japanese judge and academic; *Judge, International Court of Justice;* b. 18 Sept. 1932, Niigata; m. Yumiko Egashira 1962; three d.; (one d. Masako; m. Crown Prince Naruhito of Japan). *Education:* Univs of Tokyo and Cambridge. *Career:* Pvt. Sec. to Prime Minister 1976–78; Minister-Plenipotentiary, USSR 1981–84; Dir-Gen. Treaties Bureau and Office for Law of the Sea 1984–87; Deputy Vice-Minister, Ministry of Foreign Affairs 1987–88; Amb. to OECD 1988–89; Deputy Minister, Ministry of Foreign Affairs 1989–91, Vice-Minister for Foreign Affairs 1991–93; Adviser to Minister for Foreign Affairs 1993–94, 1999–2003; Amb. and Perm. Rep. to UN 1994–98; Sr Adviser to Pres. World Bank 1999–2003; Adjunct Prof., Tokyo Univ. 1963–88, Colo Law School 1994–98; Visiting Prof., Harvard Univ. 1979–81, 1987, 1989, 1999–2002, NY Univ. Law School 1994–; Prof., Waseda Univ. 1999–2003; Pres. Japan Inst. of Int. Affairs 1999–2003; Judge, Int. Court of Justice 2003–; Associé de l'Institut de Droit Int; Hon. LLD. *Publications:* US–Japan Economic Interaction in an Independent World 1981, Japanese Perspectives on Asian Security 1982, Practice of Japan in International Law 1984, From Involvement to Engagement: A New Course for Japanese Foreign Policy 1994, Diplomacy 1997, A Treatise on International Relations 2003.
Address: International Court of Justice, Carnegieplein 2 (Peace Palace), 2517 KJ, The Hague, Netherlands (office). *Telephone:* (70) 3022323 (office). *Fax:* (70) 3022409 (office). *E-mail:* mail@icj-cij.org (office). *Website:* www.icj-cij.org (office).

OWONO EDU, Marcelino; Equatorial Guinean politician; *Minister of Mines, Industry and Energy; Career:* Minister of Finance and of the Budget 2003–08, of Mines, Industry and Energy 2008; Alternate Gov. for Equatorial Guinea of the ADB Group.
Address: Ministry of Mines, Industry and Energy, Calle 12 de Octubre s/n, Malabo, Equatorial Guinea (office). *Telephone:* (09) 35-67 (office). *Fax:* (09) 33-53 (office). *E-mail:* d.shaw@ecqc.com (office). *Website:* www.equatorialoil.com (office).

OXHORN, Philip, MA, PhD; American academic; *Associate Professor and Director, Centre for Developing-Area Studies, McGill University; Education:* London School of Econs, UK, Univ. of Redlands, Univ. of Canterbury, NZ, Harvard Univ. *Career:* Asst Prof., McGill Univ., Montreal, Canada 1989–95, Assoc. Prof. 1996–, Assoc. Dean Grad. and Postdoctoral Studies 2001–03, Dir Centre for Developing-Area Studies 2005–; Research Consultant, IDB 1999, 2006, Woodrow Wilson Int. Center for Scholars 2000–, Canadian Int. Devt Agency 2006–; Del. of Canadian Dept of Foreign Affairs and Int. Trade to Inter-American Forum, OAS 2001; mem. Forum of Hemispheric Experts 2001–; Exec. Ed. Latin American Research Review 2007–; mem. Int. Editorial Cttee Encuentro XXI 1996–, Editorial Bd Latin American Politics and Society 1999–; mem. Latin American Studies Asscn; media appearances on nat. and int. TV and radio programmes; several fellowships, grants and academic awards. *Publications:* Organizing Civil Society: The Popular Sectors and the Struggle for Democracy in Chile 1995, What Kind of Democracy? What Kind of Market? (co-ed.) 1998, Markets and Democracy in Latin America: Conflict or Convergence? (co-ed.) 1999, Decentralization, Civil Society and Democratic Governance: Comparative Perspectives from Latin America, Africa and Asia (co-ed.) 2004, Sustaining Civil Society: Economic Change, Democracy and the Social Construction of Citizenship in Latin America 2007; numerous articles and book chapters relating to civil society and democratization in Latin America.
Address: Department of Political Science, McGill University, 855 Sherbrooke Street West, Montreal, PQ H3A 2T7, Canada (office). *Telephone:* (514) 398-8970 (office). *Fax:* (514) 398-1770 (office). *E-mail:* philip.oxhorn@mcgill.ca (office). *Website:* www.mcgill.ca/politicalscience/faculty/oxhorn (office).

OYÉ-MBA, Casimir, LLD; Gabonese banker and politician; *Senior Minister of Mining, Oil, Energy and Water;* b. 20 April 1942, Nzamaligue Village, Libreville; m. Marie-Françoise Razafimbelo 1963; three s. three d. *Education:* Univs of Rennes and Paris, France. *Career:* trainee, Banque Centrale, Libreville 1967–69, Asst Dir 1969–70, Dir 1970–73; Nat. Dir Banque pour le Gabon 1973–76; Asst Dir-Gen. Banque Centrale 1977–78; Gov. Banque des Etats de l'Afrique Centrale 1978–90; Prime Minister of Gabon 1990–94; Minister of Foreign Affairs and Co-operation 1994–99; fmr Minister of State for Planning and Devt; Sr Minister of Mining, Oil, Energy and Water 2007–; Alt. Gov. IMF for Gabon 1969–76; apptd Pres. Asscn des Banques Centrales Africaines 1987; elected mem. Parl. for Komo-Mondah dist 1990, re-elected 1996, 2001, 2006; mem. political bureau, Gabonese Democratic Party 1991; Campaign Man. for Pres. Omar Bongo 1993; Gabon mem. Bd of Govs of World Bank 1999–; mem. Ntoum City Council; Chevalier, Légion d'honneur; Gabon, Cameroon, Congo, Equatorial Guinea and Cen. African Repub. decorations.
Address: BP 874, Libreville (office); Ministry of Mining, Libreville (office); BP 13016, Libreville, Gabon (home). *Telephone:* 72-47-83. *Fax:* 72-49-90 (office).

OYUUN, Sanjaasurengin, DPhil; Mongolian politician; *Minister of Foreign Affairs;* b. 1964, Ulan Bator. *Education:* Univ. of Cambridge, UK. *Career:* worked as exploration geologist on surveys in Mongolia and for Rio Tinto-Zinc; Founder and Chair. Civil Courage Party ('Irgenii Zorig Nam') 2000–; Minister of Foreign Affairs 2007–.
Address: Ministry of Foreign Affairs, Enkh Taivny Örgön Chölöö 7A, Sükhbaatar District, Ulan Bator (office); Civil Courage Party ('Irgenii Zorig Nam'), PO Box 49, Ulan Bator (office); Ulan Bator 13, PO Box 37, Mongolia; Ulan Bator 13, Sukhbaatar District, 2-28-6 (home). *Telephone:* (11) 311311 (office); (11) 323645 (office); (91) 913964 (home). *Fax:* (11) 322127 (office); (11) 322866 (office). *E-mail:* mongmer@magicnet.mn (office); oyuna@mail.parl.gov.mn (office). *Website:* www.pmis.gov.mn (office); www.zorigfoundation.org.mn (office).

ÖZKÖK, Gen. Hilmi; Turkish army officer; b. 1940, Turgutlu, Manisa; m. Özenç Özkök; two c. *Education:* Işıklar Mil. High School, Turkish Mil. Acad., Field Artillery School, Army War Coll., NATO Defence Coll. *Career:* Artillery 3rd Lt 1959; Platoon Leader and Anti-Aircraft Battery Commdr 1972; Chief of Operations and Training Br., 15th Training Brigade; Staff Officer, Plan and Policy Dept of Shape, HQ; Chief of Defence Research Section, Plan and Policy Dept of Shape, HQ; Dir Exec. Office of Sec.-Gen. of Nat. Security Council; Commdr Cadet Regiment, Turkish Mil. Acad.; rank of Brig.-Gen. 1984; Chief of Planning and Operations Dept, Turkish Gen. Staff (TGS) 1984–86; Commdr 70th Infantry Brigade 1986–88; rank of Maj.-Gen. 1988; Commdr 28th Infantry Div. 1988–90; Chief of Personnel, Dept of TGS 1990–92; rank of Lt-Gen. 1992; Chief of Turkish Mil. Del. to NATO, Brussels 1992–95; Commdr 7th Corps 1995–96; rank of Gen. 1996; Command of Allied Land Forces South-Eastern Europe 1996–98; Deputy Chief of TGS 1998–99; 1st Army Commdr 1999–2000; Commdr of Turkish Army 2000–02; Chief of the Gen. Staff 2002–06; fmr mem. NATO Mil. Cttee; Turkish Armed Forces Medal of Honour, Turkish Armed Forces Medal of Distinguished Service, Medal of Distinguished Service and Self-Sacrifice, Chevalier, Ordre nat. du Mérite, Legion of Merit (USA), Medal of Nishan-i-Imtiaz (Pakistan), Great Cross for Military Merit (Spain), Tong-II Medal (Repub. of Korea), Eagle Golden Medal (Albania).
Address: c/o Ministry of National Defence, Milli Savunma Bakanlığı, 06100 Ankara, Turkey (office).

OZORES TYPALDOS, Carlos R.; Panamanian politician and diplomatist; *Ambassador to Colombia;* b. 7 Aug. 1940. *Career:* Minister of Foreign Affairs 1978–81; Perm. Rep. to UN 1981–84, Pres. Security Council Nov. 1982; mem. Bd Panama Canal Comm. 1983; apptd Vice-Pres. of Panama 1984; fmr Amb. to Canada, currently Amb. to Colombia; consultant to Panama-China Friendship Asscn 2002.
Address: Embassy of Panama, Calle 92, No 7a-40, Bogotá, DC, Columbia (office). *Telephone:* (1) 257-5058 (office). *Fax:* (1) 257-5067 (office). *E-mail:* embpacol@cable.net.co (office). *Website:* www.empacol.org (office).

ÖZÜLKER, Uluc; Turkish diplomatist. *Career:* fmr Deputy Under-Sec., Ministry of Foreign Affairs; fmr Perm. Rep. to EU; Amb. to France –2005. *Address:* Ministry of Foreign Affairs, Dişişleri Bakanlığı, Dr Sadık Ahmet Cad. 12, 06100 Balgat, Ankara, Turkey. *Telephone:* (312) 2921000. *Fax:* (312) 2873869. *E-mail:* webmaster@mfa.gov.tr. *Website:* www.mfa.gov.tr.

ÖZÜYE, Oktay; Turkish diplomatist; *Ambassador to People's Republic of China;* b. 1 Jan. 1944, Bursa; m.; one c. *Education:* Ankara Univ. *Career:* mil. service 1968–70; Attaché, Dept of Middle East and Africa, Ministry of Foreign Affairs 1968, Attaché, Third Sec. and Second Sec., Dept of Western Affairs 1970–71, Chief of Cabinet of Minister of State and Vice-Prime Minister 1971–72, Chief of Section, Dept of Multilateral Political Orgs 1977–79, Head Dept of Middle East and Africa 1983–85, Head Dept of Int. Econ. Orgs 1989–92, Deputy Dir-Gen., Multilateral Econ. Affairs 1992–95, Counsel to the Ministry 2000–2001, Dir-Gen., Dept of Econ. Affairs 2001–04; overseas postings include Second Sec., then First Sec., Perm. Mission of Turkey to Council of Europe 1972–74, Consul, Consulate Gen. in Strasbourg 1974–75, First Sec., Embassy in Tehran 1975–77, Counsellor, Perm. Mission to UN, Geneva 1979–83, First Counsellor and Deputy Perm. Rep., Perm. Mission to OECD 1985–89; Amb. to Singapore 1995–98, to Turkmenistan 1998–2000, to People's Repub. of China 2004–. *Address:* Embassy of Turkey, 9 Dong Wu Jie, San Li Tun, Beijing 100600, People's Republic of China (office). *Telephone:* (10) 65322490 (office). *Fax:* (10) 65325480 (office). *E-mail:* embassy@turkey.org.cn (office). *Website:* www.turkey.org.cn (office).

P

PABRIKS, Artis, PhD; Latvian politician; b. 22 March 1966, Jūrmala. *Education:* Univ. of Latvia, Univ. of Århus, Denmark. *Career:* Research Asst, Acad. of Sciences 1988–90; External Lecturer, Univ. of Århus, Denmark 1994; Lecturer, Univ. of Latvia 1995–99; First Rector, Vidzeme Univ. Coll. 1996–97, Asst Prof. 1996–2001, Assoc. Prof. 2001–; Policy Analyst, Latvian Centre for Human Rights and Ethnic Studies 2001–03, Political Educ. Foundation 2003–04; mem. Saeima (Parl.) 2004–, Chair. Foreign Affairs Comm.; Parl. Sec., Ministry of Foreign Affairs 2004, Minister of Foreign Affairs 2004–07; Deputy mem. for Latvia, European Comm. against Racism and Intolerance, Council of Europe 2002–; mem. Editorial Bd, Baltic Review magazine 2002–.
Address: Saeima (Parliament), Jekaba iela 11, Rīga 1811, Latvia (office). *Telephone:* 6708-7111 (office). *Fax:* 6708-7100 (office). *E-mail:* web@saeima.lv (office). *Website:* www.saeima.lv (office).

PACHACHI, Adnan, PhD; Iraqi politician and diplomatist; *Founder and President, Independent Democratic Movement;* b. (Adnan Muzahim al-Pachachi), 14 May 1923, Baghdad; m. Selwa Pachachi 1946; three d. *Education:* Victoria Coll., Alexandria, Egypt, American Univ., Beirut, Lebanon, Georgetown Univ, Washington, DC, USA. *Career:* Perm. Rep. to UN 1959–65, 1967–69; Minister of Foreign Affairs 1965–67; left Iraq to settle in UAE 1971, returned 2003; Founder and Pres. Ind. Democratic Movt 2003–; led Iraqi del. to UN Security Council July 2003; mem. Iraq Governing Council 2003–04, Pres. Jan. 2004; mem. Parl. 2005–; decorations from Italy and Morocco. *Publications:* Muzahim Pachachi – Political Career (in Arabic) 1990, Voice of Iraq in the UN 1959–1969 – Personal Record 1991.
Address: Independent Democratic Movement, Baghdad, Iraq (office). *E-mail:* adnan@pachachi.org (office).

PACHAURI, Rajendra K., MS, DEcon, DEng; Indian research director and international organization executive; *Chairman, Intergovernmental Panel on Climate Change;* b. 20 Aug. 1940, Nainital; m. Saroj Pachauri; three d. *Education:* North Carolina State Univ., USA. *Career:* Asst Prof. NC State Univ. 1974–75; mem. Sr Faculty, Admin. Staff Coll. of India 1975–79, Dir Consulting and Applied Research Div. 1979–81; Dir Tata Energy Research Inst. New Delhi 1981–2001, Dir-Gen. 2001–; Visiting Prof. W Va Univ. 1981–82; Visiting Fellow, Energy Dept IBRD 1990; Pres. Int. Asscn for Energy Econs 1988, Chair. 1988–90; Pres. Asian Energy Inst. 1992–; mem. World Energy Council 1990–93; Adviser on Energy and Sustainable Man. of Natural Resources to the Admin., UNDP 1994–99; Vice-Chair. Intergovernmental Panel on Climate Change (IPCC) 1997, Chair. 2002–; mem. Bd of Dirs Inst. for Global Environmental Strategies 1999, Indian Oil Corpn Ltd 1999–2003, Nat. Thermal Power Corpn Ltd 2002–, GAIL (India) Ltd 2003–; McCluskey Fellow, Yale Univ. Sept.–Dec. 2000; Millennium Pioneer Award 2000, Padma Bhushan 2001, Intergovernmental Panel on Climate Change awarded Nobel Peace Prize (shared with Albert (Al) Gore) 2007. *Publications:* The Dynamics of Electrical Energy Supply and Demand 1975, Energy and Economic Development in India 1977, International Energy Studies 1980, Energy Policy for India: An Interdisciplinary Analysis 1980, The Political Economy of Global Energy 1985, Global Energy Interactions 1986, Contemporary India 1992, Climate Change in Asia and Brazil: The Role of Technology Transfer (ed. with Preety Bhandari) 1994, Population, Environment and Development (ed. with Lubina F. Qureshy) 1997, Energy in the Indian Sub-Continent (ed. with Gurneeta Vasudeva) 2000; scientific papers and newspaper articles.
Address: Intergovernmental Panel on Climate Change, World Meteorological Organization, 7 bis, ave de la Paix, CP 2300, 1211 Geneva 2, Switzerland; 160 Golf Links, New Delhi 110003, India (home). *Telephone:* (11) 4634663 (home). *Website:* www.ipcc.ch (office).

PACHECO, Abel; Costa Rican fmr head of state, psychiatrist and writer; b. (Abel Pacheco de la Espriella), 22 Dec. 1933, San José. *Education:* Nat. Autonomous Univ. of Mexico, Louisiana State Univ., USA. *Career:* fmr TV commentator and producer of documentaries; Pres. Partido Unidad Social Cristiana (PUSC); Pres. of Costa Rica 2002–06. *Publications:* series of novels, six books on Costa Rica and several popular songs.
Address: c/o Partido Unidad Social Cristiana (PUSC), Del Restaurante Kentucky Fried Chicken 75 metros al sur, frente a la Embajada de España, Paseo Colón, Apdo 10.095, 1000 San José, Costa Rica (office).

PACHECO LUÍZ GOMES, José, LLB; Portuguese diplomat; b. 1941, Lisbon. *Education:* Univ. of Lisbon, Inst. d'Études Supérieures de Techniques d'Org., Paris, France. *Career:* Attaché, Ministry of Foreign Affairs 1967–69, Third Sec. 1969–73; Deputy Consul-Gen., Consulate-Gen. in Salisbury 1972–75, Consul-Gen. 1975–76; Counsellor for Political Affairs, Embassy in Brussels 1976–80; Diplomatic Adviser to the Prime Minister 1981–83; Dir Europe–America Dept 1983–84; Minister Counsellor and Deputy Head of Mission, Embassy in Washington, DC 1984–88; Amb. in Canberra (non-resident Amb. to NZ and Vanuatu) 1988–93, in Harare 1993–94, in Moscow (and non-resident Amb. to Georgia, Armenia, Turkmenistan, Kazakhstan, Uzbekistan, Kyrgyzstan, Tajikistan and Belarus) 1996–2001, in Ottawa 2001–03; Pres. Inst. of Portuguese Cooperation, Lisbon 1994–96; Perm. Rep. to NATO, Brussels 2003–06; Grand Cross Order of Merit (Portugal), Commdr Order of Rio Branco (Brazil), Commdr Order of Isabel the Catholic (Spain), Commdr Order of Merit (Greece, Italy), Commdr Order of the Flag (Hungary, Yugoslavia), Commdr Sovereign and Mil. Order of Malta, Commdr Order of St Sylvester of the Holy See (Vatican), Officer Légion d'Honneur (France), Order of Friendship (Russian Fed.).
Address: c/o Ministry of Foreign Affairs, Palácio das Necessidades, Largo do Rilvas, 1399-030 Lisbon, Portugal. *Telephone:* (21) 3946000. *Fax:* (21) 3946053. *E-mail:* gii@mne.gov.pt. *Website:* www.min-nestrangeiros.pt.

PADAR, Ivari, BA; Estonian politician; *Minister of Finance;* b. 12 March 1965, Navi, Võru Prov.; m.; one s. one d. *Education:* Tartu Univ. *Career:* began career as transport worker, Võru Dairy Factory 1984–88; carpenter, Võru Dept of Repairs and Construction 1988–90; teacher, Võru School 1990–92; Deputy Mayor of Võru 1993–94; Chair. Võru Farmers' Union 1994–95; Asst to Chancellor of the Exchequer 1995–97; Dir-Gen. AS HT Hulgi (customs warehouse) 1997–99; Minister of Agric. 1999–2002, of Finance 2007–; Chair. Võru City Council 2002–03; Advisor AS Tallink Duty Free 2002–03; mem. Parl. 2002–; mem. Estonian Social Democratic Party 1999– (Chair. 2003–); mem. Bd Govs Estonian Univ. of Life Sciences; Hon. Pres. Estonian Asscn of Equestrian Sports.
Address: Ministry of Finance, Suur-Ameerika 1, Tallinn 15006, Estonia (office). *Telephone:* 611-3558 (office). *Fax:* 696-6810 (office). *E-mail:* info@fin.ee (office). *Website:* www.fin.ee (office).

PADGAONKAR, Dileep, PhD; Indian journalist; *Consulting Editor and Columnist, Times of India;* b. 1 May 1944, Pune; m. Latika Tawadey 1968; two s. *Education:* Fergusson Coll., Pune, Institut des Hautes Etudes Cinématographiques, Sorbonne, France. *Career:* Paris Corresp., The Times of India 1968–73, Asst Ed., Bombay and Delhi 1973–78, Assoc. Ed. and Exec. Ed. The Times of India Group 1986–88, Ed. 1988–94, Dir (Corp.) and Exec. Man. Ed. 1998–2002, Consulting Ed. and Columnist 2002–; f. Asia Pacific Communication Assocs 1994; Information Chief for Asia and Pacific, UNESCO 1978–81; Deputy Dir Office of Public Information, Paris 1981–85, Acting Dir 1985–86, Acting Dir Communication Sector 1986; Presenter Question Time India, BBC World; Chevalier, Legion d'honneur 2001. *Television:* presenter, BBC World's Question Time India panel discussion programme. *Publication:* When Bombay Burned (ed.) 1993.
Address: The Times of India, Times House, 7 Bahadur Shah Zafar Marg, New Delhi 110002 (office); C-313, Defence Colony, New Delhi 110024, India (home). *Telephone:* (11) 3312277 (office); (11) 4697949 (home). *Fax:* (11) 3323346. *Website:* www.timesofindia.com (office).

PADILLA TOÑOS, Pedro Luciano; Dominican Republic economist and diplomatist; b. 18 Jan. 1937, Barahona; m.; two c. *Education:* Santo Domingo Autonomous Univ., Pro-Deo Social Studies Univ., Rome, Italy. *Career:* fmr Prof. of Public Int. Law and American Public Int. Law, Santo Domingo Autonomous Univ. and Pedro Henriques Urena Univ., Santo Domingo; entered foreign service 1961, served in Embassies in Italy, Venezuela, UK and Portugal; fmr Sec. of State for Foreign Affairs, Under-Sec. of State for Foreign Affairs and Dir Dept of Int. Orgs and Conferences of the State Secr. for Foreign Affairs; Perm. Rep. to UN, New York 2000–03; Amb. to Italy 2003.
Address: Secretariat of State for External Relations, Avda Independencia 752, Santo Domingo, DN, Dominican Republic. *Telephone:* 535-6280. *Fax:*

533-5772. *E-mail:* correspondencia@serex.gov.do. *Website:* www.serex .gov.do.

PADOA-SCHIOPPA, Tommaso, MSc (Econs); Italian banker, economist and government official; *Chairman, International Monetary and Financial Committee, International Monetary Fund;* b. 23 July 1940, Belluno; m. Fiorella Kostoris 1966; one s. two d. *Education:* Università Commerciale Luigi Bocconi, Milan, Massachusetts Inst. of Tech., USA. *Career:* with insurance co., Bremen, FRG 1959–60, C. & A. Brenninkmeyer 1966–68; Economist, Research Dept, Banca d'Italia, Rome 1970–79, Head, Money Market Dept 1975–79, Direttore Centrale for Econ. Research 1983–84, Deputy Dir-Gen. 1984–97; Economic Adviser, the Treasury 1978–79; Dir-Gen. Econ. and Financial Affairs, Comm. of EC 1979–83; mem. Group of Thirty; Chair. Banking Advisory Cttee, Comm. of EC 1988–91, Cen. Bank's Working Group on EC Payment Systems 1991–95, Group of Ten Basel Cttee on Banking Supervision, BIS 1993–97; mem. Exec. Bd European Cen. Bank 1998–2005; Minister of Economy and Finance 2006–08; Chair. Int. Monetary and Financial Cttee, IMF 2007–; Hon. Prof. Univ. of Frankfurt am Main 1999; Dr hc (Trieste) 1999. *Publications include:* The Management of an Open Economy with One Hundred Per Cent Plus Wage Indexation (with F. Modigliani, in Essays in International Finance) 1978, Money, Economic Policy and Europe 1985, The Road to Monetary Union in Europe 1994, Il governo dell'economia 1997, Che cosa ci ha insegnato l'avventura europea 1998.
Address: International Monetary Fund, 700 19th Street, Washington, DC 20431, USA. *Telephone:* (202) 623-7000 (office). *Fax:* (202) 623-4661 (office). *Website:* www.imf.org (office).

PADOAN, Pier Carlo; Italian economist, international organization executive and academic; *Deputy Secretary-General, Organisation for Economic Co-operation and Development; Education:* Univ. of Rome. *Career:* has held various academic positions in Italian and foreign univs including at Univ. of Rome, College of Europe (Bruges), Université Libre de Bruxelles, Univ. of Urbino, Universidad de La Plata and Univ. of Tokyo; Italian Exec. Dir at IMF, Washington, DC, with competence also for Greece, Portugal, San Marino, Albania and Timor Leste, served as mem. Bd and chaired several Bd Cttees, was also in charge of European Coordination; Econ. Adviser to Prime Ministers Massimo D'Alema and Giuliano Amato, in charge of int. econ. policies 1998–2001; Pres. of Econs, Univ. La Sapienza, Rome and Dir Fondazione Italianieuropei (policy think-tank) 2001–07; Deputy Sec.-Gen. OECD 2007–, in charge of relations with other int. orgs.
Address: OECD, 2 rue André Pascal, 75775 Paris Cedex 16, France (office). *Telephone:* 1-45-24-82-00 (office). *Fax:* 1-45-24-85-00 (office). *E-mail:* webmaster@oecd.org (office). *Website:* www.oecd.org (office).

PAEK, Yung-sun; South Korean diplomatist; *Ambassador to India;* b. 1954; m.; two s. *Education:* Seoul Nat. Univ. *Career:* fmr Counsellor, Perm. Mission to UN, New York; fmr Minister, Embassy in Moscow; Chief of Protocol, Ministry of Foreign Affairs 2006; Amb. to India (also accred to Bhutan) 2007–.
Address: Embassy of the Republic of Korea, 9 Chandragupta Marg, Chanakyapuri, POB 5416, New Delhi 110 021, India (office). *Telephone:* (11) 26885412 (office). *Fax:* (11) 26884840 (office). *E-mail:* kobe@mail .mofat.go.kr (office). *Website:* ind.mofat.go.kr (office).

PAET, Urmas; Estonian journalist and politician; *Minister of Foreign Affairs;* b. 20 April 1974, Tallinn; m. Tiina Paet; two d. *Education:* Univ. of Tartu. *Career:* Ed. Chief Editorial Office for Int. News, Estonian Radio 1991–92, Ed. News Editorial Office 1993–94; reporter, News Editorial Office, AS Postimees 1994–98, Sr Ed. and Political Journalist 1998–99; Adviser Estonian Reform Party 1999; Dist Elder, Nõmme city 1999–2003; Minister of Culture 2003–05, of Foreign Affairs 2005–.
Address: Ministry of Foreign Affairs, Islandi Väljak 1, Tallinn 15049, Estonia (office). *Telephone:* 631-7092 (office). *Fax:* 631-7099 (office). *E-mail:* vminfo@vm.ee (office). *Website:* www.vm.ee (office).

PAHAD, Aziz Goolam Hoosein, MA; South African politician; *Deputy Minister of Foreign Affairs;* b. 25 Dec. 1940, Schweizer-Reneke, Western Transvaal; m. Sandra Pahad 1994; two s. one d. *Education:* Cen. Indian High School, Johannesburg, Univ. of Witwatersrand, Univ. Coll., London, and Univ. of Sussex, UK. *Career:* in exile 1964–90; worked in London office of African Nat. Congress (ANC) from 1968, later mem. ANC Revolutionary Council until its dissolution in 1983; rep. of ANC Revolutionary Council in Angola and Zambia; mem. ANC Nat. Exec. Cttee 1985–; Deputy Head, ANC Dept of Int. Affairs 1991; mem. Nat. Peace Exec. Cttee 1991–92; mem. Sub-Council on Foreign Affairs of Transitional Exec. Council 1993–94; MP 1994–; Deputy Minister of Foreign Affairs 1994–.
Address: Room 1725, 120 Plein Street, Cape Town (office); Room 283, East Wing, Union Buildings, Pretoria, South Africa (office). *Telephone:* (21)

4643711 (Cape Town) (office); (12) 3510105 (Pretoria) (office). *Fax:* (21) 4618090 (Cape Town) (office); (12) 3510259 (Pretoria) (office). *E-mail:* dmpahad@foreign.gov.za (office). *Website:* www.dfa.gov.za (office).

PAHANG, HRH The Sultan of; Haji Ahmad Shah al-Musta'in Billah ibni al-Marhum Sultan Abu Bakar Ri'ayatuddin al-Mu'adzam Shah, DKP; Malaysian; b. 24 Oct. 1930, Istana Mangga Tunggal, Pekan; m. Tengku Hajjah Afzan binti Tengku Muhammad 1954. *Education:* Malay Coll. Kuala Kangsar, Worcester Coll., Oxford and Univ. Coll., Exeter, UK. *Career:* Tengku Mahkota (Crown Prince) 1944; Capt. 4th Battalion, Royal Malay Regt 1954; Commdr of 12th Infantry Battalion of Territorial Army 1963–65, Lt-Col; mem. State Council 1955; Regent 1956, 1959, 1965; succeeded as Sultan 1974; Timbalan Yang di Pertuan Agong (Deputy Supreme Head of State of Malaysia) 1975–79, Yang di Pertuan Agong (Supreme Head of State) 1979–84, 1985; Constitutional Head of Int. Islamic Univ. 1988; Hon. DLitt (Malaya) 1988; Hon. LLD (Northrop, USA) 1993.
Address: Istana Abu Bakar, Pekan, Pahang, Malaysia.

PAIHAMA, Gen. Kundi; Angolan politician and army general; *Minister of National Defence;* b. 1958. *Career:* with Angolan armed forces, also seconded to the Portuguese army; fmr Councillor of Benguela; fmr Minister of the Interior; Gov. of Huíla Prov. 1992–99, also of the City of Luanda; Minister of State Security 1998; elected to Congress (MPLA) 1998; Minister of Nat. Defence 1999–.
Address: Ministry of National Defence, Rua 17 de Settembro, Luanda, Angola (office). *Telephone:* 222337530 (office). *Fax:* 222334276 (office). *E-mail:* mindenl@ebonet.net (office).

PAJULA, Merle; Estonian diplomatist and government official; *Ambassador to Finland;* b. 18 Jan. 1960, Tallinn; m.; two c. *Education:* Tartu State Univ. *Career:* Sr Librarian, Estonian State Library; Sr Researcher Centre of Methodology for Folklore and Culture; Second Sec. Press and Information Dept, Ministry of Foreign Affairs 1993–95, Dir-Gen. 1998–2000; Second Sec. Embassy in Helsinki 1995–98; Perm. Rep. to UN, New York 2000–05; Head, Foreign Relations Dept, Riigikogu (Parl.) 2005–06; Amb. to Finland 2006–.
Address: Embassy of Estonia, Itäinen puistotie 10, 00140 Helsinki, Finland (office). *Telephone:* (9) 6220260 (office). *Fax:* (9) 62202610 (office). *E-mail:* Embassy.Helsinki@mfa.ee (office). *Website:* www.estemb.fi (office).

PAK, Gil-yon; North Korean diplomatist; m.; three c. *Education:* Univ. of Int. Relations. *Career:* joined Ministry of Foreign Affairs 1964, served as Officer, Consul in Singapore and Myanmar, Section Chief, Deputy Dir, Dir of Ministry 1978–1983, Vice-Minister 1983–84, 1996–; Perm. Rep. to UN, New York 1984–96, 2001–08; Kim Il Sung Order.
Address: c/o Ministry of Foreign Affairs, Pyongyang, Democratic People's Republic of Korea (office).

PAK, Pong-ju; North Korean politician. *Career:* Minister of Chemical Industry –2003; Prime Minister of Democratic People's Repub. of Korea 2003–07.
Address: c/o Office of the Premier, Pyongyang, Democratic People's Republic of Korea (office).

PAK, Song-chol; North Korean politician; *Honorary Vice-President of the Presidium;* b. 13 Jan. 1913. *Career:* Amb. to Bulgaria 1954; commanded unit in Korean War, retd as Lt-Gen.; Minister of Foreign Affairs 1959; mem. Cen. Cttee Workers' Party of Korea (WPK) 1961, mem. Political Bureau 1980–; Vice-Premier and Minister of Foreign Affairs 1966; Second Vice-Premier 1970; Political Commissar of WPK 1970; Premier 1976–77; mem. Cen. People's Cttee 1977; Vice-Pres. Democratic People's Repub. of Korea 1977–98; mem. Presidium, Democratic Front for Reunification of Fatherland 1991; Hon. Vice-Pres. Presidium, Supreme People's Ass. 1998–.
Address: c/o Supreme People's Assembly, Pyongyang, Democratic People's Republic of Korea.

PAK, Ui-chun; North Korean diplomatist; *Minister of Foreign Affairs;* *Career:* began diplomatic career at Embassy in Cameroon 1972; fmr Amb. to Algeria, Syria and Lebanon; Amb. to Russian Fed. 1998–2006; Minister of Foreign Affairs 2007–.
Address: Ministry of Foreign Affairs, Pyongyang, Democratic People's Republic of Korea (office).

PAKI, Evan Jeremy, LLM; Papua New Guinea diplomatist and lawyer; *Ambassador to USA;* b. 1973. *Education:* Univ. of Papua New Guinea, Harvard Law School (Fulbright Scholar), John F. Kennedy School of Govt, Harvard Univ., Int. Law Inst., Washington, DC. *Career:* est. law firm, Port Moresby; employed by Multilateral Investment Guarantee Agency, Washington, DC; fmr lawyer, Banking and Finance Div., Baker &

McKenzie, Sydney, Australia –2001; Special Adviser to Office of the Prime Minister 2001–03; Amb. to USA (also accred to Mexico and as High Commr to Canada) 2003–; Visiting Lecturer on Law, Univ. of Papua New Guinea 1999; represented Papua New Guinea at annual Philip C. Jessup Int. Law Moot Court Competition, Philadelphia 1994, Washington, DC 1995.
Address: Embassy of Papua New Guinea, 1779 Massachusetts Avenue, NW, Suite 805, Washington, DC 20036, USA (office). *Telephone:* (202) 745-3680 (office). *Fax:* (202) 745-3679 (office). *E-mail:* info@pngembassy .org (office). *Website:* www.pngembassy.org (office).

PAL, Shri Satyabrata; Indian diplomatist; *High Commissioner to Pakistan;* m. *Career:* Deputy Perm. Rep., UN, New York 1979–93, 1997–2002; Deputy Sec. and Dir, Ministry of External Affairs 1983–88; Deputy High Commr, Dhaka 1988–91; High Commr Gaborone, Botswana 1991–94; Jt Sec. Ministry of External Affairs 1994–97; Deputy High Commr, London 2002–05; High Commr to South Africa 2005–06, to Pakistan 2006–.
Address: High Commission of India, G-5, Diplomatic Enclave, Islamabad, Pakistan (office). *Telephone:* (51) 2828375 (office). *Fax:* (51) 2823102 (office). *E-mail:* hicomind@isb.compol.com (office).

PALACIO, Alfredo, MD; Ecuadorean politician, cardiologist and fmr head of state; b. 22 Jan. 1939, Guayaquil. *Education:* Colegio San José La Salle, Universidad de Guayaquil. *Career:* worked at various hosps in USA 1969–74, including Mount Sinai Hosp., Cleveland, OH 1969–71, Veterans Admin. Hosp., Missouri 1971–72, Barnes Hosp., Washington Univ. 1972–74; Dir Nat. Inst. of Cardiology 1980–; Prin. Prof. of Cardiology, Faculty of Medicine, Univ. of Guayaquil 1989–2003, Prof. of Public Health 2001–2003; Minister of Public Health 1994–96; Vice-Pres. of Ecuador 2003–05, Pres. 2005–07; fmr Regional Dir Ecuador Inst. of Social Security (IESS); Fellow, American Coll. of Cardiology, American Coll. of Chest Physicians, American Coll. of Physicians; mem. American Acad. of Sciences, Ecuador Acad. of Medicine, and numerous other medical socs; Dr hc (John Hopkins, USA) 2007; Commdr, Al Mérito Atahualpha, Ministry of Nat. Defence 1995, Recognition of Merit, Ecuador Nat. Civil Defence 1996, Recognition of Merit, Gran Cruz, Pres. of Ecuador 1996; American Medical Asscn Award 1976, Eugenio Espejo Award, Quito Municipality 1982, Scientific Merit Award, Guayaquil Municipality 1982, 1987. *Publications include:* Atlas de Ecocardiografía Bidimensional 1981, Atlas of 2D Echocardiography 1983, Cardiopatía Isquémica (ed.) 1985, Estudio Guayaquil 1991, Hacia un Humanisco Científico 1997.
Address: c/o Office of the President, Palacio Nacional, García Moreno 1043, Quito, Ecuador (office).

PALECKIS, Justas Vincas; Lithuanian diplomatist and politician; b. 1 Jan. 1942, Samara (Kuibyshev), Russia; m. Laima Paleckienė; two s. one d. *Education:* Univ. of Vilnius, Diplomatic Univ. of the Ministry of Foreign Affairs, USSR. *Career:* contrib. Komjaunimo Tiesa (daily), Head of Dept 1960, 1963–66; Third Sec. USSR Embassy to Switzerland; Second, First Sec., Counsellor, USSR Embassy to GDR 1969–83; Deputy Dir, Dir of sector Lithuanian CP Cen. Cttee 1983–89; Sec., Ind. Lithuanian CP Cen. Cttee 1989–90; Deputy Chair. Foreign Affairs Cttee, Lithuanian Repub. Supreme Council (Parl.) 1990–92; Lecturer, Inst. of Journalism, Vilnius State Univ. 1990–93; Lecturer, Inst. of Int. Relations and Political Science, Vilnius State Univ. 1993–95; adviser on Foreign Affairs to Lithuanian Pres. 1993–96; rank of Amb. 1993–; Amb. to UK 1996–2001 (also accred to Portugal and Ireland 1997–2001); Deputy Minister of Foreign Affairs 2002–04; mem. European Parl. (Socialist Group) 2004–, Vice-Chair. Sub-cttee on Security and Defence, mem. Cttee on Foreign Affairs, Substitute mem. Cttee on the Environment, Public Health and Food Safety, Temporary Cttee on Climate Change, Del. to EU-Russia Parl. Cooperation Cttee, Del. to EU-Fmr Yugoslav Repub. of Macedonia Jt Parl. Cttee, Del. to EU-Bulgaria Jt Parl. Cttee; Kt, Royal Swedish Order of the Northern Star 1994, Lithuanian Independence Medal 2000, Commdr, Order of Merit (Lithuania) 2003. *Publications:* Swiss Pyramids 1974, At the Foot of Swiss Pyramids 1985, Life in a Triangle. Vilnius-Brussels-Strasbourg 2007.
Address: European Parliament, Bâtiment Altiero Spinelli, ASP 13G158, 60 rue Wiertz, 1047 Brussels, Belgium (office); Europos Parlamento nario Justo Paleckio biuras, Pylimo g. 12-10, 01118 Vilnius; K. Donelaicio 20-5, 2000 Vilnius, Lithuania (home). *Telephone:* (2) 284-79-21 (office); (5) 2635445 (home). *Fax:* (2) 284-99-21 (office). *E-mail:* justasvincas.paleckis@ europarl.europa.eu (office); biuras@paleckis.lt (office). *Website:* www .europarl.europa.eu (office); www.paleckis.lt (office).

PALOCCI, António Filho; Brazilian politician and physician; b. 4 Oct. 1960; m. Margareth Rose Silva Palocci; one s. two d. *Education:* Univ. of São Paulo. *Career:* physician specializing in preventive medicine; mem. Partido dos Trabalhadores 1980–, Municipal Party Exec. 1988–89, Regional Party Directorate 1990–91 (Pres. 1997–99), Nat. Party Directorate 1996–97, Deputy Leader 2000; Pres. Rocha Lima Centre, Univ. of São Paulo 1981;

Regional Dir DCE Alexandre Vanucci Leme, Univ. of São Paulo 1982; Pres. Ass. Resident Physicians of Ribeirão Pret 1984–85; Regional Dir SIMESP 1985; Pres. Regional CUT Ribeirão Preto 1985; Regional Dir Sanitary Monitoring Service São Paulo 1986–88; Mayor of Ribeirão Preto 1993–96, 2001–02; Fed. Deputy 1999–2000, 2007–; Co-ordinator Govt transition team Oct.–Dec. 2002; Minister of Finance 2003–06; Pres. Conselho Monetário Nacional 2003–06; UNICEF Child and Peace Prize 1995, Juscelino Kubitschek Prize, Serviço Brasileiro de Apoio às Micro e Pequenas Empresas–SEBRAE 1996. *Publications include:* Saúde do trabalhador (Health of the Worker) 1994, A reforma do Estado e os municípios: a experiência de Ribeirão Preto (State and City Reform: The Experience of Ribeirão Preto) 1996, Sobre Formigas e Cigarras (auto-biography) 2007.
Address: Gabinete 548, Anexo IV, Câmara dos Deputados, Praça dos Três Poderes, 70160-900, Brasília, DF, Brazil (office). *Telephone:* (61) 3215-5548 (office). *Fax:* (61) 3215-2548 (office). *E-mail:* dep.antoniopalocci@camara .gov.br (office). *Website:* www.camara.gov.br (office).

PALSSON, Gunnar, PhD; Icelandic diplomatist; *Director, Department of Natural Resources and Environmental Affairs, Ministry of Foreign Affairs;* b. 25 Jan. 1955; m.; three c. *Education:* Univ. Coll. Dublin, Ireland, Karl Eberhardt Univ., Tübingen, Germany, State Univ. of New York, Buffalo, USA. *Career:* First Sec., Ministry of Foreign Affairs, Reykjavik 1984-86, officer, Div. of Political Affairs, NATO Int. Staff, Brussels 1986–88, Counsellor, Ministry of Foreign Affairs 1988–90, Amb. to CSCE, Negotiations on Confidence and Security-Bldg Measures (CSBM) and Negotiations on Conventional Forces in Europe (CFE), Vienna 1991–92, Deputy Perm. Under-Sec. for Political Affairs, Reykjavik 1992–94; Amb. and Perm. Rep. to UN, New York 1994–98, to NATO and WEU, Brussels and the Org. for the Prohibition of Chemical Weapons (OPCW), The Hague 1998–2002; Amb. and Dir, Dept of Natural Resources and Environmental Affairs, Ministry of Foreign Affairs 2002–; Chair. Senior Arctic Officials (SAO), Arctic Council 2002–04.
Address: Raudararsstigur 25, 13-150 Reykjavik, Iceland (office). *Telephone:* (4) 545-99-40 (office). *Fax:* (4) 562-23-73 (office). *E-mail:* gunnar.palsson@ utn.stjr.is (office). *Website:* www.mfa.is (office); www.arctic-council.org (home).

PAMIR, Mehmet Umit; Turkish diplomatist; b. 18 Sept. 1942, Istanbul; m.; two c. *Education:* Ankara Univ. *Career:* Consul then Consul-Gen., Komotini, Greece 1973–75; Counsellor to Embassies in Rome, London and Budapest and Perm. Mission to NATO, Brussels 1977–81, First Counsellor 1983–88; Dir of Dept Ministry of Foreign Affairs 1981–83, Deputy Dir-Gen. Policy and Planning Dept 1988–90; Amb. and Perm. Rep. to ICAO, Montréal 1990–91; Amb. to Algeria 1991–95, to Greece 1995–97; Chief Adviser to Prime Minister 1997–2000; Perm. Rep. to UN, New York 2000–04; Perm. Rep. to NATO, Brussels 2004–06; Nat. Dir Int. Centre for Black Sea Studies 2006–.
Address: c/o Board of Directors, International Centre for Black Sea Studies, 4 Xenophontos Str., 10557 Athens, Greece. *Telephone:* (210) 3242321. *Fax:* (210) 3242244. *E-mail:* icbss@icbss.org. *Website:* icbss.org.

PANDAY, Narendra Raj, MA; Nepalese diplomatist; b. 20 Aug. 1938, Kathmandu; m.; two c. *Education:* Tribhuvan Univ., Claremont Graduate Univ. *Career:* News Ed. and Chief, Radio Nepal –1974; entered Royal Palace Service as Asst Press Sec. to King 1974, apptd Deputy Press Sec. 1979, Jt Press Sec. 1984, Pvt. Sec. 1992, Press Sec. 1994, Principal Press Sec. 1997–99; Amb. to China (also accred to North Korea) 2003–07; Commdr of the Royal Victorian Order (UK) 1986, Orden de Isabel la Catolica (Spain) 1987, Ordre National de la Legion d'Honneur (France) 1994, Bikhyat Trishakti Patta (Nepal) 1995, Das Grosse Verdienstkruez (FRG) 1996, Prasiddha Prabal Gorkha Dakshinabahu (Nepal) 1998.
Address: Ministry of Foreign Affairs, Shital Niwas, Maharajganj, Kathmandu, Nepal. *Telephone:* (1) 4416011. *Fax:* (1) 4416016. *E-mail:* adm@mofa.gov.np. *Website:* www.mofa.gov.np.

PANDE, Kabinga; Zambian politician; *Minister of Foreign Affairs; Career:* fmr Head Public Relations, Zambian Cen. Bank; fmr Pres. Africa Travel Asscn; Minister of Science, Tech. and Vocational Training 2005, of Tourism, Environment and Natural Resources 2005–07, of Foreign Affairs 2007–; Deputy Chair. Movt for Multi-party Democracy.
Address: Ministry of Foreign Affairs, POB RW50069, Lusaka, Zambia (office). *Telephone:* (1) 213822 (office). *Fax:* (1) 222440 (office).

PANDEY, A. K.; Indian diplomatist; *High Commissioner to the Maldives; Career:* Jt Sec., Ministry of Foreign Affairs –2005; High Commr to the Maldives 2005–.
Address: Indian High Commission, H. Athireege-Aage, Ameeru Ahmed Magu, Malé, Maldives (office). *Telephone:* 3323015 (office). *Fax:* 3324778 (office).

PANDEY, Nishchal Nath, BA, LLB, MA; Nepalese academic and fmr research institute director; *Lecturer, Department of Conflict, Peace and Development Studies, Inst. of South Asia Studies, National University of Singapore;* b. 21 April 1972; m.; one d. *Education:* Tribhuvan Univ., Kathmandu. *Career:* news reporter, Nepal TV 1989; Deputy Ed. The Rising Nepal (daily newspaper) 1995–96; mem. task force to draft 9th Five Year Plan 1996–97; adviser to Nat. Planning Comm. 1997–98; Research and Documentation Officer, Inst. of Foreign Affairs, Kathmandu 1998–2001, Deputy Exec. Dir 2001–04, Officiating Exec. Dir 2004–06; Lecturer, Department of Conflict, Peace and Development Studies, Inst. of South Asia Studies, Nat. Univ. of Singapore; Head of del. to Japan Youth Forum 2002; mem. Int. Visitors Program, US Dept of State 2002; Chair. Renovation Cttee, Dhana Ganesh Temple, Handigaon 2001; mem. Renovation Cttee, Gahana Khojne Pond, Handigaon 2000; life mem. Friends of Kanti Iswari, Kathmandu; columnist for various nat. and int. news journals; Gorkha Dakchhin Bahu 1997, Birendra Aishwarya Service Medal 2002. *Publications:* Trade Facilitation: Nepal's Priorities 2005, Maoist Movement of Nepal and Implications for India and China 2005; numerous chapters in books and conf. papers. *Address:* Institute of South Asian Studies, 469A Tower Block, Bukit Timah Road 07-01, Singapore 259770, Singapore (office); Bishalnagar, Kathmandu, Nepal (home). *Telephone:* (1) 4432079 (home). *E-mail:* nina@ntc .net.np.

PANDEY, Ramesh Nath; Nepalese politician; b. Feb. 1944. *Career:* fmr Minister of Population and Devt, Information, Communication and Gen. Admin; fmr Minister for Industry and Communication; fmr Minister of State for Tourism, Labour and Social Welfare; fmr Govt Spokesman; mem. Parl.; Minister of Foreign Affairs 2005–06.
Address: c/o Ministry of Foreign Affairs, Shital Niwas, Maharajganj, Kathmandu, Nepal (office).

PANÉS CALPE, Enrique; Spanish diplomatist; *Ambassador to Portugal;* *Career:* fmr Amb. to Repub. of Korea; currently Amb. to Portugal.
Address: Embassy of Spain, Rua do Salitre 1, 1296-052 Lisbon, Portugal (office). *Telephone:* (21) 3472381 (office). *Fax:* (21) 3472384 (office). *E-mail:* emb.lisboa@mae.es (office). *Website:* www.mae.es/embajadas/lisboa (office).

PANGUENE, Armando Alexandre; Mozambican politician and diplomatist; *Ambassador to USA;* b. 18 Dec. 1942, Marracuene Dist, Maputo Prov.; m. Maria Teresa Panguene; three c. *Career:* Prov. Gov. Nampula Prov. 1974–75; Deputy Minister of Foreign Affairs 1975–77; Amb. to Portugal 1977–80; Prov. Gov. Cabo Delgado Prov. 1980–83; Deputy Minister of Defence 1984–87; Presidential Roving Amb. 1987–88; Amb. to UK 1988–96, High Commr to S Africa (also accred to Namibia and Lesotho) 1996–2001, Amb. to USA 2002– (also accred as High Commr to Canada 2003–).
Address: Embassy of Mozambique, 1525 New Hampshire Avenue, NW, Washington, DC 20036, USA (office). *Telephone:* (202) 293-7146 (office). *Fax:* (202) 835-0245 (office). *E-mail:* embamoc@aol.com (office); www .embamoc-usa.org (office).

PANITCHPAKDI, Supachai, MA, PhD; Thai banker and fmr government official and international organization official; *Secretary-General, United Nations Conference on Trade and Development (UNCTAD);* b. 30 May 1946, Bangkok; m. Mrs Sasai; one s. one d. *Education:* St Gabriel's Coll. and Trium Udom School, Bangkok, Netherlands School of Econs (now Erasmus Univ.), Rotterdam, and in UK. *Career:* worked in Research Dept, Int. Finance Div., and Financial Insts Supervision Dept, Bank of Thailand 1974–86; elected mem. Thai Parl. 1986, Deputy Minister of Finance 1986–88; Dir and Adviser, then Pres. Thai Military Bank 1988–92; apptd Senator 1992, then Deputy Prime Minister of Thailand 1992–95, Deputy Prime Minister and Minister of Commerce 1997–99; Dir-Gen. WTO 2002–05; Sec.-Gen. UNCTAD 2005–; Visiting Prof., Int. Inst. for Man. Devt, Lausanne 2001; Knight Grand Cordon (Special Class) of the Most Exalted Order of the White Elephant. *Publications include:* Globalization and Trade in the New Millennium 2001, China and WTO: Changing China Changing WTO (with Mark Clifford) 2002.
Address: United Nations Conference on Trade and Development (UNCTAD), Palais des Nations 8-14, Avenue de la Paix, 1211 Geneva 10, Switzerland (office). *Telephone:* (22) 9175806 (office). *Fax:* (22) 9170042 (office). *E-mail:* sgo@unctad.org (office). *Website:* www.unctad.org (office).

PANOS, A. James; American diplomatist; b. Los Angeles, Calif. *Education:* Princeton Univ., Johns Hopkins Univ. School of Advanced Int. Studies. *Career:* worked in pvt. business in Africa before joining the State Dept 1997, has served at embassies in Mozambique, Turkey, Haiti and US Mission to UN, Chargé d'affaires a.i., Embassy in Malabo, Equatorial Guinea –2005, Embassy in Bangui, Cen. African Repub. 2005–07.

Address: US Department of State, 2201 C Street NW, Washington, DC 20520, USA (office). *Telephone:* (202) 647-4000 (office). *Fax:* (202) 647-6738 (office). *Website:* www.state.gov (office).

PANOV, Alexander Nikolayevich, CandHistSc; Russian diplomatist; *Ambassador to Norway;* b. 6 July 1944, Moscow; m. 1967; one d. *Education:* Moscow Inst. of Int. Relations. *Career:* diplomatic service 1968–; trans., attaché Embassy in Tokyo 1968–71; teacher, Asst Prof., Moscow Inst. of Int. Relations 1971–77; Third, Second Sec., Perm. Mission to UN, New York 1977–82; First Sec., Second Far East Dept USSR Ministry of Foreign Affairs 1982–83; First Sec., Counsellor, Embassy in Tokyo 1983–88; Deputy Chief, Chief of Div., Deputy Chief, Dept of Countries of Pacific Ocean and SE Asia, USSR Ministry of Foreign Affairs 1988–90, Chief 1990–92; Amb. to Repub. of Korean 1992–94; Deputy Minister of Foreign Affairs 1994–96; Amb. to Japan 1996–2003, to Norway 2004–; Order of Merit. *Publications:* Postwar Reforms in Japan 1945–52, Japanese Diplomatic Service, Beyond Distrust to Trust; articles in periodicals.
Address: Embassy of the Russian Federation, Drammensvn 74, 0244 Oslo, Norway (office). *Telephone:* 22-55-32-78 (office). *Fax:* 22-55-00-70 (office). *E-mail:* rembassy@online.no (office). *Website:* www.norway.mid.ru (office).

PANTELIDIS, Leonidas; Cypriot diplomatist; *Ambassador to Russian Federation;* b. 11 Jan. 1953, Nicosia; m. Frosso Georgiades 1977; four c. *Education:* Univ. of Kent, UK. *Career:* joined Ministry of Foreign Affairs 1987, overseas postings include First Sec., Embassy in Washington, DC 1989–93; fmr Dir Perm Sec.'s Office, fmr Dir Office of the Foreign Minister; Amb. to Sweden (also accred to Iceland, Norway, Lativa, Denmark) 1998–2001, to Greece (also accred to Albania, Bulgaria, Romania) 2001–04, to Russian Fed. (also accred to Belarus, Kazakhstan, Armenia, Uzbekistan, Georgia Kyrgyzstan) 2004–; Grand Cross of the order of Phoenix of the Hellenic Republic.
Address: Embassy of Cyprus, 121069 Moscow, ul. Povarskaya 9, Russian Federation (office). *Telephone:* (495) 744-29-44 (office). *Fax:* (495) 744-29-35 (office). *E-mail:* moscowembassy@mfa.gov.cy (office). *Website:* www .mfa.gov.cy/embassymoscow (office).

PANTEV, Plamen I., PhD; Bulgarian research institute director and academic; *Founding Director, Institute for Security and International Studies;* b. 31 July 1952, Gradets, Vidin Dist; m. Tatyana Panteva; one d. *Education:* Sofia Univ. *Career:* fmr Researcher, Columbia Univ., New York, Johns Hopkins Univ., Washington, DC and Harvard Univ. 1988–89, Netherlands Inst. for Int. Relations 1993; Founder and Dir Inst. for Security and Int. Studies, Sofia 1994–; currently Assoc. Prof. of Law and Int. Relations and Vice-Dean of Law School, Sofia Univ. 'St Kliment Ohridsky'; Lecturer, NATO Defence Coll., Rome, Italy 2002, Henry L. Stimpson Center, Washington, DC 2003, Diplomatic Acad., Vienna July 2004, Texas A&M Univ. March 2006; Acting Co-Chair. Study Group on Regional Stability in SE Europe, Consortium of Defence Acad and Security Study Insts of PfP Countries; Ed.-in-Chief, Balkan Regional Profile (electronic periodical) –2005; mem. Int. Studies Asscn, Int. Advisory Bd Journal of Int. Negotiation, Europe's World Journal; Ford Foundation/ WEU Inst. for Security Studies Fellow, Istituto Affari Internazionali, Rome, Italy 1992, NATO Individual Fellow 1995–97, USIA Fellow, Univ. of Michigan 1997. *Publications:* seven books and more than 140 articles on int. and regional security, int. relations, int. law, foreign policy and civil–mil. relations.
Address: PO Box 231, Institute for Security and International Studies, 1c Krasno selo bl. 194, ent. B ap. 36, 1618 Sofia (office); Law School, Sofia University 'St Kliment Ohridsky', 15 Tsar Osvoboditel Blvd, 1504 Sofia, Bulgaria. *Telephone:* (2) 855-1828 (office); (2) 943-4806. *Fax:* (2) 855-1828 (office). *E-mail:* isis@mgu.bg (office). *Website:* www.isn.ethz.ch/isis (office).

PAOLILLO, Felipe; Uruguayan diplomatist and lawyer; *Vice-President, Assembly of States Parties, International Criminal Court;* b. 8 Oct. 1931. *Career:* Prof. of Int. Public Law, Univ. of Uruguay 1967–74, 1985–87; Assoc. Prof. New York Univ. School of Law 1977–84; Perm. Rep. to UN 1987–90, 2000–01, 2003, to Holy See and FAO 1996–2000; Chair. UN Gen. Ass. Credentials Cttee 2002; currently Vice-Pres. Ass. of States Parties, Int. Criminal Court, The Hague; mem. Inst. of Int. Law; mem. Interamerican Judicial Council.
Address: Secretariat of the Assembly of States Parties, International Criminal Court, Maanweg 174, 2516 AB The Hague, Netherlands (office). *Telephone:* (70) 5158097 (office). *Fax:* (70) 5158376 (office). *E-mail:* asp@ asp.icc-cpi.int (office). *Website:* www.icc-cpi.int/asp.html (office).

PAPACOSTAS, Costas; Cypriot fmr police officer and politician; *Minister of Defence;* b. 12 Nov. 1939, Agia Triada of Yialousa, Famagusta District; m. Chryso Mammidou; one s. one d. *Education:* War Coll. and Nat. Defence

Coll. of Greece, attended further special police training in crisis nan. and int. terrorism matters in Germany and USA. *Career:* served in Cyprus Army and Nat. Guard for 18 years, reaching rank of Col; seconded to Auxiliary Police Force to fight against illegal activities of EOKA B' 1973, participated in resistance against coup of 15 July 1974; seconded again to Police Force to establish and command Mobile Immediate Action Unit to fight terrorism and organized crime 1974; transferred to Police Force with rank of Chief Supt 1984, attained rank of Deputy Chief of Police, resgnd comm. in protest at state of affairs in the Force 1996; elected mem. House of Reps (AKEL-Left-New Forces) for Famagusta 1996–, Chair. House Standing Cttee on Crime and on the Fight against Drugs and Addictive Substances, Deputy Chair. House Standing Cttee on Refugees-Enclaved-Missing-Adversely Affected Persons. mem. House Standing Cttee on Defence Affairs, House Standing Cttee on Legal Affairs; Minister of Defence 2008–; Hon. Diploma and Resistance Medal for his actions towards the defence of the Repub. and the defence of law and order against the coup of 15 July 1974, Govt of Cyprus 2004, Hon. Diploma and Medal for his participation in the liberation struggle of EOKA 1955–1959, Govt of Cyprus 2006. *Publications:* two extended essays, 'The Legal and Historical Truth on the Cyprus Problem' 1985, and 'Today's Turkey-trends and Prospects' (in Greek).
Address: Ministry of Defence, 4 Emmanuel Roides Avenuw, 1432 Nicosia, Cyprus (office). *Telephone:* 22807622 (office). *Fax:* 22676182 (office). *E-mail:* defense@mod.gov.cy (office). *Website:* www.mod.gov.cy (office).

PAPADEMOS, Lucas D., PhD; Greek economist and banker; *Vice-President, European Central Bank;* b. 11 Oct. 1947, Athens. *Education:* Athens Coll., MIT, USA. *Career:* Prof. of Econs Columbia Univ., NY 1975–84, Univ. of Athens 1988–; Sr Economist Fed. Reserve Bank of Boston; Econ. Adviser Bank of Greece 1985–93, Head of Econ. Research Dept 1988–92, Deputy Gov. 1993–94, Gov. 1994–2002; Vice-Pres. ECB 2002–; mem. Cttee of Alts of Govs of EC Cen. Banks 1985–93, Council of Econ. Advisers 1985–88, 1991–94, EMI and various bds; Grand Commdr, Order of Honour 1999.
Address: European Central Bank, Kaiserstrasse 29, Postfach 160319, 60066 Frankfurt am Main, Germany (office). *Telephone:* (69) 13440 (office). *Fax:* (69) 13446000 (office). *E-mail:* info@ecb.europa.eu (office). *Website:* www .ecb.europa.eu (office).

PAPADOPOULOS, Tassos; Cypriot politician, lawyer and fmr head of state; b. 7 Jan. 1934, Nicosia; m. Photini Michaelides; two s. two d. *Career:* actively participated in EOKA struggle for independence 1955–59; Rep. of Greek Cypriot side in Constitutional Cttee (which drafted constitution); mem. House of Reps 1970–81, 1991–2003, Pres. of House 1976; elected Deputy Democratic Party (Diko) 1991, 1996, Pres. 2000–06; fmr Minister of the Interior, of Finance, of Labour and Social Insurance, of Health, of Agric. and Natural Resources; Pres. of Cyprus 2003–08; Interlocutor 1976; fmr mem. Nat. Council; fmr Chair. Standing Parl. Cttee on European Affairs, Cttee on Selection, Cttee on Financial and Budgetary Affairs; fmr Co-Chair. Jt EU–Cyprus Parl. Cttee.
Address: Dimokratiko Komma, POB 23979, 50 Grivas Dhigenis Avenue, 1080 Nicosia, Cyprus (office). *Telephone:* 2266602 (office). *Fax:* 22666488 (office). *E-mail:* diko@diko.org.cy (office). *Website:* www.diko.org.cy (office).

PAPOULIAS, Karolos, PhD; Greek politician, lawyer and head of state; *President;* b. 4 June 1929, Ioannina, Epirus; m. May Panou Papoulias; three d. *Education:* Univs of Athens, Madrid and Cologne. *Career:* fmr practising lawyer in Athens; lived in Germany 1962–74; founding mem. Socialist Democratic Union which mobilized Greeks living in W Europe against the military coup 1967; worked for Greek radio programme of Deutsche Welle; mem. Greek democratic del. at Gen. Ass. of Council of Europe during period of mil. dictatorship in Greece; mem. Parl. 1977–2004; mem. Cen. Cttee Panhellenic Socialist Movt (PASOK); Sec.-Gen. Centre for Mediterranean Studies, Athens; Deputy Minister for Foreign Affairs 1981–84, Alt. Minister 1984–85, Minister of Foreign Affairs 1985, 1993–96; Alt. Minister for Defence 1989–90; Pres. of Greece 2005–; Founder and fmr Pres. Asscn for Greek Linguistic Heritage; fmr Pres. Ethnikos athletic union.
Address: Office of the President, Odos Vassileos Georgiou 2, 100 28 Athens, Greece (office). *Telephone:* (210) 7283111 (office). *Fax:* (210) 7248938 (office). *E-mail:* publicrelationsoffice@presidency.gr (office). *Website:* www.presidency.gr (office).

PAPOUTSIS, Christos; Greek politician and economist; b. 11 April 1953, Larissa; m.; one d. *Education:* Univ. of Athens. *Career:* Pres. Greek Nat. Union of Students 1978–80; Special Adviser on Public Admin, Ministry of Presidency of Govt 1981–84; mem. Exec. Bureau Pan-Hellenic Socialist Movt (PASOK), Leader PASOK Del. to European Parl., mem. Political Council for Foreign Affairs, Security and Defence Policy; mem. European Parl. 1984–95, Vice-Pres. Socialist Group 1987–89; mem. Presidium, Party

of European Socialists 1988–; Commr for Energy and Euratom Supply Agency, Small and Medium Enterprises (SME) and Tourism, European Comm. 1995–99; Minister of Mercantile Marine 2000–01; mem. Parl. 2000, 2004; Highest Mark of Distinction with Cross (Austria), Gran Official, Orden Libertador Bernardo O'Higgins (Chile). *Publications:* European Journeys 1994, The Colour of the Future 1998, For Europe in the 21st Century 1999.
Address: Lykavittou 5, 10672 Athens, Greece (office). *Telephone:* (210) 3387700 (office). *Fax:* (210) 3387709 (office). *E-mail:* papoutsi@otenet.gr (office). *Website:* www.cpapoutsis.gr (office).

PAPPAS, Spyros; Greek lawyer, civil servant and European Union official; b. 1 Jan. 1953, Athens; m. Frady Karkanis; one s. one d. *Education:* Univ. of Athens, Panteios School of Econ. and Political Studies, Univ. of Paris, Directorate for European Affairs, INSEAD. *Career:* fmr naval Petty Officer; barrister, Athens 1976; Auditor Council of State 1978, Counsel 1983; Special Adviser in Prime Minister's Legal Office 1981; mem. Cen. Comm. for Drafting of Laws 1982; est. Nat. Centre of Public Admin., Sec.-Gen. 1985; est. Inst. of Permanent Training 1985; Assoc. Prof., European Inst. of Public Admin, Maastricht 1988, Dir of Faculty 1989, Dir-Gen. 1990, Prof. of European Law 1992; Dir-Gen. for Consumer Policy, EC 1995, for Information, Communication, Culture and Audiovisual Media 1997–99; Chair. Bd of Govs Int. East–West Acad.; mem. Supreme Council Church of Greece 1984, Comm. of Information on National Affairs, Inst. for Admin. Studies, Asscn of the Judges of the Council of State, Inst. of Public Admin., Cttee for Drafting of the Encyclopedia of Admin., Centre for European Policy Studies Int. Advisory Council, Scientific Council of Academia Istropolitana Bratislava Inst. of Advanced Studies, Foundation for Hellenic Culture; assoc. mem. Asscn of European Magistrates for Democracy and Liberty (MEDEL); substitute bd mem. Open Univ., Athens; cr. European Centre of Judges and Lawyers 1992; Hon. State Scholar 1970–73, Scholar of Council of Europe 1977; Officer Order of Merit, Luxembourg 1994; First Prize Michel Stassinopoulos Foundation for Admin. Law 1976. *Publications:* La constitution de la Grèce de 1975 1976, Le régime de planification en Grèce 1977, Le Tribunal de Première Instance 1990, Tendances actuelles et évolution de la jurisprudence de la cour de justice des Communautés européennes: suivi annuel (ed.) Vol. I 1993, Vol. II 1995, Procédures administratives nationales: préparation et mise en oeuvre des décisions communautaires: études comparatives (ed.) 1994, EC Competition Law: Financial Aspects (Co-Ed.) 1994, The Changing Role of Parliaments in the European Union (co-ed.) 1995, The European Union's Common Foreign and Security Policy: The Challenges of the Future 1996, Politiques publiques dans l'Union européenne 1996.

PAQUET-SEVIGNY, Thérèse, PhD; Canadian United Nations official, sociologist and academic; *Director, UNESCO Chair in Communication and International Development and Professor of Communications, Québec University;* b. 3 Feb. 1934, Sherbrooke, Québec; m. Robert Sévigny 1956; one s. one d. *Education:* Sorbonne-Paris Univ. and Univ. of Montreal. *Career:* journalism and communications research for La Tribune and L'Actualité, Montreal and for Montreal and Laval Univs 1952–61; Man. Dir for Consumer Research, Steinberg Limitée 1961–66; various appointments at Communications Depts Montreal Univ., McGill Univ. and Ecole des Hautes Etudes Commerciales, Montreal 1969–76; Vice-Pres. for Research and Planning, BCP Publicité Limitée 1969–71, Vice-Pres. and Man. Dir 1974–81, Pres. and Chief of Operations 1981–83; Vice-Pres. RSGL Publicité Limitée 1971–74; Vice-Pres. for Communications, Canadian Broadcasting Corpn (CBC) 1983–87; Under-Sec.-Gen. for Public Information, United Nations 1987; Prof. of Communications, Québec Univ., Montreal (UQAM) 1993–; Dir, UNESCO Chair in Communication and Int. Devt 1993–; Int. Consultant 1993–; Sec.-Gen. Orbicom (Int. Network of UNESCO Chairs in Communications) 1993–98, Sr Adviser 1999–; Dr hc (Sherbrooke, Bishop's Univ.) 1991. *Publications:* articles in books and journals.
Address: PO Box 8888, Downtown Station, Montreal, Québec, H3C 3P8 (office); 1509 Sherbrooke Street, West, Apartment 29, Montreal, Québec, H3G 1M1, Canada.

PARA, Barbara; San Marino diplomatist. *Career:* Amb. to Italy 1992–.
Address: Embassy of San Marino, Via Eleonora Duse 35, 00197 Rome, Italy (office). *Telephone:* (6) 8072511 (office). *Fax:* (6) 8070072 (office). *E-mail:* asmarino@ambrsm.it (office).

PARANHOS, Carlos Antonio da Rocha; Brazilian diplomatist; *Ambassador to Russia; Career:* fmr Spokesman for MERCOSUR; Pres. UN Conf. for Negotiation of a Successor Agreement to Int. Tropical Timber Agreement 2006; Deputy Perm. Rep. to UN and other Int. Orgs, responsible for disarmament, labour and health issues 2007–08, del. to UNCTAD, UN Conf. on Disarmament 2007–08; Amb. to Russia (also accred to Georgia) 2008–.

Address: Embassy of Brazil, 121069 Moscow, ul. B. Nikitskaya 54, Russia (office). *Telephone:* (495) 363-03-66 (office). *Fax:* (495) 363-03-67 (office). *E-mail:* brasrus@brasemb.ru (office). *Website:* www.brasemb.ru/en/embassy (office).

PARED PÉREZ, Rear-Adm. Sigfrido; Dominican Republic government official and military officer. *Career:* fmr Head Nat. Investigations Directorate; Sec. of State for Armed Forces 2004–.
Address: Secretariat of State for the Armed Forces, Plaza de la Independencia, Avda 27 de Febrero, esq. Luperón, Santo Domingo, DN, Dominican Republic (office). *Telephone:* 530-5149 (office). *Fax:* 531-1309 (office). *Website:* www.secffaa.mil.do (office).

PARHAM, Philip John; British diplomatist; *High Commissioner to Tanzania;* b. 14 Aug. 1960; m. Kasia Parham; five s. two d. *Career:* Int. Dept, Morgan Grenfell, London 1983–85, Tokyo 1986–89; Asst Dir Barclays de Zoete Wedd Ltd, Tokyo 1989–92, Dir Barclays de Zoete Wedd Ltd, London 1992–93; Head of Pakistan/Afghanistan Section, S Asia Dept, FCO 1993–94, Pvt. Sec. to Parl. Under-Sec. of State 1995, Policy Planning Staff 1995–96, seconded to US State Dept 1996, First Sec. (External), Washington, DC 1996–2000, Dir Trade and Investment Promotion, Saudi Arabia 2000–03, Head of Iraq Operations Unit, FCO 2003–04, Head of Counter-Terrorism Policy Dept 2004, High Commr to Tanzania 2006–.
Address: British High Commission, Umoja House, Garden Avenue, PO Box 9200, Dar es Salaam, Tanzania (office). *Telephone:* (22) 2110101 (office). *Fax:* (22) 2110102 (office). *E-mail:* bhc.dar@fco.gov.uk (office). *Website:* www.britishhighcommission.gov.uk/tanzania (office).

PARISI, Arturo; Italian politician and academic; b. 13 Sept. 1940, San Mango Piemonte. *Education:* Nunziatella Mil. School, Univ. of Sassari. *Career:* worked as forester and teacher at training centre for industrial workers while attending univ.; Sec., then Nat. Vice-Pres. Youth Dept, Azione Cattolica, also mem., Exec. Cttee, Int. Fed. of Catholic Youth Movt 1963–68; academic posts have included Asst Lecturer of Statistics, Univ. of Sassari, Researcher, Cattaneo Inst., Bologna 1968, Asst Prof. of Ecclesiastical Law, Univ. of Parma, Asst Prof. of History of Religious Insts, Univ. of Firenze; First Prof. of Sociology of Religions, then full Prof. of Sociology of Political Phenomena, Cattaneo Inst., Bologna 1971–, also currently Dir Cattaneo Inst.; mem. Chamber of Deputies 1999–; mem. Partito Democratico 2007–; Minister of Defence 2006–08; political adviser to Romani Prodi; Under-Sec., Presidency of Council of Ministers 1996; active in I Democratici movt 1999; Co-founder and Nat. Vice-Pres. Democrazia è Libertà – La Margherita 2001, Pres. of party in Fed. Ass. 2004–07; Vice-Pres. Il Mulino Asscn, also ed. of journal; fmr Pres. Italian Soc. of Electoral Studies; served as expert to govt cttee and parl. comm. on domestic terrorism 1987–88; active in movt for Institutional Reforms and Ulivo movt.
Address: Partito Democratico, Piazza Saint'Anastasia 7, 00186 Rome, Italy (office). *Telephone:* (06) 675471 (office). *Fax:* (06) 67547319 (office). *E-mail:* info@partitodemocratico.it (office). *Website:* www.partitodemocratico.it (office).

PARK, Geun-hye; South Korean politician; b. 2 Feb. 1952, Gumi, northern Gyeongsang Prov.. *Education:* Sogang Univ. *Career:* worked for Yukyoung Foundation and Saemaeum Hosp.; served as dir sr citizen welfare centre; Dir Korean Cultural Foundation 1993; Dir Jeongsu Scholarship Fund 1994; mem. Grand Nat. Party (GNP) 1998–2002, 2003–, Vice-Pres. 2000–02, Chair. 2004–06; mem. Nat. Ass. for Daegu 1998–; Chair. Preparatory Cttee Korean Coalition for the Future 2001, Leader 2002– (merged with GNP 2003); mem. Korean Literature Asscn 1994; Hon. Pres. Korean Girl Scouts 1974. *Publications inlcude:* four books on family and literature.
Address: National Assembly, 1 Yeouido-dong, Yeongdeungpo-gu, Seoul (office); Grand National Party, 17-7, Yeouido-dong, Yeongdeungpo-gu, Seoul 150-010, Republic of Korea. *Telephone:* (2) 3786-3373. *Fax:* (2) 3786-3610. *Website:* www.hannara.or.kr.

PARK, In-kook, BA, MA; South Korean diplomatist; *Permanent Representative, United Nations;* b. 15 Aug. 1951; m.; two s. *Education:* Seoul Nat. Univ. *Career:* Consul, Consulate-Gen. in New York 1981–84; Deputy Dir N American Div., Ministry of Foreign Affairs 1984–87; First Sec., Embassy in Saudi Arabia 1987–89; Prin. Sec. to Minister of Foreign Affairs 1989–91; First Sec., Embassy in Washington, DC 1991–94; Dir UN Div., UN Systems Bureau, Ministry of Foreign Affairs 1994, Dir Disarmament and Nuclear Energy Div. 1994–96; Dir-Gen. for Int. Co-operation, Office of Planning for Light Water Reactor Project 1996–99; Minister-Counsellor, Embassy in Brussels 1999–2002, also with Perm. Mission to EU; Aide to Minister of Foreign Affairs and Trade 2002; Sec. to Pres. for Int. Security 2002–03; Amb. to Kuwait 2003–05; Perm. Rep. to UN, Geneva 2005–06, Chair. Conf. on Disarmament 2006; Deputy Minister for Policy Planning

and Int. Orgs, Ministry of Foreign Affairs and Trade 2006–07, Deputy Minister for Multilateral and Global Issues 2007–08; Perm. Rep. to UN, New York 2008–.
Address: Permanent Mission of the Republic of Korea to the United Nations, 335 East 45th Street, New York, NY 10017, USA (office). *Telephone:* (212) 439-4000 (office). *Fax:* (212) 986-1083 (office). *E-mail:* korea@un.int (office). *Website:* www.un.int/korea (office).

PARK, Joon-woo, BA; South Korean diplomatist; b. 7 May 1953; m.; one s. one d. *Education:* Seoul Nat. Univ., Johns Hopkins Univ., USA. *Career:* joined Ministry of Foreign Affairs 1978, Staff Asst, Office of Sec. to Pres. for Foreign Affairs 1987–90, Asst Sec. to Pres. for Foreign Affairs 1996–97, Dir Northeast Asia Div. I (Japan), Ministry of Foreign Affairs and Trade 1997–99, Deputy Dir-Gen. Asian and Pacific Affairs Bureau 2004–05, Dir-Gen. 2005–06, Sr Asst to Minister 2005–06; overseas postings include Second Sec., Embassy in Washington, DC 1984–87, Counsellor, Embassy in Helsinki 1992–94, Political Officer, Embassy in Tokyo 1994–96, Minister Counsellor, Embassy in Beijing 1999–2002; Amb. to Singapore 2006.
Address: Ministry of Foreign Affairs and Trade, 95-1, Doryeom-dong, Jongno-gu, Seoul 110-787, Republic of Korea. *Telephone:* (2) 3703-2114. *Fax:* (2) 2100-7999. *E-mail:* web@mofat.go.kr. *Website:* www.mofat.go.kr.

PARKANOVÁ, Vlasta, DJur; Czech lawyer and politician; *Minister of Defence;* b. 21 Nov. 1951, Prague; m. Zdeněk Parkan; one d. *Education:* Charles Univ. *Career:* began legal career specialising in commercial law 1975–88; co-f. Civic Forum, Tábor 1989; mem. Fed. Ass. 1990–93; various positions within Ministry of Foreign Affairs and Ministry of Interior 1992–96; mem. Parl. 1996–; Minister of Justice 1997–98, Deputy Chair. Cttee on Defence and Security 1998–2002, Minister of Defence 2007–; Vice-Chair. Constitution and Legal Cttee 1998–2002, Chair. 2003–06; mem. Perm. Del. of Parl. of Czech Repub. to NATO 1998–2006; mem. Civic Democratic Alliance (ODA) 1991–98; mem. Christian Democratic Party (KDU-ČSL) 2001–.
Address: Ministry of Defence, Tychonova 1, 160 01 Prague 6, Czech Republic (office). *Telephone:* 973201111 (office). *Fax:* 973200149 (office). *E-mail:* info@army.cz (office). *Website:* www.army.cz (office).

PARKER, Lyn, LLB; British diplomatist; *Ambassador to the Netherlands;* b. 25 Nov. 1952; m. Jane Walker; two d. *Education:* Magdalen Coll., Oxford, Univ. of Manchester. *Career:* Lecturer in Law, Univ. of Manchester 1975–78; joined FCO 1978, Arms Control/Disarmament Dept 1978–79, Second, later First Sec., Chancery, Athens 1980–84, EC Dept (Internal) 1984–87, Sec. of State's Office 1987–89, on loan to European Secr., Cabinet Office 1989–92, Counsellor/Head of Chancery, New Delhi 1992–95, UK Rep. (Counsellor Political), Brussels 1995–99, Head of Whitehall Liaison Dept, FCO 1999–2001, High Commr to Cyprus 2001–05, Amb. to the Netherlands 2005–.
Address: British Embassy, Lange Voorhout 10, 2514 ED The Hague, Netherlands (office). *Telephone:* (70) 4270427 (office). *Fax:* (70) 4270345 (office). *E-mail:* library@britain.nl (office); OtherConsularEnquiries .Amsterdam@fco.gov.uk (office). *Website:* www.britain.nl (office).

PARKER, Maurice S., BA, MA; American diplomatist; *Ambassador to Swaziland;* *Education:* Univ. of California, Berkeley, San Francisco State Univ. *Career:* career mem. Sr Foreign Service with rank of Minister Counselor, Dir Office of Employee Relations and Foreign Service Assignments, Bureau of Human Resources, also fmr Dir of Consular and Int. Programs, Homeland Security Council, White House; fmr Prin. Officer in Ciudad Juarez and Barcelona; other overseas postings include Nigeria, Scotland, Colombia and Guyana; Amb. to Swaziland 2007–.
Address: US Embassy, 2350 Mbabane Place, Mbabane, Swaziland (office). *Telephone:* 4042445 (office). *Fax:* 4042059 (office). *E-mail:* usembswd@realnet.co.sz (office). *Website:* swaziland.usembassy.gov (office).

PARMLY, Michael E., MA; American diplomatist; b. St Augustine, Fla; m. Marie-Catherine Schutte; one s. one d. *Education:* St Joseph's Coll., Philadelphia and Fletcher School of Law and Diplomacy. *Career:* career mem. Sr Foreign Service with rank of Minister-Counselor; Peace Corps volunteer, Bucaramanga, Colombia 1973–75; joined the Foreign Service 1977, served in Morocco and Spain, Washington appointments have included Office Dir European Bureau and Watch Officer and Analyst, Bureau of Intelligence and Research, Political Counselor, Bucharest 1987–89, Political Counselor, US Mission to EU 1989–93, Deputy Chief of Mission and Charge d'Affaires a.i., Embassy in Sarajevo –1997, Political Minister, Embassy in Paris 1997–2000, Acting Asst Sec. of State for Democracy, Human Rights and Labor Jan.–June 2001, Prin. Deputy Asst Sec. 2000–03, State Dept Rep. in Kandahar, Afghanistan Feb.–May 2003, Sr Advisor to Amb. Khalilzad for Afghan presidential elections Aug.–Oct. 2004, Chief of Mission-Designate, US Interests Section, Havana 2005–08;

Prof. of Nat. Security Studies, Nat. War Coll., Washington, DC; Superior Honor Award.
Address: Department of State, 2201 C St, NW, Washington, DC 20520, USA. *Telephone:* (202) 647-4000. *Fax:* (202) 647-6738. *Website:* www.state.gov.

PARNOHADININGRAT, Sudjadnan; Indonesian diplomatist; *Ambassador to USA;* m. Nunung Kuncorowati; three c. *Education:* Univ. of Gajah Mada, Yogyakarta, School of Int. and Political Affairs, Columbia Univ., New York, USA. *Career:* joined Foreign Service 1981, Third Sec./Second Sec., Perm. Mission, Geneva and Vienna 1982–86, First Sec./Counselor, Perm. Mission, Geneva 1989–92, Minister Counselor, Perm. Mission, New York 1996–98, Sec. Indonesian Task Force for Implementation of Popular Consultations in East Timor 1999, Dir for Int. Orgs, Ministry of Foreign Affairs 1999–2001, Head of bilateral Indonesia-East Timor meetings 2000–01, Amb. to Australia and Vanuatu 2001–02, Sec.-Gen. Ministry of Foreign Affairs, concurrently serving as Indonesian Sr Official Meeting Leader to ASEAN 2002–05, Chair. Third Non-Proliferation Preparatory Cttee for 2005 Treaty Review Conf., New York 2004, Main Cttee Nonproliferation Treaty Review Conf. 2005, Amb. to USA 2006–.
Address: Embassy of Indonesia, 2020 Massachusetts Avenue, NW, Washington, DC 20036-1084, USA (office). *Telephone:* (202) 775-5200 (office). *Fax:* (202) 775-5256 (office). *E-mail:* information@embassyofindonesia.org (office). *Website:* www.embassyofindonesia.org (office).

PARO, Josip; Croatian diplomatist; *Ambassador to UK;* b. 2 Feb. 1955, Pag; m. Jasna Paro; two c. *Education:* Univ. of Zagreb. *Career:* after graduating from coll., worked freelance as a trans.; rep. of Atlas Airtours in Italy, France and Spain 1989–91; Ed. Filozofska istraživanja (Philosophical Research), magazine of the Croatian Soc. of Philosophy 1991–92; with Dept for Northern and Western Europe, Ministry of Foreign Affairs 1992–93, Political Advisor, Embassy in Madrid 1993–96, Head of Analytical Dept, Ministry of Foreign Affairs as Minister Counsellor 1996–97, promoted to Amb. 1997, working as Asst Minister in Div. I (Bilateral Issues) 2000–02, Amb. to UK 2002–; mem. Croatian-Yugoslav Comm. on the Return of Refugees 2000–02. *Publication:* Uspon mirna čovjeka (The Rise of a Peaceful Man).
Address: Embassy of Croatia, 21 Conway Street, London, W1T 6BN, England (office). *Telephone:* (20) 7387-2022 (office). *Fax:* (20) 7387-0310 (office). *E-mail:* vrhlon@mvpei.hr (office); croemb.london@mvpei.hr (office). *Website:* uk.mvp.hr (office).

PARRA-ARANGUREN, Gonzalo; Venezuelan judge; b. 5 Dec. 1928, Caracas. *Education:* Cen. Univ. of Venezuela, Inter-American Law Inst., Univ. of New York, USA, Ludwig-Maximilians Univ., Munich, Germany. *Career:* Prof., Cen. Univ. of Venezuela, Caracas 1956, Andrés Bello Catholic Univ., Caracas 1957; Judge, Second Court of First Instance (commercial matters), Fed. Dist and State of Miranda, Caracas 1958–71; First Assoc. Judge, Chamber of Cassation (civil, commercial and labour matters) of Supreme Court of Justice 1988–92, elected Alt. Judge 1992; mem. nat. group for Venezuela, Perm. Court of Arbitration, The Hague 1985–; Judge, Int. Court of Justice 1991–96; has acted as arbitrator in Venezuela and abroad on pvt. commercial matters; mem. Legal Advisory Cttee of Ministry of Foreign Affairs 1984–96, of Nat. Congress 1990–96; mem. Acad. of Political and Social Sciences of Caracas 1966– (Pres. 1993–95), Inst. of Int. Law 1979–; rep. Venezuela at several sessions of The Hague Conf. on Pvt. Int. Law. *Publications:* several books and numerous articles in Venezuelan and foreign journals on law of nationality, pvt. int. law and int. civil procedural law.
Address: International Court of Justice, Peace Palace, Carnegieplein 2, 2517 KJ The Hague, Netherlands (office). *Telephone:* (70) 3022323 (office). *Fax:* (70) 3022409 (office). *E-mail:* information@icj-cij.org (office). *Website:* www.icj-cij.org (office).

PARTHASARATHI, Nagesha, BE, MBA; Indian diplomatist; *Ambassador to Senegal; Education:* Univs of Bangalore and Mysore. *Career:* early career as eng exec.; joined Foreign Service 1981, served in various positions overseas including in Belgium, Senegal, Pakistan, UK, Syria; served on deputation to Ministry of Finance; fmr Jt Sec., Gulf Division, Jt Sec. Admin Ministry of External Affairs; Amb. to South Korea 2005–08, to Senegal 2008–. *Publications:* Reluctant Assassin (novel) 2005.
Address: Embassy of India, 5 rue Carde, BP 398, Dakar, Senegal (office). *Telephone:* 822-58-75 (office). *Fax:* 822-35-85 (office). *E-mail:* indiacom@sentoo.sn (office). *Website:* www.ambassadeinde.sn (office).

PARTS, Juhan, BL; Estonian politician; *Minister of Economic Affairs and Communications;* b. 27 Aug. 1966, Tallinn; m.; one s. one d. *Education:* Tallina First Secondary School, Univ. of Tartu. *Career:* Deputy Sec.-Gen.,

Ministry of Justice 1992–98; Auditor Gen. 1998–2002; Chair. Res Publica Party 2002–05; Prime Minister of Estonia 2003–05 (resgnd); Minister of Econ. Affairs and Communications 2007–.
Address: Ministry of Economic Affairs and Communications, Harju 11, Tallinn 15072 (office); Res Publica, Narva mnt. 7, Tallinn 10117, Estonia (office). *Telephone:* 625-6342 (Ministry) (office); 610-9244 (Res Publica) (office). *Fax:* 631-3660 (Ministry) (office); 610-9243 (Res Publica) (office). *E-mail:* juhan.parts@mkm.ee (office); respublica@respublica.ee (office). *Website:* www.mkm.ee (office); www.respublica.ee (office).

PARVANOV, Georgi, MA, PhD; Bulgarian historian and head of state; *President;* b. 28 June 1957, Sirishnik, Pernik Dist; m. Zorka Parvanova; two s. *Education:* mathematics college in Pernik, Sofia Univ. St Kliment Ohridski. *Career:* researcher, Inst. of History, Bulgarian CP (BCP—became Bulgarian Socialist Party—BSP 1990) 1981–91, conducted research on the nat. question and history of social democracy in Bulgaria, Sr Research Assoc. 1989–92, Dir Centre for History and Policy Studies with the Supreme Council of the Bulgarian Socialist Party (BSP) 1992–96; joined BCP 1981 first party post 1991, Deputy Chair. Supreme Council 1994–96, Chair. 1996–2001; mem. Narodno Sobraniye (Parl.) for Kurdjali (Southern Bulgaria) 1994–2001, Chair. Parl. Group for Friendship with Greece and mem. Parl. Cttee on Radio and Television 1994–97, Parl. Group of the Democratic Left, Parl. Group of Coalition for Bulgaria 1997–2001; Pres. of Bulgaria 2002–; fmr Chair. Parl. Group on Friendship between Bulgaria and Greece; Grand Gold Medal, Tomáš Garrigue Masaryk Univ., Brno, Czech Republic; Dr hc (Prešov Univ.), (Baku Univ.), (Yerevan State Univ.). *Publications:* numerous scientific articles, monographs and books, including Dimitar Blagoev and the Bulgarian National Problem 1879–1917 1988, From Bouzloudja to the Corona Theatre–An Attempt at a New Reading of Pages from the BSP's Social Democratic Period 1995, The Bulgarian Social Democracy and the Macedonian Issue at the End of the 19th Century up to 1918 1997, November 10: Before and After 2001.
Address: Office of the President, 1123 Sofia, bul. Dondukov 2, Bulgaria (office). *Telephone:* (2) 923-93-33 (office). *E-mail:* press@president.bg (office). *Website:* www.president.bg (office).

PASCHKE, Karl Theodor; German diplomatist; b. 12 Nov. 1935, Berlin; m. Pia-Irene Schwerber 1963; one s. one d. *Education:* Univs of Munich and Bonn. *Career:* Consul, New Orleans, La, USA 1964–68; Deputy Chief of Mission, Kinshasa 1968–71; Dean, Foreign Office Training School, Bonn 1972–77; Press Counsellor, Washington, DC 1977–80; Spokesman, German Foreign Office, Bonn 1980–84; Amb. to UN Orgs Vienna 1984–86; Minister, Washington, DC 1987–90; Dir-Gen. for Personnel and Man., Foreign Office, Bonn 1990–94; Under-Sec.-Gen. for Internal Oversight Services, UN, New York 1994–99; Special Insp., Foreign Office 2000; currently Chair. Cttee on Budget and Finance, Ass. of States Parties to Rome Statute of Int. Criminal Court. *Publication:* Reform der Attache-Ausbildung 1975.
Address: International Criminal Court, POB 19519, 2500 CM, The Hague, Netherlands (office); Denglerstrasse 46, 53173 Bonn, Germany (home). *Telephone:* (228) 9562032 (home). *Fax:* (228) 9562083 (home). *Website:* www.icc-cpi.int (office).

PASCOE, B. Lynn, MA; American diplomatist and UN official; *Under-Secretary-General, United Nations Department for Political Affairs;* b. 1943, Mo.; m. Diana Pascoe; two d. *Education:* Univ. of Kansas, Columbia Univ. *Career:* served on Soviet and China Desks; postings to Moscow, Hong Kong, Bangkok, Beijing (twice) and Taiwan; Prin. Deputy Asst Sec., East Asian and Pacific Bureau, State Dept; Deputy Chief of Mission, American Embassy, Beijing; Deputy Exec. Sec., Dept of State; Special Asst to Deputy Sec. of State; Dir American Inst., Taiwan 1993–96; Sr Adviser, Bureau of East African and Pacific Affairs and at US Mission to the UN; Special Negotiator for Nagorno-Karabakh and Regional Conflicts; Co-Chair. OSCE Minsk Group; apptd Amb. to Malaysia 1999; Deputy Asst Sec. for European and Eurasian Affairs, US Dept of State 2001–04; Amb. to Indonesia 2004–07; Under-Sec.-Gen., UN Dept for Political Affairs 2007–.
Address: Department of Political Affairs, United Nations, New York, NY 10017, USA (office). *Telephone:* (212) 963-1234 (office). *Fax:* (212) 963-4879 (office). *Website:* www.un.org/Depts/dpa (office).

PASHAYEV, Hafiz Mir Jalal, PhD; Azerbaijani academic and diplomatist; *Deputy Foreign Minister;* m. Rana Pashayeva; two c. *Education:* Baku State Univ., Inst. of Atomic Energy, Moscow, Russia, Univ. of Calif., Irvine, USA. *Career:* physics teacher, then Dir Metal Physics Lab., Baku State Univ.; Amb. to USA (first Azerbaijani in new post) 1993–2006; Deputy Foreign Minister 2006–. *Publications include:* numerous scientific articles and books.
Address: Ministry of Foreign Affairs, S. Qurbanov küç. 4, 1009 Baku, Azerbaijan (office). *Telephone:* (12) 492-96-92 (office). *Fax:* (12) 498-84-80

(office). *E-mail:* secretariat@mfa.gov.az (office). *Website:* www.mfa.gov.az (office).

PASINETTI, Luigi Lodovico, MA, PhD; Italian economist and academic; *Professor Emeritus of Economics, Università Cattolica del Sacro Cuore, Milan;* b. 12 Sept. 1930, Bergamo; m. Carmela Colombo 1966; one s. *Education:* Univ. Cattolica del Sacro Cuore, Milan, Univ. of Cambridge, UK, Harvard Univ., USA. *Career:* Research Fellow, Nuffield Coll., Oxford 1960–61; Fellow and Lecturer in Econs, King's Coll., Cambridge 1961–73; Lecturer, then Reader in Econs, Univ. of Cambridge 1961–76; Prof. of Econs, Università Cattolica del Sacro Cuore 1976–2007, Prof. Emer. 2007–, Chair. 1980–83; Wesley Clair Mitchell Visiting Research Prof. of Econs, Columbia Univ., New York 1971, 1975; Visiting Research Prof., Indian Statistical Inst., Calcutta and New Delhi 1979; Visiting Prof. of Econs, Univ. of Ottawa, Carleton Univ. 1981, Kyoto Univ. 1984, Univ. of Southern California 1985; Visiting Fellow, Gonville and Caius Coll., Cambridge 1989; McDonnell Distinguished Scholars Fellow, WIDER, the UN Univ., Helsinki 1991, 1992; Visiting Prof., Univ. of Sydney 1993; Visiting Fellow, Trinity Coll. Cambridge 1997, 1999; mem. Council and Exec. Cttee Int. Econ. Asscn 1980–99, Hon. Pres. 2005; Pres. Italian Econ. Asscn 1986–89, Confed. of European Econ. Asscns 1992–93, European Soc. for the History of Econ. Thought 1995–97; Fellow, Econometric Soc. 1978–; mem. Accad. Lincei, Rome 1986–, Inst. Lombardo Accad. di Scienze e Lettere, Milan 1995–; Hon. Fellow, Gonville and Caius Coll., Cambridge 1999–; Hon. Pres. European Asscn for Evolutionary Political Economy 1989, European Soc. for the History of Economic Thought 2003–, Int. Econ. Asscn 2005–; Dr hc (Fribourg) 1986; St Vincent Prize for Econs 1979, 2002, Gold Medal (First Class) for Educ., Culture and Arts 1982, 'La Madonnina' Int. Prize (Econs section), Milan 1987, Special Prize for Culture (Econs section), Presidency of the Council of Ministers 1996, Invernizzi Prize for Econs 1997. *Publications:* Growth and Income Distribution 1974, Lectures on the Theory of Production 1977, Structural Change and Economic Growth 1981, Structural Change and Adjustment in the World Economy (with P. Lloyd) 1987, Structural Economic Dynamics 1993, Economic Growth and the Structure of Long-Term Development (with R. M. Solow) 1994, The Impact of Keynes in the 20th Century (with B. Schefold) 1999, Keynes and the Cambridge Keynesians 2007; numerous articles on income distribution, capital theory, econ. growth and structural econ. dynamics. *Address:* Faculty of Economics, Università Cattolica del Sacro Cuore, Largo A. Gemelli 1, 20123 Milan, Italy (office). *Telephone:* (02) 72342470 (office). *Fax:* (02) 72342406 (office). *E-mail:* llp@unicatt.it (office). *Website:* www.unicatt.it/docenti/pasinetti (office).

PASQUA, Charles Victor; French politician; b. 18 April 1927, Grasse; m. Jeanne Joly 1947; one s. *Education:* College de Grasse, Inst. d'Etudes Juridiques, Nice and Faculté de Droit, Aix-en-Provence. *Career:* Rep. Société Ricard 1952, Insp. 1955, Regional Dir 1960, Dir French Sales 1962, Dir-Gen. French Sales and Export 1963; Pres.-Dir-Gen. Société Euralim 1967–71; Commercial Consultant 1972–; Deputy to Nat. Ass. (UDR) 1968–73; Sec.-Gen. UDR 1974–76; Senator, Hauts de Seine 1977–86, 1988–93, 1995–99, 2004–; Pres. RPR Group in Senate 1981–86, 1988–93; Minister of the Interior and Administration 1986–88, 1993–95; Political adviser Exec. Comm. of RPR 1998–99; Co-founder and Pres Rassemblement pour la France et l'Indépendance de l'Europe 1999–; mem. European Parl. 1999–2004; Chevalier, Légion d'honneur; Médaille de la France libre. *Publications:* La libre entreprise – un état d'esprit 1964, L'ardeur nouvelle 1985, Que demande le peuple 1992, Demain, la France (Vol. I): la priorité sociale (jtly) 1992, Tous pour la France 1999. *Address:* Le Rassemblement pour la France et L'Indépendance de l'Europe, 129 avenue Charles de Gaulle, 92521 Neuilly-sur-Seine Cedex; Conseil Général, Hôtel du Département, 2–16 Blvd Soufflot, 92015 Nanterre Cedex, France. *Telephone:* 1-55-62-24-24 (office). *Fax:* 1-55-62-24-44 (office). *E-mail:* infos@charles-pasqua.com (office). *Website:* www.rpfie .org (office).

PASSY, Solomon Isaac, MS, PhD; Bulgarian politician and academic; *Chairman, Foreign Affairs Committee, Bulgarian National Assembly;* b. 22 Dec. 1956, Plovdiv; m.; two s. one d. *Education:* Sofia Univ. 'St Kliment Ohridski'. *Career:* in opposition to anti-Muslim repressive policy of the Communist regime 1985–89; Asst Prof. of Math. Logic and Computer Science, Sofia Univ. 'St Kliment Ohridski' and at Bulgarian Acad. of Sciences 1984–94; participant in Nat. Round Table for transition to democracy 1989–90; activist of Ecoglasnost opposition movt 1989; Co-founder and mem. Coordinating Council of UDF 1990–91; Founding Pres. and CEO Atlantic Club of Bulgaria (first pro-Atlantic NGO ever founded in a non-NATO mem. state) 1991–2001; Founder and Spokesman, Green Party of Bulgaria 1989; Mem. Grand Nat. Ass. (Green Party, Union of Democratic Forces—UDF) 1990–91, (Nat. Movt Simeon II) 2005–, Chair. Foreign Affairs, Defence and Security Cttee, 39th Nat. Ass. July 2001,

Foreign Affairs Cttee, 40th Nat. Ass. 2005–, Bulgaria–USA caucus, 40th Nat. Ass. 2005–; Minister of Foreign Affairs 2001–05; Chair. Ad hoc Cttee on Transparency and Accountability, Parl. Ass. OSCE 2006–; Vice-Pres. Nat. Movt Simeon II 2005, mem. Political Council 2002–05; Special Adviser on NATO accession to Govt of Macedonia 2007–; mem. 2nd, 3rd, 4th and 13th Bulgarian Antarctic Expeditions to Livingston Island, Antarctica 1993–2005; Chair. Host Cttee for the Dalai Lama's visit to Sofia 1991; Leader Bulgarian Del. for the Audience with His Holiness Pope John Paul II 1994; Vice-Chair. Atlantic Treaty Asscn, Paris 1996–99; Co-Chair. Host Cttee for the visit of Pres. Bill Clinton to Bulgaria 1999; Hon. Citizen of Nedelino 2003, of State of Tex., USA 2004; Orden Infante Don Enrique (Grã-Cruz) (Portugal) 2002; Orden del Mérito Civil (Gran Cruz) (Spain) 2003; Order of Léopold II (Grand Cross) (Belgium) 2004; Ordine della Stella della Solidarieta' Italiana (I classe) (Italy) 2006; Orden de Isabel la Catolica (Gran Cruz) (Spain) 2006; Dr hc (South-West Univ. of Bulgaria) 2005; Balkan Peace Award 2004. *Publications:* numerous scientific articles on math. logic and computer science. *Address:* Foreign Affairs Committee, Bulgarian National Assembly, 1 Al. Battenberg Square, 1169 Sofia (office); National Movement Simeon II, 23 Vrabcha Street, 1000 Sofia, Bulgaria. *Telephone:* (2) 9861133 (office). *Fax:* (2) 9818568 (office). *E-mail:* kvp@parliament.bg; ndsv@ndsv.bg. *Website:* www.parliament.bg/kvp (office).

PASTORELLI, Jean, LenD; Monegasque civil servant, diplomatist and politician; *Ambassador to France;* m.; two c. *Education:* Institut d'Etudes Politiques and Ecole Nationale d'Admin (Fonctionnaire Etranger), Paris. *Career:* joined Secr., Dept of Finance and Economy 1969; Dir Budget and Treasury 1978–88; Govt Counsellor for Finance and the Economy 1988–95; Pres. Radio Monte Carlo 1995–2000, Monaco Telecom 1997–99; Perm. Del. to Posteurop 1995–; Perm. Del. to ITU, UPU 1995–2004; Pres. Tele Monte Carlo 1995–, Monte Carlo Radiodiffusion (MCR) 1995–; Minister Plenipotentiary 1995; Perm. Del. to UNESCO 2003, to French-speaking community 2003; Perm. Rep. at IAEA 2003; Nat. Authority for Principality of Monaco to Org. for Prohibition of Chemical Weapons 2003, Perm. Rep. 2003–; Pres. EUTELSAT Ass. of Parties 2001–04, INTELSAT Ass. of Parties (ITSO) 2002–04; Amb. to Belgium, the Netherlands and Grand Duchy of Luxembourg 2003–07; Head of Mission to European Communities 2003–07, Observer within Int. Criminal Court 2003–; Govt Counsellor for External Relations 2007–08; Amb. to France 2008–; Commdr, Ordre de Saint-Charles. *Address:* Embassy of Monaco, 22 boulevard Suchet, 75116 Paris, France (office). *Telephone:* 1-45-04-74-54 (office). *Fax:* 1-45-04-45-16 (office). *E-mail:* ambassade.en.france@gouv.mc (office).

PASTRANA ARANGO, Andrés, LLD; Colombian diplomatist and fmr head of state; b. 17 Aug. 1954, Bogotá; m. Nohra Puyana Bickenbach; one s. two d. *Education:* Colegio San Carlos de Bogotá, Colegio Mayor de Nuestra Señora del Rosario Law School, Harvard Univ. *Career:* Man. Dir Revista Guión (publ.) 1978–79; Man. Dir Datos y Mensajes SA News Broadcasting Co. 1979–80; Dir TV Hoy News 1980–87; Councillor Bogotá City Council 1982–86, Chair. Jan.–April 1983, 1984–85; Mayor of Bogotá 1988–90; Senator 1991–93; founder and Presidential Cand. of Nueva Fuerza Democrática 1994; Pres. of Colombia 1998–2002; Amb. to USA 2005–06 (resgnd); mem. Int. Union of Local Authorities, Exec. Cttee 1989, Pres. Latin American Chapter 1988–89; Vice-Pres. Latin American Union of Capital Cities; Co-Dir World Mayors' Conf. on Drug Addiction, New York 1989, Madrid 1990; Sec. Gen. Union of Latin American Parties 1992–; Adviser to UN Univ., Tokyo 1994; Dir and f. UN Leadership Acad., Jordan; fmr Chair. Bogotá Telephone Co., Bogotá Aqueduct and Sewerage Co., Electricity and Public Utilities Co. of Bogotá, Inst. for Urban Devt, Dist Planning; Nat. Police Distinguished Service Order, UNESCO Order, Grand Cross, Civilian Order of Merit 1988, Order of Merit, Colombian Publishing Industry 1988, Civilian Defence Order 1989, Order of Santa Bárbara, Colombian Navy 1990, José María Córdova Order of Mil. Merit 1990; Colombian Jr Chamber Exec. of the Year 1981, King of Spain Int. Journalism Award 1985, Simón Bolívar Nat. Journalism Award 1987, King of Spain Nat. Journalism Award 1987, Bogotá Circle of Journalists Nat. Award 1987. *Publication:* Hacia la formulación de un derecho ecológico (Towards the formulation of an ecological law). *Address:* c/o Ministry of Foreign Affairs, Palacio de San Carlos, Calle 10a, No 5-51, Bogotá, DC, Colombia.

PASTUSIAK, Longin, PhD; Polish politician and professor of international affairs; *Professor, Financial Academy, Warsaw;* b. 22 Aug. 1935, Łódź; m. Anna Ochab; one s. one d. *Education:* Warsaw Univ., American Univ., Washington DC, Univ. of Virginia. *Career:* Prof. and Head Dept, Polish Inst. of Int. Affairs 1963–93; Deputy to Sejm (Parl.) 1991–2001, Vice-Chair. Foreign Affairs Cttee 1993–2001; Head, Polish Del. to WEU Ass. 1993–; Head, Polish Del. to NATO Parl. Ass. 1993–, Vice-Pres. 2002–; Senator 2001–05, Pres. of the Senate 2001–05; Prof. of Int. Relations, Gdansk Univ.

1994–2005; Prof., Financial Acad., Warsaw 2005–, Higher School of Communications and Mass Media, Warsaw 2005–; Visiting Prof. Appalachian State Univ., USA; Silver Cross of Merit 1972, Kt's Cross 1985, Order of Merit (Lithuania) 2004, Grand Commdr's Cross (Lithuania) 2004; Dr hc (Naval Mil. Acad. Gdynia, Poland) 2003; Hon. DHumLitt (Appalachian State Univ.) 2004; Parliamentarian of the Year 1997, numerous scholarly awards. *Television:* various programmes on Polish public television. *Publications:* more than 70 books including Poland–Canada 1945–1961 1994, United States Diplomacy, 18th and 19th Century 1997, Chicago: Portrait of the City 1997, Will the World Come to an End? 1999, From the Secrets of the Diplomatic Archives: Polish–American Relations 1948–1954 1999, Ladies of the White House 2000, Presidents of the USA 2002; 600 scholarly pubs and more than 3,000 articles in daily and weekly journals on American history and foreign policy, German studies, East–West relations, Polish foreign policy, Polish–American relations and theoretical aspects of int. relations. *Address:* al. Niepodleglosci 151, Apt 21, 02-555 Warsaw, Poland (home). *Telephone:* (22) 8495044 (home). *Fax:* (22) 8495044 (home). *E-mail:* longin.pastusiak@mac.com (home).

PATERSON, William Edgar, OBE, MSc, PhD, FRSE, FRSA; British academic; *Director, Institute for German Studies, University of Birmingham;* b. 26 Sept. 1941, Blair Atholl, Scotland; m. 1st Jacqueline Cramb 1964 (died 1974); two s.; m. 2nd Phyllis MacDowell 1979; one d. one step-s. one step-d. *Education:* Morrison's Acad., Univ. of St Andrews, London School of Econs. *Career:* Lecturer in Int. Relations, Univ. of Aberdeen 1967–70; Volkswagen Lecturer in German Politics, Univ. of Warwick 1970–75, Sr Lecturer 1975–82, Reader 1982–89, Prof. and Chair. of Dept 1989–90; Salvesen Prof. and Dir of Europa Inst., Univ. of Edin. 1990–94; Dir Inst. for German Studies, Univ. of Birmingham 1994–; Chair. Asscn for the Study of German Politics 1974–76, Univ. Asscn for Contemporary European Studies 1989–94; Vice-Chair. German-British Forum 1996, Chair. 2005–; mem. Econ. and Social Research Council Research Priorities Bd 1994–99, British Königswinter Cttee 1995–, Kuratorium Allianz Kulturstiftung 2001–04; Co-Ed. German Politics 1991–2001, Journal of Common Market Studies 2003–; Academician, Acad. of Learned Socs in Social Sciences 2000; Bundesverdienstkreuz (Germany) 1999; Lifetime Award, Asscn for the Study of German Politics 2004, Lifetime Award, Univ. Asscn for Contemporary European Studies 2007. *Publications include:* The Federal Republic of Germany and the European Community (with Simon Bulmer) 1987, Government and the Chemical Industry (with Wyn Grant) 1988, Developments in German Politics II 1996, The Kohl Chancellorship (with Clay Clemens) 1998, The Future of the German Economy (with Rebecca Harding) 2000, Developments in German Politics 3 2003, Governance in Contemporary Germany: The Semisovereign State Revisited (co-ed.) with Simon Green) 2005; 20 other books and over 100 articles in learned journals. *Address:* Institute for German Studies, University of Birmingham, Edgbaston, Birmingham, B15 2TT (office); 220 Myton Road, Warwick, CV34 6PS, England (home). *Telephone:* (121) 414-7183 (office). *Fax:* (121) 414-7329 (office); (1926) 492492 (home). *E-mail:* williampaterson@btconnect.com (home); w.e.paterson@bham.ac.uk (office).

PATEY, William Charters, CMG; British diplomatist; *Ambassador to Saudi Arabia;* b. 11 July 1953; m. Vanessa; two s. *Career:* joined FCO 1975, Finance Dept 1975–76, Rhodesia Dept 1976–77, Attaché, Abu Dhabi 1978–81, Second Sec. (Commercial), Tripoli 1981–84, Perm. Under-Sec./Dir-Gen. Offices, FCO 1984–85, Near East and N African Dept 1986–87, Middle Eastern Dept 1987–88, First Sec., Canberra 1988–92, Asst Head, UN Dept, FCO 1992–94, Overseas Internal Audit Officer 1994–95, Deputy Head of Mission and Consul-Gen., Riyadh 1995–98, Head, Middle Eastern Dept, FCO 1998–2002, Amb. to Sudan 2002–05, to Iraq 2005–06, Dir Comprehensive Spending Review Programme, FCO 2006–07, Amb. to Saudi Arabia 2007–. *Address:* British Embassy, Diplomatic Quarter, PO Box 94351, Riyadh 11693, Saudi Arabia (office). *Telephone:* (1) 488-0077 (office). *Fax:* (1) 488-1209 (office); (1) 481-0686 (office). *E-mail:* PressOffice.Riyadh@fco.gov.uk (office). *Website:* www.britishembassy.gov.uk/saudiarabia (office).

PATHAMMAVONG, Soutsakhoru; Laotian diplomatist; m. Vanseng Pathammavong. *Career:* Amb. to France (also accred to UK) 2003–. *Address:* Embassy of Laos, 74 avenue Raymond Poincaré, 75116 Paris, France (office). *Telephone:* (1) 45-53-02-98 (office). *Fax:* (1) 47-57-27-89 (office). *E-mail:* ambalaoparis@wanadoo.fr (office). *Website:* laoparis.com (office).

PATIL, Pratibha Devisingh, LLB, MA; Indian politician and head of state; *President;* b. 19 Dec. 1934, Jalgaon, Mahar.; m. D. R. Shekhawat; one s. one d. *Career:* mem. Mahar Ass. 1962–85, Deputy Minister 1967–72, Cabinet Minister for Social Welfare 1972–74, for Public Health and Social Welfare 1974–75, for Prohibition, Rehabilitation and Cultural Affairs 1975–76, for Educ. 1977–78, for Urban Devt and Housing 1982–83; Deputy Chair. Rajya Sabha (Council of States, Parl.) 1986–88; mem. Lok Sabha 1991; Gov. of Rajasthan 2004–07; Pres. of India 2007–; Vice-Chair. Nat. Fed. for Co-op Urban Banks and Credit Soc.; Chair. Bhartiya Granin Mahila Sangh, Mahar; Organizer Women Home Guards, Jalgaon Dist 1962; mem. Standing Cttee, All India Women's Council; Convener first Women's Conf., Delhi. *Address:* Office of the President, Rashtrapati Bhavan, New Delhi 110 004 (office); 57 New Congress Nagar, Opp. Govt. Milk Scheme, Amravati, Maharashtra, India (home). *Telephone:* (11) 23015321 (office). *Fax:* (11) 23017290 (office). *E-mail:* presidentofindia@rb.nic.in (office). *Website:* www.presidentofindia.nic.in (office).

PATRIOTA, Antonio de Aguiar; Brazilian diplomatist; *Ambassador to USA;* b. 27 April 1954, Rio de Janeiro; m. Tania Cooper Patriota; two s. *Education:* Univ. of Geneva, Switzerland, Rio Branco Inst. *Career:* mem. staff, Perm. Mission to UN and other Int. Orgs, Geneva 1983–86; Political Counselor, Embassy in Beijing 1987–88; Head of Econ. Section, Embassy in Caracas 1988–90; Advisor to Sec. Gen. for Political Affairs, Ministry of Foreign Relations 1990–92; Deputy Diplomatic Advisor to fmr Pres. Itamar Franco 1992–94; Political Counselor, Perm. Mission to UN, New York 1995–99; Deputy Perm. Rep. to WTO, Geneva 2001–03; Sec. for Diplomatic Planning, Office of Minister of Foreign Relations 2003–05; Chief of Staff to Minister of Foreign Relations 2004–05; Under-Sec. Gen. for Political Affairs, Ministry of Foreign Relations 2005–06; Amb. to USA 2007–. *Address:* Embassy of Brazil, 3006 Massachusetts Avenue, NW, Washington, DC 20008, USA (office). *Telephone:* (202) 238-2700 (office). *Fax:* (202) 238-2827 (office). *E-mail:* webmaster@brasilemb.org (office). *Website:* www.brasilemb.org (office).

PATRUSHEV, Col-Gen. Nikolai Platonovich; Russian government security official; *Secretary of the Security Council;* b. 11 July 1951, Leningrad (now St Petersburg); m.; two s. *Education:* Leningrad Inst. of Vessel Construction. *Career:* on staff KGB, Kareliyan ASSR 1974; in Leningrad Oblast 1974–92; Minister of Security Republic of Kareliya 1992–94; Head Dept of Self-Security, Fed. Security Service 1994–98, Deputy Dir, then Head, Dept of Econs 1998–99, Dir 1999–; Head of Presidential Control Dept May–Aug. 1998; Deputy Head Admin. of Russian Presidency Aug.–Oct. 1998; Deputy Dir Fed. Security Service of Russia (FSB), Head of Econ. Security Dept 1998, First Deputy Dir April–Aug. 1999, Dir Aug. 1999–2008; Sec., Security Council 2008–. *Address:* Security Council, c/o Office of the President, 103132 Moscow, Staraya pl. 4, Russia (office). *Telephone:* (495) 925-35-81 (office). *Fax:* (495) 206-07-66 (office). *E-mail:* president@gov.ru (office). *Website:* www.kremlin.ru (office).

PATTAMA, Noppadon, LLB (Hons), BA, LLM, MA; Thai lawyer and politician; b. 23 April 1961, Nakorn Rachasima. *Education:* Thammasat Univ., Univs of Oxford and London, UK. *Career:* practised as barrister in Bangkok 1983–; called to the Bar, Lincoln's Inn, London 1991; Sec. to Leader of the Opposition Chuan Leekpai 1995–96; mem. Parl. (Democrat Party) 1996–2000, mem. Standing Cttee on Foreign Affairs, House of Reps 1996–2000; Parl. Sec. to Minister of Foreign Affairs 1999–2001; defected to Thai Rak Thai party 2006; Vice-Minister of Natural Resources and Environment 2006; legal adviser to fmr Prime Minister Thaksin Shinawatra (deposed in mil. coup Sept. 2006) Nov. 2006; mem. People's Power Party (successor to Thai Rak Thai); Minister of Foreign Affairs 2008; Pres. Thai Students' Asscn in UK (Samaggi Samagom) 1988–89; participant in The Ship for Southeast Asian Youth Programme 1981; Fulbright Scholarship to study in USA 1982, Ananda Mahidol Scholarship to study law in UK, King of Thailand 1984. *Address:* People's Power Party (Palang Prachachan), 1770 Thanon Petchaburi Tat Mai, Bang Gapi, Huay Kwang, Bangkok 10310, Thailand (office). *Telephone:* (2) 686–7000 (office). *Website:* www.ppp.or.th (office).

PATTERSON, Anne Woods; American diplomatist; *Ambassador to Pakistan;* b. Fort Smith, Ark.; m.; two s. *Education:* Wellesley Coll. and Univ. of N Carolina. *Career:* career minister in Foreign Service, joined Foreign Service as Econ. Officer 1973, Econ. Officer and Counsellor in Saudi Arabia 1984–88, has served as Prin. Deputy Asst Sec. and Deputy Asst Sec. of Interamerican Affairs and as Office Dir for Andean Affairs, held several other econ. and political assignments, including in Bureau of Interamerican Affairs, Bureau of Intelligence and Research, and Bureau of Econ. and Business Affairs, Political Counsellor to US Mission to UN, Geneva 1988–91, Amb. to El Salvador 1997–2000, to Colombia 2000–03, Deputy Insp. Gen. Dept of State 2003–04, Deputy Perm. Rep. and then Acting Perm. Rep., US Mission to UN, New York 2004–05, Asst Sec. of State, Bureau for Int. Narcotics and Law Enforcement Affairs, Dept of State

2005–07, Amb. to Pakistan 2007–; Order of the Congress (Colombia), Order of Boyaca (Colombia), Order of Jose Matias Delgado (El Salvador); Meritorious Award, Dept of State 1977, 1983, Superior Honor Award, Dept of State 1981, 1988, Presidential Honor Award 1993.
Address: US Embassy, Diplomatic Enclave, Ramna 5, Islamabad, Pakistan (office). *Telephone:* (51) 2080000 (office). *Fax:* (51) 2276427 (office). *E-mail:* webmasterisb@state.gov (office). *Website:* islamabad.usembassy.gov (office).

PAULS, Christian Friedemann; German lawyer and diplomatist; *Ambassador to Ireland;* b. 26 Sept. 1944, Buckow; m.; four d. *Education:* Univs of Freiburg, Montpellier, Hamburg. *Career:* military service 1963–65; served in numerous positions after joining Foreign Office in 1977, including at Foreign Office, Bonn 1977, Embassy in Athens 1977–80, Embassy in New Dehli 1980–83, Foreign Office, Bonn 1983–86, Embassy in Rome, 1986–89, Foreign Office, Bonn 1989–92, at Embassy in Washington, DC 1992–96; Ambassador, Balkan Task Force, Political Dept, Foreign Office, Bonn 1996–99; Dir-Gen., Political Dept, Foreign Office, Berlin 1999–2001; Amb. to Canada 2001–05, to Ireland 2005–.
Address: Embassy of Germany, 31 Trimleston Avenue, Booterstown, Co., Dublin, Ireland (office). *Telephone:* (1) 2693011 (office). *Fax:* (1) 2693946 (office). *E-mail:* germany@indigo.ie (office). *Website:* www.dublin.diplo.de (office).

PAULSON, Henry (Hank) Merritt, Jr, BA, MBA; American investment banker and government official; *Secretary of the Treasury;* b. 28 March 1946, Palm Beach, Fla; m. Wendy Judge 1969; one s. one d. *Education:* Dartmouth Coll., Harvard Univ. Business School. *Career:* Staff Asst to Asst Sec. of Defense (Comptroller), Pentagon, Washington, DC 1970–72; Staff Asst to Pres.'s Domestic Council, The White House, Washington, DC 1972–73; Assoc. Goldman Sachs & Co., Chicago 1974–77, Vice-Pres. 1977–82, Pnr, Investment Banking Dept 1982–, pnr in charge of investment banking, Midwest Region 1984–90, Man. Cttee Co-Head Investment Banking Div., Vice-Chair., COO 1990–99, CEO and Chair. 1999–2006; US Sec. of the Treasury 2006–; Trustee Chicago Symphony Orchestra; Dir The Peregrine Fund Inc.; Vice-Chair. Nature Conservancy and co-Chair. of Nature Conservancy Asia-Pacific Council.
Address: Department of the Treasury, 1500 Pennsylvania Avenue, NW, Washington, DC 20220 (office); 101 West 67th Street, Apt 50A, New York, NY 10023, USA (home). *Telephone:* (202) 622-2000 (office). *Fax:* (202) 622-6415 (office). *Website:* www.ustreas.gov (office).

PAWAR, Sharadchandra Govindrao, BCom; Indian politician; *Minister of Agriculture and of Consumer Affairs, Food and Public Distribution; President, Nationalist Congress Party;* b. 12 Dec. 1940, Katychiwadi, Pune; m. Pratibha Pawar 1967; one d. *Career:* Head, State Level Youth Congress; Gen. Sec. Maharashtra Pradesh Congress Cttee; elected to State Legis. 1967, held Portfolios of Home and Publicity and Rehabilitation; Minister of State and Educ. and Youth Welfare, Home, Agric. and Industries and Labour; Chief Minister of Maharashtra 1978–80, 1988–91; Minister of Defence 1991–92; Minister of Agric. and of Consumer Affairs, Food and Public Distribution 2004–; Pres. Nat. Congress (opposition) 1981–86; rejoined Congress (I) 1986; fmr Pres. Congress Forum for Socialistic Action; Sec. Defence Cttee; mem. Lok Sabha 1996–; Leader of Opposition 1998–99; Pres. Nationalist Congress Party 1999–; Pres. Maharashtra Kabbadi Asscn, Maharashtra Olympic Asscn, Agricultural Devt Foundation, Mumbai Cricket Asscn.
Address: Ministry of Agriculture, Krishi Bhavan, Dr Rajendra Prasad Road, New Delhi 110 001 (office); Nationalist Congress Party, 10 Dr Bishambhar Das Marg, New Delhi 110 001 (office); Ramalayan, 44-A Pedder Road, Mumbai 400026, India (home). *Telephone:* (11) 23383370 (office); (11) 23359218 (office); (22) 23659191 (home). *Fax:* (11) 23384129 (office); (11) 23352112 (office).

PAWLAK, Waldemar, MSc; Polish politician and business executive; *Deputy Prime Minister and Minister of the Economy;* b. 5 Sept. 1959, Pacyna, Płock Prov.; m.; two s. one d. *Education:* Warsaw Univ. of Tech. *Career:* farm man. 1984–; mem. United Peasant Party (ZSL) 1984–90; Deputy to Sejm (Parl.) 1989–; mem. Polish Peasant Party (PSL) 1992– (Chair. 1992–97); Chair. Council of Ministers (Prime Minister) of Poland June–July 1992, 1993–95; Chair. Union of Volunteer Fire Brigades 1992–; Pres. Warszawska Gielda Towarowa Spolka Akcyjna (WGT) S.A. (commodity exchange) Warsaw 2001–05; Deputy Prime Minister and Minister of the Economy 2007–.
Address: Ministry of the Economy, pl. Trzech Krzyży 3/5, 00-507 Warsaw, Poland (office). *Telephone:* (22) 6935000 (office). *Fax:* (22) 6934048 (office). *E-mail:* bpi@mgip.gov.pl (office). *Website:* www.mgip.gov.pl (office).

PAXMAN, Giles; British diplomatist; *Ambassador to Mexico;* b. 15 Nov. 1951; m. Ségolène Paxman; three d. *Education:* New Coll., Oxford. *Career:*

has served as Counsellor (Political and Institutional Affairs), UK Perm. Representation to the EU, Brussels, Counsellor (Econ. and Commercial Affairs), Rome, Head of Chancery, Singapore, worked on Environment, Consumer Affairs and the Internal Market in Brussels, Minister and Deputy Head of Mission, Paris –2005, Amb. to Mexico 2005–.
Address: British Embassy, Río Lerma 71, Col Cuauhtémoc, Del. Cuauhtémoc, 06500 México DF, Mexico (office). *Telephone:* (55) 5242-8500 (office). *Fax:* (55) 5242-8517 (office). *E-mail:* ukinmex@att.net.mx (office). *Website:* www.embajadabritanica.com.mx (office).

PAZ ZAMORA, Jaime; Bolivian politician, academic and fmr head of state; b. 15 April 1939, Cochabamba. *Education:* Colegio Jesuita, Sucre, Seminario Mayor de Villa Allende en Córdoba, Argentina and Catholic Univ. of Louvain, Belgium. *Career:* Pres. de la Fed. de Estudiantes Latino-Americanos (Belgium); Prof. of Sociology, Univ. Mayor de San Andrés; Prof. of Int. Relations, Dir Univ. Extension; f. Movimiento de la Izquierda Revolucionaria; cand. Vice-Pres. 1978 and 1980; first Vice-Pres. of the Andean Parl.; Vice-Pres. Repub. of Bolivia and Pres. Nat. Congress 1982–84; Pres. Repub. of Bolivia 1989–93; presidential cand. 2002; mem. Exec. Cttee of the Assoc. Latino-Americana de Derechos Humanos; mem. Movimiento de la Izquierda Revolucionaria (MIR).
Address: Movimiento de la Izquierda Revolucionaria, Avda América 119, 2°, La Paz, Bolivia (office). *E-mail:* mir@coibo.entelnet.bo (office); jpazamora@mail.megalinks.com (home). *Website:* www.cibergallo.org (office); www.jaimepazamora.com (home).

PEACOCK, Sir Alan, Kt, DSC, MA, FBA, FRSE; British economist and academic; *Research Professor in Public Finance, Heriot-Watt University;* b. 26 June 1922, Ryton-on-Tyne; m. Margaret Martha Astell-Burt 1944; two s. one d. *Education:* Grove Acad., Dundee High School, Univ. of St Andrews. *Career:* RN 1942–45; Lecturer in Econs, Univ. of St Andrews 1947–48; lecturer in Econs, LSE 1948–51, Reader in Public Finance 1951–56; Prof. of Econ. Science, Univ. of Edinburgh 1956–62; Prof. of Econs, Univ. of York 1962–78; Prof. of Econs and Prin. Univ. Coll. at Buckingham 1980–83, Vice-Chancellor 1983–84, Prof. Emer. 1985–; Research Prof. in Public Finance, Heriot-Watt Univ. 1987–; Chief Econ. Adviser, Dept of Trade and Industry 1973–76; Pres. Int. Inst. of Public Finance 1966–69, Hon. Pres. 1975–; mem. Royal Comm. on Constitution 1970–73, Social Science Research Council 1971–72; Trustee, Inst. of Econ. Affairs; mem. Council, London Philharmonic Orchestra 1975–79; Chair. Arts Council Enquiry into Orchestral Resources 1969–70, Cttee on Financing the BBC 1985–86, Scottish Arts Council 1986–92; mem. Bd of Dirs English Music Theatre Ltd 1975–77; Chair. Hebrides Ensemble 1994–2000; mem. Council of Man., Nat. Inst. of Econ. and Social Research 1977–86; non-exec. Dir Economist Intelligence Unit 1977–84; Exec. Dir David Hume Inst. 1985–90, Hon. Pres. 2002–(05); non-exec. Dir Caledonian Bank PLC 1989–96; Hon. mem. Royal Soc. of Musicians 1999–; Hon. Pres. Atlantic Econ. Soc. 1981–82; Hon. Fellow LSE 1980–; Foreign mem. Accademia Naz. dei Lincei, Rome 1996–; Keynes Lecturer, British Acad. 1994; Dr hc (Stirling) 1974, (Catania) 1991, (Brunel) 1989, (York) 1997, (Lisbon) 2000, (Turin) 2001; Hon. DEcon (Zürich) 1984; Hon. DSc (Buckingham) 1986; Hon. DSocSc (Edinburgh) 1990; Hon. LLD (St Andrews, Dundee) 1990; Scottish Free Enterprise Award 1987, Royal Soc. of Edinburgh 2002 (Royal Medal). *Publications:* Economics of National Insurance 1952, Growth of Public Expenditure in United Kingdom (with J. Wiseman) 1961, Economic Theory of Fiscal Policy (with G. K. Shaw) 1971, The Composer in the Market Place (with R. Weir) 1975, Welfare Economics: A Liberal Reinterpretation (with Charles Rowley), The Credibility of Liberal Economics 1977, The Economic Analysis of Government 1979, The Political Economy of Taxation (ed. with Francesco Forte) 1980, The Regulation Game (ed.) 1984, Public Expenditure and Government Growth (ed. with F. Forte) 1985, Corporate Takeovers and the Public Interest (with G. Bannock) 1991, Public Choice Analysis in Historical Perspective 1991, Paying the Piper: Culture, Music and Money 1993, Cultural Economics and Cultural Policies (ed. with Ilde Rizzo), The Political Economy of Economic Freedom 1997, The Political Economy of Heritage (ed.) 1998, What Price Civil Justice (with B. Main) 2000, Calling the Tune 2001, The Enigmatic Sailor 2003, The Political Economy of Sustainable Development 2003, Public Service Broadcasting without the BBC? 2004; and numerous articles in professional journals on economics, public finance and public policy.
Address: David Hume Institute, 25 Buccleuch Place, Edinburgh, EH8 9LD (office); 5/24 Oswald Road, Edinburgh, EH9 2HE, Scotland (home). *Telephone:* (131) 667-9609 (office); (131) 667-5677 (home). *Fax:* (131) 667-9609 (office). *E-mail:* hume.institute@ed.ac.uk (office); peacock@ebs.hw .ac.uk (home). *Website:* www.ed.ac.uk/~hume/ (office).

PEDERSEN, Geir O., MA; Norwegian diplomatist and UN official; *Special Co-ordinator for Lebanon, United Nations;* m.; five c. *Career:* diplomatic postings to China and Germany, mem. Norwegian team to secret Oslo

negotiations that led to signing of Declaration of Principles and mutual recognition between Palestine Liberation Org. (PLO) and Israel 1993, held different positions at Ministry of Foreign Affairs, including Chief of Staff 1995–98, Norwegian Rep. to Palestinian Authority 1993–2003; Dir FAFO (Norwegian Inst. for Applied Social Science) 1993–95; Dir Asia and Pacific Div., Dept of Political Affairs, UN 2003–05, Personal Rep. of Sec.-Gen. for Southern Lebanon 2005–, now Special Co-ordinator for Lebanon.
Address: Office of the United Nations Special Co-ordinator for Lebanon (UNSCOL), UN House, Riad es-Solh Sq., POB 11, 8577 Beirut, Lebanon (office).

PEDERSEN, Thor; Danish politician; *President of the Folketing;* b. 14 June 1945, Gentofte. *Education:* Copenhagen Univ. *Career:* fmr mem. staff, Assessments Div.; fmr Man. Dir of a construction co., North Zealand; fmr Mayor of Helsinge; mem. Folketing (Parl.) 1985–, Pres. 2007–; Minister of Housing 1986–87, of the Interior 1987–93, of Nordic Affairs 1988, of Econ. Affairs 1992–93, of Finance 2001–07.
Address: Graudebjerggaard, Nakke Øst Vej 49, 4500 Nykøbing Sjælland, Denmark (office). *E-mail:* thor.pedersen@ft.dk (office). *Website:* www .folketinget.dk (office).

PEIRANO, Miguel Gustavo; Argentine economist and government official; *Minister of Economy and Production; Education:* Universidad de Buenos Aires. *Career:* began career at Banco Sudameris 1989; worked for Techint Group 1990–92; various posts at Argentine Industrial Union (UIA) 1993–2004; Prof. of Political Economy, Colegio Nacional de Buenos Aires 1995–97; served as econ. adviser to Dir-Gen. of Industry of the City of Buenos Aires, Bd of Bank of the Province of Buenos Aires, Nat. Subsecretariat of Small and Medium Enterprise and Regional Devt; fmr Pres. Econs Dept, Buenos Aires City Industrial Union; fmr Sr Vice-Pres. Bank of Investment and Foreign Trade (BICE); Sec. of Industry, Commerce and Small and Medium Enterprises –2007; Minister of Economy and Production 2007–.
Address: Ministry of Economy and Production, Hipólito Yrigoyen 250, C1086AAB Buenos Aires, Argentina (office). *Telephone:* (11) 4349-5000 (office). *E-mail:* sagpya@mecon.gov.ar (office). *Website:* www.mecon.gov .ar (office).

PEIRIS, Gamini Lakshman, DPhil, PhD; Sri Lankan politician and academic; *Minister of Export Development and International Trade;* b. 13 Aug. 1946, Colombo; m. Savitri N. Amarasuriya 1971; one d. *Education:* St Thomas' Coll., Mount Lavinia, Univ. of Ceylon and New Coll., Oxford, UK. *Career:* Prof. of Law, Univ. of Colombo 1979, Dean, Faculty of Law 1982–88; Vice-Chancellor, Univ. of Colombo –1994; Dir Nat. Film Corpn of Sri Lanka 1973–88; Commr Law Comm. of Sri Lanka 1986–; mem. Inc. Soc. of Legal Educ. 1986–; Visiting Fellow, All Souls Coll. Oxford 1980–81; Butterworths Visiting Fellow, Inst. of Advanced Legal Studies, Univ. of London 1984; Distinguished Visiting Fellow, Christ's Coll. Cambridge, UK 1985–86; Smuts Visiting Fellow in Commonwealth Studies, Univ. of Cambridge 1985–86; Chair. Cttee of Vice-Chancellors of the Univs of Sri Lanka; Minister of Justice, Constitutional Affairs, Ethnic Affairs and Nat. Integration and Deputy Minister of Finance 1994–99; Minister of Enterprise Devt, Industrial Policy and Investment Promotion and of Constitutional Affairs 1999–2004, of Export Devt and Int. Trade 2007–; mem. United People's Freedom Alliance (UPFA) 2007–; Vice-Chair. Janasaviya Trust Fund; mem. Securities Council of Sri Lanka 1987–; mem. Pres. Comm. on Youth Unrest 1989; mem. Nat. Educ. Comm., Exec. Cttee of Asscn of Teachers and Researchers in Intellectual Property Law, Bd Govs Inst. of Fundamental Studies; Assoc. mem. Int. Acad. of Comparative Law; Presidential Award 1987. *Publications:* Law of Unjust Enrichment in South Africa and Ceylon 1971, General Principles of Criminal Liability in Ceylon 1972, Offences Under the Penal Code of Sri Lanka 1973, The Law of Evidence in Sri Lanka 1974, Criminal Procedure in Sri Lanka 1975, The Law of Property in Sri Lanka 1976, Landlord and Tenant in Sri Lanka 1977; numerous articles on comparative and admin. law and law of evidence.
Address: Ministry of Export Development and International Trade, 'Rakshana Mandiraya', 21 Vauxhall Street, Colombo, Sri Lanka (office); No. 37, Kirula Place, Off Kirula Road, Colombo 05, (home).

PEMAGBI, Joe Robert; Sierra Leonean diplomatist; *Permanent Representative, United Nations;* b. 22 Nov. 1945. *Career:* Head, Dept Language Educ., Njala Univ. Coll., Univ. Sierra Leone 1986–95, Dean 1988–92, Assoc. Prof. Linguistics, Communications and English 1991–95; Chair., Nat. Comm. on Democracy and Human Rights 1999–2003; Perm. Rep. to UN 2003–.
Address: Permanent Mission of Sierra Leone to the UN, 245 East 49th Street, New York, NY 10017, USA (office). *Telephone:* (212) 688-1656 (office). *Fax:* (212) 688-4924 (office). *E-mail:* sierraleone@un.int (office).

PENJO, Daw, MA; Bhutanese diplomatist; *Permanent Representative, United Nations;* b. 7 March 1958; m.; three c. *Education:* Univ. of Delhi, India, Tufts Univ., USA. *Career:* joined Ministry of Foreign Affairs 1980; assigned to Perm. Mission to UN, Geneva 1986–90; Head of Bilateral and Multilateral Div., Ministry of Foreign Affairs 1990–94; First Sec. and Deputy Chief of Mission, Dhaka, Bangldesh 1994–97; Counsellor and Deputy Chief of Mission, New Delhi 1997–2000; Dir of Bilateral Dept 2000–03; Amb. Perm. Rep. to UN, New York 2003–; Amb. (non-resident) to Canada 2003–.
Address: Permanent Mission of Bhutan, 2 United Nations Plaza, 27th Floor, New York, NY 10017, USA (office). *Telephone:* (212) 826-1919 (office). *Fax:* (212) 826-2998 (office). *E-mail:* pmbnewyork@aol.com (office). *Website:* www.un.org (office).

PENKE, Normans; Latvian diplomatist; *State Secretary, Ministry of Foreign Affairs; Education:* Univ. of Latvia, Univ. of Oxford, UK. *Career:* Amb. to UK 1997–2001 (also accred to Ireland 1998–2001); Amb. to Russian Fed. 2001–04; State Sec., Ministry of Foreign Affairs 2004–.
Address: Ministry of Foreign Affairs, Brīvības bulv. 36, Rīga 1395, Latvia (office). *Telephone:* 701-6232 (office). *Fax:* 782-8121 (office). *E-mail:* mfa .cha@mfa.gov.lv (office). *Website:* www.mfa.gov.lv (office).

PERAK, HRH The Sultan of; Tuanku Azlan Muhibuddin Shah ibni al-Marhum Sultan Yusuf Izuddin Ghafarullah Shah; Malaysian; b. 19 April 1928, Batu Gajah; m. Tuanku Bainun Mohamed Ali 1954; two s. three d. *Education:* Govt English School (now Sultan Yussuf School), Malay Coll. and Univ. of Nottingham, UK. *Career:* called to Bar, Lincoln's Inn; Magistrate, Kuala Lumpur; Asst State Sec., Perak; Deputy Public Prosecutor; Pres. Sessions Court, Seremban and Taiping; State Legal Adviser, Pahang and Johore; Fed. Court Judge 1973; Chief Justice of Malaysia 1979; Lord Pres. 1982–83; Raja Kechil Bongsu (sixth-in-line) 1962, Raja Muda (second-in-line to the throne) 1983; Sultan of Perak Jan. 1984–; Yang di-Pertuan Agong (Supreme Head of State) 1989–94; Pro-Chancellor Univ. Saina Malaysia 1971, Chancellor Univ. of Malaya 1986; Hon. Col-in-Chief Malaysian Armed Forces' Engineers Corps; Man. Malaysian Hockey Team 1972; Pres. Malaysian Hockey Fed., Asian Hockey Fed.; Vice-Pres. Int. Hockey Fed., Olympic Council of Malaysia.

PERBEN, Dominique; French politician and civil servant; b. 11 Aug. 1945, Lyon; m. 1st Annick Demoustier 1968; m. 2nd Corinne Garnier 1996; one s. two d. from previous m. *Education:* Univ. of Paris, Inst. of Political Studies, Paris. *Career:* Pvt. Sec. to Maine-et-Loire Prefect 1972–75, to Norbert Ségard (Sec. of State for Postal Services and Telecommunications) 1977; Sec.-Gen. Territoire de Belfort 1975–76; Head of Mission Del. of Devt of Belfort Region 1977, Pres.'s Office Regional Council at Rhône-Alpes 1983–86; Admin. Télédiffusion de France 1980; with Ministry of the Interior 1981; Mayor of Chalon-sur-Saône 1983–2002, Deputy Mayor 2002–04; Vice-Pres. Regional Council Saône-et-Loire 1985–88, RPR Deputy 1986–93, 1997–; mem. Regional Council Bourgogne 1992–93; Vice-Pres. Regional Council Rhône 2004–08; RPR Nat. Sec. of Local Elections 1984–86, of General Elections 1986–88, of Communication 1988–89, Asst Sec.-Gen. 1990–93; Minister of Overseas Territories 1993–95, for the Civil Service, Admin. Reform and Decentralization 1995–97; Keeper of the Seals and Minister of Justice 2002–05, Minister of Transport, Capital Works, Tourism and the Sea 2005–07; Chevalier du Mérite agricole.
Address: Assemblée nationale, 126 rue de l'Université, 75355 Paris Cedex 07 (office); Mairie, BP 92, Place de l'Hôtel de Ville, 71321 Chalon-sur-Saône Cedex, France (office).

PERERA, Air Chief Marshal G. Donald; Sri Lankan air force officer; *Chief of Defence Staff; Education:* Nat. Defence Coll., India, Air Command and Staff Coll., Air Univ., Maxwell Air Force Base, Ala, USA. *Career:* participated in Air Operations in North and East since 1983, Chief of Staff 1998–2002, Commdr Sri Lanka Air Force 2002–06, Chief of Defence Staff 2006–; Vishista Seva Vibhushanaya, Utthama Seva Padakkama, Repub. of Sri Lanka Armed Services Medal, Sri Lanka Air Force 50th Anniversary Medal, Sri Lanka Armed Services Long Service Medal, Presidential Inauguration Medal, 50th Independence Anniversary Commemoration Medal, North and East Operations Medal, Purna Bhumi Padakkama, Vadamarachchi Operations Medal, Riviresa Campaign Service Medal.
Address: c/o Group Capt. N. H. V. Gunaratne, Commanding Officer, Sri Lanka Air Force, Colombo, Sri Lanka (office). *Telephone:* (11) 2441044 (office). *E-mail:* info@airforce.lk (office). *Website:* www.airforce.lk (office).

PERES, Shimon; Israeli politician and head of state; *President;* b. 1923, Poland; m. Sonia Gelman; two s. one d. *Education:* New York Univ., Harvard Univ. *Career:* immigrated to Palestine 1934; fmr Sec. Hano'ar Ha'oved Movt; mem. Haganah Movt 1947; Israel Naval Service, Ministry of Defence 1948; Head of Defence Mission in USA; Deputy Dir-Gen. of

Ministry of Defence 1952–53, Dir-Gen. 1953–59, Deputy Minister of Defence 1959–65; mem. Knesset 1959–; mem. Mapai Party 1941–65, founder mem. and Sec.-Gen. Rafi Party 1965, mem. Labour Party after merger 1968, Chair. 1977–92, 1995–97, 2003–05, resgnd from party Nov. 2005; Minister for Econ. Devt in the Administered Areas and for Immigrant Absorption 1969–70, of Transport and Communications 1970–74, of Information March–June 1974, of Defence 1974–77, of Foreign Affairs 1992–95; Acting Prime Minister April–May 1977; Leader of the Opposition 1977–84, 1996–97; Prime Minister of Israel 1984–86, 1995–96; Minister of the Interior and of Religious Affairs 1984–85, of Defence 1995–96; Vice-Premier and Minister of Foreign Affairs 1986–88, Vice-Premier and Finance Minister 1988–90, Minister of Regional Co-operation –2001, of Foreign Affairs 2001–02; Vice-Premier –2005; Vice-Premier and Minister for Devt of the Negev and Galillee 2006–07; Pres. of Israel 2007–; shared Nobel Prize for Peace 1994; Int. Council of Christians and Jews Interfaith Gold Medallion 1997. *Publications:* The Next Step 1965, David's Sling 1970, Tomorrow is Now 1978, From These Men 1979, Witness (autobiog.) 1993, The New Middle East 1993, Battling for Peace 1995 and numerous political articles in Israeli and foreign publs.
Address: Office of the President, 3 Hanassi Street, Jerusalem 92188, Israel (office). *Telephone:* 2-6707211 (office). *Fax:* 2-5611033 (office). *E-mail:* president@president.gov.il (office). *Website:* www.president.gov.il (office).

PERETZ, Amir; Israeli politician and fmr trade union leader; b. (Armand Peretz), 1952, Morocco; m. Ahlama; four c. *Career:* emigrated to Israel at age of four; fmr Munitions Officer, Paratroopers Div., Israeli Army; fmr farmer; elected Mayor of Sderot 1983; mem. Knesset 1988–; CEO Histadrut Haovdim Haleumit 1995–2005; founder and Leader Am Ehad (One Nation) 1999–2004 (until merger with Israel Labour Party); Chair. Israel Labour Party 2005–07; Deputy Prime Minister and Minister of Defence 2006–07; mem. Peace Now.
Address: Israel Labour Party, POB 62033, Tel-Aviv 61620, Israel (office). *Telephone:* 3-6899444 (office); 3-6899431 (office). *Fax:* 3-6899420 (office); 3-6899430 (office). *E-mail:* inter@havoda.org.il (office). *Website:* www .havoda.org.il (office).

PERETZ, David Lindsay Corbett, CB, MA; British international finance official; b. 29 May 1943; m. Jane Wildman 1966; one s. one d. *Education:* The Leys School Cambridge and Exeter Coll. Oxford. *Career:* Asst Prin. Ministry of Tech. 1965–69; Head of Public Policy and Institutional Studies, Int. Bank Research Org. 1969–76; Prin. HM Treasury 1976–80, Asst Sec. External Finance 1980–84, Prin. Pvt. Sec. to Chancellor of Exchequer 1984–85, Under-Sec. (Home Finance) 1985–86, (Monetary Group, Public Finance) 1986–90; UK Exec. Dir IMF and IBRD and Econ. Minister, Washington, DC 1990–94; Deputy Dir Int. Finance, HM Treasury 1994–99; UK G7 Financial Sherpa 1994–98; Sr Adviser, World Bank Group 1999–, Exec. Sec. World Bank Joint Task Force on Small States 2001; currently mem. staff Ind. Evaluation Office of the IMF, Washington, DC.
Address: Independent Evaluation Office of the International Monetary Fund, 700 19th Street, NW, Washington, DC 20431, USA (office). *Telephone:* (202) 623-7312 (office). *Fax:* (202) 623-9990 (office). *E-mail:* dperetz@imf.org (office). *Website:* www.ieo-imf.org (office).

PÉREZ, Jésus Arnaldo; Venezuelan diplomatist and politician; *Ambassador to Canada; Career:* Amb. to France –2004; Minister of Foreign Affairs 2004; Amb. to Canada 2005–.
Address: Embassy of Venezuela, 32 Range Road, Ottawa, ON K1N 8J4, Canada (office). *Telephone:* (613) 235-5151 (office). *Fax:* (613) 235-3205 (office). *E-mail:* info.canada@misionvenezuela.org (office). *Website:* www .misionvenezuela.org (office).

PÉREZ BALLADARES, Ernesto, MBA; Panamanian fmr head of state; b. 29 June 1946, Panama City; m. Dora Boyd; two s. three d. *Education:* Univs of Notre Dame and Pennsylvania. *Career:* Dir, Corp. Credit Official for Cen. America and Panama, Citibank 1971–75; Minister of Finance and the Treasury 1976–81, of Planning and Econ. Policy 1981–82; founding mem. Partido Revolucionario Democrático (PRD) 1979, Sec.-Gen. 1982, 1992; Dir-Gen. Instituto de Recursos Hidráulicos y Electrificación (IRHE) 1983; Pres. of Panama 1994–99; Pres. Golden Fruit, SA, Inversionista el Torreón, SA; mem. Legislation Comm., PRD Political Comm.; Order of Sacred Treasure (1st class) (Japan) 1980, Orden Aguila Azteca en Grado de Bando (Mexico) 1981.
Address: c/o Office of the President, Palacio Presidencial, Valija 50, Panamá 1, Panama.

PÉREZ BRAVO, Alfredo Rogerio; Mexican diplomatist; *Ambassador to Russia;* b. 1956, México; m.; two c. *Education:* Universidad Nacional Autónoma. *Career:* joined Ministry of Foreign Affairs 1976, served as analyst and pvt. sec., Directorate-Gen. of Int. Orgs 1976–79, Head,

Personnel Dept 1979–82, Deputy Dir-Gen. of Int. Treaties 1982–83, Coordinator of Advisers to Under-Sec. of Foreign Affairs 1989–90, Adviser to Prin. Officer and Minister of Industry 1994, Dir-Gen. of Int. Scientific and Tech. Co-operation 1995–98; overseas postings include Charge d'affaires ad interim, Embassy in Stockholm 1983–87, Head of Policy and Man., Embassy in Washington, DC 1987–88, Roving Amb. for Africa (accred to 39 countries) 1990–94,; Amb. to Algeria 1991–94, to Panama (also accred to Surinam and Guyana) 1999–2001, also Perm. Rep. to CARICOM 1999–2001; Dean of Diplomatic Corps, Embassy in Kuala Lumpur 2001–07, Amb. to Russia (also accred to Armenia and Belarus) 2007–; Head of Del. to Inter-American Conf. on Narcotic Drugs 2000, Rep. to XIII Summit Meeting of Non-Aligned Movt 2003; Chair. Asscn Mexicana de Estudios Internacionales 1995–97; Vice-Chair. Advisory Council, UNESCO-Mexico 1995–98; Int. Affairs Adviser to México City Govt 1996–98; has taught at Escuela Nacional de Estudios Profesionales Acatlán, Iberoamerican Univ., Instituto Matias Romero; Grand Cross of Francisco Nunez de Balboa (Panama); Ernesto de la Guardia award, Chamber of Industry and Commerce of Panama, 25 años en el Servicio Exterior Mexicano. *Publications:* co-author: Cooperación Técnica Internacional 1998, Panamá: una transición 2001, Hecho en Asia 2004; over 30 articles in int. journals.
Address: Embassy of Mexico, 119034 Moscow, B. Levshinskii per. 4, Russia (office). *Telephone:* (495) 969-28-79 (office). *Fax:* (495) 969-28-77 (office). *E-mail:* info@embamex.ru (office). *Website:* portal.sre.gob.mx/ rusia (office).

PÉREZ DE CUÉLLAR, Javier; Peruvian politician and diplomatist (retd); b. 19 Jan. 1920, Lima; m. Marcela Temple; two c. *Education:* Catholic Univ., Lima. *Career:* joined Foreign Ministry 1940, diplomatic service 1944; served as Sec. in embassies in France, UK, Bolivia, Brazil (later Counsellor); Dir Legal and Personnel Dept, Dir of Admin., of Protocol and of Political Affairs, Ministry of External Relations 1961–63; Amb. to Switzerland 1964–66; Perm. UnderSec. and Sec.-Gen. Foreign Office 1966–69, Amb. to USSR (concurrently to Poland) 1969–71, to Venezuela 1978; Perm. Rep. to UN 1971–75; mem. UN Security Council 1973–74, Pres. 1974; Special Rep. of UN Sec.-Gen. in Cyprus 1975–77; UN Under-Sec.-Gen. for Special Political Affairs 1979–81; UN Sec.-Gen. 1982–91; Prime Minister of Peru 2000–01; Amb. to France 2001–04; Pres. World Comm. on Culture and Devt UN/UNESCO 1992–, Int. Disability Foundation 1992–, Fondation de l'Arche de la Fraternité 1993–; Dir Repub. Nat. Bank of New York 1992–; Pres. Cand. in 1995 Elections; fmr Prof. of Diplomatic Law, Acad. Diplomática del Perú and Prof. of Int. Relations, Acad. de Guerra Aérea del Perú; del. to First UN Gen. Ass. 1946–47 and other int. confs; Montague Burton Visiting Prof. of Int. Relations, Univ. of Edinburgh 1985; mem. Acad. Mexicana de Derecho Int. 1988–; Dr hc (Univ. of Nice) 1983, (Jagiellonian, Charles and Sofia Univs, Univ. of San Marcos and Vrije Univ., Brussels) 1984, (Carleton Univ., Ottawa, Sorbonne Univ., Paris) 1985, (Osnabruck) 1986, (Univs of Mich., Coimbra, Mongolian State, Humbolt, Moscow State) 1987, (Univ. of Leiden) 1988, (Cambridge) 1989, (Univ. of Kuwait) 1993, (Oxford) 1993; Olaf Palme Prize for Public Service 1989, Prince of Asturias Prize for Ibero-American Co-operation, Alexander Onassis Foundation Prize 1990, Four Freedoms Award (Franklin Delano Roosevelt Inst.) 1992. *Publication:* Manual de Derecho Diplomático 1964, Anarchy or Order 1992, Pilgrimage for Peace 1997.
Address: c/o Ministry of Foreign Affairs, Jirón Lampa 535, Lima 1; Avenida A. Miro Quesada, 1071 Lima, Peru.

PEREZ ROQUE, Felipe Ramón; Cuban politician; *Minister of Foreign Affairs;* b. 28 March 1965, Havana; m.; two c. *Education:* Superior Politécnico José A. Echeverría. *Career:* head univ. students union 1988; fmr electronics engineer; involved with biotechnology complex 1960; mem. Cen. Cttee CP of Cuba 1991–; mem. Nat. Ass. 1986–, State Council 1993–; Pvt. Sec. to Fidel Castro; Minister of Foreign Affairs 1999–; José A. Echeverría Medal.
Address: Ministry of Foreign Affairs, Calzada 360, Vedado, Havana, Cuba (office). *Telephone:* (7) 55-3537 (office). *Fax:* (7) 33-3460 (office). *E-mail:* cubaminrex@minrex.gov.cu (office). *Website:* www.cubaminrex.cu (office).

PERINA, Rudolf V., BA, MA, PhD; American diplomatist. *Education:* Univ. of Chicago and Columbia Univ., New York. *Career:* retd mem. Sr Foreign Service, joined State Dept in 1974, served at Embassy in Ottawa 1975–76, NATO Desk, State Dept 1976–78, Embassy in Moscow 1979–81, US Mission in Berlin 1981–85, US Mission to NATO, Brussels 1985–87, Dir for European and Soviet affairs, Nat. Security Council 1987–89, Deputy Chair. US Del. to Negotiations on Confidence and Security-Building Measures in Europe, Vienna 1989–92, Chief of Mission, Embassy in Belgrade 1993–96, Sr Deputy Asst Sec. of State for European and Canadian Affairs 1996–97, Amb. to Moldova 1998–2001, US Special Negotiator for

Nagorno-Karabakh and Eurasian conflicts 2001–04, Deputy Dir Policy Planning Staff, State Dept 2004–06, Chargé d'affaires a.i. in Moldova 2006–07, in Armenia July–Oct. 2007.
Address: US Department of State, 2201 C Street NW, Washington, DC 20520, USA (office). *Telephone:* (202) 647-4000 (office). *Fax:* (202) 647-6738 (office). *Website:* www.state.gov (office).

PERKINS, Edward J., DPA; American diplomatist and academic; *Professor Emeritus, University of Oklahoma;* b. 8 June 1928, Sterlington, La; m. Lucy Cheng-mei Liu; two d. *Education:* Univ. of Maryland and Univ. of Southern California. *Career:* Chief of Personnel, Army and Air Force Exchange Service, Taiwan 1958–62; Deputy Chief, Okinawa, Japan 1962–64, Chief of Personnel and Admin. 1964–66; Asst Gen. Services Officer, Far East Bureau, AID 1967–69, Man. Analyst 1969–70; Deputy Dir Man. US Operations, Mission to Thailand 1970–72; Staff Asst Office of Dir-Gen. of Foreign Service 1972; Personnel Officer 1972–74; Admin. Officer, Bureau of Near Eastern and South Asian Affairs 1974–75; Man. Analysis Officer, Office of Man. Operations, Dept of State 1975–78; Counsellor for Political Affairs, Accra 1978–81; Deputy Chief of Mission, Monrovia 1981–83; Dir Office of W African Affairs, Dept of State 1983–85; Amb. to Liberia 1985–86, to S Africa 1986–89; Dir-Gen. Foreign Service, Washington 1989–92; Perm. Rep. to UN 1992–93; Amb. to Australia 1993–96; William J. Crowe Chair Prof. of Geopolitics and Exec. Dir Int. Programs Center, Univ. of Okla 1996–2007, Prof. Emer. 2007–; Bd Dir Asscn for Diplomatic Studies and Training 1998–; Trustee Lewis and Clark Coll. 1994–, Asia Soc. 1997–2000, Inst. of Int. Educ. 1997–2000; Gov. Jt Center for Political and Econ. Studies 1996–2002; mem. Advisory Council Univ. Office of Int. Programs Pa State Univ. 1997–; mem. Advisory Bd Inst. of Int. Public Policy 1997–; Trustee Woodrow Wilson Fellowship Foundation 1999–; Bd of Visitors, Nat. Defense Univ. 2002–; mem. Pres.'s Advisory Cttee on Trade Policy ad Negotiation 2003–; Distinguished Alumni Award, Univ. of Southern Calif. 1991, Distinguished Honor Award, Dept of State 1992, Statesman of the Year Award, George Washington Univ. 1992, Dept of State Dir-Gen. Cup 2001 and numerous other awards. *Publications include:* Preparing America's Foreign Policy for the 21st Century (ed. with David L. Boren) 1999, Palestinian Refugees: Traditional Positions and New Solutions (ed. with Joseph Ginat) 1999, Democracy, Morality and the Search for Peace in America's Foreign Policy (ed. with David L. Boren) 2002, Middle East Peace Process: Vision versus Reality (ed. with Joseph Ginat and Edwin G. Corr) 2002; contribs to specialized journals and reviews.
Address: Room 105, 729 Elm Avenue, Norman, OK 73019, USA (office). *Telephone:* (405) 325-1584 (office). *Fax:* (405) 325-7738 (office).

PERMAN, Finley S.; Micronesian auditor and government official; *Secretary, Department of Finance and Administration; Education:* Hawaii Pacific Coll. *Career:* previous positions include Devt Specialist, Pohnpei Small Business Guarantee and Finance Corpn, Sr Service Asst, Bank of Hawaii, Pohnpei br.; Dir Pohnpei State Dept of Treasury and Admin 2005–07; Sec. Dept of Finance and Admin 2007–.
Address: Department of Finance and Administration, PS158, Palikir 96941, Pohnpei State, Federated States of Micronesia (office). *Telephone:* (691) 320-2640 (office). *Fax:* (691) 320-2380 (office). *E-mail:* fsmpio.fm (office). *Website:* www.fsmgov.org (office).

PERRY, June Carter, BA, MA; American diplomatist; *Ambassador to Sierra Leone;* m. Frederick M. Perry; two s. *Education:* Loyola Univ., Univ. of Chicago, State Dept Senior Seminar, Nat. Defense Univ.'s CAPSTONE program. *Career:* fmr instructor, Univ. of Maryland, N Carolina A&T State Univ.; fmr Vice-Pres. The Women's Inst., Thursday Luncheon Group; fmr Dir of Public Affairs, ACTION (national volunteer agency) including Peace Corps; Special Asst, Community Services Admin; fmr Dir of Public Affairs, WGMS/RKO Radio Corpn; Foreign Service postings have included Zambia and Zimbabwe, served as Political Affairs Officer responsible for Botswana, Lesotho, Swaziland and Zimbabwe, Sr Advisor in Africa Bureau, Special Asst to Deputy Sec., Chief of Internal Political Affairs and Narcotics Coordinator, Embassy Paris and Deputy Dir/Acting Dir Office of Policy and Plans, Political Mil. Affairs Bureau, Deputy Chief of Mission in Cen. African Repub. and Madagascar, has served on nat. security and int. affairs dels in Asia, Africa and Europe, was Diplomat-in-Residence at Howard Univ., served as Dir Office of Social and Humanitarian Affairs, Int. Orgs Bureau with responsibility for policy matters within UN Comm. on Human Rights, Econ. and Social Council and Comm. on Status of Women –2004, Amb. to Lesotho 2004–07, to Sierra Leone 2007–; Superior and Meritorious Honor Awards, Sr Performance Pay Award, citation as runner-up for Deputy Chief of Mission of the Year, Diplomat in Residence of the Year Award 2002.
Address: Embassy of the USA, Southbridge - Hill Station, Freetown, Sierra Leone (office). *Telephone:* (22) 515000 (office). *Fax:* (22) 515355 (office). *Website:* freetown.usembassy.gov (office).

PERRY, William J., BS, MS, PhD; American academic and fmr government official; *Michael and Barbara Berberian Professor, Freeman Spogli Institute for International Studies, Center for International Security and Cooperation, Stanford University;* b. 11 Oct. 1927, Vandergift, Pa; m. Leonilla Mary Green 1947; three s. two d. *Education:* Stanford Univ., Pennsylvania State Univ. *Career:* served in US Army Corps of Engineers 1946–47, Reserve Officer Training Corps 1948–55; laboratory dir General Telephone and Electronics 1954–64; f. and served as Pres. ESL, Inc. 1964–77; Exec. Vice-Pres. Hambrecht & Quist, Inc. 1981–85; f. and served as Chair. Tech. Strategies & Alliances 1985–93; Prof. (half-time) Stanford Univ. 1988–93, also Co-Dir Center for Int. Security and Arms Control; Under-Sec. of Defense for Research and Eng 1976–81; Mil. Tech. Adviser to Pres. Clinton 1993; Deputy Sec. of Defense 1993–94, Sec. of Defense 1994–97; Sr Fellow, Stanford Univ. 1997–, now also Sr Fellow, Freeman Spogli Inst. for Int. Studies (FSI) and Michael and Barbara Berberian Prof. (FSI and School of Eng), Stanford Univ., also Co-Dir Preventive Defense Project; Chair. Global Tech. Pnrs; mem. Bd of Dirs United Techs Corpn, FMC Corpn, Sylvania/General Telephone's Electronic Defense Labs, Space Foundation, Thomas Jefferson Program in Public Policy, Concord Coalition, Strategic Partnerships LLC, Center for the Study of the Presidency; mem. Pres.'s Foreign Intelligence Advisory Bd, Sec. of State's Arms Control and Nonproliferation Advisory Bd, FBI Dir's Advisory Bd, Iraq Study Group, US Inst. of Peace 2006–; fmr Chair. Bd of Visitors, US Naval Acad.; fmr Co-Chair. Pres. Comm. on Intelligence Capabilities of the US Regarding Weapons of Mass Destruction; mem. Nat. Acad. of Eng, NAS Cttee on Int. Security and Arms Control; Fellow, American Acad. of Arts and Sciences; Trustee MITRE Corpn, Carnegie Endowment for Int. Peace; fmr Fellow, Inst. of Politics, Harvard Univ., Marshall Wythe School of Law, Coll. of William and Mary; several nat. and int. honours including Outstanding Civilian Service Medals from the Army 1962, 1997, Air Force 1997, Navy (1997, Defense Intelligence Agency 1977, 1997, NASA 1981, Coast Guard 1997; Dept of Defense Distinguished Service Medal 1980, 1981, American Electronic Asscn Medal of Achievement 1980, Forrestal Medal 1994, Henry Stimson Medal 1994, Arthur Bueche Medal 1996, Eisenhower Award 1996, Marshall Award 1997, Presidential Medal of Freedom 1997,.
Address: CISAC, Encina Hall, Stanford University, Stanford, CA 94305-6165, USA (office). *Telephone:* (650) 725-6501 (office). *Fax:* (650) 725-0920 (office). *E-mail:* dcgordon@stanford.edu (office). *Website:* cisac.stanford.edu (office).

PESSOA PEREIRA DA SILVA PINTO, Ana Maria; Timor-Leste politician; *Minister for State and Internal Administration; Career:* mem. Nat. Political Comm. of Timorese Resistance 1998–2000; mem. Transitional Cabinet for Internal Admin 2000–01; Minister of Justice 2001–03; Deputy Prime Minister and Minister of State and Minister of the Presidency of the Council of Ministers 2003–05; Minister for State and Internal Admin 2005–, Sr Minister of State 2006–; cand. for Prime Minister 2006; mem. FRETILIN (Frente Revolucionaria do Timor-Leste Independente).
Address: Ministry of Internal Administration, Dili, Timor-Leste (office). *Website:* www.timor-leste.gov.tl.

PETERS, Rt Hon Winston R.; New Zealand politician and lawyer; *Minister of Foreign Affairs and for Racing;* b. 11 April 1945. *Career:* MP for Tauranga; fmr Minister of Maori Affairs, Minister in charge of the Iwi Transition Agency, Chair. Cabinet Cttee on Treaty of Waitangi Issues 1990–91; independent MP 1993–, now New Zealand First Party; Leader New Zealand First Party 1993–; Deputy Prime Minister and Treas. 1996–98; Minister of Foreign Affairs and for Racing 2005–.
Address: Ministry of Foreign Affairs, Private Bag 18901, Wellington, New Zealand. *Telephone:* (4) 439-8000 (office). *Fax:* (4) 472-9596 (office). *E-mail:* enquiries@mfat.govt.nz (office). *Website:* www.mfat.govt.nz (office).

PETERSEN, Friis Arne, MEcon; Danish diplomatist; *Ambassador to USA;* m. Birgitte Wilhelmsen; one s. two d. *Education:* Univ. of Copenhagen. *Career:* entered Danish Foreign Service 1979, Head of Dept of Relations with Russia, Eastern Europe and Balkans and OSCE 1994–95, Under-sec., responsible for European Affairs and Econ. Assistance to Russia and Cen. and Eastern Europe and for Denmark's policies on EU and NATO enlargement 1995, served as Trade Rep. in EU Trade Policy Cttee 1995–97, Perm. Sec. of State, Ministry of Foreign Affairs 1997–2005, alt. for Foreign Minister in EU Council of Foreign Ministers; mem. Bd Denmark-America Foundation 1997–; mem. Bd Danish Int. Investment Funds 1995–2000; Co-Chair. Danish-Russian Intergovernmental Council on Econ. Cooperation 1997–2005; Amb. to USA 2005–; lectures regularly at Danish univs; Hon. GCMG; Commdr, First Class of the Order of Dannebrog, Order of Merit in Gold (Greenland), Grand Cross of the Order of the White Elephant (Thailand). *Publications:* has published a number of foreign policy articles.

Address: Embassy of Denmark, 3200 Whitehaven Street, NW, Washington, DC 20008, USA (office). *Telephone:* (202) 234-4300 (office). *Fax:* (202) 328-1470 (office). *E-mail:* wasamb@um.dk (office). *Website:* www .ambwashington.um.dk (office).

PETERSEN, Jan, LLB; Norwegian politician; b. 11 June 1946, Oslo; m.; two c. *Career:* with Norwegian Consumers' Asscn, Norwegian Agency for Devt Co-operation (NORAD); Chair. Young Conservatives 1971–73; Mayor of Oppegård 1976–81; mem. Stortinget (Parl.) 1981–; mem. Standing Cttee on Local Govt and Environment 1981–84, Standing Cttee on Foreign Affairs 1984– (Chair. 1985–86, later Deputy Chair.); Leader Akershus Conservative Party 1992–94, Conservative Party (Høyre) 1994–; Chair. Political Cttee of N Atlantic Ass. 1996–2001; Minister of Foreign Affairs 2001–05. *Address:* c/o Ministry of Foreign Affairs, 7 juri pl. 1, PO Box 8114 Dep., 0032 Oslo; Høyre, Stortingst. 20, PO Box 1536 Vika, 0117 Oslo, Norway.

PETERSSON, Sven-Olof; Swedish diplomatist; *Permanent Representative, European Union;* b. 12 March 1947, Ränneslöv; m.; two c. *Education:* Lund Univ. *Career:* various posts in Ministry of Foreign Affairs including Dir Minister's Office, Dir European Integration Dept, Deputy Dir-Gen. Political Affairs, Dir-Gen., Ministry of Foreign Affairs; diplomatic posts in Lebanon, Tanzania, Algeria, France, USA; currently Perm. Rep. to EU. *Address:* Permanent Representation of Sweden to the EU, 30 square de Meeûs, 1000 Brussels, Belgium (office). *Telephone:* (2) 289-56-11 (office). *Fax:* (2) 289-56-00 (office). *E-mail:* sven-olof.petersson@foreign.ministry .se (office).

PETRAEUS, Gen. David Howell, BS, MPA, PhD; American military officer; *Commander, US Central Command;* b. 7 Nov. 1952, Cornwall on Hudson, NY; m. Holly Knowlton 1974; two c. *Education:* West Point Mil. Acad., Princeton Univ. *Career:* commissioned second lt 1974, assigned to 509th Airborne Infantry Bn, Vicenza, Italy, served in various leadership posts in airborne, mechanized and air assault infantry units in Europe and USA including Operations Officer, 3rd Infantry Div. (Mechanized) 1st Bn 1978–79, command of 101st Airborne Div. (Air Assault) 3rd Bn 1991–93, command of 82nd Airborne Div. 1st Brigade 1995–97; staff posts have included Aide to Chief of Staff of the Army, Mil. Asst to Supreme Allied Commdr —Europe, Chief Mil. Operations Officer, UN Mission, Haiti 1995, Exec. Asst to Dir of Jt Staff and subsequently Chair. Jt Chiefs of Staff, Pentagon 1997–99; promoted to Brig.-Gen. 1999; Asst Div. Commdr for Operations, 82nd Airborne Div., Fort Bragg, NC 1999–2000; Chief of Staff, XVIII Airborne Corps 2000–01; promoted to Maj.-Gen. 2001; Asst Chief of Staff for Operations, NATO Stabilization Force and Deputy Commdr, US Jt Interagency Counter-Terrorism Task Force, Bosnia 2001–02; commanded 101st Airborne Div. during Operation Iraqi Freedom, Iraq 2003; promoted to Lt-Gen. 2004; Commdr, Multi-Nat. Security Transition Command and NATO Training Mission, Iraq 2004–05; Commanding Gen. US Army Combined Arms Center and Fort Leavenworth 2005–07; promoted to Gen. 2007; Commdr Multi-Nat. Force—Iraq, overseeing all coalition forces 2007–08; Commdr US Cen. Command 2008–; Gen. George C. Marshall Award 1983, Combat Action Badge, Army Achievement Medal, Defense Distinguished Service Medal, two Distinguished Service Medals, two Defense Superior Service Medals, four Legion of Merit awards, Bronze Star Medal for Valor, State Dept Superior Honor Award, NATO Meritorious Service Medal, Gold Award of the Iraqi Order of the Date Palm. *Publication:* US Army Counterinsurgency Field Manual (co-author). *Address:* US Central Command, 7115 South Boundary Boulevard, MacDill AFB, Tampa, FL 33621-5101, USA (office). *Telephone:* (813) 827-5895 (office). *Fax:* (813) 827-2211 (office). *E-mail:* pao@centcom.mil (office). *Website:* www.centcom.mil (office).

PETRIC, Ernest, PhD; Slovenian diplomatist and academic; *Ambassador to Austria;* b. 18 Nov. 1936, Trzic; m. Silvestra Rogelj; three d. *Education:* Univ. of Ljubljana, Univ. of Vienna. *Career:* Research Asst, Inst. for Ethnic Studies, Ljubljana 1961–65; Asst Prof. of Int. Law, Univ. of Ljubljana 1965–67, Prof. 1972–83; mem. Exec. Council of Slovenia, Minister of Science and Tech. 1967–72; Prof., Univ. of Addis Ababa, Ethiopia 1983–86; Dean Faculty of Social Science, Univ. of Ljubljana 1986–89; Amb. of Yugoslavia to India (also accred to Nepal) 1989–91; Amb. to USA (also accred to Mexico) 1991–97; State Sec. Ministry of Foreign Affairs 1997–2000; Perm. Rep. to UN, New York (also Amb. to Brazil) 2000–02; Amb. to Austria, also Perm. Rep. to UN, Vienna and to OSCE 2002–; Kidric Award 1979, Yugoslav Silver Medal for Achievement 1986, Colorado Meritorious Service Medal, USA 1997. *Publications:* International Legal Protection of Minorities 1977, The International Legal Position of the Slovenian Minority in Italy 1981, The Right to Self-Determination 1984, From Emperor to Leader 1987.

Address: Embassy of Slovenia, Nibelungengasse 13/3, 1010 Vienna, Austria (office). *Telephone:* (1) 586-13-09 (office). *Fax:* (1) 586-12-65 (office). *E-mail:* vdu@gov.si (office).

PETRITSCH, Wolfgang, PhD; Austrian diplomatist; *Permanent Representative, Organisation for Economic Co-operation and Development;* b. 26 Aug. 1947, Klagenfurt. *Education:* Univs of Vienna and Southern California, USA. *Career:* Adviser, Press Sec. of Austrian Fed. Chancellor 1977–83; mem. Austrian Mission to OECD, Paris 1983–84; Head Austrian Press and Information Service, NY 1984–92; Acting Head Dept for Multilateral Econ. Co-operation, Ministry of Foreign Affairs 1992–94; Head Dept for Information on European Affairs, Fed. Chancellery 1994; Head Dept for Int. Relations, City of Vienna 1995–97; Amb. to Yugoslavia 1997–99; EU Special Envoy for Kosovo 1998–99, EU Chief Negotiator at Kosovo peace talks, France Feb.–March 1999; High Rep. of the Int. Community in Bosnia and Herzegovina 1999–2002; Perm. Rep. to UN, WTO, Geneva 2002–08, to OECD 2008–; Pres. Mine Ban Convention's First Review Conference (Nairobi Summit) 2004; Chair. Vienna Cluster Munitions Conf. 2007; mem. Bd European Cultural Foundation, Int. Advisory Bd Esterhazy Foundation (Amsterdam Chair.), Paul Lazarsfeld Soc. for Social Research (Eisenstadt Chair.), Centre for European Integration Strategies, Geneva-Vienna-Sarajevo (Vienna Chair.), Bd Sigmund Freud Soc., Vienna, Bd Bruno Kreisky Forum for Int. Dialogue, Vienna; Person of the Year, Bosnia and Herzegovina 2002, Friedrich Torberg Medal for Human Rights 2002, Strasbourg Bruno Kreisky Award for the Political Book 2004, European Award for Human Rights 2006. *Publications include:* Kosovo-Kosova. Mythen, Daten, Fakten, Bosnien und Herzegowina fünf Jahre nach Dayton – Hat der Friede eine Chance?. *Address:* Permanent Mission of Austria, 2 rue André Pascal, 75775 Paris Cedex 16, France (office). *Telephone:* 1-45-2-82-00 (office). *Fax:* 1-45-24-85-00 (office). *E-mail:* wolfgang.petritsch@bka.gv.at (office).

PETROV, Ivo; Bulgarian diplomatist; *Deputy Special Representative of the Secretary-General to Georgia, United Nations;* b. 1948. *Education:* Diplomatic Acad., Moscow, Russia. *Career:* joined Bulgarian diplomatic service 1974, served in Bonn Embassy 1986–90, Amb. and Perm. Rep. to UN Office in Vienna, OSCE and other orgs 1993–98, 2002–05, Chair. OSCE Perm. Council 2004; fmr Head of Office in charge of CSCE, Ministry of Foreign Affairs, Head of Dept for European Integration 1998–99; Head of UN Tajikistan Office of Peace-building (UNTOP) and Special Rep. of UN Sec.-Gen. to Tajikistan 1999–2002; Deputy Special Rep. of the Sec.-Gen. to Georgia 2005–. *Address:* United Nations Observer Mission in Georgia (UNOMIG), Tbilisi Headquarters, 38 Krtsanisi Street, 380060 Tbilisi, Georgia (office). *Telephone:* (32) 50-72-00 (office). *E-mail:* unomig-pio@un.org (office); envera.selimovic@un.org (office). *Website:* www.unomig.org/officials/ dsrsg (office).

PETROVSKY, Vladimir Fyodorovich, DHist; Russian diplomatist; *Senior Research Fellow, United Nations Institute for Training and Research (UNITAR);* b. 29 April 1933, Volgograd; m. Myra Mukhina; one d. *Education:* Moscow Inst. of Int. Relations. *Career:* with USSR (now Russian) Ministry of Foreign Affairs 1957–; staff mem. USSR Mission to UN 1957–61, mem. Office of the Foreign Minister, USSR Ministry of Foreign Affairs 1961–64; mem. UN Secr. 1964–71; with dept of planning of int. policy, USSR Ministry of Foreign Affairs 1971–78, Head of Dept 1978–79, Head Dept of Int. Orgs 1979–86, Deputy Minister 1986–91, First Deputy Minister Aug.–Dec. 1991; Exec. Sec. CSCE Conf. on Human Dimension 1991; UN Under-Sec.-Gen. for Political Affairs 1992; Dir-Gen. UN Office, Geneva 1993–2002; Sec.-Gen. Conf. on Disarmament 1994–2002; Sr Research Fellow, UN Inst. for Training and Research (UNITAR) 2002–; Chair. Asscn for Comprehensive Dialogue Among Civilizations 2003–; mem. Acad. of Natural Sciences of Russian Fed., Mil. Acad. of Russian Fed., Russian Acad. of Outer Space, Int. Acad. of Information; Order of Merit (Russia) 1976, Order of Labour Red Banner 1983, Polish Order of Merit 2001. *Publications:* The Foreign Service of Great Britain 1958, The Diplomacy of 10 Downing Street 1964, US Foreign Policy Thinking: Theories and Concepts 1976, The Doctrine of National Security in US Global Strategy 1980, Disarmament: Concept, Problems, Mechanisms 1983, Security in the Era of Nuclear and Outer Space Technology 1985, The Triad of Strategic Security in the Global Society 2005. *Address:* Maly Kozhinsky Perelok 4, Apt 12, 123001 Moscow, Russia (home); c/o Ministry of Foreign Affairs, Smolenskaya-Sennaya pl. 32/34, 119200 Moscow, Russia (office). *Telephone:* (495) 209-78-12 (home). *E-mail:* vpetrovs@yandex.ru (home).

PETTIGREW, Pierre S., BA, MPhil; Canadian politician; b. 18 April 1951. *Education:* Univ. du Québec à Trois-Rivières, Balliol Coll., Oxford, UK. *Career:* Dir Political Cttee NATO Ass., Brussels 1976–78; Exec. Asst to

Leader of Québec Liberal Party 1978–81; Foreign Policy Adviser to Prime Minister, Privy Council Office 1981–84; Vice-Pres. Samson Belair Deloitte and Touche Int. (Montreal) 1985–95; elected MP 1996, re-elected 1997; Minister for Int. Co-operation and Minister with special responsibility for La Francophonie 1996–97, Minister of Human Resources Devt 1997–99, of Int. Trade 1999–2003, of Health, of Intergovernmental Affairs, responsible for Official Languages 2003–04, of Foreign Affairs 2004–06; Co-Chair. First Nat. Forum on Canada's Int. Relations 1994. *Publication:* The New Politics of Confidence 1999.
Address: c/o Liberal Party of Canada, 81 Metcalfe Street, Suite 400, Ottawa, ON K1P 6M8, Canada (office). *E-mail:* pettigrew.p@parl.gc.ca (office).

PETTIT, Philip Noel, PhD; Irish/Australian philosopher and academic; *L. S. Rockefeller University Professor of Politics and Human Values, Princeton University;* b. 20 Dec. 1945, Ballinasloe, Ireland; m. Victoria McGeer; two s. *Education:* Maynooth Coll., Nat. Univ. of Ireland, Queen's Univ. Belfast, Northern Ireland. *Career:* Lecturer, Univ. Coll. Dublin 1968–72, 1975–77; Research Fellow, Trinity Hall Cambridge, UK 1972–75; Prof. of Philosophy, Univ. of Bradford, UK 1977–83; Professorial Fellow, Research School of Social Sciences, ANU, Canberra, Australia 1983–89, Prof. of Social and Political Theory 1989–2002; Visiting Prof. of Philosophy, Columbia Univ., New York, USA 1997–2001; William Nelson Cromwell Prof. of Politics, Princeton Univ., USA 2002, currently L. S. Rockefeller Univ. Prof. of Politics and Human Values; Assoc. Faculty Mem. Dept of Philosophy; Fellow, Acad. of Social Sciences, Australia, Australian Acad. of Humanities; Hon. mem. Italian Soc. for Analytical Philosophy; Hon. DLitt (Nat. Univ. of Ireland) 2000, (Queen's Univ., Belfast), Hon. PhD (Univ. of Crete) 2005, (Univ. of Montreal); Univ. Medal, Univ. of Helsinki 1992. *Publications:* Concept of Structuralism 1975, Judging Justice 1980, Semantics and Social Science (with G. Macdonald) 1981, Not Just Deserts: A Republican Theory of Criminal Justice (with J. Braithwaite) 1990, The Common Mind: An Essay on Psychology, Society and Politics 1992, Republicanism: A Theory of Freedom and Government 1997, A Theory of Freedom: From the Psychology to the Politics of Agency 2001, Rules, Reasons and Norms: Selected Essays 2002, Penser en Société 2003, Mind, Morality, and Explanation: Selected Collaborations (co-author) 2004, The Economy of Esteem (with Geoffrey Brennan) 2004, Made with Words: Hobbes on Language, Thought and Mind 2008, Examen a Zapatero 2008.
Address: UCHV, 308 Marx Hall, Princeton University, Princeton, NJ 08544-1012 (office); 16 College Road, Princeton, NJ 08540, USA (home). *Telephone:* (609) 258-4759 (office); (609) 924-3664 (home). *E-mail:* ppettit@princeton.edu (office). *Website:* www.princeton.edu/~ppettit (office).

PFANZELTER, Gerhard; Austrian diplomatist; *Permanent Representative, United Nations;* b. 1943, Innsbruck; m.; three c. *Education:* Univ. of Innsbruck, Univ. of Strasbourg, France, School of Advanced Int. Studies, Washington, DC, USA. *Career:* joined Ministry of Foreign Affairs 1969, Deputy Dir UN Dept and Head of Policy Co-ordination Unit 1979–83, Head Dept for Int. Orgs. 1993–99; First Sec. Embassy in Italy 1972–75; Counsellor and Deputy Chief Perm. Mission to UN, New York 1975–79, Perm. Rep. to UN 1999–; Amb. to Senegal, Gambia, Cape Verde, Guinea-Bissau, Mali, Guinea and Mauritania 1983–89, to Syria 1989–93.
Address: Permanent Mission of Austria to the UN, 823 United Nations Plaza, 8th Floor, New York, NY 10017, USA (office). *Telephone:* (212) 949-1840 (office). *Fax:* (212) 953-1302 (office). *E-mail:* austria@un.int (office). *Website:* www.un.int/austria (office).

PHELPS, Edmund Strother, PhD; American economist and academic; *Professor of Political Economics, Columbia University;* b. 26 July 1933, Evanston, Ill.; m. Viviana Montdor 1974. *Education:* Amherst Coll. and Yale Univ. *Career:* Research Economist, RAND Corpn 1959–60; taught Yale Univ. 1960–66; Prof., Univ. of Pennsylvania 1966–71, Columbia Univ. 1971–78, New York Univ. 1977–78, Columbia Univ. 1979–82, McVickar Prof. of Political Econs, Columbia Univ. 1982–; Sr Adviser Brookings Inst. 1976–; Econ. Adviser EBRD 1991–94; mem. NAS 1982; mem. Econ. Policy Panel, Observatoire Français des Conjonctures Economiques 1991–; Sr Adviser Consiglio Nazionale delle Ricerche 1997–2000; Distinguished Fellow, American Econ. Asscn 2000; Hon. DH (Amherst Coll.) 1985, (Univ. of Mannheim) 2001, (Univ. Tor Vergata, Rome) 2001; Kenan Enterprise Award 1996, Nobel Prize in Econ. Science 2006. *Publications:* Golden Rules of Economic Growth 1966, Microeconomic Foundations of Employment and Inflation Theory (ed.) 1970, Studies in Macroeconomic Theory: Vols 1, 2 1979, 1980, Political Economy: An Introductory Text 1985, The Slump in Europe 1988, Seven Schools of Macroeconomic Thought 1990, Structural Slumps 1994, Rewarding Work 1997.
Address: Department of Economics, Columbia University, 1004 International Affairs Building, MC 3308, 420 West 118th Street, New York, NY

10027, USA (office). *Telephone:* (212) 854-2060 (office). *Fax:* (212) 854-3735 (office). *E-mail:* esp2@columbia.edu (office). *Website:* www.columbia.edu/~esp2 (office).

PHICHIT, Maj.-Gen. Douangchai; Laotian army commander and politician; *Deputy Prime Minister and Minister of National Defence; Career:* fmr Mil. Chief of Staff; currently Deputy Prime Minister and Minister of Nat. Defence; mem. Politburo.
Address: Ministry of National Defence, rue Phone Kheng, Ban Phone Kheng, Vientiane, Laos (office). *Telephone:* (21) 412803 (office). *Fax:* (21) 412801 (office).

PHIEU, Gen. Le Kha; Vietnamese army officer and politician; b. 27 Dec. 1931, Dong Khe Commune, Dong Son Dist, Thanh Hoa Prov. *Education:* Vietnam Mil. Coll. *Career:* joined CP 1949; several positions 1964–93 including Regiment's Political Commissar and Commdr of the Regiment, Deputy Chief Army Political Dept of Second Army Corps, Deputy Political Commissar and Chief Political Dept of Ninth Mil. Zone, Maj.-Gen., Chief of Political Dept and Deputy Political Commdr of 719 Front, Lt-Gen., Deputy Chief and then Sr Lt-Gen. and Chief Gen. Political Dept Vietnamese People's Army; Sec.-Gen. CP of Viet Nam 1997–2001; mem. Politburo, Politburo Standing Bd.
Address: Communist Party of Viet Nam, 1 Hoang Van Thu, Hanoi, Viet Nam.

PHILAKONE, Phiane, LLB; Laotian diplomatist and fmr banker; *Ambassador to USA;* b. 6 July 1947, Muang Khong Dist, Champasak Prov.; m. Somchit Philakone; three c. *Education:* Int. Inst. for Public Admin, Paris, Inst. Royal de Droit et d'Admin, Vientiane. *Career:* Dir of Admin, Lao Devt Bank 1973–75; Research Dir Bank of Lao People's Democratic Repub. (cen. bank) 1976–89, Deputy Gov. 1996–99; Man. Dir Banque pour le Commerce Extérieur 1990–93; Pres. Jt Devt Bank 1990–93; Amb. to Philippines 2001–07, to USA (also accred to Canada and Mexico) 2007–.
Address: Embassy of the Lao People's Democratic Republic, 2222 S Street, NW, Washington, DC 20008, USA (office). *Telephone:* (202) 332-6416 (office). *Fax:* (202) 332-4923 (office). *E-mail:* laoemb@verizon.net (office). *Website:* www.laoembassy.com (office).

PHILEMON, Bart; Papua New Guinea politician. *Career:* Minister for Transport and Civil Aviation –2000, Minister for Foreign Affairs and Bougainville Affairs 2000–02; Caretaker Gov., Minister for Treasury, Finance, Privatisation and Agric. 2002; Minister for Finance and Treasury 2002–06; Gov. World Bank for Papua New Guinea.
Address: c/o Ministry for Finance and Treasury, POB 710, Vulpindi Haus, Waigani NCD, Papua New Guinea (office).

PHILIPPE, HRH Crown Prince (Duke of Brabant), MA; Belgian; b. 15 April 1960; m. Mathilde d'Udekem d'Acoz 1999; one d. two s. *Education:* Royal Mil. Acad., Trinity Coll., Oxford, England and Stanford Univ., USA. *Career:* apptd Second Lt Belgian armed forces 1980, subsequently obtained fighter pilot's wings and certificates as parachutist and commando, attended Royal Higher Defence Inst. 1989, apptd Col 1989, apptd Maj.-Gen. and Rear-Adm. 2001; Royal Household established 1992; Pres. Nat. Sustainable Devt Council 1993–97; apptd Senator 1994; Founder Le Fonds Prince Philippe 1998–; Hon. Pres. Bd of Dirs Foreign Trade Office 1993–, Fed. Sustainable Devt Council 1997–.
Address: Royal Palace, 16 rue Bréderode, Brussels 1000, Belgium (office). *Telephone:* (2) 5512020 (office). *Fax:* (2) 5023949 (office). *Website:* www.monarchie.be.

PHILLIPS, David L.; American international affairs scholar; *Executive Director and Director, Nobel Laureates Initiative, Elie Wiesel Foundation for Humanity; Career:* fmr positions include Exec. Dir, Int. Conflict Resolution Program, Columbia Univ., Program Dir, Int. Peace Research Inst. of Oslo, Dir, European Centre for Common Ground, Pres., Congressional Human Rights Foundation; Sr Adviser to UN 2000; Sr Adviser and mem. Future of Iraq Group, US State Dept –2003 (resgnd); Visiting Scholar, Center for Middle East Studies, Harvard Univ.; Scholar-in-Residence and Program Dir, Center for Global Peace, American Univ.; Sr Fellow, Preventive Diplomacy Program, Center for Strategic and Int. Studies; fmr Sr Fellow and Deputy Dir, Center for Preventive Action, Council on Foreign Relations; currently Exec. Dir Elie Wiesel Foundation for Humanity, also Dir Nobel Laureates Initiative. *Publications:* Unsilencing the Past: Track Two Diplomacy and Turkish-American Reconciliation 2005, Losing Iraq: Inside the Postwar Reconstruction Fiasco 2005; over 100 articles and editorials in journals and newspapers.
Address: Elie Wiesel Foundation for Humanity, 555 Madison Avenue, 20th Floor, New York, NY 10022, USA (office). *Fax:* (212) 490-6006 (office). *Website:* www.eliewieselfoundation.org (office).

PHILLIPS, Patricia Ruth (Pat); British diplomatist; *Ambassador to Angola; Education:* Univ. of Minnesota, USA. *Career:* with Ministry of Agric., Fisheries and Food 1984–91, secondment to EU Council Secr., Brussels 1988, First Sec., Agric. and Trade Policy, Embassy in Washington DC 1992–97; mem. Policy Planning staff, FCO 1997–98, Pvt. Sec. to Minister of State (Minister for Africa) 1998–2000, Deputy Head, Near East and North Africa Dept, FCO 2000–02; Counsellor (Econ.), Trade and Investment, Embassy in The Hague 2002–04, Deputy Head of Mission, Embassy in Amman 2004–07; Amb. to Angola 2007–.
Address: British Embassy, Rua Diogo Cão 4, CP 1244, Luanda, Angola (office). *Telephone:* (222) 334582 (office). *Fax:* (222) 333331 (office). *E-mail:* ppa.luanda@fco.gov.uk (office); postmaster.Luand@fco.gov.uk (office). *Website:* www.britishembassy.gov.uk/angola (office).

PHILLIPS, Stanley Davis (Dave); American business executive, government official and diplomatist; *Ambassador to Estonia;* b. High Point, N Carolina; m. Kay Phillips; four d. *Education:* Choate Rosemary Hall, Wallingford, Conn., Univ. of N Carolina, Chapel Hill, Moscow State Univ. *Career:* fmr Chair. and CEO Phillips Industries, Inc.; fmr Pnr, Market Square Partnership; served in several N Carolina govt positions including State Sec. of Commerce, Chair. State Econ. Devt Bd, and mem. Bd State Dept of Transportation; fmr Chair. Piedmont Triad Partnership, Econ. Devt Corpn, High Point and Triad Chamber of Commerce; Amb. to Estonia 2007–; fmr mem. Bd Duke Univ., Wake Forest Univ. Medical Center, Smithsonian Inst.; Chair. World Games of Special Olympics in America 1999.
Address: US Embassy, Kentmanni 20, Tallinn 15099, Estonia (office). *Telephone:* 668-8100 (office). *Fax:* 668-8134 (office). *E-mail:* USASaatkond@state.gov (office). *Website:* estonia.usembassy.gov (office).

PHILLIPS, Tom Richard Vaughan, CMG; British diplomatist; *Ambassador to Israel;* b. 21 June 1950; m. Anne; two s. *Career:* Dept of Health and Social Security 1977–83, Energy, Science and Space Dept, FCO 1983–86, First Sec., Harare 1985–88, Deputy Head of Personnel Policy Dept, FCO 1988–90, Consul Gen. and Deputy Head of Mission, Tel-Aviv 1990–93, Counsellor (External), Washington, DC 1993–97, Head of Eastern Adriatic Dept, FCO 1997–99, High Commr to Uganda 2000–02, UK Special Rep. for Afghanistan 2002, Dir S Asia and Afghanistan, FCO 2003–06, Amb. to Israel 2006–.
Address: British Embassy, 192 Rehov Hayarkon, Tel-Aviv 63405, Israel (office). *Telephone:* 3-7251222 (office). *Fax:* 3-5278574 (office). *E-mail:* webmaster.telaviv@fco.gov.uk (office). *Website:* www.britemb.org.il (office).

PHOMMACHACK, Ouan; Laotian diplomatist; *Ambassador to Thailand; Career:* fmr Amb. to USA, Amb. to Thailand 1998–; Trustee, Asian Inst. of Tech.
Address: Embassy of Laos, 500/502/1–2 Soi Sahakarnpramoon, Thanon Pracha Uthit, Wangthonglang, Bangkok 10310, Thailand (office). *Telephone:* (2) 539-6667 (office). *Fax:* (2) 539-3827 (office). *E-mail:* sabaidee@bkklaoembassy.com (office). *Website:* www.bkklaoembassy.com (office).

PHOMMACHANH, Kanika, BA, MA; Laotian diplomatist; *Permanent Representative, United Nations;* b. 8 Jan. 1951, Champassak; m.; two c. *Education:* Univ. of Montréal, Canada, Johns Hopkins Univ., USA. *Career:* Pvt. Sec. to Chief of Cabinet, Ministry of Foreign Affairs 1975, Desk Officer Eastern Europe Div. 1976–80, Dir North America Div. 1980–82, Deputy Dir-Gen. 1982–90, Dir-Gen. 1990–91; Minister Counsellor and Charge d'Affaires, Perm. Mission to UN, New York 1991–97; Dir-Gen. Ministry of Foreign Affairs 1997–2006; Perm. Rep. Desig. to UN, New York 2006–07, Perm. Rep. 2007–.
Address: Permanent Mission of Laos to the United Nations, 317 East 51st Street, New York, NY 10022, USA (office). *Telephone:* (212) 832-2734 (office). *Fax:* (212) 750-0039 (office). *E-mail:* lao@un.int (office). *Website:* www.un.int/lao (office).

PHOMMAHAXAY, Phanthong; Laotian diplomatist; b. 2 March 1941, Vientiane; m. Amphanh Phommahaxay (née Luangrath); three s. one d. *Education:* Nat. Centre for Political Studies, Vientiane. *Career:* joined Ministry of Foreign Affairs 1962, Head Passport and Political Sections 1968–73, Dir NGO Section, Dept for Int. Orgs 1978–80, Deputy Dir-Gen., then Dir-Gen. Press Dept 1984–90, Dir-Gen. Asia Pacific and Africa Dept 1994–95; Attaché in Beijing, People's Repub. of China 1965–68; Second Sec., First Sec. then Chargé d'affaires in Paris, France 1974–78; First Sec., then Deputy Head of Mission to Thailand, Bangkok 1980–84; Amb. to Indonesia 1990–94, to Australia and New Zealand 1995–98, to Germany, The Netherlands, Switzerland and Austria 1998–2001, to USA 2002–07.
Address: c/o Ministry of Foreign Affairs, rue That Luang 01004, Ban Phonxay, Vientiane, Laos. *Telephone:* (21) 413148. *Fax:* (21) 414009. *E-mail:* cabinet@mofa.gov.la. *Website:* www.mofa.gov.la.

PHOSIKHAM, Chansy; Laotian politician; *Governor of Vientiane Province; Career:* fmr Gov. Prov. of Luang Prabang; Gov. State Bank –2003; Minister of Finance 2003–07; Gov. Vientiane Prov. 2007–; mem. Seventh Party Cen. Cttee.
Address: c/o Ministry of Finance, rue That Luang, Ban Phonxay, Vientiane, Laos (office).

PHUNG, Le Cong; Vietnamese diplomatist; *Ambassador to USA;* b. 20 Feb. 1948, Thanh Hoa Prov.; m. Nguyen Thi Nhan; two s. *Education:* Coll. of Diplomacy of Viet Nam. *Career:* career diplomat, Foreign Service postings include Embassies in London 1974–77, Beijing 1978–80, Jakarta 1984–87; Amb. to Thailand 1993–97; Asst Minister of Foreign Affairs 1999–2000, Chair. Cttee on Border Affairs 2000–04, Nat. Comm. for UNESCO 2000–04; Deputy Minister of Foreign Affairs 2001–04, First Deputy Minister of Foreign Affairs 2004–07; Amb. to USA 2007–.
Address: Embassy of Viet Nam, 1233 20th Street, NW, Suite 400, Washington, DC 20036, USA (office). *Telephone:* (202) 861-0737 (office). *Fax:* (202) 861-0917 (office). *E-mail:* info@vietnamembassy.us (office). *Website:* www.vietnamembassy-usa.org (office).

PIA-COMELLA, Jelena V.; Andorran diplomatist. *Career:* fmr Minister Counsellor, Perm. Mission of Andorra to UN, New York; Chargé d'affaires a.i. in USA 2001–08; consultant for Gender Equality Architecture Reform campaign, Women's Environment and Devt Org. 2008–.
Address: WEDO, 355 Lexington Avenue, 3rd Floor, New York, NY 10017, USA (office). *Telephone:* (212) 973-0325 (office). *Fax:* (212) 973-0335 (office). *E-mail:* wedo@wedo.org (office). *Website:* www.wedo.org (office).

PIĄTAS, Gen. Czesław; Polish army officer and politician; *Secretary of State, Ministry of National Defence;* b. 20 March 1946, Germany; m. Danuta Piątas; two c. *Education:* Armour Officer's School, Acad. of Gen. Staff, USSR, US Nat. War Coll., USA. *Career:* began career in Polish Armed Forces 1968; served in variety of command and staff positions in armour units 1970s; Chief of Staff, Deputy Commdr of 10th Armoured Div. and Commdr of tank regiment 1980–82; apptd G-3 Dir Silesian Mil. Dist HQ 1982; Commdr 4th Mechanized Div.; Staff Position Silesian Mil. Dist. HQ 1993–94; Chief of Staff DCG, Warsaw Mil. Dist 1995–96; Chief of Operational and Strategic Div., Gen. Staff 1996–99; Deputy Chief of Gen. Staff of Polish Armed Forces 1999–2000, Chief of Gen. Staff Sept. 2000–06; Sec. of State, Ministry of Defence 2008–; apptd Brig.-Gen. 1992, Maj.-Gen. 1999, Lt-Gen. 2000, Gen. 2000.
Address: Ministry of National Defence, ul. Klonowa 1, 00-909 Warsaw, Poland (office). *Telephone:* (22) 6280031 (office). *Fax:* (22) 8455378 (office). *E-mail:* bpimon@wp.mil.pl (office). *Website:* www.wp.mil.pl (office).

PICADO, Sonia, LicenD; Costa Rican international civil servant and lawyer; *Chairman, Board of Directors, Inter-American Institute of Human Rights;* b. 20 Dec. 1936; m. (divorced); one s. one d. *Education:* Univ. of Costa Rica. *Career:* Dean, Law Faculty of Costa Rica 1980–84, Cathedratical Chair. 1984; Co-Chair. Int. Comm. for Central American Recovery and Devt 1987–89; mem. Cttee of Jurists, World Conf. on Refugees, UNHCR, Geneva 1988–89; Exec. Dir Inter-American Inst. of Human Rights 1988–94, currently Chair. Bd of Dirs; Vice-Pres. Inter-American Court of Human Rights 1988–94; fmr Pres. Partido de Liberación Nacional (PLN); Amb. to USA 1994–99; Head UN Comm. of Inquiry E Timor 1999; mem. Legislative Ass. for San José; currently mem. Comm. on Human Security; Max Planck/Humboldt Award (Germany) 1991, Leonidas Proaño Award (Ecuador) 1991. *Publications:* Women and Human Rights 1986, Philosophical Fundamentals of Human Rights in Latin America 1987, Religion, Tolerance and Liberty: A Human Rights Perspective 1989, Peace, Development and Human Rights 1989.
Address: Inter-American Institute of Human Rights, PO Box 10081-1000, San José, Costa Rica (office). *Telephone:* 234-0404 (office). *Fax:* 234-0955 (office). *E-mail:* instituto@iidh.ed.cr (office). *Website:* www.iidh.ed.cr (office).

PICEK, Lt-Gen. Vlastimil; Czech military officer; *Chief of General Staff;* b. 25 Oct. 1956, Turnov; m. Dagmar Picková; two c. *Education:* Mil. Acad., Brno, Czech Tech. Univ. *Career:* sr radio operator 1975–78; Deputy Battalion Commdr for Tech. Issues 1983–86, Sr Officer, Nat. Air Defence HQ 1986–89; Chief of Signal Br, Fourth Air Defence Corps HQ 1993–94; Section Chief Signal Br, Armed Forces Gen. Staff 1994–95; Deputy Chief 1995–96, Chief of Signal Br 1996–97, Chief of Operational-Tactical C2 Systems Dept 1997–2000, Chief of Command and Control Div. 2000–03; Security Dir, Ministry of Defence 2001–03; promoted to Brig. 2001; Chief of Mil. Office of Pres. 2003–07; promoted to Maj. Gen. 2003; promoted to Lt Gen. 2006; Chief of Gen. Staff 2007–; Cross of Merit of the Minister of Defence Third Grade, ACR Medal Third Grade, Nat. Service Medal, Hon. Commemorative Badge for Service in Peace Operation in the Balkans, NATO 50th Anniversary Medal.

Address: Office of the Chief of General Staff, Generální štáb AČR, Vítězné nám. 5, 160 01 Prague, Czech Republic (office). *Telephone:* 973216027 (office). *Fax:* 973216084 (office). *E-mail:* kangs@army.cz (office). *Website:* www.army.cz (office).

PICULA, Tonino; Croatian politician and historian; b. 31 Aug. 1961, Mali Losinj. *Education:* Zagreb Univ. *Career:* Assoc. Prof. and Sec. Kulturni Radnik (magazine), Cultural and Educ. Ass. 1987–89; mem. Exec. Cttee, Int. Sec. SDP of Croatia 1993–; Counsellor, SDP Co. Ass. of Zagreb, mem. Cttee for Int. Co-operation for Local Self-Govt Devt, Pres. City Org. SDP for Velika Gorica 1997–2000; mem. Croatian Parl. 2000–; Minister of Foreign Affairs 2000–03.
Address: c/o Ministry of Foreign Affairs, trg. Nikole Šubića Zrinskog 7-8, 10000 Zagreb, Croatia (office).

PIERCE, Roger Dwayne, BA, MA; American diplomatist; *Ambassador to Cape Verde;* b. Omaha, Neb.; m. Jo Ann Pierce; two s. one d. *Education:* Davis and Elkins Coll., W Va, Univ. of Maryland, Army War Coll., Pa, 44th Senior Seminar. *Career:* career mem. Sr Foreign Service, class of Counselor, entered Foreign Service 1978, Consular Officer, Mexico City 1978–79, Santiago 1979–81, Chief of Consular Section, Calcutta 1981–84, Istanbul 1986–90, Prin. Officer, Amsterdam 1990–94, served in Office of Insp.-Gen. 1995–97, Consul-Gen., Cairo 1997–2001, has held domestic assignments in State Dept's Office of Caribbean Affairs, including Desk Officer for Bahamas, Trinidad and Tobago, Netherlands Antilles, Cayman Islands, and Turks and Caicos Islands, Deputy Chief of Mission, Embassy in Tegucigalpa, Honduras 2002–05, Amb. to Cape Verde 2005–.
Address: Embassy of the USA, Rua Abílio Macedo 6, Praia, Santiago, Cape Verde (office). *Telephone:* 2615616 (office). *Fax:* 2611355 (office). *Website:* praia.usembassy.gov (office).

PIERRE-JEAN, Idalbert; Haitian diplomatist; *Ambassador to Mexico; Career:* fmr Amb. to Spain; Amb. to Mexico 2002–.
Address: Embassy of Haiti, Pres. Don Martin 53, Del. Miguel Hidalgo, 11500 México, DF, Mexico (office). *Telephone:* (55) 5557-2065 (office). *Fax:* (55) 5395-1654 (office). *E-mail:* ambadh@mail.internet.com.mx (office).

PIKIS, Georghios M., LLB; Cypriot judge; *Judge, International Criminal Court;* b. 22 Jan. 1939, Larnaca; m. Maria G. Pikis (née Papaneophytou); two s. one d. *Education:* Univ. of London, UK. *Career:* called to the Bar, Gray's Inn, London 1961; Advocate of the Cyprus Bar 1961–66; Dist Judge 1966–72; Pres. Dist Court 1972–81; Justice of Supreme Court of Cyprus 1981–95, Pres. Supreme Court 1995–2004; Judge, Int. Criminal Court (ICC), The Hague 2003–, full-time mem. 2004–; ad hoc judge European Court of Human Rights 1993, 1997; mem. UN Cttee against Torture 1996–98; mem. Bd of Dirs Int. Asscn of Supreme Admin. Jurisdictions 1999–2004; mem. Circle of Pres of Conf. of European Constitutional Courts 1999–2004, Pres. 2002–04. *Publications:* books: Criminal Procedure in Cyprus (in English, co-author) 1975, Sentencing in Cyprus (in English) 1978, The Common Law and Principles of Equity and Their Application in Cyprus (in Greek) 1981, Basic Aspects of Cyprus Law (in Greek) 2003, Constitutionalism – Human Rights – Separation of Powers, The Cyprus Precedent (in English) 2006; numerous lectures, speeches and reports (including reports to Int., European and Commonwealth Judicial Confs and Asscns) on human rights, constitutional law and the judiciary.
Address: International Criminal Court, Maanweg 174, 2516 AB The Hague, The Netherlands (office). *Telephone:* (70) 5158216 (office). *Fax:* (70) 5158789 (office). *E-mail:* georghios.pikis@icc-cpi.int (office). *Website:* www.icc-cpi.int (office).

PILDEGOVICS, Andrejs, BA, MA; Latvian civil servant and diplomatist; *Ambassador to USA;* b. 11 Aug. 1971; m. Jelena Pildegovica; three c. *Education:* Univ. of St Petersburg, USSR, Beijing Foreign Languages Inst., China, Hoover Institution, Stanford Univ., USA, Univ. of Oxford, UK. *Career:* civil servant 1994–95; Asst to State Sec., Ministry of Foreign Affairs 1995–96, Press Sec., Ministry of Foreign Affairs 1996–98, Head of Middle East and Africa Div. 1999–2000; Foreign Policy Advisor to Pres. Vaira Vike-Freiberga 2000–06, Chief of Staff, Chancery of the Pres. 2006–07; Amb. to USA 2007– (also accred to Mexico 2008–).
Address: Embassy of Latvia, 2306 Massachusetts Avenue, NW, Washington, DC 20008, USA (office). *Telephone:* (202) 328-2840 (office). *Fax:* (202) 328-2860 (office). *E-mail:* embassy@latvia-usa.org (office); embassy.usa@mfa.gov.lv (office). *Website:* www.latvia-usa.org (office).

PILGER, John Richard; Australian journalist, filmmaker and writer; b. Sydney, NSW; m. (divorced); one s. one d. *Education:* Sydney High School, Journalism Cadet Training, Australian Consolidated Press. *Career:* journalist, Sydney Daily/Sunday Telegraph 1958–62; Reuters, London 1962; feature writer, columnist and Foreign Corresp. (latterly Chief Foreign Corresp.), Daily Mirror, London 1963–86; columnist, New Statesman, London 1991–; freelance contrib., The Guardian, London, The Independent, London, New York Times, Melbourne Age, The Nation, New York, South China Morning Post, Hong Kong, Aftonbladet, Sweden; documentary filmmaker, Granada TV, UK 1969–71, Associated Television 1972–80, Central/Carlton/Granada Television, UK 1980–; credited with alerting much of int. community to horrors of Pol Pot régime in Cambodia, also occupation of Timor-Leste; Visiting Fellow, Deakin Univ., Australia 1995; Frank H. T. Rhodes Visiting Prof., Cornell Univ., USA 2003–; Hon. DLitt (Staffordshire Univ.) 1994; Hon. PhD (Dublin City Univ.) 1995, (Kingston) 1999, (Open Univ.); Hon. DArts (Oxford Brookes Univ.) 1997; Hon. DrIur (St Andrews) 1999; Hon. DUniv (Open Univ.) 2001; Descriptive Writer of the Year, UK 1966, Journalist of the Year, UK 1967, 1979, Int. Reporter of the Year, UK 1970, Reporter of the Year, UK 1974, BAFTA Richard Dimbleby Award 1991, US Acad. Award (Emmy) 1991, Reporteurs sans frontières, France 1993, George Foster Peabody Award, USA 1992, Sophie Prize for Human Rights 2003, Royal TV Soc. Award 2005. *Exhibitions:* Reporting the World: John Pilger's Great Eyewitness Photographers, The Barbican Summer Exhbn 2001. *Feature film:* The Last Day 1983. *Documentary films include:* Cambodia: Year Zero 1979 (and four other films on Cambodia), The Quiet Mutiny 1970, Japan Behind the Mask 1986, The Last Dream 1988, Death of a Nation 1994, Flying the Flag: Arming the World 1994, Inside Burma 1996, Breaking The Mirror: The Murdoch Effect 1997, Apartheid Did Not Die 1998, Welcome to Australia 1999, Paying the Price: Killing the Children of Iraq 2000, The New Rulers of the World 2001, Palestine Is Still The Issue 2002, Breaking the Silence: Truth and Lies in the War on Terror 2003, Stealing a Nation 2004, The War on Democracy 2007. *Publications:* The Last Day 1975, Aftermath: The Struggle of Cambodia and Vietnam 1981, The Outsiders 1983, Heroes 1986, A Secret Country 1989, Distant Voices 1992, Hidden Agendas 1998, Reporting the World: John Pilger's Great Eyewitness Photographers 2001, The New Rulers of the World 2002, Tell Me No Lies: Investigative Journalism and its Triumphs (ed) 2004, Freedom Next Time 2006.
Address: 57 Hambalt Road, London, SW4 9EQ, England. *Telephone:* (20) 8673-2848. *Fax:* (20) 8772-0235. *E-mail:* jpmarheine@hotmail.com (home). *Website:* www.johnpilger.com.

PILLAY, Navanethem, BA, LLM, SJD, LLB; South African judge and UN official; *High Commissioner for Human Rights, United Nations Office of the High Commissioner for Human Rights;* b. 23 Sept. 1941, Durban; m. (deceased); two d. *Education:* Natal Univ., Harvard Univ., USA. *Career:* first woman to start a law practice in Natal Prov. 1967, Sr Pnr 1967–95; first black woman apptd Acting Judge High Court of SA 1995; Judge, UN Int. Criminal Tribunal for Rwanda 1995–2003, Pres. 1999–2003; Judge, Int. Criminal Court 2003–08; UN High Commr for Human Rights, Geneva 2008–; Chair. Equality Now 1990–95, Hon. Chair. 1995–; Pres. Advice Desk for Abused Women 1989–99, Women Lawyers' Asscn 1995–98; Vice-Chair. of Council, Univ. of Durban-Westville 1995–98; Lecturer, Dept of Public Law, Natal Univ. 1980; Trustee, Legal Resources Centre 1995–98, Lawyers for Human Rights 1998–2001; mem. Women's Nat. Coalition 1992–93, Black Lawyers' Asscn 1995–98, UN Expert Groups on Refugees and on Gender Persecution 1997, Rules Bd for Courts 1997–98, Expert Group on African Perspectives on Universal Jurisdiction, Cairo and Arusha 2001–02; currently mem. Int. Criminal Law Network, Advisory Bd Journal of Int. Criminal Justice, Bd Harvard-South Africa Scholarship Cttee, Bd Dirs Nozala Investments (women's component of Nat. Econ. Initiative); Hon. mem. American Soc. of Int. Law; Unifem and Noel Foundation Life Award (Los Angeles), Award for Leadership in the Fight for Human Rights, California Legislative Assembly, Dr Edgar Brookes Award, Natal Univ., Award for Outstanding Contrib. in Raising Awareness of Women's Rights and Domestic Violence, Advice Desk for Abused Women, Award for Dedication to Human Rights, Equality Now, New York, One Hundred Heroines Award, Washington DC, Human Rights Award, Int. Asscn of Women Judges, Award for High Achievement by a Woman in the Legal Profession, Center for Human Rights and Univ. of Pretoria; further awards from Asscn of Law Soc. of SA, Black Lawyers' Asscn, Feminist Majority Foundation, Int. Bar Asscn, Peter Gruber Foundation. *Publications:* contrib.: Civilians in War 2001, Essays in Memory of Judge Cassese 2003.
Address: Office of the High Commissioner for Human Rights, Palais Wilson 52 rue des Pâquis, 1201 Geneva, Switzerland (home); 16 Lavery Crescent, Durban 4091, South Africa (home). *Telephone:* (22) 917-9011 (office). *E-mail:* InfoDesk@ohchr.org (office). *Website:* www.ohchr.org (office).

PILLAY, Patrick, MA; Seychelles politician; *Minister of Foreign Affairs;* two s. (one adopted) one d. *Career:* fmr Minister of Educ., of Youth and Culture, of Industries and Int. Business, of Health; Minister of Foreign

Affairs 2005–; fmr Seychelles Gov. to African Devt Bank; fmr Pres. Seychelles Nat. Comm. for UNESCO.
Address: Ministry of Foreign Affairs, Maison Queau de Quincy, POB 656, Mont Fleuri, Seychelles (office). *Telephone:* 283500 (office). *Fax:* 225398 (office). *E-mail:* hope@seychelles.net (home); mfapesey@seychelles.net (office); dazemia@mfa.gov.sc (office). *Website:* www.mfa.gov.sc (office).

PINDA, Mizengo Kayanza Peter; Tanzanian politician; *Prime Minister;* b. 12 Aug. 1948, Rukwa Region. *Education:* Univ. of Dar es Salaam. *Career:* State Attorney, Ministry of Justice and Constitutional Affairs 1974–78; State House Security Officer, Pres.'s Office 1978–82; Asst Pvt. Sec. to the Pres. 1982–92; State House Clerk to the Cabinet 1996–2000; MP for Mpanda East 2000–05, for Mpanda Mashariki 2005–; Deputy Minister in Prime Minister's Office for Regional Admin and Local Govt 2000–05; Minister of State for Regional Admin and Local Govt 2006–08; Prime Minister 2008–.
Address: Office of the Prime Minister, PO Box 980, Dodoma, Tanzania (office). *Telephone:* (26) 233201 (office). *Website:* www.tanzania.go.tz/pmoffice.htm (office).

PING, Jean, PhD; Gabonese economist, politician and international organization official; *Chairman, Commission of the African Union;* b. 24 Nov. 1942, Omboué; m.; c. *Education:* Univ. of Paris I (Panthéon-Sorbonne). *Career:* began career 1972 at UNESCO, Sector for External Relations and Cooperation, Paris; Perm. Rep. to UNESCO 1978–84; Dir Cabinet of the Pres. of Gabon 1984–90; Minister of Information 1990, then Minister of Mines, Energy and Water Resources and Deputy Minister, Ministry of Finance, Economy, Budget and Privatization, then Minister of Planning, Environment and Tourism –1999, Vice-Prime Minister, Minister of Foreign Affairs, Co-operation, Francophonie and Regional Integration 1999–2008; Chair. Comm. of the African Union 2008–; Pres. 59th session of UN Gen. Ass. 2004–05; mem. French Nat. Asscn of Doctors of Econs; Commdr of the Equatorial Star, Grand Officer of the Equatorial Star, Commdr of the Maritime Merit Order, Commdr of the Gabonese Nat. Order of Merit, Commdr Légion d'honneur, Officer of the Order of the Pleiad and the Order of la Francophonie, Grand Cross of the Order of Merit (Portugal); Dr hc (Inst. of Diplomacy of China), (Inst. of African Studies, Russian Acad. of Sciences).
Address: African Union (AU), PO Box 3243, Addis Ababa, Ethiopia (office). *Telephone:* (11) 5517700 (office). *Fax:* (11) 5517844 (office). *E-mail:* webmaster@africa-union.org (office). *Website:* www.africa-union.org (office).

PINTAT SANTOLÀRIA, Albert, Lic en Sc économiques; Andorran diplomatist and politician; *Cap de Govern (Head of Government);* b. 23 June 1943; m.; three c. *Education:* Catholic Univ. of Friburg, Switzerland. *Career:* Asst Consul, Sant Julià, Andorra 1982–83; Sec. to Josep Pintat, Head of Govt 1984–85; Counsellor-Gen. 1986–91; Amb. to Benelux countries and EU 1995–97; Minister of Foreign Affairs 1997–2001; Amb. to Switzerland and UK 2001–04; Cap de Govern (Head of Govt) 2005–; mem. Liberal Party of Andorra (PLA).
Address: Office of the Head of Government, Govern d'Andorra, Carrer Prat de la Creu 62–64, Edif. Administratiu, Andorra la Vella AD500, Andorra (office). *Telephone:* 875700 (office). *Fax:* 822882 (office). *E-mail:* comunicacio.gov@andorra.ad (office). *Website:* www.presidencia.ad (office).

PIOT, Baron; Peter, MD, PhD, FRCP; Belgian international development and public health official; *Executive Director, Joint United Nations Programme on HIV/AIDS (UNAIDS) and Under-Secretary-General, United Nations;* b. 17 Feb. 1949, Leuven; m. Greet Kimzeke 1975; two c. *Education:* Univs of Ghent and Antwerp, Belgium, and Washington, USA. *Career:* Asst in Microbiology, Inst. of Tropical Medicine, Antwerp 1974–78, Prof., Head Dept of Microbiology 1981–92; NATO Fellow 1978–79; Sr Fellow, Microbiology and Infectious Diseases, Washington Univ. 1978–79; Researcher, Nairobi Univ., STD/AIDS Project, Kenya 1981–92; Supervisor, Project SIDA, Kinshasa 1985–91; Asst Prof. of Public Health, Free Univ. Brussels 1989–94; Assoc. Dir Global Program AIDS, WHO 1995, Exec. Dir Jt UN Program on HIV/AIDS (UNAIDS), Geneva 1995–, Under-Sec.-Gen. UN 1995–; Dir WHO Collaborating Centre on AIDS, Antwerp; Chair. King Baudouin Foundation, Brussels; mem. Royal Acad. of Medicine, Int. AIDS Soc. (Pres. 1992–), Inst. of Medicine, Washington DC, AAAS, and numerous other socs in Europe, USA and Africa; cr. baron by King Albert II 1995; numerous decorations including, Officier, Ordre Nat. du Léopard (Zaïre) 1977, Ordre du Lion (Senegal), Nat. Order, Burkina Faso, Madagascar, Vietnam, Grand Official, Order of the Infante Don Enrique (Portugal) 2005; various hon. doctorates; numerous awards including De Kerkheer Prize for Medicine 1989, Health Research Award (Belgium) 1989, Public Health Award, Flemish Community 1990, AMICOM Award for Medicine 1991, H. Breurs Prize 1992, A. Jaunioux

Prize 1992, van Thiel Award 1993, Glaxo award for infectious diseases 1995, Nelson Mandela Award 2001, Royal Acad. of Arts and Sciences Gold Medal, Belgium 2002, E. Calderone Medal, Columbia Univ. 2003, Outstanding Physician AMA Chicago, Vlerick Award, Belgium 2004, Congressional Award of Achievement, Philippines 2005. *Publications:* author and co-author of 16 books and over 500 scientific papers on women's health, AIDS and other sexually transmitted diseases.
Address: UNAIDS, 20 Avenue Appia, 1211 Geneva 27, Switzerland (office). *Telephone:* (22) 7914510 (office). *Fax:* (22) 7914179 (office). *E-mail:* executivedirector@unaids.org (office). *Website:* www.unaids.org (office).

PIQUÉ I CAMPS, Josep, LLB, PhD; Spanish politician, business executive and economist; b. 21 Feb. 1955, Barcelona. *Education:* Univ. of Barcelona. *Career:* Lecturer in Econ. Theory, Univ. of Barcelona 1977–86, 1990–; Economist, Studies Dept, La Caixa 1984–85; Gen. Dir of Industry, Catalan Autonomous Govt 1986–88; Gen. Man. of Corp. Strategy, Ercros. SA (pvt. chemicals group) 1989–91; Man. Dir 1992, Chair. and CEO 1992–96; various posts in group including Chair. EMESA 1989–91, ERKIMIA SA 1990–96, FERTIBERIA 1993–96, FYSE 1992–93, LISAC 1992, META 1990–94, Sole Admin. FESA 1992–93, mem. Bd Prisma 1991–96, Río Tinto Minera 1991–93, Erkol 1991–96, Rhodiamul 1991–92; Minister of Industry and Energy 1996–2000; Govt Spokesman 1998–2000; Minister of Foreign Affairs 2000–02, of Science and Tech. 2002–04.
Address: c/o Ministerio de Ciencia y Tecnología, Paseo de la Castellana 160, 28071 Madrid, Spain (office). *Telephone:* (91) 3494000 (office). *Fax:* (91) 4578066 (office). *E-mail:* info@mcyt.es (office). *Website:* www.mcyt.es (office).

PIRES, Maria Madalena Emília; Timor-Leste government official; *Minister of Planning and Finance; Education:* La Trobe Univ., Australia. *Career:* came to Australia as refugee with family at age 14 in 1975; fmr Admin. Nat. Council of Timorese Resistance (CNRT) office, Darwin; fmr Pres. Timorese Asscn of Vic.; mem. World Bank jt assessment mission in Timor-Leste 1999; est. East Timor Devt Office, Melbourne; Head, Nat. Planning and Devt Agency, Timor-Leste 2000–01; joined Ministry of Planning and Finances, held several positions including Sec., East Timor Planning Comm. 2002, Advisor on Planning and External Assistance Man. 2003–04; Sr Coordination Adviser to the UN Deputy Special Representative of the Secretary-General (DSRSG) for Int. Compact on Timor-Leste –2007; Minister of Planning and Finance 2007–.
Address: Ministry of Planning and Finance, Palácio do Governo, Edif. 5, Av. Presidente Nicolau Lobato, Dili, Timor-Leste (office). *Telephone:* 3339546 (office). *E-mail:* itds@mopf.gov.tl (office).

PIRES, Gen. Pedro Verona Rodrigues; Cape Verde head of state; *President;* b. 29 April 1934, Sant' Ana, Fogo; m. Adélcia Maria da Luz Lima Barreto Pires 1975; two d. *Education:* Liceu Gil Eanes de São Vicente, Faculty of Science, Lisbon Univ., Portugal. *Career:* left Portugal to join Partido Africano da Independência da Guiné e Cabo Verde (PAIGC) 1961; mem. PAIGC dels 1961–63; involved in preparation for liberation of Cape Verde 1963–65; mem. Cen. Cttee of PAIGC 1965, of Council of War, PAIGC 1967; re-elected mem. of Commissão Permanente do Comité Executivo da Luta (CEL) and of Council of War 1970; involved in admin. of liberated areas of southern Guinea-Bissau 1971–73; Pres. Nat. Comm. of PAIGC for Cape Verde 1973 (reaffirmed as mem. of Council of War and CEL), appointed an Asst State Commr in first Govt of Repub. of Guinea-Bissau 1973–74; negotiated independence agreements of Cape Verde and Guinea-Bissau 1974; Dir PAIGC policies during transitional govt before independence of Cape Verde 1975; elected Deputy in Nat. Popular Ass. of Cape Verde June 1975–, re-elected 1980; Prime Minister of Cape Verde 1975–91, with responsibility for Finance, Planning and Co-operation; elected Deputy Gen. Sec. Partido Africano da Independência de Cabo Verde (PAICV) 1981, Sec. Gen. 1990–93, fmr Chair. Gen. 1993; Pres. of Cape Verde 2001–; mem. Perm. Comm. of CEL 1977; Amílcar Cabral Medal 1976.
Address: Presidência da República, CP 100, Plateau, Praia, Santiago (office); c/o PAICV, CP 22, Praia, Santiago, Republic of Cape Verde. *Telephone:* 2616555 (office). *Fax:* 2614356 (office). www.presidenciarepublica.cv

PIRES DE SOUZA, Waldir; Brazilian politician and government official; b. 21 Oct. 1926, Acajutiba, Bahia. *Education:* Univ. of Brasília. *Career:* Sec., State Govt of Bahia 1951–53; State Deputy, PTB party 1955–59, State Deputy, PSD party 1959–64; Gen. Consultant to the Repub. 1963–64; in exile in Uruguay and France, returned to Brazil 1970; Assoc. Prof., Univ. of Dijon, France 1966; Prof., Inst. of Higher Latin American Studies, Univ. of Paris 1968; Minister of Social Security 1985–86; Gov. State of Bahia 1987–89; State Deputy 1991–95, 1999–2003; Comptroller-Gen. 2003–06; Minister of Defence 2006–07.

Address: c/o Ministry of Defence, Esplanada dos Ministérios, Bloco Q, 70049-900 Brasília, DF, Brazil (office).

PIRZADA, Syed Sharifuddin, SPk; Pakistani politician and lawyer; b. 12 June 1923, Burhanpur; m. 1st Rafia Sultana (died 1960); m. 2nd Safiya Pirzada; m. 3rd Rashda Pirzada; two s. three d. *Education:* Univ. of Bombay. *Career:* Sec. Muslim Students Fed. 1943–45; Hon. Sec. to Quaid-i-Azam, Jinnah 1941–44; Sec. Bombay City Muslim League 1945–47; Prof., Sind Muslim Law Coll. 1947–54; Adviser to Constitution Comm. of Pakistan 1960–61; Chair. Co. Law Comm. 1962; Pres. Karachi High Court Bar Asscn, Pakistan Br. 1964–67; Attorney-Gen. of Pakistan 1965–66, 1968–72, 1977–89; Minister of Foreign Affairs 1966–68, April–Oct. 1993; Minister of Justice 1979–84; mem. or Pres. several asscns and socs; led Pakistan Del. to Session of UN Gen. Ass. 1966–67; Chair. UN Human Rights Sub-Cttee on Minorities 1977; mem. Panel of Perm. Court of Arbitration; mem. Int. Law Comm. 1981–86; Sec.-Gen. Org. of Islamic Conf. 1984–88; Chair. Heritage Council and Amb.-at-large with rank of Fed. Minister 1989–93; mem. Nat. Security Council of Pakistan 1999–; Hon. Sr Adviser to Chief Exec. on Foreign Affairs, Law, Justice and Human Rights 1999–; Judge (ad-hoc), Int. Court of Justice 2000; Chair. Nat. Cttee on Quaid-i-Azam Year 2001; Sr Adviser (Sr Fed. Minister) to Prime Minister on Foreign Affairs, Law, Justice and Human Rights 2002–08; Sr Advocate, Supreme Court. *Publications include:* Evolution of Pakistan 1962, Fundamental Rights and Constitutional Remedies in Pakistan 1966, Some Aspects of Quaid-i-Azam's Life 1978, Collected Works of Quaid-i-Azam Mohammad Ali Jinnah (Vol. I) 1985, (Vol. II) 1986, (Vol. III) 1987; Dissolution of Constituent Assembly of Pakistan 1996. *Address:* House No. 25/1–4, Phase-V, Zamzama Street, Clifton, Karachi, Pakistan (home). *Telephone:* (21) 5874183 (home).

PISANI-FERRY, Jean; French economist; *Director, Bruegel;* b. 1951. *Education:* Ecole Supérieure d'Electricité, Université Paris V, Centre d'études des programmes économiques. *Career:* served as Head, Macroeconomic Dept, Centre d'études prospectives et d'informations internationales (CEPII, Paris) 1983–92, Dir CEPII 1992–97; Econ. Adviser to Directorate-Gen. for Econ. and Financial Affairs, EC 1989–92; Sr Econ. Adviser to Minister of Finance 1997–2001; Exec. Pres. Prime Minister's Council of Econ. Analysis 2001–02; Sr Adviser to Dir of Treasury 2002–04; currently Dir Bruegel (econ. think-tank), Brussels; Prof., Université Paris-Dauphine; mem. EC Group of Econ. Policy Analysis. *Address:* Bruegel, 33 Rue de la Charité, Brussels 1210, Belgium (office). *Telephone:* (2) 227-4210 (office). *Fax:* (2) 227-4219 (office). *E-mail:* jean.pisani-ferry@bruegel.org (office). *Website:* www.bruegel.org (office); www.pisani-ferry.net (office).

PISPINIS, Vassilis-Achilleas; Greek diplomatist; *Ambassador to UK. Career:* fmr Alt. Rep. to 61st Session of UN Gen. Ass., New York; fmr Amb. to Ireland; Amb. and Dir of Political Affairs, Ministry of Foreign Affairs 2006–07; Amb. to UK 2007–, First Vice-Pres. Ass. of IMO, London 2007–. *Address:* Embassy of Greece, 1A Holland Park, London, W11 3TP, England (office). *Telephone:* (20) 7229-3850 (office). *Fax:* (20) 7229-7221 (office). *E-mail:* political@greekembassy.org.uk (office). *Website:* www.greekembassy.org.uk (office).

PITA, Afelee F., BA, MA; Tuvaluan diplomatist; *Permanent Representative, United Nations;* b. 11 Feb. 1958; m.; seven c. *Education:* Univ. of Canberra, Australia, Univ. of the S Pacific, Fiji. *Career:* Asst Sec., then Sec., Ministry of Commerce and Natural Resources 1987–88; Asst Sec. for Commerce, Ministry of Finance, Commerce and Public Corpns 1989–92; Acting Sec., Ministry of Trade, Commerce and Public Corpns 1993–94; Perm. Sec., Ministry of Health, Sports and Human Resources Devt 1994, at Ministry of Labour, World and Communications 1994–96, at Ministry of Natural Resources and Environment 1997–99, Ministry of Finance and Econ. Planning 1999–2001; Adviser to Exec. Dir Asian Devt Bank 2001–04; Perm. Sec., Ministry of Natural Resources and Lands 2004–06; Perm. Rep. to UN, New York 2006–. *Address:* Permanent Mission of Tuvalu to the United Nations, 800 Second Avenue, Suite 400b, New York, NY 10017, USA (office). *Telephone:* (212) 490-0534 (office). *Fax:* (212) 808-4975 (office).

PITANGUY, Jacqueline; Brazilian sociologist, political scientist and international organization official; *Chairwoman, Women's Learning Partnership for Rights, Development and Peace; Career:* cabinet mem. and Pres. Brazilian Nat. Council for Women's Rights 1986–89; Founder and Dir Citizenship, Studies, Information and Action (CEPIA), Rio de Janeiro, Brazil; mem. Bd Global Fund for Women 1998–2005 (Chair. 2001–2005); Chair. Women's Learning Partnership for Rights, Devt and Peace 2005–; Comm. on Citizenship and Reproduction Allen Guttmacher Inst., Inter-American Dialogue, UNESCO Inst. for Educ., Soc. for Int. Devt; mem. Int. Rights Council of the Carter Center; mem. editorial bd of several health journals; Brazilian Ministry of Foreign Affairs Medal of Rio Branco. *Publications include:* co-authored four books; numerous articles. *Address:* Women's Learning Partnership, 4343 Montgomery Avenue, Suite 201 Bethesda, MD 20814, USA (office). *Telephone:* (301) 654-2774. *Fax:* (301) 654-2775. *Website:* www.learningpartnership.org (office).

PITCHER, Frederick W.; Nauruan/Australian diplomatist and politician; *Minister of Finance and Economic Planning; Education:* educated in Australia. *Career:* early position as Exec. Dir's Adviser, Asian Devt Bank, Manila; Deputy Perm. Rep., UN, New York 2000; mem. Parl. 2004–, mem. Constitutional Review Cttee 2005; served in second Admin of fmr Pres. Ludwig Scotty; Minister for Island Devt and Industry 2004–07, of Finance and Econ. Planning 2007–; Acting Foreign Minister 2007; Pres. Nauru Island Basketball Asscn. *Address:* Ministry of Finance, Government Treasury Building, Aiwo, Nauru (office). *Telephone:* 444-3140 (office). *Fax:* 555-4477 (office). *E-mail:* minister.finance@naurugov.nr (office). *Website:* www.naurugov.nr (office).

PITRA DIAKITÉ, Josefina Perpétua; Angolan civil servant and diplomatist; *Ambassador to USA;* m. Mamadou Diakité; two s. *Education:* Agostinho Neto Univ. *Career:* Head of Contract Co-ordinating Unit, State Secr. for Co-operation 1985–87, Nat. Dir of Tech. Assistance 1987–89; Dir Western Europe Dept, Ministry of External Relations 1989–92, Dir USA and Europe Dept 1992–93; Amb. to Sweden, Norway, Denmark and Finland 1993–2000, to USA 2001–. *Address:* Embassy of Angola, 2108 16th Street, NW, Washington, DC 20009, USA (office). *Telephone:* (202) 785-1156 (office). *Fax:* (202) 822-9049 (office). *E-mail:* angola@angola.org (office). *Website:* www.angola.org (office).

PITSUWAN, Surin, PhD; Thai politician, diplomatist and international organization official; *Secretary-General, Association of South East Asian Nations (ASEAN);* b. 28 Oct. 1949, Nakhon Si Thammarat; m. Alisa Ariya 1983; three s. *Education:* Claremont McKenna Coll., Harvard Univ., USA. *Career:* taught at Thammasat Univ. 1975–86, Academic Asst to Dean of Faculty of Political Science and to Vice-Rector for Academic Affairs 1985–86; columnist, The Nation Review and Bangkok Post newspapers 1980–92; fmr corresp. and analyst, ASEAN Forecast; Congressional Fellow, Office of US Rep. Geraldine Ferraro and Senate Republican Conf. 1983–84; mem. Parl. from Nakhon Si Thammarat Prov. 1986–; Sec. to Speaker of House of Reps 1986; Asst Sec. to Minister of Interior 1988; Deputy Minister of Foreign Affairs 1992–95; Minister of Foreign Affairs 1997–2001; adviser to Int. Comm. on Intervention and State Sovereignty 1999–2001; mem. UN Comm. on Human Security 2001–03; served on ILO's World Comm. on the Social Dimension of Globalization 2002–04; Sec.-Gen. ASEAN 2008–; mem. Democratic Party (fmr Deputy Leader); mem. Advisory Bd Council on Foreign Relations, New York, Int. Advisory Bd Int. Crisis Group, Advisory Bd UN Human Security Trust Fund, 'Wise Men Group' under auspices of the Henri Dunant Centre for Humanitarian Dialogue, Geneva (advising peace negotiations between Acehnese Independence Movt (GAM) and Govt of Indonesia) 2002–04, Islamic Devt Bank's 1440 AH (2020) Vision Comm. –2005; fmr mem. Nat. Reconciliation Comm.; Int. Academic Advisor, Centre for Islamic Studies, Univ. of Oxford, UK; adviser to the Leaders Project (conf. arm of the Cohen Group of fmr US Sec. of Defense William S. Cohen), Washington, DC. *Address:* The ASEAN Secretariat, 70A Jalan Sisingamangaraja, PO Box 2072, Jakarta 12110, Indonesia (office). *Telephone:* (21) 7262991 (office). *Fax:* (21) 7398234 (office). *E-mail:* termsak@aseansec.org (office). *Website:* www.aseansec.org (office).

PLANAS PUCHADES, Luís; Spanish diplomatist and fmr politician; *Ambassador to Morocco;* b. 20 Nov. 1952, Valencia; m.; two c. *Career:* Deputy for Cordova in Congreso de los Diputados (Congress of Deputies) 1982–87; MEP 1987–93, mem. Group of Party of European Socialists; mem. Parl. of Andalucía 1994–96; Chief of Staff, Office of EC Vice Pres., Brussels 1996–99, of the Office of EC Commr for Econ. and Monetary Affairs 1999–2004; Amb. to Morocco 2004–. *Address:* Embassy of Spain, 3 rue Aïn Khalouiya, km 5.3, route des Zaêrs, Souissi, 10000 Rabat, Morocco (office). *Telephone:* (3) 7633900 (office). *Fax:* (3) 7630600 (office). *E-mail:* emb.rabat@maec.es (office). *Website:* www.mae.es/Embajadas/Rabat (office).

PLASSNIK, Ursula, DrIur; Austrian politician; *Minister for Foreign Affairs;* b. 23 May 1956, Klagenfurt; m. (divorced). *Education:* Vienna Univ., Coll. d'Europe, Bruges, Belgium. *Career:* with Ministry of Foreign Affairs, in int. law office and directorates for security policy and CSCE 1981–84; CSCE Del. to Madrid Follow-up Meeting 1981–83, Vienna 1986–87; at Embassy, Berne 1984–86; Rep. Council of Europe 1987–90; at Directorate Gen. for Econ. Policy and EU Coordination, later head of Directorate for

Gen. Affairs Council and the European Council 1994–97; at Fed. Chancellery, Cabinet Chief of Dr Wolfgang Schüssel when Fed. Vice Chancellor 1997–2000, when Chancellor 2000–04; Amb. to Switzerland Jan.–Oct. 2004; Minister for Foreign Affairs 2004–.
Address: Federal Ministry for European and International Affairs, Minoritenplatz 8, 1014 Vienna, Austria (office). *Telephone:* (5) 011-51-0 (office). *Fax:* (5) 011-59-0 (office). *E-mail:* presse@bmaa.gv.at (office). *Website:* www.bmaa.gv.at (office).

PLÉAH, Natié; Malian politician; *Minister of Defence and Veterans;* b. 1953, Moutigué, Ké-Macina Circle; m.; seven c. *Education:* secondary school in Sévaré, Markala Coll., school in Badalabougou, Ecole Nationale d'Admin, Paris, France. *Career:* began serving Gov.-Gen. Sikasso 1976, held several posts as an admin., including Second Deputy Commdr Ansongo Circle, Deputy Commdr Koulikoro then Yanfolila Circles, Commdr Circle then Koulikoro Timbuktu, Admin. Affairs Advisor to Gov. of Timbuktu, Advisor for Admin. Affairs in Ségou, Chief of Staff to Gov. of Mopti and High Commr of Kayes; Acting High Commr First Econ. Region 2002–04, Gov. of Kayes 2004–05; Gov. Dist of Bamako 2005; Minister of Youth and Sports 2005–07, of the Environment and Sanitation May 2007, of Defence and Veterans 2007–.
Address: Ministry of Defence and Veterans, route de Koulouba, BP 2083, Bamako, Mali (office). *Telephone:* 222-50-21 (office). *Fax:* 223-23-18 (office).

PLUMBLY, Sir Derek John, KCMG, BA; British diplomatist; *Chairman, Analysis and Evaluation Commission, Sudan;* b. 15 May 1948, Lyndhurst, Hants.; m. Nadia Youssef Gohar 1979; one d. two s. *Education:* Brockenhurst Grammar School, Magdalen Coll., Oxford. *Career:* with VSO, Pakistan 1970–71; joined FCO 1972; Arabic language training, MECAS, Lebanon 1973–74; Second Sec. in Jeddah 1975–77; First Sec. in Cairo 1977–80; FCO 1980–84; assigned to Washington, DC 1984–88; Counsellor in Riyadh 1988–92; with UK Mission to UN, New York 1992–96; Dir Drugs and Crime Dept, FCO 1996–97, Dir Middle East and North Africa Dept 1997–2000; Amb. to Saudi Arabia 2000–03, to Egypt 2003–07; Chair. Analysis and Evaluation Comm., established under Sudan Comprehensive Peace Agreement, Khartoum 2008–; Dr hc (Loughborough) 2007.
Address: Analysis and Evaluation Commission, Amarat Street, Khartoum, Sudan (office). *E-mail:* aec.sud@gmail.com (office).

POCAR, Fausto, LLD; Italian judge, international organization executive and academic; *President, International Criminal Tribunal for the Former Yugoslavia;* b. 21 Feb. 1939, Milan. *Education:* Univ. of Milan. *Career:* Prof. of Int. Law, Univ. of Milan, fmr Dean, Faculty of Political Sciences, fmr Vice-Rector Univ. of Milan; Judge, Int. Criminal Tribunal for the Fmr Yugoslavia (ICTY), The Hague 2000–(09), currently Judge of the Appeals Chamber and also mem. Int. Criminal Tribunal for Rwanda (ICTR), Vice-Pres. ICTY 2003–05, Pres. 2005–; mem. Human Rights Cttee under Int. Covenant on Civil and Political Rights 1984–2000, Rapporteur 1989–90, Chair. 1991–92; Special Rep. of UN High Commr for Human Rights for visits to Chechnya and Russian Fed. 1995–96; has chaired informal working group that drafted declaration on the rights of people belonging to nat. or ethnic, religious or linguistic minorities, Comm. on Human Rights 1992; Italian del. to Cttee on the Peaceful Uses of Outer Space and its Legal Sub-cttee; has lectured at The Hague Acad. of Int. Law; mem. and Treas. Institut de Droit Int.; mem. several other int. law asscn; Grand Ufficiale 2003; Dr hc (Antwerp) 2007. *Publications:* author of numerous publs on int. law, including human rights and humanitarian law, pvt. int. law and European law.
Address: International Criminal Tribunal for the Former Yugoslavia, PO Box 13888, EW, 2501 EW, The Hague, Netherlands (office). *Telephone:* (70) 512-8803 (office). *Fax:* (70) 512-5307 (office). *Website:* www.un.org/icty (office).

POČIATEK, Ján; Slovak economist and government official; *Minister of Finance;* b. 19 Sept. 1970; m. Ivana Počiatek; one d. *Education:* Slovak Tech. Univ., Univ. of Econs, Bratislava, Stockholm School of Econs, Sweden, Telenor Corp. Univ., Oslo, Norway. *Career:* Project Dir, Satellite Communications Div., Telenor Slovakia 1997–2000, Commercial Dir and Vice-Exec. Dir 2000–01, Exec. Dir 2001–06; mem. Bd Dirs Int. Satellite Communication 2001–06; Minister of Finance 2006–.
Address: Ministry of Finance, PO Box 82, Štefanovičova 5, 817 82 Bratislava, Slovakia (office). *Telephone:* (2) 5958-1111 (office). *Fax:* (2) 5249-8042 (office). *E-mail:* tlacove@mfsr.sk (office). *Website:* www.finance.gov.sk (office).

POCOCK, Andrew John, CMG, PhD; British diplomatist; *Ambassador to Zimbabwe;* b. 23 Aug. 1955; m. Julie Pocock; one s. one d. *Career:* Desk Officer, UN Dept, FCO 1981–82, Second, later First Sec., Lagos 1983–86,

Head of Section, Southern Africa Dept, FCO 1986–87, First Sec., Washington, DC 1988–92, Personnel Man. Dept, FCO 1992–94, Deputy Head of S Asia Dept 1994–95, Counsellor on loan to Royal Coll. of Defence Studies 1996, Deputy High Commr, Canberra 1997–2001, Head of African Dept (Southern), FCO 2001–03, High Commr to Tanzania 2003–06, Amb. to Zimbabwe 2006–.
Address: British Embassy, 7th Floor, Corner House, Cnr Samora Machel Avenue/Leopold Takawira Street, PO Box 4490, Harare, Zimbabwe (office). *Telephone:* (4) 772990 (office). *Fax:* (4) 774605 (office). *E-mail:* consularharare@fco.gov.uk (office). *Website:* www.britishembassy.gov.uk/zimbabwe (office).

PODBEREZKIN, Aleksei Ivanovich, DHist; Russian historian and politician; *President, International Non-Government Research and Education Organization;* b. 7 Feb. 1953, Moscow; m.; three d. *Education:* Moscow State Inst. of Int. Relations. *Career:* started career as metal worker in Moscow 1968; served in the army; referent Group of Scientific Consultants, USSR Cttee of Youth Orgs 1981–85; Sr Researcher Inst. of World Econs and Int. Relations, Diplomatic Acad., Ministry of Foreign Affairs 1985–90; f. Russian-American Univ. 1990, Pres. 1991–; Pres. Int. Non-Govt Research and Educ. Org. 1992–; adviser to Vice-Pres. of Russia 1991–93; Founder, Chair. and Sec.-Gen. All-Russian Political Movt Spiritual Heritage (Dukhovnoye Naslediye) 1994–; mem. State Duma (Parl.), mem. Communist Party faction 1995–99; Deputy Chair. Cttee on Int. Issues; Founder People's Patriotic Union of Russia 1996–; ed. Observer (analytical monthly); Ed.-in-Chief Russia: Contemporary Political History (annual) 1998–; several state decorations; Adviser of the Year 1998. *Publications:* over 1200 publs on problems of int. relations, foreign and defence policy, state construction, ideology of state patriotism, economics and financial control.
Address: Dukhovnoye Naslediye, Bakhrushina str. 32, Building 2, 113054 Moscow (office); B. Serpukovsky str. 70/44, Moscow, Russia. *Telephone:* (495) 959-20-45 (office); (495) 203-88-59 (home). *E-mail:* podberezkin_a@nasled.ru (office).

POGGIO, Albert Andrew, OBE; British diplomatist; *Representative of Government of Gibraltar in UK;* b. 18 Aug. 1946, Ballymena, N Ireland; one d. *Education:* Christian Brothers Coll., Gibraltar and City of London Coll. *Career:* Rep. of Govt of Gibraltar in UK 1988–; Chair. British Overseas Territories Asscn, Vital Health Group of Cop, Westex Group of Cos, John Mowlems-CCS Ltd; Vice-Chair. Calpe House Trust; Dir Friends of Gibraltar Heritage Soc., SVP Medcruise (Asscn of Mediterranean Ports), Med Man. Consultants Ltd; Freeman City of London.
Address: Arundel Great Court, 178–179 Strand, London, WC2R 1EL (office); The Old House, Manor Place, Chislehurst, Kent, BR7 5QJ, England (home). *Telephone:* (20) 7836-0777 (office). *Fax:* (20) 7240-6612 (office). *E-mail:* a.poggio@gibraltar.gov.uk (office). *Website:* www.gibraltar.gov.uk (office).

POHAMBA, Hifikepunye; Namibian politician and head of state; *President;* b. 18 Aug. 1935. *Career:* Sec. of Finance SWAPO 1977–89, Sec.-Gen. SWAPO 1997–2002, Vice Pres. 2002–; Minister of Home Affairs 1990–95, of Fisheries and Marine Resources 1995–98, without Portfolio 1998–2000, of Lands, Resettlement and Rehabilitation 2001–04; Pres. of Namibia 2004–; Swapo Ongulumbashe Medal 1987.
Address: Office of the President, State House, Robert Mugabe Avenue, PMB 13339, Windhoek, Namibia (office). *Telephone:* (61) 2707111 (office). *Fax:* (61) 221780 (office). *E-mail:* angolo@op.gov.na (office). *Website:* www.op.gov.na (office).

POKU, Fritz Kwabena, BA; Ghanaian diplomatist; b. 22 June 1945, Kumasi; m.; four c. *Education:* Adisadel Coll., Univ. of Ghana, Univ. of Abidjan, Ghana Inst. of Man. and Admin. *Career:* career diplomat; fmr Amb. to Switzerland and Del. to Int. Orgs in Geneva; fmr Amb. to Ethiopia, concurrently accred to Kenya, Tanzania, Uganda, Burundi, Rwanda, Eritrea; fmr Perm. Rep. to OAU, UN Econ. Comm. for Africa; Amb. to USA 2004–06; Hon. Citizen of State of Nebraska, USA.
Address: Ministry of Foreign Affairs, Treasury Road, PO Box M53, Accra, Ghana (office). *Telephone:* (21) 664951 (office). *Fax:* (21) 680017 (office). *E-mail:* ghmaf00@ghana.com (office).

POLETTI, Bernard; French diplomatist; *Ambassador to Iran;* b. 1 March 1946; m. Dagny Bjornson-Langen. *Education:* Institut d'Etudes Politiques, École Nationale des Langues Orientales. *Career:* joined Ministry of Foreign Affairs 1975, posted to Econ. Affairs Dept 1977–78, N Africa Dept 1978–82, Sec. to Prime Minister, inter-ministerial cttee on nuclear security 1982–86, Deputy Dir, N Africa and Middle East 1994–98, with Central Admin 2004–05; overseas posts include Third Sec., Embassy in Libya 1975–77, Second, later First Counsellor, Embassy in Saudi Arabia 1986–88, Second Counsellor, Mission to UN, New York 1988–91, Amb. to

UAE 1991–94, to Saudi Arabia 1998–2004, to Iran 2005–; Chevalier de la Légion d'Honneur, Officier de l'Ordre national du Mérite.
Address: Embassy of Iran, 85 Neauphle-le-Château Avenue, Tehran, Iran (office). *Telephone:* (21) 66706005 (office). *Fax:* (21) 66706543 (office). *E-mail:* consulaire@ambafrance-ir.org (office). *Website:* www.ambafrance-ir.org (office).

POLFER, Lydie; Luxembourg lawyer and politician; b. 22 Nov. 1952; m. Hubert Wurth (q.v.); one d. *Education:* Lycée Robert Schuman, Univ. of Grenoble, France, Univ. Centre for Int. and European Research, Grenoble. *Career:* admitted to Luxembourg Bar 1977; mem. Parl. 1979–; Mayor City of Luxembourg 1982–99; mem. European Parl. 1985–89, 1990–94, 2003–, mem. Group of the Alliance of Liberals and Democrats for Europe, Chair. Del. to ACP-EU Jt Parl. Ass., mem. Cttee on Foreign Affairs; Chair. Democratic Party 1994; Deputy Prime Minister, Minister of Foreign Affairs and External Trade, Minister of Civil Service and Admin. Reform 1999–2005.
Address: c/o Democratic Party, BP 510, 2015 Luxembourg (office); Bât. Altiero Spinelli, 08G258, 60, rue Wiertz 60, 1047 Brussels, Belgium. *Telephone:* (0)2 28 45621. *Fax:*)2 28 49621.

POLITI, Mauro; Italian judge and professor of law; *Judge, International Criminal Court;* b. 13 Sept. 1944, Fabrica di Roma. *Education:* Univ. of Florence. *Career:* Asst Prof. of Pvt Int. Law, Univ. of Cagliari, Sardinia 1976–79; Asst Prof. of Public Int. Law, Univ. of Urbino 1979–83, Assoc. Prof. of Int. Law 1983–86; Assoc. Prof. of Int. Law, Univ. of Trento 1986–90, Prof. 1990–; began judicial career at Tribunal of Florence 1969; Judge Tribunal of Oristano 1972, of Milan 1975–83; Deputy Prosecutor Juvenile Court, Milan 1972–75; Legal Adviser Perm. Mission to UN, NY 1992–2001; ad litem judge Int. Criminal Tribunal for fmr Yugoslavia (ICTY) 2001; Judge, Int. Criminal Court (ICC), The Hague 2003–; mem. Del. to UN Security Council 1995–96; mem. Del. to Preparatory Cttee for ICC 1995–97, 1999–2002; Chair. Sixth Legal Cttee of UN Gen. Ass. 2000–01. *Publications:* books, chapters in books and articles in professional law journals.
Address: International Criminal Court, Maanweg 174, 2516 AB The Hague, The Netherlands. *Telephone:* (70) 5158515. *Fax:* (70) 5158555. *E-mail:* pio@icc-cpi.int. *Website:* www.icc-cpi.int.

POLLARD, L. Edwin, OBE, FCIB; Barbadian banker (retd) and diplomatist; *High Commissioner to UK;* m. Deanna Winifred Warner; one s. one d. *Education:* Certified Diploma in Accounting and Finance, Asscn of Certified Accountants. *Career:* banker with Barclays Bank plc 1961–2000, managed operations in several Caribbean countries, eventually becoming Dir of Barbados business, also performed various roles in bank's regional office; has served on bds of Community Coll., Barbados Inst. of Banking and Finance, Securities Exchange of Barbados; fmr mem. Securities Comm.; High Commr to UK 2003–; Founding mem. Big Brothers and Sisters of Barbados Inc.; fmr Chair. Barclays Sports Club, Friends of Scouting; fmr Treas. Barbados Football Asscn.
Address: High Commission of Barbados, 1 Great Russell Street, London, WC1B 3ND, England (office). *Telephone:* (20) 7631-4975 (office). *Fax:* (20) 7323-6872 (office). *E-mail:* london@foreign.gov.bb (office).

POLLMANN-ZAAL, J. H. M. (Hannie); Dutch diplomatist; *Ambassador to Belgium; Career:* fmr Head, Office of Sec.-Gen., OSCE; Dir Western and Cen. Europe Dept, Ministry of Foreign Affairs 2004–07; Amb. to Belgium 2007–.
Address: Embassy of Netherlands, 48 ave Hermann Debroux, 1160 Brussels, Belgium (office). *Telephone:* (2) 679-17-11 (office). *Fax:* (2) 679-17-75 (office). *E-mail:* bru@minbuza.nl (office). *Website:* www.nederlandseambassade.be (office).

POLT, Michael Christian, MSc; American diplomatist; *Senior Transatlantic Fellow, German Marshall Fund of the United States;* b. Austria; m. Hallie Polt; two c. *Education:* Univ. of Tennessee. *Career:* 30 years in diplomatic service, posts including embassies in Mexico, Denmark, Panama, Deputy Chief of Mission, Germany and Switzerland, fmr Sr Adviser on Man. Reform to Dir-Gen. Foreign Service, fmr mem. Sr Man. Steering Bd, Prin. Deputy Asst Sec. of State for Legis. Affairs –2004, Amb. to Serbia and Montenegro 2004–06, to Serbia 2004–07, Sr Transatlantic Fellow, German Marshall Fund of the US (on loan from Dept of State) 2007–; Presidential Meritorious Service Award, American Citizens Abroad Thomas Jefferson Award for Service to US Citizens Overseas, numerous Dept of State Meritorious and Superior Honor Awards for Outstanding Policy Leadership, Management, Crisis Performance, and Political Analysis.
Address: US Department of State, 2201 C Street NW, Washington, DC 20520, USA (office). *Telephone:* (202) 647-4000 (office). *Fax:* (202) 647-6738 (office). *Website:* www.state.gov (office).

PONCE CEVALLOS, Javier; Ecuadorean journalist and government official; *Minister of National Defence;* b. 28 April 1948, Quito. *Education:* Escuela de Sociología y Ciencias Políticas, Univ. Central del Ecuador. *Career:* columnist El Tiempo newspaper 1966–70; with Ministry of Agriculture 1973–77; Dir Artes cultural review 1977–78; Sec. Gen. Ecumenical Cttee of Projects 1986–97, Coordinator 1997–; Ed. HOY 1992–99, Ed. de investigaciones 1999–2001, columnist 1989–2001; editorial writer and columnist El Universo 2001–; Ed. Enciclopedia Planeta 2002–03; Personal Sec. to Pres. Rafael Correa 2006–08; Minister of Nat. Defence 2008–.
Address: Ministry of National Defence, Exposición 208, Quito . Ecuador (office). *Telephone:* (2) 221-6150 (office). *Fax:* (2) 256-9386 (office). *Website:* www.midena.gov.ec (office).

POPENS, Normunds, MSc; Latvian diplomatist; *Permanent Representative, European Union;* b. 8 Sept. 1966; m.; one c. *Education:* Univ. of Latvia, Riga Tech. Univ. *Career:* jr researcher, Inst. of Microbiology 1987–93; English teacher, Olaine High School 1992–93; Desk Officer, Div. of America and Australia, Ministry of Foreign Affairs 1993–94, Desk Officer, Div. of Int. Econ. Relations 1994, Head of Div., Foreign Econ. Policy Dept 1998–99, Deputy Dir, Foreign Econ. Policy Dept 1999–2000, Dir, European Bilateral Relations Dept 2004–05, Dir, EU Dept 2005–06, Under-Sec. of State (EU Affairs) 2006–07; overseas postings include Trade Attaché, Embassy in Washington, DC 1994–95, Second Sec. 1995–98; Amb. to Norway 2000–04, to Iceland 2004; Perm. Rep. to EU, Brussels 2007–.
Address: Permanent Representation of Latvia to the EU, 39–41 rue d'Arlon, 1000 Brussels, Belgium (office). *Telephone:* (2) 282-03-60 (office). *Fax:* (2) 282-03-69 (office). *E-mail:* permrep.eu@mfa.gov.lv (office). *Website:* www.am.gov.lv/en/brussels (office).

POPESCU, Gen. Mihail Eugeniu, PhD; Romanian army officer; b. 1 April 1948, Carlogani, Olt County; m.; one d. *Education:* Artillery Officers Mil. School, Mil. Acad., Nat. Defence Coll. *Career:* command position, platoon artillery battalion 1969–82; Deputy Commdr and Artillery Chief of Mechanized Div. 1982–92; Artillery Chief 4th Transylvania Army 1984–92; Insp.-Gen. of Artillery, Artillery Gen. Inspectorate 1992–93; Artillery Insp., Gen. Staff Inspectorate 1993–97; Chief of Instruction and Doctrine Directorate, Chief of Army Staff 1997–2000; Chief of Gen. Staff 2000–06; apptd Gen. 2000.
Address: c/o Ministry of National Defence, 77303 Bucharest, Str. Izvor 13–15, Sector 5, Romania (office).

POPESCU-TĂRICEANU, Călin Constantin Anton, MSc; Romanian politician; *Prime Minister;* b. 14 Jan. 1952; m. Ioana Popescu-Tăriceanu; two c. *Education:* Univ. of Bucharest, Inst. of Civil Eng. *Career:* started as engineer, Nat. Water Admin, Argeş Co. 1976–77, Industrial Building Co., Bucharest 1977–79; Prof. Faculty of Hydro-technology, Inst. of Civil Eng, Bucharest 1980–91; f. Radio Contact, Romania's first pvt. radio network 1990, Gen. Man. 1992–96; f. Partidul Nat. Liberal (PNL) 1990, Exec. Sec. 1990–92, Deputy Chair. 1993–2004, Pres. 2004–05; mem. Constituent Assembly (Parl.) 1990–92, 1996–; Deputy Prime Minister 1996–97; Minister of Industry and Trade 1996–97; Prime Minister of Romania 2005–; mem. Economy, Reform and Privatization Comm. 1996–2000; Vice-Pres. Fiscal and Budgetary Policies Comm. 2000–; Assoc. Partner, Automotive Trading Services 1993–; Founding mem. and Chair. Automobile and Importers Asscn 1994–97, 2001–03, Hon. Pres. 2003–. *Publications:* 37 scientific papers and articles on water treatment and distribution.
Address: Office of the Prime Minister, 011791 Bucharest 1, Piaţa Victoriei 1, Romania (office). *Telephone:* (21) 3131450 (office). *Fax:* (21) 3122436 (office). *E-mail:* drp@pm-control.ro (office); prim.ministru@gov.ro (office). *Website:* www.cancelarie.ro (office); www.gov.ro (office).

POPOV, Gavriil Kharitonovich, DEcon; Russian politician and economist; b. 31 Oct. 1936, Moscow; m. Irina Popov 1968; two s. *Education:* Moscow State Univ. *Career:* mem. CPSU 1959–90; teacher at Moscow Univ. 1960–89, Dean of Econ. Faculty 1977–80; introduced man. and business studies to Moscow Univ., Prof. 1971–; Ed.-in-Chief of journal Voprosy ekonomiki (Questions of Economics) 1988–90; People's Deputy of USSR 1989–91; Co-Chair. Inter-regional Group of Deputies, pressing for radical change; Chair. Moscow City Soviet 1990–91; Mayor of Moscow 1991–92 (resgnd); mem. Consultative Council 1991–2000 (Chair, Foreign Policy Cttee 1996–2000); Pres. Int. Univ. 1991–, Int. Union of Economists 1991–, Free Econ. Soc. of Russia 1991–; Chair. Russian Democratic Reform Movt (RDDR) 1992–; mem. Political Council, Social Democracy Party of Russia 2001–; M. Lomonosov Prize. *Publications include:* more than a dozen books on theory of man. and current political and econ. problems.
Address: Nikitsky Pereulok 5, 103009 Moscow, Russia. *Telephone:* (495) 956-69-90. *Fax:* (495) 956-80-77.

POPOV, Mihai, DHisSc; Moldovan diplomatist and philologist; b. 1949, Chebruchi, Sloboza Region. *Education:* Kishinev State Univ., Diplomatic Acad. in Moscow. *Career:* worked as Komsomol and CSPU functionary in Kishinev 1973–83; diplomatic service since 1983; First Counsellor, USSR Embassy, Romania 1986–92; Minister-Counsellor, Moldovan Embassy, Russia 1992–93; Amb. to Belgium 1993–94; Minister of Foreign Affairs 1994–96; Amb. to France 1996–2002; Amb. to Belgium and Rep. to NATO and EU 2002–04; currently Special Advisor for Moldova and European Neighbourhood, East West Inst. (EWI), Brussels.
Address: EWI Brussels Centre, 83-85 Rue de la Loi, 1040, 1040 Brussels, Belgium (office). *Telephone:* (2) 743-46-10 (office). *Fax:* (2) 743-46-39 (office). *E-mail:* brussels@ewi.info (office). *Website:* www.ewi.info (office).

POPTODOROVA, Elena Borislavova; Bulgarian politician, diplomatist and international organization official; *Ambassador to USA;* b. 31 Aug. 1951, Sofia; m.; one s. *Education:* Univ. of Sofia, Univ. of Nat. and World Econ., Sofia. *Career:* joined Ministry of Foreign Affairs 1975, Minister Plenipotentiary Embassy in Rome (also Consul-Gen. to San Marino) 1978–90, Dir Directorate of Int. Orgs and Human Rights 2001–02; mem. Parl. 1990–2001; Vice-Chair. Del. to Inter-Parl. Union 1991–94; mem. Del. to Parl. Ass. of Council of Europe 1994–2001; mem. Jt Parl. Cttee Bulgaria–EU 1996–97; Deputy Chair. Inter-European Parl. Forum on Population and Devt, Brussels, Belgium 2000–01; Deputy Chair. Nat. Comm. for UNESCO 2001–02; Amb. to USA 2002–; mem. Bd of Dirs 21st Century Foundation 1994–, Governing Bd SOS-Kinderhorf-Bulgaria 1995–, Bd of Trustees American Univ. in Bulgaria 1995–, Governing Bd Family Planning Asscn of Bulgaria 1996–, Governing Bd Centre for Regional and Geopolitical Research 1997–; Pres. Action for Democratic Awareness in the Process of Transition Asscn 1997–.
Address: Embassy of Bulgaria, 1621 22nd Street, NW, Washington, DC 20008, USA (office). *Telephone:* (202) 387-0174 (office). *Fax:* (202) 234-7973 (office). *E-mail:* office@bulgaria-embassy.org (office). *Website:* www .webhousing.biz/~bulgaria (office).

PORCHIER, Lt-Gen. Patrick, LèsSc; French air force officer; b. 6 April 1949, Brest. *Education:* Univ. of Brest, Air Force Acad., Salon de Provence, Air War Coll., Paris, Nat. War Coll., Washington, DC, USA, NATO Defence Coll., Rome, Italy. *Career:* Fighter Pilot on Mirage III, Jaguar, Mirage F1, Mirage 2000 1972–88; Commdr 5th Wing, Orange 1987–88; Jt Chief of Staff, French Forces in Chad, Africa 1990; Deputy Commdr Air Force Acad., Salon de Provence 1990–92; Air Base Commdr, Colmar 1992–94; Commdr French Forces (Army and Air Force) in Chad 1994–95; Head of Jt and Allied Operations Team, Jt Staff, Paris 1996–97; detached to Gen.-Sec. of Nat. Defence, Prime Minister's Office 1997–99; Dir of Studies, Jt Services Defence Coll., Paris 1999–2000, Dir of Coll. 2000–02; Head of French Air S Support Command, Bordeaux 2002–03; Mil. Rep. to NATO, Brussels Sept. 2003–06; Insp. Gen. Armed Forces 2006–; Commdr Ordre Nat. du Merite, Officier Légion d'Honneur, Ordre Nat. du Tchad; Mil. Cross of Valour, Aeronautical Medal.
Address: Ministry of Defence, 14 rue Saint Dominique, 75007 Paris, France (office). *Telephone:* 1-42-19-30-11 (office). *Fax:* 1-47-05-40-91 (office). *E-mail:* courrier-ministre@sdbc.defense.gouv.fr (office). *Website:* www .defense.gouv.fr (office).

PORTAS, Paulo Sacadura Cabral, LLD; Portuguese politician and journalist; b. 12 Sept. 1962, Lisbon. *Education:* Univ. Católica de Lisboa. *Career:* began career as journalist with O Tempo (newspaper); mem. political comm. for presidential candidature of Freitas do Amaral 1986; mem. Grupo de Ofir (reform group) 1986; f. O Independente (weekly newspaper) 1988, Dir –1995; jt founder Instituto de Estudos Políticos 1995; Deputy, Assembleia da República (parl.), (CDS/Partido Popular) 1995– (Parl. Leader 1999–2001); Lecturer, Dept of Politics, Univ. Moderna 1995–97; Municipal Deputy, Oliveira de Azeméis 1997; fmr Pres. CDS/Partido Popular (now Partido Popular); fmr MEP; Speaker, Câmara Municipal de Lisboa 2001; Minister of State and of Nat. Defence 2002–05; Distinguished Public Service Award, US Defense Dept 2005.
Address: c/o Assembleia da República, Palácio de S. Bento, 1249-068 Lisbon, Portugal (office).

PORTES, Richard David, CBE, DPhil, FBA; American economist and academic; *Professor of Economics, London Business School;* b. 10 Dec. 1941, Chicago, Ill.; m. Barbara Diana Frank 1963 (divorced); one s. one d. *Education:* Yale Univ., Balliol and Nuffield Colls Oxford. *Career:* Official Fellow and Tutor in Econs, Balliol Coll. Oxford 1965–69; Asst Prof. of Econs and Int. Affairs, Princeton Univ. 1969–72; Prof. of Econs, Birkbeck Coll., London Univ. 1972–94, Head Dept 1975–77, 1980–83, 1994; Prof. of Econs, London Business School 1995–; Pres. Centre for Econ. Policy Research, London 1983–; Directeur d'Etudes, Ecole des Hautes Etudes en Sciences Sociales, Paris 1978–; fmr Rhodes Scholar, Woodrow Wilson Fellow, Danforth Fellow; Guggenheim Fellow 1977–78; British Acad. Overseas Visiting Fellow 1977–78; Research Assoc., Nat. Bureau of Econ. Research, Cambridge, Mass 1980–; Visiting Prof., Harvard Univ. 1977–78, Univ. of California 1999–2000, Columbia Univ. Business School 2003–04; Vice-Chair. Econs Cttee Social Science Research Council 1981–84; Sec.-Gen. Royal Econ. Soc. 1992–; mem. Bd of Dirs Soc. for Econ. Analysis 1967–69, 1972–80 (Sec. 1974–77); mem. Royal Inst. of Int. Affairs 1973– (Research Cttee 1982–94), Council on Foreign Relations 1978–, Hon. Degrees Cttee, Univ. of London 1984–89; Fellow Econometric Soc. 1983–; mem. Council, Royal Econ. Soc. 1986–92 (mem. Exec. Cttee 1987–); mem. Council, European Econ. Asscn 1992–96; Co-Chair. Bd of Govs and Sr Ed., Economic Policy 1985–; mem. and fmr mem. several editorial bds; mem. Franco-British Council 1996–2002, Comm. on the Social Sciences 2000–03; Hon. DSc (Univ. Libre de Bruxelles) 2000; Hon. PhD (London Guildhall) 2000. *Publications:* The Polish Crisis 1981, Deficits and Detente 1983; Threats to International Financial Stability (co-ed.) 1987; ed.: Global Macroeconomics: Policy Conflict and Cooperation 1987, Blueprints for Exchange Rate Management 1989, Macroeconomic Policies in an Interdependent World 1989, The EMS in Transition: a CEPR Report 1989, External Constraints on Macroeconomic Policy: The European Experience 1991, The Path of Reform in Central and Eastern Europe 1991, Economic Transformation of Central Europe 1993, European Union Trade with Eastern Europe 1995, Crisis? What Crisis? Orderly Workouts for Sovereign Debtors 1995, Making Sense of Globalization 2002, Crises de la Dette 2003; numerous papers and contribs to learned journals.
Address: London Business School, Regent's Park, London, NW1 4SA, England (office). *Telephone:* (20) 7706-6886 (office). *Fax:* (20) 7724-1598 (office). *E-mail:* rportes@london.edu (office). *Website:* faculty.london.edu/ rportes (office).

POSNER, Michael H., BA, JD; American lawyer and human rights activist; *President, Human Rights First; Education:* Univ. of Mich., Univ. of Calif., Berkeley. *Career:* began career as lawyer in pvt. firm Sonnenschein, Nath and Rosenthal, Chicago; Exec. Dir Human Rights First 1978–2006, Pres. 2006–; Lecturer, Yale Law School 1981–84; Visiting Lecturer, Columbia Univ. 1984–; mem. Calif. and Ill. Bars.
Address: Human Rights First, 333 Seventh Avenue, 13th Floor, New York, NY 10001-5004, USA (office). *Telephone:* (212) 845-5200 (office). *Fax:* (212) 845-5299 (office). *E-mail:* communications@humanrightsfirst.org (office). *Website:* www.humanrightsfirst.org (office).

POTAPOV, Alexander Serafimovich, CandPhil; Russian journalist; *Editor-in-Chief, Trud newspaper;* b. 6 Feb. 1936, Oktyabry, Kharkov Region, Ukraine; m.; one s. *Education:* Vilnius State Univ., Lithuania. *Career:* contrib. Leninskaya Smena (newspaper) 1958–66; Head of Dept, Deputy Ed.-in-Chief Belgorodskaya Pravda (newspaper) 1966–73; Head of Dept Belgorod Regional Exec. CPSU Cttee 1973–75; Ed. Belgorodskaya Pravda 1975–76; instructor CPSU Cen. Cttee 1976–78, 1981–85; Ed.-in-Chief Trud (Labour) newspaper 1985–; People's Deputy of Russian Fed., mem. Cttee of Supreme Soviet of Russian Fed. on Problems of Glasnost and Human Rights –1993.
Address: Trud, Nastas'yinsky per. 4, 103792 Moscow, Russia (office). *Telephone:* (495) 299-39-06 (office). *Fax:* (495) 299-47-40 (office). *E-mail:* letter@trud.ru (office). *Website:* www.trud.ru (office).

POTAPOV, Anatoly Victorovich; Russian politician and diplomatist; *Ambassador to Bulgaria;* b. 24 July 1942, Bishkek; m. Tatyana Nikolayevna Potapova; two c. *Education:* Moscow Inst. of Radio Electronics and Mine Electro Mechanics; Higher Party School at Cen. CPSU Cttee. *Career:* with Ministry of Foreign Affairs, numerous posts at home and abroad 1986–, Presidium and Ministry of CIS Countries; First Deputy Man. Ministry of Foreign Affairs 1986–92; Pro-Rector Moscow State Inst. of Int. Relations 1992; Counsellor, Russian Fed. Embassy, China 1992–96; Asst to Head of Russian Presidium 1996–98; Deputy Minister, Ministry of CIS Affairs 1998–2001; Deputy Minister of Foreign Affairs 2002–04; Amb. to Bulgaria 2004–.
Address: Embassy of the Russian Federation, 1087 Sofia, ul. D. Tsankov 28, Bulgaria (office). *Telephone:* (2) 963-16-63 (office). *Fax:* (2) 963-41-03 (office). *E-mail:* info@russia.bg (office). *Website:* www.russia.bg (office).

POTOČNIK, Janez, BA, MA, PhD; Slovenian economist and government official; *Commissioner for Science and Research, European Commission;* b. 22 March 1958. *Education:* Ljubljana Univ. *Career:* analyst SDK 1983–84; Asst Dir Inst. for Social Planning 1984–87; sr researcher Inst. for Econ. Research 1988–93; Dir Inst. of Microeconomic Analysis and Devt 1993–2001; Head negotiating team for Slovenian accession to EU 1998–2004; EU Ministerial Counsellor 2001–02, Minister without Portfolio 2002–04; EU Commr without Portfolio 2004, for Science and Research 2004–.

Address: European Commission, rue de la Loi 200, 1049 Brussels, Belgium (office). *Telephone:* (2) 299-11-11 (office). *Fax:* (2) 295-01-38 (office). *Website:* europa.eu (office).

POTTER, William C., BA, MA, PhD; American research institute director; *Director, Center for Nonproliferation Studies;* b. 8 July 1947, New Brunswick, NJ. *Education:* Southern Ill Univ., Univ. of Mich. *Career:* started career as research assoc. Univ. of Mich; lecturer Dept of Political Science, Univ. of Calif 1973–76; Post-Doctoral Fellow Stanford Univ. 1976–77; arms control consultant 1976–77; Asst Prof. Tulane Univ.; Asst Dir Center for Int. and Strategic Affairs, UCLA 1979–82, Assoc. Dir 1982–84, Exec. Dir 1984–89; Exec. Officer S Calif Consortium on Int. Studies 1982–83; Visiting Assoc. Prof. UCLA 1979–88; consultant to Lawrence Livermore Nat. Lab. 1982–89, 1992–, Jet Propulsion Lab. 1984–85, RAND Corp. 1984–86; Program Coordinator RAND/UCLA Center for the Study of Soviet Int. Behaviour 1983–85; Prof. Int. Policy Studies, Monterey Inst. of Int. Studies 1989–, Dir Center for Russian and Eurasian Studies 1989–, Dir Center for Nonproliferation Studies 1992–, Inst. Prof. 1998–; mem. several cttees Nat. Acad. of Sciences; mem. Council on Foreign Relations, Pacific Council on Int. Policy, IISS; mem. Advisory Bds UN Disarmament Matters, Center for Policy Studies in Russia; mem. Bd of Trustees UN Inst. for Disarmament Research. *Publications:* SALT and Beyond: A Handbook on Strategic Weapons and Means for Their Control (jtly) 1977, Nuclear Power and Nonproliferation: An Interdisciplinary Perspective 1982, Verification and Arms Control (ed.) 1985, International Nuclear Trade and Nonproliferation: The Challenge of the Emerging Suppliers (ed.) 1990, Nuclear Profiles of the Soviet Successor States (jtly) 1993, The International Missile Bazaar (co-ed.) 1994, Dismantling the Cold War: US and NIS Perspectives on the Nunn-Lugar Cooperative Threat Reduction Program (co-ed.) 1997, Dangerous Weapons, Desperate States (co-ed.) 1999, The Different Faces of Nuclear Terrorism (jtly) 2004; numerous chapters and articles in over eighty scholarly books and journals. *Address:* Center for Nonproliferation Studies, 460 Pierce Street, Monterey, CA 93940 (office); 52 Cuesta Drive, Monterey, CA 93940, USA (home). *Telephone:* (831) 647-3511 (office); (831) 375-3472 (home). *Fax:* (831) 647-3519 (office). *E-mail:* wpotter@miis.edu (office). *Website:* cns.miis.edu (office).

PÖTTERING, Hans-Gert, PhD; German politician; *President, European Parliament;* b. 15 Sept. 1945, Bersenbrueck; two s. *Education:* Univs of Bonn and Geneva, Institut des Hautes Études Internationales, Geneva. *Career:* Reserve Officer, Nat. Service 1966–68; European Policy Spokesman, Young Union of Lower Saxony 1974-80; Research Assistant Univ. of Osnabrueck, 1976–79, Lecturer 1989–95, Hon. Prof. 1995–; MEP 1979–, Chair. European Parl. Subcommittee on Security and Defence 1984–94, Vice-Chair. European People's Party–European Democrats Group (EPP–ED) Group 1994–99, Chair. 1999–2007; Leader EPP EU Enlargement Working Group 1996–99, Pres. 2007–; Chair. Europa-Union Deutschland 1997–99; Chair. Osnabrueck Dist CDU 1990–, mem. Exec. Cttee and Fed. Exec. CDU 1999–2007; European Hon. Senator; Grand Order of Merit of the FRG, Grand Decoration of the Repub. of Austria, Grand Cross, Order of St Gregory the Great, Grand Order of Queen Jelena with Sash and Star (Croatia); Dr hc (Babeş-Bolyai-Univ., Cluj-Napoca, Romania); Konsul-Penseler P, Artland-Gymnasium, Quakenbrück, Robert Schuman Medal, EPP-Group, Gold Medal of Mérite Européen, Luxembourg, MEP of the Year 2004 (European Voice), Walter Hallstein Prize (Frankfurt am Main) 2007. *Publications:* Adenauers Sicherheitspolitik 1955–1963. Ein Beitrag zum deutsch-amerikanischen Verhältnis (Adenauer's Security Policy 1955–1963. A Contribution to the German-American relationship) 1975, Die vergessenen Regionen: Plädoyer für eine solidarische Regionalpolitik in der Europäischen Gemeinschaft (The Forgotten Regions: for a European Community Regional Policy Based on Solidarity) (with Frank Wiehler) 1983, Europas vereinigte Staaten – Annäherungen an Werte und Ziele (Europe's United States – Approaches to Values and Objectives) (with Ludger Kühnhardt) 1993, Kontinent Europa: Kern, Übergänge, Grenzen (The Continent of Europe: Nucleus, Transitions, Borders) (with Ludger Kühnhardt) 1998, Weltpartner Europäische Union (The European Union as a World Partner) (with Ludger Kühnhardt) 2001, Von der Vision zur Wirklichkeit. Auf dem Weg zur Einigung Europas (From Vision to Reality – Towards a United Europe) 2004. *Address:* Office of the President, European Parliament, Bâtiment Paul-Henri Spaak, 11B011, 60 rue Wiertz, 1047 Brussels, Belgium (office). *Telephone:* (2) 284-57-69 (office). *Fax:* (2) 284-97-69 (office). *E-mail:* hans-gert.poettering@europarl.europa.eu (office). *Website:* www.europarl.europa.eu/president/defaulten.htm?biography (office).

POUKRE-KONO, Fernand; Central African Republic diplomatist; b. 1955, Fort-Lamy, Chad; m.; two c. *Education:* State Univ. of Kiev. *Career:* held several positions at Ministry of Foreign Affairs including Chief of UN Section 1987–90, Dir Int. Orgs 1990–91; Legal Adviser, Perm. Mission to UN, New York 1999–2001, First Councillor 2001–02, Charge d'Affaires 2002–03, Perm. Rep. 2003–. *Address:* Permanent Mission of the Central African Republic to the United Nations, 386 Park Avenue South, Room 1114, New York, NY 10016, USA (office). *Telephone:* (212) 679-8089 (office). *Fax:* (212) 545-8326 (office). *E-mail:* caf@un.int (office).

POULSEN, Ole Lønsmann, LLM; Danish diplomatist; *Ambassador to India;* b. 14 May 1945, Lyngby; m. Zareen Mehta 1973; two s. *Education:* Univs of Pune, India and Copenhagen. *Career:* with Danchurchaid 1969–73; Head of Section, Ministry of Foreign Affairs 1973–76; Asian Devt Bank, Manila 1976–77; First Sec., New Delhi 1977–80; Alt. Exec. Dir World Bank, Washington, DC 1980–83; Deputy Head of Dept, Ministry of Foreign Affairs 1983–85, Head of Dept 1985–88, Under-Sec. and Amb. 1988–92; Amb. in Vienna, Ljubljana and Sarajevo; Amb. to UN orgs in Vienna 1992–93; State Sec., Amb. 1993–96; Amb. to UK 1996–2001, to People's Repub. of China 2001–04, to Sweden 2004–06, to India 2006–; Kt Commdr of the First Class (Denmark), Grand Cross (Austria), Grand Cross (Sweden), Hon. GCVO. *Address:* Embassy of Denmark, 11 Aurangzeb Road, 110011 New Delhi, India. *Telephone:* (11) 4209-0700 (office). *Fax:* (11) 2379-2891 (office). *E-mail:* delamb@um.dk (office). *Website:* www.ambnewdelhi.um.dk (office).

POULSEN-HANSEN, Per, MA; Danish diplomatist; *Permanent Representative, NATO;* b. 14 Sept. 1946, Copenhagen; m.; three d. *Education:* Univ. of Copenhagen. *Career:* Lt and Russian language specialist, Danish Army 1967, apptd First Lt 1973; Sec. Ministry of Foreign Affairs (MOF) 1973–75; Second Sec., Embassy in Moscow 1976–79; Personal Asst to Perm. Under-Sec. of MOF 1979–81; Head of Section, Soviet and Eastern European Dept, MOF 1981–84; First Sec., Embassy in London 1984–86, Counsellor and Deputy Head of Mission 1986–87; Head of NATO and Security Policy Dept, MOF 1987–91; Amb. to Czechoslovakia 1991–93, to Czech Repub. and Slovakia 1993; Under-Sec., Political Dir, MOF 1994–99; Asst Sec. of State, Amb., Prime Minister's Office 1999–2003; Perm. Rep. to NATO, Brussels 2003–; mem. Danish Defence Comm. 1988, 1997, Interministerial Contact Group for Security Policy 1987–91, Govt Comm. on Security and Disarmament 1988–91; mem. Bd Danish Inst. of Int. Affairs 1995–99; Commdr (First Class), Order of the Dannebrog. *Address:* Danish Delegation to NATO, NATO Headquarters, Blvd Leopold III, 1110 Brussels, Belgium (office). *Telephone:* (2) 707-61-01 (office). *Fax:* (2) 707-61-15 (office). *E-mail:* brudan@um.dk (office). *Website:* www.nato.int (office).

POWELL, Gen. Colin Luther, MBA; American business executive, academic, fmr government official and fmr army officer; *Strategic Limited Partner, Kleiner Perkins Caufield and Byers;* b. 5 April 1937, New York; m. Alma V. Johnson 1962; one s. (Michael K. Powell) two d. *Education:* City Coll. of New York and George Washington Univ. *Career:* commissioned US Army 1958, Lt-Gen. 1986; Commdr 2nd Brigade, 101st Airborne Div. 1976–77; Exec. Asst to Sec. Dept of Energy 1979; Sr Mil. Asst to Sec. Dept of Defense 1979–81; Asst Div. Commdr 4th Infantry Div. Fort Carson, Colo 1981–83; Mil. Asst to Sec. of Defense 1983–86; assigned to US V Corps, Europe 1986–87; Nat. Security Adviser, White House, Washington 1987–88; C-in-C US Forces, Fort McPherson, Ga April–Sept. 1989; Chair. Jt Chiefs of Staff 1989–93; Sec. of State 2001–05 (resgnd); public speaker 1993–2000; Strategic Ltd Pnr, Kleiner Perkins Caufield & Byers (venture capital firm) 2005–; investor and mem. Bd Revolution Health Group LLC 2005–; Founder, Advisory Council Chair, Distinguished Scholar, Colin Powell Center for Policy Studies, City Coll. of New York 1997–; Chair. Pres.'s Summit For America's Future 1997–; Founding Chair. America's Promise: The Alliance for Youth 1997–2001; Hon. LLD (Univ. of West Indies) 1994; Legion of Merit, Bronze Star, Air Medal, Purple Heart, Pres. Medal of Freedom, Pres. Citizen's Medal, Hon. KCB 1993, Order of Jamaica. *Publication:* My American Journey (autobiog. with Joseph E. Persico) 1995. *Address:* Kleiner Perkins Caufield and Byers, 2750 Sand Hill Road, Menlo Park, CA 94025, USA (office). *Telephone:* (650) 233-2750 (office). *Fax:* (650) 233-0300 (office). *Website:* www.kpcb.com (office).

POWELL, David Hebbert; British diplomatist; *Ambassador to Norway;* b. 29 April 1952; m. Gillian Powell; one d. *Career:* with Ministry of Defence 1974–85; First Sec., Arms Control and Disarmament Dept, FCO 1985–88, First Sec., Chancery, Tokyo 1988–92, Asst Head of Africa Dept (Equatorial), FCO 1992–95, on loan to Cabinet Office Assessments Staff 1995–97, Political Counsellor, UK Del. to NATO, Brussels 1997–2001, Sr Staff Pay Study, FCO 2001–02, Asst Dir of Human Resources Directorate 2002–06, Amb. to Norway 2006–.

Address: British Embassy, Thomas Heftyesgate 8, 0264 Oslo, Norway (office). *Telephone:* 23-13-27-00 (office). *Fax:* 23-13-27-41 (office). *E-mail:* britemb@online.no (office). *Website:* www.britain.no (office).

POWELL, Nancy J.; American diplomatist; *Ambassador to Nepal;* b. Cedar Falls, Ia. *Education:* Univ. of Northern Iowa. *Career:* fmr high school social studies teacher, Dayton, OH 1971–77; joined Foreign Service 1977, served as Nepal Desk officer and Refugee Assistance officer, Deputy Chief of Mission in Lomé 1990–92, in Dhaka 1995–97, Consul Gen. in Calcutta 1992–93, Political Counsellor in New Delhi 1993–95, Amb. to Uganda 1997–99, to Ghana 2001–02, Prin. Deputy Asst Sec. for African Affairs, Dept of State, Washington, DC 1999–2001, Acting Asst Sec. for African Affairs Jan.–June 2001, fmr Chargé d'affaires in Pakistan, Amb. 2002–04, Prin. Deputy Asst Sec. and Acting Asst Sec. of State for Legis. Affairs, Washington, DC Nov. 2004–March 2005, Acting Asst Sec. of State, Bureau for Int. Narcotics and Law Enforcement Affairs 2005, Sr Coordinator for Avian and Pandemic Influenza 2005–06, Nat. Intelligence Officer for S Asia, Nat. Intelligence Council (NIC) 2006–07, Amb. to Nepal 2007–. *Address:* US Embassy, Maharajgunj, Kathmandu, Nepal (office). *Telephone:* (1) 4007200 (office). *Fax:* (1) 4007272 (office). *E-mail:* usembktm@state.gov (office). *Website:* nepal.usembassy.gov (office); kathmandu.usembassy.gov (office).

POWELL, Robert, BS, MPhil, PhD; American political scientist and academic; *Professor of Political Science, University of California, Berkeley; Education:* Harvey Mudd Coll., Univ. of Cambridge, UK, Univ. of California, Berkeley. *Career:* currently Prof. of Political Science, Univ. of Calif. at Berkeley; Fellow, American Acad. of Arts and Sciences; Fulbright Scholar to UK 1981–82. *Publications:* Nuclear Deterrence Theory: The Search for Credibility 1990, In the Shadow of Power: States and Strategies in International Politics 1999; numerous articles in professional journals. *Address:* International and Area Studies, 360 Stephens Hall, University of California, Berkeley, CA 94720-2300, USA (office). *Telephone:* (510) 642-4635 (office). *Fax:* (510) 642-9466 (office). *Website:* www.polisci.berkeley.edu/faculty/bio/permanent/Powell,R/index.htm (office).

POWER, Samantha; American academic and journalist; *Anna Lindh Professor of Practice of Global Leadership and Public Policy, Carr Center for Human Rights Policy, John F. Kennedy School of Government, Harvard University;* b. Ireland. *Education:* Yale Univ. and Harvard Law School. *Career:* moved to USA aged nine; early career as staff mem. CBS Sports and Atlanta affiliate; covered wars in fmr Yugoslavia as reporter for U.S. News and World Report, Boston Globe, and the Economist 1993–96; joined Int. Crisis Group (ICG) as political analyst and helped launch ICG in Bosnia 1996; also worked for Carnegie Endowment for Peace, Washington, DC; adviser to fmr Democratic presidential cand. Wesley Clark 2004; Founding Exec. Dir Carr Center for Human Rights Policy, John F. Kennedy School of Govt, Harvard Univ. 1998–2002, Lecturer in Public Policy 2002–05, Anna Lindh Prof. of Practice of Global Leadership and Public Policy 2005–, took leave of absence 2005–06 to advise US Senator Barack Obama (Democrat from Ill.) on issues of foreign policy; currently a columnist for Time Magazine. *Publications:* A Problem from Hell: America and the Age of Genocide (Pulitzer Prize for Gen. Nonfiction 2003, Nat. Book Critics' Circle Award for Gen. Nonfiction 2003, Council on Foreign Relations' Arthur Ross Prize for the best book on U.S. foreign policy) 2002; Realizing Human Rights: Moving from Inspiration to Impact (co-ed.); Chasing the Flame: Sergio Vieira de Mello and the Fight to Save the World 2008; new introduction to Hannah Arendt's Origins of Totalitarianism; numerous articles on human rights and public policy. *Address:* Carr Center for Human Rights Policy, John F. Kennedy School of Goverment, Harvard University, Rubenstein-217, Mailbox 14, 79 John F. Kennedy Street, Cambridge, MA 02138-5801, USA (office). *Telephone:* (617) 495-3140 (office). *Fax:* (617) 495-4297 (office). *E-mail:* samantha_power@ksg.harvard.edu (office). *Website:* ksgfaculty.harvard.edu/Samantha_Power (office).

PRABHAKARAN, Velupillai; Sri Lankan resistance leader; *Leader, Liberation Tigers of Tamil Eelam;* b. 26 Nov. 1954, Velvettithurai, Jaffna Penninsula; m. Mathy Parabhakaran 1984; two s. one d. *Career:* participated in Tamil protest movt 1970s, Founder and Leader Liberation Tigers of Tamil Eelam (LTTE); accused of involvement in murder of Mayor of Jaffna 1975, Indian Prime Minister Rajiv Gandhi 1991, convicted in absentia 1998; waged civil war against Sri Lankan Govt for 20 years with objective of securing ind. state for Tamil people.

PRAMUDWINAI, Don, BA, MA; Thai diplomatist; *Permanent Representative, United Nations;* b. 25 Jan. 1950; m.; one s. *Education:* Univ. of California, Tufts Univ., USA. *Career:* with East Asia Div., Ministry for Foreign Affairs 1974–76; Dir-Gen.'s Office, ASEAN 1976–81; posted to Embassy in Bonn 1981–85; Dir South-East Asia Div., Dept of Political

Affairs 1985–88; posted to Embassy in London 1988–91; Amb. attached to Office of Perm. Sec., Ministry for Foreign Affairs 1991–92, Dir-Gen. Dept for East Asian Affairs 1992–94; Amb. to Switzerland 1994–99; Dir-Gen. Dept of Information 1999–2000; Amb. to China 2000–04, to Belgium, Luxembourg and EU 2004–07; Perm. Rep. to UN, New York 2007–; Most Illustrious Order of Chula Chom Klao, Most Exalted Order of the White Elephant, Most Noble Order of the Crown of Thailand. *Address:* Permanent Mission of Thailand to the United Nations, 351 East 52nd Street, New York, NY 10022, USA (office). *Telephone:* (212) 754-2230 (office). *Fax:* (212) 754-2535 (office). *E-mail:* thailand@un.int (office).

PRASAD, Alok, BA, MA; Indian diplomatist; *High Commissioner to Sri Lanka;* m. Nandini Prasad; two c. *Education:* Delhi Univ. *Career:* joined Indian Foreign Service 1974, has represented India in various capacities in Germany, UN (New York), the Netherlands, Nepal, Burma and Botswana; also worked in Prime Minister's Office; Jt Sec. for Americas Div., Ministry of External Affairs, New Delhi 1995–2000; Deputy Chief of Mission, Washington, DC 2000–04; High Commr to Singapore 2004–06, to Sri Lanka 2006–; Fellow, Center for Int. Affairs, Harvard Univ., USA. *Address:* High Commission of India, 36–38 Galle Road, Colombo 03, Sri Lanka (office). *Telephone:* (11) 2447285 (office); (11) 2580970 (home). *Fax:* (11) 2446403 (office). *E-mail:* hc.colombo@mea.gov.in (office). *Website:* www.hcicolombo.org (office).

PRASAD, Jayant; Indian diplomatist; *Ambassador to Afghanistan; Education:* Univ. of Delhi, Jawaharlal Nehru Univ., New Delhi. *Career:* taught modern Indian history at St Stephen's Coll., Delhi 1974–76; entered Indian Foreign Service 1976, Rapporteur of UN Comm. on Human Rights, Geneva 1986–87, served as Head of Americas Div., Ministry of External Affairs, New Delhi, as Amb. to Algeria, as Staff Officer for Foreign Sec. and as First Sec., Perm. Mission of India to UN, Geneva, Amb. and Perm. Rep. to Conf. on Disarmament, Geneva 2004–07, mem. UN Sec.-Gen.'s Advisory Bd on Disarmament Matters, Amb. to Afghanistan 2008–; Fellow, Weatherhead Centre for Int. Affairs, Harvard Univ., USA 1998–99. *Address:* Embassy of India, Malalai Wat, Shar-i-Nau, Kabul, Afghanistan (office). *Telephone:* (873) 763095560 (office). *Fax:* (873) 763095561 (office). *E-mail:* embassy@indembassy-kabul.com (office).

PRAT Y COLL, Juan; Spanish civil servant and diplomatist; *Ambassador to the Netherlands;* b. 15 May 1942, Barcelona; m. Léontine van Thiel Coovels; three c. *Education:* Univs of Barcelona and Madrid. *Career:* First Sec. Embassy in Ecuador 1970–72; Deputy Head Commercial Del. to USSR 1973–75; Counsellor and Chargé d'affaires in Repub. of Korea 1975–78; Dir Regional Orgs. of Econ. Co-operation, Ministry of Foreign Affairs 1978–79; Deputy Dir-Gen., then Dir-Gen. Int. Fisheries, Ministry of Agric. and Fisheries 1979–83; Econ. and Commercial Counsellor Embassy in Morocco 1983–85; Dept Dir European Comm., Brussels, Belgium 1986–90, Dir-Gen. of North–South Relations, Mediterranean Policy and Relations with Latin America and Asia 1990–95, Dir-Gen. for External Relations 1995–96; Amb. to Italy, Albania, Malta, San Marino 1996–2000; Perm. Rep. to NATO, Brussels 2000–04; Special Amb. for Mediterranean Issues, Ministry of Foreign Affairs –2007; Amb. to the Netherlands 2007–, also Perm. Rep. to Org. for Prohibition of Chemical Weapons. *Address:* Embassy of Spain, Lange Voorhout 50, 2514 EG The Hague, Netherlands (office). *Telephone:* (70) 3024999 (office). *Fax:* (70) 3617959 (office). *E-mail:* ambassade.spanje@worldonline.nl (office); ambespnl@correo.mae.es (office). *Website:* www.mae.es/embajadas/lahaya (office).

PRAWDA, Marek Władysław; Polish diplomatist; *Ambassador to Germany;* b. 1956, Kielce; m.; two d. *Education:* Univ. of Leipzig, Polish Acad. of Sciences, Warsaw. *Career:* teacher, Univ. of Hamburg 1987–89; German Studies at Inst. of Political Studies, Polish Acad. of Sciences 1990–92; joined Ministry of Foreign Affairs 1992; served at Embassy in Bonn 1992–98; Deputy Dir Dept for Western Europe, Ministry of Foreign Affairs 1998–99, Dir 1999–2001; Amb. to Sweden 2001–05; Dir Minister's Office, Ministry of Foreign Affairs 2005–06; Amb to Germany 2006–; Sec.-Gen. Nat. Exec. Polish-German Soc. 1991–92. *Publications include:* numerous articles on social issues and German-Polish relations. *Address:* Embassy of Poland, Lassenstr. 19–21, 14193 Berlin, Germany (office). *Telephone:* (30) 22313100 (office). *Fax:* (30) 2213155 (office). *E-mail:* info@botschaft-polen.de (office). *Website:* www.berlin.polemb.net (office).

PRENDERGAST, Sir (Walter) Kieran, KCVO, CMG; British diplomatist; b. 2 July 1942, Campbeltown, Argyll; m. Joan Reynolds 1967; two s. two d. *Education:* Salesian Coll. Chertsey and St Edmund Hall, Oxford. *Career:* Asst Pvt. Sec. to successive Secs of State, FCO 1976–78; has served at Istanbul, Ankara, Nicosia, The Hague, UK Mission to UN, New York and

Tel-Aviv; seconded to staff of last gov. of Rhodesia (Lord Soames) during transition to independence in Zimbabwe; High Commr in Zimbabwe 1989–92, in Kenya 1992–95; Amb. to Turkey 1995–97; UN Under-Sec.-Gen. for Political Affairs 1997–2005 (retd); Goodman UN Fellow, Int. Security Program, Belfer Center for Science and Int. Affairs, Kennedy School of Govt, Harvard Univ. 2005–06.
Address: c/o Foreign and Commonwealth Office, King Charles Street, London, SW1A 2AH, England (office).

PRENTICE, Christopher Norman Russell, LitHum; British diplomatist; *Ambassador to Iraq;* b. 5 Sept. 1954; m. Marie-Josephine (Nina) King 1978; two s. two d. *Education:* Christ Church Coll., Oxford. *Career:* joined FCO 1977, Desk Officer (Arab-Israel, Near East N Africa Dept/NENAD) 1977–78, Arabic language training 1978–79, Third, later Second Sec., Kuwait 1980–83, Middle East Analyst, Cabinet Office, London 1983–85, First Sec. (Near East and S Asia), British Embassy, Washington, DC 1985–89, Asst Head of EC Dept (External), FCO 1989–90, Asst Pvt. Sec. to Foreign Sec. Douglas Hurd (covering Middle East, EU, W and E Europe) 1990–93, Hungarian language training 1993–94, Deputy Head of Mission, Budapest 1994–98, Head of NENAD 1998–, Amb. to Jordan 2002–06, UK Special Rep., later FCO Co-ordinator for the Sudan Peace Process 2006–07, Amb. to Iraq 2007–.
Address: Iraq Policy Unit, Foreign and Commonwealth Office, King Charles Street, London SW1A 2AH, England (office). *Telephone:* (20) 7008-1500 (office). *Fax:* (20) 7008-4119 (office). *E-mail:* britembBaghdad@fco.gov.uk (office). *Website:* www.britishembassy.gov.uk/iraq (office).

PRÉVAL, René; Haitian agronomist, politician and head of state; *President;* b. 17 Jan. 1943, Port-au-Prince; m.; two c. *Education:* Coll. of Jembloux, Belgium. *Career:* forced to leave Haiti with his family after dispute with Duvalier dictatorship 1963; returned 1975 after five years in USA; worked at Nat. Inst. for Mineral Resources 1975–77; Founding mem. Group for Defence of Constitution; Chair. Cttee Pa Blié investigating disappearance of persons under Duvalier regime 1987–91; Prime Minister Feb.–Sept. 1991; Pres. of Haiti 1996–2001, 2006–; mem. Lespwa Party.
Address: Office of the President, Palais National, rue de la République, Port-au-Prince (office); c/o La Fanmi Lavalas, blvd 15 Octobre, Tabarre, Port-au-Prince, Haiti. *Telephone:* 222-3024 (office). *E-mail:* webmestre@palaisnational.info (office).

PRICA, Milos; Bosnia and Herzegovina diplomatist; *Permanent Representative, United Nations;* b. 7 March 1961, Chicago, Ill., USA. *Education:* Univ. of Belgrade. *Career:* Chief of Staff, Pres. of Republika Srpska 1996–98; Adviser to Prime Minister on Foreign Relations, Republika Srpska 1998–99; Minister Counsellor and Deputy Perm. Rep. of Bosnia and Herzegovina to UN, New York 2000–05, Perm. Rep. 2005–; Head of Dept, Immunities and Privileges of Foreign Diplomats, Ministry of Foreign Affairs Jan.–May 2005.
Address: Office of the Permanent Representative of Bosnia and Herzegovina to the United Nations, 866 United Nations Plaza, Suite 580, New York, NY 10017, USA (office). *Telephone:* (212) 751-9015 (office). *Fax:* (212) 751-9019 (office). *E-mail:* bosnia@un.int (office). *Website:* www.un.int/bosnia (office).

PRIKHODKO, Sergey Eduardovich; Russian government official; *Adviser to the President;* b. 12 Jan. 1957, Moscow; m.; two d. *Education:* Moscow State Inst. of Int. Relations. *Career:* mem. of staff Ministry of Foreign Affairs 1980–93; Head Div. of Baltic Countries, Deputy Dir Second European Dept 1993–97; Asst to Russian Pres. on Int. Problems 1997–98, Deputy Head of Admin, Russian Presidency 1998–99, concurrently Head Dept of Admin on Int. Policy 1998; Adviser to the Pres. 2004–; Public Recognition Award 1999.
Address: Office of the President, Staraya pl. 4, 103132 Moscow, Russia (office). *Telephone:* (495) 925-35-81 (office). *Fax:* (495) 206-07-66 (office). *E-mail:* president@gov.ru (office). *Website:* www.kremlin.ru (office).

PRIMAKOV, Yevgeniy Maksimovich, DEcon; Russian politician and economist; *President, Russian Federation Chamber of Commerce and Industry;* b. 29 Oct. 1929, Kiev; m.; one d. *Education:* Moscow Inst. of Oriental Studies. *Career:* worked for State Comm. on Broadcasting and Television 1953–62; mem. CPSU 1959–91; Columnist and Deputy Ed. (Asia and Africa Desk), Pravda 1962–70; Deputy Dir Inst. of World Econ. and Int. Relations, USSR (now Russian) Acad. of Sciences 1970–77, Dir 1985–, Dir Inst. of Oriental Studies 1977–85; elected to Congress of People's Deputies of the USSR 1989; mem. CPSU Cen. Cttee 1989–91; cand. mem. Politburo 1989–90; Chair. Soviet of the Union June 1989–March 1990; mem. Presidential Council 1989–90; Pres. Gorbachev's Special Envoy to the Gulf 1990–91; Dir Central Intelligence Service of USSR 1991, Foreign Intelligence Service of Russian Fed. 1991–96; Minister of Foreign Affairs 1996–98; Chair of Govt (Prime Minister) 1998–99; Chair. Exec. Council of

Russia and Belarus Union 1998–99; mem. Security Council 1996–98; mem. State Duma (Parl.) 1999–, Head Otechestvo faction 2000–; Pres. Russian Fed. Chamber of Commerce and Industry 2001–; Corresp. mem. USSR (now Russian) Acad. of Sciences 1974, mem. 1979, Acad.-Sec., mem. of Presidium 1988–91; specialist on Egypt and other Arab countries; Chief Ed. of and contributor to a number of collective works, including: International Conflicts 1972, The Energy Crisis in the Capitalist World 1975, Years in Large-Scale Policy 1999; Nasser Prize 1975, USSR State Prize 1980, Avicenna Prize 1983. *Publications include:* Egypt under Nasser (with I. P. Belyayev) 1975, The War Which Could Be Avoided 1991, Years at the Top Level of Politics 2000, Eight Months Plus 2001.
Address: Russian Federation Chamber of Commerce & Industry, Ilyinka str. 6, 103684 Moscow, Russia. *Telephone:* (495) 929-00-01 (office). *Fax:* (495) 929-03-75 (office).

PRINCE, La Celia, LLB; Saint Vincent and the Grenadines lawyer and diplomatist; *Ambassador to USA;* b. Kingstown. *Education:* Univ. of the West Indies, Sir Hugh Wooding Law School, Trinidad, Univ. of Cambridge, UK. *Career:* practiced as barrister-at-law and solicitor; took up Fellowship in multilateral trade negotiations, assigned to CARICOM del. at Secretariat of the Free Trade Area of the Americas, Puebla Mexico, then at WTO, Geneva; worked at Secretariat of African Caribbean and Pacific Group of States, Brussels; Minister Counsellor, Embassy in Washington, DC 2005–08, Amb. to USA and Perm. Rep. to OAS, Washington, DC 2008–.
Address: Embassy of Saint Vincent and the Grenadines, 3216 New Mexico Avenue, NW, Washington, DC 20016, USA (office). *Telephone:* (202) 364-6730 (office). *Fax:* (202) 364-6736 (office). *Website:* www.embsvg.com (office).

PRINGLE, Anne Fyfe, CMG, MA; British diplomatist; *Ambassador to Russian Federation;* b. 13 Jan. 1955; m. Bleddyn Glynne Phillips 1987. *Education:* Univ. of St Andrews. *Career:* joined FCO 1977; Third Sec., Moscow 1980–83; Vice-Consul, San Francisco 1983–85, Brussels 1986–87; First Sec., FCO 1987–91, Brussels 1991–94, African Security Coordination Dept, FCO 1994–96, Head, Common Foreign and Security Policy Dept 1996–98, Head, Eastern Dept 1998–2001, Dir Directorate for Strategy and Information 2004–07; Amb. to Czech Repub. 2001–04, to Russian Fed. Oct. 2008–.
Address: British Embassy, 121099 Moscow, Smolenskaya nab. 10, Russia (office). *Telephone:* (495) 956-72-00 (office). *Fax:* (495) 956-72-01 (office). *E-mail:* moscow@britishembassy.ru (office). *Website:* www.britaininrussia.ru (office).

PRLIĆ, Jadranko, DSc; Bosnia and Herzegovina politician and university professor; b. 10 June 1959, Djakovo; m. Ankica Prlić; two d. *Education:* Univs of Mostar and Sarajevo. *Career:* worked as a journalist; joined teaching staff, Univ. of Mostar 1987, Prof. Emer. 1999–; Mayor of Mostar 1987–88; fmr Gen. Man. Apro-Mostar agricultural enterprise; Vice-Pres. Govt of Bosnia and Herzegovina 1989–91; during war 1992–95 mem. and official of highest bodies of Croatian people; following signing of Washington (1994) and Dayton (1995) Agreements: Deputy Prime Minister and Minister of Defence; mem. Parl. of Bosnia and Herzegovina and Minister of Foreign Affairs 1996–2001; mem. Council of Ministers 2001–03; Deputy Minister of Foreign Trade and Econ. Relations 2001–03; Founder and Pres. European Movement in Bosnia and Herzegovina; Gov. in IMF for Bosnia and Herzegovina; Pres. Pro-European People's Party; indicted by Int. Criminal Tribunal for the Fmr Yugoslavia for crimes against humanity and war crimes against the non-Croat population March 2005, surrendered voluntarily to Tribunal. *Publications:* Policy of Fluctuating Foreign Exchange Rates 1990, Imperfect Peace 1998, Fuga Della Storia 2000, Return to Europe 2002, Unfinished Game 2002; numerous articles in field of int. economy, particularly finance and political issues.
Address: Srosmeyorova 6, 71000 Sarajevo (office); Grbavička 21C, 71000 Sarajevo, Bosnia and Herzegovina. *Telephone:* (33) 213001 (home). *Fax:* (33) 679275 (office). *E-mail:* jprlic@bih.net.ba (office). *Website:* www.jprlic.ba (home).

PROSL, Christian, DrIur; Austrian diplomatist; *Ambassador to Germany;* b. 21 Aug. 1946, Eisenstadt; m. Patricia Prosl (née Hurni); two s. *Education:* Lycée Français de Vienne, Real-Gymnasium der Theresianischen Akad., Vienna, Univ. of Vienna, Inst. de Hautes Etudes Int., Geneva. *Career:* mil. service 1969–70; UNDP: Burkina Faso, Rwanda 1973–77; served in Fed. Ministry for Foreign Affairs, Vienna 1977–79; First Sec., Embassy in London 1979–81; Embassy in Washington, DC 1981–88 (Deputy Head of Mission 1987–88); Coordination Officer, Gen. Secr., Fed. Ministry for Foreign Affairs 1988–91; Consul Gen. in LA 1991–95; Dir Dept of Western and Northern Europe 1995–98; Dir Gen. Legal and Consular Affairs 1998–2002; Deputy Sec.-Gen. for Foreign Affairs 2000–02; Amb. to

Germany 2003–; Grosses Verdienstkreuz des Verdienstordens (Germany) 1997, Commdr de l'Ordre de la Couronne (Belgium) 2000.
Address: Embassy of Austria, Stauffenbergstr. 1, 10785 Berlin, Germany (office). *Telephone:* (30) 202870 (office). *Fax:* (30) 2290568 (office). *E-mail:* berlin-ob@bmeia.gv.at (office). *Website:* www.oesterreichische-botschaft .de (office).

PROSOR, Ron; Israeli diplomatist; *Ambassador to UK. Career:* served in USA and in major European capitals, served as spokesman in London and Bonn, as Minister-Counsellor for Political Affairs, Embassy in Washington, DC; mem. Israeli del. to Wye River Plantation talks, Md 1998; Sr Deputy Dir Gen., Ministry of Foreign Affairs and Chief of Policy Staff to the Minister –2004, Dir Gen., Ministry of Foreign Affairs 2004–06; Amb. to UK 2007–.
Address: Embassy of Israel, 2 Palace Green, Kensington, London, W8 4QB, England (office). *Telephone:* (20) 7957-9500 (office). *Fax:* (20) 7957-9555 (office). *E-mail:* info-assist@london.mfa.gov.il (office). *Website:* london.mfa.gov.il (office).

PRUAITCH, Patrick; Papua New Guinea politician; *Minister of Finance and the Treasury; Career:* mem. Parl. for Aitape-Lumi; fmr Minister for Forestry, Minister of Finance and the Treasury 2007–; mem. Nat. Alliance Party.
Address: Department of Finance and Treasury, Vulupindi Haus, Waigani Drive, POB 710, Waigani, Vulupindi Haus, National Capital District, Papua New Guinea (office). *Telephone:* 3128817 (office). *Fax:* 3128844 (office). *E-mail:* enquiries@treasury.gov.pg (office). *Website:* www.treasury .gov.pg (office).

PUAPUA, Rt Hon. Sir Tomasi, Kt, PC, KBE; Tuvaluan politician; b. 10 Sept. 1938; m. Riana Tabokai 1971; two s. two d. *Education:* Fiji School of Medicine and Univ. of Otago, NZ. *Career:* medical practitioner; Prime Minister of Tuvalu 1981–90, also Minister for Civil Service Admin., Local Govt and Minister for Foreign Affairs; Speaker of Parl. 1993–98; Gov. Gen. of Tuvalu 1998–2005.
Address: c/o Government House, Vaiaku, Funafuti, Tuvalu (office).

PUBLICOVER, Ralph Martin; British diplomatist (retd); b. 2 May 1952; m. Rosemary Veronica Publicover; one s. two d. *Career:* entered FCO 1976, Desk Officer, SE Asian Dept 1976–77, Second Sec., Dubai 1979–81, First Sec. (Econ.), Ottawa 1981–85, on loan to Cabinet Office, FCO 1985–87, First Sec., Chancery, Washington, DC and Desk Officer, EC Dept (Internal), FCO 1989–92, Asst Head, Cen. European Dept 1992–94, Deputy Head of Mission, Bucharest 1994–97, Deputy Head of Mission, Lisbon 1999–2003, Head of Consular Crisis Group, Consular Directorate, FCO 2000–03, Amb. to Angola 2005–07.
Address: c/o Foreign and Commonwealth Office, King Charles Street, London, SW1A 2AH, England. *Telephone:* (20) 7008-1500. *Website:* www .fco.gov.uk.

PUCCIO HUIDOBRO, Osvaldo, LLB, PhD; Chilean diplomatist; *Ambassador to Spain;* b. 21 Dec. 1952; three c. *Education:* Univ. of Chile, Humboldt Univ., Berlin. *Career:* counsultant, Latin-American Faculty of Social Sciences (FLASCO) 1984–86; Assoc. Researcher, Centre for Devt Studies (CED) 1986–88; consultant, UNDP 1987–88, 2000–03; Founder mem. Chilean Asscn of Political Sciences 1988; Dir Centro de Estudios Sociales AVANCE 1988–94; political advisor to Minister Sec. Gen. of the Presidency 1990–94, 2000–03; Amb. to Austria 1994–2000 (also accred to Slovakia 1995–2000, to Bosnia and Herzegovina, to Slovenia 1997–2000); Vice-Chair. Int. Cooperation Agency of Chile (AGCI) 2000–03; Amb. to Brazil 2003–05; Minister Sec. Gen. of the Presidency 2005–06; Amb. to Spain 2006–; mem. Bd of Dirs Victoria de Lebu- Carville (coal co.) 1990–92, SACOR-CORFO (agric. co.) 1992–93; mem. Academic Cttee, Santo Tomás Univ. 1992–94.
Address: Embassy of Chile, Lagasca 88, 6°, 28001 Madrid, Spain (office). *Telephone:* (91) 4319160 (office). *Fax:* (91) 5775560 (office). *E-mail:* echilees@tsai.es (office).

PUIG, Lluis de Maria; Spanish politician and historian; *President, Alexander Cirici Institute for European Co-operation;* b. 20 July 1945, Bascara, Gerona; m.; two c. *Education:* Autonomous Univ. of Barcelona, Ecole des Hautes Etudes de la Sorbonne, Paris. *Career:* worked in anti-Franco opposition as active mem. of underground Catalan and socialist orgs; Prof. of Contemporary History, Autonomous Univ. of Barcelona; Socialist mem. Cortes for Gerona 1979–; mem. Catalonian Socialist Party Bureau 1986–; Pres. Gerona Fed. of Socialist Party 1993–; mem. Council of Europe Ass. 1983–, Chair. Sub-Cttee on European Social Charter 1984–89, Vice-Pres. Ass. 1993–96; mem. Spanish del. to WEU Ass. 1990–, Vice-Chair. Socialist Group 1992–96, Defence Cttee 1992–94, Chair. Political Cttee 1994–96, mem. Presidential Cttee 1994–, Pres. WEU Ass. 1997–2000; Sec.

Alexander Cirici Inst. for European Co-operation 1986–96, Pres. 1996–; Dr hc (Ovidius Univ. of Constanta, Romania) 1998. *Publications:* several books on history of 19th and 20th century Catalonia, books and essays on Europe, articles on domestic and int. politics.
Address: c/o Assembly of Western European Union, 43 avenue du Président Wilson, 75775 Paris Cedex 16, France.

PUISSOCHET, Jean-Pierre, LLD, PhD; French international judge and lawyer; *Judge, Court of Justice of the European Communities;* b. 3 May 1936, Clermont-Ferrand; m. Eliane Millet 1973; one d. *Education:* Lycée du Parc, Lyon, Inst. for Political Studies, Lyon, School of Law, Lyon, Ecole Nat. d'Admin., Paris. *Career:* Auditeur, Conseil d'Etat 1962, Maître des Requêtes 1968, Conseiller 1985; Dir Legal Service, Council of EC 1968–70, Dir-Gen. 1970–73; Dir-Gen. Agence Nat. pour l'Emploi 1973–75; Dir Ministry of Industry and Research 1977–79; Dir of Legal Affairs, OECD 1979–85; Dir Int. Inst. of Public Admin. 1985–87; Legal Adviser, Dir of Legal Affairs, Ministry of Foreign Affairs 1987–94; Judge, Court of Justice of the European Communities 1994–; mem. Perm. Court of Arbitration, The Hague 1990–; Officier, Légion d'honneur, Grand Officier Ordre nat. du Mérite, Officier du Mérite agricole, Grand'Uffiziale dell Ordine al Merito (Italy). *Publications:* The Enlargement of the EC 1974; numerous articles on Community and int. law.
Address: Court of Justice of the European Communities, Plateau du Kirchberg, 2925 Luxembourg (office); 15 rue Jean-Pierre Brasseur, 1258, Luxembourg (home). *Telephone:* 43-03-22-46 (office). *Fax:* 43-03-20-00. *E-mail:* jean-pierre.puissochet@curia.eu.int (office).

PULIKOVSKY, Lt-Gen. Konstantin Borisovich; Russian army officer and politician; *Representative of Russian President to Far Eastern Federation District;* b. 9 Feb. 1948, Ussuriysk, Primorsk Territory. *Education:* M. Frunze Mil. Acad., Mil. Acad. of Gen. Staff. *Career:* mil. posts to rank of Army Commdr 1972; took part in conflict in Chechnya 1994–96; Commdr group of Fed. forces in Chechen Repub. 1996, Deputy Commdr., N Caucasus Mil. District 1997–; leader Krasnodar Org. All-Russian Movt of veterans of local wars and mil. conflicts Boyevoye Bratstvo; Rep. of Russian Pres. to Far Eastern Fed. Dist 2000–. *Publications include:* The Eastern Express: Through Russia With Kim Jong II 2002.
Address: Office of the Presidential Representative, Sheronova str. 22, 680030 Khabarovsk, Russia (office). *Telephone:* (4212) 31-30-44 (Khabarovsk) (office); (495) 206-73-52 (Moscow) (office).

PULLEN, Roderick Allen, BA, DPhil; British diplomatist; b. 11 April 1949; m. Karen Sketchley; four s. one d. *Education:* Mansfield Coll. and Univs of Oxford and Sussex. *Career:* with Ministry of Defence 1975–78, 1980–81; Second Sec. UK Del. to NATO 1978–80, First Sec., Del. to CSCE 1981–82, FCO 1982–84, 1988–90, Deputy High Commr, Suva 1984–88, Nairobi 1994–97, Abuja 1997–2000, High Commr to Ghana 2000–04, Amb. to Zimbabwe 2004–06, UK Special Rep. at Inter-Sudanese Peace Talks on Darfur 2006.
Address: Foreign and Commonwealth Office, King Charles Street, London, SW1A 2AH, England (office). *Telephone:* (20) 7008-1500 (office). *Website:* www.fco.gov.uk (office).

PURCELL, James Nelson, MPA; American international official and international consultant; b. 16 July 1938, Nashville, Tenn.; m. Walda Primm 1961; two d. *Education:* Furman Univ., Syracuse Univ., New York. *Career:* Budget Analyst, US Atomic Energy Comm. 1962–66; Man. Analyst, Agency for Int. Devt 1966–68; Deputy Dir Budget Preparation Staff, Office of Man. and Budget (OMB) 1968–72; Sr Examiner Int. Affairs Div. OMB 1972–74; Chief Justice, Treasury Br. OMB 1974–76; Chief Resources Programming and Man. Div., Bureau for Educ. and Cultural Affairs, Dept of State 1976–77; Deputy Budget Dir, Dept of State 1977–78; Exec. Dir Bureau of Admin., Dept of State 1978–79; Deputy Asst Sec., Programmes and Budget, Bureau for Refugee Programs, Dept of State 1979–82, Dir, Asst Sec. Bureau for Refugee Programmes 1982–87; Dir-Gen. Int. Org. for Migration 1988–98; Int. Consultant 1998–; mem. American Soc. of Public Admin.; Distinguished Honor Award, State Dept.
Address: c/o International Organization for Migration, CP 71, 17 Route des Morillons, 1211 Geneva 19, Switzerland (office); 5113 West Running Brook Road, Columbia, MD 21044, USA (home). *E-mail:* ynpatcol@aol .com.

PURI PURINI, Antonio; Italian diplomatist; *Ambassador to Germany; Career:* worked in Directorate of Political Affairs, Italian Foreign Service and in Cabinet of Foreign Affairs Minister; fmr Deputy Chief of Mission, Embassy in Washington, DC; Perm. Rep. to Council of Europe –1999; Diplomatic Adviser to Pres. 1999–2003; Amb. to Germany 2003–.
Address: Embassy of Italy, Hiroshimatr. 1, 10785 Berlin, Germany (office). *Telephone:* (30) 254400 (office). *Fax:* (30) 25440116 (office). *E-mail:*

segreteria.berlino@esteri.it (office). *Website:* www.ambberlino.esteri.it (office).

PURNELL, Jon R., BA, MA; American diplomatist; b. Norwood, Mass; m.; three c. *Education:* Norwood High School, Brown Univ., Harvard Univ. *Career:* worked as specialist in environmental educ. for Mass Audubon Soc.; career mem. Sr Foreign Service now with rank of Minister-Counselor, served in Monrovia, Liberia 1980–81, posted to Moscow 1982–84, Special Asst to Amb. Jack Matlock on Nat. Security Council 1986, mem. US conventional arms control del. in Vienna 1988–89, Deputy Prin. Officer, Consulate Gen., St Petersburg 1989–92, Dir Office of Ukraine, Belarus and Moldova 1993–96, Deputy Chief of Mission, Almaty, Kazakhstan 1997–2000, Deputy to Sec. Acting Special Advisor for Newly Independent States 2000–01, Sr Insp., Office of Insp. Gen. 2001–02, Minister-Counselor for Political Affairs, Embassy in Moscow 2002–04, Amb. to Uzbekistan 2004–07; Superior Honor Award and Meritorious Honor Award, Dept of State.
Address: US Department of State, 2201 C Street NW, Washington, DC 20520, USA (office). *Telephone:* (202) 647-4000 (office). *Fax:* (202) 647-6738 (office). *Website:* www.state.gov (office).

PUTEH, Dato' Pengiran Indera Negara P. Anak, MA, MJ; Brunei diplomatist; *Ambassador to USA;* m. Datin Kamilah binti Abdullah; two d. *Education:* Univs of London and Oxford, UK, Tufts Univ., USA, School of Law, Univ. of Birmingham, UK, School of Int. Arbitration, Centre for Commercial Law Studies, Queen Mary, Univ. of London. *Career:* various civil service posts including Sr Admin. Officer, Public Service Comm., Dir Dept of Protocol and Consular Affairs; Amb. to Japan 1986–87, Perm. Sec., Ministry of Foreign Affairs 1987–97, Amb. to USA (also accred to Mexico) 1997–; mem. Chartered Inst. of Arbitrators, London.
Address: Embassy of Brunei, 3520 International Court, Suite 300, NW, Washington, DC 20008, USA (office). *Telephone:* (202) 237-1838 (office). *Fax:* (202) 885-0560 (office). *E-mail:* info@bruneiembassy.org (office). *Website:* www.bruneiembassy.org (office).

PUTIN, Col Vladimir Vladimirovich, PhD; Russian politician and fmr head of state; *Chairman of the Government (Prime Minister);* b. 7 Oct. 1952, Leningrad (now St Petersburg); m. Lyudmila Putina 1983; two d. *Education:* Law Dept, Leningrad State Univ. *Career:* assigned to work on staff KGB USSR 1975–91, with First Chief Dept of KGB and in E Germany 1985–90; asst to Pro-Rector, Leningrad State Univ. 1990; adviser to Chair. of Leningrad City Exec. Cttee 1990–91; Chair. Cttee on Foreign Relations, St Petersburg City Council 1991–96, then also First Deputy Chair. St Petersburg City Govt (First Deputy Mayor) 1994–96; Deputy Head, Admin. of Russian Presidency, Property Man. Directorate 1996–98, then also Deputy Head, Exec. Office of Pres. (Presidential Admin) and Head, Cen. Supervision and Inspections Directorate 1997–98; First Deputy Head, Presidential Admin May–July 1998; Dir Fed. Security Service of Russian Fed. 1998–99; Sec. Security Council of Russia March–Aug. 1999; apptd Chair. of Govt (Prime Minister) Aug.–Dec. 1999, 2008–; Acting Pres. of Russian Fed. Dec. 1999–March 2000, Pres. March 2000–08; Chair. United Russia (UR) (Yedinaya Rossiya) party 2008–; Grand Cross Bundesverdienstkreuz (Germany) 2001, Grand Croix, Légion d'Honneur 2006, King Abdul Aziz Award, Saudi Arabia 2007, Order of Zayed (UAE) 2007; named Person of the Year by Time magazine 2007.
Address: Office of the Chairman of the Government, 103274 Moscow, Krasnopresnenskaya nab. 2, Russia (office). *Telephone:* (495) 205-57-35 (office). *Fax:* (495) 205-42-19 (office). *Website:* www.government.ru (office).

PUTNAM, Robert, PhD; American political scientist and academic; *Peter and Isabel Malkin Professor of Public Policy, Harvard University;* b. Rochester, NY; m. Rosemary Werner; two c. *Education:* Swarthmore Coll., Balliol Coll. Oxford, UK, Yale Univ. *Career:* mem. Faculty, Univ. of Michigan 1968–78, Prof. 1975–78; mem. staff, Nat. Security Council 1978; fmr Dean John F. Kennedy School of Govt, Harvard Univ., Prof. 1979–, later Peter and Isabel Malkin Prof. of Public Policy, and Chair. Dept of Govt; Dir Saguaro Seminar, Harvard Univ.; fmr Pres. American Political Science Asscn; mem. NAS; Corresp. Fellow, British Acad.; Fellow, American Acad. of Arts and Sciences; Harold Lasswell Fellow, American Acad. of Political and Social Science 2005; Commdr, Order of the Star of Italian Solidarity 2004; Dr hc (Swarthmore Coll., Ohio State Univ., Stockholm Univ., Univ. of Antwerp, Univ. of Edinburgh, Univ. of Manchester); Johan Skytte Prize in Political Science 2006, Charles E. Merriam Award, American Political Science Asscn 2007. *Publications:* The Comparative Study of Political Elites 1976, Bureaucrats and Politicians in Western Democracies 1981, Hanging Together: The Seven Power Summits (co-author) 1984, Double-Edged Diplomacy: International Bargaining and Domestic Politics 1993, Making Democracy Work: Civil Traditions in Modern Italy 1993, Bowling Alone: The Collapse and Revival of American Community 2000, Democracies in Flux: The Evolution of Social Capital in Contemporary Society (ed) 2002, Better Together: Restoring the American Community (co-author) 2003; numerous articles in professional journals.
Address: John F. Kennedy School of Government, Harvard University, 79 JFK Street, Cambridge, MA 02138, USA (office). *Telephone:* (617) 495-1148 (office). *Fax:* (617) 495-1589 (office). *E-mail:* robert_putnam@harvard.edu (office). *Website:* ksgfaculty.harvard.edu/Robert_Putnam (office).

PUZANOV, Col-Gen. Igor Yevgenyevich; Russian army officer; *Deputy Minister of Defence;* b. 31 Jan. 1947, Tyumen. *Education:* Omsk Gen. Army Command School, M. V. Frunze Mil. Acad., Mil. Acad. of Gen. Staff. *Career:* Commdr platoon Siberian Mil. Command –1976, Deputy Div. Commdr, then Commdr 1981–88; Deputy Regt Commdr, then Commdr Karpaty Mil. Command 1976–79; served in Afghanistan 1979–81; Head of Gen. Staff Baltic Mil. Command 1988–90; Army Commdr N Caucasian Mil. Command 1990–92; First Deputy Commdr Moscow Mil. Command 1992–2001, Statistics-Sec.; Deputy Minister of Defence 2001–; Merited Mil. Specialist.
Address: Ministry of Defence, 105175 Moscow, ul. Myasnitskaya 37, Russia (office). *Telephone:* (495) 293-38-54 (office). *Fax:* (495) 296-84-36 (office). *Website:* www.mil.ru (office).

PYNZENYK, Viktor Mikhailovich, DEcon; Ukrainian politician and economist; *Minister of Finance;* b. 15 April 1954, Smologovitsa; m. Maria Romanivna Pynzenyk; two d. one s. *Education:* Lviv State Univ. *Career:* Asst, then Docent, Sr Researcher, Prof., Chair. Lviv State Univ. 1975–92; mem. Vakhovna Rada (Parl.) 1991–2001; Deputy Chair. Bd on Problems of Econ. Policy 1992; Minister of Economy 1992–93, Deputy Prime Minister 1992–97; Pres. Foundation of Support to Reforms 1993; Chair. Council on Problems of Econ. Reforms 1994; Chair. Nat. Council on Statistics 1995; Head, State Comm. on Admin. Reform 1997–99; Head, Reforms and Order Party (Partiya 'Reformy i poryadok') 1998–; Minister of Finance 2005–06, 2007–; Dir Inst. of Reforms; Hon. Prof. Nat. Univ. of Kiev-Mogilyansk Acad. 1996–. *Publications:* over 400 papers.
Address: Ministry of Finance, 01008 Kyiv, vul. M. Hrushevskoho 12/2 (office); Reforms and Order Party (Partiya 'Reformy i poryadok'), 01021 Kyiv, vul. Instytutska 28, Ukraine (office). *Telephone:* (44) 293-74-66 (Ministry) (office); (44) 585-41-16 (office). *Fax:* (44) 293-21-78 (Ministry) (office); (44) 585-41-17 (office). *E-mail:* inform@minfin.gov.ua (office); ref_ord@i.com.ua (office). *Website:* www.minfin.gov.ua (office); www.prp .org.ua (office).

Q

QABOOS BIN SAID AS-SAID, Sultan of Oman; *Prime Minister and Minister of Foreign Affairs, Defence and Finance;* b. 18 Nov. 1940, Salalah; m. 1976. *Education:* privately in UK, RMA, Sandhurst. *Career:* 14th descendant of the ruling dynasty of Albusaid Family; Sultan of Oman (following deposition of his father) July 1970–, also Prime Minister, Minister of Foreign Affairs, Defence and Finance; Hon. KCMG.
Address: Diwan of the Royal Court, PO Box 632, Muscat 113, Sultanate of Oman. *Telephone:* 738711. *Fax:* 739427.

QADDAFI, Col Mu'ammar al- (see Gaddafi, Col Mu'ammar al-).

QADHAFI, Col Mu'ammar al- (see Gaddafi, Col Mu'ammar al-).

QARASE, Laisenia, BCom; Fijian politician; *Leader, Soqosoqo Duavata ni Lewenivanua (SDL) (Fiji United Party);* b. 4 Feb. 1941; m.; four s. one d. *Education:* Ratu Kadavulevu School, Queen Victoria School, Suva Boys' Grammar School, Univ. of Auckland, NZ, British Co-operative Coll., UK, Auckland Tech. Inst. *Career:* exec. cadet, Fijian Affairs Bd 1959–66, financial adviser 1979–99; joined Civil Service 1967, Co-operative Officer 1, Co-operatives Dept 1967–68, Asst Registrar of Co-operatives 1969–70, Sr Asst Registrar 1971–72, Chief Asst Registrar 1973–75, Registrar 1976–78; Deputy Sec. of Finance 1978–79; Perm. Sec. for Commerce and Industry 1979–80; Sec. of the Public Service Comm. 1980–83; Prime Minister and Minister for Nat. Reconciliation and Unity July 2000–06 (resigned following Court of Appeal ruling that his Govt was illegal March 7th 2001, reappointed March 15th 2001, dismissed by Acting Pres. Commodore Voreqe Bainimarama in mil. takeover of Govt Dec. 2006), also fmrly Minister for Fijian Affairs, Culture and Heritage, Multi-Ethnic Affairs and Reform of the Sugar Industry; Founder and Leader, Soqosoqo Duavata ni Lewenivanua (SDL) (Fiji United Party) 2001–; Man. Dir Fiji Devt Bank 1983–97, Merchant Bank of Fiji 1997–2000; Chair. South Pacific Fertilizers Ltd 1985–86, Fiji Post & Telecommunications Ltd 1990–91, Fiji TV Ltd 1994–98; Dir Fiji Int. Telecommunication Ltd (FINTEL) 1978–79, Foods Pacific Ltd 1985–86, Fiji Forest Industries Ltd 1988–97, Carlton Brewery (Fiji) Ltd 1989–99, Unit Trust of Fiji 1990–99, Voko Industries Ltd 1993–97, Air Pacific Ltd 1996–98, Colonial Advisory Council 1996–99; Chair. Mavanu Investments Ltd, Qalitu Enterprises Ltd; Dir Mualevu Tikina Holdings Ltd, Yatu Lau Co. Ltd.
Address: Soqosoqo Duavata ni Lewenivanua (SDL) (Fiji United Party), c/o House of Representatives, Suva, Fiji (office).

QASIMI, HH Sheikh Saqr bin Muhammad al-, (Ruler of Ras al-Khaimah); United Arab Emirates; b. 1920. *Career:* Ruler of Ras Al-Khaimah 1948–; Chair. Rulers' Council of Trucial States –1971; mem. Supreme Council of UAE 1972–.
Address: The Ruler's Palace, Ras Al-Khaimah, United Arab Emirates.

QASIMI, HH Sheikh Sultan bin Muhammad al-, (Ruler of Sharjah), PhD; United Arab Emirates; b. 1 July 1939. *Education:* Cairo Univ. and Univs of Exeter and Durham, UK. *Career:* Minister of Educ., UAE 1972; Ruler of Sharjah 1972–; Chair. Sharjah Human Soc., Arab/African Symposium; mem. Arab Historians' Union; Fellow Durham Univ.; Hon. Fellow Centre for Middle Eastern and Islamic Studies 1992; Hon. LLD (Khartoum); Hon. DSc (Univ. of Agric., Faisalabad) 1983; Distinguished Personality Prize, Univ. of Exeter 1993. *Publications:* The Myth of Arab Piracy in the Gulf, The Division of the Omani Empire, The Occupation of Aden, French-Omani Relations, The Arabian Documents in the French Archives, The White Shaikh, The Rebellious Prince, The Return of Holako, Power Struggles and Trade in the Gulf, The Gulf in Historic Maps.
Address: Ruler's Palace, Sharjah, United Arab Emirates.

QAZI, Ashraf Jehangir, MA; Pakistani diplomatist; *Special Representative of the Secretary-General for Sudan, United Nations;* b. 1942; m.; two c. *Career:* with Foreign Service of Pakistan 1965–; Amb. to Germany 1990–91, to Russia 1991–94, to People's Repub. of China 1994–97; High Commr to India 1997–2001; Amb. to USA 2002–04; Special Rep. of the UN Sec.-Gen. for Iraq 2004–07, for Sudan 2007–.
Address: United Nations Assistance Mission for Sudan (UNMIS), Ebeid Khatim Street, PO Box 69, Khartoum, 11111, Sudan (office). *Telephone:*

(187) 086000 (office). *Fax:* (917) 3673523 (office). *Website:* www.unmis.org (office).

QIRBI, Abu Bakr Abdallah al-, BSc, MB, ChB, FRCP, FRCPath, FRCP (C); Yemeni diplomatist and medical consultant; *Minister of Foreign Affairs;* b. 6 June 1941, Aden; m.; two s. *Education:* Aden Coll.; Edinburgh Univ. and Univ. of London, UK. *Career:* Prof. of Clinical Pathology, San'a Univ., Dean Faculty of Science 1979–83, Faculty of Medicine 1982–87, Univ. Vice-Rector 1982–83; Minister of Educ. 1993–94; mem. Consultative Council 1997–2001; Minister of Foreign Affairs 2001–, of Immigrants' Affairs 2006–07; Chair. People's Charitable Soc. 1995–; has made several radio and TV programmes on educ., scientific research, non-governmental work, charity and medical topics; Yemen Unification Medal; WHO Scholarship for Postgraduate Study. *Publications:* author of book on political and development issues in Yemen; more than 40 papers on the biological effects of clinical chemistry, renal disease, gastro-intestinal diseases and numerous papers on politics and social affairs.
Address: PO Box 11351, San'a, Yemen (office). *Telephone:* (1) 276555 (office). *Fax:* (1) 276618 (office). *E-mail:* aqirbi@hotmail.com (office). *Website:* www.mofa.gov.ye (office).

QOMI, Hassan Kazemi; Iranian diplomatist; *Ambassador to Iraq; Career:* fmr mem. Revolutionary Guard Corps' Quds Force; fmr Liaison of Revolutionary Guard to Hezbollah, Lebanon; Chargé d'affaires, then Amb. to Iraq 2006–.
Address: Embassy of Iran, POB 39095, Salehiya, Karadeh Maryam, Baghdad, Iraq (office). *Telephone:* (1) 884-3033 (office). *Fax:* (1) 537-5636 (office).

QUADRIO CURZIO, Alberto, Libera docenza; Italian economist and academic; *Professor of Economics, Università Cattolica del Sacro Cuore;* b. 25 Dec. 1937, Tirano-Valtellina. *Education:* Faculty of Political Sciences, Catholic Univ., Milan, St John's Coll., Cambridge, UK. *Career:* Assoc. Prof. of Econs, Univ. of Cagliari 1965–68; Assoc. Prof. of Econs, Univ. of Bologna 1968–72, Prof. 1972–75, Chair., Faculty of Political Sciences 1974–75; Prof. of Econs, Università Cattolica del Sacro Cuore, Milan 1976–, Dir Centre of Econ. Analysis 1977–, Chair. Faculty of Political Sciences 1989–; Dir Economia Politica (quarterly review) 1984–; mem. Italian Nat. Research Council 1977–88; Pres. Italian Econs Asscn 1995–98; mem. Reflection Group on Spiritual and Cultural Dimension of Europe est. by Pres. of EC 2002–04; Pres. Bd for Donato Menichella scholarships, Bank of Italy, Scientific Bd for Paolo Baffi Lectures, Bank of Italy; mem. Bd for European Investment Bank Prize 1995–2000; has delivered lectures at many Italian and foreign univs; speaker at many confs and seminars in Italy and abroad; mem. Istituto Lombardo, Accad. di Scienze e Lettere, Consult Stato Città Vaticano, Accad. Naz. dei Lincei; St Vincent Award 1984, W. Tobagi Award 1996, Cortina Ulisse Int. Award 1997, Italian Gold Medal for Contribs to Science and Culture 2000, Capri-San Michele for Econs 2003, Targa alla coerenta Zoli Foundation 2004, Cardano-Beccaria Int. Prize Rotary Pavia 2004, Assoc. Nuova Spoleto Award for Economy 2005. *Publications:* about 350, including (since 1980) Rent, Income Distribution, Order of Efficiency and Rentability 1980, The Gold Problem: Economic Perspectives 1982, Planning Manpower Education and Economic Growth 1983, Sui Momenti costitutivi della Economia Politica (co-author) 1983–84, Technological Scarcity: An Essay on Production and Structural Change 1986, The Exchange-Production Duality and the Dynamics of Economic Knowledge (co-author) 1986, Industrial Raw Materials: A Multi-Country, Multi-Commodity Analysis (co-author) 1986, The Agro-Technological System towards 2000: A European perspective (co-ed.) 1988, Produzione ed efficienza con tecnologie globali (co-author) 1987, Le scarsita relative 1988, Rent, Distribution and Economic Structure 1990, Structural Rigidities and Dynamic Choice of Technologies (co-author) 1991, Issues on International Development and Solidarity 1992, On Economic Science: Its Tools and Economic Reality 1993, The Management of Municipal Solid Waste in Europe: Economic, Technological and Environmental Perspectives (co-ed.) 1994, Innovation, Resources and Economic Growth (co-ed.) 1994, Risorse, Tecnologie, Rendita (co-author) 1996, Noi, l'Economia e l'Europa 1996, Rent Resources, Technology (co-author) 1999, Il Made in Italy oltre il 2000 2000, La Società Italiana degli Economisti 2000, Profili della Costituzione Europea 2001, Sussidiarieta e Sviluppo. Paradigmi per l'Europa e per

l'Italia 2002, Complexity and industrial clusters (co-ed.) 2002, Il Gruppo Edison: 1993–2003 (co-ed) 2003, La globalizzazione e i rapporti Nord-Est-Sud 2004, Research and Technological innovation (co-ed.) 2005, The World System in the 21st Century: Subsidiarity and Cooperation for Development (co-ed.) 2006, Research and Technological Innovation: The Challenge for a New Europe (co-ed.) 2006, Industria e Distretti. Un Paradigma di perdurante competitività italiana (co-ed.) 2006, Economisti ed Economia. Per un'Italia europea: paradigmi tra il XVIII e il XX secolo 2007, Intrapresa, sussidiarietà, sviluppo (co-ed.) 2007, Valorizzare un'economia forte. L'Italia e il ruolo della sussidiarietà (co-ed.) 2007.
Address: Facoltà di Scienze Politiche, Università Cattolica del Sacro Cuore, Largo Gemelli, 20123 Milan (office); Via A. Saffi 31, 20123 Milan, Italy (home). *Telephone:* (02) 72342474 (office). *Fax:* (02) 72342475 (office). *E-mail:* alberto.quadriocurzio@unicatt.it (office). *Website:* www.unicatt.it (office).

QUAYES, Mohamed Mijarul, MPA; Bangladeshi diplomatist; m. Naeema Chaudhury Quayes. *Education:* Univ. of Dhaka, Kennedy School of Govt, Harvard Univ., USA. *Career:* joined Foreign Service 1982; served in Missions in Tokyo, Geneva and Singapore; Dir Gen., Ministry of Foreign Affairs 2001–05; High Commr to the Maldives 2005–08; Edward S. Mason Fellow in Public Policy and Man., Harvard Inst. for Int. Devt.
Address: c/o Ministry of Foreign Affairs, Segunbagicha, Dhaka 1000, Bangladesh.

QUAYLE, Quinton Mark; British diplomatist; *Ambassador to Thailand;* b. 5 June 1955; m. Alison Quayle; two s. *Education:* School of Oriental and African Studies, London and École Nationale d'Admin, Paris. *Career:* joined FCO 1977, Cen. and Southern African Dept 1977–78, full-time language training 1979–80, Second Sec., Chancery, Bangkok 1980–83, S America Dept, FCO 1983–84, Trade Relations and Exports Dept 1984–85, First Sec., Chancery, Paris 1987–91, Deputy Head, EC Dept (External), FCO 1991–93, Dir Jt Export Promotion Directorate 1994–96, Deputy Head of Mission, Jakarta 1996–99, Int. Group Dir British Trade Int., Trade Pnrs UK 1999–2002, language training in Iasi 2002, Amb. to Romania 2002–07, to Thailand (also accred to Laos) 2007–; Sr Consultant, Price Waterhouse 1993–94.
Address: British Embassy, 14 Thanon Witthayu, Lumpini, Pathumwan, Bangkok 10330, Thailand (office). *Telephone:* (2) 305-8333 (office). *Fax:* (2) 255-8619 (office). *E-mail:* info.bangkok@fco.gov.uk (office). *Website:* www.britishembassy.gov.uk/Thailand (office).

QUETA, Adelino Mano, BA; Guinea-Bissau diplomatist; *Diplomatic Affairs Adviser, Ministry of Foreign Affairs, International Co-operation and Communities;* b. 23 June 1941, Mansoa; m.; three c. *Education:* Lisbon Tech. Univ., Portugal. *Career:* Sec.-Gen. Ministry of Economy and Finance 1981–84, Ministry of Public Works, Construction and Town Planning 1984–85; State Prosecutor 1985; Deputy Exec. Sec. ECOWAS 1985–89; Amb. to Spain, Italy, Portugal, Morocco 1989–95; Perm. Rep. to UN, New York 1995–97; Amb. to Taiwan 1997–98; Diplomatic Affairs Adviser, Ministry of Foreign Affairs, Int. Co-operation and Communities 2003–; Lecturer, Faculty of Law, Bissau; unsuccessful cand. for Pres. 2005.
Address: c/o Ministry of Foreign Affairs, International Co-operation and Communities, Rua Gen. Omar Torrijo, Bissau, Guinea-Bissau (office). *Telephone:* 204301 (office). *Fax:* 202378 (office).

QUEYRANNE, Jean-Jack; French politician; b. 2 Nov. 1945, Lyon. *Career:* First Deputy Mayor of Villeurbanne (Rhône) 1977–88; Parti Socialiste (PS) mem. Rhône Gen. Council 1979–90, Regional Council Rhône-Alps 1986–2002, Pres. 2004–; Nat. Ass. Deputy (alt.) for Rhone 1981–93; mem. PS Steering Cttee, Deputy Nat. Sec. responsible for cultural policy 1983, for press and culture 1985, Party Spokesman 1985, Nat. Del. and Spokesman 1987, Nat. Sec. responsible for audiovisual policy 1988, mem. Nat. Council 1993–94; Mayor of Bron (Rhône) 1989–97, Deputy Mayor 1997–2004; Nat. Ass. Deputy for Rhône 1997–; Minister of State attached to Minister of the Interior, with responsibility for Overseas Depts and Territories 1997–2000; Minister of Relations with Parliament 2000–02.
Address: 1 rue Roger Salengro, 69500 Bron (office); Assemblée nationale, 126 rue de l'Université, 75355 Paris 07 SP, France (office). *Telephone:* 4-72-37-50-99 (office). *Fax:* 4-72-37-58-87 (office). *E-mail:* jjqueyranne@assemblee-nationale.fr (office). *Website:* www.assemblee-nationale.fr (office).

QUIJANO CAPURRO, José Manuel; Uruguayan economist and international organization official; *Director, Mercosur; Career:* Dir Consultora Alianza Cooperativa Cooperativa Internacional, ACI, Uruguay; Advisor, Perm. Secr., Sistema Economico Latinoamericana (SELA) c. 2001; fmr consultant with Integración AFAP, Montevideo; mem. Mercosur Sectoral Comm., Dir Mercosur Secr. 2008–.

Address: Secretaría del Mercosur, Código Postal 11.200, Dr Luis Piera 1992, 1º Piso – Edificio MERCOSUR, Montevideo, Uruguay (office). *Telephone:* (2) 412-9024 (office). *Fax:* (2) 418-0557 (office). *E-mail:* secretaria@mercosur.org.uy (office). *Website:* www.mercosur.int (office).

QUILÈS, Paul; French politician; *Mayor, Cordes-sur-Ciel (Tarn);* b. 27 Jan. 1942, St Denis du Sig, Algeria; m. Josephe-Marie Bureau 1964; three d. *Education:* Ecole Polytechnique, Paris. *Career:* engineer, Shell Française 1964–78; Socialist Deputy to Nat. Ass. 1978–83, 1986–88, 1993–; Minister of Town Planning and Housing 1983–85, of Transport 1984–85, of Defence 1985–86, of Posts, Telecommunications and Space 1988–91, of Public Works, Housing, Transportation and Space Research 1991–92, of the Interior and Public Security 1992–93; Chair. Nat. Defence and Armed Forces Comm. 1997–2002; Mayor of Cordes-sur-Ciel (Tarn) 1995–; mem. Econ. and Social Council 1974–75; mem. Foreign Affairs Comm. 2002–. *Publications:* La Politique n'est pas ce que vous croyez 1985, Nous vivons une époque intéressante 1992, Les 577, Un parlement pour quoi faire 2001, Face aux désordres du monde 2005.
Address: Assemblée nationale, 75355 Paris, France. *Telephone:* (1) 40-63-68-99 (office). *Fax:* (1) 40-63-52-52 (office).

QUINLAN, Sir Michael Edward, Kt, GCB, MA; British civil servant (retd); b. 11 Aug. 1930, Hampton; m. Mary Finlay 1965; two s. two d. *Education:* Wimbledon Coll. and Merton Coll., Oxford. *Career:* civil servant 1954–92; Air Ministry 1954–64; Ministry of Defence 1964–70; Defence Counsellor, UK Del. to NATO 1970–73; Under-Sec. Cabinet Office 1974–77; Deputy Under-Sec. of State (Policy and Programmes), Ministry of Defence 1977–81; Deputy Sec. (Industry), Treasury 1981–82; Perm. Sec. Dept of Employment 1983–88; Perm. Under-Sec. of State, Ministry of Defence 1988–92; Dir Ditchley Foundation 1992–99; Dir Lloyds Bank 1992–95, Lloyds TSB Group 1996–98, Pilkington PLC 1992–99; Visiting Prof., King's Coll. London 1992–95, 2002–; Consulting Sr Fellow, IISS 2004–06; Trustee Science Museum 1992–2001; Public Policy Scholar Woodrow Wilson Center 2000. *Publications:* Thinking About Nuclear Weapons 1997, European Defence Co-operation 2001, Just War–The Just War Tradition: Ethics in Modern Warfare (with Charles Guthrie) 2007; numerous articles on defence issues and public service issues.
Address: 3 Adderbury Park, West Adderbury, Banbury, Oxon., OX17 3EN, England (home). *Telephone:* (1295) 812951 (home). *Fax:* (1295) 812951 (home). *E-mail:* michael527quinlan@btinternet.com (home).

QUINN, Martin, BA; Australian diplomatist; *Ambassador to Afghanistan;* m.; four c. *Education:* Univ. of Sydney. *Career:* served as Third Sec., Embassy in Bangkok 1987–91, First Sec., Embassy in Jakarta 1993–95; worked on Australia's first White Paper on Foreign and Trade Policy 1996–97; Counsellor (Political), Embassy in Seoul –2008, Amb. to Afghanistan 2008–; mem. negotiation and implementation team Australia–US Free Trade Agreement (AUSFTA) 2003–05.
Address: Embassy of Australia, c/o Serena Hotel, Froshgah Street, Kabul, Afghanistan (office); Department of Foreign Affairs and Trade, R. G. Casey Building, John McEwen Crescent, Barton, ACT 0221, Australia. *Telephone:* (79) 9654840 (Afghanistan) (office); (2) 6261-1111 (Australia). *Website:* www.dfat.gov.au/homs/af.html.

QUINN, Ruairi, BArch, RIBA; Irish politician, architect and town planner; *Labour Party Spokesperson on Enterprise, Trade and Employment;* b. 2 April 1946, Dublin; m. 1st Nicola Underwood 1969 (divorced) one s. one d.; m. 2nd Liz Allman 1990; one s. *Education:* Blackrock Coll. and Univ. Coll., Dublin, Athens Center of Ekistics, Greece. *Career:* Athens Center of Ekistics, Greece 1970–71; Architects' Dept, Dublin Corpn 1971–73; Partner, Burke-Kennedy Doyle and Partner 1973–82; mem. Dublin Corpn 1974–77, 1981–82; mem. Seanad Éireann 1976–77, 1981–82; mem. Dáil Éireann 1977–81, 1982–; Minister of State, Dept of the Environment 1982–83; Minister for Labour and Minister for the Public Service 1983–87; Deputy Leader Irish Labour Party 1989, Leader 1997–2002; Treas. Party of European Socialists 2000–, also Vice-Pres.; Dir of Elections for Pres. Mary Robinson (q.v.); Labour Spokesperson on Finance and Econ. Affairs 1990, on European Affairs, on Enterprise, Trade and Employment 2006–; Minister for Enterprise and Employment 1993–94, for Finance 1994–97; mem. Royal Inst. of the Architects of Ireland. *Publication:* Straight Left: A Journey in Politics 2005.
Address: Dáil Éireann, Kildare Street, Dublin 2 (office); 23 Strand Road, Sandymount, Dublin 4, Ireland (home). *Telephone:* (1) 6183434 (office). *Fax:* (1) 6184153 (office). *E-mail:* ruairi.quinn@oireachtas.ie (office). *Website:* www.ruairiquinn.ie (office).

QUIÑÓNEZ, Alfonso, MA; Guatemalan lawyer, diplomatist and international organization executive; *Executive Secretary for Integral Development and Director General, Inter-American Agency for Co-operation and Development; Education:* Francisco Marroquín Univ. of Guatemala,

Georgetown Univ., Washington, DC, Univ. of Maryland, Inter-American Defense Coll., Washington, DC. *Career:* Professor, Schools of Law and International Relations, Francisco Marroquín Univ. 2001–02; mem. Guatemalan Foreign Service for ten years, held positions of Counsellor in Spain, Minister Counsellor in USA, Amb. and Perm. Rep. to OAS 1998–2000; Exec. Dir Alvaro Arzú Foundation for Peace, Guatemala and Advisor to Mayor of Guatemala City –2001; Dir Dept of Co-operation Policies, OAS 2001, later Dir Office of Policies and Programs for Devt, OAS Exec. Secr. for Integral Devt, later Chief of Staff to Asst Sec.-Gen., Acting Exec. Sec. for Integral Devt and Acting Dir-Gen. Inter-American Agency for Integral Devt 2004–05, Exec. Sec. for Integral Devt and Dir-Gen. Inter-American Agency for Co-operation and Devt 2005–.
Address: Inter-American Agency for Co-operation and Development, 17th Street and Constitution Avenue, NW, Washington, DC 20006, USA (office). *Telephone:* (202) 458-3000 (office). *Fax:* (202) 458-6319 (office). *E-mail:* diad@oas.org (office). *Website:* www.oas.org (office).

QUIÑÓNEZ ABARCA, Anibal Enrique; Honduran diplomatist and international organization official; b. 7 Jan. 1950, Tegucigalpa; m.; four c. *Education:* Univ. Nacional Autónoma de Honduras, Univ. de El Salvador. *Career:* entered Honduran Foreign Service 1973; First Sec. in charge of Consular Affairs, Embassy in Argentina 1973–77, Embassy in Uruguay (concurrent with Paraguay) 1977–78; Amb. to Uruguay and Paraguay 1981–83, to Japan (concurrently to Singapore, Thailand, Brunei, Korea and the Philippines) 1983–85, to Japan 1985–94; Dir-Gen. Foreign Politics, Secr. of External Relations 1996–98; Consul to Greece 1999–2002; Under-Sec. of State, Office of External Relations 2002–04; Sec.-Gen. System of Cen. American Integration (SICA) 2005–08; Great Cross of Diplomatic Merit (Repub. of Korea), Order of the Rising Sun (Japan), Gran Cruz Placa de Oro de la Orden de Mayo al Mérito (Argentina), Order of the Shining Star (Taiwan), Order of Civil Merit (Spain), Order of Merit (Chile), Order of Morazán (Honduras); Hon. Diploma, Honduran Coll. of Advocates.
Address: c/o Sistema de la Integración Centroamericana y su Secretaría General, Blv. Orden de Malta No. 470, Urb. Santa Elena, Antigua Cuscatlán, El Salvador, CA, Argentina (office). *E-mail:* info@sgsica.org (office). *Website:* www.sgsica.org (office).

QUIROGA, Ernesto Araníbar, BA; Bolivian diplomatist and fmr politician; b. 24 Jan. 1951, Cochabamba; m. *Education:* Catholic Univ. of Louvain, Belgium. *Career:* economist Nat. Council of Higher Educ. 1978; fmr Prof., Faculty of Econs, Univ. of City of San Andres, La Paz; Minister of Finance 1982–83; Minister of Planning and Devt 1984; fmr Sec.-Gen. Fomento

Andina Corpn, Venezuela; Sr Regional Adviser, Regional Office for Latin America and the Caribbean, UNICEF 1988–93; consultant Market Access and Poverty Alleviation Section, USAID 2003; Perm. Rep. to UN, New York Nov. 2003–07. *Publications:* several books on econs and devt for Latin American region.
Address: c/o Ministry of Foreign Affairs and Worship, Calle Ingavi, esq. Junín, La Paz, Bolivia (office). *Website:* www.rree.gov.bo (office).

QURAY, Ahmad, (Abu Ala); Palestinian diplomatist and politician; b. 1937, Abu Dis. *Career:* joined Fatah (largest political group within PLO) 1968, currently mem. Revolutionary Council Cen. Cttee; fmr Minister of Economy and Trade and Minister of Industry, Palestinian Authority; Chief Palestinian Negotiator, Oslo Agreement 1993 and all subsequent Israeli–Palestinian talks including Taba, Cairo, Wye River, and talks in 2007; Deputy and Speaker Palestinian Legis. Council 1996–2003; Prime Minister, Palestinian Authority (PA) 2003–05 (resgnd), Head Nat. Security Council 2004–05; mem. Palestinian Nat. Council; mem. Bd Palestinian Econ. Policy Research Inst., Peres Center for Peace; mem. Bd of Advisers Gleitsman Foundation; Norwegian Royal Order of Merit 1994, Seeds of Peace Foundation Award 1996, Gleitsman Foundation Int. Activist Award 1999. *Publications include:* Hanging Peace; numerous economic essays.
Address: c/o Palestinian Authority, Jericho Area, West Bank, Palestinian Autonomous Areas. *E-mail:* info@gov.ps. *Website:* www.pna.net.

QURESHI, Makhdoom Shah Mehmu, BA, MA; Pakistani politician; *Minister of Foreign Affairs, with additional charge of Petroleum and Natural Resources;* b. 22 June 1966, Murree. *Education:* Aitchison Coll., Lahore, Forman Christian Coll., Lahore, Corpus Christi Coll., Cambridge, UK. *Career:* grew up in Multan; returned to Pakistan following law studies in UK 1983; elected to Prov. Ass. 1985; contested and won local, prov. and nat. elections from his home constituency in Multan; has served as Minister for Planning and Devt Punjab, Minister of Finance, Punjab, and Fed. Minister for Parl. Affairs in Govt of Benazir Bhutto; also served as Chair. Dist Council for Multan and first Dist Nazim under Musharraf admin; represented Pakistan People's Party (PPP) Punjab as their prime ministerial cand. 2002; sr mem. PPP and Pres. PPP Punjab; cand. for Prime Minister Feb. 2008; Minister of Foreign Affairs, with additional charge of Petroleum and Natural Resources 2008–.
Address: Ministry of Foreign Affairs, Constitution Avenue, Islamabad, Pakistan (office). *Telephone:* (51) 9210335 (office). *Fax:* (51) 9207600 (office). *E-mail:* sadiq@mofa.gov.pk (office). *Website:* www.mofa.gov.pk (office).

R

RA, Jong-yil, PhD; South Korean academic, university administrator and fmr diplomatist; *President, Woosuk University;* b. 5 Dec. 1940; m.; one s. three d. *Education:* Seoul Nat. Univ., Trinity Coll., Univ. of Cambridge, UK. *Career:* held teaching posts at several univs including Kyunghee, Southern Calif., Mich. and Stanford, USA, Cambridge and Sussex, UK; Dir Nat. Intelligence Service 1998–99; fmr mem. Exec. Cttee and fmr Dir-Gen., Millennium Democratic Party (MDP); fmr Special Asst to Pres. for Foreign and Security Affairs; Amb. to UK 2001–03; Sr Adviser to Pres. for Nat. Security 2003; Amb. to Japan 2004–07; Pres. Woosuk Univ. 2007–. *Publications include:* Politics of Western Europe 1982, Cooperation and Conflict 1986, The New Right 1990, Perestroika and its Impacts 1991, Points of Departure 1992, Unfinished War 1994, Man and Politics 1995, In Preparation for the New Millennium 1999, Advantage of Hindsight 2001, Conflict and Resolution in the Korean Church 2002. *Address:* Office of the President, Woosuk University, 585–701 490 Hujeong-ri, Samrye-eup, Wanju-kun, Jeollabuk-do, 565-701, Republic of Korea (office). *Telephone:* (63) 290-1114 (office). *Fax:* (63) 291-9312 (office). *Website:* wwws.woosuk.ac.kr (office).

RABBANI, Burhanuddin; Afghan politician and academic; *Leader, Jamiat-i-Islami;* b. 1940, Faizabad, Badakhshan Prov. *Education:* Kabul Univ., Al Azhar Univ., Cairo. *Career:* fmr Lecturer in Islamic Law, Kabul Univ.; Pres. United Nat. Islamic Front for the Salvation of Afghanistan (UNIFSA) (also known as Northern Alliance); leader Jamiat-i Islami (Islamic Soc.) 1971–; left Afghanistan 1974; made armed raids against govt of Mohammed Daoud from base in Pakistan; returned to Afghanistan 1992; elected Pres. of Afghanistan by Mujahidin Exec. Council 1992; forced to step down when Taliban occupied Kabul 1996; continued to be recognized as Pres. of Islamic State of Afghanistan by UN –2001; currently Leader Jamiat-i Islami party. *Address:* Jamiat-i-Islami, Karte Parwan, Phase 2, Badaam Bagh, Afghanistan (office). *Telephone:* (70) 278950.

RABEMANANJARA, Gen. Charles; Malagasy politician; *Prime Minister and Minister of the Interior;* b. June 1947, Antananarivo. *Career:* fmr top policemen, then Head of Gen. Armoured Corps; Dir Presidential Security Cabinet 2004–05; Minister of the Interior and Admin. Reform 2005–, Prime Minister 2007–. *Address:* Office of the Prime Minister, BP 248, Mahazoarivo, 101 Antananarivo, Madagascar (office). *Telephone:* (20) 2264498 (office). *Fax:* (20) 2233116 (office). *E-mail:* dircom@primature.gov.mg (office). *Website:* www.primature.gov.mg (office).

RABY, Geoffrey William, BEc, MEc, PhD; Australian diplomatist; *Ambassador to The People's Republic of China;* b. Sept. 1953, Melbourne. *Education:* La Trobe Univ. *Career:* fmr Sr Tutor in Econs, La Trobe Univ.; trade policy adviser, Office of Nat. Assessments 1984–86, to Minister for Trade 1993; served twice as Head, Econ. Section, Embassy in Beijing 1986–91; est. Northeast Asia Analytical Unit, Dept of Foreign Affairs and Trade (DFAT) 1991, Head of Unit 1991–93; other sr positions at DFAT include First Asst Sec., Trade Negotiations Div. 1995–98, First Asst Sec., Int. Orgs and Legal Div. 2001–02, Deputy Sec. DFAT 2002–06; Head, Trade Policy Issues Div., OECD, Paris 1993–95, Perm. Rep. to WTO, Geneva 1998–2001; Amb. to APEC, Singapore 2002–04; Amb. to The People's Repub. of China (also accred to Mongolia and North Korea) 2007–. *Address:* Embassy of Australia, 21 Dong Zhi Men Wai Dajie, San Li Tun, Beijing 100600, People's Republic of China (office). *Telephone:* (10) 51404111 (office). *Fax:* (10) 51404450 (office). *E-mail:* pubaff@dfat.gov .au (office). *Website:* www.china.embassy.gov.au (office).

RACHDI, Allal; Moroccan civil servant and international organization executive; *Director-General, Islamic Centre for the Development of Trade;* b. 17 June 1951. *Education:* Grande Ecole of Public Admin, Faculty of Law (Political Sciences), Certificate of Trade Policy, GATT, Geneva. *Career:* sr civil servant at Ministry of Foreign Trade since 1978, participated in devt and implementation of Structural Adjustment programmes, also took part in bilateral and multilateral trade negotiations, particularly in negotiations for accession of Morocco to GATT, co-operation and asscn agreements of Morocco with EU, Uruguay Round negotiations as well as negotiations of several free trade agreements, Dir Foreign Trade Policy, Ministry of Foreign Trade 1994–2000, Co-ordinator at Gen. Secr.; Chair. Nat. Comm. of Foreign Trade Facilitation 1986–2000, Nat. Imports Consultative Comm. 1992–2000; Admin., Common Fund for Commodities, Amsterdam 1998–2000, Moroccan Exports Asscn; mem. Jt Cttee of Pvt./Public Sector; Dir-Gen. Islamic Centre for the Devt of Trade, OIC 2000–. *Address:* Islamic Centre for the Development of Trade, Tours des Habous, Avenue des FAR, BP 13545, Casablanca – Principal 20000, Morocco (office). *Telephone:* (2) 314974 (office). *Fax:* (2) 310110 (office). *E-mail:* icdt@icdt-oic.org (office). *Website:* www.icdt-oic.org (office).

RACZKO, Andrzej, DEcons; Polish economist; *Alternate Executive Director (Poland), International Monetary Fund;* b. 27 Feb. 1953, Kutno; m.; two c. *Education:* Univ. of Łódź. *Career:* early career as Asst, then Asst Prof., Inst. of Econs, Univ. of Łódź 1977–86; Chief Specialist on Foreign Cooperation, Łódźkie Towarzystwo Kredytowe Bank SA 1992–93; Econ. Dir Petrobank SA 1993–97, mem. Man. Bd LG Petro Bank SA 1995–97, Dir 1997–99; Man. Mortgage Team, PKO Bank Polski SA 1999–2001; Under-Sec. of State, Ministry of Finance 2001–02, Minister of Finance 2003–04; mem. Bd of Dirs Bank Gospodarki Żywnościowej SA 2002–03; fmr mem. EU negotiating team; fmr Vice-Gov. IMF, Alt. Exec. Dir (Poland) 2004–; fmr Co-Chair. Public Debt Cttee. *Address:* Office of the Alternate Executive Director (Poland), International Monetary Fund, 700 19th Street, NW, Washington, DC 20431, USA (office). *Telephone:* (202) 623-7300 (office). *Fax:* (202) 623-6278 (office). *E-mail:* publicaffairs@imf.org (office). *Website:* www.imf.org (office).

RADAVIDSON, Benjamin Andriamparany; Malagasy politician; *Minister of National Education and Scientific Research; Career:* Minister of the Economy, Finance and the Budget 2002–07, of Nat. Educ. and Scientific Research 2007–; mem. Bd of Govs IMF. *Address:* Ministry of National Education and Scientific Research, BP 247, Anosy, 101 Antananarivo, Madagascar (office). *Telephone:* (20) 2224308 (office). *Fax:* (20) 2223897 (office). *E-mail:* mlraharimalala@yahoo.fr (office).

RADEBE, Jeffrey (Jeff) Thamsanqa, LLB; South African politician; *Minister of Transport;* b. 18 Feb. 1953, Cato Manor; m. Bridget Radebe; three c. *Education:* Isibonelo High School, Univ. of Zululand, Leipzig Univ., Germany, Lenin Int. School, Moscow. *Career:* joined Black Consciousness Movt 1970; Co-Founder Kwamashu Youth Org. 1972; articled clerk with A. J. Gumede & Phyllis Naidoo, E. S. Mchunu & Co. 1976–77; with Radio Freedom 1977–78; Deputy Chief African Nat. Congress (ANC) Rep., Tanzania 1981; headed clandestine political movt of ANC and South African Communist Party (SACP) 1986, Head Political Dept and Co-ordinator of 12 day hunger strike on Robben Island; arrested and sentenced to ten years on Robben Island 1986, sentence reduced to six years, released 1990; Sec. interim leadership group of SACP 1990–91; Deputy Chair. ANC Southern Natal Region 1990–91, Chair. 1991–94; Minister of Public Works, Govt of Nat. Unity 1994–99, of Public Enterprises 1999–2004, currently Minister of Transport, also currently mem. ANC Nat. Exec. Cttee (NEC) and Nat. Working Cttee, Head ANC Policy Unit and NEC Convener in North West Prov.; Hon. LLM (Leipzig); Dr hc (Chicago State Univ.) 1996. *Address:* Ministry of Transport, 159 Forum Bldg, 159 Struben Street, Pretoria 0002 Private Bag X193, Pretoria 0001, South Africa (office). *Telephone:* (12) 3093000 (office). *Fax:* (12) 3285926 (office). *E-mail:* khozac@dot.gov.za (office). *Website:* www.transport.gov.za (office).

RADIFERA, Jocelyn Bertin, BA; Malagasy diplomatist; *Ambassador to USA;* b. 20 Feb. 1940; m. Erna Lisa Radifera. *Education:* Howard Univ., USA, School of Banking, Banque Nationale de Paris, France, Harvard Univ., USA. *Career:* trainee in commercial and investment banking, Banque Nationale de Paris 1965–67; Leading Officer, Banque Nationale de l'Ocean Indien (Madagascar) 1967–69; Sr Financial Officer, Securities Div., Treasury Vice-Pres.'s Office, World Bank Financial Operations Dept, Washington, DC, USA 1969–74, Prin. Financial Officer 1974–81, Div. Chief 1981–97, Deputy Dir World Bank Tokyo Office, Japan 1992–97, financial and investment consultant/adviser, World Bank 1997–2003; Amb. to Japan 2003–07 (also accred to Singapore 2005–07), to USA 2007–.

Address: Embassy of Madagascar, 2374 Massachusetts Avenue, NW, Washington, DC 20008, USA (office). *Telephone:* (202) 265-5525 (office). *Fax:* (202) 265-3034 (office). *E-mail:* malagasy.embassy@verizon.net (office). *Website:* www.embassy.org/madagascar (office).

RADMANOVIĆ, Nebojša; Bosnia and Herzegovina politician; *Member of the Tripartite State Presidency;* b. 1 Oct. 1949, Gračanica; m.; two c. *Education:* Faculty of Philosophy, Univ. of Belgrade. *Career:* has held numerous positions in culture and state admin including Dir Bosanska Krajina Archives and Archives of Republika Srpska, Dir Nat. Theatre of Republika Srpska, Banja Luka, Dir and Ed.-in-Chief GLAS, Pres. Exec. Bd Town of Banja Luka, Rep. Nat. Ass., Republika Srpska and Minister of Admin and Local Self-Man.; Serb mem. Tripartite State Presidency 2006–, Chair. 2006–07; mem. Alliance of Ind. Social Democrats. *Publications include:* several books and scientific papers.
Address: Office of the State Presidency, 71000 Sarajevo, Musala 5, Bosnia and Herzegovina (office). *Telephone:* (33) 664941 (office). *Fax:* (33) 472491 (office). *Website:* www.predsjednistvobih.ba (office).

RAFAJLOVSKA, Vera, BEcons; Macedonian economist and government official; *Minister of the Economy;* b. 25 Feb. 1947, Bitola. *Education:* Univs of Bitola and Skopje. *Career:* Asst Dir and Pnr, V&F Centre for Econ. and Legal Consulting, Skopje 1991–98; Dir Rafajlovski Consulting DOO 1998–2000, Rafajlovski Revizija DOO 2000–; Minister of the Economy 2006–; fmr Ed.-in-Chief, Economic and Legal Adviser magazine; mem. NSDP party. *Publications:* author and co-author of several books in accounting, taxation, int. financial reporting.
Address: Ministry of the Economy, Bote Bocevski 9, 1000 Skopje (office); Jurij Gargarin 15, Skopje, Macedonia (office). *Telephone:* (2) 384470 (office). *Fax:* (2) 384472 (office). *E-mail:* minister@economy.gov.mk (office); ms@mt.net.mk (office). *Website:* www.ms.gov.mk (office); www .rafajlovski.com.mk (office).

RAFFARIN, Jean-Pierre; French politician; b. 3 Aug. 1948, Poitiers; m. Anne-Marie Perrier 1980; one d. *Education:* Lycée Henri IV, Poitiers, Faculté de Droit, Paris-Assas, Ecole Supérieure de Commerce, Paris. *Career:* Marketing Dept Cafés Jacques Vabre 1973–76; Adviser, Office of Minister of Labour 1976–81; Pres. Crédit Immobilier Rural de la Vienne 1978–95; Lecturer, Inst. d'Etudes Politiques, Paris 1979–88; Dir-Gen. Bernard Krief Communication 1981–88; Gen. Del. Inst. Euro-92 1988–89; Nat. Del., Deputy Sec.-Gen. and mem. Political Bureau, Parti Républicain 1977–2002; City Councillor, Poitiers 1977–95; Conseiller Régional 1986–88; Pres. Conseil Régional, Poitou-Charentes 1988–2002; mem. European Parl. 1989–95; Deputy Sec.-Gen. and Spokesman for Union pour la Démocratie Française 1993, Sec.-Gen. 1995–2002, mem. Union Pour Un Mouvement Populaire 2002–; Pres. Comm. Arc Atlantique 1994–1998; Minister of Small and Medium-Sized Businesses, of Commerce and Craft Industry 1995–97; mem. Senate (for Vienne) 1995, 1997–2002, 2005–; Vice Mayor of Chasseneuil-du-Poitou 1995–2001; Vice-Pres. Démocratie Libérale 1997–; Pres. Asscn des régions de France 1998–2002; Prime Minister of France 2002–05; Chevalier, Légion d'honneur, Grand Croix, Ordre national du Mérite, Officier, Ordre national du Québec (Canada). *Publications:* La vie en jaune 1977, La publicité nerf de la communication 1983, L'avenir a ses racines 1986, Nous sommes tous les régionaux 1988, Pour une morale de l'action 1992, Le livre de l'Atlantique 1994, Notre Contrat pour l'Alternance 2001, La Nouvelle Gouvernance 2002, La France de Mai 2003, La dernière marche 2007.
Address: Senat, 15 rue de Vaugirard, 75291 Paris Cedex 06; Union pour un Mouvement Populaire, 55 rue La Boétie 75384 Paris Cedex 08 (office); 7 route de Saint-Georges, 86360 Chasseneuil-du-Poitou, France (home). *Telephone:* 1-42-34-20-00 (Senat) (office); 1-40-76-60-00 (UMP) (office). *Fax:* 1-42-34-26-77 (office). *E-mail:* jpr@carnetjpr.com (office). *Website:* www.senat.fr (office); www.carnetjpr.com.

RAFFENNE, Gen. Jean-Paul; French army officer (retd); *Professor and Director, Senior Executive Seminar, College of International and Security Studies, George C. Marshall Center European Center for Security Studies;* b. 1944. *Career:* Liaison Officer, Fort Leavenworth, USA 1990–92; Deputy Defence Attaché, Embassy in Washington, DC 1994–96; Head, French Del. to EU Mil. Cttee 2001; Chief French Liaison Officer in unit directing Operation Enduring Freedom (mil. campaign in Afghanistan), Tampa, Fla., USA 2001; Head, Direction du renseignement militaire (mil. intelligence agency) 2002; currently Prof. and Dir, Sr Exec. Seminar, George C. Marshall Center European Center for Security Studies, Germany.
Address: George C. Marshall Center, Gernackerstrasse 2, 82467 Garmisch-Partenkirchen, Germany (office). *Telephone:* (8821) 750-2680 (office). *E-mail:* cisscontact@marshallcenter.org (office). *Website:* www .marshallcenter.org (office).

RAFSANJANI, Hojatoleslam Ali Akhbar Hashemi; Iranian ecclesiastic and politician; *Chairman, Assembly of Experts;* b. 25 Aug. 1934, Rafsanjan, Kerman prov. *Education:* Qom. *Career:* Speaker, Islamic Consultative Ass. 1980–89; MP –2000; Founding mem. Islamic Repub. Party; Acting C-in-C of the Armed Forces 1988–89; Vice-Chair. Cttee to revise the Constitution 1989; Pres. of the Islamic Repub. of Iran 1989–97; Chair. Expediency Council of Iran 2002–; mem. Ass. of Experts (Majlis-E-Khobregan) representing Tehran, Vice Chair. and First Deputy Speaker 2006–07, Chair. 2007–.
Address: Expediency Council, POB 13165-311, Pastor Street, Tehran, Iran. *E-mail:* info@maslahat.ir. *Website:* www.maslehat.ir; www .hashemirafsanjani.ir.

RAGHUNATH, Krishnan; Indian diplomatist; b. 11 Nov. 1939; m. *Career:* joined Foreign Service 1962; various overseas posts including Hong Kong 1963–65, Beijing 1965–67, San Francisco 1969–72, Moscow 1978–79; Joint Sec. E Europe Div. 1982–86; Amb. to Philippines 1986–89; High Commr to Nigeria 1989–92, to Bangladesh 1992–95; Sec. Ministry of External Affairs 1995–97, Foreign Sec. 1997–99; Amb. to Russian Fed. 2001–04.
Address: c/o Ministry of External Affairs, South Block, New Delhi, 110 011, India (office).

RAGNEMALM, Hans, LLD; Swedish judge; *Juris Ombudsman;* b. 30 March 1940, Laholm; m. Vivi Ragnemalm 1961. *Career:* Assoc. Prof. of Public Law, Univ. of Lund 1970–75; Prof. of Public Law, Univ. of Stockholm 1975–87, Dean, Faculty of Law 1984–87; Parl. Ombudsman 1987–92; Judge, Supreme Admin. Court 1992–94, Justice 1999, Pres. 2000–05; currently Juris Ombudsmen; Judge, European Court of Justice 1995–99; Alt. Mem. Court of Conciliation and Arbitration, OSCE. *Publications:* Appealability of Administrative Decisions 1970, Extraordinary Remedies in Administrative Procedure Law 1973, Elements of Administrative Procedure Law 1977, The Constitution of Sweden 1980, Administrative Justice in Sweden 1991; numerous other books and articles.
Address: c/o Regeringsrätten, PO Box 2293, 103 17 Stockholm, Sweden. *Telephone:* (8) 6176212 (office). *Fax:* (8) 6176234 (office).

RAGSDALE, Marguerita Dianne, MA, PhD, JD; American diplomatist; b. Richmond, Va. *Education:* American Univ., Washington, DC, Univ. of Va, Columbia Univ., New York. *Career:* Jr Consular and Gen. Services Officer, Embassy in Kuwait 1984, Political Officer, Embassy in Mogadishu, Somalia 1986–88, Watch Officer, Dept of State Operations Center 1988–89, Desk Officer for UAE and Oman 1989–91, Political/Econ. Officer, then Deputy Chief of Mission, Embassy in Doha, Qatar 1992–95, man. analyst for Under-Sec. of State for Man. 1996–97, mem. Senior Seminar exec. devt program 1997–98, Deputy Dir Office of Arabian Peninsula Affairs 1998–99, Head of Political Section, Embassy in Pretoria 1999–2002, Deputy Chief of Mission, Embassy in Khartoum 2002–03, Amb. to Djibouti 2003–06; mem. Nat. Trust for Historic Preservation.
Address: US Department of State, 2201 C Street NW, Washington, DC 20520, USA (office). *Telephone:* (202) 647-4000 (office). *Fax:* (202) 647-6738 (office). *Website:* www.state.gov (office).

RAHEEN, Sayed Makhdoom, MA, PhD; Afghan diplomatist; *Ambassador to India;* b. 1946, Kabul. *Education:* Tehran Univ., Iran. *Career:* apptd Lecturer, Kabul Univ. 1973; fmr Head of Bureau of Afghan Culture and Art, Ministry of Information, Culture and Tourism; fmr mem. Drafting Cttee of Constitution of Afghanistan; mem. Grand Nat. Ass. (Loya Jirga) 1976; put under house arrest following Communist coup d'etat April 1978; moved to Pakistan after Soviet invasion; apptd mem. High Council and Chair. Cttee of Culture and Publicity, Islamic Unity of Afghanistan Mujahedeen 1982; selected as Head of Radio Free Kabul by Mujahidin parties; served as adviser with rank of Minister to Pres. of Afghan Interim Govt; co-f. Nat. Islamic Movt of Afghanistan in Peshawar, Pakistan 1988; abandoned Afghan resistance and left for USA following disagreements with Jihad leaders 1991; Co-founder and first Chair. Asscn for Peace and Democracy for Afghanistan 1996; mem. Exec. Cttee Loya Jirga, Rome 1998; selected as Minister of Information, Culture and Tourism of Interim Admin, Bonn Conf. 2002; Chair. Kabul City Council 2003; Amb. to India 2007–; Medal for serving the freedom of speech and promoting cultural activities, presented by HM Zahir Shah 2004. *Publications:* Tears of Khorasan, The Mourners, reply to Khalili (poetry), Today's Muslims (in Pashto); several books and articles on culture, literature, history and Islamic Sufism, the works of Sayed Jamaludeen Afghani, Daqiqi Nama, research on Amir Khosrow, and the Relations of Afghanistan and the subcontinent; f. and published resistance magazines and papers, in Dari, Pashto, Urdu, Arabic and English.
Address: Embassy of Afghanistan, Plot No. 5, Block 50-F, Shanti Path, Chanakyapuri, New Delhi 110 021, India (office). *Telephone:* (11) 26883601 (office). *Fax:* (11) 26875439 (office). *E-mail:* embassyafghanistan@yahoo .co.in (office).

RAHIM, A. B. Manjoor, MA; Bangladeshi diplomatist; *Foreign Secretary;* b. 24 Jan. 1951; m.; one d. one s. *Education:* Univ. of Dhaka. *Career:* Lecturer, Univ. of Chittagong 1974–79; joined Bangladeshi Foreign Service 1979, served in various capacities in diplomatic and perm. missions in Rome, Seoul, New York and Stockholm; Dir-Gen. Ministry of Foreign Affairs –2000; Consul-Gen. in Jeddah, Saudi Arabia 2000–02; Amb. to Myanmar 2002–05, to Germany (also accred to Slovenia) 2005–07; Foreign Sec. 2007–.
Address: Ministry of Foreign Affairs, Segunbagicha, Dhaka 1000, Bangladesh (office). *Telephone:* (2) 9562862 (office). *Fax:* (2) 9555283 (office). *E-mail:* info@mofabd.org (office). *Website:* www.mofa.gov.bd (office).

RAHIM, Rend al-, MA; Iraqi/American diplomatist and organization official; *Executive Director, Iraq Foundation;* b. 1949; m.; one c. *Education:* Cambridge Univ., UK, Sorbonne, France. *Career:* fmr teacher, American Univ. of Beirut; worked for several cos including American Investment Co., Banque Arabe et Internationale d'Investissement, Bahrain and Chemical Bank in Beirut and London; Co-founder and Exec. Dir Iraq Foundation 1991–; Rep., Iraq Governing Council and Chief of Mission, Washington, DC 2003–04; fmr Senior Fellow, Jennings Randolph Fellowship Program, US Inst. of Peace. *Publication:* The Arab Shi'a: Forgotten Muslims (co-author) 2000.
Address: Iraq Foundation, 1012 14th Street, NW, Suite 1110, Washington, DC 20012, USA (office). *Telephone:* (202) 347-4662 (office). *Fax:* (202) 347-7897 (office). *E-mail:* iraq@iraqfoundation.org (office). *Website:* www .iraqfoundation.org (office).

RAHIMOV, Saidahmad Borievich; Uzbekistan politician and banker; *Chairman, National Bank for Foreign Economic Activity;* b. 1960. *Career:* fmr Presidential Adviser for Socioeconomic Affairs; fmr Chair., Auditing Comm.; fmr Man. Asaka Bank; Minister of Finance 2004–05; currently Chair. Nat. Bank for Foreign Economic Activity.
Address: National Bank for Foreign Economic Activity, 100047 Tashkent, Uzbekistan (office). *Telephone:* (71) 133-62-87 (office). *Fax:* (71) 132-01-72 (office). *E-mail:* webmaster@central.nbu.com (office). *Website:* www.eng .nbu.com (office).

RAHMAN, Latifur, LLB, MA; Bangladeshi judge (retd); b. 1 March 1936, Jessore Town. *Education:* Jessore Zilla School, Dhaka Coll. and Dhaka Univ. *Career:* Lecturer in English, Jagannath Coll. and Suhrawardy Coll., Dhaka; Advocate of the Dhaka High Court 1960; Advocate of the then Supreme Court of Pakistan 1965; Additional Judge, Supreme Court of Bangladesh, High Court Div. 1979, Permanent Judge 1981, Judge of the Appellate Div. 1990; Chief Justice of Bangladesh 2000–01; Chief Adviser of the Caretaker Govt of Bangladesh July–Oct. 2001; Head Interim Govt which conducted elections –2002; mem. Enquiry Comm. into train accident at Majukhan 1989; Chair. Enquiry Comm. into damage to aircraft and naval vessels in cyclone at Chittagong 1991.
Address: Dhanmondi, Dhaka, Bangladesh (office).

RAHMAN, M. Saifur; Bangladeshi chartered accountant and politician; b. March 1932, Maulvibazar, Sylhet Div.; m.; three s. one d. *Education:* Dhaka Univ. *Career:* f. chartered accountancy firm, Rahman Rahman Huq; Minister of Finance, Planning, Commerce and Foreign Trade 1976–1982, of Finance and Planning 2001–06; Chair. of various cabinet cttees 1976–1982, 1991–94; mem. Jatiyo Sangshad (Nat. Ass.) 1979–82, 1996–99, 2001; fmr Chair. Bangladesh Jatiyatabadi Dal (Bangladesh Nationalist Party); fmr Chair. Bd Govs IMF, World Bank.
Address: Bangladesh Jatiyatabadi Dal, Banani Office, House 23, Road 13, Dhaka (office); c/o Rahman Rahman Huq, 9 Mohakhali C/A, 11th floor, Dhaka, 1212 Bangladesh (office). *Telephone:* (2) 8819525 (office). *Fax:* (2) 8813063 (office). *E-mail:* bnpbd@e-fsbd.net (office). *Website:* www.bnpbd .com (office).

RAHMAN, Dato Paduka Haji Abdul; Brunei diplomatist. *Career:* currently High Commr to Malaysia.
Address: High Commission of Brunei, Suite 19-01, 19th Floor, Menara Tan & Tan, 207 Jalan Tun Razak, 50400 Kuala Lumpur, Malaysia (office). *Telephone:* (3) 21612800 (office). *Fax:* (3) 2631302 (office).

RAHMANI, Mostafa; Iranian diplomatist. *Career:* Dir Iranian Interests Section, Embassy of Pakistan, Washington, DC, USA 2007–.
Address: Iranian Interests Section, Embassy of Pakistan, 2209 Wisconsin Avenue, NW, Washington, DC 20007, USA (office). *Telephone:* (202) 965-4990 (office). *Fax:* (202) 965-1073 (office). *E-mail:* requests@daftar.org (office). *Website:* www.daftar.org (office).

RAIS, Amien; Indonesian politician; *General Chairman, Partai Amanat Nasional (PAN) (National Mandate Party);* b. 26 April 1944, Solo, Java; m. Kusnariyati Sri Rahayu; three s. two d. *Education:* Gadjah Mada Univ., Al Azhar Univ., Cairo, Egypt, Univ. of Notre Dame and Univ. of Chicago, USA. *Career:* joined Muhammadiyah (Muslim group) 1985, Vice-Chair 1990–95, 1995–98; Chair. People's Consultative Ass. (MPR) 1999–2004; co-f. Partai Amanat Nasional (PAN) (National Mandate Party), Gen. Chair. 1998–; helped found Asscn of Indonesian Muslim Intellectuals (ICMI); Prof., Gadjah Mada Univ., Jogjakarta.
Address: Partai Amanat Nasional, Jalan H. Nawi 15, Jakarta Selatan 12420, Indonesia (office). *Telephone:* (21) 72794535 (office). *Fax:* (21) 7268695 (office). *Website:* www.geocities.com/CapitolHill/Congress/6678 (office).

RAISIAN, John, BA, PhD; American economist and research institute director; *Tad and Dianne Taube Director, Hoover Institution; Education:* Ohio Univ., UCLA. *Career:* consultant to Rand Corpn 1974–75; Visiting Asst Prof. of Econs, Univ. of Wash. 1975–76; Asst Prof. of Econs, Univ. of Houston 1976–80; Sr Economist, Office of Research and Evaluation, US Bureau of Labor Statistics 1980–81; Special Asst for Econ. Policy, Office of the Asst-Sec. for Policy, US Dept of Labor 1981–83, Dir of Research and Tech. Support 1981–84; Exec. Dir Pres.'s Task Force on Food Assistance 1983; Pres. Unicorn Research Corpn (econ. consulting firm), Los Angeles 1984–86; joined Hoover Inst. on War, Revolution and Peace as Fellow, 1986, Assoc. Dir 1986–88, Deputy Dir 1988–89, Tad and Dianne Taube Dir 1989–, also currently Sr Fellow; Distinguished Teaching Award, Coll. of Social Sciences, Univ. of Houston, Distinguished Service Award, US Dept of Labor 1984. *Publications:* numerous articles on econs of labour markets.
Address: Hoover Institution, 434 Galvez Mall, Stanford University, Stanford, CA 94305-6010, USA (office). *Telephone:* (650) 723-0603 (office). *Fax:* (650) 725-8611 (office). *E-mail:* horaney@hoover.stanford.edu (office). *Website:* www.hoover.org (office).

RAJAPAKSE, Mahinda; Sri Lankan politician, lawyer and head of state; *President, Minister of Defence, Public Security, Law and Order, Religious Affairs, Nation Building and Finance and Planning;* b. 18 Nov. 1945, Hambantota. *Education:* Richmond Coll., Galle, Nalanda and Thurstan Colls, Colombo. *Career:* fmr lawyer, Tangalle; mem. Parl. for Beliatta 1970; fmr Minister of Labour, of Fisheries, of Ports and Shipping; Leader of the Opposition 2002–04; Prime Minister of Sri Lanka 2004–05; Pres. of Sri Lanka Nov. 2005–, Minister of Defence and of Finance and Planning 2005–07, of Defence, Public Security, Law and Order, Religious Affairs, Nation Building and Finance and Planning 2007–; mem. United People's Freedom Alliance; Pres. Sri Lankan Cttee for Solidarity with Palestine; Chair. Sri Lanka Freedom Party 2006–; Sri Rohana Janaranjana 2000.
Address: President's Secretariat, Republic Square, Colombo 1, Sri Lanka (office). *Telephone:* (11) 2324801 (office). *Fax:* (11) 2331246 (office). *E-mail:* gosl@presidentsl.org (office). *Website:* www.presidentsl.org (office); www .mahindarajapaksa.com.

RAJAVI, Maryam, BSc; Iranian politician; *President-Elect, National Council of Resistance of Iran;* b. (Maryam Qajar-Azedanllo), 3 Dec. 1953, Tehran; m. Massoud Rajavi 1985; one s. one d. *Education:* Sharif Univ. of Tech., Tehran. *Career:* leader anti-Shah student movt; joined Mojahedin-e Khalq Org. (People's Mojahedin of Iran, leading Iranian opposition group) 1970s, parl. cand. for Tehran in 1st post-revolutionary parl. elections 1979; official in social dept 1980–81, organized demonstrations against Khomeini Govt 1980–1981; left Iran for Paris 1982; elected jt-leader of Mojahedin 1985, Sec.-Gen. 1989–93; Deputy C-in-C Nat. Liberation Army of Iran (NLA) 1987–93, launched programme for introduction of women in front-line combat and combat pilots 1987, transformed NLA from infantry to armoured force 1989–93; Pres.-Elect, Nat. Council of Resistance of Iran (540-mem. Parl. in exile) 1993–; proposed platform for women's int. alliance against fundamentalism 1993; prominent int. campaigner for women's rights 1993–; expounded doctrine of democratic Islam as solution to Islamic fundamentalism 1995; Guest Speaker, European Parl. 2004, Int. Human Rights Conf., Paris 2004, Int. Conf. of Jurists, Paris 2004, Parls of Norway and UK 1995–96; numerous lectures, TV appearances, interviews in int. media; awards include Medal of Honour for contrib. to emancipation of women, Nat. Comm. for Gender Equality, Italy 1993, one of The Times 100 Most Powerful Women, UK 1996. *Publications:* Charter of Fundamental Freedoms in Post-dictatorship Iran 1995, Message to Fourth Int. Women's Conf., Beijing 1995, A Message of Tolerance 1995, Women, Islam and Fundamentalism 1996, Women, Voice of the Oppressed 1996, United Against Fundamentalism 1996, Message to Women in Frontline (conf.) 1997, Misogyny, Pillar of Religious Fascism 2003, Message to Int. Federation of Women against Fundamentalism and for Equality (conf.) 2004, Women and Islamic Fundamentalism 2004, Women Empowerment 2005, Women in Leadership 2006, Ten-Point Platform for Future Iran 2006; contrib.: Le Monde, De Welt, Le Figaro, International Herald Tribune.

Address: National Council of Resistance of Iran, PO Box 2516, London, NW4 2DD, England (office); National Council of Resistance of Iran, 15 rue des Gords, 95430 Auvers-sur-Oise, France (office). *Telephone:* 1-34-48-07-28 (France) (office). *Fax:* 1-34-48-04-33 (France) (office). *Website:* www.ncr-iran.org (office); www.maryam-rajavi.org.

RAJBHANDARI, Pushkar Man Singh; Nepalese diplomatist. *Career:* Jt Sec., Ministry of Foreign Affairs –2002; Amb. to Pakistan 1983–86, 2002–06 (also accred to Iraq 2003–06, to Iran 2005–06, to Russia, Syria and Afghanistan); Dean of the Asia Group.
Address: c/o Ministry of Foreign Affairs, Shital Niwas, Maharajgan, Kathmandu, Nepal. *Telephone:* (1) 4416011. *E-mail:* adm@mofa.gov.np. *Website:* www.mofa.gov.np.

RAKHIMOV, Murtaza Gubaidullovich; Russian politician and head of state; *President, Republic of Bashkortostan;* b. 7 Feb. 1934, Tavakanovo, Bashkiria; m. Luiza Galimovna Rakhimova; one s. *Education:* Ufa Oil Inst. *Career:* operator, then Chief of Oil Rig, Chief Chemist, Chief Engineer, Dir Ufa Oil Processing Plant 1956–90; USSR People's Deputy 1990–92; Chair. Supreme Soviet Repub. of Bashkortostan 1990–93, Pres. 1993–; mem. Russian Council of Fed. (Parl.) 1996–2001; Public Services to Repub. of Bashkortostan, Order of Peter the Great, Labour Red Banner, People's Friendship Order, Honour Symbol, Order of Salavat Yulayev.
Address: The Republic House, 46 Tukayev Street, 450101, Ufa, Bashkortostan, Russia. *Telephone:* (3472) 50-24-06 (office). *Fax:* (3472) 50-01-75 (office). *E-mail:* aprb@admbashkortostan.ru (office). *Website:* www.bashkortostan.ru (office).

RAKHMANIN, Vladimir Olegovich; Russian diplomatist; *Special Envoy, Ministry of Foreign Affairs;* b. 1958, Moscow. *Education:* Moscow Inst. of Int. Relations. *Career:* on staff USSR (later Russian) Ministry of Foreign Affairs 1980–; Attaché, First Far East Dept, Ministry of Foreign Affairs 1980–82; Third Sec., Embassy in People's Republic of China 1982–83, Third Secretary, Embassy in USA 1983–86, Counsellor 1992–96; Head of Secr., Deputy Foreign Minister 1986–92; Deputy Dir First Asian Dept 1996–98; Dir Dept of Information and Press 1998–2000; Chief of Protocol of the Pres. of the Russian Fed. 2000–01; Amb. to Ireland 2002–06; Special Envoy, Ministry of Foreign Affairs 2006–.
Address: Ministry of Foreign Affairs, 119200 Moscow, Smolenskaya-Sennaya pl. 32/34, Russia (office). *Telephone:* (495) 244-16-06 (office). *Fax:* (495) 230-21-30 (home). *E-mail:* ministry@mid.ru (home). *Website:* www.mid.ru (office).

RAKHMON, Emomali, BEcons; Tajikistan politician and head of state; *President;* b. (Imamali Sharipovich Rakhmonov), 5 Oct. 1952, Dangar, Kulob Oblast; m.; nine c. *Education:* Lenin Tajikistan State Univ. *Career:* served in USSR army service; worked as electrician, salesman, as trade union sec. and on various CP cttees; Dir Dangarin Sovkhoz (Soviet farm), Kulob Oblast 1982–92, Chair. Union Cttee 1976–88; Chair. Kulob Oblast Exec. Cttee 1992; Chair. Majlisi Oli (Supreme Assembly) 1992–94; Pres. of Tajikistan 1994–; World Peace Corps Acad. Gold Medal 2000.
Address: Office of the President, 734023 Dushanbe, pr. Rudaki 80, Tajikistan (office). *Telephone:* (372) 21-04-18 (office). *Fax:* (372) 21-18-37 (office). *Website:* www.president.tj (office).

RAKHMONOV, Imamali Sharipovich (see Rakhmon, Imamali Sharipovich).

RAKOWSKI, Mieczysław Franciszek, DHist; Polish politician and journalist; b. 1 Dec. 1926, Kowalewko, Szubin district; m. 1st Wanda Wiłkomirska 1952 (separated); two s.; m. 2nd Elżbieta Kępińska. *Education:* Higher School of Social Sciences, Cracow and Inst. of Social Sciences, Warsaw. *Career:* worked at Cen. Cttee of Polish United Workers' Party (PZPR) 1949–52, 1955–57; Sub-ed., Polityka 1957, Ed.-in-Chief 1958–82; Chair. Gen. Bd, Polish Journalists' Asscn 1958–61; Deputy mem. Cen. Cttee, PZPR 1964–75, mem. 1975–90; Deputy to Sejm (Parl.) 1972–89, Deputy Chair. PZPR Sejm Deputies' Club 1980; Deputy Chair. Council of Ministers 1981–85; Chair. Cttee for Trade Unions of Council of Ministers 1981–85; Vice-Marshal (Deputy Speaker) of Sejm 1985–88; Chair. Socio-Econ. Council attached to Sejm 1985–88; mem. Political Bureau PZPR Cen. Cttee 1987–90; Sec. PZPR Cen. Cttee 1988–89; First Sec. PZPR Cen. Cttee 1989–90; Chair. Council of Ministers (Prime Minister) 1988–89; Ed.-in-Chief monthly Dziś, Przegląd społeczny 1990–; Presenter, TV programme Swiat i Polityka (World and Politics); fmr Chair. Polish Yachting Union; Order of Banner of Labour 1st and 2nd Class, Gold Cross of Merit, State Prize 2nd Class 1976, Commdr's Cross with Star of Order of Polonia Restituta and other decorations. *Publications:* NRF z bliska (FRG from a Short Distance) 1958, New World 1959, Socjal demokratyczna Partia Niemiec w okresie powojennym 1949–54 (Social-Democratic Party of Germany in Post-war Period) 1960, Świat na zakręcie (The World in Turning) 1960, Zachód szuka ideologii (The West Looks for Ideology)

1961, Ameryka wielopiętrowa (Many-storied America), Klimaty w RFN (Climates of the FRG), Polityka Zagraniczna PRL (The Foreign Policy of the Polish People's Republic) 1974, Dymisja Kanclerza (Chancellor's Dismissal) 1975, Spełnione i niespełnione 1978, Przesilenie grudniowe (December Crisis) 1981, Partnerstwo (Partnership) 1982, Czas nadziei i rozczarowań (Time of Hopes and Disappointments), Vol. 1 1985, Vol. 2 1987, Ein schwieriger Dialog 1986, Jak to się stało 1992, Gorbachev: The First and the Last One 1993, People Wrote Letters to M.F. Rakowski: Years–People–Letters 1993, Es began in Polen 1995, Political Diaries (1958–62) 1998, Political Diaries (1963–66) 1999, Political Diaries (1967–68) 2000, Political Diaries (1969–72) 2001, Political Diaries (1973–75) 2002, Political Diaries (1976–78) 2002; co-author: The Polish Upswing 1971–75 1975.
Address: Miesięcznik 'Dziś', ul. Poznańska 3, 00-680 Warsaw, Poland. *Telephone:* (22) 6210121.

RALSTON, Gen. Joseph W.; American air force officer (retd); *Vice Chairman, Cohen Group;* b. 4 Nov. 1943, Hopkinsville, Ky; m. Diane Dougherty; two s. two d. *Education:* Miami Univ., Ohio, Cen. Michigan Univ., Army Command and Gen. Staff Coll., Nat. War Coll., Harvard Univ. *Career:* mem. reserve officer training program USAF 1965; Vice-Chair. of Jt Chiefs of Staff 1996–2000; concurrently Chair. Jt Requirements Oversight Council, Planning, Programming and Budgeting Systems; Vice-Chair. Defense Acquisition Bd; mem. Nat. Security Council Deputies Comm., Nuclear Weapons Council; Supreme Allied Commdr, Europe 2000–03; C-in-C, US European Command 2000–03; Vice Chair. The Cohen Group 2003–; numerous mil. decorations including Defense Distinguished Service Medal (two awards), Distinguished Service Medal.
Address: The Cohen Group, 1200 19th Street, NW, Suite 400, Washington, DC 20036, USA (office). *Telephone:* (202) 689-7900 (office). *Fax:* (202) 689-7910 (office). *E-mail:* jralston@cohengroup.net (office). *Website:* www.cohengroup.net/team-jwr.html (office).

RAM, Bal, BA, MA; Fijian diplomatist; m. Nirmala Balram; three c. *Education:* Auckland Univ., NZ. *Career:* High Commr to NZ 2002–07.
Address: Ministry of Foreign Affairs, International Co-operation and Civil Aviation, Government Bldgs, POB 2220, Suva, Fiji.

RAMDAS, Kavita N., MA; Indian international organization official; *President and CEO, Global Fund for Women;* b. 22 Sept. 1962, New Delhi; d. of Laxminarayan Ramdas and Lalita Ramdas; m. Zulfigar Ahmad 1990; one d. *Education:* Mount Holyoke Coll. and Woodrow Wilson School of Public and Int. Affairs, Univ. of Princeton, USA. *Career:* worked on issues of US poverty, econ. devt and population studies as Program Officer, John D. and Catherine T. MacArthur Foundation, Chicago; Pres. and CEO Global Fund for Women 1996–; mem. Advisory Council Woodrow Wilson School of Public and Int. Affairs, Univ. of Princeton, Advisory Council Ethical Globalization Initiative, Bd Rural Devt Inst., Seattle, Alan Guttmacher Inst., New York, Women's Edge, Washington, DC; fmr mem. Cttee on Women and Devt, Advisory Bd UN Econ. Comm. for Africa; fmr Trustee Gen. Service Foundation; Founding Bd Mem. and fmr Chair. Asian Americans and Pacific Islanders in Philanthropy (AAPIP); fmr mem. Bd Women and Philanthropy (affinity groups of the Council on Foundations); mem. Bd of Trustees Mount Holyoke Coll.; Henry Crown Fellow, Aspen Inst. 1999; Women's Funding Network Changing the Face of Philanthropy Award 1999, Santa Clara Univ. Women and Law Soc.'s Woman of the Year 2002, Nat. Women's Leadership Summit Choosing to Lead Award.
Address: Global Fund for Women, 1375 Sutter Street, Suite 400, San Francisco, CA 94109, USA (office). *Telephone:* (415) 202-7640 (office). *Fax:* (415) 202-8604 (office). *E-mail:* kavita@globalfundforwomen.org (office). *Website:* www.globalfundforwomen.org (office).

RAMDIN, Albert R.; Suriname diplomatist and international organization executive; *Assistant Secretary-General, Organization of American States (OAS);* b. 27 Feb. 1958; m. Charmaine Baksh; one s. one d. *Education:* schools in Paramaribo and the Netherlands, Univ. of Amsterdam and Free Univ. *Career:* career diplomat in public service at nat. and int. level, served as Sr Adviser to Minister of Trade and Industry; worked for two years in pvt. sector before returning to public service; apptd Adviser to Minister of Foreign Affairs and Minister of Finance; Amb. and Perm. Rep. to OAS 1997, Chair. Perm. Council Jan.–March 1998, Inter-American Council for Integral Devt 1999, coordinated Caribbean Community (CARICOM) Ambs' Caucus during Suriname's chairmanship of sub-regional group; apptd to serve concurrently as non-resident Amb. to Costa Rica 1999; Asst Sec.-Gen. for Foreign and Community Relations, CARICOM Secr. 1999; served as Amb. at Large and Special Adviser to Govt of Suriname on Western Hemispheric Affairs –2005; Adviser to OAS Sec.-Gen. with special attention to the Caribbean 2001–05, Asst Sec.-Gen. OAS 2005–.

Address: Organization of American States, 17th Street & Constitution Avenue, NW, Washington, DC 20006, USA (office). *Telephone:* (202) 458-3000 (office). *Fax:* (202) 458-6319 (office). *E-mail:* OASWeb@oas.org (office). *Website:* www.oas.org (office).

RAMGOOLAM, Hon. Navinchandra, LLB, LRCP; Mauritian physician, barrister and politician; *Prime Minister;* b. 14 July 1947, Mauritius; m. Veena Ramgoolam 1979. *Education:* Royal Coll. of Surgeons, Dublin, Ireland, London School of Econs and Inns of Court School of Law, London, UK. *Career:* called to the Bar, Inner Temple 1993; Leader, Mauritius Labour Party (MLP) 1991–, Pres. 1991–92; Leader of Opposition and mem. Nat. Ass. 1991–95; Prime Minister 1995–2000, also Minister of Defence and Home Affairs, External Communications; leader of opposition 2000–2005; Prime Minister 2005–, also Minister of Defence and Home Affairs, Civil Service and Administrative Reforms and Rodrigues and Outer Islands; acting Minister of Foreign Affairs 2008–; mem. Int. Advisory Bd Center for Int. Devt, Harvard Univ. 1999–; Licentiate, Royal College of Surgeons in Ireland; Hon. Fellow London School of Econs 1998; Dr hc (Mauritius) 1998, (Aligarh Muslim Univ.) 1998, (Jawaharlal Nehru Univ.) 2005.
Address: Prime Minister's Office, New Treasury Building, Intendance Street, Port Louis, Mauritius (office). *Telephone:* 207-9595 (office). *Fax:* 208-8619 (office). *E-mail:* primeminister@mail.gov.mu (office). *Website:* pmo.gov.mu (office).

RAMIA, José Serulle; Dominican Republic academic and diplomatist; *Ambassador to Haiti;* b. 11 June 1950, San Francisco de Macoris. *Career:* fmr Vice-Rector, teacher of int. economy, Univ. of Santo Domingo; fmr Pres., Fundación Ciencia y Arte Inc.; Amb. to Haiti 2005–. *Publications include:* 14 books; numerous newspaper articles.
Address: Embassy of Dominican Republic, rue Panaméricaine 121, BP 56, Pétionville, Port-au-Prince, Haiti (office). *Telephone:* 257-0568 (office). *Fax:* 221-8718 (office). *E-mail:* embrepdomhai@yahoo.com (office).

RAMÍREZ LEZCANO, Rubén, MA, MBA; Paraguayan economist, diplomatist and government official; b. 11 Jan. 1966; m. Adriana Cabelluzzi; two s. *Education:* Univ. of Buenos Aires, Univ. of Paris, Sorbonne, Univ. of California, Los Angeles, USA. *Career:* with Int. Econ. Affairs Counselling Dept, Pres.'s Office 1989; Sec. Embassy in Buenos Aires, in charge of Commercial Dept 1989–92; Dir Dept of Foreign Trade, Ministry of Foreign Affairs 1994–96; Exec. Sec. Nat. Council for Foreign Trade 1994–96; Counsellor Embassy in Paris and Standing Rep. at UNESCO 1996–98; Consul Gen. Los Angeles, Calif. 1998–99; Gen. Dir Export and Promotion Dept, Ministry of Foreign Affairs 1999–2000; Embassy Minister and Standing Rep. Latin American Integration Asscn, Montevideo, Uruguay 2000; Standing Rep. UN Special Orgs, Geneva, Switzerland 2001–04; Vice Minister for Econ. Relations and Integration 2004–06; Minister of Foreign Affairs 2006–08; mem. Asoc. Nacional Republicana–Partido Colorado (Nat. Republican Asscn–Colorado Party).
Address: Asociación Nacional Republicana–Partido Colorado, Casa de los Colorados, 25 de Mayo 842, Asunción, Paraguay (office). *Telephone:* (21) 44-4137 (office). *Fax:* (21) 49-7857 (office). *Website:* www.anr.org.py (office).

RAMOS-HORTA, José, MA; Timor-Leste politician and head of state; *President;* b. 26 Dec. 1949, Dili; m. Ana Pessoa 1978 (divorced); one s. *Education:* Hague Acad. of Int. Law, The Netherlands, Int. Inst. of Human Rights, Strasbourg, France, Columbia Univ., Antioch Univ., USA. *Career:* journalist and broadcaster 1969–74; Minister for External Affairs and Information, Timor-Leste 1975; Perm. Rep. of Fretilin to UN, NY 1976–89; Public Affairs and Media Dir Mozambican Embassy, Washington 1987–88; f., Dir, Lecturer Diplomacy Training Programme, Univ. of NSW 1990–, Visiting Prof. 1996–; Special Rep. Nat. Council of Maubere Resistance 1991–; returned to Timor-Leste Dec. 1999; Vice-Pres. Nat. Council of Resistance 1999–; Sr Minister for Foreign Affairs and Co-operation 2000–06 (resgnd), also Acting Defence Minister June 2006; Prime Minister of Timor-Leste 2006–07, also Minister of Defence; Pres. of Timor-Leste 2007–; served in Timor-Leste Transitional Admin. 2000–02; mem. Bd Timor-Leste Human Rights Centre, Melbourne; Sr Assoc. Mem. St Antony's Coll., Oxford 1987–; Order of Freedom (Portugal) 1996; received Unrepresented Nations and People's Org. Award 1996; shared Nobel Peace Prize 1996 (with Mgr Carlos Ximenes Belo). *Publications:* Funu: The Unfinished Saga of East Timor 1987; articles in numerous publs worldwide.
Address: Office of the President, Palácio das Cinzas, Kaikoli, Dili, Timor-Leste (office). *Telephone:* 3339011 (office). *E-mail:* presidente-tl@easttimor.minihub.org (office).

RAMPHAL, Sir Shridath Surendranath, GCMG, OE, OM, ONZ, AC, QC, SC, LLM, FRSA; Guyanese international organization official, barrister and politician; b. 3 Oct. 1928, New Amsterdam; m. Lois Winifred King 1951; two s. two d.

Education: Queen's Coll., Georgetown, King's Coll., London, Harvard Law School. *Career:* Crown Counsel, British Guiana 1953–54; Asst to Attorney-Gen. 1954–56; Legal Draftsman 1956–58; Solicitor-Gen. 1959–61; Legal Draftsman, West Indies 1958–59; Asst Attorney-Gen., West Indies 1961–62; Attorney-Gen., Guyana 1965–73; mem. Nat. Assembly 1965–75; Minister of State for External Affairs 1967–72, Minister of Foreign Affairs 1972–75, of Justice 1973–75; Commonwealth Sec.-Gen. 1975–90; Chancellor Univ. of Guyana 1988–92, Univ. of Warwick 1989–2001, Univ. of West Indies 1989–; Queen's Counsel 1965 and Sr Counsel, Guyana 1966; mem. Int. Comm. of Jurists, Ind. Comm. on Int. Devt Issues, Ind. Comm. on Disarmament and Security Issues, Ind. Comm. on Int. Humanitarian Issues, World Comm. on Environment and Devt, South Comm., Carnegie Comm. on Deadly Conflict, Bd of Govs Int. Devt Research Center, Canada, Exec. Cttee of Int. Inst. for Environment and Devt, Council of Int. Negotiation Network Carter Center, Georgia, USA 1991–97; Patron One World Broadcasting Trust; Chair. UN Cttee for Devt Planning 1984–87, West Indian Comm. 1990–92, Bd Int. Inst. for Democracy and Electoral Assistance (IDEA) 1995–2001, Advisory Cttee Future Generations Alliance Foundation 1995–97; Pres. World Conservation Union—IUCN 1990–93; Int. Steering Cttee Leadership for Environment and Devt Program Rockefeller Foundation 1991–98; Co-Chair. Comm. on Global Governance 1992–2000; Adviser to Sec.-Gen. of UNCED 1992; Chief Negotiator on Int. Econ. Issues for the Caribbean Region 1997–2001; Facilitator Belize–Guatemala Dispute 2000–02; John Simon Guggenheim Fellowship 1962; Hon. Bencher of Gray's Inn 1981; Fellow, King's Coll., London 1975, LSE 1979, RSA 1981, Magdalen Coll., Oxford 1982; Order of the Repub. (Egypt) 1973; Grand Cross, Order of the Sun (Peru) 1974; Grand Cross, Order of Merit (Ecuador) 1974, Order of Nishaan Izzuddeen (Maldives) 1989, Grand Commdr, Order of Niger 1990, Grand Commdr, Order of the Companion of Freedom (Zambia) 1990, Nishan-e-Quaid-i-Azam (Pakistan) 1990, Order of the Caribbean Community 1991, Commdr Order of the Golden Ark 1994; Hon. LLD (Panjab Univ.) 1975, (Southampton) 1976, (Univ. of The West Indies) 1978, (St Francis Xavier Univ., Halifax, Canada) 1978, (Aberdeen) 1979, (Cape Coast, Ghana) 1980, (London) 1981, (Benin, Nigeria) 1982, (Hull) 1983, (Yale) 1985, (Cambridge) 1985, (Warwick) 1988, (York Univ., Ont., Canada) 1988, (Malta) 1989, (Otago, NZ) 1990; Hon. DHL (Simmons Coll., Boston) 1982; Hon. DCL (Oxon.) 1982, (East Anglia) 1983, (Durham) 1985; Dr hc (Surrey) 1979, (Essex) 1980; Hon. DHumLitt (Duke Univ., USA) 1985; Hon. DLitt (Bradford) 1985, (Indira Gandhi Nat. Open Univ.) 1989; Hon. DSc (Cranfield Inst. of Tech.) 1987; Arden and Atkin Prize, Gray's Inn 1952, Int. Educ. Award (Richmond Coll., London) 1988, RSA Albert Medal 1988, Medal of Friendship, Cuba 2001, Pravasi Bharata Samman Award 2003. *Publications:* One World to Share: Selected Speeches of the Commonwealth Secretary-General 1975–79, Nkrumah and the Eighties (1980 Kwame Nkrumah Memorial Lectures), Sovereignty and Solidarity (1981 Callander Memorial Lectures), Some in Light and Some in Darkness: The Long Shadow of Slavery (Wilberforce Lecture) 1983, The Message not the Messenger (STC Communication Lecture) 1985, The Trampling of the Grass (Econ. Comm. for Africa Silver Jubilee Lecture) 1985, For the South, a Time to Think 1986, Making Human Society a Civilized State (Corbishley Memorial Lecture) 1987, Inseparable Humanity: An Anthology of Reflections of Shridath Ramphal 1988, An End to Otherness (six speeches) 1990, Our Country, The Planet 1992, No Island is an Island and contribs to journals of legal, political and int. affairs, including International and Comparative Law Quarterly, Caribbean Quarterly, Public Law, Guyana Journal, The Round Table, Royal Society of Arts Journal, Foreign Policy, Third World Quarterly, International Affairs.
Address: 31 St Mathew's Lodge, 50 Oakley Square, London, NW1 1NB (home); 1 The Sutherlands, 188 Sutherland Avenue, London, W9 1HR, England. *Telephone:* (20) 7266-3409. *Fax:* (20) 7286-2302. *E-mail:* ssramphal@msn.com (office).

RAMSDEN, Sir John, Kt ; British diplomatist; *Ambassador to Croatia;* m. Jane Ramsden; two d. *Career:* joined FCO 1975, UN Dept 1975-76, Second Sec., Dakar 1976–79, First Sec., Vienna 1979–80, Head of Chancery, Hanoi 1980–82, Econ. Relations Dept, FCO 1982–84, Perm. Under-Sec.'s Dept 1984–85, EC Dept (External) 1985–88, Western European Dept 1988–90, Deputy Head of Mission, Berlin 1990–93, Head of Information Dept, FCO 1993–96, Deputy Head of Mission, Geneva 1996–98, Head of Cen. and NW Europe Dept, FCO 1999–2003, Amb. to Croatia 2004–.
Address: British Embassy, 10000 Zagreb, Ivana Lučića 4, Croatia (office). *Telephone:* (1) 6009100 (office). *Fax:* (1) 6009111 (office). *E-mail:* british.embassyzagreb@fco.gov.uk (office). *Website:* www.britishembassy.gov.uk/croatia (office).

RANA, Kipkorir Aly Azad, MPolSci, PhD; Kenyan international civil servant and trade consultant. *Education:* Univ. of Nairobi, Univ. of California at Los Angeles, USA. *Career:* Deputy Head of Mission, Tokyo 1993–96;

Deputy Perm. Rep. and Alt. Del./ Co-ordinator to Security Council, UN, New York 1997; Perm. Sec. (Devt Co-ordination), Office of the Pres. of Kenya 1998; Amb. and Perm. Rep. UN, Geneva 1998–2000; Co-ordinator of African Dels to WTO and Sr Trade Policy Adviser, Minister for Trade and Industry 1999–2001; Deputy Dir-Gen. WTO 2002–05; Fulbright Hays Fellow 1973–79.
Address: c/o Ministry of Foreign Affairs, Old Treasury Bldg, Harambee Ave, POB 30551, 1211 Nairobi, Kenya (office).

RANA, Prabal Shumshere Jung Bahadur, CVO; Nepalese diplomatist. *Education:* Univ. Coll., London. *Career:* began career with Foreign Ministry, Protocol Div. 1964, subsequent posts in Italy, Pakistan, UN, New York 1977–79, Deputy Chief of Protocol 1979–1982, First Sec., then Counsellor, Embassy in London 1982–87; Under-Sec. SAARC 1987–92, Dir SAARC 1992–96; Amb. to UK 2003–06.
Address: Ministry of Foreign Affairs, Shital Niwas, Maharajganj, Kathmandu, Nepal. *Telephone:* (1) 4416011. *Fax:* (1) 4416016. *E-mail:* adm@mofa.gov.np. *Website:* www.mofa.gov.np.

RANDT, Clark Thorp, Jr, BA, JD; American lawyer and diplomatist; *Ambassador to People's Republic of China;* m. Sarah A. Talcott; two s. one d. *Education:* Hotchkiss School, Yale Univ., Univ. of Mich. Law School. *Career:* served with USAF Security Service 1968–72; China rep. Nat. Council for US-China Trade 1974; First Sec. and Commercial Attaché, US Embassy, Beijing 1982–84; pvt. law practice as Pnr, Shearman and Sterling, Hong Kong; Amb. to People's Repub. of China 2001–; mem. NY and Hong Kong Bars; fmr Gov. and First Vice-Pres. American Chamber of Commerce, Hong Kong; mem. Council on Foreign Relations.
Address: Embassy of the USA, 3 Xiu Shui Bei Jie, Chaoyang District, Beijing 100600, People's Republic of China (office). *Telephone:* (10) 65323831 (office). *Fax:* (10) 65323178 (office). *Website:* beijing.usembassy-china.org.cn (office).

RANGEL BRICEÑO, Gen.-in-Chief Gustavo; Venezuelan military officer and government official; *Minister of National Defence;* b. 16 Aug. 1955, Maracaibo. *Career:* served as Commdr of Army Infantry Div. 2004–05, Reserve and Nat. Mobilization –2007; Minister of Nat. Defence 2007–.
Address: Ministry of National Defence, Edif. 17 de Diciembre, planta baja, Base Aérea Francisco de Miranda, La Carlota, Caracas, Venezuela (office). *Telephone:* (212) 908-1264 (office). *Fax:* (212) 237-4974 (office). *E-mail:* prensamd@mindefensa.gov.ve (office). *Website:* www.mindefensa.gov.ve (office).

RANIA AL-ABDULLAH, HM Queen of Jordan, BBA; b. (Rania al-Yassin), 31 Aug. 1970, Kuwait; m. Prince Abdullah ibn al-Hussein (King Abdullah II of Jordan) 1993; two s. two d. *Education:* American Univ., Cairo. *Career:* est. support network for battered and abused children; Founder Jordan River Foundation 1995; Head Jordan Blood Disease Society, Int. Advisory Cttee of UNU's Int. Network on Water, Environment and Health (UNU/ INWEH), Arab Women Labor Affairs Cttee of Arab Labor Org., Exec. Bd Arab Network for Open and Distance Educ.; Head Queen Rania Soc. for the Support of the Mil. and their Families 2004–; Eminent Advocate for Children, UNICEF 2007–; Pres. Jordanian Soc. for Organ Donation, Nat. Council for Family Affairs, Arab Women's Summit; mem. World Econ. Forum Foundation Bd (Chair. Advisory Council for STARS), UNICEF's Global Leadership Initiative, Bd of Dirs Foundation for Int. Community Assistance, Bd of Dirs The Vaccine Fund, Bd of Dirs Int. Youth Foundation; Int. Pres. Int. Osteoporosis Foundation; Patron Jordanian Psychiatric Rehabilitation Soc.; Friend of Int. Criminal Court; Hon. Pres. Bd of Trustees, Arab Acad. for Banking and Finance, Hon. Chair. Bd of Govs Pacem In Terris Inst., La Rochelle Coll., USA, Hon. Col 2004; Dr hc (Exeter) 2001; Gold Medal of the Pres. of Italian Repub. 2002, German Media Prize 2003, ranked by Forbes magazine amongst 100 Most Powerful Women (13th) 2004, (80th) 2005, (81st) 2006, (82nd) 2007.
Address: Royal Palace, Amman, Jordan. *Website:* www.queenrania.jo.

RANIS, Gustav, PhD; American economist and academic; *Frank Altschul Professor Emeritus of International Economics, Yale University;* b. 24 Oct. 1929, Darmstadt, Germany; m. Ray Lee Finkelstein; two s. one d. *Education:* Brandeis Univ., Yale Univ. *Career:* Social Science Research Council Fellow (Japan) 1955–56; Jt Dir, Pakistan Inst. of Devt Econs, Karachi, Pakistan 1959–61; Assoc. Dir Econ. Growth Center, Yale Univ. 1961–65, Dir 1967–75; Assoc. Prof. of Econs, Yale Univ. 1961–64, Prof. of Econs 1964–82, Frank Altschul Prof. of Int. Econs 1982–2005, Prof. Emer. 2005–; Dir Yale Center for Int. and Area Studies 1996–; Dir Yale-Pakistan Project 1970–71; Asst Admin. for Program and Policy, Agency for Int. Devt, Dept of State 1965–67, Consultant 1962–65, 1967–71, 1984–; Ford Foundation Faculty Fellow, Colegio de Mexico, Mexico City 1971–72; Visiting Prof., Univ. de los Andes, Colombia 1976–77; Consultant UN FAO 1979–; Chief of Mission, ILO Comprehensive Employment Strategy

Mission to the Philippines 1973, World Bank/CARICOM Project on Production and Investment Incentives in the Caribbean 1980–82; mem. Oversight Cttee Int. Conf. on Intellectual Property Rights, Nat. Research Council 1991–; mem. Council on Foreign Relations; mem. Editorial Advisory Bd Journal of Int. Devt 1995–, Oxford Devt Studies 1996–; mem. Bd of Trustees and Brandeis Chair. Acad. Affairs Cttee Brandeis Univ.; Sterling Fellow, Yale Univ. 1953; Fellow, Inst. for Advanced Study, Berlin 1993–94; Junior Phi Beta Kappa (Brandeis Univ.) 1951; Dr hc (Brandeis Univ.) 1982. *Publications:* Development of Labor Surplus Economy: Theory and Policy (jtly) 1964, Growth with Equity: The Taiwan Case (jtly) 1979, Comparative Technology Choice in Development (jtly) 1988, Linkages in Developing Economics: A Philippine Study (jtly) 1990, The State of Development Economics, Science and Technology: Lessons for Development Policy (jtly) 1990, Taiwan: From Developing to Mature Economy (ed.) 1992, The Political Economy of Development Policy Change (jtly) 1992, Japan and the U.S. in the Developing World (ed.) 1997, Growth and Development from an Evolutionary Perspective (with John C. H. Fei) 1997, The Economics and Political Economy of Development in Taiwan into the 21st Century 1999, The Economics and Political Economy of Comparative Development into the 21st Century 1999.
Address: Economic Growth Center, P.O. Box 208269, New Haven, CT 06520-8269 (office); 7 Mulberry Road, Woodbridge, CT 06525, USA (home). *Telephone:* (203) 432-3632 (office); (203) 397-2560 (home). *Fax:* (203) 432-3635 (office). *E-mail:* gustav.ranis@yale.edu (office). *Website:* www.yale.edu/~egcenter (office).

RANJEVA, Gen. Marcel; Malagasy politician and army officer (retd); *Minister of Foreign Affairs;* b. 15 Jan. 1944, Antananarivo; m. Michele Rajaonera; two c. *Education:* Paris I (Sorbonne), France. *Career:* mem. Christian Students Youth 1960–64; assigned to Army Staff Tech. Bd 1975, then to Dept of Econ. Affairs of Ministry of Defense 1976; apptd Dir of Mil. Operations, Office of Mil. Agricultural Production 1982; Commdr Mil. Acad. 1986; Sec. Gen. Office Malagasy des Tabacs 1992; Chief of Staff, Office of the President 1995–96; Minister of Defence 1996–2002 (resgnd); Minister of Foreign Affairs 2002–; mem. Association des Anciens Elèves de Coëtquidan; Grand Croix de 2ème Classe de La République Malgache, Grand Officier de la Légion d'Honneur, Commandeur de la Légion d'honneur, Officier de l'Ordre National de Mérite.
Address: Ministry of Foreign Affairs, BP 836, Anosy, 101 Antananarivo, Madagascar (office). *Telephone:* (20) 2221198 (office). *Fax:* (20) 2234484 (office). *E-mail:* contact@madagascar-diplomatie.net (office). *Website:* www.madagascar-diplomatie.net (office).

RANJEVA, Raymond, LLD; Malagasy lawyer and international official; *Judge, International Court of Justice;* b. 31 Aug. 1942, Antananarivo; m. Yvette Madeleine R. Rabetafika 1967; five c. *Education:* Univ. of Madagascar, Madagascar Nat. School of Admin., Univ. of Paris, France. *Career:* trainee, Judicial Div., Conseil d'Etat, Paris; Civil Admin., Univ. of Madagascar 1966, Asst Lecturer 1966–72, Lecturer 1972, Dir Dept of Legal and Political Science 1973–82, Prof. 1981–91, Dean of Faculty of Law, Econs, Man. and Social Sciences 1982–88; Prof., Madagascar Mil. Acad., Madagascar School of Admin.; Dir Public Law and Political Science Study Centre; First Rector, Univ. of Antananarivo 1988–90; Man. Dir Jureco (econ., financial and legal databank for advisory and research bodies) 1986–90, Ed. Lettre mensuelle de Jureco 1986–88; Conciliator, IBRD Int. Centre for Settlement of Investment Disputes 1970–; Attorney to Mali, Border Dispute (Burkina Faso/Mali); Consultant on transfer to the State of activities of Eau-Electricité de Madagascar and Electricité de France 1973; Judge, Int. Court of Justice 1991–, Vice-Pres. 2003–06; Founder-mem. Malagasy Human Rights Cttee 1971; mem. and Vice-Pres. Malagasy Acad. 1974, Pres. Ethics and Political Science section 1975–91; mem. Nat. Constitutional Cttee 1975; mem. Court of Arbitration for Sport 1995–; legal adviser to Catholic Bishops' Conf., Madagascar; mem. Governing Body of African Soc. of Int. and Comparative Law, French Soc. of Int. Law, Québec Soc. (Canada); Sec.-Gen. Malagasy Legal Studies Soc.; mem. Pontifical Comm. 'Justice et Paix' 2002–, Curatorium de l'Acad. de Droit Int. 2002–; Commdr, Ordre Nat. Malgache of Madagascar, Chevalier, Ordre de Mérite of Madagascar, Officier, Ordre Nat. of Mali, Grand-Croix nat. malgache 2003.
Address: International Court of Justice, Peace Palace, Carnegieplein 2, 2517 KJ The Hague, Netherlands (office). *Telephone:* (70) 3022323 (office). *Fax:* (70) 3022409 (office). *E-mail:* information@icj-cij.org (office). *Website:* www.icj-cij.org (office).

RANNEBERGER, Michael E., BA, MA; American diplomatist; *Ambassador to Kenya; Education:* Towson State Univ., Baltimore, Md, Univ. of Virginia. *Career:* Angola Desk Officer 1981–84, worked as mem. of Asst Sec. Crocker's team negotiating independence for Namibia and withdrawal of Cuban troops from Angola; Special Asst to Under-Sec. Armacost 1984–85; Deputy Chief of Mission in Maputo 1986–89, included eight

months as Chargé d'affaires during civil war; Deputy Chief of Mission in Asunción 1989–92; Deputy Dir for Cen. American Affairs 1992–94; Deputy Chief of Mission in Mogadishu 1994; set up and ran inter-agency Task Force on Justice and Security-Related Issues in Haiti Jan.–June 1995; Co-ordinator for Cuban Affairs 1995–99; Amb. to Mali 1999–2002; Special Advisor on Sudan 2002–04; Prin. Deputy Asst Sec., Africa Bureau 2004–05; Sr Rep. on Sudan, Bureau of African Affairs Jan.–Aug. 2006; Amb. to Kenya with responsibility for US relations with Somalia 2006–; mem. Sr Foreign Service with rank of Minister-Counselor; Int. Affairs Fellowship, Council on Foreign Relations, seven Superior Honor Awards, State Dept, Presidential Meritorious Service Award.
Address: US Embassy, United Nations Avenue, PO Box 606, Village Market, 00621 Nairobi, Kenya (office). *Telephone:* (20) 3636000 (office). *Fax:* (20) 3633410 (office). *E-mail:* ircnairobi@state.gov (office). *Website:* nairobi.usembassy.gov (office).

RANTEKOA, David Mohlomi, BA; Lesotho diplomatist; *Ambassador to USA;* b. 2 May 1953, Ha Khopha, Pitseng, Leribe; m.; one s. two d. *Education:* St Joseph's Seminary, St Theresa's Seminary, Roma, Ha Maama, Nat. Univ. of Lesotho, Roma, Eastern and Southern African Man. Inst., Arusha, Tanzania, HM Tax Training for Commonwealth Tax Officials, UK, Irish Man. Inst., Dublin, Ireland. *Career:* served in Ministry of Finance as Sr Insp. of Income Tax, Collector of Income Tax, Deputy Commr of Income Tax, Acting Commr of Income Tax and Commr of Sales Tax 1978–92, seconded to Lesotho Electricity Corpn as Man. Dir 1992–95; served in office of Deputy Prin. Sec., Ministry of Finance, Ministry of Trade and Industry, Cabinet Office and Ministry of Trade and Industry 1995–98, Prin. Sec., Ministry of Trade and Industry 1998–2008; has served on various bds of public enterprises and cos, including Lesotho Nat. Devt Corpn, Basotho Enterprises Devt Corpn, Lesotho Highlands Devt Authority, Lesotho Floor Mills, Lesotho Sun, Maseru Sun; Amb. to USA (also accred to Brazil and Mexico) 2008–.
Address: Embassy of Lesotho, 2511 Massachusetts Avenue, NW, Washington, DC 20008, USA (office). *Telephone:* (202) 797-5533 (office). *Fax:* (202) 234-6815 (office). *E-mail:* lesothoembassy@verizon.net (office). *Website:* www.lesothoemb-usa.gov.ls (office).

RAO, Nirupama, MA; Indian diplomatist; *Ambassador to China;* b. 6 Dec. 1950; m. Sudhakar Rao; two s. *Education:* Marathwada Univ. *Career:* joined Foreign Service 1973; First Sec. (Agreement), Mission in Colombo 1981–83; Desk Officer, Southern Africa and Nepal Desks, Ministry of External Affairs, then with East Asia Div. 1984–92; Minister for Press Affairs, Embassy in Washington, DC 1993–95; Amb. to Peru 1995–98; Deputy Chief of Mission, Embassy in Moscow 1998–99; Head of Div. in charge of Multilateral Econ. Relations, Ministry of External Affairs 2000–01, Jt Sec. for External Publicity and Official Spokesperson 2001–02, Additional Sec. Human Resources Div. 2002–04, Foreign Service Inspector 2004; High Commr to Sri Lanka 2004–06; Amb. to China 2006–; fmr Fellow specializing in Asia-Pacific Security, Center for Int. Affairs (now Weatherhead Center), Harvard Univ., USA; Distinguished Int. Exec. in Residence, Univ. of Maryland, USA 1999–2000.
Address: Embassy of India, 1 Ri Tan Dong Lu, Jian Guo Men Wai, Beijing 100600, The People's Republic of China (office). *Telephone:* (10) 65321908 (office). *Fax:* (10) 65324684 (office). *Website:* www.indianembassy.org.cn (office).

RAO, Nirupama, MA; Indian diplomatist; *Ambassador to The People's Republic of China;* b. 6 Dec. 1950, Kerala; m. Sudhakar Rao; two s. *Education:* Marathwada Univ. *Career:* joined Foreign Service 1973, served in E Asia Div., Ministry of External Affairs 1984–92, Spokesperson Ministry of External Affairs 2001–02, Additional Sec., responsible for Admin and Personnel 2002–04; overseas postings include serving as Minister in charge of Press Affairs, Embassy in Washington, DC 1993–95, Amb. to Peru 1995–98, Deputy Chief of Mission, Embassy in Moscow 1998–99, High Commr to Sri Lanka 2004–06, Amb. to People's Repub. of China 2006–; Fellow, Centre for Int. Affairs, Harvard Univ., USA 1992–93; Distinguished Int. Exec.-in-Residence, Univ. of Maryland, USA 1999–2000. *Publications:* Rain Rising (poems) 2004.
Address: Embassy of India, 1 Ri Tan Dong Lu, Beijing 100600, People's Republic of China (office). *Telephone:* (10) 65321908 (office). *Fax:* (10) 65324684 (office). *E-mail:* webmaster@indianembassy.org.cn (office). *Website:* www.indianembassy.org.cn (office).

RAOULT, Eric, LèsScEcon; French politician; *Mayor of Raincy;* b. 19 June 1955, Paris; m. Béatrice Abollivier 1990. *Education:* Inst. d'Etudes Politiques, Paris and Inst. Français de Presse. *Career:* Parl. Asst to Claude Labbé; Town Councillor, Raincy 1977; Deputy Mayor of Raincy 1983–95, Mayor 1995–; mem. Cen. Cttee of RPR 1982–; Deputy to Nat. Ass. 1986–1995, 2002–, Vice-Pres. 1993–95, 2002–07; mem. Comm. on Foreign Affairs; Regional Councillor, Ile de France 1992; Minister of Integration

and the Fight against Exclusion May–Nov. 1995, Deputy Minister with responsibility for Urban Affairs and Integration 1995–97; Nat. Sec. with responsibility for elections 1998–99, with responsibility for Feds and Dom-Tom 1999–2002 (RPR).
Address: Casier de la Poste, Palais Bourbon, 75355 Paris 07 (office); Mairie, 121 avenue de la Résistance, 93340 Le Raincy, France (office). *Telephone:* 1-43-02-52-94 (office); 1-43-02-77-15 (office). *E-mail:* eraoult@assemblee-nationale.fr (office); ericraoult2007@yahoo.fr (home). *Website:* ericraoult.over-blog.com.

RAPOLAKI, Molelekeng Ernestina, MA; Lesotho diplomatist and civil servant; m. (divorced); three c. *Education:* Nat. Univ. of Lesotho, Univ. of Southern Calif., USA. *Career:* Sr Planning Officer, Ministry of Econ. Planning 1985–87, Dir of Population and Manpower Planning 1994–97; Dir Econ. Policy, Ministry of Devt Planning 1987–92, Prin. Sec. 1997–2001; Amb. to USA (also accred to Brazil and Mexico and as High Commr to Canada) 2001–08; Research Award on Population Policy Communication, Population Reference Bureau, Washington, DC 1993, Nat. Asscn of Negro Business and Professional Women's Clubs Inc. Women Who Make a Difference Award 2002. *Publications:* contrib. of chapters to Population, Health, Education and Mining Sectors in the Economic Options for Lesotho 1997.
Address: Ministry of Foreign Affairs and International Relations, PO Box 1387, Maseru 100, Lesotho (office). *Telephone:* 22311150 (office). *Fax:* 22310178 (office). *E-mail:* moear@foreign.gov.ls (office). *Website:* www.foreign.gov.ls (office).

RASHID, Ahmed; Pakistani journalist and author; b. 1948, Rawalpindi; m.; two c. *Education:* Malvern Coll., UK, Government Coll., Lahore, Fitzwilliam Coll., Univ. of Cambridge, UK. *Career:* fmr Pakistan, Afghanistan and Cen. Asia Corresp. Far Eastern Economic Review; now writes regularly for Daily Telegraph, London, International Herald Tribune, New York Review of Books, BBC Online, The Nation, Lahore and other academic and foreign affairs journals as well as several Pakistani newspapers and magazines; appears on TV and radio including BBC World Service, ABC Australia, Radio France Int. and German Radio; mem. Advisory Bd Eurasia Net of the Soros Foundation; Scholar, Davos World Econ. Forum; consultant for Human Rights Watch; mem. Bd of Advisers Int. Cttee of the Red Cross, Geneva 2004–08; f. Open Media Fund for Afghanistan (charity) 2002; Nisar Osmani Award for Courage in Journalism, Human Rights Soc. of Pakistan. *Publications include:* The Resurgence of Central Asia: Islam or Nationalism, Fundamentalism Reborn: Afghanistan and the Taliban, Jihad: The Rise of Militant Islam in Central Asia, Taliban: Islam, Oil and the New Great Game in Central Asia 2000, Descent into Chaos 2008.
Address: c/o The Daily Telegraph, 1 Canada Square, Canary Wharf, London, E14 5DT, England (office). *Telephone:* (20) 7538-5000 (office). *Fax:* (20) 7513-2506 (office). *E-mail:* dtnews@telegraph.co.uk (office). *Website:* www.telegraph.co.uk (office); www.ahmedrashid.com.

RASHID, Rashid Muhammad, BSc; Egyptian business executive and politician; *Minister of Trade and Industry;* b. 1956, Alexandria. *Education:* Alexandria Univ. *Career:* f. Fine Foods (Egypt's leading food brand) jt venture with Unilever Mashreq, later Pres. Unilever Middle East, N Africa and Turkey, London; Minister of Trade and Industry 2004–; fmr mem. Bd of Dirs Unilever.
Address: Ministry of Trade and Industry, 2 Latin America Str., Cairo, Egypt (office). *Telephone:* (2) 7921167 (office). *Fax:* (2) 7955025 (office). *E-mail:* mfti@mfti.gov.eg (office). *Website:* www.mfti.gov.eg (office).

RASI, Satu Marjatta, LLB; Finnish diplomatist; *Under-Secretary of State, Ministry of Foreign Affairs;* b. 29 Nov. 1945, Punkalaidun; m. *Education:* Helsinki Univ. *Career:* attaché, Finnish diplomatic service 1970, Second Sec., London 1972–73, Paris 1974–76, Sec. of Section, Ministry of Foreign Affairs 1977; Counsellor Perm. Mission to the UN 1979; Counsellor, Ministry of Foreign Affairs 1983–86, Dir UN Section, Political Dept 1986; Deputy Perm. Rep. to the UN 1987–91, Perm. Rep. 1997–2005; Chair. Security Council Cttee responsible for monitoring sanctions regime against Iraq 1990; Amb. to India (also accred to Bangladesh, Sri Lanka, Nepal and Bhutan) 1991–95; Dir-Gen. Dept for Int. Devt Co-operation, Ministry of Foreign Affairs 1995–97, Under-Sec. of State 2005–; Vice-Pres. ECOSOC 2002–03, Pres. 2004; Gov., Asian Devt Bank, African Devt Bank, IDB 2005–; Chair. Advisory Bd, UN Peace Building Fund 2007–.
Address: Ministry of Foreign Affairs, Merikasarmi, Laivastokatu 22, POB 176, 00161 Helsinki (office); Katajanolanlattvei 3, 00160 Helsinki, Finland (office). *Telephone:* (9) 16056400 (office). *Fax:* (9) 16056404 (office). *E-mail:* avs-keo@formin.fi (office). *Website:* formin.finland.fi (office).

RASIZADE, Artur Tahir oğlu; Azerbaijani politician and engineer; *Prime Minister;* b. 26 Feb. 1935, Ganca; m.; one d. *Education:* Azerbaijan Inst. of

Industry. *Career:* engineer, Deputy Dir Azerbaijan Inst. of Oil Machine Construction 1957–73, Dir 1977–78; chief engineer Trust Soyuzneftemash 1973–77; Deputy Head Azerbaijan State Planning Cttee 1978–81; Head of Section Cen. Cttee of Azerbaijan CP 1981–86; First Deputy Prime Minister 1986–92; adviser Foundation of Econ. Reforms 1992–96; Asst to Pres. Heydar Aliyev Feb.–May 1996; First Deputy Prime Minister May–Nov. 1996; Prime Minister 1996–, demoted and apptd Deputy Prime Minister Aug. 2003 but resumed role as Prime Minister days later.
Address: Office of the Prime Minister, 1066 Baku, Lermontov küç. 68, Azerbaijan (office). *Telephone:* (12) 492-66-23 (office). *Fax:* (12) 492-91-79 (office). *E-mail:* nk@cabmin.gov.az (office). *Website:* www.cabmin.gov.az (office).

RASMUSSEN, Anders Fogh, MSc; Danish politician; *Prime Minister;* b. 26 Jan. 1953; m. Anne-Mette Rasmussen; three c. *Education:* Econ. Univ. of Århus. *Career:* Consultant to Danish Fed. of Crafts and Small Industries 1978–87; mem. Folketing (Parl.) 1978–, mem. Econ. and Political Affairs Cttee 1982–87, Vice-Chair. 1993–98; Vice-Chair. Housing Cttee 1981–86; Minister for Taxation 1987–92, also for Econ. Affairs 1990–92; Vice-Chair. Econ. and Political Affairs Cttee 1993–98; Prime Minister of Denmark 2001–; mem. Venstre (Liberal Party), Vice-Chair. Nat. Org. Venstre 1985–98, mem. Man. Cttee Parl. Party 1984–87, 1992–2001, Spokesman for Venstre 1992–98, Vice-Chair. Foreign Policy Bd 1998–2001, Chair. Venstre 1998–; Grand Cross of the Portuguese Order of Merit 1992, Commdr (First Degree) of the Order of the Dannebrog 2002, Danish Gold Medal of Merit 2002, Grand Cross of the German Order of Merit 2002, Grand Cross of the Order of Merit of Poland 2003, Grand Cross of the Order of the Oak Crown of Luxembourg 2003, Grand Cross of the Order of Nicaragua 2003, Great Cross of the Pedro Joaquin Chamorro Order 2003, Ordinul Steaua României Mare Cruce 2004, Grand Cross of the Order of the Lithuanian Grand Duke Gediminas 2004, Three Star Order of Latvia 2005, Order of Stara Planina, First Class (Bulgaria) 2006, Grand Cross of the Nordstjär- neorden (Sweden) 2007, Grand Cross of the Order of the South Cross (Brazil) 2007; Dr hc (George Washington Univ.) 2002, Hon. DIur (Hampden-Sydney Coll., VA) 2003; Adam Smith Award 1993, Politician of the Year (Dansk Markedsfuringsforbund) 1998, Netherlands Youth Org. for Freedom and Democracy Liberal of the Year 2002, European Leader Award, Polish Leaders Forum 2003, Danish European Movement European of the Year 2003, Robert Schumann Medal 2003, Pedro Joaquin Chamorro Medal, Nicaragua 2003, Best Leader in Denmark 2005, Politician of the Year 2005, Chevalier du St-Chinian 2007. *Publications:* Oprør med skattesystemet 1979, Den truede velstand (co-author) 1980, Kampen om boligen 1982, Fra Socialstat til Minimalstat 1993, I Godvejr og storm (interviews) 2001.
Address: Office of the Prime Minister, Christiansborg, Prins Jørgens Gård 11, 1218 Copenhagen K, Denmark (office). *Telephone:* 33-92-33-00 (office). *Fax:* 33-11-16-65 (office). *E-mail:* stm@stm.dk (office). *Website:* www.stm .dk (office).

RASMUSSEN, Lars Løkke; Danish politician; *Minister of Finance;* b. 15 May 1964. *Education:* Copenhagen Univ. *Career:* mem. Venstre (Liberal Party); mem. Folketinget (Parl.) 1994–; Minister of the Interior and Health 2001–07, of Finance 2007–; Co. Mayor of Frederiksborg Co. 1998–2001.
Address: Ministry of Finance, Christiansborg Slotsplads 1, 1218 Copenha- gen K, Denmark (office). *Telephone:* 33-92-33-33 (office). *Fax:* 33-32-30-80 (office). *E-mail:* fm@fm.dk (office). *Website:* www.fm.dk (office).

RASMUSSEN, Wilkie; Cook Islands politician; *Minister of Foreign Affairs and Immigration, Tourism, Cultural Development, Marine Resources and Natural Environment Resources; Career:* practiced as barrister 1996–99; Cabinet Sec. 1999–2000; High Commr to NZ 2000–02; mem. Parl. 2002–; Minister of Foreign Affairs and Immigration, Tourism, Cultural Devt, Marine Resources and Natural Environment Resources 2005–.
Address: Ministry of Foreign Affairs and Immigration, PO Box 105, Rarotonga, Cook Islands (office). *Telephone:* 29347 (office). *Fax:* 21247 (office). *E-mail:* secfa@mfai.gov.ck (office); wilkie@omoka.co.ck (home).

RATSIFANDRIHAMANANA, HE Lila Hanitra, (Ramatoa Ratsifandriha- manana Lia), BSc; Malagasy politician and diplomatist; *Permanent Observer of the African Union, United Nations;* b. 19 Nov. 1959; m.; three c. *Education:* Leningrad (now St Petersburg) Mining School, USSR, studies in remote sensing (SITEL), Toulouse, France, Univ. of Liège, Belgium. *Career:* Minister of Scientific Research 1997–98, of Foreign Affairs 1998–2002; Amb. to Senegal (also accred to Mali, Burkina Faso, Morocco, Cape Verde and Côte d'Ivoire) 2002–06; Perm. Observer of the African Union to UN, New York 2006–; fmr mem. Indian Ocean Rim Asscn for Regional Cooperation, Common Market for Eastern and Southern Africa (COMESA), Indian Ocean Comm. (Chair. 2000).
Address: Office of the Permanent Observer for the African Union to the United Nations, 3 Dag Hammarskjöld Plaza, 305 East 47th Street, 5th

Floor, New York, NY 10017, USA (office). *Telephone:* (212) 319-5490 (office). *Fax:* (212) 319-7135 (office); (212) 319-6509 (office). *E-mail:* africanunion@un.int (office); au-newyork@africa-union-nyo.org (office). *Website:* www.un.org (office).

RATZINGER, Joseph Alois (see BENEDICT XVI, His Holiness Pope).

RAVALOMANANA, Marc; Malagasy business executive, politician and head of state; *President;* b. 12 Dec. 1949, Imerikasina; m. Lalao Rakotonirainy; three s. one d. *Education:* in Imerikasina and in Sweden. *Career:* f. TIKO (dairy and oil producing co.); owns Malagasy Broad- casting System (TV and radio stations), MAGRO (supermarket chain), FANAMBY (rice-producing co.); elected Mayor of Antananarivo 1999; following disputed victory in presidential elections Dec. 2001, declared himself Pres. of Madagascar Feb. 2002, High Constitutional Court ruled that he had won by an overall majority May 2002, Pres. of Madagascar 2002–; Vice-Pres. Protestant Church of Madagascar; Dr hc (Univ. of Antananarivo) 2007; Prix Louise Michel 2005.
Address: c/o Office of the President, Antananarivo, Madagascar (office). *E-mail:* communication@presidency.gov.mg (office). *Website:* www .madagascar-presidency.gov.mg (office).

RAVAOARIMANANA, Iary Berthine; Malagasy diplomatist; *Chargé d'affaires a.i. and First Counsellor, Embassy in London, UK. Career:* fmr Amb. to Germany, Chargé d'affaires a.i. and First Counsellor, Embassy in London, UK 2005–.
Address: Embassy of Madagascar, 8–10 Hallam Street, London, W1W 6JE, England (office). *Telephone:* (20) 3008-4550 (office). *Fax:* (20) 3008-4551 (office). *E-mail:* embamadlon@yahoo.co.uk (office). *Website:* www .embassy-madagascar-uk.com (office).

RAY, Siddhartha Shankar, BA, LLB; Indian lawyer and politician; b. 20 Oct. 1920, Calcutta; m. Maya Bhattacharya 1947. *Education:* Presidency Coll., Univ. Law Coll., Calcutta. *Career:* called to the Bar, Inner Temple, London; Sr Advocate, Supreme Court 1969; corporate, commercial and constitutional lawyer; appeared in all Courts in India including the Supreme Court, the East Pakistan High Court, the Pakistan Supreme Court (Dhaka Circuit Bench) and Tribunal of Arbitration, Int. Chamber of Commerce, Paris; mem. W Bengal Legis. Ass. 1957–71, 1972–77, 1991–92; mem. Lok Sabha 1971–72, Jr Cen. Govt Counsel 1954–57; Minister of Law and Tribal Welfare, Govt of W Bengal 1957–58; Leader of the Opposition, W Bengal Ass. 1969–71, 1991–92; Cabinet Minister for Educ., Culture, Social Welfare and W Bengal Affairs, Govt of India 1971–72; Chief Minister of W Bengal 1972–77; Gov. of Punjab and Admin. of Chandigarh 1986–89; Amb. to USA 1992–96; High Commr in the Commonwealth of the Bahamas 1994; Gen. Sec. Calcutta Univ. Law Coll. 1941–43; Under-Sec. Calcutta Univ. Inst. 1941–44; Univ. Blue in cricket, football and tennis; Individual Champion Athletics, Calcutta Univ. Law Coll. 1941, 1942; mem. Working Cttee Indian Nat. Congress, All India Congress Cttee, Congress Parl. Bd; Pres. Cricket Asscn of Bengal 1982–84; mem. Indian Nat. Trust for Art and Cultural Heritage; Trustee Jawaharlal Nehru Memorial Fund (mem. Exec. Cttee); Trustee Nehru Scholarship Trust for Cambridge Univ.; Hon. LLD (Drury Coll., Missouri) 1993.
Address: 2 Beltala Road, Kolkata 700026, India (home). *Telephone:* (33) 4753465.

RAYMOND, Valerie, BA, BJ; Canadian diplomatist; *Director General, Canadian Foreign Service Institute;* b. Winnipeg; m. Ronald Verzuh; one d. *Education:* Univ. of Guelph, Carleton Univ. *Career:* fmr journalist, Ottawa Citizen 1970s; several years at Depts of Energy, Mines and Resources, Employment and Immigration, and Status of Women Canada; joined Dept of External Affairs 1986, Dir External Communications 1986–90, Dir Human Rights, Women's Equality and Social Affairs 1992–94, Exec. Dir UN World Conf. on Women 1995, Coordinator Habitat II Summit 1996, Dir Arts and Cultural Industries Promotion 1996, Coordinator, Special Projects, Human Resources 2001; High Commr to New Zealand 1997–2001, to Sri Lanka (also accred to Maldives) 2002–05; seconded to Forum of Feds, served as Vice Pres. Governance Programs 2005–06; Dir Gen. Canadian Foreign Service Inst. 2006–; Dr hc (Univ. of Guelph) 2007.
Address: Canadian Foreign Service Institute, Department of Foreign Affairs and International Trade, 125 Sussex Drive, Ottawa, ON K1A 0G2, Canada (office). *Telephone:* (613) 944-0011 (office). *Fax:* (613) 996-4381 (office). *E-mail:* cfsi-icse.soutienwebsupport@international.gc.ca (office). *Website:* www.international.gc.ca/ifait-iaeci (office).

RAYTCHEV, Rayko Strahilov, MA; Bulgarian diplomatist; *Permanent Representative, United Nations;* b. 29 March 1955; m.; one d. *Education:* Higher Inst. of Econs, Sofia, John F. Kennedy School of Govt, Harvard Univ. *Career:* joined diplomatic corps as Attaché 1982, becoming Head

UN Dept, Co-ordination and Planning Directorate 2000–01, Head UN and Gen. Issues Dept Jan.–Nov. 2001, Deputy Perm. Rep. to UN, New York 2001–05, with Foreign Ministry's NATO and Int. Security Directorate 2005, becoming Head Global Security and Disarmament Dept March–July 2005, Head Arms Control and Int. Security Dept July–Aug. 2005, Chief of Cabinet of Minister of Foreign Affairs 2005–07, Perm. Rep. to UN, New York 2007–; Certificate in Peacekeeping Negotiations and Mediation, Pearson Peacekeeping Centre, Canada 2001.
Address: Permanent Mission of the Republic of Bulgaria to the United Nations, 11 East 84th Street, New York, NY 10028, USA (office). *Telephone:* (212) 737-4790 (office). *Fax:* (212) 472-9865 (office). *E-mail:* bulgaria@un.int (office). *Website:* www.un.int/bulgaria (office).

RAZAFINJATOVO, Haja Nirina, MA, PhD; Malagasy politician; *Minister of Finance and the Budget; Education:* Univ. of Connecticut, USA. *Career:* fmr teacher Florida International Univ., James Madison Univ., Univ. of Connecticut; served as Computer Specialist at US Embassy, Antananarivo; Minister of Telecommunications, Posts and Communication 2002–04; Minister of Nat. Educ. and Scientific Research 2004–07, of Finance and the Budget 2007–.
Address: Ministry of Finance and the Budget, BP 61, Antaninarenina, 101 Antananarivo, Madagascar (office). *Telephone:* (20) 2230173 (office). *Fax:* (20) 2264680 (office). *E-mail:* info@mefb.gov.mg (office). *Website:* www .mefb.gov.mg (office).

RAZAFY-ANDRIAMIHAINGO, Jean-Pierre; Malagasy diplomatist and lawyer; *Ambassador to France; Career:* lawyer Court of Paris; currently teaches at several French univs; conducted seminars at Institut des Hautes Etudes pour la Francophonie; consultant Intergovernmental Agency for French Speaking Countries; currently Amb. to France (concurrently non-resident Amb. to Holy See, UK, Spain, Monaco, Israel). *Publications:* La Geste Éphémère de Ranavalona Ière: l'Expédition Diplomatique Malgache en Europe, 1836–1837 1997.
Address: Embassy of Madagascar, 4 avenue Raphaël, 75016 Paris, France (office). *Telephone:* 1-45-04-62-11 (office). *Fax:* 1-45-03-58-70 (office). *E-mail:* info@ambamad-france.com (office). *Website:* www.ambamad -france.com (office).

RAZAK, Dato' Seri Mohamad Najib bin tun Haj Abdul, BA; Malaysian politician; *Deputy Prime Minister and Minister of Defence;* b. 23 July 1953, Kuala Lipis, Pahang; m. Toh Puan Indera Datin Sri Rosmah Mansor; five c. *Education:* Univ. of Nottingham. *Career:* Exec. Patronas 1974–76; Pengerusi Majuternak 1977–78; mem. Parl. 1976–; Deputy Minister of Energy, Telecommunications and Posts 1978–80, of Educ. 1980–81, of Finance 1981–82; mem. State Ass. for Pakan constituency 1982–86; Menteri Besar Pahang 1982–86; Minister of Culture, Youth and Sports 1986–87, of Youth and Sports 1987–90, of Defence 1990–95, 1999–, of Educ. 1995–99; Deputy Prime Minister 2004–; mem. UMNO Supreme Council 1981–; Vice-Pres. UMNO Youth 1982–; Chair. Pahang Foundation 1982–86; Grand Order of Youth (Korea) 1988, Kt Grand Cross, First Class (Thailand), Bintang Yudha Dharma Utama (Indonesia) 1994, Distinguished Service Order (Singapore) 1994, DUBC (Thailand) 1995; Hon. PhD (US Acad. of Sports) 1992, (Nottingham) 2004; Orang Kaya Indera Shahbandar 1976, Darjah Sultan Ahmad Shah 1978, Seri Indera Mahkota Pahang 1983, Darjah Kebesaran Seri Sultan Ahmad Shah 1985, Man of the Year Award, New Straits Times 1990, Panglima Bintang Sarawak 1990, Dato Paduka Mahkota Selangor 1992, Seri Panglima Darjah Kinabalu (SPDK) 2002.
Address: Office of the Deputy Prime Minister, Level 4, West Wing, Bangunan Perdana Putra, 62502 Putrajaya, Malaysia (office). *Telephone:* (3) 88881950 (office). *Fax:* (3) 88883973 (office). *E-mail:* najib@pmo.gov .my (office).

RAZOV, Sergey Sergeyevich, PhD; Russian diplomatist and economist; *Ambassador to People's Republic of China;* b. 28 Jan. 1953, Sochi, Krasnodar Territory; m.; two c. *Education:* Moscow Inst. of Int. Relations. *Career:* economist, sr economist USSR Trade Mission to Repub. of China 1975–79; head of div., head of group Cen. CPSU Cttee 1979–90; Head Dept of Far East Countries and Indochina, USSR Ministry of Foreign Affairs 1990–92; Amb. to Mongolia 1992–96; Dir Third Dept of CIS Countries, Russian Ministry of Foreign Affairs 1996–99; Amb. to Poland 1999–2002, to People's Repub. of China 2005–; Deputy Minister of Foreign Affairs 2002–05. *Publications:* The People's Republic of China 1991, Foreign Policy of Open Doors of People's Republic of China 1985; articles and other publs.
Address: Embassy of the Russian Federation, 4 Dong Zhi Men Nei, Bei Zhong Jie, Beijing 100600, People's Republic of China (office). *Telephone:* (10) 65322051 (office). *Fax:* (10) 65324851 (office). *E-mail:* embassy@russia .org.cn (office). *Website:* www.russia.org.cn (office).

READER, David George; British diplomatist; *Ambassador to Cambodia;* m. Elaine Reader; one s. one d. *Career:* joined FCO in 1976, early overseas postings include Attache, Embassy in Kinshasa 1979–82, Attaché Devt, Embassy in Katmandu 1982–84; at FCO 1984–87; Consul Gen. in Brisbane 1987–91, Consul and First Sec., Embassy in Belgrade 1992–95; with UK Trade and Industry, London 1996–97; Dir Trade and Investment, Embassy in Cairo 1998–2001, High Commr to Swaziland 2001–04; Amb. to Cambodia 2005–.
Address: British Embassy, 27–29 rue 75, Sangkat Sras Chak, Khan Daun Penh, Phnom-Penh, Cambodia (office). *Telephone:* (23) 427124 (office). *Fax:* (23) 427125 (office). *E-mail:* britemb@online.com.kh (office). *Website:* www.britishhembassy.gov.uk/cambodia (office).

REDDAWAY, David Norman, CMG, MBE, MA; British (b. Canadian) diplomatist; *Ambassador to Ireland;* b. 26 April 1953, Ottawa, Canada; m. Roshan Firouz 1981; two s. one d. *Education:* Oundle School, Peterborough and Univ. of Cambridge. *Career:* worked as volunteer teacher in Ethiopia before univ. studies; joined FCO 1975, First Sec. 1985–86, Pvt. Sec. in Office of Minister of State 1986–88, Head of Southern European Dept 1997–99, Dir of Public Services 1999–2001; overseas postings include Third Sec., Second Sec. then First Sec. Embassy in Tehran, Iran 1977–80, Chargé d'affaires 1990–93; First Sec. in Madrid, Spain 1980–84, in New Delhi, India 1988–90; Embassy Minister in Buenos Aires, Argentina 1993–97; Special Rep. to Afghanistan 2002; High Commr to Canada 2003–06; Amb. to Ireland 2006–; Visiting Fellow, Weatherhead Center for Int. Affairs, Harvard Univ. 2003.
Address: British Embassy, 29 Merrion Road, Dublin, 4, Ireland (office). *Telephone:* (1) 2053700 (office). *Fax:* (1) 2053893 (office). *E-mail:* publicaffairs.dublx@fco.gov.uk (office). *Website:* www.britishhembassy.ie (office).

REDDICK, Eunice S., BA, MA; American diplomatist; *Ambassador to Gabon;* b. New York, NY; m. Amb. Marc M. Wall; one s. one d. *Education:* New York Univ., School of Int. Affairs, Columbia Univ. *Career:* worked for several years at Africa-America Inst., New York and Washington, DC; career mem. Sr Foreign Service, entered Foreign Service 1980, Consular Officer, Harare 1981–83; assigned to Bureau of Population, Refugee and Migration Affairs, Dept of State 1983–86, Country Officer for Tanzania and Indian Ocean countries, Bureau of African Affairs 1986–88, Sr Watch Officer, 24-hour Operations Center 1988–89; Mandarin Chinese language training, American Inst. in Taiwan (AIT)/Taipei Language School 1989–90; assigned to Political Section, Embassy in Beijing 1990; Assoc., Inst. for Study of Diplomacy, Georgetown Univ. 1993; Deputy Dir Bureau of East Asian and Pacific Affairs Office of Burma, Cambodia, Laos, Thailand and Vietnam Affairs, Dept of State, Deputy Dir Office of Int. Devt Assistance, Bureau of Int. Org. Affairs 1993–97; Chief of Political Section, AIT, Taipei 1997–2000; Deputy Dir, later Dir Office of Philippines, Malaysia, Brunei and Singapore Affairs, Dept of State 2002–04, Dir Office of East African Affairs, Bureau of African Affairs 2005–07; Amb. to Gabon (also accred to São Tomé and Príncipe) 2007–; Dean and Virginia Rusk Fellowship 1993.
Address: US Embassy, Blvd du Bord de Mer, BP 4000, Libreville, Gabon (office). *Telephone:* 76-20-03 (office). *Fax:* 74-55-07 (office). *E-mail:* clolibreville@state.gov (office). *Website:* libreville.usembassy.gov (office).

REDING, Viviane, PhD; Luxembourg journalist and politician; *Commissioner for Information Society and Media, European Commission;* b. 27 April 1951, Esch-sur Alzette; m.; three c. *Education:* Sorbonne, Paris. *Career:* journalist, Luxemburger Wort 1978–99; mem. Parl. 1979–89; communal councillor, City of Esch 1981–99; Pres. Luxembourg Union of Journalists 1986–98; Nat. Pres. Christian-Social Women 1988–93; MEP 1989–99; Pres. Cultural Affairs Cttee 1992–99; Vice-Pres. Parti Chrétien-Social 1995–99; Vice-Pres. Civil Liberties and Internal Affairs Cttee 1997–99; EU Commr for Educ. and Culture 1999–2004, for Information Soc. and Media 2004–; mem. Benelux Parl., N Atlantic Ass. (Leader Christian Democrat/Conservative Group); Officier, Légion d'honneur; Dr hc (Hu Chen Univ. of Taiwan) 2004, (Univ. of Genoa) 2004, (Univ. of Torino) 2004; St George's Cross, Generalitat of Catalunya 1992, Gold Medal of European Merit 2001, Robert Schuman Medal 2004, Prince of Asturias Int. Cooperation Prize 2004, Gloria Artins Medal of Honour (Poland) 2005.
Address: Commission of the European Communities, 200 rue de la Loi, 1049 Brussels, Belgium (office). *Telephone:* (2) 298-16-00 (office). *Fax:* (2) 299-92-01 (office). *E-mail:* viviane.reding@ec.europa.eu (office). *Website:* ec.europa.eu/commission_barroso/reding/index_en.htm (office).

REDSHAW, Tina Susan; British diplomatist; *Ambassador to Timor-Leste;* b. 25 Jan. 1961; m. Phongphun Khogapun; one d. *Career:* joined FCO 1999, Head of Section, China and Hong Kong Dept 1999–2000, full-time language training 2000, First Sec. (Political—External), Beijing 2000–03, Amb. to Timor-Leste 2003–.

Address: British Embassy, Pantai Kelapa, Avenida de Portugal, PO Box 194 The Post Office, Dili, Timor-Leste (office). *Telephone:* 3322838 (office). *Fax:* 3312652 (office). *E-mail:* Tina.Redshaw@fco.gov.uk (office); britishembassydili@fco.gov.uk (office).

REES, Grover Joseph, III; American diplomatist; *Special Representative for Social Issues, Bureau of International Organization Affairs, US State Department;* b. La; m. Lan Dai Nguyen Rees; one s. *Education:* Yale Univ. and Louisiana State Univ. Law School. *Career:* press asst to US Rep. David C. Treen (Republican, La) 1973; law clerk to Assoc. Justice Albert Tate, Jr, Supreme Court of Louisiana 1978–79; Asst Prof. of Law, Univ. of Texas 1979–86; Chief Justice, later Assoc. Justice, High Court of American Samoa 1986–91; Gen. Counsel US Immigration and Naturalization Service 1991–93; Staff Dir and Chief Counsel Sub-cttee on Int. Operations and Human Rights, Cttee on Int. Relations, US House of Reps 1995–2001; Counsel to Cttee on Int. Relations 2001–02; Amb. to Timor-Leste 2003–06; Special Representative for Social Issues, Int. Orgs Bureau, US State Department 2006–. *Address:* Office of the Special Representative for Social Issues, Bureau of International Organization Affairs, US Department of State, 2201 C Street, NW, Washington, DC 20520, USA (office). *Telephone:* (202) 647-9034 (office). *Website:* www.state.gov/p/io (office).

REFALO, Michael A., BA, LLD, FRSA; Maltese politician, lawyer and diplomatist; *High Commissioner to UK;* b. 25 Feb. 1936; m. Blanche Smith; one s. three d. *Education:* St Aloysius Coll., Univ. of Malta. *Career:* lawyer 1961; fmr Pres. of Students' Council; MP 1971–; Parl. Sec. for Tourism 1987–94; Minister for Youth and the Arts 1994–95, for Justice and the Arts 1995–96; Shadow Minister and Opposition Spokesman on Tourism 1996–98; Minister for Tourism 1998–2005; High Commr to UK 2005–; Ed. for nine years of Sunday Nationalist Party newspaper; mem. Nationalist Party; Companion of Honour, Nat. Order of Merit (Malta) 2007. *Publications:* editorials and articles in other newspapers. *Address:* High Commission of Malta, Malta House, 36–38 Piccadilly, London, W1J 0LE, England (office). *Telephone:* (20) 7292-4800 (office). *Fax:* (20) 7734-1831 (office). *E-mail:* maltahighcommission.london@gov.mt (office).

REHN, Elisabeth, BSc, DSc; Finnish politician and international organization official; b. 6 April 1935, Helsinki; m. Ove Rehn 1955 (deceased); one s. three d. *Education:* Univ. of Helsinki. *Career:* mem. Parl. 1979–95, fmr leader Swedish People's Party; Minister of Defence 1990–95, Minister for Women's Equality 1991–95; cand. in Finnish Presidential election 1994, 2000; MEP 1995–96; fmr UN Under-Sec.-Gen.; UN Special Rapporteur for Human Rights in Fmr Yugoslavia 1995–98; UN Under-Sec.-Gen., Special Rep. of UN Sec.-Gen. in Bosnia and Herzegovina 1998–99; UNIFEM Ind. Expert on impact of war on women 2001–02; Chair. Working Table I, (Human Rights and Democratisation), Stability Pact for SE Europe, Brussels 2003–04; Chair. Finnish Asscn for Educ. and Training of Women in Crisis Prevention 1997; mem. Advisory Council Intellibridge, Washington, DC, UN Dept of Peacekeeping Review Bd, Court of Conciliation and Arbitration, OSCE 1994, Int. Steering Cttee of Engendering The Peace Process; mem. UNICEF Finnish Cttee 1982–94, Chair. 1988–93; Vice Chair. Finnish Red Cross 1984–88; Chair. Bd of Trustees, WWF Finland 2000–06; Vice Chair. Suomen Unifem ry 2003–05, Chair. of Del. 2006–; mem. Advisory Bd Femmes Africa Solidarité 2005–; Patron United World Coll. project in Bosnia and Herzegovina 2005–, Chair. Bd of Educ. from Conflict to Internationalism 2006–; hon. mem. UNICEF Finland 1994, Zonta Int. 1996; Commdr of the Order of the White Rose of Finland 1992, Cross of Liberty, First Class with Grand Star (Finland) 2002, First Class Order of the Cross of Terra Mariana (Estonia) 2003; Hon. DSc (Swedish School of Econs and Business Admin) 1994. *Address:* Saarentie 22, 02400 Kirkkonummi, Finland. *Telephone:* (9) 2952842. *E-mail:* mail@elisabethrehn.com; elisabeth.rehn@kolumbus.fi. *Website:* www.elisabethrehn.com.

REHN, Olli, DPhil; Finnish politician; *Commissioner for Enlargement, European Commission;* b. 31 March 1962, Mikkeli; m. Merja Rehn; one c. *Education:* Macalester Coll., USA, Univ. of Helsinki, Univ. of Oxford, UK. *Career:* Chair. Centre Youth of Finland 1987–89; Deputy Chair. Centre Party of Finland 1988–94; mem. Helsinki City Council 1988–94; mem. Parl. 1991–95; Special Adviser to Prime Minister 1992–93, Econ. Policy Adviser 2003–04; mem. European Parl. 1995–96; Head of Cabinet, EC 1998–2002, EU Commr for Enterprise and the Information Soc. . July–Nov. 2004, for Enlargement 2004–; Prof. and Dir of Research, Dept of Political Science and Centre for European Studies, Univ. of Helsinki 2002–03; columnist in several newspapers and magazines. *Publications:* Europe's Next Frontiers 2006, Suomen eurooppalainen valinta ei ole suhdannepolitiikkaa 2006.

Address: European Commission, 200 rue de la Loi, 1049 Brussels, Belgium (office). *Telephone:* (2) 295-79-57 (office). *Fax:* (2) 295-85-61 (office). *E-mail:* cab-rehn-web-feedback@ec.europa.eu (office). *Website:* ec.europa.eu/commission_barroso/rehn/index_en.htm (office).

REIDY, Andrea Jane, OBE; British diplomatist; *Ambassador to Eritrea;* one d. *Career:* Latin America Dept, FCO 1995–97; Second Sec., Embassy in Bratislava 1997–2000, Deputy High Commr, Embassy in Freetown 2000–02; Head of Global Opportunity Fund (Europe), EU-E, FCO 2003; Head of UK Office in Coalition Provisional Authority, Baghdad 2003–04, First Sec. (Political), Baghdad 2004–05; Communications Team Leader, Prism Programme, FCO 2005–06; Consul-Gen. for Northern Iraq, Erbil 2006–07; Amb. to Eritrea 2008–. *Address:* British Embassy, 66–68 Mariam Ghimbi Street, PO Box 5584, Asmara, Eritrea (office). *Telephone:* (1) 120145 (office). *Fax:* (1) 120104 (office). *E-mail:* asmara.enquiries@fco.gov.uk (office). *Website:* www.fco.gov.uk/eritrea (office).

REIJNDERS, Lucas, PhD; Dutch scientist and academic; *Professor of Environmental Science, University of Amsterdam;* b. 4 Feb. 1946, Amsterdam; one c. *Education:* Univ. of Amsterdam. *Career:* Dir Environmental Inst. Univ. of Groningen 1974–80, mem. staff Nat. Environmental Office 1980–, Prof. of Environmental Science Univ. of Amsterdam 1988–; Prof. of Environmental Science, Open Univ. 1999–; Winner, Gouden Ganzeveer 1990, Erewimpel ONRI 1992. *Publications:* Food in the Netherlands 1974, A Consumer Guide to Dutch Medicines 1980, Plea for a Sustainable Relation with the Environment 1984, Help the Environment 1991, Environmentally Improved Production and Products 1995, Agriculture in the Low Countries 1997, Travel Through the Ages 2000, Eating Patterns 2005, Energy 2006, Principles of Environmental Science 2008. *Address:* Anna van den Vondelstraat 10, 1054 GZ Amsterdam, Netherlands. *Telephone:* (20) 525-62-69. *Fax:* (20) 525-74-31. *E-mail:* l.reijnders@science.uva.nl (office). *Website:* www.science.uva.nl (office).

REIMAN, Leonid Dododjonovich; Russian engineer and government official; *Minister of Information and Communications Technologies;* b. 12 July 1957, Leningrad (now St Petersburg); m.; one s. one d. *Education:* Leningrad Inst. of Electro-Tech. Communications. *Career:* engineer, head of workshop Leningrad Telephone Exchange 1979–85; posts at Leningrad City Telephone Network 1985–88, later Deputy Head, Chief Eng, Dir of Int. Relations, Dir of Investments, First Deputy Dir-Gen. Jt Stock Co. Peterburgskaya Telefonnaya Set 1988–99; First Deputy Chair. State Cttee on Telecommunications Russian Fed. July–Aug. 1999; Chair. 1999–2000; Minister of Communications and Information Tech. 1999–2004; Deputy Minister for Transport and Communications April 2004; Minister of Information and Communications Techs April 2004–. *Address:* Ministry of Information and Communications Technologies, 103375 Moscow, Tverskaya str. 7, Russia (office). *Telephone:* (495) 771-81-00 (office). *Fax:* (495) 771-87-18 (office). *Website:* www.minsvyaz.ru (office).

REINA IDIAQUEZ, Jorge Arturo, LLB, DIur, PhD; Honduran academic, politician and diplomatist; *Permanent Representative, United Nations;* b. 21 March 1935, Tegucigalpa; m.; four c. *Education:* Univ. of El Salvador, Nat. Univ. of Mexico, Nat. Univ. of Honduras. *Career:* Sec., Univ. Reform Cttee 1960–63; Dean, Faculty of Humanities and Sciences, Univ. of El Salvador 1966–69; Academic Dir, Nat. Univ. of Honduras 1969–70, Dir Univ. Center for Gen. Studies 1970–73, Dean 1973–79; mem. Parl. 1990–2006, Minister Adviser to Pres. of Honduras 1994–98, 1998–2002; Pres. Liberal Party Exec. Council and Sec.-Gen. Nat. Directory 1994–2002, Sec.-Gen. Exec. Council 2005–07; Perm. Rep. to UN, New York 2008–; Cross, Fuerzas Armadas, Grand Commdr, Orden de Bernardo O'Higgins (Chile), Orden del Aguila Aztecan (Mexico); two Hon. Doctorates; Gold Medal for Academic Excellence. *Address:* Permanent Mission of Honduras to the United Nations, 866 United Nations Plaza, Suite 417, New York, NY 10017, USA (office). *Telephone:* (212) 752-3370 (office). *Fax:* (212) 223-0498 (office). *E-mail:* m.suazo@worldnet.att.net (office). *Website:* www.un.int/honduras (office).

REINART, Väino; Estonian diplomatist; *Ambassador to USA;* m. Kaire Jürgenson. *Education:* Tallinn Tech. Univ., Inst. of Chemical Physics and Biophysics, Estonian Acad. of Sciences, Grad. Inst. of Int. Studies, Geneva, Switzerland. *Career:* engineer and Research Assoc., Inst. of Chemical Physics and Biophysics, Estonian Acad. of Sciences 1984–88; held various positions in Ministry of Foreign Affairs, including Exec. Asst to Minister of Culture 1990, Sec.-Gen. 1992, Counsellor in Political Dept 1993, and Head of Div. of Int. Orgs and Security Policy 1993, Amb. and Chief Negotiator for Estonian-Russian negotiations 1994, Political Dir, Ministry of Foreign Affairs 1995, Perm. Rep. to OSCE, Vienna 1995–99, Dir-Gen. Political

Dept, Ministry of Foreign Affairs 1999–2001, Deputy Under-Sec. for Political Affairs 2001–02, Amb. and Perm. Rep. to EU 2002–07, Amb. to USA 2007–.
Address: Embassy of Estonia, 2131 Massachusetts Avenue, NW, Washington, DC 20036, USA (office). *Telephone:* (202) 588-0101 (office). *Fax:* (202) 588-0108 (office). *E-mail:* info@estemb.org (office); emb.washington@mfa .ee (office). *Website:* www.estemb.org (office).

REINFELDT, Fredrik, BS; Swedish politician; *Prime Minister;* b. 4 Aug. 1965, Stockholm; m. Filippa Reinfeldt (neé Holmberg) 1992; three c. *Education:* Stockholm Univ. *Career:* Chair. Swedish Conscripts Council, Swedish Defence Staff 1986; with Skandinaviska Enskilda Banken, Täby 1986–87; Deputy Chair. Regional Section, Young Moderates, Stockholm 1988–90, Chair. 1990–92, Chair. Exec. Cttee 1992–95; mem. Regional Section, Moderate Party, Stockholm 1992–2003, mem. Bd 1995–2002, mem. Exec. Cttee Moderate Party Group in Riksdag (Parl.) 1999–2003, Group Leader and First Deputy Chair. 2002–03, Chair. 2003–, mem. Bd Moderate Party 2002–, Party Chair. 2003–; Deputy Sec. Stockholm City Commr 1990–91, Sec. 1991; mem. Riksdag (Parl.) 1991–, Alt. Riksdag Cttee on Taxation 1991–94, mem. Cttee on Finance 1994–2001, Alt. Cttee on EU Affairs 2001–02, Chair. Cttee on Justice 2001–02, Alt. Advisory Council on Foreign Affairs 2002–03; Deputy Chair. Cttee on Finance 2002–03, mem. Advisory Council on Foreign Affairs 2003–06, Prime Minister 2006–; Deputy Chair. Swedish Central Conscripts Council 1985–86; Chair. Democratic Youth Community of Europe 1995–97; mem. Bd Swedish Nat. Union of Students 1989–90; Pres. Youth of European People's Party 1997–99.
Address: Prime Minister's Office, Rosenbad 4, 103 33 Stockholm (office); Moderata Samlingspartiet (MS) (Moderate Party), Stord Nygatan 30, POB 2080, 113 12 Stockholm, Sweden. *Telephone:* (8) 405-10-00 (office); (8) 676-80-00 (MS). *Fax:* (8) 723-11-71 (office); (8) 21-61-23 (MS). *E-mail:* registrator@primeminister.ministry.se (office); registrator@primeminister .ministry.se. *Website:* www.sweden.gov.se/sb/d/577 (office); www.moderat .se.

REINHARDT, Klaus, DrPhil; German army officer (retd); b. 15 Jan. 1941, Berlin; m. Heide-Ursula Reinhardt (née Bando) 1966; two s. *Education:* Univ. of Freiburg. *Career:* joined army as officer cadet, Mountain Infantry; Commdr Mountain Infantry 1986–88; Commdr Army Führungsakademie 1990–93; Commdg Gen. III Corps 1993–94; Gen.-Lt, Commdr German Army, Koblenz 1994–96; Commdg Gen. of NATO Peace-keeping Unit in Kosovo (Kfor) 1999–2000; Commdr NATO Forces, Heidelberg 2000; retd 2001; currently Lecturer, Univ. of Augsburg and Univ. of Munich; fmr Vice Pres. Clausewitz Soc., now Pres.; mem. Int. Advisory Bd World Security Network Foundation. *Publication:* Wende vor Moskau 1998.
Address: Karthäuserhofweg 10, 56075 Koblenz, Germany. *Telephone:* (261) 55690.

REINIG, Gen. Gaston; Luxembourg military officer; *Chief of Staff;* b. 17 Nov. 1956, Diekirch. *Education:* Royal Mil. Acad., Brussels, French Infantry School, Montpellier. *Career:* Commdr Luxembourg contingent, NATO Allied Command Europe Mobile Force Land (AMF (L)) 1984–87, Rep. to NATO Maintenance and Supply Org. Cttee 1992–95; Deputy Head of Command, Control and Communications Div., EC Monitoring Mission HQ, Sarajevo 1997; Perm. Mil. Rep. to NATO, Brussels 1998–2002, to WEU 2000–02, to EU 2000–02; Head of Mil. Centre of Diekirch (Armed Forces Operational Centre) 2002–08; Chief of Staff 2008–; Commdr, Ordre du Mérite, Officier, Ordre de la Couronne de Chêne, Croix d'Honneur et de Mérite militaire en bronze, Officier avec Couronne dans l'Ordre de Mérite civil et militaire Adolphe de Nassau, Commdr, Ordre de Mérite civil et militaire de la Couronne de Chêne; ECMM Medal for Service with the EC Monitor Mission, Army Commendation Medal.
Address: Etat-Major de l'Armée, 34–38 rue Goethe, BP 1873, 1018 Luxembourg, Luxembourg (office). *Telephone:* 26-84-82-1 (office). *Fax:* 26-84-56-06 (office). *E-mail:* secretariat.cema@ema.etat.lu (office). *Website:* www.armee.lu (office).

REITER, Janusz; Polish diplomatist and international affairs scholar; b. 6 Aug. 1952, Kościerzyna; m. Hanna Reiter 1975; two d. *Education:* Warsaw Univ. *Career:* foreign affairs commentator, Życie Warszawy (daily) 1977–81 (dismissed during martial law); Co-founder Foundation for Int. Ventures and Centre for Int. Studies in Warsaw; mem. Dziekania Club of Political Thought; staff writer, Przegląd Katolicki (weekly) 1984–89, Gazeta Wyborcza (daily) and Polish TV 1989–90, Rzeczpospolita (daily); Amb. to FRG 1990–95; Chair. Bd and Pres. Center for Int. Relations, Warsaw 1998; Amb. to USA 2005–07; Co-founder Council for Foreign Policy; mem. Council on European Integration; Great Cross of Merit with the Star and Ribbon (Germany). *Publication:* Roads to Europe.
Address: c/o Center for International Relations, Emilii Plater 25, 00-688 Warsaw, Poland (office). *E-mail:* info@reiter.org.pl (office).

REITH, Peter, BEcons, LLB; Australian company director, consultant, international organization official and fmr politician; b. 15 July 1950, Melbourne; m. Julie Treganowan 1971; four s. *Education:* Monash Univ. *Career:* Supreme Court 1975; worked as solicitor 1976–82; mem. Westernport Waterworks Trust and Cowes Sewerage Authority 1977–82; Councillor Shire of Phillip Island 1976–81, Pres. 1980–81; mem. various cttees and authorities; MP for Flinders 1982–83, 1984–2001; Deputy Leader of the Opposition 1990–93; Shadow Special Minister of State 1993, responsible for Mabo 1994; Shadow Minister for Defence Jan.–Sept. 1994, Shadow Minister with responsibility for Mabo Jan.–May 1994; Shadow Minister for Defence May–Sept. 1994; Shadow Minister for Foreign Affairs 1994–95, for Industrial Relations and Man. of Opposition Business in the House 1995–96; Minister for Industrial Relations and Leader of the House of Reps and Minister Assisting the Prime Minister for the Public Service 1996–97; Minister for Workplace Relations and Small Business and Leader of the House of Reps 1997–98, Minister for Employment, Workplace Relations and Small Business and Leader of the House of Reps 1998–2001; Minister for Defence 2001; Dir representing Australia, Repub. of Korea, New Zealand and Egypt, EBRD 2003–06, Alt. Dir 2006–; mem. Asscn of Christian Community Colls.; co-ordinator Free Legal Aid Services; Founding Sec. and mem. Newhaven Coll. *Publication:* The Reith Papers.
Address: European Bank for Reconstruction and Development (EBRD), One Exchange Square, 175 Bishopsgate, London, EC2A 2JN, England (office); 1A Camperdown Street, Brighton East, Vic. 3187, Australia (home). *Telephone:* (20) 7338-6000 (office). *Fax:* (20) 7338-6100 (office). *E-mail:* australiaoffice@ebrd.com (office); peterreith@bigpond.com.au. *Website:* www.ebrd.com (office).

REMENGESAU, Tommy E., Jr, BS; Palauan politician and head of state; *President;* b. 28 Feb. 1956, Koror; m. Debbie Mineich; two s. two d. *Education:* Grand Valley State Univ., Mich., Michigan State Univ. *Career:* Admin./Planner, Palau Bureau of Health Services 1980–81; Public Information Officer, Palau Legislature 1981–84; Senator, Nat. Congress 1984–92; Vice-Pres. and Minister of Admin. 1993–99, Pres. of Palau 2001– (re-elected 2004); rep. to IMF 1997–; twice Grand Champion All-Micronesia Fishing Derby.
Address: Office of the President, PO Box 6051, Koror, PW 96940, Palau (office). *Telephone:* 488-2403 (office). *Fax:* 488-1662 (office). *E-mail:* pres@ palaunet.com (office).

RÉMY, Pierre-Jean (see Angrémy, Jean-Pierre).

REQUEIJO GUAL, Orlando; Cuban diplomatist; b. 1957, Havana; m.; two c. *Education:* Raul Roa Carcia Higher Inst. of Int. Relations, Havana, Inst. for the Learning of Arabic Language for Foreigners, Damascus, Syria. *Career:* entered Foreign Service 1981; internal officer, Cuban Embassy, Damascus, Syria 1981; various positions, Middle East and N Africa Div., Ministry of Foreign Affairs, becoming Deputy Dir 1993–94, Dir 1998–2001; Amb. to Qatar 1994–98; Presidential Special Envoy to eight states in Persian Gulf and Arabic Peninsula 2000; Deputy Perm. Rep. to UN 2001–04, Perm. Rep. 2004–05.
Address: c/o Ministry of Foreign Relations, Calzada 360, esq. G, Vedado, Havana, Cuba (office).

RETZER, Michael L., BA; American business executive, politician and diplomatist; b. Greenville, Miss.. *Education:* Honors Coll., Univ. of Oregon. *Career:* served as Capt. in USAF; developed restaurant chain in 20 locations in Miss. and Ark.; fmr mem. Bd of Dirs and Exec. Cttee Planters Bank of Miss.; elected several times as Chair. Miss. Republican Party since 1978; elected Republican Nat. Cttee-man for Miss. 2001, Treas. Nat. Republican Party 2002, Treas. Republican Nat. Convention, New York City 2004; career mem. Sr Foreign Service with rank of Minister-Counselor, Amb. to Tanzania 2005–07; fmr mem. Chamber of Commerce, Greenville, Industrial Foundation, South Delta Planning Council; Founding mem. Delta Wildlife Foundation, Miss. Wildlife Foundation; fmr Trustee Nat. Symphony Orchestra, Washington, DC.
Address: US Department of State, 2201 C Street NW, Washington, DC 20520, USA (office). *Telephone:* (202) 647-4000 (office). *Fax:* (202) 647-6738 (office). *Website:* www.state.gov (office).

RÉWAKA, Denis Dangue; Gabonese diplomatist; *Permanent Representative, United Nations; Career:* fmr Chair. Credentials Cttee, 10th Emergency Special Session of Gen. Ass.; fmr Amb. to Slovenia; fmr Chair. ad hoc Working Group Security Council; Chair. and Pres. Security Council; Chair. Africa Group 2000; currently Perm. Rep. to UN.
Address: Permanent Mission of Gabon to the UN, 18 East 41st Street, 9th Floor, New York, NY 10017, USA (office). *Telephone:* (212) 686-9720 (office). *Fax:* (212) 689-5769 (office). *E-mail:* gabon@un.int (office).

REYELS, Rüdiger, PhD; German diplomatist; b. 29 July 1941, Salzburg, Austria; m.; three c. *Education:* Univ. of Berlin, Univs of Lausanne and Geneva, Switzerland. *Career:* trained as lawyer 1969–73; entered German Foreign Service 1973; various positions Fed. Foreign Office, Bonn 1974–76, 1979–83, 1986–90; Embassy in Tel Aviv 1976–79; Perm. Del. to NATO, Brussels 1983–86; Amb. to Zambia 1990–93; Head Personnel Admin Div., Bonn 1993–98; Deputy Fed. Govt Commr for Disarmament and Arms Control 1998–2000; Amb. to Iran 2000–03; Perm. Rep. to NATO, Brussels 2003–06.

REZAG BARA, Muhammad Kamal; Algerian diplomatist. *Career:* fmr Vice-Pres. African Comm. on Human and Peoples' Rights, later Chair.; fmr Pres. Observatoire Nat. des Droits de l'Homme; fmr Amb. to Libya; currently Adviser to the Pres.
Address: Presidency Cabinet, el-Mouradia, 16000 Algiers, Algeria (office). *Telephone:* (21) 69-53-08 (office). *Fax:* (21) 69-53-09 (office). *E-mail:* mkre3agborra@gmail.com (office). *Website:* www.el-mouradia.dz (office).

REZEK, Francisco, LLD, JSD; Brazilian lawyer, judge and fmr politician; b. 18 Jan. 1944, Cristina, Minas Gerais. *Education:* Fed. Univ. of Minas Gerais, Sorbonne, France, Univ. of Oxford, UK, Harvard Univ., USA, The Hague Acad. of Int. Law, The Netherlands. *Career:* Attorney of the Repub., Supreme Court 1972–79; Prof. of Int. and Constitutional Law Univ. of Brasília 1971–, Chair. Law Dept 1974–76, Dean, Faculty of Social Studies 1978–79; Prof. of Int., Law Rio Branco Inst. 1976–; Justice of Supreme Court 1983–90, 1992–97; Foreign Minister 1990–92; mem. Perm. Court of Arbitration 1987–2004; Judge, Int. Court of Justice, The Hague 1997–2006; currently legal adviser Advocacia Gandra Martins (law firm), São Paulo. *Publications:* Droit des traités: particularités des actes constitutifs d'organisations internationales 1968, La conduite des relations internationales dans le droit constitutionnel latino-américain 1970, Reciprocity as a Basis of Extradition 1980, Direito dos Tratados 1984, Public International Law 1989.
Address: Advocacia Gandra Martins, Alameda Jaú,1742 -11º, 13º e 14º andares, CEP:01420-002, Cerqueira César, São Paulo SP, Brazil (office). *Telephone:* (11) 3894-3333 (office). *Fax:* (11) 3894-3388 (office). *Website:* www.gandramartins.adv.br (office).

RI, Yong-ho; North Korean diplomatist; m. Ri Son Yong. *Career:* began his career at Embassy in Harare, followed by posting to Stockholm, returned to Disarmament and Security section, Ministry of Foreign Affairs, Pyongyang, participated in disarmament talks with two US Admins; Counsellor, Ministry of Foreign Affairs –2003, Amb. to UK 2003–07.
Address: Ministry of Foreign Affairs, Pyongyang, Democratic People's Republic of Korea (office).

RIBADENEIRA ESPINOSA, Diego; Ecuadorean diplomatist; *Ambassador to Peru;* m. Angela Grijalva de Ribadeneira. *Career:* Amb. to Brazil 1999–2004; Vice-Minister of Foreign Affairs 2004–07; Amb. to Peru 2007–.
Address: Embassy of Ecuador, Las Palmeras 356 y Javier Prado Oeste, San Isidro, Lima 27, Peru (office). *Telephone:* (1) 2124171 (office). *Fax:* (1) 4220711 (office). *E-mail:* embajada@mecuadorperu.org.pe (office). *Website:* www.mecuadorperu.org.pe (home).

RIBEIRO PEREIRA, Lt-Gen. Augusto Heleno; Brazilian military officer. *Career:* served in Brazilian mil. mission, Paraguay 1981–83; Mil. Attaché to France 1996–98; Head, Centro de Comunicação do Exército 2002–04; C-in-C UN Stabilization Mission in Haiti (MINUSTAH) 2004–05; Head of Cabinet for Mil. Command 2006.
Address: Quartel General do Exército, Bloco B Térreo, Setor Militário Urbano, 70630-901 Brasília, DF, Brazil (office). *Website:* www.gabcmt.eb .mil.br.

RIBEIRO VIOTTI, Maria Luiza, BEcons, MEconSc; Brazilian diplomatist; *Permanent Representative, United Nations;* b. 27 March 1954, Belo Horizonte; m.; one s. *Education:* Univ. of Brasilia, Rio Branco Inst. *Career:* Third Sec., Ministry of Foreign Affairs 1976–79, Second Sec. 1979–84, First Sec. 1984–; First Secretary, Perm. Mission to UN, New York 1985–88; Exec. Coordinator, Cabinet of Minister for External Relations 1990; Counsellor, Embassy in La Paz 1993–95; Minister Counsellor, Perm. Mission to UN, New York 1999–2004; Dir Gen. Dept of Human Rights and Social Affairs, then Dept of Int. Orgs 2004–07; Perm. Rep. to UN, New York 2007–.
Address: Permanent Mission of Brazil to the United Nations, 747 Third Avenue, 9th Floor, New York, NY 10017, USA (office). *Telephone:* (212) 372-2600 (office). *Fax:* (212) 371-5716 (office). *E-mail:* braun@delbrasonu .org (office). *Website:* www.un.int/brazil (office).

RIBERHOLDT, Gunnar; Danish diplomatist; *President, Danish-French Chamber of Commerce;* b. 7 Nov. 1933, Naestved; one s. one d. *Education:* US univs and Univ. of Copenhagen. *Career:* Ministry of Foreign Affairs 1958–62; Sec. of Embassy, Danish Perm. Mission to European Communities 1962–64, Deputy Head of Mission 1964–65; Head of Section, Ministry of Foreign Affairs 1965–69; Econ. Counsellor, Paris 1969–72; Dir Ministry of Foreign Affairs 1973–75; Dir-Gen. European Econ. Affairs 1975–77; Amb. Perm. Rep. of Denmark to European Communities (now EU) 1977–84, 1992–94; Amb. to France 1984–91; Amb., Personal Rep. of Minister for Foreign Affairs to Intergovernmental Confs on Political Union and on Econ. and Monetary Union 1991–92; Amb., Head Danish Del. to OECD 1991–92; Perm. Rep. to NATO 1995–99; Amb. to Italy (also accred to Cyprus, Malta and San Marino) 1999–2003; Pres. Danish-French Chamber of Commerce 2004–.
Address: Oestbanegade 5, 2100 Copenhagen, Denmark (home). *Telephone:* 35-43-03-05 (home). *E-mail:* clarinet@mail.dk.

RICCIARDONE, Francis Joseph; American diplomatist; b. Boston, Mass; m. Dr Marie Ricciardone; two d. *Education:* Dartmouth Coll., NH. *Career:* taught in int. schools Italy 1973–76, Iran 1976–78; entered Foreign Service 1978; served in Turkey 1979–81; research analyst for Turkey, Greece and Cyprus US Dept of State, Washington, DC 1981–82; country officer for Iraq 1982–85; political officer, Cairo 1986–89; led Civilian Observer Unit, Multi nat. Force and Observers, Sinai Desert 1989–91; Deputy Chief of Mission (desig.), Baghdad Embassy 1991–93; Political Adviser to Multi-national relief operation, Northern Iraq 1993; Office of Dir-Gen., US Dept of State, Washington, DC 1993–95; Deputy Chief of Mission and Chargé d'affaires, Ankara 1995; Sec. of State's Special Rep. for Transition in Iraq 1999–2001; Dir Task Force on the Coalition Against Terrorism 2001; Amb. to the Philippines and Palau 2002–05, to Egypt 2005–08; Meritorious Honor Award 1984, Dir-Gen.'s Award for Political Reporting 1988.
Address: Department of State, 2201 C Street NW, Washington, DC 20520, USA (office). *Telephone:* (202) 647-4000 (office). *Fax:* (202) 647-6738 (office). *Website:* www.state.gov (office).

RICE, Condoleezza, PhD; American academic and government official; *Secretary of State;* b. 14 Nov. 1954, Birmingham, Ala. *Education:* Univ. of Denver, Univ. of Notre Dame. *Career:* teacher at Stanford Univ., Calif. 1981–2001, Provost 1993–99, currently Hoover Sr Fellow and Prof. of Political Science; Special Asst to Dir of Jt Chiefs of Staff 1986; Dir, then Sr Dir of Soviet and East European Affairs, Nat. Security Council 1989–91; Special Asst to Pres. for Nat. Security Affairs 1989–91; primary foreign policy adviser to presidential cand. George W. Bush 1999–2000; Asst to Pres. for Nat. Security Affairs and Nat. Security Advisor 2001–04; Sec. of State 2004–; fmr mem. Bd of Dirs, Chevron Corpn, Charles Schwab Corpn, William and Flora Hewlett Foundation and numerous other bds; Sr Fellow, Inst. for Int. Studies, Stanford; Fellow, American Acad. of Arts and Sciences; Dr hc (Morehouse Coll.) 1991, (Univ. of Ala) 1994, (Univ. of Notre Dame) 1995, (Mississippi Coll. School of Law) 2003, (Univ. of Louisville) 2004; ranked by Forbes magazine amongst 100 Most Powerful Women (first) 2004, (first) 2005, (second) 2006, (fourth) 2007. *Publications:* Uncertain Allegiance: The Soviet Union and the Czechoslovak Army 1984, The Gorbachev Era (co-author) 1986, Germany Unified and Europe Transformed (co-author) 1995; numerous articles on Soviet and East European foreign and defence policy.
Address: Department of State, 7th Floor, 2201 C Street, NW, Washington, DC 20520, USA (office). *Telephone:* (202) 647-5291 (office). *Website:* www .state.gov (office).

RICHARD, Alain; French government official; *Mayor of Saint Ouen L'Aumône;* b. 29 Aug. 1945, Paris; m. Elisabeth Couffignal 1988; one s. one d. and one s. by previous m. *Education:* Lycée Henri IV, Paris, Institut d'Etudes Politiques, Ecole Nat. d'Admin. *Career:* Auditor, Conseil d'Etat 1971, Maître des requêtes 1978, Conseiller d'Etat 1993–95; Mayor, St Ouen l'Aumône 1977–97, 2001–; Deputy, Val d'Oise 1978–93, Senator 1995–97; Vice-Pres. Commission des lois 1981–86, Nat. Ass. 1987–88; Minister of Defence 1997–2001; Founder and Vice-Pres. Forum for Man. of Towns 1985–97; mem. Nat. Office, Parti Socialiste Unifié 1972–74; mem. Cttee Parti Socialiste 1979, Exec. Bd 1988; mem. Bd Inst. for Int. Relations 1991–97.
Address: Hôtel de Ville, 2 place Pierre Mendès-France, Saint-Ouen l'Aumône, 95318 Cergy-Pontoise Cedex (office); 28 rue René Clair, 95310 St Ouen l'Aumône, France. *Telephone:* 1-34-21-25-00 (office). *Fax:* 1-34-64-35-65 (office). *E-mail:* courrier@ville-saintouenlaumone.fr (office). *Website:* www.ville-saintouenlaumone.fr (office).

RICHARDS, Sir Francis Neville, Kt, KCMG, CVO, DL, MA; British diplomatist and academic; *Honorary Professor, School of Social Sciences and Director, Centre for Studies in Security and Diplomacy, University of Birmingham;* b. 18 Nov. 1945; m. Gillian Bruce Nevill 1971; one s. one d. *Education:* Eton Coll. and King's Coll., Cambridge. *Career:* with Royal Green Jackets 1967, served with UN Force in Cyprus (invalided 1969); joined FCO 1969, served

in Moscow 1971; UK Del. to Mutual and Balanced Force Reducations negotiations, Vienna 1973; FCO 1976–85 (Asst Pvt. Sec. to Sec. of State 1981–82); Econ. and Commercial Counsellor, New Delhi 1985–88; FCO 1988–90 (Head S Asian Dept); High Commr to Namibia 1990–92; Minister, Moscow 1992–95; Dir (Europe) FCO 1995–97, Deputy Under-Sec. of State 1997–98; Dir Govt Communications HQ (GCHQ) 1998–2003; Gov. and C-in-C of Gibraltar 2003–06; Hon. Prof., School of Social Sciences and Dir Centre for Studies in Security and Diplomacy, Univ. of Birmingham 2007–; Trustee, Imperial War Museum, London 2007–.
Address: Centre for Studies in Security and Diplomacy, European Research Institute, University of Birmingham, Edgbaston, Birmingham, B15 2TT, England (office). *Telephone:* (121) 414-6950 (office). *Fax:* (121) 414-2693 (office). *E-mail:* cssd-bham@bham.ac.uk (office). *Website:* www.cssd .bham.ac.uk (office).

RICHARDS, George Maxwell, MSc, PhD; Trinidad and Tobago professor of chemical engineering, politician and head of state; *President;* b. 1931, San Fernando; m.; two c. *Education:* Queen's Royal Coll., Port of Spain, Univs of Manchester and Cambridge, UK. *Career:* staff trainee, United British Oilfields of Trinidad, Ltd 1950–51; held several managerial posts at Shell Trinidad Ltd 1957–65; Sr Lecturer in Chemical Eng, Univ. of the West Indies (UWI), St Augustine 1965–70, Prof. 1970, later Dean Faculty of Chemical Eng, Deputy Prin. and Pro-Vice-Chancellor UWI 1980–85, Acting Prin. 1984–85, Prin. and Pro-Vice-Chancellor 1985–86, now Prof. Emer.; Chair. Salaries Review Comm. 1977–2003; Pres. Trinidad and Tobago 2003–; fmr Chair. Nat. Training Bd, Inst. of Marine Affairs; fmr mem. Bd Trinidad Publishing Co., TRINTOC, National Gas Co., etc.; fmr mem. Bd Nat. Advisory Council; mem. Asscn of Professional Engineers of Trinidad and Tobago, Inst. of Chemical Engineers, London, UK, Inst. of Petroleum, London, Royal Soc. of Chem., UK; Chaconia Medal of the Order of the Trinity (CMT), Class 1 (Gold) for public service.
Address: Office of the President, President's House, Circular Road, St Ann's, Port of Spain, Trinidad (office). *Telephone:* 624-1261 (office). *Fax:* 625-7950 (office). *E-mail:* presoftt@carib-link.net (office). *Website:* www .gov.tt (office).

RICHARDS, Simon Paul, BA, LLB, MEcon.; Dominican diplomatist and lawyer; b. 19 April 1937, Wesley. *Education:* London Univ., Univ. of the West Indies and City Univ. of New York. *Career:* Asst Master Dominica Grammar School 1958–60, Sr Master 1963–66; caseworker City of New York Dept of Social Services 1967–74; admitted to Bar of England and Wales 1975, of the State of NY 1977, of US Dist Courts for Southern and Eastern Dists of NY 1978, of Dominica 1980; practised law in New York 1977–, currently a sr trial attorney in pvt. practice; Counsellor, Deputy Perm. Rep. and Chargé d'Affaires Perm. Mission of Dominica to the UN at various times 1982–95, Perm. Rep. 1995–2002.
Address: c/o Ministry of Foreign Affairs, Government Headquarters, Kennedy Avenue, Roseau, Dominica (office).

RICHARDSON, Dennis, AO, BA; Australian diplomatist; *Ambassador to USA;* m. Betty Richardson; one s. one d. *Education:* Sydney Univ. *Career:* career public servant; joined Australian Foreign Service 1969, served in posts in Nairobi, Port Moresby and Jakarta, various sr public service roles in Depts of Prime Minister and Cabinet, Foreign Affairs, and Trade and Immigration; Head of Review of Intelligence Community Post-Cold War 1992; Prin. Adviser to Prime Minister 1990–91; Deputy Sec. Dept of Immigration and Multicultural Affairs 1993–96; Dir-Gen. Australian Security Intelligence Org. 1996–2005; Amb. to USA 2005–.
Address: Embassy of Australia, 1601 Massachusetts Avenue, NW, Washington, DC 20036-2273, USA (office). *Telephone:* (202) 797-3000 (office). *Fax:* (202) 797-3168 (office). *E-mail:* library.washington@dfat.gov .au (office). *Website:* www.usa.embassy.gov.au (office).

RICKETTS, Sir Peter, KCMG, BA; British diplomatist; *Permanent Under-Secretary and Head of Diplomatic Service;* b. 30 Sept. 1952; m.; two c. *Education:* Univ. of Oxford. *Career:* entered FCO 1974; with Mission in New York, USA 1974–75; Desk Officer, Cen. and Southern Africa Dept 1975–76; Third then Second Sec., Embassy in Singapore 1976–78; Second then First Sec., Del. to NATO, Brussels 1978–81; Desk Officer, Near East and N Africa Dept 1982–83; Asst Pvt. Sec., Office of Sec. of State 1983–86; First Sec., Chancery, Embassy in Washington, DC 1986–89; Deputy Head of Security Policy Dept 1989–91; Head, Hong Kong Dept 1991–94; Counsellor, EC and Finance, Embassy in Paris 1994–97; Deputy Political Dir 1997–99; Dir for Int. Security 1999–2000; Chair. Jt Intelligence Cttee and Intelligence Coordinator, Cabinet Office 2000–01; Dir-Gen. (Political) FCO 2001–03, Perm. Rep. to NATO, Brussels 2003–06, Perm. Under-Sec. and Head of Diplomatic Service 2006–.
Address: Foreign and Commonwealth Office, King Charles Street, London, SW1A 2AH, England (office). *Telephone:* (20) 7008-1500 (office). *E-mail:* peter.ricketts@fco.gov.uk (office). *Website:* www.fco.gov.uk (office).

RICO FRONTAURA, Victor, MA; Bolivian diplomatist and economist; *Director, Department for Sustainable Democracy and Special Missions, Organization of American States; Education:* Catholic Univ. of Bolivia, Universidad Belgrano, Buenos Aires, LSE. *Career:* Trade Adviser, Embassy in Buenos Aires 1991; Nat. Sec., Int. Econ. Relations 1996–97; Dir-Gen. Comunidad Andina (CAN), Lima, Peru 1997–2002; Vice-Minister for Exterior Relations 2002; Consul-Gen. in Santiago, Chile 2003–05; joined OAS Gen. Secr. 2005, currently Dir Dept for Sustainable Democracy and Special Missions, served as personal rep. of Sec.-Gen. in mediation process between Ecuador and Colombia 2008.
Address: Organization of American States, 17th Street & Constitution Avenue, NW, Washington, DC 20006, USA (office). *Telephone:* (202) 458-3000 (office). *Fax:* (202) 458-6319 (office). *E-mail:* pi@oas.org (office). *Website:* www.oas.org (office).

RICÚPERO, Rubens, LLB; Brazilian international organization official and fmr diplomatist and politician; b. 1 March 1937, São Paulo. *Education:* Univ. of São Paulo and Rio Branco Inst. *Career:* Prof. of Theory of Int. Relations, Univ. of Brasília 1979–95; Prof. of History of Brazilian Diplomatic Relations, Rio Branco Inst. 1980–95; with Ministry of Foreign Relations 1981–93, Minister of the Environment and Amazonian Affairs 1993–94, of Finance March–Sept. 1994; Perm. Rep. to UN, Geneva 1987–91; Chair. GATT Council of Reps 1989–91, Contracting Parties 1989–91, GATT Cttee on Trade and Devt 1989–91, GATT Informal Group of Developing Countries 1989–91 (also Spokesman); Amb. to USA 1991–93, to Italy 1995; led Brazilian dels to UN Comm. on Human Rights and Conf. on Disarmament, Geneva; Chair. Finance Cttee, UN Conf. on Environment and Devt, Rio de Janeiro 1992; Sec.-Gen. UNCTAD 1995–2004; Dir Fundação Armando Alvares Penteado 2005–; Pres. Consultative Comm. Conversando com as Nações Unidas (CNU)-Brasil 2006–; Lifetime Achievement Award, World Summit of Young Entrepreneurs of the World Trade Univ. 2004. *Publications:* several books on int. relations, econ. devt problems, int. trade and diplomatic history.
Address: c/o CNU-Brasil, Rua Plínio Barreto, 285, São Paulo Brazil (office). *Telephone:* (11) 3254-1677. *Fax:* (11) 3254-1675. *Website:* www.cnu -brasil.org.br.

RIEKSTIŅŠ, Māris; Latvian lawyer, diplomatist and politician; *Minister of Foreign Affairs;* b. 8 April 1963, Riga; m.; two c. *Education:* Univ. of Latvia. *Career:* teacher, Faculty of Pedagogy, Latvian Sports Inst. 1982–85; Deputy Chair. and Desk Officer, Cttee of Latvian Youth Orgs 1987–91; lawyer, Faculty of Law, Univ. of Latvia 1989–93; Chair. Control Cttee of Strategic Goods of Repub. of Latvia 1995–2004, Diplomatic Service Agency's Shareholders' Council 1996–2004, Advisory Council for Membership of Latvia in WTO 1999–2004, Supervisory Cttee on Org. of NATO Aspirant Countries Summit in Riga Jan.–July 2002; Head of Latvian del. for negotiations on sea border delimitations with Estonia 1995–96, Lithuania 1996–99, Latvian del. to US-Baltic Partnership Charter 1997–98, Latvian-Italian Econ. Working Group 1998–2004; several positions within Ministry of Foreign Affairs, including Desk Officer, Political Dept of Europe Div. and Dir Western Europe and Europe Divs Jan.–Nov. 1992, Under-Sec. of State 1992–93, Sec. of State 1993–2004, Head of Latvian del. for accession negotiations with NATO 2002–04, Amb. to USA 2004–07 (also accred to Mexico 2006–07); Chief of Staff to Prime Minister Jan.–Nov. 2007; Minister of Foreign Affairs Nov. 2007–; Commdr, Royal Norwegian Order of Merit 1998, Grand Officer, Royal Norwegian Order of Merit 2000, Grand Officier, Ordre nat. du Mérite 2001, Order of the Lithuanian Grand Duke Gediminas (Fourth Class) 2001, Order of the Cross of Terra Mariana (Third Class, Estonia) 2003, Ordem do Infante D. Henrique Grande Oficial (Portugal) 2003, Commdr, Three Star Order of Latvia 2003, 'Grand Official', Order of Merit of the Italian Repub. 2004.
Address: Ministry of Foreign Affairs, Brīvības bulv. 36, Rīga 1395, Latvia (office). *Telephone:* 6701-6201 (office). *Fax:* 6782-8121 (office). *E-mail:* mfa .cha@mfa.gov.lv (office). *Website:* www.mfa.gov.lv (office).

RIERA, Teodoro Maldonado, PhD; Ecuadorean diplomatist. *Career:* Amb. to UK 2006–08.
Address: Ministry of External Relations, Trade and Integration, Avenida 10 de Agosto y Carrión, Quito, Ecuador (office). *Telephone:* (2) 299-3200 (office). *Fax:* (2) 256-4873 (office). *E-mail:* webmast@mmrree.gov.ec (office). *Website:* www.mmrree.gov.ec (office).

RIES, Charles Parker, BA, MA; American diplomatist; m. Marcie Berman Ries; two c. *Education:* Johns Hopkins Univ., Baltimore, Md. *Career:* joined Foreign Service in 1977, served as a Special Asst and Exec. Asst to Under-Sec. of State for Econ. Affairs, in Energy Policy Office, in Office of Counselor of Dept, and at Embassies in Ankara and Santo Domingo, Deputy Asst US Trade Rep. for N American Affairs and mem. N American Free Trade Agreement (NAFTA) negotiating team, Office of US Trade

Rep. 1990–92, Minister Counselor for Econ. Affairs, Mission to EU 1992–96, Minister Counselor for Econ. Affairs, Embassy in London 1996–2000, Prin. Deputy Asst Sec. of State for European and Eurasian Affairs 2000–04, Amb. to Greece 2004–07.
Address: US Department of State, 2201 C Street NW, Washington, DC 20520, USA (office). *Telephone:* (202) 647-4000 (office). *Fax:* (202) 647-6738 (office). *Website:* www.state.gov (office).

RIES, Marcie Berman, BA, MA; American diplomatist; *Political-Military Counsellor, US Embassy in Baghdad;* b. Boston, Mass; m. Charles Parker Ries; one s. one d. *Education:* Oberlin Coll. and School of Advanced Int. Studies, Johns Hopkins Univ. *Career:* Man. Int. Investment Policy, Motor Vehicle Mfrs Asscn 1975–78; Consular/Political Officer, Embassy in Santa Domingo 1978–80; Int. Relations Officer, Office of Strategic Nuclear Policy 1981–83; Turkish language training, Foreign Service Inst. Arlington, Va 1983–84, Political Officer, Ankara 1984–86, Desk Officer, Malta and the Vatican, Office of Western European Affairs 1986–88, Deputy Head, Political Section, Office of European Regional Political Mil. Affairs 1988–90, Officer in Charge, French Desk, Office of Western European Affairs 1990–91, Deputy Political Counsellor, Mission to EU, Brussels 1992–96, Political Counsellor, London 1996–2000, Dir Office of UN Political Affairs, Bureau of Int. Org. Affairs 2001–03, 2003–04, Chief of Mission, Prishtina, Kosovo, Amb. to Albania 2004–07, Political-Mil. Counsellor, Embassy in Baghdad 2007–; Pearson Fellow, US House of Reps Office of Hon. Dante Fascell 1991–92; mem. Sr Seminar 2000–01; numerous awards from State Dept, including Sr Foreign Service Performance and four Superior Honor Awards.
Address: US Embassy, APO AE 09316, Baghdad, Iraq (office). *E-mail:* baghdadpressoffice@state.gov (office). *Website:* iraq.usembassy.gov (office).

RIES, Col Nico; Luxembourg army officer; b. 30 July 1953; m.; two c. *Education:* Royal Mil. Acad., Brussels, Belgium, Staff Coll., Compiegne and Ecole Supérieure de Guerre Interarmées, Paris, France. *Career:* joined Luxembourg Army 1973; apptd to Mil. Instruction Centre 1978–94, held positions successively as Infantry Platoon Leader, Co. Commdr, Personnel Officer, Deputy Commdr; Logistics Officer, Army Staff 1994–98; Asst Chief of Staff 1998–2002, Chief of Staff 2002–08; participated in EC Monitor Mission (ECMM) in fmr Yugoslavia 1991, 1997; Chevalier Ordre de Mérite civil et militaire d'Adolphe de Nassau 1994, Officier Ordre grand-ducal de la Couronne de Chêne 1994, Grand Officier, Ordre du Mérite of Grand Duchy of Luxembourg 2004, Commdr, Ordre Nat. de la Légion d'Honneur 2005, Grande Oficial da Ordem Militar de Avis (Portugal) 2005, Grand Officier Ordre de Viesturs (Latvia) 2006; Verdienstkreuz 1st Class (Germany) 1988, Croix d'Honneur et de Mérite militaire en bronze 1998, Croix de 25 ans de service 1999, Meritorious Service Medal (USA) 1998, Medal of EC Monitor Mission in fmr Yugoslavia 1998.
Address: c/o Etat-Major de l'Armée, 34–38 rue Goethe, BP 1873, 1018 Luxembourg, Luxembourg (office).

RIFAI, Omar, BA, MA, PhD; Jordanian diplomatist and academic; b. 5 Oct. 1952, Amman. *Education:* Harvard and Georgetown Univs, American University London. *Career:* career diplomat since 1975; Amb. to Israel 1996–2000, to Italy 2001–03; Sec.-Gen. Jordanian Foreign Ministry 2003–05; Amb. to Egypt 2005–07; Perm. Rep. to Arab League 2005–07.
Address: PO Box 5460, Amman 11183, Jordan (home). *Telephone:* (6) 5735150 (home). *Fax:* (6) 5412154 (home). *E-mail:* or@omarrifai.com (office).

RIIS-JØRGENSEN, Birger; Danish diplomatist; *Ambassador to UK;* m. Karin Riis-Jørgensen. *Career:* fmr Dir for West and East Africa, Ministry of Foreign Affairs, State Sec., Ministry for Foreign Affairs –2006; Amb. to UK 2006–.
Address: Royal Danish Embassy, 55 Sloane Street, London, SW1X 9SR, England (office). *Telephone:* (20) 7333-0200 (office). *Fax:* (20) 7333-0270 (office). *E-mail:* lonamb@um.dk (office). *Website:* www.amblondon.um.dk (office).

RILEY, Thomas T., BS, MBA; American diplomatist; *Ambassador to Morocco;* m. Nancy Riley; two d. *Education:* Stanford Univ., Calif. and Harvard Business School. *Career:* Assoc. Engineer, Boeing Co., Seattle, Wash. 1972–73; with TRW based in NI, England and France, including Man. of European Operations 1975–79; Co-founder General Resources Corpn 1979; worked in Silicon Valley, Calif. 1980s–2003; fmr Pres. and CEO Unity Systems, Web State, ActivePhoto; Amb. to Morocco 2004–; active in charitable orgs such as Bizworld and Hope Rehabilitation Services.
Address: US Embassy, 2 Avenue de Muhammad el-Fassi, Rabat, Morocco (office). *Telephone:* (3) 7762265 (office). *Fax:* (3) 7765661 (office). *E-mail:* ircrabat@usembassy.ma (office). *Website:* www.usembassy.ma (office).

RIMAWI, Fahid Nimer ar-, BA; Jordanian journalist; *Publisher and Editor-in-Chief, Al Majd;* b. 1942, Palestine; m.; two s. five d. *Education:* Cairo Univ., Egypt. *Career:* Ed. Difa (newspaper) 1965–67; Ed.-in-Chief, Jordan News Agency 1968–70; Sec. Editorial Bd of Afkar (magazine) 1970–73; Dir Investigating Dept of Al-Raiue (newspaper) 1975–76; writer Al-Destour (newspaper) 1978–81; Political Writer, Al-Raiue (newspaper) 1981–85; Corresp. al Talie'ah (magazine) Paris 1982–85; political writer 1985–94; Publr and Ed.-in-Chief Al Majd (weekly). *Publications:* Mawaweel Fi al Layl Al Taweel, short stories in Arabic 1982.
Address: PO Box 926856, Amman 11190 (office); Dahiyat al-Rashid, Amman, Jordan. *Telephone:* (6) 5530553 (office); (6) 5160615 (home). *Fax:* (6) 553 0352. *E-mail:* almajd@almajd.net (office). *Website:* www.almajd .net (office).

RINGBORG, Mats, MSc; Swedish diplomatist; *Ambassador to OECD and UNESCO;* b. 26 Nov. 1945; m. Catharina Nystedt; three c. *Education:* Stockholm School of Econs. *Career:* joined Ministry of Foreign Affairs 1969; First Sec. Ministry of Industry 1971–75, attaché Del. to OECD 1975, Head of Section 1977–81, Deputy Dir-Gen. 1981–84; Counsellor, Embassy in USA 1984–89, Minister 1989; Deputy Dir-Gen. Ministry of Foreign Affairs 1989–96, Dir-Gen. for Trade Policy 1996–2002; Amb. to Norway 2002–07; Amb. to OECD and UNESCO, Paris 2007–; fmr mem. Bd of Dirs Swedish Trade Council 1989–96, Swedish Export Credit Corpn 1990–96, Swedish Export Credit Guarantee Bd 1989–2002.
Address: Delegation of Sweden to the OECD, 2, rue Conseiller Collignon, 75116 Paris Cédex 16, France (office). *Telephone:* 1-45-24-98-60 (office). *Fax:* 1-45-24-18-34 (office). *E-mail:* oecd-del.paris@foreign.ministry.se (office). *Website:* www.swedenabroad.com/oecd (office).

RINI, Snyder; Solomon Islands politician; *Minister of Finance and Treasury;* b. 27 July 1948. *Education:* Univ. of Papua New Guinea, Univ. of Technology, Lae, Papua New Guinea. *Career:* Financial Controller, Brewer Solomons Agriculture Ltd. 1975–80; Perm. Sec. for Ministry of Natural Resources 1989, for Ministry of Nat. Planning and Devt 1994–95, for Ministry of Agric. and Fisheries 1997; mem. Parl. for Marovo, Western Prov. 1997–; Minister for Finance and Treasury 2000–01, Deputy Prime Minister for Nat. Planning and Devt 2001–02, Deputy Prime Minister and Minister for Finance and Treasury 2002–03, Deputy Prime Minister and Minister for Educ. and Human Resources Devt 2003–06, Prime Minister April–May 2006 (resgnd); Minister of Finance and Treasury 2007–; mem. Bd of Dirs Devt Bank of Solomon Islands 1976–84, Central Bank of Solomon Islands 1982–84, 1990–96, Solomon Islands Port Authority 1982–84, Nat. Provident Fund 1976–86 (Chair. 1990–96), Solomon Islands Electricity Authority 1988–89.
Address: Ministry of Finance and Treasury, POB 26, Honiara, Solomon Islands (office). *Telephone:* 22535 (office). *Fax:* 20392 (office). *E-mail:* finance@welkam.solomon.com.sb (office).

RINPOCHE, Samdhong; Tibetan academic and politician; *Chief Minister of Tibetan Government in Exile;* b. (Lobsang Tenzin), 5 Nov. 1939, Nagdug, Tibet. *Education:* monastic studies, Univ. of Drepung, Tibet (rehoused in India after Chinese occupation), Monastery of Gyuto, Dalhousie, India. *Career:* various positions in Tibetan colls in Simla, Darjeeling and Dalhousie, India; Vice-Pres. Congress of Tibetan Youth 1970–73; Prof. Cen. Inst. of Higher Tibetan Studies, Benares (now Varanasi), India 1971–2001, apptd Dir 1988; mem. Standing Cttee Asscn of Indian Univs 1994–, Pres. 1998–; fmr Pres. Tibetan Parl. in Exile; elected Kalon Tripa (Chief Minister) of Tibetan Govt in Exile 2001; Vice-Pres. Library of Tibetan Works and Files, Dharamsala, India; Adviser World Peace Univ., USA; mem. Cttee for Charter of Tibetans in Exile and Future Constitution of Tibet; mem. Bd of Dirs Tibetan Schools, New Delhi, India; mem. Bd of Dirs Asiatic Soc., Calcutta; mem. Bd of Dirs Foundation for Universal Responsibility, New Delhi; mem. Directorate of Indian Council for Philosophical Research; mem. Directorate Krishnamurti Foundation, India; advisory mem. Inst. of Asian Democracy, NY, USA. *Publications include:* numerous academic essays and newspaper articles.
Address: Kashag Secretariat, Central Tibetan Administration, Dharamsala 176215, Dist Kangra, H.P., India (office). *Telephone:* (18) 92222218 (office). *Fax:* (18) 92224914 (office). *E-mail:* kadrung@gov.tibet.net (home). *Website:* www.tibet.net (office).

RÍOS MONTT, Gen. Efraín; Guatemalan politician and army officer (retd); *Secretary-General, Frente Republicano Guatemalteco (FRG);* b. 1927. *Career:* joined army 1943; defence posting, Washington, DC 1973; contested presidential election for Christian Democratic coalition 1974; Mil. Attaché, Madrid; fmr Commdr Honour Guard Brigade; Dir Mil. Acad.; installed as leader of mil. junta after coup March 1982; Minister of Nat. Defence March–Sept. 1982; Pres. of Guatemala, also C-in-C of the Army 1982–83; overthrown Aug. 1983; Sec.-Gen. Frente Republicano Guatemalteco (FRG) 1988–; Pres. of Guatemalan Congress 1995–96,

2001–03; unsuccessful presidential cand. for FRG 2003 elections; mem. Parl. (FRG) 2007–.
Address: Frente Republicano Guatemalteco, 3A Calle 5-50, Zona 1, Guatemala City, Guatemala (office). *Telephone:* 2238-0826 (office). *Website:* www.frg.org.gt (office).

RIPERT, Jean Maurice; French diplomatist; *Permanent Representative, United Nations;* b. 22 June 1953; m.; one c. *Education:* Nat. School of Admin, Inst. of Political Studies. *Career:* with Directorate for Legal Affairs, Ministry of Foreign Affairs 1980–82, Directorate for Econ. and Financial Affairs 1982–83; Tech. Adviser to Minister for Co-operation and Devt 1983–84, to Minister for European Affairs 1984, to Minister for Foreign Affairs 1984–86; Second Counsellor, Embassy in Washington, DC 1986–88; Tech. Adviser to Prime Minister of France 1988–90, Diplomatic Adviser 1991; Chief of Staff to Sec. of State for Humanitarian Action 1991, Adviser to Minister for Health and Humanitarian Action 1992–1993; Consul General in Los Angeles 1993–96; Deputy Dir UN and Int. Org. Desk, Ministry of Foreign Affairs 1996–1997; Diplomatic Adviser to Prime Minister of France 1997–2000; Amb. to Greece 2000–03; Dir UN and Int. Org. Desk, Ministry of Foreign Affairs 2003–05; Perm. Rep. to UN, Geneva 2005–07, to UN, New York 2007–.
Address: Permanent Mission of France to the United Nations, 1 Dag Hammarskjöld Plaza, 245 East 47th Street, 44th Floor, New York, NY 10017, USA (office). *Telephone:* (212) 308-5700 (office). *Fax:* (212) 421-6889 (office). *E-mail:* france@un.int (office). *Website:* www.un.int/france (office).

RISDAHL JENSEN, Tom; Danish diplomatist; *Ambassador to Sweden;* b. 28 Sept. 1947, Hjørring; m. Helle Bundgaard. *Career:* Amb. to UK 2001–06, to Sweden 2006–; Hon. mem. European Affairs Soc., Univ. of Oxford; Commdr, Order of the Dannebrog 2005.
Address: Embassy of Denmark, Jakobs Torg 1, 10323 Stockholm, Sweden (office). *Telephone:* (8) 406-75-00 (office). *E-mail:* stoamb@um.dk (office). *Website:* www.ambstockholm.um.dk (office).

RISHCHYNSKI, Guillermo, BA; Canadian diplomatist; *Ambassador to Mexico;* b. 1953, Toronto; m. Jeannette Portillo Tinoco; two c. *Education:* McGill Univ., Carleton Univ. *Career:* early positions in pvt. sector marketing and project man. in Africa and Latin America; joined Foreign Service 1982, positions included Deputy Dir Mexico, Latin America and Caribbean 1989–92, Dir Team Canada Task Force 1997–98, Inspector-Gen. 2002–03; served at Consulate Gen. in Rio de Janeiro and São Paulo 1983–86, at Embassy in Amman 1986–89, Consulate in Melbourne 1992–93, Embassy in Jakarta 1993–96, Consul-Gen. in Chicago, Ill. 1997–99; Vice-Pres. for the Americas, Canadian Int. Devt Agency 2003–05; Amb. to Colombia 1999–2002, to Brazil 2005–07, to Mexico 2007–.
Address: Embassy of Canada, Schiller 529, Col. Bosque de Chapultepec (Polanco), Del. Miguel Hidalgo, 11580 México DF, Mexico (office). *Telephone:* (55) 5724-7900 (office). *Fax:* (55) 5724-7980 (office). *E-mail:* embajada@canada.org.mx (office). *Website:* www.canada.org.mx (office).

RISSE-KAPPEN, Thomas, PhD; German academic; *Professor of International Politics, University of Konstanz;* b. 17 Dec. 1955. *Education:* Univs of Frankfurt and Bonn. *Career:* Research Assoc., Peace Research Inst., Frankfurt 1981–88; Asst Prof., Cornell Univ., USA 1988–91; Visiting Asst Prof., Yale Univ. 1991–92; Assoc. Prof., Univ. of Wyoming 1992–93; Prof. of Int. Politics, Univ. of Konstanz 1993–; Visiting Prof., Stanford Univ. 1995–96. *Publications include:* Die Krise der Sicherheitspolitik 1988, The Zero Option: INF, West Germany and Arms Control 1988, Co-operation among Democracies: The European Influence on US Foreign Policy 1995, Bringing Transnational Relations Back In: Non-State Actors, Domestic Structures and International Institutions (ed.) 1995, International Relations Theory and the End of the Cold War (ed. with R. Lebow) 1995.
Address: University of Konstanz, Postfach 5560, 78434 Konstanz, Germany (office). *Telephone:* (7531) 88-2184 (office). *E-mail:* thomas.risse-kappen@uni-konstanz.de (office).

RITCHIE, David James, BA; Australian diplomatist; *Ambassador to France;* m.; two c. *Education:* Univ. of Queensland. *Career:* joined Dept of Foreign Affairs (DFA) 1975; Third Sec. in Bonn 1975–78; with S Asia, PNG and S Pacific Section, DFA 1978–81; First Sec. in Berlin 1981–83; with Commodities and Commercial Relations Section, DFA 1983–84, Head of Ministerial and Cabinet Liaison Section 1984–85, Exec. Asst to Sec., Dept of Foreign Affairs 1985–86; First Sec. in Nairobi 1986–88; Acting High Commr to Zambia 1988; Dir NZ Section, DFA 1988–92; with Asia Pacific Section, Int. Div., Dept of the Prime Minister and Cabinet 1992–93, Foreign Affairs Br. 1993–95, APEC, Trade and Multilateral Br. 1995–97, First Asst Sec., Int. Div. 1996–97; First Asst. Sec., S Pacific, Africa and Middle E Div., DFA 1997–99; Sr Adviser (Int. Relations) to the Prime

Minister 1999–2001; First Asst Sec., Int. Orgs and Legal Div., DFA 2001–02; Amb. to Indonesia 2002–08, to France 2008–.
Address: Embassy of Australia, 4 rue Jean Rey, 75724 Paris Cedex 15, France (home). *Telephone:* 1-40-59-33-00 (office). *Fax:* 1-40-59-33-10 (office). *E-mail:* info.paris@dfat.gov.au (office). *Website:* www.france.embassy.gov.au (office).

RIZA, Iqbal, MA; Pakistani UN official; *Special Advisor to the Secretary-General on the Alliance of Civilizations, United Nations;* b. 20 May 1934, Lonavla, India; m. 1959; two s. *Education:* Univ. of Punjab, Lahore, Fletcher School of Int. Law, Boston. *Career:* Pakistan Foreign Service 1958–77; served in Madrid 1959–61, Bonn 1962–64, Khartoum 1964–66, London 1966–68; Dir Foreign Service Acad., Lahore 1968–71; Deputy Chief of Mission, Paris and Deputy Perm. Rep. to UNESCO 1972–76; joined UN 1978, Sec. Cttee on the Exercise of the Inalienable Rights of the Palestinian People 1978–80, Prin. Officer, UN Dept of Public Information 1980–82; assigned to negotiations in Iran–Iraq war 1981–87; Dir Office for Special Political Affairs 1983–88, Div. for Political and Gen. Ass. Affairs 1988–89; Chief, UN Observer Mission for verification of the electoral process in Nicaragua (ONUVEN) 1989–90; Chief of Mission of UN Transition Team in El Salvador March–Aug. 1990; Special Rep. of UN Sec.-Gen. and Chief of UN Observer Mission in El Salvador (ONUSAL) 1991–93; Asst Sec.-Gen. for Peace-keeping Operations 1993–96, Coordinator of UN operations in Bosnia-Herzegovina Feb.–Dec. 1996, Under-Sec.-Gen., Chef de Cabinet in Exec. Office of Sec.-Gen. 1997–2005 (retd); currently Special Advisor to UN Sec-Gen. on the Alliance of Civilizations; mem. UN Advisory Bd on Human Security.
Address: c/o Executive Office of the UN Secretary-General, United Nations Plaza, New York, NY 10017, USA (office).

RO, Tu-chol; North Korean politician; *Vice Premier; Career:* Deputy, Supreme People's Ass.; Vice-Chair State Planning Comm. –2003; Vice Premier 2003–;.
Address: Office of the Vice Premier of the Cabinet, Pyongyang, Democratic People's Republic of Korea.

ROBERT, Lorin S.; Micronesian diplomatist; *Secretary of Foreign Affairs; Education:* American Univ. School of Int. Service, Washington, DC, Univ. of Oxford, UK. *Career:* joined Dept of Foreign Affairs 1984, posts have included Deputy Chief of Mission for Embassy in Tokyo, Deputy Asst Sec. for Asian Affairs, Asst Sec. Asia Pacific and Multilateral Affairs Div., Deputy Sec. for the Dept 2001–07, Sec. of Foreign Affairs 2007–; Chair. Bd of Trustees Micronesian Fisheries Authority; fmr Alternate Gov. IBRD and Asian Devt Bank; has represented Micronesia on various UN panels.
Address: Department of Foreign Affairs, PS123, Palikir, Pohnpei State, 96941, Federated States of Micronesia (office). *Telephone:* 320-2641 (office). *Fax:* 320-2933 (office). *E-mail:* foreignaffairs@mail.fm (office).

ROBERTS, Carl B. W., PhD; Antigua and Barbuda diplomatist; *High Commissioner to UK;* m. Pauline Roberts. *Career:* telecommunications expert with 30-year career at Cable & Wireless; fmr Deputy Perm. Rep. to WTO; High Commr to UK 2004– (also accred to Italy 2005–).
Address: High Commission of Antigua and Barbuda, 2nd Floor, 45 Crawford Place, London, W1H 4LP, England (office). *Telephone:* (20) 7258-0070 (office). *Fax:* (20) 7258-7486 (office). *E-mail:* enquiries@antigua-barbuda.com (office); antiguabarbudaUK@hotmail.com (office). *Website:* www.antigua-barbuda.com (office).

ROBERTS, Colin, CVO, MA, MPhil; British diplomatist; b. 31 July 1959; m. Camilla Roberts; two s. *Education:* King's Coll., Cambridge, Courtauld Inst. of Art. *Career:* Lecturer, Ritsumeikan Univ., Kyoto, Japan 1983–84; called to Bar of England and Wales 1986; pvt. legal practice 1986–89; entered FCO 1989, Repub. of Ireland Dept 1989–90, Second Sec. and Econ. Adviser 1990, Second, later First Sec., Political, British Embassy, Tokyo 1990–94, EU Dept-Internal 1995–96; First Sec., Political/Mil., British Embassy, Paris 1997–98; Head of Common Foreign and Security Policy Dept, FCO 1998–2000; Political Counsellor, British Embassy, Tokyo 2001–04; Amb. to Lithuania 2004–08.
Address: Foreign and Commonwealth Office, King Charles Street, London, SW1A 2AH, England (office). *Telephone:* (20) 7008-1500 (office). *Website:* www.fco.gov.uk (office).

ROBERTS, Sir Ivor Anthony, KCMG, MA; British diplomatist (retd); b. 24 Sept. 1946, Liverpool; m. Elizabeth Bray Bernard Smith 1974; two s. one d. *Education:* St Mary's Coll., Crosby, Keble Coll., Oxford. *Career:* entered diplomatic service 1968, with Middle East Centre for Arab Studies 1969, Third, then Second Sec. Paris 1970–73, Second, then First Sec. FCO 1973–78, First Sec. Canberra 1978–82, Deputy Head of News Dept FCO 1982–86, Head Security Co-ordination Dept FCO 1986–88, Minister and Deputy Head of Mission, Madrid 1989–93, Chargé d'affaires Belgrade

1994–96; Amb. to Yugoslavia 1996–97, to Ireland 1999–2003, to Italy 2003–06 (retd); Fellow, Inst. of Linguists 1991; Sr Assoc. Mem. St Antony's Coll., Oxford 1998–99; Hon. Fellow, Keble Coll., Oxford 2001.
Address: c/o Foreign and Commonwealth Office, King Charles Street, London, SW1A 2AH England.

ROBERTS, Michael John Wyn; British diplomatist; *Ambassador to Slovakia;* m. Margaret Ozanne Roberts; one s. two d. *Career:* with SE Asia Dept, FCO 1985–87; Second, later First Sec., Embassy in Athens 1987–91; with EU Dept, FCO 1991–93, Resource and Finance Dept 1993–95; First Sec. (Insts), UK Rep., Brussels 1995–99; Head of Div., European Secr., Cabinet Office 1999–2004; Deputy Head of Mission, Embassy in Ankara 2004–07; Amb. to Slovakia 2007–.
Address: British Embassy, Panská 16, 811 01 Bratislava, Slovakia (office). *Telephone:* (2) 5998-2000 (office). *Fax:* (2) 5998-2237 (office). *E-mail:* bebra@internet.sk (office). *Website:* www.britishembassy.sk (office).

ROBERTSON, Thomas Bolling, BA, MA; American diplomatist; m. Antoinette Scala Robertson; one s. one d. *Education:* Princeton Univ., Johns Hopkins School of Int. Affairs, Naval War Coll., Newport, RI, has studied in Germany, fmr Soviet Union and Italy. *Career:* guide, later exhibit man. US Information Agency, working on cultural exhibits in Soviet Union, Hungary, Romania and Zaïre 1975–81; joined State Dept in 1981, career mem. Sr Foreign Service with rank of Counselor, served overseas in Moscow 1982–84, as aide to Amb. and as Political Officer in Bonn 1984–86, Deputy Dir for Exchanges, Office of Soviet Union Affairs at State Dept 1986–89, Chief of Political Section, Embassy in Budapest 1990–93, worked in Office of Special Coordinator for Counter-terrorism 1993–94, Special Asst to Asst Sec. for European and Canadian Affairs 1994, European Specialist, Bureau of Legis. Affairs 1994–95, Law Enforcement Counselor, Embassy in Moscow 1995–97, Deputy Chief of Mission, Embassy in Budapest 1998–2001, Chargé d'affaires a.i. March–Aug. 2001, Dir for Russian Affairs, Nat. Security Council 2001–02, Career Devt Officer, Sr Level Div., Bureau of Human Resources 2002–04, Amb. to Slovenia 2004–07.
Address: US Department of State, 2201 C Street NW, Washington, DC 20520, USA (office). *Telephone:* (202) 647-4000 (office). *Fax:* (202) 647-6738 (office). *Website:* www.state.gov (office).

ROBINSON, (Arthur Napoleon) Raymond, LLB, MA, SC; Trinidad and Tobago politician, barrister, economist and fmr head of state; b. 16 Dec. 1926, Calder Hall; m. Patricia Jean Rawlins 1961; one s. one d. *Education:* Bishop's High School, Tobago, London Univ., St John's Coll., Oxford and Inner Temple, London. *Career:* MP, West Indies 1958–61; Rep. of Trinidad and Tobago Council of Univ. of West Indies 1960–62; Minister of Finance and Gov. for Trinidad Bd of Govs of IMF and IBRD 1961–67; Deputy Leader People's Nat. Movt 1967–70; Minister of External Affairs 1967–68; Dir of the Foundation for the Establishment of an Int. Criminal Court 1971; Chair. Democratic Action Congress 1971–86; Rep. for Tobago East, House of Reps 1976–80; Chair. Tobago House of Ass. 1980–86; Leader Nat. Alliance for Reconstruction 1986–91; Prime Minister of Trinidad and Tobago 1986–91, also Minister of the Economy; Minister Extraordinaire and Minister for Tobago Affairs; Adviser to the Prime Minister 1995–97; Pres. of Trinidad and Tobago 1997–2003; mem. UN Expert Group on Crime and the Abuse of Power 1979; Vice-Chair. Parliamentarians for Global Action 1993, Pres. 1995–96, Hon. Patron 1997–; Visiting Scholar, Harvard Univ. 1971; Hon. Fellow, St John's Coll., Oxford 1989; Chief of Ile Ife 1991; KStJ 1992; Hon. LLD (West Indies); Studentship Prize, Inner Temple; Distinguished Int. Criminal Law Award 1977, Defender of Democracy Award, Parliamentarians for Global Action 1997 and numerous other honours and awards. *Publications:* The New Frontier and the New Africa 1961, Fiscal Reform in Trinidad and Tobago 1966, The Path of Progress 1967, The Teacher and Nationalism 1967, The Mechanics of Independence 1971, Caribbean Man 1986; contributions to Encyclopaedia Britannica.
Address: 21 Ellerslie Park, Maraval, Trinidad, Trinidad and Tobago (home).

ROBINSON, Mary, LLM, DCL, SC, MRIA; Irish academic, international civil servant and fmr head of state; *Professor of Practice, School of International and Public Affairs, Columbia University;* b. 21 May 1944, Ballina, Co. Mayo; m. Nicholas Robinson 1970; two s. one d. *Education:* Mount Anville, Trinity Coll. Dublin, King's Inns, Dublin and Harvard Univ., USA. *Career:* Barrister 1967, Sr Counsel 1980; called to English Bar (Middle Temple) 1973; Reid Prof. of Constitutional and Criminal Law, Trinity Coll. Dublin 1969–75; lecturer in European Community Law 1975–90; Founder and Dir Irish Centre for European Law 1988–90; Senator 1969–89; Pres. of Ireland 1990–97; UN High Commr for Human Rights and UnderSec.-Gen. 1997–2002; Chancellor Dublin Univ. 1998–; mem. Dublin City Council 1979–83; mem. New Ireland Forum 1983–84;

mem. Irish Parl. Jt Cttee on EC Secondary Legislation 1973–89; mem. Vedel Cttee on Enlargement of European Parl., EC 1971–72, Saint-Geours Cttee on Energy Efficiency, EC 1978–79, Advisory Bd of Common Market Law Review 1976–90, Irish Parl. Jt Cttee on Marital Breakdown 1983–85, Editorial Bd of Irish Current Law Statutes Annotated 1984–90, Advisory Cttee of Interights, London 1984–90, Int. Comm. of Jurists, Geneva 1987–90, Cttee of Man., European Air Law Asscn 1989–90, Scientific Council of European Review of Public Law 1989–90, Euro Avocats, Brussels 1989–90; Gen. Rapporteur, Human Rights at the Dawn of the 21st Century, Council of Europe, Strasbourg 1993; Prof. of Practice Columbia Univ. School of Int. and Public Affairs (NY) 2004–; Pres. Cherish (Irish Asscn of Single Parents) 1973–90; Founder and Pres. Realizing Rights: The Ethical Globalization Initiative 2002–; founding mem. and Chair. Council of Women World Leaders 2002–; Vice Pres. Club of Madrid; mem. American Philosophical Soc.; mem. Bd of Dirs Vaccine Fund; mem. Leadership Council UN Global Coalition on Women and AIDS; mem. Advisory Bd Earth Inst.; Extraordinary Prof., Univ. of Pretoria; Hon. mem. NY Bar Asscn, American Soc. of Int. Lawyers, Bar of Tanzania; Hon. Fellow, Trinity Coll. Dublin, Inst. of Engineers of Ireland, Royal Coll. of Physicians in Ireland, Hertford Coll. Oxford, LSE, Royal Coll. of Psychiatrists, London, Royal Coll. of Surgeons, Ireland, Royal Coll. of Obstetricians and Gynaecologists, London; Hon. Bencher King's Inns, Dublin, Middle Temple, London; Dr hc (Nat. Univ. of Ireland, Cambridge, Brown, Liverpool, Dublin, Montpellier, St Andrews, Melbourne, Columbia, Nat. Univ. of Wales, Poznań, Toronto, Fordham, Queens Univ. Belfast, Northeastern Univ., Rennes, Coventry, Dublin City, Essex, Harvard, Leuven, London, Seoul, Univ. of Peace, Costa Rica, Uppsala, Yale, Basle, Nat. Univ. of Mongolia, A. Schweitzer Univ. Berne); Berkeley Medal, Univ. of Calif., Medal of Honour, Univ. of Coimbra, Medal of Honour, Ordem dos Advogados (Portugal), Gold Medal of Honour, Univ. of Salamanca, Andrés Bello Medal, Univ. of Chile, New Zealand Suffrage Centennial Medal, Freedom Prize, Max Schmidheiny Foundation (Switzerland), UNIFEM Award, Noel Foundation (USA), Marisa Bellisario Prize (Italy) 1991, European Media Prize (Netherlands) 1991, CARE Humanitarian Award (USA) 1993, Int. Human Rights Award, Int. League of Human Rights 1993, Liberal Int. Prize for Freedom 1993, Stephen P. Duggan Award (USA) 1994, Council of Europe North South Prize (Portugal) 1997, Collar of Hussein Bin Ali (Jordan) 1997, F. D. Roosevelt Four Freedoms Medal 1998, Erasmus Prize (Netherlands) 1999, Fulbright Prize (USA) 1999, Garrigues Walker Prize (Spain) 2000, William Butler Prize (USA) 2000, Indira Gandhi Peace Prize (India) 2000, Sydney Peace Prize, Amnesty Int. Amb. of Conscience Award 2004.
Address: Columbia University School of International and Public Affairs, 420 West 118th Street, New York, NY 10027 (office); Realizing Rights: The Ethical Globalization Initiative, 271 Madison Avenue, Suite 1007, New York, NY 10016, USA. *Telephone:* (212) 854-5406 (office). *Fax:* (212) 864-4847 (office). *Website:* www.sipa.columbia.edu (office); www.realizingrights.org.

ROBO, Kastriot; Albanian diplomatist; m. Teuta Robo. *Career:* fmr Chief Regional Dept, Ministry of Foreign Affairs; fmr Amb. to Cyprus and Greece, Amb. to UK (also accred to Repub. of Ireland) 2002–07.
Address: c/o Ministry of Foreign Affairs, Bulevardi Gjergj Fishta 6, Tirana, Albania (office). *Website:* www.mfa.gov.al (office).

ROCAFORT, Pilar Saborío; Costa Rican diplomatist; m. *Career:* Amb. to UK 2007–.
Address: Embassy of Costa Rica, Flat 1, 14 Lancaster Gate, London, W2 3LH, England (office). *Telephone:* (20) 7706-8844 (office). *Fax:* (20) 7706-8655 (office). *E-mail:* costaricanembassy@btconnect.com (office). *Website:* costarica.embassyhomepage.com (office).

ROCANAS, Charalambos; Greek diplomatist; *Ambassador to Italy;* b. 1949, Athens; m. Angeliki Rocanas; one d. *Education:* Univ. of Athens. *Career:* Consul in Genoa 1977–81, Consul and Consul-General in Istanbul 1981–86, Consul and Deputy Head of Mission, Washington, DC 1986–91, Consul-Gen. in New York 1993–97, Del. to 52nd and 53rd UN Gen. Ass., New York 1997–98; Amb. to Kuwait 1997–2000, to People's Repub. of China 2002–05, to Italy (also accred to San Marino) 2007–; Perm. Rep. to OAS 2007; Deputy Dir of Personnel, Ministry of Foreign Affairs 1991–93, Dir of Cultural Affairs 2000–02, Sec.-Gen. of Ministry 2005–07; Grand Cross of the Order of the Phoenix (Greece), Grand Cross of Honour (Austria), Grand Cross of the Order of Merit (Cyprus), Great Commdr of the Order of Dannebrog (Denmark), Commdr dell'Ordre du Cèdre (Lebanon).
Address: Embassy of Greece, Viale G. Rossini 4, 00198 Rome, Italy (office). *Telephone:* (06) 8537551 (office). *Fax:* (06) 85375503 (office). *E-mail:* gremroma@tin.it (office). *Website:* www.greekembassy.it (office).

ROCARD, Michel Louis Léon, LèsL; French politician; b. 23 Aug. 1930, Courbevoie (Hauts-de-Seine); m. 2nd Michèle Legendre 1972 (divorced); two s.; one s. one d. from 1st m.; m. 3rd Sylvie Geoffroy-Emmanuelli. *Education:* Lycée Louis-le-Grand, Paris, Univ. of Paris, Ecole Nat. d'Admin. *Career:* Nat. Sec. Asscn des Etudiants socialistes, French Section of Workers' Int. (Socialist Party) 1955–56; Insp. des Finances 1958, Econ. and Financial Studies Service 1962, Head of Budget Div., Forecasting Office 1965, Insp. Gen. des Finances 1985; Sec.-Gen. Nat. Accounts and Budget Comm. 1965; Nat. Sec. Parti Socialiste Unifié (PSU) 1967–73; Cand. in first round of elections for presidency of French Repub. 1969; Deputy (Yvelines) to Nat. Ass. 1969–73, 1978–81; left PSU to join Parti Socialiste (PS) 1974, mem. Exec. Bureau 1975–81, 1986–, Nat. Sec. in charge of public sector 1975–79, First Sec. 1993–94; Mayor of Conflans-Sainte-Honorine 1977–94; Minister of State, Minister of Planning and Regional Devt 1981–83, of Agric. 1983–85; Prime Minister of France 1988–91; mem. Parl. for Yvelines 1986–88; mem. European Parl. 1994–; mem. Senate 1995–97; Chair. Cttee on Devt and Co-operation 1997–99, Employment and Social Affairs 1999–2001, Culture, Educ. and Youth Matters 2001–03; Grand-Croix, Ordre nat. du Mérite, Commdr du Mérite agricole, Grand Cross, Order of Christ (Portugal), Grand Officer, Order of the Tunisian Repub. and numerous other decorations. *Publications:* Le PSU et l'avenir socialiste de la France 1969, Des militants du PSU présentés par Michel Rocard 1971, Questions à l'Etat socialiste 1972, Un député, pourquoi faire? 1973, Le marché commun contre Europe (with B. Jaumont and D. Lenègre) 1973, L'inflation au cœur (with Jacques Gallus) 1975, Parler vrai 1979, A l'épreuve des faits: textes politiques (1979–85) 1986, Le cœur à l'ouvrage 1987, Un pays comme le nôtre, textes politiques 1986–89 1989, Les Moyens d'en sortir 1996, L'art de la paix (essay) 1998, Mes idées pour demain 2000, Pour une autre Afrique 2001, Entretiens 2001, Si la gauche savait 2005. *Address:* 266 blvd Saint-Germain, 75007 Paris (office); 10 rue Philippe Paget, 78380 Bougival, France (home); European Parliament, 97–113 rue Belliard, 1047 Brussels, Belgium. *Telephone:* 1-47-05-25-00 (office). *Fax:* 1-45-51-42-04 (office). *E-mail:* mrocard.paris@noos.fr (office).

ROCCA, Christina B., BA; American diplomatist; *Representative to the United Nations Conference on Disarmament;* m.; two c. *Education:* King's Coll. London, UK. *Career:* career officer, CIA, also mem. Clandestine Operations Directorate 1982–97; Foreign Policy Adviser to Senator Sam Brownback (Republican Senator from Kansas) 1997–2001; Asst Sec. of State for S Asia Affairs 2001–06; Rep. to UN Conf. on Disarmament (with rank of Amb.) 2006–. *Address:* Department of State, Office 1113A, 2201 C Street, NW, Washington, DC 20210, USA (office); Conference on Disarmament, UNOG, 1211 Geneva 10, Switzerland. *Telephone:* (202) 647-5327 (office). *Fax:* (202) 647-6738 (office). *Website:* www.state.gov (office).

ROĆEN, Milan; Montenegrin diplomatist and politician; *Minister of Foreign Affairs;* b. 23 Nov. 1950, Žabljak; m. Stana Roćen; one s. *Education:* Belgrade Univ. *Career:* journalist, Ekonomska Politika magazine 1976–79; worked in Information and Propaganda Dept of Pres. of Cen. Cttee of League of Communists of Montenegro 1979–82, Political Chief of Staff 1982–88; Deputy Minister of Foreign Affairs 1988-92; Minister-Counsellor for Political Affairs, Fed. Repub. of Yugoslavia Embassy, Moscow 1992–97; Foreign Policy Advisor to Prime Minister of Repub. of Montenegro 1997–98, to Pres. 1998–2003; Chief Political Advisor to Prime Minister of Montenegro 2003, Feb.–Sept. 2006; Amb. of Serbia and Montenegro to Russian Fed. (also accred to Kazakhstan, Uzbekistan, Turkmenistan, Tajikistan, Kyrgyzstan and Georgia) 2003–06; Co-ordinator Pro-independence Bloc and Gen. Man. of campaign for referendum on independence Feb.–May 2006; Minister of Foreign Affairs 2006–; mem. Democratic Socialist Party of Montenegro. *Address:* Ministry of Foreign Affairs, 81000 Podgorica, Stanka Dragoje-vića 2, Montenegro (office). *Telephone:* (81) 224609 (office). *Fax:* (81) 224670 (office). *E-mail:* mip@mn.yu (office). *Website:* mip.vlada.cg.yu (office).

ROCHA, José Luis; Cape Verde diplomatist and international organization official; b. 1956, São Vicente. *Education:* Univ. of Louvain, Belgium. *Career:* joined Ministry of Planning and Co-operation 1981, Chief of Div. and Dir of Int. Co-operation Dept 1982–95; Amb. to Belgium and Luxembourg 1995–99; Perm. Rep. of Org. Int. de la Francophonie to EU 2000; currently Dir-Gen. of Political Affairs, Ministry of Foreign Affairs, Co-operation and Communities. *Address:* Ministry of Foreign Affairs, Co-operation and Communities, Palácio das Comunidades, Achada de Santo António, Praia, Santiago, Cape Verde (office). *Telephone:* 2615727 (office). *Fax:* 2616262 (office). *E-mail:* mne@gov.cv (office).

ROCHA-PARIS, João, LLB; Portuguese diplomatist; *Ambassador to the Holy See and Malta;* b. 19 April 1945; m. Ana Rocha-Paris; two d. *Education:* Univ. of Lisbon. *Career:* joined Foreign Service 1969, adviser to Deputy Minister and Minister of Foreign Affairs; Second Sec. Embassy in Madrid, Spain 1972–75; Counsellor Perm. Mission to Council of Europe, Strasbourg, France 1980–85; Counsellor Perm. Mission to NATO, Brussels, Belgium 1985–91; Amb. to Angola 1991–96, to Belgium 1996–99, to USA 1999–2002; Permanent Undersecretary, Ministry of Foreign Affairs 2002–04; Amb. to Holy See and Malta 2004–. *Address:* Embassy of Portugal, Villa Lusa, Via San Valentino 9, 00197 Rome, Italy (office). *Telephone:* (06) 8091581 (office). *Fax:* (06) 8077585 (office). *E-mail:* embportugalvatican@tiscalinet.it (office).

RODAS MELGAR, (Róger) Haroldo; Guatemalan civil servant and international organization executive; *Minister of Foreign Affairs; Career:* fmr Adviser, Ministry of Economy; Sec.-Gen. Secretaría de Integración Económica Centroamericana (SIECA) 1997–2007; Minister of Foreign Affairs 2008–. *Publications:* articles in professional journals. *Address:* Ministry of Foreign Affairs, 2a Avda La Reforma 4-47, Zona 10, Guatemala City, Guatemala (office). *Telephone:* 2331-8410 (office). *Fax:* 2331-8510 (office). *E-mail:* webmaster@minex.gob.gt (office). *Website:* www.minex.gob.gt (office).

RODAS-POSSO, Luis Antonio; Ecuadorean diplomatist; *Ambassador to Australia;* m. Dominique Hempel-Rodas-Posso. *Career:* fmr Consul Gen. in Hamburg, Germany; Amb. to Australia 2006–. *Address:* Embassy of Ecuador, 6 Pindari Crescent, O'Malley, ACT 2606, Australia (office). *Telephone:* (2) 6286-4021 (office). *Fax:* (2) 6286-1231 (office). *E-mail:* embecu@bigpond.net.au (office).

RODGERS, Jimmie, MD; Solomon Islands physician and international organization executive; *Director-General, Secretariat of the Pacific Community; Career:* holds degree in health admin; Under-Sec., later Perm. Sec. for Health, Ministry of Health and Medical Services, Solomon Islands 1990–96; joined Secr. of the Pacific Community (SPC) as Dir of Programmes in 1996, later re-designated as Deputy Dir-Gen. based in Noumea, Head of SPC Suva Regional Office 1998, later Sr Deputy Dir-Gen., Dir-Gen. SPC 2005–. *Address:* Secretariat of the Pacific Community Headquarters, BP D5, 98848 Noumea Cedex, New Caledonia (office). *Telephone:* 26-20-00 (office). *Fax:* 26-38-18 (office). *E-mail:* JimmieR@spc.int (office). *Website:* www.spc.int (office).

RODGERS, Patricia Elaine Joan, MA, DPolSc; Bahamian diplomatist; b. Nassau. *Education:* School of St Helen & St Catherine, Abingdon, Univ. of Aberdeen, Graduate Inst. of Int. Relations, St Augustine, Trinidad, Inst. Universitaire des Hautes Etudes Int., Univ. of Geneva. *Career:* Counsellor and Consul, Washington, DC 1978–83; Alt. Rep. to OAS 1982–83; Deputy High Commr (Acting High Commr) to Canada 1983–86, High Commr 1986–88; High Commr to UK (also Accred to France, Belgium and Germany) 1988–92; mem. Bahamas Del. to UN Conf. on Law of the Sea 1974, 1975, OAS Gen. Ass. 1982, Caribbean Co-ordinating Meeting (Head of Del.), OAS 1983, Canada/Commonwealth Caribbean Heads of Govt Meeting 1985, Commonwealth Heads of Govt Meeting Nassau 1985, Vancouver 1987; Adviser to Bahamas Del., Annual Gen. Meetings of World Bank and IMF 1978–82; mem. Commonwealth Observer Group, Gen. Elections Lesotho 1993; apptd. Perm. Sec., Ministry of Tourism 1995; currently Perm. Sec. Ministry of Foreign Affairs. *Publications:* Mid-Ocean Archipelagos and International Law: A Study of the Progressive Development of International Law 1981. *Address:* Ministry of Foreign Affairs and Public Service, East Hill Street, POB N-3746, Nassau, Bahamas (office). *Telephone:* 302-9300 (office). *Fax:* 328-8212 (office). *E-mail:* mfabahamas@batelnet.bs (office); carridad68@yahoo.com (home).

RODRIGO, Nihal; Sri Lankan diplomatist and international organization official; *Adviser to the President on Foreign Affairs; Career:* Asst Lecturer, Univ. of Ceylon; with Foreign Service, including diplomatic missions in Australia, Germany, India, Switzerland and USA; Deputy Perm. Rep. to UN, New York, Perm. Rep., Geneva; Dir-Gen. for S Asia, SAARC, Sec.-Gen. 1999–2002; co-ordinated activities of Non-Aligned Movt under Sri Lanka's chairmanship 1976–79, del. to summit confs 1976–, Chair. Political Cttee 1995; mem. Advisory Bd on Disarmament of UN Sec.-Gen.; mem. several presidential cttees, including Acquisition of Art Works for State Collections, Foreign Affairs, Human Rights and Information Strategy; mem. Man. Bd Bandaranaike Centre for Int. Studies; Amb. to China, Mongolia and People's Repub. of China 2004–07; Adviser to Pres. of Sri Lanka on Foreign Affairs 2007–.

Address: c/o President's Secretariat, Republic Square, Colombo 1, Sri Lanka. *Telephone:* (11) 2324801. *Fax:* (11) 2331246. *E-mail:* gosl@ presidentsl.org. *Website:* www.presidentsl.org.

RODRIGUES-BIRKETT, Carolyn; Guyanese politician; *Minister of Foreign Affairs;* b. 16 Sept. 1973, Santa Rosa, Region One; m.; two c. *Education:* Saskatchewan Federated Coll., Canada, Univ. of Guyana. *Career:* began career as teacher, Santa Rosa Primary School; Asst Co-ordinator, later Co-ordinator for Amerindian Projects, Social Impact Amelioration Program 1993–2001; Minister of Amerindian Affairs 2001–08, of Foreign Affairs 2008–.
Address: Ministry of Foreign Affairs, Takuba Lodge, 254 South Road and New Garden Street, Bourda, Georgetown, Guyana (office). *Telephone:* 226-1607 (office). *Fax:* 225-9192 (office). *E-mail:* minfor@guyana.net.gy (office). *Website:* www.sdnp.org.gy/minfor (office).

RODRÍGUEZ ARAQUE, Ali; Venezuelan politician, lawyer and diplomatist; *Minister of Finance;* b. 9 Sept. 1937, Ejido, Venezuela. *Education:* Univ. Cen. de Venezuela, Univ. de los Andes. *Career:* practised law; mem. Parl. 1983; mem. Nat. Council of Energy; Chair. Chamber of Deputies Comm. of Energy and Mines 1994–97; Vice-Chair., Bicameral Comm. of Energy and Mines; Senator 1999–2004; fmr Minister of Energy and Mines 1999–2000; Pres. of OPEC Conf. 2000, Sec.-Gen. 2001–02; Pres. and CEO Petróleos de Venezuela SA (PDVSA) 2002–04; Minister of Foreign Affairs 2004–06, of Finance 2008–; Amb. to Cuba 2006–08. *Publications:* various articles on public policy in the field of energy, including Privatisation Process of the Oil Industry in Venezuela 1997.
Address: Ministry of Finance, Edif. Ministerio de Finanzas, esq. Carmelitas, Avda Urdaneta, Caracas, Venezuela (office). *Telephone:* (212) 802-1404 (office). *Fax:* (212) 802-1413 (office). *E-mail:* consultapublica@ mf.gov.ve (office). *Website:* www.mf.gov.ve (office).

RODRÍGUEZ BARRERA, Dagoberto; Cuban diplomatist; b. 1955. *Education:* Univ. of Havana. *Career:* grad. in journalism; career diplomat, spent 20 years with Cuba's Ministry of Foreign Affairs, specializing in N America, Cuban Interests Section (Embassy of Switzerland) expert on US Congressional affairs 1995–99, Head of Section 2001–07.
Address: Ministry of Foreign Relations, Calzada 360, esq. G, Vedado, Havana, Cuba (office). *Telephone:* (7) 55-3537 (office). *Fax:* (7) 33-3460 (office). *E-mail:* cubaminrex@minrex.gov.cu (office). *Website:* www .cubaminrex.cu (office).

RODRIGUEZ CUADROS, Manuel, DJur; Peruvian diplomatist and politician; b. 1949, Cusco; m.; four c. *Education:* Universidad Nacional Mayor de San Marcos. *Career:* Asst Dir of Integration, Ministry of Foreign Affairs 1984–85, Dir Econ. Affairs 1985–86, Vice-Minister of Foreign Affairs –2003, Minister 2003–05; Perm. Rep. to UN, New York 1988–89, to Int. Orgs, Geneva –2006; Chair. 62nd Session UN Comm. on Human Rights, Geneva 2006; currrently Dir-Gen. Instituto Sudamericano de Relaciones Internacionales y Medio Ambiente. *Publication:* Delimitación Marítima con Equidad: El caso de Perú y Chile.
Address: c/o Ministry of Foreign Affairs, Jirón Lampa 535, Lima 1, Peru (office).

RODRÍGUEZ ECHEVERÍA, Miguel Angel, PhD; Costa Rican international organization official and fmr head of state, economist and business executive; b. 9 Jan. 1940, San José; m. *Education:* Univ. de Costa Rica, Univ. of Calif., Berkeley. *Career:* Lecturer and Economist, Univ. of Costa Rica 1963; Research Asst, Univ. of Calif., Berkeley 1965–66; Dir of Planning Office and Presidential Adviser on Political Econs and Planning 1966–68; Dir Cen. Bank 1967–70; columnist for La Nación 1967–68; with Ministry of Planning 1968–69; Visiting Economist, Univ. of Calif.; with Ministry of the Presidency 1970; exec. with Empacadora de Carne de Cartago and Abonos Superior SA 1970–71; Pres. Agrodinámica Int. SA and subsidiaries 1974–87; Lecturer in Econs, Univ. of Costa Rica and Univ. Autónoma de Centro América 1978; mem. of Counsel (legal and econ. advisers) 1982; mem. nat. political directorate Partido Unidad Social Cristiano 1984, mem. Exec. 1994; Dir Banco Agro Industrial y de Exportaciones SA 1986–87; gen. adviser Grupo Ganadero Int. de Costa Rica SA 1989–90; Deputy Legis. Ass. 1991–92; Vice-Pres. (for Cen. America), Christian Democratic Org. of Latin America 1991, Pres. 1995; Pres. of Costa Rica 1998–2002; Sec.-Gen. OAS Sept.–Oct. 2004 (resgnd). *Publications:* El mito de la Racionalidad del Socialismo 1963, El Orden Jurídico de la Libertad 1967, Contributions to Economic Analysis. Production Economics: A Dual Approach to Theory and Applications 1978, Nuestra Crisis Financiera: Causas y Soluciones 1979, De las Ideas a la Acción 1988, Al Progreso por la Libertad 1989, Libertad y Solidaridad: Una Política Social para el Desarrollo Humano 1992, Una Revolución Moral: Democracia, Mercado y Bien Común 1992, Por una Vida Buena, Justa y Solidaria 1993; numerous articles and contribs on econs.

Address: c/o Organization of American States, 17th Street & Constitution Avenue, NW, Washington, DC 20006, USA (office).

RODRÍGUEZ GIAVARINI, Adalberto; Argentine politician and economist. *Education:* Univ. of Buenos Aires. *Career:* fmr Comptroller Gen. Trust of State Cos.; Pres. and owner macroecons analysis co.; Chair. Microecons, Univ. of Buenos Aires 1972–78; Co-ordinator Postgrad. Studies in Econs, Univ. of Salvador 1980–83; Sec. of State for Budget, Ministry of Economy 1983–85, for Planning, Ministry of Defence 1986–89; elected mem. Chamber of Deputies 1995; Minister of Foreign Affairs, Int. Trade and Religion –2001; mem. Bd of Dirs and Exec. Cttee Fundación Carolina de Argentina, fmr Pres.; Visiting Prof., Univ. of Belgrano 1994; Prof. of Econs, School of Econs and Business Admin. 1995; mem. various academic insts and advisory bds; guest columnist maj. daily newspapers in Argentina and abroad.
Address: c/o Fundación Carolina de Argentina, Buenos Aires, Argentina. *E-mail:* info@fundacioncarolina.org.ar. *Website:* www.fundacioncarolina .org.ar.

RODRÍGUEZ IGLESIAS, Gil Carlos, PhD; Spanish judge and professor of law; b. 26 May 1946, Gijón; m. Teresa Diez Gutiérrez 1972; two d. *Education:* Univ. of Oviedo and Univ. Autónoma de Madrid. *Career:* Asst Univs of Oviedo, Freiburg, Autónoma of Madrid and Complutense of Madrid 1969–77; lecturer, Univ. Complutense of Madrid 1977–82, Prof. 1982–83, Prof. of Int. Law 2003–; Prof., Univ. of Granada 1983–2003, Dir Dept of Int. Law 1983–86; Judge, Court of Justice of European Communities 1986–2003, Pres. 1994–2003; Jean Monnet Chair of European Community Law, Dir Dept of European Studies, Instituto Universitario Ortega y Gasset 2004–05; Co-dir Revista de Derecho Comunitario Europeo; mem. Bd of Dirs Fundación Real Instituto Elcano; mem. Editorial Bds of several law reviews; mem. Curatorium, Max Planck Inst. for Int. Public Law and Comparative Law, Heidelberg;; Hon. Bencher Gray's Inn 1995, King's Inn, Dublin; Hon. Fellow, Soc. of Advanced Legal Studies, London; Hon. Mem. Academia Asturiana de Jurisprudencia; Orden de Isabel la Católica, Orden de San Raimundo de Peñafort; Dr hc (Turin) 1996, (Babeş-Bolyai Cluj-Napoca, Romania) 1996, (Sarre Univ.), (Univ. of Ohrid, Bulgaria); Walter-Hallstein Prize 2003. *Publications:* El régimen jurídico de los monopolios de Estado en la Comunidad Económica Europea 1976; numerous articles and studies on EC law and int. law.
Address: c/o Board of Directors, Fundación Real Instituto Elcano, Príncipe de Vergara, 51, 28006 Madrid, Spain. *E-mail:* info@rielcano.org. *Website:* www.realinstitutoelcano.org.

RODRÍGUEZ MENDOZA, Miguel; Venezuelan international organization official, lawyer and diplomatist; *Senior Fellow, International Centre for Trade and Sustainable Development; Education:* Cen. Univ. of Venezuela, Univ. of Manchester, UK, Ecole des Hautes Etudes en Sciences Sociales, France. *Career:* First Sec. Perm. Mission of Venezuela to UN 1978–81; Dir for Consultation and Co-ordination, Latin American Econ. System 1982–88; Special Adviser to Pres. on int. econ. affairs 1989–91; Minister of State, Pres. Inst. of Foreign Trade 1991–94; Pres. Comm. of Cartagena Agreement 1993; Chief Trade Adviser, OAS –1998; Visiting Scholar, Georgetown Univ., Washington, DC 1998–; Jt Deputy Dir-Gen. WTO 1999–2002; Of Counsel Van Bael & Bellis, Geneva 2002–04; Transatlantic Fellow, German Marshall Fund of the US 2005–; Sr Fellow, Int. Centre for Trade and Sustainable Devt, Geneva; apptd Chair. WTO panel to decide US challenge on EU system of protecting products with geographical names 2004. *Publications:* numerous articles in books and journals; has edited numerous books.
Address: International Centre for Trade and Sustainable Development, International Environment House 2, Chemin de Balexert 7, 1219 Châtelaine, Geneva, Switzerland (office). *Telephone:* (22) 917-8492 (office). *Fax:* (22) 917-8093 (office). *Website:* www.ictsd.org (office).

RODRÍGUEZ-SPITERI PALAZUELO, José, LLB; Spanish lawyer and diplomatist; b. 28 Dec. 1945, Madrid; m.; two c. *Career:* entered diplomatic corps 1972; Third Sec., later Second Sec. 1972, Spanish Embassy, New Delhi 1972–74; Vice-Consul, Munich 1975–77; Counsellor (Commercial), Spanish Embassy, Mexico City 1978–82; Diplomatic Adviser, Ministry of Foreign Affairs, Madrid 1982–86, Minister Plenipotentiary (third class) 1986, (second class) 1992; Head of N America and Asia Dept 1990–94, of European Foreign Policy Dept 1994–96, of Europe and N America Dept 1996–99; Amb. to Portugal 1999–2002, to Germany 2002–04; Amb. to Special Mission for Projects of European Integration 2005–; numerous decorations including Commdr, Order of Isabel la Católica, Order Cruceiro do Sul (Brazil), Order Infante Don Enrique (Portugal), Order of the Aztec Eagle (Mexico), Italian Service Order.
Address: Ministry of Foreign Affairs and Co-operation, Plaza de la Provincia 1, 28012 Madrid, Spain. *Telephone:* (91) 3799700. *E-mail:* informae@mae.es. *Website:* www.mae.es.

ROED-LARSEN, Terje, PhD; Norwegian diplomatist, politician and international organization official; *Under-Secretary-General and Special Envoy for the Implementation of Security Council Resolution 1559, United Nations;* b. 22 Nov. 1947; m. Mona Juul. *Career:* taught sociology and philosophy at Univs of Bergen and Oslo; Founder and Exec. Dir Inst. of Applied Social Sciences (FAFO) 1991, Hon. Chair. Programme for Int. Co-operation and Conflict Resolution; fmr Deputy Foreign Minister; facilitated negotiations between reps of Israel's Labour Govt and Palestinian Liberation Org. (PLO) leading to signing of Declaration of Principles, Washington, DC 13 Sept. 1993; Amb. and Special Adviser to Norwegian Foreign Minister for the Middle East Peace Process 1993, 1998–; UN Deputy Sec.-Gen. and Special Co-ordinator in the Occupied Territories, Gaza 1994–96; Minister of Planning 1996–98; Special Co-ordinator for the Middle East Peace Process and Personal Rep. of the UN Sec.-Gen. to the PLO and Palestinian Authority 1999–2005; Under-Sec.-Gen. and Special Envoy for the Implementation of UN Security Council Resolution 1559 (calling for Syrian withdrawal from Lebanon and disarmament of Hezbollah) 2004–; Pres. Int. Peace Acad., New York 2005–. *Address:* International Peace Academy, 777 United Nations Plaza, New York, NY 10017-3521 (office), Executive Office of the UN Secretary-General, United Nations Plaza, New York, NY 10017, USA. *Telephone:* (212) 687-4300 (office); (212) 906-5791 (UN) (office). *Fax:* (212) 983-8246 (office); (212) 906-5778 (UN) (office). *E-mail:* ipa@ipacademy.org (office). *Website:* www.ipacademy.org (office); www.un.org (office).

ROGACHEV, Igor Alekseevich, PhD; Russian diplomatist and politician; b. 1 March 1932, Moscow; m. Dioulber Rogacheva; one s. one d. (adopted). *Education:* Moscow Inst. of Int. Relations 1955, USSR Ministry of Foreign Affairs. *Career:* worked as interpreter in China 1956–58; joined diplomatic service 1958; Attaché, Embassy in China 1959–61; mem. Cen. Admin. USSR Ministry of Foreign Affairs 1961–65; First Sec. Embassy, USA 1965–69; Counsellor Embassy, China 1969–72; Deputy Head, Far Eastern Dept, Ministry of Foreign Affairs 1972–75, Head Asian Section, Dept of Planning of int. policies 1975–78, Head of South-East Asia Dept 1978–83, Head First Far East Div. 1983–86, Chief Dept of Socialist Countries of Asia 1986–87, Deputy-Minister of Foreign Affairs 1986–91; Head USSR del. Sino-Soviet talks on frontier issues 1987–91, int. talks on Cambodia 1988–91; Special Envoy to South Korea 1991; Amb.-at-Large to Democratic People's Repub. of Korea 1992; Amb. to People's Repub. of China 1992–2005; mem. Fed. Council for Amur Region 2005–; Vice-Chair. Russian–Chinese Friendship Soc. 1992–; mem. Editorial Bd Far Eastern Affairs journal; Academician Int. Acad. of Information Processes and Tech.; Order of the Badge of Honour 1971, Order of the Friendship of Peoples 1982, Order of Friendship 1996, Order of Honour 1999, Honoured Diplomatic Service Worker of Russian Fed. 2002; several medals. *Publications:* numerous articles and essays on Asian Pacific region. *Address:* Sovet Federatsii (Federation Council), 103426 Moscow, ul. B. Dmitrovka 26, Russia (office). *Telephone:* (495) 203-90-74 (office). *Fax:* (495) 203-46-17 (office). *E-mail:* post_sf@gov.ru (office). *Website:* www.council.gov.ru (office).

ROGGE, Jacques; Belgian international organization official and surgeon; *President, International Olympic Committee;* b. 1942, Ghent; m.; two c. *Career:* fmr orthopaedic surgeon and sports medicine lecturer; participated as Olympic sailing competitor 1968, 1972, 1976; Pres. Belgian Nat. Olympic Cttee 1989–92; Pres. European Olympic Cttee 1989–2001, Chef de mission, two winter and three summer Olympic Games (Chief Co-ordinator, Olympic Games 2000, 2004); mem. Int. Olympic Cttee (IOC) 1991–, Pres. 2001–; UNEP Champion of the Earth Laureate 2007. *Address:* International Olympic Committee, Château de Vidy, 1007 Lausanne, Switzerland (office). *Telephone:* (21) 6216111 (office). *Fax:* (21) 6216216 (office). *Website:* www.olympic.org (office).

ROGOFF, Kenneth S., BA, MA, PhD; American economist, international finance official and academic; *Thomas D. Cabot Professor of Public Policy, Harvard University;* b. 22 March 1953, Rochester, NY; m. Natasha Lanre; one s. one d. *Education:* Yale Univ., Massachusetts Inst. of Tech., Cambridge, Mass. *Career:* Economist, Int. Finance Div., Fed. Reserve Bd of Govs 1980–83; economist, Research Dept, IMF 1982–83; Assoc. Prof. of Econs, Univ. of Wis. 1985–88; Prof. of Econs, Univ. of Calif., Berkeley 1989–92; Prof. of Econs and Int. Affairs, Princeton Univ. 1992–94, Charles and Marie Robertson Prof. of Int. Affairs 1995–99; Prof. of Econs, Harvard Univ. 1999–, Thomas D. Cabot Prof. of Public Policy 2004–, Dir Harvard Center for Int. Devt 2003–04; Economic Counsellor and Dir, Research Dept, IMF 2001–05; Vice Pres. American Econ. Assccn 2007; Research Assoc. Nat. Bureau of Econ. Research 1985–; mem. Econ. Advisory Panel Fed. Reserve Bank of New York 2004–; mem. Academic Advisory Panel, Cen. Bank of Sweden 2005–; mem. Advisory Cttee Inst. for Int. Econs 2001–; Assoc. Ed. Review of Economics and Statistics 1993–, Economics Letters 1993–96, Journal of International Economics 1995–,

Quarterly Journal of Economics 1984–95, Journal of Economic Perspectives 1987–90; mem. Council on Foreign Relations 2004–, Trilateral Comm. 2003–; Fellow, Econometric Soc. 1990–, German Marshall Foundation 1991, American Acad. of Arts and Sciences 2001–; World Econ. Forum Fellow 2003–; Guggenheim Fellow 1998; Nat. Fellow, Hoover Inst. 1986; Alfred P. Sloan Research Fellow 1986. *Achievements include:* Int. Grandmaster of Chess (World Chess Fed.) 1978–. *Publications include:* Foundations of International Macroeconomics (with Maurice Obstfeld) 1996, Workbook for Foundations of International Macroeconomics 1998; numerous contribs to learned journals and newspapers. *Address:* Harvard University, Department of Economics, Littauer Center 232, Cambridge, MA 02138-3001 (office); 3723 Harrison Street, NW, Washington, DC 20015, USA (home). *Telephone:* (617) 495-4022 (office); (202) 363-4529 (home). *Fax:* (617) 495-7730 (office). *E-mail:* krogoff@harvard.edu (office). *Website:* www.economics.harvard.edu/faculty/rogoff (home).

ROGOV, Sergey Mikhailovich, Dr. Hist.; Russian political scientist; *Director, Institute for USA and Canadian Studies, Russian Academy of Sciences;* b. 22 Oct. 1948, Moscow; m.; one s. one d. *Education:* Moscow State Inst. of Int. Relations. *Career:* jr, sr researcher, head of sector Inst. for USA and Canadian Studies, Russian Acad. of Sciences 1976–84, Rep. of Inst. for USA and Canadian Studies to USSR Embassy, Washington, DC 1984–87, Leading Research Fellow, Moscow 1987–89, Chief Dept of Mil. and Political Studies 1989–91, Deputy Dir 1991–95, Dir 1995–; mem. Scientific Council of Ministry of Foreign Affairs, of Security Council; counsellor Cttee on Foreign Relations of State Duma; mem. Russian Acad. of Nat. Sciences; Corresp. mem. Russian Acad. of Sciences 2002–. *Publications:* 16 books on foreign policy of USSR and Russian Fed., Russian-American relationship, mil. aspects of foreign policy, problems of nat. security and over 300 scientific publs and articles. *Address:* Institute for USA and Canadian Studies, Russian Academy of Sciences, Khlebny Pereulok 2/3, 121814 Moscow, Russia (office). *Telephone:* (495) 290-58-75 (office). *Fax:* (495) 200-12-07 (office). *E-mail:* srogov@rambler.ru (office). *Website:* iskran.iip.net/engl/index-en.html (office).

ROGOZIN, Dmitry Olegovich, CandPhil; Russian journalist, politician and diplomatist; *Ambassador to NATO;* b. 21 Dec. 1963, Moscow; m. Tatyana Serebryakova; one s. *Education:* Moscow State Univ. *Career:* worked in USSR Cttee of Youth Orgs; one of founders Research and Educ. Co. RAU Corp. 1986–90; one of Party of People's Freedom 1990; Pres. Asscn of Young Political Leaders of Russia Forum-90; f. Congress of Russian Communities 1993; active in nat. movt; took part in resurrection of numerous churches; mem. State Duma (Regions of Russia, now Rodina) 1997–; Co-Founder and Leader Rodina pre-election bloc 2003, Leader Rodina—People's Patriotic Union faction 2004–; Chair. Cttee on Int. Affairs 2000–03, Deputy Chair. 2003–04; Deputy Chair. Cttee on Nationalities, State Duma; Chief Negotiator with EU on problems of Kaliningrad Region –2004; Amb. to NATO 2008–. *Publications:* Russian Answer 1996 and other books and articles on Russian people and Russian Culture. *Address:* Mission of the Russian Federation to NATO, NATO Headquarters, Blvd Leopold III, 1110 Brussels, Belgium (office). *Telephone:* (2) 707-41-11 (office). *Fax:* (2) 707-45-79 (office). *E-mail:* natodoc@hq.nato.int (home). *Website:* www.nato.int (office).

ROH, Moo-hyun; South Korean politician and fmr head of state; b. 1946, Kimhae, S. Kyonsang Prov.; m.; one s. one d. *Education:* Pusan Commercial High School. *Career:* mil. service, rank of corporal; served as judge in Taejon Dist court 1977; practised as human rights lawyer 1978; elected lawmaker 1988; elected mem. ruling Millennium Democratic Party's (MDP, later renamed Democratic Party) Supreme Council 2000–03; Minister of Maritime Affairs and Fisheries 2000–01; Pres. of the Repub. of Korea 2003–08, stripped of constitutional powers following impeachment vote March 2004, returned to office May 2004 after Constitutional Court overturned impeachment. *Address:* Democratic Party, 15, Gisan Bldg, Yeongdeungpo-gu, Seoul, Republic of Korea (office). *Telephone:* (2) 784-7007 (office). *Fax:* (2) 784-6070 (office). *Website:* www.minjoo.or.kr (office).

ROHANI, Hassan, DJur, PhD; Iranian government official; b. 1948. *Education:* Qom. *Career:* fmr Deputy Speaker, Majlis (parl.); currently mem. and rep. of Ayatollah Khamenei, Supreme Leader of Iran on Supreme Nat. Security Council (Sec. –2005); Deputy Chair. Expediency Council; Dir Center for Strategic Studies, Iran; mem. Ass. of Experts. *Address:* Center for Strategic Studies, No. 840, Opposite Niavaran Park, Tehran 19547, Iran (office). *Telephone:* (21) 2295051 (office). *Fax:* (21) 2801272 (office). *E-mail:* info@csr.ir (office). *Website:* www.csr.ir (office).

ROHOVIY, Vasyl Vasylyovich, CandEcons; Ukrainian politician and economist; b. 2 March 1953, Mirivka, Kiev region; m. Svetlana Mikhailivna Rogovaya; one s. *Education:* Kiev Inst. of National Econs, Ukrainian Acad. of Sciences. *Career:* engineer and economist Kiev Artem Production co. 1974–75, 1976–77; sr mechanic Odessa Mil. Command 1975–76; jr researcher Inst. of Econs, then Scientific Sec. Dept of Econs, Ukrainian Acad. of Sciences 1980–88; Chief Expert, Head of Sector, then Head of Div. Ukrainian Council of Ministers 1988–94; First Deputy Minister of Econs 1994–98, Minister 1998–99, 2000–01; First Deputy Head of Admin., Office of the Pres. 2000; Deputy Prime Minister for Econ. Policy 2001–02; Presidential Adviser 2002; currently Deputy Sec. of Econ, Social and Environmental Security Council, Nat. Security and Defense Council of Ukraine; apptd mem. Supervisory Council UkrExImBank JSC—State Export-Import Bank of Ukraine 2003.
Address: c/o Council of National Security and Defense of Ukraine, 11 Bankova str., 01220 Kiev, Ukraine (office). *Telephone:* (44) 254-40-25. *Website:* www.rainbow.gov.ua.

ROJAS PENSO, Juan Francisco; Venezuelan economist and consultant; b. 18 Sept. 1952. *Education:* Andrés Bello Catholic Univ., Caracas and CENDES. *Career:* Prof., Univ. Cen. de Venezuela and Univ. Simón Bolívar; Official, Council of Acuerdo de Cartagena (Cartagena Agreement, now Andean Community of Nations) 1977–79, 1982–85, Alt. Plenipotentiary Rep. and Dir Corporación Andina de Fomento 1985–87; Councillor (Econ. Affairs) to Colombia 1980–81; Dir-Gen. of Econ. Integration, Venezuelan Inst. of Foreign Trade 1985–87; Dir Commercial Policy Dept, Latin American Integration Asscn 1989–93, Deputy Sec.-Gen. 1993–99, Sec.-Gen. 1999–2005; ind. consultant to various orgs including Andean Community of Nations, OAS, Friedrich Ebert Foundation, numerous cos. and trade unions; columnist for Question (magazine), Venezuela Analítica, Aporrea.org, Tinku.org, IntegraciónyComercio.com, Redvoltairenet.org.
E-mail: jrojas_penso@yahoo.es. *Website:* www.analitica.com.

ROJAS RAMÍREZ, José Alejandro, PhD; Venezuelan politician and economist; b. 3 Sept. 1959; m.; one s. *Education:* Universidad Central de Venezuela, Inst. of Petroleum and Univ. of Paris II – Sorbonne, Paris, France. *Career:* Sr Economist Office of Programming and Macroeconomic Analysis, IDB, Gov. (for Venezuela) IDB; mem. Bd of Dirs Compañia de Energía Eléctrica del Estado Venezolano (CADAFE), Electrificación del Caroni (EDELCA) CA; Pres. Ass. of Fondo Latinoamericano de Reservas (FLAR), Consultant Council, Andean Community of Nations; Deputy Minister, then Minister of Finance; consultant several cos and orgs; currently Alt. Exec. Dir representing Mexico Costa Rica, El Salvador, Guatemala, Honduras, Nicaragua, Venezuela and Spain, World Bank, Washington, DC; Dir Quantitative Methods Dept, Universidad Central de Venezuela, mem. Postgrad. Scientific Cttee; Prof. of Econometrics and Math. Econs, Universidad Católica Andrés Bello, Caracas, of Operational Research, Instituto Politécnico de las Fuerzas Armadas, Caracas; mem. Colegio de Estadístico de Venezuela, Royal Econometric Soc., UK; fmr Vice-Pres of Finance, Petroleos de Venezuela SA. *Publications:* numerous research papers.
Address: MC12-1211, World Bank Group, 1818 H Street, NW, Washington, DC 20433, USA (office). *Telephone:* (202) 458-2095 (office). *E-mail:* jrojasramirez@worldbank.org (office). *Website:* www.worldbank.org (office).

ROKITA, Jan, LLM; Polish politician and lawyer; b. 18 June 1959, Kraków; m. Nelli Arnold 1994; one d. *Education:* Jagiellonian Univ., Pontifical Acad. of Theology, Kraków. *Career:* fmr active mem. of Independent Students' Union (NZS) 1980–82; interned under Martial Law 1982; banned by the Communist authorities from practising law 1983–89; co-founder and participant Freedom and Peace Movt 1985–88; founder and mem. Intervention and Law-abidingness Comm. of Solidarity Trade Union 1986–89; mem. Civic Cttee attached to Lech Wałęsa (q.v.) 1988–90; organizer and Chair. Int. Conf. on Human Rights, Kraków 1988; participant Round Table negotiations 1989; Chair. Special Parl. Comm. of Inquiry in respect of archives of the former Communist Security Service (Rokita Comm.) 1989–90; Deputy Chair. Civic Parl. Caucus 1989–90, Deputy Chair. Democratic Union Parl. Caucus 1991–96, Deputy Chair. Freedom Union Parl. Caucus 1996–97, mem. Solidarity Election Action Parl. Caucus 1997–2001; Deputy Chair. Civic Platform Parl. Caucus 2001–03, Chair. 2003–05; Chair. Parl. Comm. for Admin. and Internal Affairs 1997–2000; Minister-Chief of Office of Council of Ministers 1992–93; Chair. Conservative People's Party (SKL) 1998–2001; mem. Special Parl. Comm. of Inquiry into the Rywin Affair 2003–04; mem. Civic Platform (PO) (Platforma Obywatelska); POLCUL Foundation Award (Australia) 1988, Stefan Kisielewski award 2003, Edward J. Wende Award 2003, Man of the Year (Wprost weekly magazine, Poland) 2003, Top Parliamentarian (Polityka weekly magazine, Poland) 2003. *Publications:* political and historical journalism; Alfabet Rokity 2004.
Address: Biuro Posła Jana Rokity, 31-143 Kraków, ul. Basztowa 15/10, Poland. *Telephone:* (12) 4300186. *Fax:* (12) 4263560. *Website:* www.janrokita.pl.

ROLDAN-CONFESOR, Nieves; Philippine politician and international organization official. *Career:* fmr Sec. of Labour and Employment; fmr Presidential Adviser on Int. Labour Affairs; fmr Head Panel of Experts to Congressional Comm. on Labour; fmr Chair. ASEAN Labour Ministers Meeting; fmr Chair. of Governing Body ILO, Vice-Chair. Mission to Myanmar 2001; fmr mem. Bd Landbank of the Philippines, Social Security Comm., Tech. Educ. and Skills Devt Authority, Philippine Agrarian Reform Council, Nat. Econ. Planning Council; mem. Operating Council, Global Alliance for Workers and their Communities; mem. Faculty, Asian Inst. of Man.
Address: Department of Communications, International Labour Organization, 4 route des Morillons, 1211 Geneva 22, Switzerland (office). *Telephone:* (22) 799-7912 (office). *Fax:* (22) 799-8577 (office). *E-mail:* communication@ilo.org (office). *Website:* www.ilo.org (office).

ROMAÑA, Oscar Maúrtua de; Peruvian government minister, politician and diplomatist; *Representative in Mexico, Organization of American States;* b. 7 Feb. 1947; m.; three c. *Education:* Univ. Católica y San Marcos, Univ. of Oxford, Johns Hopkins Univ. *Career:* 2nd, then 1st Sec. Peruvian Embassy, USA; Consul in Belgium and at EU; Head Dept of Int. Political Econs/Econ.; Sec.-Gen. Presidency of the Repub.; Amb. to Canada, Bolivia; Dir-Gen. of Planning, of Judicial Affairs; Amb. to Thailand, concurrently to Viet Nam and Laos; Perm. Rep. ESCAP; Amb. to Ecuador; Dir Acad. of Diplomacy; Sub-Sec. for American Affairs, later Sec. for Foreign Affairs; Minister of Foreign Affairs 2005–06; OAS Rep. in Mexico 2007–; Del. to Confs of PECC, PBEC, APPF, APEC; Prof. of Int. Law Univ. Nacional de San Marcos y de Derecho; mem. Colegio de Abogados de Lima, Soc. Peruana de Derecho Int., Oxford Soc., Center of Int. Understanding; Hon. mem. Soc. Boliviana de Historia, Soc. de la Acad. Boliviana de Estudios Int., Siam Soc.; Hon. Prof., Univ. Andina Simon Bolivar, Quito; Hon. law doctorates (Winnipeg, Bangkok). *Publications:* Derecho Internacional y Política Exterior 1995, Una Visión Latinoamericana del Asia Pacifico 1999, Las Nuevas Relaciones Bilaterales Perú-Ecuador 2000, Perú y Ecuador: Socios en el siglo XXI.
Address: CDM Polanco, Apartado Postal 105-194, 11551 México, D.F., Mexico (office). *Telephone:* (55) 280-1208 (office). *Fax:* (55) 281-7390 (office). *E-mail:* OASMexico@oas.org (office). *Website:* www.oas.org (office).

ROMERO-MARTINEZ, Ivan, PhD; Honduran diplomatist; *Ambassador to UK;* b. 1 Aug. 1949, Olanchito; m. Mirian Nasser-Romero; two c. *Education:* Nat. Univ. of Honduras, Catholic Univ. of Santo Domingo, Dominican Repub., John Hopkins Univ., USA, Centre of Compared Studies, Buenos Aires, Argentina, Univ. of Brussels, Belgium. *Career:* joined Foreign Service in 1971, has served as Amb. to many countries, including Spain, Egypt, Morocco, Dominican Repub., Jamaica, Haiti, Colombia, Belgium, Netherlands, Luxembourg, UK, Sweden, Denmark, Finland, Norway and Ireland, has also served as Perm. Rep. to UN, Geneva and at EU, Brussels, other assignments have included post of Deputy Perm. Rep. to OAS, also held several positions at Embassy in Washington, DC, including Counsellor, and at Embassy in Ottawa, as Counsellor, Minister Counsellor and Chargé d'affaires a.i.; served as Special Adviser to Pres. of Honduras and Presidential Adviser with rank of Sec. of State; Perm. Rep. to UN, New York 2006–08, Amb. to UK 2008–.
Address: Embassy of Honduras, 115 Gloucester Place, London, W1U 6JT, England (office). *Telephone:* (20) 7486-4880 (office). *Fax:* (20) 7486-4550 (office). *E-mail:* hondurasuk@lineone.net (office).

ROMERO-NASSER, Ivan; Honduran diplomatist; m. Maria Del Rilar Romero-Nasser. *Career:* fmr Rep. of Inst. of Honduran Coffee (IHCAFE) in Europe; Chargé d'affaires a.i. in UK –2007.
Address: Ministry of Foreign Affairs, Centro Cívico Gubernamental, Antigua Casa Presidential, Blvd Kuwait, Contiguo a la Corte Suprema de Justicia, Tegucigalpa, Honduras (office). *Telephone:* 234-1962 (office). *Fax:* 234-1484 (office). *Website:* www.sre.hn (office).

ROMULO, Alberto (Bert) G., BSc, BL; Philippine politician; *Secretary of Foreign Affairs;* b. Camiling, Tarlac province; m. Rosie Lovely Tecson; five c. *Education:* De La Salle Univ., Universidad de Madrid, Spain. *Career:* fmr Sec. of Budget and Man., Chair. Devt Budget Co-ordinating Cttee, mem. Monetary Bd; fmr Senator, Majority Leader; Exec. Sec. –2004; Sec. of Foreign Affairs 2004–; Gintong Ama Award, Philippines Free Press Most Outstanding Senator.
Address: Department of Foreign Affairs, DFA Building, 2330 Roxas Blvd, Pasay City, 1330 Metro Manila, The Philippines (office). *Telephone:* (2)

8344000 (office). *Fax:* (2) 8321597 (office). *E-mail:* webmaster@dfa.gov.ph (office). *Website:* www.dfa.gov.ph (office).

RONDELLI, Paolo; San Marino diplomatist; *Ambassador to USA. Career:* Co-ordinator Dept of Foreign and Political Affairs and Econ. and Judicial Planning –2007; Amb. to USA 2007–.
Address: Embassy of San Marino, 888 17th Street, NW, Suite 900, Washington, DC 20006, USA (office); Via della Tana 26, 47890 San Marino, Republic of San Marino (office). *Telephone:* (202) 3372-2660 (DC) (office); (0549) 991598 (office). *Fax:* (202) 452-8938 (DC) (office). *E-mail:* rondelli@esteri.sm (office). *Website:* www.esteri.sm (office).

ROOD, John D., BS; American diplomatist; m. Jamie A. Rood; three c. *Education:* Univ. of Montana. *Career:* Founder and fmr Chair. The Vestcor Companies, Jacksonville, Fla 1983; fmr Commr and Chair. Fla Fish and Wildlife Conservation Comm.; fmr mem. Bd of Dirs James Madison Inst., Fla; Founding Bd mem. First Coast Family and Housing Foundation; fmr Visiting Prof., Univ. of N Florida; Amb. to The Bahamas 2004–07 (retd); in pvt. business 2007–.
Address: c/o US Department of State, 2201 C Street NW, Washington, DC 20520, USA. *Telephone:* (202) 647-4000.

ROONEY, L. Francis, III, AB, JD; American lawyer, business executive and diplomatist; b. 4 Dec. 1953; m. Kathleen Rooney; three c. *Education:* Georgetown Univ. and Georgetown Univ. Law Center. *Career:* fmr CEO Rooney Holdings, Inc., Naples, Fla; majority Owner Manhattan Construction Co.; fmr mem. Bd of Dirs BOK Financial Corpn, Bank of Oklahoma, Helmerich and Payne, Inc., Cimarex Energy Co.; fmr Vice-Chair. Okla Turnpike Authority; fmr Dir Okla Capital Investment Bd, 20/20 Cttee, Washington Advisory Council for Center for Strategic and Int. Studies, Washington, DC; fmr Officer, Tex. Business Hall of Fame; fmr Dir Inst. of Nautical Archaeology, Tex.; fmr mem. transition team for Gov.-Elect Brad Henry (Okla); Dir Young Pres' Org. 1992–98, Int. Pres 1997–98; mem. Leadership Task Force, Tulsa, Okla 2003; Amb. to the Holy See (Vatican) 2005–07; mem. School of Architecture Council, Univ. of Notre Dame; fmr mem. Bd and Chair. Strategic Planning Cttee St Francis Health System; fmr Chair. Cascia Hall Preparatory School; fmr mem. Bd of Advisors Panama Canal Authority; fmr Dir Newport Shipyard, RI; fmr Dir Southwest Fla Chapter, World Pres Org.; fmr Trustee Naples Winter Wine Festival, Naples Children and Educ. Foundation, Inc.; mem. Sovereign Mil. Order of Malta (Fed. Asscn), Fla Council of 100; mem. DC and Tex. Bars.
Address: US Department of State, 2201 C Street NW, Washington, DC 20520, USA (office). *Telephone:* (202) 647-4000 (office). *Fax:* (202) 647-6738 (office). *Website:* www.state.gov (office).

ROP, Anton, MA; Slovenian economist and politician; b. 27 Dec. 1960, Ljubljana. *Education:* Univ. of Ljubljana. *Career:* Asst Dir Slovene Inst. for Macroeconomic Analysis and Devt 1985–92; State Sec. Ministry of Econ. Relations and Devt 1993; Minister of Labour, Family and Social Affairs 1996–2000, of Finance 2002; Prime Minister 2002–04; Pres. Liberal Democratic Party (Liberalna Demokracija Slovenije—LDS), Leader, Parl. Group 2004–.
Address: National Assembly, Subiceva 4, 1000 Ljubljana (office); Liberalna Demokracija Slovenije, Republike trg 3, 1000 Ljubljana, Slovenia (office). *Telephone:* (1) 4789569 (office). *Fax:* (1) 4789870 (office). *E-mail:* anton .rop@dz-rs.si (office); toner@lds.si (office). *Website:* www.lds.si (office).

ROPERS, Vice Adm. Frank D. C.; German naval officer; *Military Representative, NATO;* b. Aug. 1946; m. Gabriele (Gaby); two d. *Career:* commissioned into German Navy 1969; served in Fast Patrol Boat and Destroyer Flotillas; Commdr, Fast Patrol Boat FGS Ozelot 1973–75; fmr ADC to German Mil. Rep., SHAPE; fmr Exec. Officer, FGS Lutjens; mem. Planning Staff, Defence Sec. 1983–86; Commdr, FGS Rommel 1986–89, Capt. 1989; Prin. Instructor for Maritime Warfare and Operational Planning Exec. Officer, Chief of Staff, SHAPE; fmr Head of Naval Office, Wilhelmshaven; Commdt of Naval Acad., Murwik 1994–95; Commdr NATO Standing Naval Force Mediterranean 1995–96; Commdr German Destroyer Flotilla, Wilhelmshaven 1996–98; Head of Naval Office, Rostock 1998–2001; Chief of Staff, HQ of Commdr-in-Chief, E Atlantic and Commdr Allied Naval Forces N 2001–03, Deputy Commdr 2003–05; Deputy Commdr Allied Maritime Component Command, Northwood 2005–06; Mil. Rep. to NATO 2006–.
Address: North Atlantic Treaty Organization (NATO), blvd. Léopold III, 1110 Brussels, Belgium (office). *Telephone:* (2) 707-4111 (office). *Fax:* (2) 707-4579 (office). *E-mail:* natodoc@hq.nato.int (office). *Website:* www .nato.int (office).

ROSA BAUTISTA, Leonidas; Honduran lawyer and politician; *Attorney-General;* b. 4 Feb. 1947, Lepaera; m. Abogada Irma Violeta Suazo de Rosa; three c. *Education:* Instituto Ramón Rosa, Gracias, Lempira, Universidad Nacional Autónoma de Honduras. *Career:* fmr legal adviser to Main Directorate of Transport; Vice Minister of the Interior and of Justice 1978–1980; Deputy to Constituent Nat. Ass. 1980–82; fmr Prof., Universidad Nacional Autónoma de Honduras; Minister of Foreign Affairs 2003–05; Attorney-Gen. 2005–; Sr Pnr and Dir, Bufete Rosa y Asociados, S.A. de C.V. (law firm), Tegucigalpa; Pres. Honduran Bar Asscn 1990–92; Prof., Universidad Nacional Autónoma de Honduras.
Address: Bufete Rosa y Asociados, S.A. de C.V., Edificio Rosa y Asociados, Colonia San Rafael Retorno Kobe n. 29, Tegucigalpa (office); Office of the Attorney-General, Fiscal General del Estado, Ministerio Público, Lomas del Guijarro, Tegucigalpa, Honduras (office). *Telephone:* 239-2688 (Bufete Rosa) (office). *Fax:* 239-2718 (Bufete Rosa) (office). *E-mail:* lrosab@bufeterosa.com (office). *Website:* www.bufeterosa.com (office).

ROSA LÃ, João; Portuguese diplomatist. *Career:* Perm. Rep. to UN, New York 2000; Head, OSCE Unit, Ministry of Foreign Affairs 2002; fmr Amb. to Netherlands, to Spain, Amb. to France –2006, to Morocco 2006–.
Address: c/o Embaixada do Portugal, 5, Rue Thami Lamdouar, Souissi 10100 Rabat, Morocco (office). *Telephone:* (3) 7756446 (office). *Fax:* (3) 7756445 (office). *E-mail:* ambassade.portugal@menara.ma (office).

ROSADO, Alexis; Belizean diplomatist; m. Marina Elena Rosado. *Career:* Deputy High Commr to UK –2002, High Commr to UK 2002–06.
Address: Ministry of Foreign Affairs and Foreign Trade, New Administration Building, PO Box 174, Belmopan, Belize (office). *Telephone:* 822-2167 (office). *Fax:* 822-2854 (office). *E-mail:* arosado@mfa.gov (office). *Website:* www.mfa.gov.bz (office).

ROSAS, Allan, LLD; Finnish judge and professor of law; *Judge, European Court of Justice;* b. 1948, Turku; m. Tuula Rosas, two d. one s. *Education:* Univ. of Turku. *Career:* Prof. of Law, Univ. of Turku 1978–81; Prof. of Law, Abo Akademi Univ. 1981–96, Dir Inst. for Human Rights 1985–95; Prin. Legal Adviser in charge of External Relations, Legal Service, European Comm. 1995–2001, Deputy Dir-Gen. of Legal Service 2001–02; Judge, European Court of Justice 2002–; consultant to govt agencies and UN, UNESCO, OSCE, Council of Europe; dir several int. and nat. research projects in fields of int. law, human rights law, comparative public admin; del. to int. confs and meetings; various int. and nat. academic positions of trust and mem. of several learned socs. *Publications:* more than 300 publications (books and articles), including The Legal Status of Prisoners of War 1976, Forvältningsklagav (Citizens' Complaints) 1980, Economic, Social and Cultural Rights: A Textbook 1995.
Address: Cour de justice des Communautés européennes, L-2925 Luxembourg (office). *Telephone:* 43032830 (office). *Fax:* 43033178 (office). *E-mail:* allan.rosas@curia.eu.int (office). *Website:* curia.eu.int/en/instit/presentationfr/index_cje.htm (office).

ROSATI, Dariusz Kajetan, DEcon; Polish economist and politician; b. 8 Aug. 1946, Radom; m. Teresa Nowińska 1971; one s. one d. *Education:* Main School of Planning and Statistics, Warsaw. *Career:* scientific researcher, Main School of Planning and Statistics (now Cen. School of Commerce), Warsaw 1969–, Asst Prof. 1978, Prof. 1990–; with Citibank, New York 1978–79; Visiting Prof., Princeton Univ., NJ 1986–87; Founder and first Dir Inst. of World Economy, Warsaw School of Econs 1985; Dir Foreign Trade Research Inst., Warsaw 1988–91; Partner, TKD-Ernst & Young Poland 1989–92; Head UN Section for Cen. and E Europe, Geneva 1991–95; Minister of Foreign Affairs 1995–97; mem. Council of Monetary Policy of Nat. Bank of Poland 1998–2004; mem. Bd Dirs Int. Exchange Program (IREX), Washington, DC 1998–2001; currently Chair. WTO panel on US subsidies on upland cotton; mem. Polish United Workers' Party (PZPR) 1966–90; mem. Cttee on Econ. Reform 1987–90, team of econ. advisors to Prime Minister 1988–89, Econ. Strategy Cttee to the Cabinet 1994–97; Adviser to Pres. of EC 2001–; Rector Richard Łazarski Univ. of Commerce and Law, Warsaw 2003–; mem. European Parl. (Socialist Group) 2004–, mem. Cttee on Econ. and Monetary Affairs, Substitute mem. Cttee on Foreign Affairs, Sub-cttee on Security and Defence, Vice-Chair. Temporary Cttee on Policy Challenges and Budgetary Means of the Enlarged Union 2007–2013, mem Del. to ACP-EU Jt Parl. Ass.; mem. Polish Econ. Soc. 1969–, Econ. Studies Cttee Polish Acad. of Sciences 1999–, European Econ. Asscn, European Asscn of Comparative Econ. Studies; Silver Cross of Merit 1981, Kt's Cross Order of Poland Restituta 1989, Orders of Merit from France, Italy, Greece, Ukraine and Lithuania. *Publications:* Decision-Making 1977, Inflation 1989, Export Policies 1990, Polish Way to Market 1998, An Agenda for a Growing Europe: The Sapir Report 2004, Facing the Challenge: Lisbon Strategy for growth and employment 2004, New Europe: Report from Transformation 2005; more than 250 scientific articles.

Address: ul. Bagatela 10/4, 00–585 Warsaw, Poland (office); European Parliament, Bâtiment Altiero Spinelli, 07H247, 60 rue Wiertz, 1047 Brussels, Belgium (office). *Telephone:* (22) 6215275 (Warsaw) (office). *Fax:* (2) 2847182 (Warsaw) (office). *E-mail:* piotr.stolarczyk@rosati.pl (office); dariusz@rosati.pl (office); drosati@europarl.eu.int (office). *Website:* www.rosati.pl (office).

ROSE, John, BS, MA, PhD; American research institute director and retd army officer; *Director, George C. Marshall Center; Education:* Univ. of Dayton, Univ. of Southern California, Kennedy School of Govt, Harvard Univ. *Career:* career in US Armed Forces, assignments include Dir Alliance Mil. Force Structure and Readiness Requirements, NATO, SHAPE, Belgium, Commdr NATO Air Defence Artillery Units at Brigade and Battalion level in jt combined operations, Germany; with Office of Deputy Chief of Staff for Operations and Plans, Pentagon; Asst Prof. of Int. Relations and Defense and Strategic Studies, West Point; Teacher Naval Post Grad School; retd as Brig.-Gen. 1998; Pres. Army Business Operations, Nichols Research Corpn, Arlington, Va 1998–2000; Operations Dir, Computer Sciences Corpn, Falls Church, Va 2000–02; Dir George C. Marshall Center for Security Studies, Garmisch-Partenkirchen, Germany 2002–; Pres.-elect Reagan's Defense Transition Team 1980–81; Sr Fellow, Council on Foreign Relations, NY 1991–92; Nat. Security Fellowship 1985–86. *Publications:* The Evolution of US Army Nuclear Doctrine 1945–1980 1980; journal articles on nuclear strategy, mil. doctrine and long range planning. *Address:* George C. Marshall European Center for Security Studies, Gernackerstrasse 2, 82467, Garmisch-Partenkirchen, Germany (office). *Telephone:* (8821) 750469 (office). *Fax:* (8821) 750452 (office). *E-mail:* pao@marshallcenter.org (office). *Website:* www.marshallcenter.org (office).

ROSE, Richard, BA, DPhil, FBA; American writer, academic and consultant; *Professor of Public Policy, University of Aberdeen;* b. 9 April 1933, St Louis, Mo.; m. Rosemary J. Kenny 1956; two s. one d. *Education:* Clayton High School, Mo., Johns Hopkins Univ., LSE, Oxford. *Career:* worked in political public relations, Miss. Valley 1954–55; reporter, St Louis Post-Dispatch 1955–57; Lecturer in Govt, Univ. of Manchester 1961–66; Prof. of Politics Strathclyde Univ. 1966–82, Prof. of Public Policy and Dir Centre for the Study of Public Policy 1976–2005; Prof. of Public Policy, Univ. of Aberdeen 2005–; Specialist Adviser, House of Commons Public Admin Cttee 2002–03; Consultant Psephologist, The Times, ITV, Daily Telegraph, etc. 1964–; Sec. Cttee on Political Sociology, Int. Sociology Asscn 1970–85; Founding mem. European Consortium for Political Research 1970; mem. US/UK Fulbright Comm. 1971–75; Guggenheim Fellow 1974; Visiting scholar at various insts, Europe, USA, Hong Kong; mem. Home Office Working Party on Electoral Register 1975–77; Co-Founder British Politics Group 1974–; Convenor Work Group on UK Politics, Political Studies Asscn 1976–88; mem. Council Int. Political Science Asscn 1976–82; Tech. Consultant OECD, UNDP, World Bank, Council of Europe, Int. IDEA; Dir SSRC Research Programme, Growth of Govt 1982–86; Ed. Journal of Public Policy 1985–, Chair. 1981–85; Scientific Adviser, New Democracies Barometer, Paul Lazarsfeld Soc., Vienna 1991–; Sr Fellow in Governance, Oxford Internet Inst. 2003–05; Hon. Vice-Pres. UK Political Studies Asscn; Hon. Fellow American Acad. of Arts and Sciences, Finnish Acad. of Science and Letters, Acad. of Learned Socs in the Social Sciences 2000; Hon. PhD, Örebro Univ. (Sweden); AMEX Prize in Int. Econs 1992, Lasswell Prize for Lifetime Achievement, Policy Studies Org. 1999; Lifetime Achievement Award, UK Political Studies Asscn 1990. *Publications:* numerous books on politics and public policy including Politics in England 1964, People in Politics: Observations Across the Atlantic 1970, Governing Without Consensus: An Irish Perspective 1971, International Almanack of Electoral History (co-author) 1974, The Problem of Party Government 1974, Northern Ireland: A Time of Choice 1976, Managing Presidential Objectives 1976, What is Governing? Purpose and Policy in Washington 1978, Can Government Go Bankrupt? (co-author) 1978, Do Parties Make A Difference 1984, Understanding Big Government 1984, Public Employment in Western Nations (co-author) 1985, Taxation by Political Inertia (co-author) 1987, Ministers and Ministries 1987, Presidents and Prime Ministers, The Postmodern President 1988, Ordinary People in Public Policy 1989, Training With Trainers? How Germany Avoids Britain's Supply-side Bottleneck (co-author) 1990, The Loyalties of Voters (co-author) 1990, Lesson-Drawing in Public Policy 1993 Inheritance in Public Policy (co-author) 1994, What is Europe? 1996, How Russia Votes (co-author) 1997, Democracy and Its Alternatives, Understanding Post-Communist Societies (co-author) 1998, A Society Transformed: Hungary in Time-Space Perspective, International Encyclopedia of Elections (co-author) 2000, The Prime Minister in a Shrinking World 2001, Elections without Order: Russia's Challenge to Vladimir Putin (co-author) 2002, Elections and Parties in New European Democracies 2003, Learning from Comparative Public Policy 2005; hundreds of papers in academic journals.

Address: Centre for the Study of Public Policy, University of Aberdeen, Aberdeen, AB24 3QY (office); 1 East Abercromby Street, Helensburgh, G84 7SP, Scotland (home). *Telephone:* (1436) 672164 (home). *Fax:* (1436) 673125 (home). *E-mail:* richard.rose@abdn.ac.uk (office). *Website:* www.abdn.ac.uk/cspp (office).

ROSENAU, James N., AM, PhD; American political scientist and academic; *University Professor of International Affairs, George Washington University;* b. 25 Nov. 1924, Philadelphia, Pa; m. Hongying Wang; one s. two d. *Education:* Bard Coll., Johns Hopkins, Princeton, Columbia and New York Univs. *Career:* Instructor in Political Science, Douglass Coll., Rutgers Univ. 1949–54, Asst Prof. 1954–60, Assoc. Prof. 1960–62, Prof. 1962–70, Acting Chair. 1963–64, Faculty Fellow 1965–66, Chair. New Brunswick Dept of Political Science 1968–70; Research Assoc., Center for Int. Studies, Princeton Univ. 1960–70; Prof. of Political Science, Ohio State Univ. 1970–73; Dir Inst. for Transnational Studies, Univ. of Southern Calif. 1973–92, Prof. of Political Science and Int. Relations 1973–92, Dir School of Int. Relations 1976–79; Sr Fellow, Center for Int. and Strategic Affairs, UCLA 1979–92; Univ. Prof. of Int. Affairs, George Washington Univ. 1992–; Visiting Prof. of Political Science, McGill Univ., Montréal 1990; Visiting Prof. of Int. Relations, UN Univ. for Peace, Costa Rica 1991; Co-Prin. Investigator (with Ole R. Holsti), Foreign Policy Leadership Project, NSF 1979–81, 1983–85, 1988–89, 1992–94, 1997–99; Pres. Int. Studies Asscn 1984–85; mem. Transparency Int. Council on Governance Research 1995–; Guggenheim Fellowship 1987–88. *Play:* Kwangju: An Escalatory Spree (two-act play, produced at Odyssey Theater, LA 1991). *Publications include:* Turbulence in World Politics: A Theory of Change and Continuity 1990, Governance without Government 1991, The United Nations in a Turbulent World: Engulfed or Enlarged? 1992, Global Voices 1993, International Relations Theory 1993, Thinking Theory Thoroughly: Coherent Approaches to an Incoherent World (with Mary Durfee) 1995, Along the Domestic-Foreign Frontier: Exploring Governance in a Turbulent World 1997, Strange Power: Shaping the Parameters of International Relations and International Political Economy 2000, Information Technologies and Global Politics: The Changing Scope of Power and Governance 2002, Distant Proximities: Dynamics Beyond Globalization 2003, The Study of World Politics, Vol. 1: Theoretical and Methobiological Challenge 2006, The Study of World Politics, Vol. 2: Globalization and Governance 2006; author or ed. of more than 40 books, 200 articles. *Address:* George Washington University, Gelman 709G, 2130 H Street, NW, Washington, DC 20052, USA (office). *Telephone:* (202) 994-3060 (office). *Fax:* (202) 994-0792 (office); (202) 994-4571 (office). *E-mail:* jnr@gwu.edu (office). *Website:* www.gwu.edu/~elliott/faculty/rosenau.cfm (office).

ROSENTHAL, Gert, MA; Guatemalan economist and diplomatist; *Permanent Representative, United Nations;* b. 11 Sept. 1935, Amsterdam, Netherlands; m. Margit Uhlmann; four d. *Education:* American School of Guatemala, Univ. of California, Berkeley, USA, Universidad de San Carlos de Guatemala. *Career:* worked in pvt. sector 1959–67; economist, Nat. Planning Secr. 1960–64, Head Econ. Devt Div. 1965, Sec.-Gen. (rank of Minister) 1969–70, 1973–74; Officer in charge of external financing, Ministry of Finance 1966–67; Asst to Sec.-Gen., Secr. of Cen. American Common Market (SIECA) 1968, Project Dir UNCTAD project to promote SIECA, Guatemala City 1972–73; Prof. of Econ. Devt and Public Finance, Universidad Rafael Landivar, Guatemala 1969–74; Dir Sub-regional Office UN ECLA, Mexico 1974–85, Deputy Exec. Sec. UN ECLA, Santiago, Chile 1985–87, Exec. Sec. (rank of Under-Sec.-Gen. of UN) 1988–97; mem. Oversight Comm. of Guatemalan Peace Accords 1998; Perm. Rep. to UN, New York 1998, 2008–; Pres. UN Econ. and Social Council (ECOSOC) 2003–04; Minister of Foreign Affairs 2006–08; Dr hc (Universidad del Valle) 1996. *Publications:* numerous publs on devt issues 1960–. *Address:* Permanent Mission of Guatemala to the United Nations, 57 Park Avenue, New York, NY 10016, USA (office); Calle de los Duelos #6, Antigua, Guatemala (home). *Telephone:* (212) 679-4760 (office); 832-3659 (home). *Fax:* (212) 685-8741 (office); 832-3666 (home). *E-mail:* guatemala@un.int (office); grosenthal@guate.net (home). *Website:* www.un.int/guatemala (office).

ROSENTHAL, Joel H., BA, PhD; American research institute executive and professor of politics; *President, Carnegie Council on Ethics and International Affairs; Education:* Harvard and Yale Univs. *Career:* Pres. Carnegie Council on Ethics and Int. Affairs (CCEIA) 1995–; also currently Adjunct Prof., Dept of Politics, NY Univ.; Chair. Bard Coll. Globalization and Int. Affairs Program; Ed.-in-Chief Ethics & Int. Affairs (journal); lectures and writes on ethics, US foreign policy and int. relations. *Publications:* Righteous Idealists 1991, Ethics & International Affairs: A Reader, 2nd edn, 1999; Ethics and the Future of Conflict (co-author) 2004; articles in professional journals and chapters in books.

Address: Carnegie Council on Ethics and International Affairs, Merrill House, 170 East 64th Street, New York, NY 10065-7478, USA (office). *Telephone:* (212) 838-4120 (office). *Fax:* (212) 752-2432 (office). *E-mail:* msemeniuk@cceia.org (office). *Website:* www.cceia.org (office).

ROSGAARD, Lt-Gen. Kurt Ebbe; Danish air force officer; b. 15 Nov. 1946, Næstved; m. Jytte Rosgaard (née Kjær Nielsen); one d. one s. *Education:* Royal Defence Acad., NATO Defence Coll., Rome, Italy. *Career:* began career with Danish Armed Forces 1969, assigned to Surface Air Missile Squadron 1972–77, Staff Officer, Air Force Staff 1978–80; Section Chief Hawk, NATO Programming Centre, NHMO 1980–85; Staff Officer, HQ Surface to Air Missile Group 1985, Group Commdr 1986–88, Chief Operational Br. 1988, Section Chief 1988–89; Commdr HWAK Wing E 1989–90; Asst Chief of Staff, Plans and Programmes Div., HQ Chief of Defence 1990–93, Chief of Policy Div. 1993–95; Chief of Staff, Tactical Air Command 1995–97, Tactical Air Commdr 1997–2000; Commdr Combined Air Operation Centre 1 1997–2000; Deputy Chief of Staff, Personnel, HQ Chief of Defence Command 2000–03; Mil. Rep. to NATO and EU, Brussels 2003–06; currently Royal Danish Air Force Special Rep. for Chief of Defence; Commdr 1st Class, Order of Dannebrog; Air Force Long Service Medal, Reserve Officer Asscn of Denmark Medal of Honour, Lithuanian Air Force Hon. Wings, La Médaille les services militaires voluntaires.
Address: Ministry of Defence, Holmens Kanal 42, 1060 Copenhagen K, Denmark (office). *Telephone:* 33-92-33-20 (office). *Fax:* 33-32-06-55 (office). *E-mail:* fmn@fmn.dk (home). *Website:* www.fmn.dk (office).

ROSS, Dennis B., PhD; American academic and fmr government official; *Counsellor and Ziegler Distinguished Fellow, Washington Institute for Near East Policy; Education:* UCLA. *Career:* after graduation became Exec. Dir. of program on Soviet International Behavior sponsored by Univ. Calif, Berkeley and Stanford Univ. 1984–86; Dir Near East and S Asian Affairs, Nat. Security Council (during Reagan Admin), Policy Planning Office, State Dept 1988–92, Special Middle East Co-ordinator 1997–2001, helped achieve the 1995 Interim Agreement and brokered the Hebron Accord 1997; currently Distinguished Fellow and Counsellor, Washington Inst. Near East Policy; Chair. Institute for Jewish People Policy Planning, Jerusalem; Hon. DHumLitt (Amherst Coll.) 2002, Dr hc (Jewish Theological Seminary, Syracuse Univ.); UCLA Alumnus of the Year. *Publications include:* The Missing Peace: The Inside Story of the Fight for Middle East Peace 2004, Statecraft: And How to Restore America's Standing in the World 2007; numerous articles in learned journals and newspapers.
Address: Washington Institute for Near East Policy, 1828 L Street, NW, Suite 1050, Washington, DC 20036, USA (office). *Telephone:* (202) 452-0650 (office). *Fax:* (202) 223-5364 (office). *E-mail:* dennisr@washingtoninstitute.org (office). *Website:* www.washingtoninstitute.org (office).

ROSSIER, William; Swiss economist and international organization official; b. 25 Oct. 1942. *Education:* Univ. of Lausanne. *Career:* joined Foreign Econ. Service 1970; Head Secr., Conf. on Security and Co-operation in Europe, Geneva 1972–73; Deputy Head Div. for Gen. Foreign Econ. Questions, Berne 1973–76; Counsellor, Mission to the EC, Brussels 1976–80; with Fed. Office for External Econ. Affairs 1981–88, apptd Head Div. in charge of Relations with Countries of Eastern Europe and the People's Repub. of China 1981, later Head Div. in Charge of Relations with Western Europe; fmrly involved in negotiations with GATT, OECD, UNCTAD; Plenipotentiary Amb. of Switzerland to Int. Econ. Orgs in Geneva (GATT/WTO, UNCTAD, UN-ECE, EFTA); fmr Chair. EFTA, ECE, UNCTAD Trade and Devt Bd; Chair. World Trade Org. Gen. Council 1996; Perm. Rep. to EFTA, Sec.-Gen. 2000–06.
Address: c/o Federal Department of Foreign Affairs (FDFA), Bundeshaus West, 3003 Berne 7, Switzerland (office). *Telephone:* 313222111 (office). *Fax:* 313234001 (office). *E-mail:* info@eda.admin.ch (office). *Website:* www.eda.admin.ch (office).

ROSSIN, Lawrence G., BA; American diplomatist and UN official; *Principal Deputy Special Representative of the Secretary General, Interim Admin. in Kosovo, United Nations;* b. 3 Nov. 1952; m. Debra J. McGowan; one s. one d. *Education:* Claremont Men's Coll., California, NATO Defence Coll., Rome, Massachusetts Inst. of Tech. *Career:* fmr Dir, Chief of Mission Authority and Overseas Staffing State Dept; fmr Counsellor for Political Affairs, The Hague and Port-au-Prince; fmr Peru Desk Officer; fmr Staff Asst to Secs of State for Inter-American Affairs; Dir Inter-American Affairs, Nat. Security Council 1993–94; Deputy Chief of Mission, Spain 1995–98; Dir Office S Cen. European Affairs, Dept of State, led dels to Rambouillet and Paris confs on Kosovo 1999, directed govt outreach to Kosovo Liberation Army (KLA); first Chief of Mission, Kosovo, opened and headed American Office, Pristina 1999–2000, responsible for all policy initiatives and collaboration with UN Interim Admin. in Kosovo and NATO Kosovo Force; Amb. to Croatia 2001–2003; Special Asst to Pres. and Sr Dir for Strategic Planning and Southwest Asia, Nat. Security Council 2003–04 (retd from US Sr Foreign Service); Sec.-Gen.'s Prin. Deputy Special Rep. for UN Interim Admin. in Kosovo 2004–06; Sec.-Gen.'s Prin. Deputy Special Rep. for the UN Stabilization Mission in Haiti (MINUSTAH) 2006–07; Sr Int. Coordinator, Save Darfur Coalition 2007–08; Prin. Deputy Special Rep. of the UN Sec. Gen., Interim Admin. in Kosovo 2008–; State Dept Award for Valour, three Superior Hon. Awards, Meritorious Hon. Award.
Address: Press Office, UNMIK HQ, Shop 1, Luan Haradinaj Street (Police Avenue), Pristina,, Kosovo, Serbia (office). *Telephone:* (38) 504604 (office); (212) 963-8442 (New York) (office). *Website:* www.unmikonline.org (office).

ROSTOWSKI, Jacek, BSc, MSc, MA; Polish/British economist, politician and academic; *Minister of Finance;* b. (Jan Vincent-Rostowski), 30 April 1951, London, England; m.; two c. *Education:* Univ. Coll., London, School of Slavonic and East European Studies, Univ. of London, London School of Econs and Political Science. *Career:* born into Polish immigrant family in London, grew up and educated in UK; Lecturer, School of Slavonic and East European Studies 1989–95; Adviser, Deputy Prime Minister and Minister of Finance of Poland 1989–91; worked at Centre for Econ. Performance, LSE 1992–95; Prof. of Economy, Cen. European Univ., Budapest 1995–, Dean of Faculty of Economy 1995–2000, 2005–06; Minister of Finance 2007–, Chair. Macro-econ. Policy Cttee 1997–2001; adviser to Pres. Nat. Bank of Poland 2002–04; fmr adviser to Govt of Russian Fed. on macro-econ. policy; adviser to Bd of Bank PEKAO SA 2004–; Co-founder Centre for Social and Econ. Analysis (Centrum Analiz Społeczno-Ekonomicznych—CASE), Warsaw, mem. Supervisory Council 1991–2007, Trustee CASE Foundation; mem. Supervisory Bd Polish Privatization Soc. – Kleinwort Benson (Polskie Towarzystwo Prywatyzacyjne – Kleinwort Benson), Polski Bank Rozwoju SA 1994–95. *Publications:* author or ed. of several books, book chapters and numerous articles in professional journals on an enlarged EU, monetary policy, exchange rates' policy and transformations of post-communist economies.
Address: Ministry of Finance, ul. Świętokrzyska 12, 00-916 Warsaw, Poland (office). *Telephone:* (22) 694-55-55 (office). *Fax:* (22) 827-27-22 (office). *E-mail:* kancelaria@mf.gov.pl (office). *Website:* www.mf.gov.pl (office).

ROTFELD, Adam Daniel, PhD; Polish politician and academic; *Researcher and Chairman, International Consultative Committee, Polish Institute of Foreign Affairs;* b. 1938. *Education:* Diplomatic-Consular Faculty, Main School of Foreign Service and Faculty of Journalism, Warsaw Univ., Faculty of Law and Admin, Jagiellonian Univ., Kraków. *Career:* Resident Fellow, Inst. of East-West Security Studies, New York, USA 1984–85; Assoc. Prof. and Prof. in Humanities, Univ. of Warsaw 2001–; Researcher in Int. Law and Int. Relations, Polish Inst. of Int. Affairs 1961–89; Ed. Int. Affairs magazine, Warsaw, and Head of European Security Dept 1978; Leader, Project on Building a Co-operative Security System in and for Europe, Stockholm Int. Peace Research Inst. (SIPRI) 1989, Dir SIPRI 1991–2002, apptd Personal Rep. OSCE Chairman-in-Office to settle conflicts in Trans-Dniester region of Moldova 1992; Ed. SIPRI Yearbook: Armaments, Disarmament and International Security 1991–; mem. Nat. Security Council 2001–; apptd Under-Sec. of State, Ministry of Foreign Affairs 2001, Sec. of State 2003–05; Minister of Foreign Affairs Jan.–Oct. 2005; Researcher and Chair. Int. Consultative Cttee, Polish Institute of Foreign Affairs 2006–; mem. Royal Swedish Acad. of War Studies 1996, Governing Bd of Hamburg Inst. for Peace Research and Security Policy at Univ. of Hamburg 1995, Advisory Bd to UNESCO Studies on Peace and Conflict 1993–, Advisory Bd of Geneva Centre for Democratic Control of Armed Forces 2001, and many other research centres. *Publications:* has published and ed more than 20 books and over 300 articles on legal and political aspects of relations between Germany and Cen. and Eastern Europe after World War II, human rights, cooperative security, CSBMs, multilateral security structures, and political and legal aspects of security system in Europe, including The New Security Dimensions: Europe after NATO and EU Enlargements 2001.

ROTH, Jean-Pierre, DEcon; Swiss banker; *Chairman, Bank for International Settlements;* b. 28 April 1946, Saxon, Canton of Valais; m. Floriane Tognetti; three c. *Education:* Univ. of Geneva, Institut Universitaire des Hautes Etudes Internationales, Geneva and MIT, USA. *Career:* fmr Lecturer, Univ. of Geneva and Institut Universitaire de Hautes Etudes Internationales; Scientific Collaborator, Swiss Nat. Bank (Schweizerische Nationalbank/Banque nationale suisse) 1979, mem. Bd of Dirs, Vice-Chair. and Head of Dept II (capital market, banknotes, business relations with the Confed., admin of gold holdings), Berne 1996, Chair. of Governing Bd and Head of Dept I (Int. Affairs Div., Econ. Div., Legal and Admin. Econ.),

Zurich 2001–; Chair. Bd of Dirs BIS, Basel 2006–; Gov. IMF for Switzerland, Washington, DC.
Address: Bank for International Settlements, Centralbahnplatz 2, 4002 Basel, Switzerland (office). *Telephone:* (61) 2808080 (office). *Fax:* (61) 2809100 (office). *E-mail:* press.service@bis.org (office). *Website:* www.bis.org (office).

ROTH, Kenneth, LLB, MA; American lawyer and research institute director; *Executive Director, Human Rights Watch; Education:* Brown Univ., Yale Law School. *Career:* fmrly in pvt. practice as litigator; Fed. Prosecutor, US Attorney's Office, Southern Dist. of NY; prosector, Iran-Contra Investigation, Washington, DC –1987; Deputy Dir Human Rights Watch, NY 1987–93, Exec. Dir 1993–, has conducted human rights investigations in Africa, Asia, Europe, Latin America and Middle East; contribs to The New York Times, Foreign Affairs, Int. Herald Tribune, NY Review of Books. *Publications:* over 70 articles and chapters in books on human rights topics. *Address:* Human Rights Watch, 350 Fifth Avenue, 34th Floor, New York, NY 10118-3299, USA (office). *Telephone:* (212) 290-4700 (office). *Fax:* (212) 736-1300 (office). *E-mail:* hrwnyc@hrw.org (office). *Website:* www.hrw.org (office).

ROTIMI, Brig.-Gen. Oluwole; Nigerian army officer (retd) and diplomatist; *Ambassador to USA; b.* 20 Feb. 1935, Abeokuta, Ogun; m. *Education:* King's Coll., Lagos, Cambridge Higher School, UK, Univ. Coll. of Ibadan. *Career:* joined Nigerian Army 1960, served in UN Force in the Congo, Quarter-Master Gen., Nigerian Army 1966, Commdr Ibadan Garrison 1969–70, Mil. Gov. old Western State (comprising present-day Ogun, Oyo, Ondo, Ekiti and Osun States) 1971–75, retd from Army following overthrow of Gen. Gowon 1975; SW Co-ordinator for Yar'Adua Campaign in presidential election; Amb. to USA 2008–; Grand Patron Ibadan Polo Club; Patron Abeokuta Social Club. *Address:* Embassy of Nigeria, 3519 International Court, NW, Washington, DC 20008, USA (office). *Telephone:* (202) 986-8400 (office). *Fax:* (202) 362-6541 (office). *E-mail:* babalola@nigeriaembassyusa.org (office). *Website:* www.nigeriaembassyusa.org (office).

ROUSE, Ruth Elizabeth, BA, MA; Grenadian diplomatist. *Education:* Carleton Univ., Canada, Univ. of Westminster, UK. *Career:* joined Foreign Service 1982, served in several positions including High Commr to UK, non-Resident High Commissioner to South Africa, Chief of Protocol to Govt of Grenada; served at Org. of Eastern Caribbean States High Comm., Ottawa, Canada; Perm. Rep. to UN, New York 2004–07; Grenada Independence Award for Exemplary Public Service 1998, Women Who Make A Difference Award, NGO Committee on the Status of Women, New York 2005. *Address:* c/o Ministry of Foreign Affairs, Ministerial Complex, 4th Floor, Botanical Gardens, St George's, Grenada (office).

ROWE, Leslie V., BA, MA, MEd; American diplomatist; *Ambassador to Papua New Guinea; b.* Wash.; m. Theodore Dieffenbacher; three c. *Education:* Washington State Univ., Fletcher School of Law and Diplomacy, Tufts Univ., Northeastern Univ., Univ. of the Sorbonne, Paris, France. *Career:* fmr Dir Int. Office, Tufts Univ.; taught foreign languages at secondary school level; career mem. Sr Foreign Service, joined Foreign Service 1983, assignments included Consul Gen. in Bangkok, in Lisbon; Dir Office of Children's Issues, Dept of State, Country Desk Officer for Chile; Prin. Officer, Consulate in Recife, Brazil, also served in San José, Costa Rica and in São Paulo, Brazil; Deputy Chief of Mission, Embassy in Nairobi –2006; Amb. to Papua New Guinea (also accred to Solomon Islands and Vanuatu) 2006–. *Address:* US Embassy, PO Box 1492, Douglas Street, Port Moresby, NCD, Papua New Guinea (office). *Telephone:* 3211455 (office). *Fax:* 3211593 (office). *E-mail:* png@state.gov (office). *Website:* portmoresby.usembassy.gov (office).

ROWE, Peter, BA; Australian diplomatist; *Ambassador to South Korea; b.* 1950, Sydney. *Education:* Univ. of Sydney. *Career:* early position at Office of Nat. Assessment, responsible for Korea and China, subsequently Acting Head, Asia Br. 1986–90; fmr Dir Hong Kong, Macau and Taiwan Section, Dept of Foreign Affairs and Trade; Minister and Deputy Head of Mission, Embassy in Seoul 1995–98; High Commr in Colombo 1999–2001; fmr Deputy Head of Mission, Embassy in Jakarta; has also served in Wellington, Hong Kong and Beijing; Amb. to South Korea 2006–. *Address:* Embassy of Australia, 11th Fl, Kyobo Building, 1 Jongno 1-Ga, Jongno-Gu, Seoul 110-714, Republic of Korea (office). *Telephone:* (2) 2003-0100 (office). *Fax:* (2) 722-9426 (office). *E-mail:* seoul-inform@dfat.gov.au (office). *Website:* www.southkorea.embassy.gov.au (office).

ROY-CHAUDHURY, Rahul, BA, MLitt; Indian international affairs scholar; *Senior Fellow for South Asia, International Institute for Strategic Studies (IISS); b.* 21 May 1964, Bombay; m. Minakshi Roy. *Education:* Univs of East Anglia and Oxford. *Career:* fmr faculty mem. Inst. for Defence Studies and Analyses, New Delhi; served on Nat. Security Council, Secr. of Prime Minister's Office; Sr Research Fellow, Int. Policy Inst., King's Coll. London; Sr Fellow for S Asia, IISS 2003–. *Publications:* Sea Power and Indian Security 1995, India's Maritime Security 2000. *Address:* International Institute for Strategic Studies, Arundel House, 13–15 Arundel Street, Temple Place, London, WC2R 3DX (office); 128 Hatherley Court, Hatherley Grove, London, W2 5RG, England (home). *Telephone:* (20) 7395-9179 (office). *Fax:* (20) 7395-9192 (office). *E-mail:* roy-chaudhury@iiss.org (office). *Website:* www.iiss.org (office).

ROYLE, Catherine Jane; British diplomatist; *Ambassador to Venezuela; b.* 17 Aug. 1963; m. Marcelo Camprubi; two s. *Career:* Desk Officer, Mexico and Central America Dept, FCO 1987–88, Second Sec., Embassy in Santiago 1988–91, Desk Officer, Arms Control Dept 1991–93, Head of Iraq Section, Middle East Dept 1993–95, Desk Officer, Policy Planning Dept 1996–97, Head of European and Econ. Policy, Ireland 1997–2001, Head of Convention Unit, European Directorate 2001–03, Deputy Head of Mission, Buenos Aires 2003–07, Amb. to Venezuela 2007–. *Address:* British Embassy, Torre La Castellana, 11°, Avda Principal La Castellana, Caracas, 1061, Venezuela (office). *Telephone:* (212) 263-8411 (office). *Fax:* (212) 267-1275 (office). *E-mail:* britishembassy@internet.ve (office). *Website:* www.britain.org.ve (office).

ROZENTAL, Andrés, AM, MEconSc; Mexican diplomatist and consultant; *President, Rozental & Asociados; b.* 1945, Mexico City. *Education:* Universidad de las Américas, Mexico, Univ. of Pennsylvania, USA, Univ. of Bordeaux, France. *Career:* Amb. to OAS 1971–74; Perm. Rep. to UN, Geneva 1982–83; Amb. to Sweden 1983–88; Deputy Foreign Minister 1988–94; Amb. to UK 1995–97; Amb.-at-Large and Special Presidential Envoy for Pres. Fox 2000–02; Founder and Pres. Rozental & Asociados (consultancy), Mexico City 1997–; Pres. Mexican Council on Foreign Relations 2002–06; part-time Prof. of Int. Relations, Instituto Tecnológico Autónomo de México (ITAM); Chair. Bd Latinoamericana de Duty Free, Grupo Industrial Omega; mem. Bd of Dirs New India Investment Trust, Aeroplazas de Mexico, Fumisa, Mittal Steel Mexico, Int. Inst. for Democracy and Electoral Assistance (Int. IDEA), Pacific Council on Int. Policy; mem. Bd of Govs Int. Devt Research Centre 2007–; mem. Bd of Advisors Latin America Advisor, Inter-American Dialogue 2005–; fmr mem. Editorial Bd Reforma (newspaper); Sr Nonresident Fellow, The Brookings Inst., Washington, DC 2007–; Grand Cross of the Polar Star (Sweden), Grand Cross, Civil Merit Order (Spain), Officier, Ordre Nat. du Mérite (France), Eminent Amb. of Mexico 1994. *Publications:* three books on Mexican foreign policy and numerous articles on int. affairs. *Address:* Rozental & Asociados, Campos Elíseos no 345, Edif. Omega, piso 6, Mexico City DF, Mexico (office). *Telephone:* (55) 5279-6090 (office). *Fax:* (55) 5279-6089 (office). *E-mail:* andres@mexconsult.com (office).

RUBENSTEIN, Leonard S., JD; American lawyer and international organization official; *President, Physicians for Human Rights; Education:* Wesleyan Univ., Harvard Law School. *Career:* Legal Dir, later Exec. Dir Bazelon Center for Mental Health Law, Washington, DC –1996; Pres. Physicians for Human Rights 1996–; Co-founder and Dir Mental Disability Rights Int.; Co-Founder Washington Legal Clinic for the Homeless; fmr Adjunct Prof., Georgetown Univ. Law Center; mem. Bd of Dirs Int. Fed. of Health and Human Rights Orgs; mem. Governing Council American Public Health Asscn; mem. Cttee on Scientific Freedom and Responsibility of AAAS, Council of Foreign Relations, ABA Comm. on Mental Disability Law, also Vice-Chair. Cttee on Int. Human Rights Law, Individual Rights Section; fmr mem. Ethics Cttee, DC Bar; Congressional Minority Caucuses' Healthcare Hero Award, UN Asscn of the Nat. Capital Area's Louis B. Sohn Award, Physicians Forum Edward K. Barsky Award, Nat. Mental Health Asscn's Mission Award, Political Asylum Representation Project's Outstanding Achievement Award. *Publications:* The Rights of People with Mental Disabilities (jt author), Human Rights and Health: The Legacy of Apartheid, Endless Brutality: Ongoing Human Rights Violations in Chechnya; many articles and reports on disability rights, human rights, and medical ethics. *Address:* Physicians for Human Rights, 2 Arrow Street, Suite 301, Cambridge, MA 02138, USA (office). *Telephone:* (617) 301-4200 (office). *Fax:* (617) 301-4250 (office). *E-mail:* lrubenstein@phrusa.org (office). *Website:* physiciansforhumanrights.org (office).

RUBIALES DE CHAMORRO, Maria; Nicaraguan diplomatist; *Permanent Representative, United Nations; b.* 22 Dec. 1948; three c. *Education:* Maryville Coll. of the Sacred Heart, St Louis, USA. *Career:* First Sec., Embassy in Dominican Repub. 1979–80, Embassy in Costa Rica 1980–81; Minister Counsellor, Perm. Mission to UN, New York 1981–86; Dir-Gen. of Foreign Policy for Asia, Africa and the Non-Aligned Countries,

Ministry of Foreign Affairs 1986–90; Dir-Gen. Govt Promotion Agency –2007; Perm. Rep. to UN, New York 2007–.
Address: Permanent Mission of Nicaragua to the United Nations, 820 Second Avenue, Suite 801, New York, NY 10017, USA (office). *Telephone:* (212) 490-7997 (office). *Fax:* (212) 286-0815 (office). *E-mail:* nicaragua@un .int (office). *Website:* www.un.int/nicaragua (office).

RUBIN, Hon. James P., BA, MIA; American fmr government official, academic and broadcast journalist; b. 1960, New York; m. Christiane Amanpour; one s. *Education:* Columbia Univ. *Career:* Research Dir Arms Control Asscn, Washington DC 1985–89, also consultant to US Senate Foreign Relations Cttee on nuclear arms control issues; fmr staff mem., US Senate Foreign Relations Cttee, Sr Foreign Policy Adviser to Joseph R. Biden, Jr (q.v.); Sr Adviser and spokesman for US Rep. to UN Madeleine Albright (q.v.) 1993–96; Dir of Foreign Policy and Spokesman Clinton/ Gore presidential campaign Aug.–Nov. 1996; Sr Adviser to Sec. of State 1996–97; Asst Sec. of State for Public Affairs 1997–2000; Pnr, Brunswick 2001–04; Visiting Prof. of Int. Relations, LSE 2001–04; foreign policy adviser John Kerry US presidential campaign 2004; Anchor, World News Tonight, Sky News (UK) 2005–06; World Affairs Commentator 2006–; Vice Chair. Atlantic Partnership; mem. Bd of Dirs Columbia Univ. School of Int. Affairs, Int. Rescue Cttee, UK; mem. Council on Foreign Relations; John Jay Award for Distinguished Professional Achievement (Columbia Univ.) 1998, Distinguished Service Award, Sec. of State 2000.
Address: Sky News, British Sky Broadcasting, Grant Way, Middlesex, TW7 5QD, England (office). *Telephone:* (20) 7705-3000 (office). *Website:* www.skypressoffice.co.uk/SkyNews (office).

RÜCKER, Joachim; German UN official; b. 30 May 1951; one s.; two d. *Career:* has served in several positions within Ministry of Foreign Affairs including Head, Budget and Finance Div. 2002–05; Mayor of Sindelfingen, Germany 1993–2001; Deputy High Rep. for Admin and Finance, Office of the UN High Rep., Sarajevo, Bosnia and Herzegovina 2001–02; Deputy Special Rep. of Sec.-Gen. in charge of EU Pillar for Econ. Reconstruction, UN Interim Admin Mission in Kosovo (UNMIK) 2005–06, Special Rep. of Sec.-Gen. and Head of UNMIK 2006–08.
Address: c/o United Nations Mission in Kosovo, 10000 Prishtina, Kosovo (office). *E-mail:* ruecker@un.org (office). *Website:* www.joachim-ruecker .de.

RUDD, Kevin, BA; Australian politician; *Prime Minister;* b. 21 Sept. 1957, Nambour, Queensland; m. Therese Rudd; two s. one d. *Education:* Australian Nat. Univ. *Career:* joined Dept of Foreign Affairs and Trade 1981, worked in Embassies in Stockholm and Beijing; Chief of Staff to Queensland State Opposition Leader 1988–92; Premier, Queensland State Govt 1989–92, Dir-Gen. of Cabinet 1992–95; China Consultant, KPMG 1996–98; Adjunct Prof. of Asian Languages, Univ. of Queensland 1997–; mem. Parl. (Labor Party) for Griffith 1998–, Chair. Fed. Parl. Labor Party's Cttee on Foreign Affairs, Defence and Trade 1998–2001, Shadow Minister for Foreign Affairs 2001–04, Shadow Minister for Foreign Affairs and Int. Security 2004–05, Shadow Minister for Foreign Affairs, Trade and Int. Security 2005–07; Leader, Australian Labor Party 2006–; Prime Minister 2007–; mem. Australian-American Leadership Dialogue; mem. Advisory Council, Australia-Asia Centre, Korea-Australia Centre. *Publications include:* numerous articles on Chinese politics.
Address: Australian Labor Party (ALP), POB 6222, Kingston, ACT 2604 (office); Griffith Electorate Office, POB 476A, 653 Wynnum Road, Morningside, Brisbane, Qld 4170, Australia (office). *Telephone:* (2) 6120-0800 (office); (7) 3899-4031 (office). *Fax:* (7) 3899-5755 (office). *Website:* www.pm.gov.au (office); www.kevinrudd.com.

RUESCHEMEYER, Dietrich, Dr rer. pol; American academic; *Charles C. Tillinghast Junior Professor Emeritus of International Studies, Watson Institute for International Studies, Brown University;* b. 28 Aug. 1930, Berlin, Germany; m. Marilyn Rueschemeyer; two d. *Education:* Univ. of Cologne. *Career:* Prof. of Sociology, Brown Univ. 1970–2000, Co-founder Center for the Comparative Study of Devt (merged into The Watson Inst. for Int. Studies), Head, Political Econ. and Devt Program 1997–2002, currently Charles C. Tillinghast Jr Prof. Emer. of Int. Studies; also taught at Dartmouth Coll., USA, Univ. of Toronto, Canada, Hebrew Univ. of Jerusalem, Israel, Free Univ. of Berlin, Germany and Free Univ. of Brussels, Belgium. *Publications include:* Lawyers and Their Society 1973, Power and the Division of Labour 1986, Capitalist Development and Democracy (with E. H. Stephens and J. D. Stephen) 1992; as Co-Ed.: Bringing the State Back In 1985, State and Market in Development: Synergy or Rivalry? 1992, States, Social Knowledge and the Origins of Modern Policies 1996, Participation and Democracy East and West: Comparisons and Interpretations (co-ed with M. Rueschemeyer and B. Wittrock) 1998, Comparative Historical Analysis in the Social Sciences (co-ed with J. Mahoney) 2003, Globalization and the Future of the Welfare

State (co-ed with M. Glatzer) 2005, States and Development: Historical Antecedents of Stagnation and Advance (co-ed with M. Lange) 2005.
Address: The Watson Institute, Brown University, 111 Thayer Street, Box 1970, Providence, RI 02912-1970, USA (office). *Telephone:* (401) 863-3348 (office). *E-mail:* Dietrich_Rueschemeyer@brown.edu (office). *Website:* www.brown.edu (office).

RUGGIE, John Gerard, PhD; American academic and diplomatist; *Evron and Jeanne Kirkpatrick Professor of International Affairs, John F. Kennedy School of Government, Harvard University;* *Career:* taught at Univs of Calif. at Berkeley and San Diego, also Dir Univ. of Calif. systemwide Inst. on Global Conflict and Co-operation; Dean, School of Int. and Public Affairs, Columbia Univ., NY 1991–96; Asst Sec.-Gen. of UN 1997–2001, Special Adviser to the UN Sec.-Gen. for the Global Compact 2003, Special Rep. of the Sec.-Gen. for Business and Human Rights 2005–; Evron and Jeanne Kirkpatrick Prof. of Int. Affairs, John F. Kennedy School of Govt, Harvard Univ. 2000–, also Weil Dir of Mossavar-Rahmani Center for Business and Govt; Hon. LLD (McMaster); Int. Studies Asscn's Distinguished Scholar Award, American Political Science Asscn's Hubert H. Humphrey Award.
Address: International Security Program, Belfer Center for Science and International Affairs, John F. Kennedy School of Government, Harvard University, 79 JFK Street, Cambridge, MA 02138, USA (office). *Telephone:* (617) 384-7569 (office). *Fax:* (617) 495-8963 (office). *E-mail:* john_ruggie@harvard.edu (office). *Website:* www.bcsia.ksg.harvard.edu (office).

RÜHE, Volker; German politician; *Chairman, Bundestag Foreign Policy Committee;* b. 25 Sept. 1942, Hamburg; m. Anne Rühe 1968; two s. one d. *Education:* Univ. of Hamburg. *Career:* fmr teacher; mem. Hamburg City Council 1970–76; mem. Bundestag 1976–, Chair. Foreign Policy Cttee 2002–; Deputy Chair. CDU/CSU Parl. Group 1982–89, 1998–; Sec. Gen. CDU 1989–92, Deputy Party Leader 1998–2002; Minister of Defence 1992–98.
Address: Deutscher Bundestag, Platz der Republik 1, 11011 Berlin (office). *Telephone:* (30) 22773610 (office). *E-mail:* volker.ruehe@bundestag.de (office). *Website:* www.bundestag.de (home).

RUHEE, Keerteecoomar, MSc; Mauritius academic, politician and diplomatist; *Ambassador to USA;* m.; two c. *Education:* Louisiana State Univ., USA, Univ. of Edinburgh, UK. *Career:* fmr Assoc. Prof., Univ. of Mauritius; fmr Sr Pnr, De Chazal Du Mée & Co., responsible for business devt in Africa; has held several bd memberships, including Founding mem. Transparency Mauritius, American Chamber of Commerce in Mauritius; fmr Minister of Econ. Planning and Devt, of the Civil Service and Employment, of Agric.; Chief of Staff to the Prime Minister –2007; Amb. to USA 2007–.
Address: Embassy of Mauritius, 4301 Connecticut Avenue, NW, Suite 441, Washington, DC 20008, USA (office). *Telephone:* (202) 244-1491 (office). *Fax:* (202) 966-0983 (office). *E-mail:* mauritius.embassy@prodigy.net (office). *Website:* www.maurinet.com/embasydc.html (office).

RUIZ-CABAÑAS IZQUIERDO, Miguel; Mexican diplomatist; *Ambassador to Japan;* b. 12 Jan. 1957, México; m. Martha Espinoza Cantellano; two c. *Education:* Colegio de México, Columbia Univ., USA. *Career:* joined Foreign Service 1979, Head of Dept, Ministry of Foreign Affairs 1979–81, Dir UN Dept 1989–91, Coordinator of Advisers 1991–92, Dir-Gen. Special Affairs 1995–98, Dir-Gen. for N America 1998–2001; overseas postings include at Perm. Mission to UN, New York 1981–86, Head of Migrant and Frontier Affairs, Embassy in Washington, DC 1993–95; Perm. Rep. to OAS 2001–04; Amb. to Japan 2004–; has been Prof. of Int. Relations and Foreign Policy in several Mexican acad. insts including Universidad Iberoamericana, Universidad de las Americas, El Colegio de la Defensa Nacional and Instituto Tecnológico Autónomo de México. *Publications:* numerous articles on USA–Mexico relations and worldwide illegal drug issues.
Address: Embassy of Mexico, 2-15-1, Nagata-cho, Chiyoda-ku, Tokyo 100-0014, Japan (office). *Telephone:* (3) 3581-1131 (office). *Fax:* (3) 3581-4058 (office). *E-mail:* embamex@mexicoembassy.jp (office). *Website:* www.sre .gob.mx/japon (office).

RUKINGAMA, Luc, PhD; Burundian academic and fmr politician; *Senior Programme Specialist and Chief, Higher Education Unit, Regional Office for Education in Africa, United Nations Educational, Scientific and Cultural Organization (UNESCO);* b. 1952, Kiremba; m. Thérèse Niyonzima; two s. two d. *Education:* Sorbonne, Paris. *Career:* mem. Parl.; fmr Minister for Higher Educ., for Cooperation, for Foreign Affairs and Cooperation; Minister of Communication and Govt Spokesman 2000–01; fmr Co-Pres. Union pour le Progrès National (UPRONA); unsuccessful presidential cand. 2001; currently Sr Programme Specialist and Chief of Higher Educ. Unit, UNESCO/BREDA; Chevalier, Ordre des Palmes Académiques,

Medaille de l'Unité Nationale, UNESCO Medal. *Publications:* Voyage au Congo d'André Gide ou la steréotype au cœur de l'image 1995; numerous articles.
Address: UNESCO Regional Office for Education in Africa, 12, avenue L. S. Senghor, Dakar, Senegal (office); Avenue de Juillet no 4, Kiriri, PO Box 1810, Bujumbura, Burundi (home). *Telephone:* 849-23-41 (office); 226561 (home). *Fax:* 226561 (home). *E-mail:* l.rukingama@unesco.org (office). *Website:* www.dakar.unesco.org/education_en/index.shtml (office).

RUML, Jan; Czech journalist and fmr politician; *Chairman, Olympic Watch;* b. 5 March 1953, Prague; m. Marie Ruml; two s. *Education:* grammar school, Prague, Faculty of Law, Univ. of Plzeň. *Career:* stoker, woodcutter, hosp. technician, mechanic, bookseller, cattle-minder; signed Charter 77, Feb. 1977; freelance journalist 1977–79; mem. Cttee for Protection of the Unjustly Persecuted 1979–89; in custody, indicted for subversive activities 1981–82; co-founder Lidové noviny (monthly samizdat) 1988–90; spokes-man of Charter 77 1990; First Deputy Minister of Interior of CSFR 1990–91; Deputy Minister of Interior 1991–92; mem. Civic Democratic Party (ODS) 1992–97; Deputy to House of Nations, Fed. Ass. June–Dec. 1992; Minister of Interior of Czech Repub. 1992–97; mem. Interdepart-mental Anti-drug Comm. 1993–97, Comm. for Prevention of Crime 1994–97; mem. of Parl. 1996–98, Senator 1998–2004, Vice-Pres. of Senate (Parl.) 2000–04; Founder Freedom Union (US), Chair. 1998–99; Chair. Olympic Watch; Hon. Medal of the French Nat. Police 1992. *Films:* Hledání Pevného Bodu (Looking for a Stable Point). *Publication:* (with Jana Klusáková) What Was, Is and Will Be (in Czech).
Address: Olympic Watch, Sokolska 18, 12000 Prague 2, Czech Republic (office). *E-mail:* info@olympicwatch.org (office). *Website:* www .olympicwatch.org (office); www.janruml.cz.

RUMSFELD, Donald H., BA; American business executive, fmr politician and fmr government official; *Distinguished Visiting Fellow, Hoover Institution, Stanford University;* b. 9 July 1932, Chicago; m. Joyce Pierson 1954; one s. two d. *Education:* New Trier High School, Ill., Princeton Univ. *Career:* aviator, USN 1954–57; Admin. Asst, House of Reps 1957–59; investment broker, A. G. Becker & Co., Chicago 1960–62; mem. 88th–91st Congresses; Republican; Asst to Pres. and Dir Office of Econ. Opportunity 1969–70; Dir Econ. Stabilization Program, Counsellor to Pres. 1971–72; Amb. to NATO, Brussels 1973–74; White House Chief of Staff 1974–75; Sec. of Defense 1975–77, 2001–06, currently non-paid consultant to Defense Dept; mem. Cabinet 1969–73, 1974–77; Pres., CEO then Chair. G. D. Searle and Co., Skokie, Ill. 1977–85; Sr Advisor, William Blair and Co. 1985–90; Chair. and CEO General Instrument Corpn 1990–93; Chair. Gilead Sciences, Inc. 1997–2000; Pres. Special Middle East Envoy 1983–84; Chair. Eisenhower Exchange Fellowships 1986–93, US Ballistic Missile Threat Comm. 1998–99; mem. Presidential Advisory Cttee on Arms Control 1982–86, Nat. Econ. Comm. 1988–89, Trade Deficit Review Cttee, US Comm. to Assess Nat. Security, Space Man. and Org. 2000–01; Distinguished Visiting Fellow, Hoover Inst., Stanford Univ. 2007–; f. Rumsfeld Foundation 2007; 11 hon. degrees; Presidential Medal of Freedom 1977, Woodrow Wilson Award 1985, Outstanding Pharmaceu-tical CEO 1980, Eisenhower Medal 1993, Statesmanship Award, Clar-emont Inst. 2007 and many other awards.
Address: c/o Hoover Institution, 434 Galvez Mall, Stanford University, Stanford, CA 94305-6010, USA (office). *Website:* www.hoover.org.

RUMYANTSEV, Aleksandr Yu., Dr Phys., Math., Sciences; Russian physicist and diplomatist; *Ambassador to Finland;* b. 26 July 1945, Kushka, Turkmeni-stan; m.; one d. *Education:* Moscow Inst. of Physics and Engineering. *Career:* trained as engineer; jr, then sr researcher, head of division, Dir of Scientific Devt Russian Scientific Centre, Kurchatov Inst. of Atomic Energy 1969–94, Dir 1994–2001; Minister of Atomic Energy of the Russian Fed. 2001–04; Head Fed. Agency for Atomic Energy 2004–05; Amb. to Finland 2006–; Prof. Moscow Inst. of Physics and Eng; Chair. Bd of Trustees Global Energy Int. Prize 2005–; mem. Bd of Dirs Nuclear Soc. of the Russian Fed.; mem. Russian Acad. of Sciences (corresp. mem. 1997–2000); USSR State Prize 1986; Order of Honour 2001. *Publications include:* over 100 scientific papers on new methods of solid-state physics studies by means of stationary nuclear reactors.
Address: Embassy of Russia, Tehtaankatu 1b, 00140 Helsinki, Finland (office). *Telephone:* (9) 661876 (office). *Fax:* (9) 661006 (office). *E-mail:* rusembassy@co.inet.fi (office). *Website:* www.rusembassy.fi (office).

RUPEL, Dimitrij, PhD; Slovenian politician, diplomatist and writer; *Minister of Foreign Affairs;* b. 7 April 1946, Ljubljana; m. Marjetica-Ana Rudolf-Rupel. *Education:* Ljubljana Univ., Brandeis Univ. (Mass., USA). *Career:* worked as journalist in Yugoslav newspapers and magazines; was considered as dissident for criticism of Yugoslav Communist regime; Asst Prof., Ljubljana Univ. 1980–89, Prof. 1989–; Lecturer, Queen's Univ. (Canada) 1977–78, New School for Social Research, NY (USA) 1985,

Cleveland State Univ. (USA) 1989; Co-founder Cultural-Political journal Nova Revija 1984–87; Founder and first Pres. Opposition Slovenian Democratic Alliance Party 1989–90; Minister of Foreign Affairs 1990–93, mem. first elected Govt of Slovenia 1990, Chair. Cttee for Culture, Educ. and Sports; mem. State Ass. 1992–95; elected Mayor of Ljubljana 1994–97; Amb. to USA 1997–2000; Minister of Foreign Affairs 2000–; Boris Kidrič Prize 1986, Golden Medal of Honour of the Repub. of Slovenia 1992. *Publications include:* novels: Half Way to the Horizon 1968, White Rooms 1970, Secretary of the Sixth International 1971, Tea and Guns at Four 1972, Fifth Floor of the Three-Floor House 1972, Time in It the Cruel Hangman 1974, Chi Square 1975, The Family Connection 1977, Cold Storms, Mad Homes 1978, Pleasant Life 1979, Max 1983, Follow the Addressee, Job 1984, Forgotten Invited 1985, Why is the World Upside Down? 1987, Lion's Share 1989, Story About Time 1989; non-fiction: Reading 1973, Free Words 1976, Words and Acts 1981, Reality Tests 1982, Sociology of Literature 1982, Sociology of Culture and Art 1986, Words of God and Words Divine 1987, Slovenian Intellectuals 1989, Slovenian Holidays and Everydays 1990, Slovenian Faith 1992, Slovenian Path to Independence and Recognition 1992, Secret of the State (memoirs) 1992, Disenchanted Slovenia 1993, Time of Politics 1994, Unity, Happiness, Reconciliation 1996, Freedom Against State 1998, Meetings and Partings 2001, Taking Over the Success Story 2004; plays: Less Terrible Night 1981, Job 1982, PDFS (Follow the Addressee) 1984; film screenplay: Oxygen 1971.
Address: Ministry of Foreign Affairs, 1001 Ljubljana, Prešernova 25, Slovenia (office). *Telephone:* (1) 4782231 (office). *Fax:* (1) 4782170 (office). *E-mail:* dimitrij.rupel@gov.si (office). *Website:* www.mzz.gov.si (office).

RUPÉREZ, Francisco Javier, LLB; Spanish diplomatist and politician; *Consul-General, Chicago;* b. 24 April 1941, Madrid; m. Rakela Cerovic; two d. *Education:* El Pilar Coll., Univ. of Madrid. *Career:* joined Diplomatic Service 1965, posts in Addis Ababa 1967–69, Warsaw 1969–72, Helsinki 1972–73; mem. Del. to CSCE, Helsinki 1972–73, to Int. Orgs, Geneva 1973–75; Chief of Staff of Under-Sec. of Foreign Affairs 1976; Chief of Staff of Ministry of Foreign Affairs 1976–77; mem. Exec. Cttee, Union of Democratic Centre (UCD) 1977–82; Mem. Parl. for Cuenca 1979–82, 1986–89, for Madrid 1989–93, for Ciudad Real 1993–2000; Amb. and Head of Del. to Madrid Session of CSCE 1980–82; First Spanish Amb. to NATO 1982–83; Senator and Mem. Regional Parl. of Castilla La Mancha 1983–86; Vice-Pres. Democratic People's Party (PDP) 1983–87; Pres. Christian Democratic Party 1987–89; Vice-Pres. People's Party (PP) 1989–90, Spokesman in Parl. Defence Cttee 1989–91, mem. Exec. Cttee 1990–2000, Spokesman in Parl. Foreign Affairs Cttee 1991–96; Vice-Pres. NATO Parl. Ass. 1994–96, Pres. Parl. Ass. 1998–2000; Pres. Parl. Ass. of OSCE 1996–98; Pres. Spanish Atlantic Asscn (AAE) 1996–2000; Pres. Foreign Affairs Cttee, House of Deputies 1996–2000; Pres. Christian-Democratic Int. (CDI) 1998–2000; Pres. Cttee on Defence, House of Deputies 2000; Amb. to USA 2000–04; Asst Sec.-Gen. and Exec. Dir UN Counter-Terrorism Exec. Directorate 2004–07; Consul-Gen. to Chicago 2007–; Pres. Foundation for Humanism and Democracy 1989–; Co-founder Cuadernos para el Diálogo (monthly political magazine) 1963–77; lectures regularly and directs courses at Int. Univ. Menéndez Pelayo, Univ. of Madrid and the Diplomatic School; Gran Cruz de la Orden de Isabel la Católica, Comendador de la Orden de Carlos III, Oficial de Isabel la Católica, Oficial de la Orden del Mérito Civil, Orden Bernardo O'Higgins (Chile), Gran Cruz de Vasco Núñez de Balboa (Panama), Grand Ordre de Léopold II (Belgium), Comendador con Placa de la Orden del Infante Don Enrique (Portugal), Kt Commdr of the Order of Alistical (Jordan), Kt Commdr, Order of the Arab Kingdom of Egypt, Officier, Légion d'honneur. *Publications include:* Confessional State and Religious Liberty 1970, Europe Between Fear and Hope 1976, Spain in NATO 1986, First Book of Short Stories 1987, Kidnapped by ETA: Memoirs 1990, The Price of a Shadow (novel) 2005; contribs to co-authored books and numerous articles in the Spanish press and specialized publs.
Address: Consulate-General of Spain, 180 North Michigan Avenue, Suite 1500, Chicago, IL 60601, USA (office). *Telephone:* (782) 45-89 (office). *Fax:* (312) 782-1635 (office). *E-mail:* conspainchicago@sbcglobal.net (office); javieruperez@hotmail.com (home). *Website:* www.mae.es/Consulados/ Chicago (office).

RUPNIK, Jacques, MA PhD; French political scientist and academic; *Director of Research, National Foundation for Political Science, Centre for International Studies and Research (CERI);* b. 21 Nov. 1950, Prague, Czech Republic; m. *Education:* Harvard Univ., Sorbonne, Institut d'Etudes Politiques de Paris. *Career:* Research Assoc., Russian Research Center, Harvard Univ. 1974–75; Eastern Europe specialist BBC World Service 1977–82; Prof., Institut d'Etudes Politiques de Paris 1982–96; adviser to Czech Pres. Vaclav Havel 1990–92; Exec. Dir Int. Comm. for Balkans, Carnegie Endowment for Int. Peace 1995–96; mem. Ind. Int. Comm. on Kosovo 1999–2000; Visiting Prof., Coll. of Europe 1999–, Harvard Univ.

2006; currently Research Dir Nat. Foundation for Political Science, Centre for Int. Studies and Research (CERI); adviser to EC 2007–; Ordre Nat. du Mérite 1995, Order of T.G. Maseryk, Czech Repub. 2002. *Television:* writer and presenter, The Other Europe (6-part documentary series) (Channel 4 TV, UK) 1988. *Publications:* The Other Europe 1988, Unfinished Peace 1996, Le Europe en face à l'élargissement 2004; numerous books and articles focused on central and Eastern Europe, and the Balkans. *Address:* Centre for International Studies and Research (CERI), 56 rue Jacob, 75006 Paris, France (office). *Telephone:* 1-58-71-70-51 (office); 1-49-57-08-54 (home). *Fax:* 1-58-71-70-90 (office). *E-mail:* rupnik@ceri-sciences -po.org (office); jacquesrupnik@hotmail.com (home). *Website:* www.ceri -sciencespo.com/cherlist/rupnik.htm (office).

RUTKIEWICZ, Ignacy Mikołaj; Polish journalist; *President, Foundation Press Centre for Central and Eastern Europe;* b. 15 April 1929, Vilna; m. Wilma Helena Koller 1961; two s. *Education:* Poznań Univ. *Career:* Ed., Ed.-in-Chief Wrocławski Tygodnik Katolicki (weekly) 1953–55; journalist, Zachodnia Agencja Prasowa (ZAP) 1957–66, Polska Agencja Interpress 1967–70; Ed. Odra (monthly) 1961–81, Ed.-in-Chief 1982–90, mem. Editorial Council 1991–; Co-Founder, mem. Editorial Council Więź (monthly), Warsaw 1958–; Pres.-Ed.-in-Chief Polish Press Agency (PAP), Warsaw 1990–92, 1992–94; Adviser to Prime Minister, Warsaw 1994–95; TV journalist TV Centre of Training, Polish TV (TVP) 1994–96; Sec. TV Comm. for Ethics 1996–; Ed.-in-Chief Antena (weekly) 1998; Adviser to Minister of Culture and Arts 1998–99; Sr Ed. On-line News, TVP 1999–; Co-founder and Vice-Pres. Polish-German Asscn, Warsaw 1990–2001; Vice-Pres. Alliance Européenne des Agences de Presse, Zürich 1991–92; mem. Exec. Bd, Asscn of Polish Journalists (SDP) 1980–82, Pres. 1993–95; mem. Council on Media and Information, Pres.'s Office 1993–95; mem. Euroatlantic Asscn 1995–; mem. Bd Foundation Press Centre for Cen. and Eastern Europe 1996–, (Pres. 2001–), Programme Bd Nat. Club of Friends of Lithuania 1996–, Programme Bd Polish Press Agency 1998–2002; Assoc. mem. Orbicom (int. network of UNESCO Chairs in Communications) 2000–; Kt, Order of Polonia Restituta 1981; City of Wrocław Award 1963, B. Prus Award of SDP 1990, Phil epistémoni Award, Jagiellonian Univ., Kraków 1991. *Publications:* author or co-author of more than 10 books; Transformation of Media and Journalism in Poland 1989–1996 (author and co-ed.), How to be Fair in the Media: Guidelines not only for TV journalists. *Address:* Ośrodek Nowe Media TVP, ul. Woronicza 17, 00-999 Warsaw (office); Al. Jerozolimskie 42/55, 00-024 Warsaw, Poland (home). *Telephone:* (22) 5477082 (office); (22) 8275813 (home). *E-mail:* ignacy .rutkiewicz@waw.tvp.pl (office). *Website:* www.wiadomosci.tvp.pl (office).

RWABYOMERE, Joan Kakima Nyakatuura; Ugandan diplomatist; *High Commissioner to UK. Career:* as a law student was forced to flee to Kenya to escape persecution under the Obote regime 1982, moved to Zambia before returning home when Yoweri Museveni took power in Kampala; elected MP 1989, nominated by Pres. Museveni as mem. constituent assembly to help draft Uganda's People's Constitution; del. to EEC-ACP Jt Ass.; Minister of State for Agric. 1995–96; Deputy Dir-Gen. of External Security 1996; High Commr to Nigeria 2002–06, to UK 2006–. *Address:* High Commission of Uganda, Uganda House, 58–59 Trafalgar Square, London, WC2N 5DX, England (office). *Telephone:* (20) 7839-5783 ext. 8102 (office). *Fax:* (20) 7839-8925 (office). *E-mail:* info@ ugandahighcommission.co.uk (office). *Website:* www .ugandahighcommission.co.uk (office).

RYAN, Jordan, MA; American diplomatist and UN official; *Deputy Special Representative of the Secretary-General for Recovery and Governance in Liberia, United Nations;* b. 29 Aug. 1950; m.; one d. *Education:* Columbia Univ., New York. *Career:* worked as consultant and attorney in New York and Calif.; fmr UNDP Asst Resident Rep. in China, fmr UNDP Deputy Resident Rep. and Sr Asst Resident Rep. in Viet Nam, Dir UNDP Office of the Admin., New York 1997–2001, UN Resident Coordinator and UNDP Resident Rep. in Viet Nam 2001–05, UN Resident Coordinator and Humanitarian Coordinator in Liberia and Sec.-Gen.'s Deputy Special Rep. for Recovery and Good Governance for Liberia 2006–. *Address:* UN Mission in Liberia, Pan African Plaza, Tubman Blvd, 1st Street, Monrovia, Liberia (office). *Telephone:* (212) 963-9926 (New York)

(office). *E-mail:* webmaster@unmil.org (office). *Website:* www.unmil.org (office).

RYAN, Richard, BA, MA; Irish diplomatist; *Ambassador to Netherlands;* b. 1946, Dublin; m.; three c. *Education:* Oatlands Coll. and Univ. Coll., Dublin. *Career:* joined Dept of Foreign Affairs 1973, First Sec., Perm. Mission to EC, Brussels 1980 (seconded to Comm. of EC 1982–83); Counsellor, Embassy in London 1983, Minister-Counsellor (Political) 1988, Amb. to Repub. of Korea 1989, to Spain (also accred to Algeria, Andorra and Tunisia) 1994–98; Perm. Rep. to UN, New York 1998–2005; Amb. to Netherlands 2005–; Hon. DLitt (Univ. of St Thomas) 2003. *Publications:* Ledges 1970, Ravenswood 1973. *Address:* Embassy of Ireland, Dr Kuyperstraat 9, 2514 BA The Hague, Netherlands (office). *Telephone:* (70) 3630993 (office). *Fax:* (70) 3617604 (office). *E-mail:* thehagueembassy@dfa.ie (office). *Website:* www .irishembassy.nl (office).

RYBKIN, Ivan Petrovich, DrPolitSch, CandTechSc; Russian politician; b. 20 Oct. 1946, Semigorovka, Voronezh Region; m.; two d. *Education:* Volgograd Inst. of Agric. Acad. of Social Sciences at Cen. Cttee CPSU. *Career:* Sr Engineer Kolkhoz Zavety Ilyicha Volgograd Region 1968–69; Lecturer, Prof., Head of Chair, Deputy Dean, Volgograd Inst. of Agric. 1970–87; Sec. Party Cttee 1983–87, First Sec. CPSU Dist Cttee in Volgograd, Second Sec. Volgograd Regional Cttee CPSU 1987–91; Head of Div. Cen. Cttee CP of RSFSR 1991; People's Deputy of Russia 1990–93; one of founders and Co-Chair. faction Communists of Russia 1990–91; mem. Agrarian Party, concurrently co-founder Socialist Party of Workers 1991–93; Deputy in State Duma (Parl.) 1993–96, Chair. 1994–95; mem. Council on Personnel Policy of Pres. Yeltsin 1994–95, mem. Security Council 1994–96, Sec. 1996–98; head of group negotiating with Chechen leaders 1996–98; Deputy Prime Minister 1998; Plenipotentiary Rep. of Russian Pres. to CIS states 1998; Chair. Political Union Regions of Russia, concurrently of Election Bloc 1995–96; Chair. Political Consultative Council of Pres. of Russia 1999–2000; cand. in 2004 presidential elections; Prize for Contribution to Peace with Chechnya (Ichkeria) 1996. *Publications:* State Duma, Fifth Attempt, We are Doomed to Consensus, Russia and the World: The Way to Security; numerous articles. *Address:* c/o Socialist Party, Novo-Basmannaya str. 14, Building 1, 107078 Moscow, Russia (office).

RYCROFT, Matthew John, CBE; British diplomatist; b. 16 June 1968, Southampton, England; m. Alison Rycroft; three d. *Education:* Univ. of Oxford. *Career:* joined FCO 1989; spent several months in Geneva, Switzerland and then on NATO desk in London; served at British Embassy, Paris 1991–95; Head of Political Section, Eastern Adriatic Dept, FCO 1995–96, mem. British del. to Dayton peace talks on Bosnia and Herzegovina; mem. Policy Planning Staff, FCO covering European and trans-Atlantic issues 1996–98; served at British Embassy, Washington, DC 1998–2002; Pvt. Sec. for Foreign Affairs, NI and Defence Issues to Prime Minister Tony Blair 2002–04; Amb. to Bosnia and Herzegovina 2005–08. *Address:* Foreign and Commonwealth Office, King Charles Street, London, SW1A 2AH, England (office). *Telephone:* (20) 7008-1500 (office). *Website:* www.fco.gov.uk (office).

RYTTER, Jakob, LLD; Danish diplomatist; b. 17 Dec. 1932, Århus; m. Suzanne Engelsen 1963 (died 1986); two d. *Education:* Marselisborg Gymnasium, Århus, Lycée de Fontainebleau, Univ. of Århus, Institut d'Etudes Politiques, Paris. *Career:* mil. service 1960; entered Danish Foreign Office 1961, Sec. of Embassy, Bonn 1963–66, Del. to UN Gen. Ass., New York 1966, 1968, First Sec., Tel-Aviv 1969–72, Counsellor Danish EC Representation, Brussels 1973–78, Dir EC Affairs, Danish Foreign Ministry 1978–83, Deputy Perm. Rep., Danish EC Representation 1983–86; Amb. to Israel 1986–89, 1992–96, Amb., Perm. Rep. to the EC, Brussels 1989–92; Amb. to the Netherlands 1996–2001, Perm. Rep. to OPCW, The Hague 1998–2001; Chair. Admin. and Financial Council, European Schools 1977–78; Commdr (First Class) Order of Dannebrog 1998. *Address:* Esplanaden 28, 1263 Copenhagen K, Denmark (home). *Telephone:* 33-33-97-98 (home).

S

SAAKASHVILI, Mikhail, LLM, SJD; Georgian politician, lawyer and head of state; *President;* b. 21 Dec. 1967, Tblisi; m. Sandra Roelofs; two s. *Education:* Faculty of Int. Relations, Kyiv State Univ., Ukraine, Columbia Univ. Law School, NY, USA, George Washington Univ., Washington, DC, USA, Int. Inst. of Human Rights, Strasbourg, France, Norwegian Inst. of Human Rights. *Career:* worked for Patterson, Belknap, Webb & Tyler (law firm), New York 1994; returned to Ukraine 1995; mem. Parl. (Union of Citizens of Georgia) 1995, Chair. Parl. Cttee responsible for creating new electoral system, ind. judiciary and non-political police force 1995–2000; Vice-Pres. Parl. Ass. of Council of Europe 2000; Minister for Justice 2000–01 (resgnd); resgnd from Union of Citizens of Georgia Party 2001; f. Nat. Movt opposition party 2001; elected Head, City Council of Tblisi 2002–03; Pres. of Georgia 2004–; named Man of the Year by panel of journalists and human rights activists 1997.
Address: Office of the President, 0105 Tbilisi, Ingorovka 7, Georgia (office). *Telephone:* (32) 99-00-70 (office). *Fax:* (32) 99-88-87 (office). *E-mail:* secretariat@admin.gov.ge (office). *Website:* www.president.gov.ge (office).

SAAVEDRA, Gustavo Fernández; Bolivian politician and diplomatist; b. 1941, Cochabamba; m.; three c. *Education:* San Simón Univ. *Career:* Exec. Sec., Secr. of Integration, La Paz 1969–70; Head Legal Dept, Comm. on Cartagena, Lima, Peru 1970–76; Dir of Consultation and Latin American Co-ordination, Caracas, Venezuela 1976–77; Consulting Dir-Gen. Coprinco y Asociados Consultores 1977–78, Pres. 1979–80, 1982–83; Minister of Integration 1978, of Foreign Affairs 1979, 1984–85, 2001–02; Consultant to UNCTAD 1980–83, 1987–89, 1993–98; Rep. of Ministries of Industry and Foreign Affairs, Quito, Ecuador 1980–81, Geneva, Switzerland 1985–87; Amb. to Brazil 1983–84; Exec. Dir Muller y Asociados Consultores 1987–89, Network of Advising and Man. SA 1993; Vice-Presidential cand. 1989; Minister of the Presidency 1989–93; Co-ordinator Nat. Dialogue 1997; Rep. Andean Corpn of Promotion in Peru 1998–99; Gen. Consul of Bolivia in Chile 2000–01; Special Rep. of the OAS Sec-Gen. and Head, Misión Especial de Acompañamiento al Proceso Democrático y Electoral de la República de Nicaragua (Special Mission Accompanying the Democratic Process and Elections of Repub. of Nicaragua) 2006.
Address: Casilla 7ll, La Paz, Bolivia. *Telephone:* (2) 278-2614. *Fax:* (2) 278-6793. *E-mail:* gustavof@acelerate.com.

SAAVEDRA-ALESSANDRI, Pablo, LLM, JSD; Chilean lawyer and international organization executive; *Secretary, Inter-American Court of Human Rights (Corte Interamericana de Derechos Humanos); Education:* Univ. of Notre Dame Law School, USA. *Career:* Deputy Sec. Inter-American Court of Human Rights (IACHR) (Corte Interamericana de Derechos Humanos) –2003, Sec. 2003–.
Address: Corte Interamericana de Derechos Humanos, Apdo Postal 6906-1000, San José, Costa Rica (office). *Telephone:* 234-0581 (office). *Fax:* 234-0584 (office). *E-mail:* corteidh@corteidh.or.cr (office). *Website:* www .corteidh.or.cr (office).

SABA, Elias, BLitt; Lebanese economist and politician; b. 1932; m. Hind Sabri Shurbagi 1960; five d. *Education:* American Univ. of Beirut and Univ. of Oxford, UK. *Career:* Econ. Adviser to Ministry of Finance and Petroleum, Kuwait and Kuwait Fund for Arab Econ. Devt 1961–62; Chair. Dept of Econs, American Univ. of Beirut 1963–67, Assoc. Prof. of Econs 1967–69; Deputy Prime Minister of Lebanon, Minister of Finance and of Defence 1970–72; Econ. and Financial Adviser to the Pres. 1972–73; Chair., Gen. Man. St Charles City Centre SARL 1974–; Vice-Chair. Banque du Crédit Populaire, Chair. Allied Bank, Beirut 1983; Chair., CEO The Associates, SARL 1981–; Minister of Finance 2004–05; mem. Nat. Dialogue Cttee 1975. *Publication:* Postwar Developments in the Foreign Exchange Systems of Lebanon and Syria 1962.
Address: c/o Ministry of Finance, 4e étage, Immeuble MOF, place Riad es-Solh, Beirut, Lebanon.

SABAH, Sheikh Ahmad Fahad al-Ahmad al-, BSc; Kuwaiti politician; *Director, National Security Agency;* b. 1963. *Education:* Univ. of Kuwait, Kuwait Military Acad. *Career:* officer Kuwaiti Army 1985–90, reaching rank of Maj.; Deputy Chair. Public Authority for Youth and Sports 1992–2000, Chair. (rank of cabinet minister) 2000; Minister of Information 2000; Minister of Energy 2002; fmr Chair. Kuwait Petroleum Corpn; Sec.-

Gen., OPEC Jan.–Dec. 2005; Pres. Kuwait Olympic Cttee 1990–2001; Dir Nat. Security Agency 2006–; fmr Pres. Olympic Council of Asia; mem. IOC 2001–; fmr Chair. Nat. Council for Culture, Arts and Literature; Hon. degrees from Dong-A Univ., Repub. of Korea, Taipei Univ., Taiwan, American Acad. Kingdom of Saudi Arabia Sports Medal.
Address: National Security Agency, Kuwait City, Kuwait (office).

SABAH, Sheikh Jaber Mubarek al-Hamad as-; Kuwaiti politician; *First Deputy Prime Minister, Minister of the Interior and Minister of Defence;* b. 1948. *Career:* fmr Head of Admin. Affairs, Ministry of Amiri Diwan; fmr Gov. Hawally prov., Al-Ahmadi prov.; fmr Minister of Social Affairs, of Information; Deputy Prime Minister and Minister of Defence 2001–06; First Deputy Prime Minister and Minister of the Interior and of Defence 2006–.
Address: Ministry of Defence, POB 1170, 13012 Safat, Kuwait City, Kuwait (office). *Telephone:* 4848300 (office). *Fax:* 4846059 (office). *Website:* www.mod.gov.kw (office).

SABAH, Muhammad Sabah as-Salim as-, PhD; Kuwaiti politician and diplomatist; *Deputy Prime Minister and Minister for Foreign Affairs;* b. 1955. *Education:* Univ. of Calif. and Harvard Univ., USA. *Career:* Lecturer of Econs, Faculty of Commerce, Economy and Political Sciences, Kuwait Univ. 1979–85, Kuwaiti Institute of Scientific Research 1987–88; Amb. to USA 1993–2001; Minister of State for Foreign Affairs 2001–03; Minister of Foreign Affairs 2003–; Deputy Prime Minister 2006–.
Address: Ministry of Foreign Affairs, POB 3, Gulf Street, 13001 Safat, Kuwait City, Kuwait (office). *Telephone:* 2425141 (office). *Fax:* 2412169 (office). *E-mail:* emad@mofa.org (office). *Website:* www.mofa.gov.kw (office).

SABAH, Sheikh Nasser al-Muhammad al-Ahmad as-; Kuwaiti government official and diplomat; *Prime Minister;* b. 1940. *Education:* secondary education in Britain; Univ. of Geneva. *Career:* began career at Ministry of Foreign Affairs 1964; Perm. Rep. to UN, Geneva 1965–68; Consul-Gen., Kuwaiti Embassy, Switzerland 1967–68; Amb. to Iran 1968–79; Under-Sec., Ministry of Information 1979–85; Minister of Information 1985–88, of Social Affairs and Labour 1988–90, of State for Foreign Affairs 1990–98, of Amiri Diwan Affairs 1998–2006; Prime Minister of Kuwait 2006–.
Address: Office of the Prime Minister, Council of Ministers, General Secretariat, Kuwait City, Kuwait (office). *E-mail:* info@cmgs.gov.kw (office). *Website:* www.cmgs.gov.kw (office).

SABAH, Sheikh Sabah al-Ahmad al-Jaber as-, (Amir of Kuwait); b. 1928. *Education:* Mubarakiyyah Nat. School, Kuwait and privately. *Career:* mem. Supreme Cttee 1955–62; Minister of Public Information and Guidance and of Social Affairs 1962–63, of Foreign Affairs 1963–91, acting Minister of Finance and Oil 1965, Minister of the Interior 1978; Deputy Prime Minister 1978–91; acting Minister of Information 1981–84; fmrly First Deputy Prime Minister and Minister of Foreign Affairs; Prime Minister 2003–06; Amir of Kuwait 2006–.
Address: Bayan Palace, Amiry Diwan, Kuwait.

SABAH, Salem Abdullah al-Jaber as-, MPolSc; Kuwaiti diplomatist; *Ambassador to USA;* m.; three c. *Education:* American Univ. of Beirut, Lebanon. *Career:* Diplomatic attaché for Office of Minister of State for Foreign Affairs 1986–91; First Sec. Perm. Mission of Kuwait to UN, New York 1997–98, Minister Plenipotentiary 1998; Amb. to S Korea 1998–2001, to USA 2001–.
Address: Embassy of Kuwait, 2940 Tilden Street, NW, Washington, DC 20008, USA (office). *Telephone:* (202) 966-0702 (office). *Fax:* (202) 966-0517 (office).

SABIRDINA, Maya; Kyrgyzstani diplomatist. *Career:* Chargé d'affaires a.i. in UK –2006.
Address: Ministry of Foreign Affairs, bul. Erkindik 57, 720040 Bishkek, Kyrgyzstan (office). *Telephone:* (312) 62-05-45 (office). *Fax:* (312) 66-05-01 (office). *E-mail:* gendep@mfa.gov.kg (office). *Website:* www.mfa.kg (office).

SABOURIN, Louis, LLL, PhD, FRSC; Canadian academic; *Professor of International Economic Organizations and Director, Groupe d'Etude de Recherche et de Formation Internationales, Ecole Nationale d'Administration Publique, University of Québec;* b. 1 Dec. 1935, Québec City; m. Agathe Lacerte 1959; one s. two d. *Education:* Univ. of Ottawa, Univ. of Paris, France, Institut d'Etudes Politiques de Paris, France, Columbia Univ., USA. *Career:* Prof., Dir Dept of Political Science, Univ. of Ottawa, Dean of Faculty of Social Science; Founder and Dir Inst. of Int. Co-operation and Devt, Visiting Sr Research Fellow Jesus Coll., Oxford and Queen Elizabeth House, England 1974–75; Pres. OECD Devt Centre, Paris 1977–82; Prof. of Int. Econ. Orgs, Ecole Nationale d'Admin Publique, Univ. of Québec 1983–, Dir Groupe d'Etude, de Recherche et de Formation Internationales 1983–; Visiting Prof., Univ. of Paris (Sorbonne) 1982, Univ. of Notre Dame and Stanford Univ. 1992, Hanoi, Viet Nam 2000; Founding mem. Asia-Pacific Foundation, Montreal Council of Foreign Relations; mem. Pontifical Comm. on Justice and Peace; Pres. Soc. de Droit Int. Economique 1988; Legal Counselor Hudon, Gendron, Harris, Thomas 1989–; Ford Int. Fellow 1962, Canada Council Scholar 1963; mem. Pontifical Acad. of Social Sciences, Rome 1994; Chevalier Pléiade de la Francophonie 1988; Chevalier Légion d'honneur; Dr hc (Sorbonne, Paris) 1998. *Publications:* Le système politique du Canada 1969, Dualité culturelle dans les activités internationales du Canada 1970, Canadian Federalism and International Organizations 1971, Le Canada et le développement international 1972, Allier la théorie à la pratique: le développement de la Chine nouvelle 1973, International Economic Development: Theories, Methods and Prospects 1973, The Challenge of the Less Developed Countries 1981, La crise économique: contraintes et effets de l'interdépendance pour le Canada 1984, Passion d'être, désir d'avoir, le dilemne Québec-Canada dans un univers en mutation 1992, Les organisations économiques internationales 1994, The Social Dimensions of Globalization 2000, Globalization and Inequalitites 2002, The Governance of Globalization 2004; numerous articles. *Address:* GERFI-ENAP, 4750 avenue Henri-Julien, Montreal, Québec, H2T 3E5, Canada (office). *Telephone:* (514) 849-3989 (office); (514) 735-4541 (home). *Fax:* (514) 849-3369 (office). *E-mail:* lsabourin@hotmail.com (home).

SACA GONZÁLEZ, Elías Antonio (Tony); Salvadorean politician, business executive and head of state; *President;* b. 9 March 1965, Usulután; m.; three c. *Education:* Instituto San Agustín de Usulatán, Colegio Cristóbal Colón. *Career:* fmr sports commentator and journalist; launched TV channel and several radio programmes 1990s including Radio América (with Alfonso Rivas) 1987, Radio Astral 1993; Pres. Asociación Salvadoreña de Radiodifusores (ASDER) 1997–2001, currently Vice-Pres.; Pres. Asociación Nacional de Empresa Privada (ANEP; National Private Enterprise Association) 2001–04; fmr Pres. Círculo de Informadores Deportivos (CID); currently Pres. FEDEPRICAP (Fed. of Cen. American and Dominican Repub. Business Execs); Pres. of El Salvador 2004–; mem. Alianza Republicana Nacionalista (ARENA); Micrófono de Oro 1991, Distinguished Broadcaster Award 2003. *Address:* Ministry for the Presidency, Avenida Cuba, Calle Darió González 806, Barrio San Jacinto, San Salvador, El Salvador (office). *Telephone:* 2248-9000 (office). *Fax:* 2248-9370 (office). *E-mail:* casapres@casapres.gob .sv (office). *Website:* www.casapres.gob.sv (office).

SACHS, Jeffrey David, BA, MA, PhD; American academic and economist; *Quetelet Professor of Sustainable Development and Director, The Earth Institute, Columbia University;* b. 5 Nov. 1954, Detroit, Mich.; m. Sonia Ehrlich; one s. two d. *Education:* Harvard Univ. *Career:* Research Assoc. Nat. Bureau of Econ. Research, Cambridge, Mass. 1980–85; Asst Prof. of Econs Harvard Univ. 1980–82, Assoc. Prof. 1982–83, Galen L. Stone Prof. of Int. Trade 1984–2001; Dir Harvard Inst. for Int. Devt 1995–2002, Center for Int. Devt –2002; Quetelet Prof. of Sustainable Devt and Prof. of Health Policy and Man. and Dir The Earth Inst., Columbia Univ. 2002–; advisor, Brookings Inst., Washington, DC 1982–; Special Advisor to UN Sec.-Gen. Kofi Annan on Millennium Devt Goals 2002–06, Dir Millennium Project; Founder and Chair. Exec. Cttee Inst. of Econ. Analysis, Moscow 1993–; Chair. Comm. on Macro econs and Health, WHO 2000–01; Co-Chair. Advisory Bd The Global Competitiveness Report; mem. Int. Financial Insts Advisory Comm., US Congress 1999–2000; econ. adviser to various govts in Latin America, Eastern Europe, the fmr Soviet Union, Asia and Africa, Jubilee 2000 movt; fmr consultant to IMF, World Bank, OECD and UNDP; adviser to Pres. of Bolivia 1986–90; Fellow, World Econometric Soc.; Research Assoc. Nat. Bureau of Econ. Research; syndicated newspaper column appears in more than 50 countries; mem. American Acad. of Arts and Sciences, Harvard Soc. of Fellows, Brookings Panel of Economists, Bd of Advisers, Chinese Economists Soc.; Distinguished Visiting Lecturer to LSE, Univ. of Oxford, Tel-Aviv, Jakarta, Yale Univs; BBC Reith Lecturer 2007; Commdr's Cross Order of Merit (Poland) 1999; Hon. PhD (St Gallen) 1990, (Universidad del Pacífico, Peru) 1997,

(Lingnan Coll., Hong Kong) 1998, (Varna Econs Univ., Bulgaria) 2000, (Iona Coll., New York) 2000; Frank E. Seidman Award in Political Econ. 1991, Berhard Harms Prize (Germany) 2000, Distinguished Public Service Award, Sec. of State's Open Forum 2002, Sargent Shriver Award for Equal Justice 2005. *Publications:* Economics of Worldwide Stagflation (with Michael Bruno) 1985, Developing Country Debt and the Economic Performance (Ed.) 1989, Global Linkages: Macroeconomic Interdependence and Cooperation in the World Economy (with Warwick McKibbin) 1991, Peru's Path to Recovery (with Carlos Paredes) 1991, Macroeconomics in the Global Economy (with Felipe Larrain) 1993, Poland's Jump to the Market Economy 1993, The Transition in Eastern Europe (with Olivier Blanchard and Kenneth Froot) 1994, Russia and the Market Economy (in Russian) 1995, Economic Reform and the Process of Global Integration (with A. Warner) 1995, The Collapse of the Mexican Peso: What Have We Learned? (jtly) 1995, Natural Resource Abundance and Economic Growth (with A. Warner) 1996, The Rule of Law and Economic Reform in Russia (co-ed.) 1997, Economies in Transition (co-Ed.) 1997, The End of Poverty 2005, Common Wealth: Economics for a Crowded Planet 2008; more than 200 scholarly articles. *Address:* The Earth Institute at Columbia University, 405 Low Library, 535 West 116th Street, MC 4335, New York, NY 10027, USA (office). *Telephone:* (212) 854-8704 (office). *Fax:* (212) 854-8702 (office). *E-mail:* director@ei.columbia.edu. (office). *Website:* www.earth.columbia.edu/ about/director (office).

SADANG, Elbuchel; Palauan politician; *Minister of Finance; Career:* legislator for Ngaraard State 1990–2001; Dir Bureau of Nat. Treasury, Ministry of Finance 1994–2001; Minister of Finance 2001–, also serves as Gov. for Asian Devt Bank and IMF on behalf of Palau.; mem. Asian Pacific Asscn for Fiduciary Studies, Island Govt Finance Officers Asscn; fmr mem. Bd of Trustees Civil Service Pension Plan, charged with pension fraud 2008 along with other bd mems. *Address:* Ministry of Finance, PO Box 6011, Koror, PW 96940, Palau (office). *Telephone:* 488-2561 (office). *Fax:* 488-2168 (office). *E-mail:* esadang@palaugov.net (office). *Website:* www.palaugov.net/minfinance/ mofinance.html (office).

SADCHIKOV, Nikolai Ivanovich; Russian diplomatist; *Ambassador to the Holy See;* b. 20 March 1946, Moscow; m. Olga Olegovna Sadchikova; one s. one d. *Education:* Moscow State Inst. of Int. Relations. *Career:* attaché, Dept of Middle East, USSR Ministry of Foreign Affairs 1970–72; Third Sec., USSR Embassy, North Yemen 1972–76; Counsellor, Dept of Int. Econ. Orgs, USSR Ministry of Foreign Affairs 1976–80; UN Secr. New York, 1980–83; Counsellor, USSR Mission to UN, New York 1983–86; Counsellor, Office of the Minister of Foreign Affairs 1986–90; Counsellor, Russian Embassy, UK 1990–95; Deputy Dir Dept of Consular Affairs, Ministry of Foreign Affairs 1995–97; Consul-Gen., New York 1997–99; Dir Dept of Consular Affairs, Ministry of Foreign Affairs, Russian Fed. 1999–2001; Amb. to Sweden 2001–05, to the Holy See 2005–; Order of Honour 2006. *Address:* Embassy of the Russian Federation, Via della Conciliazione 10, 00193 Rome, Italy (office). *Telephone:* (06) 6877078 (office). *Fax:* (06) 6877168 (office). *E-mail:* russsede@libero.it (office).

SADIK, Nafis, MD; Pakistani international organization official and physician; *Special Envoy of the Secretary-General for HIV/AIDS in Asia, United Nations;* b. 18 Aug. 1929, Jaunpur, India; m. Azhar Sadik 1954; one s. two d. and two adopted d. *Education:* Loretto Coll. Calcutta, Calcutta Medical Coll., Dow Medical Coll. Karachi and Johns Hopkins Univ. *Career:* Intern, Gynaecology and Obstetrics, City Hosp., Baltimore, Md 1952–54; civilian medical officer in charge of women's and children's wards in various Pakistani armed forces hosps. 1954–63; Resident, Physiology, Queen's Univ., Kingston, Ont. 1958; Head, Health Section, Planning Comm., on Health and Family Planning, Pakistan 1964; Dir of Planning and Training, Pakistan Cen. Family Planning Council 1966–68, Deputy Dir-Gen. 1968–70, Dir-Gen. 1970–71; Tech. Adviser, UN Population Fund (UNFPA) 1971–72, Chief, Programme Div. 1973–77, Asst Exec. Dir 1977–87, Exec. Dir UNFPA 1987–2000; fmrly UN Under-Sec.-Gen.; Sec.-Gen. Int. Conf. on Population and Devt 1994; UN Special Envoy for HIV/ AIDS in Asia 2002–; Pres. Soc. for Int. Devt 1994–97; Fellow ad eundem, Royal Coll. of Obstetricians and Gynaecologists; Order of Merit, First Class (Egypt) 1994, Hilal-I-Imtiaz (Pakistan); Hon. DHumLitt (Johns Hopkins) 1989, (Brown) 1993, (Duke) 1995; Hon. LLD (Wilfrid Laurier) 1995; Hon. DSc (Mich.) 1996, (Claremont) 1996, (Long Island) 1997, (Tulane) 1999, (Univ. of the West Indies) 2000; Hon. DLitt (Nepal Tribhuvan) 1998; Hon. DEcon (Nihon) 1999; Dr hc (Al-Ahfad) 2000; Bruno H. Schubert-Stiftung Prize 1995, Hugh Moore Award 1976, Women's Global Leadership Award 1994, Peace Award (UNA) 1994, Prince Mahidol Award 1995, Population Award, UN 2001, Defender of Democracy, Peoples Global Action 2006. *Publications:* Population:

National Family Planning Programme in Pakistan 1968, Population: The UNFPA Experience (ed.) 1984, Population Policies and Programmes: Lessons Learned from Two Decades of Experience 1991, Making a Difference: Twenty-five Years of UNFPA Experience 1994; articles in professional journals.
Address: Special Envoy of the UN Secretary-General for HIV/AIDS in Asia, 300 East 56th Street, 9J New York, NY 10022, USA (office). *Telephone:* (212) 826-5025 (home). *Fax:* (212) 758-1529 (office). *E-mail:* sadik@unfpa.org (office).

SADOVNIKOV, Aleksandr Alexeyevich; Russian diplomatist; *Ambassador to Iran;* b. 1948; m.; one d. *Education:* Moscow State Inst. of Int. Relations, Diplomatic Acad. *Career:* joined diplomatic service 1972, held various posts Consulate-Gen. in Isfahan, Iran 1972–76, Embassies of USSR and Russia in Iran 1979–85, 1989–93; Head Afghanistan Desk, Ministry of Foreign Affairs 1994–97, Deputy Dir Third Asian Dept 1997–99, Deputy Dir Personnel Dept 2004–05; Ambassador to Uganda 1999–2003, to Iran 2005–.
Address: Embassy of Russia, 39 Neauphle-le-Château Avenue, Tehran, Iran (office). *Telephone:* (21) 66701161 (office). *Fax:* (21) 66701652 (office). *E-mail:* rusembiran@parsonline.net (office). *Website:* www.iran.mid.ru (office).

ŠADŽIUS, Rimantas, LLM; Lithuanian politician; *Minister of Finance;* b. 8 Oct. 1960, Vilnius; m. Dalia Šadžius; one s. one d. *Education:* Lomonosov Moscow State Univ., Russia and Vilnius Univ. *Career:* began career as scientific researcher specialising in quantum chemistry and solid-state physics; Deputy Minister of Social Security and Labour 2003–04; Deputy Minister of Health 2004–06, Deputy Minister of Finance 2006–07; Minister of Finance 2007–; mem. Lithuanian Social Democratic Party (LSDP); mem. Lithuanian Asscn of Physicists.
Address: Ministry of Finance, J. Tumo-Vaižganto 8a/2, Vilnius 01512, Lithuania (office). *Telephone:* (5) 239-0005 (office). *Fax:* (5) 212-6387 (office). *E-mail:* r.sadzius@finmin.lt (office). *Website:* www.finmin.lt (office).

SÁENZ BIOLLEY, Melvin Alfredo; Costa Rican diplomatist; *Ambassador to Spain;* b. 27 April 1952, San José. *Education:* Univ. of Costa Rica. *Career:* joined Ministry of External Relations and Culture 1982, fmr Advisor to Minister of External Relations and Culture, Dir Gen. Foreign Policy Dept; Del. to UN Security Council 1997–98; fmr Consul-Gen., Consulate in Havana; Amb. to Colombia 2001–07, to Spain 2007–. *Publications:* Los Cancilleres de Costa Rica (co-author) 1986, Costa Rica y el sistema internacional 1990.
Address: Embassy of Costa Rica, Paseo de la Castellana 164, 17°, 28046 Madrid, Spain (office). *Telephone:* (91) 3459622 (office). *Fax:* (91) 3533709 (office). *E-mail:* embajada@embcr.org (office).

SAFAROV, Safar Ghaiurovich; Tajikistan diplomatist and politician; *Deputy Secretary General, Shanghai Co-operation Organization;* b. 22 May 1947, Danghara Dist; m.; five c. *Education:* Tech. Univ. of Tashkent. *Career:* fmr Chief Engineer, cotton ginning plant, Kulob; fmr Chief-Engineer-Controller, Economy of Governmental Control, Exec. Cttee of Danghara Dist; fmr Second Sec. Komsomol Cttee, Danghara Dist; fmr Head of Propaganda and Agitation Dept and Educational Works, Komsomol Cttee of Qurghonteppa Region; fmr Instructor, Org. Dept, Party Cttee of Qurghonteppa Region; fmr Deputy Head of Org. Dept of Party Cttee, Qurghonteppa Region, Second Sec. Party Cttee and First Sec. of Soviet Dist Party Cttee; fmr Deputy Chair. Majlisi Oli's Cttee on Economy and Budget, later Chair.; Deputy of Supreme Soviet, Twelfth Convocation of Tajikistan 1990–95, People's Deputy, Majlisi Oli's First Convocation 1995–2000, Chair. Cttee on Economy, Budget, Finance and Tax, Head of Exec. Apparatus of Pres.; elected Deputy for N 26 constituency, Kurgan Tube; Amb. to Russian Fed. –2007; Deputy Sec. Gen. Shanghai Co-operation Org. 2007–; Honoured Worker of Tajikistan; Glory Award (First Category).
Address: Shanghai Co-operation Organization, No 41, Liangmaqiao Road, Chaoyang Dist., Beijing 100600, People's Republic of China (office). *Telephone:* (10) 65329807 (office). *Fax:* (10) 65329808 (office). *E-mail:* sco@sectsco.org (office). *Website:* www.sectsco.org (office).

SAFAYEV, Sodyk Solihovich; Uzbekistan politician and diplomatist; *Chairman, Senat Foreign Affairs Committee;* b. 1954. *Education:* Harvard Univ. *Career:* First Deputy Minister of External Econ. Relations –1993; Minister of Foreign Affairs 1993–94, 2003–05, First Deputy Minister 2001–03; Amb. to Germany 1994–96, to USA 1996–2001; Rep. to Afghanistan 2001–03; currently Chair. Senat (Senate) Foreign Affairs Cttee.
Address: Office of the Chairman, Senat Foreign Relations Committee, Senat, 100029 Tashkent, Mustaqillik maydoni 6, Uzbekistan (office).

Telephone: (71) 138-26-66 (office). *Fax:* (71) 138-29-01 (office). *Website:* www.parliament.gov.uz (office).

SAFONOV, Col-Gen. Anatoly Yefimovich; Russian politician; *Special Representative to the President of the Russian Federation in International Co-operation for Combating Terrorism and Transitional Organized Crime;* b. 5 Oct. 1945, Krasnoyarsk; m. Galina Nikolayevna Safonova; one s. one d. *Education:* Krasnoyarsk Polytechnic Inst., Higher KGB School, Minsk. *Career:* engineer-topographer, expeditions to regions of Chukotka, Magadan, Yakutia, Krasnoyarsk –1969; KGB service –1970, Head Counter-Espionage Dept 1983–87, Head, Territorial KGB 1988–92; Deputy Minister of Security 1992–93; First Deputy Dir Fed. Service of Security, Russian Fed. 1994–97, Chair. Cttee on Security Problems of Union State of Russia and Belarus 1997; People's Deputy of Russian Fed. 1990–93; Deputy Minister of Foreign Affairs 2002–; Special Rep. to the Pres. of the Russian Fed. for int. co-operation in combating terrorism and transitional organized crime 2004–; Corresp. mem. Int. Acad. of Information Tech.; Amb. Extraordinary and Plenipotentiary; Hon. Worker of Counterespionage; Hon. Worker MFA of Russia; governmental and departmental awards.
Address: Ministry of Foreign Affairs, Smolenskaya-Sennaya pl. 32–34, 121200 Moscow, Russia (office). *Telephone:* (095) 244-95-20 (office). *Fax:* (095) 244-16-57 (office). *E-mail:* safonov@mid.ru (office).

SAGDEEV, Roald Zinnurovich, DSc; Russian physicist and academic; *Distinguished University Professor and Director, East-West Space Science Center, University of Maryland;* b. 26 Dec. 1932, Moscow; m. Susan Eisenhower (grand-d. of the late US Pres. Dwight Eisenhower) 1990. *Education:* Moscow State Univ. *Career:* Research Worker, Inst. of Atomic Energy, USSR Acad. of Sciences 1956–61; Head of Lab., Inst. of Nuclear Physics, Siberian Dept, Acad. of Sciences 1961–70, Inst. of High Temperature Physics of USSR Acad. of Sciences 1970–73; Prof. Novosibirsk State Univ. 1964–73; Dir Inst. of Space Research 1973–88, Sr Researcher 1988–; Distinguished Univ. Prof., Univ. of Md, USA 1990–, Founder and Dir East-West Space Science Center 1992–; Corresp. mem. USSR (now Russian) Acad. of Sciences 1964, mem. 1968–; specialist on global warming, plasma physics, controllable thermonuclear synthesis, cosmic ray physics; mem. Council of Dirs Int. Fund for Survival and Devt of Mankind 1988–; Head Scientific-Methodical Centre for Analytical Research, Inst. of Space Research 1988–; mem. NAS Swedish Royal Acad., Max Planck Soc.; USSR People's Deputy 1989–91; Order of October Revolution, Order of Red Banner and other decorations; Dr hc (Tech. Univ. Graz, Austria) 1984; Hero of Socialist Labour 1986; Lenin Prize 1984.
Address: 2309A Computer and Space Sciences Building, University of Maryland, College Park, MD 20742, USA (office). *Telephone:* (301) 405-8051 (office). *E-mail:* rs124@umail.umd.edu (office). *Website:* www.physics.umd.edu/people/faculty/sagdeev.html (office).

SAGUIER CABALLERO, Bernardino Hugo, PhD; Paraguayan diplomatist and international organization executive; *Secretary-General, Latin American Integration Association (Asociación Latinoamericana de Integración—ALADI);* b. 21 July 1945; m.; three c. *Education:* Catholic Univ. of Asunción, Nat. War Coll., Asunción, Acad. of Int. Law, The Hague, European Inst. of Business Admin, Fontainebleau, France. *Career:* joined Foreign Ministry, held various posts as Sec. to Comms, etc. 1962–75, Pvt. Sec. to Minister of Foreign Affairs 1965–68, Chef de Cabinet 1968–70, Dir of Int. Orgs, Treaties and Instruments 1970–75, Dir responsible for binational entity of Itaipu 1975–89, Under-Sec. of State for Foreign Affairs 1989–92; Perm. Rep. to the UN 1992–99; Amb. and Perm. Rep. to Latin American Integration Asscn (Asociación Latinoamericana de Integración—ALADI) and Mercosur c. 2005; Sec.-Gen. ALADI 2008–; fmr Head del. negotiations on Treaty of the Common Market of the Southern Cone (Mercosur), on Mercosur–US trade and investment agreement; fmr mem. del. to sessions of UN Gen. Ass. and meetings of OAS, Rio Group, River Plate Basin and Latin American Free Trade and Integration Asscns; fmr Prof., Diplomatic Acad., Ministry of Foreign Affairs; fmr Lecturer at Catholic Univ., Asunción and Higher Police Coll., Asunción; decorations from China, Brazil, S Africa, Argentina, Spain, Ecuador, Chile and others.
Address: Secretaría General, Asociación Latinoamericana de Integración, Calle Cebollati 1461, Barrio Palermo, Casilla de Correo n° 20.005, CP 11200, Montevideo, Uruguay (office). *Telephone:* (2) 419-10-14 (office); (2) 410-33-63 (office). *Fax:* (20) 418-45-66 (office). *E-mail:* sgaladi@aladi.org (office). *Website:* www.aladi.org (office).

SAHEL, El Mostafa, LenD; Moroccan politician and diplomatist; *Permanent Representative, United Nations;* b. 5 May 1946, Ouled Frej, El Jadida; m. Farida Benmansour Nejjai 1972; two s. *Education:* Lycée Mohamed V, Casablanca, Univ. Mohamed V, Rabat and Univ. de Sorbonne, Paris. *Career:* Insp. des Finances 1968–70; Financial Controller 1970–74; Head of

Service of Working Budget 1974–81, Equipment Budget 1981–86; Dir of Budget 1986–91; Sec.-Gen. Ministry of Finance 1992–93; Dir-Gen. of Communal Equipment Funds 1993–; Minister for Maritime Fisheries and Merchant Marine 1993–97, of Admin. Affairs and Relations with Parl. 1997–98; Chair. SOMED Investment Group (devt co.) 1998–2001; Prefect of Rabat region 2001–02; Minister of Interior 2002–06; Perm. Rep. to UN, New York 2006–; Ordre de Mérite, Ordre du Trône.
Address: Permanent Mission of Morocco, 866 Second Avenue, 6th and 7th Floors, New York, NY 10017, USA (office). *Telephone:* (212) 421-1580 (office). *Fax:* (212) 980-1512 (office). *E-mail:* morocco@un.int (home). *Website:* www.un.int/morocco (home).

SAHLIN, Michael, PhD; Swedish academic and diplomatist; *Ambassador to Norway;* b. 9 Jan. 1945; m.; two d. *Education:* Uppsala Univ. *Career:* Lecturer and Research Asst, Dept of Political Science, Uppsala Univ. 1973–77; with Ministry of Foreign Affairs 1977–80; Del. to CSCE 1980–82; Sec., Submarine Defence Comm. 1982–83; First Sec., Embassy in Madrid 1983–84; Chief Sec., Parl. Defence Planning Comm. 1984–87; Sec. and Head of Office, Parl. Defence Standing Cttee 1987–91, Chief Sec. 1988–90; State Sec., Ministry of Defence 1991–95; Amb. to Azerbaijan 1997–98, to Turkey 1995–98, to Fmr Repub. of Yugoslavia and Fmr Yugoslav Repub. of Macedonia 2000–02; EU Special Rep. to Macedonia 2004–05; Dir-Gen. Folke Bernadotte Acad. 2002–07; Amb. to Norway 2007–.
Address: Embassy of Sweden, Nobelsgt. 16, 0244 Oslo, Norway (office). *Telephone:* 24-11-42-00 (office). *Fax:* 22-55-15-96 (office). *E-mail:* ambassaden.oslo@foreign.ministry.se (office). *Website:* www .swedenabroad.com/oslo (office).

SAHNOUN, Mohamed; Algerian diplomatist, fmr UN official and international organization official; *President, Initiatives of Change International;* m.; three c. *Career:* Deputy Sec.-Gen. OAU (in charge of Political Affairs) 1964–73, League of Arab States (for Arab-African dialogue) 1973–75; Amb. to FRG, to France, to USA 1984–89, to Morocco 1989–1990; Perm. Rep. to the UN 1982–84; Sec. of the Maghreb Union 1989–90; Counsellor to the Pres. of Algeria for Foreign Affairs 1990–92; UN Special Rep. in Somalia 1992; OAU Special Rep. in the Congo 1993; UN/OAU Special Envoy in Great Lakes Region of Africa 1997–2006 (resgnd); fmr Special Adviser to Sec.-Gen. UN Conf. on Environment and Devt, UNCED; fmr Special Adviser to Culture of Peace Prog. UNESCO, Paris, War-Torn Societies Project UNRISD, Geneva; fmr Exec. Dir Earth Charter Project; fmr mem. World Comm. on Environment and Devt (Brundtland Comm.); mem. Bd Int. Inst. for Sustainable Devt (IISD), Winnipeg, Int. Council for Human Rights; Distinguished Fellow, US Inst. of Peace, Washington 1992–93; Pearson Fellow, Int. Devt Research Centre (IDRC), Ottawa, Canada 1993–94; mem. Univ. for Peace Council, Costa Rica and consulant on Africa Programme. *Publications:* Somalia: The Missed Opportunities 1994, Managing Conflicts in the Post-Cold War Era 1996.
Address: Initiatives of Change International, PO Box 3, 1211 Geneva 20, Switzerland (office). *Telephone:* 227335668 (office). *Fax:* 227330267 (office). *E-mail:* iofc-international@iofc.org (office). *Website:* www.iofc .org (office).

ŠAHOVIĆ, Dejan; Serbian diplomatist and lawyer; m.; two s. *Education:* School of Law, Univ. of Belgrade. *Career:* diplomatic career 1986–92, worked in Perm. Mission of fmr Yugoslavia to UN, New York; practised law in Belgrade 1992–2000; also acted as legal and political consultant and participated in UN missions in Cambodia, SA and Tajikistan; Head of Multilateral Issues, Office of the Foreign Minister 2000–01; Perm. Rep. to UN 2001–04.
Address: c/o Ministry of Foreign Affairs, 11000 Belgrade, Kneza Miloša 26, Serbia.

SAICH, Tony, BA, MSc, PhD; British academic; *Daewoo Professor of International Affairs, Harvard University;* b. 1 April 1953, London. *Education:* Univ. of Newcastle-upon-Tyne, London Univ., Univ. of Leiden. *Career:* Lecturer, Univ. of Newcastle-upon-Tyne 1978–82; Assoc. Prof., Sinological Inst., Univ. of Leiden 1982–90, Dir 1990–98; Chief Rep. of the China Office, Ford Foundation; currently Daewoo Prof. of Int. Affairs, Kennedy School of Govt, Harvard Univ., also Dir Ash Inst. for Democratic Governance and Innovation, Victor and William Fung Dir Asia Center, Dir and Faculty Chair, Asia Programs, Center for Business and Govt, Dir and Faculty Chair China Public Policy Program, Asia Programs; Chang Jiang Scholar, Ministry of Educ., People's Repub. China at Tsinghua Univ.; mem. Ed. Bds China Information, China Quarterly, Journal of Communist Studies, CCP Research Newsletter; mem. European Asscn for Chinese Studies, European Consortium for Political Research, European Network for Research on State and Soc. in East Asia, Asscn of Asian Studies, Int. Soc. for Third-Sector Research. *Publications include:* China: Politics and Government 1981, China's Science Policy in the 80s 1989, Revolutionary Discourse in Mao's China (jtly) 1994, The Rise to Power of the Chinese Communist Party 1996, The Governance and Politics of China 2001, AIDS and Social Policy in China (co-ed) 2006; numerous articles in scholarly journals.
Address: John F. Kennedy School of Government, Mailbox 130, 79 John F. Kennedy Street, Cambridge, MA 02138, USA (office). *Telephone:* (617) 495-5713 (office). *Fax:* (617) 495-4948 (office). *E-mail:* Anthony_Saich@ ksg.harvard.edu (office). *Website:* www.hks.harvard.edu (office).

SAIDI, Abdullah M. as-; Yemeni diplomatist; *Permanent Representative, United Nations; Career:* fmr Deputy Minister Foreign Affairs; Pres. Exec. Bd UNDP and UNFPA; currently Chair. Arab Group; currently Perm. Rep. to UN.
Address: Permanent Mission of Yemen to the UN, 413 East 51st Street, New York, NY 10022, USA (office). *Telephone:* (212) 355-1730 (office). *Fax:* (212) 750-9613 (office). *E-mail:* yemen@un.int (office). *Website:* www .un.int/yemen (office).

SAIF, Abdulla Hassan; Bahraini banker; *Economic Affairs Adviser to the Prime Minister;* b. 10 March 1945, Muharraq. *Education:* Inst. of Cost and Man. Accountants, UK, IMF Inst. and other int. forums. *Career:* apprentice, Bahrain Petroleum Co. 1957, served in all depts. –1971; Head of Finance and Admin. Civil Aviation Directorate 1971–74; Deputy Dir-Gen. Bahrain Monetary Agency 1974–77, Dir-Gen. 1977, fmr Gov.; Chair. Gulf Int. Bank BSC; Minister of Finance and Nat. Economy 1999–2005; Economic Affairs Adviser to Prime Minister 2005–; Chair. Specific Council for Training of Banking Sector; mem. Bd of Dirs Gulf Air Co., Org. for Social Insurance, Civil Service Pension Bd; Alt. Gov. IMF; Dr hc (DePaul Univ. Chicago) 2002.
Address: c/o Office of the Prime Minister, POB 1000, Government House, Government Road, Manama, Bahrain (office). *Telephone:* 17253361 (office). *Fax:* 17533033 (office).

SAIGA, Fumiko; Japanese diplomatist and judge; *Judge, International Criminal Court;* b. 30 Nov. 1943. *Education:* Tokyo Univ. of Foreign Studies. *Career:* with Int. Convention Div., Treaties Bureau 1980–83; First Sec., Perm. Mission to UN, New York 1983–88, Asst Dir UN Policy Div., UN Affairs Bureau Feb. 1988, Deputy Dir Social Co-operation Div., UN Affairs Bureau 1988–89, Dir Ocean Div., Econ. Affairs Bureau 1989–92, Counsellor, Embassy in Copenhagen 1992–96, Minister, Perm. Mission to UN 1996–98; Vice-Gov. Saitama Pref. 1998–2000; Consul-Gen. of Japan in Seattle 2000–02, Amb. and Perm. Rep. to UN 2002–03, Amb. to Norway (also accred to Iceland) 2003–07, Amb. in charge of Human Rights 2005–08; Judge (Pre-Trial Div.), Int. Criminal Court, The Hague, Netherlands 2008–; mem. Cttee on Elimination of Discrimination Against Women (CEDAW) 2001–.
Address: International Criminal Court, PO Box 19519, 2500 CM The Hague, The Netherlands (office). *Telephone:* (70) 515-8515 (office). *Fax:* (70) 515-8555 (office). *E-mail:* info@icc-cpi.int (office). *Website:* www.icc -cpi.int (office).

ST AIMEE, Donatus, PhD; Saint Lucia diplomatist; *Permanent Representative, United Nations;* b. 22 April 1944; m.; four c. *Education:* Florida A&M Univ., Fairleigh Dickinson Univ., New Jersey, Univ. of the West Indies, City Univ., New York. *Career:* Agricultural Extension Officer, Ministry of Agric. 1962–96; Research Asst, Coll. of the Virgin Islands, St Croix 1974–76; grad. teacher, Vieux Port Sr Secondary School 1976–78; Foreign Service Officer, Ministry of External Affairs 1980–82; Chargé d'affaires, Perm. Mission to UN, New York 1982–85, also Vice-Pres. Econ. and Social Council, OAS; Sec., Caribbean Devt and Co-operation Cttee, ECLAC 1985–96, Sec., Caribbean Council for Science and Tech. 1996–2004; Perm. Rep. to UN, New York 2008–.
Address: Permanent Mission of Saint Lucia to the United Nations, 800 Second Avenue, New York, NY 10017, USA (office). *Telephone:* (212) 697-9360 (office). *Fax:* (212) 697-4993 (office). *E-mail:* slumission@aol.com (office). *Website:* www.un.int/stlucia (office).

SAINT-JACQUES, Guy; Canadian diplomatist; *Deputy Head of Mission, Canadian Embassy, Washington DC;* m. Sylvie Saint-Jacques. *Career:* posting to Canadian Embassy, Washington, DC 1994; Dir-Gen. Personnel Man. Bureau, Dept of Foreign Affairs 2003; Deputy High Commr to UK 2003–06, Acting High Commr 2006–08; Deputy Head of Mission, Canadian Embassy, Washington, DC 2008–; Trustee Imperial War Museum.
Address: Embassy of Canada, 501 Pennsylvania Avenue, NW, Washington, DC 20001, USA (office). *Telephone:* (202) 682-1740 (office). *Fax:* (202) 682-7678 (office). *Website:* geo.international.gc.ca/can-am/washington (office).

SAINZ MUÑOZ, Most Rev. Faustino, DCL; Spanish ecclesiastic and diplomatist; *Apostolic Nuncio to UK;* b. 5 June 1937, Almadén. *Career:*

ordained priest 1964; entered diplomatic service of the Holy See 1970, served in Pontifical Representations in Senegal and Scandinavia, then in Council of Public Affairs of the Church, Vatican Secr. of State, dispatched as part of Holy See's del. to preparatory talks of CSCE 1975, returning to Vatican 1975, apptd liaison with Poland, Hungary, and later USSR and Yugoslavia, travelled to Latin America 1978, accompanied Cardinal Antonio Samoré in successfully averting war between Chile and Argentina over the Beagle conflict, accompanied Pope John Paul II on his visit to his native Poland June 1979; consecrated Titular Archbishop of Novaliciana 1988; Apostolic Pro-Nuncio to Cuba 1988–92, Apostolic Nuncio to Democratic Repub. of the Congo 1992–99, to EU 1999–2004, to UK 2005–; Hon. LLD (Aberdeen) 2007.
Address: Apostolic Nunciature, 54 Parkside, Wimbledon, London, SW19 5NE, England (office). *Telephone:* (20) 8944-7189 (office). *Fax:* (20) 8947-2494 (office). *E-mail:* nuntius@globalnet.co.uk (office).

SAITO, Yasuo; Japanese diplomatist; *Ambassador to Russia;* b. 5 Jan. 1948, Okayama; m. Chieko Saito; two c. *Career:* joined Ministry of Foreign Affairs 1971, positions included Dir-Gen. European Affairs Bureau; served as Amb. to UNESCO, Consul-Gen. in Atlanta, USA, Amb. to Saudi Arabia 2003, Amb. to Russia (also accred to Armenia, Turkmenistan, Belarus) 2006–.
Address: Embassy of Japan, 125009 Moscow, Kalashnyi per. 12, Russia (office). *Telephone:* (495) 291-85-00 (office). *Fax:* (495) 200-12-40 (office). *E-mail:* embjapan@mail.cnt.ru (office). *Website:* www.ru.emb-japan.go.jp (office).

SAJJADPOUR, Seyed Mohammad Kazem, PhD; Iranian diplomatist. *Education:* George Washington Univ., USA. *Career:* Post-doctoral Fellow, Harvard Univ.; taught at Coll. of Int. Relations, Tehran Univ., Azad Univ., National Defence Univ. of Iran; fmr Dir Inst. for Political and Int. Studies, Ministry of Foreign Affairs; fmr Amb. and Deputy Perm. Rep. to UN and other Int. Orgs, Geneva; mem. Bd of Advisers, Dialogues: Islamic World-US-The West program, New York Univ.; fmr Dir-Gen. Inst. for Political and Int. Studies (IPIS), Tehran, currently Sr Fellow.
Address: Institute for Political and International Studies, Shaheed Bahonar (Niavaran) Avenue, Shaheed Aghaee St, Tehran, Iran (office).

SAKO, Soumana, PhD, MPA; Malian politician, civil servant and international civil servant; *Executive Secretary, African Capacity Building Foundation;* b. 23 Dec. 1950, Nyamina; m. Cisse Toure; two s. two d. *Education:* Univ. of Pittsburgh, Pa, USA, Ecole Nationale d'Admin du Mali. *Career:* Staff mem. Gen. Inspectorate, Office of the Pres. of Repub. of Mali 1974; Admin. and Finance Man., Operation Puits Project 1975–76; Staff mem. Ministry of Industrial Devt and Tourism 1981; Adviser Ministry of Foreign Affairs and Int. Co-operation 1981–82; Sr Adviser Ministry of Planning and Econ. Man. 1982–84; Dir of Sr Staff, Ministry of State-Owned Enterprises 1985–87; Minister of Finance and Commerce Feb.–Aug. 1987; Deputy Controller-Gen. Office of the Pres. 1988–89; UNDP official serving in Cen. African Repub. 1989–91, Sr Economist for Madagascar and Comoros Islands 1993–97; Prime Minister of Mali 1991–92; Prof. of Devt Econs and Public Finance, Univ. of Mali 1997–2000; int. consultant 1998–; Exec. Sec. African Capacity Bldg Foundation, Harare Jan. 2000–; Commdr, Nat. Order of Mali 2000; AFGRAD Distinguished Alumnus 1992, Sennen Andriamirado Prize of Excellence 2000. *Publication:* Determinants of Public Policy–A Comparative Analysis of Public Expenditure Patterns in African States.
Address: PO Box 1502, Harare (office); The African Capacity Building Foundation, Intermarket Life Towers, 7th Floor, Corner Jason Moyo/Sam Nujoma Street, Harare, Zimbabwe; BP 433, Bamako, Mali; Villa f4 bis 48, Sema Gexco Bamako, Mali (home). *Telephone:* (4) 702931 (Harare) (office); (4) 744512 (Harare); 236196 (Bamako) (home). *Fax:* (4) 702915 (Harare) (office); 229748 (Bamako). *E-mail:* s.sako@acbf-pact.org (office); dbtymz@gmail.com. *Website:* www.acbf-pact.org (office).

SAKSKOBURGGOTSKI, Simeon; Bulgarian politician and fmr King of Bulgaria; *Leader, National Movement for Stability and Progress;* b. 16 June 1937, Sofia; m. Margarita Gómez y Acebo 1962; four s. one d. *Education:* in England, Victoria Coll., Alexandria, Egypt, Lycée Français, Spain and Valley Forge Mil. Acad., USA. *Career:* proclaimed King of Bulgaria 1943; deposed 1946; sought refuge in Egypt in 1947; has since lived mainly in Spain; Constitutional Court ruled in 1998 that confiscation of royal property by communist regime had been illegal; returned to Bulgaria 1996; Founder and Leader, Nat. Movt for King Simeon II (renamed Nat. Movt for Stability and Progress 2007) 2001–; Prime Minister of Bulgaria 2001–05.
Address: National Movement for Stability and Progress (Natsionalno dvizhenie za stabilnost i vazhod), 1000 Sofia, ul. Vrabcha 23, Bulgaria (office). *Telephone:* (2) 980-38-09 (office). *Fax:* (2) 980-38-07 (office). *E-mail:* ndsv@ndsv.bg (office). *Website:* www.ndsv.bg (office).

SALA-I-MARTÍN, Xavier, MA, PhD; Spanish (Catalan) economist and academic; *Professor of Economics, Columbia University;* b. 17 June 1963, Barcelona. *Education:* Univ. Autònoma, Barcelona, Harvard Univ., USA. *Career:* Assoc. Prof., Yale Univ., USA 1990–95; Visiting Prof., Univ. Pompeu Fabra, Barcelona 1994–2006; Prof. of Econs, Columbia Univ., USA 1996–; Visiting Prof., Harvard Univ. 2003–04; Research Assoc., Nat. Bureau of Econ. Research, Cambridge, Mass 1991–; Sr Econ. Advisor, World Econ. Forum 2002–; consultant, IMF 1993–2001, World Bank 1996–2001; Assoc. Ed. Journal of Economic Growth 1995–; Pres. Barcelona Football Club 2006, CEOs Without Borders 2006–; NSF Award 1998, King Juan Carlos I Prize for Social Sciences 1998, Kenneth Arrow Prize 1999, King Juan Carlos I Prize for Econs 2004. *Publications include:* Apuntes de Crecimiento Económico 1994, Economic Growth 1995, Economia Liberal para No Economistas y No Liberales, Converses amb Xavier Sala-i-Martin 2007; numerous articles in learned journals.
Address: Columbia University, Department of Economics, International Affairs Building, MC 3308, 420 West 118th Street #1005, New York, NY 10027, USA (office). *Telephone:* (212) 854-7055 (office). *Fax:* (212) 854-8059 (office). *E-mail:* xs23@columbia.edu (office). *Website:* www.columbia.edu/~xs23 (office).

SALAM, Nawaf A.; Lebanese lawyer, academic and diplomatist; *Permanent Representative, United Nations;* b. 15 Dec. 1953; m.; two c. *Education:* Inst. d'Etudes Politiques, Paris, Harvard Law School, Lebanese Univ., Sorbonne Univ., Paris. *Career:* fmr Assoc. Researcher, Centre d'histoire de l'Islam contemporain, Sorbonne Univ., Paris; foreign legal consultant, Edwards & Angell (law firm), Boston 1989–92; in pvt. law practice 1992–2003; part-time Lecturer, American Univ. of Beirut 1992–2003, Visiting Assoc. Prof. of Political Science 2003–05, Chair. Political Studies and Public Admin Dept 2005–07; Perm. Rep. to UN, New York 2007–.
Address: Permanent Mission of Lebanon to the United Nations, 866 United Nations Plaza, Room 531–533, New York, NY 10017, USA (office). *Telephone:* (212) 355-5460 (office). *Fax:* (212) 838-2819 (office). *E-mail:* lebanon@un.int (office).

SALAMÉ, Ghassan, MPhil, PhD; Lebanese politician, academic and fmr United Nations official; *Professor of International Relations, Institut d'Etudes Politiques, Paris;* b. 18 May 1951, Kfarzebian (Mount Lebanon); two d. *Education:* Paris III Univ., Paris I Univ., St-Joseph Univ. *Career:* taught Political Science at Saint-Joseph Univ., Beirut, American Univ. of Beirut and Paris I Univ.; Rockefeller Fellow in Int. Relations, Brookings Inst., Washington, DC 1981, Visiting Fellow 1985–86; mem. Social Science Research Council, New York 1985–90, Co-Dir 'State, Nation and Integration in the Arab World' study program 1986–91; Minister of Culture 2000–03; Prof. of Int. Relations, Institut d'Etudes Politiques, Paris, France 1988–; Co-founder and Chair. Euro-Mediterranean Studies, European Univ. Inst., Florence, Italy; Sr Adviser to UN Sec.-Gen. 2003–06; mem. Bd L'Institut du Monde Arabe, Paris 1998–2000, Arab Thought Forum 1995–98, Haut Conseil de la Francophonie 2003–06, Int. Crisis Group 2004–, Arab Anti-Corruption Org. 2005–, The Bibliotheca Alexandrina 2005–, Int. Peace Acad. 2007–; Chevalier, Légion d'honneur 2003. *Publications:* author or ed. 12 books, including Al-mujtama' wa al-dawla fi al-mashriq al-arabi (State and Society in the Arab Levant) 1987, The Foundations of the Arab State 1987, The Politics of Arab Integration 1988, Democracy without Democrats: Politics of Liberalization in the Arab and Muslim World (ed.) 1994, Appels d'empire: ingérences et résistances à l'âge de la mondialisation (Phoenix Award; APELF Award) 1996, Quand L'Amerique refait le monde 2005, and others; articles published in several periodicals, including La Revue Française de Science Politique, Foreign Policy, The Middle East Journal, Security Dialogue.
Address: Fondation Nationale des Sciences Politiques-Institut d'Etudes Politiques de Paris, 27 rue Saint-Guillaume, 75337 Paris Cedex 07, France (office). *Telephone:* 1-45-49-72-40 (office). *Fax:* 1-42-22-40-26 (office). *E-mail:* ghassan.salame@sciences-po.fr (office). *Website:* www.sciences-po.fr (office).

SALBER, Herbert; German diplomatist and international organization executive; *Director, Conflict Prevention Centre, Organization for Security and Co-operation in Europe;* b. 26 April 1954, Aachen; m.; three d. *Education:* Bonn Univ., Toulouse Univ., France. *Career:* served in Fed. Armed Forces prior to univ. studies; entered training for diplomatic service, posted to Belgrade and Nicaragua before returning to Bonn 1990, involved with Geneva Conf. on Disarmament, Nuclear Non-Proliferation Treaty and Biological Weapons Convention, Rep. to UN Special Comm. (UNSCOM) 1995, Deputy Head of German Perm. Mission to OSCE 1996–2000, Head of OSCE Centre, Almaty, Kazakhstan 2000–01, Special Adviser to Portuguese OSCE Chairmanship on Cen. Asia 2002–03; Head of Div. for EU relations with CIS, South-Eastern Europe, Turkey, Asia, Africa and Latin America, Fed. Foreign Office, Berlin 2003–04; Head of

Dept for Econ. and Scientific Relations, Embassy in Moscow 2004–06; Dir OSCE Conflict Prevention Centre 2006–.
Address: OSCE Conflict Prevention Centre, Kärntner Ring 5–7, 1010 Vienna, Austria (office). *Telephone:* (1) 514-36-122 (office). *Fax:* (1) 514-36-96 (office). *E-mail:* info@osce.org (office). *Website:* www.osce.org/cpc (office).

SALEH, Field Marshall Ali Abdullah; Yemeni army officer and head of state; *President;* b. 21 March 1942, Beit al-Ahmer, Sanhan Dist.; m.; several c. *Career:* entered mil. service 1958; participated in 1974 coup; Mil. Gov., Taiz Prov. until June 1978; mem. Provisional Presidential Council, Deputy C-in-C of Armed Forces June–July 1978; Pres. of Yemen Arab Repub. 1978–90, Pres. Presidential Council of Repub. of Yemen 1990–94, of Repub. of Yemen 1994–; C-in-C of Armed Forces 1978–90; Sec.-Gen. People's Gen. Congress 1982; rank of Marshal 1997; Hon. M.Mil.Sc.; Nat. Republican Award.
Address: Office of the President, San'a, Republic of Yemen (office). *Fax:* (1) 274147 (office).

SALEH, Maj.-Gen. Bakri Hassan; Sudanese military officer and government official; *Minister of the Presidency; Career:* Mil. Officer, Revolutionary Command Council for Nat. Salvation (RCC–NS) 1989–; Chief of Security Forces 1997; Minister of Presidential Affairs 2001; fmr Minister of Nat. Defence; currently Minister of the Presidency; mem. Nat. Congress.
Address: c/o National Congress, Khartoum, Sudan (office).

SALEH ABBAS, Youssouf, LLM; Chadian politician; *Prime Minister;* b. 1953, Abéché, Ouaddai Region. *Career:* Head, Multilateral Co-operation Div. and Dir of Int. Co-operation, Ministry of Foreign Affairs 1979–81; Diplomatic Adviser to Pres. 1981; Dir Cabinet of Head of State 1981–82; Adviser to Dir-Gen., Ministry of Foreign Affairs 1992–96; Vice-Pres. Sovereign Nat. Conf. Jan.–April 1993; Dir-Gen. Ministry of Planning and Co-operation 1996–97; mem. Movt for Democracy and Justice in Chad 1998–2001; Special Rep. to UN and EUFOR (peacekeepng force) 2007–08; Adviser to Pres. on Int. Relations and Co-operation 2006–08; Prime Minister 2008–.
Address: Office of the Prime Minister, BP 463, N'Djamena, Chad (office). *Telephone:* 52-63-39 (office). *Fax:* 52-69-77 (office). *E-mail:* cpcprimt@intnet.td (office). *Website:* www.primature-tchad.com (office).

SALIH, Barham, BE; Iraqi politician; *Deputy Prime Minister for National Security;* b. 1960, Kurdistan. *Education:* Univ. of Cardiff, Univ. of Liverpool, UK. *Career:* joined Patriotic Union Kurdistan (PUK) 1976, served as spokesman in London, UK; Rep. to US, Patriotic Union Kurdistan and Kurdistan Regional Govt 1991–2001; Regional Admin. Sulaimaniya; Deputy Prime Minister for Nat. Security Affairs 2004–05; Minister of Planning and Devt Co-operation 2005–06, Deputy Prime Minister for Nat. Security 2006–.
Address: Ministry of National Security Affairs, North Gate, Baghdad, Iraq (office). *Telephone:* (1) 888-9071 (office).

SALIH, Khaled, BA, MA, PhD; Iraqi academic and government official; *Official Spokesperson, Kurdistan Regional Government;* b. 16 Feb. 1957, Sulaimania, Kurdistan. *Education:* Gothenburg Univ., Sweden. *Career:* fmr Lecturer in Int. and Middle E Politics, Dept of Political Science, Gothenburg Univ. 1989–97; Sr Lecturer, Univ. of Linköping, Sweden 1997–98; Associate Prof. in Middle E Politics, Centre for Contemporary Middle E Studies, Univ. of Southern Denmark, Odense 1998–; mem. Kurdistan Int. Constitutional Advisory Team 2003, also served as political adviser to Kurdistan Regional Govt and Kurdistan Nat. Ass.; Official Spokesperson for Kurdistan Regional Govt 2006–; fmr Advisory Ed. Democratiya (journal). *Publications:* State-Making, Nation-Building and the Military: Iraq, 1941-1958 1996, The Future of Kurdistan in Iraq (co-ed.) 2005.
Address: Kurdistan Regional Government, Council of Ministers Building, Arbil, Kurdish Autonomous Region, Iraq; Center for Contemporary Middle East Studies, University of Southern Denmark, Campusvej 55, 5230 Odense, Denmark. *Telephone:* 6550 2183. *Fax:* 6550 2161. *E-mail:* salih@hist.ou.dk. *Website:* www.krg.org; www.humaniora.sdu.dk/middle-east.

SALIH MUHAMMAD, Osman, BSc; Eritrean politician; *Minister of Foreign Affairs;* b. 1948. *Education:* Haile Selassie I Univ. (Addis Ababa Univ.), Ethiopia. *Career:* Head, Eritrean People's Liberation Front refugee schools, Sudan 1983–87; Head, Educ. Dept 1987; Commr for Eritrean Refugees' Affairs 1987–92; mem. Nat. Ass. 1993–; Minister of Educ. 1993–2007, of Foreign Affairs 2007–; mem. People's Front for Democracy and Justice (PFDJ), mem. Exec. Bd 1993–, mem. Cen. Ass. 1993–.
Address: Ministry of Foreign Affairs, PO Box 190, Asmara, Eritrea (office). *Telephone:* (1) 127838 (office). *Fax:* (1) 123788 (office). *E-mail:* tesfai@wg.eol (office).

SALIM, Salim Ahmed; Tanzanian diplomatist; b. 23 Jan. 1942, Pemba Island, Zanzibar; m. Amne Salim; three c. *Education:* Lumumba Coll., Zanzibar, Univ. of Delhi, India, and Columbia Univ., USA. *Career:* Publicity Sec. of UMMA Party and Chief Ed. of its official organ Sauti ya UMMA 1963; Exec. Sec. United Front of Opposition Parties and Chief Ed. of its newspaper; Sec. Gen. All-Zanzibar Journalists Union 1963; Amb. to UAR 1964–65; High Commr to India 1965–68; Dir African and Middle East Affairs Div., Ministry of Foreign Affairs 1968–69; Amb. to People's Repub. of China and Democratic People's Repub. of Korea June–Dec. 1969; Perm. Rep. to UN 1970–80 (Pres. of Gen. Ass. 1979), also High Commr to Jamaica, accred to Guyana, Trinidad and Tobago, Barbados and Amb. to Cuba 1971–80; Chair. UN Special Cttee on Decolonization 1972–80; Minister of Foreign Affairs 1980–84, Prime Minister of Tanzania 1984–85, Deputy Prime Minister, Minister of Defence and Nat. Service 1986–89; Sec.-Gen. OAU 1989–2001; a fmr Vice-Pres. of Tanzania; Chair. UN Security Council Cttee on Sanctions against Rhodesia Jan.–Dec. 1975; fmr del. of Tanzania at int. confs; mem. Bd of Dirs South Centre (inter-governmental body) 2002–05; Pres. Julius K. Nyerere Foundation 2001–; African Union Special Envoy for Darfur Talks and Chief Mediator for the Inter-Sudanese Peace Talks on the Darfur Conflict 2004–08; Hon. LLD (Univ. of Philippines); Hon. DH (Univ. of Maiduguri, Nigeria) 1983; Hon. DCL (Univ. of Mauritius) 1991; Hon. Dr of Arts (Univ. of Khartoum, Sudan) 1995; Hon. PhD (Univ. of Bologna, Italy) 1996.
Address: c/o Ministry of foreign Affairs and International Co-operation, Kivukoni Road, P.O. Box 9000, Dar es Salaam, Tanzania (office). *Website:* www.nyererefoundation.or.tz (office).

SALLABANDA, Aleksander, PhD; Albanian scientist, politician and diplomatist; *Ambassador to USA;* m. Sashenka Sallabanda. *Education:* Univ. of Tirana. *Career:* Head of Microbiology Lab., Univ. of Tirana Hosp. of Pulmonary Disease and Tuberculosis 1985–93, Head of Dept of Public Health 1994–97; Head of Health Policy Dept, Democratic Party of Albania 1997–2005; mem. Council of Municipality of Tirana 2004–06; Head of Health and Environmental Comm. 2004–06; Deputy Minister of Health 2005–06; Amb. to USA 2006–.
Address: Embassy of Albania, 2100 S Street, NW, Washington, DC 20008, USA (office). *Telephone:* (202) 223-4942 (office). *Fax:* (202) 628-7342 (office). *E-mail:* info@albanianembassy.org (office). *Website:* www.albanianembassy.org (office).

SALLOUKH, Fawzi; Lebanese government official and diplomatist; *Minister of Foreign Affairs and Emigrants;* b. 1931, Qammatieh; m. Hind Basma; three c. *Education:* American Univ. Beirut. *Career:* Prof. 1955–57; Dir of Public Relations, Franklin Publishing 1957–60; Amb. to Sierra Leone 1964–71; Cen. Dept, Ministry of Foreign Affairs 1971–78; Amb. to Nigeria 1978–85, to Algeria 1985–87; Dir of Econ. Affairs 1987–90; Amb. to Austria 1990–94, to Belgium 1994–95; Sec.-Gen. Islamic Univ. 1998–; Minister of Foreign Affairs and Emigrants 2005–06 (resgnd, resignation not accepted), 2008–.
Address: Ministry of Foreign Affairs and Emigrants, rue Sursock, Achratieh, Beirut, Lebanon (office). *Telephone:* (1) 333100 (office). *E-mail:* info@emigrants.gov.lb (office). *Website:* www.emigrants.gov.lb (office).

SALLY, Razeen, PhD; British/Sri Lankan economist, academic and research institute director; *Co-Director, European Centre for International Political Economy;* b. Colombo, Sri Lanka. *Education:* St. Thomas' College, Mt Lavinia, St Mary's Coll., North Wales, LSE, INSEAD, France. *Career:* emigrated to UK 1978; Research Fellow, INSEAD European Inst. of Business Admin, Fontainebleau, France 1992–93; Lecturer, then Sr Lecturer, LSE 1993–, also Head Int. Trade Policy Unit (on leave); currently Co-Dir European Centre for Int. Political Economy, Brussels; also currently Sr Research Assoc., South African Inst. of Int. Affairs, Johannesburg; fmr Visiting Prof., Institut D'Etudes Politiques, Paris, Tallinn Tech. Univ., Estonia; Visiting Asst Prof., Dartmouth Coll., USA 1998; fmr Visiting Research Fellow, Inst. of Southeast Asian Studies, Singapore; Dir of Trade Policy, Commonwealth Business Council, London, Dir Global Dimensions trade policy programme; mem. Acad. Advisory Council, Inst. of Econ. Affairs, London; mem. Advisory Bd, Cato Center for Trade Policy Studies, Washington, DC. *Publication:* Co-publisher Ordo yearbook, Germany.
Address: European Centre for International Political Economy, Rue Belliard 4-6, 1040 Brussels, Belgium (office); London School of Economics, Houghton Street, London, WC2A 2AE, England (office). *Telephone:* (2) 289-13-50 (Brussels) (office); (20) 7955-6788 (office). *Fax:* (2) 289-13-59 (Brussels) (office); (20) 7955-7446 (office). *E-mail:* razeen.sally@ecipe.org

(office); r.sally@lse.ac.uk (office). *Website:* www.ecipe.org (office); www
.lse.ac.uk/people/r.sally@lse.ac.uk (office).

SALOMÃO, Tomaz Augusto, BA MA; Mozambican international organization official; *Executive Secretary, Southern African Development Community;* b. 16 Oct. 1954, Inhambane Prov.; m. *Education:* Commercial and
Industrial School Vasca da Gama-Inhambane, Commercial Inst. of
Lurenco Marques, Eduardo Mondlane Univ. *Career:* expert for study
unit of Montepio Savings Bank of Mozambique 1974–76; expert at
Ministry of Industry and Trade 1976–78; head of production unit at CIFEL
1978–81; Sec. of State for Nat. Defence 1983–89; lecturer Eduardo
Mondlane Univ. 1990–93; Deputy-Minister of Planning and Finance
1990–94, Minister of Planning and Finance, Gov. for Mozambique at
African Devt Bank, IMF, World Bank 1994–99; Chair. SADC Transport
and Communications Ministers' Cttee 2000–02, Chair. SADC Ministers'
Cttee on ICTs 2002–03; Chair. African Union Ministers' Cttee on ICTs
2003–04; Minister of Transport and Communications of Mozambique
2000–04; Exec. Sec. SADC 2005–; mem. Ass. of the Repub. (Parl.) 2005–.
Address: SADC House, Government Enclave, Private Bag 0095, Gaborone, Botswana. *Telephone:* 3951863 (office). *Fax:* 3972848 (office). *E-mail:*
registry@sadc.int (office). *Website:* www.sadc.int (office).

SALTANOV, Aleksander Vladimirovich; Russian diplomatist; *Deputy
Minister of Foreign Affairs;* b. 14 Feb. 1946, Moscow; m.; two s. *Education:*
Moscow State Inst. of Int. Relations. *Career:* attaché, USSR Embassy,
Kuwait 1970–74; attaché, Third then Second Sec., Dept of Near East and N
Africa, Ministry of Foreign Affairs 1974–79, Counsellor, Head of Sector,
then Head of Div. 1986–92, Dir of Dept 1999–2001; Consul then Gen.,
Consulate in Aleppo (Syria) 1979–83; First Sec. then Counsellor, USSR
Embassy, Syria 1983–86; Amb. to Jordan 1992–98; Deputy Minister of
Foreign Affairs 2001–.
Address: Ministry of Foreign Affairs, Smolenskaya-Sennaya pl. 32–34,
119200 Moscow, Russia (office). *Telephone:* (495) 244-47-15 (office). *Fax:*
(495) 244-92-39 (office). *E-mail:* saltanov@mid.ru (office). *Website:* www
.mid.ru (office).

SALVADOR CRESPO, María Isabel; Ecuadorean politician; *Minister of
External Relations, Trade and Integration;* b. 1962. *Career:* Minister of
Tourism 2005–07, of External Relations, Trade and Integration 2007–.
Address: Ministry of External Relations, Trade and Integration, Avenida
10 de Agosto y Carrión, Quito, Ecuador (office). *Telephone:* (2) 299-3201
(office). *Fax:* (2) 299-3288 (office). *E-mail:* webmast@mmrree.gov.ec
(office). *Website:* www.mmrree.gov.ec (office).

SALVESEN, (Charles) Hugh, PhD; British diplomatist; b. 10 Sept. 1955,
Scotland; m. Emilie Salvesen; two s. (twins). *Education:* Univ. of
Cambridge. *Career:* joined FCO 1982, Desk Officer, S Asian Dept
1982–84, First Sec., British Mil. Govt, Berlin 1984–85, First Sec., Chancery,
Bonn 1985–88, Desk Officer, Near East and N African Dept, FCO
1988–90, Head of Section, Western European Dept 1990–90, Head of
Political Section, UN Dept 1990–92, Asst Head of UN Dept 1992, Head of
Political Section, Buenos Aires 1993–96, Deputy High Commr, Wellington
1996–2000, Deputy Head of Econ. Policy Dept, FCO 2000–02, Sr Project
Man., later Head of FCO Services: Man. Consultancy, FCO 2002–04,
Amb. to Uruguay 2005–07 (left diplomatic service).
Address: c/o Foreign and Commonwealth Office, King Charles Street,
London, SW1A 2AH, England. *Telephone:* (20) 7008-1500.

SAMAK, Sundaravej; Thai politician; *Prime Minister;* b. 13 June 1935,
Bangkok; m. Khunying Surat Sundaravej; two c. *Education:* Thammasat
Univ. *Career:* mem. Democratic Party 1968–76; mem. Parl. 1973–76,
1979–83, 1986–90, 1992–2000, 2007–; Deputy Minister of Agriculture
1975–76, Deputy Minister of Interior 1976, Minister of Interior 1976–77, of
Transport 1983–86, 1990–91; Founder and Leader Prachakorn Thai party
1979–2000; Deputy Prime Minister 1992; Gov. of Bangkok 2000–03;
presenter of tv talk shows Chao Nee Tee Muang Thai (This Morning in
Thailand), Samak Dusit Kid Tam Wan (Daily Views) and radio talk show
Kho Tet Ching Wan Ni (The Facts of Today) 2006, also presenter tv
cooking show Tasting, Grumbling 2001–; Founder and Leader People
Power Party (PPP) (Palang Prachachan) 2007–; Prime Minister 2008–.
Address: Office of the Prime Minister, Government House, Thanon
Nakhon Pathom, Bangkok 10300 (office); People Power Party (PPP)
(Palang Prachachan), 1770 Thanon Petchaburi Tat Mai, Bang Gapi, Huay
Kwang, Bangkok 10310, Thailand. *Telephone:* (2) 280-3526 (office). *Fax:*
(2) 282-8792 (office). *E-mail:* webmaster@opm.go.th (office). *Website:*
www.opm.go.th (office); www.ppp.or.th.

SAMAR, Sima, DMed; Afghan politician and physician; *Chairperson,
Afghanistan Independent Human Rights Commission;* b. Feb. 1957,
Jaghoori, Ghazni. *Education:* Kabul Univ. *Career:* exiled in Pakistan

following Soviet invasion; Founder and Dir Shuhada Org., f. Shuhada
hosp. for Afghan women and children, Quetta, Pakistan 1989, founder of
three medical clinics, four hosps and girls' schools in rural Afghanistan
(also providing medical training, literacy programmes and food aid), f.
school for refugee girls in Quetta, f. Shuhada Org.; mem. Women Living
Under Muslim Law; political activist and opponent of women's subjuga-
tion under Taliban regime; Vice-Chair. and Minister of Women's Affairs,
Afghan Interim Authority 2001–02; currently Chair. Afghanistan Ind.
Human Rights Comm.; UN Special Rapporteur for Human Rights in
Sudan 2005–; Perdita Huston Human Rights Award, John Humphrey
Freedom Award 2001, UN Asscn of the Nat. Capital Area 2003, Jonathan
Mann Award for Health and Human Rights 2004, Profile in Courage
Award 2004, ranked by Forbes magazine amongst 100 Most Powerful
Women (74th) 2004, (28th) 2006, (92nd) 2007.
Address: Afghanistan Independent Human Rights Commission, Pul-i-
Surkh, Karti 3, Kabul (office); Shuhada Organization, Karte 3, Pule Surkh,
Kabul, Afghanistan. *Telephone:* (20) 2500676 (office); (20) 2501247. *Fax:*
(20) 2500677 (office). *E-mail:* aihrc@aihrc.org.af (office); sima_samar@
yahoo.com (home). *Website:* www.aihrc.org.af (office).

SAMARDŽIC, Vice Adm. Dragan; Montenegrin naval officer and govern-
ment official; *Chief of the General Staff of the Army of Montenegro;* b. 14
May 1963, Kotor; m. Branka Samardžic; one s. one d. *Education:* Naval
Acad., Gen. Staff School, War Coll., Belgrade. *Career:* commissioned as
Ensign in Montenegrin Navy, served aboard 401–type missile gun boats as
Weapons Officer, XO, CO and Commdr of Squadron 1985–95; various
positions in 18th Flotilla HQ including Chief of Staff and Deputy Flotilla
Commdr 1995–2001, Flotilla Commdr 2001–03; Deputy of Mil. Cabinet to
Pres. of State Union of Serbia and Montenegro, Belgrade 2003; Chief of
Staff Naval Corps and promoted to Flag Officer 2003–05; C-in-C Serbia
and Montenegro Navy 2005–06; Deputy Chief of Gen. Staff of the Army of
Montenegro 2006–07; Asst Minister for Material Resources, Ministry of
Defense 2007–08; Chief of the Gen. Staff of the Army of Montenegro
2008–; Cavaliere dell ordine al merito della erpubblica italiana; numerous
decorations from Montenegrin govt.
Address: Ministry of Defense, Jovana Tomasevica 29, 81000 Podgorica,
Montenegro (office). *Telephone:* (81) 483561 (home). *Fax:* (81) 224702
(office). *E-mail:* kabinet@mod.cg.yu (office). *Website:* www.vlada.cg.yu/
odbrana (office); www.vcg.cg.yu (office).

SAMBI, Ahmed Abdallah; Comoran politician, business executive and head
of state; *President;* b. 5 June 1958, Mutsamudu, Anjouan; m. Hadjira
Djoudi 1988; two s. five d. *Education:* in Saudi Arabia, Sudan and Hawzat
Al Qaaim Coll., Iran. *Career:* f. madras for girls 1986, imprisoned for 21
days following riot after closure of school by authorities in 1987; co-f. Ulézi
Radio and TV Ulézi 1990; co-f. National Front for Justice Party 1990, soon
left politics to concentrate on business activities; owner of factories
producing mattresses, bottled water, and perfume; Pres. of Comoros 2006–.
Address: Office of the Head of State, BP 521, Moroni, The Comoros
(office). *Telephone:* (74) 4808 (office). *Fax:* (74) 4829 (office). *Website:* www
.beit-salam.km (office).

SAMBI, Most Rev. Pietro, DST, DCL; Italian ecclesiastic and diplomatist;
Apostolic Nuncio to USA; b. 27 June 1938, Sogliano al Rubicone. *Career:*
ordained priest 1964; served in Diplomatic Corps in 1969 as attaché in
Cameroon, transferring to Jerusalem 1971, Cuba 1974, Algeria 1978,
Nicaragua 1979, Belgium 1981, India (with the rank of Counsellor) 1984;
Titular Archbishop of Bellicastrum 1985; Apostolic Pro-Nuncio to Burundi
1985–91, to Indonesia 1991–98, Apostolic Nuncio to Cyprus and Israel
(also accred as Apostolic Del. to Jerusalem and Palestine) 1998–2005,
Apostolic Nuncio to USA and Perm. Observer at OAS 2005–.
Address: Embassy of The Holy See, 3339 Massachusetts Avenue, NW,
Washington, DC 20008, USA (office). *Telephone:* (202) 333-7121 (office).
Fax: (202) 337-4036 (office). *E-mail:* nuntius@worldnet.att.net (office).

SAMBROOK, Richard, BA, MSc; British media executive; *Director, World
Service and Global News Division, BBC;* b. 24 April 1956, Canterbury; m.;
two c. *Education:* Oakwood Grammar School, Maidstone, Reading Univ.,
Birkbeck Coll. London Univ. *Career:* trainee journalist Thomson Regional
Newspapers 1977; spent three years with Celtic Press in Welsh Valleys and
South Wales Echo; joined BBC as sub-ed. in radio newsroom 1980, later
producer and programme ed. on nat. TV news, sr producer and deputy ed.
Nine O'Clock News, News Ed. BBC Newsgathering 1992–96, Head of
Newsgathering 1996–99, Deputy Dir News Div. 1999–2001, Dir BBC News
2001–04, Dir World Service and Global News Div. 2004–.
Address: BBC World Ltd, Woodlands, 80 Wood Lane, London, W12 0TT,
England (office). *Telephone:* (20) 8433-2000 (office). *Fax:* (20) 8743-9256
(office). *Website:* bbcworld.com (office).

SAMBU, Soares; Guinea-Bissau politician; *Minister of Natural Resources; Career:* Pres. Cttee on Agric., Fisheries, Natural Resources, Environment and Tourism 1997–98; mem. Cen. Cttee Partido Africano da Independência da Guiné e Cabo Verde (PAIGC), fmr Dir election campaign; mem. Nat. Ass., Deputy Speaker –2003; Minister of Foreign Affairs, Int. Co-operation and Communities 2004–05, of Natural Resources 2007–.
Address: Ministry of Natural Resources, CP 311, Bissau, Guinea-Bissau (office). *Telephone:* 215659 (office). *Fax:* 223149 (office).

SAMHAN, Mohammad Jasim, MA, MScS; United Arab Emirates diplomatist; b. 1950, Ras Al Khaimah; m.; four c. *Education:* Goddard Coll. and Syracuse Univ., USA. *Career:* worked for Dept of Water and Electricity 1966–68, with Nat. Oil Co. 1972–74; joined diplomatic corps 1974, with Consulate in Karachi 1975, then with del. to UN, rank of Counsellor 1981, with Consulate in Bombay 1981, rank of Minister Plenipotentiary; Dir Dept of Int. Orgs and Confs, Arab League 1982–84, Dept of Arab Homeland 1984–87, UAE Interests section Feb.–Nov. 1987; Perm. Rep. to Arab League 1988–90, also Amb. to Tunisia 1988–92; Perm. Rep. to UN, New York 1992–2001.
Address: c/o Ministry of Foreign Affairs, POB 1, Abu Dhabi, United Arab Emirates.

SAMORE, Gary S., BA, PhD; American academic and research institute director; *Vice President, Director of Studies, and Maurice R. Greenberg Chair, Council on Foreign Relations;* b. 31 March 1953, Brookline, Mass; m. Paula Samore; one d. *Education:* SUNY at Stony Brook, Harvard Univ. *Career:* Teaching Fellow, Govt Dept, Harvard Univ. 1979–82; worked at Rand Corpn 1980–82, at Lawrence Livermore Nat. Lab. 1984–86; Special Asst for Non-Proliferation and Nuclear Policy, US State Dept., Washington, DC 1987–92, Head of Office of Regional Non-Proliferation Affairs 1992–93, Deputy to Amb.-at-Large for Korean Affairs 1994–95; Special Asst to Pres. and Sr Dir for Non-Proliferation and Export Controls, Nat. Security Council 1996–2000; Dir of Studies and Sr Fellow for Non-Proliferation, IISS, London 2001–05; Vice-Pres. for Global Security and Sustainability, John D. and Catherine T. MacArthur Foundation, Chicago 2005–06; Vice-Pres., Dir of Studies and Maurice R. Greenberg Chair, Council on Foreign Relations 2006–; Sec. Defense Medal for Meritorious Civilian Service 1995.
Address: Council on Foreign Relations, 58 East 68th Street, New York, NY 10021, USA. *Telephone:* (212) 434-9627 (office). *E-mail:* gsamore@cfr.org (office). *Website:* www.cfr.org (office).

SAMPAIO, Jorge Fernando Branco de; Portuguese fmr head of state; b. 18 Sept. 1939; m. Maria José Ritta; one s. one d. *Career:* leader of students union and led protests against govt as student in Lisbon 1960–61; following graduation as lawyer defended several political prisoners; fmr mem. Socialist Left Movt then joined Socialist Party (PS), elected deputy Portueguese Nat. Parl. 1979, Pres. Parl. Bench 1986–87, Sec.-Gen. 1989–91; mem. European Comm. for Human Rights 1979–84; Mayor of Lisbon 1989–95; Pres. of Portugal 1996–2006; UN Special Envoy to Stop Tuberculosis 2006–07; UN High Rep. to the Alliance of Civilizations 2007–.
Address: Alliance of Civilizations, c/o United Nations, New York, NY 10017, USA (office). *Telephone:* (917) 367-5118 (office). *E-mail:* ContactAOC@unops.org (office). *Website:* www.unaoc.org (office).

SAMPERMANS, Françoise, LèsL; French business executive; *Publishing Consultant and Director, UPM-Kymmene;* b. 10 July 1947, Paris; one s. one d. *Career:* joined CIT-TRANSAC 1974; est. public relations service, Chapelle Darblay 1978; Head of Public Relations, Entreprise et Crédit 1981; Dir of Communications, Transmission, Group Thomson 1982; subsequently Deputy Dir, Dir of Communications, Alcatel CIT; Dir of Communications, Alcatel NV 1987, Alcatel Alsthom 1987; Dir-Gen. Générale Occidentale 1991–95; Pres. Dir-Gen. Groupe Express 1992–95; Vice-Pres. Québecor-Europe 1996–; Pres., Dir-Gen. Nouvel Economiste 1999–; Dir-Gen. Marianne and L'Evènement du Jeudi 1999–; Vice-Pres. Nouvelles Messageries de la Presse Parisienne 2000–04; mem. Bd UPM-Kymmene (Finland), currently Publishing Consultant, Dir; mem. Bd DATEM (France); Chevalier, Ordre des Arts et des Lettres.
Address: 18 rue Charles Silvestri, 94300 Vincennes, France.

SAMPHAN, Khieu (see Khieu Samphan).

SAMUELS, Richard J., AB, MA, PhD; American academic and research institute director; *Director, Center for International Studies, Massachusetts Institute of Technology;* b. 2 Nov. 1951; m. Debra G. Samuels; two s. *Education:* Colgate Univ., Tufts Univ., Mass Inst. of Tech. *Career:* Research Assoc., Center for Energy Policy Research, MIT 1980–86, Assoc. Prof. of Contemporary Tech. 1984–86, Asst Prof., Dept of Political Science 1980–84, Assoc. Prof. 1984–1990, Assoc. Dept. Head 1989–92, Head

1992–97, Ford Int. Prof. 1992–, Founder and Dir Japan Program 1981–, Dir MIT Center for Int. Studies 2000–; Vice-Chair. Cttee on Japan Nat. Research Council –1996; Chair. Japan-US Friendship Comm. 2001–; mem. Ed. and Advisory Bds Asian Survey, Journal of Int. and Area Studies, Social Science Japan; Outstanding Advisor of the Year MIT 2002. *Publications:* The Politics of Regional Policy in Japan: Localities Incorporated 1983, Getting America Ready for Japanese Science and Technology (co-ed.) 1986, The Business of the Japanese State: Energy Markets in Comparative and Historical Perspective (Masayoshi Ohira Prize 1988) 1987, Rich Nation, Strong Army: National security and the Technological Transformation of Japan (John Whitney Hall Prize 1996, Hiromi Arisawa Prize 1996) 1994, Crisis and Innovation in Asian Technology (co-ed.) 2003, Machiavelli's Children: Leaders and their Legacies in Italy and Japan (Marraro Prize 2004) 2003, Securing Japan: Tokyo's Grand Strategy and the Future of East Asia 2007.
Address: MIT Center for International Studies, 292 Main Street, Building E38–235, Cambridge, MA 02139 (office); 127 Woburn Street, Lexington, MA 02420, USA (home). *Telephone:* (617) 253-2449 (office); (781) 863-5181 (home). *Fax:* (617) 253-9330 (office). *E-mail:* samuels@mit.edu (office). *Website:* web.mit.edu/misti/mit-japan (office).

SAMUELSON, Paul Anthony, BA, MA, PhD, LLD, DLitt, DSc; American economist and academic; *Institute Professor Emeritus, Professor of Economics Emeritus and Gordon Y. Billard Fellow, Massachusetts Institute of Technology;* b. 15 May 1915, Gary, Ind.; m. 1st Marion E. Crawford 1938 (died 1978); four s. (including triplets) two d.; m. 2nd Risha Eckaus 1981. *Education:* Hyde Park High School Chicago, Univ. of Chicago and Harvard Univ., Cambridge, Mass. *Career:* Prof. of Econs at MIT 1940–65, Inst. Prof. 1966–85, Inst. Prof. Emer. 1986–, Gordon Y. Billard Fellow 1986, mem. Radiation Lab. Staff 1944–45; Visiting Prof. of Political Economy, New York Univ. 1987–; Consultant to Nat. Resources Planning Bd 1941–43, to War Production Bd 1945, to US Treasury 1945–52, 1961–74, to Rand Corpn 1949–75, to Council of Econ. Advisers 1960–68, to Fed. Reserve Bd 1965–, to Finance Cttee, NAS 1977–, to Loomis, Sayles & Co. Boston and to Burden Investors Services Inc.; mem. Research Advisory Bd Cttee for Econ. Devt 1960, Advisory Bd to Pres. Eisenhower's Comm. on Nat. Goals 1960, Nat. Task Force on Econ. Educ. 1960–61, Special Comm. on Social Sciences of Nat. Science Foundation 1967–68, Comm. on Money and Credit; Econ. Adviser to Pres. Kennedy during election campaign; author of report to Pres. Kennedy on State of American Economy 1961; Assoc. Ed. Journal of Public Econs, Journal of Int. Econs, Journal of Nonlinear Analysis; NAS Guggenheim Fellow 1948–49; mem. American Acad. of Arts and Sciences, American Economic Asscn (Pres. 1961), Int. Econ. Asscn (Pres. 1965–68, Lifetime Hon. Pres.); Fellow American Philosophical Soc., Econometric Soc. (Council mem., Vice-Pres. 1950, Pres. 1951); Corresp. Fellow British Acad.; Corresp. mem. Leibniz-Akad. der Wissenschaften und der Literatur; 34 hon. degrees; numerous awards including David A. Wells Prize 1941, John Bates Clark Medal 1947, Nobel Prize for Economic Science 1970, Albert Einstein Commemorative Award 1971, Alumni Medal, Univ. of Chicago 1983, Britannica Award 1989, Gold Scanno Prize, Naples 1990, Medal of Science 1996, John R. Commons Award 2000; MIT est. Paul A. Samuelson Professorship in Econs 1991. *Publications:* Foundations of Economic Analysis 1947, Economics 11 edns 1948–1980, 12th–18th edns (with William D. Norhaus) 1985–2005 (trans. into 40 languages), Readings in Economics (Ed.), seven edns 1955–73, Linear Programming and Economic Analysis (jtly) 1958, 1987, Collected Scientific Papers of Paul A. Samuelson (Vols I–V) 1966–86; author and jt author of numerous articles on econs.
Address: Massachusetts Institute of Technology, Department of Economics, E52-383, Cambridge, MA 02139, USA (office). *Telephone:* (617) 253-3368 (office). *Fax:* (617) 253-0560 (office). *Website:* econ-www.mit.edu (office).

SAMUKAI, Brownie J.; Liberian government official; *Minister of Defence; Education:* American Univ. *Career:* fmr Deputy Minister of Defense, Deputy Minister of State for Presidential Affairs; fmr Chief of Police; fled Liberia and worked with UN in East Timor and Tanzania; Minister of Defence 2006–.
Address: Ministry of Defence, Benson Street, POB 10-9007, 1000 Monrovia, Liberia (office). *Telephone:* 226077 (office).

SAN MIGUEL RODRIGUEZ, Walker, BA; Bolivian lawyer and government official; *Minister of National Defence;* b. 6 Aug. 1963, Ciudad de La Paz; m. Tatiana Núñez Ormachea. *Education:* Universidad Mayor de San Andrés, Univ. of Salamanca, Spain, Univ. of Nancy, France. *Career:* fmr Dir Lloyd Bolivian Airlines; fmr Exec. Chair. Colegio de Abogados de La Paz; Vice-Chair. Colegio Nacional de Abogados de Bolivia; Minister of Nat. Defence 2006–; mem. Nat. Acad. of Judicial Sciences of Bolivia, Inter-American Fed. of Lawyers.

Address: Ministry of National Defence, Plaza Avaroa, esq. Pedro Salazar y 20 de Octubre 2502, La Paz, Bolivia (office). *Telephone:* (2) 232-0225 (office). *Fax:* (2) 243-3153 (office). *E-mail:* comunicaciones@mindef.gov.bo (office). *Website:* www.mindef.gov.bo (office).

SANADER, Ivo, PhD; Croatian politician; *Prime Minister;* b. 8 June 1953, Split; m.; two d. *Education:* Univ. of Innsbruck, Austria. *Career:* Programme Ed., later Ed.-in-Chief Logos publishing house, Split 1983–88; mem. Editorial Bd Mogućnosti (Possibilities) magazine 1987–90; man. own cos, Innsbruck 1988–91; Gen. Man. Croatian Nat. Theatre, Split 1991–92; mem. Parl. (House of Reps of Croatian Parl.) 1992–, Minister of Science and Tech. 1992–93; Deputy Minister of Foreign Affairs 1993–95; Chief of Staff to Pres. of Repub. of Croatia and Sec.-Gen. Defence and Nat. Security Council 1995–96; Deputy Minister of Foreign Affairs 1996–2000; Prime Minister of Croatia 2003–; Pres. Croatian Democratic Union (Hrvatska Demokratska Zajednica—HDZ) 2000–; Deputy Chair. Foreign Affairs Cttee 2000; mem. Croatian Writers' Asscn, Croatian-PEN. *Publications:* author of several books on literary history and contemporary politics.
Address: Office of the Prime Minister, 10000 Zagreb, trg sv. Marka 2, Croatia (office). *Telephone:* (1) 4569220 (office). *Fax:* (1) 6303019 (office). *E-mail:* predsjednik@vlada.hr (office). *Website:* www.vlada.hr (office).

SANBERK, Özdem; Turkish diplomatist (retd); b. 1 Aug. 1938, Ankara; m. Sumru Sanberk; one d. *Education:* Lycée de Galatasaray, Faculty of Law, Univ. of Istanbul. *Career:* fmrly at Embassies in Bonn, Paris, Madrid; fmr Foreign Policy Adviser to Prime Minister Turgut Ozal; Amb. to EU 1987–91, to UK 1995–2000; fmr Under-Sec. to Ministry of Foreign Affairs 1990–95; Dir Turkish Econ. and Social Studies Foundation 2000–04, mem. Foreign Affairs Cttee 2004–; mem. Advisory Bd Euro Horizons (consulting firm); mem. Turkish-Armenian Reconciliation Comm., Turkish–Greek Forum; specialist on Turkish–EU relations, the Western Alliance, the Middle East second-track diplomacy and conflict resolution; broadcaster on domestic and foreign policy issues on radio and both Turkish and foreign TV; Comendador de la Orden de Mérito (Spain), Comendador de la Orden de Isabel la Católica (Spain); Verdienstmedaille des Verdienstordens (Germany). *Publications:* numerous articles in Turkish and int. newspapers.
Address: c/o Advisory Board, Euro Horizons, Karanfil Caddesi Mor Karanfil Sokak No:6, 34330 Levent - Istanbul, Turkey. *Website:* www.eurohorizons.com.

SANDE, Bernard Herbert, BA, MA, MBA; Malawi diplomatist; *Principal Secretary for Private Sector Development; Education:* Univ. of Malawi, Zomba, Inst. of Social Studies, The Hague, Netherlands, Univ. of Hull, UK. *Career:* fmr Prin. Sec. for Foreign Affairs; Amb. to USA 2004–06; Prin. Sec. for Pvt. Sector Devt 2006–.
Address: Ministry of Industry, Trade and Private Sector Development, PO Box 30366, Gemini House, City Centre, Lilongwe 3, Malawi (office). *Telephone:* (1) 770244 (office). *Fax:* (1) 770680 (office). *E-mail:* minci@malawi.net (office). *Website:* www.malawi.gov.mw (office).

SANDERS, Robin Renee, BA, MA, MS; American diplomatist; *Ambassador to Nigeria; Education:* Hampton Univ., Ohio Univ. *Career:* career mem. Sr Foreign Service, overseas postings have included Dominican Repub., Portugal, Sudan, Namibia, Senegal and Repub. of Congo with missions to Angola, Nigeria, S Africa, Democratic Repub. of Congo, Cameroon, Botswana, Mozambique, Rwanda, Zambia and Benin; served twice as Dir for Africa at Nat. Security Council, White House (under Pres. Bush 1988–89, and Pres. Clinton 1997–99); Chief of Staff and Sr Foreign Policy Advisor for mem. of House Int. Relations Cttee 1994–96; Special Asst for Latin America, Africa, and Int. Crime for Under-Sec. for Political Affairs, Dept of State 1996–97, Dir for Public Diplomacy for Africa 2000–02; Amb. to Repub. of Congo 2002–05; Int. Advisor and Deputy Commdt Industrial Coll. of Armed Forces, Nat. Defense Univ., Washington, DC –2007; Amb. to Nigeria 2007–; Nat. Bd mem. Operation Hope; Jt Chiefs of Staff Civilian Honor Award, three State Dept Superior Honor Awards, four State Dept Meritorious Honor Awards, 'President Merit of Honor Award' (Repub. of Congo).
Address: US Embassy, Plot 1075 Diplomatic Drive, Central District Area, Abuja, Nigeria (office). *Telephone:* (9) 4614000 (office). *Fax:* (9) 4614036 (office). *E-mail:* usabuja@pd.state.gov (office); pasinfoabuja@state.gov (office). *Website:* nigeria.usembassy.gov (office).

SANDERSON, Janet A., BA, MA; American diplomatist; *Ambassador to Haiti; Education:* Coll. of William and Mary, Williamsburg, Va, Coll. of Naval Warfare, Newport, RI. *Career:* mem. Sr Foreign Service since 1977, rank of Minister-Counselor, assigments have included Vice-Consul/Econ. Officer, Embassy in Dhaka, Agency for Int. Devt Liaison Officer in charge of US assistance programs in West Bank and Gaza, Tel-Aviv 1980–82, Petroleum Attaché, Kuwait 1982–84, Desk Officer for Kuwait and UAE

1984–86, Desk Officer, US Mission to OECD 1986–88, Econ. Counselor, Embassy in Amman 1989–92, Deputy Chief of Mission, Amman 1997–2000, Amb. to Algeria 2000–05, to Haiti 2006–; Superior Honor Award, Meritorious Honor Award, Herbert A. Salzman Award for Int. Econ. Performance 1996.
Address: Embassy of the USA, 5 Blvd Harry S. Truman, BP 1761, Bicentenaire- Port-au-Prince, Haiti (office). *Telephone:* 222-0200 (office). *Fax:* 223-9038 (office). *Website:* haiti.usembassy.gov (office).

SANDSCHNEIDER, Eberhard, PhD; German professor of international relations; *Otto Wolff Director of Research Institute, German Council on Foreign Relations; Education:* Saar Univ., Saarbrücken. *Career:* offered Chairs of Political Science by Univs of Potsdam, Erlangen-Nürnberg and Mainz; Prof. of Int. Relations, Univ. of Mainz 1995–98; Prof. of Chinese Politics and Int. Relations, Free Univ., Berlin 1998–, Dir Centre for Chinese and E Asian Politics; Otto Wolff Dir Research Inst., German Council on Foreign Relations 2003–. *Publications include:* 10 books as author or ed. including The Study of Modern China 1999, Chinese Cyberspaces: Technological Changes and Political Effects 2005; numerous contribs to academic journals.
Address: Research Institute, German Council on Foreign Relations, Rauchstr. 18, Berlin 10787, Germany (office). *Telephone:* (30) 25423125 (office). *Fax:* (30) 25423171 (office). *E-mail:* sandschneider@dgap.org (office). *Website:* www.dgap.org (office).

SANDSTRÖM, Sven, BA, MBA, PhD; Swedish banker and international finance official; *Member of the Council and Treasurer, World Conservation Union; Education:* Univ. of Stockholm, Stockholm School of Econs, Royal Inst. of Tech. *Career:* consultancy work 1966–68; Research Assoc., MIT and Harvard Business School, USA 1969–72; joined IBRD 1972, Project Analyst, Urban Projects Dept 1973, Deputy Div. Chief 1977, Div. Chief 1979, Div. Chief Urban Devt and Water Supply, S Asia Projects 1986, Dir Southern Africa Dept 1987–90, Dir Office of the Pres. 1990–91, Man. Dir 1991–2001, Chair. Operation Cttee, Chair. Information and Knowledge Man. Council; Secretariat Dir. Int. Task Force on Global Public Goods, Stockholm, 2003–06; Vice-Chair. Voluntary Replenishment Mechanism, Global Fund to Fight AIDS, Tuberculosis and Malaria; mem. Governing Council and Treas. World Conservation Union (IUCN); Coordinator and Chair. fo the replenishment of African Devt Fund of African Devt Bank; fmr Special Adviser to EU, Adviser to World Bank; mem. Bd of Dirs AES Corpn.
Address: IUCN Headquarters, Rue Mauverney 28, Gland 1196, Switzerland (office). *Telephone:* (22) 999-0000 (office). *Fax:* (22) 9990002 (office). *E-mail:* webmaster@iucn.org (office). *Website:* www.iucn.org (office).

SANÉ, Pierre Gabriel Michel, MSc, MBA; Senegalese administrator and UN official; *Assistant Director-General, United Nations Educational, Scientific and Cultural Organization (UNESCO);* b. 7 May 1948, Dakar; m. Ndeye Coumba Sow 1981; one s. one d. *Education:* Lycée Van Vollenhoven, Dakar, Ecole Supérieure de Commerce de Bordeaux, France, Ecole Nouvelle d'Organisation Economique et Sociale, Paris, London School of Econs, UK, Carleton Univ., Ottawa, Canada. *Career:* Vice-Pres. Fédération des Etudiants d'Afrique Noire en France 1971–72; auditor with audit firms in France 1973–77; Deputy Gen. Man. Société Sénégalaise Pharmaceutique (Senepharma) 1977–78; joined Int. Devt Research Centre (IDRC) 1978, various positions Ottawa, Nairobi and Dakar, to Regional Dir W and Cen. Africa, Dakar 1988–92; mem. Amnesty Int. 1988–, Sec.-Gen. 1992–2001; Asst Dir-Gen. UNESCO, Paris 2001–; Pres. PANAF 92 1991–92, Founding mem. Int. Cttee; winner, Concours Nat. de Commercialisation, France 1972. *Publications:* papers and reports on African devt, science and tech. and human rights research man. for IDRC.
Address: UNESCO, 1 rue Miollis, 75732 Paris Cedex 15, France (office). *Telephone:* 1-45-68-39-23 (office). *Fax:* 1-45-68-57-20 (office). *E-mail:* p.sane@unesco.org (office). *Website:* www.unesco.org (office).

SANFELICE DI MONTEFORTE, Vice Adm. Ferdinando; Italian naval officer; *Military Representative, NATO;* b. 18 May 1944, Rome; m. Claudia Cornaggia Medici Castiglioni; three d. *Education:* Italian Naval Acad., Jt Centre of High Defence Studies, Rome. *Career:* several appointments as Weapons Officer and Exec. Officer on board cruisers, frigates, corvettes; fmr Commdg Officer, corvette Alcione; fmr Commdg Officer, frigate Maestrale; assigned to Plans and Operations Dept, Navy Gen. Staff, Rome 1984–86; Naval Attaché and Liaison Officer to Saclant, Embassy in Washington, DC 1986–89; Commdr cruiser Andrea Doria 1989; Chief of Staff, Second Naval Div. 1990; promoted to Flag Officer 1992; fmr Head of Public Information Office and Comnavsouth, Navy Gen. Staff; ACOS Logistics and Admin Div.; fmr Multinational Logistic Commdr CTF 440 during Operation Sharp Guard; Flag Officer, Second Naval Div. 1996–98; Chief of Staff to CINC Italian Fleet/Comedcent 1998–2000; promoted to Vice Adm. 2000; Deputy Chief of Staff, SHAPE 2000–02; Commdr Naval

Forces Southern Europe 2002–04, Maritime Component Command Naples (Marcom Naples) 2004–05; Mil. Rep. to NATO and EU Mil. Cttees 2005–; Kt Commdr of Order for Merit of Repub. of Italy, Honour and Devotion Kt of Sovereign Mil. Order of Malta, Kt Commdr for Justice of Sacred Mil. Constantine Order of St Giorgio, Kt Commdr for Order of Merit of St John; Bronze Medal for Navy Merit, Silver Medal for Long Command Duty, Silver Medal for Long Sea Duty, NATO and WEU, medals for service in fmr Yugoslavia Operations, Officer US Legion of Merit.
Address: North Atlantic Treaty Organization (NATO), blvd. Léopold III, 1110 Brussels, Belgium (office). *Telephone:* (2) 707-4111 (office). *Fax:* (2) 707-4579 (office). *E-mail:* natodoc@hq.nato.int (office). *Website:* www .nato.int (office).

SANGALA, Aaron; Malawi politician; *Minister of National Defence; Career:* mem. Parl.; Deputy Minister of Health 2006–07; Deputy Minister of Women and Child Devt 2007–08; Minister of Nat. Defence 2008–.
Address: Ministry of National Defence, Private Bag 339, Capital Hill, Lilongwe 3, Malawi (office). *Telephone:* 8893906 (office). *Fax:* 1789600 (office). *E-mail:* defence@malawi.gov.mw (office). *Website:* www.malawi .gov.mw/Defence/Home%20Defence.htm (office).

SANHÁ, Issufo; Guinea-Bissau politician; *Minister of Finance; Career:* Minister of the Economy 1998–2007, of Finance 2007–; mem. Partido Africano da Independência da Guiné e Cabo Verde (PAIGC).
Address: Ministry of Finance, Rua Justino Lopes 74a, CP 67, Bissau, Guinea-Bissau (office). *Telephone:* 203670 (office). *Fax:* 203496 (office). *E-mail:* info@mail.guine-bissau.org (office). *Website:* www.guine-bissau .org (office).

SANT, Alfred, MSc, MBA, DBA; Maltese politician; *Leader, Malta Labour Party and Leader of the Opposition;* b. 28 Feb. 1948. *Education:* Univ. of Malta, Inst. Int. d'Admin Publique, Paris, Boston Univ. and Harvard Business School, USA. *Career:* Second Sec., First Sec., Malta Mission to European Communities, Brussels 1970–75; adviser on gen. and financial man. Ministry of Parastatal and People's Industries, Valletta 1977–78; Man. Dir Medina Consulting Group 1978–80; Exec. Deputy Chair. Malta Devt Corpn 1980–82; consultant to pvt. and public sectors 1982–; Chair. Metal Fond Ltd, Bottex Clothing 1982–84, First Clothing Cooperative 1983–87; Lecturer, Man. Faculty, Univ. of Malta 1984–87; Adviser to Prime Minister on econ. and diplomatic affairs 1985–87; Chair. Dept of Information, Malta Labour Party 1982–92; Pres. Malta Labour Party 1984–88, Leader 1992–; mem. Parl. 1987–; Prime Minister of Malta 1996–98; Leader of the Opposition 1998–. *Plays:* Fio. dell Tal-Katioral 1994, Oabel Tiftau L-Inujesta 1999. *Publications:* Min Hu Evelyn Costa? (plays) 1979, L-Ewwel Weraq tal-Bajtar (novel), Silg fuq Kemmuna (novel) 1985, Malta's European Challenge (essay) 1995, Bejgh u Xiri (novel) 1999, La Bidu, La Tmiem (novel) 2001, Confessions of a Maltese European 2003; contrib. articles in the press and professional publs.
Address: Malta Labour Party, National Labour Centre, Mile End Road, Hamrun HMR 02, Malta (home). *Telephone:* 21249900 (office). *Fax:* 21244204 (office). *E-mail:* segretarjat@mlp.org.mt (office); mtanti@mlp .org.mt (office); mlp@mlp.org.mt (home). *Website:* www.mlp.org.mt.

SANTAMARIA, Oscar Alfredo; Salvadorean politician and fmr international organization official. *Career:* Sec. Legislation Cttee Latin American Parl. (PARLATINO) 1977–78; Rep. Nationalist Republican Alliance at Int. Democratic Union; Presidential Chief-of-Staff and Chief Govt Negotiator with the FMLN 1993; Minister of Justice and Minister of the Presidency of the Republic 1989–94, Minister of Foreign Affairs 1994–95, also Head of Governmental Dialogue Comm. for Peace Negotiations with Farabundi Martí National Liberation Front –FMLN 1989–92 and Minister responsible for the process of Compliance with and Execution of the Peace Agreements by the Govt of El Salvador 1992–95; mem. Council of Ministers of Foreign Affairs of Cen. American Integration System (SICA) 1994–95, Sec.-Gen. 2000–04; Head of OAS Observer Mission in Nicaragua 1996.
Address: c/o Sistema de la Integración Centroamericana (SICA), boulevard de la Orden de Malta 470, Santa Elena, Antiguo Cuscatlán, San Salvador, El Salvador (office).

SANTANA CARLOS, António Nunes de Carvalho; Portuguese diplomatist; *Ambassador to UK;* b. 20 March 1945, Lisbon; m. Maria Santana Carlos; one s. *Education:* Univ. of Lisbon. *Career:* joined Foreign Service 1971, posts included Second Sec., Embassy in Tokyo 1974–76, Head of Cipher Dept, Foreign Office 1976, First Sec., Dept of Int. Econ. Orgs, Foreign Office 1979, served in Perm. Mission in Geneva, Switzerland 1982–86, Minister Counsellor, Luanda, Angola 1986–90, Dir Multilateral Affairs Dept, Foreign Office 1990–93, Deputy Dir-Gen. of Political and Econ. Affairs, Foreign Office 1993–94, Dir Office of Econ. Affairs 1994, Chargé de Mission to Minister of Foreign Affairs for Lisbon World Exhbn 1995, Sr

Rep. to China-Portugal Jt Liaison Group 1996, also served as Pres. Interministerial Comm. on Macau, Chargé de Mission to Minister of Foreign Affairs for East Timor affairs 2000–02, Dir-Gen. of Foreign Policy 2000–02, Amb. to People's Repub. of China (also accred to Mongolia) 2002–06, to UK 2006–; Grand Cross of the Order of Christ 2002, Grand Cross of the Order of Merit, Grand Officer of the Order Infante D. Henrique, Grand Officer of the Order Wissan Alouite (Morocco), Kt of the Order Rio Branco (Brazil).
Address: Embassy of Portugal, 11 Belgrave Square, London, SW1X 8PP, UK (office). *Telephone:* (20) 7235-5331 (office). *Fax:* (20) 7235-0739 (office); (20) 7245-1287 (office). *E-mail:* london@portembassy.co.uk (office).

SANTOS, Nelson, BA; Timor-Leste diplomatist; *Permanent Representative, United Nations;* b. 1968, Liquica; m.; three c. *Education:* Deakin Univ., Australia, Univ. of New South Wales. *Career:* officer, Macao Court of Relations 1995–97; Sr Officer Macao Interpol 1997–2001; Sec.-Gen. Ministry of Foreign Affairs and Co-operation 2002–06, Dir Bilateral Affairs 2002–07, Chair. successive jt ministerial comms between Timor-Leste and Indonesia; Perm. Rep. to UN, New York 2007–; . *Achievements:* successful negotiation of the Int. border between Timor-Leste and Indonesia.
Address: Permanent Mission of Timor-Leste to the United Nations, 866 Second Avenue, 9th Floor, New York, NY 10017, USA (office). *Telephone:* (212) 759-3675 (office). *Fax:* (212) 759-4196 (office). *E-mail:* timor-leste@ un.int (office). *Website:* www.un.int/timor-leste (office).

SANTOS CALDERÓN, Francisco; Colombian journalist and politician; *Vice-President;* b. 14 Oct. 1961, Bogotá. *Education:* Univ. of Kansas, Univ. of Texas at Austin, USA. *Career:* in late 1980s taught journalism and US–Latin American relations at several Colombian univs including Universidad Central, Universidad Javeriana, Universidad Jorge Tadeo Lozano; fmr Ed. El Tiempo (daily newspaper); kidnapped with other journalists by Pablo Escobar, leader of Medellín drug cartel 1990, held for eight months; Nieman Fellow, Harvard Univ. 1992; moved to Madrid, Spain and worked as journalist for daily newspaper El País 2000–02; Vice-Pres. of Colombia 2002–; co-f. Fundación Pais Libre (Free Country Foundation); Paul Harris Medal, Rotary Int.
Address: c/o Office of the President, Palacio de Nariño, Carrera 8a, No. 7–26, Bogotá, Colombia (office). *Telephone:* (1) 562-9300 (office). *Fax:* (1) 286-8063 (office).

SANTOS CALDERÓN, Juan Manuel; Colombian politician; *Minister of National Defence;* b. 10 Aug. 1951, Bogotá; m. María Clemencia Rodríguez; two s. one d. *Education:* Cartagena Naval Acad. of Colombia, Univ. of Kansas, USA, London School of Econs, UK, Harvard Univ., USA. *Career:* fmr leader Colombian Del. to Int. Coffee Org. negotiations, London; fmr journalist, Deputy Dir and Pres. Editorial Bd El Tiempo (daily); apptd Minister of Foreign Trade 1991; Vice-Pres. 1993; apptd Minister of Finance and Public Credit 2000; managed Pres. Alvaro Uribe's re-election campaign 2006; Minister of Nat. Defence 2006–; Pres. UNCTAD 1992–96, UN ECLA 1997–99; fmr Vice-Pres. Press Freedom Comm. of Inter-American Press Soc.; Founder and Chair. Fundación Buengobierno; Bernardo O'Higgins en el Grado de Comendador 1996, Gran Oficial de la Orden Nacional Francesca del Mérito 2001; Fulbright and Neiman Fellowships, King of Spain Prize for journalism. *Publications:* several books including The Third Way, An Alternative for Colombia.
Address: Ministry of National Defence, Centro Administrativo Nacional (CAN), Avda El Dorado carrera 52, Bogotá, DC, Colombia (office). *Telephone:* (1) 266-0185 (office). *Fax:* (1) 266-0351 (office). *E-mail:* yoljime@mindefensa.gov.co (office). *Website:* www.mindefensa.gov.co (office).

SANTOS LÓPEZ, Samuel; Nicaraguan politician; *Minister of Foreign Affairs;* b. 13 Dec. 1938, Managua; m. Annelly Molina de Santos. *Career:* early business career with several managerial roles including roles at Publicidad Noble y Asociados, Honduras, Hotel Best Western Las Mercedes, Inversiones Inmobiliaras Acuario S.A., Inmobiliarios Penta S.A., Inmobiliarios Alpha S.A., Inmobiliarios Beta S.A; Founder and fmr Dir Stock Market of Nicaragua; mem. Nat. Govt for Reconstruction 1979–85; Vice-Pres. Nat. Devt Bank 1979–80; Minister in charge of Reconstruction of Managua 1980–85; Mayor of Managua 1984–85; Finance Sec. Frente Sandinista de Liberación Nacional (FSLN) 1992–, Exec. Sec. –2001, Int. Relations Spokesperson 2001–06; Minister of Foreign Affairs 2007–; mem. Chamber of Commerce, Chamber of Tourism, Union of Latin American Capital Cities, Exec. Cttee of the Bolivian Congress for Town Devt, Works Comm. for the Inter-Oceanic Canal of Nicaragua.
Address: Ministry of Foreign Affairs, Del Cine González al Sur sobre Avenida Bolivar, Managua, Nicaragua (office). *Telephone:* (2) 244-8000

(office). *Fax:* (2) 228-5102 (office). *E-mail:* samuel.santos@cancilleria.gob
.ni (office). *Website:* www.cancilleria.gob.ni (office).

SANTOS-NEVES, Augusto R., BA, MBA; Brazilian diplomatist; *Ambassador to UK;* b. 1944, Rio de Janeiro; m. Mary Joan Hershberger; two s. one d. *Education:* Instituto Rio Branco, Fundação Getulio Vargas, Columbia Univ., USA. *Career:* joined diplomatic service 1966, Asst to Foreign Minister 1977–79, Chief of Staff to Sec. Gen. of Foreign Ministry 1985–88; Consul Gen. in New York 1988–92; Amb. to Mexico 1992–96 (also accred. to Belize 1995–96), to Canada 1996–99; Sec. for Policy Planning, Foreign Ministry 1999–2001, Consul Gen. in Houston, Tex. 2001–03, Amb. to Russian Fed. 2003–08 (also accred. to Kazakhstan, Belarus, Georgia, Turkmenistan and Uzbekistan), to UK 2008–; Légion d'honneur, Ordre national du Mérite, Order of Rio Branco.
Address: Embassy of Brazil, 32 Green Street, London, W1K 7AT, England (office). *Telephone:* (20) 7399-9000 (office). *Fax:* (20) 7399-9100 (office). *E-mail:* info@brazil.org.uk (office). *Website:* www.brazil.org.uk (office).

SANTOS RIVERA, Rebeca Patricia; Honduran politician; *Minister of Finance; Career:* fmr consultant, Honduran Social Security Inst.; consultant, World Bank Resident Mission in Honduras –2006; Minister of Finance 2006–.
Address: Ministry of Finance, 5A Avda, 3A Calle, Tegucigalpa, Honduras (office). *Telephone:* 222-1278 (office). *Fax:* 238-2309 (office). *E-mail:* despacho@sefin.gob.hn (office). *Website:* www.sefin.gob.hn (office).

SANTOS SIMÃO, Leonardo; Mozambican politician and medical practitioner; *Executive Director, Joaquim Chissano Foundation;* b. 6 June 1953, Mandlakaze; m. Josephine P. Simão; two d. *Education:* Liceu Salazar, Maputo, Eduardo Mondlane Univ., Univ. of London, UK, Boston Univ., USA. *Career:* Dir Centre of Dist Formation of Chicumbane, Gaza 1981–1982; Prov. Health Dir Zambezia Prov. 1982–84; Dir Prov. Hosp. of Quelimane, Zambezia Prov. 1984–88; Minister of Health 1988; apptd Prof. of Medicine, Eduardo Mondlane Univ. 1988; Minister of Foreign Affairs and Co-operation 1994–95; currently Exec. Dir Joaquim Chissano Foundation; Chair. Nat. Mine Clearance Comm.; mem. Cen. Cttee Frelimo Party; mem. Medical Asscn of Mozambique, Mozambique Asscn of Public Health; Great Cross, Order of Rio Branco (Brazil) 1996, Order of Good Hope, II Grade (South Africa) 1997, Great Cross, Order of Merit (Portugal) 1998.
Address: The Joaquim Chissano Foundation, 954, Av. Zimbabwe, Maputo, Mozambique (office). *Telephone:* (21) 484000 (office). *Fax:* (21) 484001 (office). *E-mail:* l.simao@fjchissano.org.mz (office). *Website:* www
.fjchissano.org.mz (office).

SANZ ROLDAN, Army Gen. Felix; Spanish army official; b. 20 Jan. 1945, Uclés, Cuenca; m. María del ilar Justel Parandones; three c. *Education:* Mil. Acad., Gen. Staff Coll. *Career:* First Lt in 254th Artillery Class 1966; assigned to El Aauin, Spanish Sahara 1966–67; Exec. Officer in Multiple Rocket Launcher Battery and Hawk Ada Missile Battery 1967–73; promoted to Capt. 1973, assigned to 11th Field Artillery Regiment; fmr Asst Operations Staff Officer, 12th Armoured Brigade; fmr Commdr, US-Spanish Jt Combined Planning Staff; fmr Commdr, HQ Battery; fmr Commdr, Services Battery of 11th Self-Propelled Artillery Battalion; promoted to Maj. 1983; Instructor, Field Artillery Branch, Artillery Acad. 1983–86; Asst Mil. Attaché to Embassy in Washington, DC 1986; fmr Staff Officer, Plans and Policy Div. of Army Staff, Madrid; promoted to Lt-Col 1989; fmr Br. Chief in Int. Relations, Plans and Policy Div., Army Staff; Chief of NATO/UEO Branch, Directorate for Defence Policy 1997–98; promoted to Brig.-Gen. 1998; Deputy Dir Gen. for Defence Policy (Int. Affairs), Ministry of Defence 1998–2004, Dir Gen. 2004; promoted to Maj. Gen. 2001; promoted to Lt-Gen. 2004; promoted to Army Gen. 2004; Chief of Defence Staff, NATO 2004–08.
Address: c/o Ministry of Defence, Paseo de la Castellana 109, 28071 Madrid, Spain (office).

SAPIN, Michel; French politician; b. 9 April 1952, Boulogne-Billancourt; m. Yolande Millan 1982; three c. *Education:* Ecole Normale Supérieure, Paris and Ecole Nat. d'Admin. *Career:* joined Parti Socialiste 1975; elected Deputy Nat. Ass. for Indre 1981–86, 2007–, for Hauts-de-Seine 1986–91, Sec. 1983–84, Vice-Pres. 1984, Chair. of the Cttee for Law 1988–91; town councillor, Nanterre 1989–94; Minister Del. for Justice 1991–92; Minister of Economy and Finance 1992–93, of Civil Service, of Admin. Reform 2000–02; Regional Councillor Ile de France 1992–94; mem. Council for Monetary Policy of Banque de France 1994–95; Mayor of Argenton-sur-Creuse 1995–2004; Gen. Councillor of Indre 1998–; Pres. Centre Regional Council 1998–2000, 2004–07, Vice-Pres. 2000–01; First Vice-Pres. Asscn of the Regions of France 1998–2000; Nat. Sec. on Economy, Parti Socialiste 2007–.

Address: Assemblée Nationale, 126 Rue de l'Université 753555 Paris (office). *Telephone:* 1-40-63-93-16 (office). *E-mail:* msapin@assemblee-nationale.fr (office). *Website:* www.assemblee-nationale.fr (office).

SARDO, Gabriele; Italian diplomatist; *Ambassador to Canada;* b. 9 Jan. 1944, Trieste. *Education:* Univ. of Trieste. *Career:* entered Foreign Service 1968; assigned to Directorate General for Political Affairs 1970–73, 1982–84, 1991; served in Hon. Minister's Cabinet 1975–77; posted to Mexico City 1977–82; First Counsellor in Washington, DC 1984; served in Directorate Gen. for Emigration and Social Affairs; Minister Plenipotentiary 1994–96; Deputy Head, Minister's Cabinet 1996–98; Head, Perm. Representation to UNESCO, Paris 1998–2002; Diplomatic Counsellor for Minister for Environment and Protection of Natural Resources, Rome 2002–06; Amb. to Canada 2006–.
Address: Embassy of Italy, 275 Slater Street, 21st Floor, Ottawa, ON K1P 5H9, Canada (office). *Telephone:* (613) 232-2401 (office). *Fax:* (613) 233-1484 (office). *E-mail:* ambasciata.ottawa@esteri.it (office). *Website:* www
.ambottawa.esteri.it (office).

SARKISSIAN, Serge; Armenian politician and head of state; *President;* b. 30 June 1954, Xankandi (Stepanakert, Nagornyi Karabakh ASSR, Azerbaijan SSR); m. Rita Sarkissian 1983; two d. *Education:* Yerevan State Univ. *Career:* USSR army 1972–74; metal turner, Electrical Devices Factory, Yerevan 1975–79; Komsomol Sec., Head of Propaganda section City Cttee, Xankandi 1979–88; Head Self-Defence Cttee, Nagornyi Karabakh 1989–93; Deputy Supreme Council (Parl.) 1990–93, Minister of Defence 1993–95, 2000–07, of Nat. Security 1995–96, 1999, of Internal Affairs and Nat. Security 1996–99; Chief of Staff to Pres. 1999–2000; Sec. Council of Nat. Security 1999–2007; mem. Republican Party of Armenia (RPA) 2006–, Chair. Party Council 2006–07, Chair. RPA 2007–; Prime Minister 2007–08; Pres. of Armenia 2008–; Chair. Bd of Trustees, Yerevan State Univ.; Chair. Chess Federation of Armenia; Order of Martakan Khach, Kt of the Golden Eagle Order, Hero of Artsakh, Armenian Battle Cross, Tigran Mets.
Address: Office of the President, 375077 Yerevan, Marshal Baghramian Street, Armenia (office). *Telephone:* (10) 52-02-04 (office). *Fax:* (10) 52-15-51 (office). *E-mail:* frd@gov.am (office). *Website:* www.president.am/president/eng (office). www.serzhsargsyan.com.

SARKISSIAN, Tigran, PhD; Armenian politician and central banker; *Prime Minister;* b. 29 Jan. 1960, Kirovakan (now Vanadzor); m.; two c. *Education:* Financial and Econ. Inst. after Voznesenski, Leningrad, USSR. *Career:* Chief of Dept for Foreign Econ. Relations, Scientific Researches Inst. of Econ. Planning 1987–90; Chair. Republican Council of Young Specialists and Scientists 1988–93; mem. Supreme Council of the Repub. of Armenia and Chair. of Standing Comm. for Financial, Credit and Budget Affairs 1990–95; Dir of Scientific Researches Inst. of Social Reforms 1995–98; Chair. Armenian Banks Asscn 1995–98; Chair. Cen. Bank of Armenia 1998–2008; Prime Minister 2008–.
Address: Office of the Prime Minister, 0010 Yerevan, Republic Square 1, Government House, Armenia (office). *Telephone:* (10) 52-03-60 (office). *Fax:* (10) 15-10-35 (office). *Website:* www.gov.am/enversion/premier_2/primer_home.htm (office).

SARKISYAN, Armen, CandPhys-MathSc; Armenian academic, politician and diplomatist; b. 1953, Yerevan; m.; two s. *Education:* Yerevan State Univ. *Career:* Docent, Yerevan State Univ. 1979–84; researcher Cambridge Univ. UK 1984–85; Lecturer, Yerevan State Univ. 1985–90, Head Dept of Math. Modelling; Prof., London Univ. 1992–; apptd. Chargé d'affaires, then Amb. to UK 1992–2000; Amb., Doyen of Armenian Diplomatic Corps to Europe (also accred to Belgium, Netherlands, Vatican City, Luxembourg) 1993–96; Prime Minister 1996–97; mem. IISS, London; Hon. Mem. Royal Soc. of Int. Relations and Cen. of Strategic Studies, Oxford Univ. *Publications:* author of numerous articles on politology, theoretical physics, astronomy and math. modelling.
Address: c/o Ministry of Foreign Affairs, Government House 2, Republic Square 1, 375010 Yerevan, Armenia.

SARKÖZY DE NAGY BOCSA, Nicolas Paul Stéphane; French politician, barrister, civil servant and head of state; *President;* b. 28 Jan. 1955, Paris; m. 1st Marie-Dominique Culioli 1982 (divorced 1996); two s.; m. 2nd Cecilia Ciganer-Albeniz 1996 (divorced 2007); one s.; m. 3rd Carla Bruni 2008. *Education:* Inst. of Political Studies, Paris, Paris Univ. *Career:* barrister, Paris 1981–87; Assoc., Leibovici Claude Sarközy 1987; mem. RPR Cen. Cttee 1977–, Nat. Del. 1978–79, Nat. Sec. 1988–90, Asst Sec.-Gen. 1990–93; Town Councillor, Neuilly-sur-Seine 1977–83, Mayor 1983–; Pres. Nat. Cttee Jacques Chirac's presidential campaign 1981; Regional Councillor, Ile-de-France 1983–88; RPR Deputy to Nat. Ass. from Hauts-de-Seine 1988–93, 1993–95, 1997–2007; Chief Spokesman of RPR 1997–2007; Minister of the Budget 1993–94, of Communications

1994–95, of the Interior and Security 2002–04, of the Economy, Finance and Industry 2004–05, of the Interior, Internal Security and Local Freedoms 2005–07 (resgnd); Pres. of France 2007–, Co-Prince of Andorra 2007–; mem. RPR Political Office 1995, Sec.-Gen. RPR 1998–99, Interim Pres. April–Oct. 1999, Pres. RPR Regional Cttee of Hauts-de-Seine 2000–; Leader RPR-DL List, European Elections 1999; Pres. Union pour un Mouvement Populaire (UMP) 2004–07; Chevalier, Légion d'honneur 2004, Grand Cross of the Légion d'honneur 2007, Grand Cross of the Ordre national du Mérite 2007, Stara Planina (Bulgaria) 2007, Commdr Ordre de Léopold (Belgium). *Publications:* Georges Mandel, moine de la politique 1994, Au bout de la passion, l'équilibre (co-author) 1995, Libre 2001, Témoignage 2006.
Address: Office of the President, Palais de l'Elysée, 55–57 rue du Faubourg Saint Honoré, 75008 Paris, France (office). *Telephone:* 1-42-92-81-00 (office). *Fax:* 1-47-42-24-65 (office). *Website:* www.elysee.fr (office); www .sarkozy.fr.

SARMADI, Morteza, BSc, MA; Iranian politician and diplomatist; *Deputy Foreign Minister for Euro-American Affairs;* b. July 1954, Tehran; m. Fatima Hosseini 1982; four d. *Education:* Sharif Univ., Tehran. *Career:* joined Ministry of Foreign Affairs 1981, Dir-Gen. of Press and Information 1982–89, Deputy Foreign Minister for Communication 1989–97, Deputy Foreign Minister for Europe and America 1997–, Amb. to UK 2000–05, Deputy Foreign Minister for Euro-American Affairs 2005–; Sr Del. Iran-Iraq peace talks; Trustee, Islamic Thought Foundation, Islamic Repub. News Agency, Islamic High Council of Propagation Policy, Inst. for Political and Int. Studies. *Publications:* numerous political articles.
Address: Ministry of Foreign Affairs, Shahid Abd al-Hamid Mesri Street, Ferdowsi Avenue, Tehran Iran (office). *Telephone:* (21) 61151 (office). *Fax:* (21) 33212763 (office). *E-mail:* matbuat@mfa.gov.ir (office). *Website:* www .mfa.gov.ir (office).

SARRAJ, Eyad Rajab el-, PhD; Palestinian human rights activist and psychiatrist; *Medical Director, Gaza Community Mental Health Programme;* b. Beersheva; m.; two c. *Education:* Inst. of Psychiatry, London Univ., Harvard Univ. *Career:* Founder and Medical Dir Gaza Community Mental Health Programme; Co-Founder and Commr-Gen. Palestinian Independent Comm. for Citizens' Rights; arrested three times for criticism of Palestinian Nat. Authorities; mem. Int. Rehabilitation Centre for Torture Victims; mem. Co-ordinating Cttee Campaign Against Torture Victims; Trustee Palestinian Initiative for the Promotion of Global Dialogue and Democracy (MIFTAH); fmr mem. Int. Council on Human Rights Policy; Martin Ennals Award for Human Rights Defenders 1998. *Publications:* numerous articles in journals and newspapers.
Address: Gaza Community Mental Health Programme, POB 1049, Gaza, Palestinian Autonomous Areas. *Telephone:* (7) 2865949 (office). *Fax:* (7) 2824072 (office). *E-mail:* eyad@gcmhp.net (office). *Website:* www.gcmhp .net (office).

SARUKHAN CASAMITJANA, Arturo, BA, MA; Mexican diplomatist; *Ambassador to USA;* m. Verónica Valencia. *Education:* Colegio de México, Nacional Autónoma de México, Johns Hopkins Univ., Washington, DC. *Career:* Exec. Sec., Ford Foundation Bilateral Comm. on the Future of Mexico–USA Relations 1988–89; Adviser to Sec. of Foreign Affairs 1991, Dir for Inter-American Negotiation, Ministry of Foreign Affairs 1992, Sr Adviser to Sec. of Foreign Affairs 1998, Chief of Staff to Sec. of Foreign Affairs 2000; Chief of Staff, Embassy in Washington, DC 1993, Head of counter-narcotics and law enforcement section 1994; Nat. Coordinator for Multilateral Evaluation Mechanism against Illicit Drugs (MEM), OAS 2000; Consul-Gen. in New York 2003–06, Amb. to USA 2006–; mem. Mexican Council on Foreign Relations, IISS; Fellow, Foreign Policy Asscn, USA; has lectured at Instituto Tecnológico Autónomo de México, Center for Advanced Naval Studies of Mexico, Nat. Defense Coll. of Mexico, Inter-American Defense Coll., Nat. Defense Univ., Washington, DC; Dr hc (Marian Coll., USA); Order of Civil Merit, Officers Degree (Spain), Order of the Polar Star, Commdr Degree (Sweden).
Address: Embassy of Mexico, 1911 Pennsylvania Avenue, NW, Washington, DC 20006, USA (office). *Telephone:* (202) 728-1600 (office). *Fax:* (202) 234-1698 (office). *E-mail:* mexembusa@sre.gob.mx (office). *Website:* www .sre.gob.mx/eua (office).

SASSEN, Saskia, MA, PhD; American sociologist and academic; *Robert S. Lynd Professor of Sociology, Columbia University;* b. 1949, The Hague, Netherlands; m. Richard Sennett. *Education:* Université de Poitiers, Univ. of Notre Dame. *Career:* fmr Ralph Lewis Prof. of Sociology, Univ. of Chicago; Centennial Visiting Prof., LSE; currently Robert S. Lynd Prof. of Sociology, Univ. of Columbia; Visiting Scholar Russell Sage Foundation, Woodrow Wilson Int. Center for Scholars, Center for Advanced Study in the Behavioral Sciences; Dir project on global cities and cross-border networks, Inst. of Advanced Studies, UNU, Tokyo; Co-Dir Economy

Section, Global Chicago Project; mem. Social Science Research Council (SSRC) Working Group on New York City sponsored by Russell Sage Foundation 1985–90, SSRC Cttee on Hispanic Public Policy sponsored by Ford Foundation 1987–91, New York-London Comparative Study sponsored by UK Econ. and Social Research Council, UN Centre on Regional Devt and MIT-sponsored project on Economic Restructuring in the US and Japan 1988–90, Research Working Group on Informal Sector, Stanford Univ. Project on Mexico–US Relations, Immigration and Econ. Sociology Project (Russell Sage Foundation) 1992–95, Comparative Urban Studies Project, Woodrow Wilson Center 1992–, Group of Lisbon sponsored by Science Program of EU and Gulbenkian Foundation 1993–, NAS Panel on Urban Data Sets, Council of Foreign Relations; Chair. Information Tech., Int. Co-operation and Global Security Cttee of the SSRC; mem. Advisory Panel, Queens Borough, Pres. Claire Shulman's Blue Ribbon Panel on Govt, NY State Industrial Corpn Council; mem. French Govt's Ministry of Urban Affairs scientific jury, Belgian Govt's Agency on Science and Tech. in the Office of the Prime Minister; mem. several editorial bds; Fellow American Bar Foundation, Wissenschaftszentrum, Berlin; recipient of awards from the Ford Foundation, Tinker Foundation, Revson Foundation, Chicago Inst. for Architecture and Urbanism, Twentieth Century Fund; Nat. Prize of the American Inst. of Certified Planners; Distinguished Lecturer, Inst. for Advanced Studies, Vienna, Henry Luce Lecturer, Clark Univ. *Publications include:* The Mobility of Labor and Capital 1988, The Global City 1991, Cities in a World Economy 1994, Losing Control? Sovereignty in an Age of Globalization 1996, Migranten, Siedler, Flüchtlinge, Globalization and its Discontents – Selected Essays 1984–98 1998, Guests and Aliens 1999, Global Networks/Linked Cities 2002, Denationalization: Economy and Policy in a Global Digital Age 2003, Territory, Authority, Rights: From Medieval to Global Assemblages 2006; books translated into 16 languages. *Address:* Department of Sociology, Columbia University, 412 Fayerweather Hall, 1180 Amsterdam Avenue, New York, NY 10027, USA (office). *Telephone:* (212) 854-0790 (office). *Fax:* (212) 854-2963 (office). *E-mail:* sjs2@columbia.edu (office). *Website:* www.sociology.columbia.edu (office).

SASSOU-NGUESSO, Gen. Denis; Republic of the Congo army officer and head of state; *President;* b. 1943, Edou. *Career:* joined Congolese Armed Forces 1960, mil. training in Cen. Africa, Algeria and France 1961–68; mem. Parti Congolais du Travail (PCT) 1970–, First Vice-Pres., Mil. Cttee Parti Congolais du Travail (PCT), co-ordinator of PCT activities 1977–79, Pres. PCT 1979–, Leader, Forces Démocratiques Unies (alliance of six parties including PCT) 1994–95; Minister of Defence 1975; Pres. of the Republic of the Congo 1979–92, 1997–; Chair. African Union 2006–07.
Address: Palais du Peuple, Brazzaville, Republic of the Congo (office). *Telephone:* 81-17-11 (office). *E-mail:* contact@presicongo.cg (office). *Website:* www.presidence.cg (office).

SATHIRATHAI, Surakiart, LLM, MALD, SJD; Thai politician and economist; b. 7 June 1958, Bangkok; m. Thanpuying Dr. Suthawan Sathirathai; one s. *Education:* Chulalongkorn Univ., Tufts Univ., Harvard Univ., USA. *Career:* policy adviser to Prime Minister 1988–92, to Nat. Ass. 1989–91, to Prime Minister on econ. affairs 1991–92; Co-founder Siam Premier Int. Law Office Ltd 1990, Chair. Exec. Bd 1990–2001; Dean and Assoc. Prof., Chulalongkorn Univ. 1992–95; Chair. Crown Property Bureau, Securities Exchange Comm., House Select Cttee on Budget Review 1995–96, PTTEP Co. Ltd 1998–2000, Laem Thong Bank Co. Ltd 1998–99, Petroleum Authority of Thailand, Thai Oil Co. Ltd 1999–2000; Minister of Finance 1995–96; Vice-Chair. of Prime Minister's Advisory Council on Econ. and Foreign Affairs 1996–97; Councillor of State 1997–2001; Pres. Inst. of Social and Econ. Policy (ISEP) 1997–2001; Chair. Foundation for the Inst. of Social and Econ. Policy 1999–2001; Minister of Foreign Affairs 2001–05; Deputy Prime Minister 2005–06; Kt Grand Cordon (Special Class) of the Most Noble Order of the Crown of Thailand, Kt Grand Cross (First Class) of the Most Exalted Order of the White Elephant.
Address: c/o Siam Premier International Law Office Limited, 26th Floor, The Offices at Central World, 999/9 Rama 1 Road, Pathumwan, Bangkok 10330, Thailand. *Website:* www.siamlaw.co.th.

SATOH, Yukio, BA; Japanese diplomatist; *President, Japan Institute of International Affairs;* b. 6 Oct. 1939; m.; two c. *Education:* Tokyo Univ. and Univ. of Edinburgh, UK. *Career:* entered Foreign Service 1961, with Ministry of Foreign Affairs, Tokyo, then Embassy, Washington, DC –1976, Dir Div. of Security Affairs, American Affairs Bureau, Ministry of Foreign Affairs 1976–77, Pvt. Sec. to the Foreign Minister 1977–79, Counsellor, London 1981–84, also Consul-Gen., Dir Policy Coordination Div. 1985–87, Asst Vice-Minister for Parl. Affairs, Ministry of Foreign Affairs 1987–88; Chief of Prefectural Police, Miyazaki 1984–85; Consul-Gen., Hong Kong 1988–90; Dir-Gen. North American Affairs Bureau and Dir-Gen. Information Analysis, Research and Planning Bureau, Ministry

of Foreign Affairs 1990–94, Amb. to the Netherlands 1994–96, to Australia 1996–98; Perm. Rep. to the UN 1998–2002; currently Pres. The Japan Inst. of Int. Affairs.
Address: The Japan Institute of International Affairs, Kasumigaseki Building 11 Floor, 3-2-5 Kasumigaseki, Chiyoda-ku, Tokyo, 100-6011, Japan (office). *Telephone:* (03) 3503-6625 (office). *Fax:* (03) 3503-7411 (office). *E-mail:* info@jiia.or.jp (office). *Website:* www.jiia.or.jp/en.

SATTAR, Abdul, MA; Pakistani diplomatist; b. 1931; m. Yasmine Sattar 1955; one s. two d. *Education:* Punjab Univ. and Fletcher School, USA. *Career:* served in Pakistan Missions in Saudi Arabia, Sudan and the USA; Amb. of Pakistan to Austria 1975–78, to India 1978–82, 1990–92, to USSR 1988–90; Dir, then Dir-Gen. and Additional Sec. at Foreign Office, for Asia 1982–86; Foreign Sec., Islamabad 1986–88; Sr Del. to Geneva Talks on Afghanistan 1988; Minister of Foreign Affairs 1999–2002; Distinguished Fellow, US Inst. of Peace, Washington, DC 1994; mem. Nat. Security Council. *Publications:* Pakistan in Perspective, 1947–97 (co-author); articles in learned journals on nuclear non-proliferation and regional studies.
Address: House 7, College Road, F-7/3, Islamabad, Pakistan (home). *Telephone:* (51) 2270476 (home). *Fax:* (51) 2270476 (home). *E-mail:* sattara@comsats.net.pk (home).

SATTERFIELD, David M., BA; American diplomatist; *Senior Advisor to the Secretary of State and Coordinator for Iraq;* b. Baltimore. *Education:* Univ. of Maryland, Georgetown Univ. *Career:* joined US State Dept. 1980, served in Saudi Arabia, Tunisia, Lebanon and Syria and staff mem. Bureau of Near Eastern Affairs, Bureau of East Asian and Pacific Affairs and Intelligence and Research; Dir for Exec. Secretarial Staff and for Near East and South Asian Affairs, Nat. Security Council 1993–96; Dir Office of Israel and Arab-Israeli Affairs 1996–98; Amb. to Lebanon 1998–2001, Deputy Asst Sec. for Near Eastern Affairs 2001–04, Prin. Deputy Asst. Sec. of State for Near Eastern Affairs 2004–05; Deputy Chief of Mission, Embassy in Baghdad 2005–06; Sr Advisor to Sec. of State and Coordinator for Iraq 2006–; Presidential Meritorious Exec. Rank Award, Dept of State Distinguished Honor Award, Dept Sr Performance Award, six Dept of State Superior Honor Awards.
Address: Department of State, 2201 C Street, NW, Washington, DC 20520, USA (office). *Telephone:* (202) 647-5056 (office). *Fax:* (202) 647-6738 (home). *Website:* www.state.gov (office).

SATYANAND, Hon. Anand, PCNZM, QSO, BL; New Zealand lawyer, judge and government official; *Governor-General;* b. 22 July 1944, Auckland; m. Susan Satyanand; three c. *Education:* Univ. of Auckland Law School. *Career:* admitted to the Bar 1970; practised law with Crown Solicitors' Office and Pnr, pvt. law practice; Dist Court Judge, Palmerston N and Auckland, with specialist warrant for criminal jury trials 1982–94; Parl. Ombudsman 1995–2005; Gov.-Gen. of NZ 2006–; Chair. Confidential Forum for Fmr In-Patients of Psychiatric Hosps –2006; Registrar of Pecuniary Interests of Mems of Parl. –2006; mem. Bd of Dirs NZ Inst. of Int. Affairs, Transparency Int.; fmr exec. NZ Rugby League; Prin. Companion of NZ Order of Merit 2006, KStJ; Hon. LLD (Auckland Univ.) 2006.
Address: Government House, Private Bag 39995, Wellington Mail Centre, Lower Hutt 5045, Wellington, New Zealand (office). *Telephone:* (4) 3898055 (office). *Fax:* (4) 3895536 (office). *E-mail:* info@govthouse.govt .nz (office). *Website:* www.gov-gen.govt.nz (office).

SA'UD, HM The King of Saudi Arabia; Abdullah ibn Abd al-Aziz as-; *Head of State and Prime Minister;* b. 1924, Riyadh; brother of HRH Crown Prince Sultan ibn Abd al-Aziz as-Sa'ud. *Career:* Commdr Nat. Guard 1962–2005; Second Deputy Prime Minister 1975–82, First Deputy Prime Minister and Commdr Nat. Guard 1982–2005; became Crown Prince June 1982; succeeded to throne upon death of half-brother HM King Fahd 1 Aug. 2005; Patron Nat. Heritage and Cultural Festival, Jenadriyah 1985–.
Address: Royal Diwan, Riyadh, Saudi Arabia.

SA'UD, HRH Prince Bandar ibn Sultan ibn Abd al-Aziz as-, MA; Saudi Arabian diplomatist and army officer; *Secretary-General, National Security Council;* b. 2 March 1949, Taif; m. HRH Princess Haifa bint Faisal ibn Abd al-Aziz as-Sa'ud; four s. four d. *Education:* RAF Coll., Cranwell, USAF Advanced Program and Johns Hopkins Univ. *Career:* fighter pilot, Royal Saudi Air Force 1969–82; in charge of special Saudi Arabian liaison mission to USA for purchase of AWACS and other defence equipment 1981; Defence and Mil. Attaché, Saudi Arabian Mil. Mission to USA 1982–83; Amb. to USA 1983–2005; promoted to rank of Minister 1995; Sec.-Gen. Nat. Security Council 2005–; numerous medals and decorations, including Hawk Flying Medal of Aviation, King Faisal Medal, King Abdul Aziz Sash, as well as honours from other nations.

Address: c/o Ministry of Foreign Affairs, PO Box 55937, Riyadh 11544, Saudi Arabia (office). *Telephone:* (1) 405-5000 (office).

SA'UD, HRH Prince Muhammad ibn Nawaf ibn Abd al-Aziz as-; Saudi Arabian diplomatist; *Ambassador to UK;* b. 22 May 1953, Riyadh; m. HH Princess Fadwa bint Khaled bin Abdallah as-Sa'ud; five c. *Education:* Capital Inst. High School, Riyadh, School of Foreign Service, Georgetown Univ. and Harvard Univ., USA. *Career:* worked for Ministry of Foreign Affairs where he held several positions, including the Minister's Cabinet before being promoted to Insp. Gen.; Amb. to Italy and Malta 1995–2005, to UK 2005–.
Address: Embassy of Saudi Arabia, 30 Charles Street, Mayfair, London, W1J 5DZ, England (office). *Telephone:* (20) 7917-3000 (office). *Fax:* (20) 7917-3330 (office). *E-mail:* ukemb@mofa.gov.sa (office). *Website:* www .saudiembassy.org.uk (office).

SA'UD, HRH Prince Sa'ud al-Faisal as-, BA (Econs); Saudi Arabian politician and diplomatist; *Minister of Foreign Affairs;* b. 1941, Riyadh. *Education:* Princeton Univ., USA. *Career:* fmr Deputy Minister of Petroleum and Mineral Resources 1971–74; Minister of State for Foreign Affairs March–Oct. 1975, Minister of Foreign Affairs Oct. 1975–; Leader del. to UN Gen. Ass. 1976; Special Envoy of HM King Khalid ibn Abd al-Aziz as-Sa'ud in diplomatic efforts to resolve Algerian–Moroccan conflict over Western Sahara and the civil war in Lebanon; mem. Saudi Arabian del. to Arab restricted Summit, Riyadh, Oct. 1976 and to full Summit Conf. of Arab League, Oct. 1976; Founding mem. King Faisal's Int. Charity Soc.
Address: Ministry of Foreign Affairs, Nasseriya Street, Riyadh 11124, Saudi Arabia (office). *Telephone:* (1) 401-5000 (office). *Fax:* (1) 403-0159 (office). *Website:* www.mofa.gov.sa (office).

SA'UD, HRH Crown Prince Sultan ibn Abd al-Aziz as-; Saudi Arabian politician; *First Deputy Prime Minister, Minister of Defence and Aviation and Inspector General;* b. 5 Jan. 1928, Riyadh; brother of King Abdullah ibn Abd al-Aziz as-Sa'ud; son, Prince Bandar ibn Sultan ibn Abd al-Aziz as-Sa'ud. *Education:* at court and abroad. *Career:* Gov. of Riyadh 1947; Minister of Agric. 1954, of Transportation 1955; mem. most Saudi dels to Arab and Islamic Summit confs, State visits and UN Gen. Ass. Sessions 1962–75; Vice-Pres. Supreme Cttee of Educ. Policy; Minister of Defence and Aviation and Insp. Gen. 1962–82; Chair. Ministerial Cttee for Econ. Offset Program 1982–; Chair. Bd Saudia Airlines 1963–; Chair. Council of Manpower 1980; Second Deputy Prime Minister, Minister of Defence and Civil Aviation and Insp. Gen. 1982–; Chair. Bd of Gen. Enterprise of Mil. Industries 1985–, Bd for Nat. Comm. for Wildlife Conservation and Devt 1986–, Supreme Council for Islamic Affairs 1994–; Supreme Pres. and Chair. Trustees Sultan ibn Abd al-Aziz Charity Foundation 1995–; Chair. Ministerial Cttee on Environment 1995–; Vice-Pres. Supreme Econ. Council 2000–; Chair. High Comm. for Tourism 2000–; named Crown Prince 2005; First Deputy Prime Minister, Minister of Defence and Aviation and Insp. Gen. 2005–; Order of Merit (First Class) from many countries.
Address: Ministry of Defence and Civil Aviation, PO Box 26731, Airport Road, Riyadh 11165, Saudi Arabia (office). *Telephone:* (1) 476-9000 (office). *Fax:* (1) 405-5500 (office).

SA'UD, HRH Prince Talal ibn Abd al-Aziz as-; Saudi Arabian politician and international official; *President, Arab Gulf Programme, United Nations Development Organizations (AGFUND);* b. 1934, brother of King Abdullah ibn Abd al-Aziz as-Sa'ud; son, Prince Walid ibn Talal. *Education:* Prince's School, Royal Palace, Riyadh. *Career:* positions held in his early 20s include responsibility for the Royal Palaces, Minister of Communications; fmr Minister of Economy and Finance; fmr Amb. to France; f. Riyadh's first girls' school 1957, first pvt. hosp. 1957 and Mecca's first coll. for boys 1957; passport cancelled 1962; exile in Egypt (for activities promoting human rights and democracy); returned to Saudi Arabia 1964; fmr Special Envoy, UNICEF; Pres. Arab Gulf Programme for UN Devt Orgs 'AGFUND'; Pres. Arab Council for Childhood and Devt.
Address: AGFUND, PO Box 18371, Riyadh 11415, Saudi Arabia (office); 7 rue Beaujon, 75008 Paris, France. *Telephone:* 1-43-80-22-97 (office). *E-mail:* HRH.Office@agfund.org (office). *Website:* www.princetalal.net.

SAUDABAYEV, Kanat B., PhD; Kazakhstani diplomatist; *Secretary of State;* b. 1946, Almaty region; m. Kullikhan Saudbayeva; two s. one d. *Education:* Leningrad Inst. of Culture, Acad. of Public Sciences of the Cen. Cttee of the CPSU, Kazakh State Univ., Moscow State Univ. *Career:* began career as theatrical producer; fmr Chair. State (USSR) Cttee of Culture with rank of Minister, State Film Cttee; fmr Deputy Culture Minister; Plenipotentiary Rep. of Kazakh Soviet Socialist Repub. to USSR, then to Russian Fed. 1991–92; Amb. (of Kazakhstan) to Turkey 1992–96; Minister of Foreign Affairs 1994; Amb. to UK 1996–99; Head of Prime Minister's Chancellery of Kazakhstan 1999–2000; Amb. to USA 2000–07; Sec. of State 2007–;

Order of Kurmet (Distinguished Service) 1996, Order of Otan (Mother-land) 2005.
Address: c/o Office of the Prime Minister, 010000 Astana, Beibitshilik 11, Kazkahstan (office). *Website:* www.government.kz (office).

SAUDARGAS, Algirdas; Lithuanian politician, biophysicist and diplomatist; *Ambassador to the Holy See;* b. 17 April 1948, Kaunas; m. Laima Saudargenė; one s. one d. *Education:* Kaunas Inst. of Medicine. *Career:* research Asst Inst. of Math. and Information Tech. Lithuanian Acad. of Sciences 1972–77; Sr Lecturer Lithuanian Acad. of Agric. 1977–82; researcher Kaunas Inst. of Medicine (now Acad.) 1982–90; Founder mem. Sąjūdis Movt, Chair. Sąjūdis Seimas (Parl.) Political Cttee 1988–90; elected to Supreme Soviet Repub. of Lithuania 1990; Minister of Foreign Affairs 1990–92, 1996–99; mem. official del. Repub. of Lithuania to negotiations with Soviet Union; mem. Seimas, Cttee on Foreign Affairs, mem. Seimas del. to European Parl. 1992–2004 Chair. Sub-cttee on European Affairs 1995–2004; Chair. Lithuanian Christian Democratic Party 1995– (mem. 1989–); mem. Seimas Del. to OSCE 2003–04; Amb. to the Holy See, Vatican City 2004–.
Address: Embassy of Lithuania, Via G.G. Porro 4, 00197 Rome, Italy (office); L. Stuokos-Gucevičiaus Str. B/10, Apt. 3, 2001 Vilnius, Lithuania (home). *Telephone:* (06) 8078259 (office). *Fax:* (06) 8078291 (office). *E-mail:* amb.va@urm.lt (office).

SAUER, Fernand Edmond; French international official, pharmacist and lawyer; *Honorary Director for Public Health, European Commission;* b. 14 Dec. 1947, St Avold, Moselle; m. Pamela Sheppard; one s. two d. *Education:* Univs of Strasbourg and Paris II. *Career:* fmr hosp. pharmacist and pharmaceutical insp. French Ministry of Health; joined European Comm., Brussels, Head of Pharmaceuticals 1986; Exec. Dir European Agency for Evaluation of Medicinal Products (EMEA), London 1994–2000; Dir for Public Health, EC, Luxembourg 2001–06, Hon. Dir 2006–; Hon. Fellow, School of Pharmacy, Univ. of London; Hon. mem. Royal Pharmaceutical Soc.; Chevalier, Légion d'honneur, Ordre Nat. du Mérite.
Address: DG Sanco C – Public Health and Risk Assessment, Jean Monnet Building, Office C5/120, European Commission, rue Alcide de Gasperi, 2920 Luxembourg (office). *Telephone:* 43-01-32-71-9 (office). *Fax:* 43-01-34-51-1 (office). *E-mail:* Fernand.Sauer@cec.eu.int (office). *Website:* www.ec.europa.eu.

SAUERBREY, Ellen Richmond; American politician and diplomatist; *Assistant Secretary of State for Population, Refugees and Migration;* b. 9 Sept. 1937, Baltimore. *Education:* Western Md Coll. *Career:* fmr teacher; Rep. of Northern Md District, Md State Legislature 1978–94, Minority Leader 1986–94; Nat. Chair. American Legis. Exchange Council 1990–91; US Rep., UN Comm. on Human Rights 2001; Del. to Econ. and Social Council 2002, 2003; US Rep. to UN Comm. on Status of Women –2006; Asst Sec. of State for Population, Refugees and Migration 2006–; f. Project Freedom.
Address: Bureau of Population, Refugees and Migration, Office 5824, Department of State, 2201 C Street, NW, Washington, DC 20520, USA (office). *Telephone:* (202) 647-7360 (office). *Website:* www.state.gov (office).

SAVAGE, Francis Joseph, CMG, LVO, OBE; British administrator, diplomatist and consultant; b. 8 Feb. 1943, Preston; m. Veronica Mary McAleenan 1966; two s. *Education:* St Stephen's Catholic School, Welling, N Kent Coll., Dartford. *Career:* joined Foreign Office 1961, Embassy, Cairo 1967–70, Washington, DC 1971–73, Vice-Consul, Aden 1973–74, Foreign Office 1974–78, Consul, Düsseldorf 1978–82, Consul, Peking (now Beijing) 1982–86, First Sec., Lagos and Consul, Benin 1987–90; First Sec./Counsellor, Foreign Office 1990–93; Gov. of Montserrat 1993–97, The British Virgin Islands 1998–2002; Chair. Friends of British Virgin Islands 2005–; adviser to FCO 2003–; freelance consultant 2003–; mem. Bd Visar Trust 2002–; adviser on overseas territories to FCO; Kt Commdr, Order of St Gregory the Great 2002; Montserrat Badge of Honour 2000.
Address: c/o Foreign and Commonwealth Office, King Charles Street, London, SW1A 2AH (office); 19 Cleeve Park Gardens, Sidcup, Kent, DA14 4JL, England (home). *Telephone:* (20) 8309-5061 (home). *E-mail:* frank.savage@fco.gov.uk (office); fjsavage@savagef.fsnet.co.uk (home).

SAVILLE, John; British diplomatist; *High Commissioner to Brunei;* b. 29 June 1960; m. Fabiola Moreno De Alboran; one d. *Career:* joined FCO 1981, Southern Africa Dept 1981–82, Southern European Dept 1985–88, Non-Proliferation Dept 1991–94, Head, Commonwealth and Burma Section, SE Asia Dept 1998–2000, Head, Weapons of Mass Destruction Review Unit 2004–05; Third, later Second Sec., Political, Jakarta, Indonesia 1983–85; Second, later First Sec., Press and Public Affairs, Warsaw 1988–91; First Sec., Political, Vienna 1995–98; Deputy Head of

Mission, Havana, Cuba 2000–03; High Commr to Brunei Darussalam 2005–.
Address: British High Commission, 2.01, 2nd Floor, Block D, Kompleks Yayasan Sultan Haji Hassanal Bolkiah, Jalan Pretty, PO Box 2197, Bandar Seri Begawan, BS8674, Brunei Darussalam (office). *Telephone:* (2) 222231 (office). *Fax:* (2) 234315 (office). *E-mail:* brithc@brunet.bn (office). *Website:* www.britishhighcommission.gov.uk/brunei (office).

SAVOLSKY, Igor S.; Russian diplomatist; *Ambassador to Hungary;* b. 1943; m.; one s. one d. *Education:* MGIMO. *Career:* joined Ministry of Foreign Affairs 1966; served at Embassy in Budapest 1966–72, 1986–92; Deputy Minister for CIS 1998–2000; Amb. to Czech Repub. 2000–04; Head of dels to Georgia negotiating mil. and political issues 2004–06; Amb. to Hungary 2006–; Chair. Danube Comm. 2008–.
Address: Embassy of Russia, 1062 Budapest, Bajza u. 35, Hungary (office). *Telephone:* (1) 302-5230 (office). *Fax:* (1) 353-4164 (office). *Website:* www.hungary.mid.ru (office).

SAVUA, Isikia Rabici; Fijian diplomatist and civil servant; m. Frances Savua; two s. *Career:* joined Royal Fiji Military Forces 1971, retd from forces 1988 (rank of Lt-Col); joined Fiji Diplomatic Corps 1988, Counsellor (Political), Fiji Mission to UN, New York 1988–92, Consul-Gen., Fiji Office, Sydney, Australia 1992, Perm. Rep. to UN 2003–06, Chair. of Credentials Cttee to 58th Session 2003–; Deputy Commr of Police 1992, Commr of Police 1993–2002.
Address: c/o Ministry of Foreign Affairs, International Co-operation and Civil Aviation, Government Buildings, POB 2220, Suva, Fiji (office). *Website:* www.foreignaffairs.gov.fj (office).

SAVVAIDES, George V., BSc, LLM; Greek diplomatist; b. 1945, Athens; m. Maria Savvaides (née Polyzou); one d. *Education:* Univ. of Athens, Harvard Univ. Law School, USA. *Career:* joined Foreign Ministry 1972; Attaché 1972–74; Consul in Boston 1976–77; with Dept of Bilateral Relations, Middle East and Africa 1979–81; Consul-Gen. in Skopje 1981–83; Political Adviser, Perm. Mission to NATO, Brussels 1983–87, Defence Adviser 1987–91; Dir Depts of Turkey and Cyprus 1991–96; Amb. and Perm. Rep. to NATO 1996–2000; Sec.-Gen. Ministry of Foreign Affairs 2000–02; Amb. to USA 2002–05; posting at Ministry of Foreign Affairs 2005–; Grand Cross, Order of Merit (Cyprus) 1993, Order of Madara Horsemen 1st Class (Bulgaria) 2000, Grand Cross, Order of Merit (Italy) 2001, Grand Cross, Order of the Phoenix (Greece) 2001, Grand Cross, of King Leopold II (Belgium) 2001, Grand Commdr, Order of the Cedar (Lebanon) 2001; Hon. Doctor of Humanities (Hellenic Coll./Holy Cross Greek Orthodox School of Theology) 2005.
Address: Ministry of Foreign Affairs, Odos Akadimias 1, 106 71 Athens, Greece (office). *Telephone:* (210) 3681000 (office). *Fax:* (210) 3624195 (office). *E-mail:* mfa@mfa.gr (office). *Website:* www.mfa.gr (office).

SAWERS, Sir John, KCMG, BSc; British diplomatist; *Permanent Representative, United Nations;* b. 26 July 1955; m.; three c. *Education:* Univ. of Nottingham. *Career:* Prin. Pvt. Sec. to Foreign Sec. 1992–95; Int. Fellow, Harvard Univ. 1995; served at Embassy in Washington, DC 1996–98; Foreign Affairs Adviser to Prime Minister 1999–2001; Amb. to Egypt 2001–03; Political Dir Foreign and Commonwealth Office 2003–07; Perm. Rep. to UN, New York 2007–.
Address: Permanent Mission of the United Kingdom to the United Nations, 1 Dag Hammarskjöld Plaza, 885 Second Avenue, New York, NY 10017, USA (office). *Telephone:* (212) 745-9200 (office). *Fax:* (212) 745-9316 (office). *E-mail:* uk@un.int (office). *Website:* www.ukun.org (office).

SAYACHAK, Sounthone; Laotian diplomatist. *Career:* currently Amb. to Viet Nam.
Address: Embassy of Laos, 22 Tran Binh Trong, Hanoi, Viet Nam (office). *Telephone:* (4) 9424576 (office). *Fax:* (4) 8228414 (office).

SAYEH, Antoinette Monsio, PhD; Liberian economist and government official; *Minister of Finance;* b. 12 July 1958, Monrovia; one s. *Education:* Swarthmore Coll., Fletcher School, Tufts Univ., USA. *Career:* fmrly with Ministry of Planning, Ministry of Finance; worked for 17 years at World Bank, positions included Country Dir for Benin, Niger and Togo 2000–03 and working on public finance man. and civil service reform in Pakistan; Minister of Finance 2006–; Lucretia Mott Award, Swarthmore Coll., Service to Country Award, Govt of Niger.
Address: Ministry of Finance, Broad Street, POB 10-9013, 1000 Monrovia 10, Liberia (office). *Telephone:* 47510680 (office). *Website:* www.finance.gov.lr (office).

SBAI, Abd ar-Rahman; Moroccan politician. *Career:* currently Minister-Del. to the Prime Minister, in charge of the Admin of Nat. Defence.

Address: c/o Office of the Prime Minister, Palais Royal, Le Méchouar, Rabat, Morocco (office).

SBIH, Missoum, PhD; Algerian academic and diplomatist; *Ambassador to France; Education:* Univ. of Paris (Panthéon-Sorbonne). *Career:* Founder and first Dir-Gen. Ecole Nationale d'Admin 1964–78; fmr Pres. Comm. du Plan, Social Comm. of Nat. Econ. and Social Council, Guiding Council of Nat. Inst. of Global Strategic Studies; fmr Sec.-Gen. Ministry of Foreign Affairs, fmr Amb. to Canada, to Belgium and Luxembourg, fmr Chief of Mission, Algerian Perm. Representation to EC; Pres. Nat. Reform Comm. –2005; Adviser and Special Rep. of the Pres. of Algeria –2005; Amb. to France and Perm. Del. to UNESCO 2005–; Pres. Admin. Council, Maghrébin Centre for Studies and Admin. Research; fmr Pres. Admin. Council of UN Inst. for Training and Research; mem. Nat. Council for Scientific Research; fmr mem. Comm. de la Fonction Publique Internationale, Consultative Council of UN Inst. for Research and Disarmament, ICAO Council. *Publications:* Les Institutions Administratives Du Maghreb: Le Gouvernement De L'Algerie, Du Maroc, Et De La Tunisie 1977; numerous articles on state govt and int. relations.
Address: Embassy of Algeria, 50 rue de Lisbonne, 75008 Paris, France (office). *Telephone:* 1-53-93-20-20 (office). *Fax:* 1-42-25-10-25 (office). *E-mail:* chancellerie@amb-algerie.fr (office). *Website:* www.amb-algerie.fr (office).

SCAZZIERI, Roberto, MLitt, DPhil, DrScPol; Italian economist and academic; *Professor of Economics, University of Bologna;* b. 1 May 1950, Bologna; m. Maria Cristina Bacchi 1983; one s. *Education:* Liceo Minghetti, Bologna, Univ. of Bologna, Univ. of Oxford, UK. *Career:* Asst Lecturer, Univ. of Bologna 1974–79, Lecturer in Theory and Policy of Econ. Growth 1980–83, in Econ. Principles 1983–86, in Advanced Econ. Analysis 1985–87, Assoc. Prof. of Econs, Faculty of Political Sciences 1986–87, Full Prof. of Econs, Faculty of Econs and Commerce and Dept of Econs 1990–; Prof. of Econs, Faculty of Statistics, Univ. of Padua 1987–90; Visiting Scholar, Dept of Applied Econs, Univ. of Cambridge 1987, 1989, Research Assoc. 1992–93; Visiting Fellow, Clare Hall 1992, Life mem. 1992; Visiting Fellow, Gonville and Caius Coll. 1999, mem. 1999–, Centre for Research in the Arts, Social Sciences and Humanities, Univ. of Cambridge 2004; Resident Fellow, Bologna Inst. of Advanced Study 1997, Founding Scientific Dir 2000–03, Deputy Scientific Dir 2003–06; Visiting Prof., Univ. of Lugano, Switzerland 1997; Visiting Research Fellow, Centre for History and Econs, King's Coll., Cambridge 2005, Visiting Scholar, Gonville and Caius College and Clare Hall 2007–08; Man. Ed. and Review Ed. Structural Change and Economic Dynamics; Assoc. Ed. Journal of Economic Methodology; mem. Steering Cttee Bologna-Cambridge-Harvard Sr Seminars Network, Bologna Inst. for Advanced Study, Steering Cttee European Consortium of Humanities Centres and Institutes 2002–; mem. Man. Bd European Summer School in Structural Change and Econ. Dynamics, Selwyn Coll., Cambridge 1995–; mem. Scientific Cttee Int. Centre for the History of Univs and Science 1994, Scientific Cttee Centre for Research on Complex Automated Systems (CASY), Univ. of Bologna 2002–; mem. Man. Bd 'Federigo Enriques' Centre for Epistemology and History of Sciences, Univ. of Bologna 2001–; Foundation Fellow, Kyoto Univ.; Rector's Del., Bologna-Clare Hall Fellowship 1993–; mem. Bologna Acad. of Sciences 1994; Bonaldo Stringher Prize Scholarship (Bank of Italy) 1974, St Vincent Prize for Econs 1985, Linceo Prize for Econs, Nat. Lincei Acad. 2004. *Publications:* Efficienza produttiva e livelli di attività 1981, Protagonisti del pensiero economico (co-author) 1977–82, Sui momenti costitutivi dell'economia politica 1983 (co-author), Foundations of Economics: Structures of Inquiry and Economic Theory 1986, The Economic Theory of Structure and Change 1990, A Theory of Production: Tasks, Processes and Technical Practices 1993, Production and Economic Dynamics 1996, Incommensurability and Translation. Kuhnian Perspectives on Scientific Communication and Theory Change 1999, Knowledge, Social Institutions and the Division of Labour 2001, Economics of Structural Change (co-author) 2003, Reasoning, Rationality, and Probability (co-author) 2007, Markets, Money and Capital – Hicksian Economics for the 21st Century (co-author) 2008, Capital, Time and Transitional Dynamics (co-author) 2008, Migration of Ideas (co-author) 2008; numerous articles.
Address: Università degli Studi di Bologna, Piazza Scaravilli 2, 40126 Bologna (office); Via Garibaldi 5, 40124 Bologna, Italy (home). *Telephone:* (051) 2098146 (office); (051) 2098132 (Secretary) (office). *Fax:* (051) 2098040 (office). *E-mail:* roberto.scazzieri@unibo.it (office). *Website:* www.economia.unibo.it (office); www.dse.unibo.it (office); www.crassh.cam.ac.uk (office); www.isa.unibo.it (office).

SCHABAS, William A., OC, MRIA, BA, MA, LLB, LLM, LLD; Canadian academic and lawyer; *Professor and Director, Irish Centre for Human Rights;* b. 19 Nov. 1950, Cleveland, OH, USA; m. Penelope Soterion; two d. *Education:* Univs of Toronto and Montreal. *Career:* Prof. of Law, Université du Québec à Montréal 1991–2000, Chair. Dept 1994–98; Visiting or Adjunct Prof., McGill Univ., Univ. of Montréal, Montpellier Univ., Univ. of Paris, Univ. of Rwanda, Dalhousie Univ., Cardozo School of Law, Int. Inst. for Human Rights, Canadian Foreign Service Inst.; mem. Quebec Human Rights Tribunal 1996–2000; Sr Fellow, US Inst. of Peace 1998–99; Prof. in Human Rights Law and Dir Irish Centre for Human Rights, Nat. Univ. of Ireland, Galway 2000–; Global Legal Scholar, Univ. of Warwick 2007–; Prof., Queen's Univ., Belfast 2007–; apptd Sierra Leone Truth and Reconciliation Comm. 2002; participant in numerous int. human rights missions, including Rwanda, Burundi, S Africa, Kenya, Sudan, Cambodia, Chechnya, Guyana; mem. Quebec Bar; Chair. Int. Inst. for Criminal Investigation; Treas. Int. Inst. for Human Rights; Ed.-in-Chief Criminal Law Forum; mem. Bd of Trustees, UN Voluntary Fund for Tech. Assistance in the Field of Human Rights; Dr hc (Dalhousie Univ.). *Publications include:* The Death Penalty as Cruel Treatment and Torture 1996, Int. Human Rights Law and the Canadian Charter 1996, Genocide in Int. Law 2000, The Abolition of the Death Penalty in Int. Law 2003, The UN Int. Criminal Tribunals, the former Yugoslavia, Rwanda, Sierra Leone 2006, Introduction to the Int. Criminal Court 2007; more than 200 articles in journals.
Address: Irish Centre for Human Rights, National University of Ireland Galway, University Road, Galway, Co. Galway, Ireland (office); 'Hawthorn', Oughterard, Co. Galway, Ireland (home). *Telephone:* (91) 493726 (office), (91) 557108 (home). *Fax:* (91) 494575 (office). *E-mail:* humanrights@nuigalway.ie (office). *Website:* www.nuigalway.ie (office).

SCHAEFER, Michael, PhD; German diplomatist; *Ambassador to the People's Republic of China;* b. 1949; m.; three c. *Education:* Max Planck Inst., Heidelberg, Univ. of Mannheim. *Career:* joined Foreign Service 1978, overseas postings include Bonn, UN missions in Geneva and New York, Singapore; Head, Western Balkans Task Force, Fed. Foreign Office, Berlin 1999–2001, Special Envoy for S Eastern Europe and Deputy Political Dir 2001–02, Head, Legal Dept 2002, Political Dir 2002–07; Amb. to People's Repub. of China 2007–. *Publications:* Der Sicherheitsmechanismus der Vereinten Nationen 1980, Berufsbild Diplomat: Auswahl und Ausbildung im Auswärtigen Dienst 1995; contrib. to Südosteuropa Mitteilungen, Zeitschrift Vereinte Nationen.
Address: Embassy of Germany, 17 Dong Zhi Men Wai Dajie, San Li Tun, Beijing 100600, People's Republic of China (office). *Telephone:* (10) 85329000 (office). *Fax:* (10) 65325336 (office). *E-mail:* embassy@peki.diplo.de (office). *Website:* www.beijing.diplo.de (office).

SCHÄFERS, Reinhard; German diplomatist; *Ambassador to France;* b. 27 May 1950; m.; two c. *Career:* joined Fed. Ministry of Foreign Affairs 1977, Second Sec. 1979; Consul, Embassy in Prague 1979–82; Deputy Head of Mission, Embassy in Mogadishu; First Sec. and Counsellor, Ministry of Foreign Affairs 1985–88; Counsellor, Embassy in Moscow 1988–91; Counsellor USSR Div., Ministry of Foreign Affairs 1991–92, Head of Cen., E and SE Europe Div. 1992–98; Minister, Embassy in Paris 1998–2000; Perm. Rep. to WEU 2000, to EU Political and Security Cttee 2001; Amb. to Ukraine 2006–08, to France 2008–.
Address: Embassy of Germany, 13–15 avenue Franklin D. Roosevelt, 75008 Paris, France (office). *Telephone:* 1-53-83-45-00 (office). *Fax:* 1-43-59-74-18 (office). *E-mail:* ambassade@amb-allemagne.fr (office). *Website:* www.amb-allemagne.fr (office).

SCHAPER, Herman, BA, MA; Dutch diplomatist; *Permanent Representative, NATO;* b. 24 March 1949; m. Vivian Voss; three c. *Education:* Univ. of Leiden, Univ. of Va, USA. *Career:* fmr researcher, Netherlands Soc. for Int. Affairs; Rep., Democrats '66 Party, Dutch Parl. 1981–82; fmr Dir of European Affairs Dept, Ministry of Foreign Affairs; fmr Dir, Security Policy Dept; fmr Deputy Perm. Rep. to UN; fmr Deputy Perm. Rep. to NATO, Perm. Rep. to NATO 2005–; Deputy Dir-Gen. for Political Affairs, Ministry of Foreign Affairs 2001–05. *Publications:* numerous articles on Dutch foreign policy, European security, transatlantic relations.
Address: North Atlantic Treaty Organization (NATO), blvd. Léopold III, 1110 Brussels, Belgium (office). *Telephone:* (2) 707-4111 (office). *Fax:* (2) 707-4579 (office). *E-mail:* natodoc@hq.nato.int (office). *Website:* www.nato.int (office).

SCHARIOTH, Klaus, MA, MALD, PhD; German diplomatist; *Ambassador to USA;* b. 13 March 1946, Essen, North Rhine-Westphalia; m.; three c. *Education:* studies in Caldwell, Ida, USA, in Bonn and Freiburg and in Geneva, Switzerland, Fletcher School of Law and Diplomacy, Harvard Law School, John F. Kennedy School of Govt. *Career:* nat. service 1966–67; entered Foreign Service 1976, Asia Div., Press Div. and State Sec.'s Office, Fed. Foreign Office 1977–79, Embassy in Quito, Ecuador 1979–82, Policy Planning Staff, Fed. Foreign Office 1982–86, Perm. Mission of FRG to UN, New York, Vice-Chair. UN Legal and Charter Cttees 1986–90, Int. Law Div., Fed. Foreign Office 1990–93, Chef de Cabinet (Dir pvt. office) to NATO Sec.-Gen., Brussels 1993–96, Head of

Defence and Security Policy Div., Fed. Foreign Office 1996–97, Office of the Foreign Minister 1997–98, Head of Office April 1998, Head of Int. Security and N America Directorate 1998–99, Political Dir and Head of Political Directorate-Gen. 1999–2002, State Sec. of the Foreign Office 2002–06, Amb. to USA 2006–.
Address: German Embassy, 4645 Reservoir Road NW, Washington, DC 20007-1998, USA (office). *Telephone:* (202) 298-4000 (office). *Fax:* (202) 298-4249 (office). *Website:* www.germany.info (office).

SCHELLING, Thomas Crombie, PhD; American economist; *Distinguished University Professor, Department of Economics and School of Public Affairs, University of Maryland;* b. 14 April 1921, Oakland, Calif.; m. 1st Corinne Tigay Saposs 1947 (divorced 1991); four s.; m. 2nd Alice M. Coleman 1991. *Education:* Univ. of California at Berkeley and Harvard Univ. *Career:* Fiscal Analyst, US Bureau of the Budget 1945–46; Econ. Econs Co-operation Admin., Copenhagen and Paris 1948–50, Exec. Office of the Pres. 1951–53; Assoc. Prof. and Prof. of Econs, Yale Univ. 1953–58; Lucius N Littauer Prof. of Political Economy, Harvard Univ. 1958–90; Distinguished Univ. Prof. of Econs and Public Affairs, Univ. of Md 1990–; Sr Staff mem. The Rand Corpn 1958–59; Pres. American Econ. Asscn 1991; Fellow American Acad. of Arts and Sciences; mem. NAS, Inst. of Medicine; Frank E. Seidman Distinguished Award in Political Econ. 1977, Award for Behavioral Research Relevant to the Prevention of Nuclear War 1993, Nobel Prize for Economics 2005. *Publications:* National Income Behavior 1951, International Economics 1958, Strategy of Conflict 1960, Strategy and Arms Control (with Morton H. Halperin) 1961, Arms and Influence 1967, Micromotives and Macrobehavior 1978, Choice and Consequence 1984.
Address: Department of Economics, University of Maryland, College Park, MD 20742, USA (office). *Telephone:* (301) 405-3494 (office). *Fax:* (301) 403-4675 (office). *E-mail:* tschelli@umd.edu (office). *Website:* www.puaf .umd.edu/faculty/people/schellingm.html (office).

SCHERER, Frederic M., MA, MBA, PhD; American professor of economics; *Aetna Professor Emeritus of Public Policy and Corporation Management, John F. Kennedy School of Government, Harvard University;* b. 1 Aug. 1932, Ottawa, Ill.; m. Barbara Silbermann 1957; one s. two d. *Education:* Univ. of Michigan, Harvard Univ., Hohenheim Univ. *Career:* served in US Army Counter-Intelligence Corps 1954–56; research asst. then assoc. Harvard Business School 1958–63; mem. staff, Princeton Univ. 1963–66, Univ. of Mich. 1966–72, Int. Inst. of Man. 1972–74, Northwestern Univ. 1976–82, Swarthmore Coll. 1982–89; Chief Economist, US Fed. Trade Comm. 1974–76; Aetna Prof. of Public Policy and Corp. Man., John F. Kennedy School of Govt, Harvard Univ. 1989–2000, Prof. Emer. 2000–; Ludwig Erhard Visiting Prof., Univ. of Bayreuth 2000; Lecturer, Woodrow Wilson School of Public and Int. Affairs, Princeton Univ. 2000–05; Visiting Prof., Haverford Coll., Pa 2004–06; Co-Founder European Asscn for Research in Industrial Econs; pioneering work on theory of research and devt strategy and timing; Lanchester Prize, Operations Research Soc. of America 1964, O'Melveny & Myers Centennial Research Prize 1989, Distinguished Fellow, Industrial Org. Soc. 1999, Lifetime Achievement Award, American Antitrust Inst. 2002. *Publications:* The Weapons Acquisition Process: Economic Incentives 1964, Industrial Market Structure and Economic Performance 1970, Innovation and Growth: Schumpeterian Perspectives 1984, Industry Structure, Strategy and Public Policy 1996, Quarter Notes and Bank Notes: The Economics of Music Composition in the 18th and 19th Centuries 2004.
Address: 601 Rockbourne Mills Court, Wallingford, PA 19086, USA (home). *Telephone:* (610) 872-2557 (office); (610) 872-2557 (home). *Fax:* (610) 872-2557. *E-mail:* fmscherer@comcast.net (office).

SCHIEFFER, (John) Thomas (Tom), BA, MA; American politician, diplomat-ist and business executive; *Ambassador to Japan;* b. 4 Oct. 1947, Fort Worth, Tex.; m. Susanne Silber 1979; one s. *Education:* Arlington Heights High School and Univ. of Texas. *Career:* worked in offices of State Senator Don Kennard and Gov. John Connally; elected to Texas House of Reps 1972, served three terms; admitted to Texas Bar 1979; investor and Partner, with George W. Bush and Edward W. (Rusty) Rose, Texas Rangers (professional baseball club) 1989–99, Partner-in-Charge of Ballpark Devt 1990, Pres. 1991–99; Pres. J. Thomas Schieffer Man. Co., Pablo Operating Co. –2001; Amb. to Australia 2001–05, to Japan 2005–; fmr mem. Advisory Bd JP Morgan Chase Bank, Fort Worth; fmr mem. Bd Dirs Drew Industries, White Plains, NY; fmr Tarrant Co. Coordinator for Gov. Mark White; fmr Finance Chair. for Congressman Pete Geren; was also active for many years in the campaigns of Senator Lloyd Bentsen; has served on numerous charitable and civic bds, including The Penrose Foundation, Dallas Co. Community Coll. Foundation, Dallas 2012 Olympic Cttee, Tarrant Co. Coll. Foundation, Winston School; fmr mem. Exec. Cttee Dallas Chamber of Commerce, Co-Chair. Legis. Affairs Cttee; Trustee Tarrant Co. Jr Coll. 1987; numerous civic and humanitarian awards.

Address: Embassy of the USA, 1-10-5, Akasaka, Minato-ku, Tokyo, 107-8420, Japan (office). *Telephone:* (3) 3224-5000 (office). *Fax:* (3) 3505-1862 (office). *Website:* tokyo.usembassy.gov (office).

SCHILTZ, Jean-Louis; Luxembourg lawyer and politician; *Minister for Development Cooperation and Humanitarian Action, Minister for Commu-nications and Minister of Defence;* b. 14 Aug. 1964, Luxembourg; m.; three c. *Education:* Université Paris I Panthéon Sorbonne. *Career:* worked for Schiltz & Schiltz (law firm), Luxembourg 1989–2004; Academic Asst, Law Faculty Université Paris I Panthéon Sorbonne 1989–90; mem. Cttee Young Bar Asscn 1990, Chair. 1997–98, then mem. Bar Council; MP 2004–, Minister for Devt Cooperation and Humanitarian Action, Minister for Communications and Minister of Defence 2004–; Gov. Asian Development Bank for Luxembourg 2004–; Sec.-Gen. Parti Chrétien Social (Chrësch-tlech Sozial Vollekspartei) (PCS/CSV) (Christian Social Party); First Asst, then Chargé de Cours, Centre universitaire de Luxembourg 1991–2004; co-Ed. Assurances et Responsabilité 1994–2004; mem. Editorial Bd European Lawyer, Int. Bar Asscn; fmr mem. Legal Comm., Nat. Olympic Cttee. *Sport achievements:* Luxembourg team fencing champion 1983.
Address: Parti Chrétien Social (Chrëschtlech Sozial Vollekspartei) (PCS/CSV) (Christian Social Party), 4 rue de l'Eau, BP 826, 2018, Luxembourg. *Telephone:* 22-57-311. *Fax:* 47-27-16. *E-mail:* csv@csv.lu. *Website:* www .csv.lu.

SCHINTGEN, Romain, DenD; Luxembourg judge; *Judge, Court of Justice of the European Communities;* b. 22 March 1939, Luxembourg; m. Lucie Dui 1974; one d. *Education:* Athénée Grand-Ducal de Luxembourg and Facultés de Droit, Montpellier and Paris. *Career:* advocate, Luxembourg Bar 1964, attorney-at-law 1967; Asst Ministry of Labour 1967, Counsellor 1974, Admin.-Gen. 1987; Pres. Conseil Economique et Social 1988–89; Judge, Tribunal of First Instance of the European Communities 1989–96, Court of Justice of the European Communities 1996–; Pres. Institut Universitaire Int. Luxembourg; Commdr Ordre de la Couronne de Chêne; decorations from Germany, Portugal, Spain. *Publications:* Le Droit du Travail au Grand-Duché de Luxembourg.
Address: Court of Justice of the European Communities, BP 1406, 2925; 13 rue Belle-Vue, 3345 Leudelange, Luxembourg (home). *Telephone:* 4303-2241 (office). *Fax:* 4303-3181 (office). *E-mail:* romain.schintgen@curia.eu .int (office); roschin@pt.lu (home). *Website:* europa.eu.int/cj (office).

SCHLESINGER, Stephen Cannon, BA, LLB; American research institute director and journalist; *Director, World Policy Institute, New School University;* b. 17 Aug. 1942, Boston, Mass; m. 1984; one d. *Education:* Harvard Coll., Harvard Law School, Peterhouse Coll., Cambridge, UK. *Career:* began journalism career as Special Ed., Harvard Review 1963–64; Teaching Fellow in English Composition, Harvard Univ. 1968; Legal Asst to Pres., NY State Urban Devt Corpn 1968–69; contributing writer, The Village Voice 1968–72; speech writer, McGovern presidential campaign 1972; columnist, Boston Globe 1973–74; staff writer, Time Magazine 1974–78; Adjunct Prof. in American Politics, New School for Social Research, New York 1976–77; Chief Political Corresp., New York Post 1978; Lecturer, Royce Carlton Agency 1984–88; Special Asst and Dir of Public Papers for New York Gov. Cuomo 1983–90; Dir for Int. Orgs, NY State Dept of Econ. Devt 1990–95; Special Adviser to Sec.-Gen. of Habitat II, UN 1995–97; Visiting Scholar, Taub Urban Research Center 1995–97; Dir World Policy Inst., New School Univ. 1997–; mem. Council on Foreign Relations, Author's Guild, PEN; mem. Bd Dirs Franklin & Eleanor Roosevelt Inst., Selection Cttee British Atlantic Fellowships 1995, 1996; Winner, Harry S. Truman Book Award 2004. *Publications:* The New Reformers 1975, Bitter Fruit: The Untold Story of the US Coup in Guatemala (co-author) 1982, Act of Creation: The Founding of the United Nations 2003; articles in popular publs.
Address: World Policy Institute, New School University, 66 Fifth Avenue, 9th Floor, New York, NY 10011, USA (office). *Telephone:* (212) 229-5808, ext 4266 (office). *Fax:* (212) 229-5579 (office). *E-mail:* schlesis@newschool .edu (office). *Website:* www.worldpolicy.org (office).

SCHLICHER, Ronald L.; American diplomatist; *Ambassador to Cyprus; Career:* mem. Sr Foreign Service with rank of Minister-Counselor, entered the Foreign Service in 1982, Vice-Consul, Dhahran 1982–84, Consul, Damascus 1984–86, Staff Asst, Bureau of Near Eastern Affairs 1987, Deputy Prin. Officer, Alexandria 1987–89, First Sec., Cairo 1989–91, Chief Civilian Observer, Multinational Force and Observers 1991–92, Deputy Dir for Regional Affairs, Office of Coordinator for Counter-Terrorism 1992–94, Deputy Chief of Mission, Beirut 1994–97, Dir Office of Egyptian and N African Affairs, Bureau of Near Eastern Affairs 1997–2000, Chief of Mission and Consul-Gen., Jerusalem 2000–02, Dir Iraq Task Force 2003, served for six months in Iraq with Coalition Provisional Authority, first as Regional Coordinator for the North and then as Dir Office of Prov. Outreach, Deputy Asst Sec., Dept of State, serving as Coordinator for Iraq,

Bureau of Near Eastern Affairs –2005, Amb. to Cyprus 2005–; Distinguished Honor Award, three Superior Honor Awards, two Meritorious Honor Awards, Nat. Human Intelligence Collector Award, Christian A. Herter Award, several Sr and Presidential Performance Pay awards.
Address: Embassy of the USA, Metochiou and Ploutarchou, Engomi, 2407 Nicosia, Cyprus (office). *Telephone:* 22393939 (office). *Fax:* 22780944 (office). *E-mail:* consularnicosia@state.gov (office). *Website:* cyprus .usembassy.gov (office).

SCHMID, Samuel; Swiss lawyer and politician; *Head of the Federal Department of Defence, Civil Protection and Sport;* b. 1947; m.; three s. *Education:* Univ. of Bern. *Career:* with Swiss Fed. Finance Admin 1973; joined legal practice, Bern 1973; independent advocate and notary, Lyss 1978–; solicitor with Kellerhals & Pnrs LLC, Bern 1998–; adviser to econ. and trade asscns.; local councillor 1972–74, Pres. Municipality of Rueti 1974–82; mem. Berni Greater Council 1982–93, Chair. Cttee for new Berni State Canton Constitution, mem. Finance Cttee; mem. Nat. Council 1994–98, mem. Standing Cttee for Econ. Affairs and Taxation, Cttee for Econs and Deliveries, Nat. Policy Cttee, Constitutional Affairs Cttee, Comm. for Strategic Questions, Comm. for Reorganization of the Intelligence Service; Pres. Swiss People's Party (SVP—Schweizerische Volkspartei) Parl. Group of the Presidential Election Council 1998–99; mem. Comm. for Foreign Policy 1999– (also Vice-Pres.), Comm. for Econs and Deliveries, Comm. for Social Security and Health, Nat. Political Comm.; mem. Upper House of Parl. 2001–; Head of Fed. Dept of Defence, Civil Protection and Sport 2001–; Vice-Pres. Swiss Confed. 2004, Pres. 2005; Pres. Berni Trade Asscn 1990–; mem. Exec. Cttee Swiss Trade Asscn 1991–; Col, Commdt of infantry regiment 1993–96, Commdt Stv. F Div. 3 1998–99.
Address: Federal Department of Defence, Civil Protection and Sport, Bundeshaus-Ost, 3003 Bern, Switzerland (office). *Telephone:* 313245058 (office). *Fax:* 313245104 (office). *E-mail:* samuel.schmid@gs-vbs.admin.ch (office). *Website:* www.vbs.admin.ch (office).

SCHMID, Walter Jürgen, DrIur; German lawyer and diplomatist; *Ambassador to Russia;* b. 1946. *Education:* Univ. of Tübingen. *Career:* served in mil. 1966–67; jr court lawyer 1973–75; Attaché, Minister of Foreign Affairs 1976–78, Adviser to Minister of State 1978–79; served in embassies in Montevideo 1979–82, Ankara 1982–85; Senate Dir, Senatskanzlei Freie and Hamburg 1986–91; Amb. to Guinea 1992–94; served at Royal Coll. of Defence Studies, London, UK 1995; Disarmament Dept, Ministry of Foreign Affairs 1996–2000, Deputy Rep. for Disarmament and Arms Control 2000–03, Commr for Disarmament and Arms Control 2003–05; Amb. to Russian Fed. 2005–.
Address: Embassy of Germany, 119285 Moscow, ul. Mosfilmovskaya 56, Russian Federation (office). *Telephone:* (495) 937-95-00 (office). *Fax:* (495) 938-23-54 (office). *E-mail:* germanmo@aha.ru (office). *Website:* www .moskau.diplo.de (office).

SCHMIDT, Christian, PhD, D.SC.ECON.; French economist and academic; *Director, Laboratory of Economics and Sociology of Defence Organizations (LESOD);* b. 20 July 1938, Neuilly-sur-Seine; m. Marie-Pierre de Cossè Brissac 1988. *Education:* Facultés de Lettres, Droit, Sciences, Inst. d'Etudes Politiques, Paris, Inst. des Hautes Etudes de Défense Nationale, Acad. of Int. Law, The Hague. *Career:* Research Asst Inst. of Applied Econ. Sciences Laboratoire Coll. de France 1964–67; Asst La Sorbonne 1967–70; Chargé de Mission Forecasting Admin. Ministry of Finances 1970–72; f. Dir Econ. Perspectives 1969–86; Asst Dir French Inst. of War Studies 1980–82; Pres. Charles Gide Asscn for the Study of Econ. Thought 1981–90; Consultant on Econ. Aspects of Disarmament UN 1980; Prof. of Econs Univ. of Paris IX (Paris Dauphine) 1983–; Pres., Founder Asscn française des économistes de défense 1981–, Int. Defence Econ. Asscn 1985–; Dir Lab. of Econs and Sociology of Defence Orgs. (LESOD) 1984–; Co-Dir (Research Group) CNRS 1990–; Chair. Scientific Council of European Soc. of Econ. Thought; mem. Council French Econs Asscn 2000–04, Societé d'Economie Politique 2000–; mem. various editorial bds; Croix de Chevalier, Légion d'honneur; Prix de L'institut (Acad. des Sciences Morales et Politiques) 1986, 1993. *Publications:* Conséquences Economiques et Sociales de la Course aux Armaments 1983, Essai sur l'Economie Ricardienne 1984, La Semantique Economique en Question 1985, Peace, Defence and Economic Analysis 1987, The Economics of Military Expenditures 1989, Penser la Guerre, Penser l'Economie 1991, Game Theory and International Relations 1994, Uncertainty and Economic Thought 1996, Game Theory and International Relations (co-ed.) 1996, The Rational Foundations of Economic Behaviour (co-ed.) 1996, La Theorie des Jeux: Essai d'Interpretation 2001, Game Theory and Economic Analysis 2002; numerous articles in learned journals.
Address: Université de Paris-IX Dauphine, Place du Maréchal de Lattre de Tassigny, 75775 Paris cedex 16 (office); 109 rue de Grenelle, 75007 Paris,

France (home). *Telephone:* 1-44-05-49-39 (office); 1-45-51-01-78 (home). *Fax:* 1-44-05-46-87 (office); 1-45-51-22-70 (home). *E-mail:* christian .schmidt@dauphine.fr (office); schmidt@magic.fr (home).

SCHMIT, Nicolas, PhD; Luxembourg diplomatist and politician; *Minister-delegate of Foreign Affairs and Immigration;* b. 10 Dec. 1953, Differdange. *Career:* mem. Lëtzebuerger Sozialistesch Arbechterpartei (Socialist Workers' Party of Luxembourg), Sec., Socialist Parl. Group 1989–90; adviser to Perm. Rep. to EU 1990–91; Dir Int. Econ. Relations and Co-operation, Ministry of Foreign Affairs 1992–98; Perm. Rep. to EU, Brussels 1998–2003; currently Minister-del. of Foreign Affairs and Immigration; mem. Conseil d'Etat.
Address: Ministry of Foreign Affairs and Immigration, 5 rue Notre-Dame, 2240 Luxembourg (office). *Telephone:* 478-1 (office). *Fax:* 22-31-44 (office). *E-mail:* officielle.boite@mae.etat.lu (office). *Website:* www.mae.lu (office).

SCHMÖGNEROVÁ, Brigita, PhD; Slovak international organization official and politician; *Vice-President, European Bank for Reconstruction and Development;* b. 17 Nov. 1947, Bratislava; m.; one s. *Education:* School of Econs, Bratislava. *Career:* teacher, Univ. of Athens, Greece and Georgetown Univ., Washington, DC, USA; researcher, Inst. of Econs, Slovak Acad. of Sciences; Lecturer, Univ. of Econs, Bratislava; Econ. Adviser to Pres. of Slovak Repub. 1993; Deputy Prime Minister 1994; mem. Parl. 1995–98; Minister of Finance 1998–2002; Exec. Sec. UN Econ. ECE 2002–05; adviser to IMF, IBRD and EBRD; Vice-Pres. EBRD 2005–; World Finance Minister of the Year Award, Euromoney Inst. Investor 2000.
Address: European Bank for Reconstruction and Development, One Exchange Square, London, EC2A 2JN, England (office). *Telephone:* (20) 7338-6000 (office). *Fax:* (20) 7338-6910 (office). *E-mail:* ngr@ebrd.com (office). *Website:* www.ebrd.com (office).

SCHNEIDER, Cynthia Perrin, PhD; American academic and fmr diplomatist; *Distinguished Professor in Practice of Diplomacy, School of Foreign Service, Georgetown University;* b. 16 Aug. 1953, Pa. *Education:* Harvard Univ., Oxford Univ. *Career:* Asst Curator of European Paintings, Museum of Fine Arts, Boston; Asst Prof. of Art History, Georgetown Univ. 1984–90, Assoc. Prof. 1990, Distinguished Prof. in Practice of Diplomacy, School of Foreign Service 2004–, Pfizer Medical Humanities Scholar in Residence, Public Policy Inst. and Dir Life Sciences and Society Initiative 2004–06; Amb. to Netherlands 1998–2001; Nonresident Sr Fellow, Foreign Policy, Saban Center for Middle East Policy, Brookings Inst.; Vice-Chair. Pres.'s Cttee on the Arts and Humanities; fmr mem. Bd of Dirs Nat. Museum of Women in the Arts, Australian-American Leadership Dialogue. *Publications:* Rembrandt's Landscapes 1990, Rembrandt's Landscapes: Drawing and Prints 1990.
Address: Georgetown University, Box 571444, 3300 Whitehaven Street, NW, Suite 5000, Washington, DC 20057-1485, USA (office). *Telephone:* (202) 687-0703 (office). *Fax:* (301) 924-8715 (office). *E-mail:* schneidc@ georgetown.edu (office); cpschneider@restructassoc.com. *Website:* hpi .georgetown.edu/lifesciandsociety (office).

SCHNEIDERHAN, Gen. Wolfgang; German army officer; *Inspector General of the Bundeswehr;* b. 26 July 1946, Riedlingen, Donau; m. Elke Schneiderhan (née Speckhardt); two d. three s. *Education:* Bundeswehr Command and Staff Coll., Hamburg. *Career:* began career with Bundeswehr (German Armed Forces) 1966; Youth Information Officer, 10th Armoured Div., Sigmaringen 1972–74; Co. Commdr Armoured Battalion 293, Stetten am Kalten Markt 1974–77; Asst Br. Chief, Mil. Intelligence, Armed Forces Staff 1979–81; Asst Chief of Staff, G-3 Operations, Home Defence Brigade 55, Böblingen 1981–83; Sr Officer, G-3, Operations, NATO Cen. Europe HQ, Brunssum, The Netherlands 1983–86; CO Armoured Battalion 553, Stetten am Kalten Markt 1986–88; Chief of Staff, 4th Mechanized Div., Regensburg 1988–90; Sr Officer, Arms Control, NATO HQ, Brussels 1990–92; Dir Faculty of Army Doctrine, Bundeswehr Command and Staff Coll. 1992–94; CO Armoured 39 Brigade Thüringen, Erfurt 1994–97; Asst Chief of Staff, Planning, Fed. Ministry of Defence 1997–99; Chief of Policy and Advisory Staff 2000–02; apptd Chief of Defence 2002; Inspector Gen. of the Bundeswehr 2002–; apptd Brig.-Gen. 1996, Maj.-Gen. 1999, Lt-Gen. 2000, Gen. 2002; Gold Cross of Honour of the Bundeswehr.
Address: Ministry of Defence, Stauffenbergstr. 18, 10785 Berlin, Germany (office). *Telephone:* (30) 200400 (office). *Fax:* (30) 20048333 (office). *E-mail:* poststelle@bmvg.bund400.de (office). *Website:* www.bundeswehr.de (office).

SCHOMMER, Martine; Luxembourg diplomatist; *Permanent Representative, European Union;* b. 13 July 1961. *Education:* Université de Paris III–Sorbonne. *Career:* joined Econ. Affairs office, Ministry of Foreign Affairs 1987, Diplomatic Adviser to Prime Minister 1995–98, Dir of Political

Affairs 2002–04; posted to Perm. Mission to EU 1991–95; Amb. to China 1998–2002, concurrently non-resident Amb. to Mongolia, Singapore, Vietnam; Perm. Rep. to EU 2004–; Knight, Order of the Crown (China), Chevalier de la Légion d'Honneur (France), Knight, Order of the White Rose (Finland), Knight, Order of Merit (Italy).
Address: Permanent Mission of Luxembourg, Council of the European Union, Avenue de Cortenberg 75, Brussels 1000, Belgium (office). *Telephone:* (2) 735-20-60 (office). *Fax:* (2) 736-14-29 (office). *E-mail:* secretariat@rpue.stat.lu (office).

SCHORI, (Jean) Pierre (Olov), MA; Swedish diplomatist, politician and academic; *Distinguished Visiting Professor, Adelphi University;* b. 14 Nov. 1938, Norrköping; m. Maud Edgren-Schori; three c. *Education:* Univ. of Lund and Stockholm Univ. *Career:* Licentiate in Philosophy in Social Work; Deputy Int. Sec. of Social Democratic Party 1965–68, Int. Sec. 1968–71, 1976–82; First Sec., Ministry of Foreign Affairs 1971–72; Foreign Policy Adviser to Cabinet 1973–76; Perm. Under-Sec. of State, Ministry of Foreign Affairs 1982–91; mem. Parl. for Stockholm (Social Democratic Party— SDP) 1991–99; Deputy Chair. Cttee on Foreign Affairs and Foreign Affairs Spokesman of SDP 1991–94; Minister for Int. Devt Co-operation and Deputy Foreign Minister for Co-operation with Cen. and Eastern Europe 1994–96; Minister for Int. Devt Co-operation, Migration and Asylum Policy and Deputy Foreign Minister 1996–99; mem. European Parl., Leader, Swedish Social Democrat Group, Spokesperson for Socialist Group on Foriegn Affairs and Pres. Cttee for EU–Japan Relations 1999–2000; Perm. Rep. to UN, New York 2000–04, Special Rep. for the Sec.-Gen. for Côte d'Ivoire 2004–; Distinguished Visiting Prof., Adelphi Univ., New York 2004–; mem. Local School Authority in Lidingo 1973–79, Lidingo Cultural Board 1979–82, Int. Comm. for Cen. American Recovery and Devt (The Sanford Comm.) 1987–89, Board Int. Peace Acad., New York 2000–04; Chair. Nat. Judo Fed. (Black belt, 1st Dan) 1989–96, Olof Palme Memorial Fund 1996–, Swedish Inst., Alexandria, Egypt 1999–2002, UN Cttee for Parliamentarians for Global Action 2001–04; Head, EU Election Observation Mission in Zimbabwe 2000, 2002; Pres. Solidar (ind. int. alliance of NGOs, Brussels 2004–; Ed. Tiden 1971–73.
Publications include: Latin Americans on Latin America 1968, Central America: In the Eye of the Hurricane 1981, El desafio europeo en Centroamérica 1982, Between Blocks and Bridges: Swedish Foreign Policy from Olof Palme to Post-Communism 1992, Entre Escila y Caribdis: Olof Palme, la Guerra Fría y el Poscomunismo 1994, Europe Between Maastricht and Sarajevo 1994, The Impossible Neutrality: Southern Africa 1994, Olof Palme: Reformer without Borders 1996, Olof Palme: Reformista sin Fronteras 1997, Can the United Nations Manage the New Era? 1999, From Marshall to Post-Communism: A New Deal for Internationalism, Four Years that Shook the World: The United Nations in the Shadow of 9/11 2004.
Address: Department of Political Science, Adelphi University, Blodgett Hall, Room 202D, Garden City, NY 11530-0701, USA (office). *Telephone:* (516) 877-4592 (office). *Fax:* (516) 877-4594 (office). *E-mail:* schori@adelphi.edu (office). *Website:* academics.adelphi.edu/artsci/pol (office).

SCHREIBER HUGHES, Lisa Bobbie, MS, JD; American lawyer and diplomatist; *Ambassador to Suriname;* m. Eric P. Salonen. *Education:* Rutgers School of Law, NJ, Nat. War Coll. (Nat. Defense Univ.), Washington, DC. *Career:* conducted research in Int. Commercial Arbitration, Parker School of Foreign and Comparative Law, Columbia Univ., New York; mem. Bars of NJ, Pa, DC; career mem. Sr Foreign Service, joined Foreign Service 1985, posted to Quito, later in charge of Consulate Gen. in Calgary, Alberta, also served in Havana; assignments at Dept of State have included Dir Office of Andean Affairs (Bolivia, Colombia, Ecuador, Peru and Venezuela), Post Man. Officer (Bahamas, Trinidad and Tobago), Econ. Officer (Cuba), and Chief, Agricultural Devt Div. (FAO of UN and WFP, Rome); served on Pres.'s staff at White House as Dir for Consular Affairs and Int. Programs on Homeland Security Council; Deputy Chief of Mission, Embassy in Paramaribo 2000–02; selected to represent Dept of State as Fellow in Dept of Defense 'Capstone' program for Gen. Officers 2006; Amb. to Suriname 2006–; various Dept of State Superior Honor Awards.
Address: US Embassy, PO Box 1821, Dr Sophie Redmondstraat 129, Paramaribo, Suriname (office). *Telephone:* 472900 (office). *Fax:* 425690 (office). *E-mail:* embuscen@sr.net (office). *Website:* suriname.usembassy .gov (office).

SCHREYER, Michaele, PhD; German organization official and fmr politician; *Vice-President, Netzwerks Europäische Bewegung Deutschland;* b. 9 Aug. 1951, Cologne. *Education:* Univ. of Cologne, Free Univ. of Berlin. *Career:* Research Asst, Inst. for Public Finances and Social Policy, Free Univ. of Berlin 1977–82, Lecturer 1996–99, Lecturer, Otto-Suhr-Institut 2004–; research asst and adviser for Green Caucus, Bundestag 1983–87; Researcher, Inst. for Econ. Research (IFO), Munich 1987–88;

Minister for Urban Devt and Environmental Protection in Senate of Berlin 1989–90; mem. State Parl., Berlin 1991–99, mem. Budget and Public Finance Cttee, Chair. Sub-Cttee on Funds for Public Housing 1995–97; Chair. Green Caucus, Berlin Parl. 1998–99; EU Commr for Budget, Financial Control and Fraud Prevention 1999–2004; currently Vice-Pres. Netzwerks Europäische Bewegung Deutschland (non-partisan union of European political orgs); mem. Advisory Bd for Transatlantic Relations and European Affairs, Heinrich Böll Foundation; mem. Advisory Bd Transparency Int. Germany; fmr mem. numerous co. bds; fmr mem. Bd Berlin br. of German Soc. for UN.
Address: Netzwerk Europäische Bewegung Deutschland, Sophienstr. 28/29, 10178 Berlin, Germany (office). *Telephone:* (30) 3036201 (office). *Fax:* (30) 3036201 (office). *E-mail:* netzwerk@europaeische-bewegung.de (office). *Website:* www.europaeische-bewegung.de (office).

SCHULTE, Gregory L.; American diplomatist; *Permanent Representative, United Nations, Vienna;* m. Nancy Schulte; two c. *Education:* Univ. of Calif., Berkeley, Woodrow Wilson School, Princeton Univ. *Career:* Presidential Man. Intern, Office of Sec. of Defense 1983; Dir for Strategic Forces Policy 1985, Asst for Theater Nuclear Forces Policy –1992; promoted to Sr Exec. Service 1992; assigned to NATO Int. Staff, Brussels, Belgium 1992–98; fmr Dir, Bosnia Task Force; fmr Dir Nuclear Planning; Special Asst to Pres., Implementation of Dayton Peace Accords, Nat. Security Council 1998–99, fmr Co-Chair. Exec. Cttee; Prin. Dir for Requirements, Plans and Counterproliferation Policy, Office of Sec. of Defense, Pentagon 1999–2000; Sr Dir for SE European Affairs, Nat. Security Council 2000–02, Exec. Sec. 2003–05; Perm. Rep. to UN, IAEA and Int. Orgs, Vienna 2005–; two Presidential Rank Awards.
Address: Office of the Permanent Representative of the USA to the United Nations, IZD Tower, Wagramerstrasse 17–19, 1220 Vienna, Austria (office). *Telephone:* (1) 313390 (office). *Fax:* (1) 313394873 (office). *E-mail:* pavienna@state.gov (office). *Website:* vienna.usmission.gov (office).

SCHULTZE, Charles Louis, BA, MA, PhD; American economist and fmr government official; *Senior Fellow Emeritus in Economic Studies, Brookings Institution;* b. 12 Dec. 1924, Alexandria, Va; m. Rita Irene Hertzog 1947; one s. five d. *Education:* Georgetown Univ. and Univ. of Maryland. *Career:* Economist, Office of Price Stabilization 1951–52, Council of Econ. Advisers 1952–53, 1955–59; Assoc. Prof. of Econs, Indiana Univ. 1959–61; Assoc. Prof., Adjunct Prof. of Econs, Univ. of Md 1961–87; Asst Dir, Bureau of the Budget 1962–65, Dir 1965–68; Sr Fellow, Brookings Inst., Washington, DC 1968–76, 1981–87, 1991–96, Emer. 1997–, Dir Econ. Studies 1987–90, John C. and Nancy D. Whitehead Chair 1997; Chair. Council of Econ. Advisers to Pres. 1977–81; Hon. Pres. American Econ. Asscn 1984. *Publications:* National Income Analysis 1964, The Politics and Economics of Public Spending 1969 (co-author), Setting National Priorities: The 1974 Budget, The Public Use of Private Interest 1977, Other Times, Other Places 1986, American Living Standards (co-ed. and co-author) 1988, Barriers to European Growth (co-ed. and co-author) 1989, An American Trade Strategy: Options for the 1990s (co-ed.) 1990, Memos to the President 1992.
Address: Brookings Institution, 1775 Massachusetts Avenue, NW, Washington, DC 20036 (office); 5520 33rd Street, NW, Washington, DC 20015, USA (home). *Telephone:* (202) 797-6163 (office). *Fax:* (202) 797-6181 (office). *E-mail:* escomment@brookings.edu (office). *Website:* www .brookings.org/scholars/cschultze.htm (office).

SCHUMACHER, Rolf, DrPhil; German diplomatist; *Ambassador to Argentina;* b. 21 Oct. 1943, Duisburg; m.; two c. *Education:* Univs of Tübingen, Paris, Mainz, Delhi. *Career:* studied Indian and Romance languages and literature and Islamic philology 1967–75; mem. academic staff, Univ. of Kiel 1975–76; Foreign Office training 1976–78, Cultural Attaché, Embassy in Tehran 1978–80, Consular Affairs, Embassy in Bangkok 1980–84, Adviser, Political Dept, Foreign Office, Bonn 1984–87, Counsellor (Political Dept) at German Del. to NATO, Brussels 1987–90, Deputy Head of NATO Dept (Political Dept), Foreign Office 1990–93, Deputy Head of Mission, Embassy in Algiers 1993–94, Embassy in Rabat 1994–97, Head of Dept, Fed. Presidency 1997, Head of NATO Dept, Foreign Office 1997–99, Head of N America and Security Policy Subdivision 1999–2001, Deputy Head of Political Dept 2001–03, Amb. to Argentina 2003–.
Address: Embassy of Germany, Villanueva 1055, 1426 Buenos Aires, Argentina (office). *Telephone:* (11) 4778-2500 (office). *Fax:* (11) 4778-2550 (office). *E-mail:* administracion@embajada-alemana.org.ar (office). *Website:* www.embajada-alemana.org.ar (office).

SCHÜSSEL, Wolfgang; Austrian politician; b. 7 June 1945, Vienna; m.; two c. *Education:* Univ. of Vienna. *Career:* Sec. Parl. Austrian People's Party (ÖVP) 1968, Chair. 1995–2007, Group Leader in Parl. 2007–; Sec.-Gen. Austrian Econ. Fed. 1975–89; mem. Parl. 1979–, Leader ÖVP Group of

Econ. Fed. Parl. Dels 1987; Minister of Econ. Affairs 1989–95; Vice-Chancellor of Austria and Minister of Foreign Affairs 1996–2000, Chancellor of Austria 2000–07; Minister of the Interior Jan. 1, 2007–Jan. 11, 2007; Pres. European Council Jan.– June 2006. *Publications:* several books on issues relating to democracy and economics.
Address: Austrian People's Party (ÖVP), Lichtenfelsgasse 7, 1010 Vienna, Austria (office). *Telephone:* (1) 401-26-0 (office). *Website:* www.oevp.at (office).

SCHUWIRTH, Gen. Rainer; German army officer; b. 12 July 1945, Regensburg, Bavaria; m. Barbara Hackbarth; one s., one d. *Career:* enlisted into Fed. Armed Forces 1964; trained as Artillery Officer 1964–66; assignments as Artillery Officer and Honest John Battery Commdr 1966–76; Fed. Armed Forces Command and Staff Coll., Hamburg 1976–78; G2 Staff Officer (Intelligence Estimates), HQ Centag, Heidelberg 1978–81; G3 Staff Officer (Operations) at III Corps, Koblenz 1981–83; Commdr Missile Artillery Bn 150 (Lance), Wesel 1983–85; Asst Br. Chief, Mil. Leadership and Civic Educ., Armed Forces Staff, Fed. Ministry of Defence, Bonn 1985–88, Branch Chief of Mil. Policy 1990–91; Mil. Asst to Fed. Minister of Defence 1988–90; Commdr Armoured Brigade 8, Luneberg 1991–93; Head of Mil. Policy Div., Perm. Mission to NATO 1994–96; Asst Chief of Staff, Armed Forces Staff Politico-Mil. Affairs and Operations, Ministry of Defence 1996–99; Commdg Gen. IV Corps, Potsdam 1999–2001; Dir-Gen., EU Mil. Staff 2001–04; Chief of Staff, SHAPE 2004–07 (retd); contracted by European Defence Agency to produce draft concept for EU to exploit Network Enabled Capabilities (NEC) in support of crisis-man. operations 2007; work with Stiftung Wissenschaft und Politik, Berlin 2008–; Silver Cross of Honour, Fed. Armed Forces, Gold Cross of Honour, Fed. Armed Forces, Cross of Order of Merit, Cross of Order of Merit (First Class), Commdr de l'Ordre nat. de Mérite, Gold Medal, Polish Armed Forces.
Address: c/o Stiftung Wissenschaft und Politik, Deutsches Institut für Internationale Politik und Sicherheit, Ludwigkirchplatz 3-4, 10719 Berlin, Germany.

SCHWAB, George D., BA, MA, PhD; American political scientist, editor and academic; *President, National Committee on American Foreign Policy;* b. 25 Nov. 1931; m. Eleonora Storch 1965 (died 1998); three s. *Education:* City Univ. of New York, Columbia Univ., New York. *Career:* began teaching career at Columbia Coll., Columbia Univ., New York 1959; Lecturer, Dept of History, City Coll., CUNY 1960–68, Asst Prof. of History 1968–72, Assoc. Prof. 1973–79, Prof. 1980–2000, Prof. Emer. (City Coll. and Grad. Center) 2001–; Co-founder Nat. Cttee on American Foreign Policy, later Vice-Pres. and Sr Vice-Pres., Pres. 1993–, Ed. American Foreign Policy Interests (its journal) 1976–, Global Perspectives in History and Politics series; mem. Council on Foreign Relations, German Studies Asscn, CUNY Acad. of Humanities and Sciences, Columbia Univ.'s Seminar on the History of Legal and Political Thought and Insts, United States Holocaust Memorial Museum's Cttee on Conscience, Washington, DC, Latvian Pres.'s Comm. of Int. Historians; has lectured widely on his concept of The Open-Society Bloc at Univ. of Freiburg, Bundeswehrhochschule, Hamburg, Germany and other insts; Order of the Three Stars (Latvia) 2002; Ellis Island Medal of Honor 1998. *Publications include:* Dayez: Beyond Abstract Art 1967, Enemy oder Foe 1968 (ed. English version Telos, No. 72, 1987), The Challenge of the Exception: An Introduction to the Political Ideas of Carl Schmitt 1970, 1989, Appeasement and Détente, Détente in Historical Perspective (ed. and contrib.) 1975, 1981, Ideology and Foreign Policy (ed. and contrib.) 1978, 1981, State and Nation: Towards a Further Clarification, Nationalism: Essays in Honor of Louis L. Snyder, Michael Palumbo and William O. Shausban 1981, Eurocommunism: The Ideological and Political Theoretical Foundations (ed. and contrib.) 1981, Detente in Historical Perspective 1981, Toward a New Foreign Policy, United States Foreign Policy at the Crossroads (ed. and contrib.) 1982, 1988, A Decade of the National Committee on American Foreign Policy, Power and Policy in Transition 1984, The Destruction of a Family 1987, Elie Wiesel: Between Jerusalem and New York 1990, Thoughts of a Collector 1991, Journey to Belfast and London (co-author) 1999, Carl Schmitt, a Note on a Qualitative Authoritarian Bourgeois Liberal 2000, trans.: The Leviathan in the State Theory of Thomas Hobbes 1996, The Concept of the Political 1996, Carl Schmitt's Political Theology: Four Chapters on the Concept of Sovereignty 2005; numerous articles in professional journals.
Address: National Committee on American Foreign Policy, 320 Park Avenue, Eighth Floor, New York, NY 10022-6839, USA (office). *Telephone:* (212) 224-1120 (office). *Fax:* (212) 224-2524 (office). *E-mail:* george.schwab@ncafp.org (office). *Website:* www.ncafp.org (office); www.tandf.co.uk/journals/titles/10803920.asp.

SCHWAB, Klaus, KCMG, DEcon, DrIng, MPA; German foundation director and academic; *Executive Chairman, World Economic Forum;* b. 30 March 1938, Ravensburg, Germany; m. Hilde Schwab; one s. one d. *Education:* Swiss Federal Inst. of Tech., Univ. of Fribourg, Harvard Univ. *Career:* founder and Exec. Chair. World Econ. Forum 1971–; Prof. of Business Policy, Univ. of Geneva 1972–2002; fmr mem. UN High-Level Advisory Bd on Sustainable Devt; fmr Vice-Chair. UN Cttee for Devt Planning; fmr mem. Earth Council; co-f. The Schwab Foundation for Social Entrepreneurship 1998; f. The Forum of Young Global Leaders 2004; Trustee Peres Center for Peace, Israel; Grand Cross of the Nat. Order of Merit, Germany; six hon. doctorates including from Bishops Univ., Quebec, Canada, Univ. Autonoma de Guadalajara, Mexico, LSE, UK); Hon. Prof., Ben Gurion Univ., Israel; The Candlelight Award Foundation for Prevention and Early Resolution of Conflict 2001. *Publications:* several books and The Global Competitiveness Report (annually 1979–).
Address: World Economic Forum, 91–93 route de la Capite, 1223 Cologny/ Geneva, Switzerland (office). *Telephone:* (22) 869 1212 (office). *Fax:* (22) 786 2744 (office). *E-mail:* contact@weforum.org (office). *Website:* www.weforum.org (office).

SCHWAB, Susan Carroll, PhD; American academic administrator and government official; *United States Trade Representative; Education:* Williams Coll., Stanford Univ., George Washington Univ. *Career:* agricultural trade negotiator, Office of US Trade Rep. 1977–79; Trade Policy Officer, US Foreign Service, American Embassy, Tokyo, Japan 1979–81; Chief Econ. and Legis. Asst, Office of US Senator John C. Danforth 1981–86, Legis. Dir 1986–89; Asst Sec. of Commerce and Dir Gen., US and Foreign Commercial Service, US Dept of Commerce 1989–93; Dir of Corp. Business Devt, Motorola Inc. 1993–95; Dean, School of Public Affairs, Univ. of Md 1995–2003; Pres. and CEO Univ. of Md Foundation 2004–05; Deputy US Trade Rep. 2005–06, US Trade Rep. 2006–; mem. Council on Foreign Relations; Fellow, Nat. Acad. of Public Admin. *Publications:* Trade-Offs: Negotiating the Omnibus Trade Act 1994; numerous articles in magazines and journals.
Address: Office of the United States Trade Representative, Winder Bldg, 600 17th Street, NW, Washington, DC 20508, USA (office). *Telephone:* (202) 395-3230 (office). *Fax:* (202) 395-4549 (office). *E-mail:* contactustr@ustr.eop.gov (office). *Website:* www.ustr.gov (office).

SCHWARTZ, Stephen M., BBA, MA; American diplomatist; *Chargé d'affaires in Mauritius;* b. Buffalo, NY; m. Dr Kristy Cook; one s. one d. *Education:* Miami Univ., Oxford, OH, Int. Graduate School, Stockholm, Sweden, School of Oriental and African Studies, London, UK. *Career:* served as Peace Corps volunteer in Cameroon 1981–1983, Desk Officer at HQ 1985–88, worked at Citizen's Democracy Corps in charge of volunteer programs in Cen. and Eastern Europe and fmr Soviet Union 1988–92; career mem. Sr Foreign Service since 1992, Consular Officer, Addis Ababa 1992–93, Political/Econ. section, Addis Ababa 1993–94, State Dept rep. on task force implementing Presidential Initiative for Greater Horn of Africa 1994, Gen. Services Officer, Embassy in Bujumbura, Burundi 1995–96, Desk Officer for Sudan (and three-month temporary assignment in Nairobi for southern Sudanese issues), State Dept 1996–98, Special Asst for African and Western Hemisphere issues to Under-Sec. of State for Political Affairs 1998–99, Political/Econ. Officer, US Interests Section, Havana 1999–2001, Deputy Political Counselor, Embassy in Pretoria 2001–04, Deputy Chief of Mission, Port Louis, Mauritius 2004–05, Chargé d'affaires a.i. 2005–.
Address: Embassy of the USA, Rogers House, 4th Floor, John F. Kennedy Street, PO Box 544, Port Louis, Mauritius (office). *Telephone:* 202-4400 (office). *Fax:* 208-9534 (office). *E-mail:* usembass@intnet.mu (office). *Website:* mauritius.usembassy.gov (office).

SCHWARZENBERG, Karel; Czech politician; *Minister of Foreign Affairs;* b. 10 Dec. 1937, Prague; m.; two s. one d. *Education:* Univ. of Vienna, Univ. of Graz, Univ. of Munich. *Career:* family exiled to Austria after Communist takeover of Czech Repub. 1948; Pres. Int. Helsinki Cttee for Human Rights (concerned with human rights issues in fmr USSR, Bulgaria, Kosovo and Czech Repub.) 1984–91; est. Czechoslovak Documentation Centre (archive of prohibited literature) with Dr Vilém Prečan in Bavaria, Germany 1985; returned to Czech Repub. 1990; Chancellor, Office of Pres. 1990–92; Head of first OSCE del. to Nagorno Karabakh, Azerbaijan 1992; mem. Senate (Civic Democratic Alliance, ODA) 2004–, Chair. Foreign Affairs, Defence and Security Cttee 2005–07, Alt. mem. Perm. Del. of Parl. to Parl. Ass. of Council of Europe 2005; mem. Perm. Czech del. to Parl. Ass., NATO 2006–; mem. Caucus of Open Democracy 2006–07; Minister of Foreign Affairs 2007–; mem. Bd of Dirs Forum 2000, 2005–07; Order T.G.M. (Third Class) 2002; Prize for Human Rights, Council of Europe 1989.
Address: Ministry of Foreign Affairs, Černínský Palác, Loretánské nám. 5, 118 00 Prague 1, Czech Republic (office). *Telephone:* (2) 24181111 (office). *Fax:* (2) 24182048 (office). *E-mail:* info@mzv.cz (office). *Website:* www.mzv.cz (office).

SCHWEBEL, Stephen Myron, BA, LLB; American judge, lawyer, arbitrator and mediator; *President of the Administrative Tribunal, International Monetary Fund;* b. 10 March 1929, New York City; m. Louise I. N. Killander 1972; two d. *Education:* Harvard Coll., Univ. of Cambridge, UK, Yale Law School. *Career:* attorney 1954–59; Asst Prof. of Law, Harvard Univ. 1959–61; Asst Legal Adviser, then Special Asst to Asst Sec. of State for Int. Org. Affairs 1961–67; Exec. Vice-Pres. and Exec. Dir American Soc. of Int. Law 1967–73; Consultant, then Counsellor on Int. Law, Dept of State 1967–74, Deputy Legal Adviser 1974–81; Prof. of Int. Law, then Edward B. Burling Prof. of Int. Law and Org., Johns Hopkins Univ., Washington, DC 1967–81; Legal Adviser to US Del. and Alt. Rep. in 6th Cttee, UN Gen. Ass. 1961–65; Visiting Lecturer or Prof., Univ. of Cambridge 1957, 1983, ANU 1969, Hague Acad. of Int. Law 1972, Inst. Univ. de hautes études int., Geneva 1980 and various American univs 1987–; rep. in various cttees UN 1962–74; Assoc. Rep., Rep., Counsel or Deputy Agent in cases before Int. Court of Justice 1962–80; Judge, Int. Court of Justice 1981–2000, Vice-Pres. 1994–97, Pres. 1997–2000; mem. Int. Law Comm. 1977–81, Perm. Court of Arbitration, The Hague 2006–; arbitrator or chair. in int. commercial arbitrations 1982–; mem. Tribunal in Eritrea-Yemen Arbitration 1997–99, Ethiopia-Eritrea Boundary Comm. 2000–; Pres. Barbados-Trinidad and Tobago Arbitration Tribunal 2004–; Pres. Admin. Tribunal, IMF 1994–, Southern Blue Fin Tuna Arbitration 2000; mem. Panels of Arbitrators and of Conciliators of the Int. Centre for the Settlement of Investment Disputes (ICSID) of the World Bank 2000–; mem. Bd of Eds, American Journal of Int. Law 1967–81, 1994–; mem. Council on Foreign Relations, Inst. of Int. Law; mem. Bars of State of New York, Dist of Columbia, Supreme Court of the USA; Hon. Bencher, Gray's Inn 1998–, Hon. Fellow, Lauterpacht Centre for Int. Law, Univ. of Cambridge; Hon. Fellow, Trinity Coll. Cambridge 2005; Hon. LL (Bhopal Univ.) 1983, (Hofstra Univ.) 1997, (Univ. of Miami) 2002; Gherini Prize, Yale Law School 1954, Medal of Merit, Yale Law School 1997, Manley O. Hudson Medal, American Soc. of Int. Law 2000. *Publications:* The Secretary-General of the United Nations 1952, The Effectiveness of International Decisions (ed.) 1971, International Arbitration: Three Salient Problems 1987, Justice in International Law 1994; author of some 175 articles in legal periodicals and the press on problems of international law and relations. *Address:* 1501 K Street, NW, Washington, DC 20005 (office); 1917 23rd Street, NW, Washington, DC 20008, USA (home). *Telephone:* (202) 736-8328 (office); (202) 232-3114 (home). *Fax:* (202) 736-8709 (office); (202) 797-9286 (home). *E-mail:* judgeschwebel@aol.com (office).

SCHWEISGUT, Hans Dietmar; Austrian lawyer and diplomatist; *Permanent Representative, European Union;* b. Zams; m. Kaoru Schweisgut. *Career:* Dir-Gen. European Integration, Ministry of Finance 1997; Amb. to Japan –2003, to People's Repub. of China 2003–07; Perm. Rep. to EU, Brussels 2007–. *Address:* Permanent Representation of Austria to the European Union, 30 Avenue de Cortenberg, 1040 Brussels, Belgium (office). *Telephone:* (2) 234-51-00 (office). *Fax:* (2) 234-53-00 (office). *E-mail:* bruessel-ov@bmeia.gv.at (office).

SCHWEPPE, Reinhard, LLD; German diplomatist; *Permanent Representative, United Nations, Geneva;* b. 2 April 1949, Altena, Westphalia; m. Marget Schweppe-Ebber; three c. *Education:* Univ. of Freiburg, Univ. of Hamburg. *Career:* Asst Prof. of Law, Univ. of Freiburg 1972–75; joined Foreign Service 1975, at Foreign Office, Bonn (later Berlin) 1975–1977; Third Sec., Embassy in Pretoria/Capetown 1977–80, Second Sec., Perm. Mission to EU, Brussels 1980–83; Chief of Staff of State Sec. 1983–86; Political Counsellor, Embassy in Washington, DC 1986–90, First Counsellor, Embassy in New Delhi 1990–93; Dir European Dept, Ministry of Foreign Affairs 1993–97, Deputy Dir Gen European Dept 1997–99, Head of European Directorate-Gen. 1999–2003; Amb. to Poland 2003–07; Perm. Rep. to UN, Geneva 2007–. *Address:* Permanent Mission of Germany, Chemin du Petit-Saconnex 28 c, 1209 Geneva, Switzerland (office). *Telephone:* (22) 7301111 (office). *Fax:* (22) 7343043 (office). *E-mail:* mission.germany@ties.itu.int (office). *Website:* www.genf.diplo.de (office).

SCHWIMMER, Walter, LLD; Austrian politician, international organization official and lawyer; *Chairman, International Coordination, World Public Forum – Dialogue of Civilizations;* b. 16 June 1942, Vienna; m. Martina Pucher-Schwimmer; two s. *Education:* Univ. of Vienna. *Career:* mem. Nationalrat (Austrian Parl.) 1971–99, Chair. Parl. Cttee on Health 1989–94, on Justice 1995–96; Vice-Chair. Parl. Group, Austrian People's Party (ÖVP) 1986–94; mem. Council of Europe Parl. Ass. 1991–, Vice-Pres. Council of Europe 1996, Jan.–Sept. 1999, Sec.-Gen. 1999–2004; Chair. European People's Party Group–Christian Democrats 1996–99; Dir and Exec. Vice-Pres. Vienna Health Insurance Fund; Chair. Int. Coordination, World Public Forum – Dialogue of Civilizations 2005–; mem. Bd Crans

Montana Forum 2004–; consultant on int. relations and European affairs 2004–; Hon. Sec.-Gen. Maison de la Méditerranée 2004–; Grosses Goldenes Ehrenzeichen am Bande (Austria) 2004; Grosses Silbernes Ehrenzeichen mit dem Stern (Austria), Grosses Silbernes Ehrenzeichen der Stadt Wien, Grand Cross, Order of the Star of Romania 2001, Commdr's Cross, Order of Grand Duke Gaudemes (Lithuania), Chevalier, Légion d'honneur 2003, Grand Cross of the Equestrian Order of St Agatha (San Marino) 2003, Order of the Aztec Eagle (Mexico), Grande Ufficiale dell'Ordine al Merito (Italy) 2004; Leopold-Kunschak Award 1975, Peter the Great Int. Prize of the Russian Fed., European Pro Humanitate European Foundation for Culture Prize, Germany, Medal of the European Inst. of Moscow, Person of the Year Award (Ukraine) 2002. *Publications:* Christian Trade Unions in Austria 1975, Social Consequences of Inflation 1988, A Union Goes Down in History 1993, Der Traum Europa 2003. *Address:* World Public Forum – Dialogue of Civilizations, Vienna Headquarters, Stubenring 4, 1010 Vienna, Austria (office); Crans Montana Forum, 41 Avenue Hector Otto, 98000 Monaco (office); Consultancy Office, Dresden 2B, 3400 Klosterneuburg, Austria (office). *Telephone:* (1) 513-01-38-2 (office); 97707000 (office); 224387694 (office). *Fax:* (1) 513-01-38-4 (office); 97707040 (office); 224387649 (office). *E-mail:* schwimmer@wpfdc.at (office); schwimmer.cmf@aon.at (office); schwimmer.consult@aon.at (office). *Website:* www.wpfdc.org (office); www.cmf.ch (office).

SCOBEY, Margaret, DHist; American diplomatist; *Ambassador to Egypt;* b. Memphis, Tenn. *Education:* Univ. of Tennessee, Knoxville, Univ. of Michigan, Ann Arbor. *Career:* joined Foreign Service 1981, postings to Lima, Peru and Peshawar, Pakistan, fmr Deputy Chief of Mission, Embassy in San'a, fmr Chief of Political Section, Embassy in Kuwait, Consul-Gen., Jerusalem, mem. Sr Seminar, Dept of State 1999–2000, fmr Staff Asst to Asst Sec. for Near East and S Asian Affairs, Watch Officer, Operations Center, Political-Mil. Officer for Israel and Arab-Israeli Affairs, Deputy Dir of Secr. Staff, Dir Arabian Peninsular Affairs, Near East Bureau, Deputy Chief of Mission, Embassy in Riyadh 2001–03, Amb. to Syria 2003, recalled Feb. 2005, Political Counsellor, Baghdad 2006–07, Amb. to Egypt 2008–. *Address:* US Embassy, 8 Sharia Kamal ed-Din Salah, Garden City, Cairo, Egypt (office). *Telephone:* (2) 7973300 (office). *Fax:* (2) 7973200 (office). *E-mail:* consularcairo@state.gov (office). *Website:* cairo.usembassy.gov (office).

SCOGNAMIGLIO PASINI, Carlo Luigi, DEcon; Italian politician, economist and business consultant; *President, Aspen Institute Italia;* b. 27 Nov. 1944, Varese; m. Cecilia Pirelli; one s. one d. *Education:* L. Bocconi Univ., Milan, London School of Econs. *Career:* Asst Lecturer, L. Bocconi Univ., Asst Prof. of Industrial Econs 1968–73, Prof. 1973; Asst Prof. of Finance, Univ. of Padua 1973–79; Prof. of Econs and Industrial Policy, Libera Università Int. degli Studi Sociali, Rome 1979–, Dean and Rector 1984–92; Liberal Party cand. in Milan constituency, elected to Senate 1992, Chair. European Affairs Cttee, mem. Budget Cttee, re-elected to Senate 1994; Pres. of Senate 1994–; Acting Pres. of Italy 1994–96; Pres. Rizzoli-Corriere della Sera 1983–84, Vice-Pres. 1984–; Minister of Defence 1998–99; Co-Founder, Bocconi School of Business Admin 1979; Pres. Aspen Inst. Italia 1995–; Acad. of France Award for Econs 1988. *Publications include:* The Stock Exchange 1973, Industrial Crises 1976, The White Book on PPSS 1981, The White Book on the Italian Financial Market 1982, Theory and Policy of Finance 1987, Industrial Economics 1987, Report to Minister of Treasury of Commission for Privatization of Industry 1990, The Liberal Project 1996. *Address:* Aspen Institute Italia, Piazza SS Apostoli 49, 00186 Rome, Italy (office). *Telephone:* (06) 67062835 (office). *Fax:* (06) 67063988 (office). *E-mail:* info@aspeninstitute.it (office); c.scognamigliopasini@senato.it (office). *Website:* www.aspeninstitute.it (office).

SCOPELITIS, Anastase, MEcon; Greek diplomatist; b. 1944, Port Said, Egypt; m.; three s. *Education:* Univ. of Athens. *Career:* Lecturer in Public Finance, Univ. of Athens 1969–71; Attaché, Ministry of Foreign Affairs 1971, Third Sec., Cairo 1973–76, Second Sec., London 1976–79, First Sec. 1979–80, Deputy Head of Mission, The Hague 1980–87 (Second Counsellor 1982, First Counsellor 1985), Head of EC External Relations and New Policies Units, Ministry of Foreign Affairs 1987–89, European Corresp. and Acting Dir, European Political Cooperation 1989–91, Dir 1991–93, Minister Plenipotentiary Second Class 1991, First Class 1994, Minister and Deputy Head of Mission, London 1993–96, Amb. to Denmark 1996–99, Dir-Gen. for Political Affairs and Political Dir, Ministry of Foreign Affairs 1999–2002, Sec.-Gen. 2002–03, Amb. to UK 2003–06; Grand Cross, Order of Leopold II (Belgium), Order of the Dannebrog (Denmark), Commdr, Order of Merit (Egypt), Grand Cross, Order of the White Star (Estonia), Grand Cross, Grand Commdr, Order of Merit (Germany), Grand Cross, Order of Phoenix (Greece), Grand Cross, Order of Merit (Italy), Commdr,

Order of Oranje-Nassau (Netherlands), Grand Cross, Order of Infante Dom Henrique (Portugal).
Address: c/o Ministry of Foreign Affairs, Odos Akadimias 3, 106 71 Athens, Greece. *Telephone:* (210) 3682700. *Fax:* (210) 3624195. *E-mail:* mfa@mfa.gr. *Website:* www.mfa.gr.

SCOWCROFT, Lt-Gen. Brent, PhD; American consultant and fmr government official and air force officer (retd); *President, Scowcroft Group;* b. 19 March 1925, Odgen, Utah; m. Marian Horner 1951 (died 1995); one d. *Education:* US Mil. Acad., West Point and Columbia Univ. *Career:* Operational and Admin. positions in USAF 1948–53; taught Russian history as Asst Prof., Dept of Social Sciences, US Mil. Acad., W Point 1953–57; Asst Air Attaché, US Embassy, Belgrade 1959–61; Assoc. Prof., Political Science Dept, USAF Acad., Colorado 1962–63, Prof., Head of Dept 1963–64; Plans and Operations Section, Air Force HQ, Washington 1964–66; various Nat. Security posts with Dept of Defense 1968–72; Mil. Asst to Pres., The White House 1972, Deputy Asst to Pres. for Nat. Security Affairs 1973–75, Asst to Pres. for Nat. Security Affairs 1975–77, 1989–93; Pres. Forum for Int. Policy 1993–; Pres. The Scowcroft Group 1994–; mem. Pres.'s Gen. Advisory Cttee on Arms Control 1977–81; Dir Atlantic Council, US Bd of Visitors USAF Acad. 1977–79, Council on Foreign Relations, Rand Corpn; Vice-Chair. UNA/USA; Chair. Presidential Comm. on Strategic Forces 1983–89; mem. Cttee to Advise Dir of CIA 1995–; Chair. Pres.'s Foreign Intelligence Advisory Bd 2001–04, Eisenhower Inst. 2004–; mem. Cttee of Enquiry into Nat. Security Council 1986–87; Defense DSM, Air Force DSM (with two oak leaf clusters), Legion of Merit (with oak leaf cluster), Air Force Commendation Medal, Nat. Security Medal; Hon. KBE 1993. *Publication:* A World Transformed (with George Bush) 1998.
Address: The Scowcroft Group, Suite 900, 900 17th Street, NW, Washington, DC 20006, USA (office). *Telephone:* (202) 296-9312 (office). *Fax:* (202) 296-9395 (office). *Website:* www.scowcroft.com (office).

SEA, Kosal, LLB, LLM, DIur; Cambodian diplomatist; *Permanent Representative, United Nations;* b. 4 Nov. 1965, Battambang; m.; three c. *Education:* Karl Marx Univ., Univ. of Leipzig. *Career:* Lecturer in Int. Law, Faculty of Law and Econs and the Royal School of Admin, Phnom Penh 1993–99; legal adviser, Ministry for Foreign Affairs and Int. Cooperation 1993, Chief of Bureau of Treaties and Legal Affairs 1994–98, Deputy Dir Legal and Consular Dept 1999, Dir 1999–2000, Dir Cabinet of Sr Minister and Insp. Gen. 2000–03; Minister Counsellor and Deputy Chief of Mission, Embassy in Washington, DC 2003–05; Amb. and Chargé d'Affaires ad interim, Perm. Mission to UN, New York 2006, Perm. Rep. 2007–.
Address: Permanent Mission of Cambodia to the United Nations, 866 United Nations Plaza, Suite 420, New York, NY 10017, USA (office). *Telephone:* (212) 223-0676 (office). *Fax:* (212) 223-0425 (office). *E-mail:* cambodia@un.int (office). *Website:* www.un.int/cambodia (office).

SEALY, Philip Reuben Arnott, LLB; Trinidad and Tobago diplomatist (retd); b. 1947, Barbados; m.; two c. *Education:* Univ. of Sheffield, UK, Univ. of the West Indies. *Career:* called to the UK Bar 1971, to Trinidad and Tobago Bar 1972; Legal Cadet, Ministry of Legal Affairs 1972, Foreign Service Officer, Legal Affairs Div., Ministry of External Affairs 1973–76, Chief of Protocol, Legal Affairs Div. 1992–93, Dir of Admin. Div. 1993–95, Dir Legal Affairs Div. 1995–, Amb. to Venezuela 1996–97, to Peru 1997, to Colombia 1997–98, to Ecuador 1998–2002, Perm. Rep. to UN 2002–08 (retd).
Address: c/o Ministry of Foreign Affairs, Knowsley Building, 1 Queen's Park West, Port of Spain, Trinidad and Tobago. *Telephone:* 623-4116.

SEARS, Joshua, BA; Bahamian diplomatist; b. 18 July 1952, Forbes Hill, Little Exuma; m.; four c. *Education:* Univ. of the West Indies. *Career:* participant in UNITAR 1977, Fellowship in Int. Law 1980, Advanced Dip. in Public Admin. and Policy Man. 1991; numerous appointments in Bahamas Public Service including Exec. Officer, Asst Sec., Sr Asst Sec., First Asst Sec., Deputy Perm. Sec., Under-Sec., Acting Perm. Sec., Ministry of Health and Environment, Perm. Sec., Ministry of Foreign Affairs and Perm. Sec., Ministry of Health; foreign service appointments include Rapporteur at UN Seminar 1981, First Sec. Perm. Mission to UN 1983 and Deputy High Commr to UK 1996, Amb. to USA 2000–07, Amb.-at-Large, Ministry of Foreign Affairs 2007–; Rep. of Bahamas at numerous confs including Heads of Govt of the Caribbean Community, Commonwealth Heads of Govt Meetings, meetings of Foreign Ministers of the Caribbean Community, Regular and Special Sessions of Gen. Ass. of OAS, UN Gen. Ass., World Health Ass. and Assemblies of Pan American Health Org.; Nat. Co-ordinator, first meeting of Conf. of the Parties to the Convention on Biological Diversity 1994.
Address: Ministry of Foreign Affairs, East Hill Street, PO Box N-3746, Nassau, The Bahamas (office). *Telephone:* 322-7624 (office). *Fax:* 328-8212

(office). *E-mail:* mfabahamas@batelnet.bs (office). *Website:* www.mfabahamas.org (office).

SEBASTIAN, Sir Cuthbert (Montraville), GCMG, OBE, BSc, MD, CM; Saint Christopher and Nevis government official and physician; *Governor-General;* b. 22 Oct. 1921. *Education:* Mount Allison Univ., Dalhousie Univ., Canada. *Career:* pharmacist and lab. technician, Cunningham Hosp., St Kitts 1942–43; served in RAF 1944–45; Capt. St Kitts Nevis Defence Force 1958–80; Medical Supt, Cunningham Hosp. 1966, Joseph N. France Gen. Hosp. 1967–80; Chief Medical Officer Saint Christopher and Nevis 1980–83; pvt. medical practitioner 1983–95; Gov.-Gen. of Saint Christopher and Nevis 1996–.
Address: Government House, Basseterre (office); 6 Cayon Street, Basseterre, St Kitts, Saint Christopher and Nevis, W Indies (home). *Telephone:* 465-2315 (office); 465-2344 (home).

SEBBAN, Guy; French business executive and international organization executive; *Secretary-General, International Chamber of Commerce;* b. Mostaganem; m. Michelle Sebban. *Education:* Ecole de Physique et Chimie de Paris, Univ. of Paris (Sorbonne), Université de Paris Dauphine. *Career:* fmr Man. at Rhône-Poulenc, later at Aventis, Brussels, in charge of relations with EU insts; Sr Advisor to CEO of Vivendi Universal –2005; Sec.-Gen. ICC 2005–.
Address: International Chamber of Commerce, 38 cours Albert 1er, 75008 Paris, France (office). *Telephone:* 1-49-53-28-18 (office). *Fax:* 1-49-53-28-35 (office). *E-mail:* sg@iccwbo.org (office). *Website:* www.iccwbo.org (office).

SECHE, Stephen A., BA; American journalist and diplomatist; *Ambassador to Yemen;* m. Susan Canning; three d. *Education:* Univ. of Massachusetts, Amherst. *Career:* spent four years as journalist; career mem. Sr Foreign Service, entered Foreign Service 1978, public-diplomacy positions in Guatemala, Peru and Bolivia 1978–85, other overseas assignments have included Information Officer, Embassy in Ottawa 1989–93, Press Attaché, Embassy in New Delhi 1993–97; Arabic language training in Washington, DC and at Foreign Service Inst.'s Field School, Tunis 1997–99; Counselor for Public Affairs and Dir American Cultural Center, Embassy in Damascus 1999–2002; Dir Office for Egypt and Levant Affairs, Dept of State 2002–04; Deputy Chief of Mission, Embassy in Damascus 2004–05, Chargé d'affaires a.i. 2005–06; Visiting Fellow, Univ. of Southern California 2006–07; Amb. to Yemen 2007–.
Address: US Embassy, PO Box 22347, S'awan Street, San'a, Yemen (office). *Telephone:* (1) 7552000 (office). *Fax:* (1) 303182 (office). *E-mail:* ircsanaa@state.gov (office). *Website:* yemen.usembassy.gov (office).

SECHIN, Igor Ivanovich; Russian politician and business executive; *Deputy Chairman;* b. 7 Sept. 1960, Leningrad (later St Petersburg); m.; one s. *Education:* Leningrad State Univ. *Career:* army service 1984–86; leading instructor, Exec. Cttee, Dept of Foreign Econ. Relations, Leningrad Soviet 1988–91; Chief Expert, Asst to Head of Admin to First Vice-Mayor, Chair. Cttee on Foreign Relations, Office of Mayor of Leningrad 1991–96; Expert, Deputy Head of Div., Public Relations Dept, Dept of Foreign Affairs 1996–97; Head, Gen. Admin Dept, Advisor to Deputy Head then Head Chief Control Dept, Admin of the Russian Pres. 1998–99; Head, Secr. of First Deputy Chair., later Chair., Govt of Russian Fed. 1999–2000; Deputy Chief of Staff, Presidential Exec. Office 2000–08, Aide to the Pres. 2004–08; Deputy Chairman of the Govt, in charge of industry devt, nuclear power and environment 2008–; Chair. Rosneft Oil Co. 2004–.
Address: Office of the Government, 103274 Moscow, Krasnopresnenskaya nab. 2, Russia (office). *Telephone:* (495) 205-57-35 (office). *Fax:* (495) 205-42-19 (office). *Website:* www.government.ru (office).

ŠEDIVÝ, Jiří, MA, PhD; Czech academic, international organization official and fmr government official; *Assistant Secretary General for Defence Policy and Planning, NATO;* b. 1963; m. Lucie Šedivý; one s. *Education:* King's Coll. London, UK, Charles Univ., Prague. *Career:* Reader, Int. Relations, Int. Politics and Security Studies, Charles Univ., Prague 1995–2000; Prof. of European Security, Prague Center, New York Univ., USA 2000–03; Dir Inst. of Int. Relations (IIR), Prague 1998–2004; Prof. of Cen. European Security Studies, George C. Marshall European Center for Security Studies, Germany 2004–06; Minister of Defence June–Oct. 2006 (resgnd); Asst Sec. Gen. for Defence Policy and Planning, NATO, Brussels 2007–; Chair. Czech Foundation for the Study of Int. Relations; Chair. Editorial Bd Mezinárodní vztahy (Int. Relations Quarterly), Prague; mem. Editorial Bd Contemporary Security Policy, Birmingham Univ.; mem. Council for Science, Czech Foreign Ministry; aide to fmr Pres. Vaclav Havel 1996–2000. *Publications:* Dilema rozšiřování NATO (The Dilemma of NATO Enlargement) 2001; numerous articles in professional journals on int. security, IR theory, Czech foreign and security policy.
Address: North Atlantic Treaty Organization (NATO), blvd Léopold III, 1110 Brussels, Belgium (office). *Telephone:* (2) 707-41-11 (office). *Fax:* (2)

707-45-79 (office). *E-mail:* natodoc@hq.nato.int (office). *Website:* www .nato.int (office).

SEEISO, HRH Prince Seeiso Bereng, Principal Chief of Matsieng; Lesotho diplomatist; *High Commissioner to UK;* b. 16 April 1966, Maseru; younger brother to King Letsie III (q.v.); m. HRH Princess Mabereng Seeiso Bereng Seeiso; two c. *Education:* Ampleforth Coll., Yorks. and in Birmingham. *Career:* High Commr to UK 2005–; Co-founder, with HRH Prince Harry, and Patron Sentebale (Forget-Me-Not: The Princes' Fund for Lesotho) 2006.
Address: High Commission of Lesotho, 7 Chesham Place, Belgravia, London, SW1 8HN, England (office). *Telephone:* (20) 7235-5686 (office). *Fax:* (20) 7235-5023 (office). *E-mail:* lhc@lesotholondon.org.uk (office); hicom@lesotholondon.org.uk (office). *Website:* www.lesotholondon.org .uk (office).

ŠEFČOVIČ, Maroš, JuD, PhD; Slovak diplomatist; *Permanent Representative, European Union;* b. 24 July 1966, Bratislava; m. Helena Cinová; two d. one s. *Education:* Econ. Univ., Bratislava, Comenius Univ., Bratislava, Moscow State Inst. of Int. Relations. *Career:* Adviser to First Deputy Foreign Minister, Ministry of Foreign Affairs, Prague, Czechoslovakia 1990; Desk Officer, Dept of EU and NATO countries, Ministry of Foreign Affairs, Slovak Repub., Bratislava 1995, Deputy Dir 1996, Deputy Dir, Office of the Foreign Minister 1997, Dir 1998, Dir-Gen., Bilateral Cooperation Section 2002, Dir-Gen., European Affairs Section 2003–04; overseas postings include Third Sec. and Consul, Embassy of the Czech and Slovak Fed. Repub., Zimbabwe 1991–92; Deputy Chief of Mission and Second Sec., Embassy of the Slovak Repub., Ottawa, Canada 1992, Deputy Head of Mission, Mission to the EC, Brussels 1998; Amb. to Israel 1999; Perm. Rep. to the EU 2004–. *Publications:* various articles on issues related to European integration.
Address: Permanent Representation of Slovakia to the EU, 79 Avenue Cortenberg, 1000 Brussels, Brussels (office). *Telephone:* (2) 743-68-11 (office). *Fax:* (2) 743-68-88 (office). *E-mail:* sefcovic@pmsreu.be (office). *Website:* www.eubrussels.mfa.sk (office).

SEFUE, Ombeni Yohana, BA, MA; Tanzanian diplomatist; *Ambassador to USA;* b. 26 Aug. 1954, Same Dist; m. Anita Sefue; one s. one d. *Education:* Mzumbe Univ., Inst. of Social Studies, The Hague, Netherlands, Tanzania-Mozambique Centre for Foreign Relations, Dar es Salaam. *Career:* career diplomat, Counsellor, Embassy in Stockholm 1987–1992, left Foreign Service to work for as Speechwriter and Personal Asst to then Pres. Ali Hassan Mwinyi 1993–95, retained by newly elected Pres. Benjamin William Mkapa as Speechwriter and Personal Asst with added responsibilities 1995–2005, served on Comm. for Africa (The Blair Comm.) that produced report, Our Common Interest: Report of the Commission for Africa March 2005, participated at G8 Summit session that discussed the report at Gleneagles July 2005, participated in preparation of ILO World Comm. on Social Dimension of Globalization's report, A Fair Globalization: Creating Opportunities For All 2004, involved in work of UN, OAU (later the African Union), the Commonwealth, SADC, and East African Community, worked on peace process in Great Lakes Region, World Econ. Forum, Davos and Cape Town, Sino-African Forum, as well as Tokyo Int. Conf. on African Devt process; High Commr to Canada 2005–07, Amb. to USA 2007–.
Address: Embassy of Tanzania, 2139 R Street, NW, Washington, DC 20008, USA (office). *Telephone:* (202) 939-6125 (office). *Fax:* (202) 797-7408 (office). *E-mail:* ubalozi@tanzaniaembassy-us.org (office). *Website:* www.tanzaniaembassy-us.org (office).

SEIXAS DA COSTA, Francisco, BSc; Portuguese diplomatist; *Ambassador to Brazil;* b. 28 Jan. 1948, Vila Real; m. Virginia Costa. *Education:* Univ. of Lisbon. *Career:* early career in banking 1971–75; began diplomatic career, Head Dept for Devt Co-operation, Ministry of Foreign Affairs 1975–76, Head of African Div., Dept for Econ. Affairs 1976–79, Deputy Head of Mission, Oslo 1979–82, Head of Political and Devt Co-operation Affairs, Luanda 1982–85, Head of Div., EU Devt Co-operation Affairs 1986–87, Advisor to Sec. of State for Devt Co-operation 1987–90, Dir Planning and Research Dept, Inst. for Econ. Co-operation 1989–90, Deputy Head of Mission, London 1990–94, Deputy Dir-Gen. for EU Affairs 1994–95; fmr Deputy Rep. to UNCTAD VII 1987; Head of Negotiating Team for Accession to Lomé III Convention and for Negotiation of Lomé IV 1987–90; Deputy Perm. Rep. to WEU 1990–93; Deputy Rep. to EU "Reflexion Group" to prepare Intergovernmental Conf. 1996 1995; Sec. of State for European Affairs 1995–2001, Pres. EU Internal Market Council of Ministers 2000, Chair. Intergovernmental Conf. for revision of Treaty of EU 2000; Perm. Rep. to UN, New York 2001–02; Amb. to Brazil 2004–. *Publications include:* numerous books and articles in professional journals. *Address:* Embassy of Portugal, SES, Av. das Nações, Quadra 801, Lote 02, 70402-900 Brasilia, DF Brazil (office). *Telephone:* (61) 3032-9600 (office).

Fax: (61) 3032-9642 (office). *E-mail:* embaixadadeportugal@ embaixadadeportugal.org.br (office). *Website:* www.embaixadadeportugal .org.br (office).

SEJDIU, Fatmir, PhD; Kosovo politician, academic and head of state; *President;* b. 23 Oct. 1951, Podujeva; m.; three c. *Education:* Univ. of Priština. *Career:* Prof. of Law, Univ. of Priština; mem. Ass. of Kosovo –2006, fmr mem. Cttee for Rules and Procedures of Ass., Cttee for Int. Cooperation and EU Integration; Pres. of Kosovo 2006–; mem. and fmr Chair., Democratic League of Kosovo; Dr hc (Tirana). *Publication:* Constitutional Framework of Kosovo (co-author) 2001, The History of State and Law (co-author) 2000, 2005, Agrarian Politics as an Instrument of National Repression (monograph) 2000, Glossary of Parliamentary and Legal Terms (co-author) 2005.
Address: Office of the President, 10000 Prishtina, Rruga Nëna Terezë, Kosovo (office). *Telephone:* (38) 213222 (office). *Fax:* (38) 211651 (office). *E-mail:* beqiri@president-ksgov.net (office). *Website:* www.president -ksgov.net (office).

SEKERAMAYI, Sydney Tigere, MB, ChB, DTM; Zimbabwean politician; *Minister of Defence;* b. 30 March 1944; m. *Career:* fmr govt. positions include Minister for Lands and Resettlement, Minister of State Security, Energy Minister; Intelligence Dir; Minister of Defence 2001–; mem. Parl. (Zanu-PF) for Marondera E 2005–08; Senator from Marondera-Hwedza 2008–.
Address: Ministry of Defence, Defence House, Union Avenue/Third Street, Private Bag 7713, Causeway, Harare, Zimbabwe (office). *Telephone:* (4) 700155 (office). *Fax:* (4) 727501 (office). *E-mail:* defprot@gta.gov.zw (office).

SELANGOR, HRH The Sultan of; Tuanku Sharafuddin Idris Shah Salahuddin Abdul Aziz Shah, DK, SPMS, SSIS, SPMJ; Malaysian; b. 24 Dec. 1945, Klang; m. 1st Raja Zarina binti Raja Zainul 1968 (divorced 1986); m. 2nd Lisa Davis (Puan Nur Lisa Abdullah) 1988 (divorced 1997); two d. one s. *Education:* Hale School, Perth, Australia and Langhurst Coll., Surrey, England. *Career:* fmr Regent of Selangor, proclaimed ninth Sultan of Selangor on the death of his father Nov. 2001; held various admin. posts in state and fed. govt services, including Selangor State Secr., Dist Office and Royal Malaysian Police Dept, Kuala Lumpur 1968–; mem. The Conf. of Rulers, Malaysia; Pro-Chancellor Universiti Teknologi MARA 2000; Chancellor Universiti Putra Malaysia 2002; Chair. Semi-Professional Football Asscn; Chair. Bd of Trustees Yayasan Seni Selangor (Selangor Art Foundation), Galeri Shah Alam; Patron Malaysian branch of the Royal Asiatic Soc., Royal Selangor Club; circumnavigated the world on his yacht, S. Y. Jugra 1995–96; participated in Peking to Paris Challenge vintage car race 1997; Hon. Dr of Public Admin (Universiti Teknologi MARA) 2001; Hon. Life Pres. Selangor Football Asscn. *Website:* www .selangor.gov.my.

SELIVON, Mykola Jedosovych, PhD; Ukrainian lawyer, judge and diplomatist; *Ambassador to Kazakhstan;* b. 30 Oct. 1946, Shestovytsya, Chernigiv Region; one s. one d. *Education:* Faculty of Law, Kyiv Taras Shevchenko State Univ. *Career:* Research Fellow, Inst. of State and Law, Acad. of Sciences of Ukraine 1973; apptd Sr Asst Govt Legal Group 1979, later Chief of Legal Dept; fmr Deputy Minister of Cabinet of Ministers, later First Deputy Minister –1996; Judge, Constitutional Court of Ukraine 1996–99, Deputy Chair. 1999–2002, Chair. 2002–06; Amb. to Kazakhstan 2006–; Academician, Ukrainian Acad. of Law Sciences; mem. Perm. Court of Arbitration, The Hague; Order for Service, Third Class; Distinguished Lawyer of Ukraine.
Address: Embassy of Ukraine, 010000 Astana, Auezova 57, Kazakhstan (office). *Telephone:* (7172) 32-60-42 (office). *Fax:* (7172) 32-68-11 (office). *E-mail:* embassy_ua@mbox.kz (office). *Website:* ukrembassy.kepter.kz (office).

SELLAL, Pierre, LenD; French diplomatist; *Permanent Representative, European Union;* b. 13 Feb. 1952, Mulhouse. *Education:* Lycée Albert Schweitzer, Mulhouse, Faculté de Droit et de Sciences Economiques de Strasbourg, Ecole Nationale d'Admin. *Career:* Sec. of Foreign Affairs, Ministry of Foreign Affairs 1977–80; Tech. Counsellor, Office of Minister of External Trade 1980–81; Counsellor, Perm. Mission of France to EC, Brussels, Belgium 1981–84; Head of Services, Ministry of Industrial Redeployment and Foreign Trade (Directorate of Hydrocarbons) 1984–85; Asst Sec. Gen. SGCI (Secrétariat général du comité interministériel-Interministerial Cttee for Questions of European Econ. Co-operation) 1985–90; Minister-Counsellor, Embassy of France in Italy 1990–92, Asst Perm. Rep. 1992–97; Dir European Co-operation 1997, Cabinet Dir 1997–2002, Perm. Rep. to EU 2002–.
Address: Permanent Mission of France to the European Union, 14 place de Louvain, 1000 Brussels, Belgium (office). *Telephone:* (2) 229-82-11 (office).

Fax: (2) 229-82-82 (office). *E-mail:* pierre.sellal@diplomatie.fr (office). *Website:* www.rpfrance.org (office).

SELOMA, Pelokgale; Botswana politician and diplomatist; *Ambassador to Zimbabwe; Career:* fmr mem. Parl. for Tswapong South; Asst Minister of Agric. 2001–04; Amb. to Zimbabwe (also accred to Malawi, Mozambique and Mauritius) 2005–.
Address: Embassy of Botswana, 22 Phillips Avenue, Belgravia, PO Box 563, Harare, Zimbabwe (office). *Telephone:* (4) 729551 (office). *Fax:* (4) 721360 (office).

SEMAKULA KIWANUKA, Matia Mulumba, PhD; Ugandan government official and diplomatist; *Minister of State of Investment;* m.; several c. *Education:* Makerere Univ. and Univ. of London, UK. *Career:* fmr univ. lecturer, researcher and admin.; Sr Presidential Adviser 1979–81; worked with UNEP 1985–87; Counterpart Chief Tech. Adviser and Dir of Planning and Project Co-ordination for a UNDP project on capacity-building and institutional strengthening 1988–90; Dean, Makerere Univ. School of Post grad. Studies and Research 1991–94; Exec. Dir Man. Training and Advisory Centre, Uganda 1994–96; Amb. and Perm. Rep. to UN, New York 1996–2003, Chair. Gen. Ass.'s Fourth Cttee (Special Political and Decolonization) 2000; Minister of State in Charge of Luwero 2003–05, of Investment 2005–; fmr Minister of Culture, Royal Kingdom of Buganda; mem. Royal Council.
Address: Office of the Minister of Investment, Ministry of Finance, Appollo Kaggwa Road, Plot 2/4, POB 8147, Kampala, Uganda (office). *Telephone:* (41) 2234700 (office). *Fax:* (41) 2230163 (office). *E-mail:* webmaster@finance.go.ug (office). *Website:* www.finance.go.ug (office).

SEMASHKO, Vladimir Ilich; Belarusian politician; *First Deputy Prime Minister; Career:* Minister of Energy –2003; First Deputy Prime Minister 2003–; Chair. Supervisory Bd Beltransgaz 2007–; Order of Honour 2008.
Address: Office of the Deputy Prime Ministers, vul. Savetskaya 11, 220010 Minsk, Belarus (office). *Telephone:* (17) 222-68-08 (office). *Fax:* (17) 222-66-65 (office). *Website:* www.btg.by.

SEN, Amartya Kumar, PhD, FBA; Indian economist and academic; *Lamont University Professor Emeritus and Professor of Economics and Philosophy, Harvard University;* b. 3 Nov. 1933, Santiniketan, Bengal; m. 1st Nabaneeta Dev 1960 (divorced 1975); two d.; m. 2nd Eva Colorni 1978 (died 1985); one s. one d.; m. 3rd Emma Rothschild. *Education:* Presidency Coll., Calcutta and Trinity Coll., Cambridge. *Career:* Prof. of Econs, Jadavpur Univ., Calcutta 1956–58; Fellow, Trinity Coll., Cambridge 1957–63; Prof. of Econs, Univ. of Delhi 1963–71, Chair. Dept of Econs 1966–68; Hon. Dir Agricultural Econs Research Centre, Delhi 1966–68, 1969–71; Prof. of Econs, LSE 1971–77, Univ. of Oxford 1977–80, Drummond Prof. of Political Economy 1980–88; Lamont Univ. Prof., Harvard Univ. 1987–98, 2004–, Prof. Emer. 1998–2004, Prof. of Econs and Philosophy 2004–; Master Trinity Coll., Cambridge 1998–2004; Visiting Prof., Univ. of Calif., Berkeley 1964–65, Harvard Univ. 1968–69; Andrew D. White Prof.-at-Large, Cornell Univ. 1978–84; Pres. Int. Econ. Asscn 1986–89; Fellow, Econometric Soc., Pres. 1984; Hon. Prof., Delhi Univ.; Foreign Hon. mem. American Acad. of Arts and Sciences; Hon. Fellow, Inst. of Social Studies, The Hague, Hon. Fellow LSE, Inst. of Devt Studies; Hon. CH 2000; Grand Cross, Order of Scientific Merit (Brazil) 2000; Hon. DLitt (Univ. of Saskatchewan, Canada) 1979, (Visva-Bharati Univ., India) 1983, (Oxford) 1996; Hon. DUniv (Essex) 1984, (Caen) 1987; Hon. DSc (Bath) 1984, (Bologna) 1988; Dr hc (Univ. Catholique de Louvain) 1989, (Padua) 1998; Senator Giovanni Agnelli Inst. Prize for Ethics 1989, Nobel Prize for Econs 1998, UN Econ. and Social Comm. for Asia and the Pacific (UNESCAP) Lifetime Achievement Award 2007. *Publications:* Choice of Techniques: An Aspect of Planned Economic Development 1960, Growth Economics 1970, Collective Choice and Social Welfare 1970, On Economic Inequality 1973, Employment, Technology and Development 1975, Poverty and Famines 1981, Utilitarianism and Beyond (jtly with Bernard Williams) 1982, Choice, Welfare and Measurement 1982, Resources, Values and Development 1984, Commodities and Capabilities 1985, On Ethics and Economics 1987, The Standard of Living 1988, Hunger and Public Action (with Jean Drèze) 1989, Social Security in Developing Countries (jtly) 1991, Inequality Re-examined 1992, The Quality of Life (jtly) 1993, Development as Freedom 1999, The Argumentative Indian: Writings on Indian History, Culture and Identity 2005, Identity and Violence: The Illusion of Destiny 2006; articles in various journals in econs, philosophy and political science.
Address: Department of Economics, Littauer 205, Harvard University, Cambridge, MA 02138, USA (office). *Telephone:* (617) 495-1871 (office). *Fax:* (617) 496-5942 (office). *E-mail:* slrich@fas.harvard.edu (office). *Website:* www.economics.harvard.edu/faculty/sen (office).

SEN, Nirupam; Indian diplomatist; *Permanent Representative, United Nations; Career:* joined Foreign Service 1969; served in Moscow, Warsaw, Budapest, London; fmr Amb. to Bulgaria, to Norway; fmr Minister for Commerce and Industry; High Commr to Sri Lanka 2002–04; Perm. Rep. to UN, New York 2004–.
Address: Permanent Representative of India to the United Nations, 235 East 43rd Street, New York, NY 10017, USA (office). *Telephone:* (212) 490-9660 (office). *Fax:* (212) 490-9656 (office). *E-mail:* india@un.int (office); indiaun@prodigy.net. *Website:* www.un.int/india (office).

SEN, Ranendra, (Ronen), BA; Indian diplomatist; *Ambassador to USA;* b. 9 April 1944, Pune; m. Kalpana; one d. *Career:* began diplomatic career 1966, served as Third Sec., then Second Sec., Moscow 1968–72, Consul, San Francisco, USA 1972–74, First Sec., Dhaka, Bangladesh 1974–77; with Atomic Energy Comm., Bombay 1978–80; Jt Sec. Ministry of External Affairs 1984–85; Sec. and Foreign and Defence Policy Adviser to Prime Minister 1986–91; Amb. to Mexico, Belize, El Salvador and Guatemala 1991–92, to Russia 1992–98, to Germany 1998–2002, High Commr to UK 2002–04, Amb. to USA 2004–.
Address: Embassy of India, 2107 Massachusetts Avenue, NW, Washington, DC 20008 (office); 2700 Macomb Street, NW, Washington, DC 20008, USA (home). *Telephone:* (202) 939-7010 (office). *Fax:* (202) 265-4351 (office). *E-mail:* ambassador@indiagov.org (office). *Website:* www .indianembassy.org (office).

SENČAR, Igor, BS, MS; Slovenian diplomatist; *Permanent Representative, European Union;* b. 27 Nov. 1965; m. Tatiana Bajuk, one d. *Education:* Univ. of Ljubljana. *Career:* worked in investment dept Telekom Slovenia 1990–93; First Sec. European Integration and Econ. Affairs Dept, Ministry of Foreign Affairs 1993–97; Sec. European Affairs Cttee, Nat. Ass. 1997–2000; Chief of Staff to Prime Minister 2000; State Undersecretary, Head EU Gen. Unit, Ministry of Foreign Affairs 2001–02; Counsellor, Mission to EU, Brussels 2002, Minister Plenipotentiary 2003–04, Rep. to Political and Security Cttee 2004–05, Perm. Rep. 2005–. *Publications:* book of essays and numerous articles on EU affairs.
Address: Permanent Mission of Slovenia, Council of the European Union, 30 Avenue Marnix, Brussels 1000, Belgium (office). *Telephone:* (2) 512-44-66 (office). *Fax:* (2) 512-09-97 (office).

SENDANYOYE RUGWABIZA, Valentine, BSc, MSc; Rwandan diplomatist, business executive and international organization executive; *Deputy Director-General, World Trade Organization; Education:* Nat. Univ. of Zaïre (now Democratic Repub. of the Congo). *Career:* sr man. with major Swiss multinational co., first as head of its commercial devt and marketing operations for Cen. Africa, based in Yaoundé, Cameroon, and then as its regional man. for Cen. and West Africa, based in Abidjan, Côte d'Ivoire 1989–97; managed her own co. 1997–2000; joined govt 2000, served simultaneously as Perm. Rep. to UN in Geneva, Head of Del. to WTO and Amb. to Switzerland 2002–05; Deputy Head of Del. for Rwanda's first Trade Policy Review 2004; adviser, Council of Econ. and Social Affairs, Office of Pres. of Rwanda, Kigali –2005; Deputy Dir-Gen. WTO 2005–, Coordinator of African Group in WTO; Founding mem. Rwandese Pvt. Sector Fed., Rwanda Women Entrepreneurs' Org., Rwandese Women Leaders' Caucus; one of two Ambs representing Least Developed Countries in Integrated Framework Working Group.
Address: World Trade Organization, Centre William Rappard, rue de Lausanne 154, 1211 Geneva 21, Switzerland (office). *Telephone:* (22) 739-51-11 (office). *Fax:* (22) 731-42-06 (office). *E-mail:* enquiries@wto.org (office). *Website:* www.wto.org (office).

SENDOV, Blagovest Hristov, PhD, DSc; Bulgarian mathematician, academic, politician and diplomatist; *Ambassador to Japan;* b. 8 Feb. 1932, Assenovgrad; m. 1st Lilia Georgieva 1958 (divorced 1982); two d.; m. 2nd Anna Marinova 1982; one s. *Education:* gymnasium in Assenovgrad, Sofia Univ., Moscow State Univ. and Imperial Coll., London. *Career:* cleaner in Sofia 1949–52; teacher in Boboshevo and Elin Pelin 1956–58; Asst, Dept of Algebra, Univ. of Sofia 1958–60, Asst in Numerical Analysis and Computer Science 1960-63, Asst Prof. of Computer Sciences 1963–67, Prof. of Computer Science 1967, Dean, Faculty of Math. 1970–73, Rector 1973–79; mem. Parl. 1976–90, 1994–, Pres. of Parl. 1995–97, Vice-Pres. 1997–2003; Amb. to Japan 2003–; Vice-Pres. Bulgarian Acad. of Sciences 1980–82, Vice-Pres. and Scientific Sec.-Gen. 1982–88, Dir Centre for Informatics and Computer Tech. 1985–90, Pres. 1988–91; Pres. Comm. of Science 1986–88; Vice-Pres. Int. Fed. for Information Processing 1985–88, Pres. 1989–91; Vice-Pres. World Peace Council 1983–86, IIP— UNESCO 1986–90; Extraordinary Vice-Pres. ICSU 1990–93; mem. Exec. Cttee and Bd Dirs Int. Foundation for Survival and Devt of Humanity 1988–; Hon. Pres. Int. Asscn of Univs 1985–; two Orders of People's Repub. of Bulgaria and many others; Dr hc 1969, 1977; Dimitrov Prize for Science, Honoured Scientist 1984. *Publications:* Numerical Analysis, Old and New 1973,

Hausdorff Approximation 1979, Averaged Moduli of Smoothness (mono-graph); textbooks and more than 150 articles in learned journals.
Address: Embassy of Bulgaria, 5-36-3, Yoyogi, Shibuya-ku, Tokyo 151-0053, Japan (office); 5 Plachkoviza Str., 1126 Sofia, Bulgaria (home). *Telephone:* (3) 3465-1021 (Tokyo) (office); (2) 862-60-83 (Sofia) (home). *Fax:* (3) 3465-1031 (Tokyo) (office); (2) 980-36-36 (Sofia) (office). *E-mail:* bulemb@gol.com (office); sendov2003@yahoo.com (office); bsendov@argo.bas.bg (home).

SENEWIRATNE, Kshenuka; Sri Lankan diplomatist; m. Surendra Senewiratne. *Career:* postings to UN and Brussels, Deputy High Commr to UK –2004, Head, Econ. Affairs Div., Colombo 2005, High Commr to UK 2005–08; Trustee, Imperial War Museum 2006–.
Address: Ministry of Foreign Affairs, Republic Building, Colombo 1, Sri Lanka (office). *Telephone:* (11) 2325371 (office). *Fax:* (11) 2446091 (office). *E-mail:* publicity@formin.gov.lk (office). *Website:* www.slmfa.gov.lk (office).

SENGHAAS, Dieter, DPhil; German professor of social science; *Professor of Peace, Conflict and Development Research, University of Bremen;* b. 27 Aug. 1940, Geislingen; m. Eva Knobloch 1968; one d. *Education:* Univs of Tübingen, Michigan and Frankfurt and Amherst Coll. *Career:* Research Fellow, Center for Int. Affairs, Harvard Univ. 1968–70; Research Dir, Peace Research Inst., Frankfurt (PRIF) 1971–78; Prof. of Int. Relations, Univ. of Frankfurt 1972–78; Prof. of Peace, Conflict and Devt Research, Univ. of Bremen 1978–; mem. several nat. and int. scientific orgs; Dr hc (Tübingen) 2000; Lentz Int. Peace Research Award 1987, Göttingen Peace Award 1999. *Publications:* Aggressivität und kollektive Gewalt 1972, Aufrüstung durch Rüstungskontrolle 1972, Gewalt-Konflikt-Frieden 1974, Weltwirtschaftsordnung und Entwicklungspolitik (5th edn) 1987, Abschreckung und Frieden (3rd edn) 1981, Rüstung und Militarismus (2nd edn) 1982, Von Europa lernen 1982, The European Experience 1985, Die Zukunft Europas 1986, Europas Entwicklung und die Dritte Welt 1986, Konfliktformationen im internationalen System 1988, Europa 2000: Ein Friedensplan 1990, Friedensprojekt Europa 1992, Wohin driftet die Welt 1994, Zivilisierung wider Willen 1998, Klaenge des Friedens 2001, The Clash Within Civilizations 2001, Zum ewigen Frieden 2004, On Perpetual Peace 2007; ed. or co-ed. of 33 books related to political science, int. affairs, etc.
Address: University of Bremen, 28334 Bremen (office); Freiligrathstrasse 6, 28211 Bremen, Germany (home). *Telephone:* (421) 2182281 (office); (421) 230436 (home). *Fax:* (421) 2187248 (office); (421) 249169 (home). *E-mail:* tmenge@iniis.uni-bremen.de (office). *Website:* www.iniis.uni-bremen.de/homepages/senghaas/index.php (office).

SENJUR, Marjan, BSc, MA, PhD; Slovenian economist, academic and diplomatist; *Professor, Department of Economic Theory and Policy, University of Ljubljana;* b. 12 Sept. 1944, Stara Nova vas; m.; two d. *Education:* Univ. of Ljubljana, Univ. of Zagreb. *Career:* Teaching Asst, Faculty of Econs, Univ. of Ljubljana 1967–77, Asst Dean 1979–81, Asst Prof. of Econs 1977–83, Dean, Faculty of Econs 1985–87, Prof. of Econs and Econ. Devt 1984–2002, currently Prof., Dept of Econ. Theory and Policy; Teaching and Research Asst, Florida State Univ., USA 1973–74; Lecturer in Econs, Cleveland State Univ., USA 1989; Minister for Econ. Relations and Devt 1997–2000; Amb. to UK 2002–04.
Address: Department of Economic Theory and Policy, University of Ljubljana, Kardeljeva ploščad 17, 1000 Ljubljana, Slovenia (office). *Telephone:* (1) 5892578 (office). *Fax:* (1) 5892698 (office). *E-mail:* marjan.senjur@ef.uni-lj.si (office). *Website:* www.ef.uni-lj.si/en (office).

SENKO, Vladimir Leonovich; Belarusian diplomatist; *Ambassador to Belgium and Permanent Representative to the European Union and NATO;* b. 5 Aug. 1946. *Education:* Moscow State Inst. of Int. Relations, Diplomatic Acad. *Career:* entered diplomatic service 1973, serving with USSR Embassy, Poland 1973–79, Second Sec. 1981–85, First Sec. 1988–91; Third Sec. Fourth European Div. USSR Ministry of Foreign Affairs 1979–81; First Sec. Dept of Socialist Countries, USSR Ministry of Foreign Affairs 1987–88; Deputy Minister of Foreign Affairs, Belarus, 1991–92, Minister 1994–97; Amb. to UK 1994–97, to France (also accred to Spain, Portugal and Rep. to UNESCO) 1998–2004, to Belgium and Perm. Rep. to EU and NATO 2004–.
Address: Embassy of Belarus, avenue Molière 192, 1050 Brussels, Belgium (office). *Telephone:* (2) 340-02-70 (office). *Fax:* (2) 340-02-87 (office).

ŞENSOY, Nabi; Turkish diplomatist; *Ambassador to USA;* b. 25 May 1945, Istanbul; m. *Education:* Univ. of Ankara. *Career:* Third Sec., later Second Sec., Dept of Research, Ministry of Foreign Affairs 1970–72, Vice-Consul, New York 1972–75, First Sec., Embassy in Caracas 1975–77, Head of Section, Dept of Bilateral Political Affairs for Western Europe 1977–79, Counsellor, Embassy in Havana 1979–80, Washington, DC 1980–83;

Advisor to the Prime Minister 1983–85; Consul Gen., London 1985–88; Chief of Staff to the Pres. 1988–90; Amb. to Spain 1990–95, Dir-Gen. Dept of Policy Planning, Ministry of Foreign Affairs 1995–97, Deputy Under-secretary of Political Affairs for the EU 1997–98, Amb. to Russia 1998–2002, Deputy Undersecretary of Gen. Political Affairs, Ministry of Foreign Affairs 2002–05, Amb. to USA 2006–.
Address: Embassy of Turkey, 2525 Massachusetts Avenue, NW, Washington, DC 20008, USA (office). *Telephone:* (202) 612-6700 (office). *Fax:* (202) 612-6744 (office). *E-mail:* contact@turkishembassy.org (office). *Website:* www.turkishembassy.org (office).

SEPÚLVEDA-AMOR, Bernardo, LLB; Mexican lawyer and politician; *Judge, International Court of Justice;* b. 14 Dec. 1941, Mexico City; m. Ana Yturbe 1970; three s. *Education:* Nat. Univ. of Mexico and Queen's Coll., Cambridge. *Career:* fmrly taught int. law, El Colegio de México and Faculty of Political Science, Univ. of Mexico; Asst Dir of Juridical Affairs, Ministry of Presidency 1968–70; Dir-Gen. of Int. Financial Affairs, Ministry of Finance 1976–81; Int. Adviser, Minister of Programming and Budget 1981; Amb. to USA March–Dec. 1982; Sec. of Foreign Affairs 1982–88; Amb. to UK 1989–93; Foreign Affairs Adviser to Pres. of Mexico 1993–; mem. UN Int. Law Comm. 1996–2005; fmr Judge ad hoc, Int. Court of Justice, Judge 2006–; Sec. Int. Affairs Institutional Revolutionary Party (PRI) 1981–82; Pres. to UN Sixth Comm. on Transnat. Corpns. 1977–80; Hon. Fellow Queens' Coll., Cambridge 1991; Hon. GCMG; Dr hc (Univ. of San Diego), (Univ. of Leningrad); Premio Príncipe de Asturias, Premio Simón Bolívar; Knights Grand Cross, Most Distinguished Order of St. Michael and St. George (UK), Grand Cross, Order of Isabel The Catholic (Spain), Grand Cross, Order of Civil Merit (Spain), Grand Cross, Order of Cruzeiro do Sul (Brazil), Grand Cross, Order of Rio Branco (Brazil), Grand Cross, Order of Boyacá (Columbia), Ribbon, Order of Kwang-Wha (South Korea), Grand Cross, Order of General San Martin (Argentina), Gran Cordón, Order of the Libertador (Venezuela), Grand Cross, Orden de la Bandera Yugoslava (Yugoslavia), Grand Cross Orden de Cristo (Portugal), Grand Cross, Order Infante Don Henrique (Portugal), Grand Cross, Ordre de la Couronne (Belgium), Grand Officier, Ordre d la Légion d'Honneur (France), Connander INsignia jof the Order of Merit, with the Star (Poland), Superior Commander, Grand Order of the Saviour (Greece), Grand Cross, Order of Vasco Núñez de Balboa (Panama), Grand Cross, Order of the Quetzal (Guatemala), Grand Cordon, Order of the Rising Sun (Japan), Grand Cross, Order of El Sol de Peru (Peru), Order of the Republic, First Class (Egypt), Commander, Order of Distinction (Jamaica). *Publications:* Foreign Investment in Mexico 1973, Transnational Corporations in Mexico 1974, A View of Contemporary Mexico 1979, Planning for Development 1981.
Address: International Court of Justice, Peace Palace, 2517 KJ, The Hague, Netherlands (office); Rocas 185, México, DF 01900, Mexico. *Telephone:* (70) 3022323 (office); (5) 652-0641. *Fax:* (70) 3649928 (office); (5) 652-9739. *Website:* www.icj-cij.org (office).

SERDYUKOV, Anatoly Eduardovich; Russian politician; *Minister of Defence;* b. 8 Jan. 1962, Krasnodar region. *Education:* Leningrad (now St Petersburg) Inst. of Soviet Trade and St Petersburg State Univ. *Career:* served in armed forces 1984–85; worked for furniture firm 1985–93, then Marketing Dir and Dir-Gen. St Petersburg furniture market 1993–2000; Deputy Head, Dist Inspectorate of Taxes, Ministry of Taxes and Dues 2000–01; Deputy Head then Head, St Petersburg Tax Authority 2001–04; Deputy Minister of Taxes and Dues Feb.–July 2004, Head Fed. Tax Service 2004–07; Minister of Defence 2007–.
Address: Ministry of Defence, 105175 Moscow, ul. Myasnitskaya 37, Russia (office). *Telephone:* (495) 293-38-54 (office). *Fax:* (495) 296-84-36 (office). *Website:* www.mil.ru (office).

SERETSE, Brig. Ramadeluka; Botswana lawyer, politician and army officer (retd); *Minister for Defence, Justice and Security; Career:* served as Brig. in Botswana Defence Force, now retd; mem. Parl. for Serowe North East (Botswana Democratic Party) 2004–, Minister for Lands and Housing –2008, for Defence, Justice and Security 2008–.
Address: Ministry for the Administration of Justice, Gaborone, Botswana.

SERGEEV, Yuriy A., PhD; Ukrainian diplomatist; *Permanent Representative, United Nations;* b. 5 Feb. 1956, Leninakan, Armenia; m. *Education:* T. Shevchenko Kyiv State Univ. *Career:* Dir Press Service, Ministry of Foreign Affairs 1992–93, Head, Directorate for Information 1993–94, 94–97, Dir Secr. 1994; Minister Counsellor, Embassy in London 1997; Amb. to Greece and Albania 1997–2000; Dir-Gen. for Foreign Policy, Office of Pres. of Ukraine 2000–01; First Deputy Minister for Foreign Affairs 2001, Sec. of State, Ministry for Foreign Affairs 2001–03; Amb. to France 2003–07, concurrently Perm. Rep. to UNESCO; Perm. Rep. to UN, New York 2007–.

Address: Permanent Mission of Ukraine to the United Nations, 220 East 51st Street, New York, NY 10022, USA (office). *Telephone:* (212) 759-7003 (office). *Fax:* (212) 355-9455 (office). *E-mail:* mail@uamission.org (office). *Website:* www.uamission.org (office).

SERGEYEV, Ivan Ivanovich; Russian civil servant and diplomatist; *Director General, GlavUpDK, Ministry of Foreign Affairs;* b. 7 Sept. 1941, Electrostal, Moscow Region. *Career:* Deputy, First Deputy Chair., Exec. Cttee Moscow Regional Soviet 1976–83; Deputy, First Deputy Head, Dept on Problems of Diplomatic Corps USSR (now Russian) Ministry of Foreign Affairs 1983–97; Deputy Minister of Foreign Affairs 1997–2003; Deputy Chair. Bd Black Sea Bank for Trade and Devt 1998–2003; currently Dir Gen. GlavUpDK (Main Admin. for Service to Diplomatic Corps)., Ministry of Foreign Affairs; State Prize of Russia 2002. *Address:* GlavUpDK, 119034 Moscow, Prechistenka, 20, Russia (office). *Telephone:* (495) 230-2329 (office). *Fax:* (495) 230-2329 (home). *E-mail:* info@updk.ru (office). *Website:* updk.ru (home).

SERKSNYS, Gediminas, DSc; Lithuanian diplomatist; *Ambassador to the Council of Europe;* b. 11 Feb. 1948, Kaunas; m. Elena Serksnys. *Education:* Kaunas Medical Inst., Kaunas Inst. of Physical Tech. Problems of Energetics. *Career:* Sr Scientific Worker, Kaunas Inst. of Cardiology 1981–88, later Head of Baltic Amadeus Dept; elected Deputy of the Supreme Council (Parl.) 1990, Chair. of State Re-establishing Comm.; signatory of Act of Re-establishment of Ind. Repub. of Lithuania 11 March 1990; apptd Minister without Portfolio 1992, Co-ordinator and mem. Del. State negotiations on Army Withdrawal with Russian Fed.; Deputy Foreign Minister 1991–93; Head of Br., A. Abiala and Partners Consultation Firm 1994–97; Head of Del. Preparation for Negotiations for EU Membership 1997; Amb. of Lithuania 1997; Deputy Minister of Foreign Affairs responsible for EU Integration 1998–2000; Perm. Rep. of Lithuania to UN, New York 2000–06; Head of Lithuanian Special Mission for Afghanistan 2006; Amb. to Council of Europe 2008–. *Address:* Office of the Permanent Representative of Lithuania, c/o Council of Europe, Avenue de l'Europe, 67075 Strasbourg Cedex, France.

SERYAEV, Yazmurad N.; Turkmenistan diplomatist; m. Djeunetgozel Seryaeva. *Career:* Amb. to UK 2003–. *Address:* 2nd Floor South, St George's House, 14–17 Wells Street, London, W1P 3FP, England (office). *Telephone:* (20) 7255-1071 (office). *Fax:* (20) 7323-9184 (office).

SESSA, Riccardo; Italian diplomatist; *Ambassador to The People's Republic of China;* b. 23 Sept. 1947, Massa; m. Stefania Butera; one s. one d. *Education:* La Sapienza Univ., Univ. of Paris. *Career:* fmr police officer; joined Ministry for Foreign Affairs 1973, Head, Office for Relations with Parl. 1985–89, Head, Prime Minister's Secr. 1989–92, Deputy Head, Minister of Foreign Affair's Cabinet 1992, Deputy Dir-Gen. for Emigration 1993–94, Diplomatic Adviser to Minister for Defence 1994–97, Dir-Gen. for Mediterranean and Middle East 2003–06; overseas postings include to Perm. Mission to NATO, Brussels; fmr Commercial Counsellor, Embassy in Brasília; Amb. to Fed. Repub. of Yugoslavia 1997–2000, to Iran 2000–03, to People's Repub. of China (also accred to Mongolia) 2006–; Cavaliere di Gran Croce Ordine al Merito. *Address:* Embassy of Italy, 2 Dong Er Jie, San Li Tun, Beijing 100600, People's Republic of China (office). *Telephone:* (10) 85327600 (office). *Fax:* (10) 65324676 (office). *E-mail:* ambasciata.pechino@esteri.it (office). *Website:* www.ambpechino.esteri.it (office).

SEVELE, Hon. Feleti (Fred), BSc, BA, MA, PhD; Tongan politician, business executive and academic; *Prime Minister and Minister of Communications, Civil Aviation, Marine, Ports and Disaster Relief Activities and Minister of Labour, Commerce, Industries and Tourism; Education:* Univ. of Cambridge, UK. *Career:* mem. Legis. Ass. 1999–, Minister of Labour, Commerce, Industries 2005–; Interim Prime Minister Feb.–March 2006, Prime Minister (first non-noble) March 2006–. *Address:* Office of the Prime Minister, POB 62, Taufa'ahau Road, Kolofo'ou, Nuku'alofa, Tonga (office). *Telephone:* 24644 (office). *Fax:* 23888 (office). *E-mail:* fttuita@pmo.gov.to (office). *Website:* www.pmo .gov.to (office).

SEVERIANO TEIXEIRA, Nuno, PhD; Portuguese academic and politician; *Minister of National Defence; Education:* Univ. of Lisbon, European Univ. Inst., Florence, Italy, New Univ. of Lisbon. *Career:* Researcher, European Univ. Inst., Florence 1989–92; Visiting Prof., Dept of Govt, Georgetown Univ., USA 2000; Visiting Fellow, Center for European Studies, Univ. of Calif., Berkeley, USA 2003; Prof., Dept of Political Sciences and Int. Relations, Faculty of Social and Human Sciences, New Univ. of Lisbon, Dir Portuguese Inst. of Int. Relations; Dir Inst. of Nat. Defence 1996–2000; Minister of Internal Admin 2000–02, of Nat. Defence 2006–. *Publications*

include: O Ultimatum Inglês. Política Externa e Política Interna no Portugal de 1890 1990, O Poder e a Guerra. Objectvos nacionais e estratégias políticas na entrada de Portugal na Grande Guerra 1914–1918 1996; numerous articles in professional journals. *Address:* Ministry of National Defence, Av. Ilha de Madeira 1, 1400-204, Lisbon, Portugal (office). *Telephone:* (21) 3038528 (office). *Fax:* (21) 3020284 (office). *E-mail:* gcrp@sg.mdn.gov.pt (office). *Website:* www.mdn .gov.pt (office).

SEVERIN, Anthony Bryan, BEcons, MSc; Saint Lucia civil servant and diplomatist; b. 6 Aug. 1955; m.; three c. *Education:* Univ. of W. Indies, Univ. of Bradford, UK. *Career:* joined St Lucia Public Service 1980, held several positions in Local Devt Fund 1979–80, in Ministry of Education and Culture (including Sr Exec. Officer, Finance) 1980–81, Ministry of Educ. and Culture, later Chief Economist, Cen. Planning Unit, Ministry of Planning, Establishment and Training; Perm. Sec., Ministry of Trade, Industry and Tourism 1989–92, Ministry of Trade and Industry 1992–94; Cabinet Sec. and Perm. Sec. in Office of Prime Minister 1994–2001; Amb. to CARICOM 2001–03, 2004–06; Perm. Rep. to UN, New York 2003–04, 2006–08; Founder and Assoc. Dir Folk Research Centre; Stage Man. and Financial Comptroller, St Lucia Del. to CARIFESTA, Barbados 1981; Exec. Mem. St Lucia Archaeological and Historical Soc. *Address:* c/o Ministry of External Affairs, International Financial Services, Information and Broadcasting, Conway Business Centre, Waterfront, Castries, Saint Lucia.

SEVERINO, Rodolfo, MA; Philippine diplomatist; *Visiting Senior Research Fellow, Institute of Southeast Asian Studies;* b. 22 April 1936, Manila; m. Rowena V. Romero; two s. one d. *Education:* Ateneo de Manila Univ., Johns Hopkins Univ. School of Advanced Int. Studies, Washington, DC. *Career:* Assoc. Ed. Manor Press Inc. 1956–59, Philippine Int. 1957–59, Marketing Horizons 1961–64; with Operation Brotherhood, Laos 1959–61; Special Asst to Senator Raul S. Manglapus, Philippine Senate 1961–64; information asst, UN Information Centre, Manila 1964–65; Third, then Second and First Sec., Embassy in Washington, DC 1967–74; Special Asst to Under-Sec. of Foreign Affairs 1974–76, Under-Sec. 1992–97; Chargé d'Affaires, Embassy in Beijing 1976–78; Consul-Gen., Houston, Texas 1979–86; Asst Sec. for Asian and Pacific Affairs 1986–88; Amb. to Malaysia 1988–92; Under-Sec. of Foreign Affairs 1992–97; Sec.-Gen. ASEAN 1998–2003; adviser to Cambodian Govt Jan.–June 2002; Prof., Asian Inst. of Man., Manila 2003–04; currently Visiting Sr Research Fellow, Inst. of Southeast Asian Studies, Singapore; Order of Sikatuna, rank of Datu (Philippines) 1997, rank of Rajah; Royal Award (Cambodia) 2002. *Publications include:* ASEAN Faces the Future 2001, ASEAN Today and Tomorrow 2002, Framing the ASEAN Charter 2005, Southeast Asia in Search of an ASEAN Community 2006. *Address:* Institute of Southeast Asian Studies, 30 Heng Mui Keng Terrace, Pasir Panjang, 119614 (office); 2D Hong San Walk, Palm Gardens #16-06, 689050, Singapore (home). *Telephone:* 67780955 (office); 63101794 (home). *Fax:* 67781735 (office). *E-mail:* severino@iseas.edu.sg (office); roseverino@hotmail.com (home). *Website:* www.iseas.edu.sg (office).

SEVILLA SOMOZA, Eduardo J.; Nicaraguan diplomatist; b. 26 June 1953, Washington, DC, USA; m.; three c. *Education:* Georgetown Univ. School of Foreign Service, Washington, DC and Universidad Centroamericana School of Law, Managua. *Career:* degree in int. studies 1982; First Sec., Embassy in Washington, DC 1978–79; various positions in real estate and trade firms in USA 1979–87; Amb. to Argentina (also Accred to Uruguay) 1987–2000; Perm. Rep. to UN, New York 2000–07; fmr Exec. Vice-Pres. Nicaraguan Foundation for Democracy and Devt; mem. Int. Law Asscn, Washington, DC. *Address:* c/o Ministry of Foreign Affairs, Del Cine González al Sur sobre Avda Bolivar, Managua, Nicaragua (office). *Website:* www.cancilleria.gob .ni (office).

SEYDOU, Adamou; Niger diplomatist; *Ambassador to France;* m. Fatoumata Seydou. *Career:* fmr Minister, Sport and Youth; fmr Amb. to France, UK, Italy, Spain, Switzerland, Amb. to France 2002– (also accred to UK 2003–). *Address:* Embassy of Niger, 154 rue de Longchamp, 75116 Paris, France (office). *Telephone:* 1-45-04-80-60 (office). *Fax:* 1- 45-04-79-73 (office).

SHA, Zukang; Chinese diplomatist and UN official; *Under-Secretary-General for Economic and Social Affairs, United Nations;* b. Sept. 1947, Jiangsu prov.; m.; one s. *Career:* staff mem., Embassy in London 1971–74, in Sri Lanka 1974–80; Attaché and Third Sec., Embassy in India 1980–85; Deputy Div. Dir and First Sec. Dept of Int. Orgs and Conferences 1985–88, Adviser and Deputy Dir-Gen. 1992–95; First Sec. and Adviser, Perm. Mission to UN, New York 1988–92; Amb. for Disarmament Affairs and Deputy Perm. Rep. to UN Office and Other Int. Orgs, Geneva, Switzerland

1995–97; Dir-Gen. Dept of Arms Control 1997–2001; Perm. Rep. to UN, Geneva 2001–07; UN Under-Sec.-Gen. for Econ. and Social Affairs 2007–. *Address:* Office of the Under-Secretary-General for Economic and Social Affairs, United Nations, Room DC2-2320, New York, NY 10017 USA (office). *E-mail:* esa@un.org (office). *Website:* www.un.org/esa/desa (office).

SHAABAN, Muhammad, PhD; Egyptian diplomatist and UN official; *Under-Secretary-General, United Nations Department for General Assembly and Conference Management;* b. 13 June 1942; m.; three c. *Education:* Brussels Univ. *Career:* rep. to ECOSOC, UNDP and various other cttees 1984–88; Amb. to Belgium and Luxembourg 1993–97, to Denmark and Lithuania 1998–2000; Head of Perm. Mission to EU, Brussels 1993–97; Deputy Minister of Foreign Affairs responsible for Africa 1997–98; Deputy Minister for Information, Research and Assessment 2000–01; Deputy Minister for Foreign Affairs responsible for Europe 2001–04; Nat. Co-ordinator for Reform Initiatives in Middle East 2004–07; Diplomatic Adviser to Speaker of the House, Egyptian Parl. 2004–07; Under-Sec.-Gen., Dept for Gen. Ass. and Conference Man., UN, New York 2007–; Coordinator of First Session of Euro-Mediterranean Parl. Ass. 2005; Order of Merit (Egypt) 1977, Chevalier, Ordre du Mérite (France) 1978, Grand Croix de l'Ordre de la Couronne (Belgium) 1997. *Publications:* The United Nations Secretary-General: The man and the post 1971, The Analysis of International Relations (in Arabic) 1984. *Address:* Department for General Assembly and Conference Management, United Nations, New York, NY, 10017, USA (office). *Telephone:* (212) 963-1234 (office). *Fax:* (212) 963-4879 (office). *E-mail:* shaabans@un.org (office). *Website:* www.un.org/Depts/DGACM (office).

SHAATH, Nabeel A., BA, MBA, PhD, DJur; Palestinian politician, diplomatist, consultant and academic; b. 1938, Safad; m.; two s. two d. *Education:* Univ. of Alexandria, Egypt, Univ. of Pa, Wharton School of Business, USA. *Career:* fmr Business School Prof., taught Finance and Econs, Univ. of Pa, USA 1961–65, academic positions at Univs of Cairo and Alexandria 1965–69; Dean, School of Business Admin, American Univ. in Beirut 1969–75; consultant to several govts, in Org. of Shuaiab industrial zone, Kuwait, power sector in Saudi Arabia, public transportation in Gulf Area; est. Eng and Man. Inst. and Arab Centre for Admin. Devt in Beirut, Cairo and 14 brs in other Arab countries; mem. Fatah Cen. Cttee, del. to Middle E Peace Conf., Madrid 1991; mem. PLO –Israel peace negotiations, Oslo, Norway and Washington, DC; First Head of PLO Del. to UN, Adviser to Yasser Arafat, wrote his speech to UN Gen. Ass. 1974; Palestinian Authority Minister of Planning and Int. Co-operation 1994–2003, Minister of Foreign Affairs 2003–05; Deputy Prime Minister 2005–06; elected to Palestinian Legis. Council, Rep. of Khan Younis, Gaza Strip 1996–; Rep. of Palestine to world media confs, including World Econ. Forum; acting Prime Minister of Palestinian Authority 2005–06, currently Sr Advisor to Palestinian Nat. Authority Pres. *Address:* c/o Fatah, Ramallah, Palestinian Autonomous Areas. *E-mail:* hanishka2@yahoo.com; fateh@fateh. *Website:* www.fateh.net.

SHAFEEU, Ismail; Maldivian politician; *Minister of Defence and National Security; Career:* fmr Minister of Educ. 2002–03; Minister of Home Affairs and Environment 2003–04, of Defence and Nat. Security 2004–; Chair. Dhiraagu Ltd. *Address:* Ministry of Defence and National Security, Bandaara Koshi, Ameer Ahmed Magu, Malé 20-05, Maldives (office). *Telephone:* 3322607 (office). *Fax:* 3332800 (office). *E-mail:* admin@defence.gov.mv (office). *Website:* www.defence.gov.mv.

SHAFIK, Nemat (Minouche), BA, MSc, DPhil; Egyptian/American economist and international banking official; *Permanent Secretary, Department for International Development;* b. Egypt; m.; two c. three step-c. *Education:* Univ. of Mass at Amherst, London School of Econs and St Anthony's Coll. Oxford, UK. *Career:* Econ. Policy Analyst, USAID, Cairo 1983–84, Evaluation Officer, Cairo 1984–85, Consultant, Dakar, Senegal 1986; Econs Tutor, Univ. of Oxford, UK 1987–89, Researcher, Unit for Study of African Economies, Inst. of Econs and Statistics 1989–91; Consultant, Public Econs Div., World Bank, Washington, DC 1988, Consultant, Vice Pres. for Devt Econs 1989, Economist, Int. Econs Dept 1990, Economist, World Devt Report 1992, Country Economist, Cen. European Dept 1992–94, Sr Economist, Office of the Chief Economist 1994–95, Man. Pvt. Sector Team, Middle East and N Africa (MENA) Region 1996–97, Dir Pvt Sector and Finance, MENA 1997–99, Vice-Pres. Pvt Sector Devt and Infrastructure 1999–2003, Vice-Pres. Infrastructure 2003–04; Dir-Gen. Country Programmes and mem. Man. Bd, Dept for Int. Devt (DfID), UK 2004–08, Perm. Sec. 2008–; Adjunct Prof., Econs Dept, Georgetown Univ. 1989–94; Chair. Consultive Group to Assist the Poorest 1999–2004, InfoDev 1999–2004, Global Water and Sanitation Program 1999–2004, Pvt Participation in Infrastructure Advisory Facility 1999–2004, Energy Sector

Man. and Advisory Program 1999–2004; Visiting Assoc. Prof., Wharton School, Univ. of Pennsylvania 1996; mem. Bd of Advisory Eds, The Middle East Journal 1996–2002; mem. Bd of Dirs Schutz American School in Egypt 1997–2000; mem. Bd Operating Council, Global Alliance for Workers and Communities, Int. Youth Fed. 1999–2003;. *Address:* Department for International Development, 1 Palace Street, London, SW1E 5HE (office); 61 New End, London, NW3 1HY, England. *Telephone:* (20) 7023-0000 (office). *E-mail:* n-shafik@dfid.gov.uk (office). *Website:* www.dfid.gov.uk (office).

SHAHABUDDEEN, Mohamed, LLB, LLM, BSc, PhD, LLD; Guyanese international judge; *Appeals Judge, United Nations International Criminal Tribunal for the Former Yugoslavia;* b. 7 Oct. 1931, Vreed-en-Hoop; m. Bebe Sairah 1955; two s. one d. *Education:* Univ. of London and Middle Temple London, UK. *Career:* called to the Bar, Middle Temple, London 1954; pvt. legal practice 1954–59; magistrate 1959; Crown Counsel 1959–62; Solicitor-Gen. (with rank of Justice of Appeal from 1971) 1962–73; Attorney-Gen. 1973–87; Minister of Justice and sometimes Acting Foreign Minister 1978–87; Vice-Pres. of Guyana 1983–87; Judge Int. Court of Justice 1988–97; Judge, Appeals Chamber, UN Int. Criminal Tribunal for Fmr Yugoslavia and for Rwanda 1997–; Vice-Pres. Int. Tribunal for Fmr Yugoslavia 1997–99, 2001–03; Chair. Legal Practitioners' Disciplinary Cttee, Advisory Council on the Prerogative of Mercy; mem. Guyana del. to numerous int. confs; Hon. Bencher of the Middle Temple; HQ mem. Int. Law Asscn; mem. Soc. Française pour le droit int., Advisory Bd European Journal of Int. Law, Bd of Electors of Whewell Professorship of Int. Law of Cambridge Univ., Inst. de Droit int. (first Vice-Pres. 1999–2001), Int. Acad. of Comparative Law; Hon. mem. American Soc. of Int. Law; Order of Excellence, Order of Roraima, Cacique's Crown of Honour (Guyana). *Publications:* several books and articles. *Address:* International Criminal Tribunal for the Former Yugoslavia, Churchillplein 1, 2517 JW, The Hague, Netherlands (office). *E-mail:* shahabuddeen@un.org (office). *Website:* www.un..org/icty (office).

SHAHEED, Ahmed, PhD; Maldivian government official and politician; m.; one s. two d. *Education:* Univ. of Wales, Aberystwyth, UK, Univ. of Queensland, Australia. *Career:* joined Ministry of Foreign Affairs 1982, Attaché, Perm. Mission to UN, New York 1982–84, est. Research and Analysis section, Ministry of Foreign Affairs 1989–91, Officer, Bilateral Relations Dept 1995–96, Head SAARC Div. 1996–98, Head Multilateral Affairs Dept 1998–99, Perm. Sec. 1999–2004; sSpeech writer for Pres. 1996–; Chief Govt Spokesman 2004–05; Minister of Foreign Affairs 2005–07 (resgnd); mem. Dhivehi Rayyithunge Party (DRP) (Maldivian People's Party), Co-founder and Leader New Maldives faction; Co-founder and Patron Open Soc. Asscn 2006–. *Address:* c/o Open Society Association, M. Mahi, 2nd floor, Boduthakur-ufaanu Magu, Male', 20332, Maldives (office). *Telephone:* 7671487 (office). *E-mail:* jessica@osa.org.mv (office). *Website:* osa.org.mv (office).

SHAHID, Abdulla; Maldivian politician; *Minister of Foreign Affairs;* m.; three c. *Education:* Canberra Coll. of Advanced Educ., Australia, Fletcher School of Law and Diplomacy, Tufts Univ., USA. *Career:* began civil service career in Foreign Ministry 1983; mem. Constitutional Ass. 1994; mem. Parl. 1995–; Exec. Sec. to the Pres. 1995–2005; Minister of State for Foreign Affairs 2005–07, Minister of Foreign Affairs 2007–. *Address:* Ministry of Foreign Affairs, Boduthakurufaanu Magu, Malé 10-307, The Maldives (office). *Telephone:* 3323400 (office). *Fax:* 3323841 (office). *E-mail:* ministerbureau@foreign.gov.mv (office). *Website:* www .foreign.gov.mv (office).

SHAHRANI, Nematullah, PhD; Afghan politician; *Minister of Hajj and Religious Affairs;* b. Jorm Dist, Badakhshan. *Education:* Abu Hanifa School, Kabul Univ., Al-Azhar Univ., Egypt. *Career:* fmr Prof. of Sharia, Kabul Univ.; fmr Ed.-in-Chief, Sharayat magazine; Vice-Pres., Transitional Authority 2002–04; Dir Constitutional Drafting Cttee 2002; Minister of Hajj and Religious Affairs 2004–. *Publications include:* Quran Shenaasy (Knowing the Holy Quran), Feqeh Islami Wa Qanoon e Gharb (Islamic Fiqh and Western Law); numerous articles and books on Sharia law. *Address:* Ministry of Hajj and Religious Affairs, nr District 10, Shir Pur, Shar-i-Nau, Kabul, Afghanistan (office). *Telephone:* (20) 2201338.

SHAHUMI, Suleiman Sasi ash-; Libyan politician. *Career:* currrently Sec. for Foreign Affairs. *Address:* General Secretariat of the General People's Congress, Tripoli, Libya (office).

SHAIKHLY, Salah al-, PhD; Iraqi diplomatist (retd) and economist; b. 1939, Baghdad; m. Jennifer al-Shaikhly. *Education:* in Baghdad and Kirkuk, Univ. of Manchester, UK. *Career:* early UK academic career on staff of LSE and Univ. of Oxford, Visiting Prof., Univ. of Leeds; returned to Iraq

serving in various govt positions including Deputy Minister of Planning, Head of Cen. Statistical Office, Gov. of Cen. Bank of Iraq, Head of Iraqi Fund for External Devt 1968–78; Asst Sec.-Gen., UN late 1970s; Regional Dir Arab States, UNDP 1980s; fmr Regional Advisor for Africa, UN Centre on Transnational Corpns; Spokesman, Iraqi Nat. Congress, then Spokesman on Media and Foreign Relations, Iraqi Nat. Accord 1991; ceased political activity following fall of Saddam Hussein's regime 2003; Amb. to UK 2004–07 (retd).
Address: c/o Ministry of Foreign Affairs, opp. State Org. for Roads and Bridges, Karradat Mariam, Baghdad, Iraq. *Telephone:* (1) 537-0091. *E-mail:* press@iraqmofa.net. *Website:* www.mofa.gov.iq.

SHAIMIYEV, Mintimer Sharipovich; Russian/Tatar engineer and politician; *President, Republic of Tatarstan;* b. 20 Jan. 1937, Anyakovo, Aktanyshski Dist, Tatarstan; m. Sakina Shaimiyeva; two s. *Education:* Kazan Inst. of Agric. *Career:* Engineer, Chief Engineer Service and Repair Station, Mouslyumovski Dist, Tatar ASSR 1959–62; Man. Selkhoztekhnika Regional Asscn, Tatar ASSR 1962–67; Instructor, Deputy Chief of Agricultural Dept, Tatar Regional Cttee of CPSU, Tatar ASSR 1967–69; Minister of Land Improvement and Water Man., Tatar ASSR 1969–83; First Deputy Chair. Council of Ministers, Tatar ASSR 1983, Chair. 1985–89; Sec. Tatar Regional Cttee of CPSU 1983–85, First Sec. 1989–90; Chair. Supreme Soviet, Tatar ASSR 1990–91; Pres. of Tatarstan 1991–; f. All Russia political movt 1999, now part of United Russia (Yedinaya Rossiya); mem. Acad. of Tech. Sciences; Co-Chair., Higher Council, United Russia Party; Hon. mem. Presidium, Int. Parl. of World Confed. of Kts (under auspices of UN); Hon. mem. Int. Acad. of Informatization; Hon. Prof., Moscow State Inst. of Int. Relations; Order of Lenin 1966, Order of Red Banner of Labour 1971, Order of Oct. Revolution 1976, Order of Friendship of Peoples 1987, Order for Services to the Fatherland, Grade II 1997; Silver Avitsenna Medal, UNESCO 2001.
Address: Office of the President, 420014 Tatarstan, Kazan, Kreml, Russia. *Telephone:* (843) 292-74-66 (office); (843) 291-79-01. *Fax:* (843) 292-78-66 (office). *E-mail:* secretariat@tatar.ru (office). *Website:* www.tatar.ru (office).

SHAKAR, Karim Ebrahim ash-, BA; Bahraini diplomatist; *Ambassador to People's Republic of China;* b. 23 Dec. 1945, Manama; m. Fatima Al-Mansouri 1979; three d. *Education:* Univ. of New Delhi. *Career:* joined Ministry of Foreign Affairs 1970; mem. Perm. Mission to the UN, rising to rank of Second Sec. 1972–76; apptd Chief Foreign Affairs and Int. Org., Bahrain 1977; Perm. Rep. to the UN Office, Geneva and Consul-Gen., Switzerland 1982–87; apptd Amb. (non-resident) to FRG and Austria 1984; apptd. Perm Rep. to the UN Office, Vienna 1982, Perm. Rep. (non-resident) 1984; Perm Rep. to the UN 1987–90; Amb. to UK 1990–95, Amb. (non-resident) to Ireland, Denmark and the Netherlands 1992–95; Dir Int. Directorate at Ministry of Foreign Affairs, Bahrain 1995–2001; Amb. to People's Repub. of China (also accred to Malaysia, the Philippines and Thailand) 2001–; Shaikh Isa Bin Salman Al-Khalifa Medal of Merit 2001.
Address: Embassy of Bahrain, 10-06 Liangmaqiao Diplomatic Residence Compound, 22 Dong Fang Dong Lu, Chao Yang Qu, Beijing, People's Republic of China (office). *Telephone:* (10) 65326483 (office). *Fax:* (10) 65326393 (office). *E-mail:* bahembj@yahoo.com (office).

SHAKER, Mohamed Ibrahim, LLB, DèsScPol; Egyptian diplomatist; *Vice Chairman, Egyptian Council for Foreign Affairs;* b. 16 Oct. 1933, Cairo; m. Mona El Kony 1960; one s. one d. *Education:* Cairo Univ., Inst. of Int. Studies, Univ. of Geneva, Switzerland. *Career:* Rep. of Dir-Gen. of IAEA to UN, New York 1982–83; Deputy Perm. Rep. of Egypt to UN, New York 1984–86; Amb. to Austria, Perm. Rep. to UN in Vienna, Gov. on IAEA Bd of Govs, Perm. Rep. to UNIDO 1986–88; Amb. to UK 1988–97, Dean of Diplomatic Corps; fmr mem. Core Group, Programme for Promoting Nuclear Non-proliferation (PPNN) 1987–97, UN Sec.-Gen.'s Advisory Bd on Disarmament Matters 1993–98 (Chair. 1995); Vice Chair. Egyptian Council for Foreign Affairs 1999–, Sawires Foundation for Social Devt 2001–, Regional Information Tech. Inst. 2002–; Order of the Republic (Second Grade) 1976; Order of Merit (First Grade) 1983. *Publications:* The Nuclear Non-Proliferation Treaty: Origin and Implementation, 1959–1979 1980; several articles and contribs to books on nuclear energy and nuclear non-proliferation.
Address: Egyptian Council for Foreign Affairs, Tower No.2 Osman Buildings, 12th Floor, Kornish El Nile, Maadi, Cairo 11431 (office); 120 Mohie Eldin Abou Elezz, Mohandeseen, Guizeh, Cairo (office); 9 Aziz Osman Street, Zamalek, Cairo, Egypt (home). *Telephone:* (2) 5281091 (home); (2) 3378242 (office); (2) 7359593 (home). *Fax:* (2) 7603552 (office); (2) 7359593 (home). *E-mail:* moshaker@ecfa-egypt.org (office). *Website:* www.ecfa-egypt.org (office).

SHAKERI, Mashallah; Iranian diplomatist; *Ambassador to Pakistan;* b. 1957, Yazd; m.; two c. *Career:* Tech. Expert, Ports and Shipping Org.,

Ministry of Roads and Transport 1987–90, Dir Equipment Maintenance Dept 1990–92, Dir Equipment Procurement Dept 1992–95; Head of Econ. Section, Embassy in Tokyo 1995–98; Dir Econ. Studies Dept, Ports and Shipping Org., Ministry of Roads and Transport 1998–2000, Dir-Gen. Office of the Bd 2000–04, 2005–06, Dir-Gen. Research Centre 2004–05; Advisor to Minister of Foreign Affairs 2006; Amb. to Pakistan 2006–.
Address: Embassy of Iran, Plot No. 222, 238, St 2, F-5/1, Islamabad, Pakistan (office). *Telephone:* (51) 2276270 (office). *Fax:* (51) 2824839 (office).

SHAKHRAY, Sergey Mikhailovich, LLD; Russian politician; *Head, Accountant Chamber Administration;* b. 30 April 1956, Simferopol; m. Tatyana Shakhray 1985; two s. one d. *Education:* Rostov State Univ. *Career:* Head of Law, Moscow State Univ.; People's Deputy of Russia 1990–92; Chair. of the Legis. Cttee of Russian Supreme Soviet 1990; State Councillor on legal issues of Russian Fed. 1991–92; Vice-Prime Minister of Russia 1991–92, 1993, 1994–95; Chair. State Cttee for nat. problems; Founder and Chair. Party of Russian Unity and Consent (PRES) 1993–; Head interim admin in zone of emergency situation in N Ossetia and Ingushetia 1992–93; mem. State Duma (Parl.) 1993; Minister for Nationalities and Nat. Problems 1994–95; Deputy Head of Pres. Yeltsin's Admin, Pres.'s Rep. at Constitutional Court 1996–98; Deputy Chair. Political Consultative Council of Pres. Yeltsin; adviser to Prime Minister 1998–; Prof., Moscow Inst. of Int. Relations 1999–; Deputy Head, Accountant Chamber Admin 2001–04, Head 2004–; Honoured Jurist of the Russian Fed. *Publications:* Constitution of the Russian Federation. Encyplopaedic Dictionary (co-author) 1995, Constitutional Justice in the System of Russian Federalism 2002, Constitutional Law of the Russian Federation 2003, Globalization in the Contemporary World – Political-Legal Aspects 2003, Globalization State Law 2003.
Address: Accountant Chamber of Russian Federation, Zubovskaya str. 2, 119992 Moscow, Russia (office). *Telephone:* (495) 986-00-14 (office). *Fax:* (495) 986-01-53 (office). *E-mail:* lnpautova@mail.ru (office); shahray@ach .gov.ru (office). *Website:* www.ach.gov.ru (office).

SHALA, Ahmet, BA, MBA, PhD; Kosovo politician; *Minister of Finance and the Economy;* m.; four c. *Education:* Univ. of Prishtina, Univ. Autonoma de Barcelona, Vaxjo Univ., Sweden. *Career:* fmr Policy Advisor for Econ. Devt, EU Mission in Kosovo; Deputy Head Dept for Trade and Industry 2000–02; Deputy Man. Dir Kosovo Trust Agency 2002–08; Minister of Finance and the Economy 2008–; Prof. of Marketing Modeling and Statistics, Univ. of Prishtina; f. Cambridge School (English language teaching inst.).
Address: Ministry of Finance and the Economy, Rruga Bill Klinton dhe Nënë Terezë, 10000 Prishtina, Kosovo (office). *Telephone:* (38) 213115 (office). *Fax:* (38) 213113 (office). *E-mail:* info@mfe-ks.org (office). *Website:* www.mfe-ks.org (office).

SHALGAM, Abd ar-Rahman Muhammad, BA; Libyan politician; *Secretary of the People's Committee for Foreign Liaison and International Co-operation;* b. 21 Nov. 1949, Guraifa; m. Mabrouk el-Araby; three s. *Education:* Cairo Univ., Egypt. *Career:* Sec. of the People's Cttee for Foreign Liaison and Int. Co-operation 2000–; El-Fatah Medal. *Publications include:* Africa in the Future, Religion and Politics in Islamic History, Intimacy (poetry).
Address: Secretariat of the People's Committee for Foreign Liaison and International Co-operation, Tripoli (office); El-Shat Street, Tripoli, Libya (home). *Telephone:* (21) 3400461 (office). *Fax:* (21) 3402660 (office).

SHALIKASHVILI, Gen. John, BS, MA; American army officer (retd); *Visiting Professor, Center for International Security and Cooperation, Stanford University;* b. 27 June 1936, Warsaw, Poland; m. 1st Gunhild Bartsch 1963 (died 1965); m. 2nd Joan Zimpelman 1966; one s. *Education:* Bradley Univ., Naval War Coll., US Army War Coll., George Washington Univ. *Career:* entered US army active duty 1958; various troop and staff assignments Alaska, USA, FRG, Viet Nam, Repub. of Korea 1959–75; Commdr 1st Bn, 84th Field Artillery, 9th Infantry Div., Fort Lewis, Washington 1975–77; Deputy Chief of Staff for Operations, S European Task Force, Vicenza, Italy 1978–79; Commdr Div. Artillery 1st Armored Div. US Army, Nürnberg, FRG 1979–81; Chief, Politico-Mil. Div., later Deputy Dir, Strategy, Plans and Policy, ODCSOPS, the Army Staff, Washington, DC 1981–84; rank of Brig.-Gen. 1983; Asst Div. Commdr 1st Armored Div. US Army, Nürnberg, FRG 1984–86; Dir of Strategy, Plans, Policy, ODC-SOPS, the Army Staff, Washington, DC 1986–87; rank of Maj.-Gen. 1986; Commdg Gen. 9th Infantry Div. Fort Lewis, Washington 1987–89; rank of Lt-Gen. 1989; Deputy C-in-C US Army Europe, Heidelberg, FRG 1989–91; Asst to Chair. Jt Chiefs of Staff, Washington, DC 1991–92; rank of Gen. 1992; Supreme Allied Commdr Europe and C-in-C US European Command 1992–93; Chair. Jt Chiefs of Staff 1993–97; Adviser to Pentagon 2000–; currently Visiting Prof. Center for Int. Security and Cooperation, Stanford Univ.; mem. Bd Govs of American Red Cross,

Asscn of US Army, Field Artillery Asscn, Retd Officers Asscn, Council on Foreign Relations, American Acad. of Achievement, Bradley Univ. Bd of Trustees; mem. Bd. Dirs Boeing 2000–, Frank Russell Trust Co., L-3 Communications Holdings Inc., Plug Power Inc., United Defense Industries Inc.; numerous decorations, including Mil. Order of the Carabao; Hon. LLD (Univ. of Md, Bradley Univ.; numerous awards. *Address:* Center for International Security and Cooperation, 616 Serra Street, Stanford University, Stanford, CA 94305-6055, USA. *Telephone:* (425) 882-1923. *E-mail:* brant.shali@verizon.net. *Website:* cisac.stanford .edu.

SHAMIM AHMED, F. A.; Bangladeshi diplomatist; m. Shabnam Ahmed; one s. one d. *Education:* Univ. of Dhaka. *Career:* joined Ministry of Foreign Affairs 1974, postings to Kenya, Japan, Italy, Pakistan and USA, Dir-Gen. South Asia Div., Ministry of Foreign Affairs 1995–97, Deputy Perm. Rep. to UN, New York 1997–2000, Consul Gen., New York 2000–01, Amb. to the Netherlands and Perm. Rep. to Org. for the Prohibition of Chemical Weapons 2001–03, High Commr to Pakistan 2003–07. *Address:* c/o Ministry of Foreign Affairs, Segunbagicha, Dhaka 1000, Bangladesh.

SHAMKHANI, Rear-Adm. Ali, BSc, MSc, MA; Iranian military officer; b. 1955, Ahvaz, Khuzestan. *Education:* Univ. of Ahvaz, Univ. of State Man. Org. *Career:* held various military posts in Iran-Iraq War including Cmmdr Islamic Revolution's Guards Corps (IRGC); Minister in charge of implementation of UN Resolution 598 on ending Iran-Iraq War; Cmmdr of Naval Forces and IRGC and Minister of Defence and Armed Forces Logistics –2005; currently Head, Centre for Strategic Defense Research, Tehran. *Address:* c/o Ministry of Defence, Shadid Yousuf Kaboli Street, Sayed Khandan Area, Tehran, Iran (office).

SHAMS, Mohammad Jalil, PhD; Afghan economist, academic and politician; *Minister of Economy; Education:* Sultan Ghias-ud-din Ghoori High School, Herat, Cairo Univ., Egypt, Bochum Univ., Germany. *Career:* Asst Prof., School of Econs, Kabul Univ. 1964–66; Vice-Pres. Banke Milli-e-Afghan, Hamburg, Germany 1969–71; Man. Dir Afghan Nat. Bank, London, UK 1971–74; Lecturer in Econs, Essen Polytechnic Germany 1973–74; Deputy Minister of Foreign Affairs 1992–94 (resgnd in protest against internal conflict in Afghanistan); Deputy Minister of Energy and Water 2005–06; Minister of Economy 2006–. *Address:* Ministry of Economy, 5th Floor, Malik Asghar Square, Kabul, Afghanistan (office).

SHAMSHUR, Oleh, PhD; Ukrainian academic and diplomatist; *Ambassador to USA;* b. 6 July 1956; m.; one d. *Education:* Taras Shevchenko Kyiv Univ., Kyiv Univ., Acad. of Sciences of Ukraine. *Career:* held various posts at Inst. of Social and Econ. Problems of Foreign Countries, Acad. of Sciences, including Dir of Programs 1981–93; Visiting Sholar, Univ. Coll., London, UK 1993; Sec. and Counsellor, Perm. Mission to UN and Int. Orgs, Geneva 1993–96; Deputy Chair. State Cttee for Nationalities and Migration of Ukraine and mem. Pres.'s Comm. on Citizenship 1996–98; Minister-Counsellor, Embassy to Benelux countries 1998–2003; Head of EU Dept, Ministry of Foreign Affairs 2003–04, Deputy Minister of Foreign Affairs 2003–05, Amb. to USA 2006–; Order of Merit (Third Class) 2007. *Publications:* more than 60 publs on int. migration and ethnic relations. *Address:* Embassy of Ukraine, 3350 M Street, NW, Washington, DC 20007, USA (office). *Telephone:* (202) 349-2920 (office). *Fax:* (202) 333-0817 (office). *E-mail:* letters@ukremb.com (office). *Website:* www.mfa.gov .ua/us (office).

SHAMSI, Abdulaziz Nasser R. ash-, BBA; United Arab Emirates diplomatist and civil servant; b. 1956, Ajam; m.; six c. *Education:* Univ. of Cairo, Egypt. *Career:* joined Diplomatic Service 1980; Second Sec. Embassy in Brussels 1982; served at Embassy in Tunisia 1984; Amb. to Brazil 1991–94 (also on-resident Amb. to Argentina and Chile 1993–94), to France 1995–99, (also to Switzerland 1997–99); with Ministry of Foreign Affairs, Deputy Dir Dept of Arab Nations 1990–91, Dir Int. Orgs 1999–2001, Dir of Protocol 2007–; joined Perm. Mission to UN, Geneva 1985, First Sec. 1986, Counsellor 1989; Perm. Rep. to UNESCO 1995–99, to the UN, New York 2001–07; Rio Branco Club Order of the Grand Cross 1994 (Brazil), Légion d'honneur (France) 1999. *Address:* Ministry of Foreign Affairs, POB 1, Abu Dhabi, UAE (office). *Telephone:* (2) 4444488 (office). *Fax:* (2) 4449100 (office). *E-mail:* mofa@ mofa.gov.ae (office). *Website:* www.mofa.gov.ae (office).

SHANKAR, Meera; Indian diplomatist; *Ambassador to Germany; Career:* joined Ministry of External Affairs 1973, Dir Disarmament and Policy Planning 1984–85, Dir Deputation to Prime Minister's Office 1985–91, Dir-

Gen. Deputation to Indian Council for Cultural Relations 1995–97, Jt Sec. for Nepal, Bhutan and SAARC 1997–2003; Additional Sec., UN, Disarmament and Int. Security 2003–05; Minister (Commerce), Embassy in Washington, DC 1991–95; Amb. to Germany 2005–. *Address:* Embassy of India, Tiergartenstr. 17, 10785 Berlin, Germany (office). *Telephone:* (30) 257950 (office). *Fax:* (30) 25795102 (office). *E-mail:* infowing@indianembassy.de (office). *Website:* www.indianembassy.de (office).

SHANKARDASS, Raghuvansh Kumar Prithvinath, MA, LLM; Indian lawyer; b. 9 June 1930, Nairobi, Kenya; m. Ramma Handoo 1955. *Education:* Trinity Coll., Cambridge, Lincoln's Inn, London. *Career:* Gen. Sec. Bar Asscn of India 1975–85, Vice-Pres. 1985–; Asst Sec.-Gen. Int. Bar Asscn 1980–82, Vice-Pres. 1984–86, Pres. 1986–88; Gen. Sec. Indian Law Foundation 1975–1991, Pres. 1991–; Chair. Panel of Commrs UN Compensation Comm. 1996–2005; Fellow, American Bar Foundation 1997; Ed. The Indian Advocate 1990–; Pres. Cambridge Univ. Majlis 1953; Vice-Pres. Indian Soc. of Int. Law 2003–06; Trustee India Foundation for the Arts 1994–2000, Talwar Research Foundation 1996, Nurul Hasan Educational and Research Foundation 1998–, Pratichi (India) Trust 2003–; Hon. OBE 1996. *Address:* 87 Lawyer's Chambers, Supreme Court of India, New Delhi 110 001 (office); B-12 Maharani Bagh, New Delhi 110 065, India (home). *Telephone:* (11) 23381041 (office); (11) 26830636 (home). *Fax:* (11) 26848104.

SHANMUGARATNAM, Tharman Motek, MPA; Singaporean politician; *Minister of Finance and Minister of Education;* b. 1958; m. Jane Yumiko Ittogi; three s. one d. *Education:* London School of Econs and Univ. of Cambridge, UK, Harvard Univ., USA. *Career:* early professional career at Monetary Authority of Singapore, where he was Man. Dir, currently mem. Bd and Deputy Chair.; mem. Parl. for Jurong GRC (Taman Jurong) 2001–; apptd to Cen. Exec. Cttee of People's Action Party 2002, Asst Treas. 2004–; Sr Minister of State, Ministry of Trade and Industry and Ministry of Educ. 2001–03, Acting Minister of Educ. 2003–04, Minister of Educ. 2004–, Second Minister of Finance 2006–07, Minister of Finance 2007–; Deputy Chair. Nat. Research Foundation; mem. Bd Govt of Singapore Investment Corpn; Co-Chair. Singapore-Liaoning Econ. and Trade Council 2003–; Chair. Ong Teng Cheong Inst. of Labour Studies; Life Trustee Singapore Indian Devt Asscn; Littauer Fellow Award, Harvard Univ., Singapore Public Admin Gold Medal 1999. *Address:* Ministry of Finance, The Treasury 100 High Street, #10-01, Singapore 179434 (office); Ministry of Education, 1 North Buona Vista Drive #23-00 Singapore 138675, Singapore (office). *Telephone:* 63322717 (Ministry of Finance) (office); 68796000 (Ministry of Educ.) (office). *Fax:* 63367001 (Ministry of Finance) (office); 68728924 (Ministry of Educ.) (office). *E-mail:* tharman_shanmugaratnam@mof.gov.sg (office). *Website:* www.mof.gov.sg (office); www.moe.gov.sg (office).

SHAPIRO, Charles S.; American diplomatist; *Principal Deputy Assistant Secretary of State for Western Hemisphere Affairs;* m. Robin Dickerson; two s. *Education:* Univ. of Penn., Georgia State Univ. *Career:* joined State Dept, Washington, DC 1977, postings to El Salvador and Denmark, then positions in Office of Inter-American Affairs, Bureau of Int. Narcotics Matters, Office of Andean Affairs, Dir Office of Cuban Affairs 1999–2001; Deputy Chief of Mission at US embassies in Chile and Trinidad and Tobago; Amb. to Venezuela 2002–04; Prin. Deputy Asst Sec. for Western Hemisphere Affairs 2004–; holds rank of Minister Counsellor, Sr Foreign Service. *Address:* Bureau of Western Hemisphere Affairs, Department of State, 2201 C Street, NW, Washington, DC 20520, USA (office). *Telephone:* (202) 647-6755 (office). *Fax:* (202) 647-6738 (office). *Website:* www.state.gov/p/ wha (office).

SHARANSKY, Natan; Israeli (b. Soviet) politician, human rights activist and computer scientist; *Institute Chairman and Distinguished Fellow, Adelson Institute for Strategic Studies, Shalem Center;* b. 20 Jan. 1948, Donetsk, USSR (now Ukraine); m. Natalya (now Avital) Stiglitz 1974; two d. *Career:* a leading spokesman for Jewish emigration movt in USSR; arrested by Soviet authorities for dissident activities 1977; received 13-year prison sentence on charges of treason 1978; following worldwide campaign, Soviet authorities released him in exchange for eastern spies held in West and he took up residence in Israel Feb. 1986; mem. Knesset 1996–2006 (resgnd); Minister of Trade and Industry 1996–99, of the Interior 1999–2000; Minister without Portfolio responsible for Jerusalem, Social and Diaspora Affairs 2003–05; currently Inst. Chair. and Distinguished Fellow, Adelson Inst. for Strategic Studies, Shalem Center 2006–; Pres. Beit Hatefutsot (Jewish diaspora museum); Visiting Prof., Brandeis Univ., Waltham, Mass.; fmr Leader, Israel B'Aliyah Party (merged with Likud 2003); US Congressional Gold Medal 1986. *Publications:* Fear No Evil 1988, The

Case for Democracy: the Power of Freedom to Overcome Tyranny and Terror (with Ron Dermer) 2005, Defending Identity: It's Indispensable Role in Protecting Democracy 2008.
Address: Shalem Center, 13 Yehoshua Bin-Nun Street, Jerusalem 93102, Israel (office). *Telephone:* (2) 560-5500 (office). *E-mail:* inquiries@shalem.org.il (office). *Website:* www.shalemcenter.org.il (office).

SHARIF, Ihab ash-, PhD; Egyptian diplomatist; b. 1 Jan. 1954, Cairo; m. Asmaa Hussein; two d. *Education:* Univ. of Paris (Sorbonne), Univ. of Paris XI, France. *Career:* Diplomatic Attaché, Cen. African Repub. 1981–85; Asst to Minister of State for Foreign Affairs 1985–88; First Sec., Paris 1988–92; Counsellor, Damascus 1994–98; Plenipotentiary Minister, then Head of Mission and Chargé d'affaires, Embassy in Tel-Aviv 1999; Order of Merit, Germany 1999. *Publications:* photographic travel books about 22 countries, including Europe, Myth and Reality 1997, India, Secret and Keys, Germany Today, France, A Country of Djinns and Angels.
Address: Ministry of Foreign Affairs, Corniche en-Nil, Cairo (Maspiro), Egypt (office). *Telephone:* (2) 5749820 (office). *Fax:* (2) 5748822 (office). *E-mail:* info@mfa.gov.eg (office). *Website:* www.mfa.gov.eg (office).

SHARIF, Muhammad al-Hussaini ash-; Saudi Arabian diplomatist. *Career:* currently Amb. to Turkey.
Address: Embassy of Saudi Arabia, Turan Emeksiz Sok. 6, 06700 Gaziosmanpaşa, Ankara, Turkey (office). *Telephone:* (312) 4685540 (office). *Fax:* (312) 4274886 (office). *E-mail:* tremb@mofa.gov.sa (office). *Website:* www.mofa.gov.sa (office).

SHARIFOV, Samir Rauf oğlu, MA; Azerbaijani economist and government official; *Minister of Finance;* b. 7 Sept. 1961; m.; two c. *Career:* foreign econ. relations specialist in USSR 1983–91; Deputy Chief, Dept of Int. Econ. Relations, Ministry of Foreign Affairs 1991–95; Chief of Dept, then Exec. Dir Nat. Bank of Azerbaijan 1995–2001; Exec. Dir State Oil Fund of Repub. of Azerbaijan (SOFAZ) 2001–06, also Azerbaijan Rep. and Dir Black Sea Trade and Devt Bank 2001–06; Chair. Govt Comm. on Extractive Industries Transparency Initiative 2003–06; Minister of Finance 2006–.
Address: Ministry of Finance, 1022 Baku, Samed Vurghun küç. 83, Azerbaijan (office). *Telephone:* (12) 493-30-12 (office). *Fax:* (12) 493-05-62 (office). *E-mail:* office@maliyye.gov.az (office). *Website:* maliyye.gov.az (office).

SHARMA, Kamalesh; Indian diplomatist and international organization official; *Secretary-General, Commonwealth;* m. Babli Sharma; one s. one d. *Education:* Delhi Univ., King's Coll. Cambridge, UK. *Career:* joined Foreign Service 1965; Head of Divs of Econ. Relations, Int. Orgs and Policy Planning, Foreign Office; Head of Div. Ministry of Finance; served in Bonn, Hong Kong, Saudi Arabia and Turkey; Amb. to fmr GDR, Kazakhstan, Kyrgyzstan; Amb. to UN, Geneva, also Amb. for Disarmament and Spokesman for developing countries in UNCTAD; Amb. to UN, New York 1997–2002; Special Rep. of UN Sec.-Gen. for East Timor (now Timor-Leste) and Head of UN Mission of Support in East Timor (UNMISET) 2002–04; Dir Int. Peace Acad., New York; High Commr to UK 2004–08; Sec.-Gen. The Commonwealth 2008–; Fellow, Weatherhead Center for Int. Affairs, Harvard Univ.; mem. US Foreign Policy Asscn; fmr mem. Bd Dirs Peace Academy, New York, Education Consultants India Ltd; Gov. Ditchley Foundation; Fellow, Harvard Univ., USA; Hon. LLD (De Montfort Univ., UK); Medal of US Foreign Policy Asscn. *Publications include:* Mille Fleurs: Poetry from Around the World (compilation of poems by diplomats and officials) (ed.), Imaging Tomorrow: Rethinking the Global Challange.
Address: Commonwealth Secretariat, Marlborough House, Pall Mall, London, SW1Y 5HX, England (office). *Telephone:* (20) 7747-6500 (office). *Fax:* (20) 7930-0827 (office). *E-mail:* info@commonwealth.int (office). *Website:* www.thecommonwealth.org (office).

SHARMA, Murari Raj, LLB, MA; Nepalese diplomatist and civil servant; *Ambassador to UK;* b. April 1951; m. Nila Adhikari; two s. *Education:* Tribhuvan Univ. of Nepal, Univ. of Pittsburgh, USA. *Career:* Hubert Humphrey Fellow, The American Univ., Washington, DC; taught at Tribhuvan Univ. of Nepal, Kathmandu 1974–76; worked for two parastatals 1976–78; joined Nepal Admin. Service 1978; Section Officer at Foreign Aid Co-ordination Div., Ministry of Finance 1978–82, Jt Sec. and Head of Budget Div. 1991–93; Under-Sec. Ministry of Gen. Admin 1983–89, Ministry of Home Affairs 1989–90, Jt Sec. in charge of Planning and Special Services (Drug Control and Disaster Man.) Div. 1990–91; Section Officer at Americas Section, Ministry of Foreign Affairs 1982–83, Jt Sec. and Head of UN, Int. Orgs and Int. Law Div. 1993–97, also responsible for NE Asia, SE Asia and Pacific Div. 1993–94, Special Sec. May–Nov. 1997; Acting Foreign Sec. 1997–98, Foreign Sec. 1998–2000, Perm. Rep. to UN, New York 2000–04, Chair. Fifth Cttee 2002–03, Amb.

to UK (also accred to Ireland) 2007–; mem. UN Advisory Cttee on Admin. and Budgetary Questions 2003–.
Address: Embassy of Nepal, 12A Kensington Palace Gardens, London, W8 4QU, England (office). *Telephone:* (20) 7229-1594 (office). *Fax:* (20) 7792-9861 (office). *E-mail:* eon@nepembassy.org.uk (office). *Website:* www.nepembassy.org.uk (office).

SHARMA, Sheel Kant, MS, PhD; Indian diplomatist and international organization executive; *Secretary-General, South Asian Association for Regional Cooperation (SAARC);* b. 10 Jan. 1950; m. Meenu Sharma. *Education:* Indian Inst. of Tech., Mumbai. *Career:* joined Foreign Service 1973, served as Third Sec., Embassy in Kuwait and Second Sec., Embassy in Saudi Arabia 1976–77, Under-Sec., Middle East Desk, Ministry of External Affairs 1978–81, Fellow, Inst. of Defence Studies and Analysis, New Delhi 1981–82, Deputy Sec. (North), Ministry of External Affairs 1982–83, First Sec. (Disarmament), Perm. Mission to UN, Geneva and Alt. Rep. to UN Conf. on Disarmament 1983–86, Counsellor and Deputy Chief of Mission, Embassy in Algiers 1986–89, Dir (UN Div.) and Disarmament Head, Ministry of External Affairs, New Delhi 1989–91, Jt Sec. (South and Disarmament) in charge of India's relations with ASEAN, Indo-China and South Pacific 1991–94; seconded to IAEA, Vienna, served as sr professional in External Relations and Policy Coordination Div. 1994–2000; Jt Sec. (Disarmament and Int. Security Affairs) 2000–03, Additional Sec. (Int. Orgs), Ministry of External Affairs 2003–04, Amb. to Austria and Perm. Rep. to all Int. Orgs, Vienna 2004–08, Sec.-Gen. South Asian Asscn for Regional Cooperation (SAARC) 2008–; Chair. G-77 Vienna Chapter 2005; mem. India Int. Centre, India Habitat Centre. *Publications:* articles in journals and UN reports.
Address: South Asian Association for Regional Co-operation (SAARC), PO Box 4222, Tridevi Marg, Kathmandu, Nepal (office). *Telephone:* (1) 4221785 (home). *Fax:* (1) 4227033 (office). *E-mail:* saarc@saarc-sec.org (office). *Website:* www.saarc-sec.org (office).

SHARON, Maj.-Gen. Ariel; Israeli politician and army officer (retd); b. 1928; m.; two s. *Career:* active in Hagana since early youth; Instructor, Jewish Police units 1947; Platoon Commdr Alexandroni Brigade; Regimental Intelligence Officer 1948; Co. Commdr 1949; Commdr Brigade Reconnaissance Unit 1949–50; Intelligence Officer, Cen. Command and Northern Command 1951–52; studies at Hebrew Univ. 1952–53; in charge of Unit 101, on numerous reprisal operations –1957, Commdr Paratroopers Brigade, Sinai Campaign 1956; studies at Staff Coll., Camberley, UK 1957–58; Training Commdr, Gen. Staff 1958; Commdr Infantry School 1958–69; Commdr Armoured Brigade 1962; Head of Staff, Northern Command 1964; Head, Training Dept of Defence Forces 1966; Head Brigade Group during Six-Day War 1967; resigned from Army July 1973; recalled as Commdr Cen. Section of Sinai Front during Yom Kippur War Oct. 1973, forged bridgehead across Suez Canal; founding mem. Likud party 1973, Leader 1999–2005 (resgnd from party); f. Kadima (Forward) Party 2005; mem. Knesset (Parl.) 1973–74, 1977–2006; Adviser to Prime Minister 1975–77; Minister of Agric. in charge of Settlements 1977–81, of Defence 1981–83, without Portfolio 1983–84, of Trade and Industry 1984–90, of Construction and Housing 1990–92, of Foreign Affairs and Nat. Infrastructure 1996–99; Prime Minister of Israel March 2001–06, also Minister of Immigrant Absorption (suffered stroke in Jan. 2006 and has remained in a coma since then); mem. Ministerial Defence Cttee 1990–92; Chair. Cabinet Cttee to oversee Jewish immigration from USSR 1991–96. *Publication:* Warrior (autobiog.) 1989.
Address: c/o Office of the Prime Minister, PO Box 187, 3 Rehov Kaplan, Kiryat Ben-Gurion, Jerusalem 91919, Israel (office).

SHARQI, HH Sheikh Hamad bin Muhammad ash-, (Ruler of Fujairah); United Arab Emirates; b. 25 Sept. 1948. *Education:* Mons Mil. Acad., Hendon Police Coll. *Career:* Minister of Agric. and Fisheries, UAE Fed. Cabinet 1971; Ruler of Fujairah 1974–; mem. Supreme Council 1974–.
Address: Emiri Court, PO Box 1, Fujairah, United Arab Emirates.

SHAW, Audley, BA, MA; Jamaican politician; *Minister of Finance and Public Service;* b. 13 June 1952, Christiana, Manchester. *Education:* Northern Ill. Univ., USA. *Career:* began career as Lab. Technician, Jamaica Milk Products; worked for Jamaica Promotions Ltd; fmr Area Literacy Officer, JAMAL Movt; MP for Manchester N E 1993–, served as Shadow Minister of Information and Culture, of Public Utilities and Transport, of Industry and Commerce, fmr Chair. Public Accounts Cttee, Shadow Minister of Finance and Public Service 1997–2007, Minister of Finance and Public Service 2007–; Deputy Leader, Labour Party 1999– (fmr Gen. Sec.).
Address: Ministry of Finance and the Public Service, 30 National Heroes Circle, Kingston 4 (office); The Jamaica Labour Party, 20 Belmont Road, Kingston 5, Jamaica (office). *Telephone:* 922-8600 (Ministry) (office); 929-1690 (office). *Fax:* 922-7097 (Ministry) (office). *E-mail:* info@mof.gov.jm (office); fitzalbert_2@yahoo.com (office); manchester-ne@

jamaicalabourparty.com (office). *Website:* www.mof.gov.jm (office); www .audleyshawjamaica.com (office).

SHAW, Martin, PhD; British academic; *Professor of International Relations and Politics, University of Sussex;* b. 30 June 1947, Driffield, E Yorks. *Education:* London School of Econs, Univ. of Hull. *Career:* Tutor in Sociology, LSE 1968–70; Lecturer in Sociology, Univ. of Durham 1970–72; Lecturer, then Sr Lecturer in Sociology, Univ. of Hull 1972–92, Dir Centre for Defence and Disarmament (later Security) Studies 1989–92 and Gulf War Project (funded by Joseph Rowntree and Cadbury Charitable Trusts) 1991, Head, Dept of Sociology and Social Anthropology, Reader and Prof. of Political and Int. Sociology 1992–95; Prof. of Int. Relations and Politics, Univ. of Sussex 1995–, Chair. Int. Relations and Politics Subject Group 1996–99; mem. Int. Screening Cttee SSRC –MacArthur Post-Doctoral Fellowships on Int. Peace and Security, Social Science Research Council, New York 1993–96; mem. Editorial Bds, Peace and Conflict Studies, Global Media–Global Culture, Global Society, Renewal: Journal of Labour Politics, Int. Relations; Leverhulme Research Fellow Jan.–Sept. 2000; Econ. and Social Research Council Research Fellow 2004–05. *Publications include:* Dialectics of War: An Essay of the Social Theory of War and Peace 1988, Theory of the Global State: Globality as Unfinished Revolution 2000, War and Genocide: Organized Killing in Modern Society 2003, The New Western Way of War 2005. *Address:* Department of International Relations and Politics, University of Sussex, Falmer, Brighton, BN1 9SN, England (office). *Telephone:* (1273) 678032 (office). *E-mail:* m.shaw@sussex.ac.uk (office). *Website:* www .martinshaw.org (office).

SHAW, Vernon Lorden; Dominican fmr head of state and civil servant; b. 13 May 1930; m.; four c. *Education:* Dominica Grammar School, Trinity Coll., Oxford. *Career:* various appointments at Treasury and Customs Dept, Post Office, Cen. Housing and Planning Authority, Audit Dept, Cen. Housing and Planning Authority 1948–62; Admin. Asst Ministry of Trade and Production 1962–65, Asst Sec. 1965–67; Perm. Sec., Ministry of Educ. and Health 1967, Ministry of External Affairs 1967–71; Chief Establishment Officer 1971–77; Sec. to Cabinet 1977–78 and Amb.-at-Large and Inspector of Missions 1978–90 (retd from public service); temporary resident tutor, Univ. of W Indies School of Continuing Studies 1991–93; Chair. Dominica Broadcasting Corpn 1993–95, Public Service Bd of Appeal 1993–98; Pres. of Dominica 1998–2003; mem. Inst. of Admin. Accounting; Assoc. mem. BIM; Dominica Award of Honour, Sisserou Award of Honour. *Address:* 8 Churchill Lane, Goodwill, Dominica (home). *Telephone:* 448-2361 (home).

SHAW, Yu-Ming, PhD; Taiwanese public servant and academic; b. 3 Nov. 1938, Harbin; m. Shirley Shiow-jyu Lu; one s. one d. *Education:* Nat. Chengchi Univ., Tufts Univ. and Univ. of Chicago, USA. *Career:* Asst Prof. of History, Newberry Coll., SC 1967–68, 1972–73; Assoc. Prof. of History, Univ. of Notre Dame, Ind. 1973–82; held various research posts in Asian studies in USA; Dir Asia and World Inst., Taiwan 1983–84; Dean, Grad. School of Int. Law and Diplomacy, Nat. Chengchi Univ. 1984, Dir Inst. of Int. Relations 1984–87, 1994, Prof. of History 1991; Dir-Gen. Govt Information Office and Govt spokesman 1987–91; currently Prof., Chinese Culture Univ., Pres. Cultural Foundation of the United Daily News Group 1992–; awards from American Council of Learned Socs, Asia Foundation, Inst. of Chinese Culture, USA and others. *Publications include:* China and Christianity 1979, Problems in Twentieth Century Chinese Christianity 1980, Twentieth Century Sino-American Relations 1980, History and Politics in Modern China 1982, International Politics and China's Future 1987, Beyond the Economic Miracle 1988, An American Missionary in China: John Leighton Stuart and Chinese-American Relations 1993. *Address:* Chinese Culture University, 55, Hwa-Kang Road, Yang-Ming-Shan, Taipei 111, Taiwan.

SHAWAYS, Rowsch Nouri, DEng; Iraqi engineer and politician; b. 1947. *Career:* Head, Kurdish Student Union, Germany; returned to Iraq 1979 joining Kurdish rebellion; Deputy Prime Minister, jt Kurdistan Regional Govt 1996; Prime Minister, Kurdistan Regional Govt Arbil 1996–99; Pres. Iraqi Kurdistan Nat. Ass. 1999–2004; Interim Vice-Pres. 2004–05; Deputy Prime Minister 2005; mem. Political Bureau, Kurdistan Democratic Party. *Address:* Kurdistan Democratic Party, c/o KDP Europe, PO Box 301 516, 10749 Berlin, Germany (office). *Telephone:* (30) 79743741. *Fax:* (30) 79743746. *E-mail:* KDPEurope@t-online.de; party@kdp.se. *Website:* www.kdp.se.

SHEA, Jamie Patrick, BA, PhD; British international organization official; *Director, Policy Planning, Private Office of the Secretary-General, NATO;* b. 11 Sept. 1953, London; m.; two c. *Education:* Univ. of Sussex, Lincoln Coll., Oxford. *Career:* joined NATO as minute-taker 1981, later Sr Planning Officer and Speechwriter to Sec.-Gen.; Spokesman and Deputy

Dir of Information and Press 1993–2001, Dir 2000–03, Temporary Spokesman 2003–04, Deputy Asst. Sec.-Gen. for External Relations 2003–05, Dir Policy Planning, Pvt. Office of the Sec.-Gen. 2005–; Prof. of Int. Relations, Assoc. Prof. of Int. Relations, American Univ., Washington, DC; Adjunct Assoc. Prof. of Int. Relations, James Madison Coll., Mich. State Univ., also Dir MSU Summer School in Brussels; mem. Advisory Council Int. Relations Studies and Programme of Université Libre de Bruxelles and Jean Monnet Visiting Prof.; mem. Advisory Council European Policy Centre, Brussels; Founder and mem. Security and Defence Agenda, Brussels; mem. Centre for European Policy Studies, European-Atlantic Movt, Int. Studies Asscn; Assoc. mem. Inst. Royal des Relations Internationales, Brussels; European Communicator of the Year 1999. *Address:* NATO, 1110 Brussels, Belgium (office). *Telephone:* (2) 707-44-13 (office). *Fax:* (2) 707-35-86 (office). *E-mail:* shea.jamie@hq.nato.int (office). *Website:* www.nato.int.

SHEARMAN, Martin James, CVO; British diplomatist; *High Commissioner to Uganda;* m. Miriam Shearman; two s. *Career:* EC Dept (External), FCO 1989–91; Second, later First Sec., Embassy in Tokyo 1992–96; secondment as Head of Japan Unit, Dept of Trade and Industry 1996–97; secondment to Cabinet Office Review of Trade Promotion 1998; secondment to NATO Int. Secr., Brussels 1999; Head of NATO Section, Security Policy Dept, FCO 1999–2000, Deputy Head of Common Foreign and Security Policy Dept 2001–02; Deputy High Commr, Abuja 2003–06; High Commr to Uganda 2008–. *Address:* British High Commission, PO Box 7070, Plot 4, Windsor Loop Road, Kampala, Uganda (office). *Telephone:* (31) 2312000 (office). *Fax:* (41) 2257304 (office). *E-mail:* bhcinfo@starcom.co.ug (office). *Website:* www.britishhighcommission.gov.uk/uganda (office).

SHEERAN, Josette, BA; American newspaper editor and diplomatist; *Executive Director, United Nations World Food Programme;* b. Orange, NJ. *Education:* Univ. of Colorado. *Career:* Deputy Man. Ed., Washington Times newspaper 1985–92, Man. Ed. 1992–97; Man. Dir Starpoint Solutions, NY; fmr Pres. and CEO Empower America; Deputy US Trade Rep., Office of US Trade Rep. –2005; Under-Sec. of State for Econ., Business and Agricultural Affairs, US State Dept 2005–07; Exec. Dir UN WFP 2007–; mem. Council on Foreign Relations; mem. Bd of Dirs Overseas Pvt. Investment Corpn; Press Award for Journalistic Achievement, Nat. Order of Women Legislators, nat. award for developing and promoting African-American journalists. *Address:* World Food Programme, Via Cesare Giulio Viola 68, Parco dei Medici, 00148 Rome, Italy (office). *Telephone:* (06) 65131 (office). *Fax:* (06) 6513-2840 (office). *E-mail:* wfpinfo@wfp.org (office). *Website:* www.wfp .org (office).

SHEIKH, Muhammad Majid Abbas ash-; Iraqi diplomatist. *Career:* currently Amb. to Iran. *Address:* Embassy of Iraq, Karamian Alley, No. 17, Pol-e-Roomi, Dr Shariati Avenue, Tehran, Iran (office). *Telephone:* (21) 22210672 (office). *Fax:* (21) 22233902 (office). *E-mail:* tehemb@iraqmofamail.net (office).

SHEINWALD, Sir Nigel Elton, Kt, KCMG; British diplomatist; *Ambassador to USA;* b. 26 June 1953, London; m. Dr Julia Dunne; three s. *Education:* Harrow Co. Boys' School, Balliol Coll., Oxford. *Career:* joined Diplomatic Service 1976–, Japanese Desk 1976–77, Embassy, Moscow 1978–79, mem. Lancaster House Conf. team on Zimbabwe 1979–80, Head of Anglo-Soviet Section, FCO 1981–83, Embassy in Washington, DC 1983–87, Deputy Head of Policy Planning Staff, FCO 1987–89, Deputy Head of EC Dept 1989–92, Perm. Rep. to EU, Brussels 1993–95, Head of News Dept, FCO 1995–98, Dir EU Div. 1998–2000, Amb. and Perm. Rep. to EU, Brussels 2000–03; Foreign Policy and Defence Adviser to the Prime Minister and Head, Cabinet Office Defence and Overseas Secr. 2003–07; Amb. to USA 2007–. *Address:* Embassy of the United Kingdom, 3100 Massachusetts Avenue, NW, Washington, DC 20008, USA (office). *Telephone:* (202) 588-7800 (office). *Fax:* (202) 588-7870 (office). *E-mail:* washi@fco.gov.uk (office). *Website:* www.britainusa.com (office).

SHERSTYUK, Col-Gen. Vladislav Petrovich, CandTechSc; Russian security official and academic; *Director, Institute of Information Security Issues, Lomonosov Moscow State University;* b. 16 Oct. 1940, Novoplastunovskaya, Krasnodar Region; m.; one s. *Education:* Moscow State Univ., Higher KGB School. *Career:* with KGB 1966–; Head Dept of Radioelectronic Espionage Telecommunications, Fed. Agency of Govt Telecommunications and Information 1995–98, Deputy Dir-Gen. 1998, Dir-Gen. 1998–99; First Deputy Sec., Security Council 1999; Dir Fed. Agency of Govt Communications and Information (FAPSI) 2001–02; currently Dir Inst. of Information Security Issues, Lomonosov Moscow State Univ.; Order of Labour Red Banner 1975, Order for Service to Motherland 1996

and numerous other decorations; USSR State Prize 1978, State Prize of Russian Fed. 1996, Red Star 1988.
Address: Institute of Information Security Issues, Lomonosov Moscow State University, 19234 Moscow, Michurinsky pr. 1, Russia (office). *Telephone:* (495) 932-89-58 (office). *Fax:* (495) 939-20-96 (office). *Website:* www.iisi.msu.ru (office).

SHERZOY, Mohammad Rahim, PhD; Afghan diplomatist; *Ambassador to UK;* m. Hameda Sherzoy. *Education:* studies in France and Poland. *Career:* fmr Deputy Foreign Minister for Political Affairs; fmr Political Advisor to fmr King Zahir Shah of Afghanistan; Sr mem. Afghanistan Constitution Comm. 2002–04; Amb. to UK 2007–. *Publications:* numerous articles on political, econ. and socials issues.
Address: Embassy of Afghanistan, 31 Prince's Gate, London, SW7 1QQ, England (office). *Telephone:* (20) 7589-8891 (office). *Fax:* (20) 7581-3452 (office). *E-mail:* info@afghanembassyuk.org (office). *Website:* www .afghanembassyuk.org (office).

SHETTY, Salil, MSc, MBA; Indian international organization official; *Director, Millennium Development Goals Campaign, United Nations; Education:* Bangalore Univ., Indian Inst. of Man., Ahmedabad, London School of Econs, UK. *Career:* joined ActionAid 1985, former postings include Africa and India, CEO –2004; Dir UN Millennium Devt Goals Campaign 2004–; Pres. Bd Azione Aiuto; Gov. Inst. of Devt Studies, Univ. of Sussex; mem. Council Overseas Devt Inst., UK.
Address: Millennium Development Goals Campaign, United Nations Development Programme, One United Nations Plaza, New York, NY 10017, USA (office). *Telephone:* (212) 906-5295 (office). *Fax:* (212) 906-5364 (office). *E-mail:* salil.shetty@undp.org (office). *Website:* www.undp .org/mdg/campaign.html (office).

SHEYNIS, Viktor Leonidovich, DrSc; Russian historian, politician and economist; *Chief Research Fellow, Institute of World Economy and International Relations;* b. 16 Feb. 1931, Kiev; m. Alla K. Nazimova 1953. *Education:* Leningrad Univ. *Career:* history teacher in secondary school 1953–56; manual worker, Kirov factory, Leningrad 1958–64; teacher, Leningrad Univ. 1966–75; on staff as researcher at Inst. of World Economy and Int. Relations (IMEMO) 1975–92, Chief Research Fellow 2000–; co-author of Russian Constitution and electoral laws 1993–99; People's Deputy 1990–93, mem. State Duma (Parl.) 1993–99; mem. Supreme Soviet of Russia 1991–93; Co-Founder Consent in Name of Progress faction 1992–93; mem. Council of Reps of 'Democratic Russia' Movt 1990–93, Yabloko Movt 1993–95, Yabloko Party 1995–, Political Bureau and Fed. Council; mem. Cttee on Legislation and Reform of the Judicial System; Imre Nagy Medal (Hungary) 1993. *Publications:* over 250 including Developing Nations at the Turn of the Millennium 1987, Capitalism, Socialism and Economic Mechanism of Present-day Production 1989, Die Präsidentenwahlen in Russland: Ergebnisse und Perspektiven, Osteuropa 1996, O caminho histórico da Revolução de Outubro visto sob a prisma de 1997 1997, Il tormentato cammino della Constituzione russa 1998, Wie Russland gewaklt hat: Osteuropa 2000, The Constitution: In Between Dictatorship and Democracy 2004, The Rise and Fall of Parliament: Watershed Years in Russian Politics 1985–93 (two vols) 2005.
Address: Institute of World Economy and International Relations, Profsoyuznaya str. 23, 117859 Moscow (office); Vavilova str. 91, corp. 1, Apt 41, 117335 Moscow, Russia (home). *Telephone:* (495) 128-56-46 (office); (495) 128-81-54 (office); (495) 132-73-15 (home). *Fax:* (495) 120-65-75 (office). *E-mail:* nazimova@mtu-net.ru (home). *Website:* www.imemo .ru (office).

SHI, Jiuyong, MA; Chinese lawyer and professor of international law; *Judge, International Court of Justice;* b. 9 Oct. 1926, Zhejiang; m. Zhang Guoying 1956; one s. *Education:* St John's Univ., Shanghai and Columbia Univ., New York, USA. *Career:* Asst Research Fellow, Inst. of Int. Relations, Beijing 1956–58; Sr Lecturer, Assoc. Prof. of Int. Law, Foreign Affairs Coll. Beijing 1958–64; Research Fellow in Int. Law, Inst. of Int. Law, Beijing 1964–73, Inst. of Int. Studies, Beijing 1973–80; Prof. of Int. Law, Foreign Affairs Coll. Beijing 1984–93, Foreign Econ. Law Training Centre of Ministry of Justice; Legal Adviser, Ministry of Foreign Affairs 1980–93, Chinese Centre of Legal Consultancy, Office of Chinese Sr Rep. Sino-British Jt Liaison Group (on question of Hong Kong) 1985–93; Adviser to Chinese Soc. of Int. Law –2003; mem. American Soc. of Int. Law; mem. Standing Cttee Beijing Cttee of CPPCC 1988–93, mem. 8th Nat. Cttee 1993–98; mem. Int. Law Comm. 1987–93, Chair. 1990; Judge, Int. Court of Justice 1994–, Vice-Pres. 2000–03, Pres. 2003–06; mem. Advisory Bd, The Global Community Yearbook of Int. Law and Jurisprudence; Pres. Curatorium Xiamen Acad. of Int. Law 2005–; Hon. Prof. Eastern China Univ. of Political Science and Law 2001–, Hon. Pres. Chinese Soc. of Int. Law 2004–. *Publications:* numerous publs on int. law.

Address: International Court of Justice, Peace Palace, Carnegieplein 2, 2517 KJ The Hague, Netherlands (office). *Telephone:* (70) 302-23-23 (office). *Fax:* (70) 364-99-28 (office). *E-mail:* information@icj-cij.org (office). *Website:* www.icj-cij.org (office).

SHIGEHARA, Kumiharu, BL; Japanese economist; *Head, International Economic Policy Studies Group;* b. 5 Feb. 1939, Maebashi; m. Akiko Yoshizawa 1965; one s. one d. *Education:* Maebashi High School, Univ. of Tokyo and Univ. of Poitiers. *Career:* economist, Bank of Japan 1962–70; admin. OECD 1970–71, Prin. Admin. 1971–72, Head, Monetary Div. 1972–74; Councillor for Policy Planning, Bank of Japan 1974–76, Man. Int. Affairs 1976–80; Deputy Dir Gen. Econs Branch, OECD 1980–82; Gen. Man. Bank of Japan 1983–87; Dir Gen. Econs Branch, OECD 1987–89; Dir-Gen. Inst. for Monetary and Econ. Studies and Chief Economist, Bank of Japan 1989–92; Head, Econs Dept and Chief Economist, OECD 1992–97, Deputy Sec.-Gen. 1997–99; Special Adviser Int. Friendship Exchange Council 2001; Head, Int. Econ. Policy Studies Group 2002–; Hon. PhD; Dr hc (Liège) 1998; Hozumi Special Award, Univ. of Tokyo 1960. *Publications:* The Role of Monetary Policy in Demand Management (co-author) 1975, Europe After 1992 1991, The Problems of Inflation in the 1990s (ed.) 1992, Evolving International Trade and Monetary Regimes 1992, Causes of Declining Growth in Industrialised Countries 1992, Price Stabilization in the 1990s 1993, Long-term Tendencies in Budget Deficits and Debt 1995, The Options regarding the Concept of a Monetary Policy Strategy 1996, Monetary and Economic Policy: Then and Now 1998, Causes and Implications of East Asian Financial Crises 1998, International Aspects of Competition Policy 1999, Monetary Policy and Economic Performance 2001, Looking for Models in Pursuit of Economic Prosperity 2002.
Address: 4-7-11-802, Setagaya-ku, Tokyo (office); 4-7-11-1104 Seta, Setagaya-ku, Tokyo, Japan. *Telephone:* (3) 3709-7969 (office). *Fax:* (3) 3709-7969 (office). *E-mail:* office.shigehara@online.fr (office). *Website:* office.shigehara.online.fr (office).

SHIGEIE, Toshinori; Japanese diplomatist; *Ambassador to South Korea; Career:* joined foreign service 1969; fmr Dir-Gen. Middle East and African Affairs Bureau, Ministry of Foreign Affairs; Amb. to SA 2005; fmr Minister, Embassy in Washington, DC; Amb. in Charge of Okinawa Affairs 2006–07; Amb. to South Korea 2007–; fmr Dir Japan Inst. of Int. Affairs, Tokyo.
Address: Embassy of Japan, 18-11 Junghak-dong, jongno-gu, Seoul, Republic of Korea (office). *Telephone:* (2) 2170-5200 (office). *Fax:* (2) 734-4528 (office). *E-mail:* info@japanem.or.kr (office). *Website:* www.kr .emb-japan.go.jp (office).

SHIHAB, Hussain, MSc; Maldivian politician and diplomatist; *Ambassador to Saudi Arabia;* b. 1949; m.; six c. *Education:* Kuban Agric. Inst., Russia. *Career:* Under-Sec., Ministry of Home Affairs and Social Services 1975, Ministry of Agric. 1976–78; Man. TV Maldives 1978–81, Deputy Dir, then Dir 1985; Dir of Environmental Affairs, Ministry of Home Affairs and Social Services 1986–88, Dir of Environmental Affairs, Ministry of Planning and the Environment 1988–93, Deputy Minister 1993–95, July–Sept. 1998; Dir South Asia Co-operative Environment Programme 1995–98; apptd Perm. Rep. to the UN 1998; del. to numerous UN meetings on the environment, including Conf. on Environment and Devt 1992 and Global Conf. on the Sustainable Devt of Small Island Developing States 1994; fmr Deputy Minister of Foreign Affairs; fmr Minister of State for the Arts; Amb. to Saudi Arabia 2007–; formulated Maldives' first nat. environment action plan; Silver Pen Award 1987. *Films:* Fidhaa 1985, Hadmiya 1993, Rihun 2002, Vissaradmuni 2005. *Publications:* Ochid Eyanarse Maa (short stories) 1983; papers on the environment and sustainable devt presented at int. confs.
Address: Ministry of Foreign Affairs, Boduthakurufaanu Masu, Malé 20-02, Maldives (office). *Telephone:* 3323400 (office). *E-mail:* hshihab@foreign .gov (office).

SHIHAB-ELDIN, Adnan, BSc, MSc, PhD; Kuwaiti engineer and international organization official; *Senior Research Advisor, Oxford Institute for Energy Studies;* b. 1943. *Education:* Univ. of Calif., Berkeley, USA. *Career:* trained as nuclear engineer; Asst Prof. of Physics, then Vice-Rector of Academic Affairs, Kuwait Univ. 1970–80; Dir-Gen. Kuwait Inst. for Scientific Research 1976–86; Dir of UNESCO Regional Office for Science and Tech. and UNESCO Rep. in Egypt, Sudan and Yemen 1991–99; Dir Africa, E Asia and Pacific Div., Dept of Tech. Cooperation, Int. Atomic Energy Agency (IAEA) 1999–2001; Dir Research Div., OPEC 2001–06, Acting Sec.-Gen. 2005; currently Sr Research Advisor, Oxford Inst. for Energy Studies, UK; serves as consultant to numerous public and pvt. orgs; mem. UN Advisory Cttee on Science and Tech. for Devt, NY, Arab Thought Forum, Amman, Jordan, Int. Scientific Council for Science and Tech. Policy Devt, UNESCO; mem. numerous professional socs.

Address: Oxford Institute for Energy Studies, 57 Woodstock Road, Oxford, OX2 6FA, England (office). *Telephone:* (1865) 311377. *Fax:* (1865) 310527 (office). *E-mail:* information@oxfordenergy.org (office). *Website:* www.oxfordenergy.org (office).

SHIKAKI, Khalil, BA, PhD; Palestinian research institute director and academic; *Director, Palestinian Centre for Policy and Survey Research; Education:* Columbia Univ., USA, American Univ., Beirut. *Career:* Assoc. Prof. of Political Science, al-Najah Nat. Univ. 1986–97, Dean of Scientific Research 1996–97; Senior Fellow, Crown Center for Middle East Studies, Brandeis Univ.; Visiting Prof, Columbia Univ. 1985–86, Univ. of Wis.-Milwaukee 1989–90, Univ. of S Fla 1991–92, Brookings Inst., Washington DC 2002; Dir Palestinian Centre for Policy and Survey Research 2000–. *Publications include:* Elections and the Palestinian Political System (ed) 1995, First Palestinian Elections: Political Context, Electoral Behaviour and Results (ed) 1997, Jordanian-Palestinian Relations (j jtly) 1997, Palestinian Refugee Problem and the Right of Return (jtly) 1998, Palestinian Democracy Index 1996–97 (jtly) 1999, Strengthening Palestinian Public Insts (jtly) 1999, How Palestinians View the Oslo Process 2001, Palestinians Divided 2002, Determinants of Reconciliation and Compromise Among Israelis and Palestinians (jtly) 2002, Self-Serving Perception of Terrorism Among Israelis and Palestinians (jtly) 2002, Israeli-Palestinian Peace Process: Oslo and the Lessons of Failure (jtly) 2002, Building a State, Building a Peace: How to Make a Roadmap That Works for Palestinians and Israelis 2003, Future of Palestine 2004, Public Opinion in the Israeli-Palestinian Two-Level Game (jtly) 2005, Willing to Compromise: Palestinian Public Opinion and the Peace Process 2006, Palestinian Elections: Sweeping Victory, Uncertain Mandate 2006, With Hamas in Power: Impact of Palestinian Domestic Developments on Options for the Peace Process 2007. *Address:* Palestinian Centre for Policy and Survey Research, off Irsal Street, POB 76, Ramallah, Palestinian Autonomous Areas (office). *Telephone:* (2) 2964933 (office). *Fax:* (2) 2964934 (office). *E-mail:* kshikaki@pcpsr.org (office); kshikaki@yahoo.com (home). *Website:* www.pcpsr.org (office).

SHIMALI, Mustafa Jassem ash-; Kuwaiti civil servant and politician; *Minister of Finance; Career:* served in several sr govt posts, including Under-Sec. for Econ. Affairs 1986–2006 and Under-Sec. for Finance 2006–07; Minister of Finance 2007–, Acting Minister of Commerce and Industry 2008–. *Address:* Ministry of Finance, PO Box 9, 13001 Safat, al-Morkab Street, Ministries Complex, Kuwait City, Kuwait (office). *Telephone:* 2480000 (office). *Fax:* 2404025 (office). *E-mail:* webmaster@mof.gov.kw (office). *Website:* www.mof.gov.kw (office).

SHIOJIRI, Kojiro; Japanese diplomatist; *Ambassador to Indonesia;* b. 1949, Kyoto. *Education:* Keio Univ. *Career:* joined Ministry of Foreign Affairs 1972, fmr Chief, Reform Bureau, fmr Deputy Vice-Minister for Man., Budget, Personnel and Parl. Relations; overseas postings include Mission to EC, Brussels, Counsellor, Embassy in Seoul 1997, Deputy Amb. to USA 2003–05, Amb. to Indonesia 2008–. *Address:* Embassy of Japan, Jl. M. H. Thamrin 24, Jakarta Pusat 10350, Indonesia (office). *Telephone:* (21) 31924308 (office). *Fax:* (21) 31925460 (office). *Website:* www.id.emb-japan.go.jp (office).

SHIOKAWA, Masajuro; Japanese politician; b. 1922. *Career:* mem. House of Reps for Osaka 4th Dist; fmr Minister of Transport, of Educ., Chair. Cttee on Commerce and Industry; Minister of Home Affairs 1991–92, of Finance 2001–03 (resgnd); mem. LDP, Sec.-Gen. 1995, fmr Deputy Chair. Gen. Council; fmr Pres., Toyo Univ. *Address:* c/o Office of the President, Toyo University, 28-20 Hakusan 5-chome, Bunkyo-ku, Tokyo 112-8606, Japan (office).

SHIPLEY, Rt Hon. Jennifer Mary (Jenny), PC, FNZIM; New Zealand politician and fmr prime minister and company director; b. (Jennifer Mary Robson), 1952, Gore; m. Burton Shipley 1973; one s. one d. *Career:* fmr primary school teacher; farmer 1973–88; joined Nat. Party 1975; fmr Malvern Co. Councillor; MP for Ashburton (now Rakaia) 1987–; Minister of Social Welfare 1990–93 and of Women's Affairs 1990–98, of Health 1993–96, of State Services 1996–97, also of State Owned Enterprises, of Transport, of Accident Rehabilitation and Compensation Insurance, Minister Responsible for Radio New Zealand; Minister in Charge of NZ Security Intelligence Service 1997–2000; Prime Minister of NZ 1997–99; Leader of the Opposition 1999–2001; Fellow, NZ Inst. of Man.; Distinguished Companion NZ Order of Merit. *Address:* PO Box 6636, Auckland, New Zealand (home). *Telephone:* (9) 358-5360 (office). *E-mail:* jenny@jsnz.com (office). *Website:* www.national.org.nz (office).

SHIRINOV, Abdujabbor; Tajikistan diplomatist; *Ambassador to USA;* b. 20 June 1953, Khatlon region; m.; five c. *Education:* Tajik State Nat. Univ. *Career:* computer software programmer, later Head of Dept for Designing Automatic Control Systems, Data-Processing Centre, Tajik State Univ. 1974–92; Chief Engineer, later Dir Settlement Dept, Nat. Bank of Repub. of Tajikistan 1992–98; First Deputy Chair. Exec. Bd Jt Stock Commerce Agro-Industrial Investment Bank 1998–2000; First Deputy Chair. Nat. Bank of Tajikistan 2000–06; Chair. Cttee for State Financial Control 2006; First Deputy Dir Agency for State Finance Control and Struggle Against Corruption 2006–07; Amb. to USA 2007–. *Address:* Embassy of Tajikistan, 1005 New Hampshire Avenue, NW, Washington, DC 20037, USA (office). *Telephone:* (202) 223-6090 (office). *Fax:* (202) 223-6091 (office). *E-mail:* tajikistan@verizon.net (office). *Website:* www.tjus.org (office).

SHIRLEY, Gordon, MBA, DBA; Jamaican academic and diplomatist; *Principal, University of the West Indies, Mona Campus; Education:* Univ. of the West Indies, Harvard Univ. *Career:* Sr Mechanical Engineer, Alcan Jamaica Ltd 1977–82; Asst Prof. of Operations Man., UCLA 1987–91; Head, Dept of Man. Services, Univ. of the West Indies, Mona Campus 1992–97, Prof. of Man. 1991–2004, Exec. Dir Mona School of Business 1997–2004, Academic Dir MSc Program in Computer-based Man. Information Systems 1994–2004, Pro-Vice-Chancellor and Prin. Mona Campus 2007–; Amb. to USA and Perm. Rep. to OAS 2004–07; several scholarships and awards, including Harvard Univ. Grad. School of Business Admin Doctoral Fellowship. *Address:* The University of the West Indies, Mona, Jamaica (office). *Telephone:* 927-2253 (office). *Fax:* 927-2156 (office). *E-mail:* gordon.shirley@uwimona.edu.jm (office). *Website:* myspot.mona.uwi.edu/principal/meet-the-principal/biography (office).

SHIRREFF, Lt Gen. Richard, CBE; British military officer; *Commander, Allied Rapid Reaction Corps NATO;* b. 1955, Kenya; m. Sarah-Jane Shirreff; one s. one d. *Education:* Oundle School, Exeter Coll., Univ. of Oxford, Royal Mil. Acad. Sandhurst. *Career:* commissioned from Sandhurst to 14th/20th King's Hussars 1978, regimental service in Germany, Canada, NI, the Gulf, Hong Kong, Brunei and UK; attended Army Staff Course, Camberley 1987, Higher Command and Staff Course 1999, Foundation Term, Royal Coll. of Defence Studies 2003; staff posts have included Chief of Staff, HQ 33 Armoured Brigade, Mil. Asst to C-in-C and Commdr Northern Army Group, British Army of the Rhine, Col Army Plans in Ministry of Defence, Prin. Staff Officer to Chief of Defence Staff 2000–02, Chief of Staff HQ LAND Command 2002–05; has commanded on operations in First Gulf War 1991, NI (three tours), Kosovo 1999–2000, Iraq 2006–07; commanded King's Royal Hussars 1994–96, Gen. Officer Commanding 3rd (UK) Div. 2005–07; Commdr, Allied Rapid Reaction Corps (HQ ARRC) 2007–; qualified as mil. parachutist 2005; Hon. Col, Oxford Univ. Officer Training Corps; Queen's Commendation for Valuable Service (Northern Ireland). *Address:* HQ ARRC, Public Affairs Office, Queen's Avenue, JHQ Rheindahlen, 41179 Mönchengladbach, Germany (office); Public Affairs Office, HQ ARRC, BFPO 40, England (office). *Telephone:* (2161) 5655518 (Germany) (office). *Fax:* (2161) 5655520 (Germany) (office). *Website:* www.arrc.nato.int (office).

SHMELYEV, Nikolai Petrovich, DEconSc; Russian economist and author; *Director, Institute of Europe, Russian Academy of Sciences;* b. 18 June 1936, Moscow; m. Gulia Shmelyeva 1965; one d. *Education:* Moscow Univ. *Career:* mem. CPSU 1962–91; researcher, Inst. Econ., USSR Acad. of Sciences 1958–61; Prof., Head of Dept, Inst. of Econ. of World Socialist System (IEMSS), USSR Acad. of Sciences 1961–68, 1970–82; Sr scientific researcher, Inst. of USA and Canada 1982–92; Sr Researcher, Head CIS-Europe Dept, Russian Acad. of Sciences Inst. of Europe 1992–, Dir 2000–; researcher, Slavic Research Centre, Hokkaido Univ., Japan 1995; USSR People's Deputy 1989–91; Corresp. mem. Russian Acad. of Sciences 1994–, mem. 2000–; Lecturer, Stockholm Inst. of East European Countries 1992; Lecturer, Middlebury Coll. Vt, USA 1993. *Publications:* books and articles on econ. problems, World Economic Tendencies, Progress and Contradictions 1987, Advances and Debts 1989, The Turning Point 1990; novels and stories include Pashkov House 1987, Performance for Mr. Prime Minister 1988, Pirosmani 1988, Silvestr 1991, V Puti Ya Zanemog 1995, Bezumnaya Greta 1995, Curriculum Vitae (o sebe) 2001. *Address:* Institute of Europe, Mokhovaya 11/3, 125993 Moscow (office); 3-d Frunzenskaya 7, Apt 61, 119270 Moscow, Russia (home). *Telephone:* (495) 629-45-07 (office); (495) 242-13-06 (home). *Fax:* (495) 200-42-98. *E-mail:* europe@ieras.ru (office). *Website:* www.ieras.ru (office).

SHOBOKSHI, Fawzi bin Abd al-Majeed; Saudi Arabian diplomatist; *Permanent Representative, United Nations;* b. 1938, Jeddah. *Education:* Cairo Univ. Law Coll., Egypt. *Career:* joined Ministry of Foreign Affairs

1961; Consul at Embassy in Vienna, Austria 1963–67, Head of Political Affairs in Sudan 1967–71, Chargé d'affaires in Taiwan 1971–79, Amb. to the Philippines 1979–83, to Japan (also Dean Diplomatic Corps 1994) 1983–97, to Russia 1997–99; Perm. Rep. to UN, New York 1999–; Order of Sikatuna, Rank of Data from Repub. of the Philippines; Hon. PhD (Univ. of Baguio, the Philippines) Brilliant Star of the Repub. of China.
Address: Permanent Mission of Saudi Arabia to the UN, 405 Lexington Avenue, 56th Floor, New York, NY 10017, USA (office). *Telephone:* (212) 697-4830 (office). *Fax:* (212) 983-4895 (office). *E-mail:* saudi-mission@un .int (office). *Website:* www.saudi-un-ny.org (office).

SHOBOKSHI, Osama Abd al-Majid Ali, MD; Saudi Arabian physician, academic and diplomatist; *Ambassador to Germany; Career:* Hosp Dir and Deputy Dean of the Medical Faculty; King Abdul Aziz Univ., also fmr Univ. Pres.; fmr Minister of Health; currently Amb. to Germany; Owner, Leaders insurance co.
Address: Embassy of Saudi Arabia, Kurfürstendamm 63, 10787 Berlin, Germany (office). *Telephone:* (30) 889250 (office). *Fax:* (30) 88925179 (office). *E-mail:* deemb.mofa.gov.sa (office). *Website:* www.saudibotschaft .de (office).

SHOFRY, Abdul Ghafor; Brunei diplomatist. *Career:* fmr Perm. Rep. to UN.
Address: c/o Ministry of Foreign Affairs and Trade, Jalan Subok, Bandar Seri Begawan BD 2710, Brunei (office).

SHOIGU, Col-Gen. Sergei Kuzhugetovich; Russian politician; *Minister of Civil Defence, Emergencies and Clean-up Operations;* b. 21 May 1955, Chadan, Tuva ASSR (now Republic of Tyva), Russian Fed.; m.; two d. *Education:* Krasnoyarsk Polytech. Inst. *Career:* engineer, Sr master construction trust in Krasnoyarsk 1977–78; man. construction trusts Achinskamulinstroi, Cayantyazhstroi, Abakanvagonstroi 1979–88; Second Sec. Abakan City CP Cttee, insp. CP Cttee KrasnoyarskKrai 1989–90; Deputy Chair. State Cttee on Architecture and Construction RSFSR 1990–91; Chair. State Cttee of Russian Fed. on Civil Defence, Emergencies and Natural Disasters 1991–94; Minister of Civil Defence, Emergencies and Clean-up Operations 1994–; Deputy Prime Minister Jan.–May 2000; mem. Security Council of Russia; Co-fournder and leader pre-election bloc (then party) Yedinstvo (Unity) 1999–; mem. State Duma 1999; Co-Chair. of Unity and Fatherland-United Russia (later United Russia), 2001–; Hero of Russian Fed. 1999.
Address: Ministry of Civil Defence, Emergencies and Clean-up Operations, 109012 Moscow, Teatralnyi proezd 3, Russia (office). *Telephone:* (495) 926-39-01 (office); (495) 923-57-45 (office). *E-mail:* info@mchs.gov.ru (office). *Website:* www.mchs.gov.ru (office).

SHOMAN, Assad, LLB, MA; Belizean politician, diplomatist, lawyer and writer; b. 13 Feb. 1943; four c. *Education:* Univ. of Hull and Univ. of Sussex, UK. *Career:* called to the Bar, Gray's Inn, London 1968; fmr Senator; Attorney-Gen. 1974–78; Minister of Health and Housing 1979–84; rep. of Belize in Guatemalan negotiations; fmr Head of Independence Secr.; fmr Amb. to Mexico; fmr High Commr of Belize to UK; apptd Minister of Foreign Affairs and Cooperation 2002; fmr Amb. to Cuba; fmr Minister of Nat. Devt; currently Amb. with Ministerial Rank and Chief Negotiator of Govt of Belize; Co-Founder and Leader, Soc. for the Promotion of Educ. and Research (SPEAR) 1969–, Exec. Dir 1987–92; Order of Belize. *Publications include:* Land in Belize (with Nigel Bolland) 1977, Party Politics in Belize 1987, Thirteen Chapters of a History of Belize 1994, Backtalking Belize 1995.
E-mail: assads13@yahoo.com (office).

SHOMAN, Lisa M., LLM; Belizean diplomatist and lawyer; b. 1964. *Education:* Univ. of the West Indies, Norman Manley Law School. *Career:* admitted to Bar, Belize 1988; Crown Counsel, Office of Dir of Public Prosecutions 1988–89; Assoc., Musa & Balderamos law firm 1989–90; Assoc. Young's Law Firm 1992–98; Founder and Pnr, Shoman & Chebat law firm; fmr Chair. Belize Telecommunications Ltd 2000; Amb. to USA, Perm. Rep. to OAS and High Commr to Canada 2002–07; Minister of Foreign Affairs and Foreign Trade 2007–08; mem. Bar Asscn of Belize, Exec. Cttee mem. 1993–95, Pres. 1996–97, mem. Gen. Legal Council and Disciplinary Cttee 1994–97, 1999–2000.
Address: Shoman and Chebat, 53 Barrack Road, Belize City, Belize. *Telephone:* 223-4160 (office). *Fax:* 223-4222 (office). *E-mail:* attorney@btl .net (office). *Website:* www.shomanchebat.com (office).

SHORROCKS, Anthony (Tony), BSc, MA, PhD; British research institute director; *Director, World Institute for Development Economics Research (WIDER), United Nations University; Education:* Univ. of Sussex, Brown Univ., USA, London School of Econs. *Career:* Lecturer and Reader in Econs, LSE 1972–83; Asst Prof. and Commonwealth Research Fellow, Queen's Univ., Kingston, Canada 1977, 1981; Prof. of Econs, Univ. of

Essex 1983–97, Chair. Econs Dept 1986–88, now Research Prof.; Dir of Econ. Research, British Household Panel Study 1990–93; Dir World Inst. for Devt Econs Research (WIDER), UN Univ. 2001–; Visitor, Univ. of Wisconsin 1978, Stanford Univ. 1978; Visiting Fellow, ANU 1985, 1989, Purdue Univ. 1985; Dedman Distinguished Visiting Scholar, Southern Methodist Univ. 1991–93; Sr Research Fellow, Econ. and Social Research Council 1994–95; Visiting Prof., European Univ. Inst., Florence, Italy 1998, New Econ. School, Moscow 1999, 2000; Research Fellow, Inst. for Fiscal Studies, UK 1998–; Consultant to London Weekend TV 1986, World Bank 1990, 1996–97, Russian–European Centre for Econ. Policy, Moscow 1998–2000; mem. Editorial Bd Review of Economic Studies 1977–88, Chair. Review of Economic Studies Ltd 1986–88; Fellow, Econometric Soc. 1996–; Bowley Prize for PhD Thesis 1975.
Address: World Institute for Development Economics Research of the United Nations University, Katajanokanlaituri 6 B, 00160 Helsinki, Finland (office). *Telephone:* (9) 615-9911 (office). *Fax:* (9) 615-99333 (office). *E-mail:* wider@wider.unu.edu (office). *Website:* www.wider .unu.edu (office).

SHPEK, Roman Vasilyevich; Ukrainian economist and diplomatist; *Ambassador and Head of Mission to European Union;* b. 10 Nov. 1954, Broshniv, Ivano-Frankivsk Region; m. Maria Romanivna Shpek; one s. one d. *Education:* Forestry Eng Inst., Lviv, Int. Inst. of Wood Man., Kiev, Dalover Univ. *Career:* processing engineer and head of woodworking manufacturing plant, Ivano-Frankivsk Region 1976–78, Chief Engineer, wood and woodworking plant 1978–81, Dir 1981–89; Deputy Minister of Forestry, Woodworking and Furniture Industry, Ukrainian SSR 1989–92; Minister of Privatization, Ukraine April–Oct. 1992; First Deputy Minister of the Economy of Ukraine 1992–93, Minister 1993–95, Deputy Prime Minister on Econ. Policy 1995–96; Head Nat. Agency for Devt and European Integration 1996–2000; Co-Chair. Ukrainian-German Council on Econ. Co-operation, Ukrainian-Italian Council on Econ. Co-operation, Comm Kuchma-Gor on Econ. Devt Cttee; Acting Gov., then Gov. for Ukraine, World Bank Group; Chair. Currency and Finance Council to Cabinet of Ministers of Ukraine; Nat. Co-ordinator of Tech. Assistance Programme for Ukraine 1993–2000; Ukrainian Rep. to UNDP 1996–; Amb. and Head of Mission of Ukraine to EU 2000–; Order for Merits, 3rd Degree (Ukraine).
Address: 99–101 Avenue Louis Lepoutre, 1050 Brussels (office); 29 Avenue de Saturne, 1180 Brussels, Belgium (home). *Telephone:* (2) 340-98-70 (office); (2) 379-09-87 (home). *Fax:* (2) 340-98-79 (office). *E-mail:* roman .shpek@gmail.com (home). *Website:* www.ukraine-eu.mfa.gov.ua (office).

SHRESTHA, Kedar Bhakta, MA; Nepalese diplomatist; m. Shanta Shrestha; three c. *Education:* Tri-Chandra Coll., Univ. of Bombay. *Career:* joined Ministry of Foreign Affairs 1964, Second Sec., Embassy in Bonn 1965–69, First Sec., Perm. Mission to UN, New York 1973–77, Under-sec. and Deputy Chief of Protocol 1977–80, Counsellor and Deputy Chief of Mission, Embassy in Washington, DC 1980–84; Jt Sec., Far East and SE Asia, Ministry of Foreign Affairs 1984–87, Dir S Asian Asscn for Regional Co-operation Secr., Kathmandu 1987–92, Jt Sec., Ministry of Foreign Affairs 1992–94; Foreign Sec. 1994–97; Amb. to EU and Benelux countries 1997–2002, to USA 2004, also accred to Canada 2005.
Address: c/o Ministry of Foreign Affairs, Shital Niwas, Maharajganj, Kathmandu, Nepal.

SHTAUBER, Zvi Meir, PhD; Israeli diplomatist, academic and fmr military officer; *Director, Institute for National Security Studies, Tel-Aviv University;* b. 15 July 1947; m. Nitza Rousso; two s. one d. *Education:* Harvard Business School, Fletcher School of Law and Diplomacy, Tufts Univ., USA. *Career:* with Israel Defence Forces 1970–95, Head of Strategic Planning Div. 1995, retd with rank of Brig.-Gen. 1995; Vice-Pres. Ben-Gurion Univ. of the Negev 1996–99; Foreign Policy Adviser to Prime Minister Ehud Barak (q.v.) 1999–2000; Amb. to UK 2001–04; Head, Jaffee Center for Strategic Studies, Tel-Aviv Univ. 2005, now Dir Inst. for Nat. Security Studies (incorporated Jaffee Center).
Address: Institute for National Security Studies, 40 Haim Levanon Street, Tel-Aviv 61398, Israel (office). *Telephone:* 3-6400401 (office). *E-mail:* zvis@ inss.org.il (office). *Website:* www.inss.org.il (office).

SHUKLA, Prabhat Prakash; Indian diplomatist; *Ambassador to Russia;* b. 29 March 1951; m. Amita Shukla; one d. *Career:* joined Foreign Service 1974, overseas postings include Third Sec., Embassy in Sofia 1976–77, Second Sec., Embassy in Moscow 1977–80, First Sec., Embassy in Brussels 1982–84, First Sec., Embassy in Kathmandu 1984–85, First Sec./ Counsellor, Embassy in Moscow 1985–89, Counsellor, High Comm. in London 1989–92, Counsellor, Embassy in Kiev 1992–1994; Under-Sec. (East Europe, Afghanistan), Ministry of External Affairs 1980–82, Jt Sec., Cen. Asia Div. 1994–96; Jt Sec., Office of Prime Minister 1996–2000; High

Commr to Singapore 2000–04, to Australia 2004–07; Amb. to Russia 2007–.

Address: Embassy of India, 6–8 Ulitsa Vorontsovo Polye, Moscow, Russia (office). *Telephone:* (495) 783-7535 (office). *Fax:* (495) 916-3632 (office). *Website:* www.indianembassy.ru (office).

SHULTZ, George Pratt, BA, PhD; American fmr government official, economist and academic; *Thomas W. and Susan B. Ford Distinguished Fellow, Hoover Institution, Stanford University;* b. 13 Dec. 1920, New York; m. 1st Helena M. O'Brien 1946; two s. three d.; m. 2nd Charlotte Mailliard Swig 1997. *Education:* Princeton Univ. and MIT. *Career:* Assoc. Prof. of Industrial Relations, MIT 1955–57; Sr Staff Economist, Pres.'s Council of Econ. Advisers 1955–56; Prof. of Industrial Relations, Grad. School of Business, Univ. of Chicago 1957–68, Dean, Grad. School of Business 1962–68; Pres. Industrial Research Asscn 1968; US Sec. of Labor 1969–70; Dir Office of Man. and Budget, Exec. Office of the Pres. 1970–72; US Sec. of Treasury 1972–74; Chair. Council on Econ. Policy 1973–74; Sec. of State 1982–89; Exec. Vice-Pres. Bechtel Corpn 1974–75, Pres. 1975–77, Vice-Chair. 1977–81, Pres. Bechtel Group Inc. 1981–82; Prof. of Man. and Public Policy, Grad. School of Business, Stanford Univ. 1974–82, of Int. Economy 1989–91, Prof. Emer. 1991–; Chair. JP Morgan Chase Int. Council, Accenture Energy Advisory Bd 2003–07, Advisory Council Inst. of Int. Studies, Stanford, Govs'. Econ. Policy Advisory Bd, Calif., Gov.'s Council of Econ. Advisors 2004–; mem. Bd Bechtel Group Inc. 1989–2007, Accretive Health; Chair. Pres. Reagan's Econ. Policy Advisory Bd 1981–82; Chair. Advisory Bd Precourt Inst. for Energy Efficiency; Chair. External Advisory Bd MIT Energy Initiative; mem. Bd of Trustees, Center for Advancement of Study in the Behavioral Sciences, Stanford, Calif.; Distinguished Fellow, Hoover Inst., Stanford Univ. 1989–; Thomas W. and Susan B. Ford Distinguished Fellow, Hoover Inst. 2001–, Distinguished Fellow American Econ. Asscn 2005; Jefferson Award 1989, Presidential Medal of Freedom 1989, Grand Cordon, Order of the Rising Sun 1989, Seoul Peace Prize 1992, Eisenhower Medal 2001, Reagan Distinguished American Award 2002, Ralph J. Bunche Award for Diplomatic Excellence 2002, Nat. World War II Museum American Spirit Award 2006. *Publications include:* Pressures on Wage Decisions, Labor Problems,The Dynamics of a Labor Market, Management Organization and the Computer, Strategies for the Displaced Worker, Guidelines, Informal Controls and the Market Place, Workers and Wages in the Urban Labor Market, Leaders and Followers in an Age of Ambiguity, Economic Policy beyond the Headlines (jtly), Turmoil and Triumph: My Years as Secretary of State 1993.

Address: Hoover Institution, Stanford, CA 94305-6010, USA (office). *Telephone:* (650) 725-3492 (office). *Fax:* (650) 723-5441 (office). *Website:* www-hoover.stanford.edu (office).

SHUVALOV, Igor Ivanovich; Russian politician and lawyer; *First Deputy Chairman;* b. 4 Jan. 1967, Bilibino, Magadan Region, Russia; m.; one s. two d. *Education:* Moscow State Univ. *Career:* Research Inst. EKOS, Moscow 1984–85; army service 1985–87; attaché Ministry of Foreign Affairs, Russian Fed. 1993; Sr legal adviser Stock co. (ALM) Consulting Moscow 1993–95; Dir Advocates' Bureau (ALM) 1995–97; Head Dept of State Cttee on Man. of State Property Russian Fed. 1997–98; Deputy Minister of State Property 1998; Chair. Russian Foundation of Fed. Property 1998–2000; Head of Govt Admin and Minister Without Portfolio 2000–2002, Deputy Head of Presidential Admin 2003–08; First Deputy Chair., in charge of external econ. relations and foreign trade, WTO negotiations and small business 2008–.

Address: Office of the Government, 103274 Moscow, Krasnopresnenskaya nab. 2, Russia (office). *Telephone:* (495) 205-57-35 (office). *Fax:* (495) 205-42-19 (office). *Website:* www.government.ru (office).

SHVYDKOI, Mikhail Yefimovich, PhD, DFA; Russian theatre scholar and politician; *Head, Federal Agency of Culture and Cinematography;* b. 5 Sept. 1948, Kyrgyzia; m. Marina Shvydkaya; two s. *Education:* Moscow Lunacharsky Inst. of Theatre Art. *Career:* reviewer, Radio Co., Deputy Ed.-in-Chief Theatr magazine 1973–90; Ed.-in-Chief Publrs Co. Kultura, Russian Fed. Ministry of Culture 1990–93; Deputy Minister of Culture 1993–97; Prof. of Foreign Theatre, Acad. of Humanitarian Sciences; commentator on cultural problems on Russian TV; Deputy Chair. Russian TV and Radio Co., Ed.-in-Chief Cultura TV Channel 1997–98; Chair. All-Russian State Radio and TV Holding 1998–2000; Minister of Culture 2000–04; Head, Fed. Agency of Culture and Cinematography 2004–; Chair. Nat. Comm. World Decade of Culture at UNESCO, mem. Bd of Dirs Pervyi Kanal 2004–; Govt Award of the Russian Fed. for Literature and Art 1999; numerous awards, prizes and decorations from France, Poland, Ukraine, Kazakhstan and Russian Fed. *Television:* broadcaster on Cultural Revolution (Cultura TV channel) 2002–, Life is Wonderful (STS TV channel) 2004–. *Publications:* Dramatic Composition: Theatre and Life, Secrets of Lonely Comedians, Sketches on Foreign Theatre of the Late 20th Century; numerous articles on history and contemporary state of theatre in Russian and foreign periodicals.

Address: c/o 7/6 Maliy Gnezdnikovskiy per., Moscow 125009, Russia (office). *Telephone:* (495) 629-23-11 (office). *Fax:* (495) 629-22-48 (office). *Website:* www.rosculture.ru/en (office).

SIAZON, Domingo L., Jr, BA, BSc, MPA; Philippine diplomatist and international civil servant; *Ambassador to Japan;* b. 1939, Aparri, Cagayan; m. *Education:* Ateneo de Manila Univ., Tokyo Univ., Japan, Harvard Univ., USA. *Career:* interpreter and trans., then Attaché and Third Sec. and Vice-Consul, Embassy in Tokyo 1964–68; Acting Resident Rep. to IAEA, Alt. Perm. Rep. to UNIDO, Third, Second, then First Sec., Embassy in Berne 1968–73; First Sec. and Consul-Gen., Embassy in Vienna, then Amb. to Austria, also Perm. Rep. to IAEA, UNIDO and UN at Vienna 1973–85; Dir-Gen. UNIDO 1985–93; Minister of Foreign Affairs 1995–2000; Amb. to Japan 2002–.

Address: Embassy of The Philippines, 5-15-5, Roppongi, Minato-ku, Tokyo 106-8537, Japan (office). *Telephone:* (3) 5562-1600 (office). *Fax:* (3) 5562-1603 (home). *E-mail:* info@tokyope.org (office). *Website:* www.tokyope.org (office).

SIBAL, Kanwal, MA, LLB; Indian diplomatist; b. 18 Nov. 1943, Baddomalhi (now Pakistan); m. Elizabeth; one s. one d. *Career:* Third Sec., then Second Sec., Paris 1968–73; Under-Sec. Ministry of Foreign Affairs 1973–75, Jt Sec. 1986–89; Deputy High Commr, Dar-es-Salaam 1976–79, Counsellor, Lisbon 1980–82, Deputy Chief of Mission, Kathmandu 1982–85, Amb. to Turkey 1989–92, Deputy Chief of Mission, Washington DC 1992–95, Amb. to Egypt 1995–98, to France 1998–2002, Foreign Sec. 2002–04, Amb. to Russian Fed. 2004–07.

Address: c/o Ministry of External Affairs, South Block, Room 144c, New Delhi 110 011, India (office). *Website:* meaindia.nic.in (office).

SIBANDA-THUSI, Nomasonto Mary; South African diplomatist; *Ambassador to France; Career:* Amb. to France 2004–, Perm. Del. to UNESCO, Paris 2004–.

Address: Embassy of South Africa, 59 quai d'Orsay, 75343 Paris Cedex 07, France (office). *Telephone:* 1-53-59-23-23 (office). *Fax:* 1-53-59-23-68 (office). *E-mail:* info@afriquesud.net (office). *Website:* www.afriquesud.net (office).

SIBLESZ, Hugo Hans; Dutch diplomatist; *Ambassador to France;* b. 29 March 1948, The Hague; m. Paula N. Deurloo. *Education:* Univ. of Amsterdam. *Career:* joined Foreign Service 1973, held numerous positions 1973–90; Counsellor for Political Affairs, Embassy in Paris 1990–94; Counsellor for Political Affairs, Office of the Perm. Rep. to NATO, Brussels 1994; Dir of Gen. Affairs, Ministry of Foreign Affairs 1994–96, Dir Consular Affairs 1996–98, Deputy Dir Gen. for Political Affairs 1998–2001, Dir Gen for Political Affairs 2001–06; Amb. to France, Andorra and Monaco 2006–.

Address: Embassy of the Netherlands, 7–9 rue Eblé, 75007 Paris, France (office). *Telephone:* 1-40-62-33-00 (office). *Fax:* 1-40-62-34-56 (office). *E-mail:* ambassade@amb-pays-bas.fr (office). *Website:* www.amb-pays-bas.fr (office).

SICHERMAN, Harvey, BS, PhD; American research institute director; *President and Director, Foreign Policy Research Institute; Education:* Univ. of Scranton, Univ. of Penn. *Career:* Special Asst to US Sec. of State Alexander M. Haig, Jr 1981–82; mem. Policy Planning Staff, US Sec. of State James A. Baker III; consultant to Sec. of Navy John F. Lehman, Jr 1982–87, to Sec. of State George Schultz 1988; Assoc. Dir for Research, Foreign Policy Research Institute, Philadelphia 1978–80, currently Pres. and Dir; Salvatori Fellowship. *Publications:* The Three Percent Solution and the Future of NATO 1982, Palestinian Autonomy, Self-Government and Peace 1993, New Directions in US-Chinese Relations (co-author) 1997, The Chinese Economy: A New Scenario (co-Ed.) 1999, America the Vulnerable: Our Military Problems and How to Fix Them (co-Ed.) 2002; several articles.

Address: Foreign Policy Research Institute, 1528 Walnut Street, Suite 610, Philadelphia, PA 19102, USA (office). *Telephone:* (215) 732-3774, ext. 110 (home). *Fax:* (215) 732-4401 (office). *E-mail:* frpi@frpi.org (office). *Website:* www.fpri.org (office).

SIDDIG, Omar Muhammad Ahmad; Sudanese diplomatist; *Ambassador to UK;* m. Om El Hassan Mubarak El Fadil. *Career:* Deputy Head of Mission to UN, Geneva 1999–2003, one of architects of Comprehensive Peace Agreement which ended the 20-year civil war between the state and the Sudanese People's Liberation Army of Southern Sudan in 2003, apptd Dir Dept for Peace and Humanitarian Affairs 2003, Amb. to Germany –2006, to UK (also accred to Ireland) 2006–.

Address: Embassy of Sudan, 3 Cleveland Row, St James's, London, SW1A 1DD, England (office). *Telephone:* (20) 7839-8080 (office). *Fax:* (20) 7839-7560 (office). *E-mail:* admin@sudanembassy.co.uk (office).

SIDI, Baba Ould; Mauritanian politician; b. 1946, Méderdra. *Career:* fmr Man. Soc. Mauritanienne de Commercialization de Produits Petroliers; fmr Dir Banque Int. pour la Mauritanie; Minister for Fisheries and Maritime Economy 1996, for Public Works, Employment, Youth and Sports 2000–02, for Nat. Defence 2003–07; mem. Al Jamiya al-Wataniyah (Nat. Ass.). for Méderdra.
Address: c/o Ministry of National Defence, BP 184, Nouakchott, Mauritania.

SIDIBÉ, Modibo, LLM; Malian politician; *Prime Minister;* b. 4 Nov. 1952, Bamako; m.; five c. *Education:* Univ. of Reims, Univ. of Aix-en-Provence, France. *Career:* fmr police commr; Chef de Cabinet for Minister Del. of Nat. Defence 1989–91; Cabinet Dir for Minister Del. of Internal Security 1991; Cabinet Dir for Pres. of Transitional Cttee for Health 1991–92; Minister of Health, Solidarity and the Elderly 1992–97, of Foreign Affairs and Malians Abroad 1997–2002; Sec.-Gen., Office of the Pres. 2002–07; Prime Minister 2007–; Pres. Foreign Affairs Council, ECOWAS (Econ. Community of West African States) 1999–2001, Pres. Mediation and Peace Council 1999–2001; Commandeur, Ordre National du Mali, Commandeur, Légion d'Honneur.
Address: Office of the Prime Minister, Quartier du Fleuve, BP 790, Bamako, Mali (office). *Telephone:* 223-06-80 (office). *Fax:* 222-85-83 (office).

ŠIDLAUSKAS, Rimantas; Lithuanian diplomatist; *Ambassador to Russia;* b. 14 June 1962, Bebriku, Kėdainiai District; m.; two s. *Education:* Vilnius Univ., Int. Public Admin Inst. *Career:* interpreter, Sigma (state enterprise) 1986–89; joined Ministry of Foreign Affairs 1989; First Sec. Press and Information Div., Deputy Head, then Head, Passport and Visa Div., Head Consular Treaties Div. 1989–92, Deputy Dir Consular Dept 1992–94, Deputy Minister of Foreign Affairs 1994, State Sec. 1994–97, Dir Consular Dept 1997; Head, Borders Comm. 1994–1999; Amb. to Canada 2000–02, to Russian Fed. 2002–.
Address: Embassy of Lithuania, 121069 Moscow, Borisoglebskii per. 10, Russian Federation (office). *Telephone:* (495) 785-86-05 (office). *Fax:* (495) 785-86-00 (office). *Website:* ru.mfa.lt (office).

SIDORSKY, Syarhey Syarheyovich, DEngSci; Belarusian politician; *Prime Minister;* b. 13 March 1954, Gomel; m.; two d. *Education:* Belarus Inst. of Railway Transport Engineers. *Career:* worked as electrical fitter and electrician; foreman of assembly shop, head of lab., head of dept, Deputy Dir Gomel Radio Equipment Plant 1976–91, Dir 1991–92; Gen. Man. Gomel Scientific Production Asscn RATON 1992–98; Deputy Chair. and First Deputy Chair. Gomel Oblast Admin 1998–2001; Deputy Prime Minister of Belarus 2001–02, First Deputy Prime Minister 2002–03, Acting Prime Minister July–Dec. 2003, Prime Minister Dec. 2003–; Academician, Int. Eng Acad.; Honoured Workman of Industry (Belarus). *Publications* include: more than 40 scientific publs and monographs.
Address: Office of the Prime Minister, 220010 Minsk, vul. Savetskaya 11, Belarus (office). *Telephone:* (17) 222-41-73 (office). *Fax:* (17) 222-66-65 (office). *E-mail:* timoshenko@government.by (office). *Website:* www .government.by (office).

SIEBERT, Horst, PhD; German economist; *President Emeritus, Kiel Institute of World Economics;* b. 20 March 1938, Neuwied; m. Christa Causemann 1965. *Education:* Univ. of Cologne, Wesleyan Univ., Conn., Univ. of Münster. *Career:* Asst Prof. of Econs Texas A&M Univ.; Prof. of Econs and Chair. of Econs and Int. Trade, Univ. of Mannheim 1969–84; Prof. of Econs and Chair. of Int. Econs, Univ. of Konstanz 1984–89; Chair of Theoretical Econs and Pres. Inst. of World Econs, Kiel Univ. 1989–2003, now Pres. Emer.; Prof. of Int. Econs, Johns Hopkins Univ., Bologna, Italy; mem. Council of Govt Econ. Advisers 1990–2003, Group of Econ. Analysis of EU 2001–04, Group of Econ. Policy Analysis of EU 2005–; Bundesverdienstkreuz; Dr hc (Ghent) 2000; Karl Bräuer Prize 1999, Ludwig Erhard Prize for Wirtschaftspublizistik 1999. *Publications:* Aussenwirtschaft 2000, Der Kobra-Effekt. Wie man Irrwege der Wirtschaftspolitik vermeidet 2001, The World Economy 2002, Economics of the Environment: Theory and Policy 2005, The German Economy: Beyond the Social Market 2005, Jenseits des sozialen Marktes 2005.
Address: Institute of World Economics, Kiel University, Düsternbrooker Weg 120, 24105 Kiel, Germany (office); Johns Hopkins University School of Advanced International Studies Bologna Center, Via Belmeloro 11, 40126 Bologna, Italy (office). *Telephone:* (431) 8814567 (Kiel) (office); (51) 2917821 (Bologna) (office). *Fax:* (431) 8814501 (Kiel) (office). *E-mail:* hsiebert@ifw.uni-kiel.de (office). *Website:* www.uni-kiel.de/ifw/staff/siebert.htm (office); www.jhubc.it (office).

SIEGEL, Ned L., JD; American lawyer, business executive and diplomatist; *Ambassador to the Bahamas;* m. Stephanie Moak Siegel; two s. one d. *Education:* Univ. of Connecticut, Dickinson School of Law. *Career:* served as law clerk to Chief Justice Mitchell H. Cohen in Fed. Dist Court, Camden, NJ; joined Kimmelman, Wolff & Samson law firm, NJ; joined Howard Siegel Companies 1977, Pres. and Man. Pnr, Weingarten-Siegel Group, Inc. 1980; currently Pnr, Paramount Residential, LLC; fmr Chair. The Siegel Group; apptd by Gov. Jeb Bush to Enterprise Fla's Bd of Dirs and to Space Research and Commerce Park Planning and Devt Cttee, John F. Kennedy Space Center; fmr Trustee Gov.'s Mansion Foundation, Greater Boca Raton Chamber of Commerce; apptd by Pres. George W. Bush to Bd of Dirs Overseas Pvt. Investment Corpn 2003; US Rep. to UN 2006; Amb. to the Bahamas 2007–; fmr Chair. Republican Jewish Coalition of Fla; fmr mem. Nat. Bd of Dirs Republican Jewish Coalition, Washington, DC, Bd American Jewish Cttee, S Cen. Fla Chapter; fmr Co-Pres. Bd Jewish Nat. Fund's S Palm Beach Co. Region; active in Israeli Bonds program, Temple B'nai Torah, Boca Raton, Chabad Lubavitch of Greater Boynton (served as Exec. Chair. Exec. Cttee).
Address: US Embassy, Mosmar Building, Queen Street, PO Box N-8197, Nassau, The Bahamas (office). *Telephone:* 322-1181 (office). *Fax:* 328-7838 (office). *E-mail:* embnas@state.gov (office). *Website:* nassau.usembassy .gov (office).

SIEGMAN, Henry, BA; American writer and foreign affairs analyst; *Senior Fellow and Director, US/Middle East Project, Council on Foreign Relations;* *Education:* New School for Social Research. *Career:* Dir American Asscn for Middle East Studies, also Ed. Middle East Studies (journal) 1958–63; f. Int. Jewish Cttee for Interreligious Consultations 1968; Exec. Dir American Jewish Congress 1978–94; Resident Scholar, Rockefeller Study Center, Bellagio, Italy 1992; Sr Fellow and Dir, US/Middle East Project, Council on Foreign Relations. *Publications include:* US Middle East Policy and the Peace Process 1997, Strengthening Palestinian Public Institutions 1999; contrib. essays to Wrestling with Zion, Progressive Jewish-American Responses to the Israeli-Palestinian Conflict, ed by Tony Kushner and Alisa Solomon; over 100 articles and essays on the Middle East in the New York Times, the Washington Post, Commentary Magazine, International Herald Tribune, the Nation, the Middle East Journal, Islamic World, Journal of Ecumenical Studies, Jerusalem Post, Al-Ahram, Al-Hayat, and Ashraq al-Awsat.
Address: Council on Foreign Relations, Harold Pratt House, 58 East 68th Street, New York, NY 10021, USA (office). *Telephone:* (212) 434-9658 (office). *Fax:* (212) 434-9800 (office). *E-mail:* hsiegman@crf.org. *Website:* www.cfr.org.

SIEW, Vincent C., LLM; Taiwanese diplomatist, fmr government official and research institute administrator; *Vice President;* b. 3 Jan. 1939, Chiayi City, Taiwan; m.; three d. *Education:* Nat. Chengchi Univ., Georgetown Univ. *Career:* Vice-Consul, Kuala Lumpur, Malaysia 1966–69, Consul 1969–72; Section Chief, Asia Pacific Affairs Dept, Ministry of Foreign Affairs 1972; Deputy Dir 4th Dept Bd of Foreign Trade, Ministry of Econ. Affairs 1972–74, Dir 1974–77, Deputy Dir-Gen. Bd of Foreign Trade 1977–82, Dir-Gen. 1982–88; Vice-Chair. Council for Econ. Planning and Devt, Exec. Yuan 1988–89; Dir-Gen. Dept of Organizational Affairs, Kuomintang Cen. Cttee 1989–90, Vice-Chair. Kuomintang 2000–05; Minister of Econ. Affairs 1990–93; Minister of State, Chair. Council for Econ. Planning and Devt, Exec. Yuan 1993–94; Minister of State, Chair. Mainland Affairs Council, Exec. Yuan 1994–95; legislator 1996–97; Premier of Taiwan 1997–2000; Vice Pres. of Taiwan 2008–; Eisenhower Fellow, USA 1985; Chair. Chung-Hua Inst. for Econ. Research, Convenor Presidential Econ. Advisory Panel 2003–04; fmr Chair. Cross-Straits Common Market Foundation; Prof. Nat. Chengchi Univ.; Hon. D.Man (Nat. Chia-Yi Univ.), Hon. DEcon (Sung Kyun Kwan Univ., Seoul), Hon. PhD (Rangsit Univ., Thailand), Hon. Dr Public Service (Ohio State Univ., USA). *Publications:* One Plus One is Greater than Two: The Road to the Cross-Straits Common Market, To Govern the Nation with Expertise.
Address: Office of the President, 122 Chungking South Road, Sec. 1, Taipei 10048, Taiwan (office). *Telephone:* (2) 23113731 (office). *Fax:* (2) 23311604 (office). *E-mail:* public@mail.oop.gov.tw (office). *Website:* www.president .gov.tw (office).

SIGAL, Leon V., BA, PhD; American academic and author; *Director of Northeast Asia Cooperative Security Project, Social Science Research Council;* b. 20 Aug. 1942, New Haven, Conn.; m. Meg Fidler 1983; one s. *Education:* Yale Univ., Harvard Univ. *Career:* Rockefeller Younger Scholar in Foreign Policy Studies, Brookings Inst. 1972–74, Guest Scholar 1981–84; Prof. of Govt, Wesleyan Univ. 1974–89; Adjunct Prof., Columbia Univ. School of Int. and Public Affairs 1985–89, 1996–2000; Visiting Lecturer, Woodrow Wilson School, Princeton Univ. 1988, 2000; Int. Affairs Fellow, Bureau of Politico-Mil. Affairs, Dept of State 1979, Special Asst to the Dir 1980; currently Dir Northeast Asia Cooperative Security

Project, Social Science Research Council; mem. Editorial Bd New York Times 1989–95. *Publications:* Reporters and Officials: The Organization and Politics of Newsmaking 1973, Fighting to a Finish: The Politics of War Termination in the United States and Japan 1945 1988, Disarming Strangers: Nuclear Diplomacy with North Korea (1998 Book of Distinction, American Acad. of Diplomacy) 1998, Hang Separately: Cooperative Security Between the United States and Russia 1985–1994 2000.
Address: Northeast Asia Cooperative Security Project, Social Science Research Council, 810 Seventh Avenue, New York, NY 10019, USA (office). *Telephone:* (212) 377-2700 (ext 456) (office). *Fax:* (212) 377-2727 (office). *E-mail:* sigal@ssrc.org (office). *Website:* www.ssrc.org (office).

SIKHARULIDZE, Vasil; Georgian physician, psychiatrist and diplomatist; *Ambassador to USA;* b. 30 May 1968, Tbilisi; m. Anna Tsagareli; one d. *Education:* Tbilisi State Medical Univ. *Career:* physician and psychiatrist, Inst. of Psychiatry 1993–95; Exec. Dir Atlantic Council of Georgia 1995–96; worked in Georgian Parl. as specialist on Cttee of Defense and Security 1996–2000; Head of NATO Div., Ministry of Foreign Affairs and Deputy Head of Georgian Mission to NATO, Brussels 2000–02; NATO Fellow 2001–03; Under-sec. Nat. Security Council of Georgia March–July 2004; Deputy Minister of Defence 2004–05, First Deputy Minister of Defence, responsible for Policy and Planning, Int. Relations and Legal Affairs 2005–06; Amb. to USA (also accred to Canada and Mexico) 2006–.
Address: Embassy of Georgia, 2209 Massachusetts Avenue, Washington, DC 20008, USA (office). *Telephone:* (202) 387-2390 (office). *Fax:* (202) 387-0864 (office). *E-mail:* embgeorgiausa@yahoo.com (office); consulate@georgiaemb.org (office). *Website:* embassy.mfa.gov.ge (office).

SIKKINK, Kathryn, PhD; American academic; *Professor of Political Science, University of Minnesota; Education:* Univ. of Minn., Columbia Univ. *Career:* Staff Assoc., Washington Office on Latin America, DC 1979–81; Research Asst, UN Centre on Trans nat. Corpns (UNCTC), New York June–Dec. 1982; Teaching Asst, Columbia Univ. 1983–84; Visiting Researcher, Centro de Estudios de Estado y Sociedad (CEDES) Buenos Aires, Argentina Jan.–Nov. 1985, Instituto Universitário de Pesquisa do Rio de Janeiro, Brazil 1985–86; Visiting Fellow, Center for Int. and Area Studies, Yale Univ. 1986–88; Asst Prof. of Political Science, Univ. of Minn. 1988–94, 1994–98, Prof. of Political Science 1998–, McKnight Prof., Scholar of the Coll., Arleen C. Carlson Chair in Political Science; mem. Editorial Bd Journal Int. Org.; Grawemeyer Award for Ideas Improving World Order 1999, Int. Studies Asscn Chadwick Alger Award for Best Work in the Area of Int. Org. 1999. *Publications include:* Ideas and Institutions: Developmentalism in Brazil and Argentina 1991, Activists Beyond Borders: Advocacy Networks in International Politics (co-author) 1998, The Power of Human Rights: International Norms and Domestic Change (co-ed.) 1999; numerous articles and book chapters.
Address: Political Science Department, 1414 Social Sciences, University of Minnesota, Minneapolis, MN 55455, USA (office). *Telephone:* (612) 624-7513 (office). *E-mail:* ksikkink@polisci.umn.edu (office). *Website:* www.polisci.umn.edu (office).

SIKORSKI, Radosław, BA, MA; Polish journalist and politician; *Minister of Foreign Affairs;* b. 1963, Bydgoszcz; m. Anne Applebaum; two s. *Education:* Univ. of Oxford, UK. *Career:* Chair. student strike cttee Bydgoszcz 1981; political refugee in UK 1981–89; journalist reporting on wars in Afghanistan and Angola 1986–89; adviser to Rupert Murdoch on Polish investment 1990; Deputy Minister of Nat. Defence 1992; Under-Sec. of State in Ministry of Foreign Affairs 1998–2002; Fellow, American Enterprise Inst. and Exec. Dir New Atlantic Initiative 2002–05; elected to Senate for Bydgoszcz (Law and Justice Party), Minister of Nat. Defence 2005–07 (resgnd), of Foreign Affairs 2007–; fmr commentator on Polish and int. affairs for numerous TV and radio networks; World Press Photo Prize 1988. *Television:* cr. TV programme Wywiad Miesiąca (interview of the month). *Publications:* Prochy Siętych- podróż do Heratu w czas wojny (Ashes of the Saints- a journey to Herat during the war), The Polish House: An Intimate History of Poland; ed. of series of analytical publs entitled European Outlook.
Address: Ministry of Foreign Affairs, Al. Szucha 23, 00-580 Warsaw, Poland (office). *Telephone:* (22) 5239000 (office). *Fax:* (22) 6290287 (office). *E-mail:* dsi@msz.gov.pl (office). *Website:* www.msz.gov.pl (office).

SIKUA, David Derek, DipEd, BEd, MEPA, PhD; Solomon Islands educator and politician; *Prime Minister;* b. 10 Sept. 1959. *Education:* Univ. of the South Pacific, Suva, Fiji, Univ. of Southern Queensland, Australia, Monash Univ., Univ. of Waikato, New Zealand. *Career:* teacher and Deputy Headmaster Pawa Secondary School 1982–84; teacher and Deputy Prin. Waimapuru, Nat. Secondary School 1984–86; Prin. Educ. Officer, Implementation and Planning Unit, Ministry of Educ. and Human Resources Devt 1986–87, Dir Implementation and Planning Unit 1988–90, Dir Secondary School Div. Jan. 1993–Feb. 1993, Under Sec.

Minister of Educ. and Human Resources Devt 1993–94, Perm. Sec. 1994–97; Perm. Sec., Ministry of Forests, Environment and Conservation 1997–98; Perm. Sec. (Special Duties), Ministry of Educ. and Human Resources Dev May 2003–Sept. 2003, Perm. Sec. 2003–05; mem. Parl. for North East Guadalcanal 2006–; Minister for Educ. and Human Resources Devt 2006–07; Prime Minister 2007–; Chair. Solomon Islands Nat. Comm. for UNESCO 2006–; Chair. Nat. Educ. Planning Cttee 1989–90, Nat. Library Bd 1993–94; Deputy Chair. Solomon Islands Coll. of Higher Educ. (SICHE) Council 1994–97; mem. USP Council Exec. Cttee 2007–.
Address: Office of the Prime Minister, PO Box G1, Honiara, Solomon Islands (office). *Telephone:* 22202 (office). *Fax:* 28649 (office). *Website:* www.parliament.gov.sb (office).

SILAJDŽIĆ, Haris, PhD; Bosnia and Herzegovina academic and politician; *Member of the Tripartite State Presidency;* b. 1 Oct. 1945, Sarajevo; m.; one s. *Education:* Garyounis Univ., Libya. *Career:* has held several academic positions including the Arabic Language Prof., Univ. of Prishtina, Prof., Faculty of Philosophy and Dept of History, Univ. of Sarajevo, Andrew D. White Prof. at Large, Cornell Univ., New York, Guest Lecturer, Harvard Univ. and Univ. of Maryland, Chatham House (fmrly Royal Inst. for Int. Affairs), London, Carnegie Foundation, Woodrow Wilson Center, and other univs; Minister of Foreign Affairs, Repub. of Bosnia and Herzegovina 1991–93, Prime Minister 1993–96, Co-Chair. Council of Ministers of Bosnia and Herzegovina 1996–2000; Bosniak mem. Tripartite State Presidency 2006–, Chair. 2008; fmr mem. and Vice Pres. Party of Democratic Action; Founder and Pres. Party for Bosnia and Herzegovina; Rabbi Marc H. Tanenbaum Memoral Lecturer 1997. *Publications:* several books and papers on int. relations, including relations between USA and Albania.
Address: Office of the State Presidency, 71000 Sarajevo, Musala 5, Bosnia and Herzegovina (office). *Telephone:* (33) 664941 (office). *Fax:* (33) 472491 (office). *Website:* www.predsjednistvobih.ba (office).

SILES ALVARADO, Hugo, MSc; Bolivian physicist and diplomatist; *Permanent Representative, United Nations;* m.; three c. *Education:* Universidad de San Andres, Univ. of Minnesota, USA, Univ. of Uppsala, Sweden. *Career:* Prof. at numerous Univs throughout Bolivia, including Universidad de San Andres 1973–82; medical physicist in Bolivia, Ecuador and USA, specialising in radiation therapy and radiological protection 1982–2003; Prof., Catholic Univ., Cochabamba 2004; with VARIAN Medical Systems 2004–05; Perm. Rep. to UN, New York 2007–; fmr instructor, Las Vegas Educ. Dept, USA.
Address: Permanent Mission of Bolivia to the United Nations, 211 East 43rd Street, 8th Floor, Room 802, New York, NY 10017, US (office). *Telephone:* (212) 682-8132 (office). *Fax:* (212) 682-8133 (office). *E-mail:* bolivia@un.int (office).

SILIÉ VALDEZ, Rubén Arturo; Dominican Republic international organization official, sociologist and administrator. *Career:* fmr prof. at several univs and insts; fmr Vice-Rector Nat. Univ. of Santo Domingo; Dir Latin American Faculty for Social Sciences (FLACSO), Dominican Repub. 1996–; Adviser to Vice-Pres. and Sec. of State on Educ. 2001–; apptd Amb., Ministry of Foreign Affairs 2001; Sec.-Gen. Asscn of Caribbean States 2004–08; mem. Bd Batey Relief Alliance.
Address: c/o Secretariat of State for External Relations, Avda Independencia 752, Santo Domingo, DN, Dominican Republic.

SILKALNA, Solveiga, BSc, DipEd; Latvian diplomatist; *Permanent Representative, United Nations;* b. 22 Nov. 1970, Melbourne, Australia; m.; one c. *Education:* Univ. of Melbourne, Univ. of Latvia. *Career:* Interpreter, Office of Latvian Pres. 1993–95; Desk Officer, Dept of Int. Orgs, Ministry of Foreign Affairs 1995–96, Head of Div. of Humanitarian Issues 1996–98; First Sec., Latvian Mission to EU 1998–2000, Dir of Press and Public Diplomacy Dept 2001–02, Counsellor, Policy Planning Group 2004-05; Deputy Perm. Rep. to Council of Europe 2000–01; Adviser to Prime Minister 2002–04; Perm. Rep. to UN, New York 2005–.
Address: Office of the Permanent Representative of Latvia to the United Nations, 333 East 50th Street, New York, NY 10022, USA (office). *Telephone:* (212) 838-8877 (office). *Fax:* (212) 838-8920 (office). *E-mail:* irppanony@aol.com (office).

SILLARD, Yves; French aerospace engineer; b. 5 Jan. 1936, Coutances, Manche; m. 1st Annick Legrand 1966 (divorced); m. 2nd Hélène Benech-Badiou 1982 (divorced); m. 3rd Martine Gautry 1999. *Education:* Ecole Massillon, Ecole Polytechnique, Ecole nat. Supérieure de l'Aéronautique. *Career:* Test. Eng and then Head of Colomb-Béchard unit of Centre d'Essais en Vol 1960–62, Tech. Dir of Cazeaux annex 1963–64; Head of Concorde Programme at Secrétariat général à l'Aviation civile 1965; Head of Div. setting up French Guiana Space Centre, Kourou 1966–68; Tech. Dir and then Dir Space Centre, Kourou 1968–72; Dir of Launchers, Centre

Nat. des Etudes Spatiales 1973–76, Man. Dir 1976–82; Chair. and Man. Dir Centre nat. pour l'exploitation des océans 1982–; Chair. Conseil d'administration de l'institut français de recherche pour l'exploitation de la mer 1985–89; French Nat. Co-ordinator for EUREKA Programme 1986–89; Gen. Del., Armaments 1989–93; mem. Atomic Energy Cttee 1989–93; Chair., Man. Dir Cogepag 1993–, Défence conseil international 1993–97; Asst Sec. Gen. for Scientific Affairs and Environment, NATO 1998–2001; Vice-Chair. Nat. Acad. for Aeronautics and Space; Commdr, Légion d'honneur; Chevalier, Ordre nat. du Mérite; Médaille de l'Aéronautique; Commdr Merit (FRG).
Address: 8 rue de la Forge, 17800 Brives sur Charente, France. *Telephone:* (5) 46-95-01-56 (home). *E-mail:* ysillard@club-internet.fr (home).

SILVA BARBEIRO, Marciano; Guinea-Bissau politician; *Minister of National Defence; Career:* Minister of Educ. 2004–05, Minister of Nat. Defence 2007–; mem. Partido Africano da Independência da Guiné e Cabo Verde (PAIGC).
Address: Ministry of National Defence, Amura, Bissau, Guinea-Bissau (office). *Telephone:* 223646 (office).

SILVIA, HM The Queen of Sweden; b. (Silvia Renate Sommerlath), 23 Dec. 1943, Heidelberg, Germany; m. King Carl XVI Gustaf 1976; two d., Crown Princess Victoria Ingrid Alice Désirée b. 14 July 1977, Princess Madeleine Thérèse Amelie Josephine b. 10 June 1982; one s., Prince Carl Philip Edmund Bertil b. 13 May 1979. *Education:* Munich School of Interpreting. *Career:* lived in Sao Paulo, Brazil 1947–57, returned to FRG 1957; fmr mem. staff Argentine Consulate, Munich; mem. Organizing Cttee, Munich Olympics 1971–73, Deputy Head of Protocol, Organizing Cttee, Winter Olympics, Innsbruck, Austria 1973; Chair. Royal Wedding Fund, Jubilee Fund; est. Silvia Home, Drottningholm; Patron First World Congress Against Commercial Sexual Exploitation of Children, Stockholm 1996; f. World Childhood Foundation; Hon. mem. Menton Foundation, Swedish Amateur Athletic Asscn, Children's Cancer Foundation of Sweden, Swedish Save the Children Fed.; Dr hc (Åbo Univ.) 1990, (Karolinska Institutet) 1993, (Univ. of Linköping) 1994, (Göteborg Univ.) 1999; Deutsche Kulturpreis 1990, Chancellor's Medal, Univ. of Mass, ranked by Forbes magazine amongst 100 Most Powerful Women (68th) 2004.
Address: Royal Court of Sweden, Royal Palace, Stockholm 111 30, Sweden. *Telephone:* (8) 4026000. *Fax:* (8) 4026062. *E-mail:* info@royalcourt.se. *Website:* www.royalcourt.se.

SIMAI, Mihály; Hungarian economist; *Professor of International Economics, University of Economics, Budapest;* b. 4 April 1930, Budapest; m. Vera Bence 1953; one d. *Education:* Univ. of Econs, Budapest; postgraduate studies in Geneva and Paris. *Career:* Prof. of Int. Econs and Nat. Business, Univ. of Econs, Budapest 1971–, Dir of Grad. Studies in Int. Business and Strategy 1987–, in Int. Relations 1991–; mem. Hungarian Acad. of Sciences 1979–, Deputy Dir of Research, Inst. for World Econs, Hungarian Acad. of Sciences, Budapest 1973–87, Dir 1987–91, now Research Prof.; Pres. Hungarian UN Ass., Hungarian Nat. Cttee for UNICEF 1981–; Chair. Council UN Univ. 1990–92; Vice-Pres. Int. Studies Asscn 1988–; fmr Pres. Ed. Cttee Acta Oeconomica; Dir UN Univ. World Inst. for Devt Econs Research 1993–96; mem. Governing Council, Nat. Studies Asscn 1984–, Governing Bd Karl Polanyi Inst. 1988–, Advisory Bd for UN TNCs 1990–, Editorial Bd Environmental Econs 1991–, Advisory Bd Global Governance 1993–; Peace Fellow, US Inst. for Peace 1991–92; Hon. Pres. World Fed. of UN Asscns 1982–; Labour Order of Merit (Golden Degree), Order of the Star of Hungary (Golden Degree), Order of the Flag of the Hungarian Repub. 1990. *Publications:* Capital Export in the Contemporary Capitalist System 1962, The World Economic System of Capitalism, 1965, View from the 26th Floor 1969, Joint Ventures with Foreign Partners 1971, The United States before the 200th Anniversary 1974, Planning and Plan Implementation in the Developing Countries 1975, The United Nations and the Global Problems 1977, Interdependence and Conflicts in the World Economy 1981, Economic Decolonization and the Developing Countries 1981, The United Nations Today and Tomorrow 1985, Power, Technology and the World Economy of the 1990s 1990, Foreign Direct Investments in Hungary 1991, The Future of Global Governance: Managing Risk and Change in the International System 1994, International Business Policy 1996, The Democratic Process and the Market (ed.) 1999, The Reintegration of the Former Socialist Countries in Europe, China and Vietnam into the Global Economy 2000, The Ages of Global Transformations 2001; more than 250 articles on int. econ. and political issues.
Address: Institute for World Economics, Hungarian Academy of Sciences, Országház utca 30, 1014 Budapest, Országház utca 30 (office); Budapest University of Economic Sciences and Department of World Economy, Fõvám tér 8, 1093 Budapest, Hungary. *Telephone:* (1) 224-6762 (office); (1) 218-2313. *Fax:* (1) 224-6761 (office). *E-mail:* msimai@vki.hu (office). *Website:* www.vki.hu (office).

SIMANDJUNTAK, Djisman, Diplom Rer-Pol, PhD; Indonesian economist; *Senior Economist and Chairman, Board of Trustees, Centre for Strategic and International Studies (Jakarta);* b. 1 Jan. 1947, Tapanuli; m.; two s. one d. *Education:* Parahiyangan Univ., Bandung, Univ. of Cologne, Germany. *Career:* lecturer at several Indonesian univs; currently Exec. Dir Prasetiya Mulya Business School; currently Sr Economist and Chairman Bd of Trustees, Centre for Strategic and International Studies (CSIS) Foundation. *Publications:* Indonesia's Tolerated Low-Speed Reform of Corporate Governance, in Reforming Corporate Governance in Southeast Asia, ed by Ho Khai Leong 2005.
Address: Centre for Strategic and International Studies, Jalan Tanah Abang III/27, Jakarta 10160, Indonesia (office). *Telephone:* (021) 3865532 (office). *Fax:* (021) 3809641 (office). *E-mail:* csis@csis.or.id (office). *Website:* www.csis.or.id (office).

SIMEON, Yvon; Haitian economist, politician and diplomatist; *Ambassador to Italy; Education:* France. *Career:* fmr consultant; fmr Chargé d'Affaires in France and Belgium; Democratic Convergence rep., Paris; Minister of Foreign Affairs 2004–05; Amb. to Italy 2005–, Perm.Rep. to FAO 2006–.
Address: Embassy of Haiti, Via di Villa Patrizi 7/7a, 00161 Rome, Italy (office). *Telephone:* (06) 44254106 (office). *Fax:* (06) 44254208 (office). *E-mail:* amb.haiti@tiscali.it (office).

SIMES, Dimitri K.; Russian research institute director; *Founding President, Nixon Center;* b. Moscow. *Education:* School of History, Moscow State Univ. *Career:* Research Asst, then Research Assoc. Inst. of World Economy and Int. Affairs, Moscow 1967–72; Foreign Policy Adviser to fmr Pres. Richard Nixon 1970s; fmr teacher, Univ. of Calif., Berkeley, Columbia Univ.; fmr Sr Research Fellow and Dir Soviet Studies, Center for Strategic and Int. Studies; fmr Dir Soviet and E European Studies, Paul. H. Nitze School of Advanced Int. Studies, Johns Hopkins Univ.; Chair. Center for Russian and Eurasian Programs and Sr Assoc., Carnegie Endowment for Int. Peace –1994; Founder and Pres. The Nixon Center, Washington, DC 1994–; contribs to The New York Times, Washington Post, LA Times, Foreign Affairs. *Publications:* Soviet Succession: Leadership in Transition, Détente and Conflict: Soviet Foreign Policy 1972–77, After the Collapse: Russia Seeks Its Place as a Great Power 1999.
Address: The Nixon Center, 1615 L Street, Suite 1250, Washington, DC 20036, USA (office). *Telephone:* (202) 887-1000 (home). *Fax:* (202) 887-5222 (office). *E-mail:* mail@nixoncentre.org (office). *Website:* www.nixoncenter.org (office).

SIMITIS, Constantine (Costas), DJur; Greek lawyer and politician; b. 23 June 1936, Athens; m. Daphne Arkadiou; two c. *Education:* Univ. of Marburg and London School of Econs. *Career:* lawyer at Supreme Court 1961–; taught in W German univs 1971–75; Prof. of Commercial Law, Univ. of Athens 1977; mem. Nat. Council of Panhellenic Liberation Movt (PAK) during colonels' dictatorship, mem. Pasok 1974–, mem. Cen. Cttee of Pasok, Pres. 1996–2004; mem. Parl. 1985–2004; Minister of Agric. 1981–85, of Nat. Economy 1985–87, of Educ. and Religious Affairs 1989–90, of Industry, Energy, Tech. and Trade 1993–95; Prime Minister of Greece 1996–2004. *Publications include:* Politics is a Creative Greece 1996-2004 2005, Objectives, Strategies and Prospects 2007, Democracy in Crisis? 2007; numerous articles on legal and econ. topics.
Address: Academy 35, Athens 10672, Greece. *Telephone:* (210) 3624981. *Fax:* (210) 3616527. *E-mail:* contact@costas-simitis.gr. *Website:* www.costas-simitis.gr.

SIMMA, Bruno, DJur; German professor of law and judge; *Judge, International Court of Justice;* b. 29 March 1941, Quierschied, Saar. *Education:* Univ. of Innsbruck. *Career:* called to the Bar, Innsbruck 1967; Asst, Faculty of Law, Univ. of Innsbruck 1967–72; Expert, Directorate of Legal Affairs, Council of Europe 1972; Prof. of Int. Law and EC Law, Univ. of Munich 1973–, Dir Inst. of Int. Law 1973–, Dean Faculty of Law 1995–97; Dir of Studies, Hague Acad. of Int. Law 1976, 1982, Lecturer 1995; Lecturer in Int. Law, Training Centre for Jr Diplomats, Ministry of Foreign Affairs 1981–89; Visiting Prof., Univ. of Siena, Italy 1984–85; Visiting Prof., Univ. of Michigan Law School, Ann Arbor, USA 1986, 1995, Prof. of Law 1987–92, mem. Affiliate Overseas Faculty 1997–; mem. UN Cttee on Econ., Social and Cultural Rights 1987–96, UN Int. Law Comm. 1996–2003; Judge, Int. Court of Justice, The Hague 2003–; Co-Founder and Ed. European Journal of Int. Law; Founding Pres. European Soc. of Int. Law; Assoc. Institut de Droit international; Counsel for Germany in various legal cases 1994–2003; consultant, mem. numerous legal advisory bds and professional asscns. *Publications:* articles in professional journals.
Address: International Court of Justice, Peace Palace, 2517 KJ The Hague, The Netherlands (office). *Telephone:* (70) 3022323 (office). *Fax:* (70) 3022409 (office). *E-mail:* information@icj-cij.org (office). *Website:* www.icj-cij.org (office).

SIMMONS, Robert F. Jr, BSFS, MA; American diplomatist; *Secretary General's Special Representative for Causasus and Central Asia, NATO; Education:* Georgetown Univ., School of Advanced Int. Studies, John Hopkins Univ., Washington DC. *Career:* fmr Sr Rep., Arms Control and Disarmament Agency (ACDA); fmr US Rep. to NATO; fmr Deputy Dir, Office of Regional Political and Security Issues, Bureau of European Affairs, US State Dept; worked in Disarmament and Arms Control Section, Political Affairs Div., NATO Int. Staff 1980–83; assigned to US Embassy, Pakistan 1993–95; fmr US Rep. to NATO Sr Politico–Mil. Group on Proliferation (SGP) (created by 1999 Washington Summit WMD Initiative); Sr Advisor to US Asst Sec. of State for European and Eurasian Affairs, NATO –2003, Deputy Asst Sec. Gen. for Political Affairs and Security Policy, NATO 2003–, Sec. Gen.'s Special Rep. for Causasus and Cen. Asia 2004–; fmr Chair. Verification Working Group; Superior Honor Award (four times), US State Dept, Meritorious Honor Award, ACDA. *Address:* Office of the Secretary-General, North Atlantic Treaty Organization, blvd. Léopold III, 1110 Brussels, Belgium (office). *Telephone:* (2) 707-4111 (office). *Fax:* (2) 707-4579 (office). *E-mail:* natodoc@hq.nato.int (office). *Website:* www.nato.int (office).

SIMMONS, Timothy Michael John; British diplomatist; *Ambassador to Slovenia;* b. 8 April 1960; m. Caroline Simmons; two s. *Career:* joined FCO 1982, Asst Desk Officer, Nuclear Energy Dept 1982–85, Third, later Second Sec. (Econ.), Warsaw 1985–87, Desk Officer, Middle Eastern Dept, FCO 1987–90, Desk Officer, EC Dept (External) 1990, Pvt. Sec., Perm. Under-Sec.'s Office 1990–93, First Sec., UK Mission Geneva 1993–97, on loan to Price Waterhouse 1997–99, Asst Dir (Personnel Command), FCO 1999–2001, Deputy Head of Mission, Warsaw 2001–04, Amb. to Slovenia 2005–. *Address:* British Embassy, Trg republike 3, 1000 Ljubljana, Slovenia (office). *Telephone:* (1) 2003919 (office). *Fax:* (1) 4250174 (office). *E-mail:* info@british-embassy.si (office). *Website:* info@british-embassy.si (office).

SIMONIA, Nodari Aleksandrovich, CandEconSc, DHist; Russian political economist; *Director, Institute of World Economy and International Relations (IMEMO), Russian Academy of Sciences;* b. 30 Jan. 1932, Tbilisi, Georgia; m.; one d. *Education:* Moscow Inst. of Int. Relations. *Career:* Corresp. mem. Russian Acad. of Sciences 1990, mem. 1997–; Acad. Sec., Dept of Int. Relations, Jr Researcher, Sr Researcher, Prof. and Head of Sector, Head of Div., Deputy Dir, Inst. of Oriental Studies 1955–86; Deputy Dir Inst. of World Econ. and Int. Relations, Russian Acad. of Sciences 1986–2000, Dir 2000–; Prof., Centre of Slavic Studies, Hokkaido Univ.; main research in comparative studies: Russia and developing countries; mem. Presidium, Russian Acad. of Sciences, Scientific Council Ministry of Foreign Affairs, European Acad. of Sciences, Arts and Literature; Special Rep. of Pres. of Russian Fed. for Relations with African States' Leaders. *Publications:* over 250 scientific works, including 16 books and articles and papers on the devt of capitalism in modern Russia. *Address:* IMEMO, Profsoyuznaya str. 23, 117997 Moscow, GSP-7, Russia (office). *Telephone:* (495) 120-84-50 (office); (495) 434-15-68 (home). *Fax:* (495) 310-70-27 (office). *E-mail:* imemoan@imemo.ru (office). *Website:* www.imemo.ru/eng (office).

SIMONS, Paul E., BA, MBA; American economist and diplomatist; *Ambassador to Chile;* m. Victoria Cardenas-Simons; two d. *Education:* Yale Univ., New York Univ. *Career:* fmr Asst Vice-Pres. for int. corp. lending at New York–based commercial bank; career mem. Sr Foreign Service, served as lead economist on Sec. of State's Policy Planning Staff, as Int. Economist in Treasury Dept; overseas postings include Malawi and Colombia, Econ. Counselor, Quito 1992–96, served as Deputy Chief of Mission, Tel-Aviv; Acting Asst Sec. of State for Int. Narcotics and Law Enforcement, Deputy Asst Sec. of State for Energy, Sanctions, and Commodities –2007; Amb. to Chile 2007–. *Address:* US Embassy, Avda Andrés Bello 2800, Las Condes, Santiago, Chile (office). *Telephone:* (2) 232-2600 (office). *Fax:* (2) 330-3710 (office). *E-mail:* SantiagoVisa@state.gov (office). *Website:* santiago.usembassy.gov (office).

SIMONYI, András, PhD; Hungarian economist, consultant and diplomatist; b. 16 May 1952, Budapest; m. Nada Pejak; one s. one d. *Education:* Karl Marx Univ. of Econs (now Budapest Univ.). *Career:* worked in 1980s with different orgs in field of youth exchange, particularly promoting East–West contacts, including programmes with American Council of Young Political Leaders; mem. staff Foreign Relations Dept, Socialist Workers Party 1984–89; Head of Nordic Dept, Ministry of Foreign Affairs 1989–91; Deputy Chief of Mission Embassy of Hungary, The Hague 1991–92, Hungarian Mission to EC and NATO, Brussels 1992–95; Head, Hungarian NATO Liaison Office, Brussels 1995–99; Perm. Rep. to NATO Council (first Hungarian Perm. Rep.) 1999–2001, rep. on North Atlantic Council during Kosovo campaign; Amb. to USA 2002–07; ran own consulting co.

Danison Ltd 2001–02; Imre Nagy Award, Hungary–Ohio Partnership for Educ. *Publications include:* numerous articles on the accession process to NATO, trans-Atlantic relations and European security and the war on terror. *Address:* c/o Ministry of Foreign Affairs, 1027 Budapest, Bem rkp. 47, Hungary.

SIMPSON, (Alfred William) Brian, QC, JP, MA, DCL, FBA; British legal scholar; *Charles F. and Edith J. Clyne Professor of Law, University of Michigan;* b. 17 Aug. 1931, Kendal; m. 1st Kathleen Seston 1954 (divorced 1968); one s. one d.; m. 2nd Caroline E. A. Brown 1969; one s. two d. *Education:* Oakham School, Rutland and Queen's Coll., Oxford. *Career:* Jr Research Fellow, St Edmund Hall, Oxford 1954–55; Fellow Lincoln Coll., Oxford 1955–73, Jr Proctor 1967–68; Dean Faculty of Law, Univ. of Ghana 1968–69; Prof. of Law, Univ. of Kent 1973–85, Prof. Emer. 1985–; Prof. of Law, Univ. of Chicago, USA 1983–86; Charles F. and Edith J. Clyne Prof. of Law, Univ. of Mich. 1987–; Goodhart Visiting Prof., Univ. of Cambridge, UK 1993–94; Fellow American Acad. of Arts and Sciences; Barrister-at-law, Gray's Inn. *Publications:* A History of the Common Law of Contract 1975, Cannibalism and the Common Law 1984, A Biographical Dictionary of the Common Law (Ed.) 1984, A History of the Land Law 1986, Legal Theory and Legal History 1987, Invitation to Law 1988, In the Highest Degree Odious: Detention Without Trial in Wartime Britain 1992, Leading Cases in the Common Law 1995, Human Rights and the End of Empire. Britain and the Genesis of the European Convention 2001. *Address:* University of Michigan Law School, 409 Hutchins Hall, Ann Arbor, MI 48109-1215, USA (office); 3 The Butchery, Sandwich, Kent, CT13 9DL, England. *Telephone:* (734) 763-0413 (office); (1304) 612783 (Kent). *Fax:* (734) 763-9375 (office). *E-mail:* bsimpson@umich.edu (office). *Website:* www.law.umich.edu (office).

SIMPSON, John Cody Fidler-, CBE, MA, FRGS; British broadcaster and writer; *World Affairs Editor, BBC;* b. 9 Aug. 1944, Cleveleys; m. 1st Diane Petteys 1965 (divorced 1996); two d.; m. 2nd Adèle Krüger 1996; one s. *Education:* St Paul's School, London, Magdalene Coll. Cambridge. *Career:* joined BBC 1966, Foreign Corresp. in Dublin, Brussels, Johannesburg 1972–78, Diplomatic Corresp., BBC TV 1978–80, Political Ed. 1980–81, Diplomatic Ed. 1982–88, Foreign Affairs Ed. (now World Affairs Ed.) 1988–; Contributing Ed. The Spectator 1991–95; columnist, Sunday Telegraph 1995–; Hon. Fellow Magdalene Coll. Cambridge; Hon. DLitt (De Montfort) 1995, (Univ. of E Anglia) 1998; Dr hc (Nottingham) 2000; Golden Nymph Award Cannes 1979, BAFTA Reporter of the Year 1991, 2001, Royal TV Soc. Dimbleby Award 1991, Peabody Award 1998, Emmy Award (for coverage of the fall of Kabul) 2002, Bayeux War Correspondents' Prize 2002, Int. Emmy Award, New York 2002. *Publications:* The Best of Granta 1966, The Disappeared 1985, Behind Iranian Lines 1988, Despatches from the Barricades 1990, From the House of War 1991, The Darkness Crumbles 1992, In the Forests of the Night 1993, Lifting the Veil: Life in Revolutionary Iran 1995, The Oxford Book of Exile 1995, Strange Places, Questionable People (autobiog.) 1998, A Mad World, My Masters 2000, News from No Man's Land: Reporting the World 2002, Days from a Different World: A Memoir of Childhood (autobiog.) 2005, Twenty Tales from the War Zone 2007, Not Quite World's End 2007. *Address:* c/o BBC World Affairs Unit, Television Centre, Wood Lane, London, W12 7RJ, England. *Telephone:* (20) 8743-8000. *Fax:* (20) 8743-7591.

SIMUTIS, Anicetas, MA; Lithuanian diplomatist; b. 11 Feb. 1909, Tirkšliai; m. Janina Čiurlys 1936; two c. *Education:* Univ. of Vytautas Magnus, Kaunas and Columbia Univ., New York. *Career:* joined Lithuanian Ministry of Foreign Affairs 1931; Sec. Consulate-Gen. of Lithuania 1936, Consular Attaché 1939, Vice-Consul 1951, Consul-Gen. 1967; Amb. and Perm. Rep. of Lithuania to UN 1991–93; Special Adviser to Lithuanian Mission to UN. *Publications:* The Economic Reconstruction of Lithuania after 1918 1942, Lithuanian World Directory 1953; articles in periodicals. *Address:* Permanent Mission of Lithuania to the United Nations, 420 Fifth Avenue, Third Floor, New York, NY 10018, USA.

SIN, Son-ho; North Korean diplomatist; *Permanent Representative, United Nations;* b. 5 July 1948; m.; two c. *Education:* Kim Il Sung Univ. *Career:* Third Sec., Embassy in Cairo 1972–79; Sr Officer, Ministry of Foreign Affairs 1979–83; Counsellor, Embassy in Lesotho 1983–86; Chief of Div., Ministry of Foreign Affairs 1986–90; Counsellor, Embassy in Zimbabwe 1990–95; Deputy Dir Ministry of Foreign Affairs 1995–99; Perm. Rep. to UN, New York 2000–03, 2008–; Dir-Gen. Ministry of Foreign Affairs 2003–08. *Address:* Permanent Mission of the Democratic People's Republic of Korea to the United Nations, 820 Second Avenue, 13th Floor, New York, NY 10017, USA (office). *Telephone:* (212) 972-3105 (office). *Fax:* (212) 972-3154 (office). *E-mail:* dprk@un.int (office).

SINCKLER, Christopher Peter, BA, MA; Barbadian civil servant, politician and academic; *Minister of Foreign Affairs, Foreign Trade and International Business;* m. Arlyn Mayers; two s. one d. *Education:* Univ. of the West Indies. *Career:* worked on econ. policy issues with IBRD (World Bank), IMF, IDB, WTO, CARICOM, African, Caribbean and Pacific Group of States, EU, among others; Lecturer in Small Economies and Contemporary Trade Policy Issues, Masters in Int. Trade Policy Programme, Univ. of the West Indies Cave Hill Campus; Exec. Dir Caribbean Policy Devt Centre (coalition of Caribbean non-governmental orgs) –2008; mem. Democratic Labour Party, currently Gen. Sec.; MP for St Michael NW; Minister of Foreign Affairs, Foreign Trade and Int. Business 2008–.
Address: Ministry of Foreign Affairs, Foreign Trade and International Business, 1 Culloden Road, St Michael, Bardados, BB 14018, West Indies (office). *Telephone:* 431-2200 (office). *Fax:* 429-6652 (office). *E-mail:* info@ foreign.gov.bb (office); csinckler@sunbeach.net. *Website:* www.foreign .gov.bb (office).

SINGH, Ashni Kumar, PhD; Guyanese government official; *Minister of Finance; Education:* Queens Coll., Lancaster Univ., UK. *Career:* fmr Commr Gen. Guyana Revenue Authority; Budget Dir –2006; Minister of Finance 2006–.
Address: Ministry of Finance, Main Street, Kingston, Georgetown, Guyana (office). *Telephone:* 225-6088 (office). *Fax:* (office). *E-mail:* asingh@inetguyana.net (office). *Website:* www.finance.gov.gy (office).

SINGH, Durgesh Man; Nepalese diplomatist; *Ambassador to India; Education:* student of Prime Minister of India Manmohan Singh. *Career:* fmr Amb. to Belgium, Amb. to India 2008–.
Address: Embassy of Nepal, Barakhamba Road, New Delhi 110 001, India (office). *Telephone:* (11) 23329218 (office). *Fax:* (11) 23326857 (office). *E-mail:* nepembassydelhi@bol.net.in (office).

SINGH, Harsha Vardhana, MEcon, MPhil, PhD; Indian economist and international organization executive; *Deputy Director-General, World Trade Organization;* m. Veena Jha; two c. *Education:* Delhi Univ., Univ. of Oxford, UK (Rhodes Scholar). *Career:* worked as consultant with Bureau of Industrial Costs and Prices, New Delhi and with ILO and UNCTAD, Geneva; worked in GATT/WTO Secr. in various capacities, including Econ. Research and Analysis Unit 1985–89, Trade Policy Review Div. 1989–91, Rules Div. 1991–95, Trade and Environment and Tech. Barriers to Trade Div. 1995–96, Office of WTO Dir-Gen. 1996–97, served as Chair. of dispute settlement panels, Deputy Dir-Gen. WTO 2005–; Econ. Advisor, Telecom Regulatory Authority of India (TRAI) 1997–2001, Sec. cum Prin. Advisor and Head of TRAI Secr. 2001–05; fmr mem. various trade advisory cttees of Indian Govt; mem. Visiting Faculty, TERI School of Advanced Studies for their Masters programme in Regulatory Studies; Hon. Prof., Indian Council for Research on Int. Econ. Relations. *Publications:* several papers on trade policy and regulatory issues.
Address: World Trade Organization, Centre William Rappard, rue de Lausanne 154, 1211 Geneva 21, Switzerland (office). *Telephone:* (22) 739-51-11 (office). *Fax:* (22) 731-42-06 (office). *E-mail:* enquiries@wto.org (office). *Website:* www.wto.org (office).

SINGH, Hemant Krishan, MA; Indian diplomatist; *Ambassador to Japan;* b. 1950; m. Mrinalini Singh; two c. *Education:* Univ. of Delhi. *Career:* joined Ministry of External Affairs 1974, served as Country Officer for USA 1980–81, Dir for Pakistan, Iran, Afghanistan 1991–92, Jt Sec. for Western Europe 1992–95; overseas postings include Second Sec., Embassy in Lisbon 1976–77, Embassy in Maputo 1978–80, First Sec., Embassy in Washington, DC 1981–85, Counsellor, Embassy in Kathmandu 1985–88, Embassy in Belgrade 1988–91; Deputy Perm. Rep. to UN, Geneva 1995–99; Amb. to Colombia (also accred to Ecuador and Costa Rica) 1999–2002, Amb. to Indonesia (also accred to Timor Leste) 2003–06, Amb. to Japan 2006–.
Address: Embassy of India, 2-2-11, Kudan Minami, Chiyoda-ku, Tokyo 102-0074, Japan (office). *Telephone:* (3) 3262-2391 (office). *Fax:* (3) 3234-4866 (office). *E-mail:* indembjp@gol.com (office). *Website:* www .embassyofindiajapan.org (office).

SINGH, Jaswant, BA, BSc; Indian politician and army officer; b. 3 Jan. 1938, Jasol, Rajasthan; m. Sheetal Kumari 1963; two s. *Education:* Mayo Coll., Ajmer, Jt Services Wing, Clement Town, Dehradun, Indian Mil. Acad., Dehradun. *Career:* commissioned Cen. India Horse 1957; resgnd his comm. and elected to Rajya Sabha 1980; Minister of Finance and Company Affairs 1996, 2002–04; Deputy Chair., Planning Comm. 1998–99; Minister of External Affairs 1999, 2001–02, of Electronics Feb.–Oct. 1999, of Surface Transport Aug.–Oct. 1999; Chair. Consultative Cttee for the Ministry of External Affairs 2000–01; Leader of the House, Rajya Sabha 1999–2004, Leader of the Opposition 2004. *Publications:* National Security – An Outline of Our Concerns 1996, Shauryo Tejo 1997, Defending India 1999, District Diary 2001, Khankhananama (Hindi) 2001; numerous

articles on int. affairs, security and devt issues to Indian and foreign magazines, newspapers and journals.
Address: c/o Ministry of Finance, North Block, New Delhi 110 001, India.

SINGH, K. Natwar, BA; Indian diplomatist, politician and writer; b. 6 May 1931; m. Shrimati Heminder Kumari 1967; one s. *Education:* Univ. of Delhi, Univ. of Cambridge, UK, Peking Univ., People's Repub. of China. *Career:* joined Foreign Service 1953; served in Peking 1956–58; Perm. Mission to UN 1961–66; mem. Bd UNICEF 1962–66, rapporteur 1963–65; mem. Prime Minister's Secr. 1966–71; Amb. to Poland 1971–73; Deputy High Commr to UK 1973–77; High Commr to Zambia 1977–80; Amb. to Pakistan 1980–82; mem. Lok Sabha 1984–89; Union Minister of State Dept of Steel, Dept of Fertilizers 1985–86; with Ministry of External Affairs 1986–89; mem. Cttee on External Affairs, on Public Accounts 1998–99; elected to Rajya Sabha 2002; mem. Cttee on External Affairs 2002–04; Minister of External Affairs 2004–05, Minister without Portfolio 2005 (resgnd); mem. Bd Dirs Air India 1982–84; Pres. UN Conf. on Disarmament and Devt, New York 1987; Padma Bhushan 1984, E. M. Forster's Literary Award 1989. *Publications:* E. M. Forster: A Tribute 1964, The Legacy of Nehru 1965, Tales from Modern India 1966, Stories from India 1971, Maharaja Suraj Mal: 1707–63 1981, Curtain Raisers 1984, Profiles and Letters 1997, The Magnificent Maharaja Bhupinder Singh of Patiala: 1891–1938 1997, Heart to Heart 2003; contribs to numerous newspapers and journals.
Address: 'Govind Niwas', Bharatpur, Rajasthan, 321001, India (home). *Telephone:* (11) 23013855 (home). *Fax:* (11) 23793704 (home).

SINGH, Laleshwar Kumar Narayan; Guyanese diplomatist; *High Commissioner to UK;* b. 2 April 1941; m. Latchmin Singh; two c. *Education:* Univ. of London. *Career:* trained as clerk, Inner London Magistrates' Court 1971, served in numerous positions in Magistrates' Courts in Inner London; High Commr to UK 1993– (also accred as Amb. to the Netherlands 1993–, France 1995–, Russia 1995–, Czech Repub. 1997–, the Holy See 1998–); Chair. Bd of Govs Commonwealth Secr. 2004, selection panel to appoint Dir of Commonwealth Foundation 2004; Cacique's Crown of Honour 1996.
Address: High Commission of Guyana, 3 Palace Court, Bayswater Road, London, W2 4LP, England (office). *Telephone:* (20) 7229-7684 (office). *Fax:* (20) 7727-9809 (office). *E-mail:* guyanahc1@btconnect.com (office). *Website:* www.guyanahc.com (office).

SINGH, Manmohan, PhD; Indian economist and politician; *Prime Minister and Minister-in-charge of Personnel, Public Grievances and Pensions, of Planning, of Atomic Energy, of Space, of Coal and of the Environment and Forests;* b. 26 Sept. 1932, Gah, Punjab (now Pakistan); m. Gursharan Kaur; three d. *Education:* Univ. of Punjab, Univs of Cambridge and Oxford, UK. *Career:* Lecturer, Univ. of Punjab 1957–69; Prof. Delhi School of Econs 1969–71; econ. adviser, Ministry of Foreign Trade 1971–72; Chief Econ. Adviser, Ministry of Finance 1972–76; Dir Reserve Bank of India 1976–80, Gov. 1982–85; Mem.-Sec. Planning Comm. 1980–82, Deputy Chair. 1985–87; Sec.-Gen., Commr South Comm. 1987–90; econ. adviser to Prime Minister 1990–91; Minister of Finance 1991–96; mem. Rajya Sabha (Parl.) 1991–, Leader of Opposition 1995–2004; Prime Minister of India and Minister-in-charge of Personnel, Public Grievances and Pensions, of Planning, of Atomic Energy, of Space 2004–, also Minister of External Affairs 2005–06, Minister of Coal and of the Environment and Forests 2007–; Dr hc (Univ. of Cambridge) 2006. *Publication:* India's Export Trends and Prospects for Self-Sustained Growth 1964.
Address: Prime Minister's Office, South Block, New Delhi, 110 011 (office); 7 Safdarjung Lane, New Delhi, 110011, India. *Telephone:* (11) 23013040 (office); (11) 3018668. *Fax:* (11) 23016857 (office). *E-mail:* manmohan@ sansad.nic.in (home). *Website:* www.pmindia.nic.in (office).

SINGH, Sujatha; Indian diplomatist; *High Commissioner to Australia; Career:* served as Consul-Gen. in Milan; fmr Jt Sec. (West Europe), Ministry of External Affairs –2007; High Commr to Australia 2007–.
Address: High Commission of India, 3–5 Moonah Place, Yarralumla, ACT 2600, Australia (office). *Telephone:* (2) 6273-3999 (office). *Fax:* (2) 6273-1308 (office). *E-mail:* hco@hcindia-au.org (office). *Website:* www.hcindia -au.org (office).

SINHA, Lt-Gen. (retd) Shreenivas Kumar, BA; Indian army officer; b. 7 Jan. 1926, Gaya; m. Premini Sinha; one s. three d. *Education:* Patna Univ, Officers Training School, Belgaum. *Career:* commissioned 1944, saw combat service during Second World War in Burma and Indonesia and after Independence in Kashmir, served two tenures in Nagaland and Manipur taking part in counter-insurgency operations, transferred to 5 Gorkha Rifles after Independence, fmr Col of Regt (5GR); fmr instructor, Infantry School, Mhow and Defence Services Staff Coll., Wellington; fmr Dir of Mil. Intelligence and Deputy Adjutant-Gen.; fmr Adjutant-Gen.,

Army HQ; Sec. Del. to UN Comm. for India and Pakistan for Kashmir 1949; Leader Del. UN Conf. on Application of Human Rights to Warfare 1972; Gen. Officer C-in-C, W Command 1981–82; Vice-Chief of Army Staff 1983 (retd); Amb. to Nepal 1990; Gov. of Assam 1997–2003, of Jammu and Kashmir 2003–08; Hon. ADC to Pres. of India 1979; fmr Pres. Gorkha Brigade; Param Vishist Sewa Medal 1973. *Publications:* books: Operation Rescue (on the Jammu and Kashmir operation of 1947–48), A Soldier Recalls (autobiog.), Of Matters Military, Pataliputra, Past to Present, Veer Kuer Singh; 300 articles in nat. newspapers.
Address: c/o Raj Bhawan, Guwahati, India (office).

SINHA, Yashwant, MA; Indian politician, teacher and civil servant; b. 6 Nov. 1937, Patna, Bihar; m. Nilima Sinha 1961; two s. one d. *Education:* Patna Coll., Patna Univ. Bihar. *Career:* Lecturer in Political Science, Patna Univ. 1958–60; joined IAS 1960; Deputy Comm. Santhal Paraganas; Chair. Drafting Cttee of the UNCTAD Conf. on Shipping, Geneva; Consul-Gen. of India, Frankfurt; Prin. Sec. to Chief Minister, Bihar; Jt Sec. to Govt of India, Ministry of Shipping and Transport; retd from IAS and joined Janata Party 1984, Gen. Sec. 1986–88; mem. Rajya Sabha 1988, mem. Cttee on Petitions 1989; joined Janata Dal (Samajwadi) after split in Janata Dal 1990; Minister of Finance 1998–99, 2001–02, of External Affairs 2002–04; mem. Lok Sabha 1998–; mem. Parl. Pay Cttee 1998–99.
Address: Jasol House, Paotabarea, Jodhpur (home); Vill. Hupad, Post-Morangi, Demotandh, Thana Muffassil, Hazaribagh (Bihar), India (home). *Telephone:* (11) 23012380.

SINIORA, Fouad, MBA; Lebanese banking executive and government official; *Prime Minister;* b. 19 July 1943, Sidon; m.; three c. *Education:* Nat. Evangelical Inst., American Univ. of Beirut. *Career:* various positions at First Nat. City Bank, including clerk 1967, Head Credit Dept 1970–71, Credit Account Officer, Marketing Officer, mem. Credit Cttee 1970–72; lecturer Lebanese Univ., American Univ. Beirut 1971–77; concurrently several positions at Finance Bank including Man. Industry and Tourism loans, mem. Credit Cttee, Sec. Bd of Dirs 1972–75; Financial Adviser Intra Investment 1975–77; Asst Gen. Man. Middle East Cement Co. 1975–77; Banking Control Commr Central Bank 1977–82; Dir, Arab Universal Insurance 1982–92; exec. positions at several cos including Al Mal, IRAD, Méditerranée Investors Group, Méditerranée Group Sevices, Banque de la Méditerranée, Saudi Lebanese Bank 1982–92; Minister of State for Financial Affairs, Acting Minister of Finance 1992–98; Minister of Finance –2004; Prime Minister 2005–.
Address: c/o Office of the President of the Council of Ministers, Grand Sérail, place Riad es-Solh, Beirut, Lebanon (office).

SINKINSON, Philip Andrew, OBE; British diplomatist; *High Commissioner to The Gambia;* b. 7 Oct. 1950; m. Clare Maria Jarvis; one s. *Career:* with Superannuation Section, Personnel Services Dept, FCO 1970–73, Archivist, Warsaw 1973–74, East Berlin 1974–75, Rome 1975–76, Asst Desk Officer, Recruitment Section, Personnel Policy Dept, FCO 1976–78, Deputy Man. Officer, Rio de Janeiro 1978, Accountant and Deputy Man. Officer, Quito 1978–79, Archivist, Prague 1979–81, Overseas and Interdepartmental Accounts Desk Officer, Finance Dept, FCO 1981–82, Passport Officer, Blantyre 1982–85, Lilongwe 1985–86, Desk Officer, Human Rights Section, UN Dept, FCO 1986–89, Canada Desk, N American Dept 1989–92, Vice-Consul (Commercial and Information), São Paulo 1992–95, on secondment to British Olympic Asscn, Atlanta 1995–96, Head of UK Trade and Investment for Portugal, Lisbon 1996–2001, Deputy High Commr, Kingston 2001–05, High Commr to The Gambia 2006–.
Address: British High Commission, 48 Atlantic Road, Fajara, PO Box 507, Banjul, The Gambia (office). *Telephone:* 4495133 (office). *Fax:* 4496134 (office). *E-mail:* bhcbanjul@fco.gov.uk (office). *Website:* www .britishhighcommission.gov.uk/thegambia (office).

ŠINKOVEC, Matjaz, BA, MA; Slovenian diplomatist and politician; *State Secretary, Prime Minister's Office;* b. 22 May 1951, Ljubljana; m. Magdalena Šinkovec; two s. *Education:* Lone Mountain Coll., Univ. of San Francisco, USA. *Career:* active dissident 1968–70; journalist, Daily Delo 1974; freelance trans. 1975–78; with Slovenian Foreign Office 1978–84; Int. Sec. Confed. of Slovenian Trade Unions 1984–90; Founding mem. and Vice-Pres. Social Democratic Party (SDS) 1988; first proponent of opposition coalition DEMOS 1989; Mem. Parl. and Chair. Foreign Affairs Cttee 1990–92; SDS Parl. Group Leader, mem. Council of Govt Coalition DEMOS 1990–92; Head (first) Slovenian Del. to Parl. Ass. of Council of Europe 1991–92; Amb. to Court of St James (UK) 1992–97, also accred to Ireland 1996–97; State Under-Sec. for NATO and WEU, Ministry of Foreign Affairs 1997–99; Amb. and Perm. Rep. to NATO and WEU 1999–2006; Dir Slovenian Intelligence and Security Agency 2006–07; Sec. Slovenian Nat. Security Council 2006-07; State Sec., Prime Minister's Office 2007–; Political Dir Ministry of Foreign Affairs 2008–; Golden

Signet of the Chief of Staff of the Slovenian Armed Forces 2003, Gold Medal of the Slovenian Armed Forces 2006; Pro Patria Medal, British Slovene Soc. 1997, Ministry of Foreign Affairs Award 2001. *Publications:* several books and articles on foreign relations, political campaigning, fiction and poetry.
Address: Ministry of Foreign Affairs, Prešernova 25, 1000 Ljubljana, Slovenia (office). *Telephone:* (1) 478-2000 (office). *E-mail:* matjaz@ sinkovec.com (office); sinkovec@yahoo.com (office). *Website:* www .sinkovec.com (home).

SINN, Hans-Werner, Dr rer. pol; German economist; *President, Ifo Institute for Economic Research;* b. 7 March 1948, Brake; m. Gerlinde Sinn (née Zoubek) 1971; two s. one d. *Education:* Helmholtz-Gymnasium, Bielefeld, Univ. of Münster, Univ. of Mannheim. *Career:* Lecturer, Univ. of Münster 1972–74, Univ. of Mannheim 1974–78, Sr Lecturer 1979–83, Assoc. Prof. 1983–84; Visiting Asst Prof., Univ. of Western Ont. 1978–79; Prof. of Econs and Insurance, Univ. of Munich 1984–94, Dir Centre for Econ. Studies 1991–, Prof. of Econs and Public Finance 1994–; mem. Council of Econ. Advisers, Fed. Ministry of Econs 1989–; Chair. Verein für Socialpolitik (German Econ. Asscn) 1997–2000; Pres. Ifo Inst. for Econ. Research 1999–; Pres. Int. Inst. of Public Finance 2006–(09); Order of Merit (Germany) 1999, 2005; Hon. Dr rer. pol (Univ. of Magdeburg) 1999; Venia Legendi 1983, Yrjö Jahnsson Lecturer, Univ. of Helsinki 1999, Stevenson Lecturer on Citizenship, Univ. of Glasgow 2000, Prize of Advisory Council of the Union 2003, Econ. Book Prize, Financial Times Deutschland 2003, Int. Book Prize CORINE 2004. *Publications:* Economic Decisions under Uncertainty 1980, Capital Income Taxation and Resource Allocation 1985, Jumpstart: The Economic Unification of Germany 1991, The German State Banks – Global Players in the International Financial Markets 1999, The New Systems Competition 2002, Ist Deutschland noch zu retten? 2003–05; numerous articles on public finance and other subjects; Ed. several journals including Economic Policy.
Address: Ifo Institute for Economic Research, Poschingerstr. 5, 81679 Munich (office); Centre for Economic Studies, University of Munich, Schackstr. 4, 80539 Munich, Germany (office). *Telephone:* (89) 92241276 (office). *Fax:* (89) 92241901 (office). *E-mail:* sinn@ifo.de (office). *Website:* www.cesifo-group.de/hws (office).

SISON, Michele J., BA; American diplomatist; *Chargé d'affaires a.i. in Lebanon;* b. 27 May 1959, Arlington, Va; two d. *Education:* Wellesley Coll. and London School of Econs, UK. *Career:* career mem. Sr Foreign Service with rank of Minister-Counselor, served at US Missions in Port-au-Prince, Haiti 1982–84, Lomé, Togo 1984–88, Cotonou, Benin 1988–91, Douala, Cameroon 1991–93, Abidjan, Côte d'Ivoire 1993–96, and in Washington, DC, Consul Gen., Chennai, India 1996–99, Deputy Chief of Mission and Chargé d'affaires a.i., Islamabad 1999–2002, Prin. Deputy Asst Sec., Bureau of S Asian Affairs 2002–04, Amb. to UAE 2004–08, Chargé d'affaires a.i., Beirut, Lebanon 2008–; numerous Dept of State awards for exceptional service.
Address: US Embassy, PO 70-840, Awkar facing the Municipality, Antélias, Lebanon (office). *Telephone:* (4) 542600 (office). *Fax:* (4) 544136 (office). *E-mail:* pasbeirut@state.gov (office). *Website:* lebanon.usembassy .gov (office).

SISTANI, Grand Ayatollah Sayyid Ali Husaini; Iraqi (b. Iranian) religious leader; b. 1929, Mashhad, Iran. *Career:* joined Islamic seminary, Qom 1949; fmr lecturer in jurisprudence, Najaf Ashraf; after religious training in Iran moved to Iraq to become most sr Shia cleric; apptd head of network of schools, Najaf 1992. *Publications:* numerous religious works and treatises.
Address: Office of Grand Ayatollah Sistani, Muallim Street, POB 3514\37185, Qom, Iran. *Telephone:* 251-7741415. *Fax:* 251-7741421. *E-mail:* sistani@sistani.org. *Website:* www.sistani.org.

SISULU, Sheila Violet Makate, BA; South African diplomatist and UN official; *Deputy Executive Director, United Nations World Food Programme;* d.-in-law of Walter Max Ulyate Sisulu and Albertina Nontsikelelo Sisulu; m. Mlungisi Sisulu; two s. one d. *Education:* Univ. of Witwatersrand. *Career:* various sr positions, South African Comm. for Higher Educ. 1978–88; Educ. Co-ordinator, African Bursary Fund, South African Council of Churches 1988–91; Dir Jt Enrichment Project 1991–94; Special Adviser, Ministry of Educ. 1994–97; Consul-Gen., South African Consulate-Gen., New York 1997–99; Amb. to USA 1999–2002; Deputy Exec. Dir UN World Food Programme 2003–; mem. ANC Nat. Educ. Cttee, USA–South Africa Leadership Training Program, Community Bank Foundation; Council mem. Univ. of Witwatersrand; Trustee, Equal Opportunity Foundation, Women's Devt Foundation, Women's Devt Bank, South African Broadcasting Corpn; Dr hc (Maryland, CUNY).
Address: UN World Food Programme, Via C.G. Viola 68, Parco dei Medici, 00148 Rome, Italy (office). *Telephone:* (06) 65131 (office). *Fax:* (06)

65132840 (office). *E-mail:* wfpinfo@wfp.org (office). *Website:* www.wfp.org (office).

SITHANEN, Rama Krishna, BSc, MSc; Mauritian politician and economist; *Deputy Prime Minister and Minister of Finance and Economic Development;* b. 21 April 1954. *Education:* LSE. *Career:* fmr Research Officer, Centre for Labour Econs, LSE; fmr Research Officer, OECD, Paris; Educ. Officer 1979–80; Econ. Consultant, De Chazal Du Mee & Co. 1980–82; Transport Economist, Air Mauritius 1982–87, Dir of Planning 1987–90; Gen. Man., Planning and Devt, Rogers & Co. Ltd 1990–91; MP for Belle Rose/Quatre Bornes Constituency 1991–; Minister of Finance 1991–95, Deputy Prime Minister and Minister of Finance and Econ. Devt 2005–. *Address:* Government House, Ground Floor, Port Louis, Mauritius (office). *Telephone:* 201-2557 (office). *Fax:* 208-9823 (office). *E-mail:* rsithanen@mail.gov.mu (office). *Website:* www.mof.gov.mu (office).

SITHOLE, Majozi; Swazi politician; *Minister of Finance; Career:* Minister, Econ. Planning and Devt 1999–2001; Minister Finance 2001–; mem. House of Ass. *Address:* Ministry of Finance, POB 443, Mbabane, Swaziland (office). *Telephone:* 4048148 (office). *Fax:* 4043187 (office). *E-mail:* minfin@realnet.co.sz (office).

SITRUK, Joseph; French rabbi; *Chief Rabbi of France;* b. 16 Oct. 1944, Tunis; m. Danielle Azoulay 1965; nine c. *Education:* Seminary rue Vauquelin, Paris. *Career:* Asst to Rabbi Max Warsharski, Lower Rhine region 1970–75; Rabbi, Marseilles 1975–87; Chief Rabbi of France 1987–; mem. Nat. Cttee of Human Rights; Pres. Conf. of European Rabbis 2000–; Chevalier, Ordre Nat. du Mérite, Officier, Légion d'honneur 2001, Commdr Ordre Nat. du Mérite 2003, Légion d'honneur 2007. *Publications:* Chemin faisant 1999, Dix Commandements 2000, Rien ne vaut la vie 2006. *Address:* Consistoire Central Union des Communautés Juives de France, 19 rue Saint Georges, 75009 Paris, France. *Telephone:* 1-49-70-88-00. *Fax:* 1-40-16-06-11. *E-mail:* spgrf@free.fr.

SIWIEC, Marek Maciej; Polish politician and journalist; b. 13 March 1955, Piekary Śląskie; m.; one s. one d. *Education:* Acad. of Mining and Metallurgy, Kraków. *Career:* Asst Acad. of Mining and Metallurgy, Kraków 1980–82; trainee Gas and Fuel Corpn of Victoria, Australia 1981–82; Ed.-in-Chief 'Student' (weekly) 1985–87, ITD (weekly) 1987–90, Trybuna (daily) 1990–91; Deputy to Sejm (Parl.) 1991–97; mem. Nat. Broadcasting Council 1993–96; Sec. of State in Chancellery of Pres. of Poland 1996–2004, Head Nat. Security Bureau, Nat. Security Adviser to the Pres. of Poland 1997–2004; mem. European Parl. 2004–; mem. Polish del. to Parl. Ass., Council of Europe; mem. Polish United Workers' Party (PZPR); mem. Social Democracy of Polish Repub. 1990–93, presidium of Head Council 1991–93. *Address:* ASP 126305, 60 rue Wiertz, 1097 Brussels, Poland (office). *Telephone:* (2) 284-76-53 (office). *Fax:* (2)284-36-53 (office). *E-mail:* msiwiec@europarl.eu.int (office). *Website:* www.mareksiwiec.pl (office).

SJAASTAD, Anders Christian, PhD; Norwegian politician; *Senior Adviser, Norwegian Institute of International Affairs;* b. 21 Feb. 1942, Oslo; m. Torill Oftedal Sjaastad 1969 (died 2000); one d. *Education:* Univ. of Oslo. *Career:* Pres. Norwegian Students' Asscn, Univ. of Oslo 1967; Research Asst, Inst. of Political Science, Univ. of Oslo 1968–70; Research Assoc. Norwegian Inst. of Int. Affairs (NUPI) 1970–81, Dir of Information 1973–81, Dir European Studies 1998–2004, Sr Adviser 2004–; mem. Høyre (Conservative Party), Vice-Chair. Oslo Høyre 1977–88, Chair. 1996–2000; mem. Storting (Parl.) 1981–2001; Minister of Defence 1981–86; Pres. European Movt in Norway 1989–92; Chair. Defence and Security Cttee (North Atlantic Ass.) 1994–97; Vice-Chair. Standing Cttee on Justice (Stortinget) 1993–97; mem. Norwegian Nat. Defence Comm. 1974–78, Norwegian Cttee on Arms Control and Disarmament 1976–81, 2002–06, N Atlantic Ass. 1989–97; proxy mem. Nobel Peace Prize Cttee 2004–06. *Publications:* Departmental Decision Making (co-author) 1972, Politikk og Sikkerhet i Norskehavsområdet (with J. K. Skogan) 1975, Norsk Utenrikspolitisk Arbok (ed.) 1975, Deterrence and Defence in the North (co-ed. and contrib.) 1985, Arms Control in a Multipolar World (contrib.) 1996, Maritime Security in Southeast Asia (contrib.) 2007. *Address:* NUPI – Norwegian Institute of International Affairs, C.J. Hambros plass 2D, PO Box 8159, Dep 0033, Oslo, Norway (office). *Telephone:* 22-99-40-00 (office). *Fax:* 22-36-21-82 (office). *E-mail:* internet@nupi.no (office). *Website:* www.nupi.no (office).

SKARD, Torild, BA, MEd; Norwegian academic, researcher and international organization official; *Senior Researcher, Norwegian Institute of International Relations (NUPI);* b. 29 Nov. 1936, Oslo; m. Kåre Øistein Hansen. *Education:* Univ. of Oslo. *Career:* psychologist 1965–67; Lecturer, Norwegian Post Grad. Teachers' Coll. for Special Educ. 1965–72, Inst.

for Social Sciences Univ. of Tromsø 1972–73; mem. Storting (Parl.), Pres. Lagting (Upper House) and Vice-Pres. Judiciary Cttee 1973–77; Sr Researcher, Work Research Insts, Oslo 1978–84; Dir, Co-ordinator programmes relating to the status of women, UNESCO, Paris 1984–86; Dir-Gen. Multilateral Dept for Devt Co-operation, Norwegian Ministry of Devt Co-operation/Ministry of Foreign Affairs 1986–91, Asst Sec.-Gen. 1991–94; UNICEF Regional Dir for W and Cen. Africa 1994–98; Norwegian Del. to UN Gen. Ass. 1974, UN Women's Conf. (Mexico) 1975, Int. Parl. Union, Canberra, ACT 1977; Leader Norwegian Nat. Comm. for UNESCO 1977–84, Vice-Pres. Del. to Gen. Confs 1978, 1980, 1982, 1983; Pres. UNICEF Exec. Bd 1988–89; Vice-Pres. Evaluation Supervisory Panel, UNAIDS 2000–01; Sr Adviser Ministry of Foreign Affairs 1999–2003; Sr Researcher, Norwegian Inst. of Int. Relations (NUPI), Oslo 2003–; Commdr, Ordre nat. du lion (Senegal) 1998. *Publications include:* titles in trans.: New Radicalism in Norway (ed.) 1967, Youth in Youth Clubs 1970, What is Happening in Primary Schools? 1971, Workshop for Self-Confidence – Clubs for Youth 1973, It is Oslo that is Remote: On Regional Policy in Norway 1974, Half of the Earth: Introduction to the Promotion of the Status of Women 1977, 'Women's Coup' in the Municipal Councils 1979, Elected to Parliament: A Study of Women's Progress and Men's Power 1980, Everyday Life in the Norwegian Parliament 1981, Unfinished Democracy: Women in Nordic Politics (co-ed.) 1983, Women in Power Spheres (article in International Social Science Journal, No. 4) 1983, From Harem to Equality: Women in Other Cultures 1984, You Have to Pay a Price to be a Tough Guy, Particularly if you are a Woman: Women Journalists in Norway 1984, Equality Between the Sexes: Myth or Reality in Norway? (co-author) 1984, Norwegian Municipal Councils – A Place for Women? (co-author) 1985, Continent of Mothers, Continent of Hope: Understanding and Promoting Development in Africa Today 2001. *Address:* NUPI, Postboks 8159 Dep., 0033 Oslo (office); Sandsveien, 3075 Berger i Vestfold, Norway (home). *Telephone:* 22994058 (office); 33775319 (home). *Fax:* 22362182 (office). *E-mail:* ts@nupi.no (office); toriskar@online.no (home). *Website:* www.nupi.no (office).

ŠĶĒLE, Andris; Latvian politician; *Chairman, Tautas Partija (People's Party);* b. 16 Jan. 1958, Aluksne District; m. Dzintra Skele; two c. *Education:* Latvian Acad. of Agric. *Career:* Head of Sector, Sr research Asst, Deputy Dir Research Assoc. Inst. of Latvian Agricultural Mechanization and Electrification 1981–90; First Deputy Minister of Agric. 1990–93; Prime Minister of Latvia 1995–97, 1999–2000; Founder and Chair. Tautas Partija (People's Party) 1998–; mem. Saeima (Parl.) 1998–; mem. several Parl. Comms; Chair. several bds of holding cos. *Address:* Tautas Partija, Dzir navu iela 68, Rīga, Latvia (office). *Telephone:* 6728-6441 (office). *Fax:* 6728-6405 (office). *E-mail:* koord1@tautas.lv (office). *Website:* www.tautaspartija.lv (office).

SKELEMANI, Phandu; Botswana lawyer and politician; *Minister of Foreign Affairs and International Co-operation; Career:* mem. Parl. for Francistown East, mem. Botswana Democratic Party (BDP) (Domkrag); fmr Attorney-Gen.; Minister of Presidential Affairs and Public Admin. 2004–07, of Justice, Defence and Security 2007–08, of Foreign Affairs and Int. Co-operation 2008–. *Address:* Ministry of Foreign Affairs and International Co-operation, Private Bag 00368, Gaborone, Botswana (office). *Telephone:* 3600700 (office). *Fax:* 3913366 (office). *E-mail:* csmaribe@gov.bw (office). *Website:* www.gov.bw/government/ministry_of_foreign_affairs.html (office).

SKERRIT, Roosevelt, BA; Dominican politician; *Prime Minister, Minister of Finance, Planning, Foreign Affairs and Social Security;* b. 1972. *Education:* Univ. of Mississippi, USA, New Mexico State Univ. *Career:* fmr high school teacher; Lecturer, Dominica Community Coll. –1999; mem. Dominica Labour Party; mem. House of Ass. 2000–; Minister of Educ., Sports and Youth Affairs –2004; Prime Minister of Dominica, Minister of Finance and Planning 2004–, also of Social Security and Foreign Affairs 2007–. *Address:* Office of the Prime Minister, Government Headquarters, Kennedy Avenue, Roseau, Dominica (office). *Telephone:* 4482401 (office). *Fax:* 4485200 (office).

SKIDELSKY, Baron (Life Peer), cr. 1991, of Tilton in the County of East Sussex; **Robert Jacob Alexander Skidelsky,** MA, DPhil, FBA, FRHistS, FRSL; British professor of political economy; *Professor of Political Economy, University of Warwick;* b. 25 April 1939; m. Augusta Hope 1970; two s. one d. *Education:* Brighton Coll. and Jesus Coll., Oxford. *Career:* Research Fellow, Nuffield Coll. Oxford 1965; Assoc. Prof. Johns Hopkins Univ., USA 1970; Prof. of Political Economy Univ. of Warwick 1990–; Chair. Social Market Foundation 1991–2001; Chair. Hands Off Reading Campaign 1994–97; Conservative Front Bench Spokesman on Culture, Media and Sport 1997–98, on Treasury Affairs 1998–99; mem. Lord

Chancellor's Advisory Council on Public Records 1988–93; mem. Schools Examination and Assessment Council 1992–93; mem. Bd Manhattan Inst. 1994–, Moscow School of Political Studies 1999–, Janus Capital Group Inc. 2001–; mem. House of Lords Select Cttee on Econ. Affairs 2003–; Gov. Brighton Coll. 1998–; Chair. Wilton Park Academic Council 2004–; Hon. DLitt (Buckingham) 1997; Wolfson History Prize 1993, Duff Cooper Prize 2000, Lionel Gelber Prize 2001, Council on Foreign Relations Prize 2002, James Tait Black Memorial Prize 2002. *Publications:* Politicians and the Slump 1967, English Progressive Schools 1970, Oswald Mosley 1975, John Maynard Keynes, Vol. 1 1983, Vol. 2 1992, Vol. 3 2000, (single-vol. abridgement) 2003, Interests and Obsessions 1993, The World After Communism 1995, Beyond the Welfare State 1997, The Politics of Economic Reform 1998.
Address: Tilton House, Firle, East Sussex, BN8 6LL, England. *Telephone:* (20) 7219-8721 (office); (1323) 811570. *Fax:* (1323) 811017. *E-mail:* skidelskyr@parliament.uk (home).

SKINGLE, Diana; British diplomatist (retd); b. 3 May 1947; partner Christopher Carrington. *Career:* joined FCO 1966, India Office 1966–68, Personnel Man. Dept 1968–70, Archivist, Kampala 1970–72, West African Dept, FCO 1972–73, Energy, Science and Aid Dept 1973–74, Archivist, Abidjan 1974–75, Archivist, Vila 1975–77, Admin Office, Prague 1977–79, Vice-Consul, Casablanca 1979–82, Personnel Policy Unit, FCO 1982–85, Second Sec. (Commercial and Aid), Georgetown 1985–86, Second Sec. (Devt), Bridgetown 1986–88, First Sec. (Information and Man.), UK Del. to NATO, Brussels 1988–93, Commonwealth Co-ordination Dept, FCO 1993, Western European Dept 1993–96, Personnel Policy Unit 1996–97, Personnel Man. Dept 1997–2000, Deputy Head of Mission, Addis Adaba 2001–04, High Commr to the Seychelles 2004–07 (retd).
Address: c/o Foreign and Commonwealth Office, King Charles Street, London, SW1A 2AH, England. *Telephone:* (20) 7008-1500.

SKINNER-KLÉE ARENALES, Jorge, BA, LLM; Guatemalan lawyer and diplomatist; b. 1957, Guatemala City; m.; five c. *Education:* Columbia Coll., NY, Rafael Landívar Univ., Columbia Univ. School of Law, Johns Hopkins School of Advanced Int. Studies, Washington DC. *Career:* Clerk, Skinner-Klée & Ruiz Law Office 1977–78; Court Clerk, Sec. of 1st Traffic Court, Chief Clerk of Supreme Court, Guatemalan Judiciary 1980–84; Legal Advisor, Bufete Popular (Public Defenders' Office), Rafael Landivar Univ. 1981–83; Prof. of Pvt. and Public Int. Law, Rafael Landivar Univ. 1988–92; Prof. of Int. Relations, Francisco Marroquin Univ. 2003; Minister Counsellor and Alternate Del. of Guatemala to OAS 1985–86; Deputy Chief of Mission, Embassy in Washington, DC 1987–88; Del. to Gen. Ass. of UN and OAS 1985–90; Amb. and Adviser to Minister for Foreign Affairs, Consulting Advocate to Dept of Legal Affairs and Treaties 1989–93; Int. Counsel and Alternate Del., Int. Coffee Org. 1990–93; Amb. to Germany 1993–98, to Canada 1998–2002, to Belize 2002–03, to Honduras 2003–04; Vice Minister of Foreign Relations 2004; Perm. Rep. to UN, New York 2004–08; fmr Legal Adviser, Licorera Centroamericana SA, Melazas de Secuintla SA; Great Merit Cross (Germany), Civil Merit (Chile); scholarship, Columbia Univ. School of Law. *Publications:* Habeas Corpus as a Guarantee of Effectiveness 1984, Peaceful Settlement of Disputes and the Contadora Process 1984, The Dichotomy between Human Rights and Economic Development: A Case Study in Guatemala 1985; drafted Bill of Diplomatic Service of the Repub. 1989; drafted Bill on Regime for Intellectual and Industrial Property, provision of legal advice to Agency for Int. Devt (AID) 1992, Regulations for the Consular Service of the Repub. of Guatemala (ed.) 1992.
Address: c/o Ministry of Foreign Affairs, 2a Avda La Reforma 4-47, Zona 10, Guatemala City, Guatemala (office).

SKJALDARSON, Stefán; Icelandic diplomatist; *Ambassador to Norway;* b. 10 Feb. 1955; m. Birgit Nyborg; two s. *Education:* Univ. of Oslo. *Career:* Man., Skjöldólfsstair School, Jökuldalur 1974–75; Adviser, Treasury Dept 1987; Sr Adviser, forsvarsavdelingen, Ministry of Foreign Affairs 1992–93; Sr Adviser Admin Dept 1993–94, Amb. Political Dept 1994–95; at Embassy in Oslo 1995–98, Minister 1998–99; Dir Admin. Dept, Ministry of Foreign Affairs 1999–2001, Dir Political Dept 2001–03; Amb. to Norway (also accred to Iran, Kuwait, Cyprus and Macedonia) 2003–.
Address: Embassy of Iceland, Stortingsgt 30, 0244 Oslo, Norway (office). *Telephone:* 23-23-75-30 (office). *Fax:* 22-83-07-04 (office). *E-mail:* emb .oslo@mfa.is (office). *Website:* www.island.no (office).

SKODON, Emil, BA, MBA; American diplomatist; b. 25 Nov. 1953, Chicago, Ill.; m.; two d. *Education:* Univ. of Chicago and Foreign Service Inst. *Career:* career mem. Sr Foreign Service with rank of Minister-Counselor, served in Embassy in Bridgetown, Barbados 1977–78, State Dept Office of Southern African Affairs 1982–84, assigned to econ. sections of embassies in East Berlin 1979–81, Vienna 1984–88, Counselor for Econ. Affairs, Embassy in Kuwait 1989–91, Acting Deputy Chief of Mission, Embassy in Baghdad 1990, US Consul-Gen., Perth 1991–95, Deputy Chief of Mission, Embassy in Singapore 1995–98, Dir State Dept Office of Australian, New Zealand, and Pacific Island Affairs 1998–2000, Foreign Policy Advisor to USAF Chief of Staff 2000–02, Deputy Chief of Mission, Embassy in Rome 2002–05, Amb. to Brunei 2005–08; mem. Nat. Trust for Historic Preservation; several State Dept Superior Honor and Meritorious Honor awards, US Army Outstanding Civilian Service Medal, USAF Decoration for Exceptional Civilian Service.
Address: US Department of State, 2201 C Street NW, Washington, DC 20520, USA (office). *Telephone:* (202) 647-4000 (office). *Fax:* (202) 647-6738 (office). *Website:* www.state.gov (office).

SKOL, Michael, BA; American diplomatist and business executive; *President, Skol and Associates, Inc.;* b. 15 Oct. 1942, Chicago, Ill.; m. Claudia Serwer 1973. *Education:* Yale Univ. *Career:* joined US Foreign Service 1965; served in Buenos Aires, Saigon, Santo Domingo, Naples, Rome, San José and Bogotá (Deputy Chief of Mission) and as Desk Officer for Costa Rica, Paraguay and Uruguay; Deputy Dir for Policy Planning and Dir Andean Affairs, State Dept Bureau of Inter-American Affairs; Deputy Asst Sec. of State for S America, 1988–90; Amb. to Venezuela 1990–93; Prin. Deputy Asst Sec. Latin American/Caribbean Dept of State 1993–95; Founding Chair. US-Colombia Business Partnership 1996–99; Sr Vice-Pres. Diplomatic Resolutions Inc., Washington, DC 1996–97; founder and Pres. Skol and Assocs, Inc., Washington DC 1998–; Sr Man. Dir for Latin America, DSFX, Washington DC 1998–2005; Founder and Pres. Skol, Ospina & Serna LLC, Bogotá, Colombia 2000–03; Sr Assoc. Manchester Trade Ltd; Prin., Skol and Serna, Washington, DC and Bogota 2003–; mem. Council on Foreign Relations; Order of the Liberator (Venezuela) 1993, Order of Nat. Merit (Paraguay) 1995. *Television includes:* co-creator and first co-host 'Choque de Opiniones', CNN Spanish TV network 1997.
Address: Skol and Associates, Inc., 1710 Rhode Island Avenue, NW, Suite 300, Washington, DC 20036 (office); PO Box 596, Dennis, MA 02638, USA (home). *Telephone:* (202) 331-9464 (office). *Fax:* (202) 785-0376 (office). *E-mail:* mikeskol@aol.com (office). *Website:* ssadvisors.net (office).

SKOTNIKOV, Leonid Alekseyevich; Russian diplomatist and judge; *Judge, International Court of Justice;* b. 26 March 1951, Kalinin; m.; one s. *Education:* Moscow State Inst. of Int. Relations. *Career:* mem. staff, Consular Dept Ministry of Foreign Affairs 1974–77; attaché, Perm. Mission to the UN 1977–81; mem. staff, Legal Dept, Ministry of Foreign Affairs 1981–91, Dir 1991–92, 1998–2001; Amb. to the Netherlands 1992–98; Amb. and Perm. Rep. to UN Office and other Int. Orgs in Geneva, the Disarmament Conf. 2001–05; Judge, Int. Court of Justice 2006–; Order of Friendship 2002.
Address: International Court of Justice, Peace Palace, 2517 KJ The Hague, Netherlands (office). *Telephone:* (70) 3022323 (office). *Fax:* (70) 3649928 (office). *Website:* www.icj-cij.org (office).

SKOURIS, Vassilios; Greek judge; *President, Court of Justice of the European Communities;* b. 1948. *Education:* Free Univ., Berlin, Hamburg Univ., Germany. *Career:* Asst Prof. Hamburg Univ. 1972–77; Prof. of Public Law, Bielefeld Univ. 1978, Univ. of Thessaloniki 1982; Minister of Internal Affairs 1989, 1996; Judge, Court of Justice of the European Communities 1999–, Pres. 2003–; Dir Centre for Int. and European Econ. Law, Thessaloniki 1997–; mem. Acad. Council, Acad. of European Law, Trier 1995–; mem. Greek Nat. Research Cttee 1993–95, Scientific Cttee, Ministry of Foreign Affairs 1997–99; mem. Admin. Bd, Univ. of Crete 1983–87, Higher Selection Bd for Greek Civil Servants 1994–96, Admin. Bd, Greek Nat. Judge's Coll 1995–96; Pres. Greek Asscn for European Law 1992–94, Greek Econ. and Social Council 1998.
Address: Court of Justice of the European Communities, Palais de la Cour de Justice, blvd Konrad Adenauer, 2925 Luxembourg (office). *Telephone:* 4303-1 (office). *Fax:* 4303-2600 (office). *E-mail:* info@curia.eu.int (office). *Website:* www.curia.eu.int/en/index.htm (office).

SKUBISZEWSKI, Krzysztof Jan, DrIur, LLM; Polish politician and lawyer; *President, Iran–US Claims Tribunal;* b. 8 Oct. 1926, Poznań. *Education:* Poznań Univ., Université de Nancy, France and Harvard Univ., USA. *Career:* mem. staff, Poznań Univ. (renamed Adam Mickiewicz Univ.) 1948–73, Voluntary Asst, Jr Asst, Lecturer 1948–56, Asst Prof. 1956–61, Dozent, Dept of Int. Law 1961–73, Pro-Dean Law Faculty 1961–63; Prof., Inst. of State and Law, Polish Acad. of Sciences, Warsaw 1973–96; Minister of Foreign Affairs 1989–93; Pres. Iran–US Claims Tribunal, The Hague 1994–; Judge ad hoc, Int. Court of Justice 1994–; mem. Curatorium, Hague Acad. of Int. Law 1994–, Bureau, Court of Conciliation and Arbitration, OSCE, Geneva 1995–2000; Chair., Council for Foreign Policy 1996–, Dutch–French Arbitration Tribunal 2000–; Pres. Tribunal of Arbitration in Application of the Convention of December 3, 1976 on the Protection of the Rhine against Pollution by Chlorides, Perm. Court of Arbitration 2001–04; Visiting Scholar, School of Int. Affairs, Columbia Univ., New

York 1963–64, Prof. invité, Geneva Univ. 1971, 1979; Visiting Fellow, All Souls Coll. Oxford 1971–72; Curator, Student Asscn of UN Friends, Poznań 1960–73; mem. Poznań Friends of Learning Soc. 1951–, West Inst. in Poznań 1961–, Inst. de Droit Int. 1971–, Polish Group of Int. Law Asscn 1971–, American Soc. of Int. Law, Oxford Soc., Soc. Française pour le Droit Int.; mem. Legal Sciences Cttee, Polish Acad. of Sciences 1981–, Advisory Bd European Journal of Law Reform; Corresp. mem. Polish Acad. of Sciences, Warsaw 1989–, Inst. de France 1995–; mem. Polish Acad. of Arts and Sciences, Kraków 1994–; mem. Primatial Social Council 1981–84, Consultative Council attached to Chair. of Council of State 1986–89; Hon. Prof. (Bucharest); Hon. Bencher, Gray's Inn 1990; Grand Cross of Polonia Restituta; Order of the White Eagle; Grand Officier, Légion d'honneur and other decorations; Dr hc (Ghent, Turin, Liège, Mainz, Geneva, Warsaw); Alexander von Humboldt Foundation Award 1984, R. Schuman Gold Medal 2000. *Publications:* Pieniądz na terytorium okupowanym 1960, Uchwały prawotwórcze organizacji międzynarodowych 1965, Zachodnia granica Polski 1969, Individual Rights and the State in Foreign Affairs (co-author) 1977, Resolutions of the General Assembly of the United Nations 1985, Polityka zagraniczna i odzyskanie niepodległości 1997; over 110 articles on int. law and int. relations.
Address: Iran–United States Claims Tribunal, Parkweg 13, 2585 JH The Hague (office); Parkweg, 3B, 2585 JG The Hague, Netherlands (home). *Telephone:* (70) 3520064 (office); (70) 3585195 (home). *Fax:* (70) 3502456 (office). *E-mail:* milas@iusct.nl.

SKUJA, Edgars; Latvian diplomatist; *Under-Secretary of State, Ministry of Foreign Affairs; Career:* fmr Dir Second Political Dept, Ministry of Foreign Affairs; Head of Mission, Latvian Del. to OSCE, Vienna 1992, 1999; Third Sec., Ministry of Foreign Affairs 1994; Amb. to Estonia 2003–05; Under-Sec. of State for Bilateral Relations, Ministry of Foreign Affairs 2005–; 1st Class Order of the Cross of Terra Mariana; Medal of the Baltic Ass. 2007. *Address:* Ministry of Foreign Affairs, Brīvības bulv. 36, Rīga 1395, Latvia (office). *Telephone:* 6701-6201 (office). *Fax:* 6782-8121 (office). *E-mail:* mfa .cha@mfa.gov.lv (office). *Website:* www.mfa.gov.lv (home).

SLADE, Tuiloma Neroni, LLB; Samoan diplomatist, judge and lawyer; b. 8 April 1941; m.; one d. *Education:* Hague Acad. of Int. Law. *Career:* qualified as solicitor and barrister, law practice Wellington, NZ 1967–68, legal counsel Office of Attorney-Gen., Wellington 1969–73, Parl. Counsel 1973–75; Attorney-Gen. of Western Samoa 1976–82, also Chief Justice for periods between 1980–82; Asst Dir Legal Div. Commonwealth Secr., London 1983–93; fmr Amb. to USA; Perm. Rep. to the UN 1993–2003; Head Del. UN Conf. on the Law of the Sea 1973–76; Judge, Int. Criminal Court 2003–06; Chair. first S Pacific Law Conf. 1986; legal consultant S Pacific Forum Fisheries Agency 1989; UNITAR Fellowship Hague Acad. of Int. Law and UN Legal Office. *Address:* c/o International Criminal Court, Maanweg 174, 2516 AB, The Hague, The Netherlands (office).

SLAKTERIS, Atis; Latvian agricultural engineer and politician; *Minister of Finance;* b. 21 Nov. 1956, Code Pagasts, Bauska Dist; m.; two c. *Education:* Latvian Acad. of Agric., Univ. of Minnesota, USA. *Career:* began career as mechanic, later Chief Engineer Code Co. 1980–89; First Deputy Man. Bauskas Lauktehnika (state-owned co.) 1989–90; Chief Engineer, Bauska Agric. Dept 1990–94, Head, Agric. Consultation Bureau 1994–96; Minister of State for Cooperation, Ministry of Agric. 1996–97; mem. 7th Saeima 1998–2002, serving as Chair. Cttee on Economy, Agricultural Environment and Regional Policies 1998–99, Chair. Cttee on Privatisation 1999–2000; Parl. Sec., Ministry of Agric. 2000, Minister for Agric. 2000–02; Chair. People's Party 2002–; Minister of Defence 2004, 2006–07, of Finance 2007–. *Address:* Ministry of Finance, Smilšu iela 1, Rīga 1919, Latvia (office). *Telephone:* 6709-405 (office). *Fax:* 6709-503 (office). *E-mail:* info@fm.gov .lv (office). *Website:* www.fm.gov.lv (office).

SLAUGHTER, Anne-Marie, AB, JD, DPhil; American lawyer and professor of international relations; *Bert G. Kerstetter '66 University Professor of Politics and International Affairs and Dean, Woodrow Wilson School of Public and International Affairs, Princeton University;* m. Andrew Moravcsik; two s. *Education:* Princeton Univ., Harvard Law School, Univ. of Oxford, UK,. *Career:* Summer Intern, Senate Foreign Relations Cttee, Washington, DC 1979; Summer Assoc. Bingham, Dana & Gould, Boston, Mass 1983, Thacher & Bartlett, New York 1984; Legal Asst to Prof. Abram Chayes 1984–88, to Prof. Hal S. Scott 1986–87; Ford Fellow in European Security and Western Security, Center for Int. Affairs, Harvard Univ. 1985–86, Fellow in Int. Law, Harvard Law School 1988–89, Visiting Prof. of Law 1993, Dir Grad. and Int. Legal Studies 1994–2002; Asst Prof. of Law and Int. Relations, Univ. of Chicago Law School 1989–93, Prof. 1993–94; Prof., John F. Kennedy School of Govt, Harvard Univ. and J. Sinclair Prof. of Int., Foreign and Comparative Law, Harvard

Law School 1994–2002; Allen Chair Prof., T.C. Williams School of Law, Univ. of Richmond 1994; Dean Woodrow Wilson School of Public and Int. Affairs, Princeton Univ. 2002–, Bert G. Kerstetter '66 Univ. Prof. of Politics and Int. Affairs, Princeton Univ. 2004–; Founder and Faculty Dir, Princeton Colloquium on Int. Affairs; Guest Lecturer, Nordic Acad. of Int. Law 2000, Hague Acad. of Int. Law 2000; Pres. American Soc. of Int. Law 2002–04, also Co-Chair. Research Cttee; mem. Int. Law Asscn, Council on Foreign Relations (also mem. Task Force on Expansion of NATO); mem. Cttee on Int. Security Studies, American Acad. of Arts and Sciences, Exec. Cttee, Chicago Cttee on Foreign Relations; mem. Bd of Eds Int. Org. 1995–2002, American Journal of Int. Law 1994–2003, Advisory Bd UCLA Journal of International Law and Foreign Affairs, Bd of Advisers Virginia Journal of International Law, Columbia Journal of European Law, Editorial Advisory Bd Texas International Law Journal; Trustee World Peace Foundation; contribs to The New York Times, Washington Post, Int. Herald Tribune; Women in Foreign Policy Honoree 2005; Woodrow Wilson School R.W. van de Velde Award 1979, Princeton Univ. Daniel M. Sachs Memorial Scholarship 1980, Russell Baker Scholarship, Univ. of Chicago Law School 1990. *Publications:* articles include: The Alien Tort Statute and Judiciary Act of 1789: A Badge of Honor (Francis Deak Prize, American Journal of Int. Law 1990) 1990, International Law and International Relations Theory: A Dual Agenda (co-author, Francis Deak Prize, American Journal of Int. Law 1994) 1994; books include: International Law and International Relations Theory: Millennial Lectures 2000, A New World Order: Government Networks and the Disaggregated State, A Liberal Theory of International Law.
Address: Woodrow Wilson School of Public and International Affairs, 424 Robertson Hall, Princeton University, Princeton, NJ 08544-1013, USA (home). *Telephone:* (609) 258-4800 (office). *Fax:* (609) 258-1418 (office). *E-mail:* slaughtr@princeton.edu (office). *Website:* www.wws.princeton.edu (office).

SLAVESKI, Trajko, PhD; Macedonian politician and academic; *Minister of Finance;* b. 1960, Ohrid; m.; two c. *Education:* SS Cyril and Methodius Univ., Skopje, State Univ. of Calif. and Harvard Univ., USA. *Career:* Prof., Econs Faculty, SS Cyril and Methodius Univ., Skopje; Visiting Prof., Arizona State Univ. 1997, Nat. and Capodistrian Univ., Athens 1999–; Minister of Devt 1999–2000; Adviser to Minister of Finance and Nat. Co-ordinator for Poverty Reduction Strategy 2000–02; mem. Parl. 2006–; Minister of Finance 2006–; mem. Exec. Cttee Internal Macedonian Revolutionary Organization—Democratic Party for Macedonian National Unity (VMRO—DPMNE) 2003–, Vice-Pres. 2005–.
Address: Ministry of Finance, 1000 Skopje, Dame Gruev 14, Former Yugoslav Republic of Macedonia (office). *Telephone:* (2) 3117288 (office). *Fax:* (2) 3117280 (office). *E-mail:* finance@finance.gov.mk (office). *Website:* www.finance.gov.mk (office).

SLINN, David Arthur, OBE, BA; British diplomatist; b. 16 April 1959. *Education:* Univ. of Salford. *Career:* fmr Head of British Office, Pristina, then re-assigned to Belgrade, later to Embassy in Skopje –2002; Amb. to Democratic People's Repub. of Korea 2002–06; Special Envoy to Helmand Prov. 2007–.
Address: c/o British Embassy 15th Street, Roundabout Wazir Akbar Khan, POB 334, Kabul, Afghanistan (office). *Telephone:* (70) 102000 (office). *Fax:* (70) 102250 (office). *E-mail:* britishembassy.kabul@fco.gov.uk (office). *Website:* www.britishembassy.gov.uk/afghanistan (office).

SLOBODNÍK, Igor, MA; Slovak diplomatist and fmr journalist; b. 23 Oct. 1962; m.; two s. *Education:* Comenius Univ., Bratislava. *Career:* began career with Czechoslovak Press Agency 1985–87; mil. service 1986–87; Ed. Výber (weekly newspaper) 1987–91, Ed.-in-Chief 1991–92; Pvt. Sec. to Minister of Foreign Affairs 1992; Chargé d'Affaires, Embassy in Copenhagen, Denmark 1996–97; Amb. to Court of St James (UK) 1997–2000; Chief Negotiator, EU Dept, Ministry of Foreign Affairs 2000–01; Dir Gen. Defence Policy and Int. Relations 2001–03; Amb. and Perm. Rep. to NATO 2003–08; Advisor to Minister of Foreign Affairs 2008–.
Address: Ministry of Foreign Affairs, Hlboká cesta 2, 833 36 Bratislava, Slovakia (office). *Telephone:* (2) 5978-1111 (office). *Fax:* (2) 5978-2213 (office). *E-mail:* informacie@foreign.gov.sk (office). *Website:* www.mzv.sk (office).

SLUTZ, Pamela Jo H., BA, MA; American diplomatist; *Deputy Chief of Mission, Nairobi, Kenya;* m.; two s. *Education:* Hollins Univ. and Univ. of Hawaii. *Career:* joined State Dept 1981, Office of Korea Affairs, Bureau of East Asian and Pacific Affairs 1981–82, overseas assignment in Kinshasa 1982–84, commissioned as a Foreign Service Officer 1984, overseas assignment in Jakarta 1984–87, 1999–2001, mem. US Del. to Nuclear and Space Talks with USSR, Geneva 1987–89, overseas assignment in Shanghai 1991–94, with Office of China and Mongolia Affairs, Bureau of

East Asian and Pacific Affairs 1995–97, Office of East Asian and Pacific Regional Security and Policy Planning 1997–99, overseas assignment in American Inst., Taiwan 2001–03, Amb. to Mongolia 2003–06; Deputy Chief of Mission, Embassy in Nairobi, Kenya 2006–fmr East-West Center Fellow, Univ. of Hawaii.
Address: American Embassy, United Nations Avenue, POB 606, Village Market, 00621 Nairobi, Kenya (office). *Telephone:* (20) 3636000 (office). *Fax:* (20) 537810 (office). *E-mail:* ircnairobi@state.gov (office). *Website:* nairobi.usembassy.gov (office).

SMBATYAN, Armen B.; Armenian diplomatist and musician; *Ambassador to Russian Federation;* b. 1954, Yerevan. *Education:* Yerevan State Conservatoire. *Career:* pianist and composer; Rector Yerevan State Conservatoire 1995, 1998–2002; Minister of Culture, Youth Affairs and Sport 1996–98; Amb. to Russian Fed. 2002–.
Address: Embassy of Armenia, 101990 Moscow, Armyanskii per. 2, Russia (office). *Telephone:* (495) 624-12-69 (office). *Fax:* (495) 624-45-35 (office). *E-mail:* info@armen.ru (office). *Website:* www.armenianembassy.ru (office).

SMITH, Cornelius Alvin, MBA; Bahamian diplomatist; *Ambassador to USA and Permanent Representative, Organization of American States;* b. 7 April 1937, North End, Long Island; m. Clara Elizabeth Knowles; three c. *Education:* Bahamas Teachers' Training Coll., Nassau, Univ. of Miami, USA. *Career:* public school prin., Dept of Educ. 1956–64; Sr Revenue Officer, Customs Dept of Educ. 1964–67; Human Resource Specialist, Syntex Corpn 1967–82; Pres. and CEO Smith & Assocs (consultancy) 1982–92, 2002–; Founding mem. Free Nat. Movt (FNM); elected as Opposition MP for Marco City constituency 1982, (constituency name changed to Pine Ridge 1987), re-elected for four successive terms 1982–2002, Opposition spokesperson on Educ., Public Safety and Tourism 1982–92, mem. House Select Cttee on Illicit Drug Trafficking Within and Through The Bahamas and Constituency Boundaries Comm.; Minister of Educ. 1992–95, of Public Safety and Immigration 1995–97, of Tourism 1997–2000, of Transport and Local Govt 2000–02; election campaign co-ordinator for FNM in gen. elections 2007; Perm. Rep. to OAS, Washington, DC 2007– (Chair. Perm. Council Jan.–March 2008), Amb. to USA 2008–; fmr Chair. Bahamas Jaycees, Kiwanis Club of Lucaya, Grand Bahama Chamber of Commerce, Bahamas Asscn for Manpower Training and Devt; Rotary International Paul Harris Fellow.
Address: Embassy of the Bahamas, 2220 Massachusetts Avenue, NW, Washington, DC 20008, USA (office). *Telephone:* (202) 319-2660 (office). *Fax:* (202) 319-2668 (office). *E-mail:* bahemb@aol.com (office); jsears@mfabahamas.org (office); bahamas@oas.org (office).

SMITH, Elizabeth Jean, OBE, MA; British broadcasting executive and international official; *Secretary-General, Commonwealth Broadcasting Association;* b. 15 Aug. 1936, Ajmer, India; m. Geoffrey Smith 1960; one s. one d. *Education:* Univ. of Edinburgh. *Career:* Producer, Radio News, BBC 1960; Asst Head, Cen. Talks and Features, BBC World Service 1980, Head, Current Affairs 1984, Controller, English Programmes 1987–94; Sec.-Gen. Commonwealth Broadcasting Asscn 1994–; Fellow, Radio Acad. *Publication:* as Elizabeth Hay: Sambo Sahib.
Address: Commonwealth Broadcasting Association, 17 Fleet Street, London, EC4Y 1AA, England (office). *Telephone:* (20) 7583-5550 (office). *Fax:* (20) 7583-5549 (office). *E-mail:* elizabeth@cba.org.uk (office). *Website:* www.cba.org.uk (office).

SMITH, Hon. Godfrey, BL; Belizean politician and lawyer; *Minister of Tourism and National Emergency Management; Education:* Univ. of the W Indies. *Career:* Assoc. Attorney, Barrow & Williams, Belize City 1994–97; Sec-Gen. People's United Party, Belize City 1997–98, currently Deputy Leader; Chief of Staff Office of the Prime Minister 1998–99; Attorney-Gen. 1999–2006, concurrently Minister of Information, then Minister of Foreign Affairs and Co-operation –2006; Minister of Tourism, and Nat. Emergency Man. 2006–, of Information 2006–07; currently Lecturer, Univ. Coll. Belize. *Publications include:* Belize Law Report (ed.), Practical Guide to Gross Receipt Tax.
Address: NEMO Bldg, POB 174, Belmopan, Belize. *Telephone:* 822-2167 (office). *Fax:* 822-2854 (office). *E-mail:* belizemfa@btl.net (office). *Website:* www.mfa.gov.bz (office).

SMITH, Gordon Scott, PhD; Canadian diplomatist, academic and consultant; *Executive Director, Centre for Global Studies and Adjunct Professor of Political Science, University of Victoria;* b. 19 July 1941, Montreal, Que.; m. Lise G. Lacroix; three s. one d. *Education:* Lower Canada Coll. Montreal, McGill Univ., Univ. of Chicago and MIT. *Career:* joined Defence Research Bd 1966; transferred to Dept of External Affairs 1967; mem. Canadian Del. to NATO 1968–70; Special Adviser to Minister of Nat. Defence 1970–72; joined Privy Council Office 1972; Deputy Sec. to Cabinet (Plans) 1978–79;

Deputy Under-Sec. Dept of External Affairs 1979; Assoc. Sec. to Cabinet, Privy Council Office 1980–81; Sec. Ministry of State for Social Devt 1981–84; Assoc. Sec. to Cabinet and Deputy Clerk of Privy Council 1984; Deputy Minister for Political Affairs, Dept of External Affairs 1985; Amb. and Perm. Rep. of Canada to NATO 1985–90; Sec. to the Cabinet for Fed.-Provincial Relations, Govt of Canada 1990–91; Amb. to the EC 1991–94; Deputy Minister of Foreign Affairs 1994–97; Chair. Int. Devt Research Centre 1997–; Exec. Dir Centre for Global Studies and Adjunct Prof. of Political Science, Univ. of Vic. 1997–; Pres. Gordon Smith Int. *Publication:* Altered States.
Address: Centre for Global Studies, University of Victoria, POB 1700, STN CSC, Victoria, BC V8W 2Y2 (office); Office of the Chairman, International Development Research Centre, 250 Albert Street, POB 8500, Ottawa, Ont. K1P 6M1 (office); 2027 Runnymede Avenue, Victoria, BC V8S 2V5, Canada. *Telephone:* (250) 595-8622 (office); (613) 236-2381 (office). *Fax:* (250) 595-8682 (office); (613) 238-7230 (office). *E-mail:* gssmith@uvic.ca (office); info@idrc.ca (office). *Website:* www.globalcentres.org (office); www.idrc.ca (office).

SMITH, Jennifer M., DBE; Bermudian politician; *Deputy Speaker, House of Assembly;* b. 14 Oct. 1947. *Career:* began career as journalist; reporter, Bermuda Recorder 1970–74, Ed. 1974; on staff of Fame magazine, later Ed.; joined ZBM Radio and TV; art teacher at Sr Training School (attached to Bermuda Prison Service) for eight years; represented Bermuda as an artist at CARIFESTA in Jamaica; last exhbn in 1996; contested St George's N seat for Progressive Labour Party (PLP) in House of Ass. elections 1972, 1976, 1980; mem. Senate 1980–; Shadow Minister for Educ.; mem. House of Ass. (PLP) 1989, 1993, 1998–, Deputy Speaker 2003–; Leader of PLP 1996–; Prime Minister of Bermuda 1998–2003; fmr Exec. mem. Common-wealth Parl. Asscn; Hon. DHumLitt (Mount St Vincent, Morris Brown Coll., Art Inst. of Pittsburgh) Outstanding Woman in Journalism Award 1972 and several other awards. *Publications:* Voice of Change 2003.
Address: c/o The House of Assembly, 21 Parliament Street, Hamilton HM 12 (office); POB HM 2191, Hamilton HMHX, Bermuda (home). *Website:* voiceofchange.bm (home).

SMITH, Michael (Mike), BLL; Australian diplomatist; *Ambassador for Counter-Terrorism;* b. 1949, Adelaide; m.; two c. *Education:* Adelaide Univ. *Career:* numerous positions at Dept of Foreign Affairs and Trade including Head, Multilateral and Humanitarian Legal Section 1984–86, Counsellor, Australian Perm. Mission to UN, Geneva 1986–89, Ambassador to Algeria 1989–91, Legal Adviser and Asst Sec., Refugees, Immigration and Asylum 1991–93, Minister (Political), Embassy in Washington, DC 1993–95, Amb. to Egypt 1995–98, Chief of Staff, Office of Minister for Foreign Affairs 1998–2002, Perm. Rep. to UN, Geneva 2002–06, Amb. for Counter-Terrorism 2006–.
Address: Office of the Ambassador for Counter-Terrorism, Department of Foreign Affairs and Trade, R. G. Casey Bldg, John McEwan Crescent, Barton, ACT 0221, Australia (office). *Telephone:* (2) 6261-1111 (office). *Fax:* (2) 6261-3111 (office). *Website:* www.dfat.gov.au (office).

SMITH, Ransford, MA, MBA; Jamaican diplomatist and international organization official; *Deputy Secretary-General (Economic), Common-wealth;* b. 1949. *Career:* served in several sr posts in Jamaican Foreign Service, including posts in NY, Washington,m DC and Geneva; participated in WTO Uruguay Round of multilateral trade negotiations, late 1980s; Perm. Sec., Ministry of Industry and Investment and Ministry of Commerce and Tech. –1999; Perm. Rep. of Jamaica to UN, Geneva 1999–2005; Chair. WTO Cttee on Trade and Devt 2000–01, Common-wealth Group of Developing Countries, Geneva 2001–02; led Jamaican dels to int. confs, including the Doha Ministerial Conf. of WTO; Chief Negotiator and Spokesperson for the Group of 77 and China at UNCTAD XI 2004; Pres. Trade and Devt Bd, UNCTAD 2005–06; Deputy Sec.-Gen. (Econ.), Commonwealth 2006–; Commr, Order of Distinction (Jamaica) 2005. *Publications:* Developing Countries, the WTO and a New Round: A Perspective 2001.
Address: Commonwealth Secretariat, Marlborough House, Pall Mall, London, SW1Y 5HX, England (office). *Telephone:* (20) 7747-6500 (office). *Fax:* (20) 7930-0827 (office). *E-mail:* e.delbuey@commonwealth.int (office). *Website:* www.thecommonwealth.org (office).

SMITH, Simon John Meredith; British diplomatist; *Ambassador to Austria;* b. 14 Jan. 1958, Wegberg, Germany; m. Sian Stickings; two d. *Education:* Wadham Coll., Oxford. *Career:* with East African Dept, FCO 1986–87, Japanese language training 1988–89, Head of Nuclear Policy Section, Security Policy Dept 1992–94, speech writer to the Foreign Sec. 1994–95, Deputy Head of Southern European Dept 1995–97; Counsellor, Embassy in Moscow 1998–2002; Head of NE Asia and Pacific Dept, FCO 2002–04, Head of Eastern Dept 2004–05, Dir of Russia, S Caucasus and Cen. Asia

2005–07; Perm. Rep. to UN and Int. Orgs, Vienna Aug. 2007–, Amb. to Austria Oct. 2007–.
Address: British Embassy, Jauresgasse 12, 1030 Vienna, Austria (office). *Telephone:* (1) 716-13-2202 (office). *Fax:* (1) 716-13-2206 (office). *E-mail:* info@britishembassy.at (office). *Website:* www.britishembassy.at (office).

SMITH, Stephen Francis, LLM; Australian politician; *Minister for Foreign Affairs;* b. 12 Dec. 1955, Narrogin, WA. *Education:* Univ. of Western Australia, London Univ., UK. *Career:* solicitor, lecturer and tutor 1978–83; Prin. Pvt. Sec. to State Attorney-Gen., WA 1983–87; mem. Australian Labor Party Nat. Exec. 1987–90, Jr Vice-Pres. 1989–90; Adviser to Treas. P. J. Keating 1991, to Minister for Science and Tech. R. V. Free 1991, to Prime Minister P. J. Keating 1991–92; MP for Perth 1993–, Shadow Minister for Trade 1996–97, for Resources and Energy 1997–98, for Communications 1998–2001, for Health and Ageing 2001–04, for Industry, Infrastructure and Industrial Relations 2004–06, for Educ. and Training 2006–07, Minister for Foreign Affairs 2007–.
Address: Department of Foreign Affairs and Trade, R. G. Casey Building, John McEwen Crescent, Barton ACT 0221, Australia (office). *Telephone:* (2) 6261-1111 (office). *Fax:* (2) 6261-3111 (office). *Website:* www.dfat.gov .au (office).

SNEH, Brig.-Gen. Ephraim; Israeli politician, physician and army officer (retd); *Chairman, Subcommittee on Defence Planning and Policy, Knesset;* b. 1944, Tel-Aviv; m.; two c. *Education:* Tel-Aviv Univ. Medical School. *Career:* Research Fellow, Walter Reed Army Medical Center; rank of Brig.-Gen., army service includes Medical Officer of Paratroops Brigade 1972–74; Chief Medical Officer of the Paratroops and Infantry Corps 1974–78; Commdr of the Medical Teams during the Entebbe Rescue Operation 1976; Commdr Israel Defense Forces (IDF) elite unit 1978–80; Chief Medical Officer IDF Northern Command 1980–81; Commdr of Security Zone in S Lebanon 1981–82; Head of the Civil Admin. of the West Bank 1985–87; mem. Knesset (Parl.) 1992– (Labor Party); Minister of Health 1994, of Transportation 2001–04; Deputy Minister of Defence 1999–2001, 2006–07. *Publication:* Navigating Perilous Waters 2005.
Address: The Knesset, 2 Kaplan Street, Jerusalem 91950 (office); 12 Hapalmach Street, Herzelia 46793, Israel (home). *Telephone:* (2) 6408313 (office). *Fax:* (2) 6408908 (office). *E-mail:* esneh@netvision.net.il (home). *Website:* www.sneh.org.il.

SNOWER, Dennis J., PhD; American economist, academic and research institute director; *President, Kiel Institute of World Economics;* b. 14 Oct. 1950, Vienna, Austria; m.; two c. *Education:* Univs of Oxford, UK and Princeton, NJ. *Career:* fmr Asst Prof., Univ. of Maryland and Inst. of Advanced Studies, Vienna; Prof. of Econs, Birkbeck Coll., Univ. of London, UK 1989–2004; teacher, Kiel Inst. of World Econs, Germany, mem. Int. Research Network 2001–, Pres. Inst. 2004–, also Prof. of Econs, Univ. of Kiel 2004–; numerous posts as Visiting Prof., Univ. of Stockholm, Sweden, European Univ. Inst., Florence, Italy, Columbia Univ., New York, Dartmouth Coll., NH, Hebrew Univ. of Jerusalem and Univ. of Tel-Aviv, Israel, Inst. for Advanced Studies, Vienna; Program Dir, Centre for Econ. Policy Research, London and Inst. for the Study of Labor (IZA), Bonn, Germany; known internationally as a founder of insider-outsider theory of unemployment.
Address: Kiel Institute of World Economics (IfW), Dusternbrooker Weg 120, Kiel 24105, Germany (office). *Telephone:* (431) 88141 (office). *Fax:* (431) 8814501 (office). *E-mail:* president@ifw-kiel.de (office). *Website:* www.uni-kiel.de/ifw (office).

SNOY, Bernard, DIur, PhD; Belgian economist and international organization executive; *Co-ordinator of Economic and Environmental Activities, Organization for Security and Co-operation in Europe; Education:* Catholic Univ. of Louvain, Harvard Univ., USA. *Career:* worked for World Bank 1974–86, Exec. Dir representing Austria, Belgium, Luxembourg, Turkey and countries in transition (Belarus, Czech Repub., Hungary, Kazakhstan, Slovakia and Slovenia) 1991–94; Econ. Advisor, EC 1986–88; Chief of the Cabinet, Belgian Minister of Finance, Philippe Maystadt 1988–91; mem. Bd of Dirs EBRD, London, representing Belgium, Luxembourg and Slovenia 1994–2002; Dir Working Table II (Econ. Reconstruction, Devt and Co-operation), Stability Pact for South Eastern Europe 2002–05; Co-ordinator OSCE Econ. and Environmental Activities 2005–. *Publications include:* Taxes on Direct Investment Income in the E.E.C.: A Legal and Economic Analysis 1975, Fragility of the International Financial System: How Can We Prevent New Crises in Emerging Markets? (International Financial Relations) (co-author) 2002.
Address: Office of the Co-ordinator of OSCE Economic and Environmental Activities, Kärntner Ring 5–7, 1010 Vienna, Austria (office). *Telephone:* (1) 514-36-151 (office). *Fax:* (1) 514-36-96 (office). *E-mail:* info@osce.org (office). *Website:* www.osce.org/eea (office).

SNYDER, Jack, BA, PhD; American academic; *Robert and Renée Belfer Professor of International Relations, Columbia University; Education:* Harvard and Columbia Univs. *Career:* currently Robert and Renée Belfer Prof. of Int. Relations, Dept of Political Science and Inst. of War and Peace Studies, Columbia Univ., also Dir MA Int. Affairs Program; Ed. W.W. Norton book series on World Politics; Co-Ed. Perspectives on Politics, Princeton Univ. Press book series on Int. History and Politics; mem. Editorial Bd American Political Science Review, Governing Council American Political Science Asscn (APSA); Fellow, American Acad. of Arts and Sciences. *Publications:* The Ideology of the Offensive: Military Decision Making and the Disasters of 1914 1984, Myths of Empire: Domestic Politics and International Ambition 1991, Civil Wars, Insecurity and Intervention (co-Ed.) 1999, From Voting to Violence: Democratization and Nationalist Conflict 2000; numerous articles in professional journals on anarchy and culture, democratization and war, alliances and Russian foreign relations.
Address: Columbia University, Political Science Department, International Affairs Building, Floor 7, 420 West 118th Street, New York, NY 10027, USA (office). *Telephone:* (212) 854-8290 (office). *Fax:* (212) 222-0598 (office). *E-mail:* jls6@columbia.edu (office). *Website:* www.columbia.edu/ cu/polisci (office).

SOBIR, Hassan; Maldivian diplomatist; *High Commissioner to Singapore;* m. Aminath Nasheeda. *Career:* fmr Chair. Maldives Water and Sewerage Co.; fmr Minister of Fisheries and Agric., Minister of Tourism –2004; High Commr to UK (also accred as Amb. and Perm. Rep. to EU) 2004–07, Perm. Rep. to UN, Geneva 2006–07, High Commr to Singapore 2007–.
Address: Maldives High Commission, 101 Thomson Road, 30-01A, United Square, Singapore City 307591, Singapore (office). *Telephone:* 67209012 (office). *Fax:* 67209014 (office). *E-mail:* info@maldiveshighcommission.sg (office). *Website:* maldiveshighcommission.sg (office).

SOBORUN, Somduth, BComm; Mauritian educator and diplomatist; *Permanent Representative, United Nations;* b. 27 June 1951; m.; two c. *Education:* Univ. of Delhi, Inst. of Public Admin, Kuala Lumpur, Univ. of Malta. *Career:* teacher, Ministry of Educ. 1971–74, 1977–83; Instructor, School of Business Studies and Accounting, Seychelles Polytechnic 1984–88; Second Sec., Ministry of Foreign Affairs 1988–90; Acting High Commr, High Comm. in Islamabad 1990–92, First Sec. 1992–94; First Sec., Perm. Mission to UN, New York 1994–96, Chargé d'Affaires 1996; First Sec., Multilateral Econ. Directorate, Ministry of Foreign Affairs and Int. Trade 1996–1997, Deputy Chief of Protocol 1998; Deputy Chief of Mission, Embassy in Washington, DC 1999–2001, First Sec. 1999–2000, Chargé d'Affaires 1999–2001, Minister Counsellor 2000–01; Chair. COMESA Deputy Chief of Missions and Experts Group, Washington, DC 2000–2001; Minister Counsellor, Ministry of Foreign Affairs and Regional Cooperation 2002–2003, Head of Multilateral Econ. Directorate 2002–04; Amb. to Egypt 2004–06; Chair. SADC Amb. Group to Cairo 2004–06; Perm. Rep. to UN, New York 2006–; Pres. Triolet Cultural Circle 1970–74, Community School Grads and Diplomates Asscn 1979–84, Amicale Maurice-Seychelles 1984–85.
Address: Permanent Mission of Mauritius to the United Nations, 211 East 43rd Street, 15th Floor, New York, NY 10017, USA (office). *Telephone:* (212) 949-0190 (office). *Fax:* (212) 697-3829 (office). *E-mail:* mauritius@un .int (office). *Website:* www.un.int/mauritius (office).

SOBYANIN, Sergei Semenovich, PhD; Russian politician; *Deputy Chairman;* b. 21 June 1958, Nyaksumvol, Khanty-Mansii Autonomous Okrug; m.; two d. *Education:* Kostroma State Inst. of Tech. *Career:* metalworker and then foreman at Chelyabinsk Pipe Plant 1980–82; Head of Admin. Dept Leninsky Dist Komsomol org., Chelyabinsk 1982–84; party and admin. work in Khanty-Mansii Autonomous Dist, Tyumen Region 1984–90; Head of State Tax Inspection Office, Kogalym in Khanty-Mansii Autonomous Dist 1990–91; Mayor of Kogalym 1991–93; First Deputy Head Khanty-Mansii Autonomous Dist 1993–94; Chair. Khanty-Mansii Autonomous Dist Duma, mem. Fed. Council and Chair. Fed. Council Cttee on Constitutional Legislation and Judicial-Legal Matters 1994–2000; First Deputy to Presidential Plenipotentiary Envoy in Urals Fed. Dist 2000–01; Gov. of Tyumen Region 2001–05; Chief of Staff, Presidential Exec. Office 2005–08; Deputy Chairman of the Govt, in charge of co-ordinating fed. agencies 2008–; Chair. Bd of Dirs TVEL (state nuclear power co.) 2006–; Order of Merit, Medal For Services to the Fatherland, Second Degree, Ordre du Merite Agricole, France 2003.
Address: Office of the Government, 103274 Moscow, Krasnopresnenskaya nab. 2, Russia (office). *Telephone:* (495) 205-57-35 (office). *Fax:* (495) 205-42-19 (office). *Website:* www.government.ru (office).

SÓCRATES CARVALHO PINTO DE SOUSA, José; Portuguese politician; *Prime Minister;* b. 6 Sept. 1957, Vilar de Maçada; divorced; two c. *Career:* Chair. Castelo Branco Fed., Partido Socialista (Socialist Party)

1983–96, mem. Partido Socialista Secr. 1991–, Spokesperson on Environmental Affairs 1991–95, Sec.-Gen. 2004–; mem. Parl. 1987–95; mem. Covilha Municipal Ass. 1989–96; Deputy Minister to the Prime Minister 1995–99; Minister of Environmental Affairs 1999–2002; mem. Parl. Comm. on National Defence 2002–; Prime Minister of Portugal 2005–; Pres. World Conf. of Ministers Responsible for Youth 1998.
Address: Office of the Prime Minister, Presidency of the Council of Ministers, Rua da Imprensa á Estrela 4, 1200-888 Lisbon; Partido Socialista, Largo do Rato 2, 1269-143 Lisbon, Portugal (office). *Telephone:* (213) 923500 (office); (21) 3822000 (office). *Fax:* (21) 3822016 (office). *E-mail:* relacoes.publicas@pcm.gov.pt (office); info@ps.pt (office). *Website:* www.portugal.gov.pt (office); www.ps.pt (office).

SODERBERG, Nancy E., BA, MS; American academic, international organization official, fmr diplomatist and fmr government official; *Distinguished Visiting Scholar, Department of Political Science and Public Administration, University of North Florida;* b. 13 March 1958, San Turce, Puerto Rico. *Education:* Vanderbilt Univ., Georgetown Univ. School of Foreign Service. *Career:* budget and reports analyst, Bank of New England, Boston 1980–82; Research Asst Brookings Inst., Washington, DC 1982–83; Research Asst, US Agency for Int. Devt, Washington, DC 1983; Del. Selection Asst, Mondale-Ferraro Cttee, Washington, DC 1983, Foreign Policy Adviser 1984 (unsuccessful US presidential camgaign); Deputy Issues Dir, Foreign Policy, Dukakis for Pres. Cttee, Boston 1988; Foreign Policy Adviser to Senator Edward Kennedy, Washington, DC 1985–88, 1989–92; Foreign Policy Dir Clinton/Gore Transition, Little Rock 1992–93; Special Asst to Pres. for Nat. Security Affairs, Staff Dir Nat. Security Council, Washington, DC 1993–95, Deputy Asst to Pres. for Nat. Security Affairs 1995–2001; Alt. Rep. to UN with rank of Amb. 1997–2001; Vice-Pres. (Multilateral Affairs), Int. Crisis Group, New York 2001–05; Distinguished Visiting Scholar, Univ. of North Fla, Jacksonville 2006–; Adjunct Prof. Columbia Univ. School of Int. and Public Affairs 2004; foreign policy analyst for MSNBC; mem. Council for Foreign Relations; mem. Bd of Dirs Concern Worldwide; mem. Advisory Bd Nat. Cttee on American Foreign Policy, Tannenbaum Center; Pres. Sister Cities Program of the City of New York 2002–06. *Publications:* The Superpower Myth: The Use and Misuse of American Might 2005; numerous articles in professional journals.
Address: 121 Lantern Wick Place, Ponte Vedra Beach, FL 32082; University of North Florida, Department of Political Science and Public Administration, Jacksonville, FL 32224-2645, USA. *Telephone:* (904) 620-3926; (904) 620-1000 (office). *E-mail:* nsoderberg@aol.com; n00445553@unf.edu (office). *Website:* www.unf.edu/coas/polsci-pubadmin (office).

SOEHARTO (see **SUHARTO**).

SOHLMAN, Staffan A. R., BA; Swedish diplomatist and consultant; b. 21 Jan. 1937, Rome, Italy; m. Åsa Maria Carnerud 1961; one s. one d. *Education:* Sigtuna Humanistiska Laroverk, Washington and Lee Univ., Stockholm and Lund Univs. *Career:* Nat. Inst. for Econ. Research 1962–65; Ministry of Finance 1965–68; mem. Swedish Del. to OECD 1968–70; Ministry for Foreign Affairs, Dept for Devt Co-operation 1970–75, Head Multilateral Dept 1972, Project Leader Secr. for Futures Studies 1975–77, Head Transport Div. 1977–78; Deputy Dir-Gen. Nat. Bd of Trade 1978–84; Head Multilateral Dept of Ministry for Foreign Affairs Trade Dept 1984–88; Co-ordinator for Econ. Co-operation with Cen. and Eastern Europe, Ministry for Foreign Affairs 1989–90; Dir Cen. Bank 1989; Amb., Perm. Rep. Swedish Del. to OECD 1991–95, Acting Sec.-Gen. OECD Oct.–Nov. 1994; Chair OECD Steel Cttee 1986–88, OECD Liaison Cttee with Council of Europe 1992, OECD Council Working Party on Shipbuilding 1993–95, Wassenaar Arrangement on Export Control for Conventional Arms and Dual-Use Goods and Technologies 1996–99; Amb. and Insp. Gen. of Mil. Equipment, Ministry for Foreign Affairs 1995, Amb. and Insp. Gen., Head Nat. Inspectorate of Strategic Products 1996; Amb. and Defence Co-ordinator, Ministry of Defence 2000–03; currently manages Sohlman Senior Consultants. *Publications:* Swedish Exports and Imports 1965–70, Resources, Society and the Future 1980, Swedish Defence Materials Administration 1996–2003.
Address: Hornsgatan 51, 118 49 Stockholm, Sweden (home). *Telephone:* (8) 668-53-81. *E-mail:* staffan.sohlman@comhem.se (office); sasohlman@privat.nt/ors.se.

SOILIHI, Mohamed Ali; Comoran politician; *Minister of Finance, the Budget and Planning; Career:* Gov. World Bank 1997; Minister of Finance, Economy, Budget and Home Trade 1997, of Interior Jan.–March 2002, of Finance, Economy, Planning and Employment 2002–06, of Finance, Economy, Planning and Employment 2002–06, of Finance, Economy, Planning and Employment Budget and Planning 2007–.
Address: Ministry of Finance, the Budget and Planning, BP 324, Moroni, The Comoros (office). *Telephone:* (74) 4140 (office). *Fax:* (74) 4141 (office).

SOJO GARZA-ALDAPE, Eduardo, PhD; Mexican economist, academic and government official; *Secretary of the Economy;* b. 9 Jan. 1956, León, Guanajuato. *Education:* Monterrey Inst. of Tech. and Advanced Studies, Univ. of Pennsylvania. *Career:* fmr Researcher and Prof., Monterrey Inst. of Tech. and Advanced Studies, León; has held numerous positions in Fed. Public Admin including Tech. Dir and Short-Term Statistics Dir INEGI (Nat. Geography and Statistics Inst. and Analyst Gen. Econ. and Social Policy Bureau 1979–82; Coordinator Guanajuato State Govt Econ. Cabinet during Vicente Fox Quesada admin 1995–2000; Advisors Coordinator during Fox's presidential electoral campaign, then Pres. Elect's Transition Team Econ. Coordinator –2000, Chief Econ. Advisor and Chief, Presidential Office for Public Policy 2000–06; fmr Research Analyst, Univ. of Pa Link Project. *Publications include:* Guanajuato, Century XXI Study (co-author); numerous articles in professional journals and research on combined time series and econometric modeling.
Address: Secretariat of State for the Economy, Alfonso Reyes 30, Col. Hipódromo Condesa, 06170 México DF, Mexico (office). *Telephone:* (55) 5729-9100 (office). *Fax:* (55) 5729-9320 (office). *E-mail:* fcanales@economia.gob.mx (office). *Website:* www.economia.gob.mx (office).

SULAGH, Baqir, (Bayan Jabr); Iraqi politician; *Minister of Finance; Education:* Baghdad Univ. *Career:* Sr Official Supreme Council for the Islamic Revolution in Iraq (SCIRI), fmr Head Damascus office; Minister of Construction and Housing 2003–04, of the Interior 2005–06, of Finance 2006–; mem. United Iraqi Alliance.
Address: Ministry of Finance, Khulafa St, nr ar-Russafi Square., Baghdad, Iraq (office). *Telephone:* (1) 887-4871 (office).

SOLANA MADARIAGA, Javier, PhD; Spanish politician and international organization official; *Secretary-General, Council, Western European Union; Secretary-General and High Representative for Common Foreign and Security Policy, Council of the European Union;* b. 14 July 1942, Madrid; brother of Luis Solana Madariaga; m. Concepción Giménez; two c. *Education:* Colegio del Pilar, Universidad Complutense de Madrid. *Career:* joined Spanish Socialist Party 1964; won Fulbright scholarship to study physical sciences in USA until 1968; Asst to Prof. Nicolas Cabrera, Univ. of Va 1968–71, then at Universidad Autónoma de Madrid (where contract was cancelled allegedly for political reasons); mem. Exec., Federación Socialista Madrileña and Federación de Trabajadores de la Enseñanza, Unión General de Trabajadores; Prof. of Solid State Physics, Universidad Complutense de Madrid 1977; mem. Congress of Deputies for Madrid; mem. Fed. Exec. Comm., Partido Socialista Obrero Español, fmr Press Sec. and Sec. for Research and Programmes; Minister of Culture 1982–88; Govt Spokesman 1985–88; Minister of Educ. and Science 1988–92, of Foreign Affairs 1992–95; Sec.-Gen. NATO 1995–99, responsible for NATO Defence and Foreign Policy 1999–; Sec.-Gen. and High Rep. for Common Foreign and Security Policy, Council of the EU 1999–; Sec.-Gen. WEU 1999–; Pres. European Defence Agency 2004–; Pres. Madariaga European Foundation 1998–; mem. Spanish Chapter of Club of Rome; Hon. KCMG 1999, Grand Cross of Isabel the Catholic (Spain); Manfred Wörner Medal, Ministry of Defence (Germany), Vision for Europe Award 2003, Statesman of the Year Award, EastWest Inst. 2003, Premio Carlomagno 2006, Carnegie-Wateler Peace Prize 2006, Charlemagne Prize 2007. *Publications:* more than 30 publs in field of solid-state physics.
Address: General Secretariat, Council of the European Union, rue de la Loi 175, 1048 Brussels, Belgium (office). *Telephone:* (2) 285-61-11 (office). *Fax:* (2) 285-73-97 (office). *E-mail:* public.relations@consilium.eu.int (office). *Website:* www.ue.eu.int (office).

SOLBES MIRA, Pedro, DPolSci; Spanish politician; *Second Deputy Prime Minister and Minister of the Economy and Finance;* b. 31 Aug. 1942, Pinoso, Alicante; m.; three c. *Education:* Univ. of Madrid, Inst. of European Studies of Free Univ., Brussels. *Career:* civil servant, Ministry of Trade 1968–73, Commercial Counsellor to Spain's Perm. Mission to the EC 1973–78, Special Adviser to Minister for Relations with the EC 1978–79; Dir Gen. Commercial Policy, Ministry of Econs and Trade 1979–82; Gen. Sec. Ministry of Econs and Finance and mem. of task force for Spanish Accession negotiations to EC 1982–85; Sec. of State for Relations with the EC 1985; Pres. Internal Market Council during first Spanish presidency of EC 1989; Minister of Agric., Food and Fisheries 1991–93, of Economics and Finance 1993–96; Pres. Ecofin Council during Spanish presidency of EU 1995; mem. Spanish Parl. 1996; Pres. Jt Cttee of Spanish Parl. on EU 1996; European Commr for Econ. and Monetary Affairs 1999–2004; Second Deputy Prime Minister and Minister of the Economy and Finance 2004–.
Address: Ministry of the Economy, Alcalá 9, 28014 Madrid, Spain. *Telephone:* (91) 5958000. *Fax:* (91) 5958486. *E-mail:* informacion.alcala@minhac.es. *Website:* www.minhac.es.

SOLIYEV, Khakim; Tajikistan economist and politician; *Minister of Economy and Trade;* b. 14 Sept. 1946, Dushanbe. *Education:* Far-Eastern Econ. Inst. of Russia. *Career:* currently Minister of Economy and Trade. *Address:* Ministry of the Economy and Trade, ul. Bokhtar 37, 734002 Dushanbe, Tajikistan (office). *Telephone:* (372) 27-34-34 (office). *Fax:* (372) 21-51-32 (office).

SOLJAN, Luksa; Bosnia and Herzegovina diplomatist. *Career:* currently Amb. to Italy. *Address:* Embassy of Bosnia and Herzegovina, Piazzale Clodio 12, int. 17/18, 00195 Rome, Italy (office). *Telephone:* (6) 39742817 (office). *Fax:* (6) 39030567 (office). *E-mail:* ambasciatabosnia@libero.it (office).

SOLOVTSOV, Col-Gen. Nikolai; Russian army officer; *Commander, Strategic Missile Command;* b. 1 Jan. 1949, Zaysan, USSR Kazakh Repub.; m.; two c. *Education:* Rostov Higher Eng and Command School, Dzerzhinskiy Acad., Command Dept and General Staff Acad. *Career:* First Deputy Strategic Missile Command 1998–2001, Commdr 2001–; fmr Dean SMC Acad.; Order of Honours, Distinguished Service (3rd grade), Military Merits and ten medals. *Address:* Strategic Missile Command, Ministry of Defence, 105175 Moscow, ul. Myasnitskaya 37, Russian Federation (office). *Telephone:* (495) 293-38-54 (office). *Fax:* (495) 296-84-36 (office). *Website:* www.mil.ru/eng/1862/12068/12088/12223/index.shtml (office).

SÓLYOM, László, LLD; Hungarian academic, judge, politician and head of state; *President;* b. 3 Jan. 1942, Pécs; m. Erzsébet Nagy; one s. one d. *Education:* Univ. of Pécs, Friedrich Schiller Univ., Jena, Hungarian Acad. of Sciences. *Career:* Lecturer in Civil Law, Univ. of Jena 1966–69; Research Fellow, Hungarian Acad. of Sciences 1969–82; Prof. of Law, Univ. of Budapest 1982–2002, Catholic Univ. of Budapest 1996–, Univ. of Cologne 1999–2000; Pres. Constitutional Court 1990–98; legal adviser to environmental groups and other civic movts 1982–89; Pres. of Hungary 2005–; mem. Int. Comm. of Jurists, Geneva 1994–2001, scientific council, Wissenschaftskolleg zu Berlin Inst. for Advanced Study, Berlin 1995–2001, European Comm. for Democracy Through Law (The Venice Comm.) 1998–2001; Corresp. mem. Hungarian Acad. of Sciences 2001; Grand Cross of Merit with Star (Germany) 1998; Grand Cross of Merit (Hungary) 1999; Hon. DJur (Cologne) 1999; Humboldt Research Award 1998, Nagy Imre Prize (Hungary) 2003. *Publications:* The Decline of Civil Law Liability 1980, Die Persönlichkeitsrechte: Eine vergleichend-historische Studie über ihre Grundlagen 1984, Verfassungsgerichtsbarkeit in Ungarn: Analysen und Entscheidungssammlung 1990–93 (with Georg Brunner) 1995, Constitutional Judiciary in a New Democracy: The Hungarian Constitutional Court (with Georg Brunner) 2000, The Beginnings of Constitutional Justice in Hungary (in Hungarian) 2001, The Role of Constitutional Courts in the Transition to Democracy, 18(1) Int. Sociology 2003, Politican Parties and Trade Unions in the Constitution (in Hungarian) 2004. *Address:* Office of the President, 1014 Budapest, Szent György tér 1–2, Hungary (office). *Telephone:* (1) 224-5010 (office). *Fax:* (1) 224-5002 (office). *Website:* www.keh.hu (office).

SOMARE, Rt Hon. Sir Michael Thomas, PC, CH, GCMG; Papua New Guinea politician; *Prime Minister, Minister of Autonomy and Autonomous Regions;* b. 9 April 1936, Rabaul, East New Britain Prov.; m. Veronica Bula Kaiap 1965; three s. two d. *Education:* Sogeri Secondary School, Admin. Coll. *Career:* teacher various schools 1956–64; Asst Area Educ. Officer, Madang 1962–63; Broadcasts Officer, Dept of Information and Extension Services, Wewak 1963–66, radio broadcaster and journalist 1966–67; mem. House of Ass. for East Sepik Regional 1968–; Parl. Leader Pangu Party 1968–88; Deputy Chair. Exec. Council 1972–73, Chair. 1973–75; Chief Minister Papua New Guinea 1974–75, Prime Minister 1975–80, 1982–85, 2002–; Minister for Nat. Resources 1976–77, for Public Service Comm. and Nat. Planning 1977–80; Acting Minister for Police 1978–80; Leader of the Opposition 1980–82; Minister of Foreign Affairs 1988–94, 2000–01, 2006–07, also of Bougainville Affairs 2000–01, of Defence (acting) 2007, of Autonomy and Autonomous Regions 2007–; Gov. E Sepik Prov. 1995–; Chair. Bd of Trustees, PNG; mem. Second Select Cttee on Constitutional Devt 1968–72, Australian Broadcasting Comm. Advisory Cttee; Ancient Order of Sikatuna, Title of Rajah (Philippines) 1976, Grand Cross of Equestrian Order of St Gregory the Great 1993; six hon. degrees; Queen's Silver Jubilee Medal 1977, Pacific Man of the Year Award 1983. *Publication:* Sana: An Autobiography. *Address:* Office of the Prime Minister, POB 639, Waigani, NCD (office); Karan, Murik Lakes, East Sepik, Papua New Guinea (home). *Telephone:* 3276544 (office). *Fax:* 3277380 (office). *E-mail:* primeminister@pm.gov.pg (office). *Website:* www.pm.gov.pg/pmsoffice/PMsoffice.nsf (office).

SOMAVÍA, Juan O.; Chilean diplomatist; *Director-General, International Labour Organization;* m.; two c. *Education:* Catholic Univ. of Chile, Univ. of Paris. *Career:* various posts in Ministry of Foreign Relations; Founder and Exec. Dir Latin American Inst. for Trans nat. Studies, Mexico; Coordinator Third World Forum; mem. Bd of Dirs and Vice-Pres. for Latin America of Inter-Press Service 1976–87; Sec.-Gen. South American Peace Comm. 1987; Pres. Int. Comm. of Chilean opposition No Campaign for Referendum 1988–89; Perm. Rep. to UN, New York 1990–99; Dir-Gen. ILO 1999–; fmr consultant to GATT and UNDP; mem. Bd of Dirs Int. Foundation for Devt Alternatives, mem. MacBride Comm. on communication problems; Laurea hc (Univ. of Turin) 2001; Dr hc (Connecticut Coll.) 1994, (Catholic Univ. of Lima) 1999, (Univ. of Paris I, Panthéon-Sorbonne) 2003; Leonidas Proaño Prize, Latin American Human Rights Asscn for contrib. to peace and regional security. *Address:* International Labour Organization, 4 route des Morillons, 1211 Geneva 22, Switzerland (office). *Telephone:* (22) 799-6111 (office). *Fax:* (22) 799-8533 (office). *E-mail:* cabinet@ilo.org (office). *Website:* www.ilo.org (office).

SOMMARUGA, Cornelio, LLD; Swiss diplomatist and international official; b. 29 Dec. 1932, Rome, Italy; m. Ornella Marzorati 1957; two s. four d. *Education:* Rome, Paris, Univ. of Zürich. *Career:* bank trainee, Zürich 1957–59; joined Diplomatic Service 1960; Attaché, Swiss Embassy, The Hague 1961; Sec., Swiss Embassy, Bonn 1962–64, Rome 1965–68; Deputy Head of Del. to EFTA, GATT and UNCTAD, Geneva 1969–73; Asst Sec.-Gen. EFTA 1973–75; Minister Plenipotentiary, Div. of Commerce, Fed. Dept of Public Economy, Berne 1976, Amb. 1977; del. to Fed. Council for Trade Agreements 1980–84; State Sec. for External Econ. Affairs 1984–86; Pres. ICRC 1987–99; Pres., UN Econ. Comm. for Europe 1977–78; Pres. Initiatives of Change Int., Caux 2000; Chair. Bd J. P. Morgan (Suisse) SA, Geneva 2000–03 (mem. Bd 2003–), Geneva Int. Centre for Humanitarian Demining 2000, Karl Popper Foundation 2000; mem. Panel on UN Peace Operations, Int. Comm. on Intervention and State Sovereignty; Hon. mem. ICRC 2000; Commdr, Légion d'honneur; several other state honours from Italy, Belgium, The Holy See, Luxembourg, Lithuania, Iceland, Sweden; Hon. MD; Dr hc (Fribourg) 1985, (Minho) 1990, (Nice-Sophia Antipolis, Seoul Nat. Univ.) 1992; (Bologna) 1991, (Geneva) 1997, (Webster, St Louis) 1998; North-South Prize of the Council of Europe 2001; numerous awards from Red Cross Socs. *Address:* 7bis, avenue de la Paix, 1202 Geneva, Switzerland (office); 16 chemin des Crêts-de-Champel, 1206 Geneva, Switzerland (home). *Telephone:* (22) 906-16-97 (office); (22) 347-45-52 (home). *Fax:* (22) 906-16-90 (office); (22) 347-45-55 (home). *E-mail:* c.sommaruga@gichd.org (office); cornelio.sommaruga@bluewin.ch (home). *Website:* www.gichd.ch (office); www.chaux.ch.

SOMMER, Theo, DPhil; German journalist; *Editor-at-Large, Die Zeit;* b. 10 June 1930, Constance; m. 1st Elda Tsilenis 1952; two s.; m. 2nd Heide Grenz 1976; two s.; m. 3rd Sabine Grewe 1989; one d. *Education:* Univ of Tübingen, Chicago and Harvard Univs. *Career:* Local Ed. Schwäbisch-Gmünd 1952–54; Foreign Ed. Die Zeit 1958, Deputy Ed. 1968, Ed.-in-Chief 1973–92, Publr 1992–, Ed.-at-Large 2000–; Lecturer in Int. Relations, Univ. of Hamburg 1967–70; Chief of Planning Staff, Ministry of Defence 1969–70; mem. Deutsche Gesellschaft für Auswärtige Politik; mem. Council IISS 1963–76, 1978–87, German Armed Forces Structure Comm. 1970–72, Int. Comm. on the Balkans 1995–96, Ind. Int. Comm. on the Balkans 1999–2000; Deputy Chair. Comm. on the Future on the Bundeswehr 1999–2000; Chair. Comm. Investigating Effects of DU Ammunitions, Radar and Asbestos on German Armed Forces 2002; mem. Indo-German Consultative Group 1992– (Co-Chair. 1994–), German-Japanese Dialogue Forum 1993–; mem. Bd Deutsche Welthungerhilfe 1992–, Max-Bauer Preis 1992–, German-Turkish Foundation 1998–; mem. German Foreign Policy Asscn, IISS, Königswinter Conf., Advisory Council, Mil. History Inst.; Contributing Ed. Newsweek Int. 1968–90; regular contrib. to American, British, Japanese and Korean publs; commentator German TV, radio and moderator of monthly programmes; Hon. mem. Asscn of Anciens, NATO Defense Coll. 1971, Trilateral Comm. 1993; Fed. Order of Merit (First Class) 1998, Gold Honor Cross, German Armed Forces 2002; Hon. LLD (Univ. of Maryland, USA) 1982; Theoder-Wolf Prize 1966, Int. Communications Award, People's Repub. of China 1991, Columbus Prize 1993. *Publications:* Deutschland und Japan zwischen den Mächten (Germany and Japan Between the Powers) 1935–40 1962, Vom Antikominternpakt zum Dreimächtepakt 1962, Reise in ein fernes Land 1964, Ed. Denken an Deutschland 1966, Ed. Schweden-Report 1974, Die chinesische Karte (The Chinese Card) 1979, Allianz in Umbruch (Alliance in Disarray) 1982, Blick zurück in die Zukunft (Look Back into the Future) 1984, Reise ins andere Deutschland (Journey to the Other Germany) 1986, Europa im 21. Jahrhundert 1989, Geschichte der Bonner Republik 1949–99 1999, Der Zukunft entgegen (Toward the Future) 1999,

Phoenix Europe. The European Union: Its Progress, Problems and Prospects 2000, Hamburg 2004, 1945: Biographie eines Jahres 2005.
Address: Die Zeit, Pressehaus, Speersort 1, 20079 Hamburg (office); 17 Zabelweg, 22359 Hamburg, Germany (home). *Telephone:* (40) 3280240 (office); (40) 6037300 (home). *Fax:* (40) 3280407 (office); (40) 6030044 (home). *E-mail:* sommer@zeit.de (office); tsommer01@aol.com (home). *Website:* www.zeit.de (office); www.theosommer.de.

SOMPARE, Mohamed Lamin; Guinean diplomatist. *Career:* currently Amb. to Sierra Leone.
Address: Embassy of Guinea, 6 Wilkinson Road, Freetown, Sierra Leone (office). *Telephone:* (22) 232584 (office). *Fax:* (22) 232496 (office).

SOMSAVAT, Lengsavad; Laotian politician; b. 16 June 1945, Luangphrabang; m. Bounkongmany Lengsavad; one s. two d. *Education:* Nat. Org. for the Study of Policy and Admin. *Career:* Head of the Secr., Cabinet of the Lao People's Revolutionary Party (LPRP) Cen. Cttee. 1975–82; Deputy Chief, Council of Ministers; fmr Deputy Minister; First Vice-Chair. LPRP History Research Comm. 1982–88, Chief of the Cabinet of LPRP and Cabinet of Ministers 1991–93; Amb. to Bulgaria 1989–91; Minister of Foreign Affairs 1993–2006; Deputy Prime Minister 1998–2006; Dr rer. pol (Ramkhamheng Univ., Thailand) 2000; Medal of Liberty Issara, Medal of Labour, Anti-Imperialist Cross, Revolutionary Medal, People's Repub. of Korea, Medal of Friendship Govts of Cuba and Bulgaria.
Address: c/o Ministry of Foreign Affairs, rue That Luang, 01004, Ban Phonxay, Vientiane, Laos (office).

SØNDERGAARD, Carsten; Danish diplomat; *Ambassador to Germany;* b. 8 Aug. 1952. *Education:* Univ. of Århus. *Career:* Head of Section, Ministry of Foreign Affairs 1979–83, 1986–90, Head of Dept 1992–99; First Sec., Embassy in Washington, DC 1983–86; Counsellor, Embassy in London 1990–92; Amb. to Turkey 1999–2001, to Germany 2005–; Under-Sec. for EU Policy and EU Coordination 2001; State Sec. for Foreign and Security Policy, EU Policy and EU Coordination 2001–05.
Address: Embassy of Denmark, Rauchstr. 1, 10787 Berlin, Germany (office). *Telephone:* (30) 50502000 (office). *Fax:* (30) 50502050 (office). *E-mail:* beramb@um.dk (office). *Website:* www.ambberlin.um.dk (office).

SONG, Sang-hyun, LLM, JSD; South Korean professor of law and judge; *Judge, International Criminal Court;* b. 21 Dec. 1941. *Education:* Seoul Nat. Univ., Tulane Law School, New Orleans and Cornell Law School, Ithaca, NY, USA, Univ. of Cambridge, UK. *Career:* called to the Bar, Repub. of Korea 1964; Mil. Prosecutor then Judge, Judge Advocate Office, Korean Armed Forces 1964–67; Attorney Haight, Gardner, Poor & Havens, New York 1970–72; Prof. of Law, Seoul Nat. Univ. 1972–, Dean Law School 1996–98; Lecturer in Law, Nat. Police Coll., Seoul 1983–; Judge, Int. Criminal Court, The Hague 2003–; Vice-Pres. UNICEF Korea 1998–; Pres. The Korea Childhood Leukemia Foundation 1999–; Nat. Decoration of 2nd Highest Order (Moran), Govt of Repub. of Korea 1997; Most Distinguished Alumni Medal, Cornell Univ. 1994; Legal Culture Award, Korean Fed. Bar Asscn 1998. *Publications:* books: Introduction to the Law and Legal System of Korea 1983, An Introduction to Law and Economics 1983, Korean Law in the Global Economy 1996, The Korean Civil Procedure 2004; numerous articles in professional journals.
Address: International Criminal Court, Maanweg 174, 2516 The Hague AB, The Netherlands (office); 1629-19 Seocho-dong, Seoul 137-879, Republic of Korea (home). *Telephone:* (70) 5158208 (office). *Fax:* (70) 5158789 (office); (2) 34719502 (home). *E-mail:* pio@icc-cpi.int (office). *Website:* www.icc-cpi.int (office).

SONG, Zhe, MA; Chinese diplomatist; *Permanent Representative, European Union;* b. April 1960; m.; one d. *Career:* Attaché, Third Sec., People's Inst. of Foreign Affairs 1983–88; Third, later Second Sec., Embassy in London 1988–92, Counsellor 2000–01; Second Sec., Deputy Dir, First Sec., Dir, Western European Dept, Ministry of Foreign Affairs 1992–2000, Counsellor 2001–02, Deputy Dir-Gen. 2002–03; Dir-Gen., Gen. Office of State Council 2003–08; Perm. Rep. to EU, Brussels 2008–.
Address: Permanent Mission of the People's Republic of China, 443–445 ave de Tervueren, 1150 Brussels, Belgium (office). *Telephone:* (2) 771-33-09 (office). *Fax:* (2) 772-37-45 (office). *E-mail:* chinamission_eu@mfa.gov.cn (office). *Website:* www.chinamission.be (office).

SOOD, Rakesh, PhD; Indian academic and diplomatist; *Ambassador to Nepal; Career:* joined Ministry of External Affairs 1976, has served in Missions in Brussels, Dakar, Geneva and Islamabad, Dir and Jt Sec. for Disarmament and Int. Security Affairs, Ministry of External Affairs 1992–2000, Amb. and Perm. Rep. to UN Conf. on Disarmament, UN Disarmament Comm., Geneva 2000–03; Alt. Rep. of Dept of Atomic Energy at Council of CERN 2001–03; Deputy Chief of Mission, Washington, DC 2003–04, Amb. to Afghanistan 2004–08, to Nepal

2008–; Chair. Meeting of States Parties to the Convention on Prohibitions or Restrictions on the Use of Certain Conventional Weapons Which May be Deemed to be Excessively Injurious or to Have Indiscriminate Effects 2002–03, UN Sec.-Gen.'s Group of Govt Experts to Identify and Trace, in a Timely and Reliable Manner, Illicit Small Arms and Light Weapons, in All its Aspects 2002; fmr mem. UN Sec.-Gen.'s Advisory Bd on Disarmament Matters, UN Sec.-Gen.'s Expert Groups on Conventional Arms and on Verification; has participated in negotiations on Chemical Weapons Convention and Nuclear-Test-Ban Treaty (CTBT) at Conf. on Disarmament; has represented India in UN Disarmament Comm. meetings, First Cttee of UN Gen. Ass., CTBT negotiations, Biological Weapons Convention and Inhumane Weapons Convention Review Confs, Third Special Session of UN Gen. Ass. devoted to Disarmament, Non-Aligned Movt confs and summits, ASEAN Regional Forum meetings, Middle-East Arms Control and Regional Security Working Group, India-Pakistan talks, bilateral talks with USA, UK, France, Russia, Japan, Germany and China on disarmament, nonproliferation, int. security and export control issues. *Publications:* numerous articles on disarmament, nonproliferation and security-related issues.
Address: Embassy of India, 336 Kapurdhara Marg, POB 292, Kathmandu, Nepal (office). *Telephone:* (1) 4410900 (office). *Fax:* (1) 4428279 (office). *E-mail:* pic@eoiktm.org (office). *Website:* www.south-asia.com/embassy -India (office).

SOOKLAL, Anil, PhD; South African diplomatist; *Ambassador to Belgium and Luxembourg and Permanent Representative to European Communities; Career:* served in Embassy in Delhi, Counsellor for Political Affairs, Geneva 1990s, Deputy Dir-Gen. Asia and Middle East Dept, Ministry of Foreign Affairs 2003–06, Amb. to Belgium and Luxembourg and Perm. Rep. to EU, Brussels 2006–.
Address: South African Mission to the European Union, 17–19 rue Montoyer, 1040 Brussels, Belgium (office). *Telephone:* (2) 285-44-00 (office). *Fax:* (2) 285-44-02 (office). *E-mail:* embassy@southafrica.be (office). *Website:* www.southafrica.be.

SOPE, Barak; Ni-Vanuatu politician and diplomatist; *Chairman, Melanesian Progressive Party/Leader of the Opposition; Career:* leading mem. Vanuaaku Pati (VP), Roving Amb.; mem. govts 1980–87; defected from VP, f. Melanesian Progressive Party (MPP) 1987, Chair. 1987–; mem. coalition govts 1993–96; Prime Minister of Vanuatu 1999–2001; Opposition Leader 2001–.
Address: Melanesian Progressive Pati (MPP), PO Box 39, Port Vila, Vanuatu (office). *Telephone:* 23485 (office). *Fax:* 23315 (office).

SOPER, Andrew; British diplomatist; *High Commissioner to Mozambique;* b. 6 July 1969; m. Kathryn Soper; one s. one d. *Career:* Desk Officer, Falkland Islands Dept, FCO 1985–87, Second Sec., Embassy in Mexico City 1987–90, Desk Officer, Econ. Relations Dept 1990–93, Desk Officer, Near East and N Africa Dept 1993–95, First Sec., Embassy in Washington, DC 1995–99, Deputy Head, Human Rights Policy Dept 1999–2001, Deputy Head of Mission, Brasilia 2001–04, Head of Sustainable Devt and Commonwealth Group 2004–07, High Commr to Mozambique 2007–.
Address: British High Commission, Avenue Vladimir I. Lénine 310, CP 55, Maputo, Mozambique (office). *Telephone:* 21356000 (office). *Fax:* 21356060 (office). *E-mail:* bhc.consular@tvcabo.co.mz (office). *Website:* www.britishhighcommission.gov.uk/mozambique (office).

SOPOAGA, Enele Sosene, MA; Tuvaluan diplomatist and civil servant; b. 10 Feb. 1956; m.; three c. *Education:* Univ. of Sussex and Univ. of Oxford, UK. *Career:* Educ. Admin., Ministry of Social Services 1980–86, Asst Sec. 1986, and EU Nat. Authorizing Officer with Dept of Foreign Affairs and Ministry of Foreign Affairs and Econ. Planning 1986–91, Acting Perm. Sec. 1991–92, Perm. Sec. 1992–95; Perm. Sec. Ministry of Health, Sports and Human Resource Devt Funafuti 1995–96; fmr High Comm. in Fiji, also accred to Papua New Guinea and Samoa 1996–2001; Perm. Rep. to UN, New York 2001–06; rep. on various bds of regional orgs in Pacific including Forum Officials Cttee, Pacific Islanders Forum of Leaders 1998–99, Cttee of Reps of Govts and Admins of Pacific Community (fmrly S Pacific Comm.) and Sub-cttee on Geo-scientific Research 1997–98; del. to various regional and int. confs including African, Caribbean and Pacific States, EU Jt Convention on Future of Lomé Convention, Maastricht, Netherlands, UNESCO Gen. Conf., UN World Summit on Advancement of Women, Beijing, UNDP Gen. Council; mem. Pacific Islanders Asscn, London, Oxford Univ. Soc., UK.
Address: c/o Ministry of Foreign Affairs, Vaiaku, Funafuti, Tuvalu (office).

SORENSEN, Gillian Martin; American international organization official; *Senior Adviser, United Nations;* m. Theodore C. Sorenson; one d. *Education:* Smith Coll., Sorbonne Univ., Paris, France. *Career:* served as New York City Commr for the UN and Consular Corps 1978–90, Head of

Liaison Office with Diplomatic Community 1978–90; Pres. and CEO Nat. Conf. of Christians and Jews 1990–93; Under-Sec.-Gen. and Special Adviser for Public Policy to the Sec.-Gen., UN 1993–96, responsible for worldwide Fiftieth Anniversary observances and co-ordination of UN 50 Summit at UN HQ 1995, special assignments as requested by Sec.-Gen., Asst Sec.-Gen., External Relations 1997–2003; Sr Adviser, UN 2003–; mem. Council on Foreign Relations, Women's Forum, Women's Foreign Policy Group; mem. Bd Business Council for the UN, fmr mem. Bd UN Devt Corpn (apptd by Mayor) and Corpn for Public Broadcasting (apptd by Pres. of USA); del. to three Democratic Presidential Conventions; Fellow, Kennedy School of Govt (Inst. of Politics), Harvard Univ. 2002; Peace Builder Award 2004.
Address: c/o Office of the Secretary-General, United Nations, New York, NY 10017, USA (office). *Website:* www.un.org (office).

SORO, Guillaume Kigbafori; Côte d'Ivoirian fmr rebel leader and government official; *Prime Minister;* b. 8 May 1972, Diawala; two c. *Education:* univ. studies in France. *Career:* Leader Ivorian Students' Fed. 1995–98; fmr Sec.-Gen. Mouvement patriotique de Côte d'Ivoire (MPCI); Leader, New Forces Rebels 2000–, led rebellion against Pres. Laurent Gbagbo that triggered Civil War 2002, controlled Northern Prov. of Côte d'Ivoire 2002; Minister of State for Communications 2003–05, of Reconstruction and Reinsertion 2005–07; Prime Minister 2007–.
Address: Office of the Prime Minister, blvd Angoulvant 01, BP 1533, Abidjan 01 (office); Forces Nouvelles, Bouaké, Côte d'Ivoire. *Telephone:* 20-20-04-04; 20-31-50-00 (office). *Fax:* 20-22-18-33 (office). *E-mail:* senacom@fnci.info; pm@primature.gouv.ci (office). *Website:* www.fnci.info.

SOROS, George; Hungarian investment banker and philanthropist; *Chairman, Soros Fund Management LLC;* b. 12 Aug. 1930, Budapest; m.; five c. *Education:* London School of Econs. *Career:* moved to England 1947; much influenced by work of philosopher Karl Popper; with Singer & Friedlander (merchant bankers), London; moved to Wall Street, New York 1956; set up pvt. mutual fund, Quantum Fund, registered in Curaçao 1969; since 1991 has created other funds, Quasar Int., Quota, Quantum Emerging Growth Fund (merged with Quantum Fund to form Quantum Endowment Fund 2000), Quantum Realty Trust; Pres. and Chair. Soros Fund Man. LLC, New York 1973–; philanthropist since 1979, provided funds to help black students attend Cape Town Univ., SA; Founder Open Soc. Fund (currently Chair. Open Soc. Inst.) 1979, Soros Foundations, Cen. European Univ., Budapest 1992; f. Global Power Investments 1994; Dr hc (New School for Social Research, Univ. of Oxford, Budapest Univ. of Econs, Yale Univ.); Laurea hc (Univ. of Bologna) 1995. *Publication:* The Alchemy of Finance 1987, Opening the Soviet System 1990, Underwriting Democracy 1991, Soros on Soros – Staying Ahead of the Curve (jtly) 1995, The Crisis of Global Capitalism – Open Society Engendered 1998, Open Society – Reforming Global Capitalism 2000, George Soros on Globalization 2002, The Bubble of American Supremacy – Correcting the Misuse of American Power 2004, Soros on Freedom 2006; numerous essays on politics, society and econs in major int. newspapers and magazines.
Address: Soros Fund Management LLC, 888 7th Avenue, 3300 New York, NY 10106, USA (office); Open Society Institute, 400 West 59th Street, New York, NY 10019. *Telephone:* (212) 548-0600. *Website:* www.georgesoros.com; www.soros.org.

SOROUSH, Abdolkarim, BSc; Iranian academic; *Researcher, Institute for Iranian Contemporary Historical Studies;* b. 1945, Tehran. *Education:* Mortazavi High School, Alavi High School, Univ. of London and Chelsea Coll., London, UK. *Career:* studied pharmacy and passed nat. entrance exams; left for London following graduation to continue studies; returned to Iran in 1979, and published book Knowledge and Value (Danesh va Arzesh); apptd Dir Islamic Culture Group, Teacher Training Coll., Tehran 1979; mem. Cultural Revolution Inst. 1980–83 (resgnd); Researcher, Inst. for Cultural Research and Studies (now the Inst. for Iranian Contemporary Historical Studies) 1983–; adviser to govt bodies; became more critical of political role played by Iranian clergy 1990s; co-founder monthly magazine Kiyan, and published his most controversial articles on religious pluralism, hermeneutics, tolerance, clericalism etc., magazine suppressed by direct order of supreme leader of Islamic Repub. 1998; more than 1,000 audio tapes of his speeches on various social, political, religious and literary subjects circulated world-wided, became subject to harassment and state censorship; Visiting Prof. teaching Islam and Democracy, Quranic Studies and Philosophy of Islamic Law, Harvard Univ., USA 2000–; Scholar-in-Residence, Yale Univ., USA; taught Islamic Political Philosophy at Princeton Univ. 2002–03; Visiting Scholar, Wissenschaftskolleg, Berlin, Germany 2003–04. *Publications:* Dialectical Antagonism (in Persian) 1978, Philosophy of History (in Persian) 1978, What is Science, What is Philosophy (in Persian) (11th edn) 1992, The Restless Nature of the Universe (in Persian and Turkish) 1980, Satanic Ideology (in Persian) (fifth

edn) 1994, Knowledge and Value (in Persian), Observing the Created: Lectures in Ethics and Human Sciences (in Persian) (third edn) 1994, The Theoretical Contraction and Expansion of Religion: The Theory of Evolution of Religious Knowledge (in Persian) (third edn) 1994, Lectures in the Philosophy of Social Sciences: Hermeneutics in Social Sciences (in Persian) 1995, Sagaciousness, Intellectualism and Pietism (in Persian) 1991, The Characteristic of the Pious: A Commentary on Imam Ali's Lecture About the Pious (in Persian) (fourth edn) 1996, The Tale of the Lords of Sagacity (in Persian) (third edn) 1996, Wisdom and Livelihood: A Commentary on Imam Ali's Letter to Imam Hasan (in Persian) (second edn) 1994, Sturdier than Ideology (in Persian) 1994, The Evolution and Devolution of Religious Knowledge in: Kurzman, Ch. (ed.), Intellectualism and Religious Conviction (in Persian), The World We Live (in Persian and Turkish), The Tale of Love and Servitude (in Persian), The Definitive Edition of Rumi's Mathnavi (in Persian) 1996, Tolerance and Governance (in Persian) 1997, Straight Paths, An Essay on Religious Pluralism (in Persian) 1998, Liberal Islam 1998, Political Letters (two vols) (in Persian) 1999, Expansion of Prophetic Experience (in Persian) 1999, Reason, Freedom and Democracy in Islam, Essential Writings of Adbolkarim Soroush (translated, ed with a critical introduction by M. Sadri and A. Sadri) 2000.
Address: The Institute for Iranian Contemporary Historical Studies, PO Box 19395-1975, 128 Fayyazi (Fereshteh) Avenue, Elahieh, Tehran 19649, Iran (office). *Telephone:* (21) 264037-8 (office); (21) 2003490 (office). *Fax:* (21) 262096 (office). *E-mail:* info@drsoroush.com (office). *Website:* www.drsoroush.com (office); www.iichs.org.

SOUHAIBI, Noman Taher as-, BA; Yemeni politician; *Minister of Finance;* b. 1965, Al-Sadda, Ibb. *Education:* San'a Univ. *Career:* Deputy Chair. Tax Authority 2001–05, Chair. 2005–07; Minister of Finance 2007–.
Address: Ministry of Finance, PO Box 190, San'a, Yemeni (office). *Telephone:* (1) 260370 (office). *Fax:* (1) 263040 (office).

SOULÉ MANA, Lawani; Benin government official. *Career:* previously worked in West African Devt Bank; Minister of Finance 2007–.
Address: Ministry of Finance And Economy Planning, BP 302, Cotonou, Benin (office). *Telephone:* 229-30-12-47 (office). *Fax:* 229-30-18-51 (office). *E-mail:* sgm@finance.gouv.bj (office). *Website:* www.finance.gouv.bj (office).

SOULEY, Hassane (Bonto); Niger politician. *Career:* Minister of Nat. Defence –2007.
Address: Ministry of National Defence, BP 626, Niamey, Niger (office).

SOUMARÉ, Cheikh Hadjibou; Senegalese politician; *Prime Minister;* b. 1951, Dakar. *Education:* Ecole Nationale d'Administration et de Magistrature, Univ. of Dakar. *Career:* served as municipal tax officer Kaolack, Sédhiou and Bambey 1981–85; Head Statistics Div., State Treasury 1985–90; Provisional Admin. Bank of Credit and Commerce Int., Senegal 1991–95; adviser to Minister for Finance 1995–96; Dir of the Budget 1996–2000; Dir-Gen. of Finance 2000–01; Deputy Minister for the Budget 2001–07; Prime Minister 2007–.
Address: Prime Minister's Office, Building Administratif, BP 4029, Dakar, Senegal (office). *Telephone:* 889-69-69 (office). *Fax:* 823-44-79 (office). *Website:* www.gouv.sn (office).

SOURANG, Abdou, MA; Senegalese diplomatist; *Ambassador to UK;* m.; five c. *Education:* Univ. of Senegal, Nat. Admin School, Dakar. *Career:* joined Ministry of Foreign Affairs in 1981, in charge of Bilateral Affairs Div., Direction for Econ. and Tech. Affairs; Counsellor, later First Counsellor (Political Affairs), Embassy in London 1985–91; Head of Direction for Europe, America and Oceania, Ministry of Foreign Affairs 1991–96; First Counsellor, later Minister-Counsellor, Brussels 1996–2005, served in Embassy in Paris 2005–06, Amb. to Nigeria (also accred to Benin and Togo) and Perm. Rep. to Econ. Community of West African States (ECOWAS) 2006–07, Amb. to UK 2007–.
Address: Embassy of Senegal, 39 Marloes Road, London, W8 6LA, England (office). *Telephone:* (20) 7937-7237 (office). *Fax:* (20) 7938-2546 (office). *E-mail:* mail@senegalembassy.co.uk (office). *Website:* www.senegalembassy.co.uk (office).

SOUVIRÓN CRESPO, María Beatriz; Bolivian diplomatist; *Ambassador to UK.* *Career:* fmr Co-ordinator Programa de Prevención de Desastres y Reducción del Riesgo, Ministry of Sustainable Devt; Amb. to UK (also accred to Ireland) 2006–.
Address: Embassy of Bolivia, 106 Eaton Square, London, SW1W 9AD, England (office). *Telephone:* (20) 7235-4248 (office). *Fax:* (20) 7235-1286 (office). *E-mail:* beatriz@boembassy-london.com (office). *Website:* www.boembassy-london.com (office).

SOW, Abdourahmane; Senegalese politician and diplomatist; *Ambassador to Tunisia; Career:* fmr Pres. Fédération rurale de Louga, Parti démocratique sénégalais; fmr Minister of Town Planning and Housing; fmr Minister of the Interior; fmr Financial Man. Goree Inst.; Dir WHO Office for Southern Sudan, Nairobi, Kenya 2001; currently Amb. to Tunisia; Pres. World Scout Parl. Union; Chair. Africa Scout Foundation; fmr Vice-Chair. Comm. on Human Settlements, Bureau of Preparatory Cttee for the Special Session of UN Gen. Ass. for an Overall Review and Appraisal of the Implementation of the Habitat Agenda.
Address: Embassy of Senegal, 122 avenue de la Liberté, Belvédère, Tunis, Tunisia (office). *Telephone:* (71) 802-397 (office). *Fax:* (71) 780-770 (office). *Website:* www.ambasenegal.intl.tn (office).

SOW, Alpha Ibrahima, BSc; Guinean academic and diplomatist; *Permanent Representative, United Nations;* b. 18 Dec. 1949; m.; three c. *Education:* Inst. Polytechnique de Kankan. *Career:* Prof. of Philosophy and Political Ideology, Univ. of Conakry 1972–79, Chair. Faculty of Social Sciences 1979–82, Dean 1982–83; Counsellor, Embassy in Algeria 1983–89, Embassy in Ethiopia 1989–95; Nat. Asst Dir of Political and Cultural Affairs, Ministry of Foreign Affairs 1995–96, Nat. Dir 1996–97; Amb. to Iran 1997, to Ethiopia 2003; Perm. Rep. to UN, New York 2003–.
Address: Permanent Mission of Guinea to the United Nations, 140 East 39th Street, New York, NY 10016, USA (office). *Telephone:* (212) 687-8115 (office). *Fax:* (212) 687-8248 (office). *E-mail:* guinea@un.int (office).

SOWAYEGH, Abdul Aziz H. I. as-, MA, PhD; Saudi Arabian academic and diplomatist; *Ambassador to Canada;* b. 9 Sept. 1947, Jeddah; m. *Education:* Univ. of Riyadh, Claremont Grad. School and Utah State Univ., USA. *Career:* Political Attaché, Ministry of Foreign Affairs 1969; demonstrator, Dept of Political Science, Riyadh Univ. 1969–71, Asst Prof. 1976–79, Head of Dept 1977–79, Dir of Research Centre, Coll. of Commerce 1977–79; Adviser, Ministry of Information, Riyadh 1977–79, Asst Deputy Minister 1979–86; fmr Head, Information Dept, Ministry of Foreign Affairs, fmr Ministry Spokesman; Amb. to South Korea 1994; Consul-Gen. in Houston, Tex. 1995; mem. Majlis Ash-Shura (Consultative Council) 1998–2002; Dir-Gen. Makkah Region, Ministry of Foreign Affairs 2002–06; currently Amb. to Canada. *Publications:* Arab Petropolities 1984, The Energy Crises: Where To? 1990, Oil and Arab Politics 1991, The Energy Crises: A Saudi Perspective 1992, Arab National Security: A Future Perspective 1992, The Arabs and the Peace Conference: Possible and Impossible Peace 1992, Islam in Saudi Foreign Policy 1994, Saudi Arabia and the Development of the Islamic World 2002, The Political Philosophy of King Fahd 2004.
Address: Embassy of Saudi Arabia, 201 Sussex Drive, Ottawa, ON K1N 1K6, Canada (office). *Telephone:* (613) 237-4100 (office). *Fax:* (613) 237-0567 (office). *E-mail:* caemb@mofa.gov.sa (office). *Website:* www.mofa.gov.sa (office).

SPALDING HELLMERS, James, BEcons, MEcons; Paraguayan diplomatist; *Ambassador to USA;* m. Cecilia Coello; three d. *Education:* Univ. of Massachusetts and Rutgers Univ., USA. *Career:* fmr Minister of Finance, Vice-Minister of Economy and Integration, Ministry of Finance, Vice-Minister of Commerce, Pres. of Paraguayan Petroleum, Vice-Minister of Integration; mem. Econ. Transition Comm. of Pres. Duarte Frutos 2003; Co-founder and Dir Sustainable Devt Advisory Group (GADES) –2004; fmr Gov. IDB, World Bank Group, Corporación Andina de Fomento, Financial Fund for the Devt of River Plate Basin; fmr negotiator for Paraguay in MERCOSUR process, Free Trade Area of Americas and EU; Amb. to USA 2004–.
Address: Embassy of Paraguay, 2400 Massachusetts Avenue, NW, Washington, DC 20008, USA (office). *Telephone:* (202) 483-6960 (office). *Fax:* (202) 234-4508 (office). *Website:* www.embassy.org/embassies/py.html (office).

SPANTA, Rangin Dadfar, PhD; Afghan academic and government official; *Minister of Foreign Affairs;* b. 1954, Herat prov. *Education:* Kabul Univ., Aachen Univ., Germany. *Career:* began living in Germany 1982; Prof., Inst. of Political Science, Tech. Univ. of Aachen –2005, Dir Third World Studies Inst.; returned to Afghanistan to teach at Kabul Univ. 2005; Spokesperson Alliance for Democracy; advisor to Pres. on Int. affairs 2005; Minister of Foreign Affairs 2006–.
Address: Ministry of Foreign Affairs, Malak Azghar Road, Kabul, Afghanistan (office). *Telephone:* (70) 104024 (office). *Fax:* (20) 2100360 (office). *E-mail:* contact@mfa.gov.af (office). *Website:* www.mfa.gov.af (office).

SPARKES, Andrew James, CMG; British diplomatist; *Ambassador to Kosovo;* b. 4 July 1959; m.; one s. one d. *Education:* Manchester Grammar School and Trinity Hall, Cambridge. *Career:* joined FCO 1982, Jr Desk Officer appointments 1983–85, Second Sec., Chancery, Ankara 1985–88, SE Asian

Dept 1989–90, Near East and N Africa Dept 1990–91, Cen. and Southern Africa Dept 1991–92, First Sec. (Political), Bangkok 1992–95, Grade Man., Personnel Dept 1995–96, Asst Dir, Personnel Man. 1996–97, on loan to Dept of Trade and Industry (Dir of Services Exports) 1997–99, Deputy Head of Mission, Jakarta 1999–2001, Deputy High Commr and Consul Gen., Pretoria 2001–04, Amb. to Democratic Repub. of the Congo 2004–08, to Kosovo 2008–.
Address: British Embassy, Ismail Qemajli 6, Arberi Dragodan, Pristina, Kosovo (office). *Telephone:* (38) 254700 (office). *Fax:* (38) 249799 (office). *E-mail:* britishembassy.pristina@fco.gov.uk (office).

SPASOV, Gjorgji, BSc, PhD; Macedonian academic and diplomatist; b. 11 Aug. 1949; m. Slavica Nikolovska; one s. *Education:* Belgrade Univ., Univ. of Skopje, Univ. of Oxford, UK. *Career:* started career as TV journalist 1973; Asst. Inst. for Sociological, Legal and Political Research, Univ. of Skopje 1976–1983, Sr Researcher 1983–93; Amb. to Bulgaria and Moldava 1994–97, apptd Minister of Justice 1997, Conciliator, OSCE 1998; elected mem. Parl. 1998, 2002; Prof., Univ. of Skopje 1999; Chief of Del. to European Ass. 2003; Amb. to UK 2003–08 (also accred to Iceland and Ireland) 2004–08; Madarski Konanik 1997.
Address: Ministry of Foreign Affairs, Dame Gruev 6, 1000 Skopje, Macedonia (office). *Telephone:* (2) 3110333 (office). *Fax:* (2) 3115790 (office). *E-mail:* mailmnr@mfa.gov.mk (office). *Website:* www.mfa.gov.mk (office).

SPASOVIĆ, Grujica; Serbian diplomatist; *Ambassador to Bosnia and Herzegovina; Career:* Editor-in-Chief and Exec. Ed., Danos (daily newspaper) –2006; Amb. to Bosnia and Herzegovina 2006–.
Address: Embassy of Serbia, 71000 Sarajevo, Obala Maka Dizdara 3a, Bosnia and Herzegovina (office). *Telephone:* (33) 260080 (office). *Fax:* (33) 221469 (office). *E-mail:* yugoamba@bih.net.ba (office).

SPASSKIY, Nikolay Nikolayevich, DPolSc; Russian diplomatist and government official; *Deputy Secretary, National Security Council;* b. 1961, Sevastopol. *Education:* Moscow Inst. of Int. Relations. *Career:* with USSR (later Russian) Ministry of Foreign Affairs 1983–; Deputy Head, First Deputy, Dept of N America 1992–94; Dir 1994–97; mem. Advisory Council, Ministry of Foreign Affairs 1995; Amb. to Italy (also accred to San Marino) 1997–2004; Deputy Sec., Nat. Security Council 2004–. *Publications:* La Fine del Mondo e Altri Racconti Romani 1999, Il Complotto 2000, Il Bizantino 2002, Le Reliquie di San Cirillo 2004.
Address: National Security Council, Ipat'yevski per. 4/10, 103132 Moscow, Russia (office).

SPASSOVA, Plamena; Bulgarian research institute director; *Executive Director, Economic Policy Institute; Education:* Univ. of Nat. and World Economy, Sofia. *Career:* trainee, Econ. Policy Inst., Sofia 2000–01, Library and Documentation Officer 2001–02, Research Fellow 2002–05, Project Dir 2005–06, Deputy Dir 2006, Exec. Dir 2006–.
Address: Economic Policy Institute, 2 Khan Asparouh Street, floor 4, 1463 Sofia, Bulgaria (office). *Telephone:* (2) 9522693 (office). *Fax:* (2) 9520847 (office). *E-mail:* epi@epi-bg.org (office). *Website:* www.epi-bg.org (office).

SPATAFORA, Marcello, LLB; Italian diplomatist; *Permanent Representative, United Nations;* b. 30 July 1941, Innsbruck, Austria. *Education:* Univ. of Pisa. *Career:* joined diplomatic corps 1964, Personnel Dept, Ministry of Foreign Affairs 1964–68; Vice-Consul, Paris 1968–70; First Sec., Embassy in Belgrade 1970–73; Counsellor, Embassy in Beirut 1973–77; Asst to Sec. Gen, Ministry of Foreign Affairs 1977–80; Amb. to Malaysia 1980–86, to Malta 1986–89; Head of Del. for Italian Presidency of EU 1989–91, Head of Armaments Authorization Div. 1991–93; Amb. to Australia 1993–97, to Albania 1997–98; Dir-Gen. of Econ. Affairs, Ministry of Foreign Affairs 1999–2000, Dir-Gen. for Econ. Co-operation and Multilateral Finance 2000–03; Perm. Rep. to UN, New York 2003–; Cavaliero di Gran Croce.
Address: Permanent Mission of Italy to the United Nations, 2 United Nations Plaza, 24th Floor, New York, NY 10017, USA (office). *Telephone:* (212) 486-9191 (office). *Fax:* (212) 486-1036 (office). *E-mail:* italy@un.int (office). *Website:* www.italyun.org (office).

SPECKHARD, Daniel V., BA, MA; American diplomatist; *Ambassador to Greece; Education:* Univ. of Wisconsin. *Career:* assignments have included positions in Int. Affairs Div., Office of Man. and Budget, USAID, staff mem. in US Senate, and in state and local govt 1981–90; advisor, then Dir of Policy and Resources for Deputy Sec. of State 1990–93, Deputy to Amb.-at-Large for New Ind. States 1993–97; Amb. to Belarus 1997–2000; Deputy Asst Sec.-Gen. for Political Affairs, NATO, Brussels 2000–03, Dir of Policy Planning, responsible for advising and assisting the Sec. Gen., sr NATO man., and the Council 2003–05; Dir Iraq Reconstruction Man. Office 2005–06, Deputy Chief of Mission, Baghdad 2006–07; Amb. to Greece 2007–; NATO Service Medal 2003.

Address: US Embassy, Leoforos Vassilissis Sofias 91, 101 60 Athens, Greece (office). *Telephone:* (210) 7212951 (office). *Fax:* (210) 7226724 (office). *E-mail:* AthensAmEmb@state.gov (office). *Website:* athens .usembassy.gov (office).

SPENCE, A. Michael, MA, PhD; American economist and academic; *Philip H. Knight Professor Emeritus, Graduate School of Business, Stanford University; Education:* Princeton Univ., Oxford Univ., UK, Harvard Univ. *Career:* Assoc. Prof. Harvard Univ. 1973–75, Chair. Advisory Cttee on Shareholder Responsibility 1978–79, Prof. 1979–86, Chair. Project in Industry and Competitive Analysis 1980–85, Chair. Business Econs PhD Program 1981–83, Chair. Dept of Econs 1983–84, Dean of Faculty 1984–90; Philip H. Knight Prof. Stanford Univ. 1990–2000, Dean 1990–99, Prof. Emer. 2000–; Dir Gen. Mills, Inc., Nike, Inc., Siebel Systems, Inc., Exult, Inc., Blue Martini Software, Torstar, ITI Educ.; mem. American Econ. Asscn; Fellow AAAS, Econometric Soc.; Nobel Prize in Econs 2001 (jt recipient); numerous other awards and prizes. *Address:* Graduate School of Business, 518 Memorial Way, Stanford University, Stanford, CA 94305-5015, USA (office). *Telephone:* (650) 723-2146 (office). *Website:* www.gsb.stanford.edu/news/spence_resume.html (office).

SPENCER, Baldwin; Antiguan politician and trade unionist; *Prime Minister and Minister of Foreign Affairs;* b. 8 Oct. 1948; m.; one s. one d. *Career:* Leader United Progressive Party; fmr Leader of the Opposition; Prime Minister of Antigua and Barbuda and Minister of Foreign Affairs 2004–. *Address:* Office of the Prime Minister, Queen Elizabeth Highway, St John's; United Progressive Party, Nevis Street, St John's (office); Cooks Estate, St John's, Antigua (home). *Telephone:* 462-4956 (office); 562-1049 (office); 462-1818; 461-4657 (home). *Fax:* 462-3225 (office); 462-5937 (office); 562-1065 (home). *E-mail:* pmo@candw.ag (office); upp@candw.ag (office). *Website:* www.antiguabarbuda.net/pmo (office); www.uppantigua.com (office).

ŠPIDLA, Vladimír, PhD; Czech politician; *Commissioner for Employment, Social Affairs and Equal Opportunities, European Commission;* b. 22 April 1951, Prague; m. 1st; two s.; m. 2nd Viktorie Spidlova; one s. one d. *Education:* Charles Univ., Prague. *Career:* fmr archaeologist, worker at historical monuments, sawmill, dairy and livestock industry; Vice-Pres. for Educ., Health Service, Social Affairs and Culture, Dist Cttee, Jindřichův Hradec 1990–91; Dir Labour Office, Jindřichův Hradec 1991–96; mem. Chamber of Deputies 1996–; Deputy Prime Minister and Minister of Labour and Social Affairs 1998–2002; Prime Minister of the Czech Repub. 2002–04 (resgnd); EU Commr for Employment, Social Affairs and Equal Opportunities 2004–; Founding mem. Czech Social Democratic Party Br. in S Bohemia 1989, joined party leadership 1992, Vice-Chair. 1997–2001, Chair. 2001–. *Address:* European Commission, 200 Rue de la Loi, 1040 Brussels, Belgium (office). *Telephone:* (2) 299-11-11 (office). *Fax:* (2) 295-01-38 (office). *E-mail:* V.Spidla@ec.europa.eu (office). *Website:* ec.europa.eu/ commission_barroso/spidla (office).

SPIERS, Ronald Ian, BA, MA; American diplomatist (retd.); b. 9 July 1925, Orange, NJ; m. Patience Baker 1949; one s. three d. *Education:* Dartmouth Coll., Princeton Univ. *Career:* USN 1943–46; mem. US Del. to UN 1955–58; Dir Disarmament Affairs, State Dept, Washington 1958–62, NATO Affairs 1962–66; Political Counsellor, US Embassy in London 1966–69, Minister 1974–77; Asst Sec. of State for Political-Mil. Affairs 1969–73; Amb. to the Bahamas 1973–74, to Turkey 1977–80; Asst Sec. for Intelligence and Research, Dept of State 1980–81; Amb. to Pakistan 1981–83; Under-Sec. for Man., Dept of State 1983–89; Under-Sec.-Gen. for Political and Gen. Ass. Affairs, UN, New York 1989–92; consultant to State Dept 1992–; mem. Council on Foreign Relations; Fellow, Nat. Acad. of Public Admin., American Acad. of Diplomacy; Presidential Distinguished Service Award 1984. *Address:* 1320 Middletown Road, S Londonderry, VT 05155, USA. *Telephone:* (802) 824-6482 (home). *E-mail:* rispiers@comcast.net (home).

SPINNER, Bruno, PhD; Swiss diplomatist; *Ambassador to Italy;* b. 1948, Zurich. *Career:* Minister and Deputy Head of Swiss Mission to EU, Brussels 1989–92; Head, European Integration Office, Berne 1992–2000; Amb. to UK 2000–04, to Italy (also accred to Malta and San Marino) 2004–. *Address:* Swiss Embassy, Via Barnaba Origani 61, Rome, Italy (office). *Telephone:* (6) 80957322 (office). *Fax:* (6) 8088510 (office). *Website:* www .eda.admin.ch/roma (office).

SPIROIU, Lt-Gen. Niculae, PhD; Romanian international organization official, fmr government official and fmr army officer; *Executive Director, Euro-Atlantic Council Romania, NATO;* b. 6 July 1936, Bucharest; m. 1963

(wife died 1991); one s. one d. *Education:* Tech. Mil. Acad. *Career:* scientific researcher with the Centre of Studies and Tests for Tanks and Autos Deputy Chief and Tech. Dept Chief; State Sec. and Head of the Army Supply Dept; Minister of Nat. Defence 1992–94; Counsellor Minister to UN 1994–2000; Sr Counsellor to Minister of Water and Environment Protection 2001–02; Exec. Dir Euro-Atlantic Council of Romania—Casa NATO 2005–; also currently Sr Research Fellow, EURISC Foundation; Co-Chair. US Action Comm., Center of Strategic and Int. Studies, Washington, DC 1997–99;. *Address:* Euro-Atlantic Council Romania—Casa NATO, 82-88 M. Eminescu Str., ap. 19, Sector 2, Bucharest (office); EURISC Foundation, 82-88 Mihai Eminescu Street, Entrance B, app 19, Sector 2, Bucharest, Sector 2, PO Box 2-101, Romania (office). *Telephone:* (21) 3193278 (Casa NATO) (office); (21) 2122102 (office). *Fax:* (21) 3193279 (Casa NATO) (office); (21) 3193279 (office). *E-mail:* office@casanato.org (office). *Website:* www.casanato.org (office); www.eurisc.org (office).

SPOERRI, Philip, PhD; German lawyer and international organization executive; *Director for International Law and Co-operation within the Movement, International Committee of the Red Cross;* b. 1963; m.; one s. *Education:* Göttingen, Munich and Bielefeld Univs, Geneva Univ., Switzerland. *Career:* worked as lawyer in pvt. firm in Munich; began career with ICRC in 1994, carried out first mission for ICRC in Israel (Occupied Territories), continued with missions in Kuwait and Yemen, Afghanistan and Democratic Repub. of Congo, headed legal advisers to Dept of Operations, Geneva, returned to Afghanistan as Head of Del. 2004–06, Dir for Int. Law and Co-operation within the Movt 2006–. *Address:* International Committee of the Red Cross, 9 avenue de la Paix, 1202 Geneva, Switzerland (office). *Telephone:* (22) 734-60-01 (office). *Fax:* (22) 733-20-57 (office). *E-mail:* press.gva@icrc.org (office). *Website:* www .icrc.org (office).

SPOGLI, Ronald P., AB, MBA; American diplomatist and investment banker; *Ambassador to Italy;* b. 1948, Los Angeles; m. Georgia Spogli; one d. one step-s. *Education:* Stanford Univ., Harvard Univ. *Career:* researcher, Stanford Univ. based in Milan, Italy 1972–73; fmr Man. Dir Investment Banking Div. Dean Witter Reynolds Inc.; Co-founder and Pnr, Freeman Spogli & Co. 1983–; Amb. to Italy 2005–; apptd to US State Dept's Fulbright Foreign Scholarship Bd 2002; mem. Bd of Visitors, Stanford Univ.'s Inst. for Int. Studies 2000–; mem. Bd AFC Enterprises, Regents Bancshares, Winebow. *Address:* United States Embassy, via Vittorio Veneto 119/A, 00187 Rome, Italy (office). *Telephone:* (06) 46741 (office). *Fax:* (06) 46742356 (office). *Website:* rome.usembassy.gov (office).

SPONHEIM, Lars, MSc; Norwegian politician; *Leader, Liberal Party;* b. 23 May 1957, Halden; m.; three c. *Career:* consultant 1981–84; teacher, Statens Gartnerskule Hjeltnes 1984–88, Prin. 1992–; mem. local council, Ulvik Municipality 1984–95, Mayor 1988–91; mem. County Council, Hordaland Co. 1992–93; Dir of Agric., Ulvik and Granvin Municipalities 1993; mem. Parl. for Hordaland Co. to Storting (Parl.) 1993–, mem. Parl. Finance Cttee; Leader Liberal Party 1996–; Minister of Trade and Industry 1997–2000; Minister of Food and Agric. 2001–05; mem. Parl. Foreign Cttee 2005–. *Address:* Venstre, Stortinget, 0026 Oslo, Norway. *Telephone:* 23-31-33-62 (office). *Fax:* 23-31-38-72 (office). *E-mail:* lars.sponheim@stortinget.no (office); lars@venstre.no (office). *Website:* www.venstre.no (office).

SRINIVASAN, Krishnan, MA; Indian diplomatist and writer; b. 15 Feb. 1937, Madras; m. Brinda Srinivasan 1975; one s. *Education:* Bedford School, Christ Church, Oxford, UK. *Career:* Chargé d'affaires, Libya 1969–71; High Commr in Zambia (also accred to Botswana) 1974–77, in Nigeria (also accred to Benin and Cameroon) 1980–82, in Bangladesh 1989–92; Amb. to Netherlands 1986–89; Perm. Sec. Foreign Ministry 1992–94, Foreign Sec. 1994–95; Deputy Sec.-Gen. (Political) Commonwealth 1995–2002; Visiting Fellow, Wolfson Coll., Cambridge, Centre of Int. Studies, Cambridge; Sr Fellow, Inst. of Commonwealth Studies, Univ. of London; Fellow, Netherlands Inst. of Advanced Study 2003–04, Maulana Azad Inst. of Asian Studies, Calcutta 2006–08, Swedish Collegium for Advanced Studies 2008; Hon. Mem. Christ Church Sr Common Room, Hon. Visiting Prof., Admin. Staff, Coll. of India; Hind Ratna (India) 2001, Chevalier (Cameroon) 2007; Ramsden Sermon, Univ. of Oxford 2002, Rajiv Gandhi Memorial Lecture 2006. *Publications:* The Rise, Decline and Future of the British Commonwealth 2005, The Jamdani Revolution 2008, several novels, short stories and articles on int. affairs. *Address:* Flat 8, Courtleigh, 126 Earls Court Road, London, W8 6QL, England (home). *Telephone:* (20) 7370-0339. *E-mail:* ksrinivasanuk@yahoo .co.uk.

SSEMPALA, Edith Grace, MCE; Ugandan diplomatist. *Education:* Lumumba Univ., Moscow, Russia. *Career:* Quality Controller, Rifa Electronic Co., Stockholm, Sweden 1981–86; Amb. to Denmark, Finland, Iceland, Norway and Sweden 1986–96, Dean of Diplomatic Corps, Copenhagen, Denmark 1992–96; Amb. to USA 1996–2006; Rep. to IBRD and IMF 1996–2006; mem. Advisory Bd Center for Strategic and Int. Studies—Africa Program 1998–99; lectured at numerous orgs and univs including UN on African devt and econ. reform; commentator on human rights and democracy issues; Alpha Kappa Alpha Sorority Inc. Int. Service Award to a Foreign Woman 2000, The Links Inc. Int. Trends and Services Award 2000. *Publications include:* The Road to Development: Africa in the 21st Century, Democracy – Uganda's Experience. *Address:* c/o Ministry of Foreign Affairs, Embassy House, PO Box 7048, Kampala, Uganda (office). *Telephone:* (41) 2345661 (office).

STADTHAGEN, Salvador, LLB, MA; Nicaraguan diplomatist; b. 20 April 1957, Jinotega; m. Analía Vargas; four s. *Education:* American and Harvard Univs, USA. *Career:* Official Liaison between Nicaraguan Resistance (UN) and US Dept of State 1985–86; employed by Creative Associates International, Inc., Washington, DC 1987–90; Exec. Dir Educ. for Democracy Nat. Program in Nicaragua 1992–95; Chargé d'affaires a.i. and Minister-Counsellor, Tokyo 1995–99, Amb. to Repub. of China (Taiwan) 1995–99, Sec. of Econ. Relations and Co-operation, Ministry of Foreign Affairs 1999–2000, Deputy Minister of Foreign Affairs 2000–02, Amb. to USA 2003–07. *Address:* Ministry of Foreign Affairs, Del Cine González al Sur sobre Avenida Bolivar, Managua, Nicaragua (office). *Telephone:* 244-8000 (office). *Fax:* 228-5102 (office). *E-mail:* despacho.ministro@cancilleria.gob.ni (office). *Website:* www.cancilleria.gob.ni (office).

STAFFORD, Joseph D., III, BA, MA; American diplomatist; b. 19 March 1950, Okla; m.; one s. *Education:* Univ. of Tennessee. *Career:* joined Foreign Service in 1978, Consular Officer, Tehran 1979, Admin. Officer, Palermo 1980–82, Political Officer, Cairo 1983–86, Kuwait 1986–88, Chief of Political Section, Algiers 1988–89, Political Analyst, Arabian Peninsula, Bureau of Intelligence and Research 1989–91, Deputy Dir of Maghreb Affairs 1991–93, Deputy Chief of Mission, Nouakchott 1993–96, Algiers 1996–98, Tunis 1998–2001, Abidjan 2001–04, Amb. to The Gambia 2004–07; several Superior and Meritorious Honor Awards, Award for Valor. *Address:* US Department of State, 2201 C Street NW, Washington, DC 20520, USA (office). *Telephone:* (202) 647-4000 (office). *Fax:* (202) 647-6738 (office). *Website:* www.state.gov (office).

STAGG, Sir (Charles) Richard (Vernon), KCMG, CMG; British diplomatist; *High Commissioner to India;* b. 27 Sept. 1955; m. Arabella Stagg. *Education:* Winchester Coll., Univ. of Oxford. *Career:* joined FCO 1977, served in Soviet Dept 1988–91, Pvt. Sec. to Foreign Secretary 1993–96, Head EU Dept 1996–98, Dir Public Services/Information 2001–03, Dir-Gen. of Corp. Affairs 2003–07; overseas postings include Third, later Second Sec., Embassy in Sofia 1979–82, The Hague 1982–85, Council Secr., Brussels 1987–88, Press Spokesman, Brussels 1991–93, Amb. to Bulgaria 1998–2001, High Commr to India 2007–. *Address:* British High Commission, Shantipath, Chanakyapuri, New Delhi 110021, India (office). *Telephone:* (11) 26872161 (office). *Fax:* (11) 26870065 (office). *E-mail:* postmaster.nedel@fco.gov.uk (office). *Website:* www.ukindia.com (office); www.britishhighcommission.gov.uk (office).

STAGNO UGARTE, Bruno, BSc, MSc; Costa Rican politician; *Minister of Foreign Relations;* b. 8 April 1970, Paris, France; m. Laetitia Stagno; two c. *Education:* Princeton and Georgetown Univs, USA and Sorbonne, France. *Career:* Consul-Gen. and Minister-Counsellor, Embassy in France 1994–98; Chef de Cabinet, Minister of Foreign Relations and Worship, San Jose 1998–2000; Prof., Universidad Latina 1999; Prof., School of Political Science, Univ. of Costa Rica 2000–02; adviser to legislative ass. 2000–02; Perm. Rep. to UN, New York 2002–06; Minister of Foreign Relations 2006–; Vice-Chair. Bureau of CSD-11 (Comm. on Sustainable Devt), mem. CSD-12; mem. Inst. for Democracy and Electoral Assistance 1999–2000; Pres. Ass. of State Parties, Int. Criminal Court 2005–08; mem. Advisory Bd Parliamentarians for Global Action 2005–06; Del. Bureau Int. des Expositions, 29th session of UNESCO Gen. Conference 1995–98. *Address:* Ministry of Foreign Relations, Avda 7 y 9, Calle 11 y 13, Apdo 10027, 1000 San Jose, Costa Rica (office). *Telephone:* 223-7555 (office). *Fax:* 257-6597 (office). *E-mail:* despacho.ministro@rree.go.cr (office). *Website:* www.rree.go.cr (office).

STAMATOPOULOS, Thrassyvoulos (Terry), BSc, MA; Greek diplomatist; *Permanent Representative, NATO;* m.; two s. one d. *Education:* Aristotle Univ., London School of Econs, UK, McGill Univ., Canada, Georgia State Univ., USA. *Career:* Deputy Dir Political Affairs Directorate, Ministry for Macedonia and Thrace 1979–80, Dir 1991–95; mem. Cabinet of Foreign Affairs Minister 1980–81; Consul in Atlanta, USA 1981–87; Consul Gen. in Alexandria, Egypt 1987–91; Perm. Rep. to EU, Brussels 1995–2000; Deputy Perm. Rep. to NATO, Brussels 2000–04, Perm. Rep. 2007–; Dir-Gen. for EU Affairs, Ministry of Foreign Affairs 2004–07; Grand Commdr, Order of the Phoenix, Commdr, Order of Danebrog (Denmark). *Address:* North Atlantic Treaty Organization (NATO), boulevard Léopold III, 1110 Brussels, Belgium (office). *Telephone:* (2) 707-41-11 (office). *Fax:* (2) 707-45-79 (office). *E-mail:* natodoc@hq.nato.int (office). *Website:* www.nato.int (office).

STANCZYK, Janusz, PhD; Polish diplomatist; *Ambassador to the Netherlands;* m.; two c. *Education:* Jagiellonian Univ., Kraków, Saint Louis Univ. and Univ. of Michigan, USA, Inst. of Legal Sciences, Polish Acad. of Sciences. *Career:* Dir Legal and Treaties Dept, Foreign Ministry, Poland 1992–95, Dir Gen. for Legal Affairs 1995–97, Under-Sec. of State for Legal and Econ. Affairs and for relations with int. orgs (also responsible for ministry contact with nat. parl.) 1997–2000; mem. Del. UN Gen. Ass. 1992–96, 1998–2000; Perm. Rep. to UN, New York 2000–04; Deputy Minister for Foreign Affairs and Under-Secretary of State 2004–07; Amb. to Netherlands 2007–, also Perm. Rep. to Org. for the Prohibition of Chemical Weapons. *Address:* Embassy of Poland, Alesanderstraat 25, 2514 JM, The Hague, Netherlands (office). *Telephone:* (70) 7990100 (office). *Fax:* (70) 7990137 (office). *E-mail:* ambhaga@polamb.nl (office); opcw@polamb.nl (office). *Website:* www.polamb.nl (office).

STANHOPE, Adm. Sir Mark, KCB, OBE; British naval officer; *Commander-in-Chief Fleet;* b. 1952. *Education:* Britannia Royal Naval Coll., Dartmouth, St Peter's Coll., Univ. of Oxford, Royal Coll. of Defence Studies and Higher Command and Staff Course. *Career:* fmr Jr Officer, nuclear-powered submarines HMS Swiftsure, HMS Superb, conventional submarine HMS Orpheus; qualified for submarine command 1981; Commdr HMS Orpheus 1982; joined staff of Capt. Submarine Sea Training 1984; formal staff training, Greenwich 1986; fmr Commdr HMS Splendid; fmr teacher of prospective submarine commdg officers, Perisher course; worked in Directorate of Naval Operations and Trade, Ministry of Defence; promoted to Capt. 1991; Commdr frigate HMS London 1991–93; returned to Submarine Sea Training 1993; Deputy Prin. Staff Officer to Chief of Defence Staff, Ministry of Defence 1994; Commdr HMS Illustrious 1998–2000; promoted to Rear Adm. 2000; Dir of Operational Man., HQ of NATO's Regional Command N, Netherlands 2000–01; seconded to Cabinet Office 2002; promoted to Vice-Adm. 2002; Deputy C-in-C Fleet 2002–04; promoted to Adm. 2004; Deputy Supreme Allied Commdr, Transformation (SACT), NATO 2004–07; C-in-C Fleet 2007–; Fellow, Nautical Inst.; Freeman of City of London and Guild; Younger Brother, Trinity House; mem. Upholders Livery Co.; US Legion of Merit (Officer). *Address:* Ministry of Defence, Main Bldg, Whitehall, London, SW1A 2HB, England (office). *Telephone:* (20) 7218-900 (office). *E-mail:* public@ministers.mod.uk (office). *Website:* www.royal-navy.mod.uk (office).

STANIČIĆ, Mladen, BA, MA, PhD; Croatian research institute director; *Director, Institute for International Relations (IMO);* b. 20 March 1940, Zagreb. *Education:* Faculty of Econs, Univ. of Zagreb. *Career:* journalist and columnist, Vjesnik (daily newspaper), Zagreb 1964–78; joined Inst. of Int. Relations (IMO), Zagreb 1978, currently Dir and Head of Dept for Int. Econ. and Political Reforms; Prof., Faculty of Political Science, Univ. of Zagreb; Ed.-in-Chief Croatian International Relations Review; Co-Convenor Regional Stability in SE Europe Working Group, Partnership for Peace Consortium; mem. Coordinating Council for Devt Strategy, Croatia in the 21st Century, Govt. of Croatia; mem. Council for Int. Relations, Ministry of Foreign Affairs; mem. Del. to ECOSOC Conf., New York 1994. *Address:* Institute for International Relations (IMO), Ulica Ljudevita Farkaša Vukotinovića 2, PO Box 303, 10000 Zagreb, Croatia (office). *Telephone:* (1) 4877-462 (office). *Fax:* (1) 4828-361 (office). *E-mail:* mladen@irmo.hr (office); ured@irmo.hr (office). *Website:* www.imo.hr (office).

STANKEVIČIUS, Česlovas Vytautas; Lithuanian politician, engineer and diplomatist; *Adviser to the Minister of Foreign Affairs;* b. 27 Feb. 1937, Vilkaviskis Region; m. Jadvyga Litvinaitė 1962; two s. *Education:* Kaunas Polytech. Inst. *Career:* engineer, Chief of Design, Chief Engineer, Kaunas Inst. of Urban Planning and Designing 1965–89; Chair. Kaunas Bd Sajūdis Movt 1989–90; elected Deputy and Vice-Pres. of Supreme Council, Repub. of Lithuania; signatory to March 11th Act on Re-establishment of Independence; Head official del. in negotiations with Russia 1990–93; Head, Lithuanian Parl. del. to N Atlantic Ass. 1991–92; mem. Seimas, Parl. Group of Christian Democrats 1996–2000; Minister of Defence 1996–2000; Amb. to Norway 2001–05; Adviser to the Minister of Foreign Affairs

2005–; co-author projects on nat. security and defence concept of Lithuania 1996, Law on Defence Org. 1997, Lithuanian defence strategy 2000; Order of Gediminas 2000. *Publications:* Enhancing Security of Lithuania and Other Baltic States in 1992–94 (monograph), Negotiations with Russia on Troop Withdrawal 2002.
Address: Ministry of Foreign Affairs, J. Tumo-Vaizganto 9.2, 01511 Vilnius, Lithuania (office). *Telephone:* (5) 2362861 (office). *Fax:* (5) 2362405 (office). *E-mail:* ceslovas.stankevicius@urm.lt (office); cestan@takas.lt (home). *Website:* www.urm.lt (office).

STANTON, William A., MA, PhD; American diplomatist; *Deputy Chief of Mission, Embassy in Seoul;* m. Karen Clark Stanton; two d. *Education:* Fordham Univ., New York, Univ. of N Carolina, Albert-Ludwigs Univ., Freiburg, Germany. *Career:* joined Foreign Service 1978, served in consular and political sections, Embassy in Beirut 1979–81, watch officer, Dept of State Operations Center 1981–82, staff asst to Asst Sec. for Near East and S Asian Affairs 1982–83, country officer for Lebanon 1983–85, Mandarin language training 1985–87, Political Officer, Beijing 1987–90, Chief of Internal Political Reporting 1989–90, sr training at Hoover Inst. 1990–91, Political-Mil. Affairs Officer, Islamabad 1991–93, Special Asst for E Asia and Pacific Affairs to Under-sec. for Political Affairs 1993–94, Deputy Dir Office of Chinese and Mongolian Affairs 1994–95, Minister Counsellor for Political Affairs, Beijing 1995–98, mem. Senior Seminar 1998–99, Dir Office of UN Political Affairs 1999–2001, Dir Office of Egyptian and N African Affairs 2001–03, promoted to rank of Minister-Counselor 2002, Deputy Chief of Mission, Canberra 2003–05, Chargé d'affaires a.i. in Australia 2005–06; Deputy Chief of Mission, Embassy in Seoul 2006–; three Superior Honor Awards, one Superior Group Award, three Sr Performance Awards.
Address: American Embassy, 32, Sejong-no, Jongno-gu, Seoul 110-710, Republic of Korea (office). *Telephone:* (2) 397-4114 (office). *Fax:* (2) 735-3903 (office). *E-mail:* EmbassySeoulPA@state.gov (office). *Website:* seoul .usembassy.gov (office).

STANZEL, Volker, PhD; German diplomatist; *Political Director, Ministry of Foreign Affairs;* b. 1948, Frankfurt. *Education:* Frankfurt Univ., Kyoto Univ., Cologne Univ. *Career:* joined Foreign Service 1979, worked in Embassies in Rome, Tokyo, Aden, Beijing; Head of Press and Information Dept, Embassy in Beijing 1990–93; Head of Operation Center, Foreign Office in Bonn 1993–95, Head of Dept for Non-Proliferation and Civilian Use of Nuclear Energy 1999–2001; Foreign Policy Advisor to SPD, Bundestag 1995–98; Visiting Fellow, German Marshall Fund, Washington, DC 1998–99; Dir for Asian and Pacific Affairs, Ministry of Foreign Affairs 2001–02; Dir-Gen. for Political Affairs 2002–04; Amb. to People's Repub. of China 2004–07; Political Dir Ministry of Foreign Affairs 2007–; Hon. Prof. (Zhengzhou Univ.) 2006. *Publications:* Japan: Head of the Earth 1982, Winds of Change: East Asia's New Revolution 1997, A World of Warring States: China's Perception and Possibilities of Its International Role 1997, NATO after Enlargement 1998, Dealing with the Backwoods: New Problems in Transatlantic Relations 1999, Remembering and Forgetting: But Will the Past Forget About Us? 2001, China's Foreign Policy 2001, Germany's Defense at the Hindukush: The Experiment of Afghanistan 2005.
Address: Federal Ministry of Foreign Affairs, Werderscher Markt 1, 10020 Berlin Germany (office). *Telephone:* (30) 50002677 (office). *Fax:* (30) 500052677 (office). *E-mail:* z-d@diplo.de (office). *Website:* www.diplo.de (office).

STAPLES, George M., BA, MA; American government administrator, diplomatist and academic; *Adjunct Professor, Patterson School of Diplomacy and International Commerce, University of Kentucky;* b. 1947, Knoxville, Tenn. *Education:* Univ. of Southern Calif. and Cen. Michigan Univ. *Career:* served as officer in USAF; worked as man. in pvt. industry; career member of Foreign Service, assignments have included The Bahamas, Uruguay, El Salvador, served as Deputy Chief of Mission in Bahrain and Zimbabwe, Sr Watch Officer, State Dept's Operation Center, Sr Turkey Desk Officer, Bureau of European Affairs during first Gulf War, Amb. to Rwanda 1998–2001, later to Cameroon and Equatorial Guinea, Political Advisor to Supreme Allied Commander Europe (SACEUR), NATO, Brussels –2006, Dir-Gen. Foreign Service and Dir Human Resources, US State Dept 2006–07; Adjunct Prof., Patterson School of Diplomacy and Int. Commerce, Univ. of Kentucky 2007–; fmr Nat. Security Fellow, Hoover Inst.
Address: 461 Patterson Office Tower, Patterson School of Diplomacy and International Commerce, University of Kentucky, Lexington, KY 40506-0027, USA (office). *Telephone:* (859) 257-4666 (office). *Fax:* (859) 257-4676 (office). *Website:* www.uky.edu/PattersonSchool (office).

STAPLETON, Craig Roberts, BA, MBA; American business executive and diplomatist; *Ambassador to France;* b. Kansas City, Mo.; m. Dorothy Walker Stapleton; one s. one d. *Education:* Phillips Exeter Acad., Harvard Coll. and Harvard Business School. *Career:* Pres. Marsh & McLennan Real Estate Advisors, New York 1982–2005; Pnr with George W. Bush in ownership of Texas Rangers professional baseball team 1989–98; Conn. State Chair. for re-election campaign of Pres. George W. Bush 2004; mem. Bd of Dirs Allegheny Properties 2005, Metro PCS 2005, TB Woods & Winston Pnrs 2005; Amb. to Czech Repub. 2001–04, to France 2005–; Pres. Vaclav Havel Foundation; fmr mem. Bd Peace Corps; fmr Trustee Brunswick School, Greenwich, Conn.; mem. Visiting Cttee for Harvard Coll.; Jan Masaryk Medal for service to the Czech Repub.
Address: Embassy of the USA, 2 avenue Gabriel, 75382 Paris, Cedex 08, France (office). *Telephone:* 1-43-12-22-22 (office). *Fax:* 1-42-66-97-83 (office). *Website:* france.usembassy.gov (office).

STASAVAGE, David, BA, PhD; American academic; *Professor of Politics, New York University;* *Education:* Cornell Univ., Univ. of Cambridge UK, Harvard Univ. *Career:* Consultant, World Bank Policy Research Dept 1995; Researcher, OECD Devt Centre 1995–97; Research Fellow, St Antony's Coll., Oxford 1997–99; Lecturer, Dept of Int. Relations, LSE 1999–2003, Sr Lecturer 2003–05, Reader 2005; Assoc. Prof. of Politics, Dept of Politics, New York Univ. 2006–; mem. Editorial Bd International Organization (journal); Faculty Assoc., Suntory-Toyota Centre for the Study of Econs and Related Disciplines 1999–; Consultant, Int. Econ. Analysis Div., Bank of England 2000–; Assoc. Ed. Political Studies (journal) 2000–; Visiting Scholar, French Inst. of Int. Relations 1997. *Publications:* Public Debt and the Birth of the Democratic State: France and Great Britain 1688–1789 2003, The Political Economy of a Common Currency: The CFA Franc Zone Since 1945 2003; numerous articles in political science journals.
Address: NYU Department of Politics, Room 414, 19 West 4th Street, New York, NY 10012, USA (office). *Telephone:* (212) 998-8500 (office). *Fax:* (212) 995-4184 (home). *E-mail:* david.stasavage@nyu.edu (office). *Website:* politics.as.nyu.edu (office).

STAUR, Carsten, MA; Danish diplomatist; *Permanent Representative, United Nations;* b. 9 Nov. 1954; m.; two c. *Education:* Univ. of Copenhagen. *Career:* Head of Section, Ministry of Foreign Affairs 1981–86, 1989–93, Head of Dept 1994–96; First Sec., Perm. Mission to UN, Geneva 1986–1989; Amb. to Israel 1996–98; Under-Sec. for Admin. Affairs, Ministry of Foreign Affairs 1998–2000, Under-Sec. for Bilateral Devt Co-operation 2000–2001, State Sec. for Devt Co-operation, Middle East, Africa, Asia, Latin America and UN 2001–07; Perm. Rep. to UN, New York 2007–.
Address: Permanent Mission of Denmark to the United Nations, 1 Dag Hammarskjöld Plaza, 885 Second Avenue, 18th Floor, New York, NY 10017, USA (office). *Telephone:* (212) 308-7009 (office). *Fax:* (212) 308-3384 (office). *E-mail:* nycmis@um.dk (office). *Website:* www .missionfnnewyork.um.dk/en/ (office).

STAVRAKIS, Charilaos, BA, MBA; Cypriot politician; *Minister of Finance;* b. 1956. *Education:* Univ. of Cambridge, UK, Harvard Univ. Grad. School of Business Admin, USA. *Career:* more than 25 years' experience in banking sector; undertook two-month consulting position at World Bank 1989; held various positions at Bank of Cyprus, including Head of Strategic Planning and Business Devt and Sr Man. of Treasury and Int. Services, Group Gen. Man. Int. Banking 1988–2004, Gen. Man. Cyprus Investment & Securities Corpn Ltd (CISCO) (investment banking arm of the Group) 2003–08; mem. Bd Dirs Cyprus Oil Refinery, Bank of Cyprus Australia, Bank of Cyprus (Channel Islands) Ltd, Bank of Cyprus (AEDAK), Bank of Cyprus Mutual Funds Ltd, BOC Ventures Ltd, CEO-Cyprus and Deputy Group CEO 2005–08, assumed additional duties involving man. of subsidiary cos of the Group: BOC Factors, Bank of Cyprus Finance Corpn, General Insurance of Cyprus, Eurolife, The Cyprus Investment and Securities Corpn Ltd (CISCO), BOC Mutual Funds Ltd, Bank of Cyprus UK and the setting up of banks in Russia and Ukraine; Chair. Electricity Authority Cyprus 2005–08, Cyprus Bankers Employers' Asscn 2005–08; Minister of Finance (Ind.) 2008–; mem. Chartered Inst. of Bankers (ACIB) 1988.
Address: Ministry of Finance, Cnr M. Karaolis Street and G. Afxentiou Street, 1439 Nicosia, Cyprus (office). *Telephone:* 22601192 (office). *Fax:* 22602750 (office). *E-mail:* registry@mof.gov.cy (office). *Website:* www.mof .gov.cy (office).

ŠTEFKA, Maj.-Gen. Pavel; Czech army general; *Chief of the General Staff;* b. 15 Sept. 1954, Ruda nad Modravou; m. Jirina; three d. *Education:* Mil. Coll., Vyskov, Mil. Acad., Warsaw, European Business School, Prague and American Nat. War Coll., Washington DC, USA. *Career:* Chief of Staff of motorized bn., then Deputy Chief of Staff of motorized Regt, E Mil. Dist; Chief of Staff, later Commdr of motorized Regt, Bratislava; Chief of Operations in an armoured div.; tutor Mil. Acad. Brno 1991–94; Commdr 6th Mechanized Brigade, Brno 1994; Deputy Commdr 2nd Army Corps and Chief of Staff HQ Ground Forces, Olomouc 1994–98; Chief of Operations Section of the Gen. Staff, Army of the Czech Repub. 1998–99, Chief of the Gen. Staff 2002–; Cross of Merit of Minister of Defence (Czech Republic), Medal for Service to the Nation, NATO Medal for Service for Peace and Freedom, Commemorative Medal of Minister of Defence (Slovakia), Silver Medal of Polish Army, Commemorative Medal of Auxiliary Tech. Bns, Hon. Remembrance Badge of Fifty Years of NATO. *Address:* c/o Ministry of Defence, Tychonova 1, 160 01 Prague 6, Czech Republic (office). *Telephone:* (2) 33041111 (office). *Fax:* (2) 3116238 (office). *E-mail:* stefkap@army.cz (office). *Website:* www.army.cz (office).

STEIGER, William R. (Bill), BA, PhD; American diplomatist; *Ambassador to Mozambique;* b. 1969, Arlington, Va. *Education:* St Albans School for Boys, Yale Univ., Univ. of California, Los Angeles. *Career:* Educ. Policy Advisor for Tommy G. Thompson, Gov. of Wisconsin –2001; Dir Office of Global Health Affairs and Special Asst to Sec. of US Dept of Health and Human Services 2001–08; US mem. Exec. Bd WHO; Pres. Exec. Cttee to Pan-American Health Org.; US mem. on Bd of Dirs of Global Fund to Fight AIDS, Tuberculosis, and Malaria;, Amb. to Mozambique 2008–. *Address:* US Embassy, Av. Kenneth Kaunda 193, CP 783, Maputo, Mozambique (office). *Telephone:* 21492797 (office). *Fax:* 21490114 (office). *E-mail:* maputoirc@state.gov (office). *Website:* maputo.usembassy.gov (office).

STEIN, Shimon, BA, MA; Israeli diplomatist; b. 1948; m.; two c. *Education:* Hebrew Univ. of Jerusalem. *Career:* joined Foreign Service 1974; Analyst, Centre for Political Research 1974–80; served at Embassy in Bonn 1980–85; Deputy Dir N American Dept 1985–86; Deputy Dir Office of the Under-Sec. of State 1986–88; Political Affairs Adviser, Embassy in Washington, DC 1988–93; Dir Dept of Weapons Control and Disarmament 1993–97; Deputy Under-Sec. of State 1998; Amb. to Germany 2001–07. *Address:* c/o Ministry of Foreign Affairs, 9 Yitzhak Rabin Blvd, Kiryat Ben-Gurion, Jerusalem 91035, Israel (office). *E-mail:* shimonstein@yahoo.com (office).

STEINBERG, Donald K., BA, M.ECON., MA; American diplomatist; *Vice President for Multilateral Affairs, International Crisis Group;* b. 25 March 1953, Los Angeles. *Education:* Reed Coll., Portland, Ore., Univ. of Toronto, Canada, Columbia Univ. *Career:* joined Foreign Service, rising to rank of Minister-Counselor; postings in Brazil, Malaysia, Mauritius and Cen. African Repub.; acting Chief Textile Negotiator, Office of US Trade Rep. 1988–89; first Dir House Task Force on Trade and Competitiveness 1989, Sr Policy Adviser for Foreign Affairs and Defense to Leader of House of Reps 1989–90; Officer-in-Charge and Counselor for Econ. and Commercial Affairs, US Embassy, Pretoria 1990–93; Deputy Press Sec. for Nat. Security Affairs, White House 1993; Special Asst to fmr Pres. Clinton for W African Affairs and Sr Dir for African Affairs, Sr Dir for Public Affairs, Nat. Security Council; Amb. to Angola 1995–98; Special Haiti Coordinator, Dept of State 1999–2001, Special Rep. of Pres. and Sec. of State for Global Humanitarian Demining 1998, Deputy Asst Sec. of State for Population, Refugees and Migration 2000–01, Prin. Deputy Dir . for Policy Planning 2001–03, Dir. Joint Policy Council 2003–50; Sr Fellow Jennings Randolph Fellowship Program, US Inst. of Peace 2004–05; Vice Pres. for Multilateral Affairs and Dir, New York office, Int. Crisis Group 2005–; Pulitzer Fellowship and fellowships from American Political Science Asscn, Univ. of Toronto, Uma Chapman Fox Foundation and US Dept of State; Presidential Meritorious Honor Award 1994, Hough Award for Excellence in Print, three Superior Honor Awards, Distinguished Service Award 2002, Hunt Award for Advancing Women's Role in Policy Formation 2003 US Dept of State. *Publications;* many publs on US trade policies, Africa, landmines and the role of Congress in foreign affairs. *Address:* International Crisis Group, 420 Lexington Avenue, Suite 2640, New York, NY 10170, USA (office). *Telephone:* (212) 813-0820 (office). *Fax:* (212) 813-0825 (office). *Website:* www.crisisgroup.org (office).

STEINBERG, James B., BA, JD; American fmr government official and academic administrator; *Dean, Lyndon B. Johnson School of Public Affairs, University of Texas; Education:* Harvard and Yale Univs. *Career:* Special Asst to Asst Sec. for Planning and Evaluation, Dept of Health, Educ. and Welfare 1977; law clerk US Court of Appeals, DC 1978–79; Special Asst to US Asst Attorney Gen., Civil Div. 1979–80; Minority Counsel Senate Labor and Human Resources Cttee 1981–83; Principal Aide to Senator Edward Kennedy, Senate Armed Services Cttee 1983–85; Sr Fellow IISS, London 1985–87; Sr Analyst RAND Corpn 1989–93; Deputy Asst Sec. for Intelligence and Research, State Dept 1993–94, Dir Policy Planning Staff 1994–96; Deputy Nat. Security Advisor to Pres. Clinton 1996–2000; Sr Advisor Markle Foundation 2000–01; Vice-Pres. and Dir Foreign Policy Studies, Brookings Institution 2001–05; Dean, Lyndon B. Johnson School of Public Affairs, Univ. of Tex., Austin 2006–, also J.J. "Jake" Pickle Regents Chair in Public Affairs. *Publications include:* An Ever Closer

Union: European Integration and its Implications for the Future of US–European Relations 1993, Protecting the American Homeland (jtly) 2003. *Address:* SRH 3.100, Lyndon B. Johnson School of Public Affairs, The University of Texas at Austin, PO Box Y, Austin, TX 78713-8925, USA (office). *Telephone:* (512) 471-3200 (office). *Fax:* (512) 471-4697 (office). *Website:* www.utexas.edu/lbj (office).

STEINBRÜCK, Peer; German politician; *Minister of Finance;* b. 10 Jan. 1947, Hamburg; m.; three c. *Education:* Christian-Albrechts-Univ. zu Kiel. *Career:* worked for Fed. Ministry of Planning 1974–76, Fed. Ministry of Research and Tech. 1976–77, Personal Asst to Minister 1977; mem. SPD Party; Chief of Staff for Minister-Pres., State of Nordrhein-Westfalen 1986–90; State Sec., Ministry of Natural Conservation, Environmental Protection and Regional Devt, State of Schleswig-Holstein 1990–92, State Sec., Ministry of Econs, Tech. and Transport 1992–93; State Minister of Econs, Tech. and Transport 1993–98; State Minister of Econs, Small Businesses, Tech. and Transport, State of Nordrhein-Westfalen 1998–2000, State Finance Minister 2000–02, Minister-Pres. 2002–05; Fed. Minister of Finance 2005–. *Address:* Ministry of Finance, Wilhelmstr. 97, 10117 Berlin, Germany (office). *Telephone:* (30) 22420 (office). *Fax:* (30) 22423260 (office). *E-mail:* poststelle@bmf.bund.de (office). *Website:* www.bundesfinanzministerium.de (office).

STEINBRUNER, John D., AB, PhD; American research institute director and professor of public policy; *Director, Center for International and Security Studies, University of Maryland;* b. 1941, Denver, Colo. *Education:* Stanford Univ., Calif., Massachusetts Inst. of Tech. *Career:* fmr Asst Prof. of Political Science, MIT; fmr Exec. Dir Research Seminar on Bureaucracy, Politics and Policy, Inst. of Politics, Harvard Univ.; Assoc. Prof. of Public Policy, John F. Kennedy School of Govt and Asst Dir Program for Science and Int. Affairs, Harvard Univ. 1973–76; Assoc. Prof., School of Org. and Man., Dept of Political Science, Yale Univ. 1976–78; Dir Foreign Policy Studies Program, Brookings Inst. 1978–96, currently Sr Fellow (non-resident) and Sydney Stein, Jr Chair in Int. Security; also currently Prof. of Public Policy, School of Public Affairs, Univ. of Maryland and Dir Center for Int. and Security Studies at Maryland; Chair. Arms Control Asscn; Vice-Chair. Cttee on Int. Security and Arms Control, NAS; Co-Chair. Cttee on Int. Security Studies, American Acad. of Arts and Sciences; mem. Council on Foreign Relations; fmr mem. Defense Policy Bd Dept of Defense, Carnegie Comm. on Preventing Deadly Conflict; Fellow, American Acad. of Arts and Sciences; Landmark Award and Distinguished Scholar and Teacher Award, Univ. of Maryland. *Publications:* The Cybernetic Theory of Decision: New Dimensions of Political Analysis 1974, Managing Nuclear Operations (co-ed.) 1987, Strategic Arms Reductions (co-author) 1988, Restructuring American Foreign Policy (ed.) 1989, Decisions for Defense: Prospects of a New Order (co-author) 1991, A New Concept of Cooperative Security (co-author) 1992, Principles of Global Security 2000; numerous articles in professional publications. *Address:* Center for International and Security Studies at Maryland, 4113 Van Munching Hall, School of Public Affairs, University of Maryland, College Park, MD 20742, USA (office). *Telephone:* (301) 405-4578 (office). *Fax:* (301) 403-8107 (office). *E-mail:* jsteinbr@umd.edu (office). *Website:* www.cissm.umd.edu (office).

STEINER, Achim, BA, MA; German international organization executive; *Executive Director, United Nations Environment Programme;* b. 1961, Brazil. *Education:* Univs of Oxford and London, UK, German Devt Inst., Berlin, Harvard Business School, USA. *Career:* Sr Policy Advisor, Global Policy Unit, Int. Union for the Conservation of Nature and Natural Resources (IUCN) – The World Conservation Union, Washington, DC mid-1990s, worked in SE Asia as Chief Tech. Advisor on a programme for sustainable man. of Mekong River watersheds and community-based natural resources man., worked in IUCN's Southern Africa Regional Office, Dir-Gen. IUCN 2001–06; Sec.-Gen. World Comm. on Dams, based in South Africa 1998–2001; Exec. Dir UNEP 2006–(10); Founding mem. Institut du developpement durable et des relations internationales (France); mem. several int. advisory bds including China Council for Inst. Cooperation on Environment and Devt, Environmental Advisory Council (ENVAC) of EBRD, UN Sec.-Gen.'s Advisory Council for the Global Compact, Int. Advisory Cttee of Global Environmental Action (Japan), Bd of Global Public Policy Inst. (Germany). *Address:* United Nations Environment Programme, United Nations Avenue, Gigiri, PO Box 30552, 00100 Nairobi, Kenya (office). *Telephone:* (20) 7621234 (office). *Fax:* (20) 7624275 (office). *E-mail:* executiveoffice@unep.org (office). *Website:* www.unep.org (office).

STEINER, Michael; German diplomatist and fmr government officer; *Ambassador to Italy;* b. 1949, Munich. *Education:* Munich Univ. Law

School. *Career:* joined Diplomatic Service 1981, served at Perm. Mission to UN, New York, in Embassy in Prague and later Amb. to Czech Repub.; Head of Office of German Humanitarian Aid, Zagreb, Croatia 1991–92; Head of Foreign Office Special Task Force for Peace Efforts in Bosnia and Herzegovina; Nat. Rep. at Int. Contact Group on the Balkans; Contrib. Dayton Peace Talks 1995; Prin. Deputy High Rep. in Sarajevo; apptd Foreign Policy and Security Adviser to Chancellor 1998; Special Rep. for Kosovo and Head of UN Interim Admin. Mission in Kosovo (UNMIK) 2002–03; Perm. Rep. to UN, Geneva 2003–07; Pres. Governing Council of the UN Compensation Comm. for Iraq 2004; Amb. to Italy 2007–.
Address: Embassy of Germany, Via San Martino della Battaglia 4, 00185 Rome, Italy (office). *Telephone:* (06) 492131 (office). *Fax:* (06) 49213319 (office). *E-mail:* info@rom.diplo.de (office). *Website:* www.rom.diplo.de (office).

STEINER, Sylvia Helena de Figueiredo, LLM; Brazilian judge; *Judge, International Criminal Court;* b. 19 Jan. 1953, São Paulo; m. (divorced). *Education:* Univ. of São Paulo, Univ. of Brasilia. *Career:* lawyer –1982; mem. Fed. Public Ministry 1982–95; fmr mem. and Vice-Pres. Penitentiary Council of São Paulo; Fed. Judge Regional, Court of Appeal of São Paulo 1995–2003; elected Judge Int. Criminal Court (ICC) 2003–; mem. Brazilian Del. to Preparatory Comm. of ICC 1999–2001, to Experts' Conf. on Implementation of Humanitarian Law 2001, to Meeting on Implementation of ICC Statute 2001, to First Ass. of State Parties of ICC 2002; Founding Assoc. mem. Brazilian Inst. of Criminal Sciences; Deputy Dir Brazilian Criminal Sciences Journal; mem. Admin. Council Asscn of Judges for Democracy, Exec. Council Brazilian Section of Int. Legal Comm., São Paulo Comm. for Peace and Justice; guest lecturer at numerous orgs, univs and insts. *Publications include:* articles in professional journals.
Address: International Criminal Court, Maanweg 174, 2516 AB The Hague, Netherlands (office); Rua Estado de Israel, No. 181, Apt. 13, Vila Mariana, CEP 04022-000, São Paulo, Brazil (home). *Telephone:* 70 5158515 (office); (11) 3311-4412 (home). *Fax:* 70 5158555 (office); (11) 5572-3897 (home). *E-mail:* pio@icc-cpi.int (office); sylstein@uol.com.br, ssteiner@trf3.gov.br (home). *Website:* www.icp-cpi.int (office).

STEINMEIER, Frank-Walter; German politician and lawyer; *Vice Chancellor and Minister of Foreign Affairs;* b. 5 Jan. 1956, Detmold (Dist of Lippe); m.; one d. *Education:* secondary school in Blomberg and Justus Liebig Univ., Giessen. *Career:* mil. service 1074–76; law internships in Frankfurt and Giessen 1983–86; Research Asst to Chair for Public Law and Political Science, Dept of Law, Univ. of Giessen 1986–91; mem. SPD; Head of Section for Media Law and Media Policy, Lower Saxony State Chancellery 1991; Chief-of-Staff, Office of the Premier, State of Lower Saxony 1993–94; Head of Directorate for Policy Guidelines, Interdepartmental Coordination and Planning 1994–96; State Sec. and Chief-of-Staff, Lower Saxony State Chancellery 1996–98; State Sec., Federal Chancellery and Commr for the Intelligence Services 1998; Fed. Chancellery Chief-of-Staff 1999–2005; Minister of Foreign Affairs 2005–, Vice Chancellor 2007–; Pres. European Council 2007–.
Address: Ministry of Foreign Affairs, Werderscher Markt 1, 10117 Berlin, Germany (office). *Telephone:* (30) 50000 (office). *Fax:* (30) 50003402 (office). *E-mail:* poststelle@auswaertiges-amt.de (office). *Website:* www.auswaertiges-amt.de (office).

STEMPLOWSKI, Ryszard Maria, LLM, PhD, DHabil(Hist); Polish academic, lawyer, historian and diplomatist; *Professor of History and Politics, Jagiellonian University;* b. 25 March 1939, Wygoda, Witwica; m. Irena Zasłona 1975; two d. *Education:* Tech. Lycée, Bydgoszcz, Dept of Ecological Eng, Wrocław Univ. of Tech., Dept of Law, Wrocław Univ., Inst. of History, Polish Acad. of Sciences, Warsaw. *Career:* Research Fellow, Inst. of History, Polish Acad. of Sciences 1973–90; Chief, Chancellery of Sejm (Parl.) 1990–93; Amb. to Court of St James (UK) 1994–99; Dir Polish Inst. of Int. Affairs 1999–2004; Prof., Warsaw School of Econs 2001–04; Prof. of History and Politics, Jagiellonian Univ., Kraków 2005–; Ed. Polish Diplomatic Review 2000–04; mem. Polish History Soc. 1975–, Sec.-Gen. 1976–78; Co-founder and mem. Polish Soc. of Studies of Latin America 1978–; Visiting Fellow, St Antony's Coll. Oxford 1974; Alexander von Humboldt Research Fellow, Univ. of Cologne 1981–82; Gran Croce di Merito del Ordine Constantiniano di S. Giorgio 1997; Kt, Order of Polonia Restituta 2000; Interfaith Gold Medallion Peace Through Dialogue, Int. Council of Christians and Jews 1999. *Publications:* over 150 articles; 13 books, including (in Polish) Argentina and the Rivalries among the United States, United Kingdom and Germany 1930–46 1975, State Socialism in the Actually Existing Capitalism: Chile 1932 1996, An Introduction to the Polish Foreign Policy Analysis (two vols) 2006, Government Proposals and Theoretical Concepts of Integration of European States in the 20th and 21st Centuries 2007, Normative Rules of Conducting Foreign Policy 2008.

Address: Uniwersytet Jagielloński, ul. Gronostajowa 7A, pok. nr 3.016, 30-387 Kraków (office); ul. Gubinowska 7, M. 151, 02-956, Warsaw, Poland (home). *E-mail:* ryszard.stemplowski@uj.edu.pl (office); ryszard@stemplowski.pl (home). *Website:* www.uj.edu.pl (office); www.stemplowski.pl (home).

STENSETH, Dagfinn, BA; Norwegian diplomatist; b. 28 Aug. 1936; m. Raili Stenseth. *Education:* Yale Univ., USA. *Career:* joined Dept of Foreign Affairs 1960; Emb. Sec., Moscow 1962–65, Bonn 1969–72; Bureau Chief Political Section, Dept of Foreign Affairs 1973–76, Sub-Dir Planning Dept 1973–76, Mission Chief 1986–87; Amb. to USSR 1979–1985, 1990–91, to Russian Fed. 1991–94, to Denmark 1999–2003; Political Co-ordinator 1985–86; Special Adviser for Resources and the Environment, Dept of Foreign Affairs 1997–99.
Address: PO Box 176, NO- 3321 Vestfossen, Norway (home).

STEPASHIN, Col-Gen. Sergey Vadimovich, CandHist, LLD; Russian security official; *Chairman, Accounts Chamber of the Russian Federation;* b. 2 March 1952, Port Arthur; m.; one s. *Education:* Higher Political Coll., USSR Ministry of Internal Affairs, Mil. Acad., Financial Acad. under Russian Fed. Govt. *Career:* service in Interior Forces 1973–90; Lecturer, Higher Political Coll., Leningrad 1981–90; Deputy to RSFSR Supreme Soviet 1990–93; after attempted coup Aug. 1991 Head Cttee on Defence and Security of the Russian Fed. Supreme Soviet; author programme of reorganization of state security system; Chief, Leningrad Federal Security Agency; Admin. and Deputy Chair. Russian Fed. Federal Security Agency 1991–92; First Deputy Dir Fed. Counter-Intelligence Service (later Fed. Security Service) 1993–94, Dir 1994–95; Head of Admin, Dept of Govt 1995–97; Minister of Justice 1997–98, of Internal Affairs 1998–99; First Deputy Chair. of Govt April–May 1999, Chair. of Govt (Prime Minister) May–Aug. 1999; Chair. Exec. Council of Russia and Belarus Union May–Aug. 1999; joined Yabloko Movt 1999; mem. State Duma (Parl.) 1999–2000; Chair. Accounts Chamber of Russian Fed. 2000–; Pres. European Org. of Supreme Audit Insts 2002–; Prof., Russian Fed. State Counsellor of Justice; Order of Fortitude 1998, Order 'For Merits Before Fatherland', Third Degree 2002, Légion d'honneur, Commodore degree 2005. *Publication:* Personal and Social Security (Political and Legal Issues) 1994.
Address: Accounts Chamber of the Russian Federation, Zubovskaya Str. 2, 119992 Moscow, Russia. *Telephone:* (495) 986-05-09 (office). *Fax:* (495) 986-09-52 (office). *E-mail:* info@ach.gov.ru (office). *Website:* www.ach.gov.ru (office).

STEPHANOPOULOS, Konstantinos; Greek politician, lawyer and fmr head of state; b. 1926, Patras; m. Eugenia El. Stounopoulou 1959; two s. one d. *Education:* Univ. of Athens. *Career:* pvt. law practice 1954–74; mem. Parl. for Achaia (Nat. Radical Union) 1964, (New Democracy) 1974, 1977, 1981, 1985, (Democratic Renewal) 1989; Under-Sec. of Commerce July–Nov. 1974; Minister of the Interior 1974–76, of Social Services 1976–77; in Prime Minister's Office 1977–81; Pres. of Greece 1995–2005; Parl. Rep., New Democracy Party 1981–85, Pres. Party of Democratic Renewal 1985–94; American Hellenic Inst. Hellenic Heritage Nat. Public Service Award 2005.
Address: Valaoritou 9B, 10671 Athens (office); Dafnis 0, 15452 Psyhico, Greece (home). *Telephone:* (210) 3602212 (office); (210) 6773190 (home). *Fax:* (210) 3602212 (office). *E-mail:* stephan@otenet.gr (office).

STEPHEN, Marcus; Nauruan politician, head of state and fmr weightlifter; *President;* b. 1 Oct. 1969. *Career:* participated as weightlifter for Samoa at Olympic Games in Barcelona 1992, for Nauru at Olympic Games in Atlanta 1996 and in Sydney 2000; in Commonwealth Games won one gold and two silver medals at Auckland 1990, three gold medals in Victoria 1994, three gold medals in Kuala Lumpur 1998, three silver medals at Manchester 2002; retd from sport in 2002; mem. Parl. from Ewa and Anetan 2003–07, held positions of Minister of Finance, for Sport, Telecommunications and Transport, Pres. (after vote of no confidence in Parl. against Pres. Ludwig Scotty) 2007–; Rep. at Int. Whaling Comm. 2005.
Address: Office of the President, Yaren, Nauru (office). *Telephone:* 444-3772 (office). *Fax:* 444-3776 (office). *E-mail:* the.president@naurugov.nr. *Website:* www.naurugov.nr (office).

STEPHEN, Rt Hon. Sir Ninian Martin, KG, AK, GCMG, GCVO, KBE; Australian lawyer and international official; b. 15 June 1923, Oxford, England; m. Valery Mary Sinclair 1949; five d. *Education:* George Watson's School, Edinburgh Acad., St Paul's School, UK, Chillon Coll., Switzerland, Scotch Coll., Melbourne, Melbourne Univ. *Career:* served World War II, Australian Army; admitted as barrister and solicitor, Victoria 1949; QC 1966; Judge, Supreme Court, Victoria 1970; Justice, High Court, Australia 1972–82; Gov.-Gen. of Australia 1982–89; Chair. Nat. Library of Australia 1989–94; Amb. for the Environment 1989–92; Chair. Strand Two, Northern Ireland Talks 1992, UN Group of Experts on Cambodia,

Australian Citizenship Council; Judge, Int. Criminal Tribunals for Yugoslavia 1993–97, for Rwanda 1995–97; mem. Ethics Comm. Int. Olympic Cttee 2000–; Chair. ILO High Level Team to Myanmar 2001; Hon. Bencher Gray's Inn 1981; KStJ 1982; Commdr Légion d'honneur 1993.
Address: 4 Treasury Place, Melbourne, Victoria, 3002 (office); Flat 13/1, 193 Domain Road, South Yarra, Victoria, Australia (home). *Telephone:* (3) 9650-0266 (office); (3) 9820-2787 (home). *Fax:* (3) 9650-0270 (office). *E-mail:* ninian.stephen@dpmc.gov.au.

STEPHENS, Eldridge; Saint Lucia business executive and diplomatist; *High Commissioner to UK;* m. Peternise Stephens. *Career:* Second Vice-Pres. Saint Lucia Industrial and Small Business Asscn 2003–04, First Vice-Pres. 2004–05, Pres. 2007–09; High Commr to UK 2008–.
Address: Saint Lucia High Commission, 1 Collingham Gardens, London, SW5 0HW, England (office). *Telephone:* (20) 7370-7123 (office). *Fax:* (20) 7937-6040 (office). *E-mail:* hcslu@btconnect.com (office).

STEPHENSON, Barbara J., BA, MA, PhD; American diplomatist; *Ambassador to Panama;* b. Fla. *Education:* Univ. of Florida. *Career:* career mem. Sr Foreign Service, served as a Political and Econ. Officer in Panama, later Prin. Officer, Belfast, NI; Deputy Coordinator for Iraq, Dept of State –2008; Amb. to Panama 2008–.
Address: US Embassy, PO Box 0816-02561, Building 783, Demetrio Basilio Lakas Avenue, Clayton, Panama (office). *Telephone:* 207-7000 (office). *Fax:* 317-5568 (office). *E-mail:* panamaweb@state.gov (office). *Website:* panama.usembassy.gov (office).

STEPHENSON, Thomas F., AB, MBA, JD; American business executive and diplomatist; *Ambassador to Portugal;* b. Wilmington, Del.; m.; four c. *Education:* Harvard Coll., Harvard Business School, Boston Coll. Law School. *Career:* has served on numerous pvt. and public corp. bds; fmr securities analyst, Fidelity Management Co., helped found Fidelity Ventures, Pres. Fidelity Ventures 1977–87; Pnr, Sequoia Capital (Silicon Valley venture capital co.) 1987–; Amb. to Portugal 2008–; mem. Bd of Overseers and Exec. Cttee, Harvard Univ.; fmr mem. Exec. Cttee of Bd of Overseers of Hoover Inst., Stanford Univ., Bd of Advisors of Stanford Inst. for Econ. Policy Research, Bd of Dirs of Conservation Int., Wilson Center Council; fmr Corp. Fund Vice-Chair. The Kennedy Center; fmr mem. bds and cttees Tufts New England Medical Center, Boston.
Address: US Embassy, Avenida das Forças Armadas (Sete Rios), 1600-081 Lisbon, Portugal (office). *Telephone:* (21) 7273300 (office). *Fax:* (21) 7269109 (office). *E-mail:* ref@american-embassy.pt (office). *Website:* www .american-embassy.pt (office).

STERN, Ernest, MA, PhD; American economist and academic; b. 25 Aug. 1933, Frankfurt, Germany; m. Zina Gold 1957. *Education:* Queens Coll., New York and Fletcher School of Law and Diplomacy. *Career:* Economist, US Dept of Commerce 1957–59; Program Economist, US Agency for Int. Devt (USAID) 1959–63; Instructor, Middle East Tech. Univ. 1960–61; Economist, Office of Pakistan Affairs, USAID 1963–64, Officer in Charge of Pakistan Affairs 1964–64, Asst Dir for Devt Policy USAID India 1965–67, Deputy Dir USAID Pakistan 1967–68, Deputy Staff Dir Comm. on Int. Devt (Pearson Comm.) 1968–69; Lecturer, Woodrow Wilson School of Public and Int. Affairs, Princeton 1971; Sr Staff mem. Council on Int. Econ. Policy, White House 1971; joined World Bank 1972, various posts including Deputy Chair. Econ. Cttee, Sr Adviser on Devt Policy, Dir Devt Policy, then Vice-Pres. S Asia until 1978, Vice-Pres. Operations, World Bank July 1978, Sr Vice-Pres., Operations 1980–87, Sr Vice-Pres., Finance 1987, Man. Dir 1991–95 (retd); fmr Man. Dir JP Morgan Chase; mem. Bd Advisors Inst. for Int. Econs, Washington, DC; mem. Bd of Overseers, Int. Center for Econ. Growth, Calif.; fnr mem. Bd of Dirs Center for Global Devt, US-Russian Business Council, Commonfund; mem. Council on Foreign Relations, Group of Thirty; William A. Jump Memorial Foundation Meritorious Award 1964, 1966.

STERN, Jessica, MSc; American academic and writer; *Lecturer in Public Policy, John F. Kennedy School of Government, Harvard University;* *Education:* Barnard Coll., MIT, Harvard Univ. *Career:* fmr post-doctoral Fellow, Lawrence Livermore Nat. Lab., Livermore, Calif.; Dir for Russian, Ukrainian and Eurasian Affairs, US Nat. Security Council 1994–95; Nat. Fellow, Hoover Inst., Stanford Univ. 1995–96; Superterrorism Fellow, Council on Foreign Relations 1998–99; Fellow, World Econ. Forum 2002, 2003, 2004; currently Lecturer in Public Policy, John F. Kennedy School of Govt, Harvard Univ. and Faculty Affiliate, Belfer Center for Science and Int. Affairs; mem. Trilateral Comm., Council on Foreign Relations; selected by Time Magazine as one of seven thinkers whose innovative ideas "will change the world" 2001. *Publications include:* The Utimate Terrorists 1999, Terror in the Name of God: Why Religious Militants Kill 2003; numerous articles in academic journals.

Address: John F. Kennedy School of Government, Harvard University, 79 John F. Kennedy Street, Cambridge, MA 02138, USA (office). *Telephone:* (617) 496-3623 (office). *Fax:* (617) 496-5747 (office). *E-mail:* jessica_stern@ ksg.harvard.edu (office). *Website:* www.ksgfaculty.harvard.edu (office).

STERN OF BRENTFORD, Baron (Life Peer), cr. 2007, of Elsted in the County of West Sussex and of Wimbledon in the London Borough of Merton; **Nicholas Herbert Stern,** PhD; British economist, academic and fmr government official; *IG Patel Chair in Economics and Government, London School of Economics;* b. 1946, London; m. Susan Stern; three c. *Education:* Latymer Upper School, Peterhouse Coll., Univ. of Cambridge. *Career:* taught at Univ. of Oxford, Univ. of Warwick, LSE, Sorbonne, MIT; Chief Economist, EBRD 1993–99; Sr Vice-Pres. and Chief Economist, World Bank 2000–03; Second Perm. Sec., Man. Dir, Budget and Public Finances, Treasury of the UK 2003–04, Head of Govt Econ. Service 2003–07 (retd); commissioned to compile Stern Review on the Economics of Climate Change 2005, published 2006; IG Patel Chair in Econs and Govt, LSE 2007–, Dir India Observatory, Asia Research Centre; Fellow, British Acad., Econometrics Soc.; Hon. Fellow, American Acad. of Arts and Sciences; Hon DSc (Warwick) 2006. *Publications:* Palanpur: The Economy of an Indian Village (with C. J. Bliss) 1982, The Theory and Practice of Tax Reform in Developing Countries (with E. Ahmad) 1991, A Strategy for Development 2002.
Address: House of Lords, London, SW1A 0PW; Asia Research Centre, 10th Floor, Tower 2, London School of Economics, Houghton Street, London, WC2A 2AE, England. *Telephone:* (20) 7219-5353 (House of Lords). *Fax:* (20) 7107-5285. *E-mail:* arc@lse.ac.uk. *Website:* www.lse.ac .uk/collections/IndiaObservatory (office); www.lse.ac.uk/collections/ asiaResearchCentre.

STEVENS, Bockari Kortu, BA, MA; Sierra Leonean politician and diplomatist; *Ambassador to USA;* b. Moyamba; nephew of the late Dr Siaka Probyn Stevens, fmr Pres. of Sierra Leone. *Education:* Albert Acad., Freetown, Fourah Bay Coll., Univ. of Sierra Leone, Univ. of East London, UK. *Career:* Founding mem. and Sec.-Gen. All People's Congress (APC) Nat. Youth League, mem. Governing Council APC and Cen. Cttee APC, Co-founder and Sec.-Gen. APC, UK and Ireland Br.; Personnel Man. Sierra Leone Ports Authority 1976–85; Amb. to Guinea (also accred to Mali, Guinea Bissau and Cape Verde) 1986–92; Information, Communication and Research Officer, Children's Soc. Refugee and Homelessness Team, Newham, UK; Amb. to USA 2008–.
Address: Embassy of Sierra Leone, 1701 19th Street, NW, Washington, DC 20009, USA (office). *Telephone:* (202) 939-9261 (office); (202) 723-4645 (home). *Fax:* (202) 483-1793 (office). *E-mail:* salonemb@starpower.net (office).

STEVENS, Christine, PhD; Belgian diplomatist; *Ambassador to Venezuela;* b. 1 Aug. 1951, Nairobi; m. Khalid Jehangir 1986; one s. two d. *Education:* Lycée Français de Téhéran, Iran, Monastère de Berlaymont, Waterloo and Univ. Libre de Bruxelles. *Career:* Vice-Consul, Consulate-Gen. in Amsterdam 1976–77; Second Sec., Embassy in The Hague 1977–78, in Madrid 1978–79; mem. Belgian Del. to Conf. on Security and Co-operation in Europe, Madrid 1979–81, Deputy Head of Del., Brussels 1993, Paris 1994; Deputy Spokesperson Ministry of Foreign Affairs, Brussels 1981–83; Head of Maghreb Section, Dept of the Middle East, Political Dept 1991–94; First Sec., Embassy in Brazil 1983–85; Counsellor, Embassy in Helsinki 1985–86, in Copenhagen 1986–91; Amb. to Bolivia 1994–98; Consul Gen. in Barcelona 1998–2002; Head of S American Dept 2002–05; Amb. to Venezuela 2005–; Kt of the Order of the Crown, Belgium, Orden del Merito Civil, Spain, Kt First Class of the Order of Dannebrog, Denmark. *Publication:* Parnell Square, Dublin: demeures bourgeoises du XVIIIème siècle 1976.
Address: Embassy of Belgium, Quinta la Azulita, Avda 11, entre 6a y 7a Transversales, Apdo del Este 61550, Altamira, Caracas 1060, Venezuela (office); Quinta Azaleas, Calle El Parque, Country Club, Caracas, Venezuela (home). *Telephone:* (212) 264-6056 (office); (212) 263-6392 (home). *Fax:* (212) 261-1333 (office); (212) 263-6392 (home). *E-mail:* christine.stevens@diplobel.be (office); chrstev@hotmail.com (home). *Website:* www.diplobel.org/venezuela (office).

STEVENSON, Jonathan, BA, JD; American policy analyst; *Professor of Strategic Studies, Strategic Research Department, US Naval War College;* b. 24 May 1956, New London, Conn.; m. Sharon L. Butler. *Education:* Univ. of Chicago, Boston Univ. *Career:* practised law in New York for six years, then worked as journalist including assignments in E Africa, NI; Research Assoc. IISS 1999–2000, Sr Fellow for Counter Terrorism 2001–05; Deputy Ed. Strategic Survey (journal) 2000, Ed. 2001–05; Prof. of Strategic Studies, Strategic Research Dept, US Naval War Coll., Newport 2005–. *Publications:* We Wrecked the Place: Contemplating an End to the Northern Irish Troubles 1996, Preventing Conflict: the Role of

the Bretton Woods Institutions 2000; Counter-Terrorism: Containment and Beyond 2004.
Address: Naval War College, 686 Cushing Road, Newport, RI 02841, USA (office). *Telephone:* (401) 841-6448 (office). *E-mail:* Jonathan.Stevenson@ nwc.navy.mil (office). *Website:* www.nwc.navy.mil (office).

STEWART, Brian, BA; British diplomatist (retd); b. 4 Feb. 1950, Forres, Scotland; m. Anne Stewart. *Education:* Univ. of Keele. *Career:* entered FCO 1972, Commonwealth Coordination Dept 1972–73, Overseas Language Training 1973–75; Third Sec., later Second Sec., Chancery/ Information, Embassy in Amman 1975–78; Cabinet Office 1978–80; Energy, Science and Space Dept, FCO 1980–82; First Sec., Head of Chancery, High Comm. in Singapore 1982–85; Deputy Head of Mission, Embassy in Tunis 1986–89; Narcotics Dept, FCO 1989–91, SE Asia Dept 1991–93; Deputy Head of Mission, Embassy in Damascus 1993–96; Personnel Policy Dept, FCO 1996–97, Change Man. Unit and Near East/N Africa Dept 1997–98; Deputy Head of Mission, Embassy in Kuwait 1998–2001; Acting Head of Mission, Embassy in Algiers 2002; Special Projects, Personnel Directorate, FCO 2002; Royal Coll. of Defence Studies 2003; Amb. to Algeria 2004–05.
Address: c/o Foreign and Commonwealth Office, King Charles Street, London, SW1A 2AH, England (office).

STEWART, Karen Brevard, BA, MS; American diplomatist; *Ambassador to Belarus;* b. Fla. *Education:* Wellesley Coll., Univ. of Virginia, Nat. War Coll., Nat. Defense Univ. at Fort McNair. *Career:* career mem. Sr Foreign Service, joined Foreign Service in 1977, overseas postings include Bangkok, Colombo, Vientiane (twice), Udorn, Islamabad; fmr Deputy Chief of Mission, Embassy in Minsk; Dept of State assignments have included tours as Int. Relations Officer, Office of Fisheries Affairs, Econ. Officer, Office of Energy Consuming Countries, and Econ./Commercial Desk Officer, Office of Israel and Arab-Israeli Affairs, Dir Office of Ukraine, Moldova, and Belarus Affairs, Bureau of European and Eurasian Affairs; Amb. to Belarus 2006–; Dept of State Meritorious and Superior Honor Awards.
Address: US Embassy, vul. Starovilenskaya 46, 220002 Minsk, Belarus (office). *Telephone:* (17) 210-12-83 (office). *Fax:* (17) 234-78-53 (office). *E-mail:* webmaster@usembassy.minsk.by (office). *Website:* www .usembassy.minsk.by (office).

ŠTIGLIC, Sanja, LLB; Slovenian diplomatist; *Permanent Representative, United Nations;* b. 10 March 1970, Kranj. *Education:* Univ. of Ljubljana. *Career:* attaché, Dept for Neighbouring Countries, Ministry of Foreign Affairs 1995–96, Adviser 1996–97; Second, then First Sec., Perm. Mission to UN, New York 1997–2002, Alt. Rep. to Security Council 1998, 1999; Counsellor to Govt and Deputy Head of Minister's Office, Ministry of Foreign Affairs 2002–03, State Under-Sec. and Head of Minister's Office 2003–04, Head of Div. for Relations with Western, Northern and Cen. Europe 2005–06; Perm. Rep. to UN, New York 2007–.
Address: Permanent Mission of Slovenia to the United Nations, 600 Third Avenue, 24th Floor, New York, NY 10016, USA (office). *Telephone:* (212) 370-3007 (office). *Fax:* (212) 370-1824 (office). *E-mail:* mny@mzz-dkp.gov .si (office). *Website:* www.un.int/slovenia (office).

STIGLITZ, Joseph Eugene, PhD, FBA; American economist and academic; *Professor of Economics and Finance, Graduate School of Business, Columbia University;* b. 9 Feb. 1943, Gary, Ind.; m. 1st 1978; two s. two d.; m. 2nd Anya Schiffrin 2004. *Education:* Amherst Coll., Mass. Inst. of Tech. and Univ. of Cambridge (Fulbright Scholar). *Career:* Prof. of Econs, Cowles Foundation, Yale Univ. 1970–74; Visiting Fellow, St Catherine's Coll. Oxford 1973–74; Prof. of Econs, Stanford Univ. 1974–76, Sr Fellow, Hoover Inst. 1988–2001, Joan Kenney Prof. of Econs 1992–2001; Drummond Prof. of Political Econ., Univ. of Oxford 1976–79; Oskar Morgenstern Distinguished Fellow, Inst. of Advanced Studies, Princeton 1978–79; Prof. of Econs, Princeton Univ. 1979–88; Stern Visiting Prof., Columbia Univ. 2000, Prof. of Econs and Finance, Grad. School of Business 2000, Co-Founder and Pres. Initiative for Policy Dialogue 2000–, Univ. Prof. 2000–, Chair. Cttee on Global Thought 2006–; mem. Pres.'s Council of Econ. Advisers 1993–95, Chair. (mem. of cabinet) 1995–97; Special Adviser to Pres. of World Bank, Sr Vice-Pres. and Chief Economist 1997–2000; Chair. Man. Bd and Dir Grad. Summer Programs, Brooks World Poverty Inst., Univ. of Manchester 2006–; Special Adviser, Bell Communications Research, numerous consultancies in public and pvt. sector, editorial bd memberships etc.; Sr Fellow, Brookings Inst. 2000; Fellow, American Acad. of Arts and Sciences, NAS, Econometric Soc., American Philosophical Soc., Inst. for Policy Research (Sr Fellow 1991–93); Hon. DHL (Amherst Coll.) 1974; Dr hc (Univ. of Leuven, Ben Gurion Univ.), (Oxford) 2004; Guggenheim Fellow 1969–70; John Bates Clark Award, American Econ. Asscn 1979, Int. Prize, Accad. dei Lincei, Rome 1988, UAP Scientific Prize, Paris 1989; Nobel Prize for Econs (jt recepient) 2001. *Publications include:* Globalization and its Discontents,

Economics of the Public Sector 2000, Principles of Economics 1997, Rethinking the East Asia Miracle (co-ed.) 2001, The Roaring Nineties 2003, Fair Trade for All (co-author), 2005, Making Globalization Work 2006, The Three Trillion Dollar War: The True Cost of the Iraq Conflict (co-author), 2008; other books and more than 300 papers in learned journals.
Address: Uris Hall, Room 814, Columbia University, 3022 Broadway, New York, NY 10027, USA (office). *Telephone:* (212) 854-1481 (office). *Fax:* (212) 662-8474 (office). *E-mail:* jes322@columbia.edu (office). *Website:* www.josephstiglitz.com (office).

STOBY, Miles, BA, MA; Guyanese diplomatist and international organization executive; *Permanent Observer of the Caribbean Community (CARICOM) to the United Nations;* b. 26 April 1943, Georgetown; m.; three d. *Education:* Univ. of Cambridge, UK. *Career:* served in Diplomatic Service 1966–78, postings in Washington, DC, Deputy Perm. Rep. to UN, New York 1974–76, Chargé d'affaires in Brasilia, Brazil 1976–77; Rep. at numerous intergovt. forums, including UN Gen. Ass., Security Council, Governing Council of UNDP; elected Chair. Cttee for Programme and Co-ordination (CPC); with UN Secr., on secondment as Special Asst to Asst Sec.-Gen. for Inter-Agency Affairs 1971–73; Prin. Officer in Office of Dir-Gen. for Devt and Int. Econ. Co-operation 1978–82; Dir Div. for Econ. and Social Information, Dept of Public Information 1984–87; Dir-in-Charge of Man. Advisory Service and Cen. Evaluation Unit, Dept of Admin. and Man. 1987–88; Dir Div. of Econ. and Social Council Affairs and Secr. Services, and Sec. Econ. and Social Council 1988–92; Sec. UN Conf. on Environment and Devt, Rio de Janeiro, Brazil 1992; Dir Div. for Policy Co-ordination and Econ. and Social Council Affairs, Dept for Policy Co-ordination and Sustainable Devt 1992–96; apptd Co-ordinator of Global Conf. on Sustainable Devt of Small Island Developing States, Barbados 1994; Deputy Exec. Co-ordinator for UN Reform 1997; Asst Sec.-Gen. and Exec. Dir UN Fund for Int. Partnerships 1998–99, also Co-ordinator for the Millennium Ass. 1999–2001, responsible for Millennium Summit of UN; Asst Sec.-Gen. for Gen. Ass. Affairs and Conf. Services 2001–03; Sr Adviser for UN Reform to Pres. of UN Gen. Ass. 2003–05; Perm. Observer of the Caribbean Community (CARICOM) to UN, New York 2005–.
Address: Office of the Permanent Observer for the Caribbean Community to the United Nations, 801 Second Avenue, Suite 501, New York, NY 10017, USA (office). *Telephone:* (212) 685-4313 (office). *Fax:* (212) 779-1134 (office). *E-mail:* pomcaricom@gmail.com (office).

STOIBER, Edmund, DJur; German politician and lawyer; b. 1941, Ober-audorf; m. Karin Stoiber; three c. *Education:* Univ. of Munich and Hochschule für Politische Wissenschaft. *Career:* personal counsellor to Bavarian State Minister for Devt 1972–74, Dir of Ministerial Office 1974; entered Bavarian Parl. 1974; admitted solicitor 1978; Gen. Sec. Christian Social Union (CSU) 1978–83, Chair. CSU 1999–2007; Campaign Man. for Franz Josef Strauss, Fed. Elections 1980; State Sec. and Dir Bavarian State Chancellery 1982–86, State Minister and Dir 1986–88; Bavarian State Minister for Internal Affairs 1988–93, Minister-Pres. of Bavaria 1993–2007; cand. in Chancellery elections 2002; mem. Bd Bayern Munich (football team); Bayerischer Verdienstorden. *Publications:* Politik aus Bayern 1976, Der Hausfriedensbruch im Licht akt. Probleme 1984.
Address: c/o Christlich-Soziale Union (CSU), Nymphenburger str. 64, 80335 Munich, Germany (office). *Telephone:* (89) 1243215 (office). *Fax:* (89) 1243216 (office). *Website:* www.csu.de (office); www.stoiber.de.

STOKELJ, Ciril, PhD; Slovenian diplomatist; *Deputy Head of Cabinet, Office of the President, European Parliament; Career:* Diocesan Admin., Koper 1987–93; Diplomat of Holy See in Ecuador 1993–94; Diplomatic Adviser to Prime Minister of Slovenia 1995–97; Amb. to Spain, Cuba and Andorra 1997–2002; Perm. Rep. of Slovakia to EU 2002–05; Dir of Directorate B, Interparliamentary Dels and Policy, Directorate Gen. for External Policies, European Parl., Brussels 2005–07; Deputy Head of Cabinet, Pres. of the European Parl. 2007–.
Address: Office of the President, European Parliament, Centre Européen, Plateau du Kirchberg, BP 1601, 2929 Luxembourg (office). *Telephone:* 4300-1 (office). *Fax:* 4300-29494 (office). *Website:* www.europarl.europa.eu (office).

STOKHOF, Willem Arnoldus Laurens, PhD; Dutch professor of linguistics and research institute director; *Secretary General, International Convention of Asia Scholars;* b. 25 Sept. 1941, Amsterdam; m. *Education:* Univ. of Amsterdam, Univ. of Zagreb, Yugoslavia, Univ. of Moscow, USSR. *Career:* taught at Inst. for Slavic Languages, Univ. of Amsterdam 1971–73, Nat. Center for Language Devt, Jakarta, Indonesia 1974–84, Univ. of Kupang 1974–76; Founder and Dir Int. Inst. for Asian Studies 1993–; Founding Dir Int. Inst. for the Study of Islam in the Modern World (ISIM) 1997–99, Int. Advisory Cttee 1999–; currently Sec. Gen. Int. Convention of Asia Scholars; also currently Chair. Cultural and Societal Relations between Indonesia and the Netherlands, Faculty of Arts, Leiden Univ.;

Prof. of Austronesian and Papuan Linguistics; Chair. Dept of Languages and Cultures of SE Asia and Oceania 1998–, Dir Projects Div.; Programme Dir Indonesian Linguistics Devt Project 1974–92, Project Irian Jaya Studies 1990–94, The Irian Jaya Studies: a Programme for Interdisciplinary Research 1993–97, Indonesia-Netherlands Cooperation on Public Admin 1997–2000, Dutch-Indonesian Dictionary Project 1997–, Phonetics and Phonology of (word) Prosodic Systems in the Languages of Indonesia 1997–, Indonesian-Netherlands Cooperation in Islamic Studies, Islam in Indonesia: the Dissemination of Religious Authority in the 20th Century, Royal Acad. of Arts and Sciences, Irian Jaya Studies Cluster of Research School of Asian, African and Amerindian Studies (CNWS) (mem. Bd Research School 1993–96); Dir Int. Consultancy Bureau; Vice-Chair. Wissenschaftlichen Beirates Deutsches Übersee Institut, Hamburg; Sec.-Gen. Int. Convention of Asian Scholars; mem. Bd Advisory Council for Scientific Research in Devt Problems (RAWOO) 1990–96, Cttee for the Humanities (CGW), Royal Netherlands Acad. of Arts and Sciences 1996–2001, Cttee for Publication Grants of Netherlands Org. for Scientific Research 1996–2001, Asia Cttee, European Science Foundation 1997–2001, Bd Royal Inst. of Linguistics and Anthropology (KITLV) 1997–2001, Foundation Leids Etnologisch Fonds, Comité Scientifique de l'Unité Mixte de Recherche, Institut de Recherche sur le Sud-Est Asiatique (IRSEA-CNRS; Editorial Advisor, Pacific Linguistics 1976–; mem. Editorial Bd Semaian (series) 1989–, LIPI-RUL (Lembaga Ilmu Pengetahuan Indonesia-Leiden Univ.) series 1991–2000, Data Papers on Minority Languages of Vietnam Hanoi-Leiden Series 1993–; Gen. Ed. publs of Indonesian-Netherlands Cooperation in Islamic Studies Project 1988–, publs of Irian Jaya Studies – A Programme for Interdisciplinary Research 1993–2000, Manuscripta Indonesica series 1993–, publs of Indonesian Linguistics Devt Project 1974–92; Int. Advisory Ed. WACANA 1998–; Co-Ed. Dick van der Meij, Curzon-IIAS Asian Studies Series 2001–, Manuscripta Indonesica series. *Publications:* numerous articles in int. journals and publs. *Address:* International Convention of Asis Scholars Secretariat, International Institute for Asian Studies, PO Box 9515, 2300 RA Leiden (office); Hoge Rijndijk 253, 2314 AG, Leiden, Netherlands (home). *Telephone:* (71) 5272227 (office); (71) 5894271 (home). *Fax:* (71) 5274162 (office). *E-mail:* icas@let.leidenuniv.nl (office). *Website:* www.icassecretariat.org (office).

STOLER, Andrew L., BS, MBA; American international organization official, government official and research institute administrator; *Executive Director, Institute for International Business, Economics and Law, University of Adelaide; Education:* George Washington Univ., Georgetown Univ.'s School of Foreign Service. *Career:* with Office of Int. Trade Policy, Dept of Commerce 1975–79; Dir for Canada, Australia and New Zealand, US Trade Rep. Office 1980–81, MTN Codes Co-ordinator, Geneva 1982–87, Deputy Asst US Trade Rep. for Europe and Mediterranean, Washington 1988–89, Deputy Chief of Mission, Geneva 1989–99 (concurrently Deputy Perm. Rep. to World Trade Org.); Deputy Dir-Gen. World Trade Org. 1999–2002; Exec. Dir Inst. for Int. Business, Economics and Law, Univ. of Adelaide 2002–, also Adjunct Prof. of Int. Trade; mem. Aid Advisory Council (Australia) 2004–, Advisory Cttee of Shanghai WTO Affairs Consultation Centre; Sr. Advisor, Shenzhen WTO Affairs Centre. *Address:* Institute for International Business, Economics and Law, University of Adelaide, Level 12-10, Pulteney Street, Adelaide, SA 5005, Australia (office). *Telephone:* (8) 8303-6944 (office). *Fax:* (8) 8303-6948 (office). *E-mail:* andrew.stoler@adelaide.edu.au (office). *Website:* www.iibel.adelaide.edu.au (office).

STOLFI, Fiorenzo; San Marino lawyer and politician; *Secretary of State for Foreign Affairs, Political Affairs and Economic Planning;* b. 11 March 1956, San Marino; m. Luana Dorina Console; two s. *Education:* Univ. degli Studi di Urbino. *Career:* mem. San Marino Socialist Party 1978–, fmr Vice-Pres. and Sec.-Gen.; mem. Great Council of San Marino (Parl.) 1983–, Chair. 2003–06; Sec. of State for Tourism, Commerce, Sport and Agric. 1983–86, for Industry, Handicrafts and Econ. Co-operation 1992–2000, for Internal Affairs, Posts and Telecommunications, Home Affairs and Civil Defence 2001–02, for Finance and the Budget, Transport and Relations with the Azienda Autonoma di Stato Filatelica e Numismatica (AASFN) June–Dec. 2002, for Foreign and Political Affairs, Planning and Econ. Co-operation Dec. 2002–03, for Foreign Affairs, Political Affairs and Econ. Planning 2006–; Vice-Gov. IMF for San Marino 1993–2000, Gov. 2002–03; Gov. World Bank for San Marino 2001–02. *Address:* Secretariat of State for Foreign and Political Affairs, Planning and Economic Co-operation, Palazzo Begni, Contrada Omerelli, 47890 San Marino (office). *Telephone:* 0549 882302 (office). *Fax:* 0549 882814 (office). *E-mail:* segreteriadistato@esteri.sm (office); fo.sepl@esteli.sm (office). *Website:* www.esteri.sm (office).

STOLL, Jean-François; French civil servant; *Head of General Treasury Office (departement de Seine Saint Denis);* b. 19 Jan. 1950, Isle-Adam; m. Noëlle Nicolas 1976; four c. *Education:* Institut des Etudes politiques, Paris, Ecole Nat. d'Admin. *Career:* joined Ministry of Econ., Commercial Attaché Indonesia 1982–84, Tech. Adviser 1982–86, Commercial Adviser Mexico 1987–90, Tech. Adviser for Int. Affairs, Office of the Prime Minister 1990–93, Head Service for Promotion of External Trade 1993, Dir External Econ. Relations 1998, Dir-Gen. Econ. and Trade Dept 2001–; Dir Electricité de France (EDF) 1999–2003, Head, General Treasury Office 2003–; Chevalier, Ordre Nat. du Mérite. *Address:* Ministry of the Economy, Finance and Industry, 139 rue de Bercy, 75572 Paris Cedex 12 (office); 6 rue d'Ulm, 75005 Paris, France (home). *Telephone:* 1-40-04-04-04 (office); 1-48-96-60-01 (home). *Fax:* 1-43-43-75-97 (office); 1-48-96-61-11 (home). *E-mail:* jean-francois.stoll@cp.finances.gouv.fr (office). *Website:* www.minefi.gouv.fr (office).

STOLOJAN, Theodor, PhD, DEcon; Romanian politician and economist; b. 24 Oct. 1943, Tirgoviste; m. Elena Stolojan; one s. one d. *Education:* Acad. of Econ. Studies, Coll. of Finances, Credit and Accountancy, Bucharest. *Career:* worked as economist, Ministry of the Food Industry 1966–72; first as economist and then as Chief of Division, State Budget Dept, Ministry of Finance 1972–82, then Deputy Dir, Dir of Dept Foreign Currencies and Int. Financial Relations 1982–87, Gen. Insp. Dept of State Revenues 1988–89, First Deputy Minister of Finance 1989–90, Minister of Finance 1990–91; Pres. of Nat. Agency of Privatization –1991; Prime Minister of Romania 1991–92; economist, later Sr Economist, IBRD 1992–98; Pres. Tofan Corporated Finance 1999–2000; Partner Strategic Consulting Ltd; Prof. Transylvania Univ., Brașov; Pres. Nat. Liberal Party 2002–04. *Publications:* Integration and European Fiscal Policy 2002; numerous studies. *Address:* Aurel Vlaicu 42-44, Apt 3, Sector 2, Bucharest, Romania. *Telephone:* (1) 3124343. *E-mail:* stolojan@pne (office).

STOLTENBERG, Jens; Norwegian politician; *Prime Minister;* b. 16 March 1959, Oslo; m. Ingrid Schulerud; two c. *Career:* journalist, Arbeiderbladet (nat. daily) 1979–81; Information Sec., Oslo Labour Party 1981; Exec. Officer, Statistics Norway 1989–90; Lecturer in Econs, Univ. of Oslo 1989–90; mem. Cen. Bd, Labour Youth League (AUF) 1979–89, Leader AUF 1985–89; Vice-Pres. Int. Union of Socialist Youth 1985–89; mem. Cen. Bd, Labour Party 1985–, Deputy Leader 1992–; Leader Oslo Labour Party 1990–92; mem. Storting (Parl.) for Oslo 1993–; State Sec., Ministry of Environment 1990–91; Minister of Trade and Energy 1993–96, of Finance 1996–97; Prime Minister of Norway 2000–01, 2005–; mem. Storting Standing Cttee on Social Affairs 1991–93, on Foreign Affairs 2001–; Leader Storting Standing Cttee on Oil and Energy Affairs 1997–2000; mem. Defence Comm. 1990–92; Leader, Labour Party Parl. Group 2001–. *Address:* Office of the Prime Minister, Akersgt. 42, POB 8001 Dep., 0030 Oslo, Norway (office). *Telephone:* 22–24–90–90 (office). *Fax:* 22–24–95–90 (office). *E-mail:* postmottak@smk.dep.no (office). *Website:* www.regjeringen.no/smk (home); odin.dep.no/smk (office).

STOLTENBERG, Thorvald; Norwegian politician and diplomatist; *President, Norwegian Red Cross;* b. 8 July 1931, Oslo; m. Karin Stoltenberg 1957; one s. two d. *Career:* joined Foreign Service 1959; served in San Francisco, Belgrade, Lagos and Foreign Ministry; Int. Sec. Norwegian Fed. of Trade Unions 1970–71; Under-Sec. of State, Foreign Ministry 1971–72, 1976–79; Under-Sec. of State, Ministry of Defence 1973–74, Ministry of Commerce 1974–76; Minister of Defence 1979–81, of Foreign Affairs 1987–89, 1990–93; Amb. to UN, New York 1989–90; UN High Commr for Refugees 1989–90; Special Rep. for UN Sec.-Gen. in fmr Yugoslavia 1993–94; Co-Chair. Steering Cttee, Int. Conf. on the Fmr Yugoslavia 1993–96; Amb. to Denmark 1996–99; Pres. Norwegian Red Cross; Chair. Bd of Int. Inst. for Democracy and Electoral Assistance –2003. *Address:* Norwegian Red Cross, PO Box 1, Groenland, 0133 Oslo, Norway (office). *Telephone:* 22-05-40-00 (office). *Fax:* 22-05-40-40 (office). *E-mail:* thorvald.stoltenberg@redcross.no (office). *Website:* www.redcross.no (office).

STØRE, Jonas Gahr, BSc; Norwegian politician and diplomatist; *Minister of Foreign Affairs;* b. 25 Aug. 1960; m.; three c. *Education:* Royal Norwegian Naval Acad., Institut d'Etudes Politiques de Paris, France. *Career:* Teaching Fellow, Harvard Law School, USA 1986; Researcher, Norwegian School of Man. 1986–89; Special Adviser, Office of the Prime Minister 1989–95, Dir-Gen., Int. Dept 1995–98, State Sec. and Chief of Staff 2000–01; Amb. Perm. Mission to UN, Geneva 1998; Chief of Staff, WHO 1998–2000; Working Chair., ECON Analysis 2002–03; Sec.-Gen., Norwegian Red Cross 2003–05; Minister of Foreign Affairs 2005–. *Address:* Ministry of Foreign Affairs, POB 8114 Dep., 0032 Oslo, Norway (office). *Telephone:* 22-24-36-00 (office). *Fax:* 22-24-95-80 (office). *E-mail:* post@mfa.no (office). *Website:* www.regjeringen.no (office).

STOUDMANN, Gérard, LLB; Swiss diplomatist and fmr research institute director; *Special Envoy for Francophone Africa, Federal Department of*

Foreign Affairs; b. 23 Dec. 1951, Brussels, Belgium. *Education:* Univ. of Lausanne, Inst. for Int. Studies, Geneva. *Career:* mem. gen. staff, Ministry of Defence 1977–80; with Ministry of Foreign Affairs 1981; joined Swiss Mission to EC 1982; mem. delegation to CSCE 1983–87; Deputy Head of Representation to Council of Europe 1987–89; Personal Advisor to Minister of Economy 1989–93; Man. Dir St Gallen Foundation for Int. Studies 1993–94; Minister-Counsellor OSCE 1995–97, Dir Office for Democratic Insts and Human Rights 1997–2002; Dir Geneva Centre for Security Policy 2002–06; High Rep. of the UN Sec.-Gen. for elections in Côte d'Ivoire 2006–07; currently Special Envoy for Francophone Africa, Fed. Dept of Foreign Affairs.
Address: Federal Department of Foreign Affairs, Bundeshaus West, 3003 Bern, Switzerland (office). *Telephone:* 313222111 (office). *Fax:* 313234001 (home). *E-mail:* info@eda.admin.ch (office). *Website:* www.eda.admin.ch (office).

STOYANOV, Petar Stefanov; Bulgarian fmr head of state and lawyer; b. 25 May 1952, Plovdiv; m. Antonina Stoyanova; one s. one d. *Education:* St Kliment Ohridski Univ. of Sofia. *Career:* divorce lawyer 1978–90; became politically active 1989; mem. Union of Democratic Forces (UtDF), Spokesman in Plovdiv 1990, Pres. UtDF Legal Council 1993, Deputy Chair. UtDF responsible for domestic policy 1995, Chair. 2005–07 (resgnd), mem. Nat. Exec. Council; Deputy Minister of Justice 1992–93; mem. Parl. 1994–96, Chair. UtDF Parl. Group Parl. Comm. on Youth, Sports, and Tourism; presidential cand. 1996; Pres. of Bulgaria 1997–2002.
Address: Blvd V. Levski 54, 1000 Sofia, Bulgaria (office). *Telephone:* 888-80-10-92 (mobile) (office). *Fax:* (2) 988-40-47 (office). *E-mail:* stoyanovcentre@ (office).

STOYKOV, Gen. Zlatan Kirilov; Bulgarian military officer; *Chief of General Staff;* b. 17 March 1951, Tsarvaritsa; m.; two d. *Education:* Vasil Levski Army Acad., Nat. War Coll., Gen. Staff Coll., Russia. *Career:* Platoon Commdr, 19th Motorrifle Regt 1973–74; Co. Commdr, First Motorrifle Div. 1974–78; Service Support and Guard Battalion Commdr and Commdt, First Army 1980–81, Asst Chief of Operations Dept 1981–82, Sr Asst 1982–83; Asst Chief of Operations Dept, Operations Directorate, Land Forces Command 1983–84, Sr Asst 1984–87, Deputy Chief 1987–88; Chief of Operations Dept and Deputy Chief of Staff, First Army 1988–92, Deputy Chief of Staff 1992–93; Third Motorrifle Div. Commdr 1995–98; Chief Rapid Reaction Forces HQ 1998–2000; Second Army Corps Commdr 2000–02; Deputy Chief of Gen. Staff, Armed Forces for Resources 2002–03; Chief Land Forces HQ 2003–06; Chief of Gen. Staff 2006–; promoted to Gen. 2006.
Address: Ministry of Defence, 3 Dyakon Ignatiy ul, 1000 Sofia, Bulgaria (office). *Telephone:* (2) 922-09-22 (office). *Fax:* (2) 987-32-28 (office). *E-mail:* presscntr@mod.bg (office). *Website:* www.md.government.bg (office).

STRAKER, Louis, KCMG; Saint Vincent and the Grenadines politician; *Deputy Prime Minister and Minister of Foreign Affairs, Commerce and Trade; Career:* Deputy Prime Minister of Saint Vincent and the Grenadines, Minister of Foreign Affairs, Commerce and Trade –May 2005, Deputy Prime Minister and Minister of Transport, Works and Housing May–Dec. 2005; Deputy Prime Minister and Minister of Foreign Affairs, Commerce and Trade Dec. 2005–.
Address: Ministry of Foreign Affairs, Administrative Building, 3rd Floor, Bay Street, Kingstown, Saint Vincent and the Grenadines (office). *Telephone:* 456-2060 (office). *Fax:* 456-2610 (home). *E-mail:* office .foreignaffairs@mail.gov.vc (office).

STRĂTAN, Andrei, DEcons; Moldovan government official; *Deputy Prime Minister and Minister of Foreign Affairs and European Integration;* b. 3 Sept. 1966, Chişinău; m.; two c. *Education:* Chişinău Polytechnic Inst., Moldova State Univ. *Career:* served in Soviet Customs Control Dept 1991–92, Repub. of Moldova Customs Dept 1992–2002, Head of Div. 1992–95, Deputy Dir-Gen. 1995–97, Prime Deputy Dir-Gen. 1997–99, Dir-Gen. 1999–2002; served on special missions with rank of Amb. including Head, Nat. Bureau of Stability Pact, Ministry of Foreign Affairs 2002–03; Deputy Prime Minister and Minister of Foreign Affairs 2003–04, Minister of Foreign Affairs 2004, Deputy Prime Minister and Minister of Foreign Affairs and European Integration 2005–.
Address: Ministry of Foreign Affairs, 2012 Chişinău, str. 31 August 80, Moldova (office). *Telephone:* (22) 57-82-07 (office). *Fax:* (22) 23-23-02 (office). *E-mail:* secdep@mfa.md (office). *Website:* www.mfa.md (office).

STRAUSS-KAHN, Dominique Gaston André; French economist, lawyer, politician and international organization executive; *Chairman, Executive Board and Managing Director, International Monetary Fund;* b. 25 April 1949, Neuilly-sur-Seine; m. 3rd Anne Sinclair 1991; one s. three d. from fmr marriages. *Education:* Paris Inst. for Political Studies, École des Hautes

Études Commerciales. *Career:* Lecturer, Univ. of Nancy II 1977–80; Scientific Counsellor Nat. Inst. of Statistics and Econ. Studies (INSEE) 1978–80; Dir Cerepi (CNRS) 1980–; Prof., Univ. of Paris-X Nanterre 1981; Chief of Financial Services Commissariat Gen., Plan, Asst Commr Plan 1984–86; elected Socialist Deputy Val-d'Oise 1988–91, 1997, 2001–02; Pres. of Comm. on Finances, Assemblée Nationale 1988, Minister Del. of Industry and Foreign Trade to the Minister of State, Minister of the Economy, Finance and Budget 1991–92; Minister of Industry and Foreign Commerce under Minister of Economy, Finance and Budget 1992–93; Minister of Economy, Finance and Industry 1997–99; mem. Socialist Party Cttee of Dirs 1983–, Nat. Sec. 1984–89; mem. Socialist Party Bureau 1995–; Mayor City of Sorcelles (Val d'Oise) 1995–97, apptd First Deputy Mayor 1997; Chair. Scientific Cttee Jean-Jaurès Foundation 2000; Special Councellor to Sec.-Gen. OECD 2000; Visiting Prof., Stanford Univ., USA 2000–01; fmr Dir of Research, Paris Inst. of Political Studies and Prof. of Econs; fmr Prof., École des Hautes Études Commerciales (HEC School of Man.); charged with forgery Oct. 2000; on trial for corruption Oct. 2001; Co-founder and Co-Pres. A gauche en Europe (think-tank) 2003–; Chair. Exec. Bd and Man. Dir IMF 2007–; unsuccessful cand. for Socialist Party nomination in 2007 presidential election. *Publications:* La richesse des Français 1977, Economie de la famille et accumulation patrimoniale 1977, L'epargne et la retraite 1982.
Address: International Monetary Fund, 700 19th Street, NW, Washington, DC 20431, USA (office). *Telephone:* (202) 623-7000 (office). *Fax:* (202) 623-4661 (office). *E-mail:* publicaffairs@imf.org (office). *Website:* www.imf.org (office); www.blogdsk.net (home).

STRAW, Rt Hon. John (Jack) Whitaker, PC, MP; British politician and lawyer; *Lord Chancellor and Secretary of State for Justice;* b. 3 Aug. 1946, Buckhurst Hill, Essex; m. 1st Anthea L. Weston (divorced 1978); one d. (deceased); m. 2nd Alice E. Perkins 1978; one s. one d. *Education:* Brentwood School, Univ. of Essex and Univ. of Leeds School of Law. *Career:* Pres. Nat. Union of Students 1969–71; mem. Islington Borough Council 1971–78, Inner London Educ. Authority 1971–74 (Deputy Leader 1973–74); called to Bar, Inner Temple 1972, Bencher 1997, practised as barrister 1972–74; special adviser to Sec. of State for Social Services 1974–76, to Sec. of State for Environment 1976–77; on staff of Granada TV (World in Action) 1977–79; MP for Blackburn 1979–; Opposition Treasury Spokesman 1980–83, Environment 1983–87; mem. Parl. Cttee of Labour Party (Shadow Cabinet) 1987–97; Shadow Sec. of State for Educ. 1987–92, for the Environment (Local Govt) 1992–94; Shadow Home Sec. 1994–97; Home Sec. 1997–2001; Sec. of State for Foreign and Commonwealth Affairs 2001–06; Leader of the House of Commons and Lord Privy Seal 2006–07; Lord Chancellor and Sec. of State for Justice 2007–; mem. Council, Inst. for Fiscal Studies 1983–2000, Lancaster Univ. 1989–92; Vice-Pres. Asscn of District Councils; Visiting Fellow, Nuffield Coll. Oxford 1990–98; Gov. Blackburn Coll. 1990–, Pimlico School 1994–2000 (Chair. 1995–98); Fellow Royal Statistical Soc. 1995–; Labour; Hon. LLD (Leeds) 1999. *Publications:* Policy and Ideology 1993; contribs to pamphlets, newspaper articles.
Address: Ministry of Justice, Selborne House, 54 Victoria Street, London, SW1E 6QW (office); House of Commons, Westminster, London, SW1A 0AA, England. *Telephone:* (20) 7210-8500 (office); (20) 7219-3000; (1254) 52317 (constituency office) (office). *Fax:* (20) 7210-0647 (office). *E-mail:* general.queries@justice.gsi.gov.uk (office). *Website:* www.justice.gov.uk (office).

STREISSLER, Erich W., DrIur; Austrian economist and academic; *Professor of Economics, Econometrics and Economic History, University of Vienna;* b. 8 April 1933, Vienna; m. Monika Ruppe 1961; two s. (one deceased) three d. *Education:* Vienna Law School, Univ. of Vienna, Oxford Univ., UK, Hamilton Coll., New York, USA. *Career:* studied also in France and Spain; Prof. of Statistics and Econometrics, Univ. of Freiburg Br., Germany 1962–68, twice Dean of Law and Social Science Faculty 1965–67; Prof., Univ. of Vienna 1968–, Dean of Law and Social Science Faculty 1973–74; Vice-Pres. Austrian Inst. of Econ. Research 1990–; Distinguished Austrian Visiting Prof., Stanford Univ., USA 1983; Pres. Austrian Economic Asscn 1988–94, Pres. Confed. of European Econ. Asscns 1990–91; mem. Bd of Control, Vienna Stock Exchange 1990–98; Treas. Int. Econ. Asscn 1992–99; mem. Austrian Acad. of Sciences; hon. mem. Hungarian Acad. of Sciences, Bavarian Acad. of Sciences; various science prizes. *Publications:* numerous articles in scientific journals on econ. growth, distribution, monetary matters, analysis of econ. systems and especially on the history of thought in econs.
Address: Faculty of Social Sciences and Economics, Vienna University, Hohenstaufeng 9, Vienna 1010 (office); 18 Khevenhuellerstrasse 15, 1180 Vienna, Austria (home). *Telephone:* 4277-374-25 (office); 44-05-770 (home). *Fax:* 4277-9374 (office). *E-mail:* sylvie.hansbauer@univie.ac.at (office).

STROHAL, Christian, DrIur; Austrian diplomatist and international organization executive; *Director, Office for Democratic Institutions and Human Rights, Organization for Security and Co-operation in Europe;* b. 1 May 1951, Vienna; m.; three c. *Education:* schools in Vienna, studies in law, econs and int. relations in Vienna, London and Geneva. *Career:* voluntary mil. service; with Ministry for Foreign Affairs (MFA) since 1976: Attaché, Office of Legal Adviser and Dept for Int. Orgs, postings to London, Geneva, and as First Sec. and Deputy Head of Mission to Rabat 1981–85, mem. Austrian dels to Madrid and Vienna CSCE follow-up meetings, Head of Human Rights Office, Dept of the Legal Adviser, MFA, del. to UN, Council of Europe and CSCE meetings 1985–88, Minister and Deputy Perm. Rep. at Austrian Mission at UN and int. orgs, Geneva 1988–92, Amb. and Special Rep. for World Conf. on Human Rights 1992–93, Dir for Human Rights, Int. Humanitarian Law, and Minority and Gender Issues, MFA, Austrian Rep. to UN Comm. on Human Rights, del. to UN Gen. Ass., rep. to EU Working Group on Human Rights 1994–2000, Amb. to Luxembourg 2000–03, Amb. and Dir Office for Democratic Insts and Human Rights, OSCE 2003–; del. to numerous int. confs in framework of UN, Council of Europe and OSCE; Co-convener informal East–West human rights consultations, Geneva 1988–90; rep. to Finance and Council Cttees of CERN 1988–92; Chair. Western Human Rights Group, Geneva 1990–92; Vice-Chair. UN Comm. on Human Rights 1997–98; Chair. Council of Europe Working Group for 50th anniversary of Universal Declaration of Human Rights 1997–98, EU Working Group on Human Rights 1998; Moderator OSCE supplementary human dimension meetings on human rights and inhuman treatment or punishment as well as on trafficking in human beings 2000; Lecturer, Diplomatic and Admin. Acads, Vienna, and at EU Masters Programme for Democracy and Human Rights. *Publications:* several publs on int. human rights issues. *Address:* Office for Democratic Institutions and Human Rights, Aleje Ujazdowskie 19, 00-557 Warsaw, Poland (office). *Telephone:* (22) 520-06-00 (office). *Fax:* (22) 520-06-05 (office). *E-mail:* office@odihr.pl (office). *Website:* www.osce.org/odihr (office).

STRØM-ERICHSEN, Anne-Grete; Norwegian computer engineer and politician; *Minister of Defence;* b. 1949; m.; two c. *Career:* mem., Bergen City Council 1991–2005, mem. Exec. Bd 1991–2000, Deputy Mayor, City of Bergen 1998–99, Mayor 1999–2000, Chief Commr, City of Bergen 2000–03, Commr 2003–, Councillor and Chair., Standing Cttee on Environmental Affairs and Urban Devt, City of Bergen 2003–05; Deputy Leader, Labour Party in Bergen 1992, Leader, Hordaland Labour Party 1997–99, mem. Labour Party Cen. Council 2001–; Minister of Defence 2005–. *Address:* Ministry of Defence, POB 8126 Dep., 0032 Oslo, Norway (office). *Telephone:* 23-09-80-00 (office). *Fax:* 23-09-60-51 (office). *E-mail:* postmottak@fd.dep.no (office). *Website:* odin.dep.no/fd (office); www.mod.no.

STRØMMEN, Wegger Christian; Norwegian lawyer and diplomatist; *Ambassador to USA;* m. Rev. Cecilie J. Strømmen; two d. *Education:* Univ. of Oslo Law School. *Career:* jr dist court judge 1986–87; legal adviser to Co-Chair. EU-UN Int. Conf. on the Fmr Yugoslavia 1993–95; attorney, later Pnr, Wiersholm, Mellbye & Beech (law firm) 1996–98; joined Norwegian Diplomatic Service 1984, Exec. Officer, Legal Dept 1984–86, First Sec., Tel-Aviv 1988–91, First Sec., Perm. Mission to Perm., Geneva 1991–93, Head of Div., Ministry of Foreign Affairs 1995–96, Special Advisor 1998–99, Deputy Minister of Foreign Affairs (State Sec.) 1999–2000; Deputy Perm. Rep. to UN Security Council and Chair. Security Council Working Group on Peacekeeping Operations 2000–02, Deputy Perm. Rep. to UN, New York 2002–05, Perm. Rep. to UN and other Int. Orgs, Geneva 2005–07, Amb. to USA 2007–; Visiting Fellow, IISS, London 2000; has lectured on int. law at Harvard Univ., Columbia Univ., New York Univ., Univ. of Bergen and Univ. of Oslo. *Address:* Royal Norwegian Embassy, 2720 34th Street, NW, Washington, DC 20008, USA (office). *Telephone:* (202) 333-6000 (office). *Fax:* (202) 337-0870 (office). *E-mail:* emb.washington@mfa.no (office). *Website:* www.norway.org (office).

STRONG, Rt Hon. Maurice F., CC, PC, LLD, FRS, FRSA, FRSC; Canadian environmentalist, international organization official and business executive; b. 29 April 1929, Oak Lake, Manitoba; m. 1st Pauline Olivette Williams 1950 (divorced 1980); two s. two d. one foster d.; m. 2nd Hanne Marstrand 1981. *Education:* Oak Lake High School, Manitoba. *Career:* served in UN Secr. 1947; Pres. or Dir of various Canadian and int. corpns 1954–66; also involved in leadership of various pvt. orgs in field of devt and int. affairs; Dir-Gen. External Aid Office of Canadian Govt 1966 (now Canadian Int. Devt Agency); Chair. Canadian Int. Devt Bd; Alt. Gov. IBRD, ADB, Caribbean Devt Bank; UN Under-Sec. Gen. with responsibility for environmental affairs 1970–72, Chief Exec. for 1972 Conf. on Human Environment, Stockholm, June 1972; Montague Burton Prof. of Int. Relations, Univ. of Edin. 1973; Exec. Dir UNEP 1973–75; Chair. Petro

Canada 1976–78; Pres. Stronat Investments Ltd 1976–80; Chair. Bd of Govs Int. Devt Research Centre 1977–78; Chair. Strovest Holdings Inc., Procor Inc. 1978–79, AZL Resources Inc. 1978–83, Int. Energy Devt Corpn 1980–83, NS Round Table Soc. for Int. Devt, Canadian Devt Investment Corpn, 1982–84, Supercritical Combustion Corpn, Int. Advisory Group, CH2M Hill Cos Ltd; Chair. and Dir Tech. Devt Corpn; Dir or mem. numerous business and conservation groups in Canada and internationally including Foundation Bd World Econ. Forum, Leadership for Environment and Devt, Zenon Environmental, Inc., The Humane Soc. of the US; UnderSec.-Gen., UN 1985–87, 1989; Pres. World Fed. UNA 1987, The Baca Corpn; Dir Better World Soc. 1988; Chair., Pres. American Water Devt Inc., Denver 1986–89; Sec.-Gen. UN 1992 Conf. on Environment and Devt; Chair. Ontario Hydro 1992–95, World Resources Inst.; Sr Adviser to Pres. of World Bank 1995–; UnderSec.-Gen. and Exec. Co-ordinator for UN Reform 1997; UnderSec.-Gen. and Sr Adviser to Sec.-Gen. of UN 1998–2005 (resgnd); Pres. Council UN Univ. for Peace, San José, Costa Rica 2001–; Chair. Earth Council Foundation; mem. Bd of Dirs UN Foundation, Int. Advisory Bd, Toyota Motor Corpn, Int. Advisory Bd, Center of Int. Devt at Harvard Univ., Int. Advisory Council, Liu Centre for the Study of Global Issues at Univ. of British Columbia, Lamont-Doherty Observatory Advisory Bd; Fellow Royal Agric. Soc. of Canada; hon. degrees from 49 univs; Royal Order of the Polar Star, Sweden 1996; Onassis Int. Award 1993, Jawaharlal Nehru Award for Int. Understanding 1994, Millennium Award, The Princes' Award Foundation, Denmark 2000, Global Steering Wheel Int. Prize, Russia 2001, Global Environment Leadership Award 2002, Nat. Acad. of Sciences Public Service Award, USA 2004 and numerous other awards, prizes and decorations. *Publications:* The Great Building Bee (with Jacques Hébert) 1980, A Life for the Planet 1999, Where On Earth Are We Going?; various articles in journals. *Address:* S3 Holdings Inc., 150 Isabella Street, Suite 100, Ottawa, ON K15 1V7, Canada (office). *Telephone:* (613) 232-1222 (office). *Fax:* (613) 569-4667 (office). *E-mail:* info@mauricestrong.org (office).

STROSSEN, Nadine, BA, JD; American lawyer and academic; *President, American Civil Liberties Union;* b. 18 Aug. 1950, Jersey City; m. Eli Michael Noam 1980. *Education:* Harvard Law School, Radcliffe Coll. *Career:* assoc. attorney Sullivan and Cromwell 1978–83; pnr Harvis and Zeichner 1983–84; mem. Nat. Bd Dirs American Civil Liberties Union 1983–, Pres. 1991–, mem. advisory Cttee on Reproductive Freedom Project 1983–, Nat. Exec. Cttee 1985–, Nat. Gen. Council 1986–91; Asst Prof. of Clinical Law Univ. of New York 1989–; Adjunct Prof. Grad. School of Business Univ. of Columbia 1990–; mem. Exec. Cttee Human Rights Watch 1989–91; mem. Bd Dirs Coalition to Free Soviet Jewry 1984–; mem. Asia Watch 1987–, Vice-Chair. 1989–91; mem. Nat. Coalition Against Censorship 1988, Middle East Watch 1989–91, The Fund for Free Expression 1990–; mem. Steering Cttee New York Legal Council for Soviet Jewry 1987–. *Publications include:* Regulating Campus Hate Speech – A Modest Proposal? 1990, Recent US and International Judicial Protection of Individuals Rights: A Comparative Legal Process Analysis and Proposed Synthesis 1990, In Defense of Pornography: Free Speech and the Fight for Women's Rights 1995, numerous articles in professional journals. *Address:* American Civil Liberties Union, 125 Broad Street, 18th Floor, New York, NY 10004 (office); New York Law School, 57 Worth Street, New York, NY 10013-2960 (office); 450 Riverside Drive, #51, New York, NY 10027, USA (home). *Telephone:* (212) 431-2375 (office). *Fax:* (212) 431-1992 (office). *E-mail:* nstrossen@aclu.org (office). *Website:* www.aclu.org (office).

STRUBLE, J(ames) Curtis (Curt), BA; American diplomatist; b. Visalia, CA. *Education:* Univ. of California, Berkeley. *Career:* mem. Sr Foreign Service with rank of Minister Counselor, served at Embassies in Ecuador, Thailand, Honduras, Spain, Russia and Mexico; Deputy Asst Sec., Bureau for W Hemisphere Affairs, Dept of State 2001–02, Prin. Deputy Asst Sec. July–Nov. 2002, Acting Asst Sec. 2002–03, Amb. to Peru 2003–07; Foreign Affairs Fellow, Hoover Inst., Stanford, Calif. 1988–89; eight awards for distinguished service, US State Dept. *Address:* US Department of State, 2201 C Street NW, Washington, DC 20520, USA (office). *Telephone:* (202) 647-4000 (office). *Fax:* (202) 647-6738 (office). *Website:* www.state.gov (office).

STRUCK, Peter, DJur; German lawyer and politician; b. 24 Jan. 1943, Göttingen; m.; three c. *Education:* Univs of Göttingen and Hamburg. *Career:* adviser to the govt, Hamburg 1971; personal adviser to Pres. of Univ. of Hamburg 1971–72; elected Town Councillor and Deputy Town Mayor of Uelzen 1973; admitted to Bar, 1983; worked in Dist Court of Uelzen and Regional Court of Lueneburg; mem. SDP 1964–, mem. Bundestag (representing Lower Saxony) 1980–, Chair. of Parl. Group 1998–; Minister of Defence 2002–05; mem. ÖTV (Public Workers' Union); mem. Bd Hilden AHG Gen. Hosp., Rockwool Beteiligungs GmbH, Gladbeck.

Address: c/o Sozialdemokratische Partei Deutschlands (SPD), Wilhelmstr. 141, 10963 Berlin, Germany (office). *E-mail:* peter.struck@bundestag.de (office). *Website:* www.bundestag.de/~Peter.Struck (office).

STRUYE DE SWIELANDE, Dominique, LLM, DrIur; Belgian diplomatist; *Ambassador to USA;* b. 10 July 1947, Gand. *Education:* Univ. of Gent, Univ. Coll., London, UK, Katholieke Universiteit Leuven. *Career:* entered Diplomatic Service 1974; assigned to Vienna 1975–76, Lagos 1976–70; Chargé d'affaires a.i. in Salisbury and Harare, Zimbabwe 1980–81; Counsellor in Kinshasa, Zaïre 1982–84; Counsellor, Ministry of Foreign Affairs 1984–87; Consul-Gen. and Perm. Rep. to UN and Int. Orgs, Geneva 1987–90; Dir EU Section, Ministry of Foreign Affairs 1990, Head of Cabinet 1991–92, Diplomatic Counsellor and Chief of Cabinet to the Prime Minister 1992–94, Dir-Gen. of Admin, Ministry of Foreign Affairs 1994–95, Chief of Cabinet to Sec. of State and Int. Co-operation 1995–96; Amb. to Germany 1997–2002; Perm. Rep. to NATO, Brussels 2002–06; Amb. to USA 2006–.
Address: Embassy of Belgium, 3330 Garfield Street, NW, Washington, DC 20008, USA (office). *Telephone:* (202) 333-6900 (office). *Fax:* (202) 333-3079 (office). *E-mail:* washington@diplobel.org (office). *Website:* www.diplobel.us (office).

STUBB, Cai-Göran Alexander, BA, MA, PhD; Finnish journalist, politician and academic; *Minister for Foreign Affairs;* b. 1 April 1968, Helsinki; m. Suzanne Innes-Stubb; one s. one d. *Education:* Mainland High School, Daytona Beach, Fla, USA, Gymnasiet Lärkan, Helsinki, golf scholarship to Furman Univ., S Carolina, USA, Univ. of the Sorbonne, Paris, Coll. of Europe, Belgium, London School of Econs, UK. *Career:* mil. service; researcher, Ministry of Foreign Affairs 1995–97, Finnish Acad. 1997–99; columnist for various newspapers, including APU, Ilta-Sanomat, Blue Wings, various papers in Suomen Lehtiyhtymä group, Nykypäivä and Hufvudstadsbladet 1997–; special researcher, Finland's representation to EU, Brussels 1999–2001, mem. Finnish Govt's del. to intergovernmental negotiations for Treaty of Nice; Prof., Coll. of Europe, Brussels 2000–; adviser to Pres. of EC 2001–03, mem. Comm. Task Force on European Convention; mem. Finland's representation to EU as a special expert and to intergovernmental negotiations for European Constitution 2003–04; mem. Nat. Coalition; mem. European Parl. (European People's Party) 2004–08, Vice-Pres. Cttee on Internal Market and Consumer Protection, mem. Cttee on Budgetary Control, substitute mem. Cttee on Constitutional Affairs, substitute mem. Del. to EU-Turkey Jt Parl. Cttee; Minister for Foreign Affairs 2008–. *Publications:* nine books about the EU; several articles in academic journals.
Address: Ministry of Foreign Affairs, Merikasarmi, Laivastokatu 22, PO Box 176, 00161 Helsinki, Finland (office). *Telephone:* (9) 16005 (office). *Fax:* (9) 629840 (office). *E-mail:* kirjaamo.um@formin.fi (office). *Website:* formin.finland.fi (office); www.alexstubb.com.

STULBERG, Adam, BA, MIA, MA, PhD; American academic; *Co-Director, Center for International Strategy, Technology and Policy, Georgia Institute of Technology; Education:* Univ. of Michigan, Columbia Univ., Univ. of California. *Career:* Political Consultant, RAND Corp. 1987–99; Sr Research Assoc., Center for Nonproliferation Studies, Monterey Inst. of Int. Studies 1997, Postdoctoral Research Fellow 2000–01; Asst Prof., Georgia Inst. of Tech. 1998–2006, Assoc. Prof. 2006–, Co-Dir Center for Int. Strategy, Tech. and Policy 2007–; Visiting Research Fellow, Center for Int. Security and Cooperation, Stanford Univ. 2000–01; Rapporteur Aspen Strategy Group and Council on Foreign and Defence Policy 1997–2003; mem. Project on Ferghana Valley Region of Cen. Asia 1997–98; mem. Council on Foreign Relations, Center for Preventive Action, American Asscn for the Advancement of Slavic Studies, American Political Science Asscn, Asscn for the Study of Nationalities, Int. Studies Asscn. *Publications:* Managing Military Revolutions: Agency, Culture, and Service Innovation (co-author) 2007, Well-Oiled Diplomacy: Strategic Manipulation and Russia's Energy Statecraft in Eurasia 2007; numerous contribs to academic journals.
Address: Center for International Strategy, Technology and Policy, Georgia Institute of Technology, 781 Marietta Street NW, Atlanta, GA 30332-0610, USA (office). *Telephone:* (404) 894-3195 (office). *Fax:* (404) 894-1900 (office). *E-mail:* adam.stulberg@inta.gatech.edu (office). *Website:* www.cistp.gatech.edu (office).

STUMPF, István, LLB, PhD; Hungarian politician and academic; *President, Századvég Foundation;* b. 5 Aug. 1957, Sárospatak; one s. three d. *Education:* Eötvös Lóránd Univ., John F. Kennedy School of Govt, Harvard Univ. and Grad. School of Political Man., George Washington Univ., USA. *Career:* with Eötvös Lóránd Univ., Asst Prof. of Law and Political Science 1982–87, Assoc. Prof. of Political Science 1996–, Founder and Dir Bibó István Professional Law Coll. 1988; Researcher, Inst. for Social Science, Hungarian Acad. of Studies 1987; Founder and Pres.

Századvég School of Politics and Policy Research Centre (Századvég Foundation) 1991–; Ed. and Publr Századvég Journal of Social Science; Vice-Pres. of Patriotic People's Front 1989–90; Special Adviser on youth affairs to the Pres. of Hungarian Repub. 1991–94; Minister in Charge of Prime Minister's Office, Govt of Hungary, in charge of Privatization and Telecommunications 1998–2002; Deputy Prime Minister 2001–02; Visiting Prof., Inst. for Int. Integrations Studies, Trinity Coll., Dublin, Ireland 2003; mem. Int. Political Science Asscn, Advisory Bd of Youth Centre and Youth Foundation, Council of Europe 1991–92; Pres. Nat. Council of Youth Orgs of Hungary 1989–90; German Marshall Fellowship 1991 IREX Scholarship John F. Kennedy School of Govt, Harvard Univ. *Publications include:* numerous publs on political socialization, electoral behaviour, governance and public policy.
Address: Századvég Foundation, Nagybátonyi 8-10, 1037 Budapest, Hungary (office). *E-mail:* szazadveg@szazadveg.hu (office). *Website:* www.szazadveg.hu (office).

STURZA, Vasile; Moldovan diplomatist; *Ambassador to Russian Federation; Education:* Moldova State Univ. *Career:* early career as Investigator and Prosecutor, Rybnitsa; party functionary, Cen. Cttee of CP 1988–91; worked at Gen. Prosecutor's Office 1991–94; Minister of Justice 1994–98; First Deputy Gen. Prosecutor 1998–99; Head of Moldovan Expert Team and Pres.'s Rep. at Transnistrian negotiations 2000–03; Amb. to Bulgaria 2003–05, to Russian Fed. 2005–.
Address: Embassy of Moldova, 107031 Moscow, ul. Kuznetskii most 18, Russia (office). *Telephone:* (495) 924-53-53 (office). *Fax:* (495) 924-95-90 (office). *E-mail:* moscova@mfa.md (office). *Website:* www.moldembassy.ru (office).

STÜTZLE, Walther K. A., Dr rer. pol; German journalist; *Senior Distinguished Fellow. German Institute for International and Security Affairs;* b. 29 Nov. 1941, Westerland-Sylt; m. Dr H. Kauper 1966; two s. two d. *Education:* Westerland High School and Univs of Berlin, Bordeaux and Hamburg. *Career:* researcher, Inst. for Strategic Studies, London 1967–68, Foreign Policy Inst. Bonn 1968–69; Desk Officer, Ministry of Defence, Planning Staff, Bonn 1969–72, Pvt. Sec. and Chef de Cabinet, 1973–76, Head, Planning Staff, Under-Sec. of Defence, Plans and Policy 1976–82; editorial staff, Stuttgarter Zeitung 1983–86; Dir Stockholm Int. Peace Research Inst. (SIPRI) 1986–91; Ed.-in-Chief Der Tagesspiegel 1994–98; Perm. Sec., Ministry of Defence 1998–2002, Visiting Prof., Potsdam Univ. 2004–; Sr Distinguished Fellow, German Institute for Int. and Security Affairs 2004–. *Publications:* Adenauer und Kennedy in der Berlinkrise 1961–62 1972, Politik und Kräftverhältnis 1983, Europe's Future – Europe's Choices (co-author) 1967, ABM Treaty – To Defend or Not to Defend 1987, SIPRI Yearbook (ed.) 1986–90, From Alliance to Coalition: The Future of Transatlantic Relations (contributor) 2004.
Address: Stiftung Wissenschaft und Politik, Deutsches Institut für Internationale Politik und Sicherheit, Ludwigkirchplatz 3-4, 10719 Berlin, Germany (office). *Telephone:* (30) 880070 (office). *Fax:* (30) 88007100 (office). *E-mail:* walther.stuetzle@swp-berlin.org. *Website:* www.swp-berlin.org.

SU, Chi, PhD; Taiwanese government official and academic; *Secretary General, National Security Council;* b. 1 Oct. 1949, Taichung; m. Grace Chen; one s. one d. *Education:* Nat. Chengchi Univ., Johns Hopkins and Columbia Univs, USA. *Career:* Assoc. Prof., Dept of Diplomacy Nat. Chengchi Univ. 1984–90, Prof. 1990–, Deputy Dir Inst. of Int. Relations 1990–93; Sec. Gen. Office of the Univ. Pres. 1989–90; mem. Exec. Yuan Research, Devt and Evaluation Comm. 1990–94; Sec.-Gen. China Political Science Asscn 1990–91; Deputy Dir Kuomintang Cen. Cttee Dept of Mainland Affairs 1992–93; Vice-Chair Exec. Yuan Mainland Affairs Council 1993–96; Dir-Gen. Govt Information Office 1996–97; Exec. Yuan Minister of State 1997; Nat. Policy Adviser to Pres. of Repub. 1997, Deputy Sec.-Gen. to Pres. 1997–99; fmr. Chair. Mainland Affairs Council 1999; Prof. Inst. of China Studies, Tamkang Univ. and Convener, Nat. Security Div., Nat. Policy Foundation 2000–08; Sec.-Gen. Nat. Security Council 2008–. *Publications:* The Normalization of Sino-Soviet Relations, over 20 papers and articles.
Address: Ministry of National Defense, 2/F, 164 Po Ai Road, Taipei 10048, Taiwan (office). *Telephone:* (2) 23116117 (office). *Fax:* (2) 23144221 (office). *Website:* www.mnd.gov.tw (office).

SUÁREZ DEL TORO RIVERO, Juan Manuel; Spanish international organization executive, volunteer activist, academic and engineer; *President, International Federation of Red Cross and Red Crescent Societies;* m.; two d. *Career:* fmr industrial engineer; Prof., Univ. of Las Palmas, Gran Canaria; Dir Public Transport Co.; joined local Red Cross youth br. 1979, various positions in movt including Youth Dir, Vice-Pres. and Pres. of Las Palmas Prov. Ass., Pres. of Canary Islands Br. Spanish Red Cross, mem. Nat. Cttee, Nat. Vice-Pres. and Pres. 1994; fmr mem. Governing Bd of Int.

Fed., also fmr Vice-Pres. and Chair. Devt Comm., elected Pres. of Int. Fed. of Red Cross and Red Crescent Socs at Gen. Ass., Geneva 2001–; Hon. DH (Hoseo Univ., South Korea) 2003, (Nat. Autonomous Univ. of Honduras) 2005, (Univ. of Chile) 2007, (Univ. of Panama) 2008; Spanish Red Cross Gold Medal, Grand Cross of the Ministry of Defence, Silver Medal of the Merit Order of The Civil Guard Force 2007, Infanta Cristina Imserso Award 2007.
Address: International Federation of Red Cross and Red Crescent Societies, 17 Chemin des Créts, Petit-Saconnex, CP 372, 1211 Geneva 19, Switzerland (office). *Telephone:* (22) 7304333 (office). *Fax:* (22) 7330395 (office). *E-mail:* secretariat@ifrc.org (office). *Website:* www.ifrc.org (office).

SUBASINGHE, Devinda Rohan, MA; Sri Lankan diplomatist; *President, Bridging Nations;* m. Helga Wurzer-Subasinghe; one s. *Education:* Royal Coll., Sri Lanka Law Coll., Indiana Univ. and School of Advanced Int. Studies, John Hopkins Univ., Washington, DC, USA. *Career:* success as nat. swimmer brought him to USA to pursue higher educ. as athlete/scholar; Adviser to Pres. J. R. Jayewardene and Counsellor to Pres. R. Premadasa 1977–84; Adviser on Econ. Reform to IBRD and Int. Finance Corpn in Asia Pacific and Cen. and Eastern Europe 1984–95; adviser to US Govt on foreign policy and econ. devt issues 1995–99; Founder and CEO Asia Insight 21; responsible for mandates advising UN, govts and corpns in USA, Asia, Europe, Middle East, Cen. and S America, Caribbean and Southern/S Africa on capital markets, trade liberalization and investment mobilization; fmr adviser to Pres. Chandrika Bandaranaike-Kumaratunga, fmr Prime Minister Ranil Wickremesinghe and current Minister of Foreign Affairs, Lakshman Kadirgamar; Vice-Pres. Raymond James Financial Inc., Fla 1999–2002; Amb. to USA 2003–05 (also accred to Mexico 2004–05), also Perm. Observer to OAS 2003–05; Pres. Bridging Nations (think tank), Washington, DC 2005–. *Publications:* numerous articles in newspapers and journals.
Address: Bridging Nations, 1800 K Street, NW, Suite 622, Washington, DC 20006, USA (office). *Telephone:* (202) 741-3870 (office). *Fax:* (202) 741-3871 (office). *E-mail:* phoebe.connell@bridgingnations.org (office). *Website:* www.bridgingnations.org (home).

SUCHOCKA, Hanna, DrIur; Polish diplomatist, politician and lawyer; *Ambassador to the Holy See;* b. 3 April 1946, Pleszew. *Education:* Adam Mickiewicz Univ., Poznań. *Career:* scientific worker, Dept of Constitutional Law of Adam Mickiewicz Univ., Poznań 1968–69, 1972–90, Catholic Univ. of Lublin 1988–92, Polish Acad. of Science 1990–; mem. Democratic Party (SD) 1969–84, Democratic Union 1991–94, Freedom Union 1994–; Deputy to Sejm (Parl.) 1980–85, 1989–2001; mem. Civic. Parl. Caucus 1989–91, mem. Democratic Union Parl. Caucus (now Freedom Union) 1991–, Deputy Chair. Parl. Legis. Cttee 1989–92; Chair. Council of Ministers (Prime Minister) 1992–93; Minister of Justice and Attorney-Gen. 1997–99; mem. Pontifical Acad. of Social Sciences, Rome 1994–; Amb. to the Holy See 2001–; Dr hc (Oklahoma Univ.); Max Schmidtheiny Prize 1994, Foyer Prize 2004. *Publications:* author of reports and articles for professional publs and int. confs.
Address: Polish Embassy, Via dei Delfini 16/3, 00186 Rome, Italy (office). *Telephone:* (06) 6990958 (office). *Fax:* (06) 6990978 (office). *E-mail:* polamb.wat@agora.stm.it (office).

SUDARSONO, Juwono, PhD; Indonesian government official, diplomatist and academic; *Minister of Defence;* m.; two s. one d. *Education:* Univ. of Indonesia, Univ. of Calif., Berkeley, USA, LSE, UK. *Career:* Visiting Prof. Columbia Univ. 1986–87; Dean of Social and Political Science Univ. of Indonesia 1988–94; Vice Gov. Indonesian Defence Coll. 1995–98; apptd Minister of Environment 1998, then Minister of Educ.; served as first civilian Minister of Defence 1999; returned to Univ. of Indonesia teaching part-time; fmr Commr Strategic Intelligence; Amb. to UK, Repub. of Ireland 2003–04; Minister of Defence 2004–.
Address: Ministry of Defence, Jalan Medan Merdeka Barat 13–14, Jakarta Pusat, Indonesia (office). *Telephone:* (21) 3456184 (office). *Fax:* (21) 3440023 (office). *E-mail:* postmaster@dephan.go.id (office). *Website:* www.dephan.go.id (office).

SUDRADJAT, Maj.-Gen. (retd) Edi; Indonesian politician, diplomatist and fmr army officer; *Ambassador to People's Republic of China;* b. 1938; m.; four c. *Career:* served for 31 years in Indonesian Army, more than half in combat positions; fmr Minister of Defence; Chair. Partai Keadilan dan Persatuan Indonesia; currently Amb. to People's Repub. of China (also accred to Mongolia).
Address: Embassy of Indonesia, 4 Dong Zhi Men Wai Dajie, Beijing 100600, People's Republic of China (office). *Telephone:* (10) 65325486 (office). *Fax:* (10) 65325368 (office). *E-mail:* kombei@public3.bta.net.cn (office). *Website:* www.indonesianembassy-china.com (office).

SUEBWONGLEE, Surapong; Thai physician and politician; *Deputy Prime Minister and Minister of Finance; Career:* fmr Communist rebel; trained as a medical doctor before entering politics; fmr mem. Thai Rak Thai party; Govt Spokesman 2005; Minister of Information and Communications Tech. –2006 (Govt of Prime Minister Thaksin Sinawatra deposed in mil. coup Sept. 2006); Sec.-Gen. People's Power Party 2007–; Deputy Prime Minister and Minister of Finance 2008–.
Address: Ministry of Finance, Rama 6 Road, Phayathai, Rajatevi, Bangkok 10400, Thailand (office). *Telephone:* (2) 273-9021 (office). *Fax:* (2) 273-9408 (office). *E-mail:* prinya@mof.go.th (office). *Website:* www.mof.go.th (office).

SUFAN, Ahmad Muhammad; Yemeni politician. *Career:* Deputy Prime Minister and Minister of Planning and Int. Co-operation –2007.
Address: c/o Ministry of Planning and International Co-operation, POB 175, San'a, Yemen (office).

SUHAIBI, Numan Saleh al-; Yemeni politician. *Career:* currently Minister of Finance.
Address: Ministry of Finance, PO Box 190, San'a, Yemen (office). *Telephone:* (1) 260370 (office). *Fax:* (1) 263040 (office).

SUKARNOPUTRI, Megawati (see MEGAWATI SUKARNOPUTRI).

ŠUKER, Ivan, DiplEcon; Croatian politician and economist; *Minister of Finance;* b. 12 Nov. 1957, Livno; m. Andrea Šuker; one s. one d. *Education:* Univ. of Zagreb. *Career:* Chief Accountant, City Council, Velika Gorica 1984–86, Financial Dir 1986–1990, Head of Fiscal Office 1990–2000, Deputy Mayor 1990–91, Chief of Gen. Staff, Velika Gorica (during war) 1991–92; mem. City Council, Zagreb 1993–97, Deputy Mayor 1997–2000; elected to Sabor (Parl.) for Croatian Democratic Union (Hrvatska Demokratska Zajednica—HDZ) 2000–, mem. Finance and Budget Cttee, Pres. HDZ, Velika Gorica 2000–03, mem. HDZ Nat. Bureau 2000–, Deputy Chair. HDZ 2002–; Minister of Finance 2003–.
Address: Ministry of Finance, 10000 Zagreb, ul. Katančićeva 5, Croatia (office). *Telephone:* (1) 4591300 (office). *Fax:* (1) 4922583 (office). *E-mail:* kabinet@mfin.hr (office). *Website:* www.mfin.hr (office).

SULEIMAN, Gen. Michel, BA, MA; Lebanese politician, head of state and fmr army officer; *President;* b. 21 Nov. 1948, Amchit; m. Wafaa Suleiman; three c. *Education:* Lebanese Univ. *Career:* Chief Intelligence Br., Mount Lebanon 1990–91; Army Staff Sec.-Gen. 1991–93; Commdr 11th Infantry Brigade 1993–96, Sixth Infantry Brigade 1996–98; Commdr Lebanese Armed Forces 1998–2008; Pres. of Lebanon 2008–; Kt and Grand Cordon, Nat. Order of the Cedar, First, Second, Third and Extraordinary Grade, Lebanese Order of Merit, Grade of Excellence, Syrian Order of Merit; Decoration of Mil. Pride (Silver), Medal of War, Decoration of Mil. Valor (Silver), Decoration of Nat. Unity, Decoration of the Dawn of the South, Internal Security Forces Medal, Gen. Security Medal, Commemorative Medal of Confs 2002.
Address: Presidential Palace, Baabda, Beirut, Lebanon (office). *Telephone:* (5) 920900 (office). *Fax:* (5) 922400 (office). *E-mail:* president_office@presidency.gov.lb (office). *Website:* www.presidency.gov.lb (office).

SULEIMENOV, Tuleutai Skakovich; Kazakhstani diplomatist; *Ambassador to Poland;* b. 1941, Semipalatinsk. *Education:* Karaganda Polytech. Inst., Diplomatic Acad. of USSR Ministry of Foreign Affairs. *Career:* foreman Karaganda Metallurgic factory –1969, Comsomol and CP functionary 1969–80; mem. USSR Ministry of Foreign Affairs 1980–; Counsellor USSR Embassy to Iran 1988–91; Kazakhstan Minister of Foreign Affairs 1991–94; Amb. to USA 1994–95; to Hungary 1995–2001, to Belgium 2001–03, to Poland 2003–.
Address: 14 Królowej, Marysienki str., 02–954 Warsaw, Poland; Beibit-shilik 10, Astana 473000, Kazakhstan. *Telephone:* (2) 26425388 (office). *Fax:* (2) 26423427 (office). *E-mail:* kazdipmis@hot.pl (office). *Website:* www.kazakhstan.pl (office).

SULEYMENOV, Olzhas Omarovich; Kazakhstani politician, diplomatist and writer; *Ambassador to United Nations Educational, Scientific and Cultural Organization (UNESCO);* b. 1936. *Education:* Kazak State Univ., Maxim Gorky Inst. of Literature in Moscow. *Career:* mem. CPSU 1989–90; debut as writer in 1960; Ed.-in-Chief Studio Kazakhfilm 1962–71; head of div. Prostor (magazine) 1971–; Sec. Bd Kazakh Writers' Union 1971–; Chair. Kazakh Cttee on relations with writers of Asia and Africa 1980–; actively participates in ecological movt, actions of protest against nuclear tests in Semipalatinsk since late 1980s; Deputy to USSR Supreme Soviet 1984–89; People's Deputy, mem. USSR Supreme Soviet 1989–91; Founder and Leader of People's Progress Party of Kazakhstan 1992–95; Amb. to Italy 1995–2001; currently Amb. to UNESCO; USSR Komsomol Prize, State Abai Prize of Kazakh SSR. *Publications:*

collections of poetry including Argamaki 1961, Sunny Nights 1962, The Night of Paris 1963, The Kind Time of the Sunrise 1964, The Year of Monkey 1967, Above White Rivers 1970, Each Day – Morning 1973, Repeating in the Noon 1973, A Round Star 1975, Definition of a Bank 1976 and others.
Address: Karla Marksa str. 96, Apt. 6, 480100 Almaty, Kazakhstan (home).
Telephone: (727) 268-20-65 (home).

SULLIVAN, Vice-Adm. William D.; American naval officer; *Military Representative, NATO; Education:* Florida State Univ., Officer Cand. School, Newport, RI, Georgetown Univ., Nat. War Coll. *Career:* numerous assignments at sea including Commdr guided missile destroyer USS Sampson (during Operations Desert Shield and Desert Storm), Aegis guided missile cruiser USS Cowpens (during combat operations in Persian Gulf), Flag Officer commdg Naval Forces, Korea 1999–2001; has served in Directorate for Operations, Jt Chiefs of Staff, Dir for Strategy and Plans, Pacific Command 2001–03, Vice-Dir for Strategic Plans and Policy, Jt Chiefs of Staff 2003–06; Mil. Rep. to NATO, Brussels 2006–.
Address: NATO HQ, blvd Léopold III, 1110 Brussels, Belgium (office).
Telephone: (2) 707-41-11 (office). *Fax:* (2) 707-45-79 (office). *E-mail:* natodoc@hq.nato.int (office). *Website:* www.nato.int (office).

SULTANOV, Otkir S.; Uzbekistan politician; b. 14 July 1939; m.; one d. *Education:* Tomsk State Polytech. Inst. *Career:* electrician, Tomsk plant of cutting metals 1963; master, Head of Lab., Head of Production Automatization, Deputy Chief Engineer, Deputy Dir-Gen. Tashkent Aviation Production Union 1964–85; Head Scientific Production Unit, Vostok 1985–91; Chair. State Cttee for Foreign Trade and Int. Relations 1991–92; Minister of External Econ. Relations, Deputy Prime Minister 1992–95; Prime Minister of Uzbekistan 1995–2003; fmr Deputy Prime Minister in charge of Industry; People's Deputy of Uzbekistan; awarded Mekhnat Shukhradi; Merited Engineer Repub. of Uzbekistan.
Address: c/o Office of the Cabinet of Ministers, Mustaqillik maydoni 5, 100078 Tashkent, Uzbekistan (office).

SUMAIDA'IE, Samir Shakir Mahmood, BSc; Iraqi business executive and diplomatist; *Ambassador to USA;* b. 1944, Baghdad; m.; five c. *Education:* Univ. of Durham, UK. *Career:* left Iraq after Saddam Hussein seized power 1973; Middle East Man., Nixdorf Computers, Paderborn, Germany 1973–74; Middle East Man., Logica Ltd, London 1974–78; Man. Dir Tenda Ltd, London 1978–82; Man. Dir Turath Ltd, London 1982–90; Man. Dir Samir Design Ltd, London 1991–96; Man. Dir China Business Int., Beijing 1996–2003; returned to Baghdad and was apptd mem. Iraq Governing Council July 2003; Minister of the Interior April–Aug. 2004; Perm. Rep. to UN, New York 2004–06, Amb. to USA 2006–; participant, Beirut and Vienna Opposition Confs 1991, NY Iraqi Opposition Conf. 1992; Co-founder, manifesto, Democratic Party of Iraq 1993; mem. Governing Council of Iraq 2003, fmr Chair. Media Cttee, Cttee on Provs, fmr Deputy Chair. Foreign Affairs Cttee, fmr mem. Security, Finance and Public Service Cttees. *Publication:* The Night of the Long Lament: A Day in the Life of an Iraqi Dissident, Ahmed Al-Habboubi (trans).
Address: Embassy of Iraq, 1801 P Street, Washington, DC 20036, USA (office). *Telephone:* (202) 483-7500 (office). *Fax:* (202) 462-5066 (office). *E-mail:* admin@iraqiembassy.us (office). *Website:* www.iraqiembassy.us (office).

SUMMERS, Lawrence H., PhD; American economist, academic, fmr government official and fmr university administrator; *Charles W. Eliot University Professor, Department of Economics, Harvard University;* b. 30 Nov. 1954, New Haven, Conn.; one s. two d. *Education:* Mass. Inst. of Tech and Harvard Univ. *Career:* domestic policy economist, US Council of Econ. Advisers 1982–83; Prof. of Econs Harvard Univ. 1983–93, 2002, Nathaniel Ropes Prof. of Political Economy 1987, Pres. Harvard Univ. 2002–06, Charles W. Eliot Univ. Prof. 2006–; Chief Economist and Vice-Pres. of Devt Econs IBRD 1991–93; Econ. Adviser to Pres. Bill Clinton; Treasury Under-Sec. for Int. Affairs 1993–95; Deputy Treasury Sec. 1995–99; Sec. of Treasury 1999–2001; Arthur Okun Distinguished Fellow in Econs, Globalization and Governance, Brookings Inst. 2001–02; Pres. Harvard Univ. 2002–06; Fellow, American Acad. of Arts and Sciences; mem. Nat. Acad. of Sciences 2002–; Hon. DJur (Harvard) 2007; Alan T. Waterman Award, Nat. Science Foundation 1987, John Bates Clark Medal 1993, Alexander Hamilton Medal 2001. *Publications:* Understanding Unemployment, Reform in Eastern Europe (co-author), more than 100 articles.
Address: Department of Economics, Harvard University, Littauer Center, 1875 Cambridge Street, Cambridge, MA 02138, USA (office). *Telephone:* (617) 495-1502 (office). *Fax:* (617) 495-8550 (office). *E-mail:* lawrence_summers@harvard.edu (office). *Website:* www.economics .harvard.edu (office).

SUN, Heping; Chinese diplomatist; *Ambassador to Uganda;* b. June 1951, Shangdong Prov.; m., one s. *Education:* Foreign Studies Univ., Beijing. *Career:* Third Sec. Asian Dept, Ministry of Foreign Affairs 1984–88, Second, later First Sec., later Deputy Dir Personnel Dept 1992–96, Counsellor of Gen. Office 2000–01, apptd Deputy Dir-Gen. of Gen. Office 2001; overseas posts include Desk Officer, Attaché and Third Sec., Embassy in Sudan 1978–84, Third, later Second Sec., Embassy in Philippines 1988–1992, Counsellor 1996–2000; Amb. to Nepal 2003–07, to Uganda 2007–.
Address: Embassy of the People's Republic of China, 37 Malcolm X Ave, Kololo, POB 4106, Kampala, Uganda (office). *Telephone:* (41) 4259881 (office). *Fax:* (41) 4235087 (office). *E-mail:* chinaemb_ug@mfa.gov.cn (office). *Website:* ug.china-embassy.org (office).

SUN, Jiazheng; Chinese politician; *Vice-Chairman, 11th CPPCC National Committee;* b. March 1944, Siyang, Jiangsu Prov. *Education:* Nanjing Univ., May 7th Cadre School, Jilin Prov. *Career:* joined CCP 1966; sent to do manual labour, Liuhe Co., Jilin Prov.; fmr Deputy Head, Chinese People's Armed Police Force, Fanji Commune; Deputy Head, Work Group, CCP Revolutionary Cttee, Liuhe Co. 1971; Sec. Liuhe Co. Cttee CCP Communist Youth League of China 1971; Sec. CCP Party Cttee, Ma'an Commune, Liuhe Co. 1971, mem. Standing Cttee CCP Liuhe Co. Cttee 1975; Vice-Chair. CCP Revolutionary Cttee, Liuhe Co. 1975; Sec. Jiangsu Prov. Cttee CCP Communist Youth League of China 1978; mem. Standing Cttee CCP Jiangsu Prov. Cttee 1983–89, Sec.-Gen. Jiangsu Prov. Cttee 1983–89, Head, Publicity Dept 1988; Sec. CCP Xuzhou City Cttee, Jiangsu Prov. 1984–86; Minister of Radio, Film and TV 1984–88; Minister of Culture 1998–2007; Pres. China Fed. of Literary and Art Circles in 2006–; Alt. mem. 12th CCP Cen. Cttee 1982–87, 13th CCP Cen. Cttee 1987–92, 14th CCP Cen. Cttee 1992–97, mem. 15th CCP Cen. Cttee 1997–2002, 16th CCP Cen. Cttee 2002–; Vice-Chair. 11th Nat. Cttee of the Chinese People's Political Consultative Conf. (CPPCC) at fourth plenary meeting of First Session of 11th CPPCC Nat. Cttee, Beijing 2008; Hon. Chair. Bd of Dirs Beijing Film Coll.
Address: China Federation of Literary and Art Circles, On Court North, Chaoyang District, Beijing 100029, People's Republic of China. *Telephone:* (10) 64025528. *E-mail:* webmaster@cflac.org.cn. *Website:* www.cflac.org .cn/english.htm.

SUN, Joun-yung; South Korean diplomatist and civil servant; b. 16 June 1939; m.; two c. *Education:* Seoul Nat. Univ. Coll. of Law, The American Univ. School of Int. Service, Washington, DC. *Career:* with Ministry of Foreign Affairs, Dir-Gen. Int. Econ. Affairs Bureau 1987–88, Int. Trade Bureau 1988–90, Deputy Foreign Minister for Econ. Affairs 1993–96; Vice-Minister, Ministry of Foreign Affairs and Trade 1997–2000; Counsellor for Political Affairs, Embassy in London, UK 1978; Minister, Embassy in Brasilia, Brazil 1981, for Econ. Affairs in Washington, DC 1986; apptd Amb. to Czechoslovakia 1990; Minister at Perm. Mission to UN, Geneva 1984, Amb. and Perm. Rep. 1996–98 and to other int. orgs; Perm. Rep. to UN, New York 2000–04; Amb.-at-Large for Trade Negotiations 1993, Chief Negotiator on Repub. of Korea–EC Framework Agreement for Trade and Co-operation 1994–95; Govt Co-ordinator for Accession to OECD; Co-Chair. Korea's Econ. Jt Cttees with China, Canada, Viet Nam, UK, Germany, Australia and Asscn of SE Asian Nations (ASEAN) 1993–95; Chair. World Trade Org. Council for Trade Services 1997–98, Int. Textile and Clothing Bureau and also in Geneva Co-ordinator Western Group, Conf. on Disarmament 1997 and Head of Del. at Multi-Fiber Arrangement negotiations 1985–86; Order of Civil Service Merit (Red Stripes) Civil Service Merit Medal of Honour.
Address: c/o Ministry of Foreign Affairs and Trade, 77, 1-ga, Sejong-no, Jongno-gu, Seoul, Republic of Korea (office).

SUN, Weiyan; Chinese economist; *President, University of International Business and Economics;* b. 1937, Cixi, Zhejiang Prov. *Education:* Beijing Foreign Trade Inst. *Career:* Pres. Univ. of Int. Business and Econs 1984–. *Publications:* A Handbook of International Commerce and Trade (Chief Ed.), Multi-National Management Encyclopaedia for Chinese Enterprises (Chief Ed.).
Address: University of International Business and Economics, Huixin Dong Jie, He Ping Jie N., Beijing 100029, People's Republic of China (office). *Telephone:* (10) 64965522 (office). *Fax:* (10) 64968036 (office). *E-mail:* uibe@chinaonline.com.cn.net (office).

SUN, Yuxi; Chinese diplomatist; *Ambassador to Italy;* b. 1951, Heilongjiang Prov.; m.; one d. *Education:* Beijing Foreign Studies Univ., London School of Econs, UK. *Career:* Political Officer, Embassy in France 1979–81; various positions in Ministry of Foreign Affairs 1981–88, including Desk Officer, Third Sec., Deputy Dir, First Sec., Dept of Asian Affairs; Chief of Political Section, Embassy in Pakistan 1988–91; Asst Rep., Rep. Office of People's Repub. of China, Cambodian Nat. Supreme Cttee 1991–93;

Political Counsellor, Embassy in Cambodia 1991–93; Counsellor and Dir Dept of Asian Affairs 1993–95; Minister Counsellor, Embassy in Repub. of Korea 1995–98; Spokesman and Deputy Dir-Gen., Information Dept, Ministry of Foreign Affairs 1998–2002; Amb. to Afghanistan 2002–04, to India 2004–07, to Italy 2008–, also accred to San Marino; mem. working staff, UN Gen. Ass. 1992, 1999, APEC 1994, ASEAN Regional Forum (ARF) 1994, Asia Europe Meeting (ASEM) 1996, Shanghai Cooperation Org. (SCO) Prime Minister's Meeting 2001. *Publications include:* two books in Chinese on Afghanistan and Indian Affairs; articles on world affairs to magazines and newspapers.
Address: Embassy of the People's Republic of China, Via Bruxelles 56, 00198 Rome, Italy (office). *Telephone:* (06) 8413458 (office). *Fax:* (06) 85352891 (office). *E-mail:* chinaemb_it@mfa.gov.cn (office). *Website:* it .china-embassy.org (office).

SUN, Zhenyu; Chinese economist and diplomatist; *Permanent Representative, World Trade Organization;* b. 1946, Fengrun, Hebei Prov. *Education:* Beijing Foreign Languages Inst. *Career:* joined Ministry of Foreign Trade 1969, served as Deputy Dir, Dir and Deputy Dir-Gen. Regional Policy Dept; fmr Vice-Pres. China Nat. Cereals, Oils and Foodstuffs Import and Export Corpn; Dir-Gen. Dept of American and Oceanic Affairs, Ministry of Foreign Trade and Econ. Cooperation 1990–94, Vice-Minister 1994–2002, Perm. Rep., WTO 2002–; also Deputy Perm. Rep. to UN, Geneva.
Address: Permanent Mission of China to the World Trade Organization, 11, chemin de Surville, 1213 Petit-Lancy, Geneva, Switzerland (office). *Telephone:* (22) 9097615 (office). *Fax:* (22) 9097699 (office). *Website:* www .china-un.ch/eng (office).

SUNDE, Lt-Gen. Harald; Norwegian military officer; *Military Representative, NATO;* b. 9 March 1954, Hurdal; m. Sølvi Sunde; two c. *Education:* graduated from Officer Cand. School for the Cavalry 1974, Mil. Acad. 1979, Army Staff Coll. I 1986, Führungsakademie der Bundeswehr 1989, US Army War Coll. 1999. *Career:* began mil. career as platoon officer, Recce Squadron/Brigade N; promoted to Lt 1976, Captain 1983, Maj. 1987; served as officer with Cavalry School and Training Centre and Army Special Forces, subsequently Deputy CO and CO, Recce Squadron/Brigade N; instructor, Army Staff Coll. 1987; CO, Army Special Operations Commando 1992, Chief of Staff, NORPOL BDE/IFOR 1996, CO, Armoured Brigade South Norway 1996, Inspector of Cavalry/Commdr, Cavalry Regt S 2000, ACOS J5/9, RHQ Allied Forces N, NATO 2002, Commdr Land Forces Norway 2003–05; sr staff posts included Chief, Operations Planning Br., Operations Div., HQ DEFCOMNOR 1999, Head Dept of Operations and Emergency Planning, Ministry of Defence 2005–06; Mil. Rep., NATO, Brussels 2006–; promoted to Lt-Col 1992, Col 1996, Brig.-Gen. 2000, Maj.-Gen. 2003, Lt-Gen. 2006; Nat. Service Medal 1982, NATO Medal 1997, Defence Service Medal 1999, Nat. Medal Int. Operations 2001, Defence Service Medal with Star 2004.
Address: NATO HQ, blvd Léopold III, 1110 Brussels, Belgium (office). *Telephone:* (2) 707-41-11 (office). *Fax:* (2) 707-45-79 (office). *E-mail:* natodoc@hq.nato.int (office). *Website:* www.nato.int (office).

SUNDERLAND, Eric, CBE, MA, LLD, PhD, FIBiol; British anthropologist and fmr university vice-chancellor; b. 18 March 1930, Ammanford, Carmarthenshire, Wales; m. Jean Patricia Watson 1957; two d. *Education:* Univ. of Wales, Univ. Coll., London. *Career:* Prof. of Anthropology, Univ. of Durham 1971–84, Pro-Vice-Chancellor 1979–84; Prin. Univ. Coll. of N Wales, Bangor 1984–95; Vice-Chancellor Univ. of Wales 1989–91, Prof. Emer. 1995–; Sec.-Gen. Int. Union of Anthropological and Ethnological Sciences (IUAES) 1978–98, Pres. 1998–2003; Pres. Royal Anthropological Inst., London 1989–91; Chair. of Dirs Gregynog Press 1991–; Chair. Local Govt Boundary Comm. for Wales 1994–2001, Chair. Wales Cttee; mem. Bd British Council 1996–2001, Chair. 1996; mem. BBC Broadcasting Council for Wales 1995–2000; Chair. Environment Agency Advisory Cttee for Wales 1996–2000; High Sheriff of Gwynedd 1998–99; DL; Pres. Univ. of Wales, Lampeter 1998–2002; Lord-Lt of Gwynedd 1999–2006; Chair. Wetlands for Wales Project 2001–, Comm. on Local Govt Electoral Arrangements in Wales 2001–02; Hon. mem. Gorsedd of Bards, Royal Nat. Eisteddfod of Wales; Hon. Fellow, Univ. of Wales, Lampeter, Univ. of Wales, Bangor; Gold Medal of IUAES, Zagreb XIIth Int. Congress 1988. *Publications:* Elements of Human and Social Geography: Some Anthropological Perspectives 1973, Genetic Variation in Britain (co-ed.) 1973, The Exercise of Intelligence: Biological Pre-conditions for the Operation of Intelligence (co-ed.) 1980, Genetic and Population Studies in Wales (co-ed.) 1986.
Address: Y Bryn, Ffriddoedd Road, Bangor, Gwynedd, LL57 2EH, Wales (home). *Telephone:* (1248) 353265 (home). *Fax:* (1248) 355043 (home).

SUNG, Chul-yang, PhD; South Korean diplomatist and academic; b. 20 Nov. 1939; m.; one s. one d. *Education:* Seoul Nat. Univ., Univ. of Hawaii and Univ. of Kentucky, USA. *Career:* mil. service 1960–62; taught at Eastern Kentucky Univ. and Univ. of Kentucky Fort Knox Center, USA 1970–75, Prof. of Political Science, Lexington 1978; Visiting Prof. at N Western Univ., Pembroke State Univ., Indiana Univ., USA and Seoul Nat. Univ.; taught at Grad. Inst. of Peace Studies (GIP), Kyung Hee Univ., Seoul 1986, Dean of Academic Affairs at GIP 1987–94; Sec.-Gen. Asscn of Korean Political Scientists in N America; Pres. Korean Asscn of Int. Studies; contrib. to journals and leading newspapers in Repub. of Korea; mem. Advisory Cttee, Ministry of Foreign Affairs, Ministry of Nat. Defence, Nat. Unification Bd; fmr. Amb. to USA apptd. 2000. *Publications include:* numerous articles and essays.
Address: c/o Ministry of Foreign Affairs and Trade, 77, 1-ga, Sejong-no, Jongno-gu, Seoul, Republic of Korea (office).

SUNGAR, Murat E., MA; Turkish diplomatist and international organization executive; *First Deputy Secretary-General, Organization of the Black Sea Economic Cooperation;* b. 1942, Ankara; m.; one d. *Education:* School of Political Sciences, Ankara Univ., Univ. of Cincinnati, USA. *Career:* mil. service 1966–68; joined Ministry of Foreign Affairs (MFA) 1970, Third and Second Sec., NATO Dept 1970–72, Second and First Sec., Turkish Del. to NATO, Brussels 1972–75, First Sec., Embassy in Islamabad 1975–77, Head of Section, NATO Dept, MFA 1977–79, Counsellor, Embassy in Washington, DC 1979–83, Advisor to Under-Sec. of MFA 1983–85, Consul Gen. of Turkey, New York 1985–89, Spokesman of MFA 1989–91, Amb. to India 1991–95, Sr Advisor to Prime Ministry 1995–97, Deputy Under-Sec. of MFA 1997–98, Amb. to UN Office, Geneva 1998–2002, Sec.-Gen. EU Affairs 2002–06; First Deputy Sec.-Gen. Org. of the Black Sea Econ. Co-operation (BSEC) PERMIS 2006–.
Address: Organization of the Black Sea Economic Co-operation, Sakıp Sabancı Cad., Müşir Fuad Paşa Yalısı, Eski Tersane, 34460 İstinye-İstanbul, Turkey (office). *Telephone:* (212) 229-63-30 (office). *Fax:* (212) 229-63-36 (office). *E-mail:* info@bsec-organization.org (office). *Website:* www.bsec-organization.org (office).

SUPAMONGKOL, Kantathee, MA, PhD; Thai government official; b. 3 April 1952; m. *Education:* Univ. of Calif. at LA, Univ. of Southern Calif., American Univ., USA. *Career:* fmr Prof. of Law and Int. Relations; joined Ministry of Foreign Affairs 1984; with Perm. Mission to UN, New York 1988–92; Adviser on Foreign Affairs to Speaker of House of Reps 1992; Dir. Policy and Planning Div., Ministry of Foreign Affairs 1993–94; mem. Parl. 1995, 2001; Adviser on Foreign Affairs to Prime Minister 1996; Adviser to Minister of Industry; mem. Cttee on Foreign Affairs, Cttee on Tourism, House of Reps; Trade Rep. of Thailand 2001–05; Special Envoy of the Prime Minister; Adviser on Foreign Affairs to Minister of Foreign Affairs; Minister of Foreign Affairs 2005–06; Kt Grand Cordon (Special Class) of the Most Noble Order of the Crown of Thailand.
Address: c/o Ministry of Foreign Affairs, Thanon Sri Ayudhya, Bangkok 10400, Thailand.

SURÁNYI, György, PhD, DEcon; Hungarian economist; *Chairman of the Board, Central European International Bank Limited;* b. 3 Jan. 1954, Budapest; m.; two c. *Education:* Univ. of Econs, Budapest, Hungarian Acad. of Sciences. *Career:* Research Fellow, Head of Dept, Financial Research Inst., Budapest 1977–86; consultant, World Bank, Washington, DC 1986–87; Counsellor to Deputy Prime Minister, Council of Ministers 1988–89; Sec. of State, Nat. Planning Office 1989–90; Pres. Nat. Bank of Hungary 1990–91; Man. Dir Cen. European Int. Bank Ltd 1992–95, Chair. Bd 2001–; Pres. Nat. Bank of Hungary 1995–2001; Head Multinational Banking-IntesBci Group, Italy 2001–; Pres. Supervisory Bd Privredna Banka, Zagreb 2001–; mem. Supervisory Bd VUB, Bratislava 2001–; Prof., Univ. of Econs, Budapest; mem. Bd Inst. for East-West Studies; Global Leader for Tomorrow, World Econ. Forum 1993, Leadership in Econ. Transition, EastWest Inst. New York 2001. *Publications:* author of several articles and books on monetary and financial issues.
Address: Central European International Bank Ltd, Medve u. 4-14, 1027 Budapest, Hungary (office). *Telephone:* (1) 489-6222 (office). *Fax:* (1) 489-6226 (office). *E-mail:* gsuranyi@cib.hu (office). *Website:* www.cib.hu (office).

SURDO BONETTI, Vittorio Claudio; Italian diplomatist; *Ambassador to Russia;* b. 1943, Libya; m. Roya Mirtolouei Surdo. *Career:* began Foreign Service career in Cairo 1973–76, other overseas postings include Embassy in Paris 1976–78, Embassy in Tehran 1981–85, Embassy in Bonn 1985–89; Amb. to Ukraine 1992–96; Amb. to Turkey 1999–2004; Amb. to Russia (also accred to Turkmenistan) 2006–.
Address: Embassy of Italy, 121002 Moscow, Denezhnyi per. 5, Russia. *Telephone:* (495) 796-96-91 (office). *Fax:* (495) 253-92-89 (office). *E-mail:* embitaly.mosca@esteri.it (office). *Website:* www.ambmosca.esteri.it (office).

SURIE, Nalin, MA; Indian diplomatist; b. 24 July 1951. *Education:* Univ. of Delhi. *Career:* Dir Dept of Econ. Affairs, Ministry of Finance 1989–91; Jt Sec. East Europe, Ministry of External Affairs 1991–94, Additional Sec. East Asia 2000–03, Sec. (West) Ministry of External Affairs HQ 2006–; Deputy Perm. Rep. to UN 1994–97; Amb. to Poland 1997–2004, to People's Repub. of China 2003–06.
Address: Ministry of External Affairs, South Block, Room 144c, New Delhi 110 011, India (office). *Telephone:* (11) 23011849 (office). *Fax:* (11) 23013387 (office). *E-mail:* asppr@mea.gov.in (office). *Website:* meaindia .nic.in (office).

SURUMA, Ezra, PhD, MA, BSc; Ugandan economist; *Minister of Finance, Planning and Economic Development;* b. 11 Nov. 1945; m. Specioza Suruma; four s. *Education:* Fordham Univ., Univ. of Conn. *Career:* previous positions include Dir of Econ. Affairs, Movement Secr., Chair. and Man. Dir, Uganda Commercial Bank, Deputy Gov. and Dir of Research, Bank of Uganda; Minister of Finance, Planning and Econ. Devt 2005–.
Address: Ministry of Finance, Planning and Economic Development, Appollo Kaggwa Road, Plot 2/4, POB 8147, Kampala, Uganda (office). *Telephone:* (41) 2234700 (office). *Fax:* (41) 2230163 (office). *E-mail:* webmaster@finance.go.ug (office). *Website:* www.finance.go.ug (office).

SUSSANGKARN, Chalongphob, PhD; Thai government official and economist; b. 16 April 1950. *Education:* Univ. of Cambridge, UK. *Career:* Lecturer in Econs, Univ. of Calif., Berkeley, USA 1977–79; Economist, World Bank, USA 1979–85; Research Fellow, Macroeconomic Policy Program, Thailand Devt Research Inst. 1985–86, Dir Human Resources and Social Devt Program 1987–95, Pres. 1996–2007; Minister of Finance 2007–08; mem. Bd Econ. Soc. of Thailand, Exec. Cttee Global Devt Network –2005, Exec. Cttee Nat. Centre for Genetic Eng and Biotechnology; Law Devt Cttee, Office of the Council of State; mem. Advisory Bd Asia-Pacific Devt Journal, ASEAN Econ. Bulletin, Asian Devt Review, Asian Econ. Policy Review; Regional Co-ordinator, East Asian Devt Network 2004–; Nat. Outstanding Researcher Award, Nat. Research Council of Thailand 2004. *Publications:* numerous research papers and contribs to professional publs.
Address: c/o Ministry of Finance, Thanon Rama VI, Samsennai, Phaya Thai, Bangkok, 10400, Thailand (office).

ŠUTANOVAC, Dragan; Serbian politician; *Minister of Defence;* b. 1968, Belgrade; m.; two c. *Education:* Faculty of Mechanical Eng, Univ. of Belgrade, Marshall Centre for Security Studies, Germany. *Career:* MEP April–May 2000; Deputy, Belgrade City Ass. 2000–; Special Adviser, Ministry of Internal Affairs 2000–01; mem. Parl. 2000–, Pres. Parl. Cttee for Defence and Security 2002–03; Deputy Minister of the Interior 2001–06; Minister of Defence 2007–; mem. Demokratska Stranka, DS (Democratic Party).
Address: Ministry of Defence, 11000 Belgrade, Birčaninova 5, Serbia (office). *Telephone:* (11) 3006323 (office). *Fax:* (11) 3000328 (office). *E-mail:* minstar.odbrane@mod.gov.yu (office). *Website:* www.mod.gov.yu (office).

SUTOYO, Susanto; Indonesian diplomatist; *Ambassador to Italy;* b. 4 July 1947, Kendal; m. Endang H. Sutoyo; three c. *Education:* Diponegoro Univ. *Career:* joined Dept of Foreign Affairs 1974, Jr Staff, Directorate of Information and Cultural Relations 1974–75, Head, Section of Social and Cultural Relations, Asia-Pacific, Directorate of Social and Cultural Relations 1975–79, Head, Section of GATT Trade Co-operation, Directorate of Multilateral Econ. Co-operation 1983–86, Head, Sub-Directorate of Trade, Finance and Devt Co-operation, Directorate of Multilateral Econ. Co-operation 1991–93, Dir ASEAN Econ. Co-operation 1995–99, fmr Dir-Gen. for Multilateral Econ., Finance and Devt Affairs; overseas postings include Attaché, later Third Sec., Embassy in Addis Ababa 1979–82, Second Sec., later First Sec. and Counsellor, Perm. Mission to UN and Other Int. Orgs, Geneva 1986–89, Deputy Perm. Rep. 1999; Counsellor, later Minister-Counsellor, Perm. Mission to UN, New York (Chair. Comm. on Social Devt 1995) 1993–95, Amb. to Italy (also accred. to Malta and Cyprus) 2005–; also Perm. Rep. to FAO, IFAD, WFP.
Address: Embassy of Indonesia, Via Campania 53–55, 00187 Rome, Italy (office). *Telephone:* (06) 4200911 (office). *Fax:* (06) 4880280 (office). *E-mail:* indorom@indonesianembassy.it (office); indorom@uni.net (office). *Website:* www.indonesianembassy.it (office).

SUTRESNA, Nana S., MA; Indonesian diplomatist; *Special Envoy of the President of Indonesia on Co-operation between Asian-African Countries and among members of the Non-Aligned Movement;* b. 21 Oct. 1933, Ciamis, Jawa Barat; m. 1973; two s. one d. *Education:* Acad. for Foreign Affairs, Jakarta, Univ. of Wales, Aberystwyth, UK. *Career:* foreign news for the Indonesian News Agency, ANTARA 1955–57; joined Dept of Foreign Affairs 1957, Head of Public Relations and Spokesman 1972–76, Dir for European Affairs 1979–81, Dir-Gen. for Political Affairs 1984–88, served at Embassy in Washington, DC and in Mexico City, as Minister Counsellor then Minister in Vienna 1976–79, Head of Indonesian Del. to Disarmament Conf., Geneva 1981–83, Deputy Perm. Rep. to UN, Geneva 1981–84, Perm. Rep. to UN (also accred to Bahamas, Jamaica and Nicaragua) 1988–92, Amb.-at-Large 1992–99, Amb. to UK (also accred to Ireland) 1999–2002, Special Envoy of Pres. of Indonesia to N and S Korea 2002–06, Special Envoy of Pres. on Co-operation between Asian-African Countries and among mems of the Non-Aligned Movt 2006–.
Address: Ministry of Foreign Affairs, Jalan Taman Pejambon 6, 10th Floor, Jakarta Pusat 10110, Indonesia (office). *Telephone:* (21) 3813453 (office). *Fax:* (21) 3857316 (office). *E-mail:* infomed@deplu.go.id (office). *Website:* www.deplu.go.id (office).

SVERRISDÓTTIR, Valgerur; Icelandic politician; b. 23 March 1950; m. Arvid Kro; three d. *Education:* Reykjavik Women's School. *Career:* Sec., Agricultural Research Labs 1967–68; Sec. to Man. Dir KEA Cooperative 1969–70; Sec., Akureyri Regional Hosp. 1970–71; teacher, Grenivík School, 1972–82; has worked as farmer 1974–; Deputy Mem. Althingi (Parl.) 1984–87, mem. Parl. for NE Iceland constituency 1987–, Second Deputy Speaker 1988–89, 1990–91, Deputy Speaker 1992–95; Minister of Industry and Commerce 1999–2005, for Nordic Cooperation 2004–05, of Foreign Affairs 2006–07; mem. Progressive Party NE Iceland Constituency Cttee 1983–87, Chair. 1985-86, mem. Cen. Cttee 1983–, Deputy Sec. 1990–92, Parl. Group Leader 1995–99; mem. Nordic Council 1987–90, 1995–99, Chair. Parl. Group 1995–99; mem. Bd of Dirs KEA Cooperative 1981–92, SÍS (Fed. of Iceland Cooperative Socs) 1985–92, Akureyri Ship Repair Yard 1989–91, Bifröst Cooperative Coll. 1990–96 (Chair. 1995–96), Nordic Cultural Fund 1991–93, 1995–99 (Chair. 1995).
Address: Framsóknarflokkurinn (Progressive Party), Hverfisgata 33, POB 453, 121 Reykjavík, Iceland (office). *Telephone:* 5404300 (office). *Fax:* 5404301 (office). *E-mail:* framsokn@framsokn.is (office). *Website:* www .framsokn.is (office).

SVILANOVIĆ, Goran, LLM; Serbian politician and lawyer; *Chairman of Working Table I, Stability Pact for South Eastern Europe;* b. 22 Oct. 1963, Gnjilane, Kosovo; m.; two c. *Education:* Belgrade Univ., Inst. of Law, Strasbourg, Saarbrücken Univ., European Univ. of Peace, Austria. *Career:* worked as Asst Researcher, Belgrade Univ. 1986–98, discharged following protest against controversial univ. law 1998; collaborator with Yugoslavian Forum on Human Rights 1989–93; head of telephone service for rescue of victims of nat., ethnic, religious and other discrimination, Centre for Anti-war Action 1993–97; Chair. Council on Human Rights 1996–98; Official Rep. of Civic Alliance of Serbia (Građanski savez Srbije—GSS) 1997, Vice-Pres. 1998, Pres. 1999, left party 2004; Fed. Minister of Foreign Affairs 2000–04; mem. Parl. (nominated for Democratic Party) 2004–; Chair. Working Table I, Stability Pact for South Eastern Europe 2004–; mem. Int. Comm. on the Balkans. *Publications:* Civil and Civil Process Law; books and numerous articles on the situation of refugees and problems of citizenship.
Address: Working Table I, Stability Pact for South Eastern Europe, 50 Rue Wiertz, 1050 Brussels, Belgium (office). *Telephone:* (2) 401-87-00 (office). *Fax:* (2) 401-87-12 (office). *E-mail:* scsp@stabilitypact.org (office). *Website:* www.stabilitypact.org (office).

SWE, Kyaw Tint, BA; Myanma diplomatist and civil servant; *Permanent Representative, United Nations;* b. 19 March 1945; m.; two c. *Education:* Univ. of Yangon, Inst. of Social Studies, The Hague, Netherlands. *Career:* with Ministry of Foreign Affairs, positions including Dir Econ. Div. 1990–93, Deputy Dir-Gen. Asscn SE Asian Nations (ASEAN) Affairs Dept 1997–98, Dir-Gen. Int. Orgs. and Econ. Dept 1998–2001; Sec. Nat. Comm. for Environmental Affairs 1990–93, 1997–98; Del. of Myanmar to UN Gen. Ass.; rep. to various int. meetings including UN Conf. on Environment and Devt (UNCED), World Conf. on Human Rights, World Conf. on Women; served with Embassies in Israel, Malaysia and Germany; Minister-Counsellor and Deputy Perm. Rep. to Econ. and Social Comm. for Asia and Pacific (ESCAP), Bangkok, Thailand 1993–94; Deputy Chief of Mission in Tokyo 1994–97; Perm. Rep. to UN, New York 2001–.
Address: Permanent Representative of Myanmar to the UN, 10 East 77th Street, New York, NY 10021, USA (office). *Telephone:* (212) 535-1310 (office). *Fax:* (212) 737-2421 (office). *E-mail:* myanmar@eu.int (office).

SWING, William Lacy, BA, BD; American diplomatist; *Director-General, International Organization for Migration;* b. 11 Sept. 1934, Lexington, N Carolina; m. Yuen Cheong 1993; one s. one d. from previous marriage. *Education:* Catawba Coll., Yale Univ., Tübingen Univ., Harvard Univ. *Career:* Vice-Consul, Port Elizabeth, S. Africa 1963–66; int. economist, Bureau of Econ. Affairs, Dept of State 1966–68; Consul, Hamburg 1968–72; Desk Officer for FRG, Dept of State 1972–74; Deputy Chief of

Mission, US Embassy, Bangui, Cen. African Repub. 1974–76; Sr Fellow, Center for Int. Affairs, Harvard Univ. 1976–77; Deputy Dir, Office of Cen. African Affairs, Dept of State 1977–79; Amb. to People's Repub. of Congo 1979–81, to Liberia 1981–85, to S Africa 1989–93, to Nigeria 1992–93, to Haiti 1993–98, to Democratic Repub. of Congo 1998–2001; Special Rep. of UN Sec.-Gen. for Western Sahara 2001–03; Democratic Repub. of Congo 2003–08; Dir-Gen. Int. Org. for Migration 2008–; Dir Office of Foreign Service Assignments and Career Devt 1985–87; Deputy Asst Sec. for Personnel 1987–89; Fellow, Harvard Univ.; Hon. LLD (Catawba Coll.) 1980; Hon. DHumLitt (Hofstra) 1994; Presidential Distinguished Service Award 1985; Distinguished Honor Award 1994, Award for Valor 1995, Presidential Meritorious Service Award 1987, 1990, 1994, 1998, Presidential Certificate of Commendation 1998. *Publications:* Education for Decision 1963, U.S. Policy Towards South Africa: Dilemmas and Priorities 1977, Liberia: The Road to Recovery 1982, Haiti: In Physical Contact with History 1994; book chapter in Challenges of Peace Implementation 2004.
Address: International Organization for Migration, 17 route des Morillons, CP 71, 1211 Geneva 19, Switzerland (office). *Telephone:* 227179111 (office). *Fax:* 227986150 (office). *E-mail:* info@iom.int (office). *Website:* www.iom .int (office).

SYCHOV, Alyaksandr; Belarusian diplomatist; *Ambassador to Austria;* b. 19 Sept. 1951, Gomel, Belarus; m. Natalia Vedmedenko 1976; one s. one d. *Education:* Moscow State Inst. of Int. Relations. *Career:* Third then Second Sec., Ministry of Foreign Affairs 1979–84; Del. Perm. Mission of the Repub. of Belarus to UN office and other int. orgs., Geneva 1984–90; Head Dept of Foreign Econ. Relations, Ministry of Foreign Affairs 1991–92, Deputy Minister for Foreign Affairs 1992–94; Perm. Rep. to UN, New York 1994–2000; Deputy Minister of Foreign Affairs 2000–05; Amb. to Austria 2005–, also Perm. Rep. to OSCE, JCG, OSCC and other int. orgs in Vienna; Chair. First Cttee of the 51st session of the UN Gen. Ass., 19th Special Session 1996–97; Vice-Pres. ECOSOC 1998–99. *Publications:* numerous articles on Belarus foreign policy and int. affairs.
Address: Embassy of Belarus, Hüttelbergstr. 6, 1140 Vienna, Austria (office). *Telephone:* (1) 419-96-30-11 (office). *Fax:* (1) 416-96-30-30 (office). *E-mail:* mail@byembassy.at (office). *Website:* www.byembassy.at (office).

SYDYKOVA, Zamira Beksultanovna; Kyrgyzstani journalist and diplomatist; *Ambassador to USA. Education:* Moscow State Univ. *Career:* est. ind. Respublica newspaper 1992, Ed.-in-Chief 1992–, accused of slander against regime of Askar Akayev 1995, deprived of right to practise journalism; mem. Political Council of Kyrgyzstan; Amb. to USA 2005–; Award for Courage in Journalism, Int. Women's Mass Media Group 2000.
Address: Embassy of Kyrgyzstan, 2360 Massachusetts Avenue, NW, Washington, DC 20008, USA (office). *Telephone:* (202) 449-9822 (office). *Fax:* (202) 386-7550 (office). *E-mail:* consul@kgembassy.org (office). *Website:* www.kgembassy.org (office).

SYKES, Roger Michael Spencer; British diplomatist; *High Commissioner to Fiji;* b. 22 Oct. 1948; m. Annie Sykes; three s. *Career:* joined FCO 1968–71, postings to Caracas 1971–72, Freetown 1972–75, Visa Officer, Karachi 1976–78, Admin Attaché, later Cultural Attaché, Valletta 1978–81; with Press Office, FCO 1981–82; Attaché, Embassy in Lagos 1982–86; Deputy High Commr, Vila 1986–90; S Asian Dept, FCO 1990–93; Political and Econ. Sec., later Commercial Sec., Embassy in Amman 1993–97; Head of British Trade Office, Al Khobar 1997–2001; Deputy Head of Mission, Embassy in Karachi 2002–05; High Commr to Fiji 2006–.
Address: British High Commission, Victoria House, 47 Gladstone Road, PO Box 1355, Suva, Fiji (office). *Telephone:* 3229100 (office). *Fax:* 3229132 (office). *E-mail:* publicdiplomacysuva@fco.gov.uk (office). *Website:* www .britishhighcommission.gov.uk/fiji (office).

SYLLA, Jacques Hugues, LLB; Malagasy politician and lawyer; *President, National Assembly;* b. 1946, Holy Marie, Toamasina Prov.; m. Yvette Rakoto; four c. *Career:* practised as lawyer; Co-founder Toamasina Br. of Nat. Cttee for Observation of the Elections (CNOE), First Foreign Minister of fmr Pres. Albert Zafy 1992–93; Minister of Foreign Affairs 1993–96; Prime Minister of Madagascar 2002–07; Pres. Nat. Ass. 2007–.
E-mail: poste@assemblee-nationale.mg (office). *Website:* www.assemblee -nationale.mg (office).

SYLVESTER, Lawrence; Belizean diplomatist; *High Commissioner to UK;* m. Pauline Williams-Sylvester. *Career:* CEO Ministry of Foreign Affairs and Tourism 2000–06, Amb. to CARICOM, Georgetown, Guyana 2002–06, High Commr to UK (also accred as Amb. and Perm. Rep. to EU) 2006–.
Address: Belize High Commission, Third Floor, 45 Crawford Place, London, W1H 4LP, England (office). *Telephone:* (20) 7723-3603 (office). *Fax:* (20) 7723-9637 (office). *E-mail:* bzhc-lon@btconnect.com (office). *Website:* www.belizehighcommission.com (office).

SYMINGTON, W. Stuart, BA, JD; American lawyer and diplomatist; *Ambassador to Djibouti;* b. Mo. *Education:* Brown Univ., Columbia Univ. *Career:* worked as clerk to Chief Judge of Eastern Dist of Missouri, then litigated and practised corp. law in New York, London, Paris and St Joseph, Mo.; joined Foreign Service 1986, began his diplomatic career by tracking protests and politics in Honduras, moved to Spain 1989, worked on econ. issues before serving as Amb.'s aide during Operation Desert Shield and Desert Storm, then posting to Mexico; worked for Under-Sec. for Political Affairs on Latin American and African Issues, Dept of State; served on staff of Congressman Ike Skelton studying US mil. jt operations and educ.; travelled to Sudan and N Korea on teams negotiating to free American captives, later acted as aide to US Perm. Rep. to UN; fmr Political Officer, Embassy in Quito; Deputy Chief of Mission, Embassy in Niamey 2001–03; Deputy Dir West African Affairs, Africa Bureau, Dept of State 2003–04; worked for Amb. Negroponte in Iraq on election process and political issues 2004–05; taught at Jt Forces Staff Coll., Nat. Defense Univ., Norfolk, Va 2005–06; Amb. to Djibouti 2006–; Pearson Fellowship.
Address: US Embassy, Villa Plateau du Serpent, boulevard du Maréchal Joffre, BP 185, Djibouti, Djibouti (office). *Telephone:* 353995 (office). *Fax:* 353940 (office). *E-mail:* amembadm@bow.intnet.dj (office). *Website:* djibouti.usembassy.gov (office).

SYMONETTE, Theodore Brent; Bahamian politician; *Deputy Prime Minister and Minister of Foreign Affairs;* b. 2 Dec. 1954, Nassau; m. Robin Mactaggart; one s. two d. *Education:* St Andrew's School, Nassau, Leys School, Cambridge, Brunel Univ., London, UK. *Career:* called to Bahamas Bar 1978; fmr Senator; fmr Minister of Tourism; fmr Attorney-Gen.; Deputy Leader, Free Nat. Movt; Deputy Prime Minister and Minister of Foreign Affairs 2007–; fmr Chair. Hotel Corpn, Airport Authority, Public Accounts Cttee.
Address: Ministry of Foreign Affairs, East Hill Street, PO Box N-3746, Nassau, The Bahamas (office). *Telephone:* 322-7624 (office). *Fax:* 328-8212 (office). *E-mail:* mfabahamas@batelnet.bs (office). *Website:* www .mfabahamas.org (office).

SYQUIA, Enrique, LLD; Philippine lawyer and professor of international law; b. 22 May 1930, Manila; m. Leticia Corpus Syquia 1964; five s. *Education:* Univ. of Santo Tomas, Univ. of Madrid and Hague Acad. of Int. Law. *Career:* Head Syquia Law Offices, Manila 1954–; Prof. of Law 1976–; Publr The Lawyers Review 1987–, The Diplomats Review 1989–91; Dir Philippine Bar Asscn 1971–92, Pres. 1981–84; mem. Exec. Council, Int. Bar Asscn 1974–92, Vice-Pres. 1982–84; Pres. Int. Law Asscn 1978–80, Vice-Chair. 1989–; Pres. Philippines Council for Foreign Relations 1987–94; Vice-Pres. Union Int. des Avocats 1989–; Pres. Int. Inst. of Humanitarian Law 1991–93; Special Adviser Philippine Del. to UN Gen. Ass. 1989–92; mem. and/or officer of numerous nat. and int. law orgs including ABA, American Judicature Soc., American Soc. of Int. Law; mem. Inst. Hispano-Luso-Americano de Derecho Internacional 1980–, Dir 1991–, Pres. 1998–2000; Hon. Consul-Gen. of Kingdom of Jordan in the Philippines 1987–96; del. to numerous law confs at home and abroad since 1953; Patron American Soc. of Int. Law 1989–; various hon. trusteeships etc.; Sovereign Mil. Order of Malta, Order de Isabel la Católica (Spain) 1999; Kt Pontifical Equestrian Order of Gregory the Great 1996, Kt Illustrious Spanish Order of Corpus Christi 1997 and numerous other awards and decorations. *Publications:* The Tokyo Trial 1955, A Manual on International Law 1957, Twenty Papers on World Affairs 1989; about 100 articles on law, especially int. law.
Address: 6th Floor, Cattleya Condominium, 235 Salcedo Street, Legaspi Village, Makati, Manila (office); 127 Cambridge Circle, North Forbes, Makati, Manila, Philippines (home). *Telephone:* (2) 817-1095/1098 (office); (2) 810-7975 (home); (2) 810-7975; (2) 817-1089. *Fax:* (2) 817-1089 (office); (2) 817-1724 (home). *E-mail:* syquia@intlaw.com.ph (office).

SZÉKELY, Árpád; Hungarian diplomatist; *Ambassador to Russian Federation;* b. 1957, Miskolc; m.; three c. *Education:* Moscow State Univ. of Int. Relations. *Career:* joined Ministry of Foreign Affairs 1981, posted to Embassy in Bonn 1984–89; Special Asst to the Prime Minister for Home Policy and Trade 1990–92, Rep. to Hungarian-Bavarian Intergovernmental Council 1990; Amb. to Russian Fed. 2005–, also accred to Armenia 2006–.
Address: Embassy of Hungary, 119590 Moscow, ul. Mosfilmovskaya 62, Russia (office). *Telephone:* (495) 796-93-70 (office). *Fax:* (495) 796-93-80 (office). *E-mail:* mow.missions@kum.hu (office). *Website:* www.mfa.gov .hu/emb/moscow (office).

SZEKERES, Imre, PhD; Hungarian engineer and politician; *Minister of Defence;* b. 9 Sept. 1950, Szolnok; m.; two c. *Education:* Veszprém Univ. *Career:* sec. of communist youth org. at Univ.; Asst Lecturer, Cybernetics Inst., Veszprém Univ. 1974–77; mem. Veszprém City Council 1986, later Deputy Chair. responsible for culture and finances; co-f. Reformkömök movt; Chair. Hungarian Socialist Party (HSP) Org. in Veszprém Co. 1989,

headed electoral list during first parl. elections 1990, Nat. Sec. 1990, Vice-Chair. 1990–2004, Deputy Chair. 2004–, electoral campaign chief 1994; mem. Parl. 1994–, Head, HSP parl. group 1994–98; Chair. Parl. Budget and Finance Cttee 1998-2002; Political State Sec., Cabinet of Prime Minister 2002–04; Minister of Defence 2006–; Pres. Hungarian Triathlon Asscn 2003–.
Address: Ministry of Defence, 1055 Budapest, Balaton u. 7–11, Hungary (office). *Telephone:* (1) 474-1114 (office). *Fax:* (1) 474-1285 (office). *E-mail:* media@hm.gov.hu (office). *Website:* www.hm.gov.hu (office).

SZENES, Lt-Gen. Zoltán, MSc, PhD, CSc; Hungarian army officer (retd); *Associate Professor, Zrínyi Miklós National Defence University;* b. 23 July 1951, Köcsk; m. Ibolya Szenes; one d. *Education:* Mil. Tech. Acad., Budapest, War Coll. of Logistics and Transportation, Leningrad (now St Petersburg), Russia, Hungarian Acad. of Science, Budapest Univ. of Econs, Royal Coll. of Defence Studies, London, UK. *Career:* joined Hungarian People's Army 1969; assigned to 25th Tank Regt, Tata 1973–74; staff officer, 11th Tank Div. 1974–75; Chief of Staff for Logistics, 9th Mechanized Div., Kaposvár 1979–82; Sr Lecturer, Zrínyi Miklós Nat. Defence Univ., Budapest 1985–86, Assoc. Prof. 2005–; Head of Logistics Dept 1986–91; Chief of Supply Services of Defence Staff 1991–92; Fellow, Royal Coll. of Defence Studies, London 1995–96; Head of Educ. and Science Dept, Ministry of Defence 1996–98; Mil. Rep. to NATO and WEU, Brussels, Belgium 1998–99; ACOS Logistics, AFSOUTH HQ, Naples, Italy 1999–2002; Dir of Defence Staff 2002–03, Chief of Defence Staff 2003–05; apptd Maj.-Gen. 2002, Lt-Gen. 2003–05 (retd); Co-Pres. Budapesti Honvéd Sport Club; Cross of the Legion of Honour (Officer Grade) 2004, Commdr's Cross, Order of Merit (Mil. Div.) 2004; Meritorious Service Award, Pro Scientia Gold Medal, Tanárky Sándor Price Award, Hungarian Asscn of Mil. Sciences, Budapest, Hungarian NATO Enlargement Medal, NATO KFOR and SFOR Medals, Officer Service Medal (First Class), Andrássy Gyula Price Award 2001, NATO Service Award for the Period 1998–2002 2004. *Publications:* The Implications of NATO for Civil-Military Relations in Hungary 2001, Future of NATO (in Academic and Applied Research in Military Science journal) 2005, The Effects of Peacekeeping on the HDF (in Peacekeeping Today and Tomorrow) 2006. *Address:* Zrínyi Miklós Nat. Defence Univ., 1101, Budapest, Hungary (office). *Telephone:* (1) 432-9087 (office); (30) 2428914 (mobile) (office). *Fax:* (1) 432-9217 (office). *E-mail:* szenes.zoltan@zmne.hu (office); szenes@hotmail.com (home). *Website:* www.zmne.hu (office).

SZENTIVÁNYI, Gábor; Hungarian economist and diplomatist; *State Secretary and Political Director, Ministry of Foreign Affairs;* b. 9 Oct. 1952, Vaskút; m. Gabriella Gönczi; one s. one d. *Education:* Univ. of Econ. Sciences, Budapest. *Career:* joined Foreign Service 1975, positions in Baghdad 1976–81, Washington, DC 1986–91; mem. staff Protocol Dept, Ministry of Foreign Affairs 1982–85, Spokesman and Dir Gen. for Press and Int. Information Dept 1994–97, Deputy State Sec. 2002–06, State Sec. and Political Dir 2007–; Amb. to UK 1997–2002, to the Netherlands 2004–07; Man. Dir Burson-Marsteller's Budapest office 1991–94; mem.

Hungarian Foreign Affairs Soc., Hungarian Atlantic Council; Freeman, City of London 2000; Hon. GCVO, Officer, Order of Prince Henry the Navigator 1982, Grand Cross of Merit (Chile) 2002, Middle Cross of the Order of Merit (Hungary) 2004, Kt Grand Cross, Order of Oranje-Nassau (Netherlands) 2007.
Address: Ministry of Foreign Affairs, Bem rkp. 47, 1027 Budapest, Hungary (office). *Telephone:* (1) 458-1936 (office). *Fax:* (1) 458-1811 (office). *E-mail:* GSzentivanyi@kum.hu (office).

SZOMBATI, Béla, MA; Hungarian diplomatist; b. 16 July 1955, Tel-Aviv, Israel; m. Zsusza Mihályi 1978; two s. *Education:* Univ. of London, UK, Eötvös Loránd Univ. *Career:* joined Ministry of Foreign Affairs 1980, Dept of Int. Security 1980–82, Dept of Asia 1982; Attaché, later Sec., Embassy in Vietnam 1982–86; US Desk Officer 1986–88; Sec. Embassy in USA 1998–91; Head, Foreign Relations Dept and Adviser to Pres. 1991–94; Amb. to France 1994–99; Deputy Head, State Secr. for Integration 1999–2002; Amb. to UK 2002–06, with Ministry of Foreign Affairs 2006–; Commdr's Cross, Order of Merit (Poland) 2001, Officier, Légion d'honneur 2002.
Address: Ministry of Foreign Affairs, Bem rkp. 47, 1027 Budapest, Hungary (office). *Telephone:* (1) 458-1000 (office). *Fax:* (1) 212-5981 (office). *E-mail:* iroda.konz@kum.hu (office). *Website:* www.mfa.gov.hu (office).

SZURÖS, Mátyás, PhD; Hungarian politician and diplomatist; b. 11 Sept. 1933, Püspökladány. *Education:* Moscow Univ. Inst. of Int. Relations, Budapest Univ. of Econ. Sciences. *Career:* on staff of Foreign Ministry 1959–65; staff mem. HSWP 1965–74, Deputy Leader Foreign Dept HSWP Cen. Cttee 1974–75, Head 1982–83; Amb. to GDR 1975–78, to USSR 1978–82; mem. Cen. Cttee HSWP 1978, Secr. 1983–89; mem. Parl. 1985–, Chair. Foreign Relations Parl. Cttee 1985–89 (mem. 1998–), Pres. of Parl. March–Oct. 1989, Acting Pres. 1989–90, Deputy Speaker 1990–94; Chair. Hungarian Group of IPU 1989–90, 1994–2002, mem. Exec. Cttee IPU 1994–96; Gen. Pres. SDP 2003–05; Chair. Ópusztaszer Historical Commemorative Cttee 1989–98, Bd Trustees Illyés Foundation 1994–99, Trustee 1999–; mem. Council of Hundreds (World Fed. of Hungarians) 1997–; Freeman of Püspökladány 1996, of Beregszász 1997; Bocskai Award 1996. *Publications:* Hazánk és a nagyvilág (Homeland and World) 1985, Hazánk és Európa (Homeland and Europe) 1987, Magyarságról-Külpolitikáról (On Being Hungarian and on Foreign Policy) 1989, Cselekvo politikával a magyarságért-Politikai portré (1988–96) (Active policy for Hungary, portrait of a politician) 1996, Köztársaság született harangszavú délben (1989. október 23) (The Republic Was Born and the Bells Rang at Noon, 23 October 1989) 1999, National Politics and Joining. Questions of Integration 2001, Hoggan tovább a rogos utakon (How Much Marching Further on the Thorny Way) 2003.
Address: Hungarian National Assembly, 1055 Budapest, Kossuth Lajos tér 1-3, Hungary (office). *Telephone:* (1) 441-5067 (office); (1) 441-5068 (office). *Fax:* (1) 441-5972 (office). *E-mail:* secretariate@ipu.parlament.hu (office).

T

TABECARU, Nicolae; Moldovan politician and diplomatist; b. 20 Aug. 1955, Nadrechnoye, Odessa Region, Ukraine; m.; two c. *Education:* Moldovan State Univ., Moscow Diplomatic Acad. *Career:* diplomatic service 1989–; Head Protocol Dept, Ministry of Foreign Affairs 1990; First Sec. Perm. Mission of Repub. of Moldova to UN 1991–92; Head, Dept for UN and Disarmament, Ministry of Foreign Affairs 1992–93; Head, Protocol Diplomatic Dept 1993; Counsellor, Minister-Counsellor, Embassy in Belgium (also accred to Luxembourg, UK, NATO and EC) 1993–96; Head, Dept of Europe and N America, Ministry of Foreign Affairs 1996–97; Adviser on Problems of Foreign Policy to Moldovan Pres. 1997–; Minister of Foreign Affairs 1997–99; fmr Amb. to Germany. *Address:* c/o Ministry of Foreign Affairs, Piaţa Marii Adunari Nationale 1, 2033 Chişinău, Moldova.

TADIĆ, Boris; Serbian politician, psychologist and head of state; *President;* b. 15 Jan. 1958, Sarajevo, Bosnia and Herzegovina; m.; two c. *Education:* Univ. of Belgrade. *Career:* convicted for student political activities; several positions as prof. of psychology, army clinical psychologist, researcher on devt and social psychology projects; Prof. of Politics and Advertising, Univ. for Drama and Arts, Belgrade 2003; Founder and Dir Centre for the Devt of Democracy and Political Skills 1997–2002; mem. Democratic Party 1990–, later Sec. of Gen. Cttee, Vice-Pres. Exec. Bd, Acting Pres. Exec. Bd, Vice-Pres. of Democratic Party (twice), Pres. 2004–; Rep. to Nat. Ass 1996–97, 2004–; mem. Council for Science and Tech.; Rep. in Council of Fed. Ass. 2000; Minister of Telecommunications, Fed. Repub. of Yugoslavia 2002–03; Minister of Defence, Council of Ministers of Serbia and Montenegro 2003–04; elected Rep. to Ass. of Serbia and Montenegro 2003, Acting Head of Group of Democratic Party Reps; Pres. of Repub. of Serbia 2004–; mem. Bd for Defence and Security; first Pres. Comm. for the Supervision of Security Service. *Address:* Office of the President, 11000 Belgrade, Andrićev venac 1, Serbia (office). *Telephone:* (11) 3030866 (office). *Fax:* (11) 3030868 (office). *Website:* kontakt.predsednik@predsednik.yu (office); www.boristadic.org (office); www.predsednik.yu (office).

TAEL, Kaja, PhD; Estonian diplomatist and academic; *Under Secretary for European Union Affairs, Ministry of Foreign Affairs;* b. 24 July 1960, Tallinn. *Education:* Tartu Univ. *Career:* Researcher, Inst. of Language and Literature, Acad. of Sciences, Tallinn 1984–90; Visiting Scholar, Uppsala Univ., Sweden 1990–91; Dir Estonian Inst., Tallinn 1991–95, Chair. 1995–; Foreign Policy Adviser to Pres. of Estonia 1995–98; Prof., Dept of Nordic Languages, Tallinn Pedagogical Univ. 1995–2000; joined Foreign Ministry 1998, Exec. Sec. Estonian—Russian Intergovernmental Comm. 1998–99; Dir-Gen. of Policy Planning Dept, Ministry of Foreign Affairs 1999–2001, Amb. to UK 2001–06, Under-sec. for EU Affairs 2006–; Order of the Polar Star (Sweden) 1995, Order of the Lion (Finland) 1995, Order of Aguila Azteca (Mexico) 1996, Order of the White Star (Estonia) 2000. *Publications:* several articles in specialist linguistic journals and translations of various works of philosophy, including John Stuart Mill's On Liberty 1996, Henry Kissinger's Diplomacy 2000 and Eric Hobsbawm's The Age of Extremes 2002. *Address:* Ministry of Foreign Affairs, Islandi väljak 1, 15049 Tallinn, Estonia (office). *Telephone:* 637-7023 (office). *Fax:* 631-7099 (office). *E-mail:* vminfo@vm.ee (office). *Website:* www.vm.ee (office).

TAFIDA, Dalhatu Sarki, MB BS, MRCP; Nigerian physician, politician and diplomatist; *High Commissioner to UK;* b. 24 Nov. 1940, Zaria, Kaduna State; m. Salamatu Ndana Tafida; nine c. *Education:* Middle School, Zaria, Barewa Coll., Zaria, Govt Coll., Keffi, Coll. of Medicine, Univ. of Lagos, Royal Victoria Infirmary, Newcastle upon Tyne and Univ. of Liverpool, UK, John Hopkins Univ., USA. *Career:* House Officer, Ahmadu Bello Univ. 1967–68, Sr House Officer 1968–69, Registrar from 1969–70; Clinical Asst in Medicine, Royal Victoria Infirmary, Newcastle upon Tyne 1970–71; Sr Registrar in Medicine, Katsina Specialist Hosp. 1972–73; Consultant Physician, Ministry of Health, Kaduna State 1973–76; Perm. Sec., Ministry of Health, Kaduna 1976–80; Chief Physician to Pres. of Nigeria 1980–83; Commr for Health, Agric. and Educ., Kaduna State 1984–87; Pro-Chancellor Univ. of Agriculture, Makurdi 1989–91; Fed. Minister of Health 1993–95; represented Kaduna North in Senate 2003–07, Senate Majority Leader 2003–07; High Commr to UK 2008–; Fellow, Nigerian

Medical Coll. of Physicians 1975, West African Coll. of Physicians 1975; conferred with traditional title of Tafidan Zazzau 1983; Order of the Fed. Rep. 1983. *Address:* Nigeria House, 9 Northumberland Avenue, London, WC2N 5BX, England (office). *Telephone:* (20) 7839-1244 (office). *Fax:* (20) 7839-8746 (office). *E-mail:* information@nigeriahc.org.uk (office). *Website:* www .nigeriahc.org.uk (office).

TAFROV, Stefan; Bulgarian diplomatist; b. 11 Feb. 1958, Sofia. *Education:* Lycée de langue française, Sofia, Univ. of Sofia. *Career:* staff writer, weekly newspaper ABV, Sofia 1983–87; First Deputy Minister of Foreign Affairs 1991–92, April–Dec. 1997; Amb. to Italy 1992–95, to UK 1995–97, to France 1998–2001; Perm. Rep. to UN, New York 2001–06; Commdr Légion d'honneur (France). *Address:* c/o Ministry of Foreign Affairs, ul. Al. Zhendov 2 1040 Sofia, Bulgaria (office). *Telephone:* (2) 971-14-08 (office). *Fax:* (2) 870-30-41 (office). *E-mail:* iprd@mfa.government.bg (office).

TAGLIAVINI, Heidi, PhD; Swiss diplomatist and United Nations official. *Education:* Geneva Univ. *Career:* joined Diplomatic Service 1982; with Dept of Foreign Affairs, worked in Directorate of Political Affairs, Head of Human Rights and Humanitarian Policy 1999; staff mem. Embassy in The Hague, Netherlands; Deputy Head of Mission, Embassy in Moscow, Russia 1996; Amb. to Bosnia and Herzegovina 2001–02; mem. first OSCE Assistance Group to Chechnya 1995, Personal Rep. of OSCE and Chair.-in-Office for the Caucasus 2000–01; Deputy Head of UN Observer Mission in Georgia (UNOMIG) 1998–99, Special Rep. of UN Sec.-Gen. for Georgia and Head of Mission 2002–06. *Publications include:* Defence of the Future: The Caucasus in the Search for Peace (co-ed with F. Duve). *Address:* c/o Department of Peace-keeping Operations, Room S-3727-B, United Nations, New York, NY 10017 USA (office).

TAHA, Hissène Brahim; Chadian diplomat; *Ambassador to France;* b. 1951, Abéché; m.; six c. *Education:* Inst. Nat. des Langues et Civilisations Orientales, Paris. *Career:* Counsellor, Ministry of Foreign Affairs 1979–89, Chef du Bureau 1990–91; Counsellor, Embassy in Riyadh 1991–2001; Amb. to Taiwan 2001–06, to France 2006– (also accred to Portugal and Vatican City 2008–). *Address:* Embassy of Chad, 65 rue des Belles Feuilles, 75116 Paris, France (office). *Telephone:* 1-45-53-36-75 (office). *Fax:* 1-45-53-16-09 (office). *E-mail:* ambassadedutchad@wanadoo.fr (office).

TAHERIAN, Mohammad-Ebrahim; Iranian diplomatist; *Head of Afghanistan Affairs Department, Ministry of Foreign Affairs; Career:* served in Afghanistan and Tajikistan; Amb. to Bosnia 1994–98, to Afghanistan 2001–03, to Pakistan 2003–06; Head of Afghanistan Affairs Dept, Ministry of Foreign Affairs 2006–. *Address:* Afghanistan Affairs Department, Ministry of Foreign Affairs, Shahid Abd al-Hamid Mesri St, Ferdowsi Ave, Tehran, Iran (office). *Telephone:* (21) 61151 (office). *Fax:* (21) 66743149 (office). *E-mail:* matbuat@mfa.gov.ir (office). *Website:* www.mfa.gov.ir (office).

TAIANA, Jorge; Argentine academic, politician and diplomatist; *Minister of Foreign Affairs, International Trade and Worship;* b. 31 May 1950, Buenos Aires; m.; three c. *Education:* Bachiller Colegio Nacional, Buenos Aires, Univ. of Buenos Aires. *Career:* Adjunct Prof., Univ. of Buenos Aires 1985–91; Titular Prof., Univ. of Lomas de Zamora 1987; Prof., Univ. Rafael Landívar, Guatemala 1994; Titular Prof., Nat. Univ. of Quilmes 1995–2001; Head of Cabinet, Ministry of Education 1973–74; Under-Sec., Ministry of Economy 1974–75; Regional Dir Servicio Universitario Mundial (non-Govt Org.) 1986–89; advisor to Foreign Affairs Cttee, Chamber of Deputies 1987–89; Under-Sec. for Foreign Policy, Ministry of Foreign Affairs 1989–90, Dir Int. Orgs 1990–91; Amb. to Guatemala and Belize 1992–96; Exec. –Sec. Inter-American Comm. on Human Rights, OAS 1996–2001; Sec. for Human Rights, Govt of Buenos Aires Province 2002–03; Vice-Minister of Foreign Affairs 2003–05, Minister of Foreign Affairs, Int. Trade and Worship 2005–; Grand Cross, Order of Quetza (Guatemala) 1996, Order of El Sol del Peru (Peru) 2003, Order of Antonio José de Irisarri (Guatemala) 2003, Order of Baron de Rio Branco (Brazil)

2005, Officer, Order of Wissam Al Alaoui (Morocco) 2004. *Publications:* author of several publications on human rights and labour movements. *Address:* Ministry of Foreign Affairs, International Trade and Worship, Esmerelda 1212, 1007 Buenos Aires, Argentina (office). *Telephone:* (11) 4819-7000 (office). *E-mail:* web@mrecic.gov.ar (office). *Website:* www .mrecic.gov.ar (office).

TAIT, Alan A., MA, PhD; British international civil servant, academic and consultant; b. 1 July 1934, Edinburgh, Scotland; m. Susan Somers 1963; one s. *Education:* Heriots School, Univs of Edinburgh and Dublin. *Career:* Lecturer, Trinity Coll., Dublin 1959–70, Fellow 1967, Sr Tutor 1968; Prof. of Money and Finance, Univ. of Strathclyde 1970–76; Visiting Scholar, IMF 1971; Consultant to Sec. of State for Scotland 1972–76; Adviser to Pakistan Taxation Comm. 1973; Chief Fiscal Analysis Div., IMF 1975–82, Deputy Dir Fiscal Affairs Dept 1982–94, Dir of Geneva Office 1994–98; Co-Chair. Working Group, WHO Cttee on Macroeconomics and Health 2000–02; mem. Review Cttee GAVI 2003–04; Hon. Fellow, Trinity Coll. Dublin 1996; Hon. Prof., Univ. of Kent at Canterbury 1999–2007. *Publications:* Taxation of Personal Wealth 1967, Economic Policy in Ireland (ed. with J. Bristow) 1968, Value-Added Tax 1988; contribs to numerous academic journals on public finance, macroecons, econs of health. *Address:* Cramond House, Harnet Street, Sandwich, Kent, CT13 9ES, England (home). *Telephone:* (1304) 621038 (home). *E-mail:* alan@ataits .plus.com (home).

TAJ, Lt-Gen. Nadeem; Pakistani military and intelligence officer; *Director, Inter-Services Intelligence Directorate; Career:* fmr Mil. Sec. to fmr Pres. Musharraf; fmr Dir-Gen. of Mil. Intelligence; fmr Gen. Officer Commdt, Lahore; Commandant Pakistan Mil. Acad., Kakul –2007; Dir, Inter-Services Intelligence Directorate (Pakistan's largest intelligence agency) 2007–, promoted to Lt-Gen. *Address:* c/o Ministry of Defence, Pakistan Secretariat, No. II, Rawalpindi 46000, Pakistan.

TAKAGI, Seiichiro, PhD; Japanese professor of politics; *Professor, School of International Politics, Economics and Communication, Aoyama Gakuin University; Education:* Univ. of Tokyo, Stanford Univ., Calif., USA. *Career:* Asst Prof., School of Liberal Arts and Grad. School of Policy Science, Saitama Univ. 1978–79, Assoc. Prof. 1979–86, Assoc. Prof., Grad. School of Policy Science April–June 1986, Prof. 1986–99; Dir Second Research Dept (Area Studies), Nat. Inst. for Defence Studies 1999–2003; Prof., School of Int. Politics, Econs and Business, Aoyama Gakuin Univ., Tokyo 2003–; Visiting Scholar, Northeast Asia-US Forum on Int. Policy, Stanford Univ. 1983, 1985; Guest Scholar, The Brookings Inst. 1987–88; Dir for the Japanese Side, Contemporary Japanese Studies Program, Beijing Univ., People's Repub. of China 1991–92; Dir Inst. for Policy Science, Saitama Univ. 1996–97; fmr mem. Bd Assocn for Political and Econ. Studies on Asia; mem. Japanese Cttee, Council for Security Cooperation in Asia-Pacific, Japan Assocn for Int. Relations, Japan Political Science Assocn, Int. Studies Assocn; Fulbright Grad. Fellowship 1967, Ford Foundation Special Research Grant 1971, Fulbright Sr Researcher Grant 1987, Ohira Masayoshi Memorial Foundation Research Grant 1988. *Publications:* numerous articles on foreign policies and relations and security issues in East Asia and the Pacific, particularly China, Japan, and USA. *Address:* School of International Politics, Economics and Communication, Aoyama Gakuin University, 4-4-25 Shibuya, Shibuya-ku, Tokyo 150-8366, Japan (office). *Telephone:* (3) 3409-8111 (office). *Fax:* (3) 3409-0927 (office). *Website:* www.sipeb.aoyama.ac.jp (office).

TAKANO, Toshiyuki; Japanese diplomatist; *Ambassador to Germany;* b. 1944. *Career:* fmr Counsellor, Embassy in USA; fmr Amb. to Singapore, to S Korea –2005, Amb. to Germany 2005–; fmr Deputy Foreign Minister. *Address:* Embassy of Japan, Hiroshimstr. 6, 10785 Berlin, Germany (office). *Telephone:* (30) 210940 (office). *Fax:* (30) 21094222 (office). *E-mail:* info@botschaft-japan.de (office). *Website:* www.botschaft-japan.de (office).

TAKASU, Yukio, LLB; Japanese diplomatist; *Permanent Representative, United Nations; Education:* Univ. of Tokyo, Merton Coll., Oxford. *Career:* First Sec., then Counsellor, Perm. Mission to UN, New York 1981–88; Dir W Europe Div., Ministry of Foreign Affairs 1989–92; Deputy Chief of Mission, Embassy in Indonesia 1992–93; Asst Sec.-Gen. and Controller, UN, New York 1993–97; Perm. Rep. to UN, New York 1997–2000, 2007–; Dir-Gen. Multilateral Co-operation Dept 2000–01, Ministry of Foreign Affairs; Perm. Rep. to IAEA and UNIDO 2001–05; Amb. responsible for Human Security, Science and Tech. Co-operation, also Special Envoy for UN Reform 2005–06; Visiting Fellow, Harvard Univ. 2006–07.

Address: Permanent Mission of Japan to the United Nations, 866 United Nations Plaza, 2nd Floor, New York, NY 10017, USA (office). *Telephone:* (212) 223-4300 (office). *Fax:* (212) 751-1966 (office). *E-mail:* mission@un -japan.org (office). *Website:* www.un.int/japan (office).

TALABANI, Jalal; Iraqi politician and head of state; *President;* b. 1933, Kelkan. *Education:* high schools in Erbil and Kirkuk. *Career:* f. secret student asscn at age of 13; mem. Kurdish Democratic Party 1947, elected to Cen. Cttee 1951; denied admission to medical school by govt due to political activities; allowed to enter law school 1953; forced to go into hiding to escape arrest for founding and becoming Sec.-Gen. of Kurdistan Student Union 1956; following overthrow of Hashemite monarchy, returned to law school 1958; pursued career as journalist and ed. of Khabat and Kurdistan; mil. service 1959, later Commdr of tank unit; organized and led Kurdish revolt against Govt in Mawat, Rezan and Karadagh regions 1961; rep. Kurdish leadership on numerous diplomatic missions in Europe and Middle East 1960s; Founder and Sec.-Gen. Patriotic Union of Kurdistan 1975–; apptd mem. Iraqi Governing Council 2003; President of Iraq 2005–. *Address:* Office of the President, Baghdad, Iraq (office).

TALAEI, Mohsen, MA, BA; Iranian diplomatist; *Deputy Foreign Minister for Economic Affairs;* b. 1954. *Education:* Univ. of Tehran. *Career:* Sr Research Expert, Supreme Inst. of Planning 1977–79; Sr Macro Econ. Programming Expert, Man. and Planning Org. 1980–84, Sec. to State Planning HQ 1980–92, Dir Econ. Planning Office 1984–92, Dir-Gen. Enterprise Coordination Office 1986–92, Adviser to Econ. Deputy 1996–98, Adviser to Head 2002–04; Chief of Secr., Council of Free Trade Areas 1986–92; Head Cttee on Privatization Studies 1986–92; Econ. Counsellor, Embassy in Rome, Italy 1992–96, Deputy Amb. 1994–96; Adviser on Europe and USA to Deputy Minister of Foreign Affairs 1996–98; Dir-Gen. Strategic and Econ. Coordination Office, Ministry of Foreign Affairs 1996–98; Amb. to S Korea 1998–2002; Special Asst to Minister for Foreign Affairs 2002–04; Amb. to Japan 2006–08; Deputy Foreign Minister for Econ. Affairs 2008–. *Address:* Ministry of Foreign Affairs, Shahid Abd al-Hamid Mesri Street, Ferdowsi Avenue, Tehran, Iran (office). *Telephone:* (21) 61151 (office). *Fax:* (21) 66743149 (office). *E-mail:* matbuat@mfa.gov.ir (office). *Website:* www .mfa.gov.ir (office).

TALAGI, Grace Sisilia Tupou, BSc; Niuean civil servant and diplomat; *High Commissioner to New Zealand;* b. 27 Feb. 1952, Niue; m. Takili Talagi; one s. three d. *Career:* food technologist 1976–81, food industry trainer 1981–83; Agric. Projects Man. and Exports Promoter 1983–88; Dir of Agric. and Fisheries 1988–94; Asst Head of External Affairs 1994–99; Sec. to the Govt 1999–2005; High Commr to NZ (first woman diplomat) 2005–. *Address:* High Commission of Niue, Molesworth House, 101 Molesworth Street, Thorndon, Wellington, New Zealand (office); PO Box 175, Alofi, Niue (home). *Telephone:* (4) 499-4515 (office). *Fax:* (4) 499-4516 (office). *E-mail:* komisina@niuhicom.co.nz (office).

TALAT, Mehmet Ali, MSc; Turkish Cypriot politician; *President, 'Turkish Republic of Northern Cyprus';* b. 6 July 1952, Kyrenia; m.; one s. one d. *Education:* Middle East Tech. Univ., Ankara, Eastern Mediterranean Univ., Famagusta. *Career:* began career as self-employed electrical engineer; active in Turkish Cypriot orgs, co-founder and first Chair. Cypriots Educ. and Youth Fed. (KÖGEF), Turkey; joined youth div. Republican Turkish Party (Cumhuriyetçi Türk Partisi, CTP), mem. CTP Party Council, and Cen. Exec. Cttee, also CTP Sec., becoming Chair. 1996–; Minister of Educ. and Culture 1994, later Minister of State and Deputy Prime Minister; MP for Nicosia 1998–; Prime Minister of 'Turkish Repub. of Northern Cyprus' 2004–05, Pres. 2005–. *Address:* c/o Office of the President, Lefkosa (Nicosia), Mersin 10 (office); Mersin Cad 12, Kyrenia, Mersin 10, Turkey (home). *Telephone:* 2283444 (office); (392) 8154866 (home). *Fax:* 2272252 (office). *E-mail:* info@kktc-cb .org (office). *Website:* www.tncpresidency.org.

TALBOTT, Strobe; American journalist and fmr government official; *President, Brookings Institution;* b. 25 April 1946, Dayton, Ohio; m. Brooke Lloyd Shearer 1971; two s. *Education:* Hotchkiss School, Connecticut, Yale Univ. and Univ. of Oxford, UK. *Career:* joined Time magazine; Diplomatic Corresp., White House Corresp., Eastern Europe Corresp., Washington Bureau Chief 1984–89, Ed.-at-Large 1989–94; Amb.-at-Large State Dept Feb.–Dec. 1993; Deputy Sec. of State 1994–2001; Pres. The Brookings Inst. 2002–; Rhodes Scholar, Univ. of Oxford 1969; Dir Carnegie Endowment for Int. Peace; mem. Council on Foreign Relations. *Publications:* Khrushchev Remembers 1970, Khrushchev Remembers: The Last Testament (jtly) 1974, Endgame: The Inside Story of Salt II 1979, Deadly Gambits: The Reagan Administration and the Stalemate in Nuclear Arms Control 1984, The Russians and Reagan 1984, Reagan and

Gorbachev (jtly) 1987, The Master of the Game: Paul Nitze and the Nuclear Peace 1988, At the Highest Levels: The Inside Story of the End of the Cold War (jtly) 1993, The Age of Terror: America and The World After September 11 (co-ed.) 2001, The Russia Hand: A Memoir of Presidential Diplomacy 2002, Engaging India 2005, The Great Experiment 2008. *Address:* The Brookings Institution, 1775 Massachusetts Avenue, NW, Washington, DC 20036, USA (office). *Telephone:* (202) 797-6000 (office). *Fax:* (202) 797-6004 (office). *E-mail:* communications@brookings.edu (office). *Website:* www.brookings.edu (office).

TALLA, Maj.-Gen. István; Hungarian air force officer; b. 11 April 1954; m. Valentina; one s. *Education:* Mil. Aviation Coll., Szolnok, Mil. Aviation Coll., USSR, Zrinyi Miklós Mil. Acad., Budapest, USAF Air War Coll., USA. *Career:* served in air force as Flight Leader, Deputy Squadron Commdr, Squadron Commdr, Wing Weapon Officer, Weapon Officer at Hungarian Defence Forces (HDF) Aviation Directorate, Chief of Army Aviation at Corps HDF, Deputy Chief of Aviation HDF, Deputy Chief of Hungarian AF Staff, Chief of Staff; currently Deputy Commdr CAOC-5, Poggio Renatico (IT); Mil. Rep. to NATO 2005–07; numerous medals and decorations. *Address:* c/o Ministry of Defence, 1055 Budapest, Balaton u. 7–11 Hungary (office). *Telephone:* (1) 236-5111 (office). *Fax:* (1) 474-1111 (office). *E-mail:* honvedelem@armedia.hu (office). *Website:* www.honvedelem.hu (office).

TALLAWY, Mervat; Egyptian diplomatist and international organization official; b. 1 Dec. 1937, Menya; m. Dr Ali Abdel-Rahman Rahmy 1964; one d. *Education:* American Univ. Cairo, Inst. for Diplomatic Studies, Cairo and Grad. Inst. of Int. Studies, Geneva. *Career:* joined Ministry of Foreign Affairs 1963; served Geneva, New York and Caribbean countries, Vienna and Tokyo; Deputy Dir UN Inst. for the Advancement of Women 1982–85; Minister Plenipotentiary, Deputy Dir Dept of Int. Orgs. Ministry of Foreign Affairs 1985–88; Amb. to Austria and Resident Rep. to IAEA, UNIDO and UN Centre for Social and Humanitarian Affairs 1988–91; Dir of Int. Econ. Dept, Ministry of Foreign Affairs 1991; Asst Minister for Int. Political and Econ. Affairs 1992–93; Amb. to Japan 1993–97; Minister of Insurance and Social Affairs 1997–99; Asst UN Sec. for UNDP, Arab countries 1997; Sec.-Gen. Nat. Council for Women 2000; Exec. Sec. UN Econ. and Social Comm. for Western Asia (ESCWA) 2000–07; Rapporteur-Gen. UN Conf. on Adoption of Int. Convention on Prevention of Illicit Drug Trafficking, Vienna 1988; mem. UN Cttee on Elimination of Discrimination against Women (CEDAW) (Chair. 1990–92); Chair. UN Comm. on Status of Women 1991–93; Chair. workshop on Women and Violence leading to adoption of UN Declaration on Elimination of Violence Against Women, Vienna 1992; Chair. Working Group on Health, UN Int. Conf. for the Advancement of Women, Beijing 1995; Head Egyptian Del. to Multilateral Middle East Peace Talks Working Group on Econ. Regional Co-operation, Brussels 1992, Paris 1992, Rome 1993 and to Steering Cttee of Multilateral Middle East Talks, Tokyo 1994; Head Egyptian Del. to UN World Conf. on Natural Disasters, Yokohama 1994; Del. to UN Environment Conf., Rio de Janeiro 1992, to UN Int. Conf. on Population and Devt, Cairo 1994; initiator of proposal leading to adoption of UN Declaration for the Protection of Women and Children in Time of Armed Conflicts 1974; mem. Club of Rome; Amb. of the Year (Austria) 1991. *Address:* 18 el-Mansour Mohammed Street, Apt 15, Zamalek, 11211 Cairo, Egypt (home). *Telephone:* (2) 735-8102 (home). *Fax:* (2) 735-8102 (home).

TAMARÓN, Marqués de Santiago de Mora-Figueroa, 9th Marqués de Tamarón; Spanish diplomatist; b. 18 Oct. 1941, Jerez de la Frontera; m. Isabelle de Yturbe 1966; one s. one d. *Education:* Univ. of Madrid and Escuela Diplomática. *Career:* Lt Spanish Marine Corps 1967; Sec. Embassy, Nouakchott 1968–70, Paris 1970–73; Banco del Noroeste 1974; Counsellor, Copenhagen 1975–80; Minister-Counsellor, Ottawa 1980–81; Pvt. Sec. to Minister of Foreign Affairs 1981–82; Head of Studies and Deputy Dir Escuela Diplomática 1982–88; Dir Inst. de Cuestiones Internacionales y Política Exterior (INCIPE) 1988–96; Dir Instituto Cervantes 1996–99; Amb. to UK 1999–2004; mem. Trilateral Comm. 1989–96; Commdr Order of Carlos III, Officier, Ordre nat. du Mérite (France), Commdr Order of Dannebrog, Commdr Order of Merit (Germany), Gran Cruz Mérito Naval (Spain). *Publications:* Pólvora con Aguardiente 1983, El Guirigay Nacional 1988, Trampantojos 1990, El Siglo XX y otras Calamidades 1993, El Peso de la Lengua Española en el Mundo (co-author) 1995, El Rompimiento de Gloria 2003.

TANAKA, Nobuaki, BA, MA; Japanese diplomatist and international organization official; *Ambassador to Turkey;* b. 26 Aug. 1946, Chiba; m.; one s. *Education:* Tokyo Univ., King's Coll., Cambridge, UK. *Career:* on staff, Ministry of Foreign Affairs Japan 1970–78, First Sec., Washington, DC 1978–86, Dir Oceania Div., Ministry of Foreign Affairs 1986–88, Dir Policy Planning Div. 1990, Dir First N America Div. 1990–92, Minister,

Embassy of Japan to Thailand 1992–94, Deputy Dir-Gen. N American Affairs Bureau and Deputy Press Sec., Ministry of Foreign Affairs 1997–99, Deputy Dir-Gen. Foreign Policy Bureau 1999–2000, Consul-Gen., San Francisco, USA 2000–02, Amb. to Pakistan 2004–06, to Turkey 2008–; Asst Dir-Gen. for Man. and Admin, UNESCO, Paris 1994–97, UN Under-Sec.-Gen. for Disarmament Affairs 2006–07; Lecturer, Waseda Univ. 1986–91; Sr Researcher, Int. Inst. of Peace Studies, Japan (Asst to fmr Prime Minister Nakasone for the Trilateral Comm) 1988–90; Prof., Doshisha Women's Coll., Japan 2002–04. *Address:* Embassy of Japan, Reşit Galip Caddesi 81, GOP 06692, Ankara, Turkey (office). *Telephone:* (312) 4460500 (office). *Fax:* (312) 4371812 (office). *E-mail:* culture@jpn-emb.org.tr (office). *Website:* www.tr.emb -japan.go.jp (office).

TANAKA, Nobuo, MBA; Japanese international organization official; *Executive Director, International Energy Agency;* b. 3 March 1950; m. Gloria Tanaka; two c. *Education:* Univ. of Tokyo, Case Western Reserve Univ., Ohio, USA. *Career:* began career with Ministry of Economy, Trade and Industry (METI) 1973, held posts including Deputy Dir Gen. Affairs Div., Machinery and Information Industries Bureau, Personnel Div., Dir of Int. Nuclear Energy Affairs, Natural Resources and Energy Agency; Deputy Dir for Science, Tech. and Industry, OECD 1989–91, Dir for Science, Tech. and Industry 1991–95, 2004–07, also Head Steering Group of Centre for Entrepreneurship 2004–07; Dir for Industrial Finance Div. and Dir for Policy Planning and Coordination Div., METI 1995–98; Minister for Energy, Trade and Industry, Embassy in Washington, DC 1998–2000; Exec. Vice-Pres. Research Inst. of Economy Trade and Industry, Japan 2000–02; Dir-Gen. Multilateral Trade System Dept, METI 2002–04; Exec. Dir IEA 2007–. *Address:* The International Energy Agency, 9 rue de la Fédération, 75015 Paris, France (office). *Telephone:* 1-40-57-65-00 (office). *Fax:* 1-40-57-65-59 (office). *E-mail:* info@iea.org (office). *Website:* www.iea.org (office).

TANDJA, Col Mamadou; Niger army officer (retd) and head of state; *President; Career:* mem. Nat. Movt for the Devt of Soc. (MNSD); Pres. of Niger 1999– (re-elected 2004). *Address:* Office of the President, BP 550, Niamey, Republic of Niger (office). *Telephone:* 20-72-23-80 (office). *Fax:* 20-72-33-96 (office). *Website:* www.delgi.ne/presidence (office).

TANG, Ignacio Milam; Equatorial Guinean politician and diplomatist; *Prime Minister; Career:* fmr Minister for Youth and Sports; fmr Second Vice-Pres. Chamber of People's Reps; Deputy Prime Minister 2001–03; Sec.-Gen. of the Presidency 2003–06; Amb. to Spain 2006–08; Prime Minister 2008–; mem. Democratic Party of Equatorial Guinea. *Address:* Office of the Prime Minister, Malabo, Equatorial Guinea (office).

TANG, Pascal Biloa, BA; Cameroonian diplomatist; *Ambassador to France;* b. 20 Nov. 1937, Ebolowa; m.; six c. *Education:* Univs of Aix-en-Provence and Grenoble, France, Institut Universitaire des Hautes Etudes Internationales, Geneva, Switzerland. *Career:* Dir Dept of Admin., Consular and Cultural Affairs, Ministry of Foreign Affairs 1965, Dept of African and Asian Affairs 1976–77, Dept of Legal Affairs and Treaties 1985–86; served in Embassy in Addis Ababa and London, then First Counsellor, Embassy in Bonn 1979–81, Chargé d'Affaires, Algiers 1982, First Counsellor, Brussels 1982–85; Chargé de Mission, Presidency of Repub. 1977–79, Diplomatic Adviser to Pres. and Tech. Adviser to Presidency 1986–90; Perm. Rep. of Cameroon to UN, New York 1990–95; currently Amb. to France. *Address:* Embassy of Cameroon, 73 rue d'Auteuil, 75116 Paris, France. *Telephone:* 1-47-43-98-33. *Fax:* 1-46-51-24-52.

TANG YING YEN, Henry, JP, GBS; Hong Kong business executive and government official; *Chief Secretary for Administration, Hong Kong Special Administrative Region;* b. 6 Sept. 1952, Hong Kong; m. Lisa Kuo; four c. *Education:* Univ. of Michigan. *Career:* Man. Dir Peninsula Knitters Ltd; Chair. Fed. of Hong Kong Industries; Dir Meadville Ltd; Hong Kong Affairs Adviser to Chinese Govt; fmr mem. Legis. Council; mem. Exec. Council Hong Kong Special Admin. Region July 1997–, Sec. for Commerce, Industry and Technology July 2002–Aug. 2003, Financial Sec. Aug. 2003–2007, Chief Sec. for Admin 2007–; mem. Selection Cttee for First Govt of the Hong Kong Special Admin. Region, CPPCC Shanghai Cttee, Hong Kong Trade Devt Council, Liberal Party. *Address:* Central Government Offices, Lower Albert Road, Central, Hong Kong Special Administrative Region, People's Republic of China. *Telephone:* (852) 28102545 (office). *Fax:* (852) 28450176 (office).

TANIGUCHI, Makoto, BA, MA; Japanese diplomatist and university professor; *Director, Research Institute of Current Chinese Affairs, Waseda University;* b. 1930, Osaka; m. Hiroko Kanari 1972; one s. *Education:*

Hitotsubashi Univ., St John's Coll. Cambridge, UK. *Career:* joined Ministry of Foreign Affairs 1959; specialized in econ. affairs; Dir for UN Specialized Agencies 1972, Dir for UN Econ. Affairs 1973–74, Counsellor of Japanese Mission to Int. Orgs, Geneva, in charge of UNCTAD Affairs 1974–76, Minister and Consul-Gen., Manila 1976–79, Minister, Japanese Mission to UN, in charge of Econ. Matters 1979–83; Amb. to Papua New Guinea 1983–86, to UN, New York 1986–90; Deputy Sec.-Gen. OECD 1990–96; External Auditor Hitachi Metals 1995–; Special Adviser to Sec.-Gen. OECD 1997; Prof. Inst. of Asia-Pacific Studies, Waseda Univ., Tokyo 1998–2000, Dir Research Inst. of Current Chinese Affairs, Waseda Univ. 2000–; Prof., Toyo Eiwa Women's Univ., Tokyo 1997–; Chair. Preparatory Cttee for UN Conf. on New and Renewable Sources of Energy 1980–81, Chair. Cttee I 1981; Chair. Cttee I, UNCTAD VII; Vice-Pres., Pres. Exec. Bd UNICEF 1987–88; Visiting Prof. Univ. of Int. Trade and Econs Beijing 1995; Head Japanese Del. to UN Comm. on Human Rights 1987–89; Second Order of Merit 1999. *Publications:* North-South Issues: A Path to Global Solutions (in Japanese) 1993, North-South Issues in the 21st Century: A Challenge of Globalization (in Japanese) 2001, Japan and Asia in a New Global Age 2001; many articles. *Address:* Research Institute of Current Chinese Affairs, Waseda University, Bokusha Building 2F 1-101, Totsuka-machi, Shinjuku-ku, Tokyo 169-0071 (office); Azabu House 901, 1-7-13 Roppongi, Minato-ku, Tokyo 106-0032, Japan (home). *Telephone:* (3) 5286-3987 (office); (3) 3585-2879 (home). *Fax:* (3) 5286-3987 (office); (3) 3585-2879 (home). *E-mail:* xxchiang@mn .waseda.ac.jp (office).

TANIN, Zahir, MD; Afghan journalist, physician and diplomatist; *Permanent Representative, United Nations;* b. 1 May 1956; m.; two c. *Education:* Kabul Medical Univ., BBC Leadership Programme. *Career:* began career as journalist in Kabul 1980; freelance writer in France 1992–93; fmr Ed.-in-Chief Afkbar-e-Haftah and Sabawoon Magazine; Research Fellow, Int. Relations Dept, LSE, UK 1994–95; Producer, BBC World Service 1995–2000, Sr Producer 2000–01, Ed. Afghanistan and Cen. Asia (Persian Section) 2001–03, Persian/Pashto Section in Afghanistan 2003–06; Perm. Rep. to the UN, New York 2006–. *Radio:* The Oral History of Afghanistan in the 20th Century (29-part series; BBC). *Publications include:* The Communist Regime in Afghanistan (co-author), Afghanistan in the Twentieth Century. *Address:* Permanent Mission of Afghanistan to the United Nations, 360 Lexington Avenue, 11th Floor, New York, NY 10017, USA (office). *Telephone:* (212) 972-1212 (office). *Fax:* (212) 972-1216 (office). *E-mail:* afgwatan@aol.com (office). *Website:* www.mfa.gov.af (office).

TANNER, Fred, PhD; Swiss academic and international organisation official; *Director, Geneva Centre for Security Policy; Education:* Univ. of Geneva, Fletcher School of Law and Diplomacy, Tufts Univ. *Career:* fmr Lecturer and Researcher, Harvard Univ, Johns Hopkins Univ. Princeton Univ, USA; Dir Mediterranean Acad. of Diplomatic Studies, Malta 1994–97; Deputy Dir Geneva Centre for Security Policy 1997–2006, Dir 2006–; Hon. Chair. Cttee for Security Studies in Bosnia and Herzegovina, OSCE 1999–2001; mem. Governing Council Int. Security Studies Section, Int. Studies Asscn; mem. Governing Bd Programme for Strategic and Security Studies, Graduate Inst. for Int. Studies, Geneva; mem. Advisory Bd Swiss Asscn of Foreign Affairs; mem. Scientific Comm. Ministry of Defence, Austria. *Publications:* From Versailles to Baghdad 1993, EU as a Security Actor in the Mediterranean 2001, Refugee Manipulation Refugee Manipulation 2002, Promoting Security Sector Governance in the EU's Neighbourhood 2005, The Iraq Crisis and World Order 2006. *Address:* Geneva Centre for Security Policy, 7 bis, Avenue de la Paix, PO Box 1295, 1211 Geneva, Switzerland (office). *Telephone:* 229061600 (office). *Fax:* 229061649 (office). *E-mail:* director@gcsp.ch (office). *Website:* www .gcsp.ch (office).

TANNER, Lindsay, MA; Australian politician; *Minister for Finance and Deregulation;* b. 26 April 1956, Orbost, Vic.; m. Andrea Tanner; two d. *Education:* Univ. of Melbourne. *Career:* Articled Clerk and Solicitor, Holding Redlich 1982–85; Electorate Asst for Senator Barney Cooney 1986; Asst Sec., Federated Clerks Union, Vic. 1987–88, State Sec. 1988–93; MP (Australia Labor Party) for Melbourne 1993–, Shadow Minister for Transport 1996–98, for Finance and Consumer Affairs 1998, for Communications 2001–04, for Finance 2005–07, Minister for Finance and Deregulation 2007–. *Publications:* The Politics of Pollution (jt author) 1978, The Last Battle 1996, Open Australia 1999, Crowded Lives 2003; numerous articles in journals and newspapers. *Address:* Department of Finance and Administration, John Gorton Building, King Edward Terrace, Parkes ACT 2600, Australia (office). *Telephone:* (2) 6215-2222 (office). *Fax:* (2) 6273-3021 (office). *E-mail:* Lindsay.Tanner.MP@aph.gov.au (office). *Website:* www.finance.gov.au (office); www.lindsaytanner.com.

TANTAWI, Field Marshal Muhammad Hussain; Egyptian army officer and government official; *Minister of Defence and Military Production; Career:* served in Suez war 1956, six-days war 1967, October 1973 war; currently Minister of Defence and Mil. Production. *Address:* Ministry of Defence and Military Production, Sharia 23 July, Kobri el-Kobba, Cairo, Egypt (office). *Telephone:* (2) 4032159 (office). *Fax:* (2) 2916227 (office). *E-mail:* mod@idsc.gov.eg (office).

TANZI, Vito, PhD; American economist; *Senior Consultant in Trade and Integration, Inter-American Development Bank;* b. 29 Nov. 1935, Italy; m. Maria T. Bernabé 1997; three s. *Education:* George Washington and Harvard Univs. *Career:* Chair. of Econs Dept, American Univ. 1971–74, Prof. of Econs 1970–74; Head of Tax Policy Div. IMF 1974–81, Dir Fiscal Affairs Dept 1981–2000; Pres. Int. Inst. of Public Finance 1990–94; Sr Assoc. Carnegie Endowment for Int. Peace 2001; Under-Sec. of State, Ministry of Economy and Finance, Italy 2001–03; Sr Consultant in Trade and Integration, IDB 2003–; Dr hc (Córdoba, Argentina) 1998, (Liège) 1999, (Turin) 2001, (BARI) 2003; Commendatore della Repubblica Italiana. *Publications:* ten books, over 200 articles in professional journals. *Address:* Inter-American Development Bank, 1300 New York Avenue, NW, Washington, DC 20577 (office); 5912 Walhonding Road, Bethesda, MD 20816, USA (home). *Telephone:* (202) 623-3442 (office). *Fax:* (202) 623-3096 (office); (301) 229-4106 (home). *E-mail:* vivot@contractual.iadb .org (office); vitotanzi@msn.com (home). *Website:* www.iadb.org (office).

TAO, Dayong; Chinese economist; *Professor of Economics, Beijing Normal University;* b. 12 March 1918, Shanghai; m. Niu Ping-Qing 1942; one s. one d. *Education:* Nat. Cen. Univ. *Career:* Lecturer, Nat. Sun Yat-sen Univ. 1942–43; Assoc. Prof., Nat. Guangxi Univ. 1943–44, Nat. Jiaotong Univ. 1944–45; Prof., Nat. Szechwan Univ. 1945–46; Visiting Prof. (invited by British Council) 1946–48; Prof., Beijing Univ. 1949–51; Prof., Beijing Normal Univ. 1952–; Ed.-in-Chief, New Construction 1951–54, Qunyan 1985–; mem. 5th CPPCC Nat. Cttee 1978–83, Standing Cttee 6th CPPCC Nat. Cttee 1983–88; mem. Standing Cttee 6th, 7th, 8th NPC 1983–98; Vice-Chair. 5th, 6th, 7th Cen. Cttee Chinese Democratic League 1985–97, Hon. Vice-Chair. 8th Cen. Cttee 1997–; Vice-Pres. World Econs Soc. of China 1980–85, Chinese Soc. of Foreign Econ. Theories 1983–; Adviser, Centre for Hongkong and Macao Studies 1982; Int. Order of Merit 1990, Medal of The First Five Hundred 1991, Int. Register of Profiles 1993, 20th Century Award for Achievement 1993. *Publications:* Economic Reconstruction of Post-War Eastern Europe 1948, Post-war Capitalism 1950, History of Socialism 1949, Introduction to World Economy 1951, Studies in Contemporary Capitalistic Economy 1985, A Critique of Henry George's Economic Thought 1982, History of Social Development 1982, A New History of Foreign Economic Thoughts 1990, Selected Works of Tao Dayong (Vols I and II) 1992, (Vol. III) 1998, Outline of New Democratic Economics 2002. *Address:* Economics Department, Beijing Normal University, Xinjiekou-wai Street 19, Beijing 100875, People's Republic of China (office). *Telephone:* (10) 62200012 (office).

TAPAGARARUA, Willie Jimmy; Ni-Vanuatu politician; *Minister for Finance and Economic Management; Career:* fmr Deputy Prime Minister and Minister for Industry and Commerce; currently Minister for Finance and Econ. Man. *Address:* Ministry of Finance, PMB 058, Port Vila, Vanuatu (office). *Telephone:* 23032 (office). *Fax:* 27937 (office). *Website:* www .vanuatugovernment.gov.vu (office).

TAPIA ROA, Ruth Esperanza; Nicaraguan government official; *Secretary-General, Ministry of National Defence;* b. 21 Nov. 1960, Masaya. *Education:* Centre D' Etudes Diplomatiques et Strategiques, France, Universidad Centroamericana, Managua. *Career:* First Sec. at Embassy in Paris 1985–90; Spokesperson, Supreme Court of Justice 2002–07; Sec.-Gen. Ministry of Nat. Defence 2007–. *Address:* Ministry of National Defence, Casa de la Presidencia, Managua, Nicaragua (office). *Telephone:* 266-3580 (office). *Fax:* 228-7911 (office). *E-mail:* webmaster@midef.gob.ni (office). *Website:* www.midef.gob.ni (office).

TARAND, Andres; Estonian politician; b. 11 Jan. 1940, Tallinn; m. Mari (née Viiding) Tarand 1963; two s. *Education:* Tartu State Univ. *Career:* hydrometeorologist 1963; Research Asst, Tallinn Botanical Gardens 1965–68, Sr Engineer 1970–73, Sr Researcher 1973–76, Sector Dir 1976–79, 1981–88, Dir of Research 1979–81, Dir Tallinn Botanical Gardens 1988–90; researcher, Antarctic Expedition 1968–70; Chair. Environment Cttee Supreme Soviet Estonian SSR 1990; mem. Council of Estonia 1990–92; mem. Constitutional Ass. 1991–92; mem. Riigikogu (Parl.) 1992, 1995–2004; Minister for the Environment 1992–94, 1994–95; Prime Minister of Estonia 1994–95; mem. People's Party Moderates (Rahvaer-

akond Mõõdukad, renamed Sotsiaaldemokraatlik Erakond 2004) 1996–, Chair. 1996–2002, Chair. Cttee of Foreign Affairs 1999–2002; mem. European Parl. (Socialist Group) 2004–, mem. Cttee on Industry, Research and Energy, Del. for Relations with the Korean Peninsula, Substitute mem. Cttee on the Environment, Public Health and Food Safety, Del. for Relations with Australia and NZ; Regional Vice-Pres. Globe International Europe 1999–; mem. Estonian Geographical Asscn 1966–, Bd Estonian Inst. for Sustainable Devt, Stockholm Environment Inst.'s Centre, Tallinn 1988–, Bd Univ. of Tartu 1996–, Bd Estonian Nature Fund 1998–; Badge of the Order of Nat. Coat of Arms (Second Class) 2001, Commdr, Légion d'honneur 2001; Panda Award, Danish Section of WWF 1998. *Publications:* Neljakümne kiri 1991, Cassiopeia 1992, Kiri ei Põle Ära 2005; numerous articles on climatology, urban ecology, politics.
Address: European Parliament, Bâtiment Altiero Spinelli, 12G165, 60 rue Wiertz, 1047 Brussels, Belgium (office); Harju 1-1, 10 146 Tallinn Estonia. *Telephone:* (2) 284-5429 (office). *Fax:* (2) 284-9429 (office). *E-mail:* andres .tarand@europarl.europa.eu (office). *Website:* www.europarl.europa.eu (office); www.atarand.eu.

TARAR, Muhammad Rafiq; Pakistani politician and lawyer; b. 2 Nov. 1929, Pir Kot, Gujranwala Dist; m.; three s. one d. *Education:* Govt Islamia High School, Gujranwala, Guru Nanak Khalsa Coll., Gujranwala, Punjab Univ. Law Coll. *Career:* legal practice, Gujranwala; Additional Sessions Judge, Gujranwala, Bahawalnagar, Sargodha; mem. Lahore High Court 1974, Chief Justice of Punjab 1989; mem. Electoral Comm. of Pakistan 1980–89; mem. Supreme Court 1991–94; Senator, Pakistan Muslim League March–Dec. 1997; Pres. of Pakistan 1998–2001.
Address: House 457, G-3, Johar Town, Lahore, Pakistan.

TARASOFSKY, Richard G., BA, LLB, LLM; Canadian international lawyer; *Head of Sustainable Development Programme, Chatham House; Education:* McGill Univ., Montreal, Canada, Osgoode Hall Law School, Toronto, Canada, London School of Econs. *Career:* mem. Ontario Bar 1990–; Lecturer/Researcher (ad hoc), Foundation for Int. Environmental Law and Devt (FIELD), King's Coll., Univ. of London 1992–93; Legal Officer, Environmental Law Centre, IUCN—The World Conservation Union, Bonn, Germany 1993–98; ind. consultant on int. law of sustainable devt, Berlin 1998–2004, Sr Policy Advisor to Ecologic; Head of Sustainable Devt Programme, Chatham House (fmrly Royal Inst. of Int. Affairs) 2004–; mem. IUCN Comm. on Environmental Law. *Publications:* numerous articles on sustainable devt.
Address: Chatham House, 10 St James's Square, London, SW1Y 4LE, England (office). *Telephone:* (20) 7957-5751 (office). *Fax:* (20) 7957-5710 (office). *E-mail:* rtarasofsky@chathamhouse.org.uk (office). *Website:* www .chathamhouse.org.uk (office).

TARASOV, Gennady Pavlovich; Russian diplomatist; *Ambassador to Israel;* b. 14 Sept. 1947. *Education:* Moscow State Inst. of Int. Relations. *Career:* on staff Ministry of Foreign Affairs 1970–; worked in Egypt, USSR Mission in UN and other posts –1986; Deputy Head of Dept Near E and S African Countries, USSR Ministry of Foreign Affairs 1986–90; Amb. of USSR, then of Russia to Saudi Arabia 1990–96; Dir Dept of Information and Press, Ministry of Foreign Affairs 1996–98; Amb. to Portugal 1998–2001, to Israel 2002–.
Address: Embassy of Russia, 120 Rehov Hayarkon, Tel Aviv 63753, Israel. *Telephone:* 3-35226736 (office). *Fax:* 3-35226713 (office). *E-mail:* amb_ru@ mail.netvision.net.il (office). *Website:* www.israel.mid.ru (office).

TARJANNE, Pekka, DTech; Finnish international telecommunications official; *Executive Co-ordinator, United Nations Information and Communication Technologies Task Force;* b. 19 Sept. 1937, Stockholm; m. Aino Kairamo 1962; two s. one d. *Education:* Helsinki Univ. of Tech. *Career:* research and teaching at univs in Denmark and USA 1961–66; Prof. of Theoretical Physics, Univ. of Oulu 1965–66, Univ. of Helsinki 1967–77; mem. Parl. 1970–77; Minister for Transport and Communications 1972–75; Dir-Gen. of Posts and Telecommunications, Finland 1977–89; Sec.-Gen. ITU 1989–98; Vice-Chair. Project Oxygen 1999–2000; Exec. Co-ordinator, UN Information and Communication Technologies Task Force 2001–; Commdr Order of White Rose of Finland; Commdr Légion d'honneur; Grand Cross, Order of Finnish Lion 1998. *Publication:* A Group Theoretical Model for Strong Interaction Dynamics 1962.
Address: United Nations Information and Communication Technologies Task Force, United Nations Plaza, New York, NY 10017, USA.

TARSCHYS, Daniel, PhD; Swedish politician and political scientist; *Professor of Political Science and Public Administration, University of Stockholm;* b. 21 July 1943, Stockholm; m. Regina Rehbinder 1970; two d. *Education:* Univ. of Stockholm, Univ. of Leningrad, USSR, Univ. of Princeton, USA. *Career:* Prof. of Political Science and Public Admin., Stockholm Univ. 1985–; adviser with Ministry of Finance 1976–78, 1979–83; Sec. of State,

Prime Minister's Office 1978–79; Prof. of Soviet and E European Studies, Uppsala Univ. 1983–85; mem. Parl. 1976–82, 1985–94; Chair. Parl. Social Affairs Cttee 1985–91, Foreign Affairs Cttee 1991–94; Vice-Pres. Liberal Int. 1992–94; mem. Council of Europe Parl. Ass. 1986–94, Alt. mem. 1981–83; Sec.-Gen. Liberal, Democratic and Reformers Group (LDR) 1987–91, Chair. 1991–94; Sec.-Gen. Council of Europe 1994–99; Chair. Bank of Sweden Tercentenary Foundation 2006–; chair. of several insts and govt cttees; Grand Crosses of Germany, Liechtenstein, Romania, San Marino and Spain; King's Medal (Sweden). *Publications:* books and articles on political philosophy, budgetary policy, public admin. and comparative politics.
Address: University of Stockholm, 10691 Stockholm, Sweden (office). *E-mail:* daniel.tarschys@statsvet.su.se (office).

TARZI, Nangyalai, PhD; Afghan diplomatist; *Permanent Representative, United Nations, Geneva;* m.; one s. one d. *Education:* Kabul Univ. and Faculté de Droit et Sciences Économiques, Paris, France. *Career:* Prof. of Law and Political Science, Kabul Univ. 1964–70; joined Ministry of Foreign Affairs 1970; Political Observer of OIC, Perm. Mission to UN 1979–86; Deputy Perm. Observer of OIC to UN, New York 1986–92; Perm. Observer of OIC to UN, Geneva 1992–2000; Dir UN Information Centre, Tehran 2001–02; mem. Emergency Loya Jirga 2002; Amb. to Pakistan 2002–06; Perm. Rep. to UN and other Int. Orgs, Geneva 2007–.
Address: Permanent Mission of Afghanistan to the United Nations, 63 rue de Lausanne, 1202 Geneva, Switzerland (office). *Telephone:* (22) 731-16-16 (office). *Fax:* (22) 731-45-10 (office). *E-mail:* ambassador@mission -afghanistan.ch (office); nstarzil@yahoo.com (office). *Website:* www .mission-afghanistan.ch (office).

TAŞKENT, Kurtuluş; Turkish diplomatist; *Ambassador to Russia; Career:* Deputy Under-Sec., Ministry of Foreign Affairs 2001–02; Head, del. to UN Conf. on Comprehensive Nuclear Test Ban Treaty, New York 2001; Amb. to Russia (also accred to Kazakhstan) 2002–.
Address: Embassy of Turkey, 119121 Moscow, 7-i Rostovskii per. 12, Russia (office). *Telephone:* (495) 956-55-95 (office). *Fax:* (495) 956-55-97 (office). *E-mail:* turemb@co.ru (office).

TAŠOVSKI, Slobodan, BA; Macedonian diplomatist; *Permanent Representative, United Nations;* b. 9 July 1954. *Education:* Univ. of Belgrade. *Career:* Desk Officer, Directorate for US and Canada, Fed. Secr. for Foreign Affairs 1978–92, Head Dept for Multilateral Affairs 1992–94; Deputy Perm. Rep. to UN, New York 1994–98; Head, NGO Section, Dept for Multilateral Affairs, Ministry of Foreign Affairs 1998–2001; Counsellor, Embassy in Washington, DC 2001–03, Deputy Head of Mission 2003–05; Head, US Section, Dept for Bilateral Affairs, Ministry of Foreign Affairs 2005–07; Minister Counsellor, Embassy in the Netherlands 2007–08; Perm. Rep. to UN, New York 2008–.
Address: Permanent Mission of the Former Yugoslav Republic of Macedonia to the United Nations, 866 United Nations Plaza, Suite 517, New York, NY 10017, USA (office). *Telephone:* (212) 308-8504 (office). *Fax:* (212) 308-8724 (office). *E-mail:* macedonia@un.int (office). *Website:* www.un.int/macedonia (office).

TATHAM, Michael Harry; British diplomatist; *Ambassador to Bosnia and Herzegovina;* m. Belinda Tatham; one d. *Career:* Desk Officer for Namibia, Southern African Dept, FCO 1988–89; Second Sec. (Press and Political), Embassy in Prague 1989–93; Desk Officer for Gibraltar, EU Dept (Internal), FCO 1993–95; Pvt. Sec. to Minister of State for Europe 1995–96; Deputy Head of Mission, Embassy in Sofia 1997–99; Pvt. Sec. (Foreign Affairs) to the Prime Minister 1999–2002; Deputy Head of Mission, Embassy in Prague 2002–05; Head of Western Balkans Group and Balkans Co-ordinator, FCO 2006–08; Amb. to Bosnia and Herzegovina 2008–.
Address: British Embassy, Tina Ujevića 8, 71000 Sarajevo, Bosnia and Herzegovina (office). *Telephone:* (33) 282200 (office). *Fax:* (33) 282203 (office). *E-mail:* britemb@bih.net.ba (office). *Website:* www .britishembassy.ba (office).

TAUBMAN, Nicholas F., BS.; American business executive and diplomatist; *Ambassador to Romania;* m. Jenny Taubman. *Education:* Wharton School of Finance and Commerce, Univ. of Pennsylvania. *Career:* served in US Army 1957–58, 1960–61; mem. Roanoke, Va City Council 1976–78; Pres. Mozart Investments, Roanoke; fmr Dir Roanoke Valley Industries, Roanoke Merchants Asscn, Alliance Tire & Rubber Co., Hadera, Israel, Shenandoah Life Insurance Company; fmr Dir Cen. YMCA, Roanoke, Va, Junior Achievement, Roanoke, Virginia Coll. Fund, Richmond, Va, Blue Ridge Mountains Council, American Boy Scouts, Roanoke Symphony Orchestra; fmr Pres. and Dir Roanoke Valley Chamber of Commerce; fmr Chair. Brotherhood Week; fmr Pres. Automotive Assocs, Rochester, NY, Automotive Exec. Asscn; fmr mem. Legis. Study Cttee, Roanoke Valley

Chamber of Commerce, City of Roanoke Admin. Man. Study Cttee, Young Presidents' Org.; fmr Chair. and Dir Advance Auto Parts; fmr mem. Bd of Regents Mercersburg Acad., Pa, Temple Emanuel, World Presidents' Org.; Amb. to Romania 2005–; Trustee or fmr Trustee Virginia Historical Soc., Burrell Memorial Hosp., Hollins Univ., Va; hon. degree (Hollins Univ.) 2005; Distinguished Service Award, Roanoke Jaycees 1978, Brotherhood Citation, Nat. Conf. of Christians and Jews 1981.
Address: Embassy of the USA, 70132 Bucharest, Str. Tudor Arghezi 7–9, Romania (office). *Telephone:* (21) 2003300 (office). *Fax:* (21) 2003442 (office). *Website:* www.usembassy.ro (office).

TAUMOEPEAU TUPOU, Sonatane Tu'akinamolahi; Tongan diplomatist; *Minister of Foreign Affairs;* m.; four c. *Education:* Newington Coll., Sydney, Australia, East–West Centre, Univ. of Hawaii, USA. *Career:* commissioned Lt in Tongan Defence Services 1971, attained rank of Capt.; First Sec. in High Comm. to UK 1973, High Commr to UK (also accred to other European countries, EEC and USA) 1979–83; Asst Sec. in Prime Minister's Office 1977; apptd. Deputy Sec. to the Govt 1978; Sec. of Foreign Affairs 1979–83, 1986–2000; Perm. Rep. to UN, New York (also accred as Amb. to USA and High Commr to Canada) 1999–2004; Minister of Foreign Affairs 2004–, Acting Minister of Defence 2005–; Acting Gov. of Vava'u 2005–.
Address: Ministry of Foreign Affairs, National Reserve Bank Building, Salote Road, Kolofo'ou, Nuku'alofa, Tonga (office). *Telephone:* 23600 (office). *Fax:* 23360 (office). *E-mail:* secfo@candw.to (office).

TAURANTAS, Aurimas; Lithuanian diplomatist; *Special Ambassador of the Ministry of Foreign Affairs;* b. 1956, Vilnius; m. Gražina Taurantienė; one d. *Career:* mem. Lithuanian Greens' Party and Jt Sajudis faction; Speaker, Lituanian Parl. 1991; fmr Perm. Rep. to Council of Europe; Dir Second Bilateral Relations Dept, Ministry of Foreign Affairs –2002, Amb. to UK 2002–06 (also accred to Ireland 2003–06); Special Amb. of Ministry of Foreign Affairs 2007–.
Address: Ministry of Foreign Affairs, J. Tumo-Vaižganto g. 2, Vilnius 01511, Lithuania (office). *Telephone:* (5) 236-2444 (office). *Fax:* (5) 231-3090 (office). *E-mail:* urm@urm.lt (office). *Website:* www.urm.lt (office).

TAVOLA, Kaliopate, MAgrSc; Fijian politician and economist; b. 10 Oct. 1946, Dravuni; m. Helen Tavola; two d. one s. *Education:* Massey Univ., New Zealand, Australian Nat. Univ., Australia. *Career:* Agric. Officer Ministry of Primary Industries 1973–77, Sr Agric. Officer 1977–79, Prin. Economist 1979, Prin. Agric. Officer Eastern Div./Projects 1980, Chief Economist 1980–81, 1982–84, Dir of Agric. (acting) 1981–82, later Minister of Primary Industries; London Rep. Fiji Sugar Marketing (FSM) Co. Ltd 1984–88, Deputy CEO 1998–2000; Commercial Counsellor Fiji High Comm. 1984–88; Head of Mission, EU, Brussels 1988–98; Amb. to Belgium, Luxembourg, Netherlands, France, Italy, Spain, Portugal, Greece 1988–98; Perm. Rep. to UNESCO, FAO, WTO, WCO, OPCW; responsible for IFAD, MFO, PCA 1988–98; Commr-Gen. S Pacific Pavilion, EXPO '92, Seville, Spain 1992; Minister of Foreign Affairs and External Trade 2000–06; mem. Senate.
Address: c/o The Senate, Parliament of Fiji Islands, Government Buildings, Suva, Fiji (office). *E-mail:* ktavola@govnet.gov.fj.

TAY, Simon SC, LLB, LLM; Singaporean academic; *Chairman, Singapore Institute of International Affairs;* m. Siow Jin Hua; one s. *Education:* Nat. Univ. of Singapore, Harvard Univ., USA. *Career:* served as Nominated Mem. of Parl. 1997–2001; Chair. Nat. Environment Agency 2002–; Visiting Prof. Harvard Law School 2003; currently Chair. Singapore Inst. of Int. Affairs; teaches int. law at Nat. Univ. of Singapore; serves on numerous expert panels, ASEAN Regional Forum, APEC Independent Experts, Energy City Center Int. Advisory Bd; Fulbright Fellow, Harvard 1993–94; Laylin Prize, Harvard 1994, Singapore Young Artist of the Year 1995, Eisenhower Fellowship 2002, National Day Award PBM 2006. *Publications:* Stand Alone 1993, Asian Dragons and Green Trade 1996, Reinventing ASEAN 2001, The Enemy Within: Combating Corruption in Asia 2003, Sketching Regional Futures 2005, A Mandarin and the Making of Public Policy 2006.
Address: Singapore Institute of International Affairs, 2 Nassim Road, Singapore, 258370 (office). *Telephone:* 67349600 (office). *Fax:* 67336217 (office). *E-mail:* chairman@siiaonline.org (office). *Website:* www.siiaonline.org (office).

TAYLOR, Duncan John Rushworth, CBE; British diplomatist; *High Commissioner to Barbados;* b. 17 Oct. 1958, New Malden, Surrey; m. Marie-Beatrice (Bebe) Taylor 1981; two s. three step-d. *Education:* in French lycées, Highgate School, London, Trinity Coll., Cambridge. *Career:* joined FCO 1982, Asst Desk Officer, West African Dept 1982–83, Head of Japan Section, Far Eastern Dept 1987–89, Personnel Operations Dept 1989–90, Head of Personnel Man. Review Implementation Task Force 1990–91,

Head of Consular Div. 1997–2000; Third, later Second Sec., Chancery, British Embassy, Havana, Cuba 1983–87; Head of Commercial Section, British Embassy, Budapest, Hungary 1992–96; Dir Latin American Affairs (on loan to Rolls Royce) 1996–97; Deputy Consul-Gen., Press and Public Affairs and Deputy Head of Mission, British Consulate Gen., New York, USA 2000–05; High Commr to Barbados (also accred to Antigua and Barbuda, Dominica, Grenada, Saint Kitts and Nevis, Saint Lucia, and Saint Vincent and the Grenadines) 2005–.
Address: British High Commission, Lower Collymore Rock, PO Box 676, Bridgetown, BB 11000, Barbados (office). *Telephone:* 430-7800 (office). *Fax:* 430-7815 (office). *E-mail:* britishhcb@sunbeach.net (office). *Website:* www.britishhighcommission.gov.uk/barbados (office).

TAYLOR, John B., BA, DEcon; American economist and government official; *Mary and Robert Raymond Professor of Economics, Stanford University;* b. 8 Dec. 1946, Yonkers, NY; m. Allyn Taylor; two c. *Education:* Princeton Univ., Stanford Univ. *Career:* Mary and Robert Raymond Prof. of Econs, Stanford Univ., also Sr Fellow, Hoover Inst., fmr Dir Stanford Inst. for Econ. Policy Research, fmr Dir Introductory Econs Center, fmr Chair. Stanford Cttee on Undergraduate Studies; Sr Staff Economist and mem. Presidential Council of Econ. Advisers under Pres Gerald Ford and George Bush, Sr; Under-Sec. of Treasury for Int. Affairs 2001–05; mem. California Council of Econ. Advisers under Gov. Arnold Shwarzenegger 2005–; Fellow, American Acad. of Arts and Sciences; Medal of Repub. of Uruguay 2005; Hoagland Prize 1992, Lilian and Thomas B. Rhodes Prize 1997, Alexander Hamilton Award 2005, George Shultz Award 2005, Adam Smith Award 2007.
Address: Stanford University, Department of Economics, Stanford, CA 94305, USA (office). *Telephone:* (650) 723-9677 (office). *E-mail:* JohnBTaylor@stanford.edu (office). *Website:* www.stanford.edu/ ~johntayl (office).

TAYLOR, Lance Jerome, BS, PhD; American economist and academic; *Arnhold Professor of International Co-operation and Development, New School University;* b. 25 May 1940, Montpelier, Idaho; m. Yvonne S. M. Taylor 1963; one s. one d. *Education:* Calif. Inst. of Tech., Harvard Univ. *Career:* Asst then Assoc. Prof., Harvard Univ. 1968–74; Prof., MIT 1974–93; Arnhold Prof. of Int. Co-operation and Devt, New School for Social Research (now New School Univ.), New York 1993–, also Dir Center for Econ. Policy Analysis –2008, now Faculty Research Fellow; Visiting Prof., Univ. of Brasília 1973–74, Delhi School of Econs 1987–88, Stockholm School of Econs 1990; consultant for UN agencies and over 25 govts and agencies; Marshall Lecturer, Univ. of Cambridge 1987; V. K. Ramaswamy Lecturer, Delhi School of Econs 1988. *Publications:* Structuralist Macroeconomics 1983, Varieties of Stabilization Experience 1988, Income Distribution, Inflation and Growth 1991, The Market Meets its Match: Restructuring the Economies of Eastern Europe 1994, Global Finance at Risk 2000, Reconstructing Macroeconomics 2003.
Address: Center for Economic Policy Analysis, New School University, 80 Fifth Avenue 5th Floor, Room 509, New York, NY 10011 (office); 15 Old County Road, P.O. Box 378, Washington, ME 04574, USA (home). *Telephone:* (212) 229-5901 ext. 352 (office); (207) 845-2722 (home). *Fax:* (212) 229-5903 (office); (207) 845-2589 (home). *E-mail:* taylorl@newschool .edu (office); lance@blacklocust.com (home). *Website:* www.newschool .edu/cepa (office).

TAYLOR, Terence; British international organization executive; *Director, International Council for the Life Sciences; Career:* fmr career officer, British Army, counter-terrorist operations and UN peace-keeping; on staff, Ministry of Defence, UK 1985–92; Commr, UN Special Comm. on Iraq 1993–95, Chief Inspector 1993–97; Research Fellow, Science Program, Center for Int. Security and Co-operation, Stanford Univ., CA 1993–94; consultant to US Dept of Energy, Int. Cttee of the Red Cross; Political Affairs Officer, Dept of Disarmament Affairs, UN HQ, New York 1994–95; joined IISS 1995, Asst Dir, Pres. and Exec. Dir IISS-US 2001–05; Dir Int. Council for Life Sciences 2006–; fmr mem. UK Dels at UN Gen. Ass.'s Cttee on Disarmament, UN Disarmament Comm.
Address: International Council for the Life Sciences, 1747 Pennsylvania Avenue, NW, 7th Floor, Washington, DC, 20006, USA (office). *Telephone:* (202) 659-8058 (office). *Fax:* (202) 659-8074 (office); (20) 7836 3108 (London) (office). *E-mail:* taylor@iclscharter.org (office).

TAYLOR, William B., Jr; American diplomatist; *Ambassador to Ukraine;* m. two c. *Education:* US Mil. Acad., West Point and Kennedy School of Govt, Harvard Univ. *Career:* served as infantry officer in US Army in Vietnam and Germany; Foreign Service postings as Deputy Defense Advisor, US Mission to NATO, in Washington on staff of US Senator Bill Bradley, at Nat. Defense Univ. and in Dept of Energy, coordinator (with rank of Amb.) of US Govt assistance to fmr Soviet Union and Eastern Europe 1992–2002, coordinator of US Govt and int. assistance to Afghanistan,

Kabul 2002–03, Dir Iraq Reconstruction Man. Office, Baghdad 2004–05, US Rep. to Quartet's effort to facilitate Israeli disengagement from Gaza and parts of West Bank 2005–06, Amb. to Ukraine 2006–.
Address: US Embassy, vul. Yuriya Kotsyubynskoho 10, 01901 Kiev, Ukraine (office). *Telephone:* (44) 490-40-00 (office). *Fax:* (44) 490-40-85 (office). *E-mail:* press@usembassy.kiev.ua (office). *Website:* kiev .usembassy.gov (office).

TAZHIN, Marat Muhanbetkaziyevich, PhD; Kazakhstani politician; *Minister of Foreign Affairs;* b. 8 April 1960, Aktubinsk. *Education:* Almaty Inst. of Nat. Economy and Kazakh State Univ. *Career:* began career as scientific researcher –1992; First Deputy Head, then Head of Internal Policy Dept, Deputy Chief of Presidential Apparatus, Head of Information and Analysis Center, Office of the Pres. 1992–94; State Adviser to Pres. 1994–95; Deputy Head, Admin of Pres. and Head, Analysis and Strategic Research Center 1995–99; Nat. Security Asst to Pres. 1999–2001, 2002, 2006–07; Sec., Security Council 1999–2001, Chair. 2001; First Deputy Chief, Admin of Pres. 2002–06; Minister of Foreign Affairs 2007–; Order of Kurmet, Order of Barys.
Address: Ministry of Foreign Affairs, 010000 Astana, 35 Street No. 1, Left Bank of Essil River, Kazakhstan (office). *Telephone:* (3172) 72-05-18 (office). *Fax:* (3172) 72-05-16 (office). *E-mail:* midrk@mid.kz (office). *Website:* www.mfa.kz (office).

TEA BANH, Lt-Gen.; Cambodian politician; *Deputy Prime Minister and Minister of Defence;* b. 5 Nov. 1945, Koh Kong Prov.; m. Tao Toeun 1955; three c. *Career:* platoon Commdr Koh Kong Prov. 1962–69, Co. Commdr 1969–70, Mil. Commdr and Dir Training 1973–79; Deputy Chief of Staff in charge of Telecommunications and Air Force 1979–80, Deputy Minister of Nat. Defence in charge of Telecommunications and Air Force 1980–82; Minister of Communications Transport and Posts 1982–87; Vice-Chair. Council of Ministers 1984–88; mem. Parl. for Siem Reap Prov. 1988–; Minister of Nat. Defence 1987–88, 1993–94, 2006–, Deputy Minister 1988–93, Co-Minister 1994–2006; Deputy Prime Minister 2006–; Co-Deputy C-in-C Nat. Armed Forces 1994–95.
Address: blvd Confederation de la Russie, cnr rue 175, Phnom-Penh, Cambodia (office). *Telephone:* (23) 883184 (office). *Fax:* (23) 366169 (office). *E-mail:* info@mond.gov.kh (office). *Website:* www.mond.gov.kh (office).

TEEWE, Natan; I-Kiribati lawyer and politician; *Minister of Finance and Economic Development; Career:* Minister for Communications, Transport and Tourism Devt –2007, of Finance and Econ. Devt 2007–; mem. Boutokaan Te Koaua Party.
Address: Ministry of Finance and Economic Development, POB 67, Bairiki, Tarawa, Kiribati (office). *Telephone:* 21802. *Fax:* 21307.

TEFFT, John F., BA, MA; American diplomatist; *Ambassador to Georgia;* m. Mariella Cellitti Tefft; two d. *Education:* Marquette Univ., Milwaukee and Georgetown Univ., Washington, DC. *Career:* mem. Sr Foreign Service since 1973, rank of Minister-Counselor, overseas assignments in Jerusalem, Budapest and Rome, Chargé d'affaires a.i., Embassy in Moscow 1996–97, Deputy Chief of Mission, Moscow 1996–99, Amb. to Lithuania 2000–03, Int. Affairs Advisor, Nat. War Coll., Washington, DC 2003–04, Deputy Asst Sec. of State for European and Eurasian Affairs 2004, Amb. to Georgia 2004–; Distinguished Honor Award 1992, Deputy Chief of Mission of the Year Award 1999, Presidential Meritorious Service Award 2001, 2005.
Address: Embassy of the USA, 0131 Tbilisi, George Balanchine 11, Georgia (office). *Telephone:* (32) 27-70-00 (office). *Fax:* (32) 53-23-10 (office). *E-mail:* consulate-tbilisi@state.gov (office). *Website:* georgia.usembassy .gov (office).

TEIKMANIS, Andris; Latvian civil servant and diplomatist; *Ambassador to Russian Federation;* b. 29 Nov. 1959, Riga; m.; one s. one d. *Education:* Latvian State Univ. *Career:* inspector, Riga Dept of Internal Affairs 1983–88; judge, Kirov area of Riga 1988–89; elected to Council of People's Deputies of Riga 1989, Chair. 1990; remained in Riga admin 1991–92; Chair. Riga's Duma (Mayor of Riga) 1992; mem. Supreme Council of the Latvian Repub. (Latvijas Republikas Augstakaja padome) 1990–93; Co-founder Awakening (Atmoda), Latvian Popular Front (Lavijas Tautas fronte) (later Head of); Special Envoy to European Council, Strasbourg 1994–95, Perm. Rep. to Council of Europe 1995–98, Amb. to Germany 1998–2002, Under-Sec. of State, Ministry of Foreign Affairs 2002–05, Amb. to Russian Fed. 2005–; mem. Soviet Del. to Int. Youth Meeting For 'Freedom and Democracy', Paris 1989; Three Star Order 2000.
Address: Embassy of Latvia, 105062 Moscow, ul. Chaplygina 3, Russian Federation (office). *Telephone:* (495) 232-97-60 (office). *Fax:* (495) 232-97-50 (office). *E-mail:* embassy.russia@am.gov.lv (office). *Website:* www.am .gov.lv/lv/moscow (office).

TEIRLINCK, Luc; Belgian diplomatist; b. 1950. *Career:* over 30 years with Belgian diplomatic service, including fmr Amb. to SA, Amb. to Netherlands 2003–07.
Address: Belgian Federal Foreign Office, Karmelietenstraat 15, 1000 Brussels, Belgium (office). *Telephone:* (2) 501-81-11 (office). *Website:* www.diplomatie.be (office).

TEIXEIRA DOS SANTOS, Fernando, PhD; Portuguese government official and economist; *Minister of State and of Finance;* b. 13 Sept. 1951; m. Maria Clementina Pereira Nunes. *Education:* Univ. of Porto, Univ. of SC, USA. *Career:* Chair. European Regional Cttee, Int. Org. of Securities Comms (IOSCO) 2004–05, Instituto Iberoamericano de Mercado de Valores, Cttee of European Securities Regulators Expert Group, Portuguese Securities Exchange Comm.; Prof. of Economics, Univ. of Porto 1986–95; Sec. of State for the Treasury and Finance 1995–99; Pres. Comissão do Mercado de Valores Mobiliários 2000–05; Minister of State and of Finance 2005–; Gov. for Portugal, EIB; Grand Official of the Order Infante D. Henrique 2005.
Address: Ministry of Finance, Rua da Alfândega 5, 1149-006 Lisbon, Portugal (office). *Telephone:* (21) 8846600 (office). *Fax:* (21) 8846651 (office). *E-mail:* relacoes.publicas@sgmf.pt (office). *Website:* www.min -financas.pt (office).

TEIXEIRA PINTO, Elsa; São Tomé and Príncipe politician; *Minister of Defence and Internal Order; Career:* Sec. of State for State Reforms and Public Admin 2002–04; fmr Minister for Justice, State Reforms and Public Admin; Minister of Defence and Internal Order 2008–; mem. Movimento de Libertação de São Tomé e Príncipe—Partido Social Democrata.
Address: Ministry of Defence and Internal Order, Av. 12 de Julho, CP 427, São Tomé, São Tomé and Príncipe (office). *Telephone:* 222041 (office). *E-mail:* midefesa@cstome.net (office). *Website:* www.mindefordInterna .gov.st (office).

TEJAN-JALLOH, (Alhaji) Sulaiman; Sierra Leonean diplomatist and politician; m. Mariama Tejan-Jalloh. *Career:* early career as barrister; Minister of Transport and Communications 1996–97; Deputy High Commr to UK –2000, High Commr to UK (also accred as Amb. to Ireland and Denmark) 2000–06, to USA 2006–08 (recalled following allegations of obtaining false passports).
Address: Ministry of Foreign Affairs, Gloucester Street, Freetown, Sierra Leone (office). *Telephone:* (22) 223260 (office). *Fax:* (22) 225615 (office). *E-mail:* mfaicsl@yahoo.com (office).

TELES CARREIRA, Ana Maria; Angolan diplomatist; *Ambassador to UK;* m. Mario Afonso D'Almeida. *Career:* Amb. to India (also accred to Thailand) 2001–05, to UK (also accred to Ireland) 2005–; fmr Chair. Southern African Devt Community.
Address: Embassy of Angola, 22 Dorset Street, London, W1U 6QY, England (office). *Telephone:* (20) 7299-9850 (office). *Fax:* (20) 7486-9397 (office). *E-mail:* embassy@angola.org.uk (office). *Website:* www.angola .org.uk (office).

TELIČKA, Pavel; Czech diplomatist, lawyer and university teacher; *Partner, BXL Consulting;* b. 24 Aug. 1965, Washington, USA; m. Eva Teličková; one s. one d. *Education:* Charles Univ., Prague. *Career:* joined Ministry of Foreign Affairs 1986, mem. of del. for talks on Czech membership of EU 1991, with Czech Standing Mission to EU 1991–95, Deputy Amb. to Brussels 1993–95; Dir of Dept in Ministry of Foreign Affairs 1995–98, Dir-Gen. Dept for EU and NATO 1998; Deputy Chair. Comm. for Czech Integration to EU 1998, Chief Negotiator 1998–99; Deputy Minister for Foreign Affairs 1998–99; apptd State Sec. for European Affairs 1999; Amb. and Head, Perm. Mission of Czech Repub. to European Communities 2003–04, EU Commr without Portfolio 2004; currently Co-founder and Pnr, BXL Consulting (consults on EU affairs); Sr External Adviser, European Policy Centre; mem. Admin. Council, Notre Europe Foundation, Paris; mem. Europe-USA-Asia Trilateral Comm.; Hon. mem. Man. Bd Nat. Training Fund 1999–2003, Centre of Good Will 2001–; mem. Bd Govs Univ. of Tomase Bati 2001–03; mem. Tomáš Bata Foundation 1997–; Pres. Václav Havel Commemorative Medal 2003, Commemorative Medal of King Jiří z Poděbrad 2003. *Publications:* (with K. Barták) How Were We Entering the EU? 2003.
Address: BXL Consulting, Rond-Point Schuman 11, 1040 Brussels, Belgium (office). *Telephone:* (2) 256-75-15 (office). *Fax:* (2) 256-75-18 (office). *E-mail:* office@bxl.cz (office). *Website:* www.bxl.cz (office).

TELITO, Rev. and Rt Hon. Sir Filoimea, GCMG, MBE; Tuvaluan government official; *Governor-General;* b. Vaitupu Island. *Career:* fmr school prin. and church pastor; Gov.-Gen. of Tuvalu 2005–.

Address: Office of the Governor-General, Private Mail Bag, Vaiaku, Funafuti, Tuvalu (office). *Telephone:* 20715 (office). *Website:* www .tuvaluislands.com (office).

TEMARU, Oscar Manutahi; French Polynesian politician; *President;* b. 1 Nov. 1944, Faa'a Dist, Tahiti; m. Marie Temaru; seven c. *Career:* in French Navy 1961–63; customs officer 1964–99; f. Front de Libération de la Polynésie—FLP (Polynesia Liberation Front) 1977 (changed party name to Tavini Huiraatira no te ao maohi—Serve the Polynesian People 1983); Mayor of Faa'a 1983; elected mem. Territorial Ass. 1986; mem. UPD Party (Union for Democracy); Pres. of French Polynesia June–Oct. 2004, 2005–06, 2007–.
Address: Office of the President of the Government, BP 2551, 98713 Papeete, French Polynesia (office). *Telephone:* 472121 (office). *Fax:* 472210 (office). *Website:* www.presidence.pf (office).

TEO, Rear-Adm. (retd) Chee Hean, MSc, MPA; Singaporean politician and fmr naval officer; *Minister for Defence;* b. 27 Dec. 1954; m. Chew Poh Yim; one s. one d. *Education:* St Michael's School, St Joseph's Inst., Singapore Armed Forces Training Inst., UMIST, Manchester, Imperial Coll., London, Kennedy School of Govt, Harvard Univ. *Career:* various command and staff appointments in Repub. of Singapore Navy and Jt Staff 1977–86, Chief of Navy 1991, rank of Rear-Adm. 1991, retd 1992; MP for Marine Parade Group Representation Constituency 1992–97, becoming Minister of State in Ministries of Finance, Communications and Defence; Acting Minister for Environment and Sr Minister of State for Defence 1995–96, Minister for Environment and Second Minister for Defence 1996–97, MP for Pasir Ris Group Representation Constituency 1997–, Minister for Educ. and Second Minister for Defence 1997–2001, Minister for Defence 2003–.
Address: Ministry of Defence, Gombak Drive, off Upper Bukit Timah Road, Mindeg Building, Singapore 669645, Singapore (office). *Telephone:* 67608844 (office). *Fax:* 67646119 (office). *Website:* www.mindef.gov.sg (office).

TEO, Michael Eng Cheng, BBA, MA; Singaporean diplomatist and air force officer (retd); *High Commissioner to UK;* b. 19 Sept. 1947, Sarawak; m. Joyce Teo (née Ng Sinn Toh); one s. one d. *Education:* Auburn Univ., Fletcher School of Law and Diplomacy, Tufts Univ., USAF War Coll., USA. *Career:* joined Repub. of Singapore Air Force 1968, Commdr 1985, Brig.-Gen. 1987, Chief of Air Force 1990 (retd); joined Diplomatic Sevice 1993, High Commr to NZ 1994–96, Amb. to Repub. of Korea 1996–2001, High Commr to UK (also accred as Amb. to Ireland) 2002–; The Most Noble Order of the Crown (Thailand) 1981, Legion of Merit, Degree of Commdr (USA) 1991, Order of Diplomatic Service Merit Gwanghwa Medal (Repub. of Korea) 2002; Public Admin Medal (Singapore) 1989, Outstanding Achievement Award (Philippines) 1989, Bintang Swa Bhuana Paksa Utama (Indonesia) 1991.
Address: Singapore High Commission, 9 Wilton Crescent, London, SW1X 8SP, England (office). *Telephone:* (20) 7201-5850 (office). *Fax:* (20) 7245-6583 (office). *E-mail:* info@singaporehc.org.uk (office); singhc_lon@sgmfa .gov.sg (office). *Website:* www.mfa.gov.sg/london (office).

TEODORO, Gilberto ('Gilbert') Cojuangco, Jr, BSc, LLB, LLM; Philippine lawyer, politician and air force officer; *Secretary of National Defense;* b. 14 June 1964, Manila; m. Monica Prieto-Teodoro; one s. *Education:* Xavier School, De La Salle Univ., Univ. of the Phillipines (UP), Harvard Law School, USA, Air Command and Staff Coll. of the Philippine Air Force, Jt Command and Staff Coll. *Career:* Pres. Kabataang Barangay for Cen. Luzon 1980–85, for Prov. of Tarlac 1980–85; mem. Sangkuniang Panlalawigan, for Prov. of Tarlac 1980–86; called to the Phillipines Bar 1989; lawyer, EP Mendoza Law firm 1990–97; admitted to State Bar of NY, USA 1997; Congressman of First Dist of Tarlac 1998–, Asst Majority Leader (11th Congress), Head of Nationalist People's Coalition House mems and mem. House contingent to Legis.-Exec. Devt Advisory Council; Sec. of Nat. Defense (youngest Sec. to hold Defense portfolio) 2007–; licensed commercial pilot; Col, Philippine Air Force, 0-133104 E (Reserve Force); Asst Faculty mem. Command and Gen. Staff Course; Lecturer, Air Command Staff Coll.; Chair. Philippine Nat. Police Foundation Inc.; mem. Integrated Bar of the Philippines, UP Alumni Asscn, UP Law Alumni Asscn, Harvard Alumni Asscn, Harvard Law Alumni Asscn; Lifetime mem. Armor-Cavalry Asscn of the Philippines; Hon. Command Pilot, Philippine Air Force; Hon. mem. PMA Alumni Asscn Sponsoring Class – '76, Philippine Air Force Aviation Cadet Alumni Asscn Sponsoring Class – '80, Asscn of Chiefs of Police of the Philippines, Inc.; Mil. Merit Medal, Philippine Air Force Gen. Staff Course Badge, Presidential Flight Crew Badge, Mil. Civic Action Medal (Plain), Mil. Civic Action Medal with Bronze Service Star, Mil. Civic Action Medal with Second Service Star; Dean's Medal for Academic Excellence, Univ. of the Phillipines 1989, Leadership and Seminar Academic Excellence Awardee, Air Command and Staff Coll. of the Philippine Air Force 2001, Leadership Award, Jt Command and Staff Coll. 2003; numerous mil. awards and commendations, including Basic RASS Aeronautical Badge, Caliber .45 Pistol Expert Marksmanship Badge, M-16 Rifle Marksmanship Badge.
Address: Department of National Defense, DND Building, 3rd Floor, Camp Aguinaldo, Quezon City, 1100 Metro Manila, The Phillipines (office). *Telephone:* (2) 9113300 (office). *Fax:* (2) 9116213 (office). *E-mail:* webmaster@dnd.gov.ph (office). *Website:* www.dnd.gov.ph (office).

TER-MINASSIAN, Teresa, MS (Econs); Italian economist and international finance official; *Director, Fiscal Affairs Department, International Monetary Fund; Education:* Univ. of Rome, Harvard Univ., USA. *Career:* began career in Research Dept Bank of Italy 1967–71; joined IMF as economist in Fiscal Affairs Dept 1971, Deputy Dir 1988–97, Dir 2001–, also experience in fmr European Dept, Deputy Dir Western Hemisphere Dept 1997–2001. *Publication:* Fiscal Federalism in Theory and Practice 1997.
Address: IMF, 700 19th Street, NW, Washington, DC 20431, USA (office). *Telephone:* (202) 623-8844 (office). *Fax:* (202) 623-4259 (office). *E-mail:* tterminassian@imf.org (office).

TERENGGANU, HM The Sultan of; Tuanku Mizan Zainal Abidin; Malaysian; *Yang di-Pertuan Agong (Supreme Head of State);* b. 22 Jan. 1962, Kuala Terengganu; m. Permaisuri Nur Zahirah Cik Puan Seri Rozita Adil Bakeri 1996; one s. one d. *Career:* apptd Heir Apparent Yang di-Pertuan Muda of Terengganu 1979; 16th Sultan of Terengganu 1998–; Timbalan Yang di-Pertuan Agong (Deputy Supreme Head of State) 1999–2006; Col-in-Chief Royal Armoured Corps; elected as 13th Yang di-Pertuan Agong (Supreme Head of State) 13 Dec. 2006, crowned 26 April 2007.
Address: Istana Badariah, 20500 Kuala Terengganu, Malaysia (office).

TERESHKOVA, Maj.-Gen. Valentina Vladimirovna, CandTechSc; Russian politician and fmr cosmonaut; *Head, Russian Centre for International Scientific and Cultural Co-operation;* b. 6 March 1937, Maslennikovo, Yaroslavl Region; m. 1963 (divorced); one d. *Education:* Yaroslavl Textile Coll. and Zhukovsky Air Force Engineering Acad. *Career:* fmr textile worker, Krasny Perekop textile mill, Yaroslavl; Textile Mill Sec., Young Communist League 1960; joined Yaroslavl Air Sports Club 1959 and started parachute jumping; mem. CPSU 1962–91, Cen. Cttee CPSU 1971–90; began cosmonaut training March 1962; made 48 orbits of the Earth in spaceship Vostok VI 16–19 June 1963; first woman in world to enter space; Deputy to USSR Supreme Soviet 1966–90; USSR People's Deputy 1989–91; Chair. Soviet Women's Cttee 1968–87; mem. Supreme Soviet Presidium 1970–90; Head Union of Soviet Socs. for Friendship and Cultural Relations with Foreign Countries 1987–92; Chair. then Dir of Presidium, Russian Asscn of Int. Co-operation (now Russian Centre of Int. Scientific and Cultural Co-operation) 1992–; Pres. Moscow House of Europe 1992–; Head Russian Centre for Int. Scientific and Cultural Co-operation 1994–; visit to UK 1977; Pilot-Cosmonaut of USSR, Hero of Soviet Union, Joliot-Curie Gold Medal, World Peace Council 1966, Order of the Nile (Egypt) 1971 and other decorations.
Address: Russian Centre of International Co-operation, 103885 Moscow, Vozdvizhenka Str. 14–18, Russia. *Telephone:* (495) 290-12-45.

TESAURO, Giuseppe; Italian professor of international law; *President, Autorità Garante della Concorrenza e del Mercato;* b. 15 Nov. 1942, Naples; m. Paola Borrelli 1967; three c. *Education:* Liceo Umberto, Naples, Univ. of Naples, Max Planck Inst. Volkerrecht-Heidelberg. *Career:* Asst Prof. of Int. Law, Univ. of Naples 1965–71; Prof. of Int. Law and Int. Org., Univs of Catania, Messina, Naples, Rome 1971–88; Dir EEC Law School, Univ. of Rome 1982–88; mem. Council Legal Affairs, Ministry of Foreign Affairs 1986–; Judge, First Advocate Gen. European Court of Justice 1988–98; Pres. Italian Competition Authority 1998–. *Publications:* Financing International Institutions 1968, Pollution of the Sea and International Law 1971, Nationalizations and International Law 1976, Movements of Capital in the EEC 1984, Course of EEC Law 1988.
Address: Autorità Garante della Concorrenza e del Mercato, Piazza Verdi 6/A, 00198 Rome, Italy (office). *Telephone:* (06) 858211 (office). *Fax:* (06) 85821256 (office). *E-mail:* antitrust@agcm.it (office). *Website:* www.agcm .it (office).

TESFAY, Girma Asmerom, MA; Eritrean diplomatist; *Permanent Representative to the European Union;* b. 10 Dec. 1949. *Education:* Bowdoin Coll., Brunswick, Me, Grad. School, American Univ., School of Int. Service, Washington, DC, USA. *Career:* mem. Ethiopian Olympic Nat. Soccer Team 1968; soccer coach, Washington, DC Summer Program 1970–74; Asst Soccer Coach, Federal City Coll., Washington, DC 1973–74; Researcher, Nicholson & Carter (law firm), Washington, DC 1974–75; contrib., Monthly Newsletter, Pride Inc., Washington, DC 1975–76; joined Eritrean People's Liberation Front (EPLF) 1977, mem. EPLF Dept of

Educ. Editorial Bd 1977–79, Head, Amharic Radio Programme and Amharic Newsletter, EPLF Dept of Information 1979–87, Head of Information, EPLF Dept of Foreign Relations 1987–90, Head of Protocol 1990–91, Chief of Protocol, State and Ministry of Foreign Affairs 1991–92, Head of Eritrean TV, Ministry of Information and Culture 1992–93, Head of African Affairs, Ministry of Foreign Affairs 1993–96; Amb. to Ethiopia 1997–99, to S Africa 1999–2001, to USA and Canada 2001–06, Amb. and Perm. Rep. to EU 2007–.
Address: Ministry of Foreign Affairs, PO Box 190, Asmara, Eritrea (office). *Telephone:* (1) 127838 (office). *Fax:* (1) 123788 (office). *E-mail:* tesfai@wg.eol (office).

TESHABAEV, Fatikh G., PhD; Uzbekistan diplomatist; *Special Adviser in Uzbekistan, United Nations Development Programme (UNDP);* b. 18 Oct. 1939, Tashkent; m. Mauluda Teshabaev 1966; two s. one d. *Education:* Univs. of Tashkent and Delhi. *Career:* First Deputy Minister for Foreign Affairs 1991–93; Amb. to USA and Perm. Rep. to UN 1993–96; Amb.-at-Large 1996–97; Amb. to UK 1997–99; Special Adviser, UNDP in Uzbekistan 2000–; Nehru Award. *Publications:* articles on political thought in oriental countries.
Address: United Nations Development Programme, 4 T. Shevchenko Street, 100029 Tashkent; Birinchitor Kucha Topqairagoch 12, 100081 Tashkent, Uzbekistan (home). *Telephone:* (71) 2791786 (home); (71) 1055860. *E-mail:* fatih.teshabaev@undp.org (office); teshabaev2002@yahoo.com.

TESORIERE, (Harcourt) Andrew (Pretorius), BSc, FRGS; British diplomatist; *OSCE Ambassador to Kyrgyzstan;* b. 2 Nov. 1950; m. Dr Alma Gloria Vasquez. *Education:* Nautical Coll., Pangbourne, Britannia Royal Naval Coll., Dartmouth, Univ. Coll. of Wales, Aberystwyth, Ecole Nat. d'Admin, Paris, France. *Career:* RN Officer, attachments to army 1969–74; joined FCO 1974, language student, SOAS, 1975, British Embassy, Tehran 1975, Oriental Sec., British Embassy, Kabul 1976–79, British Embassy, Nairobi 1979–81, Second Sec. and Vice-Consul, British Embassy, Abidjan 1981–85, FCO 1985–87, First Sec. and Head of Chancery, later Charge d'Affaires, British Embassy, Damascus, Syria 1987–91, First Sec., FCO 1991–94; Head, UN Humanitarian Field Operations Afghanistan 1994–95; Amb. to Albania 1996–98; Head, UN Special Mission to Afghanistan 1998–2000; Chargé d'Affaires, Afghanistan 2001–02; Amb. to Latvia 2002–05, to Algeria 2005–07; Special Advisor to NATO Commander in Afghanistan (South) 2007–08; OSCE Ambassador to Kyrgyzstan 2008–; NATO Medal (ISAF).
Address: c/o Foreign and Commonwealth Office, King Charles St, London, SW1A 2AH, England (office). *Telephone:* (20) 7008-1500 (office). *Website:* www.fco.gov.uk (office).

TEVES, Margarito B., BA, MSc; Philippine government official and economist; *Secretary of Finance; Education:* Universidad Cen. de Madrid, Spain, Williams Coll., USA. *Career:* mem. Congress 1987–98, Chair. Cttee on Rural Devt, on Econ. Affairs; Chair. and CEO Think Tank Inc. 1998–2000; Pres. and CEO Land Bank of the Philippines 2000–05; Sec. of Finance 2005–; Chair. People's Credit and Finance Corpn, Philippine Crop Insurance Corpn; mem. Bd Manila Electric Co., PhilEquity Fund Inc.; mem. Council, Nat. Food Authority, Food Terminal Inc.; f. Corporate Planning Soc. of the Philippines; fmr Pres. Philippine Econ. Soc.; fmr Trustee Philippine Futuristics Soc.
Address: Department of Finance, DOF Building, Roxas Boulearvd, cnr Pablo Ocampo Street, 1004 Metro Manila, Philippines (office). *Telephone:* (2) 4041774 (office). *Fax:* (2) 5219495 (office). *E-mail:* hotline@dof.gov.ph (office). *Website:* www.dof.gov.ph (office).

TÉVOÉDJRÈ, Albert, LèsL; Benin politician and international civil servant; *Ombudsman, Presidential Mediation Board;* b. 10 Nov. 1929, Porto Novo; m. Isabelle Ekué 1953; three s. *Education:* Toulouse Univ., France, Fribourg Univ., Switzerland, Institut Universitaire de Hautes Etudes Internationales, Geneva, Sloan School of Management and MIT, USA. *Career:* teaching assignments include Lycée Delafosse, Dakar, Senegal 1952–54, Ecole Normale d'Institutrices, Cahors, France 1957–58, Lycée Victor Ballot, Porto Novo 1959–61, Geneva Africa Inst. 1963–64, Georgetown Univ., Washington, DC 1964; Sec. of State for Information 1961–62; Sec.-Gen. Union Africaine et Malgache (UAM) 1962–63; Research Assoc., Center for Int. Affairs, Harvard Univ. 1964–65; joined Int. Labour Office 1965, Regional Dir for Africa March 1966, Asst Dir-Gen. 1969–75, Deputy Dir-Gen. 1975; Dir Int. Inst. for Labour Studies 1975–84; Sec.-Gen. World Social Prospects Asscn (AMPS) 1980–; fmr Chief Ed. L'Etudiant d'Afrique Noire; Minister of Planning and Employment Promotion 1997–99; Chair. Millennium for Africa Comm. –2002; Special Envoy of the UN Sec.-Gen. in Ivory Coast 2003–05; Ombudsman, Presidential Mediation Bd (OPM) 2006–; Founding mem. Promotion Africaine (soc. to combat poverty in Africa); Founding mem. Nat.

Liberation Movt and mem. Cttee 1958–60; Deputy Sec.-Gen. of Nat. Syndicate of Teachers, Dahomey 1959–60; Visiting Prof., Sorbonne, Paris 1979–, Univ. des Mutants, Dakar 1979–, Nat. Univ. of Côte d'Ivoire 1979–, Northwestern Univ. 1980; Int. Humanitarian Medal 1987. *Publications:* L'Afrique revoltée 1958, La formation des cadres africains en vue de la croissance économique 1965, Pan-Africanism in Action 1965, L'Afrique face aux problèmes du socialisme et de l'aide étrangère 1966, Une stratégie du progrès social en Afrique et la contribution de l'OIT 1969, Pour un contrat de solidarité 1976, La pauvreté—richesse des peuples 1978, etc.
Address: Place de la République, 01BP, 1501 Port-Novo, Benin (office). *Telephone:* 20-21-20-22 (office). *Fax:* 20-21-44-36 (office). *E-mail:* webmaster@mediateur.gouv.bj (office). *Website:* www.mediateur.gouv.bj (office).

THAÇI, Hashim, PhD; Kosovo politician and fmr guerrilla leader; *Prime Minister;* b. 24 April 1968, Burojë; m.; one s. *Education:* Univ. of Zurich, Switzerland. *Career:* fmr Commdr Kosovo Liberation Army, fmr Dir Political Group; Chair. Partia Demokratike e Kosovës (PDK—Democratic Party of Kosovo–fmrly Party for the Democratic Progress of Kosovo) 2000–, mem. Parl. Group 2006–; mem. and Prime Minister, Interim Admin. Council, Kosovo 1999–2001, Prime Minister of Kosovo 2008–.
Address: Office of the Government of Kosovo, 10000 Prishtina, Rruga Nënë Terezë (office); Partia Demokratike e Kosovës, 10000 Prishtina, Rruge Nënë Terezë 20; Arbëria, Rruge Metush Krasniqi 22, 10000 Prishtina, Kosovo. *Telephone:* (38) 224262. *Fax:* (38) 223769. *E-mail:* webmaster@ks-gov.net (office); pdk@pdk-ks.org. *Website:* www.ks-gov.net/pm (office); www.pdk-ks.org.

THAHANE, Timothy T., BComm, MA; Lesotho government official and diplomatist; *Minister of Finance and Development Planning;* b. 2 Nov. 1940, Leribe; m. Dr Edith Mohapi 1972; one s. one d. *Education:* Lesotho High School, Univs of Newfoundland and Toronto, Canada. *Career:* Asst Sec., Prin. Asst Sec., Cen. Planning Office 1968–70, Dir of Planning 1968–73; Amb. to EEC for Negotiations of Lomé Convention 1973–74; Alt. Exec. Dir (Africa Group 1) World Bank 1974–76, Exec. Dir 1976–78, representing 15 African countries and Trinidad and Tobago; Vice-Chair. and Chair., Jt Audit Cttee of World Bank Group 1976–78; Amb. to the USA 1978–80; Vice-Pres. UN Affairs, IBRD 1990–96; Deputy Gov. South African Reserve Bank 1996–2002; Minister of Finance and Devt Planning 2002–; Vice-Pres. and Sec., IBRD 1980–96; Dir Bd of Global Coalition for Africa, Washington 1992–; mem. Bd of Lesotho Bank (Vice-Chair. 1972–73), Third World Foundation, Centre for Econ. Devt and Population Activities, Washington, DC. *Publications:* articles on econ. planning and investment in Lesotho, Southern Africa and Africa in general.
Address: Ministry of Finance and Development Planning, POB 395, Maseru 100, Lesotho (office). *Telephone:* 22310826 (office). *Fax:* 22310411 (office). *E-mail:* hmf@finance.gov.ls (office); thahanet@finance.gov.ls (office). *Website:* www.finance.gov.ls (office).

THAM, Carl Gustav Wilhelm; Swedish diplomatist (retd); b. 5 July 1939, Stockholm. *Education:* Univ. of Stockholm. *Career:* Gen. Sec. Liberal Party 1969–76; State Sec., Ministry of Employment 1976–78; Minister of Energy 1978–79; Special Adviser on Devt Assistance Issues 1979–81, State Sec. for Devt Assistance Issues, State Dept 1981–82; Gen. Man. SIDA 1985–94; Minister of Educ. and Science 1994–98; Chair. Social Democratic Culture Asscn 1999–2002; Gen. Sec. Olof Palme Int. Centre 1999–2002; Amb. to Germany 2002; Chair. Action Aid Sweden; Adviser, Arbetarnas Bildningsförbund (ABF, Workers Educ. Asscn).
Address: c/o Arbetarnas Bildningsförbund, Schleegatan 18, 112 28 Stockholm, Sweden (office). *E-mail:* carl.tham@gmail.com.

THAN, Sr Gen. Shwe; Myanma politician and army officer; *Minister of Defence;* b. 2 Feb. 1933, Kyaukse; m. Daw Kyaing Kyaing. *Career:* joined army aged 20; positions included time spent in dept of psychological warfare; several other positions in army after mil. coup that ousted Prime Minister U Nu in 1962, including promotion to Lt-Col 1972, to Col 1978, to Commdr of Mil. Dist of South West 1983, Asst Man. of Gen. Staff of the Army, Brig.-Gen. and Vice-Minister of Defence 1985, Maj.-Gen. 1986; mem. Cen. Exec. Cttee 1986; Prime Minister 1992–2003, Minister of Defence 1992–; Chair. State Law and Order Restoration Council (SLORC) 1992–97, Chair. State Peace and Devt Council (SDP) 1997–.
Address: Ministry of Defence, Ahlanpya Phaya Street, Yangon; Office of the Chairman of the State Peace and Development Council, 15–16 Windermere Park, Yangon, Myanmar. *Telephone:* (1) 281611 (Ministry); (1) 282445.

THANH, Lt-Gen. Phung Quang; Vietnamese military officer and government official; *Minister of Defence;* b. 2 Feb. 1949, Vin Phuc Prov. *Education:* Univ. of Mil. Science. *Career:* fmr Commdr First Mil. Zone; fmr Chief of Gen. Staff, People's Army of Viet Nam and Deputy Minister of Defence;

Minister of Defence 2006–; mem. CP of Viet Nam Central Cttee (CPVCC); mem. Politburo.
Address: Ministry of National Defence, 1a Hoang Dieu, Ba Dinh District, Hanoi, Viet Nam (office). *Telephone:* (4) 069 882041 (office). *Fax:* (4) 069 532090 (office).

THANI, Sheikh Abdul Aziz ibn Khalifa ath-, BS; Qatari politician, international official and petroleum industry executive; *Chairman, State of Qatar Investment Board;* b. 12 Dec. 1948, Doha; one s. three d. *Education:* Northern Indiana Univ., USA. *Career:* Deputy Minister of Finance and Petroleum June–Dec. 1972, Minister of Finance and Petroleum, State of Qatar 1972; Chair. State of Qatar Investment Bd 1972–, Qatar Nat. Bank 1972, Qatar Gen. Petroleum Corpn 1973–; Gov. IMF and IBRD (World Bank) 1972; rep. at numerous int. confs including OPEC, OAPEC and Arab, Islamic and non-aligned summit confs.
Address: c/o Qatar General Petroleum Corporation, PO Box 3212, Doha, Qatar.

THANI, Sheikh Abdullah bin Khalifa ath-; Qatari politician; b. 25 Dec. 1959, Doha. *Education:* Royal Military Acad., Sandhurst UK. *Career:* various positions within Qatar Armed Forces 1976–89; Minister of the Interior 1989–96; Deputy Prime Minister 1995–96; Prime Minister of Qatar 1996–2007 (resgnd); Chair. Qatari Olympic Cttee 1979–89.
Address: c/o Office of the Prime Minister, PO Box 923, Doha, Qatar.

THANI, Sheikh Hamad bin Jasim bin Jaber ath-; Qatari politician; *Prime Minister and Minister of Foreign Affairs;* b. 1959. *Career:* Dir Office of the Minister of Municipal Affairs and Agric. 1982–89, Minister of Municipal Affairs and Agric. 1989–92; Deputy Minister of Electricity and Water 1990–92; Minister of Foreign Affairs 1992–; First Deputy Prime Minister 2003–07; Prime Minister 2007–; Head Perm. Cttee for the Support of Al Quds 1998–; mem. Supreme Defence Council 1996–, Parl. Constitution Cttee 1999–, Ruling Family Council 2000–; CEO Supreme Council for the Investment of the Reserves of State (Qatar Investment Authority) 2000–; fmr Chair. Qatar Electricity and Water Co.; fmr Pres. Cen. Municipal Council, Special Emiri Projects Office; fmr Dir Special Emiri Projects Office; fmr mem. Bd of Dirs Qatar Petroleum, Supreme Council for Planning.
Address: Ministry of Foreign Affairs, POB 250, Doha (office); Qatar Investment Authority, PO Box 23224, Doha, Qatar. *Telephone:* 4334334 (office). *Fax:* 4442777 (office). *E-mail:* webmaster@mofa.gov.qa (office). *Website:* www.mofa.gov.qa (office).

THANI, Sheikh Hamad bin Khalifa ath-, (Amir of Qatar); b. 1952, Doha; m. Sheikha Mozah bint Nasser al-Missned; five s. (including Sheikh Tamim bin Hamad bin Khalifa ath-Thani) two d. *Education:* Royal Mil. Coll., Sandhurst, UK. *Career:* apptd Heir-Apparent May 1977; Commdr First Mobile Bn (now Hamad Mobile Bn); Maj., then Maj.-Gen., C-in-C Armed Forces of Qatar; Minister of Defence May 1977–; Amir of Qatar 27 June 1995–; Prime Minister 1995–96; Supreme Pres. Higher Planning Council; Pres. Higher Youth Council 1979–91; f. Mil. Sports Fed.; mem. Int. Mil. Sports Fed.; Pres. Qatari Nat. Olympic Cttee 2000–; mem. IOC (mem. Sports for All Cttee.); Chair. Organizing Cttee. 15th Asian Games 2006; Head, Upper Council of Environment and Natural Sanctuaries; Orders of Merit from Egypt, France, Indonesia, Lebanon, Morocco, Oman, Saudi Arabia, UK, Venezuela.
Address: The Royal Palace, PO Box 923, Doha, Qatar.

THANI, HH Sheikh Tamim bin Hamad bin Khalifa ath-; Qatari; *Heir Apparent and Commander-in-Chief of the Armed Forces;* b. 3 June 1980, Doha; m. Sheikha Jawahar bint Hamad bin Sohaim ath-Thani 2005. *Education:* Sherborne School and Royal Mil. Acad., Sandhurst, UK. *Career:* proclaimed Heir Apparent 8 Aug. 2003; Officer Qatar Armed Forces 1997– (now C-in-C of the Armed Forces); Head Upper Council of the Environment and Natural Sanctuaries; Pres. as-Sadd Sports Club 1999–2000; Chair. Qatar Nat. Olympic Cttee 2000–, Organizing Cttee Asian Games, Doha 2006; mem. IOC, Supreme Educ. Council; Chair. ictQATAR programme 2005–; Sheikh Zayed bin Sultan al-Nahyan Medal of Honor, UAE 2004, Issa bin Salman al-Khalifa Order of Merit – Excellence Class, Bahrain 2004.
Address: The Royal Palace, POB 923, Doha, Qatar (office). *Website:* www.diwan.gov.qa.

THAPA, Bhek Bahadur; Nepalese diplomatist and politician. *Career:* fmr Amb. to USA, Amb. to India 1997–2003; Special Rep. for Foreign Affairs 2003–04, Minister of Foreign Affairs 2004; Amb.-at-Large 2004–.
Address: Shital Niwas, Maharaganj, Kathmandu, Nepal (office). *Telephone:* (1) 4416011 (office). *Fax:* (1) 4416016 (office). *E-mail:* mofa@mos.com.np (office). *Website:* www.mofa.gov.np (office).

THAPA, Surya Bahadur; Nepalese politician; *President, Rashtriya Janashakti Party;* b. 20 March 1928, Muga, East Nepal; m. 1953; one s. three d. *Education:* Allahabad Univ., India. *Career:* House Speaker, Advisory Ass. to King of Nepal 1958; mem. Upper House of Parl. 1959; Minister of Forests, Agric., Commerce and Industry 1960, of Finance and Econ. Affairs 1962; Vice-Chair. Council of Ministers, Minister of Finance, Econ. Planning, Law and Justice 1963; Vice-Chair. Council of Ministers, Minister of Finance, Law and Gen. Admin. 1964–65; Chair. Council of Ministers, Minister of Palace Affairs 1965–69; Prime Minister of Nepal and Minister of Palace Affairs 1979–83; Minister of Finance 1979–80, of Defence 1980–81, 1982–83, of Foreign Affairs 1982; Prime Minister of Nepal 1997–98, Prime Minister and Minister of Royal Palace Affairs, of Defence, of Home Affairs, of Foreign Affairs, of Industry, Commerce and Supplies, of Law, Justice and Parl. Affairs, of Agric. and Co-operatives, of Population and the Environment, of Water Resources, of Land Reforms and Man., of Women, Children and Social Welfare, of Forest and Soil Conservation, of Science and Tech., of Labour and Transport Man., of Gen. Admin, of Local Devt and of Health, Interim Govt 2003–04 (resgnd); Pres. Rashtriya Prajatantra Party 1990–2002; Pres. Rashtriya Janashakti Party (split from Rashtriya Prajatantra Party Nov. 2004) 2005–; mem. Royal Advisory Cttee 1969–72; arrested and released 1972, 1975; Hon. DLitt (Kurukshetra Univ.); Tri-Sahkti-Patta 1963, Gorkha Dakshinbahu I 1965, Om Rama Patta 1980; several Nepalese and foreign awards.
Address: Rashtriya Janashakti Party (National People's Power Party), Ramalphokhari, Kathmandu, Nepal (office). *Telephone:* (1) 4437063 (office). *Fax:* (1) 4437064 (office). *E-mail:* rjpnepal@info.com.np (office).

THAYEB, Mohammad Hamzah; Indonesian diplomatist; *Ambassador to Australia;* b. 31 May 1952, Paris, France; m. Lastry Thayeb; three c. *Education:* Jayabaya Univ. *Career:* public relations officer, ASEAN Nat. Secr. 1975–78, Gen. Affairs Officer 1978–83, Econ. Bureau Officer 1983–86, Political Officer, Perm. Mission of Indonesia to UN Geneva 1986–90, Officer at Foreign Minister's Secr. 1990–93, 1997–99, Political Officer, Task Force of Non-Aligned Movt, Perm. Mission of Indonesia to UN, New York 1993–95, Coordinator Task Force of UN Security Council, Perm. Mission, New York 1995–97, Head of Political Div., Perm. Mission, New York 1999–2002, Dir for Int. Security and Disarmament, Directorate Gen. for Multilateral Political, Social and Security Affairs 2002–04, Dir for E Asia and the Pacific, Directorate Gen. for Asia Pacific and African Affairs 2004–05, Amb. to Australia (also accred to Vanuatu) 2005–.
Address: Embassy of Indonesia, 8 Darwin Avenue, Yarralumla, ACT 2600, Australia (office). *Telephone:* (2) 6273-8600 (office). *Fax:* (2) 6250-6017 (office). *Website:* www.kbri-canberra.org.au (office).

THEIN SEIN, Gen. U; Myanma army officer and politician; *Prime Minister;* m. Daw Khin Khin Win. *Education:* Defence Services Academy 9. *Career:* held positions of Second and First Sec. in ruling State Peace and Devt Council junta; also serves as Chair. govt-sponsored Nat. Convention Convening Comm.; Acting Prime Minister April–Oct. 2007, Prime Minister Oct. 2007–; promoted to rank of full Gen. from Lt-Gen. (Myanmar's fourth-highest ranking gen.) 2007.
Address: Prime Minister's Office, Theinbyu Street, Botahtaung Township, Yangon, Myanmar (office). *Telephone:* (1) 283742 (office).

THÉMEREAU, Marie-Noëlle; New Caledonian politician; b. 1949; m.; two c. *Career:* served as Rep. Southern Prov. and Congress 1989–2001, Vice-Pres. Southern Prov. 1996–99, Vice-Pres. Congress of New Caledonia 1999–2001; also fmr Head Admin; Pres. New Caledonia 2004–07 (resgnd).
Address: c/o Présidence du Gouvernement, 8 route des Artifices, BP M2, 98849 Nouméa Cédex, New Caledonia (office).

THIBAULT, Paul, MA; Canadian international organization official (retd); b. April 1945; m. Denyse Dufresne; one d. *Education:* Univ. of Ottawa, Carlton Univ., Ecole nationale d'administration, Paris, France. *Career:* with Dept of External Affairs 1968–85, various positions in Ottawa and abroad including Geneva, Tehran and Paris; Dir of Operations, Priorities and Planning Secr., Privy Council Office 1985–88; Asst Sec. to the Cabinet (Security and Intelligence) 1988–92; Asst Sec. Program Br. (Govt Operations, Foreign and Defence), Treasury Bd Secr. 1992–96, Acting Deputy Sec. Program Br. 1996; Exec. Dir Immigration and Refugee Bd 1997–98; Fed. Coordinator, Year 2000 Nat. Contingency Planning for Dept of Nat. Defence 1998–2000; Assoc. Deputy Minister of Industry 2000–01, of Foreign Affairs 2001–03; Pres. Canadian Int. Devt Agency 2003–05.
Address: c/o Canadian International Development Agency, 200 Promenade du Portage, Gatineau, PQ K1A 0G4, Canada (office).

THINLEY, Lyonchhen Jigmi Yozer, MA; Bhutanese politician; *Prime Minister and Chairman;* b. 1952, Bumthang. *Education:* St Stephen's Coll., India, Pennsylvania State Univ., USA. *Career:* mem. civil service

1954–1983, Head, Royal Civil Service Comm. Secr., Dir Educ. Dept; fmr Perm. Rep. to UN, New York; fmr Chair. Council of Ministers; Minister of Foreign Affairs 1998–2003; Prime Minister, Chair. and Minister of Home and Cultural Affairs 2003–04; Minister of Home and Cultural Affairs 2004–07 (resgnd), Prime Minister and Chair. 2008–; Founder and Pres. Druk Phuensum Tshogpa (DPT) party 2007–; Red Scarf 1987, Druk Thuksey and Coronation Medals 1999.
Address: Cabinet Secretariat, Tashichhodzong, Thimphu (office); Druk Phuensum Tshogpa (DPT), Thimphu; Druk Phuensum Tshogpa (DPT), Chang Lam, Thimphu, Bhutan (office). *Telephone:* (2) 321437 (office); (2) 336336 (DPT) (office). *Fax:* (2) 321438 (office); (2) 335845 (DPT) (office). *E-mail:* cabinet@druknet.bt (office); dpt@druknet.bt (office). *Website:* www.dpt.bt (office).

THOMAS, Alan William; Australian diplomatist; *Ambassador to European Union, Belgium and Luxembourg; Career:* positions at Dept of Foreign Affairs included Head, Staffing Br 1995–97, N Asia Div. 1997–98, Corp. Man. Div. 1998–2000, Deputy Sec. –2006; fmr Head, Americas and Defence Br., Dept of Prime Minister; Amb. to Singapore 1979–83, to Japan 1986–89, to Brazil 1992–95, to People's Repub. of China 2003–06, to EU, Belgium and Luxembourg 2007–.
Address: Embassy of Australia, Centre Guimard, 6–8 rue Guimard, 1040 Brussels, France (office). *Telephone:* (2) 286-05-00 (office). *Fax:* (2) 230-68-02 (office). *E-mail:* austemb.brussels@dfat.gov.au (office). *Website:* www .belgium.embassy.gov.au (office).

THOMAS, Tillman; Grenadian politician; *Prime Minister;* b. 13 June 1945, Hermitage, St Patrick. *Career:* mem. House of Reps for St Patrick E 1984–90, 2003–; Jr Minister, Ministry of Legal Affairs 1984–90; Founder mem. Nat. Democratic Congress Party 1987, Asst Gen. Sec. 1987–90, Leader 2000–; Leader of Opposition 2003–08; Prime Minister 2008–.
Address: Office of the Prime Minister, Ministerial Complex, 6th Floor, Botanical Gardens, St George's, Grenada (office). *Telephone:* 440-2255 (office). *Fax:* 440-4116 (office). *E-mail:* pmoffice@gov.gd (office). *Website:* www.pmoffice.gov.gd (office).

THOMPSON, David; Barbadian lawyer and politician; *Prime Minister and Minister of Finance, Economic Affairs and Development, Labour, Civil Service and Energy; Education:* Combermere School, Hugh Wooding Law School, Trinidad and Tobago, Univ. of the W Indies. *Career:* in pvt. law practice 1986–91; Pnr, Thompson & Patterson 1994–; mem. House of Ass.; Minister of Community Devt and Culture 1991; Minister of Finance 1992–93; Leader of Democratic Labour Party 1994–2001, fmr Leader of the Opposition; Prime Minister and Minister of Finance, Econ. Affairs and Devt, Labour, Civil Service and Energy 2008–; mem. Barbados Bar Asscn, Barbados Museum and Historical Soc.
Address: Office of the Prime Minister, Government Headquarters, Bay Street, St. Michael (office); Democratic Labour Party, George Street, Belleville, St Michael, Barbados (office). *Telephone:* 436-6435 (office); 429-3104 (office). *Fax:* 436-9280 (office); 427-0548 (office). *E-mail:* info@primeminister.gov.bb (office); dlp@sunbeach.net (office). *Website:* www .primeminister.gov.bb (office).

THOMPSON-FLÔRES, Francisco, BA (Phil), BA (Econs); Brazilian international trade official. *Education:* Univ. of Poitiers, France and London School of Econs, UK. *Career:* joined Minister of External Affairs 1959, Under-Sec.-Gen. 1985–88; seconded to London, UK 1961–64, Brussels, Belgium 1964–67, Washington, DC, USA 1973–76; Amb. to Argentina 1988–92, to Germany 1992–95, to the Holy See 1995–98, to Uruguay 2000–02; Sec. for Econ. and Tech. Int. Co-operation to the Presidency 1979; Co-ordinator of Int. Affairs, Ministry of Agric. 1979–83; Chief Negotiator Mercosur framework 1985–88; Personal Rep. of the Pres. to Latin America and the Caribbean–EU Summit 1998–99; Deputy Dir-Gen. WTO 2002–05; fmr mem. Advisory Cttee for Integration Affairs Inter-American Devt Bank Presidency, Advisory Bd Mercosur Econ. Research Network; Chair. Negotiating Group on Agric. Americas Free Trade Area 1999–2000.
Address: c/o World Trade Organization, Centre William Rappard, 154 rue de Lausanne, 1211 Geneva, Switzerland (office).

THOMSON, James Alan, BS, MS, PhD; American business executive and security expert; *President and CEO, RAND Corporation;* b. 21 Jan. 1945, Boston, Mass. *Education:* Univ. of New Hampshire and Purdue Univ. *Career:* Research Fellow, Univ. of Wisconsin, Madison 1972–74; Systems Analyst, Office of Sec. of Defense, US Dept of Defense, Washington, DC 1974–77; staff mem. Nat. Security Council, Washington, DC 1977–81; Vice-Pres. RAND Corpn, Santa Monica, Calif. 1981–88, Pres. and CEO 1989–; Dir LA World Affairs Council, Object Reservoir Inc., AK Steel Holdings Corpn, Encysive Pharmaceuticals Inc.; mem. Int. Inst. for Strategic Studies (UK), Council on Foreign Relations 1985–, Bd Los Angeles World Affairs Council; Hon. DSc (Purdue) 1992, (New Hamp-

shire); Hon. LLD (Pepperdine) 1996. *Publications:* Conventional Arms Control and the Security of Europe 1988; articles on defence issues.
Address: RAND Corporation, 1776 Main Street, Santa Monica, CA 90401, USA (office). *Telephone:* (310) 451-6936 (office). *Fax:* (310) 451-6972 (office). *E-mail:* thomson@rand.org (office). *Website:* www.rand.org (office).

THONGLOUN, Sisolit; Laotian politician; *Deputy Prime Minister and Minister of Foreign Affairs;* b. 10 Nov. 1945. *Education:* Pedagogical Coll., Neo Lao Hak Sat, Houaphanh, Pedagogical Inst., St Petersburg, Russia, Acad. of Social Science, Moscow. *Career:* Staff Officer, Educational Div., Neo Lao Hak Sat (Lao Nat. Patriotic Front), Houaphanh Prov. 1967–69; Staff Officer, Rep. Office, Neo Lao Hak Sat (LNPE), Hanoi 1969–73; Instructor, Vientiane Univ. 1978–79; Sec. to Ministry of Educ. and Chief, External Relations Div., Ministry of Educ. 1979–81; Dir Public Research Dept, Minister Council Bd, Office of the Prime Minister 1985–86; Vice-Minister, Ministry of Foreign Affairs 1987–92; Minister of Labour and Social Welfare 1993–97; mem. Parl. 1998–2000; Deputy Prime Minister of Laos 2001–, Minister of Foreign Affairs 2006–; Pres. Cttee for Planning and Cooperation, Cttee for Investment and Cooperation, Lao Nat. Cttee for Energy; Hon. Pres., SOS of Lao PDR1–.
Address: Ministry of Foreign Affairs, rue That Luang 01004, Ban Phonxay, Vientiane, Laos (office). *Telephone:* (21) 413148 (office). *Fax:* (21) 414009 (office). *E-mail:* souknivone@mofa.gov.la (office). *Website:* www.mofa .gov.la (office).

THORENS, Justin Pierre, DenD; Swiss professor of law and attorney; *President, Latsis International Foundation;* b. 15 Sept. 1931, Collonge-Bellerive; m. Colette F. Vecchio 1963; one s. one d. *Education:* Univ. of Geneva, Freie Univ. Berlin and Univ. Coll. London. *Career:* attorney-at-law, Geneva Bar 1956–; Alt. Pres. Jurisdictional Court, Geneva 1971–78; Lecturer, Faculty of Law, Univ. of Geneva 1967, Assoc. Prof. 1970, Prof. 1973–96, Dean 1974–77, Hon. Prof. 1996–; Rector, Univ. of Geneva 1977–83; Visiting Scholar, Stanford Univ. 1983–84, Univ. of Calif., Berkeley 1983–84; Guest Prof., Univ. of Munich, Germany 1984; mem. Cttee European Centre for Higher Educ. (CEPES), Bucharest 1981–95, Pres. 1986–88; mem. Admin. Council Asscn des Universités Partiellement ou Entièrement de Langue Française (AUPELF), Montreal 1978–87, Vice-Pres. 1981–87, Hon. Vice-Pres. 1987–, mem. Gov. Council 1987–; Pres. Bd Int. Asscn of Univs (AIU), Paris 1985–90, Hon. Pres. 1990–; mem. Council UN Univ. Tokyo 1986–92, Pres. 1988–89; mem. UNESCO Swiss Nat. Comm. 1989–2001, Int. Acad. of Estate and Trust Law; Pres. Latsis Int. Foundation 1989–; various prizes, awards and distinctions. *Publications:* publs on pvt. law, civil procedure, arbitration, Anglo-American property law, univ. politics, cultural questions.
Address: 18 chemin du Nant d'Aisy, 1246 Corsier (Geneva), Switzerland. *Telephone:* (22) 7518081 (office); (22) 7511262 (home). *Fax:* (22) 7518082 (office); (22) 7518082 (home). *E-mail:* etude.jthorens@bluewin.ch (office); justin.thorens@bluewin.ch (home).

THUNELL, Lars H., PhD; Swedish international organization executive; *Executive Vice-President, International Finance Corporation, World Bank Group; Education:* Univ. of Stockholm. *Career:* fmr Research Fellow, Harvard Univ. Center for Int. Affairs, USA; fmr CEO Trygg-Hansa insurance co.; fmr Deputy CEO Nordbanken; fmr Pres. and CEO Securum (asset man. co.), Stockholm; CEO Skandinaviska Enskilda Banken AB 1997–2005; Chair. Bd IBX Integrated Business Exchange AB; mem. or fmr mem. Bd of Dirs Svenska Cellulosa AB, Swedish Bankers Asscn, Akzo Nobel NV, Mentor Foundation; worked at ABB Zurich and American Express, New York; has also held numerous non-exec. bd positions with int. cos and non-governmental orgs; Exec. Vice-Pres. IFC (pvt. sector arm of World Bank Group) 2006–. *Publications:* author of books and articles on risk and risk man. in int. business.
Address: International Finance Corporation, 2121 Pennsylvania Avenue, NW, Washington, DC 20433, USA (office). *Telephone:* (202) 473-1000 (office). *Website:* www.ifc.org (office).

TIBAIJUKA, Anna Kajumulo; Tanzanian agricultural economist and United Nations official; *Under-Secretary-General and Executive Director, United Nations Centre for Human Settlements (Habitat);* m. (deceased); four c. *Education:* Swedish Univ. of Agricultural Sciences, Uppsala. *Career:* Assoc. Prof. Dar-es-Salaam Univ. 1993–98; Founding Chair. Tanzanian Nat. Women's Council; UNCTAD Special Co-ordinator for Least Developed Countries, Landlocked and Small Island Developing Countries 1998–2000; Exec. Dir UN Centre for Human Settlements (Habitat) 2000–, Under-Sec.-Gen. 2002–, Dir-Gen. UN Office, Nairobi 2006–; Exec. Sec. for Third UN Conf. on Least Developed Countries, Brussels, Belgium 2001.
Address: PO Box 30030, Nairobi, Kenya (office). *Telephone:* (20) 623141 (office). *Fax:* (20) 624265 (office). *E-mail:* habitat@unchs.org (office). *Website:* www.unchs.org (office).

TICHENOR, Warren W., BS; American business executive and diplomatist; *Permanent Representative, United Nations, Geneva;* b. 1960, Harlingen, Tex.; m. Rhonda Tichenor; one s. *Education:* Univ. of Southern California. *Career:* early career working in various positions in family's media co. Tichenor Media System, Inc. (later renamed Hispanic Broadcasting Corpn, merged with Univision Communications 2003, sold 2007); Pres. W.W. Tichenor & Co., Inc. (pvt. investment firm), San Antonio, Tex. –2006; Dir Hispanic Campaign 2000 (served in similar capacity in George W. Bush's re-election campaign for Gov. of Tex. 1998); has served on bds and in other capacities of various charitable, political, business and civic orgs; Amb. and Perm. Rep. to UN and other Int. Orgs, Geneva 2006–.
Address: US Permanent Mission to the United Nations, Route de Pregny 11, 1292 Chambesy, Switzerland (office). *Telephone:* (22) 749-41-11 (office). *Fax:* (22) 749-48-80 (office). *E-mail:* info@usmission.ch (office). *Website:* www.usmission.ch (office).

TIEN, Hung-Mao, MA, PhD; Taiwanese academic and diplomatist; *Representative to UK;* b. 7 Nov. 1938, Tainan; m. Amy Tien; one s. one d. *Education:* Tunghai Univ. and Univ. of Wisconsin, USA. *Career:* fmr Prof. of Political Science, Univ. of Wisconsin; Pres. Inst. for Nat. Policy Research 1991–; mem. Nat. Unification Research Council, Office of Pres. of Taiwan 1994–; Nat. Policy Adviser to Pres. of Taiwan 1996–; Dir Foundation for Int. Co-operation and Devt 1996–, Minister of Foreign Affairs 2000–02; Rep. to UK 2002–. *Publications include:* Government and Politics in Kuomintang China 1927–37, The Great Transition, Social and Political Change in the Republic of China, Taiwan's Electoral Politics and Democratic Transition: Riding the Third Wave 1995.
Address: Taipei Representative Office in the UK, 50 Grosvenor Gardens, London, SW1W 0EB, England (office); #225, Tung-shih Street, Hsi-chih, Taipei County, Taiwan (home). *Telephone:* (20) 7881-2650 (office); (2) 660-0145 (home). *Website:* www.taiwanembassy.org/uk (office).

TIIDO, Harri, MA; Estonian diplomatist and fmr journalist; *Undersecretary for Political Affairs;* b. 8 Oct. 1953, Jõhvi; m. Anna Tiido; one d. *Education:* Tallinn Secondary School, Tartu Univ. *Career:* journalist Estonian Nat. Public Radio and Radio Kuku, Tallinn 1980–96; worked for Voice of America 1996–97; Chief Ed. Radio Kuku 1997–2000; Deputy Under-Sec. of Security Policy, Ministry of Foreign Affairs 2000–03; Perm. Rep. to NATO, Brussels, 2003–07; Under-Sec. for Political Affairs 2007–.
Address: Ministry of Foreign Affairs, Islandi valjak 1, Tallinn, Estonia (office). *Telephone:* 637-7011 (office). *Fax:* 637-7099 (office). *E-mail:* harri.tiido@mfa.ee (office). *Website:* www.vm.ee (office).

TIKOISUVA, Pio Bosco; Fijian fmr rugby player and diplomatist; *High Commissioner to UK;* b. 1947, Taveuni. *Career:* played for Harlequins rugby team, London while undertaking a printing course 1974–77, fmr nat. rugby capt., captained Fiji in 25–21 win over British and Irish Lions 1977, Man. and Coach of winning Fiji team to Hong Kong Sevens 1978, retd from int. rugby 1979, continued to play for St John Marist team until mid-1980s, apptd CEO Fiji Rugby Union 2001; High Commr to UK (also accred as Amb. to Ireland) 2008–; inducted into Fiji Sports Hall of Fame 2002.
Address: High Commission of Fiji, 34 Hyde Park Gate, London, SW7 5DN, England (office). *Telephone:* (20) 7584-3661 (office). *Fax:* (20) 7584-2834 (office). *E-mail:* mail@fijihighcommission.org.uk (office). *Website:* www.fijihighcommission.org.uk (office).

TIMERMAN, Héctor Marcos; Argentine diplomatist and journalist; *Ambassador to USA;* b. 16 Dec. 1953, Buenos Aires; m. Anabelle Sielecki; two d. *Education:* Columbia Univ., USA. *Career:* in political exile in USA 1978–84; lecturer on human rights, New York 1979–83, 2005–06; fmr Dir Trespuntos magazine, fmr Co-Dir Debate magazine, fmr columnist Noticias magazine, Ambito Financiero newspaper; Co-founder and mem. Bd of Dirs Human Rights Watch, New York 1981–89; Dir Fund for Free Expression, London 1983–89; mem. Bd of Dirs Asamblea Permanente por los Derechos Humanos (Perm. Ass. for Human Rights), Buenos Aires 2002–04; Consul-Gen. in New York 2004–07, Amb. to USA 2007–; Pres. Int. Coalition of Historic Site Museums of Conscience. *Publications:* Torture (co-author) 2005.
Address: Embassy of Argentina, 1600 New Hampshire Avenue, NW, Washington, DC 20009-2512, USA (office). *Telephone:* (202) 238-6401 (office). *Fax:* (202) 332-3171 (office). *Website:* www.embassyofargentina.us (office).

TIMKEN, William R., Jr, BA, MBA; American diplomatist; *Ambassador to Germany;* b. Canton, Ohio; m. Sue Timken; six c. *Education:* Stanford Univ. and Harvard Business School. *Career:* various exec. positions, including Pres. and CEO Timken Co. 1962–2003, Chair. 1973–2003, Chair. (non-exec.) 2004–05; mem. Bd of Dirs numerous public cos; fmr Chair. Nat. Asscn of Mfrs, The Manufacturing Inst., Ohio Business Roundtable; fmr mem. Advisory Council, Stanford Univ. School of Business; fmr mem. US-Japan Business Council; apptd by Pres. George W. Bush as Chair. Securities Investor Protection Corpn 2003; Amb. to Germany 2005–; Hon. Citizen of Colmar, France; Chevalier, Légion d'honneur; Woodrow Wilson Award for Corp. Citizenship, Adam Smith Award, Ellis Island Medal of Honor, named Ohio Business Statesman of the Year, Ohio Gov.'s Award.
Address: Embassy of the USA, Neustädtische Kirche 4/5, 10117 Berlin, Germany (office). *Telephone:* (30) 2385174 (office). *Fax:* (30) 2386290 (office). *Website:* berlin.usembassy.gov (office).

TINY, Carlos Alberto Pires; São Tome and Príncipe politician; *Minister of Foreign Affairs, Co-operation and Communities; Career:* fmr Minister of Health; fmr Pres. Assembleia Nacional; unsuccessful cand. for Pres. 2001; Minister of Foreign Affairs, Co-operation and Communities 2008–; mem. Movimento de Libertação de São Tomé e Príncipe—Partido Social Democrata.
Address: Ministry of Foreign Affairs, Co-operation and Communities, Av. 12 de Julho, CP 111, São Tomé, São Tomé and Príncipe (office). *Telephone:* 221017. *Fax:* 222597 (office). *E-mail:* minecoop@cstome.net (office). *Website:* www.mnecc.gov.st (office).

TITARENKO, Mikhail Leontyevich, PhD; Russian academic; *Director, Institute of Far East Studies, Russian Academy of Sciences;* b. 27 April 1934, Bryansk region; m. Galina Titarenko 1957 (died 1997); two s. *Education:* Moscow State Univ., Beijing Univ., Fudan Univ., Shanghai. *Career:* diplomatic service 1961–65; researcher and consultant in govt bodies 1965–85; Dir Inst. of Far East Studies, Russian Acad. of Sciences 1985–; mem. Editorial Bd, Far Eastern Affairs 1986–; Chair. Academic Council on Problems of Modern China, Russian Acad. of Sciences 1987–; Pres. All-Russian Asscn of Sinologists 1988–; Corresp. mem. Russian Acad. of Sciences 1997–, Academician 2003–; mem. Russia Acad. of Natural Sciences, Int. Acad. of Informatization; Honour of the Russian Fed. 1994, Merited Scholar of Russia 1995, 200 Years of Russian Foreign Service Medal 2002. *Publications:* Anthology of Ancient Chinese Philosophy (two vols), Ancient Chinese Philosopher Mo Di 1985, Development of Productive Forces in China 1989, History of Chinese Philosophy 1989, Economic Reform in China: Theory and Practice 1990, Russia and East Asia: Issues of International and Cross-Civilization Relations 1994, Russia Towards Asia 1998, China: Civilization and Reforms 1999, Russia's Co-operative Security: East Asian Vector 2003; and numerous articles.
Address: Institute of Far East Studies, Russian Academy of Sciences, 32 Nakhimovsky pr., 117218 Moscow, Russia (office). *Telephone:* (495) 124-01-17 (office); (495) 198-55-38 (home). *Fax:* (495) 718-96-56 (office). *E-mail:* ifes@cemi.rssi.ru (office). *Website:* www.ifes-ras.ru (office).

TITOV, Konstantin Alekseyevich, CandEconSc; Russian politician; b. 30 Oct. 1944, Moscow; m. Natalia Borisovna Titova; one s. *Education:* Kuybyshev (now Samara) Aviation Inst., Kuybyshev Inst. of Planning. *Career:* milling-machine operator, Kuybyshev aviation factory 1962–63, flight engineer 1968–69, Deputy Sec. Komsomol Cttee 1969–70; Deputy Head Students Div., Kuybyshev City Komsomol Cttee 1970–73; Sec. Komsomol Cttee, Jr, Sr Researcher, Head of Group, Head Research Lab. Kuybyshev Inst. of Planning 1973–88; Deputy Dir Research Cen. Informatika (Samara br.) 1988–90; Chair. Samara City Council 1990–91; Head of Admin. Samara Region 1991–96; Gov. Samara Region 1996–2007; mem. Council of Fed. of Russia 1993–2001, Chair. Cttee on Budget, Taxation Policy, Finance and Customs Regulation 1996–2001; Pres. Interregional Asscn of Econ. Interaction 'Bolshaya Volga' 1994; Deputy Chair. 'Our Home Is Russia' political movt 1995; Chair. of Council, Union of Right Forces 1998–; Cand. for Pres. of Russian Fed. 2000; Chair. Russian Party of Social Democracy 2000, Co-Founder Union of Social Democratic Parties 2001; mem. Russian Acad. of Natural Sciences; Golden Mask Prize, Russian Theatre Artists Union; Order of St Faithful Prince Daniil Moskovsky (3rd Degree), Order of St Grand Duke Vladimir (2nd Degree); Order of Friendship, Green Man of the Year, Russian Ecological Union 1996, Honoured Economist of the Russian Fed., Gov. of the Year 1998, National Prize of Peter the Great 2002, Order Glory of Russia 2002, National Olympus Laureate 2003.
Address: c/o Office of the President, 103132 Moscow, Staraya pl. 4, Russia (office). *Website:* www.kremlin.ru (office).

TKESHELASHVILI, Ekaterine (Eka), LLM; Georgian lawyer and government official; *Minister of Foreign Affairs;* b. 23 May 1977, Tbilisi; m. *Education:* Tbilisi State Univ., Univ. of Notre Dame, USA. *Career:* lawyer, Int. Cttee of Red Cross 1999–2000; intern, Appeals Office, Int. Tribunal of fmr Yugoslavia 2001–02; lawyer and Dir Institutional Reform and Non-governmental Sector, IRIS Georgia 2002–04; Deputy Minister of Justice 2004–05; Deputy Minister of Internal Affairs 2005–06; Chair. Tbilisi Court of Appeals 2006–07; Minister of Justice 2007; Gen. Prosecutor Jan.-May 2008; Minister of Foreign Affairs May 2008–.

Address: Ministry of Foreign Affairs, 0108 Tbilisi, Sh. Chitadze 4, Georgia (office). *Telephone:* (32) 28-47-47 (office). *Fax:* (32) 28-46-78 (office). *E-mail:* inform@mfa.gov.ge (office). *Website:* www.mfa.gov.ge (office).

TLOU, Thomas, MA, PhD, MAT; Botswana historian, academic and diplomatist; *Chairman, Botswana Institute of Development Policy Analysis;* b. 1 June 1932, Gwanda, Southern Rhodesia (now Zimbabwe); m. Sheila Dinotshe 1977; two s. one d. *Education:* schools in Rhodesia, Luther Coll., Decorah, Iowa, Johns Hopkins Univ., Baltimore and Univ. of Wisconsin. *Career:* primary school teacher, Rhodesia 1957–62; Lecturer in History, Luther Coll. 1969, Univ. of Wis. 1970–71; Lecturer in History, Univ. of Botswana, Lesotho and Swaziland (UBLS) 1971, later Prof., Dean of Faculty of Humanities and Head of History; mem. Bd Nat. Museum and Art Gallery of Botswana 1974–76, 1981–; mem. Univ. Senate and Council of UBLS 1974–76; Acting Dir Nat. Research Inst. 1976; Perm. Rep. to UN 1977–80; Deputy Vice-Chancellor Univ. of Botswana 1980, Vice-Chancellor 1984–98, mem. Senate and Council of Univ. of Botswana and Swaziland (now Univ. of Botswana) 1980–, mem. Nat. Archives Advisory Council, mem. Univ. of Botswana Review Comm.; mem. Pres.'s Comm. on Incomes Policy 1989–90; mem. Namibian Pres. Comm. on Higher Educ. 1991, Univ. of Botswana Review Comm. 1990, UNESCO Bd 1992–95; Chair. SADCC Consultancy on Human Resources Devt 1991, Asscn of Eastern and Southern African Univs 1992–93; Vice-Chair. Asscn of Commonwealth Univs 1993, Chair. 1994; mem. Bd Botswana Tech. Centre; mem. Nat. Employment, Manpower and Incomes Council; Chair. Asscn of Eastern and Southern Africa Univs; mem. Exec. Bd Asscn of African Univs 1993–96, Botswana Inst. of Devt Policy Analysis (Chair. 1999–), Botswana Nat. Council on Educ. (Chair. 1999–2003); mem. Council, Univ. of Swaziland 1993–95; mem. American-African Studies Asscn; Life mem. Botswana Soc.; mem. Bd Lutheran World Fed. (LWF) 1998–2002; mem. LWF Study Group on African Religion 1998–2000; Chair. Tertiary Educ. Council 2002–; mem. Evangelical Lutheran Church 2003–; Chevalier des Palmes académiques 1982, Presidential Order of Honour 1994; Hon. DLitt (Luther Coll.) 1978, Hon. LLD (Ohio) 1986. *Publications:* History of Botswana (co-author) 1984, A History of Ngamiland 1750–1906: The Formation of an African State 1985, Biography of Seretse Khama 1995; and several articles and book chapters on history of Botswana and Ngamiland.
Address: PO Box 1004, Gaborone, Botswana. *Telephone:* 3927645 (office); 3927645 (home). *Fax:* 3185098. *E-mail:* tlout@mopipi.ub.bw (office).

TODD, Damian Roderic (Ric), BA; British diplomatist; *Ambassador to Poland;* b. 29 Aug. 1959, Crawley, Surrey; m. Alison Todd; one s. two d. *Education:* Worcester Coll., Oxford. *Career:* FCO 1980–81, Third then Second Sec., Cape Town and Pretoria 1981–84, EC Dept, FCO 1984–87, First Sec. and Consul, Prague 1987–89, Econ. Relations Dept 1989–91, First Sec. (Econ.), Embassy in Bonn 1991–95; seconded to HM Treasury, London 1995–97; Head, Agricultural Team 1996–97; Head, EU Coordination and Strategy Team 1998–2001; Amb. to Slovakia 2001–04, to Poland 2007–; Finance Dir FCO 2004–07; Head, Agric. Spending Team, HM Treasury 1995–97,.
Address: British Embassy, Aleje Róż 1, Warsaw 00-556, Poland (office). *Telephone:* (22) 3110000 (office). *Fax:* (22) 3110311 (office). *E-mail:* info@britishembassy.pl (office). *Website:* www.britishembassy.pl (office).

TODD, William E., BA; American diplomatist; *Ambassador to Brunei;* b. Va. *Education:* Longwood Coll. *Career:* career mem. Sr Exec. Service, has served as Prin. Deputy Asst Sec. and later as Deputy Asst Sec. for Civilian Police, Rule of Law, Asia, Africa, and Europe, Bureau of Int. Narcotics and Law Enforcement Affairs, Dept of State, Deputy Insp. Gen., Dept of State –2008; Amb. to Brunei Darussalam 2008–.
Address: US Embassy, Teck Guan Plaza, 3rd Floor, Jalan Sultan, PO Box 2991, Bandar Seri Begawan BS 8811, Brunei (office). *Telephone:* 2220384 (office). *Fax:* 2225293 (office). *E-mail:* amembassy_bsb@state.gov (office). *Website:* bandar.usembassy.gov (office).

TOIHIRI, Mohamed, BA, MA, PhD; Comoran academic and diplomatist; *Permanent Representative, United Nations;* b. 20 Aug. 1955; m.; two c. *Education:* Univ. of Bordeaux III, France. *Career:* Cultural Dir Radio Comoros 1978; Lecturer in French and African, North African and Caribbean literature, Nat. Coll. of Comoros 1983–84; Dir and Public Relations Dir Sony Corpn then TDK, France 1986–88; Ed.-in-Chief Le Comorien 1990–92; Prof., French School of Comoros and Academic Insp. of high school French teachers 2001–02; Prof. of French, WHO in Comoros 2002; Lecturer in French, Univ. of Michigan, USA 2002–03; Sr Lecturer and French Literature Chair., Univ. of Comoros 2004–07; Perm. Rep. to UN, New York 2007–, also Amb. to USA; contrib. to nat. newspapers including Alwatwan 1994–, Kashkazi 2006–. *Publications:* several novels and plays and articles in academic journals.

Address: Permanent Mission of Comoros to the United Nations, 336 East 45th Street, 2nd Floor, New York, NY 10017, USA (office). *Telephone:* (212) 750-1637 (office).

TOLBA, Mohamed Ould, MSc; Mauritanian diplomatist; b. 31 Dec. 1962, R'Kiz; m.; two c. *Education:* École Normale Supérieure de Nouakchott, Univ. of Dijon, Institut Int. de Planification, Paris. *Career:* several positions in Ministry of Educ. 1984–2002, Sec.-Gen., Ministry of Educ. 2002; fmr Minister of Foreign Affairs and Cooperation; fmr Minister of Communication and Relations with Parl.; Perm. Rep. to UN, New York 2005–07.
Address: c/o Ministry of Foreign Affairs and Co-operation, BP 230, Nouakchott, Mauritania (office).

TOLGFORS, Sten, BSc; Swedish politician; *Minister of Defence and of Foreign Trade;* b. 17 July 1966, Forshaga. *Education:* Karlberg Upper Secondary School and Örebro Univ. *Career:* mem. Örebro City Ass. 1991–94; Special Adviser, Ministry of Defence 1992–93, Ministry of Industry and Commerce 1992–94; mem. Nat. Bd Moderate Party Youth Org. 1990–95, Nat. Exec. 2002–, Spokesperson for Social Insurance 2002–03, Spokesperson for Educ. 2003–06; mem. Riksdag (Parl.) 1994–, Alt. mem. Cttee on Educ. 1994–2002, Cttee on Foreign Affairs 1994–98, Cttee on Industry and Trade 1998–2002, Del. to OSCE Parl. Ass. 1998–2002; mem. Del. to Nordic Council 1998–2002, Cttee on Foreign Affairs 1998–2002, Cttee on Social Insurance 2002–03, Cttee on Educ. 2003–06, Advisory Council on Foreign Affairs 2006; Minister for Foreign Trade 2006–, of Defence 2007–.
Address: Ministry of Defence, Jakobsgt. 9, 103 33 Stockholm, Sweden (office). *Telephone:* (8) 405-10-00 (office). *Fax:* (8) 723-11-89 (office). *E-mail:* registrator@defence.ministry.se (office). *Website:* forsvar.regeringen.se (office).

TÓMASSON, Tómas Ármann, MA; Icelandic diplomatist; b. 1 Jan. 1929, Reykjavik; m. Heba Jónsdóttir 1957 (divorced); three s. one d. *Education:* Reykjavik Grammar Schoo and Univ. of Illinois, Fletcher School of Law and Diplomacy and Columbia Univ., USA. *Career:* entered Icelandic foreign service 1954; Sec. Moscow 1954–58; Ministry for Foreign Affairs 1958–60; Deputy Perm. Rep. to NATO and OECD 1960–66; Chief of Div., Ministry for Foreign Affairs 1966–69, Deputy Sec.-Gen. of Ministry 1970–71; Amb. to Belgium and EEC and Perm. Rep. on N Atlantic Council 1971–77, 1984–86, also accred to Luxembourg 1976–77, 1984–86; Perm. Rep. to UN 1977–82, 1993–94; Amb. to France (also accred to Portugal, Spain, Cape Verde) 1982–84, to USSR (also accred to Bulgaria, GDR, Hungary, Mongolia and Romania) 1987–90; Amb., Head of Del. to CSBMs and CFE negotiation, Vienna 1990; Amb. to USA (also accred to Canada) 1990–93; Amb., Head of Del. to CSCE Review Conf. and Summit, Budapest Oct.–Dec. 1994; mem. staff, Ministry for Foreign Affairs, Reykjavik 1994–; Order of the Falcon (Iceland) and decorations from France, Belgium, Luxembourg, Portugal and Sweden.
Address: Ministry for Foreign Affairs, 150 Reykjavik; Espigerdi 4/9H, 108 Reykjavik, Iceland (home). *Telephone:* 5459900 (office); 5534918 (home). *Fax:* 5526247 (office); 5623152 (office). *E-mail:* tomas.a.tomasson@utn.stjr.is (office); tat@islandia.is (home).

TOMBIŃSKI, Jan, MA; Polish diplomatist and writer; *Permanent Representative, European Union;* b. 4 Oct. 1958, Kraków; m.; ten c. *Education:* Jagiellonian Univ. *Career:* librarian, Jagiellonian Univ. 1985–87, Asst Lecturer, later Sr Lecturer 1987–89; int. affairs commentator, clandestine journal Świat, Krakow 1989–90; overseas postings include Embassy in Prague 1990–95, Minister-Counsellor, Embassy in Ljubljana 1995–96; Amb. to Slovenia (also accred to Bosnia and Herzegovina) 1995–98, to France 2001–07; Counsellor to Minister, Depts of Western Europe, Cen. Europe and Southern Europe, Dir Depts of Cen. Europe and Southern Europe, Dir, European Policy Dept, Ministry of Foreign Affairs 1998–2001; Perm. Rep. to EU, Brussels 2007–; Founder and Pres. Asscn for European Integration, Kraków 1989. *Publications:* Hitler and the Swiss neutrality 1933–35 1989, Austria and European Integration 1926–32 1989, Poland: Six Months after the Elections 1989, Polish Television Towards Choice 1990, Debate on the Project of the European Union in the League of Nations 1991, Polish Election Law 1992, Polish–German Relations 1945–91 1994, The Response of Austria to the Briand Plan 1994.
Address: Permanent Representation of Poland to the EU, 282–284 Avenue de Tervuren, 1150 Brussels, Belgium (office). *Telephone:* (2) 777-72-00 (office). *Fax:* (2) 777-72-97 (office). *E-mail:* mail@polrepeu.be (office). *Website:* www.pol-mission-eu.be (office); www.brukselaeu.polemb.net (office).

TOMEING, Litokwa; Marshall Islands politician and head of state; *President;* b. Ratak Chain; m. *Career:* traditional tribal chief; apptd Minister for Ratak 1997; mem. Nitijela (Parl.) for Wotje Atoll, fmr Vice-

Speaker, later Speaker –2007; fmr mem. United Democratic Party, now mem. United People's Party 2007–; Pres. Marshall Islands 2008–.
Address: Office of the President, Government of the Republic of the Marshall Islands, POB 2, Majuro MH 96960, Marshall Islands (home). *Telephone:* (625) 3445 (office). *Fax:* (625) 4021 (office). *E-mail:* pressoff@ntamar.net (office). *Website:* www.rmigovernment.org (office).

TOMKA, Peter, LLM, PhD; Slovak diplomatist, lawyer, arbitrator and judge; *Judge, International Court of Justice;* b. 1 June 1956, Banska Bystrica; m. Zuzana Halgasová 1990; one s. one d. *Education:* Charles Univ., Prague. *Career:* Asst. Faculty of Law, Charles Univ., Prague 1980–84, Lecturer 1985–86, Adjunct Lecturer 1986–91; Asst Legal Adviser, Ministry of Foreign Affairs, Czechoslovakia 1986–90, Head of Public Int. Law Div. 1990–91; Counsellor and Legal Adviser, Czechoslovakian Mission to the UN 1991–92; Deputy Perm. Rep. of Slovakia to the UN 1993–97, Perm. Rep. 1999–2003; Agent of Slovakia before the Int. Court of Justice 1993–2003, Judge, Int. Court of Justice 2003–; Legal Adviser to Slovak Ministry of Foreign Affairs 1997–99; Chair. UN Legal Cttee 1997, Cttee of Advisers on Public Int. Law, Council of Europe 2001–02; mem. Perm. Court of Arbitration, The Hague 1994–, UN Int. Law Comm. 1999–2003; Arbitrator in the Iron Rhine case (Belgium/Netherlands) 2003–05, in Annex VII to the UN Convention on the Law of the Sea 2004–, and in Int. Centre for Settlement of Investment Disputes 2005–.
Address: International Court of Justice, Peace Palace, 2517 KJ The Hague, Netherlands (office). *Telephone:* (70) 3022323 (office). *Fax:* (70) 3649928 (office). *E-mail:* mail@icj-cij.org (office). *Website:* www.icj-cij.org (office).

TOMMASI, Mariano, MA, PhD; Argentine economist and academic; *Professor, Department of Economics, Universidad de San Andrés;* m. Paula Tommasi; three c. *Education:* Univ. of Chicago, USA, Catholic Univ. of Argentina. *Career:* Asst Prof. UCLA 1991–94; Research Fellow Harvard-MIT 1994–95; Assoc. Prof. Universidad de San Andrés 1995–2000, Prof. 2000–, Chair. Econs Dept 1995–97, 2001–06, Dir Center of Studies for Institutional Devt 1997–; Visiting Prof. Tel-Aviv Univ. 1993, 1994, UCLA 1997, Harvard 2000, Yale 2003, 2007; Dir Centre of Studies for Institutional Devt 1997–; Vice Pres. Latin American and Caribbean Econ. Assoc. at UCLA 2002–03, Pres. 2004–05; Co-Dir Task Force on Decentralization, Columbia Univ.; Assoc. Ed. Estudios de Economica; mem. Latin America Chapter, Econometric Soc.; mem. advisory bds Centre for Econ. Devt, Israel, Inst. of Public Policy and Devt Studies, Universidad de las Américas-Puebla.
Address: Vito Dumas 284, Victoria, B1644BID Buenos Aires, Argentina (office). *Telephone:* (11) 4725-7020 (office). *Fax:* (11) 4725-2211 (office). *E-mail:* tamara@udesa.edu.ar (office). *Website:* www.udesa.edu.ar (office).

TONELLI, Gilles; Monegasque civil servant and politician; *Government Counsellor for Finance and the Economy;* m.; three c. *Education:* Ecole des Travaux Publiques. *Career:* engineer in Paris 1983–84, section head at public works service 1984–87; Official Rep. at Dept of Public Works and Social Affairs 1987–90, Dir of Urban Planning and Construction 1990–93, Dir-Gen. Dept Public Works and Social Affairs 1993–95, 1995–99; Tech. Advisor, Dept of Finance 1995; Gen. Controller of Expenditure 1999–2000; Sec.-Gen. Ministry of State 2000–05; Govt Counsellor for Facilities, the Environment and Urban Planning 2005–06, for Finance and the Economy 2006–.
Address: Department of Finance and the Economy, Ministère d'Etat, place de la Visitation, Monte Carlo, MC 98000, Monaco (office). *Telephone:* 98-98-82-56 (office). *E-mail:* dfin@troisseptsept.mc (office).

TONG, Anote, MSc; I-Kiribati head of state and politician; *President and Minister for Foreign Affairs and Immigration;* b. 1952; m. Meme Bernadette Tong; eight c. *Education:* Univ. of Canterbury, Christchurch, NZ, LSE, UK. *Career:* Sr Asst Sec., Ministry of Educ. 1976–77; Sec. Ministry of Communication and Works 1980–82; Minister for Natural Resources Devt 1994–96; mem. Parl. for Maiana Island 1996–2003; Sr mem. Boutokaan Te Koaua Party 1996–2003; Beretitenti (Pres.) of Kiribati and Minister for Foreign Affairs and Immigration 2003–; fmr Chair. National Fishing Co., Development Bank of Kiribati, Otintai Hotel Ltd, Air Tungaru Co-operative.
Address: Office of the President (Beretitenti), POB 68, Bairiki, Tarawa, Kiribati (office). *Telephone:* 21183 (office). *Fax:* 21145 (office).

TONG, Zhiguang; Chinese international official and professor of economics; *Chairman, Research Society of China, World Trade Organization;* b. 1933. *Education:* Beijing Inst. of Foreign Trade and Univ. of Int. Business and Econs, Bombay Univ., India. *Career:* joined CCP 1973; Deputy Head State Council Leading Group for Right to Intellectual Property 1991–; Vice-Minister of Foreign Trade and Econ. Co-operation 1991–93; Chair. Bd The Export-Import Bank of China 1994–99; Chair. WTO Research Soc. of China 2001–; Vice-Chair. China-UK Friendship Group; mem. China-US

Inter-parliamentarian Exchange Group of the NPC; fmr Chief Negotiator and Del. Leader for China's accession to GATT/WTO and Sino-US Trade Negotiations; fmr sr diplomat to India, Myanmar, USA and UN; fmr Adviser to Chinese Del. of UN Gen. Ass.; fmr Chair. China Exim Bank; fmr Pres. and CEO of China Resources (Holdings) Co. Ltd, Hong Kong; mem. 8th Standing Cttee NPC 1993–98, mem. NPC Foreign Affairs Cttee, del. of Hebei Prov. to 8th NPC 1993–98, 9th Standing Cttee NPC 1998–2003; Del., 15th CCP Nat. Congress 1997–2002. *Publications:* several articles on foreign trade, int. econs and the WTO.
Address: 2212, 28 Dong Holi Xiang, Anwai Beijing 100710 (office); 7202 Yin Zha Hu Tong, Xicheng Qu, Beijing (home); c/o The Export-Import Bank of China, 75 Chongnei Street, Beijing 100005, People's Republic of China. *Telephone:* (10) 84255121 (office); (10) 64259703 (home). *Fax:* (10) 84255122 (office). *E-mail:* wtori@sina.com.cn (office).

TONG SANG, Gaston, DipEng; French Polynesian engineer, politician and head of state; *President;* b. 7 Aug. 1949, Bora Bora; two c. *Education:* Collège La Mennais, Papeete, Lycée Montaigne, Bordeaux, Ecole des Hautes études industrielles (HEI), Centre des Hautes Etudes de la Construction, Paris. *Career:* engineer, Road Infrastructure Dept, Polynesian Dept of Works 1976–80, Head, Maritime Works Dept 1980–82; Cabinet Dir for Govt Counsellors 1982–84; Cabinet Dir for Minister of Works 1984–86; Minister of Works, Supplies, Energy and Mines 1986–89; Mayor of Bora Bora 1989–91; Regional Councillor for Iles sous le Vent and Minister of Supplies, Urban Areas, Works and Energy 1991–95; Minister of Works, Energy and Ports 1995–96, of Housing, Territories, Urban Areas and Real Estate 1996–98, of Property Affairs, Land Man. and Urban Areas 1998–2000, of Land Man. and Land Redistribution 2001–04, of Energy, Commerce, Industry and Small Businesses 2004–07; Pres. of French Polynesia 2007, 2008–, also Minister for External Relations, Int. Transport and Communication; mem. To Tatou Ai'a party; Chevalier de l'ordre Nat. du Mérite 1996, Chevalier des Palmes académiques 2000, Chevalier de la Légion d'honneur 2004.
Address: Office of the President of the Government, BP 2551, 98713 Papeete, French Polynesia (office). *Telephone:* 472121 (office). *Fax:* 472210 (office). *Website:* www.presidence.pf (office).

TØNNESSON, Stein, CandPhil, DPhil; Norwegian research institute director; *Director, International Peace Research Institute, Oslo;* b. 2 Dec. 1953, Copenhagen, Denmark; m.; one c. *Education:* Univ. of Århus, Denmark, Univ. of Oslo. *Career:* taught Norwegian and History at Univ. of Oslo 1983; historian for Norwegian Asscn of Sports 1983–85; wrote doctoral thesis on Vietnam Revolution of 1945 1986–92; Research Fellow, Int. Peace Research Inst., Oslo (PRIO) 1990–92, Dir 2001–09; Research Prof. Nordic Inst. of Asian Studies 1992–95, Sr Research Fellow 1995–98; consultant to Statoil 1996–2000; Prof. of Human Devt Studies, Univ. of Oslo; mem. Advisory Bd Norwegian Forum for Research in US; mem. Bd CARE Norway, Swedish School of Advanced Asia Pacific Studies, Bd NOR-FUND 2007–. *Publications include:* The Vietnamese Revolution of 1945 1991, Imperial Policy and Southeast Asian Nationalism 1930–1957 (co-ed.) 1995, Asian Forms of the Nation (co-ed.) 1996, Vietnam 1946: How the War Began 2008; book chapters and articles in scholarly journals.
Address: Jacob Aalls gt. 13, 0368 Oslo (home); International Peace Research Institute, Fuglehauggata 11, 0260 Oslo, Norway (office). *Telephone:* 22-54-77-31 (office). *Fax:* 22-54-77-01 (office). *E-mail:* stein@prio.no (office). *Website:* www.prio.no (office).

TOPAN, Sanné Mohamed; Burkinabè diplomatist; *Ambassador to Mali;* b. 1 Jan. 1955, Kiembara prov., Sourou; m.; three c. *Career:* fmr. Prof.; Deputy Sec.-Gen., Nat. Comm. for UNESCO 1987–95; Nat. Corresp. Islamic Org. for Educ., Science and Culture 1989–91; Dir Office of the Pres. of Burkina Faso 1996–99; Minister of Employment, Labour and Social Security 1999–2000, of Parl. Relations 2000–02; Amb. to Mali (also accred to Guinea and Niger) 2002–; Officier de l'Ordre Nat. du Burkina Faso.
Address: ACI-2000, Commune III, BP 9022, Bamako, Burkina Faso (office). *Telephone:* 223-31-71 (office). *Fax:* 221-92-66 (office). *E-mail:* ambafaso@experco.net (office).

TOPI, Bamir, PhD, DrSc; Albanian politician, biologist and head of state; *President;* b. 24 April 1957, Tirana; m. Teuta Topi; two d. *Education:* Veterinary Medicine Faculty, Agricultural Univ. of Tirana. *Career:* joined Inst. for Veterinary Studies, Tirana as Scientific Researcher 1984–87, Dir 1990–96; elected to Nat. Ass. 1996, re-elected twice; Minister of Agric. and Food 1996–97; Pres. 2007–; fmr Deputy Chair. Democratic Party, resgnd on taking office 2007.
Address: Office of the President, Bulevardi Dëshmorët e Kombit, Tirana, Albania (office). *Telephone:* (4) 228437 (office). *Fax:* (4) 236925 (office). *E-mail:* info@president.al (office). *Website:* www.president.al (office).

TOPOLÁNEK, Mirek; Czech politician; *Prime Minister;* b. 15 May 1956, Vsetín; m.; three c. *Education:* Brno Univ. of Tech. *Career:* Project Designer, later Ind. Designer, OKD Ostrava 1980–87; Head Designer Specialist, Energoproject Praha, Ostrava Works 1987–91; Exec. Dir then Man. Dir VAE Ltd (later VAE Inc.) 1991–96, Chair. Bd of Dirs 1996; active in citizens forum 1989; mem. Municipal Corpn of Ostrava-Poruba 1990–94; Senator 1995–2004; mem. Civil Democratic Party (ODS) 1994–, Vice-Chair. 1996–98, Chair. 2002–; mem. Cttee for Economy, Agriculture and Transport, Organization Cttee and Chair. of the Sub-cttee for Power Eng, Vice-Pres. of Senate 2002–04; Chair. ODS Senate Club 1990–2002; Prime Minister June–Oct. 2006 (resgnd), reinstated Jan. 2007–; mem. Bd Asscn for Restoration and Devt of Northern Moravian Region and Silesia, Mining Coll., Univ. of Tech., Ostrava, Jagello Asscn.
Address: Office of the Government, náb. E. Beneše 4, 118 01 Prague 1 (office); Civic Democratic Party (Občanská demokratická strana), Jánský vršek 13, 110 00 Prague 1, Czech Republic (office). *Telephone:* 224002111 (office); 234707188 (ODS) (office). *Fax:* 224003090 (office); 234707103 (ODS) (office). *E-mail:* ochvat.radim@vlada.cz (office); hk@ods.cz (office). *Website:* www.vlada.cz (office); www.ods.cz (office); www.topolanek.cz (office).

TOR FAUS, Imma, DEA, Agrégation; Andorran diplomatist; *Ambassador to Belgium;* b. 12 April 1966, Sant Julia de Loria. *Education:* Lycée Comte de Foix, Lycée Saint Sernin de Toulouse, Toulouse Le Mirail Univ., Univ. of Sorbonne, Paris, France. *Career:* teacher training course Centre Pédagogique Régional de Toulouse 1989–90; Teacher of French Language and Literature, Lycée Comte de Foix 1990–98; Amb. and Perm. Rep. to Council of Europe 1998–2004; Minister Counsellor responsible for Consular Affairs, Embassy in Paris, France 1998–99; Amb. to France 1999–, to Belgium 2007–, also Perm. Rep. to EC 2007–; Perm. Rep. to UNESCO 2004–07; Rep. to Francophonie 2004–07.
Address: Embassy of Andorra, 10 rue de la Montagne, 1000 Brussels, Belgium (office). *Telephone:* (2) 513-28-06 (office). *Fax:* (2) 513-07-41 (office). *E-mail:* ambassade@andorra.be (office). *Website:* www.andorra.be (office).

TORLOT, Timothy Achille (Tim); British diplomatist; *Ambassador to Yemen;* b. 17 Sept. 1957; m. Bridie Torlot; one d. *Education:* Trinity School of John Whitgift, Croydon, Worcester Coll., Oxford. *Career:* Desk Officer, N America Dept, FCO 1982–82, Third Sec., Embassy in Muscat 1984–87, Second Sec., Embassy in Wellington 1987–92, Personnel Man. Dept 1992–95, Head of Commonwealth Section, South East Asia Dept 1995–97, Dir, Tech. and Sector Partnership, UK Trade and Investment 1997–2001, Deputy Head of Mission to Iraq 2005–06, Amb. to Yemen 2007–.
Address: British Embassy, PO Box 1287, 938 Dhahr Himiyar, East Ring Road, San'a, Yemen (office). *Telephone:* (1) 308100 (office). *Fax:* (1) 302454 (office). *E-mail:* britishembassysanaa@fco.gov.uk (office). *Website:* www.britishembassy.gov.uk/yemen (office).

TÖRNUDD, Klaus, PhD; Finnish diplomatist and academic; b. 26 Dec. 1931, Helsinki; m. Mirja Siirala 1960; one s. one d. *Education:* Univ. of Helsinki, Univ. of Paris and School of Advanced Int. Studies, Johns Hopkins Univ., Washington DC. *Career:* entered Finnish Foreign Service 1958, served at Finnish Mission to UN 1961–64, Cairo Embassy 1964–66, Moscow Embassy 1971–73, CSCE 1973–74; Prof. of Int. Politics, Univ. of Tampere, Finland 1967–71; Deputy Dir of Political Affairs in the Ministry for Foreign Affairs 1974–77, Dir 1977–81, Under-Sec. of State for Political Affairs 1983–88; Perm. Rep. to the UN 1988–91; Fellow, Harvard Univ., USA 1991–92; Sr Adviser, Ministry for Foreign Affairs 1992–93; Amb. to France and to UNESCO 1993–96; mem. Sr Faculty, Geneva Centre for Security Policy 1997–98; Visting Prof. Nat. Defence Coll. of Finland 1998–2003; Ed. Co-operation and Conflict (Nordic Journal of Int. Politics) 1968–70, mem. Editorial Bd 1976–79; mem. Editorial Bd of Ulkopolitiikka-Utrikespolitik 1983–87; Chair. of Bd Tampere Peace Research Inst. 1978–82; Chair. UN Study Group on Nuclear Weapon-Free Zones 1983–85; mem. Bd of Trustees UNITAR 1984–88; mem. of Bd of Govs IAEA 1985–87; mem. UN Sec.-Gen.'s Advisory Bd on Disarmament Matters 1991–96; Dr hc (Åbo Akademi Univ., Finland) 2002. *Publications:* several books on Finnish politics and int. affairs.
Address: Tempelgatan 8A, 00100 Helsinki, Finland (home). *Telephone:* (9) 490159 (home). *Fax:* (9) 448849 (home). *E-mail:* klaus.toernudd@kolumbus.fi (home).

TORO-HARDY, Alfredo; Venezuelan diplomatist; m. Gabriela Gaxiola de Toro 2001; two s. one d. *Education:* Cen. Univ. of Venezuela, Univ. of Paris II, Int. Inst. of Public Admin, Paris, France, Univ. of Pennsylvania, USA. *Career:* Dir Diplomatic Acad. with rank of Amb., Ministry of Foreign Affairs 1992–94; Adviser to Minister of Foreign Affairs 1992–94; Amb. to Brazil 1994–97, to Chile 1997–99; Rep. to Latin American Econ. Council of the UN, Santiago de Chile 1997–99; Amb. to USA 1999–2001 (also accred

to Bahamas), to UK 2001–07 (also accred to Ireland 2002–07); Rep. to Int. Orgs for Coffee and Cocoa 2003–; mem. Consultative Bd Nat. Security and Defence Council 1988–2000; Adviser to Foreign Affairs Cttee, Chamber of Deputies, Congress of Venezuela 1986–92, to Presidential Comm. for Reform of the State 1989–91, for Borders Affairs 1991–92; Visiting Scholar/Sr Fulbright Scholar, Princeton Univ., USA 1986–87; Assoc. Prof., Simón Bolívar Univ., Caracas, Coordinator Latin American Studies Inst. and Dir N American Studies Centre 1989–91; prof. and guest speaker in several univs and academic insts of Venezuela, USA, Chile, Brazil, UK and other countries; columnist and collaborator, El Universal, Caracas 1994–2000, El Globo, Caracas 1989–97, El Diario de Caracas, 1989–94, Visión, México City 1989–90, Gazeta Mercantil, Sao Paulo 1994–97, Folha de Sao Paulo 1995–97, El Mercurio, Santiago de Chile 1997–99; mem. Editorial Bd Economía Hoy, Caracas 1990–91, Política Internacional, Caracas 1992–2003; mem. Chairmans Club, London, UK, Royal Inst. of Int. Affairs, London, Global Dimensions/LSE, London, Windsor Energy Group, London, Inter-American Dialogue, Washington, DC, USA, Inter-American Peace and Justice Comm., Santiago, Chile; Ad honorem Prof., Univ. of Brasilia 1996–97; several foreign and Venezuelan decorations. *Television:* host of weekly TV program, Radio Caracas Televisión 1992–94. *Publications:* 24 published books on foreign affairs and int. trade relations 1983–2003.
Address: Ministry of Foreign Affairs, Torre MRE, esq. Carmelitas, Avenida Urdaneta, Caracas 1010, Venezuela (office). *Telephone:* (212) 862-1085 (office). *Fax:* (212) 864-3633 (office). *E-mail:* criptogr@mre.gov.ve (office). *Website:* www.mre.gov.ve (office).

TORO JIMENEZ, Fermin; Venezuelan diplomatist; b. 1933, Caracas; m.; four c. *Education:* Cen. Univ. of Venezuela. *Career:* Counsellor to Mission, UN, Geneva 1958–59; fmr Sr Prof., School of Law and Political Science, Cen. Univ. of Venezuela, taught in Int. Public Law, Admin., Civil and Labour Law 1959–2003; Prof., Universidad José Maria Vargas, Escuela Superior de Guerra Naval 2002–03; Dir Inst. of Superior Diplomatic Studies, Ministry of Foreign Relations 1994–99; Legal Advisor to Pres. 2002–03; Dir of Int. Relations in Pres.'s Office 2003; State Agent on Human Rights for Int. System 2003, 2004; Perm. Rep. to UN, New York 2004–06; fmr Head of Human Rights Section, Pres.'s Office of Int. Affairs; mem. American Asscn of Jurists; founding mem. American Asscn of Jurists (Venezuelan chapter), Sec.-Gen. 1986–. *Publications:* several articles and books on politics, diplomacy, int. public law, human rights, foreign policy.
Address: c/o Ministry of Foreign Affairs, Torre MRE, esq. Carmelitas, Avda Urdaneta, Caracas, Venezuela (office). *Website:* www.mre.gov.ve (office).

TORRIJOS ESPINO, Martin; Panamanian business executive, politician and head of state; *President;* b. 18 July 1963, Panama City; m. Vivian de Torrijos; one s. *Education:* Texas A&M Univ., USA. *Career:* fmr man. McDonald's, Chicago, USA; Sec.-Gen. Democratic Revolutionary Party (PRD) 1999–; cand. for presidential elections 1999; Pres. of Panama 2004–; Vice-Pres. Conference of Political Parties of Latin America and the Caribbean (COPPAL) 2002–.
Address: Office of the President, Palacio Presidencial, Valija 50, Panamá 1, Panama (office). *Telephone:* 227-4062 (office). *Fax:* 227-0076 (office). *Website:* www.presidencia.gob.pa (office).

TORRY, Sir Peter James, KCMG, KCVO; British diplomatist; b. 1948, Berlin, Germany; m. Angela Torry; three d. *Education:* Dover Coll., New Coll., Oxford. *Career:* joined FCO 1970, Third Sec., Havana 1971–74, Second Sec. (Econ.), Jakarta 1974–77, First Sec., FCO 1977–81, 1985–89 (later also Counsellor), First Sec. (Political), Bonn 1981–85, Counsellor, Washington, DC 1989–93, Dir for Personnel and Security, FCO 1993–98, Amb. to Spain 1998–2003, to Germany 2003–07.
Address: c/o Foreign and Commonwealth Office, King Charles Street, London SW1A 2AH, England (office). *Website:* www.fco.gov.uk (office).

TORSTILA, Pertti, MPolSci; Finnish diplomatist; *Secretary of State, Ministry of Foreign Affairs;* b. 13 Feb. 1946; m.; two c. *Education:* Univ. of Helsinki, Ecole Nat. d'Admin, Paris. *Career:* joined Finnish Foreign Service 1970, Preparatory Negotiations, CSCE 1972–73, Summit Meeting, Helsinki 1975, Second Sec., Finnish Embassy, Paris 1973–76, First Sec., Finnish Embassy, Budapest 1976–78, Political Dept, Foreign Ministry, Helsinki 1979–80, Counsellor, Finnish Embassy, Paris 1981–84, Dir Disarmament and Security Policy, CSCE, Foreign Ministry 1984–88, Deputy Dir-Gen. Political Dept 1988–89, Amb. and Head of Finnish Del. to CSCE Negotiations, Vienna 1989–92, Amb. to Hungary and Croatia 1992–96, Dir-Gen. for Political Affairs, Foreign Ministry 1996–2000, Under-Sec. of State 2000– (Acting Sec. of State Oct.–Dec. 2001), Amb. to Sweden 2002–06; Sec. of State, Ministry of Foreign Affairs 2006–.
Address: Ministry of Foreign Affairs, Merikasarmi, Laivastokatu 22, Merikasarminkatu 5f, PO Box 176, 00161 Helsinki, Finland (office).

Telephone: (9) 16055010 (office). *Fax:* (9) 16056555 (office). *E-mail:* pertti .torstila@formin.fi (office). *Website:* formin.finland.fi (office).

TOŠOVSKÝ, Josef, BCom; Czech banker; *Chairman, Financial Stability Institute;* b. 28 Sept. 1950, Náchod; m. Bohdana Světlíková; two d. *Education:* Univ. of Econs Prague. *Career:* Assoc. Prof. Univ. of Econs, Prague; banker with Czechoslovak State Bank 1973–, Deputy Dir 1978–, consultant to Bank Chair. 1982; Chief Economist, Živnostenská banka, London 1984–85, Deputy Dir June–Dec. 1989; Consultant to Bank Chair., Prague 1986–89; Chair. Czechoslovak State Bank 1989–92, Gov. 1992, for Czech Nat. Bank 1993–97, 1998–2000; Prime Minister of Czech Repub. 1997–98; Chair. Financial Stability Inst., BIS, Basel, Switzerland 2000–; Dr hc (Mendelova Univ. Brno) 2002; Cen. Banker of the Year, IMF 1993, European Man. of the Year, European Business Press Fed. 1994, Karel Engliš Prize 1994, European Banker of the Year, Group 20 + 1 1996, East-West Inst. Award for Leadership in Transition (USA) 2001. *Publications:* numerous articles in professional press.
Address: Financial Stability Institute, Bank for International Settlements, Centralbahnplatz 2, 4002 Basel, Switzerland (office). *Telephone:* (61) 2808074 (office). *Fax:* (61) 2809100 (office). *E-mail:* josef.tosovsky@bis .org (office). *Website:* www.bis.org (office).

TOUABOY, Emmanuel; Central African Republic diplomatist; *Ambassador to USA;* m. Mireille Nathalie Touaboy; several c. *Career:* Amb. to USA and Perm. Rep. to UN, New York 2001–; mem. Advisory Bd Jarch Management 2008–; High Steward Euclid Univ.
Address: Embassy of Central African Republic, 1618 22nd Street, NW, Washington, DC 20008, USA (office). *Telephone:* (202) 483-7800 (office). *Fax:* (202) 332-9893 (office). *Website:* www.embassy.org/embassies/cf.html (office).

TOUADÉRA, Faustin-Archange, BSc, MSc, PhD; Central African Republic mathematician, university vice-chancellor and politician; *Prime Minister;* b. 21 April 1957, Bangui. *Education:* Barthelemy Boganda Coll., Bangui, Univ. of Bangui, Univ. of Abidjan, Côte d'Ivoire, Lille Univ. of Science and Tech. (Lille I), France, Univ. of Yaoundé I, Cameroon. *Career:* Asst Lecturer in Math., Faculty of Science, Univ. of Bangui 1987, Vice-Dean Faculty of Science 1989–92, apptd Dir Coll. for Training of Teachers (ENS) 1992, Vice-Chancellor Univ. of Bangui 2004–08; mem. Inter-state Cttee for Standardization of Math. Programmes in French-speaking countries and Indian Ocean (CIEHPM) 1992–2002, Pres. CIEHPM 2001–03; mem. African Network of Math. and Applications for Devt (RAMAD) 2001–; Vice-Pres. Math. Union of Cen. African Repub. (UMAC) 2003–; Prime Minister of Cen. African Repub. 2008–; Chevalier of the Order, Officer of the Order, Kt of the Order (all for services to educ.).
Address: Office of the Prime Minister, c/o Office of the President, Palais de la Renaissance, Bangui, Central African Republic (office). *Telephone:* 61-46-63 (office).

TOUNGUI, Paul; Gabonese politician; *Minister of State for Economic Affairs, Finance, the Budget and Privatization;* s.-in-law of Pres. Omar Bongo. *Career:* fmr Univ. Prof. of Math.; Minister of Mines, Energy Resources, Oil and Hydro Resources 2001; Minister of State for Econ. Affairs, Finance, the Budget and Privatization 2002–; First Vice-Chair. IMF Intergovernmental Group of 24 on Int. Monetary Affairs and Devt; mem. Bd of Govs African Devt Bank, Islamic Devt Bank.
Address: Ministry of Economic Affairs, Finance, the Budget and Privatization, BP 165, Libreville, Gabon (office). *Telephone:* 76-12-10 (office). *Fax:* 76-59-74 (office).

TOURAY, Omar Alieu, MA, PhD; Gambian diplomatist; *Secretary of State for Foreign Affairs;* b. Farafenni; m.; three c. *Education:* Grad. Inst. of International Studies, Univ. of Geneva. *Career:* joined diplomatic corps as Sr Asst Sec., Ministry of External Affairs 1995, served at Embassy in Brussels and at Mission to EU 1995–2002; Amb.to Ethiopia, Perm. Rep.to African Union and High Commr to South Africa and Kenya 2002–07; Perm. Rep. to UN, New York.2007; Coordinator, Nat. Authority Officer System Support Unit 2008; Head, Food and Trade Asscn 2008; Sec. of State for Foreign Affairs 2008–; fmr Pres. GAM-Solar Energy; mem. Bd of Dirs Nat. Centre for Arts and Culture. *Publications:* The Gambia and the World: A History of the Foreign Policy of Africa's Smallest State, 1965–1995 2000; numerous papers on int. econ. relations.
Address: Department of State for Foreign Affairs, 4 Col. Muammar Ghadaffi Avenue, Banjul, Gambia (office). *Telephone:* 4223577 (office). *Fax:* 4223578 (office).

TOURÉ, Lt-Col Amadou Toumani; Malian army officer and head of state; *President;* b. 4 Nov. 1948, Mopti; m.; two d. *Education:* Ecole Normale Secondaire de Badalabougou, Bamako. *Career:* with Armed Forces of Mali, Lt 1974–78, Capt. 33rd Parachute Bn 1978–84, Commdr 1984–88,

rank of Lt-Col 1988, Brigade General 1992–96, Army General 1996–; Commdr Presidential Guard 1981–84; led coup which overthrew Gen. Moussa Traoré March 1991; Leader Nat. Reconciliation Council 1991–92; Chair. Transition Cttee for the Salvation of the People (acting Head of State) 1991–92; participated in diplomatic initiatives in Rwanda, Burundi, Togo 1996, Cen. African Repub. 1997; Head Inter-African Mission to Monitor the Implementation of the Bangui Agreements 1997–; Pres. of Mali 2002–; Rotary Int. Paul Harris Fellow; Chevalier, National Order of Mali 1981, Grand Cross 1993, Gold Medal of Independence, Mali 1992, Commander, Légion d'Honneur 1994, Grand Officier 1998, Grand Officier, Central African Order of Merit 1996, Grand Officer, Order of Merit of Chad 1997, Grand Medal, Int. Order of Lawyers 2005; Laureate Prize for the Promotion of Democracy in Africa, Observatoire Panafricain de la Démocratie (OPAD) 1996, Prix du Ciwara d'Exception 1997, Prix Chaba Sangare 2001.
Address: Office of the President, B.P. 1463, Koulouba, Bamako, Mali. *Telephone:* 222-25-72 (office). *Fax:* 223-00-26 (office). *E-mail:* presidence@ koulouba.pr.ml (office). *Website:* www.koulouba.pr.ml (office).

TOURÉ, Aminata Djibrilla Maiga, BA; Niger diplomatist; *Ambassador to USA. Education:* Univ. of Togo, postgraduate studies in Paris and Cameroon. *Career:* joined Ministry of Foreign Affairs 1979, served in Dept of Legal and Consular Affairs –1991, posting to Embassy in Bonn 1991–95; Mayor of Niamey Commune II under supervision of Ministry of Interior 1996–2000; Parl. Sec., Ministry of Foreign Affairs 2000–03, Gen. Sec. Nat. Francophony Comm. 2003–05, Amb. to USA 2006–.
Address: Embassy of Niger, 2204 R Street, NW, Washington, DC 20008, USA (office). *Telephone:* (202) 483-4224 (office). *Fax:* (202) 483-3169 (office). *E-mail:* ambassadeniger@hotmail.com (office). *Website:* www .nigerembassyusa.org (office).

TOURÉ, Modibo, BSc, MBA; Malian international organization official; *Secretary General, African Development Bank;* m.; three c. *Education:* Ecole Nationale d'Admin, Bamako, Vanderbilt Univ., USA. *Career:* consultant with Shell Oil, Mali 1982–84; Inspecteur des Finances, Bamako 1984–87; Man. United Parcel Service, Nashville, Tenn., USA 1989–90; UNDP Program Officer and later Asst Resident Rep., Burkina Faso 1991–94, Deputy Resident Rep., Djibouti 1994–97, Program Man., New York 1997–98, Sr Deputy Resident Rep., Rwanda 1998–99, Sr Country Program Man., New York 1999–2001, Special Advisor to Dir, Regional Bureau for Africa, New York 2000–01, UN Resident Coordinator, Humanitarian Coordinator and UN Resident Rep., Chad 2001–04, UNDP Resident and Humanitarian Coordinator, Ethiopia 2004–05, mem. UNDP Transition Team 2005–06; Dir UN Mine Action Service 2005–06; Sec. Gen. African Devt Bank (ADB) 2006–.
Address: African Development Bank, 15 avenue du Ghana, angle des rues Pierre de Coubertin et Hedi Nouira, BP 323, 1002 Tunis Belvédère, Tunisia (office); ADB Headquarters, Rue Joseph Anoma, 01 BP 1387, Abidjan 01, Côte d'Ivoire. *Telephone:* (71) 333-511 (Tunis) (office). *Fax:* (71) 351-933 (Tunis) (office). *E-mail:* afdb@afdb.org (office). *Website:* www.afdb.org (office).

TOWPIK, Andrzej, DJur; Polish diplomatist and civil servant; *Permanent Representative, United Nations;* b. 1939; m.; two s. *Education:* Main School of Foreign Service, Warsaw, Columbia Univ., New York, USA, Jagiellonian Univ., Kraków. *Career:* Research Fellow Polish Inst. of Int. Affairs 1962–75; with Ministry of Foreign Affairs 1975–, positions including Sec. of Embassy in Madrid, Spain 1977–81, Deputy Dir Policy Planning Dept 1981–86, Counsellor-Minister Perm. Mission to UN, Geneva 1986–90, Dir Dept of European Inst. 1990, Amb. (ad personam) 1993, Political Dir 1994, Under-Sec. of State for Polish Security Policy 1994–97, Perm. Rep. and Head of Mission to NATO and WEU 1997–2002; Under-Sec. of State for Defence Policy, Ministry of Nat. Defence 2002; currently Perm. Rep. to UN, New York.
Address: Permanent Mission of Poland to the UN, 9 East 66th Street, New York, NY 10021, USA. *Telephone:* (212) 744-2506. *Fax:* (212) 517-6771. *E-mail:* poland@un.int. *Website:* www.un.int/poland.

TRAAVIK, Kim; Norwegian diplomatist; *Permanent Representative, NATO; Career:* joined Ministry of Foreign Affairs 1977; numerous overseas postings including Embassy in Helsinki 1979–82, Perm. Mission to UN, New York 1982–85, Perm. Mission to NATO, Brussels 1987–89; Head of Security Policy and Arms Control Divs, Ministry of Foreign Affairs 1989–92, Asst Dir Gen. and Head of European Political Affairs Section 1992–94; DCM, Perm. Mission to EU, Brussels 1994–97; Amb. to OSCE 1997–99; Dir Gen. European for European Political Affairs, Ministry of Foreign Affairs 2000–01; Chair Working Table III (Security Issues), Stability Pact for Southeastern Europe 2000–01; State Sec. and Deputy Foreign Minister 2001–05; Perm. Rep. to NATO, Brussels 2006–.

Address: North Atlantic Treaty Organization, blvd Léopold III, 1110 Brussels, Belgium (office). *Telephone:* (2) 707-41-11 (office). *Fax:* (2) 707-45-79 (office). *E-mail:* natodoc@hq.nato.int (office). *Website:* www.nato.int (office).

TRAD, Faisal Hassan, BA; Saudi Arabian diplomatist; *Ambassador to Japan;* b. 12 Feb. 1956, Al Medina Al Monawara; m.; five c. *Education:* King Abdel-Aziz Univ., Jeddah. *Career:* Attaché, Econ. Section, Ministry of Foreign Affairs 1978, Head, Dept for Bilateral Econ. Relations 1990–98, Head, Dept for Multilateral Econ. Relations 1998–2001; overseas postings include Second Sec., Embassy in London 1981–85, First Sec., Embassy in Brussels 1985–90, Perm. Rep. to Arab League, Cairo 2001–04; currently Amb. to Japan.
Address: Embassy of Saudi Arabia, 1-8-4, Roppongi, Minato-ku, Tokyo 106-0032, Japan (office). *Telephone:* (3) 3589-5241 (office). *Fax:* (3) 3589-5200 (office). *E-mail:* info@saudiembassy.or.jp (office). *Website:* www.saudiembassy.or.jp (office).

TRAORÉ, Aboubacar; Malian government official. *Career:* Minister of the Economy and Finance 2004–.
Address: Ministry of the Economy and Finance, BP 234, Koulouba, Bamako, Mali (office). *Telephone:* 222-51-56 (office). *Fax:* 222-01-92 (office).

TRAORÉ, Mamady; Guinean diplomatist; *Minister of Trade and Industry, Tourism and Crafts;* b. 1952, Sareya; m.; four c. *Education:* Polytechnic Inst. of Conakry, Oxford Univ., UN Inst. for Training and Research (UNITAR), Geneva. *Career:* teacher, Teacher Training Coll. of Econ., Econ. Law School, Lola, Yomou, Conakry; joined Ministry of Foreign Affairs 1980, Head of African and OAU Div., Dept of Political and Cultural Affairs 1980–84, Head of Asia and Middle E Div. 1986–88, Head of Africa and Asia Div. 1988–89, Counsellor, Guinea Embassy, Tripoli, Libya 1989–92, Chargé d'affaires 1992–93, Amb. to Nigeria 1998–2002, to Mali 2003–07, Perm. Rep. to UN, NY 2002–03, Pres. UN Security Council 2003; Minister of Industry, Tourism and Crafts 2007–.
Address: Ministry of Trade and Industry, BP 468, Conakry, Guinea (office). *Telephone:* 30-44-26-06 (office). *Fax:* 30-44-49-90 (office).

TRECHSEL, Stefan, DIur; Swiss lawyer; *Judge ad litem, International Criminal Tribunal for the former Yugoslavia;* b. 25 June 1937, Berne; m. Franca Julia Kinsbergen 1967; two d. *Education:* Univ. of Berne and Georgetown Univ., Washington, DC. *Career:* Asst and Main Asst for Criminal Law, Univ. of Berne 1964–71; Swiss Fed. Dept for Tech. Cooperation 1966–67; Public Prosecutor, Dist of Bern-Mittelland 1971–75; Guest Prof. of Criminal Law and Procedure, Univ. of Fribourg 1975–77; Prof., Hochschule St Gallen 1979–99; Prof. of Criminal Law and Legal Instruction, Univ. of Zurich 1999–2004, Prof. Emer. 2004–; Judge ad litem, Int. Criminal Tribunal for the fmr Yugoslavia, The Hague, Netherlands 2004–; mem. European Comm. of Human Rights 1975–99, 2nd Vice-Pres. 1987, Chamber Pres. 1993–94, Pres. 1995–99; Council of Europe Medal pro merito 2004; Dr hc (New York Univ. Law School) 1975. *Publications:* Der Strafgrund der Teilnahme 1967, Die Europäische Menschenrechtskonvention, ihr Schutz der persönlichen Freiheit und die Schweizerischen Strafprozessrechte 1974, Strafrecht Allgemeiner Teil I (6th edn of textbook by Peter Noll) 1994, Schweizerisches Strafgesetzbuch, Kurzkommentar 1997, Human Rights in Criminal Proceedings 2005.
Address: Rabbentalstrasse 63, 3013 Bern, Switzerland (home). *Telephone:* (3170) 306-15-11 (home). *E-mail:* trechsel@gmx.net (office). *Website:* www.rws.unizh.ch (office); www.un.org/icty.

TREKY, Ali Abdussalam, PhD; Libyan diplomatist and politician; b. 10 Oct. 1938, Misurata; m. Aisha Dihoum 1969; one s. three d. *Education:* Univ. of Benghazi, Libya and Toulouse Univ., France. *Career:* joined Foreign Ministry 1970; Minister Plenipotentiary 1970, Dir of Political Admin 1970–73, Dir of African Admin 1973–74, Asst Deputy for Political Affairs 1974–76; Sec. of State for Foreign Affairs 1971–77, Foreign Sec. 1977–81, Sec. of Liaison for Foreign Affairs 1981–86; Foreign Minister 1984–86; Head of Libyan del. to UN Gen. Ass. 1977–80; Perm. Rep. of Libya to the UN 1982–84, 1986–91, 2003–07, to League of Arab States, Cairo 1991–93; Amb. to France 1995–2001; Minister of African Affairs –2003; Sec. Libyan Popular Cttee for African Unity 2000–.
Address: c/o Secretariat of the People's Committee for Foreign Liaison and International Co-operation, Tripoli, Libya (office).

TREMONTI, Giulio; Italian politician and lawyer; *Minister of Finance;* b. 18 Aug. 1947, Sondrio, Lombardy. *Education:* Univ. of Pavia. *Career:* teacher of tax law, Univ. of Pavia; fmr Sr Teaching Fellow, Inst. of European and Comparative Law, Univ. of Oxford, UK; mem. Camera dei Deputati (Parl.) (Forza Italia) 1994–, mem. Parl. Special Cttee for Reform of Italian Constitution; Minister of Finance 1994–95, 2008–, of Economy and Finance 2001–04 (resgnd), Sept. 2005–06, Deputy Prime Minister 2005–06; Pres. Comm. for Monetary Reform 1994–95; 1994–95; fmr Vice-Pres. Aspen Inst. Italia; mem. Italy/Vatican Cttee for Treaty on Financing of Ecclesiastical Insts, Comm. on Deregulation; Ed. Rivista di Diritto Finanziario e Scienza delle Finanze; regular contrib., Corriere della Sera. *Publications:* several books on tax and public policy.
Address: Ministry of Finance, Via XX Settembre 97, 00187 Rome, Italy (office). *Telephone:* (06) 476111 (office). *Fax:* (06) 5910993 (office). *E-mail:* pubblicazione.sito@tesoro.it (office). *Website:* www.mef.gov.it (office).

TRENDAFILOVA, Ekaterina Panayotova, PhD; Bulgarian barrister and judge; *Judge, International Criminal Court;* b. 20 June 1953, Sofia; m. Emil Roussev Bachvarov; one d. *Education:* Sofia Univ. 'St Kliment Ohridski'. *Career:* legal internship, Sofia City Court 1977–78; Deputy Dist Attorney, Sofia Dist Court 1985–89; specialization at Inst. of State and Law, Moscow, USSR 1983, 1985; Prof., Faculty of Law, Sofia Univ. 'St Kliment Ohridski' 1984–, Assoc. Prof. (Docent) 1996–2001, Full Prof. 2001–; Prof., Faculty of Law, Veliko Turnovo Univ. 'Sts Cyril and Methodius' 1995–; Visiting Prof., Tokai Univ., Japan 1993; called to the Bar of Bulgaria 1995; advised the Ministry of Foreign Affairs on the establishment of the Int. Criminal Court (ICC) and served as an expert to the Ministry of Justice, Ministry of Interior, Constitutional Court, Supreme Court of Cassation and Parl. of Bulgaria where she chaired the Criminal Div. of the Legis. Consultative Council; Judge, Pre-Trial Div., ICC 2003–(12); mem. Intergovernmental Comm. entrusted with the preparation of the ratification of the European Convention on Human Rights and Fundamental Freedoms 1991; Bulgarian Rep. to UN Comm. for Crime Prevention and Criminal Justice, Vienna 1992–94; Chair. Program and Analytical Center for European Law 1999–, Modern Criminal Procedure Foundation 1999–; Vice-Pres. Specialized Scientific Council on Legal Science 2003–04; mem. Comm. for Social Sciences at the Higher Accreditation Agency with the Council of Ministers of Bulgaria 2000–03, Legal Comm. Nat. Higher Attestation Comm. with the Council of Ministers of Bulgaria 2004–05; scientific advisor, Students' Internship Program between the American Govt and Bulgarian Parl. 2000–05; Head, Criminal Div. Legis. Consultative Council with the Speaker of the Bulgarian Parl. 2001–05; Middle-term expert under the PHARE Twinning project (Bulgaria–Austria) 2002–03; mem. Consultative Council Open Soc. Inst. Project "Access to Justice" 2002–05, Advisory Bd Open Soc. Inst. Int. Project "Independence and Accountability of Prosecution" 2003–05; European expert within EC CARDS Regional Project 2004–; Head of Working Group on Judicial Reform, Open Soc. Inst. Project Strategy for the Socio-econ. and Political Devt of Bulgaria 2005–2010 2004–05; mem. Editorial Bd Human Rights Review 2003–; mem. Union of Bulgarian Lawyers 1980–, Union of Bulgarian Scholars 1984– (Chair. legal section 2001–03), Bulgarian Humboldt Soc. 1994–, Bulgarian Fulbright Soc. 1997–, Women with Int. Societal Expertise (WISE), Paris 2004–; Hon. mem. European Correspondents Scientific Cttee, Centre Int. Constats et Prospective, Paris 1991; Best Young Lecturer of the Year Award, Nat. Soc. for Dissemination of Legal Knowledge 1984, Alexander von Humboldt Scholarship, Augsburg Univ., Germany 1993–94, Fulbright Scholarship, Univ. of California, USA 1997, Author of the Year Award for contrib. to the legal literature 2000, Legal Initiative for Training and Devt Award 2004. *Publications:* more than 70 publs in Bulgaria, USA, France, Italy and the Netherlands in the field of human rights law, criminal procedural law, int. criminal procedural law, comparative law and constitutional law.
Address: International Criminal Court, PO Box 19519, 2500 CM, The Hague (office); International Criminal Court, Maanweg 174, 2516 AB, The Hague, Netherlands (office). *Telephone:* (70) 515-8515 (office). *Fax:* (70) 515-8555 (office). *E-mail:* eptrend@abv.bg (office); pio@icc-cpi.int (office). *Website:* www.icc-cpi.int (office); www.icc-cpi.int/library/asp/ICC-ASP_ej2_bul-cv.pdf (office).

TREVIÑO, Adm. Jose Maria; Spanish naval officer; *Military Representative, NATO;* b. Granada; m. Lola Portela 1973; one s. two d. *Education:* Naval Acad., Naval War Coll., NATO Defence Coll., Rome. *Career:* served on surface ships and submarines as Ensign, Temerario, Poseidon, as Lt, Narciso Monturiol, Cosme Garcia, Delfin, as Exec. Officer, Tonina, Communications Officer, sailing training ship Juan Sebastián Elcano; commands at sea included Lt, MCM diving unit UBMCM and minesweeper Odiel, Lt-Commdr, submarine Marsopa, Commdr, FFG class frigate Navarra (took part in Sharp Guard Operation, Adriatic Sea, during Yugoslavian conflict), Capt., Spanish Submarine Flotilla, Commdr CVBG Group (as Rear-Adm.) and Spanish–Italian Amphibious Force (SIAF) (including tour of Persian Gulf) 2002–04, also served as Chief of Staff of Spanish Fleet; posts ashore included Intelligence Div., Jt Defence Staff HQ, Madrid, Dir of Naval Intelligence, Gen. Naval Staff HQ, Chief of Cabinet of Minister of Defence, Chief of Staff of Jt Command, Lisbon; promoted to Adm. 2006; Mil. Rep., NATO, Brussels 2006–; Grand Crosses of Saint Hermenegildo, Navy and Air Merit, Commdr de l'Ordre National

du Mérite, Honour Sword of Republic of Argentina; NATO Medal, WEU medal, Army Merit Cross, four Navy Merit Crosses.
Address: NATO HQ, blvd Léopold III, 1110 Brussels, Belgium (office). *Telephone:* (2) 707-41-11 (office). *Fax:* (2) 707-45-79 (office). *E-mail:* natodoc@hq.nato.int (office). *Website:* www.nato.int (office).

TRICHET, Jean-Claude, LèsSc (Econ); French banker; *President, European Central Bank;* b. 20 Dec. 1942, Lyon; m. Aline Rybalka 1965; two s. *Education:* Ecole des Mines, Nancy, Univ. of Paris, Inst. d'Etudes Politiques, Paris, Faculté Sciences Economiques, Paris and Ecole Nat. d'Admin. *Career:* Engineer, competitive sector 1966–68, Insp. of Finances 1971–76; assigned to Gen. Inspectorate of Finance 1974, assigned to Treasury Dept 1975, Sec.-Gen. Business Restructuring Interministerial Cttee 1976–78; Adviser, Minister of Economic Affairs 1978; Adviser to Pres. of Repub. 1978–81; Head of Devt Aid Office and Deputy Dir of Bilateral Affairs, Treasury Dept 1981, Head of Int. Affairs, Treasury Dept 1985; Chief of Staff to Minister of Finance 1986–87; Dir Treasury Dept 1987; Alternate Gov. IMF and World Bank 1987, Under-Sec. of Treas. and Censor Bank of France 1987–93; Gov. Bank of France 1993–2003; Chair. Paris Club 1985–93; mem. Bd of Dirs BIS 1993–2003, EMI 1994–98; a Gov. IBRD 1993–95; Vice-Gov. IMF 1995–2003; Chair. Monetary Cttee of EC 1992–93; Dir European Cen. Bank 1998–2003, Pres. 2003–; Chair. Group of Ten Central Bank Govs 2003–; Officier, Légion d'honneur, Ordre nat. du Mérite; decorations (Commdr) from Austria, Argentina, Belgium, Brazil, Ecuador, Germany, Ivory Coast, Yugoslavia; Policy Maker of the Year, Int. Economy Magazine 1991, Prize Zebilli Marimo, Acad. des Sciences Morales et Politiques 1999, Int. Prize Pico della Mirandola 2002. *Publications:* various articles on finance and economy.
Address: European Central Bank, Kaiserstrasse 29, 60311 Frankfurt am Main, Germany (office). *Telephone:* (69) 1344-7301 (office). *Fax:* (69) 1344-7305 (office). *E-mail:* info@ecb.europa.eu (office). *Website:* www.ecb.europa.eu (office).

TRIESMAN, Baron (Life Peer), cr. 2004, of Tottenham in the London Borough of Haringey; **David Maxim Triesman,** MA, FRSA; British politician and trade unionist; *Prime Minister's Special Envoy on Returns;* b. 30 Oct. 1943, Hertfordshire; m. Lucy Hooberman 2004. *Education:* Stationers' Co. School, London, Univ. of Essex and King's Coll., Cambridge. *Career:* Sr Research Officer in Addiction, Inst. of Psychiatry 1970–74; secondment to Asscn of Scientific, Tech. and Managerial Staff 1974–75; Sr Lecturer and Co-ordinator Post grad. Research, Poly tech. of South Bank 1975–84; Deputy Sec.-Gen. (Nat. Negotiating Sec.) Nat. Asscn of Teachers in Further and Higher Educ. 1984–93; Gen. Sec. Asscn of Univ. Teachers 1993–2001; Gen. Sec. Labour Party 2001–03, Govt Whip and Lord-in-Waiting 2004–05; Parl. Under-Sec. of State for Foreign and Commonwealth Affairs 2005–07; Govt Spokesman on Higher Educ., Trade and Industry, Foreign Affairs and Aid 2004–; Prime Minister's Special Envoy on Returns 2007–; Visiting Prof. in Social Econs, St Lawrence Univ. 1977; Visiting Fellow in Econs, Wolfson Coll., Cambridge 2000–; Sr Visiting Fellow, Univ. of Warwick 2003–; Visiting Fellow, LSE 2004–; mem. Greater London Manpower Bd 1981–86, Home Office Consultative Cttee on Prison Educ. 1980–83, Burnham Further and Higher Educ. Cttee 1980–84, Univ. Entrance and Schools Exams Bd for Social Science 1980–84, Standing Cttee on Business and the Community, Higher Educ. Funding Council for England 1999–; mem. Kensington, Chelsea and Westminster Area Health Authority 1976–82; mem. Industrial Relations Public Appointments Panel, Dept of Trade and Industry 1996–2001, Ind. Review of Higher Educ. Pay and Conditions 1998–99, Cabinet Office Better Regulation Task Force 2000–03, Treasury Public Services Productivity Panel 2000–03, British N American Cttee 1999–; Chair. (non-exec.) Mortgage Credit Corpn 1978–2001, Vic. Man. Ltd 2000–01; Chair. Usecolor Foundation 2001; mem. Fabian Soc. 1974–, Charles Rennie Mackintosh Soc., Glasgow 1986–, Highgate Literary and Scientific Inst. 1990–; mem. Council Ruskin Coll., Oxford 2000–03; Hon. Fellow, Univ. of Northampton 1995. *Publications include:* The Medical and Non-Medical Use of Drugs 1969, Football Mania (with G. Viani) 1972, Football in London 1985, College Administration (co-author) 1988, Managing Change 1991, Can Unions Survive (Staniewski Memorial Lecture) 1999, Higher Education for the New Century 2000.
Address: House of Lords, Westminster, London, SW1A 0PW, England (office). *Telephone:* (20) 7219-1114 (office). *E-mail:* triesman@parliament.uk (office).

TRIET, Nguyen Minh, BS; Vietnamese politician and head of state; *President;* b. 8 Oct. 1942, Ben Cat dist., Binh Duong Prov. *Education:* Nguyen Ai Quoc Party School, Saigon Univ. *Career:* active in Sai Gon Students' Movt 1960–63; mem. Cadre of Cen. Cttee of the People's Revolutionary Youth Union and Youth Mobilisation of Party Cen. Cttee's Dept for S Vietnam, also Sec.Agency's Youth Union 1963–73, Deputy Dir.Office of Youth Union and Deputy Chief Youth Union Cen. Cttee's Bd for Voluntary

Young People 1974–79; apptd additional mem. Party Cttee of Song Be Prov., Perm. Deputy Sec. 1989–91; mem. Party Cen. Cttee 1991–; Deputy Nat. Ass. 1991–2006; mem. Politburo 1997–; Dir Cen. Party Cttee's Comm. for Mass Mobilisation 1997–2000; Sec. Ho Chi Minh City Party Cttee 1997–2000, Gen. Sec. 2000–06; Pres. of Viet Nam 2006–.
Address: c/o Dang Cong San Viet Nam (Communist Party of Viet Nam), 1 Hoang Van Thu, Hanoi, Viet Nam. *E-mail:* cpv@hn.vnn.vn. *Website:* www.cpv.org.vn.

TRIVELLI, Paul A., BA, MA; American diplomatist; b. 1953, New York City; m. Evangelina Valle; one s. one d. *Education:* Williams Coll., Univ. of Denver, Naval War Coll. *Career:* entered Foreign Service in 1978, served as Econ./Commercial Officer for most of career, has been posted to Mexico City, Quito, Panama City, El Salvador, Monterrey, Managua and State Dept Bureau of Western Hemisphere Affairs, Deputy Chief of Mission, Embassy in Tegucigalpa, Honduras 1998–2002, Dir Office of Cen. American Affairs 2002–03, Dir Office of Policy Planning and Coordination, Bureau of Western Hemisphere Affairs 2003–05, Amb. to Nicaragua 2005–08.
Address: Department of State, 2201 C St, NW, Washington, DC 20520, USA (office). *Telephone:* (202) 647-4000 (office). *Fax:* (202) 647-6738 (office). *Website:* www.state.gov (office).

TROTT, Christopher John; British diplomatist; *Ambassador to Senegal;* b. 14 Feb. 1966; m. Sunna Park; one s. *Career:* Desk Officer, Middle East Dept, FCO 1991–92, Deputy Head of Mission, Embassy in Rangoon (now Yangon) 1993–96, First Sec., Commercial Dept, Embassy in Tokyo 1996–99, Political Dept 1999–2002, temp. appointments as Deputy Head of Mission, Kabul, Afghanistan and Head of Consular Assistance Team, London 2002–03, Desk Officer, Human Rights Policy Dept 2003–04, Secondment to Interdepartmental Post Conflict Reconstruction Unit 2004–07, Amb. to Senegal 2007–.
Address: British Embassy, 20 rue du Dr Guillet, BP 6025, Dakar, Senegal (office). *Telephone:* 823-73-92 (office). *Fax:* 823-27-66 (office). *E-mail:* britemb@sentoo.sn (office). *Website:* www.britishembassy.gov.uk/senegal (office).

TROVOADA, Patrice Emery; São Tomé and Príncipe politician; b. 18 March 1962, Libreville, Gabon. *Career:* Minister of Foreign Affairs 2001–02; oil adviser to Pres. Fradique de Menezes –2005 (sacked by Pres.); Sec.-Gen. Independent Democratic Action (ADI) Party; cand. in presidential election July 2006; Prime Minister 2008.
Address: Acção Democrática Independente (ADI), Av. Marginal 12 de Julho, Edif. C. Cassandra, São Tomé, São Tomé and Príncipe (office). *Telephone:* 222201 (office).

TRUBNIKOV, Gen. Vyacheslav Ivanovich; Russian security officer, politician and diplomatist; *Ambassador to India;* b. 25 April 1944, Irkutsk; m.; one d. *Education:* Moscow State Inst. of Int. Relations. *Career:* served in USSR KGB (First Main Directorate, intelligence) 1967–91; staff mem. HQ of First Main Dept (intelligence) 1977–84; KGB station officer in India (as corresp. Press Agency Novosti) 1971–77; mem. Union of Journalists 1973; resident in Bangladesh and India 1984–90; Head Div. of America KGB 1990–92; First Deputy Dir Russian Intelligence Service 1992–96, Dir 1996–2000; mem. Security Council, Defence Council and Foreign Policy Council of Russia 1996; First Deputy Minister of Foreign Affairs 2000–04; Amb. to India 2004–.
Address: Embassy of the Russian Federation, Shanti Path, Chanakyapuri, New Delhi, 110 021, India. *Telephone:* (11) 26873799 (office). *Fax:* (11) 26876823 (office). *E-mail:* indrusem@del2.vsnl.net.in (office). *Website:* www.india.mid.ru (office).

TRUMAN, Edwin Malcolm, BA, MA, PhD; American economist and academic; *Senior Fellow, Peterson Institute for International Economics;* b. 6 June 1941, Albany, NY; m. Tracy P. Truman; one s. one d. *Education:* Amherst Coll., Yale Univ. *Career:* trained as economist; fmr Lecturer, Yale Univ.; joined Div. of Int. Finance, Bd of Govs of Fed. Reserve System 1972, Dir (later Staff Dir) 1977–98; Asst Sec., US Treasury for Int. Affairs 1998–2001; Asst Sec. (Int. Affairs), Senate Finance Cttee 1999–; Sr Fellow, Peterson Inst. for Int. Econs, Washington, DC; mem. G-7 Working Group on Exchange Market Intervention 1982–83, G-10 Working Group on the Resolution of Sovereign Liquidity Crises 1995–96, G-10-sponsored Working Party on Financial Stability in Emerging Market Econs 1996–97, G-22 Working Party on Transparency and Accountability 1998, Financial Stability Forum's Working Group on Highly Leveraged Insts 1999–2000; Hon. LLD (Amherst Coll.) 1988. *Publications:* Inflation Targeting in the World Economy 2003, Chasing Dirty Money: The Fight Against Money Laundering (co-author) 2004, A Strategy for IMF Reform 2006; numerous articles on int. monetary econs, int. debt problems, econ. devt and European econ. integration.

Address: Peterson Institute for International Economics, 1750 Massachusetts Avenue, NW, Washington, DC 20036-1903, USA (office). *Telephone:* (202) 328-9000 (home). *Fax:* (202) 659-3225 (office). *E-mail:* ttruman@iie .com (office); tnttruman@yahoo.com (home). *Website:* www.iie.com (office).

TSANG, Sir Donald Yam-kuen, Kt, KBE, JP, MPA; Hong Kong government official; *Chief Executive;* b. (Tsang Yam-kuen), 7 Oct. 1944, Hong Kong; m.; two s. *Education:* in Hong Kong and Harvard Univ., USA. *Career:* joined Govt of Hong Kong 1967; served in various govt depts and brs of Govt Secr.; attached to Asian Devt Bank, Manila 1977; Dist Officer, Shatin; Deputy Dir of Trade responsible for trade relations with N America; Deputy Sec. of Gen. Duties Br. responsible for Sino-British Jt Declaration 1985–89; Dir of Admin. Office of Chief Sec. 1989–91; Dir-Gen. of Trade 1991–93; Sec. for the Treasury 1993–95; Financial Sec. 1995–2001; Chief Sec. for Admin. 2001–05, Acting Chief Exec. March–May 2005 (resgnd to campaign for election as Chief Exec.), Chief Exec. 2005–; Grand Bauhinia Medal 2002; Hon. LLD 1999; Hon. DBA 1999; Dr hc (Chinese Univ. of Hong Kong, Hong Kong Polytechnic Univ., Univ. of Hong Kong).
Address: Office of the Chief Executive, 5/F Main Wing, Central Government Offices, Lower Albert Rd, Central, Hong Kong Special Administrative Region, People's Republic of China (office). *Telephone:* 28783300 (office). *Fax:* 25090577 (office). *E-mail:* ceo@ceo.gov.hk (office). *Website:* www.ceo.gov.hk (office).

TSANG, John, JP, MPA; Hong Kong ; *Financial Secretary;* b. 1951; m.; two c. *Education:* La Salle Coll., Hong Kong, Boston State Coll., Massachusetts Inst. of Tech., Kennedy School of Govt, Harvard Univ., USA. *Career:* began career working in Boston Public Schools, USA; joined Hong Kong civil service 1982, Admin. Asst to the Financial Sec. 1987–91, Asst Dir-Gen. of Trade 1991–95, Pvt. Sec. to Gov. Chris Patten 1995–97, Dir-Gen. Econ. and Trade Office, London 1997–99, Commr of Customs and Excise 1999–2002, Perm. Sec. for Housing, Planning and Lands 2002–03, Sec. for Commerce, Industry and Tech. 2003–06; Dir Office of the Chief Exec. of Hong Kong 2006–07, Financial Sec. 2007–, mem. Exec. Council, Hong Kong Special Admin. Region; Chair. Sixth Ministerial Conference (MC6), WTO 2005.
Address: Executive Council, Central Government Offices, Lower Albert Road, Central, Hong Kong Special Administrative Region, People's Republic of China (office). *Telephone:* 28102545 (office). *Fax:* 28450176 (office). *Website:* www.gov.hk (office).

TSCHÜTSCHER, Klaus, LLM, DrIur; Liechtenstein politician and academic; *Deputy Prime Minister and Minister of Economic Affairs, of Justice and of Sports;* b. 8 July 1967; m. Jeanette Tschütscher; two c. *Education:* Univs of St Gallen and Zurich, Switzerland. *Career:* Leader Liechtenstein Fiscal Admin Sept. 1995; mem. Exec. Cttee Liechtenstein Steuerwaltung 1996–; Dozent, Univ. of Liechtenstein 1998–; mem. Vaterländische Union (Patriotic Union); mem. Liechtenstein Del. to OECD (Harmful Tax Practices) 1999, to EU (EU tax topics, in particular EU interest taxation) 1999, for legal aid negotiations with USA 2001; Chair. Standing Working Group 'International Developments of the Tax Law' 2001–; mem. MWS Mixed Comm. 2001–; mem. Future Finance Plan Liechtenstein 2002; currently Deputy Prime Minister and Minister of Econ. Affairs, of Justice and of Sports.
Address: Regierungsgebäude, Postfach 684, 9490 Vaduz, Liechtenstein (office). *Telephone:* 2366180 (office). *Fax:* 2366022 (office). *E-mail:* office@ liechtenstein.li (office). *Website:* www.liechtenstein.li (office).

TSEKOA, Mohlabi Kenneth, BEd, MA; Lesotho politician, educator and diplomatist; *Minister of Foreign Affairs and International Relations;* b. 13 Aug. 1945; m.; two s. one d. *Education:* Nat. Univ. of Lesotho, Univ. of Botswana, Lesotho and Swaziland, Univ. of Newcastle-upon-Tyne, Univ. of London, UK, Univ. of Mass, USA. *Career:* teacher, Hlotse High School 1970–74; Deputy Headmaster, St Agnes High School 1974–76; Sr Educ. Officer, Lesotho Distance Teaching Centre 1976–78, Dir 1978–84; Deputy Prin. Sec., Ministry of Educ. 1984–86, Prin. Sec. 1986–89; High Commr to UK and Amb. to Ireland, Spain and Portugal 1989–96; Govt Sec. and Head of the Public Service 1996–2001; Minister of Finance and Devt Planning 2001–02, of Foreign Affairs 2002–04, of Educ. and Training 2004–07, of Foreign Affairs and Int. Relations 2007–.
Address: Ministry of Foreign Affairs and International Relations, POB 1387, Maseru 100, Lesotho (office). *Telephone:* 22311746 (office). *Fax:* 22310527 (office). *E-mail:* dps@foreign.gov.ls (office). *Website:* www .lesotho.gov.ls/foreign (office).

TSEPOV, Boris Anatolyevich, CJur; Russian diplomatist; *Ambassador to Lithuania;* b. 13 June 1948. *Education:* Moscow Inst. of Int. Relations, Diplomatic Acad. *Career:* entered diplomatic service 1971; posts in USSR

Embassy, Kuwait 1971–76; in Third African Div., USSR Ministry of Foreign Affairs 1976–78; Secr. of Deputy Minister 1978–86, with Dept for Int. Humanitarian Cooperation and Human Rights 1986–90; Counsellor Perm. USSR (now Russian) Mission to UN New York 1991–94; Dir of Dept, concurrently Exec. Sec. Russian Ministry of Foreign Affairs 1994–98; Amb. to Kenya (also accred Perm. Rep. to int. orgs, Nairobi) 1998–2001; Dir Dept of Compatriots' Affairs and Human Rights 2001; currently Amb. to Lithuania.
Address: Embassy of the Russian Federation, Latviu 53/54, Vilnius 2600, Lithuania (office). *Telephone:* (5) 272-1763 (office). *Fax:* (5) 272-3877 (office). *E-mail:* rusemb@rusemb.lt (office).

TSHERING, Lyonpo Dago; Bhutanese diplomatist and politician; *Ambassador to India;* b. (Dago Tshering), 17 July 1941, Paro. *Education:* Univ. of Bombay, Indian Admin. Service Training, Mussoorie and Indian Audit and Accounts Service Training, Simla, India, Univ. of Manchester, UK, Nat. Admin, Tokyo. *Career:* Asst, Ministry of Devt 1961–62; Asst, Office of the Chief Sec. 1962–63; returned to Ministry of Devt 1963, Sec. 1965–71; mem. Nat. Ass. 1968–1990; mem. Royal Advisory Council 1968–70; First Sec., Bhutan Embassy in India 1971–73; Deputy Perm. Rep. to UN 1973–74, Perm. Rep. 1974–80, 1984–85; Amb. to Bangladesh 1980–84; Minister of Home Affairs 1985–98; Amb. to India 1998–; Orange Scarf.
Address: Embassy of Bhutan, Chandragupta Marg, Chanakyapuri, New Delhi 110 021, India (office). *Telephone:* (11) 26889807 (office). *Fax:* (11) 26876710 (office). *E-mail:* bhutan@vsnl.com (office).

TSHERING, Lyonpo Ugyen, BA; Bhutanese politician and diplomatist; *Minister of Foreign Affairs;* b. 8 Aug. 1954, Thimphu; m. *Education:* Univ. of Calif., Berkeley, USA. *Career:* joined Govt Planning Comm. 1978, apptd Co-ordinator bilateral and multilateral assistance to Govt 1983, Project Co-ordinator, Computer Support Centre 1984, apptd Sec. Computerization Cttee 1983, Dir Planning Comm. 1986–89, now Vice-Chair.; Perm. Rep. to UN, New York 1989–98; apptd Editorial Adviser to Nat. Ass. 1980; fmr Chair. Asian Devt Bank; apptd Chair. World Bank Projects Implementation Cttee 1984; Chair. Tech. Cttee on Rural Devt, SAARC 1988–89; Sec., Ministry of Foreign Affairs 2001–03; Minister of Labour and Human Resources 2003–07 (resgnd); Minister of Foreign Affairs 2008–; Red Scarf 1998.
Address: Ministry of Foreign Affairs, Convention Centre, POB 103, Thimphu, Bhutan (office). *Telephone:* (2) 321413 (office). *Website:* www .mfa.gov.bt (office).

TSHIELA COMPTON, Eugénie; Democratic Republic of the Congo diplomatist; *Ambassador to UK;* b. 20 Jan. 1962, Kananga; m. Guy Robin Compton. *Education:* Institut catholique de Tshidimba, Facultés de théologie catholique, Kinshasa, Univ. of Liège, Belgium, Univ. of Westminster, UK. *Career:* organizer of socio-cultural activities, Kananga 1985–87; elected Commissaire du Peuple (Nat. Deputy) for Kananga 1987; Regional Pres. Parti pour la démocratie sociale et chrétienne 1990, mem. Nat. Directory; Conseillère de la République (Nat. Deputy), Haut Conseil de la République Parlement de transition 1993–97; mem. collective of the political opposition of the diaspora in Europe, with responsibility for foreign relations 1997–98; Rep. Rassemblement congolais pour la démocratie in UK 1998–2000, in Europe 2000–02; Nat. Deputy 2002–05; Amb. to UK 2005–.
Address: Embassy of Democratic Republic of the Congo, 281 Gray's Inn Road, London, WC1X 8QF, England (office). *Telephone:* (20) 7278-9825 (office). *Fax:* (20) 7833-9967 (office). *E-mail:* info@ambardcongo.org.uk (office). *Website:* www.ambardcongo.org.uk (office).

TSONEV, Nikolai Georgiev, PhD; Bulgarian economist, academic, politician and fmr army officer; *Minister of Defence;* b. 9 June 1956, Pernik. *Education:* Nat. Artillery Mil. School, Shumen, Vassilyevski Air Defence School, Kyiv, Ukrainian SSR, Univ. for Nat. and World Economy, Sofia, Sofia Univ. St Kliment of Ohrid. *Career:* officer in Bulgarian Army 1978–92; man. of several limited liability firms 1992–99; Dir Public Procurement Directorate, Ministry of Defence 1999–2000, adviser to Minister of Defence 2001–02, Dir of Social Activities Directorate 2002–08, Minister of Defence 2008–; Prof. of Strategic Planning, Civic Admin and European Integration Inst. 2002–; Prof., Univ. for Nat. and World Economy, Sofia 2004–.
Address: Ministry of Defence, 1000 Sofia, ul. Dyakon Ignatiy 3, Bulgaria (office). *Telephone:* (2) 922-09-22 (office). *Fax:* (2) 987-32-28 (office). *E-mail:* presscntr@mod.bg (office). *Website:* www.md.government.bg (office).

TSVANGIRAI, Morgan; Zimbabwean trade unionist and politician; *President, Movement for Democratic Change;* b. 1952, Gutu, Masvingo; m. Susan Tsvangirai 1978; six c. *Education:* Silveria and Gokomere High Schools, Harvard Univ., USA. *Career:* with Mutare Clothing Co. 1972–74;

mem. local textile union; rose from plant operator to foreman Trojan Nickel Mine, Bindura 1974–84; mem. Associated Mine Workers' Union, apptd Br. Chair. 1984; fmr exec. mem. Nat. Mine Workers' Union; elected Sec.-Gen. Zimbabwe Congress of Trade Unions (ZCTU) 1988; charged with being a spy for SA, imprisoned for six weeks 1989; Founder and Chair. Nat. Constitutional Ass.; organized series of anti-Govt strikes against tax rises 1997; Founder and Pres. Movement for Democratic Change (MDC) 1999–; Parl. Opposition Leader 2000–; unsuccessful Presidential cand. 2002; charged with treason Feb. 2002 and put on trial for allegedly plotting the assassination of Pres. Robert Mugabe (q.v.), acquitted Oct. 2004.
Address: Movement for Democratic Change, Harvest House, 6th Floor, cnr Angwa St and Nelson Mandela Ave, Harare, Zimbabwe (office). *Website:* www.mdczimbabwe.org (office).

TUCHMAN MATHEWS, Jessica, PhD; American research centre executive and journalist; *President, Carnegie Endowment for International Peace;* b. 1946, New York; m. Colin D. Mathews 1978; two s. one step-s. one step-d. *Education:* The Brearley School, New York, Radcliffe Coll., MA and Calif. Inst. of Tech. *Career:* professional mem. staff, House Interior Cttee on Energy and Environment 1973–74; Issues Dir for Morris Udall's presidential campaign, Washington, DC 1975–76; Dir Office of Global Issues, mem. staff Nat. Security Council, The White House, Washington, DC 1977–79, Undersecretary of State for Global Affairs 1993; mem. Editorial Bd The Washington Post, Washington, DC 1980–82, columnist 1990–97; Founding Vice-Pres. and Research Dir World Resources Inst., Washington, DC 1982–93; Sr Fellow, Council on Foreign Relations 1993–97, Dir Council's Washington program; Pres. Carnegie Endowment for Int. Peace 1997–; Dir Somalogic Inc.; mem. Council on Foreign Relations, Trilateral Comm.; fmr mem. Bd Brookings Inst., Radcliffe Coll., Rockefeller Brothers Fund, Surface Transportation Policy Project, Joyce Foundation; Trustee, Rockefeller Foundation, The Century Foundation, Nuclear Threat Initiative; Hon. DSc (Claremont Grad. School) 1990, (Hood Coll.) 1992.
Address: Carnegie Endowment for International Peace, 1779 Massachusetts Avenue, NW, Washington, DC 20036-2103, USA (office). *Telephone:* (202) 939-2210 (office). *Fax:* (202) 332-0925 (office). *E-mail:* jmathews@ CarnegieEndowment.org (office). *Website:* www.carnegieendowment.org (office).

TUDELA, Luis Solari; Peruvian diplomatist; b. 5 Dec. 1935, Lima; m. Martha Reinoso de Solari. *Education:* Pontificia Universidad Católica de Lima, Diplomatic Acad. of Peru, Inst. of Higher Int. Studies, Ginebra. *Career:* Prof. of Int. Public Law, Univ. of Lima, Universidad Nacional Federico Villareal, Universidad San Martín de Porres, Diplomatic Acad. of Peru, Universidad Cen. de Panamá; held various positions, including Dir of Evaluation, Chancellery, Dir of Dir Orgs, Under-sec., later Sec. for External Policy, Under-sec. for Bilateral Affairs; Amb. to Panama, Italy and the Holy See (also accred to Croatia, Cyprus, Malta and the Sovereign Mil. Order of Malta) 1997; fmr Legal Consultant, Ministry of Foreign Affairs; Vice-Minister and Sec.-Gen. of Foreign Affairs 2003–04; Amb. to UK (also accred to Ireland) 2004–06; mem. Drafting Cttee Int. Law Comm. 1987–91; contrib. to El Comercio daily newspaper; mem. Colegio de Abogados de Lima; Titular mem. Peruvian Soc. of Int. Law; Hon. mem. Colegio de Abogados de Panamá; Caballero de la Orden Cóndor de los Andes (Bolivia), Gran Cruz de las Ordenes El Sol del Perú y al Mérito por Servicios Distinguidos (Peru), Vasco Núñez de Balboa (Panama), Gran Cruz de la Orden del Piano (Holy See), Gran Cruz de la Orden de Malta, Gran Cruz de la Orden de Río Branco (Brazil). *Publications:* Texto de Derecho Internacional Público; numerous publs in specialist magazines.
Address: Ministry of Foreign Affairs, Jirón Lampa 535, Lima, 1, Peru (office). *Telephone:* (1) 3112402 (office). *Fax:* (1) 3112406 (office). *Website:* www.rree.gob.pe (office).

TUGE-ERECIŃSKA, Barbara, MA; Polish diplomatist; *Ambassador to UK;* b. 24 March 1956, Gdansk. *Education:* Univ. of Gdansk. *Career:* with Foreign Dept, Nat. Exec. Comm., Solidarity 1981; mem. Primate's Cttee of Help to Victimized People 1982–87; Hon. Sec., Consular Agency of Sweden, Denmark and Norway 1987–90; Plenipotentiary for Foreign Contacts, Gdansk 1990–91; Amb. to Sweden 1991–97; Dir Dept of Europe (West), Ministry of Foreign Affairs 1997–98, Dir Dept of European Policy 1998–99, Under-Sec. of State 1999–2001; Amb. to Denmark 2001–05; Sec. of State, Ministry of Foreign Affairs 2005–06; Amb. to UK 2006–.
Address: Embassy of Poland, 47 Portland Place, London, W1B 1JH, England (office). *Telephone:* (870) 774-2700 (office). *Fax:* (20) 7291-3573 (office). *E-mail:* polishembassy@polishembassy.org.uk (office). *Website:* www.london.polemb.net (office).

TUIMEBAYEV, Zhanseit K.; Kazakhstani diplomatist. *Career:* Amb. to Russian Fed. 2006–07; Minister of Education and Science 2007–.

Address: Ministry of Education and Science, Beibitshilik 11, 101000 Astana, Kazakhstan (office). *Telephone:* (7172) 75-20-27 (office). *Fax:* (7172) 75-28-71 (office). *E-mail:* pressa@edu.gov.kz (office). *Website:* www .edu.gov.kz (office).

TULIN, Dmitri Vladislavovich, MBA, PhD; Russian economist; b. 26 March 1956, Moscow; m. Vera Nerod 1977; two s. *Education:* Moscow Financial Inst. and USSR Inst. of Econs and Finance. *Career:* economist, Int. Monetary and Econ. Dept USSR State Bank (Gosbank) 1978, Sr Economist 1980, Chief Economist 1985, Man. 1989, Man. Dir, mem. Bd Securities Dept 1990; Deputy Chair. Cen. Bank of Russian Fed. 1991–94; Exec. Dir for Russian Fed. IMF 1994–96; Chair. Bd Vneshtorgbank (Bank for Foreign Trade) 1996–98; Sr Adviser EBRD 1999–2004; Deputy Chair. Cen. Bank of Russian Fed. 2004. *Publications:* articles on monetary econs and banking in Russian professional journals.
Address: c/o Central Bank of the Russian Federation, 12 Neglinnaya Street, Moscow, 107016, Russian Federation (office).

TUMANOV, Vladimir Aleksandrovich, DJur; Russian lawyer; *Member, European Court of Human Rights;* b. 20 Oct. 1926, Kropotkin, Krasnodar Dist; m. 1948; one s. *Education:* Inst. of Foreign Trade, USSR Ministry of Foreign Trade, All-Union Inst. of Law. *Career:* Scientific Researcher All-Union Inst. of Law 1952–59; Chief Scientific Researcher, Head of Comparative Law Dept, Inst. of State and Law USSR (now Russian) Acad. of Sciences; Pres. Int. Asscn of Legal Science at UNESCO (resgnd); mem. State Duma (Russian Parl.) 1993–94; mem. Constitutional Court of Russian Fed. 1994–, Chair. 1995–97, Adviser 1997–; mem. European Court of Human Rights 1997–, Acad. of Comparative Rights; Pres. Int. Asscn of Legal Sciences; Chair. Council on Problems of Improving Legal System, Admin. of Russian Pres. 2000–. *Publications include:* Force-majeure in Civil Law 1958, Constitutional Law of Foreign Countries (Vols 1, 2) 1987–88, Legal Nihilism and Prospects of the Rule of Law 1991, Constitution of the Russian Federation of 1993 (an encyclopaedic guide) 1994.
Address: 13th Parkovaya str. 25, Korp. 1, Apt. 40, 105215 Moscow, Russia (home). *Telephone:* (495) 206-18-39 (home).

TUN, Maj.-Gen. Hla; Myanma politician; *Minister of Finance and Revenue;* b. 11 July 1951, Yangon; m. Daw Khin Than Win; two c. *Education:* Defence Services Acad., Pyin-Oo-Lwin. *Career:* Minister of Finance and Revenue 2003–; General Service Medal, People's War Medal, State Peace and Tranquility Medal, Maing Yan/Me Tha Waw Battle Star, Distinguished Service Medal, Service Medal.
Address: Ministry of Finance and Revenue, 26(A) Setmu Road, Yankin Township, Yangon, Myanmar (office); No. 28, Pan Wah Street, Kamayut Tsp., Yangon, Myanmar (home). *Telephone:* (1) 274894 (office). *Fax:* (1) 543632 (office). *Website:* www.myanmar.com/Ministry/finance (office).

TUOMIOJA, Erkki Sakari, MBA, Dr rer. pol; Finnish politician; b. 1 July 1946, Helsinki; m. Marja-Helena Rajala 1979. *Career:* reporter 1967–69; econ. researcher Rautaruuki 1975–77; Chief Ed. Ydin magazine 1977–91; MP 1970–79, 1991–; Deputy Mayor of Helsinki 1979–91; Minister of Trade and Industry 1999–2000, of Foreign Affairs 2000–07; Pres. European Council July–Dec. 2006; Chair. Parl. Grand (European Affairs) Cttee 1995–99; lecturer Helsinki Univ. 1997–. *Publications:* 18 books on history, politics and int. affairs.
Address: c/o Ministry of Foreign Affairs, Merikasarmi, PO Box 176, 00161 Helsinki, Finland (office). *Website:* www.tuomioja.org (office).

TUPOUTO'A LAVAKA, HRH Crown Prince; Tongan politician and army officer; b. 12 July 1959, Nuku'alofa; m. Nanasipau'u Vaea 1982; three c. *Education:* in New Zealand, Britannia Royal Naval Coll., Dartmouth, Univ. of New South Wales, Australian Jt Services Staff Coll., US Naval War Coll. *Career:* fmrly known as Aho'eitu' Unuaki'otonga Tuku'aho, then HRH Prince 'Ulukalala-Lavaka-Ata; joined Tonga Defence Services 1981, Second-in-Command 1995; CO, Navy 1993; Minister of Foreign Affairs and Defence 1998–06; Prime Minister of Tonga 2000–06, also fmr Minister of Civil Aviation and Telecommunications; proclaimed Crown Prince 11 Sept. 2006.

TURK, Brig. Anton; Slovenian army officer; *Military Representative, NATO;* b. 10 Dec. 1951, Novo Mesto; m. Zora; two d. *Education:* Teacher Training Coll., Ljubljana, Faculty of Organisational Sciences, Kranj, Reserve Officers School, Gen. Staff Course of Slovenian Mil. Educ. Centre. *Career:* Commdg Officer, reserve units of fmr Yugloslav Fed. Armed Forces 1977; fmr Chief of Staff, HQ of Infantry Brigade Service; Commdr, Armed Forces Training Centre, Vrhnika 1992–94; Head of Conscript Training Dept, Gen. Staff 1994–96; Chief of Office, Chief of Gen. Staff 1996; ADC, Pres. of Repub. of Slovenia 1996–2003; Deputy Chief, Gen. Staff (ranked Maj.-Gen.) 2001; Nat. Mil. Rep., Allied Command of Operations, NATO 2004–06, Mil. Rep. to NATO and EU 2006–; Silver Medal of Slovenian

Armed Forces 1993, Bronze Medal of Gen. Maister 1996, Silver Medal of Gen. Maister 1998, Ordre Nat. du Mérite 2002, Golden Medal of Slovenian Armed Forces 2003, Golden Medal of Gen. Maister 2004, Order for 10 Years of Service 2005, Golden Medal of Slovenian CHOD 2005.
Address: North Atlantic Treaty Organization (NATO), blvd. Léopold III, 1110 Brussels, Belgium (office). *Telephone:* (2) 707-4111 (office). *Fax:* (2) 707-4579 (office). *E-mail:* natodoc@hq.nato.int (office). *Website:* www .nato.int (office).

TÜRK, Danilo, PhD; Slovenian academic, diplomatist, lawyer, politician and head of state; *President;* b. 19 Feb. 1952, Maribor; m. Barbara Miklic Türk; one d. *Education:* Ljubljana and Belgrade Univs. *Career:* Lecturer in Public Int. Law, Univ. of Ljubljana 1978–88, Prof. of Int. Law 1988–, Head Inst. of Int. Law and Int. Relations 1983–95; mem. UN Sub-comm. on Prevention of Discrimination and Protection of Minorities 1984–92; Special Rapporteur 1989–92, Chair. 1990; Perm. Rep. of Slovenia to the UN 1992–2000; mem. UN Security Council 1998–99, Pres. Aug. 1998, Nov. 1999; mem. Security Council Mission to Jakarta and East Timor, Indonesia Sept. 1999, Asst Sec.-Gen. of UN for Political Affairs 2000–05; active in the field of human rights with several NGOs; Chair. Int. Law Asscn, Slovenia 1990–; Pres. of Slovenia 2007–. *Publications:* book on the principle of non-intervention in int. relations and int. law and over 100 articles in legal journals and other publs.
Address: Office of the President, 1000 Ljubljana, Erjavčeva 17 (office); Faculty of Law, University of Ljubljana, Kongresni trg 12, 1000 Ljubljana, Slovenia. *Telephone:* (1) 4781222 (office); (1) 2418500. *Fax:* (1) 4781357 (office); (1) 2418660. *E-mail:* gp.uprs@up-rs.si (office); rektorat@uni-lj.si. *Website:* www.up-rs.si (office); www.uni-lj.si.

TURKI, Abdul Aziz al-Abdullah at-, BA; Saudi Arabian international organization official; *Secretary-General, Organization of Arab Petroleum Exporting Countries;* b. 12 Aug. 1936, Jeddah; m.; two d. *Education:* Univ. of Cairo. *Career:* with US Embassy, Jeddah 1953–54, ARAMCO 1954–66; Dir Office of Minister of Petroleum and Mineral Resources 1966–68; Dir of Gen. Affairs, Directorate of Mineral Resources 1968–70; Asst Sec.-Gen. OAPEC 1970–75, Sec.-Gen. 1990–; Sec.-Gen. Supreme Advisory Council for Petroleum and Mineral Affairs, Saudi Arabia 1975–90; Saudi Gov. for OPEC 1975–90; Deputy Minister, Ministry of Petroleum and Mineral Resources 1975; Chair. Arab Maritime Petroleum Transport Co., Kuwait 1981–87, Pemref 1982–89; mem. Bd of Dirs Petromin 1975–89, ARAMCO 1980–89.
Address: Organization of Arab Petroleum Exporting Countries, PO Box 20501, Safat 13066, Kuwait (office). *Telephone:* 4959000 (office). *Fax:* 4959755 (office). *E-mail:* oapec@oapecorg.org (office). *Website:* www .oapecorg.org (office).

TURKMANI, Lt-Gen. Hasan at-; Syrian government official and politician; *Minister of Defence;* b. 1935, Aleppo. *Education:* Syrian Mil. Acad. *Career:* various mil. posts including command of mechanical div. during 1973 War, Chief Commdr Cen. Staff 2002-04; fmr. Vice-Pres., Council of Ministers; Minister of Defence 2004–.
Address: Ministry of Defence, place Omayad, Damascus, Syria (office). *Telephone:* (11) 7770700 (office). *Fax:* (11) 2237842 (office).

TURKOVIĆ, Bisera, PhD; Bosnia and Herzegovina diplomatist; *Ambassador to USA; Education:* Univ. of Sarajevo, Philip Inst. of Technology and Univ. of LaTrobe, Melbourne, Australia, Pacific Western Univ., USA. *Career:* Lecturer in Criminal Justice, Univ. of Sarajevo 2001–04; Minister of European Integration 2000–01; Amb. to Croatia 1993–94, to Hungary 1994–96, to OSCE 1996–2000; fmr Exec. Dir Centre for Security Studies in Bosnia and Herzegovina; Perm. Rep. to UN and Amb. to OSCE, Vienna –2005, Amb. to USA and Perm. Observer to OAS, Washington, DC 2005– (also accred to Mexico 2006–).
Address: Embassy of Bosnia and Herzegovina, 2109 E Street, NW, Washington, DC 20037, USA (office). *Telephone:* (202) 337-1500 (office). *Fax:* (202) 337-1502 (office). *E-mail:* turkovic.bisera@bhembassy.org (office). *Website:* www.bhembassy.org (office).

TURNER, (Robert) Leigh; British diplomatist; *Ambassador to Ukraine;* m. Pamela Major; one s. one d. *Career:* with Dept of Transport 1979, Property Services Agency 1980, Dept of the Environment 1981, HM Treasury 1982; with Personnel, Cen. America, FCO 1983; Second Sec. (Chancery), Embassy in Vienna 1984–87; Second, Sec., Counter-terrorism, EU Budget and Finance, FCO 1987–91; language training 1991; First Sec. (Econ.), Embassy in Moscow 1992–95; Deputy, then Head of Hong Kong Dept, FCO 1995–98; Counsellor (EU/Econ.), Embassy in Bonn (later Berlin) 1998–2002, Special Unpaid Leave in Berlin 2002–06; Dir Overseas Territories, FCO 2006–08; Amb. to Ukraine 2008–.
Address: British Embassy, vul. Desyatinna 9, 01025 Kiev, Ukraine (office). *Telephone:* (44) 490-36-60 (office). *Fax:* (44) 490-36-62 (office). *E-mail:*

ukembinf@sovamua.com (office). *Website:* www.britemb-ukraine.net (office).

TURNER, Adm. Stansfield, MA; American naval officer (retd), lecturer and author; b. 1 Dec. 1923, Chicago, Ill.; m. 1st Eli Karin Gilbert 1985 (died 2000); m. 2nd Marion Weiss 2002. *Education:* Amherst Coll., US Naval Acad., Annapolis, Univ. of Oxford, UK (Rhodes Scholar). *Career:* active duty, USN, serving minesweeper, destroyers, USS Horne (guided missile cruiser in action in Vietnamese conflict); served in Office of Chief of Naval Operations, then in Office of Asst Sec. of Defense for Systems Analysis; Advanced Man. Program, Harvard Business School; Exec. Asst and Naval Aide to Sec. of the Navy 1968–70; Rear Adm. 1970; CO Carrier Task Group in USS Independence, US Sixth Fleet 1970; Dir Systems Analysis Div. of Office of Chief of Naval Operations, Dept of the Navy 1971–72; Vice-Adm. 1972; Pres. US Naval War Coll., Newport, RI 1972–74; Commdr US Second Fleet and NATO Striking Fleet Atlantic 1974–75; Adm. 1975; C-in-C Allied Forces Southern Europe, NATO 1975–77; Dir Cen. Intelligence (CIA) 1977–81; Sr Research Scholar, Center for Int. and Security Studies, Univ. of Maryland 1991–2007; Hon. Fellow, Exeter Coll., Oxford 1981–; Nat. Security Medal, Legion of Merit, Bronze Star. *Publications:* Secrecy and Democracy: The CIA in Transition 1985, Terrorism and Democracy 1991, Caging the Nuclear Genie: An American Challenge for Global Security 1997, Caging the Genies: A Workable Plan for Nuclear, Chemical and Biological Weapons 1998, Burning Before Reading 2005.
Address: 488 River Bend Road, Great Falls, VA 22066, USA (home). *E-mail:* admturner@aol.com.

TURNQUEST, Orville A. T. (Tommy); Bahamian politician; *Minister of National Security and Immigration;* b. 16 Nov. 1959, Nassau; m. Shawn Carey; two s. one d. *Education:* St Anne's School, Nassau, Malvern Coll., UK and Univ. of Western Ont., Canada. *Career:* began career with Canadian Imperial Bank of Commerce; mem. Free Nat. Movt (FNM) 1985–, fmr Vice-Pres., Leader 2002–05; mem. Parl. 1992–2002, 2007–; Parl. Sec., Office of the Prime Minister 1992–95; Minister of State for Public Service and Labour 1995–96, for Public Works 1996–97; Minister of Works 1997–98, of Public Service, Immigration and Nat. Insurance 1998–2000, of Tourism 2000–02, of Nat. Security and Immigration 2007–.
Address: Ministry of National Security and Immigration, Churchill Building, 3rd Floor, PO Box N-3217, Nassau, The Bahamas (office). *Telephone:* 356-6792 (office). *Fax:* 356-6087 (office). *E-mail:* psmns@ hotmail.com (office); tommyt@tommyturnquest.org. *Website:* www .tommyturnquest.org.

TUSK, Donald Franciszek; Polish politician; *Prime Minister;* b. 22 April 1957, Gdańsk; m.; one s. one d. *Education:* Gdańsk Univ. *Career:* journalist Maritime Publishing House, with magazines Pomerania and Samorząd-ność; with Gdańsk Height Services Work Co-operative; Deputy ed. Gazeta Gdańska 1989; mem. Liquidation Cttee RSW Press-Books-Ruch; assoc. Free Trade Unions by the Coast; co.-f. Independent Students Union (NZS); mem. Solidarity Trade Union 1980–89; Founder and Ed. underground Publ Przegląd Polityczny; Leader Programme Council for Liberals Foundation; Leader Congress of Liberals 1989, later the Liberal-Democratic Congress (Kongres Liberalno-Demokratyczny—KLD), Chair. 1991–94; Vice-Chair. Freedom Union (Unia Wolnosci—UW) 1994 following the merger with Democratic Union (UD); Deputy to Sejm (Parl.) (Gdynia/Słupsk constituency) 1991–93, 2001–, Deputy Marshal of Sejm 2001–, mem. Civic Platform Parl. Caucus 2001–; Chair. Parl. Liberal-Democratic Caucus and Special Cttee for Consideration of Constitutional Acts 1991–93; Senator (Gdańsk Voivodship) and Vice-Marshal of Senate 1997–2001; Co-Founder Civic Platform (Platforma Obywatelska—PO) 2001, Leader 2005–; Prime Minister 2007–; unsuccessful cand. in presidential elections 2006; Silver Mouth Award, Radio Three (Sweden) 2004. *Publications:* Kashubian Lake District 1985, Once There Was Gdańsk 1996, Gdańsk 1945, 1998, Old Sopot 1998, Ideas of Gdańsk's Liberalism 1998.
Address: Chancellery of the Prime Minister, 00-583 Warsaw, Al. Ujazdowskie 1/3 (office); Civic Platform (Platforma Obywatelska), 00-159 Warsaw, ul. Andersa 21, Poland (office). *Telephone:* (22) 8413832 (Prime Minister's Office) (office); (22) 6357879 (Civic Platform) (office). *Fax:* (22) 6284821 (Prime Minister's Office) (office); (22) 6357641 (Civic Platform) (office). *E-mail:* cirinfo@kprm.gov.pl (office); poczta@ platforma.org (office). *Website:* www.kprm.gov.pl (office); www.platforma .org (office).

TUTKUS, Lt Gen. Valdas; Lithuanian military officer; *Chief of Defence, Armed Forces;* b. 27 Dec. 1960; m.; one s. *Education:* Frunze Mil. Acad., NATO Defence Coll., Rome. *Career:* Second Lt Motorised Infantry Battalion 1982; served in Afghanistan 1983–85; promoted to First Lt 1984; Founding mem. Lithuanian Armed Forces 1991; Chief of Jt Staff, Ministry

of Defence 1992–94; First Deputy Commdr, Armed Forces 1994–96, Deputy Commdr 1996–99; Mil. Rep. to NATO, Brussels, to EU, to WEU 1999–2001; Commdr Land Forces 2001–04; Chief of Defence, Armed Forces 2004–.
Address: Ministry of National Defence, Totorių 25/3, Vilnius 01121, Lithuania (office). *Telephone:* (5) 262-4821 (office). *Fax:* (5) 212-6082 (office). *E-mail:* vis@kam.lt (office). *Website:* www.kam.lt (office).

TUTTLE, Robert Holmes, MBA; American diplomatist and business executive; *Ambassador to UK;* m. Maria Hummer; two d. *Education:* Stanford Univ., Univ. of Southern Calif. *Career:* Asst to Pres. Reagan 1982–85, Dir of Presidential Personnel 1985–89; Co-Man. Pnr Tuttle-Click Automotive Group; Amb. to UK 2005–; fmr mem. Bd Woodrow Wilson Int. Center for Scholars, Ronald Reagan Presidential Library Foundation, Annenberg School of Communication, Univ. of Southern Calif., Los Angeles Museum of Contemporary Art (Chair. 2001–04).
Address: Embassy of the United States, 24 Grosvenor Square, London, W1A 1AE, England (office). *Telephone:* (20) 7499-9000 (office). *Website:* www.usembassy.org.uk (office); london.usembassy.gov (office).

TUTU, Most Rev. Desmond Mpilo, MTh; South African ecclesiastic (retd) and academic; b. 7 Oct. 1931, Klerksdorp; m. Leah Nomalizo Tutu 1955; one s. three d. *Education:* Bantu High School, Bantu Normal Coll., Univ. of South Africa, St Peter's Theological Coll., Rosettenville, King's Coll., Univ. of London. *Career:* schoolmaster 1954–57; parish priest 1960; Theological Seminary Lecturer 1967–69; Univ. Lecturer 1970–71; Assoc. Dir Theological Educ. Fund, World Council of Churches 1972–75; Dean of Johannesburg 1975–76; Bishop of Lesotho 1977–78, of Johannesburg 1984–86; Archbishop of Cape Town, Metropolitan of the Church of the Prov. of Southern Africa 1986–95, Archbishop Emer. 1995–; Chancellor Univ. of Western Cape 1988–; Chair. Truth and Reconciliation Comm. 1995–99; Pres. All Africa Conf. of Churches 1987–97; Sec.-Gen. South African Council of Churches 1979–84; Visiting Prof. of Anglican Studies, New York Gen. Theological Seminary 1984; elected to Harvard Univ. Bd of Overseers 1989; Dir Coca-Cola 1986–; Visiting Prof., Emory Univ., Atlanta 1998–2000; Visiting Prof. in Post-Conflict Studies, King's Coll., London 2004–; f. Desmond Tutu Peace Centre, Cape Town, supported by Desmond Tutu Peace Trust; mem. Third Order of the Soc. of St Francis; Freedom of Borough of Merthyr Tydfil (Wales), Durham, Hull, Borough of Lewisham (UK), Florence, Lecco (Italy), Kinshasa (Democratic Repub. of Congo), Krugersdorp, Cape Town (SA); Order of Jamaica; Hon. DD, DCL, LLD, ThD (Gen. Theol. Sem. New York, Kent Univ., Harvard Univ., Ruhr Bochum Univ.); Hon. DDiv (Aberdeen) 1981; Hon. STD (Columbia) 1982; Dr hc (Mount Allison Univ., Sackville, NB, Strasbourg) 1988, (Oxford) 1990; Hon. LLD (South Bank Univ.) 1994; Hon. DD (Exeter) 1997; FKC (Fellow of King's Coll. London); numerous awards including Onassis Award, Family of Man Gold Medal 1983, Nobel Peace Prize 1984, Carter-Menil Human Rights Prize 1986, Martin Luther King Jr Humanitarian Award 1986, Third World Prize (jt recipient) 1989, Grand Cross of Merit, Germany 1996, Bill of Rights Award, American Civil Liberation Union Fund 1997, Henry W. Edgerton Civil Liberties Award, American Civil Liberties Union 1997, One Hundred Black Men Award, USA 1997, Peace Prize, Int. Community of UNESCO, Athens 1997, Gandhi Peace Prize 2007. *Publications:* Crying in the Wilderness 1982, Hope and Suffering 1983 (both collections of sermons and addresses), The Rainbow People of God 1994, An African Prayer Book 1996, No Future Without Forgiveness 1999.
Address: c/o Desmond Tutu Peace Trust, PO Box 8428, Roggebaai, 8012 Cape Town, South Africa. *Telephone:* (21) 4257002. *Fax:* (21) 4189468. *E-mail:* info@tutu.org. *Website:* www.tutu.org.

TUWAIJRI, Abdulrahman at-, PhD; Saudi Arabian economist; *Secretary-General, Supreme Economic Council;* b. 23 Feb. 1955, Almajmaah; m. Norah Alabdulatif 1982; three s. two d. *Education:* King Saud Univ. and Iowa State Univ., USA. *Career:* grad. asst Dept of Econs, King Saud Univ. 1978–84, Asst Prof. 1985–88; Econ. Adviser Gen. Secr. Cooperation Council for the Arab States of the Gulf 1988–90; Alt. Exec. Dir IMF 1991–95, Exec. Dir 1995–2001; Sec.-Gen., Supreme Econ. Council 2002–.
Address: c/o Ministry of Finance and National Economy, Airport Road, Riyadh 11177, Saudi Arabia. *Telephone:* (1) 405-0000. *Fax:* (1) 401-0583.

TWEGRI, Muhammad Ibrahim at-, PhD; Egyptian academic and international organization executive; *Assistant General Secretary for Economic Affairs, League of Arab States; Career:* Dir-Gen. Arab Admin. Devt Org. (ARADO) –2007; Asst Gen. Sec. for Econ. Affairs, League of Arab States (Arab League) 2007–; Mem.-at-Large Int. Fed. of Training and Devt Orgs; mem. Preparatory Cttee Int. Conf. of Cyberlaw (ICCY) 2005. *Publications:* numerous papers in professional journals.
Address: League of Arab States, PO Box 11642, Arab League Bldg, Tahrir Square, Cairo, Egypt (office). *Telephone:* (2) 575-0511 (office). *Fax:* (2) 574-0331 (office). *E-mail:* info@arableagueonline.org (office). *Website:* www .arableagueonline.org (office).

TYMOSHENKO, Yuliya Volodymyrivna, CandEcon; Ukrainian business executive and politician; *Prime Minister;* b. 27 Nov. 1960, Dnipropetrovsk; m. Oleksandr Hennadyovych Tymoshenko; one d. *Education:* Dnipropetrovsk State Univ. *Career:* planning engineer, Dnipropetrovsk Machine-Construction Plant 1984–89; Commercial Dir Dnipropetrovsk Youth Centre Terminal 1989–91; Dir-Gen. Ukraine Benzine Corpn 1991–95; Pres. Union Unified Energy Systems of Ukraine (UES), First Deputy Chair. Bd of Dirs, Head Cttee on Budgetary Issues 1995–97; elected to Verkhovna Rada (parl.) 1996, joined political union Community (Hromada—with Pavlo Lazarenko), left Hromada to form and lead Fatherland (Batkivish-china) faction 1999; Deputy Prime Minister of Ukraine responsible for energy issues 1999–2001 (resgnd); joined opposition Nat. Salvation Forum 2001; arrested on charge of corruption March 2001, released due to pressure of opposition; led Yuliya Tymoshenko Bloc in 2002 and 2006 elections; Prime Minister of Ukraine Jan.–Sept. 2005, 2007–; Higher Order of Orthodox Church St Barbara Great Martyr 1997; ranked third by Forbes magazine amongst 100 Most Powerful Women 2005. *Publications:* about 50 papers on econs.
Address: Office of the Cabinet of Ministers, 01008 Kyiv, vul. M. Hrushevskoho 12/2 (office); Fatherland (Batkivshchyna), 0408 Kyiv, vul. Turovska 13, Ukraine. *Telephone:* (44) 293-21-71 (office); (44) 462-58-39. *Fax:* (44) 293-20-93 (office). *E-mail:* web@kmu.gov.ua (office). *Website:* www.kmu.gov.ua (office); www.tymoshenko.com.ua.

TYSON, Robert (Bob), BA; Australian diplomatist; *Ambassador to Russia;* m.; two c. *Education:* Australian Nat. Univ. *Career:* Third/Second Sec., Embassy in Wellington 1972–75; First Sec., Embassy in Bangkok 1976–79; Dir Foreign Service Training 1979–80; Head, Int. Div., Dir of the Cabinet Unit and Prin. Adviser, Inter-governmental Relations, Dept of the Premier and Cabinet, Melbourne 1980–83; Counsellor and Deputy Head of Mission, Embassy in Moscow 1984–87; Sr Adviser, N America and Defence Br., Dept of the Prime Minister and Cabinet 1987–89; Consul-General in Honolulu 1989–93; Minister, Congressional Liaison, Embassy in Washington DC 1993–97; Asst Sec., Passports Branch 1997–99, Nuclear Policy Br. 1999–2000; Amb. to Saudi Arabia 2000–04, to Russian Fed. 2005–.
Address: Embassy of Australia, 109028 Moscow, Podkolokolii per. 10a/2, Russian Federation (office). *Telephone:* (495) 956-60-70 (office). *Fax:* (495) 956-61-70 (office). *E-mail:* austembmos@dfat.gov.au (office). *Website:* www.russia.embassy.gov.au (office).

U

UBAIDI, Gen. Abd al-Qader Jasim al-; Iraqi army officer and government official; *Minister of Defence;* b. Ramadi. *Career:* fmr Gen. in Iraqi army under Saddam Hussein, rejoined army 2003, served as Commdr of Operations Centre, then Mil. Commdr in western Iraq, then Commdr infantry commando units; Minister of Defence 2006–.
Address: Ministry of Defence, Baghdad, Iraq (office). *E-mail:* webmaster@mod.iraqiaf.org (office). *Website:* www.iraqmod.org (office).

UBEDA RIVERA, Gioconda, LLB; Costa Rican diplomatist; *Ambassador to Mexico;* b. 23 Dec. 1959; m.; one d. *Education:* Univ. of Costa Rica. *Career:* fmr Lecturer in Int. Law, Univ. of Costa Rica; overseas postings include Embassy in Argentina 1988–90, 1994–96, Embassy in Mexico 1986–88; Dir Dept of Judicial Affairs, Ministry of Foreign Affairs 1997–2006; Amb. to Mexico 2006–; Co-founder Int. Centre for Rights of Migrants (CIDE-HUM), Centre for Int. Studies (CEI); fmr consultant to UN, UNDP, UNHCR, ICRC, Inter-American Inst. for Human Rights.
Address: Embassy of Costa Rica, Río Po 113, Col. Cuauhtémoc, Del., Cuauhtémoc 06500, Mexico (office). *Telephone:* (55) 5525-7764 (office). *Fax:* (55) 5511-9240 (office). *E-mail:* embcrica@ri.redint.com (office).

UCH, Kiman; Cambodian diplomatist; *Ambassador to France;* b. 1 Jan. 1943, Kratie; m. *Education:* Univ. of Adelaide, Australia. *Career:* English teacher 1967–70; fmr spokesman for Govt of Prime Minister Hun Sen; Sec. of State and Acting Minister of Foreign Affairs and Int. Co-operation 1993–2002; Amb. to France (also accred to Spain, Italy, Portugal, Greece, and Andorra) 2003–.
Address: Embassy of Cambodia, 4 rue Adolphe Yvon, 75116 Paris, France (office). *Telephone:* 1-45-03-47-20 (office). *Fax:* 1-45-03-47-40 (office). *E-mail:* ambcambodgeparis@mangoosta.fr (office). *Website:* www.ambcambodgeparis.info (office).

UDEN, Martin, LLB; British diplomatist; *Ambassador to South Korea;* m. Fiona Uden; two s. *Education:* Queen Mary Coll., Univ. of London. *Career:* called to the Bar 1977; joined FCO 1977, held numerous positions in areas such as nuclear non-proliferation, Japan, Yugoslavia and Albania, CSCE; fmr Dir of Inward Investment, UK Trade and Investment HQ; Second Sec., Embassy in Seoul 1978–81, Political Counsellor 1994–97, served in Embassy in Bonn 1986–90, High Comm. in Ottawa 1997–2001, fmr Consul-Gen. in San Francisco, Amb. to South Korea 2008–. *Publications:* Times Past in Korea 2003.
Address: British Embassy, Taepyungro 40, 4 Jeong-dong, Jung-gu, Seoul 100-120, Republic of Korea (office). *Telephone:* (2) 3210-5500 (office). *E-mail:* bembassy@uk.or.kr (office). *Website:* www.britishembassy.or.kr (office).

UEDA, Hideaki; Japanese diplomatist; m.; three c. *Education:* Tokyo Univ., Harvard Univ., USA. *Career:* joined Ministry of Foreign Affairs 1967, served at Embassy in Moscow; fmr First Sec., Embassy in Australia; Dir, Press Div., Ministry of Foreign Affairs 1986–88; Counsellor and Minister for Public Affairs, Embassy in Washington, DC 1990–92; Deputy Dir-Gen., Econ. Cooperation Bureau, Ministry of Foreign Affairs, Tokyo 1992–95, Dir-Gen., Multilateral Cooperation Dept 1998–2000; Amb. to Japanese Secr. for Osaka APEC 1995; Consul Gen., Hong Kong 1995–98; Amb. to Poland 2000–03, to Australia 2004–07. *Publication:* Rise and Fall of the Far Eastern Republic 1990.
Address: c/o Ministry of Foreign Affairs, 2-11-1, Shiba-Koen, Minato-ku, Tokyo 105-8519, Japan.

UGALDE, Sylvia; Costa Rican diplomatist; m. *Career:* Chargé d'affaires a.i. in UK –2006, Minister Counsellor 2007–.
Address: Embassy of Costa Rica, Flat 1, 14 Lancaster Gate, London, W2 3LH, England (office). *Telephone:* (20) 7706-8844 (office). *Fax:* (20) 7706-8655 (office). *E-mail:* costaricanembassy@btconnect.com (office). *Website:* costarica.embassyhomepage.com (office).

UHL, Petr; Czech human rights activist; *Editor, Právo;* b. 8 Oct. 1941, Prague; m. Anna Šabatová 1974; three s. one d. *Education:* Czech. Univ. of Tech., Prague. *Career:* designer and patent clerk 1964–66; teacher, Coll. of Tech. Prague 1966–69; imprisoned for political activities 1969–73; designer 1974–78; Co-Founder Charter 77; Co-Founder Cttee for Protection of the

Unjustly Prosecuted 1978; imprisoned for political activities 1979–84; stoker 1984–89; ed. of East European Information Agency 1988–90; leading rep. of Civic Forum, Prague 1989–90; Dir-Gen., Czechoslovak News Agency 1990–92, Ed. 1992–94; Ed.-in-Chief Listy (magazine) 1994–96; Ed. Právo (daily) 1996–98, 2001–; Commr of Govt of Czech Repub. for Human Rights 1998–2001; Deputy to House of the Nations, Fed. Ass. 1990–92; Chair., Control and Auditing Comm. of Prison Staff Corps, Czech Repub. 1990; mem. Working Group on Arbitrary Detention of UN Comm. on Human Rights 1991–2001, Chair., Cttee for Prevention of Torture of Human Rights Council of Czech Govt 2002–, mem. Council of Czech TV 2003–, mem. Monitoring Centre for Racism and Xenophobia 2004–; State Honours of Czech Repub. 1998, of Poland 2000, of Germany 2001, Order of Merit, France 2002; Press Freedom Award, Reporter without Borders, Austria 2002. *Publications:* The Programme of Social Self-government 1982, On Czechoslovak Prison System (co-author) 1998, Justice and Injustice in the Eyes of Petr Uhl 1999, and numerous articles in Czech and foreign press.
Address: Právo, Slezská 13, 121 50 Prague (office); Anglická 8, 120 00 Prague 2, Czech Republic (home). *Telephone:* (2) 24228865 (home); (2) 606662279. *Fax:* (2) 21001276 (office). *E-mail:* uhl@seznam.cz (home).

UHLIG, Harald Friedrich Hans Volker Sigmar, PhD; German economist; *Professor of Macroeconomic and Economic Policy, Humboldt University;* b. 26 April 1961, Bonn. *Education:* Technische Univ., Berlin, Univ. of Minnesota. *Career:* Research Asst, Fed. Reserve Bank of Minneapolis and Inst. for Empirical Macroeconomics 1986–89; teaching asst, Univ. of Minn. 1987; Asst Prof., Dept of Econs, Princeton Univ. 1990–94; Research Prof. for Macroeconomics, Center for Econ. Research, Tilburg Univ., Netherlands 1994–2000; Prof. of Macroecon. and Econ. Policy, Humboldt Univ. 2000–; main field of work macroecons, secondary fields Bayesian time series econometrics and financial econs; assoc. ed., Journal of Econ. Dynamics and Control 1995–98, Macroecon. Dynamics 1997–, Computational Econs 1998–, Econometric Theory 2000–; Asst, Review of Econ. Studies 1998–; co-ed. European Econ. Review 1997–; mem. Econometric Soc., American Econ. Asscn, European Econ. Asscn; Alfred P. Sloan Doctoral Dissertation Fellowship 1989–90, Gossenpreis 2003, Fellow of the Econometric Soc. 2003. *Publications:* numerous articles in econ. journals.
Address: Department of Business Administration and Economics, Spandauer Str. 1, 10178 Berlin (office); Neidenburger Allee 22, 14055 Berlin, Germany (home). *Telephone:* (30) 20935926 (office). *Fax:* (30) 20935934 (office). *E-mail:* uhlig@wiwi.hu-berlin.de. *Website:* www.wiwi.hu-berlin.de/wpol.

UKEC LUETH UKEC, John; Sudanese diplomatist. *Career:* chargé d'affaires ad interim to USA 2006–.
Address: Embassy of Sudan, 2210 Massachusetts Avenue, NW, Washington, DC 20008, USA (office). *Telephone:* (202) 338-8565 (office). *Fax:* (202) 667-2406 (office). *E-mail:* info@sudanembassy.org (office). *Website:* www.sudanembassy.org (office).

ULAAN, Chultemiin, MSc; Mongolian economist and politician; *Minister of Finance;* b. 22 April 1954, Baruun, Sukhbaatar Prov.; m. Baldan-Osor Bud; three c. *Education:* Irkhutsk Inst. of Nat. Economy, Irkhutsk, Acad. of Social Sciences, Moscow, Russia, Acad. of Social Sciences, Sofia, Bulgaria. *Career:* Officer State Planning Dept 1977–82, Head of Div. 1982–85; Instructor, Cen. Cttee, Mongolian People's Revolutionary Party (MPRP) 1985–89, Deputy Dir 1989–90, Adviser to Sec.-Gen. 1990; Cabinet mem. and Minister, Nat. Devt Bd 1992–96; mem. Parl. 1996–; Minister of Finance and Economy 2000–04; Deputy Prime Minister 2004–06; Minister of Finance 2007–.
Address: Ministry of Finance, Government Building 2, Negsden Ündestnii Gudmaj 5/1, Chingeltei District, Ulan Bator (office). *Telephone:* (11) 320247 (office). *Fax:* (11) 320247 (office). *E-mail:* webmaster@pmis.gov.mn (office). *Website:* www.pmis.gov.mn (office).

UNAKITAN, Kemal; Turkish politician; *Minister of Finance;* b. 1946, Edirne; m.; three c. *Education:* Ankara Econ. and Commerical Sciences Acad. *Career:* fmr Financial Comptroller Ministry of Finance, Minister of Finance 2002–; fmr mem. Exec. Bd SEKA Directorate Gen., Albaraka Türk and Family Finance.

Address: Ministry of Finance, Maliye Bakanlığı, Dikmen Cad., Ankara, Turkey (office). *Telephone:* (312) 4250018 (office). *Fax:* (312) 4250058 (office). *E-mail:* bshalk@maliye.gov.tr (office). *Website:* www.maliye.gov .tr (office).

UNG SEAN; Cambodian diplomatist; *Ambassador to Thailand;* m. Ung Sean Soka. *Career:* fmr Deputy Foreign Minister; Amb. to Thailand 1999–; also Perm. Rep. to ESCAP; mem. Asian Inst. of Tech.; Trustee Asian Disaster Preparedness Center.
Address: Embassy of Cambodia, 518/4, Thanon Pracha Uthit, Ramkhamhaeng Soi 39, Wangtonglang, Bangkok, 10310, Thailand (office). *Telephone:* (2) 957-5851 (office). *Fax:* (2) 957-5850 (office). *E-mail:* recbkk@ cscoms.com (office).

UNTERMEYER, Chase; American diplomatist; b. 7 March 1946; m. Diana Cumming Kendrick; one d. *Education:* Harvard Coll. *Career:* served in USN during Vietnam War as destroyer officer in Pacific and as aide to Commdr of US naval forces in the Philippines; early career as political reporter for Houston Chronicle newspaper; elected mem. Tex. House of Reps for dist in Houston 1976; Exec. Asst to Vice-Pres. George Bush 1981–84; apptd Asst Sec. of the Navy for manpower and reserve affairs 1984; Dir Presidential Personnel, The White House 1988–91; Dir Voice of America 1991–93; fmr mem. and Chair. Bd of Visitors, US Naval Acad.; fmr mem. Bd Nat. Public Radio; fmr mem. Houston Port Comm.; fmr Chair. Tex. State Bd of Educ.; Prof. of Public Policy and Vice-Pres. for government affairs, Univ. of Tex. Health Science Center, Houston –2004; Amb. to Qatar 2004–08.
Address: US Department of State, 2201 C Street NW, Washington, DC 20520, USA (office). *Telephone:* (202) 647-4000 (office). *Fax:* (202) 647-6738 (office). *Website:* www.state.gov (office).

UNWIN, Peter William, CMG, MA; British writer and diplomatist (retd) and international official (retd); b. 20 May 1932, Middlesbrough; m. Monica Steven 1955; two s. two d. *Education:* Ampleforth Coll., York, Open Scholar in History, Christ Church, Oxford. *Career:* joined HM Foreign Service 1956, British Legation, Budapest 1958, British Embassy, Tokyo 1961, FCO 1963, British Information Services, New York, 1967, FCO 1970, British Embassy, Bonn 1973, Head of Personnel Policy Dept, FCO 1976, Harvard Univ., USA 1979, Minister (Econ.), British Embassy, Bonn 1980, Amb. to Hungary 1983–86, to Denmark 1986–88; Commonwealth Deputy Sec.-Gen. 1989–93; Chair. British-Hungarian Soc. 1993–2000 (Pres. 2000–03), Abbeyfield Int. 1996–2001; Vice-Chair. Anglo-Danish Soc. 1997–99, UK Cttee UNICEF 1997–2000; Dir David Davies Memorial Inst. of Int. Studies, Univ. of Wales, Aberystwyth 1995–2001, Chair 2001–07; Order of Merit (Hungary). *Publications:* Voice in the Wilderness, Imre Nagy and the Hungarian Revolution 1991, Baltic Approaches 1996, Hearts, Minds & Interests 1998, Where East Met West 2000, The Narrow Sea: The History of the English Channel 2003, 1956: Power Defied 2006.
Address: 30 Kew Green, Richmond, Surrey TW9 3BH, England (home). *Telephone:* (20) 8940-8037 (home).

URBAIN, Robert; Belgian politician; *Minister of State;* b. 24 Nov. 1930, Hornu; three s. *Education:* Ecole Normale, Mons. *Career:* math. teacher 1950–58; Deputy for Mons 1971–95; Sec. of State for Planning and Housing 1973, for Econ. Affairs (French region) 1977–78; Minister of Posts and Telephones 1979, of Foreign Trade 1980–81, of Health and Educ. (French sector) 1981–85, of Social Affairs and Health Feb.–May 1988, of Foreign Trade 1988–92, of Foreign Trade and European Affairs 1992–95; mem. Senate 1995–99; Minister of State 1998–; Prés. du Conseil d'Admin. de la Faculté Polytechnique de Mons; Grand-Croix Ordre de Léopold II, Croix civique (1st Class); Officier Ordre de la Pléiade, Grand-Croix Ordre de la Couronne, and numerous foreign awards.
Address: Hôtel de Ville, 7300 Boussu (office); Rue de Bavay 42, 7301 Hornu, Belgium (home). *Telephone:* (65) 71-73-11 (office); (65) 63-07-38 (home). *Fax:* (65) 79-36-14 (office); (65) 65-02-65 (home). *E-mail:* r.urbain@boussu.be (office).

URBAN, Carol J.; American diplomatist; b. Long Island, NY; m. Richard Gilbert. *Education:* St Bonaventure Univ. and Univ. of Maryland. *Career:* joined US Information Agency (USIA) in 1975, held several sr man. positions including Exec. Officer, Bureau of American Republics Affairs, Exec. Officer, Bureau of Asia and Pacific Affairs and Exec. Dir Resource Man. Cttee, served abroad in Moscow 1986–89, Madrid 1992–95, Bonn 1998–99, following merger of USIA into State Dept, overseas assignments have included Berlin 1999–2001, second tour in Madrid, Counselor for Man., Embassy in Madrid 2001–04, Deputy Chief of Mission, Bern 2004–06, Chargé d'affaires a.i. in Switzerland 2006; career mem. Sr Foreign Service with rank of Minister-Counselor; numerous awards including Meritorious and Superior Honor Awards from USIA and State Dept.

Address: c/o US Department of State, 2201 C Street NW, Washington DC 20520, USA (office).

URBINA, Jorge, LLM, DIur; Costa Rican professor of law and diplomatist; *Permanent Representative, United Nations;* b. 2 May 1946; m.; two c. *Education:* Univ. of Costa Rica, Univ. of Bordeaux, France. *Career:* Prof. of Law, Univ. of Costa Rica 1970–82; Prof., Int. Affairs School, Heredia Nat. Univ. 1990–93; Deputy Perm. Rep. to UN, New York 1982–84; Vice Minister for Foreign Affairs 1984–86; Exec. Pres. Nat. Inst. for Municipal Counselling and Promotion 1986–90; Minister of Information 1989–90; Assoc. Researcher, Centro de Investigaciones Económicas y Sociales 1990–93; Perm. Consultant, Programme for Democratic Governance in Cen. America, UNDP 1993–98; Programme Coordinator, Int. Centre for Human Devt 1998–2006; Perm. Rep. to UN, New York 2006–; mem. Costa Rica Bar Asscn, Cen. American Asscn of Ciculo de Copán.
Address: Permanent Mission of Costa Rica to the United Nations, 211 East 43rd Street, Room 903, New York, NY 10017, USA (office). *Telephone:* (212) 986-6373 (office). *Fax:* (212) 986-6842 (office). *E-mail:* pmnu@rree.go .cr (office). *Website:* www.un.int/costarica (office).

URIBE ECHAVERRÍA, Jorge Alberto; Colombian business executive and politician; b. 30 Oct. 1940, Rionegro, Antioquia. *Education:* Collegio Jorge Robledo Ortiz, Culver Military Acad., Ind., Cheshire Acad., Conn, George Washington Univ., Washington DC, USA, Univ. of Besancôn, France. *Career:* Nat. Dir Compañia de Exportaciones Comex 1963; Nat. Dir Instituto Colombiano de Administración, Incolda 1964–65; joined DeLima Marsh SA (insurance co.), becoming Man., Medellín br., later Gen. Man., Exec. Vice-Pres., Pres. 1991–2003; Minister of Nat. Defence 2003–05 (resgnd); Estrella de Antioquía, Distinción Especial Policía Nacional y Ejecutivo 1973.
Address: c/o Ministry of National Defence, Centro Administrativo Nacional (CAN), 2, Avda El Dorado, Bogotá, DC, Colombia (office).

URIBE VÉLEZ, Alvaro, LLB; Colombian politician and head of state; *President;* b. 4 July 1952, Medellín; m. Lina Moreno; two s. *Education:* Univ. of Antioquia, Harvard Univ., Mass., USA, Univ. of Oxford, UK. *Career:* Sec.-Gen. Ministry of Labour 1977–78; Dir of Civil Aviation 1980–82; Mayor of Medellín 1982, Councillor 1984–86, Senator of Antioquia Prov. 1986–90, 1990–94; Gov. of Antioquia 1995–97; Presidential cand. for Movimiento Primero Colombia 2002, Pres. 2002–; Light Unto The Nations Award 2007.
Address: Office of the President, Palacio de Nariño, Carrera 8A, No. 7–26, Bogotá, Colombia. *Telephone:* (1) 562-9300. *Fax:* (1) 286-8063. *E-mail:* primerocolombia@md.impsat.net.co (office). *Website:* web.presidencia .gov.co (office).

URRUTIA GARCÍA, Edmundo René; Guatemalan diplomatist; m. Yolanda Aguilar de Urrutia. *Career:* Amb. to UK 2006–08.
Address: Ministry of Foreign Affairs, 2A Avda La Reforma 4-47, Zona 10, Guatemala City, Guatemala (office). *Telephone:* 2331-8410 (office). *Fax:* 2331-8510 (office). *E-mail:* webmaster@minex.gob.gt (office). *Website:* www.minex.gob.gt (office).

UŠACKA, Anita, DrIur; Latvian professor of law and judge; *Judge, International Criminal Court;* b. 26 April 1952, Rīga. *Education:* Moscow State Univ., Univ. of Latvia. *Career:* Asst, Dept for Fundamental Legal Studies, Univ. of Latvia 1975–76, Prin. Lecturer 1980–82, Docent 1982–99, Head of Dept 1989–96, Assoc. Prof. 1999–, Prof. Dept for State Law 2002–; Assoc. Prof. Rīga Grad. School of Law 1999–2001; Exec. Dir Latvian Br., UNICEF 1994–96; Judge Constitutional Court of Repub. of Latvia 1996–; Judge, Int. Criminal Court 2003–; mem. Ed. Bd Law and the Rights journal; mem. Bd Lawyers Training Centre of Latvia, Sub-Comm. Constitutional Legal Procedure, Council of Europe, Int. Women Lawyers Asscn 1997–. *Publications:* numerous articles in professional journals, reports to int. scientific confs.
Address: International Criminal Court, Maanweg 174, 2516 AB, The Hague, Netherlands (office); Constitutional Court of the Republic of Latvia, 1 J. Alumana Str., Rīga, 1010, Latvia (office). *Telephone:* (70) 5158515 (The Hague) (office); 733-1516 (Rīga) (office). *Fax:* (70) 5158555 (The Hague) (office); 722-0572 (Rīga) (office). *Website:* www.icc-cpi.int (office).

UŠACKAS, Vygaudas, LLB; Lithuanian diplomatist; *Ambassador to UK;* b. 16 Dec. 1964, Skuodas; m. Loreta Ušackienė-Bilkstyte; one s. one d. *Education:* Vilnius Univ., Univ. of Oslo, Norway, Århus Univ., Denmark. *Career:* Counsellor, Lithuanian Mission to EU 1992–94, Rep. for Relations with NATO 1994–96, mem. Del. to WEU 1995–96, Political Dir, Ministry of Foreign Affairs 1996–99, Deputy Minister of Foreign Affairs 1999–2000, also served as Chief Negotiator for Lithuania accession to EU, Amb. to

USA (also accred to Mexico and for Special Missions at Ministerial Advisory Group) 2001–06, to UK 2006–.
Address: Embassy of Lithuania, 84 Gloucester Place, London, W1U 6AU, England (office). *Telephone:* (20) 7486-6401 (office). *Fax:* (20) 7486-6403 (office). *E-mail:* chancery@lithuanianembassy.co.uk (office). *Website:* uk .mfa.lt (office).

USHAKOV, Yurii Viktorovich, PhD; Russian diplomatist; *Ambassador to USA;* b. 13 March 1947, Moscow; m.; one d. *Education:* Moscow State Inst. of Int. Relations, Diplomatic Acad. *Career:* joined diplomatic service 1970; trans., expert, attaché USSR Embassy in Denmark 1970–75, Second then First Sec. 1978–82, Minister-Counsellor 1986–92; adviser Gen. Secr. USSR Ministry of Foreign Affairs 1982–86; Head Dept of All-Europe Co-operation, Ministry of Foreign Affairs 1992–96; Perm. Rep. of Russia to Org. for Security and Co-operation in Europe (OSCE) 1996–98; Deputy Minister of Foreign Affairs 1998; Amb. to USA 1999–.
Address: Embassy of the Russian Federation, 2650 Wisconsin Ave, NW, Washington, DC 20007, USA (office). *Telephone:* (202) 298-5700 (office). *Fax:* (202) 298-5749 (office). *E-mail:* rusembus@erols.com (office). *Website:* www.russianembassy.org (office).

USMAN, Nenadi E., BSc; Nigerian politician; b. 12 Nov. 1966, Jere, Kaduna State. *Education:* Ahmadu Bello Univ., Univ. of Jos. *Career:* served as Commr of Health, for Environment and Natural Resources, for Women's Affairs, Youth and Social Devt; fmr Exec. Advisor for Youth, for Information, Home Affairs and Culture; Minister of State for Finance 2003–06, Minister of Finance 2006–07; Chair. Fed. Accounts Allocation Cttee 2003–06; mem. Govt Econ. Man. Team 2003–06; mem. House of Reps for Kachia/Kagarko Fed. Constituency; mem. Kaduna State Caucus, Defunct Nat. Republican Convention; f. Educ. and Empowerment for Women in Kaduna State.
Address: c/o National Assembly of Nigeria, National Assembly Complex, Three Arms Zone, POB 141, Abuja, Nigeria (office).

USMAN, Shamsudeen, BSc, MSc, PhD; Nigerian economist and government official; *Minister of Finance;* m. Nenadi Usman. *Education:* Ahmadu Bello Univ., Zaria, LSE, UK. *Career:* Planning Officer, Kano State Ministry of Econ. Planning 1974–76; Lecturer, Ahmadu Bello Univ., Zaria 1976–81; Controller, Nigerian Industrial Devt Bank 1981–85; Gen. Man. Corp. Banking, NAL Merchant Bank 1985–98; Dir-Gen. Tech. Cttee on Privatization and Commercialization (TCPC) 1989–91; Exec. Dir, United Bank of Africa Plc and later Union Bank of Nigeria 1992–94; Deputy Gov. Cen. Bank of Nigeria 1999–2007; Minister of Finance 2007–; Pres. Nigerian Econ. Soc. 1986–87, Fellow 1995; Officer of the Order of the Fed. Repub.
Address: Ministry of Finance, Ahmadu Bello Way, Central Area, PMB 14, Garki, Abuja, Nigeria (office). *Telephone:* (9) 2346290 (office). *Website:* fmf .gov.ng (office).

UTKAN, Necati; Turkish diplomatist. *Career:* fmr Dir Turkish Co-operation and Devt Agency; fmr spokesman, Ministry of Foreign Affairs; fmr Amb. to Italy; currently serves at various times as Special Envoy.
Address: Ministry of Foreign Affairs, Dişişleri Bakanlığı, Yeni Hizmet Binası, 06100 Balgat, Ankara, Turkey (office). *Telephone:* (312) 2921000 (office). *Fax:* (312) 2873869 (office). *Website:* www.mfa.gov.tr (office).

'UTOIKAMANU, Fekitamoeloa Tupoupai; Tongan diplomatist; *Ambassador to USA and Permanent Representative, United Nations;* b. Dec. 1959; m.; one d. *Education:* Univ. of Auckland, NZ. *Career:* Macroeconomist, Cen. Planning Dept, Foreign Ministry 1983–86, Acting Planning Officer 1988–91; Acting Deputy Sec., Ministry of Finance 1987; Deputy Sec. of Foreign Affairs and Deputy Nat. Authorizing Officer 1991–2002; Sec. of Foreign Affairs and Nat. Authorizing Officer 2002–05; Perm. Rep. to UN, New York 2005–, concurrently Amb. to USA.
Address: Office of the Permanent Representative of Tonga to the United Nations, 250 East 51st Street, New York, NY 10022, USA (office). *Telephone:* (917) 369-1025 (office). *Fax:* (917) 369-1024 (office). *E-mail:* tongaunmission@aol.com (office). *Website:* www.tongausun.org (office).

UZAWA, Hirofumi, PhD; Japanese economist and academic; *Professor Emeritus of Economics, University of Tokyo;* b. 21 July 1928, Tottori Province; m. Hiroko Aoyoshi 1957; two s. one d. *Education:* Univ. of Tokyo. *Career:* Research Assoc., Lecturer, Asst Prof., Dept of Econs, Stanford Univ., Calif. 1956–60, Assoc. Prof. of Econs and Statistics 1961–64; Asst Prof. of Econs and Math., Univ. of Calif., Berkeley 1960–61; Prof. of Econs, Univ. of Chicago 1964–68, Univ. of Tokyo 1969–89, Prof. Emer. 1989–; Prof. of Econs, Niigata Univ. 1989–94; mem. The Japan Acad. 1989–; Matsunaga Memorial Prize 1969, Yoshino Prize 1971, Mainichi Prize 1974, desig. as Person of Cultural Merits 1983, Order of Culture 1997. *Publications:* in English: Studies in Linear and Nonlinear Programming (co-author) 1958; in Japanese: Economic Development and Fluctuations (co-author) 1972, Social Costs of the Automobile 1974, A Re-examination of Modern Economic Theory 1977, Transformation of Modern Economics 1986, A Critique of Japanese Economy 1987, Towards a Theory of Public Economics 1987, Preference, Production and Capital 1988, Optimality, Equilibrium and Growth 1988, A History of Economic Thought (in Japanese) 1989, Poverty Amid Economic Prosperity (in Japanese) 1989, Economic Analysis (in Japanese) 1990, Collected Papers of Hirofumi Uzawa (12 vols) 1994–95, Introduction to Mathematics (six vols) 1997–2000.
Address: Kamiyama-cho 20-23, Shibuya-ku, Tokyo, Japan (home).

UZUMCU, Ahmet, BA; Turkish diplomatist; *Permanent Representative, United Nations, Geneva;* b. 30 Aug. 1951, Armutlu; m.; one d. *Education:* Ankara Univ. *Career:* Attaché, Protocol Dept, Ministry of Foreign Affairs 1976; mil. service 1976–78; Attaché, then Second Sec., Bilateral Cultural Relations Dept 1978–79; Second, then First Sec., Embassy in Vienna, Austria 1979–82; Consul, Consulate-Gen. in Aleppo, Syria 1982–84; Chief of Section, Personnel Dept, Ministry of Foreign Affairs 1984–86; Counsellor, Del. to NATO, Brussels 1986–89, mem. Int. Staff 1989–94; Head of NATO Dept, Ministry of Foreign Affairs 1994–96; Minister, Head of Personnel Dept 1996–99; Amb. to Israel 1999–2002; Perm. Rep. to NATO 2002–04; Deputy Under-Sec., Ministry of Foreign Affairs for Bilateral Political Affairs 2004–06; Perm. Rep. to UN, Geneva 2006–; Pres. UN Disarmament Conference 2008.
Address: Permanent Mission of Turkey to the United Nations Office at Geneva and other International Organizations, Chemin du Petit-Saconnex 28b, 1211 Geneva 19, Switzerland (office). *Telephone:* 229185080 (office). *Fax:* 227340859 (office). *E-mail:* mission.turkey@ties.itu.int (office).

UZUN, Ahmet, BSc; Turkish-Cypriot civil servant and politician; *Minister of Finance, 'Turkish Republic of Northern Cyprus';* b. 1950, Lefkoşa (Nicosia); m.; two c. *Education:* Ankara Univ. *Career:* held various political roles since 1975, including Under-Sec. to Deputy Prime Minister; Minister of Finance, 'Turkish Repub. of Northern Cyprus' 2004–; fmr Pres. Public Officers' Union (KTAMS); mem. Cen. Admin. Council Republican Turkish Party (Cumhuriyetci Turk Partisi).
Address: Ministry of Finance, Lefkoşa (Nicosia), Mersin 10, Turkey (office). *Telephone:* 2283116 (office). *Fax:* 2278230 (office). *E-mail:* bim@ kktcmaliye.com (office). *Website:* www.kktcmaliye.com (office).

V

VAAHTORANTA, Tapani, CandPolit, MA, PhD; Finnish research institute director. *Education:* Univ. of Turku, Princeton Univ., USA. *Career:* Asst Prof., Univ. of Turku 1986–89; Sr Research Fellow, Finnish Inst. of Int. Affairs 1989–90, Research Dir 1990–91, later Dir; mem. faculty, Geneva Centre for Security Policy 1998–2001. *Publications:* Finnish and Swedish Security: Comparing National Policies (co-ed.) 2001, Charting a New Course: Globalisation, African Recovery and the New African Initiative (co-ed.) 2002.
Address: Finnish Institute of International Affairs, Mannerheimintie 15 A, Helsinki 00260, Finland (office). *Telephone:* (9) 43420722 (office). *Fax:* (9) 43420769 (office). *E-mail:* tapani.vaahtoranta@upi-fiia.fi (office). *Website:* www.upi-fiia.fi.

VAIKŠNORAS, Maj. Gen. Vitalijus; Lithuanian military officer; *Chief of Defence Staff, Ministry of National Defence;* b. 23 April 1961, Dusetos, Zarasai dist.; m.; one d. *Education:* Naval Academy in Kaliningrad,. *Career:* Chair. Lithuanian Interdepartmental Comm.; Chief of Defence Staff, Ministry of Nat. Defence 2003–; promoted to Maj. Gen. 2007; NATO Individual Fellowship, Latvian Armed Forces Commdr 2nd grade Medal of Merit 2008.
Address: Ministry of National Defence, Totorių str. 25/3, 01121 Vilnius, Lithuania (office). *Telephone:* (5) 262-4821 (office). *Fax:* (5) 212-6082 (office). *E-mail:* vis@kam.lt (office). *Website:* www.kam.lt (office).

VAITIEKŪNAS, Petras, PhD; Lithuanian diplomatist and politician; *Minister of Foreign Affairs;* b. 26 March 1953; m.; three c. *Education:* Vilnius Univ., Acad. of Sciences of Repub. of Lithuania, Coll. of Strategic Studies and Defence Econs, Germany. *Career:* scientific researcher, Inst. of Physics, Acad. of Sciences of Repub. of Lithuania 1976–90; mem. Supreme Council, Restoration Seimas (Parl.) of Repub. of Lithuania 1990–92, adviser to Chair. of Seimas 1992–93; Sr Asst for Foreign Affairs to Pres. 1993–98; Head, Cen. European Div., Political Dept, Ministry of Foreign Affairs 1998; Adviser to Minister of Foreign Affairs 1998–99; Amb. to Latvia 1999–2004; Foreign Affairs Adviser to Pres. 2004; Amb.-at-Large, Foreign Policy and Analysis Planning Dept, Ministry of Foreign Affairs 2004–05; Amb. to Belarus 2005–06; Minister of Foreign Affairs 2006–.
Address: Ministry of Foreign Affairs, J. Tumo-Vaižganto g. 2, Vilnius 01511, Lithuania (office). *Telephone:* (5) 236-2401 (office). *Fax:* (5) 231-3090 (office). *E-mail:* petras.vaitiekunas@urm.lt (office). *Website:* www .urm.lt (office).

VAJPAYEE, Atal Bihari, MA; Indian politician; b. 25 Dec. 1924, Gwalior, MP. *Education:* Victoria (now Laxmibai) Coll., Gwalior, D.A.V. Coll., Kanpur. *Career:* mem. Rashtriya Swayamsewak Sangh 1941, Indian Nat. Congress 1942–46; mem. Lok Sabha 1957–62, 1967–84 (for New Delhi 1977–84), 1991–, Rajya Sabha 1962–67, 1986; Founder-mem. Bharatiya Jana Sangh 1951, Parl. Leader 1957–77; Chair. Cttee on Govt Assurance 1966–67, Public Accounts Cttee, Lok Sabha 1967–70, 1991–93; detained during Emergency 1975–77; Founder-mem. Janata Party 1977, Pres. Bharatiya Janata Party 1980–86, Parl. Leader 1980–84, 1986; Minister of External Affairs 1977–79; Leader of Opposition, Lok Sabha 1993–98, Chair. Standing Cttee on External Affairs 1993–96; Minister of External Affairs 1998; Prime Minister of India 15–28 May 1996, 1998–2004, also Minister of Health and Family Welfare, Atomic Energy and Agric. 1998–2004; Chair. Nat. Security Council 1998–2004; mem. Nat. Integration Council 1961–; fmr Ed. Rastradharma (monthly), Panchjanya (weekly), Swadesh and Veer Arjun (dailies); Dr hc (Kanpur Univ.) 1993; Bharat Ratna Pte Govind Ballabh Pant Award 1994, Padma Vibhushan 1992, Lokmanya Tilak Puruskar. *Publications:* New Dimensions of India's Foreign Policy, Jan Sangh Aur Musalmans, Three Decades in Parliament; collections of poems and numerous articles.
Address: c/o Bharatiya Janata Party (BJP) (Indian People's Party), 11 Ashok Rd, New Delhi 110 001 (office); 7 Race Course Road, New Delhi 110011, India (home). *Telephone:* (11) 23018939 (home). *Fax:* (11) 23019545 (home).

VALDÉS, Juan Gabriel, PhD; Chilean politician and diplomatist; b. June 1947; m. Antonia Echenique Celis; four c. *Education:* Catholic Univ. of Chile, Santiago, Univ. of Essex, UK, Princeton Univ., USA. *Career:* Researcher, Political Science Inst. of Catholic Univ. of Chile, Inst. for Policy Studies, Washington, DC 1972–76; Officer, Latin American Inst. for Transnational Studies, Prof. of Int. Relations, Econ. Research and Devt Centre, Mexico City, Mexico 1976–1984; Research Fellow, Kellogg Inst. of Int. Studies, Notre Dame Univ., USA, Center for Latin American Studies, Princeton Univ. 1984, 1987; Consultant, Econ. Comm. for Latin America 1985; Amb. to Spain 1990–94; Dir Int. Div. and Co-ordinator NAFTA Negotiating Team, Ministry of Finance 1994–96, Lead Negotiator Chile–Canada Free Trade Agreement 1996; Consultant, UN Programme for Devt, Santiago 1994; mem. Nat. TV Council 1995; Vice-Minister Int. Econ. Affairs, Ministry of Foreign Affairs 1996–99, Minister 1999–2000; Perm. Rep. to UN, New York 2000–03, concurrently Amb. to Iran 2001; Amb. to Argentina 2003–04; Sec.-Gen.'s Special Rep., UN Stabilization Mission in Haiti (MINUSTAH) 2004–06; Dir Public Diplomacy Program, Ministry of Foreign Affairs 2006–. *Publications include:* Movimiento Sindical Y Empresas Transnacionales 1979, Chile 2000: Encuentro En Caceres De Politicos E Intelectuales Chilenos 1994, Pinochet's Economists : The Chicago School of Economics in Chile 1995; numerous articles on int. relations.
Address: Ministry of Foreign Affairs, Catedral 1158, Santiago, Chile (office). *Telephone:* (2) 679-4200 (office). *Fax:* (2) 699-4202 (office). *Website:* www.minrel.gov.cl (office).

VALDEZ CUETO, Sixto Julio; Bolivian diplomatist and fmr journalist; *Chargé d'affaires, Embassy in Buenos Aires; Career:* fmr journalist; fmr Head, Empresa Nacional de Television (state broadcasting corpn); fmr Amb., responsible for integration issues; Chargé d'affaires, Embassy in Buenos Aires 2007–; mem. Movimento al political party.
Address: Embassy of Bolivia, Corrientes 545, 2°, C1043AAF Buenos Aires, Argentina (office). *Telephone:* (11) 4394-6042 (office). *Fax:* (11) 5217-1070 (office). *E-mail:* svaldez@embajadadebolivia.com.ar (office). *Website:* www.embajadadebolivia.com.ar (office).

VALENÇA PINTO, Gen. Luis, BEng; Portuguese military officer; *Chief of Defence;* b. Lisbon; m. Maria de Lourdes; two s. one d. *Education:* Tech. Univ. of Lisbon, NATO Defence Coll., Rome. *Career:* Engineer Platoon Leader during combat tour in Angola 1971–72, Engineer Co. Commdr 1973–75; Mil. Rep. to NATO, Brussels 1978–84; Mil. Counsellor, Del. to NATO, Brussels 1990–93; Mil. Rep. to SHAPE 1997–2000; Dir Nat. Defence Inst. 2000; Army Logistics Commdr 2001–03; Chief of Staff 2003–06; Chief of Defence 2006–; seven Distinguished Service Medals (five Gold and two Silver), Mil. Merit Medal (three classes). *Publications:* articles on security and defence issues in mil. and academic journals.
Address: Ministry of National Defence, Av. Ilha de Madeira 1, 1400-204 Lisbon, Portugal (office). *Telephone:* (21) 3038528 (office). *Fax:* (21) 3020284 (office). *E-mail:* gcrp@sg.mdn.gov.pt (office). *Website:* www.mdn .gov.pt (office).

VALENCIA BENAVIDES, Andrés; Mexican diplomatist; *Ambassador to Brazil; Career:* joined Foreign Service 1973, overseas postings include Perm. Rep. to OAS, Consul-Gen. in Atlanta, Ga; fmr Amb. to Colombia, to Israel; fmr Dir of Bilateral Affairs, Ministry of Foreign Affairs, fmr Sr Adviser to Under-Sec. of Foreign Affairs; currently Amb. to Brazil.
Address: Embassy of Mexico, SES, Av. das Nações, Quadra 805, Lote 18, 70412-900 Brasilia, DF, Brazil (office). *Telephone:* (61) 3244-1011 (office). *Fax:* (61) 3244-1755 (office). *E-mail:* embamexbra@cabonet.com.br (office). *Website:* www.mexico.org.br (office).

VALERE, Marina Annette, BA; Trinidad and Tobago diplomatist; *Permanent Representative, United Nations; Education:* Univ. of Manchester, UK. *Career:* entered Foreign Service 1971, served at Perm. Mission to UN 1978–81, Acting High Commr, Kingston 1993–94, Amb. to USA and Perm. Rep. to OAS 2003–08, Chair. Cttee on Inter-American Summits Man., OAS, Perm. Rep. to UN 2008–.
Address: Permanent Mission of Trinidad and Tobago to the United Nations, 820 Second Avenue, 5th Floor, New York NY 10017, USA (office). *Telephone:* (212) 697-7620 (office). *Fax:* (212) 682-3580 (office). *E-mail:* tto@un.int (office).

VALLO, Stanislav, PhD; Slovak diplomatist; *Ambassador to Italy;* b. 15 Nov. 1950, Zálesie. *Education:* Comenius Univ., Bratislava. *Career:* mil. service

1975–76; worked at Ministry of Foreign Affairs, First Counsellor, later Chargé d'affaires a.i., Embassy in Rome, First Counsellor, Embassy to Holy See 1995–96, Head of Directorate Gen. for Culture, Countrymen, Press and Human Dimension, Ministry of Foreign Affairs 1996–97, Head of Dept of Culture and Countrymen 1997–99, First Counsellor, Embassy in Paris 1999–2003, Head of Dept of Culture and Countrymen, Ministry of Foreign Affairs 2003–06, Amb. to Italy (also accred to Malta) 2006–. *Publications:* has translated numerous Italian authors into Slovakian. *Address:* Embassy of Slovakia, Via dei Colli della Farnesina 144, 00194 Rome, Italy (office). *Telephone:* (06) 3671500 (office). *Fax:* (06) 36715265 (office). *E-mail:* embassy@rome.mfsa.sk (office); amb.slovac@virgilio.it (office).

VAN DAELE, Gen. August; Belgian army officer; *Chief of Defence Staff;* b. 25 Feb. 1944, Sint-Niklaas. *Education:* Royal Cadet Training School, Royal Mil. Acad., Defence Coll. *Career:* tech. officer, Proficiency Training Centre, Brustem 1967–69; with Mobile Training Unit 1969–71; assigned as line man. Inspection and Tech. Acceptance Testing Service 1971; CO Air Maintenance Squadron, 10th Fighter-Bomber Wing, Kleine-Brogel 1980–83, CO Maintenance Group 1985–87; Deputy CO of Inspection and Tech. Acceptance Testing Service 1983–84, Head of Service 1987–88; Head of Equipment Inspection Service 1988–89, Inspection Service 1989–92, Aviation Equipment Section 1992–94; apptd Deputy Chief of Staff, Logistics, Air Force HQ 1994; Dir-Gen. for Material Resources, Defence Staff 2000–02; Chief of Defence Staff 2003–; mem. NATO Mil. Cttee; Aide to the King of Belgium. *Address:* Ministry of Defence, 8 rue Lambermont, 1000 Brussels, Belgium (office). *Telephone:* (2) 550-28-11 (office). *Fax:* (2) 550-29-19 (office). *E-mail:* cabinet@mod.mil.be (office). *Website:* mod.fgov.be (office).

VAN DAELE, Baron Franciskus; Belgian diplomatist; *Permanent Representative, NATO;* m. Baroness Christiane van Daele; one s. two d. *Career:* joined Belgian Foreign Service in 1971, served in Athens 1977–81, Rome 1986–89; Deputy Perm. Rep. to UN, New York 1989–93; Dir Gen. for Political Affairs, Ministry of Foreign Affairs 1993–97; Perm. Rep. to EU, Brussels 1997–2002; Amb. to USA 2002–06; Perm. Rep. to NATO, Brussels 2006–. *Address:* Office of the Permanent Representative of Belgium, blvd Léopold III, 1110 Brussels, Belgium (office). *Telephone:* (2) 707-41-11 (home). *Fax:* (2) 707-45-79 (office). *E-mail:* natodoc@hq.nato.int (office). *Website:* www .nato.int (office).

VAN DAM, Nikolaos, DLitt; Dutch diplomatist; *Ambassador to Indonesia;* b. 1 April 1945, Amsterdam; m. Marinka van Dam-Bogaerts; three s. one d. *Education:* Univ. of Amsterdam. *Career:* taught Modern Middle Eastern History at Univ. of Amsterdam 1970–75; with Middle East Bureau, Ministry of Foreign Affairs 1975–80; First Sec., Embassy in Beirut 1980–83; Charge d'Affaires, Libya 1983–85; Asst Dir Africa and Middle East Dept, Ministry of Foreign Affairs 1985–88; Amb. to Iraq 1988–91, to Egypt 1991–96, to Turkey 1996–99, to Germany 1999–2005, to Indonesia (also accred to Timor-Leste) 2005–; Kt, Order of Orange Nassau 1983, Officer, Order of Orange Nassau 1991, Grand Officer, Order of Merit of Grand Duchy of Luxembourg 2003, Kt Commdr Cross, Order of Merit of FRG 2005. *Publications:* The Netherlands and the Arab World: From the Middle Ages Until the Twentieth Century 1987, The Struggle for Power in Syria: Politics and Society Under Asad and the Ba'th Party 1997, The Peace That Did Not Come: Twenty Years as a Diplomat in the Middle East 1998; numerous articles in professional journals. *Address:* Embassy of the Netherlands, Jalan H. R. Rasuna Said, Kav. S/3, Kuningan, Jakarta 12950, Indonesia (office). *Telephone:* (21) 5241009 (office). *Fax:* (21) 5700734 (office). *E-mail:* jak-ca@minbuza.nl (office). *Website:* www.mfa.nl/jak (office).

VAN DEN HOUT, Tjaco T., JD; Dutch lawyer, diplomatist and international organization executive; *Secretary-General, Permanent Court of Arbitration, The Hague; Education:* Leiden Univ., Harvard Univ., USA. *Career:* joined Foreign Service 1974; has served in numerous diplomatic positions including mem. Del. to CSCE, Geneva and at embassies in Africa and Asia; Deputy Dir for Int. Orgs, Ministry of Foreign Affairs 1989–91, Deputy Dir of Foreign Service 1991–94, Deputy Sec.-Gen. 1996-99; Sec.-Gen. Perm. Court of Arbitration, The Hague 1999–. *Address:* Permanent Court of Arbitration, Peace Palace, Carnegieplein 2, 2517 KJ The Hague, Netherlands (office). *Telephone:* (70) 3024165 (office). *Fax:* (70) 3024167 (office). *E-mail:* secgen@pca-cpa.org (office). *Website:* www.pca-cpa.org (office).

VAN DER GEEST, Willem, MPhil, PhD; Dutch research institute director; *Director, European Institute for Asian Studies;* b. 8 June 1954, Leiden. *Education:* Univ. of Leiden, Univ. of Stockholm, Sweden, Univ. of Cambridge, UK. *Career:* Research Asst Nat. Inst. of Econ. Research,

Sweden 1979; Research Officer Inst. of Social Studies, The Hague 1980–82; part-time lecturer at Univ. of Leiden 1981–82; tutor in Econs Cambridge Univ. 1983–84; economist Ministry of Finance, Bangladesh 1984–86; Sr Research Economist Oxford Univ. 1987–91, Research Assoc. 1992–95; Sr Consultant Pakistan Inst. of Devt Econs 1992–95; Sr Economist Int. Labour Org., Geneva 1995–97; Visiting Prof. Univ. Libre de Bruxelles 2001–; Sr Adviser Bangladesh Inst. of Devt Studies 2002–03; currently Dir European Inst. for Asian Studies; mem. Royal Econ. Soc.; Vice-Pres. EU-Japan Assoc., Brussels. *Publications:* Negotiating Structural Adjustment in Africa (ed.) 1994, Adjustment, Employment and Missing Institutions in Sub-Saharan Africa (co-ed.) 1999, Economic Reform and Trade Performance in South Asia (co-ed.) 2004, numerous chapters and articles in books and journals. *Address:* European Institute for Asian Studies, 35 Rue des Deux Eglises, 1000 Brussels, Belgium (office). *Telephone:* (2) 230-81-22 (office). *Fax:* (2) 230-54-02 (office). *E-mail:* w.vandergeest@eias.org (office). *Website:* www .eias.org (office).

VAN DER MEULEN, Robert Paul, LLM, MCL; Dutch diplomatist; *Ambassador and Head, European Commission Delegation to Jordan;* b. 25 May 1950, Eindhoven; m. Christine Bayle 1982; two d. *Education:* Univ. of Leyden. *Career:* Asst, European Inst., Univ. of Leyden 1974–76; Dir European Integration, Foreign Econ. Relations Dept, Ministry of Econ. Affairs 1976, Head of Bureau, Accession of Greece, Spain and Portugal, Co-operation with Mediterranean cos and EFTA cos 1979; with Perm. Representation of Netherlands to EC, Brussels 1981–82; First Sec. Embassy in Washington, DC 1982–84, Counsellor 1984–85; Deputy Head Office of Vice-Pres. of EC 1985–88; Amb., Head of Del. of European Comm. to Brunei, Indonesia and Singapore 1989–94, to Tunisia 1994–98, to Jordan 2002–; Head, Maghreb Div. (DG RELEX-F3), European Comm. 1998–2001, Acting Dir S Mediterranean and Middle East 2001–02; Grand Officier, Ordre de la Répub. Tunisienne. *Address:* Delagation of the European Commission, 15, Al-Jahiz Street, Shmeisani, PO Box 926794, Amman 11110, Jordan (office); 1 rue du Genève (valise diplomatique), 1049 Brussels, Belgium (home). *Telephone:* (6) 5668191 (office); (6) 5931042 (home). *E-mail:* robert.van-der-meulen@ cec.eu.int (office); delegation-jordan@cec.eu.int (office); vdmeulen@go .com.jo (home). *Website:* www.deljor.cec.eu.int (office).

VAN DER STOEL, Max, LLM, MA; Dutch politician; b. 3 Aug. 1924, Voorschoten; one s. four d. *Education:* Univ. of Leiden. *Career:* Int. Sec. Labour Party (Partij van de Arbeid) 1958–65; mem. Exec. Bd Socialist Int. 1958–65; mem. First Chamber of States-Gen. (Parl.) 1960–63, Second Chamber 1963–65, 1967–73, 1978–80; State Sec. of Foreign Affairs 1965–66; mem. Ass. Council of Europe 1967–72; N Atlantic Ass., European Parl. 1972–73; Minister of Foreign Affairs 1973–77, 1981–82; Perm. Rep. to the UN 1983–86; mem. Council of State 1986–92; OSCE High Commr on Nat. Minorities 1993–2001; Minister of State of the Netherlands 1991; apptd. Special Rapporteur of UN Comm. on Human Rights on the situation of human rights in Iraq 1991–99; Special Rep. of Chair. of OSCE on Macedonia 2001–03; Hon. KCMG, UK 2006; Dr hc (Athens) 1997, (Charles Univ. Prague) 1993, (Utrecht) 1994, (Péter Pázmány Catholic Univ., Budapest) 1999, (Univ. Coll. London) 2001, (SouthEast Europe Univ., Skopje) 2003; Gold Medal, Comenius Univ., Bratislava, Slovakia 1998. *Address:* Lubeckstr. 138, 2517 SV The Hague, Netherlands.

VAN DIJK, Petrus, LLM, SJD; Dutch state councillor and fmr professor of international law; *President, Administrative Jurisdiction Division, Council of State;* b. 21 Feb. 1943, De Lier; m. Francisca G. M. Lammerts 1969; one s. one d. *Education:* Utrecht and Leyden Univs. *Career:* Lecturer in Int. Law, Utrecht Univ. 1967–76, Prof. 1976–90; State Councillor 1990–, Pres. Admin. Jurisdiction Div., Council of State 2000–03, 2006–; Judge, European Court of Human Rights 1996–98, Deputy Pres. Admin. Tribunal of Council of Europe 2001–; Fullbright-Hays Scholar, Univ. of Mich. Law School 1970–71; Visiting Prof. Wayne State Univ. Law School 1978; Chair. Netherlands Inst. of Human Rights 1982–97, Netherlands Inst. of Social and Econ. Law 1986–90; Deputy Judge, Court of Appeal of The Hague 1986, Court of Appeal for Business and Industry 1992–, Cen. Appeal Bd Social Affairs 2006–; mem. Perm. Court of Arbitration 2002–; mem. Bd Trustees Inst. of Social Sciences 1992–98, Anne Frank Foundation 1994–; mem. various advisory cttees; mem. Royal Netherlands Acad. of Arts and Sciences; mem. Netherlands Del. to UN Gen. Ass. 1981, 1983, 1986; Kt, Order of the Netherlands Lion. *Publications include:* Theory and Practice of the European Convention on Human Rights (with G. J. H. van Hoof) 1979, The Final Act of Helsinki: Basis for a Pan-European System? 1980, Contents and Function of the Principle of Equity in International Economic Law 1987, Normative Force and Effectiveness of International Economic Law 1988, Access to Court 1993, Universality of Human Rights 1994; book chapters and ed. of numerous legal publs.

Address: Council of State, PO Box 20019, 2500 EA The Hague, Netherlands (office). *Telephone:* (70) 4264645 (office). *Fax:* (70) 4264716 (office). *E-mail:* pvandijk@raadvanstate.nl (office). *Website:* www.raadvanstate.nl (office).

VAN EEKELEN, Willem Frederik, D.LL.; Dutch politician and diplomatist; *Chairman, European Movement in the Netherlands;* b. 5 Feb. 1931, Utrecht; m. Johanna Wentink; two c. *Education:* Utrecht Univ. and Princeton Univ., USA. *Career:* diplomatic service 1957–77; mem. Consultative Ass. Council of Europe and WEU 1981–82; Sec. Gen. WEU 1989–94; Sec. of State for Defence 1978–81, for Foreign Affairs 1982–86; Minister of Defence 1986–88; Senator 1995–; Chair. European Movt in the Netherlands 1995–; mem. Governing Bd Stockholm Int. Peace Research Inst. (SIPRI) 1999–; mem. Advisory Bd Geneva Centre for Democratic Control of Armed Forces (DCAF); Grand Officer Légion d'honneur, Grand Cross of Germany, Belgium, Luxembourg. *Publications:* The Security Agenda for 1996, Debating European Security 1948–1998, From Words to Deeds 2006. *Address:* European Movement in the Netherlands, Het Kleine Loo 414, unit H, 2592 CK The Hague (office); Else Mauhslaan 187, 2595 HE The Hague, Netherlands. *Telephone:* (70) 3541144 (office); (70) 3241103. *Fax:* (70) 3587606 (office); (70) 3241103. *E-mail:* ebn@xs4all.nl (office); derotte@wanadoo.nl (home). *Website:* www.europese-beweging.nl (office).

VAN EENENNAAM, Boudewijn Johannes; Dutch diplomatist; *Permanent Representative, United Nations, Geneva;* b. 1946; m. Jellie van der Steeg. *Education:* Univ. of Leiden, Clingendael Inst. for Int. Affairs, The Hague. *Career:* numerous positions with Ministry of Foreign Affairs, including Dir Atlantic Co-operation and Security Affairs Dept 1990–93, Deputy Dir-Gen. for Political Affairs 1993–97, Dir-Gen. 1997–2002, Counsellor (Political Affairs), Washington, DC 1984–88, Political Adviser, Netherlands Del. to NATO 1989, Amb. to USA 2002–06, Perm. Rep. to UN, Geneva 2006–. *Publications include:* numerous articles on int. security issues. *Address:* Permanent Mission of the Netherlands, Avenue Giuseppe-Motta 31-33, 1202 Geneva, Switzerland (office). *Telephone:* 227481800 (office). *Fax:* 227481818 (office). *E-mail:* mission.netherlands@ties.itu.int (office). *Website:* www.pvgeneve.org (office).

VAN MIDDELKOOP, Eimert; Dutch politician; *Minister of Defence;* b. 14 Feb. 1949, Berkel en Rodenrijs; m.; three s. one d. *Education:* Netherlands School of Econs, Rotterdam. *Career:* Lecturer, Reformed School of Social Work, Zwolle 1971–72; Asst, Calvinist Political Union (GPV) 1973–89; mem. House of Reps (GPV) 1989–2001, for Christian Union 2001–02; mem. Senate 2003–07; Minister of Defence 2007–; fmr mem. Supervisory Cttee, Social and Cultural Planning Office; fmr Chair. Policy Review Cttee European Defence; fmr Sec. Centre for Parl. History, Nijmegen; fmr mem. Advisory Board, East-West Parl. Practice Project, Royal Netherlands Air Force, Netherlands Inst. of Int. Relations, Inst. for Multiparty Democracy. *Address:* Ministry of Defence, Plein 4, POB 20701, 2500 ES The Hague, Netherlands (office). *Telephone:* (70) 3188188 (office). *Fax:* (70) 3187888 (office). *E-mail:* defensievoorlichting@mindef.nl (office). *Website:* www .mindef.nl (home).

VAN OSCH, Lt-Gen. A. G. D.; Dutch military officer; *Military Representative, NATO;* b. 1955; m.; two d. *Education:* Royal Netherlands Mil. Acad., Leiden Univ., US Army Command and Gen. Staff Coll. *Career:* began mil. training 1974, commissioned 1978, assignments have included long-term planner, Army Staff, Lecturer in Strategy, Nat. Defence Coll.; Commander 41 Field Artillery Bn, Germany 1993–95; fmr Head of Operational Policy and Training, Army Staff; Chief Ops (Land), HQ SFOR (Stabilization Force in Bosnia and Herzegovina) 1999; Operational Planner, Coalition Co-ordination Center, Tampa, Fla, USA 2001; served as Head of Policy Devt, Directorate of Personnel and Org., Ministry of Defence, Deputy Chief of Defence Staff Operations 2002–03, Deputy Chief of Defence Staff for Int. Planning and Co-operation 2003–04; Commdt Royal Mil. Acad. and Netherlands Higher Defence Coll. 2004; Mil. Rep. to NATO, Brussels 2007–, also to EU. *Address:* NATO HQ, blvd Léopold III, 1110 Brussels, Belgium (office). *Telephone:* (2) 707-41-11 (office). *Fax:* (2) 707-45-79 (office). *E-mail:* natodoc@hq.nato.int (office). *Website:* www.nato.int (office).

VAN UHM, Gen. P.J.M.; Dutch military officer; *Chief of Defence;* b. 1955, Nijmegen. *Education:* Royal Mil. Acad., Breda, Royal Netherlands Army Staff Coll. *Career:* Co. Commdr 43th Armoured Infantry Battalion 1982–84, deployed to Lebanon 1983; Deputy Head of Operations, 1 Div. "7 December" 1986; Head of Training Policy Office, then Head of Training Section, Royal Netherlands Army Staff Coll. 1986–91; Defence Liaison Officer, Ministry of Foreign Affairs 1991; Head of Plans Div., 1 (NL) Corps Staff 1991–94; Commdr 11 Infantry Battalion, Grenadiers and Rifles Guards, Airmobile Brigade 1994–95; Head of Personal Office of C-in-C of Royal Netherlands Army, then Head of Gen. Policy Div., Army Staff, then Head of Mil.-Strategic Affairs Div., Defence Staff 1995–2000; Asst Chief of Staff for Jt Mil. Affairs, UN Stabilisation Force (SFOR), Sarajevo 2000–01; Commdr 11 Airmobile Brigade 2001–02, 11 Air Manoeuvre Brigade 2002–03, Operational Command '7 December' 2005; Commdr Royal Netherlands Army 2005–08; Chief of Defence 2008–. *Address:* Ministry of Defence, Plein 4, POB 20701, 2500 The Hague, The Netherlands (office). *Telephone:* (70) 3188188 (office). *Fax:* (70) 3187888 (office). *E-mail:* defensievoorlichting@mindef.nl (office). *Website:* www .mindef.nl (office).

VAN VOORST, Carol, MA, PhD; American academic and diplomatist; *Ambassador to Iceland;* m. William A. Garland. *Education:* Hope Coll., Mich., Nat. War Coll., Washington, DC, Princeton Univ. *Career:* taught American history at CUNY; edited colonial-era historical papers at New York Univ.; worked as congressional aide for Helsinki Comm., Washington, DC; joined Foreign Service in 1980, assigned to The Netherlands 1981–82, Special Asst to Deputy Sec. of State 1984–85, Desk Officer for Germany 1985–87, assigned to Sinai Multinational Force and Observers 1987–88, Desk Officer for Norway/Denmark 1989–91, Special Asst to Under-Sec. for Political Affairs 1991–92, Desk Officer for Panama 1992–95, Dir Office of Nordic and Baltic Affairs, Bureau of European Affairs 1995–97, Chief of Political Dept and subsequently Deputy High Rep. at Office of the High Rep., Sarajevo 1998–99, Deputy Chief of Mission, Embassy in Helsinki 1999–2002, Dir of Austrian, German, and Swiss Affairs, Bureau of European and Eurasian Affairs 2002–04, Deputy Chief of Mission in Vienna 2004–05, Amb. to Iceland 2006–. *Address:* Embassy of the USA, Laufásvegur 21, 101 Reykjavík, Iceland (office). *Telephone:* 5629100 (office). *Fax:* 5629118 (office). *E-mail:* reykjavikprotocol@state.gov (office). *Website:* reykjavik.usembassy.gov (office).

VAN WALSUM, (Arnold) Peter, LLB; Dutch diplomatist; *Secretary-General's Personal Envoy for Western Sahara, United Nations;* b. 25 June 1934, Rotterdam; m.; four c. *Education:* Univ. of Utrecht. *Career:* First Sec. Perm. Mission to UN 1970–74, First Sec. New Delhi 1974–79, Counsellor, London 1975–79, Counsellor Perm. Mission to EC 1979–81, Head Western Hemisphere Dept, Ministry of Foreign Affairs 1981–85; Amb. to Thailand 1985–89, to Germany 1993–98; Dir-Gen. Political Affairs, Ministry of Foreign Affairs 1989–93; Perm. Rep. to UN 1998–2001, Chair. Iran Sanctions Cttee 1999–2000; UN Sec.-Gen.'s Personal Envoy for Western Sahara 2005–. *Address:* United Nations Mission for the Referendum in Western Sahara (MINURSO), PO Box 80,000, Laayoune, Western Sahara, Morocco (office); United Nations Mission for the Referendum in Western Sahara (MINURSO), PO Box 5846, Grand Central Station, New York, NY 10163-5846, USA (office). *Telephone:* (48) 893828 (office). *Fax:* (48) 892893 (office). *Website:* www.minurso.unlb.org (office).

VAN WULFFTEN PALTHE, Peter P.; Dutch diplomatist; *Ambassador to Germany;* b. 30 April 1950. *Education:* Univs of Lausanne and Leiden. *Career:* joined Foreign Service 1977; has served in Embassies in Yaoundé, Bogota, Manila, Havana, UN offices in New York and Geneva; fmr mem. UN Comm. on Human Rights (Chair. 1994); Dir for Movements of Persons, Migration and Consular Affairs, Ministry of Foreign Affairs 1998–2001, Dir Gen. for Regional Policy and Consular Affairs 2001–05; Amb. to Germany 2005–. *Address:* Embassy of the Netherlands, Klosterstr. 50, 10179 Berlin, Germany (office). *Telephone:* (30) 209560 (office). *Fax:* (30) 20956441 (office). *E-mail:* nlgovbln@bln.nlamb.de (office). *Website:* www .niederlandeweb.de (office).

VANHANEN, Matti Taneli, MScS; Finnish politician; *Prime Minister;* b. 4 Nov. 1955, Jyväskylä; two c. *Career:* journalist, Kehäsanomat (local newspaper) 1985–88, Ed.-in-Chief 1988–91; mem. Centre Party 1976–, mem. Bd and Chair. Youth League 1980–83, Vice-Chair. Party 2000–2003, Chair. 2003–; mem. Espoo City Council 1981–84; mem. Bd Helskinki Metropolitan Area Council YTV 1983–84; mem. Nurmijärvi Municipal Council 1989–; mem. Bd Uusimaa Regional Council 1997–2000; mem. Parl. 1991–; Vice-Chair. Centre Party Parl. Group 1994–2001, Parl. Environment Cttee 1991–95; Chair. Parl. Grand Cttee 2000–01; Rep. of Parl. to European Convention on the Future of the EU 2002–03; Minister of Defence April–June 2003; Prime Minister 2003–; Vice-Chair. Housing Foundation for the Young 1981–97, Chair. 1998–2003; Chair. State Youth Council 1987–90; Vice-Chair. Housing Council 1991–2003; Chair. Union for Rural Educ. 1998–2003; Vice-Chair. Pro Medi-Heli Asscn 1995–2003; mem. Supervisory Bd Neste/Fortum 1991–2003, Helsingin Osuuskauppa (Cooperative) 2002–03.

Address: Prime Minister's Office, Snellmaninkatu 1A, 00023 Government, Finland (office). *Telephone:* (9) 16001 (office). *Fax:* (9) 16022165 (office). *E-mail:* kirjaamo@vnk.fi (office). *Website:* www.vnk.fi (office).

VANIN, Mikhail Valentinovich; Russian diplomatist and fmr civil servant; *Ambassador to Slovenia;* b. 1960, Moscow Region. *Education:* Moscow State Univ., Acad. of State Service. *Career:* Insp., then Head of Div. against Contraband, Deputy Head Customs, Sheremetyevo Airport 1982–91; Chief Counsellor Div. of Contracts and Legal Problems, Ministry of Foreign Affairs 1991–92; Head Div. for Fight Against Contraband and Violation of Customs Law, State Customs Cttee 1992–98, Vice-Chair. 1998, Chair. Customs Inspection 1999, Chair. State Customs Cttee May 1999–2004; Rep. Russian Customs Service, Kyrgyzstan 1998–99; Amb. to Slovenia 2004–. *Address:* Embassy of Russia, Tomšičeva 9, 1000 Ljubljana, Slovenia (office). *Telephone:* (1) 4256875 (office). *Fax:* (1) 4256878 (office). *E-mail:* ambrus.slo@siol.net (office). *Website:* www.rus-slo.mid.ru (office).

VANSTONE, Amanda Eloise, BA, LLB; Australian politician; *Ambassador to Italy;* b. 7 Dec. 1952, Adelaide; m. *Education:* S Australian Inst. Tech. and Univ. of Adelaide. *Career:* retailer, wholesaler; pvt. practice barrister and solicitor, S Australia; mem. Senate for S Australia 1984–, Shadow Special Minister of State 1987, Spokesperson on the Status of Women 1987; Parl. Sec. to Deputy Leader of the Opposition; Minister for Employment, Educ., Training and Youth Affairs 1996–97, for Justice 1997–98, for Justice and Customs 1998–2001, for Family and Community Services 2001; Minister assisting the Prime Minister for the Status of Women 2001–03; Minister of Immigration and Multicultural and Indigenous Affairs 2003–06, also Minister Assisting the Prime Minister for Reconciliation 2003–04, Minister Assisting the Prime Minister for Indigenous Affairs 2004–06; Amb. to Italy 2007–; mem. Australian War Memorial Foundation, Flinders Univ. Foundation, Adelaide Univ. Alumni Asscn. *Address:* Embassy of Australia, via A. Bosio 5, 00161 Rome, Italy (office). *Telephone:* (06) 852721 (office). *Fax:* (06) 85272300 (office). *E-mail:* info-rome@dfat.gov.au (office). *Website:* www.italy.embassy.gov.au (office).

VARELA FERNANDEZ, Ricardo Javier, MPolSci, PhD; Uruguayan diplomatist; *Ambassador to UK;* m. Maria Jesus de Cores; two s. *Education:* Univ. of Uruguay, Georgetown Univ., USA. *Career:* Protocol Officer, Ministry of Foreign Affairs, Montevideo 1979–82, Third Sec., Washington, DC 1982–88, Political Affairs Dept Officer, Montevideo 1988–89, First Sec., Perm. Del. to UNESCO, Paris 1989–95, Deputy Chief, Multilateral Political Orgs Dept, Montevideo 1995–96, Chief of Staff, Under-Sec. of State Office 1996–97, Counsellor, Mission to OAS, Washington, DC 1997–2002, Head of Protocol, Montevideo 2002–04, Amb. to UK 2004– (also accred to Ireland 2006–); Gran Official (Italy). *Address:* Embassy of Uruguay, 2nd Floor, 140 Brompton Road, London, SW3 1HY, England (office). *Telephone:* (20) 7589-8835 (office). *Fax:* (20) 7581-9585 (office). *E-mail:* emburuguay@emburuguay.org.uk (office).

VÁŠÁRYOVÁ, Magdaléna; Slovak actress, writer, politician and diplomatist; b. 26 Aug. 1948, Banská Štiavnica; m. Milan Lasica; two d. *Education:* Comenius Univ., Bratislava. *Career:* actress with Nová Scéna, Bratislava 1971–83, Slovak Nat. Theatre 1984–90; fmr Amb. to Austria, fmr Amb. to Poland; currently mem. of Parl., State Sec. of Ministry of Foreign Affairs 2005–06; mem. Slovak Democratic and Christian Union-Democratic Party (Slovenská demokratická a kresťanská únia-Demokratická strana); Artist of Merit 1988, Prize for Dramatic Performance in …a pozdravuji vlaštovky, Italy 1972, Gold Crocodile for Za frountou 1974, Andrea 1993, Silver Medal 2000. *Films include:* Senzi mama 1964, Markéta Lazarová 1967, Sladký cas Kalimagdory 1968, Zbehovia a pútnici 1968, Královská polovacka 1969, Na komete 1970, Radúz a Mahulena 1970, Princ Bajaja 1971, …a pozdravuji vlaštovky 1972, Rusalka 1977, Postřižiny 1980. *Plays include:* Ubohý moj Marat 1970, Woyzeck 1971, Three Sisters 1972, Hamlet 1074, Clavio 1976, Výnosné miesto 1984, Sleena Júlia 1986, Samovrah 1989. *Publications include:* Short Sheets to One City 1988, Diskrétní pruvodce - co možná nevíte o spolecesnkém chování. *Address:* c/o Slovak Democratic and Christian Union-Democratic Party (Slovenská demokratická a kresťanská únia-Demokratická strana), Ružinovská 28, 827 35 Bratislava, Slovakia. *Telephone:* (2) 4341-4102. *Fax:* (2) 4341-4106. *E-mail:* sdku@sdkuonline.sk. *Website:* www.sdkuonline.sk.

VASQUEZ, Gaddi H.; American diplomatist; *Permanent Representative, United Nations, Rome;* b. Carrizo Springs, Tex. *Education:* Univ. of Redlands. *Career:* fmr Trustee Prof., Chapman Univ.; early career as police officer in Orange, California; served as appointee of three fmr California Govs; apptd by fmr Pres. George H. W. Bush to several fed. comms; Dir US Peace Corps –2006; Amb. and Perm. Rep. to UN, Rome 2006–; three hon. doctorates; numerous awards for leadership and community service, including Outstanding Alumni Award, American Asscn of Community

Colls, Coro Foundation Crystal Eagle Award, Marine Corps Scholarship Fund Globe and Anchor Award, Jewish Nat. Fund Tree of Life Award, Salvation Army's William H. Booth Award for Service. *Address:* US Mission to the UN Agencies in Rome, Via Sallustiana 49, 00187 Rome, Italy (office). *Telephone:* (06) 4674-3500 (office). *Fax:* (06) 4674-3535 (office). *E-mail:* InfoUSUNRome@state.gov (office). *Website:* usunrome.usmission.gov (office).

VÁSQUEZ MORALES, Ricaurte, PhD; Panamanian government official and economist; *Chairman, Panama Canal Authority; Education:* Villanova Univ., Pa, N Carolina State Univ., Rensselaer Polytechnic Inst., NY, USA. *Career:* Minister of Planning and Econ. Policy 1984–88; Pres. Sigma Man. Corpn 1988–96; Vice-Pres. Asesores y Gestores Bursátiles 1992–94; Dir Panama Holdings Inc. 1994–96; fmr econ. analyst Chase Manhattan Bank, econ. consultant Cámara Panameña de la Construcción, economist Corporación de Cobre de Cerro Colorado; Dir Office of Financial Admin, Panama Canal Comm. 1996; Vice-Admin. Panama Canal Authority –2004; Minister of Finance and the Treasury and Chair. Panama Canal Authority 2004–07; has taught econs, econometrics and finance at Universidad Santa María La Antigua, Florida State Univ. Panamá, Universidad del Istmo. *Address:* c/o Ministry of Finance and the Treasury, Edif. Ogawa, Vía España, Apdo 5245, Panamá 5, Panama (office).

VASSILAKIS, Adamantios Th.; Greek diplomatist; m.; two c. *Education:* Free Univ. of Brussels, Belgium. *Career:* Third Sec., Embassy of Greece in Tirana, Albania 1975–77, Head of Section for USSR and Eastern Europe, Ministry of Foreign Affairs 1977–85; Consul Gen., San Francisco, Calif. 1985–89; Minister Plenipotentiary (1st class), 1998–, Dir-Gen. for European Affairs, also Dir, Center for Analysis and Planning, Ministry of Foreign Affairs 1999–2002; Perm. Rep. to UN 2002–07. *Address:* c/o Ministry of Foreign Affairs, Odos Akadimias 3, 106 71 Athens, Greece (office). *Website:* www.mfa.gr (office).

VASSILIOU, Georghios Vassos, DEcon; Cypriot politician and economist; *Leader, United Democrats Movement;* b. 20 May 1931, Famagusta; m. Androulla Georgiadou 1966; one s. two d. *Education:* Univ. of Budapest, Hungary. *Career:* Market Researcher, Reed Paper Group, London 1960–62; Founder Middle East Marketing Research Bureau (now MEMRB Int.) and Ledra Advertising Co. 1962; f. Inst. of Dirs (Cyprus Br.); mem. Exec. Cttee Cyprus Chamber of Commerce 1970–86; mem. Bd and Exec. Cttee Bank of Cyprus 1981–88; mem. Econ. Advisory Council Church of Cyprus 1982–88, Educational Advisory Council 1983–88; Pres. of Cyprus 1988–93; Leader, United Democrats Movt 1993–; Chair. World Inst. for Devt Econ. Research, UN Univ., Helsinki 1995–2000; mem. Parl. 1996–99; Chief Negotiator for the Accession of Cyprus to the EU 1998–2003; Visiting Prof., Cranfield School of Man., UK; mem. InterAction Council 1998–, Trilateral Comm. 2000–; Hon. Prof., Cyprus Int. Inst. of Man.; Dr hc (Univs of Cyprus, Athens, Salonica, Budapest, Belgrade); Grand Cross, Order of Merit (Cyprus), Grand Cross, Légion d'honneur, Grand Cross of the Saviour (Greece), Grand Cross of the Order of the Repub. of Italy, Grand Star (Austria), Grand Collar, Order of Infante D. Henrique (Portugal), Grand Collar of the Nile (Egypt), Standard (Flag) Order decorated with diamonds (Hungary), and other distinctions, awards and decorations. *Publications:* Marketing in the Middle East 1976, The Middle East Markets Up to 1980 1977, Moyen Orient: Le Consommateur des années '80 1980, Towards the Solution of the Cyprus Problem 1992, Modernisation of the Civil Service 1992, Overcoming Indifference 1994, Tourism and Sustainable Development 1995, Towards a Larger, Yet More Effective European Union 1999, Cyprus-European Union: From the First Steps to Accession 2004; numerous articles in various int. publs. *Address:* PO Box 22098, 1583 Nicosia (office); 9A Orpheos Street, 1070 Cyprus (home). *Telephone:* (2) 2336142 (office); (2) 2374888 (home). *Fax:* (2) 2336301 (office). *E-mail:* gvassiliou@memrb.com.cy (office).

VÁZQUEZ ROSAS, Tabaré Ramón, PhD; Uruguayan politician, physician and head of state; *President;* b. 17 Jan. 1940, Montevideo; m. Maria Auxiliadora Delgado; three c. *Education:* Universidad de la Republica, Gustave Roussy Inst., Paris. *Career:* Prof. Faculty of Medicine, Universidad de la Republica 1987–; Mayor of Montevideo 1990–95; Leader, Encuentro Progresista-Frente Amplio (Broad Front) coalition 2001–; unsuccessful presidential cand. 2000; Pres. of Uruguay 2005–; WHO Dir-Gen's Award for coordinating tobacco control in Uruguay 2006. *Address:* Office of the President, Casa de Gobierno, Edif. Libertad, Avenida Luis Alberto de Herrera 3350, Montevideo; Encuentro Progresista-Frente Amplio, Colonia 1367, 2° Montevideo, Uruguay (office). *Telephone:* (2) 4872110 (office); (2) 9022176 (office). *Fax:* (2) 4809397 (office). *Website:* www.presidencia.gub.uy (office).

VÉDRINE, Hubert; French politician, lawyer and civil servant; *Managing Director, Hubert Védrine Conseil;* b. 31 July 1947, Saint-Silvain-Bellegarde;

m. Michèle Froment; two s. *Education:* Lycée Albert Camus, Univ. of Nanterre, Institut d'Etudes Politiques, Paris, Ecole Nat. d'Admin. *Career:* Sr Civil Servant, Ministry of Culture 1974–78, Ministry for Capital Works 1978–79; Co-ordinator for Cultural Relations, Near and Middle East, Ministry of Foreign Affairs 1979–81; Technical Adviser External Affairs, Office of the Sec.-Gen. of the Pres. 1981–86, Legal Adviser, Conseil d'Etat 1986, 1995–96; Spokesman for Presidency of Repub. 1988–91, Sec.-Gen. 1991–95; Minister of Foreign Affairs 1997–2002; Man. Dir Hubert Védrine Conseil 2003–; Pnr, Jeantet et Associés (law firm) 1996–97. *Publications:* Mieux aménager sa ville 1979, Les Mondes de François Mitterrand, A l'Elysée 1981–95 1996, Dialogue avec Dominique Moïsi: Les Cartes de la France à l'heure de la mondialisation 2000, Face à l'Hyperpuissance 2003, Multilateralisme – une reforme possible 2004, François Mitterand – un dessein, un destin 2006.
Address: Hubert Védrine Conseil, 21 rue Jean Goujon, 75008 Paris (office); 6 rue de Luynes, 75007 Paris, France (home). *Telephone:* 1-45-63-32-82 (office). *Fax:* 1-45-63-38-29 (office). *E-mail:* bureau.hv@hvconseil.com (office). *Website:* www.hvconseil.com (office); www.hubertvedrine.net.

VEGA GARCÍA, Gen. Gerardo Clemente Ricardo; Mexican politician and army officer; b. 28 March 1940, Puebla City. *Career:* nat. security studies in USA and Panama and fmr Dir of Mil. Educ.; fmr Rector Army and Air Force Univ.; fmr Deputy Chief of Mil. Doctrine, Estado Mayor of SEDENA; fmr Mil. Attaché, embassies in USSR, Poland, and Germany; fmr Deputy Dir and Dir Nat. Defence Coll.; promoted to Div. Gen. with command of Mil. Zone One 2000; Sec. of Nat. Defence –2006.
Address: c/o Secretariat of State for National Defence, Manuel Avila Camacho, esq. Avda Industria Militar, 3°, Col. Lomas de Sotelo, Del. Miguel Hidalgo, 11640, México, DF, Mexico (office).

VEKARIC, Vatroslav, MA, PhD; Croatian research institute director; *Director, Institute for International Politics and Economics;* b. 4 March 1944, Dubrovnik. *Education:* Univ. of Belgrade. *Career:* began career as journalist with Radio Zagreb 1967–68; Research Fellow, Inst. for Int. Politics and Econs (IIPE) 1968–77, Dir Centre for Regional Studies 1977–80, Deputy Dir IIPE (Dir of Research) 1980–85, Dir IIPE 2000–; Dir Centre for Strategic Studies, Belgrade 1985–2000; conducted UN research projects 1981–83; Lecturer, Univ. of Belgrade 1982–84, Centre for Post-Grad. Studies, Dubrovnik 1985–, Univ. of Bari 1997, 1999, Univ. of Sant Angelo, Rome 1998, Univ. of Florence 1998; Ed.-in-Chief Review of International Affairs 2001–; mem. Bd Dirs Diplomatic Acad., Serbia and Montenegro 2001–; mem. Int. Advisory Bd Journal of International Relations; mem Int. Studies Asscn, USA 1986–, Cttee for Mediterranean Studies, Sassari, Italy 1983– (Deputy Sec.-Gen. 1984–87), Contemplating Group for Scenarios of Devt of the Mediterranean (UN-UNEP), Cannes, France 1983–87, Governing Bd AIRI, Rome 1989–, Int. Law Asscn 1993–, Editorial Bd Nuova Fase review, Edizioni Democrazia Domani, Rome 1994–, Scientific Council Inst. for the Study of the Greek Economy, Athens 1994–, Programme Cttee Centre for Euro-Mediterranean Studies, Rome 1997–99. *Publications:* seven books and more than 130 essays and articles.
Address: Institute for International Politics and Economics, Makedonska 25, 11000 Belgrade, Serbia (office). *Telephone:* (11) 3373824 (office); (11) 3110917 (home). *Fax:* (11) 3373835 (office). *E-mail:* amarcord@eunet.yu (office). *Website:* www.diplomacy.bg.ac.yu (office).

VELASCO BRANES, Andres, PhD; Chilean government official and economist; *Minister of Finance; Education:* Yale and Columbia Univs, USA. *Career:* Chief of Staff to Minister of Finance 1990–92, later Dir of Int. Finance; Postdoctoral Fellow in Political Economy, Harvard Univ. and MIT 1994–95; Chief Economist and Deputy Lead Negotiator NAFTA accession team, Chile 1995; fmr adviser to govts of Ecuador and El Salvador; fmr consultant World Bank, IMF, Inter-American Devt Bank, UN Econ. Comm. for Latin America, Fed. Research Bank of Atlanta; fmr Dir Center for Latin American and Caribbean Studies, New York Univ.; Sumitomo-FASID Prof. of Int. Finance and Devt, Harvard Univ. 2000–06; Minister of Finance 2006–. *Publications:* Trade, Development and the World Economy: Selected Essays of Carlos Díaz-Alejandro (ed.) 1988, Vox Populi (novel) 1995, Lugares Comunes (novel) 2003, Free Trade and Beyond: Prospects for Integration in the Americas (co-ed.) 2004.
Address: Ministry of Finance, Teatinos 120, 12°, Santiago, Chile (office). *Telephone:* (2) 675-5800 (office). *Fax:* (2) 671-8064 (office). *E-mail:* webmaster@minhda.cl (office). *Website:* www.minhda.cl (office); ksghome .harvard.edu/~avelasco.

VELDRE, Vinets; Latvian veterinarian and politician; *Minister for Defence;* b. 26 March 1971. *Education:* Latvian Univ. of Agriculture, Faculty of Veterinary Medicine, Uppsala Univ., Sweden, Free Univ. of Berlin, Danish Meat Trade Coll., A & G Univ., Tex., USA, Massey Univ., New Zealand. *Career:* Lab Asst, Latvian Univ. of Agriculture, Faculty of Veterinary Medicine, Dept of Epizootics 1993–95; Sr Inspector State Veterinary

Service, Rīga Dist Veterinary Authority 1995–97, Head, Control Div. for Food of Animal Origin 1997–99, Dir and State Chief Veterinary Inspector 1999–2001, Dir-Gen. Food and Veterinary Service 2001–07; Minister for Health Jan. 2007–Dec. 2007, for Defence Dec. 2007–; mem. People's Party (TP) (Tautas partija); Award On Diligence, Ministry of Agriculture 2005.
Address: Ministry of Defence, K. Valdemāra iela 10–12, Rīga 1473, Latvia (office). *Telephone:* 6721-0124 (office). *Fax:* 6721-2307 (office). *E-mail:* kanceleja@mod.gov.lv (office). *Website:* www.mod.gov.lv (office).

VELHO RODRIGUES, Frances Vitória; Mozambican diplomatist and politician; *Permanent Representative, United Nations, Geneva;* b. 30 April 1952, Maputo; m. Isaac Murargy; one s. one d. *Education:* Geneva and Florence. *Career:* Expert Researcher in Econ. Planning, Ministry of Foreign Affairs 1977–79, Dir Int. Econ. Relations Dept 1979–85; Amb. 1980, to Belgium 1985, concurrently to the EU (fmrly EC) 1985, to Luxembourg and the Netherlands 1988–95, to Austria 1990–95, to Greece 1992–95, to Switzerland 2006–; Deputy Minister of Foreign Affairs and Cooperation 1994–99, 2000–05; Perm. Rep. to UN, Geneva 2006–, also Perm. Rep. to WTO and Amb. to Switzerland; mem. Standing Cttee Southern Africa Devt Co-ordination Conf. 1980–85; mem. Nat. Exec. Council UNESCO, Mozambique 1990; Pres. Asscn Mozambican Diplomats (ADIMO) 2004–; Chevalier, Légion d'Honneur 1999, Order of Eduardo Mondlane (Mozambique) 2005; Distinction Roll of Honour, Ministry of Foreign Affairs 1981.
Address: Permanent Mission of Mozambique, Rue Gautier 13, 1st Floor, 1201 Geneva, Switzerland (office); Av Lucas Elias Kumato 243, Sommershild, Maputo, Mozambique (home). *Telephone:* 229011783 (office). *Fax:* 229011784 (office). *E-mail:* mission.moza@bluewin.ch (office).

VELICHKO, Valentyn V.; Belarusian diplomatist; *Ambassador to Ukraine; Career:* fmr Minister for CIS Affairs; fmr Deputy Minister of Foreign Affairs; fmr Amb. to Latvia; currently Amb. to Ukraine; Order of Honor (Belarus) 2006.
Address: Embassy of Belarus, vul. M. Kotsyubynskogo 3, 01030 Kiev, Ukraine (office). *Telephone:* (44) 537-52-00 (office). *E-mail:* belarus@visti .com (office). *Website:* www.belembassy.org.ua (office).

VENDRELL, Francesc, LLB, MA; Spanish United Nations official and academic; *EU Special Representative in Afghanistan,*b. 15 June 1940. *Education:* Univ. of Barcelona, Univs of London and Cambridge, UK. *Career:* joined UN 1968; Chief, then Dir for Europe and the Americas Office of Research and Collection of Information, Office of the UN Sec.-Gen. 1987–92; Deputy Personal Rep. of Sec.-Gen. for Cen. American Peace Process 1989–91; rep. Sec.-Gen. during first phase of Guatemala peace negotiations 1990–92; Dir for Special Political Assignments 1992; Sr Political Adviser to Special Envoy in Haiti 1993; Dir E Asia and Pacific Div., Dept of Political Affairs 1993–97; Dir Combined Asia and Pacific Div. 1998–99; Officer-in-Charge, Office of Asst Sec.-Gen. for Political Affairs (Asia, Pacific, the Americas and Europe) 1999–2000; apptd Deputy Personal Rep. of Sec.-Gen. for E Timor (now Timor-Leste) 1999; Special Rep. of Sec.-Gen. and Head of Special Mission to Afghanistan (UNSMA) with rank of Asst Sec.-Gen. 2000–02; EU Special Rep. in Afghanistan 2002–; Visiting Prof., Rutgers Univ. Law School, NJ, USA 1972–74, Yale Univ. Law School, CT 1977, 1979; Dir of Studies, The Hague Acad. of Int. Law, Netherlands 1979.
Address: Council of the European Union, Rue de la Loi, 175, 1048 Brussels, Belgium (office). *Telephone:* (2) 281-61-11 (office). *Fax:* (2) 281-69-34 (office). *Website:* www.consilium.europa.eu (office).

VENEMAN, Ann M., MA, JD; American government official, lawyer and international organization official; *Executive Director, United Nations Children's Fund (UNICEF);* b. 29 June 1949, Modesto, Calif.. *Education:* Univ. of California, Davis, Univ. of California, Berkeley and Univ. of California, Hastings Coll. of Law. *Career:* staff attorney, Gen. Counsel's Office, Bay Area Rapid Transit Dist, Oakland, Calif. 1976–78; Deputy Public Defender, Modesto 1978–80; Assoc., later Pnr, Damrell, Damrell & Nelson (law firm), Modesto 1980; Assoc. Admin. Foreign Agric. Service, US Dept of Agric. 1986–89, Deputy Under-Sec. of Agric. for Int. Affairs and Commodity Programs 1989–91, Deputy Sec. of Dept 1991–93; with Patton, Boggs & Blow (law firm), Washington, DC 1993–95; Sec. Calif. Dept of Food and Agric. 1995–99; Pnr, Nossaman, Guthner, Knox & Elliott (law firm) 1999–2001; US Sec. of Agric. 2001–05 (resgnd); Exec. Dir UNICEF 2005–; fmr mem. Bd of Dirs Calgene (first co. to market genetically engineered food); mem. Bd Close Up Foundation; Hon. mem. US Afghan Women's Council, US State Dept 2004; Dr hc (California Polytechnic State Univ., San Luis Obispo) 2001, (Lincoln Univ. of Mo.) 2003, (Delaware State Univ.) 2004; Outstanding Woman in Int. Trade Award 2001, Outstanding Alumna of the Year Award, Univ. of California, Davis 2001, Food Research and Action Center Award 2001, Nat. 4-H

Alumni Recognition Award 2002, Dutch American Heritage Award 2002, Statesman of the Year Award, Jr Statesman Foundation 2002, Alumnus of the Year Award, Goldman School of Public Policy 2003, American PVO Partners Award for Service to People in Need 2004, Richard E. Lyng Award for Public Service 2005, Sesame Workshop's Leadership Award for Children 2006.
Address: United Nations Children's Fund (UNICEF), 3 United Nations Plaza, New York, NY 10017, USA (office). *Telephone:* (212) 326-7000 (office). *Fax:* (212) 887-7465 (office). *E-mail:* info@unicef.org (office). *Website:* www.unicef.org (office).

VENETIAAN, Runaldo Ronald; Suriname mathematician and head of state; *President;* b. 1936, Paramaribo. *Education:* Leiden Univ. *Career:* moved to Netherlands to further educ.; early career as math. lecturer; fmr Minister of Educ.; fmr mem. Exec. Bd UNESCO; Leader Suriname Nat. Party; Pres. of Suriname 1991–96, 2000–.
Address: Office of the President, Paramaribo, Suriname.

VERANNEMAN DE WATERVLIET, Jean-Michel; Belgian diplomatist; *Ambassador to UK;* b. 1947, Bruges; m. Maria do Carmo Neves da Silveira; three s. *Education:* Institut d'Etudes Politiques, Paris, Université Libre de Bruxelles, Vrije Universiteit Brussel. *Career:* six months as trainee European Comm., Brussels; mil. service with Chasseurs Ardennais Regt; joined Diplomatic Corps 1976, postings include Bonn, Brasilia, La Paz, UN, New York, EU, Brussels, Amb. to Mozambique 1983–86, Consul Gen., São Paulo 1991–94, Minister Plenipotentiary, London 1994–97, Amb. to Brazil 2000–03, to Israel 2004–06, to UK 2006–.
Address: Belgian Embassy, 17 Grosvenor Crescent, London, SW1X 7EE, England (office). *Telephone:* (20) 7470-3700 (office). *Fax:* (20) 7470-3795 (office). *E-mail:* london@diplobel.be (office). *Website:* www.diplomatie.be/london (office).

VERBEKE, Johan C., LLD, LLM, MA; Belgian diplomatist and lawyer; *Special Representative in Georgia, United Nations;* b. 9 July 1951, Ghent; m.; three c. *Education:* Univ. of Ghent, Yale Univ., USA, Université de Nancy, France. *Career:* Asst Prof. in European Econ. Law, Univ. of Ghent 1975–77; Jr Assoc. Cleary, Gottlieb, Steen and Hamilton (law firm), New York 1978–81; joined Ministry of Foreign Affairs 1981, Chief Spokesman 1990–92, Chief of Staff to Perm. Rep. to EU 1992–94, First Deputy Dir for Political Affairs 1998–99, Dir-Gen. European Affairs 1999–2000, Chef de Cabinet 2000–04; overseas posts include Lebanon, Jordan, Burundi, Chile, Deputy Chief of Mission, Embassy in Washington, DC 1994–98, Perm. Rep., UN, New York 2004–08; Special Coordinator for Lebanon, UN 2008; Special Rep. in Georgia and Head UN Mission in Georgia (UNOMIG) 2008–.
Address: United Nations, New York, NY 10017, USA (office). *Telephone:* (212) 963-1234 (office). *Fax:* (212) 963-4879 (office). *Website:* www.un.org (office).

VERES, János, PhD; Hungarian politician; *Minister of Finance;* b. 5 Feb. 1957, Nyírbátor; m. Éva Szabó; two c. *Education:* Univ. of Agriculture, Debrecen and Karl Marx Univ. of Econs. *Career:* began career in business sector 1981–2002; mem. Nyírbátor local govt 1990–94; mem. Parl. 1994–; Chair., Chamber of Commerce and Trade, Szabolcs-Szatmár-Bereg County 1997–2002; Mayor of Nyírbátor 2002–03; mem. Exec. Cttee, Socialist Party of Hungary 2004–; Sec. of State for Political Affairs, Ministry of Finance 2003–04; Chief of Staff, Office of the Prime Minister 2004–05; Minister of Finance 2005–.
Address: Ministry of Finance, 1051 Budapest, József Nádor tér 2–4, Hungary (office). *Telephone:* (1) 318-2066 (office). *Fax:* (1) 318-2570 (office). *E-mail:* kommunikacio@pm.gov.hu (office). *Website:* www1.pm.gov.hu (office).

VERESHCHETIN, Vladlen Stepanovich, DJur; Russian judge; b. 8 Jan. 1932, Briansk; m.; one d. *Education:* Moscow Inst. of Int. Relations. *Career:* mem. staff, Presidium of USSR Acad. of Sciences 1958–67; First Vice-Chair. and Legal Counsel, Intercosmos, USSR Acad. of Sciences 1967–81; Prof. of Int. Law, Univ. of Friendship of Peoples 1979–82; Deputy Dir and Head, Dept of Int. Law, Inst. of State and Law, Russian Acad. of Sciences 1981–95; mem. Perm. Court of Arbitration, The Hague 1984–95; judge, Int. Court of Justice, The Hague 1995–2006; Vice-Pres. Russian (fmrly Soviet) UN Asscn 1984–97; Vice-Pres. Russian (fmrly Soviet) Asscn of Int. Law 1985–97; mem. UN Int. Law Comm. 1992–95; Hon. Dir Int. Inst. of Space Law 1995–; Hon. Foreign Mem. Bulgarian Acad. of Sciences 2006; Order of Friendship of Peoples 1975, October Revolution Order 1981; Hon. Master of Sciences, Russian Fed. 1995; Hon. Awards from German Acad. of Sciences 1978, Bulgarian Acad. of Sciences 1979, Int. Acad. of Astronautics 1987, 1994, Badge of Honour 1967, Hugo Grotius Award 2001. *Publications:* books and more than 150 articles on int. law, law of the sea, space law, state responsibility, int. criminal law.

Address: Profsouyaznaya str. 43, Bldg 1, Apt 255, 117420 Moscow, Russian Federation (home).

VERHAGEN, Maxime Jacques Marcel; Dutch politician; *Minister of Foreign Affairs;* b. 14 Sept. 1956, Maastricht; m.; two s. one d. *Education:* Leiden Univ. *Career:* began career as Asst at Christian Democratic Alliance (CDA) 1984–87, Head of European Affairs, Devt, Cooperation and Trade Policy 1987–89; mem. Oegstgeest Municipal Council 1986–89; MEP 1989–94; mem. House of Reps 1996–, Chair. Christian Democratic Appeal (CDA) 2002–; Minister of Foreign Affairs 2007–; fmr Vice-Chair. ACP-EU Joint Ass., Parl. Cttee on Foreign Affairs; fmr Bd mem. Eduardo Frei Foundation, Netherlands Atlantic Asscn, European Movt, Univ. of Nijmegen Parl. History Foundation, Free Voice.
Address: Ministry of Foreign Affairs, Bezuidenhoutseweg 67, POB 20061, 2500 EB The Hague, Netherlands (office). *Telephone:* (70) 3486486 (office). *Fax:* (70) 3484848 (office). *E-mail:* minbuza@buza.minbuza.nl (office). *Website:* www.minbuza.nl (office).

VERHEUGEN, Günter; German politician; *Commissioner for Enterprise and Industry and Vice-President, European Commission;* b. 28 April 1944, Bad Kreuznach; m. Gabriele Verheugen (née Schäfer). *Education:* in Cologne and Bonn. *Career:* trainee, Neue Rhein-Neue Ruhr-Zeitung 1963–65; Head of Public Relations Div., Fed. Ministry of the Interior 1969–74; Head of Analysis and Information Task Force, Fed. Foreign Office 1974–76; Fed. Party Man., Free Democratic Party (FDP) 1977–78; Gen. Sec. FDP 1978–82; joined Sozialdemokratische Partei Deutschlands (SPD) 1982; mem. Bundestag 1983–99, Chair. EU Special Cttee 1992, mem. Foreign Affairs Cttee 1983–98; Spokesman, SPD Nat. Exec. 1986–87; Ed.-in-Chief Vorwärts (SPD newspaper) 1987–89; Chair. Radio Broadcasting Council, Deutsche Welle 1990–99; Fed. Party Man. SPD 1993–95; Deputy Chair. SPD Parl. Group for Foreign, Security and Devt Policy 1994–97; Chair. Socialist Int. Peace, Security and Disarmament Council 1997–; mem. SPD Nat. Exec.; Minister of State, Fed. Foreign Office 1998–99; EU Commr for Enlargement 1999–2004, for Enterprise and Industry 2004–, Vice-Pres EU Comm. 2004–; Commdr Distinguished Service Cross (Italy). *Publications:* Eine Zukunft für Deutschland 1980, Das Programm der Liberalen Baden-Baden 1980, Der Ausverkauf-Macht und Verfall der FDP 1984, Apartheid-Südafrika und der Deutschen Interessen am Kap 1986.
Address: European Commission, 200 rue de la Loi, 1049 Brussels, Belgium (office). *Telephone:* (2) 298-11-00 (office). *Fax:* (2) 299-18-27 (office). *Website:* europa.eu (office).

VERHOFSTADT, Guy, LLB; Belgian politician; b. 11 April 1953, Dendermonde; m. Dominique Verkinderen 1981; one s. one d. *Education:* Koninklijk Atheneum, Ghent and Univ. of Ghent. *Career:* began career as attorney-at-law Ghent Bar; Pres. Flemish Liberal Students' Union, Ghent 1972–73 and 1974–75; Councillor Ghent 1976–82; Political Sec. to Willy De Clerq, Nat. Pres. Party for Freedom and Progress (PVV) 1977–81; mem. House of Reps Ghent-Eeklo Dist 1978–84; Vice-Pres. PVV Ghent-Eeklo Dist Fed. 1979; Nat. Pres. PVV Youth Div. 1979–81, Nat. Pres. PVV 1982–85; Deputy Prime Minister and Minister for the Budget, Scientific Research and the Nat. Plan 1985–88; Pres. of Shadow Cabinet 1988–91; Nat. Pres. of PVV 1989–92, of Flemish Liberals and Democrats (VLD) 1992–95, 1997–99; Minister of State 1995–99; Senator VLD 1995–99, Vice-Pres. of Senate 1995–99; Prime Minister of Belgium 1999–2007 (resgnd), reappointed Dec. 2007, resgnd March 2008. *Publications:* Het Radicaal Manifest: Handvest voor een nieuwe liberaale omwenteling 1979, Burgermanifest 1991, De Weg naar politieke vernieuwing: Het tweede burgermanifest 1992, Angst, afgunst en het algemeen belang 1994, De Belgische Ziekte: Diagnose en remedies 1997, In goede banen: VLD-plan voor meer tewerks telling 1999; De vierde golf – een liberaal project voor de nieuwe eeuw 2002; contribs to books and articles in periodicals.
Address: Vlaamse Liberalen en Demokraten (VLD, Flemish Liberals and Democrats—Liberal Party), Melsensstraat 34, 1000 Brussels, Belgium (office). *Telephone:* (2) 549-00-20 (office). *Fax:* (2) 512-60-25 (office). *E-mail:* contact@openvld.be (office). *Website:* www.openvld.be (office); www.guyverhofstadt.be (home).

VERSHBOW, Alexander R., BA, MA; American diplomatist; *Ambassador to South Korea;* b. 3 July 1952, Boston, Mass; m. Lisa K. Vershbow 1976; two s. *Education:* Yale Coll. and School of Int. Affairs, Columbia Univ. *Career:* joined Foreign Service 1977, Bureau of Politico-Military Affairs 1977–79, US Embassy, Moscow 1979–81, Office of Soviet Union Affairs 1981–85, US Embassy, London 1985–88; adviser US Del. to SALT II and START negotiations; Dir State Dept's Office of Soviet Union Affairs 1988–91; US Deputy Perm Rep. to NATO and Chargé d'affaires US Mission 1991–93; Prin. Deputy Asst Sec. of State for European and Canadian Affairs (responsibilities covered the Balkan conflict) 1993–94; Special Asst to the Pres. and Sr Dir for European Affairs at Nat. Security Council 1994–97 (worked on US policy which laid foundations of the Dayton Peace

Agreement, adaptation and enlargement of NATO and its new relationship with Russia); Perm. Rep. to NATO 1998–2001; Amb. to Russian Fed. 2001–05, to S Korea 2005–; Anatoly Sharansky Freedom Award, Union of Councils of Soviet Jews 1990, first Joseph J. Kruzel Award for contribs to the cause of peace, US Dept of Defense 1997, Distinguished Service Award for Work at NATO, US State Dept 2001, ABA Amb.'s Award 2004. *Publications:* articles on arms control, speeches on Russia and NATO issues.
Address: Embassy of the United States, 32 Sejongno, Jongno-gu, Seoul 110-710, South Korea (office). *Telephone:* (2) 397-4200 (office). *Fax:* (2) 725-0152 (office). *E-mail:* EmbassySeoulPA@state.gov (office). *Website:* seoul .usembassy.gov (office).

VESTERDORF, Bo; Danish judge and international official; *President, Court of First Instance of the European Communities;* b. 11 Oct. 1945. *Career:* fmr Jurist-Linguist Court of Justice; fmr Admin. Ministry of Justice, later Head Constitutional and Admin. Law Dept, then apptd Dir Ministry of Justice; fmr Legal Attaché with Perm. Representation of Denmark to European Communities; fmr temporary judge Eastern Regional Court; fmr mem. Human Rights Steering Cttee, then Bureau, Council of Europe; Judge Court of First Instance of the European Communities 1989–, Pres. 1998–.
Address: Court of the First Instance of the European Communities, rue du Fort Niedergrünewald, 2925 Luxembourg, Luxembourg (office). *Telephone:* 4303-1 (office). *Fax:* 4303-2100 (Registry) (office). *Website:* www .curia.eu.int (office).

VESTMANN, Bjarni, BA; Icelandic diplomatist and fmr journalist; *Icelandic Representative, Financial Mechanism Committee, European Free Trade Association;* b. 24 May 1961; m. Rakel Árnadóttir; three d. *Education:* Univ. of Iceland, Coll. of Europe, Bruges, Brussels, Belgium, Diploma of Advanced European Studies. *Career:* radio journalist, Raykjavík 1987–88; News Ed., Icelandic Broadcasting Service State TV 1988–90, TV and radio corresp., Brussels, Belgium 1990–91, News Ed. 1991–92; Head of Press, Information and Culture, Ministry of Foreign Affairs 1992–94; Deputy of Defence Dept 1994–95, Minister-Counsellor and Deputy Dir 2004–07; with Embassy in Stockholm, Sweden 1995–98, Counsellor 1999–2002; Political Adviser, Icelandic Del. to NATO 1998–2002; Icelandic Rep. to Mil. Cttee of NATO, Brussels 2002–04; Icelandic Rep. to Financial Mechanism Cttee, EFTA 2007–.
Address: Department of European Affairs, Ministry of Foreign Affairs, Raudarástíg 25, 150 Reykjavík, Iceland (office). *Telephone:* 5459923 (office). *Fax:* 5624878 (office). *E-mail:* bjarni.vestmann@utn.stjr.is (office). *Website:* www.mfa.is (office).

VEZZAZ, Abderrahmane Ould Hamma, MBA; Mauritanian politician; b. 1956, Tidjikja; m.; six c. *Education:* Institut Supérieur de Commerce et d'Administration des Entreprises, Casablanca, Morocco and Univ. of Paris IX, France. *Career:* Dir Overseas Trade Dept, Ministry of Trade 1992–97; Adviser on Public Sector, Office of the Prime Minister 1997–98; Minister of Rural Devt and the Environment Jan.–July 1998; also worked with Arab Bank for Econ. Devt in Africa (BADEA), Tech. Advisor to Prime Minister of Niger 2002–06; Exec. Dir private credit business 2006–07; Minister of the Economy and Finance 2007–08.
Address: c/o Ministry of the Economy and Finance, BP 181, Nouakchott, Mauritania (office).

VICENOVÁ, Milena; Czech veterinary surgeon, diplomatist and fmr government official; *Permanent Representative, European Union;* b. 12 Aug. 1955, Prerov; m. Milan Vicena; two d. *Education:* Univ. of Veterinary Medicine, Brno. *Career:* early career as veterinary surgeon, Ceska Lipa 1980; Ed. State Agricultural Publishing House 1985–89; Ed.-in-Chief, Our Breed Livestock agricultural magazine 1990–96, Strategy Ltd 1993–96; Head of Territorial Div., External Relations Dept, Ministry of Agric. 1996–98, Head of Structural Funds Div. 1998–2000, Dir of Implementation, Structural Policy Dept, then Dir, Man. Authority Dept and Deputy Dir-Gen., SAPARD Programme 2000–03, Dir, EU Relations Dept and Rep. to EU Special Agric. Cttee 2003–04, Dir, Food Safety Dept, Vice Dir-Gen., Food Authority and Rep. to European Food Safety Authority Advisory Forum 2004–06, Minister of Agric. 2006–08; Dir Nat. Training Fund 2007; Perm. Rep. to EU, Brussels 2008–; fmr Chair. Guild of Agricultural Journalists; fmr Rep. to Int. Fed. of Agricultural Journalists.
Address: Permanent Representation of The Czech Republic to the EU, 92–98 Rue de Trèves, 1040 Brussels, Belgium (office). *Telephone:* (2) 234-12-00 (office). *Fax:* (2) 372-07-84 (office). *E-mail:* sec.beu@kum.hu (office). *Website:* www.hunrep.be (office).

VICTORIA INGRID ALICE DÉSIRÉE, HRH Crown Princess (Duchess of Västergötland); Swedish; b. 14 July 1977, Stockholm. *Education:* Enskilda Gymnasiet, Stockholm, Université Catholique de l'Ouest, Angers, France,

Yale Univ., USA and Nat. Defence Coll., Stockholm. *Career:* internships at the Swedish Embassy, Washington, DC 1999, UN, New York 2002, Swedish Trade Council, Berlin and Paris 2002; has completed study programmes at the Offices of the Swedish Govt and the Swedish Int. Devt Co-operation Agency; participated in state visits to study int. aid efforts.
Address: c/o Information and Press Department, Kungl. Slottet, Stockholm 111 30, Sweden (office). *E-mail:* info@royalcourt.se (office). *Website:* www.royalcourt.se.

VIEGAS FILHO, José; Brazilian politician and diplomatist; *Ambassador to Spain;* b. 14 Oct. 1942, Campo Grande; m. 1st Rosa Maria Amorim (died 1999); three c.; m. 2nd Erika Stockholm. *Career:* joined Instituto Rio Branco 1964; apptd consul-aid, New York 1969; responsible for Brazilian businesses in Cuba 1987–90; apptd Chief Dept of Int. Bodies within Foreign Office 1992; Amb. to Denmark 1995–98, to Peru 1998–2001, to Russia 2001–02; Minister of Defence 2003–04 (resgnd); Amb. to Spain 2004–.
Address: Embassy of Brazil, Fernando el Santo 6, 28010 Madrid, Spain (office). *Telephone:* (91) 7004650 (office). *Fax:* (91) 7004660 (office). *E-mail:* adm@embajadabrasil.es (office). *Website:* www.brasil.es (office).

VIEIRA, Brig.-Gen. João Bernardo; Guinea-Bissau politician and head of state; *President;* b. 1939, Bissau. *Career:* joined Partido Africano da Independencia da Guiné e Cabo Verde (PAIGC) 1960; Political and Mil. Chief of Catió 1961–64; Mil. Chief of the Southern Front and mem. Political Bureau 1964–65; Vice-Pres. Council of War 1965–67; Rep. of the Political Bureau for the Southern Front 1967–70; mem. Council of War, responsible for mil. operations 1970–71; mem. Exec. Cttee and Council of War 1971–73; mem. Perm. Secr. of PAIGC 1973; Pres. of People's Nat. Ass. 1973–78; Prime Minister 1987–80; Pres. of Guinea-Bissau 1980–99; Chair. of Council of Revolution 1980–84; Chair. Council of State 1984–94; State Commr for the Armed Forces Sept. 1973–78; Chief State Commr 1978–84; C-in-C of Armed Forces 1982, Minister of Defence and of Interior 1982–92; deposed May 1999 and went into exile in Portugal; returned to Guinea-Bissau April 2005 to stand election; Pres. of Guinea-Bissau Oct. 2005–.
Address: c/o Office of the Prime Minister, Avda Unidade Africana, CP 137, Bissau, Guinea-Bissau.

VIEIRA, Mauro; Brazilian diplomatist; *Ambassador to Argentina;* b. 15 Feb. 1952. *Education:* Fluminense Fed. Univ., Inst. Rio Branca, Cambridge Univ., UK, Univ. of Mich., USA, Univ. of Nancy, France. *Career:* joined Foreign Service 1974; Asst to Chief Political Finance Div. 1975–77; Third Sec. Embassy in USA 1978, Second Sec. 1978–80, First Sec. 1980–82; First Sec. ALADI Uruguay 1982–85; consultant, Sec.-Gen. Foreign Affairs 1985; Adjunct Sec.-Gen. Ministry of Science and Tech. 1986–87; Nat. Sec. of Admin, Nat Inst. of Social Pensions, Ministry of Pensions and Social Welfare 1987–88; consultant, Chief Dept of Culture 1989; Adviser, Embassy in Mexico 1990–92; Diplomatic Adviser to Minister of State for Foreign Affairs 1993–94; Minister Counsellor, Embassy in France 1995–99; Chief of Cabinet of Sec.-Gen. Foreign Affairs 1999–2002; Amb. to Switzerland 2002; Special Envoy of Pres. to Syria and Palestine 2003; Amb. to Argentina 2004–; Grand Cross, Order of Rio Branca, Order of Merit of Brazil, Commdr, Naval Order of Merit, Military Order of Merit, Medalla del Pacificador (Brazil); Grand Cross, Order of Bernardo O'Higgins (Chile), National Order of Merit (Romania), Order of Merit (Poland), Order of Infante D. Henrique (Portugal), Order of Civil Merit (Spain), Order of Águila Azteca (Mexico), Grand Official of the Order of Danneborg (Denmark), Légion d'Honneur (France).
Address: Embassy of Brazil, Cerrito 1350, 1010 Buenos Aires, Argentina (office). *Telephone:* (11) 4515-2400 (office). *Fax:* (11) 4515-2401 (office). *E-mail:* embras@embrasil.org.ar (office). *Website:* www.brasil.org.ar (office).

VIEIRA DE LA IGLESIA, Lt Gen. Ángel; Spanish air force officer; b. 23 Jan. 1944, Salamanca; m. Ma del Carmen Lista Alfonso; four c. *Education:* Air Force Acad., Spanish Flying Combat School, French Air Force, US Marine Corps, Air Staff Coll. *Career:* Tactics Teacher, Air Force Staff School 1991–93; assigned to WEU Planning Cell, Brussels 1993–96, promoted to Col; Commdr, 35th Transport Wing, Spain 1996–99; promoted to Brig. Gen. 1999; Chief of Operations Div., Spanish Jt Staff 1999; promoted to Maj. Gen. 2001; Vice-Chief, Spanish Air Force Staff 2001–03; Chief, Canary Islands Air Command 2003–04; promoted to Lt-Gen. 2004; Mil. Rep. to NATO 2005–06; Great Cross, Commendation, Cross and Badge of S. Hermenegildo, Great Cross of Aeronautical Merit, Great Cross of Mil. Merit, other nat. and foreign medals.
Address: c/o Ministry of Defence, Paseo de la Castellana 109, 28071 Madrid, Spain (office). *Website:* www.mde.es (office).

VIERITA, Adrian Cosmin, BA, MA; Romanian diplomatist; *Ambassador to USA;* m. Codrina Eugenia Vierita; two c. *Education:* Diplomatic Acad. of

Vienna, Romanian Inst. of Int. Studies, Bucharest, Polytechnic Univ., Bucharest, Acad. of Econ. Studies, Bucharest. *Career:* joined Foreign Service 1991, held various exec. positions within Ministry of Foreign Affairs, including Chief of Staff to State Sec. co-ordinating relations with Asia, Africa, the Middle East and Latin America, Deputy Dir UN and Int. Orgs Directorate, Dir Cen. and SE Europe Directorate, Gen. Dir for European and trans-Atlantic Affairs; overseas postings include four-year tour with Perm. Mission to Int. Orgs, Vienna, Deputy Perm. Rep. to IAEA and to UNIDO, Amb. to Germany 2002–06; State Sec. for European Affairs, Ministry of Foreign Affairs 2006–08; Amb. to USA 2008–; Visiting Lecturer, European Coll. for Liberal Arts, Berlin. *Publications:* Romania in the United Nations Organization (co-author).
Address: Embassy of Romania, 1607 23rd Street, NW, Washington, DC 20008, USA (office). *Telephone:* (202) 332-4829 (office). *Fax:* (202) 232-4748 (office). *E-mail:* info@roembus.org (office). *Website:* www.roembus .org (office).

VĪĶE-FREIBERGA, Vaira, MA, PhD; Latvian fmr head of state and psychologist; b. 1 Dec. 1937, Rīga; m. Imants Freibergs 1960; one s. one d. *Education:* Univ. of Toronto and McGill Univ., Canada. *Career:* Prof. of Psychology Univ. of Montréal 1965–98; Prof. Emer. 1998–; Vice-Chair. Science Council of Canada 1988–97; Dir Latvian Inst., Rīga 1998–99; Pres. of Latvia 1999–2007; fmr Pres. Canadian Psychological Asscn; Pres. Social Science Fed. of Canada; Chair. Asscn for Advancement of Baltic Studies, USA; Pres. Acad. des Lettres et des Sciences Humaines, RSC; mem. Latvian Acad. of Sciences, Council of Women Leaders 1999–; lectures and seminars on Latvian culture in USA, Canada, Latvia and numerous countries; Hon. Prof., Victoria Univ., Canada 2000, Latvia Univ.; decorations include Three Star Order of Latvia 1995, Dame of GCB 2006, Officer of the National Order of Québec, Canada 2006; Hon. LLD (Latvia) 1991, Hon. DLitt (Victoria Univ., Toronto) 2000, Hon. DSci (McGill Univ.) 2002, Dr hc (Latvia) 2000, (Vytautas Magnus Univ., Lithuania) 2002, (Eurasian Nat. Univ.) 2004, (Baku, Azerbaijan) 2005, (Tbilisi) 2005, (Yerevan) 2005, (Ottawa) 2006, (Liege) 2006; numerous prizes include Anna Abele Prize 1979, Marcel-Vincent Prize and Medal 1992, Pierre Chauveau Medal 1995, awards from Latvian Acad. of Science 1992, American Acad. of Achievement Gold Plate 2000, McGill Univ., Canada 2002, Kaunas Vytautas Magnus Univ., Lithuania 2002, Georgetown Univ., USA 2002, Free Univ. of Berlin 2003, Grand Prize of Folklore, Ministry of Culture, Latvia 2003, Award of Distinction of the Canadian Psychological Asscn 2004, Forbes Executive Women's Forum Trailblazer Award 2005, Medal of the American Jewish Cttee 2005, Hannah Arendt Prize for Political Thought 2005, Coudenhove-Kalergi Foundation Europa Prize, Pan-Europa Union 2006, Baltic Statesmanship Award of the US-Baltic Foundation 2006, J.W. Goethe Univ. Medal and Walter Hallstein Prize 2006, UN FAO Ceres Medal 2007. *Publications include:* La Frequence Lexicalle des Mots au Québec 1974, Latvian Sun-Songs (co-author) 1988, Linguistic and Poetics of Latvian Folk Songs 1989, On the Amber Mountain 1993, Against the Current 1993, The Cosmological Sun 1997, The Chronological Sun 1999, The Warm Sun 2002, Latvian Sun Song Melodies 2005; contrib. more than 400 articles and papers.
Address: c/o Chancery of the President, Pils lauk. 3, Rīga 1050, Latvia. *E-mail:* chancery@president.lv (office). *Website:* www.president.lv.

VILA COMA, Julià; Andorran government official and diplomatist. *Career:* Dir of Customs, Ministry of Finance, Andorra 1980–2004; Perm. Rep. to UN, New York 2004–07; Chevalier, Ordre National du Mérite, France 2000.
Address: c/o Ministry of Foreign Affairs, Carrer Prat de la Creu 62–64, Edif. Administratiu, Andorra la Vella AD500, Andorra (office).

VILHJALMSSON, Thor, Cand. juris; Icelandic judge (retd) and professor of law; b. 9 June 1930, Reykjavik; m. Ragnhildur Helgadóttir 1950; one s. three d. *Education:* Reykjavik Grammar School, St Andrews Univ., Scotland, Univ. of Iceland, New York Univ. and Univ. of Copenhagen. *Career:* Asst Lecturer, Univ. of Iceland 1959–62, part-time Lecturer 1962–67, Prof. 1967–76 and Dean, Faculty of Law 1968–70, Dir Inst. of Law 1974–76; Deputy Judge Reykjavik Civil Court 1960–62, Judge 1962–67; Judge, European Court of Human Rights 1971–98, Vice-Pres. 1998; Assoc. Justice of the Supreme Court of Iceland 1976–93, Pres. 1983–84, 1993; Judge, EFTA Court, Geneva 1994–96, Luxembourg 1996–2002 (Pres. 2000–02); mem. Icelandic Del. to UN Gen. Ass. 1963, UN Sea-Bed Cttee 1972, 1973 to Law of the Sea Conf. 1974, 1975 and other int. confs; Pres. Asscn of Icelandic Lawyers 1971–74; Ed. Icelandic Law Review 1973–83; Commdr, Order of the Icelandic Falcon. *Publications:* Civil Procedure I–IV and several studies and articles on constitutional law, human rights and legal history.
Address: Midleiti 10, 1S 103 Reykjavik, Iceland (home). *Telephone:* 5535330 (home). *Fax:* 5535330 (home). *E-mail:* thorhv@vortex.is (home).

VILLAGRÁN DE LEÓN, Francisco; Guatemalan diplomatist; *Ambassador to USA. Career:* career diplomat in Guatemalan Foreign Service since 1985, has served as Amb. to UN, OAS, Canada, Norway and Germany; worked as consultant on institutional devt for OAS –2003; Chair. Cttee on Juridical and Political Affairs and Perm. Rep. of Guatemala to OAS 2006–08, Amb. to USA 2008–; Reagan-Fascell Democracy Fellow, Nat. Endowment for Democracy 2003–04.
Address: Embassy of Guatemala, 2220 R Street, NW, Washington, DC 20008, USA (office). *Telephone:* (202) 745-4952 (office). *Fax:* (202) 745-1908 (office). *E-mail:* info@guatemala-embassy.org (office). *Website:* www .guatemala-embassy.org (office).

VILLALTA, Vladimiro P.; Salvadorean diplomatist; *Ambassador to UK;* m. Adrienne Ribas de P. Villalta; one s. one d. *Career:* fmr Pres. Comisión de Seguimiento Honduras-El Salvador; fmr Dir of Grants, Ministry of Foreign Affairs; Amb. to UK 2005–; mem. Comisión Presidencial para Asuntos Limítrofes.
Address: Embassy of El Salvador, 1st and 2nd Floors, 8 Dorset Square, London, NW1 6PU, England (office). *Telephone:* (20) 7224-9800 (office). *Fax:* (20) 7224-9878 (office). *E-mail:* elsalvadorembassy@rree.gob.sv (office); Elsalvador.embassy@gmail.com (office).

VILLAR Y ORTIZ DE URBINA, Francisco; Spanish diplomatist; *Ambassador to France;* b. 8 Jan. 1945, Salamanca. *Education:* Univ. of Salamanca. *Career:* Perm. Rep. to UN 1987–91; Political Dir and Rep. to Comité politique de la Coopération Politique Européenne (CPE) 1991–93; Perm. Rep. to OAS 1996–2000; Perm. Rep. to UNESCO 2000–03; Amb. to France 2004–.
Address: Embassy of Spain, 22 ave Marceau, 75008 Paris, France (office). *Telephone:* (1) 44-43-18-00 (office). *Fax:* (1) 47-23-59-55 (office). *E-mail:* ambespfr@mail.mae.es (office). *Website:* www.amb-espagne.fr (office).

VILLAROSA, Shari, BA, BL; American diplomatist; *Chargé d'affaires in Myanmar; Education:* William and Mary Coll. and Univ. of N Carolina. *Career:* overseas assignments have included Songkhla, Thailand, Brasília, Brazil, Quito, Ecuador and Bogotá, Colombia, State Dept assignments include Special Asst to Under-Sec. for Econ. Affairs, Deputy Dir Office of Burma, Cambodia, Laos, Thailand and Vietnam Affairs, Singapore and Indonesia Desk Officer, and in Office of Investment Affairs, spent a year as Diplomat-in-Residence, East-West Center, Honolulu, most recently served as Dir Philippines, Malaysia, Brunei, Singapore Affairs, Bureau of E Asia and Pacific Affairs, as Econ. Counselor, Embassy in Jakarta, and as Chargé d'affaires a.i., Embassy in Dili, East Timor –2005, Chargé d'affaires a.i. in Myanmar 2005–.
Address: Embassy of the USA, 581 Merchant Street, Kyauktada Township, PO Box 521, Yangon, Myanmar (office). *Telephone:* (1) 379880 (office). *Fax:* (1) 256018 (office). *E-mail:* info.rangoon@state.gov (office). *Website:* rangoon.usembassy.gov (office).

VILLAS-BOAS, José Manuel P. de; Portuguese diplomatist and academic; *Professor, Department of Political Science and International Relations, Universidade do Minho;* b. 23 Feb. 1931, Oporto; m. Maria do Patrocinio de Almeida Braga 1956. *Education:* Lisbon Univ. *Career:* Attaché, Ministry of Foreign Affairs 1954; Embassies, Pretoria 1959, London 1963; Counsellor 1969; Head of African Dept, Ministry of Foreign Affairs 1970–72; Consul-Gen., Milan 1972–74; Minister Plenipotentiary, Asst Dir-Gen. of Political Affairs, Ministry of Foreign Affairs 1974–77, Dir-Gen. of Political Affairs 1977–79; Amb. and Perm. Rep. to NATO 1979–84, Amb. to South Africa 1984–89, to People's Repub. of China 1989–93, to Russia 1993–97; Prof., Dept of Political Science and Int. Relations, Univ. of Minho, Braga 1997–, mem. Strategic Council 2003–; Grand Cross Order of Merit (Portugal), Hon. KCMG (UK), Grand Cross of St Olav (Norway), of Merit (Spain), Cruzeiro do Sul (Brazil), of Rio Branco (Brazil), of Good Hope (S Africa), Grand Officer of the Order of Merit (FRG), of the Lion (Senegal), Commdr, Légion d'honneur (France), Order of Merit (Italy), etc. *Publication:* Orthodoxy and Political Power in Russia 1999, Caderno de Memórias 2003.
Address: Casa de Esteiro, Vilarelho 4910 Caminha (home); Department of Political Science and International Relations, Universidade do Minho, Campus de Gualtar, 4710-057 Braga, Portugal (office). *Telephone:* (258) 721333 (home); (253) 604518 (office). *Fax:* (258) 921356 (home). *E-mail:* casaesteiro@iol.pt (home). *Website:* www.eeg.uminho.pt (office).

VILLIGER, Kaspar; Swiss former head of state; b. 5 Feb. 1941, Pfeffikon, Lucerne; m.; two d. *Education:* Swiss Fed. Inst. of Tech., Zürich. *Career:* Man. of cigar factory Villiger Söhne AG, Pfeffikon 1966; subsequently bought bicycle factory in Buttisholz; fmr Vice-Pres. Chamber of Commerce of Cen. Switzerland and mem. Cttee Swiss Employers' Cen. Asscn; mem. Lucerne Cantonal Parl. 1972–82; mem. Nat. Council, Liberal Party of Switzerland (FDP) 1982; mem. Council of States 1987; Swiss Fed.

Councillor 1989–2003; Head, Fed. Mil. (Defence) Dept 1989–95, Dept of Finance 1996–2001, 2003; Vice-Pres. of Swiss Confed. 1994, 2001; Pres. Swiss Confed. Jan.–Dec. 1995, 2002; Dir Nestlé 2004–, Swiss Re 2004–, Neue Zürcher Zeitung.
Address: c/o Swiss Reinsurance Company, Mythenquai 50/60, PO Box 8022, 3003 Zurich, Switzerland (office).

VIMONT, Pierre; French diplomatist; *Ambassador to USA;* b. 15 June 1949. *Education:* Institut d'Etudes Politiques and Ecole nationale d'Admin, Paris. *Career:* Sec., Ministry of Foreign Affairs 1977, Sec., London 1977–78, Information and Press matters, Ministry of Foreign Affairs 1981–85; with Inst. for East-West Security Studies, New York 1985–86; Second Counsellor, French Perm. Representation to European Communities, Brussels 1986–90; Head of Pvt. Office, Minister of European Affairs 1990–93; Dir for Devt and Scientific, Tech. and Educational Cooperation 1993–97; Dir for European Cooperation 1997–99, Ministry of Foreign Affairs; Amb. and Perm. Rep. to EU 1999–2002; Prin. Pvt. Sec., Minister of Foreign Affairs 2002–07; Amb. to USA 2007–; fmr Pres. Group of Personal Reps to Intergovernmental Conf.; Chevalier, Ordre nat. du Mérite 1993. *Address:* Embassy of France, 4101 Reservoir Road, NW, Washington DC 20007, USA (office). *Telephone:* (202) 944-6166 (office). *Fax:* (202) 944-6072 (office). *E-mail:* info@ambafrance-us.org (office). *Website:* www .ambafrance-us.org (office).

VINCHON, Lt-Gen. Pascal; French military officer; *Military Representative, NATO;* b. Nîmes; m. Carine Boissonnet; four c. *Education:* Air Force Acad., Centre for Advanced Mil. Studies, Paris, US Air War Coll. *Career:* promoted to Second Lt 1974, First Lt 1976, Captain 1979, participated in various operational missions over Mauritania and Chad 1980–81; Flight Commdr, Tactical Fighter Squadron 1/11 1982–84, Deputy Commdr, Fighter Squadron 2/12 1984–85, Commdr, Fighter Squadron 1/12 1985–87, Commdr, Air Force Acad. cadet class 1987–89, Deputy Commdr, 3rd Tactical Fighter Wing 1989–91, Commdr, 3rd Tactical Fighter Wing 1991–92; Mil. Adviser to Rep., Balkan Contact Group 1994, mem. French negotiating team, Dayton Peace Agreement 1995; Mil. Adviser to Perm. Rep. to UN, New York 1995–98; mem. French negotiating team for Kosovo, Rambouillet 1999; served in staff positions including Head of Balkan crisis action team, French Jt Command Centre, Asst Dir European and NATO Affairs, Ministry of Defence Policy Directorate, Chief of Personal Staff to Chief of Staff of French Air Force 2001–03; Defence attaché, Embassy in Washington, DC 2003–06, Mil. Rep., NATO, Brussels 2006–; promoted to Major 1984, Lt-Col 1988, Col 1992, Brig.-Gen. 2001, Maj.-Gen. 2003, Lt-Gen. 2006; Officier, Légion d'honneur, Ordre national du Mérite; Medal of the Combatant, Overseas Operations Medal, Nat. Defence Medal.
Address: NATO HQ, blvd Léopold III, 1110 Brussels, Belgium (office). *Telephone:* (2) 707-41-11 (office). *Fax:* (2) 707-45-79 (office). *E-mail:* natodoc@hq.nato.int (office). *Website:* www.nato.int (office).

VINES, David Anthony, PhD; British/Australian economist and academic; *Professor of Economics, University of Oxford;* b. 8 May 1949, Oxford; m. 1st Susannah Lucy Robinson 1979 (divorced 1992); three s.; m. 2nd Jane E. Bingham 1995; two step-s. *Education:* Scotch Coll. Melbourne and Univs of Melbourne and Cambridge. *Career:* Fellow, Pembroke Coll. Cambridge 1976–85; Research Officer, Sr Research Officer, Dept of Applied Econs, Univ. of Cambridge 1979–85; Adam Smith Prof. of Political Econ. Univ of Glasgow 1985–92; Fellow and Tutor in Econs Balliol Coll. Oxford 1992–, Prof. of Econs, Univ. of Oxford 2000–; Adjunct Prof. of Econs, Inst. of Advanced Studies, ANU 1991–; Dir ESRC Research Programme on Global Econ. Insts 1993–2000; mem. Bd Channel 4 TV 1986–92, Glasgow Devt Agency 1990–92, Analysis, Scottish Early Music Asscn 1988–95; econ. consultant to Sec. of State for Scotland 1988–92; consultant to IMF 1988, 1989; mem. Acad. Panel, HM Treasury 1986–; mem. Research Programmes Bd, ESRC 1990–92; mem. Int. Policy Forum, HM Treasury 1999–; Houblon Norman Fellow, Bank of England 2001–02. *Publications:* Stagflation, Vol. II: Demand Management (with J. E. Meade and J. M. Maciejowski) 1983, Macroeconomic Interactions Between North and South (with D. A. Currie) 1988, Macroeconomic Policy: inflation, wealth and the exchange rate (jtly) 1989, Deregulation and the Future of Commercial Television (with G. Hughes) 1989, Information, Strategy and Public Policy (with A. Stevenson) 1991, North South Macroeconomic Interactions and Global Macroeconomic Policy (ed. with D. A. Currie) 1995, Europe, East Asia and APEC: a Shared Global Agenda (with P. Drysdale) 1998, The Asian Financial Crisis: Causes Contagion and Consequences (ed., with P. Agenor, M. Miller and A. Weber) 1999, Integrity in the Public and Private Domains (ed. with A. Montefiore) 1999, The World Bank: Structure and Policies (ed. with C. L. Gilbert) 2000, papers in professional journals. *Address:* Balliol College, Oxford, OX1 3BJ; Department of Economics, Manor Road, Oxford, OX1 3UQ, England. *Telephone:* (1865) 277719

(Coll.); (1865) 271067 (Dept). *Fax:* (1865) 277803 (Coll.); (1865) 271094 (Dept). *E-mail:* david.vines@economics.ox.ac.uk. *Website:* www .economics.ox.ac.uk.

VITORINO, António, LLM; Portuguese politician and lawyer; b. 12 Jan. 1957, Lisbon; m.; two c. *Education:* Lisbon Law School. *Career:* fmr Prof., Lisbon Autonomous Univ.; mem. Parl. (Partido Socialista) 1981, 2005–; Sec. of State for Parl. Affairs 1984–85, for Admin and Justice of Macao Govt 1986–87; Judge, Portuguese Constitutional Court 1989–94; Minister for Defence and the Presidency 1995–97; Vice-Pres. Portugal Telecom Internacional 1998–99; EU Commr for Freedom, Security and Justice 1999–2004.
Address: c/o Partido Socialista, Assembleia da República, Palácio de San Bento, 1249–068 Lisbon, Portugal (office).

VITUSAGAVULU, Jesoni, BA, MA; Fijian business executive and diplomatist; m. Silina Vitusagavulu; three d. *Education:* Univ. of the South Pacific, Univ. of Sussex, UK, Univ. of Bar Ilan, Israel, Australian Grad. School of Man., Univ. of New South Wales. *Career:* Chief Exec. Fiji Trade and Investment Bureau 1996–2003; Founder and Man. Dir TOPtier Man. Consultancy 2003–05; Lecturer, MBA programme, Univ. of the South Pacific 2003–05; held sr man. positions in Air Pacific, Fiji Devt Bank, Unit Trust of Fiji, Suva Stock Exchange, Fijian Property Trust; fmr Trustee Fijians Trust Fund; fmr mem. Prime Minister's Think Tank Advisory Group; fmr Dir Kadavu Devt Co.; fmr Chair. Food Processors (Fiji) Ltd, Agricultural Marketing Authority, Kontiki Growth Fund; Amb. to USA (also accred to Cuba and Mexico) 2005–07 (accred as High Commr to Canada 2006–07).
Address: Ministry of Foreign Affairs, International Co-operation and Civil Aviation, Government Bldgs, PO Box 2220, Suva, Fiji (office). *Telephone:* 3309631 (office). *Fax:* 3301741 (office). *E-mail:* info@foreignaffairs.gov.fj (office). *Website:* www.foreignaffairs.gov.fj (office).

VIVES, Xavier, MA, PhD; Spanish economist; *Professor of Economics and Finance, Institut Européen d'Administration des Affaires (INSEAD);* b. 23 Jan. 1955, Barcelona; m. Aurora Bastida; two s. *Education:* Autonomous Univ. of Barcelona, Univ. of Calif. at Berkeley, USA. *Career:* Sr Researcher, Fundación de Estudios de Economía Aplicada (FEDEA); Programme Dir Applied Microecons. and Industrial Org. Programmes, Centre for Econ. Policy Research, London; Dir Institut d'Analisi Económica, Barcelona 1991–2001; Prof. of Econs and Finance, Institut Européen d'Admin des Affaires (INSEAD) 2001–; Visiting Prof., Harvard Univ., Univs of Pa, Calif., Berkeley and New York Univ.; Fellow, Econometric Soc. 1992; Premio Extraordinario de Licenciatura, Autonomous Univ. of Barcelona 1978, King Juan Carlos I Prize for Research in Social Science 1988, Societat Catalana d'Economía Prize 1996. *Publications:* Monitoring European Integration: The Future of European Banking (co-author) 1999, Oligopoly Pricing: Old Ideas and New Tools 2000, Corporate Governance: Theoretical and Empirical Perspectives (ed.) 2000, Politicas Publicas y Equilibrio Territorial en el Stado Autonomico. *Address:* INSEAD, boulevard de Constance, 77305 Fontainebleau Cedex (office); Bat. C, Royal Paic, Appt 138, 39, Rue Royal, 77300 Fontainebleau France (home). *Telephone:* 1-60-72-42-79 (office); 1-60-72-83-01 (home). *Fax:* 1-60-74-67-19 (office). *E-mail:* xavier.vives@insead.edu (office). *Website:* faculty.insead.edu/vives (office).

VIVIAN, Young; Niuean politician; *Premier;* b. 1935. *Career:* Leader Niue People's Party; Premier Dec. 1992–March 1993, May 2002–, also Minister responsible for Legis. Ass., Premier's Dept and Cabinet, Civil Aviation, Crown Law Office, Econ. Devt Planning and Statistics, External Affairs and Niueans Abroad, Niue Public Service Comm., Niue Broadcasting Corpn, Finance, Customs and Revenue, Police, Prison and Nat. Security, Environment, Niue Tourism, Public Works (Civil and Quarry, Outside Services and Heavy Plant) and Recovery Task Force.
Address: Niue People's Party, Alofi, Niue (office).

VIZJAK, Andrej, MEng; Slovenian politician and engineer; *Minister of the Economy;* b. 6 Aug. 1964, Brežice. *Education:* Brežice Gymnasium, Faculty of Electrical Eng and Computing, Univ. of Ljubljana. *Career:* began career as electrical engineer, Litostroj, Ljubljana; researcher in computer automatisation of industrial processes, Jožef Stefan Inst. –1994; Labour Insp., Krško Unit, Nat. Labour Inspectorate 1994–2000; State Sec., Ministry of Labour, Family and Social Affairs 2000; elected to Nat. Ass. 2000–04, 2004–, Minister of Economy 2004–; Leader of Social Democratic Party (SDP) Parl. Group 2000–04; elected Mayor of Brežice 2002.
Address: Ministry of the Economy, 1000 Ljubljana, Kotnikova 5, Slovenia (office). *Telephone:* (1) 4783600 (office). *Fax:* (1) 4331031 (office). *E-mail:* info.mg@gov.si (office). *Website:* www.mg-rs-si (office).

VLAHOVIĆ, Miodrag; Montenegrin politician and diplomatist; *Ambassador to USA;* b. 1961, Djakovica; m.; three d. *Education:* Univ. of Montenegro, Podgorica, Univ. of Belgrade, Luxembourg Int. Univ. *Career:* f. STUDEKS Cultural Centre, Podgorica 1985; mem. Fed. Presidency and Int. Sec., Socialist Youth Union of Yugoslavia 1986–88; Sec. for Montenegro Asscn for Yugoslav Democratic Unity 1989; co-f. Citizens Cttee for Peace 1991–92, organized first peace rally in Montenegro 1991; mem. Parl., Repub. of Montenegro, mem. Parl. Cttee for Int. Relations, Cttee for Political System, Cttee for Legal and Admin. Matters 1992–94 (resgnd); Liberal Party of Montenegro Int. Sec. 1992–93; columnist for ind. weekly "Monitor" 1991–93, 1999–2000; Founder-mem. Montenegrin Centre for Democracy and Human Rights (CEDEM) 1998; co-author of new Montenegrin law on NGOs; Dir Centre for Regional and Security Studies (CeRS) 1999; Minister of Foreign Affairs, Repub. of Montenegro 2004–06; Amb. to USA 2006–; Owner MConsult Ltd 1990–; mem. Socialiat Democratic Party of Montenegro.
Address: Embassy of Montenegro, 1610 New Hampshire Avenue, NW, Washington, DC 20009, USA (office). *Telephone:* (202) 234 6108 (office). *Fax:* (202) 234 6109 (office).

VOGEL, Bernhard, DPhil; German politician; *Chairman, Konrad Adenauer Foundation;* b. 19 Dec. 1932, Göttingen. *Education:* Univs of Heidelberg and Munich. *Career:* Lecturer, Inst. for Political Sciences, Heidelberg 1961–67; mem. Bundestag (Parl.) 1965–67, Speaker of Bundesrat (Upper House) 1976–77, 1987–88; Minister of Educ. and Culture, Rhineland-Palatinate 1967–76; Chairman / Deputy Chairman of the Joint Commission of the Federal and State Governments for Education Planning and Research Development 1970-1976; mem. Rhineland-Palatinate State Parl. 1971–88, Thuringia State Parl. 1994–2004; Chair. CDU, Rhineland-Palatinate 1974–88, mem. Fed. Exec. Cttee of CDU 1975–, Chair. CDU, Thuringia 1993–2000; Minister-Pres., Rhineland-Palatinate 1976–88, Thuringia 1992–2003, Chair. Conf. of State Prime Ministers 1981–82, 1996–97; Rep. for Cultural Affairs of FRG within framework of Agreement on German-French Co-operation 1979–82; Chair. Advisory Bd of German TV Broadcasting/Second Channel (ZDF) 1979–92, Deputy Chair. 1992–2007; Chair. Konrad Adenauer Foundation 1989–95, 2001–; Pres. Cen. Cttee of German Catholics 1972–76; Hon. Prof., award by State of Baden-Wurttemberg; Grosses Bundesverdienstkreuz; decorations from France, Luxembourg, Poland, UK, and the Vatican; Grosskreuz St Gregorius; Gold Medal of Strasbourg; Dr hc (Catholic Univ. of America, Catholic Univ. of Lublin, German Coll. for Admin. Sciences, Speyer). *Publications:* Die Unabhangigen in den Kommunalwahlen westdeutscher Lander 1960, Wahlen und Wahlsysteme 1961, Kontrolliert der Bundestag die Regierung? 1964, Wahlkampf und Wählertradition. Eine Studie zur Bundestagswahl von 1961 1965, Wahlen in Deutschland 1848–1970 (with D. Noheln and R.-O. Schultze), Schule am Scheideweg 1974, Die Wahl der Parlamente und anderer Staatsorgane 1969–1978 (co-ed. with Dolf Sternberger), Neue Bildungspolitik (ed.) 1975, Foderalismus in der Bewahrung (ed.) 1992, Sorge tragen fur die Zukunft 2002, Religion und Politik (ed.) 2003, Im Zentrum: Menschenwürde. Politisches Handeln aus christlicher Verantwortung, christliche Ethik als Orientierungshilfe (ed.) 2006, Deutschland aus der Vogel Perspektive. Eine kleine Geschichte der Bundesrepublik Deutschland (zusammen mit Hans-Jochen Vogel) 2007; Ed. Politische Meinung; numerous essays and speeches.
Address: Konrad-Adenauer-Stiftung e.V., Der Vorsitzende, Rathausallee 12, 53757 Sankt Augustin, Germany (office). *Telephone:* (2241) 2462420 (office). *Fax:* (2241) 2462675 (office). *E-mail:* bernhard.vogel@kas.de (office).

VOHIDOV, Alisher; Uzbekistan economist and diplomatist; *Permanent Representative, United Nations;* b. 24 Dec. 1951; m.; two c. *Education:* Tashkent State Univ., Acad. of Foreign Trade and Diplomatic Acad., Moscow, Russia. *Career:* Researcher Inst. of Econs, Acads of Sciences, Tashkent 1974, Moscow 1975–79; Sr Expert Ministry of Foreign Trade, Moscow 1982–84; Researcher Diplomatic Acad., Ministry of Foreign Affairs 1986–92; Dir Int. Orgs Dept, Ministry of Foreign Affairs 1992–93; Chief Adviser to Resident Co-ordinator UN Office, Tashkent 1993–94; First Sec., Counsellor and Chargé d'affaires, Perm. Mission to UN, New York 1994–1997, Perm. Rep. to UN New York 1997–.
Address: Permanent Mission of Uzbekistan to the UN, 801 Second Ave, 20th Floor, New York, NY 10017, USA (office). *Telephone:* (212) 486-4242 (office). *Fax:* (212) 486-7998 (office). *E-mail:* uzbekistan@un.int (office).

VOLK, Vojko, BA; Slovenian diplomatist; *Head, Policy Planning and Research Department, Ministry of Foreign Affairs;* m. Ana Kosor-Volk. *Career:* fmr State Under-Sec., Ministry of Foreign Affairs, later State Sec.; fmr Amb. to Italy; currently Head of Policy Planning and Research Dept, Ministry of Foreign Affairs; Medal of Independence of Slovenia. *Publications:* Slovenija Proti Jugoslaviji (Slovenia Against Yugoslavia) 1992.

Address: Ministry of Foreign Affairs of the Republic of Slovenia, Prešernova cesta 25, 1001 Ljubljana, P.P. 481; Presernova 25, 1000, Ljubljana, Slovenia (home). *Telephone:* (01) 4782000 (office); (01) 4782369 (home). *Fax:* (01) 4782340 (office). *E-mail:* info.mzz@gov.si (office); vojko.volk@gov.si (home). *Website:* www.mzz.gov.si (office).

VOLKOVA, Tatyana Gellar; American diplomatist; *Ambassador to Kyrgyzstan; Career:* fmr Local Faculty Fellow, Kazakhstan; Project Coordinator, Rapid Environment and Health Risks Assessment; Amb. to Kyrgyzstan 2008–.
Address: US Embassy, pr. Mira 171, 720016 Bishkek, Kyrgyzstan (office). *Telephone:* (312) 55-12-41 (office). *Fax:* (312) 55-12-64 (office). *Website:* bishkek.usembassy.gov (office).

VOLLEBAEK, Knut, MSc; Norwegian diplomatist; *High Commissioner on National Minorities, Organization for Security and Co-operation in Europe;* b. 11 Feb. 1946, Oslo; m. Ellen Sofie Aadland Vollebaek; one s. *Education:* Inst. Catholique de Paris, Univ of Oslo, Univ of California, Santa Barbara, USA, Univ Complutense, Madrid, Spain and, Norwegian School of Econs and Business Admin, Bergen. *Career:* joined Foreign Service 1973; Second Sec. Embassy of Norway, Delhi 1975–78, First Sec. Embassy of Norway, Madrid 1978–81, Exec. Officer, then Sr Exec. Officer, Ministry of Foreign Affairs 1981–84, Counsellor Embassy of Norway, Harare 1984–86; Head First Political Affairs Div., Ministry of Foreign Affairs 1986–89, State Sec. and Deputy Minister of Foreign Affairs 1989–90; Amb. to Costa Rica 1991–93; Dir Gen. Dept of Bilateral Devt Cooperation, Ministry of Foreign Affairs 1993–94; Gov. Inter-Amercian Devt Bank, Asian Devt Bank and African Devt Bank 1994–97; Deputy Co-Chair. Int. Conf. on the Fmr Yugoslavia, Geneva 1993; Asst Sec. Gen. for Devt Cooperation 1994–97; Minister of Foreign Affairs 1997–2000; Chair. Barents Euro-Arctic Council 1997–98; Chair. Council of Baltic Sea States 1999–2000; Chair.-in-Office OSCE 1999; Amb. to USA 2001–07; High Commr on Nat. Minorities, OSCE 2007–; Commdr of the Royal Norwegian Order of St Olav 2001; Hon. DJur (St Olaf Coll., Minn., USA) 2003; Hon. DHumLitt (Concordia Coll., Minn., USA) 2003.
Address: High Commissioner on National Minorities, PO Box 20062, 2500 EB The Hague, Netherlands (office). *Telephone:* (70) 3125500 (office). *Fax:* (70) 3635910 (office). *E-mail:* hcnm@hcnm.org (office). *Website:* www.osce.org/hcnm (office).

VOLTEN, Peter M. E., MA, PhD; Dutch research institute director; *Director, Centre for European Security Studies;* m. Karin Deen; four c. *Education:* Free Univ. of Amsterdam. *Career:* Visiting Scholar, Stanford Univ., USA 1975–77; Sr Staff mem. Dutch Ministry of Defence 1977–85, Dir of Studies and Strategic Planning 1987–89; Prof. of History, Univ. of Utrecht 1984–89; Sr Research Fellow, Netherlands Inst. of Int. Relations 1985–87; Dir of Research, Inst. for East-West Security Studies 1989–92, Sr Vice-Pres. and Dir Netherlands Centre 1992–93; Prof. of Int. Relations, Univ. of Groningen 1994–, Dir Centre for European Security Studies 1994–; mem. Bd Dirs Free Univ. of Amsterdam. *Publications include:* Brezhnev's Peace Program: a Study of Soviet Domestic Political Process and Power 1982, Uncertain Futures: Eastern Europe and Democracy (ed.) 1990, The Guns Fall Silent: the End of the Cold War and the Future of Conventional Disarmament (co-ed.) 1990, Bound to Change: Consolidating Democracy in East Central Europe (ed.) 1992; numerous articles on security and defence policy in learned journals.
Address: Centre for European Security Studies, PO Box 716, Groningen, 9700, Netherlands (office). *Telephone:* (50) 3132520 (office). *Fax:* (50) 3132506 (office). *E-mail:* p.m.e.volten@let.rug.nl (office). *Website:* www.let.rug.nl/cess (office).

VON BRAUN, Joachim, PhD; German agricultural economist, research institute director and academic; *Director General, International Food Policy Research Institute;* b. 10 July 1950, Brakel; m. Dr Barbara von Braun; three d. *Education:* Univ. of Göttingen. *Career:* Dir Food Consumption and Nutrition Div., Int. Food Policy Research Inst. (IFPRI), Washington, DC 1990–93, Dir-Gen. IFPRI 2002–; Prof. and Dir Inst. for Food Econs and Consumer Analyses, Univ. of Kiel 1993–97; Dir Centre for Devt Research and Head of Dept of Econs and Technological Change, Univ. of Bonn 1997–2002; Pres. Int. Asscn of Agricultural Economists 2000–03; mem. Hunger Task Force, UN Millennium Devt Project 2003–05; Fellow, German Economics Association 1996, AAAS 2006; Hon. Prof., Int. Research Center for Food and Agric. Econs, Nanjing Agricultural Univ., China 2004–; Dr hc (Stuttgart-Hohenheim) 2005; Josef G. Knoll Science Prize 1988. *Publications:* Famine in Africa: Causes, Responses and Prevention (co-author) 1999, Russia's Agro-Food Sector: Towards Truly Functioning Markets (co-ed.) 2000, Agricultural Biotechnology in Developing Countries: Towards Optimizing the Benefits for the Poor (co-author) 2000, Villages in the Future: Crops, Jobs and Livelihood (co-ed.) 2001, Information and Communication Technologies for Development and

Poverty Reduction – The Potential of Telecommunications (co-ed.) 2005, Globalization of Food and Agriculture and the Poor (co-ed.) 2008.
Address: International Food Policy Research Institute, 2033 K Street, NW, Washington, DC 20006, USA (office). *Telephone:* (202) 862-5600 (office). *Fax:* (202) 467-4439 (office). *E-mail:* j.vonbraun@cgiar.org (office). *Website:* www.ifpri.org (office).

VON DER SCHULENBURG, Michael; German UN official and diplomatist; *Deputy Special Representative for Political Affairs in Iraq, United Nations; Career:* served in various capacities with UN in New York, Vienna, Haiti, Pakistan, Afghanistan, Kuwait, Iraq, Iran and Syria, Dir Office of Special Rep. of Sec.-Gen. Afghanistan and as Dir with OSCE in Vienna –2005, Deputy Special Rep. for Political Affairs with UN Assistance Mission in Iraq (UNAMI) 2005–.
Address: c/o Office of the Secretary-General, UN Headquarters, First Avenue at 46th Street, New York, NY 10017, Jordan (office). *Website:* www.uniraq.org (office).

VON NORDENSKJÖLD, Fritjof, LLB; German diplomatist and organization official; *Executive Vice-President, Deutsche Gesellschaft für Auswärtige Politik eV;* b. 23 Dec. 1938, Hildesheim; m.; two c. *Education:* Univ. of Tübingen, Univ. of Munich. *Career:* legal practise, Munich 1969–70; joined Ministry of Foreign Affairs 1971, service in Minister's Office 1971–74, Minister Plenipotentiary, German Embassy, Antananarivo 1974–77, Head of Foreign Minister's Office 1977–82, Amb. to Haiti 1982–85, Deputy Dir in charge of parl. affairs, Ministry of Foreign Affairs 1985–88, Minister Counsellor and Head of Political Service, German Embassy, Paris 1988–90, Minister Plenipotentiary, German Embassy, Washington 1990–94, Dir Gen. of Econ. Affairs, Ministry of Foreign Affairs 1994, Dir Gen. of Admin. 1994–98, Amb. to Italy 1998–2001, to France 2001–04; currently Exec. Vice-Pres. Deutsche Gesellschaft für Auswärtige Politik eV.
Address: Deutsche Gesellschaft für Auswärtige Politik eV, Rauchstr. 17/18, 10787 Berlin, Germany (office). *Telephone:* (30) 254231 (office). *Fax:* (30) 254216 (office). *E-mail:* nordenskjold@dgap.org (office). *Website:* www.dgap.org (office).

VONDRA, Alexandr, RNDr; Czech diplomatist, academic and consultant; *Deputy Prime Minister, responsible for European Affairs;* b. 17 Aug. 1961, Prague; m. Martina Vondrova; three c. *Education:* Charles Univ. *Career:* worked at Naprstek Museum of Asian, African and American Cultures, Prague 1985–87; also active in Czechoslovakia's democratic opposition mid-1980s; fmr man. rock band Narodni trida; Spokesperson for Charter 77 1989; Co-founder Civic Forum movt 1989; Foreign Policy Adviser to Pres. Václav Havel 1990–92; First Deputy Minister of Int. Affairs 1992, First Deputy Minister of Foreign Affairs 1993–97, chief negotiator in process of preparing Czech-German Declaration 1995–96; Amb. to USA 1997–2001; Czech Govt Commr to Prague NATO Summit (coordinated Prague NATO Summit 2002) 2001–02; Deputy Minister of Foreign Affairs 2003; Asst Lecturer, German Marshall Fund 2003–04; Man. Dir Dutko Worldwide (consulting firm), Prague 2004–06; Minister of Foreign Affairs June–Oct. 2006 (resgnd); elected Senator (ODS) for Litoměřice, Roudnice and Slaný regions 2006; Deputy Prime Minister, responsible for European Affairs 2007–; Adjunct Prof., New York Univ. in Prague; Pres. Czech Euro-Atlantic Council; mem. Bd of Dirs Program of Atlantic Security Studies (PASS), Prague; Hon. Chair. Czech Euro-Atlantic Council 2004–06; Gold Plaque (Slovakia) 2001, Cross of Merit (Czech Repub.) 2002, Cross of Order of Merit (Poland) 2004, Commdr of the Three Stars (Latvia) 2005; US Nat. Endowment for Democracy Medal 1999, NATO Meritorious Service Medal 2005, Award for Human Understanding, Tolerance and Peace 2006.
Address: Office of the Government, náb. E. Beneše 4, 118 01 Prague 1, Czech Republic (office). *Telephone:* 224002111 (office). *Fax:* 224003090 (office). *E-mail:* posta@vlada.cz (office). *Website:* www.vlada.cz (office).

VORONIN, Vladimir Nikolayevich; Moldovan politician and head of state; *President;* b. 25 May 1941, Corjova, Chişinău Dist; m.; two c. *Education:* Tech. Coll., Chişinău, Union Inst. of the Alimentary Industry, Acad. of Social Sciences, Cen. CPSU Cttee, Acad. of Ministry of Internal Affairs. *Career:* bakery man., Criuleni 1961–66, Dubăsari 1966–71; fmr Deputy to Supreme Council, Moldovan SSR, First Sec., Party Cttee, Bender (Tighina) 1985–89, Minister of Internal Affairs, Moldovan SSR 1989–90; mem. Police Reserve, Russian Fed. 1989–93; Co-Pres. Organizational Cttee for Consolidation of CP 1993; revived CP Party of Moldova as Party of Communists of the Republic of Moldova 1994; presidential cand. (placed third) 1996; Deputy in Parl. Repub. of Moldova 1998; Pres. of Moldova 2001–.
Address: Office of the President, 2073 Chişinău, bd Ştefan cel Mare 154, Moldova (office). *Telephone:* (22) 23-47-93 (office). *E-mail:* president@prm.md (office). *Website:* www.president.md (office).

VOSGANIAN, Varujan, PhD; Romanian politician; *Minister of the Economy and Finance;* b. 25 July 1958, Craiova; m. Mihaela Vosganian; one d. *Education:* Acad. of Econ. Sciences, Bucharest and Bucharest Univ. *Career:* Assoc. Prof., Acad. of Econ. Sciences, Bucharest; Sr Researcher, Nat. Inst. of Economy; Deputy, Romanian Parl. 1990–96, Senator 1996–2000, 2004–, Chair. Cttee on Budget, Finances, Banking Activity and Capital Markets 1996–98; mem. Romanian Del. to Parl. Ass. of the Council of Europe (APCE) 2004–, mem. Political and Econ. Comms 2004–; Minister of the Economy 2006–, also of Finance 2007–; mem. Nat. Liberal Party (PNL), Vice-Pres. 2007–; Founding mem. Romanian Soc. of the Economy (SOREC); Vice-Pres. Romanian Writers Union 2005–; Hon. mem. Scientific Council, Nat. Inst. of Prognosis, Romania; Dr hc (Vasile Goldis Univ.) 2006, (Leibniz Univ., Milan) 2006; Special Prize for Poetry, Nichita Stanescu Int. Poem Festival 2006, Prize for Excellency for Contrib. to the Devt of Capital Markets in Romania, Bucharest Stock Exchange 2006, Prize for Contrib. to Devt of Romanian Science and Culture, Romanian Acad. 2006. *Publications include:* more then 500 econ., political and literary articles, studies, essays and poems.
Address: Ministry of the Economy and Finance, 050741 Bucharest 5, Str. Apolodor 17, Romania (office). *Telephone:* (21) 3199759 (office). *Fax:* (21) 3122509 (office). *E-mail:* presamfp@mfinante.gv.ro (office). *Website:* www.mfinante.ro (office); www.varujanvosganian.ro.

VOTO BERNALES, Jorge, BEcons, MA; Peruvian diplomatist; *Permanent Representative, United Nations;* b. 19 Jan. 1944, Lima; m.; three c. *Career:* Third Sec., Gen. Div. of Planning, Ministry of Foreign Affairs 1971, Chief of Cabinet to Sec.-Gen. of Foreign Affairs 1980, Dir of the Americas Gen. Div. of Political Affairs 1987–90, Dir-Gen. of Planning 1993, Dir-Gen. of Bilateral Political Affairs 1994–95, Vice-Minister and Sec.-Gen. of Foreign Affairs 1995–97; Perm. Rep. to UN, Geneva 1997–2004, also Vice Pres. Human Rights Comm., Chair. Agric. Cttee, WTO, Perm. Rep. to UNEP and UN Human Settlements Programme (non-resident) 1998–2004; Exec.-Sec., Fund for Peace and Devt Peru-Ecuador 2004–06; Perm. Rep. to UN, New York 2006–.
Address: Permanent Mission of Peru to the United Nations, 820 Second Avenue, Suite 1600, New York, NY 10017, USA (office). *Telephone:* (212) 687-3336 (office). *Fax:* (212) 972-6975 (office). *E-mail:* peru@un.int (office).

VRAALSEN, Tom Eric, MEcon; Norwegian diplomatist; *Special Envoy for Humanitarian Affairs for the Sudan, United Nations Department of Peacekeeping Operations;* b. 26 Jan. 1936, Oslo; m.; five c. *Education:* Århus School of Econs and Business Admin., Denmark. *Career:* joined Norwegian Foreign Service 1960; various diplomatic positions, Beijing 1962–64, 1969–70, Cairo 1964–67, Manila 1970–71, Jakarta 1971; in charge of Norwegian relations with Africa, Asia and Latin America, Political Dept, Ministry of Foreign Affairs 1971–73, in charge of UN and int. org. affairs 1973–75; Deputy Perm. Rep. to UN 1975–79, Perm. Rep. 1982–89; Dir-Gen. Political Dept, Ministry of Foreign Affairs 1981–82; Minister for Devt Co-operation, for Nordic Co-operation 1989–90; Sr Vice-Pres. Saga Petroleum 1991–92; Asst Sec.-Gen. Ministry of Foreign Affairs 1992–94; Amb. to UK 1994–96, to USA 1996–2001, to Finland 2001–03; UN Special Envoy for Humanitarian Affairs for the Sudan 1998–; Dr hc (Augustana Coll.) 2000. *Publications:* UN in Focus (co-author) 1975, The UN: Dream and Reality 1984.
Address: Department of Peace-Keeping Operations, Room S-3727-B, United Nations, New York, NY 10017, USA (office). *Telephone:* (212) 963-8079 (office). *Fax:* (212) 963-9222 (office). *Website:* www.un.org/Depts/dpko (office).

VRABIE, Vitalie; Moldovan politician; *Minister of Defence;* b. 2 Oct. 1964, Costuleni Village, Ungheni Dist; m.; two c. *Education:* Agricultural Inst., Chişinău, Acad. of Public Admin, Moscow. *Career:* began career as Sr Agronomist, Prut Farm; Dir JSV Garant-impex, Ungheni 1994–99; mem. Ungheni City Council 1995–99, fmr Dir Office of Chamber of Commerce and Industry; elected Mayor of Ungheni 1999, re-elected 2003; Chair. Asscn of Mayors and Local Communities 2003–06; fmr mem. Council of Europe Congress of Local and Regional Authorities, fmr Head Nat. Del.; Minister of Local Public Admin 2006–07; Minister of Defence 2007–.
Address: Ministry of Defence, 2021 Chişinău, şos. Hînceşti 84, Moldova (office). *Telephone:* (22) 25-22-22 (office). *Fax:* (22) 23-26-31 (office). *E-mail:* ministru@army.md (office). *Website:* www.army.gov.md (office).

VRANKIĆ, Dragan; Bosnia and Herzegovina politician; *Minister of Finance and the Treasury;* b. 23 Jan. 1955, Trebižatu; m.; three c. *Education:* Univ. of Dubrovnik. *Career:* fmr Gov. of Herzegovina-Neretva canton; Deputy Prime Minister and Minister of Finance, Fed. of Bosnia and Herzegovina 2003–07; Minister of Finance and the Treasury, Bosnia and Herzegovina 2007–.

Address: Ministry of Finance and the Treasury, 71000 Sarajevo, trg Bosne i Hercegovine 1, Bosnia and Herzegovina (office). *Telephone:* (33) 205345 (office). *Fax:* (33) 471822 (office). *E-mail:* trezorbih@trezorbih.gov.ba (office). *Website:* www.trezorbih.gov.ba (office).

VRBOŠIĆ, Josip, DrSci; Croatian academic and diplomatist; *Ambassador to Bosnia and Herzegovina;* b. 27 June 1951, Kršinci-Našice. *Career:* Prof., School of Law, Univ. of Osijek 1997–2001; Amb. to Bosnia and Herzegovina 2001–.
Address: Embassy of Croatia, Mehmeda Spahe 20, 71000 Sarajevo, Bosnia and Herzegovina (office). *Telephone:* (33) 444330 (office). *Fax:* (33) 472434 (office).

VUČINIĆ, Boro, PhD; Montenegrin politician; *Minister of Defence;* b. 1954, Podgorica; m.; four c. *Education:* Faculty of Law, Montenegrin State Univ. *Career:* started career at Titograd Civil Eng Org.; Dir Social Fund for Building Land, Business Premises and Roads; Deputy Municipal Ass. of Podgorica; mem. Parl. (Democratic Socialist Party), mem. Constitutional Affairs Cttee, Cttee for Drafting of Constitutional Charter of State Union of Serbia and Montenegro; Minister of Environmental Protection and Urban Planning 2004–06, of Defence 2006–; fmr Chair. Nat. Rifle Ass. of Yugoslavia; fmr Vice-Chair. Yugoslav Olympic Cttee; Head, Yugoslav Sports Del., Mediterranean Games 1997; Chair. Montenegrin Olympic Cttee.
Address: Ministry of Defence, Jovana Tomasevica 29, 81000 Podgorica, Montenegro (office). *Telephone:* (81) 483561 (office). *Fax:* (81) 224702 (office). *E-mail:* kabinet@mod.cg.yu (office). *Website:* www.vlada.cg.yu/odbrana (office).

VUJAČIĆ, Ivan, DEcon; Serbian diplomatist; *Ambassador to USA. Education:* Univ. of Belgrade, Univ. of Michigan, USA. *Career:* fmr Prof. of Econs, Univ. of Belgrade; joined Democratic Party 1990, served as first Pres. Bd of Econ. Advisors, mem. Exec. Cttee 1990–92, mem. Foreign Relations Cttee, Political Council 1993–97, Pres. local cttee, Belgrade 1995–2001, Pres. Political Council, mem. Presidency 2000–02; served as mem. of Parl. 1992–96; one of founders G17 group of ind. economists 1998; mem. Centre for Liberal Democratic Studies; Amb. to USA 2002–.
Address: Embassy of Serbia, 2134 Kalorama Road, NW, Washington, DC 20008, USA (office). *Telephone:* (202) 332-0333 (office). *Fax:* (202) 332-3933 (office). *E-mail:* ambassador@serbiaembusa.org (office). *Website:* www.serbiaembusa.org (office).

VUJANOVIĆ, Filip; Montenegrin politician, lawyer and head of state; *President;* b. 1 Sept. 1954, Belgrade, Serbia; m.; one s. two d. *Education:* Univ. of Belgrade. *Career:* began career with First Municipal Court; Official Assoc., Dist Attorney's Office, Belgrade 1978–80; Sec. to Dist Court, Titograd (now Podgorica) 1980–81, mem. Attorney's Chamber, Chair. Chamber 1989; Lawyer, private legal practice 1982–93; Minister of Justice, Repub. of Montenegro 1992–95, of the Interior 1995–98; Prime Minister of the Repub. of Montenegro, with responsibility for Religious Affairs 2001–02; Pres. Parl. Ass. 2002–; Pres. of Repub. of Montenegro 2003–; mem. Democratic Party of Socialists of Montenegro, currently Deputy Chair.
Address: Office of the President, 81000 Podgorica, Sveti Petar Cetinjski 3, Montenegro (office). *Telephone:* (81) 242388 (office). *Fax:* (81) 246608 (office). *E-mail:* predsjednik@cg.yu (office). *Website:* www.predsjednik.cg .yu (office).

VUKELIĆ, Branko; Croatian politician; *Minister of Defence;* b. 9 March 1958, Karlovac; m. Đurđica Vukelić; one c. *Education:* Faculty of Electrical Eng, Univ. of Zagreb. *Career:* project engineer, Chief of Preparation and Installation, EAB, Karlovac 1982–90; Man. INA Br. Office, Karlovac 1991–97; Pres. Karlovac City Croatian Democratic Union (CDU) Cttee 1993–; mem. Karlovac City Council 1993–97, 2001–, Mayor of Karlovac 1997–2001; Pres. Karlovac Co. CDU Cttee March 2002; Gen. Sec. CDU June 2002; Minister of Economy, Labour and Entrepreneurship 2003–08, of Defence 2008–.
Address: Ministry of Defence, Trg Petra Krešimira IV. br. 1, 10000 Zagreb, Croatia (office). *Telephone:* (1) 4567111 (office). *Fax:* (1) 4567963 (office). *E-mail:* infor@morh.hr (office). *Website:* www.morh.hr (office).

VUKIČEVIĆ, Stanimir; Serbian diplomatist; *Assistant Minister and Director-General for Bilateral Relations, Ministry of Foreign Affairs;* b. 28 May 1948, Djurakovac, Istok; m.; one c. *Career:* worked in Dept for Property and Legal Affairs, Ministry of Foreign Affairs 1978–83, Second Sec., Department for Africa and Middle East 1983–86; First Sec., Embassy in Mogadisho, Somalia 1986–90; Counsellor, Dept for S and Southeast Asia 1990–95; Minister Counsellor, Embassy in Tirana, Albania (Charge d'affaires a.i.) 1995–99; Amb. and Pres. Cttee for Cooperation with UNMIK and KFOR 1999–2000; Amb. to Bosnia and Herzegovina 2001–06; Asst Minister and Dir-Gen. for Bilateral Relations 2006–.
Address: Ministry of Foreign Affairs, 11000 Belgrade, Kneza Miloša 26, Serbia (office). *Telephone:* (11) 3615666 (office). *Fax:* (11) 3618366 (office). *E-mail:* mfa@smip.sv.gov.yu (office). *Website:* www.mfa.gov.yu (office).

VYAS, Sudhir; Indian diplomatist; *Ambassador to Bhutan;* b. 1953. *Career:* joined the foreign service 1977, has held diplomatic posts in Cairo, Algiers, Nepal, Islamabad, Mission to UN, New York; Deputy Sec. for Bhutan, Ministry of External Affairs 1984–86; Amb. to UAE –2005, to Bhutan 2005–.
Address: Embassy of India, India House, Jungshina, Thimphu, Bhutan (office). *Telephone:* (2) 322162 (office). *Fax:* (2) 323195 (office). *E-mail:* hocbht@druknet.bt (office).

W

WADE, Abdoulaye; Senegalese lawyer and head of state; *President;* b. 29 May 1926, Saint-Louis; m.; two c. *Education:* Univs of Besançon and Dijon, France, Univ. of Dakar. *Career:* fmr univ. teacher of law in Senegal and abroad; barrister, Court of Appeal, Senegal; Founder and Pres., Senegalese Democratic Party 1974–; mem. Parl. 1974–; Minister of State 1991–92, 1995–97; Pres. of Senegal 2000–; mem. Int. Acad. of Trial Lawyers; Commander, Order of Merit (Senegal); Grand Officer, Légion d'Honneur; UNESCO Félix Houphouët-Boigny Peace Prize 2005. *Publications:* author of several books and essays on law, economics and political science. *Address:* Office of the President, Avenue Léopold Sédar Senghor, BP 168, Dakar, Senegal (office). *Telephone:* 823-10-88 (office). *Website:* www.gouv .sn/institutions/president (office).

WAENA, Sir Nathaniel Rahumaea, GCMG; Solomon Islands politician and government official; *Governor-General; Career:* Minister of Prov. Govt and Rural Devt *c.* 2001; Minister for Nat. Unity, Reconciliation and Peace –2004; Gov.-Gen. Solomon Islands 2004–; Patron St Martins, Tenar 2004, Stuyvenberg Rural Training Centre, Nana 2006, Pawa Prov. Secondary School Fund Raising Drive 2007; Solomon Island Cross (CSI), KStJ. *Address:* Office of the Governor-General, Honiara, Solomon Islands (office).

WAGNER, Ann Louise, BS; American diplomatist; *Ambassador to Luxembourg;* m. Ray Wagner; two s. one d. *Education:* Univ. of Missouri-Columbia (vocal music scholarship). *Career:* served for nine years as a local cttee-woman in Lafayette Township, Mo.; Co-Chair. Republican Nat. Cttee; Chair. Mo. Republican Party for six years; held man. positions at Hallmark Cards, Kansas City, Mo., Ralston Purina, St Louis, Mo.; served on bds of Campfire USA, St Louis Children's Hosp., Catholic Charities of Archdiocese of St Louis; active in St Louis Forum, United Way, American Red Cross, St Patrick's Center for Homeless; Amb. to Luxembourg 2005–. *Address:* Embassy of the USA, 22 Blvd Emmanuel Servais, 2535 Luxembourg, Luxembourg (office). *Telephone:* 46-01-23 (office). *Fax:* 46-14-01 (office). *Website:* luxembourg.usembassy.gov (office).

WAGNER TIZÓN, Allan; Peruvian politician and diplomatist; b. 7 Feb. 1942, Lima; m. Julia de la Guerra Urquiaga; five d. *Education:* Nat. Univs of Trujillo and of Engineering, Lima, Universidad Católica and Universidad de San Marcos. *Career:* joined Ministry of Foreign Affairs 1963; joined Diplomatic Service 1968; Chief of Econ. Dept, Embassy in Washington, DC 1972–74, Deputy Chief of Mission and Chargé d'affaires 1983–85; Chief of Political Dept, Embassy in Chile 1978–79; Minister of Foreign Affairs 1985–88, 2002–03; Amb. to Spain 1988–90, to Venezuela 1991–92 (resgnd); Prof. Diplomatic Acad. 1991; Dir of Devt and Adviser to Latin American Econ. System (SELA) 1992–98; Founder-mem. Peruvian Centre of Int. Studies (CEPEI), Pres. 1999–; Founder-mem. Inst. of European–Latin American Relations (IRELA); Amb. to USA 2001–02; Adviser to Sec.-Gen. of Andean Community of Nations –2002, Sec.-Gen. 2004–06; Minister of Defence 2006–07; Del. of Peru, Int. Court of Justice trying land and maritime boundary dispute with Chile 2007–; Orden Bernardo O'Higgins (Chile) 2001, Orden en el Grado de Gran Cruz (Chile) 2001, Gran Cruz de la Orden El Sol del Perú, Orden al Mérito por Servicios Distinguidos. *Address:* c/o Ministry of Defence, Avda Arequipa 291, Lima 1, Peru.

WAJED, Sheikh Hasina; Bangladeshi politician; *President, Awami League;* b. 28 Sept. 1947, Tungipara, Gopalganj Dist, E Pakistan (now Bangladesh); m. M. A. Wazed Miah; one s. one d. *Education:* Univ. of Dhaka. *Career:* active in politics as a student; arrested during civil war 1971; assumed leadership of opposition Awami League from her father, first elected Pres. 1981, fifth time in 2002–; lived in exile 1975–81; arrested and placed under house arrest on several occasions during 1980s; Prime Minister of Bangladesh 1996–2001, also Minister of the Armed Forces Div., of the Cabinet Div., of Special Affairs, of Defence, of Power, Energy and Mineral Resources and of the Establishment; charged with corruption and alleged plundering of state funds while in office Dec. 2001; Leader of official parl. opposition 2001–; arrested on extortion charges July 2007; shared Houphouet-Boigny Peace Prize 1999. *Publications:* several books and numerous articles.

Address: Bangladesh Awami League (AL), 23 Bangabandhu Avenue, Dhaka, Bangladesh (office). *E-mail:* president@albd.org (office). *Website:* www.albd.org (office).

WALD, Patricia McGowan, LLB; American lawyer and judge; b. 16 Sept. 1928, Torrington, Conn.; m. Robert L. Wald 1952; two s. three d. *Education:* Connecticut Coll. for Women, Yale Law School. *Career:* Law Clerk, US Court of Appeals for the Second Circuit 1951–52; Assoc., Arnold, Fortas and Porter (law firm), Washington, DC 1952–53; mem. Nat. Conf. on Bail and Criminal Justice 1963–64; Consultant, Nat. Conf. on Law and Poverty 1965; mem. President's Comm. on Crime in the Dist of Columbia 1965–66, on Law Enforcement and Admin. of Criminal Justice 1966–67; Attorney, Office of Criminal Justice, US Dept of Justice 1967–68, Neighborhood Legal Services Program 1968–70; Co-Dir, Ford Foundation Drug Abuse Research Project 1970; Attorney, Center for Law and Social Policy 1971–72, Mental Health Law Project 1972–77; Asst Attorney for Legis. Affairs, Dept of Justice 1977–79; Circuit Judge, US Court of Appeals for the DC Circuit 1979–99, Chief Judge 1986–91; First Vice-Pres. American Law Inst. 1993–98; mem. Exec. Bd CEELI (ABA) 1994–97; Judge Int. Criminal Tribunal for Fmr Yugoslavia, The Hague, Netherlands 1999–2001; Chair. Open Soc. Inst. Justice Initiative 2002–04, now mem. Bd of Dirs; Commr, Pres.'s Comm. on Intelligence Capabilities of US Regarding Weapons of Mass Destruction 2004–05; numerous hon. degrees including Hon. LLD (Yale) 2001; August Voelmer Award, American Soc. of Criminology 1976, Woman Lawyer of the Year, Women's Bar Asscn 1984; Sandra Day O'Connor Medal of Honor (Seton Hall Law School) 1993; Margaret Brent Award for Distinguished Women in the Legal Profession 1994, American Inns of Court Award for Ethics 2003, American Lawyer Lifetime Achievement Award 2004. *Publications:* Bail in the United States (with Daniel J. Freed) 1964, Law and Poverty: Report to the Nat. Conf. on Law and Poverty 1965, Bail Reform: A Decade of Promise Without Fulfillment, Vol. 1 1972, Dealing with Drug Abuse: A Report to the Ford Foundation (with Peter Barton Hutt) 1972, Juvenile Detention in 'Pursuing Justice for the Child' 1977, The Rights of Children and the Rites of Passage in 'Child Psychiatry and the Law' 1980, Provisional Release at the ICTY: A Work in Progress in Essays on ICTY, Procedure and Evidence 2001; and numerous learned articles and contribs to journals. *Address:* 2101 Connecticut Avenue, NW, Apartment 38, Washington, DC 20008, USA (home). *Telephone:* (202) 232-1158 (home). *Fax:* (202) 232-2360 (home). *E-mail:* patwald2@cs.com (home).

WALDECK, Pieter Willem; Dutch diplomatist; *Ambassador to UK;* b. 6 Nov. 1947, The Hague; m. Cordula Catharina Agatha Quarles van Ufford 1976; one s. two d. *Education:* secondary school in The Hague, Leiden Univ. *Career:* mem. Bd (for sales and publicity) Dutch Student Travel Agency (NBBS) –1973; mil. service in Royal Netherlands Navy 1973–75, trained as interpreter/trans. in Russian at Harderwijk and Amsterdam, worked for naval intelligence service, left Navy with rank of Lt, Special Services 1975; joined Ministry of Foreign Affairs 1975, served in Embassies in Moscow (Political and Cultural Affairs), Bangkok (Devt Co-operation) and Cairo (Trade Promotion); Pvt. Sec. to HM Majesty Queen Beatrix and HRH Prince Claus 1984–88; Head of EC External Relations Section, European Integration Dept, Ministry of Foreign Affairs 1988–92; Counsellor at Perm. Representation of the Netherlands to EU, Brussels, responsible for Community relations with Mediterranean countries and with European Parl. 1992–97; Head of Information and Communication Dept and Spokesman for two successive Ministers of Foreign Affairs 1997–2000; Grand Master Royal Household and Counsellor to HM Queen Beatrix 2002–06; Amb. to UK 2007–. *Address:* Embassy of The Netherlands, 38 Hyde Park Gate, London, SW7 5DP, England (office). *Telephone:* (20) 7590-3200 (office). *Fax:* (20) 7225-0947 (office). *E-mail:* london@netherlands-embassy.org.uk (office). *Website:* www.netherlands-embassy.org.uk (office).

WALDRON, Arthur, PhD; American academic; *Lauder Professor of International Relations, University of Pennsylvania;* b. 13 Dec. 1948, Boston, Mass.; m.; two s. *Education:* Harvard Univ., Mass., Leningrad State Univ., Russia, Nat. Normal Univ., Taiwan. *Career:* Mellon Fellow, Princeton Univ. 1980; Visiting Fellow, Inst. of SE Asian Studies, Singapore 1983; Fellow in Chinese Studies, American Council of Learned Socs 1984–85; Asst Prof. of

History and East Asian Studies, Princeton Univ. 1985–91; Prof. of Strategy and Policy, US Naval War Coll. 1991–97; Adjunct Prof. of East Asian Studies, Brown Univ., RI 1992; Research Assoc., Harvard Univ. Olin Inst. for Strategic Studies 1994–, Harvard Univ. Fairbank Center for East Asian Research 1994–; Dir of Asian Studies American Enterprise Inst. 1996–2003; Lauder Prof. of Int. Relations, Univ. of Pennsylvania 1997–; Commr US–China Security Review Comm., US Congress 2001–; consultant Defense Policy Bd, Office of Sec. of Defense; mem. Editorial Bds War in History, American Asian Review, Int. History Review; Visiting Fellow, The Heritage Foundation; adviser and fmr mem. Nat. Security Advisory Council, Center for Security Policy; mem. Bd Freedom House, Jamestown Foundation. *Publications include:* The Great Wall of China: From History to Myth 1989, The Modernization of Inner Asia (ed.) 1991, How the Peace Was Lost: The 1935 Memorandum "Developments Affecting American Policy in the Far East" 1992, From War to Nationalism: China's Turning Point 1924–1925 1995; numerous academic and popular articles and reviews. *Address:* Department of History, University of Pennsylvania, College Hall 311C, Philadelphia, PA 19104-6379, USA (office). *Telephone:* (215) 898-6565 (office). *Fax:* (215) 473-2089 (office). *E-mail:* awaldron2@mac.com (office). *Website:* www.history.upenn.edu (office).

WALES, HRH The Prince of; (Prince Charles Philip Arthur George), (Earl of Chester (cr.1958), Duke of Cornwall, Duke of Rothesay, Earl of Carrick, Baron Renfrew, Lord of the Isles and Great Steward of Scotland (cr.1952), KG, KT, GCB, OM, PC, MA; b. 14 Nov. 1948, London; m. 1st Lady Diana Spencer (subsequently Diana, Princess of Wales) 29 July 1981 (divorced 28 Aug. 1996, died 31 Aug. 1997); two s., HRH Prince William Arthur Philip Louis, b. 21 June 1982, HRH Prince Henry Charles Albert David, b. 15 Sept. 1984; m. 2nd Camilla Parker Bowles (subsequently The Duchess of Cornwall) 9 April 2005. *Education:* Cheam School, Gordonstoun School, Geelong Grammar School, Trinity Coll. Cambridge and Univ. Coll. of Wales, Aberystwyth. *Career:* mem. Gray's Inn 1974, Hon. Bencher 1975; Personal ADC to HM the Queen 1973–; Capt. RN 1988, Rear Adm. 1998–, Vice-Adm. 2002–; Maj.-Gen. Army 1998–, Lt-Gen. 2002–; Group Capt. RAF 1988–, Air Vice-Marshal 1998–, Air Marshal 2002–; Col-in-Chief The Royal Regt of Wales (24th/41st Foot) 1969–; Col Welsh Guards 1975–; Col-in-Chief The Cheshire Regt 1977–, Lord Strathcona's Horse (Royal Canadian) Regt 1977–, The Parachute Regt 1977–, The Royal Australian Armoured Corps 1977–, The Royal Regt of Canada 1977–, The Royal Winnipeg Rifles 1977–, Royal Pacific Islands Regt, Papua New Guinea 1984–, Royal Canadian Dragoons 1985–, Army Air Corps 1992–, Royal Dragoon Guards 1992–, Royal Gurkha Rifles 1994–; Deputy Col-in-Chief The Highlanders (Seaforth, Gordons, Camerons) 1994–; Air Cdre-in-Chief RNZAF 1977–; Col-in-Chief Air Reserve 1977–; Pres. Soc. of St George's and Descendants of Knights of the Garter 1975–; Adm. Royal Thames Yacht Club 1974–; High Steward, Royal Borough of Windsor and Maidenhead 1974–; Chair. The Mountbatten Memorial Trust 1979–, The King's Fund 1986; Pres. The Prince's Trust 1976–, The Prince's Scottish Youth Business Trust, Business in the Community 1985, Prince of Wales's Foundation for Architecture and the Urban Enviroment 1992–, Prince of Wales's Business Leaders Forum 1990–; Chancellor, Univ. of Wales 1976–; mem. Bd Commonwealth Devt Corpn 1979–89; Hon. Pres. Royal Acad. Trust 1993–; Trustee Gurkha Welfare Trust 1989; Patron Royal Opera, Oxford Centre for Islamic Studies 1993–, British Orthopaedic Asscn 1993–, Royal Coll. of Music 1993–, Nat. Gallery 1993–, ActionAid 1995–, Help the Aged 1997–, Welsh Nat. Opera 1997–, Guinness Trust 1997–; represented HM the Queen at Independence Celebrations in Fiji 1970, at Requiem Mass for Gen. Charles de Gaulle 1970, at Bahamas Independence Celebrations 1973, at Papua New Guinea Independence Celebrations 1975, at Coronation of King of Nepal 1975, at funeral of Sir Robert Menzies 1978, at funeral of Jomo Kenyatta 1978, at funeral of Rajiv Gandhi 1990, at funeral of King Olav of Norway 1991; Pres. Royal Ballet, Birmingham Royal Ballet 2003–; Hon. FRCS 1978; Hon. FRAeS 1978; Hon. FIMechE 1978; Royal Fellowship of the Australian Acad. of Science 1977; Hon. Fellow, Trinity Coll. Cambridge 1989; Hon. mem. Hon. Company of Master Mariners 1977 (Master 1988), Company of Merchants of City of Edinburgh 1979; Hon. Life mem. Incorporation of Gardeners of Glasgow 1987; Hon. Air Cdre RAF Valley 1993–; received Freedom of City of Cardiff 1969, of Royal Borough of New Windsor 1970, of City of London 1971, of Chester 1973, of City of Canterbury 1978, of City of Portsmouth 1979, of City of Lancaster 1993, of City of Swansea 1994; Liveryman of Fishmongers' Co. 1971; Freeman of Drapers' Co. 1971; Freeman of Shipwrights' Co. 1978; Hon. Freeman and Liveryman of Goldsmiths Co. 1979, Liveryman of Farmers' Co. 1980, of Pewterers' Co. 1982, of Fruiterers' Co. 1989; Hon. Liveryman of Worshipful Co. of Carpenters 1992; Grand Cross of The Southern Cross of Brazil 1978, Grand Cross of The White Rose of Finland 1969, Grand Cordon of the Supreme Order of the Chrysanthemum of Japan 1971, Grand Cross of The House of Orange of the Netherlands 1972, Grand Cross Order of Oak Crown of

Luxembourg 1972, Kt of The Order of Elephant of Denmark 1974, Grand Cross of The Order of Ojasvi Rajanya of Nepal 1975, Order of the Repub. of Egypt (First Class) 1981; Grande Croix, Légion d'honneur 1984; Order of Mubarak the Great of Kuwait 1993; cr. Prince of Wales and Earl of Chester (invested July 1969); KG 1958 (invested and installed 1968), KT 1977, PC 1977, GCB and Great Master of Order of the Bath 1975; Dr hc (Royal Coll. of Music) 1981; Hon. DCL (Durham) 1998; Spoleto Prize 1989, Author of the Year 1989, Premio Fregene 1990, Coronation Medal 1953, The Queen's Silver Jubilee Medal 1977, Global Environmental Citizen Prize 2007. *Publications:* The Old Man of Lochnagar 1980, A Vision of Britain 1989, HRH The Prince of Wales Watercolours 1990, Urban Villages 1992, Highgrove: Portrait of an Estate 1993, Prince's Choice: A Selection from Shakespeare by the Prince of Wales 1995, Travels with the Prince 1998, The Garden at Highgrove (with Candida Lycett Green) 2000, The Elements of Organic Gardening (with Stephanie Donaldson) 2007. *Address:* Clarence House, London, SW1A 1BA; Highgrove House, Doughton, Nr Tetbury, Gloucestershire, GL8 8TN, England. *Website:* www.princeofwales.gov.uk (office).

WAŁĘSA, Lech; Polish fmr politician and trade union activist; b. 29 Sept. 1943, Popowo; m. Danuta Wałęsa 1969; four s. four d. *Education:* primary and tech. schools. *Career:* electrician, Lenin Shipyard, Gdańsk 1966–76, 1983–; Chair. Strike Cttee in Lenin Shipyard 1970; employed Zremb and Elektromontaż 1976–80; Chair. Inter-institutional Strike Cttee, Gdańsk Aug.–Sept. 1980; Co-Founder and Chair. Solidarity Ind. Trade Union 1980–90, Chair. Nat. Exec. Comm. of Solidarity 1987–90; interned 1981–82; Founder of Civic Cttee attached to Chair. of Solidarity 1988–90; participant and Co-Chair. Round Table debates 1989; Pres. of Polish Republic 1990–95, Chair. Country Defence Cttee 1990–95, Supreme Commdr of Armed Forces of Polish Republic for Wartime 1990–95; Founder of Lech Wałęsa Inst. Foundation 1995; Founder Christian Democratic Party of the Third Republic (ChDTRP) 1997, apptd Pres. 1998, Chair. –2000, Hon. Chair. 2000–; retd from politics; resgnd from Solidarity 2006; Order of the Bath 1991, Grand Cross of Légion d'honneur 1991, Grand Order of Merit (Italy) 1991, Order of Merit (FRG) 1991, Great Order of the White Lion 1999, Orden Heraldica do Cristobal Colon 2001; 100 hon. doctorates including Harvard Univ. and Univ. of Paris; Man of the Year, Financial Times 1980, The Observer 1980, Die Welt 1980, Die Zeit 1981, L'Express 1981, Le Soir 1981, Time 1981, Le Point 1981; awarded Let Us Live Peace Prize of Swedish journal Arbetet 1981, Love International Award (Athens) 1981, Freedom Medal (Philadelphia) 1981, Medal of Merit (Polish American Congress) 1981, Free World Prize (Norway) 1982, Int. Democracy Award 1982, Social Justice Award 1983, Nobel Peace Prize 1983, Humanitarian Public Service Medal 1984, Int. Integrity Award 1986, Phila Liberty Medal 1989, Human Rights Prize, Council of Europe 1989, White Eagle Order (Poland) 1989, US Medal of Freedom 1989, Meeting-90 Award (Rimini) 1990, Path for Peace Award, Apostolic Nuncio to the UN 1996, Freedom Medal of Nat. Endowment for Democracy (Washington USA) 1999, Int. Freedom Award (Memphis USA), and other awards, orders and prizes. *Publications:* autobiogs: Droga nadziei (A Path of Hope) 1987, Droga do wolności (The Road to Freedom) 1991, The Struggle and the Triumph 1992, Wszystko co robię, robię dla Polski (Everything I Do, I Do for Poland) 1995. *Address:* Lech Wałęsa Institute Foundation, Al. Jerozolimskie 11/19, 00 508 Warsaw, Poland. *Telephone:* (22) 622 22 20 (office). *Fax:* (22) 625 14 14 (office). *E-mail:* sekretariat@ilw.org.pl (office). *Website:* www.ilw.org.pl (office).

WALI, Aminu Bashir; Nigerian diplomatist and business executive; b. 3 Aug. 1941, Kano; m.; two s. *Education:* School of Arabic Studies, Kano, Fed. Training Centre, Lagos, North-Western Polytechnic, N London Univ., Nat. Inst. for Policy and Strategic Studies, Kuru. *Career:* Co. Sec. to Sayen Nagari Co. Ltd 1962–69; Gen. Man., Nigerian Match and Chemical Industries, Kano 1969–72; Man. Dir, Intersales W Africa Ltd, Kano 1972–86; founding mem., Democratic Party of Nigeria (PDP), Deputy Nat. Chair. 1998; Special Adviser to Pres. on Nat. Ass. Matters 1999–2003; Perm. Rep. to UN, New York 2004–08; serves as Chair. for numerous cos including Philip Morris Nigeria Ltd, Int. Tobacco Co. Ltd, Int. Bank for W Africa Ltd, Nigerian Eng and Construction Co. Ltd; fmr Dir Barclays Bank of Nigeria Ltd, Nigeria Hotels Ltd, Nigerbras Shipping Line; mem. Nat. Inst. for Policy and Strategic Studies 1986; mem. Bd of Trustees, Democratic Party of Nigeria 1998. *Address:* c/o Ministry of Foreign Affairs, Maputo St, Zone 3, Wuse District, PMB 130, Abuja, USA (office).

WALKER, Neil, LLB, PhD; British academic; *Professor of European Law, European University Institute;* b. 5 July 1960; m.; three c. *Education:* Univ. of Strathclyde. *Career:* research work and part-time lecturing at Univ. of Strathclyde 1981–86; Lecturer, Faculty of Law, Univ. of Edin. 1986–92, Sr Lecturer 1992–95, Prof. of Legal and Constitutional Theory 1996–2006,

Hon. Tercentenary Prof. of Law 2007–; Visiting Prof., Univ. of Puerto Rico, Univ. of Tilburg 2000; Prof. of European Law European Univ. Inst. 2000–, Dean of Studies 2003–; mem. Ed. Bds Edin. Law Review, European Law Journal; mem. Ed. Cttee European Law series, Cambridge Univ. Press. *Publications:* Managing the Police: Law, Organisation and Democracy (jtly) 1986, The Scottish Community Charge (jtly) 1989, Edinburgh Essays in Public Law (co-ed.) 1991, Policing the European Union (jtly) 1996, Legal Aspects of the European Single currency (co-ed.) 1999, Policing in a Changing Constitutional Order 2000, Convergence and Divergence in European Public Law (co-ed.) 2002, Sovereignty in Transition (ed.) 2003, The Area of Freedom, Security and Justice (ed.) 2004.
Address: Via Giovanni Dupre, 19A, Fiesole, Toscana, Italy (home); European University Institute, Badi Fiesolana, Via del Roccettini 9, 50016, San Domenico di Fiesole, Italy (office). *Telephone:* (55) 4685529 (office). *Fax:* (55) 4685298 (office). *E-mail:* neil.walker@iue.it (office). *Website:* www.iue.it (office).

WALKLEY, R. Barrie; American diplomatist; b. Gasquet, Calif.; m. Annabelle Walkley; one s. one d. *Education:* Univ. of California, Santa Barbara, Univ. of California, Los Angeles, Univ. of Southern California. *Career:* Peace Corps volunteer in Somalia 1967–69; mem. Sr Foreign Service since 1982, rank of Minister-Counsellor, assigned to Yaoundé, Cameroon 1982, assignments at State Dept, has also served in Lahore, Pretoria and Islamabad, seconded to UN 1993, served as UN Spokesman in Mogadishu, Somalia, Deputy Chief of Mission, Embassy in Kinshasa 1998–2001, Amb. to Guinea 2001–04, to Gabon (also accred to São Tomé and Príncipe) 2004–07; Superior Honor Award, Presidential Performance Award, Meritorious Honor Award, Dir's Award for Writing on Public Diplomacy, US Information Agency.
Address: US Department of State, 2201 C Street NW, Washington, DC 20520, USA (office). *Telephone:* (202) 647-4000 (office). *Fax:* (202) 647-6738 (office). *Website:* www.state.gov (office).

WALL, Frank A., BCL, LLB, LLM; Irish public official and solicitor; *Director, Fisheries Policy, General Secretariat of Council, European Union;* b. 10 Oct. 1949, Limerick; m. Margot Hourigan 1977; three s. one d. *Education:* Mungret Coll., Limerick, Univ. Coll., Cork, Inc. Law Soc., Dublin and Free Univ. of Brussels. *Career:* Adviser Group of European Progressive Democrats, European Parl. 1974–79; Adviser to Minister for Agric., Dublin 1980; Nat. Dir of Elections 1982; Senator 1982–83; mem. Exec. Cttee, Irish Council of the European Movt 1980–91; Gen. Sec. Fianna Fáil 1981–91; mem. Bd, Friends of Fianna Fáil Inc., USA 1986–91; Chair. Irish Council of European Movt 1987–91; Co-Founder Inst. of European Affairs 1990, Chair. Brussels Br. 1998–2001; Dir Inter-Institutional Affairs, Council of the EU 1991–2004, Dir Fisheries Policy 2004–. *Publications:* European Regional Policy (with Sean Brosnan) 1978, Changing Balance between European Institutions 1999.
Address: Council of the European Union, rue de la Loi 175, 1048 Brussels, Belgium (office). *Telephone:* (2) 285-80-55 (office). *Fax:* (2) 285-82-61 (office). *E-mail:* frank.wall@consilium.europa.eu (office).

WALL, Marc M.; American diplomatist; m. Eunice S. Reddick; one s. one d. *Career:* career officer, Sr Foreign Service, with rank of Minister-Counselor, has served in Côte d'Ivoire and Zimbabwe, several assignments with Bureau of Econ. and Business Affairs, Special Asst to Under-sec. for Econ., Business, and Agricultural Affairs, several tours dealing with Asia, including Chief of Econ. Office, Mission to Taiwan and of Trade Unit, Embassy in Beijing, Deputy Dir Bureau of Asian and Pacific Affairs' Office of Econ. Policy, has also been mem. Sec. of State's Policy Planning Council, Dir Bureau of African Affairs' Econ. Policy Staff –2004, Amb. to Chad 2004–07, Diplomat in Residence, Univ. of Pennsylvania 2007–.
Address: US Department of State, 2201 C Street NW, Washington, DC 20520, USA (office). *Telephone:* (202) 647-4000 (office). *Fax:* (202) 647-6738 (office). *Website:* www.state.gov (office).

WALLACE, George W., Jr; Liberian diplomatist. *Career:* joined Dept of State (now Ministry of Foreign Affairs) 1954, numerous positions including Amb. to UK, to USA; Sr Amb.-at-Large –2006; Minister of Foreign Affairs 2006–07.
Address: c/o Ministry of Foreign Affairs, POB 10-9002, 1000 Monrovia, Liberia (office).

WALLACE, Helen, CMG, PhD, FBA; British professor of European studies; *Centennial Professor, European Institute, London School of Economics;* b. 25 June 1946, Manchester; m. William Wallace (now Lord Wallace of Saltaire) 1968; one s. one d. *Education:* Univs of Oxford, Bruges, Belgium and Manchester. *Career:* Lecturer in European Studies, UMIST 1974–78, Visiting Prof., Coll. of Europe, Bruges 1976–2001; in Public Admin., Civil Service Coll. 1978–85; mem. Planning Staff, FCO 1979–80; Head W European Programme, Royal Inst. of Int. Affairs 1985–92; Prof. of Contemporary European Studies and Dir Sussex European Inst., Univ. of Sussex 1992–2001, Professorial Fellow 2001–06; Dir Robert Schuman Centre for Advanced Studies, European Univ. Inst. 2001–06; Centennial Professor, European Inst., LSE 2006–; mem. Better Regulation Comm. 2006–07 mem. Acad. for Learned Socs for the Social Sciences 2000; Ordre nat. du Mérite 1996; Hon. LLD (Sussex) 2002; Hon. DLitt (Loughborough) 2004; Lifetime Achievement in European Studies, Univ. Asscn for Contemporary European Studies 2006. *Publications:* French and British Foreign Policies in Transition (co-author) 1990, The Wider Western Europe (ed.) 1991, The European Community: The Challenge of Enlargement (co-author) 1992, Participation and Policy-Making (co-author) 1997, Interlocking Dimensions of European Integration (ed.) 2001, Policy Making in the European Union (ed.) 2005, The Council of Ministers (co-author) 2006.
Address: Room J216, European Institute, London School of Economics, Houghton Street, London, WC2A 2AE, England (office). *Telephone:* (20) 7955-7301 (office). *Fax:* (20) 7955-7546 (office). *E-mail:* h.s.wallace@btopenworld.com (office); h.wallace@lse.ac.uk (office). *Website:* www.lse.ac.uk (office).

WALLACE OF SALTAIRE, Baron (Life Peer) cr. 1995, of Shipley in the County of West Yorkshire; **William John Lawrence Wallace,** BA, PhD; British academic; *Professor of International Relations, London School of Economics; Education:* Cambridge Univ., Cornell Univ., USA. *Career:* Dir of Studies, Royal Inst. of Int. Affairs 1978–90; Walter F. Hallstein Fellow St Antony's Coll., Oxford 1990–95; Prof. of Int. Studies, Central European Univ., Budapest 1994–97; currently Prof. of Int. Relations, LSE; nominated to House of Lords 1995, mem. European Union Cttee 1996–2001, Chair. Sub-Cttee on Justice and Home Affairs 1997–2000; Ordre pour le Mérite, France 1995. *Publications include:* Regional Integration: the West European Experience 1994, Integration in a Larger and More Diverse European Union (jtly) 1995, Policy-making in the European Union (jtly) 2000, Rethinking European Order: West European Responses, 1989–97 (jtly) 2001, Non-State Actors in International Relations (jtly) 2001.
Address: Department of International Relations, London School of Economics, Houghton Street, London, WC2A 2AE, England (office). *Telephone:* (20) 7955-7166 (office). *Fax:* (20) 7405-1305 (office). *E-mail:* w.wallace@lse.ac.uk (office). *Website:* www.lse.ac.uk (office).

WALLENBERG, Marcus; Swedish international organization executive; *Chairman, International Chamber of Commerce; Education:* Edmund A. Walsh School of Foreign Service, Georgetown Univ., USA. *Career:* fmr Dir Stora Feldmühle, Düsseldorf; Exec. Vice-Pres. Investor AB –1999, Pres. and CEO 1999–2005; Chair. Saab, Skandinaviska Enskilda Banken; Vice-Chair. L. M. Ericsson; mem. Bd of Dirs AstraZeneca, Electrolux, Stora Enso Oyj, Knut and Alice Wallenberg Foundation; Chair. ICC 2005–; fmr mem. Advisory Council Stanford Grad. School of Business, Founder Wallenberg Global Learning Center at Stanford Univ.; mem. Royal Swedish Acad. of Eng and Sciences; European Business Leadership Award, Stanford Business School Alumni Asscn 2003.
Address: International Chamber of Commerce, 38 cours Albert 1er, 75008 Paris, France (office). *Telephone:* 1-49-53-28-28 (office). *Fax:* 1-49-53-28-59 (office). *Website:* www.iccwbo.org (office).

WALLERSTEIN, Immanuel, PhD; American sociologist and academic; *Senior Research Scholar, Yale University;* b. 28 Sept. 1930, New York; m. Beatrice Wallerstein; three c. *Education:* Columbia Univ., New York. *Career:* Instructor to Assoc. Prof., Columbia Univ. 1958–71; Prof., McGill Univ., Montreal, Canada 1971–76; Pres. African Studies Asscn 1972–73; Pres. Comm. de Recherche, Centre Québécoise des relations internationales 1974–75; Visiting Dir of Studies, École des Hautes Études en Sciences Sociales, Paris, France 1975–76, 1980–81, 1983–95; mem. Scientific Cttee Istituto Int. di Storia Economica Francesco Datini, Prato, Italy 1977–; Distinguished Prof. of Sociology, Binghamton Univ. 1976–99 and Dir Fernand Braudel Center for the Study of Econs, Historical Systems and Civilizations 1976–2005; Sr Research Scholar, Yale Univ. 2000–; mem. Exec. Council Int. African Inst. 1978–84; mem. Bd of Dirs Social Science Research Council 1979–85; Chair. Gulbenkian Comm. on Restructuring of Social Sciences 1993–95; Pres. Int. Sociological Asscn 1994–98; Visiting Prof. at numerous univs; Ed. Review 1977–2005, Studies in Modern Capitalism 1979–; Fellow, American Acad. of Arts and Sciences 1998; Hon. LittD (York) 1995; Dr hc (Paris-Denis Diderot) 1976, (Univ. Libre de Bruxelles) 1996, (Universidad Nacional Autónoma de México) 1998, (ISCTE, Lisbon) 1999, (Benemérita Universidad Autónoma de Puebla) 1999, (Bucharest) 2001, (Alicante) 2002, (San Marcos) 2004, (Lund) 2005, (Higher School of Econs, Moscow) 2005, (Kharkov Nat. Univ., Ukraine) 2005, (Univ. of Coimbra, Portugal) 2006. *Publications include:* The Modern World-System (three vols) 1974, 1980, 1989, The Capitalist World-Economy 1979, Race, Nation, Class (with E. Balibar) 1991, Geopolitics

and Geoculture 1991, Unthinking Social Science 1991, After Liberalism 1995, Historical Capitalism, with Capitalist Civilization 1995, Open the Social Sciences 1996, El futuro de la civilización capitalista 1997, Utopistics: Or, Historical Choices of the Twenty-first Century 1998, The End of the World As We Know It: Social Science for the Twenty-first Century 1999, The Essential Wallerstein 2000, Decline of American Power 2003, Uncertainties of Knowledge 2004, Alternatives: The US Confronts the World 2004, World-Systems Analysis: An Introduction 2004, Africa: The Politics of Independence and Unity 2005, European Universalism: The Rhetoric of Power 2006, numerous others.
Address: Sociology Department, Yale University, PO Box 208265, New Haven, CT 06520-8265, USA (office). *Telephone:* (203) 432-3334 (office). *Fax:* (203) 432-6976 (office). *E-mail:* immanuel.wallerstein@yale.edu (office). *Website:* www.yale.edu/socdept/faculty/wallerstein.html; fbc.binghamton.edu/commentr.htm (office).

WALLSTRÖM, Margot; Swedish politician; *Vice-President and Commissioner for Institutional Relations and Communication Strategy, European Commission;* b. 28 Sept. 1954, Kåge, Västerbotten Co.; m. Håkan Wallström; two s. *Career:* Organizing Sec. Värmland br., Social Democratic Youth League; bank clerk, Sparbanken Alfa, Värmland 1977–79; Chief Accountant 1986–88; MP 1979–85; fmr mem. Värmland Co. Council, Directorate of Bd of Civil Aviation, Directorate of Nat. Environment Protection Bd etc.; Minister with responsibility for Ecclesiastical, Consumers, Equality and Youth Affairs, Ministry of Public Admin 1988–92; Minister of Cultural Affairs 1994–96, of Health and Social Affairs 1996–98; EC Commr for the Environment 1999–2004, Vice-Pres. and Commr for Institutional Relations and Communication Strategy 2004–; Chair. of Ministerial Initiative, Council of World Women Leaders 2007; Dr hc (Chalmers Univ.) 2001, (Mälardalen Univ.) 2004, (Univ. of Mass, Howell) 2005.
Address: Commission of the European Communities, 200 rue de la Loi, 1049 Brussels, Belgium (office). *Telephone:* (2) 2981800 (office). *Fax:* (2) 2981899 (office). *Website:* ec.europa.eu/commission_barroso/wallstrom/index.htm (office).

WALT, Stephen Martin, BA, MA, PhD; American academic; *Professor of International Affairs, John F. Kennedy School of Government, Harvard University;* b. 2 July 1955; m.; two c. *Education:* Stanford Univ., Univ. of Calif. *Career:* part-time mem. Professional Staff Center for Naval Analyses 1980–82; Research Fellow, Center for Science and Int. Affairs, Harvard Univ. 1981–84, now Prof. of Int. Affairs, Academic Dean, John F. Kennedy School of Govt 2002–06; Asst Prof., Princeton Univ. 1984–89; Resident Assoc., Carnegie Endowment for Int. Peace 1986–87; Guest Scholar Brookings Inst. 1988; Assoc. Prof., Univ. of Chicago 1989–95, Prof. 1995–99, Master, Social Sciences Collegiate Div. and Deputy Dean, Div. of Social Sciences 1996–99; Visiting Prof., Nanyang Tech. Univ. Singapore 2000; mem. Editorial Bds Security Studies, Foreign Policy, Bulletin of the Atomic Scientists, Columbia Int. Affairs Online Service, Journal of Cold War Studies; Co-Ed. Cornell Studies in Security Affairs; mem. American Political Science Asscn, Int. Studies Asscn, Soc. of Historians of American Foreign Relations, IISS. *Publications:* The Origins of Alliances 1987, Revolution and War 1996, Taming American Power: The Global Response to US Primacy 2006, The Israel Lobby and U.S. Foreign Policy (with John Mearsheimer) 2007; numerous articles and chapters in journals and books.
Address: John F. Kennedy School of Government, Harvard University, 79 John F. Kennedy Street, Cambridge, MA 02138, USA (office). *Telephone:* (617) 495-5712 (office). *Fax:* (617) 495-8963 (office). *E-mail:* stephen_walt@harvard.edu (office). *Website:* ksghome.harvard.edu (office).

WALTER, Andrew, DPhil; Australian academic; *Senior Lecturer in International Relations, London School of Economics;* b. 5 Sept. 1961. *Education:* Univ. of Western Australia, Univ. of Oxford, UK. *Career:* Tutor in Int. Relations, Univ. of Oxford 1985–86, Lecturer in Int. Relations, Lady Margaret Hall, Oxford 1987–88, Univ. Lecturer in Int. Relations and Fellow, St Anthony's Coll., Oxford 1990–97, European Studies Centre Fellow, Lecturer in Int. Trade and Finance, Univ. of Oxford Foreign Service Programme 1990–97; Assoc., European Mergers and Acquisitions Group, Leveraged Finance Group, JP Morgan, London 1987–90, JP Morgan Finance Program, New York, USA 1989; Sr Lecturer in Int. Relations and Dir MSc Politics of the World Economy Programme, LSE 1997–, London Academic Dir TRIUM Exec. MBA Programme, Dir Int. Relations Summer School Programme; Sr Visiting Fellow, Inst. of Defence and Strategic Studies, Nat. Technological Univ., Singapore 2001–02; other visiting fellowships include Univ. of British Columbia 1994, Int. Univ. of Japan 1994, Pacific Council on Int. Policy and Center for Int. Studies (Univ. of Southern Calif., Los Angeles) 1996. *Publications:* World Power and World Money; The Role of Hegemony and International Monetary

Order (revised edn) 1993; numerous articles on political economy of int. finance and investment and history of thought.
Address: Department of International Relations, London School of Economics, Room D507, Houghton Street, London, WC2A 2AE, England (office). *Telephone:* (20) 7955-6338 (office). *Fax:* (20) 7955-7446 (office). *E-mail:* a.walter@lse.ac.uk (office). *Website:* www.lse.ac.uk (office).

WALTZ, Kenneth N., PhD; American academic; *Adjunct Professor of Political Science, Columbia University; Education:* Columbia Univ., New York. *Career:* teaching positions at Swarthmore Coll., PA and Brandeis Univ., MA; fmrly Ford Prof. of Political Science, Univ. of Calif., Berkeley; Adjunct Prof. of Political Science, Columbia Univ. 1997–, currently also Sr Research Assoc., Saltzman Inst. of War and Peace Studies; Fellow, American Acad. of Arts and Sciences; Hon. degrees from Univ. of Copenhagen, Oberlin Coll., Nankai Univ. Heinz Eulau Award for Best Article 'Nuclear Mythos and Political Realities', American Political Science Review 1990, James Madison Award, American Political Science Asscn 1999. *Publications include:* Man, the State and War: A Theoretical Analysis 1959, Foreign Policy and Democratic Politics: the American and British Experience 1967, Theory of International Politics 1979, The Spread of Nuclear Weapons: A Debate (with Scott Sagan) 1995, The Spread of Nuclear Weapons: A Debate Renewed 2003.
Address: Institute of War and Peace Studies, Columbia University, 420 West 118th Street, New York, NY 10027, USA (office). *Telephone:* (212) 854-4573 (office). *Fax:* (212) 864-1686 (office). *Website:* www.columbia.edu (office).

WALUBITA, Sipakeli Keli, BA; Zambian police official, politician and diplomatist; *High Commissioner to India;* b. 23 Dec. 1943, Senanga; m. I. Walubita; four c. *Education:* Mongu and Munali Secondary Schools, Univ. of Zambia, Lusaka, Int. Police Acad., Washington DC, USA, Citizenship Coll., Kabwe, Nat. Inst. of Public Admin, Lusaka, Barclays Bank Training Schools, Lusaka. *Career:* Cadet Supt, Zambia Police 1968–74, Supt of Police and Second-in- Command, Luanshya Dist Police 1974–75, Sr Supt, Zambia Police Prin., Zambia Police Coll. 1975–78, Asst Commr of Police 1978–81, Police Sec., Office of the Sec. of Defence and Security, later Security Research Officer, Defence and Security Bureau 1981–85 (resgnd from Zambia Police Service); Bank Man., Barclays Bank (Z) Ltd, in charge of Security and Frauds Investigations 1985–89; Security Man. Consultant Founder Socrats Man. Consultancy, Lusaka 1989–90; Founding mem. Movt for Multiparty Democracy 1990, Interim Chair. Nat. Security Cttee 1990, Chair. 1991; First Minister of Environment and Natural Resources 1991–93; Minister of Works and Supply 1993–94, 1996–97, of Information and Broadcasting Services and Chief Government Spokesman 1994–95; re-elected mem. Parl. for Sinjembela Constituency, Shangombo Dist 1996; Minister of Foreign Affairs 1997–2002; High Commr to India (also accred to Malaysia, Myanmar, Nepal, Sri Lanka and the Maldives) 2004–, also accred to Singapore 2005–.
Address: High Commission of Zambia, D-5/4, Vasant Vihar, New Delhi, 110 057, India (office). *Telephone:* (11) 26145883 (office). *Fax:* (11) 26145764 (office). *E-mail:* zambiand@sify.com (office).

WALZER, Michael, BA, PhD; American academic, editor and writer; *Professor of Social Science, School of Social Science, Institute for Advanced Study;* b. 3 March 1935, New York, NY; m. Judith Borodovko 1956; two d. *Education:* Brandeis and Harvard Univs, Univ. of Cambridge, UK. *Career:* Asst Prof. of Politics, Princeton, NJ 1962–66; Assoc. Prof., Harvard Univ. 1966–68, Prof. of Govt 1968–80; Ed. Dissent 1964–; Prof. of Social Science, School of Social Science, Inst. for Advanced Study, Princeton, NJ 1980–; mem. Conf. on the Study of Political Thought, Soc. of Ethical and Legal Philosophy; mem. Editorial Bd Political Theory; Contributing Ed. The New Republic (weekly newsmagazine); mem. Bd of Govs Hebrew Univ.; Dr hc (Lawrence Univ.) 1980, (Brandeis Univ.) 1981, (Georgetown Univ.) 1992, (Kalamazoo Coll.) 1994, (Tel-Aviv Univ.) 2003, Brandeis Univ. Doctorate Alumni Award 2001; Fulbright Fellow, Univ. of Cambridge 1956–57, Harbison Award 1971. *Publications:* The Revolution of the Saints: A Study in the Origins of Radical Politics 1965, The Political Imagination in Literature (co-ed. with Philip Green) 1968, Obligations: Essays on Disobedience, War and Citizenship 1970, Political Action: A Practical Guide to Movement Politics 1971, Regicide and Revolution: Speeches at the Trial of Louis XVI (ed.) 1974, Just and Unjust Wars: A Moral Argument with Historical Illustrations 1977, Radical Principles: Reflections of an Unreconstructed Democrat 1977, Spheres of Justice: A Defense of Pluralism and Equality 1983, Exodus and Revolution 1985, Interpretation and Social Criticism 1987, The Company of Critics: Social Criticism and Political Commitment in the Twentieth Century 1988, Civil Society and American Democracy (selected essays in German) 1992, What it Means to be an American 1992, Thick and Thin: Moral Argument at Home and Abroad 1994, Pluralism, Justice and Equality (with David Miller) 1995, Toward a Global Civil Society (ed.) 1995, On Toleration 1997,

Arguments from the Left (selected essays in Swedish) 1977, Pluralism and Democracy (selected essays in French) 1997, Reason, Politics and Pasion (The Horkheimer Lectures, in German) 1999, The Jewish Political Tradition, Vol. 1 Authority (co-ed with Menachem Lorberbaum, Noam Zohar and Yair Lorberbaum) 2000, Exilic Politics in the Hebrew Bible 2001, War, Politics, and Morality (selected essays in Spanish) 2001, The Thread of Politics: Democracy, Social Criticism, and World Government (selected essays in Italian) 2002, Erklärte Kriege—Kriegserklärungen (selected essays in German) 2003, Arguing About War (selected essays and articles) 2004, Politics and Passion 2004; contribs to professional journals.
Address: School of Social Science, Institute for Advanced Study, Einstein Drive, Princeton, NJ 08540, USA (office). *Telephone:* (609) 734-8256 (office). *Fax:* (609) 951-4434 (office). *E-mail:* walzer@ias.edu (office). *Website:* www.sss.ias.edu/home/walzer.html (office).

WANG, Chen, MScS; Chinese journalist and editor; *President, Renmin Ribao (People's Daily);* b. 1950, Wen'an Co., Hebei Prov. *Education:* School of Postgradruate Studies, Chinese Acad. of Social Sciences, Beijing. *Career:* joined CCP CCP; fmr reporter, CCP Yijun Co. Cttee, CCP Yan'an Municipal Cttee, Shaanxi Prov.; reporter, Guangming Daily, then successively Ed., Dir Chief Ed.'s Office, Assoc. Chief Ed. 1982–95, Chief Ed. 1995–2000; Deputy Dir Dept of Propaganda, CCP Cen. Cttee 2000; Ed.-in-Chief Renmin Ribao (People's Daily) 2001–02, Pres. 2002–; mem. CPPCC Nat. Cttee 1998–2003; mem. 16th CCP Cen. Cttee 2002–.
Address: Renmin Ribao (People's Daily), 2 Jin Tai Xi Lu, Chao Yang Men Wai, Beijing 100733, People's Republic of China (office). *Telephone:* (10) 65092121 (office). *Fax:* (10) 65091982 (office). *E-mail:* info@peopledaily .com.cn (office). *Website:* www.people.com.cn (office).

WANG, Guangya; Chinese diplomatist; *Permanent Representative, United Nations;* b. 1950, Jiangsu Prov.; m.; one s. *Education:* Atlantic United Coll., Wales and London School of Econs, UK, Johns Hopkins Univ., USA. *Career:* mem. Dept of Translation and Interpretation, Ministry of Foreign Affairs (MFA) 1975–77; Attaché, Perm. Mission to UN, New York 1977–81, 1982–83; Counsellor 1988–92; Third Secretary, then Deputy Div. Chief, then Div. Chief, Dept of Int. Orgs and Confs, MFA 1983–88, Deputy Dir 1992–93, Dir 1993–98; Asst Minister of Foreign Affairs 1998–99, Vice-Minister (in charge of Depts of Int. Orgs, Arms Control, and Treaties and Law) 1999–2003; Amb., Perm. Rep. to UN, New York 2003–.
Address: Permanent Mission of the People's Republic of China to the UN, 350 East 35th Street, New York, NY 10016, USA (office). *Telephone:* (212) 655-6100 (office). *Fax:* (212) 634-7626 (office). *E-mail:* chinamission_un@ fmprc.gov.cn (office). *Website:* www.china-un.org (office).

WANG, Gungwu, CBE, PhD, FAHA; Australian historian, academic and university vice-chancellor; *Director, East Asian Institute, National University of Singapore;* b. 9 Oct. 1930, Indonesia; m. Margaret Lim Ping-Ting 1955; one s. two d. *Education:* Nat. Cen. Univ., Nanjing, Univ. of Malaya and Univ. of London. *Career:* Asst Lecturer Univ. of Malaya, Singapore 1957–59, lecturer 1959; lecturer, Univ. of Malaya, Kuala Lumpur 1959–61, Sr Lecturer 1961–63, Dean of Arts 1962–63, Prof. of History 1963–68; Rockefeller Fellow, Univ. of London 1961–62, Sr Visiting Fellow 1972; Prof. of Far Eastern History, ANU 1968–86, Prof. Emer. 1986–, Dir Research School of Pacific Studies 1975–80; Visiting Fellow, All Souls Coll. Oxford 1974–75; John A. Burns Distinguished Visiting Prof. of History, Univ. of Hawaii 1979; Rose Morgan Visiting Prof. of History, Univ. of Kansas 1983; Vice-Chancellor, Univ. of Hong Kong 1986–95; Chair. Inst. of E Asian Political Economy, Nat. Univ. of Singapore 1996–97, Dir East Asian Inst. 1997–; Distinguished Sr Fellow Inst. of Southeast Asian Studies, Singapore 1996–99, Distinguished Professorial Fellow 1999–2003; Fellow and Hon. Corresp. mem. for Hong Kong of Royal Soc. of Arts 1987–95; Pres. Australian Acad. of the Humanities 1980–83, Asian Studies Asscn of Australia 1978–80; Chair. Australia-China Council 1984–86, Environmental Pollution Advisory Cttee (Hong Kong) 1988–95, Council for the Performing Arts (Hong Kong) 1989–94, Asia-Pacific Council, Griffith Univ. 1997–2001, Inst. of Southeast Asian Studies, Singapore; mem. Exec. Council, Hong Kong 1990–92; Adviser Chinese Heritage Centre, Nanyang Tech. Univ. 1995–2000 (Vice-Chair.) 2000–, Southeast Asian Studies, Academia Sinica, Taipei 1994–; mem. Council Int. Inst. for Strategic Studies, London 1992–2001; mem. Nat. Arts Council, Singapore 1996–2000, Nat. Heritage Bd 1997–99 (Adviser 2000–), Nat. Library Bd 1997–2003; mem. Academia Sinica, Taipei, DD Social Science Research Council, NY 1999–; Foreign Hon. mem. American Acad. of Arts and Science; Hon. Fellow SOAS, London; Hon. Sr Fellow Chinese Acad. of Social Sciences, Beijing; Hon. Prof. Beijing Univ., Fudan Univ., Hong Kong Univ., Nanjing Univ., Tsinghua Univ.; Hon. DLitt (Sydney, Hull, Hong Kong); Hon. LLD (Monash, ANU, Melbourne); Hon. DUniv (Griffith, Soka). *Publications:* 21 books, including The Chineseness of China 1991, China and the Chinese Overseas 1991, Community and

Nation: China, South-East Asia and Australia 1992, Zhongguo yu Haiwai Huaren 1994, The Chinese Way: China's Position in International Relations 1995; Hong Kong's Transition: A Decade after the Deal (ed.) 1995, Global History and Migrations (ed.) 1997, The Nanhai Trade 1998, The Chinese Overseas: From Earthbound China to the Quest for Autonomy 2000, Joining the Modern World: Inside and Outside China 2000, Only Connect: Sino-Malay Encounters 2001, Don't Leave Home: Migration and the Chinese 2001, To Act is to Know: Chinese Dilemmas 2002, Bind Us in Time: Nation and Civilisation in Asia 2002, Anglo-Chinese Encounters since 1800: War, Trade, Science and Governance 2003, Ideas Won't Keep: the Struggle for China's Future 2003, Reform, Legitimacy and Dilemmas: China's politics and Society (ed.) 2003, Damage Control: the Chinese Communist Party in the era of Jiang Zeming (ed.) 2004, Diasporic Chinese Ventures 2004; also numerous articles on Chinese and South-East Asian history; Gen. Ed. East Asian Historical Monographs series.
Address: East Asian Institute, Block AS5, 7 Arts Link, National University of Singapore, Kent Ridge, Singapore 117571. *Telephone:* 7752033. *Fax:* 7793409. *E-mail:* eaiwgw@nus.edu.sg (office). *Website:* nus.edu.sg/ nusinfo/eai (office).

WANG, Jin-Pyng, BS; Taiwanese politician; *President of the Li-Fa Yuan (Legislative Yuan);* b. 17 March 1941, Kaohsiung Co.; m. Chen Tsai-Lien; one s. two d. *Education:* Nat. Taiwan Normal Univ. *Career:* mem. Legis. Yuan 1975–, various positions including Sec.-Gen. of KMT Caucus, Dir and Dir-Gen. Dept of Party–Govt Co-ordination, Convenor Finance Cttee 1981–88, Vice-Pres. 1993–99, Pres. Li-Fa Yuan (Legis. Yuan) 1999–; Vice-Chair. Cen. Policy Cttee of Kuomintang (KMT) 1990, Chair. Finance Cttee 1990–92; Vice-Chair. KMT 2000–; mem. CSC 1993–; Pres. Sino–Japanese Inter-Parl. Friendship Asscn 1992–99, Taiwan Maj. League of Professional Baseball 1997–2002, Volunteer Fire-Fighter Asscn of the ROC 1997–, Taiwan Foundation for Democracy 2003–; Chair. Nat. Biotech and Health Care Industries Promotion Cttee 2001–, Foundation for the Promotion of Biotech Industries Devt 2001–.
Address: Legislative Yuan, 1 Chuanshan S. Road, Taipei, Taiwan (office). *Telephone:* (2) 23586011/15 (office). *Fax:* (2) 23955317 (office). *Website:* www.ly.gov.tw.

WANG, Jisi, MA; Chinese professor of international relations; *Dean, School of International Studies, Peking University;* b. 1948, Guangzhou City. *Education:* Beijing Univ. *Career:* worked as herdsman, peasant and factory worker, Inner Mongolia and cen. China 1968–78; taught at Dept of Int. Politics, Peking Univ. 1983–91; Visiting Fellow, St Anthony's Coll., Oxford, UK 1982–83; Visiting Scholar, Univ. of Calif., Berkeley 1984–85; Visiting Assoc. Prof., Univ. of Michigan 1990–91; Sr Researcher and Dir Inst. of American Studies, Chinese Acad. of Social Sciences, Beijing 1991–2005; Pres. Inst. of Int. Studies, Peking Univ. 2005–; Dir Inst. of Int. and Strategic Studies, Party School of the Cen. Cttee, CCP; Guest Prof., Peking Univ., Tsinghua Univ.; Pres. Chinese Asscn for American Studies; Founding-mem. Pacific Council on Int. Policy, Los Angeles; mem. Int. Council Asia Soc., New York; mem. Advisory Council Center for NE Asian Policy Studies, Brookings Inst., Washington, DC; Adviser, Asia Center, Harvard Univ. *Publications include:* Yu lun xuan qu lun san bian 1988, Wang Jisi xue shu lun zhu zi xuan ji 1991, Yu Lunxuan hou ji 1994, Yu lun xuan qian ji 1993, Wang Jisi jiao shou gu dian wen xue lun wen xuan 1996, China-Japan-U.S.: Managing the Trilateral Relationship (co-author with Morton I. Abramowitz) 1998, China-Japan-U.S. Relations: Meeting New Challenges (co-author with Morton Abramowitz and Funabashi Yoichi) 2002, Rise of China and a Changing East Asian Order (co-author with Kokubun Ryosei) 2004.
Address: Office of the Dean, Institute of International Studies, Peking University, Beijing 100871, People's Republic of China (office). *Telephone:* (10) 6400-0228 (office). *Fax:* (10) 6400-0021 (office). *E-mail:* sis@pku.edu .cn (office). *Website:* www.sis.pku.edu.cn (office).

WANG, Luolin; Chinese economist; *Vice-President, Chinese Academy of Social Sciences;* b. June 1938, Wuchang City, Hunan Prov. *Education:* Beijing Univ. *Career:* joined CCP 1978; Asst Lecturer, Lecturer, Assoc. Prof., Amoy Univ. 1961–84; Deputy Dean, later Vice-Pres. Amoy Univ. 1984; Vice-Pres. Chinese Acad. of Social Sciences 1993–; Vice-Chair. State Academic Degrees Cttee 1999; Alt. mem. 13th CCP Cen. Cttee 1987–92, 14th CCP Cen. Cttee 1992–97, mem. 15th CCP Cen. Cttee 1997–2002; Hon. PhD (Hong Kong Lingnan Univ.). *Publications:* Blue Book of China's Economy (co-ed. annually).
Address: Chinese Academy of Social Sciences, Jianguomennei Dajie 5 Hao, Beijing 100732, People's Republic of China (office). *Telephone:* (10) 65137744 (office). *Fax:* (10) 65138154 (office). *E-mail:* wangll@cass.net .cn (office). *Website:* www.cass.net.cn (office).

WANG, Gen. Maorun; Chinese army officer; *Political Commissar, National Defence University;* b. May 1936, Rongcheng, Shandong Prov. *Education:* Mil. Acad. of the Chinese PLA. *Career:* joined PLA 1951, CCP 1956; staff officer, Qingdao Garrison 1962; various posts in a corps political dept 1969–73; Deputy Sec.-Gen. Political dept Jinan Mil. Region 1973–76; Dir of a corps political dept 1976–83; corps deputy political commissar 1983–85; Dir Political Dept PLA Lanzhou Mil. Region 1985–90; Deputy Political Commissar and Sec. CCP Comm. for Inspecting Discipline, Lanzhou Mil. Region 1990; Political Commissar, Nat. Defence Univ. 1990–; rank of Maj.-Gen. 1988, Lt-Gen. 1993, Gen. 1998; mem. 15th CCP Cen. Cttee 1997–2002; Del., 11th CCP Nat. Congress 1977–82.
Address: National Defence University, Beijing, People's Republic of China (office).

WANG, Mengkui; Chinese academic; *President, Development Research Centre of the State Council;* b. April 1938, Wenxian Co., Henan Prov. *Education:* Beijing Univ. *Career:* joined CCP 1956; Ed. Red Flag Magazine 1964–69; Assoc. Research Fellow then Research Fellow, Research Dept of Secr. CCP Cen. Cttee 1981–87; Exec. Vice-Dir Econs Research Centre of State Planning Comm. 1987; Deputy Dir Research Office of State Council 1990–95, Dir 1995–98, Dir Devt Research Centre of the State Council 1998–; Alt. mem. 14th CCP Cen. Cttee 1992–97, mem. 15th CCP Cen. Cttee 1997–2002.
Address: Development Research Centre of the State Council, Number 225, Chaoyangmen Nei Dajie, Beijing 100010, People's Republic of China (office). *E-mail:* drc@drc.gov.cn (office). *Website:* www.drc.gov.cn (office).

WANG, Qishan; Chinese economist and politician; *Vice-Premier, State Council;* b. July 1948, Tianzhen, Shanxi Prov. *Education:* Northwest China Univ. *Career:* Researcher, Modern History Inst., Chinese Acad. of Social Sciences 1982, Researcher, Secr. (Rural Policies Dept) CCP Cen. Cttee Politboro 1982; joined CCP 1983; Div. Head, Rural Devt Research Centre of State Council, Acting Dir then Dir Rural Devt Inst. 1982–87; Gen. Man. China Rural Trust and Investment Corpn 1988–89; Vice-Pres. Construction Bank of China 1989–93, Pres. 1994–97; Vice-Gov. People's Bank of China 1993–94, Gov. 1994 (Sec. CCP Party Cttee); Chair. of China Investment Bank 1994–97; Chair. China Int. Capital Corpn Ltd 1995–97; mem. CCP Standing Cttee Guangdong Prov. Cttee 1997–2000; Exec. Vice-Gov. Guangdong Prov. 1998–2000; Dir Econ. Restructuring Office of the State Council 2000–; Sec. Econ. System Reform Scheme Office, CCP Party Cttee 2000–02; Sec. CCP Hainan Prov. Cttee 2002–03; Chair. Standing Cttee Hainan Prov. People's Congress 2003; mem. Standing Cttee CCP Beijing Municipal Cttee 2003–, Deputy Sec. CCP Beijing Municipal Cttee 2003–; apptd Acting Mayor of Beijing 2003–04, elected Mayor and Exec. Chair. Beijing Organizing Committee for XXIX Olympiad and Deputy Sec. Leading Party Mems' Group 2004–07;; Alt. mem. 15th CCP Cen. Cttee 1997–2002, mem. 16th and 17th CCP Cen. Cttee 2002–07; mem. Political Bureau of CPC Cen. Cttee 2007–; Vice-Premier State Council and mem. Leading Party Members' Group 2008–.
Address: Office of the Vice-Premier, Great Hall of the People, West Edge, Tiananmen Square, Beijing, People's Republic of China (office). *Website:* english.gov.cn/links/statecouncil.htm (office).

WANG, Wenyuan; Chinese politician and economist; b. Feb. 1931, Huangpi, Hubei Prov. *Education:* Northeast China Inst. of Finance and Econs. *Career:* teaching asst, Lecturer, Assoc. Prof., Prof. and Pres. Econs Coll., Liaoning Univ. 1958–88; Deputy Sec.-Gen. CPPCC, Shenyang City Cttee, Liaoning Prov., 1982–88; mem. Standing Cttee CPPCC Liaoning Prov. Cttee 1982–92; Vice-Chair. Shenyang City Cttee Jiusan Soc. 1982–88, Liaoning Prov. Cttee Jiusan Soc. 1988–92, Cen. Jiusan Soc. 1988–; Vice-Gov. of Liaoning Prov. 1988–92; Deputy Procurator Gen. Supreme People's Procuratorate 1992–98; Vice-Pres. China Sr Procurators' Training Centre 1992–98; mem. 7th CPPCC Nat. Cttee 1988–93, 8th CPPCC Nat. Cttee 1993–98, 9th CPPCC Nat. Cttee 1998–2003; Pres. 6th Council of China Council for the Promotion of Peaceful Reunification 1999–.
Address: c/o National Committee of Chinese People's Political Consultative Conference, 23 Taipingqiao Street, Beijing, People's Republic of China (office).

WANG, Yi; Chinese diplomatist; *Vice-Minister for Foreign Affairs;* b. 1953, Beijing. *Career:* clerk, Asian Affairs Dept, Ministry of Foreign Affairs, subsequently served as Deputy Chief and Chief 1982–89; Counsellor, Embassy in Japan 1989–94; returned to Asian Affairs Dept as Deputy Chief 1994–95, Chief 1995–98, Asst to Minister for Foreign Affairs 1998–2001, Vice-Minister for Foreign Affairs 2001–04, 2007–; Amb. to Japan 2004–07.
Address: Ministry of Foreign Affairs, 225 Chaoyangmen Nan Dajie, Chaoyang Qu, Beijing 100701, People's Republic of China. *Telephone:* (10) 65961114 (office). *Fax:* (10) 65962146 (office). *E-mail:* webmaster@mfa.gov.cn (office). *Website:* www.fmprc.gov.cn (office).

WANG, Ying-Fan, BA; Chinese diplomatist and politician; *Vice-Chairman, Foreign Affairs Committee, National People's Congress;* m.; one d. *Education:* Beijing Univ. *Career:* on staff, Office of Chargé d'Affaires of People's Repub. of China, London 1964; joined Dept of Translation and Interpreting, Ministry of Foreign Affairs 1967; attaché, Embassy, Ghana then Embassy, Philippines; Deputy Div. Dir, Dept of Asian Affairs, Foreign Ministry 1978, Deputy Dir-Gen. 1988; Amb. to the Philippines 1988–90; Dir-Gen. Dept of Asian Affairs, Foreign Ministry 1990–94, Asst Foreign Minister 1994–95, Vice-Minister for Foreign Affairs 1995–2000; Perm. Rep. to UN 2000–03; currently Vice-Chair. Foreign Affairs Cttee, Nat. People's Congress.
Address: c/o Foreign Affairs Committee, National People's Congress, Great Hall of the People, Beijing, People's Republic of China (office).

WANG, Gen. Zuxun; Chinese army officer; *President, Academy of Military Science;* b. May 1936, Qujing, Yunnan Prov. *Career:* joined PLA 1951; Vice-Commdr, then Commdr Yunnan Mil. Command 1984–89; Commdr Army Group 1989–93; Vice-Pres. PLA Acad. of Mil. Science 1993–99, Pres. 1999–; rank of Gen. 2000.
Address: Xianghongqi, Beijing 100091, People's Republic of China (office).

WANGCHUCK, HM Dasho Jigme Khesar Namgyal, (The Druk Gyalpo — 'Dragon King'— of Bhutan), MPhil; b. 21 Feb. 1980. *Education:* Cushing Acad. and Wheaton Coll., USA, Magdalen Coll., Oxford, UK. *Career:* proclaimed Crown Prince Oct. 2004; succeeded to throne 14 Dec. 2006, on the abdication of his father; participated in official visits; Chair. Bhutan Trust Fund for Environmental Conservation; Pres. Bhutan-India Friendship Asscn; Chancellor Royal Univ. of Bhutan; Chief Patron Scouts Asscn of Bhutan; Patron Royal Soc. for the Protection of Nature, Bhutan Chamber of Commerce and Industry, India-Bhutan Foundation, European Convention of Bhutan Socs, Oxford Centre for Buddhist Studies, Bhutan Shooting Fed.; Red Scarf 2002.
Address: Royal Palace, Thimphu, Bhutan. *Website:* www.bhutan.gov.bt.

WANGCHUCK, HM Jigme Singye; Bhutanese fmr ruler; b. 11 Nov. 1955; m.; ten c. (including HM King Dasho Jigme Khesar Namgyal Wangchuck). *Education:* North Point, Darjeeling, Ugyuen Wangchuk Acad., Paro, also in UK. *Career:* Crown Prince March 1972; succeeded to throne 24 July 1972, crowned 2 June 1974, abdicated 14 December 2006; Chair. Planning Comm. of Bhutan 1972–; C-in-C of Armed Forces; Chair. Council of Ministers 1972–98.
Address: Royal Palace, Thimphu, Bhutan (office). *Website:* www.bhutan.gov.bt.

WANGCHUCK, Lyonpo Khandu, BA; Bhutanese politician; *Minister of Economic Affairs;* b. 24 Nov. 1950. *Education:* St Stephen's Coll., India. *Career:* Asst Sec., Ministry of Trade, Industry and Forests 1974, Deputy Dir 1976, Man. Dir Industrial Devt Corpn 1978, Dir of Trade and Commerce 1980–84; Dir of Agric. 1986, Dir Gen. 1987–89, Sec. 1989–1991; Sec. Royal Civil Service Comm. 1991–94; Prime Minister and Chair. 2001–02, 2006–July 2007 (resgnd); Minister of Trade and Industry 1998–2003, of Foreign Affairs 2003–07 (resgnd), of Econ. Affairs 2008–; mem. Nat. Ass. for Lamgong-Wangchang constituency; mem. Druk Phuensum Tshogpa party; fmr Chair. Bhutan Nat. Bank; Red Scarf 1987, Orange Scarf 1998, Coronation Medal 1999.
Address: Ministry of Economic Affairs, Tashichhodzong, POB 141, Thimphu (office); Jangsa, Shari Geog, Paro, Bhutan (home). *Telephone:* (2) 322211 (office). *Fax:* (2) 323617 (office). *E-mail:* kdorjee@druknet.bt (office). *Website:* www.mti.gov.bt (office).

WANIEK, Danuta, DJur; Polish politician and political scientist; b. 26 Oct. 1946, Włocławek; m. (husband deceased); two s. *Education:* Warsaw Univ., Institut für Höhere Studien und Wissenschaft, Vienna. *Career:* Inst. of Political Studies, Polish Acad. of Sciences (PAN) 1989–; mem. Polish United Workers' Party (PZPR) 1967–90; mem. Social Democracy of Polish Repub. (SDRP) 1990–; Deputy to Sejm (Parl.) 1991–2001, mem. Parl. Cttee of Nat. Defence; Chair. Women's Democratic Union 1990–; Deputy Minister of Nat. Defence 1994–95; Minister of State and Head of Chancellery of Pres. of Poland 1995–97; mem. Nat. Broadcasting Council 2001–, Pres. 2003–05; with Instytut Problemów Strategicznych 2007–; Krzyz Zaslugi (Cross of Merit). *Publications:* Compromise within the Political System of Germany: Partnership or Struggle? 1988, Constitution and Political Reality 1989, Debate over 'Little Constitution' (ed.) 1992, Creating New Constitutional Order in Poland (ed.) 1993.
Address: Instytut Problemów strategicznych, Al. Ujazdowskie 20/6, 00-478 Warsaw, (office); ul. Protazego 61, 03-606, Warsaw, Poland (home). *Telephone:* (22) 622-07-35 (office). *E-mail:* zarzad@ips.org.pl (office). *Website:* www.krrit.gov.pl (office).

WARD, Adam Patrick, BA, MA; British academic and think tank administrator; *President and Executive Director, US Office, International Institute for Strategic Studies (IISS);* b. 12 Aug. 1972, Liverpool. *Education:* Univ. of Warwick, Univ. of Salzburg, Austria. *Career:* Asia Pacific Ed. and Analyst, Oxford Analytica consulting firm 1997–2001; Sr Fellow for East Asian Security, IISS, London 2001–06, currently Pres. and Exec. Dir US Office of IISS, Washington, DC. *Publications include:* numerous articles on foreign policy, political and econ. issues affecting Asia-Pacific region. *Address:* International Institute for Strategic Studies— US, 1850 K Street, NW, Suite 300, Washington, DC 20006, USA (office). *Telephone:* (202) 659-1490 (office). *Fax:* (202) 296-1134 (office). *E-mail:* ward@iiss.org (office). *Website:* www.iiss.org (office).

WARDAK, Gen. Abdul Rahim; Afghan government official and military officer; *Minister of Defence;* b. 1945, Wardak Prov.. *Education:* Habibia High School, Ali Naser Acad. of Cairo, Egypt. *Career:* previous positions include Lecturer Cadet Univ., Asst of Protocol, Ministry of Defence, Mil. Attaché, India, Dir Mil. Officers Soc., Educ. Comm., Disarmament Program; apptd Chief of Army Staff 1992; fmr Deputy Minister of Defence, Minister of Defence 2004–. *Address:* Ministry of Defence, Shash Darak, Kabul, Afghanistan (office). *Telephone:* (20) 2100451 (office). *Fax:* (20) 2104172 (office).

WARE, Marilyn; American diplomatist; m.; three c. *Career:* Chair. American Water Works Co. 1988–2003; fmr mem. Econ. Advisory Bd RWE AG, Germany, Int. Advisory Council of Thames Water plc; Amb. to Finland 2006–08; fmr mem. Bd of Dirs The Vice-President's Residence Foundation, Int. Republican Inst.; fmr mem. Bd of Trustees American Enterprise Inst. for Public Policy Research, Washington, DC; fmr Vice-Chair. Eisenhower Fellowships Program, Phila; Chair. statewide study of early childhood care and educ. practices in Pa 2002; Co-Chair. Gov. of Pa Tom Ridge's successful election campaigns 1993, 1998; Co-founder Janus School, Lancaster Farmland Trust; fmr Hon. Pres. WaterAid America; Hon. LLD (Franklin & Marshall Coll., Lancaster, Pa) 2004. *Address:* US Department of State, 2201 C Street NW, Washington, DC 20520, USA (office). *Telephone:* (202) 647-4000 (office). *Fax:* (202) 647-6738 (office). *Website:* www.state.gov (office).

WARREN, David Alexander, CMG; British diplomatist; *Ambassador to Japan;* m. Pamela Warren. *Career:* began FCO career at S East Asian Dept 1975–76, Head of Recruitment Section, Personnel Policy Dept 1981–83, EC Dept (External) 1983–86, Asst Head of Far East Dept 1990–91, Head of China Hong Kong Dept 1998–2000, Dir Human Resources 2004–07; Second, later First Sec., Embassy in Tokyo 1976–81, First Sec. and Head of Chancery, Embassy in Nairobi 1987–90, Commercial Counsellor, Embassy in Tokyo 1993–98, Amb. to Japan 2008–; Dir Int. Div. Office of Science and Tech., Cabinet Office 1991–93; Dir UK Trade and Investment 2000–04. *Address:* British Embassy, 1 Ichiban-cho, Chiyoda-ku, Tokyo 102-8381, Japan (office). *Telephone:* (3) 5211-1100 (office). *Fax:* (3) 5275-3164 (office). *E-mail:* public-affairs.tokyo@fco.gov.uk (office). *Website:* www.uknow.or.jp (office).

WARREN-GASH, Haydon Boyd; British diplomatist (retd); b. 8 Aug. 1949; m. Caroline Emma Bowring; one s. one d. *Career:* joined FCO 1971, Latin America Dept 1971–72, Third Sec., Chancery, Ankara 1973–76, Rhodesia Dept 1976–77, Second Sec., Chancery, Madrid 1977–81, Perm. Under-Sec.'s Dept 1981–82, Pvt. Sec., Minister of State's Office 1982–85, Asst Head, Southern European Dept 1989–90, Deputy High Commr, Nairobi 1991–94, Head of Southern European Dept 1994–97, Amb. to Côte d'Ivoire (also accred to Liberia, Niger and Burkina Faso) 1997–2001, HIV/AIDS Special Project Coordinator 2001–02, Amb. to Morocco (also accred to Mauritania) 2002–05, to Colombia 2005–08. *Address:* c/o Foreign and Commonwealth Office, King Charles Street, London, SW1A 2AH, England. *Telephone:* (20) 7008-1500.

WASINONDH, Kitti; Thai diplomatist; *Ambassador to UK;* m. Nutchanart Wasinondh; one d. *Career:* Dir-Gen. Dept of Information, Ministry of Foreign Affairs –2007, Amb. to UK (also accred to Ireland) 2007–. *Address:* Embassy of Thailand, 29–30 Queen's Gate, London, SW7 5JB, England (office). *Telephone:* (20) 7589-2944 (office); (20) 7225-5500 (office). *Fax:* (20) 7823-7492 (office); (20) 7823-9695 (office). *E-mail:* csinfo@thaiembassyuk.org.uk (office). *Website:* www.thaiembassyuk.org.uk (office).

WÄSTBERG, Olof (Olle), BA; Swedish politician, writer and banker; *Director-General, Swedish Institute;* b. 6 May 1945, Stockholm; m. Inger Claesson 1968; two s. *Education:* Univ. of Stockholm. *Career:* Vice-Pres. Liberal Youth Sweden 1968–71; mem. Bd Liberal Party 1972–93, 1997–, Pres. Exec. Cttee 1982–83, teacher of political science, Univ. of Stockholm 1967–68; journalist, political Dept Expressen 1968–71, Ed. 1994–95;

Research Fellow, Business and Social Research Centre 1971–76; Pres. Akieframjandet 1976–82; mem. Parl. 1976–82; Pres. Swedish Newspaper Promotion Asscn 1983–91; Under-Sec. of State, Ministry of Finance 1991–93; Consul Gen. of Sweden in NY 1999–2004; Dir-Gen. Swedish Inst., Stockholm 2005–; Dir Stockholm Stock Exchange 1977–82, 1988–94; Pres. Nordic Investment Bank 1992–94; Chair. Bd Swedish Broadcasting Corpn 1996–99, Stockholm City Theatre 1998–99; mem. Govt comms on S African consumer politics, stock market and media; Gold Medal, Swedish Marketing Group 1982. *Publications:* books on African problems, immigration policies and economic topics; articles in professional journals. *Address:* Swedish Institute, Slottsbacken 10, Box 7434, 103 91 Stockholm (office); Bellmangatan 6, 11820 Stockholm, Sweden. *Telephone:* (8) 453-78-00 (office). *Fax:* (8) 20-72-48 (office). *E-mail:* margareta.engholm@si.se (office). *Website:* www.si.se (office).

WATHELET, Melchior, LenD, LLM; Belgian politician and judge; *Professor of European Law, Catholic University of Louvain;* b. 6 March 1949, Petit-Rechain; m.; one c. *Education:* Univ. of Liège, Harvard Univ., USA. *Career:* researcher, Univ. of Liège 1973–77; Sec. of State for Regional Economy (French Sector) and for Housing 1980–81; Minister of New Tech., Planning and Forestry (French Sector) 1981–85; Minister and Chair. French Regional Exec. responsible for New Tech., Foreign Affairs, Gen. Affairs and Personnel 1985–88; Deputy Prime Minister and Minister of Justice and of the Middle Classes 1988–92, Vice-Prime Minister 1992–95, Minister of Justice and of Economic Affairs 1992–95, of Nat. Defence June–Sept. 1995; Pres. Parti Social Chrétien (PSC) 1992–94; Judge, Court of Justice of the European Communities 1995–2003, later Pres. of the First Chamber, Judge Emeritus 2003–; currently Prof. of European Law, Catholic University of Louvain, Belgium; Visiting Prof. of European Law, Louisiana State Univ., USA 2003. *Address:* Catholic University of Louvain, International Law Department Charles De Visscher - Budg. INT, Place Montesquieu 2, 1348 Louvain-la-Neuve, Belgium (office). *Telephone:* 10-47-84-53 (office). *E-mail:* Melchior .Wathelet@uclouvain.be (office). *Website:* www.uclouvain.be/int (office).

WATT, James Wilfrid, CVO, BA, MA; British diplomatist; *Ambassador to Jordan;* b. 5 Nov. 1951; m. 1st Amal Saad Watt (died 1998); one s. one d.; m. 2nd; three step-c. *Education:* Univ. of Oxford. *Career:* worked for investment bank in London and as conf. interpreter in Spain; joined British Diplomatic Service in 1977, First Sec. (Political), Abu Dhabi 1981–85, served in UK Perm. Mission to UN, New York, responsible in Security Council for Middle East matters and UN Peacekeeping doctrine 1985–89, Deputy Head of UN Dept, FCO and Head, Human Rights Unit 1989–92, Deputy Head of Mission in Jordan 1992–96, Deputy High Commr, Islamabad (concurrently responsible for relations with Afghanistan) 1996–98, on sabbatical at SOAS, London 1999, Dir of Consular Services, FCO 2000–03, Amb. to Lebanon 2003–06, to Jordan 2006–. *Address:* British Embassy, PO Box 87, Abdoun, Ammam, 11118, Jordan (office). *Telephone:* (6) 5909200 (office). *Fax:* (6) 5909279 (office). *E-mail:* info@britain.org.jo (office). *Website:* www.britain.org.jo (office).

WATTS, Michael J., BSc, PhD; American academic; *Professor of Geography, University of California, Berkeley; Education:* Univ. Coll. London, Univ. of Mich. *Career:* Chair. Berkeley-Stanford African Studies Center 1980–84; served on African Studies Cttee of Social Science Research Council 1980–87; Nat. Science Foundation 1987–89; visiting appointments at Museum of Natural History, Smithsonian Inst., Univ. of Bergen, Univ. of Bologna, Penn State Univ.; currently Prof., Class of 1963 Chair in Undergraduate Studies and Chancellor's Prof., Univ. of California, Berkeley, fmr Dir Inst. of Int. Studies; Guggenheim Fellow 2003. *Publications:* Reworking Modernity 1992, Silent Violence 1993, Geographies of Global Change (co-ed.) 1995, Liberation Ecologies (co-ed.) 1995, Globalizing Agro-Food (co-ed.) 1997, Liberation Ecologies: Environment, Development, Social Movements 2004, Afflicted Powers 2005; numerous articles and chapters in scholarly journals and books. *Address:* Department of Geography, University of California, 555 McCone Hall, Berkeley, CA 94720, USA (office). *Telephone:* (510) 642-3902. *Fax:* (510) 642-3370 (office). *E-mail:* mwatts@berkeley.edu (office). *Website:* geography.berkeley.edu (office).

WAYNE, Earl Anthony, BA, MA, MPA; American diplomatist; *Ambassador to Argentina;* m.; one d. one s. *Education:* Harvard, Princeton and Stanford univs, Univ. of Calif., Berkeley. *Career:* joined the Foreign Service 1975, Special Asst to Secs of State Haig and Shultz 1981–83, Dir for Regional Affairs for Amb.-at-Large for Counter-Terrorism 1989–91, Dir for Western European Affairs, Nat. Security Council 1991–93, Deputy Asst Sec. for Europe and Canada, Dept of State 1996–1997, Prin. Deputy Asst Sec. for European Affairs 1997–2000, Asst Sec. of State for Econ. and Business Affairs 2000–06; overseas postings include First Sec., Embassy in Paris 1984–87, Deputy Chief of Mission, Mission to EU, Brussels 1993–96,

Amb. to Argentina 2006–; Nat. Security Corresp., Christian Science Monitor 1987–89; Presidential Distinguished Service Award 2001, Distinguished Honor Award, Dept of State 2005, Presidential Meritorious Service Award 2005.
Address: US Embassy, Colombia 4300, C1425GMN Buenos Aires, Argentina (office). *Telephone:* (11) 5777-4533 (office). *Fax:* (11) 5777-4212 (office). *E-mail:* BuenosAires-GSO@state.gov (office). *Website:* buenosaires.usembassy.gov (office).

WEALE, Martin Robert, CBE, MA, ScD; British economist; *Director, National Institute of Economic and Social Research;* b. 4 Dec. 1955, Barnet, Herts.. *Education:* Clare Coll., Cambridge. *Career:* Overseas Devt Inst. Fellow, Nat. Statistical Office, Malawi 1977–79; researcher and lecturer, Faculty of Econs and Politics, Univ. of Cambridge 1979–95, Econs Fellow, Clare Coll. 1981–95; Dir Nat. Inst. of Econ. and Social Research 1995–, Statistics Commr 2000–; mem. Bd for Actuarial Standards 2006–; Hon. Fellow, Inst. of Actuaries 2001; Hon. DSc (City Univ.) 2007. *Publications include:* Macroeconomic Policy: Inflation, Wealth and the Exchange Rate (co-author) 1989, Reconciliation of National Income and Expenditure (co-author) 1995, Econometric Modelling: Techniques and Applications (co-ed.) 2000; numerous journal articles.
Address: National Institute of Economic and Social Research, 2 Dean Trench Street, London, SW1P 3HE (office); 63 Noel Road, London, N1 8HE, England (home). *Telephone:* (20) 7654-1945 (office). *E-mail:* mweale@niesr.ac.uk (office). *Website:* www.niesr.ac.uk (office).

WEEFUR, Kronyanh M.; Liberian diplomatist; *Ambassador to Côte d'Ivoire; Career:* fmr Chargé d'Affaires, Rome, Italy, currently Amb. to Côte d'Ivoire.
Address: Embassy of Liberia, Immeuble La Symphonie, avenue Général de Gaulle, 01 BP 2514, Abidjan 01, Côte d'Ivoire (office). *Telephone:* 20-22-23-59 (office). *Fax:* 22-44-14-75 (office).

WEERAMANTRY, Christopher Gregory, BA, LLD; Sri Lankan judge; *Judge (ad-hoc), International Court of Justice;* b. 17 Nov. 1926, Colombo. *Education:* Univ. of London. *Career:* advocate Supreme Court of Sri Lanka 1948–65, Commr of Assize 1965–67, Justice of Supreme Court 1967–72; Sir Hayden Starke Prof. of Law, Monash Univ., Melbourne, Australia 1972–91, Prof. Emer. of Law 1991–; Judge Int. Court of Justice 1991–2000 (ad-hoc 1999–2000), Vice-Pres. 1997–99; lecturer and Examiner, Council of Legal Educ. 1951–56; mem. Council of Legal Educ. 1967–72; Visiting Prof. Univs. of Tokyo 1978, Stellenbosch 1979, Papua New Guinea 1981, Fla 1984, Lafayette Coll., Pa 1985, Hong Kong 1989; Hon. Visiting Prof. Univ. of Colombo 1984; Chair Comm. of Inquiry into Int. Responsibility for Phosphate Mining on Nauru 1987–88; mem. Editorial Bd Sri Lankan Journal of Int. Law, Human Rights Quarterly (Johns Hopkins Univ.), Interdisciplinary Peace Research (La Trobe Univ.), Journal of Ceylon Law; mem. Advisory Bd China Law Reports; Vice Chair. UN Centre against Apartheid/Govt. of Nigeria Conf. on Legal Status of Apartheid Regime, Lagos 1984; Co-ordinator UN Univ./Netherlands Inst. of Human Rights Workshop on Science, Tech. and Human Rights, Utrecht 1989; Assoc. Academician, Int. Acad. of Comparative Law, Paris; Vice-Pres. Int. Comm. of Jurists, Vic.; Past Pres. World Fed. of Overseas Sri Lankan Orgs.; Vice-Patron UN Asscn of Sri Lanka; Chair. Cttee of Chief Justices of Asia and Africa; mem. Europa Mundi (UNESCO project), Club of Rome (Australia), Commonwealth Lawyers' Asscn and other professional bodies; Hon. Life mem. Bar Asscn of Sri Lanka; Hon. LLD (Colombo), Dr. hc (Monash Univ.) 2000; Mohamed Sahabdeen Award for Int. Understanding in the SAARC Region 1993; Order of Deshamanya. *Publications:* numerous books on law, human rights and other topics; numerous articles in law journals worldwide and published lectures.
Address: 5/1 Roland Towers, Dharmaraja Mawatha, off Alfred House Avenue, Colombo 3, Sri Lanka. *Telephone:* (1) 555028. *Fax:* (74) 720480. *E-mail:* cgw@lanka.ccom.lk.

WEHBE, Mikhail, PhD; Syrian diplomatist and civil servant; *Permanent Observer of the League of Arab States, United Nations, Vienna;* b. 27 Feb. 1942, Damascus; m.; two c. *Education:* Univ. of Lebanon, Sofia Univ., Bulgaria. *Career:* Third Sec. Perm. Mission to UN, Geneva 1969–71; Second, then First Sec. Embassy in London, UK 1974–79, Counsellor, then Minister Counsellor in Bulgaria 1982–88; served at Ministry of Foreign Affairs, positions including Minister of State's Chief of Cabinet 1979–82, Chief of Pvt. Offices Dept, mem. Consultative Council for Admin. and Man. Affairs 1988–96; Rep. to UN Gen. Ass. 1992–95; Rep. to Summit Confs of Non-Aligned Movt, Indonesia and Colombia; Perm. Rep. to UN, New York 1996–2003, Pres. Security Council Aug. 2003, mem. Comm. on Human Rights 2003; Perm. Rep. to UN, Geneva 2003–05; Perm. Observer of the League of Arab States to UN, Vienna 2005–, Rep. of League of Arab States to Preparatory Comm. for the Comprehensive Nuclear-Test-Ban

Treaty Org. (CTBTO Preparatory Comm.) 2005–, Perm. Observer of League of Arab States to UNIDO 2005–.
Address: Permanent Delegation of the League of Arab States, c/o United Nations Office at Vienna (UNOV), Vienna International Centre, POB 500, 1400 Vienna, Austria (office). *Telephone:* (1) 26060 (office). *Fax:* (1) 263-33-89 (office). *Website:* www.arableagueonline.org (office).

WEIDENBAUM, Murray Lew, BBA, MA, PhD, LLD; American economist, academic and fmr government official; *Mallinckrodt Distinguished University Professor and Honorary Chairman, Weidenbaum Center on the Economy, Government and Public Policy, Washington University;* b. 10 Feb. 1927, Bronx, New York; m. Phyllis Green 1954; one s. two d. *Education:* City Coll. New York, Columbia Univ., New York and Princeton Univ. *Career:* Fiscal Economist, Budget Bureau, Washington, DC 1949–57; Corpn Economist, Boeing Co., Seattle 1958–62; Sr Economist, Stanford Research Inst., Palo Alto, Calif. 1962–63; mem. Faculty, Washington Univ., St Louis, Mo. 1964–, Dir of Center for Study of American Business at Washington Univ. 1975–81, 1982–95, Chair. 1995–2000, Prof. and Chair. Dept of Econs 1966–69, Mallinckrodt Distinguished Univ. Prof. 1971–; Asst Sec. for Econ. Policy, Treasury Dept, Washington 1969–71; Head, Council of Econ. Advisers, US Govt 1981–82; Chair. Research Advisory Cttee, St Louis Regional Industrial Devt Corpn 1965–69; Pres. Midwest Econ. Asscn 1985; Chair. US Trade Deficit Review Comm 1999–2000; Exec. Sec. Pres.'s Cttee on Econ. Impact of Defense and Disarmament 1964; mem. US Financial Investment Advisory Panel 1970–72; mem. Pres.'s Econ. Policy Advisory Bd 1982–89, Bd of Dirs Harbour Group Ltd 1982–, May Dept Stores Co. 1982–99, Tesoro Petroleum Corpn 1992–2002, Macroeconomic Advisers 1996–; consultant to various firms and insts; Fellow, Nat. Asscn of Business Economists, Int. Acad. of Management; mem. Acad. of Missouri Squires; Hon. Chair. Weidenbaum Center on the Econ., Govt and Public Policy 2001; Hon. Fellow Soc. for Tech. Communication; Townsend Harris Medal for Distinguished Achievement, City Coll. of NY 1970, Treasury Dept Alexander Hamilton Medal 1971, Distinguished Writer Award, Georgetown Univ. 1975, Free Market Hall of Fame 1983, Officier, Ordre nat. du Mérite 1985, Founder's Day Medal, Washington Univ. 1998. *Publications:* Federal Budgeting 1964, Economic Impact of the Vietnam War 1967, Modern Public Sector 1969, Economics of Peacetime Defense 1974, Government-Mandated Price Increases 1975, The Future of Business Regulation 1979, Business, Government and the Public 1990, Rendezvous with Reality: The American Economy After Reagan 1990, Small Wars, Big Defense 1992, Bamboo Network 1996, Business and Government in the Global Marketplace 2004, One-Armed Economist 2004; articles in econ. journals.
Address: Weidenbaum Center on the Economy, Government and Public Policy, Washington University, Box 1027, One Brookings Drive, St Louis, MO 63130 (office); 303 N Meramec No. 103, St Louis, MO 63105, USA (home). *Telephone:* (314) 727-8950 (home); (314) 935-5662 (office). *Fax:* (314) 935-5688 (office). *E-mail:* moseley@wc.wustl.edu (office). *Website:* wc.wustl.edu (office).

WEIDENFELD, Werner, DPhil; German political scientist and academic; *Professor of Political Science and Director, Center for Applied Policy Research, Geschwister Scholl Institute for Political Science, Ludwig-Maximilians-Universität München;* b. 2 July 1947, Cochem; m. Gabriele Kokott-Weidenfeld 1976. *Education:* Univ. of Bonn. *Career:* Prof. of Political Science, Univ. of Mainz 1976–95; Assoc. Prof., Sorbonne, Paris 1986–88; Co-ordinator for German-American Co-operation 1987–99; Prof. of Political Science, Ludwig-Maximilians-Universität München 1995–, Dir Centre for Applied Policy Research; Perm. Guest Prof., Remnim Univ., Beijing 2000–; mem. Exec. Bd Bertelsmann Foundation Gütersloh 1992–2007; Bundesverdienstkreuz (First Class) 1998, Commdr, Ordinul serviciul Credincios of the Repub. of Romania; Dr hc; Columbus Medal, German-American Soc., Munich 1991, Europe Medal (Bavaria) 1996, Bavarian Europe-Schoolbook Award 1997, Gen. Lucius D. Clay Medal, Assn of German-American Clubs 1998, World of Difference Award, Anti-Defamation League 1999, European Cultural Award, European Cultural Foundation 2001. *Publications:* Die Englandpolitik Gustav Stresemanns 1972, Konrad Adenauer und Europa 1976, Europa 2000 1980, Die Frage nach der Einheit der deutschen Nation 1981, Die Identität der Deutschen 1983, Die Bilanz der Europäischen Integration 1984, Nachdenken über Deutschland 1985, 30 Jahre EG 1987, Geschichtsbewusstsein der Deutschen 1987, Der deutsche Weg 1990, Jahrbuch der Europäischen Integration (ed.), Die Deutschen–Profil einer Nation 1991, Handwörterbuch zur deutschen Einheit 1992, Osteuropa: Herausforderungen-Probleme-Strategien 1992, Technopoly, Europa im globalen Wettbewerb 1993, Maastricht in der Analyse, Materialien zur Europäischen Union (ed.) 1994, Europa '96: Reformprogramm für die Europäische Union (ed.) 1994, Reform der Europäischen Union 1995, Kulturbruch mit Amerika? 1996, Handbuch zur deutschen Einheit 1996, Demokratie am Wendepunkt? (ed.) 1996, Europa öffnen–Anforderungen an die Erweiterung (ed.) 1997,

Aussenpolitik für die deutsche Einheit: Die Entscheidigungsjahre 1989/90 1998, Amsterdam in der Analyse: Strategien für Europa (ed.) 1998, Handbuch zur deutschen Einheit 1949–1989–1999 (ed.) 1999, Deutschland-Trendbuch (ed.) 2001, Herausforderung Terrorismus 2004, Wie Zukunft ensteht 2002, Europa-Handbuch (ed.) 2004, Die Europäische Verfassung in der Analyse (ed.) 2005, Managing Integration (ed.) 2005, Rivalität der Partner (ed.) 2005, Die Europäische Verfassung verstehen 2006, Partners at Odds 2006, Werte 2006, Understanding the European Constitution 2007, Europa leicht gemacht 2007, Reformen kommunizieren (ed.) 2007, Reformvertrag in der Analyse (ed.) 2008.
Address: Center for Applied Policy Research, Geschwister Scholl Institute for Political Science, Ludwig-Maximilians-Universität München, Maria-Theresia-Str. 21, 81675 Munich (office); Oettingenstr. 67, 80538 Munich, Germany. *Telephone:* (89) 21809040 (office). *Fax:* (89) 21809042 (office). *E-mail:* cap.office@lrz.uni-muenchen.de (office). *Website:* www.cap-lmu .de/english/index.php (office).

WEILER, Joseph H. H., BA, LLB, LLM, PhD; Israeli academic and lawyer; *Joseph Straus Professor of Law and Director, Jean Monnet Center for International and Regional Economic Law and Justice, New York University;* b. South Africa. *Education:* Sussex Univ., Univ. of Cambridge, UK, The Hague Acad. of Int. Law, European Univ. Inst. *Career:* mem. Law Dept, European Univ. Inst. 1978–85, Co-f. Acad. of European Law 1989; Prof. of Law, Univ. of Michigan 1985–92; Prof., Harvard Law School 1992–2001; currently Univ. Prof., New York Univ., also Joseph Straus Prof. of Law and EU Jean Monnet Chair, NYU School of Law, Chair. Hauser Global Law School Program and Dir Jean Monnet Center for Int. and Regional Econ. Law and Justice; also currently Prof., Coll. of Europe in Bruges, Belgium and Natolin, Poland; Hon. Prof., Univ. Coll. London, Univ. of Copenhagen; Co-Dir Acad. of Int. Trade Law, Macao; fmr. mem. Cttee of Jurists of the Inst. Affairs Cttee of European Parl.; Panel Mem. WTO; Founding Ed. European Journal of International Law, European Law Journal, World Trade Review; mem. Advisory Board or Scientific Cttee of Journal of Common Market Studies, Cahiers de Droit Européen, Common Market Law Review, European Foreign Affairs Review, Maastricht Journal of European and Comparative Law, Columbia Journal of European Law, Harvard International Review, Harvard Journal of International Law, (Australian) Federal Law Review, Journal of European Integration, European Foreign Policy Bulletin (online), ELSA-Selected Papers of European Law; Council Mem. Centre for European Econ. and Public Affairs, Univ. Coll., Dublin, Asscn for Hebraic Studies, AHS Inst.; mem. Bd Centre for Law of EU, Univ. Coll., London; Fellow, American Acad. of Arts and Sciences; Reporter, American Law Inst.; Dr hc (London, Sussex). *Publications:* The European Court and National Courts: Doctrine and Jurisprudence (co-ed.) 1998, Der Fall Steinmann 1998, Kompetenzen und Grundrechte (jtly) 1999, The Constitution of Europe: Essays on European Integration 1999, The EU, the WTO, and the NAFTA: Towards a Common Law of International Trade 2000, L'Italia in Europa (jtly) 2000. *Address:* Jean Monnet Center, NYU School of Law, Vanderbilt Hall, Room 109, 40 Washington Square South, New York, NY 10012, USA (office). *Telephone:* (212) 992-8912 (office). *Fax:* (212) 995-4343 (office). *E-mail:* weiler@jeanmonnetprogram.org (office). *Website:* www .jeanmonnetprogram.org (office).

WELCH, C. David, MA; American diplomatist; *Assistant Secretary, Bureau of Near Eastern Affairs;* b. 1953, Munich, Germany; m. Gretchen Gerwe Welch; three d. *Education:* London School of Econs, UK, Georgetown Univ., Washington, DC, Fletcher School of Law and Diplomacy, Tufts Univ., Medford, Mass. *Career:* Officer responsible for Syria, Bureau of Near Eastern Affairs and South Asian Affairs, Dept of State, Washington, DC 1981–82, for Lebanon 1982–83, Chief of Political Section, US Embassy, Damascus, Syria 1984–86, Political Counselor, US Embassy, Amman, Jordan 1986–88, mem. staff, Nat. Security Council, White House, Washington, DC 1989–91, Exec. Asst to Under-Sec. of State for Political Affairs 1991–92, Chargé d'Affaires, US Embassy, Riyadh, Saudi Arabia 1992–94, Deputy Chief of Mission 1994–95, Prin. Deputy Asst Sec., Bureau of Near Eastern Affairs 1995–98, Asst Sec. of State for Int. Org. Affairs 1998–2001, Amb. to Egypt 2001–05, Asst Sec., Bureau of Near Eastern Affairs 2005–; mem. Council on Foreign Relations, American Foreign Service Asscn; several State Dept Awards for exceptional service. *Address:* Bureau of Near Eastern Affairs, Office 6242, US Department of State, 2201 C Street, NW, Washington, DC 20520, USA (office). *Telephone:* (202) 647-7209 (office). *Website:* www.state.gov (office).

WELCH, Gen. Larry D., BA, MS; American research institute director and air force officer (retd); *President and CEO, Institute for Defense Analyses;* b. 1934, Guymon, Okla. *Education:* Univ. of Maryland, George Washington Univ., Armed Forces Staff Coll., Va, Nat. War Coll., Washington, DC. *Career:* enlisted in Kan. Nat. Guard 1951, served with 161st Armored Field Artillery; joined aviation cadet program, promoted to Second Lt 1953,

served as flight instructor 1953–58; assigned to HQ Air Training Command, Randolph Air Force Base, Tex. 1958; served in tactical fighter units in Europe, USA and Vietnam; Insp. Gen., then Deputy Chief of Staff for Plans and Deputy Chief of Staff for Operations, HQ Tactical Air Command 1977–81; Commdr Ninth Air Force and Air Force Component Commdr, Rapid Deployment Jt Task Force 1981; Deputy Chief of Staff for Programs and Resources, Air Force HQ 1982–84, Vice Chief of Staff 1984–85; promoted to Gen. 1984; C-in-C Strategic Air Command and Dir Jt Strategic Target Planning Staff, Offutt Air Force Base, Neb. 1985–86; Air Force Chief of Staff 1986–90; Pres. Inst. for Defense Analyses 1990–2003, Pres. and CEO 2006–; mem. Bd of Dirs Henry L. Stimson Center, Sandia Corpn; mem. Defense Science Bd; Defense Distinguished Service Medal, Distinguished Service Medal, Legion of Merit, Distinguished Flying Cross, Meritorious Service Medal, Air Medal, Air Force Commendation Medal, Jt Meritorious Unit Award, Air Force Outstanding Unit Award. *Address:* Institute for Defense Analyses, 4850 Mark Center Drive, Alexandria, VA 22311-1882, USA (office). *Telephone:* (703) 845-2000 (office). *Website:* www.ida.org (office).

WELLS, Barry Leon, BA, MA; American diplomatist; *Ambassador to The Gambia;* m. Winsome Wells; two d. *Education:* Fed. Exec. Inst., Exec. Seminar, Aspen Inst. *Career:* served as Country Dir for US Peace Corps in Belize followed by a tour in Jamaica; fmr Assoc. Prof. and Asst Dean, Howard Univ. Grad. School of Social Work, Washington, DC; has lectured at Univ. of Pittsburgh, Youngstown State Univ. and Univ. of the West Indies; career mem. Sr Exec. Service, joined Foreign Service Inst. (FSI), Dept of State 1988, assignments included Assoc. Dean of School of Professional and Area Studies, Assoc. Dean of Sr Seminar and The Leadership and Man. School, Deputy Dir FSI 2001–05, Acting Dir 2005–06; Dir Office of Civil Rights, Dept of State 2006–07, first Chief Diversity Officer 2007–08; Amb. to The Gambia 2008–; mem. Thursday Luncheon Group, Bd of Dirs Nat. MultiCultural Inst. *Address:* US Embassy, PMB 19, The White House, Kairaba Avenue, Fajara, Banjul, The Gambia (office). *Telephone:* 4392856 (office). *Fax:* 4392475 (office). *E-mail:* ConsularBanjul@state.gov (office). *Website:* www.usembassybanjul.gm (office).

WELLS, George; Ni-Vanuatu politician; *Minister of Foreign Affairs; Career:* fmr Minister of Internal Affairs, fmr Minister of Nat. Defence; Minister of Foreign Affairs 2007–; mem. Parl. for Luganville; fmr mem. Vanuaaku Pati party, currently mem. Nat. United Party. *Address:* Ministry of Foreign Affairs, PMB 051, Port Vila, Vanuata (office). *Telephone:* 27750 (office). *Fax:* 27832 (office). *Website:* www .vanuatugovernment.gov.vu (office).

WEN, Jiabao; Chinese party and state official; *Premier of State Council (Prime Minister);* b. Sept. 1942, Tianjin; m.; one s. one d. *Education:* Beijing Geological Coll. *Career:* joined CCP 1965; technician and political instructor, Geomechanics Survey Team, Gansu Prov. Geological Bureau, Ministry of Land and Resources 1968–1978, Deputy Head 1978–79; Engineer and Deputy Section Head, Gansu Prov. Geological Bureau 1979–81, Deputy Dir-Gen. 1981–82; Dir Reform Research Office of the Geological and Mining Bureau of the State Council 1982–83; Deputy Minister of Geology and Mining 1983–85; Deputy Dir, Gen. Office of 12th CCP Cen. Cttee 1985–86, Dir, Gen. Office of 13th and 14th CCP Cen. Cttee 1986–97; Alt. mem. Secr. of Cen. Cttee 1987; Sec. CCP Cen. Organs Working Cttee 1988; mem. 13th CCP Cen. Cttee 1987–92, 14th CCP Cen. Cttee 1992–97, Alt. mem. CCP Politburo 1992–97, mem. 1997–; Sec. Secr. of Cen. Cttee 1992; mem. 15th CCP Cen. Cttee 1997–2002, 16th CCP Cen. Cttee 2002–07 (mem. Standing Cttee of the Politburo 2002–07), 17th CCP Cen. Cttee 2007– (mem. Standing Cttee of the Politburo 2007–); Sec. Financial Work Cttee of Cen. Cttee 1998–2002; Vice-Premier State Council 1998–2003, Premier State Council (Prime Minister), People's Repub. of China 2003–. *Address:* Office of the Premier, Great Hall of the People, West Edge, Tiananmen Square, Beijing, People's Republic of China (office). *Website:* www.gov.cn (office).

WENAWESER, Christian; Liechtenstein diplomatist; *Permanent Representative, United Nations;* b. 16 Nov. 1963, Zurich, Switzerland. *Education:* Gymnasium Freudenberg, Zurich, Zurich Univ., Institut Universitaire de Hautes Etudes Internationales, Geneva, Switzerland. *Career:* teaching asst, Zurich Univ. 1987–88; Swiss Nat. Foundation Scholarship, Bayerische Akad. der Wissenschaften, Munich, Germany 1989–90; diplomatic training, Ministry of Foreign Affairs, Bern, Switzerland and Perm. Mission of Liechtenstein to UN, New York 1991–92, later Desk Officer (Human Rights, Disarmament, Int. Law), First Sec. (based at Office for Foreign Affairs, Vaduz) 1992–98, Counsellor and Deputy Perm. Rep. 1998–2002, Perm. Rep. 2002–; Chair. Third Cttee of Gen. Ass., 57th Session 2002–03,

ad hoc Cttee on the Scope of Protection of UN Personnel 2003–, Special Working Group on the Crime of Aggression 2003–; Pres. Meeting of States Parties of the Convention on the Rights of the Child Feb. 2003; Vice-Chair. Open-Ended Working Group of the Questions on Security Council Report 2004–.
Address: Permanent Mission of Liechtenstein to the UN, 633 Third Avenue, 27th Floor, New York, NY 10017, USA. *Telephone:* (212) 599-0220 (office). *Fax:* (212) 599-0064 (office). *E-mail:* liechtenstein@un.int (office). *Website:* www.un.int/liechtenstein (office).

WENDT, Alexander, BA, PhD; American professor of political science; *Ralph D. Mershon Professor of International Security, Department of Political Science, Ohio State University;* b. 1958, Mainz, Germany. *Education:* Macalester Coll., Univ. of Minnesota. *Career:* Asst Prof., Dept of Political Science, Yale Univ. 1989–95, Assoc. Prof. 1995–97; Assoc. Prof., Dept of Govt, Dartmouth Coll. 1997–99; Assoc. Prof. of Political Science, Univ. of Chicago 1999–2004; Ralph D. Mershon Prof. of Int. Security, Dept of Political Science, Ohio State Univ. 2004–. *Publications include:* Social Theory of International Politics 1999, Kurt Biedenkopf: Ein Politisches Porträt; various articles on int. relations theory.
Address: Department of Political Science, Ohio State University, 2105 Derby Hall, 154 North Oval Mall, Columbus, OH 43210, USA (office). *Telephone:* (614) 292-9219 (office). *Fax:* (614) 292-1146 (office). *E-mail:* wendt.23@osu.edu (office). *Website:* psweb.sbs.ohio-state.edu/faculty/wendt (office).

WENSLEY, Penelope Anne, AO, BA; Australian diplomatist; *Governor of Queensland;* b. 18 Oct. 1946, Toowoomba; m. Dr Stuart McCosker 1974; two d. *Education:* Univ. of Queensland. *Career:* diplomatic service 1968–, Paris 1969–72, Mexico City 1975–77, Wellington, NZ 1982–85, Consul Gen. Hong Kong 1986–88; Head Int. Orgs. Div., Dept of Foreign Affairs and Trade 1991–92, Perm. Rep. to UN, Geneva 1993–95, also Amb. for Environment, UN 1992–95, Head N Asia Div. 1996–97; Perm. Rep. to UN, New York 1997–2002; High Commr to India 2002–04; Amb. to Bhutan 2002–04, to France (also accred to Algeria, Mauritania, Morocco, Monaco) 2005–08; Gov. of Queensland 2008–; Sr Adviser, Australian del. to UN Conf. on Environment and Devt 1992; Vice-Pres. World Conf. on Human Rights, Vienna 1993; Vice-Chair. UN Climate Change Convention Negotiations 1993–96; Coordinator Western Group Negotiations on UN Conventions on Biodiversity and Desertification 1994–96; Chair. Preparatory Process UN Conf. for the Sustainable Devt of Small Island Developing States 1993–94; Chair. Int. Coral Reef Initiative Conf. 1995; Vice-Chair. UN Inst. for Training and Research; mem. WHO High Level Advisory Council on Health and the Environment; Chair. UN Gen. Ass. Fifth Cttee (Admin. and Budgetary) 1999; Co-Chair. Preparatory Process for UN Gen. Ass. Special Session on HIV/AIDS 2001; Patron UN Youth Asscn of Australia; Fellow, Women's Coll., Univ. of Queensland; Adjunct Prof. Univ. of Queensland 2000; Hon. PhD, Alumnus of the Year (Univ. of Queensland) 1994.
Address: Government House, GPOB 434, Brisbane, Queensland, 4001, Australia (office). *Telephone:* (7) 3858-5700 (office). *Fax:* (7) 3858-5701 (office). *E-mail:* govhouse@govhouse.qld.gov.au (office). *Website:* www.govhouse.qld.gov.au (office).

WERLEIGH, Claudette Antoine; Haitian politician, educator, lawyer and organization official; *Secretary-General, Pax Christi International;* b. 26 Sept. 1946, Cap-Haitien; m. Georges Werleigh; two d. *Career:* worked for Caritas (Catholic aid org.) 1976–87; Minister of Social Affairs March–Aug. 1990, of Foreign Affairs 1993–95; Prime Minister of Haiti 1995–96; Rep. to OAS summit 1998; Dir of Conflict Transformation Programmes, Life and Peace Inst., Uppsala, Sweden –2007; Sec.-Gen. Pax Christi International 2007–; fmr Vice-Pres. Pax Christi Int.; fmr Bd mem. Forum on Early Warning and Early Response (FEWER), London, UK.
Address: Pax Christi International, 21 rue Vieux Marche aux Grains, 1000 Brussels, Belgium (office). *Telephone:* (2) 502-55-50 (office). *Fax:* (2) 502-46-26 (office). *E-mail:* claudette@paxchristi.net (office). *Website:* www.paxchristi.net (office).

WESSELS, Wolfgang, Dr rer. pol; German academic; *Professor of European Politics, University of Cologne;* b. 19 Jan. 1948, Cologne; m. Aysin Wessels 1973; two d. *Career:* Dir Institut für Europäische Politik, Bonn 1973–94; Dir Admin. Studies and Prof., Coll. of Europe, Bruges, Belgium 1980–96; Jean Monnet Prof., Univ. of Cologne 1994–; Jean Monnet – European Studies GOLD Lifelong Learning Award, European Comm. 2007. *Publications include:* The European Council, Decision-Making in European Politics (with Simon Bulmer) 1987; Co-Ed.: Die Europäische Politische Zusammenarbeit in den achtziger Jahren—Eine gemeinsame Aussenpolitik für Westeuropa? 1989, Jahrbuch der Europäischen Integration 1980–, Europa vom A–Z. Taschenbuch der Europäischen Integration 1991–, Foreign Policy of the European Union. From EPC to CFSP and Beyond

1997, Die Öffnung des Staates. Modelle und Wirklichkeit grenzüberschreitender Verwaltungspraxis 2000, Das politische System der Europäischen Union. Die institutionelle Architektur des EU-Systems 2008; papers and articles on European integration.
Address: Forschungsinstitut für Politische Wissenschaft und Europäische Fragen, University of Cologne, Gottfried-Keller-Strasse 6, 50931 Cologne, Germany (office). *Telephone:* (221) 4704131 (office). *Fax:* (221) 9402542 (office). *E-mail:* wessels@uni-koeln.de (office). *Website:* www.politik.uni-koeln.de/wessels (office).

WESTCOTT, Nicholas James, CMG, BA, PhD; British diplomatist; *High Commissioner to Ghana;* b. 20 July 1956; m. Miriam Pearson 1989; one s. one d. *Education:* Epsom Coll., Univ. of Dar es Salaam, Tanzania (Research Assoc.), Sidney Sussex Coll., Cambridge. *Career:* joined FCO 1982, with Cultural Relations Dept 1982–84; secondment to EC (DG VIII), Brussels 1984–85, First Sec., Perm. Rep. to the European Communities 1985–89; with Europe Communities Dept (Internal), FCO 1990–91, European Corresp. and Head of Common Foreign and Security Policy Unit 1992–93; Deputy High Commr, Dar es Salaam 1993–96; Head of Econ. Relations Dept, FCO 1996–98, Counsellor, Resource Planning Dept 1999; Minister-Counsellor (Trade and Transport), Embassy in Washington, DC 1999–2002; Chief Information Officer, FCO 2002–07; High Commr to Ghana (also accred as Amb. to Cote d'Ivoire, Burkina Faso, Niger and Togo) 2008–. *Publications:* Managed Economies in World War II (with G. Teidemans) 1983; numerous articles on African and Commonwealth history in various journals.
Address: British High Commission, Osu Link, off Gamel Abdul Nasser Avenue, PO Box 296, Accra, Ghana (office). *Telephone:* (21) 221665 (office). *Fax:* (21) 7010650 (office). *E-mail:* high.commission@accra.fco.gov.uk (office). *Website:* www.britishhighcommission.gov.uk/ghana (office).

WESTDAL, Christopher, BA, MBA; Canadian diplomatist. *Education:* St John's Coll., Univ. of Man. *Career:* previous positions beginning 1973 with Canadian Int. Devt Agency (CIDA); Amb. to Bangladesh and Burma 1982–85, to South Africa 1991–93, to Ukraine 1995–98, to UN, Geneva 1999–2003, to Russian Fed. 2003–06; currently mem. Bd of Dirs Silver Bear Resources Inc.
Address: Silver Bear Resources, 2 Bloor Street West, Suite 2102, P.O. Box 110, Toronto, Ontario, M4W 3E2, Canada (office). *Website:* www.silverbearresources.com (office).

WESTENDORP Y CABEZA, Carlos; Spanish diplomatist. *Career:* joined Diplomatic Service 1966, Consul, São Paulo 1966–69, Dir Econ. Studies, Diplomatic School, Madrid 1969–70; Head of Tech. Cabinet, Ministry of Industry 1974–75; Head of Commercial Office, Embassy in The Hague 1975–79; various posts for EC including Pres. Exec. Bd for Relations with EC 1983–85, Sec.-Gen. 1985, Perm. Rep. 1985–91, State Sec. 1991–95; Minister of Foreign Affairs 1995–96; Perm. Rep. to UN 1996–97, High Rep. for implementation of peace agreement in Bosnia and Herzegovina 1997–99; mem. European Parl. 1999–2003; mem. Autonomous Community of the Madrid Parl. Ass. 2003–04; Amb. to USA 2004–08.
Address: Ministry of Foreign Affairs, Plaza de la Provincia 1, 28012 Madrid, Spain (office). *Telephone:* (91) 3799700 (office). *E-mail:* informae@mae.es (office). *Website:* www.mae.es (office).

WESTMACOTT, Sir Peter John, Kt, KCMG, LVO; British diplomatist; *Ambassador to France;* b. 23 Dec. 1950; m. Susan Nemazee; two s. one d. *Career:* joined FCO 1972, Second Sec., British Embassy, Tehran 1974–78, Perm. Mission to EU, Brussels 1978–80, First Sec. for Econs, British Embassy, Paris 1980–84, FCO, London 1984–87, Head of Chancery, British Embassy, Ankara 1987–90, Deputy Pvt. Sec. to HRH Prince of Wales 1990–93, Counsellor, British Embassy, Washington, DC 1993–97, Dir for Americas, later Deputy Under-Sec., FCO 1997–2002, Amb. to Turkey 2002–07, to France 2007–.
Address: British Embassy, 35 rue du Faubourg Saint Honoré, 75383 Paris, 08, France (office). *Telephone:* 1-44-51-31-00 (home). *Fax:* 1-44-51-41-27 (office). *E-mail:* britembinf@turk.net (office). *Website:* www.amb-grandebretagne.fr (office).

WETANG'ULA, Moses Masika, LLB; Kenyan lawyer and politician; *Minister of Foreign Affairs;* b. 13 Sept. 1956, Western Kenya; m.; c. *Education:* Univ. of Nairobi, Kenya School of Law. *Career:* Professional Dist. Magistrate, Chief Magistrate's Court, Nakuru 1982, Dist. Magistrate's Court, Rongo, South Nyanza 1983; Sole Practioner, M. M Wetang'ula Advocate Chambers, Nairobi 1983–85, currently Proprietor, Wetang'ula & Co. Advocates; mem. Parl. (FORD–Kenya) 1993–97, 2002–07, fmr mem. Parl. Cttee on Legal and Constitutional Affairs, Foreign Affairs and Standing Orders, Chair Electricity Regulatory Bd 1998–2001; fmr mem. Jt Ass. of African Caribbean and Pacific/EU, Pres. Jt

Ass Working Group on Regional Cooperation; Asst Minister for Int. Affairs –2008, Minister of Foreign Affairs 2008–; mem. Law Soc. of Kenya, Commonwealth Parl. Asscn, Int. Bar Asscn, Int. Comm. of Jurists, Kenya Chapter; Parliamentarians for Global Action, Inter-Parl. Union.
Address: Ministry of Foreign Affairs, Old Treasury Bldg, Harambee Avenue, POB 30551, Nairobi, Kenya (office). *Telephone:* (20) 334433 (office). *E-mail:* mfapress@nbnet.co.ke (office); mwetangula@hotmail .com (office). *Website:* www.mfa.go.ke (office).

WETHERELL, Gordon L.; British diplomatist; *Governor, Turks and Caicos Islands;* b. 11 Nov. 1948, Addis Ababa, Ethiopia; m.; four d. *Career:* joined FCO 1973, W Africa Dept 1973–74, Third Sec., East Berlin 1974–75, Second Sec. 1975–77, Arms Control/Disarmament Dept, FCO 1977–79, First Sec., Comprehensive Test Ban Negotiations, Geneva 1979–80, First Sec., Chancery, British High Comm., New Delhi 1980–83, NATO Desk, FCO 1983–86, on loan to HM Treasury 1986–87, Asst Head, EC Dept (External), FCO 1987–88, Counsellor and Head of Chancery, Warsaw 1988–92, Political/Mil. Counsellor, Bonn 1992–94, Head of Personnel Services Dept, FCO 1994–97, Amb. to Ethiopia 1997–2000, to Luxembourg 2000–04, High Commr to Ghana (also accred as Amb. to Niger) 2004–07, Gov. Turks and Caicos Islands 2008–.
Address: Office of the Governor, Government House, Waterloo, Grand Turk, Turks and Caicos Islands (office). *Telephone:* 946-2309 (office). *Fax:* 946-2903 (office). *E-mail:* Governor_Office@gov.tc (office).

WEYLAND, Joseph, DIur; Luxembourg diplomatist; b. 24 April 1943; m.; two s. *Education:* Institut d'Etudes Politiques, Paris, France. *Career:* Attaché, Ministry of Foreign Affairs 1967, First Sec., Bonn 1969–72, Deputy Dir of Protocol and Legal Matters, Ministry of Foreign Affairs 1972–76, Deputy Perm. Rep. to EEC, Brussels 1976–79, Dir Econ. Relations and Co-operation, Ministry of Foreign Affairs 1979–83, Amb. and Perm. Rep. to UN, New York 1983–84, to EEC, Brussels 1984–91, Rep. to Inter-Governmental Conf. on Single European Act 1985, Chair. Cttee on Political Union at Inter-Governmental Conf. on Maastricht Treaty 1991, Sec.-Gen. Ministry of Foreign Affairs 1991–92, Amb. to UK (also accred to Ireland and Iceland) 1993–2002, Amb. to Belgium and Perm. Rep. to NATO, Brussels 2003–05, Amb. to USA (also accred to Canada, Mexico and OAS) 2005–08; mem. Bd Luxair 1979–83, 1991–92; mem. Bd SNCI and CFL 1979–83; Grand Officer, Order of Merit (Luxembourg), Commdr, Order of the Crown of Oak (Luxembourg), Commdr, Légion d'honneur, Grand Cross of the Order of Merit (Spain), Grand Cross (Belgium, Italy, Netherlands, Portugal).
Address: Ministry of Foreign Affairs and Immigration, Hôtel St Maximin, 5 rue Notre-Dame, 2240 Luxembourg-Ville, Luxembourg (office). *Telephone:* 478-1 (office). *Fax:* 22-31-44 (office). *E-mail:* officielle.boite@mae .etat.lu (office). *Website:* www.mae.lu (office).

WHEELER, Fraser William; British diplomatist; *High Commissioner to Guyana;* b. 23 March 1957; m. Sarah Wheeler; one s. one d. *Career:* Finance Dept, FCO 1980–81, Defence Dept 1981–82, Entry Clearance/Consular Officer, Accra 1982–84, Third Sec., UK Mission to UN, Geneva 1984–87, Soviet Dept, FCO 1987–91, Second Sec. (Trade), Moscow 1991–94, Deputy Consul Gen., Vancouver 1994–98, Strategic Policy Adviser, Directorate for Strategy and Innovation, FCO 2000–02, Head of Partnerships and Networks Devt Unit, Directorate for Strategy and Innovation 2002–04, Deputy Head of Mission, Basra 2004–06, High Commr to Guyana (also accred as Amb. to Suriname) 2006–; Vice-Pres. Nat. Communications plc (Canada) 1998–2000.
Address: British High Commission, 185 Jalan Ampang, 50450 Kuala Lumpur (office); British High Commission, PO Box 11030, 50732 Kuala Lumpur, Malaysia. *Telephone:* (3) 21702200 (office). *Fax:* (3) 21702303 (office). *E-mail:* political.kualalumpur@fco.gov.uk (office). *Website:* www .britain.org.my (office).

WHEELER, Graeme; New Zealand banker and international organization executive; *Managing Director, World Bank Group; Career:* fmr Dir of Macroeconomic Policy and Strategy, NZ Treasury, fmr Treas. NZ Debt Man. Office and Deputy Sec. NZ Treasury; Dir Financial Products and Services Dept, World Bank (IBRD) 1997–2001, Vice-Pres. and Treas. 2001–05, Acting Man. Dir, then Man. Dir 2005–.
Address: The World Bank Group, 1818 H Street, NW, Washington, DC 20433, USA (office). *Telephone:* (202) 473-1000 (office). *Fax:* (202) 477-6391 (office). *E-mail:* pic@worldbank.org (office). *Website:* web .worldbank.org (office).

WHITE, Hugh John, BA, BPhil; Australian academic and research institute director; *Professor of Strategic Studies and Head, Strategic and Defence Studies Centre, Australian National University;* b. 15 Oct. 1953, Melbourne; m.; two c. *Education:* Scotch Coll., Melbourne, Univ. of Melbourne, Univ. of Oxford, UK. *Career:* Intelligence Analyst, Office of Nat. Assessments

1980–83; with Dept of Int. Relations, ANU 1983–84; Foreign Affairs and Defence Corresp., Sydney Morning Herald 1984–85; Private Sec.and Consultant to Minister for Defence 1985–90; Sr Adviser to Prime Minister on Int. Relations 1990–91; Head of Strategic Analysis Branch, Office of Nat. Assessments 1992; Head of Int. Policy, Dept of Defence 1993–95, Deputy Sec. for Strategy 1995–2000; Dir Australian Strategic Policy Inst. 2000–04; Prof. of Strategic Studies, ANU 2004–, also Head of Strategic and Defence Studies Centre, Assoc. Dean (Research), ANU Coll. of Asia and the Pacific, Visiting Fellow, Lowy Inst. of Int. Policy; John Locke Prize in Mental Philosophy 1978.
Address: Strategic and Defence Studies Centre, Australian National University, Canberra, ACT 0200, Australia (office). *Telephone:* (2) 6125-9921 (office). *Fax:* (2) 6125-9926 (office). *E-mail:* Hugh.White@anu.edu.au (office). *Website:* rspas.anu.edu.au/sdsc (office).

WHITEMAN, Hon. Burchell Anthony, OJ; Jamaican diplomatist; *High Commissioner to UK;* b. May Pen, Clarendon; m. Joline Whiteman. *Education:* Univ. Coll. of the West Indies. *Career:* fmr Prin. York Castle High School and Brown's Town Community Coll.; worked at community level for People's Nat. Party (PNP) 1980s, later PNP Gen. Sec.; elected mem. Parl. for NW St Ann 1989; State Minister of Educ. 1989–93, apptd Minister of Educ. 1993; fmr Special Advisor to Gov.-Gen. Prof. Kenneth Hall; served as Senator and Minister of Information –2006; High Commr to UK (also accred as Amb. to Denmark, Finland, Norway, Sweden, Portugal and Spain) 2007–.
Address: Jamaican High Commission, 1–2 Prince Consort Road, London, SW7 2BZ, England (office). *Telephone:* (20) 7823-9911 (office). *Fax:* (20) 7589-5154 (office). *E-mail:* hc@jhcuk.com (office). *Website:* jhcuk.org (office).

WHITESIDE, Bernard Gerrard, MBE; British diplomatist; *Ambassador to Ecuador;* b. 3 Oct. 1954. *Career:* Third Sec. (Commercial), Moscow 1983–86, Third, later Second Sec., UK Del. to Conf. on Disarmament, Geneva 1986–89, Press Officer, FCO 1989–90, Second Sec. (Aid/Chancery), Bogota 1991–95, First Sec. (Justice and Home Affairs), UK Representation to EU, Brussels 1996–97, Head of Policy Section, Migration and Visa Dept, FCO 1997–99, seconded to Dept for Int. Devt as Russia Programme Man. 1999–2001, Amb. to Moldova 2002–06, to Ecuador 2007–.
Address: British Embassy, Edif. Citiplaza, 14°, Avda Naciones Unidas y República de El Salvador, Casilla 17-17-830, Quito, Ecuador (office). *Telephone:* (2) 297-0800 (office). *Fax:* (2) 297-0809 (office). *E-mail:* consuio@uio.satnet.net (office). *Website:* www.britembquito.org.ec (office).

WHITMAN, Marina von Neumann, PhD; American economist and academic; *Professor of Business Administration and Public Policy, Gerald R. Ford School of Public Policy, University of Michigan;* b. 6 March 1935, New York; m. Robert F. Whitman 1956; one s. one d. *Education:* Radcliffe Coll. and Columbia Univ. *Career:* Lecturer in Econs, Univ. of Pittsburgh 1962–64, Asst Prof. 1964–66, Assoc. Prof. 1966–71, Prof. of Econs 1971–73, Distinguished Public Service Prof. 1973–79; Sr Staff Economist, Council of Econ. Advisers 1970–71; mem. President's Price Comm. 1971–72; mem. President's Council of Econ. Advisers (with special responsibility for int. monetary and trade problems) 1972–73; Vice-Pres., Chief Econ. Gen. Motors Corpn, New York 1979–85, Group Exec. Vice-Pres. for Public Affairs 1985–92; Distinguished Visiting Prof. of Business Admin. and Public Policy, Univ. of Mich. 1992–94, Prof. 1994–; mem. Trilateral Comm. 1973, Bd of Dirs Council on Foreign Relations 1977–87; mem. Bd of Dirs J. P. Morgan Chase Corpn 1973–2002, Procter and Gamble Co. 1976–2003, Alcoa 1993–2002, Unocal 1993–2005; mem. Bd of Overseers Harvard Univ. 1972–78, Bd of Trustees, Princeton Univ. 1980–90; mem. Consultative Group on Int. Econ. and Monetary Affairs 1979–; more than 20 hon. degrees. *Publications:* New World, New Rules: The Changing Role of the American Corporation 1999; many books and articles on econ. topics.
Address: Gerald R. Ford School of Public Policy, University of Michigan, Weill Hall, 735 South State Street, Ann Arbor, MI 48109-3091, USA (office). *Telephone:* (734) 763-4173 (office). *Fax:* (734) 763-9181 (office). *E-mail:* marinaw@umich.edu (office). *Website:* www.fordschool.umich .edu (office).

WHITMAN, Richard G., PhD; British professor of European studies; *Professor of Politics, University of Bath;* b. 2 Nov. 1965, Ipswich, Suffolk. *Career:* Sr Lecturer, Univ. of Westminster 1995–2000, Prof. of European Studies 2000–04, Dir Centre for the Study of Democracy 2000–04; Head of European Programme, Royal Inst. of Int. Affairs (now Chatham House) 2004–06; Prof. of Politics, Univ. of Bath 2006–; NATO Int. Research Fellow 1997–99; Visiting Fellow, Western European Union Inst. for Security Studies 1998, Copenhagen Peace Research Inst. (COPRI) 2000; mem. Acad. of Social Sciences 2007–, American Acad. of Social Sciences. *Publications:* Rethinking the European Union – Institutions, Interests and

Identities 1997, From Civilian Power to Superpower? – The International Identity of the European Union 1998, The Enlargement of the European Union – Issues and Strategies 1999, The Foreign Policies of European Union Member States (co-ed. with I. Manners and D. Allen) 2000; several book chapters and articles in learned journals. *Address:* Department of European Studies and Modern Languages, University of Bath, Bath, BA2 7AY, England (office). *Telephone:* (1225) 386490 (office). *Fax:* (1225) 386987 (office). *E-mail:* r.g.whitman@bath.ac.uk (office). *Website:* people.bath.ac.uk/rgw22 (office).

WHITNEY, Benson K., BA, JD; American business executive, lawyer and diplomatist; *Ambassador to Norway;* m. Mary Whitney; four c. *Education:* Vassar Coll., Poughkeepsie, NY, University of Minnesota Law School, Minneapolis. *Career:* fmr Ed. Order of the Coif law review; practised law with Popham, Haik, Schnobrich, Kaufman & Doty Ltd; fmr Man. Gen. Pnr, Gideon Hixon Fund; fmr Pres. Minn. Venture Capital Asscn; fmr CEO Whitney Man. Co.; Minn. Exec. Dir and Minn. Finance Chair. for Bush-Cheney '04; fmr Minn. Finance Chair. Republican Nat. Cttee; fmr trustee, dir, chair. or advisor of several orgs, including Guthrie Theater, Wilderness Inquiry, Persephone Fund, Headwaters Fund, Minnesotans for Term Limits, Minneapolis Acad. Amb. to Norway 2005–; Amos Deinard Award for Scholarship. *Address:* Embassy of the USA, Henrik Ibsens gate 48, 0244 Oslo, Norway (office). *Telephone:* 22-44-85-50 (office). *Fax:* 22-43-07-77 (office). *E-mail:* oslo@usa.no (office). *Website:* norway.usembassy.gov (office).

WHITTING, Ian Robert; British diplomatist; *Ambassador to Iceland;* m. Tracy Gallagher; two d. *Career:* Desk Officer, Personnel Services Dept, FCO 1972–74; Attaché (Visas), Embassy in Moscow 1975–76, Third Sec. (Commercial and Information), Embassy in Tunis 1976–78, Press Attaché, Embassy in Athens 1980–83; Desk Officer, Soviet Dept, FCO 1983–85; Second Sec. (Political Bilateral and European Affairs), Embassy in Moscow 1985–88; Desk Officer (S Africa), S African Dept, FCO 1988–90; First Sec. (EU and Econ.), Embassy in Dublin 1990–94, Deputy Head of Mission and HM's Consul, Abidjan 1994–97; Conf. Media Co-ordinator (Commonwealth Heads of Govts Meeting, G8 and EU Presidency), FCO 1997–98, Sec. of State's Special Rep. to Great Lakes Region and Deputy Head of Africa Equatorial Dept 1998–2002, Head of EU Dept (Bilateral) 2002–03; First Sec. (EU and Econ. Affairs), later Deputy Head of Mission and HM's Consul Gen., Embassy in Athens 2003–07; Amb. to Iceland 2008–. *Address:* British Embassy, PO Box 460, 121 Reykjavik, Iceland (office). *Telephone:* 5505100 (office). *Fax:* 5505105 (office). *E-mail:* alp.mehmet@fco.gov.uk (office). *Website:* www.britishembassy.is (office).

WIATR, Jerzy Józef, MPh; Polish politician and sociologist; b. 17 Sept. 1931, Warsaw; m. Ewa Żurowska-Wiatr; one s. *Education:* Warsaw Univ. *Career:* asst, Warsaw Univ. 1951–59; Mil. Political Acad. 1959–65; Polish Acad. of Sciences (PAN) 1965–69; Prof., Warsaw Univ. 1969–2001, Dean of Social Sciences 1977–80; participant Round Table debates 1989; Deputy to Sejm (Parl.) 1991–2001; mem. Cttee for Nat. Defence and Cttee for Constitutional Responsibility 1991–97; Minister of Educ. 1996–97; Dir Inst. for Social and Int. Studies, Keller-Krauz Foundation 1998–; Pres. Cen. European Political Science Asscn 2000–03; Vice Pres. Int. Political Science Asscn 1979–82; Vice-Pres. Int. Studies Asscn 1980–81; mem. Polish United Workers Party (PZPR) 1949–90; mem. Social Democracy of Polish Repub. (SdRP) 1990–99; mem. Democratic Left Alliance 1999–; Commdr's Cross with Star of Polonia Restituta Order 1996; Dr hc. *Publications:* over 30 books including Education For and In the 21st Century 1997; numerous articles on sociology and political science. *Address:* ul. Komisji Edukacji Narodowej 98/49, 02 777 Warsaw, Poland (home). *Telephone:* (22) 619-90-11 (office); (22) 643-54-41 (home). *Fax:* (22) 643-54-41 (home). *E-mail:* jwiatr@ewspa.edu.pl (office).

WICKRAMASURIYA, Jaliya; Sri Lankan business executive and diplomatist; *Ambassador to USA;* m. Priyanga Wickramasuriya. *Career:* worked in tea business from age of 18, worked for Dilmah for 18 years, then for Standard Trading Co., Colombo; Founder, Man. Dir and CEO Ceylon Royal Tea, Atlanta, Ga, USA, brands introduced to Australia, Europe and Japan; Consular Gen. in Los Angeles –2008, Amb. to USA (also accred to Mexico) 2008–. *Address:* Embassy of Sri Lanka, 2148 Wyoming Avenue, NW, Washington, DC 20008, USA (office). *Telephone:* (202) 483-4025 (office). *Fax:* (202) 232-7181 (office). *E-mail:* slembassy@slembassyusa.org (office). *Website:* www.slembassyusa.org (office).

WICKREMANAYAKE, Ratnasiri; Sri Lankan politician; *Prime Minister and Minister of Internal Administration; Career:* elected mem. Mahajana Eksath Peramuna for Horana 1960; apptd Deputy Minister of Justice 1970; Gen. Sec. Sri Lankan Freedom Party 1977; won Kalutara Dist seat 1994; apptd Minister of Public Admin, Home Affairs and Plantation and Leader of the

House 1994; Prime Minister of Sri Lanka 2000–01; Minister of Buddha Sasana and Religious Affairs 2000–02; Chair. United People's Freedom Alliance; Prime Minister and Minister of Internal Admin 2005–; ex-officio Chair. Bd of Govs Cen. Cultural Fund. *Address:* Prime Minister's Office, 58, Sir Ernest de Silva Mawatha, Colombo 7, Sri Lanka (office). *Telephone:* (11) 2575317 (office). *Fax:* (11) 2575454 (office). *Website:* www.pmoffice.gov.lk (office).

WICKREMASINGHE, Ranil, LLB; Sri Lankan politician and lawyer; *Leader, United National Party;* b. 24 March 1949, Colombo; m. Maithree Wickremasinghe 1995. *Education:* Royal Coll. of Colombo, Univ. of Colombo and Sri Lanka Law Coll. *Career:* attorney-at-law, Supreme Court; elected mem. Parl. 1977, 1989; Leader of House 1989–93; Deputy Minister of Foreign Affairs 1977–79; Minister of Youth Affairs and Employment 1978–89, of Educ. 1980–89, of Industries 1989–90, of Industries, Science and Tech. 1990–94; Prime Minister of Sri Lanka 1992, 2001–04, also Minister of Policy Devt and Implementation 2001–04; Leader, United Nat. Party 1994–, Leader of the Opposition 1994–2001, 2006–; cand. in presidential elections 1999, 2005. *Address:* United National Party (UNP), 30 Sir Marcu Fernando Mawatha, Colombo 7, Sri Lanka (office). *Telephone:* (11) 5636551 (office). *Fax:* (11) 2682905 (office). *E-mail:* info@unp.lk (office). *Website:* www.unp.lk (office).

WIDHYA, Chem, MPolSci; Cambodian diplomatist; *Ambassador to Germany;* b. 6 Dec. 1958, Phnom Penh; m.; three c. *Education:* Inst. of Int. Relations, Potsdam-Babelsberg, E Germany. *Career:* Pvt. Sec. to Prime Minister Hun Sen 1990–91; Secr. of Supreme Nat. Council 1991–93; Deputy Sec.-Gen. to Constituent Ass. 1993; Perm. Sec., Ministry of Foreign Affairs and Int. Cooperation 1993–96, Under-Sec. of State 1996–97, Sec. of State 1997–2004; Perm. Rep. to UN, New York 2004–06; Amb. to Germany (also accred to Cyprus, Malta and Slovenia) 2007–; mem. Bd of Dirs Royal School of Admin 1995–, Cambodia Devt Resource Inst. 2000–; Order of Chevalier and Commdr, Royal Order of Mony Saraphoan 2003. *Address:* Embassy of Cambodia, Benjamin-Vogelsdorf-Strasse, 13187 Berlin Germany (office). *Telephone:* (30) 48637901 (office). *Fax:* (30) 48637973 (office). *E-mail:* rec-berlin@t-online.de (office). *Website:* www.kambodscha-botschaft.de (office).

WIDODO, Makmur, MA; Indonesian diplomatist and civil servant; *Ambassador to Germany;* b. 1 Aug. 1945, Surakarta, Solo; m.; three c. *Education:* Gadjah Mada Univ., Jogjakarta and Ohio Univ., USA. *Career:* journalist Nat. News Agency (Antara) 1970–74; with Dept of Foreign Affairs (DFA) 1975–, positions included Head Cen. America and Caribbean Affairs Section 1977, Second Sec. Head of Section, Nat. Secr. of ASEAN 1980, Counsellor and Head Sub-Directorate of Non-UN Int. Orgs 1991–93, Minister and Dir for Int. Orgs 1997–99; Third Sec. Head of Information Dept, Embassy in Stockholm, Sweden 1980–84; First Sec. and Head Dept of Disarmament, Perm. Mission to UN, New York 1986–91; Minister Counsellor in Geneva 1993–97; Amb. and Deputy Perm. Rep. to UN 1999–2001, Perm. Rep. 2001–02; Dir Gen. for Multilateral Political, Social and Security Affairs, Ministry of Foreign Affairs 2002–04; Amb. to Germany 2004–; mem. Cttee on Palestine, Non-Aligned Movement. *Address:* Embassy of Indonesia, Lehrter Str. 16–17, 10557 Berlin, Germany (office). *Telephone:* (30) 478070 (office). *Fax:* (30) 44737142 (office). *Website:* www.kbri-berlin.org (office).

WIEBES, Cees, PhD; Dutch academic; *Senior Lecturer, University of Amsterdam;* b. 1 July 1950. *Education:* Univ. of Amsterdam. *Career:* Sr Researcher concerned with circumstances surrounding fall of Srebrenica, Netherlands Inst. of War Documentation (NIOD) 1999–2003; currently Sr Lecturer, Dept of Int. Relations and Int. Public Law, Univ. of Amsterdam; freelance writer and researcher for nat. and int. media; mem. Archival Cttee, Ministry of Foreign Affairs; mem. Ed. Bd Global Intelligence Monthly, Journal of Intelligence History; Hon. Sec. Netherlands Intelligence Studies Asscn (NISA) 1991–99. *Publications:* Intelligence and the War with Bosnia 1992–1995 2003, The Netherlands and the Oil Crisis of 1973/74 2004; 22 books and monographs, numerous journal articles and contribs to books. *Address:* University of Amsterdam, O. Z. Achterburgwal 237, 1012 DL Amsterdam, Netherlands (office). *Telephone:* (20) 525-2153 (office). *E-mail:* C.Wiebes@uva.nl (office).

WIJEWARDENA, Jayalatha D. A.; Sri Lankan diplomatist; *Ambassador to Thailand; Career:* fmr High Commr in Kenya, Tanzania and Uganda; Chargé d'affaires a.i. in USA 2000–03; Additional Sec., Ministry of Foreign Affairs, Bangkok 2003; Perm. Rep. to EU and Amb. to Belgium 2003–04; Amb. to Thailand 2004–; Trustee Asian Inst. of Tech. 2004–.

Address: Embassy of Sri Lanka, Ocean Tower II, 13th Floor, 75/6–7 Sukhumvit, Soi 19, Bangkok 10110, Thailand (office). *Telephone:* (2) 261-1934 (office). *Fax:* (2) 261-1936 (office). *E-mail:* slemb@ksc.th.com (office).

WIKTORIN, Gen. Owe Erik Axel; Swedish army officer; b. 7 May 1940, Motala; m. Cajs Gårding 1965; two s. *Education:* AF Flying Training School, AF Acad., Armed Forces Staff and War Coll., USAF Air Command and Staff Coll. *Career:* fighter pilot, Skaraborg Wing 1964–69, CO squadron 1969–71; staff officer, Swedish Defence Staff 1973–79, Head of Planning Section 1980–83, Dir of Plans and Policy and Deputy Chief 1986–91, Chief 1991–92; Deputy CO Jämtland (Sector) Wing 1983–84; Head of Planning Section AF Staff 1984–86; CO Southern Jt Command Swedish Armed Forces 1992–94, apptd Supreme Commdr 1994; Fellow Royal Swedish Acad. of War Sciences 1985; Kt Commdr of White Rose of Finland; Chevalier, Légion d'honneur; Gold Medal for Merit, Southern Skåne Regt, Swedish Home Guard; Gold Medal for Merit, Nat. Fed. of AF Asscns.

WILCOX, Philip C., Jr, BA, LLB; American lawyer and diplomatist; *President, Foundation for Middle East Peace;* b. 1 Feb. 1937, Denver, Colo. *Education:* Williams Coll., Stanford Univ. Law School. *Career:* fmr teacher in Sierra Leone; fmr lawyer, Holme, Roberts and Owen LLP; joined Foreign Service 1966, numerous postings abroad including Press Attache, Embassy in Vientiane, Laos, Political and Econ. Officer, Embassy in Jakarta, Indonesia, Chief of Econ. Section, Embassy in Dhaka, Bangladesh, Chief of Mission and Consul Gen., Jerusalem; served in several sr positions at Dept of State including Special Asst to Under-Sec. for Man., Deputy Dir for UN Political Affairs, Bureau of Int. Org. Affairs, Dir for Regional Affairs, for Israeli and Arab-Israeli Affairs and Deputy Asst Sec. of State for Middle Eastern Affairs, Bureau for Middle Eastern and South Asian Affairs, Prin. Deputy Asst Sec. of State for Intelligence and Research and Coordinator for Counter Terrorism; currently Pres. Foundation for Middle East Peace; fmr mem. Accountability Review Bd (concerning terrorist attack in Nairobi, Kenya 1998); mem. Bd of Dirs Middle East Inst., Americans for Near East Refugee Aid, Washington Inst. for Foreign Affairs; Meritorious Award, Superior Award, Presidential Honor Award. *Address:* Foundation for Middle East Peace, 1761 N Street, NW, Washington, DC 20036, USA (office). *Telephone:* (202) 835-3650 (office). *Fax:* (202) 835-3651 (office). *E-mail:* info@fmep.org (office). *Website:* www.fmep.org (office).

WILDASH, Richard, LVO, MA (Cantab.), FRGS; British diplomatist; *High Commissioner to Malawi;* b. 24 Dec. 1955, London; m. Jane Wildash; two d. *Education:* St Paul's School, Barnes, London and Corpus Christi Coll., Cambridge. *Career:* Third Sec., British Embassy, East Berlin 1979–81, Third Sec., Abidjan 1981–84, First Sec., Harare 1988–92, First Sec., New Delhi 1994–98, Deputy High Commr, Kuala Lumpur 1998–2002, High Commr to Cameroon 2002–06 (also accred as Amb. to Equatorial Guinea, Chad, Gabon and Cen. African Repub.), High Commr to Malawi 2006–; Chair. Int. Natural Rubber Council 2000–02; mem. Chartered Inst. of Linguists. . *E-mail:* wildash@fish.co.uk (office); richard.wildash@fco.gov.uk (office); wildash@fish.co.uk (home). *Address:* British High Commission, Off Convention Road, PO Box 30042, Lilongwe 3, Malawi (office). *Telephone:* 1772400 (office). *Fax:* 1772657 (office). *Website:* www.britishhighcommission.gov.uk/malawi (office).

WILDHABER, Luzius, DrIur, LLM, JSD; Swiss judge and professor of law; b. 18 Jan. 1937, Basle; m. 1st Simone Wildhaber-Creux 1963 (died 1994); two d.; m. 2nd Gill Reilly 1998 (divorced 2004). *Education:* Basle, Paris, Heidelberg, London and Yale Univs. *Career:* Int. Law Div. Fed. Dept of External Affairs 1968–71; Prof. of Int. Constitutional and Admin. Law, Univ. of Fribourg 1971–77; Prof. of Int. and Constitutional Law, Univ. of Basle 1977–98, Rector (desig.) 1990–92, Rector 1992–94, Pro-Rector 1994–96; Judge, Supreme Court of Liechtenstein 1975–88, Admin. Tribunal, IDB 1989–94, European Court of Human Rights 1991–2007; Pres. European Court of Human Rights 1998–2007; Hon. Bencher of the Inner Temple 2002; Star of Romania 2000; Order of Merit of Lithuania 2003, Great Gold Badge of Honour with Sash, Austria 2006, Commander, Order of Orange-Nassau, Netherlands 2007; Dr hc (Charles Univ., Prague) 1999, (Sofia Univ.) 1999, (American Univ. in Bulgaria) 1999, (Bratislava) 2000, (State Univ. of Moldova) 2000, (Bucharest) 2000, (Russian Acad. of Sciences) 2000, (Law Univ. of Lithuania) 2000, (Tbilisi) 2001, (Nat. Law Acad. of Ukraine) 2001, (Neuchâtel); Hon. LLD (McGill Univ., Montreal) 2001; Marcel Benoist Prize 1999. *Publications:* Advisory Opinions – Rechtsgutachten höchster Gerichte 1962, Treaty-making Power and Constitution 1971, Erfahrungen mit der Europäischen Menschenrechts-konvention 1979, Wechselspiel zwischen Innen und Aussen 1996, Praxis des Völkerrechts (with J. P. Müller, 3rd edn) 2001, The European Court of

Human Rights: History, Achievements, Reform 2006; more than 200 articles. *Address:* Auf der Wacht 21, 4104 Oberwil, Switzerland (home). *Telephone:* 614012521 (home). *E-mail:* luzius.wildhaber@unibas.ch (office).

WILKES, Gen. Sir Michael (John), KCB, CBE; British army officer; b. 11 June 1940, Steep, Hants.; m. Anne Jacqueline Huelin 1966; two s. *Education:* Royal Mil. Acad., Sandhurst. *Career:* commissioned RA 1960; joined 7 Para Regt, Royal Horse Artillery 1961; served Middle East Troop, Commdr Special Forces, Radfan, Saudi Arabia, Borneo 1964–67; Staff Coll. 1971–72; Brig. Maj. RA, HQ 3 Armoured Div. 1973–74; Battery Commdr Chestnut Troop, 1 Royal Horse Artillery (BAOR) 1975–76, CO 1977–79; Mil. Asst to Chief of Gen. Staff 1980–81; Chief of Staff, 3 Armoured Div. 1982–83; Commdr 22 Armoured Brigade 1984–85; Arms Dir, Ministry of Defence 1986–88; Gen. Officer Commdg 3 Armoured Div. 1988–90; Commdr UK Field Army and Insp.-Gen., TA 1990–93; Middle East Adviser to Ministry of Defence 1992–95; Adjutant-Gen. 1993–95; Lt-Gov. and C-in-C, Jersey 1995–2000; Col Commdt and Pres., Hon. Artillery Co. 1992–98; Pres. Army Cadet Force Asscn 1999–; Kermit Roosevelt Lecturer 1995; Order of Mil. Merit 1st Class (Jordan) 1994, Freeman City of London 1993; KStJ. *Address:* c/o Le Riche House, PO Box 4, 1-3 l'avenue le Bas, Longveville, St Saviour, JE4 8NB, Jersey (office).

WILKINS, David Horton, BA, JD; American politician and diplomatist; *Ambassador to Canada;* b. 12 Oct. 1946; m. Susan Clary; two c. *Education:* Clemson Univ., Univ. of S Carolina. *Career:* Chair. Greenville Co. Legis. Del. 1985–86, 1989–94; Chair. Judicial Comm. 1986–92; Chair. Southern Legis. Conf. 1998; Pres. Nat. Speakers Conf. 2001; Speaker Pro Tempore S Carolina Legislature 1992–94, Speaker 1994–2005; State Chair. Bush-Cheney Re-election Campaign; Amb. to Canada 2005–; William M. Bulger Excellence in State Legis. Leadership Award 2004. *Address:* Embassy of the USA, 490 Sussex Drive, PO Box 866, Station B, Ottawa, ON K1P 5T1, Canada (office). *Telephone:* (613) 238-5335 (office). *Fax:* (613) 688-3080 (office). *Website:* www.usembassycanada.gov (office).

WILKINSON, Paul, MA, FRSA; British political scientist and academic; *Professor of International Relations and Chairman, Centre for the Study of Terrorism and Political Violence, University of St Andrews;* b. 9 May 1937, Harrow, Middx; m. Susan Wilkinson 1960; two s. one d. *Education:* Lower School of John Lyon, Harrow, Univ. Coll., Swansea and Univ. of Wales. *Career:* regular officer RAF 1959–65; Asst Lecturer in Politics, Univ. Coll., Cardiff 1966–68, Lecturer 1968–75, Sr Lecturer 1975–78; Reader in Politics, Univ. of Wales 1978–79; Chair. in Int. Relations, Aberdeen Univ. 1979–89; Head Dept of Int. Relations, Univ. of St Andrews 1990–94, Prof. of Int. Relations 1990–, Head School of History and Int. Relations 1994–96, Dir Centre for the Study of Terrorism and Political Violence 1998–2002, Chair. 2002–; Dir Research Inst. for the Study of Conflict and Terrorism 1989–94; Visiting Fellow, Trinity Hall, Cambridge 1997–98; Hon. Fellow, Univ. Coll., Swansea 1986. *Publications:* Social Movement 1971, Political Terrorism 1974, Terrorism versus Liberal Democracy 1976, Terrorism and the Liberal State (revised edn) 1986, British Perspectives on Terrorism 1981, Terrorism: Theory and Practice (jtly) 1978, The New Fascists (revised edn) 1983, Contemporary Research on Terrorism 1987, Lessons of Lockerbie 1989, Terrorism and Political Violence (co-ed. with David Rapoport) 1990, Technology and Terrorism (ed.) 1993, Terrorism: British Perspectives (ed.) 1993, Research Report (Vol. Two) Lord Lloyd's Inquiry into Legislation Against Terrorism 1996, Aviation Terrorism and Security Versus (co-ed. with Brian Jenkins) 1998, Terrorism Versus Democracy: The Liberal State Response 2000 (second revised edn 2006), Addressing The New International Terrorism (co-author) 2003, Homeland Security in the UK 2007, Very Short Introduction to International Relations 2007; numerous articles in specialist journals. *Address:* Department of International Relations, University of St Andrews, New Arts Building, The Scores, St Andrews, Fife, KY16 9AX, Scotland (home). *Telephone:* (1334) 462935 (office). *Fax:* (1334) 461922 (office). *E-mail:* gm39@st-andrews.ac.uk (office). *Website:* www.st-andrews.ac.uk/academic/intrel/research/cstpv (office).

WILKINSON, Richard Denys, CVO; British diplomatist (retd); b. 11 May 1946; m.; two s. one d. *Career:* joined FCO 1972, E Europe and Soviet Desk 1972–73, First Sec., Chancery, British Embassy, Madrid 1973–77, EC Dept, FCO 1977–79, Rhodesia Dept 1979, Deputy Head, Dept of Political Planning 1980–83, First Sec. (Econ. and Commercial), British Embassy, Ankara 1983–85, Head of Chancery, British Embassy, Mexico City 1985–88, Counsellor (Information), British Embassy, Paris 1988–92, Head, Dept of Political Planning, FCO 1993–94, Head of Asian Dept 1994–96, Dir Americas Dept 2000–03; Amb. to Venezuela 1997–2000, to Chile 2003–05.

Address: c/o Foreign and Commonwealth Office, King Charles Street, London, SW1A 2AH, England. *Telephone:* (20) 7008-1500.

WILLEMS, Lodewijk; Belgian diplomatist; *Ambassador to Germany; Career:* fmr Chair. ECE; Amb. to UK 1997–2002, to Germany 2002–.
Address: Embassy of Belgium, Jägerstr. 52–53, 10117 Berlin, Germany (office). *Telephone:* (30) 206420 (office). *Fax:* (30) 20642200 (office). *E-mail:* berlin@diplobel.org (office). *Website:* www.diplomatie.be/berlin (office).

WILLETT, Lee, BA, MA, PhD; British academic; *Head of Maritime Studies Programme, Military Sciences Department, Royal United Services Institute; Career:* Leverhulme Research Fellow, Centre for Security Studies, Univ. of Hull, seconded to Naval Staff Directorate, Ministry of Defence as Research Assoc.; fmr Head of Mil. Capabilities Programme, Mil. Sciences Dept, Royal United Services Inst. for Defence and Security Studies, currently Head of Maritime Studies Programme.
Address: Royal United Services Institute for Defence and Security Studies, Whitehall, London, SW1A 2ET, England (office). *Telephone:* (20) 7747-2611 (office). *Fax:* (20) 7321-0943 (office). *E-mail:* dr.leewillett@rusi.org (office). *Website:* www.rusi.org (office).

WILLIAMS, Sir Daniel Charles, GCMG, QC, LLB; Grenadian government official and fmr lawyer; *Governor-General;* b. 4 Nov. 1935; m. Cecilia Patricia Gloria Modeste 1970; two s. four d. *Education:* Univ. of London. *Career:* called to Bar, Lincoln's Inn, London 1968; barrister 1969–70, 1974–84, 1990–96; magistrate, St Lucia 1970–74; MP (New Nat. Party) 1984–89; Minister of Health, Housing and Environment 1984–89, of Legal Affairs and Attorney-Gen. 1988–89; Acting Prime Minister July 1988; Gov.-Gen. of Grenada 1996–; fmrly several lay positions in RC Church; Chief Scout. *Publications:* Index of Laws of Grenada 1959–79, The Office and Duties of the Governor-General of Grenada 1998, A Synoptic View of the Public Service of Grenada 1999, Prescription of a Model Grenada 2000, God Speaks 2001, The Layman's Lawbook 2002, The Love of God 2003, Government of the Global Village 2007; (contrib.) Modern Legal Systems Cyclopedia: Central America and the Caribbean, Vol. 7 1985.
Address: Government House, St George's, Grenada (office). *Telephone:* 4402401 (office). *Fax:* 4406688 (office).

WILLIAMS, Izben Cordinal; Saint Christopher and Nevis diplomatist, psychiatrist and foundation administrator; *Ambassador to USA;* m.; two s. *Education:* Univ. of Toronto, Canada, Univ. of the West Indies, Univ. of Miami, USA. *Career:* training in family medicine and psychiatry; f. own pvt. practice; consultant psychiatrist to several E Caribbean govts; prin. partner of condominium hotel resort; f. Outreach Foundation (community devt agency); Amb. to USA and OAS 2001–.
Address: Embassy of Saint Christopher and Nevis, 3216 New Mexico Avenue, NW, Washington, DC 20016, USA (office). *Telephone:* (202) 686-2636 (office). *Fax:* (202) 686-5740 (office). *E-mail:* info@stkittsnevis.org (office). *Website:* www.stkittsnevis.org (office).

WILLIAMS, James Ernest; Saint Christopher and Nevis diplomatist; m. Valerie Williams. *Career:* High Commr to UK (also accred to Sweden) 2001–.
Address: Saint Christopher and Nevis High Commission, 2nd Floor, 10 Kensington Court, London, W8 5DL, England (office). *Telephone:* (20) 7937-9718 (office). *Fax:* (20) 7937-7484 (office). *E-mail:* sknhighcomm@btconnect.com (office).

WILLIAMS, Jody, BA, MA; American international organization official, campaigner, academic and writer; *Chairman, Nobel Women's Initiative;* b. 9 Oct. 1950, Poultney, Vt; m. Stephen D. Goose 2001. *Education:* Univ. of Vermont, School for Int. Training, Brattleboro, Vt, Johns Hopkins School of Advanced Int. Studies, Washington, DC. *Career:* English teacher, Mexico, UK and Washington DC 1978–81; campaigned to spread awareness of US policy in Cen. America 1981–92; Co-ordinator Nicaragua-Honduras Educ. Project 1984–86; Deputy Dir Medical Aid for El Salvador, Los Angeles 1986–92; Founding Co-ordinator Int. Campaign to Ban Landmines (ICBL) 1992, currently ICBL Campaign Amb.; Tech. Adviser, UN Study on Impact of Armed Conflict on Children; Head, UN Human Rights Council High-Level Mission to Darfur 2007; Visiting Prof. of Social Work, Univ. of Houston 2003–; Founder-mem. and Chair. Nobel Women's Initiative 2006–; more than 15 hon. degrees in USA and Canada, including from the Royal Mil. Coll. of Canada, Smith Coll., Wesleyan Univ., Penn State Univ.; Nobel Peace Prize (jt recipient with ICBL) 1997, Distinguished Peace Leadership Award, Nuclear Age Peace Foundation 1998, Olender Foundation Peacemaker of the Year 1999, Eleanor Roosevelt Global Women's Rights Award 2004, ranked 100th by Forbes magazine amongst 100 Most Powerful Women in the World 2004. *Publications:* After the Guns Fall Silent: The Enduring Legacy of Landmines (with Shawn Roberts) 1995, Banning Landmines: Disarma-

ment, Citizen Diplomacy and Human Security 2008; more than 24 chapters and articles for books and journals; numerous articles for newspapers around the world, including The Wall Street Journal, The Independent (UK), the Economist.
Address: Nobel Women's Initiative, 151 Slater Street, Suite 408, Ottawa, ON K1P 5H3, Canada (office). *Telephone:* (613) 569-8400 (office). *Fax:* (613) 563-0682 (office). *E-mail:* jwilliams@nobelwomensinitiative.org (office). *Website:* www.nobelwomensinitiative.org (office); www.icbl.org.

WILLIAMS, Lorraine Bernadine, LLB; Saint Lucia politician, lawyer, diplomatist and UN official; *Assistant Director-General, Knowledge and Communication Department, United Nations Food and Agriculture Organization;* b. 20 May 1958, St Lucia; m. Basil Williams 1983; one s. *Education:* St Joseph's Convent and Advanced Level Coll. (Castries) and Univ. of the West Indies (Barbados). *Career:* attorney in pvt practice 1983–90; Magistrate, then Chief Magistrate 1990–92; Attorney-Gen. and Minister of Legal Affairs 1992–97, Minister of Women's Affairs 1994–97; High Commr for Eastern Caribbean States, Ottawa, Canada –2007; Asst Dir-Gen. Knowledge and Communication Dept, FAO, Rome 2007–; Prin. Del. from St Lucia to Inter-American Comm. on Women 1995; Degree of Excellence Award 1995.
Address: Knowledge and Communication Department, Food and Agriculture Organization of the United Nations (FAO), Viale delle Terme di Caracalla, 00100 Rome, Italy (office); Rodney Heights, Quarter of Gros Islet, POB 433, Castries, Saint Lucia (home). *Telephone:* (06) 5705-1 (office). *Fax:* (06) 5705-3152 (office). *E-mail:* fao-hq@fao.org (office). *Website:* www.fao.org (office).

WILLIAMS, Martin John, CVO, OBE, BA; British consultant and diplomatist (retd); *United Kingdom Consultant, New Zealand Antarctic Heritage Trust;* b. 3 Nov. 1941; m. Susan Dent 1964; two s. *Education:* Manchester Grammar School, Corpus Christi Coll. Oxford. *Career:* joined Commonwealth Relations Office 1963; various posts including service at Embassy in Manila 1966–69, Consulate-Gen. in Milan 1970–72, Embassy in Tehran 1977–80, High Comm. in New Delhi 1982–86, Embassy in Rome 1986–90; Head of S. Asian Dept, FCO 1990–92; seconded to NI Office, Belfast as Asst Under-Sec. (Political Affairs) 1993–95; High Commr in Zimbabwe 1995–98, in NZ (also accred to Samoa and Gov. Pitcairn Island) 1998–2001; UK Consultant to New Zealand Antarctic Heritage Trust 2002; Chair. Link Foundation for UK –NZ Relations 2004–.
Address: Russet House, Lughorse Lane, Yalding, Kent, ME18 6EG, England (home). *Telephone:* (1622) 815403 (home).

WILLIAMS, Penny, BA; Australian diplomatist; *High Commissioner to Malaysia;* m.; four c. *Career:* Dir Staffing Operations Section, Dept of Foreign Affairs and Trade 2001–02, Asst Sec. Staffing Branch 2003–04, First Asst Sec., Diplomatic Security Information Man. and Services Div. 2004–05, First Asst Sec. Corp. Man. Div. 2005–07; overseas postings include First Sec., Embassy in Damascus 1992–94, Counsellor, Embassy in Santiago 1997–2000; High Commr to Malaysia 2007–.
Address: High Commission of Australia, 6 Jalan Yap Kwan Seng, 50450 Kuala Lumpur, Malaysia (office). *Telephone:* (3) 21465555 (office). *Fax:* (3) 21415773 (office). *E-mail:* Public-Affairs-KLPR@dfat.gov.au (office). *Website:* www.australia.org.my (office).

WILLIAMS, Steve; British diplomatist; *Ambassador to Bulgaria;* m. Fiona Williams; one s. two d. *Career:* Third Sec., FCO 1981–83; Second Sec. (Political and Cultural), Embassy in Sofia 1984–87; Second Sec., EC (External) Dept, FCO 1987–90; secondment to Barclays Bank, London 1990–91; Head of Econ. and Commercial Section, Embassy in Oslo 1991–95, First Sec. (External Relations), UK Rep. to EU, Brussels 1995–98; Deputy Head of EU (Internal) Dept, FCO 1998– 2000; Deputy Head of Mission, Embassy in Buenos Aires 2001–03; Head of Latin America and Caribbean Dept, FCO 2003–05, Dir Americas 2005–07; Amb. to Bulgaria 2007–.
Address: British Embassy, ul. Moskovska 9, 1087 Sofia, Bulgaria (office). *Telephone:* (2) 933-92-22 (office). *Fax:* (2) 933-92– (office). *E-mail:* britembcon@mail.orbitel.bg (office). *Website:* www.british-embassy.bg (office).

WILLIAMS OF CROSBY, Baroness (Life Peer), cr. 1993, of Stevenage in the County of Hertfordshire; **Rt Hon. Shirley Williams,** PC, MA; British politician and academic; *Public Service Professor of Electoral Politics, Emerita, John F. Kennedy School of Government, Harvard University;* b. 27 July 1930, London; m. 1st Bernard Williams 1955 (divorced 1974, died 2003); one d.; m. 2nd Prof. Richard Neustadt 1987 (died 2003). *Education:* Summit School, Minn., USA, St Paul's Girls' School, Somerville Coll. Oxford and Columbia Univ., New York. *Career:* Gen. Sec. Fabian Soc. 1960–64; Labour MP for Hitchin 1964–74, for Hertford and Stevenage 1974–79; SDP MP for Crosby 1981–83; Parl. Pvt. Sec., Minister of Health

1964–66; Parl. Sec. Minister of Labour 1966–67; Minister of State, Dept of Educ. and Science 1967–69; Minister of State, Home Office 1969–70; Opposition Spokesman on Health and Social Security 1970–71, on Home Affairs 1971–73, on Prices and Consumer Affairs 1973–74; Sec. of State for Prices and Consumer Protection 1974–76, for Educ. and Science 1976–79; Paymaster-Gen. 1976–79; Sr Research Fellow (part-time) Policy Research Inst. 1979–85; mem. Labour Party Nat. Exec. Cttee 1970–81; mem. Council for Social Democracy Jan.–March 1981; left Labour Party March 1981; Co-Founder SDP March 1981, Pres. 1982–88; Public Service Prof. of Elective Politics, John F. Kennedy School of Govt, Harvard Univ. 1988–2000, Prof. Emer. 2000–, Dir Inst. of Politics 1988–89; mem. Social and Liberal Democratic Party 1988–; Deputy Leader Liberal Democrat Party, House of Lords 1999–2001, Leader Nov. 2001–; Visiting Fellow, Nuffield Coll., Oxford 1967–75; Fellow, Inst. of Politics, Harvard 1979–80 (mem. Sr Advisory Council 1986–); Regents Lecturer and Fellow, Inst. of Politics, Univ. of Calif., Berkeley; Dir Turing Inst., Glasgow 1985–90, Learning by Experience Trust 1986–94, Project Liberty 1990–98; Janeway Lecturer, Princeton Univ., NJ; Pick Lecturer, Chicago Univ.; Godkin Lecturer, Harvard Univ.; Montgomery Lecturer, Dartmouth Coll.; Heath Fellow, Grinell Coll.; Rede Lecturer and Darwin Lecturer, Univ. of Cambridge; Hoover Lecturer, Strathclyde Univ.; Dainton Lecturer, British Library; Gresham Lecturer, Mansion House; mem. EC Comité des Sages 1996–97, Council Int. Crisis Group 1998–, Int. Advisory Council, Council on Foreign Relations (US); Chair. EC Job Creation Competition 1997–98; Trustee The Century Foundation, New York, Inst. for Public Policy Research, London, RAND Europe UK; Gov. The Ditchley Foundation; mem. Bd Moscow School of Political Studies; lecture series: Who's Who plus 2001: Erasmus, Notre Dame; Hon. Fellow Somerville Coll., Oxford, Newnham Coll., Cambridge; Grand Cross (FRG); Hon. DEd, CNAA; Hon. DrPolEcon (Univ. of Leuven, Belgium, Radcliffe Coll., Harvard, USA); Hon. LLD (Leeds) 1979, (Southampton) 1981, (Ulster) 1997; Dr hc (Aston, Bath, Essex, Heriot-Watt, Napier, Sheffield, Washington Coll. (USA)); RSA Silver Medal. *Radio:* Snakes and Ladders – A Political Diary (BBC Radio 4) 1996, Women in the House (BBC Radio 4) 1998. *Television:* Shirley Williams in Conversation (BBC series) 1979. *Publications:* Youth Without Work (OECD Study) 1981, Politics is for People 1981, A Job to Live 1985, 'Human Rights in Europe' for Human Rights: What Work? (ed. Power and Alison) 2000, Making Globalisation Good (Chapter 15: Global Social Justice – The Moral Responsibilities of the Rich to the Poor) (ed. John Dunning) 2003, God and Caesar 2003; pamphlets on EC and economics of Central Africa; articles for The Times, Guardian, Independent, Int. Herald Tribune, Political Quarterly, Prospect etc.
Address: House of Lords, Westminster, London, SW1A 0PW, England (office). *Telephone:* (20) 7219-5850 (home); (20) 7219-3242 (home); (617) 495-8866 (Harvard). *Fax:* (20) 7219-1174 (office). *E-mail:* williamss@ parliament.uk (office); shirley_williams@ksg.harvard.edu. *Website:* ksgfaculty.harvard.edu/shirley_williams.

WILLIAMSON, John, PhD; British economist and academic; *Senior Fellow, Peterson Institute for International Economics;* b. 7 June 1937, Hereford; m. Denise R. de Souza 1974; two s. one d. *Education:* London School of Econs and Princeton Univ. *Career:* Lecturer, Reader, Univ. of York 1963–68; HM Treasury 1968–70; Prof., Univ. of Warwick 1970–77; adviser, IMF 1972–74; Prof., Catholic Univ. of Rio de Janeiro 1978–81; Sr Fellow, Inst. for Int. Econs (now Peterson Inst. for Int. Econs) 1981–; Chief Economist South Asia, World Bank 1996–99; Project Dir UN High-Level Panel on Financing for Devt 2001. *Publications:* The Crawling Peg 1965, The Failure of World Monetary Reform 1977, The Exchange Rate System 1983, Targets and Indicators (with M.H. Miller) 1987, Latin American Adjustment: How Much Has Happened? 1990, The Political Economy of Policy Reform 1993, The Crawling Band as an Exchange Rate Regime 1996, A Survey of Financial Liberalization (co-author) 1998, Exchange Rate Regimes for Emerging Markets 2000, After the Washington Consensus: Restarting Growth and Reform in Latin America (co-ed.) 2003, Dollar Adjustment: How Far? Against What? (co-ed.) 2004.
Address: Institute for International Economics, 1750 Massachusetts Avenue, NW, Washington, DC 20036-1903 (office); 3919 Oliver Street, Chevy Chase, MD 20815, USA. *Telephone:* (202) 454-1340 (office); (301) 654-5312 (home). *Fax:* (202) 328-5432 (office). *E-mail:* jwilliamson@iie .com (office). *Website:* www.iie.com/jwilliamson.htm (office).

WILLIBIRIO SAKO, Jean; Central African Republic diplomatist; *Ambassador to France; Career:* Co-ordinator for Cen. African Repub., Nat. AIDS Comm., World Bank 2002; fmr Chair. Ind. Jt Electoral Comm.; Amb. to France, also Perm. Rep. to UNESCO, Paris 2006–.
Address: Embassy of the Central African Republic, 30 rue des Perchamps, 75116 Paris, France (office). *Telephone:* 1-45-25-39-74 (office). *Fax:* 1-45-27-48-11 (office). *E-mail:* accueil@amb-rcaparis.org (office). *Website:* www .amb-rcaparis.org (office).

WILSON, Fraser Andrew, MBE; British diplomatist; *Ambassador to Albania;* b. 6 May 1949; m. Janet; two s. *Career:* archivist, Havana 1970–71, SE Asia Floater 1971–73, Man. Officer, Seoul 1973–77, unofficial rep., then mem. Gov.'s staff, Salisbury 1977–80, Desk Officer, Western European Dept, FCO 1980–82, Desk Officer, Eastern European and Soviet Dept 1982–84, Second Sec. (Commercial), Moscow 1984–85, Vice-Consul, then Commercial Sec., Rangoon 1986–90, Desk Officer, Eastern European and Soviet (later Eastern) Dept 1990–92, Asst Insp., Diplomatic Service Overseas Inspectorate 1992–94, Deputy Consul Gen., São Paulo 1994–97, Amb. to Turkmenistan 1998–2002, High Commr to Seychelles 2002–04, Deputy Head of Overseas Territories Dept, FCO 2004–06, Amb. to Albania 2006–.
Address: British Embassy, Rruga Skënderbeu 12, Tirana, Albania (office). *Telephone:* (4) 234973 (office). *Fax:* (4) 247697 (office). *E-mail:* tiran@fco .gov.uk (office). *Website:* www.uk.al (office).

WILSON, Hon. Margaret, LLB, M.jur; New Zealand politician; *Speaker, House of Representatives;* b. 20 May 1947, Gisborne. *Education:* St Dominic's Coll., Northcote, Morrinsville Coll., Univ. of Auckland. *Career:* sec. for Legal Employers Union 1970–1971; law clerk and solicitor, Peter Jenkins, barrister and solicitor in Auckland 1970–72; taught at Univ. of Auckland; Founder-mem. Industrial Relations Soc. 1973; Acting Ed. Recent Law 1974; Founding Ed. New Zealand Journal of Industrial Relations 1976–77, mem. Editorial Bd 1994–; Exec. mem., Vice-Chair. and Chair. Auckland Br., Asscn of Univ. Teachers 1976–84; Founder-mem. and Vice-Pres. Auckland Women Lawyers' Asscn 1984, Life mem. 1985–; Convenor, Govt Working Party on Equal Pay and Equal Opportunities 1988; Dir Reserve Bank of New Zealand 1985–89; Chief Political Adviser and Head of Prime Minister's Office 1987–89; Chair. Nat. Advisory Council on Employment of Women 1987–91; Chair. TV3 News Ltd 1988–89; Law Commr of the Law Comm. 1988–89; apptd Foundation Dean and Prof. of Law, Univ. of Waikato 1990; mem. Advisory Cttee to establish the Ministry of Women's Affairs 1985, Advisory Group on restructuring of the Ministry of Justice 1995, team to review the Crown Forestry Rental Trust 1995, Judicial Working Group on Gender Equality 1995–97; Chief Govt Law Officer; Attorney-Gen. 1999–2005; Minister of Labour 1999–2004; Minister in Charge of Treaty of Waitangi Negotiations 1999–2005; Assoc. Minister of Justice 1999–2004, Assoc. Minister of State Services 2000–02; Minister responsible for the Law Comm. 2001–02; Minister for Courts 2002–03, Assoc. Minister 2003–04; Minister of Commerce 2004; Speaker of House of Reps 2005–; Pres. NZ Labour Party 1984–87; Hon. LLD (Waikato) 2004.
Address: Parliament Buildings, Wellington, New Zealand (office). *Telephone:* (4) 471-9999 (office). *Fax:* (4) 472-2055 (office). *Website:* www .parliament.govt.nz (office).

WILSON, Hon. Michael, PC, OC; Canadian business executive, diplomatist and fmr politician; *Ambassador to USA;* b. 4 Nov. 1937, Toronto. *Education:* Univ. of Toronto, LSE. *Career:* MP for Etobicoke Centre 1979–93, Minister of Finance 1984–91, Minister of Industry, Science and Tech. and Minister for Int. Trade –1993, represented Canada at IMF, IBRD, OECD, GATT and G-7 Ministers meetings; Vice Chair. RBC Dominion Securities and institutional asset management business 1993; Chair. UBS Canada 2001–06; Amb. to USA 2006–; mem. Bd of Dirs BP plc 1998–2006; Chair. Council for Public-Private Partnerships 2001–06, Canadian Coalition for Good Governance; Chancellor Trinity Coll. (Univ. of Toronto) 2003–06; Dr hc (Univ. of Toronto), (York Univ.).
Address: Embassy of Canada, 501 Pennsylvania Avenue, NW, Washington, DC 20001, USA (office). *Telephone:* (202) 682-1740 (home). *Fax:* (202) 682-7726 (office). *E-mail:* webmaster@canadianembassy.org (office). *Website:* www.canadianembassy.org (office).

WILSON, Ross L., BA, MA; American diplomatist; *Ambassador to Turkey;* b. 1955, Minneapolis, Minn.; m. Margo Squire; two s. *Education:* Univ. of Minnesota, Columbia Univ., New York, Nat. War Coll., Washington, DC. *Career:* joined State Dept 1979, now career mem. Sr Foreign Service with rank of Minister-Counselor, served in Offices of Soviet Union and Egyptian Affairs, twice at Embassy in Moscow 1980–82 and 1987–90, Embassy in Prague 1985–87, Special Asst to Under-Sec. of State for Econ. Affairs and Counselor Dept Zoellick 1990–92, Deputy Exec. Sec. Dept of State 1992–94, Consul Gen., Melbourne 1995–97, Prin. Deputy to Amb.-at-Large and Special Advisor to Sec. of State for New Ind. States of fmr Soviet Union 1997–2000, Amb. to Azerbaijan 2000–03, US Sr Negotiator for Free Trade Area of the Americas, Office of US Trade Rep. 2003–05, Exec. Asst and Chief of Staff for Deputy Sec. of State Robert B. Zoellick Feb.–Aug. 2005, Amb. to Turkey 2005–; Order of Honor (Azerbaijan); numerous State Dept awards, President's Meritorious Service Award 2005.
Address: Embassy of the USA, Atatürk Bul. 110, Kavaklıdere, 06100 Ankara, Turkey (office). *Telephone:* (312) 4555555 (office). *Fax:* (312) 4670019 (office). *E-mail:* webmaster_ankara@state.gov (office). *Website:* ankara.usembassy.gov (office).

WIN, U Nay; Myanmar diplomatist; *Ambassador to UK;* m. Daw Nwe Nwe Hlaing. *Career:* Amb. to Nepal 2001–05, to UK (also accred to Denmark, Norway and Sweden) 2005–; Patron, Britain-Burma Soc.
Address: Embassy of Myanmar, 19A Charles Street, Berkeley Square, London, W1J 5DX, England (office). *Telephone:* (20) 7499-4340 (office). *Fax:* (20) 7409-7043 (office). *E-mail:* memblondon@aol.com (office); melondon@btconnect.com (office).

WIN, U Ye; Myanma diplomatist; *Ambassador to Thailand;* m. Daw Ei Ei Khaing. *Career:* fmr Project Man., Myanma Posts and Telecommunications; Amb. to Thailand 2005–.
Address: Embassy of Myanmar, 132 Thanon Sathorn Nua, Bangkok, 10500, Thailand (office). *Telephone:* (2) 234-0278 (office). *Fax:* (2) 236-6898 (office). *E-mail:* mebkk@asianet.co.th (office).

WINCKLER, Georg; Austrian university rector and academic; *Professor of Economics, University of Vienna;* b. 27 Sept. 1943, Ostrava, Czechoslovakia; m.; two d. *Education:* Princeton Univ., USA, Univ. of Vienna. *Career:* Prof. of Econs, Univ. of Vienna 1978–, Univ. Rector 1999–; with Research Dept IMF 1990–91; Visiting Prof. of Econs, Georgetown Univ., USA 1995; Pres. Austrian Rectors' Conf. 2000–; Vice-Pres. European Univ. Asscn 2001–. *Publications:* Central and Eastern Europe: Roads to Growth 1992, Central Banks and Seigniorage: A Study of Three Economies in Transition (European Econ. Review) 1996, Grundzüge der Wirtschaftspolitik Österreichs (co-author) 2001.
Address: Office of the Rector, University of Vienna, Dr Karl Lueger-Ring, 1010 Vienna, Austria (office). *Telephone:* (1) 4277-10010 (office); (1) 328-12-72 (home). *Fax:* (1) 4277-9100 (office). *E-mail:* georg.winckler@univie.ac.at (office). *Website:* www.univie.ac.at (office).

WINID, Bogusław W., MA; Polish diplomatist; *Permanent Representative, NATO;* b. 3 Nov. 1960, Warsaw; m. Beata Winid; one s. *Education:* History Inst., Univ. of Warsaw, Indiana Univ., USA. *Career:* Asst, American Studies Centre, Univ. of Warsaw 1984–88; joined Dept of N and S America, Ministry of Foreign Affairs 1991, Deputy Dir 1997–98, Dir 1998–2001; First Sec., later Counsellor, Embassy in Washington, DC 1992–97, Deputy Chief of Mission 2001–06, Under-Sec. of State for Int. Relations, Ministry of Defence 2006–07, Perm. Rep. to NATO and WEU, Brussels 2007–. *Publications:* In the Capitol's Shadow: Polish Diplomacy towards the United States of America 1919–1939, Santiago 1898, NATO Expansion in the United States Congress 1993–1998; numerous journal articles.
Address: Permanent Mission of Poland to NATO, blvd Léopold III, 1110, Brussels, Brussels (office). *Telephone:* (2) 707-13-88 (office). *Fax:* (2) 707-13-89 (office). *E-mail:* poland@skynet.be (office). *Website:* www.brukselanato.polemb.net (office).

WINKLER, Jan; Czech politician and diplomatist; *Ambassador to UK;* b. 1957, Pardubice; m. Jana Winklerová; three c. *Education:* Charles Univ., Prague, Univ. of Sussex, UK, Basel Univ., Switzerland, Univ. of Pittsburgh, USA. *Career:* co. lawyer for Czechoslovak State Railways 1981–90; Registrar and Sec. Charles Univ. 1990–95; Dir Analyses and Planning Dept, Ministry of Foreign Affairs 1995–97, Deputy Minister of Foreign Affairs 1997–99, Deputy Minister of Foreign Affairs (Security Policy) 2003–05; Amb. to UK 2005–; Sr Man., Andersen Consulting/Accenture 1999–2002; Prin. Consultant, PricewaterhouseCoopers Consulting/IBM Business Consulting 2002–03; Chair. Nat. Gallery Bd 1994–99; mem. Masaryk Democratic Movt 1991–; mem. Civic Inst. 1991–, Asscn of Univ. Admins, UK 1991–95, European Higher Educ. Soc., Netherlands 1992–97, OECD Programme on Institutional Man. in Higher Educ., Paris 1993–97, Duke of Edinburgh Award Programme in Czech 1997–.
Address: Embassy of the Czech Republic, 26 Kensington Palace Gardens, London, W8 4QY, England (office). *Telephone:* (20) 7243-1115 (office). *Fax:* (20) 7727-9654 (office). *E-mail:* london@embassy.mzv.cz (office). *Website:* www.mzv.cz/london (office).

WINTERS, L. Alan, MA, PhD; British economist and academic; *Director, World Bank Development Research Group;* b. 8 April 1950, London; m. 1st Margaret Elizabeth Griffin 1971; m. 2nd Zhen Kun Wang 1997; one s. two d. *Education:* Chingford Co. High School, Univs. of Bristol and Cambridge. *Career:* Jr, Research Office, Dept of Applied Econs, Univ. of Cambridge 1971–80; lecturer in econs, Univ. of Bristol 1980–86; economist, World Bank 1983–85, Div. Chief/Research Man. 1994–99; Prof. of Econs, Univ. of Wales at Bangor 1986–90, Univ. of Birmingham 1990–94, Univ. of Sussex 1999–; currently Dir, World Bank Development Research Group, Washington DC. *Publications:* Econometric Model of the British Export Sector 1981, International Economics 1984, Europe's Domestic Market 1987, Eastern Europe's International Trade 1994, Sustainable Development 1995, The Uruguay Round and the Developing Countries 1996, Trade Liberalisation and Poverty 2001.

Address: World Bank, Mailstop MC3–304, 1818 H Street, NW, Washington, DC 20433, USA (office). *Telephone:* (202) 458-8208 (office). *Fax:* (202) 522-1150 (office). *E-mail:* lwinters@worldbank.org (office). *Website:* econ.worldbank.org (office).

WIRAJUDA, Nur Hassan, MA, LLM, SJD; Indonesian politician; *Minister of Foreign Affairs;* b. 9 July 1948, Tangerang; m.; four c. *Education:* Univ. of Indonesia, Univ. of Oxford, UK, Tufts Univ., Harvard Univ. and Univ. of Virginia, USA. *Career:* practising lawyer (legal aid) and univ. lecturer, Jakarta 1972–75; Legal Council Corp. Sec., Dockyard State Enterprise, Jakarta 1972–73; Head of Section, Secr. of the Foreign Affairs Cttee of the Nat. Council for Political and Security Stabilization, Secr. Gen., Dept of Foreign Affairs 1974–75; Third Sec., then Second Sec. for Political Affairs, Indonesian Embassy, Cairo 1977–81; Head of Section, Politics-Legal Affairs, Directorate of Int. Orgs, Dept of Foreign Affairs 1981, Dir for Int. Orgs 1993–97, Deputy Dir for Territorial Treaties, Directorate of Legal and Treaty Affairs 1998, Dir Gen. for Political Affairs 2000–01; Counsellor, later Minister Counsellor for Political Affairs, Perm. Mission in Geneva 1989–93; Amb. to Egypt (also accred to Djibouti) 1997–98; Amb. and Perm. Rep. to the UN, Geneva, WTO and the Conf. on Disarmament 1998–2000; Personal Rep. of the Pres. to the Group of Fifteen Developing Countries (G-15) 1998–2000; represented the Govt in the sovereignty case concerning Pulau Ligitan and Pulau Sipadan before Int. Court of Justice, The Hague 2000; Leading Govt Negotiator in the Dialogue on Aceh with Free Aceh Movt Reps, Switzerland 2000; Minister of Foreign Affairs 2001–.
Address: Ministry of Foreign Affairs, Jalan Taman Pejambon 6, 10th Floor, Jakarta 10110, Indonesia (office). *Telephone:* (21) 3813453 (office). *Fax:* (21) 3857316 (office). *E-mail:* ditpen1@deplu.go.id (office). *Website:* www.deplu.go.id (office).

WIRTH, Timothy Endicott, PhD; American fmr politician; *President, United Nations Foundation;* b. 22 Sept. 1939, Santa Fe, NM; m. Wren Winslow 1965; one s. one d. *Education:* Harvard and Stanford Univs. *Career:* Special Asst to Sec. Dept of Health, Educ. and Welfare 1967, Deputy Asst Sec. for Educ. 1969; Asst to Chair., Nat. Urban Coalition 1968; Vice-Pres. Great Western United Corpn, Denver 1970; Man. Arthur D. Little Inc. 1971–73; mem. 94th–99th Congresses from 2nd Dist Colo; Senator from Colorado 1987–92; Counsellor Dept of State 1993–97; Pres. UN Foundation 1998–, Better World Fund 1998–; Ford Foundation Fellow 1964–66; Pres. White House Fellows Asscn 1968–69; mem. Exec. Cttee Denver Council Foreign Relations 1974–75; mem. Bd of Visitors, USAF Acad. 1978–; Adviser, Pres. Comm. on the 80s 1979–80; Democrat.
Address: United Nations Foundation, 1800 Massachusetts Avenue, NW, Washington, DC 20036, USA (office). *Telephone:* (202) 887-9040 (office). *Fax:* (202) 887-9021 (office). *Website:* www.unfoundation.org (office).

WISE, James, BA; Australian diplomatist; m.; two c. *Education:* Univ. of Tasmania. *Career:* numerous positions at Dept of Foreign Affairs and Trade including Third Sec., Embassy in Port Moresby 1983–85, Second and First Sec., Embassy in Moscow 1987–91; Sr Analyst, Office of Nat. Assessments 1991–94; Dir Russia, E Europe and Cen. Asia Section 1994–95; Deputy Head of Mission and Perm. Rep. to ESCAP, Bangkok 1995–98; Asst Sec., NZ and Papua New Guinea Br 1998–99; Asst Sec., Staffing Br 1999–2001; First Asst Sec., S Pacific, Africa and Middle East Div. 2001–02; High Commr to Malaysia 2002–07; First Asst Sec., Corp. Man. Div., Dept of Foreign Affairs and Trade 2007–.
Address: Corporate Management Division, Department of Foreign Affairs and Trade, R. G. Casey Bldg, John McEwen Crescent, Barton, ACT 0221, Australia (office). *Telephone:* (2) 6261-1111 (office). *Fax:* (2) 6261-3111 (office). *Website:* www.dfat.gov.au (office).

WISZNIEWSKI, Andrzej, PhD, DSc; Polish academic, electrical engineer and politician; *Professor, Institute of Power Engineering, Technical University of Wrocław;* b. 15 Feb. 1935, Warsaw; m. Ewa Lutosławska; one d. *Education:* Tech. Univ. of Wrocław. *Career:* researcher, Wrocław Univ. of Tech. 1957–, Extraordinary Prof. 1972, Ordinary Prof. 1990–, Rector 1990–96; Univ. of Garyounis Benghazi, Libya 1976–79; Head of Scientific Research Cttee and mem. Council of Ministers 1997–99; Minister of Science 1999–2001; mem. Speech Communication Asscn, USA, Solidarity Trade Union 1980–, Social Movt of Solidarity Election Action 1998–2001; Hon. Mem. Inst. of Electrical Engineers 1999, Distinguished Mem. Int. Conf. on Large Electric Systems 2000; Kt's Cross, Order of Polonia Restituta 1979; Grand Cross, Order of Saint Stanisław with Star 1998; Commdr, Order of Saint Sylvester 1998; Grand Cross, Order of Merit (Peru) 2001; Dr hc (Cen. Conn. State Univ.) 1993, (Tech. Univ. of Lvov) 1999, (Tech. Univ. of Wrocław) 2001; City of Wrocław Award 1996, Council of Rectors Award 1998. *Publications:* Measuring Transformers 1983, Algorithms of Numeral Measurements in Electroenergetic Automatics 1990, Schutztechnik in Elektroenergiesystemen (co-author) 1994, Protective Automatics in Electroenergetics Systems 1998, How to Speak and Make Speeches Convincingly 1994, Aphorisms and Quotations: for Orators, Disputants and Banqueters 1997, Measuring and Decision Making Algorithms (jtly), Art of Writing 2003; over 130 articles on electrotechnics and electroenergetics. *Address:* Technical University of Wrocław Institute of Power Engineering, Grunwaldski Square 13, 50-370 Wrocław (office); Krasickiego 18, 51-144 Wrocław, Poland (home). *Telephone:* (71) 3203487 (office); (71) 3726477 (home); (601) 381944 (home). *Fax:* (71) 3202656 (office). *E-mail:* andrzej .wiszniewski@pwr.wroc.pl (office); awiszniewski@wr.home.pl (home). *Website:* www.pwr.wroc.pl/~i-8zas (office).

WITHERS, John L., II, BA, MA, PhD; American diplomatist; *Ambassador to Albania;* m. Maryruth Coleman. *Education:* Harvard Univ., McGill Univ., Canada, Yale Univ., grad.-level research at Nanjing Univ., People's Repub. of China. *Career:* began his career in Foreign Service in 1984, Political Officer, Embassy in The Hague 1985–86; Desk Officer, Office of Chinese Affairs, Dept of State 1986–88; Political Officer, Embassy in Lagos 1988–90, Political Officer, Embassy in Moscow 1991–93; with Office of Northern European Affairs on Ireland and Iceland desks, Dept of State 1993, Special Asst to Office of Deputy Sec. 1993–96; Deputy Chief of Mission, Embassy in Riga 1997–2000; Dir Office of N Cen. European Affairs, Dept of State 2001–02, Dir Operations Center 2003–05; Amb. to Albania 2007–. *Address:* US Embassy, Rruga Elbasanit 103, Tirana, Albania (office). *Telephone:* (4) 247285 (office). *Fax:* (4) 232222 (office). *E-mail:* wm_tirana@pd.state.gov (office). *Website:* tirana.usembassy.gov (office).

WLOSOWICZ, Zbigniew; Polish diplomatist and United Nations official. *Career:* fmr UN Rep. from Poland, UN Envoy Feb. 1993; mem. UN Security Council; Special Adviser on Inter-Governmental Affairs UNDP 1998–2000; UN Special Rep. of the Sec.-Gen. in Cyprus and Chief of Mission, UNFICYP 2000–05. *Address:* c/o Ministry of Foreign Affairs, 00-580 Warsaw, Al. Szucha 23, Poland.

WOLDE-GIORGIS, Girma; Ethiopian head of state; *President;* b. Dec. 1925, Addis Ababa; m.; five c. *Education:* School of Social Science, Netherlands, Air Traffic Man. School, Sweden, Air Traffic Control Man. School, Canada. *Career:* served in Ethiopian Army, rank of Lt 1941–45; trainee, Ethiopian Air Force 1946–47; Instructor in Air Navigation and Air Traffic Control 1948–54; Head Civil Aviation Authority, Eritrean Fed. State, Asmara 1955–57; Dir-Gen. Ethiopian Civil Aviation, mem. Bd Ethiopian Airlines 1958; Dir-Gen. Ministry of Commerce, Industry and Planning 1959–60; elected mem. Parl., Pres. 1st Session 1961; Vice-Pres. 52nd Int. Parl. Ass., Belgrade 1961; mem. Bd Ethiopian Chamber of Commerce 1967, Civil Advisory Council 1973; Vice-Commr to Peace Comm. 1974; Rep. of Ministry of Transport and Communications to Northern Region of Eritrea and Tigrai 1974; mem. Int. Cttee of the Red Cross, Head of Logistics to Demobilize ex-Army Personnel 1990; mem. House of People's Reps Econ. Cttee 2000–01; Pres. of Ethiopia 2001–; Medal of Genet, Mil. Officers' Acad. 1944, Haile Selassie Star, Cavalry 1956, Minilik Star, Cavalry 1960, Haile Selassie Gold Medal 1960, City Council Gold Medal 1971, Red Cross Silver Medal 1988. *Publication:* Air and Men (in Amharic) 1954. *Address:* Office of the President, PO Box 1362, Addis Ababa, Ethiopia (office). *Telephone:* (1) 518677 (office); (1) 518890 (home). *Fax:* (1) 518656 (office).

WOLFE, Raymond, BSc; Jamaican diplomatist; *Permanent Representative, United Nations;* b. 4 May 1941; m.; two c. *Education:* Univ. of the West Indies, York Univ., Canada. *Career:* joined Ministry of Foreign Affairs 1973; served in Embassy in Moscow 1977–81, in Nigeria 1990–92, in Japan 1992–94; held several sr positions at Ministry of Foreign Affairs 1994–98, including Dir European Affairs Dept and Dir Africa, Asia and Pacific Affairs Dept; served at Perm. Mission to UN, New York 1984–90; High Commr to Canada 1998–2003; Under-Sec. for Multilateral Affairs, Ministry of Foreign Affairs and Foreign Trade 2003–06; Perm. Rep. to UN, New York 2006–. *Address:* Permanent Mission of Jamaica to the United Nations, 767 Third Avenue, 9th Floor, New York, NY 10017, USA (office). *Telephone:* (212) 935-7509 (office). *Fax:* (212) 935-7607 (office). *E-mail:* jamaica@un.int (office). *Website:* www.un.int/jamaica (office).

WOLFSON, Dirk Jacob, PhD; Dutch economist; *Professor Emeritus of Economics, Erasmus University;* b. 22 June 1933, Voorburg; m. Anna Maaike Hoekstra 1960; three c. *Education:* Univ. of Amsterdam. *Career:* Teaching Asst Univ. of Amsterdam 1961–63; Economist, IMF, Washington, DC 1964–70; Dir (Chief Economist), Econ. Policy Div. Netherlands Treasury Dept 1970–75; Prof. of Public Finance, Erasmus Univ., Rotterdam 1975–86, Prof. of Econs 1992–99, Prof. Emer. 1999–; Rector,

Inst. of Social Studies, The Hague 1986–90; mem. Social and Econ. Council 1982–96, Scientific Council for Govt Policy 1990–98; Royal Supervisor, Netherlands Cen. Bank and Chair. Banking Council 1990–99; mem. Senate (Social Democratic Party) 1999–; mem. Royal Netherlands Acad. of Arts and Sciences 1989–; Kt, Order of the Netherlands Lion; Commdr, Order of Orange Nassau. *Publications:* Public Finance and Development Strategy 1979; numerous books and articles on econ. theory and policy. *Address:* Aelbrechtskolk 41A, 3025 HB Rotterdam, Netherlands (home). *Telephone:* (10) 4779497 (home). *Fax:* (10) 4764667 (home). *E-mail:* dwolfson@xs4all.nl (home).

WOLLACK, Kenneth; American national organization executive and fmr journalist; *President, National Democratic Institute for International Affairs; Education:* Earlham Coll., Richmond, Ind., Univ. of London, UK. *Career:* served on nat. staff of McGovern presidential campaign 1972; Legis. Dir American Israel Public Affairs Cttee 1973–80; Co-Ed. Middle East Policy Survey, Washington, DC 1980–86; Exec. Vice-Pres. Nat. Democratic Inst. for Int. Affairs 1986–93, Pres. 1993–; currently Sr Fellow, UCLA School of Public Policy and Social Research; mem. Advisory Cttee on Voluntary Foreign Aid; Chair. US Cttee for UNDP; fmr regular contrib. on foreign affairs to Los Angeles Times. *Address:* National Democratic Institute for International Affairs, 2030 M Street, NW, Fifth Floor, Washington, DC 20036-3306, USA (office). *Telephone:* (202) 728-5500 (office). *Fax:* (20) 728-5520 (office). *E-mail:* contact@ndi.org (office). *Website:* www.ndi.org (office).

WOLOU, B. Mayanendja Nonon Saa Wolou; Togolese diplomatist; *Chargé d'affaires in USA. Career:* Minister-Counsellor, Embassy in Washington, DC, Chargé d'affaires a.i. 2005–. *Address:* Embassy of Togo, 2208 Massachusetts Avenue, NW, Washington, DC 20008, USA (office). *Telephone:* (202) 234-4212 (office). *Fax:* (202) 232-3190 (office).

WOLPE, Howard, BA, PhD; American research director and fmr politician; *Africa Program Director, Woodrow Wilson International Center for Scholars;* b. 11 Feb. 1939, Los Angeles, Calif. *Education:* Reed Coll., MIT. *Career:* served in Mich. House of Reps, then seven terms as mem. US Congress, Chair. Sub cttee on Africa, Investigations and Oversight Sub cttee on Science, Space and Tech.; fmr Presidential Envoy to Africa; taught at W Mich. Univ. and Univ. of Mich.; fmr Visiting Fellow Brookings Inst.; currently Africa Program Dir, Woodrow Wilson Int. Center for Scholars, Washington, DC; mem. Council on Foreign Relations; mem. Bd of Dirs Nat. Endowment for Democracy, Africare; African-American Inst. Star Crystal Award for Excellence, Sierra Club Lifetime Achievement Award. *Publications include:* Nigeria: Modernization and the Politics of Communalism (co-ed.) 1971, Urban Politics in Nigeria 1973, The United States and Africa: A Post-War Perspective (co-author) 1998. *Address:* Woodrow Wilson International Center for Scholars, One Woodrow Wilson Plaza, 1300 Pennsylvania Avenue, NW, Washington, DC 20004-3027 (office); 11616 Chapel Cross Way, Reston, VA 20194, USA (home). *Telephone:* (202) 691-4046 (office); (703) 736-0314 (home). *Fax:* (202) 691-4001 (office); (703) 736-0815 (home). *E-mail:* wolpehe@wwic.si .edu (office); hwolpe@aol.com (home). *Website:* www.wilsoncenter.org/ africa (office).

WOLZFELD, Jean-Louis; Luxembourg diplomatist; *Ambassador to Italy;* b. 5 July 1951. *Career:* entered diplomatic service 1976; Amb. to Japan 1987–93, Perm. Rep. to UN 1993–98, Amb. to UK 2002–08 (also accred to Ireland and Iceland 2003–08), to Italy 2008–; Dir for Political Affairs, Ministry of Foreign Affairs 1998–2002; jury mem., Golden Bridge Award 2003; Commdr Order of the Oak Crown (Luxembourg), Officer Order of Merit (Luxembourg), Grand Cordon Order of the Sacred Treasure (Japan), Grand Officer Order of Leopold II (Belgium), Grand Officer Order of Merit (Spain), Commdr Order of the Phoenix (Greece). *Address:* Embassy of Luxembourg, Via S. Croce in Gerusalemme 90, 00185 Rome, Italy (office). *Telephone:* (06) 77201177 (office). *Fax:* (06) 77201055 (office). *E-mail:* rome.amb@mae.etat.lu (office). *Website:* www .ambasciatalussemburgo.it (office).

WOOD, Adam Kenneth Compton; British diplomatist; *High Commissioner to Kenya;* b. 13 March 1955; m. Catherine Richardson. *Career:* Aid Policy, Overseas Devt Admin (ODA), FCO, laterly Asst Desk Officer, Zimbabwe 1977–80; Asst Pvt. Sec. to the Lord Privy Seal, London 1980–83; Asst to UK Exec. Dir World Bank, Washington, DC 1983–86; Head of Lomé Section, EC Dept, ODA 1986–88, Kenya Programme Man., ODA Regional Office, Nairobi 1988–93, Adviser to Dir-Gen., EC, Brussels 1993–96, Head, Dept for Int. Devt, SE Asia, Bangkok 1996–2000, Devt Counsellor, UK Rep., Brussels 2000–02, High Commr to Uganda 2002–05, to Kenya 2005–.

Address: British High Commission, Upper Hill Road, PO Box 30465-00100 GPO, 00100 Nairobi, Kenya (office). *Telephone:* (20) 2844000 (office). *Fax:* (20) 2844033 (office). *E-mail:* nairobi-chancery@fco.gov.uk (office). *Website:* www.britishhighcommission.gov.uk/kenya (office).

WOOD, Adrian John Bickersteth, CBE, MA, MPA, PhD; British economist; *Professor of International Development, University of Oxford;* b. 25 Jan. 1946, Woking; m. Joyce M. Teitz 1971; two d. *Education:* Bryanston School, King's Coll. Cambridge and Harvard Univ. *Career:* Fellow, King's Coll. Cambridge 1969–77; Asst Lecturer, Lecturer, Univ. of Cambridge 1973–77; Economist, Sr Economist, IBRD 1977–85; Professorial Fellow, Inst. of Devt Studies, Univ. of Sussex 1985–2000; Chief Economist Dept for Int. Devt 2000–05; Prof. of Int. Devt, Univ. of Oxford 2005–; Harkness Fellowship 1967–69. *Publications:* A Theory of Profits 1975, A Theory of Pay 1978, Poverty and Human Development (with others) 1981, China: Long-Term Development Issues and Options (with others) 1985, North-South Trade, Employment and Inequality 1994. *Address:* Queen Elizabeth House, 3 Mansfield Road, Oxford, OX1 3TB, England (office). *Telephone:* (1865) 281837 (office). *Fax:* (1865) 281801 (office). *E-mail:* adrian.wood@qeh.ox.ac.uk (office). *Website:* www.qeh.ox.ac.uk (office).

WOOD, L. John, MA (Hons); New Zealand diplomatist and academic; *Adjunct Professor of Political Science, University of Canterbury;* b. 31 March 1944, Kaikoura; m. 1st Rosemary Taunt 1969 (died 1995); one s.; m. 2nd Rose Newell. *Education:* Lincoln Country Dist High School, Christchurch Boys' High School, Univ. of Canterbury and Balliol Coll., Oxford. *Career:* joined Ministry of Foreign Affairs 1969; seconded to Treasury 1971–72; Second Sec., later First Sec. Tokyo 1973–76; seconded to Prime Minister's Dept 1976–78; First Sec., later Counsellor and Consul-Gen. Bonn 1978–82; Ministry of Foreign Affairs 1982–83; Minister, Deputy Chief of Mission, Washington, DC 1984–87; Amb. to Iran (also accred to Pakistan and Turkey) 1987–90; Dir N Asia Div. Ministry of External Relations and Trade 1990–91, Deputy Sec. Econ. and Trade Relations 1991–94; Amb. to USA 1994–98, 2001–06; Deputy Sec. External Econ. and Trade Policy, Ministry of Foreign Affairs and Trade 1991–94, 1998–2002; Adjunct Prof. of Political Science, University of Canterbury 2006–; mem. Advisory Bd, NZ/US Council 2006–; Paul Harris Fellow, Rotary International 2005; Trustee, Univ. of Canterbury Foundation 2006–; elected by Court of Convocation to Univ. of Canterbury Council 2007–; Companion of the Queen's Service Order for Public Service 2006; Hon. DLit (Canterbury) 2006; Consumers for World Trade Hall of Fame 2004. *Address:* 215 Bay Paddock Road, R.D.I Hapuku, Kaikoura (home); School of Political Science and Communications, University of Canterbury, Private Bag 4800, Christchurch, New Zealand (office). *Telephone:* (3) 319-7074 (home). *Fax:* (3) 319-7073 (home). *E-mail:* blue-duck@xtra.co.nz (home). *Website:* www.posc.canterbury.ac.nz (office).

WOOD, Michael M.; American business executive and diplomatist; *Ambassador to Sweden;* m. Judy Wood; one s. one d. *Career:* Co-founder and CEO Hanley Wood, LLC 1976–2005, mem. Bd 2005–; mem. Bd of Advisors, Veronis Suhler Stevenson 2005–; f. Redwood Investments, LLC 2005; mem. US del. attending inauguration of Pres. Lucio Gutierrez Borbua of Ecuador 2003; organized Building the American Dream housing industry round table with Pres. Ronald Reagan 1984; fmr mem. Harvard Jt Center for Housing Studies; has served on Nat. Asscn of Home Builders Long-Range Planning Cttee; Amb. to Sweden 2006–; Top Executive of the Year Award, Media Business magazine 2005. *Address:* US Embassy, Dag Hammarskjölds Väg 31, 115 89 Stockholm, Sweden (office). *Telephone:* (8) 783-53-00 (office). *Fax:* (8) 661-19-64 (office). *E-mail:* StockholmWeb@state.gov (office). *Website:* stockholm.usembassy.gov (office).

WOOD, William Braucher, BA, MBA; American diplomatist; *Ambassador to Afghanistan;* b. 7 Aug. 1950, Indiana. *Education:* Bucknell Univ., George Washington Univ. *Career:* diplomatic career includes service in Uruguay, Argentina, El Salvador, Italy; mem. US negotiating team at CSCE Summit, Helskinki 1992; lead US negotiator at NATO High Level Task Force on conventional arms control; Political Counselor, US Perm. Mission to UN –1998, Chief US Negotiator in Security Council; served on Policy Planning Staff for Latin America, Dept of State, Washington, DC, as Special Asst in Bureau of Political-Mil. Affairs, as expert on Latin American Affairs for Under-Sec. for Political Affairs, Prin. Deputy Asst Sec. of State and Acting Asst Sec. of State, Bureau of Int. Org. Affairs 1998–2002, Amb. to Colombia 2003–07, to Afghanistan 2007–; Meritorious and Superior Honor Awards, Dept of State (several times), James Clement Dunn Award for Excellence 1998, Distinguished Service Award 2002. *Address:* US Embassy, Great Masoud Road, Kabul, Afghanistan (office). *Telephone:* (20) 2300436 (office). *Fax:* (20) 2301364 (office). *E-mail:* kabulwebmaster@state.gov (office). *Website:* kabul.usembassy.gov (office).

WOODLAND, Alan Donald, PhD, FASSA; Australian economist and academic; *Professor and Australian Professorial Fellow, Faculty of Economics and Business, University of Sydney;* b. 4 Oct. 1943, Dorrigo, NSW; m. Narelle Todd 1966; one s. two d. *Education:* Univ. of New England. *Career:* Lecturer, Univ. of New England 1967–69; Asst Prof., Univ. of British Columbia 1969–74, Assoc. Prof. 1974–78, Prof. of Econs 1978–81; Prof. of Econometrics and and Australian Professorial Fellow, Faculty of Econs and Business, Univ. of Sydney 1982–; Jt Ed. The Economic Record 1987–92; Fellow, Reserve Bank 1981; Fellow, Econometric Soc. *Publication:* International Trade and Resource Allocation 1982, International Trade Policy and the Pacific Rim, Institute of Economic Affairs Conference Vol. No. 120, (co-ed.) 1999, Economic Theory and International Trade: Essays in Honour of Murray C. Kemp (ed.) 2002, The Economics of Illegal Immigration (co-author) 2005. *Address:* Faculty of Economics and Business, Room 487 H04, Merewether Building, University of Sydney, Sydney, NSW 2006 (office); 5 Rosebery Road, Killara, NSW 2071, Australia (home). *Telephone:* (2) 9351-6825 (office); (2) 9416-3100 (home). *Fax:* (2) 9351-6409 (office). *E-mail:* a.woodland@econ.usyd.edu.au (office). *Website:* www.econ.usyd.edu.au/ecmt (office).

WOOLCOTT, Richard, AC, AO, BA; Australian consultant, company director and fmr diplomatist; b. 11 June 1927, Sydney; m. Birgit Christensen 1952; two s. one d. *Education:* Frankston High School, Geelong Grammar School, Univ. of Melbourne and London Univ. School of Slavonic and E European Studies. *Career:* joined Australian Foreign Service 1951; served in Australian missions in London, Moscow (twice), S Africa, Malaya, Singapore and Ghana; attended UN Gen. Ass. 1962; Acting Commr to Singapore 1963–64; High Commr to Ghana 1967–70; accompanied Prime Ministers Menzies 1965, Holt 1966, McMahon 1971, 1972, Whitlam 1973, 1974 and Hawke 1988–91 on visits to Asia, Europe, the Americas and the Pacific; Adviser at Commonwealth Heads of Govt Confs London 1965, Ottawa 1973, Kuala Lumpur 1989; Pacific Forum 1972, 1973, 1988; Australia-Japan Ministerial Cttee 1972, 1973, 1988, 1989; Head, S Asia Div., Dept of Foreign Affairs 1973; Deputy Sec. Dept of Foreign Affairs 1974; Amb. to Indonesia 1975–78, to Philippines 1978–82; Perm. Rep. to UN 1982–88; Sec. of Dept of Foreign Affairs and Trade 1988–92; Prime Minister's Special Envoy to develop Asia Pacific Econ. Co-operation 1989; Australian Rep. on UN Security Council 1985–86; rep. of Australia at Non-aligned Summit meeting, Harare 1986; ASEAN Post-Ministerial Conf. 1989, 1990, 1991; Alt. Australian Gov., inaugural EBRD meeting 1991; Chair. Australia Indonesia Inst. 1992–98, Official Establishments Trust 1992–99, Nat. Cttee on Population and Devt 1993–95, Across Asia Multimedia (Hong Kong) 2000–; Dir Auric Pacific (Singapore) 2001–02; mem. int. council of The Asia Soc.; Vice-Pres. Multiple Sclerosis Soc. of Australia 1995–2000; Founding Dir Australasia Centre, Asia Soc. 1997–; Founding Dir or consultant several firms; mem. Bd of Commrs, Lippo Bank, Indonesia 1999–2002; Life Fellow, Trinity Coll., Melbourne Univ. 1995; Bintang Mahaputra Utama (Indonesia) 2000. *Publications:* Australian Foreign Policy 1973, The Hot Seat: Reflections on Diplomacy From Stalin's Death to the Bali Bombings 2003; numerous articles, including special features for The Australian, articles for International Herald Tribune, Time. *Address:* Asia Society, AustralAsia Centre, Level 1, 175 Collins Street, Melbourne, Vic. 3000 (office); PO Box 3926, Manuka, Canberra, ACT 2603 (office); 19 Talbot Street, Forrest, Canberra, ACT 2603, Australia. *Telephone:* (2) 6295-3206 (office). *Fax:* (2) 6295-3066 (office). *E-mail:* rwoolcot@ozemail.com.au (home). *Website:* www.asiasociety.org.

WOONTON, Robert Philip, PhD; Cook Islands politician; b. 1949; m. Sue Woonton. *Career:* Minister of Foreign Affairs and Immigration 1999–; Prime Minister Feb. 2002–04, portfolio also includes Police, Parl., House of Ariki, Tourism, Agric., Marine Resources, Transport, Airport and Ports Authorities, Nat. Disaster Man. *Address:* c/o Office of the Prime Minister, Government of the Cook Islands, Private Bag, Avarua, Rarotonga, Cook Islands (office). *E-mail:* rwoonton@oyster.net.ck (home).

WORDSWORTH, Stephen John, LVO, MA; British diplomatist; *Ambassador to Serbia;* b. 17 May 1955; m. Nichole Wordsworth; one s. *Education:* Univ. of Cambridge. *Career:* Asst Desk Officer, E European and Soviet Dept, FCO 1977–79, 1981, Third, later Second Sec., Moscow 1979–81, Desk Officer, UK EC Presidency Secr. 1981, Desk Officer, E European and Soviet Dept, FCO 1982–83, First Sec. (Econ./Commercial), Lagos 1983–86, seconded to Cabinet Office Assessments Staff 1986–88, Head of GDR/Berlin Section, Western European Dept, FCO 1988–90, First Sec. (Political), Bonn 1990–94, Counsellor seconded to NATO 1994–98,

conducted Review of the Work of the British Council 1998–99, Head of Eastern Adriatic Dept, FCO 1999–2002, Minister/Deputy Head of Mission, Moscow 2003–05, Amb. to Serbia 2006–.
Address: British Embassy, Resavska 46, 11000 Belgrade, Serbia (office). *Telephone:* (11) 2645055 (office). *Fax:* (11) 659651 (office). *E-mail:* stephen.wordsworth@fco.gov.uk (office). *Website:* www.britishembassy.gov.uk/serbiaandmontenegro (office).

WORTHINGTON, Ian Alan; British diplomatist; *Ambassador to Dominican Republic;* b. 9 Aug. 1958. *Career:* Finance Dept, FCO 1977–78, Third Sec. (Scientific), Moscow 1980–82, Man. Officer, Lusaka 1982–85, Press Facilities Officer, News Dept, FCO 1985–88, Second Sec. (Commercial), Seoul 1988–91, Deputy Head of Mission, Vilnius 1991–92, Second Sec. (Political), Kingston 1992–95, Head of Trade Offic, later Consul Gen., Ekaterinburg 1995–98, Inspector/Reviewer, Man. Consultancy Services, FCO 1998–2001, Head of Trade and Investment, Berlin 2001–06, Amb. to Dominican Repub. 2006–.
Address: British Embassy, Edif. Corominas Pepin, 7°, Avda 27 de Febrero 233, Santo Domingo, DN, Dominican Republic (office). *Telephone:* 472-7111 (office). *Fax:* 472-7574 (office). *E-mail:* brit.emb.sadom@codetel.net.do (office).

WOS, Aldona Zofia; American physician, diplomatist and philanthropist; b. Warsaw, Poland; m. Louis DeJoy; two twin c. *Education:* Warsaw Medical Acad. *Career:* spent childhood on Long Island, NY; completed her internship and residency in internal medicine and fellowship in Pulmonary Medicine in New York; apptd to serve on US Holocaust Memorial Council 2002–; N Carolina State Chair. of Women for Senator Elizabeth Dole 2001; N Carolina Finance Co-Chair. for 2004 Bush-Cheney campaign 2003; Amb. to Estonia 2004–06; mem. Bd numerous philanthropic and community orgs including United Way of Greater Greensboro, Family Services of the Piedmont, Hospice Palliative Care of Greensboro, Nat. Conf. of Community of Justice; mem. American Coll. of Physicians, American Women's Medical Asscn, American Coll. of Chest Physicians, Medical Soc. of State of NY, N Carolina Medical Soc., Greater Greensboro Soc. of Medicine; Hon. mem. Jr League of Greensboro 2004; Hon. LLD (Inst. of World Politics, Washington, DC) 2006; Singular Sensations Award for Woman of Outstanding Achievement, Nat. Glaucoma Foundation 1990.
Address: US Department of State, 2201 C Street NW, Washington, DC 20520, USA (office). *Telephone:* (202) 647-4000 (office). *Fax:* (202) 647-6738 (office). *Website:* www.state.gov (office).

WOSCHNAGG, Gregor, PhD; Austrian diplomatist and civil servant; b. 23 Aug. 1939, Bern, Switzerland; m.; three c. *Education:* Univ. of Vienna, Univ. of Grenoble, France, Trinity Coll. Cambridge, UK, Coll. of Europe, Bruges, Belgium. *Career:* with Fed. Ministry for Foreign Affairs, positions included Dir Press and Information Dept 1975–81, Dir-Gen. of Secr. 1986–87, served in Dept of Econ. Integration 1966–68, later Dir, Deputy in EU Accession negotiations 1987–96, Deputy Head Econ. and Integration Political Section 1993–96, Head 1997–99; Rep. of Austria to UN, New York 1968–73; with Embassy in Cairo, Egypt 1973–75; Amb. to Kenya and Perm. Rep. UNEP and HABITAT 1981–86; Perm. Rep. to EU 1999–2007. *Publications include:* several Publs on econ. and foreign policy issues; book on Kenya.
Address: c/o Federal Ministry of European and International Affairs, Minoritenplatz 8, 1014 Vienna, Austria (office).

WRIGHT, David S., BSc, MBA; Canadian diplomatist and academic; *Kenneth and Patricia Taylor Distinguished Professor of Foreign Affairs, Victoria College, University of Toronto;* b. Montréal; m. Ilze Skuja; one s. *Education:* Lower Canada Coll., McGill Univ. Montréal, Columbia Univ., New York, USA. *Career:* joined Foreign Service 1968; Second Sec. Embassy in Rome 1969–72; First Sec. Perm. Mission to UN, New York 1972–75; Econ. Bureau External Affairs 1975–78; Counsellor (Econs and Finance) Embassy in Tokyo 1978–82; Dir Policy Planning Bureau 1982–85; Dir-Gen. Econ. Policy Bureau External Affairs 1985–87; Minister and Deputy Chief of Mission, Embassy in Paris 1987–90; Asst Deputy Minister for Europe, Dept of Foreign Affairs and Int. Trade 1990–94; Amb. to Spain 1994–97; Perm. Rep. to NATO, Brussels 1997–2003, fmr Dean North Atlantic Council; Kenneth and Patricia Taylor Distinguished Prof. of Foreign Affairs, Victoria Coll., Univ. of Toronto 2003–. *Publications include:* publs on various foreign affairs and econ. issues.
Address: Victoria College, University of Toronto, 73 Queen's Park Crescent, Toronto, ON M5S 1K9, Canada (office). *Telephone:* (416) 585-4434 (office). *Fax:* (416) 813-4072 (office). *E-mail:* d.wright@utoronto.ca (office). *Website:* www.utoronto.ca (office).

WRIGHT, James R., BA, MA; Canadian diplomatist; *High Commissioner to UK;* b. Montreal; m. Donna Thomson; two c. *Education:* McGill Univ.,

Montreal. *Career:* joined Dept of Foreign Affairs 1976, fmr Dir of Personnel, Dir-Gen. for Cen., East and South Europe Bureau 1996–2000, Political Dir and Asst Deputy Minister, Int. Security Br. 2000–06; served at Embassy in Moscow 1978–80, Embassy in Washington, DC 1983–87, Minister Political and Public Affairs, High Comm. in London 1992–96, High Commr to UK 2006–; ex officio Gov. Ditchley Foundation; mem. Bd of Dirs, Commonwealth War Graves Comm., Imperial War Museum.
Address: Canadian High Commission, Macdonald House, 38 Grosvenor Street, London W1K 4AA, England (office). *Telephone:* (20) 7258-6600 (office). *Fax:* (20) 7258-6506 (office). *E-mail:* ldn@international.gc.ca (office). *Website:* www.dfait-maeci.gc.ca (office); www.canada.org.uk (office).

WRIGHT, Robert G., BS; Canadian diplomatist; *Ambassador to People's Republic of China;* m. Carol Smith; two c. *Education:* McGill Univ. *Career:* Trade Policy Officer, Dept of Industry, Trade and Commerce 1971; del. Tokyo Round of multilateral trade negotiations, Geneva 1977–80; apptd Chief W Europe Div., Dept of Industry, Trade and Commerce 1980, later Dir Pacific Trade Relations and Dir GATT Div.; Deputy Head del. Uruguay Round, Geneva 1985–91; Dir-Gen. US Trade and Econ. Policy, Dept of Int. Trade and External Affairs 1991–93; Deputy Head and Minister, Embassy in USA 1993–95; Deputy Minister for Int. Trade 1995; Amb. to Japan 2001–05, to People's Repub. of China 2005–.
Address: Embassy of Canada, 19 Dong Zhi Men Wai Dajie, Chao Yang Qu, Beijing 100600, People's Republic of China (office). *Telephone:* (10) 65323536 (office). *Fax:* (10) 65324311 (office). *Website:* www.beijing.gc.ca (office).

WRIGHT, Sir Stephen J. L., Kt, KCMG, CMG, BA; British diplomatist and business executive; *CEO, International Financial Services London;* b. 1946, Quito, Ecuador; m. Abbey Wright; four c. *Education:* Shrewsbury School, Univ. of Oxford. *Career:* served in Havana, Cuba 1969–71, New York, Brussels and London, then at UK High Comm., New Delhi, India 1988–91; Counsellor, UK Perm. Mission to EU, Brussels, Belgium 1991–94; Dir for EU Affairs, London 1994–97; Minister and Deputy Head of Mission, Washington, DC 1997–99; Dir for Wider Europe, FCO, London 1999–2000, Dir-Gen. for Defence and Intelligence Affairs 1999–2002; Amb. to Spain (also accred to Andorra) 2003–07; CEO International Financial Services London 2007–.
Address: International Financial Services London, 29–30 Cornhill, London, EC3V 3NF, England (office). *Telephone:* (20) 7213-9100 (office). *E-mail:* info@ifsl.org.uk (office). *Website:* www.ifsl.org.uk (office).

WU, Dawei; Chinese diplomatist and politician; *Vice-Minister of Foreign Affairs;* b. 1946, Heilongjiang Prov.; m.; one d. *Career:* Attaché, Chinese Embassy, Tokyo, Japan 1973–79, Deputy Section Chief, Gen. Office of State Council 1980–85, Second Sec., later First Sec., Chinese Embassy, Tokyo 1985–89, Section Chief, Asian Affairs Dept, Ministry of Foreign Affairs 1989–92, Deputy Dir-Gen. 1992–94, Minister-Counsellor, Chinese Embassy, Tokyo 1994–98, Amb. to Repub. of Korea 1998–2001, to Japan 2001–04; Vice-Minister of Foreign Affairs in charge of affairs of Asia, Treaty and Law 2004–.
Address: Ministry of Foreign Affairs, 225 Chaoyangmennei Dajie, Dongsi, Beijing 100701, People's Republic of China (office). *Telephone:* (10) 65961114 (office). *Fax:* (10) 65962146 (office). *E-mail:* webmaster@fmprc.gov.cn (office). *Website:* www.fmprc.gov.cn (office).

WU, Donghe; Chinese diplomatist; *Ambassador to North Korea;* b. May 1940, Hebei Prov. *Career:* mem. Dept of Translation and Interpretation, Ministry of Foreign Affairs 1966–69, Protocal Dept 1969–74, Third Sec., Chinese Embassy, Togo 1974–78, Second Sec., later First Sec., Chinese Embassy, Antananarivo, Madagascar 1978–83, Deputy Dir, later Dir and Counsellor, Dept of African Affairs, Ministry of Foreign Affairs 1983–89, Amb. to Niger 1989–92, to Mali 1993–95, Dir-Gen., Gen. Office, Ministry of Foreign Affairs 1995–98, Asst Foreign Minister 1998–99, Sec. Discipline Comm., Ministry of Foreign Affairs 1999–2001, Amb. to Democratic People's Repub. of Korea 2001–.
Address: Embassy of the People's Republic of China, Kin Mal Dong, Maolangbong District, Pyongyang, Democratic People's Republic of Korea (office). *Telephone:* (2) 3823316 (office). *Fax:* (2) 3813425 (office).

WU, Guanzheng; Chinese government official; b. 25 Aug. 1938, Yugan Co., Jiangxi Prov.; m. Zhang Jinshang 1959; three s. *Education:* Tsinghua Univ., Beijing. *Career:* joined CCP 1962; Deputy Sec. CCP Party Br., Tsinghua Univ. 1965–68; mem. CCP Cttee of Wuhan Gedian Chemical Plant, Deputy Dir Revolutionary Cttee of Wuhan Gedian Chemical Plant 1968–75; Deputy Dir Wuhan Science and Tech. Cttee, Vice-Chair. Wuhan City Asscn of Science and Tech., Deputy Commdr and Dir of Gen. Office, Wuhan City Technical Innovation Headquarters; Dir, Sec. CCP Cttee of Wuhan City Eng Science and Tech. Research Centre 1975–82; Standing

mem. CCP Cttee of Wuhan City 1982–83; Sec. CCP Cttee and Mayor of Wuhan City 1983–86; Deputy Sec. Jiangxi Prov. CCP Cttee, Acting Gov., Gov. Jiangxi Prov. 1986–95; Sec. CCP Cttee Jiangxi Prov., First Sec. CCP Cttee Jiangxi Prov. Mil. Command 1995–97, Sec. CCP Cttee Shandong Prov. and Prin. of School for CCP Shandong Cttee 1997–07; Alt. mem. 12th CCP Cen. Cttee 1982–87, mem. 13th CCP Cen. Cttee 1987–92, 14th CCP Cen. Cttee 1992–97, 15th CCP Cen. Cttee 1997–2002, 16th CCP Cen. Cttee 2002–07; mem. CCP Cen. Cttee Politburo 1997–2007, Standing Cttee CCP Cen. Cttee Politburo 2002–07; Sec. 16th CCP Cen. Cttee Cen. Comm. for Discipline Inspection 2002–07.
Address: 482 Weiyi Road, Jinan City, Shandong, People's Republic of China. *Telephone:* (531) 2033333.

WU, Jianmin; Chinese diplomatist and international organization official; *President, China Foreign Affairs University;* b. 30 March 1939, Jiangsu Prov. *Education:* Beijing Foreign Languages Inst. *Career:* translator at Ministry of Foreign Affairs 1959–71; with Perm. Mission to UN, New York 1971–90, Counsellor 1985–89, Deputy Chief of Mission 1989–90; Political Counsellor, Embassy in Brussels 1989–90, Amb. to The Netherlands 1991–94; Perm. Rep. to UN, New York 1996–98; Amb. to France 1998–2003; Pres. China Foreign Affairs Univ. 2003–; Chair. Int. Exhibitions Bureau 2003–; Vice–Dir CPPCC Foreign Affairs Cttee 2003–.
Address: Office of the President, China Foreign Affairs University, Xicheng District, Beijing 100037, People's Republic of China (office); Bureau of International Expositions, 34 Avenue d'Iéna, Paris 75116, France. *Telephone:* 1-45-00-38-63 (office). *Fax:* 1-45-00-96-15 (office). *E-mail:* info@bie-paris.org (office). *Website:* www.bie-paris.org (office); www.cfau .edu.cn (office).

WU, Jinglian; Chinese economist; *Professor of Economics, Chinese Academy of Social Sciences;* b. Jan. 1930, Nanjing, Jiangsu Prov. *Education:* Fudan Univ. *Career:* Asst Research Fellow, Econs Research Inst. of Chinese Acad. of Sciences 1954–79; Assoc. Research Fellow, Econs Inst. of Chinese Acad. of Social Sciences 1979–83, Research Fellow and Prof. 1983–; Vice-Dir Office for Econ. Reform Programmes of State Council; mem. Standing Cttee 9th CPPCC Nat. Cttee 1998–2003, Vice-Chair. Econ. Cttee of CPPCC 1984–; elected one of China's Top Ten Econ. Figures 2000. *Publications:* Explorations into Problems of Economic Reform, Planned Economy or Market Economy.
Address: c/o Chinese Academy of Social Sciences, Beijing, People's Republic of China (office).

WU, Rong-i, MA, MS, PhD; Taiwanese government official and economist; *Vice-Premier and Minister of the Consumer Protection Commission;* b. 15 Dec. 1939; m.; one d. one s. *Education:* Nat. Taiwan Univ., Université Catholique de Louvain, Belgium. *Career:* Prof. and Dir Dept of Econs, Nat. Chung Hsing Univ. 1975–93; Visiting Scholar, Yale Univ., USA 1982–83; Vice-Pres. Taiwan Inst. of Econ. Research 1991–92, Pres. 1993–; Commr Fair Trade Comm., Exec. Yuan 1992–93, mem. Science and Tech. Advisory Group 2004–; Nat. Policy Adviser to Pres. 2000–, mem. Econ. Advisory Group to Pres. 2000–; Vice-Premier and Minister of the Consumer Protection Commission 2005–; mem. Eminent Persons Group, Asia-Pacific Econ. Co-operation 1993–94.
Address: Executive Yuan, No. 1 Jhongsiao East Road, Taipei 10058, Taiwan. *Telephone:* (2) 33566500 (office). *Fax:* (2) 33566920 (office). *Website:* www.ey.gov.tw (office).

WURTH, Hubert, LLB; Luxembourg painter and diplomatist; *Ambassador to UK;* b. 15 April 1952; m. Lydie Polfer (q.v.); two c. *Education:* Univ. de Paris II, Inst. d'Etudes Politiques, Paris. *Career:* called to the Luxembourg Bar 1977; Attaché, Dept of Int. Econ. Relations, Ministry of Foreign Affairs 1978, Deputy Perm. Rep. to Council of Europe 1979, Chief Sec. to Vice-Pres. of the Govt and Minister for Foreign Affairs, Econ. Affairs and Justice 1981, Deputy Dir of Political Affairs 1986; Amb. to USSR (also

accred to Poland, Finland and Mongolia) 1988–92, to the Netherlands 1992–98 (also served as rep. for the Pact on Stability in Europe 1993–95 and on special mission in Fmr Yugoslavia 1996), Perm. Rep. to UN, New York 1998–2003, to OECD 2003–, to UNESCO 2003–07, Amb. to France 2003–07, to UK (also accred to Ireland) 2007–. *Exhibitions:* exhbns in Luxembourg, Moscow, Helsinki, Amsterdam, The Hague, New York (Abstract Painting). *Publication:* Monography on Hubert Wurth as a Painter 1998.
Address: Embassy of Luxembourg, 27 Wilton Crescent, London, SW1X 8SD, England (office). *Telephone:* (20) 7235-6961 (office). *Fax:* (20) 7235-9734 (office). *E-mail:* londres.amb@mae.etat.lu (office).

WYATT, Matthew; British diplomatist; *Permanent Representative, United Nations, Rome; Career:* Asst Pres. for External Affairs, UN Int. Fund for Agricultural Devt (IFAD) 2006–, Chair. IFAD Governing Council 2006–; Amb. and Perm. Rep. to UN Agencies, Rome 2006–.
Address: UK Representation to UN Agencies for Food and Agriculture, Via de Monserrato 48/1, 00186 Rome, Italy (office). *Telephone:* (06) 6840-0901-3 (office). *Fax:* (06) 6840-0920 (office). *Website:* www.ifad.org (office).

WYPLOSZ, Charles, PhD, DipEng; French professor of economics; *Professor of Economics, Graduate Institute of International Studies, Geneva;* b. 5 Sept. 1947, Vichy; m. Claire-Lise Monod 1967; one s. three d. *Education:* Univ. of Paris, Harvard Univ. *Career:* Asst, Assoc., then Full Prof. of Econs, Institut Européen d'Admin des Affaires (INSEAD), Fontainebleau 1978–, Assoc. Dean (Research and Devt) 1986–89; Directeur d'études, EHESS, Paris 1988–95; Prof. of Econs, Grad. Inst. of Int. Studies, Geneva 1995–; Man. Ed. Econ. Policy 1984–2001; mem. Council of Econ. Advisers to Prime Minister of France 1999–, Comm. Economique, Ministry of Finance, France 1999–; mem. Panel of Econ. and Monetary Experts, Cttee for Econ. and Monetary Affairs, European Parl. 2000–; mem. Group of Econ. Analysis, EC 2001–. *Publications:* numerous publs in professional journals; occasional contribs to press.
Address: Graduate Institute of International Studies, 11 avenue de la Paix, 1202 Geneva (office); 3 rue du Valais, 1202 Geneva, Switzerland (home). *Telephone:* (22) 9085946 (office). *Fax:* (22) 7333049 (office). *E-mail:* wyplosz@hei.unige.ch (office). *Website:* heiwww.unige.ch/~wyplosz (office).

WYZNER, Eugeniusz, LLM; Polish diplomatist; *Vice-Chairman, International Civil Service Commission;* b. 1931, Chełmno; m. Elżbieta Laudańska 1961; one s. *Education:* Jagiellonian Univ., Kraków, Warsaw Univ. and Acad. of Int. Law, The Hague. *Career:* Deputy Perm. Rep. to UN 1961–68; Deputy Dir of Dept at Ministry of Foreign Affairs 1968–71, Dir of Dept 1971–73; Amb., Perm. Rep. to UN, Geneva 1973–78; Dir of Dept, Ministry of Foreign Affairs 1978–81; UN Under-Sec.-Gen. 1982–94; Deputy Minister for Foreign Affairs and Parl. Sec., Ministry of Foreign Affairs 1994–95, Acting Minister for Foreign Affairs Dec. 1995; Amb. and Rep. to UN 1998–99; Vice-Chair. Int. Civil Service Comm. 1999–; mem. Bd of Dirs Int. Inst. of Space Law, Paris, Int. Peace Acad., New York, Int. Congress Inst. 1987–; Chair. UN Steering Cttee on Status of Women 1989–91, UN Appointments and Promotion Bd 1991–94, UN Exhibits Cttee 1992–94; mem. UN Sr Bd on Services to the Public 1989–94; Amb. ad personam; Gold Cross of Merit; Grand Commdr's Cross, Order of Polonia Restituta; Grand Commdr Order of the Phoenix (Greece); Commdr Légion d'honneur and other decorations. *Publications:* Wybrane zagadnienia z działalności ONZ w dziedzinie kodyfikacji i postępowego rozwoju prawa międzynarodowego, Niektóre aspekty prawne finansowania operacji ONZ w Kongo i na Bliskim Wschodzie, Poland and 50 Years of the United Nations Existence 1995.
Address: International Civil Service Commission, 2 United Nations Plaza, New York, NY 10017, USA (office). *Telephone:* (212) 963-8465 (office). *Fax:* (212) 963-1717 (office). *E-mail:* wyzner@un.org (office). *Website:* icsc .un.org (office).

X

XI, Jinping; Chinese politician; *Secretary, Chinese Communist Party Shanghai Municipal Committee;* b. 1953, Fuping, Shaanxi Prov.; m. Peng Liyuan; one d. *Education:* Tsinghua Univ., Beijing. *Career:* sent to do manual labour, Yanchuan Co., Shaanxi Prov. 1969; joined CCP 1974; served as Sec. to Geng Biao 1982; Vice-Sec., Sec. CCP Zhengding Co. Cttee 1982–85; First Political Commissar, Chinese People's Armed Police Force; Vice-Mayor of Xiamen, Fujian Prov. 1985–88; Sec. CCP Ningde Pref. Cttee 1988–90; First Sec. Fujian Mil. Dist (Ningde Mil. Sub-Area Command), PLA Nanjing Mil. Region 1988; Sec. CCP Fuzhou Municipal Cttee, Chair. Standing Cttee Fuzhou Municipal People's Congress 1990–96; Deputy Sec. CCP Fujian Prov. Cttee 1995–2002; Vice-Gov. of Fujian Prov. 1999–2000, Gov. 2000–02; Acting Gov. of Zhejiang Prov. 2002; Deputy Sec. CCP Zhejiang Prov. Cttee 2002, Sec. 2002–07; Chair. Standing Cttee of Prov. People's Congress 2003–; Sec. CCP Shanghai Municipal Cttee 2007–; Del., 14th CCP Nat. Congress 1992; Alt. mem. 15th CCP Cen. Cttee 1997–2002, mem. 16th CCP Cen. Cttee 2002–07, Standing Cttee Politburo 17th CCP Cen. Cttee 2007–; considered an emerging mem. of China's fifth generation of leadership. *Publications include:* Research on Developing Chinese Rural Market-orientated Economy, Science and Patriotism (Chief Ed.).
Address: Office of the Chairman, Chinese Communist Party Shanghai Municipal Committee, Shanghai, Shanghai Province, People's Republic of China (office).

XIAO, Yang; Chinese party and government official; *President, Supreme People's Court;* b. Aug. 1938, Heyuan Co., Guangdong Prov. *Education:* People's Univ. of China, Beijing. *Career:* joined CCP 1966; imprisoned during 'Cultural Revolution' 1968–71; teacher of political science and law, Heyuan Co. 1969–75; Deputy Dir Qujiang Co. CCP Cttee Office, then various party posts 1971–81; Sec. CCP Cttee of Wujiang Dist, Shaoguan City, Guangdong Prov. 1981–83; Deputy Sec. Qingyuang Prefectural CCP Cttee, Guangdong 1983; Deputy Chief, Guangdong Prov. Procurator's Office, Deputy Sec. CCP Leadership Group 1983–86; Procurator-Gen. Guangdong Prov. Procurator's Office 1986–90; Deputy Procurator-Gen. Supreme Procurator's Office, Deputy Sec. CCP Leadership Group 1990–92; teacher, China Univ. of Political Science and Law, Beijing 1990; Minister of Justice 1993–98; Pres. Supreme People's Court 1998–, China Asscn of Judges 1999; Alt. mem. 14th CCP Cen. Cttee 1992–97, mem. 15th CCP Cen. Cttee 1997–2002, 16th CCP Cen. Cttee 2002–; Vice-Chair. Cen. Cttee for Comprehensive Man. of Public Security 1998.
Address: Supreme People's Court, 27 Dongjiaominxiang, Beijing 100745, People's Republic of China (office). *Telephone:* (10) 65136195 (office).

XIE, Xuren; Chinese economist and government official; *Minister of Finance;* b. 1947, Ningbo City, Zhejiang Prov. *Education:* Zhejiang Univ. *Career:* began career as technician, Ningbo Zhenhai Machinery Factory, Ningbo City 1967, served as Section Chief and later Deputy Dir –1981; Magistrate, People's Court, Zhejiang Prov. 1984–85; Dir Investment and Planning Offices, Prov. Planning and Econ. Comm., Zhejiang Prov. 1985–88; Deputy Dir Prov. Planning and Econ. Comm. 1988–90; Deputy Dir Budget Dept, Ministry of Finance 1990–91, Deputy Dir Planning Dept 1990–93, Dir Planning Dept and Asst to Minister 1993–94, Dir Reforms Dept 1994–95, Vice-Minister 1995–98; Pres. Agricultural Devt Bank of China 1998–2000; Vice-Minister, State Econ. and Trade Comm. 2001–03; Dir State Admin of Taxation 2003–07; Minister of Finance 2007–; joined CCP 1980, Deputy Sec., Yinxian Co. Cttee 1984–85, Deputy Sec., Work Cttee Depts, Financial Work Cttee, CCP Cen. Cttee (CCPCC) 2000–01, Deputy Sec., Leading Party Group, CCPCC 2001–03, Alt. mem. CCPCC 2002–.
Address: Ministry of Finance, 3 Nansanxiang, Sanlihe, Xicheng Qu, Beijing 100820, People's Republic of China (office). *Telephone:* (10) 68551888 (office). *Fax:* (10) 68533635 (office). *E-mail:* webmaster@mof.gov.cn (office). *Website:* www.mof.gov.cn (office).

XIONG, Gen. Guangkai; Chinese diplomatist and army officer; *Deputy Chief of the General Staff, Armed Forces, People's Liberation Army;* b. March 1939, Nanchang City, Jiangxi Prov. *Education:* August 1st Middle School, Beijing, PLA Training School for Foreign Languages, PLA Mil. Acad. *Career:* joined PLA 1956, CCP 1959; worker, Data Office, Intelligence Dept, PLA HQ of the Gen. Staff, 1957–60; translator, secretarial Asst Office of Mil. Attaché, Chinese Embassy, GDR 1960–72; Asst Mil. Attaché, Chinese Embassy, FRG 1972–80; Asst Div. Chief, Intelligence Dept, Gen. Staff HQ 1983–85, Deputy Dir 1985–87, Dir 1987–88, Asst to Chief of Gen. Staff 1988–92, Deputy Chief of Gen. Staff 1996–; Alt. mem. 14th CCP Cen. Cttee 1992–97, mem. 15th CCP Cen. Cttee 1997–2002, 16th CCP Cen. Cttee 2002–; mem. Cen. Cttee Leading Group on Taiwan 1993–; rank of Maj.-Gen. 1988, Lt-Gen. 1993, Gen. 2000; Head of mil. del. to USA 1995.
Address: c/o Ministry of National Defence, 20 Jingshanqian Jie, Beijing 100009, People's Republic of China (office).

XODJAYEV, Batir Asadillaevich; Uzbekistan politician. *Career:* fmr Prof., Univ. of World Economy and Diplomacy, Tashkent; Minister of the Economy 2006–.
Address: Ministry of the Economy, 100003 Tashkent, O'zbekiston shox ko'ch. 45a, Uzbekistan (office). *Telephone:* (71) 132-63-20 (office). *Fax:* (71) 132-63-72 (office). *E-mail:* mineconomy@mmes.gov.uz (office). *Website:* www.mineconomy.uz (office).

Y

YA'ALON, Lt-Gen. Moshe, BA; Israeli army officer; b. 1950, Kiryat Haim; m.; three c. *Education:* Command and Staff Coll., Camberley, UK, Univ. of Haifa. *Career:* drafted into Israeli Defence Forces (IDF) 1968, served in Nahal Paratroop Regt; reserve paratrooper during Yom Kippur War 1973, participated in liberation of Suez Canal; held several command positions in IDF Paratroop Brigade, Commdr reconnaisance unit during Litani Operation 1978, later Deputy Commdr, apptd Commdr 1990; served in elite unit 1979–82, later Deputy Commdr; fought in Operation Peace for Galilee; retrained in IDF Armoured Corps 1989–90; apptd CO Judea and Samaria, promoted Brig.-Gen. 1992; Commdr of Ground Forces, Tze'elim 1993; apptd CO Intelligence, rank Maj.-Gen. 1995; apptd CO Cen. Command 1998, IDF Deputy Chief-of-Staff 2000, Chief-of-Staff 2002–05. *Address:* Ministry of Defence, Kaplan Steet, Hakirya, Tel-Aviv 67659, Israel. *Telephone:* 3-5692010. *Fax:* 3-6916940. *E-mail:* public@mod.gov.il. *Website:* www.mod.gov.il.

YADAV, Ram Baran, MBBS, MD; Nepalese physician, politician and head of state; *President;* b. 4 Feb. 1948, Sapahi, Dhanusa dist. *Education:* Calcutta Medical Coll., Inst. of Medical Educ. and Research, India. *Career:* worked as physician for more than two decades in hospitals in south Nepal's Terai region; joined Nepali Congress Party 1987, Gen. Sec. –2008 (resgnd); elected to House of Reps 1991, 1994; Minister for Health 1991–94; Pres. of Nepal (first elected Pres.) 2008–. *Address:* Office of the President, Kathmandu, Nepal (office).

YADE, Ramatoulaye (Rama); French politician; *Minister of State, attached to the Ministry of Foreign and European Affairs, responsible for Foreign Affairs and Human Rights;* b. 13 Dec. 1976, Dakar, Senegal; m. Joseph Zimet. *Education:* Institut d'études politiques, Paris. *Career:* immigrated to France with family 1987; Admin. Sénat Local Authorities Dept 2002–07, Deputy Dir Programmes Public Sénat (Parl. TV channel), becoming Dir of Communication 2005–07; Exec. Sec. France–W Africa Friendship Group; joined UMP (Union pour un Mouvement Populaire) 2005, UMP Nat. Sec. for Francophone Affairs 2006; Minister of State, attached to Ministry of Foreign and European Affairs, responsible for Foreign Affairs and Human Rights 2007–; cand. for municipal elections, Colombes 2008. *Publication:* Noirs de France 2007. *Address:* Ministry of Foreign and European Affairs, 37 quai d'Orsay, 75351 Paris Cedex 07, France (office). *Telephone:* 1-43-17-53-53 (office). *Fax:* 1-43-17-52-03 (office). *Website:* www.diplomatie.gouv.fr (office).

YAKOVENKO, Alexander Vladimirovich, CandJurSc; Russian diplomatist; *Deputy Minister of Foreign Affairs;* b. 1954; m.; one d. *Education:* Moscow State Inst. of Int. Relations. *Career:* with USSR Mission to UN, New York 1981–86; Head of Div., Dept on Security and Co-operation in Europe, Ministry of Foreign Affairs, Russian Fed. 1986–92; Deputy Dir Dept on Problems of Security and Disarmament, Ministry of Foreign Affairs 1992–97; Perm. Rep. to int. orgs in Vienna 1997–2000; Dir Information and Press Dept Ministry of Foreign Affairs 2000–04, currently Deputy Minister of Foreign Affairs. *Address:* Ministry of Foreign Affairs, Smolenskaya-Sennaya pl. 32/34, 121200 Moscow, Russia (office). *Telephone:* (495) 244-41-19 (office). *Fax:* (495) 244-41-12 (office). *Website:* www.mid.ru (office).

YAKOVLEV, Gen. Vladimir Nikolayevich, CAND.MIL.SC.; Russian army officer; *Head of Staff for Co-ordination of Military Co-operation within Commonwealth of Independent States;* b. 17 Aug. 1954, Tver; m. Raisa Anatolyevna Yakovleva; two d. *Education:* Dzerzhinsky Mil. Acad., Mil. Acad. of Gen. Staff. *Career:* served with strategic rocket forces incl. Commdr rocket regt 1985–89; Deputy Commdr rocket div. 1989–91, Commdr 1991–93; Head of Staff Rocket Army 1993–94, Commdr 1994–97; Head of Gen. Staff Rocket Troops Jan. 1999–; C-in-C Rocket Strategic Forces of Russian Fed. 1997–2001; Head of Staff for Co-ordination of Mil. Co-operation within CIS 2001–; Prof. Acad. of Mil. Sciences; mem. Russian Acad. of Eng; corresp. mem. Russian Acad. of Rocket and Artillery Sciences; Order of Red Star, Order for Mil. Service, Prize of Russian Pres. for Achievement in Educ. 1998. *Publications include:* Military Work: Science, Art, Vocation 1998, Organizational Activities of General Staff in Rocket Strategic Forces 1999, Rocket Shield of the Motherland 1999, co-author Mil. Encyclopaedic Dictionary of Rocket Strategic Forces.

Address: Ministry of Defence, Bolshaya Pirogovskaya str. 23, K-160 Moscow, Russia (office). *Telephone:* (495) 244-62-14 (office).

YAKUB ALI, A. M., MA; Bangladeshi diplomatist; m.; two c. *Education:* Dhaka Univ. *Career:* apptd Asst Sec., Ministry of Foreign Affairs 1981, Sr Asst Sec. (Int. Orgs) 1985–87; First Sec., Embassy in Paris 1987; First Sec., Embassy in Rabat 1991–93; Dir (Int. Orgs), Ministry of Foreign Affairs 1993–96; Counsellor/Minister and Deputy Chief of Mission, Embassy in Washington, DC 1996–2001; Dir-Gen. and Chief of Protocol, Ministry of Foreign Affairs 2001–03; High Commr to Sri Lanka 2003–06. *Address:* c/o Ministry of Foreign Affairs, Segunbagicha, Dhaka 1000, Bangladesh.

YAMAMOTO, Donald Y., BA, MA; American diplomatist; *Ambassador to Ethiopia;* b. Seattle, Wash.; m.; two c. *Education:* Columbia Coll., Columbia Univ., Nat. War Coll. *Career:* career mem. Sr Foreign Service, entered Foreign Service 1980, assignments have included staff aide to Amb. to People's Repub. of China and Human Rights Officer during Tiananmen Square demonstrations 1989, Prin. Officer, Fukuoka Consulate, Japan, Chargé d'affaires a.i., Embassy in Eritrea; Deputy Dir for East African Affairs, Dept of State 1998–2000; Amb. to Djibouti 2000–03; Deputy Asst Sec. of State, Bureau of African Affairs 2003–06; Amb. to Ethiopia 2006–07; Congressional Fellowship 1991, three individual Superior Honor Awards, two Group Awards. *Address:* US Embassy, PO Box 1014, Entoto Street, Addis Ababa, Ethiopia (office). *Telephone:* (11) 5174000 (office). *Fax:* (11) 5174001 (office). *E-mail:* pasaddis@state.gov (office). *Website:* addisababa.usembassy.gov (office).

YAMAMOTO, Tadashi, MBA; Japanese research institute director; *President, Japan Center for International Exchange; Education:* Sophia Univ., St Norbert Coll., Marquette Univ., USA. *Career:* Founder and Pres. Japan Center for Int. Exchange 1970–; Exec. Dir Japan–USA Econ. Relations Group 1979–81, USA–Japan Advisory Comm. 1983–84, Korea–Japan 21st Century Cttee 1988–91; mem. Prime Minister's Council on Int. Cultural Exchange 1988–89, 1993–94; Exec. Dir Prime Minister's Comm. on Japan's Goals in 21st Century 1999–2000; Pacific Asia Dir Trilateral Comm.; Dir UK–Japan 21st Century Group, German–Japan Forum, Korea–Japan Forum, Friends of Global Fund; decorations from govts of Australia, Germany, Japan, UK; USA–Japan Foundation Distinguished Service Award 2008. *Publications:* Emerging Civil Society in the Asia Pacific Community (Masayoshi Ohira Award) 1995, The Nonprofit Sector in Japan 1998, Corporate-NGO Partnership in Asia Pacific 1999, Deciding the Public Good: Governance and Civil Society in Japan 1999, Governance and Civil Society in a Global Age 2001, Philanthropy and Reconciliation: Rebuilding Postwar US-Japan Relations 2006. *Address:* Japan Center for International Exchange, 4-9-17 Minami Azabu, Minato-ku, Tokyo 106-0047, Japan (office). *Telephone:* (3) 3446-7781 (office). *Fax:* (3) 3443-7580 (office). *E-mail:* admin@jcie.or.jp (office). *Website:* www.jcie.or.jp (office).

YAMASHITA, Shoichi, PhD; Japanese research institute director; *Director, International Centre for the Study of East Asian Development; Education:* Univ. of Penn. *Career:* researcher Inst. of Developing Economies, Tokyo 1965–79; Hiroshima Univ. 1979–2002, Prof. of Econs 1983–94, Dean, Graduate School for Int. Devt and Cooperation 1994–98, Councillor 1994–99, Prof. Emer 2002–; Advisory Prof. Fudan Univ., China 1996–; Pres. Japan Soc. for Int. Devt 1999–2002; Dir. Int. Centre for the Study of East Asian Devt 2002–. *Publications include:* Transfer of Japanese Technology and Management to the ASEAN Countries (ed.) 1991, Japan's Options for the Asian Age (ed.) 1997. *Address:* The International Centre for the Study of East Asian Development, 11–4 Otemachi, Kokurakita, Kitakyushu, Fukuoka, 803–0814, Japan (office). *Telephone:* (93) 583-6202 (office). *Fax:* (93) 583-6576 (office). *E-mail:* office@icsead.or.jp (office). *Website:* www.icsead.or.jp (office).

YAMASSOUM, Nagoum; Chadian politician; b. 1954; m. Brigitte Boukar Belingar; two s. *Education:* Univ. of Bordeaux, Univ. of Paris XI, France. *Career:* Prime Minister of Chad Aug. 1999–2002; Minister of State,

Minister of Foreign Affairs and African Integration 2003–05; Nat. Order of Chad, Nat. Order of Taiwan.
Address: POB 4321, N'Djamena, Moursal, Chad (home). *Telephone:* 51-51-59 (home). *Fax:* 51-70-21 (home). *E-mail:* nagoumy@hotmail.com (home).

YAÑEZ-BARNUEVO, Juan Antonio, LLB, DipIL; Spanish diplomatist; *Permanent Representative, United Nations;* b. 15 Feb. 1942, Coria del Río, Seville; m. Isabel Sampedro 1969; one s. *Education:* Univs of Seville, Madrid and Cambridge, School for Int. Civil Servants, Madrid, Hague Acad. of Int. Law and Diplomatic School, Madrid. *Career:* Sec. of Embassy, Perm. Mission of Spain to UN, New York 1970–73; Deputy Head, Office of Int. Legal Affairs, Ministry of Foreign Affairs 1975–78; Deputy Perm. Rep. to Council of Europe, Strasbourg 1978–82; Dir of Int. Dept of Presidency of Govt (Foreign Policy Adviser to Prime Minister) 1982–91; Amb. and Perm. Rep. of Spain at UN, New York 1991–96; Deputy Dir Diplomatic School 1996–98; Amb.-at-Large 1998–2004; Head Spanish Del. to UN negotiations on the Int. Criminal Court 1998–2004; Head Legal Dept, Foreign Ministry 2002–04; Perm. Rep. to UN 2004–; mem. Int. Humanitarian Fact-finding Comm. 2002–; Francisco Tomás y Valiente Prize (Seville) 1998, Jurist of the Year (Madrid Law School) 1999. *Publications:* La Justicia Penal Internacional: Una perspectiva iberoamericana 2001.
Address: Permanent Mission of Spain to the United Nations, 345 East 46th Street, New York, NY 10017, USA (office); Carretera de Húmera, 1 (Aravaca), 28023 Madrid, Spain (home). *Telephone:* (212) 661-1050 (office). *Fax:* (212) 949-7247 (office). *E-mail:* spain@spainum.org (office). *Website:* www.spainun.org (office).

YANG, Huaiqing; Chinese naval officer; *Political Commissar, Navy, People's Liberation Army;* b. Feb. 1939, Shouguang Co., Shandong Prov. *Career:* joined PLA 1958, CCP 1960; served as Asst of Org. Section under political dept of frigate detachment; Asst, section chief, deputy Dir and Dir of Cadre Dept of Navy Fleet; dir political dept of a naval base; political commissar of a naval base; Deputy Dir Political Dept of PLA Navy, Dir 1992–95; Political Commissar PLA Navy 1995–; rank of Rear-Adm. 1990, Vice Adm. 1994, Adm. 2000; Deputy to 8th NPC 1993; mem. 15th CCP Cen. Cttee 1997–2002, 16th CCP Cen. Cttee 2002–.
Address: Ministry of National Defence, Beijing, People's Republic of China (office).

YANG, Jiechi; Chinese diplomatist and government official; *Minister of Foreign Affairs;* b. May 1950, Shanghai; m. *Education:* Univ. of Bath and London School of Econs, UK. *Career:* staff mem., later Second Sec. Trans. and Interpretation Dept, Ministry of Foreign Affairs 1975–84, Counsellor, later Div. Dir 1987–90, Counsellor, later Div. Dir, later Dir-Gen. North American and Oceania Affairs Dept 1990–93, Asst Minister, Ministry of Foreign Affairs 1995–98, Vice-Minister 1998–2000; Second Sec., later First Sec., later Counsellor, Chinese Embassy, Washington, DC, USA 1983–87, Minister and Deputy Chief of Mission 1993–95, Amb. to USA 2001–05; Vice-Minister of Foreign Affairs in charge of region of N America and Oceania and Latin America, foreign-related affairs involving Hong Kong, Macao and Taiwan, work of translation and interpretation 2005–07, Minister of Foreign Affairs 2007–.
Address: Ministry of Foreign Affairs, 225 Chaoyangmen Nan Dajie, Chaoyang Qu, Beijing 100701, People's Republic of China (office). *Telephone:* (10) 65961114 (office). *Fax:* (10) 65962146 (office). *E-mail:* webmaster@mfa.gov.cn (office). *Website:* www.fmprc.gov.cn (office).

YAPP, John William; British diplomatist; *High Commissioner to Belize; Career:* with Estate and Services, FCO 1971–73; Chancery, Embassy in Islamabad 1973–75, Consular, Embassy in Kuala Lumpur 1976–77; Asst Pvt. Sec. to Ministers of State, FCO 1978–80; Second Sec. (Commercial), Embassy in Dubai 1980–84, Second Sec. (Econ./Commercial), Embassy in The Hague 1984–88; Section Head, Jt Export Promotion Directorate, FCO/Dept of Trade and Industry 1988–91; First Sec. (Political/Press) and Deputy Gov. Pitcairn Islands, Wellington 1991–95; Deputy Head N America Dept, FCO 1995–97; High Commr to the Seychelles 1998–2002, Political-Mil. attachment, Embassy in Washington, DC 2003; Deputy Head of S Asia Group, FCO 2004–07; High Commr to Belize 2007–.
Address: British High Commission, Embassy Square, PO Box 91, Belmopan, Belize (office). *Telephone:* 822-2146 (office). *Fax:* 822-2761 (office). *E-mail:* brithicom@btl.net (office). *Website:* www.britishhighbze .com (office).

YAQUB, Muhammad, PhD; Pakistani banker and economist; b. 1937, Jalandar, India; m. Nasreen Yaqub; two s. one d. *Education:* Punjab Univ., Yale Univ., Princeton Univ., USA. *Career:* Asst Dir, Research Dept State Bank of Pakistan 1966–68, Deputy Dir 1968–69, Sr Deputy Dir 1969–72, Sr Prin. Officer, Dir Research Dept 1975, Gov. 1993–99; Sr Economist and Resident Rep., IMF, Saudi Arabia 1975, Fund Resident

Adviser to Saudi Arabian Govt, IMF 1977, Div. Chief, Middle Eastern Dept IMF 1977–80, Asst Dir 1981–82, IMF Rep. to Paris Club, London Club, OECD and co. aid consortia; Consultant IMF, Washington; Prin. Econ. Adviser, Special Section, Ministry of Finance 1992–93; has headed IMF missions to numerous Middle Eastern countries. *Publications:* Major-Macro Economic Policy Issues in Pakistan.
Address: IMF, 700 19th Street, NW, Washington, DC 20431, USA (office). *Website:* www.imf.org (office).

YAR'ADUA, Alhaji Umaru Musa, MSc; Nigerian politician and head of state; *President;* b. 1951, Katsina; brother of the late Shehu Yar'Adua; m. Hajia Turai Umaru Yar'Adua. *Education:* Barewa Coll., Zaria and Ahmadu Bello Univ. *Career:* mem. Nat. Youth Service Corps, Holy Child Coll., Lagos 1975–76; Lecturer in Chem., Katsina Coll. of Arts, Science and Tech. 1976–79, Katsina Polytechnic 1979–83; Gen. Man., Sambo Farms Ltd, Funtua 1983–89; Chair. Katsina State Investment and Property Devt Co. (KIPDECO) 1994–96, Nation House Press Ltd 1995–99; Dir Hamada Holdings 1983–99, Madara Ltd 1987–99, Lodigiani Nigeria Ltd 1987–99, Habib Nigeria Bank Ltd 1995–99; fmr mem. Peoples' Redemption Party (PRP); Founding mem. Peoples' Front (later Social Democratic Party, SDP) 1987–95; mem. Constituent Ass. 1988; f. K34 Political Asscn (later People's Democratic Party, PDP) 1998; Gov., Katsina state 1999–2007; Pres. of Nigeria 2007–; Nat. Primary Educ. Productivity Merit Award 2004, Cen. Bank of Nigeria Best Gov. Award 2005.
Address: Office of the President, New Federal Secretariat Complex, Shehu Shagari Way, Central Area District, Abuja, Nigeria (office). *Telephone:* (9) 5233536 (office). *E-mail:* maimaje@yaradua2007.com (office). *Website:* www.yaradua2007.com (office); www.nigeria.gov.ng (office).

YASTRZHEMBSKY, Sergey Vladimirovich, CandHistSc; Russian politician, journalist and diplomatist; *Assistant to the President of the Russian Federation;* b. 4 Dec. 1953, Moscow; m. Anastassia Yastrzhembskaya; three c. *Education:* Moscow State Inst. of Int. Relations, Inst. of Int. Workers' Movt. *Career:* jr researcher, Acad. of Social Sciences Cen. Cttee CPSU 1979–81; on staff journal Problems of the World and Socialism (Prague) 1981–89; Sr staff-mem. Int. Div. Cen. Cttee CPSU 1989–90; Deputy Ed.-in-Chief Megapolis (journal) 1990–91, Ed.-in-Chief VIP journal 1991–92; Dir Dept of Information and Press, Russian Ministry of Foreign Affairs 1992–93; Amb. to Slovakia 1993–96; Press Sec. to Pres. Boris Yeltsin 1996; Deputy Head Pres. Yeltsin's Admin. 1997–98; Vice-Chair. Moscow Govt 1998–99; Asst to Pres. Vladimir Putin (q.v.) 2000–; Special Envoy to the EU 2004; Rank II Order of the White Cross (Slovakia); Russian Orthodox Church Order of St Daniil; 850th Anniversary of Moscow Commemorative Medal. *Exhibitions:* four photography exhibitions including one at Tretiakov Art Gallery. *Publications:* Social Democracy in the Contemporary World 1991; essays and articles on current events, contemporary devt of Portugal and European social democracy, and relations between Russia and EU.
Address: Office of the President, Staraya pl. 4, 103132 Moscow, Russia (office). *Telephone:* (495) 606-08-31 (office). *Fax:* (495) 606-91-93 (office). *E-mail:* president@gov.ru (office). *Website:* www.kremlin.ru (office).

YATIM, Dato' Rais bin, MA, LLB, PhD; Malaysian politician; *Minister of Foreign Affairs;* b. 15 April 1942, Jelebu, Negeri Sembilan; m. Datin Masnah Mohamat; three s. one d. *Education:* Univs of Northern Illinois, Singapore and London. *Career:* lecturer at ITM, School of Law and also managed own law firm in Kuala Lumpur 1973; mem. Bar Council 1973; mem. Parl. 1974; Parl. Sec. Ministry of Youth, Sport and Culture 1974; Deputy Minister of Law 1976, of Home Affairs 1978; elected to State Ass., Negeri Sembilan 1978; Menteri Besar, Negeri Sembilan 1978; Minister of Land and Regional Devt 1982, of Information 1984–86, of Foreign Affairs 1986–87; Advocate and Solicitor, High Court of Malaysia 1988–; returned to law practice, Kuala Lumpur 1988–; mem. United Malays' Nat. Org. (UMNO) Supreme Council of Malaysia 1982–; Deputy Pres. Semangat 1989–; Minister in Prime Minister's Dept 1999; Minister of Foreign Affairs 2008–; mem. Civil Liberty Cttee Bar Council, Kuala Lumpur 1996–98. *Publications:* Faces in the Corridors of Power 1987, Freedom under Executive Power in Malaysia 1995, Zaman Beredar Pesaka Bergilir 1999.
Address: Ministry of Foreign Affairs, Wisma Putra, 1 Jalan Wisma Putra, Presint 2, 62602 Putrajaya (office); 41 Road 12, Taman Grandview, Ampang Jaya, 68000 Ampang, Selangor, Malaysia (home). *Telephone:* (3) 88874000 (office); (3) 4569621 (home). *Fax:* (3) 88891717 (office). *E-mail:* webmaster@kln.gov.my (office); drrais@pc.jaring.my (home). *Website:* www.kln.gov.my (office).

YAVLINSKII, Grigorii Alekseevich, PhD, CEconSc; Russian politician and economist; *Leader, Yabloko Russian Democratic Party (Rossiisskaya demokraticheskaya partiya);* b. 10 April 1952, Lviv, Ukrainian SSR; m.; two s. *Education:* Plekhanov Inst. of Econ., Moscow. *Career:* electrician Lviv Co., Raduga 1968–69; Sr Researcher, Research Inst. of Man.,

Ministry of Coal Industry, Moscow 1976–80; Head of Div. Research Inst. of Labour 1980–84; Deputy Chief, Chief of Div., Chief of Dept of Man. USSR State Labour Cttee 1984–89; Chief of Div. State Cttee on Econ. Reform USSR Council of Ministers 1988–90; mem. Pres.'s Political Advisory Council 1990–; Deputy Chair. Council of Ministers of Russian Fed., Chair. State Cttee on Econ. Reform 1990, author of econ. programme 500 days July–Nov. 1990; Econ. Counsellor of Prime Minister of Russia 1991; Chair. of Council of Scientific Soc. EPI-CENTRE (Cen. for Political and Econ. Studies) 1991–; mem. Econ. Council of Pres. of Kazakhstan 1991–; Deputy Chair. USSR Cttee on Operational Man. of Nat. Econ. Aug.–Dec. 1991; mem. Political Advisory Council of Pres. Gorbachev Oct.–Dec. 1991; co-leader (with Y.U. Boldyrev and V. Lukin) of pre-election bloc (later political movt then political party) Yabloko Russian Democratic Party (Rossiisskaya demokraticheskaya partiya 'Yabloko') 1993, Leader 1995–, currently also party Chair. in Duma; mem. State Duma (Parl.) 1993–; cand. in presidential elections 1996, 2000; Int. Prize for Freedom 2004. *Achievements:* Ukraine Jr Boxing Champion 1967, 1968. *Publications:* Russia–The Search for Landmarks 1993, Incentives and Institutions: The Transition to a Market Economy in Russia 2000; over 60 books on economy of USSR, numerous articles.
Address: Yabloko Russian Democratic Party (Rossiisskaya demokraticheskaya partiya 'Yabloko'), 119034 Moscow, per. M. Levshinskii 7/3, Russia (office). *Telephone:* (495) 201-43-79 (office). *Fax:* (495) 292-34-50 (office). *E-mail:* info@yabloko.ru (office). *Website:* www.yabloko.ru (office).

YAZDI, Mehdi Danesh; Iranian diplomatist. *Career:* fmr Dir-Gen. for Int. Legal Affairs, Ministry of Foreign Affairs; currently Deputy Perm. Rep. to UN, New York, Pres. of Exec. Bd UNICEF –2006, Vice Chair. UN Disarmament Comm. 2006–.
Address: Permanent Mission of Iran to the United Nations, 622 Third Avenue, 34th Floor, New York, NY 10017, USA (office). *Telephone:* (212) 687-2020 (office). *Fax:* (212) 867-7086 (office). *E-mail:* iran@un.int (office). *Website:* www.un.int/iran (office).

YEH, Chu-Lan, LLB; Taiwanese politician; b. 13 Feb. 1949, Miaoli County; m.; one d. *Education:* Fu Jen Catholic Univ. *Career:* Dir Business Dept, United Advertising Co. Ltd 1979–89; mem. Legislative Yuan 1990–2000, Convener Home and Nations Cttee, Foreign and Overseas Chinese Affairs Cttee, Judiciary Cttee, Deputy Convener Democratic Progressive Party Caucus 1992, General Convener 1995; Minister of Transportation and Communications 2000–02; Chair. Council for Hakka Affairs 2002–04; Vice-Premier and Minister of Consumer Protection Comm. 2004–05; Acting Mayor of Kaohsiung 2005–06.
Address: c/o Democratic Progressive Party (DPP), 10/F, 30 Beiping East Road, Taipei 10051, Taiwan. *Telephone:* (2) 23929989. *E-mail:* foreign@dpp.org.tw. *Website:* www.dpp.org.tw.

YEKHANUROV, Yuriy Ivanovych; Ukrainian politician and economist; *Minister of Defence;* b. 23 Aug. 1948, Belkachi, Yakut ASSR (now the Republic of Sakha—Yakutiya) Russian Fed.; m. Olena Lvivna Yekhanurova; one s. *Education:* Kyiv Construction Tech. Coll.; Higher School of Econ. State Planning, Kyiv Inst. of Nat. Econs, Academic Research Econ. Inst. of State Planning. *Career:* master, then head of workshop, Chief Engineer, Dir, Kyivmiskbur Co. 1967–77, Head, Kyivmiskbudkomplekt Co. 1977–88; Head, Buddetal Co. 1977–88; Deputy Chief, Golovkyivmiskbud Co. 1988–91; elected to Kyiv City Rada (Council) 1990; Head, State Econ. Council, Cabinet of Ministers 1991–92; Deputy Head, Bd of Verkhovna Rada 1992; Deputy Head, Kyiv City Admin. 1992–93; Deputy Minister of the Economy 1993–94; Head of State Property Fund 1994–97; Minister of Economy Feb.–July 1997; Head of State Cttee on Entrepreneurship Devt 1997–98; mem. Verkhovna Rada (Parl.) 1998–, Deputy Head, Cttee on Econ. Policy, Man. Economy, Property and Investment 1998–99; First Deputy Prime Minister 1999–2001; Deputy Head of Presidential Admin 2001, 2004, re-elected mem. Verkhovna Rada for Our Ukraine bloc 2002, Head of Parl. Cttee on Industrial Policy and Entrepreneurship 2002; Deputy Head of Viktor Yushchenko's presidential campaign team 2004; Head, Cen. Exec. Cttee, Our Ukraine People's Union party March 2005; Gov. Dnipropetrovsk Oblast April–Sept. 2005; apptd acting Prime Minister Sept. 2005, Prime Minister Sept. 2005–06; Minister of Defence 2007–. *Publications:* more than 60 publs on econs.
Address: Ministry of Defence, 03168 Kyiv, Povitroflotskyi pr. 6 (office); Verkhovna Rada, 01008 Kyiv, vul. M. Hrushevskoho 5, Ukraine (office). *Telephone:* (44) 226-26-56 (Ministry) (office); (44) 255-31-57 (office). *Fax:* (44) 226-20-15 (Ministry) (office). *E-mail:* pressmou@pressmou.kiev.ua (office); yekhanurov.yurii@rada.gov.ua (office). *Website:* www.mil.gov.ua (office); www.rada.gov.ua (office).

YEN, Ching-Chang, LLB, MA; Taiwanese politician; b. 7 April 1948, Tainan; m.; one s. one d. *Education:* Nat. Taiwan Univ., Univ. of Michigan, USA.

Career: joined Ministry of Finance 1972, Sr Customs Officer, Taipei Customs Bureau 1972–73, Specialist, Dept of Customs Admin. 1973–77, Sr Specialist in Secr. 1977–78, 1980–84, Exec. Sec. Legal Comm. 1984–85, Taxation and Tariff Comm. 1985–92, Deputy Minister of Finance 1996–2000, Minister of Finance 2000–02; Deputy Dir-Gen. First Bureau, Office of the Pres. 1992–93; Dir-Gen. 1993–96; Prof., Nat. Taiwan Univ., Nat. Chengchi Univ. and Soochoe Univ. 1981–86; first Amb. of Taiwan WTO 2002–05; Chair. and CEO Yuanta Financial Holding Co., Ltd (fmrly Fuhwa Financial Holding Co.) 2005–; Eisenhower Fellowship, USA 1995; Chevalier Ordre nat. du Mérite 1998; Class One Merit Medal, Exec. Yuan 2000, Order of Brilliant Star with Grand Cordon in 2005. *Publications:* Anti-dumping Act and Customs Policy 1981, Legal Problems of Sino-American Trade Negotiations 1987, Unveiling GATT: Order and Trend of Global Trade 1989, International Economic Law 1991, Laws and Regulations of International Economic Relations 1995, Taxation Law 1998, Understanding and Appreciating French Wines 1997; (in English) Taiwan Trade and Investment Law 1994.
Address: Yuanta Financial Holding Co., Ltd, 9F, No. 4, Section 1, Chung-Hsiao W. Road, Taipei, Taiwan (office).

YENNIMATAS, George; Greek diplomatist; *Ambassador to Turkey;* m. *Career:* Gen. Sec., Ministry of Foreign Affairs –2005, Amb. to Turkey 2005–.
Address: Embassy of Greece, Zia ür-Rahman Caddesi 9–11, 06700 Gaziosmanpaşa, Ankara, Turkey (office). *Telephone:* (312) 4368860 (office); (312) 4480647; (312) 4480387. *Fax:* (312) 4463191 (office). *E-mail:* greekembassy@ttnet.net.tr (office); greekemb@superonline.com.

YEO, George Yong-Boon, BA, MBA; Singaporean politician; *Minister of Foreign Affairs;* b. 13 Sept. 1954, Singapore; m. Jennifer Leong Lai Peng 1984; one d. three s. *Education:* Univ. of Cambridge, UK, Singapore Command and Staff Coll., Harvard Business School, USA. *Career:* fmr Signals Officer, Singapore Air Force, later Head Air Plans Dept, Chief of Air Staff 1985; Dir Jt Operations and Planning, Ministry of Defence 1986–88, rank of Brig.-Gen. 1988; mem. Parl. 1988–; Minister of State for Finance and Minister of State for Foreign Affairs 1988–90; Acting Minister for Information and the Arts and Sr Minister of State for Foreign Affairs 1990–91; Minister for Information and the Arts 1991–99; Second Minister for Foreign Affairs 1991–94; Minister for Health 1994–97; Second Minister for Trade and Industry 1997–99, Minister for Trade and Industry 1999–2004; Minister of Foreign Affairs 2004–; mem. Harvard Business School Visiting Cttee 1998–2004; Adviser Sun Yat Sen Nanyang Memorial Hall.
Address: Ministry of Foreign Affairs, Tanglin, 248163 Singapore (office). *Telephone:* 63798000 (office). *Fax:* 64747885 (office). *E-mail:* mfa@mfa .gov.sg (office). *Website:* www.mfa.gov.sg (office).

YEROCOSTOPOULOS, Constantin; Greek diplomatist; *Permanent Representative, Council of Europe; Career:* Perm. Rep. to Council of Europe 2004–.
Address: Office of the Permanent Representative of Greece, Council of Europe, Avenue de l'Europe, 67075 Strasbourg Cedex, France (office).

YERXA, Rufus H., MJur; American international organization official and lawyer; *Deputy Director-General, World Trade Organization; Education:* Univ. of Washington, Univ. of Puget Sound, Cambridge Univ., UK. *Career:* congressional expert on int. trade; Legal Counsel, Ways and Means Cttee, US House of Reps. 1981–89; Amb. and Perm. Rep. to GATT, Geneva 1989–93; Sr Deputy Trade Rep. 1993–95; lawyer in pvt. practice 1995–98; European Gen. Counsel, then Int. Counsel Monsanto Co. 1998–2002; Deputy Dir-Gen. WTO 2002–.
Address: World Trade Organization, Centre William Rappard, 154 rue de Lausanne, 1211 Geneva, Switzerland (office). *Telephone:* (22) 7395111 (office). *Fax:* (22) 7314206 (office). *E-mail:* enquiries@wto.org (office). *Website:* www.wto.org (office).

YESENBAYEV, Mazhit Tulenbekovich; Kazakhstani politician, engineer and economist; b. 28 April 1949, Pavlodar. *Education:* Kazakh Polytech. Inst., Almaty. *Career:* fmr Gov. Cen. Karaganda Region; apptd Minister of Finance 1999–2001, of Economy and Trade 2002–03; Presidential Aide on Econ. Affairs 2003–; Order of Parasat 1999. *Publications:* 34 publs on problems of territorial org. of production and optimization of teaching and educational process.
Address: c/o Ministry of Economy and Trade, Beibitshilik 2, 473000 Astana, Kazakhstan (office).

YI DAN; Cambodian diplomatist. *Career:* Amb. to Laos 2007–.
Address: Embassy of Cambodia, rue Thadeua, Km 3, BP 34, Vientiane, Laos (office). *Telephone:* (21) 314952 (office). *Fax:* (21) 314951 (office). *E-mail:* recamlao@laotel.com (office).

YIMER ABOYE, Fisseha, LLB, LLM; Ethiopian diplomatist and civil servant; *Permanent Representative, United Nations, Geneva;* b. 2 Aug. 1940; m.; two c. *Education:* Addis Ababa Univ., Univ. of Pa, USA. *Career:* legal expert in Office of Auditor-Gen. 1970–71; High Court Judge 1975; Lecturer, then Asst Prof. of Public Int. Law, Addis Ababa Univ. School of Law 1972–77, Deputy Dean 1974–77; with Ministry of Foreign Affairs, positions including Head of Legal Dept 1977–90, Deputy Minister in Govt 1990–91; Perm. Rep. to UN, Vienna 1992–96, Geneva 1996–.
Address: Permanent Mission of Ethiopia, 56 Rue de Moillebeau-1209, PO Box 338, 1221 Geneva 19, Switzerland (office). *Telephone:* (22) 919-7010 (office). *Fax:* (22) 740-1129 (office). *E-mail:* mission.ethiopia@ties.itu.int (office).

YOMA, Jorge Raúl; Argentine diplomatist and fmr politician; *Ambassador to Mexico;* m. Monica Mariel Perafán de Yoma. *Career:* fmr Senator; Amb. to Mexico 2006–.
Address: Embassy of Argentina, Blvd Manuel Avila Camacho 1, 7°, Plaza Comermex, Col. Lomas de Chapultepec, Del. Miguel Hidalgo, 11009 México, DF, Mexico (office). *Telephone:* (55) 5520-9430 (office). *Fax:* (55) 5540-5011 (office). *E-mail:* embajadaargentina@prodigy.net.mx (office). *Website:* www.cancilleria.gov.ar (office).

YONLI, Paramanga Ernest, PhD; Burkinabè politician, agricultural economist and diplomatist; *Ambassador to USA;* b. 1956, Tansarga, Tapoa Prov. *Education:* Univ. of Benin, Univ. of Paris I (Panthéon-Sorbonne), Nat. Inst. of Agric., Paris-Grignon, Ouagadougou Univ. *Career:* conducted research into food security and marketing; fmr Minister of the Civil Service and Institutional Devt; fmr Minister of Econ. and Finance; Prime Minister of Burkina Faso 2000–07 (resgnd); Amb. to USA 2008–.
Address: Embassy of Burkina Faso, 2340 Massachusetts Avenue, NW, Washington, DC 20008, USA (office). *Telephone:* (202) 332-5577 (office). *Fax:* (202) 667-1882 (office). *E-mail:* ambawdc@verizon.net (office). *Website:* www.burkinaembassy-usa.org (office).

YORK, HRH The Duke of; (Prince Andrew Albert Christian Edward), (Earl of Inverness, Baron Killyleagh), KCVO, ADC, KG; British; *Special Representative for International Trade and Investment, Ministry of Defence;* b. 19 Feb. 1960, London; m. Sarah Ferguson 1986 (divorced 1996); two d., Beatrice Elizabeth Mary, b. 8 Aug. 1988, Eugenie Victoria Helena, b. 23 March 1990. *Education:* Heatherdown Preparatory School, Ascot, Gordonstoun School, Scotland, Lakefield Coll. School, Ont., Canada, Britannia Royal Naval Coll., Dartmouth. *Career:* joined Royal Navy as Seaman Officer, specializing as a pilot 1979, before entering Royal Naval Coll.; flying training with RAF Leeming, Yorks. and helicopter training at Royal Naval Air Station (RNAS) Culdrose, Cornwall; received Wings 1981; joined front-line unit 820 Naval Air Squadron and embarked in Anti-Submarine Warfare Carrier HMS Invincible; participated in Falklands conflict; rank of Lt 1984; Personal ADC to HM The Queen 1984; served as Flight Pilot in NAS, Type 22 Frigate HMS Brazen 1984–86; returned to 702 NAS as Helicopter Warfare Instructor 1987; joined Type 42 Destroyer HMS Edinburgh as Officer of the Watch 1988–89; returned to RNAS Portland to form HMS Campbeltown Flight; served as Flight Commdr, 829 NAS 1989–91; Army Command and Staff Course, Staff Coll., Camberley 1992; rank of Lt Commdr 1992; commanded Hunt Class Minehunter HMS Cottesmore 1993–94; Sr Pilot, 815 NAS, RNAS Portland 1995–96; joined Ministry of Defence, London as a staff officer, Directorate of Naval Operations 1997–99; rank of Commdr, with Diplomacy Section of Naval Staff, London 1999–2001; Special Rep. for Int. Trade and Investment 2001–; Adm. of the Sea Cadet Corps 1992–; Col-in-Chief Staffordshire Regt 1989–, Royal Irish Regt 1992–, Royal NZ Army Logistic Regt, Small Arms School Corps, Royal Highland Fusiliers (Princess Margaret's Own and Ayrshire Regt), 9th/12th Royal Lancers (Prince of Wales's); Hon. Air Commodore RAF Lossiemouth, Morayshire; Patron of over 90 orgs, including Greenwich Hosp., Fight for Sight, Defeating Deafness, Jubilee Sailing Trust, Royal Aero Club; Trustee Nat. Maritime Museum, Greenwich; Chair. Trustees Outward Bound Trust; Capt. Royal and Ancient Golf Club of St Andrews; mem. Advisory Bd of Govs, Lakefield Coll. School; Commodore Royal Thames Yacht Club; Elder Brother Trinity House.
Address: Buckingham Palace, London, SW1A 1AA, England. *Website:* www.royal.gov.uk.

YOU, Si-Kun; Taiwanese politician; b. 1948, Yilan Co. *Education:* Chih-Leei Coll. of Business, Tung-hai Univ. Dept of Political Science. *Career:* mem. Seventh Taiwan Prov. Ass. 1981, Eighth 1985; co-f. Democratic Progressive Party (DPP) 1986, elected to First Cen. Standing Cttee 1986, Second 1987, Third 1988, Fourth 1989, Sec. Gen. DPP HQ 1999–2000, Chair. 2006–07 (resgnd); Yilan Co. Magistrate 1990–97; Exec. Campaign Man. and Chief Spokesperson for DPP cand. Chen Shui-bian's Presidential Campaign 2000; Vice-Premier of Taiwan 2000, also Sec. Gen. Office of the Pres. 2001–05; Premier of Taiwan 2002–05; Sec.-Gen. to the Pres. 2005–;

Founder and Chair. Lan-yang Cultural and Educ. Foundation 1990–97, Chair. Taipei Rapid Transit Corpn 1998; Chair. Taiwan-India Co-operation Council 2006–. *Publications:* The Resignation of Tangwai Assemblymen 1985, The Road to Democracy: The Love for Native Land 1989.
Address: Democratic Progressive Party (DPP), 10/F, 30 Beiping East Road, Taipei, Taiwan (office). *Telephone:* (20) 23929989 (office). *E-mail:* foreign@dpp.org.tw (office). *Website:* www.dpp.org.tw (office).

YOUNG, Sir Colville Norbert, Kt, GCMG, MBE, JP, DPhil; Belizean government official and academic; *Governor-General;* b. 20 Nov. 1932, Belize City; m. Norma Eleanor Trapp 1956; three s. one d. *Education:* Univ. of West Indies, Univ. of York. *Career:* Prin. St Michael's Coll., Belize 1974–76; Lecturer in English and Gen. Studies Belize Tech. Coll. 1976–86; Pres. Univ. Coll. of Belize 1986–90, lecturer 1990–93; Gov.-Gen. of Belize 1993–; Hon. PhD (York) 2003; Arts Faculty Prize, Univ. Coll. of the West Indies 1959, Student of the Year, Univ. Coll. of the West Indies 1960, Outstanding Teacher's Award 1987. *Compositions include:* Misa Caribeña, Tiger Dead (folk opera), Ode to Independence (secular cantata for mixed voices and orchestra). *Publications:* Creole Proverbs of Belize 1980, Caribbean Corner Calling 1988, Language and Education in Belize 1989, Pataki Full 1990, From One Caribbean Corner (poetry) 1983, contrib. drama and poetry in various anthologies, articles in various publs.
Address: Belize House, Belmopan, Belize. *Telephone:* (8) 22521; (2) 30881. *Fax:* (8) 22050.

YOUNG, Johnny, BA; American diplomatist; m. Angelena Clark; one s. one d. *Education:* Temple Univ., Pa. *Career:* began Foreign Service career as budget and fiscal officer, Antananarivo 1967; Supervisory Gen. Services Officer, Conakry 1970, Nairobi 1972; Admin. Officer and Chargé d'Affaires, Doha 1974; Admin. Counsellor, Bridgetown; Career Devt Officer, Bureau of Personnel 1979; Exec. Dir, Office of the Insp.-Gen. 1981; Admin. Counsellor, Amman 1984; served at The Hague 1985; Amb. (with rank of Minister Counsellor) to Togo, Amb. to Bahrain 1997–2001, to Slovenia 2001–04; mem. American Acad. of Diplomacy 2005–; Meritorious Honor Award, two Group Honor Awards.
Address: c/o US Department of State, 2201 C Street, NW, Washington, DC 20520, USA (office).

YOUNG KIM FAT, Shiu Ching; Mauritian diplomatist. *Career:* fmr Adviser to Rep. to UNIDO; fmr Second Sec., Perm. Mission of Mauritius, Geneva; currently First Sec. and Deputy Chief of Mission, Embassy in Washington, DC, Chargé d'affaires a.i. 2005–07.

YOUSFI, Youcef, PhD; Algerian politician and diplomatist; *Permanent Representative, United Nations;* b. 2 Oct. 1941, Batna; m.; three c. *Education:* Ecole Nationale Supérieure des Industries Chimiques, France, Université de Nancy, France. *Career:* fmr sr lecturer, then Prof. of Chemical Eng Ecole Nationale Polytechnic d'Alger; fmr Prof. of Chemical Eng and Dir Chem. Inst., Houari Boumediene Univ. of Science and Tech., concurrently served as adviser on petroleum affairs to Ministry of Industry and Energy; fmr Vice-Pres. of Marketing, Sonatrach (nat. petroleum co.), CEO 1985; Chair. Bd, Mines, Petroleum and Hydraulics Participating Fund 1988; Chief of Staff to the Pres. Liamine Zéroual 1996–97; mem. Nat. Peoples's Ass. 1997; Minister of Energy and Mines 1997–99; Chair. OPEC 1998–99; Minister of Foreign Affairs 1999–2000, Minister-Del. to Chief of Govt 2000–01; Amb. to Canada 2001–06; Perm. Rep. to UN, New York 2006–.
Address: Mission of Algeria, United Nations Headquarters, 326 East 48th Street, New York, NY 10017, USA (office). *Telephone:* (212) 750-1960 (office). *Fax:* (212) 759-5274 (office). *E-mail:* mission@algeria-un.org (office). *Website:* www.algeria-un.org (office).

YOUSSEF, Maj.-Gen. Nasser; Palestinian government official and military officer; *Minister of the Interior; Career:* Head of Security Forces in Gaza Strip and West Bank 1994; Minister of the Interior, Palestinian Authority (PA) 2005–.
Address: Ministry of the Interior, Gaza, Palestinian Autonomous Areas (office). *Telephone:* (8) 2829185 (office). *Fax:* (8) 2862500 (office).

YOUSSOUF, Mahamoud Ali; Djibouti politician; *Minister of Foreign Affairs and International Cooperation; Career:* Amb. to Egypt, Cairo –2001; Minister-Del. of Int. Cooperation 2001; Minister of Foreign Affairs and Int. Cooperation 2005–.
Address: Ministry of Foreign Affairs, International Cooperation and Parliamentary Relations, Bd Cheick Osman, BP 1863, Djibouti (office). *Telephone:* 352471 (office). *Fax:* 353049 (office).

YOVANOVITCH, Marie L., BA, MS; American diplomatist; *Ambassador to Armenia; Education:* Princeton Univ., Pushkin Inst., Nat. War Coll.

Career: entered Foreign Service in 1986, career mem. Sr Foreign Service with rank of Counselor, overseas assignments have included Ottawa, Moscow, London and Mogadishu, Deputy Dir Russian Desk 1998–2000, Deputy Chief of Mission, Embassy in Kiev 2001–04, Sr Advisor to Under-Sec. of State for Political Affairs 2004–05, Amb. to Kyrgyzstan 2005–08, to Armenia 2008–.
Address: US Embassy, American Avenue 1, 0082 Yerevan, Armenia (office). *Telephone:* (10) 46-47-00 (office). *Fax:* (10) 46-47-42 (office). *E-mail:* usinfo@usa.am (office). *Website:* yerevan.usembassy.gov (office).

YU, Myung-hwan; South Korean diplomatist and politician; *Minister of Foreign Affairs and Trade;* b. 8 April 1946; m.; one s. one d. *Education:* Seoul Nat. Univ., Inst. of Social Studies, The Hague, Netherlands. *Career:* joined Ministry of Foreign Affairs (MFA) 1973; Third Sec., Embassy in Tokyo 1976–79; Asst Sec., Office of the Pres. 1979–81; First Sec., Embassy in Singapore 1981–83; Counsellor, Embassy in Barbados 1983–85; Asst Sec., Office of the Pres. 1985–86; Dir N America Div., American Affairs Bureau, MFA 1986–88, Exec. Sec. to Minister of Foreign Affairs Jan.–Oct. 1988; Counsellor, Embassy in Washington, DC 1988–91; Deputy Dir-Gen. American Affairs Bureau 1991–92, Spokesperson, MFA 1992–94; Minister, Perm. Mission to UN, New York 1994–95; Sec. to the Pres. for Foreign Affairs, Office of the Pres. 1995–96; Dir-Gen. American Affairs Bureau, MFA 1996–98; Minister, Embassy in Washington, DC 1998–2001; Special Aide to Minister of Foreign Affairs and Trade Aug.–Dec. 2001, Amb. for Anti-Terrorism and Afghanistan Issues, Ministry of Foreign Affairs and Trade 2001–02; Amb. to Israel 2002–04, to the Philippines 2004–05; Vice-Minister of Foreign Affairs 2005–07; Amb. to Japan 2007–08; Minister of Foreign Affairs and Trade 2008–; Order of Service Merit Red Stripes 1996, Grand Cross, Order of Sikatuna (Philippines) 2005.
Address: Ministry of Foreign Affairs and Trade, 37 Sejongno (Doryeom-dong), Jongno-gu, Seoul 110-787, Republic of Korea (office). *Telephone:* (2) 2100-2114 (office). *Fax:* (2) 2100-7999 (office). *E-mail:* web@mofat.go.kr (office). *Website:* www.mofat.go.kr (office).

YU, Xintian; Chinese research institute director; *President, Shanghai Institute for International Studies; Career:* Dir Inst. of Asia-Pacific Studies 1992–94; Vice-Pres. Shanghai Acad. of Social Sciences 1994–2000; currently Pres. Shanghai Inst. for Int. Studies (SIIS); Sec. CCP Leadership Group of SIIS; Vice Pres. China Asscn of Int. Relations; Pres. Shanghai Asscn of Int. Relations; Pres. Shanghai Asscn of Taiwan Studies; Visiting Scholar SAIS, Johns Hopkins Univ. and Inst. for East Asia Study, Univ. of Calif., Berkeley 1990–91; Fellow, Eisenhower Exchange 1997. *Publications include:* Manufacturing Miracles: Paths of Industrialization in Latin America and East Asia, The South Side: the Impact of Developing Countries on International Relations 1993, Taking Our Own Road: Overall Design of Modernization of China 1994, Opportunity and Limitation: Comparative Conditions of Modernization in Developing Countries 1998.
Address: Shanghai Institute for International Studies, No. 1, Lane 845, Julu Road, Shanghai 200040, People's Republic of China (office). *Telephone:* (21) 54031148 (office). *Fax:* (21) 54030272 (office). *E-mail:* siis@public.sta.net.cn (office). *Website:* www.siis.org.cn (office).

YU, Yongding, MA, PhD; Chinese economist; *Director and Senior Fellow, Institute of World Economics and Politics, Chinese Academy of Social Sciences;* b. 18 Nov. 1948, Jiangsu Prov. *Education:* Beijing Electronic Science and Tech. Coll., Chinese Acad. of Social Sciences, Univ. of Oxford, UK. *Career:* worker, Beijing Heavy Machinery Factory 1969–79; researcher, Inst. of World Econs and Politics (IWEP), Chinese Acad. of Social Sciences (CASS) 1979–88, Research Fellow 1983–87, Sr Fellow 1987–, Dir 1994–; Prof., Dept of World Econs, Post-Grad. School, CASS; Vice-Pres. China Soc. of World Econs 1997–; Lecturer, Univ. of West of England 1993–94; fellow of several research insts and adviser to several govt depts. *Publications:* General Theory on Trade (trans.) 1984, Rational Expectations (trans.) 1988, Post-Keynesian Monetary Economics (trans.) 1989, China's Inflation and Its Control (co-ed.) 1996, Western Economics (ed.) 1997, The World Economy 1998–1999 (co-ed.) 1998, The World Economy 1999–2000 (co-ed.) 1999, The Impact of China's Entry into WTO on its Industries (co-ed.) 1999; numerous articles on macro-econs and int. finance in learned journals.
Address: Institute of World Economics and Politics, Chinese Academy of Social Sciences, 5 Jiangguomenwai Dajie, Beijing 100732, People's Republic of China (office). *Telephone:* (10) 65126180 (office). *Fax:* (10) 65126105 (office). *E-mail:* yuyd@cass.org.cn (office). *Website:* www.iwep.org.cn (office).

YUMKELLA, Kandeh, PhD; Sierra Leonean politician and international organization executive; *Director-General, United Nations Industrial Development Organization;* m.; one s. one d. *Education:* Univ. of Illinois, USA. *Career:* held several academic and research positions in USA; Minister for Trade, Industry and State Enterprises, Sierra Leone 1994–95; Special

Advisor to Dir-Gen. UNIDO 1996, Dir Africa and Least Developed Countries Regional Bureau 1996–2000, UNIDO Rep. and Dir Regional Industrial Devt Centre 2000–03, Sr Advisor to Dir-Gen. 2003–05, Dir-Gen. UNIDO 2005–. *Publications:* co-author of numerous books, articles and staff papers on int. trade and devt issues.
Address: UNIDO Headquarters, PO Box 300, Vienna International Centre, Wagramerstr. 5, 1400 Vienna, Austria (office). *Telephone:* (1) 26026-0 (office). *Fax:* (1) 2692669 (office). *E-mail:* unido@unido.org (office). *Website:* www.unido.org (office).

YUNUS, Pengiran Haji; Brunei diplomatist; *Ambassador to Belgium; Career:* Amb. to Cambodia –2001; High Commr to UK 2001–06; Amb. to Belgium 2006–.
Address: Embassy of Brunei, 238 avenue F. D. Roosevelt, 1050 Brussels, Belgium (office). *Telephone:* (2) 675-08-78 (office). *Fax:* (2) 672-93-58 (office). *E-mail:* kedutaan-brunei.brussels@skynet.be (office).

YUNUS, Muhammad; Bangladeshi banker and academic; *Managing Director and CEO, Grameen Bank;* m. Afrizi Yunus; one d. *Education:* Vanderbilt Univ., USA. *Career:* Prof. of Econs, Chittagong Univ. 1976; f. Grameen Bank Project, pioneering microcredit loans to those in extreme poverty Dec. 1976, changed to ind. bank, Grameen Bank Sept. 1983, now Man. Dir, CEO; f. Nagorik Shakti political party 2007; Dir UN Foundation; mem. Int. Advisory Group, Fourth World Conf. on Women, Beijing 1993–95, Advisory Council for Sustainable Econ. Devt 1993, UN Expert Group on Women and Finance; Founding Man. Dir German Telephones 1998–; Hon. LLD (Warwick) 1996; Independence Day Award, Pres.'s Award and Cen. Bank Award (all Bangladesh), Ramon Magsaysay Award (Philippines), Aga Khan Award for Architecture, Mohamed Shabdeen Award for Science (Sri Lanka), World Food Prize (USA), Nobel Peace Prize (jtly with Grameen Bank) 2006. *Publications include:* Creating a World Without Poverty: How Social Business Can Transform Our Lives 2008.
Address: Grameen Bank, Mirpur 1, Dhaka 1216, Bangladesh (office). *Telephone:* (2) 801138 (office). *Fax:* (2) 803559 (office). *E-mail:* grameen.bank@grameen.net (office). *Website:* www.grameen-info.org (office).

YUSGIANTORO, Purnomo, BSc, MS, PhD; Indonesian international organization official and government official; *Minister for Energy and Mineral Resources;* b. 16 June 1951, Semarang, Cen. Java; m.; three c. *Education:* Bandung Inst. of Tech., Univ. of Colorado, USA. *Career:* worked with several int. think tanks during 1980s; energy consultant with World Bank (IBRD) and Asian Devt Bank 1988–2000; fmr Deputy Gov. Nat. Resilience Inst. (Lemhannas); adviser, Minister of Energy 1993–98; Minister for Energy and Mineral Resources 2000–; fmr Gov. OPEC, Vienna, Pres. OPEC Conf. and Acting Sec.-Gen. OPEC 2004; fmr Lecturer in Econs and Man., Atmajaya Univ., Jakarta and univs in USA; Co-founder Indonesian Inst. for Energy Econs.
Address: Ministry of Energy and Mineral Resources, Jalan Merdeka Selatan 18, Jakarta 10110, Indonesia (office). *Telephone:* (21) 3804242 (office). *Fax:* (21) 3847461 (office). *E-mail:* pulahta@setjen.dpe.go.id (office). *Website:* www.dpe.go.id (office).

YUSHCHENKO, Viktor Andriyovich, CandEconSc; Ukrainian economist, banker, politician and head of state; *President;* b. 23 Feb. 1954, Khoruzhivka, Sumy Oblast; m. Kateryna Mykhailivna Yushchenko; two s. three d. *Education:* Ternopil Inst. of Finance and Econ., Ukrainian Inst. of Econs and Agricultural Man. *Career:* economist, Br. Dir USSR State Bank, Ulianivskyi Dist, Sumy Oblast 1976–85, Deputy Dir of Agric. Credits, Ukrainian Br. of USSR State Bank 1985–87; Dept Dir Ukrainian Bank (fmrly Ukrainian Agro-Industrial Bank) 1987–91, First Deputy Chair. 1991–93; Gov. Nat. Bank of Ukraine 1993–99; Prime Minister of Ukraine 1999–2001; founder and Chair. Our Ukraine coalition 2002, mem. Parl. 2002–; Pres. of Ukraine 2005–; mem. Ukrainian Acad. of Econ. Sciences, Acad. of Econ. and Cybernetics; Dr hc (Mohyla Acad. — National University of Kyiv), (Ostroh Acad.); Global Finance Award 1997, State Prize Laureate Science and Technology 1999, Chatham House Prize, UK 2005. *Publications:* over 250 articles and research papers in Ukrainian and int. journals.
Address: Office of the President, 01220 Kyiv, vul. Bankova 11, Ukraine (office). *Telephone:* (44) 291-53-33 (office). *Fax:* (44) 293-61-61 (office). *E-mail:* president@adm.gov.ua (office); viktor@yuschenko.com.ua. *Website:* www.president.gov.ua (office); www.yuschenko.com.ua.

YUSHKIAVITSHUS, Henrikas Alguirdas; Russian/Lithuanian international civil servant; *Chargé de mission, United Nations Educational, Scientific and Cultural Organization (UNESCO);* b. (Henrikes Alguirdas Yushkiavitshus), 30 March 1935, Šiauliai, Lithuania; m. Elena Samuilytė 1961; one d. *Education:* Leningrad Electrotechnical Communication Inst. *Career:* Dir Technological Dept Lithuanian Radio and TV 1960–66; Dir Tech. Centre, Int. Radio and TV Org. 1966–71; Vice-Chair USSR State

Cttee for TV and Radio 1971–90; Chair. Interministerial Cttee for Radio and TV Devt and mem. Interministerial Cttee for Satellite Communications 1971–90; Asst Dir-Gen. for Communication, Information and Informatics, UNESCO 1990–2001, Chargé de mission UNESCO 2001–; Corresp. mem. Russian Eng Acad.; mem. Int. Acad. of Electrotechnical Sciences, Fed. Tenders Comm. 2004–; Fellow, Soc. of Motion Picture and TV Engineers, USA; Hon. Academician, Russian Acad. of Information; recipient of several Soviet and Russian decorations etc.; Order of Gediminas, Lithuania 1996; Dr hc (Int. Inst. for Advanced Studies in Systems Research and Cybernetics, Canada); Emmy Directorate Award, US Nat. Acad. of TV Arts and Sciences. *Publications:* contribs to professional journals.
Address: c/o UNESCO, 1 rue Miollis, 75732 Paris, Cedex 15 (office); 23 rue Ginoux, 75015 Paris, France (home). *Telephone:* 1-45-68-13-08 (office); 1-45-77-20-84 (home). *Fax:* 1-45-68-57-89 (office); 1-45-75-21-82 (home). *E-mail:* henrikas@noos.fr (home).

YUSUF AHMED, Col Abdullahi; Somali politician, military leader and head of state; *President;* b. 15 Dec. 1934, Galkayo, Puntland; m.; four c. *Education:* Italy, USSR. *Career:* served in Somali army; fmr Deputy Chief SSDF faction; Co-Chair. Somali Reconciliation Council 1997; declared Puntland region autonomous 1998, Pres. of 'Puntland' 1998–2001; Pres. Transitional Admin of Somalia 2004–; mem. Darod clan.

Address: Office of the President, People's Palace, Mogadishu, Somalia (office). *E-mail:* info@somali-gov.info (office). *Website:* www.somali-gov.info (office).

YUZHANOV, Ilya Arturovich, CandEcon; Russian economist, politician and business executive; b. 7 Feb. 1960, Leningrad (now St Petersburg); m.; three c. *Education:* Leningrad State Univ. *Career:* teacher, lecturer in Leningrad insts 1982–90; Chief Specialist, Leningrad Cttee on Econ. Reforms 1990–91; Head of Dept, First Deputy Chair. Cttee on Econ. Devt, St Petersburg 1991–94; Chair. Cttee on Land Resources of St Petersburg 1994–97; Chair. State Cttee on Land Resources of Russian Fed. 1997–98; Minister on Land Policy, Construction and Communal Econs May–Sept. 1998; Minister of Antimonopoly Policy and Support for Entrepreneurship 1999–2004; Chair. Supervisory Council NOMOS-Bank 2004–06, mem. Bd Dirs 2006–; mem. Bd Dirs jt stock cos, including Unified Energy System of Russia 2000–, NOVATEK 2006–, Uralkalii 2006–, Kirovsky Zavod 2006–; Medal in Commemoration of 850th Anniversary of Founding of Moscow 1997, Merited Economist of Russian Fed. 2000, Best Independent Director in Russia 2007. *Publications:* monographs and numerous articles in journals and newspapers on antimonopoly and other problems in econs.
Address: NOMOS-Bank, Verkhnyaya Radishchevskaya str. 3, Moscow 109240, Russia (office). *Telephone:* (495) 725-32-30 (office). *Fax:* (495) 797-32-50 (office). *E-mail:* yuzhanov_ia@nomos.ru (office). *Website:* www.nomos.ru (office).

Z

ZACKHEOS, Sotirios, MA; Cypriot diplomatist; *President, European Arab Interactive Forum;* b. 24 Jan. 1950, Nicosia; m.; two c. *Education:* Univ. of Athens and Stanford Univ., USA. *Career:* Counsellor Embassy, Moscow 1979–85; Amb. to China (also accred to Japan, Pakistan, The Philippines and Mongolia) 1989–93; Dir of Econ. Affairs, Foreign Ministry 1993, of Political Affairs 1995; Perm. Rep. to UN, Geneva 1996–97, Amb., Perm. Rep. to UN, New York 1997–2003, Perm. Sec. 2003–; Chair. Fourth Cttee (Special Political and Decolonization) 1999; High Commr (non-resident) to St Lucia, Grenada and Trinidad & Tobago 1997–2003; Amb. (non-resident) to Suriname 1997–2003; Perm. Sec., Ministry of Foreign Affairs 2003–07; Pres. European Arab Interactive Forum; Chair. S. Zackheos & Assocs Ltd (consulting office); Adviser to CEO, Russian Commercial Bank; Pres. Donalink; Dir Otkritie UES Capital Partners Fund PLC, EP Global Energy Ltd, Sharelink Financial Services Group; Adviser J&P Group; ad hoc special envoy of Pres. of Cyprus to Russia and Middle East; Grand Cross, Order of the Phoenix (Greece), Golden Order for Services in Diplomacy (Slovenia); Pancyprian Asscn of Florida Man of the Year Award 2003. *Publications:* contribs to Anthology of Young Cypriot Poets, Justice Pending: Indigenous Peoples and Other Good Causes; numerous articles in Cypriot newspapers.
Address: Palais d'Ivoire, 12 Themistoklis Dervis Street, Apt 304, 1066 Nicosia, Cyprus (office). *Telephone:* 22818385 (office). *Fax:* 22666744 (office). *E-mail:* s.zackheos@cytanet.com.cy (office).

ZACKIOS, Gerald M.; Marshall Islands government minister and lawyer. *Education:* Int. Maritime Law Inst. *Career:* Attorney-Gen. 1995–2001; Minister of Foreign Affairs and Minister in Assistance to the Pres., then Minister of Foreign Affairs 2001–08, also of Trade 2001–07.
Address: c/o Ministry of Foreign Affairs and Trade, PO Box 1349, Majuro, MH 96960, Marshall Islands.

ZADORNOV, Mikhail Mikhailovich, Cand.Econ.; Russian politician; b. 4 May 1963, Moscow; m. Natalya Zadornova 1982; one d. *Education:* G. Plekhanov Inst. of Nat. Econ. *Career:* one of authors Programme of Econ. Reforms 500 Days; mem. State Comm. on Econ. Reform, Russian Council of Ministers 1990–91; mem. State Duma (Parl.) (Yabloko faction) 1993–97, 1999–2003, re-elected as ind. 2003–; Chair., Cttee on Budget, Taxation, Banks and Finances 1994–97; Minister of Finance 1997–99; Special Rep. of Pres. Boris Yeltsin, rank of First Deputy Prime Minister, in negotiations with int. financial orgs 1998–99; Deputy Chair. Cttee on Budget and Taxes, Chair. Sub-Cttee on Monetary Policy, Exchange and Capital Control and the Activities of the Cen. Bank of the Russian Fed. 1999–2003. *Publications:* more than 20 books; numerous articles on Russia's financial problems.
Address: State Duma, 103265 Moscow, Okhotny ryad 1, Russia. *Telephone:* (495) 292-71-98 (office). *Fax:* (495) 292-90-00 (office). *E-mail:* zadornov@duma.gov.ru (office).

ZAHIR, Maj.-Gen. Mohamed; Maldivian army officer; *Chief of Staff, Maldives National Defence Force;* m. Fathimath Amira; four s. one d. *Education:* Hendon Police Coll., London, UK, Naval Postgraduate School, Monterey, Calif., USA, Sr Execs in Nat. and Int. Security Program, John F. Kennedy School of Govt, USA. *Career:* joined civil service and worked in various Govt Depts before enlisting in Maldives Nat. Defence Force (MNDF— fmrly Nat. Security Service (NSS)) 1978, promoted to rank of Sergeant and commissioned as officer 1980, undertook various command positions within different units of MNDF, Deputy Chief of Staff, MNDF –1996, also commanded MNDF Defence Inst. for Training and Educ. (fmrly known as NSS Training Unit), promoted to rank of Brig., Chief of Staff, MNDF 1996–, promoted to rank of Maj.-Gen. 2004, Chair. MNDF Advisory Council; Medal for Exceptional Bravery 1988, Presidential Medal, Distinguished Service Medal, Dedicated Service Medal.
Address: Office of the Chief of Staff, Maldives National Defence Force, Bandaara koshi, Ameer Ahmed Magu, Malé, Maldives (office). *Telephone:* 3322607 (office). *Fax:* 3322496 (office). *E-mail:* media@mndf.gov.mv (office). *Website:* www.mndf.gov.mv (office).

ZAKARIA, Fareed, BA, PhD; American editor, academic, writer and television presenter; *Editor, Newsweek International;* b. India; m.; one s. one d. *Education:* Yale and Harvard Univs. *Career:* Lecturer on Int. Politics and Econs, Harvard Univ., also Head of Project on the Changing Security Environment; Adjunct Prof., Columbia Univ., New York, Case Western Reserve Univ., Cleveland, OH; Man. Ed. Foreign Affairs journal 1992–2000; Ed. Newsweek Int. 2000–; columnist, Newsweek (USA), Newsweek Int., The Washington Post 2001–; Host and Man. Ed. Foreign Exchange with Fareed Zakaria (PBS Series) 2006–07; political commentator, ABC News 2006–07; host of TV show on foreign affairs for CNN 2008–; speaker at World Econ. Forum, Davos, Switzerland and various univs; wine columnist for Slate (webzine); mem. Bd Trilateral Comm., IISS, Shakespeare and Co., The Century Asscn; Overseas Press Club Award, Deadline Club Award, Edwin Hood Award. *Publications include:* From Wealth to Power: The Unusual Origins of America's World Role, The American Encounter: The United States and the Making of the Modern World (co-ed.), The Future of Freedom 2003, The Post-American World 2008; contrib. to publs including The New York Times, The New Yorker and The Wall Street Journal.
Address: Newsweek International, Newsweek Building, 251 West 57th Street, New York, NY 10019-1894, USA (office). *E-mail:* editors@newsweek.com (office). *Website:* www.newsweek.com (office); www.fareedzakaria.com.

ZAMA, Francis; Solomon Islands politician. *Career:* fmrly with Solomon Islands Cen. Bank; fmr Minister of Educ.; Minister of Finance and Treasury 2003–06; Chair. Public Accounts Comm., Ministry of Finance, Nat. Reform and Planning 2007–; mem. People's Alliance Party.
Address: c/o Ministry of Finance, National Reform and Planning, POB 26, Honiara, Solomon Islands (office). *Telephone:* 22535 (office). *Fax:* 20392 (office). *E-mail:* finance@welkam.solomon.com.sb (office).

ZAMAGNI, Stefano; Italian economist; *Professor of Economics, University of Bologna;* b. 4 Jan. 1943, Rimini; m. Vera Negri 1968; two d. *Education:* Univ. of Milan, Univ. of Oxford, UK. *Career:* Assoc. Dir and Adjunct Prof., Bologna Center, Johns Hopkins Univ. 1977–; Prof. of Econs, Univ. of Bologna 1985–, Chair. Dept of Econs 1985–88, 1991–94, Dean Faculty of Econs 1994–96, Co-ordinator PhD Programme in Econs 1989–93; Pres. Int. Catholic Migration Comm., Geneva 1999–; Vice-Pres. Italian Econ. Asscn 1989–92, State Vic. Bank Visiting Prof., Deakin Univ., Geelong, Australia; McDonnell Visiting Scholar, Wider, Helsinki, Finland; Co-Ed. Economia Politica (quarterly) 1983–, Italian Economic Papers 1990–, Journal of International and Comparative Economics, Ricerche Economiche; mem. Exec. Cttee Int. Econ. Asscn 1989–, Pontifical Council on Justice and Peace 1992–, Scientific Cttee, J. Maritain Int. Inst. 1995–, Bd of Dirs UNIBANCA 1999–, Scientific Cttee, Rosselli Foundation, Turin, Bd of Dirs Hosp. Bambino Gesù, Rome 2000–; pres. not-for profit governmental agency 2007–; mem. Acad. of Sciences; Paul Harris Fellow, Rotary International 1995; Hon. Citizen of Rosario and Mar del Plata, Argentina; Accad. Lincei Award, St Vincent Prize in Econs, Capri Prize in Econs 1995, Golden Sigismondo Prize 1997, Gold Medal, Pio Manzu Int. Centre 1998, Gold Medal, Cooperative Credit 2005. *Publications:* Microeconomic Theory 1987, The Economic Theories of Production 1989, History of Economic Thought 1991, Value and Capital—Fifty Years Later (with L. McKenzie) 1991, Firms and Markets 1991, Man – Environment and Development: Toward a Global Approach 1991, Market, State and the Theory of Public Intervention 1992, The Economics of Crime and Illegal Markets 1993, Towards a One World Development Path 1993, The Economics of Altruism 1995, An Evolutionary Dynamic Approach to Altruism 1996, Technological Change: Time-Use Policies and Employment 1996, Globalization as Specificity of Post-Industrial Economy 1997, Civil Economy and Paradoxes of Growth in Post-Fordist Societies 1997, Living in the Global Society 1997, Civil Economy, Cultural Evolution and Participatory Development 1999, The Economics of Corruption and Illegal Markets (co-author) 1999, Financial Globalization and the Emerging Economies (co-author) 2000, Time in Economic Theory (with E. Agliardi) 2004, Economic Theory and Interpersonal Relations (with P. Sacco) 2006, Toward a New Economic Theory of Cooperative Firm 2005, Civil Economy (with L. Bruni) 2007.
Address: Department of Economics, University of Bologna, Piazza Scaravilli 2, 40126 Bologna, Italy (office). *Telephone:* (051) 2098132 (office). *Fax:* (051) 2098040 (office). *E-mail:* bruna.bordoni@unibo.it (office); stefano.zamagni@unibo.it (home).

ZAMMIT, Tarcisio, BA, MA; Maltese diplomatist; *Ambassador to Belgium and Luxembourg;* b. 1947, B'kara; m. Theresa Mercieca 1979; one d. *Education:* Lyceum, Malta, Univ. of Malta, Univ. of London, UK. *Career:* fmr teacher, St Aloysius Coll., Malta; joined Ministry of Foreign Affairs 1977; First Sec. Embassy of Malta, Brussels 1981–90; EU Directorate, Ministry of Foreign Affairs, Malta 1991–95; Amb. to Tunisia 1995–96; Deputy Head, Mission of Malta to EU 1998–2003; Rep. to EU Political and Security Cttee 2003–; Amb. to Belgium and Luxembourg 2003–. *Address:* Embassy of Malta, 65–67 rue Belliard, 1040 Brussels, Belgium (office). *Telephone:* (2) 343-01-95 (office). *Fax:* (2) 343-01-06 (office). *E-mail:* tarcisio.zammit@gov.mt (office).

ZANNIER, Lamberto, DIur; Italian lawyer and diplomatist; *Special Representative of the Secretary-General and Head of Mission, United Nations Interim Administration in Kosovo;* m.; two s. two d. *Education:* Trieste Univ., Italian Diplomatic Inst. *Career:* served with FAO Legal Office, Rome 1976–78; joined Ministry of Foreign Affairs in 1978, worked on Multilateral Econ. Co-operation Desk; Second Sec., Embassy in Abu Dhabi 1979–82; First Sec., for Multilateral Affairs, Embassy in Vienna 1982–87; with Political Affairs Div. then Office of the Sec.-Gen. Ministry of Foreign Affairs 1987–91; seconded to NATO as Head of Disarmament, Arms Control and Cooperative Security Section 1991–97; Deputy Chief of Mission, Perm. Mission to OSCE, Chair. for negotiations on Adaptation of the Treaty on Conventional Armed Forces in Europe 1997–2000; Rep. Exec. Council of Org. for Prohibition of Chemical Weapons 2000–02; Dir OSCE Conflict Prevention Centre 2002–06; worked on EU common foreign and security policy, Ministry of Foreign Affairs 2006–08; Special Rep. of the UN Sec.-Gen. and Head of Mission, Interim Admin. Mission in Kosovo (UNMIK) 2008–. *Publications:* numerous publs and articles on arms control, peacekeeping and security co-operation. *Address:* UNMIK Administrative Headquarters, Prishtina, Kosovo (office). *Website:* www.unmikonline.org (office).

ŽANTOVSKÝ, Michael; Czech diplomatist, politician, scientist and translator; *Ambassador to Israel;* b. 3 Jan. 1945, Prague; m. 1st Kristina Žantovská (divorced 1999); one s. one d.; m. 2nd Jana Žantovský; one s. *Education:* Charles Univ., Prague, McGill Univ., Montreal. *Career:* scientific worker in a research inst., Prague 1973–; freelance translator and interpreter 1980–89; activist for ind. creative org. Open Dialogue 1988; Founder mem. restored PEN 1989; Press Spokesman for Centre of Civic Forum 1989–90; mem. Advisory Bd to Pres. Václav Havel (q.v.) 1990–91; Press Spokesman to Pres. 1991–92; with Ministry of Foreign Affairs Aug. 1992; Amb. to USA 1993–97; mem. Senate 1996–2002, Chair. Senate Comm. for Foreign Affairs, Defence and Security 1996–2002; Amb. to Israel 2004–; mem. Civic Democratic Alliance (ODA) 1997–, Chair. March–Nov. 1997, 2001, Vice-Chair. 1998–2001; mem. Bd of Supervisors OPS Prague – 'European City of Culture 2000' 1999–2001. *Publications:* papers in scientific journals on psychological motivation and sexual behaviour, author of plays and translator of numerous papers. *Address:* Embassy of the Czech Republic, PO Box 16361, 23 Rehov Zeitlin, Tel-Aviv 61664, Israel (office). *Telephone:* (3) 6911031 (office). *Fax:* (3) 6918286 (office). *E-mail:* telaviv@embassy.mzv.cz (office). *Website:* www .mfa.cz/telaviv (office); www.mzv.cz (office).

ZAPATA, José Benjamin, BA; Honduran diplomatist; *Permanent Representative, United Nations, Geneva;* m.; two c. *Education:* Universidad Autonoma de Guadalajara, Jalisco, Mexico. *Career:* fmr Econ. Attaché covering all Benelux countries; fmr Econ. and Commercial Counsellor then Counsellor, Embassy in Brussels; Minister Counsellor for Econ. Affairs then Minister and Deputy Chief of Mission, Embassy in Washington, DC 1989–2002; Perm. Rep. to UN, Geneva 2003–, Vienna 2004–. *Address:* Permanent Mission of Honduras to the UN, Ch. de Taverney 13, 1211 Grand-Seconnex, Switzerland (office). *Telephone:* (22) 710-07-60 (office). *Fax:* (22) 710-07-66 (office). *E-mail:* mission.honduras@ties.itu.int (office).

ZAPATERO, José Luis Rodríguez; Spanish politician and lawyer; *Prime Minister and President of the Council;* b. 4 Aug. 1960, Valladolid; m. 1990; two d. *Career:* worked as a teacher of law; joined Partido Socialista Obrero Español (PSOE) 1978, Leader, Socialist Youth Org., León 1982, mem. Parl. 1986–, Leader PSOE Regional Chapter for León 1988, mem. PSOE Fed. Exec. Cttee 1997, Sec.-Gen. 2000–; Prime Minister of Spain and Pres. of the Council 2004–. *Address:* Prime Minister's Chancellery and Ministry of the Presidency, Complejo de la Moncloa, 28071 Madrid; Partido Socialista Obrero Español, Ferraz 68 y 70, 28008, Madrid, Spain (office). *Telephone:* (91) 3353535 (office); (91) 5820444 (office). *Fax:* (91) 5492739 (office); (91) 5820422 (office). *Website:* www.mpr.es (office); www.psoe.es (office).

ZAPRIANOV, Lt-Gen. Atanas Dimitrov; Bulgarian military officer; *Military Representative, NATO;* b. 16 April 1950, Dragoinovo; m. Ivanka Vasileva Zaprianova; one s. one d. *Education:* V. Levski Army Acad., Signal Officers War Coll., Russia, G. S. Rakovski Nat. War Coll., Nat. Defense Univ., USA. *Career:* began mil. career with Signal Regt, serving as Signal Platoon Commdr 1974–75, Signal Co. Commdr 1975–77, Deputy Commdr for Tech. Support, Signal Bn 1977–79, Chief of Staff 1982–84, Deputy Commdr 1984–86; promoted to Second Lt 1974, First Lt 1977, Captain 1981, Major 1986, Lt-Col 1991, Col 1995, Maj.-Gen. 1999, Lt-Gen. 2003; staff positions include Asst Chief of Dept, Land Forces HQ 1986–87, Sr Asst Chief of Dept, Signal Directorate 1987–90, Deputy Chief of Dept, Signal Directorate 1990–91, Chief of Operations Dept, Signal Directorate 1991–94, Deputy Chief of Communications and Electronics Directorate 1995–98, Chief of Communications and Information Systems Directorate 1998–2000, Chief of Communications and Information Systems Main Directorate 2000–02, Deputy Chief of Gen. Staff 2003–06; Commdt G. S. Rakovski War Coll. 2002–03; Mil. Rep., NATO 2006–, also to EU; Orders First and Second Class of Loyal Service with Colours, special awards from Minister of Defence. *Address:* NATO HQ, blvd Léopold III, 1110 Brussels, Belgium (office). *Telephone:* (2) 707-41-11 (office). *Fax:* (2) 707-45-79 (office). *E-mail:* natodoc@hq.nato.int (office). *Website:* www.nato.int (office).

ZARIF, Mohammad Javad, BA, MA, PhD; Iranian diplomatist; b. 8 Jan. 1960; m., two c. *Education:* San Francisco State Univ., Univ. of Denver, USA. *Career:* served as Adviser, later Counsellor and Charge d'Affaires, Perm. Mission to UN, New York 1982–89, Deputy Perm. Rep. 1989–92, Chair. Sixth (Legal) Cttee, UN Gen. Ass. 1992–93, Perm. Rep. 2002–07, Vice-Pres. UN Gen. Ass. 2003–05, Chair. Governmental Expert Cttee on Confidence Building 1998, OIC Expert Cttee on Dialogue among Civilizations 2000–02, UN Disarmament Comm. 2000, UNESCO Culture Comm. 2007–, mem. UN Group of Eminent Persons on Dialogue among Civilizations 2000–02; Adviser to Foreign Minister, Tehran 1988–89, Deputy Foreign Minister 1992–2002; Visiting Prof., Coll. of Int. Relations, Tehran 1989–, Univ. of Tehran 1997–; Pres. Asian African Legal Consultative Cttee, New Delhi 1997–98. *Publications:* numerous articles on int. affairs in journals and newspapers. *Address:* United Nations Educational, Scientific and Cultural Organization (UNESCO), 7 place de Fontenoy, 75352 Paris SP, France (office). *Telephone:* 1-45-68-10-00 (office). *Fax:* 1-45-67-16-90 (office). *E-mail:* bpi@unesco.org (office). *Website:* www.unesco.org (office); www.zarif.net (office).

ZARIFI, Hamrokhon; Tajikistan diplomatist; *Minister of Foreign Affairs;* b. (Hamrokhon Zaripov), 25 Dec. 1948; m.; two c. *Education:* Kulob State Univ., Nat. Inst. of Modern Language, Pakistan, Korean Inst. for Econs and Trade. *Career:* Lecturer in Math., Kulob State Univ. 1971–74; Co-ordinator, Kulob Oblast Exec. Cttee 1974–84; held various posts in party org. and Tajikistan govt 1984–93; Deputy Chief Personnel Dept, Ministry of Foreign Affairs 1993–94, Chief of Dept 1994–96, Deputy Minister of Foreign Affairs 1995–97; Perm. Rep. to UN, Vienna 1996–2003, also Head of del. to OSCE, also Chargé d'Affaires, Embassy in Vienna 1996–97, Head of Mission to EEC 1997–2001, Amb. to Austria 1997–2003, to Switzerland 1998–2003, to Hungary 1999–2002, to USA 2003–06; Minister of Foreign Affairs 2006–. *Address:* Ministry of Foreign Affairs, 734051 Dushanbe, pr. Rudaki 42, Tajikistan (office). *Telephone:* (372) 21-18-08 (office). *Fax:* (372) 21-02-59 (office). *E-mail:* dushanbe@mfaumo.td.silk.org (office). *Website:* www.mid .tj (office).

ZARROUK, Nazhia; Tunisian diplomatist and fmr government official; *Ambassador to Lebanon; Career:* Minister for Family and Women 1995–97, for Family and Women's Affairs 1997–99; Minister-Del. at the Premier Minister's Office in charge of Family and Women's Affairs 1999, Minister 1999–2001; Minister of Vocational Training and Employment 2001–03; Minister of Women's Affairs, Family and Children 2003; Amb. to Lebanon 2003–. *Address:* Embassy of Tunisia, Hazmieh, Mar-Takla, Beirut, Lebanon (office). *Telephone:* (5) 457431 (office). *Fax:* (5) 950434 (office).

ZASYPKIN, Alexander; Russian diplomatist; *Ambassador to Yemen; Career:* joined Ministry of Foreign Affairs 1973; served in Embassy in Damascus –1990, then Charge d' affaires, Embassy in Riyadh; Minister Plenipotentiary, Embassy in Sanaa 1994–95; Deputy Dir Middle East and N African Office, Ministry of Foreign Affairs 1995–2002; Amb. to Yemen 2002–. *Address:* Embassy of Russia, POB 1087, 26 September Street, San'a, Yemen (office). *Telephone:* (1) 278719 (office). *Fax:* (1) 283142 (office).

ZATLERS, Valdis; Latvian surgeon and head of state; *President;* b. 22 March 1955, Rīga; m. Lilita Zatlere; three c. *Education:* Rīga Inst. of

Medicine, Univs of Yale and Syracuse, USA. *Career:* served in Latvian Nat. Front 1988–89; practiced medicine at Yale Univ., Syracuse Univ. and Keggi Orthopaedic Foundation, USA 1990–91; traumatologist and orthopaedist, Riga Hospital No.2 1979–85, Head of Traumatology Dept 1985–94; Dir Latvian Hosp. of Traumatology and Orthopaedics, Rīga 1994–2007, Chair. of Bd 1998–2007; Bd mem. Latvian Popular Front 1988–89; Pres. of Latvia 2007–; Chair. Latvian Asscn for Traumatology and Orthopaedics 2003–; f. Latvian Arthroscopy Asscn, Pres. 1990–93, Vice-Pres. 1994–98; mem. Int. Soc. of Arthroscopy, Knee Surgery and Orthopaedic Sports Medicine (ISACOS) 1993–; Hon. mem. Georgian Asscn of Orthopaedics and Traumatology 1992; Order of Three Stars (Fourth Degree), Latvia 2007; Int. Arthroscopy Asscn Prize 1993. *Address:* Office of the President, Pils lauk. 3, Rīga 1050, Latvia (office). *Telephone:* 6737-7548 (office). *Fax:* 6709-2106 (office). *E-mail:* chancery@president.lv (office). *Website:* www.president.lv (office).

ZAVGAYEV, Doku Gapurovich, CandEcon; Russian/Chechen politician; *Director General, Ministry of Foreign Affairs;* b. 22 Dec. 1940. *Career:* mem. CPSU 1966–91; teacher at elementary school, mechanic, engineer of sovkhoz, man. Regional Union Selkhoztechnika, Dir sovkhoz Znamensky, Chair. Nadterechny Regional Exec. Cttee 1971–72; Chief Repub. Union of Sovkhozes 1972–75; Minister of Agric. of Checheno-Ingush SSR 1975–77; head of div., Second Sec. Checheno-Ingush Regional CP Cttee 1977–89; First Sec. Repub. CP Cttee 1989–91; Chair. Supreme Soviet of Checheno-Ingush Autonomous SSR 1990–91, mem. Cen. CPSU Cttee 1990–91; People's Deputy of RSFSR 1990–93; in Admin. of Pres. of Russia 1994–95; elected Pres. of Chechen Repub. 1995–96; Deputy, Council of Russian Fed. 1995–97; Amb. to Tanzania 1997–2004; Deputy Minister of Foreign Affairs 2004, Dir Gen. Ministry of Foreign Affairs 2004–; Order of Red Banner of Labour, Badge of Honour; awarded four medals. *Publication:* System of Agric. in Checheno-Ingush Republic. *Address:* Ministry of Foreign Affairs, Smolenskaya–Sennaya pl. 32/34, 119200 Moscow, Russia. *Telephone:* (095) 244-16-06 (office). *Fax:* (095) 230-21-30 (office). *E-mail:* ministry@mid.ru (office). *Website:* www.mid.ru (office).

ZAWAHIRI, Ayman az-, MS, DMed; Egyptian guerrilla leader and physician; b. 19 June 1951, grandson of Rabi'a Zawahiri. *Education:* Cairo Univ. *Career:* paediatrician; mem. The Muslim Brotherhood (arrested for membership 1966); Founder Egyptian Islamic Jihad; imprisoned on firearms charge following Egyptian Pres. Sadat's assassination 1981–84; joined mujahidin troops fighting Soviet occupation forces in Afghanistan 1984; co-f. Int. Front for Fighting Jews and Crusaders (with Osama bin Laden q.v.) 1998; co-f. al Qa'ida; accused of planning bombings of US embassies in E Africa 1998; personal physician and political adviser to Osama bin Laden; fmr Leader Vanguards of Conquest Movt.

ŽBOGAR, Samuel, BA; Slovenian diplomatist; *Ambassador to USA. Career:* Chargé d'affaires a.i. and First Sec., Embassy in Beijing, Sec. at Slovenian Rep. Office to Monitoring Mission of EC in Zagreb, Adviser to Dept for Neighbouring Countries in the Republican Cttee for Int. Cooperation, Ljubljana, Sec. to Slovenian Del. at Int. Conf. on Fmr Yugoslavia, various positions within Ministry of Foreign Affairs, including Counsellor, State Under-Sec., Dir Dept for Africa, Asia, Latin America and the Pacific, Counsellor to the Minister and Sec. in Office of Sec.-Gen., and Third Sec. in Dept for Neighbouring Countries, Minister Plenipotentiary and Deputy Perm. Rep. of Slovenian Mission to UN 1997–2001, Deputy to UN Security Council 1998–99, Head of Task Force for Slovenia's OSCE presidency in 2005 2001–04, Amb. to USA (also accred to Mexico) 2004–. *Address:* Embassy of Slovenia, 2410 California Street, NW, Washington, DC 20008, USA (office). *Telephone:* (202) 386-6601 (office). *Fax:* (202) 386-6633 (office). *E-mail:* vwa@gov.si (office). *Website:* washington.embassy.si (office).

ZEBARI, Hoshyar, BA, MA; Iraqi politician; *Minister of Foreign Affairs;* b. 1953, Aqra, Iraqi Kurdistan; four s. one d. *Education:* Univ. of Jordan, Univ. of Essex, UK. *Career:* responsible for Kurdish Student Soc. in Europe, Chair. Overseas Student Cttee, UK 1978–80; participated in armed resistance campaign against regime of Saddam Hussein 1980–88; elected to Cen. Cttee, Kurdistan Democratic Party (KDP) 1979, Chief Foreign Rep. 1988–91 (acted as a spokesman during the 1991 Gulf War), mem. Political Bureau and Chief Rep. of Kurdistan Front in Europe 1989, liaised with coalitions' Operation Provide Comfort and Mil. Coordinating Centre, Zakho, Iraqi Kurdistan 1991–95, Head of KDP Int. Relations Bureau 1992–2003; mem. Kurdistani Nat. Ass. 1992–; elected to Exec. Council Iraqi Nat. Congress (INC) 1992, Head of Int. Relations of the Iraqi Opposition 1992, mem. INC Leadership Council 1999, mem. Iraqi Opposition Coordination and Follow-Up Cttee 2002; Prin. Negotiator in Kurdish peace talks that produced Washington Peace Agreement between

KDP and Patriotic Union of Kurdistan 1998; Interim Minister of Foreign Affairs 2003–05, Minister of Foreign Affairs 2005–. *Address:* Ministry of Foreign Affairs, opposite State Organization for Roads and Bridges, Karradat Mariam, Baghdad, Iraq (office). *Telephone:* (1) 537-0091 (office). *E-mail:* contact@iraqmofa.net (office). *Website:* www.iraqmofa.net (office).

ZECCHINI, Salvatore, MBA; Italian economist, government official and university professor; *Economic Adviser to Minister of Industry and Trade;* b. 17 Nov. 1943, Palermo; m. Eliana de Leva 1971; one s. one d. *Education:* Columbia Univ. and Univ. of Pennsylvania, USA. *Career:* economist, Research Dept Banca d'Italia, Dir Research Dept 1972–81, Dir 1981–84; Adviser to Govt of Italy 1978–84; Exec. Dir IMF 1984–89; Special Counsellor, OECD 1989–90, Asst Sec.-Gen. 1990–96, then Deputy Sec.-Gen.; Dir Centre for Co-operation of Economies in Transition 1990–96; Prof. of Int. Econ. Policy, Univ. of Rome 1997–; Econ. Adviser to Minister of Finance 1997–2000, to Minister of Industry and Trade 2001–; Dir Public Investment Evaluation Centre 1997–98, Chair. Advisory Council of ICE (External Trade Agency) 2002–. *Publications:* The Transition to a Market Economy (co-ed.) 1991, Lessons from The Economic Transition (ed.) 1996; articles in professional journals and books on econs and int. finance. *Address:* Ministry of Industry and Trade, Via Molise 2, 00187 Rome, Italy (office). *Telephone:* (06) 420434448 (office). *Fax:* (06) 420434025 (office). *E-mail:* zecchini@flashnet.it (home).

ZEDILLO PONCE de LEÓN, Ernesto, MA, MPhil, PhD, DEcon; Mexican fmr head of state, economist and academic; *Director, Center for the Study of Globalization, Yale University;* b. 27 Dec. 1951, Mexico City; m. Nilda Patricia Velasco Núñez; five c. *Education:* Instituto Nacional Politécnico, Yale Univ., USA. *Career:* joined Partido Revolucionario Institucional (PRI) 1971, with Instituto de Estudios Políticos, Económicos y Sociales (Iepes) (affil. to PRI); econ. researcher, Dirección Gen. de Programación Económica y Social; economist, Deputy Man. Econ. Research, Gen. Dir Trust Fund for the Renegotiation of Pvt. Firms' External Debt and Deputy Dir, Banco de Mexico (BANXICO) 1978–87; Prof. of Macroeconomics and Int. Econs, Instituto Nacional Politécnico and Colegio de México 1979–87; Under-Sec. of the Budget 1987–88, Sec. Budget and Econ. Planning 1988–92, Sec. of Educ. 1992–93; campaign man. for the late Luis Donaldo Colosio (fmr presidential cand.) 1993–94; Pres. of Mexico 1994–2000; Chair. UN High Level Panel on Financing for Devt 2000–01; Co-Chair. UN Comm. on Pvt. Sector and Devt 2004; Jt Coordinator UN Millennium Project's Task Force on Trade; Co-Chair. Int. Task Force on Global Public Goods (sponsored by Govts of Sweden and France); mem. Advisory Panel to Dir-Gen. WTO 2001–02, Trilateral Comm., Int. Advisory Bd of Council on Foreign Relations and Bd Dirs Inst. for Int. Econs, High-Level Panel on Legal Empowerment of the Poor, Foundation Bd of the World Econ. Forum, Club de Madrid; UN Special Envoy for 2005 World Summit; Distinguished Visiting Fellow, Centre for Global Governance, LSE 2001; Distinguished Lecturer, Univ. of Miami 2001; Distinguished Collins Fellow, John F. Kennedy School of Govt, Harvard Univ. 2001; Prof. in the Field of Int. Econs and Politics and Dir Yale Center for the Study of Globalization, Yale Univ., USA 2002–; mem. Bd Dirs Procter and Gamble, ALCOA, Union Pacific Corpn, Inst. for Int. Economics; mem. int. advisory Bd Daimler-Chrysler, Coca Cola Co., MAGNA; Trustee Fundacion Carolina, Madrid; decorations from govts of 32 countries; Hon. LLD (Yale) 2001, (Harvard) 2003; Hon. DHumLitt (Miami) 2002; Wilbur Cross Medal 2001, Democracy and Peace Award, Inst. of the Americas, Univ. of California, San Diego 2001, Landon Distinguished Lecturer, Kansas State Univ. 2001, Franklin D. Roosevelt Freedom from Fear Award 2002, Tribuna Americana Award, Casa de America, Madrid, Spain 2003, Gold Insigne, Council of the Americas 2003, Berkeley Medal, Univ. of California, Berkeley 2004. *Address:* Yale Center for the Study of Globalization, Betts House, 393 Prospect Street, New Haven, CT 06511, USA (office). *Telephone:* (203) 432-1900 (office). *Fax:* (203) 432-1200 (office). *E-mail:* ernesto.zedillo@yale.edu (office). *Website:* www.ycsg.yale.edu (office).

ZEIBOTS, Rear Vice-Adm. Gaidis Andrejs; Latvian naval officer; *Advisor to Minister of Defence;* b. 26 June 1945, Valka Dist; m.; one d. *Education:* Naval Acad. of Radioelectronics, Leningrad (now St Petersburg), Russia, Coll. of Strategic Studies, George C. Marshall Centre, US Army War Coll., USA. *Career:* Chief of Radio Eng Service of destroyer, Tallinn Naval Base, Estonia 1969–70, Liepaja Naval Base 1970–72; Exec. Officer of destroyer, Liepaja 1975–76, Commdr 1976–78; Deputy Chief of Staff, Missile Carrier Div., Baltic Naval Base 1980–86; Deputy Commdr Naval Base 1986–88; Commdr Naval Div., Gdynia, Poland 1988–91; C-in-C Latvian Naval Forces 1991–99; Exec. Sec. NATO Integration, Ministry of Defence 1999–2002; Deputy Commdr and Operational Commdr Latvian Nat. Armed Forces 2002–03, Chief of Defence 2003–06; Advisor to Minister of Defence 2007–; Norwegian Order of Royal Kts, Order of King Gedimins

(Fourth Class); Medal of Order of Three Stars, two Ministry of Defence Awards, NAF Commdr Medal, Naval Commdr Medal.
Address: Ministry of Defence, K. Valdemāra iela 10/12, Rīga 1473, Latvia (office). *Telephone:* 67335017 (office). *E-mail:* gaidis.zeibots@mod.gov.lv (office); kanceleja@mod.lv (office). *Website:* www.mod.lv (office).

ZEIGERMAN, Dror, PhD; Israeli diplomatist and politician; b. 14 May 1948; m. Asi Sherf; two s. one d. *Education:* Hebrew Univ., Jerusalem, George Washington Univ., USA. *Career:* mil. service 1966–69; Chair. Students' Union, Hebrew Univ., Jerusalem 1969–70; Sec. Israeli Liberal Party, Jerusalem Br. 1970–73; Gen. Sec. Zionist Council in Israel; Head Students' Dept, Jewish Agency and World Zionist Org. 1977–81; Likud Party mem. Knesset (Parl.) 1981–84, mem. Cttees on Foreign Relations and Security, Immigration and Absorption, Educ.; Head, Students' Dept, Zionist Org. in Israel, Special Adviser on Student and Youth Matters to Head of Exec. Cttee and Zionist Org. 1987–88; Gen. Man. Israel School of Tourism; Consul-Gen. of Israel, Toronto, Canada 1992–95; Amb. to UK 1998–2000. *Address:* c/o Ministry of Foreign Affairs, Hakirya, Romema, Jerusalem 91950, Israel (office).

ZEINE, Ali Mahamane Lamine; Niger politician. *Career:* currently Minister of the Economy and Finance.
Address: Ministry of the Economy and Finance, BP 389, Niamey, Niger (office). *Telephone:* 72-23-74 (office). *Fax:* 73-59-34 (office).

ZELAYA ROSALES, José Manuel; Honduran politician; *President;* b. 20 Sept. 1952, Catacamas, Olancho; m. Xiomara Castro Sarmiento; four c. *Education:* Nat. Honduran Univ. *Career:* trained as civil engineer; ranch owner; mem. Liberal Party of Honduras; Deputy in Nat. Congress 1985–, Chair. Natural Resources and Petroleum Cttee 1985–89; Minister for Investment, in charge of Honduran Investment Fund 1994–2002; Sec. Cen. Exec. Council for Advertising and Org. 1999–2004; Founder and Leader, Movimiento Esperanza Liberal (faction within Liberal Party) 2005–; Pres. of Honduras 2005–; Chair. Bd of Dirs Asociación de Industriales de la Madera 1987–94; mem. Honduran Nat. Business Council (COEHP) 1987–94, Bd of Dirs Sogerin Bank.
Address: Office of the President, Palacio José Cecilio del Valle, Blvd Juan Pablo II, Tegucigalpa (office); Partido Liberal, Col. Miramonte, Tegucigalpa, Honduras (office). *Telephone:* 232-6282 (office); 232-0520 (home). *Fax:* 231-0097 (office); 232-0797 (office). *Website:* www.presidencia.gob.hn (office).

ZENAWI, Meles; Ethiopian politician and fmr guerrilla fighter; *Prime Minister;* b. 1956. *Career:* leader of Ethiopian People's Revolutionary Democratic Front (EPRDF) that overthrew regime of Mengistu Haile Mariam 1991; Acting Head of State of Ethiopia May–June, Pres. 1991–95; Prime Minister of Ethiopia 1995–.
Address: Office of the Prime Minister, PO Box 1013, Addis Ababa, Ethiopia. *Telephone:* (11) 552044. *Fax:* (11) 1552020.

ZENELI, Bashkim; Albanian diplomatist; *Ambassador to Greece; Career:* fmr Deputy Head, Parl. Foreign Relations Cttee; fmr Amb. to Germany, Amb. to Greece –2005; Medal of Gratitude (Albania) 2006.
Address: Ministry of Foreign Affairs, Bulevardi Gjergj Fishta 6, Tirana, Albania (office). *Telephone:* (4) 364090 (office). *Fax:* (4) 362084 (office). *E-mail:* info@mfa.gov.al (office). *Website:* www.mfa.gov.al (office).

ZENG, Qinghong; Chinese politician; b. July 1939, Ji, Jiangxi Prov.. *Education:* Beijing Inst. of Tech. *Career:* joined CCP 1960; technician, No. 743 Army Unit, Group Army, PLA Services and Arms 1963–65; technician, No. 6 Office, No. 2 Dept, Second Acad., Seventh Ministry of Machine-Building Industry 1965–69, No. 2 Dept 1970–73; sent to do manual labour, Chikan Base, Army (or Ground Force), PLA Services and Arms 1969–70, Xihu Production Base, Hunan Prov. 1969–70; technician, Production Div., Comm. of Science, Tech. and Industry for Nat. Defence, Beijing 1973–79; Sec. Gen. Office, State Devt and Reform Comm. 1979–81; Deputy Div. Dir Gen. Office, State Energy Comm. 1981–82; worked in Liaison Dept, Foreign Affairs Bureau, Ministry of Petroleum Industry 1982–83; Deputy Man. Liaison Dept, China Nat. Offshore Oil Corpn 1983–84; Deputy Dir Foreign Affairs Bureau, Ministry of Petroleum Industry 1983–84; Sec. CCP Party Cttee, South and Yellow Seas Petroleum Corpn 1983–84; Deputy Head, later Head, Org. Dept, CCP Shanghai Municipal Cttee 1984–86, Sec.-Gen. Standing Cttee 1984–86, Deputy Sec. CCP Shanghai Municipal Cttee 1986–89; Deputy Dir, Gen. Office, 13th and 14th CCP Cen. Cttees 1989–93, Dir, Gen. Office, 14th CCP Cen. Cttee 1993–97, Sec. Work Cttee, Offices Under Cen. Cttee 1993–97, mem. 15th CCP Cen. Cttee 1992–97, Dir, Gen. Office, 15th CCP Cen. Cttee 1997–99, Dir Work Cttee, Offices Under Cen. Cttee 1997–99, Head, Org. Dept 1999–2002, Alt. mem. Politburo 1997–2002, mem. Politburo Secr. 1997, mem. 16th CCP Cen. Cttee 2002–07, Standing Cttee Politburo 2002–07;

Chief Strategist to Pres. Jiang Zemin –2002; Vice-Pres. People's Repub. of China 2003–07 (retd).
Address: c/o Central Committee of Chinese Communist Party, Beijing, People's Republic of China (office).

ZEPOS, Yannis-Alexis; Greek diplomatist; *Ambassador to Egypt;* m. Daphne Zepos. *Education:* Univ. of Athens. *Career:* mem. Bar Asscn of Athens 1970–74; Attaché, Western European Political Affairs Directorate, Ministry of Foreign Affairs 1974–75, various positions 1981–82; Diplomatic Cabinet of Pres. of Repub. 1975–76; Sec., Embassy in Lisbon, Portugal 1976–77, Minister-Counsellor and Chargé d'Affaires 1991–92; mem. Del. to 32nd Gen. Ass. of UN, NY 1977–81; Gen. Consul in Cairo, Egypt 1982–87; Minister-Counsellor and Deputy Head of Mission, Embassy in Madrid, Spain 1987–90; Deputy Dir Balkan, Cen.-Eastern European and USSR Political Affairs Directorate 1990–91; Consul-Gen. in Chicago, USA 1992–95; Minister and Deputy Perm. Rep. to NATO, Brussels, Belgium 1995–97, Amb. and Perm. Rep. 2004–07; Amb. to India (non-resident to Nepal, Bangladesh, Sri Lanka and Maldives) 1997–2001; Dir Diplomatic Cabinet for Minister of Foreign Affairs 2001–04; Amb. to Egypt 2007–; Grand Commdr Order of the Phoenix (Greece), Grand Cross Order of Honour (Portugal), Grand Cordon Order of Merit (Egypt), Grand Commdr Order of Isabel II (Spain), Grand Commdr Order of Merit (Italy), Grand Commdr Order of Makarios III (Cyprus), Commdr Order of Christ (Portugal), Commdr Order of Merit (France), Commdr Order of Henri the Navigator (Portugal).
Address: Embassy of Greece, 18 Sharia Aicha at-Taimouria, Cairo 11451 (Garden City), Egypt (office). *Telephone:* (2) 7950443 (office). *Fax:* (2) 7963903 (office). *E-mail:* grembcai@internetgypt.com (office).

ZERI, Pavli; Albanian diplomatist; b. May 1945, Tirana; m.; two c. *Education:* Univ. of Tirana. *Career:* worked at Inst. of Pedagogical Studies 1973–75, High School Pres. 1975–79, then served in Directotate of High Educ. and Directorate of Int. Relations, Ministry of Educ.; Lecturer, Univ. of Tirana; Foreign State Sec., Govt of Nat. Reconciliation 1997; Diplomatic Adviser to Prime Minister 1997–98; mem. Parl. Comm. for Foreign Policy; Deputy Minister of Defence 2001–04; Amb. to Italy (also accred to Malta) 2004.
Address: c/o Ministry of Foreign Affairs, Bulevardi Gjergj Fishta 6, Tirana, Albania. *Telephone:* (4) 364090. *Fax:* (4) 362084. *E-mail:* info@mfa.gov.al. *Website:* www.mfa.gov.al.

ZERIHOUN, Tayé-Brook, MPhil; Ethiopian UN official and diplomatist; *Head Peace-keeping Force in Cyprus, United Nations;* m.; one s. three d. *Education:* Columbia University, New York. *Career:* joined UN 1981, worked on special assignments on decolonization, trusteeship, conflict prevention and resolution, peacemaking and peace-building, New York, Deputy Dir, then Dir Africa I Div., Dept of Political Affairs, with responsibility for countries of Horn of Africa, Great Lakes and Southern Africa regions and regional orgs including Inter-Governmental Authority on Devt and Southern African Devt Community 1995–2003, Chair. Inter-departmental Task Force for Sudan 2003–04, Sec.-Gen.'s Prin. Deputy Special Rep. for Sudan with rank of Asst Sec.-Gen. 2004–; Special Rep. of Sec.-Gen. and Head UN Peacekeeping Force in Cyprus (UNFICYP) 2008–.
Address: United Nations Peace Keeping Force in Cyprus, P.O. Box 21642, 1590 Nicosia, Cyprus (office); Department of Peace-keeping Operations, Room S-3727-B, United Nations, New York, NY 10017, USA (office). *Telephone:* 22614527 (Nicosia) (office); (212) 963-8077 (New York) (office). *Fax:* (212) 963-9222 (office). *E-mail:* unficyp-public-information-office@un .org (office). *Website:* www.unficyp.org (office).

ZERMEÑO INFANTE, Jorge; Mexican politician and diplomatist; *Ambassador to Spain;* b. 23 Jan. 1949, Mexico City. *Education:* Univ. Iberoamericana. *Career:* mem. Partido Acción Nacional 1968–; mem. Chamber of Deputies 1991–94, Pres. 2006–07; Municipal Pres. Torreón 1997–99; Senator for Coahuila 2000–05; Amb. to Spain 2007–.
Address: Embassy of Mexico, Carrera de San Jerónimo 46, 28014 Madrid, Spain (office). *Telephone:* (91) 3692814. *Fax:* (91) 4202292 (office). *E-mail:* embamex@embamex.es (office). *Website:* www.embamex.es (office).

ZERVAN, Juraj; Slovak lawyer, human rights activist and diplomatist; *Ambassador to UK;* m. Mária Zervanová. *Career:* family emigrated to Canada to escape Communism when he was a child; fmr Dir Dept for Nat. Minorities, Ministry of Foreign Affairs; First Sec., Embassy in London 2002–04; Shadow Foreign Minister (Direction-Social Democracy party) 2004–07; Amb. to UK 2007–.
Address: Embassy of Slovakia, 25 Kensington Palace Gardens, London, W8 4QY, England (office). *Telephone:* (20) 7313-6470 (office). *Fax:* (20) 7313-6481 (office). *E-mail:* mail@slovakembassy.co.uk (office). *Website:* www.slovakembassy.co.uk (office).

ZHA, Peixin; Chinese diplomatist; b. April 1946, Jiangsu Prov.; m. Zhang Xiaokang; one s. *Education:* univ. grad. *Career:* staff mem., Perm. Mission of People's Repub. of China to UN 1972–73, attaché, Liaison Office to USA 1973–78; staff mem. N American and Oceania Affairs Dept, Ministry of Foreign Affairs, later Deputy Div. Chief, later Deputy Dept Chief 1978–1990; Counsellor, then Minister Counsellor, Embassy in Ottawa 1990–93; Amb. to Canada 1996–98; Deputy Dir, then Dir-Gen. Foreign Affairs Office of the State Council 1993–96, Vice-Minister 1998–2002; Amb. to UK (also accred to Ireland) 2002–07.
Address: Ministry of Foreign Affairs, 225 Chaoyangmen Nan Dajie, Chaoyang Qu, Beijing 100701, People's Republic of China (office). *Telephone:* (10) 65961114 (office). *Fax:* (10) 65962146 (office). *E-mail:* webmaster@mfa.gov.cn (office). *Website:* www.fmprc.gov.cn (office).

ZHAMISHEV, Bolat Bidahmetovich, PhD; Kazakhstani banker and politician; *Minister of Finance; Education:* Kazakh Inst. of Agric. *Career:* First Vice-Minister of Finance 1999–2001, 2002–03; Vice-Minister of Internal Affairs 2001–02; Deputy Chair. Nat. Bank of Kazakhstan 2003–04; Chair. Agency for Regulation and Oversight of Financial Orgs 2004–06; Deputy Chair. Exec. Bd Russian-Kazakh Eurasian Devt Bank 2006–07; Minister of Finance 2007–.
Address: Ministry of Finance, pl. Respubliki 60, 010000 Astana, Kazakhstan (office). *Telephone:* (7172) 28-00-65 (office). *Fax:* (7172) 32-40-89 (office). *E-mail:* info@minfin.kz (office). *Website:* www.minfin.kz (office).

ZHANG, Deguang; Chinese diplomatist; *Secretary-General, Shanghai Co-operation Organization;* b. 10 Feb. 1941, Jining. *Education:* Beijing Inst. of Foreign Languages. *Career:* joined Ministry of Foreign Affairs 1965, worked in translation branch 1965–73, held posts of Second Sec., First Sec. and Deputy Dir of Chancery, Sino-Russian Negotiations, Dept of USSR and European affairs 1977–87, Head Dept of Eastern Europe and Cen. Asia 1993–95, Deputy Minister of Foreign Affairs 1995–2001; overseas posts include Attaché Embassy in USSR 1973–77, Counsellor Embassy in USA 1987–92, Amb. to Kazakhstan 1992–93; Amb. Extraordinary and Plenipotentiary 2001–03; Sec.-Gen. Shanghai Co-operation Org. 2004–; Academician, Russian Acad. of Social Sciences 2003–; Friendship Order (Russia) 1999, First Grade Friendship Order (Kazakhstan), Commemorative Diploma for special contribution to Sino-Russian friendship 2003 (Russia), 300th Anniversary of St Petersburg Commemorative Medal (Russia) 2004; Dr hc Inst. of Far Eastern Studies 2003.
Address: Secretariat of the Shanghai Co-operation Organization, 41 Liangmaqiao Road, Choyang District, Beijing 100600, People's Republic of China (office). *Telephone:* (10) 65329806 (office). *Fax:* (10) 65329808 (office). *E-mail:* sco@sectsco.org (office). *Website:* www.sectsco.org/html/00034.html (office).

ZHANG, Dejiang; Chinese politician; *Vice Premier, State Council;* b. Nov. 1946, Tai'an Co., Liaoning Prov. *Education:* Yanbian Univ., Kim Il Sung Comprehensive Univ., Pyongyang, N Korea. *Career:* sent to countryside, Taiping Brigade, Luozigou Commune, Wangqing Co., Jilin Prov. 1968–70; Sec. Propaganda Dept, CCP Communist Youth League of China Wangqing Co. Cttee 1970–72; mem. CCP 1971–; mem. Standing Cttee, CCP Party Cttee, Yanbian Univ. 1975–78, 1980–83, Vice-Chair CCP Revolutionary Cttee 1975–78, Vice-Pres. Yanbian Univ. 1980–83; Deputy Sec. CCP Yanji City Cttee 1983–85; Deputy Sec. CCP Yanbian Korean Autonomous Prefectural Cttee 1985–86, Sec. 1990–95; Vice-Minister of Civil Affairs 1986–90; Deputy Sec. CCP Jilin Prov. Cttee 1990–95, Sec. 1995–98; Chair. Jilin Prov. People's Congress 1998; Alt. mem. 14th CCP Cen. Cttee 1992–97, mem. 15th CCP Cen. Cttee 1997–2002, 16th CCP Cen. Cttee 2002–07, Political Bureau 2002–07; Sec., CCP Zhejiang Prov. Cttee 1998–2002, Guandong Prov. 2002–07; mem. 17th CCP Cen. Cttee 2007–, Political Bureau 2007–; Vice Premier State Council 2008–.
Address: Office of the Vice-Premier, Great Hall of the People, West Edge, Tiananmen Square, Beijing, People's Republic of China (office). *Website:* english.gov.cn (office).

ZHANG, Guoying; Chinese party official; *Chairman of Standing Committee, Guangdong Provincial People's Congress;* b. 1937, Dongguan Co., Guangdong Prov. *Career:* joined CCP 1954; Section Chief, Posts and Telecommunications Admin, Hainan Prov.; Deputy Sec. CCP Baoting Co. Cttee, Hainan Prov.; Deputy Sec., later Sec. CCP Renhua Co. Cttee, Guangdong Prov.; Deputy Sec. CCP Huiyang Prefectural Cttee, Guangdong Prov.; Vice-Chair. All-China Women's Fed. Exec. Cttee 1988–, later Sec. Secr.; Deputy Sec. CCP 7th Guangdong Prov. Cttee 1990–98; Political Commissar Unit in Tibet 1992–; Vice-Chair. Standing Cttee of Prov. People's Congress, Guangdong Prov. 1998–2001, Chair. 2001–; mem. 12th CCP Cen. Cttee 1982–87, 13th CCP Cen. Cttee 1987–92, 14th CCP Cen. Cttee 1992–97; Del., 15th CCP Nat. Congress 1997–2002; Deputy, 9th NPC 1998–2003.

Address: All-China Women's Federation, Beijing, People's Republic of China (office).

ZHANG, Junsai, MA; Chinese diplomatist; *Ambassador to Australia;* b. Oct. 1953, Shanghai; m.; one d. *Education:* Beijing Foreign Studies Univ., Tufts Univ., USA. *Career:* Attaché and Third Sec., N American and Oceanian Affairs Dept, Ministry of Foreign Affairs 1983–88, Second Sec. 1990–91, First Sec. and Dir 1995–97, Deputy Dir-Gen. 2003–07; Attaché, Embassy in New Zealand 1979–83; Consul in Sydney 1991–95, Counsellor, Embassy in Australia 1997–2000, Amb. 2007–; Amb. to Fiji 2000–03.
Address: Embassy of The People's Republic of China, 15 Coronation Drive, Yarralumla, ACT 2600, Australia (office). *Telephone:* (2) 6273-4780 (office). *Fax:* (2) 6273-4878 (office). *E-mail:* chinaemb_au@mfa.gov.cn (office). *Website:* au.china-embassy.org/eng (office).

ZHANG, Qiyue, BA; Chinese diplomatist; *Ambassador to Belgium;* b. Oct. 1959, Beijing; m.; one s. *Education:* Univ. of Foreign Studies, Beijing, UN Program for Int. Orgs and Interpretation. *Career:* interpreter, UN Secr., New York and Geneva 1983–87, Third Sec., then Second Sec., then Deputy Dir, then First Sec., Dept of Int. Orgs and Confs, Ministry of Foreign Affairs 1987–95, First Sec. and Political Counsellor, Perm. Mission to UN 1995–98, Spokesperson and Deputy Dir-Gen. Information Dept, Ministry of Foreign Affairs 1998–2005, Amb. to Belgium 2005–.
Address: Embassy of People's Republic of China, 463 avenue de Tervueren, 1160 Brussels, Belgium (office). *Telephone:* (2) 771-14-95 (office). *Fax:* (2) 779-28-95 (office). *E-mail:* chinaemb_be@mfa.gov.cn (office). *Website:* www.chinaembassy-org.be (office).

ZHANG, Yan; Chinese diplomatist and government official; *Ambassador to India;* b. 3 Nov. 1950; m. Chen Wangxia; one d. *Career:* served with mission to Liberia 1978–83; with Ministry of Foreign Affairs 1983–96, Counsellor, Dept of Int. Orgs and Confs, Ministry of Foreign Affairs March–Aug. 1998; Dir-Gen. Foreign Affairs Office, Yunnan 1996–98; Sr Official, Asia Pacific Econ. Co-operation (APEC) 1998–99, Deputy Exec. Dir 2000, Exec. Dir 2001; Amb. to UN 2001–05; Dir-Gen. Dept of Arms Control and Disarmament, Ministry of Foreign Affairs 2005–07; Amb. to India 2007–.
Address: Embassy of the People's Republic of China, Chanakyapuri, New Delhi 110 021, India (office). *Telephone:* (11) 26112345 (home). *Fax:* (11) 26885486 (office). *E-mail:* chinaemb_in@mfa.gov.cn (office). *Website:* www.chinaembassy.org.in (office).

ZHAO, Jinjun; Chinese diplomatist; b. 24 Dec. 1945, Shandong Prov.; m. Marie; one s. *Education:* Beijing Foreign Studies Univ. *Career:* staff mem., Chinese Embassy, Brussels, Belgium 1973–79; staff mem., W European Affairs Dept, Ministry Foreign Affairs 1979–83; Third Sec., later Second Sec., Chinese Embassy, Paris, France 1983–87, Counsellor and Minister-Counsellor 1993–97, Consul Gen. 1999–2002; Deputy Dir, Dir, First Sec. and Counselor, Ministry Foreign Affairs, W European Affairs Dept 1987–93; Deputy Dir-Gen., Ministry Foreign Affairs, W European Affairs Dept 1997–99; Asst Minister (in charge of W European and Hong Kong, Macao and Taiwan Affairs), Ministry Foreign Affairs 2002–03; Amb. to France 2003–08.
Address: c/o Ministry of Foreign Affairs, 225 Chaoyangmen Nan Dajie, Chaoyang Qu, Beijing 100701 People's Republic of China (office). *Website:* www.fmprc.gov.cn (office).

ZHAO, Leji; Chinese politician; *Secretary, Shaanxi Provincial People's Congress;* b. March 1957, Xi'ning, Qinghai Prov. *Education:* Peking Univ., Beijing. *Career:* joined CCP 1975; teacher, later Deputy Dir Dean's Office, Qinghai Prov. Commerce School 1980–83; Deputy Dir Political Div., Commerce Dept, Qinghai Prov. 1983–84, Deputy Dir, later Dir Commerce Dept 1986–93 (also Sec. CCP Party Cttee), Dir Financial Dept 1993–94; Sec. CCP Qinghai Prov. Cttee 1984–86, 2003–, Deputy Sec. 2000–03; Asst Gov. of Qinghai Prov. 1993–94, Vice-Gov. 1994–99, Acting Gov. 1999–2000, Gov. 2000–03; Sec. CCP Xining City Cttee, Qinghai Prov. 1997–98; Chair. Standing Cttee Qinghai Prov. People's Congress 2004–07; Sec. CCP Shaanxi Prov. Cttee 2007–; mem. 16th CCP Cen. Cttee 2000–.
Address: Shaanxi Provincial People's Congress, Xi'ning, Shaanxi Province, People's Republic of China (office). *Website:* www.shaanxi.gov.cn (office).

ZHAO, Qizheng; Chinese politician; *Vice-Chairman, Foreign Affairs Committee, Chinese People's Political Consultative Conference (CPPCC);* b. Jan. 1940, Beijing; s. of Zhao Jingyuan and Wan Shuxian; m. Zheng Shiting; one d. *Education:* China Univ. of Science and Tech. *Career:* joined CCP 1979; technician, later Sr Engineer 1963–74; Deputy Dir Shanghai Broadcasting Materials Factory 1982–84; Deputy Sec. Industrial Work Cttee, CCP Shanghai Municipal Cttee 1984, Deputy Head, later Head, Org. Dept 1984–86, mem. Standing Cttee 1986–91, Dir Dist Admin. Cttee 1993; Sec. Work Cttee CCP Pudong Dist Cttee, Shanghai 1992; Vice-Mayor of Shanghai 1993–98; Deputy Dir then Dir CCP Cen. Cttee Int. Commu-

nications Office 1998–; Deputy Dir, then Dir Information Office of State Council 1998–2005; mem. 16th CCP Cen. Cttee 2002–07; Vice-Chair. Foreign Affairs Cttee, CCP Cen. Cttee 2005–; Dean, School of Journalism and Communication, Renmin Univ. of China. *Publications:* America and American People in Chinese People's Eyes, Introducing China to the Rest of the World.
Address: c/o State Council Information Office, 225 Chaoyangmen Neidajie, Beijing 100010, People's Republic of China. *Telephone:* (10) 6559-2339 (office). *Fax:* (10) 6559-2364 (office). *E-mail:* xuying@scio.gov.cn (office).

ZHENG, Xianglin; Chinese diplomatist; *Ambassador to Nepal;* b. 1954 June , Liaoning. *Career:* staff mem., Embassy in Tokyo 1997; fmr Deputy Dir-Gen. Dept Foreign Affairs Man., Ministry of Foreign Affairs; Amb. to Nepal 2007–.
Address: Embassy of China, Baluwatar, POB 4234, Kathmandu, Nepal (office). *Telephone:* (1) 4419053 (office). *Fax:* (1) 4414045 (office). *E-mail:* chinaemb_np@mfa.gov.cn (office). *Website:* www.fmprc.gov.cn/ce/cenp (office).

ZHONG, Jianhua; Chinese diplomatist; *Ambassador to South Africa;* b. Dec. 1950, Jiangsu Prov.; m.; one s. one d. *Education:* Tufts Univ., USA. *Career:* Diplomatic Courier, Ministry of Foreign Affairs 1977–79, Attaché, Dept of Consular Affairs 1983–84, Third Sec. 1985–87; First Sec., Office of the Chinese Sr Rep., Sino-British Jt Liaison Group 1991–93, Div. Chief Dept of Consular Affairs 1993–94, Deputy Dir-Gen. 1994–99, Dir-Gen. 1999–2001; overseas postings include staff mem., later Attaché, Embassy in London 1979–83, Third, later Second Sec. 1987–91; Consul-Gen. in Los Angeles 2001–07; Amb. to South Africa 2007–.
Address: Embassy of The People's Republic of China, 965 Church Street, Arcadia, Pretoria 0083, South Africa (office). *Telephone:* (12) 3424194 (office). *Fax:* (12) 3424154 (office). *E-mail:* reception@chinese-embassy.org .za (office). *Website:* www.chinese-embassy.org.za (office).

ZHOU, Wenzhong; Chinese diplomatist; *Ambassador to USA;* m.; one d. *Education:* Univ. of Bath and London School of Econs, UK. *Career:* Attaché, then Third Sec., Washington, DC 1978–83, Second Sec., Deputy Div. Dir, then Div. Dir Dept of Translation and Interpretation, Ministry of Foreign Affairs 1983–87, Deputy Consul Gen., San Francisco 1987–90, Amb. to Barbados and Antigua and Barbuda 1990–93, Deputy Dir-Gen. N American and Oceanic Affairs Dept, Ministry of Foreign Affairs 1993–94, Consul Gen., Los Angeles 1994–95, Deputy Chief of Mission, Embassy in Washington, DC 1995–98, Amb. to Australia 1998–2001; Asst Minister of Foreign Affairs 2001–03, Vice-Minister of Foreign Affairs 2003–05; Amb. to USA 2005–.
Address: Embassy of the People's Republic of China, 2300 Connecticut Avenue, NW, Washington, DC 2008, USA (office). *Telephone:* (202) 558-0032 (office). *Fax:* (202) 232-7855 (office). *E-mail:* webmaster@china -embassy.org (office). *Website:* www.china-embassy.org (office).

ZHU, Yinghuang, MA; Chinese journalist; *Professor of Journalism and Communications, Tsinghua University;* b. 28 Dec. 1943, Shanghai; m. Yao Xiang 1972; one d. *Education:* Stanford Univ., USA. *Career:* fmr Ed.-in-Chief China Daily, now Ed.-in-Chief Emer.; Prof. of Journalism and Communications, Tsinghua Univ.; Prof. of Communication, Univ. of China; mem. CPPCC; Outstanding Journalist of China 1984.
Address: China Daily, 15 Huixin Dongjie, Chao Yang Qu, Beijing 100029, People's Republic of China (office). *Telephone:* (10) 64995027 (office); (10) 64280990 (home). *Fax:* (10) 64918377 (office). *E-mail:* yhzhu@chinadaily .com.cn (office). *Website:* www.chinadaily.com.cn (office).

ZIADEH, Khaled; Lebanese diplomatist. *Career:* Amb. to Egypt 2006–.
Address: Embassy of Lebanon, 22 Sharia Mansour Muhammad, Cairo, Egypt (office). *Telephone:* (2) 7382823 (office). *Fax:* (2) 7382818 (office).

ZIEGLER, Jean, DenD, DenScPol; Swiss academic, writer and politician; *Special Rapporteur for the Right to Food, United Nations;* b. 19 April 1934, Berne; m.; one s. *Education:* Univs of Geneva, Berne, Paris-Sorbonne and Columbia Univ. New York. *Career:* with Swiss American Corpn New York 1959; Jr lawyer in training with Theodor Haffner, New York; Asst to Sec.-Gen. of Int. Comm. of Jurists; UN expert, Léopoldville and Elisabethville, Congo 1961–62; Research Assoc., Faculté de Droit, Inst. Africain de Geneva 1963; Prof., Inst. d'Etudes Politiques, Univ. of Grenoble 1967; Faculty of Law and Social and Econ. Sciences, Univ. of Berne 1969; Prof., Faculty of Econ. and Social Sciences, Univ. of Geneva and Univ. Inst. of Devt Studies 1975; Prof., Univ. of Paris I—Sorbonne 1983; numerous research tours in Africa, Latin America and Asia since 1963; City Councillor, Geneva 1967–83; mem. Swiss Nat. Council 1967–83, 1987–99; mem. Fed. Parl. for Geneva; mem. Cen. Cttee Swiss Socialist Party; mem. Exec. Council, Socialist Int.; UN Special Rapporteur for the Right to Food; Chevalier, Ordre des Arts et des Lettres; Dr hc (Univ.

Mons-Hainault); Adlai Stevenson Peace Award 1964, Bruno Kreisky Peace Prize 2000, President's Gold Medal, Italy. *Publications include:* La contre-révolution en Afrique 1963, Vive le pouvoir! ou les délices de la raison d'Etat 1985, Sankara. Un nouveau pouvoir africain (with J. P. Rapp) 1986, Dialogue Est-Ouest (with Y. Popov) 1987, La Suisse lave plus blanc 1990, La victoire des vaincus, oppression et résistance culturelle 1991, Le bonheur d'être Suisse 1993, Il s'agit de ne pas se rendre (with Régis Debray) 1994, L'or du Maniéma (novel) 1996, La Suisse, l'or et les morts 1997, Les seigneurs du crime, les nouvelles mafia contre la démocratie 1999, La faim dans le monde racontée à mon fils 2001, Les Nouveaux Maîtres du Monde 2003, L'Empire de la honte 2005; numerous book chapters, articles in reviews, journals, newspapers etc.
Address: University of Geneva, 1211 Geneva 4, Switzerland (office). *Telephone:* (22) 9065964 (office); (22) 9065956 (office). *Fax:* (22) 9065983 (office). *E-mail:* jeziegler@vtxnet.ch (home). *Website:* www.unhchr.ch (office); www.righttofood.org (office).

ZIMBA, Lyonpo Yeshey, MA (Econs); Bhutanese politician; *Minister of Works and Human Settlements;* b. 10 Oct. 1952, Omladama, Punakha Dist; m. Thuji Zangmo; one s. three d. *Education:* Univ. of Wisconsin. *Career:* joined civil service in the Royal Secr. 1974, planning officer, Ministry of Planning 1977, Jt Sec. 1991; apptd Chair. Royal Monetary Authority (Cen. Bank) 1986; Chair. Bank of Bhutan; Minister of Finance 1998–2003; Prime Minister and Chair. Council of Ministers 2000–01, 2004–05; Minister of Trade and Industry 2003–04, 2005–07 (resgnd), of Works and Human Settlements 2008–; Silver Medal for Scholastic Achievement, Gold Medal for Best All-Round Coll. Student, Red Scarf 1991, Druk Thuksey and Coronation Medals 1999.
Address: Ministry of Works and Human Settlements, POB 791, Thimphu, Bhutan. *Telephone:* (2) 327998 (office). *Fax:* (2) 323122 (office). *E-mail:* mowhs@mowhs.gov.bt (office). *Website:* www.mowhs.gov.bt (office).

ZIMMERMANN, Klaus F., Dr rer. pol, Dr rer. pol habil.; German professor of economics; *President, DIW Berlin, German Institute for Economic Research;* b. 2 Dec. 1952; m. Dr Astrid Zimmermann-Trapp; two c. *Education:* Univ. of Mannheim. *Career:* CORE Research Fellow, Université Catholique de Louvain, Belgium 1986; Research Fellow, Social Science Research Centre (WZB), Berlin 1986; Visiting Assoc. Prof., Univ. of Pennsylvania, Philadelphia, USA, 1987; Heisenberg Fellow, German Research Foundation (DFG) 1988–89; Full Prof. of Econ. Theory, Univ. of Munich and Dir SELAPO Centre for Human Resources, Munich 1989–98, Dean, Faculty of Econs, Univ. of Munich 1993–95; Research Fellow, Centre for Econ. Policy Research, London, UK 1990–, Programme Dir for Human Resources 1991–98, Labour Econs 1998–2001; Full Prof. of Econs, Bonn Univ. and Dir Inst. for the Study of Labour (IZA Bonn) 1998–; Pres. German Inst. for Econ. Research (DIW Berlin) 2000–; Assoc. Research Fellow, Centre for European Policy Studies, Brussels, Belgium 2001–; Research Assoc., Center for Comparative Immigration Studies, Univ. of Calif., San Diego 2001–; Visiting Prof., Univs of Dortmund and Munich 1989, Humboldt Univ., Berlin 1991, Kyoto Univ., Japan 1995, Dartmouth Coll., USA 1997, Univ. of Munich 1998; Founder and Sec. European Soc. for Population Econs 1986–1992, Pres. 1994; Man. Ed. Journal of Population Economics 1988–95, Ed.-in-Chief 1996–; Man. Ed. Econ. Policy 1995–98; Assoc. Ed. Recherches Economiques de Louvain 1991–, Journal of Applied Econometrics 1992–, Labour Economics 1992–2000, European Economic Review 1993–98, International Journal of Manpower 1999–, Economic Bulletin 2000–, DIW-Wochenbericht 2000–, DIW-Vierteljahrsfahrte 2002–; Advisor to Pres. of EU 2001–03, 2005–; mem. Council of the Verein für Socialpolitik (German Econ. Asscn) 2003–06; Fellow, European Econ. Asscn 2004–; mem. German Econ. Research Insts (ARGE) 2005–; Hon. Prof. of Econs, Free Univ. of Berlin 2001–; Picard Lecturer, Dartmouth Coll. 1994, Distinguished John G. Diefenbaker Award, Canada Council for the Arts 1998. *Publications:* author or ed. of 33 books including Familienökonomie. Theoretische und empirische Untersuchungen zur Frauenerwerbstätigkeit und Geburtenentwicklung (Economics of the Family. Theoretical and Empirical Investigations on Female Labour Supply and Fertility) 1985, Demographische Probleme der Haushaltsökonomie (Demographic Problems of Household Economics) (ed.) 1986, Arbeitsbuch Makroökonomie (Macroeconomics) (with Thomas Bauer) 1997, Employment Policy in Transition: The Lessons of German Integration for the Labour Market (ed. with R. T. Riphahn and D. J. Snower) 2001, Perspektiven der Arbeitsmarktpolitik. Internationaler Vergleich und Empfehlungen für Deutschland (Perspectives of Labour Market Policies. International Comparisons and Recommendations for Germany) (with C. M. Schmidt, M. Fertig and J. Kluve) 2001, Neue Entwicklungen in der Wirtschaftswissenschaft (New Developments in Economics) (ed.) 2001, Arbeitskräftebedarf bei hoher Arbeitslosigkeit. Ein ökonomisches Zuwanderungskonzept für Deutschland (Labour Demand in Face of High Unemployment. An Economic Immigration Concept for Germany) (with T. Bauer, H. Bonin, R. Fahr and H. Hinte) 2002, Frontiers in Economics (ed.) 2002, The

Economics of Migration Vol. I-IV (ed. with T. Bauer) 2002, Family, Household and Work (ed. with M. Vogler) 2003, Arbeit in einer alternden Gesellschaft: Problembereiche und Entwicklungstendenzen der Erwerbssituation Älterer (Jobs in an Aging Society: Problems and Trends in the Labour Market Situation of the Elderly) (ed. with M. Herfurth and M. Kohli) 2003, Reformen jetzt! So geht es mit Deutschland wieder aufwärts (Rapid Implementation of Reforms! By this way the situation is getting better for Germany) (ed.) 2003, How Labour Markets Fare (ed. with A. Constant) 2004, Zuwanderung und Arbeitsmarkt: Deutschland und Dänemark im Vergleich (Immigration and the Labour Market: Germany and Denmark in Comparison) (with H. Hinte) 2004, Migrants, Work and the Welfare State (ed. with T. Tranes) 2004, European Migration: What Do We Know? (ed.) 2005, Deutschland – was nun? Reformen für Wirtschaft und Gesellschaft (Germany – What Now?) (ed.) 2006, Immigration Policy and the Labour Market: The German Experience and Lessons for Europe (ed with H. Bonin, R. Fahr and H. Hinte.) 2007; over 180 papers in refereed journals and collected vols on labour econs, population econs, migration, industrial org., econometrics.
Address: DIW Berlin, Mohrenstrasse 58, Berlin 10117 (office); IZA, Schaumburg-Lippe-Str. 5–9, 53113 Bonn, Germany (office). *Telephone:* (30) 89789212 (DIW) (office); (228) 3894200 (IZA) (office). *Fax:* (30) 89789100 (DIW) (office); (228) 3894210 (office). *E-mail:* kzimmermann@ diw.de (office); zimmermann@iza.org (office). *Website:* www.diw.de (office); www.iza.org (office).

ZINNI, Gen. Anthony, BA, MA; American diplomatist, academic and fmr military commander; *Distinguished Advisor, Center for Strategic and International Studies;* b. 1947, Philadelphia. *Education:* Vilanova Univ. *Career:* joined marines 1961, infantry officer 1965, rising to rank of Gen.; active service in Viet Nam (injured 1970), Philippines, Mediterranean, Caribbean, Korea, Turkey, Iraq, Soviet Union, Kenya; Head Unified Task Force Somalia in Operation Restored Hope 1992–93, supervised withdrawal of US forces 1995, also Asst to Special Envoy to Somalia; Deputy Commanding Gen. US Marine Corps. Combat Devt Command, Quantico, Va 1992–94, Commanding Gen. 1st Marine Expeditionary Force 1994–96; Commdr US Cen. Command 1997–2000, in charge of mil. forces in 25 countries in Middle East, Africa and fmr USSR; Head of Persian Gulf forces 1997–2000, Commdr in charge of Operation Desert Fox, Iraq 1998; retd from mil. Aug. 2000; fmr academic positions include Stanley Chair in Ethics, Va Mil. Inst., Nimitz Chair, Univ. of Calif., Berkeley, Hofheimer Chair, Jt Forces Staff Coll., Weissberg Chair in Int. Studies, Beloit Coll., Harriman Prof. of Govt, Coll. of William and Mary; mem. Bd Reves Center for Int. Studies, Coll. of William and Mary, Center for Responsible Leadership and Governance, Villanova Univ.; has worked with Inst. on Global Conflict and Cooperation, Univ. of Calif., US Inst. of Peace and Henri Dunant Centre for Humanitarian Dialogue, Geneva; Pres. Center for Middle East Devt, UCLA; Distinguished Advisor, Center for Strategic and Int. Studies, Washington 2000–; US Envoy to Middle East 2001–03; has participated in diplomatic missions to Somalia, Pakistan, Ethiopia and Eritrea; mem. mem. Council on Foreign Relations; Bd of Dirs several US cos; Defense Distinguished Service Medal, Defense Superior Service Medal (with two oak leaf clusters), Bronze Star Medal with Combat "V", Purple Heart; non-military awards include Papal Gold Cross of Honor, Union League's Abraham Lincoln Award, Italic Studies Institute's Global Peace Award, Distinguished Sea Service Award from Naval Order of US, Eisenhower Distinguished Service Award from Veterans of Foreign Wars, Chapman Award from Marine Corps Univ Foundation, Penn Club Award, St. Thomas of Villanova Alumni Medal. *Publications:* Battle Ready (with Tom Clancy and Tony Koltz) 2004, The Battle for Peace (with Tony Koltz) 2006.
Address: Center for Strategic and International Studies, 1800 K Street, NW, Suite 400, Washington, DC 20006, USA (office). *Telephone:* (202) 887-0200 (office). *Fax:* (202) 775-3199 (office). *Website:* www.csis.org (office); www.generalzinni.com.

ZISWILER, Urs Johann; Swiss diplomatist; *Ambassador to USA;* b. 1949, Muri, Canton of Argovi; m. Ronit Ziswiler; two c. *Education:* Univs of Geneva and Zurich, Fed. Inst. of Tech., Zurich. *Career:* early career as jr expert for World Bank in Madagascar; later served as del. of ICRC in Beirut, Gaza, Tel-Aviv and Kampala; joined Foreign Service in 1979, Deputy Chief of Mission, Embassies in Kinshasa, Lagos and Oslo 1980–85, Tel-Aviv 1988–90, Spokesman and Head of Information Dept, European Integration Office 1990–92, Chargé d'affaires a.i. for Yugoslavia and Bosnia and Herzegovina 1993, Deputy Chief of Mission, Embassy in Buenos Aires 1994–95, Head of Political Div. for Human Rights and Humanitarian Policy and Coordinator for Int. Refugee Policy 1995–99, Amb. to Canada and the Bahamas 1999–2004, Head of Directorate of Political Affairs, Fed. Dept of Foreign Affairs and Sr Diplomatic Advisor to Minister of Foreign Affairs 2004–06, Amb. to USA 2006–.

Address: Embassy of Switzerland, 2900 Cathedral Avenue, NW, Washington, DC 20008, USA (office). *Telephone:* (202) 745-7900 (office). *Fax:* (202) 387-2564 (office). *E-mail:* was.vertretung@eda.admin.ch (office). *Website:* www.swissemb.org (office).

ZIVKOVIC, Ivan; Serbian diplomatist; *Ambassador to Ethiopia; Career:* fmr Chargé d'affaires in Washington, DC, then Amb. to USA 2002–04; Amb. to Ethiopia 2004–.
Address: Embassy of Serbia and Montenegro, POB 1341, Addis Ababa, Ethiopia (office). *Telephone:* (1) 517804 (office). *Fax:* (1) 514192 (office). *E-mail:* serbembaddis@ethionet.et (office).

ZIYAD, Abu Amr, BA, MA, PhD; Palestinian academic, politician and government official; b. 1950, Gaza City; m.; four c. *Education:* Damascus Univ., Syria, Georgetown Univ., USA. *Career:* early career as teacher, Bahrain, Oman, Syria; elected mem. Palestinian Legis. Council (PLC) 1996 (ind.), re-elected 2006, Chair. PLC Political Cttee, mem. PLO-CC; Minister of Culture 2003, of Foreign Affairs March–June 2007; Prof. of Political Science, Birzeit Univ., Ramallah, West Bank 1985–; has done work for Centre for Policy Analysis on Palestine, Washington, DC and Centre for Palestine Research and Studies, Nablus; Pres. Palestinian Council on Foreign Relations; organised talks between the 12 major Palestinian factions within West Bank and Gaza to determine direction of intifada 2002; frequently serves as mediator between Hamas and Fatah. *Publications:* several books on books on Islamist movts and politics in Gaza 1948-67 including Islamic Fundamentalism in the West Bank and Gaza: Muslim Brotherhood and Islamic Jihad, Civil Society and Democratization in Palestine, The Significance of Jerusalem: A Muslim's Perspective and Emerging Trends in Palestinian Strategic Thinking and Practice.
Address: c/o Ministry of Foreign Affairs POB 1336, Ramallah; POB 4017, Gaza, Palestinian Autonomous Areas (office).

ZIYAL, Ugur; Turkish diplomatist; *Ambassador to Italy;* b. Aug. 1944, Istanbul; m.; one d. *Education:* Univ. of Ankara. *Career:* Third Sec., Dept of Cyprus in Greece, Ministry of Foreign Affairs 1967; mil. service 1969; various high-ranking diplomatic positions including Consul at Consulate Gen. in Geneva 1973–76, Chief of Cabinet, Sec. Gen. of Ministry of Foreign Affairs 1976–80, First Sec. and Counsellor, Embassy in Washington, DC 1980–88, Chief of Dept of Aviation and Maritime Affairs 1988, Deputy Dir-Gen. Directorate Gen. for Multilateral Political Affairs, Amb. to Jordan 1997–98, Advisor to Ministry of Foreign Affairs 1998–2001, Deputy Undersecretary for Political Affairs 2001–04, Undersecretary for Political Affairs 2004–05, Amb. to Italy 2005–.
Address: Embassy of Turkey, Palazzo Gamberini, Via Palestro 28, 00185 Rome, Italy (office). *Telephone:* (06) 445941 (office). *Fax:* (06) 4941526 (office). *E-mail:* roma.be@libero.it (office). *Website:* www .ambasciataditurchia.it (office).

ZLENKO, Anatoliy Maksimovich; Ukrainian diplomatist; b. 2 June 1938, Stavistichl, Kiev Region; m. Ludmila Ivanovna Zlenko; two d. *Education:* Kiev Taras Shevchenko Univ. *Career:* mem. CPSU 1959–91; diplomatic service since 1967, attaché, Third, Second Sec., Ministry of Foreign Affairs of Ukraine 1967–73; mem. UNESCO Secr., Paris 1973–79; Exec. Sec. Ukrainian Comm. on UNESCO Problems 1979–83; Perm. Rep. of Ukraine in UNESCO 1983–87; Deputy Minister of Foreign Affairs of Ukraine 1987–89, First Deputy Minister 1989–90, Minister 1990–94, 2000; Perm. Rep. to UN, New York 1994–97; Amb. to France 1997–2000 (concurrently to UNESCO and to Portugal 1998–2000); Chevalier de la Légion d'honneur 2000; Order of Merit (Portugal) 2000; Grand Cross, Order of Bernardo O'Higgins (Chile) 2001. *Publications:* Foreign Policy of Ukraine: From Romanticism to Pragmatism 2001, From Nation's Needs to Foreign Policy Priorities 2002; articles in Ukrainian and foreign press on int. relations.
Address: c/o Ministry of Foreign Affairs, No. 1 Mykhailivska Square, 01018 Kiev, Mykhaylivska pl. 1, Ukraine (office).

ZOELLICK, Robert Bruce, BA, MPP, JD; American lawyer, business executive and fmr government official; *President, World Bank Group;* b. 25 July 1953, Evergreen Park, Ill.; m. Sherry Lynn Ferguson 1980. *Education:* Swarthmore Coll., Harvard Law School and Kennedy School of Govt, Harvard Univ. *Career:* Special Asst to Asst Attorney-Gen., Criminal Div., Dept of Justice 1978–79; fellowship to Hong Kong 1980; pvt. law practice 1981–82; Vice-Pres., Asst to Chair. and CEO Bd Fannie Mae 1983–85, Exec. Vice-Pres. Housing and Law 1993–97; Special Asst to Deputy Sec., Deputy Asst Sec. for Financial Insts Policy, Counsellor to Sec. and Exec. Sec. Treasury Dept 1985–88; Counsellor with rank of Under-Sec. Dept of State 1989–92, Under-Sec. for Econ. and Agricultural Affairs 1991–92; Deputy Chief of Staff, Asst to Pres. 1992–93; Olin Prof. of Nat. Security Affairs, US Naval Acad. 1997–98; Pres. and CEO Center for Strategic and Int. Studies 1998–99; US Trade Rep. 2001–05; Deputy Sec. of State and

COO Dept of State 2005–06; Vice-Chair., Int., Goldman Sachs Group Inc., New York 2006–07; Pres. World Bank Group (IBRD) 2007–; mem. Bd of Dirs Alliance Capital, Said Capital, German Marshall Fund US; Dir Aspen Inst. Strategy Group; Sr Int. Adviser, Goldman Sachs; Research Scholar, Harvard Univ.; Kt Commdr's Cross (Germany); Hon. DHumLitt (St Joseph's Coll., Rensselaer, Ind.); Distinguished Service Award, Treasury Dept, Alexander Hamilton Award, State Dept, Department of Defense Medal for Distinguished Public Service.
Address: The World Bank, 1818 H Street, NW, Washington, DC 20433, USA (office). *Telephone:* (202) 473-1000 (office). *Fax:* (202) 477-6391 (office). *Website:* www.worldbank.org (office).

ZOGBY, James, BA, PhD; American international organization executive and analyst; *President, Arab American Institute;* m. Eileen Patricia McMahon; five c. *Education:* Le Moyne Coll., Temple Univ. *Career:* Nat. Endowment for the Humanities post-doctoral fellow Princeton Univ. 1976; co-f. Palestinian Human Rights Campaign; co-founder and Exec. Dir American-Arab Anti-Discrimination Cttee; co-f. and Pres. Arab American Inst. 1985–; Co-Pres. Builder's for Peace Cttee 1993; Chair. Forum on Palestinian Economy, Casablanca Econ. Summit 1994; Co-convenor Nat. Democratic Ethnic Coordinating Cttee; elected to Democratic Nat. Cttee's Exec. Cttee as Rep. of Nat. Democratic Ethnic Coordinating Cttee 1999; mem. Bd American Civil Liberties Union, Nat. Immigration Forum, Central Asian-American Enterprise Fund 2001–; mem. Human Rights Watch Middle East Advisory Cttee; mem. Council on Foreign Relations; currently Senior Analyst Zogby Int.; lectured on Middle East Issues, US-Arab relations, and history of Arab American community; Hon. LLD (Le Moyne); Distinguished Public Service Award. *Television:* host of A Capital View, and Viewpoint with James Zogby. *Publications:* books include What Ethnic Americans Really Think, and What Arabs Think: Values, Beliefs and Concerns; author of "Washington Watch" newspaper column 1992–.
Address: Arab American Institute, 1600 K Street NW, Suite 601, Washington DC, 20006, USA (office). *Telephone:* (202) 429-9210 (office). *Fax:* (202) 429-9214 (office). *E-mail:* jzogby@aaiusa.org (office). *Website:* www.aaiusa.org (office).

ZONGO, Tertius, MEconSc; Burkinabè diplomatist, civil servant and academic; *Prime Minister;* b. 18 May 1957, Kougoudgou, Boulkiemdé Prov.; m.; three c. *Education:* Inst. of Enterprises Admin., Nantes, France. *Career:* Head of Accounts, Nat. Office of Crops 1983–85, Dir-Gen. 1985–88; Sec.-Gen. Chamber of Commerce, Industry and Crafts 1986; Prof. of Accounting, Business Economy and Financial Analysis, Univ. of Ouagadougou; Chief of Dept Multilateral Co-operation 1988–92; Dir-Gen. of Co-operation, Ministry of Finances and Planning 1992; Gov. of Burkina Faso to World Bank (IBRD), Int. Monetary Fund (IMF), African Devt Bank, Islamic Devt Bank; Minister of Budget and Planning 1996–97, of Economy and Finance 1997–2000; Govt Spokesman 1996–2000; Amb. to USA 2002–07; Prime Minister of Burkina Faso 2007–; Knight and Officer of the Nat. Order. *Publications:* numerous contribs to papers on agric. and devt.
Address: Office of the Prime Minister, 03 BP 7027, Ouagadougou 03, Burkina Faso (office). *Telephone:* 50-32-48-89 (office). *Fax:* 50-31-47-61 (office). *E-mail:* webmaster@primature.gov.bf (office). *Website:* www.primature.gov.bf (office).

ZOUMARA, Côme; Central African Republic government official. *Career:* fmr Adviser to Pres. on Global Defence and Coordinator of Nat. Comm. on Disarmament, Demobilization and Rehabilitation of Ex-Fighters of Central African Repub.; Minister of Foreign and Francophone Affairs and Regional Integration 2006.
Address: c/o Ministry of Foreign and Francophone Affairs and Regional Integration, Bangui, Central African Republic (office).

ZUBAKOV, Vice-Adm. Yurii Antonovich; Russian politician and diplomatist; *Deputy Secretary, National Security Council;* b. 27 Nov. 1943, Chita; m. Tatiana Michailovna; one s. one d. *Education:* KGB Higher School. *Career:* on staff USSR KGB 1966–89; Deputy Head of sector Cen. CPSU Cttee 1989–90; on staff USSR Security Council 1990–91; Deputy Dir Foreign Intelligence Service USSR (later Russia) 1991–96; Deputy Minister of Foreign Affairs 1996–98; Minister 1998–99; Amb. to Lithuania 2000–03, to Moldova 2003–04; Deputy Sec. Nat. Security Council 2004–.
Address: National Security Council, Ipat'yevski per. 4/10, 103132 Moscow, Russia.

ZUBKOV, Viktor Alekseyevich; Russian government official; *First Deputy Chairman;* b. 15 Sept. 1941, Arbat village, Sverdlovsk Oblast; m.; one d. *Education:* Leningrad (now St Petersburg) Agricultural Inst. *Career:* began career in state farm network, Leningrad Oblast including Gen. Dir Pervomaiskoye Sovkhoz Union 1967–85; various roles within CP including First Sec. Priozersk Cttee and First Deputy Chair. Leningrad regional Cttee

1985–91; Deputy Chair. External Relations Cttee, St Petersburg City Council 1992–93; Deputy Chair. Fed. Tax Service and Head, State Tax Inspectorate, St Petersburg 1993–99; Deputy Minister for Tax 1999–2001; Deputy Minister of Finance 2001–04; Chair. Financial Monitoring Service, Ministry of Finance 2004–07; Chair. Govt of the Russian Fed. (Prime Minister) 2007–08, First Deputy Chair. 2008–; Chair. OAO Gazprom 2008–.
Address: Office of the Chairman, Government of the Russian Federation, 103274 Moscow, Krasnopresnenskaya nab. 2, Russia (office). *Telephone:* (495) 205-57-35 (office). *Fax:* (495) 205-42-19 (office). *Website:* www.government.ru (office).

ZULEEG, Manfred (Friedrich), DJur; German academic and fmr international judge; *Jean Monnet Professor of European Law, University of Frankfurt;* b. 21 March 1935, Creglingen; m. Sigrid Feuerhahn 1965; three s. one d. *Education:* Univs of Erlangen and Hamburg and Bologna Center, Johns Hopkins Univ. *Career:* Research Asst, Inst. for Law of the European Communities, Univ. of Cologne 1962–68, Sr Lecturer 1968–71; Prof. of Public Law and Law of the European Communities, Univ. of Bonn 1971–78; Prof. of Public Law, including European and Public Int. Law, Univ. of Frankfurt 1978–88, Jean Monnet Chair of European Law 1998–; Judge, Court of Justice, European Communities 1988–94; Research Fellow, Univ. of California, Berkeley 1969–70, Visiting Prof. 1996; Dr hc (Athens). *Publications:* Die Rechtsform der Subventionen 1965, Das Recht der Europaïschen Gemeinschaften im innerstaatlichen Bereich 1969, Subventionskontrolle durch Konkurrentenklage 1974, Der rechliche Zusammenhalt der Europäischen Union 2004; contrib. to other works.
Address: J. W. Goethe-Universität, Senckenberganlage 31, 60054 Frankfurt am Main, Germany (office). *Telephone:* (69) 79828071 (office). *Fax:* (69) 79828089 (office). *E-mail:* m.zuleeg@jur.uni-frankfurt.de (office).

ZULFACAR, Maliha, MA, MS, PhD; Afghan/American diplomatist, academic, film maker and fmr government official; *Ambassador to Germany;* b. Kabul; two c. *Education:* Western Coll. for Women, Oxford, OH, Univ. of Cincinnati, USA, Paderborn Univ., Germany. *Career:* Assoc. Prof. of Sociology, Univ. of Kabul –1979; Assoc. Prof., Social Sciences Dept, Calif. Polytechnic State Univ.; Chair Gender Studies Dept, Faculty of Social Sciences, Univ. of Educ., Kabul; Deputy Minister of Higher Educ. of Afghanistan 2002; Sr Research Fellow and Dir American Inst. of Afghanistan Studies 2003–04, Dir oral history project; Amb. of Afghanistan to Germany 2006–; Distinguished Teaching Award 2000–01, Outstanding Faculty Award, Coll. of Liberal Arts 2000–01, Pres.'s Community Service Award 2002, Calif. Faculty Asscn Distinguished Award 2002, Faculty Women of the Year 2004. *Films:* Guftugo: An Interview with Afghan Villagers (documentary) 2000, Kabul Transit 2006. *Publications:* Afghan Immigrants in the USA and Germany: A Comparative Analysis of the Use of Ethnic Social Capital 1998, Countries and Cultures (children's book); several articles in academic journals.
Address: Embassy of Afghanistan, Taunusstr. 3, Ecke Kronbergerstr. 5, 14193 Berlin, Germany (office); Social Sciences Department, California Polytechnic State University, San Luis Obispo, CA 93407, USA (office). *Telephone:* (30) 206-73-50 (Berlin) (office); (805) 756-2260 (San Luis Obispo) (office). *Fax:* (30) 229-15-10 (Berlin) (office). *E-mail:* info@botschaft-afghanistan.de (office); mzulfaca@calpoly.edu (office). *Website:* www.botschaft-afghanistan.de (office); www.cla.calpoly.edu (office).

ZULFUGAROV, Tofik Nadir oglu; Azerbaijani diplomatist; b. 1 Nov. 1959, Rostov-on-Don; m. *Education:* Baku State Univ. *Career:* researcher, Inst. of Oriental Studies Azerbaijan Acad. of Sciences 1985–91; researcher, Inst. of History Azerbaijan Acad. of Sciences 1991–92; diplomatic service 1992–; took part in negotiations on regulating Nagorny Karabakh conflict, Head of Azerbaijan del. 1992–; Head, Dept of Conflict Problems, Azerbaijan Ministry of Foreign Affairs 1993–94, Minister of Foreign Affairs 1998–2000.
Address: c/o Ministry of Foreign Affairs, Gendjler Maydani 3, Baku, Azerbaijan.

ZULUAGA ESCOBAR, Oscar Iván, BA, MA; Colombian business executive and politician; *Minister of Finance and Public Credit;* b. 3 Feb. 1957, Pensilvania, Caldas. *Education:* Liceo de Cervantes, Universidad Javeriana, Univ. of Exeter, UK. *Career:* elected Councillor in Pensilvania 1988–90, Mayor of Pensilvania 1990–92; Chair. ACESCO SA steel co. 1992–2001; launched campaign for Senate and won one of biggest votes in country 2001; supported candidacy of Alvaro Uribe Velez for Pres. of Colombia, Presidential Sr Advisor 2006–07; Minister of Finance and Public Credit 2007–; fmr mem. several bds, including Nat. Fed. of Merchants (Federación Nacional de Comerciantes—FENALCO), Colombian Fed. of Metalworkers (Federación Colombiana de Industrias Metalúrgicas—Fedemetal), Colombo-Venezuelan Chamber of Commerce; fmr rep. of Colombian Iron and Steel Industry; fmr Nat. Pres. Asscn Internationale

des Étudiants en Sciences Economiques et Commerciales (AIESEC)-COLOMBIA; winner, Concurso Nacional de Tesis Universitarias under the heading 'Portfolio Investment Actions', Nat. Asscn of Financial Insts 1983, honoured as one of "10 Best Young Executives of Colombia", Jr Chamber of Colombia (Bogotà Chapter) 1997, chosen by Congress as Best Minister of the Cabinet 2007, selected as one of five Best Finance Ministers of Latin America.
Address: Ministry of Finance and Public Credit, Carrera 8A, No. 6-64, Of. 305, Bogotá, DC, Colombia (office). *Telephone:* (1) 381-1700 (office). *Fax:* (1) 350-9344 (office). *Website:* www.minhacienda.gov.co (office).

ZUMA, Jacob; South African politician; *President, African National Congress of South Africa;* b. 12 April 1942, Inkandla, KwaZulu-Natal. *Career:* joined African Nat. Congress (ANC) 1959; mem. Umkhonto WeSizwe 1962 after ANC banned 1960, arrested 1963, sentenced to ten years' imprisonment; helped re-establish ANC underground structures, Natal Prov. 1973–75; left S Africa 1975; mem. ANC Nat. Exec. Cttee 1977, Deputy Chief Rep., Mozambique –1984, Chief Rep. 1984–87; Head of Underground Structures ANC Head Office, Lusaka, Zambia, 1987, Chief Intelligence Dept, mem. political and mil. council mid-1980s; returned to S Africa after legalization of ANC 1990, Chair. S Natal Region 1990, Deputy Sec.-Gen. ANC 1991, Nat. Chair. 1994–97, Deputy Pres. 1997–2007, Pres. 2007–; Deputy Pres. of S Africa 1999–2005; mem. Exec. Cttee Econ. Affairs and Tourism for KwaZulu Natal Gov. 1994–99, Chair. ANC in KwaZulu 1994–, est. and patron KwaZulu Reconstruction and Devt Project Bursary Fund; arrested and charged with rape Dec. 2005, found not guilty May 2006, charges of corruption dropped Sept. 2006; Hon. DLitt (Fort Hare Univ.) 2001, Hon. DBA (Univ. of Zululand) 2001, Hon. DPhil (Medical Univ. of Southern Africa) 2001; Nelson Mandela Award for Outstanding Leadership (USA) 1998.
Address: African National Congress of South Africa, PO Box 61884, Marshalltown 2107, South Africa (office). *Telephone:* (11) 3761000 (office). *Fax:* (11) 3761134 (office). *Website:* www.anc.org.za (office).

ZÚÑIGA CHAVES, Guillermo, MSc; Costa Rican politician; *Minister of Finance; Career:* early position with Fitch Cen. America (business ratings co.); served as Costa Rican Gov. at IBRD and Inter-American Devt Bank (IABD); mem. Bd of Dirs Banco Central de Costa Rica, Nat. Comm. on Prevention of Risks and Attention of Emergencies; Minister of Finance 2006–.
Address: Ministry of Finance, Edif. Antigüo Banco Anglo, Avda 2a, Calle 3a, San José, Costa Rica (office). *Telephone:* 255-4874 (office); 257-9333 (office). *Fax:* 255-4874 (office). *E-mail:* WebMaster1@hacienda.go.cr (office). *Website:* www.hacienda.go.cr (office).

ŻYGULSKI, Kazimierz, HHD; Polish professor and politician; *President, Warsaw School of Socioeconomic Science;* b. 8 Dec. 1919, Wolanka; m. Helena Gutkowa 1955; one s. *Education:* Univ. of Lwów (now Lvov, Ukraine). *Career:* in resistance movt in Lwów Voivodship during Nazi occupation; imprisoned in USSR 1944–56; researcher, Sociology and History of Culture Research Centre of Polish Acad. of Sciences, Łódź 1956–59; scientific worker, Philosophy and Sociology Inst. of Polish Acad. of Sciences, Warsaw 1959–90, Head Culture Research Centre 1961–90, Chair. Scientific Council 1987–90, Extraordinary Prof. 1973–83, Ordinary Prof. 1983–; Pro-Rector, State Film, TV and Theatrical Higher School, Łódź 1970–71; Counsellor to Deputy Chair. of Council of Ministers 1971–72; Minister of Culture and Art 1982–86; Pro-Rector, Dir Scientific Research Centre, Warsaw School of Socioeconomic Science 1997–2002; Pres. Warsaw School of Socioeconomic Science 2002–; mem. Polish Cttee ICOM 1972–90, Presidium State Prizes Cttee 1975–83, Presidium Nat. Council for Culture 1983–86; Amb. ad personam 1987; Chair. Polish Nat. Comm. for UNESCO 1987–90; mem. UNESCO Exec. Bd 1987–90, Chair. Int. Cttee of Extra Govt Org., UNESCO 1989–90; mem. European Acad. of Arts, Sciences and Humanities 1989–; Hon. Academician Int. Personnel Acad. (Ukraine) 1999; Officer's Cross Order of Polonia Restituta. *Television:* European Culture Past and Present (series). *Publications:* Drogi rozwoju kultury masowej (Mass Cultural Ways of Development) 1962, Wstęp do zagadnień kultury (Introduction to the Problems of Culture) 1972, Wartości i wzory kultury (Values and Models of Culture) 1975, Wspólnota śmiechu: Socjologiczne studium komizmu (Community of Laughter: A Sociological Study of the Comical) 1976, Święto i kultura (Holiday and Culture) 1981, Jestem z lwowskiego etapu (I am from Lwów) 1994, Widmo Przyszłości: nowa fala okrucieństwa (Ghost of the Future: New Wave of Atrocities) 1996, Globalne problemy współczesnego świata (The Global Problems of the Contemporary World) 1996, Uwagi o ekstremalnych zjawiskach w kulturze współczesnej (Notes on Extreme Phenomena in Contemporary Culture) 1998, Socialne i ekonomiczne aspekty globalizacji (The Socio-economic Aspects of Globalization) 1999, Czytając tajne polskie teczki J. Stalina (Reading Secret Materials Concerning Poles from Stalin Times) 1999, Etos edukacji w XXI wieku. Uwagi socjologa (Ethos of Education in the 21st Century. Sociologist Remarks) 2000, Myśliciel i bieg stuleci (A Thinker and the Course of Centuries) 2004; The Problems of Contemporary Sociology 2006, numerous research works and monographs on sociology of culture 2003–08.
Address: Wyższa Szkoła Społeczno-Ekonomiczna, ul. M. Kasprzaka 29/31, 01-234 Warsaw (office); ul. Madalińskiego 50/52 m. 23, 02-581 Warsaw, Poland (home). *Telephone:* (22) 8770720 (office); (22) 8498179 (home). *Fax:* (22) 8770720 (office).

APPENDIX: Directory of Diplomatic Missions

DIPLOMATIC MISSIONS OF AFGHANISTAN

United Nations: 360 Lexington Ave, 11th Floor, New York, NY 10017; tel. (212) 972-1212; fax (212) 972-1216; e-mail afgwatan@aol.com; Permanent Representative Dr Zahir Tanin.

Australia: POB 155, Deakin West, ACT 2600; tel. (2) 6282-7311; fax (2) 6282-7322; e-mail ambassador@afghanembassy.net; internet www.afghanembassy.net; Ambassador AMANULLAH JAYHOON.

Austria: Lackierergasse 9/9, 1090 Vienna; tel. (1) 524-78-06; fax (1) 406-02-19; e-mail afg.emb.vie@chello.at; internet www.embassyofafghanistan.com; Chargé d'affaires a.i. Wahid Monawar.

Bangladesh: House CWN(C) 2A, 24 Gulshan Ave, Gulshan Model Town, Dhaka 1212; tel. (2) 9895994; fax (2) 9884767; e-mail afghanembassydhaka@yahoo.com; Ambassador AHMAD KARIM NAWABI.

Belgium: 61 ave de Wolvendael, 1180 Uccle; tel. (2) 761-31-66; fax (2) 761-31-67; e-mail ambassade.afghanistan@skynet.be; Ambassador Zia Nezam.

Bulgaria: 1618 Sofia, Ovcha Kupel, ul. Boryana 61/216A/15; tel. (2) 955-61-96; fax (2) 955-99-76; e-mail ariana@sofianet.net; Ambassador KARSIMIR TULECHKI.

Canada: 240 Argyle Ave, Ottawa, ON K2P 1B9; tel. (613) 563-4223; fax (613) 563-4962; e-mail contact@afghanemb-canada.net; internet www.afghanemb-canada.net; Ambassador Omar Samad.

China, People's Republic: 8 Dong Zhi Men Wai Dajie, Chao Yang Qu, Beijing 100600; tel. (10) 65321532; fax (10) 653226603; e-mail afgemb.beijing@gmail.com; Ambassador AHMAD EKLIL HAKIMI.

Czech Republic: Na Kazance 634/7, 171 00 Prague 7; tel. 233544228; fax 233542009; e-mail afg.prague@centrum.cz; Ambassador Mohammad Kacem Fazelly.

Egypt: 59 Sharia el-Orouba, Cairo (Heliopolis); tel. (2) 4177236; fax (2) 4177238; e-mail afghan_emb_cairo@hotmail.com; Ambassador DR M. RAHIM SHERZOY.

France: 32 ave Raphaël, 75016 Paris; tel. 1-45-25-05-29; fax 1-45-24-60-68; e-mail ambafghane@wanadoo.fr; internet www.ambafghane-paris.com; Ambassador Dr Assad Omer.

Germany: Taunusstr. 3, Ecke Kronbergerstr. 5, 14193 Berlin; tel. (30) 2067350; fax (30) 2291510; e-mail info@botschaft-afghanistam.de; internet www.botschaft-afghanistan.de; Ambassador PROF. DR MALIHA ZULFACAR.

India: 5/50f Shanti Path, Chanakyapuri, New Delhi 110 021; tel. (11) 2410331; fax (11) 26875439; e-mail afghanspirit@yahoo.com; Ambassador Dr Sayed Makhdoom Raheen.

Indonesia: Jalan Dr Kusuma Atmaja 15, Jakarta Pusat 10310; tel. (21) 3143169; fax (21) 31935390; e-mail afghanembassy_jkk@yahoo.com; Ambassador BESMULLAH BESMEL.

Iran: Dr Beheshti Ave, Cnr of 4th St, Pakistan St, Tehran; tel. (21) 88737050; fax (21) 88735600; e-mail afghaembassytehran@hotmail.com; Ambassador Yahya Maroufi.

Italy: Via Nomentana 120, 00161 Roma; tel. (06) 8611009; fax (06) 86322939; e-mail afghanembassy.rome@flashnet.it; Ambassador MUHAMMAD MUSA MAROOFI.

Japan: Matsumoto International House (MIH), 3-37-8, Nishihara, Shibuya-ku, Tokyo 151-0066; tel. (3) 5465-1219; fax (3) 5465-1229; e-mail info@afghanembassyjp.com; internet www.afghanembassyjp.com; Ambassador Haron Amin.

Kazakhstan: 010000 Astana, Diplomatiyalyk kalashyk C-10; tel. (727) 224-29-46; fax (727) 224-30-25; e-mail aziz59@mail.ru; Ambassador AZIZ ARYANFAR.

Korea, Republic: 27-2, Hannam-dong, Yeongsan-gu, Seoul 140-210; tel. (2) 793-3535; fax (2) 795-2662; e-mail info@afghanistanembassy.or.kr; internet www.afghanistanembassy.or.kr; Ambassador Mohammad Karim Rahimi.

Kuwait: POB 33186, 73452 Rawdah, Block 6, Surra St, Across Surra Co-op Society House 16, Kuwait City; tel. 5329461; fax 5326274; e-mail afg_emb_kuw@hotmail.com; Ambassador MUHAMMAD YOUSUF SAMAD.

Kyrgyzstan: 720040 Bishkek, Gorkogo 210; tel. (312) 69-01-76; fax (312) 69-03-30; e-mail afghanemb_bishkek@yahoo.com; Ambassador Shahjahan Ahmadi.

Libya: POB 4245, Sharia Mozhar al-Aftes, Tripoli; tel. (21) 4775192; fax (21) 609876; Chargé d'affaires MUHAMMAD AMER ALZAIDY.

Malaysia: 2nd Floor, Wisma Chinese Chamber, 258 Jalan Ampang, 50450 Kuala Lumpur; tel. (3) 42569400; fax (3) 42566400; e-mail consular@afghanembassykl.org; internet www.afghanembassykl.org; Ambassador Mohammad Yunos Farman.

Norway: Kronprinsensgt. 17, 0251 Oslo; tel. 22-83-84-10; fax 22-83-84-11; e-mail info@afghanemb.com; internet www.afghanistanembassy.no; Ambassador JAVID LODIN.

Pakistan: 8, St 90, G-6/3, Islamabad 44000; tel. (51) 2824505; fax (51) 2824504; e-mail afghanem@yahoo.com; Ambassador Majnoon Ghulab.

Poland: 02-954 Warsaw, ul. Goplańska 1; tel. (22) 8855410; fax (22) 8856500; e-mail warsaw@afghanembassy.com.pl; internet www.afghanembassy.com.pl; Ambassador ZIAUDDIN MOJADEDI.

Qatar: POB 22104, Isteolal St, West Bay, Doha; tel. 4930821; fax 4930819; e-mail afgembqatar@hotmail.com; Ambassador Wali Monawar.

Russian Federation: 121069 Moscow, ul. Povarskaya 42; tel. (495) 290-16-80; fax (495) 290-01-46; e-mail safarat_moscow@yahoo.com; Ambassador ZALMAI AZIZ.

Saudi Arabia: POB 93337, Riyadh 11673; tel. (1) 480-3459; fax (1) 480-3451; e-mail afgembriyad@hotmail.com; Ambassador Kabir Farahi.

Spain: Umbría 8, 28043 Madrid; tel. (91) 7218581; fax (91) 7216832; e-mail embajadadeafganistanenmadrid@gmail.com; Chargé d'affaires GUL AHMAD SHERZADA.

Sudan: Madinatol Riyadh, Shareol Moshtal Sq. 10, House No. 81, Khartoum; tel. (183) 221852; fax (183) 222059; e-mail afembsudan@hotmail.com; Chargé d'affaires a.i. Khalilurrahman Hanani.

Switzerland: 63 rue de Lausanne, 1202 Geneva; tel. 227311616; fax 227314510; e-mail mission.afghanistan@bluewin.ch; internet www.mission-afghanistan.ch; Ambassador NANGUYULAI TARZI.

Syria: BP 12217, ave Secretariat, Mezzeh Ouest, Damascus; tel. (11) 6112910; fax (11) 6133595; Ambassador Muhammadullah Haidari.

Tajikistan: 734000 Dushanbe, Kuchai Pushkin 34; tel. (372) 221-67-35; fax (372) 251-00-96; e-mail afghanemintj@yahoo.com; Ambassador SAYED MUHAMMAD KHAIRKHOH.

Turkey: Cinnah Cad. 88, 06551 Çankaya, Ankara; tel. (312) 4422523; fax (312) 4422269; Ambassador Masood Khalili.

Turkmenistan: 744000 Aşgabat, Gerogly 14; tel. (12) 39-58-21; fax (12) 39-58-20; Ambassador ABDUL KARIM KHADAM.

Ukraine: 01037 Kyiv, pr. Chervonozoryanyi 42; tel. (44) 245-81-04; e-mail sm_kh2003@yahoo.com; Ambassador Mohammed Asif Dilawar.

United Arab Emirates: POB 5687, Abu Dhabi; tel. (2) 6655560; fax (2) 6655576; Ambassador FARID ZEKRIA.

United Kingdom: 31 Prince's Gate, London, SW7 1QQ; tel. (20) 7589-8891; fax (20) 7584-4801; e-mail london@mfa.gov.af; internet www.afghanembassyuk.org; Ambassador Dr Muhammad Rahim Sherzoy.

United States of America: 2341 Wyoming Ave, NW, Washington, DC 20008; tel. 483-6410; fax 483-6488; e-mail info@embassyofafghanistan.org; internet www.embassyofafghanistan.org; Ambassador SAID TAYEB JAWAD.

Uzbekistan: 100047 Tashkent, Gulomov ko'ch. 73; tel. (71) 234-84-58; fax (71) 234-84-65; e-mail afgemuz@mail.tps.uz; Ambassador Farooq Baraki.

DIPLOMATIC MISSIONS OF ALBANIA

United Nations: 320 East 79th St, New York, NY 10075; tel. (212) 249-2059; fax (212) 535-2917; e-mail albania@un.int; Permanent Representative ADRIAN NERITANI.

Argentina: Juez Tedín 3036, 4°, C1425CWH Buenos Aires; tel. (11) 4809-3574; fax (11) 4815-2512; e-mail ambasada.bue@netsat.com.ar; Ambassador Rezar Bregu.

Austria: Prinz-Eugen-Str. 18/1/5, 1040 Vienna; tel. (1) 328-86-56; fax (1) 328-86-58; e-mail albemb.vie@chello.at; Ambassador VALTER IBRAHIMI.

Belgium: 30 rue Tenbosch, 1000 Brussels; tel. (2) 644-33-29; fax (2) 640-31-77; e-mail amba.brux@skynet.be; Ambassador Mimoza Halimi.

Bulgaria: 1504 Sofia, ul. Krakra 10; tel. (2) 943-38-57; fax (2) 943-30-69; e-mail aembassy.sofia@mfa.gov.al; Ambassador BUJAR SKENDO.

Canada: 130 Albert St, Suite 302, Ottawa, ON K1P 5G4; tel. (613) 236-4114; fax (613) 236-0804; e-mail embassyrepublicofalbania@on.aivn.com; Ambassador Besnik Konçi.

China, People's Republic: 28 Guang Hua Lu, Jian Guo Men Wai, Beijing 100600; tel. (10) 65321120; fax (10) 65325451; e-mail embassy.beijing@mfa.gov.al; Ambassador MAXHUN PEKA.

Croatia: 10000 Zagreb, Jurišićeva 2a; tel. (1) 4810679; fax (1) 4810682; e-mail ambasada.shqiptare@inet.hr; Ambassador Pëllumb Qazimi.

Czech Republic: Pod kaštany 22, 160 00 Prague 6; tel. 233370594; fax 233377232; e-mail alembprg@mbox.vol.cz; Ambassador QAZIM TEPSHI.

Denmark: Fredriksholms Kanal 4, 1220 Copenhagen K; tel. 33-91-79-79; fax 33-91-79-69; e-mail embassyofalbania@mail.dk; Ambassador Afërdita Dalla.

Egypt: Ground Floor, 27 Sharia Gezira al-Wissta, Cairo (Zamalek); tel. (2) 7361815; fax (2) 7356966; e-mail embassy.cairo@mfa.gov.al; Chargé d'affaires a.i. ELIR HOXHA.

France: 57 ave Marceau, 75116 Paris; tel. 1-47-23-31-00; fax 1-47-23-59-85; e-mail ambassade.paris@mfa.gov.al; Chargé d'affaires a.i. Ylljet Aliçka.

Germany: Friedrichstr. 231, 10969 Berlin; tel. (30) 2593040; fax (30) 25931890; e-mail kanzlei@botschaft-albanien.de; internet www.botschaft-albanien.de; Ambassador GAZMEND TURDIU.

Greece: Odos Vekiareli 7, Filothei, 152 37 Athens; tel. (210) 6876200; fax (210) 6876223; e-mail albem@ath.forthnet.gr; Ambassador Vili Minarolli.

Hungary: 1026 Budapest, Gábor Áron u. 55; tel. (1) 326-8905; fax (1) 326-8904; e-mail aalbemb@enternet.hu; Ambassador EDUARD SULO.

Israel: 54/26 Pinkas St, Tel-Aviv 62261; tel. 3-5465866; fax 3-5444545; e-mail alb_emb@netvision.net.il; Ambassador Tonin Gjuraj.

Italy: Via Asmara 3–5, 00199 Roma; tel. (06) 86224110; fax (06) 86224120; e-mail embassy.rome@mfa.gov.al; internet www.ambalbania.it; Ambassador LLESH KOLA.

Japan: 4/F Hokkoku Shimbun Bldg, 6-4-8, Tsukiji, Chuo-ku, Tokyo 104-0045; tel. (3) 3543-6861; fax (3) 3543-6862; e-mail embassy.tokyo@mfa.gov.al; Chargé d'affaires a.i. Fatos Kerciku.

Kosovo: Prishtina, Qyteza Pejton, Rruga Mujo Ulqinaku 18; tel. (38) 248208; fax (38) 248209; e-mail mission.kosova@mfa.gov.al; Ambassador ISLAM LAUKA.

Macedonia, former Yugoslav Republic: 1000 Skopje, Majka Tereza 22; tel. (2) 3246726; fax (2) 3246727; e-mail ambshquip@mt.net.mk; Ambassador Vladimir Prelja.

Malaysia: UBN Tower 10, 31st Floor, Jalan P. Pamlee, 50250 Kuala Lumpur; tel. (3) 20788690; fax (3) 20702285; e-mail albania@streamyx.com; Chargé d'affaires a.i. DILAVER QESJA.

Montenegro: 81000 Podgorica, Zmaj Jovina br. 30, Stari Aerodrom; tel. (81) 652796; fax (81) 652798; Chargé d'affaires Saimir Bala.

Netherlands: Anna Paulownastraat 109B, 2518 BD The Hague; tel. (70) 4272101; fax (70) 4272083; e-mail embalba@xs4all.nl; Ambassador ROLAND BIMO.

Poland: 02-386 Warsaw, ul. Altowa 1; tel. (22) 8241427; fax (22) 8241426; e-mail embassy.warsaw@mfa.gov.al; Ambassador Florent Çeliku.

Romania: 011811 Bucharest, Str. Duiliu Zamfirescu 7, Sector 1; tel. (21) 2119829; fax (21) 2108039; Ambassador DASHNOR DERVISHI.

Russian Federation: 119049 Moscow, ul. Mytnaya 3/8; tel. (495) 230-77-32; fax (495) 230-76-35; e-mail embassy.moscow@mfa.gov.al; Ambassador Teodor Laco.

Serbia: 11000 Belgrade, bul. Kneza Aleksandra Karađorđevića 25A; tel. (11) 3066642; fax (11) 2665439; e-mail albembassy_belgrade@hotmail.com; Ambassador SPIRO KOÇI.

Spain: María de Molina 64, 5°b, 28006 Madrid; tel. (91) 5612118; fax (91) 5613775; e-mail embassy.madrid@mfa.gov.al; Ambassador Anila Bitri Lani.

Sweden: Capellavägen 7, 181 32 Lidingö; tel. (8) 731-09-20; fax (8) 767-65-57; Ambassador RUHI HADO (designate).

Switzerland: Pourtalèsstr. 45a, 3074 Muri bei Bern; tel. 319526010; fax 319526012; e-mail emalb.ch@bluewin.ch; Ambassador Mehmet Elezaj.

Turkey: Ebuziya Tevfik Sok. 17, Çankaya, Ankara; tel. (312) 4416103; fax (312) 4416109; e-mail embassy.ankara@mfa.gov.al; Ambassador ALTIN KODRA.

United Kingdom: 2nd Floor, 24 Buckingham Gate, London, SW1E 6LB; tel. (20) 7828-8897; fax (20) 7828-8869; e-mail embassy.london@mfa.gov.al; internet www.albanianembassy.co.uk; Ambassador Zef Mazi.

United States of America: 2100 S St, NW, Washington, DC 20008; tel. (202) 223-4942; fax (202) 628-7342; e-mail info@albanianembassy.org; internet www.albanianembassy.org; Ambassador ALEKSANDER SALLABANDA.

Vatican City: Via Silla 7/1, 00192 Rome, Italy; tel. (06) 39754085; fax (06) 39733150; e-mail embassy.vatican@mfa.gov.al; Ambassador Rrok Logu.

DIPLOMATIC MISSIONS OF ALGERIA

United Nations: 326 East 48th St, New York, NY 10017; tel. (212) 750-1960; fax (212) 759-5274; e-mail mission@algeria-un.org; internet www.algeria-un.org; Permanent Representative YOUCEF YOUSFI.

Angola: Rua Edif. Siccal, Rainha Ginga, CP 1389, Luanda; tel. 222332881; fax 222334785; e-mail ambalg@netangola.com; Ambassador Toufik Dahmani.

Argentina: Montevideo 1889, C1021AAE Buenos Aires; tel. (11) 4815-1271; fax (11) 4815-8837; e-mail argeliae@interserver.com.ar; Ambassador AHCÈNE BOUKHELFA.

Australia: 9 Terrigal Crescent, O'Malley, ACT 2606; tel. (2) 6286-7355; fax (2) 6286-7037; e-mail info@algeriaemb.org.au; internet www.algeriaemb.org.au; Ambassador Kamerzamane Belramoul.

Austria: Rudolfinergasse 18, 1190 Vienna; tel. (1) 369-88-53; fax (1) 369-88-56; e-mail office@algerische-botschaft.at; internet www.algerische-botschaft.at; Ambassador TAOUS FEROUKHI.

Bahrain: POB 26402, Villa 579, Rd 3622, Adliya, Manama; tel. 17713669; fax 17713662; e-mail abdemyh@hotmail.com; Ambassador Ahmad Bouziane.

Belgium: 207–209 ave Molière, 1050 Brussels; tel. (2) 343-50-78; fax (2) 343-51-68; e-mail info@algerian-embassy.be; internet www.algerian-embassy.be; Ambassador HALIM BENATTALLAH.

Brazil: SHIS, QI 09, Conj. 13, Casa 01, Lago Sul, 70472-900 Brasília, DF; tel. (61) 3248-4039; fax (61) 3248-4691; e-mail sanag277@bsb.terra.com.br; Ambassador Mohammed Achache.

Bulgaria: 1000 Sofia, ul. Slavyanska 16; tel. (2) 980-22-50; Ambassador ZINE EL-ABIDINE HACHICHI.

Burkina Faso: Secteur 13, Zone du Bois, 295 ave Babanguida, 01 BP 3893, Ouagadougou 01; tel. 50-36-81-81; fax 50-36-81-79; Ambassador Mohamed El Amine Ben Cherif.

Cameroon: 433 rue 1828, Quartier Bastos, BP 1619, Yaoundé; tel. 2221-5351; fax 2231-5354; Ambassador BAALLAL AZZOUZ.

Canada: 500 Wilbrod St, Ottawa, ON K1N 6N2; tel. (613) 789-8505; fax (613) 789-1406; e-mail ambalgcan@rogers.com; internet www.embassyalgeria.ca; Ambassador Smail Benamara.

Chad: BP 178, rue de Paris, N'Djamena; tel. 52-38-15; fax 52-37-92; e-mail amb.algerie@intnet.td; Ambassador BOUBAKEUR OGAB.

China, People's Republic: 2 Dong Zhi Men Wai Dajie, Chao Yang Qu, Beijing 100600; tel. (10) 65321231; fax (10) 65321648; Ambassador Djamel Eddine Grine.

Colombia: Carrera 11, No 93-53, Of. 302, Bogotá, DC; tel. (1) 635-0520; fax (1) 635-0531; e-mail ambalgbg@cable.net.co; Ambassador OMAR BENCHEHIDA.

Congo, Republic: rue Col Brisset, BP 2100, Brazzaville; tel. 81-17-37; fax 81-54-77; Ambassador Abdelah Laouari.

Côte d'Ivoire: 53 blvd Clozel, 01 BP 1015, Abidjan 01; tel. 20-21-23-40; fax 20-22-37-12; Ambassador SALEH LEBDIOUI.

Cuba: Avda 5, No 2802, esq. 28, Miramar, Havana; tel. (7) 204-2835; fax (7) 204-2702; Ambassador Ahcene Kerman.

Czech Republic: V tišině 483/10, POB 204, 160 41 Prague 6; tel. 233371142; fax 233371144; e-mail ambalger@mbox.vol.cz; internet www.algerie.cz; Chargé d'affaires a.i. HICHEM KIMOUCHE.

Denmark: Hellerupvej 66, 2900 Hellerup; tel. 33-11-94-40; fax 33-11-58-50; e-mail ambalda@mail.tele.dk; internet www.algerianembassy.dk; Ambassador Latifa Benazza.

Egypt: 14 Sharia Bresil, Cairo (Zamalek); tel. (2) 3418527; fax (2) 3414158; Ambassador ABD AL-QADER HAGGAR.

Ethiopia: Woreda 23, Kebele 13, House No. 1819, POB 5740, Addis Ababa; tel. (11) 3719666; fax (11) 3719669; Ambassador Noureddine Aouam.

France: 50 rue de Lisbonne, 75008 Paris; tel. 1-53-93-20-20; fax 1-42-25-10-25; e-mail chancellerie@amb-algerie.fr; internet www.amb-algerie.fr; Ambassador MISSOUM SBIH.

Gabon: Batterie 4, BP 4008, Libreville; tel. 73-23-18; fax 73-14-03; e-mail ambalgabon@komo.tiggabon.com; Ambassador (vacant).

Germany: Görschstr. 45–46, 13187 Berlin; tel. (30) 437370; fax (30) 48098716; e-mail info@algerische-botschaft.de; internet www.algerische-botschaft.de; Ambassador HOCINE MEGHAR.

Ghana: 22 Josif Broz Tito Ave, POB 2747, Cantonments, Accra; tel. (21) 776719; fax (21) 776828; Ambassador Lakhal Benkelai.

Greece: Leoforos Vassileos Konstantinou 14, 116 35 Athens; tel. (210) 7564191; fax (210) 7018681; e-mail ambdzath@otenet.gr; Ambassador AHMED BENYAMINA.

Guinea: Cité des Nations, Quartiers Kaloum, BP 1004, Conakry; tel. 30-44-15-05; fax 30-41-15-35; .

Hungary: 1121 Budapest, Zugligeti u. 27; tel. (1) 200-6860; fax (1) 200-6781; e-mail ambalbud@axelero.hu; Ambassador BACHIR ROUIS.

India: E-6/5 Vasant Vihar, New Delhi 110 057; tel. (11) 26147036; fax (11) 26147033; internet www.embalgind.com; Ambassador Dr Noureddine Bardad Dajdj.

Indonesia: Jalan H. R. Rasuna Said, Kav. 10-1, Kuningan, Jakarta 12950; tel. (21) 5254719; fax (21) 5254654; e-mail ambaljak@rad.net.id; internet www .algeria-id.org; Ambassador HAMZA YAHIA-CHERIF.

Iran: Tehran; tel. (21) 22420017; fax (21) 22420015; e-mail ambalg_teheran@ yahoo.fr; Ambassador Muhammad Amin Dragi.

Iraq: 13/14/613 Hay ad-Daoudi, Baghdad; tel. (1) 543-4137; fax (1) 542-5829; Ambassador (vacant).

Italy: Via Bartolomeo Eustachio 12, 00161 Roma; tel. (06) 44202533; fax (06) 44292744; Ambassador Rachid Marif.

Japan: 2-10-67, Mita, Meguro-ku, Tokyo 153-0062; tel. (3) 3711-2661; fax (3) 3710-6534; Ambassador SID ALI KETRANDJI.

Jordan: POB 830375, Amman 11183; tel. (6) 4641271; fax (6) 4616552; e-mail ambalg@go.com.jo; Ambassador Ali Arroudy.

Kenya: 37 Muthaiga Rd, POB 53902, Nairobi; tel. (20) 310440; fax (20) 310450; e-mail algerianembassy@mitsuminett.com; Ambassador MUHAMMAD-HACENE ECHARIF.

Korea, Republic: 2-6, Itaewon 2-dong, Yeongsan-gu, Seoul 140-857; tel. (2) 794-5034; fax (2) 794-5040; e-mail sifdja01@kornet.net; internet www .algerianemb.or.kr; AmbassadorRabah Hadid.

Kuwait: POB 578, 13006 Safat, Istiqlal St, Kuwait City; tel. 2519220; fax 2519497; e-mail ambalgkt@qualitynet.net; Ambassador MUHAMMAD BURUBA.

Lebanon: POB 4794, face Hôtel Summerland, rue Jnah, Beirut; tel. (1) 826712; fax (1) 826711; Ambassador Ahmad Boutehri.

Liberia: Capitol By-Pass, POB 2032, Monrovia; tel. 224311; Chargé d'affaires a.i. MUHAMMAD AZZEDINE AZZOUZ.

Libya: Sharia Kairouan 12, Tripoli; tel. (21) 4440025; fax (21) 3334631; Ambassador Muhammad Seghir Kara.

Malaysia: 5 Jalan Mesra, off Jalan Damai, 55000 Kuala Lumpur; tel. (3) 21488159; fax (3) 21488154; e-mail enquiries@algerianembassy.org.my; internet www.algerianembassy.org.my; Ambassador AMAR BELANI.

Mali: Daoudabougou, BP 02, Bamako; tel. 220-51-76; fax 222-93-74; Ambassador Abdelkrem Ghraieb.

Mauritania: Ilot A, Tevragh Zeina, BP 625, Nouakchott; tel. 525-35-69; fax 525-47-77; Ambassador ABDELKRIM BEN HOCINE.

Mexico: Sierra Madre 540, Col. Lomas de Chapultepec, Del. Miguel Hidalgo, 11000 México, DF; tel. (55) 5520-6950; fax (55) 5540-7579; e-mail embajadadeargelia@yahoo.com.mx; Ambassador Merzak Belhimeur.

Morocco: 46–48 blvd Tariq ibn Ziad, BP 448, 10001 Rabat; tel. (3) 7661574; fax (3) 7762237; e-mail algerabat@iam.net.ma; Ambassador LARBI BELKHEIR.

Mozambique: Rua de Mukumbura 121–125, CP 1709, Maputo; tel. 21492070; fax 21490582; e-mail ab220261@virconn.com; Ambassador Fouad Bouttoura.

Namibia: 111A Gloudina St, Ludwigsdorf, POB 3079, Windhoek; tel. (61) 221507; fax (61) 236376; Chargé d'affaires a.i. YOUCEF DELILECHE.

Netherlands: Van Stolklaan 1–3, 2585 JS The Hague; tel. (70) 3522954; fax (70) 3061961; e-mail ambalg1@wanadoo.nl; internet www.embalgeria.nl; Ambassador Benchaâ Dani.

Niger: route des Ambassades-Goudel, BP 142, Niamey; tel. 20-72-35-83; fax 20-72-35-93; Ambassador HAMID BOUKRIF.

Nigeria: Plot 203, Etim Inyang Cres., POB 55238, Falomo, Lagos; tel. (1) 612092; fax (1) 2624017; Ambassador El-Mihoub Mihoubi.

Oman: POB 216, Muscat 115; tel. 24601698; fax 24694419; e-mail algeria@ omantel.net.om; Ambassador TAYEB SAÂDI.

Pakistan: 107, St 9, E-7, POB 1038, Islamabad; tel. (51) 2653793; fax (51) 2820912; Ambassador Nadir Larbaoui.

Poland: 03-932 Warsaw, ul. Dąbrowiecka 21; tel. (22) 6175855; fax (22) 6160081; e-mail ambalgva@zigzag.pl; Ambassador ABDELAZIZ LAHIOUEL.

Portugal: Rua Duarte Pacheco Pereira 58, 1400-140 Lisbon; tel. (21) 3041520; fax (21) 3010393; e-mail embaixada-argelia@clix.pt; internet www.emb -argelia.pt; Ambassador Sabri Boukadoum.

Qatar: POB 2494, Doha; tel. 4831186; fax 4836452; Ambassador MUHAM-MAD BOUROUBA.

Romania: 010663 Bucharest, Bd. Lascăr Catargiu 29; tel. (21) 2124185; fax (21) 2115695; e-mail ambalgerie@roumanie.eunet.ro; Ambassador Abdel Hamid Senouci Bereksi.

Russian Federation: 103051 Moscow, Krapivinskii per. 1A; tel. (495) 937-46-00; fax (495) 937-46-25; e-mail algamb@ntl.ru; internet www .algerianembassy.ru; Ambassador AMAR ABBA.

Saudi Arabia: POB 94388, Riyadh 11693; tel. (1) 488-7171; fax (1) 482-1703; Ambassador Abd al-Karim Gharib.

Senegal: 5 rue Mermoz, Plateau, Dakar; tel. 33-849-5700; fax 33-849-5701; e-mail ambalgdak@orange.sn; 1963Ambassador DR ABDELHAMID CHEBCHOUB.

Serbia: 11000 Belgrade, Maglajska 26 b; tel. (11) 3671211; e-mail ambalg@ eunet.yu; Ambassador Boudjemaa Delmi.

South Africa: 950 Arcadia St, Hatfield, Pretoria 0083; POB 57480, Arcadia 0007; tel. (12) 3425074; fax (12) 3426479; Ambassador MOURAD BENCHEIKH.

Spain: General Oráa 12, 28006 Madrid; tel. (91) 5629705; fax (91) 5629877; e-mail embargel@tsai.es; Ambassador Mohammed Haneche.

Sudan: Blvd El-Mechtel Eriad, POB 80, Khartoum; tel. (183) 234773; fax (183) 224190; Ambassador SALIH BEN KOBBI.

Sweden: Danderydsgt. 3–5, POB 26027, 100 41 Stockholm; tel. (8) 679-91-30; fax (8) 611-49-57; e-mail embassy.algeria@telia.com; internet www .embalgeria.se; Ambassador Merzak Bedjaoui.

Switzerland: Willadingweg 74, 3000 Bern 15; tel. 313501050; fax 313501059; e-mail ambalg.berne@bluewin.ch; Ambassador KAMEL HOUHOU.

Syria: Immeuble Noss, Raouda, Damascus; tel. (11) 3331446; fax (11) 3334698; Ambassador Lahsan Abu Faris.

Tanzania: 34 Ali Hassan Mwinyi Rd, POB 2963, Dar es Salaam; tel. (22) 2117619; fax (22) 2117620; e-mail algemb@twiga.com; Ambassador ABDELMOUN'AAM AHRIZ.

Tunisia: 18 rue de Niger, 1002 Tunis; tel. (71) 783-166; fax (71) 788-804; Ambassador Abdelaziz Maoui.

Turkey: Şehit Ersan Cad. 42, 06680 Çankaya, Ankara; tel. (312) 4687719; fax (312) 4687593; e-mail cezayirbe@yahoo.fr; Ambassador SMAÏL ALLAOUA.

Uganda: 14 Acacia Ave, Kololo, POB 4025, Kampala; tel. (41) 4232918; fax (41) 4341015; e-mail ambalgka@imul.com; Ambassador Abdelkader Aziria.

Ukraine: 01001 Kyiv, vul. B. Khmelnytskoho 64; tel. (44) 216-70-79; fax (44) 216-70-08; e-mail ambkv@ksv.net.ua; Ambassador MOKADDEM BAFDAL.

United Arab Emirates: POB 3070, Abu Dhabi; tel. (2) 448949; fax (2) 4470686; Ambassador Hamid Chebira.

United Kingdom: 54 Holland Park, London, W11 3RS; tel. (20) 7221-7800; fax (20) 7221-0448; e-mail info@algerianembassy.org.uk; internet www .algerianembassy.org.uk; Ambassador MUHAMMAD SALAH DEMBRI.

United States of America: 2118 Kalorama Rd, NW, Washington, DC 20008; tel. (202) 265-2800; fax (202) 667-2174; e-mail ambalg2004@yahoo.com; internet www.algeria-us.org; Ambassador Amine Kherbi.

Uzbekistan: 100000 Tashkent, Murtozaev ko'ch. 6; tel. (71) 134-17-74; fax (711) 120-62-75; Ambassador HASEN LASKRI.

Venezuela: 8a Transversal con 3a Avda, Quinta Azahar, Urb. Altamira, Caracas 1060; tel. (212) 263-2092; fax (212) 261-4254; e-mail ambalgcar@ cantv.net; Ambassador Mohammed Khelladi.

Viet Nam: 13 Phan Chu Trinh, Hanoi; tel. (4) 8253865; fax (4) 8260830; e-mail ambalghanoi@ambalgvn.org.vn; internet www.ambalgvn.org.vn; Ambassador NACEUR BOUCHERIT.

Yemen: POB 509, 67 Amman St, San'a; tel. (1) 209689; fax (1) 209688; Ambassador Ben Saad bin al-Abed.

DIPLOMATIC MISSIONS OF ANDORRA

United Nations: 2 United Nations Plaza, 25th Floor, New York, NY 10017; tel. (212) 750-8064; fax (212) 750-6630; e-mail andorra@un.int; Permanent Representative CARLES FONT-ROSSELL.

Austria: Kärntner Ring 2a/13, 1010 Vienna; tel. (1) 961-09-09; fax (1) 961-09-09-50; e-mail office@ambaixada-andorra.at; Ambassador Joan Pujal Laborda.

Belgium: 10 rue de la Montagne, 1000 Brussels; tel. (2) 513-28-06; fax (2) 513-07-41; e-mail ambassade@andorra.be; internet www.andorra.be; Ambassador IMMA TOR FAUS.

France: 51 bis rue de Boulainvilliers, 75016 Paris; tel. 1-40-06-03-30; fax 1-40-06-03-64; e-mail ambaixada@andorra.ad; internet www.amb-andorre.fr; Ambassador Vicenç Mateu Zamora.

Portugal: Rua do Possolo 76, 2350-251 Lisbon; tel. (21) 3913740; fax (21) 3913749; Ambassador ANTONI CALVÓ ARMENGOL.

Spain: Alcalá 73, 28009 Madrid; tel. (91) 4317453; fax (91) 5776341; e-mail embajada@embajadaandorra.es; Ambassador Xavier Espot Miró.

United Kingdom: 63 Westover Rd, London, SW18 2RF; tel. (20) 8874-4806; fax (20) 8874-4902; Ambassador MARIA ROSA PICART DE FRANCIS.

United States of America: 2 United Nations Plaza, 25th Floor, New York, NY 10017; tel. (212) 750-8064; fax (212) 750-6630; Ambassador Carles Font-Rossell.

DIPLOMATIC MISSIONS OF ANGOLA

United Nations: 125 East 73rd St, New York, NY 10021; tel. (212) 861-5656; fax (212) 861-9295; e-mail ang-un@angolamissionun.org; internet www.angolamissionun.org; Permanent Representative ISMAEL ABRAÃO GASPAR MARTINS.

Algeria: 12 rue Mohamed Khoudi, el-Biar, Algiers; tel. (21) 92-53-37; fax (21) 92-04-18; Ambassador Hermínio Escórcio.

Argentina: La Pampa 3452–56, C1430BXD Buenos Aires; tel. (11) 4554-8383; fax (11) 4554-8998; Ambassador FERNANDO DITO.

Austria: Seilerstätte 15/10–11, 1010 Vienna; tel. (1) 718-74-88; fax (1) 718-74-86; e-mail embangola.viena@embangola.at; internet www.embangola.at; Ambassador Dr Fidelino Loy de Jesus Figueiredo.

Belgium: 182 rue Franz Merjay, 1050 Brussels; tel. (2) 346-18-72; fax (2) 344-08-94; e-mail angola.embassy.belgium@skynet.be; Ambassador TOKO DIAKENGA SERÃO.

Botswana: 2715 Phala Cres., Private Bag BR 111, Gaborone; tel. 3900204; fax 3975089; e-mail angolaemb@info.bw; Ambassador José Agostinho Neto.

Brazil: SHIS, QL 06, Conj. 5, Casa 01, 71620-055 Brasília, DF; tel. (61) 3248-4489; fax (61) 3248-1567; e-mail emb.angola@tecnolink.com.br; internet www.angola.org.br; Ambassador LEOVIGILDO DA COSTA E SILVA.

Canada: 189 Laurier Ave East, Ottawa, ON K1N 6P1; tel. (613) 234-1152; fax (613) 234-1179; e-mail info@embangola-can.org; internet www.embangola-can.org; Ambassador Miguel Maria N'Zau Puna.

Cape Verde: Av. OUA, Achada de Santo António, CP 78A Praia, Santiago; tel. 2623235; fax 2623234; e-mail emb.angola@cv.telecom.cv; Ambassador JOSÉ AUGUSTO CÉSAR 'KILUANGE'.

China, People's Republic: 1-8-1 Tayuan Diplomatic Office Bldg, Beijing 100600; tel. (10) 65326968; fax (10) 65326992; internet www.angolaembassychina.com; Ambassador João Manuel Bernardo.

Congo, Democratic Republic: 4413–4429 blvd du 30 juin, BP 8625, Kinshasa; tel. (12) 32415; fax (12) 98971; e-mail consangolakatanga@voila.fr; Ambassador MAWETE JOÃO BAPTISTA.

Congo, Republic: BP 388, Brazzaville; tel. 81-47-21; fax 81-52-87; e-mail miranotom@yahoo.fr; Ambassador Dr Pedro Fernando Mavunza.

Côte d'Ivoire: Lot 2461, rue des Jardins, Cocody-les-Deux-Plateaux, 01 BP 1734, Abidjan 01; tel. 22-41-38-79; fax 22-41-28-89; Ambassador GILBERTO BUTA LUTUKUTA.

Cuba: Avda 5, No 1012, entre 10 y 12, Miramar, Havana; tel. (7) 204-2474; fax (7) 204-0487; e-mail embangol@ceniai.inf.cu; Ambassador Antonio J. Condesse D. Carvahlo.

Egypt: 12 Midan Fouad Mohi ed-Din, Mohandessin, Cairo; tel. (2) 3377602; fax (2) 708683; Ambassador PEDRO HENDRICK VAAL NETO.

Equatorial Guinea: Malabo; Ambassador Emilio José do Carvalho.

Ethiopia: Woreda 18, Kebele 26, House No. 6, POB 2962, Addis Ababa; tel. (11) 5510085; fax (11) 5514922; Ambassador MANUEL DOMINGOS AUGUSTO.

France: 19 ave Foch, 75116 Paris; tel. 1-45-01-58-20; fax 1-45-00-33-71; e-mail barreira.ramiromanuel_@libertysurf.fr; Ambassador Victor Manuel Rita da Fonseca Lima.

Gabon: BP 4884, Libreville; tel. 73-04-26; fax 73-78-24; Ambassador EMILIO JOSÉ DE CARVALHO GUERRA.

Germany: Wallstr. 58, 10179 Berlin; tel. (30) 2408970; fax (30) 24089712; e-mail botschaft@botschaftangola.de; internet www.botschaftangola.de; Ambassador Alberto do Carmo Bento Ribeiro.

Ghana: Accra; Ambassador EARISTO D. KIMBA.

India: 5/50f, Nyaya Marg, Chanakyapuri, New Delhi 110 021; tel. (11) 26882680; fax (11) 24673785; e-mail xietuang@del2.vsnl.net.in; internet www.angolaembassyindia.com; Ambassador Antonio Fwaminy Dacosta Fernandes.

Israel: 8 Shaul Hamelech Blvd, Tel-Aviv 64733; tel. 3-6912093; fax 3-6912094; e-mail embangi@zahav.net.il; Ambassador JOSÉ JOÃO MANUEL.

Italy: Via Druso 39, 00184 Roma; tel. (06) 7726951; fax (06) 77590009; e-mail ambasciata@ambasciatangola.it; internet www.ambasciatangola.com; Ambassador Manuel Pedro Pacavira.

Japan: 2-10-24, Daizawa, Setagaya-ku, Tokyo 155-0032; tel. (3) 5430-7879; fax (3) 5712-7481; e-mail embassy@angola.or.jp; internet www.angola.or.jp; Ambassador ALBINO MALUNGO.

Mexico: Gaspar de Zúñiga 226, Col. Lomas de Chapultepec, Sección Virreyes, Del. Miguel Hidalgo, 11000 México, DF; tel. (55) 5202-4421; fax (55) 5540-5928; e-mail info@embangolamex.org; Ambassador José Jaime Furtado Gonçalvez.

Morocco: km 5, 53 Ahmed Rifaï, BP 1318, Souissi, Rabat; tel. (3) 7659239; fax (3) 7653707; e-mail amb.angola@iam.net.ma; Ambassador DR LUIS JOSÉ DE ALMEIDA.

Mozambique: Av. Kenneth Kaunda 783, CP 2954, Maputo; tel. 21493139; fax 21493930; Ambassador João Garcia Bires.

Namibia: Angola House, 3 Dr Agostinho Neto St, Ausspannplatz, PMB 12020, Windhoek; tel. (61) 227535; fax (61) 221498; Ambassador MANUEL A. D. RODRIGUEZ.

Nigeria: 5 Kasumu Ekomode St, Victoria Island, POB 50437, Falomo Ikoyi, Lagos; tel. (9) 4135121; fax (9) 4134082; Ambassador Evaristo Domingos Kimba.

Poland: 02-635 Warsaw, ul. Balonowa 20; tel. (22) 6463529; fax (22) 8447452; e-mail embaixada@emb-angola.pl; Ambassador LIZETH NAWANGA SATUMBO PENA.

Portugal: Av. da República 68, 1069-213 Lisbon; tel. (21) 7961830; fax (21) 7971238; e-mail embaixadadeangola@mail.telepac.pt; internet www.embaixadadeangola.org; Ambassador Assunção Afonso Sousa dos Anjos.

Russian Federation: 119590 Moscow, ul. U. Palme 6; tel. (495) 939-95-18; fax (495) 956-18-80; e-mail angomosc@col.ru; Ambassador SAMUEL TITO ARMANDO.

São Tomé and Príncipe: Av. Kwame Nkrumah 45, CP 133, São Tomé; tel. 222400; fax 221362; e-mail embrang@cstome.net; Ambassador Pedro Fernando Mavunza.

Serbia: 11000 Belgrade, Vase Pelagića 32; tel. (11) 3690241; fax (11) 3690191; Ambassador ANTÓNIO MANUEL BENJAMIN.

Singapore: 9 Temasek Blvd, 44-03 Suntec Tower Two, Singapore 038989; tel. 63419360; fax 63419367; e-mail embangola@pacific.net.sg; Ambassador Flávio Saraiva de Carvalho Fonseca.

Slovakia: Mudroňova 47, 811 03 Bratislava 1; tel. (2) 5441-2164; fax (2) 5441-2182; e-mail embangola1@embangola.sk; Ambassador ALBERTO CORREIA NETO.

South Africa: 1030 Schoeman St, Hatfield, Pretoria 0083; POB 8685, Pretoria 0001; tel. (12) 3420049; fax (12) 3427039; Ambassador Miguel Gaspar Fernandes Neto.

Spain: Serrano 64, 3°, 28001 Madrid; tel. (91) 4356430; fax (91) 5779010; e-mail gabinete@embajadadeangola.com; internet www.embajadadeangola.com; Ambassador ARMANDO DA CRUZ NETO.

Sweden: Skeppsbron 8, POB 3199, 103 64 Stockholm; tel. (8) 24-28-90; fax (8) 34-31-27; e-mail info@angolaemb.se; internet www.angolaemb.se; Ambassador Domingos Culolo.

Switzerland: Laubegstr. 18, 3006 Bern; tel. 313518585; fax 313518586; e-mail berna@ambassadeangola.ch; internet www.ambassadeangola.ch; Ambassador APOLINARIO JORGE CORREIA.

Tanzania: Plot 78, Lugalo Rd, POB 20793, Dar es Salaam; tel. (22) 2117674; fax (22) 2132349; Ambassador (vacant).

United Kingdom: 22 Dorset St, London, W1U 6QY; tel. (20) 7299-9850; fax (20) 7486-9397; e-mail embassy@angola.org.uk; internet www.angola.org.uk; Ambassador ANA MARIA TELES CARREIRA.

United States of America: 2108 16th St, NW, Washington, DC 20009; tel. (202) 785-1156; fax (202) 822-9049; e-mail angola@angola.org; internet www.angola.org; Ambassador Josefina Perpétua Pitra Diakité.

Vatican City: Palazzo Odeschalchi, Piazza SS. Apostoli 81, 00166 Rome, Italy; tel. (06) 69190650; fax (06) 69788483; Ambassador ARMINDO FERNANDES DO ESPÍRITO SANTO VIEIRA.

Zambia: Plot 108, Great East Rd, Northmead, POB 31595, 10101 Lusaka; tel. (1) 34764; fax (1) 221210; Ambassador Pedro de Morais Neto.

Zimbabwe: 26 Speke Ave, POB 3590, Harare; tel. (4) 770075; fax (4) 770077; Ambassador FILIPE MONIMAMBU.

DIPLOMATIC MISSIONS OF ANTIGUA AND BARBUDA

United Nations: 610 Fifth Ave, Suite 311, New York, NY 10020; tel. (212) 541-4117; fax (212) 757-1607; e-mail antigua@un.int; internet www.un.int/antigua; Permanent Representative John W. Ashe.

France: 43 ave de Friedland, 75008 Paris; tel. 1-53-96-93-96; fax 1-53-75-15-69; e-mail carl.roberts@antigua-barbuda.com; Ambassador DR CARL ROBERTS (resident in London, United Kingdom).

United Kingdom: 2nd Floor, 45 Crawford Pl., London, W1H 4LP; tel. (20) 7258-0070; fax (20) 7258-7486; e-mail enquiries@antigua-barbuda.com; internet www.antigua-barbuda.com; High Commr Dr Carl Roberts.

United States of America: 3216 New Mexico Ave, NW, Washington, DC 20016; tel. (202) 362-5122; fax (202) 362-5225; e-mail embantbar@aol.com; Ambassador DEBORAH MAE LOVELL.

DIPLOMATIC MISSIONS OF ANTIGUA AND BARBUDA, DOMINICA, GRENADA, MONTSERRAT, SAINT CHRISTOPHER AND NEVIS, SAINT LUCIA AND SAINT VINCENT AND THE GRENADINES

Canada: 130 Albert St, Suite 700, Ottawa, ON K1P 5G4; tel. (613) 236-8952; fax (613) 236-3042; e-mail echcc@travel-net.com; High Commissioner Brendon Calvert Browne.

DIPLOMATIC MISSIONS OF ARGENTINA

United Nations: 1 United Nations Plaza, 25th Floor, New York, NY 10017; tel. (212) 688-6300; fax (212) 980-8395; e-mail argentina@un.int; internet www.un.int/argentina; Permanent Representative JORGE ARGÜELLO.

Algeria: 5 chemin Mohamed Drareni, Djenane, El Malik, Hydra, Algiers; tel. (21) 54-86-65; fax (21) 54-86-47; e-mail eargel@mrecic.gov.ar; Ambassador Bibiana Lucía Jones.

Australia: John McEwen House, Level 2, 7 National Circuit Barton, ACT 2600; tel. (2) 6273-9111; fax (2) 6273-0500; e-mail info@argentina.org.au; internet www.argentina.org.au; Ambassador PEDRO VILLAGRA DELGADO.

Austria: Goldschmiedgasse 2/1, 1010 Vienna; tel. (1) 533-84-63; fax (1) 533-87-97; e-mail embargviena@embargviena.at; Ambassador Eugenio Maria Curia.

Belgium: 225 ave Louise, 3e étage, 1050 Brussels; tel. (2) 647-78-12; fax (2) 647-93-19; e-mail info@embargentina.be; Ambassador GUILLERMO MARCOS JACOVELLA.

Bolivia: Calle Aspiazú 497, esq. Sánchez Lima, Casilla 64, La Paz; tel. (2) 241-7737; fax (2) 242-2727; e-mail ebolv@mrecic.gov.ar; Ambassador Horacio Antonio Macedo.

Brazil: SHIS, QL 02, Conj. 01, Casa 19, Lago Sul, 70442-900 Brasília, DF; tel. (61) 3364-7600; fax (61) 3364-7666; e-mail ebras@mrecic.gov.br; internet www.brasil.embajada-argentina.gov.ar; Ambassador JUAN PABLO LOHLÉ.

Bulgaria: 1000 Sofia, ul. D. Tsankov 36, POB 635; tel. (2) 971-25-39; e-mail arebulg@mbox.contact.bg; Ambassador Gerónimo Cortés Funes.

Canada: 81 Metcalfe St, 7th Floor, Ottawa ON K1P 6K7; tel. (613) 236-2351; fax (613) 235-2659; e-mail embargentina@argentina-canada.net; internet www.argentina-canada.net; Ambassador ARTURO G. BOTHAMLEY.

Chile: Miraflores 285, Santiago; tel. (2) 582-2500; fax (2) 639-3321; e-mail embajador@embargentina.cl; internet www.embargentina.cl; Ambassador Carlos Enrique Abihaggle.

China, People's Republic: Bldg 11, 5 Dong Wu Jie, San Li Tun, Beijing 100600; tel. (10) 65322090; fax (10) 65322319; e-mail echin@public.bta.net.cn; Chargé d'affaires a.i. MARÍA ISABEL RENDÓN.

Colombia: Avda 40a, No 13-09, 16°, Apdo Aéreo 53013, Bogotá, DC; tel. (1) 288-0900; fax (1) 288-8868; e-mail embargentina@etb.net.co; Ambassador Martín Antonio Balza.

Costa Rica: Curridabat, Apdo 1963, 1000 San José; tel. 234-6520; fax 283-9983; e-mail embarg@racsa.co.cr; Ambassador JUAN JOSÉ ARCURI.

Cuba: Calle 36, No 511, entre 5 y 7, Miramar, Havana; tel. (7) 204-2565; fax (7) 204-2140; e-mail ecuba@enet.cu; Chargé d'affaires a.i. Pedro von Eyken.

Czech Republic: Panská 6, 110 00 Prague 1; tel. 224212448; fax 222241246; e-mail embar@iol.cz; Ambassador JUAN EDUARDO FLEMING.

Denmark: Borgergade 16, 4th Floor, 1300 Copenhagen K; tel. 33-15-80-82; fax 33-15-55-74; e-mail edina@mrecic.gov.ar; Ambassador Juan Carlos Kreckler.

Dominican Republic: Avda Máximo Gómez 10, Apdo 1302, Santo Domingo, DN; tel. 682-2977; fax 221-2206; e-mail edomi@mreic.gov.ar; Ambassador JORGE J. A. ROBALLO.

Ecuador: Avda Amazonas 477 y Roca, 8°, Quito; tel. (2) 256-2292; fax (2) 256-8177; e-mail embarge2@uio.satnet.net; Ambassador Carlos Piñeiro Iñiguez.

Egypt: 1st Floor, 8 Es-Saleh Ayoub St, Cairo (Zamalek); tel. (2) 27351501; fax (2) 27364355; e-mail argemb@idsc.gov.eg; Ambassador LUIS ENRIQUE CAPPAGLI.

El Salvador: Calle La Sierra 3-I-B, Col. Escalón, San Salvador; tel. 2263-3638; fax 2263-3687; e-mail esalv@mrecic.gov.ar; Ambassador Rubén Néstor Patto.

Finland: Bulevardi 5A 11, 00120 Helsinki; tel. (9) 42428700; fax (9) 42428701; e-mail embassy@embargentina.fi; internet www.embargentina.fi; Ambassador LILA SUBIRÁN DE VIANA.

France: 6 rue Cimarosa, 75116 Paris; tel. 1-44-05-27-00; fax 1-45-53-46-33; e-mail efranpol@noos.fr; internet www.ambassadeargentine.net; Ambassador Eric Calcagno y Maillmann.

Germany: Kleiststr. 23–26, 10787 Berlin; tel. (30) 2266890; fax (30) 2291400; e-mail info@argentinische-botschaft.de; internet www.argentinische-botschaft.de; Chargé d'affaires a.i. MAGDALENA DOLORES SUSANA VON BECKH WIDMANSTETTER.

Greece: Leoforos Vassilissis Sofias 59, 115 21 Athens; tel. (210) 7224753; fax (210) 7227568; e-mail egrecmrs@compulink.gr; Ambassador Jorge Alejandro Mastropietro.

Guatemala: Edif. Europlaza 1703, 5 Avda 5-55, Zona 14, Apdo 120, Guatemala City; tel. 2385-3786; e-mail embajadadeargentina@hotmail.com; Ambassador ANÍBAL GABRIEL GUTIÉRREZ.

Haiti: 50 rue Lamarre, Pétionville, BP 1755, Port-au-Prince; tel. 256-6414; e-mail embarghaiti@hainet.net; Ambassador Ernesto López.

Honduras: Calle Palermo 302, Col. Rubén Darío, Apdo 3208, Tegucigalpa; tel. 232-3376; fax 231-0376; e-mail ehond@mrecic.gov.ar; Chargé d'affaires a.i. ALEJANDRO JOSÉ AMURA.

Hungary: 1023 Budapest, Vérhalom u. 12–16, II, 3a; tel. (1) 325-0492; fax (1) 326-0494; Ambassador Domingo Santiago Cullen.

India: A-2/6, Vasant Vihar, New Delhi 110 057; tel. (11) 41661982; fax (11) 41661988; Ambassador ERNESTO CARLOS ALVAREZ.

Indonesia: Menara Thamrin, Suite 1602, 16th Floor, Jalan M. H. Thamrin, Kav. 3, Jakarta; tel. (21) 2303061; fax (21) 2303962; e-mail embargen@cbn.net.id; Ambassador Javier A. Sanz de Urquiza.

Iran: POB 15875-4335, 11 Ghoo Alley, Yar Moh., Darrous, Tehran; tel. (21) 22577433; fax (21) 22577432; e-mail eiran@mrecic.gov.ar; Chargé d'affaires MARIO QUINTEROS.

Ireland: 15 Ailesbury Dr., Dublin 4; tel. (1) 2691546; fax (1) 2600404; e-mail embassyofargentina@eircom.net; Chargé d'affaires a.i. Ana C. Pisano.

Israel: Apt 3, Medinat Hayeudim 85, Herzliya Business Park, Herzliya Pitauch 46120; tel. 9-9702740; fax 9-9702747; e-mail embarg@netvision.net .il; Ambassador ATILIO NORBERTO MOLTENI.

Italy: Piazza dell'Esquilino 2, 2°, 00185 Roma; tel. (06) 48073300; fax (06) 4819787; e-mail ambasciata.argentina@ambargentina.mysam.it; Ambassador Victorio María José Taccetti.

Jamaica: Dyoll Life Bldg, 6th Floor, 40 Knutsford Blvd, Kingston 5; tel. 926-5588; fax 926-0580; e-mail embargen@cwjamaica.com; Ambassador MARIO JOSÉ PINO.

Japan: 2-14-14, Moto Azabu, Minato-ku, Tokyo 106-0046; tel. (3) 5420-7101; fax (3) 5420-7173; e-mail ejapo@mb.rosenet.ne.jp; internet www .embargentina.or.jp; Ambassador Daniel Adán Dziewezo Polski.

Kenya: Posta Sacco, 6th Floor, University Way, POB 30283, 00100 Nairobi; tel. (20) 339949; fax (20) 217693; e-mail argentina@form-net.com; Ambassador DANIEL CHUBURU.

Korea, Republic: Chun Woo Bldg, 5th Floor, 534 Itaewon-dong, Yeongsan-gu, Seoul 140-861; tel. (2) 793-4062; fax (2) 792-5820; e-mail info@argentina .or.kr; internet www.argentina.or.kr; Ambassador Alfredo A. Alcorta.

Kuwait: POB 3788, 40188 Mishref, Kuwait City; tel. 5379211; fax 5379212; e-mail ekuwa@mrecic.gov.ar; Ambassador RICARDO E. INSUA.

Lebanon: 2nd Floor, Residence des Jardins, Immeuble Moutran, 161 rue Sursock, Achrafieh, Beirut; tel. (1) 210800; fax (1) 210802; e-mail elbno@ mrecic.gov.ar; Chargé d'affaires a.i. Guillermo Luis Nicolás.

Libya: POB 932, Gargaresh, Madina Syahia, Tripoli; tel. (21) 4834956; fax (21) 4840928; e-mail embartrip@hotmail.com; Ambassador JUAN CARLOS VALLE RALEIGH.

Malaysia: Suite 16-03, 16th Floor, Menara Keck Seng, 203 Jalan Bukit Bintang, 55100 Kuala Lumpur; tel. (3) 21441451; fax (3) 21441428; e-mail emsia@pd.jaring.my; Ambassador Alfredo Morelli.

Mexico: Avda Palmas 910, Col. Lomas de Chapultepec, Del. Miguel Hidalgo, 11000 México, DF; tel. (55) 5520-9430; fax (55) 5540-5011; e-mail embajadaargentina@prodigy.net.mx; Ambassador JORGE RAÚL YOMA.

Morocco: 4 ave Mehdi Ben Barka, Souissi, 10000 Rabat; tel. (3) 7755120; fax (3) 7755410; e-mail emarr@mrecic.gov.ar; Ambassador Alberto de Núñez.

Netherlands: Javastraat 20, 2585 AN The Hague; tel. (70) 3118411; fax (70) 3118410; e-mail argentina@xs4all.nl; internet www.embassyargentina.nl; Ambassador SANTOS GOÑI MARENCO.

New Zealand: Sovereign Assurance House, 14th Floor, 142 Lambton Quay, POB 5430, Lambton Quay, Wellington; tel. (4) 472-8330; fax (4) 472-8331; e-mail enzel@arg.org.nz; internet www.arg.org.nz; Ambassador Pedro R. Herrera.

Nicaragua: Semáforos de Villa Fontana, 2 c. abajo, 1 al sur, 1 abajo, 75 varas oeste, Casa 133, Apdo 703, Managua; tel. 283-7066; fax 270-2343; e-mail embargentina@cablenet.com.ni; Chargé d'affaires a.i. NICOLÁS SERGIO REBOK.

Nigeria: 2 Abubakar Koko Cres., Asokoro District, Abuja; tel. (9) 3148680; fax (9) 3148683; e-mail enige@mrecic.gov.ar; Chargé d'affaires a.i. Ricardo Jorge Monticelli.

Norway: Drammensvn 39, 0244 Oslo; tel. 22-55-24-49; fax 22-44-16-41; e-mail enoru@online.no; internet argentour.com/embajada; Ambassador JUAN MANUEL ORTIZ DE ROSAS.

Pakistan: 20, Hill Rd, Shalimar F-6/3, POB 1015, Islamabad; tel. (51) 2821242; fax (51) 2825564; e-mail epaki@mrecic.gov.ar; Ambassador Rodolfo Martin Saravia.

Panama: Edif. del Banco de Iberoamérica, 7°, Avda 50 y Calle 53, Apdo 1271, Panamá 1; tel. 264-6561; fax 269-5331; e-mail embargen@c-com.net.pa; Ambassador JORGE ALBERTO ARGUINDEGUI.

Paraguay: Avda España, esq. Avda Perú, Casilla 757, Asunción; tel. (21) 21-2320; fax (21) 21-1029; e-mail embarpy@supernet.com.py; internet www .embajada-argentina.org.py; Ambassador Rafael Edgardo Romá.

Peru: Arequipa 121, Lima 1; tel. (1) 4339966; fax (1) 4330769; e-mail embajada@terra.com.pe; Chargé d'affaires a.i. HÉCTOR ISAAC NIKI.

Philippines: 8th Floor, Liberty Center, 104 H. V. de la Costa St, Salcedo Village, Makati City, 1227 Metro Manila; tel. (2) 8453218; fax (2) 8453220; e-mail embarfil@eastern.com.ph; Ambassador Ismael Mario Schuff.

Poland: 03-973 Warsaw, ul. Brukselska 9; tel. (22) 6176028; fax (22) 6177162; e-mail epolo@home.pl; Ambassador CARLOS ALBERTO PASSALACQUA.

Portugal: Av. João Crisóstomo 8, r/c esq., 1000-178 Lisbon; tel. (21) 7977311; fax (21) 7959225; e-mail eport@mrecic.gov.ar; Ambassador Jorge Marcelo Faurie.

Romania: 010031 Bucharest, Union Internacional Centre, Str. Ion Campineanu 11, 3rd Floor, Rm 101; tel. (21) 3122626; fax (21) 3120116; e-mail eruma@mrecic.gov.ar; Chargé d'affaires a.i. MIGUEL ANGEL SUAREZ.

Russian Federation: 119017 Moscow, ul. B. Ordynka 72; tel. (495) 502-10-20; fax (495) 502-10-21; e-mail efrus@co.ru; Ambassador Leopoldo Bravo.

Saudi Arabia: POB 94369, Riyadh 11693; tel. (1) 465-2600; fax (1) 465-3057; e-mail earab@nesma.net.sa; Ambassador ENRIQUE ANTONIO PAREJA.

Serbia: 11000 Belgrade, Kneza Mihajlova 24/I; tel. (11) 2623569; fax (11) 2622630; e-mail embaryu@eunet.yu; Ambassador Mario Eduardo Bossi de Ezcurra.

South Africa: 200 Standard Plaza, 440 Hilda St, Hatfield, Pretoria 0083; POB 11125, Pretoria 0028; tel. (12) 4303524; fax (12) 4303521; e-mail argembas@ global.co.za; Ambassador CARLOS SERSALE DI CERISANO.

Spain: Pedro de Valdivia 21, 28006 Madrid; tel. (91) 7710519; fax (91) 7710526; e-mail embajada@portalargentino.net; internet www .portalargentino.net; Ambassador Carlos Antonio Bettini.

Sweden: POB 14039, 104 40 Stockholm; Narvavägen 32, 3rd Floor, Apartment 3, 115 22 Stockholm; tel. (8) 663-19-65; fax (8) 661-00-09; e-mail cancilleria@argemb.se; Ambassador HERNÁN MASSINI EZCURRA.

Switzerland: Jungfraustr. 1, 3005 Bern; tel. 313564343; fax 313564340; e-mail esuiz@mrecic.gov.ar; internet www.embargentina-suiza.org; Chargé d'affaires a.i. Fernando Raúl Lerena.

Syria: BP 116, Damascus; tel. (11) 3334167; fax (11) 3327326; e-mail easir@ net.sy; Ambassador HERNÁN ROBERTO PLORUTTI.

Thailand: 16th Floor, Suite 1601, Glas Haus Bldg, 1 Soi Sukhumvit 25, Klongtoey, Bangkok 10110; tel. (2) 259-0401; fax (2) 259-0402; e-mail embtail@mozart.inet.co.th; Ambassador Felipe Frydman.

Trinidad and Tobago: TATIL Bldg, 4th Floor, 11 Maraval Rd, POB 162; Port of Spain; tel. 628-7557; fax 628-7544; e-mail etrin@mrecic.gov.ar; internet www.trinidadytobago.embajada-argentina.gov.ar; Ambassador JOSÉ LUIS VIGNOLO.

Tunisia: 10 rue al-Hassan et Houssaine, BP 9, al-Menzah IV, 1002 Tunis; tel. (71) 231-222; fax (71) 750-058; e-mail etune@emb_argentina.intl.tn; Ambassador Jesús Fernando Taboada.

Turkey: Uğar Mumcu Cad. 60/3, 06700 Gaziosmanpaşa, Ankara; tel. (312) 4462062; fax (312) 4462063; e-mail embargturquia@yahoo.com.ar; Ambassador SEBASTIÁN BRUGO MARCÓ.

Ukraine: 01901 Kyiv, vul. Ivana Franka 36, POB 217; tel. (44) 490-25-16; fax (44) 238-69-22; e-mail eucra@mrecic.gov.ar; Ambassador Olga Lila Roldán Vázquez.

United Arab Emirates: POB 3325, Abu Dhabi; tel. (2) 4436838; fax (2) 4431392; e-mail embar@emirates.net.ae; Ambassador RUBÉN EDUARDO CARO.

United Kingdom: 65 Brook St, London, W1K 4AH; tel. (20) 7318-1300; fax (20) 7318-1301; e-mail info@argentine-embassy-uk.org; internet www .argentine-embassy-uk.org; Ambassador Federico Mirré.

United States of America: 1600 New Hampshire Ave, NW, Washington, DC 20009; tel. (202) 238-6401; fax (202) 332-3171; internet www .embassyofargentina.us; Ambassador HÉCTOR MARCOS TIMERMAN.

Uruguay: Cuareim 1470, 11800 Montevideo; tel. (2) 9028166; fax (2) 9028172; e-mail emargrou@adinet.com.uy; internet emb-uruguay.mrecic.gov.ar; Ambassador Hernán María Patiño Mayer.

Vatican City: Via del Banco di Santo Spirito 42, 00186 Rome, Italy; tel. (06) 68801701; fax (06) 6879021; e-mail emba.argentina@flashnet.it; Ambassador CARLOS LUIS CUSTER.

Venezuela: Edif. Fedecámaras, 3°, Avda El Empalme, El Bosque, Apdo 569, Caracas; tel. (212) 731-3311; fax (212) 731-2659; e-mail argentina@impsat .net.ve; internet www.venezuela.embajada-argentina.gov.ar; Ambassador Alicia Amalia Castro.

Viet Nam: 8th Floor, Office Tower, Daeha Business Centre, 360 Kim Ma, Ba Dinh District, Hanoi; tel. (4) 8315262; fax (4) 8315577; e-mail embarg@hn .vnn.vn; internet www.embargentina.org.vn; Ambassador TOMÁS FERRARI.

DIPLOMATIC MISSIONS OF ARMENIA

United Nations: 119 East 36th St, New York, NY 10016; tel. (212) 686-9079; fax (212) 686-3934; e-mail armenia@un.int; internet www.un.int/armenia; Permanent Representative Armen Martirosian.

Argentina: José Andrés Pacheco de Melo 1922, C1126AAD Buenos Aires; tel. (11) 4812-2803; fax (11) 4816-8710; e-mail armenia@teletel.com.ar; Ambassador VLADIMIR KARMIRSHALYAN.

Austria: Hadikgasse 28, 1140 Vienna; tel. (1) 522-74-79; fax (1) 522-74-81; e-mail armenia@armembassy.at; Ambassador Dr Ashot Hovakimian.

Belarus: 220050 Minsk, vul. Kirava 17; tel. (17) 227-51-53; e-mail armrep@cis.minsk.by; Ambassador OLEG YESAIAN.

Belgium: 28 rue Montoyer, 1000 Brussels; tel. (2) 348-44-00; fax (2) 348-44-01; e-mail armembel@sknet.be; internet www.armembassy.be; Ambassador Viguen Tchitetchian.

Bulgaria: 1606 Sofia, ul. 20-ti April 11; tel. (2) 952-60-46; e-mail armembsof@omega.bg; Ambassador SERGEI MANASERIAN.

Canada: 7 Delaware Ave, Ottawa, ON K2P 0Z2; tel. (613) 234-3710; fax (613) 234-3444; e-mail embottawa@rogers.com; internet www.armembassycanada.ca; Chargé d'affaires a.i. Arman Akopian.

China, People's Republic: 9-2-62 Tayuan Diplomatic Compound, Beijing 100600; tel. (10) 65325677; fax (10) 65325654; e-mail armemb@public3.bta.net.cn; Ambassador MOVSISIAN VAHAGN.

Egypt: 20 Sharia Muhammad Mazhar, Cairo (Zamalek); tel. (2) 7374157; fax (2) 7374158; e-mail hovakimyan_liana@yahoo.com; internet www.armembegypt.com; Ambassador Dr Rouben Karapetian.

France: 9 rue Viète, 75017 Paris; tel. 1-42-12-98-00; fax 1-42-12-98-03; e-mail ambarmen@wanadoo.fr; Ambassador EDVARD NALBANDIAN.

Georgia: 0102 Tbilisi, Tetelashvili 4; tel. (32) 95-17-23; fax (32) 96-42-87; e-mail armemb@caucasus.net; Ambassador Hrach Silvanian.

Germany: Nussbaumallee 4, 14050 Berlin; tel. (30) 4050910; fax (30) 40509125; e-mail armgermanyembassy@mfa.am; Ambassador KARINE KAZINIAN.

Greece: Leoforos Sygrou 159, 171 21 Athens; tel. (210) 9345727; fax (210) 9352187; Ambassador Vahran Kazgoian.

India: E-1/20, Vasant Vihar, New Delhi 110 057; tel. (11) 24112851; fax (11) 24112853; e-mail armemb@vsnl.com; Ambassador ASHOT KOCHARYAN.

Iran: 1 Ostad Shahriar St, Razi St, Jomhouri Islami Ave, Tehran 11337; tel. (21) 66704833; fax (21) 66700657; e-mail emarteh@yahoo.com; Ambassador Karen Nazarian.

Italy: Via dei Colli della Farnesina 174, 00194 Roma; tel. (06) 3296638; fax (06) 3297763; e-mail ambarmit@tin.it; Ambassador ROUBEN SHUGARIAN.

Kazakhstan: 050025 Almaty, Seyfulin 57/9; tel. (727) 291-71-26; e-mail armeniaemb_kz@hotmail.com; Ambassador Levon Khachatrian.

Lebanon: POB 70607, rue Jasmin, Rabieh, Mtaileb, Beirut; tel. (4) 402952; fax (4) 418860; e-mail armenia@dm.net.lb; Ambassador VAHAN TER-GHEVONDYAN.

Poland: 02-908 Warsaw, ul. Woziwody 15; tel. (22) 8408130; fax (22) 6420643; e-mail main@embarmenia.it.pl; Ambassador Ashot Galoyan.

Romania: Bucharest, Str. Intr. Poiana 27, Sector 1; tel. (21) 3197604; fax (21) 3197603; e-mail armembro@starnets.ro; Ambassador YEGISHE SARKISSIAN.

Russian Federation: 101990 Moscow, Armyanskii per. 2; tel. (495) 924-32-43; fax (495) 924-45-35; e-mail armrep@armen.ru; internet www.armenianembassy.ru; Ambassador Armen B. Smbatian.

Switzerland: 28 ave du Mail, 1205 Geneva; tel. 223201100; fax 223206148; e-mail arm.mission@deckpoint.ch; Ambassador ZOHRAB MNATSAKANIAN.

Syria: BP 33241, Ibrahim Hanono St, Malki, Damascus; tel. (11) 6133560; fax (11) 6130952; e-mail am309@net.sy; Ambassador Archad Boladian.

Turkmenistan: 744000 Aşgabat, Gerogly 14; tel. (12) 35-44-18; fax (12) 39-55-38; e-mail eat@online.tm; Ambassador (vacant).

Ukraine: 01901 Kyiv, vul. Volodymyrska 45; tel. (44) 224-90-05; fax (44) 235-05-00; e-mail despanut@visti.com; Ambassador Armen Khachatrian.

United Kingdom: 25A Cheniston Gdns, London, W8 6TG; tel. (20) 7938-5435; fax (20) 7938-2595; e-mail armemb@armenianembassyuk.com; Ambassador DR VAHE GABRIELYAN.

United States of America: 2225 R St, NW, Washington, DC 20008; tel. (202) 319-1976; fax (202) 319-2982; e-mail armecon@speakeasy.net; internet www.armeniaemb.org; Ambassador Tatoul Markarian.

DIPLOMATIC MISSIONS OF AUSTRALIA

United Nations: 150 East 42nd St, 33rd Floor, New York, NY 10017; tel. (212) 351-6600; fax (212) 351-6610; e-mail australia@un.int; internet www.unny.mission.gov.au; Permanent Representative ROBERT HILL.

Afghanistan: c/o Serena Hotel, Froshgah St, Kabul; tel. (79) 9654840; Ambassador Martin Quinn.

Argentina: Villanueva 1400, C1426BMJ Buenos Aires; tel. (11) 4779-3500; fax (11) 4779-3581; e-mail info.ba.general@dfat.gov.au; internet www.argentina.embassy.gov.au; Ambassador PETER HUSSIN.

Austria: Mattiellistr. 2, 1040 Vienna; tel. (1) 506-74-0; fax (1) 504-11-78; e-mail austemb@aon.at; internet www.australian-embassy.at; Ambassador Peter James Shannon.

Bangladesh: 184 Gulshan Ave, Gulshan 2, Dhaka 1212; tel. (2) 8813101; fax (2) 8811125; e-mail ahc.dhaka@dfat.gov.au; internet www.bangladesh.embassy.gov.au; High Commissioner DOUGLAS FOSKETT.

Belgium: Centre Guimard, 6–8 rue Guimard, 1040 Brussels; tel. (2) 286-05-00; fax (2) 230-68-02; e-mail austemb.brussels@dfat.gov.au; internet www.belgium.embassy.gov.au; Ambassador Alan William Thomas.

Brazil: SES, Av. Das Nações, Quadra 801, Conj. K, Lote 7, 70200-010 Brasília, DF; tel. (61) 3226-3111; fax (61) 3226-1112; e-mail embaustr@dfat.gov.au; internet www.brazil.embassy.gov.au; Ambassador NEIL ALLAN MULES.

Brunei: Level 6, DAR Takaful IBB Utama, Jalan Pemancha, Bandar Seri Begawan BS 8711; tel. 2229435; fax 2221652; e-mail austhicom.brunei@dfat.gov.au; internet www.bruneidarussalam.embassy.gov.au; High Commissioner Ruth Adler.

Cambodia: Villa 11, R. V. Senei Vinnavaut Oum (rue 254), Sangkat Chaktomouk, Khan Daun Penh, Phnom-Penh; tel. (23) 213470; fax (23) 213413; e-mail australian.embassy.cambodia@dfat.gov.au; internet www.cambodia.embassy.gov.au; Ambassador MARGARET ANNE ADAMSON.

Canada: 50 O'Connor St, Suite 710, Ottawa, ON K1P 6L2; tel. (613) 236-0841; fax (613) 236-4376; internet www.ahc-ottawa.org; High Commissioner William Norman Fisher.

Chile: Isidora Goyenechea 3621, 12° y 13°, Casilla 33, Correo 10 Las Condes, Santiago; tel. (2) 550-3500; fax (2) 331-5960; e-mail consular.santiago@dfat.gov.au; internet www.chile.embassy.gov.au; Ambassador CRISPIN CONROY.

China, People's Republic: 21 Dong Zhi Men Wai Dajie, San Li Tun, Beijing 100600; tel. (10) 51404111; fax (10) 51404450; e-mail pubaff.beijing@dfat.gov.au; internet www.china.embassy.gov.au; Ambassador Geoffrey William Raby.

Croatia: 10000 Zagreb, Nova Ves 11, 3 Kaptol Centar; tel. (1) 4891200; fax (1) 4891216; e-mail australian.embassy@zg.t-com.hr; internet www.auembassy.hr; Ambassador TRACY REID.

Cyprus: 4 Annis Komninis St, 2nd Floor, 1060 Nicosia; tel. 22753001; fax 22766486; e-mail auscomm@logos.cy.net; internet www.cyprus.embassy.gov.au; High Commr Garth Leslie Hunt.

Denmark: Dampfærgevej 26, 2100 Copenhagen Ø; tel. 70-26-36-76; fax 70-26-36-86; e-mail australianembassydenmark@gmail.com; internet www.denmark.embassy.gov.au; Ambassador SHARYN JANE MINAHAN.

Egypt: 11th Floor, World Trade Centre, Corniche en-Nil, Cairo 11111 (Boulac); tel. (2) 5750444; fax (2) 5781638; e-mail cairo.austremb@dfat.gov.au; internet www.egypt.embassy.gov.au; Ambassador Dr Robert Bowker.

Fiji: 37 Princes Rd, POB 214, Suva; tel. 3382211; fax 3382065; e-mail public-affairs-suva@dfat.gov.au; internet www.fiji.embassy.gov.au; High Commissioner JAMES BATLY.

France: 4 rue Jean Rey, 75724 Paris Cedex 15; tel. 1-40-59-33-00; fax 1-40-59-33-10; e-mail info.paris@dfat.gov.au; internet www.france.embassy.gov.au; Ambassador David A. Ritchie.

Germany: Wallstr. 76–79, 10179 Berlin; tel. (30) 8800880; fax (30) 880088210; e-mail info.berlin@dfat.gov.au; internet www.germany.embassy.gov.au; Ambassador IAN FERGUSON KEMISH.

Greece: Thon Bldg, Odos Kifisias & Odos Alexandras, Ambelokipi, POB 14070, 115 10 Athens; tel. (210) 8704000; fax (210) 8704111; e-mail ae.athens@dfat.gov.au; internet www.ausemb.gr; Ambassador Paul Tighe.

Hungary: 1126 Budapest, Királyhágó tér 8–9; tel. (1) 457-9777; fax (1) 201-9792; e-mail ausembbp@mail.datanet.hu; internet www.ausembbp.hu; Ambassador ALEX BROOKING.

India: 1/50-g Shanti Path, Chanakyapuri, New Delhi 110 021; tel. (11) 41399900; fax (11) 41494490; e-mail austhighcom.newdelhi@dfat.gov.au; internet www.ausgovindia.com; High Commissioner John McCarthy.

Indonesia: Jalan H. R. Rasuna Said, Kav. C15–16, Kuningan, Jakarta 12940; tel. (21) 25505555; fax (21) 25505467; e-mail public-affairs-jakt@dfat.gov.au; internet www.austembjak.or.id; Ambassador BILL FARMER.

Iran: POB 15875-4334, No. 13, 23rd St, Intifada Ave, Tehran 15138; tel. (21) 88724456; fax (21) 88720484; e-mail dfat-tehran@dfat.gov.au; internet www.iran.embassy.gov.au; Ambassador Greg Moriarty.

Iraq: International Zone, Baghdad; tel. (1) 538-2103; e-mail austemb.baghdad@dfat.gov.au; internet www.iraq.embassy.gov.au; Ambassador MARC INNES-BROWN.

Ireland: Fitzwilton House, 7th Floor, Wilton Terrace, Dublin 2; tel. (1) 6645300; fax (1) 6785185; e-mail austemb.dublin@dfat.gov.au; internet www.ireland.embassy.gov.au; Ambassador Anne Plunkett.

Israel: Europe House, 4th Floor, 37 Shaul Hamelech Blvd, Tel-Aviv 64928; tel. 3-6935000; fax 3-6935002; e-mail info@australianembassy.org.il; internet www.australianembassy.org.il; Ambassador JAMES LARSEN.

Italy: Via A. Bosio 5, 00161 Roma; tel. (06) 852721; fax (06) 85272300; e-mail info-rome@dfat.gov.au; internet www.italy.embassy.gov.au; Ambassador Amanda Vanstone.

Japan: 2-1-14, Mita, Minato-ku, Tokyo 108-8361; tel. (3) 5232-4111; fax (3) 5232-4149; internet www.australia.or.jp; Ambassador ALISTAIR MURRAY McLEAN.

Jordan: POB 35201, Amman 11180; tel. (6) 5807000; fax (6) 5807001; e-mail amman.austremb@dfat.gov.au; internet www.jordan.embassy.gov.au; Ambassador Trevor Peacock.

Kenya: ICIPE House, Riverside Dr., off Chiromo Rd, POB 39341, Nairobi; tel. (20) 445034; fax (20) 444718; internet www.kenya.embassy.gov.au; High Commissioner LISA FILIPETTO.

Kiribati: POB 77, Bairiki, Tarawa; tel. 21184; fax 21904; internet www.kiribati.embassy.gov.au; High Commissioner Anne Quinane.

Korea, Republic: Kyobo Bldg, 11th Floor, 1, 1-ga, Jongno-gu, Seoul 110-714; tel. (2) 2003-0100; fax (2) 722-9264; e-mail seoul-inform@dfat.gov.au; internet www.southkorea.embassy.gov.au; Ambassador PETER ROWE.

Kuwait: Dar al-Awadi Complex (Level 12), Ahmad al-Jaber St, Sharq, Kuwait City; tel. 2322422; fax 2322430; e-mail austemb.kuwait@dfat.go.au; internet www.kuwait.embassy.gov.au; Ambassador Glenn Miles.

Laos: rue Pandit J. Nehru, quartier Phonxay, BP 292, Vientiane; tel. (21) 413600; fax (21) 413601; e-mail austemb.laos@dfat.gov.au; internet www.laos.embassy.gov.au; Ambassador MICHELE FORSTER.

Lebanon: Embassy Complex, Semail Hill, Beirut; tel. (1) 974030; fax (1) 974029; e-mail austemle@dfat.gov.au; internet www.lebanon.embassy.gov.au; Ambassador Lyndall Sachs.

Malaysia: 6 Jalan Yap Kwan Seng, 50450 Kuala Lumpur; tel. (3) 21465555; fax (3) 21415773; e-mail Public-Affairs-KLPR@dfat.gov.au; internet www.australia.org.my; High Commissioner PENNY WILLIAMS.

Malta: Villa Fiorentina, Ta'Xbiex Terrace, Ta'Xbiex XBX 1034; tel. 21338201; fax 21344059; e-mail aushicom@onvol.net; internet www.malta.embassy.gov.au; High Commissioner Jurek Juszczyk.

Mauritius: Rogers House, 2nd Floor, John F. Kennedy St, POB 541, Port Louis; tel. 202-0160; fax 208-8878; e-mail ahc.portlouis@dfat.gov.au; internet www.mauritius.embassy.gov.au; High Commissioner CATHERINE JOHNSTONE.

Mexico: Rubén Darío 55, Col. Polanco, Del. Miguel Hidalgo, 11580 México, DF; tel. (55) 1101-2200; fax (55) 1101-2201; e-mail dima-mexico.city@dfat.gov.au; internet www.mexico.embassy.gov.au; Ambassador Katrina Anne Cooper.

Micronesia, Federated States: POB S, Kolonia, Pohnpei, FM 96941; tel. 320-5448; fax 320-5449; e-mail australia@mail.fm; internet www.australianembassy.fm; Ambassador SUSAN COX.

Myanmar: 88 Strand Rd, Yangon; tel. (1) 251810; fax (1) 246159; internet www.burma.embassy.gov.au; Ambassador Bob Davis.

Nepal: Suraj Niwas, Bansbari, POB 879, Kathmandu; tel. (1) 4371678; fax (1) 4371533; internet www.nepal.embassy.gov.au; Ambassador GRAEME LADE.

Netherlands: Carnegielaan 4, 2517 KH The Hague; tel. (70) 3108200; fax (70) 3107863; e-mail austemb_thehague@dfat.gov.au; internet www.netherlands.embassy.gov.au; Ambassador Lydia Morton.

New Zealand: 72–76 Hobson St, Thorndon, POB 4036, Wellington; tel. (4) 473-6411; fax (4) 498-7135; e-mail nzinbox@dfat.gov.au; internet www.australia.org.nz; High Commissioner JOHN DAUTH.

Nigeria: 5th Floor, Oakland Centre, 48 Aguiyi Ironsi St, Maitama, Abuja; PMB 5152, Abuja; tel. (9) 4135226; fax (9) 4135227; e-mail ahc.abuja@dfat.gov.au; internet www.nigeria.embassy.gov.au; High Commissioner Jeff Hart.

Pakistan: Diplomatic Enclave 1, Constitution Ave and Isphani Rd, G-5/4, POB 1046, Islamabad; tel. (51) 2824345; fax (51) 2820112; e-mail consular.islm@dfat.gov.au; internet www.pakistan.embassy.gov.au; High Commissioner ZORICA McCARTHY.

Papua New Guinea: Godwit Rd, Waigani, NCD; tel. 3259333; fax 3259183; internet www.png.embassy.gov.au; High Commissioner Chris Moraitis.

Philippines: 23rd Floor, Tower II, RCBC Plaza, 6819 Ayala Ave, Makati City, 1200 Metro Manila; tel. (2) 7578100; fax (2) 7578268; e-mail public-affairs-MNLA@dfat.gov.au; internet www.australia.com.ph; Ambassador ROD SMITH (designate).

Poland: 00-513 Warsaw, ul. Nowogrodzka 11, Nautilus Bldg, 3rd Floor; tel. (22) 5213444; fax (22) 6273500; e-mail ambasada.australia@dfat.gov.au; internet www.poland.embassy.gov.au; Ambassador Ian K. Forsyth.

Portugal: Av. da Liberdade 200, 2°, 1250-147 Lisbon; tel. (21) 33101500; fax (21) 3101555; e-mail austemb.lisbon@dfat.gov.au; internet www.portugal.embassy.gov.au; Ambassador LUKE WILLIAMS.

Russian Federation: 109028 Moscow, Podkolokolii per. 10a/2; tel. (495) 956-60-70; fax (495) 956-61-70; e-mail austembmos@dfat.gov.au; internet www.russia.embassy.gov.au; Ambassador Robert Tyson.

Samoa: Beach Rd, POB 704, Apia; tel. 23411; fax 23159; internet www.samoa.embassy.gov.au; High Commissioner MATT ANDERSON.

Saudi Arabia: POB 94400, Riyadh 11693; tel. (1) 488-7788; fax (1) 488-7973; internet www.saudiarabia.embassy.gov.au; Ambassador Kevin Magee.

Serbia: 11000 Belgrade, Čika Ljubina 13; tel. (11) 3303400; fax (11) 3303409; e-mail belgrade.embassy@dfat.gov.au; internet www.serbia.embassy.gov.au; Ambassador CLARE BIRGIN.

Singapore: 25 Napier Rd, Singapore 258507; tel. 68364100; fax 67375481; e-mail public-affairs-sing@dfat.gov.au; internet www.australia.org.sg; High Commissioner Miles Kupa.

Solomon Islands: Hibiscus Ave, POB 589, Honiara; tel. 21561; fax 23691; e-mail austhoniara.enquiries@dfat.gov.au; internet www.solomonislands.embassy.gov.au; High Commissioner PETER HOOTON.

South Africa: 292 Orient St, Arcadia, Pretoria; Private Bag X150, Pretoria 0001; tel. (12) 4236000; fax (12) 3428442; e-mail pretoria.info@dfat.gov.au; internet www.australia.co.za; High Commissioner Philip Green.

Spain: Plaza del Descubridor Diego de Ordás 3, 28003 Madrid; tel. (91) 3536600; fax (91) 3536692; e-mail pilar.sanchez@dfat.gov.au; internet www.spain.embassy.gov.au; Ambassador NOEL CAMPBELL.

Sri Lanka: 21 Gregory's Rd, Colombo 7; tel. (11) 2463200; fax (11) 2686453; e-mail austcom@sltnet.lk; internet www.srilanka.embassy.gov.au; High Commissioner Kathy Klugman.

Sweden: Sergels Torg 12, POB 7003, 103 86 Stockholm; tel. (8) 613-29-00; fax (8) 613-29-82; e-mail reception@austemb.se; internet www.sweden.embassy.gov.au; Ambassador HOWARD CRAIG BROWN.

Thailand: 37 Thanon Sathorn Tai, Bangkok 10120; tel. (2) 344-6300; fax (2) 344-6593; e-mail austembassy.bangkok@dfat.gov.au; internet www.austembassy.or.th; Ambassador Bill Paterson.

Timor-Leste: Av. dos Mártires da Pátria, Dili; tel. 3322111; fax 3322247; e-mail austemb_dili@dfat.gov.au; internet www.easttimor.embassy.gov.au; Ambassador PETER HEYWARD.

Tonga: Salote Rd, Private Bag 35, Nuku'alofa; tel. 23244; fax 23243; e-mail ahctonga@kalianet.to; internet www.tonga.embassy.gov.au; High Commissioner Bruce Hunt.

Turkey: Uğur Mumcu Cad. 88, 7th Floor, 06700 Gaziosmanpaşa, Ankara; tel. (312) 4599500; fax (312) 4464827; e-mail dima-ankara@dfat.gov.au; internet www.turkey.embassy.gov.au; Ambassador PETER LEO DOYLE.

United Arab Emirates: POB 32711, Al-Muhairy Centre, Level 14, Sheikh Zayed I St, Abu Dhabi; tel. (2) 6346100; fax (2) 6393525; e-mail abudhabi.embassy@dfat.gov.au; internet www.uae.embassy.gov.au; Ambassador Jeremy Bruer (also accredited to Qatar).

United Kingdom: Australia House, Strand, London, WC2B 4LA; tel. (20) 7379-4334; fax (20) 7240-5333; internet www.uk.embassy.gov.au; High Commr FRANCES ADAMSON (acting).

United States of America: 1601 Massachusetts Ave, NW, Washington, DC 20036-2273; tel. (202) 797-3000; fax (202) 797-3168; internet www.austemb.org; Ambassador Dennis Richardson.

Vanuatu: Winston Churchill Ave, Port Vila; tel. 22777; fax 23948; e-mail australia_vanuatu@dfat.gov.au; internet www.vanuatu.embassy.gov.au; High Commissioner JOHN PILBEAM.

Vatican City: Via Paola 24/10, 00186 Rome, Italy; tel. (06) 6877688; fax (06) 6896255; e-mail holysee.embassy@dfat.gov.au; internet www.holysee .embassy.gov.au; Ambassador Anne Plunkett (resident in Dublin, Ireland).

Viet Nam: 8 Dao Tan, Ba Dinh District, Hanoi; tel. (4) 8317755; fax (4) 8317711; e-mail austemb@fpt.vn; internet www.vietnam.embassy.gov.au; Ambassador BILL TWEDDELL.

Zimbabwe: 1 Green Close, Borrowdale, Harare, POB 4541, Harare; tel. (4) 852471; fax (4) 870566; e-mail zimbabwe.embassy@dfat.gov.au; internet www.dfat.gov.au/missions/countries/zw.html; Ambassador Jon Courtney.

DIPLOMATIC MISSIONS OF AUSTRIA

United Nations: 823 United Nations Plaza, 8th Floor, New York, NY 10017; tel. (212) 949-1840; fax (212) 953-1302; e-mail austria@un.int; internet www .un.int/austria; Permanent Representative GERHARD PFANZELTER.

Albania: Rruga Frederik Shiroka 3, Tirana; tel. (4) 274855; fax (4) 233140; e-mail tirana-ob@bmaa.gv.al; Ambassador Klaus Derkowitsch.

Algeria: 17 chemin Abd al-Kader Gadouche, 16035 Hydra, Algiers; tel. (21) 69-10-86; fax (21) 69-12-32; e-mail algier-ob@bmeia.gov.at; Ambassador SYLVIA MEIER-KAJBIC.

Argentina: French 3671, C1425AXC Buenos Aires; tel. (11) 4807-9185; fax (11) 4805-4016; e-mail buenos-aires-ob@bmaa.gv.at; internet www.austria .org.ar; Ambassador Dr Gudrun Graf.

Australia: POB 3375, Manuka, ACT 2603; tel. (2) 6295-1533; fax (2) 6239-6751; e-mail canberra-ob@bmeia.gv.at; internet www.austria.org.au; Ambassador DR HANNES PORIAS.

Belgium: 5 place du Champ de Mars, BP 5, 1050 Brussels; tel. (2) 289-07-00; fax (2) 513-66-41; e-mail bruessel-ob@bmeia.gv.at; internet www .aussenministerium.at/bruessel; Ambassador Franz Cede.

Bosnia and Herzegovina: 71000 Sarajevo, Džidžikovac 7; tel. (33) 279400; fax (33) 668339; e-mail sarajewo-ob@bmaa.gv.at; internet www.austrijska -ambasada.ba; Ambassador WERNER ALMHOFER.

Brazil: SES, Av. das Nações, Quadra 811, Lote 40, 70426-900 Brasília, DF; tel. (61) 3443-3111; fax (61) 3443-5233; e-mail brasilia-ob@bmaa.gv.at; Ambassador Werner Brandstetter.

Bulgaria: 1000 Sofia, ul. Shipka 4; tel. (2) 932-90-32; fax (2) 981-05-67; e-mail sofia-ob@bmaa.gov.at; Ambassador DR KARL DIEM.

Canada: 445 Wilbrod St, Ottawa, ON K1N 6M7; tel. (613) 789-1444; fax (613) 789-3431; e-mail ottawa-ob@bmeia.gv.at; internet www.austro.org; Ambassador Otto Ditz.

Chile: Barros Errazuriz 1968, 3°, Santiago; tel. (2) 223-4774; fax (2) 204-9382; e-mail santiago-de-chile-ob@bmaa.gv.at; Ambassador WOLFGANG ANGERHOLZER.

China, People's Republic: 5 Xiu Shui Nan Jie, Jian Guo Men Wai, Beijing 100600; tel. (10) 65322061; fax (10) 65321505; e-mail peking-ob@bmaa.gv.at; internet www.aussenministerium.at/peking; Ambassador Martin Sajdik.

Colombia: Edif. Fiducafe, 4°, Carrera 9, No 73-44, Bogotá, DC; tel. (1) 326-2680; fax (1) 317-7639; e-mail bogota-ob@bmeia.gv.at; internet www .embajadadeaustria.org.co; Ambassador HANS PETER GLANZER.

Croatia: 10000 Zagreb, Jabukovać 39; tel. (1) 4881050; fax (1) 4834461; e-mail agram.ob@bmaa.gv.at; internet www.bmaa.gv.at; Ambassador Helga Konrad.

Cuba: C6617 Avda 5a A, esq. 70, Miramar, Havana; tel. (7) 204-2394; fax (7) 204-1235; e-mail havanna-ob@bmeia.gv.at; Ambassador JOHANNES SKRIWAN.

Cyprus: POB 23961, 34 Demosthenis Severis Ave, 1687 Nicosia; tel. 22410151; fax 22680099; e-mail nicosia-ob@bmeia.gv.at; Ambassador Eva Hager.

Czech Republic: Viktora Huga 10, 151 15 Prague 5; tel. 257090511; fax 257316045; e-mail austrianembassy@vol.cz; internet www.austria.cz; Ambassador MARGOT KLESTIL-LÖFFLER.

Denmark: Sølundsvej 1, 2100 Copenhagen Ø; tel. 39-29-41-41; fax 39-29-20-86; e-mail kopenhagen-ob@bmeia.gv.at; Ambassador Dr Erwin Kubesch.

Egypt: 5th Floor, Riyadh Tower, 5 Sharia Wissa Wassef, cnr of Sharia en-Nil, Cairo 11111 (Giza); tel. (2) 5702975; fax (2) 5702979; e-mail kairo-ob@ bmaa.gv.at; internet www.austriaegypt.org; Ambassador DR KURT SPALLINGER.

Estonia: Vambola 6, Tallinn 10114; tel. 627-8740; fax 631-4365; e-mail tallinn -ob@bmeia.gv.at; Ambassador Dr Angelika Saupe-Berchthold.

Ethiopia: POB 1219, Addis Ababa; tel. (11) 3712144; fax (11) 3712140; e-mail addis-abeba-ob@bmeia.gv.at; internet www.aussenministerium.at/ addisabeba; Ambassador RUDOLF AGSTNER.

Finland: Unioninkatu 22, 00130 Helsinki; tel. (9) 6818600; fax (9) 665084; e-mail helsinki-ob@bmeia.gv.at; Ambassador Dr Lorenz Graf.

France: 6 rue Fabert, 75007 Paris; tel. 1-40-63-30-63; fax 1-45-55-63-65; e-mail paris-ob@bmeia.gv.at; internet www.amb-autriche.fr; Ambassador HUBERT HEISS.

Germany: Stauffenbergstr. 1, 10785 Berlin; tel. (30) 202870; fax (30) 2290569; e-mail berlin-ob@bmeia.gv.at; internet www.oesterreichische-botschaft.de; Ambassador Dr Christian Prosl.

Greece: Leoforos Vassilissis Sofias 4, 106 74 Athens; tel. (210) 7257270; fax (210) 7257292; e-mail athen-ob@bmeia.gv.at; Ambassador DR MICHAEL LINHART.

Hungary: 1068 Budapest, Benczúr u. 16; tel. (1) 479-7010; fax (1) 352-8795; e-mail budapest-ob@bmeia.gv.at; internet www.austrian-embassy.hu; Ambassador Dr Ferdinand Mayrhofer-Grünbühel.

India: EP-13 Chandragupta Marg, Chanakyapuri, New Delhi 110 021; tel. (11) 26889037; fax (11) 26886929; e-mail new-delhi-ob@bmeia.gv.at; internet www.aussenministerium.at/newdelhi; Ambassador DR FERDINAND MAULTASCHL.

Indonesia: Jalan Terusan Denpasar Raya, Kuningan, Jakarta 12950; tel. (21) 2593037; fax (21) 52920651; e-mail jakarta-ob@bmeia.gv.at; internet www .austrian-embassy.or.id; Ambassador Dr Klaus Wölfer.

Iran: 3rd Floor, 78 Argentine Sq., Tehran; tel. (21) 88710753; fax (21) 88710778; e-mail teheran-ob@bmaa.gv.at; Ambassador MICHAEL POSTL.

Iraq: 929/30/38 Hay Babel, Baghdad; tel. (1) 719-9049; fax (1) 718-2427; Chargé d'affaires Gudrun Harrer.

Ireland: 15 Ailesbury Court, 93 Ailesbury Rd, Dublin 4; tel. (1) 2694577; fax (1) 2830860; e-mail dublin-ob@bmeia.gv.at; Ambassador DR WALTER HAGG.

Israel: Beit Crystal, 12 Hahilazon, Ramat-Gan 52522; tel. 3-6120924; fax 3-7510716; e-mail tel-aviv-ob@bmaa.gv.at; internet www.austrian-embassy .org.il; Ambassador Michael Rendi.

Italy: Via G. B. Pergolesi 3, 00198 Roma; tel. (06) 8440141; fax (06) 8543286; e-mail rom-ob@bmaa.gv.at; internet www.austria.it; Ambassador CHRISTIAN BERLAKOVITS.

Japan: 1-1-20, Moto Azabu, Minato-ku, Tokyo 106-0046; tel. (3) 3451-8281; fax (3) 3451-8283; e-mail tokio-ob@bmaa.gv.at; internet www.bmeia.gv.at/ tokio; Ambassador Dr Jutta Stefan-Bastl.

Jordan: POB 830795, Jabal Amman, Amman 11183; tel. (6) 4601101; fax (6) 4612725; e-mail amman-ob@bmeia.gv.at; Ambassador FRANZ HÖRLBERGER.

Kazakhstan: 010000 Astana, Saryarka 6/1310, Arman Business Centre; tel. (727) 299-01-44; fax (727) 299-02-27; e-mail astana-ob@bmeia.gv.at; Ambassador Ursula Faringer.

Kenya: City House, 2nd Floor, Wabera St, POB 30560, 00100 Nairobi; tel. (20) 319076; fax (20) 342290; e-mail nairobi-ob@bmeia.gv.at; internet www .aussenministerium.at/nairobi; Ambassador ROLAND HAUSER.

Korea, Republic: Kyobo Bldg, Rm 1913, 1-1, 1-ga, Jongno, Jongno-gu, Seoul 110-714; tel. (2) 732-9071; fax (2) 732-9486; e-mail seoul-ob@bmeia.gv.at; internet www.bmeia.gv.at/seoul; Ambassador Wilhelm Donko.

Kosovo: 38000 Prishtina, Fan Noli 22, Dragodan I; tel. (38) 249284; fax (38) 249285; e-mail pristina-as@bmeia.gv.at; .

Kuwait: POB 15013, Daiyah, Area 3, Shawki St, House 10, 35451 Kuwait City; tel. 2552532; fax 2563052; e-mail kuwait-ob@bmaa.gv.at; Ambassador Georg Stillfried.

Latvia: Elizabetes iela 21A/11, Rīga 1010; tel. 6721-6125; fax 6721-4401; e-mail riga-ob@bmaa.gv.at; Ambassador HERMINE POPPELLER.

Lebanon: POB 11-3942, 8th Floor, Immeuble Tabaris, 812 ave Charles Malek, Achrafieh, Beirut; tel. (1) 217360; fax (1) 217772; e-mail beirut-ob@ bmeia.gv.at; Chargé d'affaires a.i. Gerhard Lutz.

Libya: POB 3207, Sharia Khalid ibn al-Walid, Garden City, Tripoli; tel. (21) 4443379; fax (21) 4440838; e-mail tripolis-ob@bmaa.gv.at; Ambassador DR THOMAS WUNDERBALDINGER.

Lithuania: Gaono g. 6, Vilnius 01131; tel. (5) 266-0580; fax (5) 279-1363; e-mail wilna-ob@bmaa.gv.at; Ambassador Andrea Wicke.

Luxembourg: 3 rue des Bains, 1212 Luxembourg; tel. 47-11-88; fax 46-39-74; e-mail luxemburg-ob@bmeia.gv.at; internet www.bmeia.gv.at/luxemburg; Ambassador DR CHRISTINE STIX-HACKL.

Macedonia, former Yugoslav Republic: 1000 Skopje, Mile Popjordanov 8; tel. (2) 3083400; fax (2) 3083150; e-mail skopje-ob@bmeia.gv.at; Ambassador Dr Alois Kraut.

Malaysia: Suite 10.01–02, Level 10, Wisma Goldhill 67, Jalan Raja Chulan, 50200 Kuala Lumpur; tel. (3) 20570020; fax (3) 23817168; e-mail kuala-lumpur-ob@bmeia.gv.at; Ambassador DR DONATUS KOECK.

Malta: Whitehall Mansions, 3rd Floor, Ta'Xbiex Seafront, Ta'Xbiex XBX 1034; tel. 23279000; fax 21317430; e-mail valletta-ob@bmaa.gv.at; Ambassador Caroline Gudenus.

Mexico: Sierra Tarahumara 420, Col. Lomas de Chapultepec, Del. Miguel Hidalgo, 11000 México, DF; tel. (55) 5251-1606; fax (55) 5245-0198; e-mail mexiko-ob@bmaa.gv.at; internet www.embajadadeaustria.com.mx; Ambassador DR WERNER DRUML.

Moldova: 2009 Chişinău, Mateevici 23b; tel. (22) 73-93-70; fax (22) 72-14-11; e-mail chisinau@ada.gv.at; .

Montenegro: 81000 Podgorica, Kralja Nikole 104; tel. (81) 601580; fax (81) 624344; e-mail podgorica-ob@bmeia.gv.at; Ambassador FLORIAN RAUNIG.

Morocco: 2 rue Tiddas, BP 135, 10000 Rabat; tel. (3) 7761698; fax (3) 7765425; e-mail rabat-ob@bmeia.gv.at; Ambassador Dr Georg Mautner-Markhof.

Netherlands: Van Alkemadelaan 342, 2597 AS The Hague; tel. (70) 3245470; fax (70) 3282066; e-mail den-haag-ob@bmeia.gv.at; internet www.bmeia.gv.at/denhaag; Ambassador WOLFGANG PAUL.

Nigeria: Plot 9, Usuma St, Maitama, Abuja; tel. (9) 4130772; fax (9) 4612715; e-mail abuja-ob@bmeia.gv.at; Ambassador Dr Peter Christian Fellner.

Norway: Thomas Heftyesgt. 19–21, 0244 Oslo; tel. 22-54-02-00; fax 22-55-43-61; e-mail oslo-ob@bmeia.gv.at; Ambassador DR ANTON KOZUSNIK.

Oman: Moosa Complex Bldg, No. 477, 2nd Floor, Way No. 3109, POB 2070, Ruwi 112; tel. 24793135; fax 24793669; e-mail maskat-ob@bmaa.gv.at; Ambassador Dr Andreas Karabaczek.

Pakistan: 13, St 1, F-6/3, POB 1018, Islamabad 44000; tel. (51) 2209710; fax (51) 2828306; e-mail islamabad-ob@bmeia.gv.at; Ambassador DR MICHAEL STIGELBAUER.

Peru: Avda Central 643, 5°, San Isidro, Lima 27; tel. (1) 4420503; fax (1) 4428851; e-mail lima-ob@bmaa.gv.at; Ambassador Georg Woutsas.

Philippines: Prince Bldg, 4th Floor, 117 Rada St, Legaspi Village, Makati City, 1200 Metro Manila; tel. (2) 8179191; fax (2) 8134238; e-mail manila-ob@bmaa.gv.at; Ambassador HERBERT JÄGER.

Poland: 00-748 Warsaw, ul. Gagarina 34; tel. (22) 8410081; fax (22) 8410085; e-mail warschau-ob@bmaa.gv.at; internet www.ambasadaaustrii.pl; Ambassador Alfred Längle.

Portugal: Av. Infante Santo 43, 4°, 1399-046 Lisbon; tel. (21) 3943900; fax (21) 3958224; e-mail lissabon-ob@bmeia.gv.at; Ambassador EWALD JÄGER.

Romania: 020461 Bucharest, Str. Dumbrava Roşie 7; tel. (21) 2015612; fax (21) 2100885; e-mail bukarest-ob@bmeia.gv.at; Ambassador Martin Eichtinger.

Russian Federation: 119034 Moscow, Starokonyushennyi per. 1; tel. (495) 502-95-12; fax (495) 937-42-69; e-mail moskau-ob@bmeia.gv.at; internet www.aussenministerium.at/moskau; Ambassador DR MARTIN VUKOVICH.

Saudi Arabia: POB 94373, Riyadh 11693; tel. (1) 480-1217; fax (1) 480-1526; e-mail riyadh-ob@bmeia.gv.at; internet www.bmeia.gv.at/riyadh; Ambassador Dr Friedrich Stift.

Senegal: 18 rue Emile Zola, BP 3247, Dakar; tel. 33-849-4000; fax 33-849-4370; e-mail dakar-ob@bmaa.gv.at; Ambassador GERHARD DOUJAK.

Serbia: 11000 Belgrade, Kneza Sime Markovića 2; tel. (11) 3336500; fax (11) 635606; e-mail belgrade-ob@bmeia.gv.at; internet www.aussenministerium.at/belgrad; Ambassador Gerhard Jandl.

Slovakia: Ventúrska 10, 811 01 Bratislava; tel. (2) 5930-1500; fax (2) 5443-2486; e-mail pressburg-ob@bmeia.gv.at; internet www.rakusko.eu; Ambassador DR HELMUT WESSELY.

Slovenia: 1000 Ljubljana, Prešernova cesta 23; tel. (1) 4790700; fax (1) 2521717; e-mail laibach-ob@bmaa.gv.at; internet www.aussenministerium.at/laibach; Ambassador Dr Valentin Inzko.

South Africa: Momentum Office Park, 1109 Duncan St, Brooklyn, Pretoria 0181; POB 95572, Waterkloof 0145; tel. (12) 4529155; fax (12) 4601151; e-mail pretoria-ob@bmeia.gv.at; internet www.bmeia.gv.at/pretoria; Ambassador DR HELMUT FREUDENSCHUSS.

Spain: Paseo de la Castellana 91, 9°, 28046 Madrid; tel. (91) 5565315; fax (91) 5973579; e-mail madrid-ob@bmeia.gv.at; internet www.bmeia.gv.at/madrid; Ambassador Dr Ulrike Tilly.

Sweden: Kommendörsgt. 35, 5th Floor, 114 58 Stockholm; tel. (8) 665-17-70; fax (8) 662-69-28; e-mail stockholm-ob@bmeia.gv.at; internet www.aussenministerium.at/stockholm; Ambassador STEPHAN TOTH.

Switzerland: Kirchenfeldstr. 77–79, 3005 Bern; tel. 313565252; fax 313515664; e-mail bern-ob@bmeia.gv.at; internet www.aussenministerium.at/bern; Ambassador Hans Peter Manz.

Syria: BP 5634, Immeuble Mohamed Naim ad-Deker, 1 rue Farabi, Mezzeh Est, Damascus; tel. (11) 6116730; fax (11) 6116734; e-mail damaskus-ob@bmaa.gv.at; Ambassador DR IUR. KARL SHRAMEK.

Thailand: 14 Soi Nandha, off Thanon Sathorn Tai, Soi 1, Bangkok 10120; tel. (2) 303-6057; fax (2) 287-3925; e-mail bangkok-ob@bmaa.gv.at; Ambassador Arno Riedel.

Tunisia: 16 rue ibn Hamdiss, BP 23, al-Menzah, 1004 Tunis; tel. (71) 751-091; fax (71) 767-824; e-mail tunis-ob@bmeia.gv.at; Ambassador DR JOHANN FRÖHLICH.

Turkey: Atatürk Bul. 189, Kavaklıdere, Ankara; tel. (312) 4190431; fax (312) 4189454; e-mail ankara-ob@bmeia.gv.at; Ambassador Dr Heidemaria Gürer.

Ukraine: 01030 Kyiv, vul. Ivana Franka 33; tel. (44) 288-09-43; fax (44) 230-23-52; e-mail kiew-ob@bmeia.gv.at; internet www.aussenministerium.at/kiew; Ambassador JOSEF MARKUS WUKETICH.

United Arab Emirates: POB 35539, Al-Khazna Tower, 7th Floor, Najda St, Abu Dhabi; tel. (2) 6766611; fax (2) 6715551; internet www.austrianembassy.ae; Ambassador Dr Gerald Kriechbaum.

United Kingdom: 18 Belgrave Mews West, London, SW1X 8HU; tel. (20) 7344-3250; fax (20) 7344-0292; e-mail london-ob@bmeia.gv.at; internet www.bmeia.gv.at/london; Ambassador DR GABRIELE MATZNER-HOLZER.

United States of America: 3524 International Court, NW, Washington, DC 20008-3022; tel. (202) 895-6700; fax (202) 895-6750; e-mail obwas@sysnet.net; internet www.austria.org; Ambassador Eva Nowotny.

Vatican City: Via Reno 9, 00198 Rome, Italy; tel. (06) 853725; fax (06) 8543058; e-mail vatikan-ob@bmeia.gv.at; Ambassador DR MARTIN BOLLDORF.

Venezuela: Edif. Torre Las Mercedes, 4°, Of. 408, Avda La Estancia, Chuao, Apdo 61381, Caracas 1060-A; tel. (212) 991-3863; fax (212) 993-2753; e-mail caracas-ob@bmaa.gv.at; Ambassador Marianne Feldmann.

Viet Nam: Prime Centre, 8th Floor, 53 Quang Trung, Hai Ba Trung District, Hanoi; tel. (4) 9433050; fax (4) 9433055; e-mail hanoi-ob@bmeia.gv.at; internet www.aussenministerium.at/hanoi; Ambassador DR JOHANNES PETERLIK.

Zimbabwe: 13 Duthie Rd, Alexandra Park, POB 4120, Harare; tel. (4) 702921; fax (4) 705877; e-mail harare-ob@bmeia.gv.at; Ambassador Dr Gerhard Ziegler.

DIPLOMATIC MISSIONS OF AZERBAIJAN

United Nations: 866 United Nations Plaza, Suite 560, New York, NY 10017; tel. (212) 371-2559; fax (212) 371-2784; e-mail azerbaijan@un.int; Permanent Representative AGSHIN MEHDIYEV.

Austria: Hügelgasse 2, 1130 Vienna; tel. (1) 403-13-22; fax (1) 403-13-23; e-mail vienna@mission.mfa.gov.az; Ambassador Fuad Ismayilov.

Belarus: 220029 Minsk, vul. Vostochnaya 133/167; tel. (17) 293-32-99; fax (17) 237-27-51; e-mail azoffice_minsk@avilink.net; Ambassador ALI NAGHIYEV.

Belgium: 464 ave Molière, 1050 Brussels; tel. (2) 345-26-60; fax (2) 345-91-58; e-mail office@azembassy.be; internet www.azembassy.be; Ambassador Emin Eyyubov.

Canada: 275 Slater St, Suite 904, Ottawa, ON K1P 5H9; tel. (613) 288-0497; fax (613) 230-8089; e-mail azerbaijan@azembassy.ca; internet www.azembassy.ca; Chargé d'affaires FARID SHAFIYEV.

China, People's Republic: 3-2-31 San Li Tun Diplomatic Compound, Beijing 100600; tel. (10) 65324614; fax (10) 65324615; e-mail mailbox@azerbembassy.org.cn; internet www.azerbembassy.org.cn; Ambassador Yashar Tofigi Aliyev.

Czech Republic: Na Míčánce 32, 160 00 Prague 6; tel. 246032422; fax 246032423; ; TAHIR TAGHIZADE.

Egypt: Villa 16/24, Rd 10, Maadi Sarayat, Cairo; tel. (2) 23583790; fax (2) 23583725; e-mail azsefqahira@link.net; internet www.azembassy.org.eg; Ambassador Faig Bagirov.

France: 78 ave d'Iéna, 75016 Paris; tel. 1-44-18-60-20; fax 1-44-18-60-25; e-mail ambazer@wanadoo.fr; Ambassador Tarık Ismaïl Oglou Alıyev.

Georgia: 0177 Tbilisi, Nutsubidze 47; tel. (32) 25-26-39; fax (32) 25-00-13; e-mail secretariat@azembassy.ge; internet www.azembassy.ge; Ambassador Namiq Aliyev.

Germany: Hubertusallee 43, 14193 Berlin; tel. (30) 2191613; fax (30) 21916152; e-mail office@azembassy.de; internet www.azembassy.de; Ambassador Parviz Shahbazov.

Greece: Skoufa 10, Kolonaki, 106 73 Athens; tel. (210) 3632721; fax (210) 3639087; e-mail embassy@azembassy.gr; internet www.azembassy.gr; Ambassador Mir-Hamza Efendiyev.

Hungary: 1054 Budapest, Szabadság tér 7, Bank Center, Platina Tower, 5th floor; tel. (1) 374-6070; fax (1) 302-3535; e-mail bakybudapest@azerembassy.hu; Ambassador Hasan Hasanov.

India: Vasant Marg, Vasant Vihar E-70, New Delhi; tel. (11) 26152228; fax (11) 26152227; e-mail azembassy@airtelbroadband.in; Ambassador Tamerlan Garayev.

Indonesia: Jalan Mas Putih D, Persil 29, Grogol Utara Kebayoran Lama, Jakarta Selatan 12210; tel. (21) 5491939; fax (21) 5491745; e-mail azerbembjkt@u.net.id; internet www.azembassy.or.id; Ambassador Ibrahim Hajiyev.

Iran: 10 Akdsihi St, Tehran; tel. (21) 22215191; fax (21) 22217504; e-mail info@azembassy.ir; internet www.azembassy.ir; Ambassador Abbasali K. Hasanov.

Italy: Via Regina Margherita 1, Piano 2, 00198 Roma; tel. (06) 85305557; fax (06) 85231448; e-mail azerb.roma@azembassy.it; internet www.azembassy.it; Ambassador Emil Zulfgar Oğlu Karimov.

Japan: 1-19-15, Higashigaoka, Meguro-ku, Tokyo; tel. (3) 5486-4744; fax (3) 5486-7374; e-mail info@azerbembassy.jp; Ambassador Azer Huseyn.

Jordan: Muhammad Ali Bdeir St, Abdoun, Amman; tel. (6) 5935525; fax (6) 5932826; e-mail azerbaijan@azembassy.com.jo; internet www.azembassyjo.org; Ambassador Elman Arasli.

Kazakhstan: 010000 Astana, Diplomatiyalyk kalashyk C-14; tel. (7172) 24-15-81; fax (7172) 24-15-32; e-mail astana@azembassy.kz; Ambassador Latif Gandilov.

Korea, Republic: 3/F, Annex Bldg, Hannam Tower, 730 Hannam-dong, Yeongsan-gu, Seoul 140-893; tel. (2) 797-1765; fax (2) 792-1767; e-mail seoul@mission.mfa.gov.az; internet www.azembassy.co.kr; Ambassador Rovshan Jamshidov.

Kuwait: Al-Yarmouk, Block No. 2, St 1, Bldg 15, Kuwait City; tel. 5355247; fax 535546; e-mail embazerbaijan@yahoo.com; internet www.azerembassy-kuwait.org; Ambassador Shahin Abdullayev.

Kyrgyzstan: 720040 Bishkek; ; Arif Aghayev.

Latvia: Raiņa bulv. 3/1, Rīga 1050; tel. 6714-2889; fax 6714-2896; e-mail office@azembassy.lv; 2005Ambassador Tofiq Zulfugarov.

Lithuania: Olimpiečių g. 5-7, Vilnius; tel. (5) 219-0042; fax (5) 279-1504; Ambassador Naira Shakhtakhtinskaya.

Malaysia: 2nd Floor, Wisma Chinese Chamber, 258 Jalan Ampang, 50450 Kuala Lumpur; tel. (3) 42526800; e-mail azembkl@streamyx.com; Ambassador Tahir Karimov.

Moldova: 2012 Chişinău, str. Kogelnichanu 64; tel. (22) 23-22-77; fax (22) 22-75-58; e-mail chisinau@mission.mfa.gov.az; Ambassador Isfendiyar Vahabzadeh.

Morocco: rue 3 Abu Hanifa, Aqdal, Rabat; tel. (3) 7671915; fax (3) 7671918; e-mail azembma@menara.ma; Ambassador Sabir Aghabayov.

Netherlands: Laan Copes van Cattenburch 127, 2585 EZ The Hague; tel. (70) 3538205; fax (70) 3469604; e-mail info@azembassy.nl; Ambassador Fuad Iskandarov.

Pakistan: House 14, St 87, G-6/3, Atatürk Ave, Islamabad; tel. (51) 2829345; fax (51) 2820898; e-mail azeremb@isb.paknet.com.pk; internet www.azembassy.com.pk; Ambassador Dr Eynulla Yadalla Oglu Madatli.

Poland: 03-941 Warsaw, ul. Zwycięców 12; tel. (22) 6162188; fax (22) 6161949; e-mail info@azer-embassy.pl; internet www.azer-embassy.pl; Ambassador Vilayat Guliyev.

Romania: 014132 Bucharest 1, Str. Grigore Gafencu 10; tel. (21) 2332484; fax (21) 2332465; e-mail azsefroman@azembassy.ro; internet www.azembassy.ro; Ambassador Eldar Hasanov.

Russian Federation: 125009 Moscow, Leontyevskii per. 16; tel. (495) 629-43-32; fax (495) 202-50-72; e-mail azerirus@cnt.ru; internet www.azembassy.msk.ru; Ambassador Polad Bulbuloğlu.

Saudi Arabia: 59 Al-Worood Quarter St, off Amir Failsal bin Sa'ud Abd ar-Rahman, Aloroba Rd, Riyadh; tel. (1) 419-2382; fax (1) 419-2260; e-mail asim67@awalnet.net.sa; Ambassador Elman Arasli.

Spain: Ronda de la Avutarda 38, 28043 Madrid; tel. (91) 7596010; fax (91) 7597056; Ambassador Mammad Novruz oğlu Aliyev.

Sweden: Stockholm; e-mail azerembassy@gmail.com; Ambassador Rafael Ibrahimov.

Switzerland: Dalmaziquai 27, 3005 Bern; tel. 313505040; fax 313505041; e-mail bern@mission.mfa.gov.az; internet www.azembassy.ch; Ambassador Elchin Amirbayov.

Turkey: Cemal Nadir Sok. 20 Celikler Apt, Çankaya, Ankara; tel. (312) 4412620; fax (312) 4412600; e-mail azer-tr@tr.net; internet www.azembassy.org.tr/english.htm; Ambassador Zakir Hashimov.

Turkmenistan: 744000 Aşgabat, M. Kosayev 62a; tel. (12) 39-11-02; fax (12) 39-14-47; e-mail azsefir_ashg@online.tm; internet www.azembassyashg.com; Ambassador Elkhan Bakhadur oğlu Guseyinov.

Ukraine: 04050 Kyiv, vul. Hlubochytska 24; tel. (44) 484-69-39; fax (44) 484-69-46; e-mail embass@faust.kiev.ua; internet www.azembassy.org.ua; Ambassador Talyat Museib oğlu Aliyev.

United Arab Emirates: POB 45766, Plot N-297, Villa Sector W/16, Al-Bateen Area, Abu Dhabi; tel. (2) 6662848; fax (2) 6663150; e-mail azembassy@emirates.net.ae; Ambassador (vacant).

United Kingdom: 4 Kensington Court, London, W8 5DL; tel. (20) 7938-3412; fax (20) 7937-1783; e-mail london@mission.mfa.gov.az; internet www.azembassy.org.uk; Ambassador Fakhraddin Gurbanov.

United States of America: 2741 34th St, NW, Washington, DC 20008; tel. (202) 337-3500; fax (202) 337-5911; e-mail azerbaijan@azembassy.com; internet www.azembassy.com; Ambassador Yashar Aliyev.

Uzbekistan: 100000 Tashkent, Sharq Tongi ko'ch. 25; tel. (71) 173-61-67; fax (71) 173-26-58; e-mail sefir@tsk.sarkor.uz; Ambassador Namiq Abbasov.

DIPLOMATIC MISSIONS OF BAHAMAS

United Nations: 231 East 46th St, New York, NY 10017; tel. (212) 421-6925; fax (212) 759-2135; e-mail bahamas@un.int; Permanent Representative Paulette A. Bethel.

Canada: 50 O'Connor St, Suite 1313, Ottawa, ON K1P 6L2; tel. (613) 232-1724; fax (613) 232-0097; e-mail ottawa-mission@bahighco.com; High Commissioner Philip Patric Smith.

China, People's Republic: 4/F, Tayuan Diplomatic Office Bldg, 14 Liang Ma He Lu, Beijing 100600; tel. (10) 65322922; fax (10) 65322304; e-mail pmiller@mfabahamas.org; internet www.bahamasembassy.cn; Chargé d'affaires a.i. Philip Miller.

Cuba: 3006 Avda 5, No 3006, entre 30 y 32, Miramar, Playa, Havana; tel. (7) 206-9700; fax (7) 206-9701; e-mail embahamas@enet.cu; Ambassador Carlton Wright.

Haiti: 12 rue Goulard, pl. Boyer, Pétionville, Port-au-Prince; tel. 257-8782; fax 256-5729; e-mail bahamasembassy@hainet.net; Ambassador Dr Eugene Newry.

United Kingdom: 10 Chesterfield St, London, W1J 5JL; tel. (20) 7408-4488; fax (20) 7499-9937; e-mail information@bahamashclondon.net; internet www.bahamashclondon.net; High Commr Basil G. O'Brien.

United States of America: 2220 Massachusetts Ave, NW, Washington, DC 20008; tel. (202) 319-2660; fax (202) 319-2668; e-mail bahemb@aol.com; Ambassador Cornelius A. Smith.

DIPLOMATIC MISSIONS OF BAHRAIN

United Nations: 866 Second Ave, 14th/15th Floor, New York, NY 10017; tel. (212) 223-6200; fax (212) 319-0687; e-mail bahrain@un.int; internet www.un.int/bahrain; Permanent Representative Tawfeeq Ahmed Khalil Almansoor.

China, People's Republic: 10-06 Liangmaqiao Diplomatic Residence Compound, 22 Dong Fang Dong Lu, Chao Yang Qu, Beijing; tel. (10) 65326483; fax (10) 65326393; e-mail beijing.mission@mofa.gov.bh; Ambassador Bibi Sharaf al-Alalawi.

Egypt: 15 Sharia Bresil, Cairo (Zamalek); tel. (2) 3407996; fax (2) 3416609; Ambassador Khalil Ibrahim ath-Thawadi.

France: 3 bis place des Etats-Unis, 75116 Paris; tel. 1-47-23-48-68; fax 1-47-20-55-75; e-mail ambassade@ambahrein-france.com; internet www.ambahrein-france.com; Ambassador Dr Hashim Hassan al-Bash.

Germany: Klingelhöfer Str. 7, 10785 Berlin; tel. (30) 86877777; fax (30) 86877788; Chargé d'affaires a.i. Khalil Ibrahim Muhammad Butarada.

India: 4 A-4, Palam Marg, Vasant Vihar, New Delhi 110 057; tel. (11) 26154153; fax (11) 26146731; e-mail newdelhi.mission@mofa.gov.bh; Ambassador MOHAMMED GHASSAN SHAIKHO.

Iran: Intifada Ave, 31st St, No. 16, Tehran; tel. (21) 88773383; fax (21) 88779112; e-mail bahmanama@neda.net; Ambassador Rashid bin Saad ad-Dosari.

Iraq: 41/6/605 Hay al-Mutanabi, Baghdad; tel. (1) 541-0841; fax (1) 541-2027; Chargé d'affaires HASSAN AL-ANSARI.

Japan: Residence Viscountess 720, 1-11-36, Akasaka, Minato-ku, Tokyo 107-0052; tel. (3) 3584-8001; e-mail info@bahrain-embassy.or.jp; internet www.bahrain-embassy.or.jp; Ambassador Dr Khalil Hassan.

Jordan: POB 5220, Faris Al-Khoury St, Shmeisani Amman 11183; tel. (6) 5664148; fax (6) 5664190; e-mail bahemb@maktoob.com; Ambassador NASSER RASHID AL-KAABI.

Kuwait: POB 196, 13002 Safat, Area 6, Surra Rd, Villa 35, Kuwait City; tel. 5318530; fax 5330882; e-mail b111b@kems.net; Ambassador Sheikh Khalifa bin Hamad al-Khalifa.

Lebanon: Sheikh Ahmed ath-Thani Bldg, Raoucheh, Beirut; tel. (1) 805495; Ambassador MUHAMMAD BAHLOUL.

Morocco: rue beni Hassan, km 6.5, route des Zaêrs, Souissi, Rabat; tel. (3) 7633500; fax (3) 7630732; e-mail bahrain@mtds.com; Ambassador Khalid bin Salman al-Khalifa.

Oman: POB 66, Madinat Qaboos, Al-Khuwair; tel. 24605912; fax 24605072; Ambassador ISMAIL SALIM ALI.

Pakistan: House 5, St 83, G-6/4, Islamabad; tel. (51) 2831114; fax (51) 2206732; Ambassador Mohammed Ebrahim Mohammed Abd al-Qadir.

Qatar: POB 24888, Doha; tel. 4839360; fax 4831018; e-mail doha.mission@mofa.gov.bh; Ambassador KHALID MUHAMMAD JABER AL-MUSALEM.

Russian Federation: 109017 Moscow, ul. B. Ordynka 18/1; tel. (495) 953-00-22; fax (495) 953-74-74; e-mail moscowbah@yahoo.com; Ambassador Abdulhameed Ali Hasan Ali.

Saudi Arabia: POB 94371, Riyadh 11693; tel. (1) 488-0044; fax (1) 488-0208; Ambassador RASHID SAAD AD-DOSERI.

Syria: BP 36225, Damascus; tel. (11) 6132314; fax (11) 6130502; e-mail bed@net.sy; Ambassador Wahid Mubarak Sayyar.

Tunisia: 72 rue Mouaouia ibn Soufiane, BP 79, al-Menzah VIII, 2019 Tunis; tel. (71) 750-865; fax (71) 766-549; e-mail tunis.mission@mofa.gov.bh; Ambassador ABD AR-RAHMAN MUBARAK AS-SULAITI.

United Arab Emirates: POB 3367, Abu Dhabi; tel. (2) 6657500; fax (2) 6674141; e-mail bahrain1@emirates.net.ae; Ambassador Muhammad Saqr al-Maawda.

United Kingdom: 30 Belgrave Sq., London, SW1X 8QB; tel. (20) 7201-9170; fax (20) 7201-9183; e-mail information@bahrainembassy.co.uk; internet www.bahrainembassy.co.uk; Ambassador (vacant).

United States of America: 3502 International Dr., NW, Washington, DC 20008; tel. (202) 342-1111; fax (202) 362-2192; e-mail info@bahrainembassy.org; internet www.bahrainembassy.org; Ambassador Nasser Mohamed Al Belooshi.

DIPLOMATIC MISSIONS OF BANGLADESH

United Nations: 227 East, 45th Street, 14th Floor, New York, NY 10017; tel. (212) 867-3434; fax (212) 972-4038; e-mail bangladesh@un.int; internet www.un.int/bangladesh; Permanent Representative ISMAT JAHAN.

Australia: POB 5, Red Hill, ACT 2603; tel. (2) 6290-0511; fax (2) 6290-0544; e-mail info@bangladoot-canberra.org; internet www.bangladoot-canberra.org; High Commissioner Md Restadul Islam (acting).

Bahrain: POB 26718, House 2280, Rd 2757, Area 327, Adliya, Manama; tel. 17714717; fax 17710031; e-mail bangla@batelco.com.bh; internet www.banglaembassy.com.bh; Ambassador M. A. K. MAHMOOD.

Belgium: 29–31 rue Jacques Jordaens, 1000 Brussels; tel. (2) 640-55-00; fax (2) 646-59-98; e-mail bdootbrussels@skynet.be; internet www.bangladeshembassy.be; Ambassador A. H. M. Moniruzzaman.

Bhutan: POB 178, Upper Choubachu, Thimphu; tel. (2) 322539; fax (2) 322629; e-mail bdoot@druknet.bt; Ambassador A. K. M. ATIQUR RAHMAN.

Brunei: 10 Simpang 83-20, Jalan Sungai Akar, Kampong Sungai Akar, Bandar Seri Begawan BC 3915; tel. 2342420; fax 2342421; e-mail bdoot@brunet.bn; High Commissioner Mohammad Hedayatul Islam Chowdhury.

Canada: 275 Bank St, Suite 302, Ottawa, ON K2P 2L6; tel. (613) 236-0138; fax (613) 567-3213; e-mail bangla@rogers.com; internet www.bdhc.org; High Commissioner SYED MASUD MAHMOOD KHUNDOKER (acting).

China, People's Republic: 42 Guang Hua Lu, Beijing 100600; tel. (10) 65321819; fax (10) 65324346; e-mail bdemb@public3.bta.net.cn; internet www.bangladeshembassy.com.cn; Ambassador Munshi Faiz Ahmad.

Egypt: POB 136, 20 Sharia Gezeret El Arab, Mohandessin, Cairo; tel. (2) 33462003; fax (2) 33462008; e-mail bdoot@link.net; Ambassador NASIM FIRDAUS.

France: 39 rue Erlanger, 75016 Paris; tel. 1-46-51-90-33; fax 1-46-51-90-35; e-mail bangembpar@yahoo.com; Ambassador Ruhul Amin.

Germany: Dovestr. 1, 5th Floor, 10587 Berlin; tel. (30) 3989750; fax (30) 39897510; e-mail bdootbn@aol.com; internet www.bangladeshembassy.de; Chargé d'affaires a.i. ZAKIR AHMED.

India: EP-39 Dr S. Radhakrishnan Marg, Chanakyapuri, New Delhi 110 021; tel. (11) 24121389; fax (11) 26878953; e-mail bhcdelhi@mantraonline.com; internet www.bhcdelhi.org; High Commissioner Liaquat Ali Choudhury.

Indonesia: Jalan Denpasar Raya 3, Block A-13, Kav. 10, Kuningan, Jakarta 12950; tel. (21) 5221574; fax (21) 5261807; Ambassador SALMA KHAN.

Iran: POB 11365-3711, Gandhi Ave, 5th St, Bldg No. 14, Tehran; tel. (21) 88772979; fax (21) 88778295; e-mail banglaemb@irtp.com; Ambassador Shameem Ashan.

Iraq: 6/14/929 Hay Babel, Baghdad; tel. (1) 719-0068; fax (1) 718-6045; Ambassador MUHAMMAD FAZLUR RAHMA.

Italy: Via Antonio Bertoloni 14, 00197 Roma; tel. (06) 8078541; fax (06) 8084853; e-mail embangrm@mclink.it; Ambassador Karim Fazlul.

Japan: 4-15-15, Meguro, Meguro-ku, Tokyo 153-0063; tel. (3) 5704-0216; fax (3) 5704-1696; e-mail bdootjp@gol.com; internet www.bdembjp.com; Ambassador ASHRAF UD-DOULA.

Jordan: POB 5685, 10 Muzdalifa St, Ar-Rabiya, Amman 11183; tel. (6) 5529192; fax (6) 5529194; e-mail embangl@wanadoo.jo; Ambassador Muhammad Ghulam.

Kenya: Lenana Rd, POB 41645, Nairobi; tel. (20) 562816; fax (20) 562817; High Commissioner YAKUB ALI.

Korea, Republic: 7-18, Woo Sung Bldg, Dongbinggo-dong, Yeongsan-gu, Seoul; tel. (2) 796-4056; fax (2) 790-5313; Ambassador Mohammad Shahidul Islam.

Kuwait: POB 22344, 13084 Safat, Khaldya, Block 6, Ali bin Abi Taleb St, House 361, Kuwait City; tel. 5316042; fax 5316041; e-mail bdoot@ncc.moc.kw; Ambassador NAZRUL ISLAM KHAN.

Libya: POB 5086, Hi Damasq, Tripoli; tel. (21) 4911198; fax (21) 4906616; e-mail bdtripoli@bsisp.net; Ambassador Jamiluddin Ahsan.

Malaysia: Block 1, Lorong Damai 7, Jalan Damai, 55000 Kuala Lumpur; tel. (3) 21487940; fax (3) 21413381; e-mail bddoot@streamyx.com; internet www.bangladesh-highcomkl.com; High Commissioner M. KHAIRUZZAMAN.

Maldives: M. Kurinbee Lodge, 5th Floor, Izzudheen Magu, Malé; tel. 3315541; fax 3315543; e-mail bdootmal@dhivehinet.net.mv; High Commissioner Mohamed Mijarul Quayes.

Morocco: 25 ave Tarek ibn Ziad, BP 1468, Rabat; tel. (3) 7766731; fax (3) 7766729; e-mail bdoot@mtds.com; Ambassador MOHAMMAD AL-HAROON.

Myanmar: 11b Than Lwin Rd, Yangon; tel. (1) 515275; fax (1) 515273; e-mail bdootygn@mptmail.net.mm; Ambassador Maj.-Gen. Abu Roshde Rokonuddawla.

Nepal: Maharajgunj Ring Rd, POB 789, Kathmandu; tel. (1) 4372843; fax (1) 4373265; e-mail bdootktm@wlink.com.np; Ambassador IMTIAZ AHMED.

Netherlands: Wassenaarseweg 39, 2596 CG The Hague; tel. (70) 3283722; fax (70) 3283524; e-mail amb.vanbangladesh@wanadoo.nl; internet www.bangladeshembassy.nl; Ambassador Mizanur Rahman.

Oman: POB 3959, Ruwi 112, St 664, Bldg 5903, Muscat; tel. 24707462; fax 24708495; e-mail bangla@omantel.net.om; Ambassador GOLAM AKBAR KHANDAKAR.

Pakistan: 1, St 5, F-6/3, Islamabad; tel. (51) 2279267; fax (51) 2279266; e-mail bdhcisb@sat.net.pk; High Commissioner Yasmeen Murshed.

Philippines: Universal-Re Bldg, 2nd Floor, 106 Paseo de Roxas, Legaspi Village, Makati City, Metro Manila; tel. (2) 8175001; fax (2) 8164941; Ambassador (vacant).

Qatar: POB 3080, Doha; tel. 4671927; fax 4671190; e-mail bdootqat@qatar.net.qa; Ambassador Maroof Zaman.

Russian Federation: 119121 Moscow, Zemledelcheskii per. 6; tel. (495) 246-78-04; fax (495) 248-31-85; e-mail moscow.bangla@com2com.ru; internet www.bangladeshembassy.ru; Ambassador AMIR HUSSAIN SIKDER.

Saudi Arabia: POB 94395, Riyadh 11693; tel. (1) 419-6665; fax (1) 419-3555; e-mail bdootriyadh@zajil.net; Ambassador Muhammad Akram ul-Haq.

Singapore: 91 Bencoolen St, 6 Sunshine Plaza, Singapore 189652; tel. 62550075; fax 62551824; e-mail bdoot@singnet.com.sg; internet www .bangladesh.org.sg; High Commissioner KAMRUL AHSAN.

South Africa: 410 Farenden St, Sunnyside, Pretoria 0002; tel. (12) 3432105; fax (12) 3435222; e-mail bdoot@mweb.co.za; High Commissioner MD Shahidul Islam.

Spain: Diego de León 69, 2°D, 28006 Madrid; tel. (91) 4019932; fax (91) 4029564; e-mail chancery@bdoot-mad.e.telefonica.net; Ambassador SAIFUL AMIN KHAN.

Sri Lanka: 85 Dharmapala Mawatha, Colombo 7; tel. (11) 2303943; fax (11) 2303942; e-mail bdootlanka@eureka.lk; High Commissioner Mohammed Shahadat Hossain.

Sweden: Anderstorpsvägen 12, 1st Floor, 171 54 Solna; tel. (8) 730-58-50; fax (8) 730-58-70; e-mail banijya@bangladeshembassy.se; Ambassador MUHAMMAD AZIZUL HAQUE.

Thailand: 727 Soi Thonglor, Thanon Sukhumvit 55, Bangkok 10110; tel. (2) 392-9437; fax (2) 391-8070; e-mail bdoot@samart.co.th; Ambassador Mustafa Kamal.

Turkey: Cinnah Cad. 78/7–10, 06690 Çankaya, Ankara; tel. (312) 4392750; fax (312) 4422561; e-mail bdootankara@superonline.com; Ambassador MAJ.-GEN. MUHAMMAD ISHTIAQ.

United Arab Emirates: POB 2504, Villa 32, Khlaidya, Abu Dhabi; tel. (2) 668375; fax (2) 667324; e-mail banglaad@emirates.net.ae; Ambassador A. T. M. Nazimullah Chowdhury.

United Kingdom: 28 Queen's Gate, London, SW7 5JA; tel. (20) 7584-0081; fax (20) 7581-7477; e-mail bhclondon@btconnect.com; internet www.bhclondon .org.uk; High Commr SHAFI U. AHMED.

United States of America: 3510 International Dr., NW, Washington, DC 20008; tel. (202) 244-0183; fax (202) 244-2771; e-mail info@bangladoot.org; internet www.bangladoot.org; Ambassador M. Humayun Kabir.

Uzbekistan: 100015 Tashkent, 1-chi Kunaev ko'ch. 17; tel. (71) 152-26-92; fax (71) 120-67-11; e-mail bdoot.tas@online.ru; Ambassador A. B. M. ABDUS SALAM.

Viet Nam: 7th Floor, Daeha Business Centre, 360 Kim Ma, Ba Dinh District, Hanoi; tel. (4) 7716625; fax (4) 7716628; Ambassador Mohd Enamul Kabir.

Zimbabwe: 9 Birchenough Rd, POB 3040, Harare; tel. (4) 727004; Ambassador NASIMA HAIDER.

DIPLOMATIC MISSIONS OF BARBADOS

United Nations: 800 Second Ave, 2nd Floor, New York, NY 10017; tel. (212) 867-8431; fax (212) 986-1030; e-mail barbados@un.int; Permanent Representative Christopher F. Hackett.

Belgium: 100 ave F. D. Roosevelt, 1050 Brussels; tel. (2) 732-17-37; fax (2) 732-32-66; e-mail brussels@foreign.gov.bb; Ambassador ERROL HUMPHREY.

Canada: 55 Metcalfe St, Suite 470, Ottawa, ON K1P 6L5; tel. (613) 236-9517; fax (613) 230-4362; e-mail ottawa@foreign.gov.bb; High Commissioner Glyne Samuel Murray.

United Kingdom: 1 Great Russell St, London, WC1B 3ND; tel. (20) 7631-4975; fax (20) 7323-6872; e-mail london@foreign.gov.bb; High Commr L. EDWIN POLLARD.

United States of America: 2144 Wyoming Ave, NW, Washington, DC 20008; tel. (202) 939-9200; fax (202) 332-7467; e-mail washington@foreign.gov.bb; Ambassador Michael Ian King.

Venezuela: Edif. Los Frailes, 5°, Of. 501, Avda Principal con Calle La Guairita, Chuao, Caracas 1060; tel. (212) 992-0545; fax (212) 991-0333; e-mail caracas@foreign.gov.bb; Ambassador KEITH FRANKLIN.

DIPLOMATIC MISSIONS OF BELARUS

United Nations: 136 East 67th St, 4th Floor, New York, NY 10021; tel. (212) 535-3420; fax (212) 734-4810; e-mail belarus@un.int; internet missions.un .int/belarus; Permanent Representative Andrei Dapkiunas.

Argentina: Cazadores 2166, C1428AVH Buenos Aires; tel. (11) 4788-9394; fax (11) 4788-2322; e-mail argentina@belembassy.org; Chargé d'affaires a.i. OLEG MALAEV.

Armenia: 0028 Yerevan, N. Duman St 12–14; tel. (10) 27-56-11; fax (10) 26-03-84; e-mail armenia@belembassy.org; Ambassador Marina Dolgopolova.

Austria: Hüttelbergstr. 6, 1140 Vienna; tel. (1) 419-96-30-11; fax (1) 416-96-30-30; e-mail mail@byembassy.at; internet www.byembassy.at; Ambassador ALYAKSANDR SYCHOV.

Belgium: 192 ave Molière, 1050 Brussels; tel. (2) 340-02-70; fax (2) 340-02-87; e-mail embbel@skynet.be; internet www.belembassy.org/belgium; Ambassador Vladimir Senko.

Bulgaria: 1113 Sofia, ul. Kokiche 20; tel. (2) 965-28-43; e-mail embassyblr@ omega.bg; internet www.belembassy.org/bulgaria; Ambassador VYACHESLAV H. KACHANOV.

Canada: 130 Albert St, Suite 600, Ottawa, K1P 5G4; tel. (613) 233-9994; fax (613) 233-8500; e-mail belamb@igs.net; Ambassador Nina Nikolaevna Mazai.

China, People's Republic: 1 Dong Yi Jie, Ri Tan Lu, Beijing 100600; tel. (10) 65321691; fax (10) 65326417; e-mail china@belembassy.org; internet www .belembassy.com; Ambassador ANATOLY AFANASYEVICH TOZIK.

Cuba: Calle 5, No 3802, entre 38 y 40, Miramar, Havana; tel. (7) 204-7330; fax (7) 204-7332; e-mail cuba@belembassy.org; Ambassador Poluyan Igor Ivanovich.

Czech Republic: Sádky 626, 171 00 Prague 7; tel. 233540899; fax 233540925; Chargé d'affaires a.i. VASIL MARKOVICH.

Egypt: 26 Sharia Gaber Ibn Hayan, Cairo (Dokki); tel. (2) 7499171; e-mail egypt@belembassy.org; Ambassador Sergei Mikhnevich.

France: 38 blvd Suchet, 75016 Paris; tel. 1-44-14-69-79; fax 1-44-14-69-70; e-mail france@belembassy.org; internet www.france.belembassy.org; Ambassador VIKTAR SHYKH.

Germany: Am Treptower Park, 12345 Berlin; tel. (30) 5363590; fax (30) 53635923; e-mail info@belarus-botschaft.de; internet www.belarus-botschaft .de; Ambassador Vladimir Skvortsov.

Hungary: 1126 Budapest, Agárdi u. 3B; tel. (1) 214-0553; fax (1) 214-0554; e-mail hungary@belembassy.org; internet belembassy.org/hungary; Ambassador ALENA KUPCHYNA.

India: 163 Jor Bagh, New Delhi 110 003; tel. (11) 24697025; fax (11) 24697029; e-mail india@belembassy.org; Ambassador Oleg Laptenok.

Iran: 1 Azar St, Aban St, Shahid Taheri St, Zafaranieyeh Ave, Tehran 19887; tel. (21) 22708829; fax (21) 22718682; e-mail iran@belembassy.org; Ambassador LEONID V. RACHKOV.

Israel: POB 11129, 3 Reines St, Tel-Aviv 64381; tel. 3-5231069; fax 3-5231273; e-mail press@belembassy.co.il; internet www.belembassy.co.il; Ambassador Igor Leshchenya.

Italy: Via delle Alpi Apuane 16, 00141 Roma; tel. (06) 8208141; fax (06) 82002509; e-mail italy@belembassy.org; internet www.belembassy.it; Ambassador ALEKSEI SKRIPKO.

Japan: 4-14-12, Shirogane K House, Shirogane, Minato-ku, Tokyo 108-0072; tel. (3) 3448-1623; fax (3) 3448-1624; e-mail japan@belembassy.org; internet www.belarus.jp; Chargé d'affaires a.i. Leonid I. Batyanovsky.

Kazakhstan: 010000 Astana, Kenesary 35; tel. (7172) 32-48-29; fax (7172) 32-06-65; e-mail kazakhstan@belembassy.org; internet kazakhstan.belembassy .org; Ambassador VASILII I. HAPEYEV.

Korea, Republic: 432-1636 Sindang 2-dong, Jung-gu, Seoul; tel. (2) 2237-8171; fax (2) 2237-8174; e-mail korea@belembassy.org; internet korea .belembassy.org; Ambassador Aleksandr Guryanov.

Kyrgyzstan: 720040 Bishkek, Moskovskaya 210; tel. (312) 65-13-65; fax (312) 65-11-77; e-mail kyrgyzstan@belembassy.org; Ambassador VALERY A. BRYLYOV.

Latvia: Jēzusbaznīcas iela 12, Rīga 1050; tel. 6722-2560; fax 6732-2891; e-mail latvia@belembassy.org; internet belembassy.org/latvia; Ambassador Alyaksandr Gerasimenka.

Libya: POB 1530, Tripoli; tel. (21) 4444708; fax (21) 3332994; e-mail libya@ belembassy.org; Ambassador DEREVYASHKO ALEKSANDR NIKOLAEVICH.

Lithuania: Mindaugo g. 13, Vilnius 03225; tel. (5) 266-2200; fax (5) 266-2212; e-mail lithuania@belembassy.org; internet www.belarus.lt; Ambassador Uladzimir Drazhin.

Moldova: 2012 Chişinău, str. Mateevici 35; tel. (22) 23-83-02; fax (22) 23-83-00; e-mail moldova@belembassy.org; internet www.belembassy.org/ moldova; Ambassador VASILIY A. SAKOVICH.

Netherlands: Anna Paulownastraat 34, 2518 BE The Hague; tel. (70) 3631566; fax (70) 3640555; e-mail info@witrusland.com; internet www.witrusland .com; Ambassador Vladimir Gerasimovich.

Poland: 02-952 Warsaw, ul. Wiertnicza 58; tel. (22) 7420990; fax (22) 7420980; e-mail poland@belembassy.org; internet www.belembassy.org/poland; Ambassador PAVEL P. LATUSHKA.

Romania: Bucharest, Str. Tuberozelor 6, Sector 1; tel. (21) 2231776; fax (21) 2231763; e-mail romania@belembassy.org; Chargé d'affaires a.i. Dmitriy Shemetov.

Russian Federation: 101990 Moscow, ul. Maroseika 17/6; tel. (495) 777-66-44; fax (495) 777-66-33; e-mail mail@embassybel.ru; internet www.embassybel .ru; Ambassador VASIL DALHALYOV.

Serbia: 11000 Belgrade, Deligradska 13; tel. (11) 3616836; fax (11) 3616938; e-mail sam@belembassy.org; Chargé d'affaires a.i. Siarhei Chichuk.

Slovakia: Kuzmányho 3A, 811 06 Bratislava; tel. (2) 5441-6325; fax (2) 5441-6328; e-mail slovakia@belembassy.org; internet www.belembassy.org/ slovakia; Chargé d'affaires a.i. VIKTOR NAVROTSKY.

South Africa: 327 Hill St, Arcadia, Pretoria 0083; POB 4107, Pretoria 0001; tel. (12) 4307664; fax (12) 3426280; e-mail sa@belembassy.org; Ambassador Dr Anatolii Akhramchuk.

Sweden: Herserudsvägen 5, 4th Floor, 181 34 Lidingö; tel. (8) 731-57-45; fax (8) 767-07-46; e-mail sweden@belembassy.org; internet www.belembassy .org/sweden; Ambassador ANDREI M. GRINKEVICH.

Switzerland: Quartierweg 6, CP 438, 3074 Muri bei Bern; tel. 319527914; fax 319527616; e-mail swiss@belembassy.org; Chargé d'affaires a.i. Alyaksandr Ganevich.

Syria: BP 16239, 27 rue Qurtaja, Mezzeh Est, Damascus; tel. (11) 6118097; fax (11) 6132802; e-mail syria@belembassy.org; Ambassador VLADIMIR N. LOPATO-ZAGORSKII.

Turkey: Abidin Daver Sok. 17, 06550 Çankaya, Ankara; tel. (312) 4416769; fax (312) 4416674; e-mail turkey@belembassy.org; Ambassador Natalya Zhylevich.

Turkmenistan: 744000 Aşgabat, ul. Esgerler 35; tel. (12) 36-46-88; fax (12) 36-46-91; e-mail turkmenistan@belembassy.org; Ambassador YURIY H. MALUMOV.

Ukraine: 01030 Kyiv, vul. M. Kotsyubynskogo 3; tel. (44) 537-52-00; fax (44) 537-52-13; e-mail inbox@belembassy.org.ua; internet www.belembassy.org .ua; Ambassador Valentyn V. Velichko.

United Arab Emirates: POB 30337, Villa 434, 26th St, Ar-Rouda Area, Abu Dhabi; tel. (2) 4453399; fax (2) 4451131; e-mail uae@belembassy.org; Ambassador VLADIMIR SULIMSKY.

United Kingdom: 6 Kensington Court, London, W8 5DL; tel. (20) 7937-3288; fax (20) 7361-0005; e-mail uk@belembassy.org; internet www.uk.belembassy .org; Ambassador Aleksandr Mikhnevich.

United States of America: 1619 New Hampshire Ave, NW, Washington, DC 20009; tel. (202) 986-1604; fax (202) 986-1805; e-mail usa@belarusembassy .org; internet www.belarusembassy.org; Ambassador MIKHAIL KHVOSTOV.

Uzbekistan: 100047 Tashkent, Ya. G'ulomov ko'ch. 75; tel. (71) 120-72-54; fax (71) 120-72-53; e-mail uzbekistan@belembassy.org; internet www .uzbekistan.belembassy.org; Ambassador Dr Nikolai N. Demchuk.

Viet Nam: 11th Floor, 44b Ly Thuong Kiet, Hanoi; tel. (4) 9344416; fax (4) 9344417; e-mail check@hn.vnn.vn; Ambassador ALYAKSANDR KUTSALAY.

DIPLOMATIC MISSIONS OF BELGIUM

United Nations: 823 United Nations Plaza, 4th Floor, New York, NY 10017; tel. (212) 378-6300; fax (212) 681-7618; e-mail belgium@un.int; internet www .un.int/belgium; Permanent Representative Johan C. Verbeke.

Afghanistan: House 1–3, St 1, Taimani Wat, Qala-i-Fathullah, Kabul; tel. (70) 294149; e-mail kabul@diplobel.org; internet www.diplomatie.be/kabul; Ambassador PIETER LEENKNEGT.

Algeria: BP 341, 16030 el-Biar, Algiers; tel. (21) 92-26-60; fax (21) 92-50-36; e-mail algiers@diplobel.be; internet www.diplomatie.be/algiersfr; Ambassador Baudouin Vanderhulst.

Angola: Av. 4 de Fevereiro 93, 3° andar, CP 1203, Luanda; tel. 222336437; fax 222336438; e-mail luanda@diplobel.org; internet www.diplomatie.be/ luanda; Ambassador HUBERT COOREMAN.

Argentina: Defensa 113, 8°, C1065AAA Buenos Aires; tel. (11) 4331-0066; fax (11) 4311-0814; e-mail buenosaires@diplobel.org; internet www.diplobel .org/argentina; Ambassador Koenraad Rouvroy.

Australia: 19 Arkana St, Yarralumla, ACT 2600; tel. (2) 6273-2501; fax (2) 6273-3392; e-mail canberra@diplobel.org; internet www.diplomatie.be/ canberra; Ambassador FRANK CARRUET.

Austria: Wohllebengasse 6, 1040 Vienna; tel. (1) 502-07-0; fax (1) 502-07-22; e-mail vienna@diplobel.org; internet www.diplomatie.be/vienna, Ambassador Cristina Funes-Noppen.

Azerbaijan: 1073 Baku, Suleyman Dadaşov 19; tel. (12) 437-37-70; Ambassador FRANK GEERKENS.

Brazil: SES, Av. das Nações, Quadra 809, Lote 32, 70422-900 Brasília, DF; tel. (61) 3443-1133; fax (61) 3443-1219; e-mail brasilia@diplobel.org; internet www.belgica.org.br; Ambassador Johan Ballegeer.

Bulgaria: 1164 Sofia, ul. V. Zavera 1; tel. (2) 988-72-90; fax (2) 963-36-38; e-mail sofia@diplobel.be; internet www.diplomatie.be/sofia; Ambassador PHILIPPE BEKE.

Burkina Faso: Immeuble Me Benoit Sawadogo, 994 rue Agostino Neto, Koulouba, 01 POB 1624, Ouagadougou 01; tel. 50-31-21-64; fax 50-31-06-60; e-mail ouagadougou@diplobel.org; internet www.diplomatie.be/ ouagadougou; Ambassador Jansen Paul.

Burundi: 9 blvd de la Liberté, BP 1920, Bujumbura; tel. 22226176; fax 22223171; e-mail bujumbura@diplobel.org; Ambassador FRANÇOIS CORNET D'ELZIUS.

Cameroon: rue 1792, Quartier Bastos, BP 816, Yaoundé; tel. 2220-0519; fax 2220-0521; e-mail yaounde@diplobel.org; internet www.diplomatie.be/ yaounde/; Ambassador Franck Carruet.

Canada: 360 Albert St, 8th Floor, Suite 820, Ottawa, ON K1R 7X7; tel. (613) 236-7267; fax (613) 236-7882; e-mail ottawa@diplobel.org; internet www .diplomatie.be/ottawa; Ambassador JEAN L. A. LINT.

Chile: Edif. Forum, Providencia 2653, 11°, Of. 1103, Santiago; tel. (2) 232-1070; fax (2) 232-1073; e-mail santiago@diplobel.org; internet www .diplomatie.be/santiago; Ambassador Francis de Sutter.

China, People's Republic: 6 San Li Tun Lu, Beijing 100600; tel. (10) 65321736; fax (10) 65325097; e-mail Beijing@diplobel.org; internet www.diplomatie.be/ beijing; Ambassador BERNARD PIERRE.

Colombia: Calle 26, No 4a-45, 7°, Apdo Aéreo 3564, Bogotá, DC; tel. (1) 380-0370; fax (1) 380-0340; e-mail bogota@diplobel.org; internet www.diplobel .org/colombia; Ambassador Jean-Luc Bodson.

Congo, Democratic Republic: Immeuble Le Cinquantenaire, pl. du 27 octobre, BP 899, Kinshasa; tel. (12) 20110; fax (12) 21058; e-mail kinshasa@diplobel.org; internet www.diplobel.org/congo; Ambassador JOHAN SWINNEN.

Congo, Republic: ave Patrice Lumumba, BP 225, Brazzaville; tel. 81-37-12; fax 81-37-04; e-mail brazzaville@diplobel.org; internet www.diplomatie.be/ brazzaville; Ambassador Michel Tilemans.

Costa Rica: Los Yoses, 4a entrada, 25 m sur, Apdo 3725, 1000 San José; tel. 225-6633; fax 225-0351; e-mail sanjose@diplobel.be; internet www.diplobel .org/costarica; Ambassador BARON OLIVIER GILLÈS DE PÉLICHY.

Côte d'Ivoire: Immeuble Alliance, ave Terrasson des Fougères, 01 BP 1800, Abidjan 01; tel. 20-21-00-88; fax 20-22-41-77; e-mail abidjan@diplobel.org; internet www.diplomatie.be/abidjan; Ambassador Dirk Verheyen.

Croatia: 10000 Zagreb, Pantovčak 125; tel. (1) 4578901; fax (1) 4578903; e-mail ambabel@zg.htnet.hr; Ambassador MARC DE SCHOUTHEETE DE TERVARENT.

Cuba: Calle 8, No 309, entre 3 y 5, Miramar, Havana; tel. (7) 204-2410; fax (7) 204-1318; e-mail havana@diplobel.org; internet www.diplomatie.be/havana; Ambassador Claudia de Maesschalck.

Cyprus: 2A Chilonos St, Office 102, 1101 Nicosia; tel. 22449020; fax 22774717; e-mail nicosia@diplobel.be; internet www.diplomatie.be/nicosia; Chargé d'affaires a.i. PIERRE GILLON.

Czech Republic: Valdštejnská 6, 118 01 Prague 1; tel. 257533524; fax 257533750; e-mail prague@diplobel.org; Ambassador Raf Van Hellemont.

Denmark: Øster Allé 7, 2100 Copenhagen Ø; tel. 35-25-02-00; fax 35-25-02-11; e-mail copenhagen@diplobel.be; internet www.diplomatie.be/ copenhagen; Ambassador MARC VAN CRAEN.

Egypt: POB 37, 20 Sharia Kamal esh-Shennawi, Cairo 11511 (Garden City); tel. (2) 7947494; fax (2) 7943147; e-mail cairo@diplobel.org; internet www .diplomatie.be/cairo; Ambassador Daniel Leroy.

Estonia: Rataskaevu 2, Tallinn 10123; tel. 627-4100; fax 627-4101; e-mail tallinn@diplobel.be; internet www.diplomatie.be/tallinn; Ambassador PIERRE DUBUISSON.

Ethiopia: Comoros St, Kebele 8, POB 1239, Addis Ababa; tel. (11) 6611813; fax (11) 6613646; e-mail addisababa@diplobel.org; internet www.diplomatie.be/addisababa; Ambassador Gunther Sleeuwagen.

Finland: Kalliolinnantie 5, 00140 Helsinki; tel. (9) 170412; fax (9) 628842; e-mail helsinki@diplobel.be; internet www.diplomatie.be/helsinki; Ambassador GUIDO COURTOIS.

France: 9 rue de Tilsitt, 75840 Paris Cedex 17; tel. 1-44-09-39-39; fax 1-47-54-07-64; e-mail paris@diplobel.org; internet www.diplomatie.be/paris; Ambassador Pierre-Dominique Schmidt.

Gabon: Quartier Bas de Gué-Gué, Bord de Mer à côté de la Délégation de la Commission Européenne, BP 4079, Libreville; tel. 73-29-92; fax 73-96-94; e-mail libreville@diplobel.org; internet www.diplomatie.be/libreville; Ambassador IVO GOEMANS.

Germany: Jägerstr. 52–53, 10117 Berlin; tel. (30) 206420; fax (30) 20642200; e-mail berlin@diplobel.org; internet www.diplomatie.be/berlin; Ambassador Mark Geleyn.

Greece: Odos Sekeri 3, 106 71 Athens; tel. (210) 3617886; fax (210) 3604289; e-mail athens@diplobel.org; internet www.diplomatie.be/athens; Ambassador PIERRE VAESEN.

Hungary: 1027 Budapest, Kapás u. 11–15; tel. (1) 457-9960; fax (1) 375-1566; e-mail budapest@diplobel.org; internet www.diplomatie.be/budapest; Ambassador Marc Trenteseau.

India: 50N Shanti Path, Chanakyapuri, New Delhi 110 021; tel. (11) 42428000; fax (11) 42428002; e-mail newdelhi@diplobel.be; internet www.diplomatie.be/newdelhi; Ambassador JEAN M. DEBOUTTE.

Indonesia: Deutsche Bank Bldg, 16th Floor, Jalan Imam Bonjol 80, Jakarta 10310; tel. (21) 3162030; fax (21) 3162035; e-mail jakarta@diplobel.org; internet www.diplomatie.be/jakarta; Ambassador Marc Trenteseau.

Iran: POB 11365-115, 155–157 Shahid Fayyaz Bakhsh Ave, Shemiran, Elahieh, Tehran 16778; tel. (21) 22041617; fax (21) 22044608; e-mail teheran@diplobel.be; internet www.diplomatie.be/tehran; Ambassador HERVÉ GOYENS.

Ireland: 2 Shrewsbury Rd, Dublin 4; tel. (1) 2057100; fax (1) 2057106; e-mail dublin@diplobel.org; internet www.diplomatie.be/dublin; Ambassador Leopold Carrewyn.

Israel: 12 Hahilazon St, Ramat-Gan 52522; tel. 3-6138130; fax 3-6138160; e-mail telaviv@diplobel.org; internet www.diplomatie.be/telaviv; Ambassador DANIELLE DEL MARMOL.

Italy: Via dei Monti Parioli 49, 00197 Roma; tel. (06) 3609511; fax (06) 3226935; e-mail ambelrom@tin.it; internet www.diplomatie.be/romeit; Ambassador Jean de Ruyt.

Japan: Shiba Daimon Front Bldg, 1-7-13, Shiba Koen, Minato-ku, Tokyo 105-0011; tel. (3) 3262-0191; fax (3) 3262-0651; e-mail tokyo@diplobel.be; internet www.diplomatie.be/tokyo; Ambassador JOHAN MARICOU.

Jordan: POB 942, Amman 11118; tel. (6) 5932683; fax (6) 5930487; e-mail ambabelamman@wanadoo.jo; internet www.diplomatie.be/amman; Ambassador Johan Indekeu.

Kazakhstan: 010000 Astana, Kosmonavtov 62; tel. (7172) 97-78-48; fax (7172) 97-78-49; e-mail embassy.astana@diplobel.fed.be; Ambassador CHRISTIAN MEERSCHMAN.

Kenya: Muthaiga, Limuru Rd, POB 30461, Nairobi; tel. (20) 741564; fax (20) 442701; e-mail nairobi@diplobel.be; internet www.diplomatie.be/nairobi; Ambassador Leo Willems.

Korea, Republic: 737-10, Hannam-dong, Yeongsan-gu, Seoul 140-895; tel. (2) 749-0381; fax (2) 797-1688; e-mail seoul@diplobel.org; internet www.belgium.or.kr; Ambassador VICTOR WEI.

Kuwait: POB 3280, 13033 Safat, Baghdad St, Block 8, House 15, Kuwait City; tel. 5722014; fax 5748389; e-mail kuwait@diplobel.org; internet www.diplomatie.be/kuwait; Ambassador Giles Heyvaert.

Latvia: Alberta iela 13, Rīga 1010; tel. 6711-4852; fax 6711-4855; e-mail riga@diplobel.be; internet www.diplomatie.be/riga; 2004Ambassador CHRISTIAN VERDONCK.

Lebanon: POB 11-1600, Riad es-Solh, Beirut; tel. (1) 976001; fax (1) 976007; e-mail beirut@diplobel.org; internet www.diplomatie.be/beirut; Ambassador Stéphane De Loecker.

Libya: POB 91650, Jasmin St, Hay Andalus, Tripoli; tel. (21) 4782044; fax (21) 4782046; e-mail tripoli@diplobel.be; internet www.diplomatie.be/tripoli; Ambassador ALPHONSE CREUSEN.

Lithuania: Kalinausko g. 2b, Vilnius 03107; tel. (5) 266-0820; fax (5) 212-6444; e-mail vilnius@diplobel.org; internet www.diplomatie.be/vilnius; Ambassador Filnius Cumps.

Luxembourg: 4 rue des Girondins, 1626 Luxembourg; tel. 44-27-46-1; fax 45-42-82; e-mail luxembourg@diplobel.org; internet www.diplomatie.be/luxemburg; Ambassador ALAIN KUNDYCKI.

Malaysia: Suite 10-02, 10th Floor, Menara Tan & Tan, 207 Jalan Tun Razak, 50400 Kuala Lumpur; tel. (3) 21620025; fax (3) 21620023; e-mail kualalumpur@diplobel.org; internet www.diplomatie.be/kualalumpur; Ambassador Frank Van de Craen.

Malta: Europa Centre, 8–9 John Lopez St., Floriana FLN 1400; tel. 21228214; fax 21243246; internet www.diplomatie.be/valletta; e-mail valletta@diplobel.be; Ambassador THOMAS BAEKELANDT.

Mexico: Alfredo Musset 41, Col. Polanco, Del. Miguel Hidalgo, 11550 México, DF; tel. (55) 5280-0758; fax (55) 5280-0208; e-mail mexico@diplobel.org; internet www.diplomatie.be/mexico; Ambassador Gustavus J. M. Dierckx.

Morocco: 6 ave de Muhammad el-Fassi, Tour Hassan, Rabat; tel. (3) 7268060; fax (3) 7767003; e-mail rabat@diplobel.org; internet www.diplomatie.be/rabat; Ambassador PATRICK VERCAUTEREN DRUBBEL.

Netherlands: Alexanderveld 97, 2585 DB The Hague; tel. (70) 3123456; fax (70) 3645579; e-mail thehague@diplobel.org; internet www.diplomatie.be/thehague; Ambassador Luc Carbonez.

Nigeria: 9 Usuma St, Maitama, Abuja; tel. (9) 4131859; fax (9) 4132015; e-mail abuja@diplobel.org; internet www.belgiumvisas.org; Ambassador DIRK VAN EECKHOUT.

Norway: Drammensvn 103d, 0244 Oslo; tel. 23-13-32-20; fax 23-13-32-32; e-mail oslo@diplobel.org; internet www.diplomatie.be/oslo; Ambassador Frank Recker.

Pakistan: 14, St 17, F-7/2, Islamabad; tel. (51) 2652635; fax (51) 2652631; e-mail islamabad@diplobel.org; internet www.diplomatie.be/islamabad; Ambassador MICHEL GOFFIN.

Philippines: Multinational Bancorporation Center, 9th Floor, 6805 Ayala Ave, Makati City, Metro Manila; tel. (2) 8451869; fax (2) 8452076; e-mail manila@diplobel.org; internet www.diplomatie.be/manila; Ambassador Grégoire Vardakis.

Poland: 00-095 Warsaw, ul. Senatorska 34; tel. (22) 5512800; fax (22) 8285711; e-mail warsaw@diplobel.org; internet www.diplomatie.be/warsawfr; Ambassador JAN LUYKX.

Portugal: Praça Marquês de Pombal 14, 6°, 1269-024 Lisbon; tel. (21) 3170510; fax (21) 3561556; e-mail lisbon@diplobel.org; internet www.diplomatie.be/lisbon; Ambassador Rudy Huygelen.

Qatar: POB 24418, As-Sanaa St, District 64, Doha; tel. 4931542; fax 4930151; e-mail doha@diplobel.be; Ambassador GUY DE LAUWER.

Romania: 020061 Bucharest, Bd. Dacia 58, Sector 2; tel. (21) 2102970; fax (21) 2102803; e-mail bucharest@diplobel.org; internet www.diplobel.org/romania; Ambassador Philippe Roland.

Russian Federation: 121069 Moscow, ul. M. Molchanovka 7; tel. (495) 780-03-31; fax (495) 780-03-32; e-mail moscow@diplobel.org; internet www.diplomatie.be/moscow; Ambassador VINCENT MERTENS DE WILMARS.

Rwanda: rue Nyarugenge, BP 81, Kigali; tel. 575551; fax 573995; e-mail kigali@diplobel.be; Ambassador François Roux.

Saudi Arabia: POB 94396, Riyadh 11693; tel. (1) 488-2888; fax (1) 488-2033; e-mail ambelriyad@nesma.net.sa; Ambassador MICHEL LASTSCHENKO.

Senegal: ave des Jambaars, BP 524, Dakar; tel. 33-889-4390; fax 33-889-4398; e-mail ambeldak@orange.sn; internet www.diplomatie.be/dakar; Ambassador Luc Willemarck.

Serbia: 11000 Belgrade, Krunska 18; tel. (11) 3230018; fax (11) 3244394; e-mail belgrade@diplobel.org; Ambassador DENISE DE HAUWERE.

Singapore: 8 Shenton Way, 14-01 Temasek Tower, Singapore 068811; tel. 62207677; fax 62226976; e-mail singapore@diplobel.org; internet www.diplomatie.be/singapore; Ambassador Marc A. M. Calcoen.

Slovakia: Fraňa kráľa 5, 811 05 Bratislava; tel. (2) 5710-1211; fax (2) 5249-4296; internet www.diplomatie.be/bratislava; Ambassador ALAIN COOLS.

Slovenia: 1000 Ljubljana, trg Republike 3/IX; tel. (1) 2006010; fax (1) 4266395; e-mail ljubljana@diplobel.org; internet www.diplomatie.be/ljubljanafr; Ambassador Louis Mouraux.

South Africa: 625 Leyds St, Muckleneuk, Pretoria 0002; tel. (12) 4403201; fax (12) 4403216; e-mail pretoria@diplobel.org; internet www.diplomatie.be/pretoria; Ambassador JAN MUTTON.

Spain: Paseo de la Castellana 18, 6°, 28046 Madrid; tel. (91) 5776300; fax (91) 4318166; e-mail madrid@diplobel.org; internet www.diplobel.org/spain; Ambassador Claude Rijmenans.

Sweden: POB 1040, 101 38 Stockholm; Kungsbroplan 2, 2nd Floor, 112 27 Stockholm; tel. (8) 534-802-00; fax (8) 534-802-07; e-mail stockholm@diplobel.org; internet www.diplomatie.be/stockholm; Ambassador MARC BAPTIST.

Switzerland: Jubiläumstr. 41, 3005 Bern; tel. 313500150; fax 313500165; e-mail bern@diplobel.org; internet www.diplomatie.be/bern; Ambassador Régine De Clercq.

Syria: 3 rue Salaam, Bâtiment 101, 2e–3e étage, Mezzeh Est, Damascus; tel. (11) 61399931; fax (11) 61399977; e-mail damascus@diplobel.org; internet www.diplomatie.be/damascus; Ambassador DERRICK LUNCK.

Tanzania: Ocean Rd, POB 9210, Dar es Salaam; tel. (22) 2112688; fax (22) 2117621; e-mail daressalaam@diplobel.be; internet www.diplomatie.be/dar-es-salaam; Ambassador Peter Maddens.

Thailand: 17th Floor, Sathorn City Tower, 175 Thanon Sathorn Tai, Tungmahamek, Sathorn, Bangkok 10120; tel. (2) 679-5454; fax (2) 679-5467; e-mail bangkok@diplobel.org; internet www.diplomatie.be/bangkok; Ambassador JAN MATTHYSEN.

Tunisia: 47 rue du 1er juin, BP 24, 1002 Tunis; tel. (71) 781-655; fax (71) 792-797; e-mail tunis@diplobel.org; internet www.diplomatie.be/tunis; Ambassador Michel Carlier.

Turkey: Mahatma Gandhi Cad. 55, Gaziosmanpaşa, Ankara; tel. (312) 4056166; fax (312) 4468251; e-mail ankara@diplobel.org; internet www.diplomatie.be/ankara; Ambassador MARC VAN RYSELBERGHE.

Uganda: Rwenzori House, 3rd Floor, Plot 1, Lumumba Ave, POB 7043, Kampala; tel. (41) 4345559; fax (41) 4347212; e-mail kampala@diplobel.org; internet www.diplomatie.be/kampala; Ambassador Jan de Bruyne.

Ukraine: 01030 Kyiv, vul. Leontovicha 4; tel. (44) 238-26-00; fax (44) 238-26-01; e-mail kiev@diplobel.org; internet www.diplomatie.be/kiev; Ambassador MARC VINCK.

United Arab Emirates: POB 3686, Al-Masood Tower, 6th Floor, Hamdan St, Abu Dhabi; tel. (2) 6319449; fax (2) 6319353; e-mail abudhabi@diplobel.org; internet www.diplomatie.be/abudhabi; Ambassador Philippe Dartois.

United Kingdom: 17 Grosvenor Cres., London, SW1X 7EE; tel. (20) 7470-3700; fax (20) 7470-3795; e-mail london@diplobel.be; internet www.diplomatie.be/london; Ambassador JEAN-MICHEL VERANNEMAN DE WATERVLIET.

United States of America: 3330 Garfield St, NW, Washington, DC 20008; tel. (202) 333-6900; fax (202) 333-3079; e-mail washington@diplobel.org; internet www.diplobel.us; Ambassador Dominicus Struye de Swielande.

Vatican City: Via Giuseppe de Notaris 6A, 00197 Rome, Italy; tel. (06) 3224740; fax (06) 3226042; e-mail vatican@diplobel.be; internet www.diplomatie.be/vaticanfr; Ambassador FRANK DE CONINCK.

Venezuela: Quinta la Azulita, Avda 11, entre 6a y 7a Transversales, Apdo del Este 61550, Altamira, Caracas 1060; tel. (212) 263-3334; fax (212) 261-0309; e-mail caracas@diplobel.org; internet www.diplomatie.be/caracas; Ambassador Christine Stevens.

Viet Nam: 9th Floor, Hanoi Towers, 49 Hai Ba Trung, Hanoi; tel. (4) 9346179; fax (4) 9346183; e-mail hanoi@diplobel.be; internet www.diplomatie.be/hanoi; Ambassador HUBERT COOREMAN.

DIPLOMATIC MISSIONS OF BELIZE

United Nations: 800 Second Ave, Suite 400g, New York, NY 10017; tel. (212) 593-0999; fax (212) 593-0932; e-mail blzun@undp.org; Permanent Representative Stuart Leslie.

Austria: Franz Josefs Kai 13/5/16, Postfach 982, 1011 Vienna; tel. (1) 533-76-63; fax (1) 533-81-14; e-mail belizeembassy@utanet.at; Ambassador ALEXANDER PILETSKY.

Belgium: 136 blvd Brand Witlock, 1200 Brussels; tel. (2) 732-62-04; fax (2) 732-62-46; e-mail embelize@skynet.be; Ambassador Alexis Rosado.

China (Taiwan): 11/F, 9 Lane 62, Tien Mou West Rd, Taipei 11156; tel. (2) 28760894; fax (2) 28760896; e-mail embelroc@ms41.hinet.net; internet www.embassyofbelize.org.tw; Ambassador WILLIAM QUINTO.

Cuba: Avda 5, No 3608, entre 36 y 36a, Miramar, Havana; tel. (7) 204-3504; fax (7) 204-3506; e-mail belize.embassy@ip.etecsa.cu; Chargé d'affaires a.i. Margaret Juan.

Dominican Republic: Carretera La Isabela, Calle Proyecto 3, Arroyo Manzano 1, Santo Domingo, DN; tel. 567-7146; fax 567-7159; e-mail domrep@embelize.org; internet www.embelize.org; Ambassador R. EDUARDO LAMA S.

El Salvador: Calle el Bosque Norte y Calle Lomas de Candelaria 1, Bloque P, Col. Jardines de la Cima, 1a Etapa, San Salvador; tel. 2248-1423; fax 2273-6244; e-mail embassyofbelizeinelsal@yahoo.com; Ambassador Darwin Gabourel.

Guatemala: Edif. El Reformador, Suite 803, 8°, Avda de la Reforma 1-50, Zona 9, Guatemala City; tel. 2334-5531; fax 2334-5536; e-mail info@embajadadebelize.org; internet www.embajadadebelize.org; Ambassador ALFREDO MARTÍN MARTÍNEZ.

Italy: Piazza di Spagna 81, 00187 Roma; tel. (06) 69190776; fax (06) 69925794; Ambassador Nunzio Alfredo D'Angieri.

Mexico: Bernardo de Gálvez 215, Col. Lomas de Chapultepec, Del. Miguel Hidalgo, 11000 México, DF; tel. (55) 5520-1274; fax (55) 5520-6089; e-mail embelize@prodigy.net.mx; Ambassador SALVADOR AMÍN FIGUEROA.

Panama: Villa de la Fuente 1, F-32, Calle 22, POB 0819-12255, Panamá; tel. 236-3762; fax 236-4132; e-mail nmusag@cwpanama.net; Ambassador Alma Musa.

United Kingdom: 3rd Floor, 45 Crawford Pl., London, W1H 4LP; tel. (20) 7723-3603; fax (20) 7723-9637; e-mail bzhc-lon@btconnect.com; internet www.belizehighcommission.com; High Commr LAWRENCE SYLVESTER.

United States of America: 2535 Massachusetts Ave, NW, Washington, DC 20008; tel. (202) 332-9636; fax (202) 332-6888; e-mail chancery@embassyofbelize.org; internet www.embassyofbelize.org; Chargé d'affaires a.i. Nestor Mendez.

DIPLOMATIC MISSIONS OF BENIN

United Nations: 4 East 73rd St, New York, NY 10021; tel. (212) 249-6014; fax (212) 988-3714; e-mail benin@un.int; internet www.un.int/benin; Permanent Representative JEAN-MARIE EHOUZOU.

Algeria: BP 103, 16 Lot du Stade Birkhadem, Algiers; tel. (21) 56-52-71; Ambassador Leonard Adjin.

Belgium: 5 ave de l'Observatoire, 1180 Brussels; tel. (2) 374-91-92; fax (2) 375-83-26; e-mail ambabenin_benelux@yahoo.fr; Chargé d'affaires a.i. DÉSIRÉ AUGUSTE ADJAHI.

Brazil: SHIS, QI 9, Conj. 11, Casa 24, Lago Sul, 71625-110 Brasília, DF; tel. (61) 3248-2192; fax (61) 3248-5440; e-mail ambabeninbrasilia@yahoo.fr; Ambassador Isidore Benjamin Amédée Monsi.

Canada: 58 Glebe Ave, Ottawa, ON K1S 2C3; tel. (613) 233-4429; fax (613) 233-8952; e-mail ambaben@benin.ca; internet www.benin.ca; internet www.benin.ca; Chargé d'affaires a.i. AWAHOU LABOUDA.

China, People's Republic: 38 Guang Hua Lu, Jian Guo Men Wai, Beijing 100600; tel. (10) 65323054; fax (10) 65325103; Ambassador Sedozan Apithy.

Congo, Democratic Republic: 3990 ave des Cliniques, BP 3265, Kinshasa-Gombe; tel. (98) 128659; e-mail abkin@raga.net; Ambassador GEORGES S. WHANNOU DE DRAVO.

Côte d'Ivoire: rue des Jasmins, Lot 1610, Cocody-les-Deux-Plateaux, 09 BP 283, Abidjan 09; tel. 22-41-44-13; fax 22-42-76-07; Ambassador Omer Jean-Gilles de Souza.

Cuba: Calle 20, No 119, entre 1 y 3, Miramar, Havana; tel. (7) 204-2179; fax (7) 204-2334; e-mail ambencub@ceniai.inf.cu; Ambassador GRÉGOIRE LAITIAN HOUDÉ.

Denmark: Gamlehave Allé 12, 2920 Charlottenlund; tel. 39-68-10-30; fax 39-68-10-32; e-mail ambabenin@c.dk; internet www.ambabenin.dk; Chargé d'affaires a.i. Zacharie Richard Akplogan.

Ethiopia: Addis Ababa; Ambassador EDOUARD AHO-GELLE.

France: 87 ave Victor Hugo, 75116 Paris; tel. 1-45-00-98-82; fax 1-45-01-82-02; e-mail ambassade@ambassade-benin.org; internet www.ambassade-benin.org; Ambassador Edgar Yves Monnou.

Gabon: BP 3851, Akebe, Libreville; tel. 73-76-82; fax 73-77-75; Ambassador EL HADJ LASSISSI ADÉBO.

Germany: Englerallee 23, 14195 Berlin; tel. (30) 23631470; fax (30) 236314740; Ambassador Issa Kpara.

Ghana: 19 Volta St, Second Close, Airport Residential Area, POB 7871, Accra; tel. (21) 774860; fax (21) 774889; Ambassador PIERRE SADELER.

Japan: Shokokusha Bldg 6/F, 2-16-9, Hirakawachu, Chiyoda-ku, Tokyo 102-0093; tel. (3) 3556-2562; fax (3) 3556-2563; e-mail abenintyo@mist.ocn.ne.jp; Ambassador Allassane Yasso.

Libya: POB 6676, Sharia Ghout ash-Shaal, Tripoli; tel. (21) 4837663; fax (21) 834569; Ambassador LAFIA CHABI.

Morocco: 30 ave Mehdi ben Barka, BP 5187, Souissi, 10105 Rabat; tel. (3) 7754158; fax (3) 7754156; e-mail benin@menara.ma; Ambassador Issiradjou Ibrahim Gomina.

Niger: BP 11544, Niamey; tel. 20-72-28-60; Ambassador TAÏROU MAMADOU DJAOUGA.

Nigeria: 4 Abudu Smith St, Victoria Island, POB 5705, Lagos; tel. (1) 2614411; fax (1) 2612385; Ambassador Patrice Houngavou.

Russian Federation: 127006 Moscow, Uspenskii per. 7; tel. (495) 299-23-60; fax (495) 200-02-26; e-mail ambabeninmoscou@hotmail.com; Ambassador VISSINTO AYI D'ALMEIDA.

South Africa: 900 Park St, cnr Orient and Park Sts, Arcadia, Pretoria 0083; POB 26484, Arcadia 0007; tel. (12) 3426978; fax (12) 3421823; e-mail embbenin@yebo.co.za; Chargé d'affaires a.i. Pamphile C. Goutondji.

United States of America: 2124 Kalorama Rd, NW, Washington, DC 20008; tel. (202) 232-6656; fax (202) 265-1996; Ambassador SÈGBÉ CYRILLE OGUIN.

DIPLOMATIC MISSIONS OF BHUTAN

United Nations: 2 United Nations Plaza, 27th Floor, New York, NY 10017; tel. (212) 826-1919; fax (212) 826-2998; e-mail pmbnewyork@aol.com; Permanent Representative Daw Penjo.

Bangladesh: House 12, Rd 107, Gulshan 2, Dhaka 1212; tel. (2) 8826863; fax (2) 8823939; e-mail bhtemb@bdmail.net; Ambassador DASHO TSHERING DORJI.

India: Chandragupta Marg, Chanakyapuri, New Delhi 110 021; tel. (11) 26889807; fax (11) 26876710; e-mail bhutan@vsnl.com; Ambassador Lyonpo Dago Tshering.

Kuwait: POB 1510, 13016 Safat, Adailiya-Block 3, Issa Abd ar-Rahman al-Assoussi St, Jadda 32, Villa 7, Kuwait City; tel. 2516640; fax 2516550; e-mail bhutankuwait@hotmail.com; Ambassador TSHERING WANGDI.

Thailand: 375/1 Soi Ratchadanivej, Thanon Pracha-Uthit, Huay Kwang, Bangkok 10320; tel. (2) 274-4740; fax (2) 274-4743; e-mail bht_emb_bkk@yahoo.com; Ambassador Singye Dorji.

DIPLOMATIC MISSIONS OF BOLIVIA

United Nations: 211 East 43rd St, 8th Floor, Rm 802, New York, NY 10017; tel. (212) 682-8132; fax (212) 682-8133; e-mail bolivia@un.int; Permanent Representative E. HUGO SILES-ALVARADO.

Argentina: Corrientes 545, 2°, C1043AAF Buenos Aires; tel. (11) 4394-6042; fax (11) 5217-1070; internet www.embajadadebolivia.com.ar; Chargé d'affaires a.i. Sixto Julio Valdez Cueto.

Austria: Waaggasse 10/4, 1040 Vienna; tel. (1) 587-46-75; fax (1) 586-68-80; e-mail embolaustria@of-viena.at; Ambassador DR HORACIO BAZOBERRY OTERO.

Belgium: 176 ave Louise, BP 6, 1050 Brussels; tel. (2) 627-00-10; fax (2) 647-47-82; e-mail embajada.bolivia@embolbrus.be; internet www.embolbrus.be; Ambassador Cristian Manuel Inchauste Sandoval.

Brazil: SHIS, QI 19, Conj. 13, Casa 19, 71655-130 Brasília, DF; tel. (61) 3366-3432; fax (61) 3366-3136; e-mail embolivia-brasilia@embolivia-brasil.org.br; internet www.embolivia-brasil.org.br; Ambassador RENÉ MAURICIO DORFLER OCAMPO.

Canada: 130 Albert St, Suite 416, Ottawa, ON K1P 5G4; tel. (613) 236-5730; fax (613) 236-8237; e-mail bolivianembassy@bellnet.ca; Ambassador Edgar José Torrez-Mosqueira.

China, People's Republic: 2-3-2 Tayuan Diplomatic Office Bldg, Beijing 100600; tel. (10) 65323074; fax (10) 65324686; e-mail embolch@public3.bta.net.cn; Ambassador LUIS FERNANDO RODRÍGUEZ UREÑA.

Colombia: Transversal 14a, No 118a-26, Apdo Aéreo 96219, Santa Barbara, Bogotá, DC; tel. (1) 629-8237; fax (1) 619-4940; e-mail embolivia-bogota@rree.gov.bo; Ambassador Carlos Vladimir Schmidt Colque.

Costa Rica: Barrio Rohrmoser 669, Apdo 84810, 1000 San José; tel. 296-3747; fax 232-7292; e-mail embocr@racsa.co.cr; Ambassador MARTÍN CALLISAYA COAQUIRA.

Cuba: Calle 26, No 113, entre 1 y 3, Miramar, Havana; tel. (7) 204-2426; fax (7) 204-2127; e-mail emboliviahabana@cubacel.net; Ambassador Saúl Chávez Orozco.

Denmark: Store Kongensgade 81, 2nd Floor, 1264 Copenhagen K; tel. 33-12-49-00; fax 33-12-49-03; e-mail embocopenhagen@mail.dk; Ambassador EUGENIO POMA AÑAGUAYA.

Ecuador: Avda Eloy Alfaro 2432 y Fernando Ayarza, Apdo 17-210003, Quito; tel. (2) 244-4830; fax (2) 224-4833; e-mail embolivia-quito@andinanet.net; Ambassador Juan Xavier Zarate Rivas.

Egypt: 21 New Ramses Centre, Sharia B. Oman, Cairo 11794 (Dokki); tel. (2) 7624362; fax (2) 7624360; e-mail embolivia_cairo@yahoo.com; Chargé d'affaires a.i. RAÚL PALZA ZEBALLOS.

France: 12 ave Président Kennedy, 75016 Paris; tel. 1-42-24-93-44; fax 1-45-25-86-23; e-mail ambassade@amb-bolivie.fr; internet www.amb-bolivie.fr; Ambassador Luzmila Carpio Sangûeza.

Germany: Wichmannstr. 6, 10787 Berlin; tel. (30) 2639150; fax (30) 26391515; e-mail embajada.bolivia@berlin.de; internet www.bolivia.de; Ambassador WALTER PRUDENCIO MAGNE VÉLIZ.

Israel: Toyota Bldg, 13th Floor, 65 Yigal Alon St, Tel-Aviv 67443; tel. 3-5621992; fax 3-5621990; e-mail embolivia-telaviv@emb.co.il; Ambassador Gen. Reynaldo Caceres Quiroga.

Italy: Via Brenta 2A, int. 18, 00198 Roma; tel. (06) 8841001; e-mail embolivia-roma@rree.gov.bo; Ambassador ESTEBAN ELMER CATARINA MAMANI.

Japan: Kowa Bldg, No. 38, Room 804, 4-12-24, Nishi Azabu, Minato-ku, Tokyo 106-0031; tel. (3) 3499-5441; fax (3) 3499-5443; e-mail emboltk1@ad.il24.net; Ambassador Masakatsu Jaime Ashimine Oshiro.

Mexico: Goethe 104, Col. Anzures, Del. Miguel Hidalgo, 11590 México, DF; tel. (55) 5255-3620; e-mail embajada@embol.org.mx; internet www.embol.org.mx; Ambassador JORGE MANSILLA TORRES.

Netherlands: Nassaulaan 5, 2514 JS The Hague; tel. (70) 3616707; fax (70) 3620039; e-mail embolned@xs4all.nl; Ambassador Roberto Calzadilla Sarmiento.

Panama: Calle Eric Arturo del Valle, Bella Vista 1, Panamá; tel. 269-0274; fax 264-3868; e-mail emb_bol_pan@cwpanama.net; Ambassador EDGAR SOLIZ MORALES.

Paraguay: Calle Campos Cervera 6421, Asunción; tel. (21) 61-4984; fax (21) 60-1999; e-mail embolivia.asuncion@personaldata.net.py; Ambassador Marco Antonio Vidaurre Noriega.

Peru: Los Castaños 235, San Isidro, Lima 27; tel. (1) 4402095; fax (1) 4402298; e-mail jemis@emboli.attla.com.pe; Ambassador FRANZ SOLANO CHUQUIMIA.

Russian Federation: 115191 Moscow, ul. Serpukhovskii Val 8/135–137; tel. (495) 954-06-30; fax (495) 958-07-55; e-mail embolrus@online.ru; internet www.emborus.com; Ambassador Sergio Sánchez Ballivián.

Spain: Velázquez 26, 3°, 28001 Madrid; tel. (91) 5780835; fax (91) 5773946; e-mail embajada@embajadadebolivia.es; internet www.embajadadebolivia.es; Ambassador MARÍA DEL CARMEN ALMENDRAS CAMARGO.

Sweden: Södra Kungsvägen 60, 181 32 Lidingö; tel. (8) 731-58-30; fax (8) 767-63-11; e-mail embolivia-estocolmo@telia.com; Chargé d'affaires a.i. María Elena García de Baccino.

United Kingdom: 106 Eaton Sq., London, SW1W 9AD; tel. (20) 7235-4248; fax (20) 7235-1286; e-mail info@embassyofbolivia.co.uk; internet www.embassyofbolivia.co.uk; Ambassador MARÍA BEATRIZ SOUVIRON CRESPO.

United States of America: 3014 Massachusetts Ave, NW, Washington, DC 20008; tel. (202) 483-4410; fax (202) 328-3712; e-mail webmaster@bolivia-usa.org; internet www.bolivia-usa.org; Ambassador Mario Gustavo Guzmán Saldaña.

Uruguay: Dr Prudencio de Peña 2469, 11300 Montevideo; tel. (2) 7083573; fax (2) 7080066; e-mail embouy@adinet.com; Ambassador MARCELO JANKO ALVAREZ.

Vatican City: Via di Porta Angelica 15/2, 00193 Rome, Italy; tel. (06) 6874191; fax (06) 6874193; e-mail embolivat@rdn.it; Ambassador Carlos Federico de la Riva Guerra.

Venezuela: Avda Luis Roche con 6a Transversal, Altamira, Caracas; tel. (212) 263-3015; fax (212) 261-3386; e-mail emboliviaven@cantv.net; Ambassador JORGE ALVARO RIVAS.

DIPLOMATIC MISSIONS OF BOSNIA AND HERZEGOVINA

United Nations: 866 United Nations Plaza, Suite 580, New York, NY 10017; tel. (212) 751-9015; fax (212) 751-9019; e-mail bosnia@un.int; internet www.un.int/bosnia; Permanent Representative Milos Prica.

Argentina: 14 de Julio 1656, C1430END Buenos Aires; tel. (11) 4554–9257; e-mail embajadabh@embajadabh.org.ar; internet www.embajadabh.org.ar; Chargé d'affaires a.i. MARIO ĐURAGIĆ.

Australia: 5 Beale Crescent, Deakin, ACT 2600; tel. (2) 6232-4646; fax (2) 6232-5554; e-mail embaucbr@tpg.com.au; internet www.bosnia.webone.com .au; Ambassador Amira Kapetanović.

Austria: Tivoligasse 54, 1120 Vienna; tel. (1) 811-85-55; fax (1) 811-85-69; e-mail bihembassyvienna@diplomats.com; Ambassador Tomislav Limov.

Belgium: 15–17 rue Belliard, 7e étage, 1040 Brussels; tel. (2) 502-01-88; fax (2) 644-32-54; e-mail info@bh-embassy-belgium.org; internet www.bh-embassy -belgium.org; Ambassador Nikola Radovanović.

Canada: 130 Albert St, Suite 805, Ottawa, ON K1P 5G4; tel. (613) 236-0028; fax (613) 236-1139; e-mail embassyofbih@bellnet.ca; internet www .bhembassy.ca; Ambassador Milenko Misić.

China, People's Republic: 1-5-1 Tayuan Diplomatic Office Bldg, Beijing 100600; tel. (10) 65326587; fax (10) 65326418; Ambassador Pero Barunčić.

Croatia: 10000 Zagreb, Josipa Torbara 9; tel. (1) 4683761; fax (1) 4683764; e-mail ambasada-bh-zg@zg.htnet.hr; Ambassador Aleksandar Dragičević.

Czech Republic: Opletalova 27, 110 00 Prague 1; tel. 224422510; fax 222210183; e-mail embbh@iol.cz; Ambassador Ivan Orlić.

Denmark: H. C. Andersens Blvd 48, 2nd Floor, 1553 Copenhagen V; tel. 33-33-80-40; fax 33-33-80-17; e-mail info@embassybh.dk; internet www .embassybh.dk; Ambassador Sead Maslo.

Egypt: 42 Sharia as-Sawra, Cairo (Dokki); tel. (2) 7499191; fax (2) 7499190; e-mail ambbih@link.net; Ambassador Radomir Kosić.

France: 174 rue de Courcelles, 75017 Paris; tel. 1-42-67-34-22; fax 1-40-53-85-22; e-mail amb.pariz@mvp.gov.ba; Ambassador Željana Zovko.

Germany: Ibsenstr. 14, 10439 Berlin; tel. (30) 81471210; fax (30) 81471211; Ambassador Mitar Kujundžić.

Greece: Filaellinon 25, 105 57 Athens; tel. (210) 6410788; fax (210) 6411978; e-mail ambasbih@otenet.gr; Ambassador Milovan Blagojević.

Hungary: 1026 Budapest, Pasaréti u. 48; tel. (1) 212-0106; fax (1) 212-0109; Ambassador Branimir Mandić.

India: E-9/11 Vasant Vihar, New Delhi 110 057; tel. (11) 51662481; fax (11) 51662482; e-mail bosher@airtelbroadband.in; Ambassador Kemal Muftić.

Indonesia: Menara Imperium, 11th Floor, Suite D-2, Metropolitan Kuningan Super Blok, Kav. 1, Jalan H. R. Rasuna Said, Jakarta 12980; tel. (21) 83703022; fax (21) 83703029; Chargé d'affaires a.i. Dinko Tomac.

Iran: No. 485, Aban Alley, 4th St, Iran Zamin Ave, Shahrak-e-Ghods, Tehran; tel. (21) 88086929; fax (21) 88092120; e-mail ba-emb-ir-teh@kavosh .net; Ambassador Senahid Bristrić.

Israel: 13th Floor, 7 Menachim Begin Rd, Ramat-Gan 52681; tel. 3-6124499; fax 3-6124488; Ambassador Nedeljko Masleška.

Italy: Piazzale Clodio 12, int. 17/18, 00195 Roma; tel. (06) 39742817; fax (06) 39030567; e-mail ambasciata@ambih.191.it; Ambassador Midhat Haracic.

Japan: 3-4, Rokuban-cho, Chiyoda-ku, Tokyo 102-0085; tel. (3) 3556-4151; fax (3) 3556-4152; e-mail bih8emb@gol.com; Chargé d'affaires a.i. Mithat Pašić.

Jordan: POB 850836, Amman 11185; tel. (6) 5856921; fax (6) 5856923; e-mail ambamman@wanadoo.jo; Ambassador Vasilj Krunoslav.

Kuwait: POB 6131, 32036 Hawalli, Bayan, Block 6, St 4, House 25, Kuwait City; tel. 5392637; fax 5392106; Ambassador Šerif Mujkanović.

Libya: POB 6946, Sharia Abd al-Melik bin Kutn, Tripoli; tel. (21) 4776442; Ambassador Šeta Ferhat.

Macedonia, former Yugoslav Republic: 1000 Skopje, Mile Popjordanov 56; tel. (2) 3086216; fax (2) 3086221; Ambassador Milan Balaban.

Malaysia: JKR 854, Jalan Bellamy, 50460 Kuala Lumpur; tel. (3) 21440353; fax (3) 21426025; e-mail hsomun@hotmail.com; Ambassador Mustafa Mujezinović.

Montenegro: 81000 Podgorica, Atinska 58; tel. (81) 618105; fax (81) 618016; Ambassador Branimir Jukić.

Netherlands: Bezuidenhoutseweg 223, 2495 AL The Hague; tel. (70) 3588505; fax (70) 3584367; e-mail fuad.sabeta@mfa.gov.ba; internet www.xs4all.nl/ ˜bih; Ambassador Fuad Sabeta.

Norway: Bygdøy allé 10, POB 2407 Solli, 0201 Oslo; tel. 22-54-09-63; fax 22-55-27-50; e-mail ambasadagkbih@gkbih.com; internet www.gkbih.com; Ambassador Faik Uzonović.

Pakistan: House No. 1, Kaghan Rd, F-8/3, Islamabad; tel. (51) 2261003; fax (51) 2261004; e-mail ambassador@bosnianembassypakistan.org; internet www.bosnianembassypakistan.org; Ambassador Damir Dzanko.

Poland: 00-789 Warsaw, ul. Humanska 10; tel. (22) 8569935; fax (22) 8481521; Ambassador Zoran Skenderija.

Qatar: POB 876, Doha; tel. 4670194; fax 4670595; e-mail ambasada@qatar .net.qa; internet www.bhembassyqatar.org; Ambassador Azra Kalajdžisalihović.

Romania: 011786 Bucharest 1, Str. Stockholm 12; tel. (21) 4092601; fax (21) 4092603; Ambassador Branko T. Nešković.

Russian Federation: 119590 Moscow, ul. Mosfilmovskaya 50/1/484; tel. (499) 147-64-88; fax (499) 147-64-89; e-mail embassybih@mail.cnt.ru; Ambassador Enver Halilović.

Saudi Arabia: POB 94301, Riyadh 11693; tel. (1) 456-7914; fax (1) 454-4360; e-mail baembsaruh@awalnet.net.sa; Ambassador Razim Čolić.

Serbia: 11000 Belgrade, Krunska 9; tel. (11) 3241170; fax (11) 3241057; Chargé d'affaires a.i. Amira Arifović-Harms.

Slovenia: 1000 Ljubljana, Korlajeva 26; tel. (1) 2343259; fax (1) 2343261; Ambassador Izmir Talić.

South Africa: 25 Stella St, Brooklyn, Pretoria 0181; POB 11464, Hatfield 0028; tel. (12) 3465547; fax (12) 3462295; e-mail bih@mweb.co.za; Ambassador Dragan Pjević.

Spain: Lagasca 24, 2°, 28001 Madrid; tel. (91) 5750870; fax (91) 4355056; e-mail ambasada@ctv.es; Ambassador Josip Brkić.

Sweden: Birger Jarlsgt. 55, POB 7102, 103 87 Stockholm; tel. (8) 440-05-40; fax (8) 24-98-30; e-mail amb.bih.sto@telia.com; Ambassador Jakov Skočibušić.

Switzerland: Thorackerstr. 3, 3074 Muri bei Bern; tel. 313511052; fax 313511079; e-mail emb-ch-brn@vtxmail.ch; Ambassador Jasmina Pašalić.

Turkey: Turan Emeksiz Sok. 3/9, Park Evleri B Blok, Gaziosmanpaşa, Ankara; tel. (312) 4273602; fax (312) 4273604; e-mail bh_emb@kablonet .com.tr; Ambassador Nada Janković.

United Arab Emirates: POB 43362, Abu Dhabi; tel. (2) 6444164; fax (2) 6443619; e-mail abhad@bhmc.ae; internet www.bhmc.ae; Ambassador Milutin Vasiljević.

United Kingdom: 5–7 Lexham Gdns, London, W8 5JJ; tel. (20) 7373-0867; fax (20) 7373-0871; e-mail embassy@bhembassy.co.uk; internet www .bhembassy.co.uk; Ambassador Tanja Milasinović.

United States of America: 2109 E St, NW, Washington, DC 20037; tel. (202) 337-1500; fax (202) 337-1502; e-mail info@bhembassy.org; internet www .bhembassy.org; Ambassador Bisera Turković.

Vatican City: Piazzale le Clodio 12, 00195 Rome, Italy; tel. (06) 39742411; fax (06) 39742484; e-mail embvavat@tin.it; Ambassador (vacant).

DIPLOMATIC MISSIONS OF BOTSWANA

United Nations: 103 East 37th St, New York, NY 10016; tel. (212) 889-2277; fax (212) 725-5061; e-mail botswana@un.int; Permanent Representative Samuel Otsile Outlule.

Australia: 52 Culgoa Circuit, O'Malley, ACT 2606; tel. (2) 6290-7500; fax (2) 6286-2566; High Commissioner Molosiwa Selepeng.

Belgium: 169 ave de Tervueren, 1150 Brussels; tel. (2) 735-20-70; fax (2) 735-63-18; e-mail botswana@brutele.be; Ambassador Claurinah Tshenolo Modise.

China, People's Republic: Unit 811, IBM Tower, Pacific Century Place, 2A Gong Ti Bei Lu, Beijing 100027; tel. (10) 65391616; fax (10) 65391199; Ambassador Naomi E. Majinda.

Ethiopia: POB 22282, Addis Ababa; tel. (11) 715422; fax (11) 714099; Ambassador Zibane John Ntakhwana.

Japan: 6F Kearny Place, 4-5-10, Shiba, Minato-ku, Tokyo 108-0014; tel. (3) 5440-5676; fax (3) 5765-7581; e-mail botjap@sepia.ocn.ne.jp; internet www .botswanaembassy.or.jp; Ambassador Oscar Motswagae.

Namibia: 101 Nelson Mandela Ave, POB 20359, Windhoek; tel. (61) 221942; fax (61) 221948; High Commissioner Norman Moleboge.

South Africa: 24 Amos St, Colbyn, Pretoria 0083; POB 57035, Arcadia 0007; tel. (12) 4309640; fax (12) 3421845; High Commissioner Motlhagodi Molomo.

Sweden: Tyrgt. 11, POB 26024, 100 41 Stockholm; tel. (8) 545-258-00; fax (8) 723-00-87; Ambassador Bernadette Sebage Rathedi.

United Kingdom: 6 Stratford Pl., London, W1C 1AY; tel. (20) 7499-0031; fax (20) 7495-8595; e-mail bohico@govbw.com; High Commr Roy Blackbeard.

United States of America: 1531-1533 New Hampshire Ave, NW, Washington, DC 20036; tel. (202) 244-4990; fax (202) 244-4164; e-mail cratsiripe@gov.bw; internet www.botswanaembassy.org; Ambassador Lapologang Caesar Lekoa.

Zambia: 5201 Pandit Nehru Rd, Diplomatic Triangle, POB 31910, 10101 Lusaka; tel. (1) 250555; fax (1) 250804; High Commissioner LAPOLOGANG CAESAR LEKOA.

Zimbabwe: 22 Phillips Ave, Belgravia, POB 563, Harare; tel. (4) 729551; fax (4) 721360; Ambassador Pelokgale Seloma.

DIPLOMATIC MISSIONS OF BRAZIL

United Nations: 747 Third Ave, 9th Floor, New York, NY 10017; tel. (212) 372-2600; fax (212) 371-5716; e-mail braun@delbrasonu.org; internet www .un.int/brazil; Permanent Representative MARIA LUIZA RIBEIRO VIOTTI.

Algeria: BP 246, 55 chemin Cheikh Bachir El-Ibrahimi, el-Biar, Algiers; tel. (21) 92-44-37; fax (21) 92-41-25; e-mail brasilia@wissal.dz; internet www .ambresil.dz; Ambassador Sérgio França Danese.

Angola: Rua Houari Boumedienne 132, Miramar, CP 5428, Luanda; tel. 222441307; fax 222444913; e-mail emb.bras@ebonet.net; Ambassador MARCELO DA SILVA VASCONCELOS.

Argentina: Cerrito 1350, C1010ABB Buenos Aires; tel. (11) 4515-2400; fax (11) 4515-2401; e-mail info@embrasil.org.ar; internet www.brasil.org.ar; Ambassador Mauro Vieira.

Armenia: 0010 Yerevan, S. Yerevantzu 57; tel. (10) 50-02-09; fax (10) 53-69-55; .

Australia: GPOB 1540, Canberra, ACT 2601; tel. (2) 6273-2372; fax (2) 6273-2375; e-mail brazilemb@brazil.org.au; internet www.brazil.org.au; Ambassador Fernando de Mello Barreto.

Austria: Pestalozzigasse 4/2, 1010 Vienna; tel. (1) 512-06-31; fax (1) 513-83-74; e-mail mail@brasilemb.at; Ambassador JULIO CEZAR ZELNER GONÇALVES.

Barbados: Sunjet House, 3rd Floor, Fairchild St, Bridgetown; tel. 427-1735; fax 427-1744; e-mail brembarb@sunbeach.net; internet www.brazilbb.org; Ambassador Orlando Galvêas Oliveira.

Belgium: 350 ave Louise, 6e étage, BP 5, 1050 Brussels; tel. (2) 640-20-15; fax (2) 640-81-34; e-mail brasbruxelas@beon.be; Ambassador ALMIR FRANCO DE SÁ BARBUDA.

Belize: 12 Floral Park Ave, POB 548, Belmopan; tel. 822-0460; fax 822-8461; e-mail embbrazil@btl.net; internet www.abe.mre.gov.br; Ambassador Roberto Coutinho.

Bolivia: Edif. Multicentro, Torre B, Avda Arce s/n, esq. Rosendo Gutiérrez, Sopocachi, La Paz; tel. (2) 244-0202; fax (2) 244-0043; e-mail webmaster@ brasil.org.bo; internet www.brasil.org.bo; Ambassador FREDERICO CEZAR DE ARAUJO.

Bulgaria: 1113 Sofia, ul. F. Zh. Kyuri 19/1/6; tel. (2) 971-98-19; fax (2) 971-28-18; internet www.brazil-bg.info; Ambassador Paulo Américo Veiga Wolowski.

Cameroon: rue 1828, Bastos, BP 16227, Yaoundé; tel. 2220-1085; fax 2220-2048; e-mail embiaunde@cameroun-online.com; Ambassador ROBERTO PESSOA DACOSTA.

Canada: 450 Wilbrod St, Ottawa, ON K1N 6M8; tel. (613) 237-1090; fax (613) 237-6144; e-mail mailbox@brasembottawa.org; internet www .brasembottawa.org; Ambassador Valdemar Carneiro Leão Neto.

Cape Verde: Chã de Areia 2, CP 93, Praia, Santiago; tel. 2615607; fax 2615609; e-mail contato@embrasilpraia.org; Ambassador MARIA DULCE SILVA BARROS.

Chile: Alonso Ovalle 1665, Casilla 1497, Santiago; tel. (2) 698-2486; fax (2) 671-5961; e-mail embrasil@brasembsantiago.cl; internet www .brasembsantiago.cl; Ambassador Mario Vilalva.

China, People's Republic: 27 Guang Hua Lu, Jian Guo Men Wai, Beijing 100600; tel. (10) 65322881; fax (10) 65322751; e-mail empequim@public.bta .net.cn; internet www.brazil.org.cn; AmbassadorLUIZ CASTRO NEVES.

Colombia: Calle 93, No 14-20, 8°, Bogotá, DC; tel. (1) 218-0800; fax (1) 218-8393; internet www.brasil.org.co; Ambassador Valdemar Carneiro Leão.

Costa Rica: Edif. Torre Mercedes, 6°, Apdo 10132, 1000 San José; tel. 295-6875; fax 295-6874; e-mail embajador@embrasil.co.cr; Ambassador HILDEBRANDO TADEU NASCIMENTO VALADARES.

Côte d'Ivoire: Immeuble Alpha 2000, rue Gourgas, 01 BP 3820, Abidjan 01; tel. 20-22-23-41; fax 22-22-64-01; e-mail brascote@aviso.ci; Ambassador Fausto Carmello.

Croatia: 10000 Zagreb, trg Nikole Šubića Zrinskog 10/I; tel. (1) 4002250; e-mail brasemb@zg.primatel.hr; Ambassador HAROLDO VALLADAO.

Cuba: Calle Lamparilla, No 2, 4°K, Habana Vieja, Havana; tel. (7) 66-9052; fax (7) 66-2912; e-mail embhavana@brasil.co.cu; Ambassador Bernardo Pericás Neto.

Czech Republic: Panská 5, 110 00 Prague 1; tel. 224321910; fax 224312901; e-mail chebrem@mbox.vol.cz; AmbassadorLEDA LUCIA MARTINS CAMARGO.

Denmark: Kastelsvej 19, 3rd and 4th Floors, 2100 Copenhagen Ø; tel. 39-20-64-78; fax 39-27-36-07; e-mail ambassade@brazil.dk; internet www.brazil .dk; Ambassador Georges Lamazière.

Dominican Republic: Eduardo Vicioso 64, esq. Avda Winston Churchill, Apdo 1655, Santo Domingo, DN; tel. 532-0868; fax 532-0917; e-mail contacto@embajadadebrasil.org.do; internet www.embajadadebrasil.org .do; Ambassador RONALDO EDGAR DUNLOP.

Ecuador: Edif. España, Avda Amazonas 1429 y Colón, 9° y 10°, Apdo 17-01-231, Quito; tel. (2) 256-3142; fax (2) 250-4468; e-mail ebrasil@ embajadadelbrasil.org.ec; internet www.embajadadelbrasil.org.ec; Ambassador Antonino Marques-Porto.

Egypt: 1125 Corniche en-Nil Ave, Cairo 11561 (Maspiro); tel. (2) 5773013; fax (2) 5774860; e-mail brasemb@soficom.com.eg; internet www .brazilembcairo.org; Ambassador ELIM SATURNINO FERREIRA DUTRA.

El Salvador: Blvd de Hipódromo 132, Col. San Benito, San Salvador; tel. 2298-1993; fax 2279-3934; e-mail brasemb@es.com.sv; Ambassador Eduardo Prisco Paraiso Ramos.

Ethiopia: Bole Sub-City, Kebele 2, House No. 2830, POB 2458, Addis Ababa; tel. (11) 6620401; fax (11) 6620412; e-mail embradisadm@ethionet.et; Ambassador RENATO XAVIER.

Finland: Itäinen puistotie 4b 1, 00140 Helsinki; tel. (9) 6841500; fax (9) 650084; e-mail brasemb.helsinki@kolumbus.fi; internet www.brazil.fi; Ambassador Luiz Sérgio Gama Figueira.

France: 34 cours Albert 1er, 75008 Paris; tel. 1-45-61-63-00; fax 1-42-89-03-45; e-mail imprensa@bresil.org; internet www.bresil.org; Ambassador JOSÉ MAURICIO BUSTANI.

Gabon: blvd de l'Indépendance, BP 3899, Libreville; tel. 76-05-35; fax 74-03-43; e-mail emblibreville@inet.ga; internet www.ambassadedubresil-gabon .org; Ambassador Carlos A. Ferreira Guimarães.

Germany: Wallstr. 57, 10179 Berlin; tel. (30) 726280; fax (30) 72628320; e-mail brasil@brasemberlin.de; internet www.brasilianische-botschaft.de; Ambassador LUIZ FELIPE DE SEIXAS CORRÊA.

Ghana: Millennium Heights Bldg 2a, 14 Liberation Link, Airport Commercial Area, POB CT3859, Accra; tel. (21) 774908; fax (21) 778566; Ambassador Louis Fernando de Andradi Serra.

Greece: Plateia Philikis Etairias 14, 106 73 Athens; tel. (210) 7213039; fax (210) 7244731; e-mail embagre@embratenas.gr; Ambassador AFFONSO EMILIO DE ALENCASTRO MASSOT.

Guatemala: 18a Calle 2-22, Zona 14, Apdo 196-a, Guatemala City; tel. 2337-0949; fax 2337-3475; e-mail braembx@intelnet.net.gt; internet www .embajadadebrasil.com.gt; Ambassador Renan Paes Barreto.

Guinea-Bissau: Rua São Tomé, Esquina Rua Moçambique, CP 29, Bissau; tel. 201327; fax 201317; e-mail embaixada-brasil@bissau.net; internet www .guine.org; Ambassador JOÃO BATISTA CRUZ.

Guyana: 308 Church St, Queenstown, POB 10489, Georgetown; tel. 225-7970; fax 226-9063; e-mail guibrem@solutions2000.net; Ambassador Arthur V. C. Meyer.

Haiti: Immeuble Héxagone, 3ème étage, angle des rues Clerveaux et Darguin, Pétion-Ville, BP 15845, Port-au-Prince; tel. 256-9662; fax 256-0900; e-mail haibrem@accesshaiti.com; Ambassador IGOR KIPMAN.

Honduras: Col. Palmira, Calle República del Brasil, Apdo 341, Tegucigalpa; tel. 221-4432; fax 236-5873; e-mail brastegu@sigmanet.hn; Ambassador Brian Michael Fraser Neele.

Hungary: 1123 Budapest, Alkotás u. 50; tel. (1) 351-0060; fax (1) 351-0066; internet www.brazil.hu; Ambassador JOSÉ AUGUSTO LINDGREN ALVES.

India: 8 Aurangzeb Rd, New Delhi 110 011; tel. (11) 23017301; fax (11) 23793684; e-mail brasindi@vsnl.com; Ambassador José Vicente De Sa Pimentel.

Indonesia: Menara Mulia, Suite 1602, Jalan Jenderal Gatot Subroto, Kav. 9–11, Jakarta 12390; tel. (21) 5265656; fax (21) 5265659; internet www .brazilembassy.or.id; Ambassador EDMUNDO SUSSUMU FUJITA.

Iran: POB 19886-3854, 26 Yekta St, Zafaranieh, Tehran; tel. (21) 22743996; fax (21) 22744009; e-mail emb_brazil@yahoo.com; internet www.braziliran .com; Ambassador Luiz Antônio Fechini Gomez.

Ireland: HSBC House, 5th Floor, 41–54 Harcourt St, Dublin 2; tel. (1) 4756000; fax (1) 4751341; e-mail brasembdublin@brazil-ie.org; internet www .brazil.ie; Ambassador STÉLIO MARCOS AMARANTE.

Israel: 2 Beit Yachin, 8th Floor, Kaplan St, Tel-Aviv 64734; tel. 3-6919292; fax 3-6916060; e-mail embrisra@netvision.net.il; Ambassador Sergio Moreira Lima.

Italy: Palazzo Pamphili, Piazza Navona 14, 00186 Roma; tel. (06) 683981; fax (06) 6867858; e-mail info@ambrasile.it; internet www.ambasciatadelbrasile .it; Ambassador ADHEMAR GABRIEL BAHADIAN.

Jamaica: Pan Caribbean Bldg, 10th Floor, 60 Knutsford Blvd, Kingston 5; tel. 929-8607; fax 968-5897; Ambassador (vacant).

Japan: 2-11-12, Kita Aoyama, Minato-ku, Tokyo 107-8633; tel. (3) 3404-5211; fax (3) 3405-5846; e-mail brasemb@brasemb.or.jp; internet www .brasemb.or.jp; Ambassador ANDRÉ MATTOSO MAIA AMADO.

Jordan: POB 5497, Amman 11183; tel. (6) 4642183; fax (6) 4641328; e-mail jorbrem@wanadoo.jo; Ambassador Antônio Carlos Coelho da Rocha.

Kazakhstan: 010000 Astana, Kabanbai Batyr 6/1; tel. (7172) 92-51-12; fax (7172) 92-51-17; e-mail brasembastana@mre.gov.br; Ambassador ESTRADA MEYER.

Kenya: Tanar Center, UN Crescent Rd, UN Close, Gigiri, Nairobi; tel. (20) 7125765; fax (20) 7125767; Ambassador Joaquim Augusto Whitaker Salles.

Korea, Republic: Ihn Gallery Bldg, 4th and 5th Floors, 141 Palpan-dong, Jongno-gu, Seoul; tel. (2) 738-4970; fax (2) 738-4974; e-mail braseul@kornet .net; internet www.brasemb.or.kr; Ambassador CELINA ASSUMPÇÃO DO VALLE PEREIRA.

Kuwait: POB 39761, 73058 Nuzha, Block 2, St 1, Jadah 1, Villa 8, Kuwait City; tel. 5328610; fax 5328613; e-mail brasemkw@qualitynet.net; internet www.brazilianembassykw.com; Ambassador Mario da Graça Roiter.

Lebanon: POB 40242, Baabda, Beirut; tel. (5) 921255; fax (5) 923001; e-mail braemlib@dm.net.lb; Ambassador EDUARDO AUGUSTO IBIAPINA DE SEIXAS.

Libya: POB 2270, Sharia ben Ashour, Tripoli; tel. (21) 3614894; fax (21) 3614895; e-mail brcastripoli@Ittnet.net; Ambassador Joaquim Palmeiro.

Malaysia: Suite 20-01, 20th Floor, Menara Tan & Tan, 207 Jalan Tun Razak, 50400 Kuala Lumpur; tel. (3) 21711420; fax (3) 21711427; e-mail brazil@po .jaring.my; internet www.brazilembassy.org.my; Chargé d'affaires a.i. CESAR DE PAULA CIDADE.

Mexico: Lope de Armendáriz 130, Col. Lomas Virreyes, Del. Miguel Hidalgo, 11000 México, DF; tel. (55) 5201-4531; fax (55) 5520-4929; e-mail embrasil@brasil.org.mx; internet www.brasil.org.mx; Ambassador Iván Oliveira Cannabrava.

Morocco: 10 ave el-Jacaranda, Secteur 2, Hay Riad, 10000 Rabat; tel. (3) 7714663; fax (3) 7714808; e-mail brabat@menara.ma; internet www .ambassadedubresil.org; Ambassador CARLOS ALBERTO SIMAS MAGALHÃES.

Mozambique: Av. Kenneth Kaunda 296, CP 1167, Maputo; tel. 21484800; fax 21484806; e-mail ebrasil@teledata.mz; Ambassador Leda Camargo.

Namibia: 52 Bismarck St, POB 24166, Windhoek; tel. (61) 237368; fax (61) 233389; e-mail brasemb@mweb.com.na; Ambassador CHRISTIANO WINDHOEK.

Netherlands: Mauritskade 19, 2514 HD The Hague; tel. (70) 3023959; fax (70) 3023950; e-mail brasil@brazilianembassy.nl; internet www.brazilianembassy .nl; Ambassador Gilberto Vergne Saboia.

New Zealand: Level 9, Deloitte House, 10 Brandon St, Wellington 6011; tel. (4) 473-3516; fax (4) 473-3517; e-mail brasemb@brazil.org.nz; internet www .brazil.org.nz; Ambassador MANOEL GOMES-PEREIRA.

Nicaragua: Km 7³/₄, Carretera Sur, Quinta los Pinos, Apdo 264, Managua; tel. 265-0035; fax 265-2206; e-mail ebrasil@ibw.com.ni; Ambassador Victoria Alice Cleaver.

Nigeria: Plot 324, Diplomatic Dr., Zone Central, Area District, Abuja; tel. (9) 4618688; fax (9) 4618687; Ambassador ALBERTO FERREIRA GUIMARAES.

Norway: Sigurd Syrsgt. 4, 0244 Oslo; tel. 22-54-07-30; fax 22-44-39-64; e-mail consular@brasil.no; internet www.brasil.no; Ambassador Sérgio Eduardo Moreira Lima.

Pakistan: 50, Atatürk Ave, G-6/3, POB 1053, Islamabad; tel. (51) 2279690; fax (51) 2823034; e-mail brasembp@isb.compol.com; Ambassador CARLOS EDUARDO SETTE CAMARA DA FONSECA COSTA.

Panama: Edif. El Dorado, 1°, Calle Elvira Méndez y Avda Ricardo Arango, Urb. Campo Alegre, Apdo 4287, Panamá 5; tel. 263-5322; fax 269-6316; e-mail embrasil@embrasil.org.pa; Ambassador Luíz Tupy Caldas de Moura.

Paraguay: Col Irrazábal, esq. Eligio Ayala, Casilla 22, Asunción; tel. (21) 21-4466; fax (21) 21-2693; e-mail acesar@embajadabrasil.org.py; internet www .embajadabrasil.org.py; Ambassador WALTER PECLY MOREIRA.

Peru: Avda José Pardo 850, Miraflores, Lima; tel. (1) 5120830; fax (1) 4452421; e-mail embajada@embajadabrasil.org.pe; internet www .embajadabrasil.org.pe; Ambassador Jorge d'Escragnolle Taunay, Filho.

Philippines: 16th Floor, Liberty Center, 104 H. V. de la Costa St, Salcedo Village, Makati City, 1227 Metro Manila; tel. (2) 8453651; fax (2) 8453676; e-mail brascom@info.com.ph; internet www.brasemb.org.ph; Ambassador ALCIDES G. R. PRATES.

Poland: 03-931 Warsaw, ul. Poselska 11, Saska Kepa; tel. (22) 6174800; fax (22) 6178689; e-mail brasil@brasil.org.pl; internet www.brasil.org.pl; Ambassador Marcelo Andrade de Moraes Jardim.

Portugal: Quinta de Mil Flores, Estrada das Laranjeiras 144, 1649-021 Lisbon; tel. (21) 7248510; fax (21) 7267623; e-mail geral@embaixadadobrasil .pt; internet www.embaixadadobrasil.pt; Ambassador CELSO MARCOS VIEIRA DE SOUZA.

Romania: Bucharest, Bd Aviatorilor 40, Sector 1; tel. (21) 2301130; fax (21) 2301599; e-mail braembuc@starnets.ro; Ambassador Vitor Candido Paim Gobato.

Russian Federation: 121069 Moscow, ul. B. Nikitskaya 54; tel. (495) 363-03-66; fax (495) 363-03-67; e-mail brasrus@brasemb.ru; internet www.brasemb .ru; Ambassador CARLOS AUGUSTO REGO SANTOS-NEVES.

São Tomé and Príncipe: Av. Marginal de 12 de Julho 20, São Tomé; tel. 226060; fax 226895; e-mail brasembsaotome@cstome.net; Ambassador Manuel Innocencio de Lacerda Santos, Jr.

Saudi Arabia: POB 94348, Riyadh 11693; tel. (1) 488-0018; fax (1) 488-1073; e-mail arabras@shabakah.net.sa; Ambassador LUÍS SÉRGIO GAMA FIGUEIRA.

Senegal: Immeuble Fondation Fahd, 4e étage, blvd Djily Mbaye, angle rue Macodou Ndiaye, BP 136, Dakar; tel. 33-823-1492; fax 33-823-7181; e-mail embdakar@sentoo.sn; Ambassador Kátia Godinho Gilaberte do Nascimento Borges.

Serbia: 11000 Belgrade, Krunska 14; tel. (11) 3239781; fax (11) 3230653; e-mail brasbelg@eunet.yu; Ambassador DANTE COELHO DE LIMA.

Singapore: 101 Thomson Rd, 10-05 United Sq., Singapore 307591; tel. 62566001; fax 62564565; e-mail cinbrem@brazil.org.sg; internet www.brazil .org.sg; Ambassador Paulo Alberto de Silveira Soares.

South Africa: Hillcrest Office Park, Woodpecker Pl., 1st Floor, 177 Dyer Rd, Hillcrest, Pretoria 0083; POB 3269, Pretoria 0001; tel. (12) 3665200; fax (12) 3665299; e-mail pretoria@brazilianembassy.org.za; internet www .brazilianembassy.org.za; Ambassador JOSÉ VICENTE DE SÁ PIMENTEL.

Spain: Fernando el Santo 6, 28010 Madrid; tel. (91) 7004650; fax (91) 7004660; e-mail adm@embajadadebrasil.es; internet www.brasil.es; Ambassador José Viegas Filho.

Suriname: Maratakkastraat 2, POB 925, Paramaribo; tel. 400200; fax 420774; e-mail brasemb@sr.net; internet www2.mre.gov.br/suriname/index.asp; Ambassador RICARDO LUIZ VIANA DE CARVALHO.

Sweden: Odengt. 3, 114 24 Stockholm; tel. (8) 545-163-00; fax (8) 545-163-14; e-mail stockholm@brazilianembassy.se; internet www.brazilianembassy.se; Ambassador Antonino Lisboa Mena Gonçalves.

Switzerland: Monbijoustr. 68, 3007 Bern; tel. 313718515; fax 313710525; e-mail info@brasbern.ch; internet www.brasbern.ch; Ambassador EDUARDO DOS SANTOS.

Syria: BP 2219, 39 rue Al-Farabi, Mezzeh Est, Damascus; tel. (11) 6124551; fax (11) 6124553; e-mail braemsyr@net.sy; Ambassador Eduardo Monteiro de Barros Roxo.

Thailand: 34th Floor, Lumpini Tower, 1168/101 Thanon Rama IV, Sathorn, Bangkok 10120; tel. (2) 679-8567; fax (2) 679-8569; e-mail embrasbkk@inet .co.th; internet www.brazilembassy.or.th; Ambassador EDGARD TELLES RIBEIRO.

Timor-Leste: Av. Governador Serpa Rosa, POB 157, Farol, Dili; tel. 3324203; fax 3324620; e-mail esctimor@office.net.au; Ambassador Edson Marinho Duarte Monteiro.

Trinidad and Tobago: 18 Sweet Briar Rd, St Clair, POB 382, Port of Spain; tel. 622-5779; fax 622-4323; e-mail embassyofbrazil@tstt.net.tt; internet www .brazilembtt.org; Ambassador LUIZ FERNANDO DE ATHAYDE.

Tunisia: 5 rue Sufétula, BP 83, 1002 Tunis; tel. (71) 893-569; fax (71) 846-995; e-mail brasemb.tunis@gnet.tn; internet www.ambassadedubresil.com; Ambassador Marilia Sardenberg Zelner Gonçalves.

Turkey: Reşit Galip Cad., İlkadım Sok. 1, 06700 Gaziosmanpaşa, Ankara; tel. (312) 4481840; fax (312) 4481838; e-mail brasemb@brasembancara.org; internet www.brasembancara.org; Ambassador CESÁRIO MELANTONIO NETO.

Ukraine: 01010 Kyiv, vul. Suvorova 14/12, POB 471; tel. (44) 280-63-01; fax (44) 280-95-68; e-mail kievbrem@brasil.kiev.ua; internet brasil.kiev.ua; Ambassador Renato Luiz Rodrigues Marques.

United Arab Emirates: POB 3027, St 5, Villa 3, Madinat Zayed, Abu Dhabi; tel. (2) 6320606; fax (2) 6327727; e-mail abubrem@emirates.net.ae; internet www.brazilembuae.ae; Ambassador FLAVIO MOREIRA SAPHA.

United Kingdom: 32 Green St, London, W1K 7AT; tel. (20) 7399-9000; fax (20) 7399-9100; e-mail info@brazil.org.uk; internet www.brazil.org.uk; Ambassador Carlos Augusto Rego Santos-Neves.

United States of America: 3006 Massachusetts Ave, NW, Washington, DC 20008; tel. (202) 238-2700; fax (202) 238-2827; e-mail webmaster@brasilemb.org; internet www.brasilemb.org; Ambassador ANTONIO PATRIOTA.

Uruguay: Blvr Artigas 1328, 11300 Montevideo; tel. (2) 7072119; fax (2) 7072086; e-mail montevideu@brasemb.org.uy; internet www.brasil.org.uy; Ambassador José Eduardo Felicio.

Vatican City: Via della Conciliazione 22, 00193 Rome, Italy; tel. (06) 6875252; fax (06) 6872540; e-mail embaixada@vatemb.it; internet www.vatemb.it; Ambassador VERA BARROUIN MACHADO.

Venezuela: Avda Mohedano con Calle Los Chaguaramos, Centro Gerencial Mohedano, 6°, La Castellana, Caracas; tel. (212) 261-5505; fax (212) 261-9601; e-mail brasembcaracas@cantv.net; internet www.embajadabrasil.org.ve; Ambassador Antonio Ferreira Simões.

Viet Nam: 14 Thuy Khue, T72 Hanoi; tel. (4) 8430817; fax (4) 8432542; e-mail vetbrem@netnam.org.vn; internet www.brazil.org.vn; Ambassador JOÃO DE MENDONÇA LIMA NETO.

Zambia: 74 Anglo American Bldg, Independence Ave, POB 33300; tel. (1) 250400; fax (1) 251652; e-mail brasemblusaca@iconnect.zm; Chargé d'affaires a.i. Paulo M. G. de Sousa.

Zimbabwe: Old Mutual Centre, 9th Floor, Jason Moyo Ave, POB 2530, Harare; tel. (4) 790740; fax (4) 790754; e-mail brasemb@ecoweb.co.zw; Chargé d'affaires a.i. FRANCISCO CARLOS SOARES LUZ.

DIPLOMATIC MISSIONS OF BRUNEI

United Nations: 771 First Ave, New York, NY 10017; tel. (212) 697-3465; fax (212) 697-9889; e-mail info@bruneimission-ny.org; Permanent Representative Emran Bahar.

Australia: 10 Beale Crescent, Deakin, ACT 2600; tel. (2) 6285-4500; fax (2) 6285-4545; e-mail canberra.australia@mfa.gov.bn; High Commissioner MOHAMMAD SAHRIP BIN OTHMAN.

Bahrain: POB 15700, House 892, Rd 3218, Block 332, Mahooz, Manama; tel. 17720222; fax 17741757; e-mail kbbhhom@batelco.com.bh; Chargé d'affaires Haji Ahmad Haji Jumaat.

Bangladesh: House 26, Rd 6, Baridhara, Dhaka; tel. (2) 8819552; fax (2) 8819551; e-mail bruhcomm@citechco.net; High Commissioner DATO' HAJI ABDUL RAHMAN BIN ABDUL HAMID.

Belgium: 238 ave F. D. Roosevelt, 1050 Brussels; tel. (2) 675-08-78; fax (2) 672-93-58; e-mail kedutaan-brunei.brussels@skynet.be; Ambassador Pengiran Haji Alihashim bin Pengiran Haji Yusuf.

Cambodia: 237 rue Pasteur 51, Sangkat Boeung Keng Kang 1, Khan Chamkarmon, Phnom-Penh; tel. (23) 211457; fax (23) 211456; e-mail brunei@bigpond.com.kh; Ambassador PENGIRAN HAJAH BASMILLAH ABBAS.

Canada: 395 Laurier Ave East, Suite 400, Ottawa, ON K1N 6R4; tel. (603) 234-5656; fax (603) 234-4397; e-mail bhco@bellnet.ca; High Commissioner Faizal Bahrin Haji Bakri (acting).

China, People's Republic: 1 Liang Ma Qiao Bei Jie, Chao Yang Qu, Beijing 100600; tel. (10) 65329773; fax (10) 65324097; e-mail beb@public.bta.net.cn; Ambassador MAGDALENE TEO CHEE SIONG.

Egypt: 24 Sharia Hassan Assem, Cairo (Zamalek); tel. (2) 7380097; fax (2) 7366375; e-mail ebdic@intouch.com; Ambassador Haji Muharram bin Haji Piah.

France: 7 rue de Presbourg, 75116 Paris; tel. 1-53-64-67-60; fax 1-53-64-67-83; e-mail ambassade.brunei@wanadoo.fr; Ambassador DATO' PADUKA ZAINIDI HAJI SIDUP.

Germany: Kronenstr. 55–58, 10117 Berlin; tel. (30) 2060760; fax (30) 20607666; e-mail berlin@brunei-embassy.de; Ambassador Dato' Paduka Haji Ali Haji Hassan.

India: 4 Poorvi Marg, Vasant Vihar, New Delhi 110 057; tel. (11) 26148340; fax (11) 26142101; e-mail newdelhi.india@mfa.gov.bn; High Commissioner DATO' PADUKA HAJI ABDUL GHAFAR BIN HAJI ISMAIL.

Indonesia: Jalan Tanjung Karang 7, Jakarta Pusat 10230; tel. (21) 31906080; fax (21) 31905070; Ambassador Dato' Paduka Seri Haji Husin Ahmad.

Iran: 6/1, Mina Blvd, Africa Ave, Tehran; tel. (21) 88797946; fax (21) 88770162; e-mail bruneiran@hotmail.com; Ambassador PENGIRAN HAJI SAHARI PENGIRAN HAJI SALEH.

Japan: 6-5-2, Kita Shinagawa, Shinagawa-ku, Tokyo 141-0001; tel. (3) 3447-7997; fax (3) 3447-9260; e-mail contact@bruemb.jp; internet www.bruemb.jp; Ambassador Dato'Paduka Haji Adnan Buntar.

Jordan: POB 851752, Amman 11185; tel. (6) 5928021; fax (6) 5928024; e-mail kbnbdjor@cyberia.jo; Ambassador PEHIN DATO HARIMAUPADANG.

Korea, Republic: 737-11, Hannam-dong, Yeongsan-gu, Seoul 140-210; tel. (2) 790-1078; fax (2) 790-1084; e-mail kbnbd_seoul@yahoo.com; Ambassador Dato' Paduka Haji Harun bin Hj Ismail.

Laos: Unit 12, Ban Thoungkang, Lao-Thai Friendship Rd, Sisathanak, Vientiane; tel. (21) 352294; fax (21) 352291; e-mail embdlaos@laotel.com; Ambassador HAJIK SIDEK ALI.

Malaysia: Suite 19-01, 19th Floor, Menara Tan & Tan, 207 Jalan Tun Razak, 50400 Kuala Lumpur; tel. (3) 21612800; fax (3) 2631302; High Commissioner Dato' Paduka Haji Abdul Rahman.

Myanmar: 317/319 U Wisara Rd, Sanchaung Township, Yangon; tel. (1) 524285; fax (1) 512854; Ambassador BRIG.-GEN. DATO' PADUKA HAJI MOHAMAD YUSOF BIN ABU BAKAR.

Oman: POB 91, Ruwi 112, Shati al-Qurum, St 3050, Villa 4062, Muscat; tel. 24603533; fax 24605910; e-mail kbopuni@omantel.net.om; Ambassador Dato Seri Setia Haji Adam bin Haji Ahmad.

Pakistan: House 5, St 6, F-6/3, Islamabad; tel. (51) 2879636; fax (51) 2823688; High Commissioner PEHIN DATO' HAJI PANGLIMA COL (RETD) HAJI ABDUL JALIL BIN HAJI AHMAD.

Philippines: Bank of the Philippine Islands Bldg, 11th Floor, Ayala Ave, cnr Paseo de Roxas, Makati City, 1227 Metro Manila; tel. (2) 8162836; fax (2) 8916646; Ambassador Emaleen Abdul Rahman Teo.

Qatar: POB 22772, Doha; tel. 4831956; fax 4836798; e-mail bruemb@qatar.net.qa; Chargé d'affaires HAJI ALI HASSAN HAJI MUHAMMAD SALLEH.

Russian Federation: 121059 Moscow, Berezhkovskaya nab. 2, Radisson-Slavyanskaya Hotel, kom. 440–441; tel. (495) 941-82-16; fax (495) 941-82-14; e-mail moscow.russia@mfa.gov.bn; Ambassador Janin bin Erih.

Saudi Arabia: POB 94314, al-Warood, Area 29, al-Fujairah St, Riyadh 11693; tel. (1) 456-0814; fax (1) 456-1594; e-mail brunei@shabakah.net.sa; Ambassador PENGIRAN HAJI JABARUDDIN BIN PENGIRAN HAJI MUHAMMAD SALLEH.

Singapore: 325 Tanglin Rd, Singapore 247955; tel. 67339055; fax 67375275; High Commissioner Abdul Ghafar bin Ismail.

Thailand: 12 Soi Ekamai 2, Thanon Sukhumvit 63, Prakanong Nua, Wattana, Bangkok 10110; tel. (2) 714-7395; fax (2) 714-7383; Ambassador PENGIRAN DATO' PADUKA HAJI SHARIFUDDIN BIN HAJI YUSSOF.

United Arab Emirates: POB 5836, Plot 8, Villa 1, St 27, E-33, Abu Dhabi; tel. (2) 4486999; fax (2) 4486333; e-mail kbdauh98@emirates.net.ae; Ambassador Dato Paduka Haji Adnan bin Haji Zainal.

United Kingdom: 19–20 Belgrave Sq., London, SW1X 8PG; tel. (20) 7581-0521; fax (20) 7235-9717; e-mail bhcl@brunei-high-commission.co.uk; High Commr PENGIRAN DATO' MAIDIN HASHIM.

United States of America: 3520 International Court, NW, Washington, DC 20008; tel. (202) 237-1838; fax (202) 885-0560; e-mail info@bruneiembassy.org; internet www.bruneiembassy.org; Ambassador Pengiran Indera Negara P. A. Puteh.

Viet Nam: Villa No. 8 & 9, Van Phuc Diplomatic Quarter, 44/8 Van Bao, Ba Dinh District, Hanoi; tel. (4) 7262001; fax (4) 7262010; e-mail bruemviet@hn.vnn.vn; Ambassador DATO PADUKA HAJI MAHADI BIN WASLI (designate).

DIPLOMATIC MISSIONS OF BULGARIA

United Nations: 11 East 84th St, New York, NY 10028; tel. (212) 737-4790; fax (212) 472-9865; e-mail bulgaria@un.int; internet www.un.int/bulgaria; Permanent Representative Rayko Strahilov Raytchev.

Afghanistan: St 15, Shirpur St, Wazir Akbar Khan, Kabul; tel. (20) 2103257; fax (20) 2101089; e-mail bgembkabul@yahoo.com; Ambassador KRASIMIR TULECHKI.

Albania: Rruga Skënderbej 12, Tirana; tel. (4) 233155; fax (4) 232272; e-mail bgemb@interalb.net; internet www.mfa.bg/tirana; Ambassador Teodor Spasov Rusinov.

Algeria: 13 blvd Col Bougara, Algiers; tel. (21) 23-00-14; fax (21) 23-05-33; Ambassador DIMITAR DIMITROV.

Angola: Rua Fernão Mendes Pinto 35/37, Alvalade, CP 2260, Luanda; tel. 222324213; fax 222321010; e-mail bulgemb@ebonet.net; Ambassador Elenko Andreev.

Argentina: Mariscal A. J. de Sucre 1568, C1428DUT Buenos Aires; tel. (11) 4781-8644; fax (11) 4781-1214; e-mail info@embular.int.ar; internet www.embular.int.ar; Ambassador STEPHAN APOSTOLOV.

Armenia: Yerevan, Nor Aresh, Sofia St 16; tel. (10) 45-82-33; fax (10) 45-46-02; e-mail bulembassy@arminco.com; internet www.mfa.bg/yerevan; Ambassador Todor Staikov.

Australia: 33 Culgoa Circuit, O'Malley, ACT 2606; tel. (2) 6286-9711; fax (2) 6286-9600; e-mail embassy@bulgaria.org.au; Ambassador DR LUBOMIR TODOROV.

Austria: Schwindgasse 8, 1040 Vienna; tel. (1) 505-31-13; fax (1) 505-14-23; e-mail amboffice@aon.at; Ambassador Radi Naidenov.

Azerbaijan: 1069 Baku-34, Oktai Kerimov küç. 34; tel. (12) 441-43-81; fax (12) 440-81-82; e-mail balkan@bg.embassy.in-baku.com; internet www.mfa.bg/baku; Ambassador IVAN K. PALCHEV.

Belarus: 220030 Minsk, pl. Svoboda 11; tel. (17) 328-65-58; fax (17) 328-65-59; e-mail embassy@bulgaria.by; internet www.mfa.bg/minsk; Ambassador Petko Ganchev.

Belgium: 58 ave Hamoir, 1180 Brussels; tel. (2) 374-59-63; fax (2) 375-84-94; e-mail embassy@bulgaria.be; internet www.bulgaria.be; Ambassador HRISTO GEORGIEV.

Bosnia and Herzegovina: 71000 Sarajevo, Soukbunar 5; tel. (33) 668191; fax (33) 668182; e-mail possar@bih.net.ba; Ambassador (vacant).

Brazil: SEN, Av. das Nações, Quadra 801, Lote 08, 70432-900 Brasília, DF; tel. (61) 3223-6193; fax (61) 3323-3285; e-mail bulgaria@linkexpress.com.br; Ambassador NIKOLAY TZATCHEV.

Cambodia: 227/229 blvd Norodom, Phnom-Penh; tel. (23) 217504; fax (23) 212792; e-mail bulgembpnp@online.com.kh; internet www.mfa.bg/phnom-penh; Chargé d'affaires Krasimir Tulechki.

Canada: 325 Stewart St, Ottawa, ON K1N 6K5; tel. (613) 789-3215; fax (613) 789-3524; e-mail mailmn@storm.ca; Ambassador EVGUENI S. STOYTCHEV.

Chile: Rodolfo Bentjerodt 4895, Vitacura, Santiago; tel. (2) 228-3110; fax (2) 208-0404; e-mail embul@entelchile.net; Chargé d'affaires a.i. Peter D. Atanassov.

China, People's Republic: 4 Xiu Shui Bei Jie, Jian Guo Men Wai, Beijing 100600; tel. (10) 65321946; fax (10) 65324502; e-mail bulemb@public.bta.net.cn; internet www.mfa.bg/beijing; Ambassador ANGEL ORBETSOV.

Croatia: 10000 Zagreb, Gornje Prekrižje 28; tel. (1) 4646625; fax (1) 4823338; e-mail veleposlanstvo.republike.bugarske@zg.t-com.hr; Ambassador Ivan Sirakov.

Cuba: Calle B, No 252, entre 11 y 13, Vedado, Havana; tel. (7) 33-3125; fax (7) 33-3297; e-mail embulhav@ceniai.inf.cu; Ambassador TCHAVDAR MLADENOV NIKOLOV.

Cyprus: POB 24029, 13 Konst. Paleologos St, 2406 Engomi, Nicosia; tel. 22672486; fax 22676598; e-mail bulgaria@cytanet.com.cy; Ambassador Peter Georgiev Vodenski.

Czech Republic: Krakovská 6, 110 00 Prague 1; tel. 222211258; fax 222211728; e-mail bulvelv@mbox.vol.cz; Ambassador ZDRAVKO POPOV.

Denmark: Gamlehave Allé 7, 2920 Charlottenlund; tel. 39-64-24-84; fax 39-63-49-23; e-mail bg-embassy@mail.tdcadsl.dk; Ambassador Ivan I. Dimitrov.

Egypt: 6 Sharia el-Malek el-Ajdal, Cairo (Zamalek); tel. (2) 3413025; fax (2) 3413826; e-mail mka@link.com.eg; Ambassador ALEXANDAR OLSHEVSKI.

Ethiopia: Haile Gabreselassie Rd, Woreda 17, Kebele 13, POB 987, Addis Ababa; tel. (11) 6610032; fax (11) 6613373; e-mail bulemba@ethionet.et; Chargé d'affaires a.i. Emil Trifonov.

Finland: Kuusisaarentie 2B, 00340 Helsinki; tel. (9) 4584055; fax (9) 4584550; e-mail bulembfi@yahoo.com; internet www.mfa.bg/helsinki; Ambassador DR PLAMEN LUBOMIROV BONCHEV.

France: 1 ave Rapp, 75007 Paris; tel. 1-45-51-85-90; fax 1-45-51-18-68; e-mail bulgamb@wanadoo.fr; internet www.amb-bulgarie.fr; Ambassador Irina Bokova.

Georgia: 0102 Tbilisi, D. Aghmashenebeli 61; tel. (32) 91-01-94; fax (32) 91-02-70; e-mail bgembassy.georgia@gol.ge; internet www.mfa.bg/tbilisi; Chargé d'affaires a.i. IAHOR SAHARIEV.

Germany: Mauerstr. 11, 10117 Berlin; tel. (30) 2010922; fax (30) 2086838; e-mail info@botschaft-bulgarien.de; internet www.botschaft-bulgarien.de; Ambassador Meglena Ivanova Plugtschieva-Alexandrova.

Ghana: 3 Kakramadu Rd, POB 3193, East Cantonments, Accra; tel. (21) 772404; fax (21) 774231; e-mail bulembgh@ghana.com; Chargé d'affaires a.i. GEORGE MITEV.

Greece: Odos Stratigou Kallari 33a, Palaio Psychiko, 154 52 Athens; tel. (210) 6478068; fax (210) 6478130; e-mail embassbg@otenet.gr; internet www.bulgaria.bg/Europe/Atina; Ambassador Andrei Karaslavov.

Hungary: 1062 Budapest, Andrássy u. 115; tel. (1) 322-0824; fax (1) 322-5215; e-mail bgembhu@axelero.hu; Ambassador GIRNO GYAVROV.

India: 16/17 Chandragupta Marg, Chanakyapuri, New Delhi 110 021; tel. (11) 26115550; fax (11) 26876190; e-mail bulemb@bulgariaembindia.com; internet bulgariaembindia.com; Ambassador Dragovest Goranov.

Indonesia: Jalan Imam Bonjol 34–36, Menteng, Jakarta Pusat 10310; tel. (21) 3904048; fax (21) 3904049; e-mail bgemb.jkt@centrin.net.id; Ambassador BOYKO MIRCHEV.

Iran: POB 11365-7451, Vali-e-Asr Ave, Dr Abbaspour Ave, 82 Nezami-e-Ganjavi St, Tehran; tel. (21) 88775662; fax (21) 88779680; e-mail bulgr.tehr@neda.net; Ambassador Plamen Georgiev Shukyurliev.

Iraq: 12/25/624 al-Ameriya, Baghdad; tel. (1) 556-8197; fax (1) 556-4182; e-mail bulgemb@uruklink.net; Ambassador NIKOLAY GEORGIEV NICOLOV.

Ireland: 22 Burlington Rd, Dublin 4; tel. (1) 6603293; fax (1) 6603915; e-mail bulgarianembassydublin@eircom.net; internet www.mfa.bg/dublin; Ambassador Emil Savov Yalnazov.

Israel: 21 Leonardo da Vinci St, Tel-Aviv 64733; tel. 3-6961361; fax 3-6961430; e-mail bgemtlv@netvision.net.il; Chargé d'affaires a.i. SERGEI TASSEV.

Italy: Via Pietro Paolo Rubens 21, 00197 Roma; tel. (06) 3224640; fax (06) 3226122; e-mail embassy@bulemb.it; internet www.bulemb.it; Ambassador Atanas Mladenov.

Japan: 5-36-3, Yoyogi, Shibuya-ku, Tokyo 151-0053; tel. (3) 3465-1021; fax (3) 3465-1031; e-mail bulemb@gol.com; internet www.mfa.bg/tokyo; Ambassador PROF. BLAGOVEST SENDOV.

Jordan: POB 950578, 7 al-Mousel St, Amman 11195; tel. (6) 5529391; fax (6) 5539393; e-mail bulembjord@joinnet.com.jo; Ambassador Nikolai Nikolov.

Kazakhstan: 050000 Almaty, Gornyi Gigant, 8-oi Gvardeiskoi Divizii; tel. (727) 264-67-10; fax (727) 262-99-56; e-mail bulgarianembassy@rambler.ru; internet www.mfa.bg/almaty; Ambassador NIKOLA F. BORISOV.

Korea, Republic: 723-42, Hannam 2-dong, Yeongsan-gu, Seoul 140-894; tel. (2) 794-8626; fax (2) 794-8627; e-mail ebdy1990@unitel.co.kr; Ambassador Alexander Savov.

Kuwait: POB 12090, 71651 Shamiya, Jabriya, Block 11, St 107 and St 1, Villa 272, Kuwait City; tel. 5314458; fax 5321453; e-mail bgembkw@qualitynet.net; Ambassador ANGEL N. MANTCHEV.

Lebanon: POB 11-6544, Immeuble Hibri, rue de l'Australie 55, Raouche, Beirut; tel. (1) 452883; fax (1) 452892; Ambassador Vanelin Dimitrov Lazarov.

Libya: POB 2945, Sharia Selma ben Al-Ukua, Ben Ashour Area No. 58-6, Tripoli; tel. (21) 3609988; fax (21) 3609990; e-mail tripoli@embassy.transat.bg; Ambassador DR ZDRAVKO VELEV.

Lithuania: Pylimo 8, Palangos 2, 01118 Vilnius; tel. (5) 249-9274; fax (5) 261-9174; e-mail vilnius@bgembassy.lt; Ambassador Ivan Pentchev Dantchev.

Macedonia, former Yugoslav Republic: 1000 Skopje, Ivo Ribar Lola 40; tel. (2) 3229444; fax (2) 3246491; e-mail bgemb@unet.com.mk; Ambassador MIHO MIHOV.

Mexico: Paseo de la Reforma 1990, Col. Lomas de Chapultepec, Del. Miguel Hidalgo, 11000 México, DF; tel. (55) 5596-3283; fax (55) 5596-1012; e-mail ebulgaria@yahoo.com; Ambassador Sergey Penchev Michev.

Moldova: 2012 Chişinău, str. Bucureşti 92; tel. (22) 23-79-83; fax (22) 23-79-78; e-mail ambasada-bulgara@meganet.md; internet www.mfa.bg/kishinev; Ambassador NIKOLAI ILIYEV.

Mongolia: Olimpiin Gudamj 8, Ulan Bator (CPOB 702); tel. (11) 322841; fax (11) 324841; e-mail posolstvobg@magicnet.mn; Ambassador Mircho Ivanov.

Montenegro: 81000 Podgorica, Vukice Mitrovića 10; tel. (81) 655009; fax (81) 655008; e-mail bg.embassy.me@abv.bg; Ambassador SNEZHANA NAYDENOVA.

Morocco: 4 ave Ahmed el-Yazidi, BP 1301, 10000 Rabat; tel. (3) 7765477; fax (3) 7763201; e-mail bulemrab@wanadoo.net.ma; Ambassador Katia Petrova Todorova.

Netherlands: Duinroosweg 9, 2597 KJ The Hague; tel. (70) 3503051; fax (70) 3584688; e-mail info@embassy-bulgaria.nl; internet www.embassy-bulgaria.nl; Ambassador ZLATIN V. TRAPKOV.

Nigeria: 10 Euphrates St, cnr Aminu Kano Cres., Maitama, Abuja; tel. (9) 4130034; fax (9) 4132741; e-mail bulgarian@nigtel.com; Ambassador (vacant).

Norway: Tidemandsgt. 11, 0244 Oslo; tel. 22-55-40-40; fax 22-55-40-24; e-mail bulgemb@online.no; Ambassador NIKOLAS IVANOV KARADIMOV.

Pakistan: Plot No. 6-11, Diplomatic Enclave, Ramna 5, POB 1483, Islamabad; tel. (51) 2279196; fax (51) 2279195; e-mail bul@isb.compol.com; Ambassador Georgi Grancharov.

Poland: 00-540 Warsaw, Al. Ujazdowskie 33/35; tel. (22) 6294071; fax (22) 6282271; e-mail office@bgemb.com.pl; Ambassador IVAN A. NAYDENOV.

Portugal: Rua do Sacramento à Lapa 31, 1200-792 Lisbon; tel. (21) 3976364; fax (21) 3979272; e-mail ebul@mail.telepac.pt; Ambassador Maksim Georgiev Gaytandzhiev.

Romania: 011835 Bucharest, Str. Rabat 5; tel. (21) 2302150; fax (21) 2307654; e-mail bulembassy@pcnet.ro; internet www.bgembassy-romania.org; Ambassador KONSTANTIN ANDREEV.

Russian Federation: 119590 Moscow, ul. Mosfilmovskaya 66; tel. (495) 143-67-00; fax (495) 232-33-02; e-mail bulemrus@bolgaria.ru; internet www.bolgaria.ru; Ambassador Plamen I. Grozdanov.

Serbia: 11000 Belgrade, Birčaninova 26; tel. (11) 3613980; fax 3611136; e-mail bulgamb@eunet.yu; Ambassador GEORGI DIMITROV.

Slovakia: Kuzmányho 1, 811 06 Bratislava; tel. (2) 5441-5308; fax (2) 5441-2404; e-mail bulharskoet@stonline.sk; internet www.bulgarianembassy.sk; Ambassador Ognian Galkov.

Slovenia: 1000 Ljubljana, Rožna dolina XV/18; tel. (1) 4265744; fax (1) 4258845; e-mail bgembassysl@siol.net; Ambassador VLADIMIR A. ATANASOV.

South Africa: 1071 Church St, Hatfield, Pretoria 0083; POB 29296, Arcadia 0007; tel. (12) 3423720; fax (12) 3423721; e-mail embulgsa@iafrica.com; internet www.bulgarianembassy.co.za; Ambassador V. C. Neykov.

Spain: Santa María Magdalena 15, 28016 Madrid; tel. (91) 3455761; fax (91) 3591201; e-mail embulmad@tyahoo.es; Ambassador IVAN YANKOV HRISTOV.

Sudan: St 31, House No. 9, Block 10, al-Amarat, POB 1690, 11111 Khartoum; tel. (183) 560106; fax (183) 560107; e-mail bgembsdn@yahoo.co.uk; Chargé d'affaires a.i. Svilen Bozhanov.

Sweden: Karlavägen 29, 114 31 Stockholm; tel. (8) 723-09-38; fax (8) 21-45-03; e-mail bg.embassy@telia.com; internet www.bulgarien.se; Ambassador GORAN YONOV.

Switzerland: Bernastr. 2–4, 3005 Bern; tel. 313511455; fax 313510064; e-mail bulembassy@bluewin.ch; internet www.bulembassy.ch; Ambassador Atanas Pavlov.

Syria: BP 2732, 8 rue Pakistan, place Arnous, Damascus; tel. (11) 3318445; fax (11) 4419854; e-mail bul-emb@scs-net.org; Ambassador GEORGI YANKOV.

Thailand: 83/24 Soi Witthayu 1, Thanon Whitthayu, Lumpini, Pathumwan, Bangkok 10330; tel. (2) 627-3872; fax (2) 627-3874; e-mail bulgemth@csloxinfo.com; Chargé d'affaires Mima Dimitrova Stoilova-Nikolova.

Tunisia: 5 rue Ryhane, BP 6, Cité Mahragène, 1082 Tunis; tel. (71) 798-962; fax (71) 791-667; e-mail bgtunis.amb@planet.tn; Ambassador (vacant).

Turkey: Atatürk Bul. 124, 06680 Kavaklıdere, Ankara; tel. (312) 4672071; fax (312) 4672574; e-mail bulankemb@ttnet.com; Ambassador Branimir Mladenov.

Ukraine: 01023 Kyiv, vul. Hospitalna 1; tel. (44) 246-72-37; fax (44) 235-51-19; e-mail embuln@i.kiev.ua; internet www.mfa.bg/kyiv; Ambassador DIMITAR VLADIMIROV.

United Kingdom: 186–188 Queen's Gate, London, SW7 5HL; tel. (20) 7584-9400; fax (20) 7584-4948; e-mail ambass.office@bulgarianembassy.org.uk; internet www.bulgarianembassy.org.uk; Ambassador Dr Lachezar Nikolov Matev.

United States of America: 1621 22nd St, NW, Washington, DC 20008; tel. (202) 387-0174; fax (202) 234-7973; e-mail office@bulgaria-embassy.org; internet www.bulgaria-embassy.org; Ambassador ELENA POPTODOROVA.

Uzbekistan: 100000 Tashkent, Rakatboshi ko'ch. 52; tel. (71) 158-48-88; fax (71) 152-39-52; e-mail misiyabg@bcc.com.uz; internet www.mfa.bg/tashkent; Chargé d'affaires Stoyanka G. Rusinova.

Vatican City: Via di Porta Angelica 63, 00193 Roma, Italia; tel. (06) 6875717; fax (06) 6865233; e-mail ambulvat@yahoo.it; internet www.mfa.bg/vatican; Ambassador VALENTIN VASSILEV BOZHILOV.

Venezuela: Quinta Sofía, Calle Las Lomas, Urb. Las Mercedes, Apdo 68389, Caracas; tel. (212) 993-2714; fax (212) 993-4839; e-mail embulven@cantv.net; internet www.mfa.bg/caracas; Ambassador Kiril Georgiev Kotsaliev.

Viet Nam: Van Phuc Quarter, 5 Nui Truc, Hanoi; tel. (4) 8452095; fax (4) 8460856; e-mail bgremb@fpt.vn; internet www.mfa.bg/hanoi; Ambassador GEORGI VASSILIEV.

Yemen: POB 1518, Asr, St 4, Residence 5, San'a; tel. (1) 208469; fax (1) 207924; e-mail bgemb_yem@y.net.ye; Chargé d'affaires a.i. Alexi Alaxiev.

Zimbabwe: 15 Maasdorp Ave, Alexandra Park, POB 1809, Harare; tel. (4) 730509; fax (4) 732504; e-mail bgembhre@ecoweb.co.zw; Ambassador CHRISTO TEPAVITCHAROV.

DIPLOMATIC MISSIONS OF BURKINA FASO

United Nations: 115 East 73rd St, New York, NY 10021; tel. (212) 288-7515; fax (212) 772-3562; e-mail burkinafaso@un.int; Permanent Representative Michel Kafando.

Algeria: BP 212, 23 Lot el-Feth, chemin ibn Badis el-Mouiz (ex Poirson), el-Biar, Didouche Mourad, Algiers; tel. (21) 92-33-39; fax (21) 92-73-90; e-mail abfalger@yahoo.fr; Ambassador MAMADOU SERME.

Austria: Prinz-Eugen-Str. 18/3a, 1040 Vienna; tel. (1) 503-82-64; fax (1) 503-82-64-20; e-mail s.r@abfvienne.at; internet www.abfvienne.at; Ambassador Noellie Marie Béatrice Damiba.

Belgium: 16 place Guy d'Arezzo, 1180 Brussels; tel. (2) 345-99-12; fax (2) 345-06-12; e-mail ambassade.burkina@skynet.be; internet www.ambassadeduburkina.be; Ambassador KADRÉ DÉSIRÉ OUEDRAOGO.

Canada: 48 Range Rd, Ottawa, ON K1N 8J4; tel. (613) 238-4796; fax (613) 238-3812; e-mail burkina.faso@sympatico.ca; internet www.burkinafaso.ca; Ambassador Juliette Bonkoungou-Yameogo.

China (Taiwan): 6/F, 9-1 Lane 62, Tien Mou West Rd, Taipei 11156; tel. (2) 28733096; fax (2) 28733071; e-mail abftap94@ms17.hinet.net; Ambassador JACQUES Y. SAWADOGO.

Côte d'Ivoire: Immeuble SIDAM, 5e étage, 34 ave Houdaille, 01 BP 908, Plateau, Abidjan 01; tel. 20-21-15-01; fax 20-21-66-41; e-mail amba.bf@africaonline.ci; Ambassador Emile Ilboudo.

Cuba: Calle 40, No 516, entre 5 y 7, Miramar, Havana; tel. (7) 204-2217; fax (7) 204-1942; e-mail ambfaso@ceniai.inf.cu; Ambassador DANIEL OUEDRAOGO.

Denmark: Svanemøllevej 20, 2100 Copenhagen Ø; tel. 39-18-40-22; fax 39-27-18-86; e-mail mail@ambaburkina.dk; internet www.ambaburkina.dk; Ambassador Céline M. Yoda.

Egypt: POB 306, Ramses Centre, 22 Sharia Wadi en-Nil, Mohandessin, Cairo 11794; tel. (2) 3808965; fax (2) 3806974; Ambassador SOPHIE SOW.

Ethiopia: Kebele 19, House No. 281, POB 19685, Addis Ababa; tel. (11) 6615863; fax (11) 6625857; e-mail ambfet@telecom.net.et; Ambassador Bruno Zidouemba.

France: 159 blvd Haussmann, 75008 Paris; tel. 1-43-59-90-63; fax 1-42-56-50-07; e-mail amba.burkina.faso@wanadoo.fr; internet www.ambaburkinafrance.org; Chargé d'affaires a.i. PIABIÉ FIRMIN GRÉGOIRE N'DO.

Germany: Karolingerpl. 10–11, 14052 Berlin; tel. (30) 30105990; fax (30) 301059920; e-mail embassy_burkina_faso@t-online.de; Ambassador Xavier Niodogo.

Ghana: 772 Asylum Down, off Farrar Ave, POB 65, Accra; tel. (21) 221988; fax (21) 777490; e-mail ambafaso@ghana.com; Ambassador PIERRE SEM SANOU.

India: P 3/1 Vasant Vihar, New Delhi 110 057; tel. (11) 26140641; fax (11) 26140630; e-mail emburnd@bol.net.in; internet www.embassyburkinaindia.com; Chargé d'affaires Ousman Nacambo.

Italy: Via XX Settembre 86, 00187 Roma; tel. (06) 42010611; fax (06) 48903514; e-mail ambabf.roma@tin.it; Ambassador MAMADOU SISSOKO.

Japan: Apt 301, Hiroo Glisten Hills, 3-1-17, Hiroo, Shibuya-ku, Tokyo 150-0012; tel. (3) 3400-7919; fax (3) 3400-6945; e-mail faso-amb@khaki.plala.or.jp; internet www.embassy-avenue.jp/burkina; Chargé d'affaires a.i. Patrice Kafando.

Libya: POB 81902, Route de Gargeresh, Tripoli; tel. (21) 4771221; fax (21) 4778037; Ambassador YOUSSOUF SANGARE.

Mali: ACI-2000, Commune III, BP 9022, Bamako; tel. 223-31-71; fax 221-92-66; e-mail ambafaso@experco.net; Ambassador Prof. Sanné Mohamed Topan.

Morocco: 7 rue al-Bouziri, BP 6484, Agdal, 10101 Rabat; tel. (3) 7675512; fax (3) 7675517; e-mail ambfrba@smirt.net.ma; Ambassador BRIG.-GEN. IBRAHIM TRAORÉ.

Nigeria: 15 Norman Williams St, Ikoyi, Lagos; tel. (1) 617985; e-mail ebfn@nova.net.ng; Ambassador Dramane Yaméogo.

Saudi Arabia: POB 94330, Riyadh 11693; tel. (1) 465-2244; fax (1) 465-3397; e-mail burkinafaso.ksa@arab.net.sa; Ambassador OUMAR DIAWARA.

Senegal: Sicap Sacré Coeur III, Extension VDN No. 10628B, BP 11601, Dakar; tel. 33-864-5824; fax 33-864-5823; e-mail ambabf@sentoo.sn; Ambassador Salamata Sawadogo.

United States of America: 2340 Massachusetts Ave, NW, Washington, DC 20008; tel. (202) 332-5577; fax (202) 667-1882; e-mail ambawdc@verizon.net; internet www.burkinaembassy-usa.org; Ambassador PARMANGA ERNEST YONLI.

DIPLOMATIC MISSIONS OF BURUNDI

United Nations: 336 East 45th St, 12th Floor, New York, NY 10017; tel. (212) 499-0001; fax (212) 499-0006; e-mail burundi@un.int; Permanent Representative Joseph Ntakirutimana.

Belgium: 46 square Marie-Louise, 1000 Brussels; tel. (2) 230-45-35; fax (2) 230-78-83; e-mail ambassade.burundi@skynet.be; internet www.amb-burundi.be; Ambassador LAURENT KAVAKURE.

Canada: 325 Dalhousie St, Suite 815, Ottawa, ON K1N 7G2; tel. (613) 789-0414; fax (613) 789-9537; e-mail ambabucanada@infonet.ca; Ambassador Appolonie Simbizi.

China, People's Republic: 25 Guang Hua Lu, Jian Guo Men Wai, Beijing 100600; tel. (10) 65321801; fax (10) 65322381; e-mail ambbubei@yahoo.fr; Ambassador GABRIEL SABUSHIMIKE.

Egypt: 22 Sharia en-Nakhil, Madinet ed-Dobbat, Cairo (Dokki); tel. (2) 3373078; fax (2) 3378431; Ambassador Gervais Ndikumagnege.

Ethiopia: POB 3641, Addis Ababa; tel. (11) 4651300; e-mail burundi.emb@telecom.net.et; Ambassador PHILIPPE NTAHONKURIYE.

France: 10–12 rue de l'Orme, 75019 Paris; tel. 1-45-20-60-61; fax 1-45-20-02-54; e-mail ambabu.paris@wanadoo.fr; Ambassador Ildephonse Nkeramihigo.

Germany: Berliner Str. 36, 10715 Berlin; tel. (30) 2345670; fax (30) 23456720; e-mail info@burundi-embassy-berlin.com; internet www.burundi-embassy-berlin.com; Ambassador DOMITILLE BARANCIRA.

Italy: Corso Francia 221, 00919 Roma; tel. (06) 36381786; fax (06) 36381511; Ambassador Leopold Ndayisaba.

Kenya: Development House, 14th Floor, Moi Ave, POB 44439, Nairobi; tel. (20) 575113; fax (20) 219005; Ambassador JEREMIE NGENDAKUMANA.

Libya: POB 2817, Sharia Ras Hassan, Tripoli; tel. (21) 608848; Ambassador Raphaël Bitariho.

Russian Federation: 119049 Moscow, Kaluzhskaya pl. 1/226–227; tel. (495) 230-25-64; fax (495) 230-20-09; e-mail bdiam@mail.cnt.ru; Ambassador RENOVAT NDAYIRUKIYE.

Rwanda: rue de Ntaruka, BP 714, Kigali; tel. 575010; Chargé d'affaires a.i. (vacant).

South Africa: 20 Glyn St, Colbyn, Pretoria 0083; POB 12914, Hatfield 0028; tel. (12) 3424881; fax (12) 3424885; Ambassador PATRICE RWIMO.

Tanzania: Plot 1007, Lugalo Rd, POB 2752, Upanga, Dar es Salaam; tel. (22) 238608; e-mail burundemb@raha.com; Ambassador Leandre Amuri Bangengwanubusa.

United States of America: 2233 Wisconsin Ave, NW, Suite 212, Washington, DC 20007; tel. (202) 342-2574; fax (202) 342-2575; e-mail burundiembassy@erols.com; internet www.burundiembassy-usa.org; Ambassador CELESTIN NIYONGABO.

DIPLOMATIC MISSIONS OF CAMBODIA

United Nations: 866 United Nations Plaza, Suite 420, New York, NY 10017; tel. (212) 223-0676; fax (212) 223-0425; e-mail cambodia@un.int; internet www.un.int/cambodia; Permanent Representative Sea Kosal.

Australia: 5 Canterbury Crescent, Deakin, ACT 2600; tel. (2) 6273-1259; fax (2) 6273-1053; e-mail cambodianembassy@ozemail.com.au; internet www.embassyofcambodia.org.nz/au.htm; Ambassador MEAS KIM HENG.

Belgium: 264 ave de Tervueren, 1150 Brussels; tel. (2) 772-03-72; fax (2) 772-03-76; e-mail amcambel@skynet.be; AmbassadorSun Saphoeun.

Brunei: 8 Simpang 845, Kampong Tasek, Meradun, Jalan Tutong, Bandar Seri Begawan BF 1520; tel. 2654046; fax 2650646; e-mail cambodia@brunet.bn; Ambassador NAN SY.

China, People's Republic: 9 Dong Zhi Men Wai Dajie, Beijing 100600; tel. (10) 65321889; fax (10) 65323507; e-mail cambassybeijing@sohu.com; Ambassador Khek Caimealy.

Cuba: Avda 5, No 7001, entre 70 y 72, Miramar, Havana; tel. (7) 204-1496; fax (7) 204-6400; e-mail cambohav@enet.cu; Ambassador PRES MANOLA.

Egypt: 2 Sharia Tahawia, Cairo (Giza); tel. (2) 3489966; Ambassador In Sopheap.

France: 4 rue Adolphe Yvon, 75116 Paris; tel. 1-45-03-47-20; fax 1-45-03-47-40; e-mail ambcambodgeparis@mangoosta.fr; internet www.ambcambodgeparis.info; Ambassador UCH KIMAN.

Germany: Benjamin-Vogelsdorf-Str., 13187 Berlin; tel. (30) 48637901; fax (30) 48637973; e-mail rec-berlin@t-online.de; internet www.kambodscha-botschaft.de; AmbassadorWidhya Chem.

India: N-14 Panchsheel Park, New Delhi 110 017; tel. (11) 26495092; fax (11) 26495093; e-mail camboemb@bol.net.in; Ambassador CHOEUNG BUNTHENG.

Indonesia: Jalan T. B. Simatupang, Kav. 13, Jakarta Selatan 12520; tel. (21) 7812523; fax (21) 7812524; e-mail recjkt@cabi.net.id; Ambassador Khem Bunneang.

Japan: 8-6-9, Akasaka, Minato-ku, Tokyo 107-0052; tel. (3) 5412-8521; fax (3) 5412-8526; e-mail aap33850@hkg.odn.ne.jp; internet www.cambodianembassy.jp; Ambassador POU SOTHIREAK.

Korea, Democratic People's Republic: Munsudong, Taedongkang District, Pyongyang; tel. (2) 3817283; fax (2) 3817625; e-mail recpyongyang@gmail.com; Ambassador Chhorn Hay.

Korea, Republic: 657-162, Hannam-dong, Yeongsan-gu, Seoul 140-910; tel. (2) 3785-1041; fax (2) 3785-1040; e-mail camboemb@korea.com; Ambassador LIM SAMKOL.

Laos: rue Thadeua, Km 3, BP 34, Vientiane; tel. (21) 314952; fax (21) 314951; e-mail recamlao@laotel.com; Ambassador Dan Yi.

Malaysia: 46 Jalan U Thant, 55000 Kuala Lumpur; tel. (3) 42573711; fax (3) 42571157; e-mail reckl@tm.net.my; Ambassador HRH SAMDECH PREAH ANOCH NORODOM ARUNRASMY.

Myanmar: 34 Kaba Aye Pagoda Rd, Yangon; tel. (1) 549609; fax (1) 546156; e-mail recyangon@mptmail.net.mm; Ambassador Hul Phany.

Philippines: Unit 7A, 7th Floor, Country Space One Bldg, Sen. Gil J. Puyat Ave, Makati City, Metro Manila; tel. (2) 8189981; fax (2) 8189983; e-mail cam.emb.ma@netasia.net; Ambassador IN MAY.

Poland: 03-969 Warsaw, ul. Drezdeńska 3; tel. (22) 6165231; fax (22) 6161836; e-mail royalembassyofcambodia@neostrada.pl; Ambassador Chan Ky Sim.

Russian Federation: 121002 Moscow, Starokonyushennyi per. 16; tel. (495) 637-47-36; fax (495) 956-65-73; e-mail cambemoscow@stream.ru; AmbassadorKHIEU THAVIKA.

Singapore: 400 Orchard Rd, 10-03/04 Orchard Towers, Singapore 238875; tel. 63419785; fax 63419201; e-mail cambodiaembasy@pacific.net.sg; internet www.recambodia.net; Ambassador Serey Sin.

Thailand: 518/4, Thanon Pracha Uthit, Ramkhamhaeng Soi 39, Wangtonglang, Bangkok 10310; tel. (2) 957-5851; fax (2) 957-5850; e-mail recbkk@cscoms.com; Ambassador UNG SEAN.

United Kingdom: 64 Brondesbury Park, Willesden Green, London, NW6 7AT; tel. (20) 8451-7850; fax (20) 8451-7594; e-mail cambodianembassy@btconnect.com; internet www.cambodianembassy.org.uk; Ambassador Hor Nambora.

United States of America: 4530 16th St, NW, Washington, DC 20011; tel. (202) 726-7742; fax (202) 726-8381; e-mail mail@embassyofcambodia.org; internet www.embassyofcambodia.org; Ambassador SEREYWATH EK.

Viet Nam: 71 Tran Hung Dao, Hanoi; tel. (4) 8253788; fax (4) 9423225; e-mail arch@fpt.vn; Ambassador (vacant).

DIPLOMATIC MISSIONS OF CAMEROON

United Nations: 22 East 73rd St, New York, NY 10021; tel. (212) 794-2296; fax (212) 249-0533; e-mail info@cameroonmission.org; internet www.cameroonmission.org; Permanent Representative MARTIN BELINGA EBOUTOU.

Algeria: 26 chemin Cheikh Bachir El-Ibrahimi, 16011 el-Biar, Algiers; tel. (21) 92-11-24; fax (21) 92-11-25; e-mail ambacam_alger@yahoo.fr; Chargé d'affaires Jean Missoup.

Belgium: 131–133 ave Brugmann, 1190 Brussels; tel. (2) 345-18-70; fax (2) 344-57-35; Chargé d'affaires a.i. JACQUES ALFRED NDOUMBE EBOULÉ.

Brazil: SHIS, QI 09, Conj. 07, Casa 01, 71625-070 Brasília, DF; tel. (61) 3248-5403; fax (61) 3248-0443; e-mail embcameroun@embcameroun.org.br; internet www.embcameroun.org.br; Ambassador Martin Mbarga Nguele.

Canada: 170 Clemow Ave, Ottawa, ON K1S 2B4; tel. (613) 236-1522; fax (613) 238-3885; e-mail cameroun@rogers.com; High Commissioner MARTIN AGBOR MBENG (acting).

Central African Republic: rue du Languedoc, BP 935, Bangui; tel. 61-18-57; fax 61-16-87; Chargé d'affaires a.i. Gilbert Noula.

Chad: rue des Poids Lourds, BP 58, N'Djamena; tel. 52-28-94; Chargé d'affaires a.i. ABBAS IBRAHIMA SALAHEDDINE.

China, People's Republic: 7 Dong Wu Jie, San Li Tun, Beijing 100600; tel. (10) 65321771; fax (10) 65321761; e-mail acpk71@hotmail.com; Ambassador Eleih-Elle Etian.

Congo, Democratic Republic: 171 blvd du 30 juin, BP 10998, Kinshasa; tel. (12) 34787; Chargé d'affaires a.i. DOMINIQUE AWONO ESSAMA.

Congo, Republic: BP 2136, Brazzaville; tel. 81-10-08; fax 81-56-75; Chargé d'affaires a.i. Guillaume Nseke.

Côte d'Ivoire: Immeuble le Général, blvd Botreau Roussel, 06 BP 326, Abidjan 06; tel. 20-21-33-31; fax 20-21-66-11; Ambassador (vacant).

Egypt: POB 2061, 15 Sharia Muhammad Sedki Soliman, Mohandessin, Cairo; tel. (2) 3441101; fax (2) 3459208; Ambassador Mouchili Nji Mfouayo Ismaila.

Equatorial Guinea: 37 Calle Rey Boncoro, Apdo 292, Malabo; tel. (09) 22-63; Ambassador JOHN NCHOTU AKUM.

Ethiopia: Bole Rd, Woreda 18, Kebele 26, House No. 168, POB 1026, Addis Ababa; tel. (11) 5504488; fax (11) 5518434; Ambassador Jean-Hilaire Mbéa Mbéa.

France: 21 quai Alphonse Le Gallo, 92100 Boulogne-Billancourt; tel. 1-47-43-98-33; fax 1-46-51-24-52; Ambassador LEJEUNE MBELLA MBELLA.

Gabon: BP 14001, Libreville; tel. 73-28-00; Ambassador Jean Koé Ntonga.

Germany: Rheinallee 76, 53173 Bonn; tel. (228) 356038; fax (228) 359058; e-mail botschaftkamerun@yahoo.fr; Ambassador JEAN MELAGA.

Israel: 28 Moshe Sharet St, Ramat-Gan 52425; tel. 3-5298401; fax 3-5270352; Ambassador Henri Etoundi Essomba.

Italy: Via Siracusa 4–6, 00161 Roma; tel. (06) 44291285; fax (06) 44291323; internet www.cameroonembassy.it; Ambassador MICHAEL TABONG KIMA.

Japan: 3-27-16, Nozawa, Setagaya-ku, Tokyo 154-0003; tel. (3) 5430-4381; fax (3) 5430-6489; e-mail ambacamtokyo@gol.com; Chargé d'affaires a.i. Apollinaire Essomba.

Liberia: 18th St and Payne Ave, Sinkor, POB 414, Monrovia; tel. 261374; Ambassador VICTOR E. NDIBA.

Morocco: 20 rue du Rif, BP 1790, Souissi, Rabat; tel. (3) 7754194; fax (3) 7750540; e-mail ambacamrabat@ifrance.com; Ambassador Mahamat Paba Salé.

Netherlands: Amaliastraat 14, 2514 JC The Hague; tel. (70) 3469715; fax (70) 3652979; e-mail ambacam-la-haye@planet.nl; internet www.cameroon-embassy.nl; Chargé d'affaires a.i. MATHIEU BLAISE BANOUM.

Nigeria: 5 Elsie Femi Pearse St, Victoria Island, PMB 2476, Lagos; tel. (1) 2612226; fax (1) 7747510; High Commissioner André E. Kendeck Mandeng.

Russian Federation: 121069 Moscow, ul. Povarskaya 40, BP 136; tel. (495) 290-65-49; fax (495) 290-61-16; Ambassador ANDRÉ NGONGANG OUANDJI.

Saudi Arabia: POB 94336, Riyadh 11693; tel. (1) 488-0022; fax (1) 488-1463; e-mail ambacamriyad@ifrance.com; internet www.ambacamriyad.org.sa; Ambassador Dr Mohamadou Labarang.

Senegal: 157–9 rue Joseph Gomis, BP 4165, Dakar; tel. 33-849-0292; fax 33-823-3396; Ambassador EMMANUEL MBONJO-EJANGUE.

South Africa: 924 Pretorius St, Arcadia 0083; POB 13790, Hatfield 0028; tel. (12) 3624731; fax (12) 3624732; e-mail hicocam@cameroon.co.za; High Commissioner Njoteh Albert Fobatong (acting).

Spain: Rosario Pino 3, 28020 Madrid; tel. (91) 5711160; fax (91) 5712504; e-mail ambcammadrid@telefonica.net; Ambassador (vacant).

Switzerland: Brunnadernrain 29, 3006 Bern; tel. 313524734; fax 313524736; e-mail ambacam.berne@yahoo.fr; Ambassador Jean Simplice Ndjemba Endezoumou.

United Kingdom: 84 Holland Park, London, W11 3SB; tel. (20) 7727-0771; fax (20) 7792-9353; High Commr SAMUEL LIBOCK MBEI.

United States of America: 2349 Massachusetts Ave, NW, Washington, DC 20008; tel. (202) 265-8790; fax (202) 387-3826; e-mail cdm@ambacam-usa.org; internet www.ambacam-usa.org; Ambassador Jerome Mendouga.

DIPLOMATIC MISSIONS OF CANADA

United Nations: 1 Dag Hammarskjöld Plaza, 885 Second Ave, 14th Floor, New York, NY 10017; tel. (212) 848-1100; fax (212) 848-1195; e-mail canada@un.int; internet www.un.int/canada; Permanent Representative JOHN MCNEE.

Afghanistan: House 256, St 15, Wazir Akbar Khan, POB 2052, Kabul; tel. (79) 9742800; fax (79) 9742805; e-mail kabul@international.gc.ca; internet www.international.gc.ca/afghanistan; Ambassador Arif Lalani.

Algeria: BP 48, 18 rue Mustapha Khalef, Ben Aknoun, 16000 Algiers; tel. (21) 91-49-51; fax (21) 91-49-73; e-mail alger@international.gc.ca; internet www.international.gc.ca/world/embassies/algeria; Ambassador PATRICK PARISOT.

Argentina: Tagle 2828, C1425EEH Buenos Aires; Casilla 1598, Correo Central 1000, Buenos Aires; tel. (11) 4808-1000; fax (11) 4808-1111; e-mail bairs-webmail@dfait-maeci.gc.ca; internet www.buenosaires.gc.ca; Ambassador Timothy Joseph Martin.

Australia: Commonwealth Ave, Canberra, ACT 2600; tel. (2) 6270-4000; fax (2) 6273-3285; e-mail cnbra@international.gc.ca; internet www.canada.org.au; High Commissioner MICHAEL LEIR.

Austria: Laurenzerberg 2/III, 1010 Vienna; tel. (1) 531-38-30-00; fax (1) 531-38-33-21; e-mail vienn@international.gc.ca; internet www.kanada.at; Ambassador Marie Gervais-Vidricaire.

Bangladesh: House 16A, Rd 48, Gulshan 2, Dhaka 1212; tel. (2) 9887091; fax (2) 8823043; e-mail dhaka@international.gc.ca; internet www.international.gc.ca/bangladesh; High Commissioner BARBARA RICHARDSON.

Barbados: Bishops Court Hill, Pine Rd, POB 404, Bridgetown; tel. 429-3550; fax 429-3780; e-mail bdgtn@international.gc.ca; internet geo.international.gc.ca/latin-america/barbados; High Commissioner David Marshall.

Belgium: 2 ave de Tervueren, 1040 Brussels; tel. (2) 741-06-11; fax (2) 741-06-43; e-mail bru@international.gc.ca; internet www.ambassade-canada.be; Ambassador LAURETTE GLASGOW.

Bosnia and Herzegovina: 71000 Sarajevo, Grbavička 4/II; tel. (33) 222033; fax (33) 222044; e-mail sjevo@international.gc.ca; Ambassador David Hutchings.

Brazil: SES, Av. das Nações, Quadra 803, Lote 16, 70410-900 Brasília, DF; tel. (61) 3424-5400; fax (61) 3424-5490; e-mail brsla@international.gc.ca; internet www.dfait-maeci.gc.ca/brazil; Ambassador PAUL HUNT.

Brunei: 5th Floor, Jalan McArthur Bldg, 1 Jalan McArthur, Bandar Seri Begawan BS 8711; tel. 2220043; fax 2220040; e-mail bsbgn@international.gc.ca; internet www.dfait-maeci.gc.ca/Brunei; High Commissioner Léopold Battel.

Burkina Faso: rue Agostino Neto, 01 BP 548, Ouagadougou 01; tel. 50-31-18-94; fax 50-31-19-00; e-mail ouaga@dfait-maeci.gc.ca; internet www.dfait-maeci.gc.ca/burkina_faso; Ambassador LOUIS-ROBERT DAIGLE.

Cambodia: Villa 9, R. V. Senei Vinnavaut Oum (rue 254), Sangkat Chaktomouk, Khan Daun Penh, Phnom-Penh; tel. (23) 213470; fax (23) 211389; e-mail pnmpn@international.gc.ca; internet www.dfait-maeci.gc.ca/cambodia; Chargé d'affaires a.i. Ernest Loignon.

Cameroon: Immeuble Stamatiades, pl. de l'Hôtel de Ville, BP 572, Yaoundé; tel. 2223-2311; fax 2222-1090; e-mail yunde@international.gc.ca; High Commissioner JULES SAVARIA.

Chile: Edif. World Trade Center, Torre Norte, 12°, Nueva Tajamar 481, Santiago; tel. (2) 362-9660; fax (2) 362-9663; e-mail stago@international.gc.ca; internet geo.international.gc.ca/latin-america/chile; Ambassador Norbert Kalisch.

China, People's Republic: 19 Dong Zhi Men Wai Dajie, Chao Yang Qu, Beijing 100600; tel. (10) 65323536; fax (10) 65324311; internet www.beijing.gc.ca; Ambassador ROBERT WRIGHT.

Colombia: Carretera 7, No 115-33, 14°, Apdo Aéreo 110067, Bogotá, DC; tel. (1) 657-9800; fax (1) 657-9912; e-mail bgota@dfait-maeci.gc.ca; internet www .bogota.gc.ca; Ambassador Matthew Levin.

Congo, Democratic Republic: 17 ave Pumbu, Commune de la gombe, BP 8341, Kinshasa 1; tel. (89) 50310; fax (99) 75403; e-mail kinshasa@ international.gc.ca; Ambassador SIGRID JOHNSON.

Costa Rica: Oficentro Ejecutivo La Sabana, Edif. 5, 3°, detrás de la Contraloría, Centro Colón, Apdo 351, 1007 San José; tel. 242-4400; fax 242-4410; e-mail sjcra@international.gc.ca; internet www.sanjose.gc.ca; Ambassador Neil Reeder.

Côte d'Ivoire: Immeuble Trade Center, 23 ave Noguès, 01 BP 4104, Abidjan 01; tel. 20-30-07-00; fax 20-30-07-20; e-mail abdjn@dfait-maeci.gc.ca; internet www.dfait-maeci.gc.ca/abidjan; Ambassador MARIE-ISABELLE MASSIP.

Croatia: 10000 Zagreb, prilaz Đure Deželića 4; tel. (1) 4881200; fax (1) 4881230; e-mail zagreb@dfait-maeci.gc.ca; Ambassador Thomas Marr.

Cuba: Calle 30, No 518, esq. 7, Miramar, Havana; tel. (7) 204-2516; fax (7) 204-2044; e-mail havan@international.gc.ca; internet www.dfait-maeci.gc .ca/cuba; Ambassador ALEXANDRA BUGAILISKIS.

Czech Republic: Muchova 6, 160 00 Prague 6; tel. 272101800; fax 272101890; e-mail canada@canada.cz; internet www.canada.cz; Ambassador Michael Calcott.

Denmark: Kr. Bernikowsgade 1, 1105 Copenhagen K; tel. 33-48-32-00; fax 33-48-32-20; e-mail copen@international.gc.ca; internet www.canada.dk; Ambassador FREDERICKA GREGORY.

Dominican Republic: Apdo 2054, Santo Domingo, DN; tel. 685-1136; fax 682-2691; e-mail sdmgo@international.gc.ca; internet www.dominicanrepublic .gc.ca; Ambassador Patricia Fortier.

Ecuador: Edif. Eurocenter, 3°, Avda Amazonas 4153, Apdo 17-11-6512, Quito; tel. (2) 250-6162; fax (2) 250-3108; e-mail quito@international.gc.ca; internet www.dfait-maeci.gc.ca/ecuador; Ambassador CHRISTIAN LAPOINTE.

Egypt: POB 1667, 26 Kamel esh-Shenawy, Cairo (Garden City); tel. (2) 7943110; fax (2) 7963548; e-mail cairo@dfait-maeci.gc.ca; internet www.dfait -maeci.gc.ca/cairo/menu-en.asp; Ambassador Philip MacKinnon.

El Salvador: Centro Financiero Gigante, Torre A, Lobby 2, Alameda Roosevelt y 65 Avda Sur, Col. Escalón, San Salvador; tel. 2279-4655; fax 2279-0765; e-mail ssal@dfait-maeci.gc.ca; internet www.dfait-maeci.gc.ca/ elsalvador; Ambassador STÉPHANIE ALLARD-GOMEZ.

Ethiopia: Nefas Silk Lafto Kifle Ketema 3, Kebele 4, House No. 122, POB 1130, Addis Ababa; tel. (11) 3713022; fax (11) 3713033; e-mail addis@ international.gc.ca; internet www.dfait-maeci.gc.ca/africa/ethiopia-contact -en.asp; Ambassador Yves Boulanger.

Finland: Pohjoisesplanadi 25B, 00100 Helsinki; tel. (9) 228530; fax (9) 601060; e-mail hsnki@international.gc.ca; internet www.canada.fi; Ambassador SCOTT FRASER.

France: 35 ave Montaigne, 75008 Paris; tel. 1-44-43-29-00; fax 1-44-43-29-99; e-mail paris_webmaster@international.gc.ca; internet www.amb-canada.fr; Ambassador Marc Lortie.

Germany: Leipziger Pl. 17, 10117 Berlin; tel. (30) 203120; fax (30) 20312590; e-mail brlin@international.gc.ca; internet www.kanada-info.de; Ambassador PAUL DUBOIS.

Ghana: 42 Independence Ave, Sankara Interchange, POB 1639, Accra; tel. (21) 211521; fax (21) 211523; e-mail accra@international.gc.ca; internet www .accra.gc.ca; High Commissioner Darren Schemmer.

Greece: Odos Ioannou Ghennadiou 4, 115 21 Athens; tel. (210) 7273400; fax (210) 7273480; e-mail athns@dfait-maeci.gc.ca; internet www.dfait-maeci.gc .ca/canadaeuropa/greece; Ambassador RENATE ELISABETH WIELGOSZ.

Guatemala: Edif. Edyma Plaza, 8°, 13a Calle 8-44, Zona 10, Apdo 400, Guatemala City; tel. 2363-4348; fax 2365-1210; e-mail gtmla@international .gc.ca; internet www.guatemala.gc.ca; Ambassador Kenneth M. Cook.

Guyana: High and Young Sts, POB 10880, Georgetown; tel. 227-2081; fax 225-8380; e-mail grgtn@international.gc.ca; internet www.dfait-maeci.gc.ca/ guyana; High Commissioner CHARLES COURT.

Haiti: route de Delmas, entre Delmas 71 et 75, BP 826, Port-au-Prince; tel. 249-9000; fax 249-9920; e-mail prnce@international.gc.ca; internet www .dfait-maeci.gc.ca/haiti; Ambassador Claude Boucher.

Hungary: 1027 Budapest, Ganz utca 12–14; tel. (1) 392-3360; fax (1) 392-3390; internet www.canadaeuropa.gc.ca/hungary; Ambassador PIERRE GUIMOND.

Iceland: POB 1510, 121 Reykjavík; Túngata 14, 101 Reykjavík; tel. 5756500; fax 5756501; e-mail rkjvk@international.gc.ca; internet www.canada.is; Ambassador Anna Blauveldt.

India: 7/8 Shanti Path, Chanakyapuri, New Delhi 110 021; tel. (11) 41782000; fax (11) 41782020; e-mail delhi@international.gc.ca; internet www.india.gc .ca; High Commissioner DAVID MALONE.

Indonesia: World Trade Center, 6th Floor, Jalan Jenderal Sudirman, Kav. 29–31, POB 8324/JKS.MP, Jakarta 12920; tel. (21) 25507800; fax (21) 25507811; e-mail canadianembassy.jkrta@international.gc.ca; internet www .international.gc.ca/asia/jakarta/; Ambassador John T. Holmes.

Iran: POB 11365-4647, 57 Shahid Sarafraz St, Ostad Motahari Ave, Tehran 15868; tel. (21) 81520000; fax (21) 81523900; e-mail teran@international.gc .ca; internet www.iran.gc.ca; Chargé d'affaires JAMES CARRICK.

Ireland: 7–8 Wilton Terrace, 3rd Floor, Dublin 2; tel. (1) 2344000; fax (1) 2344001; e-mail dubln@international.gc.ca; internet www.canada.ie; Ambassador Patrick G. Binns.

Israel: POB 9442, 3/5 Nirim St, Tel-Aviv 67060; tel. 3-6363300; fax 3-6363380; e-mail taviv@international.gc.ca; internet www.international.gc .ca/telaviv; Ambassador JON ALLEN.

Italy: Via Salaria 243, 00199 Roma; tel. (06) 854441; fax (06) 854443915; e-mail rome@international.gc.ca; internet www.canada.it; Ambassador Alexander Himmelfarb.

Jamaica: 3 West Kings House Rd, POB 1500, Kingston 10; tel. 926-1500; fax 511-3493; e-mail kngtn@international.gc.ca; internet www.kingston.gc.ca; High Commissioner DENIS KINGSLEY.

Japan: 7-3-38, Akasaka, Minato-ku, Tokyo 107-8503; tel. (3) 5412-6200; fax (3) 5412-6249; internet www.canadanet.or.jp; Ambassador Joseph Caron.

Jordan: POB 815403, Amman 11180; tel. (6) 5666124; fax (6) 5689227; e-mail amman@dfait-maeci.gc.ca; internet amman.gc.ca; Ambassador MARGARET HUBER.

Kazakhstan: 050010 Almaty, Karasai Batyr 34; tel. (727) 250-11-51; fax (727) 258-24-93; e-mail almat@international.gc.ca; internet www.dfait-maeci.gc .ca/canadaeuropa/kazakhstan; Ambassador Margaret Skok.

Kenya: Limuru Rd, POB 1013, 00621 Gigiri, Nairobi; tel. (20) 3663000; fax (20) 3663900; e-mail nrobi@international.gc.ca; High Commissioner ROSS HYNES.

Korea, Republic: POB 6299, 9/F Kolon Bldg, 45, Mugyo-dong, Jung-gu, Seoul; tel. (2) 3455-6000; fax (2) 3455-6123; e-mail canada@cec.or.kr; internet www.korea.gc.ca; Ambassador Ted Lipman.

Kuwait: POB 25281, 13113 Safat, Daiyah, Area 4, 24 al-Mutawakkel St, Kuwait City; tel. 2563025; fax 2560173; e-mail kwait@international.gc.ca; internet www.dfait-maeci.gc.ca/kuwait; Ambassador DENIS THIBAULT.

Latvia: Baznicas iela 20–22, Rīga 1010; tel. 6781-3945; fax 6781-3960; e-mail riga@international.gc.ca; internet www.dfait-maeci.gc.ca/dfait/missions/ baltiks; Ambassador Claire A. Poulin.

Lebanon: POB 60163, 1e étage, Immeuble Coolrite, Autostrade Jal ed-Dib 43, Beirut; tel. (4) 713900; fax (4) 710595; e-mail berut.webmaster@dfait-maeci .gc.ca; internet www.dfait-maeci.gc.ca/beirut; Ambassador LOUIS DE LORIMIER.

Libya: POB 93392, Al-Fateh Tower Post Office, Tripoli; tel. (21) 3351633; fax (21) 3351630; e-mail trpli@dfait-maeci.gc.ca; internet www.dfait-maeci.gc .ca/libya; Ambassador Haig Sarafian.

Malaysia: 17th Floor, Menara Tan & Tan, 207 Jalan Tun Razak, 50400 Kuala Lumpur; tel. (3) 27183333; fax (3) 27183391; e-mail klmpr@dfait -maeci.gc.ca; internet www.dfait-maeci.gc.ca/kualalumpur; High Commissioner DAVID SUMMERS.

Mali: route de Koulikoro, Immeuble Séméga, Hippodrome, BP 198, Bamako; tel. 221-22-36; fax 221-43-62; e-mail bmako@international.gc.ca; internet www.bamako.gc.ca; Ambassador Isabelle Roy.

Mexico: Schiller 529, Col. Polanco, Del. Miguel Hidalgo, 11560 México, DF; tel. (55) 5724-7900; fax (55) 5724-7980; e-mail embajada@canada.org.mx; internet www.canada.org.mx; Ambassador GUILLERMO E. RISHCHYNSKI.

Morocco: 13 bis rue Jaâfar as-Sadik, BP 709, Agdal, Rabat; tel. (3) 7687400; fax (3) 7687430; e-mail rabat@dfait-maeci.gc.ca; internet www.dfait-maeci .gc.ca/morocco; Ambassador Michèle Lévesque.

Netherlands: Sophialaan 7, POB 30820, 2500 GV The Hague; tel. (70) 3111600; fax (70) 3111620; e-mail info@canada.nl; internet www.canada.nl; Ambassador JAMES CORNELIUS WALL.

New Zealand: Level 11, 125 The Terrace, POB 8047, Wellington; tel. (4) 473-9577; fax (4) 471-2082; e-mail wlgtn@international.gc.ca; internet www .wellington.gc.ca; High Commissioner Penny Reedie.

Nigeria: 15 Bobo St, Maitama, POB 5144, Abuja; tel. (9) 4139910; fax (9) 4139932; e-mail abuja@international.gc.ca; internet nigeria.gc.ca; High Commissioner CAROLINE CHRÉTIEN.

Norway: Wergelandsvn 7, 0244 Oslo; tel. 22-99-53-00; fax 22-99-53-01; e-mail oslo@international.gc.ca; internet www.canada.no; Ambassador Jillian Stirk.

Pakistan: Diplomatic Enclave, Sector G-5, POB 1042, Islamabad; tel. (51) 2086000; fax (51) 2279188; e-mail isbad@international.gc.ca; High Commissioner DAVID B. COLLINS.

Panama: Edif. World Trade Center, Galería Comercial, 1°, Urb. Marbella, Apdo 0832-2446, Panamá; tel. 264-7115; fax 263-8083; e-mail panam@international.gc.ca; internet www.dfait-maeci.gc.ca/panama; Ambassador José Herrán Lima.

Peru: Casilla 18-1126, Correo Miraflores, Lima; tel. (1) 4444015; fax (1) 4444347; e-mail lima@dfait-maeci.gc.ca; internet www.dfait-maeci.gc.ca/peru; Ambassador GENEVIÈVE DES RIVIÈRES.

Philippines: Floors 6–8, Tower 2, RCBC Plaza, 6819 Ayala Ave, Makati City, 1200 Metro Manila; tel. (2) 8579000; fax (2) 8431082; e-mail manil@dfait-maeci.gc.ca; internet www.dfait-maeci.gc.ca/manila; Ambassador Robert Desjardins.

Poland: 00-481 Warsaw, ul. Matejki 1/5; tel. (22) 5843100; fax (22) 5843190; e-mail wsaw@international.gc.ca; internet www.canada.pl; Ambassador DAVID PRESTON.

Portugal: Av. da Liberdade 196–200, 3°, 1269-121 Lisbon; tel. (21) 3164600; fax (21) 3164691; e-mail lsbon.ag@dfait-maeci.gc.ca; internet international.gc.ca/lisbon; Ambassador Anne-Marie Bourcier.

Romania: 011411 Bucharest, Str. Tuberozelor 1–3, Sector 1; tel. (21) 3075000; fax (21) 3075010; e-mail bucst@dfait-maeci.gc.ca; internet www.dfait-maeci.gc.ca; Ambassador MARTA MOSZCZENSKA.

Russian Federation: 119002 Moscow, Starokonyushennyi per. 23; tel. (495) 925-60-00; fax (495) 925-60-25; e-mail mosco@international.gc.ca; internet www.dfait-maeci.gc.ca/missions/russia-russie/menu.asp; Ambassador Ralph James Lysyshyn.

Saudi Arabia: POB 94321, Riyadh 11693; tel. (1) 488-2288; fax (1) 488-1997; e-mail ryadh@international.gc.ca; internet www.saudiarabia.gc.ca; Ambassador RODERICK BELL.

Senegal: rue Galliéni angle rue Amadou Cissé Dia, BP 3373, Dakar; tel. 33-889-4700; fax 33-889-4720; e-mail dakar@international.gc.ca; internet www.dakar.gc.ca; Ambassador Jean-Pierre Bolduc.

Serbia: 11000 Belgrade, Kneza Miloša 75; tel. (11) 3063000; fax (11) 3063042; e-mail bgrad@international.gc.ca; internet www.canada.org.yu; Ambassador ROBERT MCDOUGALL.

Singapore: 1 George St 11-01, Singapore 049145; tel. 68545900; fax 68545930; e-mail echiesg@pacific.net.sg; internet www.dfait-maeci.gc.ca/singapore; High Commissioner Alan Virtue.

South Africa: 1103 Arcadia St, cnr Hilda St, Hatfield, Pretoria 0083; Private Bag X13, Hatfield 0028; tel. (12) 4223000; fax (12) 4223052; e-mail pret@international.gc.ca; internet www.dfait-maeci.gc.ca/southafrica/menu-en.asp; High Commissioner RUTH ARCHIBALD.

Spain: Núñez de Balboa 35, 28001 Madrid; tel. (91) 4233250; fax (91) 4233251; e-mail madrid@international.gc.ca; internet www.canada-es.org; Ambassador Malcolm McKechnie.

Sri Lanka: 6 Gregory's Rd, Cinnamon Gdns, POB 1006, Colombo 7; tel. (11) 5326232; fax (11) 5226299; e-mail clmbo@international.gc.ca; internet www.dfait-maeci.gc.ca/world/embassies/srilanka; High Commissioner ANGELA BOGDAN.

Sweden: Tegelbacken 4, 7th Floor, POB 16129, 103 23 Stockholm; tel. (8) 453-30-00; fax (8) 453-30-16; e-mail stkhm@international.gc.ca; internet www.canadaemb.se; Ambassador Alexandra Volkoff.

Switzerland: Kirchenfeldstr. 88, 3005 Bern; tel. 313573200; fax 313573210; e-mail bern@international.gc.ca; internet www.canada-ambassade.ch; Ambassador ROBERT COLLETTE.

Syria: BP 3394, Damascus; tel. (11) 6116692; fax (11) 6114000; e-mail dmcus@dfait-maeci.gc.ca; internet www.dfait-maeci.gc.ca/syria; Ambassador Mark Bailey.

Tanzania: 38 Mirambo St, Garden Ave, POB 1022, Dar es Salaam; tel. (22) 2163300; fax (22) 2116897; e-mail dslam@international.gc.ca; internet www.dfait-maeci.gc.ca/tanzania; High Commissioner JANET SIDDALL.

Thailand: Abdulrahim Bldg, 15th Floor, 990 Thanon Rama IV, Bangrak, Bangkok 10500; tel. (2) 636-0540; fax (2) 636-0565; e-mail bngkk@international.gc.ca; internet geo.international.gc.ca/asia/bangkok; Ambassador David Sproule.

Trinidad and Tobago: Maple House, 3–3A Sweet Briar Rd, St Clair, POB 1246, Port of Spain; tel. 622-6232; fax 628-1830; e-mail pspan@international.gc.ca; internet www.portofspain.gc.ca; High Commissioner HOWARD STRAUSS.

Tunisia: 3 rue du Sénégal, place d'Afrique, BP 31, Belvédère, 1002 Tunis; tel. (71) 104-000; fax (71) 104-190; e-mail tunis@international.gc.ca; internet www.dfait-maeci.gc.ca/tunisia; Ambassador Bruno Picard.

Turkey: Cinnah Cad. 58, 06690 Çankaya, Ankara; tel. (312) 4092700; fax (312) 4092811; e-mail ankra@international.gc.ca; internet geo.international.gc.ca/canada-europa/turkey; Chargé d'affaires a.i. GRAEME MCINTYRE.

Ukraine: 01901 Kyiv, vul. Yaroslaviv Val 31; tel. (44) 590-31-00; fax (44) 590-31-57; e-mail kyiv@international.gc.ca; internet www.kyiv.gc.ca; Ambassador Abina M. Dann.

United Arab Emirates: POB 6970, Abu Dhabi Trade Towers, West Tower, 9th and 10th Floors, Abu Dhabi; tel. (2) 4071300; fax (2) 4071399; e-mail abdbi@international.gc.ca; internet www.dfait-maeci.gc.ca/abudhabi; Ambassador SARA HRADECKY.

United Kingdom: MacDonald House, 1 Grosvenor Sq., London, W1K 4AB; tel. (20) 7258-6600; fax (20) 7258-6533; e-mail ldn@international.gc.ca; internet www.dfait-maeci.gc.ca/london; High Commr James R. Wright.

United States of America: 501 Pennsylvania Ave, NW, Washington, DC 20001; tel. (202) 682-1740; fax (202) 682-7701; e-mail canada@canadianembassy.org; internet www.canadianembassy.org; Ambassador MICHAEL WILSON.

Uruguay: Plaza Independencia 749, Of. 102, 11100 Montevideo; tel. (2) 9022030; fax (2) 9022029; e-mail mvdeo@international.gc.ca; internet www.dfait-maeci.gc.ca/uruguay; Ambassador Alain Latulippe.

Vatican City: Palazzo Pio, Via della Conciliazione 4D, 00193 Rome, Italy; tel. (06) 68307316; fax (06) 68806283; e-mail vatcn@international.gc.ca; internet geo.international.gc.ca/canada-europa/holysee; Ambassador DONALD W. SMITH.

Venezuela: Edif. Embajada de Canadá, Avda Francisco de Miranda con Avda Sur, Altamira, Apdo 62302, Caracas 1060-A; tel. (212) 600-3101; fax (212) 261-8741; e-mail crcas@international.gc.ca; internet www.caracas.gc.ca; Ambassador Perry Calderwood.

Viet Nam: 31 Hung Vuong, Hanoi; tel. (4) 7345000; fax (4) 7345049; e-mail hanoi@international.gc.ca; internet www.dfait-maeci.gc.ca/vietnam; Ambassador GABRIEL M. LESSARD.

Zambia: Plot 5199, United Nations Ave, POB 31313, 10101 Lusaka; tel. (1) 250833; fax (1) 254176; e-mail lsaka@international.gc.ca; High Commissioner John Deyell.

Zimbabwe: 45 Baines Ave, POB 1430, Harare; tel. (4) 252181; fax (4) 252186; e-mail hrare@dfait-maeci.gc.ca; internet www.harare.gc.ca; Ambassador ROXANNE DUBÉ.

DIPLOMATIC MISSIONS OF CAPE VERDE

United Nations: 27 East 69th St, New York, NY 10021; tel. (212) 472-0333; fax (212) 794-1398; e-mail capeverde@un.int; Permanent Representative Antonio Pedro Monteiro Lima.

Angola: Rua Oliveira Martins 3, Luanda; tel. 222321765; fax 222320832; Ambassador DOMINGOS MASCARENHAS.

Austria: Schwindgasse 20, 1040 Vienna; tel. (1) 503-87-27; fax (1) 503-87-29; e-mail embcviena@nnweb.at; Chargé d'affaires a.i. Hercules do Nascimento Cruz.

Belgium: 29 ave Jeanne, 1050 Brussels; tel. (2) 646-62-70; fax (2) 646-33-85; e-mail emb.caboverde@skynet.be; Ambassador FERNANDO JORGE WAHNON FERREIRA.

Brazil: SHIS, QL 14, Conj. 03, Casa 08, Lago Sul, 71640-035 Brasília, DF; tel. (61) 3248-0543; fax (61) 3364-4059; e-mail embcvbrasil@embcv.org.br; internet www.embcv.org.br; Ambassador Daniel António Pereira.

China, People's Republic: 6-2-121 Tayuan Diplomatic Office Bldg, Beijing; tel. (10) 65327547; fax (10) 65327546; e-mail ecvb@163bj.com; internet www.embcvchina.com; Ambassador JULIO CESAR FREIRE DE MORAIS.

Cuba: Calle 20, No 2001, esq. 7, Miramar, Havana; tel. (7) 204-2979; fax (7) 204-1072; e-mail embajadora@caboverde.co.cu; Ambassador Crispina Almeida Gomes.

Ethiopia: Kebele 3, House No. 107, POB 200093, Addis Ababa; tel. (11) 6635466; Chargé d'affaires a.i. CUSTODIA LIMA.

France: 3 rue de Rigny, 75008 Paris; tel. 1-42-12-73-50; fax 1-40-53-04-36; e-mail ambassade-cap-vert@wanadoo.fr; internet perso.orange.fr/ambassade-cap-vert; Ambassador José Armado Duarte.

Germany: Stavangerstr. 16, 10439 Berlin; tel. (30) 20450955; fax (30) 20450966; e-mail info@embassy-capeverde.de; internet www.embassy-capeverde.de; Ambassador JORGE HOMERO TOLENTINO ARAÚJO.

Italy: Via Giosuè Carducci 4, 1°, 00187 Roma; tel. (06) 4744678; fax (06) 4744643; Ambassador José Eduardo Dantas Ferreira Barbosa.

Luxembourg: 46 rue Goethe, 1637 Luxembourg; tel. 26-48-09-48; fax 26-48-09-49; e-mail ambcvlux@pt.lu; Chargé d'affaires FERNANDA TAVARES FERNANDES.

Portugal: Av. do Restelo 33, 1449-025 Lisbon; tel. (21) 3041440; fax (21) 3041466; e-mail emb.caboverde@netcabo.pt; Ambassador Arnaldo Andrade Ramos.

Senegal: 3 blvd El-Hadji Djilly M'Baye, BP 11269, Dakar; tel. 33-822-4285; fax 33-821-0697; e-mail acvc.sen@metissacana.sn; Ambassador RAÚL JORGE VERA CRUZ BARBOSA.

United States of America: 3415 Massachusetts Ave, NW, Washington, DC 20007; tel. (202) 965-6820; fax (202) 965-1207; e-mail ambacvus@sysnet.net; internet www.virtualcapeverde.net; Ambassador Jose Brito.

DIPLOMATIC MISSIONS OF CENTRAL AFRICAN REPUBLIC

United Nations: 386 Park Ave South, Rm 1114, New York, NY 10016; tel. (212) 679-8089; fax (212) 545-8326; e-mail caf@un.int; Permanent Representative FERNAND POUKRE-KONO.

Belgium: 416 blvd Lambermont, 1030 Brussels; tel. (2) 242-28-80; fax (2) 215-13-11; e-mail ambassade.centrafrique@skynet.be; Ambassador Armand-Guy Zounguere-Sokambi.

Cameroon: 41 rue 1863, Quartier Bastos, Montée du Carrefour de la Vallée Nlongkak, BP 396, Yaoundé; tel. 2220-5155; Chargé d'affaires a.i. JEAN WENZOUÏ.

Chad: rue 1036, près du Rond-Point de la Garde, BP 115, N'Djamena; tel. 52-32-06; Ambassador David Nguindo.

China, People's Republic: 1-1-132 Tayuan Diplomatic Office Bldg, No. 1 Xin Dong Lu, Chao Yang Qu, Beijing; tel. 65327353; fax 65327354; e-mail centra_chine@yahoo.fr; Ambassador (vacant).

Congo, Democratic Republic: 11 ave Pumbu, BP 7769, Kinshasa; tel. (12) 30417; Ambassador Bernard Le Sissa.

Congo, Republic: BP 10, Brazzaville; tel. 83-40-14; .

Côte d'Ivoire: 9 rue des Jasmins, Cocody Danga Nord, 01 BP 3387, Abidjan 01; tel. 20-21-36-46; fax 22-44-85-16; Ambassador Yagao-N'Gama Lazare.

Egypt: 41 Sharia Mahmoud Azmy, Mohandessin, Cairo (Dokki); tel. (2) 3446873; Ambassador HENRY KOBA.

France: 30 rue des Perchamps, 75116 Paris; tel. 1-45-25-39-74; fax 1-45-27-48-11; e-mail accueil@amb-rcaparis.org; internet www.amb-rcaparis.org; Ambassador Jean Willibiro Sako.

Gabon: Libreville; tel. 72-12-28; Ambassador (vacant).

Germany: Johanniterstr. 19, 53113 Bonn; tel. (228) 233564; fax (228) 6195928; e-mail rca@botschaft-zentralafrika.de; internet www.botschaft-zentralafrika.de; Ambassador (vacant).

Morocco: Villa No 4, ave Souss, Cité Saâda, Quartier Administratif, BP 770, Agdal, 10000 Rabat; tel. (3) 7631654; fax (3) 7631655; e-mail centrafricaine@iam.net.ma; Ambassador ISMAÏLA NIMAGA.

Russian Federation: 117571 Moscow, ul. 26-i Bakinskikh Kommissarov 9/124–125; tel. (495) 434-45-20; fax (495) 933-28-99; Ambassador Claude Bernard Beloum.

United States of America: 1618 22nd St, NW, Washington, DC 20008; tel. (202) 483-7800; fax (202) 332-9893; e-mail car@ambrca.org; Ambassador EMMANUEL TOUABOY.

DIPLOMATIC MISSIONS OF CHAD

United Nations: 211 East 43rd St, Suite 1703, New York, NY 10017; tel. (212) 986-0980; fax (212) 986-0152; e-mail chad@un.int; Permanent Representative Mahamat Ali Adoum.

Algeria: Villa no 18, Cité DNC, chemin Ahmed Kara, Hydra, Algiers; tel. (21) 69-26-62; fax (21) 69-26-63; Ambassador EL-HADJ MAHAMOUD ADJI.

Belgium: 52 blvd Lambermont, 1030 Brussels; tel. (2) 215-19-71; fax (2) 216-35-26; e-mail ambassade.tchad@chello.be; Ambassador Maïtine Djoumbe.

Burkina Faso: Ouagadougou; Ambassador AGNÈS MAÏMOUNA ALLAH.

Cameroon: Quartier Bastos, BP 506, Yaoundé; tel. 2221-0624; fax 2220-3940; e-mail ambatchad_yaounde@yahoo.fr; Ambassador André Sekimbaye Bessane.

Central African Republic: ave Valéry Giscard d'Estaing, BP 461, Bangui; tel. 61-46-77; fax 61-62-44; Ambassador MAHAMAT YAYA DAGACHE.

China, People's Republic: 21 Guanghua Lu, Beijing 100600; tel. (10) 65321296; fax (10) 5323638; e-mail ambatchad.beijing@yahoo.fr; Ambassador Ahmed Soungui.

Congo, Democratic Republic: 67–69 ave du Cercle, BP 9097, Kinshasa; tel. (12) 22358; Ambassador (vacant).

Egypt: POB 1869, 12 Midan ar-Refaï, Cairo 11511 (Dokki); tel. (2) 3373379; fax (2) 3373232; Ambassador Ousman Kalibou Bella.

Ethiopia: Bole Rd, Woreda 17, Kebele 20, House No. 2583, POB 5119, Addis Ababa; tel. (11) 6613819; fax (11) 6612050; Ambassador MAITINE DJOUMBE.

France: 65 rue des Belles Feuilles, 75116 Paris; tel. 1-45-53-36-75; fax 1-45-53-16-09; e-mail ambassadedutchad@wanadoo.fr; Ambassador Hissène Brahim Taha.

Libya: POB 1078, Sharia Muhammad Mussadeq 25, Tripoli; tel. (21) 4443955; Ambassador IBRAHIM MAHAMAT TIDEI.

Niger: POB 12820, Niamey; tel. 20-75-34-64; fax 20-72-43-61; Ambassador Youssouf Mbodou Mbami.

Nigeria: 2 Goriola St, Victoria Island, PMB 70662, Lagos; tel. (1) 2622590; fax (1) 2618314; Ambassador MAHAMAT HABIB DOUTOUM.

Russian Federation: 117393 Moscow, ul. A. Pilyugina 14/3/895–896; tel. (495) 936-17-63; fax (495) 936-11-01; Ambassador Djibrine Abdoul.

Saudi Arabia: POB 94374, Riyadh 11693; tel. (1) 465-7702; .

Sudan: St 57, al-Amarat, Khartoum; tel. (183) 471612; Ambassador Moussa Mahamat Seid Medela.

United States of America: 2002 R St, NW, Washington, DC 20009; tel. (202) 462-4009; fax (202) 265-1937; e-mail info@chadembassy.org; internet www.chadembassy.org; Ambassador HASSABALLAH AHMAT SOUBIANE.

DIPLOMATIC MISSIONS OF CHILE

United Nations: 3 Dag Hammarskjöld Plaza, 305 East 47th St, 10th/11th Floor, New York, NY 10017; tel. (212) 832-3323; fax (212) 832-0236; e-mail chile@un.int; internet www.un.int/chile; Permanent Representative Juan Gabriel Valdes.

Algeria: 8 rue F. les Crêtes, Hydra, Algiers; tel. (21) 48-31-63; fax (21) 60-71-85; e-mail embchile@gecos.net; Ambassador PABLO MUÑOZ ROMERO.

Argentina: Tagle 2762, C1425EEF Buenos Aires; tel. (11) 4808-8600; fax (11) 4804-5927; e-mail data@embajadadechile.com.ar; internet www.embajadadechile.com.ar/home.asp; Ambassador Luis Osvaldo Maira Aguirre.

Australia: 10 Culgoa Circuit, O'Malley, ACT 2606; tel. (2) 6286-2098; fax (2) 6286-1289; e-mail echileau@embachile-australia.com; internet www.embachile-australia.com; Ambassador JOSÉ BALMACEDA SERIGÓS.

Austria: Lugeck 1/3/10, 1010 Vienna; tel. (1) 512-92-08; fax (1) 512-92-08-33; e-mail echileat1@chello.at; Ambassador Milenko Esteban Skoknic Tapia.

Belgium: 106 rue des Aduatiques, 1040 Brussels; tel. (2) 743-36-60; fax (2) 736-49-94; e-mail embachile@embachile.be; internet www.embachile.be; Ambassador JUAN SALAZAR SPARKS.

Brazil: SES, Av. das Nações, Quadra 803, Lote 11, 70407-900 Brasília, DF; tel. (61) 2103-5151; fax (61) 3322-0714; e-mail embchile@embchile.org.br; Ambassador Alvaro Humberto Abel Diaz Pérez.

Canada: 50 O'Connor St, Suite 1413, Ottawa, ON K1N 6L2; tel. (613) 235-4402; fax (613) 235-1176; e-mail echileca@chile.ca; internet www.chile.ca; Ambassador EUGENIO LUIS ORTEGA RIQUELME.

China, People's Republic: 1 Dong Si Jie, San Li Tun, Beijing 100600; tel. (10) 65321591; fax (10) 65323170; e-mail embachile@echilecn.com; Ambassador Fernando Reyes Matta.

Colombia: Calle 100, No 11B-44, Bogotá, DC; tel. (1) 214-7990; fax (1) 619-3863; e-mail embajadachile@cable.net.co; Ambassador GASPAR TAPIA GABRIEL.

Costa Rica: Los Yoses, del Automercado Los Yoses 225 m sur, Apdo 10102, 1000 San José; tel. 280-0037; fax 253-7016; e-mail echilecr@racsa.co.cr; internet www.embachile.co.cr; Ambassador Mendoza Negri Gonzalo.

Croatia: 10000 Zagreb, Smičiklasova 23/II; tel. (1) 4611958; fax (1) 4610328; e-mail embajada@echile.hr; internet www.clembassy.hr; Ambassador EMILIO JOSÉ PEDRO RUIZ-TAGLE ORREGO.

Cuba: Avda 33, No 1423, entre 14 y 18, Miramar, Havana; tel. (7) 204-1222; fax (7) 204-1694; e-mail embachilecu@echile.cu; internet www.conchile-lahabana.cu; Ambassador Jaime Manuel Toha González.

Czech Republic: U Vorlíků 4/623, 160 00 Prague 6; tel. 224315064; fax 224316069; e-mail echilecz@mbox.vol.cz; Ambassador MARCELO ROZAS LÓPEZ.

Denmark: Kastelsvej 15, 3rd Floor, 2100 Copenhagen Ø; tel. 35-38-58-34; fax 35-38-42-01; e-mail embassy@chiledk.dk; internet www.chiledk.dk; Ambassador Ricardo Concha.

Dominican Republic: Avda Anacaona 11, Mirador del Sur, Santo Domingo, DN; tel. 532-7800; fax 530-8310; e-mail embaj.chile@codetel.net.do; Ambassador ERIC CAMPAÑA BARRIOS.

Ecuador: Edif. Xerox, 4°, Juan Pablo Sanz 3617 y Amazonas, Quito; tel. (2) 224-9403; fax (2) 244-4470; e-mail embachileecu@trans-telco.net; Ambassador Enrique Krauss.

Egypt: El-Asmak Bldg, 1 Sharia Saleh Ayoub, Cairo (Zamalek); tel. (2) 7358711; fax (2) 7353716; e-mail embchile@link.net; Ambassador SAMUEL FERNÁNDEZ ILLAMES.

El Salvador: Pasaje Bellavista 121, 9a Calle Poniente, Col. Escalón, San Salvador; tel. 2263-4285; fax 2263-4308; e-mail conchile@conchileelsalvador.com.sv; internet www.conchileelsalvador.com.sv; Ambassador Manuel Matta Aragay.

Finland: Erottajankatu 11, 00130 Helsinki; tel. (9) 6126780; fax (9) 61267825; e-mail info@embachile.fi; internet www.embachile.fi; Ambassador CARLOS PARRA MERINO.

France: 2 ave de la Motte-Picquet, 75007 Paris; tel. 1-44-18-59-60; fax 1-44-18-59-61; e-mail echile@amb-chili.fr; internet www.amb-chili.fr; Ambassador María Pilar Armanet.

Germany: Mohrenstr. 42, 10117 Berlin; tel. (30) 7262035; fax (30) 726203603; e-mail comunicaciones@echilealemania.de; internet www.embajadaconsuladoschile.de; Ambassador ÁLVARO ROJAS MARÍN.

Greece: Odos Rigillis, 3rd Floor, 106 74 Athens; tel. (210) 7252574; fax (210) 7252536; e-mail embachilegr1@ath.forthnet.gr; Ambassador Sofia Prats.

Guatemala: 14 Calle 15-21, Zona 13, Guatemala City; tel. 2334-8273; fax 2334-8276; e-mail echilegu@intelnet.net.gt; Ambassador JORGE MARIO SAAVEDRA CANALES.

Haiti: 2 rue Coutilien, Musseau, Port-au-Prince; tel. 256-7960; fax 257-0623; e-mail echileht@acn2.net; Ambassador Alain Marcel Young Debeuf.

Honduras: Calle Oslo C-4242, Col. Lomas del Guijarro, Tegucigalpa; tel. 232-2114; fax 239-7925; e-mail echilehn@123.hn; Ambassador SERGIO VERDUGO NEIRA.

Hungary: 1024 Budapest, Rózsahegy u. 1b; tel. (1) 326-3054; fax (1) 326-3056; e-mail echilehu@axelero.hu; internet www.chile.hu; Ambassador Joaquín Montes Larraín.

India: 146 Jorbagh, New Delhi 110 003; tel. (11) 24617123; fax (11) 24617102; e-mail embchile@airtelbroadband.in; internet www.echileindia.com; Ambassador OSCAR ALFONSO SILVA.

Indonesia: Bina Mulia Bldg, 7th Floor, Jalan H. R. Rasuna Said, Kav. 10, Kuningan, Jakarta 12950; tel. (21) 5201131; fax (21) 5201955; e-mail emchijak@indosat.net.id; Ambassador Rolando Drago Rodríguez.

Ireland: 44 Wellington Rd, Dublin 4; tel. (1) 6675094; fax (1) 6675156; e-mail echile@eircom.net; internet www.embachile-irlanda.ie; Ambassador ALBERTO YOACHAM SOFFIA.

Israel: Beit Sharbat, 8th Floor, 4 Kaufman St, Tel-Aviv 68012; tel. 3-5102751; fax 3-5100102; e-mail echileil@inter.net.il; Ambassador Irene Faivovich Bronfman.

Italy: Via Po 23, 00198 Roma; tel. (06) 844091; fax (06) 8841452; e-mail echileit@flashnet.it; internet www.chileit.it; Ambassador GABRIEL VALDES SUBERCASEAUX.

Jamaica: Island Life Centre, 5th Floor, South Sixth St, Lucia Ave, Kingston 5; tel. 968-0260; fax 968-0265; e-mail chilejam@cwjamaica.com; Ambassador Pedro García Castelblanco.

Japan: Nihon Seimei Akabanebashi Bldg, 8th Floor, 3-1-14, Shiba, Minato-ku, Tokyo 105-0014; tel. (3) 3452-7561; fax (3) 3452-4457; e-mail embajada@chile.or.jp; internet www.chile.or.jp; Ambassador DANIEL CARVALLO.

Jordan: POB 830663, 28 Hussein Abu Ragheb St, Abdoun, Amman 11183; tel. (6) 5923360; fax (6) 5924263; e-mail echile@batelco.jo; Ambassador Luis Palam.

Kenya: Riverside Dr. 66, Riverside, POB 45554, 00100 Nairobi; tel. (20) 4452950; fax (20) 4443209; e-mail echile@echile.co.ke; Ambassador GAETE VIDAL PABLO RODRIGO.

Korea, Republic: 1801 Coryo Daeyungak Tower, 25-5 Chungmoro 1-ga, Jung-gu, Seoul 100-706; tel. (2) 779-2610; fax (2) 779-2615; e-mail echilekr@yahoo.co.kr; internet www.echilecor.or.kr; Ambassador Adolfo Carafí Melero.

Lebanon: Nouvelle Naccache, 21 Bifurcation après La Belle Antique avant Carpacio, Beirut; tel. (4) 418670; fax (4) 418672; e-mail echilelb@dm.net.lb; Ambassador FELIPE DU MONCEAU DE BERGENDAL.

Malaysia: 8th Floor, West Block, Wisma Selangor Dredging, 142-C Jalan Ampang, Peti Surat 27, 50450 Kuala Lumpur; tel. (3) 21616203; fax (3) 21622219; e-mail eochile@ppp.nasionet.net; Ambassador Patricio Torres.

Mexico: Andrés Bello 10, 18°, Col. Polanco, Del. Miguel Hidalgo, 11560 México, DF; tel. (55) 5280-9681; fax (55) 5280-9703; e-mail echilmex@prodigy.net.mx; internet www.embajadadechile.com.mx; Ambassador GERMÁN GUERRERO PAVEZ.

Morocco: 35 ave Ahmed Balafrej, Souissi, Rabat; tel. (3) 7636065; fax (3) 7636067; e-mail echilema@menara.net.ma; Ambassador Marcia Covarrubias.

Netherlands: Mauritskade 51, 2514 HG The Hague; tel. (70) 3123640; fax (70) 3616227; e-mail echilenl@echile.nl; internet www.echile.nl; Ambassador CECILIA MACKENNA ECHAURREN.

New Zealand: 19 Bolton St, POB 3861, Wellington; tel. (4) 471-6270; fax (4) 472-5324; e-mail echile@embchile.co.nz; internet www.embchile.co.nz; Ambassador Juan A. Salazar Sparks.

Nicaragua: Entrada principal los Robles, 1 c. abajo, 1 c. al sur, Apdo 1289, Managua; tel. 278-0619; fax 270-4073; e-mail echileni@cablenet.com.ni; internet www.embachileni.com; Ambassador NATACHA MOLINA GARCÍA.

Norway: Meltzersgt. 5, 0244 Oslo; tel. 22-44-89-55; fax 22-44-24-21; e-mail embassy@chile.no; internet www.chile.no; Ambassador Roberto Eduardo Alonso Budge.

Panama: Edif. Banco de Boston, 11°, Calle Elvira Méndez y Vía España, Apdo 7341, Panamá 5; tel. 223-9748; fax 263-5530; e-mail echilepa@cw.panama.net; internet www.embachilepanama.com; Ambassador CARLOS KLAMMER BORGOÑO.

Paraguay: Capital Emilio Nudelman 351, Asunción; tel. (21) 61-3855; fax (21) 66-2755; e-mail echilepy@conexion.com.py; Ambassador Fabio Vio Ugarte.

Peru: Avda Javier Prado Oeste 790, San Isidro, Lima; tel. (1) 6112211; fax (1) 6112223; e-mail embajada@embachileperu.com.pe; Ambassador CRISTIÁN BARROS MELET.

Philippines: 17th Floor, Liberty Center, 104 H. V. de la Costa St, cnr Leviste St, Salcedo Village, Makati City, 1227 Metro Manila; tel. (2) 8433461; fax (2) 8431976; e-mail echileph@meridiantelekoms.net; internet www.embachileph.com; Ambassador (vacant).

Poland: 02-925 Warsaw, ul. Okrężna 62; tel. (22) 8582330; fax (22) 8582329; e-mail embachile@onet.pl; internet www.embachile.pl; Ambassador JOSÉ MANUEL OVALLE BRAVO.

Portugal: Av. Miguel Bombarda 5, 1°, 1000-207 Lisbon; tel. (21) 3148054; fax (21) 3150909; e-mail embachile@net.novis.pt; internet www.emb-chile.pt; Ambassador Francisco Pérez Walker.

Romania: 010991 Bucharest, Str. Sevastopol 13–17/111; tel. (21) 3127239; fax (21) 3127246; e-mail info@chile.ro; Ambassador CARLOS PARKER.

Russian Federation: 119002 Moscow, Denezhnii per. 7/1; tel. (495) 241-01-45; fax (495) 241-68-67; e-mail echileru@col.ru; internet www.embachilerusia.ru; Ambassador Cesar Augusto Parra Muñoz.

Singapore: 105 Cecil St, 25-00 The Octagon, Singapore 069534; tel. 62238577; fax 62250677; e-mail echilesg@pacific.net.sg; Ambassador GRACIELA MERCEDES FERNÁNDEZ SOBARZO.

South Africa: Brooklyn Gardens, cnr Veale St and Middle St, Block B, 1st Floor, New Muckleneuk, Pretoria; POB 2449, Brooklyn Sq. 0075; tel. (12) 4608090; fax (12) 4608093; e-mail chile@iafrica.com; internet www.embchile.co.za; Ambassador Claudio E. Herrera Alamos.

Spain: Lagasca 88, 6°, 28001 Madrid; tel. (91) 4319160; fax (91) 5775560; e-mail echilees@tsai.es; Ambassador OSVALDO PUCCIO HUIDOBRO.

Sweden: Sturegt. 8, 3rd Floor, 114 35 Stockholm; tel. (8) 679-82-80; fax (8) 679-85-40; e-mail echilese@embassyofchile.se; internet www.embassyofchile.se; Ambassador Ovid Harasich.

Switzerland: Eigerpl. 5, 12th Floor, 3007 Bern; tel. 313700058; fax 313720025; e-mail embajada@embachile.ch; Ambassador MARÍA CAROLINA ROSETTI GALLARDO.

Syria: 6 rue Ziad Bin Abi Soufian, Rawda, Damascus; tel. (11) 3338443; fax (11) 3331563; e-mail echilesy@scs-net.org; Ambassador Ricardo Fiegelist.

Thailand: 83/17 Witthayu Place, Soi Witthayu 1, Thanon Witthayu, Lumpini, Pathumwan, Bangkok 10330; tel. (2) 251-9470; fax (2) 2251-9475; e-mail embajada@chile-thai.com; internet www.chile-thai.com; Ambassador JOAQUÍN MONTES.

Turkey: Reşit Galip Cad., İrfanli Sok. 14/1–3, 06700 Gaziosmanpaşa, Ankara; tel. (312) 4473418; fax (312) 4474725; e-mail embassy@chile.org.tr; internet www.chile.org.tr; Ambassador Francisco Marambio.

United Kingdom: 12 Devonshire St, London, W1G 7DS; tel. (20) 7580-6392; fax (20) 7436-5204; e-mail embachile@embachile.co.uk; internet www.echileuk.demon.co.uk; Ambassador RAFAEL MORENO.

United States of America: 1732 Massachusetts Ave, NW, Washington, DC 20036; tel. (202) 785-1746; fax (202) 887-5579; e-mail embassy@embassyofchile.org; internet www.chile-usa.org; Ambassador Mariano Fernández Amunategui.

Uruguay: 25 de Mayo 575, Montevideo; tel. (2) 9164090; fax (2) 9153804; e-mail echileuy@netgate.com.uy; Ambassador EDUARDO ARAYA ALEMPARTE.

Vatican City: Piazza Risorgimento 55, 00192 Rome, Italy; tel. (06) 6861232; fax (06) 6874992; e-mail echileva@uni.net; Ambassador Pedro Pablo Cabrera Gaete.

Venezuela: Edif. Torre La Noria, 10°, Calle Paseo Enrique Eraso, Las Mercedes, Caracas; tel. (212) 992-3378; fax (212) 992-0614; e-mail echileve@cantv.net; internet www.embachileve.org; Ambassador ROLANDO DRAGO RODRÍGUEZ.

Viet Nam: Suite 1201–1203, 12th Floor, 2 Ngo Quyen, Tung Shing Sq. Bldg, Hoan Kiem District, Hanoi; tel. (4) 9351147; fax (4) 9351150; e-mail embajada1@chile.org.vn; Ambassador Jorge Canelas Ugalde.

DIPLOMATIC MISSIONS OF CHINA, PEOPLE'S REPUBLIC

United Nations: 350 East 35th St, New York, NY 10016; tel. (212) 655-6100; fax (212) 634-7626; e-mail chinamission_un@fmprc.gov.cn; internet www.china-un.org; Permanent Representative WANG GUANGYA.

Afghanistan: Sardar Shah Mahmoud Ghazi Wat, Kabul; tel. (20) 2102545; fax (20) 2102728; e-mail chinaemb_af@mfa.gov.cn; Ambassador Yang Houlan.

Albania: Rruga Skënderbej 57, Tirana; tel. (4) 232385; fax (4) 233159; e-mail chinaemb_al@mfa.gov.cn; Ambassador WANG JUNLING.

Algeria: 34 blvd des Martyrs, Algiers; tel. (21) 69-27-24; fax (21) 69-30-56; e-mail chinaemb_dz@mfa.gov.cn; internet dz.chineseembassy.org; Ambassador Zhang Shixian.

Angola: Rua Houari Boumedienne 196, Miramar, CP 52, Luanda; tel. 222341683; fax 222344185; e-mail shiguan@netangola.com; Ambassador ZHANG BEISAN.

Antigua and Barbuda: Cedar Valley, POB 1446, St John's; tel. 462-1125; fax 462-6425; e-mail chinaemb_ag@mfa.gov.cn; internet ag.chineseembassy.org/eng; Ambassador Chen Ligang.

Argentina: Crisólogo Larralde 5349, C1431APM Buenos Aires; tel. (11) 4543-8862; fax (11) 4545-1141; e-mail embchinaargentina@hotmail.com; internet ar.chineseembassy.org/esp; Ambassador GANG ZENG.

Armenia: 0019 Yerevan, Marshal Baghramian St 12; tel. (10) 56-00-67; fax (10) 54-57-61; e-mail chiemb@arminco.com; internet am.chineseembassy.org; AmbassadorHong Jiuyin.

Australia: 15 Coronation Drive, Yarralumla, ACT 2600; tel. (2) 6273-4780; fax (2) 6273-4878; e-mail chinaemb_au@mfa.gov.cn; internet au.china-embassy.org/eng; Ambassador ZHANG JUNSAI.

Austria: Metternichgasse 4, 1030 Vienna; tel. (1) 714-31-49; fax (1) 713-68-16; e-mail chinaemb_at@mfa.gov.cn; internet www.chinaembassy.at; AmbassadorWu Ken.

Azerbaijan: 1000 Baku, Khagani küç. 67; tel. (12) 493-65-87; fax (12) 498-00-10; e-mail chinaemb@azeurotel.com; Ambassador ZHANG HAIZHOU.

Bahamas: 3 Orchard Terrace, Village Rd, POB SS-6389, Nassau; tel. 393-1415; fax 393-0733; e-mail chinaemb_bs@mfa.gov.cn; internet bs.china-embassy.org; Ambassador Hu Dingxian.

Bahrain: POB 3150, Bldg 158, Rd 4156, Juffair Ave, Block 341, Manama; tel. 17723800; fax 17727304; e-mail chinaemb_bh@mfa.gov.cn; Ambassador LI ZHIGUO.

Bangladesh: Plots 2 and 4, Rd 3, Block 1, Baridhara, Dhaka; tel. (2) 8824862; fax (2) 8823004; e-mail chinaemb@bdmail.net; internet bd.china-embassy.org; Ambassador Zheng Qingdian.

Barbados: 17 Golf View Terrace, Golf Club Rd, POB 428, Rockley, Christ Church; tel. 435-6890; fax 435-8300; e-mail chinaemb_bb@mfa.gov.cn; internet bb.chineseembassy.org; Ambassador LIU HUANXING.

Belarus: 220071 Minsk, vul. Brestyanskaya 22; tel. (17) 284-97-28; fax (17) 210-58-41; e-mail chinaemb_by@mfa.gov.cn; internet by.china-embassy.org; Ambassador Wu Hongbin.

Belgium: 463 ave de Tervueren, 1160 Brussels; tel. (2) 771-14-95; fax (2) 779-28-95; e-mail chinaemb_be@mfa.gov.cn; internet wwww.chinaembassy-org.be; Ambassador ZHANG QIYUE.

Benin: 2 route de l'Aéroport, 01 BP 196, Cotonou; tel. 21-30-07-65; fax 21-30-08-41; e-mail prcbenin@serv.eit.bj; internet bj.chineseembassy.org; AmbassadorLi Beifen.

Bolivia: Calle 1, Los Pinos 8532, Casilla 10005, La Paz; tel. (2) 279-3851; fax (2) 279-7121; e-mail emb-china@kolla.net; Ambassador ZHAO WUYI.

Bosnia and Herzegovina: 71000 Sarajevo, Braće Begića 17; tel. (33) 215102; fax (33) 215108; e-mail chinaemb_ba@mfa.gov.cn; Ambassador Liu Wenxin.

Botswana: 3096 North Ring Rd, POB 1031, Gaborone; tel. 3953270; fax 3900147; e-mail chinaemb_bw@mfa.gov.cn; internet bw.china-embassy.org; AmbassadorDING XIAOWEN.

Brazil: SES, Av. das Nações, Quadra 813, Lote 51, 70443-900 Brasília, DF; tel. (61) 2198-8200; fax (61) 3346-3299; e-mail chinaemb_br@mfa.gov.cn; internet www.embchina.org.br; Ambassador Chen Duqing.

Brunei: 1, 3 & 5 Simpang 462, Kampong Sungai Hanching, Jalan Muara, Bandar Seri Begawan BC 2115; tel. 2334163; fax 2335710; e-mail chinaemb.bn@mfa.gov.cn; internet bn.china-embassy.org/eng; AmbassadorTONG XIAOLING.

Bulgaria: 1113 Sofia, ul. A. von Khambolt 7; tel. (2) 973-38-73; fax (2) 971-10-81; e-mail webmaster@chinaembassy.bg; internet bg.chineseembassy.org; Ambassador Zhang Wanxue.

Burundi: 675 sur la Parcelle, BP 2550, Bujumbura; tel. 22224307; fax 22213735; AmbassadorZENG XIANQI.

Cambodia: 156 blvd Mao Tse Toung, Phnom-Penh; tel. (23) 720920; fax (23) 364738; e-mail chinaemb_kh@mfa.gov.cn; Ambassador Zhang Jinfeng.

Cameroon: Nouveau Bastos, BP 1307, Yaoundé; tel. 2221-0083; fax 2221-4395; e-mail chinaemb_cm@mfa.gov.cn; Ambassador HUANG CHANG QING.

Canada: 515 St Patrick St, Ottawa, ON K1N 5H3; tel. (613) 789-3434; fax (613) 789-1911; e-mail chinaemb_ca@mfa.gov.cn; internet www.chinaembassycanada.org; AmbassadorLu Shumin.

Cape Verde: Achada de Santo António, CP 8, Praia, Santiago; tel. 2623029; fax 2623047; e-mail chinaemb_cv@mfa.gov.cn; Ambassador WU YUANSHAN.

Central African Republic: ave des Martyrs, BP 1430, Bangui; tel. 61-27-60; fax 61-31-83; e-mail chinaemb_cf@mfa.gov.cn; Ambassador Shi Hu.

Chad: BP 735, N'Djamena; tel. 52-29-49; fax 53-00-45; internet td.china-embassy.org; AmbassadorWANG YINGWU.

Chile: Pedro de Valdivia 550, Santiago; tel. (2) 233-9880; fax (2) 335-2755; e-mail embajadachina@entelchile.net; internet cl.china-embassy.org/esp; Ambassador Li Changhua.

Colombia: Carrera 16, No 98-30, Bogotá, DC; tel. (1) 622-3215; fax (1) 622-3114; e-mail chinaemb_co@mfa.gov.cn; internet co.china-embassy.org/chn; Ambassador WU CHANGSHENG.

Comoros: Coulée de Lave, C109, BP 442, Moroni; tel. (73) 2521; fax (73) 2866; e-mail chinaemb_km@mfa.gov.cn; Ambassador Tao Weiguang.

Congo, Republic: blvd du Marechal Lyauté, BP 213, Brazzaville; tel. 81-11-32; fax 81-11-35; e-mail chinaemb_cg@mfa.gov.cn; AmbassadorLI SHULI.

Costa Rica: De la casa de D. Oscar Arias, 100 m sur y 50 m este, Rohrmoser, Pavas, Apdo 1518, 1200 San José; tel. 291-4811; fax 291-4820; Ambassador Wang Xiaoyuan.

Côte d'Ivoire: Lot 45, ave Jacques Aka, Cocody, 01 BP 3691, Abidjan 01; tel. 22-44-59-00; fax 22-44-67-81; e-mail chinaemb_ci@mfa.gov.cn; AmbassadorWEI WENHUA.

Croatia: 10000 Zagreb, Mlinovi 132; tel. (1) 4637011; fax (1) 4637012; e-mail veleposlanstvo.nr.kine1@zg.t-com.hr; Ambassador Wu Lianqi.

Cuba: Calle 13, No 551, entre C y D, Vedado, Havana; tel. (7) 33-3005; fax (7) 33-3092; e-mail chinaemb_cu@mfa.gov.cn; Ambassador ZHAO RONGXIAN.

Cyprus: POB 24531, 30 Archimedes St, 2411 Engomi, Nicosia; tel. 22352182; fax 22353530; e-mail eocinc@spidernet.com.cy; internet cy.china-embassy.org; Ambassador Zhao Yali.

Czech Republic: Pelléova 18, 160 00 Prague 6; tel. 224311323; fax 224319888; e-mail chinaemb-cz@mfa.gov.cn; internet www.chinaembassy.cz; Ambassador HUO YUZHEN.

Denmark: Øregårds Allé 25, 2900 Hellerup; tel. 39-46-08-89; fax 39-62-54-84; e-mail mail@chinaembassy.dk; internet www.chinaembassy.dk; Ambassador Xie Hangsheng.

Djibouti: BP 2021, rue Addis Ababa, Lotissement Heron, Djibouti; tel. 352246; fax 354833; e-mail chinaemb_dj@mfa.gov.cn; AmbassadorWANG XIAODU.

Dominica: Ceckhall, Morne Daniel, POB 2247, Roseau; tel. 4490080; fax 4400088; internet dm.chineseembassy.org; Ambassador Deng Boqing.

Ecuador: Avda Atahualpa 349 y Amazonas, Quito; tel. (2) 245-8927; fax (2) 244-4364; e-mail embchina@uio.telconet.net; Ambassador LIU YUQIN.

Egypt: 14 Sharia Bahgat Ali, Cairo (Zamalek); tel. (2) 7361219; fax (2) 7359459; e-mail webmaster_eg@mfa.gov.cn; internet eg.china-embassy.org/eng; Ambassador Wu Sike.

Equatorial Guinea: Carretera del Aeropuerto, Apdo 44, Malabo; tel. (09) 35-05; fax (09) 23-81; e-mail chinaemb_gq@mfa.gov.cn; AmbassadorYAN XIAOMIN.

Eritrea: 16 Ogaden St, POB 204, Asmara; tel. (1) 185271; e-mail chemb@eol.com.er; Ambassador Shu Zhan.

Estonia: Narva mnt. 98, Tallinn 15009; tel. 601-5830; fax 601-5833; e-mail chinaemb@online.ee; internet www.chinaembassy.ee; Ambassador XIE JUNPING.

Ethiopia: Jimma Rd, Woreda 24, Kebele 13, House No. 792, POB 5643, Addis Ababa; tel. (11) 3711960; fax (11) 3712457; e-mail chinaemb_et@mfa.gov.cn; internet et.china-embassy.org; Ambassador Lin Lin.

Fiji: 147 Queen Elizabeth Dr., PMB, Nasese, Suva; tel. 3300215; fax 3300950; e-mail chinaemb_fj@mfa.gov.cn; internet fj.china-embassy.org/chn; Ambassador CAI JINBIAO.

Finland: Vanha Kelkkamäki 9–11, 00570 Helsinki; tel. (9) 22890110; fax (9) 22890168; e-mail chinaemb_fi@mfa.gov.cn; internet www.chinaembassy-fi.org; AmbassadorMa Keqing.

France: 11 ave George V, 75008 Paris; tel. 1-49-52-19-50; fax 1-47-20-24-22; e-mail chinaemb_fr@mfa.gov.cn; internet www.amb-chine.fr; AmbassadorKONG QUAN.

Gabon: blvd Triomphale Omar Bongo, BP 3914, Libreville; tel. 74-32-07; fax 74-75-96; e-mail gzy@internetgabon.com; Ambassador Xue Jinwei.

Georgia: 0108 Tbilisi, Barnov 52, POB 224; tel. (32) 25-26-71; fax (32) 44-13-83; e-mail yfarm@access.sanet.ge; internet ge.china-embassy.org; Ambassador WANG KAIWEN.

Germany: Märkisches Ufer 54, 10179 Berlin; tel. (30) 275880; fax (30) 27588221; e-mail chinesischebotschaft@debital.net; internet www.china-botschaft.de; Ambassador Ma Canrong.

Ghana: 6 Agostino Neto Rd, Airport Residential Area, POB 3356, Accra; tel. (21) 777073; fax (21) 774527; e-mail chinaemb_gh@mfa.gov.cn; internet gh.china-embassy.org; AmbassadorYU WENZHE.

Greece: Odos Demokratias 10, Palaio Psychiko, 154 52 Athens; tel. (210) 6723282; fax (210) 6723819; e-mail embchina@otenet.gr; Ambassador Luo Linquan.

Grenada: Azar Villa, Calliste St, St George's; tel. 414-1228; fax 439-6231; internet gd.china-embassy.org; Ambassador QIAN HONGSHAN.

Guinea: Quartier Donka, Cité Ministérielle, Commune de Dixinn, BP 714, Conakry; tel. 30-41-48-35; fax 30-45-15-26; e-mail chinaemb_gn@mfa.gov.cn; internet gn.chineseembassy.org; AmbassadorHuo Zhengde.

Guinea-Bissau: Av. Francisco João Mendes, Bissau; tel. 203637; fax 203590; e-mail chinaemb_gw@mail.mfa.gov.cn; AmbassadorYAN BANGHUA.

Guyana: Lot 2, Botanic Gardens, Mandella Ave, Georgetown; tel. 225-9228; fax 231-6602; e-mail prcemb@networks.gy.com; internet gy.china-embassy.org/eng; Ambassador Zhang Jungao.

Hungary: 1068 Budapest, Benczúr u. 15; tel. (1) 413-2400; fax (1) 413-2451; e-mail chinaemb_hu@mfa.gov.cn; internet hu.chineseembassy.org/hu; Ambassador ZHANG CHUNXIANG.

Iceland: Víimelur 29, 107 Reykjavík; tel. 5526751; fax 5626110; e-mail chinaemb_is@mfa.gov.cn; internet is.china-embassy.org; AmbassadorZhang Keyuan.

India: 50D Shanti Path, Chanakyapuri, New Delhi 110 021; tel. (11) 26112345; fax (11) 26885486; e-mail chinaemb_in@mfa.gov.cn; internet www.chinaembassy.org.in; Ambassador ZHANG YAN.

Indonesia: Jalan Mega Kuningan 2, Karet Kuningan, Jakarta 12950; tel. (21) 5761038; fax (21) 5761034; e-mail enbsychn@cbn.net.id; internet id.china-embassy.org/eng/; AmbassadorLan Lijun.

Iran: 13 Narenjestan 7th, Pasdaran Ave, Tehran; tel. (21) 22291242; fax (21) 22291243; e-mail chinaemb_ir@mfa.gov.cn; internet www.chinaembassy.ir; Ambassador XIE XIAOYAN.

Iraq: POB 15097, 624 New Embassy Area, Hitteen Quarter, Baghdad; tel. (1) 556-2741; fax (1) 556-9721; e-mail chinaemb_iq@mfa.gov.cn; Ambassador Chen Yiau Dong.

Ireland: 40 Ailesbury Rd, Dublin 4; tel. (1) 2691707; fax (1) 2839938; e-mail chinaemb_ie@mfa.gov.cn; internet ie.china-embassy.org; AmbassadorLIU BIWEI.

Israel: POB 6067, 222 Ben Yehuda St, Tel-Aviv 61060; tel. 3-5467277; fax 3-5467311; e-mail chnemb@isdn.net.il; internet www.chinaembassy.org.il; Ambassador Chen Yonglong.

Italy: Via Bruxelles 56, 00198 Roma; tel. (06) 8413458; fax (06) 85352891; e-mail chinaemb_it@mfa.gov.cn; internet it.china-embassy.org; AmbassadorSUN YUXI.

Jamaica: 8 Seaview Ave, POB 232, Kingston 10; tel. 927-3871; fax 927-6920; e-mail chinaemb_jm@mfa.gov.cn; internet jm.chineseembassy.org/eng; Ambassador Chen Jinghua.

Japan: 3-4-33, Moto Azabu, Minato-ku, Tokyo 106-0046; tel. (3) 3403-3380; fax (3) 3403-3345; e-mail lsb@china-embassy.or.jp; internet www.china-embassy.or.jp; AmbassadorCUI TIANKAI.

Jordan: POB 7365, 9 Jakarda St, Amman 11118; tel. (6) 5515151; fax (6) 5518713; e-mail chinaemb_jo@mfa.gov.cn; internet jo.china-embassy.org; Ambassador Gong Xiaosheng.

Kazakhstan: 010000 Astana, Kabanbai batyr 37; tel. (7172) 79-35-70; fax (7172) 79-35-67; e-mail chinaemb_kz@mfa.gov.cn; internet kz.china-embassy.org; Ambassador ZHANG XIYUN.

Kenya: Woodlands Rd, Kilimani District, POB 30508, Nairobi; tel. (20) 2722559; fax (20) 2726402; e-mail chinaemb_ke@mfa.gov.cn; internet ke.china-embassy.org; AmbassadorZhang Ming.

Korea, Democratic People's Republic: Kinmauldong, Moranbong District, Pyongyang; tel. (2) 3823316; fax (2) 3813425; e-mail chinaemb_kp@mfa.gov.cn; internet kp.china-embassy.org; Ambassador LIU XIAOMING.

Korea, Republic: 54, Hyoja-dong, Jongno-gu, Seoul; tel. (2) 738-1038; fax (2) 738-1059; e-mail chinaemb_kr@mfa.gov.cn; internet www.chinaemb.or.kr; Ambassador Ning Fukui.

Kuwait: POB 2346, 13024 Safat, Yarmouk, Sheikh Ahmad al-Jaber Bldgs 4 & 5, St 1, Villa 82, Kuwait City; tel. 5333340; fax 5333341; e-mail chinaemb_kw@mfa.gov.cn; Ambassador WU JIUHONG.

Kyrgyzstan: 720001 Bishkek, Toktogula 196; tel. (312) 61-08-58; fax (312) 66-30-14; e-mail chinaemb_kg@mfa.gov.cn; Ambassador Zhang Yannian.

Laos: rue Wat Nak, Muang Sisattanak, BP 898, Vientiane; tel. (21) 315100; fax (21) 315104; e-mail embassyprc@laonet.net; Ambassador PAN GUANGXUE.

Latvia: Ganību dambis 5, Rīga 1045; tel. 6735-7023; fax 6735-7025; e-mail chinaemb_lv@mfa.gov.cn; Ambassador Zhang Limin.

Lebanon: POB 11-8227, 72 rue Nicolas Ibrahim Sursock, Ramletbaida, Beirut 1107 2260; tel. (1) 850314; fax (1) 822492; e-mail chinaemb_lb@mfa.gov.cn; internet lb.china-embassy.org; Ambassador LIU ZHIMING.

Lesotho: POB 380, Maseru 100; tel. 22316521; fax 22310489; e-mail chinaemb_ls@mfa.gov.cn; internet ls.china-embassy.org; Ambassador Qiu Bohua.

Liberia: Tubman Blvd, Congotown, POB 5970, Monrovia; tel. 228024; fax 226740; e-mail Chinaemb_lr@mfa.gov.cn; internet lr.china-embassy.org; Ambassador ZHOU YUXIAO.

Libya: POB 5329, Sharia Menstir, Andalus, Gargaresh, Tripoli; tel. (21) 4832914; fax (21) 4831877; e-mail chinaemb_ly@mfa.gov.cn; Ambassador Huang Jiemen.

Lithuania: Algirdo g. 36, Vilnius 03218; tel. (5) 216-2861; fax (5) 216-2682; e-mail chinaemb_lithuania@mfa.gov.cn; internet www.chinaembassy.lt; AmbassadorYANG XIUPING.

Luxembourg: 2 rue Van der Meulen, Dommeldange, 2152 Luxembourg; tel. 43-69-91-1; fax 42-24-23; e-mail ambchine@pt.lu; internet lu.china-embassy.org; AmbassadorMa Zhixue.

Macedonia, former Yugoslav Republic: 1000 Skopje, 474 No 20; tel. (2) 3213163; fax (2) 3212500; Ambassador DONG CHUNFENG.

Madagascar: Ancien Hôtel Panorama, BP 1658, 101 Antananarivo; tel. (20) 2240129; fax (20) 2240215; e-mail chinaemb_mg@mfa.gov.cn; internet mg .china-embassy.org; Ambassador Li Shuli.

Malawi: Lilongwe; ; FAN GUIJIN (designate).

Malaysia: 229 Jalan Ampang, 50450 Kuala Lumpur; tel. (3) 21428495; fax (3) 21414552; e-mail cn@tm.net.my; internet my.china-embassy.org/eng; Ambassador Cheng Yonghua.

Mali: route de Koulikoro, Hippodrome, BP 112, Bamako; tel. 221-35-97; fax 222-34-43; e-mail chinaemb_ml@mfa.gov.cn; AmbassadorZHANG GUOQING.

Malta: Karmnu Court, Lapsi St, St Julian's STJ 1264; tel. 21384889; fax 21344730; e-mail chinaemb--mt@mfa.gov.cn; internet mt.chineseembassy .org; AmbassadorChai Xi.

Mauritania: rue 42-133, Tevragh Zeina, BP 257, Nouakchott; tel. 525-20-70; fax 525-24-62; e-mail chinaemb_mr@mfa.gov.cn; internet mr.china-embassy .org; AmbassadorZHANG XUN.

Mauritius: Royal Rd, Belle Rose, Rose Hill; tel. 454-9111; fax 464-6012; e-mail chinaemb_mu@mfa.gov.cn; internet www.ambchine.mu; Ambassador Gao Yuchen.

Mexico: Avda San Jerónimo 217B, Del. Alvaro Obregón, 01090 México, DF; tel. (55) 5616-0609; fax (55) 5616-0460; e-mail embchina@adetel.net.mx; internet www.embajadachina.org.mx; Ambassador YIN HENGMIN.

Micronesia, Federated States: POB 1530, Kolonia, Pohnpei, FM 96941; tel. 320-5575; fax 320-5578; e-mail chinaemb@mail.fm; internet fm .chineseembassy.org/eng; AmbassadorLiu Fei.

Moldova: 2004 Chişinău, str. Mitropolit Dosoftei 124; tel. (22) 24-85-51; fax (22) 29-59-60; e-mail chinaembassy@mtc.md; internet md.chineseembassy .org; Ambassador REN MINGGONG.

Mongolia: Zaluuchuudyn Örgön Chölöö 5, Ulan Bator (CPOB 672); tel. (11) 320955; fax (11) 311943; internet mn.chineseembassy.org; AmbassadorYu Hongyao.

Montenegro: 81000 Podgorica, Radosava Burića 4A; tel. (81) 609275; Ambassador LI MANCHANG.

Morocco: 16 ave Ahmed Balafrej, 10000 Rabat; tel. (3) 7754056; fax (3) 7757519; e-mail chinaemb_ma@mfa.gov.cn; internet ma.china-embassy.org; Ambassador Cheng Tao.

Mozambique: Av. Julius Nyerere 3142, CP 4668, Maputo; tel. 21491560; fax 21491196; e-mail emb.chi@tvcabo.co.mz; AmbassadorTIAN GUANGFENG.

Myanmar: 1 Pyidaungsu Yeiktha Rd, Yangon; tel. (1) 221281; fax (1) 227019; e-mail chinaemb_mm@mfa.gov.cn; internet mm.china-embassy.org; Ambassador Guan Mu.

Namibia: 13 Wecka St, POB 22777, Windhoek; tel. (61) 222089; fax (61) 225544; e-mail chinaemb@iafrica.com.na; internet na.chineseembassy.org; Ambassador REN XIAOPING.

Nepal: Baluwatar, POB 4234, Kathmandu; tel. (1) 4419053; fax (1) 4414045; e-mail chinaemb_np@mfa.gov.cn; internet www.fmprc.gov.cn/ce/cenp; Ambassador Zheng Xianglin.

Netherlands: William Lodewijklaan 10, 2517 JT The Hague; tel. (70) 3065091; fax (70) 3551651; e-mail chinaemb_nl@mfa.gov.cn; internet www .chinaembassy.nl; AmbassadorZHANG JUN.

New Zealand: 2–6 Glenmore St, POB 17-257, Karori, Wellington; tel. (4) 472-1382; fax (4) 499-0419; e-mail administration@chinaembassy.org.nz; internet www.chinaembassy.org.nz; Ambassador Zhang Yuanyuan.

Niger: BP 873, Niamey; tel. 20-72-32-83; fax 20-72-32-85; e-mail embchina@ intnet.ne; AmbassadorCHEN GONGLAI.

Nigeria: Plot 302–303, Central Area, Abuja; tel. (9) 4618661; fax (9) 4618660; e-mail chinaemb_ng@mfa.gov.cn; internet ng.china-embassy.org; AmbassadorXu Jianguo.

Norway: Tuengen allé 2B, Vinderen, 0244 Oslo; tel. 22-49-20-52; fax 22-92-19-78; e-mail webmaster@chinese-embassy.no; internet www.chinese-embassy .no; Ambassador GAO JIAN.

Oman: Al-Ansherah St, Way No. 1507, House No. 465, Madinat Alalam, POB 315, Muscat 112; tel. 24696698; fax 24602322; e-mail chinaemb_om@ mfa.gov.cn; Ambassador Pan Weifang.

Pakistan: Ramna 4, Diplomatic Enclave, Islamabad; tel. (51) 2877279; fax (51) 2279600; e-mail chinaemb_pk@mfa.gov.cn; internet pk.china-embassy .org; Ambassador LUO ZHAOHUI.

Papua New Guinea: POB 1351, Boroko, NCD; tel. 3259836; fax 3258247; internet www.chinaembassy.org.pg; Ambassador Wei Ruixing.

Peru: Jirón José Granda 150, San Isidro, Apdo 375, Lima 27; tel. (1) 2220841; fax (1) 4429467; e-mail chinaemb_pe@mfa.gov.cn; internet www .embajadachina.org.pe; AmbassadorGAO ZHENGYUE.

Philippines: 4896 Pasay Rd, Dasmariñas Village, Makati City, Metro Manila; tel. (2) 8443148; fax (2) 8452465; e-mail chinaemb_ph@mfa.gov.cn; internet ph.chineseembassy.org; Ambassador Song Tao.

Poland: 00-203 Warsaw, ul. Bonifraterska 1; tel. (22) 8313836; fax (22) 6354211; e-mail ambchina@pol.pl; internet www.chinaembassy.org.pl; AmbassadorSUN RONGMIN.

Portugal: Rua do Pau de Bandeira 11–13, 1200-756 Lisbon; tel. (21) 3928430; fax (21) 3975632; e-mail chinaemb_pt@mfa.gov.cn; internet pt.china -embassy.org/pot; Ambassador Gao Kexiang.

Qatar: POB 17200, Doha; tel. 4934203; fax 4934201; e-mail chinashi@qatar .net.qa; internet www.mfa.gov.cn/eng/wjb/zwjg/2490/2492/t14412.htm; AmbassadorYUE XIAOYONG.

Romania: 014103 Bucharest, Şos. Nordului 2; tel. (21) 2334188; fax (21) 2334189; e-mail chinaemb_ro@mfa.gov.cn; internet www.chinaembassy.org .ro; Ambassador Liu Zengwen.

Russian Federation: 117330 Moscow, ul. Druzhby 6; tel. (495) 956-11-68; fax (495) 956-11-69; e-mail chiemb@microdin.ru; internet ru.china-embassy.org; AmbassadorLIU GUCHANG.

Samoa: Private Bag, Vailima, Apia; tel. 22474; fax 21115; e-mail tce@samoa .ws; AmbassadorShi Longzhuang.

Saudi Arabia: POB 75231, Riyadh 11578; tel. (1) 483-2126; fax (1) 281-2070; e-mail chinaemb_sa@mfa.gov.cn; internet www.chinaembassy.org.sa; Ambassador YANG HONGLIN.

Senegal: rue 18 prolongée, BP 342, Dakar-Fann; tel. 33-864-7775; fax 33-864-7780; AmbassadorLu Shaye.

Serbia: 11000 Belgrade, Augusta Cesarca 2v; tel. (11) 3695057; fax (11) 3066001; e-mail chinaemb_yu@mail.mfa.gov.cn; Ambassador LI GUOBANG.

Seychelles: POB 680, St Louis; tel. 266588; fax 266866; e-mail china@ seychelles.net; internet sc.china-embassy.org/eng/; Ambassador Wang Weiguo.

Sierra Leone: 29 Wilberforce Loop, POB 778, Freetown; tel. (22) 231797; e-mail chinaemb_sl@mfa.gov.cn; internet sl.china-embassy.org; Ambassador CHENG WENJU.

Singapore: 150 Tanglin Rd, Singapore 247969; tel. 64712117; fax 64795345; e-mail chinaemb_sg@fmprc.gov.cn; internet www.chineseembassy.org.sg; Ambassador Zhang Xiaokang.

Slovakia: Jančova 8, 811 02 Bratislava; tel. (2) 6280-3348; fax (2) 6280-4285; AmbassadorHUANG ZHONGPO.

Slovenia: 1000 Ljubljana, Koblarjeva 3; tel. (1) 4202855; fax (1) 2822199; e-mail kitajsko.veleposlanistvo@siol.net; internet si.china-embassy.org; Ambassador Zhi Zhaolin.

South Africa: 965 Church St, Arcadia, Pretoria 0083; POB 95764, Waterkloof 0145; tel. (12) 3424194; fax (12) 3424154; e-mail reception@chinese-embassy .org.za; internet www.chinese-embassy.org.za; AmbassadorZHONG JIANHUA.

Spain: Arturo Soria 113, 28043 Madrid; tel. (91) 5194242; fax (91) 5192035; e-mail embajadachina@embajadachina.es; internet www.embajadachina.es; AmbassadorQiu Xiaoqi.

Sri Lanka: 381/A Bauddhaloka Mawatha, Colombo 7; tel. (11) 2694491; fax (11) 2693799; e-mail chinaemb_lk@mfa.gov.cn; internet lk.china-embassy .org; Ambassador YE DABO.

Sudan: POB 1425, Khartoum; tel. (183) 272730; fax (183) 271138; e-mail ssddssgg@yahoo.com.cn; AmbassadorLi Chengwen.

Suriname: Anton Dragtenweg 154, POB 3042 Paramaribo; tel. 451570; fax 452540; e-mail chinaemb_sr@mfa.gov.cn; internet sr.chineseembassy.org; Ambassador SU GE.

Sweden: Lidovägen 8, 115 25 Stockholm; tel. (8) 579-364-37; fax (8) 579-364-54; e-mail protocol@chinaembassy.se; internet www.chinaembassy.se; AmbassadorChen Mingming.

Switzerland: Kalcheggweg 10, 3006 Bern; tel. 313527333; fax 313514573; e-mail chinaemb_ch@mfa.gov.cn; internet www.china-embassy.ch; AmbassadorDONG JINYI.

Syria: BP 2455, 83 rue Ata Ayoubi, Damascus; tel. (11) 3339594; fax (11) 3338067; e-mail chinaemb_sy@mfa.gov.cn; internet sy.chineseembassy.org; AmbassadorLi Huaxin.

Tajikistan: 734002 Dushanbe, Khiyoboni Rudaki 143; tel. (372) 224-20-07; fax (372) 251-00-24; e-mail chinaembassy@tajnet.com; internet tj.china -embassy.org; AmbassadorZUO XUELIANG.

Tanzania: 2 Kajificheni Close at Toure Dr., POB 1649, Dar es Salaam; tel. (22) 2667212; Ambassador Liu Xisheng.

Thailand: 57 Thanon Ratchadaphisek, Bangkok 10310; tel. (2) 245-7043; fax (2) 246-8247; e-mail chinaemb_th@mfa.gov.cn; internet www.chinaembassy .or.th/eng; Ambassador ZHANG JIUHUAN.

Timor-Leste: Av. Governador Serpa Rosa, Farol, Dili; tel. 3325168; fax 3325166; e-mail chinaemb_tp@mfa.gov.cn; Ambassador Su Jian.

Togo: 1381 rue de l'Entente, BP 2690, Lomé; tel. 222-38-56; fax 221-40-75; e-mail chinaemb_tg@mfa.gov.cn; AmbassadorYANG MIN.

Tonga: Vuna Rd, POB 877, Nuku'alofa; tel. 24554; fax 24595; e-mail chinaemb_to@mfa.gov.cn; Ambassador Hu Yeshun.

Trinidad and Tobago: 39 Alexandra St, St Clair, Port of Spain; tel. 622-6976; fax 622-7613; e-mail tian@wow.net; internet tt.chineseembassy.org; Ambassador HUANG XING.

Tunisia: 22 rue Dr Burnet, 1002 Tunis; tel. (71) 780-064; fax (71) 792-631; e-mail ambassade.chine@ati.tn; Ambassador Liu Yuhe.

Turkey: Gölgeli Sok. 34, 06700 Gaziosmanpaşa, Ankara; tel. (312) 4360628; fax (312) 4464248; e-mail chinaemb_tr@mfa.gov.cn; internet www .chinaembassy.org.tr; Ambassador SUN GUOXIANG.

Turkmenistan: 744036 Aşgabat, Berzengi raion, ul. Archabil, Hotel 'Kuwwat'; tel. (12) 48-81-31; fax (12) 48-18-13; e-mail chemb@online.tm; Ambassador Lu Guicheng.

Uganda: 37 Malcolm X Ave, Kololo, POB 4106, Kampala; tel. (41) 4259881; fax (41) 4235087; e-mail chinaemb_ug@mfa.gov.cn; internet ug.china -embassy.org; AmbassadorSUN HEPING.

Ukraine: 01901 Kyiv, vul. M. Hrushevskoho 32; tel. (44) 253-31-54; fax (44) 253-73-71; internet ua.china-embassy.org; AmbassadorZhou Li.

United Arab Emirates: POB 2741, Plot 26, W-22, Abu Dhabi; tel. (2) 4434276; fax (2) 4436835; e-mail chinaemb_ae@mfa.gov.cn; internet ae .chineseembassy.org; Ambassador GAO YUNSHENG.

United Kingdom: 49–51 Portland Pl., London, W1B 4JL; tel. (20) 7299-4049; fax (20) 7636-5578; e-mail press@chinese-embassy.org.uk; internet www .chinese-embassy.org.uk; AmbassadorFu Ying.

United States of America: 2300 Connecticut Ave, NW, Washington, DC 20008; tel. (202) 558-0032; fax (202) 232-7855; e-mail chinaembassy_us@ fmprc.gov.cn; internet www.china-embassy.org; Ambassador ZHOU WENZHONG.

Uruguay: Miraflores 1508, Carrasco, Casilla 18966, Montevideo; tel. (2) 6016126; fax (2) 6018508; e-mail embchina@adinet.com.uy; internet uy.china -embassy.org; AmbassadorLi Zhongliang.

Uzbekistan: 100047 Tashkent, Ya. G'ulomov ko'ch. 79; tel. (71) 133-80-88; fax (71) 133-47-35; e-mail chinaemb@bcc.com.uz; internet uz.china-embassy .org; AmbassadorYU HONGJUN.

Vanuatu: PMB 071, Rue d'Auvergne, Nambatu, Port Vila; tel. 23598; fax 24877; Ambassador Cheng Shuping.

Venezuela: Avda El Paseo, Quinta El Oriente, Prados del Este, Caracas; tel. (212) 977-4949; fax (212) 978-0876; e-mail embcnven@cantv.net; internet ve .chineseembassy.org; AmbassadorZHANG TUO.

Viet Nam: 46 Hoang Dieu, Hanoi; tel. (4) 8453736; fax (4) 8232826; e-mail eossc@hn.vnn.vn; internet vn.chineseembassy.org; Ambassador Hu Qianwen.

Yemen: POB 482, az-Zubairy St, San'a; tel. (1) 275337; fax (1) 275341; e-mail chinaem@y.net.ye; internet ye.chineseembassy.org; Ambassador LUO XIAOGUANG.

Zambia: Plot 7430, United Nations Ave, Longacres, POB 31975, 10101 Lusaka; tel. (1) 251169; fax (1) 251157; Ambassador Li Qiangmin.

Zimbabwe: 30 Baines Ave, POB 4749, Harare; tel. (4) 794155; e-mail chinaemb_zw@mfa.gov.cn; internet www.chinaembassy.org.zw; Ambassador NANSHENG YUAN.

DIPLOMATIC MISSIONS OF CHINA (TAIWAN)

Belize: 20 North Park St, POB 1020, Belize City; tel. 227-8744; fax 223-3082; e-mail embroc@btl.net; internet come.to/ROCBelize; Ambassador Ting Joseph Shih.

Burkina Faso: 994 rue Agostino Neto, 01 BP 5563, Ouagadougou 01; tel. 50-31-61-95; fax 50-31-61-97; e-mail ambachine@fasonet.bf; Ambassador TAO WEN-LUNG.

Dominican Republic: Avda Rómulo Betancourt 1360, Secto Bella Vista, Santo Domingo, DN; tel. 532-5461; fax 532-5649; e-mail dom@mofa.gov.tw; internet www.roc-taiwan-do.com; Ambassador Tsai Meng-hung.

El Salvador: Avda La Capilla 716, Col. San Benito, Apdo 956, San Salvador; tel. 2263-1330; fax 2263-1329; e-mail sinoemb3@intercom.com.sv; Ambassador CARLOS S. C. LIAO.

Gambia: 26 Radio Gambia Rd, Kanifing South, POB 916, Banjul; tel. 4374046; fax 4374055; e-mail rocemb@gamtel.gm; AmbassadorPatrick Chang Pei-chi.

Guatemala: 4a Avda 'A' 13-25, Zona 9, Apdo 1646, Guatemala City; tel. 2339-0711; fax 2332-2668; e-mail echina@intelnet.net.gt; Ambassador HONG-LIEN OU.

Haiti: 16 rue Léon Nau, Pétionville, BP 655, Port-au-Prince; tel. 257-2899; fax 256-8067; e-mail haiti888@gmail.com; AmbassadorYang Cheng-ta.

Honduras: Col. Lomas del Guijarro, Calle Eucaliptos 3750, Apdo 3433, Tegucigalpa; tel. 239-5837; fax 232-5103; e-mail hnd@mofa.gov.tw; Ambassador LAI CHIEN-CHUNG.

Kiribati: Bairiki, Tarawa; tel. 22557; fax 22535; e-mail Kir@mofa.gov.tw; AmbassadorChen Shih-liang.

Marshall Islands: A5-6, Lojkar Village, Long Island, POB 1229, Majuro, MH 96960; tel. (247) 4141; fax (247) 4143; e-mail eoroc@ntamar.net; Ambassador BRUCE J. D. LINGHU.

Nauru: Civic Center, 1st Floor, Aiwo; tel. 444-3239; fax 444-3846; e-mail nru@mofa.gov.tw; .

Nicaragua: Optica Matamoros, 2 c. abajo, $\frac{1}{2}$ c. al lago, Carretera a Masaya, Planes de Altamira, Apdo 4653, Managua; tel. 277-1333; fax 267-4025; e-mail nic@mofa.gov.tw; internet www.roc-taiwan.org.ni; AmbassadorWU CHIN-MU.

Palau: WCTC Bldg, Of. 3f, POB 9087, Koror, PW 96940; tel. 488-8150; fax 488-8151; e-mail embrocb@palaunet.com; Ambassador Matthew S. Lee.

Panama: Edif. Torre Hong Kong Bank, 10°, Avda Samuel Lewis, Panamá; tel. 223-3424; fax 269-8757; e-mail embchina@cableonda.net; Ambassador TOMAS PING-FU HOU.

Paraguay: Avda Mariscal López 1143 y Mayor Bullo, Casilla 503, Asunción; tel. (21) 21-3362; fax (21) 21-2373; e-mail embroc01@highway.com.py; Ambassador David C. Y. Hu.

Saint Christopher and Nevis: Taylor's Range, POB 119, Basseterre; tel. 465-2421; fax 465-7921; e-mail rocemb@caribsurf.com; Ambassador RONG-CHUEN WU.

Saint Lucia: Reduit Beach Ave, Rodney Bay; tel. 452-8105; fax 458-0441; Ambassador Tom Chou.

Saint Vincent and the Grenadines: Murray Rd, POB 878, Kingstown; tel. 456-2431; fax 456-2913; e-mail rocemsvg@caribsurf.com; Ambassador LEO LEE.

São Tomé and Príncipe: Av. Marginal de 12 de Julho, CP 839, São Tomé; tel. 223529; fax 221376; e-mail rocstp@cstome.net; AmbassadorYang Ching-yuen.

Solomon Islands: Panatina Plaza, POB 586, Honiara; tel. 38050; fax 38060; e-mail embroc@solomon.com.sb; Ambassador GEORGE CHAN.

Swaziland: Makhosikhosi St, Mbabane; tel. 4044739; fax 4046688; e-mail rocembassy@africaonline.co.sz; Ambassador Leonard Chao.

Vatican City: Via della Conciliazione 4D, 00193 Rome, Italy; tel. (06) 68136206; fax (06) 68136199; e-mail taiwan@embroc.it; internet www .taiwanembassy.org/va; Ambassador CHU-SENG TOU.

DIPLOMATIC MISSIONS OF COLOMBIA

United Nations: 140 East 57th St, 5th Floor, New York, NY 10022; tel. (212) 355-7776; fax (212) 371-2813; e-mail colombia@colombiaun.org; internet www.colombiaun.org; Permanent Representative Claudia Blum.

Argentina: Carlos Pellegrini 1363, 3°, C1011AAA Buenos Aires; tel. (11) 4325-0258; fax (11) 4322-9370; e-mail rodrigoholguin@embajadacolombia .int.ar; internet www.embajadacolombia.int.ar; Ambassador JAIME BERMÚDEZ MERIZALDE.

Austria: Stadiongasse 6–8/15, 1010 Vienna; tel. (1) 406-44-46; fax (1) 408-83-03; e-mail embcolviena@aon.at; internet www.embcol.or.at; Ambassador Rosso José Serrano Cadena.

Belgium: 96A ave F. D. Roosevelt, 1050 Brussels; tel. (2) 649-56-79; fax (2) 646-54-91; e-mail colombia@emcolbru.org; internet www.emcolbru.org; Ambassador CARLOS HOLMES TRUJILLO GARCÍA.

Bolivia: Calle 9, 7835 Calacoto, La Paz; tel. (2) 278-4491; fax (2) 278-6510; e-mail elapaz@minrelext.gov.co; Ambassador Jesús Edgar Papamija Diago.

Brazil: SES, Av. das Nações, Quadra 803, Lote 10, 70444-900 Brasília, DF; tel. (61) 3226-8997; fax (61) 3224-4732; e-mail embjcol@embcol.org.br; internet www.embcol.org.br; Ambassador TONY JOZAME AMAR.

Bulgaria: Sofia, ul. Al. Zhendov 1; tel. (2) 971-31-03; fax (2) 972-76-60; .

Canada: 360 Albert St, Suite 1002, Ottawa, ON K1R 7X7; tel. (613) 230-3760; fax (613) 230-4416; e-mail embajada@embajadacolombia.ca; internet www .embajadacolombia.ca; Ambassador JAIME GIRÓN DUARTE.

Chile: Presidente Errázuriz 3943, Las Condes, Santiago; tel. (2) 206-1314; fax (2) 208-0712; e-mail esantiag@cancilleria.gov.co; Ambassador Jesús Alberto Vallejo Mejía.

China, People's Republic: 34 Guang Hua Lu, Jian Guo Men Wai, Beijing 100600; tel. (10) 65321713; fax (10) 65321969; e-mail ebeijing@minrelext.gov .co; Ambassador GUILLERMO RICARDO VÉLEZ LONDOÑO.

Costa Rica: Barrio Dent de Taco Bell, San Pedro, Apdo 3154, 1000 San José; tel. 283-6871; fax 283-6818; e-mail esanjose@cancilleria.gov.co; Ambassador Luis Guillermo de San Francisco Fernández Correa.

Cuba: Calle 14, No 515, entre 5 y 7, Miramar, Havana; tel. (7) 204-1246; fax (7) 204-1249; e-mail embacub@cancilleria.gov.co; Ambassador JULIO LONDOÑO PAREDES.

Dominican Republic: Avda Abraham Lincoln 502, 2°, Santo Domingo, DN; tel. 562-1670; e-mail erdomini@cancilleria.gov.co; Chargé d'affaires a.i. Diana Mercedes Carvajal Toscano.

Ecuador: Edif. Arista, Avda Colón 1133 y Amazonas, 7°, Apdo 17-07-9164, Quito; tel. (2) 222-8926; e-mail equito@cancilleria.gov.co; internet www .cancilleria.gov.co; Ambassador CARLOS JOSÉ HOLGUÍN MOLINA (expelled March 2008).

Egypt: 6 Sharia Gueriza, Cairo (Zamalek); tel. (2) 3414203; fax (2) 3407429; e-mail colombemb@idsc.gov.eg; Ambassador Jaime Girón Duarte.

El Salvador: Calle El Mirador 5120, Col. Escalón, San Salvador; tel. 2263-1936; fax 2263-1942; e-mail elsalvador@minrelext.gov.co; Ambassador FABIO TORRIJOS QUINTERO.

France: 22 rue de l'Elysée, 75008 Paris; tel. 1-42-65-46-08; fax 1-42-66-18-60; e-mail eparis@minrelext.gov.co; internet www.embcolfrancia.com; Ambassador Fernando Cepeda Ulloa.

Germany: Kurfürstenstr. 84, 10787 Berlin; tel. (30) 2639610; fax (30) 26396125; e-mail info@botschaft-kolumbien.de; internet www.botschaft -kolumbien.de; Ambassador DR MARÍA DORA VICTORIANA MEJÍA MARULANDA.

Guatemala: Edif. Europlaza 1603, 5a Avda 5-55, Zona 14, Guatemala City; tel. 2385-3432; fax 2335-3603; e-mail eguatemala@minrelext.gov.co; Ambassador Eduardo López Sabogal.

Honduras: Edif. Palmira, 3°, Col. Palmira, Apdo 468, Tegucigalpa; tel. 239-9324; fax 232-9324; e-mail ehonduras@cancilleria.gov.co; internet www .embajadadecolombia.hn; Ambassador MIGUEL CAMILO RUIZ BLANCO.

India: 3 Palam Marg, Vasant Vihar, New Delhi 110 057; tel. (11) 51662106; fax (11) 51662108; e-mail edelhi@minrelext.gov.co; Ambassador Juan Alfredo Pinto Saavedra.

Iran: 5 Faryar St, Hedayat St, Darrous, Tehran; tel. (21) 22541981; e-mail emteh@apadana.com; Ambassador PEDRO PUBLO BRUT GOUR.

Israel: Shekel Bldg, 8th Floor, 111 Arlozovov St, Tel-Aviv 62068; tel. 3-6953416; fax 3-6957847; e-mail emcolis@netvision.net.il; Ambassador Juan Hurtado.

Italy: Via Giuseppe Pisanelli 4, 00196 Roma; tel. (06) 3612131; fax (06) 3225798; e-mail info@embajadadecolombia.it; internet www .ambasciatadicolombia.it; Ambassador SABAS EDUARDO PRETELT DE LA VEGA.

Jamaica: Victoria Mutual Bldg, 3rd Floor, 53 Knutsford Blvd, Kingston 5; tel. 929-1701; fax 968-0577; e-mail ekingston@cancilleria.gov.co; Ambassador Ventura Emilio Diaz Mejía.

Japan: 3-10-53, Kami Osaki, Shinagawa-ku, Tokyo 141-0021; tel. (3) 3440-6451; fax (3) 3440-6724; e-mail embajada@emcoltokyo.or.jp; internet www .colombiaembassy.org; Ambassador PATRICIA CÁRDENAS.

Kenya: International House, 6th Floor, Mam Ngina St, POB 48494, 00100 Nairobi; tel. (20) 246770; fax (20) 246771; e-mail enairobi@cancilleria.gov .co; Ambassador María Victoria Díaz de Suárez.

Korea, Republic: Kyobo Bldg, 13th Floor, 1-ga, Jongno, Jongno-gu, Seoul; tel. (2) 720-1369; fax (2) 725-6959; e-mail eseul@cancilleria.gov.co; Ambassador ALEJANDRO BORDA ROJAS.

Lebanon: 5th Floor, Mazda Centre, Jal ed-Dib, Beirut; tel. (4) 712646; fax (4) 712656; e-mail ebeirut@minrelext.gov.co; Ambassador Georgine Mallat.

Malaysia: Level 28, UOA Centre, 19 Jalan Pinang, 50450 Kuala Lumpur; tel. (3) 21645488; fax (3) 21645487; e-mail emcomal@streamyx.com; internet www.embcolombia.com.my; Ambassador SILVIA CASTAÑO DE GONZÁLEZ.

Mexico: Paseo de la Reforma 379, 1°, 5° y 6°, Col. Cuauhtémoc, Del. Cuauhtémoc, 06500 México, DF; tel. (55) 5525-0277; fax (55) 5208-2876; e-mail emcolmex@prodigy.net.mx; internet www.colombiaenmexico.org; Ambassador Luis Camilo Osorio Isaza.

Netherlands: Groot Hertoginnelaan 14, 2517 EG The Hague; tel. (70) 3614545; fax (70) 3614636; e-mail info@colombiaemb.nl; internet www .colmbiaemb.nl; Chargé d'affaires a.i. SONIA MARINA PEREIRA PORTILLA.

Nicaragua: 2da Entrada a las Colinas, 1 c. arriba, $\frac{1}{2}$ c. al lago, Casa 97, Apdo 1062, Managua; tel. 276-2149; fax 276-0644; e-mail emanagua@cancilleria .gov.co; Ambassador Antonio González Castaño.

Panama: Edif. World Trade Center, Of. 1802, Calle 53, Urb. Marbella, Panamá; tel. 264-9644; fax 223-1134; e-mail epanama@minrelext.gov.co; Ambassador GINA BENEDETTI DE VÉLEZ.

Paraguay: Calle Coronel Brizuela, esq. Ciudad del Vaticano, Asunción; tel. (21) 22-9888; fax (21) 22-9703; e-mail easuncio@cancilleria.gov.co; Ambassador Mauricio González López.

Peru: Avda J. Basadre 1580, San Isidro, Lima 27; tel. (1) 4410954; fax (1) 4419806; e-mail emperu@embajadacolombia.org.pe; Ambassador ÁLVARO PAVA CAMELO.

Poland: 03-936 Warsaw, ul. Zwycięzców 29; tel. (22) 6170973; fax (22) 6176684; e-mail embcol@medianet.pl; Ambassador Jorge Alberto Barrantes Ulloa.

Portugal: Palácio Sottomayor, 6°, Av. Fontes Pereira de Melo 16, 1050-021 Lisbon; tel. (21) 3188480; fax (21) 3188499; e-mail elisboa@cancilleria.gov .co; Ambassador FUAD RICARDO CHAR ABDALA.

Russian Federation: 119121 Moscow, ul. Burdenko 20/2; tel. (495) 248-30-42; fax (495) 248-30-25; e-mail emoscu@cancilleria.gov.co; Ambassador Diego José Tóbon Echeverri.

South Africa: 1105 Park St, 3rd Floor, Hatfield, Pretoria 0083; POB 12791, Hatfield 0028; tel. (12) 3420211; fax (12) 3420216; e-mail info@ embassyofcolombia.co.za; Ambassador CARLOS MOREÑO DE CARO.

Spain: General Martínez Campos 48, 28010 Madrid; tel. (91) 7004770; fax (91) 3102869; e-mail emadrid@cancilleria.gov.co; Chargé d'affaires a.i. Luis Armando Soto Boutin.

Sweden: Östermalmsgt. 46, 3rd Floor, POB 5627, 114 86 Stockholm; tel. (8) 21-43-20; fax (8) 21-84-90; e-mail embcol@telia.com; Ambassador FERNANDO ALZATE DONOSO.

Switzerland: Dufourstr. 47, 3005 Bern; tel. 313511700; fax 313527072; e-mail colombie@iprolink.ch; internet www.emcol.ch; Ambassador Claudia Elena Jiménez Jaramillo.

United Kingdom: 3 Hans Cres., London, SW1X OLN; tel. (20) 7589-9177; fax (20) 7589-4718; e-mail mail@colombianembassy.co.uk; internet www .colombianembassy.co.uk; Ambassador NOEMÍ SANÍN POSADA.

United States of America: 2118 Leroy Pl., NW, Washington, DC 20008; tel. (202) 387-8338; fax (202) 232-8643; e-mail enwas@colombiaemb.org; internet www.colombiaemb.org; Ambassador Carolina Barco Isakson.

Uruguay: Edif. Tupí, Juncal 1305, 18°, 11000 Montevideo; tel. (2) 9161592; fax (2) 9161594; e-mail embajada@colombia.com.uy; internet www .colombia.com.uy; Ambassador CLAUDIA TURBAY QUINTERO.

Vatican City: Via Cola di Rienzo 285/4b, 00192 Rome, Italy; tel. (06) 3211681; fax (06) 3211703; e-mail estasede@minrelext.gov.co; Ambassador Juan Pablo María Gómez Martínez.

Venezuela: Torre Credival, 11°, 2A Calle de Campo Alegre con Avda Francisco de Miranda, Apdo 60887, Caracas; tel. (212) 261-6596; fax (212) 261-1358; e-mail ecaracas@minrelext.gov.co; Ambassador FERNANDO MARÍN VALENCIA.

DIPLOMATIC MISSIONS OF COMOROS

United Nations: 420 East 50th St, New York, NY 10022; tel. (212) 972-8010; fax (212) 983-4712; e-mail comoros@un.int; internet www.un.int/comoros; Permanent Representative Mohamed Toihiri.

Belgium: 63 rue Berthelot, 1190 Brussels; tel. and fax (2) 779-58-38; e-mail ambacom.bxl@skynet.be; Ambassador SULTAN CHOUZOUR.

France: 20 rue Marbeau, 75116 Paris; tel. 1-40-67-90-54; fax 1-40-67-72-96; Ambassador Soulaimana Mohamed Ahmed.

Madagascar: Antananarivo; tel. (20) 2265819; Ambassador COL HALIDI CHARIF.

South Africa: 817 Thomas St, cnr Church and Eastwood Sts, Arcadia, Pretoria 0083; tel. (12) 3439483; fax (12) 3420138; Chargé d'affaires Bacar Salim.

United States of America: 336 East 45th St, 2nd Floor, New York, NY 10017; tel. (212) 750-1637; e-mail comun@undp.org; Ambassador MOHAMED TOIHIRI.

DIPLOMATIC MISSIONS OF CONGO, DEMOCRATIC REPUBLIC

United Nations: 866 United Nations Plaza, Suite 511, New York, NY 10017; tel. (212) 319-8061; fax (212) 319-8232; e-mail drcongo@un.int; internet www .un.int/drcongo; Permanent Representative Christian Ileka Atoki.

Algeria: 111 Parc Ben Omar Kouba, Algiers; tel. (21) 59-12-27; Ambassador IKAKI BOMELE MOLINGO.

Angola: Rua Cesário Verde 24, Luanda; tel. 222361953; Ambassador Bolangambe Yongo.

Argentina: Callao 322, 2°, C1022AAQ Buenos Aires; tel. (11) 4552-3942; e-mail rdcbuenos@hotmail.com; Chargé d'affaires a.i. YEMBA LOHAKA.

Belgium: 30 rue Marie de Bourgogne, 1040 Brussels; tel. (2) 213-49-81; fax (2) 213-49-95; e-mail secretariat.cmd@amba-rdcongo.be; Ambassador Jean-Pierre Mutamba Tshampanga.

Benin: Carré 221, Ayélawadjè, Cotonou; tel. 21-30-00-01; .

Brazil: SHIS, QL 06, Conj. 04, Casa 15, Lago Sul, CP 71620-045 Brasília, DF; tel. (61) 3365-4822; fax (61) 3365-4823; e-mail ambaredeco@ig.com.br; Chargé d'affaires a.i. Baudouin Mayola ma Lulendo.

Cameroon: BP 632, Yaoundé; tel. 2220-5103; Chargé d'affaires a.i. KUSAMBILA ZOLA WAY.

Canada: 18 Range Rd, Ottawa, ON K1N 8J3; tel. (613) 230-6391; fax (613) 230-1945; e-mail info@ambassadesrdcongo.org; Chargé d'affaires a.i. Louise Nzanga Ramazani.

Central African Republic: Ambassador EMBE ISEA MBAMBE.

Chad: ave du 20 août, BP 910, N'Djamena; tel. 52-21-83; .

China, People's Republic: 6 Dong Wu Jie, San Li Tun, Beijing 100600; tel. (10) 65320321; fax (10) 65321360; Ambassador CHARLES MUMBALA NZANKU.

Congo, Republic: Brazzaville; tel. 83-29-38; Ambassador Félix Mumengui Otthuw.

Côte d'Ivoire: Carrefour France-Amérique, RAN Treichville, ave 21, 01 BP 541, Abidjan 01; tel. 21-24-69-06; Ambassador ISABELLE I. NGANGELLI.

Czech Republic: Soukenická 34, 110 00 Prague 1; tel. 222314656; fax 286850898; e-mail ambrdcpraha@hotmail.com; Chargé d'affaires a.i. Pierre Kabeya Milambu.

Egypt: 5 Sharia Mansour Muhammad, Cairo (Zamalek); tel. (2) 3403662; fax (2) 3404342; Ambassador KAMIMBAYA WA DJONDO.

Ethiopia: Makanisa Rd, Woreda 23, Kebele 13, House No. 1779, POB 2723, Addis Ababa; tel. (11) 3710111; fax (11) 3713485; Ambassador Gérard Mapango Kemishanga.

France: 32 cours Albert 1er, 75008 Paris; tel. 1-42-25-57-50; fax 1-45-62-16-52; e-mail contact@ambardcparis.com; internet www.ambardcparis.com; Chargé d'affaires a.i. JEAN BUESSO SAMBA.

Gabon: BP 2257, Libreville; tel. 74-32-53; Ambassador Kabangi Kaumbu Bula.

Germany: Im Meisengarten 133, 53179 Bonn; tel. (228) 858160; fax (228) 349989; Chargé d'affaires a.i. PIERRE YVON MALAMBA OSANG-A-BULL.

Greece: Odos Iras 3a, Palaio Psychiko, 154 52 Athens; tel. (210) 6776123; fax (210) 6776124; e-mail ambathenes@minaffecirdc.cd; Chargé d'affaires a.i. Marie-Jeanne Nkale Keta.

Guinea: Quartier Almamya, ave de la Gare, Commune du Kaloum, BP 880, Conakry; tel. 30-45-15-01; .

India: B-2/6, Vasant Vihar, New Delhi 110 057; tel. (11) 51660976; fax (11) 51663152; e-mail congoembassy@yahoo.co.in; Ambassador Balumuene Nkuna Francois.

Israel: Rehov Rachel 1/2, Tel-Aviv 64584; tel. 3-5248306; fax 3-5292623; Chargé d'affaires a.i. KIMBOKO MA MAKENGO.

Italy: Via Barberini 3, 00187 Roma; tel. (06) 42010779; Ambassador Albert Tshiseleka Fehla.

Japan: Harajuku Green Heights, Room 701, 3-53-17, Sendagaya, Shibuya-ku, Tokyo 151-0051; tel. (3) 3423-3981; fax (3) 3423-3984; Ambassador MARCEL MULUMBA TSHIDIMBA.

Kenya: Electricity House, Harambee Ave, POB 48106, 00100 Nairobi; tel. (20) 2229772; fax (20) 3754253; e-mail ambardckenyal@yahoo.com; Ambassador Tadumi On'Okoko.

Korea, Republic: 702, Daewoo Complex Bldg, 167 Naesu-dong, Jongno-gu, Seoul; tel. (2) 722-7958; fax (2) 722-7998; e-mail congokoreambassy@yahoo .com; Ambassador N. CHRISTOPHE NGWEY.

Liberia: Spriggs Payne Airport, Sinkor, POB 1038, Monrovia; tel. 261326; Ambassador (vacant).

Mauritania: Tevragh Zeina, BP 5714, Nouakchott; tel. 525-46-12; fax 525-50-53; e-mail ambardc.rim@caramail.com; Chargé d'affaires a.i. TSHIBASU MFUAD.

Morocco: 34 ave de la Victoire, BP 553, 10000 Rabat; tel. (3) 7262280; Chargé d'affaires a.i. Wawa Bamialy.

Mozambique: Av. Kenneth Kaunda 127, CP 2407, Maputo; tel. 21497154; fax 21494929; Chargé d'affaires a.i. MULUMBA TSHIDIMBA MARCEL.

Netherlands: Violenweg 2, 2597 KL The Hague; tel. (70) 3547904; fax (70) 3541373; Ambassador Jacques Masangu-a-Mwanza.

Poland: 02-637 Warsaw, ul. Miączyńska 50; tel. (22) 8496999; fax (22) 8485215; e-mail ambardcvarsovie@yahoo.fr; Ambassador ISIDORE MAVAMBU MATUMONA.

Portugal: Av. Fontes Pereira de Melo 31, 7°, 1050-117 Lisbon; tel. (21) 3522895; fax (21) 3544862; e-mail ambalisbonne@minaffecirde.cd; Chargé d'affaires Lokosu N'Kulufa.

Romania: 010517 Bucharest, Str. Mihai Eminescu 50–54/15/7, Sector 1; tel. (21) 2105498; e-mail ambardcbuc@yahoo.fr; Chargé d'affaires a.i. PHOBA KI KUMBU.

Russian Federation: 117556 Moscow, Simferopolskii bulv. 7a/49-50; tel. (495) 113-83-48; e-mail rdcambamoscou@yahoo.fr; Ambassador Raphaël Mutombo Tshitambwe.

Senegal: Fenêtre Mermoz, Dakar; tel. 33-825-1280; Chargé d'affaires a.i. FATAKI NICOLAS LUNGUELE MUSAMBYA.

Serbia: 11000 Belgrade, Moravska 5; tel. (11) 3446431; Chargé d'affaires a.i. Paul Emile Tshinga Ahuka.

South Africa: 791 Schoeman St, Arcadia, Pretoria 0083; POB 28795, Sunnyside 0132; tel. (12) 3441478; fax (12) 3441510; e-mail rdcongo@lantic .net; Ambassador BENE M'POKO.

Spain: Paseo de la Castellana 255, 1°, 28046 Madrid; tel. (91) 7332647; fax (91) 3231575; e-mail ambardcmadrid@hotmail.com; Ambassador (vacant).

Sudan: St 13, Block 12 CE, New Extension, 23, POB 4195, Khartoum; tel. (183) 471125; Chargé d'affaires a.i. BAWAN MUZURI.

Sweden: Stockholmsvägen 33, 4th Floor, POB 1171, 181 23 Lidingö; tel. (8) 765-83-80; fax (8) 765-85-91; e-mail rdcongo6@hotmail.com; Chargé d'affaires a.i. Henri Mbayahe Ndungo.

Switzerland: Sulgenheimweg 21, 3007 Bern; tel. 313713538; fax 313727466; e-mail rdcambassy@bluewin.ch; Ambassador KESIA-MBE MINDUA.

Tanzania: 438 Malik Rd, POB 975, Upanga, Dar es Salaam; tel. (22) 2150282; fax (22) 2153341; Chargé d'affaires a.i. Nsingi Zi Lubaki.

Togo: Lomé; tel. 221-51-55; Ambassador LOKOKA IKUKELE BOMOLO.

Tunisia: 11 rue Tertullien, Notre Dame, Tunis; tel. (71) 281-833; Ambassador Mboladinga Katako.

Uganda: 20 Philip Rd, Kololo, POB 4972, Kampala; tel. (41) 4250099; fax (41) 4340140; Chargé d'affaires a.i. BISELELE WA MUTSHIPAYI.

United Kingdom: 281 Gray's Inn Rd, London, WC1X 8QF; tel. (20) 7278-9825; fax (20) 7833-9967; Ambassador Eugénie Tshiela Compton.

United States of America: 1800 New Hampshire Ave, NW, Washington, DC 20009; tel. (202) 234-7690; fax (202) 237-0748; Ambassador FAIDA MITIFU.

Vatican City: Via del Castro Pretorio 28/2, 00185 Rome, Italy; tel. (06) 45447860; Chargé d'affaires a.i. Edouard Kambembo Ngunza.

Zambia: Plot 1124, Parirenyatwa Rd, POB 31287, 10101 Lusaka; tel. (1) 235679; Ambassador JOHNSON WA BINANA.

Zimbabwe: 5 Pevensey Rd, Highlands, POB 2446, Harare; tel. (4) 481172; fax (4) 796421; Ambassador Dr Kikaya bin Karub (acting).

DIPLOMATIC MISSIONS OF CONGO, REPUBLIC

United Nations: 14 East 65th St, New York, NY 10021; tel. (212) 744-7840; fax (212) 744-7975; e-mail congo@un.int; Permanent Representative BASILE IKOUEBE.

Algeria: 111 Parc Ben Omar Kouba, Algiers; tel. (21) 58-68-00; Ambassador Pierre N'Gaka.

Angola: Av. 4 de Fevereiro 3, Luanda; tel. 222310293; Ambassador CHRISTIAN GILBERT BEMBET.

Belgium: 16–18 ave F. D. Roosevelt, 1050 Brussels; tel. (2) 648-38-56; fax (2) 648-42-13; e-mail ambassade.congobrazza@skynet.be; Ambassador Jacques Obia.

Cameroon: Rheinallée 45, BP 1422, Yaoundé; tel. 2221-2458; Chargé d'affaires a.i. JOSEPH NZIÉFÉ.

Central African Republic: BP 1414, Bangui; tel. 61-20-79; Ambassador Likibi Tsiba Nobert.

China, People's Republic: 7 Dong Si Jie, San Li Tun, Beijing 100600; tel. (10) 65321658; fax (10) 65322915; Ambassador PIERRE PASSI.

Congo, Democratic Republic: 179 blvd du 30 juin, BP 9516, Kinshasa; tel. (12) 34028; Ambassador Edouard Roger Okoula.

Cuba: Avda 5, No 1003, Miramar, Havana; tel. (7) 204-9055; Ambassador PASCAL ONGEMBY.

Ethiopia: Woreda 3, Kebele 51, House No. 378, POB 5639, Addis Ababa; tel. (11) 5514188; fax (11) 5514331; Ambassador Raymond Serge Bale.

France: 37 bis rue Paul Valéry, 75116 Paris; tel. 1-45-00-60-57; fax 1-40-67-17-33; e-mail ambacongo_france@yahoo.fr; internet www.ambacongo.org; Ambassador HENRI LOPES.

Gabon: BP 269, Libreville; tel. 07-85-26-11; e-mail ambacobrazzalibreville@yahoo.fr; Ambassador Edouard Roger Okoula.

Germany: Grabbeallee 47, 13156 Berlin; tel. (30) 49400753; fax (30) 49918063; e-mail botschaftkongobrzv@thotmail.de; Chargé d'affaires a.i. SERGE MICHEL ODZOCKI.

Israel: POB 12504, 9 Maskit St, Herzliya Pitauch 46120; tel. 9-9577130; fax 9-9577216; Chargé d'affaires a.i. David Madouka.

Italy: Via Ombrone 8–10, 00198 Roma; tel. (06) 8417422; Ambassador MAMADOU DEKAMO KAMARA.

Morocco: 197 ave Général Abdendi Britel, Souissi II, Rabat; tel. (3) 7659966; fax (3) 7659959; Ambassador Jean-Marie Ewengue.

Mozambique: Av. Kenneth Kaunda 783, CP 4743, Maputo; tel. 21490142; Chargé d'affaires a.i. MONSEGNO BASHA OSHEFWA.

Namibia: 9 Korner St, POB 22970, Windhoek; tel. (61) 257517; fax (61) 240796; Ambassador Patrice Ndounga.

Romania: 021412 Bucharest 2, Bd. Pache Protopopescu 14; tel. (21) 3153371; e-mail ambacobuc@yahoo.fr; Chargé d'affaires GEORGES AMBARA.

Russian Federation: 119034 Moscow, Kropotinskii per. 12; tel. (495) 236-33-68; fax (495) 236-41-16; Ambassador Jean-Pierre Louyébo.

Senegal: Statut Mermoz, BP 5242, Dakar; tel. 77-634-5022; fax 33-825-7856; Ambassador VALENTIN OLLESSONGO.

South Africa: 960 Arcadia St, Arcadia, Pretoria 0083; POB 40427, Arcadia 0007; tel. (12) 3425508; fax (12) 3425510; Ambassador Roger Issombo.

United States of America: 4891 Colorado Ave, NW, Washington, DC 20011; tel. (202) 726-5500; fax (202) 726-1860; e-mail info@embassyofcongo.org; internet www.embassyofcongo.org; Ambassador SERGE MOMBOULI.

Vatican City: Rome, Italy; Ambassador Pierre-Claver Akouala.

DIPLOMATIC MISSIONS OF COSTA RICA

United Nations: 211 East 43rd St, Rm 903, New York, NY 10017; tel. (212) 986-6373; fax (212) 986-6842; e-mail pmnu@rree.go.cr; internet www.un.int/costarica; Permanent Representative JORGE URBINA.

Argentina: Avda Callao 1769, 7°b, C1024AAD Buenos Aires; tel. (11) 4815-0072; fax (11) 4814-1660; e-mail embarica@fibertel.com.ar; Ambassador Maritza Castro Salazar.

Austria: Wagramerstr. 23/1/1 Top 2–3, 1220 Vienna; tel. (1) 263-38-24; fax (1) 263-38-24-5; e-mail embajadaaustria_costa.rica@chello.at; Ambassador ANA TERESA DENGO BENAVIDES.

Belgium: 489 ave Louise, BP 13, 1050 Brussels; tel. (2) 640-55-41; fax (2) 648-31-92; e-mail info@costaricaembassy.be; internet www.costaricaembassy.be; Ambassador Roberto Echandi.

Belize: 10 Unity Blvd, POB 288, Belmopan; tel. 822-1582; fax 822-1583; e-mail fborbon@btl.net; Ambassador FERNANDO BORBÓN ARIAS.

Bolivia: Edif. San Miguel Arcángel 1420, 1°, Of. 102, Avda Montenegro en Calacoto, La Paz; tel. (2) 279-8930; e-mail embcrbo@entelnet.bo; Ambassador María de los Angeles Gutiérrez Vargas.

Brazil: SRTV/N 701, Conj. C, Ala A, Salas 308/310, Edif. Centro Empresarial Norte, 70710-200 Brasilia, DF; tel. (61) 328-32219; fax (61) 3328-2243; e-mail embcostaricabr@solar.com.br; Ambassador JORGE ALFREDO ROBLES ARIAS.

Canada: 325 Dalhousie St, Suite 407, Ottawa, ON K1N 7G2; tel. (613) 562-2855; fax (613) 562-2582; e-mail embcr@costaricaembassy.com; internet www.costaricaembassy.com; Ambassador Emilia María Alvarez Navarro.

Chile: Calle Zurich 255, Dpto 85, Las Condes, Santiago; tel. (2) 334-9486; fax (2) 334-9490; e-mail embacostarica@adsl.tie.cl; Ambassador EDGAR GARCÍA MIRANDA.

China, People's Republic: Jian Guo Men Wai, 1-5-41 Jiao Gong Lu, Beijing 100600; tel. (10) 65324157; fax (10) 65324546; e-mail embajadacrchina@gmail.com; Ambassador Antonio Burgués Terán.

Colombia: Carrera 8, No 95-48, Bogotá, DC; tel. (1) 623-0205; fax (1) 691-8558; e-mail embacosta@andinet.com; internet www.embajadacostarica.netfirms.com/funcionarios.htm; Ambassador MELVIN ALFREDO SÁENZ BIOLLEY.

Czech Republic: Hellichova 458/1, 118 00 Prague 1; tel. 257310582; fax 257310572; e-mail embcr_rc@rree.go.cr; Chargé d'affaires a.i. William José Calvo Calvo.

Dominican Republic: Ensanche Serralles, entre Abraham Lincoln y Lope de Vega, Calle Malaquías Gil 11 Altos, Santo Domingo, DN; tel. 683-7209; fax 565-6467; e-mail embarica@codetel.net.do; Ambassador MARTA EUGENIA NÚÑEZ MADRIZ.

Ecuador: Rumipamba 692 y República, 1°, Apdo 17-03-301, Quito; tel. (2) 225-4945; fax (2) 225-4087; e-mail embajcr@uio.satnet.net; Ambassador Luz Argentina Calderón Gei.

El Salvador: 85 Avda Sur y Calle Cuscatlán 4415, Col. Escalón, San Salvador; tel. 2264-3863; fax 2264-3866; e-mail embajada@embajadacostarica.org.sv; internet www.embajadacostarica.org.sv; Ambassador INGRID HERRMANN ESCRIBANO.

France: 78 ave Emile Zola, 75015 Paris; tel. 1-45-78-96-96; fax 1-45-78-99-66; e-mail embcr@wanadoo.fr; Ambassador Roxana Pinto López.

Germany: Dessauer Str. 28–29, 10963 Berlin; tel. (30) 26398990; fax (30) 26557210; e-mail emb@botschaft-costarica.de; internet www.botschaft-costarica.de; Ambassador DR BERND NIEHAUS QUESADA.

Guatemala: 15 Calle 5-59, Zona 10, Guatemala City; tel. 2366-9918; fax 2368-0705; e-mail embarica@intelnet.net.gt; Ambassador Lidiette Brenes Arguedas.

Honduras: Residencial El Triángulo, 1a Calle, Lomas del Guijarro, Apdo 512, Tegucigalpa; tel. 232-1768; fax 232-1876; e-mail embacori@amnettgu.com; Ambassador JAVIER GUERRA LASPIUR.

Israel: 14 Abba Hillel St, 15th Floor, Ramat-Gan 52506; tel. 3-6135061; fax 3-6134779; e-mail emcri@netvision.net.il; Ambassador Noemí Judith Baruch Goldberg.

Italy: Viale Liegi 2, int. 8, 00198 Roma; tel. (06) 84242853; fax (06) 85355956; e-mail embcosta@tiscalinet.it; internet www.ambasciatacostarica.org; Ambassador (vacant).

Jamaica: Belvedere House, Beverly Dr., Hopedale, Old Hope Rd, Kingston 6; tel. 927-5988; fax 978-3946; e-mail cr_emb_jam14@hotmail.com; Ambassador Nidia Lorena Sandoval Arce.

Japan: Kowa Bldg, No. 38, Room 901, 4-12-24, Nishi Azabu, Minato-ku, Tokyo 106-0031; tel. (3) 3486-1812; fax (3) 3486-1813; e-mail ecrj@tky3.web3.ne.jp; Ambassador MARIO FERNÁNDEZ SILVA.

Korea, Republic: Iljin Bldg, 7, 50-1, Dohwa-dong, Mapo-gu, Seoul 121-040; tel. (2) 707-9248; fax (2) 707-9255; e-mail embajadacr@ecostarica.or.kr; internet www.ecostarica.or.kr; Ambassador Fernando Borbón Arias.

Mexico: Río Po 113, Col. Cuauhtémoc, Del. Cuauhtémoc, 06500 México, DF; tel. (55) 5525-7764; fax (55) 5511-9240; e-mail embcrica@ri.redint.com; Ambassador GIOCONDA UBEDA RIVERA.

Netherlands: Laan Copes van Cattenburch 46, 2585 GB The Hague; tel. (70) 3540780; fax (70) 3584754; e-mail embajada@embacrica.demon.nl; Ambassador Francisco José Aguilar Urbina.

Nicaragua: Reparto las Colinas, Prado Ecuestre 304, 1°, Managua; tel. 276-1352; fax 276-0115; e-mail infembcr@cablenet.com.ni; Ambassador ANTONIO TACSAN LAM.

Norway: Skippergt. 33, 8th Floor, 0154 Oslo; tel. 22-42-58-23; fax 22-33-04-08; e-mail embassy@costarica.no; internet www.costarica.no; Ambassador Dr Claudio Bogantes Zamora.

Panama: Edif. Plaza Omega, 3°, Calle Samuel Lewis, Apdo 8963, Panamá; tel. 264-2980; fax 264-4057; e-mail embarica@cwp.net.pa; Ambassador EKHART PETERS SEVEERS.

Paraguay: Shopping del Sol 13104, Avda Antonio Mena Porta, casi Dr Manuel Peña, Asunción; tel. (21) 29-7158; e-mail embarica@tigo.com.py; Ambassador Esteban Arias Monge.

Peru: Baltazar La Torre 828, San Isidro, Lima; tel. (1) 2642999; fax (1) 2642799; e-mail costarica.peru@hotmail.com; Ambassador SARA FAIGENZICHT WEISLEDER.

Poland: 02-954 Warsaw, ul. Kubickiego 9/5; tel. (22) 8589112; fax (22) 6427832; e-mail emcoripol@neostrada.pl; Chargé d'affaires a.i. Hilda María Santiesteban Montero.

Russian Federation: 121615 Moscow, Rublevskoye shosse 26/1/23–24; tel. (495) 415-40-14; fax (495) 415-40-42; e-mail consulcr@rol.ru; Ambassador ISABEL MONTERO DE LA CÁMARA.

Singapore: 271 Bukit Timah Rd, 04-08 Balmoral Plaza, Singapore 259708; tel. 67380566; fax 67380567; e-mail embassycostarica@singnet.com.sg; Ambassador Juan Fernando Cordero Arias.

Spain: Paseo de la Castellana 164, 17°, 28046 Madrid; tel. (91) 3459622; fax (91) 3533709; e-mail embajada@embcr.org; Ambassador MELVIN ALFREDO SÁENZ BIOLLEY.

Switzerland: Schwarztorstr. 11, 3007 Bern; tel. 313727887; fax 313727834; e-mail costarica@bluewin.ch; Ambassador Edgar Mohs Villalta.

United Kingdom: Flat 1, 14 Lancaster Gate, London, W2 3LH; tel. (20) 7706-8844; fax (20) 7706-8655; e-mail costarica@btconnect.com; Ambassador PILAR SABORÍO DE ROCAFORT.

United States of America: 2114 S St, NW, Washington, DC 20008; tel. (202) 234-2945; fax (202) 265-4795; e-mail embassy@costarica-embassy.org; internet www.costarica-embassy.org; Ambassador Tomás Dueñas.

Uruguay: Casilla 12242, Montevideo; tel. (2) 7083645; fax (2) 7089727; e-mail embarica@adinet.com.uy; Ambassador MARCO VINICIO VARGAS PEREIRA.

Vatican City: Via G.B. Benedetti 3, 00197 Rome, Italy; tel. (06) 80660390; e-mail embcr.vaticano@iol.it; Ambassador Luis París Chaverri.

Venezuela: Edif. For You P.H., Avda San Juan Bosco, entre 1a y 2a Transversal, Altamira, Apdo 62239, Caracas; tel. (212) 267-1104; fax (212) 265-4660; e-mail embaricavene@yahoo.com.mx; Ambassador WALTER RUBÉN HERNÁNDEZ JUÁREZ.

DIPLOMATIC MISSIONS OF CÔTE D'IVOIRE

United Nations: 46 East 74th St, New York, NY 10021; tel. (212) 717-5555; fax (212) 717-4492; e-mail ivorycoast@un.int; internet www.un.int/cotedivoire; Chargé d'affaires Ilahiri Alcide Djedje.

Algeria: BP 260, Immeuble 'Le Bosquet', Parc Paradou, Hydra, Algiers; tel. (21) 69-23-78; fax (21) 69-30-32; e-mail acialg@yahoo.fr; Ambassador AMONCASSI SYLVESTRE AKA.

Angola: Rua Eng Armindo de Andrade 75, Miramar, CP 432, Luanda; tel. 222440878; fax 222440907; e-mail aciao@ambaci-angola.org; internet www.ambaci-angola.org; Ambassador Anne Gnahouret Tatret.

Austria: Stadiongasse 4/5, 1010 Vienna; tel. (1) 406-50-51; fax (1) 409-77-15; Ambassador YOUSSOUFOU BAMBA.

Belgium: 234 ave F. D. Roosevelt, 1050 Brussels; tel. (2) 672-23-57; fax (2) 672-04-91; e-mail mailbox@ambcibnl.be; internet www.ambacibnl.be; Ambassador Marie Gosset.

Brazil: SEN, Av. das Nações, Lote 09, 70473-900 Brasília, DF; tel. (61) 3321-7320; fax (61) 3321-1306; e-mail cotedivoire@cotedivoire.org.br; internet www.cotedivoire.org.br; Ambassador DAOUDA DIABATE.

Burkina Faso: pl. des Nations Unies, 01 BP 20, Ouagadougou 01; tel. 50-31-82-28; fax 50-31-82-30; Ambassador Richard Kodjo.

Cameroon: BP 11354, Yaoundé; tel. 2221-3291; fax 2221-3295; Ambassador PAUL AYOMAN AMBOHALÉ.

Canada: 9 Marlborough Ave, Ottawa, ON K1N 8E6; tel. (613) 236-9919; fax (613) 563-8287; e-mail acica@ambaci-ottawa.org; internet www.ambaci-ottawa.org; Ambassador Diénébou Kaba.

China, People's Republic: 9 San Li Tun, Bei Xiao Jie, Beijing 100600; tel. (10) 65321223; fax (10) 65322407; Ambassador COFFIE ALAIN NICAISE PAPATCHI.

Congo, Democratic Republic: 68 ave de la Justice, BP 9197, Kinshasa; tel. (12) 21208; Ambassador Guillaume Ahipeau.

Denmark: Gersonsvej 8, 2900 Hellerup; tel. 39-62-88-22; fax 39-62-01-62; e-mail ambaivoire@mail.tele.dk; internet www.ambacotedivoire.org; Ambassador DJÉROU ROBERT LY.

Egypt: 9 ave Shehab, rue Ibrahim Soliman, Mohandessin, Cairo; tel. (2) 3034373; fax (2) 3050148; e-mail acieg@ambaci-egypte.org; internet www.ambaci-egypte.org; Ambassador N'Guessan Marcel Konan.

Ethiopia: Woreda 23, Kebele 13, House No. 1308, POB 3668, Addis Ababa; tel. (11) 3711213; fax (11) 3712178; Ambassador MDALO GBOUAGBRE.

France: 102 ave Raymond Poincaré, 75116 Paris; tel. 1-53-64-62-62; fax 1-45-00-47-97; e-mail bureco-fr@cotedivoire.com; Ambassador Hyacinthe Marcel Kouassi.

Gabon: Charbonnages, BP 3861, Libreville; tel. 73-82-70; fax 73-82-87; Ambassador CLAUDINE YAPOBI RICCI.

Germany: Schinkelstr. 10, 14193 Berlin; tel. (30) 8906960; fax (30) 890696206; e-mail ambic@t-online.de; internet www.ambaci.de; Chargé d'affaires a.i. Serges Gba.

Ghana: 9 18th Lane, off Cantonments Rd, POB 3445, Christiansborg, Accra; tel. (21) 774611; fax (21) 773516; e-mail acigh@ambaci-ghana.org; Ambassador PAUL KAKOULANGBA.

Guinea: blvd du Commerce, BP 5228, Conakry; tel. 30-45-10-82; fax 30-45-10-79; Ambassador Jeannot Zoro Bi Bah.

India: B-9/6, Vasant Vihar, New Delhi 110 057; tel. (11) 51704234; fax (11) 51704236; e-mail embassy@amb2ci-inde.org; Ambassador GILBERT BLEU-LAINE.

Israel: South Africa Bldg, 12 Menachim Begin St, Ramat-Gan 52521; tel. 3-6126677; fax 3-6126688; e-mail ambacita@netvision.net.il; Ambassador Léon H. Kacou Adom.

Italy: Via Guglielmo Saliceto 6–10, 00161 Roma; tel. (06) 44231129; fax (06) 44292531; Ambassador RICHARD GBAKA ZADY.

Japan: 2-19-12, Uehara, Shibuya-ku, Tokyo 151-0064; tel. (3) 5454-1401; fax (3) 5454-1405; e-mail ambacijn@yahoo.fr; internet www.ahibo.com/ambaci-jp; Chargé d'affaires a.i. Tui Digbe.

Korea, Republic: Chungam Bldg, 2nd Floor, 794-4, Hannam-dong, Yeong-san-gu, Seoul; tel. (2) 3785-0561; fax (2) 3785-0564; e-mail abenikof@hotmail.com; Ambassador HONORAT ABENI KOFFI.

Liberia: Tubman Blvd, Sinkor, POB 126, Monrovia; tel. 261123; Ambassador Clément Kaul Meledje.

Mali: square Patrice Lumumba, Immeuble CNAR, BP E 3644, Bamako; tel. 222-03-89; fax 222-13-76; Ambassador ABOUBACAR SIRIKI DIABATÉ.

Mexico: Tennyson 67, Col. Polanco, Del. Miguel Hidalgo, 11560 México, DF; tel. 5280-8573; fax 5282-2954; Ambassador Anne Gnahouret Tatret.

Morocco: 21 rue de Tiddas, BP 192, 10001 Rabat; tel. (3) 7763151; fax (3) 7762792; e-mail ambcim@clam.net.ma; Ambassador AKE CHARLES DARIUS ATCHIMON.

Nigeria: 3 Abudu Smith St, Victoria Island, POB 7786, Lagos; tel. (1) 610936; fax (1) 2613822; e-mail cotedivoire@micro.com.ng; Ambassador Aiko Zike Marc.

Russian Federation: 119034 Moscow, Korobeinikov per. 14/9; tel. (495) 637-24-00; fax (495) 637-21-57; e-mail ambacimow@hotmail.com; internet ambaci-russie.org; Ambassador GNAGNO PHILIBERT FAGNIDI.

Saudi Arabia: POB 94303, Riyadh 11693; tel. (1) 482-5582; fax (1) 482-9629; e-mail ambciryd@digi.net.sa; Ambassador Lancina Dosso.

Senegal: ave Birago Diop, BP 359, Dakar; tel. 33-869-0270; fax 33-825-2115; e-mail cmrci@ambaci-dakar.org; internet www.ambaci-dakar.org; Ambassador FATIMATA TANOE TOURÉ.

South Africa: 795 Government Ave, Arcadia, Pretoria 0083; POB 13510, Hatfield 0028; tel. (12) 3426913; fax (12) 3426713; Ambassador Boubakar Kone.

Spain: Serrano 154, 28006 Madrid; tel. (91) 5626916; fax (91) 5622193; e-mail costamarfil@ic1.inycom.es; Ambassador JEANNE GUEHE MOULOT.

Switzerland: Thormannstr. 51, 3005 Bern; tel. 313508080; fax 313508081; e-mail acibe-1@acibe.org; internet www.acibe.org; Ambassador Mamadou Diarrassouba.

Tunisia: 17 rue el-Mansoura, BP 21, Belvédère, 1002 Tunis; tel. (71) 755-911; fax (71) 755-901; e-mail acitn@ambaci-tunis.org; Ambassador YAPO ATCHAPO THOMAS.

United Kingdom: 2 Upper Belgrave St, London, SW1X 8BJ; tel. (20) 7235-6991; fax (20) 7259-5320; e-mail info@ambaci-uk.org; internet www.ambaci-uk.org; Ambassador Philippe D. Djangoné-Bi.

United States of America: 3421 Massachusetts Ave, NW, Washington, DC 20007; tel. (202) 797-0300; fax (202) 462-9444; Ambassador CHARLES KOFFI.

Vatican City: Via Sforza Pallavicini 11, 00193 Rome, Italy; tel. (06) 6877503; fax (06) 6867925; e-mail ambco.va@flashnet.it; Ambassador Kouamé Benjamin Konan.

DIPLOMATIC MISSIONS OF CROATIA

United Nations: 820 Second Ave, 19th Floor, New York, NY 10017; tel. (212) 986-1585; fax (212) 986-2011; e-mail croatia@un.int; internet www.un.int/croatia; Permanent Representative NEVEN JURICA.

Albania: Rruga A. Toptani, Torre Drin 4, Tirana; tel. (4) 256948; fax (4) 230578; e-mail croemb.tirana@mvpei.hr; Ambassador Darko Javorski.

Algeria: Algiers; Ambassador MIRKO BOLFEK.

Argentina: Gorostiaga 2104, C1426CTN Buenos Aires; tel. (11) 4777-6409; fax (11) 4777-9159; e-mail embajadada@embajadadacroacia.org.ar; Ambassador Mira Martinec.

Australia: 14 Jindalee Crescent, O'Malley, ACT 2606; tel. (2) 6286-6988; fax (2) 6286-3544; e-mail croemb@bigpond.com; Chargé d'affaires a.i. LJUBINKO MATEŠIĆ.

Austria: Heuberggasse 10, 1170 Vienna; tel. (1) 485-95-24; fax (1) 480-29-42; e-mail vlprhbec@reinprecht.at; internet at.mfa.hr; Ambassador Prof. Dr Zoran Jašić.

Belgium: 425 ave Louise, 1050 Brussels; tel. (2) 639-20-36; fax (2) 512-03-38; e-mail croemb.bruxelles@mvp.hr; internet be.mfa.hr; Ambassador BORIS GRIGIĆ.

Bosnia and Herzegovina: 71000 Sarajevo, Mehmeda Spahe 20; tel. (33) 444330; fax (33) 472434; e-mail croemb.sarajevo@mvpei.hr; internet ba.mvp.hr; Ambassador Dr Josip Vrbošić.

Brazil: SHIS, QI 09, Conj. 11, Casa 03, 71625-110 Brasília, DF; tel. (61) 3248-0610; fax (61) 3248-1708; e-mail embaixada.croacia@terra.com.br; Ambassador RADE MARÉLIC.

Bulgaria: 1504 Sofia, ul. Veliko Tarnovo 32; tel. (2) 943-32-25; fax (2) 946-13-55; e-mail croemb.sofia@mvp.hr; Ambassador Dražen Vukov Colić.

Canada: 229 Chapel St, Ottawa, ON K1N 7Y6; tel. (613) 562-7820; fax (613) 562-7821; e-mail croemb.ottawa@mvpei.hr; internet ca.mfa.hr; Ambassador VESELA MRĐEN KORAĆ.

Chile: Ezequias Alliende 2370, Providencia, Santiago; tel. (2) 269-6141; fax (2) 269-6092; e-mail embajada@croacia.cl; Ambassador Boris Maruna.

China, People's Republic: 2-72 San Li Tun Diplomatic Office Bldg, Beijing 100600; tel. (10) 65326241; fax (10) 65326257; e-mail vrhpek@public.bta.net.cn; Ambassador BORIS VELIĆ.

Czech Republic: V Průhledu 9, 162 00 Prague 6; tel. 233340479; fax 233343464; e-mail velrhprag@vol.cz; internet www.cz.mvp.hr; Ambassador Marijan Ramušćak.

Denmark: Frederiksgade 19, 1st Floor, 1265 Copenhagen K; tel. 33-91-90-95; fax 33-91-71-31; e-mail croemb.denmark@mvp.hr; Ambassador ALEKSANDAR HEINA.

Egypt: 3 Sharia Abou el-Feda, Cairo (Zamalek); tel. (2) 7383155; fax (2) 7355812; e-mail croemb.cairo@mvpei.hr; internet eg.mfa.hr; Ambassador Dražen Margeta.

Finland: Kruunuvuorenkatu 5, 00160 Helsinki; tel. (9) 6222232; fax (9) 6222221; e-mail croemb.helsinki@mvpei.hr; Ambassador DR DAMIR KUŠEN.

France: 39 ave Georges Mandel, 75116 Paris; tel. 1-53-70-02-80; fax 1-53-70-02-90; e-mail redaction@amb-croatie.fr; internet www.amb-croatie.fr; Ambassador Mirko Galič.

Germany: Ahornstr. 4, 10787 Berlin; tel. (30) 21915514; fax (30) 23628965; e-mail info@kroatische-botschaft.de; internet de.mfa.hr; Ambassador DR VESNA CVJETKOVIĆ KURELEC.

Greece: Tzavela 4, Neo Psychiko, 154 51 Athens; tel. (210) 6777059; fax (210) 6711208; Ambassador Neven Madey.

Hungary: 1063 Budapest, Munkácsy Mihály u. 15; tel. (1) 354-1315; fax (1) 354-1319; e-mail croemb.bp@mvpei.hr; Ambassador IVAN BANDIĆ.

India: A-15 West End, New Delhi 110 021; tel. (11) 41663101; fax (11) 24116873; e-mail croemb.new-delhi@mvpei.hr; Ambassador (vacant).

Indonesia: Menara Mulia, Suite 2101, Jalan Gatot Subroto, Kav. 9–11, Jakarta 12930; tel. (21) 5257822; fax (21) 5204073; e-mail embassy@croatemb.or.id; internet www.croatemb.or.id; Ambassador ALEKSANDAR BROZ.

Iran: No. 25, 1st Behestan, Pasdaran St, Tehran; tel. (21) 22589923; fax (21) 22549199; e-mail vrh.teheran@mvp.hr; Ambassador Esad Prohić.

Ireland: Adelaide Chambers, Peter St, Dublin 8; tel. (1) 4767181; fax (1) 4767183; e-mail croatianembassy@eircom.net; internet ie.mfa.hr; Ambassador VESELKO GRUBIŠIĆ.

Israel: 40 Einstein St, Canion Ramat Aviv, 40 Einstein St, Tel-Aviv 69101; tel. 3-6438654; fax 3-6438503; e-mail croemb.israel@mvpei.hr; Ambassador Ivan del Vechio.

Italy: Via Luigi Bodio 74–76, 00191 Roma; tel. (06) 36307650; fax (06) 36303405; e-mail vhrim@mvpei.hr; internet it.mfa.hr; Ambassador TOMISLAV VIDOŠEVIĆ.

Japan: 3-3-10, Hiroo, Shibuya-ku, Tokyo 150-0012; tel. (3) 5469-3014; fax (3) 5469-3015; e-mail croemb.tokyo@mvpei.hr; Ambassador Drago Štambuk.

Libya: Great al-Fatah Towers, Floor 12, Room 125, Tripoli; tel. (21) 3351381; fax (21) 3351486; e-mail croemb.tripoli@mvpei.hr; Ambassador JOVAN VEJNOVIĆ.

Macedonia, former Yugoslav Republic: 1000 Skopje, Mitropolit Teodosij Gologanov 44; tel. (2) 3246012; fax (2) 3246004; e-mail croemb.skopje@mvpei.hr; Ambassador Ivan Kujundžić.

Malaysia: 3 Jalan Menkuang, off Jalan Ru Ampang, 55000 Kuala Lumpur; tel. (3) 42535340; fax (3) 42535217; e-mail kuala-lumpur@mvpei.hr; Ambassador ZELJKO CIMBUR.

Montenegro: 81000 Podgorica, Vladimira Ćetkovića 2; tel. (81) 269760; fax (81) 269810; Ambassador Petar Turčinović.

Morocco: 73 rue Marnissa, Souissi, Rabat; tel. (3) 7638824; fax (3) 7638827; e-mail croamb@menara.ma; Ambassador DARKO BEKIĆ.

Netherlands: Amaliastraat 16, 2514 JC The Hague; tel. (70) 3623638; fax (70) 3623195; e-mail croemb.haag@mvp.hr; internet nl.mfa.hr; Ambassador Frane Krnić.

Norway: Drammensvn 82, 0244 Oslo; tel. 23-01-40-50; fax 23-01-40-60; e-mail croemb.oslo@mvpei.hr; Ambassador DOBROSLAV SILOBRČIĆ.

Poland: 02-611 Warsaw, ul. Ignacego Krasickiego 25; tel. (22) 8442393; fax (22) 8444808; e-mail croemb.warszawa@mvpei.hr; internet pl.mvp.hr; Ambassador Nebojša Koharović.

Portugal: Rua D. Lourenço de Almeida 24, 1400-126 Lisbon; tel. (21) 3021033; fax (21) 3021251; e-mail croemb.lisboa@mvpei.hr; Ambassador ŽELJKO VUKOSAV.

Romania: 024031 Bucharest, Str. Dr Burghelea 1, Sector 2; tel. (21) 3130457; fax (21) 3130384; e-mail croemb.bucharest@mvp.hr; Ambassador Ivica Maštruko.

Russian Federation: 119034 Moscow, Korobeinikov per. 16/10; tel. (495) 637-38-68; fax (495) 637-46-24; e-mail croemb.russia@mvpei.hr; internet ru.mvp.hr; Ambassador Božo Kovačević.

Serbia: 11000 Belgrade, Kneza Miloša 62; tel. (11) 3610535; fax (11) 3610032; e-mail croambg@eunet.yu; internet rs.mvp.hr; Ambassador Tonči Staničić.

Slovakia: Mišikova 21, 811 06 Bratislava; tel. (2) 5443-3647; fax (2) 5443-5365; e-mail croemb.bratislava@mvpei.hr; Ambassador TOMISLAV CAR.

Slovenia: 1000 Ljubljana, Gruberjevo nabrežje 6; tel. (1) 4256220; fax (1) 4258106; e-mail croemb.slovenia@mvp.hr; internet si.mvp.hr; Ambassador Dr Mario Nobilo.

South Africa: 1160 Church St, Colbyn, Pretoria 0083; POB 11335, Hatfield 0028; tel. (12) 3421206; fax (12) 3421819; Ambassador IVAN PICUKARIĆ.

Spain: Claudio Coello 78, 2°, 28001 Madrid; tel. (91) 5776881; fax (91) 5776905; e-mail croemb.madrid@mvp.hr; internet es.mvp.hr; Ambassador Filip Vučak.

Sweden: Birger Jarlsgt. 13, 1st Floor, 111 45 Stockholm; tel. (8) 678-42-20; fax (8) 678-83-20; e-mail croemb.stockholm@mvpei.hr; Ambassador DR SVJETLAN BERKOVIĆ.

Switzerland: Thunstr. 45, 3005 Bern; tel. 313520275; fax 313520373; e-mail croemb.bern@mvpei.hr; Ambassador Jakša Muljačić.

Turkey: Kelebek Sok. 15/A, 06700 Gaziosmanpaşa, Ankara; tel. (312) 4469460; fax (312) 4464700; e-mail ankara@mvpei.hr; internet tr.mvp.hr; Ambassador GORDAN BAKOTA.

Ukraine: 01091 Kyiv, vul. Artema 51/50; tel. (44) 486-58-62; fax (44) 484-69-43; e-mail croemb.ukraine@mvpei.hr; internet ua.mvp.hr; Ambassador Željko Kirinčić.

United Kingdom: 21 Conway St, London, W1T 6BN; tel. (20) 7387-2022; fax (20) 7387-0310; e-mail croemb.london@mvpei.hr; internet uk.mfa.hr; Ambassador Joško Paro.

United States of America: 2343 Massachusetts Ave, NW, Washington, DC 20008-2803; tel. (202) 588-5899; fax (202) 588-8936; e-mail public@croatiaemb.org; Ambassador Kolinda Grabar-Kitarović.

Vatican City: Via della Conciliazione 44, 00193 Rome, Italy; tel. (06) 6877000; fax (06) 6877003; e-mail velrhvat@tin.it; internet va.mfa.hr; Ambassador Prof. Emilio Marin.

DIPLOMATIC MISSIONS OF CUBA

United Nations: 315 Lexington Ave and 38th St, New York, NY 10016; tel. (212) 689-7215; fax (212) 779-1697; e-mail cuba@un.int; internet www.un.int/cuba; Permanent Representative Orlando Requeijo Gual.

Algeria: 22 rue Larbi Alik, Hydra, Algiers; tel. (21) 69-21-48; fax (21) 69-32-81; e-mail ambcuba@wissal.dz; Ambassador Roberto Blanco Domínguez.

Angola: Rua Che Guevara 42, Ingombotas, Luanda; tel. 222336749; fax 222339165; e-mail embcuba.ang@ebonet.net; Ambassador Pedro Ross Leal.

Antigua and Barbuda: Embassy of the Republic of Cuba, Longfords Main Rd, St John's; tel. 562-5864; Ambassador Dr Marcelino Fajardo Delgado.

Argentina: Virrey del Pino 1810, Belgrano, C1426DXH Buenos Aires; tel. (11) 4782-9049; fax (11) 4786-7713; e-mail argoficemb@ecuargentina.minrex.gov.cu; internet www.embacuba.com.ar; Ambassador Aramis Fuente Hernández.

Austria: Kaiserstr. 84, 1070 Vienna; tel. (1) 877-81-98; fax (1) 877-81-98-30; e-mail secembajador@ecuaustria.at; internet emba.cubaminrex.cu/austria; Ambassador Norma Miguelina Goicochea Estenoz.

Bahamas: Cash Fountain Bldg, Armstrong and Shirley Sts, POB EE-15679, Nassau; tel. 356-3473; fax 356-3472; e-mail cubanembassy@coralwave.com; Ambassador Félix Wilson Hernández.

Barbados: Palm View, Erdiston Dr., Pine Hill, St Michael; tel. 435-2769; fax 435-2534; e-mail embajadadecuba@sunbeach.net; Ambassador Pedro Andrés García Roque.

Belarus: 220005 Minsk, vul. Krasnozvezdnaya 13; tel. (17) 200-03-83; fax (17) 200-23-45; e-mail oficome@belsonet.net; Ambassador Omar Senón Medina Quintero.

Belgium: 77 rue Roberts-Jones, 1180 Brussels; tel. (2) 343-00-20; fax (2) 344-96-91; e-mail mision@embacuba.be; internet www.embacuba.be; Ambassador Elio Eduardo Rodríguez Perdomo.

Belize: 6087 Manatee Dr., Buttonwood Bay, POB 1775, Belize City; tel. 223-5345; fax 223-1105; e-mail embacuba@btl.net; internet embacu.cubaminrex.cu/beliceing; Ambassador Eugenio Martínez Enríquez.

Benin: ave de la Marina, face Hôtel du Port, 01 BP 948, Cotonou; tel. 21-31-52-97; fax 21-31-65-91; e-mail ecubaben@leland.bj; Ambassador Marta Fernández Peraza.

Bolivia: Bajo Irpavi Avda Gobles 20, entre 13 y 14, La Paz; tel. (2) 272-1157; fax (2) 272-3419; e-mail embacuba@acelerate.com; Ambassador Luis Felipe Vásquez Vásquez.

Botswana: Plot 5198, Village, POB 40261, Gaborone; tel. 3951750; fax 3911485; Ambassador Jorge Luis López Tormo.

Brazil: SHIS, QI 05, Conj. 18, Casa 01, 71615-180 Brasília, DF; tel. (61) 3248-4710; fax (61) 3248-6778; e-mail embacuba@uol.com.br; internet www.embaixadacuba.org.br; Ambassador Pedro Juan Núñez Mosquera.

Bulgaria: 1113 Sofia, ul. K. Sharkelov 1; tel. (2) 972-09-96; fax (2) 972-04-60; e-mail consulado@embacuba.bg.com; Ambassador Gerardo Suárez Álvarez.

Burkina Faso: rue 4/64, La Rotonde, Secteur 4, Ouagadougou; tel. 50-30-64-91; fax 50-31-73-24; e-mail embacuba.bf@fasonet.bf; Ambassador Fernando Prats Mari.

Cambodia: 96/98 rue 214, Sangkat Veal Vong, Khan 7 Makara, Phnom-Penh; tel. (23) 213212; fax (23) 217428; Ambassador Bárbara Gilda López Armenteros.

Canada: 388 Main St, Ottawa, ON K1S 1E3; tel. (613) 563-0141; fax (613) 563-0068; e-mail cuba@embacubacanada.net; internet embacu.cubaminrex.cu/Default.aspx?tabid=73; Ambassador Ernesto Antonio Sentí Darias.

Cape Verde: Achada de Santo António, Praia, Santiago; tel. 2619048; fax 2617527; e-mail ecubacpv@cvtelecom.cv; Ambassador Pedro Evelio Dorta González.

Chile: Avda Los Leones 1346, Providencia, Santiago; tel. (2) 494-1485; fax (2) 494-1495; e-mail afragap@vtr.net; Ambassador Alfonso Fraga Pérez.

China, People's Republic: 1 Xiu Shui Nan Jie, Jian Guo Men Wai, Beijing 100600; tel. (10) 65321714; fax (10) 65322656; e-mail earufe@public3.bta.net.cn; Ambassador Carlos Miguel Pereira.

Colombia: Carrera 9, No 92-54, Bogotá, DC; tel. (1) 621-7054; fax (1) 611-4382; e-mail embacu@cable.net.co; internet embacu.cubaminrex.cu/colombia; Ambassador José Antonio Pérez Novoa.

Congo, Democratic Republic: 4660 ave Cateam, BP 10699, Kinshasa; tel. (12) 8803823; Ambassador Luis Castillo.

Congo, Republic: 28 rue Lacien Fourneaux, BP 80, Brazzaville; tel. 81-03-79; e-mail embacuba@congonet.cg; Ambassador Sidenio Acosta Aday.

Cyprus: POB 28923, 1 Androcleous St, 1060 Nicosia; tel. 22769743; fax 22753820; e-mail embacuba@spidernet.com.cy; Ambassador Pablo Rodríguez Vidal.

Czech Republic: Sibiřské nám. 1, 160 00 Prague 6; tel. 224311253; fax 233341029; e-mail embacubapraga@embacuba.cz; Chargé d'affaires a.i. Barbara Elena Montalvo Álvarez.

Denmark: Kastelsvej 19, 3rd Floor, 2100 Copenhagen Ø; tel. 39-40-15-06; e-mail embadin@hotmail.com; internet www.cubaembassy.dk; Ambassador Guillermo Vázquez Moreno.

Dominican Republic: Francisco Prats Ramírez 808, El Millón, Santo Domingo, DN; tel. 537-2113; fax 537-9820; e-mail embadom@verizon.net.do; internet embacu.cubaminrex.cu/dominicana; Ambassador Juan Domingo Astiasarán Ceballo.

Ecuador: Mercurio 365, entre La Razón y El Vengador, Quito; tel. (2) 245-6936; fax (2) 243-0594; e-mail embajada@ecuecuador.minrex.gov.cu; Ambassador Benigno Pérez Fernández.

Egypt: Apartment 1, 13th Floor, 10 Sharia Kamel Muhammad, Cairo (Zamalek); tel. (2) 7360651; fax (2) 7360656; e-mail cubaemb@link.net; Ambassador Angel Dalmau Fernández.

Ethiopia: Woreda 17, Kebele 19, House No. 197, POB 5623, Addis Ababa; tel. (11) 620459; fax (11) 620460; e-mail embacuba@ethiopia.cubaminrex.cu; Ambassador Ricardo García Díaz.

Finland: Frederikinkatu 61, 3rd Floor, 00100 Helsinki; tel. (9) 6802022; fax (9) 643163; e-mail cuba@cuba.fi; internet emba.cubaminrex.cu/finlandia; Ambassador Sergio González González.

France: 16 rue de Presles, 75015 Paris; tel. 1-45-67-55-35; fax 1-45-66-80-92; e-mail embacu@ambacuba.fr; Ambassador Rogelio Placido Sánchez Levis.

Gambia: C/801, POB 1487, Banjul; tel. 4460789; e-mail embacuba@ganet.gm; Ambassador Jorge Martínez Salsamendi.

Germany: Stavangerstr. 20, 10439 Berlin; tel. (30) 44717319; fax (30) 9164553; e-mail embacuba-berlin@t-online.de; internet www.botschaft-kuba.de; Ambassador Gerardo Peñalver Portal.

Ghana: 20 Amilcar Cabral Rd, Airport Residential Area, POB 9163 Airport, Accra; tel. (21) 775868; fax 774998; e-mail embghana@africaonline.com.gh; Ambassador Miguel Pérez Gruz.

Greece: Odos Sofokleos 5, Filothei, 152 37 Athens; tel. (210) 6855550; fax (210) 6842807; Ambassador Hermes Herrera Hernandez.

Grenada: L'Anse aux Epines, St George's; tel. 444-1884; fax 444-1877; e-mail embacubagranada@caribsurf.com; Ambassador Margarita Delgado.

Guatemala: Avda las Américas 20-72, Zona 13, Guatemala City; tel. 2332-4066; fax 2332-5525; e-mail embagua@intelnet.net.gt; Ambassador Omar Morales Bazo.

Guinea: rue DI 256, Corniche Nord, Conakry; tel. 30-46-95-25; fax 30-46-95-28; e-mail embagcon@sotelgui.net.gn; Ambassador Marcello Caballero Torres.

Guinea-Bissau: Rua Joaquim N'Com 1, y Victorino Costa, CP 258, Bissau; tel. 213579; fax 201301; e-mail embcuba@sol.gtelecom.gw; Ambassador Pedro Féliz Doña Santana.

Guyana: 46 High St, POB 10268, Kingston, Georgetown; tel. 225-1881; fax 226-1824; e-mail emguyana@networksgy.com; internet www.cubanembassy.org.gy; Ambassador Francisco Alejandro Marchante Castellanos.

Haiti: 18 rue Marion, Peguy Ville, POB 15702, Port-au-Prince; tel. 256-3812; fax 257-8566; e-mail embacuba@hughes.net; Ambassador Raúl Barzaga Navas.

Honduras: Col. Loma Linda Norte, Calle Diangonal Huri 2255, contiguo a Residencial Torres Blancas, Tegucigalpa; tel. 239-3778; fax 235-7624; e-mail embacuba@amnettgu.com; internet embacu.cubaminrex.cu/honduras; Ambassador Juan Carlos Hernández Padrón.

Hungary: 1026 Budapest, Harangivrág u. 5; tel. (1) 325-7290; fax (1) 438-5956; e-mail ildiko@embacuba.hu; internet www.embacuba.hu; Chargé d'affaires a.i. BLAS NABEL PÉREZ.

India: W-124a, Greater Kailash Part I, New Delhi 110 048; tel. (11) 26222467; fax (11) 26222469; e-mail embcuind@del6.vsnl.net.in; Ambassador Miguel Angel Ramirez Ramos.

Indonesia: Taman Puri, Jalan Opal, Blok K-1, Permata Hijau, Jakarta 12210; tel. (21) 5304293; fax (21) 53676906; e-mail cubaindo@cbn.net.id; Ambassador JORGE LEÓN.

Iran: Africa Ave, Shahid Azafi Sharqi St, No. 21, Tehran; tel. (21) 22257809; fax (21) 22222989; e-mail embacuba-iran@apadana.com; Ambassador Fernando Néstor García Ricardo.

Ireland: 2 Adelaide Court, Adelaide Rd, Dublin 2; tel. (1) 4752999; fax (1) 4763674; e-mail carillo@eircom.net; Ambassador PEDRO NOEL CARRILLO ALFONSO.

Italy: Via Licinia 7, 00153 Roma; tel. (06) 5717241; fax (06) 5745445; e-mail embajada@ecuitalia.it; internet www.ambasciatacuba.com; Ambassador Rodney Alejandro López Clemente.

Jamaica: 9 Trafalgar Rd, Kingston 10; tel. 978-0931; fax 978-5372; e-mail embacubajam@cwjamaica.com; Ambassador GISELA BEATRIZ GARCÍA RIVERA.

Japan: 1-28-4, Higashi-Azabu, Minato-ku, Tokyo 106-0044; tel. (3) 5570-3182; fax (3) 5570-8566; e-mail embajada@ecujapon.jp; internet embacuba .cubaminrex.cu/japon; Ambassador José Fernández de Cossio.

Kazakhstan: 010005 Astana, pr. Respublika 10/1; tel. (7172) 22-14-19; e-mail embacuba@cubakaz.com; internet www.cubakaz.com; Ambassador TERESITA CAPOTE CAMACHO.

Kenya: International House, Mama Ngina St, 13th Floor, POB 41931, Nairobi; tel. (20) 241003; fax (20) 241023; e-mail embacuba@swiftkenya .com; Ambassador Julio César González Marchante.

Korea, Democratic People's Republic: Munsudong, Taedongkang District, Pyongyang; tel. (2) 3827380; fax (2) 3817703; e-mail embarpdc@di.chesin .com; Ambassador JOSÉ MANUEL GALEGO MONTANO.

Laos: Ban Saphanthong Neua 128, BP 1017, Vientiane; tel. (21) 314902; fax (21) 314901; e-mail embacuba@laonet.net; Ambassador Eduardo Valido García.

Lebanon: Center Farrania, Saïd Freiha St, Mar-Takla, Hazmieh, Beirut 2901 6727; tel. (1) 459925; fax (1) 950070; e-mail libancub@cyberia.net.lb; internet www.embacubalebanon.com; Ambassador DARÍO DE URRA TORRIENTE.

Liberia: 17 Kennedy Ave, Congotown, POB 3579, Monrovia; tel. 262600; Ambassador Dr Miguel Gustavo Pérez Cruz.

Libya: POB 83738, Sharia ibn al-Youmin, Ahmed al-Mahzumi, Tripoli; tel. (21) 4775216; fax (21) 4776294; e-mail embacuba.libia@lttnet.net; Ambassador PABLO ÁNGEL REYES DOMÍNGUEZ.

Malaysia: 10 Lorong Gurney, 54100 Kuala Lumpur; tel. (3) 26911066; fax (3) 26911141; e-mail admin@cubemb.com.my; internet www.cubaemb.com.my; Ambassador Carlos A. Amores.

Mali: porte 31, rue 328, Niarela, Bamako; tel. 221-02-89; fax 221-02-93; e-mail emcuba.mali@malinet.ml; Ambassador ALBERTO MIGUEL OTERO LÓPEZ.

Mexico: Presidente Masaryk 554, Col. Polanco, Del. Miguel Hidalgo, 11560 México, DF; tel. (55) 5280-8039; e-mail cancilleria@embacuba.com.mx; internet www.embacuba.com.mx; Ambassador Manuel Francisco Aguilera de la Páz.

Mongolia: Negdsen Ündestnii Gudamj 18, Ulan Bator (CPOB 710); tel. (11) 323778; fax (11) 327709; Ambassador EDUARDO CASTELLANOS SOTO.

Mozambique: Av. Kenneth Kaunda 492, CP 387, Maputo; tel. 21492444; fax 21491905; e-mail residcuba.mozambique@tvcabo.co.mz; Ambassador Marcelina Evangelina Seoane Domínguez.

Namibia: 31 Omuramba Rd, Eros, POB 23866, Windhoek; tel. (61) 227072; fax (61) 231584; Ambassador ANA VILMA VALLEJERA RODRÍGUEZ.

Netherlands: Scheveningseweg 9, 2517 KS The Hague; tel. (70) 3606061; fax (70) 3647586; e-mail embacuba@cistron.nl; internet www.embacuba.nl; Ambassador Oscar de los Reyes Ramos.

New Zealand: 35 Hobson St, Thorndon, Wellington; tel. (4) 472-3748; fax (4) 473-2958; e-mail embajada@xtra.co.nz; Ambassador JOSÉ LUIS ROBAINA GARCÍA.

Nicaragua: Carretera a Masaya, 3a Entrada a las Colinas, 400 varas arriba, 75 al sur, Managua; tel. 276-0742; fax 276-0166; e-mail embacuba@ embacuba.net.ni; internet embacu.cubaminrex.cu/nicaragua; Ambassador Luis Hernández Ojeda.

Niger: rue Tillaberi, angle rue de la Cure Salée, face lycée Franco-Arabe, Plateau, BP 13886, Niamey; tel. 20-72-46-00; fax 20-72-39-32; e-mail embacuba@niger.cubaminrex.cu; Ambassador SERAFIN GIL RODRÍGUEZ VALDÉS.

Nigeria: Plot 935, Idejo St, Victoria Island, POB 328, Victoria Island, Lagos; tel. (1) 2614836; fax (1) 2617036; Ambassador Elio Savón Oliva.

Pakistan: House 37, School Rd, F-6/2, Islamabad; tel. (51) 2824077; fax (51) 2824076; e-mail embacubapakistan@yahoo.com; Ambassador GUSTAVO MACHÍN GÓMEZ.

Panama: Avda Cuba y Ecuador 33, Apdo 6-2291, Bellavista, Panamá; tel. 227-5277; fax 225-6681; e-mail embacuba@cableonda.net; Ambassador Carlos Eloy García Trápaga.

Paraguay: Luis Morales 757, esq. Luis León y Luis Granado, Barrio Jara, Asunción; tel. (21) 22-2763; fax (21) 21-3879; e-mail embacuba@cmm.com .py; internet www.embacuba.org.py; Ambassador IRMA GONZÁLEZ CRUZ.

Peru: Coronel Portillo 110, San Isidro, Lima; tel. (1) 2642053; fax (1) 2644525; e-mail embacuba@ecuperu.minrex.gov.cu; internet embacu .cubaminrex.cu/peru; Ambassador Luis Delfín Pérez Osorio.

Philippines: 101 Aguirre St, cnr Trasierra St, Cacho-Gonzales Bldg Penthouse, Legaspi Village, Makati City, Metro Manila; tel. (2) 8171192; fax (2) 8164094; Ambassador RAMÓN ALONSO MEDINA.

Poland: 02-516 Warsaw, ul. Rejtana 15/8; tel. (22) 8481715; fax (22) 8482231; e-mail embacuba@medianet.pl; internet emba.cubaminrex.cu/polonia; Ambassador Rosario Cristina Navas Morata.

Portugal: Rua Pero da Covilhã 14 (Restelo), 1400-297 Lisbon; tel. (21) 3015317; fax (21) 3011895; e-mail embaixada.cuba@netcabo.pt; internet pwp .netcabo.pt/embaixada.cuba; Ambassador JORGE CASTRO BENÍTEZ.

Qatar: POB 12017, Saha 76, New Dafna, West Bay Lagoon, Doha; tel. 4110713; fax 4110387; e-mail embacuba@qatar.net.qa; internet www .embacubaqatar.com; Ambassador Armando Vergara Bueno.

Romania: 010516 Bucharest, Str. Mihai Eminescu 44–48, 2nd Floor, Rm 5; tel. (21) 2118916; e-mail embacuba@kappa.ro; Ambassador MANUEL ISMAEL HERMIDA MEDINA.

Russian Federation: 119017 Moscow, ul. B. Ordynka 66; tel. (495) 933-79-57; e-mail embsecret@ecurusia.ru; Ambassador Jorge Martí Martínez.

Saint Christopher and Nevis: 34 Bladen Housing Devt, POB 600, Basseterre; tel. 466-3374; fax 465-8072; e-mail cubask@caribsurf.com; Ambassador ANA MARÍA GONZÁLEZ SUÁREZ.

Saint Lucia: Rodney Heights, Gros Islet, POB 2150, Castries; tel. 458-4665; fax 458-4666; e-mail embacubasantalucia@candw.lc; Ambassador Hugo Ruiz Cabrera.

Saint Vincent and the Grenadines: Ratho Mill, Kingstown; tel. 458-5844; fax 456-9344; e-mail embacubasvg@gmail.com; internet www.embacu .cubaminrex.cu/sanvicenteing; Ambassador OLGA CHAMERO TRÍAS.

Senegal: 43 rue Aimé Césaire, BP 4510, Dakar-Fann; tel. 33-869-0240; fax 33-864-1063; e-mail embacubasen@sentoo.sn; Ambassador Llusif Sadin Tasse.

Serbia: 11000 Belgrade, Ljube Jovanovića 9B; tel. (11) 3692441; fax (11) 3692442; e-mail emcubayu@eunet.yu; internet www.kubabeograd.org.yu; Ambassador JULIO CÉSAR CANCIO FERRER.

Seychelles: Belle Eau, POB 730, Victoria; tel. 224094; fax 224376; e-mail cubasey@seychelles.net; Ambassador Domingo Angel García Rodríguez.

Slovakia: Somolického 1A, 811 05 Bratislava; tel. (2) 5249-2777; fax (2) 5249-4200; Ambassador DAVID PAULOVICH ESCALONA.

Somalia: Mogadishu; .

South Africa: 45 Mackenzie St, Brooklyn, Pretoria 0181; POB 11605, Hatfield 0028; tel. (12) 3462215; fax (12) 3462216; e-mail sudafri@iafrica.com; Ambassador ESTHER ARMENTEROS CÁRDENAS.

Spain: Paseo de la Habana 194, 28036 Madrid; tel. (91) 3592500; fax (91) 3596145; e-mail secreembajada@ecubamad.com; internet emba.cubaminrex .cu/espana; Ambassador Alberto Velazco San José.

Sri Lanka: 15/9 Maitland Crescent, Colombo 7; tel. (11) 2677170; fax (11) 2669380; e-mail cubaembalk@sltnet.lk; internet embacuba.cubaminrex.cu/ srilankaing; Ambassador ENNA VIANT VALDÉS.

Suriname: Brokopondolaan 4, Paramaribo; tel. 434917; fax 432626; e-mail embacubasuriname@gmail.com; internet embacu.cubaminrex.cu/ surinaming; Ambassador Andrés Marcelo González Garrido.

Sweden: Sturevägen 9, 182 73 Stocksund; tel. (8) 545-83-277; fax (8) 545-83-270; e-mail primero.enero59@swipnet.se; internet home.swipnet.se/embacubasuecia; Ambassador ERNESTO MÉLENDEZ BACHS.

Switzerland: Gesellschaftsstr. 8, CP 5275, 3012 Bern; tel. 313022111; fax 313029830; e-mail embacuba.berna@bluewin.ch; internet emba.cubaminrex.cu/suiza; Ambassador Ana María Rovira Ingidua.

Syria: Immeuble Istouani and Charbati, 40 rue ar-Rachid, Damascus; tel. (11) 3339624; fax (11) 3333802; e-mail embacubasy@net.sy; Ambassador LUIS MAIRISI VIGIRDO.

Tanzania: Plot 313, Lugalo Rd, POB 9282, Upanga, Dar es Salaam; tel. (22) 2115928; fax (22) 2115927; e-mail embacuba.tz@raha.com; Ambassador Felipe Ruiz O'Farrill.

Thailand: Mela Mansion Apartment 3C, 5 Soi Sukhumvit 27, Klongtoey Nua, Wattana, Bangkok 10110; tel. (2) 665-2803; fax (2) 661-6560; e-mail cubaemb1@loxinfo.co.th; internet embacuba.cubaminrex.cu/tailandiaing; Ambassador MARÍA LUISA FERNÁNDEZ.

Trinidad and Tobago: Furness Bldg, 2nd Floor, 90 Independence Sq., Port of Spain; tel. 627-1306; fax 627-3515; e-mail embajador@tstt.net.tt; Ambassador Sergio Oliva Guerra.

Tunisia: 1 rue Amilcar, al-Menzah VIII, 1004 Tunis; tel. (71) 767-235; fax (71) 755-922; e-mail embajador-tunez@topnet.tn; internet emba.cubaminrex.cu/tunezar; Ambassador ROLANDO GONZÁLEZ TÉLLEZ.

Turkey: Şölen Sok. 8, 06550 Çankaya, Ankara; tel. (312) 4428970; fax (312) 4414007; e-mail embacubatur@tr.net; Ambassador Ernesto Gómez Abascal.

Uganda: KAR Dr., 16 Lower Kololo Terrace, POB 9226, Kampala; tel. (41) 4233742; fax (41) 4233320; e-mail ecuba@africaonline.co.ug; Ambassador RICARDO ANTONIO DANZA SIGAS.

Ukraine: 01901 Kyiv, prov. Bekhterevskyi 5; tel. (44) 486-57-43; fax (44) 486-19-07; e-mail embacuba@naverex.kiev.ua; Ambassador Julio Garmendía Peña.

United Kingdom: 167 High Holborn, London, WC1V 6PA; tel. (20) 7240-2488; fax (20) 7836-2602; e-mail embacuba@cubaldn.com; internet www.cubaldn.com; Ambassador RENÉ JUAN MUJICA CANTELAR.

United States of America: 'Interests section' in the Embassy of Switzerland, 2630 16th St, NW, Washington, DC 20009; tel. (202) 797-8518; fax (202) 797-8521; e-mail consulcuba@sicuw.org; internet www.eda.admin.ch/eda/en/home/reps/nameri/vusa/wasemb/wacuba.html; Counsellor Jorge Alberto Bolaños Suárez.

Uruguay: Echevarriarza 3471, Montevideo; tel. (2) 6232803; fax (2) 6232805; e-mail cancilleria@netgate.com.uy; Ambassador MARIELENA RUIZ CAPOTE.

Vatican City: Via Aurelia 137/5a, 00165 Rome, Italy; tel. (06) 39366680; fax (06) 636685; e-mail embajada@cubassede.com; Ambassador Raúl Roa Kourí.

Venezuela: Calle Roraima e Rio de Janeiro y Choroni, Chuao, Caracas 1060; tel. (212) 991-6611; fax (212) 993-5695; e-mail embacubavzla@cantv.net; Ambassador GERMÁN SÁNCHEZ OTERO.

Viet Nam: 65a Ly Thuong Kiet, Hanoi; tel. (4) 9424775; fax (4) 9422426; e-mail embacuba@netnam.org.vn; internet embacuba.cubaminrex.cu/vietnaming; Ambassador Jesús Aise Sotolongo.

Yemen: POB 15256, St 6B, Block 9, House 3, Safia Zone, nr Amman St, San'a; tel. (1) 442321; fax (1) 442322; e-mail embacubayemen@y.net.ye; Ambassador BIENVENIDO GARCÍA NEGRÍN.

Zambia: 5574 Mogoye Rd, Kalundu, POB 33132, 10101 Lusaka; tel. (1) 291308; fax (1) 291586; e-mail ambassador@iconnect.zm; Ambassador Narciso Martín Mora Díaz.

Zimbabwe: 5 Phillips Ave, Belgravia, POB 4139, Harare; tel. (4) 720256; Ambassador BUENAVENTURA REYES ACOSTA.

DIPLOMATIC MISSIONS OF CYPRUS

United Nations: 13 East 40th St, New York, NY 10016; tel. (212) 481-6023; fax (212) 685-7316; e-mail cyprus@un.int; internet www.un.int/cyprus; Permanent Representative Andreas D. Mavroyiannis.

Australia: 30 Beale Crescent, Deakin, ACT 2600; tel. (2) 6281-0832; fax (2) 6281-0860; e-mail press@cyprus.org.au; internet www.cyprus.org.au; High Commissioner PHILIPPOS K. KRITIOTIS.

Austria: Parkring 20, 1010 Vienna; tel. (1) 513-06-30; fax (1) 513-06-32; e-mail embassy2@cyprus.vienna.at; Ambassador Kornelios S. Korneliou.

Belgium: 61 ave de Cortenbergh, 1000 Brussels; tel. (2) 650-06-10; fax (2) 650-06-20; e-mail ambassade.cyprus@skynet.be; Ambassador CONSTANTINOS ELIADES.

Bulgaria: 1164 Sofia, ul. Dzheimz Baucher i Plachkovitsa 1a/1; tel. (2) 961-77-30; fax (2) 862-94-70; e-mail cyprusembasofia@netbg.com; Ambassador Giorgos Giorgis (resident in Athens, Greece).

China, People's Republic: 2-13-2 Tayuan Diplomatic Office Bldg, Liang Ma He Nan Lu, Chao Yang Qu, Beijing 100600; tel. (10) 65325057; fax (10) 65324244; e-mail cyembpek@public3.bta.net.cn; Ambassador MARIOS IERONYMIDES.

Czech Republic: Pod Hradbami 9, 160 00 Prague 6; tel. 224316833; fax 224317529; e-mail embassy@kypros.cz; Ambassador Achilleas Antoniades.

Denmark: Borgergade 28, 1st Floor, 1300 Copenhagen K; tel. 33-91-58-88; fax 33-91-58-77; e-mail consulate@cyprus-embassy.dk; Ambassador ANTONIS TOUMAZIS.

Egypt: 17 Sharia Omar Tosson, Ahmed Orabi, Mohandessin, Cairo; tel. (2) 3455967; fax (2) 3455969; Ambassador Phaedon Anastasiou.

Finland: Bulevardi 5A 19, 00120 Helsinki; tel. (9) 6962820; fax (9) 677428; e-mail mail@cyprusembassy.fi; internet www.cyprusembassy.fi; Ambassador THALIA PETRIDES.

France: 23 rue Galilée, 75116 Paris; tel. 1-47-20-86-28; fax 1-40-70-13-44; e-mail paris@mfa.gov.cy; Ambassador Pericles Nearkou.

Germany: Wallstr. 27, 10179 Berlin; tel. (30) 3086830; fax (30) 27591454; e-mail info@botschaft-zypern.de; internet www.botschaft-zypern.de; Ambassador PANTELAKIS ELIADES.

Greece: Odos Herodotou 16, 106 75 Athens; tel. (210) 7232727; fax (210) 4536373; Ambassador Georgios Georgis.

Hungary: 1051 Budapest, Dorottya u. 3, III, 2–3u.; tel. (1) 266-1330; fax (1) 266-0538; Ambassador GEORGE SHIAKALLIS.

India: 106 Jor Bagh, New Delhi 110 003; tel. (11) 24697503; fax (11) 24628828; e-mail cyprus@del3.vsnl.net.in; High Commissioner Andreas G. Zenonos.

Iran: 328 Shahid Karimi, Dezashib, Tajrish, Tehran; tel. (21) 22219842; fax (21) 22219843; Ambassador GEORGE LIKOURGUS.

Ireland: 71 Lower Leeson St, Dublin 2; tel. (1) 6763060; fax (1) 6763099; e-mail dublinembassy@mfa.gov.cy; internet www.mfa.gov.cy/embassydublin; Ambassador Sotos A. Liassides.

Israel: Top Tower, 14th Floor, Dizengoff Centre, 50 Dizengoff St, Tel-Aviv 64322; tel. 3-5250212; fax 3-6290535; e-mail cyprus@netvision.net.il; Ambassador GEORGE ZODIATES.

Italy: Via Francesco Denza 15, 00197 Roma; tel. (06) 8088365; fax (06) 8088338; e-mail ciproamb@tin.it; Ambassador Athena K. Mavronicola.

Kenya: Eagle House, 5th Floor, Kimathi St, POB 30739, 00100 Nairobi; tel. (20) 220881; fax (20) 312202; e-mail cyphc@nbnet.co.ke; High Commissioner VASSOS CHAMBERLEN.

Libya: POB 3284, Sharia adh-Dhul 60, Ben Ashour, Tripoli; tel. (21) 3601274; fax (21) 3613516; e-mail cyprusembassy@mail.lttnet.net; Ambassador Yannis Iacovou.

Mexico: Sierra Gorda 370, Col. Lomas de Chapultepec, Del. Miguel Hidalgo, 11000 México, DF; tel. (55) 5202-7600; fax (55) 5520-2693; e-mail chipre@att.net.mx; Ambassador ANTONIS GRIVAS.

Netherlands: Surinamestraat 15, 2585 GG The Hague; tel. (70) 3466499; fax (70) 3924024; e-mail cyprus@xs4all.nl; internet www.mfa.gov.cy/embassythehague; Ambassador James Droushiotis.

Poland: 02-629 Warsaw, ul. Pilicka 4; tel. (22) 8444577; fax (22) 8442558; e-mail embassyofcyprus@neostrada.pl; Ambassador KALLIOPI AVRAAM.

Portugal: Av. da Liberdade 229, 1°, 1250-142 Lisbon; tel. (21) 3194180; fax (21) 3194189; e-mail chipre@netcabo.pt; internet www.mfa.gov.cy/embassylisbon; Ambassador Nearchos Palas.

Qatar: POB 24482, 3 Saba Saha 12 St, District 63, West Bay, Doha; tel. 4934390; fax 4933087; e-mail kyprosdoha@qatar.net.qa; Ambassador GEORGE C. KASOULIDES.

Romania: 050726 Bucharest, J. W. Marriot Grand Hotel, Calea 13 Septembrie 90, Sector 5; tel. (21) 4034900; fax (21) 4034901; Ambassador Spyros Attas.

Russian Federation: 121069 Moscow, ul. Povarskaya 9; tel. (495) 744-29-44; fax (495) 744-29-45; e-mail moscowembassy@mfa.gov.cy; internet www.mfa.gov.cy/embassymoscow; Ambassador LEONIDAS PANTELIDES.

Serbia: 11040 Belgrade, Diplomatska Kolonija 9; tel. (11) 3672725; fax (11) 3671348; e-mail cyprus@eunet.yu; Ambassador Homer Mavrommatis.

Slovenia: 1000 Ljubljana, Komenskega 12; tel. (1) 2321542; fax (1) 2302002; e-mail embassy.cyprus@siol.net; Ambassador CHARALAMBOS PANAYIDES.

South Africa: cnr Church St and Hill St, Arcadia, Pretoria 0083; POB 14554, Hatfield 0028; tel. (12) 3425258; fax (12) 3425596; e-mail cyprusjb@mweb.co.za; High Commissioner Costa Leontiou.

Spain: Paseo de la Castellana 45, 4–5°, 28046 Madrid; tel. (91) 5783114; fax (91) 5782189; e-mail embajadachipre@telefonica.net; internet www.mfa.gov.cy/embassymadrid; Ambassador REA YIORDAMLIS.

Sweden: Birger Jarlsgt. 37, 4th Floor, POB 7649, 103 94 Stockholm; tel. (8) 24-50-08; fax (8) 24-45-18; e-mail info@cyprusemb.se; internet www.cyprusemb.se; Ambassador Pavlos Anastasiades.

Syria: BP 9269, 278G rue Malek bin Rabia, Mezzeh Ouest, Damascus; tel. (11) 6130812; fax (11) 6130814; e-mail syriapio@scs-net.org; Ambassador EFSTATHIOS ORPHANIDES.

United Kingdom: 13 St James' Sq., London, SW1Y 4LB; tel. (20) 7321-4100; fax (20) 7321-4164; e-mail cyphclondon@dial.pipex.com; internet www.mfa.gov.cy/highcomlondon; High Commr Dimitris Hatziargirou (acting).

United States of America: 2211 R St, NW, Washington, DC 20008; tel. (202) 462-5772; fax (202) 483-6710; e-mail cypembwash@earthlink.net; internet www.cyprusembassy.net; Ambassador ANDREAS KAKOURIS.

DIPLOMATIC MISSIONS OF CZECH REPUBLIC

United Nations: 1109–1111 Madison Ave, New York, NY 10028; tel. (646) 981-4000; fax (646) 981-4099; e-mail un.newyork@embassy.mzv.cz; internet www.mfa.cz/un.newyork; Permanent Representative Martin Palous.

Albania: Rruga Skënderbej 10, Tirana; tel. (4) 234004; fax (4) 232159; e-mail tirana@embassy.mzv.cz; internet www.mzv.cz/tirana; Ambassador MARKÉTA FIALKOVÁ.

Algeria: BP 358, Villa Koudia, 3 chemin Ziryab, Alger-Gare, Algiers; tel. (21) 23-00-56; fax (21) 23-01-03; e-mail algiers@embassy.mzv.cz; internet www.mzv.cz/algiers; Ambassador Milan Šarapatka.

Angola: Rua Companhia de Jesus 43–45, Miramar, Luanda; tel. 222430646; fax 222447676; e-mail luanda@embassy.mzv.cz; Ambassador VLADIMÍR VÁLKY.

Argentina: Junín 1461, C1113AAM Buenos Aires; tel. (11) 4807-3107; fax (11) 4807-3109; e-mail buenosaires@embassy.mzv.cz; internet www.mfa.cz/buenosaires; Ambassador Blanka Kováksová.

Australia: 8 Culgoa Circuit, O'Malley, ACT 2606; tel. (2) 6290-1386; fax (2) 6290-0006; e-mail canberra@embassy.mzv.cz; internet www.mzv.cz/canberra; Ambassador KAREL PAŽOUREK.

Austria: Penzingerstr. 11–13, 1140 Vienna; tel. (1) 899-58-0; fax (1) 894-12-00; e-mail vienna@embassy.mzv.cz; internet www.mzv.cz/vienna; Ambassador Dr Jan Koukal.

Belarus: 220030 Minsk, Muzykalny per. 1/2; tel. (17) 226-52-44; fax (17) 211-01-37; e-mail minsk@embassy.mzv.cz; internet www.mzv.cz/minsk; Chargé d'affaires VLADIMÍR RUML.

Belgium: Czech House, 60 rue du Trône, 1050 Brussels; tel. (2) 213-94-01; fax (2) 213-94-02; e-mail brussels@embassy.mzv.cz; internet www.mzv.cz/brussels; Ambassador Vladimír Müller.

Bosnia and Herzegovina: 71000 Sarajevo, Franjevačka 19; tel. (33) 447525; fax (33) 447526; e-mail sarajevo@embassy.mzv.cz; internet www.mzv.cz/wwwo/?zu=sarajevo; Ambassador JIŘÍ KUDĚLA.

Brazil: SES, Via L3 Sul, Quadra 805, Lote 21, CP 170, 70414-900 Brasília, DF; tel. (61) 3242-7785; fax (61) 3242-7833; e-mail brasilia@embassy.mzv.cz; internet www.mzv.cz/brasilia; Chargé d'affaires a.i. Jana Chaloupková.

Bulgaria: 1504 Sofia, ul. Ya. Sakazov 9; tel. (2) 946-11-11; fax (2) 946-18-00; e-mail sofia@embassy.mzv.cz; internet www.mzv.cz/sofia; Ambassador MARTIN KLEPETKO.

Canada: 251 Cooper St, Ottawa, ON K2P 0G2; tel. (613) 562-3875; fax (613) 562-3878; e-mail ottawa@embassy.mzv.cz; internet www.czechembassy.org; Ambassador Pavel Vošalík.

Chile: Avda El Golf 254, Santiago; tel. (2) 232-1066; fax (2) 232-0707; e-mail santiago@embassy.mzv.cz; internet www.mfa.cz/santiago; Ambassador LUBOMÍR HLADÍK.

China, People's Republic: Ri Tan Lu, Jian Guo Men Wai, Beijing 100600; tel. (10) 85329500; fax (10) 65325653; e-mail beijing@embassy.mzv.cz; internet www.mzv.cz/beijing; Ambassador Dr Viteslav Grepl.

Colombia: Carrera 7, No 114-33, Ofs 603 y 604, Bogotá, DC; tel. (1) 640-0600; fax (1) 640-0599; e-mail bogota@embassy.msv.cz; internet www.mzv.cz/bogota; Ambassador ZDENĚK KREJČÍ.

Costa Rica: 75 m oeste de la entrada principal del Colegio Humboldt, Apdo 12041, 1000 San José; tel. 296-5671; fax 296-5595; e-mail sanjose@embassy.mzv.cz; internet www.mzv.cz/sanjose; Ambassador Milan Jakobec.

Croatia: 10000 Zagreb, Savska cesta 41; tel. (1) 6177246; fax (1) 6176630; e-mail zagreb@embassy.mzv.cz; internet www.mzv.cz/zagreb; Ambassador KAREL KÜHNL.

Cuba: Avda Kohly, No 259, entre 41 y 43, Nuevo Vedado, CP 10600, Havana; tel. (7) 883-3201; fax (7) 883-3596; e-mail havana@embassy.mzv.cz; internet www.czechembassy.org/wwwo/?zu=havana; Chargé d'affaires a.i. Vít Korselt.

Cyprus: POB 5202, 48 Arsinois St, 1307 Nicosia; tel. 22421118; fax 22421059; e-mail nicosia@embassy.mzv.cz; internet www.mzv.cz/nicosia; Ambassador JAN BONDY.

Denmark: Ryvangs Allé 14–16, 2100 Copenhagen Ø; tel. 39-10-18-10; fax 39-29-09-30; e-mail copenhagen@embassy.mzv.cz; internet www.mfa.cz/copenhagen; Ambassador Ivan Jančárek.

Egypt: 1st Floor, 4 Sharia Dokki, Cairo 12511 (Giza); tel. (2) 37485531; fax (2) 37485892; e-mail cairo@embassy.mzv.cz; internet www.mfa.cz/cairo; Ambassador MILOSLAV STAŠEK.

Estonia: Lahe 4, Tallinn 10150; tel. 627-4400; fax 631-4716; e-mail tallinn@embassy.mzv.cz; internet www.mfa.cz/tallinn; Ambassador Miloš Lexa.

Ethiopia: Kebele 15, House No. 29, POB 3108, Addis Ababa; tel. (11) 5516132; fax (11) 5513471; e-mail addisabeba@embassy.mzv.cz; internet www.mzv.cz/addisababa; Ambassador ZDENĚK DOBIÁŠ.

Finland: Armfeltintie 14, 00150 Helsinki; tel. (9) 6120880; fax (9) 630655; e-mail helsinki@embassy.mzv.cz; internet www.mfa.cz/helsinki; Ambassador Vladimír Kotzy.

France: 15 ave Charles Floquet, 75007 Paris; tel. 1-40-65-13-00; fax 1-40-65-13-13; e-mail paris@embassy.mzv.cz; internet www.mzv.cz/paris; Ambassador PAVEL FISCHER.

Georgia: 0162 Tbilisi, Chavchavadze 37/6; tel. (32) 91-67-40; fax (32) 91-67-44; e-mail tbilisi@embassy.mzv.cz; internet www.mzv.cz/tbilisi; Ambassador Jozef Vrabec.

Germany: Wilhelmstr. 44, 10117 Berlin; tel. (30) 226380; fax (30) 2294033; e-mail berlin@embassy.mzv.cz; internet www.mfa.cz/berlin; Ambassador RUDOLF JINDRÁK.

Ghana: C260/5, 2 Kanda High Rd, POB 5226, Accra-North; tel. (21) 223540; fax (21) 225337; e-mail accra@embassy.mzv.cz; internet www.mzv.cz/accra; Ambassador Miroslav Křenek.

Greece: Odos Georgiou Seferis 6, Palaio Psychiko, 154 52 Athens; tel. (210) 6713755; fax (210) 6710675; e-mail athens@embassy.mzv.cz; internet www.mzv.cz/athens; Ambassador HANA MOTTLOVÁ.

Hungary: 1064 Budapest, Rózsa u. 61; tel. (1) 351-0539; fax (1) 351-9189; e-mail budapest@embassy.mzv.cz; internet www.mzv.cz/wwwo/?zu=budapest; Ambassador Jaromír Plíšek.

India: 50M Niti Marg, Chanakyapuri, New Delhi 110 021; tel. (11) 26110205; fax (11) 26886221; e-mail newdelhi@embassy.mzv.cz; internet www.mfa.cz/newdelhi; Ambassador HYNEK KMONÍČEK.

Indonesia: Jalan Gereja Theresia 20, Menteng, Jakarta Pusat 10350; tel. (21) 3904075; fax (21) 3904078; e-mail jakarta@embassy.mzv.cz; internet www.mfa.cz/jakarta; Ambassador Pavel Řezáč.

Iran: POB 11365-4457, No. 199, Lavasani Ave, Cnr of Yas St, Tehran 195376-4358; tel. (21) 22288149; fax (21) 22802079; e-mail teheran@embassy.mzv.cz; internet www.mfa.cz/tehran; Chargé d'affaires a.i. MICHAL ČERNÝ.

Iraq: POB 27124, 37/11/601 Hay al-Mansour, Baghdad; tel. (1) 542-4868; fax (1) 214-2621; e-mail baghdad@embassy.mzv.cz; Ambassador Peter Voznica.

Ireland: 57 Northumberland Rd, Dublin 4; tel. (1) 6681135; fax (1) 6681660; e-mail dublin@embassy.mzv.cz; internet www.mfa.cz/dublin; Ambassador JOSEF HAVLAS.

Israel: POB 16361, 23 Zeitlin St, Tel-Aviv; tel. 3-6918282; fax 3-6918286; e-mail telaviv@embassy.mzv.cz; internet www.mfa.cz/telaviv; Ambassador Michael Žantovský.

Italy: Via dei Gracchi 322, 00192 Roma; tel. (06) 36309571; fax (06) 3244466; e-mail rome@embassy.mzv.cz; internet www.mzv.cz/rome; Ambassador VLADIMÍR ZAVÁZAL.

Japan: 2-16-14, Hiroo, Shibuya-ku, Tokyo 150-0012; tel. (3) 3400-8122; fax (3) 3400-8124; e-mail tokyo@embassy.mzv.cz; internet www.mzv.cz/tokyo; Ambassador Jaromir Novotny.

Jordan: POB 2213, Amman 11181; tel. (6) 5927051; fax (6) 5927053; e-mail amman@embassy.mzv.cz; internet www.mzv.cz/amman; Chargé d'affaires a.i. IVANA HOLOUBKOVA.

Kazakhstan: 010000 Astana, Sary-Arka 6, Biznes-Tsentr Arman, 13th floor; tel. (7172) 99-01-43; fax (7172) 99-01-42; e-mail astana@embassy.mzv.cz; internet www.mzv.cz/astana; Ambassador (vacant).

Kenya: Jumia Pl., Lenana Rd, POB 48785, 00100 Nairobi; tel. (20) 2731010; fax (20) 2731013; e-mail nairobi@embassy.mzv.cz; internet www.mzv.cz/nairobi; Ambassador PETER KOPØIVA.

Korea, Democratic People's Republic: Taedongkang Guyok 38, Taehakgori, Puksudong, Pyongyang; tel. (2) 3817021; fax (2) 3817022; e-mail pyongyang@embassy.mzv.cz; internet www.mzc.cz/pyongyang; Ambassador Martin Tomčo.

Korea, Republic: 1-121, 2-ga, Shinmun-ro, Jongno-gu, Seoul 110-062; tel. (2) 725-6765; fax (2) 734-6452; e-mail seoul@embassy.mzv.cz; internet www.mzv.cz/seoul; Ambassador TOMÁŠ SMETÁNKA.

Kuwait: al-Nuzha, Block 3, St 34, Bldg 13, Kuwait City; tel. 2529018; fax 2529021; e-mail kuwait@embassy.mzv.cz; internet www.mzv.cz/kuwait; Ambassador Antonín Blažek.

Latvia: Elizabetes iela 29A, Rīga 1010; tel. 6721-7814; fax 6721-7821; e-mail riga@embassy.mzv.cz; internet www.mfa.cz/riga; Ambassador TOMÁŠ PŠTROSS.

Lebanon: POB 40195, Baabda, Beirut; tel. (5) 929010; fax (5) 922120; e-mail beirut@embassy.mzv.cz; internet www.mzv.cz/beirut; Ambassador Jan Čížek.

Libya: POB 1097, Sharia Ahmad Lutfi Sayed, Sharia ben Ashour, Tripoli; tel. (21) 3615436; fax (21) 3615437; e-mail tripoli@embassy.mzv.cz; internet www.mzv.cz/tripoli; Ambassador DUŠAN ŠTRAUCH.

Lithuania: Birutės g. 16, Vilnius 08117; tel. (5) 266-1040; fax (5) 266-1066; e-mail vilnius@embassy.mzv.cz; internet www.mzv.cz/vilnius; Ambassador Alois Buchta.

Luxembourg: 2 rond-point Robert Schuman, 2525 Luxembourg; tel. 26-47-78-11; fax 26-47-78-20; e-mail luxembourg@embassy.mzv.cz; internet www.mzv.cz/luxembourg; Ambassador KATEŘINA LUKEŠOVÁ.

Macedonia, former Yugoslav Republic: 1000 Skopje, Salvador Aljende 35; tel. (2) 3109805; fax (2) 3178380; e-mail skopje@embassy.mzv.cz; internet www.mzv.cz/belgrade; Ambassador Jozef Braun.

Malaysia: 32 Jalan Mesra, off Jalan Damai, 55000 Kuala Lumpur; tel. (3) 21427185; fax (3) 21412727; e-mail kualalumpur@embassy.mzv.cz; internet www.mzv.cz/kualalumpur; Ambassador DANA HUNÁTOVÁ.

Mexico: Cuvier 22, Col. Nueva Anzures, Del. Miguel Hidalgo, 11590 México, DF; tel. (55) 5531-2777; fax (55) 5531-1837; e-mail mexico@embassy.mzv.cz; internet www.mzv.cz/mexico; Ambassador Jiří Havlík.

Moldova: 2005 Chişinău, str. Moara Roşie 23; tel. (22) 29-65—04; fax (22) 29-64-37; e-mail chisinau@embassy.mzv.cz; internet www.mzv.cz/chisinau; Ambassador PETR KYPR.

Mongolia: Olimpiin Gudamj 12, Ulan Bator (CPOB 665); tel. (11) 321886; fax (11) 323791; e-mail czechemb@magicnet.mn; internet www.mzv.cz/ulaanbaatar; Ambassador (vacant).

Morocco: Villa Merzaa, km 4.5, route des Zaêrs, BP 410, Zankat Aït Melloul, Souissi, 10200 Rabat; tel. (3) 7755421; fax (3) 7755493; e-mail rabat@embassy.mzv.cz; internet www.mzv.cz/rabat; Ambassador ELEONORA URBANOVÁ.

Netherlands: Paleisstraat 4, 2514 JA The Hague; tel. (70) 3130031; fax (70) 3563349; e-mail hague@embassy.mzv.cz; internet www.mfa.cz/hague; Ambassador Petr Mareš.

Nigeria: Plot 1223, Gnassingbé Eyadéma St, Asokoro District, POB 4628, Abuja; tel. (9) 3141245; fax (9) 3141248; e-mail abuja@embassy.mzv.cz; internet www.mzv.cz/abuja; Ambassador ALEXANDR KARYCH.

Norway: Fritznersgt. 14, 0244 Oslo; tel. 22-12-10-31; fax 22-55-33-95; e-mail oslo@embassy.mzv.cz; internet www.mzv.cz/oslo; Ambassador Luboš Nový.

Pakistan: 49, St 27, Shalimar F-6/2, POB 1335, Islamabad; tel. (51) 2274304; fax (51) 2825327; e-mail islamabad@embassy.mzv.cz; internet www.mzv.cz/islamabad; Ambassador ALEXANDR LANGER.

Peru: Baltazar La Torre 398, San Isidro, Lima 27; tel. (1) 2643374; fax (1) 2641708; e-mail lima@embassy.mzv.cz; internet www.mfa.cz/lima; Ambassador Věra Zemanová.

Philippines: 30th Floor, Rufino Pacific Tower, 6784 Ayala Ave, 1200 Makati City, Metro Manila; tel. (2) 8111155; fax (2) 8111020; e-mail manila@embassy.mzv.cz; internet www.mzv.cz/manila; Ambassador JAROSLAV LUDVA.

Poland: 00-555 Warsaw, ul. Koszykowa 18; tel. (22) 5251850; fax (22) 5251898; e-mail warsaw@embassy.mzv.cz; internet www.mfa.cz/warsaw; Ambassador (vacant).

Portugal: Rua Pero de Alenquer 14, 1400-294 Lisbon; tel. (21) 3010487; fax (21) 3010629; e-mail lisbon@embassy.mzv.cz; internet www.mfa.cz/lisbon; Ambassador LADISLAV ŠKEŘÍK.

Romania: 030045 Bucharest, Str. Ion Ghica 11, Sector 3; tel. (21) 3039230; fax (21) 3122539; e-mail bucharest@embassy.mzv.cz; internet www.mzv.cz/bucharest; Ambassador Dr Petr Dokládal.

Russian Federation: 123056 Moscow, ul. Yu. Fuchika 12/14; tel. (495) 251-05-44; fax (045) 250-15-23; e-mail moscow@embassy.mzv.cz; internet www.mfa.cz/moscow; Ambassador MIROSLAV KOSTELKA.

Serbia: 11000 Belgrade, bul. Kralja Aleksandra 22; tel. (11) 3230133; fax (11) 3236448; e-mail belgrade@embassy.mzv.cz; internet www.mzv.cz/belgrade; Ambassador Hana Hubáčková.

Slovakia: POB 208, Hviezdoslavovo nám. 8, 810 00 Bratislava; tel. (2) 5920-3303; fax (2) 5920-3330; e-mail bratislava@embassy.mzv.cz; internet www.mzv.cz/bratislava; Ambassador VLADIMÍR GALUŠKA.

Slovenia: 1000 Ljubljana, Riharjeva 1; tel. (1) 4202450; fax (1) 2839259; e-mail ljubljana@embassy.mzv.cz; internet www.mzv.cz/ljubljana; Ambassador Ivana Hlavsová.

South Africa: 936 Pretorius St, Arcadia, Pretoria 0083; POB 13671, Hatfield 0028; tel. (12) 4312380; fax (12) 4302033; e-mail pretoria@embassymzv.cz; Ambassador MARTIN POHL.

Spain: Avda Pío XII 22–24, 28016 Madrid; tel. (91) 3531880; fax (91) 3531885; e-mail madrid@embassy.mzv.cz; internet www.mfa.cz/madrid; Ambassador Martin Košatka.

Sweden: Villagt. 21, POB 26156, 100 41 Stockholm; tel. (8) 440-42-10; fax (8) 440-42-11; e-mail stockholm@embassy.mzv.cz; internet www.mzv.cz/stockholm; Ambassador JAN KÁRA.

Switzerland: Muristr. 53, Postfach 537, 3000 Bern 31; tel. 313504070; fax 313504098; e-mail bern@embassy.mzv.cz; internet www.mfa.cz/bern; Ambassador Dr Boris Lazar.

Syria: BP 2249, place Abou al-Ala'a al-Maari, Damascus; tel. (11) 3331383; fax (11) 3338268; e-mail damascus@embassy.mzv.cz; internet www.mzv.cz/damascus; Ambassador TOMÁŠ ULIČNÝ.

Thailand: 71/6 Soi Ruamrudi 2, Thanon Ploenchit, Bangkok 10330; tel. (2) 255-3027; fax (2) 253-7637; e-mail bangkok@embassy.mzv.cz; internet www.mfa.cz/bangkok; Ambassador Ivan Hotěk.

Tunisia: 98 rue de Palestine, BP 53, Belvédère, 1002 Tunis; tel. (71) 780-456; fax (71) 793-228; e-mail tunis@embassy.mzv.cz; internet www.mzv.cz/tunis; Ambassador JAROMÍR PŘÍVRATSKÝ.

Turkey: Kaptanpaşa Sok. 15, 06700 Gaziosmanpaşa, Ankara; tel. (312) 4056139; fax (312) 4463084; e-mail ankara@embassy.mzv.cz; internet www.mzv.cz/ankara; Ambassador Eva Filipi.

Ukraine: 01901 Kyiv, vul. Yaroslaviv Val 34A; tel. (44) 272-04-31; fax (44) 272-62-04; e-mail kiev@embassy.mzv.cz; internet www.mzv.cz/kiev; Ambassador JAROSLAV BAŠTA.

United Arab Emirates: POB 27009, City Bank Bldg, Corniche Plaza, Abu Dhabi; tel. (2) 6782800; fax (2) 6795716; e-mail abudhabi@embassy.mzv.cz; internet www.mzv.cz; Ambassador Dr Věra Jeřábková.

United Kingdom: 26 Kensington Palace Gdns, London, W8 4QY; tel. (20) 7243-1115; fax (20) 7727-9654; e-mail london@embassy.mzv.cz; internet www.mzv.cz/london; Ambassador JAN WINKLER.

United States of America: 3900 Spring of Freedom St, NW, Washington, DC 20008; tel. (202) 274-9100; fax (202) 966-8540; e-mail washington@embassy.mzv.cz; internet www.mzv.cz/washington; Ambassador Petr Kolar.

Uruguay: Luis B. Cavia 2996, Casilla 12262, 11300 Montevideo; tel. (2) 7087808; fax (2) 7096410; e-mail montevideo@embassy.mzv.cz; internet www.mzv.cz/montevideo; Ambassador PETR STIEGLER.

Uzbekistan: 100041 Tashkent, Mirzo-Ulugbek Tumani, Navnihol ko'ch. 6; tel. (71) 120-60-71; fax (71) 120-60-75; e-mail tashkent@embassy.mzv.cz; internet www.mzv.cz/tashkent; Ambassador Aleš Fojtík.

Vatican City: Via Crescenzio 91/1B, 00193 Rome, Italy; tel. (06) 6874696; fax (06) 6879731; e-mail vatican@embassy.mzv.cz; internet www.mzv.cz/vatican; Ambassador PAVEL JAJTNER.

Venezuela: Calle Los Cedros, Quinta Isabel, Urb. Country Club, Altamira, Caracas 1060; tel. (212) 261-8528; fax (212) 266-3987; e-mail caracas@embassy.mzv.cz; internet www.mfa.cz/caracas; Ambassador Dr Jiří Jiránek.

Viet Nam: 13 Chu Van An, Hanoi; tel. (4) 8454131; fax (4) 8233996; internet www.mfa.cz/hanoi; Ambassador IVO ŽDÁREK.

Yemen: POB 2501, Safiya Janoobia, St 16, House 6, San'a; tel. (1) 440946; fax (1) 440762; e-mail sanaa@embassy.mzv.cz; internet www.mzv.cz/sanaa; Ambassador Jozef Vrabec.

Zimbabwe: 4 Sandringham Dr., Alexandra Park, GPO 4474, Harare; tel. (4) 700636; fax (4) 720930; e-mail harare@embassy.mzv.cz; internet www.mzv .cz/harare; Ambassador VÁCLAV JÍLEK.

DIPLOMATIC MISSIONS OF DENMARK

United Nations: 1 Dag Hammarskjöld Plaza, 885 Second Ave, 18th Floor, New York, NY 10017; tel. (212) 308-7009; fax (212) 308-3384; e-mail nycmis@um.dk; internet www.missionfnnewyork.um.dk/en/; Permanent Representative Carsten Staur.

Afghanistan: House 35–36, Road 13, Lane 1, Wazir Akbar Khan, Kabul; tel. (20) 2300968; e-mail kblamb@um.dk; internet www.ambkabul.um.dk; Head of Mission JENS HAARLOV.

Albania: Rruga Nikolla Tupe 1/4, POB 1743, Tirana; tel. (4) 280600; fax (4) 280630; e-mail tiaamb@um.dk; internet www.ambtirana.um.dk; Ambassador Niels Severin Munk.

Algeria: BP 384, 12 ave Emile Marquis, Lot Djenane el-Malik, Hydra, 16035 Algiers; tel. (21) 54-82-28; fax (21) 69-29-09; e-mail algamb@um.dk; internet www.ambalgier.um.dk; Ambassador OLE WØHLERS OLSEN.

Argentina: Avda Leandro N. Alem 1074, 9°, 1001 Buenos Aires; tel. (11) 4312-6901; fax (11) 4312-7857; e-mail bueamb@um.dk; internet www .buenosaires.um.dk; Ambassador Henrik Bramsen Hahn.

Australia: 15 Hunter St, Yarralumla, ACT 2600; tel. (2) (2) 6270-5333; fax (2) 6270-5324; e-mail cbramb@um.dk; internet www.canberra.um.dk; Ambassador SUSANNE HOFFMANN SHINE.

Austria: Führichgasse 6, 1010 Vienna; tel. (1) 512-79-04-0; fax (1) 513-81-20; e-mail vieamb@um.dk; internet www.ambwien.um.dk; Ambassador Hugo Ostergaard-Andersen.

Bangladesh: House (NW) H 1, Rd 51, Gulshan Model Town, POB 2056, Dhaka 1212; tel. (2) 8811799; fax (2) 8813638; e-mail dacamb@um.dk; internet www.ambdhaka.um.dk; Ambassador EINAR H. JENSEN.

Belgium: 73 rue d'Arlon, 1040 Brussels; tel. (2) 233-09-00; fax (2) 233-09-32; e-mail bruamb@um.dk; internet www.ambbruxelles.um.dk; Ambassador Jørgen Molde.

Benin: Lot P7, Les Cocotiers, 04 BP 1223, Cotonou; tel. 21-30-38-62; fax 21-30-38-60; e-mail cooamb@um.dk; internet www.ambcotonou.um.dk; Ambassador GERT MEINECKE.

Bolivia: Edif. Fortaleza, Avda Arce 2799, esq. Cordero, 9°, Casilla 9860, La Paz; tel. (2) 243-2070; fax (2) 243-3150; e-mail lpbamb@um.dk; internet www .amblapaz.um.dk; Ambassador Charlotte Slente.

Bosnia and Herzegovina: 71000 Sarajevo, Splitska 9; tel. (33) 665901; fax (33) 665902; e-mail sijamb@um.dk; internet www.danishembassy.ba; Ambassador NIELS-JORGEN NEHRING.

Brazil: SES, Av. das Nações, Quadra 807, Lote 26, 70416-900 Brasília, DF; tel. (61) 3445-3443; fax (61) 3445-3509; e-mail bsbamb@um.dk; internet www .ambbrasilia.um.dk; Ambassador Christian Kønigsfeldt.

Bulgaria: 1000 Sofia, bul. Dondukov 54, POB 1393; tel. (2) 917-01-00; fax (2) 980-99-01; e-mail sofamb@um.dk; internet www.ambsofia.um.dk; Ambassador SVEND BOJE MADSEN.

Burkina Faso: 316, ave Blaise Compaoré, 01 BP 1760, Ouagadougou 01; tel. 50-32-85-40; fax 50-32-85-77; e-mail ouaamb@um.dk; internet www .ambouagadougou.um.dk; Ambasssador Mogens Pedersen.

Canada: 47 Clarence St, Suite 450, Ottawa, ON K1N 9K1; tel. (613) 562-1811; fax (613) 562-1812; e-mail ottamb@um.dk; internet www.ambottawa .um.dk; Ambassador POUL ERIK DAM KRISTENSEN.

Chile: Jacques Cazotte 5531, Casilla 13430, Vitacura, Santiago; tel. (2) 941-5100; fax (2) 218-1736; e-mail sclamb@um.dk; internet www.ambsantiago .um.dk/la; Ambassador Kim Højlund Christensen.

China, People's Republic: 1 Dong Wu Jie, San Li Tun, Beijing 100600; tel. (10) 85329900; fax (10) 85329916; e-mail bjsamb@um.dk; internet www .ambbeijing.um.dk; Ambassador JEPPE TRANHOLM-MIKKELSEN.

Croatia: 10000 Zagreb, trg Nikole Šubića Zrinskog 10; tel. (1) 4924530; fax (1) 4924554; e-mail zagreb@um.dk; Ambassador Berno Kjeldsen.

Cyprus: POB 20995, 7 Dositheou St, Parabldg Block C, 4th Floor, 1071 Nicosia; tel. 22377417; fax 22377472; e-mail nicamb@um.dk; internet www .ambnicosia.um.dk; Ambassador SVEND WAEVER.

Czech Republic: Maltézské nám. 5, POB 25, 118 01 Prague 1; tel. 257531600; fax 257531609; e-mail prgamb@um.dk; internet www.ambprag.um.dk; Chargé d'affaires a.i. Malene Hedlund.

Egypt: 12 Sharia Hassan Sabri, Cairo 11211 (Zamalek); tel. (2) 7396500; fax (2) 7396588; e-mail caiamb@um.dk; internet www.ambkairo.um.dk; Ambassador TORBEN BRYLLE.

Estonia: Wismari 5, Tallinn 15047; tel. 630-6400; fax 630-6421; e-mail tllamb@um.dk; internet www.ambtallinn.um.dk; Ambassador Kirsten Geelan.

Ethiopia: c/o Embassy of Norway, Nefas Silk Lafto Kifle Ketema, Kebele 3, House No. 1019, POB 12955, Addis Ababa; tel. (11) 3711377; fax (11) 3711399; e-mail addambdk@ethionet.et; internet www.ambaddisababa.um .dk; Ambassador PERNILLE DAHLER KARDEL.

Finland: Keskuskatu 1a, POB 1042, 00100 Helsinki; tel. (9) 6841050; fax (9) 68410540; e-mail helamb@um.dk; internet www.ambhelsingfors.um.dk; Ambassador Niels Kaas Dyrlund.

France: 77 ave Marceau, 75116 Paris; tel. 1-44-31-21-21; fax 1-44-31-21-88; e-mail paramb@um.dk; internet www.ambparis.um.dk; Ambassador NIELS EGELUND.

Germany: Rauchstr. 1, 10787 Berlin; tel. (30) 50502000; fax (30) 50502050; e-mail beramb@um.dk; internet www.ambberlin.um.dk; Ambassador Carsten Søndergaard.

Ghana: 67 Dr Isert Rd, North Ridge, POB CT 596, Accra; tel. (21) 253473; fax (21) 228061; e-mail accamb@um.dk; internet www.ambaccra.um.dk; Ambassador FLEMMING BJØRK PEDERSEN.

Greece: Mourouzilo 10, 106 74 Athens; tel. (210) 7256440; fax (210) 7256473; e-mail athamb@athamb.um.dk; internet www.ambathen.um.gr; Ambassador Tom Helge Nørring.

Hungary: 1122 Budapest, Határor u. 37; tel. (1) 487-9000; fax (1) 487-9045; e-mail budamb@um.dk; internet www.ambbudapest.um.dk; Ambassador MADS SANDAU-JENSEN.

Iceland: Hverfisgata 29, 101 Reykjavík; tel. 5750300; fax 5750310; e-mail rekamb@um.dk; internet www.ambreykjavik.um.dk; Ambassador Lasse Reimann.

India: 11 Aurangzeb Rd, New Delhi 110 011; tel. (11) 42090700; fax (11) 23792019; e-mail delamb@um.dk; internet www.ambnewdelhi.um.dk; Ambassador OLE LØNSMANN-POULSEN.

Indonesia: Menara Rajawali, 25th Floor, Jalan Mega Kuningan, Lot 5.1, Jakarta 12950; tel. (21) 5761478; fax (21) 5761535; e-mail jktamb@um.dk; internet www.ambjakarta.um.dk/en; Ambassador Niels Erik Andersen.

Iran: POB 19395-5358, 18 Dashti St, Dr Shariati Ave, Tehran 19148; tel. (21) 22640009; fax (21) 22640007; e-mail thramb@um.dk; internet www .ambteheran.um.dk; Ambassador SØREN HASLUND.

Iraq: Al-Jana'a Quarter, Hay at-Tashriya, Baghdad; tel. (1) 778-8440; e-mail bgwamb@um.dk; internet www.ambbagdad.um.dk; Ambassador Bo Eric Weber.

Ireland: 7th Floor, Block E, Iveagh Court, Harcourt Rd, Dublin 2; tel. (1) 4756404; fax (1) 4784536; e-mail dubamb@um.dk; internet www.ambdublin .um.dk; Ambassador HENRIK RÉE IVERSEN.

Israel: POB 21080, Museum Tower, 4 Berkowitz St, Tel-Aviv 61210; tel. 3-6085850; fax 3-6085851; e-mail tlvamb@um.dk; internet www.ambtelaviv .um.dk; Ambassador A. Carsten Damsgaard.

Italy: Via dei Monti Parioli 50, 00197 Roma; tel. (06) 9774831; fax (06) 97748399; e-mail romamb@um.dk; internet www.ambrom.um.dk; Ambassador GUNNAR ORTMANN.

Japan: 29-6, Sarugaku-cho, Shibuya-ku, Tokyo 150-0033; tel. (3) 3496-3001; fax (3) 3496-3440; e-mail tyoamb@um.dk; internet www.ambtokyo.um.dk; Ambassador Freddy Svane.

Kenya: Cassia House, Westlands Office Park, POB 40412, 00100 Nairobi; tel. (20) 4451460; fax (20) 4451474; e-mail nboamb@um.dk; internet www .ambnairobi.um.dk; Ambassador BO JENSEN.

Korea, Republic: Namsong Bldg, 5th Floor, 260-199, Itaewon-dong, Yeongsan-gu, Seoul 140-200; tel. (2) 795-4187; fax (2) 796-0986; e-mail selamb@um.dk; internet www.ambseoul.um.dk; Ambassador Poul O. G. Hoiness.

Latvia: Pils iela 11, Rīga 1863; tel. 6722-6210; fax 6722-9218; e-mail rixamb@ um.dk; internet www.ambriga.um.dk; Ambassador ARNOLD CHRISTIAN DE FINE SKIBSTED.

Lebanon: POB 11-5190, Immeuble 812 Tabaris, 4e étage, ave Charles Malek, Achrafieh, Beirut; tel. (1) 335828; fax (1) 335851; e-mail dk-emb@dm.net.lb; internet www.ambbeirut.um.dk; Ambassador Jan Top Christensen.

Lithuania: T. Kosciuškos g. 36, Vilnius 01100; tel. (5) 264-8760; fax (5) 231-2300; e-mail vnoamb@um.dk; internet www.ambvilnius.um.dk; Ambassador LAURIDS MIKAELSEN.

Luxembourg: 4 rue des Girondins, 1626 Luxembourg; tel. 22-21-22-1; fax 22-21-24; e-mail luxamb@um.dk; internet www.ambluxembourg.um.dk; Ambassador Ole Lisborg.

Malaysia: Wisma Denmark, 22nd Floor, 86 Jalan Ampang, 50450 Kuala Lumpur; tel. (3) 20322001; fax (3) 20322012; e-mail kulamb@um.dk; internet www.ambkualalumpur.um.dk; Ambassador BØRGE PETERSEN.

Mexico: Tres Picos 43, Col. Chapultepec Morales, Del. Miguel Hidalgo, 11580 México, DF; tel. (55) 5255-3405; fax (55) 5545-5797; e-mail mexamb@um.dk; internet www.ambmexicocity.um.dk; Ambassador Johannes Dahl-Hansen.

Mozambique: Av. Julius Nyerere 1162, CP 4588, Maputo; tel. 21480000; fax 21480010; e-mail mpmamb@um.dk; internet www.ambmaputo.um.dk; Ambassador MADS SANDAU-JENSEN.

Nepal: 761 Neel Saraswati Marg, Lazimpat, POB 6332, Kathmandu; tel. (1) 4413010; fax (1) 4411409; e-mail ktmamb@um.dk; internet www.ambkathmandu.um.dk; Ambassador Finn Thilsted.

Netherlands: Koninginnegracht 30, 2514 AB The Hague; tel. (70) 3025959; fax (70) 3025950; e-mail haaamb@um.dk; internet www.ambhaag.um.dk; Ambassador KIRSTEN BIERING.

Nicaragua: De la Plaza España, 1 c. abajo, 2 c. al lago, $\frac{1}{2}$ c. abajo, Apdo 4942, Managua; tel. 268-0250; fax 266-8095; e-mail mgaambu@um.dk; internet www.ambmanagua.um.dk; Ambassador Søren Vøhtz.

Norway: Olav Kyrresgt. 7, 0244 Oslo; tel. 22-54-08-00; fax 22-55-46-34; e-mail oslamb@um.dk; internet www.amboslo.um.dk; Ambassador THEIS TRUELSEN.

Pakistan: House No. 16, Street 21, F-6/2, POB 1118, Islamabad; tel. (51) 2824078; fax (51) 2824076; e-mail isbamb@um.dk; internet www.ambislamabad.um.dk; Ambassador Bent Wigotski.

Poland: 02-517 Warsaw, ul. Rakowiecka 19; tel. (22) 5652900; e-mail wawamb@um.dk; internet www.ambwarszawa.um.dk; Ambassador HANS MICHAEL KOFOED-HANSEN.

Portugal: Rua Castilho 14, 3°c, 1269-077 Lisbon; tel. (21) 3512960; fax (21) 3554615; e-mail lisamb@um.dk; internet www.amblissabon.um.dk; Ambassador Dr Lars Vissing.

Romania: 024031 Bucharest, Str. Dr Burghelea 3; tel. (21) 3000800; fax (21) 3120358; e-mail buhamb@um.dk; internet www.ambbukarest.um.dk; Ambassador ULRIK HELWEG-LARSEN.

Russian Federation: 119034 Moscow, Prechistenskii per. 9; tel. (495) 642-68-00; fax (495) 775-01-91; e-mail mowamb@um.dk; internet www.ambmoskva.um.dk; Ambassador Per Carlsen.

Saudi Arabia: POB 94398, Riyadh 11693; tel. (1) 488-0101; fax (1) 488-1366; e-mail ruhamb@um.dk; internet www.ambriyadh.um.dk; Ambassador HANS KLINGENBERG.

Serbia: 11040 Belgrade, Neznanog Junaka 9a; tel. (11) 3679500; fax (11) 3679502; e-mail begamb@um.dk; internet www.ambbeograd.um.dk; Ambassador Mette Kjuel Nielsen.

Singapore: 101 Thomson Rd, 13-01/02 United Sq., Singapore 307591; tel. 63555010; fax 62533764; e-mail sinamb@um.dk; internet www.denmark.com.sg; Ambassador VIBEKE ROVSING LAURITZEN.

Slovakia: Panská 27, 816 06 Bratislava; tel. (2) 5930-0200; fax (2) 5443-3656; e-mail btsamb@um.dk; internet www.denmark.sk; Ambassador Jorgen Munk Rasmussen.

Slovenia: 1000 Ljubljana, Tivolska 48, EuroCenter; tel. (1) 4380800; fax (1) 4317417; e-mail ljuamb@um.dk; internet www.ambljubljana.um.dk; Ambassador ANITA HUGAU.

South Africa: iParioli Office Park, Block B2, Ground Floor, 1166 Park St, Hatfield, Pretoria; POB 11439, Hatfield 0028; tel. (12) 4309340; fax (12) 3427620; e-mail pryamb@um.dk; internet www.ambpretoria.um.dk; Ambassador Dan E. Frederiksen.

Spain: Serrano 26, 7°, 28001 Madrid; tel. (91) 4318445; fax (91) 4319168; e-mail madamb@um.dk; internet www.embajadadinamarca.es; Ambassador NIELS PULTZ.

Sweden: Jakobs Torg 1, POB 16119, 103 23 Stockholm; tel. (8) 406-75-00; fax (8) 791-72-20; e-mail stoamb@um.dk; internet www.ambstockholm.um.dk; Ambassador Tom Risdahl Jensen.

Switzerland: Thunstr. 95, 3006 Bern; tel. 313505454; fax 313505464; e-mail brnamb@um.dk; internet www.ambbern.um.dk; Ambassador LARS MØLLER.

Syria: BP 2244, Fatmeh Idriss 6, rue al-Ghazzawi, Mezzeh Ouest, Damascus; tel. (11) 61909000; fax (11) 61909033; e-mail damamb@um.dk; internet www.ambdamaskus.um.dk; Ambassador Ole Egberg Mikkelsen.

Tanzania: Ghana Ave, POB 9171, Dar es Salaam; tel. (22) 2113887; fax (22) 2116433; e-mail daramb@um.dk; internet www.ambdaressalaam.um.dk; Ambassador BJARNE HENNEBERG SØRENSEN.

Thailand: 10 Soi Attakarn Prasit, Thanon Sathorn Tai, Bangkok 10120; tel. (2) 343-1100; fax (2) 213-1752; e-mail bkkamb@um.dk; internet www.ambbangkok.um.dk; Ambassador Michael Sternberg.

Turkey: Mahatma Gandhi Cad. 74, 06700 Gaziosmanpaşa, Ankara; tel. (312) 4466141; fax (312) 4472498; e-mail ankamb@um.dk; internet www.ambankara.um.dk; Ambassador JESPER VAHR.

Uganda: Plot 3, Lumumba Ave, POB 11243, Kampala; tel. (31) 2263211; fax (31) 2264624; e-mail kmtamb@um.dk; internet www.ambkampala.um.dk; Ambassador Stig Barlyng.

Ukraine: 01901 Kyiv, vul. B. Khmelnytskoho 56; tel. (44) 200-12-60; fax (44) 200-12-81; e-mail ievamb@um.dk; Ambassador UFFE ANDERSSON BALSLEV.

United Kingdom: 55 Sloane St, London, SW1X 9SR; tel. (20) 7333-0200; fax (20) 7333-0270; e-mail lonamb@um.dk; internet www.amblondon.um.dk; Ambassador Birger Riis-Jørgensen.

United States of America: 3200 Whitehaven St, NW, Washington, DC 20008-3616; tel. (202) 234-4300; fax (202) 328-1470; e-mail wasamb@um.dk; internet www.ambwashington.um.dk; Ambassador FRIIS ARNE PETERSEN.

Viet Nam: 19 Dien Bien Phu, Hanoi; tel. (4) 8231888; fax (4) 8231999; e-mail hanamb@um.dk; internet www.ambhanoi.um.dk; Ambassador Peter Lysholt Hansen.

Zambia: 4 Manenekela Rd, POB 50299, Lusaka; tel. (1) 254277; fax (1) 254618; e-mail lunamb@um.dk; internet www.amblusaka.um.dk/en; Ambassador ORLA BAKDAL.

DIPLOMATIC MISSIONS OF DJIBOUTI

United Nations: 866 United Nations Plaza, Suite 4011, New York, NY 10017; tel. (212) 753-3163; fax (212) 223-1276; e-mail djibouti@nyct.net; Permanent Representative Roble Olhaye.

Belgium: 204 ave F. D. Roosevelt, 1050 Brussels; tel. (2) 347-69-67; fax (2) 347-69-63; e-mail amb_djib@yahoo.fr; Ambassador MOHAMMED MOUSSA CHEHEM.

China, People's Republic: 2-2-102 Tayuan Diplomatic Office Bldg, Beijing; tel. (10) 65327857; fax (10) 65327858; Ambassador Moussa Bouh Odowa.

Egypt: 11 Sharia el-Gazaer, Aswan Sq., Cairo (Agouza); tel. (2) 3456546; fax (2) 3456549; Ambassador SHEIKH MOUSSA MOHAMED AHMED.

Eritrea: POB 5589, Asmara; tel. (1) 354961; fax (1) 351831; Ambassador Ahmad Issa.

Ethiopia: POB 1022, Addis Ababa; tel. (11) 6613200; fax (11) 6612786; Ambassador ISMAÏL GOULAL BOUDINE.

France: 26 rue Emile Ménier, 75116 Paris; tel. 1-47-27-49-22; fax 1-45-53-50-53; e-mail ambassadeur@ambdjibouti.org; Ambassador Rachad Farah.

India: c/o A 2–20 Sarfarjung Enclave, New Delhi 110 029; tel. (11) 41354491; fax (11) 41354490; e-mail info@embassyofdjibouti.org; internet embassyofdjibouti.org/EmbasyNewDelhi.htm; Ambassador YOUSSOUF OMAR DOUALEH.

Japan: 5-18-10, Shimo Meguro, Meguro-ku, Tokyo 153-0064; tel. (3) 5704-0682; fax (3) 5725-8305; internet www.angelfire.com/de3/djibouti-embassy-tok; Ambassador Ahmed Araita Ali.

Kenya: Comcraft House, 2nd Floor, Haile Selassie Ave, POB 59528, Nairobi; tel. (20) 339640; Ambassador ADEN HOUSSEIN ABDILLLAHI.

Saudi Arabia: POB 94340, Riyadh 11693; tel. (1) 454-3182; fax (1) 456-9168; e-mail dya_bamakhrama@hotmail.com; Ambassador Dya-Eddine Said Bamakhrama.

Somalia: Mogadishu; .

United States of America: 1156 15th St, NW, Suite 515, Washington, DC 20005; tel. (202) 331-0270; fax (202) 331-0302; Ambassador Roblé Olhaye.

Yemen: POB 3322, 6 Amman St, San'a; tel. (1) 445236; fax (1) 445237; e-mail youssouf@y.net.ye; Ambassador YOUSSOUF OMAR DOUALEH.

DIPLOMATIC MISSIONS OF DOMINICAN REPUBLIC

United Nations: 144 East 44th St, 4th Floor, New York, NY 10017; tel. (212) 867-0833; fax (212) 986-4694; e-mail drun@un.int; internet www.un.int/dr; Permanent Representative Erasmo Lara-Peña.

Argentina: Santa Fe 830, 7°, C1059ABP Buenos Aires; tel. (11) 4312-9378; fax (11) 4894-2078; e-mail consuldo@hotmail.com; Ambassador RAFAEL CALVENTI.

Belgium: 12 ave Bel Air, 1180 Brussels; tel. (2) 346-49-35; fax (2) 346-51-52; e-mail embajadombxl@brutele.be; Ambassador Federico Alberto Cuello Camilo.

Brazil: SHIS, QL 06, Conj. 07, Casa 02, 71626-075 Brasília, DF; tel. (61) 3248-1405; fax (61) 3364-3214; e-mail embdombrasil@serex.gov.do; Ambassador MANUEL MORALES LAMA.

Canada: 130 Albert St, Suite 418, Ottawa, ON K1P 5G4; tel. (613) 569-9893; fax (613) 569-8673; e-mail info@drembassy.org; internet www.drembassy.org; Ambassador Luis Arias Nuñez.

Chile: Candelaria Goyenechea 4153, Vitacura, Santiago; tel. (2) 953-7570; e-mail mvelazquez@serex.gov.do; Ambassador CÉSAR MEDINA ABREU.

China (Taiwan): 6/F, Lane 62, Tien Mou West Rd, Taipei 11156; tel. (2) 28751357; fax (2) 28752661; e-mail embajada_dom_entaipei@hotmail.com; Ambassador Víctor Manuel Sánchez.

Colombia: Calle 100, No 19-61, Of. 402, Bogotá, DC; tel. (1) 635-3627; fax (1) 635-3884; e-mail embajado@cable.net.co; Ambassador RAÚL FERNANDO DE JESÚS BARRIENTO LARA.

Costa Rica: McDonald's de Curridabat 400 sur, 90 m este, Apdo 4746, 1000 San José; tel. 283-8103; fax 280-7604; e-mail embdominicanacr@racsa.co.cr; Ambassador Adonaida Medina Rodríguez.

Cuba: Avda 5, No 9202, entre 92 y 94, Miramar, Havana; tel. (7) 204-8429; fax (7) 204-8431; Ambassador DANIEL GUERRERO TAVERAS.

Ecuador: Edif. Albatros, Avda de los Shyris 1240 y Portugal, 2°, Apdo 17-01-387-A, Quito; tel. (2) 243-4232; e-mail emrepdom@interactive.net.ec; Ambassador Néstor Juan Cerón Suero.

El Salvador: Edif. Colinas 1°, Blvd El Hipódromo 253, Zona Rosa, Col. San Benito, San Salvador; tel. 2223-4036; fax 2223-3109; e-mail endosal@saltel.net; Ambassador ROBERTO VICTORIA.

France: 45 rue de Courcelles, 75008 Paris; tel. 1-53-63-95-95; fax 1-45-63-35-63; e-mail embajadom@wanadoo.fr; internet www.amba-dominicaine-paris.com; Ambassador Guillermo Piña-Contreras Zeller.

Germany: Dessauer Str. 28–29, 10963 Berlin; tel. (30) 25757760; fax (30) 25757761; e-mail embajadomal@t-online.de; Ambassador PEDRO LUCIANO VERGES CIMAN.

Guatemala: Edif. Géminis 10, Suite 804, Torre Sur, 12 Calle 1-25, Zona 10, Guatemala City; tel. 2338-2170; fax 2338-2171; e-mail embardom@intelnet.net.gt; Ambassador Teresa Migdalia Torres García.

Haiti: rue Panaméricaine 121, BP 56, Pétionville, Port-au-Prince; tel. 257-0568; fax 221-8718; e-mail embrepdomhai@yahoo.com; Ambassador JOSÉ SERULLE RAMIA.

Honduras: Calle Principal frente al Banco Continental, Col. Miramontes, Tegucigalpa; tel. 239-0130; fax 239-1594; e-mail embadom@compunet.hn; Ambassador José del Carmen Acosta Carrasco.

India: 1st Floor, 4 Munirka Marg, Vasant Vihar, New Delhi 110 057; tel. (11) 46015000; fax (11) 46015004; e-mail info@dr-embassy-india.com; Ambassador FRANK HANS DANNENBERG.

Israel: 19/1 Soutine St, Tel-Aviv 64884; tel. 3-5277073; fax 3-5277074; e-mail embajdom@netvision.net.il; Ambassador Leonardo Cohen.

Italy: Via Giuseppe Pisanelli 1, int. 8, 00196 Roma; tel. (06) 36004377; fax (06) 36004380; e-mail embajadadominicana@yahoo.it; Chargé d'affaires a.i. IGNACIO MANUEL GONZÁLEZ FRANCO.

Jamaica: 32 Earls Court, Kingston 8; tel. 755-4155; fax 755-4156; e-mail domemb@cwjamaica.com; Ambassador Filomena Altagracia Navarro Tavarez.

Japan: Kowa Bldg, No. 38, Room 904, 4-12-24, Nishi Azabu, Minato-ku, Tokyo 106-0031; tel. (3) 3499-6020; fax (3) 3499-2627; e-mail embdomjapon@serex.gov.do; Ambassador JOSÉ UREÑA.

Korea, Republic: Taepyeong-no Bldg, 19th Floor, 2-ga, 310 Taepyeong-no, Jung-gu, Seoul; tel. (2) 756-3513; fax (2) 756-3514; e-mail embadom@kornet.net; Ambassador Héctor Galuán.

Mexico: Bahía Magdalena 148, Of. 307, (entre Bahía de Caracas y Bahía de las Palmas), Col. Verónica Anzures, Del. Miguel Hidalgo, 11300 México, DF; tel. (55) 5260-7262; e-mail embajada@ambadom.org.mx; internet www.embadom.org.mx; Ambassador PABLO A. MARIÑEZ ALVAREZ.

Netherlands: Raamweg 21–22, 2596 HL The Hague; tel. (70) 3317553; fax (70) 4049890; e-mail embajada@embajadadominicana.nl; Ambassador Guido d'Alessandro.

Nicaragua: Reparto Las Colinas, Prado Ecuestre 100, con Curva de los Gallos, Apdo 614, Managua; tel. 276-2029; fax 276-0654; e-mail embdom@alfanumeric.com.ni; Ambassador PEDRO BLANDINO.

Panama: Casa 40a, Calle 75, Apdo 6250, Panamá 5; tel. 270-3884; fax 270-3886; e-mail embajdom@sinfo.net; Ambassador Virgilio Augusto Alvarez Bonilla.

Peru: Calle Tudela y Varela 360, San Isidro, Lima; tel. (1) 4219765; fax (1) 4219763; e-mail embdomperu@terra.com.pe; Ambassador RAFAEL JULIÁN CEDANO.

Portugal: Av. das Forças Armadas 133, Quinta das Mil Flores, Bloco B, Escritório 3, 1600-081 Lisbon; tel. (21) 7247030; fax (21) 7247039; e-mail embdomportugal@serex.gov.do; Ambassador Marina Isabel Cáceres Estévez.

Spain: Paseo de la Castellana 30, 28046 Madrid; tel. (91) 4315395; fax (91) 4358139; e-mail embajada@embajadadominicana.es; internet www.embajadadominicana.es; Ambassador ALEJANDRO GONZÁLEZ PONS.

Sweden: Sibyllegt. 13, 4th Floor, POB 5584, 114 85 Stockholm; tel. (8) 667-46-11; fax (8) 667-51-05; e-mail stockholm@domemb.se; Ambassador Marina Isabel Cacres de Estvez.

Switzerland: Wettpoststr. 4, Postfach 22, 3000 Bern 15; tel. 313511585; fax 313511587; e-mail embaj.rep-dom@freesurf.ch; Ambassador JOSÉ TOMÁS ARES GERMÁN.

Trinidad and Tobago: Suite 8, 1 Dere St, Queen's Park West, Port of Spain; tel. 624-7930; fax 623-7779; e-mail embdomtrinidadytobago@serex.gov.do; Ambassador José Manuel Castillo Betances.

United Kingdom: 139 Inverness Terrace, London, W2 6JF; tel. (9065) 508945; fax (20) 7727-3693; e-mail info@dominicanembassy.org.uk; internet www.dominicanembassy.org.uk; Ambassador ANÍBAL DE CASTRO.

United States of America: 1715 22nd St, NW, Washington, DC 20008; tel. (202) 332-6280; fax (202) 265-8057; e-mail embassy@us.serex.gov.do; internet www.domrep.org; Ambassador Flavio Dario Espinal.

Uruguay: Tomás de Tezanos 1186, 11300 Montevideo; tel. (2) 6287766; fax (2) 6289655; e-mail embajadomuruguay@hotmail.com; Ambassador SILVIO ANTONIO HERASME PEÑA.

Vatican City: Lungotevere Marzio 3, 00186 Rome, Italy; tel. (06) 6864084; e-mail embajadardss@tiscali.it; Ambassador Rafael Marion-Landais.

Venezuela: Edif. Argentum, Ofs 1 y 2, 2a Transversal, entre 1a Avda y Avda Andrés Bello, Los Palos Grandes, Caracas 1060; tel. (212) 283-3709; fax (212) 283-3965; e-mail embdomvenezuela@serex.gov.do; Ambassador JAIME DURÁN HERNÁNDEZ.

DIPLOMATIC MISSIONS OF DOMINICA

United Nations: 800 Second Ave, Suite 400h, New York, NY 10017; tel. (212) 949-0853; fax (212) 808-4975; e-mail dominica@un.int; Permanent Representative Simon Paul Richards.

Canada (see entry for Antigua and Barbuda).

China, People's Republic: 1-12-1, Tayuan Diplomatic Office Bldg, 14 Liangmahe Lu, Chao Yang Qu, Beijing; e-mail dominica@dominicaembassy.com; AmbassadorDavid King Hsiu.

United Kingdom: 1 Collingham Gdns, London, SW5 0HW; tel. (20) 7370-5194; fax (20) 7373-8743; e-mail dominicahighcom@btconnect.com; High Commr AGNES ADONIS (acting).

United States of America: 3216 New Mexico Ave, NW, Washington, DC 20016; tel. (202) 364-6781; fax (202) 364-6791; e-mail embdomdc@aol.com; Chargé d'affaires a.i. Judith Ann Rolle.

DIPLOMATIC MISSIONS OF ECUADOR

United Nations: 866 United Nations Plaza, Rm 516, New York, NY 10017; tel. (212) 935-1680; fax (212) 935-1835; e-mail ecuador@un.int; internet www.un.int/ecuador; Permanent Representative MARIA FERNANDA ESPINOSA GARCES.

Argentina: Quintana 585, 9° y 10°, C1129ABB Buenos Aires; tel. (11) 4804-0073; fax (11) 4804-0074; e-mail embecuador@embecuador.com.ar; Ambassador Francisco Ernesto Proaño Arandi.

Australia: 6 Pindari Crescent, O'Malley, ACT 2606; tel. (2) 6286-4021; fax (2) 6286-1231; e-mail embecu@bigpond.net.au; internet www .embassyecuadoraustralia.org.au; Ambassador LUIS ANTONIO RODAS-POSSO.

Austria: Goldschmiedgasse 10/2/24, 1010 Vienna; tel. (1) 535-32-08; fax (1) 535-08-97; e-mail mecaustria@chello.at; Ambassador Byron Morejon Almeida.

Belgium: 363 ave Louise, 1050 Brussels; tel. (2) 644-30-50; fax (2) 644-28-13; e-mail amb.equateur@skynet.be; internet www.ecuador.be; Ambassador FERNANDO YÉPEZ LASSO.

Bolivia: Edif. Hermman, 14°, Plaza Venezuela 1440, Casilla 406, La Paz; tel. (2) 278-4422; fax (2) 277-1043; e-mail eecuabolivia@mmrree.gov.ec; Ambassador Leonardo Carrión Eguigurren.

Brazil: SHIS, QI 11, Conj. 09, Casa 24, 71625-290 Brasília, DF; tel. (61) 3248-5560; fax (61) 3248-1290; e-mail embeq@solar.com.br; internet www .embequador.org.br; Ambassador EDUARDO RODRIGO ALFONSO MORA-ANDA.

Canada: 50 O'Connor St, Suite 316, Ottawa, ON K1P 6L2; tel. (613) 563-8206; fax (613) 235-5776; e-mail mecuacan@rogers.com; internet www .vivecuador.com; Ambassador Fernando Ribadeneira Fernández Salvador.

Chile: Avda Providencia 1979 y Pedro Valdivia, 5°, Santiago; tel. (2) 231-5073; fax (2) 232-5833; e-mail embajadaecuador@adsl.tie.cl; internet www .embajadaecuador.cl; Ambassador FRANCISCO BORJA CEVALLOS.

China, People's Republic: 2-62 San Li Tun Office Bldg, Chaoyang Qu, 100600 Beijing; tel. (10) 65323158; fax (10) 65324371; e-mail embecuch@public3bta .net.cn; Ambassador Washington Hago.

Colombia: Edif. Fernando Mazuera, 7°, Calle 72, No 6-30, Bogotá, DC; tel. (1) 212-6549; fax (1) 212-6536; e-mail eecucolombia@mmrree.gov.ec; internet www.embajadaecuacol.net; Ambassador FRANCISCO SUÉSCUM OTTATI.

Costa Rica: Edif. de la esq. sureste del Museo Nacional, 125 m al este, Avda 2, Calles 19 y 21, Apdo 1374, 1000 San José; tel. 232-1503; fax 232-1503; e-mail cecusanjose@mmrree.gov.ec; internet www.consuladoecuadorsj.com; Ambassador Dr Juan Leoro Almeida.

Cuba: Avda 5A, No 4407, entre 44 y 46, Miramar, Havana; tel. (7) 204-2034; fax (7) 204-2868; e-mail embecuad@ceniai.inf.cu; Chargé d'affaires a.i. OSCAR GARCÍA ENDARA.

Dominican Republic: Rafael Augusto Sánchez 17, Edif. Profesional Saint Michel, Of. 301, Ensanche Naco, Apdo 808, Santo Domingo, DN; tel. 563-8363; fax 563-8153; e-mail mecuador@yahoo.com; Ambassador Carlos Alonso Manrique Muñoz.

Egypt: Suez Canal Bldg, 4 Sharia Ibn Kasir, Cairo (Giza); tel. (2) 3496782; fax (2) 3609327; e-mail ecuademb@idsc.gov.eg; Ambassador FRANKLIN BAHAMONDE.

El Salvador: Pasaje Los Pinos 241, entre 77 y 79 Avda Norte, San Salvador; tel. 2263-5258; e-mail ecuador@integra.com.sv; Ambassador Dr Galo Larenas Serrano.

France: 34 ave de Messine, 75008 Paris; tel. 1-45-61-10-21; fax 1-42-56-06-64; e-mail embajadaenfrancia@ambassade-equateur.fr; internet www .ambassade-equateur.fr; Ambassador MARCO ERAZO BOLAÑOS.

Germany: Joachimstaler Str. 10–12, 10719 Berlin; tel. (30) 8009695; fax (30) 800969699; e-mail alemania@embassy-ecuador.org; Ambassador Horacio Hernán Sevilla Borja.

Guatemala: 4 Avda 12-04, Zona 14, Guatemala City; tel. 2337-2994; fax 2368-1831; e-mail embecuad@guate.net; Ambassador ROBERTO PONCE ALVAREDO.

Honduras: Casa 2968, Sendero Senecio, Col. Castaños Sur, Apdo 358, Tegucigalpa; tel. 221-1049; fax 235-4074; e-mail mecuahon@multivisionhn .net; Ambassador Fernando Chávez Dávila.

Hungary: 1023 Budapest, Levél u. 4; tel. (1) 315-2114; fax (1) 315-2104; e-mail embajada@ecuador.hu; internet www.ecuador.hu; Ambassador DR ALFONSO LÓPEZ ARAUJO.

India: C-156 Second Floor, Defence Colony, New Delhi 110 014; tel. (11) 51555602; fax (11) 51555604; e-mail eecuindia@mmrree.gov.ec; Chargé d'affaires Carlos Abad Ortiz.

Indonesia: World Trade Center, 17th Floor, Jalan Jenderal Sudirman, Kav. 31, Jakarta 12920; tel. (21) 5211484; fax (21) 5226954; e-mail ecuadorinindonesia@gmail.com; Ambassador RODRIGO YÉPEZ ENRÍQUEZ.

Israel: Asia House, 4 Rehov Weizman, Tel-Aviv 64239; tel. 3-6958764; fax 3-6913604; e-mail mecuaisr@infolink.net.il; Ambassador Francisco Riofrío Maldonado.

Italy: Via Antonio Bertoloni 8, 00197 Roma; tel. (06) 45439007; fax (06) 8076271; e-mail mecuroma@flashnet.it; Ambassador GEOCONDA GALÁN CASTELO.

Japan: Kowa Bldg, No. 38, Room 806, 4-12-24, Nishi Azabu, Minato-ku, Tokyo 106-0031; tel. (3) 3499-2800; fax (3) 3499-4400; e-mail ecujapon@alto .ocn.ne.jp; internet www.ecuador-embassy.or.jp; Chargé d'affaires a.i. Juan Larrea Miño.

Korea, Republic: Korea First Bldg, 19th Floor, 100, Gongpyeong-dong, Jongno-gu, Seoul; tel. (2) 739-2401; fax (2) 739-2355; e-mail mecuadorcor1@ kornet.net; Ambassador JOSÉ ENRIQUE NÚÑEZ TAMAYO.

Malaysia: 10th Floor, West Block, Wisma Selangor Dredging, 142c Jalan Ampang, 50450 Kuala Lumpur; tel. (3) 21635078; fax (3) 21635096; e-mail embecua@po.jaring.my; Ambassador Manuel Pesantes.

Mexico: Tennyson 217, Col. Polanco, Del. Miguel Hidalgo, 11560 México, DF; tel. (55) 5545-3141; fax (55) 5254-2442; e-mail mecuamex@prodigy.net .mx; Ambassador GALO GALARZA DÁVILA.

Netherlands: Koninginnegracht 84, 2514 AJ The Hague; tel. (70) 3463763; fax (70) 3658910; e-mail ambassade@ambassadevanecuador.nl; internet www .embajadaecuador.nl; Ambassador Dr Rodrigo Guillermo Riofrío Machuca.

Nicaragua: De los Pipitos $1\frac{1}{2}$ c. abajo, Apdo C-33, Managua; tel. 268-1098; fax 266-8081; e-mail ecuador@ibw.com.ni; Ambassador GONZALO ANDRADE RIVERA.

Panama: Edif. Torre 2000, 6°, Calle 50, Marbella, Bellavista, Panamá; e-mail eecuador@cwpanama.net; tel. 264-2654; fax 223-0159; Ambassador Elsa Beatriz Villacís Roca.

Paraguay: Justo Román y Julio C. Escobar, esq. Barrio Manorá, Casilla 13162, Asunción; tel. (21) 61-4814; fax (21) 61-4813; e-mail mecuapy@ conexion.com.py; Ambassador JULIO CÉSAR PRADO ESPINOSA.

Peru: Las Palmeras 356 y Javier Prado Oeste, San Isidro, Lima 27; tel. (1) 2124171; fax (1) 4220711; e-mail embajada@mecuadorperu.org.pe; internet www.mecuadorperu.org.pe; Ambassador Diego Ribadeneira Espinosa.

Poland: 02-516 Warsaw, ul. Rejtana 15/15; tel. (22) 8487230; fax (22) 8488196; e-mail eccupolonia@mmrree.gov.ec; Ambassador FERNANDO FLORES MACÍAS.

Russian Federation: 103064 Moscow, Gorokhovskii per. 12; tel. (499) 261-55-27; fax (499) 267-70-79; e-mail embajada@ecuaemb.ru; internet www .ecuaemb.ru; Ambassador Patricio Chávez.

Spain: Velázquez 114, 2°, 28006 Madrid; tel. (91) 5627215; fax (91) 7450244; e-mail embajada@mecuador.es; Ambassador NICOLÁS ISSA OBANDO.

Sweden: Engelbrektsgt. 13, 114 32 Stockholm; tel. (8) 679-60-43; fax (8) 611-55-93; e-mail suecia@embajada-ecuador.se; internet www.embajada-ecuador .se; Ambassador Roberto Betancourt Ruales.

Switzerland: Kramgasse 54, 3011 Bern; tel. 313516254; fax 313512771; e-mail embecusuiza@bluewin.ch; Ambassador JAIME MARCHAN ROMERO.

United Kingdom: Flat 3b, 3 Hans Cres., Knightsbridge, London, SW1X 0LS; tel. (20) 7584-1367; fax (20) 7823-9701; e-mail eecugranbretania@mmrree .gov.ec; Chargé d'affaires a.i. Déborah Salgado Campaña.

United States of America: 2535 15th St, NW, Washington, DC 20009; tel. (202) 234-7200; fax (202) 667-3482; e-mail embassy@ecuador.org; internet www.ecuador.org; Ambassador LUIS BENIGNO GALLEGOS CHIRIBOGA.

Uruguay: Pedro Berro 1217, entre Guayaquí y Pereira, Montevideo; tel. (2) 7076463; fax (2) 7076465; e-mail embajadaecuador@netgate.com.uy; Ambassador Edmundo Vera Manzo.

Vatican City: Via di Porta Angelica 64, 00193 Rome, Italy; tel. (06) 6897179; fax (06) 68892786; e-mail mecuadorsantasede@ecuaemss.it; Ambassador FAUSTO CÓRDOVEZ CHIRIBOGA.

Venezuela: Centro Andrés Bello, Torre Oeste, 13°, Avda Andrés Bello, Maripérez, Apdo 62124, Caracas 1060; tel. (212) 265-0801; fax (212) 264-6917; e-mail embajadaecuador@cantv.net; Ambassador Gen. (retd) René Vargas Pazos.

DIPLOMATIC MISSIONS OF EGYPT

United Nations: 304 East 44th St, New York, NY 10017; tel. (212) 503-0300; fax (212) 949-5999; e-mail egypt@un.int; Permanent Representative MAGED ABDELFATTAH ABDELAZIZ.

Afghanistan: Road 15, Wazir Akbar Khan, Kabul; tel. (20) 2021901; fax (20) 2104064; e-mail egypt_kabul@mfa.gov.eg; Ambassador Mohammad Sharif Hassan Rayhan.

Albania: Rruga Skënderbej 43, Tirana; tel. (4) 233022; fax (4) 232295; Ambassador REFAAT AL-ANSARI.

Algeria: BP 297, 8 chemin Abd al-Kader Gadouche, 16300 Hydra, Algiers; tel. (21) 69-16-73; fax (21) 69-29-52; Ambassador Abd al-Aziz Shawki Seif an-Nasr.

Angola: Rua Comandante Stona 247, Alvalade, CP 3704, Luanda; tel. 222321590; fax 222323285; e-mail embegipto@ebonet.net; Ambassador BELAL ABD EL-WAHED EL-MASRY.

Argentina: Virrey del Pino 3140, C1426EHF Buenos Aires; tel. (11) 4553-3311; fax (11) 4553-0067; e-mail embegypt@fibertel.com.ar; Ambassador Youssef Hassan Shawki.

Armenia: Yerevan, Sepuhi St 6A; tel. (10) 22-01-17; fax (10) 22-64-25; e-mail egyemb@arminco.com; Ambassador WAHID GALAL.

Australia: 1 Darwin Ave, Yarralumla, ACT 2600; tel. (2) 6273-4437; fax (2) 6273-4279; Ambassador Mohamed M. Tawfik.

Austria: Hohe Warte 50–54, 1190 Vienna; tel. (1) 370-81-04; fax (1) 370-81-04-27; e-mail egyptembassyvienna@egyptembassyvienna.at; internet www.egyptembassyvienna.at; Ambassador EHAB MUHAMMAD MOSTAFA FAWZI.

Azerbaijan: 1000 Baku, Hasan Aliyev küç. 7; tel. (12) 498-79-06; fax (12) 498-79-54; e-mail emb.egypt@azeuro.net; Ambassador Youssef Ahmed Ibrahem Ash-Sharkawy.

Bahrain: POB 818, Mahouz, Manama; tel. 17720005; fax 17721518; e-mail egyembbh@batelco.com.bh; internet www.geocities.com/egyptemb; Ambassador DR AZMY HASSAN KHALIFA.

Bangladesh: House NE (N) 9, Rd 90, Gulshan Model Town, Dhaka 1212; tel. (2) 8858737; fax (2) 8858747; e-mail egypt_embassy_dhaka@themail.com; Ambassador Fayez Mustafa Noseir.

Belgium: 19 ave de l'Uruguay, 1000 Brussels; tel. (2) 663-58-00; fax (2) 675-58-88; e-mail eg.sec.be@hotmail.com; Ambassador DR MAHMOUD KAREM MAHMOUD.

Benin: Lot G26, route de l'Aéroport, BP 1215, Cotonou; tel. 21-30-08-42; fax 21-30-14-25; Ambassador Osama Tawfeek Badr.

Bolivia: Avda Ballivián 599, Casilla 2956, La Paz; tel. (2) 278-6511; fax (2) 278-4325; e-mail embajadaegipto@acelerate.com; Ambassador NAGWA MOHAMED AFIFI.

Bosnia and Herzegovina: 71000 Sarajevo, Nurudina Gackića 58; tel. (33) 666498; fax (33) 666499; e-mail eg.em.sa@bih.net.ba; Ambassador Ahmed el-Sayed Khattab.

Brazil: SEN, Av. das Nações, Lote 12, 70435-900 Brasília, DF; tel. (61) 3323-8800; fax (61) 3323-1039; e-mail embegito@opengate.com.br; internet www.opengate.com.br/embegito; Ambassador MUHAMMAD ABD AL-FATTAH ABDALLAH.

Bulgaria: 1000 Sofia, ul. 6-ti Septemvri 5, POB 1025; tel. (2) 987-02-15; fax (2) 980-12-63; e-mail egembsof@spnet.net; Ambassador Heba Salah ad-Din al-Marassy.

Burkina Faso: Zone du Conseil de L'Entente, blvd du Faso, 04 BP 7042, Ouagadougou 04; tel. 50-30-66-39; fax 50-31-38-36; e-mail egyptianembassy@liptinfor.bf; Ambassador MUHAMMAD MAMDOUH ALI EL-ASHMAWI.

Burundi: 31 ave de la Liberté, BP 1520, Bujumbura; tel. 22223161; fax 22222918; Ambassador Muhammad Abdul el-Khader el-Khasab.

Cameroon: 718 rue 1828, Quartier Bastos, BP 809, Yaoundé; tel. 2220-3922; fax 2220-2647; Ambassador MOHAMED SA'AD M. AKL.

Canada: 454 Laurier Ave East, Ottawa, ON K1N 6R3; tel. (613) 234-4931; fax (613) 234-9347; e-mail egyptemb@sympatico.ca; Ambassador Mahmoud F. es-Saeed.

Central African Republic: angle ave Léopold Sédar Senghor et rue Emile Gentil, BP 1422, Bangui; tel. 61-46-88; fax 61-35-45; e-mail ambassadedEgypt_Centreafrique@excite.com; Ambassador HANI RIAD MO'AWAD.

Chad: Quartier Clemat, ave Georges Pompidou, auprès rond-point de la SONASUT, BP 1094, N'Djamena; tel. 51-09-73; fax 51-09-72; e-mail ambegyndj@africamail.com; Ambassador Khaled Abdallah Shehata.

Chile: Roberto del Río 1871, Providencia, Santiago; tel. (2) 274-8881; fax (2) 274-6334; e-mail egipto@ctcinternet.cl; Ambassador ASHRAF YOSSEF ZA'ZA.

China, People's Republic: 2 Ri Tan Dong Lu, Jian Guo Men Wai, Beijing 100600; tel. (10) 65321825; fax (10) 65325365; Ambassador Mahmoud Allam.

Colombia: Transversal 19A 101-10, Bogotá, DC; tel. (1) 256-2940; fax (1) 256-9255; e-mail embegyptbta@unete.com; Ambassador MOHAMED AHDY KHAIRAT.

Congo, Democratic Republic: 519 ave de l'Ouganda, BP 8838, Kinshasa; tel. (51) 10137; fax (88) 03728; Ambassador Mortda Aly Mohamed Lashin.

Congo, Republic: 7 bis ave Bayardelle, BP 917, Brazzaville; tel. 81-07-94; fax 81-15-33; Ambassador MEDHAT KAMAL ABD EL-RAOF EL-KADI.

Côte d'Ivoire: Immeuble El Nasr, rue du Commerce, 01 BP 2104, Abidjan 01; tel. 20-32-79-25; fax 20-22-30-53; e-mail amegypteci@afnet.net; Ambassador Sherif Youssef Abbas Soliman.

Croatia: 10000 Zagreb, Petrova 51B; tel. (1) 2310781; fax (1) 2310619; e-mail veleposlanstvo.egipat@zg.t-com.hr; Chargé d'affaires a.i. EMAN MOHAMED ZAKI MOHARRAM.

Cuba: Avda 5, No 1801, esq. 18, Miramar, Havana; tel. (7) 204-2441; fax (7) 204-0905; e-mail emegipto@enet.cu; Ambassador Abdel Fattah Moustafa Ezz Eldin.

Cyprus: POB 21752, 14 Ayios Prokopios St, Engomi, 2406 Nicosia; tel. 22449050; fax 22449081; e-mail info@egyptianembassy.org.cy; internet www.egyptianembassy.org.cy; Ambassador AHMAD IBRAHIM RAGHEB.

Czech Republic: Pelléova 14, 160 00 Prague 6; tel. 224311506; fax 224311157; e-mail embassyegypt@centrum.cz; Ambassador Amal Mostafa K. Mourad.

Denmark: Kristianiagade 19, 2100 Copenhagen Ø; tel. 35-43-70-70; fax 35-25-32-62; e-mail egyptembassydenmark@yahoo.com; Ambassador AFAF ALI SAYED AL-MAZARIKI.

Djibouti: BP 1989, Djibouti; tel. 351231; fax 356657; e-mail ambegypte2004@gawab.com; Ambassador Ahmed Abdel Wahed Zein.

Ecuador: Avda Tarqui 4-56 y Avda 6 de Diciembre, Apdo 9355, Quito; tel. (2) 222-5240; fax (2) 256-3521; e-mail embegipto@ecnet.ec; Ambassador SUZANNE MOHAMED GAMIL NOAH.

Eritrea: 5 Dej Afworki St, POB 5570, Asmara; tel. (1) 123294; Ambassador Ibrahim Khalil Abdallah.

Ethiopia: POB 1611, Addis Ababa; tel. (11) 1226422; fax (11) 1226432; Ambassador SHAMEL NASSER.

Finland: Itäinen puistotie 2, POB 183, 00140 Helsinki; tel. (9) 4777470; fax (9) 47774721; e-mail secretaryofembassy@hotmail.com; Ambassador Maasoum Mostafa Marzouk.

France: 56 ave d'Iéna, 75116 Paris; tel. 1-53-67-88-30; fax 1-47-23-06-43; e-mail ambassadedegypteaparis@hotmail.com; internet www.ambassade-egypte.com; Ambassador NASSER KAMEL.

Gabon: Immeuble Floria, 1 blvd de la Mer, Quartier Batterie IV, BP 4240, Libreville; tel. 73-25-38; fax 73-25-19; Ambassador Ahmed Muhammad Taha Awad.

Germany: Stauffenbergstr. 6–7, 10785 Berlin; tel. (30) 4775470; fax (30) 4771049; e-mail embassy@egyptian-embassy.de; internet www.egyptian-embassy.de; Ambassador MUHAMMAD ABD AL-HAY M. AL-ORABI.

Ghana: 38 Senchi St, Airport Residential Area, Accra; tel. (21) 776795; fax (21) 777579; e-mail boustaneaccra@hotmail.com; Ambassador Seif Allah Mostafa Abdul Maguid Noseir.

Greece: Leoforos Vassilissis Sofias 3, 106 71 Athens; tel. (210) 3618612; fax (210) 3603538; Ambassador HAMDY SANAD LOZA.

Guatemala: Edif. Cobella, 5°, 5 Avda 10-84, Zona 14, Apdo 502, Guatemala City; tel. 2333-6296; fax 2368-2808; e-mail egyptemb@gold.guate.net.gt; Ambassador Maher Ibrahim Youssef Badar.

Guinea: Corniche Sud, BP 389, Conakry; tel. 30-41-23-94; e-mail ambconakry@hotmail.com; Ambassador MOHAMED ABD ELHAY HASSOUNA.

Hungary: 1125 Budapest, Istenhegyi u. 7b; tel. (1) 225-2150; fax (1) 225-8596; e-mail egyemb@pronet.hu; Ambassador Hisham el-Zimaity.

India: 1/50M Niti Marg, Chanakyapuri, New Delhi 110 021; tel. (11) 26114096; fax (11) 26885355; e-mail egypt@del2.vsnl.net.in; Ambassador MUHAMMAD ABDUL HAMEED HIJAZI.

Indonesia: Jalan Denpasar Raya, Blok A12, No. 1, Kuningan Timur, Setiabudi, Jakarta Selatan 12950; tel. (21) 5204359; fax (21) 5204792; e-mail egypt@indosat.net.id; internet www.mfa.gov.eg/missions/indonesia/jakarta/embassy/en-gb/; Ambassador Mohamed El Sayed Taha.

Iraq: 103/11/601 Hay al-Mansour, Baghdad; tel. (1) 543-0572; fax (1) 242-5839; e-mail egypt@uruklink.net; Ambassador (vacant).

Ireland: 12 Clyde Rd, Dublin 4; tel. (1) 6606566; fax (1) 6683745; e-mail info@embegyptireland.ie; internet www.embegyptireland.ie; Ambassador Amr Mostafa Helmy.

Israel: 54 Rehov Bazel, Tel-Aviv 62744; tel. 3-5464151; fax 3-5441615; e-mail egypem.ta@zahav.net.il; Ambassador MUHAMMAD ASIM IBRAHIM.

Italy: Villa Savoia, Via Salaria 267, 00199 Roma; tel. (06) 84401976; fax (06) 8554424; e-mail amb.egi@pronet.it; internet www.mfa.gov.eg/missions/italy/ rome/embassy/en-gb; Ambassador Muhammad Ashraf Gaml Eldin Rashed.

Japan: 1-5-4, Aobadai, Meguro-ku, Tokyo 153-0042; tel. (3) 3770-8022; fax (3) 3770-8021; e-mail egyptemb@mc.kcom.ne.jp; internet www.embassy -avenue.jp/egypt/index.htm; AmbassadorWALID ABDELNASSER.

Jordan: POB 35178, 14 Riyad el-Mefleh St, Amman 11180; tel. (6) 5605202; fax (6) 5604082; e-mail egypt@embegyptjordan.com; Ambassador Ahmad Rezeq.

Kazakhstan: 050010 Almaty, Muhammed Haidar Dulati 80; tel. (727) 269-15-93; fax (727) 291-10-22; e-mail egyptianemb_kz@yahoo.com; Ambassador ABDEL MAWJOOD AHMED AL-HABASHI.

Kenya: Kingara Rd, Lavington, POB 30285, Nairobi; tel. (20) 570360; fax (20) 570383; Ambassador Saher Hasaneen Tawfeek Hamza.

Korea, Democratic People's Republic: 39 Munsudong, Taedongkang District, Pyongyang; tel. (2) 3817414; fax (2) 3817611; Ambassador (vacant).

Korea, Republic: POB 3734, 46-1, Hannam-dong, Yeongsan-gu, Seoul 140-210; tel. (2) 749-0787; fax (2) 795-2588; e-mail embassyegyptkorea@yahoo .com; Ambassador Mohamed Reda Kamel el-Taify.

Kuwait: POB 11252, 35153 Dasmah, Istiqlal St, Kuwait City; tel. 2519955; fax 2563877; Ambassador ABD ELRAHIM ISMAIL SHALABY.

Lebanon: POB 5037, rue Thomas Eddison, ar-Ramla el-Baida, Beirut; tel. (1) 862917; fax (1) 863751; Ambassador Ahmad al-Bidyawi.

Liberia: Coconut Plantation, Randal St, Mamba Point, POB 462, Monrovia; tel. 226226; fax 226122; Ambassador OMAR ABD EL AZIZ EL SHEEMY.

Libya: POB 1105, The Grand Hotel, Tripoli; tel. (21) 4448909; fax (21) 4449262; e-mail egyembib@hotmail.com; Ambassador Muhammad Fatihy Refa'a et-Tahtawi.

Madagascar: Lot MD 378 Ambalatokana Mandrosoa Ivato, BP 4082, 101 Antananarivo; tel. (20) 2245497; fax (20) 2245379; Ambassador MAGID FOAD SALEH FOAD.

Malawi: 10/247 Tsoka Rd, POB 30451, Lilongwe 3; tel. 1780668; fax 1780691; Ambassador Adel el-Hamid Ahmed Marzouk.

Malaysia: 12 Jalan Rhu, off Jalan Ampang, 55000 Kuala Lumpur; tel. (3) 42568184; fax (3) 42573515; e-mail egyembkl@tm.net.my; Ambassador HANI ABDEL KADER AHMED SHASH.

Mali: Badalabougou-est, BP 44, Bamako; tel. 222-35-65; fax 222-08-91; e-mail mostafa@datatech.net.ml; Ambassador Mostafa Abdel Hamid Gendy.

Malta: Villa Mon Rêve, 10 Sir Temi Zammit St, Ta'Xbiex XBX 1013; tel. 21314158; fax 21319230; e-mail embegmlt@onvol.net; Ambassador ABD AL-KARIM MAHMOUD SOLIMAN.

Mauritania: Villa no. 468, Tevragh Zeina, BP 176, Nouakchott; tel. 525-21-92; fax 525-33-84; Ambassador Bahaa Eddin Mokhtar Mowafi.

Mauritius: Sun Trust Bldg, 2nd floor, Edith Cavell St, Port Louis; tel. 213-1765; fax 213-1768; Ambassador BAKRY ROSHDY EL-AMARY.

Mexico: Alejandro Dumas 131, Col. Polanco, Del. Miguel Hidalgo, 11560 México, DF; tel. (55) 5281-0823; fax (55) 5282-1294; e-mail embofegypt@ prodigy.net.mx; Ambassador Aly Hosussam Eldin Elhefny Mahmoud.

Morocco: 31 rue al-Jazair, 10000 Rabat; tel. (3) 7731833; fax (3) 7706821; e-mail embegypt@mtds.com; Ambassador ACHRAF YOUSUF ABDELHALIM ZAÂZAÂ.

Mozambique: Av. Mao Tse Tung 851, CP 4662, Maputo; tel. 21491118; fax 21491489; e-mail egypt2@tropical.co.mz; Ambassador Hamdy Abd Elwahab Saleh.

Myanmar: 81 Pyidaungsu Yeiktha Rd, Yangon; tel. (1) 222886; fax (1) 222865; Ambassador YOUSSEF KAMAL BOUTROS HANNA.

Namibia: 10 Berg St, POB 11853, Windhoek; tel. (61) 221501; fax (61) 228856; Ambassador Mohamed Hadi Mostafa El-Tonsi.

Nepal: Pulchowk, Lalitpur, POB 792, Kathmandu; tel. (1) 5524812; fax (1) 5522975; Ambassador ABDUL HAMEED MAHMOUD SOLIMAN.

Netherlands: Badhuisweg 92, 2587 CL The Hague; tel. (70) 3542000; fax (70) 3543304; e-mail ambegnl@wanadoo.nl; Ambassador Ahmed Amin Fathallah.

Niger: Terminus Rond-Point Grand Hôtel, BP 254, Niamey; tel. 20-73-33-55; fax 20-73-38-91; Ambassador MOHAMED MAHMOUD MOUSTAFA EL-ASH-MAWI.

Nigeria: Plot 3319, Barada Close, Abuja; tel. (9) 4136091; fax (9) 4132602; Ambassador Mohamed Ashraf Harby Salama.

Norway: Drammensvn 90A, 0244 Oslo; tel. 23-08-42-00; fax 22-56-22-68; e-mail information@egypt-embassy.no; internet www.egypt-embassy.no; Ambassador WAGUIH SAID HANAFI.

Oman: Jamiat ad-Dowal al-Arabiya St, Diplomatic City, Al-Khuwair, POB 2252, Ruwi 112; tel. 24600411; fax 24603626; e-mail egyembmuscat@hotmail .com; Ambassador Izzadin Fahmy Mahmoud.

Pakistan: 38–51, UN Blvd, Diplomatic Enclave, Ramna 5/4, POB 2088, Islamabad; tel. (51) 2209072; fax (51) 2279552; Ambassador HUSSEIN KAMEL HARIDY.

Panama: Calle 55, No 15, El Cangrejo, Apdo 7080, Panamá 5; tel. 263-5020; fax 264-8406; Chargé d'affaires a.i. Tarek Sirag.

Peru: Avda Jorge Basadre 1470, San Isidro, Lima 27; tel. (1) 4402642; fax (1) 4402547; e-mail emb-egypt@amauta.rcp.net.pe; Ambassador DESOUKY ALI FAYED.

Philippines: 2229 Paraiso St, cnr Banyan St, Dasmariñas Village, Makati City, Metro Manila; tel. (2) 8439232; fax (2) 8439239; Ambassador Salwa Moufid Kamel Magarious.

Poland: 03-972 Warsaw, ul. Alzacka 18; tel. (22) 6176973; fax (22) 6179058; e-mail embassyofegypt@neostrada.pl; Ambassador FAHMY AHMED FAYED SALAMA.

Portugal: Av. D. Vasco da Gama 8, 1400-128 Lisbon; tel. (21) 3018301; fax (21) 3017909; e-mail gabemh@egyemb.jazznet.pt; Ambassador Amgad Maher Abdel Ghaffar.

Qatar: POB 2899, Doha; tel. 4832555; fax 4832196; e-mail info@ egyptmbqatar.com; Ambassador ABD AL-AZIZ DAWOUD.

Romania: 010407 Bucharest 1, Bd. Dacia 67; tel. (21) 2110938; fax (21) 2100337; e-mail egyptemb@canad.ro; Ambassador Muhammad al-Sayyid Gohar.

Russian Federation: 119034 Moscow, Kropotkinskii per. 12; tel. (495) 246-02-34; fax (495) 246-10-64; e-mail egyemb_moscow@yahoo.com; Ambassador EZZAT SAAD AS-SAYED AL-BURAEY.

Rwanda: BP 1069, Kigali; tel. 82686; fax 82686; e-mail egypt@rwanda1.com; Ambassador Ahmed Rami Awwad El Hoseni.

Saudi Arabia: POB 94333, Riyadh 11693; tel. (1) 481-0464; fax (1) 481-0463; Ambassador MUHAMMAD ABD AL-HAMID KASSEM.

Senegal: 22 ave Brière de l'Isle, Plateau, BP 474, Dakar; tel. 33-889-2474; fax 33-821-8993; e-mail ambegydk@telecomplus.sn; Ambassador Sanaa Ismail Atta Allah.

Serbia: 11000 Belgrade, Andre Nikolića 12; tel. (11) 2650585; fax (11) 2652036; Ambassador ADEL AHMED NAGUIB.

Sierra Leone: 174c Wilkinson Rd, POB 652, Freetown; tel. (22) 231245; fax (22) 234297; Ambassador Mahmoud Yehia M. Ezzat.

Singapore: 75 Grange Rd, Singapore 249579; tel. 67371811; fax 67323422; e-mail admin@egyptemb-sin.org; Ambassador MOHAMED ELZORKANY.

South Africa: 270 Bourke St, Muckleneuk, Pretoria 0002; POB 30025, Sunnyside 0132; tel. (12) 3431590; fax (12) 3431082; e-mail egyptemb@global .co.za; Ambassador Mona Omar Muhammad Attia.

Spain: Velázquez 69, 28006 Madrid; tel. (91) 5776308; fax (91) 5781732; Ambassador YASSER MORAD HOSSNY.

Sri Lanka: 39 Dickman's Rd, Colombo 5; tel. (11) 2583621; fax (11) 2585292; e-mail egyptemb@sltnet.lk; Ambassador Gihan Amin Mohamed Ali.

Sudan: University St, POB 1126, Khartoum; tel. (183) 777646; fax (183) 778741; e-mail sphinx-egysud@yahoo.com; Ambassador MOHAMED ABDEL MONEIM EL SHAZLY.

Sweden: Strandvägen 35, POB 14230, 104 40 Stockholm; tel. (8) 459-98-60; fax (8) 661-26-64; e-mail egypt.embassy@chello.se; Ambassador Samah Muhammad Sotouhi.

Switzerland: Elfenauweg 61, 3006 Bern; tel. 313528012; fax 313520625; Ambassador NIHAD ZIKRY.

Syria: BP 12443, rue al-Gala'a, Abou Roumaneh, Damascus; tel. (11) 3330756; fax (11) 3337961; fax egyemb@syria.net; Ambassador Shawki Ismail Ali Soliman.

Tanzania: 24 Garden Ave, POB 1668, Dar es Salaam; tel. (22) 2117622; fax (22) 2112543; e-mail egypt.emb.tz@Cats-net.com; Ambassador SABRY MAGDY SABRY.

Thailand: 6 Las Colinas Bldg, 42nd Floor, Sukhumvit 21, Wattana, Bangkok 10110; tel. (2) 661-7184; fax (2) 262-0235; e-mail egyptemb@loxinfo.co.th; Ambassador Mohamed Ashraf Mohamed Kamal El Kholy.

Togo: 1163 rue de l'OCAM, BP 8, Lomé; tel. 221-24-43; fax 221-10-22; Ambassador ADEL MOSTAFA AHMED EL-SALASY.

Tunisia: ave Muhammad V, Quartier Montplaisir, rue 8007, Tunis; tel. (71) 792-233; fax (71) 794-389; e-mail egyembassy.tunis@planet.tn; Ambassador Shadia Hussein Farraq.

Turkey: Atatürk Bul. 126, 06680 Kavaklıdere, Ankara; tel. (312) 4261026; fax (312) 4270099; e-mail egankara@yahoo.com; Ambassador DR ALAA ELDIN A. SHAWKY ELHADIDI.

Uganda: 33 Kololo Hill Dr., POB 4280, Kampala; tel. (41) 4254525; fax (41) 4232103; e-mail egyembug@utlonline.co.ug; Ambassador Reda Abdel Rahman Bebars.

Ukraine: 01901 Kyiv, vul. Observatorna 19; tel. (44) 212-13-27; fax (44) 216-94-28; e-mail eg.emb_kiev@mfa.gov.eg; internet www.mfa.gov.eg/Missions/ukraine/kiev/embassy/en-GB/default; Ambassador YOUSSEF MOUSTAFA ZADA.

United Arab Emirates: POB 4026, Abu Dhabi; tel. (2) 4445566; fax (2) 4449878; e-mail egemb_abudhabi@mfa.gov.eg; Ambassador Muhammad Said Obaid.

United Kingdom: 26 South St, London, W1K 1DW; tel. (20) 7499-3304; fax (20) 7491-1542; e-mail embassy@embassyofegypt.co.uk; internet www.egyptianconsulate.co.uk; Ambassador GEHAD MADI.

United States of America: 3521 International Court, NW, Washington, DC 20008; tel. (202) 895-5400; fax (202) 244-4319; e-mail Embassy@egyptembassy.net; internet www.egyptembassy.net; Ambassador Nabil M. Fahmy.

Uruguay: Avda Brasil 2663, 11300 Montevideo; tel. (2) 7096412; fax (2) 7080977; e-mail boustanemontevideo@easymail.com.uy; Ambassador DR OHIB ANWAR ES-SOUKKARY.

Uzbekistan: 100115 Tashkent, Chilonzor ko'ch. 53a; tel. (71) 120-50-08; fax (71) 120-64-52; Ambassador Nadia Ibrahim Kfafi.

Vatican City: Piazza della Città Leonina 9, 00193 Rome, Italy; tel. (06) 6865878; fax (06) 6832335; e-mail ambegyptvatican@tiscali.it; Ambassador NEVINE SIMAIKA HALIM ABDALLA.

Venezuela: Calle Caucagua con Calle Guaicaipuro, Quinta Maribel, Urb. San Román, Apdo 490007, Caracas; tel. (212) 992-6259; fax (212) 993-1555; e-mail egyptianembassy@cantv.net; Ambassador Essam Saleh Awad Moustafa.

Viet Nam: 63 To Ngoc Van, Quang An, Tay Ho District, Hanoi; tel. (4) 8294999; fax (4) 8294997; e-mail arabegypt@ftp.vn; Ambassador MUHAMMAD ALAA EL-DEIN SAAD EL-LEISI.

Yemen: POB 1134, Gamal Abd an-Nasser St, San'a; tel. (1) 275948; fax (1) 274196; Ambassador Muhammad Morsy Muhammad Awad.

Zambia: Plot 5206, United Nations Ave, Longacres, POB 32428, Lusaka 10101; tel. (1) 250229; fax (1) 254149; Ambassador MOHAMED TAMER SAAD ELDIN MANSOUR.

Zimbabwe: 7 Aberdeen Rd, Avondale, POB A433, Harare; tel. (4) 303445; fax (4) 303115; Ambassador Muhammad Fared Moneib.

DIPLOMATIC MISSIONS OF EL SALVADOR

United Nations: 46 Park Ave, New York, NY 10016; tel. (212) 679-1616; fax (212) 725-7831; e-mail elsalvador@un.int; Permanent Representative CARMEN MARÍA GALLARDO HERNÁNDEZ.

Argentina: Suipacha 1380, 2°, C1011ACD Buenos Aires; tel. (11) 43251-0849; fax (11) 4328-7428; e-mail elsalvador@fibertel.com.ar; internet wwww.embajadaelsalvador.com.ar; Ambassador Guillermo Rubio Funes.

Austria: Prinz-Eugen-Str. 72/2/1, 1040 Vienna; tel. (1) 505-38-74; fax (1) 505-38-76; e-mail sgutierrez@rree.gob.sv; Ambassador VANESSA EUGENIA INTERIANO TOBAR.

Belgium: 171 ave de Tervueren, 1150 Brussels; tel. (2) 733-04-85; fax (2) 735-02-11; e-mail embajadabruselas@rree.gob.sv; Ambassador Héctor González Urrutia.

Belize: 49 Nanche St, POB 215, Belmopan; tel. 823-3404; fax 823-3569; e-mail embasalva@btl.net; Ambassador DR JOSE SERGIO MENA.

Brazil: SHIS, QL 10, Conj. 01, Casa 15, Lago Sul, 71630-100 Brasília, DF; tel. (61) 3364-4141; fax (61) 3364-2459; e-mail elsalvador@embelsalvador.brte.com.br; Ambassador César Edgardo Martínez Flores.

Canada: 209 Kent St, Ottawa, ON K2P 1Z8; tel. (613) 238-2939; fax (613) 238-6940; e-mail embajada@elsalvador-ca.org; Ambassador MAURICIO ROSALES RIVERA.

Chile: Coronel 2330, 5°, Of. 51, Santiago; tel. (2) 233-8324; fax (2) 231-0960; e-mail embasalva@adsl.tie.cl; internet www.rree.gob.sv/embajadas/chile.nsf; Ambassador Aida Elena Minero Reyes.

China (Taiwan): 2/F, 9 Lane 62, Tien Mou West Rd, Shih Lin, Taipei 11156; tel. (2) 28763606; fax (2) 28763514; e-mail embasal.taipei@msa.hinet.net; Ambassador FRANCISCO RICARDO SANTANA BERRÍOS.

Colombia: Edif. El Nogal, Of. 503, Carrera 9a, No 80-15, Bogotá, DC; tel. (1) 349-6765; fax (1) 349-6670; e-mail elsalvador@supercable.net.co; Ambassador Joaquín Alexander Maza Martelli.

Costa Rica: Paseo Colón, Calle 30, Avda 1, No 53, Apdo 1378, 1000 San José; tel. 257-7855; fax 257-7683; e-mail embasacr@sol.racsa.co.cr; Ambassador MILTON JOSÉ COLINDRES UCEDA.

Dominican Republic: Haim López Penha 32, Santo Domingo, DN; tel. 565-4311; fax 541-7503; e-mail emb.salvador@verizon.net.do; Ambassador Ernesto Ferreiro Rusconi.

Ecuador: Edif. Gabriela III, 3°, Avda República de El Salvador 733 y Portugal, Quito; tel. (2) 243-3070; fax (2) 224-2829; e-mail embajada@elsalvador.com.ec; internet www.elsalvador.com.ec; Ambassador RAFAEL ANGEL ALFARO PINEDA.

France: 12 rue Galilée, 75116 Paris; tel. 1-47-20-42-02; fax 1-40-70-01-95; e-mail embparis@wanadoo.fr; Ambassador Joaquín Rodezno Munguia.

Germany: Joachim-Karnatz-Allee 47, 10557 Berlin; tel. (30) 2064660; fax (30) 22488244; e-mail embasalvarfa@googlemail.com; internet www.botschaft-elsalvador.de; Ambassador EDGARDO CARLOS SUÁREZ MALLAGRAY.

Guatemala: Avda las Américas 16-40, Zona 13, Guatemala City; tel. 2360-7660; fax 2334-2069; e-mail emsalva@intelnet.net.gt; Ambassador Gen. (retd) Juan Antonio Martínez Varela.

Honduras: Col. Altos de Miramontes, Casa 2952, Diagonal Aguan, Tegucigalpa; tel. 232-4947; fax 239-6556; e-mail embasalhonduras@rree.gob.sv; internet www.rree.gob.sv/embajadas/honduras.nsf; Ambassador SIGIFREDO OCHOA PÉREZ.

Israel: 6 Hamada St, Herzliya Pituach; tel. 9-9556342; fax 9-9556603; e-mail embassy@el-salvador.org.il; internet www.el-salvador.org.il; Ambassador Suzana Gun de Hasenson.

Italy: Via G. Castellini 13, 00197 Roma; tel. (06) 8076605; fax (06) 8079726; e-mail embasalvaroma@iol.it; internet www.embasalvaroma.com; Ambassador JOSÉ ROBERTO ANDINO SALAZAR.

Japan: Kowa Bldg, No. 38, 8th Floor, 4-12-24, Nishi Azabu, Minato-ku, Tokyo 106-0031; tel. (3) 3499-4461; fax (3) 3486-7022; e-mail embesaltokio@gol.com; Ambassador José Ricardo Paredes-Osorio.

Korea, Republic: Samsung Life Insurance Bldg, 20th Floor, Taepyeong-no 2-ga, Jung-gu, Seoul 100-716; tel. (2) 753-3432; fax (2) 753-3456; e-mail koembsal@hananet.net; Ambassador ZOILA DEL CARMEN AGUIRRE DE MAY.

Mexico: Temístocles 88, Col. Polanco, Del. Miguel Hidalgo, 11560 México, DF; tel. (55) 5281-5725; fax (55) 5280-0657; e-mail embesmex@webtelmex.net.mx; Ambassador Hugo Roberto Carrillo Corleto.

Netherlands: Riouwstraat 137, 2585 HP The Hague; tel. (70) 3249855; fax (70) 3247842; Ambassador EDGAR HERNÁN VARELA ALAS.

Nicaragua: Reparto Las Colinas, Avda del Campo y Pasaje Los Cerros 142, Apdo 149, Managua; tel. 276-0712; fax 276-0711; e-mail embelsa@cablenet.com.ni; internet www.embelsanica.org.ni; Ambassador Alfredo Francisco Ungo Rivas Laguardia.

Panama: Edif. Metropolis, 4°, Avda Manuel Espinosa Batista, Panamá; tel. 223-3020; fax 264-1433; e-mail embasalva@cwpanama.net; Ambassador GERARDO SOL MIXCO.

Peru: Avda Javier Prado 2108, San Isidro, Lima 27; tel. (1) 4403500; fax (1) 2212561; e-mail embajadasv@terra.com.pe; Ambassador Raúl Soto-Ramírez.

Spain: General Oraá 9, 28006 Madrid; tel. (91) 5628002; fax (91) 5630584; e-mail madrid@embasalva.com; Ambassador DR ENRIQUE BORGO BUSTAMANTE.

Sweden: Herserudsvägen 5a, 5th Floor, 181 34 Lidingö; tel. (8) 765-86-21; fax (8) 731-72-42; e-mail embassy@elsalvador.se; internet www.elsalvador.se; Ambassador Martin Rivera Gómez.

Trinidad and Tobago: 29 Long Circular Rd, St James, Port of Spain; tel. 628-4454; fax 622-8314; Ambassador CARLOS MAURICIO PINEDA.

United Kingdom: 1st and 2nd Floors, 8 Dorset Sq., London, NW1 6PU; tel. (20) 7224-9800; fax (20) 7224-9878; e-mail elsalvador.embassy@gmail.com; Ambassador Dr Vladimiro P. Villalta.

United States of America: 1400 16th St, NW, Suite 100, Washington, DC 20036; tel. (202) 265-9671; fax (202) 232-3763; e-mail correo@elsalvador.org;

internet www.elsalvador.org; Ambassador RENÉ ANTONIO LEÓN RODRÍGUEZ.

Uruguay: Melitón González 1157, Apto 501, Montevideo 11300; tel. (2) 6222005; fax (2) 6226842; e-mail embasauy@dedicado.net.uy; Ambassador José Mario Avila Romero.

Vatican City: Via Panama 22/2, 00198 Rome, Italy; tel. (06) 8540538; fax (06) 85301131; e-mail embasalssede@iol.it; Ambassador FRANCISCO SOLER.

Venezuela: Centro Comercial Ciudad Tamanaco (CCCT), Torre C, 4°, Of. 406, Chuao, Caracas; tel. (212) 959-0817; fax (212) 959-3920; e-mail embsalv@viptel.com; Chargé d'affaires a.i. Rafael Hernández.

DIPLOMATIC MISSIONS OF EQUATORIAL GUINEA

United Nations: 57 Magnolia Ave, Mount Vernon, NY 10553; tel. (914) 667-8999; fax (914) 667-8778; e-mail eqguinea@un.int; Permanent Representative LINO SIMA EKUA AVOMO.

Angola: Luanda; Ambassador Gen. Eustaquio Nzeng Esono.

Belgium: 6 place Guy Arezzo, 1180 Brussels; tel. (2) 346-25-09; fax (2) 346-33-09; e-mail guineaaecuatorial.brux@skynet.be; Ambassador VITORINO NKA OBIANG MAYE.

Brazil: SHIS, QL 10, Conj. 09, Casa 01, 70630-095 Brasília, DF; tel. (61) 3364-4185; fax (61) 3364-1641; Ambassador Teodoro Biyogo Nsué Okomo.

Cameroon: 82 rue 1851, Quartier Bastos, BP 277, Yaoundé; tel. 2221-0804; Ambassador FLORENCIO MAYE ELA MANGUE.

China, People's Republic: 2 Dong Si Jie, San Li Tun, Beijing; tel. (10) 65323709; fax (10) 65323805; e-mail ntugabeso@hotmail.com; AmbassadorNarciso Ntugu Abeso Oyana.

Ethiopia: Bole Rd, Woreda 17, Kebele 23, House No. 162, POB 246, Addis Ababa; tel. (11) 6626278; Ambassador (vacant).

France: 29 blvd de Courcelles, 75008 Paris; tel. 1-45-61-98-20; fax 1-45-61-98-25; e-mail embarege_paris@hotmail.com; Ambassador Eduardo Ndong Elo Nzang.

Gabon: BP 1462, Libreville; tel. 75-10-56; Ambassador JOSÉ ESONO BACALE.

Germany: Rohlfsstr. 17–19, 14195 Berlin; tel. (30) 88663877; fax (30) 88663879; e-mail botschaft@guinea-ecuatorial.de; internet www.botschaft-aequatorialguinea.de; Ambassador Cándido Muatetema Rivas.

Libya: Tripoli; .

Morocco: ave President Roosevelt, angle rue d'Agadir 9, Rabat; tel. (3) 7769454; Ambassador Juan Ndong Nguema Mbengono.

Nigeria: 7 Bank Rd, Ikoyi, POB 4162, Lagos; tel. (1) 2683717; Ambassador A. S. DOUGAN MALABO.

Russian Federation: 119017 Moscow, Pogorelskii per. 7/1; tel. (495) 953-27-66; Ambassador Fausto Abeso Fuma.

São Tomé and Príncipe: Rua Ex-Adriano Moreira, São Tomé; tel. 225427; .

South Africa: 48 Florence St, Colbyn, Pretoria; POB 12720, Hatfield 0028; tel. (12) 3429945; fax (12) 3427250; Ambassador Juan Antonio Bibang Nchuchuma.

Spain: Avda Pio XII 14, 28016 Madrid; tel. (91) 3532169; fax (91) 3532165; Ambassador IGNACIO MILAN TANG.

United Kingdom: 13 Park Pl., St. James's, London, SW1A 1LP; tel. (20) 7499-6867; fax (20) 7499-6782; internet www.embarege-londres.org; Ambassador Agustin Nze Nfumu.

United States of America: 2020 16th St, NW, Washington, DC 20009; tel. (202) 518-5700; fax (202) 518-5252; Ambassador PURIFICACIÓN ANGUE ONDO.

DIPLOMATIC MISSIONS OF ERITREA

United Nations: 800 Second Ave, 18th Floor, New York, NY 10017; tel. (212) 687-3390; fax (212) 687-3138; e-mail eritrea@un.int; internet www.un.int/eritrea; Permanent Representative Araya Desta.

Australia: 16 Bulwarra Close, O'Malley, ACT 2606; tel. (2) 6290-1991; fax (2) 6286-8902; Ambassador DR ANDEAB GHEBREMESKEL.

Belgium: 15–17 ave Wolvendael, 1180 Brussels; tel. (2) 374-44-34; fax (2) 372-07-30; e-mail eri_emba_brus@hotmail.com; Ambassador Girma Asmeron Tesfay.

Canada: 75 Albert St, Suite 610, Ottawa, ON K1P 5E7; tel. (613) 234-3989; fax (613) 234-6213; Ambassador AHFEROM BERHANE GHEBREMEDHIN.

China, People's Republic: 2-10-1 Tayuan Diplomatic Office Bldg, Beijing 100600; tel. (10) 65326534; fax (10) 65326532; AmbassadorTseggai Tesfatsion Sereke.

Djibouti: BP 1944, Djibouti; tel. 354961; fax 351831; Ambassador MOHAMED SAÏD MANTAY.

Egypt: 6 Sharia el-Fallah, Mohandessin, Cairo; tel. (2) 3033503; fax (2) 3030516; e-mail eritembe@yahoo.com; Ambassador Mahmoud Omar Chirum.

Ethiopia: POB 2571, Addis Ababa; tel. (11) 5512844; fax (11) 5514911; Chargé d'affaires a.i. SAHIH OMER.

France: 1 rue de Staël, 75015 Paris; tel. 1-43-06-15-56; fax 1-43-06-07-51; Ambassador Ahmed Hassan Dehli.

Germany: Stavangerstr. 18, 10439 Berlin; tel. (30) 4467460; fax (30) 44674621; e-mail embassyeritrea@t-online.de; internet www.botschaft-eritrea.de; Ambassador PETROS TSEGGAI ASGHEDOM.

India: C-7/9, Vasant Vihar, New Delhi 110 057; tel. (11) 26146336; fax (11) 26146337; e-mail eriindia@yahoo.co.in; internet www.eritreaembindia.com; Ambassador Alem Tsehaye Woldemariam.

Israel: 33 Jabotinsky St, Ramat-Gan 52511; tel. 3-6120039; fax 3-5750133; Ambassador TESFAMARIAM TEKESTE.

Italy: Via Boncompagni 16, int. 6, 00187 Roma; tel. (06) 42741293; fax (06) 42741514; e-mail segretaria@embassyoferitrea.it; Ambassador Zemede Tekle Woldetatios.

Japan: Shirokanedai ST Bldg, Room 401, 4-7-4, Shirokanedai, Minato-ku, Tokyo, 108-0071; tel. (3) 5791-1815; fax (3) 5791-1816; e-mail eritrea-embassy@excite.co.jp; internet www.embassy-avenue.jp/eritrea; Ambassador ESTIFANOS AFEWORKI.

Kenya: New Rehema House, 2nd Floor, Westlands, POB 38651, Nairobi; tel. (20) 443164; fax (20) 443165; e-mail eriembk@africaonline.co.ke; Ambassador Salih Omar Abdu.

Kuwait: POB 53016, 73015 Nuzha, Jabriya, Block 9, St 21, House 9, Kuwait City; tel. 5317427; fax 6631304; Ambassador MAHMOUD OMAR CHIROUM.

Libya: POB 91279, Tripoli; tel. (21) 4773568; fax (21) 4780152; Ambassador Abdallah Mussa.

Netherlands: Nassauplein 13, 2585 EB The Hague; tel. (70) 4276812; fax (70) 4277236; e-mail eritrea@xs4all.nl; Ambassador MOHAMMED SULEIMAN AHMED.

Qatar: POB 4309, D-Ring Rd 14, Doha; tel. 4667934; fax 4664139; Ambassador Ali Ibrahim Ahmed.

Russian Federation: 129090 Moscow, ul. Meshchanskaya 17; tel. (495) 631-06-20; fax (495) 631-37-67; Ambassador TEKLAY MINASSIE ASGEDOM.

South Africa: 1281 Cobham Rd, Queenswood, Pretoria 0186; POB 11371, Queenswood 0121; tel. (12) 3331302; fax (12) 3332330; Ambassador Tesfamicael Gerahtu Ogbaghiorghis.

Sudan: St 39, House No. 26, POB 1618, Khartoum 2; tel. (183) 483834; fax (183) 483835; e-mail erena@sudanet.net; Ambassador GEN. ISSA AHMED ISSA.

Sweden: Stjärnvägen 2b, 4th Floor, POB 1164, 181 23 Lidingö; tel. (8) 441-71-70; fax (8) 446-73-40; e-mail info@eritrean-embassy.se; internet www.eritrean-embassy.se; Chargé d'affaires a.i. Yonas Manna Bairu.

Syria: BP 12846, Autostrade Al-Mazen West, 82 rue Akram Mosque, Damascus; tel. (11) 6112357; fax (11) 6112358; Chargé d'affaires a.i. HUMMED MOHAMED SAEED KULU.

United Arab Emirates: POB 2597, Abu Dhabi; tel. (2) 6331838; fax (2) 6346451; Ambassador Osman Muhammad Omar.

United Kingdom: 96 White Lion St, London, N1 9PF; tel. (20) 7713-0096; fax (20) 7713-0161; e-mail eriemba@erimbauk.com; Ambassador TESFAMICAEL GERAHTU OGBAGHIORGHIS.

United States of America: 1708 New Hampshire Ave, NW, Washington, DC 20009; tel. (202) 319-1991; fax (202) 319-1304; Ambassador Ghirmai Ghebremariam.

Yemen: POB 11040, Western Safia Bldg, San'a; tel. (1) 209422; fax (1) 214088; Ambassador MOUSA YASSIN SHEIKH.

DIPLOMATIC MISSIONS OF ESTONIA

United Nations: 600 Third Ave, 26th Floor, New York, NY 10016; tel. (212) 883-0640; fax (212) 883-0648; e-mail mission.newyork@mfa.ee; Permanent Representative Tina Intelmann.

Austria: Wohllebengasse 9/13, 1040 Vienna; tel. (1) 503-77-61; fax (1) 503-77-61-20; e-mail saatkond@estwien.at; Ambassador KATRIN SAARSALU-LAYACHI.

Belgium: 1 ave Isidore Gérard, 1160 Brussels; tel. (2) 779-07-55; fax (2) 779-28-17; e-mail saatkond@estemb.be; internet www.estemb.be; Ambassador Malle Talvet-Mustonen.

Canada: 260 Dalhousie St, Suite 210, Ottawa, ON K1N 7E4; tel. (613) 789-4222; fax (613) 789-9555; e-mail embassy.ottawa@mfa.ee; internet www.estemb.ca; Chargé d'affaires a.i. RASMUS LUMI.

China, People's Republic: Office Building C-617/618, Kempinski Hotel, Beijing Lufthansa Center, Beijing 100016; tel. (10) 64637913; fax (10) 64637908; e-mail embassy.beijing@mfa.ee; internet www.peking.vm.ee; Ambassador Andres Unga.

Czech Republic: Na Kampě 1, 118 00 Prague 1; tel. 257011180; fax 257011181; e-mail embassy.prague@estemb.cz; internet www.estemb.cz; Ambassador MATI VAARMANN.

Denmark: Aurehøjvej 19, 2900 Hellerup; tel. 39-46-30-70; fax 39-46-30-76; e-mail sekretar@estemb.dk; internet www.estemb.dk; Ambassador Meelike Palli.

Finland: Itäinen puistotie 10, 00140 Helsinki; tel. (9) 6220260; fax (9) 62202610; e-mail helen.naarits@estemb.fi; internet www.estemb.fi; Ambassador MERLE PAJULA.

France: 17 rue de la Baume, 75008 Paris; tel. 1-56-62-22-00; fax 1-49-52-05-65; e-mail estonie@mfa.ee; internet www.est-emb.fr; Ambassador Margus Rava.

Georgia: 0171 Tbilisi, Saburtalo, Likhauri 4; tel. (32) 36-51-22; fax (32) 36-51-38; e-mail tbilisisaatkond@mfa.ee; Chargé d'affaires a.i. HARRY LAHTEIN.

Germany: Hildebrandstr. 5, 10785 Berlin; tel. (30) 25460600; fax (30) 25460601; e-mail embassy.berlin@mfa.ee; internet www.estemb.de; Ambassador Clyde Kull.

Greece: Patriarchou Ioakeim 48, 106 76 Athens; tel. (210) 7229803; fax (210) 7229804; e-mail estemb@otenet.gr; internet www.estemb.gr; Ambassador PEEP JAHILO.

Hungary: 1062 Budapest, Lendvay u. 12, Fsz. 3; tel. (1) 354-2570; fax (1) 354-2571; Ambassador Toivo Tasa.

Ireland: Riversdale House, St Ann's, Ailesbury Rd, Dublin 4; tel. (1) 2196730; fax (1) 2196731; e-mail embassy.dublin@mfa.ee; internet www.estemb.ie; Ambassador ANDRE PUNG.

Italy: Viale Liegi 28, int. 5, 00198 Roma; tel. (06) 84407510; fax (06) 84407519; e-mail embassy.rome@mfa.ee; internet www.estemb.it; Ambassador Andres Tomasberg.

Japan: 2-6-15, Jingu-mae, Shibuya-ku 150-0001; tel. (3) 5412-7281; fax (3) 5412-7282; e-mail embassy.tokyo@mfa.ee; internet www.estemb.or.jp; Ambassador PEETER MILLER.

Latvia: Skolas iela 13, Rīga 1010; tel. 6781-2020; fax 6781-2029; e-mail embassy.riga@mfa.ee; internet www.estemb.lv; Ambassador Jaak Jõerüüt.

Lithuania: Mickevičiaus g. 4A, Vilnius 08119; tel. (5) 278-0200; fax (5) 278-0201; e-mail sekretar@estemb.lt; internet www.estemb.lt; Ambassador ANDRES TROPP.

Netherlands: Zeestraat 92, 2518 AD The Hague; tel. (70) 3029050; fax (70) 3029051; e-mail embassy.haag@mfa.ee; internet www.estemb.nl; Ambassador Gita Kalmet.

Norway: Parkvn 51A, 0244 Oslo; tel. 22-54-00-70; fax 22-54-00-71; e-mail Embassy.Oslo@mfa.ee; internet www.estemb.no; Ambassador JUHAN HARAVEE.

Poland: 02-639 Warsaw, ul. Karwińska 1; tel. (22) 8811810; fax (22) 8811812; e-mail embassy@estemb.pl; internet www.estemb.pl; Ambassador Ants Frosch.

Portugal: Rua Filipe Folque 10J, 2° esq., 1050-113 Lisbon; tel. (21) 3194150; fax (21) 3194155; e-mail embest@embest.pt; internet www.embest.pt; Ambassador MART TARMAK.

Russian Federation: 125009 Moscow, M. Kislovskii per. 5; tel. (495) 737-36-40; fax (495) 737-36-46; e-mail embassy.moskva@mfa.ee; internet www.estemb.ru; Ambassador Marina Kaljurand.

Spain: Claudio Coello 91, 28006 Madrid; tel. (91) 4261671; fax (91) 4261672; e-mail embassy.madrid@mfa.ee; internet www.estemb.es; Ambassador ANDRES RUNDU.

Sweden: Tyrgt. 3, 114 27 Stockholm; POB 26076, 100 41 Stockholm; tel. (8) 545-122-80; fax (8) 545-122-99; e-mail info@estemb.se; internet www.estemb.se; Ambassador Alar Streimann.

Turkey: Gölgeli Sok. 16, 06700 Gaziosmanpaşa, Ankara; tel. (312) 4056970; fax (312) 4056976; e-mail embassy.ankara@mfa.ee; internet www.estemb.org.tr/embassy; Ambassador MÄRT VOLMER.

Ukraine: 01901 Kyiv, vul. Volodymyrska 61/11–37; tel. (44) 590-07-80; fax (44) 590-07-81; e-mail embassy.kiev@mfa.ee; internet www.estemb.kiev.ua; Ambassador Jaan Hein.

United Kingdom: 16 Hyde Park Gate, London, SW7 5DG; tel. (20) 7589-3428; fax (20) 7589-3430; e-mail embassy.london@estonia.gov.uk; internet www.estonia.gov.uk; Ambassador DR MARGUS LAIDRE.

United States of America: 2131 Massachusetts Ave, NW, Washington, DC 20008; tel. (202) 588-0101; fax (202) 588-0108; e-mail info@estemb.org; internet www.estemb.org; Ambassador Väino Reinart.

DIPLOMATIC MISSIONS OF ETHIOPIA

United Nations: 866 Second Ave, 3rd Floor, New York, NY 10017; tel. (212) 421-1830; fax (212) 754-0360; e-mail ethiopia@un.int; internet www.un.int/ethiopia; Permanent Representative DAWIT YOHANNES.

Austria: Wagramerstr. 14/1/2, 1223 Vienna; tel. (1) 710-21-68; fax (1) 710-21-71; e-mail office@ethiopianembassy.at; internet www.ethiopianembassy.at; Ambassador Kongit Woldemariam Sinegiorgis.

Belgium: 231 ave de Tervueren, 1150 Brussels; tel. (2) 771-32-94; fax (2) 771-49-14; e-mail etebru@brutele.be; Ambassador BERHANE GEBRE-CHRISTOS.

Canada: 151 Slater St, Suite 210, Ottawa, ON K1P 5H3; tel. (613) 235-6637; fax (613) 235-4638; internet www.ethiopia.ottawa.on.ca; Ambassador Getachew Hamussa Hailemariam.

China, People's Republic: 3 Xiu Shui Nan Jie, Jian Guo Men Wai, Beijing 100600; tel. (10) 65325258; fax (10) 65325591; e-mail ethchina@public3.bta.net.cn; internet www.ethiopiaemb.org.cn; Ambassador HAILEKIROS GESSESSE.

Congo, Democratic Republic: BP 8435, Kinshasa; tel. (12) 23327; Ambassador Dieudeonne A. Ganga.

Côte d'Ivoire: Immeuble Nour Al-Hayat, 01 BP 3712, Abidjan 01; tel. 20-21-33-65; fax 20-21-37-09; e-mail ambethio@gmail.com; Ambassador ABDULAZIZ AHMED ADEM.

Djibouti: rue Clochette, BP 230, Djibouti; tel. 350718; fax 354803; e-mail ethemb@intnet.dj; Ambassador Shemsudin Ahmed.

Egypt: Mesaha Sq., Villa 11, Cairo (Dokki); tel. (2) 3353693; fax (2) 3353699; e-mail ethio@ethioembassy.org.eg; Ambassador IBRAHIM IDRIS.

France: 35 ave Charles Floquet, 75007 Paris; tel. 1-47-83-83-95; fax 1-43-06-52-14; e-mail embeth@free.fr; Ambassador Tadelech Haïle-Mikael.

Germany: Boothstr. 20A, 12207 Berlin; tel. (30) 772060; fax (30) 7720626; e-mail emb.ethiopia@t-online.de; internet www.aethiopien-botschaft.de; Ambassador KASSAHUN AYELE TESEMMA.

Ghana: 2 Milne Close, Airport Residential Area, POB 1646, Accra; tel. (21) 775928; fax (21) 776807; e-mail ethioemb@ghana.com; Ambassador Ato Cham Ugala Uriat.

India: 7/50G Satya Marg, Chanakyapuri, New Delhi 110 021; tel. (11) 26119513; fax (11) 26875731; e-mail delethem@yahoo.com; Ambassador GENET ZEWDIE.

Ireland: 1–3 Merrion House, Fitzwilliam St Lower, Dublin 2; tel. (1) 6787062; fax (1) 6787065; e-mail info@ethiopianembassy.ie; Ambassador Ato Zerihun Retta.

Israel: Bldg B, Floor 8B, 48 Darech Menachem Begin, Tel-Aviv 66184; tel. 3-6397831; fax 3-6397837; e-mail ethembis@netvision.net.il; internet www.ethioemb.org.il; Ambassador FESSEHA ASGHEDOM TESSEMA.

Italy: Via Andrea Vesalio 16–18, 00161 Roma; tel. (06) 4416161; fax (06) 4403676; Ambassador Grum Abay Teshome.

Japan: 2F Takanawa Kaisei Bldg, 3-4-1, Takanawa, Minato-ku, Tokyo 108-0074; tel. (3) 5420-6860; fax (3) 5420-6866; e-mail info@ethiopia-emb.or.jp; internet www.ethiopia-emb.or.jp; Ambassador ABDIRASHID DULANE.

Kenya: State House Ave, POB 45198, Nairobi; tel. (20) 2732054; Ambassador Dissasa Dirbissa Winsa.

Korea, Democratic People's Republic: POB 55, Munsudong, Taedongkang District, Pyongyang; tel. (2) 3827554; fax (2) 3827550; Chargé d'affaires FEKADE S. G. MESKEL.

Kuwait: POB 939, 45710 Safat, Jabriya, Block 10, St 107, Villa 30, Kuwait City; tel. 5330128; fax 5331179; e-mail ethiokuwait@yahoo.com; Ambassador Kadafou Muhammad Hanfary.

Nigeria: 19 Ona Cres., Maitama, POB 2488, Abuja; tel. (1) 4131691; fax (1) 4131692; e-mail etabuja@primair.net; Ambassador YOHANESS GENDA.

Russian Federation: 129041 Moscow, Orlovo-Davydovskii per. 6; tel. (495) 680-16-16; fax (495) 680-66-08; e-mail eth-emb@col.ru; Ambassador Dr Teketel Forsido.

Saudi Arabia: POB 94341, Riyadh 11693; tel. (1) 477-5285; fax (1) 476-8020; e-mail ethiopian@naseej.com.sa; Ambassador Ato MUHAMMAD ALI.

Senegal: 18 blvd de la République, BP 379, Dakar; tel. 33-821-9896; fax 33-821-9895; e-mail ethembas@sentoo.sn; Ambassador Ato Hassen Abdulkadik.

South Africa: 47 Charles St, Bailey's Muckleneuk, Brooklyn 0181; POB 11469, Hatfield 0028; tel. (12) 3463542; fax (12) 3463867; e-mail ethiopia@sentechsa.com; Ambassador MELESE MARIMO MARASSO.

Sudan: Plot No. 4, Block 384bc, POB 844, Khartoum; tel. (183) 471379; fax (183) 471141; e-mail eekrt@hotmail.com; Ambassador Dr Kadafo Mohammed Hanfare.

Sweden: Löjtnantsgt. 17, POB 10148, 100 55 Stockholm; tel. (8) 665-60-30; fax (8) 660-81-77; e-mail ethio.all@telia.com; internet www.ethemb.se; Ambassador DINA MUFTI.

Turkey: Reşit Galip Cad., Gökçek Sok. 11, Ankara; tel. (312) 4360400; fax (312) 4481938; e-mail ethembank@ttnet.net.tr; Ambassador Mulatu Teshome Wirtu.

Uganda: 3L Kitante Close, off Kira Rd, POB 7745, Kampala; tel. (41) 4348340; fax (41) 4341885; Ambassador ATO TERFA MENEGESHA.

United Kingdom: 17 Prince's Gate, London, SW7 1PZ; tel. (20) 7589-7212; fax (20) 7584-7054; e-mail info@ethioembassy.org.uk; internet www .ethioembassy.org.uk; Ambassador Berhanu Kebede.

United States of America: 3506 International Dr., NW, Washington, DC 20008; tel. (202) 364-1200; fax (202) 587-0195; e-mail info@ ethiopianembassy.org; internet www.ethiopianembassy.org; Ambassador SAMUEL ASSEFA.

Yemen: POB 234, Al-Hamadani St, San'a; tel. (1) 208833; fax (1) 213780; e-mail ethoembs@y.net.ye; Ambassador Tofiki Abdulahi.

Zimbabwe: 14 Lanark Rd, Belgravia, POB 2745, Harare; tel. (4) 701514; fax (4) 701516; e-mail embassy@ecoweb.co.zw; Ambassador DINA MUFTI.

DIPLOMATIC MISSIONS OF FIJI

United Nations: 630 Third Ave, 7th Floor, New York, NY 10017; tel. (212) 687-4130; fax (212) 687-3963; e-mail fiji@un.int; internet www.fijiprun.org; Permanent Representative Dr Tupeni Baba.

Australia: POB 159, Deakin West, ACT 2600; tel. (2) 6260-5115; fax (2) 6260-5105; e-mail admin@aus-fhc.org; High Commissioner EVISAKE KEDRAYATE (acting).

Belgium: 92–94 square Eugène Plasky, 5e étage, 1030 Brussels; tel. (2) 736-90-50; fax (2) 736-14-58; e-mail embassy@be; internet www.fijiembassy .be; Ambassador Seremaia Tuinausori Cavuilati.

China, People's Republic: 1-15-2 Tayuan Diplomatic Office Bldg, Beijing 100600; tel. (10) 65327305; fax (10) 65327253; e-mail info@fijiembassy.org .cn; internet www.fijiembassy.org.cn; Ambassador SIR JAMES AH KOY.

India: N-87, Panchsheel Park, New Delhi 110 017; tel. (11) 41751092; fax (11) 41751095; e-mail fijihighcommission@yahoo.co.in; High Commissioner Savenaca Kaunisela.

Japan: Noa Bldg, 14th Floor, 2-3-5, Azabudai, Minato-ku, Tokyo 106-0041; tel. (3) 3587-2038; fax (3) 3587-2563; e-mail info@fijiembassy.jp; internet www.fijiembassy.jp; Ambassador RATU INOKE KUBUABOLA.

Malaysia: Level 2, Menara Chan, 138 Jalan Ampang, 50450 Kuala Lumpur; tel. (3) 27323335; fax (3) 27327555; e-mail fhckl@pd.jaring.my; High Commissioner (vacant).

New Zealand: 31 Pipitea St, Thorndon, POB 3940, Wellington; tel. (4) 473-5401; fax (4) 499-1011; e-mail viti@paradise.net.nz; internet www.fiji.org.nz; High Commissioner SAKIUSA RAKAI (acting).

Papua New Guinea: Defence House, 4th Floor, Champion Parade, Port Moresby, NCD; tel. 3211914; fax 3217220; e-mail rakaie@fijihighcom.org .pg; High Commissioner Ratu Isoa Tikoca.

United Kingdom: 34 Hyde Park Gate, London, SW7 5DN; tel. (20) 7584-3661; fax (20) 7584-2838; e-mail mail@fijihighcommission.org.uk; internet www.fijihighcommission.org.uk; High Commr MACA TULAKEPA (acting).

United States of America: 2000 M St, NW, Suite 710, Washington, DC 20036; tel. (202) 466-8320; fax (202) 466-8325; e-mail info@fijiembassydc.com; internet www.fijiembassy.org; Ambassasdor Ratu Finau Mara.

DIPLOMATIC MISSIONS OF FINLAND

United Nations: 866 United Nations Plaza, Suite 222, New York, NY 10017; tel. (212) 355-2100; fax (212) 759-6156; e-mail sanomat.yke@formin.fi; internet www.un.int/finland; Permanent Representative KIRSTI LINTONEN.

Afghanistan: House 39, Street 10, Lane 1, Wazir Akbar Khan, Kabul; tel. (20) 2103051; fax (60) 581504; e-mail sanomat.kab@formin.fi; internet www .finland.org.af; Ambassador Timo Oula.

Algeria: 10 rue des Cèdres, el-Mouradia, Algiers; tel. (21) 69-29-25; fax (21) 69-16-37; e-mail finamb@wissal.dz; Ambassador KAIJA ILANDER.

Argentina: Santa Fe 846, 5°, C1059ABP Buenos Aires; tel. (11) 4312-0600; fax (11) 4312-0670; e-mail sanomat.bue@formin.fi; internet www.finlandia.org .ar; Ambassador Ritva Anneli Jolkkonen.

Australia: 12 Darwin Ave, Yarralumla, ACT 2600; tel. (2) 6273-3800; fax (2) 6273-3603; e-mail sanomat.can@formin.fi; internet www.finland.org.au; Ambassador GLEN LINDHOLM.

Austria: Gonzagagasse 16, 1010 Vienna; tel. (1) 531-59-0; fax (1) 535-57-03; e-mail sanomat.wie@formin.fi; internet www.finnland.at; Ambassador Kirsti Helena Kauppi.

Belgium: 58 ave des Arts, 5e étage, 1000 Brussels; tel. (2) 287-12-12; fax (2) 287-12-00; e-mail sanomat.bry@formin.fi; internet www.finlande.be; Ambassador AAPO PÕLHÖ.

Brazil: SES, Av. das Nações, Quadra 807, Lote 27, 70417-900 Brasília, DF; tel. (61) 3443-7151; fax (61) 3443-3315; e-mail brasilia@finlandia.org.br; internet www.finlandia.org.br; Ambassador Ilpo Ilmari Manninen.

Bulgaria: 1000 Sofia, Bacho Kiro 26; tel. (2) 810-21-10; fax (2) 810-21-11; e-mail sanomat.sof@formin.fi; internet www.finland.bg; Ambassador KAUKO JÄMSÉN.

Canada: 55 Metcalfe St, Suite 850, Ottawa, ON K1P 6L5; tel. (613) 288-2233; fax (613) 288-2244; e-mail embassy@finland.ca; internet www.finland.ca; Ambassador Pasi Mikael Patokallio.

Chile: Alcántara 200, Of. 201, Las Condes, Santiago; tel. (2) 263-4917; fax (2) 263-4701; e-mail sanomat.snt@formin.fi; Ambassador IIVO SALMI.

China, People's Republic: Beijing Kerry Centre, 26/F South Tower, 1 Guanghua Lu, Beijing 100020; tel. (10) 85298541; fax (10) 85298547; e-mail sanomat.pek@formin.fi; internet www.finland.cn; Ambassador Antti Kuosmanen.

Croatia: 10000 Zagreb, Miramarska 23; tel. (1) 6312080; fax (1) 6312090; e-mail sanomat.zag@formin.fi; internet www.finland.hr; Ambassador ANN-MARIE NYROOS.

Cyprus: POB 21438, Arch. Makarios III Ave 9, 1508 Nicosia; tel. 22458020; fax 22477880; e-mail sanomat.nic@formin.fi; internet www.finland.org.cy; Ambassador Risto Piipponen.

Czech Republic: Hellichova 1, 118 00 Prague 1; tel. 251177251; fax 251177241; e-mail sanomat.pra@formin.fi; internet www.finland.cz; Ambassador HANNU VEIKKO KYRÖLÄINEN.

Denmark: Skt Annæ Pl. 24, 1250 Copenhagen K; tel. 33-13-42-14; fax 33-32-47-10; e-mail sanomat.kob@formin.fi; internet www.finlandsambassade.dk; Ambassador Eero Kalevi Salovaara.

Egypt: 13th Floor, 3 Sharia Abou el-Feda, Cairo 11511 (Zamalek); tel. (2) 7363722; fax (2) 7371376; e-mail sanomat.kai@formin.fi; internet www .finland.org.eg; Ambassador HANNU HALINEN.

Estonia: Kohtu 4, Tallinn 15180; tel. 610-3200; fax 610-3281; e-mail sanomat .tal@formin.fi; internet www.finland.ee; Ambassador Jaakko Kalela.

Ethiopia: Mauritania St, Kebele 12, House No. 1431, POB 1017, Addis Ababa; tel. (11) 3205920; fax (11) 3205923; e-mail sanomat.add@formin.fi; Ambassador KIRSTI AARNIO.

France: 1 place de Finlande, 75007 Paris; tel. 1-44-18-19-20; fax 1-45-55-51-57; e-mail sanomat.par@formin.fi; internet www.amb-finlande.fr; Ambassador Charles Murto.

Germany: Rauchstr. 1, 10787 Berlin; tel. (30) 505030; fax (30) 5050333; e-mail sanomat.ber@formin.fi; internet www.finnland.de; Ambassador ERNST RENÉ ANSELM NYBERG.

Greece: Odos Eratosthenous 1, 116 35 Athens; tel. (210) 7010444; fax (210) 7515064; e-mail sanomat.ate@formin.fi; internet www.finland.gr; Ambassador Erkki Väinö Juhani Huittinen.

Hungary: 1118 Budapest, Kelenhegyi u. 16 A; tel. (1) 279-2500; fax (1) 385-0843; e-mail sanomat.bud@formin.fi; internet www.finland.hu; Ambassador Jari Vilén.

Iceland: Túngata 30, 101 Reykjavík; tel. 5100100; fax 5623880; e-mail sanomat.rey@formin.fi; internet www.finland.is; Ambassador Kai Granholm.

India: E-3 Nyaya Marg, Chanakyapuri, New Delhi 110 021; tel. (11) 41497500; fax (11) 41497555; e-mail sanomat.NDE@formin.fi; internet www .finland.org.in; Ambassador Asko Numminem.

Indonesia: Menara Rajawali, 9th Floor, Lot 5.1, Jalan Mega Kuningan, Kawasan Mega Kuningan, Jakarta 12950; tel. (21) 5761650; fax (21) 5761631; e-mail sanomat.jak@formin.fi; internet www.finland.or.id; Ambassador Antti Koistinen.

Iran: No. 4, Shirin Alley, Agha Bozorgi St, Elahiyeh, Tehran; tel. (21) 22230979; fax (21) 22210948; e-mail finlandiran@hotmail.com; Ambassador Heikki Puurunen.

Iraq: POB 2041, 86/25/925 Hay Babel, Baghdad; tel. (1) 776-6271; fax (1) 778-0488; e-mail fin-emb@yahoo.com; .

Ireland: Russell House, Stokes Place, St Stephen's Green, Dublin 2; tel. (1) 4781344; fax (1) 4783727; e-mail sanomat.dub@formin.fi; internet www .finland.ie; Ambassador Seppo Kauppila.

Israel: Canion Ramat Aviv, 40 Einstein St, Tel-Aviv 69101; tel. 3-7456600; fax 3-7440314; e-mail sanomat.tel@formin.fi; internet www.finland.org.il; Ambassador Kari Veijalainen.

Italy: Via Lisbona 3, 00198 Roma; tel. (06) 852231; fax (06) 8540362; e-mail sanomat.roo@formin.fi; internet www.finland.it; Ambassador Pauli Antero Mäkelä.

Japan: 3-5-39, Minami Azabu, Minato-ku, Tokyo 106-8561; tel. (3) 5447-6000; fax (3) 5447-6042; e-mail sanomat.tok@formin.fi; internet www.finland .or.jp; Ambassador Jorma Kari Johannes Julin.

Kenya: International House, 2nd Floor, Mama Ngina St, POB 30379, 00100 Nairobi; tel. (20) 334777; fax (20) 335986; Ambassador Heli Sirve.

Korea, Republic: POB 1602, Kyobo Bldg 15/F, Suite 1602, 1-1, 1-ga, Jongno, Jongno-gu, Seoul 110-714; tel. (2) 732-6737; fax (2) 723-4969; e-mail sanomat .seo@formin.fi; internet www.finland.or.kr; Ambassador Kim Luotonen.

Latvia: Kalpaka bulv. 1, Rīga 1605; tel. 6707-8800; fax 6707-8814; e-mail sanomat.rii@formin.fi; internet www.finland.lv; Ambassador Pekka Wuoristo.

Lithuania: Klaipėdos g. 6, Vilnius 01117; tel. (5) 212-1621; fax (5) 212-2463; e-mail sanomat.vil@formin.fi; internet www.finland.lt; Ambassador Timo Lahelma.

Luxembourg: 2 rue Heine, 1720 Luxembourg; tel. 49-55-51; fax 49-46-40; e-mail sanomat.lux@formin.fi; internet www.finlande.lu; Ambassador Tarja Laitiainen.

Malaysia: Wisma Chinese Chamber, 5th Floor, 258 Jalan Ampang, 50450 Kuala Lumpur; tel. (3) 42577746; fax (3) 42577793; e-mail sanomat.kul@ formin.fi; internet www.finland.or.my; Ambassador Lauri Korpinen.

Mexico: Monte Pelvoux 111, 4°, Col. Lomas de Chapultepec, Del. Miguel Hidalgo, 11000 México, DF; tel. (55) 5540-6036; fax (55) 5540-0114; e-mail finmex@prodigy.net.mx; internet www.finlandia.org.mx; Ambassador Ulla Marianna Vaisto.

Morocco: 145 rue Soufiane Ben Wahb, BP 590, 10002 Rabat; tel. (3) 7658775; fax (3) 7658904; e-mail sanomat.rab@formin.fi; Ambassador Sauli Erik Feodorow (resident in Lisbon, Portugal).

Mozambique: Av. Julius Nyerere 1128, CP 1663, Maputo; tel. 21482400; fax 21491662; e-mail sanomat.map@formin.fi; Ambassador Kari Alanko.

Namibia: 2 Crohn St (cnr Bahnhof St), POB 3649, Windhoek; tel. (61) 221355; fax (61) 221349; e-mail sanomat.win@formin.fi; internet www .finland.org.na; Chargé d'affaires a.i. Seija Kinni-Huttunen.

Nepal: Bishalnagar, POB 2126, Kathmandu; tel. (1) 4416636; fax (1) 4416703; e-mail sanomat.kat@formin.fi; internet www.finland.org.np; Chargé d'affaires a.i. Pirkko-Liisa Kyöstilä.

Netherlands: Groot Hertoginnelaan 16, 2517 EG The Hague; tel. (70) 3469754; fax (70) 3107174; e-mail info.haa@formin.fi; internet www.finlande .nl; Ambassador Mikko Jokela.

Nicaragua: Sucursal Jorge Navarro, Apdo 2219, Managua; tel. 266-3415; fax 266-3416; e-mail sanomat.mgu@formin.fi; internet www.finlandia.org.ni; Ambassador Marja Luoto.

Nigeria: Maputo St Wuse, Zone 3, PMB 5140, Abuja; tel. (9) 3147256; fax (9) 3147252; e-mail sanomat.aba@formin.fi; Ambassador Anna-Liisa Korhonen.

Norway: Thomas Heftyesgt. 1, 0244 Oslo; tel. 22-12-49-00; fax 22-12-49-49; e-mail sanomat.osl@formin.fi; internet www.finland.no; Ambassador Peter Stenlund.

Pakistan: House No. 24, St 89, G-6/3, Islamabad; tel. (51) 2828426; fax (51) 2828427; e-mail finnemb@isd.wol.net.pk; Ambassador Pirjo Irmeli Mustonen.

Peru: Avda Víctor Andrés Belaúnde 147, Edif. Real Tres, Of. 502, San Isidro, Lima; tel. (1) 2224466; fax (1) 2224463; e-mail sanomat.lim@formin.fi; internet www.finlandiaperu.org.pe; Ambassador Pekka Orpana.

Philippines: 21st Floor, BPI Buendia Center, Sen. Gil J. Puyat Ave, Makati City, Metro Manila; tel. (2) 8915011; fax (2) 8914106; e-mail sanomat.mni@ formin.fi; internet www.finland.ph; Ambassador Ritta Resch.

Poland: 00-559 Warsaw, ul. Chopina 4/8; tel. (22) 5989500; fax (22) 6213442; e-mail sanomat.var@formin.fi; internet www.finland.pl; Ambassador Jan Store.

Portugal: Rua do Possolo 76, 1°, 1350-251 Lisbon; tel. (21) 3933040; fax (21) 3904758; e-mail sanomat.lis@formin.fi; internet www.finlandia.org.pt; Ambassador Sauli Erik Feodorow.

Romania: 011832 Bucharest, Str. Atena 2 bis; tel. (21) 2307504; fax (21) 2307505; e-mail sanomat.buk@formin.fi; internet www.finlandia.ro; Ambassador Tapio Saarela.

Russian Federation: 119034 Moscow, Kropotkinskii per. 15/17; tel. (495) 787-41-74; fax (495) 247-33-80; e-mail sanomat.mos@formin.fi; internet www .finland.org.ru; Ambassador Harry Gustaf Helenius.

Saudi Arabia: POB 94363, Riyadh 11693; tel. (1) 488-1515; fax (1) 488-2520; e-mail sanomat.ria@formin.fi; Ambassador Martti Isoaro.

Serbia: 11001 Belgrade, Birčaninova 29, POB 926; tel. (11) 3065400; fax (11) 3065375; e-mail sanomat.beo@formin.fi; Ambassador Kari Johannes Veijalainen.

Singapore: 101 Thomson Rd, 21-03 United Sq., Singapore 307591; tel. 62544042; fax 62534101; e-mail sanomat.sin@formin.fi; internet www .finland.org.sg; Ambassador Satu Mattila.

Slovakia: Palisády 29, 811 06 Bratislava; tel. (2) 5980-5111; fax (2) 5980-5120; e-mail sanomat.brt@formin.fi; internet www.finlandembassy.sk; Ambassador Rauno Viemerö.

Slovenia: 1000 Ljubljana, Ajdovščina 4/8; tel. (1) 3002120; fax (1) 3002139; e-mail sanomat.lju@formin.fi; internet www.finland.si; Ambassador Birgitta Stenius-Mladenov.

South Africa: 628 Leyds St, Muckleneuk, Pretoria 0002; POB 443, Pretoria 0001; tel. (12) 3430275; fax (12) 3433095; e-mail sanomat.pre@formin.fi; internet www.finland.org.za; Ambassador Heikki Tuunanen.

Spain: Paseo de la Castellana 15, 28046 Madrid; tel. (91) 3196172; fax (91) 3083901; e-mail sanomat.mad@formin.fi; internet www.finlandia.es; Ambassador Maija Lahteenmaki.

Sweden: Gärdesgt. 11, POB 24285, 104 51 Stockholm; tel. (8) 676-67-00; fax (8) 20-74-97; e-mail info@finland.se; internet www.finland.se; Ambassador Alec Aalto.

Switzerland: Weltpoststr. 4, Postfach 11, 3015 Bern; tel. 313504100; fax 313504107; e-mail sanomat.brn@formin.fi; internet www.finlandia.ch; Ambassador Pekka Ojanen.

Syria: BP 3893, Immeuble 164a, rue Doha, Area 3, Mezzeh Est, Damascus; tel. (11) 6127570; fax (11) 6119777; Ambassador Pertti Harvola.

Tanzania: cnr Mirambo St and Garden Ave, POB 2455, Dar es Salaam; tel. (22) 2196565; fax (22) 2196573; e-mail sanomat.dar@formin.fi; internet www .finland.or.tz; Ambassador Juhani Toivonen.

Thailand: Amarin Tower, 16th Floor, 500 Thanon Ploenchit, Bangkok 10330; tel. (2) 250-8801; fax (2) 250-8802; e-mail sanomat.ban@formin.fi; internet www.finland.or.th; Ambassador Lars Erik Backström.

Tunisia: Dar Nordique, rue du Lac Neuchâtel, Les Berges du Lac, 1053 Tunis; tel. (71) 861-777; fax (71) 961-080; e-mail sanomat.tun@formin.fi; internet www.finlandtunis.org; Ambassador Laura Reinilä.

Turkey: Kader Sok. 44, 06700 Gaziosmanpaşa, Ankara; tel. (312) 4261930; fax (312) 4680072; e-mail sanomat.ank@formin.fi; internet www.finland.org .tr; Ambassador Maria Serenius.

Ukraine: 01901 Kyiv, vul. Striletska 14; tel. (44) 278-70-49; fax (44) 278-20-32; e-mail sanomat.kio@formin.fi; internet www.finland.org.ua; Ambassador Christer Michelsson.

United Arab Emirates: POB 3634, Al-Masood Tower, Hamdan St, Abu Dhabi; tel. (2) 6328927; fax (2) 6325063; e-mail sanomat.abo@formin.fi; internet www.finland.ae; Chargé d'affaires a.i. Esa Hurtig.

United Kingdom: 38 Chesham Pl., London, SW1X 8HW; tel. (20) 7838-6200; fax (20) 7235-3680; e-mail sanomat.lon@formin.fi; internet www.finemb.org .uk; Ambassador JAAKKO LAAJAVA.

United States of America: 3301 Massachusetts Ave, NW, Washington, DC 20008; tel. (202) 298-5800; fax (202) 298-6030; e-mail sanomat.was@formin .fi; internet www.finland.org; Ambassador Pekka Lintu.

Venezuela: Apdo 61118, Chacao, Caracas 1060; tel. (212) 952-4111; fax (212) 952-7536; e-mail sanomat.car@formin.fi; internet www.finland.org.ve/es; Ambassador MIKKO PYHÄLÄ.

Viet Nam: Suite 63, 6th Floor, Central Bldg, 31 Hai Ba Trung, Hanoi; tel. (4) 8266788; fax (4) 8266766; e-mail sanomat.han@formin.fi; internet www .finland.org.vn; Ambassador Pekka Hyvönen.

Zambia: Haile Selassie Ave, opp. Ndeke House, Longacres, POB 50819, 15101 Lusaka; tel. (1) 251988; fax (1) 253783; e-mail sanomat.lus@formin.fi; internet www.finland.org.zm; Ambassador SINIKKA ANTILA.

DIPLOMATIC MISSIONS OF FRANCE

United Nations: 1 Dag Hammarskjöld Plaza, 245 East 47th St, 44th Floor, New York, NY 10017; tel. (212) 308-5700; fax (212) 421-6889; e-mail france@un.int; internet www.un.int/france; Permanent Representative Jean-Maurice Ripert.

Afghanistan: Cherpour Ave, Shar-i-Nau, POB 62, Kabul; tel. (70) 284032; e-mail chancellerie.kaboul-amba@diplomatie.gouv.fr; internet www .ambafrance-af.org; Ambassador RÉGIS KOETSCHET.

Albania: Rruga Skënderbej 14, Tirana; tel. (4) 234054; fax (4) 234442; e-mail ambafrance.tr@adanet.com.al; internet www.ambafrance-al.org; Ambassador Maryse Daviet.

Algeria: chemin Abd al-Kader Gadouche, 16035 Hydra, Algiers; tel. (21) 69-24-88; fax (21) 69-13-69; e-mail contact@ambafrance-dz.org; internet www .ambafrance-dz.org; Ambassador BERNARD BAJOLET.

Andorra: Carrer les Canals 38–40, POB 155, Andorra la Vella AD500; tel. 736700; fax 736731; e-mail ambassade.de.france@andorra.ad; internet www .ambafrance-ad.org; Ambassador Gilles Chouraqui.

Angola: Rua Reverendo Pedro Agostinho Neto 31–33, CP 584, Luanda; tel. 222334841; fax 222391949; e-mail cad.luanda-amba@diplomatie.gouv.fr; internet www.ambafrance-ao.org; Ambassador FRANCIS BLONDET.

Argentina: Cerrito 1399, C1010ABA Buenos Aires; tel. (11) 4515-2930; fax (11) 4515-0120; e-mail ambafr@abaconet.com.ar; internet www.embafrancia -argentina.org; Ambassador Frédéric Gabriel Charles Baleine du Laurens.

Armenia: 0015 Yerevan, Grigor Lusavorichi St 8; tel. (10) 56-11-03; fax (10) 56-98-31; e-mail cad.erevan@diplomatie.gouv.fr; internet www.ambafrance -am.org; Ambassador SERGE SMESSOW.

Australia: 6 Perth Ave, Yarralumla, ACT 2600; tel. (2) 6216-0100; fax (2) 6216-0127; e-mail embassy@ambafrance-au.org; internet www.ambafrance -au.org; Ambassador François Descoueyte.

Austria: Technikerstr. 2, 1040 Vienna; tel. (1) 502-75-0; fax (1) 502-75-16-8; e-mail presse@ambafrvienne.at; internet www.ambafrance-at.org; Ambassador PIERRE VIAUX.

Azerbaijan: 1000 Baku, Rasul Rza küç. 7, POB 36; tel. (12) 490-81-00; fax (12) 490-81-01; e-mail ambafranbakou@azerin.com; internet www.ambafrance .az; Chargé d'affaires a.i. Jean-Yves Berthault.

Bahrain: POB 11134, Rd 1901, Bldg 51A, Block 319, Diplomatic Area, Manama; tel. 17298600; fax 17298607; e-mail chancellerie.manama -AMBA@diplomatie.gouv.fr; internet www.ambafrance-bh.org; Ambassador MALIKA BERAK.

Bangladesh: House 18, Rd 108, Gulshan Model Town, POB 22, Dhaka 1212; tel. (2) 8813811; fax (2) 8813812; internet www.ambafrance-bd.org; Ambassador Charley Causeret.

Belarus: 220030 Minsk, pl. Svabody 11; tel. (17) 210-28-68; fax (17) 210-25-48; e-mail webmestreby@diplomatie.fr; internet www.ambafrance-by.org; Ambassador MIREILLE MUSSO.

Belgium: 65 rue Ducale, 1000 Brussels; tel. (2) 548-87-11; fax (2) 548-87-32; e-mail ambafr@ambafrance-be.org; internet www.ambafrance-be.org; Ambassador Dominique Boché.

Benin: ave Jean-Paul II, BP 966, Cotonou; tel. 21-30-02-25; fax 21-30-07-57; e-mail ambafrance.cotonou@diplomatie.gouv.fr; internet www.ambafrance -bj.org; Ambassador HERVÉ BESANCENOT.

Bolivia: Avda Hernando Silés 5390, esq. Calle 8, Obrajes, Casilla 717, La Paz; tel. (2) 214-9900; fax (2) 214-9904; e-mail information@ambafrance-bo.org; internet www.ambafrance-bo.org; Ambassador Alain Fouquet.

Bosnia and Herzegovina: 71000 Sarajevo, Kapetanović Ljubušaka 18; tel. (33) 668149; fax (33) 668103; e-mail ambsarajevo.presse@diplomatie.gouv.fr; internet www.ambafrance.ba; Ambassador MARYSE BERNIAU.

Botswana: 761 Robinson Rd, POB 1424, Gaborone; tel. 3973863; fax 3971733; e-mail frambbots@info.bw; Ambassador Jean-Pierre Courtois.

Brazil: SES, Av. das Nações, Quadra 801, Lote 04, 70404-900 Brasília, DF; tel. (61) 3312-9100; fax (61) 3312-9103; e-mail france@ambafrance.org.br; internet www.ambafrance.org.br; Ambassador ANTOINE POUILLIEUTE.

Brunei: Kompleks Jalan Sultan, Units 301–306, 3rd Floor, 51–55 Jalan Sultan, Bandar Seri Begawan BS 8811; tel. 2220960; fax 2243373; e-mail france@brunet.bn; internet www.ambafrance-bn.org; Ambassador Patrick Bonneville.

Bulgaria: 1504 Sofia, ul. Oborishte 27–29; tel. (2) 965-11-00; fax (2) 965-11-20; internet www.ambafrance-bg.org; Ambassador ETIENNE DE PONCINS.

Burkina Faso: ave du Trésor, 01 BP 504, Ouagadougou 01; tel. 50-49-66-66; fax 50-49-66-09; e-mail ambassade@ambafrance-bf.org; internet www .ambafrance-bf.org; Ambassador François Goldblatt.

Burundi: 60 ave de l'UPRONA, BP 1740, Bujumbura; tel. 22203000; fax 22203010; Ambassador JOËL LOUVET.

Cambodia: 1 blvd Monivong, Phnom-Penh; tel. (23) 430020; fax (23) 430037; e-mail ambafrance.phnom-penh-amba@diplomatie.gouv.fr; internet www .ambafrance-kh.org; Ambassador Jean-François Desmazières.

Cameroon: Plateau Atémengué, BP 1631, Yaoundé; tel. 2222-7900; fax 2222-7909; e-mail chancellerie.yaounde-amba@diplomatie.gouv.fr; internet www .ambafrance-cm.org; Ambassador GEORGES SERRE.

Canada: 42 Sussex Dr., Ottawa, ON K1M 2C9; tel. (613) 789-1795; fax (613) 562-3735; e-mail politique@ambafrance-ca.org; internet www.ambafrance -ca.org; Ambassador Daniel Jouanneau.

Cape Verde: Achada de Santo António, CP 192, Praia, Santiago; tel. 2615591; fax 2615590; internet www.ambafrance-cv.org; Ambassador BERNARD DEMANGE.

Central African Republic: blvd du Général de Gaulle, BP 884, Bangui; tel. 61-30-05; fax 61-74-04; e-mail chancellerie.bangui-amba@diplomatie.gouv.fr; internet www.ambafrance-cf.org; Ambassador Alain-Jean Girma.

Chad: rue du Lt Franjoux, BP 431, N'Djamena; tel. 52-25-75; fax 52-28-55; e-mail amba.france@intnet.td; internet www.ambafrance-td.org; Ambassador BRUNO FOUCHER.

Chile: Condell 65, Casilla 38d, Providencia, Santiago; tel. (2) 470-8000; fax (2) 470-8050; e-mail ambassade@ambafrance-cl.org; internet www.france.cl; Ambassador Elisabeth Beton-Délègue.

China, People's Republic: 3 Dong San Jie, San Li Tun, Chao Yang Qu, Beijing 100600; tel. (10) 65321331; fax (10) 65324841; e-mail secretariat@ambafrance -cn.org; internet www.ambafrance-cn.org; Ambassador HERVÉ LADSOUS.

Colombia: Carrera 11, No 93-12, Bogotá, DC; tel. (1) 638-1400; fax (1) 638-1430; internet www.ambafrance-co.org; Ambassador Jean-Michel Marlaud.

Comoros: blvd de Strasbourg, BP 465, Moroni; tel. (73) 0615; fax (73) 3347; e-mail pierre.lanners@snpt.km; internet www.ambafrance-km.org; Ambassador CHRISTIAN JOB.

Congo, Democratic Republic: 97 ave de la République du Tchad, BP 3093, Kinshasa; tel. (81) 5559999; fax (81) 5559937; e-mail ambafrance@ic.cd; internet www.ambafrance-cd.org; Ambassador Bernard Prevost.

Congo, Republic: rue Alfassa, BP 2089, Brazzaville; tel. 81-55-41; e-mail webmestre@mail.com; internet www.ambafrance-cg.org; Ambassador NICHOLAS NORMAND.

Costa Rica: Carretera a Curridabat, del Indoor Club 200 m sur y 25 m oeste, Apdo 10177, 1000 San José; tel. 234-4167; fax 234-4195; e-mail sjfrance@sol .racsa.co.cr; internet www.ambafrance-cr.org; Ambassador Jean-Paul Monchau.

Côte d'Ivoire: rue Lecoeur, 17 BP 175, Abidjan 17; tel. 20-20-04-04; fax 20-20-04-47; e-mail scac.abidjan-amba@diplomatie.gouv.fr; internet www .ambafrance-ci.org; .

Croatia: 10000 Zagreb, Hebrangova 2; tel. (1) 4893600; fax (1) 4893660; e-mail presse@ambafrance.hr; internet www.ambafrance.hr; Ambassador François Saint-Paul.

Cuba: Calle 14, No 312, entre 3 y 5, Miramar, Havana; tel. (7) 201-3131; fax (7) 201-3107; e-mail internet.la-havane-amba@diplomatie.fr; internet www .ambafrance-cu.org; Ambassador FRÉDÉRIC DORÉ.

Cyprus: 14–16 Saktouri St, 2nd Floor, Agioi Omologitai, 1080 Nicosia; tel. 22585300; fax 22585335; e-mail ambafrance@cytanet.com.cy; internet www .ambafrancechypre.org; Ambassador Nicolas Galey.

Czech Republic: Velkopřevorské nám. 2, POB 102, 118 000 Prague 1; tel. 251171711; fax 251171720; e-mail ambafrcz@france.cz; internet www.france .cz; Ambassador CHARLES FRIES.

Denmark: Kongens Nytorv 4, 1050 Copenhagen K; tel. 33-67-01-00; fax 33-93-97-52; e-mail presse@ambafrance-dk.org; internet www.ambafrance-dk .org; Ambassador Bérengère Quincy.

Djibouti: 45 blvd du Maréchal Foch, BP 2039, Djibouti; tel. 350963; fax 350272; e-mail ambfrdj@intnet.dj; internet www.ambafrance-dj.org; Ambassador DOMINIQUE DECHERF.

Dominican Republic: Calle Las Damas 42, Zona Colonial, Santo Domingo, DN; tel. 695-4300; fax 695-4311; e-mail ambafrance@ambafrance-do.org; internet www.ambafrance-do.org; Ambassador Cécile Pozzo di Borgo.

Ecuador: Calle Leonidas Plaza 107 y Avda Patria, CP 536, Quito; tel. (2) 294-3800; fax (2) 294-3809; e-mail francie@andinanet.net; internet www .ambafrance-ecu.org; Ambassador DIDIER LOPINOT.

Egypt: POB 1777, 29 Sharia Charles de Gaulle, Cairo (Giza); tel. (2) 5703916; fax (2) 5718498; e-mail questions@ambafrance-eg.org; internet www .ambafrance-eg.org; Ambassador Philippe Coste.

El Salvador: 1 Calle Poniente 3718, Col. Escalón, Apdo 474, San Salvador; tel. 2279-4016; fax 2298-1536; e-mail ambafrance@es.com.sv; internet www .embafrancia.com.sv; Ambassador FRANCIS ROUDIÈRE.

Equatorial Guinea: Carretera del Aeropuerto, Apdo 326, Malabo; tel. (09) 20-05; fax (09) 23-05; e-mail chancellerie.malabo-amba@diplomatie.gouv.fr; internet www.ambafrance-gq.org; Ambassador Henri Deniaud.

Eritrea: POB 209, Asmara; tel. (1) 126599; fax (1) 123298; Ambassador PIERRE COULONT.

Estonia: Toom-Kuninga 20, Tallinn 15185; tel. 631-1492; fax 631-1385; e-mail france@datanet-ee.org; internet www.ambafrance-ee.org; Ambassador Daniel Labrosse.

Ethiopia: Kabana, POB 1464, Addis Ababa; tel. (11) 1236022; fax (11) 1236029; e-mail scacamb@ethionet.et; internet www.ambafrance-ethiopie .org; Ambassador STÉPHANE GOMPERTZ.

Fiji: Dominion House, 7th Floor, Thomson St, Suva; tel. 3312233; fax 3301894; internet www.ambafrance-fj.org; Ambassador Jean-François Bouffandeau.

Finland: Itäinen puistotie 13, 00140 Helsinki; tel. (9) 618780; fax (9) 61878342; e-mail ambassade@france.fi; internet www.france.fi; Ambassador GÉRARD CROS.

Gabon: 1 rue du pont Pirah, BP 2125, Libreville; tel. 79-70-00; fax 79-70-09; e-mail ambafran@inet.ga; internet www.ambafrance-ga.org; Ambassador Jean Marc Simon.

Georgia: 0108 Tbilisi, Gogebashvili 15; tel. (32) 99-99-76; fax (32) 95-33-75; e-mail ambafrance@access.sanet.ge; internet www.ambafrance-ge.org; Ambassador ERIC FOURNIER.

Germany: Pariser Pl. 5, 10117 Berlin; tel. (30) 590039000; fax (30) 590039110; e-mail info@botschaft-frankreich.de; internet www.ambafrance-de.org; Ambassador Bernard de Montferrand.

Ghana: 12th Rd, off Liberation Ave, POB 187, Accra; tel. (21) 214550; fax (21) 214589; e-mail info@ambafrance-gh.org; internet www.ambafrance-gh .org; Ambassador PIERRE JACQUEMOT.

Greece: Leoforos Vassilissis Sofias 7, 106 71 Athens; tel. (210) 3391000; fax (210) 3391009; internet www.ambafrance-gr.org; Ambassador Christophe Farnaud.

Guatemala: Edif. COGEFAR, 5a Avda 8-59, Zona 14, Apdo 971-A, 01014 Guatemala City; tel. 2421-7370; fax 2421-7409; e-mail ambfrguate@intelnet .net.gt; internet www.ambafrance.org.gt; Ambassador NORBERT CARRASCO-SAULNIER.

Guinea: ave du Commerce, BP 373, Conakry; tel. 30-47-10-00; fax 30-47-10-15; internet www.ambafrance-gn.org; Ambassador Jean-Michel Berrit.

Guinea-Bissau: Av. Immeuble des 8 logements, ave Francisco Mendez, Bissau; tel. 201312; fax 205094; e-mail chancellerie@ambafrance-gw.org; internet www.ambafrance-gw.org; Ambassador JEAN-FRANÇOIS PAROT.

Haiti: 51 pl. des Héros de l'Indépendance, BP 1312, Port-au-Prince; tel. 222-0952; fax 223-8420; e-mail ambafrance@hainet.net; internet www.diplomatie .gouv.fr/fr/pays-zones-geo_833/haiti_513/index.html; Ambassador Christian Connan.

Honduras: Col. Palmira, Avda Juan Lindo, Callejón Batres 337, Apdo 3441, Tegucigalpa; tel. 236-6800; fax 236-8051; e-mail info@ambafrance-hn.org; internet www.ambafrance-hn.org; Ambassador LAURENT DOMINATI.

Hungary: 1062 Budapest, Lendvay u. 27; tel. (1) 332-4980; fax (1) 311-8291; e-mail ambasfn-presse@matavnet.hu; internet www.ambafrance.hu; Ambassador René Roudaut.

Iceland: Túngata 22, 101 Reykjavík; tel. 5759600; fax 5759604; e-mail alain .fortin@diplomatie.gouv.fr; internet www.ambafrance.is; Ambassador OLIVIER MAUVISSEAU.

India: 2/50e Shanti Path, Chanakyapuri, New Delhi 110 021; tel. (11) 24196100; fax (11) 24196119; e-mail webmaster@france-in-india.org; internet www.france-in-india.org; Ambassador Jérôme Bonnafont.

Indonesia: Jalan M. H. Thamrin 20, Jakarta Pusat 10350; tel. (21) 23557601; fax (21) 23557600; e-mail ambassade@ambafrance-id.org; internet www .ambafrance-id.org; Ambassador CATHERINE BOIVINEAU.

Iran: 85 Neauphle-le-Château Ave, Tehran; tel. (21) 66706005; fax (21) 66706543; e-mail consulaire@ambafrance-ir.org; internet www.ambafrance -ir.org; Ambassador Bernard Poletti.

Iraq: POB 118, 7/55/102 Abu Nawas, Baghdad; tel. (1) 790-6061; fax (1) 718-1975; Ambassador JEAN FRANÇOIS GIRAULT.

Ireland: 36 Ailesbury Rd, Dublin 4; tel. (1) 2775000; fax (1) 2775001; e-mail chancellerie@ambafrance.ie; internet www.ambafrance-ie.org; Ambassador Yvon Roé d'Albert.

Israel: 112 Tayelet Herbert Samuel, Tel-Aviv 63572; tel. 3-5208300; fax 3-5208342; e-mail diplomatie@ambafrance-il.org; internet www.ambafrance-il .org; Ambassador JEAN-MICHEL CASA.

Italy: Piazza Farnese 67, 00186 Roma; tel. (06) 686011; fax (06) 68601418; e-mail fatima.madjer@diplomatie.gouv.fr; internet www.ambafrance-it.org; Ambassador Jean-Marc de La Sablière.

Jamaica: 13 Hillcrest Ave, POB 93, Kingston 6; tel. 978-0210; fax 927-4998; e-mail frenchembassy@cwjamaica.com; internet www.ambafrance-jm-bm .org; Ambassador FRANCIS HURTUT.

Japan: 4-11-44, Minami Azabu, Minato-ku, Tokyo 106-8514; tel. (3) 5420-8800; fax (3) 5420-8847; e-mail ambafrance.tokyo@diplomatie.fr; internet www.ambafrance-jp.org; Ambassador Philippe Faure.

Jordan: POB 5348, Amman 11183; tel. (6) 4604630; fax (6) 4604638; e-mail webmestre@mail.com; internet www.ambafrance-jo.org; Ambassador DENYS GAUER.

Kazakhstan: 010000 Astana, Kosmonavtov 62; tel. (7172) 79-51-00; fax (7172) 79-51-01; e-mail ambafrance@mail.ru; internet www.ambafrance-kz .kz; Ambassador Alain Couanon.

Kenya: Barclays Plaza, 9th Floor, Loita St, POB 41784, Nairobi; tel. (20) 2778000; fax (20) 2778180; e-mail ambafrance.nairobi@diplomatie.gouv.fr; internet www.ambafrance-ke.org; Ambassador ELIZABETH BARBIER.

Korea, Republic: 30, Hap-dong, Seodaemun-gu, Seoul 120-030; tel. (2) 3149-4300; fax (2) 3149-4328; e-mail ambafrance@korea.com; internet www .ambafrance-kr.org; Ambassador Philippe Thiébaud.

Kuwait: POB 1037, 13011 Safat, Mansouriah, Block 1, St 13, Villa 24, Kuwait City; tel. 2582020; fax 2571058; e-mail cad.koweit-amba@diplomatie.gouv .fr; internet www.ambafrance-kwt.org; Ambassador CORINNE BREUZÉ.

Laos: rue Setthathirath, BP 06, Vientiane; tel. (21) 215253; fax (21) 215250; e-mail contact@ambafrance-laos.org; internet www.ambafrance-laos.org; Ambassador François Sénémaud.

Latvia: Raiņa bulv. 9, Rīga 1050; tel. 6703-6600; fax 6703-6615; e-mail webmastre.ambafrance-lv@diplomatie.gouv.fr; internet www.ambafrance-lv .org; Ambassador ANDRÉ-JEAN LIBOUREL.

Lebanon: rue de Damas, Beirut; tel. (1) 420000; fax (1) 420013; e-mail ambafr@ciberia.net.lb; internet www.ambafrance-lb.org; Chargé d'affaires a.i André Parant.

Libya: POB 312, Sharia Beni al-Amar, Hay Andalus, Tripoli; tel. (21) 4774891; fax (21) 4778266; e-mail info@ambafrance-ly.org; internet www .ambafrance-ly.org; Ambassador JEAN-LUC SIBIUDE.

Lithuania: Švarco g. 1, Vilnius 01131; tel. (5) 212-2979; fax (5) 212-4211; e-mail ambafrance.vilnius@diplomatie.gouv.fr; internet www.ambafrance-lt .org; Ambassador Guy Yelda.

Luxembourg: 8B blvd Joseph II, BP 359, 2013 Luxembourg; tel. 45-72-71; fax 45-72-71-227; e-mail ambassade@ambafrance-lu.org; internet www .ambafrance-lu.org; Ambassador CHARLES DE BANCALIS.

Macedonia, former Yugoslav Republic: 1000 Skopje, Salvador Aljende 73; tel. (2) 3244300; fax (2) 3117760; e-mail franamba@mt.net.mk; internet www .ambafrance-mk.org; Ambassador Bernard Valero.

Madagascar: 3 rue Jean Jaurès, BP 204, 101 Antananarivo; tel. (20) 2239898; fax (20) 2239927; e-mail ambatana@wanadoo.mg; internet www.ambafrance-mada.org; Ambassador GILDAS LE LIDEC.

Malaysia: 192–196 Jalan Ampang, 50450 Kuala Lumpur; tel. (3) 20535500; fax (3) 20535501; e-mail ambassade.kuala-lumpur-amba@diplomatie.gouv.fr; internet www.ambafrance-my.org; Ambassador Alain du Boispéan.

Mali: square Patrice Lumumba, BP 17, Bamako; tel. 497-57-57; fax 222-31-36; e-mail ambassade@france-mali.org.ml; internet www.ambafrance-ml.org; Ambassador MICHEL REVEYRAND DE MENTHON.

Malta: POB 408, Valletta CMR 01; 130 Melita St, Valletta CMR 01; tel. 21233430; fax 21233528; e-mail france@global.net.mt; internet www.ambafrance-mt.org; Ambassador Jean-Marc Rives.

Mauritania: rue Ahmed Ould Hamed, Tevragh Zeina, BP 231, Nouakchott; tel. 529-96-99; fax 529-69-38; e-mail ambafrance.nouakchott-amba@diplomatie.gouv.fr; internet www.france-mauritanie.mr; Ambassador PATRICK NICOLOSO.

Mauritius: 14 St George St, Port Louis; tel. 202-0100; fax 202-0110; e-mail ambafr@intnet.mu; internet www.ambafrance-mu.org; Ambassador Jacques Maillard.

Mexico: Campos Elíseos 339, Col. Polanco, Del. Miguel Hidalgo, 11560 México, DF; tel. (55) 9171-9700; fax (55) 9171-9703; e-mail prensa@ambafrance-mx.org; internet www.ambafrance-mx.org; Ambassador ALAIN LE GOURRIÉREC.

Moldova: Chişinău, str. Vlaicu Pîrcălab 6; tel. (22) 20-04-00; fax (22) 20-04-01; e-mail amb-fr@cni.md; internet www.ambafrance.md; Ambassador Pierre Andrieu.

Monaco: Le Roc fleuri, 1 rue du Tenao, BP 345, MC 98006 Cedex; tel. 92-16-54-60; fax 92-16-54-64; e-mail courrier@ambafrance.mc; internet www.ambafrance.mc; Ambassador ODILE REMIK-ADIM.

Mongolia: 3 Peace Ave, Ulan Bator (CPOB 687); tel. (11) 324519; fax (11) 319176; e-mail ambafrance@magicnet.mn; internet www.ambafrance-mn.org; Ambassador Patrick Chrismant.

Montenegro: 81000 Podgorica, Atinska 35; tel. (81) 665348; e-mail france@cg.yu; Ambassador BERNARD GARANCHER.

Morocco: 3 rue Sahnoun, BP 602, Rabat; tel. (3) 7689700; fax (3) 7689701; internet www.ambafrance-ma.org; Ambassador Jean-François Thibault.

Mozambique: Av. Julius Nyerere 2361, CP 4781, Maputo; tel. 21484600; fax 21484680; e-mail ambafrancemz@tvcabo.co.mz; internet www.ambafrance-mz.org; Ambassador THIERRY VITEAU.

Myanmar: 102 Pyidaungsu Yeiktha Rd, POB 858, Yangon; tel. (1) 212523; fax (1) 212527; e-mail ambafrance-rangoun@diplomatie.gouv.fr; internet www.ambafrance-mm.org; Ambassador Jean-Pierre Lafosse.

Namibia: 1 Goethe St, POB 20484, Windhoek; tel. (61) 2276700; fax (61) 231436; e-mail frambwdk@iafrica.com.na; internet www.ambafrance-na.org; Ambassador PHILIPPE BOSSIÈRE.

Nepal: Lazimpat, POB 452, Kathmandu; tel. (1) 4412332; fax (1) 4419968; e-mail consulat@ambafrance-np.org; internet www.ambafrance-np.org; Ambassador Gilles-Henry Garault.

Netherlands: Smidsplein 1, 2514 BT The Hague; tel. (70) 3125800; fax (70) 3125824; e-mail info@ambafrance-nl.org; internet www.ambafrance-nl.org; Ambassador JEAN-MICHEL GAUSSOT.

New Zealand: Sovereign House, 13th Floor, 34–42 Manners St, POB 11-343, Wellington; tel. (4) 384-2555; fax (4) 384-2579; e-mail amba.france@actrix.co.nz; internet www.ambafrance-nz.org; Ambassador Michel Legras.

Nicaragua: Iglesia el Carmen 1½ c. abajo, Apdo 1227, Managua; tel. 222-6210; fax 268-5630; e-mail info@ambafrance-ni.org; internet www.ambafrance-ni.org; Ambassador THIERRY PIERRE FRAYSSÉ.

Niger: route de Tondibia, Quartier Yantala, BP 10660, Niamey; tel. 20-72-24-32; fax 20-72-25-18; e-mail webmestre@mail.com; internet www.ambafrance-ne.org; Ambassador François Ponge.

Nigeria: 37 Udi Hills St, Abuja; tel. (9) 5231055; fax (9) 5235482; e-mail ambafrance.abj@micro.com.ng; internet www.ambafrance-ng.org; Ambassador YVES GAUDEUL.

Norway: Drammensvn 69, 0244 Oslo; tel. 23-28-46-00; fax 23-28-46-70; e-mail ambafrance.oslo@diplomatie.gouv.fr; internet www.ambafrance-no.org; Ambassador Chantal Poiret.

Oman: Diplomatic City, Al-Khuwair, POB 208, Madinat Qaboos 115; tel. 24681800; fax 24681843; e-mail diplofr1@omantel.net.om; internet www.ambafrance-om.org; Ambassador MARC BARETY.

Pakistan: Constitution Ave, G-5, Diplomatic Enclave 1, POB 1068, Islamabad; tel. (51) 2278730; fax (51) 2823236; e-mail Ambafrance.ISLAMABAD@diplomatie.gouv.fr; Ambassador Régis de Belenet.

Panama: Plaza de Francia 1, Las Bovedas, San Felipe, Apdo 869, Panamá 1; tel. 211-6200; fax 211-6201; e-mail pierre_henri.guignard@diplomatie.gouv.fr; internet www.ambafrance-pa.org; Ambassador PIERRE HENRI GUIGNARD.

Papua New Guinea: Defens Haus, 6th Floor, Cnr of Hunter St and Champion Parade, POB 1155, Port Moresby; tel. 3215550; fax 3215549; e-mail ambfrpom@global.net.pg; internet www.ambafrance-pg.org; Ambassador Patrick Boursin.

Paraguay: Avda España 893, Calle Pucheu, Casilla 97, Asunción; tel. (21) 21-2449; fax (21) 21-1690; e-mail chancellerie@ambafran.gov.py; internet www.ambafran.gov.py; Ambassador GILLES BIENVENUE.

Peru: Avda Arequipa 3415, Lima 27; tel. (1) 2158400; fax (1) 2158410; e-mail france.consulat@ambafrance-pe.org; internet www.ambafrance-pe.org; Ambassador Pierre Charrasse.

Philippines: Pacific Star Bldg, 16th Floor, Makati Ave, cnr Sen. Gil J. Puyat Ave, 1200 Makati City, Metro Manila; tel. (2) 8576900; fax (2) 8576951; e-mail consulat@ambafrance-ph.org; internet www.ambafrance-ph.org; Ambassador GÉRARD CHESNEL.

Poland: 00-477 Warsaw, ul. Piękna 1; tel. (22) 5293000; fax (22) 5293001; e-mail presse@ambafrance-pl.org; internet www.ambafrance-pl.org; Ambassador Barry Delongchamps.

Portugal: Rua de Santos-o-Velho 5, 1249-079 Lisbon; tel. (21) 3939100; fax (21) 3939151; e-mail consulat.lisbonne@ambafrance-pt.org; internet www.ambafrance-pt.org; Ambassador PATRICK GAUTRAT.

Qatar: POB 2669, Doha; tel. 4832283; fax 4832254; e-mail ambadoha@qatar.net.qa; internet www.ambafrance-qa.org; Ambassador Antoine Sivan.

Romania: 010392 Bucharest, Str. Biserica Amzei 13–15; tel. (21) 3031000; fax (21) 3031090; e-mail chancellerie.bucarest-amba@diplomatie.gouv.fr; internet www.ambafrance-ro.org; Ambassador HENRI PAUL.

Russian Federation: 119049 Moscow, ul. B. Yakimanka 45; tel. (495) 937-15-00; fax (495) 937-14-46; e-mail amba@ambafrance.ru; internet www.ambafrance.ru; Ambassador Stanislas Lefebvre de Laboulaye.

Saint Lucia: French Embassy to the OECS, GPO Private Box 937, Vigie, Castries; tel. 455-6060; fax 455-6056; e-mail frenchembassy@candw.lc; internet www.ambafrance-lc.org; Ambassador MICHÈLE SAUTERAUD.

Saudi Arabia: POB 94367, Riyadh 11693; tel. (1) 488-1255; fax (1) 488-2882; e-mail diplomatie@ambafrance.org.sa; internet www.ambafrance.org.sa; Ambassador Bertrand Besancenot.

Senegal: 1 rue El Hadj Amadou Assane Ndoye, BP 4035, Dakar; tel. 33-839-5100; fax 33-839-5181; e-mail webmestre.dakar-amba@diplomatie.gouv.fr; internet www.ambafrance-sn.org; Ambassador JEAN-CHRISTOPHE RUFIN.

Serbia: 11000 Belgrade, Pariska 11, POB 283; tel. (11) 3023500; fax (11) 3023510; e-mail amba_fr@eunet.yu; internet www.ambafrance-srb.org; Ambassador Jean-François Terral.

Seychelles: La Ciotat Bldg, Mont Fleuri, POB 478, Victoria; tel. 382500; fax 382510; e-mail ambafrance@intelvision.net; internet www.ambafrance-sc.org; Ambassador MICHEL TRÉTOUT.

Singapore: 101–103 Cluny Park Rd, Singapore 259595; tel. 68807800; fax 68807801; e-mail ambassadeur@france.org.sg; internet www.france.org.sg; Ambassador Pierre Buhler.

Slovakia: Hlavné nám. 7, 812 83 Bratislava; tel. (2) 5934-7111; fax (2) 5934-7199; e-mail diplo@france.sk; internet www.france.sk; Ambassador HENRY CUNY.

Slovenia: 1000 Ljubljana, Barjanska cesta 1; tel. (1) 4790400; fax (1) 4790410; e-mail info@ambafrance.si; internet www.ambafrance.si; Ambassador Chantal de Ghaisne de Bourmont.

South Africa: 250 Melk St, cnr Melk and Middle Sts, New Muckleneuk, Pretoria 0181; tel. (12) 4251600; fax (12) 4251689; e-mail france@ambafrance-rsa.org; internet www.ambafrance-rsa.org; Ambassador DENIS PIETTON.

Spain: Salustiano Olózaga 9, 28001 Madrid; tel. (91) 4238900; fax (91) 4238908; e-mail chancellerie@ctv.es; internet www.ambafrance-es.org; Ambassador Bruno Delaye.

Sri Lanka: 89 Rosmead Place, POB 880, Colombo 7; tel. (11) 2698815; fax (11) 2699039; e-mail ambfrclb@sltnet.lk; internet www.ambafrance-lk.org; Ambassador MICHEL LUMMAUX.

Sudan: al-Amarat, St 13, Plot No. 11, Block 12, POB 377, 11111 Khartoum; tel. (183) 471082; fax (183) 465928; e-mail cad.khartoum@diplomatie.gouv.fr; internet www.ambafrance-sd.org; Ambassador Christine Robichon.

Suriname: Henck Arronstraat 5–7 boven, POB 2648, Paramaribo; tel. 476455; fax 471208; e-mail ambafrance.paramaribo@diplomatie.gouv.fr; internet www.ambafrance-sr.org; Ambassador RICHARD BARBEYRON.

Sweden: Kommendörsgt. 13, POB 5135, 102 43 Stockholm; tel. (8) 459-53-00; fax (8) 459-53-41; e-mail presse@ambafrance-se.org; internet www.ambafrance-se.org; Ambassador Joël De Zorzi.

Switzerland: Schosshaldenstr. 46, 3006 Bern; tel. 313592111; fax 313592191; e-mail scac@ambafrance-ch.org; internet www.ambafrance-ch.org; Ambassador JEAN-DIDIER ROISIN.

Syria: BP 769, rue Ata al-Ayoubi, al-Afif, Damascus; tel. (11) 3390200; fax (11) 3390221; e-mail ambafr@net.sy; Ambassador Michel Duclos.

Tajikistan: 734025 Dushanbe, Kuchai Rakhimi 17; tel. (372) 21-78-55; fax (372) 51-00-82; e-mail ambassade.douchanbe@diplomatie.gouv.fr; Ambassador OLIVIER MAITLAND PELEN.

Tanzania: Ali Hassan Mwinyi Rd, POB 2349, Dar es Salaam; tel. (22) 2198800; fax (22) 2198815; e-mail ambfrance@africaonline.co.tz; internet www.ambafrance-tz.org; Ambassador Jacques Champagne de Labriolle.

Thailand: 35 Soi Rong Phasi Kao, Thanon Charoenkrung, Bangkok 10500; tel. (2) 657-5100; fax (2) 657-5111; e-mail ambassade@ambafrance-th.org; internet www.ambafrance-th.org; Ambassador LAURENT AUBLIN.

Togo: rue de la Marina, BP 7485, Lomé; tel. 223-46-40; fax 223-46-56; e-mail Eric.BOSC@diplomatie.fr; internet www.ambafrance-tg.org; Ambassador Alain Holleville.

Trinidad and Tobago: TATIL Bldg, 6th Floor, 11 Maraval Rd, Port of Spain; tel. 622-7447; fax 628-2632; e-mail francett@wow.net; internet www.ambafrance-tt.org; Ambassador CHARLEY CAUSERET.

Tunisia: 2 place de l'Indépendence, 1000 Tunis; tel. (71) 105-111; fax (71) 105-100; e-mail courier@ambassadefrance-tn.org; internet www.ambassadefrance-tn.org; Ambassador Serge Degallaix.

Turkey: Paris Cad. 70, 06540 Kavaklıdere, Ankara; tel. (312) 4554545; fax (312) 4554527; e-mail ambaank@yahoo.fr; internet www.ambafrance-tr.org; Ambassador BERNARD EMIÉ.

Turkmenistan: 744000 Aşgabat, ul. Esgerler 35; tel. (12) 36-35-50; fax (12) 36-36-40; e-mail cad.achgabat-amba@diplomatie.gouv.fr; Ambassador Christian Lechervy.

Uganda: 16 Lumumba Ave, Nakasero, POB 7212, Kampala; tel. (41) 4342120; fax (41) 4341252; e-mail ambafrance.kampala@diplomatie.gouv.fr; internet www.ambafrance-ug.org; Ambassador BERNARD GARANCHER.

Ukraine: 01034 Kyiv, vul. Reitarska 39; tel. (44) 590-36-00; fax (44) 590-36-24; e-mail pressefr@carrier.kiev.ua; internet www.ambafrance-ua.org; Ambassador Jean-Paul Veziant.

United Arab Emirates: POB 4014, Abu Dhabi; tel. (2) 4435100; fax (2) 4434158; e-mail ambafr@emirates.net.ae; internet www.ambafrance-eau.org; Ambassador PATRICE PAOLI.

United Kingdom: 58 Knightsbridge, London, SW1X 7JT; tel. (20) 7073-1000; fax (20) 7073-1004; e-mail presse.londres-amba@diplomatie.fr; internet www.ambafrance-uk.org; Ambassador Maurice Gordault-Montagne.

United States of America: 4101 Reservoir Rd, NW, Washington, DC 20007; tel. (202) 944-6166; fax (202) 944-6072; e-mail info@ambafrance-us.org; internet www.ambafrance-us.org; Ambassador PIERRE VIMONT.

Uruguay: Avda Uruguay 853, Casilla 290, 11100 Montevideo; tel. (2) 9020077; fax (2) 9023711; e-mail ambafranceuruguay@gmail.com; internet www.ambafranceuruguay.org; Ambassador Jean-Claude Moyret.

Uzbekistan: 100041 Tashkent, Oxunboboev ko'ch. 25; tel. (71) 133-53-82; fax (71) 133-51-97; e-mail presse@ambafrance-uz.org; internet www.ambafrance-uz.org; Ambassador HUGUES PERNET.

Vanuatu: Kumul Highway, POB 60, Port Vila; tel. 22353; fax 22695; e-mail ambafra@vanuatu.com.vu; internet www.ambafrance-vu.org; Ambassador Pierre Mayaudon.

Vatican City: Villa Bonaparte, Via Piave 23, 00186 Rome, Italy; tel. (06) 42030900; fax (06) 42030968; e-mail ambfrssg@tin.it; internet www.france-vatican.org; Chargé d'affaires a.i. PIERRE COCHARD.

Venezuela: Calle Madrid con Avda Trinidad, Las Mercedes, Apdo 60385, Caracas 1060; tel. (212) 909-6500; fax (212) 909-6630; e-mail infos@francia.org.ve; internet www.francia.org.ve; Ambassador Hadelin de La Tour-du-Pin.

Viet Nam: 57 Tran Hung Dao, Hanoi; tel. (4) 9437719; fax (4) 9437236; internet www.ambafrance-vn.org; Ambassador HERVÉ BOLOT.

Yemen: POB 1286, cnr Sts 2 and 21, San'a; tel. (1) 268888; fax (1) 269160; e-mail ambaf@y.net.ye; internet www.ambafrance-ye.org; Ambassador Gilles Gauthier.

Zambia: Anglo American Bldg, 4th Floor, 74 Independence Ave, POB 30062, 10101 Lusaka; tel. (1) 251322; fax (1) 254475; e-mail france@ambafrance-zm.org; internet www.ambafrance-zm.org; Ambassador FRANCIS SAUDUBRAY.

Zimbabwe: Bank Chambers, 11th Floor, 74–76 Samora Machel Ave, POB 1378, Harare; tel. (4) 703216; fax (4) 730078; internet www.ambafrance-zw.org; Ambassador Gabriel Jugnet.

DIPLOMATIC MISSIONS OF GABON

United Nations: 18 East 41st St, 9th Floor, New York, NY 10017; tel. (212) 686-9720; fax (212) 689-5769; e-mail gabon@un.int; Permanent Representative DENIS DANGUE RÉWAKA.

Algeria: BP 125, Rostomia, 21 rue Hadj Ahmed Mohamed, Hydra, Algiers; tel. (21) 69-24-00; fax (21) 60-25-46; Ambassador Yves Ongollo.

Angola: Av. 4 de Fevereiro 95, Luanda; tel. 222372614; Ambassador RAPHAËL NKASSA-NZOGHO.

Belgium: 112 ave Winston Churchill, 1180 Brussels; tel. (2) 340-62-10; fax (2) 346-46-69; e-mail ambagabbelg@yahoo.fr; Ambassador René Makongo.

Brazil: SHIS, QL 08, Conj. 03, Casa 01, Lago Sul, 71620-235 Brasília, DF; tel. (61) 3248-3536; fax (61) 3248-2241; e-mail mgabao@terra.com.br; Ambassador BENJAMIN LEGNONGO-NDUMBA.

Cameroon: Quartier Bastos, Ekoudou, BP 4130, Yaoundé; tel. 2220-2966; fax 2221-0224; Ambassador Michel Mandougoua.

Canada: 4 Range Rd, Ottawa, ON K1N 8J5; tel. (613) 232-5301; fax (613) 232-6916; e-mail ambgabon@sprint.ca; Ambassador JOSEPH OBIANG NDOUTOUME.

China, People's Republic: 36 Guang Hua Lu, Jian Guo Men Wai, Beijing 100600; tel. (10) 65322810; fax (10) 65322621; Ambassador Emmanuel Mba-Allo.

Congo, Democratic Republic: ave du 24 novembre, BP 9592, Kinshasa; tel. (12) 68325; Ambassador MICHEL MADOUNGOU.

Côte d'Ivoire: Immeuble Les Heveas, blvd Carde, 01 BP 3765, Abidjan 01; tel. 22-44-51-54; fax 22-44-75-05; Ambassador Henri Bekalé-Akwé.

Egypt: 17 Sharia Mecca el-Moukarama, Cairo (Dokki); tel. (2) 3379699; Ambassador JOSEPH MAMBOUNGOU.

Equatorial Guinea: Calle de Argelia, Apdo 18, Malabo; Ambassador Jean-Baptiste Mbatchi.

Ethiopia: Woreda 17, Kebele 18, House No. 1026, POB 1256, Addis Ababa; tel. (11) 6611075; fax (11) 6613700; Ambassador EMMANUEL ISSOZE-NGONDET.

France: 26 bis ave Raphaël, 75016 Paris; tel. 1-72-70-01-50; fax 1-72-81-05-89; e-mail hditsougou@caramail.com; Ambassador Jean-Marie Adzé.

Germany: Hohensteinerstr. 16, 14197 Berlin; tel. (30) 89733440; fax (30) 89733444; e-mail info@botschaft-gabun.de; internet www.botschaft-gabun.de; Ambassador JEAN-CLAUDE BOUYOBART.

Italy: Via San Marino 36a, 00198 Roma; tel. (06) 85358970; fax (06) 8417278; e-mail ambagabon@tiscali.net; Ambassador Noel Baiot.

Japan: 1-34-11, Higashigaoka, Meguro-ku, Tokyo 152-0021; tel. (3) 5430-9171; fax (3) 5430-9175; e-mail info@gabonembassy-tokyo.org; internet www.geocities.jp/gabontky; Ambassador JEAN-CHRISTIAN OBAME.

Korea, Republic: Yoosung Bldg, 4th Floor, 738-20, Hannam-dong, Yeong-san-gu, Seoul; tel. (2) 793-9575; fax (2) 793-9574; e-mail amgabsel@unitel.co.kr; Ambassador Jean-Pierre Sole-Emane.

Lebanon: POB 11-1252, Riad es-Solh, Hadath, Beirut 1107 2080; tel. (5) 924649; fax (5) 924643; Ambassador SIMON NTOUTOUME EMANE.

Morocco: km 3.5, route des Zaêrs, BP 1239, 10100 Rabat; tel. (3) 7751950; fax (3) 7757550; Ambassador François Banga Eboumi.

Nigeria: 8 Norman Williams St, SW Ikoyi, POB 5989, Lagos; tel. (1) 2684673; fax (1) 2690692; Ambassador E. AGUEMINYA.

Russian Federation: 119002 Moscow, Denezhnyi per. 16; tel. (495) 241-00-80; fax (495) 244-06-94; Ambassador Paul Bié Eyené.

São Tomé and Príncipe: Rua Damão, CP 394, São Tomé; tel. 224434; fax 223531; e-mail ambagabon@cstome.net; Ambassador BEKALÉ MICHEL.

Saudi Arabia: POB 94325, Riyadh 11693; tel. (1) 456-7171; fax (1) 453-6121; e-mail ambagabonriyad@yahoo.com; Ambassador Nabil Koussou Inama.

Senegal: ave Cheikh Anta Diop, cnr Fann Résidence, BP 436, Dakar; tel. 33-865-2234; fax 33-864-3145; Ambassador VINCENT BOULE.

South Africa: 921 Schoeman St, Arcadia, Pretoria 0083; POB 9222, Pretoria 0001; tel. (12) 3424376; fax (12) 3424375; Ambassador Marcel-Jules Odongui-Bonnard.

Spain: Francisco Alcántara 3A, 28002 Madrid; tel. (91) 4138211; fax (91) 4131153; e-mail emb-gabon-es@nemo.es; Ambassador CARLOS VICTOR BOUNGOU.

Togo: Lomé; tel. 222-18-93; fax 222-18-92; Ambassador (vacant).

United Kingdom: 27 Elvaston Pl., London, SW7 5NL; tel. (20) 7823-9986; fax (20) 7584-0047; Ambassador (vacant).

United States of America: 2034 20th St, NW, Suite 200, Washington, DC 20009; tel. (202) 797-1000; fax (202) 332-0668; Ambassador Carlos Boungou.

Vatican City: Piazzale Clodio 12, 00195 Rome, Italy; tel. (06) 39721584; fax (06) 39724847; Ambassador DÉSIRÉ KOUMBA.

DIPLOMATIC MISSIONS OF THE GAMBIA

United Nations: 800 Second Ave, Suite 400f, New York, NY 10017; tel. (212) 949-6640; fax (212) 808-4975; e-mail gambia@un.int; Permanent Representative Tamsir Jallow.

Belgium: 126 ave F. D. Roosevelt, 1050 Brussels; tel. (2) 640-10-49; fax (2) 646-32-77; e-mail info@gambiaembassy.be; internet www.gambiaembassy .be; Chargé d'affaires a.i. AMIE NYAN-ALABOSON.

China (Taiwan): 9/F, 9-1 Lane 62, Tien Mou West Rd, Taipei 11156; tel. (2) 28753911; fax (2) 28752775; e-mail gm.roc@msa.hinet.net; Ambassador Mawdo Corajiki Juwara.

Cuba: Calle 24, No 307, entre 3 y 5, Miramar, Havana; tel. (7) 204-5315; fax (7) 204-5316; Ambassador PA-MODOU NJIE.

Ethiopia: Kebele 3, House No. 79, POB 60083, Addis Ababa; tel. (11) 6624647; fax (11) 6627895; e-mail gambia@ethionet.et; Ambassador Dr Omar A. Touray.

France: 117 rue St Lazare, 75008 Paris; tel. 1-72-74-82-61; fax 1-53-04-05-99; e-mail ambgambia_france117@hotmail.com; Chargé d'affaires a.i. MOSES BENJAMIN JALLOW.

Guinea-Bissau: 47 Victorino Costa, Chao de Papel, CP 529, 1037 Bissau; tel. 205085; fax 251099; e-mail gambiaembbissau@hotmail.com; Ambassador Cherno B. Touray.

Morocco: 11 rue Cadi ben Hammadi Senhaji, Souissi, Rabat; tel. (3) 7638045; fax (3) 7638189; Ambassador MAUDO HARLEY NURU TOURAY.

Nigeria: 162 Awolowo Rd, SW Ikoyi, POB 873, Lagos; tel. (1) 682192; High Commissioner Angela Colley.

Qatar: POB 22377, Doha; tel. 4651429; fax 4651705; Chargé d'affaires BASSIROU DRAMMEH.

Saudi Arabia: POB 94322, Riyadh 11693; tel. (1) 205-2158; fax (1) 456-2024; e-mail gamextriyadh@yahoo.com; Ambassador Lamin Jabang.

Senegal: 11 rue Elhadji Ismaïla Guèye (Thiong), BP 3248, Dakar; tel. 33-821-4416; fax 33-821-6279; Ambassador GIBRIL SEMAN JOOF.

Sierra Leone: 6 Wilberforce St, Freetown; tel. (22) 225191; fax (22) 226846; High Commissioner Dembo Badjie.

United Arab Emirates: Abu Dhabi; tel. (2) 6678030; Ambassador KEBBA NJIE.

United Kingdom: 57 Kensington Court, London, W8 5DG; tel. (20) 7937-6316; fax (20) 7937-9095; e-mail gambia@gamhighcom.wanadoo.co.uk; High Commr Elizabeth Ya Eli Harding.

United States of America: 1155 15th St, NW, Suite 1000, Washington, DC 20005-2076; tel. (202) 785-1399; fax (202) 785-1430; e-mail info@ gambiaembassy.us; internet www.gambiaembassy.us; Chargé d'affaires a.i. ABDUL RAHMAN COLE.

DIPLOMATIC MISSIONS OF GEORGIA

United Nations: 1 United Nations Plaza, 26th Floor, New York, NY 10021; tel. (212) 759-1949; fax (212) 759-1832; e-mail georgia@un.int; internet www .un.int/georgia; Permanent Representative Irakli Alasania.

Armenia: 0010 Yerevan, Aram St 42; tel. (10) 56-43-57; fax (10) 56-41-83; e-mail geoemb@netsys.am; internet www.armenia.mfa.gov.ge; Ambassador REVAZ GACHECHILADZE.

Austria: Doblhoffgasse 5/5, 1010 Vienna; tel. (1) 403-98-48; fax (1) 403-98-48-20; e-mail vienna.emb@mfa.govge; internet www.austria.mfa.gov.ge; Ambassador Victor Dolidze.

Azerbaijan: 1073 Baku, Yasamal rayon, section 523, S. Dadashev küç. 29; tel. (12) 497-45-60; fax (12) 497-45-61; e-mail embgeo@azeurotel.com; internet www.az.mfa.gov.ge; Ambassador NIKOLOZ NATBILADZE.

Belgium: 62 ave de Tervueren, 1040 Brussels; tel. (2) 761-11-90; fax (2) 761-11-99; e-mail info@georgia-embassy.be; internet www.belgium.mfa.gov.ge; Ambassador Salome Samadashvili.

Bulgaria: 1113 Sofia, ul. Krichim 65; tel. (2) 862-54-04; fax (2) 868-42-98; e-mail saelcho.sofia@mbox.contact.bg; internet www.bulgaria.mfa.gov.ge; Ambassador TEIMURAZ SHARASHENIDZE.

China, People's Republic: LA 03-02, Section A, Liangmaqiao Diplomatic Compound, Beijing; tel. (10) 65327518; fax (10) 65327519; e-mail geobeijing@gmail.com; internet www.china.mfa.gov.ge; Ambassador Mikheil Ukleba.

Cyprus: 26 Eleonon St, Strovolos, 2057 Nicosia; tel. 22357327; fax 22357307; e-mail geoembassy@cytanet.com.cy; Ambassador LASHA ZHVANIA.

Czech Republic: Na Zátorce 13, 160 00 Prague 6; tel. 233311749; fax 233383291; e-mail prague.emb@mfa.gov.ge; Ambassador Vladimer Chipashvili.

Denmark: Nybrogade 10, 1st Floor, 1203 Copenhagen K; tel. 39-11-00-00; fax 39-11-00-01; e-mail copenhagen.emb@mfa.gov.ge; internet www .denmark.mfa.gov.ge; Ambassador DAVID T. KERESELIDZE.

Egypt: 28 Sharia Sad el-Aali, Cairo (Dokki); tel. (2) 3359024; fax (2) 3366129; e-mail geoembeg@link.com.eg; Ambassador Giorgi Janjghava.

Estonia: Koidu 70/7, Tallinn 10129; tel. 698-8590; e-mail embassy.georgia@ mail.ee; Chargé d'affaires ZURAB MARSHANIA.

France: 104 ave Raymond Poincaré, 75116 Paris; tel. 1-45-02-16-16; fax 1-45-02-16-01; e-mail ambassade.georgie@mfa.gov.ge; internet www.france.mfa .gov.ge; Ambassador Mamuka Kudava.

Germany: Heinrich-Mann-Str. 32, 13156 Berlin; tel. (30) 4849070; fax (30) 48490720; e-mail info@botschaftvongeorgien.de; internet www .botschaftvongeorgien.de; Ambassador LEVAN DUCHIDZE.

Greece: Odos Agiou Dimitriou 24, Palaio Psychiko, 154 52 Athens; tel. (210) 6716737; fax (210) 6716722; Ambassador Irakli Tavartkiladze.

Iran: POB 19575-379, Elahiyeh, Tehran; tel. (21) 22211470; fax (21) 22206848; e-mail georgia@apadana.com; Ambassador LEVAN ASATIANI.

Israel: 3 Daniel Frisch St, Tel-Aviv; tel. 3-6093206; fax 3-6093205; e-mail geoemba@netvision.net.il; Ambassador Lasha Zhvania.

Italy: Corso Vittorio Emanuele II 21, III piano, 00186 Roma; tel. (06) 69925809; fax (06) 69941942; e-mail amgeorgia@libero.it; internet www.italy .mfa.gov.ge; Ambassador ZAAL GOGSADZE.

Japan: 2/F, Nanbu Bldg, 3-3, Kioi-cho, Chiyoda-ku, Tokyo 102-0094; tel. (3) 5226-5011; fax (3) 5226-5014; e-mail tokio.emb@mfa.gov.ge; Ambassador Ivane Machavariani.

Jordan: POB 851903, 31 Odeh Abu Tayeh, Shmeisani, Amman 11185; tel. (6) 5603793; fax (6) 5603819; e-mail geoemb@wanadoo.jo; internet www.mfa .gov.ge; Ambassador EKATERINE MEIERING-MIKADZE.

Kazakhstan: 010000 Astana, Diplomatiyalyk kalashyk C-4; tel. (7172) 24-32-58; fax (7172) 24-34-26; e-mail geoembassy@mail.online.kz; Ambassador Zurab Shurghaia.

Kuwait: Qurtoba, Block 2, Area 1, Ave 3, Villa 6, Kuwait City; tel. 5352909; fax 5354707; e-mail kuwait.emb@mfa.gov.ge; Ambassador GOCHA JAPARIDZE.

Latvia: Raiņa bulv. 3–19, Rīga 1050; tel. 6722-5812; e-mail riga.emb@mfa .gov.ge; Ambassador Konstantin Korkelia.

Lithuania: Poškos g. 13, Vilnius 08123; tel. (5) 273-6959; fax (5) 272-3623; e-mail vilnius.emb@mfa.gov.ge; Ambassador DAVIT APSIAURI.

Netherlands: Groot Hertoginnelaan 28, 2517 EG The Hague; tel. (70) 3029081; fax (70) 3029080; e-mail thehague.emb@mfa.gov.ge; internet www .netherlands.mfa.gov.ge; Ambassador Dr Maia Panjikidze.

Poland: 03-934 Warsaw, ul. Wąchocka 1s; tel. (22) 6166221; fax (22) 6166226; e-mail warsaw.emb@mfa.gov.ge; Ambassador KONSTANTIN KAVTARADZE.

Romania: 010516 Bucharest 1, Str. Mihai Eminescu 44–48, ap. 8; tel. (21) 2100602; fax (21) 2113999; Ambassador Zurab Beridze.

Russian Federation: 121069 Moscow, M. Rzhevskii per. 6; tel. (495) 291-13-59; fax (495) 291-21-36; e-mail ineza@got.mmtel.ru; Ambassador IRAKLI CHUBINASHVILI.

Spain: Felipe IV 10, 28014 Madrid; tel. (91) 4293329; fax (91) 4296883; e-mail embassymadrid@mfa.gov.ge; internet www.spain.mfa.gov.ge; Ambassador Zurab Pololikashvili.

Sweden: Humlegårdsgt. 19, 1st Floor, 114 46 Stockholm; tel. (8) 678-02-60; fax 678-02-64; e-mail geoemb.sweden@telia.com; internet www.sweden.mfa .gov.ge; Ambassador AMIRAN KAVADZE.

Switzerland: 1 rue Richard Wagner, 1202 Geneva; tel. 229191010; fax 227339033; e-mail geomission.geneva@bluewin.com; internet www .switzerland.mfa.gov.ge; Chargé d'affaires a.i. Teimuraz Bakradze.

Turkey: Kılıç Ali Sok. 12, Oran, Ankara; Ankara; tel. (312) 4918030; fax (312) 4426507; e-mail ankara.emb@mfa.gov.ge; Ambassador GRIGOL MGALOBLISHVILI.

Turkmenistan: 744000 Aşgabat, ul. Azadi 139a; tel. (12) 34-48-38; fax (12) 34-32-48; e-mail georgia@online.tm; internet www.turkmenistan.mfa.gov.ge; Ambassador Aleksi Petriashvili.

Ukraine: 04119 Kyiv, vul. Melnikov 83D; tel. (44) 451-43-53; fax (44) 451-43-56; e-mail posta@georgia.com.ua; Ambassador MERAB ANTADZE.

United Kingdom: 4 Russell Gdns, London, W14 8EZ; tel. (20) 7603-7799; fax (20) 7603-6682; e-mail embassy@geoemb.plus.com; internet www.geoemb .org.uk; Ambassador Gela Charkviani.

United States of America: 1101 15th St, NW, Suite 602, Washington, DC 20005; tel. (202) 387-2390; fax (202) 387-0864; e-mail embgeorgiausa@yahoo .com; internet www.use.mfa.gov.ge; Ambassador VASIL SIKHARULIDZE.

Uzbekistan: 100170 Tashkent, A. Muhitdinov ko'ch. 6; tel. (711) 62-62-43; fax (711) 62-91-39; e-mail gruzemb@geo-embassy.co.uz; Chargé d'affaires Giorgi Chkheidze.

Vatican City: Via Emilia 25, 00187 Rome, Italy; tel. (06) 42010664; e-mail georgiasantasede@gmail.com; Ambassador KETEVAN BAGRATION-MUKHRANBATONI.

DIPLOMATIC MISSIONS OF GERMANY

United Nations: 871 United Nations Plaza, New York, NY 10017; tel. (212) 940-0400; fax (212) 940-0402; e-mail germany@un.int; internet www .germany-info.org/un; Permanent Representative Dr Thomas Matussek.

Afghanistan: Wazir Akbar Khan, Mena 6, POB 83, Kabul; tel. (20) 2101512; fax (30) 50007518; e-mail zreg@kabu.auswaertiges-amt.de; internet www .kabul.diplo.de; Ambassador DR HANS-ULRICH SEIDT.

Albania: Rruga Skënderbej 8, Tirana; tel. (4) 274505; fax (4) 233497; e-mail info@tira.diplo.de; internet www.tirana.diplo.de; Ambassador Bernd Borchardt.

Algeria: BP 664, 165 chemin Sfindja, Alger-Gare, 16000 Algiers; tel. (21) 74-19-56; fax (21) 74-05-21; e-mail zreg@algi.diplo.de; internet www.algier.diplo .de; Ambassador DR JOHANNES WESTERHOFF.

Angola: Av. 4 de Fevereiro 120, CP 1295, Luanda; tel. 222334516; fax 222399269; e-mail germanembassy.luanda@ebonet.net; internet www .luanda.diplo.de; Ambassador Dr Ingo Winkelmann.

Argentina: Villanueva 1055, C1426BMC Buenos Aires; tel. (11) 4778-2500; fax (11) 4778-2550; e-mail administracion@embajada-alemana.org.ar; internet www.embajada-alemana.org.ar; Ambassador DR ROLF SCHUMACHER.

Armenia: 0025 Yerevan, Charents St 29; tel. (10) 52-32-79; fax (10) 52-47-81; e-mail info@eriw.diplo.de; internet www.eriwan.diplo.de; Ambassador Andrea Wiktorin.

Australia: 119 Empire Circuit, Yarralumla, ACT 2600; tel. (2) 6270-1911; fax (2) 6270-1951; e-mail info1@germanembassy.org.au; internet www .germanembassy.org.au; Ambassador DR MARTIN LUTZ.

Austria: Metternichgasse 3, 1030 Vienna; tel. (1) 711-54-0; fax (1) 713-83-66; e-mail info@wien.diplo.de; internet www.wien.diplo.de; Ambassador Dr Gerhard Westdickenberg.

Azerbaijan: 1005 Baku, Nizami küç. 340, ISR Plaza; tel. (12) 465-41-00; fax (12) 498-54-19; e-mail zreg@bakudiplo.org; internet www.baku.diplo.de; Ambassador DR PEER STANCHINA.

Bahrain: POB 10306, Al-Hasan Bldg, 1st Floor, Sheikh Hamad Causeway, Area 317, Manama; e-mail germemb@batelco.com.bh; internet www .manama.diplo.de; tel. 17530210; fax 17536282; Ambassador Dr Hubert Lang.

Bangladesh: 178 Gulshan Ave, Gulshan 2, Dhaka 1212; tel. (2) 8853521; fax (2) 8853528; e-mail aadhaka@optimaxbd.net; internet www.dhaka.diplo.de; Ambassador FRANK MEYKE.

Belarus: 220034 Minsk, vul. Zakharava 26; tel. (17) 217-59-00; fax (17) 294-85-52; e-mail germanembassy@mail.belpak.by; internet www.minsk.diplo .de; Ambassador Dr Gebhardt Weiss.

Belgium: 8–14 rue Jacques de Lalaing, 1040 Brussels; tel. (2) 787-18-00; fax (2) 787-28-00; e-mail info@bruessel.diplo.de; internet www.bruessel.diplo.de; Ambassador PROF. DR REINHARD BETTZEUGE.

Benin: 7 ave Jean-Paul II, BP 504, Cotonou; tel. 21-31-29-67; fax 21-31-29-62; e-mail info@cotonou.diplo.de; internet www.cotonou.diplo.de; Ambassador Dr Albrecht Conze.

Bolivia: Avda Arce 2395, esq. Belisario Salinas, Casilla 5265, La Paz; tel. (2) 244-0066; fax (2) 244-1441; e-mail info@la-paz.diplo.de; internet www.la-paz .diplo.de; Ambassador ERICH RIEDLER.

Bosnia and Herzegovina: 71000 Sarajevo, ul. Buka bb; tel. (33) 275000; fax (33) 652978; e-mail info@sarajewo.diplo.de; internet www.sarajewo.diplo .de; Ambassador Michael Georg Schmunk.

Botswana: Professional House, 3rd Floor, Segoditshane Way, Broadhurst, POB 315, Gaborone; tel. 3953143; fax 3953038; e-mail info@gaborone.diplo .de; internet www.gaborone.diplo.de; Ambassador ULF HANEL.

Brazil: SES, Av. das Nações, Quadra 807, Lote 25, 70415-900 Brasília, DF; tel. (61) 3442-7000; fax (61) 3443-7508; e-mail info.brasilia@alemanha.org .br; internet www.brasilia.diplo.de; Ambassador Friedrich Prot von Kunow.

Brunei: Kompleks Bangunan Yayasan Sultan Haji Hassanal Bolkiah, Unit 2.01, Block A, 2nd Floor, Jalan Pretty, Bandar Seri Begawan BS 8711; tel. 2225547; fax 2225583; e-mail prgerman@brunet.bn; internet www.bandar -seri-begawan.diplo.de; Ambassador CONRAD KARL CAPPELL.

Bulgaria: 1113 Sofia, ul. F. Zh. Kyuri 25, POB 869; tel. (2) 918-38-00; fax (2) 963-16-58; e-mail reg1@sofi.diplo.de; internet www.sofia.diplo.de; Ambassador Michael Geier.

Burkina Faso: 399 ave Joseph Badoua, 01 BP 600, Ouagadougou 01; tel. 50-30-67-31; fax 50-31-39-91; e-mail amb.allemagne@fasonet.bf; Ambassador ULRICH HOCHSCHILD.

Burundi: 22 rue 18 septembre, BP 480, Bujumbura; tel. 22226412; fax 22221004; e-mail info@buju.diplo.de; Ambassador Thomas Mangartz.

Cambodia: 76–78 rue Yougoslavie (rue 214), BP 60, Phnom-Penh; tel. (23) 216381; fax (23) 427746; e-mail germanembassy@everyday.com.kh; internet www.phnom-penh.diplo.de; Ambassador FRANK MANN.

Cameroon: Nouvelle Bastos, Bastos-Usine, BP 1160, Yaoundé; tel. 2221-0566; fax 2220-7313; e-mail info@jaun.diplo.de; internet www.jaunde.diplo .de; Ambassador Volker Seitz.

Canada: 1 Waverley St, Ottawa, ON K2P 0T8; tel. (613) 232-1101; fax (613) 594-9330; e-mail germanembassyottawa@on.aibn.com; internet www .ottawa.diplo.de; Ambassador MATTHIAS MARTIN A. HÖPFNER.

Chile: Las Hualtatas 5677, Vitacura, Santiago; tel. (2) 463-2500; fax (2) 463-2525; e-mail reg1@santi.diplo.de; internet www.santiago.diplo.de; Ambassador Dr Peter Scholz.

China, People's Republic: 17 Dong Zhi Men Wai Dajie, San Li Tun, Beijing 100600; tel. (10) 85329000; fax (10) 65325336; e-mail embassy@peki.diplo.de; internet www.beijing.diplo.de; Ambassador DR MICHAEL SCHAEFER.

Colombia: Apdo 98833, Bogotá, DC; tel. (1) 423-2600; fax (1) 429-3145; e-mail info@bogota.diplo.de; internet www.bogota.diplo.de; Ambassador Michael Glotzbach.

Congo, Democratic Republic: 82 ave Roi Baudouin, BP 8400, Kinshasa-Gombe; tel. (81) 5561380; e-mail amballemagne@ic.cd; internet www .kinshasa.diplo.de; Ambassador KARL-ALBRECHT RICHARD WOKALEK.

Costa Rica: Barrio Rohrmoser, de la Casa de Oscar Arias 200 m norte, 75 m este, Apdo 4017, 1000 San José; tel. 290-9091; fax 231-6403; e-mail info@ embajada-alemana-costarica.org; internet www.embajada-alemana-costarica .org; Ambassador Volker Fink.

Côte d'Ivoire: 39 blvd Hassan II, Cocody, 01 BP 1900, Abidjan 01; tel. 22-44-20-41; e-mail d.bo.abj@africaonline.co.ci; internet www.abidjan.diplo.de; Ambassador ROLF ULRICH.

Croatia: 10000 Zagreb, ul. grada Vukovara 64; tel. (1) 6300100; fax (1) 6155536; e-mail deutsche.botschaft.zagreb@inet.hr; internet www.zagreb .diplo.de; Ambassador Hans Jochen Peters.

Cuba: Calle 13, No 652, esq. B, Vedado, Havana; tel. (7) 833-2460; e-mail info@havanna.diplo.de; internet www.havanna.diplo.de; Ambassador CLAUDE ROBERT ELLNER.

Cyprus: 10 Nikitaras St, Ay. Omoloyitae, 1080 Nicosia; POB 25705, 1311 Nicosia; tel. 22451145; fax 22665694; e-mail info@nikosia.diplo.de; internet www.nikosia.diplo.de; Ambassador Dr Rolf Kaiser.

Czech Republic: Vlašská 19, POB 88, 118 01 Prague 1; tel. 257113111; fax 257534056; e-mail zreg@prag.auswaertiges-amt.de; internet www.deutsche -botschaft.cz; Ambassador HELMUT ELFENKÄMPER.

Denmark: Stockholmsgade 57, POB 2712, 2100 Copenhagen Ø; tel. 35-45-99-00; fax 35-26-71-05; e-mail tyskeamba@email.dk; internet www.kopenhagen .diplo.de; Ambassador Dr Gerhard Nourney.

Dominican Republic: Edif. Torre Piantini, 16°, Calle Gustavo Mejía Ricart 196, esq. Avda Abraham Lincoln, Santo Domingo, DN; tel. 542-8949; fax 542-8955; e-mail info@santo-domingo.diplo.de; internet www.santo -domingo.diplo.de; Ambassador CHRISTIAN GERMANN.

Ecuador: Edif. Citiplaza, 13° y 14°, Avda Naciones Unidas y República de El Salvador, Apdo 17-17-536, Quito; tel. (2) 297-0820; fax (2) 297-0815; e-mail alemania@interactive.net.ec; internet www.quito.diplo.de; Ambassador Christian Berger.

Egypt: 8B Sharia Berlin (off Sharia Hassan Sabri), Cairo (Zamalek); tel. (2) 27282000; fax (2) 27282159; e-mail germemb@tedata.net.eg; internet www .cairo.diplo.de; Ambassador BERND ERBEL.

El Salvador: 7a Calle Poniente 3972, esq. 77a Avda Norte, Col. Escalón, Apdo 693, San Salvador; tel. 2247-0000; fax 2247-0099; e-mail info@san -salvador.diplo.de; internet www.san-salvador.diplo.de; Ambassador Jürgen Steinkrüger.

Eritrea: SABA Building, 8th Floor, Warsay St, POB 4974, Asmara; tel. (1) 186670; fax (1) 186900; e-mail info@asmara.diplo.de; internet www.asmara .diplo.de; Ambassador ALEXANDER BECKMANN.

Estonia: Toom-Kuninga 11, Tallinn 15048; tel. 627-5300; fax 627-5304; e-mail tallinn@germany.ee; internet www.tallinn.diplo.de; Ambassador Julius Bobinger.

Ethiopia: Yeka Kifle Ketema, Kebele 6, POB 660, Addis Ababa; tel. (11) 1235139; fax (11) 1235152; e-mail germemb@ethionet.et; internet www.addis -abeba.diplo.de; Ambassador DR CLAAS DIETER KNOOP.

Finland: POB 5, 00331 Helsinki; Krogiuksentie 4b, 00340 Helsinki; tel. (9) 458580; fax (9) 45858258; e-mail info@deutschland.fi; internet www.helsinki .diplo.de; Ambassador Wilfried Grolig.

France: 13–15 ave Franklin D. Roosevelt, 75008 Paris; tel. 1-53-83-45-00; fax 1-43-59-74-18; e-mail ambassade@amb-allemagne.fr; internet www.amb -allemagne.fr; Ambassador DR PETER AMMON.

Gabon: blvd de l'Indépendance, Immeuble les Frangipaniers, BP 299, Libreville; tel. 76-01-88; fax 72-40-12; e-mail amb-allegmagne@inet.ga; Ambassador Hans-Dietrich Bernhard.

Georgia: 0103 Tbilisi, Telavi 20, Sheraton Metekhi Palace Hotel; tel. (32) 44-73-00; fax (32) 44-73-64; e-mail info@tiflis.diplo.de; internet www.tiflis.diplo .de; Ambassador DR PATRICIA FLOR.

Ghana: 6 Ridge St, North Ridge, POB 1757, Accra; tel. (21) 211000; fax (21) 221347; e-mail info@accra.diplo.de; internet www.accra.diplo.de; Ambassador Dr Marius Haas.

Greece: Odos Karaoli & Dimitriou 3, 106 75 Athens; tel. (210) 7285111; fax (210) 7251205; e-mail boathens@internet.gr; internet www.athen.diplo.de; Ambassador DR WOLFGANG SCHULTHEISS.

Guatemala: Edif. Plaza Marítima, 2°, 20 Calle 6-20, Zona 10, Guatemala City; tel. 2364-6700; fax 2333-6906; e-mail embalemana@intelnet.net.gt; internet www.guatemala.diplo.de; Ambassador Peter Linder.

Guinea: 2e blvd, Kaloum, BP 540, Conakry; tel. 30-41-15-06; fax 30-45-22-17; e-mail amball@sotelgui.net.gn; internet www.conakry.diplo.de; Ambassador KARL PRINZ.

Haiti: 2 impasse Claudinette, Bois Moquette, Pétionville, BP 1147, Port-au-Prince; tel. 257-7280; fax 257-4131; e-mail amballemagne@hainet.net; Ambassador Dr Hubertus Thoma.

Honduras: Edif. Paysen, 3°, Blvd Morazán, Apdo 3145, Tegucigalpa; tel. 232-3161; fax 239-9018; e-mail embalema@amnettgu.com; internet www .tegucigalpa.diplo.de; Ambassador PAUL ALBERT RESCH.

Hungary: 1014 Budapest, Úri u. 64–66; tel. (1) 488-3500; fax (1) 488-3523; e-mail info@deutschebotschaft-budapest.hu; internet www .deutschebotschaft-budapest.hu; Ambassador Hans Peter Schiff.

Iceland: Laufásvegur 31, 101 Reykjavík; tel. 5301100; fax 5301101; e-mail info@reykjavik.diplo.de; internet www.reykjavik.diplo.de; Ambassador DR KARL-ULRICH MÜLLER.

India: 6 Block 50g, Shanti Path, Chanakyapuri, POB 613, New Delhi 110 021; tel. (11) 44199199; fax (11) 26873117; internet www.new-delhi.diplo.de; Ambassador Bernd Mützelburg.

Indonesia: Jalan M. H. Thamrin 1, Jakarta 10310; tel. (21) 39855000; fax (21) 3901757; e-mail germany@rad.net.id; internet www.jakarta.diplo.de; Ambassador PAUL FREIHERR VON MALTZAHN.

Iran: POB 11365-179, 320–324 Ferdowsi Ave, Tehran; tel. (21) 39990000; fax (21) 39991899; e-mail info@tehe.diplo.de; internet www.teheran.diplo.de; Ambassador Herbert Honsowitz.

Iraq: POB 2036, Hay al-Mansour, Baghdad; tel. (1) 543-1470; fax (1) 541-5840; e-mail info@bagdad.diplo.de; internet www.bagdad.diplo.de; Ambassador DR HANNS SCHUMACHER.

Ireland: 31 Trimleston Ave, Booterstown, Blackrock, Co Dublin; tel. (1) 2693011; fax (1) 2693946; e-mail info@dublin.diplo.de; internet www.dublin .diplo.de; Ambassador Christian Pauls.

Israel: POB 16038, 19th Floor, 3 Daniel Frisch St, Tel-Aviv 64731; tel. 3-6931313; fax 3-6969217; e-mail ger_emb@netvision.net.il; internet www.tel -aviv.diplo.de; Ambassador DR HARALD KINDERMANN.

Italy: Via San Martino della Battaglia 4, 00185 Roma; tel. (06) 492131; fax (06) 49213319; e-mail info@rom.diplo.de; internet www.rom.diplo.de; Ambassador Michael Steiner.

Jamaica: 10 Waterloo Rd, POB 444, Kingston 10; tel. 926-6728; fax 929-8282; e-mail germanembassa.kingston@gmail.com; internet www.kingston .diplo.de; Ambassador JÜRGEN ENGEL.

Japan: 4-5-10, Minami Azabu, Minato-ku, Tokyo 106-0047; tel. (3) 5791-7700; fax (3) 3473-4243; e-mail germtoky@ma.rosenet.ne.jp; internet www .tokyo.diplo.de; Ambassador Hans-Joachim Daerr.

Jordan: POB 183, 25 Benghazi St, Jabal Amman 11118; tel. (6) 5930351; fax (6) 5929413; e-mail germaemb@wanadoo.jo; internet www.amman.diplo.de; Ambassador DR KLAUS BURKHARDT.

Kazakhstan: 010000 Astana, Kosmonavtov 62; tel. (7172) 79-12-00; fax (7172) 79-12-13; e-mail info@astana.diplo.de; internet www.astana.diplo.de; Ambassador Rainer Eugen Schlageter.

Kenya: Ludwig Krapf House, Riverside Dr. 113, POB 30180, Nairobi; tel. (20) 4262100; fax (20) 4262129; e-mail info@nairobi.diplo.de; internet www .nairobi.diplo.de; Ambassador WALTER JOHANNES LINDNER.

Korea, Democratic People's Republic: Munsudong District, Pyongyang; tel. (2) 3817385; fax (2) 3817397; e-mail zreg@pjoe.auswaertiges-amt.de; Ambassador Thomas Schafer.

Korea, Republic: 308-5, Dongbinggo-dong, Yeongsan-gu, Seoul 140-816; tel. (2) 748-4114; fax (2) 748-4161; e-mail info@seoul.diplo.de; internet www .seoul.diplo.de; Ambassador NORBERT BAAS.

Kosovo: 10000 Prishtina, Arbëri, Rruga Azem Jashanica 17; tel. (38) 254500; fax (38) 254536; e-mail info@pris.auswaertiges-amt.de; internet www .pristina.diplo.de; Ambassador Hans-Dieter Steinbach.

Kuwait: POB 805, 13009 Safat, Dahiya Abdullah as-Salem, Area 1, Ave 14, Villa 13, Kuwait City; tel. 2520857; fax 2520763; e-mail info@kuwait.diplo .de; internet www.kuwait.diplo.de; Ambassador DR MICHAEL WORBS.

Kyrgyzstan: 720040 Bishkek, Razzakova 28; tel. (312) 90-50-00; fax (312) 66-66-30; e-mail info@bischkek.diplo.de; internet www.bischkek.diplo.de; Ambassador Prof. Dr Klaus Werner Grewlich.

Laos: rue Sok Paluang 26, Muang Sisattanak, BP 314, Vientiane; tel. (21) 312110; fax (21) 351152; e-mail info@vien.diplo.de; Ambassador PETER WIENAND.

Latvia: Raiņa bulv. 13, Rīga 1050; tel. 6708-5100; fax 6708-5149; e-mail mailbox@deutschebotschaft-riga.lv; internet www.deutschebotschaft-riga .lv; Ambassador Eberhard Schuppius.

Lebanon: POB 11-2820, Riad es-Solh, Beirut 1102 2110; tel. (4) 929600; fax (4) 929616; e-mail info@beirut.diplo.de; internet www.beirut.diplo.de; Ambassador HANSJOERG HABER.

Libya: POB 302, Sharia Hassan al-Mashai, Tripoli; tel. (21) 3330554; fax (21) 4448968; e-mail info@tripolis.diplo.de; internet www.tripolis.diplo.de; Ambassador Bernd Westphal.

Lithuania: Z. Sierakausko g. 24/8, Vilnius 03105; tel. (5) 210-6400; fax (5) 210-6446; e-mail info@wilna.diplo.de; internet www.deutschebotschaft-wilna.lt; Ambassador VOLKER HEINSBERG.

Luxembourg: 20–22 ave Emile Reuter, BP 95, 2010 Luxembourg; tel. 45-34-45-1; fax 45-56-04; internet www.luxemburg.diplo.de; Ambassador Dr Hubertus von Morr.

Macedonia, former Yugoslav Republic: 1000 Skopje, Leninska 59; tel. (2) 3093900; fax (2) 3093899; e-mail dtboskop@unet.com.mk; internet www .deutschebotschaft-skopje.com.mk/mk; Ambassador RALF ANDREAS BRETH.

Madagascar: 101 rue du Pasteur Rabeony Hans, BP 516, Ambodirotra, 101 Antananarivo; tel. (20) 2223802; fax (20) 2226627; e-mail amballem@ wanadoo.mg; internet www.antananarivo.diplo.de; Ambassador Dr Wolfgang Moser.

Malawi: Convention Dr., POB 30046, Lilongwe 3; tel. 1772555; fax 1770250; e-mail info@lilongwe.diplo.de; internet www.lilongwe.diplo.de; Ambassador ALBERT JOSEF GISY.

Malaysia: 26th Floor, Menara Tan & Tan, 207 Jalan Tun Razak, 50400 Kuala Lumpur; tel. (3) 21709666; fax (3) 21619800; e-mail contact@german-embassy.org.my; internet www.kuala-lumpur.diplo.de; Ambassador Herbert D. Jess.

Mali: Badalabougou-est, rue 14, porte 334, BP 100, Bamako; tel. 222-32-99; fax 222-96-50; e-mail allemagne.presse@afribonemali.net; internet www.bamako.diplo.de; Ambassador DR REINHARD SCHWARZER.

Malta: 'Il-Piazzetta', Entrance B, 1st Floor, Tower Rd, Sliema SLM 1605; tel. 21336531; fax 21341271; e-mail info@valletta.diplo.de; internet www.valletta.diplo.de; Ambassador Karl Andreas von Stenglin.

Mauritania: Tevragh Zeina, BP 372, Nouakchott; tel. 525-17-29; fax 525-17-22; e-mail amb-allemagne@toptechnology.mr; Ambassador EBERHARD SCHANZE.

Mexico: Horacio 1506, Col. Los Morales, Del. Miguel Hidalgo, 11530 México, DF; tel. (55) 5283-2200; fax (55) 5281-2588; e-mail info@mexi.diplo.de; internet www.mexiko.diplo.de; Ambassador Dr Roland Michael Wegener.

Moldova: 2012 Chişinău, str. Maria Cibotari 35; tel. (22) 20-06-00; fax (22) 23-46-80; e-mail info@chisinau.diplo.de; internet www.chisinau.diplo.de; Ambassador NIKOLAUS VON DER WENGE GRAF LAMBSDORFF.

Mongolia: Negdsen Ündestnii Gudamj 7, Ulan Bator (CPOB 708); tel. (11) 323325; fax (11) 323905; internet www.ulan-bator.diplo.de; Ambassador Pius A. Fischer.

Montenegro: 81000 Podgorica, Hercegovačka 10; tel. (81) 667285; e-mail l@podg.diplo.de; internet www.beograd.diplo.de; Ambassador THOMAS SCHMITT.

Morocco: 7 Zankat Madnine, BP 235, 10001 Rabat; tel. (3) 7709662; fax (3) 7706851; e-mail amballma@mtds.com; internet www.rabat.diplo.de; Ambassador Dr Gottfried Haas.

Mozambique: Rua Damião de Góis 506, CP 1595, Maputo; tel. 21492700; fax 21492888; e-mail germaemb@tvcabo.co.mz; internet www.maputo.diplo.de; Ambassador KLAUS-CHRISTIAN KRAEMER.

Myanmar: 9 Bogyoke Aung San Museum Rd, POB 12, Yangon; tel. (1) 548951; fax (1) 548899; e-mail info@rangun.diplo.de; internet www.rangun.diplo.de; Ambassador Dietrich Andreas.

Namibia: Sanlam Centre, 6th Floor, 154 Independence Ave, POB 231, Windhoek; tel. (61) 273100; fax (61) 222981; e-mail germany@iway.na; internet www.windhuk.diplo.de; Ambassador ARNE FREIHERR VON KITTLITZ UND OTTENDORF.

Nepal: Gyaneshwar, POB 226, Kathmandu; tel. (1) 4412786; fax (1) 4416899; e-mail info@kathmandu.diplo.de; internet www.kathmandu.diplo.de; Ambassador Franz Ring.

Netherlands: Groot Hertoginnelaan 18–20, 2517 EG The Hague; tel. (70) 3420600; fax (70) 3651957; e-mail ambduits@euronet.nl; internet www.den-haag.diplo.de; Ambassador DR THOMAS LÄUFER.

New Zealand: 90–92 Hobson St, POB 1687, Wellington; tel. (4) 473-6063; fax (4) 473-6069; e-mail german.embassy@iconz.co.nz; internet www.wellington.diplo.de; Ambassador Jörg Hans Zimmermann.

Nicaragua: Bolonia, de la Rotonda El Güegüense, 1½ c. al lago, contiguo a Optica Nicaragüense, Apdo 29, Managua; tel. 266-3917; fax 266-7667; e-mail alemania@cablenet.com.ni; internet www.managua.diplo.de; Ambassador GREGOR KOEBEL.

Niger: 71 ave du Général de Gaulle, BP 629, Niamey; tel. 20-72-35-10; fax 20-72-39-85; e-mail amballny@intnet.ne; Ambassador Heike Thiele.

Nigeria: 9 Lake Maracaibo Close, off Amazon St, Maitama, Abuja; tel. (9) 4130962; fax (9) 4130949; e-mail info@abuja.diplo.de; internet www.abuja.diplo.de; Ambassador JOACHIM CHRISTOPH SCHMILLEN.

Norway: Oscarsgt. 45, 0244 Oslo; tel. 23-27-54-00; fax 22-44-76-72; e-mail info@oslo.diplo.de; internet www.oslo.diplo.de; Ambassador Roland Mauch.

Oman: POB 128, Ruwi 112, Muscat; tel. 24832482; fax 24835690; e-mail info@maskat.diplo.de; internet www.maskat.diplo.de; Ambassador KLAUS GEYER.

Pakistan: Ramna 5, Diplomatic Enclave, POB 1027, Islamabad 44000; tel. (51) 2007100; fax (51) 2279436; e-mail info@isla.diplo.de; internet www.islamabad.diplo.de; Ambassador Dr Günter Mulack.

Panama: Edif. World Trade Center, 20°, Calle 53E, Marbella, Apdo 0832-0536, Panamá 5; tel. 263-7733; fax 223-6664; e-mail germpanama@cwp.net.pa; internet www.panama.diplo.de; Ambassador BORUSSO VON BLÜCHER.

Paraguay: Avda Venezuela 241, Casilla 471, Asunción; tel. (21) 21-4009; fax (21) 21-2863; e-mail aaasun@pla.net.py; internet www.pla.net.py/embalem; Ambassador Dietmar Blaas.

Peru: Avda Arequipa 4210, Miraflores, Lima 18; tel. (1) 2125016; fax (1) 4226475; e-mail kanzlei@embajada-alemana.org.pe; internet www.embajada-alemana.org.pe; Ambassador CHRISTOPH MÜLLER.

Philippines: 25th Floor, Tower 2, RCBC Plaza, 6819 Ayala Ave, Makati City, Metro Manila; tel. (2) 7023000; fax (2) 7023015; e-mail deboma@pldtdsl.net; internet www.manila.diplo.de; Ambassador Christian-Ludwig Weber-Lortsch.

Poland: 00-467 Warsaw, ul. Jazdów 12; tel. (22) 5841700; fax (22) 5841739; e-mail warszawa@wars.diplo.de; internet www.ambasadaniemiec.pl; Ambassador DR MICHAEL H. GERDTS.

Portugal: Campo dos Mártires da Pátria 38, 1169-043 Lisbon; tel. (21) 8810210; fax (21) 8853846; e-mail info@lissabon.diplo.de; internet www.lissabon.diplo.de; Ambassador Joachim Broudré-Gröger.

Qatar: POB 3064, 6 Al-Jazeera al-Arabiya St, Doha; tel. 4876959; fax 4876949; e-mail germany@qatar.net.qa; internet www.doha.diplo.de; Ambassador DR DIRK BAUMGARTNER.

Romania: 011849 Bucharest, Str. Capt. Aviator Gh. Demetriade 6–8; tel. (21) 2029830; fax (21) 2305846; e-mail botschaft@deutschebotschaft-bukarest.ro; internet www.bukarest.diplo.de; Ambassador Roland Lohkamp.

Russian Federation: 119285 Moscow, ul. Mosfilmovskaya 56; tel. (495) 937-95-00; fax (495) 938-23-54; e-mail germanmo@aha.ru; internet www.moskau.diplo.de; Ambassador DR WALTER SCHMID.

Rwanda: 8 rue de Bugarama, BP 355, Kigali; tel. 575141; fax 502087; internet www.kigali.diplo.de; Ambassador Dr Christian Clages.

Saudi Arabia: POB 94001, Riyadh 11693; tel. (1) 488-0700; fax (1) 488-0660; e-mail info@riad.diplo.de; internet www.riad.diplo.de; Ambassador JÜRGEN KRIEGHOFF.

Senegal: 20 ave Pasteur, angle rue Mermoz, BP 2100, Dakar; tel. 33-889-4884; fax 33-822-5299; e-mail reg1@daka.auswaertiges-amt.de; internet www.dakar.diplo.de; Ambassador Doretta Loschelder.

Serbia: 11000 Belgrade, Kneza Miloša 76; tel. (11) 3064300; fax (11) 3064303; e-mail germany@sbb.co.yu; internet www.belgrad.diplo.de; Ambassador WOLFRAM JOSEF MAAS.

Singapore: 12-00 Singapore Land Tower, 50 Raffles Place, Singapore 048623; tel. 65336002; fax 65331132; e-mail germany@singnet.com.sg; internet www.sing.diplo.de; Ambassador Folkmar Stoecker.

Slovakia: Hviezdoslavovo nám. 10, 813 03 Bratislava; tel. (2) 5920-4400; fax (2) 5441-9634; e-mail info@germanembassy.sk; internet www.germanembassy.sk; Ambassador DR JOCHEN TREBESCH.

Slovenia: 1000 Ljubljana, Prešernova cesta 27; tel. (1) 4790300; fax (1) 4250899; e-mail germanembassy-slovenia@siol.net; internet www.ljubljana.diplo.de; Ambassador Dr Hans-Joachim Goetz.

South Africa: 180 Blackwood St, Arcadia, Pretoria 0083; POB 2023, Pretoria 0001; tel. (12) 4278900; fax (12) 3433606; e-mail GermanEmbassyPretoria@gonet.co.za; internet www.pretoria.diplo.de; Ambassador DIETER WALTER HALLER.

Spain: Fortuny 8, 28010 Madrid; tel. (91) 5579000; fax (91) 3102104; e-mail zreg@madri.auswaertiges-amt.de; internet www.madrid.diplo.de; Ambassador Wolf-Ruthart Born.

Sri Lanka: 40 Alfred House Ave, POB 658, Colombo 3; tel. (11) 2580431; fax (11) 2580440; e-mail info@colombo.diplo.de; internet www.colombo.diplo.de; Ambassador JÜRGEN WEERTH.

Sudan: 53 Baladia St, Block No. 8d, Plot 2, POB 970, Khartoum; tel. (183) 777990; fax (183) 777622; e-mail reg1@khar.auswaertiges-amt.de; internet www.khartum.diplo.de; Ambassador Dr Stephan Keller.

Sweden: Artillerigt. 64, POB 27832, 115 93 Stockholm; tel. (8) 670-15-00; fax (8) 670-15-72; e-mail zreg@stoc.diplo.de; internet www.stockholm.diplo.de; Ambassador WOLFGANG TRAUTWEIN.

Switzerland: Willadingweg 83, Postfach 250, 3000 Bern 15; tel. 313594111; fax 313594444; e-mail vw-pfb1@bern.diplo.de; internet www.bern.diplo.de; Ambassador Andreas von Stechow.

Syria: BP 2237, 16 rue Abd al-Mun'im Riyad, al-Malki, Damascus; tel. (11) 37900000; fax (11) 3323812; e-mail germemb@scs-net.org; internet www.damaskus.diplo.de; Ambassador VOLKMAR KARL WENZEL.

Tajikistan: 734017 Dushanbe, Kuchai Varzov 16; tel. (372) 221-21-89; fax (372) 224-03-90; e-mail info@dusc.diplo.de; internet www.duschanbe.diplo.de; Ambassador Rainer Müller.

Tanzania: Umoja House, Mirambo St/Garden Ave, 2nd Floor, POB 9541, Dar es Salaam; tel. (22) 2117409; fax (22) 2112944; e-mail german.embassy@bol.co.tz; internet www.daressalam.diplo.de; Ambassador WOLFGANG RINGE.

Thailand: 9 Thanon Sathorn Tai, Bangkok 10120; tel. (2) 287-9000; fax (2) 287-1776; e-mail info@german-embassy.or.th; internet www.bangkok.diplo.de; Ambassador Dr Christoph Brümmer.

Togo: blvd de la République, BP 1175, Lomé; tel. 221-23-70; fax 222-18-88; e-mail amballtogo@cafe.tg; Ambassador HELMUT KOLB.

Trinidad and Tobago: 7–9 Marli St, Newtown, POB 828, Port of Spain; tel. 628-1630; fax 628-5278; e-mail germanembassy@tstt.net.tt; internet www.port-of-spain.diplo.de; Ambassador Dr Ernst Martens.

Tunisia: 1 rue al-Hamra, BP 35, Mutuelleville, 1002 Tunis-Mutuelleville; tel. (71) 786-455; fax (71) 788-242; e-mail reg1@tunis.diplo.de; internet www.tunis.diplo.de; Ambassador DR HORST-WOLFRAM KERLL.

Turkey: Atatürk Bul. 114, 06690 Kavaklıdere, Ankara; tel. (312) 4555100; fax (312) 4266959; e-mail infomail@germanembassyank.com; internet www.ankara.diplo.de; Ambassador Dr Eckart Cuntz.

Turkmenistan: 744000 Aşgabat, ul. Hydyr Derzhazhev, Hotel 'Ak Altin'; tel. (12) 36-35-15; fax (12) 36-35-22; e-mail grembtkm@online.tm; Ambassador HANS MONDORF.

Uganda: 15 Philip Rd, Kololo, POB 7016, Kampala; tel. (41) 4501111; fax (41) 4501115; e-mail info@kampala.diplo.de; internet www.kampala.diplo.de; Ambassador Reinhard Buchholz.

Ukraine: 01901 Kyiv, vul. B. Khmelnytskoho 25; tel. (44) 247-68-00; fax (44) 247-68-18; e-mail kanzlei@german-embassy.kiev.ua; internet kiew.diplo.de; Ambassador REINHARD SCHAEFERS.

United Arab Emirates: POB 2591, Abu Dhabi Mall, West Tower, 14th Floor, Abu Dhabi; tel. (2) 6446693; fax (2) 6446942; e-mail info@abu-dhabi.diplo.de; internet www.abu-dhabi.diplo.de; Ambassador Klaus-Peter Brandes.

United Kingdom: 23 Belgrave Sq., London, SW1X 8PZ; tel. (20) 7824-1300; fax (20) 7824-1449; e-mail mail@german-embassy.org.uk; internet www.london.diplo.de; Ambassador (vacant).

United States of America: 4645 Reservoir Rd, NW, Washington, DC 20007-1998; ; tel. (202) 298-4000; fax (202) 298-4249; internet www.germany.info; Ambassador Klaus Scharioth.

Uruguay: La Cumparsita 1417/1435, Casilla 20014, 11200 Montevideo; tel. (2) 9025222; fax (2) 9023422; e-mail info@montevideo.diplo.de; internet www.montevideo.diplo.de; Ambassador BERNHARD GRAF VON WALDERSEE.

Uzbekistan: 100017 Tashkent, Sh. Rashidov ko'ch. 15, POB 4337; tel. (71) 120-84-40; fax (71) 120-66-93; e-mail info@taschkent.diplo.de; internet www.taschkent.diplo.de; Ambassador Matthias Meyer.

Vatican City: Via di Villa Sacchetti 4–6, 00197 Rome, Italy; tel. (06) 809511; fax (06) 80951227; internet www.vatikan.diplo.de; Ambassador HANS-HENNING HORSTMANN.

Venezuela: Torre La Castellana, 10°, Avda Eugenio Mendoza, cruce con Avda José Angel Lamas, La Castellana, Caracas 1010-A; tel. (212) 261-0181; fax (212) 261-0641; e-mail info@caracas.diplo.de; internet www.caracas.diplo.de; Ambassador Georg-Clemens Dick.

Viet Nam: 29 Tran Phu, Hanoi; tel. (4) 8453836; fax (4) 8453838; e-mail germanemb.hanoi@fpt.vn; internet www.hanoi.diplo.de; Ambassador ROLF SCHULZE.

Yemen: POB 2562, Hadda, San'a; tel. (1) 413174; fax (1) 413179; e-mail info@sanaa.diplo.de; internet www.sanaa.diplo.de; Ambassador Michael Klor-Berchtold.

Zambia: Plot 5209, United Nations Ave, POB 50120, 15101 Ridgeway, Lusaka; tel. (1) 250644; fax (1) 254014; e-mail info@lusaka.diplo.de; internet www.lusaka.diplo.de; Ambassador DR IRENE HINRICHSEN.

Zimbabwe: 30 Ceres Rd, Avondale, Harare; tel. (4) 308655; fax (4) 303455; e-mail botschaft_harare@gmx.de; Ambassador Karin Blumberger-Sauerteig.

DIPLOMATIC MISSIONS OF GHANA

United Nations: 19 East 47th St, New York, NY 10017; tel. (212) 832-1300; fax (212) 751-6743; e-mail ghanaperm@aol.com; Permanent Representative LESLIE KOJO CHRISTIAN.

Algeria: 62 rue des Frères Benali Abdellah, Hydra, Algiers; tel. (21) 60-64-44; fax (21) 69-28-56; Ambassador Lawrence R. A. Satuh.

Angola: Rua Cirilo da Conceição E Silva 5, 1A, CP 1012, Luanda; tel. 222338239; fax 222338235; e-mail embassyghana@ebonet.net; Ambassador KWASI BAAH-BOAKYE.

Australia: 13 Numeralla St, O'Malley, ACT 2606; tel. (2) 6290-2110; fax (2) 6290-2115; e-mail info@ghanahighcom.org.au; internet www.ghanahighcom.org.au; High Commissioner Kofi Sekyiamah.

Belgium: blvd Général Wahis 7, 1030 Brussels; tel. (2) 705-82-20; fax (2) 705-66-53; e-mail ghanaemb@chello.be; internet www.ghanaembassy.be; Ambassador NANA BEMA KUMI.

Benin: route de l'Aéroport, Lot F, Les Cocotiers, BP 488, Cotonou; tel. 21-30-07-46; fax 21-30-03-45; e-mail ghaemb02@leland.bj; Ambassador M. Adu.

Brazil: SHIS, QL 10, Conj. 08, Casa 02, 70466-900 Brasília, DF; tel. (61) 3248-6047; fax (61) 3248-7913; e-mail ghaembra@zaz.com.br; Ambassador SAMUEL KOFI DADEY.

Burkina Faso: 22 ave d'Oubritenga, 01 BP 212, Ouagadougou 01; tel. 50-30-76-35; e-mail embagna@fasonet.bf; Ambassador Mogtari Sahanun.

Canada: 1 Clemow Ave, Ottawa, ON K1S 2A9; tel. (613) 236-0871; fax (613) 236-0874; e-mail ghanacom@ghc-ca.com; internet www.ghanahighcommission-canada.com; High Commissioner MARGARET IVY AMOAKOHENE.

China, People's Republic: 8 San Li Tun Lu, Beijing 100600; tel. (10) 65321319; fax (10) 65323602; Ambassador Afare Apeadu Donkor.

Côte d'Ivoire: Lot 2393, rue J 95, Cocody-les-Deux-Plateaux, 01 BP 1871, Abidjan 01; tel. 20-33-11-24; fax 20-22-33-57; Ambassador KABRAL BLAY-AMIHERE.

Cuba: Avda 5, No 1808, esq. 20, Miramar, Havana; tel. (7) 204-2153; fax (7) 204-2317; e-mail eghana@ceniai.inf.cu; internet www.ghanaembassy.cu; Ambassador Cecilia Gyan Amoah.

Czech Republic: V tišině 4, 160 00 Prague 6; tel. 233377236; fax 233375647; e-mail ghanaemb@mbox.vol.cz; Ambassador VERONICA SHARON BOAKYE KUFUOR.

Denmark: Egebjerg Allé 13, 2900 Hellerup; tel. 39-62-82-22; fax 39-62-16-52; e-mail ghana@mail.dk; Ambassador Maureen Abla Amematekpor.

Egypt: 1 Sharia 26 July, Cairo (Zamalek); tel. (2) 3444455; fax (2) 3032292; Ambassador AKILAJA O. AKIWUMI.

Ethiopia: Jimma Rd, Woreda 24, Kebele 13, House No. 108, POB 3173, Addis Ababa; tel. (11) 3711402; fax (11) 3712511; Ambassador John Evonlah Aggrey.

France: 8 Villa Saïd, 75116 Paris; tel. 1-45-00-09-50; fax 1-45-00-81-95; e-mail ambghanaparis@yahoo.fr; Ambassador PROF. ALBERT OWUSU-SARPONG.

Germany: Stavangerstr. 17 and 19, 10439 Berlin; tel. (30) 5471490; fax (30) 44674063; e-mail chancery@ghanaemberlin.de; internet www.ghanaemberlin.de; Ambassador Grant Ohemeng Kesse.

Guinea: Immeuble Ex-Urbaine et la Seine, BP 732, Conakry; tel. 30-44-15-10; Ambassador LAMISI MBILAH.

India: 50-N Satya Marg, Chanakyapuri, New Delhi 110 021; tel. (11) 26883298; fax (11) 26883202; High Commissioner (vacant).

Israel: 3rd Floor, 12 Hahilazon St, Ramat-Gan 52522; tel. 3-7520834; fax 3-7520827; e-mail chancery@ghanaemb.co.il; Ambassador LT-COL LAWRENCE KPABITEY KODJIKU.

Italy: Via Ostriana 4, 00199 Roma; tel. (06) 86217191; fax (06) 86325762; e-mail ghembrom@rdn.it; Ambassador Charles Agyei Amoama.

Japan: 1-5-21, Nishi Azabu, Minato-ku, Tokyo 106-0031; tel. (3) 5410-8631; fax (3) 5410-8635; e-mail mission@ghanaembassy.or.jp; internet www.ghanaembassy.or.jp; Ambassador DR BARFUOR ADJEI-BARWUAH.

Korea, Republic: 5-4, Hannam-dong, Yeongsan-gu, Seoul (CPOB 3887); tel. (2) 3785-1427; fax (2) 3785-1428; e-mail ghana3@kornet.net; internet www.ghanaembassy.or.kr; Ambassador (vacant).

Liberia: cnr 11th St and Gardiner Ave, Sinkor, POB 471, Monrovia; tel. 261477; Ambassador MAJ.-GEN. FRANCIS ADU-AMANFOH.

Libya: POB 4169, Andalus 21/a, nr Funduk Shati Gargaresh, Tripoli; tel. (21) 4772534; fax (21) 4773557; e-mail ghaemb@all-computers.com; Ambassador George Kumi.

Malaysia: 14 Ampang Hilir, off Jalan Ampang, 55000 Kuala Lumpur; tel. (3) 42526995; fax (3) 42578698; e-mail ghcomkl@tm.net.my; High Commissioner NANA KWADWO SEINTI.

Mali: BP 3161, Bamako; Ambassador Maj.-Gen. C. B. Yaachie.

Morocco: 27 rue Ghomara, La Pinede, Souissi, Rabat; tel. (3) 7757620; fax (3) 7757630; Ambassador KOBINA ANNAN.

Namibia: 5 Nelson Mandela Ave, POB 24165, Windhoek; tel. (61) 221341; fax (61) 221343; High Commissioner Maureen A. Amematekpor.

Netherlands: Laan Copes van Cattenburch 70, 2585 GD The Hague; tel. (70) 3384380; fax (70) 3062800; e-mail gaababio@ghanaembassy.nl; internet www.ghanaembassy.nl; Ambassador DR GRACE AMPONSAH-ABABIO.

Nigeria: 21–25 King George V Rd, POB 889, Lagos; tel. (1) 2630015; fax (1) 2630338; High Commissioner Lt-Gen. Joshua Hamidu.

Russian Federation: 121069 Moscow, Skatertnyi per. 14; tel. (495) 202-18-71; fax (495) 202-18-89; e-mail embghmos@astelit.ru; Ambassador AIR VICE-MARSHALL EDWARD A. MANTEY.

Saudi Arabia: POB 94339, Riyadh 11693; tel. (1) 454-5122; fax (1) 450-9819; e-mail ghanaemb@naseej.com; Ambassador Alhaji Rashid Bawa.

Senegal: Lot 27, Parcelle B, Almadies, BP 25370, Dakar; tel. 33-869-1990; fax 33-820-1950; Ambassador FREDERICK DANIEL LARYEA.

Serbia: 11000 Belgrade, Đorđa Vajferta 50; tel. (11) 3440856; fax (11) 3440071; e-mail ghana@eunet.yu; internet www.ghanaembelgrade.com; Ambassador Dr Nyaho Nyaho-Tamakloe.

Sierra Leone: 13 Walpole St, Freetown; tel. (22) 223461; fax (22) 227043; High Commissioner KABRAL BLAY-AMIHERE.

South Africa: 1038 Arcadia St, Hatfield, Pretoria 0083; POB 12537, Hatfield 0028; tel. (12) 3425847; fax (12) 3425863; High Commissioner Dr Jimmy B. Heymann.

Spain: Capitán Haya 38, 10°A, 28020 Madrid; tel. (91) 5670390; fax (91) 5670393; e-mail mission@ghanaembassyspain.com; Ambassador FRANCIS TSEGAH.

Switzerland: Belpstr. 11, Postfach, 3001 Bern; tel. 313817852; fax 313814941; e-mail ghanaemb@tcnet.ch; internet www.ghanaembassy.ch; Ambassador Kwabena Baah-Duodu.

Togo: 8 rue Paulin Eklou, Tokoin-Ouest, BP 92, Lomé; tel. 221-31-94; fax 221-77-36; e-mail ghmfa01@cafe.tg; Ambassador KWABENA MENSA-BONSU.

United Kingdom: 13 Belgrave Sq., London, SW1X 8PN; tel. (20) 7235-4142; fax (20) 7245-9552; e-mail information@ghanahighcommissionuk.com; internet www.ghanahighcommissionuk.com; High Commr Annan Arkyin Cato.

United States of America: 3512 International Dr., NW, Washington, DC 20008; tel. (202) 686-4520; fax (202) 686-4527; e-mail info@ghanaembassy.org ; internet www.ghana-embassy.org; Ambassador DR KWAME BAWUAH-EDUSEI.

Zimbabwe: 11 Downie Ave, Belgravia, POB 4445, Harare; tel. (4) 700982; fax (4) 701014; e-mail ghcom25@africaonline.co.zw; Ambassador John K. Gbenah.

DIPLOMATIC MISSIONS OF GREECE

United Nations: 866 Second Ave, 13th Floor, New York, NY 10017; tel. (212) 888-6900; fax (212) 888-4440; e-mail mission@greeceun.org; internet www.greeceun.org; Permanent Representative JOHN MOURIKIS.

Albania: Rruga Frederik Shiroka 3, Tirana; tel. (4) 274670; fax (4) 234290; e-mail gremb.tir@mfa.gr; internet www.greekembassy.al; Ambassador Konstantin Kokossis.

Algeria: 60 blvd Col Bougara, 16030 el-Biar, Algiers; tel. (21) 92-34-91; fax (21) 92-34-90; e-mail gremb.alg@mfa.gr; Ambassador IOANNIS NEONAKIS.

Argentina: Arenales 1658, C1061AAT Buenos Aires; tel. (11) 4811-4811; fax (11) 4816-2600; e-mail secretariagr@fibertel.com.ar; Ambassador Michael B. Christides.

Armenia: 0002 Yerevan, Demirchian St 6; tel. (10) 53-00-51; fax (10) 53-00-49; e-mail embassy@greekembassy.am; internet www.greekembassy.am; Ambassador IOANNIS KORINTHIOS.

Australia: 9 Turrana St, Yarralumla, ACT 2600; tel. (2) 6273-3011; fax (2) 6273-2620; e-mail greekemb@bigpond.net.au; Ambassador George Zois.

Austria: Argentinierstr. 14, 1040 Vienna; tel. (1) 506-15-0; fax (1) 505-62-17; e-mail gremb@griechischebotschaft.at; internet www.griechische-botschaft.at; Ambassador PANAGOTIS ZOGRAFOS.

Azerbaijan: 1004 Baku, Icheri Şeher, Kichik Gala küç. 86/88; tel. (12) 492-46-80; fax (12) 492-48-35; e-mail greekemb@azeurotel.com; Ambassador Dimidis Temistokles.

Belgium: 10 rue des petits Carmes, 1000 Brussels; tel. (2) 545-55-00; fax (2) 545-55-85; e-mail ambagre@skynet.be; Ambassador GEORGE PAPADOPOULOS.

Bosnia and Herzegovina: 71000 Sarajevo, Obala Maka Dizdara I; tel. (33) 203516; fax (33) 203512; e-mail greekemb@bih.net.ba; Ambassador Constantina Mauroskelidou.

Brazil: SES, Av. das Nações, Quadra 805, Lote 22, 70480-900 Brasília, DF; tel. (61) 3443-6573; fax (61) 3443-6902; e-mail info@emb-grecia.org.br; internet www.emb-grecia.org.br; Ambassador ANDONIOS NICOLAIDIS.

Bulgaria: 1504 Sofia, ul. San Stefano 33; tel. (2) 843-30-85; fax (2) 843-30-86; e-mail info@greekembassy-sofia.bg; internet info.greekembassy-sofia.org; Ambassador Danae-Magdalene Koumanakou.

Cameroon: Quartier Mont Fébé, BP 82, Yaoundé; tel. 2221-0195; fax 2220-3936; e-mail ambgrece@camnet.cm; Ambassador CHARAKAMBOUS PAUL.

Canada: 76–80 MacLaren St, Ottawa, ON K2P 0K6; tel. (613) 238-6271; fax (613) 238-5676; e-mail embassy@greekembassy.ca; internet www.greekembassy.ca; Ambassador Nikolaos Matsis.

Chile: Jorge Sexto 306, Las Condes, Santiago; tel. (2) 212-7900; fax (2) 212-8048; e-mail embassygr@tie.cl; internet www.grecia.cl; Ambassador CHRYSSOULA KARYKOPOULOU-VLAVIANOU.

China, People's Republic: 19 Guang Hua Lu, Jian Guo Men Wai, Beijing 100600; tel. (10) 65321588; fax (10) 65321277; e-mail gremb.pek@mfa.gr; internet www.grpressbeijing.com; Ambassador Michel Kambanis.

Congo, Democratic Republic: Immeuble de la Communauté Hellénique, 3ème étage, blvd du 30 juin, BP 478, Kinshasa; tel. (99) 70521; e-mail gremb.kin@mfa.gr; Ambassador IOANNIS CHRISTOPHILIS.

Croatia: 10000 Zagreb, Opatička 12; tel. (1) 4810444; fax (1) 4810419; e-mail greece-embassy@grembassy.hr; internet www.grembassy.hr; Ambassador Ourania Arvaniti.

Cuba: Avda 5, No 7802, esq. 78, Miramar, Havana; tel. (7) 204-2995; fax (7) 204-1784; e-mail gremb@enet.cu; Ambassador ILIAS MALTEZOS.

Cyprus: POB 21799, 8–10 Byron Ave, 1096 Nicosia; tel. 22445111; fax 22680649; e-mail info@greekembassy-cy.org; internet www.greekembassy-cy.org; Ambassador Demetrios Rallis.

Czech Republic: Na Ořechovce 19, 162 00 Prague 2; tel. 222250943; fax 222253686; e-mail greekemb@czn.cz; Ambassador VASSILIOS IKOSSIPENTARCHOS.

Denmark: Hammerensgade 4, 1267 Copenhagen K; tel. 33-11-45-33; fax 33-93-16-46; e-mail greekembcop@post.tele.dk; Ambassador Dimitris Contoumas.

Egypt: 18 Sharia Aicha at-Taimouria, Cairo 11451 (Garden City); tel. (2) 7950443; fax (2) 7963903; e-mail grembcai@internetgypt.com; Ambassador PANAYOTIS VLASSOPOULOS.

Estonia: Pärnu mnt. 12, Tallinn 10148; tel. 640-3560; fax 640-3561; e-mail grembest@yahoo.com; Ambassador Christos Karapanos.

Ethiopia: off Debre Zeit Rd, POB 1168, Addis Ababa; tel. (11) 4654911; fax (11) 4654883; internet www.telecom.net.et/~greekemb; Ambassador DIONISIOS KOUNTOUREAS.

Finland: Maneesikatu 2a 4, 00170 Helsinki; tel. (9) 6229790; fax (9) 2781200; e-mail info@greekembassy.fi; internet www.greekembassy.fi; Ambassador Dimitrios-Michail Loundras.

France: 17 rue Auguste Vacquerie, 75116 Paris; tel. 1-47-23-72-28; fax 1-47-23-73-85; e-mail gremb.par@mfa.gr; internet www.amb-grece.fr; Ambassador DIMITRIOS PARASKEVOPOULOS.

Georgia: 0179 Tbilisi, T. Tabldze 37d; tel. (32) 91-49-70; fax (32) 91-49-80; e-mail grembgeo@access.sanet.ge; internet www.greekembassy.ge; Ambassador Georgios Chatzimihelakis.

Germany: Jägerstr. 55, 3rd Floor, 10117 Berlin; tel. (30) 206260; fax (30) 20626444; e-mail greekembassyberlin@t-online.de; internet www.griechenland-botschaft.de; Ambassador ANASTASSIOS KRIEKOUKIS.

Hungary: 1063 Budapest, Szegfu u. 3; tel. (1) 413-2600; fax (1) 342-1934; e-mail greekemb@axelero.hu; Ambassador Dimitris Contumas.

India: EP–32, Dr S. Radhakrishnan Marg, Chanakyapuri, New Delhi 110 021; tel. (11) 26880700; fax (11) 26888010; e-mail gremb@bol.net.in; internet www.greeceinindia.com; Ambassador STAVROS LYKIDIS.

Indonesia: Plaza 89, 12th Floor, Suite 1203, Jalan H. R. Rasuna Said, Kav. X-7 No. 6, Kuningan, Jakarta Selatan 12940; tel. (21) 5207776; fax (21) 5207753; e-mail grembas@cbn.net.id; internet www.greekembassy.or.id; Ambassador Charalambos Christopoulos.

Iran: POB 11365-8151, Africa Ave, Esfandiar St, No. 43, Tehran; tel. (21) 22050533; fax (21) 22057431; e-mail embgreece@parsonline.net; Ambassador MARCARIOUS KARAFOTIAS.

Iraq: 63/13/913 Hay Babel, Baghdad; tel. (1) 718-2433; fax (1) 718-8729; e-mail greekembirq@hotmail.com; Ambassador Panayotis Makris.

Ireland: 1 Upper Pembroke St, Dublin 2; tel. (1) 6767254; fax (1) 6618892; e-mail embgr@eircom.net; Ambassador GEORGIOS-ALEXANDROS VALLINDAS.

Israel: 3 Daniel Frisch St, Tel-Aviv 64731; tel. 3-6953060; fax 3-6951329; e-mail gremb.tlv@mfa.gr; Ambassador Michail Spinelis.

Italy: Viale G. Rossini 4, 00198 Roma; tel. (06) 8537551; fax (06) 85375503; e-mail gremroma@tin.it; internet www.greekembassy.it; Ambassador CHARALAMBOS ROCANAS.

Japan: 3-16-30, Nishi Azabu, Minato-ku, Tokyo 106-0031; tel. (3) 3403-0871; fax (3) 3402-4642; e-mail gremb.tok@mfa.gr; internet www.greekemb.jp; Ambassador Ioannis Vavvas.

Jordan: POB 35069, 7 Iskandaronah St, Abdoun, Amman 11180; tel. (6) 5922724; fax (6) 5927622; e-mail greekemb@nol.com.jo; Ambassador TRYPHON PARASKEVOPOULOS.

Kazakhstan: 050020 Almaty, Kyz Zhibek 80, mer Kok-Tobe; tel. (727) 250-39-61; fax (727) 250-39-38; e-mail hellenic.embassy@ducatmail.com; Chargé d'affaires Georgios Partheniou.

Kenya: Nation Centre, 13th Floor, Kimathi St, POB 30543, Nairobi; tel. (20) 340722; fax (20) 216044; e-mail embgr@kenyaweb.com; Ambassador IOANNIS KORINTHIOS.

Korea, Republic: Hanwha Bldg, 27th Floor, 1, Janggyo-dong, Jung-gu, Seoul 100-797; tel. (2) 729-1401; fax (2) 729-1402; e-mail greekemb@kornet.net; Ambassador Konstantinos Drakakis.

Kuwait: POB 23812, 13099 Safat, Khaldiya, Block 4, St 44, House 4, Kuwait City; tel. 4817100; fax 4817103; e-mail grembkw@hotmail.com; Ambassador STAVROS LYKIDIS.

Latvia: Elizabetes iela 11–5, 1010 Rīga; tel. 6735-6345; fax 6735-6351; e-mail greekemb-riga@mfa.gr; internet www.greekembassy.se; Ambassador Chryssanthie Panayotopoulou.

Lebanon: POB 11-0309, Immeuble Boukhater, rue des Ambassades, Nouvelle Naccache, Beirut; tel. (4) 418772; fax (4) 418774; e-mail hellas.emb@inco.com.lb; Ambassador NIKOLAOS VAMVOUNAKIS.

Libya: POB 5147, Sharia Jalal Bayar 18, Tripoli; tel. (21) 3338563; fax (21) 4441907; e-mail grembtri@hotmail.com; Ambassador Chrysanthi Panagiotopoulou.

Lithuania: Didžioji 33/Rūdininkų 2; tel. (5) 261-0526; fax (5) 261-0536; e-mail embassy@grembvil.w3.lt; Ambassador GEORGE CHRISTOFIS.

Luxembourg: 27 rue Marie-Adélaïde, 2128 Luxembourg; tel. 44-51-93; fax 45-01-64; e-mail ambgrec@pt.lu; Ambassador Dionysios Kodelas.

Malta: Villino Fondgalland, 6 Ir-Rampa Ta'Xbiex, Ta'Xbiex XBX 1035; tel. 21320998; fax 21320788; e-mail embassy.malta@mfa.gr; Ambassador DOROTHEA TSIMBOUKELI-DOUVOS.

Mexico: Sierra Gorda 505, Col. Lomas de Chapultepec, Del. Miguel Hidalgo, 11010 México, DF; tel. (55) 5520-2070; fax (55) 5202-4080; e-mail grecemb@prodigy.net.mx; Ambassador Alexander Migliaressis.

Montenegro: 81000 Podgorica, Atinska 4; tel. (81) 655544; fax (81) 655543; Chargé d'affaires a.i. NIKOLAOS KAYMENAKIS.

Morocco: km 5, route des Zaêrs, Villa Chems, Souissi, 10000 Rabat; tel. (3) 7638964; fax (3) 7638990; e-mail ambagrec@iam.net.ma; Ambassador Michel Cambanis.

Netherlands: Amaliastraat 1, 2514 JC The Hague; tel. (70) 3638700; fax (70) 3563040; e-mail grembhag@planet.nl; internet www.greekembassy.nl; Ambassador CONSTANTINOS IOANNIS RALLIS.

New Zealand: 5–7 Willeston St, 10th Floor, POB 24-066, Wellington; tel. (4) 473-7775; fax (4) 473-7441; e-mail info@greece.org.nz; Ambassador Evangelos Damianakis.

Nigeria: No 6, Takum Close, Wuse II, Abuja; tel. (9) 4139433; fax (9) 4139435; e-mail grembabuja@mfa.gr; internet grembnigeria.mfa.gr; Ambassador HARALAMBOS DAFARANOS.

Norway: Nobelsgt. 45, 0244 Oslo; tel. 22-44-27-28; fax 22-56-00-72; e-mail gremb@online.no; Ambassador Jean Boucaouris.

Pakistan: 22, Margalla Rd, F-6/3, Islamabad; tel. (51) 2822558; fax (51) 2825161; e-mail greece@isb.paknet.com.pk; internet www.greekembassy.org.pk; Ambassador ATHANASIOS VALASIDIS.

Peru: Avda Principal 190, 6°, Urb. Santa Catalina, Lima 13; tel. (1) 4761548; fax (1) 4761329; e-mail emgrecia@terra.com.pe; Ambassador Vassilos Simantirakis.

Poland: 00-432 Warsaw, ul. Górnośląska 35; tel. (22) 6229460; fax (22) 6229464; e-mail gremb.war@mfa.gr; internet www.greece.pl; Ambassador PANTELIS CARCABASSIS.

Portugal: Rua do Alto do Duque 13, 1449-026 Lisbon; tel. (21) 3031260; fax (21) 3011205; e-mail gremb.lis@mfa.gr; Ambassador Spyridon Theocharopoulos.

Romania: 021403 Bucharest, Bd. Pache Protopopescu 1–3, Sector 2; tel. (21) 2094170; fax (21) 2094175; e-mail grembassy@grembassy.ro; internet www.grembassy.ro; Ambassador GEORGIOS POUKAMISSAS.

Russian Federation: 103009 Moscow, Leontiyevskii per. 4; tel. (495) 290-14-46; fax (495) 771-65-10; e-mail gremb.mow@mfa.gr; internet www.hellas.ru; Ambassador Ilias Klis.

Saudi Arabia: POB 94375, Riyadh 11693; tel. (1) 480-1975; fax (1) 480-1969; e-mail gremb.ria@mfa.gr; Ambassador IOANNIS-THEODOROS ECONOMOU.

Serbia: 11000 Belgrade, Francuska 33; tel. (11) 3226523; fax 3344746; internet www.greekemb.co.yu; Ambassador Christos Panagopoulos.

Slovakia: Hlavné nám. 4, 811 01 Bratislava; tel. (2) 5443-4143; fax (2) 5443-4064; e-mail embassy@greece.sk; internet www.greece.sk; Ambassador KONSTANTINOS KARABETSIS.

Slovenia: 1000 Ljubljana, Trnovski Pristan 14; tel. (1) 4201400; fax (1) 2811114; e-mail emb.gr.slo@siol.net; Ambassador Dionyssios Coundoureas.

South Africa: 1003 Church St, Arcadia, Pretoria 0083; tel. (12) 3427136; fax (12) 4304313; e-mail embgrsaf@global.co.za; Ambassador ARISTIDIS SANDIS.

Spain: Avda Dr Arce 24, 28002 Madrid; tel. (91) 5644653; fax (91) 5644668; e-mail embajadadegrecia@telefonica.net; internet www.embagrec.org; Ambassador Geórgios Gabrielides.

Sudan: Sharia al-Gamhouria, Block 5, No. 30, POB 1182, Khartoum; tel. (183) 765902; fax (183) 765901; e-mail grembkrt@mfa.gr; Ambassador GEORGIOS VEIS.

Sweden: Kommendörsgt. 16, POB 55565, 102 04 Stockholm; tel. (8) 545-660-10; fax (8) 660-54-70; e-mail grembstockholm@greekembassy.se; internet www.greekembassy.se; Ambassador Evangelos Carokis.

Switzerland: Weltpostr. 4, 3015 Bern; tel. 313561414; fax 313681272; e-mail gremb.brn@mfa.gr; internet www.greekembassy.ch; Ambassador CONSTANTINE TRITARIS.

Syria: BP 30319, Immeuble Pharaon, 11 rue Farabi, Mezzeh Est, Damascus; tel. (11) 6113035; fax (11) 6114920; e-mail gremb.dam@mfa.gr; Ambassador Konstantina Zagorianou-Prifti.

Thailand: Unit 25/5-9, 9th Floor, BKI/YWCA Bldg, 25 Thanon Sathorn Tai, Bangkok 10120; tel. (2) 679-1462; fax (2) 679-1463; e-mail embgrbkk@ksc.th.com; Ambassador IOANNIS PAPADOPOULOS.

Tunisia: 6 rue Saint Fulgence, Notre Dame, 1082 Tunis; tel. (71) 288-411; fax (71) 789-518; e-mail gremb.tun@mfa.gr; Ambassador Dimitrios Karatidis.

Turkey: Zia ür-Rahman Cad. 9–11, 06670 Gaziosmanpaşa, Ankara; tel. (312) 4480873; fax (312) 4463191; e-mail gremb.ank@mfa.gr; Ambassador FOTIOS-JEAN XYDAS.

Ukraine: 01901 Kyiv, vul. Panfilovtsev 10; tel. (44) 254-54-71; fax (44) 254-39-98; e-mail greece@kiev.relc.com; internet www.greece.kiev.ua; Ambassador Charalambos Dimitriou.

United Arab Emirates: POB 5483, Plot 141, Villa 1, E-48, Moroor, Abu Dhabi; tel. (2) 6654847; fax (2) 6656008; e-mail grembauh@emirates.net.ae; Ambassador GEORGE KOSTOLAS.

United Kingdom: 1a Holland Park, London, W11 3TP; tel. (20) 7229-3850; fax (20) 7229-7221; e-mail political@greekembassy.org.uk; internet www.greekembassy.org.uk; Ambassador Vassilis-Achilleas Pispinis.

United States of America: 2217 Massachusetts Ave, NW, Washington, DC 20008; tel. (202) 939-1300; fax (202) 939-1324; e-mail greece@greekembassy.org; internet www.greekembassy.org; Ambassador ALEXANDROS P. MALLIAS.

Uruguay: Edif. Artigas, Rincón 487, 2°, 11100 Montevideo; tel. (2) 9165191; fax (2) 9150795; e-mail gremb.mvd@mfa.gr; Ambassador Nicolaos Dictakis.

Vatican City: Via Giuseppe Mercalli 6, 00197 Rome, Italy; tel. (06) 8070786; fax (06) 8079862; e-mail grembassyvat@grembassyvat.191.it; Ambassador MILTIADIS HISKAKIS.

Venezuela: Quinta Maryland, Avda Principal del Avila, Alta Florida, Caracas 1050; tel. (212) 730-3833; fax (212) 731-0429; e-mail embgrccs@cantv.net; Ambassador Efstathios Daras.

Zimbabwe: 8 Deary Ave, Belgravia, POB 4809, Harare; tel. (4) 793208; fax (4) 703662; e-mail grembha@zol.co.zw; Ambassador DIMITRI M. ALEXANDRAKIS.

DIPLOMATIC MISSIONS OF GRENADA

United Nations: 800 Second Ave, Suite 400k, New York, NY 10017; tel. (212) 599-0301; fax (212) 599-1540; e-mail grenada@un.int; Permanent Representative Dr Angus Friday.

Belgium: 123 rue de Laeken, 1e étage, 1000 Brussels; tel. (2) 223-73-03; fax (2) 223-73-07; e-mail embassyofgrenadabxl@skynet.be; Ambassador JOAN-MARIE COUTAIN.

Canada (see entry for Antigua and Barbuda).

China, People's Republic: T5-2-52, Tayuan Diplomatic Office Building, Chaoyang Qu, Beijing 100600; tel. (10) 65321208; fax (10) 65321015; e-mail grenembbeijing@yahoo.com; Ambassador JOSLYN R. WHITEMAN.

United Kingdom: The Chapel, Archel Rd, West Kensington, London, W14 9QH; tel. (20) 7385-4415; fax (20) 7381-4807; e-mail grenada@high -commission.demon.co.uk; High Commr Joseph Stephen Charter.

United States of America: 1701 New Hampshire Ave, NW, Washington, DC 20009; tel. (202) 265-2561; fax (202) 265-2468; internet www .grenadaembassyusa.org; Ambassador DENIS G. ANTOINE.

Venezuela: Avda Norte 2, Quinta 330, Los Naranjos del Cafetal, Caracas; tel. (212) 985-5461; fax (212) 985-6391; e-mail mcphail@spiceisle.com; internet www.grenadaembassycaracas.org; Ambassador Richard Paul McPhail.

DIPLOMATIC MISSIONS OF GUATEMALA

United Nations: 57 Park Ave, New York, NY 10016; tel. (212) 679-4760; fax (212) 685-8741; e-mail guatemala@un.int; internet www.un.int/guatemala; Permanent Representative JORGE SKINNER-KLÉE ARENALES.

Argentina: Avda Santa Fe 830, 5°, C1059ABP Buenos Aires; tel. (11) 4313-9160; fax (11) 4313-9181; e-mail embagua@peoples.com.ar; Ambassador Luis Fernando González Davison.

Austria: Landstr. Hauptstr. 21/Top 9, 1030 Vienna; tel. (1) 714-35-70; fax (1) 714-35-70-15; e-mail embajada@embaguate.co.at; Ambassador LUIS ALBERTO PADILLA MENÉNDEZ.

Belgium: 185 ave Winston Churchill, 1180 Brussels; tel. (2) 345-90-58; fax (2) 344-64-99; e-mail embaguate.belgica@skynet.be; Ambassador Antonio Fernando Arenales Forno.

Belize: 8 'A' St, King's Park, POB 1771, Belize City; tel. 233-3150; fax 235-5140; e-mail embbelice1@minex.gob.gt; Ambassador MANUEL ARTURO TÉLLEZ MIRALDA.

Brazil: SHIS, QI 03, Conj. 10, Casa 01, Lago Sul, 71605-001 Brasília, DF; tel. (61) 3365-1908; fax (61) 3365-1906; e-mail embaguate-brasil@minex.gob.gt; Ambassador Carlos Jiménez Licona.

Canada: 130 Albert St, Suite 1010, Ottawa, ON K1P 5G4; tel. (613) 233-7237; fax (613) 233-0135; e-mail embassy1@embaguate-canada.com; internet www .embaguate-canada.com; Ambassador MANUEL ESTUARDO ROLDÁN BARILLAS.

Chile: Séptimo de Línea 1262, Providencia, Santiago; tel. (2) 264-0525; fax (2) 264-1146; e-mail embajada@guatemala.cl; internet www .embajadadeguatemala.cl; Ambassador Antonio R. Castellanos López.

China (Taiwan): 3/F, 9-1 Lane 62, Tien Mou West Rd, Taipei 11156; tel. (2) 28756952; fax (2) 28740699; e-mail embaguat.tw@iname.com; internet www .geocities.com/WallStreet/Floor/8227; Ambassador FRANCISCO BERMÚDEZ AMADO.

Colombia: Diagonal 145a, No 32-37, Bogotá, DC; tel. (1) 636-1724; fax (1) 274-1196; e-mail embcolombia@minex.gob.gt; Ambassador Manlio Fernando Sesenna Olivero.

Costa Rica: De Pops Curridabat 500 m sur y 30 m este, 2a Casa Izquierda, Apdo 328, 1000 San José; tel. 291-6208; fax 290-4111; e-mail costarica@ minex.gob.gt; Ambassador JUAN JOSÉ BARRIOS TARACENA.

Cuba: Calle 16, No 505, entre 3 y 5, Miramar, Havana; tel. (7) 204-3417; fax (7) 204-3200; e-mail embagucu@ceniai.inf.cu; Ambassador Herbert Estuardo Meneces Coronado.

Dominican Republic: Edif. Corominas Pepín, 9°, Avda 27 de Febrero 233, Santo Domingo, DN; tel. 381-0249; fax 381-0278; e-mail guaterd@ codetel_net.do; Ambassador CÉSAR AUGUSTO MÉNDEZ PINELO.

Ecuador: Edif. Gabriela III, 3°, Of. 301, Avda República de El Salvador 733 y Portugal, Apdo 17-03-294, Quito; tel. (2) 245-9700; e-mail embecuador@ minex.gob.gt; Ambassador Juan León Alvarado.

Egypt: 5th Floor, 17 Sharia Port Said, Maadi, Cairo; tel. (2) 3802914; fax (2) 3802915; e-mail embegipto@minex.gob.gt; Ambassador FLORIDALMA FRANCO PAIZ.

El Salvador: 15 Avda Norte 135, San Salvador; tel. 2271-2225; fax 2221-3019; e-mail embelsalvador@minex.gob.gt; Ambassador Dr José Luis Chea Urruela.

France: 2 rue Villebois-Marueil, 75017 Paris; tel. 1-42-27-78-63; fax 1-47-54-02-06; e-mail embaguatefrancia@wanadoo.fr; internet www .ambassadeduguatemala.com; Ambassador ANAISABEL PRERA FLORES.

Germany: Joachim-Karnatz-Allee 45–47, 10557 Berlin; tel. (30) 2064363; fax (30) 20643659; e-mail embaguate.alemania@t-online.de; internet www .botschaft-guatemala.de; Chargé d'affaires a.i. Nelson Rafael Olivero Garcia.

Honduras: Col. Lomas del Guijaro, Calle Alfonso XIII, Casa 3716, Tegucigalpa; tel. 232-5018; fax 232-1580; Ambassador ANGELA GAROZ CABRERA.

Israel: 103 Medinat Hayehudim St, Herzliya Pitauch 46766; tel. 9-9577335; fax 9-9518506; e-mail embguate@netvision.net.il; Ambassador Moisés Russ Topolsky.

Italy: Via dei Colli della Farnesina 128, 00194 Roma; tel. (06) 36381143; fax (06) 3291639; e-mail embaguate.italia@tin.it; Ambassador FRANCISCO EDUARDO BONIFAZ RODRÍGUEZ.

Japan: Kowa Bldg, No. 38, Room 905, 4-12-24, Nishi Azabu, Minato-ku, Tokyo 106-0031; tel. (3) 3400-1830; fax (3) 3400-1820; e-mail embguate@ vega.ocn.ne.jp; internet www.embassy-avenue.jp/guatemala; Ambassador Arturo Duarte.

Korea, Republic: 614, Lotte Hotel, 1, Sogong-dong, Jung-gu, Seoul 100-635; tel. (2) 771-7582; fax (2) 771-7584; e-mail embcorea@minex.gob.gt; Ambassador RAFAEL A. SALAZAR.

Mexico: Explanada 1025, Col. Lomas de Chapultepec, Del. Miguel Hidalgo, 11000 México, DF; tel. (55) 5540-7520; fax (55) 5202-1142; e-mail embaguatemx@minex.gob.gt; Chargé d'affaires a.i. Eduardo Antonio Escobedo Sanabria.

Netherlands: Javastraat 44, 2585 AP The Hague; tel. (70) 3020253; fax (70) 3602270; e-mail embpaisesbajos@minex.gob.gt; Ambassador CARLA MARÍA RODRÍGUEZ MANCÍA.

Nicaragua: Km 11½, Carretera a Masaya, Apdo E-1, Managua; tel. 279-9609; fax 279-9610; e-mail embnic@minex.gob.gt; Ambassador Jorge Rolando Echeverría Roldán.

Norway: Oscarsgt. 59, 0258 Oslo; tel. 22-55-60-04; fax 22-55-60-47; e-mail guatemala@embajada.no; Ambassador LUIS RAÚL ESTÉVEZ LÓPEZ.

Panama: Edif. Altamira, Of. 925, Vía Argentina, El Cangrejo, Corregimiento de Bella Vista, Panamá 9; tel. 269-3475; fax 223-1922; Ambassador Lionel Valentín Maza Luna.

Peru: Inca Ripac 309, Jesús María, Lima 11; tel. (1) 4602078; fax (1) 4635885; e-mail embperu@minex.gob.gt; Ambassador LUIS PEDRO QUEZADA CÓRDOVA.

Russian Federation: 119049 Moscow, ul. Korovii Val 7/98; tel. (495) 238-22-14; fax (495) 238-14-46; e-mail embrusia@minex.gob.gt; Ambassador Lars Henrik Pira Pérez.

Spain: Rafael Salgado 3, 10° dcha, 28036 Madrid; tel. (91) 3441722; fax (91) 4587894; e-mail informacion@embajadaguatemala.es; internet www .embajadaguatemala.es; Ambassador (vacant).

Sweden: Munkbron 3, 111 28 Stockholm; tel. (8) 660-52-29; fax (8) 660-42-29; e-mail embassy@guatemala.se; internet www.guatemala.se; Ambassador Susana Barrios Beltranena.

United Kingdom: 13 Fawcett St, London, SW10 9HN; tel. (20) 7351-3042; fax (20) 7376-5708; e-mail ambassador.gtm@btconnect.com; Ambassador EDMUNDO RENÉ URRUTIA GARCIA.

United States of America: 2220 R St, NW, Washington, DC 20008; tel. (202) 745-4952; fax (202) 745-1908; e-mail info@guatemala-embassy.org; internet www.guatemala-embassy.org; Ambassador Francisco Villagrán de León.

Uruguay: Costa Rica 1538, Carrasco, Montevideo; tel. (2) 6012225; fax (2) 6014057; e-mail embajadaguatemala@netgate.com.uy; Ambassador RICARDO PUTZEYS.

Vatican City: Piazzale Gregorio VII 65a, 00165 Rome, Italy; tel. (06) 6381632; fax (06) 39376981; e-mail embsantasede@minex.gob.gt; Ambassador Acisclo Valladares Molina.

Venezuela: Avda de Francisco de Miranda, Torre Dozsa, 1°, Urb. El Rosal, Caracas; tel. (212) 952-1166; fax (212) 954-0051; e-mail embaguat@cantv .net; Ambassador IVAN ESPINOZA FARFÁN.

DIPLOMATIC MISSIONS OF GUINEA

United Nations: 140 East 39th St, New York, NY 10016; tel. (212) 687-8115; fax (212) 687-8248; e-mail guinea@un.int; Permanent Representative Mamady Traoré.

Algeria: 43 blvd Central Saïd Hamdine, Hydra, Algiers; tel. (21) 69-20-66; fax (21) 69-34-68; Ambassador MAMADY CONDÉ.

Angola: Luanda; .

Belgium: 108 blvd Auguste Reyers, 1030 Brussels; tel. (2) 771-01-26; fax (2) 762-60-36; e-mail ambasssadedeguinee.bel@skynet.be; Ambassador AHMED TIDIANE SAKHO.

Brazil: SHIS QL 02, Conj. 07, Casa 09, Lago Sul, 71610-075 Brasília, DF; tel. (61) 3365-1301; fax (61) 3365-4921; e-mail ambaguibrasil@terra.com.br; Ambassador Fodé Touré.

Canada: 483 Wilbrod St, Ottawa, ON K1N 6N1; tel. (613) 789-8444; fax (613) 789-7560; e-mail ambassadedeguinea@bellnet.ca; Chargé d'affaires a.i. KABA HAWA DIAKITE.

China, People's Republic: 2 Xi Liu Jie, San Li Tun, Beijing 100600; tel. (10) 65323649; fax (10) 65324957; Ambassador Diare Mamady.

Congo, Republic: Brazzaville; tel. 81-24-66; .

Côte d'Ivoire: Immeuble Duplessis, 08 BP 2280, Abidjan 08; tel. 20-22-25-20; fax 20-32-82-45; Ambassador (vacant).

Cuba: Calle 20, No 504, entre 5 y 7, Miramar, Havana; tel. (7) 204-2003; fax (7) 204-2380; Ambassador HADIATOU SOW.

Egypt: 46 Sharia Muhammad Mazhar, Cairo (Zamalek); tel. (2) 7358109; fax (2) 7361446; Ambassador El Hadj Ousmane Camara.

Equatorial Guinea: Malabo; .

Ethiopia: Debre Zeit Rd, Woreda 18, Kebele 14, House No. 58, POB 1190, Addis Ababa; tel. (11) 4651308; fax (11) 4651250; Ambassador Sekou Camara.

France: 51 rue de la Faisanderie, 75116 Paris; tel. 1-47-04-81-48; fax 1-47-04-57-65; e-mail accueil@ambaguinee-paris.org; internet www.ambaguinee-paris.org; Ambassador KEITA MAKALÉ CAMARA.

Gabon: BP 4046, Libreville; tel. 73-85-09; Ambassador Mohamed Sampil.

Germany: Jägerstr. 67–69, 10117 Berlin; tel. (30) 20074330; fax (30) 200743333; e-mail berlin@embaguinee.de; Ambassador ALEXANDRE CECE LOUA.

Ghana: 11 Osu Badu St, Dzorwulu, POB 5497, Accra-North; tel. (21) 777921; fax (21) 760961; e-mail embagui@ghana.com; Ambassador Mamadou Falilou Bah.

Guinea-Bissau: Rua 14, no. 9, CP 396, Bissau; tel. 212681; Ambassador TAMBA TIENDO MILLIMONO.

Iran: POB 11365-4716, Dr Shariati Ave, Malek St, No. 10, Tehran; tel. (21) 77535744; fax (21) 77535743; e-mail ambaguinee_thr@hotmail.com; Ambassador Olia Kamara.

Italy: Via Adelaide Ristori, 9B 13, 00197 Roma; tel. (06) 8078989; fax (06) 8077588; e-mail ambaguineerome1@virgilio.it; Ambassador EL HADJ THIERNO MAMADOU CELLOU DIALLO.

Japan: 12-9, Hachiyama-cho, Shibuya-ku, Tokyo 150-0035; tel. (3) 3770-4640; fax (3) 3770-4643; e-mail ambagui-tokyo@gol.com; Ambassador Ousmane Tolo Thiam.

Liberia: Monrovia; Ambassador ABDOULAYE DORÉ.

Libya: POB 10657, Hay Andalus, Tripoli; tel. (21) 4772793; fax (21) 4773441; e-mail magatte@lttnet.net; Ambassador Abdul Aziz Soumah.

Malaysia: 5 Jalan Kedondong, off Jalan Ampang Hilir, 55000 Kuala Lumpur; tel. (3) 42576500; fax (3) 42511500; e-mail mwcnakry@sotelgui.net.gn; Ambassador MOHAMED SAMPIL.

Mali: Immeuble Saybou Maïga, Quartier du Fleuve, BP 118, Bamako; tel. 222-30-07; fax 221-08-06; Ambassador (vacant).

Morocco: 15 rue Hamzah, Agdal, 10000 Rabat; tel. (3) 7674148; fax (3) 7672513; Ambassador MAHMADOU SALIOU SYLA.

Nigeria: 8 Abudu Smith St, Victoria Island, POB 2826, Lagos; tel. (1) 2616961; Ambassador Komo Beavogui.

Russian Federation: 119034 Moscow, Pomerantsev per. 6; tel. (495) 201-36-01; fax (502) 220-21-38; Ambassador LT-COL AMARA BANGOURA.

Saudi Arabia: POB 94326, Riyadh 11693; tel. (1) 488-1101; fax (1) 482-6757; Ambassador el-Hadj Aboul Karim Dioubatè.

Senegal: rue 7, angle B&D, point E, BP 7123, Dakar; tel. 33-824-8606; fax 33-825-5946; Ambassador HADJA KOUMBA DIAKITÉ.

Serbia: 11000 Belgrade, Ohridska 4; tel. (11) 431830; fax (11) 451391; Ambassador El Hadj Muhammad Issiaga Kourouma.

Sierra Leone: 6 Wilkinson Rd, Freetown; tel. (22) 232584; fax (22) 232496; Ambassador MOHAMED LAMIN SOMPARE.

South Africa: 336 Orient St, Arcadia, Pretoria 0083; POB 13523, Hatfield 0028; tel. (12) 3420893; fax (12) 3427348; e-mail embaguinea@iafrica.com; Chargé d'affaires a.i. Bouram-Ciré Diakite.

Togo: Lomé; tel. 221-74-98; fax 221-81-16; .

United Kingdom: 48 Onslow Gdns, London, SW7 3PY; tel. (20) 7594-4819; e-mail ambaguineeuk@yahoo.co.uk; Ambassador Lansana Keïta.

United States of America: 2112 Leroy Pl., NW, Washington, DC 20008; tel. (202) 483-9420; fax (202) 483-8688; Ambassador (vacant).

DIPLOMATIC MISSIONS OF GUINEA-BISSAU

United Nations: 211 East 43rd St, Rm 704, New York, NY 10017; tel. (212) 338-9394; fax (212) 293-0264; e-mail guinea-bissau@un.int; Chargé d'affaires a.i. Alfredo Lopes Cabral.

Algeria: BP 32, 17 rue Ahmad Kara, Colonne Volrol, Hydra, Algiers; tel. (21) 60-01-51; fax (21) 60-97-25; Ambassador JOSÉ PEREIRA BATISTA.

Belgium: 80 ave Brugmann, 1190 Brussels; tel. (2) 347-72-76; Ambassador Henrique Adriano Da Silva.

Bosnia and Herzegovina: 71000 Sarajevo, Radnička 2; tel. (33) 660948; fax (33) 655524; Ambassador DESIDERIUS OSTROGON DA COSTA.

China, People's Republic: 2-2-101 Tayuan Diplomatic Compound, Beijing; tel. (10) 65327393; fax (10) 65327106; Chargé d'affaires Carrington Ca.

Cuba: Calle 14, No 313, entre 3 y 5, Miramar, Havana; tel. (7) 204-2689; fax (7) 204-2794; Chargé d'affaires a.i. MALAM DJASSI.

Egypt: 37 Sharia Lebanon, Madinet el-Mohandessin, Cairo (Dokki); .

France: 94 rue Saint Lazare, 75009 Paris; tel. 1-48-74-36-39; fax 1-48-78-36-39; e-mail ambaguineebxo@wanadoo.fr; Ambassador JOÃO SOARES DA GAMA.

Guinea: Quartier Bellevue, Commune de Dixinn, BP 298, Conakry; Ambassador Malam Camara.

Portugal: Rua de Alcolena 17, 1400-004 Lisbon; tel. (21) 3030440; fax (21) 3019653; Ambassador CONSTANTINO LOPES DA COSTA.

Russian Federation: 117556 Moscow, Simferopolskii bulv. 7a/183; tel. (495) 317-95-82; Ambassador Rogerio Araujo Adolpho Herbert.

Senegal: rue 6, angle B, point E, BP 2319, Dakar; tel. 33-823-0059; fax 33-825-2946; Ambassador LANSANA TOURÉ.

United States of America: POB 33813, Washington, DC 20033-3813; tel. (301) 947-3958; Chargé d'affaires a.i. (vacant).

DIPLOMATIC MISSIONS OF GUYANA

United Nations: 866 United Nations Plaza, Suite 555, New York, NY 10017; tel. (212) 527-3232; fax (212) 935-7548; e-mail guyana@un.int; Permanent Representative SAMUEL R. INSANALLY.

Belgium: 12 ave du Brésil, 1000 Brussels; tel. (2) 672-62-16; fax (2) 675-55-98; e-mail embassy_guyana@skynet.be; Ambassador Patrick Ignasius Gomes.

Brazil: SHIS, QI 05, Conj. 19, Casa 24, 71615-190 Brasília, DF; tel. (61) 3248-0874; fax (61) 3248-0886; e-mail embguyana@embguyana.org.br; internet www.embguyana.org.br; Ambassador MARILYN CHERYL MILES.

Canada: Burnside Bldg, 151 Slater St, Suite 309, Ottawa, ON K1P 5H3; tel. (613) 235-7249; fax (613) 235-1447; e-mail guyanahcott@rogers.com; High Commissioner Rajnarine Singh.

China, People's Republic: 1 Xiu Shui Dong Jie, Jian Guo Men Wai, Beijing 100600; tel. (10) 65321601; fax (10) 65325741; e-mail guyemb@public3.bta.net.cn; Chargé d'affaires CECIL POLLYDORE.

Cuba: Calle 18, No 506, entre 5 y 7, Miramar, Havana; tel. (7) 204-2249; fax (7) 204-2867; e-mail embguyana@ip.etecsa.cu; Ambassador Dr Timothy N. Critchlow.

India: F-8/22, Vasant Vihar, New Delhi 110 057; tel. (11) 41669717; fax (11) 41669714; e-mail hcommguy.del@gmail.com; High Commissioner J. RONALD GAJRAJ.

Suriname: Gravenstraat 82, POB 785, Paramaribo; tel. 477895; fax 472679; e-mail guyembassy@sr.net; Ambassador Karshanje Arjun.

United Kingdom: 3 Palace Court, Bayswater Rd, London, W2 4LP; tel. (20) 7229-7684; fax (20) 7727-9809; e-mail ghc.l@ic24.net; High Commr LALESHWAR K. N. SINGH.

United States of America: 2490 Tracy Pl., NW, Washington, DC 20008; tel. (202) 265-6900; fax (202) 232-1297; e-mail guyanaembassydc@verizon.net; internet www.guyanaembassyusa.com; Ambassador Bayney Ram Karran.

Venezuela: Quinta 'Roraima', Avda El Paseo, Prados del Este, Apdo 51054, Caracas 1050; tel. (212) 977-1158; fax (212) 976-3765; e-mail embaguy@caracas.org.ve; Ambassador ODEEN ISHMAEL.

DIPLOMATIC MISSIONS OF HAITI

United Nations: 801 Second Ave, Rm 600, New York, NY 10017; tel. (212) 370-4840; fax (212) 661-8698; e-mail haiti@un.int; Permanent Representative Léo Mérorès.

Argentina: Avda Figueroa Alcorta 3297, C1425CKL Buenos Aires; tel. (11) 4802-0211; fax (11) 4802-3984; e-mail embajadahaiti@fibertel.com.ar; Ambassador JEAN MARIE MICHEL RAYMOND MATHIEU.

Bahamas: Sears House, Shirley St and Sears Rd, POB N-3036, Nassau; tel. 326-0325; fax 322-7712; Ambassador Louis Harold Joseph.

Belgium: 139 chaussée de Charleroi, 1060 Brussels; tel. (2) 649-73-81; fax (2) 640-60-80; e-mail ambassade@amb-haiti.be; Ambassador RAYMOND LAFONTANT, Jr.

Brazil: SHIS, QL 10, Conj. 06, Casa 16, Lago Sul, 71630-065 Brasília, DF; tel. (61) 3248-6860; fax (61) 3248-7472; e-mail embhaiti@terra.com.br; Ambassador (vacant).

Canada: 130 Albert St, Suite 1500, Ottawa, ON K1P 5G4; tel. (613) 238-1628; fax (613) 238-2986; e-mail bohio@bellnet.ca; Chargé d'affaires a.i. MARIE NATHALIE MENOS-GISSEL.

Chile: Zurich 255, Of. 21, Las Condes, Santiago; tel. (2) 650-8180; fax (2) 334-0384; e-mail embhai@terra.cl; Ambassador Guy G. Lamothe.

China (Taiwan): 8/F, 9-1 Lane 62, Tien Mou West Rd, Taipei 11156; tel. (2) 28766718; fax (2) 28766719; e-mail haiti@ms26.hinet.net; Ambassador PAUL RAYMOND PERODIN.

Cuba: Avda 7, No 4402, esq. 44, Miramar, Havana; tel. (7) 204-5421; fax (7) 204-5423; e-mail embhaiti@enet.cu; internet www.embhaiti.cu; Ambassador Marie Carmele Andrine Constant.

Dominican Republic: Avda Juan Sánchez Ramírez 33, Santo Domingo, DN; tel. 686-5778; fax 686-6096; e-mail amb.haiti@codetel.net.do; Ambassador FRITZ CENEAS.

France: 10 rue Théodule Ribot, BP 275, 75017 Paris; tel. 1-47-63-47-78; fax 1-42-27-02-05; e-mail ambhaitiparis@noos.fr; Ambassador Lionel Etienne.

Germany: Uhlandstr. 14, 10623 Berlin; tel. (30) 88554134; fax (30) 88554135; e-mail haibot@aol.com; Ambassador JEAN ROBERT SAGET.

Italy: Via di Villa Patrizi 7/7a, 00161 Roma; tel. (06) 44254106; fax (06) 44254208; e-mail amb.haiti@tiscali.it; Ambassador Yvon Simeon.

Jamaica: 2 Munroe Rd, Kingston 6; tel. 927-7595; fax 978-7638; Ambassador JEAN-GABRIEL AUGUSTIN.

Japan: Kowa Bldg, No. 38, Room 906, 4-12-24, Nishi Azabu, Minato-ku, Tokyo 106-0031; tel. (3) 3486-7096; fax (3) 3486-7070; Chargé d'affaires a.i. Jean-Claude Bordes.

Mexico: Presa Don Martín 53, Col. Irrigación, Del. Miguel Hidalgo, 11500 México, DF; tel. (55) 5557-2065; fax (55) 5395-1654; e-mail ambadh@mail.internet.com.mx; Ambassador IDALBERT PIERRE-JEAN.

Panama: Edif. Dora Luz, 2°, Calle 1, El Cangrejo, Apdo 442, Panamá 9; tel. 269-3443; fax 223-1767; Chargé d'affaires a.i. Bocchit Edmond.

South Africa: 808 George St, Arcadia, Pretoria 0007; POB 14362, Hatfield 0028; tel. (12) 4307560; fax (12) 3427042; Ambassador YOLETTE AZOR-CHARLES.

Spain: Marques del Duero 3, 1°, 28001 Madrid; tel. (91) 5752624; fax (91) 4314600; e-mail ambhaities@yahoo.es; Ambassador Yolette Azor Charles.

United States of America: 2311 Massachusetts Ave, Washington, DC 20008; tel. (202) 332-4090; fax (202) 745-7215; e-mail embassy@haiti.org; internet www.haiti.org; Ambassador RAYMOND A. JOSEPH.

Vatican City: Via de Villa Patrizi 5b, 00161 Roma, Italy; tel. (06) 44242749; fax (06) 44236637; Chargé d'affaires a.i. Patrick Saint-Hilaire.

Venezuela: Quinta Flor 59, Avda Las Rosas, La Florida, Caracas; tel. (212) 730-7220; fax (212) 730-4605; Chargé d'affaires a.i. GANDY THOMAS.

DIPLOMATIC MISSIONS OF HOLY SEE

Albania: Rruga e Durrësit 13, POB 8355, Tirana; tel. (4) 233516; fax (4) 232001; e-mail nunpal@icc-al.org; Apostolic Nuncio Most Rev. Giovanni Bulaitis (Titular Archbishop of Narona).

Algeria: 1 rue Noureddine Mekiri, 16021 Bologhine, Algiers (Apostolic Nunciature); tel. (21) 95-45-20; fax (21) 95-40-95; e-mail nuntiusalger2@yahoo.fr; Apostolic Nuncio MOST REV. THOMAS YEH SHENG-NAN (Titular Archbishop of Leptis Magna).

Angola: Rua Luther King 123, CP 1030, Luanda; tel. 222330532; fax 222332378; e-mail nunc.nuncio@snet.co.ao; Apostolic Nuncio Most Rev. Giovanni Angelo Becciu (Titular Archbishop of Roselle).

Argentina: Alvear 1605, C1014AAD Buenos Aires; tel. (11) 4813-9697; fax (11) 4815-4097; e-mail nunciaturaapostolica@speedy.com.ar; Apostolic Nuncio MOST REV. ADRIANO BERNARDINI (Titular Archbishop of Faleri).

Australia: POB 3633, Manuka, ACT 2603 (Apostolic Nunciature); tel. (2) 6295-3876; fax (2) 6295-3690; Apostolic Nuncio Most Rev. Giuseppe Lazzarotto (Titular Archbishop of Numana).

Austria: Theresianumgasse 31, 1040 Vienna; tel. (1) 505-13-27; fax (1) 505-61-40; e-mail nuntius@nuntiatur.at; internet www.nuntiatur.at; Apostolic Nuncio MOST REV. EDMOND FARHAT (Titular Archbishop of Byblos).

Bangladesh: United Nations Rd 2, Diplomatic Enclave, Baridhara Model Town, POB 6003, Dhaka 1212; tel. (2) 8822018; fax (2) 8823574; e-mail nuntius@dhaka.net; Apostolic Nuncio Joseph Marino.

Belarus: 220050 Minsk, vul. Valadarskaga 6; tel. (17) 289-15-84; fax (17) 289-15-17; e-mail nuntius@catholic.by; internet nunciature.catholic.by; Apostolic Nuncio MARTIN VIDOVIĆ (Titular Archbishop of Nona).

Belgium: 9 ave des Franciscains, 1150 Brussels; tel. (2) 762-20-05; fax (2) 762-20-32; e-mail nonciature.ue.chencellerie@pro.tiscali.be; internet www.vatican.va; Apostolic Nuncio Most Rev. Karl-Josef Rauber.

Benin: blvd de France, Quartier Awhouanléko/Djoméhountin, Zone des Ambassades, 08 BP 400, Cotonou; tel. 21-30-03-08; fax 21-30-03-10; e-mail noncia@intnet.bj; Apostolic Nuncio MICHAEL AUGUST BLUME (Titular Bishop of Alexanum).

Bolivia: Avda Arce 2990, Casilla 136, La Paz; tel. (2) 243-1007; fax (2) 243-2120; e-mail nunapobol@acelerate.com; Apostolic Nuncio Most Rev. Ivo Scapolo (Titular Archbishop of Tagaste).

Bosnia and Herzegovina: 71000 Sarajevo, Pehlivanuša 9; tel. (33) 551055; fax (33) 207863; e-mail nunbosnia@bih.net.ba; Apostolic Nuncio ALESSANDRO D'ERRICO (Titular Archbishop of Hyccarum).

Brazil: SES, Av. das Nações, Quadra 801, Lote 01, 70401-900 Brasília, DF; tel. (61) 3223-0794; fax (61) 3224-9365; e-mail nunapost@solar.com.br; Apostolic Nuncio Most Rev. Lorenzo Baldisseri (Titular Archbishop of Diocletiana).

Bulgaria: 1000 Sofia, ul. 11-ti Avgust 6, POB 9; tel. (2) 981-21-97; fax (2) 981-61-95; e-mail nuntius@mbox.digsys.bg; Apostolic Nuncio GIUSEPPE LEANZA (Titular Archbishop of Lilibeo).

Burundi: 46 ave des Travailleurs, BP 1068, Bujumbura; tel. 22225415; fax 22223176; e-mail nonciat@cbinf.com; Apostolic Nuncio Most Rev. Paul Richard Gallagher (Titular Archbishop of Hodelm).

Cameroon: rue du Vatican, BP 210, Yaoundé (Apostolic Nunciature); tel. 2220-0475; fax 2220-7513; e-mail nonce.cam@sat.signis.net; Apostolic Pro-Nuncio MOST REV. ELISEO ANTONIO ARIOTTI (Titular Archbishop of Vibiana).

Canada: Apostolic Nunciature, 724 Manor Ave, Rockcliffe Park, Ottawa, ON K1M 0E3; tel. (613) 746-4914; fax (613) 746-4786; e-mail nuntius@rogers.com; Nuncio Most Rev. Luigi Ventura (Titular Archbishop of Equilio).

Central African Republic: ave Boganda, BP 1447, Bangui; tel. 61-26-54; fax 61-03-71; e-mail nonrca@intnet.cf; Apostolic Nuncio MOST REV. PIERRE NGUYÊN VAN TOT (Titular Archbishop of Rusticiana).

Chad: rue de Béguinage, BP 490, N'Djamena; tel. 52-31-15; fax 52-38-27; e-mail nonceapo@intnet.td; Apostolic Nuncio Most Rev. Pierre Nguyên Van Tot (Titular Archbishop of Rusticiana).

Chile: Calle Nuncio Sótero Sanz 200, Casilla 16.836, Correo 9, Santiago (Apostolic Nunciature); tel. (2) 231-2020; fax (2) 231-0868; e-mail nunciatu@entelchile.net; Nuncio MOST REV. ALDO CAVALLI (Titular Archbishop of Vibo Valentia).

China (Taiwan): 87 Ai Kuo East Rd, Taipei 10642 (Apostolic Nunciature); tel. (2) 23216847; fax (2) 23911926; Chargé d'affaires a.i. Mgr Ambrose Madtha.

Colombia: Carrera 15, No 36-33, Apdo Aéreo 3740, Bogotá, DC (Apostolic Nunciature); tel. (1) 320-0289; fax (1) 285-1817; e-mail nunciatura@cable.net.co; Apostolic Nuncio MOST REV. BENIAMINO STELLA.

Congo, Democratic Republic: 81 ave Goma, BP 3091, Kinshasa; tel. (88) 08814; fax (88) 48483; e-mail nuntius@raga.net; Apostolic Nuncio Most Rev. Giovanni d'Aniello (Titular Archbishop of Paestum).

Congo, Republic: rue Col Brisset, BP 1168, Brazzaville; tel. 81-55-80; fax 81-55-81; e-mail nonapcg@yahoo.com; Apostolic Nuncio MOST REV. ANDRES CARRASCOSA COSO (Titular Archbishop of Elo).

Costa Rica: Urb. Rohrmoser, Sabana Oeste, Centro Colón, Apdo 992, 1007 San José (Apostolic Nunciature); tel. 232-2128; fax 231-2557; e-mail nuapcr@racsa.co.cr; Apostolic Nuncio Most Rev. Osvaldo Padilla (Titular Archbishop of Pia).

Côte d'Ivoire: Apostolic Nunciature, rue Jacques Aka, 08 BP 1347, Abidjan 08; tel. 22-40-17-70; fax 22-40-17-74; e-mail nuntius@aviso.ci; Apostolic Nuncio MGR MARIO ROBERTO CASSARI.

Croatia: 10000 Zagreb, Ksaverska cesta 10 a; tel. (1) 4673996; fax (1) 4673997; e-mail apostolska.nuncijatura.rh@inet.hr; Apostolic Nuncio Most Rev. Francisco-Javier Lozano (Titular Archbishop of Penafiel in Tripolitania).

Cuba: Calle 12, No 514, entre 5 y 7, Miramar, Havana (Apostolic Nunciature); tel. (7) 204-2700; fax (7) 204-2257; e-mail csa@pcn.net; Apostolic Nuncio MOST REV. LUIGI BONAZZI (Titular Archbishop of Atella).

Cyprus: POB 21964, Holy Cross Catholic Church, Paphos Gate, 1010 Nicosia (Apostolic Nunciature); tel. 22662132; fax 22660767; e-mail holcross@logos.cy.net; Apostolic Nuncio Most Rev. Antonio Franco (Titular Archbishop of Gallese—resident in Jerusalem) (designate).

Czech Republic: Voršilská 12, 110 00 Prague 1; tel. 224999811; fax 224999833; e-mail nunciatgc@mbox.vol.cz; Apostolic Nuncio MOST REV. DIEGO CAUSERO (Titular Archbishop of Gradum).

Dominican Republic: Avda Máximo Gómez 27, Apdo 312, Santo Domingo, DN (Apostolic Nunciature); tel. 682-3773; fax 687-0287; Apostolic Nuncio Most Rev. Józef Wesołowski (Titular Archbishop of Slebte).

Ecuador: Avda Orellana 692, Apdo 17-07-8980, Quito; tel. (2) 250-5200; fax (2) 256-4810; e-mail nunapec@impsat.net.ec; Apostolic Nunciature Apostolic Nuncio MOST REV. GUIDO GIACOMO OTTONELLO (Titular Archbishop of Sasabe).

Egypt: Apostolic Nunciature, Safarat al-Vatican, 5 Sharia Muhammad Mazhar, Cairo (Zamalek); tel. (2) 7352250; fax (2) 7356152; e-mail nunteg@yahoo.com; Apostolic Nuncio Most Rev. Michael Louis Fitzgerald (Titular Archbishop of Nepte).

El Salvador: 87 Avda Norte y 7a Calle Poniente, Col. Escalón, Apdo 01-95, San Salvador (Apostolic Nunciature); tel. 2263-2931; fax 2263-3010; e-mail nunels@telesal.net; Apostolic Nuncio MOST REV. LUIGI PEZZUTO (Titular Archbishop of Torre di Proconsolare).

Ethiopia: POB 588, Addis Ababa (Apostolic Nunciature); tel. (11) 3712100; fax (11) 3711499; Apostolic Nuncio Most Rev. Moliner Inglés Ramiro (Titular Archbishop of Sarda).

France: 10 ave du Président Wilson, 75116 Paris (Apostolic Nunciature); tel. 1-53-23-01-50; fax 1-47-23-65-44; e-mail noncapfr@wanadoo.fr; Apostolic Nuncio MOST REV. FORTUNATO BALDELLI (Titular Archbishop of Mevania).

Gabon: blvd Monseigneur Bessieux, BP 1322, Libreville (Apostolic Nunciature); tel. 74-45-41; e-mail nonapcg@yahoo.com; Apostolic Nuncio Mgr Andrés Carrascosa Coso (Titular Archbishop of Elo).

Georgia: 0108 Tbilisi, Jenti 40, Nutsubidze Plateau; tel. (32) 53-76-01; fax (32) 53-67-04; e-mail nuntius@access.sanet.ge; Apostolic Nuncio MOST REV. CLAUDIO GUGEROTTI (Titular Archbishop of Ravello).

Germany: Lilienthalstr. 3a, 10965 Berlin; tel. (30) 616240; fax (30) 61624300; e-mail apostolische@nuntiatur.de; internet www.nuntiatur.de; Apostolic Nuncio Most Rev. Jean-Claude Périsset (Titular Archbishop of Iustiniana Prima).

Ghana: 8 Drake Ave, Airport Residential Area, POB 9675, Accra; tel. (21) 777759; fax (21) 774019; e-mail nuncio@ghana.com; Apostolic Nuncio MOST REV. GEORGE KOCHERRY (Titular Archbishop of Othona).

Greece: POB 65075, Odos Mavili 2, Palaio Psychiko, 154 52 Athens; tel. (210) 6722728; fax (210) 6742849; e-mail nunate@ath.forthnet.gr; Apostolic Nuncio Most Rev. Patrick Coveney (Titular Archbishop of Satriano).

Guatemala: 10a Calle 4-47, Zona 9, Apdo 22, Guatemala City (Apostolic Nunciature); tel. 2332-4274; fax 2334-1918; e-mail nuntius@c.net.gt; Apostolic Nuncio MOST REV. BRUNO MUSARÒ (Titular Archbishop of Abari).

Guinea: La Minière, BP 2016, Conakry; tel. 30-42-26-76; fax 30-46-36-71; e-mail nonce@biasy.net; Apostolic Nuncio Most Rev. George Antonysamy (Titular Archbishop of Sulci).

Haiti: rue Louis Pouget, Morne Calvaire, BP 326, Port-au-Prince; tel. 257-6308; fax 257-3411; e-mail nonciature@haitiworld.com; Apostolic Nuncio MOST REV. MARIO GIORDANA (Titular Archbishop of Minora).

Honduras: Palacio de la Nunciatura Apostólica, Col. Palmira, Avda Santa Sede 412, Apdo 324, Tegucigalpa; tel. 232-6613; fax 239-8869; e-mail nunciature@amnettgu.com; Apostolic Nuncio Most Rev. Antonio Arcari (Titular Archbishop of Ceciti).

Hungary: 1126 Budapest, Gyimes u. 1–3; tel. (1) 355-8979; fax (1) 355-6987; e-mail nunciatura@nunciatura.axelero.net; Apostolic Nuncio MOST REV. JULIUSZ JANUSZ (Titular Archbishop of Caprulae).

India: 50c Niti Marg, Chanakyapuri, New Delhi 110 021 (Apostolic Nunciature); tel. (11) 26889184; fax (11) 26874286; e-mail nuntius@apostolicnunciatureindia.com; internet www.apostolicnunciatureindia.com; Nuncio Most Rev. Pedro López Quintana (Titular Archbishop of Agropoli).

Indonesia: Jalan Merdeka Timur 18, POB 4227, Jakarta Pusat (Apostolic Nunciature); tel. (21) 3841142; fax (21) 3841143; e-mail vatjak@cbn.net.id; Apostolic Nuncio MOST REV. LEOPOLDO GIRELLI (Titular Archbishop of Capri).

Iran: Apostolic Nunciature, POB 11365-178, Razi Ave, 97 Neauphle-le-Château Ave, Tehran; tel. (21) 66403574; fax (21) 66419442; e-mail apnun-thr@parsonline.net; Apostolic Nuncio Most Rev. Jean-Paul Gobel (Titular Archbishop of Galazia in Campania).

Iraq: POB 2090, Saadoun St, 904/2/46, Baghdad; tel. (1) 719-5183; e-mail nuntiusiraq@yahoo.com; Apostolic Nuncio MOST REV. FRANCIS ASSISI CHULLIKATT (Titular Archbishop of Ostra).

Ireland: 183 Navan Rd, Dublin 7; tel. (1) 8380577; fax (1) 8380276; e-mail nuncioirl@eircom.net; Apostolic Nuncio Most Rev. Giuseppe Leanza (Titular Archbishop of Lilybaeum).

Israel: 1 Netiv Hamazalot, Old Jaffa 68037; tel. 2-6835658; fax 2-6835659; e-mail vatge@netvision.net.il; Apostolic Nuncio MOST REV. ANTONIO FRANCO (Titular Archbishop of Gallese).

Italy: Via Po 27–29, 00198 Roma; tel. (06) 8546287; fax (06) 8549725; e-mail nunzio@nunziatura.it; Apostolic Nuncio Most Rev. Giuseppe Bertello (Titular Archbishop of Urbisaglia).

Japan: Apostolic Nunciature, 9-2, Sanban-cho, Chiyoda-ku, Tokyo 102-0075; tel. (3) 3263-6851; fax (3) 3263-6060; Apostolic Nuncio MOST REV. ALBERTO BOTTARI DE CASTELLO (Titular Archbishop of Oderzo).

Jordan: POB 142916, 14 Anton an-Naber St, Amman 11814; tel. (6) 5929934; fax (6) 5929931; e-mail nuntius@nol.com.jo; Apostolic Nuncio Most Rev. Francis Assisi Chullikatt.

Kazakhstan: 010000 Astana, Zelenaya Alleya 20; tel. (7172) 24-12-69; fax (7172) 24-16-04; e-mail nuntius_kazakhstan@lycos.com; Apostolic Nuncio (vacant).

Kenya: Apostolic Nunciature, Manyani Rd West, Waiyaki Way, POB 14326, 00800 Nairobi; tel. (20) 4442975; fax (20) 4446789; e-mail nunciokenya@nunciokenya.org; Apostolic Nuncio Most Rev. Alain Paul Charles Lebeaupin (Titular Archbishop of Vico Equense).

Korea, Republic: POB 393, Kwang Hwa Mun, Seoul 110-603 (Apostolic Nunciature); tel. (2) 736-5725; fax (2) 739-5738; e-mail nunseoul@kornet.net; Apostolic Nuncio MOST REV. EMIL PAUL TSCHERRIG (Titular Archbishop of Voli).

Lebanon: POB 1061, Jounieh (Apostolic Nunciature); tel. (9) 263102; fax (9) 264488; e-mail naliban@terra.net.lb; Apostolic Nuncio Most Rev. Luigi Gatti (Titular Archbishop of Santa Giusta).

Libya: Tripoli; Apostolic Nuncio MOST REV. FÉLIX DEL BLANCO PRIETO (Titular Archbishop of Vannida, resident in Malta).

Lithuania: Kosciuškos g. 28, Vilnius 01100; tel. (5) 212-3696; fax (5) 212-4228; e-mail nuntiusbalt@aiva.lt; Apostolic Nuncio Most Rev. Peter Stephan Zurbriggen (Titular Archbishop of Glastonia).

Madagascar: Amboniloha Ivandry, BP 650, 101 Antananarivo; tel. (20) 2242376; fax (20) 2242384; e-mail nuntiusantana@wanadoo.mg; Apostolic Nuncio MOST REV. AUGUSTINE KASUJJA (Titular Archbishop of Caesarea de Numidia).

Malta: V20/22 Pietru Caxaru St, Tal-Virtù, Rabat RBT 2604; tel. 21453422; fax 21453423; e-mail apost@keyworld.net; Apostolic Nuncio Most Rev. Félix del Blanco Prieto (Titular Archbishop of Vannida).

Mexico: Juan Pablo II 118, Col. Guadalupe Inn, Del. Alvaro Obregón, 01020 México, DF; tel. (55) 5663-3999; fax (55) 5663-5308; Apostolic Nuncio MOST REV. CHRISTOPHE PIERRE (Titular Archbishop of Gunela).

Morocco: rue Béni M'tir, BP 1303, Souissi, Rabat (Apostolic Nunciature); tel. (3) 7772277; fax (3) 7756213; e-mail nuntius@iam.net.ma; Apostolic Nuncio Most Rev. Antonio Sozzo (Titular Archbishop of Concordia).

Mozambique: Av. Kwame Nkrumah 224, CP 2738, Maputo; tel. 21491144; fax 21492217; Apostolic Nuncio MOST REV. GEORGE PANIKULAM (Titular Archbishop of Caudium).

Netherlands: Carnegielaan 5 (Apostolic Nunciature), 2517 KH The Hague; tel. (70) 3503363; fax (70) 3521461; e-mail apost.nuntiatuur@inter.nl.net; Apostolic Nuncio Most Rev. François Bacqué (Titular Archbishop of Gradisca).

New Zealand: Apostolic Nunciature, 112 Queen's Drive, Lyall Bay, POB 14-044, Wellington 6041; tel. (4) 387-3470; fax (4) 387-8170; e-mail nuntius@ihug.co.nz; Apostolic Nuncio MOST REV. CHARLES D. BALVO (Titular Archbishop of Castello).

Nicaragua: Apostolic Nunciature, Km 10.8, Carretera Sur, Apdo 506, Managua; tel. 265-8657; fax 265-7416; e-mail nuntius@cablenet.com.ni; Apostolic Nuncio Most Rev. Henryk Józef Nowacki (Titular Archbishop of Blera).

Nigeria: Pope John Paul II Cres., Maitama, PMB 541, Garki, Abuja; tel. (9) 4138381; fax (9) 4136653; e-mail nuntiusabj@hotmail.com; Apostolic Nuncio MOST REV. RENZO FRATINI (Titular Archbishop of Botriana).

Pakistan: Apostolic Nunciature, St 5, G-5, Diplomatic Enclave 1, POB 1106, Islamabad 44000; tel. (51) 2278218; fax (51) 2820847; e-mail vatipak@dsl.net.pk; Apostolic Nuncio Most Rev. Adolfo Tito Yllana (Titular Archbishop of Montecorvino).

Panama: Punta Paitilla, Avda Balboa y Vía Italia, Apdo 4251, Panamá 5 (Apostolic Nunciature); tel. 269-2102; fax 264-2116; e-mail nuncio@cableonda.net; Apostolic Nuncio MOST REV. GIAMBATTISTA DIQUATTRO (Titular Archbishop of Giru Mons).

Papua New Guinea: POB 98, Port Moresby; tel. 3256021; fax 3252844; e-mail nunciaturepng@datec.net.pg; Apostolic Nuncio Archbishop Francisco Montecillo Padilla.

Paraguay: Calle Ciudad del Vaticano 350, casi con 25 de Mayo, Casilla 83, Asunción (Apostolic Nunciature); tel. (21) 21-5139; fax (21) 21-2590; e-mail nunapos@conexion.com.py; Apostolic Nuncio MOST REV. ORLANDO ANTONINI (Titular Archbishop of Formia).

Peru: Avda Salaverry, 6a cuadra, Apdo 397, Lima 100 (Apostolic Nunciature); tel. (1) 4319436; fax (1) 4315704; e-mail nunciatura@speedy.com.pe; Apostolic Nuncio Most Rev. Rino Passigato (Titular Archbishop of Nova Caesaris).

Philippines: 2140 Taft Ave, POB 3364, 1099 Metro Manila (Apostolic Nunciature); tel. (2) 5210306; fax (2) 5211235; e-mail nuntiusp@info.com.ph; Apostolic Nuncio MOST REV. FERNANDO FILONI (Titular Archbishop of Volturnum).

Poland: 00-582 Warsaw, Al. J. Ch. Szucha 12, POB 163; tel. (22) 6288488; fax (22) 6284556; e-mail nuncjatura@episkopat.pl; Apostolic Nuncio Most Rev. Józef Kowalczyk (Titular Archbishop of Heraclea).

Portugal: Av. Luís Bivar 18, 1069-147 Lisbon; tel. (21) 3171130; fax (21) 3171149; e-mail nunciatura@netcabo.pt; Apostolic Nuncio MOST REV. ALFIO RAPISARDA (Titular Archbishop of Cannae).

Romania: 010187 Bucharest, Str. Pictor C. Stahi 5–7; tel. (21) 3123883; fax (21) 3120316; e-mail nuntius@rdslink.ro; Apostolic Nuncio Most Rev. Francisco-Javier Lozano (Titular Archbishop of Penafiel).

Russian Federation: 127055 Moscow, Vadkovskii per. 7/37; tel. (495) 726-59-30; fax (495) 726-59-32; e-mail nuntius@cityline.ru; Apostolic Nuncio MOST REV. ANTONIO MENNINI (Titular Archbishop of Ferentium).

Rwanda: 49 ave Paul VI, BP 261, Kigali (Apostolic Nunciature); tel. 575293; fax 575181; e-mail nuntrw@rwandatel1.rwanda1.com; Apostolic Nuncio Most Rev. Anselmo Guido Pecorari (Titular Archbishop of Populonia).

San Marino: Domus Plebis 1, 47890 San Marino; tel. 0549 992448; Apostolic Nuncio Most Rev. GIUSEPPE BERTELLO (Titular Archbishop of Urbs Salvia) (resident in Rome, Italy).

Senegal: rue Aimé Césaire, angle Corniche-Ouest, Fann Résidence, BP 5076, Dakar; tel. 33-824-2674; fax 33-824-1931; e-mail vatemb@orange.sn; Apostolic Nuncio Most Rev. Giuseppe Pinto (Titular Archbishop of Anglona).

Serbia: 11000 Belgrade, Svetog Save 24; tel. (11) 3085356; fax (11) 3085216; e-mail nunbel@eunet.yu; Apostolic Nuncio MOST REV. EUGENIO SBARBARO (Titular Archbishop of Tiddi).

Slovakia: Nekrasovova 17, 811 04 Bratislava; tel. (2) 5479-3528; fax (2) 5479-3529; e-mail nunziatura@nunziatura.sk; Apostolic Nuncio (vacant).

Slovenia: 1000 Ljubljana, trg Krekov 1; tel. (1) 4339204; fax (1) 4315130; e-mail nunaplub@yahoo.com; Apostolic Nuncio MOST REV. ABRIL Y CASTELLÓ SANTOS (Titular Archbishop of Tamada).

South Africa: 800 Pretorius St, Arcadia, Pretoria 0083; POB 26017, Arcadia 0007; tel. (12) 3443815; fax (12) 3443595; e-mail nunziosa@iafrica.com; Apostolic Nuncio Most Rev. James Patrick Green.

Spain: Avda de Pío XII 46, 28016 Madrid; tel. (91) 7668311; fax (91) 7667085; e-mail nunap@planalfa.es; Apostolic Nuncio MOST REV. MANUEL MONTEIRO DE CASTRO (Titular Archbishop of Benevento).

Sri Lanka: 220 Bauddhaloka Mawatha, Colombo 7 (Apostolic Nunciature); tel. (11) 2582554; fax (11) 2580906; e-mail aponun@sri.lanka.net; Apostolic Nuncio Most Rev. Dr Mario Zenari (Titular Archbishop of Zuglio).

Sudan: Kafouri Belgravia, POB 623, Khartoum (Apostolic Nunciature); tel. (183) 330037; fax (183) 330692; e-mail kanuap@yahoo.it; Apostolic Nuncio MOST REV. LEO BOCCARDI (Titular Archbishop of Bitettum).

Sweden: Svalnäsvägen 10, 182 63 Djursholm; tel. (8) 446-51-10; fax (8) 622-51-10; e-mail nunciature@telia.com; Charge d'affaires a.i. Rev. Dagoberto Campos Salas.

Switzerland: Thunstr. 60, 3006 Bern (Apostolic Nunciature); tel. 313526040; fax 313525064; e-mail nunziaturach@yahoo.com; Apostolic Nuncio MOST REV. FRANCESCO CANALINI (Titular Archbishop of Valeria).

Syria: BP 2271, 1 place Ma'raket Ajnadin, al-Malki, Damascus (Apostolic Nunciature); tel. (11) 3332601; fax (11) 3327550; e-mail noncesy@mail.sy; Apostolic Nuncio Most Rev. Morandini Giovanni Battista (Titular Archbishop of Grado).

Tanzania: Oyster Bay, Plot 146, Haile Selassie Rd, POB 480, Dar es Salaam (Apostolic Nunciature); tel. (22) 2666422; fax (22) 2668059; e-mail nunzio@cats-net.com; Apostolic Nuncio MOST REV. JOSEPH CHENNOTH (Titular Archbishop of Milevum).

Thailand: 217/1 Thanon Sathorn Tai, POB 12-178, Bangkok 10120 (Apostolic Nunciature); tel. (2) 212-5853; fax (2) 212-0932; e-mail nuntiusth@csloxinfo.com; Apostolic Nuncio Most Rev. Salvatore Pennacchio (Titular Archbishop of Montemarano).

Trinidad and Tobago: 11 Mary St, St Clair, POB 854, Port of Spain; tel. 622-5009; fax 628-5457; e-mail apnun@tstt.net.tt; Apostolic Nuncio MOST REV. THOMAS EDWARD GULLICKSON (Titular Archbishop of Bomarzo).

Turkey: Apostolic Nunciature, Birlik Mah. 3, Cad. 37, PK 33, 06552 Çankaya, Ankara; tel. (312) 4953514; fax (312) 4953540; e-mail vatican@tr.net; Apostolic Nuncio Most Rev. Antonio Lucibello (Titular Archbishop of Thurio).

Turkmenistan: 744000 Aşgabat, Merkezi Poçta, POB 98; tel. (12) 39-11-40; fax (12) 35-36-83; e-mail aszomi@online.tm; internet www.catholic-turkmenistan.org; Apostolic Nuncio ANTONIO LUCIBELLO (Titular Archbishop of Thurio) (resident in Ankara, Turkey).

Uganda: Chwa II Rd, Mbuya Hill, POB 7177, Kampala (Apostolic Nunciature); tel. (41) 4505619; fax (41) 4441774; Apostolic Nuncio (vacant).

Ukraine: 01901 Kyiv, vul. Turhenyevska 40; tel. (44) 482-35-57; fax (44) 482-35-53; e-mail nuntius@visti.com; internet www.nuntiatura.kiev.ua; Apostolic Nuncio MOST REV. IVAN JURKOVIČ (Titular Archbishop of Corbavia).

United Kingdom: 54 Parkside, London, SW19 5NE (Apostolic Nunciature); tel. (20) 8944-7189; fax (20) 8947-2494; e-mail nuntius@globalnet.co.uk; Apostolic Nuncio Most Rev. Faustino Sainz Muñoz (Titular Archbishop of Novaliciana).

United States of America: 3339 Massachusetts Ave, NW, Washington, DC 20008-3687; tel. (202) 333-7121; fax (202) 337-4036; e-mail nuntius@worldnet.att.net; Apostolic Nuncio MOST REV. PIETRO SAMBI (Titular Archbishop of Bellicastrum).

Uruguay: Blvr Artigas 1270, Casilla 1503, Montevideo (Apostolic Nunciature); tel. (2) 7072016; fax (2) 7072209; Apostolic Nuncio Most Rev. Janusz Bolonek (Titular Archbishop of Madaurus).

Venezuela: Avda La Salle, Los Caobos, Apdo 29, Caracas 1010-A (Apostolic Nunciature); tel. (212) 781-8939; fax (212) 793-2403; e-mail nunapos@cantv.net; Apostolic Nuncio MOST REV. GIACINTO BERLOCO (Titular Archbishop of Fidene).

Zambia: 283 Los Angeles Blvd, POB 31445, 10101 Lusaka; tel. (1) 251033; fax (1) 250601; e-mail nuntius@coppernet.zm; Apostolic Nuncio Most Rev. Nicola Girasoli (Titular Archbishop of Egnazia Appula).

Zimbabwe: 5 St Kilda Rd, Mount Pleasant, POB MP191, Harare (Apostolic Nunciature); tel. (4) 744547; fax (4) 744412; e-mail nunzim@zol.co.zw; Apostolic Nuncio MOST REV. EDWARD JOSEPH ADAMS (Titular Archbishop of Scala).

DIPLOMATIC MISSIONS OF HONDURAS

United Nations: 866 United Nations Plaza, Suite 417, New York, NY 10017; tel. (212) 752-3370; fax (212) 223-0498; e-mail m.suazo@worldnet.att.net; internet www.un.int/honduras; Permanent Representative Jorge Arturo Reina Idiaquez.

Argentina: Avda Callao 1564, 2A, C1024AAO Buenos Aires; tel. (11) 4803-0077; fax (11) 4807-5710; e-mail embajadadehonduras@fibertel.com.ar; Ambassador CARMEN ELEONORA ORTEZ WILLIAMS.

Belgium: 3 ave des Gaulois, 5e étage, 1040 Brussels; tel. (2) 734-00-00; fax (2) 735-26-26; e-mail ambassade.honduras@chello.be; internet www.honduras.be; Ambassador Ramón Custodio Espinoza.

Belize: 22 Gabourel Lane, POB 285, Belize City; tel. 224-5889; fax 223-0562; e-mail embahonbe@sre.hn; Ambassador MANUEL SANDOVAL CABRERA.

Brazil: SHIS, QI 19, Conj. 07, Casa 34, Lago Sul, 71655-070 Brasília, DF; tel. (61) 3366-4082; fax (61) 3366-4618; e-mail embhonduras@ig.com.br; Ambassador Victor Manuel Lozano Urbina.

Canada: 151 Slater St, Suite 805, Ottawa, ON K1P 5H3; tel. (613) 233-8900; fax (613) 232-0193; e-mail embhonca@embassyhonduras.ca; internet www.embassyhonduras.ca; Ambassador DELIA BEATRIZ VALLE MARICHAL.

Chile: Zurich 255, Of. 51, Las Condes, Santiago; tel. (2) 234-4069; fax (2) 334-7946; e-mail honduras@entelchile.net; Ambassador Francisco Martínez.

China (Taiwan): 9/F, 9 Lane 62, Tien Mou West Rd, Taipei 11156; tel. (2) 28755507; fax (2) 28755726; e-mail honduras@ms9.hinet.net; Ambassador MARLENE VILLELA-TALBOTT.

Colombia: Calle 121, No 11d-23, Bogotá, DC; tel. (1) 215-4259; fax (1) 637-0686; e-mail info@embajadadehonduras.org.co; internet www.embajadadehonduras.org.co; Ambassador Rafael Murillo Selva Rendón.

Costa Rica: Pavas, del Parque de la Amistad en Rohrmoser, 100 m sur y 50 m este, Apdo 2239, 1000 San José; tel. 231-1642; fax 253-2209; e-mail embhoncr@embajadahonduras.co.cr; internet www.sre.hn/costarica.html; Ambassador GEN. (RETD) ALVARO ROMERO.

Cuba: Edif. Santa Clara, 1°, 123 Centro de Negocios Miramar, 3a Avda, 78 y 80 Calles, Miramar, Havana; tel. (7) 204-5496; fax (7) 204-5497; e-mail embhocu@enet.cu; Ambassador Juan Ramón Elvir Salgado.

Dominican Republic: Calle Arístides García Mella, esq. Rodríguez Objío, Edif. El Buen Pastor VI, Apt 1B, 1°, Mirador del Sur, Santo Domingo, DN; tel. 482-7992; fax 482-7505; e-mail e.honduras@codetel.net.do; Ambassador NERY MAGALY FÚNES.

Ecuador: Edif. World Trade Center, Torre A, 5°, Of. 501, Avda 12 de Octubre 1942 y Luis Cordero, Apdo 17-03-4753, Quito; tel. (2) 222-3985; fax (2) 222-0441; e-mail embhquito@yahoo.com; Ambassador Hernán Antonio Bermúdez Aguilar.

Egypt: 21 Sharia Aicha at-Taimouria, Cairo (Garden City); tel. (2) 3409510; fax (2) 3413835; .

El Salvador: 89 Avda Norte 561, entre 7 y 9 Calle Poniente, Col. Escalón, San Salvador; tel. 2263-2808; fax 2263-2296; Ambassador José Salomón Farjado Bueso.

France: 8 rue Crevaux, 75116 Paris; tel. 1-47-55-86-45; fax 1-47-55-86-48; e-mail ambassade.honduras@yahoo.com; Ambassador MAX VELÁSQUEZ DIAZ.

Germany: Cuxhavenerstr. 14, 10555 Berlin; tel. (30) 39743711; fax (30) 39749712; e-mail embahonduras@ngi.de; Ambassador Roberto Augusto Martínez Castañeda.

Guatemala: 19 Avda 'A', 20-19, Zona 10, Guatemala City; tel. 2366-5640; fax 2368-0062; e-mail embhond@intelnet.net.gt; Ambassador BESSY ROSSANA VALENZUELA ULLOA DE FUENTES.

Israel: Zohar Tal St 1, Herzliya Pituach 46766; tel. 9-9577686; fax 9-9577457; e-mail honduras@netvision.net.il; Chargé d'affaires Dennis Weizenblut.

Italy: Via Giambattista Vico 40, int. 8, 00197 Roma; tel. (06) 3207236; fax (06) 3207973; e-mail embhon@fastwebnet.it; Ambassador ROBERTO OCHOA MADRID.

Jamaica: 7 Lady Kay Dr., Norbrook, Kingston 8; tel. 941-1790; fax 941-6470; e-mail eduardonorris@hotmail.com; Ambassador José Eduardo Norris Madrid.

Japan: Kowa Bldg, No. 38, Room 802, 8/F, 4-12-24, Nishi Azabu, Minato-ku, Tokyo 106-0031; tel. (3) 3409-1150; fax (3) 3409-0305; e-mail honduras@interlink.or.jp; Ambassador NADINA JOYCE LEFEBVRE LABRO.

Jordan: POB 840526, Amman 33384; tel. (6) 5856414; fax (6) 5853501; Chargé d'affaires a.i. Faiz Roberto Elmadi.

Korea, Republic: Jongno Tower Bldg, 2nd Floor, 6, Jongno 2-ga, Jongno-gu, Seoul 110-160; tel. (2) 738-8402; fax (2) 738-8403; e-mail hondseul@kornet.net; Ambassador RENE FRANCISCO UMANA CHINCHILLA.

Mexico: Alfonso Reyes 220, Col. Condesa, Del. Cuauhtémoc, 06170 México, DF; tel. (55) 5211-5747; fax (55) 5211-5425; e-mail emhonmex@prodigy.net.mx; Ambassador Rosalinda Bueso Asfura.

Netherlands: Burgemeester Patijnlaan 1932, 2585 CB The Hague; tel. (70) 3641684; fax (70) 3649134; e-mail eholan@honduras.demon.nl; Ambassador JULIO ANTONIO RENDÓN BARNICA.

Nicaragua: Reparto Las Colinas, Prado Ecuestre 298, frente a Residencia de la Embajada de China (Taiwán), Apdo 321, Managua; tel. 276-2406; fax 276-1998; e-mail embhonduras@cablenet.com.ni; Ambassador Jorge Alberto Milla Reyes.

Panama: Edif. Bay Mall, 1°, Avda Balboa 112, Apdo 8704, Panamá 5; tel. 264-5513; fax 224-5513; e-mail ehpan@cableonda.net; Ambassador JUAN ALFARO POSADAS.

Peru: Avda Las Camelias 491, Of. 202, San Isidro, Lima; tel. (1) 4228111; fax (1) 2211677; internet www.embhonpe.org; Ambassador Juán José Cueva Membreño.

Spain: Rafael Calvo 15, 6°D, 28010 Madrid; tel. (91) 7025157; fax (91) 7025158; e-mail info@embahonduras.es; internet www.embahonduras.es; Ambassador JOSÉ EDUARDO MARTELL MEJÍA.

Sweden: Stjärnvägen 2, 7th Floor, 181 34 Lidingö; tel. (8) 731-50-84; fax (8) 636-99-83; e-mail hondurasembassy@telia.com; internet www.hondurasembassy.se; Chargé d'affaires a.i. Iliana Waleska Pastor Melghem.

United Kingdom: 115 Gloucester Pl., London, W1U 6JT; tel. (20) 7486-4880; fax (20) 7486-4550; e-mail hondurasuk@lineone.net; Ambassador IVÁN ROMERO-MARTÍNEZ.

United States of America: 3007 Tilden St, NW, Suite 4-M, Washington, DC 20008; tel. (202) 966-7702; fax (202) 966-9751; e-mail embassy@hondurasemb.org; internet www.hondurasemb.org; Ambassador Roberto Flores Bermudez.

Vatican City: Via Boezio 45, 00192 Rome, Italy; tel. (06) 6876051; e-mail honvati@fastwebnet.it; Ambassador ALEJANDRO EMILIO VALLADARES LANZA.

Venezuela: Edif. Banco de Lara, 8°, Of. b2, Avda Principal de la Castellana con 1a Transversal de Altamira, La Castellana, Apdo 68259, Caracas; tel. (212) 264-0606; fax (212) 263-4379; e-mail honduven@cantv.net; Chargé d'affaires a.i. Fernando Suárez Loco.

DIPLOMATIC MISSIONS OF HUNGARY

United Nations: 227 East 52nd St, New York, NY 10022; tel. (212) 752-0209; fax (212) 755-5395; e-mail hungary@un.int; internet www.un.int/hungary; Permanent Representative GÁBOR BRÓDI.

Afghanistan: c/o Embassy of the Federal Republic of Germany, Zanbaq Sq., Wazir Akbar Khan, Mena 6, POB 83, Kabul; tel. (79) 7035375; e-mail huembkbl@gmail.com; Chargé d'affaires a.i. Sandor Matyus.

Albania: Rruga Skënderbej 16, Tirana; tel. (4) 232238; fax (4) 233211; e-mail mission.tia@kum.hu; internet www.mfa.gov.hu/emb/tirana; Ambassador SÁNDOR MOLNÁRI.

Algeria: BP 68, 18 ave des Frères Oughlis, el-Mouradia, Algiers; tel. (21) 69-79-75; fax (21) 69-81-86; e-mail huembalgoffice@djazairconnect.com; Ambassador Dr Béla Marton.

Argentina: Plaza 1726, C1430DGF Buenos Aires; tel. (11) 4553-3536; e-mail hungria@escape.com.ar; Ambassador MÁTYÁS JÓZSA.

Australia: 17 Beale Crescent, Deakin, ACT 2600; tel. (2) 6282-3226; fax (2) 6285-3012; e-mail cbr.missions@kum.hu; internet www.hunconsydney.com; Ambassador Gábor Csaba.

Austria: Bankgasse 4–6, 1010 Vienna; tel. (1) 537-80-30-0; fax (1) 535-99-40; e-mail kom@huembvie.at; Ambassador DR ISTVÁN HORVÁTH.

Belgium: 44 ave du Vert Chasseur, 1180 Brussels; tel. (2) 348-18-00; fax (2) 347-60-28; e-mail titkarsag.bxl@kum.be; Ambassador Ferenc Robák.

Bosnia and Herzegovina: 71000 Sarajevo, Hasana Bibera 53; tel. (33) 205302; fax (33) 268930; e-mail hung.emb@bih.net.ba; internet www.mfa.gov.hu/emb/sarajevo; Ambassador IMRE VARGA.

Brazil: SES, Av. das Nações, Quadra 805, Lote 19, 70413-900 Brasília, DF; tel. (61) 3443-0836; fax (61) 3443-3434; e-mail huembbrz@terra.com.br; internet www.hungria.org.br; Ambassador Dr Csaba Pólyi.

Bulgaria: 1000 Sofia, ul. 6-ti Septemvri 57; tel. (2) 963-11-35; fax (2) 963-21-10; e-mail embassy.sof@kum.hu; internet www.mfa.gov.hu/emb/sofia; Ambassador DR JENO FALLER.

Canada: 299 Waverley St, Ottawa, ON K2P 0V9; tel. (613) 230-2717; fax (613) 230-7560; e-mail mission.ott@kum.hu; internet www.mfa.gov.hu/emb/ottawa; Ambassador Pal Vastagh.

Chile: Avda Los Leones 2279, Providencia, Santiago; tel. (2) 247-2210; fax (2) 234-1227; e-mail huembstg@entelchile.net; internet www.mfa.gov.hu/kulkepviselet/CL/HU; Ambassador JÓZSEF KOSÁRKA.

China, People's Republic: 10 Dong Zhi Men Wai Dajie, San Li Tun, Beijing 100600; tel. (10) 65321431; fax (10) 65325053; e-mail titkarsag.pek@kum.hu; internet www.huemb.org.cn; Ambassador Sándor Mészáros.

Croatia: 10000 Zagreb, Pantovčak 255–257A; tel. (1) 4890900; fax (1) 4579301; e-mail mission.zgb@kum.hu; Ambassador PÉTER IMRE GYÖRKÖS.

Cuba: Calle G, No 458, entre 19 y 21, Vedado, Havana; tel. (7) 833-3365; fax (7) 833-3286; e-mail oficina@embajadadehungria.cu; internet www.mfa.gov.hu/kulkepviselet/cu/hu; Ambassador János Horvát.

Cyprus: 2 Prigkipos Karolou St, Ayios Dhometios, 2373 Nicosia; tel. 22459130; fax 22459134; e-mail huembnic@cytanet.com.cy; Ambassador JANOS KISFALVI.

Czech Republic: Pod Hradbami 17, 160 00 Prague 6; tel. 220317200; fax 233322104; e-mail huembprg@vol.cz; internet www.mfa.gov.hu/kulkepviselet/cz/hu; Ambassador István Szabó.

Denmark: Strandvejen 170, 2920 Charlottenlund; tel. 39-63-16-88; fax 39-63-00-52; e-mail missioncph@kum.hu; internet www.mfa.gov.hu/kulkepviselet/dk/hu; Ambassador DR ANDRÁS JÁNOS TÓTH.

Egypt: 29 Sharia Muhammad Mazhar, Cairo (Zamalek); tel. (2) 7358659; fax (2) 7358648; e-mail huembcai@soficom.com.eg; Ambassador László Kádár.

Estonia: Narva mnt. 122, Tallinn 15025; tel. 605-1880; fax 605-4088; e-mail mission.tal@kum.hu; internet www.mfa.gov.hu/kulkepviselet/ee/ee; Ambassador JÓZSEF VIG.

Finland: Kuusisaarenkuja 6, 00340 Helsinki; tel. (9) 484144; fax (9) 480497; e-mail office@unkari.fi; internet www.mfa.gov.hu/emb/helsinki; Ambassador Dr András Hajdu.

France: 7 sq. Vergennes, 75015 Paris; tel. 1-56-36-07-54; fax 1-56-36-02-68; e-mail mission.par@kum.hu; internet www.mfa.gov.hu/emb/paris; Ambassador LÁSZLÓ NIKICSER.

Germany: Unter den Linden 74–76, 10117 Berlin; tel. (30) 203100; fax (30) 2291314; e-mail infober@kum.hu; internet www.mfa.gov.hu/kulkepviselet/de; Ambassador Dr Sándor Peisch.

Greece: Odos Karneadou 25–29, Kolonaki, 106 75 Athens; tel. (210) 7256800; fax (210) 7256840; e-mail mission.ath@kum.hu; internet www.hunembassy.gr; Ambassador JÓZSEF TÓTH.

India: Plot 2, 50m Niti Marg, Chanakyapuri, New Delhi 110 021; tel. (11) 26114737; fax (11) 26886742; e-mail mission.del@kum.hu; Ambassador Dr Iván Németh.

Indonesia: 36 Jalan H. R. Rasuna Said, Kav. X/3, Kuningan, Jakarta 12950; tel. (21) 5203459; fax (21) 5203461; e-mail huembjkt@telkom.net; internet www.huembjkt.or.id; Ambassador MIHÁLY ILLÉS.

Iran: POB 6363-19395, Darrous, Hedayat Sq., Shadloo St, No. 16, Tehran; tel. (21) 22550460; fax (21) 22550503; e-mail huembthr@neda.net; Ambassador Giorgy Boustin.

Iraq: POB 2065, 43/4/609 al-Mansour, Hay al-Mutanabi, Baghdad; tel. (1) 543-2956; fax (1) 541-4766; e-mail huembbgd@hotmail.com; Chargé d'affaires ANDRÁS NAGY.

Ireland: 2 Fitzwilliam Place, Dublin 2; tel. (1) 6612902; fax (1) 6612880; e-mail mission.dub@kum.hu; internet www.mfa.gov.hu/kulkepviselet/ie; Ambassador Ferenc Jári.

Israel: POB 21095, 18 Pinkas St, Tel-Aviv 62661; tel. 3-5466985; fax 3-5467018; e-mail huembtlv@bezeqint.net; internet www.hungaryemb.org.il; Ambassador DR ANDRÁS GYENGE.

Italy: Via dei Villini 12–16, 00161 Roma; tel. (06) 4402032; fax (06) 4403270; e-mail mission.rom@kum.hu; internet www.huembit.it; Ambassador Miklós Merényi.

Japan: 2-17-14, Mita, Minato-ku, Tokyo 108-0073; tel. (3) 3798-8801; fax (3) 3798-8812; e-mail huembtio@gol.com; internet www.mfa.gov.hu/kulkepviselet/JP/HU; Ambassador GYULA DABRÓNAKI.

Jordan: POB 3441, Amman 11181; tel. (6) 5925614; fax (6) 5930836; e-mail mission.amm@kum.hu; internet www.mfa.gov.hu/emb/amman; Ambassador Dr Géza Mihályi.

Kazakhstan: 050000 Almaty, ul. Musabayeva 4, POB 166; tel. (727) 255-12-06; fax (727) 258-18-37; e-mail mission.ala@kum.hu; Ambassador JÁNOS NÉMETH.

Kenya: Kabarsiran Ave, off James Gichuru Rd, Lavington, POB 61146, Nairobi; tel. (20) 560060; fax (20) 560114; e-mail huembnai@africaonline.co.ke; internet www.mfa.gov.hu/kulkepviselet/KE/en/; Ambassador Gábor Sági.

Korea, Republic: 1-103, Dongbinggo-dong, Yeongsan-gu, Seoul 140-230; tel. (2) 792-2105; fax (2) 792-2109; e-mail mission.sel@kum.hu; internet www.mfa.gov.hu/emb/seoul; Ambassador MIKLÓS LENGYEL.

Kuwait: POB 23955, 13100 Safat, Bayan, Block 13, St 13, Villa 381, Kuwait City; tel. 5379351; fax 5379350; e-mail huembkwi@quality.net; internet www.mfa.gov.hu/kulkepviselet/Kuwait/en; Ambassador János Gyuris.

Latvia: Alberta iela 4, Rīga 1010; tel. 6721-7500; fax 6721-7878; e-mail mission.rix@kum.hu; internet www.mfa.gov.hu/emb/riga; Ambassador DR ISTVÁN MOHÁCSI.

Lebanon: POB 90618, Centre Massoud, 2e étage, Fanar, Beirut; tel. (1) 898840; fax (1) 873391; e-mail mission.bej@kum.hu; internet www.mfa.gov.hu/kulkepviselet/LB/en; Ambassador Lajos Tamás.

Libya: POB 4010, Sharia Talha ben Abdullah, Tripoli; tel. (21) 3618218; fax (21) 3618220; e-mail hutpi9@hotmail.com; Ambassador DR ISTVAN CSEJTEI.

Lithuania: Jojailos g. 4, Vilnius 01116; tel. (5) 269-0038; fax (5) 269-0041; e-mail vilnius@kum.hu; Ambassador Péter Noszkó-Horvath.

Luxembourg: 36 rue Marie-Adélaïde, 2128 Luxembourg; tel. 45-91-77; fax 45-82-89; e-mail ambhongr@pt.lu; internet www.mfa.gov.hu/kulkepviselet/lu; Ambassador TIBOR KECSKÉS.

Macedonia, former Yugoslav Republic: 1000 Skopje, Mirka Ginova 27; tel. (2) 3063423; fax (2) 3063070; e-mail hungemb@mt.net.mk; Ambassador Dr Ferenc Kékesi.

Malaysia: Menara Tan & Tan, 10th Floor, Suite 10-04, Jalan Tun Razak, 50400 Kuala Lumpur; tel. (3) 21637914; fax (3) 21637918; e-mail mission.kul@kum.hu; Ambassador TAMÁS TÓTH.

Mexico: Paseo de las Palmas 2005, Col. Lomas de Chapultepec, Del. Miguel Hidalgo, 11000 México, DF; tel. (55) 5596-0523; fax (55) 5596-2378; internet www.mfa.gov.hu/kulkepviselet/MX/hu; Ambassador György Tibor Herczsg.

Moldova: 2004 Chişinău, bd Ştefan cel Mare 131; tel. (22) 22-34-04; fax (22) 22-45-13; e-mail hu.emb@cni.md; Ambassador MIHÁLY BAYER.

Montenegro: 81000 Podgorica, Kralja Nikole 104; tel. (81) 602910; fax (81) 625243; e-mail mission.pdg@kum.hu; Ambassador Dr Zoltán Somogyi.

Morocco: route des Zaêrs, 17 Zankat Aït Melloul, BP 5026, Souissi, Rabat; tel. (3) 7750757; fax (3) 7754123; e-mail ambhongrie@menara.ma; internet www.mfa.gov.hu/emb/rabat; Ambassador LÁSZLÓ VÁRADI.

Netherlands: Hogeweg 14, 2585 JD The Hague; tel. (70) 3500404; fax (70) 3521749; e-mail mission.hga@kum.hu; internet www.hungarianembassy.nl; Ambassador Iván Udvardi.

Nigeria: Plot 1685, Jose Marti Cres., Asokoro, Abuja; tel. (1) 3141180; fax (1) 3141177; e-mail huemblgs@nova.net.ng; internet www.mfa.gov.hu/emb/abuja; Ambassador DR FERENC KATÓ.

Norway: Sophus Liesgt. 3, 0244 Oslo; tel. 22-55-24-18; fax 22-44-76-93; e-mail huembosl@online.no; Ambassador Lajos Bozi.

Pakistan: 12, Margalla Rd, F-6/3, POB 1103, Islamabad; tel. (51) 2823352; fax (51) 2825256; e-mail hungemb@comsats.net.pk; Ambassador BELA FAZEKAS.

Poland: 00-559 Warsaw, ul. Chopina 2; tel. (22) 6284451; fax (22) 6218561; e-mail mission.vao@kum.hu; internet www.mfa.gov.hu/emb/warsaw; Ambassador Róbert Kiss.

Portugal: Calçada de Santo Amaro 85, 1349-042 Lisbon; tel. (21) 3630395; fax (21) 3632314; e-mail mission.lis@kum.hu; internet www.mfa.gov.hu/emb/lisbon; Ambassador ATTILA GECSE.

Qatar: POB 23525, Doha; tel. 4932531; fax 4932537; e-mail mission.doh@kum.hu; internet www.mfa.gov.hu/kulkepviselet/qu; Ambassador Ferenc Csillag.

Romania: 020027 Bucharest, Str. Dimitrie Gerotă 63–65; tel. (21) 3120073; fax (21) 3120467; e-mail hunembro@ines.ro; internet hungaryemb.ines.ro; Ambassador JÁNOS TERÉNYI.

Russian Federation: 119590 Moscow, ul. Mosfilmovskaya 62; tel. (495) 796-93-70; fax (495) 796-93-80; e-mail mow.missions@kum.hu; internet www.mfa.gov.hu/emb/moscow; Ambassador Árpád Székely.

Saudi Arabia: POB 94014, al-Waha District, Ahmad Tonsy St 23, Riyadh 11693; tel. (1) 454-6707; fax (1) 456-0834; e-mail huemb.ryd@nournet.com .sa; Ambassador ISTVÁN TÖLLI.

Serbia: 11000 Belgrade, Krunska 72; tel. (11) 2440472; fax (11) 3441876; e-mail hunemblg@eunet.yu; internet www.hunemblg.hu; Ambassador Sándor Papp.

Singapore: 250 North Bridge Rd, 29-01 Raffles City Tower, Singapore 179101; tel. 68830882; fax 68830177; e-mail mission.sin@kum.hu; internet www.mfa.gov.hu/emb/singapore; Ambassador TAMAS MAGDA.

Slovakia: Sedlárska 3, 814 25 Bratislava; tel. (2) 5920-5200; fax (2) 5443-5484; e-mail pozsony@embhung.sk; Ambassador Antal Heizer.

Slovenia: 1210 Ljubljana, ul. Konrada Babnika 5; tel. (1) 5121882; fax (1) 5121878; e-mail huemblju@siol.net; internet www.hu-embassy.si; Ambassador DR JÓZSEF CZUKOR.

South Africa: 959 Arcadia St, Hatfield, Pretoria 0083; POB 13843, Hatfield 0028; tel. (12) 4303020; fax (12) 4303029; e-mail huembprt@mweb.co.za; Ambassador István Emri.

Spain: Fortuny 6, 4°, 28010 Madrid; tel. (91) 4137011; fax (91) 4134138; e-mail info@embajada-hungria.org; internet www.mfa.gov.hu/emb/madrid; Ambassador GÁBOR TÓTH.

Sweden: Dag Hammarskjölds Väg 10, POB 24125, 104 51 Stockholm; tel. (8) 661-67-62; fax (8) 660-29-59; e-mail embassy.stockholm@kum.hu; internet www.mfa.gov.hu/kulkepviselet/se; Ambassador Gábor Iklódy.

Switzerland: Muristr. 31, Postfach 216, 3000 Bern 15; tel. 313528572; fax 313512001; e-mail huembbrn@bluemail.ch; internet www.mfa.gov.hu/emb/bern; Ambassador JENO BOROS.

Syria: BP 2607, 12 rue as-Salam, Mezzeh Est, Damascus; tel. (11) 6117966; fax (11) 6117917; e-mail mission.dam@kum.hu; internet www.mfa.gov.hu/kulkepviselet/sy; Ambassador Prof. Péter Medgyes.

Thailand: Oak Tower, 20th Floor, President Park Condominium, 95 Sukhumvit Soi 24, Prakhanong, Bangkok 10110; tel. (2) 661-1150; fax (2) 661-1153; e-mail huembbgk@mozart.inet.co.th; internet www.mfa.gov.hu/kulkepviselet/TH/hu; Ambassador DR ANDRAS BALOGH.

Tunisia: 12 rue Achtart, 1082 Nord Hilton, BP 572, Tunis; tel. (71) 780-544; fax (71) 781-264; e-mail huembtun@planet.tn; internet www.mfa.gov.hu/emb/tunis; Ambassador Dr Pál Pataki.

Turkey: Sancak Mah. Layoş, Koşut Cad. 2, Yıldız, Çankaya, Ankara; tel. (312) 4422273; fax (312) 4415049; e-mail huembtur@isnet.net.tr; internet www.mfa.gov.hu/kulkepviselet/TR/hu; Ambassador ISTVÁN SZABÓ.

Ukraine: 01034 Kyiv, vul. Reitarska 33; tel. (44) 230-80-00; fax (44) 272-20-90; e-mail kev.missions@kum.hu; internet www.mfa.gov.hu/emb/kiev; Ambassador András Bársony.

United Arab Emirates: POB 44450, Abu Dhabi; tel. (2) 6766190; fax (2) 6766215; e-mail mission.abu@kum.hu; Ambassador JÁNOS GÖNCI.

United Kingdom: 35 Eaton Pl., London, SW1X 8BY; tel. (20) 7235-5218; fax (20) 7823-1348; e-mail office@huemblon.org.uk; internet www.mfa.gov.hu/emb/london; Ambassador Borbála Czakó.

United States of America: 3910 Shoemaker St, NW, Washington, DC 20008; tel. (202) 362-6730; fax (202) 966-8135; e-mail informacio.was@kum.hu; internet www.huembwas.org; Ambassador DR FERENC SOMOGYI.

Vatican City: Piazza Girolamo Fabrizio 2, 00161 Rome, Italy; tel. (06) 4402167; fax (06) 4402312; e-mail mission.vat@kum.hu; Ambassador Gabór Erdödy.

Viet Nam: Daeha Business Centre, 12th Floor, 360 Kim Ma, Ba Dinh District, Hanoi; tel. (4) 7715714; fax (4) 7715716; e-mail hungemb@hn.vnn .vn; internet www.mfa.gov.hu/emb/hanoi; Ambassador LASZLO VIZI.

Zimbabwe: 20 Lanark Rd, Belgravia, POB 3594, Harare; tel. (4) 733528; fax (4) 730512; Ambassador Tamás Gáspár Gál.

DIPLOMATIC MISSIONS OF ICELAND

United Nations: 800 Third Ave, 36th Floor, New York, NY 10022; tel. (212) 593-2700; fax (212) 593-6269; e-mail icecon.ny@utn.stjr.is; internet brunnur .stjr.is/embassy/newyork.nsf/pages/index.html; Permanent Representative HJALMAR W. HANNESSON.

Austria: Naglergasse 2/8, 1010 Vienna; tel. (1) 533-27-71; fax (1) 533-27-74; e-mail emb.vienna@mfa.is; internet www.iceland.org/at; Ambassador Sveinn Björnsson.

Belgium: 11 rond point Robert Schuman, 1040 Brussels; tel. (2) 238-50-00; fax (2) 230-69-38; e-mail emb.brussels@mfa.is; internet www.iceland.org/be; Ambassador STEFÁN HAUKUR JÓHANNESSON.

Canada: 360 Albert St, Suite 710, Ottawa, ON K1R 7X7; tel. (613) 482-1944; fax (613) 482-1945; e-mail icemb.ottawa@utn.stjr.is; internet www.iceland .org/ca; Ambassador Markus Orn Antonsson.

China, People's Republic: Landmark Tower 1, 802, 8 North Dongsanhuan Lu, Beijing 100004; tel. (10) 65907795; fax (10) 65907801; e-mail icemb .beijing@utn.stjr.is; internet www.iceland.org/cn; Ambassador GUNNAR SNORRI GUNNARSSON.

Denmark: Strandgade 89, 1401 Copenhagen K; tel. 33-18-10-50; fax 33-18-10-59; e-mail icemb.coph@utn.stjr.is; Ambassador Svavar Gestsson.

Finland: Pohjoisesplanadi 27C, 00100 Helsinki; tel. (9) 6122460; fax (9) 61224620; e-mail icemb.helsinki@utn.stjr.is; internet www.iceland.org/fi; Ambassador HANNES HEIMISSON.

France: 8 ave Kléber, 75116 Paris; tel. 1-44-17-32-85; fax 1-40-67-99-96; e-mail icemb.paris@utn.stjr.is; internet www.iceland.org/fr; Ambassador Tómas Ingi Olrich.

Germany: Rauchstr. 1, 10787 Berlin; tel. (30) 50504000; fax (30) 50504300; e-mail icemb.berlin@utn.stjr.is; internet www.botschaft-island.de; Ambassador ÓLAFUR DAVISSON.

India: 11 Aurangzeb Rd, New Delhi 110 011; tel. (11) 43530300; fax (11) 42403001; e-mail emb.newdelhi@mfa.is; internet www.iceland.org/in; Ambassador Dr Gunnar Pálsson.

Iran: 30–32 Fayazi St (Fereshteh), Vali-e-Asr Ave, Tehran; tel. (21) 22039990; fax (21) 22040640; e-mail info@consulate-of-iceland-tehran.com; Ambassador STEFAN SKJALDARSON.

Italy: Via di San Saba 12, int 7, 00153 Roma; tel. (06) 57250509; fax (06) 5758012; e-mail gudni@mfa.is; internet www.iceland.org/it; Chargé d'affaires Guni Bragason.

Japan: 4-18-26, Takanawa, Minato-ku, Tokyo 108-0074; tel. (3) 3447-1944; fax (3) 3447-1945; e-mail icemb.tokyo@utn.stjr.is; internet www.iceland.org/jp; Ambassador THORDUR AEGIR OSKARSSON.

Mozambique: Av. Zimbabwe 1694, Maputo; tel. 21483509; fax 21483511; e-mail mozambique@iceida.is; internet www.iceland.org/mo; Chargé d'affaires a.i. Jóhann Pálsson.

Norway: Stortingsgt. 30, 0244 Oslo; tel. 23-23-75-30; fax 22-83-07-04; e-mail emb.oslo@mfa.is; internet www.island.no; Ambassador STEFÁN SKJALDARSON.

Russian Federation: 121069 Moscow, Khlebnyi per. 28; tel. (495) 956-76-04; fax (495) 956-76-12; e-mail emb.moscow@mfa.is; internet www.iceland.org/ru; Ambassador Benedikt Ásgeirsson.

South Africa: iParioli Office Park, Phase II, Block A2, 1166 Park St, Pretoria; POB 14325 Hatfield 0028; tel. (12) 3425885; fax (12) 3420883; e-mail emb .pretoria@mfa.is; internet www.iceland.org/za; Ambassador DR SIGRIDUR DUNA KRISTMUNDSDOTTIR.

Sweden: Kommendörsgt. 35, 114 58 Stockholm; tel. (8) 442-83-00; fax (8) 660-74-23; e-mail icemb.stock@utn.strj.is; internet www.iceland.org/se; Ambassador Gumundur Árni Stefánsson.

United Kingdom: 2A Hans St, London, SW1X 0JE; tel. (20) 7259-3999; fax (20) 7245-9649; e-mail icemb.london@utn.stjr.is; internet www.iceland.org/uk; Ambassador SVERRIR HAUKUR GUNNLAUGSSON.

United States of America: 1156 15th St, NW, Suite 1200, Washington, DC 20005-1704; tel. (202) 265-6653; fax (202) 265-6656; e-mail icemb.wash@utn .stjr.is; internet www.iceland.org/us; Ambassador Albert Jónsson.

DIPLOMATIC MISSIONS OF INDIA

United Nations: 235 East 43rd St, New York, NY 10017; tel. (212) 490-9660; fax (212) 490-9656; e-mail india@un.int; internet www.un.int/india; Permanent Representative NIRUPAM SEN.

Afghanistan: Malalai Wat, Shar-i-Nau, Kabul; tel. (873) 763095560; fax (873) 763095561; e-mail embassy@indembassy-kabul.com; Ambassador Rakesh Sood.

Algeria: BP 108, 14 rue des Abassides, 16030 el-Biar, Algiers; tel. (21) 92-32-88; fax (21) 92-40-11; e-mail indembalg@hotmail.com; Ambassador DR ASHOK KUMAR AMROHI.

Angola: Rua Marquês das Minas 18a, Macalusso, CP 6040, Luanda; tel. 222392281; fax 222371094; e-mail indembluanda@ebonet.net; Ambassador (vacant).

Argentina: Avda Eduardo Madero 942, C1106ACW Buenos Aires; tel. (11) 4393-4001; fax (11) 4393-4063; e-mail indemb@indembarg.org.ar; internet www.indembarg.org.ar; Ambassador RENGARAJ VISWANATHAN.

Armenia: 0019 Yerevan, Dzorapi St 50/2; tel. (10) 53-91-73; fax (10) 53-39-84; e-mail hoc@embassyofindia.am; internet www.indianembassy.am; Ambassador Reena Pandey.

Australia: 3–5 Moonah Place, Yarralumla, ACT 2600; tel. (2) 6273-3999; fax (2) 6273-1308; e-mail hco@hcindia-au.org; internet www.hcindia-au.org; High Commissioner SUJATHA SINGH.

Austria: Kärntner Ring 2, 1015 Vienna; tel. (1) 505-86-66; fax (1) 505-92-19; e-mail indemb@eoivien.vienna.at; internet www.indianembassy.at; Ambassador Saurabh Kumar.

Azerbaijan: 1069 Baku, Sabayel rayon, Oktay Karimov küç. 31/39; tel. (12) 447-41-86; fax (12) 447-25-72; e-mail eibaku@adanet.az; Ambassador B. R. MUTHU KUMAR.

Bahrain: POB 26106, Bldg 182, Rd 2608, Area 326, Adliya, Manama; tel. 17712785; fax 17715527; e-mail indemb@batelco.com.bh; internet www .indianembassy-bah.com; Ambassador Dr Balakrishna Shetty.

Bangladesh: House 2, Rd 142, Gulshan-I, Dhaka; tel. (2) 9889339; fax (2) 8817487; e-mail hc@hcidhaka.org; internet www.hcidhaka.org; High Commissioner PINAK RANJAN CHAKRAVARTY.

Belarus: 220090 Minsk, vul. Kaltsova 4, kor. 5; tel. (17) 262-93-99; fax (17) 262-97-99; e-mail amb@indemb.bn.by; internet www.indembminsk.org; Ambassador R. K. Tyagi.

Belgium: 217 chaussée de Vleurgat, 1050 Brussels; tel. (2) 640-91-40; fax (2) 648-96-38; e-mail admin@indembassy.be; internet www.indembassy.be; Ambassador DIPAK CHATTERJEE.

Bhutan: India House, Jungshina, Thimphu; tel. (2) 322162; fax (2) 323195; e-mail hocbht@druknet.bt; Ambassador Sudhir Vyas.

Botswana: Plot 5375, President's Dr., Private Bag 249, Gaborone; tel. 3972676; fax 3974636; e-mail administration@hci.org.bw; internet www .highcommissionofinida.org.bw; High Commissioner V. N. HADE.

Brazil: SHIS, QL 08, Conj. 08, Casa 01, 71620-285 Brasília, DF; tel. (61) 3248-4006; fax (61) 3248-7849; e-mail indemb@indianembassy.org.br; internet www.indianembassy.org.br; Ambassador Hardeep Singh Puri.

Brunei: 'Baitussyifaa', Simpang 40–22, Jalan Sungai Akar, Bandar Seri Begawan BC 3915; tel. 2339947; fax 2339783; e-mail hicomind@brunet.bn; internet www.brunet.bn/gov/emb/india; High Commissioner R. V. WARJRI.

Bulgaria: 1000 Sofia, bul. Patriarkh Evtimii 31; tel. (2) 986-76-72; fax (2) 980-12-89; e-mail ambsofia@inet.bg; internet www.indembsofia.org; Ambassador Lal Dingliana.

Cambodia: 5 rue 466, Phnom-Penh; tel. (23) 210912; fax (23) 213640; e-mail embindia@online.com.kh; Ambassador ALOKE SEN.

Canada: 10 Springfield Rd, Ottawa, ON K1M 1C9; tel. (613) 744-3751; fax (613) 744-0913; e-mail hicomind@hciottawa.ca; internet www.hciottawa.ca; High Commissioner Rajamani Lakshmi Narayan.

Chile: Triana 871, Casilla 10433, Santiago; tel. (2) 235-2005; fax (2) 235-9607; e-mail info@embajadaindia.cl; internet www.embajadaindia.cl; Ambassador SUSMITA GONGULEE THOMAS.

China, People's Republic: 1 Ri Tan Dong Lu, Jian Guo Men Wai, Beijing 100600; tel. (10) 65321908; fax (10) 65324684; internet www.indianembassy .org.cn; Ambassador Nirupama Rao.

Colombia: Edif. Bancafe, Torre B, Carrera 7, No 71-21, Of. 1001, Bogotá, DC; tel. (1) 317-4865; fax (1) 317-4976; e-mail indembog@cable.net.co; internet www.embajadaindia.org; Ambassador DEEPAK BHOJWANI.

Côte d'Ivoire: Cocody Danga Nord, 06 BP 318, Abidjan 06; tel. 22-42-37-69; fax 22-42-66-49; Ambassador Amarendra Khatua.

Croatia: 10000 Zagreb, ul. Boškovićeva 7 A; tel. (1) 4873239; fax (1) 4817907; e-mail embassy.india@zg.htnet.hr; internet www.indianembassy.hr; Ambassador RAJIVA MISRA.

Cuba: Calle 21, No 202, esq. K, Vedado, Havana; tel. (7) 833-3777; fax (7) 833-3287; e-mail hoc@indembassyhavana.cu; internet www .indembassyhavana.cu; Ambassador Mitra Vasisht.

Cyprus: POB 25544, 3 Indira Gandhi St, Engomi, 2413 Nicosia; tel. 22351741; fax 22352062; e-mail hicomind@spidernet.com.cy; internet www .hcinicosia.org.cy; High Commr LAVANYA PRASAD.

Czech Republic: Valdštejnská 6, 118 00 Prague 1; tel. 257533490; fax 257533378; e-mail indembprague@bohem-net.cz; internet www.india.cz; Ambassador Dinkar Prakash Srivastava.

Denmark: Vangehusvej 15, 2100 Copenhagen Ø; tel. 39-18-28-88; fax 39-27-02-18; e-mail india@email.dk; internet www.indian-embassy.dk; Ambassador PARTHA SARATHI RAY.

Egypt: 5 Sharia Aziz Abaza, Cairo (Zamalek); tel. (2) 3927702; e-mail infoemb@indembcairo.com; internet www.indembcairo.com; Ambassador Achamkulangare Gopinathan.

Ethiopia: Kabena, POB 528, Addis Ababa; tel. (11) 1552100; fax (11) 1552521; Ambassador GURJIT SINGH.

Fiji: POB 471, Suva; tel. 3301125; fax 3301032; e-mail hicomindsuva@is.com .fj; High Commissioner Ishwar Singh Chauhan.

Finland: Satamakatu 2A 8, 00160 Helsinki; tel. (9) 2289910; fax (9) 6221208; e-mail indianembassy@indianembassy.fi; internet www.indianembassy.fi; Ambassador PRADEEP SINGH.

France: 15 rue Alfred Dehodencq, 75016 Paris; tel. 1-40-50-70-70; fax 1-40-50-09-96; e-mail eiparis.admin@wanadoo.fr; internet www.amb-inde.fr; Ambassador Ranjan Mathai.

Germany: Tiergartenstr. 17, 10785 Berlin; tel. (30) 257950; fax (30) 25795102; e-mail infowing@indianembassy.de; internet www.indianembassy.de; Ambassador MEERA SHANKAR.

Ghana: 9 Ridge Rd, Roman Ridge, POB 5708, Cantonments, Accra; tel. (21) 775601; fax (21) 772176; e-mail indiahc@ncs.com.gh; internet www.indiahc -ghana.com; High Commissioner Rajesh N. Prasad.

Greece: Odos Kleanthous 3, 106 74 Athens; tel. (210) 7216227; fax (210) 7211252; e-mail indembassy@ath.forthnet.gr; internet www .indembassyathens.gr; Ambassador DILIP SINHA.

Guyana: Bank of Baroda Bldg, 10 Ave of the Republic, POB 101148, Georgetown; tel. 226-3996; fax 225-7012; e-mail hoc.georgetown@mea.gov .in; High Commissioner Avinash C. Gupta.

Hungary: 1025 Budapest, Búzavirág u. 14; tel. (1) 325-7742; fax (1) 325-7745; e-mail chancery@indianembassy.hu; internet www.indianembassy.hu; Ambassador MANBIR SINGH.

Indonesia: Jalan H. R. Rasuna Said, Kav. S/1, Kuningan, Jakarta 12950; tel. (21) 5204150; fax (21) 5204160; e-mail eoijakarta@indo.net.id; internet www .embassyofindiajakarta.org; Ambassador Navrekha Sharma.

Iran: POB 15875-4118, 46 Mir-Emad St, Cnr of 9th St, Dr Beheshti Ave, Tehran; tel. (21) 88755103; fax (21) 88755973; e-mail indemteh@dpimail.net; internet www.indianembassy-tehran.com; Ambassador MANBIR SINGH.

Iraq: 6/25/306 Hay al-Maghrib, Baghdad; tel. (1) 422-2014; fax (1) 422-9549; Ambassador R. Dayakar.

Ireland: 6 Leeson Park, Dublin 6; tel. (1) 4966792; fax (1) 4978074; e-mail indembassy@eircom.net; internet indianembassy.ie; Ambassador P. S. RAGHAVAN.

Israel: POB 3368, 140 Hayarkon St, Tel-Aviv 61033; tel. 3-5291999; fax 3-5291953; e-mail indemtel@indembassy.co.il; internet www.indembassy.co.il; Ambassador Arun Kumar Singh.

Italy: Via XX Settembre 5, 00187 Roma; tel. (06) 4884642; fax (06) 4819539; e-mail gen.email@indianembassy.it; internet www.indianembassy.it; Ambassador RAJIV DOGRA.

Jamaica: 4 Retreat Ave, POB 446, Kingston 6; tel. 927-4480; fax 978-2801; e-mail hicomindkin@cwjamaica.com; High Commissioner M. S. Grover.

Japan: 2-2-11, Kudan Minami, Chiyoda-ku, Tokyo 102-0074; tel. (3) 3262-2391; fax (3) 3234-4866; e-mail indembjp@gol.com; internet www .embassyofindiajapan.org; Ambassador HEMANT KRISHAM SINGH.

Jordan: POB 2168, Amman 11181; tel. (6) 4622098; fax (6) 4659540; e-mail amb.amman@mea.gov.in; Ambassador Ratakonda Dayakar.

Kazakhstan: 010000 Astana, pr. Kabanbai Batyr 6/1, Kaskad Business Centre, 5th Floor; tel. (7172) 92-57-10; fax (7172) 92-57-16; e-mail admn .astana@mea.gov.in; internet www.indembassy.kz; Ambassador ASHOK SAJJANHAR.

Kenya: Jeevan Bharati Bldg, 2nd Floor, Harambee Ave, POB 30074, Nairobi; tel. (20) 225104; fax (20) 316242; e-mail hcindia@kenyaweb.com; internet www.hcinairobi.co.ke; High Commissioner Parampreet Singh Randhawa.

Korea, Democratic People's Republic: Block 53, Munsudong, Taehak St, Taedongkang District, Pyongyang; tel. (2) 3817274; fax (2) 3817619; e-mail indemhoc@di.chesin.com; Ambassador ZILE SINGH.

Korea, Republic: 37-3, Hannam-dong, Yeongsan-gu, CPOB 3466, Seoul 140-210; tel. (2) 798-4257; fax (2) 796-9534; e-mail eoiseoul@sinbiro.com; internet www.indembassy.or.kr; Ambassador N. Parthasarathi.

Kuwait: POB 1450, 13015 Safat, Diplomatic Enclave, Arabian Gulf St, Kuwait City; tel. 2530600; fax 2525811; e-mail contact@indembkwt.org; internet www.indembkwt.org; Ambassador M. GANAPATHI.

Kyrgyzstan: 720044 Bishkek, ul. Aeroportinskaya 15a; tel. (312) 54-92-14; fax (312) 54-32-45; e-mail indembas@infotel.kg; Ambassador Jyoti Swarup Pande.

Laos: 2 Ban Wat Nak, rue Thadeua, Km 3, Sisattanak District, Vientiane; tel. (21) 352301; fax (21) 352300; e-mail indiaemb@laotel.com; internet indemblao.nic.in; Ambassador SHRI SURESH K. GOEL.

Lebanon: POB 113-5240, Immeuble Sahmarani, rue Kantari 31, Hamra, Beirut; tel. (1) 353892; fax (1) 869806; e-mail indembei@dm.net.lb; Ambassador Nantu Sarkar.

Libya: POB 3150, 16 Sharia Mahmud Shaltut, Tripoli; tel. (21) 4441835; fax (21) 3337560; e-mail indembtrip@hotmail.com; Ambassador D. P. SRIVASTAVA.

Madagascar: 4 Làlana Emile Rajaonson, Tsaralalana, BP 1787, 101 Antananarivo; tel. (20) 2223334; fax (20) 2233790; e-mail indembmd@wanadoo.mg; Ambassador Diljit Singh Pannun.

Malaysia: 2 Jalan Taman Duta, off Jalan Duta, 50480 Kuala Lumpur; tel. (3) 20933510; fax (3) 20933507; e-mail highcomm@po.jaring.my; internet www.indianhighcommission.com.my; High Commissioner ASHOK K. KANTHA.

Maldives: H. Athireege-Aage, Ameeru Ahmed Magu, Malé; tel. 3323015; fax 3324778; High Commissioner A. K. Pandey.

Mauritius: Life Insurance Corpn of India Bldg, 6th Floor, John F. Kennedy St, POB 162, Port Louis; tel. 208-3775; fax 208-6859; e-mail hicom.ss@intnet.mu; internet indiahighcom.intnet.mu; High Commissioner BONDAL JAISHANKAR.

Mexico: Musset 325, Col. Polanco, Del. Miguel Hidalgo, 11550 México, DF; tel. (55) 5531-1050; fax (55) 5254-2349; e-mail indembmx@prodigy.net.mx; internet www.indembassy.org; Ambassador Rinzing Wangdi.

Mongolia: Zaluuchuudyn Örgön Chölöö 10, Ulan Bator (CPOB 691); tel. (11) 329522; fax (11) 329532; e-mail indembmongolia@magicnet.mn; Ambassador YOGESHWAR VARMA.

Morocco: 13 ave de Michlifen, Agdal, 10000 Rabat; tel. (3) 7671339; fax (3) 7671269; e-mail india@menara.ma; internet www.indianembassymorocco.ma; Ambassador Prabhu Dayal.

Mozambique: Av. Kenneth Kaunda 167, CP 4751, Maputo; tel. 21492437; fax 21492364; e-mail hicomind@tvcabo.co.mz; internet www.hicomind-maputo.org; High Commissioner RAJINDER BHAGAT.

Myanmar: 545–547 Merchant St, POB 751, Yangon; tel. (1) 282552; fax (1) 254086; e-mail amb.indembygn@mptmail.net.mm; internet www.indiaembassy.net.mm; Ambassador Bhaskar Kumar Mitra.

Namibia: 97 Nelson Mandela Ave, POB 1209, Windhoek; tel. (61) 226037; fax (61) 237320; e-mail hicomind@mweb.com.na; internet www.highcommissionofindia.web.na; High Commissioner TSEWANG TOPDEN.

Nepal: 336 Kapurdhara Marg, POB 292, Kathmandu; tel. (1) 4410900; fax (1) 4428279; e-mail pic@eoiktm.org; internet www.south-asia.com/embassy-India; Ambassador Shiv Shankar Mukherjee.

Netherlands: Buitenrustweg 2, 2517 KD The Hague; tel. (70) 3469771; fax (70) 3617072; e-mail ambassador@indianembassy.nl; internet www.indianembassy.nl; Ambassador NEELAM D. SABHARWAL.

New Zealand: 180 Molesworth St, POB 4045, Wellington 1; tel. (4) 473-6390; fax (4) 499-0665; e-mail hicomind@hicomind.org.nz; internet www.hicomind.org.nz; High Commissioner K. P. Ernest.

Nigeria: 15 Rio Negro Close, off Yedseram St, Maitama, Abuja; tel. (9) 4132323; fax (9) 4132324; e-mail hoc.abuja@mea.gov.in; internet www.hicomindlagos.com; High Commissioner HARIHARA SUBRAMANIAM VISWANATHAN.

Norway: Niels Juelsgt. 30, 0244 Oslo; tel. 24-11-59-10; fax 24-11-59-12; e-mail amb.oslo@mea.gov.in; internet www.indemb.no; Ambassador Mahesh Kumar Sachdev.

Oman: POB 1727, Ruwi 112; tel. 24813838; fax 24811607; e-mail indiamct@omantel.net.om; internet www.indemb-oman.org; Ambassador ANIL WADHWA.

Pakistan: G-5, Diplomatic Enclave, Islamabad; tel. (51) 2206950; fax (51) 2823102; e-mail hicomind@isb.compol.com; High Commissioner Satyabrata Pal.

Panama: Avda Federico Boyd y Calle 51, Bella Vista, Apdo 8400, Panamá 7; tel. 264-3043; fax 264-2855; e-mail indempan@c-com.net.pa; internet www.indempan.org; Ambassador ASHOK TOMAR.

Papua New Guinea: Lot 20, Section 8, Unit 2, Tanatana St, Boroko, POB 86, Waigani, NCD, Port Moresby; tel. 3254757; fax 3253138; e-mail hcipom@datec.net.pg; High Commissioner S. P. Mann.

Peru: Avda Salaverry 3006, San Isidro, Lima 27; tel. (1) 4602289; fax (1) 4610374; e-mail hoc@indembassy.org.pe; internet www.indembassy.org.pe; Ambassador APPUNNI RAMESH.

Philippines: 2190 Paraiso St, Dasmariñas Village, POB 2123, Makati City, Metro Manila; tel. (2) 8430101; fax (2) 8158151; e-mail amb@embindia.org.ph; internet www.embindia.org.ph; Ambassador Shri Rajeet Mitter.

Poland: 02-516 Warsaw, ul. Rejtana 15, m. 2–7; tel. (22) 8495800; fax (22) 8496705; e-mail hoc.warsaw@mea.gov.in; internet www.indianembassy.pl; Ambassador CHANDRA MOHAN BHANDARI.

Portugal: Rua Pêro da Covilhã 16, 1400-297 Lisbon; tel. (21) 3041090; fax (21) 3016576; e-mail main@indembassy-lisbon.org; internet www.indembassy-lisbon.org; Ambassador Nilima Mitra.

Qatar: POB 2788, Doha; tel. 4255777; fax 4670448; e-mail indembdh@qatar.net.qa; internet www.indianembassy.gov.qa; Ambassador GEORGE JOSEPH.

Romania: 020078 Bucharest 3, Str. Mihai Eminescu 183; tel. (21) 2115451; fax (21) 2110614; e-mail office@embassyofindia.ro; internet www.embassyofindia.ro; Ambassador Debashish Chakravarti.

Russian Federation: 101000 Moscow, ul. Vorontsovo Pole 6/8; tel. (495) 783-75-35; fax (495) 975-23-37; e-mail india@online.ru; internet www.indianembassy.ru; Ambassador PRABHAT SHUKLA.

Saudi Arabia: POB 94387, Riyadh 11693; tel. (1) 488-4144; fax (1) 488-4189; e-mail info@indianembassy.org.sa; internet www.indianembassy.org.sa; Ambassador M. O. H. Farouk.

Senegal: 5 rue Carde, BP 398, Dakar; tel. 33-822-5875; fax 33-822-3585; e-mail indiacom@sentoo.sn; internet www.ambassadeinde.sn; Ambassador PARBATI SEN VYAS.

Serbia: 11040 Belgrade, Ljutice Bogdana 8,; tel. (11) 2661029; fax (11) 3674209; e-mail indemb@eunet.yu; internet www.embassyofindiabelgrade.org; Ambassador Ajay Swarup.

Seychelles: Le Chantier, POB 488, Francis Rachel St, Victoria; tel. 610301; fax 610308; e-mail hicomind@seychelles.net; internet www.seychelles.net/hicomind; High Commissioner MALAY MISHRA.

Singapore: 31 Grange Rd, India House, Singapore 239702; tel. 67376777; fax 67326909; e-mail indiahc@pacific.net.sg; internet www.embassyofindia.com; High Commissioner Subrahmanyam Jaishankar.

Slovakia: Dunajská 4, 811 08 Bratislava; tel. (2) 5296-2915; fax (2) 5296-2921; e-mail eindia@slovanet.sk; internet www.indianembassy.sk; Ambassador HOMAI SAHA.

South Africa: 852 Schoeman St, Arcadia, Pretoria 0083; POB 40216, Arcadia 0007; tel. (12) 3425392; fax (12) 3425310; e-mail polinf@hicomind.co.za; High Commissioner R. K. Bhatia.

Spain: Avda Pío XII 30–32, 28016 Madrid; tel. (91) 1315114; fax (91) 3451112; internet www.embajadaindia.com; Ambassador SURYAKANTHI TRIPATTHI.

Sri Lanka: 36–38 Galle Rd, Colombo 3; tel. (11) 2421605; fax (11) 2446403; e-mail cpic@sltnet.lk; internet www.hcicolombo.org; High Commissioner Alok Prasad.

Sudan: 61 Africa Rd, POB 707, Khartoum II; tel. (183) 574001; fax (183) 574050; e-mail ambassador.office@indembsdn.com; internet www.indembsdn.com; Ambassador DEEPAK VOHRA.

Suriname: Rode Kruislaan 10, POB 1329, Paramaribo; tel. 498344; fax 491106; e-mail india@sr.net; internet www.indembassysuriname.com; Ambassador Ashok Kumar Sharma.

Sweden: Adolf Fredriks Kyrkogt. 12, POB 1340, 111 83 Stockholm; tel. (8) 10-70-08; fax (8) 24-85-05; e-mail information@indianembassy.se; internet www.indianembassy.se; Ambassador DEEPA GOPALAN WADHWA.

Switzerland: Kirchenfeldstr. 28, 3006 Bern; tel. 313511110; fax 313511557; e-mail india@spectraweb.ch; internet www.indembassybern.ch; Chargé d'affaires a.i. Ajaneesh Kumar.

Syria: BP 685, Immeuble Yassin Noueilati, 40/46 ave Adnan al-Malki, Damascus; tel. (11) 3739082; fax (11) 3326231; e-mail indemcom@scs-net.org; Ambassador GOTAM MOKOBAD HAYA.

Tajikistan: 734000 Dushanbe, Kuchai Buxoro 45; tel. (372) 221-71-72; fax (372) 251-00-45; e-mail hocdushanbe@tojikiston.com; Ambassador Amar Sinha.

Thailand: 46 Soi Prasarnmitr, 23 Thanon Sukhumvit, Bangkok 10110; tel. (2) 258-0300; fax (2) 258-4627; e-mail indiaemb@mozart.inet.co.th; internet indianembassy.gov.in/bangkok; Ambassador VIJAYA LATHA REDDY.

Trinidad and Tobago: 6 Victoria Ave, POB 530, Port of Spain; tel. 627-7480; fax 627-6985; e-mail hcipos@tstt.net.tt; High Commissioner Jagjit Singh Sapra.

Tunisia: 4 place Didon, Notre Dame, 1002 Tunis; tel. (71) 787-819; fax (71) 783-394; e-mail embassy.india@email.ati.tn; Ambassador BASANT K. GUPTA.

Turkey: Cinnah Cad. 77/a, 06680 Çankaya, Ankara; tel. (312) 4382195; fax (312) 4403429; e-mail chancery@indembassy.org.tr; internet www .indembassy.org.tr; Ambassador Chitra Narayanan.

Turkmenistan: 744000 Aşgabat, ul. Yu. Emre 2/1, Imperial International Business Centre; tel. (12) 45-81-52; fax (12) 45-61-56; e-mail indembhoc@ online.tm; Ambassador PROF. RAM PAL KAUSHIK.

Uganda: 11 Kyaddondo Rd, Nakasero, POB 7040, Kampala; tel. (41) 4457368; fax (41) 4454943; e-mail hoc@hicomindkampala.org; High Commissioner Sibarata Tripathi.

Ukraine: 01901 Kyiv, vul. Teryokhina 4; tel. (44) 468-66-61; fax (44) 468-66-19; e-mail india@public.ua.net; internet www.indianembassy.org.ua; Ambassador DEBABRATA SAHA.

United Arab Emirates: POB 4090, Abu Dhabi; tel. (2) 4492700; fax (2) 4444685; e-mail indiauae@indembassyuae.org; internet www.indembassyuae .org; Ambassador Talmiz Ahmad.

United Kingdom: India House, Aldwych, London, WC2B 4NA; tel. (20) 7836-8484; fax (20) 7836-4331; e-mail india@hcilondon.net; internet www .hcilondon.net; High Commr SHIV SHANKAR MUKHERJEE.

United States of America: 2107 Massachusetts Ave, NW, Washington, DC 20008; tel. (202) 939-7000; fax (202) 265-4351; e-mail information@indiagov .org; internet www.indianembassy.org; Ambassador Ronen Sen.

Uzbekistan: 100000 Tashkent, Qarabulak ko'ch. 15–16; tel. (71) 140-09-83; fax (71) 140-09-99; e-mail indhoc@buzton.com; internet www.indembassy .uz; Ambassador SKAND RANJAN TAYAL.

Venezuela: Quinta Tagore, No. 12, Avda San Carlos, La Floresta, Caracas; tel. (212) 285-7887; fax (212) 286-5131; e-mail info@embindia.org; internet www.embindia.org; Ambassador Yashvardhan Kumar Sinha.

Viet Nam: 58–60 Tran Hung Dao, Hanoi; tel. (4) 8244990; fax (4) 8244998; e-mail india@netnam.org.vn; internet www.indembassy.com.vn; Ambassador LAL THLA MUANA.

Yemen: POB 1154, Bldg 12, Djibouti St, San'a; tel. (1) 441251; fax (1) 441257; e-mail indiaemb@y.net.ye; internet www.eoisanaa.com.ye; Ambassador R. M. Aggarwal.

Zambia: 1 Pandit Nehru Rd, POB 32111, 10101 Lusaka; tel. (1) 253159; fax (1) 254118; High Commissioner YOGESH K. GUPTA.

Zimbabwe: 12 Natal Rd, Belgravia, POB 4620, Harare; tel. (4) 795955; fax (4) 722324; e-mail hci@samara.co.zw; Ambassador Ajit Kumar.

DIPLOMATIC MISSIONS OF INDONESIA

United Nations: 325 East 38th St, New York, NY 10016; tel. (212) 972-8333; fax (212) 972-9780; e-mail ptri@indonesiamission-ny.org; internet www .indonesiamission-ny.org; Permanent Representative RADEN MOHAMMAD MARTY MULIANA NATALEGAWA.

Afghanistan: Interior Ministry St, Shar-i-Nau, POB 532, Kabul; tel. (20) 2201066; e-mail kabul.kbri@deplu.go.id; internet www.kbri-kabul.go.id; Chargé d'affaires Brig.-Gen. Erman Hidayat.

Algeria: BP 62, 17 chemin Abd al-Kader Gadouche, 16070 el-Mouradia, Algiers; tel. (21) 69-49-15; fax (21) 69-49-16; e-mail kbrial@wissal.dz; Ambassador YULI MUMPUNI WIDARSO.

Argentina: Mariscal Ramón Castilla 2901, C1425DZE Buenos Aires; tel. (11) 4807-2211; fax (11) 4802-4448; e-mail emindo@tournet.com.ar; internet www.indonesianembassy.org.ar; Ambassador Sunten Zephyrimus Manurung.

Australia: 8 Darwin Ave, Yarralumla, ACT 2600; tel. (2) 6250-8600; fax (2) 6273-6017; internet www.kbri-canberra.org.au; Ambassador MOHAMMAD HAMZAH THAYEB.

Austria: Gustav-Tschermak-Gasse 5–7, 1180 Vienna; tel. (1) 479-23-0; fax (1) 479-05-57; e-mail unitkom@kbriwina.at; internet www.kbriwina.at; Ambassador Triyono Wibowo.

Bangladesh: Plot No. 14, Rd 53, Gulshan 2, Dhaka 1212; tel. (2) 9881640; fax (2) 8810993; e-mail indhaka@bangla.net; internet www.jakarta-dhaka.com; Ambassador WARMAS HASAN SAPUTRA.

Belgium: 294 ave de Tervueren, 1150 Brussels; tel. (2) 771-20-14; fax (2) 772-82-10; e-mail kbribxl@brutele.be; internet www.indonesian-embassy.be; AmbassadorNadjib Riphat Kesoema.

Brazil: SES, Av. das Nações, Quadra 805, Lote 20, 70479-900 Brasília, DF; tel. (61) 3443-8800; fax (61) 3443-6732; e-mail kbribrasilia@persocom.com .br; internet www.indonesia-brasil.org.br; Ambassador BALI MONIAGA.

Brunei: Simpang 528, Lot 4498, Kampong Sungai Hanching Baru, Jalan Muara, Bandar Seri Begawan BC 2115; tel. 2330180; fax 2330646; e-mail kbribsb@brunet.bn; Ambassador Herijanto Soeprapto.

Bulgaria: 1087 Sofia, bul. Simeonovsko shose 53/4; tel. (2) 962-52-40; fax (2) 962-58-42; e-mail kbrisofia@indonesia.bg; internet www.indonesia.bg; Ambassador R. BROTO UTOMO.

Cambodia: 90 blvd Norodom, Phnom-Penh; tel. (23) 216148; fax (23) 216571; e-mail kukppenh@bigpond.com.kh; Ambassador Nurrachman Oerip.

Canada: 55 Parkdale Ave, Ottawa, ON K1Y 1E5; tel. (613) 724-1100; fax (613) 724-1105; e-mail info@indonesia-ottawa.org; internet www.indonesia -ottawa.org; Ambassador DJOKO HARDONO.

Chile: Nueva Costanera 3318, Vitacura, Santiago; tel. (2) 207-6266; fax (2) 207-9901; e-mail kbristgo@mi-mail.cl; Ambassador Ibrahim Ambong.

China, People's Republic: 4 Dong Zhi Men Wai Dajie, Beijing 100600; tel. (10) 65325486; fax (10) 65325368; e-mail kombei@public3.bta.net.cn; internet www.indonesianembassy-china.com; AmbassadorSUDRADJAT.

Colombia: Carrera 9, No 76-27, Bogotá, DC; tel. (1) 217-6738; fax (1) 326-2165; e-mail info@indonesiabogota.org.co; internet www.indonesiabogota .org.co; Chargé d'affaires a.i. Meity Suhariah Ichwanu.

Cuba: Avda 5, No 1607, esq. 18, Miramar, Havana; tel. (7) 204-9618; fax (7) 204-9617; e-mail indonhav@ceniai.inf.cu; internet www.indohav.cu; Chargé d'affaires a.i. YOEL ROHROHMANA.

Czech Republic: Nad Budánkami II/7, 150 21 Prague 5; tel. 257214388; fax 257212105; e-mail informace@indonesian-embassy.cz; internet www .indonesian-embassy.cz; Ambassador Salim Said.

Denmark: Ørehøj Allé 1, 2900 Hellerup; tel. 39-62-44-22; fax 39-62-44-83; e-mail unitkomkph@kbricph.dk; internet www.kbricph.dk; Ambassador ABDUL RAHMAN SALEH.

Egypt: POB 1661, 13 Sharia Aicha at-Taimouria, Cairo (Garden City); tel. (2) 7947200; fax (2) 7962495; e-mail pwkcairo@access.com.eg; Ambassador Dr Bachtiar Aly.

Ethiopia: Mekanisa Rd, POB 1004, Addis Ababa; tel. (11) 3712104; fax (11) 3710873; e-mail indoeth@hotmail.com; Ambassador DEDDY SUDARMAN.

Finland: Kuusisaarentie 3, 00340 Helsinki; tel. (9) 4470370; fax (9) 4582882; e-mail info@indonesian-embassy.fi; internet www.indonesian-embassy.fi; Ambassador Iris Indira Murti.

France: 47–49 rue Cortambert, 75016 Paris; tel. 1-45-03-07-60; fax 1-45-04-50-32; e-mail kasubpen@amb-indonesie.fr; internet www.amb-indonesie.fr; Ambassador ARIZAL EFFENDI.

Germany: Lehrter Str. 16–17, 10557 Berlin; tel. (30) 478070; fax (30) 44737142; internet www.botschaft-indonesien.de; Ambassador Makmur Widodo.

Greece: Odos Marathonodromou 99, Palaio Psychiko, 154 52 Athens; tel. (210) 6742345; fax (210) 6756955; Ambassador FAISHA H. SOEFTENDY.

Hungary: 1068 Budapest, Városligeti fasor 26; tel. (1) 413-3800; fax (1) 322-8669; e-mail kbribud@indonesia.hu; internet www.indonesia.hu; Ambassador Sapartini Singgih Kuntjoro Jakti.

India: 50A Kautilya Marg, Chanakyapuri, New Delhi 110 021; tel. (11) 26118642; fax (11) 26874402; e-mail iembassy@giasdl01.vsnl.net.in; internet www.indonesianembassy.org.in; Chargé d'affaires a.i. RIZALI W. INDRAKESUMA.

Iran: POB 11365-4564, Ghaem Magham Farahani Ave, No. 210, Tehran; tel. (21) 88716865; fax (21) 88718822; e-mail kbritehran@safineh.net; internet www.indonesian-embassy.ir; Chargé d'affaires a.i. Sugeng Wahono.

Italy: Via Campania 55, 00187 Roma; tel. (06) 4200911; fax (06) 4880280; e-mail indorom@uni.net; internet www.indonesianembassy.it; Ambassador SUSANTO SUTOYO.

Japan: 5-2-9, Higashi Gotanda, Shinagawa-ku, Tokyo 141-0022; tel. (3) 3441-4201; fax (3) 3447-1697; e-mail info@indonesian-embassy.or.jp; internet www.indonesian-embassy.or.jp; Ambassador Jusuf Anwar.

Jordan: POB 811784, Amman 11181; tel. (6) 5538911; fax (6) 5528380; e-mail amman96@go.com.jo; Ambassador ABD AR-RAHMAN SABRAN.

Kenya: Menengai Rd, Upper Hill, POB 48868, Nairobi; tel. (20) 2714196; fax (20) 2713475; e-mail indonbi@indonesia.or.ke; internet www.indonesia.or .ke; Ambassador Djismun Kasri.

Korea, Democratic People's Republic: 5 Foreigners' Bldg, Munsudong, Taedongkang District, Pyongyang; tel. (2) 3827439; fax (2) 3817620; e-mail kompyg2@public2.bta.net.cn; AmbassadorDAULAT HOTMA AUDISON PASSARIBU.

Korea, Republic: 55, Yeouido-dong, Yeongdeungpo-gu, Seoul 150-010; tel. (2) 783-5675; fax (2) 780-4280; e-mail komsel@soback.kornet.nm.kr; internet www.indonesiaseoul.org; Ambassador Jakob Tobing.

Kuwait: POB 21500, 13076 Safat, Kaifan, Block 6, Al-Andalus St, House 29, Kuwait City; tel. 4839927; fax 4819250; e-mail unitkom@kbrikuwait.org; internet www.kbrikuwait.org; Ambassador SUDIRMAN FAISAL ISMAIL.

Laos: ave Phone Keng, BP 277, Vientiane; tel. (21) 413909; fax (21) 214828; e-mail kbrivte@laotel.com; Ambassador Sutjiptorahhardjo Donokusumo.

Lebanon: POB 40007, ave Palais Presidential, rue 68, Secteur 3, Baabda, Beirut; tel. (5) 924682; fax (5) 924678; e-mail indobey@cyberia.net.lb; internet www.welcome.to/indobey; Ambassador SYAM SOEMANAGARA.

Libya: POB 5921, Tripoli; tel. (21) 4842067; fax (21) 4842069; e-mail indonesia@bsisp.net; Ambassador Achmad Nawawi Hasbi.

Madagascar: 26–28 rue Patrice Lumumba, BP 3969, 101 Antananarivo; tel. (20) 2224915; fax (20) 2232857; Chargé d'affaires a.i. SLAMET SUYATA SASTRAMIHARDZA.

Malaysia: 233 Jalan Tun Razak, POB 10889, 50400 Kuala Lumpur; tel. (3) 21452011; fax (3) 21417908; e-mail dubresi_kul@kbrikl.org.my; internet www.kbrikl.org.my; Chargé d'affaires a.i. Tatang B. Razak.

Mexico: Julio Verne 27, Col. Polanco, Del. Miguel Hidalgo, 11560 México, DF; tel. (55) 5280-6363; fax (55) 5280-7062; e-mail kbrimex@prodigy.net.mx; Ambassador ANDUNG ABDULLAH NITIMIHARDJA.

Morocco: 63 rue Béni Boufrah, km 5.9, route des Zaêrs, BP 576, 10105 Rabat; tel. (3) 7757860; fax (3) 7757859; e-mail kbrirabat@iam.net.ma; internet www.indonesie.ma; Ambassador Sjachwien Adenan.

Myanmar: 100 Pyidaungsu Yeiktha Rd, POB 1401, Yangon; tel. (1) 254465; fax (1) 254468; e-mail kbriygn@indosat.net.id; internet www.indonesia.com.mm; Ambassador WYOSO PROJOWARSITO.

Namibia: 103 Nelson Mandela Ave, POB 20691, Windhoek; tel. (61) 2851000; fax (61) 2851231; e-mail kbri@iafrica.com.na; internet www.indonesiawindhoek.org; Ambassador (vacant).

Netherlands: Tobias Asserlaan 8, 2517 KC The Hague; tel. (70) 3108100; fax (70) 3643331; e-mail bidpen@indonesia.nl; internet www.indonesia.nl; Ambassador JUNUS EFFENDI HABIBIE.

New Zealand: 70 Glen Road, Kelburn, POB 3543, Wellington; tel. (4) 475-8698; fax (4) 475-9374; e-mail kbriwell@ihug.co.nz; internet www.indonesianembassy.org.nz; Ambassador Amris Hassan.

Nigeria: 5 Anifowoshe St, Victoria Island, POB 3473, Marina, Lagos; tel. (1) 2614601; fax (1) 2613301; e-mail indlgs@infoweb.abs.net; Ambassador SUSANTO ISMODIRDJO.

Norway: Fritznersgt. 12, 0244 Oslo; tel. 22-12-51-30; fax 22-12-51-31; e-mail kbrioslo@online.no; internet www.indonesia-oslo.no; Ambassador Retno L. P. Marsudi.

Pakistan: St 5, G-5/4, Diplomatic Enclave 1, POB 1019, Islamabad; tel. (51) 2832017; fax (51) 2832013; e-mail unitkom@kbri-islamabad.go.id; internet www.kbri-islamabad.go.id; Ambassador ANWAR SANTOSO.

Papua New Guinea: 1-2/410 Kiroki St, Sir John Guise Dr., Waigani, NCD; tel. 3253116; fax 3253544; e-mail kbripom@daltron.com.pg; internet www.kbripng.gov.pg; Ambassador Bom Soejanto.

Peru: Avda Las Flores 334, San Isidro, Lima; tel. (1) 2220308; fax (1) 2222684; e-mail kbrilima@indonesia-peru.org.pe; internet www.indonesia-peru.org.pe; Ambassador I GDE DJELANTIK.

Philippines: 185 Salcedo St, Legaspi Village, Makati City, Metro Manila; tel. (2) 8925061; fax (2) 8925878; e-mail bidpen_manila@yahoo.com; internet www.kbrimanila.org.ph; Ambassador Dr Irzan Tanjung.

Poland: 03-903 Warsaw, ul. Estońska 3, POB 33; tel. (22) 6175179; fax (22) 6178451; e-mail info@indonesianembassy.pl; internet www.indonesianembassy.pl; Ambassador HAZAIRIN POHAN.

Portugal: Rua Miguel Lupi 12, 1°, 1249-080 Lisbon; tel. (21) 3932070; fax (21) 3932079; e-mail info@indonesianembassy-lisbon.org; internet www.indonesianembassy-lisbon.org; Ambassador Francisco Xavier Lopes da Cruz.

Qatar: POB 22375, Al-Maheed St, Doha; tel. 4657945; fax 4657610; e-mail inemb@qatar.net.qa; internet www.kbridoha.com; Ambassador ROZY MUNIR.

Romania: 010488 Bucharest 1, Str. Gina Patrichi 10; tel. (21) 3120742; fax (21) 3120214; e-mail indobuch@indonezia.ro; Ambassador Nuni Turnijati Djoko.

Russian Federation: 109017 Moscow, ul. Novokuznetskaya 12; tel. (495) 951-95-50; fax (495) 230-64-31; e-mail kbrimos@online.ru; internet www.kbrimoskow.org; Ambassador (vacant).

Saudi Arabia: POB 94343, Riyadh 11693; tel. (1) 488-2800; fax (1) 488-2966; e-mail contact@kbri-riyadh.org.sa; internet www.kbri-riyadh.org.sa; Ambassador Dr Ismail Suny.

Senegal: ave Cheikh Anta Diop, BP 5859, Dakar; tel. 33-825-7316; fax 33-825-5896; e-mail kbri@sentoo.sn; internet www.indonesia-senegal.org; Ambassador AHZAM BAHDARI RAZIF.

Serbia: 11000 Belgrade, bul. Kneza Aleksandra Karađorđevića 18; tel. (11) 3674062; fax (11) 3672984; e-mail kombeojo@eunet.yu; Ambassador Muhammad Abduh Dalimunthe.

Singapore: 7 Chatsworth Rd, Singapore 249761; tel. 67377422; fax 67375037; e-mail info@kbrisingapura.com; internet www.kbrisingapura.com; AmbassadorWARDANA.

Slovakia: Mudroňova 51, 811 03 Bratislava; tel. (2) 5441-9886; fax (2) 5441-9890; e-mail indonesia@indonesia.sk; internet www.indonesia.sk; Ambassador Lutfi Rauf.

South Africa: 949 Schoeman St, Arcadia, Pretoria 0082; POB 13155, Hatfield, Pretoria 0028; tel. (12) 3423350; fax (12) 3423369; e-mail fpanggabean@indonesia-pretoria.org.za; internet www.indonesia-pretoria.org.za; 1995Ambassador SUGENG RAHARDJO.

Spain: Agastia 65, 28043 Madrid; tel. (91) 4130294; fax (91) 4138994; e-mail kbri@embajadadeindonesia.es; internet www.embajadadeindonesia.es; Ambassador Slamet Santoso Mustafa.

Sri Lanka: 400/50 Sarana Rd, off Bauddhaloka Mawatha, Colombo 7; tel. (11) 2674337; fax (11) 2678668; e-mail pensosbud@kbrilk.org; internet www.kbrilk.org; Chargé d'affaires a.i. SUHARDI CONDROSENTONO.

Sudan: St 60, 84, Block 12, ar-Riyadh, POB 13374, Khartoum; tel. (183) 225106; fax (183) 225528; e-mail kbri_khartoum@sudanmail.com; Ambassador Syamsudin Yahya.

Suriname: Van Brussellaan 3, Uitvlugt, POB 157, Paramaribo; tel. 431230; fax 498234; e-mail indonemb@sr.net; Ambassador SUPRIJANTO MUHADI.

Sweden: Sysslomansgt. 18/I, POB 12520, 102 29 Stockholm; tel. (8) 545-55-880; fax (8) 650-87-50; e-mail kbri@indonesiskaambassaden.se; internet www.indonesiskaambassaden.se; Ambassador Linggawaty Hakim.

Switzerland: Elfenauweg 51, 3006 Bern; tel. 313520983; fax 313516765; e-mail kbribern@bgb.ch; internet www.indonesia-bern.org; Ambassador LUCIA HELWINDA RUSTAM.

Syria: BP 3530, Immeuble 26, Bloc 270a, 132 rue Al-Madina al-Munawar, Mezzeh Est, Damascus; tel. (11) 6119630; fax (11) 6119632; e-mail kbridams@net.sy; internet kbri-damascus.go.id; Ambassador Muhammad Basyouni.

Tanzania: 299 Ali Hassan Mwinyi Rd, POB 572, Dar es Salaam; tel. (22) 2119119; fax (22) 2115849; e-mail kbridsm@raha.com; Ambassador TRIJONO MARJONO.

Thailand: 600–602 Thanon Phetchaburi, Ratchathewi, Bangkok 10400; tel. (2) 252-3135; fax (2) 255-1267; e-mail kukbkk@ksc11.th.com; internet www.kbri-bangkok.com; Ambassador Ibrahim Yusuf.

Timor-Leste: Farol, Palapaco, POB 207, Dili; tel. 3317107; fax 3312332; e-mail kukridil@hotmail.com; internet www.kbridili.org; Ambassador AHMED BEY SOFWAN.

Tunisia: BP 63, al-Menzah, 1004 Tunis; tel. (71) 860-377; fax (71) 861-758; e-mail kbritun@gnet.tn; Ambassador Hertomo Reksodiputro.

Turkey: Abdullah Cevdet Sok. 10, 06680 Çankaya, Ankara; tel. (312) 4382190; fax (312) 4382193; e-mail indoank@indoank.org; Ambassador AWANG BAHRIN.

Ukraine: 04107 Kyiv, vul. Nahirna 27b; tel. (44) 206-54-46; fax (44) 206-54-40; e-mail kbri@indo.ru.kiev.ua; internet www.kbri.kiev.ua; Ambassador Albertus Emanuel Alexander Laturiuw.

United Arab Emirates: POB 7256, Abu Dhabi; tel. (2) 4454448; fax (2) 4455453; e-mail indoemb@emirates.net.ae; internet www.indoemb.org/kbri; Chargé d'affaires a.i. JOKO SANTOSO.

United Kingdom: 38 Grosvenor Sq., London, W1X 2HW; tel. (20) 7499-7661; fax (20) 7491-4993; e-mail kbri@btconnect.com; internet www.indonesianembassy.org.uk; Ambassador Yuri Octavian Thamrin.

United States of America: 2020 Massachusetts Ave, NW, Washington, DC 20036-1084; tel. (202) 775-5200; fax (202) 775-5256; e-mail information@embassyofindonesia.org; internet www.embassyofindonesia.org; Ambassador SUDJADNAN PARNOHADININGRAT.

Uzbekistan: 100000 Tashkent, Ya. G'ulomov ko'ch. 73; tel. (71) 132-02-36; fax (71) 120-65-40; e-mail tashkent@indonesia.embassy.uz; internet www .indonesia.embassy.uz; Ambassador Sjahril Sabarudin.

Vatican City: Piazzale Roberto Ardigò 42, 00142 Rome, Italy; tel. (06) 5940441; fax (06) 5417934; e-mail indonesia.vat@agora.stm.it; Ambassador SUPRAPTO MARTOSEMOTO.

Venezuela: Quinta La Trinidad, Avda El Paseo, Prados del Este, Apdo 80807, Caracas 1080; tel. (212) 976-2725; fax (212) 976-0550; e-mail kbri@telcel.net .ve; Ambassador Alfred T. Palembangan.

Viet Nam: 50 Ngo Quyen, Hanoi; tel. (4) 8253353; fax (4) 8259274; e-mail komhan@hn.vnn.vn; internet www.indonesia-hanoi.org.vn; Ambassador ARTAULI RATNA MENARA PANGGABEAN TOBING.

Yemen: POB 19873, Bldg 16, Beirut St, Haddah, San'a; tel. (1) 414633; fax (1) 412956; e-mail indosan@y.net.ye; Ambassador Kemas Fachruddin.

Zimbabwe: 3 Duthie Ave, Belgravia, POB CY 69 Causeway, Harare; tel. (4) 251799; fax (4) 796587; e-mail indohar@ecoweb.co.zw; internet www .indonesia-harare.org; Ambassador HUPUDIO SUPARDI.

DIPLOMATIC MISSIONS OF IRAN

United Nations: 622 Third Ave, 34th Floor, New York, NY 10017; tel. (212) 687-2020; fax (212) 867-7086; e-mail iran@un.int; internet www.un.int/iran; Permanent Representative Mohammad Khazaee.

Afghanistan: Charahi Shir Pur, Kabul; tel. (20) 2101393; Ambassador FADA-HOSSEIN MALEKI.

Albania: Rruga Mustafa Matohiti 20, Tirana; tel. (4) 255038; fax (4) 230409; Ambassador Habibollah Biazar.

Argentina: Avda Figueroa Alcorta 3229, CP 396, C1425CKL Buenos Aires; tel. (11) 4802-1470; fax (11) 4805-4409; e-mail embajadairan@fibertel.com .ar; Chargé d'affaires a.i. MOHSEN BAHARVAND.

Armenia: Yerevan, Budaghian St 1; tel. (10) 28-04-57; fax (10) 23-00-52; e-mail info@iranembassy.am; internet www.iranembassy.am; Ambassador Alireza Haghighian.

Australia: POB 705, Mawson, ACT 2607; tel. (2) 6290-2427; fax (2) 6290-2431; e-mail ambassador@iranembassy.org.au; internet www.iranembassy .org.au; Ambassador MAHMOUD MOVAHHEDI.

Austria: Strohgasse 14c, 1030 Vienna; tel. (1) 712-26-50; fax (1) 713-57-33; e-mail public@iranembassy-wien.at; Chargé d'affaires a.i. Ali Meshkin Mehr.

Azerbaijan: 1000 Baku, B. Sadarov küç. 4; tel. (12) 492-64-53; fax (12) 498-07-33; e-mail iranemb@azerin.com; Ambassador NASIR HAMIDI ZARE.

Bahrain: POB 26365, Building 1034, Rd 3221, Area 332, Mahooz, Manama; tel. 17722880; fax 17722101; Chargé d'affaires Reza Honarvar Nazari.

Bangladesh: House No. 7, Rd 6, Baridhara Model Town, Dhaka; tel. (2) 8825896; fax (2) 8828780; e-mail dacembiran@yahoo.com; Ambassador HASSAN FARAZANDEH.

Belarus: 220049 Minsk, vul. Suvorava 2; tel. (17) 207-66-99; fax (17) 207-61-99; Ambassador Abdulhamid Fekri.

Belgium: 15 ave F. D. Roosevelt, 1050 Brussels; tel. (2) 627-03-50; fax (2) 762-39-15; e-mail secretariat@iranebassy.be; internet www.iranembassy.be; Ambassador ALIASGHAR KHAJI.

Bosnia and Herzegovina: 71000 Sarajevo, Obala Maka Dizdara 6; tel. (33) 650210; fax (33) 663910; e-mail iries1@bih.net.ba; Ambassador Mohammed Reza Morshed Zadeh.

Brazil: SES, Av. das Nações, Quadra 809, Lote 31, 70421-900 Brasília, DF; tel. (61) 3242-5733; fax (61) 3224-9640; e-mail webiran@webiran.org.br; internet www.webiran.org.br; Ambassador (vacant).

Brunei: 400 Kampong Anggerek Desa, Berakas, Bandar Seri Begawan BB 3717; tel. 2330020; fax 2330021; Ambassador Abolfazl Khazaei Tarshizi.

Bulgaria: 1087 Sofia, ul. V. Levski 77; tel. (2) 987-61-73; fax (2) 980-22-60; Ambassador FEREIDUN HAKBIN.

Canada: 245 Metcalfe St, Ottawa, ON K2P 2K2; tel. (613) 235-4726; fax (613) 232-5712; e-mail iranemb@salamiran.org; internet www.salamiran.org; Chargé d'affaires a.i. Seyed Mahdi Mohebi.

China, People's Republic: 13 Dong Liu Jie, San Li Tun, Beijing 100600; tel. (10) 65322040; fax (10) 65321403; Ambassador JAVAD MANSOURI.

Colombia: Calle 96, No 11a-16/20, Apdo 93854, Bogotá, DC; tel. (1) 610-3064; fax (1) 610-2556; e-mail embajadairan@andinet.com.co; Ambassador Abdoulazim Hasheminik.

Croatia: 10000 Zagreb, Pantovčak 125C; tel. (1) 4578981; fax (1) 4578987; Ambassador MOHAMMAD HASSAN FADAIFARD.

Cuba: Avda 5, No 3002, esq. 30, Miramar, Havana; tel. (7) 204-2675; fax (7) 204-2770; e-mail embairan@ip.etecsa.cu; Ambassador Mostafa Alaei.

Cyprus: POB 8145, 42 Armenias St, Akropolis, Nicosia; tel. 22314459; fax 22315446; e-mail iranemb@cytanet.com.cy; Ambassador DR SAYED REZA HADJ-ZARGARBASHI.

Czech Republic: Na Zátorce 18, 160 00 Prague 6; tel. 220570454; fax 233380255; e-mail embircz@volny.cz; Chargé d'affaires a.i. Majid Nili Ahmadabadi.

Denmark: Svanemøllevej 48, 2100 Copenhagen Ø; tel. 39-16-00-03; fax 39-16-00-75; e-mail info@iran-embassy.dk; internet www.iran-embassy.dk; Ambassador MUHAMMAD REZA MORSHEDZADEH.

Eritrea: Asmara; Ambassador Reza Ameri.

Ethiopia: 317–318 Jimma Rd, POB 1144, Addis Ababa; tel. (11) 3710037; fax (11) 3712299; internet www.iranembassy-addis.net; Ambassador ABABA KIUMARS FOTOUHI QIYAM.

Finland: Kulosaarentie 9, 00570 Helsinki; tel. (9) 6869240; fax (9) 68692410; e-mail embassy@iran.fi; internet www.iran.fi; Ambassador Dr Reza Nazarahari.

France: 4 ave d'Iéna, 75116 Paris; tel. 1-40-69-79-00; fax 1-40-70-01-57; e-mail contact@amb-iran.fr; internet www.amb-iran.fr; Ambassador DR ALI AHANI.

Georgia: 0160 Tbilisi, Zovreti 16; tel. (32) 98-69-90; fax (32) 98-69-93; e-mail iranemb@caucasus.net; Ambassador Mojtaba Damirchilou.

Germany: Podbielskiallee 65–67, 14195 Berlin; tel. (30) 843530; fax (30) 54353535; e-mail iran.botschaft@t-online.de; internet berlin.mfa.gov.ir; Ambassador MUHAMMAD MEHDI AKHOUNDZADEH BASTI.

Ghana: 12 Arkusah St, Airport Residential Area, POB 12673, Accra-North; tel. (21) 774474; fax (21) 777043; Ambassador Valiollah Mohammadi Nasrabadi.

Greece: Odos Kalari 16, Palaio Psychiko, 154 52 Athens; tel. (210) 6471436; fax (210) 6477945; e-mail irembatn@compulik.gr; Ambassador MEHDI MOHTASHAMI.

Guinea: Donka, Cité Ministerielle, Commune de Dixinn, BP 310, Conakry; tel. 30-22-01-97; fax 30-46-56-38; e-mail ambiran_guinea@yahoo.com; Ambassador Bakhtiar Asadzadeh Sheikhjani.

Hungary: 1143 Budapest, Stefánia u. 97; tel. (1) 460-9260; fax (1) 460-9430; e-mail embiran@iranembassy.hu; internet www.iranembassy.hu; Ambassador ABULFAZ RAHNAMA HEZAVEI.

India: 5 Barakhamba Road, New Delhi 110 001; tel. (11) 23329600; fax (11) 23325493; e-mail info@iran-embassy.org.in; internet www.iran-embassy.org .in; Ambassador Sayed Mahdi Nabizadeh.

Indonesia: Jalan Hos Cokroaminoto 110, Menteng, Jakarta Pusat 10310; tel. (21) 31931378; fax (21) 3107860; e-mail irembjkt@indo.net.id; internet www .iranembassy.or.id; Ambassador BEHROUZ KAMALVANDI.

Iraq: POB 39095, Salehiya, Karadeh Maryam, Baghdad; tel. (1) 884-3033; fax (1) 537-5636; Ambassador Hassan Kazemi Qomi.

Ireland: 72 Mount Merrion Ave, Blackrock, Co Dublin; tel. (1) 2880252; fax (1) 2834246; e-mail iranemb@indigo.ie; Ambassador EBRAHIM RAHIMPOUR.

Italy: Via Nomentana 361, 00162 Roma; tel. (06) 86328485; fax (06) 86328492; e-mail info@iranembassy.it; internet www.iranembassy.it; Ambassador Abolfazl Zohrevand.

Japan: 3-13-9, Minami Azabu, Minato-ku, Tokyo 106-0047; tel. (3) 3446-8011; fax (3) 3446-9002; e-mail sjei@gol.com; internet www.iranembassyjp .com; Ambassador ABBAS ARAQCHI.

Jordan: POB 173, Amman 11118; tel. (6) 4641281; fax (6) 4641383; e-mail pub -rel@iranembassyjordan.org; internet www.iranembassyjordan.org; Ambassador Muhammad Irani.

Kazakhstan: 050000 Almaty, ul. Luganskogo 31–33; tel. (727) 254-19-74; fax (7272) 254-27-54; e-mail iranembassy@itte.kz; Ambassador RAMIN MEHMAN PARAST.

Kenya: Dennis Pritt Rd, POB 49170, Nairobi; tel. (20) 711257; fax (20) 339936; Ambassador Mohammad Raesi.

Korea, Democratic People's Republic: Munhungdong, Monsu St, Taedong-kang District, Pyongyang; tel. (2) 3817492; fax (2) 3817612; Ambassador MORTEZA MORADIAN.

Korea, Republic: 726-126, Hannam-dong, Yeongsan-gu, Seoul; tel. (2) 793-7751; fax (2) 792-7052; e-mail iranemb@hotmail.com; Ambassador Mohammad Reza Bakhtiari.

Kuwait: POB 4686, 13047 Safat, Daiyah, Embassies Area, Block B, Kuwait City; tel. 2560694; fax 2529868; e-mail iranebassy@hotmail.com; Ambassador ALI JANNATI.

Kyrgyzstan: 720026 Bishkek, Razzakova 36; tel. (312) 62-49-17; fax (312) 22-74-98; e-mail sefabish@amil.elcat.gg; Ambassador Muhammad Reza Sabouri.

Lebanon: POB 5030, Bir Hassan, Beirut; tel. (1) 821224; fax (1) 821230; Ambassador MUHAMMAD-REZA RAOUF SHEIBANI.

Libya: POB 6185, Tripoli; tel. (21) 3609552; fax (21) 3611674; e-mail iran_em_tripoli@hotmail.com; Ambassador Muhammad Menhaj.

Madagascar: route Circulaire, Lot II L43 ter, Ankadivato, 101 Antananarivo; tel. (20) 2228639; fax (20) 2222298; Ambassador ABDOL RAHIM HOMATASH.

Malaysia: 1 Lorong U Thant Satu, off Jalan U Thant, 55000 Kuala Lumpur; tel. (3) 42514824; fax (3) 42562904; e-mail ir_emb@tm.net.my; internet www.iranembassy.com.my; Ambassador Mahdi Khandaghabadi.

Mali: ave al-Quds, Hippodrome, BP 2136, Bamako; tel. 221-76-38; fax 221-07-31; Ambassador MOHAMMED SOLEIMANI.

Mexico: Paseo de la Reforma 2350, Col. Lomas Altas, Del. Miguel Hidalgo, 11950 México, DF; tel. (55) 9172-2691; fax (55) 9172-2694; e-mail iranembmex@hotmail.com; Ambassador Mohammad Hassan Ghadiri Abyaneh.

Morocco: ave Imam Malik, BP 490, 10001 Rabat; tel. (3) 7752167; fax (3) 7659118; e-mail iranembassy@iam.net.ma; Ambassador WAHID AHMADI.

Netherlands: Duinweg 20–22, 2585 JX The Hague; tel. (70) 3548483; fax (70) 3503224; e-mail info@iranembassy.nl; internet www.iranianembassy.nl; Ambassador Bozorgmehr Ziaran.

New Zealand: POB 14733, Kilbirnie, Wellington; tel. (4) 386-2983; fax (4) 386-3065; e-mail info@iranembassy.org.nz; internet www.iranembassy.org.nz; Ambassador MORTEZA RAHMANI-MOVAHED.

Nicaragua: Managua; Ambassador Akbar Esmaeil Pour.

Niger: 11 rue de la Présidence, BP 10543, Niamey; tel. 20-72-21-98; fax 20-72-28-10; Ambassador MOHAMMAD AMIN NEJAD.

Nigeria: 2 Udi St, Maitama, Abuja; tel. (1) 5238048; fax (1) 5237785; e-mail irembassy_abuja@yahoo.com; Ambassador Jawad Torkabadi.

Norway: Drammensvn 88E, 0244 Oslo; tel. 23-27-29-60; fax 22-55-49-19; e-mail iremb@iran-embassy-oslo.no; internet www.iran-embassy-oslo.no; Ambassador ABDUL REZA FARAJI RAD.

Oman: Diplomatic Area, Jamiat ad-Dowal al-Arabiya St, POB 3155, Ruwi 112; tel. 24696944; fax 24696888; e-mail iranembassy@hotmail.com; internet www.iranembassy.gov.om; Ambassador Morteza Rahimi.

Pakistan: Plot No. 222, 238, St 2, F-5/1, Islamabad; tel. (51) 2276270; fax (51) 2824839; Ambassador MASHALLAH SHAKERI.

Philippines: 2224 Paraiso St, cnr Pasay Rd, Dasmariñas Village, Makati City, Metro Manila; tel. (2) 8884757; fax (2) 8884777; Ambassador Ali Mojtaba Rouzbehani.

Poland: 03-928 Warsaw, ul. Królowej Aldony 22; tel. (22) 6171585; fax (22) 6178452; e-mail iranemb@iranemb.warsaw.pl; internet www.iranemb.warsaw.pl; Ambassador HADI FARAJVAND.

Portugal: Rua do Alto do Duque 49, 1400-009 Lisbon; tel. (21) 3010871; fax (21) 3010777; e-mail iranembassy@emb-irao.pt; internet www.emb-irao.pt; Ambassador Muhammad Taheri.

Qatar: POB 1633, Doha; tel. 4835300; fax 4831665; e-mail irembsdoha@yahoo.com; internet www.iranembassy.org.qa; Ambassador MUHAMMAD TAHER RABBANI.

Romania: 010633 Bucharest, Bd. Lascar Catargiu 39, Sector 1; tel. (21) 3120495; fax (21) 3120496; e-mail office@iranembassy.ro; internet www.iranembassy.ro; Ambassador Hamid Reza Arshadi.

Russian Federation: 117292 Moscow, Pokrovskii bulv. 7; tel. (495) 917-72-82; fax (495) 230-28-97; Ambassador GHOLMREZA SHAFEHEE.

Saudi Arabia: POB 94394, Riyadh 11693; tel. (1) 488-1916; fax (1) 488-1890; Ambassador Sayed Muhammad Hosseini.

Senegal: rue AX8, point E, BP 735, Dakar; tel. 33-825-2528; fax 33-824-2314; e-mail ambiiran@telecomplus.sn; Ambassador MOHAMMAD HOSEINI.

Serbia: 11000 Belgrade, Ljutice Bogdana 40; tel. (11) 3674360; fax (11) 3674363; Ambassador Seyed Mir Heydari.

Somalia: Via al-Mukarah, POB 1166, Mogadishu; tel. (1) 80881; .

South Africa: 1002 Schoeman St, Hatfield, Pretoria 0083; POB 12546, Hatfield 0083; tel. (12) 3425880; fax (12) 3421878; internet www.iranembassy.org.za; Ambassador Asghar Ebrahimi Asl.

Spain: Jerez 5, Villa El Altozano, Chamartín, 28016 Madrid; tel. (91) 3450112; fax (91) 3451190; e-mail embiran@hotmail.com; Ambassador SEYED DAVOUD MOHSENI SALEHI MONFARED.

Sri Lanka: 17 Bullers Lane, Colombo 7; tel. (11) 2501137; fax (11) 2502691; e-mail emb_colombo@mfa.gov.ir; Ambassador Behnam Behruz.

Sudan: Sq. 15, House No. 4, Mogran, POB 10229, Khartoum; tel. (183) 781490; fax (183) 778668; e-mail iranemb_khartoum@mfa.gov.ir; Ambassador Reza Ameri.

Sweden: Västra Yttringe Gård, Elfviksvägen, POB 6031, 181 06 Lidingö; tel. (8) 636-36-77; fax (8) 636-36-13; internet www.iran.se; Ambassador Hassan Ghashghavi.

Switzerland: Thunstr. 68, 3006 Bern; tel. 313510801; fax 313515652; e-mail secretariat@iranembassy.ch; internet www.iranembassy.ch; Ambassador KEYVAN IMANI.

Syria: BP 2691, Autostrade Mezzeh, nr ar-Razi Hospital, Damascus; tel. (11) 6117675; fax (11) 6110997; e-mail iran-dam@net.sy; Ambassador Sayed Ahmad Moussavi.

Tajikistan: 734000 Dushanbe, Kuchai Boxtar 18; tel. (372) 221-00-74; fax (372) 251-00-89; e-mail iran-embassy@tajnet.com; Chargé d'affaires AHMADI AJALLUYON.

Thailand: 215 Thanon Sukhumvit, Soi 49, Klongtan Nua, Wattana, Bangkok 10110; tel. (2) 390-0871; fax (2) 390-0867; e-mail info@iranembassy.or.th; internet www.iranembassy.or.th; Ambassador Majid Bizmark (designate).

Tunisia: 10 rue de Docteur Burnet, Belvédère, 1002 Tunis; tel. (71) 790-084; fax (71) 793-177; Ambassador MUHAMMAD TAGHI MOAYED.

Turkey: Tahran Cad. 10, Kavaklıdere, Ankara; tel. (312) 4682821; fax (312) 4682823; e-mail iranembassy_ankara@hotmail.com; Ambassador Gholamreza Baqeri-Moqaddam (acting).

Turkmenistan: 744000 Aşgabat, ul. 2072 3; tel. (12) 35-02-37; fax (12) 35-05-65; e-mail isroiref@online.tm; Ambassador MOHAMMAD REZA FORQANI.

Uganda: 9 Bandali Rise, Bugolobi, POB 24529, Kampala; tel. (41) 4441689; fax (41) 4443590; Ambassador Aboutalebi Morteza.

Ukraine: 01901 Kyiv, vul. Kruhlouniversytetska 12; tel. (44) 229-44-63; fax (44) 229-32-55; Ambassador SEYYED MUSSA KAZEMI.

United Arab Emirates: POB 4080, Abu Dhabi; tel. (2) 4447618; fax (2) 4448714; e-mail iranemb@eim.ae; internet www.iranembassy.org.ae; Ambassador Hamid Reza Asefi.

United Kingdom: 16 Prince's Gate, London, SW7 1PT; tel. (20) 7225-3000; fax (20) 7589-4440; e-mail info@iran-embassy.org.uk; internet www.iran-embassy.org.uk; Ambassador RASOUL MOVAHEDIAN ATTAR.

United States of America: 'Interests section' in the Embassy of Pakistan, 2209 Wisconsin Ave, NW, Washington DC 20007; tel. (202) 965-4990; fax (202) 965-1073; e-mail requests@daftar.org; internet www.daftar.org; Dir Ali Jazini.

Uruguay: Blvr Artigas 531, Montevideo; tel. (2) 7116657; fax (2) 7116659; e-mail embajada.iran@adinet.com.uy; Ambassador MORTEZA TAFRISHI.

Uzbekistan: 100007 Tashkent, Parkent ko'ch. 20; tel. (71) 268-69-68; fax (71) 120-67-61; e-mail iriemuz@hotmail.com; Ambassador Mohammad Fathali.

Vatican City: Via Bruxelles 57, 00198 Rome, Italy; tel. (06) 8450443; e-mail chalac@libero.it; Ambassador MAHDI FARDI ZADEH.

Venezuela: Quinta Ommat, Calle Kemal Ataturk, Valle Arriba, Apdo 68460, Caracas; tel. (212) 992-3575; fax (212) 992-9989; e-mail embairanve@cantv.net; Ambassador Abdollah Zifan.

Viet Nam: 54 Tran Phu, Ba Dinh District, Hanoi; tel. (4) 8232068; fax (4) 8232120; e-mail iriemb@fpt.vn; Ambassador JAVAD GHAVAM SHAHIDI.

Yemen: POB 1437, Haddah St, San'a; tel. (1) 413552; fax (1) 414139; e-mail iriranemb@y.net.ye; internet www.iranyemen.com.ye; Ambassador Hossein Kamalian.

Zimbabwe: 8 Allan Wilson Ave, Avondale, POB A293, Harare; tel. (4) 726942; Ambassador RASOUL MOMENI.

DIPLOMATIC MISSIONS OF IRAQ

United Nations: 14 East 79th St, New York, NY 10021; tel. (212) 737-4433; fax (212) 772-1794; e-mail missionofiraq@nyc.rr.com; internet www.iraqi-mission.org; Permanent Representative Hamid al-Bayati.

Algeria: 4 rue Abri Arezki, Hydra, Algiers; tel. (21) 69-31-25; fax (21) 69-10-97; e-mail algemb@iraqmofamail.net; Ambassador DR ZIAD KHALID ABDALLI.

Australia: 48 Culgoa Circuit, O'Malley, ACT 2606; tel. (2) 6286-2744; fax (2) 6286-8744; e-mail iraqembcnb@hotmail.com; internet www .iraqembassyaustralia.org; Ambassador Ghanim T. ash-Shibli.

Austria: Johannesgasse 26, Postfach 599, 1010 Vienna; tel. (1) 713-81-95; fax (1) 713-67-20; e-mail office@iraqembassy.at; Ambassador TARIQ AQRAWI.

Azerbaijan: 1000 Baku, Khagani küç. 9; tel. (12) 498-14-47; fax (12) 498-14-37; e-mail iraqyia@azeri.com; Ambassador Arshad Omar Ismayil.

Bahrain: Al-Mahawez, Bldg 396, Rd 3207, Manama; tel. 17741472; fax 17720756; e-mail bhremb@iraqmofamail.net; Ambassador GHASSAN MUHSEN HUSSAIN.

Belgium: 115 ave F. D. Roosevelt, 1050 Brussels; tel. (2) 374-59-92; fax (2) 374-76-15; e-mail ambassade.irak@skynet.be; Ambassador Muhammad Jawan ad-Doreky.

Brazil: SES, Av. das Nações, Quadra 815, Lote 64, 70430-900 Brasília, DF; tel. (61) 3346-2822; fax (61) 3346-7034; e-mail embaixadairaque@terra.com .br; Chargé d'affaires a.i. HUSSEIN ALI ABD AL-BAQI RAMMAH.

Bulgaria: 1113 Sofia, ul. A. P. Chekhov 21-23; tel. (2) 973-33-48; fax (2) 971-11-97; e-mail sofemb@iraqmofamail.net; Ambassador Haider Shaiaa al-Barak.

Canada: 215 McLeod St, Ottawa, ON K2P 0Z8; tel. (613) 236-9177; fax (613) 236-9641; e-mail media@iraqembassy.ca; internet www.iraqembassy.ca; Ambassador HOWAR M. ZIAD.

China, People's Republic: 25 Xiu Shui Bei Jie, Jian Guo Men Wai, Beijing 100600; tel. (10) 65324355; fax (10) 65321599; e-mail iraqbeijing@yahoo .com; AmbassadorMohammad Sabir Ismail.

Czech Republic: Na Zátorce 10, 160 00 Prague 6; tel. 224326976; fax 224321715; e-mail iraqiembassy@volny.cz; AmbassadorDHIA AL-DABBASS.

Denmark: Granhøjen 18, 2900 Hellerup; tel. 39-45-02-70; fax 39-40-69-97; e-mail kbnemb@iraqmofamail.net; Chargé d'affaires a.i. Faris Fatouhi.

Egypt: Cairo; tel. (2) 7358087; fax (2) 7366956; e-mail caiemb@iraqmofamail .net; Ambassador SAFIA TALEB AS-SOUHAIL.

Finland: Lars Sonckin tie 2, 00570 Helsinki; tel. (9) 6818870; fax (9) 6848977; e-mail hlsemb@iraqmofamail.net; Ambassador Mebjil Jasim Muhammad as-Samrrai.

France: 53 rue de la Faisanderie, 75016 Paris; tel. 1-45-53-33-70; fax 1-45-53-33-80; e-mail paremb@iraqmofamail.net; Ambassador MOUAFAK MEHDI ABOUD HAMOUD.

Germany: Riemeisterstr. 20, 14169 Berlin; tel. (30) 814880; fax (30) 81488222; e-mail info@iraqiembassy-berlin.de; internet www.iraqiembassy-berlin.de; Ambassador Alaa A. Hussain al-Hashimi.

Greece: Odos Mazaraki 4, Palaio Psychiko, 154 52 Athens; tel. (210) 6722330; fax (210) 6717185; e-mail iraqvia@otenet.gr; Ambassador HATIM ABDUL HASSAN AL-KHAWAM.

India: B-5/8, Vasant Vihar, New Delhi 110 057; tel. (11) 26149085; fax (11) 26149076; e-mail dlhemb@iraqmofamail.net; Chargé d'affaires a.i. Muayad Hussain.

Indonesia: Jalan Teuku Umar 38, Jakarta 10350; tel. (21) 3904067; fax (21) 3904066; Chargé d'affaires a.i. FALIH ABDULKADIR AL-HAYALI.

Iran: Karamian Alley, No. 17, Pol-e-Roomi, Dr Shariati Ave, Tehran; tel. (21) 22210672; fax (21) 22233902; e-mail tehemb@iraqmofamail.net; Ambassador Muhammad Majid Abbas ash-Sheikh.

Italy: Via della Camilluccia, 355, 00135 Roma; tel. (06) 3014508; fax (06) 3014445; e-mail romemb@iraqmofamail.net; Ambassador MUHAMMAD MAHMOUD AL-AMILI.

Japan: 2-16-11, Takanawa, Minato-ku, Tokyo 108-0074; tel. (3) 5449-3231; fax (3) 5449-7719; e-mail tokemb@iraqmofamail.net; internet www.iraqi -japan.com; Ambassador Ghanim Alwan al-Jumaily.

Jordan: POB 2025, Amman; tel. (6) 4623175; fax (6) 4619172; e-mail baghdad@nets.com.jo; Ambassador SAAD J. AL-HAYYANI.

Korea, Republic: 310-49, Dongbinggo-dong, Yeongsan-gu, Seoul; tel. (2) 792-6671; fax (2) 792-6674; .

Lebanon: Beirut; tel. (1) 453209; fax (1) 459850; e-mail brtemb@ iraqmofamail.net; Ambassador JAWAD AL-HA'IRI.

Malaysia: 2 Jalan Langgak Golf, off Jalan Tun Razak, 55000 Kuala Lumpur; tel. (3) 21480555; fax (3) 21414331; Chargé d'affaires Dr Hoshiar H. S. Dazayi.

Mexico: Paseo de la Reforma 1875, Col. Lomas de Chapultepec, Del. Miguel Hidalgo, 11000 México, DF; tel. (55) 5596-0933; fax (55) 5596-0254; Chargé d'affaires a.i. SABIR MAHMOUD ABDULRAZZAK AL-ANI.

Morocco: 39 blvd Mehdi ben Barka, 10100 Rabat; tel. (3) 7754466; fax (3) 7759749; e-mail rbtemb@iraqmofamail.net; Ambassador Abd al-Muhsin Muhammad Said.

Netherlands: Johan de Wittlaan 16, 2517 JR The Hague; tel. (70) 3101260; fax (70) 3924958; e-mail info@embassyofiraq.nl; internet www.embassyofiraq.nl; Ambassador SIAMAND BANAA.

Oman: POB 262, Way 1737, House No. 2803, Ruwi 112; tel. 604178; fax 602026; e-mail musemb@iraqmofamail.net; Ambassador Abd ar-Rasoul Kadhim Aloush.

Pakistan: 57, St 48, F-8/4, Islamabad; tel. (51) 2253734; fax (51) 2253688; e-mail iraqiya@sat.net.pk; Ambassador KAIS SUBHI AL-YACOUBI.

Poland: 03-932 Warsaw, ul. Dąbrowiecka 9a; tel. (22) 6175773; fax (22) 6177065; e-mail iraqembassy@ambasadairaku.pl; Ambassador Dr Walid Hamid Shiltagh.

Portugal: Rua do Arriaga à Lapa 9, 1200-608 Lisbon; tel. (21) 3933310; fax (21) 3977052; e-mail lisemb@iraqmofa.net; Ambassador HUSSAIN MUAALA.

Qatar: POB 1526, Doha; tel. 4672237; fax 4673347; e-mail dohemb@ iraqmofamail.net; Ambassador Sadiq Hameedi ar-Rakawi.

Romania: 011834 Bucharest 1, Str. Venezuela 6–8; tel. (21) 2339008; fax (21) 2339007; e-mail bkremb@iraqmofamail.net; Ambassador ABDEL MURAD ALI.

Russian Federation: 119121 Moscow, ul. Pogodinskaya 12; tel. (495) 246-55-07; fax (495) 230-29-22; e-mail mosemb@iraqmofamail.net; Ambassador Dr Abdul-Karim Hashim.

Saudi Arabia: Riyadh; .

Serbia: 11000 Belgrade, Neznanog Junaka 27a; tel. (11) 2662681; fax (11) 2668068; e-mail bgremb@iraqmofamail.net; Chargé d'affaires a.i. May Khalid Omran al-Bayati.

South Africa: 803 Duncan St, Brooklyn, Pretoria 0181; POB 11089, Hatfield 0028; tel. (12) 3622048; fax (12) 3622027; Ambassador QASIM ABDLBAQI SHAKIR.

Spain: Ronda de Sobradiel 67, 28043 Madrid; tel. (91) 7591282; fax (91) 7593180; e-mail mdremb@iraqmofamail.net; Ambassador Talal H. al-Khudairi.

Sudan: Sharia ash-Shareef al-Hindi, POB 1969, Khartoum; tel. (183) 271867; fax (183) 271855; e-mail krtemb@iraqmofamail.net; Ambassador SAMIR KHAIREE ALNEEMA.

Sweden: Baldersgt. 6a, POB 26031, 100 41 Stockholm; tel. (8) 411-44-43; fax (8) 796-83-66; Ambassador Ahmad A. Bamarni.

Switzerland: Elfenstr. 6, 3006 Bern; tel. 313514043; fax 313518312; e-mail bernemb@iraqmofamail.net; Chargé d'affaires a.i. AHMED KHALIL AHMED AL-ANI.

Syria: Damascus; tel. (11) 3341290; fax (11) 3341291; e-mail dmkemb@ iraqmofamail.net; Ambassador Sabah Abd al-Wahab al-Imam.

Tunisia: ave Tahar B. Achour, route X2 m 10, Mutuelleville, Tunis; tel. (71) 962-480; fax (71) 963-737; e-mail tunemb@iraqmofamail.net; Ambassador GHAZI TAHIR KHALID.

Turkey: Turan Emeksiz Sok. 11, 06700 Gaziosmanpaşa, Ankara; tel. (312) 4687421; fax (312) 4684832; e-mail ankemb@iraqmofamail.net; Ambassador Sabah J. Omran.

United Arab Emirates: Manhal St, Haoudh 55, St 32, Abu Dhabi; tel. (2) 6655215; fax (2) 6655214; e-mail iraqiemb@emirates.net.ae; Ambassador FARES UJAIL AL-YAWER.

United Kingdom: 9 Holland Villas Rd, London, W14 8BP; tel. (20) 7602-8456; fax (20) 7371-1652; e-mail lonemb@iraqmofamail.net; Chargé d'affaires a.i. Abd al-Muhaimen al-Oraibi.

United States of America: 1801 P St, Washington, DC 20036; tel. (202) 483-7500; fax (202) 462-5066; e-mail admin@iraqiembassy.us; internet www .iraqiembassy.us; Ambassador SAMIR SHAKIR MAHMOOD AS-SUMAIDAIE.

Vatican City: Via della Camilluccia 355, 00135 Rome, Italy; tel. (06) 3014508; fax (06) 35506416; e-mail ftkemb@iraqmofamail.net; Ambassador Albert Edward Ismail Yelda.

Venezuela: Quinta Babilonia, Avda Nicolás Cópernico con Calle Los Malabares, Valle Arriba, Caracas; tel. (212) 991-1627; fax (212) 992-0268; .

Viet Nam: 66 Tran Hung Dao, Hanoi; tel. (4) 9424141; fax (4) 9424055; e-mail hanemb@iraqmofamail.net; Ambassador Amal Abood Fairooz.

Yemen: POB 498, South Airport Rd, San'a; tel. (1) 440184; fax (1) 440187; e-mail snaemb@iraqmofamail.net; Ambassador TALAL JAMEEL SALEH AL-OBAYDI.

DIPLOMATIC MISSIONS OF IRELAND

United Nations: 1 Dag Hammarskjöld Plaza, 885 Second Ave, 19th Floor, New York, NY 10017; tel. (212) 421-6934; fax (212) 752-4726; e-mail ireland@un.int; internet www.un.int/ireland; Permanent Representative Paul Kavanagh.

Argentina: Avda del Libertador 1068, 6°, C1112ABN Buenos Aires; tel. (11) 5787-0801; fax (11) 5787-0802; e-mail info@irlanda.org.ar; internet www.irlanda.org.ar; Ambassador PHILOMENA MURNAGHAN.

Australia: 20 Arkana St, Yarralumla, ACT 2600; tel. (2) 6273-3022; fax (2) 6273-3741; e-mail canberraembassy@dfa.ie; Ambassador Máirtín O'Fainnín.

Austria: Rotenturmstr. 16–18, 5th Floor, 1010 Vienna; tel. (1) 715-42-46; fax (1) 713-60-04; e-mail vienna@dfa.ie; Ambassador FRANK COGAN.

Belgium: 50 rue Wiertz, 1050 Brussels; tel. (2) 235-66-76; fax (2) 235-66-71; e-mail embassybrussels@dfa.ie; Ambassador Brian Nason.

Brazil: SHIS QL 12, Conj. 05, Casa 09, Lago Sul, Brasília, DF; tel. (61) 3248-8800; fax (61) 3248-8816; e-mail brasiliaembassy@dfa.ie; Ambassador MICHAEL HOEY.

Bulgaria: 1000 Sofia, Platinum Business Centre, ul. Bacho Kiro 26–28; tel. (2) 985-34-25; fax (2) 983-33-02; e-mail info@embassyofireland.bg; Ambassador Geoffrey Keating.

Canada: 130 Albert St, Suite 1105, Ottawa, ON K1P 5G4; tel. (613) 233-6281; fax (613) 233-5835; e-mail embassyofireland@rogers.com; Ambassador DECLAN MICHAEL KELLY.

China, People's Republic: 3 Ri Tan Dong Lu, Jian Guo Men Wai, Beijing 100600; tel. (10) 65322691; fax (10) 65326857; e-mail beijingembassy@dfa.ie; internet www.embassyofireland.cn; Ambassador Declan Kelleher.

Cyprus: 7 Aiantas St, Ayios Omoloyites, 1082 Nicosia; POB 23848, 1686 Nicosia; tel. 22818183; fax 22660050; e-mail nicosiaembassy@dfa.ie; Ambassador TOM BRADY.

Czech Republic: Tržiště 13, 118 00 Prague 1; tel. 257530061; fax 257531387; e-mail pragueembassy@dfa.ie; internet www.embassyofireland.cz; Ambassador Donal Hamill.

Denmark: Østbanegade 21, 2100 Copenhagen Ø; tel. 35-42-32-33; fax 35-43-18-58; e-mail ireland@mail.dk; Ambassador JOSEPH HAYES.

Egypt: POB 2681, 3 Sharia Abou el-Feda, Cairo (Zamalek); tel. (2) 7358264; fax (2) 7362863; e-mail irishemb@rite.com; Ambassador Gerry Corr.

Estonia: Demini Bldg, Viru 1/Vene 2, Tallinn 10123; tel. 681-1888; fax 681-1889; e-mail tallinnembassy@dfa.ie; Ambassador NOEL KILKENNY.

Ethiopia: Sierra Leone St, Kebele 6, House No. 21, POB 9585, Addis Ababa; tel. (11) 4665050; fax (11) 4665020; e-mail ireland.emb@ethionet.et; Chargé d'affaires a.i. Don Sexton.

Finland: Erottajankatu 7A, 00130 Helsinki; tel. (9) 646006; fax (9) 646022; e-mail helsinki@dfa.ie; Ambassador PHILIP MCDONAGH.

France: 12 ave Foch, 75116 Paris; tel. 1-44-17-67-00; fax 1-44-17-67-60; e-mail paris@dfa.ie; internet www.embassyofirelandparis.com; Ambassador Anne Anderson.

Germany: Friedrichstr. 200, 10117 Berlin; tel. (30) 220720; fax (30) 22072299; e-mail berlin@dfa.ie; Ambassador DAVID DONOGHUE.

Greece: Leoforos Vassileos Konstantinou 7, 106 74 Athens; tel. (210) 7232771; fax (210) 7293383; e-mail athensembassy@dfa.ie; Ambassador Antóin Mac Unfraidh.

Hungary: 1944 Budapest, Bank Center Gránit Torony, VII; tel. (1) 302-9600; fax (1) 302-9599; e-mail iremb@hu.inter.net; Ambassador MARTIN GREENE.

India: 230 Jor Bagh, New Delhi 110 003; tel. (11) 24626733; fax (11) 24697053; e-mail ireland@ndf.vsnl.net.in; internet www.irelandinindia.com; Ambassador Kieran Dowling.

Iran: Bonbast Nahid St, North Kamranieh Ave, No. 9, Tehran 19369; tel. (21) 22803835; fax (21) 22286933; e-mail irelembteh@padisar.net; Ambassador JOHN DEADY.

Israel: The Tower, 17th Floor, 3 Daniel Frisch St, Tel-Aviv 64731; tel. 3-6964166; fax 3-6964160; e-mail telavivembassy@dfa.ie; Ambassador Michael Forbes.

Italy: Piazza di Campitelli 3, 00186 Roma; tel. (06) 6979121; fax (06) 6792354; e-mail romeembassy@dfa.ie; internet www.ambasciata-irlanda.it; Ambassador SEÁN Ó HUIGINN.

Japan: Ireland House, 2-10-7, Kojimachi, Chiyoda-ku, Tokyo 102-0083; tel. (3) 3263-0695; fax (3) 3265-2275; e-mail irljapan@gol.com; internet www.irishembassy.jp; Ambassador Brendan Scannell.

Korea, Republic: Daehan Fire and Marine Insurance Bldg, 15th Floor, 51-1, Namchang-dong, Jung-gu, Seoul; tel. (2) 774-6455; fax (2) 774-6458; e-mail irelandkor@kornet.net; internet www.irelandhouse-korea.com/embassy.html; Ambassador CONOR MURPHY.

Latvia: Valdemara Centrs 632, Kr. Valdemara iela 21, Rīga 1010; tel. 6703-5286; fax 6703-5323; e-mail irijas.vestnieciba@gmail.com; Ambassador Tim Mawe.

Lithuania: Gedimino pr.1, Vilnius 01103; tel. (5) 262-9460; fax (5) 262-9462; e-mail vilniusembassy@dfa.ie; 2005Ambassador DÓNAL DENHAM.

Luxembourg: 28 route d'Arlon, 1140 Luxembourg; tel. 45-06-10-1; fax 45-88-20; e-mail luxembourg@dfa.ie; Ambassador Martin Burke.

Malawi: Lilongwe; tel. 1706405; e-mail lilongweemdiplomats@dfa.ie; Ambassador LIAM MACGABHANN.

Malaysia: Ireland House, The Amp Walk, 218 Jalan Ampang, POB 10372, 50450 Kuala Lumpur; tel. (3) 21612963; fax (3) 21613427; e-mail info@ireland-embassy.com.my; internet www.ireland-embassy.com.my; Ambassador Eugene Hutchinson.

Malta: Whitehall Mansions, Ta'Xbiex Seafront, Ta'Xbiex XBX 1026; tel. 21334744; fax 21334755; e-mail vallettaembassy@dfa.ie; Chargé d'affaires GERALD O'CONNOR.

Mexico: Cerrada Blvd Manuel Avila Camacho 76, 3°, Col. Lomas de Chapultepec, Del. Miguel Hidalgo, 11000 México, DF; tel. (55) 5520-5803; fax (55) 5520-5892; e-mail emexicoembassy@dfa.ie; Ambassador Dermot Brangan.

Mozambique: Av. Julius Nyerere 3332, Maputo; tel. 21491440; fax 21493023; e-mail maputoembassy@dfa.ie; Ambassador FRANK SHERIDAN.

Netherlands: Dr Kuyperstraat 9, 2514 BA The Hague; tel. (70) 3630993; fax (70) 3617604; e-mail thehagueembassy@dfa.ie; internet www.irishembassy.nl; Ambassador Richard Ryan.

Nigeria: Plot 415, Negro Cres., Maitama District, Abuja; tel. (9) 4131751; fax (9) 4131805; e-mail abujaembassy@dfa.ie; internet www.irishembassy-nigeria.net; Ambassador LIAM CANNIFFE.

Norway: Haakon VIIs gt. 1, 0244 Oslo; tel. 22-01-72-00; fax 22-01-72-01; e-mail osloembassy@dfa.ie; Ambassador Thelma Maria Doran.

Poland: 00-496 Warsaw, ul. Mysia 5; tel. (22) 8496633; fax (22) 8498431; e-mail warsawembassy@dfa.ie; internet www.irlandia.pl; Ambassador DECLAN O'DONOVAN.

Portugal: Rua da Imprensa à Estrela 1, 4°, 1200-684 Lisbon; tel. (21) 3929440; fax (21) 3977363; e-mail lisbon@dfa.ie; Ambassador James Brennan.

Romania: 011015 Bucharest 1, Str. Buzesti 50–52, 3rd Floor; tel. (21) 3102131; fax (21) 3112285; e-mail bucharestembassy@dfa.ie; Ambassador PÁDRAIC CRADOCK.

Russian Federation: 129010 Moscow, Grokholskii per. 5; tel. (495) 937-59-11; fax (495) 680-06-23; e-mail moscowembassy@dfa.ie; Ambassador Justin Harman.

Saudi Arabia: POB 94349, Riyadh 11693; tel. (1) 488-2300; fax (1) 488-0927; e-mail riyadhembassy@dfa.ie; internet www.embassyofireland-riyadh.com; Ambassador TOM RUSSELL.

Singapore: Ireland House, 541 Orchard Rd, 8th Floor, Liat Towers, Singapore 238881; tel. 62387616; fax 62387615; e-mail singaporeembassy@dfa.ie; internet www.embassyofireland.sg; Ambassador Richard O'Brien.

Slovakia: Carlton Savoy Bldg, Mostavá 2, 811 02 Bratislava 1; tel. (2) 5930-9611; fax (2) 5443-0690; e-mail bratislava@dfa.ie; Ambassador DECLAN CONNOLLY.

South Africa: Southern Life Plaza, 1st Floor, 1059 Schoeman St, cnr Festival and Schoeman Sts, Arcadia, Pretoria 0083; POB 4174, Arcadia 0001; tel. (12) 3425062; fax (12) 3424752; e-mail pretoria@dfa.ie; internet www.embassyireland.org.za; Ambassador Colin Wrafter.

Spain: Paseo de la Castellana 46, 4°, 28046 Madrid; tel. (91) 4364093; fax (91) 4351677; internet www.dfa.ie/home/index.aspx?id=33979; Ambassador PETER GUNNING.

Sweden: Östermalmsgt. 97, POB 10326, 100 55 Stockholm; tel. (8) 661-80-05; fax (8) 660-13-53; e-mail stockholmembassy@dfa.ie; Ambassador Barrie Robinson.

Switzerland: Kirchenfeldstr. 68, 3005 Bern; tel. 313521442; fax 313521455; e-mail berneembassy@dfa.ie; Ambassador JAMES STARKEY.

Tanzania: 353 Toure Dr., POB 9612, Oyster Bay, Dar es Salaam; tel. (22) 2602355; fax (22) 2602362; e-mail embassydaresalaam@dfa.ie; Ambassador Anne Barrington.

Turkey: Uğur Mumcu Cad. 88, MNG Binası B Blok Kat 3, Gaziosmanpaşa 06700 Ankara; tel. (312) 4466172; fax (312) 4468061; e-mail ankaraembassy@dfa.ie; Ambassador ANTONY MANNIX.

Uganda: 25 Yusuf Lule Rd, Nakasero, POB 7791, Kampala; tel. (41) 4340400; fax (41) 4344353; e-mail kampalaembassy@dfa.ie; Chargé d'affaires a.i. Aine Hearns.

United Kingdom: 17 Grosvenor Pl., London, SW1X 7HR; tel. (20) 7235-2171; fax (20) 7245-6961; internet www.embassyofireland.co.uk; Ambassador DAVID COONEY.

United States of America: 2234 Massachusetts Ave, NW, Washington, DC 20008; tel. (202) 462-3939; fax (202) 232-5993; e-mail embirlus@aol.com; internet www.irelandemb.org; Ambassador Michael Collins.

Vatican City: Villa Spada, Via Giacomo Medici 1, 00153 Rome, Italy; tel. (06) 5810777; fax (06) 5895709; Ambassador NOEL FAHEY.

Viet Nam: Vincom City Towers, 8th Floor, 191 Ba Trieu, Hai Ba Trung District, Hanoi; tel. (4) 9743291; fax (4) 9743295; e-mail irishembassyhanoi@dfanet.ie; Ambassador Maeve Collins.

Zambia: 6663 Katima Mulilo Rd, Olympia Park, POB 34923, 10101 Lusaka; tel. (1) 290650; fax (1) 290482; Ambassador BILL NOLAN.

DIPLOMATIC MISSIONS OF ISRAEL

United Nations: 800 Second Ave, New York, NY 10017; tel. (212) 499-5510; fax (212) 499-5516; e-mail israel@un.int; internet www.israel-un.org; Permanent Representative Dan Gillerman.

Angola: Edif. Siccal, 11° andar, Rua Rainha Ginga, Luanda; tel. 222395295; fax 222396366; e-mail info@luanda.mfa.gov.il; internet luanda.mfa.gov.il; Ambassador BAHIJ MANSOUR.

Argentina: Avda de Mayo 701, 10°, C1084AAC Buenos Aires; tel. (11) 4338-2500; fax (11) 4338-2624; e-mail info@buenosaires.mfa.gov.il; internet buenosaires.mfa.gov.il; Ambassador Rafael Eldad.

Australia: 6 Turrana St, Yarralumla, ACT 2600; tel. (2) 6215-4500; fax (2) 6215-4555; e-mail info@canberra.mfa.gov.il; internet canberra.mfa.gov.il; Ambassador YUVAL ROTEM.

Austria: Anton-Frank-Gasse 20, 1180 Vienna; tel. (1) 476-46-0; fax (1) 476-46-55-5; e-mail info-sec@vienna.mfa.gov.il; internet vienna.mfa.gov.il; Ambassador Dan Ashbel.

Azerbaijan: 1065 Baku, Izmir küç. 1033, Hyatt Tower III, 7th Floor; tel. (12) 490-78-81; fax (12) 490-78-92; e-mail info@baku.mfa.gov.il; internet baku.mfa.gov.il; Ambassador ARTHUR LENK.

Belarus: 220033 Minsk, pr. Partizansky 6a; tel. (17) 298-43-92; fax (17) 298-44-03; e-mail info@minsk.mfa.gov.il; Ambassador Ze'ev Ben Arie.

Belgium: 40 ave de l'Observatoire, 1180 Brussels; tel. (2) 373-55-00; fax (2) 373-56-17; e-mail info@brussels.mfa.gov.il; internet brussels.mfa.gov.il; Ambassador TAMAR SAMASH.

Brazil: SES, Av. das Nações, Quadra 809, Lote 38, 70424-900 Brasília, DF; tel. (61) 2105-0500; fax (61) 2105-0555; e-mail info@brasilia.mfa.gov.il; internet brasilia.mfa.gov.il; Ambassador Tzipora Rimon.

Bulgaria: 1463 Sofia, pl. Balgaria 1, NDK Administration Bldg; tel. (2) 951-50-44; fax (2) 952-11-01; e-mail info@sofia.mfa.gov.il; internet sofia.mfa.gov.il; Ambassador NOAH GAL-GENDLER.

Cameroon: rue du Club Olympique à Bastos 154, Longkak, BP 5934, Yaoundé; tel. 2221-1291; fax 2221-0823; e-mail info@yaounde.mfa.gov.il; internet yaounde.mfa.gov.il; Ambassador Avraham Nir.

Canada: 50 O'Connor St, Suite 1005, Ottawa, ON K1P 6L2; tel. (613) 567-6450; fax (613) 567-9878; e-mail info@ottawa.mfa.gov.il; internet www.embassyofisrael.ca; Ambassador ALAN BAKER.

Chile: San Sebastián 2812, 5°, Las Condes, Santiago; tel. (2) 750-0500; fax (2) 750-0555; e-mail info@santiago.mfa.gov.il; internet santiago.mfa.gov.il; Ambassador David Cohen.

China, People's Republic: 17 Tian Ze Lu, Chao Yang Qu, Beijing 100600; tel. (10) 65327788; fax (10) 65327781; e-mail israemb@public.bta.net.cn; internet beijing.mfa.gov.il; Ambassador AMOS NADAI.

Colombia: Calle 35, No 7-25, 14°, Bogotá, DC; tel. (1) 327-7500; fax (1) 327-7555; e-mail info@bogota.mfa.gov.il; internet bogota.mfa.gov.il; Ambassador Meron Reuben.

Congo, Democratic Republic: 141 blvd du 30 juin, BP 8343, Kinshasa; tel. (99) 87218; fax (88) 07494; e-mail daniel.saada@mfa.gov.il; Ambassador DANIEL SAADA.

Costa Rica: Edif. Centro Colón, 11°, Calle 38 Paseo Colón, Apdo 5147, 1000 San José; tel. 221-6444; fax 257-0867; e-mail ambassador.sec@sanjose.mfa.gov.il; internet sanjose.mfa.gov.il; Ambassador Ehud Moshe Eitam.

Côte d'Ivoire: Immeuble Nour Al-Hayat, 01 BP 1877, Abidjan 01; tel. 20-21-49-53; fax 20-21-87-04; e-mail info@abidjan.mfa.gov.il; Ambassador MICHAËL ARBEL.

Croatia: 10000 Zagreb, ul. grada Vukovara 271/11; tel. (1) 6169500; fax (1) 6169555; e-mail ambassador@zagreb.mfa.gov.il; Ambassador Shmuel Meirom.

Cyprus: POB 25159, 4 Ioanni Grypari St, 1090 Nicosia; tel. 22369500; fax 22666338; e-mail ambassadorsec3@nicosia.mfa.gov.il; internet nicosia.mfa.gov.il; Ambassador AVRAHAM HADDAD.

Czech Republic: Badeniho 2, 170 06 Prague 7; tel. 233325109; fax 233320092; e-mail ambassador-sec@prague.mfa.goo.il; internet prague.mfa.gov.il; Ambassador Arie Arazi.

Denmark: Lundevangsvej 4, 2900 Hellerup; tel. 88-15-55-00; fax 88-15-55-55; e-mail reception@copenhagen.mfa.gov.il; internet copenhagen.mfa.gov.il; Ambassador DAVID WALZER.

Dominican Republic: Pedro Henríquez Ureña 80, Santo Domingo, DN; tel. 472-0774; fax 472-1785; e-mail ambassador@santodomingo.mfa.gov.il; internet santodomingo.mfa.gov.il; Ambassador Amos Radian.

Ecuador: Edif. Plaza 2000, Avda 12 de Octubre y General Francisco Salazar, Apdo 17-21-08, Quito; tel. (2) 223-7474; fax (2) 223-8055; e-mail info@quito.mfa.gov.il; internet quito.mfa.il; Ambassador DANIEL SABBAN.

Egypt: 6 Sharia Ibn el-Malek, Cairo (Giza); tel. (2) 33321500; fax (2) 33321555; e-mail info@cairo.mfa.gov.il; Ambassador Shalom Cohen.

El Salvador: Centro Financiero Gigante, Torre B, 11°, Alameda Roosevelt y Avda Sur 63, San Salvador; tel. 2211-3434; fax 2211-3443; e-mail info@sansalvador.mfa.gov.il; internet sansalvador.mfa.gov.il; Ambassador MATTANYA COHEN.

Eritrea: 32 Abo St, POB 5600, Asmara; tel. (1) 188521; fax (1) 188550; e-mail info@asmara.mfa.gov.il; Ambassador Menahem Kanafi.

Ethiopia: Woreda 16, Kebele 22, House No. 283, POB 1266, Addis Ababa; tel. (11) 6460999; fax (11) 64619619; e-mail embassy@addisababa.mfa.gov.il; internet addisababa.mfa.gov.il; Ambassador YAACOV AMITAI.

Finland: Yrjönkatu 36a, 00100 Helsinki; tel. (9) 6812020; fax (9) 1356959; e-mail info@helsinki.mfa.gov.il; internet helsinki.mfa.gov.il; Ambassador Avi Granot.

France: 3 rue Rabelais, 75008 Paris; tel. 1-40-76-55-00; fax 1-40-76-55-55; e-mail information@paris.mfa.gov.il; internet paris.mfa.gov.il; Ambassador DANIEL SHEK.

Georgia: 0102 Tbilisi, D. Aghmashenebeli 61; tel. (32) 94-27-05; fax (32) 95-52-09; e-mail press@tbilisi.mfa.gov.il; internet tbilisi.mfa.gov.il; Ambassador Shabtai Tsur.

Germany: Auguste-Viktoria-Str. 74–76, 14193 Berlin; tel. (30) 89045500; fax (30) 89045222; e-mail botschaft@israel.de; internet www.israel.de; Ambassador YORAM BEN ZEEV.

Greece: Odos Marathonodromou 1, Palaio Psychiko, 154 52 Athens; tel. (210) 6719530; fax (210) 6479510; e-mail info@athens.mfa.gov.il; internet athens.mfa.gov.il; Ambassador Ali Yahya.

Guatemala: 13a Avda 14-07, Zona 10, Guatemala City; tel. 2333-4624; fax 2333-6950; e-mail info@guatemala.mfa.gov.il; Ambassador ISAAC BACHMAN.

Hungary: 1026 Budapest, Fullánk u. 8; tel. (1) 392-6200; fax (1) 200-0783; e-mail info@budapest.mfa.gov.il; internet budapest.mfa.gov.il; Ambassador David Admon.

India: 3 Aurangzeb Rd, New Delhi 110 011; tel. (11) 23013238; fax (11) 23014298; e-mail info@newdelhi.mfa.gov.il; internet delhi.mfa.gov.il; Ambassador MARK SOFER.

Ireland: Carrisbrook House, 122 Pembroke Rd, Dublin 4; tel. (1) 2309400; fax (1) 2309446; e-mail info@dublin.mfa.gov.il; internet dublin.mfa.gov.il; Ambassador Zion Evrony.

Italy: Via Michele Mercati 12, 00197 Roma; tel. (06) 36198500; fax (06) 36198555; e-mail adm-sec@roma.mfa.gov.il; internet roma.mfa.gov.il; Ambassador GIDEON MEIR.

Japan: 3, Niban-cho, Chiyoda-ku, Tokyo 102-0084; tel. (3) 3264-0911; fax (3) 3264-0791; e-mail consular@tky.mfa.gov.il; internet tokyo.mfa.gov.il; Ambassador Nissim Ben Sheetrit.

Jordan: POB 95866, 47 Maysaloon St, Dahiat ar-Rabieh, Amman 11195; tel. (6) 5503500; fax (6) 5524689; e-mail embassy@amman.mfa.gov.il; Ambassador YAAKOV ROSEN.

Kazakhstan: 010000 Astana, ul. Auezova 8; tel. (7172) 68-87-38; e-mail info@almaty.mfa.gov.il; internet www.almaty.mfa.gov.il; Ambassador Ran Ichay.

Kenya: Bishop's Rd, POB 30354, Nairobi; tel. (20) 2722182; fax (20) 2715966; e-mail info@nairobi.mfa.gov.il; internet nairobi.mfa.gov.il; Ambassador EMMANUEL SERI.

Korea, Republic: 18th Fl., Kabool Bldg, 149 Seorin-dong, Jongno-gu, Seoul 110-726; tel. (2) 739-8666; fax (2) 739-8667; e-mail seoul@israel.org; internet seoul.mfa.gov.il; Ambassador Yigal B. Caspi.

Latvia: Elizabetes iela 2, Rīga 1010; tel. 6732-0739; fax 6783-0170; e-mail press@rig.mfa.gov.il; internet riga.mfa.gov.il; Ambassador CHEN IVRI.

Mauritania: Ilot A516, Tevragh Zeina, BP 5714, Nouakchott; tel. 525-82-35; fax 525-46-12; e-mail info@nouakchott.mfa.gov.il; Ambassador Boaz Besmuth Bismuth.

Mexico: Sierra Madre 215, Col. Lomas de Chapultepec, Del. Miguel Hidalgo, 11000 México, DF; tel. (55) 5201-1500; fax (55) 5201-1555; e-mail embisrael@prodigy.net.mx; internet mexico-city.mfa.gov.il; Ambassador YOSEF LIVNE.

Myanmar: 15 Khabaung Road, Hlaing Township, Yangon; tel. (1) 515115; fax (1) 515116; e-mail info@yangon.mfa.gov.il; internet yangon.mfa.gov.il; Ambassador Ruth Schatz.

Nepal: Bishramalaya House, Lazimpat, POB 371, Kathmandu; tel. (1) 4411811; fax (1) 4413920; e-mail info@kathmandu.mfa.gov.il; internet kathmandu.mfa.gov.il; Ambassador DAN STAV.

Netherlands: Buitenhof 47, 2513 AH The Hague; tel. (70) 3760500; fax (70) 3760555; e-mail info@hague.mfa.gov.il; internet thehague.mfa.gov.il; Ambassador Harry Kney-Tal.

Nigeria: Plot 12, Mary Slessor St, Asokoro, POB 10924, Abuja; tel. (9) 3143170; fax (9) 3143177; e-mail info@abuja.mfa.gov.il; internet abuja.mfa.gov.il; Ambassador NOAM KATZ.

Norway: Parkvn 35, POB 534 Skøyen, 0214 Oslo; tel. 21-01-95-00; fax 21-01-95-30; e-mail israel@oslo.mfa.gov.il; internet oslo.mfa.gov.il; Ambassador Miryam Shomrat.

Panama: Panamá; tel. 208-4700; fax 208-4755; Ambassador MENASHE BAR-ON.

Peru: Edif. El Pacifico, 6°, Plaza Washington, Natalio Sánchez 125, Santa Beatriz, Lima; tel. (1) 4334431; fax (1) 4338925; e-mail info@lima.mfa.gov.il; internet lima.mfa.gov.il; Ambassador Walid Mansour.

Philippines: Trafalgar Plaza, 23rd Floor, 105 H. V. de la Costa St, Salcedo Village, Makati City, 1227 Metro Manila; tel. (2) 8925330; fax (2) 8941027; e-mail info@manila.mfa.gov.il; internet manila.mfa.gov.il; Ambassador ZVI VAPNI.

Poland: 02-078 Warsaw, ul. Krzywickiego 24; tel. (22) 5970500; fax (22) 8251607; e-mail publicaffairs@warsaw.mfa.gov.il; internet www.israel.pl; Ambassador David Abraham Akiva Peleg.

Portugal: Rua António Enes 16, 4°, 1050-025 Lisbon; tel. (21) 3553640; fax (21) 3553658; e-mail israemb@lisboa.mfa.gov.il; internet lisbon.mfa.gov.il; Ambassador AHARON RAM.

Romania: 040231 Bucharest 4, Bd. Dimitrie Cantemir 1, Bl. b2, 5th Floor; tel. (21) 3304149; fax (21) 3300750; e-mail israel.embassy@algoritma.ro; Ambassador Oren David.

Russian Federation: 115095 Moscow, ul. B. Ordynka 56; tel. (495) 660-27-00; fax (495) 660-27-68; e-mail info@moscow.mfa.gov.il; internet moscow.mfa.gov.il; Ambassador ANNA AZARI.

Senegal: Immeuble SDIH, 3 pl. de l'Indépendance, BP 2096, Dakar; tel. 33-823-7965; fax 33-823-6490; e-mail info@dakar.mfa.gov.il; internet dakar.mfa.gov.il; Ambassador Daniel Pinhasi.

Serbia: 11000 Belgrade, bul. Kneza Aleksandra Karađorđevića 47; tel. (11) 3672400; fax (11) 3670304; e-mail info@belgrade.mfa.gov.il; Ambassador ARTHUR KOLL.

Singapore: 24 Stevens Close, Singapore 257964; tel. 68349200; fax 67337008; e-mail press@singapore.mfa.gov.il; internet singapore.mfa.gov.il; Ambassador Ilan Ben-dov.

Slovakia: Sláviče údolie 106, POB 6, 811 02 Bratislava; tel. (2) 5441-0557; fax (2) 5441-0850; e-mail cao-sec@bratislava.mfa.gov.il; Ambassador ZEEV BOKER.

South Africa: 428 King's Hwy, Elizabeth Grove St, Lynnwood, Pretoria; POB 3726, Pretoria 0001; tel. (12) 3480470; fax (12) 3488594; e-mail operator@pretoria.mfa.gov.il; internet pretoria.mfa.gov.il; Ambassador Ilan Baruch.

Spain: Velázquez 150, 7°, 28002 Madrid; tel. (91) 7829500; fax (91) 7829555; e-mail embajada@embajada-israel.es; internet www.embajada-israel.es; Ambassador RAPHAEL SCHUTZ.

Sweden: Storgt. 31, POB 14006, 104 40 Stockholm; tel. (8) 528-065-00; fax (8) 528-065-55; e-mail info@stockholm.mfa.gov.il; internet stockholm.mfa.gov.il; Ambassador Eviatar Manor.

Switzerland: Alpenstr. 32, 3006 Bern; tel. 313563500; fax 313563556; e-mail info@bern.mfa.gov.il; internet bern.mfa.gov.il; Ambassador ILAN ELGAR.

Thailand: Ocean Tower II, 25th Floor, 75 Sukhumvit, Soi 19, Thanon Asoke, Bangkok 10110; tel. (2) 204-9200; fax (2) 204-9255; e-mail info@bangkok.mfa.gov.il; internet bangkok.nfa.gov.il; Ambassador Yael Rubinstein.

Turkey: Mahatma Gandhi Cad. 85, 06700 Gaziosmanpaşa, Ankara; tel. (312) 4597500; fax (312) 4597555; e-mail info@ankara.mfa.gov.il; internet ankara.mfa.gov.il; Ambassador GAVRIEL LEVY.

Ukraine: 01901 Kyiv, bulv. L. Ukrainky 34; tel. (44) 586-15-00; fax (44) 586-15-55; e-mail info@kiev.mfa.gov.il; internet ukraine.mfa.gov.il; Ambassador Zina Kalay-Kleitman.

United Kingdom: 2 Palace Green, Kensington, London, W8 4QB; tel. (20) 7957-9500; fax (20) 7957-9555; e-mail public3@london.mfa.gov.il; internet london.mfa.gov.il; Ambassador RON PROSOR.

United States of America: 3514 International Dr., NW, Washington, DC 20008; tel. (202) 364-5590; fax (202) 364-5566; e-mail ask@israelemb.org; internet www.israelemb.org; Ambassador Sallai Meridor.

Uruguay: Blvr Artigas 1585, 11200 Montevideo; tel. (2) 4004164; fax (2) 4095821; e-mail info@montevideo.mfa.gov.il; internet montevideo.mfa.gov.il; Ambassador YOEL BARNEA.

Uzbekistan: 100000 Tashkent, A. Kahhor ko'ch. 3; tel. (71) 140-75-00; fax (71) 140-75-55; e-mail info@tashkent.mfa.gov.il; internet tashkent.mfa.gov.il; Ambassador Ami Mel.

Vatican City: Via Michele Mercati 12, 00197 Rome, Italy; tel. (06) 36198690; fax (06) 36198626; e-mail info-vat@holysee.mfa.gov.il; internet vatican.mfa.gov.il; Ambassador MORDECHAI LEWY.

Venezuela: Centro Empresarial Miranda, 4°, Avda Principal de los Ruices cruce con Francisco de Miranda, Apdo 70081, Los Ruices, Caracas; tel. (212) 239-4511; fax (212) 239-4320; e-mail info@caracas.mfa.gov.il; internet caracas.mfa.gov.il; Ambassador Shlomo Cohen.

Viet Nam: 68 Nguyen Thai Hoc, Dong Da, Hanoi; tel. (4) 8433141; fax (4) 8435760; e-mail info@hanoi.mfa.gov.il; internet hanoi.mfa.gov.il; Ambassador EPHRAIM BEN-MATITYAU.

DIPLOMATIC MISSIONS OF ITALY

United Nations: 2 United Nations Plaza, 24th Floor, New York, NY 10017; tel. (212) 486-9191; fax (212) 486-1036; e-mail italy@un.int; internet www.italyun.org; Permanent Representative Marcello Spatafora.

Afghanistan: Great Masoud Rd, Kabul; tel. (20) 2103144; e-mail ambasciata.kabul@esteri.it; internet www.ambkabul.esteri.it; Ambassador ETTORE FRANCESCO SEQUI.

Albania: Rruga Lek Dukagjini 2, Tirana; tel. (4) 234045; fax (4) 250921; e-mail segreteriaambasciata.tirana@esteri.it; internet www.ambtirana.esteri.it; Ambassador Saba D'Elia.

Algeria: 18 rue Muhammad Ouidir Amellal, 16030 el-Biar, Algiers; tel. (21) 92-23-30; fax (21) 92-59-86; e-mail segretaria.algeri@esteri.it; internet www.ambalgeri.esteri.it; Ambassador GIAMPAOLO CANTINI.

Angola: Rua Americo Boavida 49–51, Ingombotas, CP 6220, Luanda; tel. 222331245; fax 222333743; e-mail segreteria.luanda@esteri.it; internet www.ambluanda.esteri.it; Ambassador Torquato Cardilli.

Argentina: Billinghurst 2577, C1425DTY Buenos Aires; tel. (11) 4011-2100; fax (11) 4804-4914; e-mail ambasciata.buenosaires@esteri.it; internet www.ambbuenosaires.esteri.it; Ambassador STEFANO RONCA.

Armenia: 0010 Yerevan, Italiayi St 5; tel. (10) 54-23-35; fax (10) 54-23-41; e-mail segreteria.jerevan@esteri.it; internet www.ambjerevan.esteri.it; Ambassador Massimo Cassinelli.

Australia: 12 Grey St, Deakin, ACT 2600; tel. (2) 6273-3333; fax (2) 6273-4223; e-mail ambasciata.canberra@esteri.it; internet www.ambcanberra.esteri.it; Ambassador STARACE JANFOLLA.

Austria: Rennweg 27, 1030 Vienna; tel. (1) 712-51-21; fax (1) 713-97-19; e-mail ambasciata.vienna@esteri.it; internet www.ambvienna.esteri.it; Ambassador Dr Massimo Spinetti.

Azerbaijan: 1004 Baku, Icheri Şeher, Kichik Gala küç. 44; tel. (12) 497-51-33; fax (12) 497-52-02; e-mail ambasciata.baku@esteri.it; internet www .ambbaku.esteri.it; Ambassador GIAN-LUIGI MASCIA.

Bahrain: PO Box 397, Villa 1554, Rd 5647, Block 356, Manama; tel. 17252424; fax 17277060; e-mail ambasciata.manama@esteri.it; internet www .italian-embassy.org.ae/Ambasciata_Manama; Ambassador Calogero di Gesu.

Bangladesh: Plots 2 and 3, Rd 74/79, Gulshan Model Town, POB 6062, Dhaka 1212; tel. (2) 8822781; fax (2) 8822578; e-mail ambdhaka@dominox .com; internet dominox.com/italydhaka; Ambassador ITALA MARIA MARTA OCCHI.

Belarus: 220004 Minsk, vul. Rakovskaya 16b; tel. (17) 220-29-69; fax (17) 306-20-37; e-mail ambasciata.minsk@esteri.it; internet www.ambminsk .esteri.it; Ambassador Norberto Cappello.

Belgium: 28 rue Emile Claus, 1050 Brussels; tel. (2) 643-38-50; fax (2) 648-54-85; e-mail ambbruxelles@esteri.it; internet www.ambbruxelles.esteri.it; Ambassador SANDRO MARIA SIGGIA.

Bolivia: Calle 5 (Jordán Cuellar) 458, Obrajes, La Paz; tel. (2) 278-8506; fax (2) 278-8178; e-mail segreteria.lapaz@esteri.it; internet www.italian-embassy .org.ae/ambasciata_lapaz; Ambassador Silvio Mignano.

Bosnia and Herzegovina: 71000 Sarajevo, Čekaluša 39; tel. (33) 218022; fax (33) 659368; e-mail ambsara@bih.net.ba; Ambassador ALESSANDRO FALLAVOLLITO.

Brazil: SES, Av. das Nações, Quadra 807, Lote 30, 70420-900 Brasília, DF; tel. (61) 3442-9900; fax (61) 3443-1231; e-mail embitalia@embitalia.org.br; internet www.italian-embassy.org.ae/ambasciata_brasilia; Ambassador Michele Valensise.

Bulgaria: 1000 Sofia, ul. Shipka 2; tel. (2) 921-73-00; fax (2) 980-37-17; e-mail ambasciata.sofia@esteri.it; internet www.ambsofia.esteri.it; Ambassador GIOVAN BATTISTA CAMPAGNOLA.

Cameroon: Plateau Bastos, BP 827, Yaoundé; tel. 2220-3376; fax 2221-5250; e-mail ambasciata.yaounde@esteri.it; internet www.ambyaounde.esteri.it; Ambassador Antonio Bellavia.

Canada: 275 Slater St, 21st Floor, Ottawa, ON K1P 5H9; tel. (613) 232-2401; fax (613) 233-1484; e-mail ambasciata.ottawa@esteri.it; internet www .ambottawa.esteri.it; Ambassador GABRIELE SARDO.

Chile: Clemente Fabres 1050, Providencia, Santiago; tel. (2) 470-8400; fax (2) 223-2467; e-mail info.santiago@esteri.it; internet www.ambsantiago.esteri.it; Ambassador Paolo Casardi.

China, People's Republic: 2 Dong Er Jie, San Li Tun, Beijing 100600; tel. (10) 85327600; fax (10) 65324676; e-mail ambasciata.pechino@esteri.it; internet www.ambpechino.esteri.it; Ambassador RICCARDO SESSA.

Colombia: Calle 93b, No 9-92, Apdo Aéreo 50901, Bogotá, DC; tel. (1) 218-6604; fax (1) 610-5886; e-mail ambbogo.mail@esteri.it; internet www .ambbogota.esteri.it; Ambassador Antonio Tarelli.

Congo, Republic: 2 blvd Lytautey, BP 2484, Brazzaville; tel. 81-58-41; fax 81-11-52; e-mail ambasciata.brazzaville@esteri.it; internet www.ambbrazzaville .esteri.it/Ambasciata_Brazzaville; Ambassador ANGELO TRAVAGLINI.

Costa Rica: Los Yoses, 5a entrada, Apdo 1729, 1000 San José; tel. 224-6574; fax 225-8200; e-mail ambasciata.sanjose@esteri.it; internet www.ambsanjose .esteri.it; Ambassador Leonardo Sampoli.

Côte d'Ivoire: 16 rue de la Canebière, Cocody, 01 BP 1905, Abidjan 01; tel. 22-44-61-70; fax 22-44-35-87; e-mail ambitali@aviso.ci; internet www .ambabidjan.esteri.it; Ambassador GIOVANNI POLIZZI.

Croatia: 10000 Zagreb, Medulićeva 22; tel. (1) 4846386; fax (1) 4846384; e-mail amb.zagabria@esteri.it; Ambassador Alessandro Pignatti Morano di Custoza.

Cuba: No 5, Avda 402, Calle 4, Miramar, Havana; tel. (7) 204-5615; fax (7) 204-5659; e-mail ambasciata.avana@esteri.it; internet sedi.esteri.it/avana; Ambassador DOMENICO VECCHIONI.

Cyprus: POB 27695, 11 25th March St, Engomi, 2408 Nicosia; tel. 22357635; fax 22357616; e-mail ambnico.mail@esteri.it; internet www.ambnicosia .esteri.it; Ambassador Luigi Napolitano.

Czech Republic: Nerudova 20, 118 00 Prague 1; tel. 233080111; fax 257531522; e-mail ambasciata.praga@esteri.it; internet www.ambpraga .esteri.it; Ambassador FABIO PIGLIAPOCO.

Denmark: Gammel Vartov Vej 7, 2900 Hellerup; tel. 39-62-68-77; fax 39-62-25-99; e-mail info.copenaghen@esteri.it; internet www.ambcopenaghen .esteri.it; Ambassador Andrea Giuseppe Mochi Onory di Saluzzo.

Dominican Republic: Rodríguez Objío 4, Santo Domingo, DN; tel. 682-0830; fax 682-8296; e-mail ambital@verizon.net.do; internet www .ambsantodomingo.esteri.it; Ambassador ENRICO GUICCIARDI.

Ecuador: Calle La Isla 111 y Humberto Alborñoz, Apdo 17-03-72, Quito; tel. (2) 256-1077; fax (2) 250-2818; e-mail archivio.quito@esteri.it; internet www .ambitalquito.org; Ambassador Giulio Cesare Piccirilli.

Egypt: 15 Sharia Abd ar-Rahman Fahmi, Cairo (Garden City); tel. (2) 7943194; fax (2) 7940657; e-mail ambasciata.cairo@esteri.it; internet www .ambilcairo.esteri.it; Ambassador ANTONIO BADINI.

El Salvador: Calle la Reforma 158, Col. San Benito, Apdo 0199, San Salvador; tel. 2223-4806; fax 2298-3050; e-mail ambasciatore.sansalvador@ esteri.it; internet www.ambsansalvador.esteri.it; Ambassador Caterina Bertolini.

Eritrea: POB 220, 11 171–1 St, Asmara; tel. (1) 120160; fax (1) 121115; e-mail ambasciata.asmara@esteri.it; internet www.ambasmara.esteri.it; Ambassador GAETANO MARTINEZ TAGLIAVIA.

Estonia: Vene 2, Tallinn 10123; tel. 627-6160; fax 631-1370; e-mail ambasciata .tallinn@esteri.it; internet www.ambtallinn.esteri.it; Ambassador Fabrizio Piaggesi.

Ethiopia: Villa Italia, POB 1105, Addis Ababa; tel. (11) 1235717; fax (11) 1235689; e-mail ambasciata.addisabeba@esteri.it; Ambassador RAFFAELE DE LUTIO.

Finland: Itäinen puistotie 4, 00140 Helsinki; tel. (9) 6811280; fax (9) 6987829; e-mail ambasciata.helsinki@esteri.it; internet www.ambhelsinki.esteri.it; Ambassador Elisabetta Kelescian.

France: 51 rue de Varenne, 75343 Paris Cedex 07; tel. 1-49-54-03-00; fax 1-45-54-04-10; e-mail ambasciata.parigi@esteri.it; internet www.ambparigi.esteri .it; Ambassador LUDOVICO ORTONA.

Gabon: Immeuble Personnaz et Gardin, rue de la Mairie, BP 2251, Libreville; tel. 74-28-92; fax 74-80-35; e-mail ambasciata.libreville@esteri.it; internet www.amblibreville.esteri.it; Ambassador Raffaele De Benedictis.

Georgia: 0108 Tbilisi, Chitadze 3A; tel. (32) 99-64-18; fax (32) 99-64-15; e-mail embassy.tbilisi@esteri.it; internet www.ambtbilisi.esteri.it; Chargé d'affaires a.i. VITTORIO SANDALLI.

Germany: Hiroshimastr. 1, 10785 Berlin; tel. (30) 254400; fax (30) 25440116; e-mail segreteria.berlino@esteri.it; internet www.ambberlino.esteri.it; Ambassador Antonio Puri Purini.

Ghana: Jawaharlal Nehru Rd, POB 140, Accra; tel. (21) 775621; fax (21) 777301; e-mail ambasciata.accra@esteri.it; internet www.ambaccra.esteri.it; Ambassador FABRIZIO DE AGOSTINI.

Greece: Odos Sekeri 2, 106 74 Athens; tel. (210) 3617260; fax (210) 3617330; e-mail ambasciata.atene@esteri.it; internet www.ambatene.esteri.it; Ambassador Gianpaolo Scarante.

Guatemala: 12 Calle 6-49, Zona 14, Guatemala City; tel. 2337-4557; fax 2337-0795; e-mail ambasciata.guatemala@esteri.it; internet www.ambguatemala .esteri.it; Ambassador PIO LUIGI TEODORANI FABBRI POZZO.

Honduras: Edif Plaza Azul, 4°, Col. Lomas Del Guijarro Sur, Apdo U-9093, Tegucigalpa; tel. 239-5790; fax 239-5737; e-mail ambasciata.tegucigalpa@ esteri.it; internet www.ambtegucigalpa.esteri.it; Ambassador Giuseppe Magno.

Hungary: 1143 Budapest, Stefánia u. 95; tel. (1) 460-6200; fax (1) 460-6260; e-mail ambasciata.budapest@esteri.it; internet www.ambitalia.hu; Ambassador PAOLO GUIDO SPINELLI.

India: 50e Chandragupta Marg, Chanakyapuri, New Delhi 110 021; tel. (11) 26114355; fax (11) 26873889; e-mail ambasciata.newdelhi@esteri.it; internet www.ambnewdelhi.esteri.it; Ambassador Antonio Armellini.

Indonesia: Jalan Diponegoro 45, Menteng, Jakarta Pusat 10310; tel. (21) 31937445; fax (21) 31937422; e-mail embitaly@italambjkt.or.id; internet www.ambjakarta.esteri.it; Ambassador ROBERTO PALMIERI.

Iran: POB 11365-7863, 81 Neauphle-le-Château Ave, Tehran; tel. (21) 66726955; fax (21) 66726961; e-mail segreteria.teheran@esteri.it; internet www.ambteheran.esteri.it; Ambassador Roberto Toscano.

Iraq: 33/7/15 Hay al-Maghrib, Mahala 304, Baghdad; tel. (1) 425-0720; e-mail ambasciata.baghdad@esteri.it; internet www.italian-embassy.org.ae/ ambasciata_baghdad; Ambassador MAURIZIO MELANI.

Ireland: 63–65 Northumberland Rd, Dublin 4; tel. (1) 6601744; fax (1) 6682759; e-mail ambasciata.dublino@esteri.it; internet www.ambdublino .esteri.it; Ambassador Dr Lucio Alberto Savoia.

Israel: Trade Tower Bldg, 25 Hamered St, Tel-Aviv 68125; tel. 3-5104004; fax 3-5100235; e-mail info@telaviv.esteri.it; internet www.ambtelaviv.esteri.it; Ambassador SANDRO DE BERNARDIN.

Japan: 2-5-4, Mita, Minato-ku, Tokyo 108-8302; tel. (3) 3453-5291; fax (3) 3456-2319; e-mail ambasciata.tokyo@esteri.it; internet www.ambtokyo .esteri.it/ambasciata_tokyo; Ambassador Mario Bova.

Jordan: POB 9800, Jabal al-Weibdeh, 5 Hafiz Ibrahim St, Amman 11191; tel. (6) 4638185; fax (6) 4659730; e-mail info.amman@esteri.it; internet www .ambmman.esteri.it; Ambassador GIANFRANCO GIORGOLO.

Kazakhstan: 010000 Astana, Kosmonavtov 62; tel. (7172) 24-33-90; fax (7172) 24-38-68; e-mail ambasciata.astana@esteri.it; internet www .ambastana.esteri.it; Chargé d'affaires Bruno Antonio Pasquino.

Kenya: International House, 9th Floor, Mama Ngina St, POB 30107, Nairobi; tel. (20) 247750; fax (20) 247086; e-mail ambasciata.nairobi@esteri .it; internet www.ambnairobi.esteri.it; Ambassador PIERANDREA MAGISTRATI.

Korea, Republic: 1-398, Hannam-dong, Yeongsan-gu, Seoul 140-210; tel. (2) 796-0491; fax (2) 797-5560; e-mail embassy.seoul@esteri.it; internet www .ambseoul.esteri.it; Ambassador Massimo Andrea Leggeri.

Kuwait: POB 4453, 13045 Safat, Kuwait City; tel. 5356010; fax 5356030; e-mail ambasciata.alkuwait@esteri.it; internet www.ambalkuwait.esteri.it; Ambassador GIORGIO DI PIETROGIACOMO.

Latvia: Teātra iela 9, Rīga 1050; tel. 6721-6069; fax 6721-6084; e-mail ambitalia.riga@apollo.lv; internet www.ambriga.esteri.it; Ambassador Francesco Puccio.

Lebanon: rue du Palais Présidentiel, Baabda, Beirut; tel. (5) 954955; fax (5) 959616; e-mail amba.beirut@esteri.it; internet www.ambbeirut.esteri.it; Ambassador GABRIELE CHECCHIA.

Libya: POB 912, Sharia Vahran 1, Tripoli; tel. (21) 3334133; fax (21) 3331673; e-mail ambasciata.tripoli@esteri.it; internet www.ambtripoli.esteri.it; Ambassador Francesco Trupiano.

Lithuania: Vytauto g. 1, Vilnius 08118; tel. (5) 212-0620; fax (5) 212-0405; e-mail ambasciata.vilnius@esteri.it; internet www.ambvilnius.esteri.it; Ambassador DR GIULIO PRIGIONI.

Luxembourg: 5–7 rue Marie-Adélaïde, 2128 Luxembourg; tel. 44-36-44-1; fax 45-55-23; e-mail ambasciata.lussemburgo@esteri.it; internet www .amblussemburgo.esteri.it; Ambassador Roberto Bettarini.

Macedonia, former Yugoslav Republic: 1000 Skopje, VIII Udarna brig. 22; tel. (2) 3236500; fax (2) 3117087; Ambassador DONATINO MARCON.

Malaysia: 99 Jalan U Thant, 55000 Kuala Lumpur; tel. (3) 42565122; fax (3) 42573199; e-mail embassyit@italy-embassy.org.my; internet www .ambkualalumpur.esteri.it; Ambassador Alessandro Busacca.

Malta: 5 Vilhena St, Floriana FRN 1111; tel. 21233157; fax 21239217; e-mail ambasciata.lavalletta@esteri.it; internet www.amblavalletta.esteri.it; Ambassador PAOLO ANDREA TRABALZA.

Mexico: Paseo de las Palmas 1994, Col. Lomas de Chapultepec, Del. Miguel Hidalgo, 11000 México, DF; tel. (55) 5596-3655; fax (55) 5596-2472; e-mail segreteria.messico@esteri.it; internet www.ambcittadelmessico.esteri.it; Ambassador Felice Scauso.

Monaco: L'Annonciade, 17 ave de l'Annonciade, MC 98000; tel. 93-50-22-71; fax 93-50-06-89; e-mail ambasciata.montecarlo@esteri.it; internet www .ambprincipatomonaco.esteri.it; Ambassador MARIO POLVERINI.

Montenegro: 81000 Podgorica, Džordža Vašingtona 83; tel. (81) 234661; fax (81) 234663; e-mail segreteria.podgorica@esteri.it; internet www .conspodgorica.esteri.it; Ambassador Gabriele Meucci.

Morocco: 2 rue Idriss al-Azhar, BP 111, 10001 Rabat; tel. (3) 7219730; fax (3) 7706882; e-mail ambasciate.rabat@esteri.it; internet www.ambrabat.esteri.it; Ambassador UMBERTO LUCCHESI PALLI.

Mozambique: Av. Kenneth Kaunda 387, CP 976, Maputo; tel. 21492229; fax 21492046; e-mail ambasciata.maputo@esteri.it; internet www.ambmaputo .esteri.it; Ambassador Guido Larcher.

Myanmar: 3 Inya Myaing Rd, POB 866, Golden Valley, Bahan Township, Yangon 11201; tel. (1) 527100; fax (1) 514565; e-mail ambitaly@ambitaly.net .mm; internet www.italian-embassy.org.ae/ambasciata_yangon; Ambassador GIUSEPPE CINTI.

Netherlands: Alexanderstraat 12, 2514 JL The Hague; tel. (70) 3021030; fax (70) 3614932; e-mail embitaly.denhaag@esteri.it; internet www.amblaja .esteri.it; Ambassador Gaetano Cortese.

New Zealand: 34–38 Grant Rd, Thorndon, POB 463, Wellington 1; tel. (4) 473-5339; fax (4) 472-7255; e-mail ambasciata.wellington@esteri.it; internet www.ambwellington.esteri.it/ambasciata_wellington; Ambassador DR GIOACCHINO TRIZZINO.

Nicaragua: Rotonda El Güegüense, 1 c. al norte, Apdo 2092, $\frac{1}{2}$ c. abajo, Managua 4; tel. 266-2961; fax 266-3987; e-mail embitaliasegr@cablenet.com .ni; internet www.ambmanagua.esteri.it; Ambassador Dr Alberto Boniver.

Nigeria: 21st Cres., off Constitution Ave, Central Business District, Abuja; tel. (9) 5244036; fax (9) 5244034; e-mail ambasciata.abuja@esteri.it; internet www.ambabuja.esteri.it; Ambassador MASSIMO BAISTROCCHI.

Norway: Inkognitogt. 7, 0244 Oslo; tel. 22-55-22-33; fax 22-44-34-36; e-mail ambasciata.oslo@esteri.it; internet www.amboslo.esteri.it; Ambassador Rosa Anna Coniglio Papalia.

Oman: Shati al-Qurum, Way No. 3034, House No. 2697, POB 3727, Ruwi 112; tel. 24693727; fax 24695161; e-mail ambasciata.mascate@esteri.it; internet www.ambmascate.esteri.it; Ambassador CESARE CAPITANI.

Pakistan: 54 Margalla Rd, F-6/3, POB 1008, Islamabad; tel. (51) 2828982; fax (51) 2829026; e-mail segreteria.ambislamabad@esteri.it; internet www.italian -embassy.org.ae/Ambasciata_Islamabad; Ambassador Vincenzo Prati.

Panama: Torre Banco Exterior, 25°, Avda Balboa, Apdo 2369, Panamá 9; tel. 225-8950; fax 227-4906; e-mail ambpana.mail@esteri.it; internet www .ambpanama.esteri.it; Ambassador PLACIDO VIGO.

Paraguay: Quesada 5871 con Bélgica, Asunción; tel. (21) 61-5620; fax (21) 61-5622; e-mail ambitalia@cmm.com.py; internet www.embajadadeitalia.org .py; Ambassador Giovanni Marocco.

Peru: Avda Gregorio Escobedo 298, Apdo 0490, Lima 11; tel. (1) 4632727; fax (1) 4635317; e-mail segretaria@italembperu.org.pe; internet www .italembperu.org.pe; Ambassador FABIO CLAUDIO DE NARDIS.

Philippines: Zeta II Bldg, 6th Floor, 191 Salcedo St, Legaspi Village, Makati City, Metro Manila; tel. (2) 8924531; fax (2) 8171436; e-mail informazioni .manila@esteri.it; internet www.ambmanila.esteri.it; Ambassador Rubens Anna Fedele.

Poland: 00-055 Warsaw, pl. Dąbrowskiego 6; tel. (22) 8263471; fax (22) 8278507; e-mail ambasciata.varsavia@esteri.it; internet www.ambvarsavia .esteri.it; Ambassador ANNA BLEFARI MELAZZI.

Portugal: Largo Conde de Pombeiro 6, 1150-100 Lisbon; tel. (21) 3515320; fax (21) 3521516; e-mail ambasciata.lisbona@esteri.it; internet www .amblisbona.esteri.it; Ambassador Luca del Balzo di Presenzano.

Qatar: POB 4188, Doha; tel. 4831828; fax 4831909; e-mail ambasciata .doha@esteri.it; internet sedi.esteri.it/doha; Ambassador GIUSEPPE BUCCINO GRIMALDI.

Romania: 010667 Bucharest, Str. Henri Coandă 7–9; tel. (21) 3052100; fax (21) 3120422; e-mail ambasciata.bucarest@esteri.it; internet www .ambbucarest.esteri.it; Ambassador Daniele Mancini.

Russian Federation: 121002 Moscow, Denezhnyi per. 5; tel. (495) 796-96-91; fax (495) 253-92-89; e-mail embitaly.mosca@esteri.it; internet www .ambmosca.esteri.it; Ambassador VITTORIO CLAUDIO SURDO.

San Marino: Viale Antonio Onofri 117, 47890 San Marino; tel. 0549 991146; fax 0549 992229; e-mail ambasciata.sanmarino@esteri.it; internet www .ambsanmarino.esteri.it; Ambassador Fabrizio Santurro.

Saudi Arabia: POB 94389, Riyadh 11693; tel. (1) 488-1212; fax (1) 480-6964; e-mail segreteria1.riad@esteri.it; internet www.ambriad.esteri.it; Ambassador EUGENIO D'AURIA.

Senegal: rue Alpha Achamiyou Tall, BP 348, Dakar; tel. 33-822-0578; fax 33-821-7580; e-mail ambasciata.dakar@esteri.it; internet sedi.esteri.it/dakar; Ambassador Agostino Mathis.

Serbia: 11000 Belgrade, ul. Birčaninova 11; tel. (11) 3066100; fax (11) 3249413; e-mail office@italy.org.yu; internet www.italy.org.yu; Ambassador ALESSANDRO MEROLA.

Singapore: 101 Thomson Rd, 27-02/03 United Sq., Singapore 307591; tel. 62506022; fax 62533301; e-mail ambitaly@italyemb.org.sg; internet www .italyemb.org.sg; Ambassador Folco de Luca Gabrielli.

Slovakia: Palisády 49, 811 06 Bratislava; tel. (2) 5980-0011; fax (2) 5441-3202; e-mail amb.bratislava@esteri.it; internet www.ambbratislava.esteri.it; Ambassador ANTONINO PROVENZANO.

Slovenia: 1000 Ljubljana, Snežniška 8; tel. (1) 4262194; fax (1) 4253302; e-mail archivio.lubiana@esteri.it; internet www.amblubiana.esteri.it; Ambassador Dr Daniele Verga.

South Africa: 796 George Ave, Arcadia, Pretoria 0083; tel. (12) 4230000; fax (12) 4305547; e-mail segreteria.pretoria@esteri.it; internet www.ambpretoria .esteri.it; Ambassador ALESSANDRO CEVESE.

Spain: Lagasca 98, 28006 Madrid; tel. (91) 4233300; fax (91) 5757776; e-mail archivio.ambmadrid@esteri.it; internet www.ambmadrid.esteri.it; Ambassador Pasquale Terracciano.

Sri Lanka: 55 Jawatta Rd, Colombo 5; tel. (11) 2588388; fax (11) 2596344; e-mail ambasciata.colombo@esteri.it; internet www.ambcolombo.esteri.it; Ambassador PIO MARIANI.

Sudan: St 39, Block 61, POB 793, Khartoum; tel. (183) 471615; fax (183) 471217; e-mail ambasciata.khartoum@esteri.it; internet www.ambkhartoum .esteri.it; Ambassador Lorenzo Angeloni.

Sweden: Oakhill, Djurgården, 115 21 Stockholm; tel. (8) 545-671-00; fax (8) 660-05-05; e-mail info.stockholm@esteri.se; internet www.ambstoccolma .esteri.it; Ambassador ANNA DELLA CROCE BRIGANTE COLONNA.

Switzerland: Elfenstr. 14, 3000 Bern 16; tel. 313500777; fax 313500711; e-mail ambasciata.berna@esteri.it; internet www.ambberna.esteri.it; Ambassador GIUSEPPE DEODATO.

Syria: BP 2216, rue al-Ayoubi, Damascus; tel. (11) 3338338; fax (11) 3320325; e-mail ambasciata.damasco@esteri.it; internet www.ambdamasco.esteri.it; Ambassador AKELLI FRANCO LUIGI AMIRIO.

Tanzania: Plot 316, Lugalo Rd, POB 2106, Dar es Salaam; tel. (22) 2115935; fax (22) 2115938; e-mail segr.dar@esteri.it; internet www.ambdaressalaam .esteri.it; Ambassador Francesco Catania.

Thailand: 399 Thanon Nang Linchee, Thungmahamek, Yannawa, Bangkok 10120; tel. (2) 285-4090; fax (2) 285-4793; e-mail ambasciata.bangkok@esteri .it; internet www.italian-embassy.org.ae/Ambasciata_Bangkok; Ambassador IGNAZIO DI PACE.

Tunisia: 37 rue Jamal Abdelnaceur, 1000 Tunis; tel. (71) 321-811; fax (71) 324-155; e-mail ambitalia.tunisi@esteri.it; internet www.ambtunisi.esteri.it; Ambassador Antonio D'Andria.

Turkey: Atatürk Bul. 118, 06680 Kavaklıdere, Ankara; tel. (312) 4574200; fax (312) 4574280; e-mail ambasciata.ankara@esteri.it; internet www.italian -embassy.org.ae/Ambasciata_Ankara; Ambassador CARLO MARSILI.

Uganda: 11 Lourdel Rd, Nakasero, POB 4646, Kampala; tel. (41) 4250442; fax (41) 4250448; e-mail segreteria.kampala@esteri.it; internet www .ambkampala.esteri.it; Ambassador Umberto Plaja.

Ukraine: 01901 Kyiv, vul. Yaroslaviv Val 32B; tel. (44) 230-31-00; fax (44) 230-31-03; e-mail ambasciata.kiev@esteri.it; internet www.ambkiev.esteri.it; Ambassador PETRO GIOVANNI DONNICI.

United Arab Emirates: POB 46752, Villa 438–439, St 26, Al-Manaseer Area, Abu Dhabi; tel. (2) 4435622; fax (2) 4434337; e-mail italianembassy .abudhabi@esteri.it; internet www.ambabudhabi.esteri.it; Ambassador Paolo Dionisi.

United Kingdom: 14 Three Kings Yard, London, W1K 4EH; tel. (20) 7312-2200; fax (20) 7312-2230; e-mail ambasciata.londra@esteri.it; internet www .amblondra.esteri.it; Ambassador GIANCARLO ARAGONA.

United States of America: 3000 Whitehaven St, NW, Washington, DC 20008; tel. (202) 612-4400; fax (202) 518-2151; e-mail stampa@itwash.org; internet www.ambwashingtondc.esteri.it; Ambassador Giovanni Castellaneta.

Uruguay: José Benito Lamas 2857, Casilla 268, 11300 Montevideo; tel. (2) 7084916; fax (2) 7084148; e-mail ambasciata.montevideo@esteri.it; internet www.ambmontevideo.esteri.it; Ambassador GUIDO SCALICI.

Uzbekistan: 100031 Tashkent, Yusuf Xos Hojib ko'ch. 40; tel. (71) 152-11-19; fax (71) 120-66-06; e-mail segreteria.tashkent@esteri.it; internet www .ambtashkent.esteri.it; Ambassador Giovanni Ricciulli.

Vatican City: Palazzo Borromeo, Viale delle Belle Arti 2, 00196 Rome, Italy; tel. (06) 3264881; fax (06) 3201801; e-mail amb.scv@esteri.it; Ambassador ANTONIO ZANARDI LANDI.

Venezuela: Edif. Atrium, Calle Sorocaima, entre Avdas Tamanaco y Venezuela, El Rosal, Apdo 3995, Caracas; tel. (212) 952-7311; fax (212) 952-4960; e-mail ambcaracas@esteri.it; internet www.ambcaracas.esteri.it; Ambassador Luigi Maccotta.

Viet Nam: 9 Le Phung Hieu, Hoan Kiem District, Hanoi; tel. (4) 8256256; fax (4) 8267602; e-mail ambasciata.hanoi@esteri.it; internet www.ambhanoi .esteri.it; Ambassador ALFREDO MATACOTTA CORDELLA.

Yemen: POB 1152, No. 5 Bldg, St No. 29, San'a; tel. (1) 269164; fax (1) 266137; e-mail ambasciata.sanaa@esteri.it; internet www.ambsanaa.esteri.it; Ambassador Mario Boffo.

Zambia: Plot 5211, Embassy Park, Diplomatic Triangle, POB 50497, Lusaka; tel. (1) 250781; fax (1) 254929; e-mail ambasciata.lusaka@esteri.it; internet www.amblusaka.esteri.it; Ambassador DR GIOVANNI CERUTI.

Zimbabwe: 7 Bartholomew Close, Greendale North, POB 1062, Harare; tel. (4) 498190; fax (4) 498199; e-mail segreteria.ambzimbabwe@esteri.it; internet www.ambitalia.co.zw; Ambassador Mario Bologna.

DIPLOMATIC MISSIONS OF JAMAICA

United Nations: 767 Third Ave, 9th Floor, New York, NY 10017; tel. (212) 935-7509; fax (212) 935-7607; e-mail jamaica@un.int; internet www.un.int/ jamaica; Permanent Representative RAYMOND OSBOURNE WOLFE.

Belgium: 77 ave Hansel Soulie, 1000 Brussels; tel. (2) 230-11-70; fax (2) 234-69-69; e-mail emb.jam.brussels@skynet.be; Ambassador Marcia Yvette Gilbert-Roberts.

Canada: 275 Slater St, Suite 800, Ottawa, ON K1P 5H9; tel. (613) 233-9311; fax (613) 233-0611; e-mail hc@jhcottawa.ca; internet www.jhcottawa.ca; High Commissioner RUBY VIOLET EVADNE COYE.

China, People's Republic: Office 6-2-72, Jian Guo Men Wai Diplomatic Compound, 1 Xiu Shui Jie, Beijing 100600; tel. (10) 65320667; fax (10) 65320669; e-mail embassy@jamaicagov.cn; internet www.jamaicagov.cn; Ambassador Wayne McCook.

Cuba: Avda 5, No 3608, entre 36 y 36A, Miramar, Havana; tel. (7) 204-2908; fax (7) 204-2531; e-mail embjmcub@enet.cu; Ambassador ELINOR FELIX-SHERLOCK.

Dominican Republic: Avda Enriquillo 61, Los Cacicazgos, Santo Domingo, DN; tel. 482-7770; fax 482-7773; e-mail emb.jamaica@verizon.net.do; Chargé d'affaires a.i. Thomas F. Allan Marley.

Germany: Schmargendorfer Str. 32, 12159 Berlin; tel. (30) 85994511; fax (30) 85994540; e-mail info@jamador.de; internet www.jamador.de; Ambassador JOY ELFREDA WHEELER.

Japan: Toranomon Yatsuka Bldg, 2nd Floor, 1-1-11, Atago, Minato-ku, Tokyo 105-0002; tel. (3) 3435-1861; fax (3) 3435-1864; e-mail mail@ jamaicaemb.jp; internet www.jamaicaemb.jp; Ambassador (vacant).

Mexico: Schiller 326, 8°, Col. Chapultepec Morales, Del. Miguel Hidalgo, 11570 México, DF; tel. (55) 5250-6804; fax (55) 5250-6160; e-mail embajadadejamaica@prodigy.net.mx; Ambassador SHEILA IVOLINE SEALY-MONTEITH.

Nigeria: Plot 77, Samuel Adedoyin Ave, Victoria Island, POB 75368, Lagos; tel. (1) 2611085; fax (1) 2610047; High Commissioner Robert Miller (acting).

South Africa: 1119 Burnett St, Hatfield, Pretoria 0083; tel. (12) 3626667; fax (12) 3668510; e-mail jhcpretoria@telkomsa.net; High Commissioner JOAN THOMAS (acting).

Trinidad and Tobago: 2 Newbold St, St Clair, Port of Spain; tel. 622-4995; fax 628-9043; e-mail jhctnt@tstt.net.tt; High Commissioner Peter Black.

United Kingdom: 1–2 Prince Consort Rd, London, SW7 2BZ; tel. (20) 7823-9911; fax (20) 7589-5154; e-mail jamhigh@jhcuk.com; internet www.jhcuk .com; High Commr BURCHELL ANTHONY WHITEMAN.

United States of America: 1520 New Hampshire Ave, NW, Washington, DC 20006; tel. (202) 452-0660; fax (202) 452-0081; e-mail info@emjamusa.org; internet www.jamaicaembassy.org; Ambassador Anthony Johnson.

Venezuela: Edif. Los Frailes, 5°, Calle La Guairita, Urb. Chuao, Caracas 1062; tel. (212) 991-6741; fax (212) 991-5708; e-mail embjaven@cantv.net; Ambassador AUDLEY RODRÍQUEZ.

DIPLOMATIC MISSIONS OF JAPAN

United Nations: 866 United Nations Plaza, 2nd Floor, New York, NY 10017; tel. (212) 223-4300; fax (212) 751-1966; e-mail mission@un-japan.org; internet www.un.int/japan; Permanent Representative Yukio Takasu.

Afghanistan: House 83, St 15, Wazir Akbar Khan, Kabul; tel. (873) 762853777; fax (873) 761218272; e-mail ejafg1@web-sat.com; Ambassador JUNICHI KASUGE.

Algeria: BP 80, 1 chemin el-Bakri (ex Macklay), Ben Aknoun, Algiers; tel. (21) 91-20-04; fax (21) 91-20-46; Ambassador Shimizu Kumio.

Angola: Rua Armindo de Andrade 183–185, Miramar, Luanda; tel. 222442007; fax 222449888; Chargé d'affaires a.i. HIROAKI SANO.

Argentina: Bouchard 547, 17°, C1106ABG Buenos Aires; tel. (11) 4318-8200; fax (11) 4318-8210; e-mail taishikan@japan.org.ar; internet www.ar.emb -japan.go.jp; Ambassador Shinya Nagai.

Australia: 112 Empire Circuit, Yarralumla, ACT 2600; tel. (2) 6273-3244; fax (2) 6273-1848; e-mail cultural@japan.org.au; internet www.au.emb-japan.go .jp; Ambassador TAKA-AKI KOJIMA.

Austria: Hessgasse 6, 1010 Vienna; tel. (1) 531-92-0; fax (1) 532-05-90; e-mail info@embjp.at; internet www.at.emb-japan.go.jp; Ambassador Akio Tanaka.

Azerbaijan: 1065 Baku, Izmir küç. 1033, Hyatt Tower III, 6th Floor; tel. (12) 490-78-18; fax (12) 490-78-20; e-mail japan@emb.baku.az; Ambassador TADAKHIRU ABE.

Bahrain: POB 23720, 55 Salmaniya Ave, Salmaniya 327, Manama; tel. 17716565; fax 17715059; e-mail jpembbh@batelco.com.bh; internet www.bh .emb-japan.go.jp; Ambassador Takeshi Kondo.

Bangladesh: 5 and 7, Dutabash Rd, Baridhara, Dhaka 1212; tel. (2) 8810087; fax (2) 8826737; e-mail information@embjp.accesstel.net; internet www.bd.emb-japan.go.jp; Ambassador MASAYUKI INOUE.

Belarus: 220004 Minsk, pr. Pobeditelei 23/1; tel. (17) 223-62-33; fax (17) 210-21-69; Chargé d'affaires a.i. Naotake Yamashita.

Belgium: 58 ave des Arts, 6e étage, BP 17/18, 1000 Brussels; tel. (2) 513-23-40; fax (2) 513-15-56; e-mail info.embjapan@skynet.be; internet www.be.emb-japan.go.jp; Ambassador AZUZA HAYASHI.

Bolivia: Calle Rosendo Gutiérrez 497, esq. Sánchez Lima, Casilla 2725, La Paz; tel. (2) 241-9110; fax (2) 241-1919; e-mail coopjapon@acelerate.com; internet www.bo.emb-japan.go.jp; Ambassador Mitsunori Shirakawa.

Bosnia and Herzegovina: 71000 Sarajevo, Bistrik 9; tel. (33) 209580; fax (33) 209583; Ambassador ITARU UMEZU.

Brazil: SES, Av. das Nações, Quadra 811, Lote 39, 70425-900 Brasília, DF; tel. (61) 3442-4200; fax (61) 3242-0738; e-mail consularjapao@yawl.com.br; internet www.br.emb-japan.go.jp; Ambassador Ken Shimanouchi.

Brunei: 1 & 3 Jalan Jawatan Dalam, Lot 37355, 33 Simpang 122, Kampong Kiulap, Bandar Seri Begawan BE 1518; tel. 2229265; fax 2229481; e-mail embassy@japan.com.bn; internet www.bn.emb-japan.go.jp; AmbassadorNISAKA YOSHINOBU.

Bulgaria: 1087 Sofia, ul. Lyulyakova gradina 14; tel. (2) 971-27-08; fax (2) 971-10-95; internet www.bg.emb-japan.go.jp; Ambassador Tsuneharu Takeda.

Cambodia: 194 blvd Norodom, Sangkat Tonle Bassac, Khan Chamkarmon, Phnom-Penh; tel. (23) 217161; fax (23) 216162; e-mail eojc@online.com.kh; internet www.kh.emb-japan.go.jp; Ambassador KATSUHIRO SHINOHARA.

Cameroon: 1513 rue 1828, Quartier Bastos, Ekoudou, BP 6868, Yaoundé; tel. 2220-6202; fax 2220-6203; Ambassador Tsuzuki Kensu Ke.

Canada: 255 Sussex Dr., Ottawa, ON K1N 9E6; tel. (613) 241-8541; fax (613) 241-7415; e-mail infocul@embjapan.ca; internet www.ca.emb-japan.go.jp; Ambassador TSUNEO NISHIDA.

Central African Republic Temporarily closed; affairs handled through the Embassy of Japan, Yaoundé, Cameroon, since October 2003.

Chile: Avda Ricardo Lyon 520, Santiago; tel. (2) 232-1807; fax (2) 232-1812; e-mail embajada.dejap001@chilnet.cl; internet www.cl.emb-japan.go.jp; Ambassador WATARU HAYASHI.

China, People's Republic: 7 Ri Tan Lu, Jian Guo Men Wai, Beijing 100600; tel. (10) 65322361; fax (10) 65324625; e-mail info@eoj.cn; internet www.cn.emb-japan.go.jp; AmbassadorYuji Miyamoto.

Colombia: Carrera 7A, No 71-21, 11°, Torre B, Bogotá, DC; tel. (1) 317-5001; fax (1) 317-5007; e-mail info@embjp-colombia.com; internet www.colombia.emb-japan.go.jp; Ambassador TATSUMARO TERAZAWA.

Congo, Democratic Republic: Immeuble Citibank, 2ème étage, ave Colonel Lukusa, BP 1810, Kinshasa; tel. (81) 8845305; fax (satellite) 871-761-21-41-42; e-mail ambassadedujapon@yahoo.co.jp; internet www.rdc.emb-japan.go.jp; Ambassador Yasuo Takano.

Costa Rica: Oficentro Ejecutivo La Sabana, Edif. 7, 3º, detrás de la Contraloría, Sabana Sur, Apdo 501, 1000 San José; tel. 232-1255; fax 231-3140; e-mail embjapon@sol.racsa.co.cr; internet www.cr.emb-japan.go.jp; Ambassador HIDEKAZU YAMAGUCHI.

Côte d'Ivoire: Immeuble Alpha 2000, ave Chardy, 01 BP 1329, Abidjan 01; tel. 20-21-28-63; fax 20-21-30-51; Ambassador Tetsuo Shioguchi.

Croatia: 10000 Zagreb, Boškovićeva 2; tel. (1) 4870650; fax (1) 4667334; e-mail embassy@jpemb.htnet.hr; Ambassador TETSUHISA SHIRAKAWA.

Cuba: Centro de Negocios Miramar, Avda 3, No 1, 5°, esq. 80, Miramar, Havana; tel. (7) 204-3355; fax (7) 204-8902; Ambassador Akira Takamatsu.

Czech Republic: Maltézské nám. 6, 118 01 Prague 1; tel. 257533546; fax 257532377; e-mail info@japanembassy.cz; internet www.cz.emb-japan.go.jp; Ambassador HIDEAKI KUMAZAWA.

Denmark: Pilestræde 61, 1112 Copenhagen K; tel. 33-11-33-44; fax 33-11-33-77; e-mail info@embjapan.dk; internet www.embjapan.dk; Ambassador Masaki Okada.

Dominican Republic: Torre BHD, 8°, Avda Winston Churchill, esq. Luis F. Thomén, Santo Domingo, DN; tel. 567-3365; fax 566-8013; internet www.do.emb-japan.go.jp; Ambassador HARUO OKAMOTO.

Ecuador: Juan León Mera 130 y Avda Patria, 7°, Quito; tel. (2) 256-1899; fax (2) 250-3670; e-mail japembec@uio.satnet.net; Ambassador Hiroyuki Hiramatsu.

Egypt: 9th Floor, Cairo Centre Bldg, 2 Sharia Abd al-Kader Hamza; tel. (2) 7953962; fax (2) 7963540; e-mail center@embjapan.org.eg; internet www.eg.emb-japan.go.jp; Ambassador KAORU ISHIKAWA.

El Salvador: World Trade Center, Torre 1, 6°, 89 Avda Norte y Calle El Mirador, Col. Escalón, Apdo 115, San Salvador; tel. 2224-4740; fax 2298-6685; internet www.sv.emb-japan.go.jp; Ambassador Shisei Kaku.

Estonia: Harju 6, Tallinn 15069; tel. 631-0531; fax 631-0533; e-mail jaapansk@online.ee; internet www.japemb.ee; Chargé d'affaires a.i. TOSHIKO SHIMIZU.

Ethiopia: Woreda 18, Kebele 7, House No. 653, POB 5650, Addis Ababa; tel. (11) 5511088; fax (11) 5511350; e-mail japan-embassy@telecom.net.et; Ambassador Kinichi Komano.

Fiji: Dominion House, 2nd Floor, POB 13045, Suva; tel. 3304633; fax 3302984; e-mail eojfiji@is.com.fj; internet www.fj.emb-japan.go.jp; Ambassador MASASHI NAMEKAWA.

Finland: Unioninkatu 20–22, 00130 Helsinki; tel. (9) 6860200; fax (9) 633012; e-mail inquiry.fi@jpnembassy.fi; internet www.fi.emb-japan.go.jp; Ambassador Hitoshi Honda.

France: 7 ave Hoche, 75008 Paris; tel. 1-48-88-62-00; fax 1-42-27-50-81; e-mail info-fr@amb-japon.fr; internet www.fr.emb-japan.go.jp; Ambassador YUTAKA IIMURA.

Gabon: blvd du Bord de Mer, BP 2259, Libreville; tel. 73-22-97; fax 73-60-60; Ambassador Sadamu Fujiwara.

Germany: Hiroshimastr. 6, 10785 Berlin; tel. (30) 210940; fax (30) 21094222; e-mail info@botschaft-japan.de; internet www.botschaft-japan.de; Ambassador TOSHIYUKI TAKANO.

Ghana: Fifth Ave, POB 1637, West Cantonments, Accra; tel. (21) 765060; fax (21) 762553; Ambassador Massamichi Ishikawa.

Greece: Odos Ethnikis Antistasseos, Halandri, 152 31 Athens; tel. (210) 6709900; fax (210) 6709980; e-mail embjapan@otenet.gr; internet www.embjapan.gr; Ambassador TAKANORI KITAMURA.

Guatemala: Edif. Torre Internacional, 10°, Avda de la Reforma 16-85, Zona 10, Guatemala City; tel. 2367-2244; fax 2367-2245; e-mail embjpn@intelnet.net.gt; internet www.gt.emb-japan.go.jp; Ambassador Kazumi Suzuki.

Guinea: Lanseboundji, Corniche Sud, Commune de Matam, BP 895, Conakry; tel. 30-46-85-10; fax 30-46-85-09; Ambassador KEIICHI KITABAN.

Haiti: Villa Bella Vista, 2 Impasse Tulipe Desprez, BP 2512, Port-au-Prince; tel. 245-3333; fax 245-8834; Ambassador Haruo Okomoto.

Honduras: Col. San Carlos, Calzada Rep. Paraguay, Apdo 3232, Tegucigalpa; tel. 236-2628; fax 236-6100; e-mail gerardo@graduate.chiba-u.jp; internet www.hn.emb-japan.go.jp; Ambassador TAKASHI KOEZUKA.

Hungary: 1125 Budapest, Zalai u. 7; tel. (1) 398-3100; fax (1) 275-1281; e-mail japan.embassy@mail.datanet.hu; internet www.hu.emb-japan.go.jp; Ambassador Teruyoshi Inagawa.

Iceland: Laugavegur 182, POB 5380, 105 Reykjavík; tel. 5108600; fax 5108605; e-mail japan@itn.is; Ambassador HISAO YAMAGUCHI (resident in Oslo, Norway).

India: Plots 4–5, 50g Shanti Path, Chanakyapuri, New Delhi 110 021; tel. (11) 26876581; fax (11) 26885587; e-mail jpembjic@bol.net.in; internet www.in.emb-japan.go.jp; Ambassador Hideaki Domichi.

Indonesia: Menara Thamrin, 7th–10th Floors, Jalan M. H. Thamrin 24, Kav. 3, Jakarta Pusat 10350; tel. (21) 31924308; fax (21) 31925460; internet www.id.emb-japan.go.jp; Ambassador SHIN EBIHARA.

Iran: POB 11365-814, Bucharest Ave, Cnr of 5th St, Tehran; tel. (21) 88713396; fax (21) 88713515; internet www.ir.emb-japan.go.jp; Ambassador Akio Shirota.

Iraq: 50/21/929 Hay Babel, Baghdad; tel. (1) 776-6791; e-mail azza_fh@yahoo.com; Ambassador KENJIRO MONJI.

Ireland: Nutley Bldg, Merrion Centre, Nutley Lane, Dublin 4; tel. (1) 2028300; fax (1) 2838726; e-mail protocol@embip.ie; internet www.ie.emb-japan.go.jp; AmbassadorToshinao Urabe.

Israel: 4 Berkowitz St, Museum Tower, Tel-Aviv 64238; tel. 3-6957292; fax 3-6910516; e-mail embjpcul@netvision.net.il; internet www.israel.emb-japan.go.jp; Ambassador YOSHINORI KATORI.

Italy: Via Quintino Sella 60, 00187 Rome; tel. (06) 487991; fax (06) 4873316; internet www.it.emb-japan.go.jp; Ambassador Yuki Nakamura.

Jamaica: Mutual Life Centre, North Tower, 6th Floor, 2 Oxford Rd, POB 8104, Kingston 5; tel. 929-3338; fax 968-1373; internet www.jamaica.emb-japan.go.jp; Ambassador MASAHIRO OBATA.

Jordan: POB 2835, Ibn al-Furat St, Sweifiyeh, Amman 11181; tel. (6) 5932005; fax (6) 5931006; e-mail mail@embjapan.org.jo; internet www.jordan.emb-japan.go.jp; AmbassadorShigenobu Kato.

Kazakhstan: 010000 Astana, Chubar sh-a, Kosmonavtov 62; tel. (7172) 97-78-43; fax (7172) 97-78-42; internet www.kz.emb-japan.go.jp/jp/index_r.htm; Ambassador TETSUO ITO.

Kenya: Mara Rd, Upper Hill, POB 60202, Nairobi; tel. (20) 2898000; fax (20) 2898220; e-mail jinfocul@eojkenya.org; internet www.ke.emb-japan.go.jp; Ambassador Satoru Miyamura.

Korea, Republic: 18-11, Junghak-dong, Jongno-gu, Seoul; tel. (2) 2170-5200; fax (2) 734-4528; e-mail info@japanem.or.kr; internet www.kr.emb-japan.go.jp; Ambassador TOSHINORI SHIGEIE.

Kuwait: POB 2304, 13024 Safat, Jabriya, Area 9, Plot 496, St 101, Kuwait City; tel. 5312870; fax 5326168; e-mail info@embjp-kw.org; internet www.kw.emb-japan.go.jp; Ambassador Masatoshi Muto.

Kyrgyzstan: 720033 Bishkek, Frunze 503; tel. (312) 61-18-75; fax (312) 61-18-82; Ambassador TETSUO ITO.

Laos: rue Sisangvone, Vientiane; tel. (21) 414401; fax (21) 414406; internet www.la.emb-japan.go.jp; Ambassador Masaaki Miyashita.

Latvia: Kr. Valdemāra iela 21, Rīga 1010; tel. 6781-2001; fax 6781-2004; e-mail eoj.001@latnet.lv; Ambassador AKIRA NAKAJIMA.

Lebanon: POB 11-3360, Army St, Zkak al-Blat, Serail Hill, Beirut; tel. (1) 985751; fax (1) 989754; e-mail japanemb@japanemb.org.lb; internet www.lb.emb-japan.go.jp; Ambassador Yoshihisa Kuroda.

Libya: POB 3265, Sharia Jamal ad-Din al-Waeli, Hay Andalus, Tripoli; tel. (21) 4781041; fax (21) 4781044; Ambassador AKIRA WATANABE.

Lithuania: M. K. Čiurlionio g. 82b, Vilnius 03100; tel. (5) 231-0462; fax (5) 231-0461; Ambassador Masaki Okada.

Luxembourg: 62 ave de la Faïencerie, BP 92, 2010 Luxembourg; tel. 46-41-51-1; fax 46-41-76; e-mail embjapan@pt.lu; internet www.lu.emb-japan.go.jp; Ambassador KAZUHITO TATEBE.

Madagascar: 8 rue du Dr Villette, BP 3863, Isoraka, 101 Antananarivo; tel. (20) 2226102; fax (20) 2221769; Ambassador Tetsuro Kawaguchi.

Malaysia: 11 Pesiaran Stonor, off Jalan Tun Razak, 50450 Kuala Lumpur; tel. (3) 21427044; fax (3) 21672314; internet www.my.emb-japan.go.jp; Ambassador MASAHIKO HORIE.

Marshall Islands: A-1 Lojkar Village, POB 300, Majuro, MH 96960; tel. (247) 7463; fax (247) 7493; Ambassador Kenro Iino.

Mexico: Paseo de la Reforma 395, Apdo 5-101, Col. Cuauhtémoc, Del. Cuauhtémoc, 06500 México, DF; tel. (55) 5211-0028; fax (55) 5207-7743; e-mail embjapmx@mail.internet.com.mx; internet www.mx.emb-japan.go.jp; Ambassador MASAAKI ONO.

Micronesia, Federated States: Pami Bldg, 3rd Floor, POB 1847, Kolonia, Pohnpei, FM 96941; tel. 320-5465; fax 320-5470; Chargé d'affaires a.i. Toshio Omura.

Mongolia: Olimpiin Gudamj 8, Ulan Bator (CPOB 1011); tel. (11) 320777; fax (11) 313332; e-mail eojmongol@magicnet.mn; internet www.eojmongolia.mn; Ambassador YASUYOSHI ICHIHASHI.

Morocco: 39 ave Ahmed Balafrej, Souissi, 10100 Rabat; tel. (3) 7631782; fax (3) 7750078; e-mail amb-japon@fusion.net.ma; internet www.ma.emb-japan.go.jp; Ambassador Haruku Hirose.

Mozambique: Av. Julius Nyerere 2832, CP 2494, Maputo; tel. 21499819; fax 21498957; Ambassador TATSUYA MIKI.

Myanmar: 100 Natmauk Rd, POB 841, Bahan Township, Yangon 11021; tel. (1) 549644; fax (1) 549643; e-mail jembassy@baganmail.net.mm; internet www.mm.emb-japan.go.jp; Ambassador Yasuaki Nogawa.

Nepal: Panipokhari, POB 264, Kathmandu; tel. (1) 4426680; fax (1) 4414101; e-mail comjpn@mos.com.np; internet www.np.emb-japan.go.jp; Ambassador TATSUO MIZUNO.

Netherlands: Tobias Asserlaan 2, 2517 KC The Hague; tel. (70) 3469544; fax (70) 3106341; e-mail japan.cultural@planet.nl; internet www.nl.emb-japan.go.jp; Ambassador Minoru Shibuya.

New Zealand: Majestic Centre, Levels 18–19, 100 Willis St, POB 6340, Wellington 1; tel. (4) 473-1540; fax (4) 471-2951; e-mail japan.emb@eoj.org.nz; internet www.nz.emb-japan.go.jp; Ambassador TAKAHASHI TOSHIHIRO.

Nicaragua: Plaza España, 1 c. abajo y 1 c. al lago, Bolonia, Apdo 1789, Managua; tel. 266-8668; fax 266-8566; e-mail embjpnic@cablenet.com.ni; internet www.ni.emb-japan.go.jp; Ambassador Shinichi Saito.

Nigeria: Plot 585 Bobo St, Maitama, PMB 5070, Abuja; tel. (9) 4138898; fax (9) 4137667; Ambassador AKIO TANAKA.

Norway: Wergelandsveien 15, 0244 Oslo; tel. 22-99-16-00; fax 22-44-25-05; e-mail info@japan-embassy.no; internet www.no.emb-japan.go.jp; Ambassador Hisao Yamaguchi.

Oman: Shati al-Qurum, Villa No. 760, Way No. 3011, Jamiat ad-Dowal al-Arabiya St, POB 3511, Ruwi 112; tel. 24601028; fax 24698720; internet www.oman.emb-japan.go.jp; Ambassador KEIJI OMORI.

Pakistan: Plot No. 53-70, Ramna 5/4, Diplomatic Enclave 1, Islamabad 44000; tel. (51) 2279320; fax (51) 2279340; e-mail japanemb@comsats.net.pk; internet www.pk.emb-japan.go.jp; Ambassador Seiji Kojima.

Palau: POB 6050, Palau Pacific Resort, Arakebesang, Koror, PW 96940; tel. 488-6455; fax 488-6458; Ambassador MASASHI NAMEKAWA (resident in Fiji).

Panama: Calle 50 y 60e, Obarrio, Apdo 1411, Panamá 1; tel. 263-6155; fax 263-6019; e-mail taiship2@cwpanama.net; internet www.panama.emb-japan.go.jp; Ambassador Shuji Shimokoji.

Papua New Guinea: Cuthbertson House, Cuthbertson St, POB 1040, Port Moresby; tel. 3211800; fax 3217906; Ambassador HASHIME NISHIYAMA.

Paraguay: Avda Mariscal López 2364, Casilla 1957, Asunción; tel. (21) 60-4616; fax (21) 60-6901; e-mail japoncul@rieder.net.py; internet www.py.emb-japan.go.jp; Ambassador Kenro Iino.

Peru: Avda San Felipe 356, Apdo 3708, Jesús María, Lima 11; tel. (1) 2181130; fax (1) 4630302; internet www.pe.emb-japan.go.jp; Ambassador SHUICHIRO MEGATA.

Philippines: 2627 Roxas Blvd, Pasay City, 1300 Metro Manila; tel. (2) 5515710; fax (2) 5515780; e-mail jicc-mnl@japanembassy.ph; internet www.ph.emb-japan.go.jp; Ambassador Makoto Katsura.

Poland: 00-464 Warsaw, ul. Szwoleżerów 8; tel. (22) 6965000; fax (22) 6965001; e-mail info-cul@emb-japan.pl; internet www.pl.emb-japan.go.jp; Ambassador RYUICHI TANABE.

Portugal: Av. da Liberdade 245–6, 1269-033 Lisbon; tel. (21) 3110560; fax (21) 3534802; e-mail bunka@ip.pt; internet www.pt.emb-japan.go.jp; Ambassador Satoshi Hara.

Qatar: POB 2208, Doha West Bay, Diplomatic Area, Doha; tel. 4840888; fax 4832178; Ambassador YUKIO KITAZUME.

Romania: 011141 Bucharest 1, America House East Wing, Şos. Nicolae Titulescu 4–8; tel. (21) 3191890; fax (21) 3191895; e-mail embassy@embjpn.ro; internet www.ro.emb-japan.go.jp; Ambassador Kanji Tsushima.

Russian Federation: 129090 Moscow, Grokholskii per. 27; tel. (495) 229-25-50; fax (495) 229-25-55; e-mail embjapan@mail.cnt.ru; internet www.ru.emb-japan.go.jp; Ambassador YASUO SAITO.

Saudi Arabia: POB 4095, Riyadh 11491; tel. (1) 488-1100; fax (1) 488-0189; e-mail info@jpn-emb-sa.com; internet www.ksa.emb-japan.go.jp; Ambassador Shigeru Nakamura.

Senegal: blvd Martin Luther King, Corniche-Ouest, BP 3140, Dakar; tel. 33-849-5500; fax 33-849-5555; AmbassadorAKIRA NAKAJIMA.

Serbia: 11070 Novi Belgrade, Vladimira Popovića 6; tel. (11) 3012800; fax (11) 3118258; Ambassador Tadashi Ngai.

Singapore: 16 Nassim Rd, Singapore 258390; tel. 62358855; fax 67331039; e-mail eojsingfv@vsystem.com.sg; internet www.sg.emb-japan.go.jp; Ambassador MAKOTO YAMANAKA.

Slovakia: Hlavné nám. 2, 813 27 Bratislava; tel. (2) 5980-0100; fax (2) 5443-2771; internet www.sk.emb-japan.go.jp; Ambassador Makoto Washizu.

Slovenia: 1000 Ljubljana, trg Republike 3/XI; tel. (1) 2008281; fax (1) 2511822; internet www.si.emb-japan.go.jp; Ambassador TSUNESHIGE IIYAMA.

Solomon Islands: National Provident Fund Bldg, Mendana Ave, POB 560, Honiara; tel. 22953; fax 21006; Chargé d'affaires Iwanda Akira.

South Africa: 259 Baines St, cnr Frans Oerder St, Groenkloof, Pretoria 0181; Private Bag X999, Pretoria 0001; tel. (12) 4521500; fax (12) 4603800; e-mail info@embjapan.org.za; internet www.japan.org.za; Ambassador AKIHIKO FURUYA.

Spain: Serrano 109, 28006 Madrid; tel. (91) 5907600; fax (91) 5901321; internet www.es.emb-japan.go.jp; Ambassador Motohide Yoshikawa.

Sri Lanka: 20 Gregory's Rd, POB 822, Colombo 7; tel. (11) 2693831; fax (11) 2698629; e-mail cultujpn@sltnet.lk; internet www.lk.emb-japan.go.jp; Ambassador KIYOSHI ARAKI.

Sudan: St 43, House No. 67, POB 1649, Khartoum; tel. (183) 471601; fax (183) 471600; Ambassador Yuichi Ishii.

Suriname: Henck Arronstraat 23–25, POB 2921, Paramaribo; tel. 474860; fax 412208; e-mail eojparbo@sr.net; Ambassador YASUO MATSUI (resident in Venezuela).

Sweden: Gärdesgt. 10, 115 27 Stockholm; tel. (8) 579-353-00; fax (8) 661-88-20; e-mail protocol@japansamb.se; internet www.se.emb-japan.go.jp; Ambassador Akira Nakajima.

Switzerland: Engestr. 53, 3000 Bern 9; tel. 313002222; fax 313002255; e-mail eojs@bluewin.ch; internet www.ch.emb-japan.go.jp; Ambassador NOBUYASU ABE.

Syria: BP 3366, 3537 Sharkasiya, rue al-Jala'a, Abou Roumaneh, Damascus; tel. (11) 3338273; fax (11) 3339920; Ambassador Masaki Kuneida.

Tajikistan: 734000 Dushanbe, Kuchai X. Nazarov 80A; tel. (372) 21-39-70; fax (44) 600-54-78; e-mail embjpn@embjpn.tojikiston.com; Ambassador YUICHI KUSUMOTO.

Tanzania: 1018 Ali Hassan Mwinyi Rd, POB 2577, Dar es Salaam; tel. (22) 2115827; fax (22) 2115830; internet www.tz.emb-japan.go.jp; Ambassador Makoto Ito.

Timor-Leste: Pertamina 6, Dili; tel. 3323131; fax 3323130; e-mail japrepet@yahoo.co.jp; Ambassador KENJI SHIMIZU.

Trinidad and Tobago: 5 Hayes St, St Clair, POB 1039, Port of Spain; tel. 628-5991; fax 622-0858; e-mail embassyofjapan@tstt.net.tt; internet www.tt.emb-japan.go.jp; Ambassador Koichiro Seki.

Tunisia: 9 rue Apollo XI, BP 163, Cité Mahrajène, 1082 Tunis; tel. (71) 791-251; fax (71) 786-625; internet www.tn.emb-japan.go.jp; Ambassador SHIGERU ENDO.

Turkey: Reşit Galip Cad. 81, 06692 Gaziosmanpaşa, Ankara; tel. (312) 4460500; fax (312) 4371812; e-mail culture@jpn-emb.org.tr; internet www.tr.emb-japan.go.jp; Ambassador Nobuaki Tanaka.

Turkmenistan: 744000 Aşgabat, ul. Hydyr Derzhazhev, Hotel 'Ak Altin'; tel. (12) 47-70-81; fax (12) 47-70-83; Ambassador YASUO SAITO (resident in Moscow, Russia).

Uganda: Plot 8, Kyaddondo Rd, Nakasero, POB 23553, Kampala; tel. (41) 4349542; fax (41) 4349547; e-mail jembassy@jembassy.co.ug; Ambassador Ryuuzi Kikuchi.

Ukraine: 01901 Kyiv, Muzeiniy prov. 4; tel. (44) 490-55-00; fax (44) 490-55-02; e-mail jpembua7f@sovamua.com; internet www.ua.emb-japan.go.jp; Ambassador MUTSUO MABUCHI.

United Arab Emirates: POB 2430, Abu Dhabi; tel. (2) 4435696; fax (2) 4434219; e-mail embjpn@japanembassyauh.com; internet www.uae.emb-japan.go.jp; Ambassador Takuma Hatano.

United Kingdom: 101–104 Piccadilly, London, W1J 7JT; tel. (20) 7465-6500; fax (20) 7491-9348; e-mail info@jpembassy.org.uk; internet www.uk.emb-japan.go.jp; Ambassador YOSHIJI NOGAMI.

United States of America: 2520 Massachusetts Ave, NW, Washington, DC 20008-2869; tel. (202) 238-6700; fax (202) 238-2187; e-mail jicc@embjapan.org; internet www.us.emb-japan.go.jp; Ambassador Ryozo Kato.

Uruguay: Blvr Artigas 953, 11300 Montevideo; tel. (2) 4187645; fax (2) 4187980; e-mail embjapon@adinet.com.uy; internet www.uy.emb-japan.go.jp; Ambassador MASAMI TAKEMOTO.

Uzbekistan: 100047 Tashkent, S. Azimov ko'ch., 1-tor 28; tel. (71) 120-80-60; fax (71) 120-80-77; internet www.uz.emb-japan.go.jp; Ambassador Tsytomu Hiraoka.

Vatican City: Via Virgilio 30, 00193 Rome, Italy; tel. (06) 6875828; fax (06) 68807543; Ambassador KAGEFUMI UENO.

Venezuela: Edif. Bancaracas, 10°, Avda San Felipe con 2a Transversal, La Castellana, Caracas; tel. (212) 261-8333; fax (212) 261-6780; e-mail ajapon@genesisbci.net; internet www.ve.emb-japan.go.jp; Ambassador Shuji Shimokoji.

Viet Nam: 27 Lieu Giai, Ba Dinh District, Hanoi; tel. (4) 8463000; fax (4) 8463043; e-mail soumuhan@vnn.vn; internet www.vn.emb-japan.go.jp; Ambassador MITSUO SAKABA.

Yemen: POB 817, Haddah Area, San'a; tel. (1) 423700; fax (1) 417850; internet www.ye.emb-japan.go.jp; Ambassador Masakazu Toshikage.

Zambia: Plot 5218, Haile Selassie Ave, POB 34190, 10101 Lusaka; tel. (1) 251555; fax (1) 254425; internet www.zm.emb-japan.go.jp; Ambassador MASAAKI MIYASHITA.

Zimbabwe: Social Security Centre, 4th Floor, cnr Julius Nyerere Way and Sam Nujoma St, POB 2710, Harare; tel. (4) 250025; fax (4) 250111; internet www.zw.emb-japan.go.jp; Ambassador Takeo Yoshikawa.

DIPLOMATIC MISSIONS OF JORDAN

United Nations: 866 United Nations Plaza, Suite 552, New York, NY 10017; tel. (212) 832-9553; fax (212) 832-5346; e-mail jordan@un.int; Permanent Representative MOHAMMED F. AL-ALLAF.

Algeria: 47 rue Ammani Belkalem, Hydra, Algiers; tel. (21) 69-20-31; fax (21) 69-15-54; e-mail jordan@wissal.dz; Ambassador Abdullah el-Ayyam.

Australia: 20 Roebuck St, Red Hill, ACT 2603; tel. (2) 6295-9951; fax (2) 6239-7236; e-mail jordan@jordanembassy.org.au; internet www.jordanembassy.org.au; Ambassador RAJAB SUKAYRI.

Austria: Rennweg 17/4, 1030 Vienna; tel. (1) 405-10-25; fax (1) 405-10-31; e-mail info@jordanembassy.at; internet www.jordanembassy.at; Ambassador Makram Queisi.

Bahrain: POB 5242, Villa 43, Rd 1901, Area 319, Manama; tel. 17291109; fax 17291980; e-mail jordemb@batelco.com.bh; Ambassador HUSSAIN AL-MAJALI.

Belgium: 104 ave F. D. Roosevelt, 1050 Brussels; tel. (2) 640-77-55; fax (2) 640-27-96; e-mail jordan.embassy@skynet.be; internet www.jordanembassy.be; Ambassador Ahmad Khalaf Masaadeh.

Brazil: SHIS, QI 09, Conj. 18, Casa 14, 70483-900 Brasília, DF; tel. (61) 3248-5414; fax (61) 3248-1698; e-mail emb.jordania@apis.com.br; Ambassador RAMEZ ZAKI ODEH GOUSSOUS.

Canada: 100 Bronson Ave, Suite 701, Ottawa, ON K1R 6G8; tel. (613) 238-8090; fax (613) 232-3341; e-mail jordan@on.aibn.com; internet www.embassyofjordan.ca; Ambassador Nabil Ali Mohamed Barto.

Chile: Rosa O' Higgins 287, Las Condes, Santiago; tel. (2) 325-7748; fax (2) 325-7754; e-mail jordanem@vtr.net; Ambassador NABIL MASARWEH.

China, People's Republic: 5 Dong Liu Jie, San Li Tun, Beijing 100600; tel. (10) 65323906; fax (10) 65323283; e-mail beijingmission@jordan-embassy.com; AmbassadorAnmar Abdulhalim Namir Harmud.

Egypt: 6 Sharia Juhaini, Cairo; tel. (2) 7499912; fax (2) 7601027; e-mail jocairo2@ie-eg.com; Ambassador OMAR RIFAI.

France: 80 blvd Maurice Barrès, 92200 Neuilly-sur-Seine; tel. 1-55-62-00-00; fax 1-55-62-00-06; e-mail amjo.paris@wanadoo.fr; Ambassador Dina Kawar.

Germany: Heerstr. 201, 13595 Berlin; tel. (30) 36996051; fax (30) 36996011; e-mail jordan@jordanembassy.de; internet www.jordanembassy.de; Ambassador ISSA NASSER TAWFIQ AYYOUB.

Greece: Odos Papadiamnti 21, Palaio Psychiko, 154 52 Athens; tel. (210) 6744161; fax (210) 6740578; e-mail jor_embl@otenet.gr; Ambassador Zaid Abdullah Zuraikat.

India: 30 Golf Links, New Delhi 110 003; tel. (11) 24653318; fax (11) 24653353; e-mail jordan@jordanembassyindia.org; internet www.jordanembassyindia.org; Ambassador MOHAMMAD ALI DAHER.

Indonesia: Artha Graha Tower, 9th Floor, Sudirman Central Business District, Jalan Jenderal Sudirman, Kav. 52–53, Jakarta 12190; tel. (21) 5153483; fax (21) 5153482; e-mail jordanem@cbn.net.id; internet www.jordanembassy.or.id; Ambassador Mohammad Hassan Dawodieh.

Iran: POB 14665-835, Shahrak-e-Ghods, Faz 4, Khayaban Flamk, Khayaban 8, Block 1647, Tehran 009821; tel. (21) 88088356; fax (21) 88080496; e-mail jordanemb-teh@hotmail.com; Ambassador AHMAD JALAL AL-MEFLAH.

Iraq: POB 6314, 145/49/617 Hay al-Andalus, Baghdad; tel. (1) 541-2892; fax (1) 541-2009; e-mail jordan@uruklink.net; Ambassador Ahmad al-Lozi.

Israel: 14 Abba Hillel, Ramat-Gan 52506; tel. 3-7517722; fax 3-7517712; Ambassador ALI HAMDAN ABD AL-QADER AL-AYED.

Italy: Via G. Marchi 1b, 00161 Roma; tel. (06) 86205303; fax (06) 8606122; e-mail embroma@jordanembassy.it; Ambassador HRH Princess Wijdan bint Fawaz al-Hashimi.

Japan: Chiyoda House, 4th Floor, 2-17-8, Nagata-cho, Chiyoda-ku, Tokyo 100-0014; tel. (3) 3580-5856; fax (3) 3593-9385; e-mail jor-emb@mc.kcom.ne.jp; internet www18.ocn.ne.jp/~jor-emb; Ambassador SAMIR NAOURI.

Kazakhstan: 010000 Astana; tel. (7172) 24-52-54; fax (7172) 24-52-53; Chargé d'affaires a.i. Suleiman Arabiat.

Kuwait: POB 39891, 73059 Kuwait City; tel. 2533261; fax 2533270; e-mail kujor@qualitynet.net; Ambassador MUHAMMAD AL-QURAAN.

Lebanon: POB 109, Beirut 5113; tel. (5) 922500; fax (5) 922502; e-mail joremb@dm.net.lb; Ambassador Ziyad Majali.

Malaysia: 2 Jalan Kedondong, off Jalan Ampang Hilir, 55000 Kuala Lumpur; tel. (3) 42521268; fax (3) 42528610; e-mail general@jordanembassy.org.my; internet www.jordanembassy.org.my; Ambassador HASSAN MAHMOUD MOHAMMAD AL-JAWARNEH.

Morocco: 65 Villa al-Wafaa, Souissi, 10000 Rabat; tel. (3) 7759270; fax (3) 7758722; Ambassador (vacant).

Netherlands: Badhuisweg 79, 2587 CD The Hague; tel. (70) 4167200; fax (70) 4167209; e-mail info@jordanembassy.nl; internet www.jordanembassy.nl; Ambassador AHMAD S. AL-HASSAN.

Oman: Diplomatic City, Arab League St, POB 70, Al-Adhaiba 130; tel. 24692760; fax 24692762; e-mail embhkjom@omantel.net.om; Ambassador Mazin Midhat Jumah.

Pakistan: 99, Main Double Rd, F-10/1, Islamabad; tel. (51) 2297383; fax (51) 2211630; e-mail jordanem@isb.paknet.com.pk; Ambassador SALEH JAWARNEH.

Qatar: POB 2366, Doha; tel. 4832202; fax 4832173; e-mail jordand@qatar .net.qa; internet www.jordanembassy.com.qa; Ambassador Omar Ibrahim al-Ahmad (recalled Oct. 2006).

Romania: 020461 Bucharest 2, Str. Dumbrava Roşie 1; tel. (21) 2104705; fax (21) 2100320; e-mail jordan.embassy@pcnet.ro; Ambassador RASSEM YAQOUB HASHEM.

Russian Federation: 123001 Moscow, Mamonovskii per. 3; tel. (495) 699-12-42; fax (495) 699-43-54; e-mail emjordan@umail.ru; Ambassador Abdelilah Muhammad Ali al-Kurdi.

Saudi Arabia: POB 94316, Riyadh 11693; tel. (1) 488-0051; fax (1) 488-0072; e-mail jordan.embassy@nesma.net.sa; Ambassador HANI KHALIFAH.

South Africa: 252 Olivier St, Brooklyn, Pretoria 0075; POB 14730, Hatfield 0028; tel. (12) 346861517; fax (12) 3468611; e-mail embjordpta@telkomsa .net; Ambassador Dr Mazen Izzedine Tal.

Spain: General Martínez Campos 41, 28010 Madrid; tel. (91) 3191100; fax (91) 3082536; e-mail jordania@telefonica.net; internet www.embjordaniaes .org; Ambassador ZAID M. AL-LOZI.

Sudan: St 33, House No. 13, POB 1379, Khartoum; tel. (183) 483125; fax (183) 471038; Ambassador Munther Qubaah.

Switzerland: Belpstr. 11, 3007 Bern; tel. 313840404; fax 313840405; e-mail jordanie@bluewin.ch; internet www.jordanie.ch; Ambassador SHEHAB AD-DIN MADI.

Syria: rue Abou Roumaneh, Damascus; tel. (11) 3334642; fax (11) 3336741; Ambassador Dr Hashem Muhammad Taleb ash-Shabboul.

Tunisia: 10 Nahj ash-Shankiti, 1002 Tunis; tel. (71) 785-829; fax (71) 786-461; e-mail emb.jordan@planet.tn; Ambassador SAMIR MUSTAPHA KHALIFA.

Turkey: Dede Korkut Sok. 18 Mesnevi, 06690 Çankaya, Ankara; tel. (312) 4402054; fax (312) 4404327; e-mail jordembank@superonline.com; Ambassador Faris Shawkat al-Mufti.

United Arab Emirates: POB 4024, Abu Dhabi; tel. (2) 4447100; fax (2) 4449157; e-mail jordan2@emirates.net.ae; Ambassador EID KAMAL AR-RODAN.

United Kingdom: 6 Upper Phillimore Gdns, London, W8 7HA; tel. (20) 7937-3685; fax (20) 7937-8795; e-mail info@jordanembassyuk.org; internet www .jordanembassyuk.org; Ambassador Dr Alia Bouran.

United States of America: 3504 International Dr., NW, Washington, DC 20008; tel. (202) 966-2664; fax (202) 966-3110; e-mail hkjembassydc@ jordanembassyus.org; internet www.jordanembassyus.org; Ambassador HRH PRINCE ZEID RA'AD AL-HUSSEIN.

Uzbekistan: 100000 Tashkent, Farhod ko'ch. 9; tel. (71) 274-24-79; fax (71) 120-66-44; e-mail jordanembuzb@mail.ru; Ambassador Muhammad Nour Othman Yousef Balkar.

Yemen: POB 2152, Hadat Damascus St, San'a; tel. (1) 413276; fax (1) 414516; e-mail sanaa@fm.gov.jo; Ambassador AHMAD ALI JARADAT.

DIPLOMATIC MISSIONS OF KAZAKHSTAN

United Nations: 866 United Nations Plaza, Suite 586, New York, NY 10017; tel. (212) 230-1900; fax (212) 230-1172; e-mail kazakhstan@un.int; internet www.un.int/kazakhstan; Permanent Representative Byrganym Aitimova.

Afghanistan: House 1, St 10, Wazir Akbar Khan, Kabul; tel. (70) 284296; e-mail sher60@mail.ru; Ambassador AGYBAY SMAGULOV.

Armenia: 0019 Yerevan, Marshal Baghramian 2–oi per. 1; tel. (10) 21-13-33; fax (10) 27-14-74; e-mail kazembassy@web.am; Ambassador Aiymdoc Ye. Bozzhigitov.

Austria: Felix-Mottl-Str. 23, 1190 Vienna; tel. (1) 367-66-57-11; fax (1) 367-91-75-33; e-mail embassy@kazakhstan.at; internet www.kazakhstan.at; Ambassador KAIRAT ABDRAKHMANOV.

Azerbaijan: 1000 Baku, Inglab küç. 90; tel. (12) 465-62-48; fax (12) 465-62-49; e-mail embassyk@azdata.net; Ambassador (vacant).

Belarus: 220029 Minsk, vul. Kuibysheva 12; tel. (17) 234-30-23; fax (17) 334-96-50; e-mail kazemb@nsys.by; internet www.kazembassy.by; Ambassador BULAT G. ISKAKOV.

Belgium: 30 ave Van Bever, 1180 Brussels; tel. (2) 373-38-90; fax (2) 374-50-91; e-mail info@kazakhstanembassy.be; internet www.kazakhstanembassy .be; Ambassador Konstantin V. Zhigalov.

China, People's Republic: 9 Dong Liu Jie, San Li Tun, Beijing 100600; tel. (10) 65324189; fax (10) 65326183; e-mail kz@kazembchina.org; internet www .kazembchina.org; Ambassador IKRAM ADYRBEKOV.

Czech Republic: Romaina Rollanda 12, 160 00 Prague 6; tel. 233375642; fax 233371019; e-mail kzembas@bon.cz; internet www.kazembassy.cz; Ambassador Anarbek Karashev.

Egypt: 9 Wahib Doss St, Maadi, Cairo; tel. (2) 3809804; fax (2) 3586546; e-mail kazaemb@link.net; Ambassador BAGDAD K. AMREYEV.

France: 59 rue Pierre Charron, 75008 Paris; tel. 1-45-61-52-00; fax 1-45-61-52-01; e-mail info@amb-kazakhstan.fr; internet www.amb-kazakhstan.fr; Ambassador Amanzhol Zhankuliev.

Germany: Nordendstr. 14–17, 13156 Berlin; tel. (30) 47007111; fax (30) 47007125; e-mail info@botschaft-kaz.de; internet www.botschaft-kasachstan .de; Ambassador NURLAN ONZHANOV.

Hungary: 1025 Budapest, II ker., Kapy u. 59; tel. (1) 275-1300; fax (1) 275-2092; e-mail kazak@axelero.hu; internet www.kazembassy.hu; Ambassador Rashid Ibraev.

India: 61 Poorvi Marg, Vasant Vihar, New Delhi 110 057; tel. (11) 46007700; fax (11) 46007701; e-mail embassy@kazind.com; internet www.kazind.com; Ambassador KAIRAT UMAROV.

Iran: 4 North Hedayet St, Cnr of Masjed Alley, Darrus, Tehran; tel. (21) 22565933; fax (21) 22546400; e-mail kazembir@apadana.com; internet www .kazembassy-iran.org; Ambassador Erik M. Utembayev.

Israel: 52A Rehov Hayarkon, Tel-Aviv 63432; tel. 3-5163411; fax 3-5163437; e-mail kzisrael@netvision.net.il; internet www.kazakhemb.org.il; Ambassador VADIM P. ZVERKOV.

Italy: Via della Camilluccia 693, 00135 Roma; tel. (06) 36301130; fax (06) 36292675; e-mail kazakstan.emb@agora.it; internet www.embkaz.it; Ambassador Almaz N. Khamzayev.

Japan: 5-9-8, Himonya, Meguro-ku, Tokyo 152-0003; tel. (3) 3791-5273; fax (3) 3791-5279; e-mail embkazjp@gol.com; internet www.embkazjp.org; Ambassador AKYLBEK KAMALDINOV.

Jordan: Abu Bakir Nabaty St, Amman; tel. (6) 5927953; fax (6) 5927952; e-mail kazemb@orange.jo; Ambassador Bolat S. Sarsenbayev.

Korea, Republic: 484-24, Bukak Village 11, Pyeongchang-dong, Jongno-gu, Seoul; tel. (2) 379-9714; fax (2) 395-9719; e-mail kazkor@chollian.net; internet www.kazembassy.org; Ambassador DULAT BAKISHEV.

Kyrgyzstan: 720040 Bishkek, pr. Mira 95 a; tel. (312) 66-21-01; fax (312) 69-20-94; e-mail kaz_emb@kazemb.elcat.kg; Ambassador Umirzak U. Uzbekov.

Lithuania: Birutès g. 20A/35, Vilnius 08117; tel. (5) 212-2123; fax (5) 231-3580; e-mail kazemb@iti.lt; internet kazakhstan.embassy.lt; Ambassador TLEUKHAN KABDRAKHMANOV.

Malaysia: 115 Jalan Ampang Hilir, 55000 Kuala Lumpur; tel. (3) 42522999; fax (3) 42523999; e-mail kuala-lumpur@kazembassy.org.my; internet www .kazembassy.org.my; Ambassador Mukhtar Tileuberdi.

Mongolia: Diplomatic Corps Bldg 95, Apartment 2-11, Chingeltei District, Ulan Bator (CPOB 291); tel. (11) 312240; fax (11) 312204; e-mail kzemby@ mbox.mn; Ambassador ORMAN NURBAYEV.

Netherlands: Nieuwe Parklaan 69, 2597 LB The Hague; tel. (70) 3634757; fax (70) 3657600; e-mail info@kazakhembassy.nl; internet www.kazakhembassy .nl; Ambassador Mainura S. Murzamadiyeva.

Pakistan: House 11, St 45, F-8/1, Islamabad; tel. (51) 2262926; fax (51) 2262806; e-mail embkaz@isb.comsats.net.pk; Ambassador VAKYTBEK S. SHABARBAYEV.

Poland: 02-954 Warsaw, ul. Królowej Marysieńki 14; tel. (22) 6425388; fax (22) 6423427; e-mail kazdipmis@hot.pl; internet www.kazakhstan.pl; Ambassador Aleksei Volkov.

Qatar: POB 25513, Doha; tel. 4128015; e-mail kazembassyqatar@mail.ru; Ambassador AZAMAT R. BERDYBAI.

Romania: Bucharest, Str. Av. Traian Vasile 76, Sector 1; tel. (21) 6657828; fax (21) 2243512; Chargé d'affaires a.i. Bakytzhan Ordabayev.

Russian Federation: 101000 Moscow, Chistoprudnyi bulv. 3A; tel. (495) 927-17-01; fax (495) 608-15-49; e-mail kazembassy@kazembassy.ru; internet www.kazembassy.ru; Ambassador NURTAI A. ABYKAYEV.

Saudi Arabia: POB 94012, Riyadh 11693; tel. (1) 480-6406; fax (1) 480-9106; e-mail office@kazembgulf.net; internet www.kazembgulf.net; Ambassador Muhammed Khojamuhamedovich Abalakov.

Singapore: 20 Raffles Place, 14-06 Ocean Towers, Singapore 048620; tel. 65366100; fax 64388990; e-mail office@kazakhstan.org.sg; internet www.kazakhstan.org.sg; Ambassador YERLAN BAUDARBEK-KOZHATAYEV.

Spain: Cascanueces 25, 28043 Madrid; tel. (91) 7216290; fax (91) 7219374; e-mail embajada@kazesp.org; internet www.kazesp.org; Ambassador Nurlan Danenov.

Switzerland: Alleeweg 15, 3006 Bern; tel. 313517972; fax 313517975; e-mail kasachische.botschaft@freesurf.ch; Ambassador AMANZHOL ZHANKULIYEV.

Tajikistan: 734000 Dushanbe, Kuchai Xuseinzoda 31/1; tel. (372) 221-11-08; fax (372) 251-01-08; e-mail dipmiskz7@tajnet.com; Ambassador Yerlan A. Abildayev.

Turkey: Kiliç Ali Sok. 6, Oran Sitesi, Çankaya, Ankara; tel. (312) 4919100; fax (312) 4904455; e-mail kazank@kazakhstan.org.tr; internet www.kazakhstan.org.tr; Chargé d'affaires a.i. YERZHAN ISSIN.

Turkmenistan: 744036 Aşgabat, ul. Garaşizlik 11/13; tel. (12) 48-04-68; fax (12) 48-04-76; e-mail embkaz@online.tm; Ambassador Murat M. Atanov.

Ukraine: 01901 Kyiv, vul. Melnykova 26; tel. (44) 489-18-58; fax (44) 483-11-98; e-mail post@kazakh.kiev.ua; internet www.kazembassy.com.ua; Ambassador AMANGELDY ZH. ZHUMABAYEV.

United Arab Emirates: POB 39556, Al-Mushrif, W-52, Villa 61b, Abu Dhabi; tel. (2) 4476623; fax (2) 4476624; e-mail kazemb@emirates.net.ae; Ambassador Aslar A. Musinov.

United Kingdom: 33 Thurloe Sq., London, SW7 2SD; tel. (20) 7581-4646; fax (20) 7584-8481; e-mail london@kazakhstan-embassy.org.uk; internet www.kazakhstanembassy.org.uk; Chargé d'affaires a.i. DR DASTAN YELEUNEKOV.

United States of America: 1401 16th St, NW, Washington, DC 20036; tel. (202) 232-5488; fax (202) 232-5845; e-mail zakh.embusa@verizon.net; internet www.kazakhembus.com; Ambassador Erlan A. Idrissov.

Uzbekistan: 100015 Tashkent, Chekhov ko'ch. 23; tel. (71) 152-16-54; fax (71) 152-16-50; e-mail kazembassy@kaz.uz; Ambassador ASKAR I. MYRZAHMETOV.

DIPLOMATIC MISSIONS OF KENYA

United Nations: 866 United Nations Plaza, Rm 486, New York, NY 10017; tel. (212) 421-4740; fax (212) 486-1985; e-mail kenya@un.int; internet www.un.int/kenya/; Permanent Representative Zachary Dominic Muburi-Muita.

Australia: POB 1990, Canberra, ACT 2601; tel. (2) 6247-4788; fax (2) 6257-6613; e-mail khc-canberra@kenya.asn.au; High Commissioner JOHN L. LANYASUNYA.

Austria: Neulinggasse 29/8, 1030 Vienna; tel. (1) 712-39-19; fax (1) 712-39-22; e-mail kenyarep-vienna@aon.at; Ambassador Julius Kiplagat Kandie.

Belgium: 208 ave Winston Churchill, 1180 Brussels; tel. (2) 340-10-40; fax (2) 340-10-50; e-mail info@kenyabrussels.com; internet www.kenyabrussels.com; Ambassador MARX G. N. KAHENDE.

Botswana: Plot 786, Independence Ave, Private Bag 297, Gaborone; tel. 3951408; fax 3951409; e-mail kenya@info.bw; internet www.kenyamission-botswana.com; High Commissioner Charles Mbaka.

Brazil: SHIS, QL 10, Conj. 08, Casa 08, Lago Sul, 71630-085 Brasilia, DF; tel. (61) 3364-0691; fax (61) 3364-0978; e-mail brazil@mfa.go.ke; Ambassador PIUS NAMACHANJA.

Burundi: Bujumbura; Ambassador Benjamin A. W. Mweri.

Canada: 415 Laurier Ave East, Ottawa, ON K1N 6R4; tel. (613) 563-1773; fax (613) 233-6599; e-mail kenyahighcommission@rogers.com; internet www.kenyahighcommission.ca; High Commissioner PROF. JUDITH M. BAHEMUKA.

China, People's Republic: 4 Xi Liu Jie, San Li Tun, Beijing 100600; tel. (10) 65323381; fax (10) 65321770; e-mail kenrepbj@hotmail.com; Ambassador Ruth Sereti Solitei.

Congo, Democratic Republic: 4002 ave de l'Ouganda, BP 9667, Kinshasa; tel. (81) 5554797; fax (81) 5554805; e-mail kinshasa@mfa.go.ke; Ambassador KARUCHU SYLVESTER GAKUMU.

Egypt: POB 362, 7 Sharia el-Mohandes Galal, Cairo (Dokki); tel. (2) 3453628; fax (2) 3443400; Ambassador Bishar Abdirahman Hussein.

Ethiopia: Woreda 16, Kebele 1, POB 3301, Addis Ababa; tel. (11) 610033; fax (11) 611433; Ambassador FRANKLIN ESIPILA.

France: 3 rue Freycinet, 75116 Paris; tel. 1-56-62-25-25; fax 1-47-20-44-41; e-mail paris@amb-kenya.fr; internet www.kenyaembassyparis.org; Ambassador Raychelle Awuor Omamo.

Germany: Markgrafenstr. 63, 10969 Berlin; tel. (30) 2592660; fax (30) 25926650; e-mail office@kenyaembassyberlin.de; internet www.kenyaembassyberlin.de; Ambassador HARRY MUTUMA KATHURIMA.

India: 34 Paschimi Marg, New Delhi 110 057; tel. (11) 26146537; fax (11) 26146550; e-mail info@kenyamission-delhi.com; internet www.kenyamission-delhi.com; High Commissioner Prof. Festus Kaberia.

Iran: POB 19395-4566, 46 Gulshar St, Africa Ave, Tehran; tel. (21) 22059154; fax (21) 22053372; e-mail kenmteh@irtp.com; Ambassador ALI ABBAS ALI.

Ireland: Dublin; Ambassador Catherin Muigai Mwangi.

Israel: 15 Aba Hillel Silver St, Ramat-Gan 52136; tel. 3-5754633; fax 3-5754788; e-mail info@kenyaembassytlv.org; internet www.kenyaembassyisrael.org; Ambassador FELISTAS VUNORO KHAYUMBI.

Italy: Via Archimede 164, 00197 Roma; tel. (06) 8082717; fax (06) 8082707; e-mail info@embassyofkenya.it; internet www.embassyofkenya.it; Ambassador Ann Belinda Nyikuli.

Japan: 3-24-3, Yakumo, Meguro-ku, Tokyo 152-0023; tel. (3) 3723-4006; fax (3) 3723-4488; e-mail info@kenrep-jp.com; internet www.kenyarep-jp.com; Ambassador DENNIS N.O. AWORI.

Malaysia: 8 Jalan Taman U Thant, 55000 Kuala Lumpur; tel. (3) 21461163; fax (3) 21451087; e-mail kenya@po.jaring.my; High Commissioner David Gachoki Njoka.

Namibia: Kenya House, 5th Floor, 134 Robert Mugabe Ave, POB 2889, Windhoek; tel. (61) 226836; fax (61) 221409; e-mail rboit@mfa.go.ke; High Commissioner ROSE BOIT.

Netherlands: Nieuwe Parklaan 21, 2597 LA The Hague; tel. (70) 3504215; fax (70) 3553594; e-mail info@kenya-embassy.nl; Ambassador Prof. Ruthie Chepkoech Rono.

Nigeria: 18 Yedseram St, Maitama, PMB 5160, Abuja; tel. (9) 4139155; fax (9) 4139157; e-mail abuja@mfa.go.ke; High Commissioner DANIEL MEPUKORI KOIKAI.

Pakistan: 8a, Embassy Rd, F-6/4, POB 2097, Islamabad; tel. (51) 2876024; fax (51) 2876027; e-mail kenreppk@apollo.net.pk; High Commissioner Mishi Masika Mwatsahu.

Russian Federation: 119034 Moscow, Lopukhinskii per. 5; tel. (495) 637-21-86; fax (495) 637-54-63; e-mail kenemb@kenemb.ru; internet www.kenemb.ru; Ambassador DR SOSPETER MAGITA MACHAGE.

Rwanda: BP 1215, Kigali; tel. 583332; fax 510919; e-mail kigali@mfa.go.ke; Ambassador Ketter A. Alex.

Saudi Arabia: POB 94358, Riyadh 11693; tel. (1) 488-1238; fax (1) 488-2629; Ambassador YUSUF ABD AR-RAHMAN NZIBO.

South Africa: 302 Brooks St, Menlo Park, Pretoria 0081; POB 35954, Menlo Park 0012; tel. (12) 3622249; fax (12) 3622252; e-mail info@kenya.org.za; High Commissioner Tabitha J. Seii.

Sudan: St 3, POB 8242, Khartoum; tel. (183) 265163; fax (183) 281233; Ambassador COL (RETD) ELIJAH MALEKYA MATIBO.

Sweden: Birger Jarlsgt. 37, 2nd Floor, POB 7694, 103 95 Stockholm; tel. (8) 21-83-04; fax (8) 20-92-61; e-mail kenya.embassy@telia.com; Ambassador Purity W. Muhindi.

Tanzania: Plot 127 Mafinga St, Kinondoni, POB 5231, Dar es Salaam; tel. (22) 2668285; fax (22) 2668213; e-mail info@kenyahighcom.tz.org; internet www.kenyahighcomtz.org; High Commissioner BOAZ KIDIGA MBAYA.

Thailand: 62 Thonglor Soi 5, Thanon Sukhumvit 55, Klongtan, Wattana, Bangkok 10110; tel. (2) 712-5721; fax (2) 712-5720; Ambassador Richard Titus Ekai.

Uganda: 41 Nakasero Rd, POB 5220, Kampala; tel. (41) 4458235; fax (41) 4458239; e-mail kenyahicom@africaonline.co.ug; High Commissioner JAPHETH R. GETUGI.

United Arab Emirates: POB 3854, Abu Dhabi; tel. (2) 6666300; fax (2) 6652827; e-mail kenyarep@emirates.net.ae; Ambassador Bishar Abdi Rahman Hussein.

United Kingdom: 45 Portland Pl., London, W1N 4AS; tel. (20) 7636-2371; fax (20) 7323-6717; e-mail knganga@kenyahighcommission.net; internet www.kenyahighcommission.net; High Commr JOSEPH KIRUGUMI MUCHEMI.

United States of America: 2249 R St, NW, Washington, DC 20008; tel. (202) 387-6101; fax (202) 462-3829; e-mail information@kenyaembassy.com; internet www.kenyaembassy.com; Ambassador Peter N. Rateng 'Oginga Ogego.

Zambia: 5207 United Nations Ave, POB 50298, 10101 Lusaka; tel. (1) 250722; fax (1) 253829; e-mail kenhigh@zamnet.zm; High Commissioner LAZARUS O. AMAYO.

Zimbabwe: 95 Park Lane, POB 4069, Harare; tel. (4) 704820; fax (4) 723042; Ambassador Prof. John Abduba.

DIPLOMATIC MISSIONS OF KOREA, DEMOCRATIC PEOPLE'S REPUBLIC

United Nations: 820 Second Ave, 13th Floor, New York, NY 10017; tel. (212) 972-3105; fax (212) 972-3154; e-mail dprk@un.int; Permanent Representative (vacant).

Algeria: Algiers; tel. (21) 62-39-27; Ambassador Pak Ho Il.

Australia: 57 Culgoa Circuit, O'Malley, ACT 2606; tel. (2) 6286-4770; fax (2) 6286-4795; e-mail dprkembassy@hotmail.com; AmbassadorPANG SONG HAE.

Austria: Beckmanngasse 10–12, 1140 Vienna; tel. (1) 894-23-13; fax (1) 894-31-74; e-mail d.v.r.korea.botschaft@chello.at; Ambassador Kim Gwang Sop.

Bangladesh: House 6, Rd 7, Baridhara Model Town, Dhaka; tel. (2) 601250; Ambassador MUN SONG MO.

Benin: Cotonou; AmbassadorKim Pyong Gi.

Brazil: SHIS, QI 25, Conj. 10, Casa 11, Brasília, DF; tel. (61) 3367-1940; fax (61) 3367-3177; e-mail embcorea@hotmail.com; Ambassador PAK HYOK.

Bulgaria: 1087 Sofia, bul. A. Sakharov 4; tel. (2) 977-53-48; Ambassador Jo Sung Ju.

Burkina Faso: Ouagadougou; AmbassadorKIL MUN YONG.

Burundi: BP 1620, Bujumbura; tel. 22222881; Ambassador Soon Chun Lee.

Cambodia: 39 rue 268, Phnom-Penh; tel. (15) 912567; fax (23) 426230; Ambassador RI IN SOK.

Cameroon: Yaoundé; Ambassador Kim Ryong Yong.

Cape Verde: Praia; Ambassador RI IN SOK.

Chad: N'Djamena; AmbassadorKim Pyong Gi.

Chile: Santiago; Ambassador YU CHANG UN (resident in Peru).

China, People's Republic: Ri Tan Bei Lu, Jian Guo Men Wai, Beijing 100600; tel. (10) 65321186; fax (10) 65326056; Ambassador Choe Jin Su.

Congo, Democratic Republic: 168 ave de l'Ouganda, BP 16597, Kinshasa; tel. (81) 8801443; fax (81) 5300194; e-mail ckc.kin168@yahoo.com; AmbassadorRI WON SON.

Congo, Republic: Brazzaville; tel. 83-41-98; AmbassadorRi Won Son.

Côte d'Ivoire: Abidjan; AmbassadorRI JAE RIM.

Cuba: Calle 17, No 752, Vedado, Havana; tel. (7) 66-2313; fax (7) 33-3073; Ambassador Pak Dong Chun.

Czech Republic: Na Větru 395/18, 162 00 Prague 6; tel. 224320783; fax 224318817; e-mail vel.kldr@seznam.cz; Ambassador PYONG GAP RI.

Egypt: 6 Sharia as-Saleh Ayoub, Cairo (Zamalek); tel. (2) 3408219; fax (2) 3414615; Ambassador Jang Myong Son.

Equatorial Guinea: Malabo; tel. (09) 20-47; Ambassador (vacant).

Ethiopia: Woreda 20, Kebele 40, House No. 892, POB 2378, Addis Ababa; tel. (11) 6182828; Ambassador O Ul Rok.

Gabon: Ambassador KIM RYONG YONG.

Germany: Glinkastr. 5–7, 10117 Berlin; tel. (30) 2293189; fax (30) 2293191; AmbassadorHong Chang Il.

Ghana: 139 Nortei Ababio Loop, Ambassadorial Estate, Roman Ridge, POB 13874, Accra; tel. (21) 777825; Ambassador KIM PYONG GI.

Guinea: BP 723, Conakry; AmbassadorRi Kyong Son.

Guinea-Bissau: Bissau; Ambassador KIM KYONG SIN.

India: D-14 Maharani Bagh, New Delhi 110 065; tel. (11) 26829644; fax (11) 26829645; e-mail dprk194899@yahoo.com; Ambassador Han Chang On.

Indonesia: Jalan Teluk Betung 1–2, Jakarta Pusat 12050; tel. (21) 31908425; fax (21) 31908427; e-mail dprkorea@rad.net.id; Ambassador JONG CHUN GUN.

Iran: 349 Shahid Dastjerdi Ave, Africa Ave, Tehran; tel. (21) 88783341; Ambassador Kim Chang Ryong.

Italy: Via dell'Esperanto 26, 00144 Roma; tel. (06) 54220749; fax (06) 54210090; e-mail permerepun@hotmail.com; AmbassadorHAN TAE SONG.

Jordan: POB 799, Amman; tel. (6) 4417614; fax (6) 4424735; e-mail dprk-embv@scs-net.org; Ambassador Kim Hyong Jun.

Laos: quartier Wat Nak, Vientiane; tel. (21) 315261; fax (21) 315260; Ambassador PAK MYONG GU.

Libya: Tripoli; Ambassador Kim Tong Je.

Madagascar: 101 Antananarivo; tel. (20) 2244442; Ambassador RI YONG HAK.

Malaysia: 4 Jalan Persiaran Madge, off Jalan U Thant, 55000 Kuala Lumpur; tel. (3) 42569913; fax (3) 42569933; AmbassadorPak Ryong Yon.

Mali: Bamako; AmbassadorKIM PONG HUI.

Mauritania: Nouakchott; AmbassadorPak Ho Il.

Mexico: Eugenio Sue 332, Col. Polanco, Del. Miguel Hidalgo, 11550 México, DF; tel. (55) 5545-1871; fax (55) 5203-0019; e-mail dpkoreaemb@prodigy.net.mx; Ambassador SO JAE MYONG.

Mongolia: Khuvisgalchdyn Gudamj, Ulan Bator (CPOB 1015); tel. (11) 326153; fax (11) 330529; AmbassadorPak Jong Do.

Mozambique: Rua da Kaswende 167, Maputo; tel. 21491482; Ambassador PAK KUN GWANG.

Nepal: Jhamsikhel, Lalitpur, Kathmandu; tel. (1) 5521855; fax (1) 5525394; Ambassador Jang Yong Chol.

Niger: Niamey; AmbassadorPAK SONG IL.

Nigeria: 31 Akin Adesola St, Victoria Island, Lagos; tel. (1) 2610108; Ambassador Kim Pyong Gi.

Pakistan: House 16 A-B, Park Rd, F-B/2, Islamabad; tel. (51) 2252756; AmbassadorRI YONG HWAN.

Peru: Los Nogales 227, San Isidro, Lima; tel. (1) 4411120; fax (1) 4409877; e-mail embcorea@hotmail.com; Ambassador Yu Chang Un.

Poland: 00-728 Warsaw, ul. Bobrowiecka 1A; tel. (22) 8405813; fax (22) 8405710; e-mail korembpl@yahoo.com; Ambassador KIM PYONG IL.

Qatar: POB 799, Doha; tel. 4417614; fax 4424735; Ambassador Ho Jong.

Romania: 014103 Bucharest, Şos. Nordului 6; tel. (21) 2329665; Ambassador HA PYONG GUK.

Russian Federation: 107140 Moscow, ul. Mosfilmovskaya 72; tel. (499) 143-62-49; fax (499) 143-63-12; AmbassadorKim Yong Jae.

Rwanda: Kigali; Ambassador KIM PONG GI.

Singapore: 7500 Beach Rd, 09-320 The Plaza, Singapore 199591; tel. 64403498; fax 63482026; e-mail embdprk@singnet.com.sg; Ambassador Ji Jae Suk.

Somalia: Via Km 5, Mogadishu; Ambassador KIM RYONG SU.

South Africa: 958 Waterpoort St, Faerie Glen, Pretoria; POB 1238, Garsfontein 0042; tel. (12) 9918661; fax (12) 9918662; e-mail dprkembassy@lantic.net; AmbassadorAn Hui Jong.

Sri Lanka: Colombo; Ambassador HAN CHANG-ON.

Sweden: Norra Kungsvägen 39, 181 31 Lidingö; tel. (8) 767-38-36; fax (8) 767-38-35; e-mail koscom@telia.com; Ambassador Jon In Chan.

Switzerland: Pourtalèsstr. 43, 3074 Muri bei Bern; tel. 319516621; fax 319515704; e-mail dprk.embassy@bluewin.ch; Ambassador RI CHOL.

Syria: rue Fares al-Khouri-Jisr Tora, Damascus; Ambassador Kim Pyongnam.

Tanzania: Plot 5, Ursino Estate, Kawawa Rd, Msasani, POB 2690, Dar es Salaam; tel. (22) 2775395; fax (22) 2700838; AmbassadorSOON CHUN LEE.

Thailand: 14 Mooban Suanlaemthong 2, Thanon Pattanakarn, Suan Luang, Bangkok 10250; tel. (2) 319-2686; fax (2) 318-6333; Ambassador O Yong Son.

Togo: Lomé; AmbassadorKIM PYONG GI.

Uganda: 10 Prince Charles Dr., Kololo, POB 5885, Kampala; tel. (41) 4546033; fax (41) 4450224; AmbassadorPak Hyon Jae.

United Kingdom: 73 Gunnersbury Ave, London, W5 4LP; tel. (20) 8992-4965; fax (20) 8992-2053; AmbassadorJA SONG-NAM.

Uzbekistan: 100000 Tashkent, Usmon Nosir ko'ch. 95a; tel. (71) 152-63-16; fax (71) 152-63-15; Ambassador Ri Tong Phal.

Viet Nam: 25 Cao Ba Quat, Hanoi; tel. (4) 8453008; fax (4) 8231221; e-mail emb.dprk@hn.vnn.vn; Ambassador MA CHOL SU.

Yemen: POB 1209, al-Hasaba, Mazda Rd, San'a; tel. (1) 232340; Ambassador Chang Myong Son.

Zimbabwe: 102 Josiah Chinamano Ave, Greenwood, POB 4754, Harare; tel. (4) 724052; Ambassador RI MYONG CHOL.

DIPLOMATIC MISSIONS OF KOREA, REPUBLIC

United Nations: 335 East 45th St, New York, NY 10017; tel. (212) 439-4000; fax (212) 986-1083; e-mail korea@un.int; internet www.un.int/korea; Permanent Representative Hyun Chong Kim.

Afghanistan: Wazir Akbar Khan, St 10, House 34, Kabul; tel. (932) 02102481; fax (873) 762728481; e-mail kabul@mofat.go.kr; Ambassador SUNG-ZU KANG.

Algeria: BP 92, 17 chemin Abd al-Kader Gadouche, Hydra, Algiers; tel. (21) 69-36-20; fax (21) 69-16-03; Ambassador Kim Deng-Ji.

Argentina: Avda del Libertador 2395, C1425AAJ Buenos Aires; tel. (11) 4802-9665; fax (11) 4803-6993; e-mail embcorea@cscom.com.ar; internet www.embcorea.org.ar; Ambassador EUI-SEUNG HWANG.

Australia: 113 Empire Circuit, Yarralumla, ACT 2600; tel. (2) 6270-4100; fax (2) 6273-4839; e-mail info@korea.org.au; internet www.korea.org.au; Ambassador Cho Chang-Beom.

Austria: Gregor-Mendel-Str. 25, 1180 Vienna; tel. (1) 478-19-91; fax (1) 478-10-13; e-mail mail@koreaemb.at; internet www.mofat.go.kr/austria; AmbassadorKIM SUNG-HWAN.

Azerbaijan: 1000 Baku; internet aze.mofat.go.kr; .

Bangladesh: 4 Madani Ave, Diplomatic Enclave, Baridhara, Dhaka; tel. (2) 8812088; fax (2) 8823871; e-mail embdhaka@embdhaka.org; internet bgd .mofat.go.kr; Ambassador SUK BUM PARK.

Belgium: 175 chaussée de la Hulpe, 1170 Brussels; tel. (2) 662-57-77; fax (2) 675-52-21; e-mail eukorea@mofat.go.kr; Ambassador Chong Woo-Seong.

Brazil: SEN, Av. das Nações, Lote 14, 70436-900 Brasília, DF; tel. (61) 3321-2500; fax (61) 3321-2508; e-mail emb-br@mofat.go.kr; internet bra-brasilia .mofat.go.kr; AmbassadorCHOI JONG-HWA.

Brunei: 17 Simpang 462, Kampong Hancing Baru, Jalan Muara, Bandar Seri Begawan BC 2115; tel. 2330248; fax 2330254; e-mail koreaemb@brunet.bn; Ambassador Hwang Wong-kun.

Bulgaria: 1414 Sofia, pl. Balgaria 1, NDK Administration Bldg; tel. (2) 965-01-62; e-mail korean-embassy@mofat.go.kr; Ambassador CHEONG JAI-SIK.

Cambodia: 50 rue 214, Sangkat Boeung Raing, Khan Daun Penh, BP 2433, Phnom-Penh; tel. (23) 211900; fax (23) 219200; e-mail cambodia@mofat.go .kr; internet khm.mofat.go.kr; Ambassador Shin Hyun-Suk.

Canada: 150 Boteler St, Ottawa, ON K1N 5A6; tel. (613) 244-5010; fax (613) 244-5043; internet www.emb-korea.ottawa.on.ca; Ambassador SOO DONG KIM.

Chile: Alcántara 74, Casilla 1301, Santiago; tel. (2) 228-4214; fax (2) 206-2355; e-mail corembad@tie.cl; Ambassador Shin Jang-bum.

China, People's Republic: 3rd–4th Floors, China World Trade Centre, 1 Jian Guo Men Wai Dajie, Beijing 100600; tel. (10) 65053171; fax (10) 65053458; e-mail consul@koreanembassy.cn; internet www.koreaemb.org.cn; Ambassador (vacant).

Colombia: Calle 94, No 9-39, Bogotá, DC; tel. (1) 616-7200; fax (1) 610-0338; e-mail embcorea@mofat.go.kr; internet col.mofat.go.kr/index.jsp; Ambassador Song Ki-Do.

Congo, Democratic Republic: 65 blvd Tshatshi, BP 628, Kinshasa; tel. (81) 9820302; e-mail amb-rdc@mofat.go.kr; AmbassadorKIM YOUNG-JUN.

Costa Rica: Oficentro Ejecutivo La Sabana, Edif. 2, 3º, Sabana Sur, Apdo 838, 1007 San José; tel. 220-3160; fax 220-3168; e-mail koreasec@sol.racsa.co .cr; internet cri.mofat.go.kr; Ambassador Cho Byoung-Lip.

Côte d'Ivoire: Immeuble le Mans, 8e étage, 01 BP 3950, Abidjan 01; tel. 20-32-22-90; fax 20-22-22-74; e-mail ambcoabj@mofat.go.kr; AmbassadorKIM JONG-IL.

Croatia: 10000 Zagreb, Novi Goljak 25; tel. (1) 4821282; fax (1) 4821274; Ambassador Dae-Ho Byun.

Czech Republic: Slavíčkova 5, 160 00 Prague 6; tel. 2234090411; fax 2234090450; Ambassador CHO SEONG-YONG.

Denmark: Svanemøllevej 104, 2900 Hellerup; tel. 39-46-04-00; fax 39-46-04-22; e-mail korembdk@mofat.go.kr; internet www.mofat.go.kr/denmark; Ambassador Myung-Soo Lee.

Dominican Republic: Avda Sarasota 98, Santo Domingo, DN; tel. 532-4314; fax 532-3807; e-mail embcod@mofat.go.kr; internet dom.mofat.go.kr; AmbassadorLIN BYUNG-TAIK.

Ecuador: Edif. Citiplaza, 8°, Avda Naciones Unidas y Avda de El Salvador, Quito; tel. (2) 297-0625; fax (2) 297-0630; e-mail embajadadecorea@mail .com; Ambassador Kyung Surk Kin.

Egypt: 3 Sharia Boulos Hanna, Cairo (Dokki); tel. (2) 3611234; fax (2) 3611238; Ambassador CHOI SEUNG-HOH.

El Salvador: 5a Calle Poniente 3970, entre 75 y 77 Avda Norte, Col. Escalón, San Salvador; tel. 2263-9145; fax 2263-0783; e-mail embcorea@mofat.go.kr; Ambassador Oh Dae-Sung.

Ethiopia: Jimma Rd, Old Airport Area, POB 2047, Addis Ababa; tel. (11) 4655230; e-mail skorea.emb@telecom.net.et; Ambassador JHUNG BYUNG KUCK.

Fiji: Vanua House, 8th Floor, PMB, Suva; tel. 3300977; fax 3303410; e-mail korembfj@mofat.go.kr; Ambassador Bong Joo Kim.

Finland: Fabianinkatu 8A, 00130 Helsinki; tel. (9) 2515000; fax (9) 25150055; e-mail korembfi@mofat.go.kr; internet fin.mofat.go.kr; Ambassador PARK HEUNG-SHIN.

France: 125 rue de Grenelle, 75007 Paris; tel. 1-47-53-01-01; fax 1-47-53-00-41; e-mail koremb-fr@mofat.go.kr; internet www.amb-coreesud.fr; AmbassadorCho Il-hwan.

Gabon: BP 2620, Libreville; tel. 73-40-00; fax 73-99-05; e-mail gabon -ambcoree@mofat.go.kr; internet gab.mofat.go.kr; Ambassador EOM SUNG-JUN.

Germany: Stülerstr. 8–10, 10787 Berlin; tel. (30) 260650; fax (30) 2606551; e-mail koremb-ge@mofat.go.kr; internet www.koreaemb.de; AmbassadorJung-Il Choi.

Ghana: 3 Abokobi Rd, POB GP13700, East Cantonments, Accra-North; tel. (21) 776157; fax (21) 772313; Ambassador WI KEYEI-CHUI.

Greece: Leoforos Kifissias 124, 115 26 Athens; tel. (210) 6984080; fax (210) 6984083; e-mail gremb@mofat.go.kr; Ambassador Young-Han Bae.

Guatemala: Edif. El Reformador, 7°, Avda de la Reforma 1-50, Zona 9, Apdo 1649, Guatemala City; tel. 2334-5480; fax 2334-5481; e-mail korembsy@ mofat.go.kr; internet gtm.mofat.go.kr; Ambassador YU JI-EUN.

Honduras: Edif. Plaza Azul, 5°, Col. Lomas del Guijarro Sur, Tegucigalpa; tel. 235-5561; fax 235-5564; e-mail info@koreaemb.hn; internet www .koreaemb.hn; AmbassadorSun Kiu Kim.

Hungary: 1062 Budapest, Andrássy u. 109; tel. (1) 351-1179; fax (1) 351-1182; e-mail hungary@mofat.go.kr; internet www.mofat.go.kr/hungary; Ambassador LEE HO-JIN.

India: 9 Chandragupta Marg, Chanakyapuri, POB 5416, New Delhi 110 021; tel. (11) 26885412; fax (11) 26884840; e-mail kobe@mail.mofat.go.kr; internet ind.mofat.go.kr; Ambassador Paek Yung-Sun.

Indonesia: Jalan Jenderal Gatot Subroto 57, Jakarta Selatan; tel. (21) 5201915; fax (21) 5254159; e-mail koemb@indo.net.id; Ambassador LEE SUN-JIN.

Iran: No. 37, Ahmad Ghasir Ave, Tehran; tel. (21) 88711125; fax (21) 88737917; e-mail korth@dpi.net.ir; AmbassadorKim Young-Moke.

Iraq: Baghdad; e-mail kembiraq@mofat.go.kr; Ambassador HA CHAN-HO.

Ireland: Clyde House, 15 Clyde Rd, POB 2101, Dublin 4; tel. (1) 6608800; fax (1) 6608716; e-mail irekoremb@mofat.go.kr; AmbassadorTae-Yong Cho.

Israel: 38 Sderot Chen, Tel-Aviv 64166; tel. 3-6963244; fax 3-6963243; e-mail israel@mofat.go.kr; AmbassadorKAK SOO SHIN.

Italy: Via Barnaba Oriani 30, 00197 Roma; tel. (06) 802461; fax (06) 802462259; Ambassador Young Jae Cho.

Japan: 1-2-5, Minami Azabu, Minato-ku, Tokyo 106-0047; tel. (3) 3452-7611; fax (3) 5232-6911; internet jpn-tokyo.mofat.go.kr; AmbassadorYU MYUNG-HWAN.

Jordan: POB 3060, Bahjat Homsi St, Amman 11181; tel. (6) 5930745; fax (6) 5930280; e-mail jordan@mofat.go.kr; Ambassador Yeon-Sung Shin.

Kazakhstan: 050000 Almaty, Jarkentskaya 2/77; tel. (727) 253-26-60; fax (727) 250-70-59; e-mail koreaemb-kz@mofat.go.kr; internet kaz.mofat.go .kr; Ambassador KIM IL-SOO.

Kenya: Anniversary Towers, 15th Floor, University Way, POB 30455, Nairobi; tel. (20) 333581; fax (20) 217772; e-mail emb-ke@mofat.go.kr; Ambassador Yum Ki-syub.

Kuwait: POB 20771, 13068 Safat, Rawda, Block 1, St 10, House 17, Kuwait City; tel. 2554206; fax 2526874; AmbassadorSONG KEUN HO.

Laos: rue Lao-Thai Friendship, Ban Wat Nak, Sisattanak District, BP 7567, Vientiane; tel. (21) 415833; fax (21) 415831; e-mail koramb@laotel.com; internet lao.mofat.go.kr; Ambassador Park Jae-hyun.

Lebanon: POB 40-290, Baabda, Beirut; tel. (5) 953167; fax (5) 953170; e-mail koremadm@dm.net.lb; Ambassador YOUNG-SUN KIM.

Lesotho: Maseru; Ambassador Kim Eun Soo.

Libya: POB 4781, Gargaresh, Tripoli; tel. (21) 4831322; fax (21) 4831324; Ambassador KIM JOONG-JAE.

Malaysia: Lot 9 and 11, Jalan Nipah, off Jalan Ampang, 55000 Kuala Lumpur; tel. (3) 42512336; fax (3) 42521425; e-mail korem-my@mofat.go.kr; internet mys.mofat.go.kr/eng/index.jsp; Ambassador Bong Ryull-Yang.

Mexico: Lope de Armendáriz 110, Col. Lomas Virreyes, Del. Miguel Hidalgo, 11000 México, DF; tel. (55) 5202-9866; fax (55) 5540-7446; e-mail coremex@prodigy.net.mx; internet mex.mofat.go.kr; AmbassadorWON JONG-CHAN.

Mongolia: Olimpiin Gudamj 10, Ulan Bator (CPOB 1039); tel. (11) 321548; fax (11) 311157; AmbassadorPark Jin-Ho.

Morocco: 41 ave Mehdi ben Barka, Souissi, 10100 Rabat; tel. (3) 7756791; fax (3) 7750189; e-mail morocco@mofat.go.kr; internet mar.mofat.go.kr; Ambassador YOO JUNG-HEE.

Myanmar: 97 University Ave, Yangon; tel. (1) 515190; fax (1) 513286; e-mail hankuk@koremby.net.mm; internet mmr.mofat.go.kr; Ambassador Park Gi-Jong.

Nepal: Red Cross Marg, Tahachal, POB 1058, Kathmandu; tel. (1) 4270172; fax (1) 4272041; e-mail koreaemb@mos.com.np; Ambassador NAM SANG-JUNG.

Netherlands: Verlengde Tolweg 8, 2517 JV The Hague; tel. (70) 3586076; fax (70) 3504712; e-mail koremb@euronet.nl; internet www.mofat.go.kr/ netherlands; AmbassadorJong-Moo Choi.

New Zealand: ASB Bank Tower, Level 11, 2 Hunter St, POB 11-143, Wellington; tel. (4) 473-9073; fax (4) 472-3865; e-mail info@koreaembassy .org.nz; internet www.koreaembassy.org.nz; Ambassador LEE JOON-GYU.

Nicaragua: De la Plaza España, 3 c. abajo, 500 m al sur, casa A-45, Managua; tel. 254-8107; fax 254-8131; e-mail hrlee92@mofat.go.kr; AmbassadorLee Sang-Pal.

Nigeria: Plot 934, Idejo St, Victoria Island, POB 4668, Lagos; tel. (1) 2615353; Ambassador KIE DONG-LEE.

Norway: Inkognitogt. 3, 0244, Oslo; tel. 22-54-70-90; fax 22-56-14-11; e-mail kornor@mofat.go.kr; internet nor.mofat.go.kr; Ambassador Byung-Koo Choi.

Oman: POB 377, Madinat Qaboos 115; tel. 24691490; fax 24691495; e-mail emboman@mofat.go.kr; AmbassadorCHO SUNG-HWAN.

Pakistan: Block 13, St 29, G-5/4, Diplomatic Enclave 2, POB 1087, Islamabad; tel. (51) 2279380; fax (51) 2279391; e-mail emb-pk@mofat.go .kr; Ambassador Kim Joo-seok.

Panama: Edif. Plaza, planta baja, Calle Ricardo Arias y Calle 51E, Campo Alegre, Apdo 8096, Panamá 7; tel. 264-8203; fax 264-8825; e-mail panama@ mofat.go.kr; Ambassador GWANG-KEUN KIM.

Papua New Guinea: POB 381, POM, 4th Floor, Pacific MMI Bldg, sec. 21, Allotments 2 & 3, Champion Parade, Granville, Port Moresby; tel. 3215822; fax 3215828; e-mail hkkim68@mofat.go.kr; internet png.mofat.go.kr; Ambassador Park Sang-Yoon.

Paraguay: Avda Rep. Argentina Norte 678, esq. Pacheco, Casilla 1303, Asunción; tel. (21) 60-5606; fax (21) 60-1376; e-mail paraguay@mofat.go.kr; internet pry.mofat.go.kr; AmbassadorJOO TECK KIM.

Peru: Avda Principal 190, 7°, Urb. Santa Catalina, La Victoria, Lima; tel. (1) 4760815; fax (1) 4760950; e-mail korembj-pu@mofat.go.kr; internet per .mofat.go.kr; AmbassadorHahn Young-Hee.

Philippines: Pacific Star Bldg, 10th Floor, Sen. Gil J. Puyat Ave, cnr Makati Ave, Makati City, 1226 Metro Manila; tel. (2) 8116139; fax (2) 8116148; internet phl.mofat.go.kr; AmbassadorHONG JONG-KI.

Poland: 00-464 Warsaw, ul. Szwoleżerów 6; tel. (22) 5592906; fax (22) 5592905; e-mail koremb_waw@mofat.go.kr; AmbassadorSi-hyung Lee.

Portugal: Edif. Presidente 7°, Av. Miguel Bombarda 36, 1051-802 Lisbon; tel. (21) 7937200; fax (21) 7977176; e-mail embpt@mofat.go.kr; internet prt .mofat.go.kr; AmbassadorCHUNG EUI-MIN.

Qatar: POB 3727, West Bay Diplomatic Area, Doha; tel. 4832238; fax 4833264; e-mail koemb_ga@mofa.go.kr; Ambassador Kim Jong Yong.

Romania: 012013 Bucharest, Bd. Mircea Eliade 14; tel. (21) 2307198; fax (21) 2307629; e-mail koerom@mofat.go.kr; Ambassador IHL SONG CHOI.

Russian Federation: 131000 Moscow, ul. Plyushchikha 56/1; tel. (495) 783-27-27; fax (495) 783-27-77; e-mail info@koreaemb.ru; internet rus-moscow .mofat.go.kr; AmbassadorKim Jae-Sup.

Saudi Arabia: POB 94399, Riyadh 11693; tel. (1) 488-2211; fax (1) 488-1317; Ambassador KANG GWANG-WON.

Senegal: 4e étage, Immeuble Fayçal, 3 rue Parchappe, BP 3338, Dakar; tel. 33-822-5822; fax 33-821-6600; e-mail senegal@mofat.go.kr; internet www .mofat.go.kr/senegal; AmbassadorJae Chol Hahn.

Serbia: 11070 Belgrade, Užička 32; tel. (11) 3674225; fax (11) 3674229; Ambassador DR KIM YOUNG-HEE.

Singapore: 47 Scotts Rd, 08-00 Goldbell Towers, Singapore 228233; tel. 68362263; fax 62352581; e-mail info@koreaembassy.org.sg; internet www .koreaembassy.org.sg; AmbassadorKim Joong-Keun.

South Africa: Greenpark Estates, Bldg 3, 27 George Storrar Dr., Groenkloof, Pretoria 0081; POB 939, Groenkloof 0027; tel. (12) 4602508; fax (12) 4601158; AmbassadorKIM KYUN-SEOP.

Spain: González Amigó 15, 28033 Madrid; tel. (91) 3532000; fax (91) 3532001; e-mail embspain.adm@mofa.go.kr; Ambassador Chun-seun Lee.

Sri Lanka: 98 Dharmapala Mawatha, Colombo 7; tel. (11) 2699036; fax (11) 2696699; e-mail kesl@koreanembassy.net; Ambassador LIM JAE-HONG.

Sudan: House No. 2, St 1, New Extension, POB 2414, Khartoum; tel. (183) 451136; fax (183) 452822; e-mail ssudan@mofat.go.kr; Ambassador Dong Eok Kim.

Sweden: Laboratoriegt. 10, POB 27237, 102 53 Stockholm; tel. (8) 545-894-00; fax (8) 660-28-18; e-mail koremb.sweden@mofat.go.kr; internet www .mofat.go.kr/sweden; AmbassadorLEE JOON-HEE.

Switzerland: Kalcheggweg 38, 3006 Bern; tel. 313562444; fax 313562450; e-mail swiss@mofat.go.kr; internet www.mofat.go.kr/switzerland; AmbassadorChang Chul-Kyoon.

Tanzania: Plot 97, Msese Rd, Kingsway, Kinondoni, POB 1154, Dar es Salaam; tel. (22) 2668788; fax (22) 2667509; e-mail embassy-tz@mofat.go.kr; internet tza.mofat.go.kr; Ambassador KIM YOUNG-JUN.

Thailand: 23 Thanon Thiam-Ruammit, Huay Kwang, Bangkok 10320; tel. (2) 247-7537; fax (2) 247-7535; e-mail korea_emb_th@yahoo.co.kr; AmbassadorHan Tae-Kyu.

Timor-Leste: Av. de Portugal, Motael, Dili; tel. 3321635; fax 3323636; e-mail koreadili@mofat.go.kr; Ambassador RYU JIN-KYU.

Tunisia: 16 rue Caracalla, BP 297, Notre Dame, 1082 Tunis; tel. (71) 799-905; fax (71) 791-923; e-mail tunisie@mofat.go.kr; Ambassador Son Se-Joo.

Turkey: Cinnah Cad., Alaçam Sok 5, 06690 Çankaya, Ankara; tel. (312) 4684822; fax (312) 4682279; e-mail turkey@mofat.go.kr; internet tur-ankara .mofat.go.kr; Ambassador KIM CHANG-YEOB.

Turkmenistan: Aşgabat; Ambassador Kim Chong Yul.

Ukraine: 01034 Kyiv, vul. Volodymyrska 43; tel. (44) 246-37-59; fax (44) 246-37-57; e-mail korea@koremb.kiev.ua; internet ukr.mofat.go.kr; AmbassadorHUR SEUNG-CHUL.

United Arab Emirates: POB 3270, Abu Dhabi; tel. (2) 4435337; fax (2) 4435348; e-mail keauhlee@emirates.net.ae; Ambassador Joon-Jae Lee.

United Kingdom: 60 Buckingham Gate, London, SW1E 6AJ; tel. (20) 7227-5500; fax (20) 7227-5503; internet www.koreanembassy.org.uk; Chargé d'affaires a.i.SUK-IN CHOI.

United States of America: KORUS House, 2370 Massachusetts Ave, NW, Washington, DC 20008; tel. (202) 939-5600; fax (202) 797-0595; e-mail webmaster@dynamic-korea.com; internet www.koreaembassyusa.org; Ambassador Tae-Sik Lee.

Uruguay: Edif. World Trade Center, Avda Luis Alberto de Herrera 1248, Torre 2, 10°, Montevideo; tel. (2) 6289374; fax (2) 6289376; e-mail ecorea@ adinet.com.uy; Ambassador TAE-SHIN JAN.

Uzbekistan: 100000 Tashkent, Afrosiab ko'ch. 7; tel. (71) 152-31-51; fax (71) 120-62-48; e-mail admin1@korea.anet.uz; internet uzb.mofat.go.kr; Ambassador Kyun Je-Min.

Venezuela: Avda Francisco de Miranda, Centro Lido, Torre B, 9°, Ofs 91-B y 92-B, El Rosal, Caracas; tel. (212) 954-1270; fax (212) 954-0619; e-mail venadmi@2net-uno.net; Ambassador SHIN SOONG CHULL.

Viet Nam: 4th Floor, Daeha Business Centre, 360 Kim Ma, Ba Dinh District, Hanoi; tel. (4) 8315111; fax (4) 8315117; e-mail korembviet@mofat.go.kr; internet vnm-hanoi.mofat.go.kr; Ambassador Im Hong-Jae.

DIPLOMATIC MISSIONS OF KUWAIT

United Nations: 321 East 44th St, New York, NY 10017; tel. (212) 973-4300; fax (212) 370-1733; e-mail kuwait@kuwaitmission.com; internet www .kuwaitmission.com; Permanent Representative ABDULLAH AHMED MOHAMED AL-MURAD.

Algeria: chemin Abd al-Kader Gadouche, Hydra, Algiers; tel. (21) 59-31-57; Ambassador Saud Faisal Saud ad-Daweesh.

Argentina: Uruguay 739, C1015ABO Buenos Aires; tel. (11) 4374-7202; fax (11) 4374-8718; e-mail info@kuwait.com.ar; internet www .embajadadekuwait.com.ar; Ambassador SAUD ABD AL-AZIZ AR-ROUMI.

Australia: 5 Callemonda Rise, O'Malley, ACT 2606; tel. (2) 6286-7777; fax (2) 6286-3733; e-mail Kuwaitcan_2002@yahoo.com.au; internet www .kuwaitemb-australia.com; Ambassador Jamal al-Ghunaim.

Austria: Universitätsstr. 5/2, 1010 Vienna; tel. (1) 405-56-46; fax (1) 405-56-46-13; e-mail kuwaitem@eunet.at; Ambassador FAWZI ABD AL-AZIZ AL-JASEM.

Bahrain: POB 786, Rd 1703, Diplomatic Area, Manama; tel. 17534040; fax 17530278; Ambassador Sheikh Azzam Mubarak as-Sabah.

Bangladesh: Plot 39, Rd 23, Block J, Banani, Dhaka 13; tel. (2) 8822700; fax (2) 8823753; e-mail dhaka@mofa.gov.kw; Ambassador ABDULLATIF AL-MAWASH.

Belgium: 43 ave F. D. Roosevelt, 1050 Brussels; tel. (2) 647-79-50; fax (2) 646-12-98; e-mail embassy.kwt@euronet.be; Ambassador Nabila Abdulla al-Mulla.

Brazil: SHIS, QI 05, Chácara 30, Lago Sul, 71600-550 Brasília, DF; tel. (61) 3213-2333; fax (61) 3248-0969; e-mail kuwait@opendf.com.br; Ambassador WALEED AHMAD MUHAMMAD AHMAD AL-KANDARI.

Bulgaria: 1700 Sofia, bul. Simeonovsko shose 15; tel. (2) 962-56-89; fax (2) 962-45-84; e-mail kuwaitembassy-bulgaria@spnet.net; Ambassador Ahmad Abdullah A. Buzuobar.

Canada: 333 Sussex Dr., Ottawa, ON K1N 1J9; tel. (613) 780-9999; fax (613) 780-9905; e-mail info@embassyofkuwait.ca; internet www.embassyofkuwait .ca; Ambassador MUSAED RASHED A. AL-HAROUN.

China, People's Republic: 23 Guang Hua Lu, Jian Guo Men Wai, Beijing 100600; tel. (10) 65322216; fax (10) 65321607; AmbassadorFaisal Rashed Al-Ghais.

Czech Republic: Na Zátorce 26, 160 00 Prague 6; tel. 2205707781; fax 220570787; Ambassador ABDULAZIZ ABDULLAH AD-DUAIJ.

Egypt: 12 Sharia Nabil el-Wakkad, Cairo (Dokki); tel. (2) 3602661; fax (2) 3602657; Ambassador Ahmad Khalid al-Kalib.

Ethiopia: Woreda 17, Kebele 20, House No. 128, POB 19898, Addis Ababa; tel. (11) 6615411; fax (11) 6612621; Ambassador FAISAL MUTLAQ AL-ADWAHI.

France: 25 rue Chateaubriand, 75008 Paris; tel. 1-47-23-54-25; fax 1-47-20-33-59; Ambassador Ali Sulaiman as-Saeid.

Germany: Griegstr. 5–7, 14193 Berlin; tel. (30) 8973000; fax (30) 89730010; e-mail info@kuwait-botschaft.de; internet www.kuwait-botschaft.de; Ambassador ABD AL-HAMID ABDULLAH AL-AWADHI.

Greece: Odos Marathonodromou 27, Palaio Psychiko, 154 52 Athens; tel. (210) 6473593; fax (210) 6875875; e-mail kuwemath@otenet.gr; Ambassador Khaled Mutlaq al-Duwailah.

India: 11 Olof Palme Marg, Vasant Vihar, New Delhi 110 057; tel. (11) 26150124; fax (11) 26873516; e-mail kuinfo@kuwait-info.com.com; internet www.kuwait-info.com; Ambassador KHALAF ABBAS KHALAF AL-FOUDARI.

Indonesia: Jalan Teuku Umar 51, Menteng, Jakarta 10310; tel. (21) 3919916; fax (21) 3912285; e-mail ami@Kuwait-toplist.com; Ambassador Mohammed Fadel Khalaf.

Iran: Africa Ave, Mahiyar St, No. 15, Tehran; tel. (21) 88785997; Ambassador MAJDI ADH-DHUFAIRI.

Italy: Via Archimede 124–126, 00197 Roma; tel. (06) 8078415; fax (06) 8076651; Chargé d'affaires a.i. Ahmad Saleh Ahmad as-Salem al-Wehaib.

Japan: 4-13-12, Mita, Minato-ku, Tokyo 108-0073; tel. (3) 3455-0361; fax (3) 3456-6290; e-mail ask.kwt@kuwait-embassy.or.jp; internet kuwait-embassy .or.jp; Ambassador SHEIKH ABDUL RAHMAN AL-OTAIBI.

Jordan: POB 2107, Amman 11181; tel. (6) 5675135; fax (6) 5681971; e-mail q8@kuwaitembassyamman.org; Ambassador Sheikh Faisal al-Humoud al-Malek as-Sabah.

Kenya: Muthaiga Rd, POB 42353, Nairobi; tel. (20) 761614; fax (20) 762837; Chargé d'affaires a.i. JABER SALEM HUSSAIN EBRAHEEM.

Korea, Republic: 309-15, Dongbinggo-dong, Yeongsan-gu, Seoul; tel. (2) 749-3688; fax (2) 749-3687; Ambassador Mohammed Abdulrasul al-Awadi.

Lebanon: POB 4530, Rond-point du Stade, Bir Hassan, Beirut; tel. (1) 756100; fax (1) 756103; e-mail info@kuwaitinfo.net; internet www .kuwaitinfo.net; Ambassador ALI SULEIMAN AS-SAID.

Libya: POB 2225, Beit al-Mal Beach, Tripoli; tel. (21) 4440281; fax (21) 607053; Chargé d'affaires (vacant).

Malaysia: 229 Jalan Tun Razak, 50400 Kuala Lumpur; tel. (3) 21410033; fax (3) 21456121; e-mail kuwait@streamyx.com; Ambassador MONTHER BADER SULAIMAN AL-EISSA.

Mauritania: Tevragh Zeina, BP 345, Nouakchott; tel. 525-33-05; fax 525-41-45; .

Morocco: km 4.3, route des Zaêrs, BP 11, 10001 Rabat; tel. (3) 7631111; fax (3) 7753591; Ambassador SALAH MUHAMMAD AL-BIJAN.

Netherlands: Carnegielaan 9, 2517 KH The Hague; tel. (70) 3123400; fax (70) 3924588; e-mail info@kuwaitembassy.nl; Ambassador Yousef Abdullah Ahmad al-Onaizi al-Qenaei.

Oman: Al-Khuwair Diplomatic Area, Arab League St, Block No. 13, Bldg No. 58, POB 1798, Ruwi 112; tel. 24699626; fax 24604732; Ambassador SHAMLAN AR-ROUMI.

Pakistan: Plot Nos 1, 2 and 24, University Rd, G-5, Diplomatic Enclave, POB 1030, Islamabad; tel. (51) 229413; fax (51) 2829487; Ambassador Faisal Abdulaziz al-Mulaifi.

Philippines: 1230 Acacia Rd, Dasmariñas Village, Makati City, Metro Manila; tel. (2) 8876880; fax (2) 8876666; Ambassador BADER NASSER AL-HOUTI.

Poland: 00-486 Warsaw, ul. Franciszka Nullo 13; tel. (22) 6222860; fax (22) 6274314; e-mail embassy@kue.com.pl; Ambassador Khaled Mohammed Ash-Shaibani.

Qatar: POB 1177, Doha; tel. 4832111; fax 4832042; e-mail kuwaitembassy@ qatar.net.qa; Ambassador SULEIMAN IBRAHIM AL-MARJAN.

Romania: 011751 Bucharest 1, Str. Louis Blanc 19a-b; tel. (21) 2309980; fax (21) 2309992; e-mail kuwaitstampa@tiscalinet.it; internet www .kuwaitembassy.ro; Ambassador Yaqoub Yousef al-Ateeqi.

Russian Federation: 119285 Moscow, ul. Mosfilmovskaya 44A; tel. (499) 147-00-40; fax (495) 956-60-32; Ambassador SULEIMAN IBRAHIM AL-MORJAN.

Saudi Arabia: POB 94304, Riyadh 11693; tel. (1) 488-3401; fax (1) 488-3682; Ambassador Sheikh Hamad Jaber al-Ali as-Sabah.

Senegal: blvd Martin Luther King, Dakar; tel. 33-824-1723; fax 33-825-0899; Ambassador MUHAMMAD AZ-ZUWAIKH.

Singapore: c/o The Ritz-Carlton Millenia Singapore, 7 Raffles Ave, Suite 3108, Singapore 039799; tel. 64345388; fax 64345387; Ambassador Abdulaziz Ahmed S. al-Adwani.

Somalia: First Medina Rd, Km 5, POB 1348, Mogadishu; .

South Africa: 890 Arcadia St, Arcadia, Pretoria 0083; Private Bag X920, Pretoria 0001; tel. (12) 3420877; fax (12) 3420876; e-mail safarku@global.co .za; Ambassador Hassan Bader Kareem al-Oqab.

Spain: Paseo de la Castellana 141, 16°, 28046 Madrid; tel. (91) 5792467; fax (91) 5702109; Ambassador ADIL HAMAD M. AL-AYYAR.

Sri Lanka: 292 Bauddhaloka Mawatha, Colombo 7; tel. (11) 2597958; fax (11) 2597954; e-mail cmb@kuwaitembassysl.org; Ambassador Fahid Hajar Shaouf al-Mutairi.

Sudan: Africa Ave, near the Tennis Club, POB 1457, Khartoum; tel. (183) 781525; Ambassador MUNTHIR BADR SALMAN.

Sweden: Banérgt. 37, POB 10030, 100 55 Stockholm; tel. (8) 450-99-80; fax (8) 450-99-55; e-mail kuwaitambassad@telia.com; Ambassador Sami Muhammad al-Sulaiman.

Switzerland: Brunadernrain 19, 3006 Bern; tel. 313567000; fax 313567001; internet www.kuwaitembassy.ch; Ambassador SUHAIL KHALIL YOUSEF SHUHAIBER.

Syria: rue Ibrahim Hanano, Damascus; Ambassador Fahed Ahmad al-Awadhi.

Thailand: 100/44 Sathorn Nakhon Tower, 24th Floor, Thanon Sathorn Nua, Bangrak, Bangkok 10500; tel. (2) 636-6600; fax (2) 636-7360; e-mail kwembasy@inet.co.th; Ambassador HAFEEZ MOHAMMED SALEM AL-AJMI.

Tunisia: 40 route Ariane, al-Menzah, Tunis; tel. (71) 236-811; Ambassador (vacant).

Turkey: Reşit Galip Cad. Kelebek Sok. 110, Gaziosmanpaşa, Ankara; tel. (312) 4450576; fax (312) 4466839; e-mail kuwait@ada.net.tr; Ambassador ABDULLAH ABD AL-AZIZ AD-DUWAIKH.

Ukraine: 04210 Kyiv, vul. Obolonska nab. 19; tel. (44) 391-51-60; fax (44) 391-51-64; e-mail kuwait_embassy@ukr.net; Ambassador Hamood Youssef al-Roudhan.

United Arab Emirates: POB 926, Abu Dhabi; tel. (2) 4446888; fax (2) 4444990; Ambassador FAISAL ABDULLAH IBRAHIM AL-MISHAAN.

United Kingdom: 2 Albert Gate, London, SW1X 7JU; tel. (20) 7590-3400; fax (20) 7823-1712; e-mail kuwait@dircon.co.uk; internet www.kuwaitinfo.org.uk; Ambassador Khalid ad-Duwaisan.

United States of America: 2940 Tilden St, NW, Washington, DC 20008; tel. (202) 966-0702; fax (202) 966-0517; e-mail kio@kuwait-info.org; internet www.kuwait-info.org; Ambassador SHEIKH JABER AL-AHMED AL-SABAH.

Uzbekistan: 100000 Tashkent, Batumi ko'ch. 2; tel. (71) 120-58-88; fax (71) 120-84-96; Ambassador Valid Ahmad al-Kandari.

Venezuela: Quinta El-Kuwait, Avda Las Magnolias con Calle Los Olivos, Los Chorros, Caracas; tel. (212) 239-4234; fax (212) 238-3878; Ambassador (vacant).

Yemen: POB 3746, South Ring Rd, San'a; tel. (1) 268876; fax (1) 268875; Ambassador Abd ar-Rahman Sayed al-Otaebi.

Zimbabwe: 1 Bath Rd, Avondale, POB A485, Harare; Ambassador SAUD FAISAL AL-DAWESS.

DIPLOMATIC MISSIONS OF KYRGYZSTAN

United Nations: 866 United Nations Plaza, Suite 477, New York, NY 10017; tel. (212) 486-4214; fax (212) 486-5259; e-mail kyrgyzstan@un.int; Permanent Representative Nurbek Jeenbaev.

Austria: Invalidenstr. 3/8, 1030 Vienna; tel. (1) 535-03-79; fax (1) 535-03-79-13; e-mail kyrbot@nnweb.at; Ambassador RINA N. PRIZHIVOIT.

Belarus: 220002 Minsk, vul. Starovilenskaya 57; tel. (17) 234-91-17; fax (17) 234-16-02; e-mail manas@nsys.minsk.by; internet kgembassy.by; Ambassador Lidiya A. Imanaliyeva.

Belgium: 47 rue de l'Abbaye, 1050 Brussels; tel. (2) 640-18-68; fax (2) 640-01-31; e-mail kyrgyz.embassy@skynet.be; Ambassador CHINGIZ AITMATOV.

China, People's Republic: 2-4-1 Tayuan Diplomatic Office Bldg, Beijing 100600; tel. (10) 65326458; fax (10) 65326459; e-mail tianshan@kyrgyzstan.link263.com; Ambassador Kadyrbek T. Sarbayev.

Germany: Otto-Suhr-Allee 146, 10585 Berlin; tel. (30) 34781338; fax (30) 34781362; e-mail info@botschaft-kirgisien.de; internet www.botschaft-kirgisien.de; Ambassador MARATBEK BAKIEV.

India: C-93 Anand Niketan, New Delhi 110 021; tel. (11) 24108008; fax (11) 24108009; e-mail alatoo@starith.net; Ambassador Irina A. Orolbayeva.

Iran: POB 19579-3511, Bldg 12, 5th Naranjestan Alley, Pasdaran St; tel. (21) 22830354; fax (21) 22281720; e-mail krembiri@mydatak.net; Ambassador MEDETKAN SH. SHERIMKULOV.

Japan: 5-6-16, Shimomeguro, Meguro-ku, Tokyo 153-0064; tel. (3) 3719-0828; fax (3) 3719-0868; e-mail chancery@kyrgyzemb.jp; internet www.kyrgyzemb.jp; Ambassador Askar Kutanov.

Kazakhstan: 010000 Astana, Diplomatiyalyk kalashyk B-5; tel. (7172) 24-20-24; fax (7172) 24-24-12; e-mail kz@mail.online.kz; Ambassador JANUSH RUSTENBEKOV.

Malaysia: 10 Lorong Damai 9, 55000 Kuala Lumpur; tel. (3) 21649862; fax (3) 21632024; e-mail kyrgyz@tm.net.my; internet www.kyrgyz.net.my; Ambassador Jeenbek Kulubaev (designate).

Pakistan: House 163, Street 36, F-10/1, Islamabad; tel. (51) 2212196; fax (51) 2212169; e-mail kyrgyzembassy@dsl.net.pk; Ambassador NURLAN T. AITMURZAYEV.

Russian Federation: 119017 Moscow, ul. B. Ordynka 64; tel. (495) 237-48-82; fax (495) 951-60-62; e-mail embassy@embas-kyrg.msk.ru; Chargé d'affaires a.i. Raimkul A. Attakurov.

Saudi Arabia: POB 75871, 32 Muhammad Khamid al-Fikki St, Riyadh; tel. (1) 229-3272; fax (1) 229-3274; Ambassador ZHUSUPBEK SHARIPOV.

Tajikistan: 734000 Dushanbe, Kuchai Studentcheskaya 67; tel. (372) 224-26-11; e-mail kyremb@tajnet.com; Ambassador Turatbek E. Junushaliyev.

Turkey: Boyabat Sok. 11, Ankara; tel. (312) 4468408; fax (312) 4468411; e-mail kirgiz-o@tr.net; Ambassador MAMBETJUNUS ABYLOV.

Turkmenistan: 744000 Aşgabat, ul. Gerogly 85; tel. (12) 35-55-06; e-mail kg@online.tm; internet kyrgtm.by.ru; Ambassador Borubek Ashirov.

Ukraine: 01901 Kyiv, vul. Artema 51/50; tel. (44) 482-08-89; fax (44) 482-13-97; e-mail embassy.kg.kiev@silvercom.net; Ambassador ERKIN B. MAMKULOV.

United Kingdom: Ascot House, 119 Crawford St, London, W1U 6BJ; tel. (20) 7935-1462; fax (20) 7935-7449; e-mail mail@kyrgyz-embassy.org.uk; internet www.kyrgyz-embassy.org.uk; Ambassador Dr Kuban Ilyasovich Mambetaliev.

United States of America: 2360 Massachusetts Ave, NW, Washington, DC 20008; tel. (202) 449-9822; fax (202) 386 7550; e-mail consul@kgembassy.org; internet www.kgembassy.org; Ambassador ZAMIRA BEKSULTANOVNA SYDYKOVA.

Uzbekistan: 100000 Tashkent, X. Samatov ko'ch. 30; tel. (71) 137-47-94; fax (71) 120-72-94; e-mail erkindik@sarkor.uz; Ambassador Azizbek M. Madmarov.

DIPLOMATIC MISSIONS OF LAOS

United Nations: 317 East 51st St, New York, NY 10022; tel. (212) 832-2734; fax (212) 750-0039; e-mail lao@un.int; internet www.un.int/lao; Permanent Representative PHOMMACHANH KANIKA.

Australia: 1 Dalman Crescent, O'Malley, ACT 2606; tel. (2) 6286-4595; fax (2) 6290-1910; e-mail laoemb@bigpond.net.au; internet www.laosembassy.net; Ambassador Khenthong Nuanthosing.

Belgium: 19–21 ave de la Brabançonne, 1000 Brussels; tel. (2) 740-09-50; fax (2) 734-16-66; e-mail ambalaobx@yucom.be; Ambassador THONGPHACHANH SONNASINH.

Brunei: Lot 19824, 11 Simpang 480, Jalan Kebangsaan Lama, off Jalan Muara, Bandar Seri Begawan BC 4115; tel. 2345666; fax 2345888; e-mail LAOSEMBA@brunet.bn; Ambassador Bounthong Vongsaly.

Cambodia: 15–17 blvd Mao Tse Toung, POB 19, Phnom-Penh; tel. (23) 997931; fax (23) 720907; e-mail laoembpp@camintel.com; Ambassador CHANTAVY BODHISANE.

China, People's Republic: 11 Dong Si Jie, San Li Tun, Chao Yang Qu, Beijing 100600; tel. (10) 65321224; fax (10) 65326748; e-mail laoemcn@public.east.cn.net; Ambassador Vichit Xindavong.

Cuba: Avda 5, No 2808, esq. 30, Miramar, Havana; tel. (7) 204-1056; fax (7) 204-9622; e-mail embalao@ip.etecsa.cu; Ambassador PHOUANGKEO LANGSY.

France: 74 ave Raymond Poincaré, 75116 Paris; tel. 1-45-53-02-98; fax 1-47-57-27-89; e-mail ambalaoparis@wanadoo.fr; internet www.laoparis.com; Ambassador Soutsakhone Pathammavong.

Germany: Bismarckallee 2A, 14193 Berlin; tel. (30) 89060647; fax (30) 89060648; Ambassador BOUNTHONG VONGSALY.

India: A-104/7 Parmanand Estate, Maharani Bagh, New Delhi 110 065; tel. (11) 26933319; fax (11) 26323048; Ambassador Ly Bun Kham.

Indonesia: Jalan Patra Kuningan XIV 1-A, Kuningan, Jakarta 12950; tel. (21) 5229602; fax (21) 5229601; e-mail laoemjktof@hotmail.com; Chargé d'affaires a.i. OUKHAM SENGKEOMIXAY.

Japan: 3-3-22, Nishi Azabu, Minato-ku, Tokyo 106-0031; tel. (3) 5411-2291; fax (3) 5411-2293; Ambassador Sithong Chitnhothinh.

Korea, Democratic People's Republic: Munhungdong, Taedongkang District, Pyongyang; tel. (2) 3827363; fax (2) 3817722; Ambassador CHALEUNE WARINTHRASAK.

Korea, Republic: 657-93, Hannam-dong, Yeongsan-gu, Seoul; tel. (2) 796-1713; fax (2) 796-1771; e-mail laoseoul@korea.com; Ambassador Soukthavone Keola.

Malaysia: 12A Persiaran Madge, off Jalan Ampang Hilir, 55000 Kuala Lumpur; tel. (3) 42511118; e-mail embassylao-kualalumpur@hotmail.com; Ambassador DR BOUNTHEUANG MOUNLASY.

Mongolia: Ikh Toiruu 59, Ulan Bator (CPOB 1030); tel. (11) 322834; fax (11) 321048; Ambassador Peng Intarat.

Myanmar: A1 Diplomatic Quarters, Franser Rd, Yangon; tel. (1) 222482; fax (1) 227446; Ambassador KOUILY SOUPHAKET.

Philippines: 34 Lapu-Lapu St, Magallanes Village, Makati City, Metro Manila; tel. (2) 8525759; Ambassador Leuane Sombounkhan.

Poland: 02-516 Warsaw, ul. Rejtana 15/26; tel. (22) 8484786; fax (22) 8497122; e-mail sotholaw@yahoo.com; Chargé d'affaires a.i. SENGPHET HOUNGBOUNGNUANG.

Russian Federation: 121069 Moscow, ul. Kachalova 18; tel. (495) 203-14-54; fax (495) 203-01-58; e-mail thingsavanh_ph@yahoo.com; Ambassador Thongsavanh Phomvihane.

Singapore: 101 Thomson Rd, 03-05A United Sq., Singapore 307591; tel. 62506044; fax 62506014; e-mail laoembsg@singnet.com.sg; Ambassador THOUANE VORASARN.

Sweden: Badstrandsvägen 11, POB 34050, 112 65 Stockholm; tel. (8) 618-20-10; fax (8) 618-20-01; e-mail info@laoembassy.se; internet www.laoembassy.se; Ambassador Done Somvorachit (designate).

Thailand: 502/502/1–3 Soi Sahakarnpramoon, Thanon Pracha Uthit, Wangthonglang, Bangkok 10310; tel. (2) 539-6667; fax (2) 539-3827; e-mail sabaidee@bkklaoembassy.com; internet www.bkklaoembassy.com; Ambassador OUAN PHOMMACHACK.

United States of America: 2222 S St, NW, Washington, DC 20008; tel. (202) 332-6416; fax (202) 332-4923; e-mail laoemb@verizon.net; internet www .laoembassy.com; Ambassador Phiane Philakone.

Viet Nam: 22 Tran Binh Trong, Hanoi; tel. (4) 9424576; fax (4) 8228414; Ambassador SOUNTHONE SAYACHAK.

DIPLOMATIC MISSIONS OF LATVIA

United Nations: 333 East 50th St, New York, NY 10022; tel. (212) 838-8877; fax (212) 838-8920; e-mail irppanony@aol.com; Permanent Representative Solveiga Silkalna.

Austria: Stefan-Esders-Pl. 4, 1190 Vienna; tel. (1) 403-31-12; fax (1) 403-31-12-27; e-mail embassy.austria@mfa.gov.lv; Ambassador AVIARS GROZA.

Azerbaijan: 1065 Baku, J. Jabbarli küç. 44; tel. (12) 436-67-78; fax (12) 436-67-79; e-mail embassy.azerbaijan@mfa.gov.lv; Ambassador Mihails Popkovs.

Belarus: 220013 Minsk, vul. Doroshevicha 6A; tel. (17) 211-30-33; fax (17) 284-74-94; e-mail embassy.belarus@mfa.gov.lv; internet www.am.gov.lv/belarus; Ambassador MAIRA MORA.

Belgium: 158 ave Molière, 1050 Brussels; tel. (2) 344-16-82; fax (2) 344-74-78; e-mail embassy.belgium@mfa.gov.lv; internet www.mfa.gov.lv/belgium; Ambassador Raimonds Jansons.

Canada: 350 Sparks St, Suite 1200, Ottawa, ON K1R 7S8; tel. (613) 238-6014; fax (613) 238-7044; e-mail embassy.canada@mfa.gov.lv; internet www .ottawa.am.gov.lv; Ambassador MARĢERS KRAMS.

China, People's Republic: Unit 71, Green Land Garden, No. 1A Green Land Rd, Chao Yang Qu, Beijing 100016; tel. (10) 64333863; fax (10) 64333810; e-mail embassy.china@mfa.gov.lv; internet www.latvianembassy.org.cn; Ambassador Janis Lovniks.

Czech Republic: Hradešínská 3, POB 54, 101 00 Prague 10; tel. 255700881; fax 255700880; e-mail embassy.czech@mfa.gov.lv; internet www.latvia.cz; Ambassador ARGITA DAUDZE.

Denmark: Rosbæksvej 17, 2100 Copenhagen Ø; tel. 39-27-60-00; fax 39-27-61-73; e-mail embassy.denmark@mfa.gov.lv; Ambassador Andris Razans.

Estonia: Tõnismägi 10, Tallinn 10119; tel. 627-7850; fax 625-7855; e-mail embassy.estonia@mfa.gov.lv; Ambassador INESE SEGLIŅA.

Finland: Armfeltintie 10, 00150 Helsinki; tel. (9) 4764720; fax (9) 47647288; e-mail embassy.finland@mfa.gov.lv; internet www.mfa.gov.lv/fi/helsinki; Ambassador Dr Einars Semanis.

France: 6 villa Saïd, 75116 Paris; tel. 1-53-64-58-10; fax 1-53-64-58-19; e-mail embassy.france@mfa.gov.lv; internet www.am.gov.lv/paris; Ambassador JĀNIS KĀRKLIŅŠ.

Georgia: 0160 Tbilisi, Odessa 60; tel. (32) 24-48-58; fax (32) 38-14-06; e-mail embassy.georgia@mfa.gov.lv; .

Germany: Reinerzstr. 40–41, 14193 Berlin; tel. (30) 82600222; fax (30) 82600233; e-mail embassy.germany@mfa.gov.lv; internet www.mfa.gov.lv/berlin; Ambassador DR MĀRTIŅŠ VIRSIS.

Greece: Odos Irodotou 9, Kolonaki, 106 74 Athens; tel. (210) 7294483; fax (210) 7294479; e-mail latvia@otenet.gr; Ambassador Līga Bergmane.

Ireland: 92 St Stephen's Green, Dublin 2; tel. (1) 4283320; fax (1) 4283311; e-mail embassy.ireland@mfa.gov.lv; internet www.am.gov.lv/en/ireland; Ambassador INDULIS ĀBELIS.

Israel: Europe Israel Tower, 15th Floor, Rehov Weizman, Tel-Aviv 64239; tel. 3-7775800; fax 3-6953101; e-mail embassy.israel@mfa.gov.lv; Ambassador Kārlis Eihenbaums.

Italy: Viale Liegi 42, 00198 Roma; tel. (06) 8841227; fax (06) 8841239; e-mail embassy.italy@mfa.gov.lv; internet www.mfa.gov.lv/rome; Ambassador ASTRA KURME.

Japan: 37-11, Kamiyama-cho, Shibuya-ku, Tokyo 150-0047; tel. (3) 3467-6888; e-mail embassy.jp@mfa.gov.lv; Ambassador Pēteris Vaivars.

Kazakhstan: 010000 Astana, Kabanbai Batyr 6/1/122, Kaskad Business Centre; tel. (7172) 92-53-16; fax (7172) 92-53-19; Ambassador RETS PLĒSUMS.

Lithuania: M. K. Čiurlionio g. 76, Vilnius 03100; tel. (5) 213-1260; fax (5) 213-1130; e-mail embassy.lithuania@mfa.gov.lv; internet www.am.gov.lv/vilnius; Ambassador Hardijs Baumanis.

Netherlands: Balistraat 88, 2585 XX The Hague; tel. (70) 3063934; fax (70) 3062858; e-mail embassy.netherlands@mfa.gov.lv; Ambassador BAIBA BRAŻE.

Norway: Bygdøy allé 76, POB 3163 Elisenberg, 0208 Oslo; tel. 22-54-22-80; fax 22-54-64-26; e-mail embassy.norway@mfa.gov.lv; Ambassador Māris Klišāns.

Poland: 03-928 Warsaw, ul. Królowej Aldony 19; tel. (22) 6174389; fax (22) 6174289; e-mail embassy.poland@mfa.gov.lv; internet www.latvia.pl; Ambassador ALBERTS SARKANIS.

Portugal: Travessa da Palmeira 31a, 1200-315 Lisbon; tel. (21) 3407170; fax (21) 3469045; e-mail embassy.portugal@mfa.gov.lv; Ambassador Artis Bertulis.

Russian Federation: 105062 Moscow, ul. Chaplygina 3; tel. (495) 232-97-60; fax (495) 232-97-50; e-mail embassy.russia@am.gov.lv; internet www.am.gov .lv/lv/moscow; Ambassador ANDRIS TEIKMANIS.

Slovenia: 1000 Ljubljana, Ajdovščina 4; tel. (1) 4341620; fax (1) 4341622; e-mail juris.poikans@mfa.gov.lv; Chargé d'affaires a.i. Aivars Groza.

Spain: Alfonso XII 52, 1°, 28014 Madrid; tel. (91) 3691362; fax (91) 3690020; e-mail lespan@telefonica.net; Ambassador MĀRTIŅŠ PERTS.

Sweden: Odengt. 5, POB 19167, 104 32 Stockholm; tel. (8) 700-63-00; fax (8) 14-01-51; e-mail embassy.sweden@mfa.gov.lv; internet www.stockholm.mfa .gov.lv; Ambassador Elita Kuzma.

Turkey: Reşit Galip Cad. 95, Çankaya, Ankara; tel. (312) 4056136; fax (312) 4056137; e-mail embassy.turkey@mfa.gov.lv; Ambassador IVARS PUNDURS.

Ukraine: 01901 Kyiv, vul. I. Mazepy 6b; tel. (44) 490-70-30; fax (44) 490-70-35; e-mail embassy.ukraine@mfa.gov.lv; internet www.am.gov.lv/ukraine; Ambassador Atis Sjanits.

United Kingdom: 45 Nottingham Pl., London, W1U 5LY; tel. (20) 7312-0040; fax (20) 7312-0042; e-mail embassy.uk@mfa.gov.lv; internet www.london .mfa.gov.lv; Ambassador INDULIS BĒRZINŠ.

United States of America: 2306 Massachusetts Ave, NW, Washington, DC 20008; tel. (202) 328-2840; fax (202) 328-2860; e-mail embassy@latvia-usa .org; internet www.latvia-usa.org; Ambassador Andrejs Pildegovics.

Uzbekistan: 100000 Tashkent, A. Lashkarbegi ko'ch. 16A; tel. (71) 137-22-15; fax (71) 120-70-36; e-mail amblatv@bcc.com.uz; Ambassador IGORS APOKINS.

DIPLOMATIC MISSIONS OF LEBANON

United Nations: 866 United Nations Plaza, Rm 531–533, New York, NY 10017; tel. (212) 355-5460; fax (212) 838-2819; e-mail lebanon@un.int; Permanent Representative Nawaf A. Salam.

Algeria: 9 rue Kaïd Ahmad, el-Biar, Algiers; tel. (21) 78-20-94; Ambassador BASSAM ALI TARABAH.

Argentina: Avda del Libertador 2354, C1425AAW Buenos Aires; tel. (11) 4802-0466; fax (11) 4802-2909; e-mail embajada@ellibano.com.ar; internet www.ellibano.com.ar; Ambassador Hicham Salim Hamdan.

Armenia: 0010 Yerevan, Vardanants St 7; tel. (10) 52-65-40; fax (10) 52-69-90; e-mail libarm@arminco.com; Ambassador TONY BADAWI.

Australia: 27 Endeavour St, Red Hill, ACT 2603; tel. (2) 6295-7378; fax (2) 6239-7024; e-mail lebanemb@tpg.com.au; internet www.lebanemb.org.au; Ambassador Jean Daniel.

Austria: Oppolzergasse 6/3, 1010 Vienna; tel. (1) 533-88-21; fax (1) 533-49-84; e-mail embassy.lebanon@inode.at; Chargé d'affaires a.i. ISHAYA AL-KHOURY.

Bahrain: Villa 1556, Rd 5647, Area 356, Manama; tel. 17579001; fax 17232535; e-mail lebem@batelco.com.bh; Ambassador Aziz Kazzi.

Belgium: 2 rue Guillaume Stocq, 1050 Brussels; tel. (2) 645-77-65; fax (2) 645-77-69; e-mail ambassade.liban@brutele.be; Chargé d'affaires a.i. ADNAN MANSOUR.

Brazil: SES, Av. das Nações, Quadra 805, Lote 17, 70411-900 Brasília, DF; tel. (61) 3443-5552; fax (61) 3443-8574; e-mail embaixada@libano.org.br; internet www.libano.org.br; Ambassador Fouad el-Khoury Ghanem.

Bulgaria: 1113 Sofia, ul. F. Zh. Kyuri 19; tel. (2) 971-31-69; fax (2) 973-32-56; Ambassador HIKMAT AWWAD.

Canada: 640 Lyon St, Ottawa, ON K1S 3Z5; tel. (613) 236-5825; fax (613) 232-1609; e-mail info@lebanonembassy.ca; internet www.lebanonembassy .ca; Chargé d'affaires a.i. Massoud Maalouf.

Chile: Alianza 1728, Casilla 1950, Santiago; tel. (2) 219-9724; fax (2) 219-3502; e-mail libano@netline.cl; Ambassador MOURAD JAMMAL.

China, People's Republic: 10 Dong Liu Jie, San Li Tun, Beijing 100600; tel. (10) 65322197; fax (10) 65322770; e-mail lebanon@public.bta.net.cn; Ambassador Sleiman Rassi.

Colombia: Calle 74, No 11-88, CP 51084, Bogotá, DC; tel. (1) 212-8360; fax (1) 347-9106; e-mail emblibanco@hotmail.com; Chargé d'affaires a.i. Hassan Muslimani.

Congo, Democratic Republic: 3 ave de l'Ouganda, Kinshasa; tel. (12) 82469; Chargé d'affaires a.i. Chehade Mouallem.

Côte d'Ivoire: Immeuble Trade Center, ave Noguès, 01 BP 2227, Abidjan 01; tel. 20-33-28-24; fax 20-32-11-37; Ambassador Ali Ajami.

Cuba: Calle 17a, No 16403, entre 164 y 174, Siboney, Havana; tel. (7) 208-6220; fax (7) 208-6432; e-mail lbcunet@ceniai.inf.cu; Chargé d'affaires a.i. Namir Noureddine.

Cyprus: POB 21924, 6 Chiou St, Ayios Dhometios, 1515 Nicosia; tel. 22878282; fax 22878293; Ambassador Michel el-Khoury.

Czech Republic: Lazarská 6, 120 00 Prague 2; tel. 224930495; fax 224934534; e-mail czklebemb@vol.cz; Ambassador Jaad el-Hassan.

Egypt: 22 Sharia Mansour Muhammad, Cairo (Zamalek); tel. (2) 7382823; fax (2) 7382818; Ambassador Khaled Ziadeh.

France: 3 villa Copernic, 75116 Paris; tel. 1-40-67-75-75; fax 1-40-67-16-42; e-mail na@ambliban.fr; internet www.ambassadeliban.fr; Ambassador Boutros Assaker.

Gabon: BP 3341, Libreville; tel. 73-14-77; Ambassador Michelin Baz.

Germany: Berliner Str. 127, 13187 Berlin; tel. (30) 4749860; fax (30) 47487858; e-mail lubnan@t-online.de; internet www.libanesische-botschaft.info; Chargé d'affaires a.i. Ramez Dimechkié.

Ghana: F864/1, off Cantonments Rd, Osu, POB 562, Accra; tel. (21) 776727; fax (21) 764290; e-mail lebanon@its.com.gh; Ambassador Jawdat el-Hajjar.

Greece: 6 Odos Maritou 25, Palaio Psychiko, 154 52 Athens; tel. (210) 6755873; fax (210) 6755612; e-mail grlibemb@otenet.gr; Ambassador Gibran Soufan.

Hungary: 1112 Budapest, Sasadi u. 160; tel. (1) 249-0900; fax (1) 249-0901; e-mail amblib@axelero.hu; .

India: H-1, Anand Niketan, New Delhi 110 021; tel. (11) 24111415; fax (11) 24110818; e-mail lebemb@bol.net.in; Ambassador Khaled Salman.

Indonesia: Jalan YBR V 82, Kuningan, Jakarta 12950; tel. (21) 5253074; fax (21) 5207121; e-mail lebanon_embassy_jkt@yahoo.com; Ambassador Victor Zmeter.

Iran: No. 31, Shahid Kalantari St, Gharani Ave, Tehran; tel. (21) 88908451; fax (21) 88907345; Ambassador Zain el-Musawi.

Iraq: 51/116, Askari St, Al-Liwadiat, Baghdad; tel. (1) 416-7850; fax (1) 416-8092; Chargé d'affaires Hassan Hujazi.

Italy: Via Giacomo Carissimi 38, 00198 Roma; tel. (06) 8537211; fax (06) 8411794; e-mail liban@tiscali.it; internet www.liban.it; Ambassador Melhem Nasri Mistou.

Japan: Chiyoda House, 5th Floor, 2-17-8, Nagata-cho, Chiyoda-ku, Tokyo 100-0014; tel. (3) 3580-1227; fax (3) 3580-2281; e-mail ambaliba@cronos.ocn.ne.jp; Ambassador Mohammed Harake.

Jordan: POB 811779, Amman 11181; tel. (6) 5929111; Ambassador Adib Charbel Aoun.

Kazakhstan: 010000 Astana, Riksos Prezident Hotel, kom. 5013; tel. (7172) 24-50-50; Chargé d'affaires a.i. Vazken Kavlakian.

Korea, Republic: 310-49, Dongbinggo-dong, Yeongsan-gu, Seoul 140-230; tel. (2) 794-6482; fax (2) 794-6485; e-mail emleb@lebanonembassy.net; internet www.lebanonembassy.net; Ambassador Issam Mustapha.

Kuwait: POB 253, 13003 Safat, Da'Yiah Diplomatic Area Plot 6, Kuwait City; tel. 2562103; fax 2571682; Ambassador Bassam Na'amani.

Liberia: 12th St, Monrovia; tel. 262537; Ambassador Mansour Abdallah.

Libya: POB 927, Auss bin al-Arkam, Ben Achour 10, Tripoli; tel. (21) 3615744; fax (21) 3611740; e-mail emblebanon_ly@hotmail.com; Chargé d'affaires a.i. Nazih Achour.

Malaysia: 56 Jalan Ampang Hilir, 55000 Kuala Lumpur; tel. (3) 42516690; fax (3) 42603426; e-mail lebanon@streamyx.com; Ambassador Khaled Al Kilani.

Mexico: Julio Verne 8, Col. Polanco, Del. Miguel Hidalgo, 11560 México, DF; tel. (55) 5280-5614; fax (55) 5280-8870; e-mail embalib@prodigy.net.mx; Ambassador Nouhad Mahmoud.

Morocco: 19 ave Abd al-Karim ben Jalloun, 10000 Rabat; tel. (3) 7760728; fax (3) 7766667; Ambassador Ahmad Othmane Abdellah.

Netherlands: Frederikstraat 2, 2514 LK The Hague; tel. (70) 3658906; fax (70) 3620779; e-mail amb.lib@wanadoo.nl; Ambassador Zeidan as-Saghir.

Oman: Shati al-Qurum, Way No. 3019, Villa No. 1613, POB 67, Al-Harthy Complex, Muscat 118; tel. 24695844; fax 24695633; e-mail lebanon1@omantel.net.om; Ambassador Afif Ayyub.

Pakistan: House 6, Street 27, F-6/2, Islamabad; tel. (51) 2278338; fax (51) 2826410; e-mail lebemb@comsats.net.pk; internet www.lebanonembassy.pak.4t.com; Ambassador Wafic Muhammad Rehaime.

Paraguay: San Francisco 629, esq. República Siria y Juan de Salazar, Asunción; tel. 22-9375; fax 23-2012; e-mail embajadadelibano@tigo.com.py; Ambassador Faras Eid.

Poland: 02-516 Warsaw, ul. Starościńska 1B/10–11; tel. (22) 8445065; fax (22) 6460030; e-mail embassy@lebanon.com.pl; internet www.lebanon.com.pl; Chargé d'affaires a.i. Kabalan Frangieh.

Qatar: POB 2411, 63 United Nations St, Al-Haditha Area, Doha; tel. 4933330; fax 4933331; e-mail embleb@qatar.net.qa; Ambassador Hassan Saad.

Romania: 011817 Bucharest 1, Str. Paris 46, ap.1; tel. (21) 2309205; fax (21) 2307534; e-mail emblebanon@k.ro; Ambassador Muhammad el-Dib.

Russian Federation: 103051 Moscow, ul. Sadovaya-Samotechnaya 14; tel. (495) 200-00-22; fax (495) 200-32-22; Ambassador Dr Assem Jaber.

Saudi Arabia: POB 94350, Riyadh 11693; tel. (1) 480-4060; fax (1) 480-4703; Ambassador Merwan Zaid.

Senegal: 56 ave Jean XXIII, BP 234, Dakar; tel. 33-822-0255; fax 33-823-5899; e-mail ambaliban@sentoo.sn; Ambassador Michel Haddad.

Serbia: 11000 Belgrade, Diplomatska kolonija 5; tel. (11) 3691178; fax (11) 3690155; e-mail ambaleb@eunet.yu; Ambassador Chéhadé Mouallem.

Sierra Leone: 22a Spur Rd, Wilberforce, Freetown; tel. (22) 222513; fax (22) 234665; Ambassador Ghassan Abdel Sater.

South Africa: 290 Lawley St, Waterkloof, Pretoria 0081; POB 941, Groenkloof 0027; tel. (12) 3467020; fax (12) 3467022; Chargé d'affaires a.i. Michel Katra.

Spain: Paseo de la Castellana 178, 3° izqda, 28046 Madrid; tel. (91) 3451368; fax (91) 3455631; e-mail leem-e@teleline.es; Chargé d'affaires a.i. Choucri Fathalla Abboud.

Sudan: Khartoum; Ambassador Ahmad Shammatt.

Sweden: Kommendörsgt. 35, POB 5360, 102 49 Stockholm; tel. (8) 665-19-65; fax (8) 662-68-24; Ambassador Nasrat al-Assad Bassile.

Switzerland: Thunstr. 10, 3074 Muri bei Bern; tel. 319506565; fax 319506566; e-mail ambalibch@hotmail.com; Chargé d'affaires a.i. Hussein Rammal.

Tunisia: Nahj 7037, no 3, al-Menzah, Tunis; tel. (71) 754-011; fax (71) 750-724; Ambassador Farid Abboud.

Turkey: Kızkulesi Sok. 44, Gaziosmanpaşa, 06700 Ankara; tel. (312) 4467487; fax (312) 4461023; e-mail lebembas@ttnet.net.tr; Chargé d'affaires Wajib Abd as-Samad.

United Arab Emirates: POB 4023, Abu Dhabi; tel. (2) 4492100; fax (2) 4493500; e-mail libanamb@emirates.net.ae; Ambassador Fauzi Fawaz.

United Kingdom: 21 Palace Gardens Mews, London, W8 4RB; tel. (20) 7227-6696; fax (20) 7243-1699; e-mail emb.leb@btinternet.com; Chargé d'affaires a. i. Inaam Osseiran.

United States of America: 2560 28th St, NW, Washington, DC 20008; tel. (202) 939-6300; fax (202) 939-6324; e-mail info@lebanonembassyus.org; internet www.lebanonembassyus.org; Chargé d'affaires a.i. Dr Antoine Chedid.

Uruguay: Avda General Rivera 2278, Montevideo; tel. (2) 4086640; fax (2) 4086365; e-mail embliban@adinet.com.uy; Ambassador Victor Georges Bitar Ghanem.

Vatican City: Via di Porta Angelica 15, 00193 Rome, Italy; tel. (06) 6833512; fax (06) 6833507; Ambassador Assi Naji Abi.

Venezuela: Edif. Embajada del Líbano, Prolongación Avda Parima, Colinas de Bello Monte, Calle Motatán, Caracas 1050; tel. (212) 751-5943; fax (212) 753-0726; e-mail emblibano@telcel.net.ve; Ambassador Nicolas Bechara Khawaja.

Yemen: POB 38, St 3, San'a; tel. (1) 203959; fax (1) 201120; e-mail lebem@y.net.ye; Ambassador Hassan Musilmani.

DIPLOMATIC MISSIONS OF LESOTHO

United Nations: 204 East 39th St, New York, NY 10016; tel. (212) 661-1690; fax (212) 682-4388; e-mail lesotho@un.int; internet www.un.int/lesotho; Permanent Representative LEBOHANG FINE MAEMA.

Belgium: 45 blvd Général Wahis, 1030 Brussels; tel. (2) 705-39-76; fax (2) 705-67-79; e-mail lesothobrussels@hotmail.com; Ambassador 'Mamoruti Tiheli.

Canada: 130 Albert St, Suite 1820, Ottawa, ON K1P 5G4; tel. (613) 234-0770; fax (613) 234-5665; e-mail lesotho.ottawa@bellnet.ca; High Commissioner MOTSEOSA PHILADEL SENYANE.

China, People's Republic: 302 Dongwai Diplomatic Office Bldg, 23 Dong Zhi Men Wai Dajie, Chaoyang Qu, Beijing 100600; tel. (10) 65326843; fax (10) 65326845; e-mail boemeli@public.bta.net.en; Ambassador Rachobokoane Anthony Thibeli.

Egypt: 10 Sharia Bahr al-Ghazal, Sahafeyeen, Cairo; tel. (2) 3447025; fax (2) 3025495; .

Ethiopia: Asmara Rd, Woreda 17, Kebele 16, House No. 157, POB 7483, Addis Ababa; tel. (11) 6614368; fax (11) 6612837; Ambassador Motlatsi Ramafole.

Germany: Kurfürstenstr. 84, 10787 Berlin; tel. (30) 2575720; fax (30) 25757222; e-mail embleso@yahoo.com; Ambassador DR MAKASE NYAPHISI.

Ireland: 2 Clanwilliam Sq., Grand Canal Quay, Dublin 2; tel. (1) 6762233; fax (1) 6762258; e-mail lesothodublin@eircom.net; Ambassador Mannete Malethole Ramaili.

Italy: Via Serchio 8, 00198 Roma; tel. (06) 8542496; fax (06) 8542527; e-mail les.rome@flashnet.it; Ambassador JONAS SPONKIE MALEWA.

Japan: U & M Akasaka Bldg, 3/F, 7-5-47, Akasaka, Minato-ku, Tokyo 107-0052; tel. (3) 3584-7455; Ambassador Mokhele Likate.

Kenya: Nairobi; tel. (20) 224876; fax (20) 337493; High Commissioner (vacant).

Libya: Ambassador Paul Khoashane Motholo.

South Africa: 391 Anderson St, Menlo Park, Pretoria 0081; POB 55817, Arcadia 0007; tel. (12) 4607648; fax (12) 4607469; Chargé d'affaires a.i. M KUMI.

United Kingdom: 7 Chesham Pl., London, SW1 8HN; tel. (20) 7235-5686; fax (20) 7235-5023; e-mail lhc@lesotholondon.org.uk; internet www.lesotholondon.org.uk; High Commissioner Prince Seeiso Bereng Seeiso.

United States of America: 2511 Massachusetts Ave, NW, Washington, DC 20008; tel. (202) 797-5533; fax (202) 234-6815; e-mail lesothoembassy@verizon.net; internet www.lesothoemb-usa.gov.ls; Chargé d'affaires a.i. MABASIA MOHOBANE.

DIPLOMATIC MISSIONS OF LIBERIA

United Nations: 820 Second Ave, 13th Floor, New York, NY 10017; tel. (212) 687-1033; fax (212) 687-1035; e-mail liberia@un.int; Permanent Representative Nathaniel Barnes.

Belgium: 50 ave du Château, 1081 Brussels; tel. (2) 411-01-12; fax (2) 411-09-12; e-mail liberia.embassy@scarlet.be; Ambassador YOUNGOR S. TELEWODA.

Cameroon: Quartier Bastos, Ekoudou, BP 1185, Yaoundé; tel. 2221-1296; fax 2220-9781; Ambassador Massa James.

China, People's Republic: Rm 013, Gold Island Diplomatic Compound, 1 Xi Ba He Nanlu, Beijing 100028; tel. (10) 64403007; fax (10) 64403918; Ambassador NEH RITA SANGAI DUKULY TOLBERT.

Congo, Democratic Republic: 3 ave de l'Okapi, BP 8940, Kinshasa; tel. (12) 82289; Ambassador Jalla D. Lansanah.

Côte d'Ivoire: Immeuble La Symphonie, ave Général de Gaulle, 01 BP 2514, Abidjan 01; tel. 20-22-23-59; fax 22-44-14-75; Ambassador KRONYANH M. WEEFUR.

Egypt: 11 Sharia Bresil, Cairo (Zamalek); tel. (2) 3419864; fax (2) 3473074; Ambassador Dr Brahima D. Kaba.

Ethiopia: Roosevelt St, Woreda 21, Kebele 4, House No. 237, POB 3116, Addis Ababa; tel. (11) 5513655; Ambassador DR EDWARD GBOLOCO HOWARD CLINTON.

France: 12 place du Général Catroux, 75017 Paris; tel. 1-47-63-58-55; fax 1-42-12-76-14; e-mail libem.paris@wanadoo.fr; Ambassador Dudley McKinley Thomas.

Germany: Kurfürstenstr. 84, 10787 Berlin; tel. (30) 26391194; Ambassador SEDIA MASSAQUOI-BANGOURA.

Ghana: 10 Odoi Kwao St, Airport Residential Area, POB 895, Accra; tel. (21) 775641; fax (21) 775987; Ambassador Rudolph P. von Ballmoos.

Guinea: Cité Ministérielle, Donka, Commune de Dixinn, BP 18, Conakry; tel. 30-42-26-71; Chargé d'affaires a. i. SIAKA FAHNBULLEH.

Israel: 74 Derech Menachim Begin, Tel-Aviv 67215; tel. 3-5611068; fax 3-5610896; .

Italy: Piazzale delle Medaglie d'Oro 7, 00136 Roma; tel. (06) 35453399; fax (06) 35344729; e-mail info@liberiaembassy.it; internet www.liberiaembassy.it; Chargé d'affaires a.i. MUSU JATU RUHLE.

Japan: Sugi Terrace 201, 3-13-11, Okusawa, Setagaya-ku, Tokyo 158; tel. (3) 3726-5711; fax (3) 3726-5712; Chargé d'affaires a.i. Adam Bility.

Morocco: Lot no 7, Napabia, rue Ouled Frej, Souissi, Rabat; tel. (3) 7638426; Ambassador (vacant).

Nigeria: 3 Idejo St, Plot 162, off Adeola Odeku St, Victoria Island, POB 70841, Lagos; tel. (1) 2618899; Ambassador Prof. James Tapeh.

Sierra Leone: 10 Motor Rd, Brookfields, POB 276, Freetown; tel. (22) 230991; Chargé d'affaires a.i. SAMUEL PETERS.

South Africa: Suite 9 Section 7, Schoeman St Forum, 1157 Schoeman St, Hatfield, Pretoria; POB 14082, Hatfield, Pretoria; tel. (12) 3422734; fax (12) 3422737; e-mail libempta@pta.lia.net; Ambassador Lois Lewis Bruthus.

United Kingdom: 23 Fitzroy Sq., London, W1 6EW; tel. (20) 7388-5489; fax (20) 7380-1593; e-mail liberianembassy@yahoo.co.uk; internet www.embassyofliberia.org.uk; Ambassador WESLEY MOMO JOHNSON.

United States of America: 5201 16th St, Washington, DC 20011; tel. (202) 723-0437; fax (202) 723-0436; e-mail info@liberiaemb.org; internet www.embassyofliberia.org; Ambassador Charles A. Minor.

DIPLOMATIC MISSIONS OF LIBYA

United Nations: 309–315 East 48th St, New York, NY 10017; tel. (212) 752-5775; fax (212) 593-4787; e-mail libya@un.int; internet www.libya-un.org; Permanent Representative GIADALLA AZZUZ BELGASSEM ETTALHI.

Afghanistan: Charahi Zanbaq, Wazir Akbar Khan, Kabul; tel. (20) 2101084; fax (20) 290160; Chargé d'affaires Mohammad Amer Alzaidy.

Albania: Rruga Dëshmorët e 4 Shkurtit 48, Tirana; tel. (4) 228101; fax (4) 232098; e-mail amblibi@abissnet.com.al; Chargé d'affaires a.i. MOULOUD O. A. AL-HAMUDI.

Algeria: 15 chemin Cheikh Bachir El-Ibrahimi, Algiers; tel. (21) 92-15-02; fax (21) 92-46-87; Ambassador Abd al-Moula el-Ghadhbane.

Argentina: 3 de Febrero 1358/62, C1426BJN Buenos Aires; tel. (11) 4788-3760; fax (11) 4784-9895; e-mail oficinapopularlibia@hotmail.com; Ambassador DR ALI Y. GIUMA BEN GIUMA.

Australia: 50 Culgoa Circuit, O'Malley, ACT 2606; tel. (2) 6290-7900; fax (2) 6286-4522; Chargé d'affaires a.i. Mohamed A. K. Dalla.

Austria: Blaasstr. 33, 1190 Vienna; tel. (1) 367-76-39; fax (1) 367-76-01; e-mail office@libyanembassyvienna.at; Sec. of the People's Bureau AHMED M. A. MENESI.

Azerbaijan: 1000 Baku, H. Javid pr. 520, apt 20; tel. (12) 493-23-65; fax (12) 498-12-47; e-mail libyabak@azerin.com; Chargé d'affaires a.i. Muhammad al-Giledi Jabir.

Bahrain: POB 26015, Manama; tel. 17722252; fax 17722911; Chargé d'affaires ABD AL-HAMID M. AL-WINDI.

Bangladesh: NE(D), 3a Gulshan Ave (N), Gulshan Model Town, Dhaka 1212; tel. (2) 600141; Chargé d'affaires Lutfi Alamin M. Mughrabi.

Belarus: 220000 Minsk, vul. Belaruskaya 4; tel. (17) 201-39-88; fax (17) 206-39-97; Ambassador ABDALLAH AL-MAGRAVI.

Belgium: 28 ave Victoria, 1000 Brussels; tel. (2) 647-37-37; fax (2) 640-90-76; e-mail tripoli@diplobel.org; Chargé d'affaires a.i. Yousuf Sifaw Hafiani.

Benin: Carré 36, Cotonou; tel. 21-30-04-52; fax 21-30-03-01; Ambassador TOUFIK ASHOUR ADAM.

Bosnia and Herzegovina: 71000 Sarajevo, Tahtali sokak 17; tel. (33) 657534; fax (33) 663620; Ambassador Ibrahim Ali Tagiuri.

Botswana: Plot 8851 (Government Enclave), POB 180, Gaborone; tel. 3952481; fax 356928; Ambassador ASSED MOHAMED ALMUTAA.

Brazil: SHIS, QI 15, Chácara 26, Lago Sul 71600-750 Brasília, DF; tel. (61) 3248-6710; fax (61) 3248-0598; e-mail emblibia@terra.com.br; Ambassador Salem Omar Abdullah Az-Zubaidi.

Bulgaria: 1784 Sofia, bul. A. Sakharov 1; tel. (2) 974-35-56; fax (2) 974-32-73; Ambassador TAHIR BENSHABAN.

Burkina Faso: 01 BP 1601, Ouagadougou 01; tel. 50-30-67-53; fax 50-31-34-70; Ambassador Abd an-Nasser Saleh Muhammad Younes.

Cameroon: Quartier Nylon Nlongkak, Quartier Bastos, BP 1980, Yaoundé; tel. 2220-4138; fax 2221-4298; Chargé d'affaires a.i. IBRAHIM O. AMAMI.

Canada: 81 Metcalfe St, Suite 1000, Ottawa, ON K1P 6K7; tel. (613) 230-0919; fax (613) 230-0683; e-mail info@libya-canada.org; internet www.libya-canada.org; Ambassador Ahmed Ali Jarrud.

Central African Republic: Bangui; tel. 61-46-62; fax 61-55-25; Ambassador (vacant).

Chad: BP 1096, N'Djamena; tel. 51-92-89; e-mail alibya1@intnet.td; Ambassador Ghayth Salim.

China, People's Republic: 3 Dong Liu Jie, San Li Tun, Beijing 100600; tel. (10) 65323666; fax (10) 65323391; Secretary of the People's Bureau MUSTAFA M. EL-GUELUSHI.

Congo, Republic: BP 920, Brazzaville; .

Côte d'Ivoire: Immeuble Shell, 01 BP 5725, Abidjan 01; tel. 20-22-01-27; fax 20-22-01-30; Ambassador FATHI NASHAD.

Croatia: 10000 Zagreb, Gornje Prekrižje 51b; tel. (1) 4629250; fax (1) 4629279; e-mail lnb@zg.htnet.hr; Ambassador (vacant).

Cuba: Avda 7, No 1402, esq. 14, Miramar, Havana; tel. (7) 204-2192; fax (7) 204-2991; e-mail oficinalibia@ip.etecsa.cu; Ambassador SAAD DAHER ZAMUNA.

Cyprus: POB 22487, 7 Stassinos Ave, 1060 Nicosia; tel. 22460055; fax 22452710; e-mail lapbcy@cytanet.com.cy; Ambassador Khalifa M. Fergiani.

Djibouti: BP 2073, Djibouti; tel. 350202; Ambassador KAMEL AL-HADI ALMARASH.

Egypt: 7 Sharia as-Saleh Ayoub, Cairo (Zamalek); tel. (2) 3401864; Ambassador Saleh ad-Droufi.

Eritrea: Asmara; .

Ethiopia: Ras Tessema Sefer, Woreda 3, Kebele 53, House No. 585, POB 5728, Addis Ababa; tel. (11) 5511077; fax (11) 5511383; Ambassador Ali Abdalla Awidan.

France: 2 rue Charles Lamoureux, 75116 Paris; tel. 1-47-04-71-60; fax 1-47-55-96-25; Sec. of the People's Bureau DR MUHAMMAD AL-HARARI.

Gambia: Independence Dr., Banjul; tel. 4223213; fax 4223214; Chargé d'affaires a.i. Taher S. Daloub.

Germany: Podbielskiallee 42, 14195 Berlin; tel. (30) 2005960; fax (30) 20059699; e-mail info@libysche-botschaft.de; internet www.libysche-botschaft.de; Chargé d'affaires a.i. HASSAN A. H. MAAWAL.

Ghana: 14 Sixth St, Airport Residential Area, POB 9665, Accra; tel. (21) 774819; fax (21) 774953; Secretary of People's Bureau Muhammad al-Gamudi.

Greece: Odos Vironos 13, Palaio Psychiko, 154 52 Athens; tel. (210) 6472120; Ambassador (vacant).

Guinea: Commune de Kaloum, BP 1183, Conakry; tel. 30-41-41-72; Ambassador B. Ahmed.

Guinea-Bissau: Rua 16, CP 362, Bissau; tel. 212006; Representative DOKALI ALI MUSTAFA.

Hungary: 1143 Budapest, Stefánia u. 111; tel. (1) 343-6076; fax (1) 343-1583; Head of People's Bureau (Ambassador) Omar Muftah Dallal.

India: 22 Golf Links, New Delhi 110 003; tel. (11) 24697717; fax (11) 24633005; e-mail libya@bol.net.in; Chargé d'affaires MAHFUD R. M. RAHIAM.

Indonesia: Jalan Pekalongan 24, Jakarta Pusat 10310; tel. (21) 31935308; fax (21) 31935726; Ambassasdor Salaheddin Mohamed El Bishari.

Iran: No. 163, Ostad Motahari Ave, Shahid Muftahi Ave, Tehran; tel. (21) 88742572; Ambassador ALI MARIA.

Italy: Via Nomentana 365, 00162 Roma; tel. (06) 86320951; fax (06) 86205473; Ambassador Abd al-Hafid Gaddur.

Japan: 10-14, Daikanyama-cho, Shibuya-ku, Tokyo 150-0034; tel. (3) 3477-0701; fax (3) 3464-0420; Secretary of the People's Bureau MUFTAH M. H. FAITOURI.

Jordan: POB 2987, Amman; tel. (6) 5693101; fax (6) 5693404; Ambassador Muhammad Hussein Bargathi.

Kazakhstan: 010000 Astana, Mikroraion Karaotkel-2 sh-a, kot. 110; tel. (7172) 24-18-79; fax (7172) 24-27-57; e-mail libya@nursat.kz; Chargé d'affaires a.i. AHMED ADDEB.

Korea, Democratic People's Republic: Munsudong, Taedongkang District, Pyongyang; tel. (2) 3827544; fax (2) 3817267; Secretary of People's Bureau Bashir Ramadan Khalifa Abu Janah.

Kuwait: POB 21460, 13075 Safat, 27 Istiqlal St, Kuwait City; tel. 2575183; fax 2575182; Chargé d'affaires ALI JAFFERE.

Liberia: Monrovia; Ambassador Muhammad Umarat-Tabi.

Madagascar: Lot IIB, 37A route Circulaire Ampandrana-Ouest, 101 Antananarivo; tel. (20) 2221892; Chargé d'affaires a.i. DR MOHAMED ALI SHARFEDIN AL-FITURI.

Malaysia: 6 Jalan Madge, off Jalan U Thant, 55000 Kuala Lumpur; tel. (3) 21411293; fax (3) 21413549; Chargé d'affaires a.i. Ahmad Masaoud B. Alghali.

Mali: Badalabougou-ouest, face Palais de la Culture, BP 1670, Bamako; tel. 222-34-96; fax 222-66-97; Ambassador DR SALAHEDDIN AHMED ZAREM.

Malta: Dar Jamahariya, Notabile Rd, Balzan BZN 01; tel. 21486347; fax 21483939; e-mail libyanpeople@waldonet.net.mt; Sec. of People's Bureau Dr Saad A. F. esh-Shlmani.

Mauritania: BP 673, Nouakchott; tel. 525-52-02; fax 525-50-53; .

Mexico: Horacio 1003, Col. Polanco, Del. Miguel Hidalgo, 11550 México, DF; tel. (55) 5545-5725; fax (55) 5545-5677; e-mail libia.mexico@yahoo.com; .

Morocco: 1 rue Chouaïb Doukkali, BP 225, 10000 Rabat; tel. (3) 7769566; fax (3) 7705200; Ambassador MUHAMMAD BELKACEM EZZAOUI.

Namibia: 69 Burg St, Luxury Hill, POB 124, Windhoek; tel. (61) 234454; fax (61) 234471; Ambassador Salam Mohammed Krayem (designate).

Netherlands: 15 Parkweg, 2585 JH The Hague; tel. (70) 355886; fax (70) 3559075; e-mail libyanembassy@wanadoo.nl; Sec. of the People's Bureau ZAKIA ABDUSSALAM M. SAHLI.

Nicaragua: Mansión Teodolinda, 1 c. al sur, $\frac{1}{2}$ c. abajo, Managua; tel. (2) 66-8540; fax (2) 66-8542; e-mail ofilibia@ibw.com.ni; Sec. of the People's Bureau Abdullah Muhammad Matoug.

Niger: route de Goudel, BP 683, Niamey; tel. 20-72-40-19; fax 20-72-40-97; e-mail boukhari@intnet.ne; Ambassador BOUKHARI SALEM HODA.

Nigeria: 46 Raymond Njoku Rd, SW Ikoyi, Lagos; tel. (1) 2680880; Chargé d'affaires a.i. Ibrahim al-Bashar.

Pakistan: House 736, Margalla Rd, F-10/2, Islamabad; tel. (51) 2214378; fax (51) 2290093; Ambassador MOHAMMAD ALI WARSHFANI.

Panama: Avda Balboa y Calle 32 (frente al Edif. Atalaya), Apdo 6-894 El Dorado, Panamá; tel. 227-3342; fax 227-3886; Chargé d'affaires a.i. Abdulmajid Milud Shahin.

Philippines: 1644 Dasmarinas St, cnr Mabolo St, Dasmariñas Village, Makati City, Metro Manila; tel. (2) 8177331; fax (2) 8177337; e-mail lpbmanila@skynet.net; Chargé d'affaires a.i. SADEK A. A. OMAN.

Portugal: Av. das Descobertas 24, 1400-092 Lisbon; tel. (21) 3016301; fax (21) 3012378; e-mail bureau.popular.libia@clix.pt; Chargé d'affaires Ali Emdored.

Qatar: POB 574, Doha; tel. 4429546; fax 4429548; Chargé d'affaires AL-MABROUK MUHAMMAD AL-MUADANE.

Romania: 010633 Bucharest 1, Bd. Lascar Catargiu 15; tel. (21) 2127832; fax (21) 3120232; Chargé d'affaires Ahmad Ibrahim al-Faqih.

Russian Federation: 131940 Moscow, ul. Mosfilmovskaya 38; tel. (495) 143-03-54; fax (495) 938-21-62; Ambassador ABDUL-ADIM KHIMALI.

Rwanda: BP 1152, Kigali; tel. 576470; Secretary of the People's Bureau Moustapha Masand El-Ghailushi.

Saudi Arabia: POB 94365, Riyadh 11693; tel. (1) 488-9757; fax (1) 488-3252; Ambassador MUHAMMAD SA'ID AL-QASHAT.

Senegal: route de Ouakam, Dakar; tel. 33-824-5710; fax 33-824-5722; AmbassadorAl Hady Salem Hammad.

Serbia: 11000 Belgrade, Sime Lozanića 6; tel. (11) 2663445; fax (11) 3670805; e-mail libyaamb@eunet.yu; Chargé d'affaires a.i. HANAN KHALED ZOGHBIA.

Sierra Leone: 1a and 1b P. Z. Compound, Wilberforce, Freetown; tel. (22) 235231; fax (22) 234514; Chargé d'affaires a.i. Ali Tellisi.

Slovakia: Révova ul. 45, 811 02 Bratislava 1; tel. (2) 5441-0324; fax (2) 5441-0730; e-mail lpb@stonline.sk; Sec. of People's Bureau AHMED KHALIFA.

Somalia: Via Medina, POB 125, Mogadishu; Ambassador Mohamed Zubeyd.

South Africa: 900 Church St, Arcadia, Pretoria 0083; POB 40388, Arcadia 0007; tel. (12) 3423902; fax (12) 3423904; Ambassador DR ABDULLAH ABDUSSALAM AL-ZUBEDI.

Spain: Pisuerga 12, 28002 Madrid; tel. (91) 5635753; fax (91) 5643986; e-mail oficinapopularlibia-madrid@hotmail.com; Ambassador Abdulwahed R. Gammudi.

Sri Lanka: 120 Horton Pl., POB 155, Colombo 7; tel. (11) 2693700; fax (11) 2695671; e-mail libya@eureka.lk; Sec. of the People's Bureau ABD-AL KARIM ALI ABD-AL KARIM.

Sudan: 50 Africa Rd, POB 2091, Khartoum; Secretary of People's Bureau Gumma al-Fazani.

Sweden: Valhallavägen 74, POB 10133, 100 55 Stockholm; tel. (8) 14-34-35; fax (8) 10-43-80; e-mail libyanembassy06@hotmail.com; Chargé d'affaires a.i. HAGI DHAN.

Switzerland: Tavelweg 2, 3006 Bern; tel. 313513076; fax 313511325; Chargé d'affaires a.i. Ibrahim ad-Dredi.

Syria: Abou Roumaneh, Damascus; Head of People's Bureau AHMAD ABD AS-SALAM BIN KHAYAL.

Tanzania: 386 Mtitu St, POB 9413, Dar es Salaam; tel. (22) 2150188; fax (22) 2150068; Secretary of People's Bureau Dr Ahmed Ibrahim el-Ashhab.

Togo: Cite OUA, BP 4872, Lomé; tel. 261-47-08; fax 261-47-10; Chargé d'affaires a.i. AHMED M. ABDULKAFI.

Tunisia: 48 bis rue du 1er juin, Mutuelle ville, 1002 Tunis; tel. (71) 780-866; fax (71) 795-338; .

Turkey: Cinnah Cad. 60, 06690 Çankaya, Ankara; tel. (312) 4381110; fax (312) 4403862; e-mail ashaabiankara@hotmail.com; Chargé d'affaires a.i. MUHAMMAD ZENATI.

Turkmenistan: 744000 Aşgabat, ul. Azad 17a; tel. (12) 35-49-17; fax (12) 39-35-26; Chargé d'affaires a.i. Ragab ben Khamadi.

Uganda: 26 Kololo Hill Dr., POB 6079, Kampala; tel. (41) 4344924; fax (41) 4344969; Sec. of People's Bureau ABDALLA ABDULMAULA BUJELDAIN.

Ukraine: 04050 Kyiv, vul. Ovrutska 6; tel. (44) 238-60-70; fax (44) 238-60-68; Chargé d'affaires Furjani Abd as-Salam.

United Arab Emirates: POB 5739, Abu Dhabi; tel. (2) 4450030; fax (2) 4450033; e-mail libyandh@emirates.net.ae; Chargé d'affaires ABD AL-HAMID ALI SHAIKHY.

United Kingdom: 15 Knightsbridge, London, SW1X 7LY; tel. (20) 7201-8280; fax (20) 7245-0588; Chargé d'affaires a.i. Omar R. Jelban.

United States of America: Liaison Office, 2600 Virginia Ave, NW, Suite 705, Washington, DC 20037; tel. (202) 944-9601; fax (202) 944-9606; e-mail libya@libyanbureau-dc.org; Chief of Office ALI SULEIMAN AUJALI.

Vatican City: Via Orazio 31b, 00193 Rome, Italy; tel. (06) 97605051; fax (06) 45433476; Sec. of the People's Bureau Abd al-Hafid Gaddur.

Viet Nam: A3 Van Phuc Residential Quarter, Hanoi; tel. (4) 8453379; fax (4) 8454977; e-mail libpbha@yahoo.com; Secretary SALEM ALI SALEM DANNAH.

Yemen: POB 1506, Ring Rd, St No. 8, House No. 145, San'a; Secretary of Libyan Brotherhood Office Mustafa Hwaidi.

Zambia: 251 Ngwee Rd, off United Nations Ave, Longacres, POB 35319, 10101 Lusaka; tel. (1) 253055; fax (1) 251239; Ambassador KHALIFA OMER SWIEXI.

Zimbabwe: 124 Harare St, POB 4310, Harare; tel. (4) 728381; Ambassador Mahmoud Yousef Azzabi.

DIPLOMATIC MISSIONS OF LIECHTENSTEIN

United Nations: 633 Third Ave, 27th Floor, New York, NY 10017; tel. (212) 599-0220; fax (212) 599-0064; e-mail liechtenstein@un.int; internet www.un.int/liechtenstein; Permanent Representative CHRISTIAN WENAWESER.

Austria: Löwelstr. 8/7, 1010 Vienna; tel. (1) 535-92-11; fax (1) 535-92-11-4; e-mail info@vie.rep.llv.li; internet www.liechtenstein.li/fl-aussenstelle-wien; Ambassador Princess Maria-Pia Kothbauer of Liechtenstein.

Belgium: 1 place du Congrès, 1000 Brussels; tel. (2) 229-39-00; fax (2) 219-35-45; e-mail ambassade.liechtenstein@bbru.llv.li; Ambassador HSH PRINCE NIKOLAUS OF LIECHTENSTEIN.

Germany: Mohrenstr. 42, 10117 Berlin; tel. (30) 52000630; fax (30) 52000631; e-mail vertretung@ber.rep.llv.li; internet www.berlin.liechtenstein.li; Ambassador PrinceStefan of Liechtenstein.

Switzerland: Willadingweg 65, Postfach, 3000 Bern 15; tel. 313576411; fax 313576415; e-mail info@bbrn.liv.li; internet www.bern.liechtenstein.li; Ambassador HUBERT FERDINAND BÜCHEL.

United States of America: 888 17th St, NW, Suite 1250, Washington, DC 20006; tel. (202) 331-0590; fax (202) 331-3221; e-mail tamara.brunhart@was.rep.llv.li; internet www.liechtenstein.li; Ambassador Claudia Fritsche.

DIPLOMATIC MISSIONS OF LITHUANIA

United Nations: 420 Fifth Ave, 3rd Floor, New York, NY 10018; tel. (212) 354-7820; fax (212) 354-7833; e-mail lithuania@un.int; internet www.un.int/lithuania; Permanent Representative DALIUS CEKUOLIS.

Afghanistan: House 2, St 1, Wazir Akbar Khan, Kabul; tel. (79) 9740521; e-mail biruteatiene@yahoo.com; Head of Mission and Chargé d'affaires Birutė Abraitienė.

Argentina: Mendoza 1018, C1428DJD, Buenos Aires; tel. (11) 4788-2153; fax (11) 4785-7915; e-mail embajada@lituania.org.ar; internet ar.mfa.lt; Chargé d'affaires a.i. LAURA TUPE.

Armenia: Yerevan, Noy 86; tel. (10) 74-19-64; fax (10) 74-19-63; Chargé d'affaires a.i. Kęstutis Stankevičius.

Austria: Löwengasse 47/4, 1030 Vienna; tel. (1) 718-54-67; fax (1) 718-54-69; e-mail amb.at@urm.lt; internet at.mfa.lt; Ambassador GIEDRIUS PUODŽIŪNAS.

Azerbaijan: 1000 Baku, Istiglaliyat küç. 15; tel. (12) 498-71-91; fax (12) 493-03-48; e-mail amb.az@urm.lt; Ambassador Kęstutis Kudzmanas.

Belarus: 220088 Minsk, vul. Zakharava 68; tel. (17) 285-24-48; fax (17) 285-33-37; e-mail amb.by@urm.ly; internet by.urm.lt; Ambassador EDMINAS BAGDONAS.

Belgium: 48 rue Maurice Liétart, 1150 Brussels; tel. (2) 772-27-50; fax (2) 772-17-01; e-mail info@lt-embassy.be; internet be.mfa.lt; Ambassador Nijolė Žambaitė.

Canada: 130 Albert St, Suite 204, Ottawa, ON K1P 5G4; tel. (613) 567-5458; fax (613) 567-5315; e-mail litemb@storm.ca; internet www.lithuanianembassy.ca; Ambassador GINTĖ BERNADETA DAMUŠIS.

China, People's Republic: B30 King's Garden, 18 Xiaoyun Lu, Chao Yang Qu, Beijing 100016; tel. (10) 84518520; fax (10) 84514442; e-mail amb.cn@urm.lt; internet cn.mfa.lt; Ambassador Rokas Bernotas.

Czech Republic: Pod Klikovkou 1916/2, 150 00 Prague 5; tel. 257210122; fax 257210124; e-mail amb.cz@urm.lt; internet cz.mfa.lt; Ambassador OSVALDAS ČIUKŠYS.

Denmark: Bernstorffsvej 214, 2920 Charlottenlund; tel. 39-63-62-07; fax 39-63-65-32; e-mail amb.dk@urm.lt; internet dk.mfa.lt; Ambassador Rasa Kairienė.

Egypt: 47 Sharia Ahmed Heshmat, Cairo (Zamalek); tel. (2) 7364329; fax (2) 7364326; e-mail amb.eg@urm.lt; Ambassador GINUTIS DAINIUS VOVERIS.

Estonia: Uus 15, Tallinn 15070; tel. 616-4990; fax 641-2013; e-mail amb.ee@urm.lt; internet www.ee.mfa.lt; Ambassador Juozas Bernatonis.

Finland: Rauhankatu 13A, 00170 Helsinki; tel. (9) 6844880; fax (9) 68448820; e-mail amb.fi@urm.lt; internet fi.mfa.lt; Ambassador HALINA KOBECKAITĖ.

France: 22 blvd de Courcelles, 75017 Paris; tel. 1-40-54-50-50; fax 1-40-54-50-75; e-mail chancellerie@amb-lituanie.fr; internet fr.mfa.lt; Ambassador Giedrius Čekuolis.

Georgia: 0162 Tbilisi, T. Abuladze 27; tel. (32) 91-29-33; fax (32) 22-17-93; e-mail amb.ge@urm.lt; Ambassador RIČARDAS DEGUTIS.

Germany: Charitéstr. 9, 10117 Berlin; tel. (30) 8906810; fax (30) 89068115; e-mail amb@botschaft-litauen.de; internet de.mfa.lt; Ambassador Evaldas Ignatavičius.

Greece: Leoforos Vassilissis Sofias 49, 106 76 Athens; tel. (210) 7294356; fax (210) 7294347; e-mail amb.gr@urm.lt; Ambassador ARTŪRAS ŽURAUSKAS.

Hungary: 1124 Budapest, Dobsinai u. 4a; tel. (1) 224-7910; fax (1) 202-3995; e-mail litvania@litvania.hu; internet hu.mfa.lt; Ambassador Darius Jonas Semaška.

Ireland: 90 Merrion Rd, Dublin 4; tel. (1) 6688292; fax (1) 6680004; e-mail amb.ie@urm.lt; internet ie.mfa.lt; Ambassador IZOLDA BRIČKOVSKIENĖ.

Israel: 8 Shaul Ha Meleh, Tel-Aviv 64733; tel. 3-6958685; fax 3-6958691; e-mail lrambizr@netvision.net.il; internet il.mfa.lt; Ambassador Asta Skaisgiryte-Liauskiene.

Italy: Viale di Villa Grazioli 9, 00198 Roma; tel. (06) 8559052; fax (06) 8559053; e-mail amb.it@urm.lt; internet it.mfa.lt; Ambassador ŠARŪNAS ADOMAVIČIUS.

Japan: 3-7-18, Moto Azabu, Minato-ku, Tokyo 106-0046; tel. (3) 3408-5091; fax (3) 3408-5092; e-mail linfo@lithemb.or.jp; internet www.lithemb.or.jp; Ambassador Dainius Petras Kamaitis.

Kazakhstan: 050059 Almaty, Iskanderova 15, Gornyi Gigant; tel. (727) 293-46-06; fax (727) 293-51-53; e-mail amb.kz@urm.lt; internet kz.mfa.lt; Ambassador ROMUALDAS KOZYROVIČIUS.

Latvia: Rūpniecibas iela 24, Rīga 1010; tel. 6732-1519; fax 6732-1589; e-mail lt@apollo.lv; internet lv.urm.lt; Ambassador Antanas Vinkus.

Moldova: 2001 Chişinău, str. I. Valilenco 24/1; tel. (22) 54-31-94; fax (22) 23-42-87; e-mail amb.md@urm.lt; Ambassador VYTAUTAS ŽALYS.

Netherlands: Laan van Meerdervoort 20, 2517 AK The Hague; tel. (70) 3855418; fax (70) 3853940; e-mail amb.nl@urm.lt; internet nl.mfa.lt; Ambassador Vaidotas Verba.

Norway: Henrik Ibsensgt. 100, 0244 Oslo; tel. 22-12-92-00; fax 22-12-92-01; e-mail amb.no@urm.lt; internet no.mfa.lt; Ambassador ALFONTAS EIDINTAS.

Poland: 00-478 Warsaw, Al. Ujazdowskie 14; tel. (22) 6253368; fax (22) 6253440; e-mail ambasada@lietuva.pl; internet www.lietuva.pl; Ambassador Egidijus Meilūnas.

Portugal: Av. 5 de Outubro 81, 1°, 1050-050 Lisbon; tel. (21) 7990110; fax (21) 7996363; e-mail ambasadorius@mail.telepac.pt; internet pt.mfa.lt; Ambassador ALGIMANTAS RIMKŪNAS.

Romania: 011973 Bucharest, Bd. Primăverii, 51, Sector 1; tel. (21) 3115997; fax (21) 3115919; e-mail amb.ro@urm.lt; internet www.ro.mfa.lt; Ambassador Vladimir Jarmolenko.

Russian Federation: 121069 Moscow, Borisoglebskii per. 10; tel. (495) 785-86-05; fax (495) 785-86-00; internet ru.mfa.lt; Ambassador RIMANTAS ŠIDLAUSKAS.

Slovenia: 1000 Ljubljana, Kongresni trg 3; tel. (1) 2442611; fax (1) 2442619; e-mail amb.si@urm.lt; Ambassador Rimutis Klevečka.

Spain: Pisuerga 5, 28002 Madrid; tel. (91) 7022116; fax (91) 3104018; e-mail amb.es@urm.lt; internet es.mfa.lt; Ambassador MEČYS LAURINKUS.

Sweden: Grevgt. 5, 114 53 Stockholm; tel. (8) 667-54-55; fax (8) 667-54-56; e-mail info@litemb.se; internet www.litemb.se; Ambassador Remigijus Motuzas.

Switzerland: Kramgasse 12, 3011 Bern; tel. 313525291; fax 313525292; e-mail amb.ch@urm.lt; internet ch.mfa.lt; Ambassador VYTAUTAS PLEČKAITIS.

Turkey: Mahatma Gandhi Cad. 17/8–9, 06700 Gaziosmanpaşa, Ankara; tel. (312) 4470766; fax (312) 4470663; e-mail lrambasd@ada.net.tr; Ambassador Darius Pranckevičius.

Ukraine: 01901 Kyiv, vul. Buslivska 21; tel. (44) 254-09-20; fax (44) 254-09-28; e-mail amb.ua@urm.lt; internet ua.mfa.lt; Ambassador ALGIRDAS KUMŽA.

United Kingdom: 84 Gloucester Pl., London, W1U 6AU; tel. (20) 7486-6401; fax (20) 7486-6403; e-mail amb.uk@urm.lt; internet uk.mfa.lt; Ambassador Vygaudas Ušackas.

United States of America: 4590 MacArthur Blvd, NW, Washington, DC 20007; tel. (202) 234-5860; fax (202) 328-0466; e-mail info@ltembassyus.org; internet www.ltembassyus.org; Ambassador AUDRIUS BRUZGA.

Vatican City: Corso Vittorio Emanuele II 308, 00186 Rome, Italy; tel. (06) 68192858; fax (06) 68809596; e-mail amb.va@urm.lt; internet va.mfa.lt; Ambassador Algirdas Saudargas.

DIPLOMATIC MISSIONS OF LUXEMBOURG

United Nations: 17 Beekman Pl., New York, NY 10022; tel. (212) 935-3589; fax (212) 935-5896; e-mail luxun@undp.org; internet www.un.int/luxembourg; Permanent Representative JEAN-MARC HOSCHEIT.

Austria: Sternwartestr. 81, 1180 Vienna; tel. (1) 478-21-42; fax (1) 478-21-44; e-mail vienne.amb@mae.etat.lu; Ambassador Arlette Conzemius.

Belgium: 75 ave de Cortenbergh, 1000 Brussels; tel. (2) 737-57-00; fax (2) 737-57-10; e-mail bruxelles.amb@mae.etat.lu; Ambassador ALPHONSE BERNS.

China, People's Republic: 21 Nei Wu Bu Jie, Beijing 100600; tel. (10) 65135937; fax (10) 65137268; e-mail pekin.amb@mae.etat.lu; Ambassador Carlo Krieger.

Czech Republic: Tržiště 13, 118 00 Prague 1; tel. 257181800; fax 257532537; e-mail alena.veliskova@mae.etat.lu; internet www.ambalux.cz; Ambassador JEAN FALTZ.

Denmark: Fridtjof Nansens Pl. 5, 1st Floor, 2100 Copenhagen Ø; tel. 35-26-82-00; fax 35-26-82-08; e-mail copenhague.amb@mae.etat.lu; internet www.luxembourgembassy.dk; Ambassador Pierre-Louis Lorenz.

France: 33 ave Rapp, 75007 Paris; tel. 1-45-55-13-37; fax 1-45-51-72-29; e-mail paris.amb@mae.etat.lu; internet www.ambassade-luxembourg.fr; Ambassador GEORGES SANTER.

Germany: Klingelhöfer Str. 7, 10785 Berlin; tel. (30) 2639570; fax (30) 26395727; e-mail berlin.amb@mae.etat.lu; Ambassador Jean Auguste Joseph Welter.

Greece: Leoforos Vassilissis Sofias 23A & Odos Neophytou Vamva 2, 10674 Athens; tel. (210) 7256400; fax (210) 7256405; e-mail athenes.amb@mae.etat.lu; internet www.mae.lu/grece; Ambassador CONRAD BRUCH.

India: 730 Gadaipur Rd, Branch Post Office, Gadaipur, New Delhi 110 030; tel. (11) 26801966; fax (11) 26801971; e-mail vm.bharathi@mae.etat.lu; internet www.luxembourgindia.org; Ambassador Marc Courte.

Italy: Via Santa Croce in Gerusalemme 90, 00185 Roma; tel. (06) 77201177; fax (06) 77201055; e-mail rome.amb@mae.etat.lu; internet www.ambasciatalussemburgo.it; Ambassador JEAN FALTZ.

Japan: 1/F Luxembourg House, 1st Floor, 8–9, Yonban-cho, Chiyoda-ku, 102-0081; tel. (3) 3265-9621; fax (3) 3265-9624; internet www.luxembourg.or.jp; Ambassador Paul Steinmetz.

Malaysia: Menara Keck Seng Bldg, 16th Floor, 203 Jalan Bukit Bintang, 55100 Kuala Lumpur; tel. (3) 21433134; fax (3) 21433157; e-mail emluxem@po.jaring.my; Chargé d'affaires CHARLES SCHMIT.

Netherlands: Nassaulaan 8, 2514 JS The Hague; tel. (70) 3647589; fax (70) 3462000; e-mail lahaye.amb@mae.etat.lu; Ambassador Jean Graff.

Poland: 00-789 Warsaw, ul. Słoneczna 15; tel. (22) 5078650; fax (22) 5078661; e-mail varsovie.amb@mae.etat.lu; Ambassador RONALD DOFING.

Portugal: Rua das Janelas Verdes 43, 1200-690 Lisbon; tel. (21) 3931940; fax (21) 3901410; e-mail lisbonne.amb@mae.etat.lu; Ambassador Alain de Muyser.

Russian Federation: 119034 Moscow, Khrushchevskii per. 3; tel. (495) 203-53-81; e-mail moscou.amb@mae.etat.lu; Ambassador CARLO KRIEGER.

Spain: Claudio Coello 78, 1°, 28001 Madrid; tel. (91) 4359164; fax (91) 5774826; e-mail madrid.amb@mae.etat.lu; internet www.mae.lu/espagne; Ambassador Jean-Paul Senninger.

Switzerland: Kramgasse 45, 3000 Bern 8; tel. 313114732; fax 313110019; e-mail berne.am@mae.etat.lu; Ambassador GÉRARD PHILIPPS.

United Kingdom: 27 Wilton Cres., London, SW1X 8SD; tel. (20) 7235-6961; fax (20) 7235-9734; e-mail londres.amb@mae.etat.lu; Ambassador Hubert Wurth.

United States of America: 2200 Massachusetts Ave, NW, Washington, DC 20008; tel. (202) 265-4171; fax (202) 328-8270; e-mail washington.info@mae.etat.lu; internet www.luxembourg-usa.org; Ambassador JOSEPH WEYLAND.

Vatican City: Via Casale di S. Pio V 20, 00165 Rome, Italy; tel. (06) 660560; fax (06) 66056309; Ambassador Georges Santer (resident in Paris, France).

DIPLOMATIC MISSIONS OF MACEDONIA, FORMER YUGOSLAV REPUBLIC

United Nations: 866 United Nations Plaza, Suite 517, New York, NY 10017; tel. (212) 308-8504; fax (212) 308-8724; e-mail macedonia@un.int; internet www.un.int/macedonia; Permanent Representative SLOBODAN TASOVSKI.

Albania: Rruga Kavajes 116, Tirana; tel. (4) 230909; fax (4) 232514; e-mail makambas@albnet.net; Ambassador Blagorodna Mingova-Krepieva.

Australia: POB 1890, Canberra, ACT 2601; tel. (2) 6282-6220; fax (2) 6282-6229; e-mail info@macedonianemb.org.au; internet www.macedonianemb.org.au; Ambassador VIKTOR GABER.

Austria: Maderstr. 1/10, 1040 Vienna; tel. (1) 524-87-56; fax (1) 524-87-53; e-mail macembassy@24on.cc; Ambassador Dr Vesna Borozan.

Belgium: 209A ave Louise, 1050 Brussels; tel. (2) 734-56-87; fax (2) 732-07-17; e-mail ambassade.mk@skynet.be; Chargé d'affaires a.i. JORDAN PANEV.

Bosnia and Herzegovina: 71000 Sarajevo, Splitska 57; tel. (33) 206004; e-mail maк.amb@bih.net.ba; Ambassador Mihailo Trpkoski.

Bulgaria: 1113 Sofia, ul. F. Zh. Kyuri 17/2/1; tel. (2) 870-15-60; fax (2) 971-28-32; e-mail todmak@bgnet.bg; Ambassador ABDIRAMAN ALITI.

Canada: 130 Albert St, Suite 1006, Ottawa, ON K1P 5G4; tel. (613) 234-3882; fax (613) 233-1852; e-mail emb.macedonia.ottawa@sympatico.ca; Ambassador Sasko Nasev.

China, People's Republic: 3-2-21 San Li Tun Diplomatic Office Bldg, Beijing 100600; tel. (10) 65327846; fax (10) 65327847; e-mail macdebas@public3.bta

.net.cn; internet www.macedonianembassy.com.cn; Ambassador FATMIR DZELADINI.

Croatia: 10000 Zagreb, Kralja Zvonimira 6; tel. (1) 4620261; fax (1) 4617369; e-mail veleposlanstvo.republike.makedonije@zg.t-com.hr; Chargé d'affaires a.i. Stojan Rumenovski.

Czech Republic: Balbínova 392/4, 120 00 Prague 2; tel. 222521093; fax 222521108; e-mail prague@mfa.gov.mk; Chargé d'affaires a.i. GOCE KARAJANOV.

Denmark: Skindergade 28a, 1st Floor, 1159 Copenhagen K; tel. 39-76-69-20; fax 39-76-69-23; e-mail copenhagen@mfa.gov.mk; Chargé d'affaires a.i. Salim Kjerimi.

France: 5 rue de la Faisanderie, 75116 Paris; tel. 1-45-77-10-50; fax 1-45-77-14-84; e-mail paris@mfa.gov.mk; Ambassador JON IVANOVSKI.

Germany: Koenigsallee 2–4, 14193 Berlin; tel. (30) 89069522; fax (30) 89541194; e-mail amba.berlin@t-online.de; Ambassador Gjorgji Filipov.

Hungary: 1024 Budapest, Margit Körut u. 43-45; tel. (1) 336-0510; fax (1) 315-1921; e-mail macedonia.embassy@axelero.hu; Chargé d'affaires a.i. SAŠO VELJANOVSKI.

Iran: No. 7, 4th Alley, Intifada Ave, Tehran; tel. (21) 88720810; .

Italy: Viale Bruxelles 73–75, 00198 Roma; tel. (06) 84241109; fax (06) 84241131; e-mail rome@mfa.gov.mk; Ambassador LJUPCO TOZIJA.

Montenegro: 81000 Podgorica, Hercegovačka 49/III; tel. (81) 667415; fax (81) 667205; e-mail mkgkpodgorica@cg.yu; Ambassador Stefan Nikolovski.

Netherlands: Laan van Meerdervoort 50C, 2517 AM The Hague; tel. (70) 4274464; fax (70) 4274469; e-mail repmak@wanadoo.nl; Ambassador DR DOBRINKA TASKOVSKA.

Poland: 02-954 Warsaw, ul. Królowej Marysieńki 40; tel. (22) 6517291; fax (22) 6517292; e-mail ambrmwar@zigzag.pl; internet www.ambasadarm.zigzag.pl; Ambassador Dimko Kokarovski.

Romania: 020083 Bucharest, Str. Mihai Eminescu 144; tel. (21) 2100880; fax (21) 2117295; e-mail ammakbuk@rdsmail.ro; Ambassador LJUPČO ARSOVSKI.

Russian Federation: 117292 Moscow, ul. D. Ulyanova 16/2/8/509–510; tel. (495) 124-33-57; fax (495) 982-36-34; e-mail mkambmos@mail.tascom.ru; Ambassador Zlatko Lečevski.

Serbia: 11000 Belgrade, Gospodar Jevremova 34; tel. (11) 3284924; fax (11) 3285076; e-mail macemb@eunet.yu; Ambassador ALEKSANDAR VASILEVSKI.

Slovenia: 1000 Ljubljana, Prešernova cesta 2; tel. (1) 4210021; fax (1) 4210023; e-mail makamb@siol.net; Ambassador Samoil Josif Filipovski.

Spain: Don Ramón de la Cruz 107, 2°B, 28006 Madrid; tel. (91) 5717298; fax (91) 5713481; e-mail emb.mkd.madrid@gmail.com; Chargé d'affaires a.i. DANICA RUZIN.

Sweden: Riddargt. 35, POB 10128, 100 55 Stockholm; tel. (8) 661-18-30; fax (8) 661-03-25; e-mail macedonian.embassy@telia.com; Ambassador Agon Demjaha.

Switzerland: Kirchenfeldstr. 30, 3005 Bern; tel. 313520002; fax 313520037; e-mail makedamb@bluewin.ch; Chargé d'affaires a.i. KENAN RAMADANI.

Turkey: Karaca Sok. 24/5–6, 06700 Gaziosmanpaşa, Ankara; tel. (312) 4399204; fax (312) 4399206; e-mail macemb@ttnet.net.tr; Ambassador Melpomeni Korneti.

Ukraine: 03150 Kyiv, vul. I. Fedorova 12; tel. (44) 238-66-16; fax (44) 238-66-17; e-mail embmac@carrier.kiev.ua; Ambassador (vacant).

United Kingdom: Suites 2.1 and 2.2, 2nd Floor, Buckingham Court, Buckingham Gate, London, SW1E 6PE; tel. (20) 7976-0535; fax (20) 7976-0539; e-mail info@macedonianembassy.org.uk; internet www.macedonianembassy.org.uk; Ambassador Marija Efremova.

Vatican City: Via di Porta Cavalleggeri 143, 00165 Rome, Italy; tel. (06) 635878; fax (06) 634826; e-mail vatican@mfa.gov.mk; Ambassador BARTOLOMEJ KAJTAZI.

United States of America: 2129 Wyoming Ave, NW, Washington, DC 20008; tel. (202) 667-0501; fax (202) 667-2131; e-mail usoffice@macedonianembassy.org; internet www.macedonianembassy.org; Ambassador Dr Zoran Jolevski.

DIPLOMATIC MISSIONS OF MADAGASCAR

United Nations: 820 Second Ave, Suite 800, New York, NY 10017; tel. (212) 986-9491; fax (212) 986-6271; e-mail repermad@ren.com; internet www.un.int/madagascar; Permanent Representative ZINA ANDRIANARIVELO-RAZAFY.

Algeria: BP 65, 22 rue Abd al-Kader Aouis, 16090 Bologhine, Algiers; tel. (21) 95-03-74; fax (21) 95-17-76; e-mail ambamadalg@yahoo.fr; Ambassador Vola Dieudonné Razafindralambo.

Belgium: 276 ave de Tervueren, 1150 Brussels; tel. (2) 770-17-26; fax (2) 772-37-31; e-mail info@ambassademadagascar.be; internet www.ambassademadagascar.be; Ambassador JEANNOT RAKOTOMALALA.

Canada: 3 Raymond St, Ottawa, ON K1R 1A3; tel. (613) 567-0505; fax (613) 567-2882; e-mail ambamadcanada@bellnet.ca; internet www.madagascar-embassy.ca; Ambassador Simon Constant Horace.

China, People's Republic: 3 Dong Jie, San Li Tun, Beijing 100600; tel. (10) 65321353; fax (10) 65322102; e-mail ambpek@public2.bta.net.cn; Ambassador VICTOR SIKONINA.

Ethiopia: Woreda 17, Kebele 19, House No. 629, POB 60004, Addis Ababa; tel. (11) 612555; fax (11) 610127; e-mail emb.mad@telecom.net.et; Ambassador Jean Pierre Rakotoarivony.

France: 4 ave Raphaël, 75016 Paris; tel. 1-45-04-62-11; fax 1-45-03-58-70; e-mail accueil@ambassade-madagascar.fr; internet www.ambassade-madagascar.fr; Ambassador JEAN-PIERRE RAZAFY-ANDRIAMIHAINGO.

Germany: Seepromenade 92, 14612 Falkensee (Brandenburg); tel. (3322) 23140; fax (3322) 231429; e-mail info@botschaft-madagaskar.de; internet www.botschaft-madagaskar.de; Ambassador Alphonse Sem Ralison.

Italy: Via Riccardo Zandonai 84A, 00194 Roma; tel. (06) 36307797; fax (06) 3294306; e-mail ambamad@hotmail.com; Ambassador AUGUSTE RICHARD PARAINA.

Japan: 2-3-23, Moto Azabu, Minato-ku, Tokyo 106-0046; tel. (3) 3446-7252; fax (3) 3446-7078; Ambassador Jimmy Ramiandrisoa.

Libya: POB 652, Maidane az-Zajeir, Tripoli; tel. (21) 3408257; fax (21) 3408256; e-mail ambamtri@yahoo.fr; Ambassador DIEUDONNÉ MARIE MICHEL RAZAFINDRANDRIATSIMANIRY.

Mauritius: Guiot Pasceau St, Floreal, POB 3, Port Louis; tel. 686-5015; fax 686-7040; e-mail madmail@intnet.mu; Ambassador Bruno Ranarivelo.

Russian Federation: 119034 Moscow, Kursovoi per. 5; tel. (495) 290-02-32; fax (495) 202-34-53; e-mail info@ambamadagascar.ru; internet www.ambamadagascar.ru; Ambassador ELOI MAXIME DOVO.

Senegal: Immeuble rue 2, angle Ellipse, Point E, BP 25395, Dakar; tel. 33-825-2666; fax 33-864-4086; e-mail ambadak@yahoo.fr; internet www.ambamad.sn; Ambassador Lila Hanitra Ratsifandrihamanana.

South Africa: 90B Tait St, Colbyn, Pretoria; POB 11722, Queenswood 0121; tel. (12) 3420983; fax (12) 3420995; e-mail consul@infodoor.co.za; Ambassador DENIS ANDRIAMANDROSO.

United Kingdom: 8–10 Hallam St, London W1W 6JE; tel. (20) 3008-4550; fax (20) 3008-4551; e-mail embamadlon@yahoo.co.uk; internet www.embassy-madagascar-uk.com; Chargé d'affaires Iary Berthine Ravaoarimanana.

United States of America: 2374 Massachusetts Ave, NW, Washington, DC 20008; tel. (202) 265-3034; fax (202) 483-7603; e-mail malagasy.embassy@org; internet www.kln.gov.my/perwakilan/washington; Ambassador JOCELYN RADIFERA.

DIPLOMATIC MISSIONS OF MALAWI

United Nations: 600 Third Ave, 21st Floor, New York, NY 10016; tel. (212) 949-0180; fax (212) 599-5021; e-mail malawiun@aol.com; Permanent Representative Steve Dick Tennyson Matenje.

Belgium: 46 ave Hermann Debroux, 1160 Brussels; tel. (2) 231-09-80; fax (2) 231-10-66; e-mail embassy.malawi@skynet.be; internet www.embassymalawi.be; Ambassador BRAVE NDISALE.

China, People's Republic: Beijing; Ambassador Thengo Maloya.

Ethiopia: Bole Rd, Woreda 23, Kebele 13, House No. 1021, POB 2316, Addis Ababa; tel. (11) 3711280; fax (11) 3719742; e-mail malemb@telecom.net.et; Ambassador JAMES DONALD KALILAGNWE.

Germany: Westfälische Str. 86, 10709 Berlin; tel. (30) 8431540; fax (30) 84315430; e-mail malawibonn@aol.com; internet www.malawi-botschaft.de; Ambassador Issac Chikwekwere Lamba.

Japan: Takanawa-Kaisei Bldg, 7th Floor, 3-4-1, Takanawa, Minato-ku, Tokyo 108-0074; tel. (3) 3449-3010; fax (3) 3449-3220; e-mail malawi@luck.ocn.ne.jp; internet www.malawiembassy.org; Ambassador ROOSEVELT LASTON GONDWE.

Mozambique: Av. Kenneth Kaunda 75, CP 4148, Maputo; tel. 21492676; fax 21490224; High Commissioner Martin O. Kansichi.

Namibia: 56 Bismarck St, POB 13254, Windhoek 9000; tel. (61) 221391; fax (61) 227056; e-mail mhc@mweb.co.na; High Commissioner F. CHIKUTA.

South Africa: 770 Government Ave, Arcadia, Pretoria 0083; POB 11172, Hatfield 0028; tel. (12) 3421759; High Commissioner Agrina Mussa.

Tanzania: Plot 38, Ali Hassan Mwinyi Rd, POB 7616, Dar es Salaam; tel. (22) 2666284; fax (22) 2668161; e-mail mhc@africaonline.co.tz; High Commissioner (vacant).

United Kingdom: 70 Winnington Rd, London, N2 0TX; tel. (20) 8455-5624; fax (20) 3235-1066; e-mail malawihighcom@btconnect.com; internet www .malawihighcom.org.uk; High Commr Dr Francis Moto.

United States of America: 1029 Vermont Ave, NW, Suite 1000, Washington, DC 20005; tel. (202) 721-0270; fax (202) 721-0288; e-mail malawidc@aol .com; internet www.malawiembassy-dc.org; Ambassador HAWA NDILOWE.

Zambia: 31 Bishops Rd, Kabulonga, POB 50425, Lusaka; tel. (1) 213750; fax (1) 265764; e-mail mhcomm@zamtel.zm; High Commissioner Dr Chrissie Mughogho.

Zimbabwe: 9–11 Duthie Rd, Alexandra Park, POB 321, Harare; tel. (4) 798584; fax (4) 799006; e-mail malahigh@africaonline.co.zw; Ambassador DR BENSON M. TEMBO.

DIPLOMATIC MISSIONS OF MALAYSIA

United Nations: 313 East 43rd St, New York, NY 10017; tel. (212) 986-6310; fax (212) 490-8576; e-mail malaysia@un.int; internet www.un.int/malaysia; Permanent Representative Hamidon bin Ali.

Argentina: Nicolás Villanueva 1040–48, C1426BMD Buenos Aires; tel. (11) 4776-0504; fax (11) 4776-0604; e-mail mwbaires@fibertel.com.ar; Ambassador ROHANA RAMLI.

Australia: 7 Perth Ave, Yarralumla, ACT 2600; tel. (2) 6273-1543; fax (2) 6273-2496; e-mail malcanberra@netspeed.com.au; internet www.malaysia .org.au; High Commissioner Dato' Haji Salim Hashim.

Austria: Floridsdorfer Hauptstr. 1–7, Florida Tower, 24th Floor, 1210 Vienna; tel. (1) 505-10-42-0; fax (1) 505-79-42; e-mail mwvienna@utanet.at; Ambassador MOHD ARSHAD MANZOOR HUSSAIN.

Bahrain: Bldg 2771, Rd 2835, Block 428, as-Seef District, Manama; tel. 17564551; fax 17564552; e-mail malmnama@kln.gov.my; internet www.kln .gov.my/perwakilan/manama; Ambassador Naimun Ashakli bin Muhammad.

Bangladesh: House 19, Rd 6, Baridhara, Dhaka 1212; tel. (2) 8827759; fax (2) 8823115; e-mail mwdhaka@citech-bd.net; internet www.kln.gov.my/ perwakilan/dhaka; High Commissioner ABDUL MALEK ABDUL AZIZ.

Belgium: 414a ave de Tervueren, 1150 Brussels; tel. (2) 776-03-40; fax (2) 762-50-49; e-mail mwbrusel@euronet.be; Ambassador Dato Muhammad Kamal bin Yan Yahaya.

Bosnia and Herzegovina: 71000 Sarajevo, Radnicka 4A; tel. (33) 201578; fax (33) 667713; e-mail malsrjevo@bih.net.ba; Ambassador RAMLAN BIN IBRAHIM.

Brazil: SHIS, QI 05, Chácara 62, 70477-900 Brasília, DF; tel. (61) 3248-5008; fax (61) 3248-6307; e-mail mwbrasilia@persocom.com.br; Ambassador Dato' Ismail bin Mustapha.

Brunei: 61 Simpang 336, Jalan Kebangsaan, Kampong Sungai Akar, Bandar Seri Begawan BC 1211; tel. 2345652; fax 2345654; e-mail mwbrunei@brunet .bn; High Commissioner DATUK ALI ABDULLAH.

Cambodia: 5 rue 242, Sangkat Chaktomouk, Khan Daun Penh, Phnom-Penh; tel. (23) 216176; fax (23) 216004; e-mail mwppenh@online.com.kh; internet www.kln.gov.my/perwakilan/phnompenh; Ambassador Dato' Adnan Haji Othman.

Canada: 60 Boteler St, Ottawa, ON K1N 8Y7; tel. (613) 241-5182; fax (613) 241-5214; e-mail malottawa@kln.gov.my; High Commissioner DATO' DENNIS J. IGNATIUS.

Chile: Tajamar 183, 10° y 11°, Of. 1002, Correo 35, Las Condes, Santiago; tel. (2) 233-6698; fax (2) 234-3853; e-mail mwstg@embdemalasia.cl; internet www.kln.gov.my/perwakilan/santiago; Ambassador Abdullah Faiz Mohd Zain.

China, People's Republic: 2 Liang Ma Qiao Bei Jie, Chao Yang Qu, San Li Tun, Beijing 100600; tel. (10) 65322531; fax (10) 65325032; e-mail mwbjing@ kln.gov.my; Ambassador DATO' SYED NORULZAMAN.

Croatia: 10000 Zagreb, Slavujevac 4a; tel. (1) 4834346; fax (1) 4834348; e-mail malzagreb@kln.gov.my; Ambassador Aminahtun Karim Shaharudin.

Cuba: Avda 5 y 68, No 6612, Miramar, Havana; tel. (7) 204-8883; fax (7) 204-6888; e-mail malhavana@kln.gov.my; Ambassador DATO' MOHAMED KAMAL BIN YAN YAHAYA.

Czech Republic: Washingtonova 25, 110 00 Prague 1; tel. 234706611; fax 296326192; e-mail mwprague@mwprague.cz; Ambassador Salman Ahmad.

Egypt: 21 El Aanab, Mohandessin, Cairo (Giza); tel. (2) 7610013; fax (2) 7610216; e-mail mwcairo2@soficom.com.eg; Ambassador DATUK ZAINAL ABIDIN ABDUL KADIR.

Fiji: Pacific House, 5th Floor, POB 356, Suva; tel. 3312166; fax 3303350; e-mail mwsuva@connect.com.fj; High Commissioner Nafisah Mohamed.

Finland: Aleksanterinkatu 17, 00100 Helsinki; tel. (9) 69697142; fax (9) 69697144; e-mail malhsinki@kln.gov.my; internet www.kln.gov.my/ perwakilan/helsinki; Ambassador SYED SULTAN IDRIS.

France: 2 bis rue Bénouville, 75116 Paris; tel. 1-45-53-11-85; fax 1-47-27-34-60; e-mail malparis@kln.gov.my; Ambassador Dato' S. Thanarajasingam.

Germany: Klingelhöferstr. 6, 10785 Berlin; tel. (30) 8857490; fax (30) 88574950; e-mail info@malemb.de; internet www.malemb.de; Ambassador ZAKARIA BIN SULONG.

Ghana: 18 Templesi Lane, Airport Residential Area, POB 16033, Accra; tel. (21) 763691; fax (21) 764910; e-mail mwaccra@africaonline.com.gh; Chargé d'affaires a.i. Yaacob Awang Chik.

Guinea: Quartier Mafanco, Corniche Sud, BP 5460, Conakry; tel. 30-22-17-54; e-mail mwcky@sotelgui.net.gn; Ambassador (vacant).

Hungary: 1026 Budapest, Pasaréti u. 29; tel. (1) 488-0810; fax (1) 488-0824; e-mail mwbdpest@axelero.hu; Ambasssador Wan Yusof Embong.

India: 50M Satya Marg, Chanakyapuri, New Delhi 110 021; tel. (11) 26111291; fax (11) 26881538; e-mail maldelhi@kln.gov.my; internet www.kln .gov.my/perwakilan/newdelhi; High Commissioner DATUK TAN SENG SUNG.

Indonesia: Jalan H. R. Rasuna Said, Kav. X/6, 1–3 Kuningan, Jakarta 12950; tel. (21) 5224947; fax (21) 5224974; e-mail maljakarta@kln.gov.my; internet www.kln.gov.my/perwakilan/jakarta; Ambassador Dato' Zainal Abidin Mohamad Zain.

Iran: POB 11365-8518, No. 6, Shahid Akhgan St, Fereshteh Ave, Tehran; tel. (21) 22010016; fax (21) 22010477; e-mail mwtehran@parsonline.net; internet myperwakilan.mfa.gov.my/me/tehran; Ambassador DATO SYED MUNSHE AFDZARUDDIN BIN SYED HASSAN.

Ireland: Level 3a–5a Shelbourne House, Shelbourne Rd, Dublin 4; tel. (1) 6677280; fax (1) 6677283; e-mail mwdublin@mwdublin.ie; Ambassador Dato' Siddiq Firdause Haji Mohd Ali.

Italy: Via Nomentana 297, 00162 Roma; tel. (06) 8415764; fax (06) 8555040; e-mail mw.rome@embassymalaysia.it; Ambassador DATO' LILY ZACHARIAH.

Japan: 20-16, Nanpeidai-cho, Shibuya-ku, Tokyo 150-0036; tel. (3) 3476-3840; fax (3) 3476-4971; e-mail maltokyo@kln.gov.my; Ambassador Dato' Mohd Radzi Abdul Rahman.

Jordan: POB 5351, Tayser Na'na'ah St, off Umawiyyeen St, Abdoun, Amman 11183; tel. (6) 5902400; fax (6) 5934343; e-mail mwamman@kln.gov .my; Ambassador HASNUDIN BEN HAMZAH.

Kazakhstan: 050051 Almaty, Rubenshtein 9 a; tel. (727) 333-44-83; fax (727) 387-28-25; e-mail mwalmaty@nursat.kz; Ambassador Dato Than Tai Hing.

Korea, Democratic People's Republic: Munhungdong Diplomatic Enclave, Pyongyang; tel. (2) 3817125; fax (2) 3817845; e-mail malpygyang@kln.gov .my; Chargé d'affaires a.i.JAMAL SHARIFUDDIN BIN JOHAN.

Korea, Republic: 4-1, Hannam-dong, Yeongsan-gu, Seoul 140-884; tel. (2) 795-9203; fax (2) 794-5480; e-mail mwseoul@kornet.net; internet www .malaysia.or.kr; Ambassador Dato' M. Santhananaban.

Kuwait: POB 4105, 13042 Safat, Daiya, Diplomatic Enclave, Area 5, Istiqlal St, Plot 5, Kuwait City; tel. 2550394; fax 2550384; e-mail malkuwait@kln .gov.my; internet www.kln.gov.my/perwakilan/kuwait; Ambassador DATO' ASHAARY BIN SANI.

Laos: 23 rue Singha, quartier Phonxay, BP 789, Vientiane; tel. (21) 414205; fax (21) 414201; e-mail mwvntian@laopdr.com; internet www.kln.gov.my/ perwakilan/vientiane; Ambassador Zainal Abidin Ahmad.

Libya: POB 6309, Hay Andalus, Tripoli; tel. (21) 4830854; fax (21) 4831496; e-mail mwtripoli@lttnet.net; Ambassador DATO' ZULKIFLI YAACOB.

Mexico: Sierra Nevada 435, Col. Lomas de Chapultepec, Del. Miguel Hidalgo, 11000 México, DF; tel. (55) 5202-4923; fax (55) 5282-4910; e-mail mwmexico@prodigy.net.mx; Chargé d'affaires a.i. Harris bin Alwi.

Morocco: 17 ave Bir Kacem, Souissi, Rabat; tel. (3) 7658324; fax (3) 7658363; e-mail malrabat@kln.gov.my; internet www.kln.gov.my/perwakilan/rabat; Ambassador OTHMAN SAMIN.

Myanmar: 82 Pyidaungsu Yeiktha Rd, Dagon Township, Yangon; tel. (1) 220249; fax (1) 221840; e-mail mwkyangon@mptmail.net.mm; internet www .kln.gov.my/perwakilan/yangon; Ambassador Datuk Mazlan Muhammad.

Namibia: 12 Babs Street, Ludwigsdorf, POB 312, Windhoek; tel. (61) 259344; fax (61) 259343; e-mail malwdhoek@kln.gov.my; High Commissioner HAYATI BT ISMAIL.

Nepal: Block B, 2nd Floor, Karmachari Sanchaya Kosh Bldg, Pulchowk, POB 24372, Lalitpur, Kathmandu; tel. (1) 5010004; fax (1) 5010492; e-mail malkatmandu@kln.gov.my; internet www.kln.gov.my/perwakilan/kathmandu; Ambassador Mahinder Singh.

Netherlands: Rustenburgweg 2, 2517 KE The Hague; tel. (70) 3506506; fax (70) 3506536; e-mail malaysia@euronet.nl; internet www.kln.gov.my/perwakilan/thehague; Chargé d'affaires a.i. MOHAMAD RAZDAN BIN JAMIL.

New Zealand: 10 Washington Ave, Brooklyn, POB 9422, Wellington; tel. (4) 385-2439; fax (4) 385-6973; e-mail mwwelton@xtra.co.nz; internet www.kln .gov.my/perwakilan/wellington; High Commissioner Dato' Sopian bin Ahmad.

Nigeria: 2 Pechora Close, Maitama PMB 5217, Abuja; tel. (9) 4133918; fax (9) 413 3922; e-mail malabuja@kln.gov.my; Chargé d'affairs a.i MELVIN CASTELINO.

Oman: Shati al-Qurum, Villa No. 1611, Way No. 3019, POB 3939, Ruwi 112; tel. 24698329; fax 24605031; e-mail mwmuscat@omantel.net.om; internet www.kln.gov.my/perwakilan/muscat; Ambassador Dato Muhammad Zamri Muhammad Kassim.

Pakistan: House 34, St 56, F-7/4, Islamabad; tel. (51) 2279570; fax (51) 2824761; e-mail malislamb@kln.gov.my; internet www.kln.gov.my/perwakilan/islamabad; High Commissioner AHMAD SHAHIZAN ABD SAMAD.

Papua New Guinea: POB 1400, Pacific View Apts, Units 201/203, 2nd floor, Pruth St, Korobosea, Port Moresby; tel. 3252076; fax 3252784; internet www .kln.gov.my/perwakilan/portmoresby; High Commissioner (vacant).

Peru: Avda Daniel Hernández 350, San Isidro, Lima 27; tel. (1) 4220297; fax (1) 2210786; e-mail mallima@kln.gov.my; internet www.kln.gov.my/perwakilan/lima; Ambassador DATUK HAJI MOHAMMED NOR BIN HAJI ATAN.

Philippines: 107 Tordesillas St, Salcedo Village, Makati City, 1200 Metro Manila; tel. (2) 8174581; fax (2) 8163158; e-mail mwmanila@indanet.com; internet www.kln.gov.my/perwakilan/manila; Ambassador Ahmad Rasidi Hazizi.

Poland: 03-902 Warsaw, Saska-Kepa, ul. Gruzińska 3; tel. (22) 6174413; fax (22) 6176256; e-mail mwwarsaw@poczta.neostrada.pl; Ambassador ROSMIDAH BINTE ZAHID.

Qatar: POB 23760, Doha; tel. 4836463; fax 4836453; e-mail maldoha@kln .gov.my; Ambassador Dato' Muhammad Shahrul Ikram Yaakob.

Romania: 020025 Bucharest 2, Str. Pta Cantacuzino 1, 3rd Floor, Rm 8; tel. (21) 2113801; fax (21) 2100270; e-mail mwbucrst@itcnet.ro; Ambassador DATIN PADUKA HALIMAH ABDULLAH.

Russian Federation: 119192 Moscow, ul. Mosfilmovskaya 50; tel. (499) 147-15-14; fax (495) 937-96-02; e-mail malmoscow@kln.gov.my; Ambassador Dato' Muhammad Khalis Ali Hassan.

Saudi Arabia: POB 94335, Riyadh 11693; tel. (1) 488-7100; fax (1) 482-4177; e-mail malriyadh@kln.gov.my; internet www.kln.gov.my/perwakilan/riyadh; Ambassador DATUK ISMA'IL IBRAHIM.

Senegal: 7 Extension VDN, Fann Mermoz, BP 15057, Dakar; tel. 33-825-8935; fax 33-825-4719; e-mail mwdakar@sentoo.sn; Chargé d'affaires a.i. Sharwana bin Idriss.

Singapore: 30 Hill St, 02-01, Singapore 179360; tel. 62350111; fax 67336135; e-mail mwspore@singnet.com.sg; High Commissioner DATO' NAGALINGAM PARAMESWARAN.

South Africa: 1007 Schoeman St, Arcadia, Pretoria 0083; POB 11673, Hatfield 0028; tel. (12) 3425990; fax (12) 4307773; High Commissioner Yahaya bin Abdul Jabar.

Spain: Paseo de la Castellana 91, Edif. Centro 23, 10°, 28046 Madrid; tel. (91) 5550684; fax (91) 5555208; e-mail mwmadrid@adv.es; Ambassador NAIMUN ASHAKLI.

Sri Lanka: 33 Bagatalle Rd, Colombo 3; tel. (11) 2554681; fax (11) 2554684; e-mail malcolmbo@eureka.lk; internet www.kln.gov.my/perwakilan/colombo; High Commissioner Rosli Ismail.

Sudan: St 3, Block 2, al-Amarat, POB 11668, Khartoum; tel. (183) 482763; fax (183) 482762; e-mail mwktoum@kln.gov.my; Ambassador HAJI ZAINAL HAMZAH.

Sweden: Karlavägen 37, POB 26053, 100 41 Stockholm; tel. (8) 791-76-90; fax (8) 791-87-60; e-mail mwstholm@algohotellet.se; Ambassador Dato' Kamarudin Mustafa.

Switzerland: Jungfraustr. 1, 3005 Bern; tel. 313504700; fax 313504702; e-mail malberne@greenmail.ch; Ambassador DATO' MOHD YUSOF BIN AHMAD.

Syria: Immeuble 15, Abd al-Kader al-Jazairy St, Abou Roumaneh, Damascus; tel. (11) 3343388; fax (11) 3341002; e-mail mwsyria@scs-net .org; Ambassador Zein Eddin Yehya.

Thailand: 35 Thanon Sathorn Tai, Tungmahamek, Sathorn, Bangkok 10120; tel. (2) 679-2190; fax (2) 679-2208; e-mail malbangkok@kln.gov.my; internet www.kln.gov.my/mission/bangkok; Ambassador DATO' SHARAANI BIN IBRAHIM.

Timor-Leste: Rua Almirante Américo Thomás, Mandarin, Dili; tel. 3311141; fax 3321805; e-mail mwdili@mail.timortelecom.tp; internet www.kln.gov .my/perwakilan/dili; Chargé d'affaires a. i. Azri Mat Yacob.

Turkey: Mahatma Gandhi Cad. 58, 06700 Gaziosmanpaşa, Ankara; tel. (312) 4463547; fax (312) 4464130; e-mail malankara@kln.gov.my; internet www .kln.gov.my/perwakilan/ankara; Ambassador DATO' SAIPUL ANWAR ABD AL-MUIN.

Ukraine: 1042 Kyiv, vul. Rayevskoho 4; tel. (44) 390-95-43; fax (44) 390-95-45; e-mail malkiev@kln.gov.my; internet www.kln.gov.my/perwakilan/kiev; Ambassador Dato Abdullah Sani Omar.

United Arab Emirates: POB 3887, Abu Dhabi; tel. (2) 4482775; fax (2) 4482779; e-mail mwabudhabi@eim.ae; internet www.kln.gov.my/perwakilan/abudhabi; Ambassador DATO' ABD AL-MUBIN RAZALI.

United Kingdom: 45 Belgrave Sq., London, SW1X 8QT; tel. (20) 7235-8033; fax (20) 7235-5161; e-mail mwlon@btconnect.com; internet www.kln.gov .my/mission/london; High Commr Datuk Abd Aziz Mohammed.

United States of America: 3516 International Court, NW, Washington, DC 20008; tel. (202) 572-9700; fax (202) 572-9882; e-mail mwalsh@kln.gov.my; Ambassador DATIN PADUKA RAJMAH HUSSAIN.

Uzbekistan: 100031 Tashkent, M. Yaqubov ko'ch. 28–30; tel. (71) 133-32-27; fax (71) 133-32-71; e-mail mwtskent@rol.uz; Ambassador (vacant).

Venezuela: Centro Profesional Eurobuilding, 6°, Ofs 6D-G, Calle La Guairita, Apdo 65107, Chuao, Caracas 1060; tel. (212) 992-1011; fax (212) 992-1277; e-mail malcaracas@kln.gov.my; internet www.embajadamalasia.com; Ambassador RAMLAN KIMIN.

Viet Nam: 43-45 Dien Bien Phu, Ba Dinh District, Hanoi; tel. (4) 7343836; fax (4) 7343832; e-mail mwhanoi@hn.vnn.vn; internet www.kln.gov.my/perwakilan/hanoi; AmbassadorLim Kim Eng.

Yemen: POB 16157, San'a; tel. (1) 415605; fax (1) 416181; e-mail mwsanaa@y .net.ye; Ambassador DATO' ABD-ASSAMD BIN OTHMAN.

Zimbabwe: 40 Downie Ave, Avondale, POB 5570, Harare; tel. (4) 334413; fax (4) 334415; e-mail malharare@kln.gov.my; AmbassadorCheah Choong Kit.

DIPLOMATIC MISSIONS OF MALDIVES

United Nations: 820 Second Ave, Suite 800C, New York, NY 10017; tel. (212) 599-6195; fax (212) 661-6405; e-mail mdv@undp.org; internet www.un.int/maldives; Permanent Representative AHMED KHALEEL.

China, People's Republic: 1-5-31 Jian Guo Men Wai Diplomatic Compound, Jianwai Xiushui Lu, Chao Yang Qu, Beijing 100600; tel. (10) 85323847; fax (10) 85323746; e-mail admin@maldivesembassy.cn; Ambassador Ahmed Latheef.

India: B–2, Anand Niketan, New Delhi 110 021; tel. (11) 41435701; fax (11) 41435709; e-mail admin@maldiveshighcom.co.in; internet www .maldiveshighcom.co.in; High Commissioner LT-GEN. (RETD) ABDUL SATTAR ADAM.

Japan: Iikura MINT Bldg, 8/F, 1-9-10, Azabudai, Minato-ku, Tokyo 106-0041; tel. 6234-4315; fax 6234-4316; e-mail info@maldivesembassy.jp; internet www.maldivesembassy.jp; Ambassador Abdul Hameed Zakariyya.

Malaysia: Suite 07-01, Menara See Hoy Chan, 374 Jalan Tun Razak, 50400 Kuala Lumpur; tel. (3) 21637244; fax (3) 21647244; e-mail mail@maldives .org.my; High Commissioner MIDHATH HILMY.

Singapore: 101 Thomson Rd, 30-01a, United Sq., Singapore 307591; tel. 67209012; fax 67209014; e-mail info@maldiveshighcommission.sg; High Commissioner Hassan Sobir.

Sri Lanka: 25 Melbourne Ave, Colombo 4; tel. (11) 2587827; fax (11) 2581200; e-mail info@maldiveshighcom.lk; internet www.maldiveshighcom .lk; High Commissioner ALI HUSSAIN DIDI.

United Kingdom: 22 Nottingham Pl., London, W1U 5NJ; tel. (20) 7224-2135; fax (20) 7224-2157; e-mail info@maldiveshighcommission.org; internet www .maldiveshighcommission.org; High Commr Dr Mohamed Asim.

United States of America: 800 Second Ave, Suite 400E, New York, NY 10017; tel. (212) 599-6195; fax (212) 661-6405; e-mail maldives@un.int; internet www.maldivesembassy.us; Ambassador MOHAMED HUSSAIN MANIKU.

DIPLOMATIC MISSIONS OF MALI

United Nations: 111 East 69th St, New York, NY 10021; tel. (212) 737-4150; fax (212) 472-3778; e-mail malionu@aol.com; Permanent Representative Cheick Sidi Diarra.

Algeria: Villa 15, Cité DNC/ANP, chemin Ahmed Kara, Hydra, Algiers; tel. (21) 69-13-51; fax (21) 69-20-82; Ambassador MAHAMADOU MAGASSOUBA.

Angola: Rua Padre Manuel Pombo 81, Maianga, Luanda; e-mail ambamali@netangola.com; Ambassador Farouk Camara.

Belgium: 487 ave Molière, 1050 Brussels; tel. (2) 345-74-32; fax (2) 344-57-00; e-mail mali@skynet.be; Ambassador IBRAHIM BOCAR BA.

Burkina Faso: 2569 ave Bassawarga, 01 BP 1911, Ouagadougou 01; tel. 50-38-19-22; Ambassador Col Toumany Sissoko.

Canada: 50 Goulburn Ave, Ottawa, ON K1N 8C8; tel. (613) 232-1501; fax (613) 232-7429; e-mail ambassadedumali@rogers.com; internet www .ambamalicanada.org; Ambassador MAMADOU BANDIOUGOU DIAWARA.

China, People's Republic: 8 Dong Si Jie, San Li Tun, Beijing 100600; tel. (10) 65321704; fax (10) 65321618; e-mail ambamali@163bj.com; Ambassador N'Tji Laico Traoré.

Côte d'Ivoire: 46 blvd Lagunaire, 01 BP 2746, Abidjan 01; tel. 20-32-31-47; fax 20-21-55-14; Ambassador SADA SAMAKÉ.

Cuba: Calle 36a, No 704, entre 7 y 9, Miramar, Havana; tel. (7) 204-5321; fax (7) 204-5320; e-mail ambamali@ceniai.inf.cu; Ambassador Fidèle Diarra.

Egypt: POB 844, 3 Sharia al-Kansar, Cairo (Dokki); tel. (2) 3371841; e-mail mali.eg@ie.eg.com; Ambassador MAMADOU KABA.

Ethiopia: Kebele 03, House No. 418, Addis Ababa; tel. (11) 168990; fax (11) 162838; e-mail keitamoone@maliembassy-addis.org; internet www .maliembassy-addis.org; Ambassador Al-Maamoun Baba Lamine Keïta.

France: 89 rue du Cherche-Midi, 75263 Paris Cedex 06; tel. 1-45-48-58-43; fax 1-45-48-55-34; e-mail ambamali.paris@wanadoo.fr; Ambassador MOHAMED SALIA SOKONA.

Gabon: BP 4007, Quartier Batterie IV, Libreville; tel. 82-73-82; fax 73-82-80; e-mail ambamaga@yahoo.fr; Ambassador Traoré Rokiatou Guikine.

Germany: Kurfürstendamm 72, 10709 Berlin; tel. (30) 3199883; fax (30) 31998848; e-mail ambmali@1019freenet.de; internet www.ambamali.de; Ambassador FATOUMATA SIRE DIAKITE.

Ghana: 1st Bungalow, Liberia Rd, Airport Residential Area, POB 1121, Accra; tel. (21) 666942; Ambassador Muphtah Ag Hairy.

Guinea: rue D1–15, Camayenne, Corniche Nord, BP 299, Conakry; tel. 30-46-14-18; fax 30-46-37-03; e-mail ambamaliguinee@yahoo.fr; Ambassador HAMADOUN IBRAHIMA ISSEBERE.

Iran: 3/F, 10 Maleck Ave, Tehran; tel. (21) 77500074; e-mail ambmali_teheran@yahoo.fr; Ambassador Amadou Mody Diall.

Italy: Via Antonio Bosio 2, 00161 Roma; tel. (06) 44254068; fax (06) 44254029; e-mail amb.malirome@tiscalinet.it; Ambassador IBRAHIM BOCAR DAGA.

Japan: 3-12-9, Kamiosaki, Shinagawa-ku, Tokyo 141-0021; tel. (3) 3705-3437; fax (3) 3705-3489; e-mail info@ambamali-jp.org; internet www .ambamali-jp.org; Ambassador Guisse Maïmouna Dial.

Korea, Democratic People's Republic: Pyongyang; Ambassador NAKOUNTE DIAKITÉ.

Libya: POB 2008, Sharia Jaraba Saniet Zarrouk, Tripoli; tel. (21) 4444924; Ambassador Ousmane Tandia.

Mauritania: Tevragh Zeina, BP 5371, Nouakchott; tel. 525-40-81; fax 525-40-83; e-mail ambmali@hotmail.com; Ambassador MOUSSA KALILOU COULIBALY.

Morocco: 58 cité Olm, Souissi, Rabat; tel. (3) 7759125; fax (3) 7754742; Ambassador Moussa Coulibaly.

Russian Federation: 113184 Moscow, ul. Novokuznetskaya 11; tel. (495) 951-06-55; fax (495) 230-28-89; e-mail amaliru@mail.ru; Ambassador GEN. BRÉHIMA SIRÉ TRAORÉ.

Saudi Arabia: POB 94331, Riyadh 11693; tel. (1) 464-5640; fax (1) 419-5016; Ambassador Muhammad Mahmoud Ould Bouya.

Senegal: Fann Résidence, Corniche-Ouest, rue 23, BP 478, Dakar; tel. 33-824-6252; fax 33-825-9471; e-mail ambamali@sentoo.sn; Ambassador N'TJI LAÏCO TRAORÉ.

South Africa: 876 Pretorius St, Arcadia 0083; POB 12978, Hatfield, Pretoria 0028; tel. (12) 3427464; fax (12) 3420670; Ambassador Sinaly Coulibaly.

Tunisia: 117 ave Jugurtha Matuelleville, BP 54, Nouvelle Ariana, 1002 Tunis; tel. (71) 792-589; fax (71) 791453; e-mail ambamali@wanadoo.tn; Ambassador ARAFA M'BARAKOU ASKIA TOURÉ.

United States of America: 2130 R St, NW, Washington, DC 20008; tel. (202) 332-2249; fax (202) 332-6603; e-mail info@maliembassy.us; internet www .maliembassy.us; Ambassador Abdoulaye Diop.

DIPLOMATIC MISSIONS OF MALTA

United Nations: 249 East 35th St, New York, NY 10016; tel. (212) 725-2345; fax (212) 779-7097; e-mail mltun@un.int; Permanent Representative SAVIOUR F. BORG.

Australia: 38 Culgoa Circuit, O'Malley, ACT 2606; tel. (2) 6290-1724; fax (2) 6290-2453; e-mail maltahighcommission.canberra@gov.mt; High Commissioner Francis Tabone.

Austria: Opernring 5/1, 1010 Vienna; tel. (1) 586-50-10; fax (1) 586-50-10-9; e-mail maltaembassy.vienna@gov.mt; Ambassador CHRISTOPHER GRIMA.

Belgium: 25 rue Archimède, 5e étage, 1000 Brussels; tel. (2) 238-27-04; fax (2) 238-27-07; e-mail tarcisio.zammit@gov.mt; Ambassador Tarcisio Zammit.

Bosnia and Herzegovina: 71000 Sarajevo, Mula Mustafe Bašeskije 12; tel. (33) 668632; e-mail lor.tac@tiscalinet.it; Ambassador DR LORENZO TACCHELLA.

China, People's Republic: 1-52 San Li Tun Diplomatic Compound, Beijing 100600; tel. (10) 65323114; fax (10) 65326125; e-mail maltamembassy .beijing@gov.mt; Ambassador Karl Xuereb.

Czech Republic: Lázeňská 4, 118 00 Prague 1; tel. 257531874; fax 257530968; e-mail srmr@seznam.cz; Ambassador MARIO QUAGLIOTTI.

Denmark: Amaliegade 8b, 2nd Floor, 1256 Copenhagen K; tel. 33-15-30-90; fax 33-15-30-91; e-mail maltaembassy.copenhagen@gov.mt; Ambassador Dr Noel Buttigieg-Scicluna.

Egypt: 1 Sharia es-Saleh Ayoub, Cairo (Zamalek); tel. (2) 7362368; fax (2) 7362371; e-mail maltaembassy.cairo@gov.mt; Ambassador GIOVANNI MICELI.

France: 92 ave des Champs Elysées, 75008 Paris; tel. 1-56-59-75-90; fax 1-45-62-00-36; e-mail maltaembassy.paris@gov.mt; Ambassador Dr Vicky-Ann Cremona.

Germany: Klingelhöfer Str. 7, 10785 Berlin; tel. (30) 2639110; fax (30) 26391123; e-mail maltaembassy.berlin@gov.mt; Ambassador JOHN PAUL GRECH.

Greece: Leoforos Vassilissis Sofias 96, 115 28 Athens; tel. (210) 7785138; fax (210) 7785242; e-mail maltaembassy.athens@gov.mt; Ambassador Richard Vella Laurenti.

India: D70 East of Kailash, New Delhi 110 065; tel. (11) 26439090; fax (11) 41659090; e-mail malta@kathpalia.in; High Commissioner WILFRED KENNELY.

Ireland: 17 Earlsfort Terrace, Dublin 2; tel. (1) 6762340; fax (1) 6766066; e-mail maltaembassy.dublin@gov.mt; Chargé d'affaires Ruth Farrugia.

Italy: Lungotevere Marzio 12, 00186 Roma; tel. (06) 6879990; fax (06) 6892687; e-mail maltaembassy.rome@gov.mt; Ambassador WALTER BALZAN.

Libya: POB 2534, Sharia Ubei ben Ka'ab, Tripoli; tel. (21) 3611181; fax (21) 3611180; e-mail maltaembassy.tripoli@gov.mt; Ambassador Dr Joseph Cassar.

Netherlands: Carnegielaan 4–14, 2517 KH The Hague; tel. (70) 3561252; fax (70) 3648789; e-mail maltaembassy.thehague@gov.mt; Ambassador DR IVAN FSADNI.

Portugal: Av. da Liberdade 49, 5°, 1250-139 Lisbon; tel. (21) 3405470; fax (21) 3405479; e-mail maltaembassy.lisbon@mail.telepac.pt; Ambassador Salv Stellini.

Russian Federation: 119049 Moscow, ul. Korovii Val 7/219; tel. (495) 237-19-39; fax (495) 237-21-58; e-mail maltaembassy.moscow@gov.mt; Ambassador DR MARIO COSTA.

Saudi Arabia: POB 94361, Riyadh 11693; tel. (1) 463-2345; fax (1) 463-3993; e-mail maltaembassy.riyadh@gov.mt; Ambassador Godwin Montanaro.

Spain: Paseo de la Castellana 45, 6° dcha, 28046 Madrid; tel. (91) 3913061; fax (91) 3913066; e-mail maltaembassy.madrid@gov.mt; Ambassador GAETAN A. NAUDI.

United Kingdom: Malta House, 36–38 Piccadilly, London, W1J 0LE; tel. (20) 7292-4800; fax (20) 7734-1831; e-mail maltahighcommission.london@gov.mt; High Commr Dr Michael Refalo.

United States of America: 2017 Connecticut Ave, NW, Washington, DC 20008; tel. (202) 462-3611; fax (202) 387-5470; e-mail maltaembassy.washington@gov.mt; internet www.foreign.gov.mt; Ambassador MARK MICELI-FARRUGIA.

DIPLOMATIC MISSIONS OF MARSHALL ISLANDS

United Nations: 800 Second Ave, 18th Floor, New York, NY 10017; tel. (212) 983-3040; fax (212) 983-3202; e-mail marshallislands@un.int; Permanent Representative Alfred Capelle.

China (Taiwan): 4/F, 9-1 Lane 62, Tien Mou West Rd, Shi-lin, Taipei 111; tel. (2) 28734884; fax (2) 28734904; e-mail rmiembtp@ms41.hinet.net; Ambassador ALEXANDER CARTER BING.

Fiji: 41 Borron Rd, Government Bldgs, POB 2038, Suva; tel. 3387899; fax 3387115; Ambassador Mack Kaminaga.

Indonesia: Jalan Pangeran Jayakarta 115, Blok A-11, Jakarta Pusat 10730; tel. (21) 7248565; fax (21) 7248566; e-mail marshall@idola.net.id; Ambassador CARL L. HEINE.

Japan: Meiji Park Heights 101, 9-9, Minamimoto-machi, Shinjuku-ku, Tokyo 106; tel. (3) 5379-1701; fax (3) 5379-1810; e-mail ambassador@rmiembassyjp.org; Ambassador Phillip Kabua.

United States of America: 2433 Massachusetts Ave, NW, Washington, DC 20008; tel. (202) 234-5414; fax (202) 232-3236; e-mail info@rmiembassyus.org; internet www.rmiembassyus.org; Ambassador BENJAMIN GRAHAM.

DIPLOMATIC MISSIONS OF MAURITANIA

United Nations: 116 East 38th St, New York, NY 10017; tel. (212) 986-7963; fax (212) 986-8419; e-mail mauritania@un.int; internet www2.un.int/public/mauritania; Permanent Representative Abderrahim Ould Hadrami.

Algeria: 107 Lot Baranès, Aire de France, Bouzaréah, Algiers; tel. (21) 79-21-39; fax (21) 78-42-74; Ambassador MOHAMED LEMINE OULD MOHAMED VAL DIT ISSELMOU BABAMINE.

Belgium: 6 ave de la Colombie, 1000 Brussels; tel. (2) 672-47-47; fax (2) 672-20-51; e-mail info@amb-mauritania.be; Ambassador Moulaye Ould Muhammad Laghdaf.

Brazil: Hotel Meliá Comfort, apt. 1606, SHS, Quadra 6, Conj. A, Bloco D, Asa Sul, 70316-000 Brasília, DF; tel. (61) 3218-4700; Ambassador N'DIAYE KANE.

Burkina Faso: Ouagadougou; Ambassador Mohamed Ould Sid Ahmed Lekhal.

China, People's Republic: 9 Dong San Jie, San Li Tun, Beijing 100600; tel. (10) 65321346; fax (10) 65321685; Ambassador OULD TALEB AMAR SIDI MOHAMED.

Congo, Democratic Republic: BP 16397, Kinshasa; tel. (12) 59575; Ambassador Lt-Col M'Bareck Ould Bouna Mokhtar.

Côte d'Ivoire: rue Pierre et Marie Curie, 01 BP 2275, Abidjan 01; tel. 22-41-16-43; fax 22-41-05-77; Ambassador ABDERRAHIM OULD HADRAMI.

Egypt: 114 Mohi ed-Din, Abou-el Ezz, Mohandessin, Cairo; tel. (2) 3490671; fax (2) 3489060; Ambassador Muhammad Lemine Ould.

Ethiopia: Lidete Kifle Ketema, Kebele 2, House No. 431 A, POB 200015, Addis Ababa; tel. (11) 3729165; fax (11) 3729166; Ambassador MOHAMED ABDELLAHI OULD BABANA.

France: 5 rue de Montévidéo, 75116 Paris; tel. 1-45-04-88-54; fax 1-40-72-82-96; e-mail ambassade.mauritanie@wanadoo.fr; Ambassador Matt Mint Mohamed el-Mokhtar Ould Ewnene.

Gabon: BP 3917, Libreville; tel. 74-31-65; Ambassador EL HADJ THIAM.

Germany: Kommandantenstr. 80, 10117 Berlin; tel. (30) 2065863; fax (30) 20674750; e-mail ambarim.berlin@gmx.de; Ambassador Mamadou Diakité.

Israel: Rehov Arlosoroff 111, Tel-Aviv 62098; tel. 3-6916820; fax 3-6957046; Ambassador AHMAD OULD TEGUEDDI.

Italy: Via Giovanni Paisiello 26, 00198 Roma; tel. (06) 85351530; fax (06) 85351441; Ambassador Yahya Ngam.

Japan: 5-17-5, Kita Shinagawa, Shinagawa-ku, Tokyo 141-0001; tel. (3) 3449-3810; fax (3) 3449-3822; e-mail ambarim@seagreen.ocn.ne.jp; internet www.amba-mauritania.jp; Ambassador MUHAMMAD MAHMOUD OULD JAAFAR.

Jordan: POB 851594, Saleh Zakee St, Villa 19, Sweifiyeh, Amman 11185; tel. (6) 5855146; fax (6) 5855148; e-mail muritanyaembassy_amman1@hotmail.com; Ambassador Muhammad al-Ameen Yahia.

Libya: Sharia Aïssa el-Wakwak, Tripoli; tel. (21) 4443223; Ambassador YAHIA MUHAMMAD EL-HADI.

Mali: route de Koulikoro, Hippodrome, BP 135, Bamako; tel. 221-48-15; fax 222-49-08; Ambassador Sidamine Ould Ahmed Challa.

Morocco: 6 rue Thami Lamdour, BP 207, Souissi, 10000 Rabat; tel. (3) 7656678; fax (3) 7656680; e-mail ambassadeur@mauritanie.org.ma; Ambassador CHAIKH OULD AÂL.

Qatar: POB 3132, Doha; tel. 4836003; fax 4836015; Ambassador Muhammad al-Amin as-Salem Ould Dada.

Russian Federation: 119049 Moscow, ul. B. Ordynka 66; tel. (495) 237-37-92; fax (495) 237-28-61; e-mail m_embassy@oss.ru; Ambassador MUHAMMAD MAHMOUD OULD DAHI.

Saudi Arabia: POB 94354, Riyadh 11693; tel. (1) 464-6749; fax (1) 465-8355; Ambassador Muhammad Walad Muhammad Fal.

Senegal: 37 blvd Charles de Gaulle, Dakar; tel. 33-823-5344; fax 33-823-5311; Ambassador MOHAMED EL-MOCTAR OULD MOHAMED YAHYA.

South Africa: 146 Anderson St, Brooklyn, Pretoria; tel. (12) 3623578; fax (12) 3623304; e-mail rimambapretoria@webmail.co.za; Ambassador Mohammed Lemine Ould Mohamed Salem Ould Selamane.

Spain: Velázquez 90, 3°, 28006 Madrid; tel. (91) 5757006; fax (91) 4359531; Ambassador SALEM OULD MEMMOU.

Syria: ave al-Jala'a, rue Karameh, Damascus; Ambassador (vacant).

Tunisia: 17 rue Fatma Ennechi, BP 62, al-Menzah, Tunis; tel. (71) 234-935; Ambassador AHMED S. OULD SALECK.

United Arab Emirates: POB 2714, Abu Dhabi; tel. (2) 4462724; fax (2) 4465772; Ambassador Muhammad al-Mukhtar Ould M. Yahaya.

United Kingdom: 8 Carlos Pl., London, W1K 3AS; tel. (20) 7478-9323; fax (20) 7478-9339; e-mail ambarim@aol.com; Ambassador OULD MOCTAR NECHE MÉLAÏNINE.

United States of America: 2129 Leroy Pl., NW, Washington, DC 20008; tel. (202) 232-5700; fax (202) 319-2623; e-mail info@mauritaniembassy-usa.org; Ambassador Ibrahima Dia.

Yemen: POB 19383, No. 6, Algeria St, San'a; tel. (1) 264188; fax (1) 215926; Ambassador AHMED OULD SIDY.

DIPLOMATIC MISSIONS OF MAURITIUS

United Nations: 211 East 43rd St, 15th Floor, New York, NY 10017; tel. (212) 949-0190; fax (212) 697-3829; e-mail mauritius@un.int; internet www.un.int/mauritius; Permanent Representative Somduth Soborun.

Australia: 2 Beale Crescent, Deakin, ACT 2600; tel. (2) 6281-1203; fax (2) 6282-3235; e-mail mhccan@cyberone.com.au; High Commissioner MARIE FRANCE ROUSSETY.

Belgium: 68 rue des Bollandistes, 1040 Brussels; tel. (2) 733-99-88; fax (2) 734-40-21; e-mail ambmaur@skynet.be; Ambassador Sutiawan Gunessee.

China, People's Republic: 202 Dong Wai Diplomatic Office Bldg, 23 Dong Zhi Men Wai Dajie, Chao Yang Qu, Beijing 100600; tel. (10) 65325695; fax (10) 65325706; e-mail mebj@public.bta.net.cn; Ambassador PAUL REYNOLD LIT FONG CHONG LEUNG.

Egypt: 156 Sharia es-Sudan, Mohandessin, Cairo; tel. (2) 7618102; fax (2) 7618101; e-mail embamaur@thewayout.net; Ambassador R. Soobadar.

Ethiopia: Kebele 03, House No. 750, POB 200222, Kifle Ketema, Addis Ababa; tel. (1) 6615997; fax (1) 6614704; e-mail mmaddis@ethionet.et; Ambassador TAYE WAN CHAT KWONG.

France: 127 rue de Tocqueville, 75017 Paris; tel. 1-42-27-30-19; fax 1-40-53-02-91; e-mail ambassade.maurice@online.fr; Ambassador Dr Mohammad Houssein Ismaël Dilmahomed.

Germany: Kurfürstenstr. 84, 10787 Berlin; tel. (30) 2639360; fax (30) 26558323; e-mail berlin@mauritius-embassy.de; internet www.mauritius-embassy.de; Ambassador MARIE GHISELAINE HENRISON.

India: 41 Jesus and Mary Marg, Chanakyapuri, New Delhi 110 021; tel. (11) 24102161; fax (11) 24102194; e-mail mhcnd@bol.net.in; High Commissioner M. Choonee.

Madagascar: Anjaharay, route Circulaire, BP 6040, Ambanidia, 101 Antananarivo; tel. (20) 2221864; fax (20) 2221939; Ambassador ERNEST GÉRARD LEMAIRE.

Malaysia: 17th Floor, West Block, Wisma Selangor Dredging, Jalan Ampang, 50450 Kuala Lumpur; tel. (3) 21411870; e-mail maurhckl@streamyx.com; Chargé d'affaires a.i. D. P. Gokulsing.

Mozambique: Rua Dom Carlos 42, Av. de Zimbabwe, Sommerscheid, Maputo; tel. 21494624; fax 21494729; e-mail mhcmoz@intra.co.mz; High Commissioner ALAIN LARIDON.

Pakistan: House 13, St 26, F-6/2, POB 1084, Islamabad; tel. (51) 2824657; fax (51) 2824656; e-mail mauripak@dsl.net.pk; High Commissioner Abdool Raschid Meerun.

South Africa: 1163 Pretorius St, Hatfield, Pretoria 0083; tel. (12) 3421283; fax (12) 3421286; e-mail mhcpta@mweb.co.za; High Commissioner MOHAMED ISMAEL DOSSA.

United Kingdom: 32–33 Elvaston Pl., London, SW7 5NW; tel. (20) 7581-0294; fax (20) 7823-8437; e-mail londonmhc@btinternet.com; High Commr Abhimanu Mahendra Kundasamy.

United States of America: 4301 Connecticut Ave, NW, Suite 441, Washington, DC 20008; tel. (202) 244-1491; fax (202) 966-0983; e-mail mauritius.embassy@prodigy.net; Ambassador KEERTEECOOMAR RUHEE.

DIPLOMATIC MISSIONS OF MEXICO

United Nations: 2 United Nations Plaza, 28th Floor, New York, NY 10017; tel. (212) 752-0220; fax (212) 688-8862; e-mail mexico@un.int; internet www.un.int/mexico; Permanent Representative Claude Heller.

Algeria: BP 329, 25 chemin El-Bakri, Ben Aknoun, 16306 Algiers; tel. (21) 91-46-00; fax (21) 91-46-01; e-mail embamexargelia@gmail.com; Ambassador EDUARDO ROLDÁN ACOSTA.

Argentina: Arcos 1650, C1426BGL Buenos Aires; tel. (11) 4789-8800; fax (11) 4789-8836; e-mail embamexarg@interlink.com.ar; internet www.embamex.int.ar; Ambassador María Cristina de la Garza Sandoval.

Australia: 14 Perth Ave, Yarralumla, ACT 2600; tel. (2) 6273-3963; fax (2) 6273-1190; e-mail embamex@mexico.org.au; internet www.mexico.org.au; Ambassador MARTHA ORTIZ DE ROSAS.

Austria: Operngasse 21/10, 1040 Vienna; tel. (1) 310-73-83; fax (1) 310-73-87; e-mail embamex@embamex.or.at; Ambassador Alejandro Díaz y Pérez Duarte.

Belgium: 94 ave F. D. Roosevelt, 1050 Brussels; tel. (2) 629-07-77; fax (2) 644-08-19; e-mail embamex@embamex.eu; internet www.embamex.eu; Ambassador SANDRA FUENTES-BERAIN.

Belize: 3 North Ring Road, Embassy Sq., Belmopan; tel. 822-2480; fax 822-2487; e-mail embamexbze@btl.net; internet www.sre.gob.mx/belice; Ambassador José Arturo Trejo Nava.

Bolivia: Sánchez Bustamante 509, Casilla 430, La Paz; tel. (2) 277-2133; fax (2) 277-6085; e-mail embamex@acelerate.com; internet www.sre.gob.mx/bolivia; Ambassador ROBERTA LAJOUS VARGAS.

Brazil: SES, Av. das Nações, Quadra 805, Lote 18, 70412-900 Brasília, DF; tel. (61) 3244-1011; fax (61) 3244-1755; e-mail embamexbra@cabonet.com.br; internet www.mexico.org.br; Ambassador Andrés Valencia Benavides.

Canada: 45 O'Connor St, Suite 1000, Ottawa, ON K1P 1A4; tel. (613) 233-8988; fax (613) 235-9123; e-mail info@embamexcan.com; internet www.sre.gob.mx/canada; Ambassador EMILIO RAFAEL JOSÉ GOICOECHEA LUNA.

Chile: Félix de Amesti 128, Las Condes, Santiago; tel. (2) 583-8400; fax (2) 583-8484; e-mail info@emexico.cl; internet www.emexico.cl; Ambassador Ricardo Villanueva Hallal.

China, People's Republic: 5 Dong Wu Jie, San Li Tun, Beijing 100600; tel. (10) 65321717; fax (10) 65323744; e-mail embmxchn@public.bta.net.cn; internet www.sre.gob.mx/china; Ambassador JORGE EUGENIO GUAJARDO GONZÁLEZ.

Colombia: Edif. Teleport Business Park, Calle 114, No 9-01, Of. 204, Torre A, Bogotá, DC; tel. (1) 629-4989; fax (1) 629-5121; e-mail emcolmex@etb.net.co; internet www.sre.gob.mx/colombia; Ambassador (vacant).

Costa Rica: Avda 7, No 1371, Apdo 10107, 1000 San José; tel. 257-0633; fax 258-2437; e-mail residencia@embamexico.or.cr; internet portal.sre.gob.mx/costarica; Ambassador MARÍA CARMEN OÑATE MUÑOZ.

Cuba: Calle 12, No 518, Miramar, Playa, Havana; tel. (7) 204-2553; fax (7) 204-2717; e-mail embamex@ip.etecsa.cu; Ambassador Gabriel Jiménez Remus.

Czech Republic: Nad Kazankou 8, 171 00 Prague 7; tel. 283061530; fax 233550477; e-mail embamex@rep-checa.cz; internet www.rep-checa.cz; Ambassador JOSÉ LUIS BERNAL RODRÍGUEZ.

Denmark: Bredgade 65, 1st Floor, 1260 Copenhagen K; tel. 39-61-05-00; fax 39-61-05-12; e-mail info@mexican-embassy.dk; internet www.sre.gob.mx/dinamarca; Ambassador Martha Elena Federica Bárcena Coqui.

Dominican Republic: Arzobispo Meriño 265, esq. Las Mercedes, Zona Colonial, Santo Domingo, DN; tel. 687-6444; fax 687-7872; e-mail embamex@codetel.net.do; Ambassador ENRIQUE MANUEL LOAEZA TOVAR.

Ecuador: Avda 6 de Diciembre 4843 y Naciones Unidas, Apdo 17-11-6371, Quito; tel. (2) 292-3770; fax (2) 244-8245; e-mail embajadamexico@embamex.org.ec; internet www.sre.gob.mx/ecuador; Ambassador Héctor Romero Barraza.

Egypt: 5th Floor, Apartment 502–503, 17 Sharia Port Said, 11431 Cairo (Maadi); tel. (2) 3580256; fax (2) 3591887; e-mail mexemb@idsc.gov.eg; internet www.sre.gob.mx/egipto; Ambassador JAIME NUALART.

El Salvador: Calle Circunvalación y Pasaje 12, Col. San Benito, Apdo 432, San Salvador; tel. 2243-3190; fax 2243-0437; e-mail embamex@intercom.com.sv; internet portal.sre.gob.mx/elsalvador; Ambassador Berenice Rendón Talavera.

Finland: Simonkatu 12A, 7th Floor, 00100 Helsinki; tel. (9) 5860430; fax (9) 6949411; e-mail mexican.embassy@welho.com; Ambassador (vacant).

France: 9 rue de Longchamp, 75116 Paris; tel. 1-53-70-27-70; fax 1-47-55-65-29; e-mail embfrancia@sre.gob.mx; internet www.sre.gob.mx/francia; Ambassador Carlos de Icaza González.

Germany: Klingelhöfer Str. 3, 10785 Berlin; tel. (30) 2693230; fax (30) 269323700; e-mail mail@embamexale.de; internet www.embamex.de; Ambassador JORGE CASTRO-VALLE KUEHNE.

Greece: Plateia Philikis Etairias 14, 106 73 Athens; tel. (210) 7294780; fax (210) 7294783; e-mail embgrecia@sre.gob.mx; Ambassador Manuel Cosío Durán.

Guatemala: 2a Avda 7-57, Zona 10, Apdo 1455, Guatemala City; tel. 2420-3400; fax 2420-3410; e-mail embamexguat@itelgua.com; internet www.sre.gob.mx/guatemala; Ambassador EDUARDO IBARROLA NICOLÍN.

Haiti: Delmas 60, 2, BP 327, Port-au-Prince; tel. 257-8100; fax 256-6528; e-mail embmxhai@yahoo.com; Ambassador Zadalinda González y Reynero.

Honduras: Col. Lomas del Guijarro, Avda Eucalipto 1001, Tegucigalpa; tel. 232-4039; fax 232-4719; e-mail embamexhonduras@gmail.com; internet www.sre.gob.mx/honduras; Ambassador TARCISIO NAVARRETE MONTES DE OCA.

Hungary: 1024 Budapest, Rómer Flóris u. 58; tel. (1) 326-0447; fax (1) 326-0485; e-mail embamexhu@axelero.hu; internet www.sre.gob.mx/hungria; Ambassador José Luis Martínez y Hernández.

India: C-8 Anand Niketan, New Delhi 110 021; tel. (11) 24107182; fax (11) 24117193; e-mail embamexindia@airtelbroadband.in; internet www.sre.gob.mx/india; Ambassador ROGELIO GRANGUILLHOME MORFIN.

Indonesia: Menara Mulia, Suite 2306, Jalan Jenderal Gatot Subroto, Kav. 9–11, Jakarta Selatan 12930; tel. (21) 5203980; fax (21) 5203978; Ambassador Pedro González-Rubio Sánchez.

Iran: No. 41, Golfam St, Africa Ave, Tehran POB 19156-74741; tel. (21) 22057586; fax (21) 22057589; e-mail embiran@sre.gob.mx; Ambassador ÁNGEL LUIS ORTIZ MONASTERIO CASTELLANOS.

Ireland: 19 Raglan Rd, Dublin 4; tel. (1) 6673105; fax (1) 6641013; e-mail info@embamex.ie; internet www.sre.gob.mx/irlanda; Ambassador Cecilia Jaber Breceda.

Israel: Trade Tower, 5th Floor, 25 Hamered St, Tel-Aviv 68125; tel. 3-5163938; fax 3-5163711; e-mail embamex@netvision.net.il; internet portal.sre.gob.mx/israel; Ambassador CARLOS RICO-FERRAT.

Italy: Via Lazzaro Spallanzani 16, 00161 Roma; tel. (06) 44115204; fax (06) 4403876; e-mail ofna.embajador@emexitalia.it; internet www.sre.gob.mx/italia; Ambassador Jorge Eduardo Chen Charpentier.

Jamaica: PCJ Bldg, 36 Trafalgar Rd, Kingston 10; tel. 926-4242; fax 929-7995; e-mail embamexj@cwjamaica.com; Ambassador ROSAURA LEONORA RUEDA GUTIÉRREZ.

Japan: 2-15-1, Nagata-cho, Chiyoda-ku, Tokyo 100-0014; tel. (3) 3581-1131; fax (3) 3581-4058; e-mail embamex@mexicoembassy.jp; internet www.sre.gob.mx/japon; AmbassadorMiguel Ruiz-Cabañas Izquierdo.

Kenya: Kibagare Way, off Loresho Ridge, POB 14145, Nairobi; tel. (20) 4182593; fax (20) 4181500; e-mail mexico@embamexken.com; Ambassador JUAN CARLOS CUE VEGA.

Korea, Republic: 33-6, Hannam 1-dong, Yeongsan-gu, Seoul 140-885; tel. (2) 798-1694; fax (2) 790-0939; e-mail srecor@uriel.net; internet portal.sre.gob .mx/corea; Ambassador Leandro Arellano.

Lebanon: POB 70-1150, Antélias; tel. (4) 418871; fax (4) 418873; e-mail mail@embassyofmexicoinlebanon.org; internet www .embassyofmexicoinlebanon.org; Ambassador JORGE ÁLVAREZ FUENTES.

Malaysia: Suite 22-05, 22nd Floor, Menara Tan & Tan, 207 Jalan Tun Razak, 50400 Kuala Lumpur; tel. (3) 21646362; fax (3) 21640964; e-mail embamex@po.jaring.my; internet www.embamex.org.my; Ambassador Jorge Alberto Lozoya Legorreta.

Morocco: 6 rue Cadi Mohamed Brebi, BP 1789, Souissi, Rabat; tel. (3) 7631969; fax (3) 7631971; e-mail embamexmar@smirt.net.ma; Ambassador JUAN ANTONIO MATEOS CICERO.

Namibia: Southern Life Tower, 3rd Floor, 39 Post St Mall, POB 13220, Windhoek; tel. (61) 229082; fax (61) 229180; Ambassador Mauricio de María y Campos.

Netherlands: Nassauplein 28, 2585 EC The Hague; tel. (70) 3602900; fax (70) 3560543; e-mail embamex@embamex-nl.com; internet www.embamex-nl .com; Ambassador JORGE LOMÓNACO TONDA.

New Zealand: AMP Chambers, Level 2, 185–187 Featherston St, POB 11-510, Wellington; tel. (4) 472-0555; fax (4) 496-3559; e-mail mexico@xtra.co .nz; internet www.sre.gob.mx/nuevazelandia; Ambassador María Angélica Arce Mora.

Nicaragua: Contiguo a Optica Matamoros, Km $4\frac{1}{2}$, Carretera a Masaya, Apdo 834, Managua; tel. 278-1859; fax 278-2886; e-mail embamex@ turbonett.com.ni; Ambassador RAÚL LÓPEZ-LIRA NAVA.

Panama: Edif. Torre ADR, 10°, Avda Samuel Lewis y Calle 58, Urb. Obarrio, Corregimiento de Bella Vista, Panamá; tel. 263-4900; fax 263-5446; e-mail embamexpan@cwpanama.net; internet www.sre.gob.mx/panama; Ambassador Yanerit Cristina Morgan Sotomayor.

Paraguay: Avda España 1428, casi San Rafael, Casilla 1184, Asunción; tel. (21) 618-2000; fax (21) 618-2500; e-mail evamx@embamex.com.py; internet www.embamex.com.py; Ambassador ERNESTO CAMPOS TENORIO.

Peru: Avda Jorge Basadre 710, esq. Los Ficus, San Isidro, Lima; tel. (1) 2211100; fax (1) 4404740; e-mail info@mexico.org.pe; internet www.mexico .org.pe; Ambassador Antonio Guillermo Villegas Villalobos.

Philippines: 2157 Paraiso St, Dasmariñas Village, Makati City, Metro Manila; tel. (2) 8122211; fax (2) 8929824; e-mail ebmexfil@info.com.ph; internet portal.sre.gob.mx/filipinaseng/; Ambassador ERENDIRA ARACELI PAZ CAMPOS.

Poland: 02-516 Warsaw, ul. Starościńska 1b/4–5; tel. (22) 6468800; fax (22) 6464222; e-mail embamex@ikp.pl; Ambassador Raphael Steger Cataño.

Portugal: Estrada de Monsanto 78, 1500-462 Lisbon; tel. (21) 7621290; fax (21) 7620045; e-mail embamex.port@mail.telepac.pt; internet www.sre.gob .mx/portugal; Ambassador MAURICIO TOUSSAINT RIBOT.

Romania: 020082 Bucharest, Str. Mihai Eminescu 124c, Rm 13–14, Sector 2; tel. (21) 2104577; fax (21) 2104713; internet www.embamex.ro; Chargé d'affaires a.i. Luis Alberto Barrero Stahl.

Russian Federation: 119034 Moscow, B. Levshinskii per. 4; tel. (495) 969-28-79; fax (495) 969-28-77; e-mail info@embamex.ru; Ambassador ALFREDO ROGERIO PÉREZ BRAVO.

Saudi Arabia: POB 94391, Riyadh 11693; tel. (1) 480-8822; fax (1) 480-8833; e-mail embasaudita@sre.gob.mx; Ambassador Raúl López Lira Nava.

Serbia: 11000 Belgrade, Ljutice Bogdana 5, Savski venac; tel. (11) 3674170; fax (11) 3675013; e-mail embamex@net.yu; internet www.mexican-embassy .org.yu; Chargé d'affaires a.i. EDUARDO HÉCTOR MOGUEL FLORES.

Singapore: 152 Beach Rd, 06-07/08, 6th Floor, Gateway East Tower, Singapore 189721; tel. 62982678; fax 62933484; e-mail embamexsing@ embamexsing.org.sg; internet www.embamexsing.org.sg; Ambassador Juan José Gomez Camacho.

South Africa: 1 Hatfield Sq., 3rd Floor, 1101 Burnett St, Hatfield, Pretoria 0083; POB 9077, Pretoria 0001; tel. (12) 3622822; fax (12) 3621380; e-mail embamexza@mweb.co.za; Ambassador LUIS CABRERA CUARON.

Spain: Carrera de San Jerónimo 46, 28014 Madrid; tel. (91) 3692814; fax (91) 4202292; e-mail embamex@embamex.es; internet www.embamex.es; Ambassador Jorge Zermeño Infante.

Sweden: Grevgt. 3, 114 53 Stockholm; tel. (8) 663-51-70; fax (8) 663-24-20; e-mail suecia.embamex@telia.com; internet www.sre.gob.mx/suecia; Ambassador NORMA BERTHA PENSADO MORENO.

Switzerland: Bernastr. 57, 3005 Bern; tel. 313574747; fax 313574748; e-mail embamex1@swissonline.ch; internet www.sre.gob.mx/suiza; Ambassador Luciano Joublanc Montano.

Thailand: 20/60–62 Thai Wah Tower I, 20th Floor, Thanon Sathorn Tai, Bangkok 10120; tel. (2) 285-0995; fax (2) 285-0667; e-mail mexthai@loxinfo .co.th; internet www.sre.gob.mx/tailandia; Ambassador LUIS ARTURO PUENTE ORTEGA.

Trinidad and Tobago: 12 Hayes St, St Clair, Port of Spain; tel. 622-1422; fax 628-8488; e-mail info@mexico.tt; Ambassador Ricardo Villanueva Hallal.

Turkey: Kırkpınar Sok. 8/6, 06540 Çankaya, Ankara; tel. (312) 4423033; fax (312) 4420221; e-mail mexico@embamextur.com; internet www.mexico.org .tr; Ambassador SALVADOR CAMPOS ICARDO.

United Kingdom: 16 St George St, Hanover Sq., London, W1S 1FD; tel. (20) 7499-8586; fax (20) 7495-4035; e-mail mexuk@sre.gob.mx; internet www.sre .gob.mx/reinounido; Ambassador Juan José Bremer de Martino.

United States of America: 1911 Pennsylvania Ave, NW, Washington, DC 20006; tel. (202) 728-1600; fax (202) 234-1698; e-mail mexembusa@sre.gob .mx; internet www.sre.gob.mx/eua; Ambassador ARTURO SARUKHAN CASAMITJANA.

Uruguay: 25 de Mayo 512/514 esq. Treinta y Tres, 11100 Montevideo; tel. (2) 9166034; fax (2) 9166098; e-mail embajada-mexico@techtelnet.com.uy; internet www.sre.gob.mx/uruguay; Ambassador Cassio Manuel Luiselli Fernández.

Vatican City: Via Ezio 49, 00192 Rome, Italy; tel. (06) 3230360; fax (06) 3230361; e-mail embamex-s.sede@mclink.it; internet portal.sre.gob.mx/ vaticano; Ambassador LUIS FELIPE BRAVO MENA.

Venezuela: Edif. Forum, Calle Guaicaipuro con Principal de las Mercedes, 5°, El Rosal, Apdo 61371, Caracas; tel. (212) 952-5777; fax (212) 952-3003; e-mail mexico@embamex.com.ve; internet www.embamex.com.ve; Ambassador Jesús Mario Chacón Carrillo.

Viet Nam: 14 Thuy Khue, T-11, Hanoi; tel. (4) 8470948; fax (4) 8470949; e-mail embvietnam@sre.gob.mx; Ambassador RICARDO CÁMARA SÁNCHEZ.

DIPLOMATIC MISSIONS OF MICRONESIA, FEDERATED STATES

United Nations: 820 Second Ave, Suite 17a, New York, NY 10017; tel. (212) 697-8370; fax (212) 697-8295; e-mail fsmun@fsmgov.org; internet www .fsmgov.org/fsmun; Permanent Representative Masao Nakayama.

China, People's Republic: 1-1-11 Jian Guo Men Wai Diplomatic Compound, Chao Yang Qu, Beijing 100010; e-mail embassy@fsmembassy.cn; Chargé d'affaires CARLSON D. APIS.

Fiji: 37 Loftus St, POB 15493, Suva; tel. 304566; fax 3304081; e-mail fsmsuva@sopacsun.sopac.org.fj; Ambassador Samson Pretrick.

Japan: Reinanzaka Bldg, 2nd Floor, 1-14-2, Akasaka, Minato-ku, Tokyo 107-0052; tel. (3) 3585-5456; fax (3) 3585-5348; e-mail fsmemb@fsmemb.or .jp; Ambassador JOHN FRITZ.

United States of America: 1725 N St, NW, Washington, DC 20036; tel. (202) 223-4383; fax (202) 223-4391; e-mail firstsecretary@fsmembassydc.org; internet www.fsmembassydc.org; Ambassador Yosiwo P. George.

DIPLOMATIC MISSIONS OF MOLDOVA

United Nations: 35 East 29th St, New York, NY 10016; tel. (212) 447-1867; fax (212) 447-4067; e-mail unmoldova@aol.com; internet www.un.int/ moldova; Permanent Representative ALEXEI TULBURE.

Austria: Löwengasse 47/10, 1030 Vienna; tel. (1) 961-10-30; fax (1) 961-10-30-34; e-mail viena@mfa.md; Ambassador Victor Postolachi.

Azerbaijan: 1073 Baku, H. Javid pr. 520, Block 12; tel. (12) 510-15-38; fax (12) 403-52-91; e-mail baku@mfa.md; Ambassador ION ROBU.

Belarus: 220030 Minsk, vul. Belaruskaya 2; tel. (17) 289-14-41; fax (17) 289-11-47; e-mail emmdby@anitex.by; Ambassador Ion Filimon.

Belgium: 57 ave F. D. Roosevelt, 1050 Brussels; tel. (2) 732-96-59; fax (2) 732-96-60; e-mail bruxelles@mfa.md; Ambassador VICTOR GAICIUC.

Bulgaria: 1142 Sofia, bul. G.S. Rakovski 152; tel. (2) 935-60-11; fax (2) 980-64-75; e-mail sofia@mfa.md; Ambassador Veaceslav Madan.

China, People's Republic: 2-9-1 Tayuan Diplomatic Office Bldg, Beijing 100600; tel. (10) 65325494; fax (10) 65325379; e-mail beijing@mfa.md; Ambassador IACOV TIMCIUC.

Czech Republic: Na Zátorce 12, 160 00 Prague 6; tel. 233323762; fax 233323765; e-mail secretariat@ambasadamoldova.cz; internet www.ambasadamoldova.cz; Ambassador Valerian Cristea.

France: 1 rue de Sfax, 75116 Paris; tel. 1-40-67-11-20; fax 1-40-67-11-23; e-mail ambassade.moldavie@wanadoo.fr; internet www.ambassade-moldavie.com; Ambassador VICTORIA IFTODI.

Germany: Gotlandstr. 16, 10439 Berlin; tel. (30) 44652970; fax (30) 44652972; e-mail office@botschaft-moldau.de; internet www.botschaft-moldau.de; Ambassador Igor Corman.

Greece: G. Bacu 20, 115 24 Athens; tel. (210) 699-0372; fax (210) 699-0371; e-mail atena@mfa.md; Ambassador IULIAN MAGALEAS.

Hungary: 1111 Budapest, Budafoki u. 9–11; tel. (1) 209-1191; fax (1) 209-1195; Ambassador Valeriu Bobutac.

Israel: 38 Rembrandt St, Tel-Aviv 64045; tel. 3-5231000; fax 3-5233000; Ambassador LARISA MICULET.

Italy: Via Montebello 8, 00185 Roma; tel. (06) 4740210; fax (06) 47881092; e-mail roma@mfa.md; internet www.ambmoldova.it; Ambassador Nicolae Dudău.

Latvia: Basteja bulv. 14, 1050 Rīga; tel. 6735-9160; fax 6735-9165; e-mail riga@moldovaembassy.lv; Ambassador EDUARD MELNIC.

Lithuania: Miglos g. 61a, Vilnius; tel. (5) 260-7914; fax (5) 260-7915; e-mail ambasada.vilnius@gmail.com; Ambassador Ion Ciornii.

Poland: 02-710 Warsaw, ul. Imielińska 1; tel. (22) 6462099; e-mail embassy@moldova.pl; internet www.moldova.pl; Ambassador BORIS GAMURARI.

Portugal: Rua Gonçalo Velho Cabral 31a, 1400-188 Lisbon; tel. (21) 3009064; fax (21) 3009067; e-mail lisabona@mfa.md; Ambassador Mihael Camarzan.

Romania: 011824 Bucharest 1, Al. Alexandru 40; tel. (21) 2300474; fax (21) 2307790; e-mail ambasadamoldova@zappmobile.ro; Ambassador LIDIA GUȚU.

Russian Federation: 107031 Moscow, ul. Kuznetskii most 18; tel. (495) 924-53-53; fax (495) 924-95-90; e-mail moscova@mfa.md; internet www.moldembassy.ru; Ambassador Vasile Sturza.

Sweden: Engelbrektsgt. 10, 114 32 Stockholm; tel. (8) 411-40-64; fax (8) 411-40-74; e-mail stockholm@moldovaembassy.se; internet www.moldovaembassy.se; Ambassador NATALIA GHERMAN.

Turkey: Kaptanpaşa Sok. 49, 06700 Gaziosmanpaşa, Ankara; tel. (312) 4465527; fax (312) 4465816; e-mail ankara@mfa.md; Ambassador Mihail Barbulat.

Ukraine: 01010 Kyiv, vul. I. Mazepy 6; tel. (44) 290-77-21; fax (44) 290-77-22; e-mail moldoukr@sovamua.com; Ambassador SERGIU STATI.

United Kingdom: 5 Dolphin Sq., Edensor Rd, London, W4 2ST; tel. (20) 8995-6818; fax (20) 8995-6927; e-mail londra@mfa.md; internet www.moldovanembassy.org.uk; Ambassador Mariana Durleşteanu.

United States of America: 2101 S St, NW, Washington, DC 20008; tel. (202) 667-1130; fax (202) 667-1204; e-mail washington@mfa.md; internet www.embassyrm.org; Ambassador NICOLAE CHIRTOACA.

DIPLOMATIC MISSIONS OF MONACO

United Nations: 866 United Nations Plaza, Suite 520, New York, NY 10017; tel. (212) 832-0721; fax (212) 832-5358; e-mail monaco@un.int; internet www.un.int/monaco; Permanent Representative Gille Noghes.

Belgium: 17 place Guy d'Arezzo, BP 7, 1180 Brussels; tel. (2) 347-49-87; fax (2) 343-49-20; e-mail ambassade.monaco@skynet.be; Ambassador JOSÉ BADIA.

France: 22 blvd Suchet, 75116 Paris; tel. 1-45-04-74-54; fax 1-45-04-45-16; e-mail ambassade.en.france@gouv.mc; Ambassador Jacques Boisson.

Germany: Klingelhöferstr. 7, 10785 Berlin; tel. (30) 2639033; fax (30) 2690344; e-mail ambassademonaco@aol.com; Ambassador CLAUDE JOËL GIORDAN.

Italy: Via Antonio Bertoloni 36, 00197 Roma; tel. (06) 8083361; fax (06) 8077692; e-mail monaco@ambasciatadimonaco.it; Ambassador Philippe Blanchi.

Spain: Villanueva 12, 28001 Madrid; tel. (91) 5782048; fax (91) 4357132; e-mail ambmonacomad@hotmail.com; Ambassador JOSÉ BADIA.

Switzerland: Hallwylstr. 34, 3005 Bern; tel. 313562858; fax 313562855; e-mail ambassademonaco@bluewin.ch; Ambassador Robert Fillon.

United States of America: 2314 Wyoming Ave, NW, Washington, DC 20008; tel. (202) 234-1530; Ambassador GILLES ALEXANDRE NOGHES.

Vatican City: Largo Nicola Spinelli 5, 00198 Rome, Italy; tel. (06) 8414357; fax (06) 8414507; e-mail ambmonacovat@alice.it; Ambassador Jean-Claude Michel.

DIPLOMATIC MISSIONS OF MONGOLIA

United Nations: 6 East 77th St, New York, NY 10021; tel. (212) 737-3874; fax (212) 861-9460; e-mail mongolia@un.int; internet www.un.int/mongolia; Permanent Representative OCHIR ENKHTSETSEG.

Austria: Fasangartengasse 45–47, 1130 Vienna; tel. (1) 535-30-13; fax (1) 535-30-06; e-mail office@embassymon.at; internet www.embassymon.at; Ambassador Luvsandagva Enkhtaivan.

Belgium: 18 ave Besme, 1190 Brussels; tel. (2) 344-69-74; fax (2) 344-32-15; e-mail brussels.mn.embassy@chello.be; Ambassador AVIRMEDIIN BATTÖR.

Bulgaria: 1113 Sofia, ul. F. Zh. Kyuri 52; tel. (2) 865-90-12; fax (2) 963-07-45; e-mail mongemb@gmail.com; Ambassador Badamdorj Batkhishig.

Canada: 151 Slater St, Suite 503, Ottawa, ON K1P 5H3; tel. (613) 569-3830; fax (613) 569-3916; internet mail@mongolembassy.org; internet www.mongolembassy.org; Ambassador DUGERJAV GOTOV.

China, People's Republic: 2 Xiu Shui Bei Jie, Jian Guo Men Wai, Beijing 100600; tel. (10) 65321203; fax (10) 65325045; e-mail mail@mongolembassychina.org; internet www.mongolembassychina.org; Ambassador Galsangiin Batsükh.

Cuba: Calle 66, No 505, esq. 5, Miramar, Havana; tel. (7) 204-2763; fax (7) 204-0639; e-mail monelch@ceniai.inf.cu; Ambassador GOMBO BYAMBADORJ.

Czech Republic: Na Marně 5, 160 00 Prague 6; tel. 224311198; fax 224314827; e-mail monemb@bohem-net.cz; internet www.mongolembassy.net; Ambassador Enkhtur Ochir.

Egypt: 3 Midan en-Nasr, Cairo (Dokki); tel. (2) 3460670; Ambassador D. BAYARKHÜÜ.

France: 5 ave Robert Schuman, 92100 Boulogne-Billancourt; tel. 1-46-05-28-12; fax 1-46-05-30-16; e-mail ambassademongolie@yahoo.fr; internet www.ambassademongolie.fr; Ambassador Radnaabazar Altangerel.

Germany: Dietzgenstr. 31, 13156 Berlin; tel. (30) 4748060; fax (30) 47480616; e-mail mongolbot@aol.com; internet www.botschaft-mongolei.de; Ambassador TUVDENDORJ GALBAATAR.

Hungary: 1022 Budapest II, K. Bogár u. 14c; tel. (1) 212-4579; fax (1) 212-5731; e-mail mnk@mail.matavnet.hu; Ambassador Omboosrengiin Erdenechimeg.

India: 34 Archbishop Makarios Marg, New Delhi 110 003; tel. (11) 24631728; fax (11) 24633240; e-mail mongemb@vsnl.net; internet www.mongemb.com; Ambassador VIKTORYN ENKHBOLD.

Japan: Pine Crest Mansion, 21-4, Kamiyama-cho, Shibuya-ku, Tokyo 150-0047; tel. (3) 3469-2088; fax (3) 3469-2216; e-mail embmong@gol.com; Ambassador Rentsendoogiin Jigjid.

Kazakhstan: 050000 Almaty, Musabayev 1; tel. (727) 269-35-70; fax (727) 258-17-27; e-mail monkazel@kazmail.asdc.kz; Ambassador RAVDANGIIN KHATANBAATAR.

Korea, Democratic People's Republic: Munsudong, Taedongkang District, Pyongyang; tel. (2) 3827322; fax (2) 3817323; Ambassador Sodovjamtsyn Khürelbaatar.

Korea, Republic: 33-5, Hannam-dong, Yeongsan-gu, Seoul 140–885; tel. (2) 794-1350; fax (2) 794-7605; e-mail mongol5@kornet.net; internet www.mongolembassy.com; Ambassador DORJPALAMYN GEREL.

Laos: rue Wat Nak, Km 3, BP 370, Vientiane; tel. (21) 315220; fax (21) 315221; e-mail embmong@laotel.com; Ambassador Togtokhyn Batbaatar.

Poland: 02-516 Warsaw, ul. Rejtana 15/16; tel. (22) 8482063; fax (22) 8499391; e-mail mongamb@ikp.atm.com.pl; internet www.ambmong.net7.pl; Chargé d'affaires a.i. BARKHAS DORJ.

Russian Federation: 121069 Moscow, Borisoglebskii per. 11; tel. (495) 290-67-92; fax (495) 291-46-36; e-mail mongolia@online.ru; Ambassador Luvsandandaryn Khangai.

Singapore: 600 North Bridge Rd, 24-08 Parkview Sq., Singapore 188778; tel. 63480745; fax 63481753; e-mail consulmn@singnet.com.sg; internet www.mongoliaembassysingapore.com; Ambassador PÜREVJAVYN GANSÜKH (designate).

Thailand: 100/3, Soi Ekamai 22, Thanon Sukhumvit 63, Prakanong Nua, Wattana, Bangkok 10110; tel. (2) 381-1400; fax (2) 392-1499; e-mail mongemb@loxinfo.co.th; internet www.mongolmissionbkk.com; Ambassador Yaichil Batsuuri.

Turkey: Koza Sok. 109, 06700 Gaziosmanpaşa, Ankara; tel. (312) 4467977; fax (312) 4467791; e-mail mogolelc@ttnet.net.tr; internet web.ttnet.net.tr/mogolelc; Ambassador OCHIRYN OCHIRJAV.

United Kingdom: 7 Kensington Court, London, W8 5DL; tel. (20) 7937-0150; fax (20) 7937-1117; e-mail office@embassyofmongolia.co.uk; internet www.embassyofmongolia.co.uk; Ambassador Bulgaagiin Altangerel.

United States of America: 2833 M St, NW, Washington, DC 20007; tel. (202) 333-7117; fax (202) 298-9227; e-mail esyam@mongolianembassy.us; internet www.mongolianembassy.us; Ambassador KHASBAZAR BEKHBAT.

Viet Nam: Villa 5, Van Phuc Diplomatic Quarter, Hanoi; tel. (4) 8453009; fax (4) 8454954; e-mail mongembhanoi@hn.vnn.vn; Ambassador Ganbold Baasanjav.

DIPLOMATIC MISSIONS OF MONTENEGRO

United Nations: 420 East 54th St, Apt. 18H, New York, NY 10022; tel. (212) 753-9255; Permanent Representative NEBOYŠA KALUDJEROVIĆ.

Austria: Niebelungengasse 13, 1010 Vienna; tel. (1) 715-31-02; fax (1) 715-31-02-20; e-mail diplomat-mn@me-austria.eu; Ambassador Vesko Garčević.

Bosnia and Herzegovina: 71000 Sarajevo, Talirovića 4; tel. (33) 239925; fax (33) 239928; e-mail ambcg1@bih.net.ba; Ambassador RAMIZ BAŠIĆ.

China, People's Republic: 3-1-12 San Li Tun Diplomatic Compound, Beijing 100600; tel. (10) 65327610; fax (10) 65327690; e-mail embmontenegro@yahoo.com; Chargé d'affaires a.i. Ljiljana Tosković.

Croatia: 10000 Zagreb, trg Nikole Šubića Zrinskog 1/IV; tel. (1) 4573362; fax (1) 4573423; e-mail ambacrnegore@rcg.hr; Ambassador BRANKO LUKOVAC.

France: 216 blvd Saint-Germain, 75007 Paris; tel. 1-53-63-80-30; fax 1-42-22-83-90; e-mail ambasadacg@orange.fr; Ambassador Milica Pejanović-Đurišić.

Germany: Dessauerstr. 28–29, 10963 Berlin; tel. (30) 25291996; fax (30) 25292334; Chargé d'affaires a.i. ABID CRNOVRŠANIN.

Italy: Via Antonio Gramsci 9, 00197 Roma; tel. (06) 45471660; fax (06) 45443800; e-mail montenegro-roma@libero.it; Ambassador Darko Uskoković.

Macedonia, former Yugoslav Republic: 1000 Skopje, Vasil Stefanovski 7; tel. (2) 3227277; fax (2) 3227254; Ambassador DUŠKO LALIČEVIĆ.

Russian Federation: 117049 Moscow, ul. Korovyi Val 7/97; tel. (495) 237-71-34; Chargé d'affaires a.i. Miodrag Koljević.

Serbia: Belgrade, Užička 1; tel. (11) 2668975; e-mail ambasadacg@gmail.com; Ambassador ANKA VOJVODIĆ.

Slovenia: 1000 Ljubljana, Reseljeva cesta 40; tel. (1) 4395365; fax (1) 4395360; e-mail embamon-lj@t-2.net; Ambassador Branko Perović.

United Kingdom: 11 Waterloo Pl., London, SW1Y 4AU; tel. (20) 7863-8806; fax (20) 7863-8807; Ambassador DRAGIŠA BURZAN.

United States of America: 1610 New Hampshire Ave, NW, Washington, DC 20009; tel. (202) 234 6108; fax (202) 234 6109; Ambassador Miodrag Vlahović.

Vatican City: Via Crescenzio 97/II, 00193 Rome, Italy; tel. (06) 68134897; fax (06) 68130569; e-mail ambmont.vat@hotmail.it; Ambassador ANTUN SBUTEGA.

DIPLOMATIC MISSIONS OF MONTSERRAT

Canada (see entry for Antigua and Barbuda).

DIPLOMATIC MISSIONS OF MOROCCO

United Nations: 866 Second Ave, 6th and 7th Floors, New York, NY 10017; tel. (212) 421-1580; fax (212) 980-1512; e-mail morocco@un.int; internet www.un.int/morocco; Permanent Representative AL MUSTAPHA SAHEL.

Algeria: Villa nos 21 et 22, Cité al-Fath, Sable Rouge, el-Biar, Algiers; tel. (21) 69-14-08; fax (21) 69-29-00; e-mail ambmaroc@wissal.dz; Ambassador Abdellah Belkeziz.

Angola: Edif. Siccal, 10° andar, Rua Rainha Ginga, Luanda; tel. 222393708; fax 222338847; e-mail aluanda@supernet.ao; Ambassador ABDELLAH AIT EL HAJ.

Argentina: Castex 3461, C1425CDG Buenos Aires; tel. (11) 4801-8154; fax (11) 4802-0136; e-mail sifamarruecos@fibertel.com.ar; Ambassador Larbi Reffouh.

Australia: 17 Terrigal Crescent, O'Malley, ACT 2606; tel. (2) 6290-0755; fax (2) 6290-0744; e-mail sifmacan@bigpond.com; internet www.moroccoembassy.org.au; Ambassador BADRE EDDINE ALLALI.

Austria: Opernring 3–5, 1010 Vienna; tel. (1) 586-66-50; fax (1) 586-76-67; e-mail emb-pmissionvienna@morocco.at; Ambassador Dr Omar Zniber.

Bahrain: POB 26229, Villa 415, Rd 3207, Block 332, Mahooz, Manama; tel. 17740566; fax 17740178; e-mail sifamana@batelco.com; Ambassador MUHAMMAD AIT OUALI.

Bangladesh: House 44, United Nations Rd, POB 6112, Baridhara, Dhaka; tel. (2) 8823176; fax (2) 8810028; e-mail sifmadac@citechco.net; internet www.morocco-dhaka.com; Ambassador Mohamed Houroro.

Belgium: 29 blvd St-Michel, 1040 Brussels; tel. (2) 736-11-00; fax (2) 734-64-68; e-mail sifamabruxe@euronet.be; Ambassador MUSTAPHA SALAHDINE.

Brazil: SEN, Av. das Nacões, Quadra 801, Lote 02, 70432-900 Brasília, DF; tel. (61) 3321-4487; fax (61) 3321-0745; e-mail sifamarbr@onix.com.br; Ambassador Farida Jaidi.

Bulgaria: 1407 Sofia, bul. Tchervena Stena 1/1; tel. (2) 865-11-26; fax (2) 865-48-11; e-mail ambmarsofia@mbox.contact.bg; Ambassador GHAILANI DLIMI.

Burkina Faso: Ouaga 2000 Villa B04, place de la Cotière, 01 BP 3438, Ouagadougou 01; tel. 50-37-40-16; fax 50-37-41-72; e-mail maroc1@fasonet.bf; Ambassador Ali Ahmaoui.

Cameroon: 32 rue 1793, Quartier Bastos, BP 1629, Yaoundé; tel. 2220-5092; fax 2220-3793; e-mail ambmaroccam@yahoo.fr; Ambassador ABDELFATTAH AMOUR.

Canada: 38 Range Rd, Ottawa, ON K1N 8J4; tel. (613) 236-7391; fax (613) 236-6164; e-mail info@ambamaroc.ca; internet www.ambamaroc.ca; Ambassador Mohamed Tangi.

Chile: Avda Luis Pasteur 5850, Of. 203, Vitacura, Santiago; tel. (2) 218-0311; fax (2) 219-4280; e-mail ambmarch@terra.cl; Ambassador ABDELHADI BOUCETTA.

China, People's Republic: 16 San Li Tun Lu, Beijing 100600; tel. (10) 65321489; fax (10) 65321453; e-mail embmor@public.bta.net.cn; Ambassador Mohamed Cherti.

Colombia: Carrera 6A, No 113-37, Bogotá, DC; tel. (1) 620-5888; fax (1) 634-9477; e-mail embamarruecost@etb.net.co; Ambassador MOHAMED KHATTABI.

Côte d'Ivoire: 24 rue de la Canebière, 01 BP 146, Cocody, Abidjan 01; tel. 22-44-58-73; fax 22-44-60-58; e-mail sifmaabj@aviso.ci; Ambassador Hassan Bennani.

Czech Republic: Mickiewiczova 6, 160 00 Prague 6; tel. 233325656; fax 233322634; e-mail sifamapragu@iol.cz; Ambassador MOHAMMED RACHID IDRISSI KAITOUNI.

Denmark: Øregårds Allé 19, 2900 Hellerup; tel. 39-62-45-11; fax 39-62-24-49; e-mail sifamaeco@yahoo.fr; Ambassador Aïcha al-Kabbaj.

Egypt: 10 Sharia Salah ed-Din, Cairo (Zamalek); tel. (2) 7364718; fax (2) 7361937; e-mail morocemb@link.net; Ambassador MUHAMMAD FARAG AD-DOKALI.

Equatorial Guinea: Avda Enrique, Apdo 329, Malabo; tel. (09) 26-50; fax (09) 26-55; Chargé d'affaires a.i. Elhassan Dahman.

Ethiopia: 210 Bole Rd, POB 60033, Addis Ababa; tel. (11) 5508440; fax (11) 5511828; e-mail morocco.emb@ethionet.et; Ambassador ABDELJEBBAR BRAHIME.

Finland: Runeberginkatu 4c, 00100 Helsinki; tel. (9) 6122480; fax (9) 635160; e-mail embassy.of.morocco@co.inet.fi; Chargé d'affaires a.i. Tayeb Raouf.

France: 5 rue Le Tasse, 75016 Paris; tel. 1-45-20-69-35; fax 1-45-20-22-58; e-mail info@amb-maroc.fr; internet www.amb-maroc.fr; Ambassador FATHALLAH SIJILMASSI.

Gabon: blvd de l'indépendance, Immeuble CK 2, BP 3983, Libreville; tel. 77-41-51; fax 77-41-50; e-mail sifamalbv@inet.ga; Ambassador Ali Boji.

Germany: Niederwallstr. 39, 10117 Berlin; tel. (30) 2061240; fax (30) 20612420; e-mail marokko-botschaft@t-online.de; internet www.maec.gov.ma/berlin; Ambassador MUHAMMAD RACHAD BOUHLAL.

Greece: Odos Marathonodromou 5, Palaio Psychiko, 154 52 Athens; tel. (210) 6744209; fax (210) 6749480; e-mail sifamath@otenet.gr; Ambassador Muhammad Lofti Aouad.

Guinea: Cité des Nations, Villa 12, Commune du Kaloum, BP 193, Conakry; tel. 30-41-36-86; fax 30-41-38-16; e-mail ambargu@sotelgui.net.gn; Ambassador MOHAMED LASFAR.

Hungary: 1026 Budapest, Törökvész Lejto u. 12a; tel. (1) 200-7855; fax (1) 275-1437; e-mail sifamabudap@axelero.hu; Ambassador Lemhouer al-Hassane.

India: 33 Golf Links, New Delhi 110 003; tel. (11) 24636920; fax (11) 24636925; e-mail sifamand@giasdl01.vsnl.net.in; internet www.moroccoembindia.com; Ambassador LARBI MOUKHARIQ.

Indonesia: Menara Mulia, 19th Floor, Suite 1901, Kav. 9–11, Jakarta 12930; tel. (21) 5200773; fax (21) 5200586; e-mail sifamaind@telkomvision.com; Ambassador M. Abderrahmane Drissi Alami.

Iran: 5 Lavasani Ave, Davoud Barati, Tehran; tel. (21) 22206731; fax (21) 22210162; e-mail sifamateh@sefaratmaghreb.com; internet www.sefaratmaghreb.com; Ambassador MUHAMMAD LOUFA.

Iraq: POB 6039, 27/11/601 Hay al-Mansour, Baghdad; tel. (1) 542-1779; fax (1) 542-3030; Chargé d'affaires Essadek Abdelkrim.

Ireland: 39 Raglan Rd, Dublin 4; tel. (1) 6609449; fax (1) 6609468; e-mail sifamdub@indigo.ie; Chargé d'affaires MINA TOUNSI.

Italy: Via Lazzaro Spallanzani 8, 00161 Roma; tel. (06) 4402524; fax (06) 4402695; e-mail sifaroma@ambasciatadelmarocco.it; internet www.ambasciatadelmarocco.it; Ambassador Tajeddine Baddou.

Japan: 5-4-30, Minami Aoyama, Minato-Ku, Tokyo 107-0062; tel. (3) 5485-7171; fax (3) 5485-7173; e-mail sifamato@circus.ocn.ne.jp; internet www.morocco-emba.jp; Ambassador ABDELKADER LECHEHEB.

Jordan: POB 2175, Amman 11183; tel. (6) 5680591; fax (6) 5680253; e-mail ambmaroc@batelco.jo; Ambassador Muhammad Mael-Ainin.

Kenya: Diamond Trust House, 3rd Floor, Moi Ave, POB 61098, Nairobi; tel. (20) 710647; fax (20) 222364; Ambassador ABDELILAH BENRYANE.

Korea, Republic: S-15, UN Village, 270-3, Hannam-dong, Yeongsan-gu, Seoul; tel. (2) 793-6249; fax (2) 792-8178; e-mail sifamase@kornet.net; internet www.moroccoemb.or.kr; Ambassador Ahmed Bourzaim.

Kuwait: Yarmouk, Block 2, St 2, Villa 14, Kuwait City; tel. 5312980; fax 5317423; e-mail ambkow@yahoo.fr; Ambassador MUHAMMAD BELAICH.

Lebanon: Bir Hassan, Beirut; tel. (1) 859829; fax (1) 859839; e-mail sifmar@cyberia.net.lb; Ambassador Ali Oumlil.

Liberia: Tubman Blvd, Congotown, Monrovia; tel. 262767; Ambassador MOHAMED LASFAR.

Libya: POB 908, Ave 7 Avril, Tripoli; tel. (21) 3617809; fax (21) 3614752; e-mail sifmatripo@hotmail.com; Ambassador Driss Alaoui.

Madagascar: Bâtiment D1, Rez-de-chaussée, Ankorondrano, BP 12, 104 Antananarivo; tel. (20) 2221347; fax (20) 2221124; e-mail amar_med@hotmail.com; Ambassador MUHAMMAD AMAR.

Malaysia: Unit 9, 3rd Floor, East Block, Wisma Selangor Dredging, 142b Jalan Ampang, 50450 Kuala Lumpur; tel. (3) 21610701; fax (3) 21623081; e-mail sifmakl@po.jaring.my; Ambassador Ahmed Amaziane.

Mali: Badalabougou-est, rue 25, porte 80, BP 2013, Bamako; tel. 222-21-23; fax 222-77-87; e-mail sifamali@afribone.net.ml; Ambassador MOULAY DRISS FADHILL.

Mauritania: 569 ave de Gaulle, Tevragh Zeina, BP 621, Nouakchott; tel. 525-14-11; fax 529-72-80; e-mail sifmanktt@mauritel.mr; Ambassador Abderrahmane Benomar.

Mexico: Paseo de las Palmas 2020, Col. Lomas de Chapultepec, Del. Miguel Hidalgo, 11000 México, DF; tel. (55) 5245-1786; fax (55) 5245-1791; e-mail sifamex@infosel.net.mx; internet www.marruecos.org.mx; Ambassador MAHMOUD RMIKI.

Netherlands: Oranjestraat 9, 2514 JB The Hague; tel. (70) 3469617; fax (70) 3562829; e-mail ambamar.lahaye@wanadoo.nl; Ambassador Ali al-Mhamdi.

Niger: ave du Président Lubke, face Clinique Kaba, BP 12403, Niamey; tel. 20-73-40-84; fax 20-73-80-27; e-mail ambmang@intnet.ne; Ambassador MOHAMED JABER.

Nigeria: 5 Mary Slessor St, Asokoro, Abuja; tel. (9) 3141961; fax (9) 3141959; e-mail mcherkaoui45@yahoo.fr; Ambassador Mustapha Cherqaoui.

Norway: Holtegt. 28, 0355 Oslo; tel. 23-19-71-50; fax 23-19-71-51; e-mail sifamoslo@c2i.net; Ambassador BOUCHAÂB YAHDIH.

Oman: Shati al-Qurum, Villa No. 2443, Way No. 3030, POB 3125, Ruwi 112; tel. 24696152; fax 24601114; e-mail sifamamu@omantel.net.om; Ambassador Dr Noureddine Benomar.

Pakistan: 6, Gomal Rd, E-7, POB 1179, Islamabad; tel. (51) 2829656; fax (51) 2822745; e-mail sifamapak@morocco-embassy.com.pk; internet www.morocco-embassy.com.pk; Ambassador MOHAMMAD RIDA EL FASSI.

Peru: Calle Manuel Ugarte y Morosco 790, San Isidro, Lima; tel. (1) 2643323; fax (1) 2640006; e-mail sifamlim@chavin.rcp.net.pe; internet www.embajadamarruecoslima.com; Ambassador Abderrahim Mohandis.

Poland: 02-516 Warsaw, ul. Starościńska 1/11–12; tel. (22) 8496341; fax (22) 8481840; e-mail info@moroccoembassy.org.pl; internet www.moroccoembassy.org.pl; Ambassador ABDESSELAM ALEM.

Portugal: Rua Alto do Duque 21, 1400-099 Lisbon; tel. (21) 3020842; fax (21) 3020935; e-mail sifmar@emb-marrocos.pt; internet www.emb-marrocos.pt; Ambassador Samir Arrour.

Qatar: POB 3242, Doha; tel. 4831885; fax 4833416; e-mail moroccoe@qatar.net.qa; Ambassador ABDELADIM TABIR.

Romania: 010459 Bucharest 1, Str. Dionisie Lupu 78; tel. (21) 2102945; fax (21) 2102767; e-mail ambamarbuc@ambasadamaroc.ro; internet www.ambasadamaroc.ro; Ambassador Lahcen Azouly.

Russian Federation: 121069 Moscow, bulv.·B. Nikitskaya 51; tel. (495) 291-17-62; fax (495) 291-16-42; e-mail sifmamos@df.ru; Ambassador NOUREDDINE SEFIANI.

Saudi Arabia: POB 94392, Riyadh 11693; tel. (1) 481-1858; fax (1) 482-7016; e-mail moembassy@hotmail.com; Ambassador Abd al-Krim Semmar.

Senegal: 73 ave Cheikh Anta Diop, BP 490, Dakar; tel. 33-824-6927; fax 33-825-7021; e-mail ambmadk@sentoo.sn; Ambassador MOHA OUALI TAGMA.

Serbia: 11000 Belgrade, Sanje Živanović 4; tel. (11) 3691866; fax (11) 3690499; e-mail sifamabe@eunet.yu; Ambassador Kamal Faqir Benaissa.

South Africa: 799 Schoeman St, cnr Farenden St, Arcadia, Pretoria 0083; POB 12382, Hatfield 0028; tel. (12) 3430230; fax (12) 3430613; e-mail sifmapre@mwebbiz.co.za; Chargé d'affaires HABIB DEFOUAD.

Spain: Serrano 179, 28002 Madrid; tel. (91) 5631090; fax (91) 5617887; e-mail correo@embajada-marruecos.es; internet www.embajada-marruecos.es; Ambassador Omar Azziman.

Sudan: St 19, 32, New Extension, POB 2042, Khartoum; tel. (183) 473068; fax (183) 471053; e-mail sifmasoud@sudan.mail.net; Ambassador MUHAMMAD MAA EL-AININE.

Sweden: Kungsholmstorg 16, 112 21 Stockholm; tel. (8) 545-511-30; fax (8) 545-511-39; e-mail sifamastock@stockholm.mail.telia.com; internet www.marockosambassad.com; Ambassador Zohour Alaoui.

Switzerland: Helvetiastr. 42, 3005 Bern; tel. 313510362; fax 313510364; e-mail sifamaberne2@bluewin.ch; internet www.amb-maroc.ch; Ambassador MUHAMMAD GUEDIRA.

Syria: 35 rue Abu Bakr Al Karkhi-Villas, Mezzeh Ouest, Damascus; tel. (11) 6110451; fax (11) 6117885; e-mail sifmar@scs-net.org; Ambassador Abdelouahab Bellouki.

Thailand: Sathorn City Tower, 12th Floor, 175 Thanon Sathorn Tai, Sathorn, Bangkok 10120; tel. (2) 679-5604; fax (2) 2679-5603; e-mail sifambkk@samarts.com; internet www.moroccoembassybangkok.org; Ambassador EL HASSANE ZAHID.

Tunisia: 39 ave du 1er juin, 1002 Tunis; tel. (71) 782-775; fax (71) 787-103; e-mail ambamaroc@sifamatunis.net; Ambassador Najib Zerouali el-Ouariti.

Turkey: Reşit Galip Cad., Rabat Sok. 11, 06700 Gaziosmanpaşa, Ankara; tel. (312) 4376020; fax (312) 4471405; e-mail sifamatr@tr.net; Ambassador ABDELLAH ZAGOUR.

Ukraine: 03680 Kyiv, pr. Fedorov 12; tel. (44) 284-33-26; fax (44) 568-58-84; e-mail morocco@voilacable.com; Ambassador Abdeljalil Saubry.

United Arab Emirates: POB 4066, Abu Dhabi; tel. (2) 4433963; fax (2) 4433917; e-mail sifmabo@emirates.net.ae; Ambassador ABDELKADER AZ-ZAOUI.

United Kingdom: 49 Queen's Gate Gdns, London, SW7 5NE; tel. (20) 7581-5001; fax (20) 7225-3862; e-mail mail@sifamaldn.org; Ambassador Muhammad Belmahi.

United States of America: 1601 21st St, NW, Washington, DC 20009; tel. (202) 462-7980; fax (202) 265-0161; Ambassador AZIZ MEKOUAR.

Vatican City: Via delle Fornaci 203, 00165 Rome, Italy; tel. (06) 39388398; fax (06) 6374459; e-mail sifamavat@marocco.191.it; Ambassador Ali Achour.

Venezuela: Torre Multinvest, Plaza Isabel La Católica, Avda Eugenio Mendoza, 2°, La Castellana, Caracas; tel. (212) 265-9573; fax (212) 266-4681; e-mail embamaroccaracas@cantv.net; Ambassador DR IBRAHIM HOUSSEIN MOUSSA.

Viet Nam: Sofitel Plaza, 1 Thanh Nien, Hanoi; tel. (4) 7345586; fax (4) 7345589; e-mail embamaroc-hanoi@vnn.vn; Ambassador El Houcine Fardani.

Yemen: Faj Attan, Hay Assormi, ave Beyrouth, San'a; tel. (1) 426628; fax (1) 426627; e-mail sifama_yemen@hotmail.com; Ambassador MUHAMMAD TOUHAMI.

DIPLOMATIC MISSIONS OF MOZAMBIQUE

United Nations: 420 East 50th St, New York, NY 10022; tel. (212) 644-5965; fax (212) 644-5972; e-mail mozambique@un.int; internet www.un.int/mozambique; Permanent Representative Filipe Chidumo.

Angola: Rua Amílcar Cabral 102, R/C CP 12117, Luanda; tel. 222330811; fax 222332883; e-mail embamoc.lda@netangola.com; Ambassador ANTÓNIO MATOSE.

Belgium: 97 blvd St-Michel, 1040 Brussels; tel. (2) 736-25-64; fax (2) 732-06-64; e-mail maria_manuelalucas@yahoo.com; internet www.mozambiqueembassy.be; Ambassador Maria Manuela dos Santos Lucas.

Brazil: SHIS, QL 12, Conj. 07, Casa 09, 71630-275 Brasília, DF; tel. (61) 3248-4222; fax (61) 3248-3917; e-mail embamoc-bsb@uol.com; Ambassador MURADE ISAAC MIGUIGY MURARGY.

China, People's Republic: 1-7-2 Tayuan Diplomatic Office Bldg, Beijing 100600; tel. (10) 65323664; fax (10) 65325189; e-mail embamoc@public.bta.net.cn; AmbassadorAntónio Inácio Júnior.

Cuba: Avda 7, No 2203, entre 22 y 24, Miramar, Havana; tel. (7) 204-2443; fax (7) 204-2232; e-mail embamoc@ceniai.inf.cu; Ambassador AMADEU PAULO SAMUEL DA CONCEICAO.

Egypt: 9th Floor, 3 Sharia Abu el-Feda, Cairo (Zamalek); tel. (2) 3320647; fax (2) 3320383; e-mail emozcai@intouch.com; Ambassador Daniel Eduardo Mondlane.

Ethiopia: Woreda 17, Kebele 23, House No. 2116, POB 5671, Addis Ababa; tel. (11) 3712905; fax (11) 3710021; e-mail embamoc-add@telecom.net.et; Ambassador MANUEL TOMÁS LUBISSE.

France: 82 rue Laugier, 75017 Paris; tel. 1-47-64-91-32; fax 1-44-15-90-13; e-mail embamoc.franca@minec.gov.mz; Ambassador Ana Nemba Uaene.

Germany: Stromstr. 47, 10551 Berlin; tel. (30) 39876506; fax (30) 39876503; e-mail emoza@aol.com; Ambassador CARLOS DOS SANTOS.

India: B-3/24, Vasant Vihar, New Delhi 110 057; tel. (11) 26156663; fax (11) 26156665; e-mail salvaro64@hotmail.com; High Commissioner Carlos A. do Rosario.

Indonesia: Wisma GKBI, 37th Floor, Suite 3709, Jalan Jenderal Sudirman 28, Jakarta 10210; tel. (21) 5740901; fax (21) 5740907; e-mail embamoc@cbn.net.id; Ambassador GERALDO ANTONIO CHIRINZA.

Italy: Via Filippo Corridoni 14, 00195 Roma; tel. (06) 37514852; fax (06) 37514699; e-mail segretaria@ambasciatamozambico.it; Chargé d'affaires a.i. Laurinda Fernando Saide Banze.

Japan: Shiba Amerex Bldg, 6th Floor, 3-12-17 Mita, Minato-ku, Tokyo 108-0073; tel. (3) 5419-0973; fax (3) 5442-0556; e-mail mozambiq@tkk.att.ne.jp; internet www.embamoc.jp; Ambassador DANIEL ANTÓNIO.

Kenya: Bruce House, 3rd Floor, Standard St, POB 66923, Nairobi; tel. (20) 221979; fax (20) 222446; High Commissioner Marcos Namachulua (temporarily closed in January 2008).

Malawi: POB 30579, Lilongwe 3; tel. 1774100; fax 1771342; High Commissioner JORGE DE SOUSA MATEUS.

Portugal: Av. de Berna 7, 1050-036 Lisbon; tel. (21) 7961672; fax (21) 7932720; e-mail embamoc.portugal@minec.gov.mz; Ambassador Miguel da Costa Mkaima.

Russian Federation: 129090 Moscow, ul. Gilyarovskogo 8/25; tel. (495) 684-40-07; fax (495) 684-36-54; e-mail embamocru@hotmail.com; Ambassador BERNARDO MARCELINO CHERINDA.

South Africa: 529 Edmund St, Arcadia, Pretoria 0083; POB 40750, Arcadia 0007; tel. (12) 4010300; fax (12) 3266388; High Commissioner Fernando Andrade Fazenda.

Spain: Goya 67, 1° izqda, 28001 Madrid; tel. (91) 5776382; fax (91) 5776705; e-mail embamocmadrid@worldonline.es; Ambassador ALVARO MANUEL T. DA SILVA.

Swaziland: Princess Dr., POB 1212, Mbabane; tel. 4043700; fax 4048402; Ambassador Amour Zacarias Kapela.

Sweden: Sturegt. 46, 4th Floor, POB 5801, 102 48 Stockholm; tel. (8) 666-03-50; fax (8) 663-67-29; e-mail info@embassymozambique.se; internet www.embassymozambique.se; Ambassador PEDRO COMISSÁRIO AFONSO.

Tanzania: 25 Garden Ave, POB 9370, Dar es Salaam; tel. (22) 2116502; High Commissioner Zacarias Kupela.

United Kingdom: 21 Fitzroy Sq., London, W1T 6EL; tel. (20) 7383-3800; fax (20) 7383-3801; e-mail sandra@mozambiquehc.co.uk; internet www.mozambiquehc.org.uk; High Commr ANTÓNIO GUMENDE.

United States of America: 1525 New Hampshire Ave, NW, Washington, DC 20036; tel. (202) 293-7146; fax (202) 835-9245; e-mail embamoc@aol.com; internet www.embamoc-usa.org; Ambassador Armando Alexandre Panguene.

Zambia: Kacha Rd, Plot 9592, POB 34877, 10101 Lusaka; tel. (1) 220333; fax (1) 220345; High Commissioner SHAHARUDDIN MOHAMMED SOM.

Zimbabwe: 152 cnr Herbert Chitepo Ave, and Leopold Takawira St, POB 4608, Harare; tel. (4) 790837; fax (4) 732898; Ambassador Vincente Mebunia Vekoso.

DIPLOMATIC MISSIONS OF MYANMAR

United Nations: 10 East 77th St, New York, NY 10021; tel. (212) 535-1310; fax (212) 737-2421; e-mail myanmar@un.int; Permanent Representative KYAW TINT SWE.

Australia: 22 Arkana St, Yarralumla, ACT 2600; tel. (2) 6273-3811; fax (2) 6273-3181; e-mail mecanberra@bigpond.com; internet www.myanmarembassycanberra.com; Ambassador U Thet Win.

Bangladesh: NE(L) 3, Rd 84, Gulshan 2, Dhaka 1212; tel. (2) 600988; fax (2) 8823740; e-mail mofa.aung@mptmail.net.mm; Ambassador U NYAN LYNN.

Belgium: 9 blvd Général Wahis, 1030 Brussels; tel. (2) 701-93-80; fax (2) 705-50-48; Chargé d'affaires a.i. Han Thu.

Brazil: SHIS, QI 13, Conj. 08, Casa 09, Lago Sul, 71615-340 Brasília, DF; tel. (61) 3248-3747; fax (61) 3364-2747; e-mail mebrsl@brnet.com.br; Ambassador U HTEIN WIN.

Brunei: 14 Lot 2185/46292, Simpang 212, Jalan Kampong Rimba, Gadong, Bandar Seri Begawan BE 3119; tel. 2450506; fax 2451008; e-mail myanmar@brunet.bn; Ambassador U Tin Htun.

Cambodia: 181 blvd Norodom, Sangkat Boeung Keng Kang 1, Khan Chamkarmon, Phnom-Penh; tel. (23) 213663; fax (23) 213665; e-mail m.e.phnompenh@bigpond.com.kh; AmbassadorHLA MIN.

Canada: 85 Range Rd, Suite 902/903, Ottawa, ON K1N 8J6; tel. (613) 232-6434; fax (613) 232-6435; e-mail meott@magma.ca; Chargé d'affaires a.i. U Maung Maung.

China, People's Republic: 6 Dong Zhi Men Wai Dajie, Chao Yang Qu, Beijing 100600; tel. (10) 65321425; fax (10) 65321344; e-mail info@myanmarembassy.com; internet www.myanmarembassy.com; AmbassadorU THEIN LWIN.

Egypt: 24 Sharia Muhammad Mazhar, Cairo (Zamalek); tel. (2) 3404176; fax (2) 3416793; Ambassador U Aung Gyi.

France: 60 rue de Courcelles, 75008 Paris; tel. 1-56-88-15-90; fax 1-45-62-13-30; e-mail me-paris@wanadoo.fr; AmbassadorU SAW HLA MIN.

Germany: Thielallee 19, 14195 Berlin; tel. (30) 2061570; fax (30) 20615720; e-mail info@botschaft-myanmar.de; internet www.botschaft-myanmar.de; AmbassadorU Tin Win.

India: 3/50F Nyaya Marg, Chanakyapuri, New Delhi 110 021; tel. (11) 26889007; fax (11) 26877942; e-mail myandeli@nda.vsnl.net.in; Ambassador U KYI THEIN.

Indonesia: Jalan Haji Agus Salim 109, Jakarta Selatan; tel. (21) 327684; fax (21) 327204; e-mail myanmar@cbn.net.id; Ambassador U Khin Zaw Win.

Israel: Textile Centre Bldg, 12th Floor, 2 Kaufman St, Tel-Aviv 68012; tel. 3-5170760; fax 3-5163512; e-mail teltaman@zahav.net.il; Ambassador U MYINT SWE.

Italy: Viale Gioacchino Rossini 18, int. 2, I piano, 00198 Roma; tel. (06) 8543974; fax (06) 8413167; e-mail meroma@tiscali.it; AmbassadorU Khin Maung Aye.

Japan: 4-8-26, Kita Shinagawa, Shinagawa-ku, Tokyo 140-0001; tel. (3) 3441-9291; fax (3) 3447-7394; e-mail contact@myanmar-embassy-tokyo.net; internet www.myanmar-embassy-tokyo.net; Ambassador U HLA MYINT.

Korea, Republic: 724-1, Hannam-dong, Yeongsan-gu, Seoul 140-210; tel. (2) 792-3341; fax (2) 796-5570; e-mail myanmare@ppp.kornet.net; Ambassador U Nyo Win.

Laos: Ban Thong Kang, rue Sok Palaung, BP 11, Vientiane; tel. (21) 314910; fax (21) 314913; e-mail mev@loxinfo.co.th; Ambassador U TIN OO.

Malaysia: 1 Lorong Ru Kedua, off Jalan Ampang Hilir, 55000 Kuala Lumpur; tel. (3) 42560280; fax (3) 42568320; e-mail mekl@tm.net.my; Ambassador U Tin Latt.

Nepal: Chakupath, Patan Gate, Lalitpur, POB 2437, Kathmandu; tel. (1) 5521788; fax (1) 5523402; Ambassador U AUNG KHIN SOE.

Pakistan: 43, St 26, F-6/2, Islamabad; tel. (51) 2879612; fax (51) 2879616; e-mail embassy_myanmar@yahoo.com; Ambassador U Maung Nyo.

Philippines: Xanland Center, 4th Floor, 152 Amorsolo St, Legaspi Village, Makati City, Metro Manila; tel. (2) 8931944; fax (2) 8928866; e-mail embmyanmnl@mindgate.net; Ambassador U HIN TUN.

Russian Federation: 119049 Moscow, ul. Korovii Val 7/135; tel. (495) 230-24-26; fax (495) 730-96-46; e-mail mofa.aung@mptmail.net.mm; Ambassador U Tin Soe.

Serbia: 11000 Belgrade, Kneza Miloša 72; tel. (11) 3617165; fax (11) 3614968; e-mail mebel@sezampro.yu; Ambassador SOE NWE.

Singapore: 15 St Martin's Drive, Singapore 257996; tel. 67350209; fax 67356236; e-mail ambassador@mesingapore.org.sg; internet www.mesingapore.org.sg; Ambassador Win Myint.

South Africa: 201 Leyds St, Arcadia, Pretoria 0083; POB 12121, Queenswood 0121; tel. (12) 3415207; fax (12) 3413867; e-mail euompta@global.co.za; Ambassador U OHN THWIN.

Sri Lanka: 4a Rosmead Ave, Rosmead Place, Colombo 7; tel. (11) 2696440; fax (11) 2682052; e-mail mmembcmb@eureka.lk; Ambassador U Than Tun.

Thailand: 132 Thanon Sathorn Nua, Bangkok 10500; tel. (2) 233-2237; fax (2) 236-6898; Ambassador U YE WIN.

United Kingdom: 19a Charles St, London, W1J 5DX; tel. (20) 7499-4340; fax (20) 7409-7043; e-mail melondon@btconnect.com; Ambassador U Nay Win.

United States of America: 2300 S St, NW, Washington, DC 20008; tel. (202) 332-9044; fax (202) 332-9046; e-mail thuriya@aol.com; Chargé d'affaires a.i. LWIN MYINT.

Viet Nam: A-3 (101–104), Van Phuc Diplomatic Quarter, Kim Ma, Hanoi; tel. (4) 8453369; fax (4) 8452404; e-mail myan.emb@fpt.vn; Ambassador U Khin Aung.

DIPLOMATIC MISSIONS OF NAMIBIA

United Nations: 135 East 36th St, New York, NY 10016; tel. (212) 685-2003; fax (212) 685-1561; e-mail namibia@un.int; internet www.un.int/namibia; Permanent Representative DR KAIRE MUNIONGANDA MBUENDE.

Angola: Rua dos Coqueiros 37, CP 953, Luanda; tel. 222395483; fax 222339234; e-mail embnam@netangola.com; Ambassador Lineekela Mboti.

Austria: Ungargasse 33/5, 1030 Vienna; tel. (1) 402-93-71; fax (1) 402-93-70; e-mail nam.emb.vienna@speed.at; internet www.embnamibia.at; Ambassador SELMA ASHIPALA-MUSAVYI.

Belgium: 454 ave de Tervueren, 1150 Brussels; tel. (2) 771-14-10; fax (2) 771-96-89; e-mail info@namibiaembassy.be; internet www.namibiaembassy.be; Ambassador Hanno Burkhard Rumpf.

Botswana: Plot 186, Morara Close, POB 987, Gaborone; tel. 3902181; fax 3902248; High Commissioner TSUKHOE GOWASES.

Brazil: SHIS QI 09, Conj. 08, Casa 11, Lago Sul, 71625-080 Brasília, DF; tel. (61) 3248-6274; fax (61) 3248-7135; e-mail info@embassyofnamibia.org.br; internet www.embassyofnamibia.org.br; Ambassador Hopelong Uushona Ipinge.

China, People's Republic: 2-9-2 Tayuan Diplomatic Office Bldg, Beijing 100600; tel. (10) 65324810; fax (10) 65324549; e-mail namemb@eastnet.com.cn; Ambassador LEONARD NAMBAHU.

Cuba: Avda 5, No 4406, entre 44 y 46, Miramar, Havana; tel. (7) 204-1430; fax (7) 204-1431; e-mail embnamib@ceniai.inf.cu; Ambassador Claudia Grace Uushona.

Ethiopia: Woreda 17, Kebele 19, House No. 2, POB 1443, Addis Ababa; tel. (11) 6611966; fax (11) 6612677; Ambassador GEORGE LISWANISO.

France: 80 ave Foch, 75016 Paris; tel. 1-44-17-32-65; fax 1-44-17-32-73; e-mail namparis@club-internet.fr; Ambassador Panduleni-Kaino Shingenge.

Germany: Wichmannstr. 5, 10787 Berlin; tel. (30) 2540950; fax (30) 25409555; e-mail namibia@home.ivm.de; internet www.namibia-botschaft.de; Ambassador PROF. PETER KATJAVIVI.

India: E-2/6, Poorvi Marg, Vasant Vihar, New Delhi 110 057; tel. (11) 26140389; fax (11) 26146120; e-mail nhcdelhi@del2.vsnl.net.in; High Commissioner Marten Kapewasha.

Malaysia: 11 Jalan Mesra, off Jalan Damai, 55000 Kuala Lumpur; tel. (3) 21433593; e-mail namhckl@streamyx.com; High Commissioner NEVILLE MELVIN GERTZE.

Nigeria: Plot 1738 T. Y., Danyuma St, Cadasdral Zone, Asokoro, Abuja; tel. (9) 3142740; fax (9) 3142743; e-mail namibiahighcomabuja@yahoo.com; Ambassador David Smith.

Russian Federation: 113096 Moscow, 2-i Kazachii per. 7; tel. (495) 230-32-75; fax (495) 230-22-74; e-mail namembrf@online.ru; Ambassador DR SAMUEL K. MBAMBO.

South Africa: 197 Blackwood St, Arcadia, Pretoria 0083; POB 29806, Sunnyside 0132; tel. (12) 4819100; fax (12) 3445998; e-mail secretary@namibia.org.za; High Commissioner Philemon Kambala.

Sweden: Luntmakargt. 86–88, POB 19151, 104 32 Stockholm; tel. (8) 442-98-00; fax (8) 612-66-55; e-mail info@embassyofnamibia.se; internet www.embassyofnamibia.se; Ambassador THERESIA SAMARIA.

United Kingdom: 6 Chandos St, London, W1G 9LU; tel. (20) 7636-6244; fax (20) 7637-5694; e-mail namibia.hicom@btconnect.com; High Commr George Mbanga Liswaniso.

United States of America: 1605 New Hampshire Ave, NW, Washington, DC 20009; tel. (202) 986-0540; fax (202) 986-0443; e-mail info@namibiaembassyusa.org; internet www.namibianembassyusa.org; Ambassador PATRICK NANDAGO.

Zambia: 30b Mutende Rd, Woodlands, POB 30577, 10101 Lusaka; tel. (1) 260407; fax (1) 263858; High Commissioner Frieda Nangula Ithete.

DIPLOMATIC MISSIONS OF NAURU

United Nations: 800 Second Ave, Suite 400D, New York, NY 10017; tel. (212) 937-0074; fax (212) 937-0079; Permanent Representative MARLENE INEMWIN MOSES.

China (Taiwan): Room C, 9/F, 247 Chung Cheng Rd, Sec. 2 Shi-lin, Taipei; tel. (2) 8736121; fax (2) 8736125; Ambassador Ludwig D. Keke.

Fiji: Ratu Sukuna House, 7th Floor, Government Bldgs, POB 2420, Suva; tel. 3313566; fax 3302861; High Commissioner KENNAN RANIBOK ADEANG.

United States of America: 800 Second Ave, New York, NY 10017; tel. (212) 937-0074; fax (212) 937-0079; Ambassador Marlene Moses.

DIPLOMATIC MISSIONS OF NEPAL

United Nations: 820 Second Ave, Suite 17B, New York, NY 10017; tel. (212) 370-3988; fax (212) 953-2038; e-mail nepal@un.int; internet www.un.int/nepal; Permanent Representative MADHU RAMAN ACHARYA.

Australia: Suite 2.02, 24 Marcus Clarke St, Canberra, ACT 2601; tel. (2) 6162-1554; fax (2) 6162-1557; e-mail info@necan.gov.np; internet www.necan.gov.np; Ambassador Yogendra Dhakal.

Bangladesh: United Nations Rd, Rd 2, Diplomatic Enclave, Baridhara, Dhaka; tel. (2) 601790; fax (2) 8826401; e-mail rnedhaka@bdmail.net; Ambassador PRADEEP KHATIWADA.

Belgium: 210 ave Brugmann, 1050 Brussels; tel. (2) 346-26-58; fax (2) 344-13-61; e-mail embn@skynet.be; internet www.nepalembassy.be; Chargé d'affaires a.i. Ambika D. Luintel.

China, People's Republic: 1 Xi Liu Jie, San Li Tun Lu, Beijing 100600; tel. (10) 65322739; fax (10) 65323251; e-mail beijing@nepalembassy.org.cn; internet www.nepalembassy.org.cn; Ambassador TANKA KARKI.

Denmark: Svanemøllervej 92, 2900 Hellerup; tel. 44-44-40-26; fax 44-44-40-27; e-mail embdenmark@gmail.com; Ambassador Vijaykant Lal Karna.

Egypt: 9 Sharia Tiba, Madinet el-Kobah, Cairo (Dokki); tel. (2) 3603426; fax (2) 704447; Ambassador RAMBHAKTA P. B. THAKUR.

France: 45 bis rue des Acacias, 75017 Paris; tel. 1-46-22-48-67; fax 1-42-27-08-65; e-mail ambassadedunepal@noos.fr; internet www.nepalembassy.org; Ambassador (vacant).

Germany: Guerickestr. 27, 2nd Floor, 10587 Berlin; tel. (30) 34359920; fax (30) 34359906; e-mail neberlin@t-online.de; internet www.nepalembassy-germany.de; Ambassador MADAN KUMAR BHATTARAI.

India: Barakhamba Rd, New Delhi 110 001; tel. (11) 23329218; fax (11) 23326857; e-mail nepembassydelhi@bol.net.in; Ambassador Dr Durgesh Man Singh.

Japan: 7-14-9, Todoroki, Setagaya-ku, Tokyo 158-0082; tel. (3) 3705-5558; fax (3) 3705-8264; e-mail nepembjp@big.or.jp; internet www.nepal.co.jp/embassy; Ambassador Ganesh Yonzan Tamang.

Korea, Republic: 244-143, Huam-dong, Yeongsan-gu, Seoul; tel. (2) 3789-9770; fax (2) 736-8848; e-mail info@nepembseoul.gov.np; internet www.nepembseoul.gov.np; Ambassador Kamal Koirala.

Malaysia: Suite 13A-01, 13th Floor, Wisma MCA, 163 Jalan Ampang, 50450 Kuala Lumpur; tel. (3) 21645934; fax (3) 21648659; e-mail mekl_88@streamyx.com; internet www.nepalembassy.com.my; Ambassador Rishiraj Adhikari.

Myanmar: 16 Natmauk Yeiktha Rd, POB 84, Tamwe, Yangon; tel. (1) 545880; fax (1) 549803; e-mail nepemb@mptmail.net.mm; Ambassador Guna Laxmi Sharma Biswakarma.

Pakistan: 2, St 8, F-8/3, Islamabad; tel. (51) 2854696; fax (51) 2854722; e-mail nepem@isb.comsats.net.pk; Ambassador Bal Bahadur Kunwar.

Qatar: POB 23002, Doha; tel. 4675681; fax 4675680; e-mail nembdoha@qatar.net.qa; internet www.rnedoha.org.qa; Ambassador Shyamananda Suman.

Russian Federation: 119121 Moscow, 2-i Neopalimovskii per. 14/7; tel. (495) 244-02-15; fax (495) 244-00-00; e-mail nepalemb@mtu-net.ru; internet www.nepalembassyrus.org; Chargé d'affaires a.i. Achyut Bhakta Poudel.

Saudi Arabia: POB 94384, Riyadh 11693; tel. (1) 461-1108; fax (1) 464-0690; e-mail neksa@zajil.net; internet www.neksa.org; Ambassador Hamid Ansari.

Sri Lanka: 153 Kynsey Rd, Colombo 8; tel. (11) 2689657; fax (11) 2689655; e-mail mecolombo@eureka.lk; Ambassador Durga Prasad Bhattarai.

Thailand: 189 Soi 71, Thanon Sukhumvit, Prakanong, Bangkok 10110; tel. (2) 390-2280; fax (2) 381-2406; e-mail nepembkk@asiaaccess.net.th; Ambassador Navin Prakash Jung Shah.

United Kingdom: 12A Kensington Palace Gdns, London, W8 4QU; tel. (20) 7229-1594; fax (20) 7792-9861; e-mail eon@nepembassy.org.uk; internet www.nepembassy.org.uk; Ambassador Murari Raj Sharma.

United States of America: 2131 Leroy Pl., NW, Washington, DC 20008; tel. (202) 667-4550; fax (202) 667-5534; e-mail info@nepalembassyusa.org; internet www.nepalembassyusa.org; Ambassador Suresh Chandra Chalise.

DIPLOMATIC MISSIONS OF NETHERLANDS

United Nations: 235 East 45th St, 16th Floor, New York, NY 10017; tel. (212) 697-5547; fax (212) 370-1954; e-mail netherlands@un.int; internet www.pvnewyork.org; Permanent Representative Franciscus Antonius Maria Majoor.

Afghanistan: House 2 and 3, St 4, Ansari and Ghiassudin Wat, Shar-i-Nau, Kabul; tel. (70) 286847; e-mail kab@minbuza.nl; internet www.mfa.nl/kab-en; Ambassador Hans Blankenberg.

Albania: Rruga Asim Zeneli 10, Tirana; tel. (4) 240828; fax (4) 232723; e-mail tir@minbuza.nl; internet www.mfa.nl/tir; Ambassador Sweder van Voorst tot Voorst.

Algeria: BP 72, 23 chemin Cheikh Bachir El-Ibrahimi, el-Biar, Algiers; tel. (21) 92-28-28; fax (21) 92-29-47; e-mail alg@minbuza.nl; internet www.mfa.nl/alg; Ambassador Henk Revis.

Angola: Edif. Secil, 6°, Av. 4 de Fevereiro 42, CP 3624, Luanda; tel. 222310686; fax 222310966; e-mail lua@minbuza.nl; internet mfa.nl/lua-en; Ambassador Jan Gijs Schouten.

Argentina: Edif. Porteño II, Olga Cossenttini 831, 3°, C1107BVA Buenos Aires; tel. (11) 4338-0050; fax (11) 4338-0060; e-mail bue@minbuza.nl; internet www.embajadaholanda.int.ar; Ambassador Hendrik Jacob Willem Soeters.

Australia: 120 Empire Circuit, Yarralumla, ACT 2600; tel. (2) 6220-9400; fax (2) 6273-3206; e-mail can@minbuza.nl; internet www.netherlands.org.au; Ambassador Niek van Zutphen.

Austria: Opernring 5, 7th Floor, 1010 Vienna; tel. (1) 589-39; fax (1) 589-39-26-5; e-mail wen-public@minbuza.nl; internet www.mfa.nl/wen; Ambassador Justus Jonathan de Visser.

Bangladesh: House 49, Rd 90, Gulshan Model Town, POB 166, Dhaka 1212; tel. (2) 8822715; fax (2) 8823326; e-mail dha@minbuza.nl; internet www.netherlandsembassydhaka.org; Ambassador Berendina Maria (Bea) ten Tusscher.

Belgium: 48 ave Hermann Debroux, 1160 Brussels; tel. (2) 679-17-11; fax (2) 679-17-75; e-mail bru@minbuza.nl; internet www.nederlandseambassade.be; Ambassador Rudolf Bekink.

Benin: ave Pape Jean Paul II, Route de l'aeroport, derrière le Tri Postal, 08 BP 0783, Cotonou; tel. 21-30-04-39; fax 21-30-41-50; e-mail cot@minbuza.nl; internet www.mfa.nl/cot; Ambassador C. G. Weijers.

Bolivia: Edif. Hilda, 7°, Avda 6 de Agosto 2455, La Paz; tel. (2) 244-4040; fax (2) 244-3804; e-mail nllap@caoba.entelnet.bo; internet www.mfa.nl/lap-es; Ambassador Martin de la Bey.

Bosnia and Herzegovina: 71000 Sarajevo, Grbavička 4; tel. (33) 562600; fax (33) 223413; e-mail sar@minbuza.nl; internet www.netherlandsembassy.ba; Ambassador Karel E. Vosskühler.

Brazil: SES, Av. das Nações, Quadra 801, Lote 05, 70405-900 Brasília, DF; tel. (61) 3961-3200; fax (61) 3961-3234; e-mail bra@minbuza.nl; internet www.mfa.nl/brasil; Ambassador Onno Hattinga van't Sant.

Bulgaria: 1504 Sofia, ul. Oborishte 15, POB 91; tel. (2) 816-03-00; fax (2) 816-03-01; e-mail sof@minbuza.nl; internet www.netherlandsembassy.bg; Ambassador Willem Van Ee.

Burkina Faso: 415 ave Dr Kwamé N'Krumah, 01 BP 1302, Ouagadougou 01; tel. 50-30-61-34; fax 50-30-76-95; e-mail oua@minbuza.nl; Ambassador Dr Han Gerard Duijfjes.

Canada: 350 Albert St, Suite 2020, Ottawa, ON K1R 1A4; tel. (613) 237-5030; fax (613) 237-6471; e-mail nlgovott@netcom.ca; internet www.netherlandsembassy.ca; Ambassador Karel P. M. de Beer.

Chile: Las Violetas 2368, Casilla 56-D, Santiago; tel. (2) 756-9200; fax (2) 756-9226; e-mail stg@minbuza.nl; internet www.holanda-paisesbajos.cl; Ambassador Hero de Boer.

China, People's Republic: 4 Liang Ma He Nan Lu, Beijing 100600; tel. (10) 65321131; fax (10) 65324689; e-mail pek-cdp@minbuza.nl; internet www.hollandinchina.org; Ambassador Dirk Jan van den Berg.

Colombia: Carrera 13, No 93-40, 5°, Apdo Aéreo 43585, Bogotá, DC; tel. (1) 638-4200; fax (1) 623-3020; e-mail bog@minbuza.nl; internet colombia.nlembajada.org; Ambassador Frans B. A. M. van Haren.

Congo, Democratic Republic: 11 ave Zongontolo, 55 Immeuble Residence, BP 10299, Kinshasa; tel. (99) 8001140; fax (99) 9975326; e-mail kss@minbuza.nl; Ambassador E. C. W. van der Laan.

Costa Rica: Los Yoses, Avda 8, Calles 35 y 37, Apdo 10285, 1000 San José; tel. 296-1490; fax 296-2933; e-mail nethemb@racsa.co.cr; internet www.nethemb.or.cr; Ambassador S. T. Blankhart.

Croatia: 10000 Zagreb, Medvešćak 56; tel. (1) 4642200; fax (1) 4642211; e-mail zag@minbuza.nl; internet www.netherlandsembassy.hr; Ambassador Catharina Maria Trooster.

Cuba: Calle 8, No 307, entre 3 y 5, Miramar, Havana; tel. (7) 204-2511; fax (7) 204-2059; e-mail hav@minbuza.nl; internet cuba.nlambassade.org; Ambassador W. W. Wildeboer.

Cyprus: POB 23835, 34 Demosthenis Severis Ave, 1080 Nicosia; tel. 22873666; fax 22872399; e-mail nic@minbuza.nl; internet www.nlembassy.org.cy; Ambassador Jan Eric van den Berg.

Czech Republic: Gotthardská 6/27, 160 00 Prague 6; tel. 233015200; fax 233015254; e-mail nlgovpra@ti.cz; internet www.netherlandsembassy.cz; Ambassador Jan-Lucas van Hoorn.

Denmark: Toldbodgade 33, 1253 Copenhagen K; tel. 33-70-72-00; fax 33-14-03-50; e-mail kop@minbuza.nl; internet www.nlembassy.dk; Ambassador Gerard Johan Hendrik Christiaan Kramer.

Dominican Republic: Max Henríquez Ureña 50, entre Avda Winston Churchill y Abraham Lincoln, Ensanche Piantini, Apdo 855, Santo Domingo, DN; tel. 262-0320; fax 565-4685; e-mail std@minbuza.nl; internet www.holanda.org.do; Chargé d'affaires a.i. N. J. van Dam.

Ecuador: Edif. World Trade Center, Torre 1, 1°, Avda 12 de Octubre 1942 y Luis Cordero, Quito; tel. (2) 222-9229; fax (2) 256-7917; e-mail nlgovqui@embajadadeholanda.com; internet www.embajadadeholanda.com; Ambassador Kornelis Spaans.

Egypt: 18 Sharia Hassan Sabri, Cairo (Zamalek); tel. (2) 7395500; fax (2) 7365249; e-mail kai-ca@minbuza.nl; internet www.mfa.nl/cai-en/homepage; Ambassador Tjeerd de Zwaan.

Eritrea: 16 Bihat Street, POB 5860, Asmara; tel. (1) 127628; fax (1) 127591; e-mail asm@minibuza.nl; internet www.mfa.nl/asm; Ambassador Nelleke Linssen.

Estonia: Rahukohtu 4-I, Tallin 10130; tel. 680-5500; fax 680-5501; e-mail info@netherlandsembassy.ee; internet www.netherlandsembassy.ee; Ambassador Henk Van Der Zwan.

Ethiopia: Woreda 24, Kebele 13, House No. 1, POB 1241, Addis Ababa; tel. (11) 3711100; fax (11) 3711577; e-mail add@minbuza.nl; internet www .netherlandsembassyethiopia.org; Ambassador ALPHONS HENNEKENS.

Finland: Erottajankatu 19b, 00130 Helsinki; tel. (9) 228920; fax (9) 22892228; e-mail hel@minbuza.nl; internet www.netherlands.fi; Ambassador Robert J. H. Engels.

France: 7–9 rue Eblé, 75007 Paris; tel. 1-40-62-33-00; fax 1-40-62-34-56; e-mail ambassade@amb-pays-bas.fr; internet www.amb-pays-bas.fr; Ambassador HUGO HANS SIBLESZ.

Georgia: 0103 Tbilisi, Telavi 20, Sheraton Metekhi Palace Hotel; tel. (32) 27-62-00; fax (32) 27-62-32; e-mail tbi@minbuza.nl; internet www .dutchembassy.ge; Ambassador O. F. G. Elderenbosch.

Germany: Klosterstr. 50, 10179 Berlin; tel. (30) 209560; fax (30) 20956441; e-mail nlgovbln@bln.nlamb.de; internet www.niederlandeweb.de; Ambassador DR PETER PAUL VAN WULFFTEN PALTHE.

Ghana: 89 Liberation Rd, Ako Adjei Interchange, POB CT1647, Accra; tel. (21) 214350; fax (21) 773655; e-mail acc@minbuza.nl; internet www .ambaccra.nl; Ambassador Lidi Remmelzwaal.

Greece: Leoforos Vassileos Konstantinou 5–7, 106 74 Athens; tel. (210) 7239701; fax (210) 7248900; e-mail ath@minbuza.gr; internet www .dutchembassy.gr; Ambassador JOHANNES ANTHONIUS FRANCISCUS MARIA FORSTER.

Guatemala: Edif. Torre Internacional, 13°, 16 Calle 0-55, Zona 10, Guatemala City; tel. 2381-4300; fax 2381-4350; e-mail nlgovgua@intelnet .net.gt; internet www.embajadadeholanda-gua.org; Ambassador Teunis Kamper.

Hungary: 1022 Budapest, Füge u. 5–7; tel. (1) 336-6300; fax (1) 326-5978; e-mail bdp@minbuza.nl; internet www.netherlandsembassy.hu; Ambassador RONALD ALEXANDER MOLLINGER.

India: 6/50f Shanti Path, Chanakyapuri, New Delhi 110 021; tel. (11) 24197600; fax (11) 24197710; e-mail nde@minbuza.nl; internet www.holland -in-india.org; Ambassador Bob H. Hiensch.

Indonesia: Jalan H. R. Rasuna Said, Kav. S/3, Kuningan, Jakarta 12950; tel. (21) 5248200; fax (21) 5700734; e-mail jak@minbuza.nl; internet indonesia .nlembassy.org; Ambassador DR NIKOLAOS VAN DAM.

Iran: POB 11365-138, Darrous, Shahrzad Blvd, Kamasaie St, 1st East Lane, No. 33, Tehran 19498; tel. (21) 22567005; fax (21) 22566990; e-mail teh@ minbuza.nl; internet www.mfa.nl/teh; Ambassador Radink van Vollenhoven.

Iraq: Park as-Sadoun, 10/38/103, Hay an-Nidhal, Baghdad; tel. (1) 7782571; e-mail bad@minbuza.nl; internet www.mfa.nl/bag; Ambassador ROBERT KABRELSEH.

Ireland: 160 Merrion Rd, Dublin 4; tel. (1) 2693444; fax (1) 2839690; e-mail info@netherlandsembassy.ie; internet www.netherlandsembassy.ie; Ambassador (vacant).

Israel: Beit Oz, 14 Abba Hillel St, Ramat-Gan 52506; tel. 3-7540777; fax 3-7540748; e-mail nlgovtel@012.net.il; internet www.netherlands-embassy.co .il; Ambassador MICHIEL DEN HOND.

Italy: Via della Camilluccia 701–3, 00135 Roma; tel. (06) 367671; fax (06) 36767256; e-mail rom-az@minbuza.nl; internet www.olanda.it; Ambassador Egbert Frederik Jacobs.

Japan: 3-6-3, Shiba Koen, Minato-ku, Tokyo 105-0011; tel. (3) 5401-0411; fax (3) 5401-0420; e-mail nlgovtok@oranda.or.jp; internet www.oranda.or .jp; Ambassador ALPHONS HAMER.

Jordan: POB 941361, 22 Ibrahim Ayoub St, 4th Circle, Amman 11194; tel. (6) 5902200; fax (6) 5930161; e-mail amm@minbuza.nl; internet www .netherlandsembassy.com.jo; Ambassador Joanna Maria Petronella Francisca van Vliet.

Kazakhstan: 010000 Astana, Kosmonavtov 62/801; tel. (7172) 97-44-82; fax (7172) 97-44-80; e-mail ast@minbuza.nl; Ambassador PETER VAN LEEUWEN.

Kenya: Riverside Lane, off Riverside Dr., POB 41537, Nairobi; tel. (20) 4288000; fax (20) 4447416; e-mail nlgovnai@africaonline.co.ke; internet www.netherlands-embassy.or.ke; Ambassador Maria Alice Crispina Van den Assum.

Korea, Republic: Kyobo Bldg, 14th Floor, 1-ga, Jongno, Jongno-gu, Seoul 110-714; tel. (2) 737-9514; fax (2) 735-1321; e-mail seo@minbuza.nl; internet www.nlembassy.or.kr; Ambassador HANS HEINSBROEK.

Kuwait: POB 21822, 13079 Safat, Jabriya, Area 9, St 1, Plot 40a, Kuwait City; tel. 5312650; fax 5326334; e-mail kwe@minbuza.nl; internet www .netherlandsembassy.gov.kw; Ambassador Dr Cornelis G. J. Van Honk.

Latvia: Torņu iela 4, Jēkaba Kazarmas 1A, Rīga 1050; tel. 6732-6147; fax 6732-6151; e-mail info@netherlandsembassy.lv; internet www .netherlandsembassy.lv; Ambassador ROBERT SCHUDDEBOOM.

Lebanon: POB 167190, Netherlands Tower, ave Charles Malek, Achrafieh, Beirut; tel. (1) 204663; fax (1) 204664; e-mail nlgovbei@sodetel.net.lb; internet www.netherlandsembassy.org.lb; Ambassador Robert Zeldenrust.

Libya: POB 3801, Sharia Jalal Bayar 20, Tripoli; tel. (21) 4441549; fax (21) 4440386; e-mail tri@minbuza.nl; internet www.mfa.nl/tri-uk; Ambassador BART VON BARTHELD.

Lithuania: Business Centre 2000, 4th Floor, Jogailos g. 4, Vilnius 01116; tel. (5) 269-0072; fax (5) 269-0073; e-mail vil@minbuza.nk; internet www .netherlandsembassy.lt; Ambassador Johanna Gerarda Maria Ruigrok.

Luxembourg: 6 rue Ste Zithe, 2763 Luxembourg; tel. 22-75-70; fax 40-30-16; e-mail lux@minbuza.nl; internet www.paysbas.lu; Ambassador GERTJAN STORM.

Macedonia, former Yugoslav Republic: 1000 Skopje, Leninova 69–71; tel. (2) 3129319; fax (2) 3129309; e-mail sko@minbuza.nl; internet www.nlembassy .org.mk; Ambassador Simone Filippini.

Malaysia: The Amp Walk, 7th Floor, South Block, 218 Jalan Ampang, POB 10543, 50450 Kuala Lumpur; tel. (3) 21686200; fax (3) 21686240; e-mail kll@ minbuza.nl; internet www.netherlands.org.my; Ambassador LODY EMBRECHTS.

Mali: rue 437, BP 2220, Hippodrome, Bamako; tel. 221-56-11; fax 221-36-17; e-mail bam@minbuza.nl; internet www.mfa.nl/bam; Ambassador Ellen van der Laan.

Malta: Whitehall Mansions, 3rd Floor, Ta'Xbiex Seafront, Ta'Xbiex XBX 1026; tel. 21313980; fax 21313990; e-mail val@minbuza.nl; internet www.mfa .nl/val; Ambassador JAN HEIDSMA.

Mexico: Edif. Calakmul 7°, Avda Vasco de Quiroga 3000, Col. Santa Fe, Del. Alvaro Obregón, 01210 México, DF; tel. (55) 5258-9921; fax (55) 5258-8138; e-mail nlgovmex@nlgovmex.com; internet www.paisesbajos.com.mx; Ambassador Cornelia Minderhoud.

Morocco: 40 rue de Tunis, BP 329, Hassan, 10001 Rabat; tel. (3) 7219600; fax (3) 7219665; e-mail nlgovrab@mtds.com; internet www .ambassadepaysbasrabat.org; Ambassador SJOERD LEENSTRA.

Mozambique: Av. Kwame Nkrumah 324, CP 1163, Maputo; tel. 21484200; fax 21484248; e-mail map@minbuza.nl; internet www.hollandinmozambique .org; Ambassador Frans Bijvoet.

New Zealand: Investment House, 10th Floor, cnr Featherston and Ballance Sts, POB 840, Wellington; tel. (4) 471-6390; fax (4) 471-2923; e-mail wel@ minbuza.nl; internet www.netherlandsembassy.co.nz; Ambassador HENRICA E. C. M. TER BRAACK.

Nicaragua: Calle Erasmus de Rotterdam, Carretera a Masaya km 5, del Colegio Teresiano 1 c. al sur, 1 c. abajo, Apdo 3688, Managua; tel. 276-8630; fax 276-0399; e-mail mng@minbuza.nl; internet www.embajadaholanda-nic .com; Ambassador Lambertus Christiaan Grijns.

Nigeria: 21st Cres., Central Business District, Abuja; tel. (9) 5244024; fax (9) 5244030; Ambassador ARIE VAN DER WIEL.

Norway: Oscarsgt. 29, 0244 Oslo; tel. 23-33-36-00; fax 23-33-36-01; e-mail nlgovosl@online.no; internet www.netherlands-embassy.no; Ambassador Ronald van Roeden.

Oman: Shati al-Qurum, Way No. 3017, Villa No. 1366, POB 3302, Ruwi 112; tel. 24603706; fax 24603778; e-mail mus@minbuza.nl; internet www.mfa.nl/ mus; Ambassador ANNELIES BOOGAERDT.

Pakistan: House No. 28, Margalla Rd, F-7/3, POB 1065, Islamabad; tel. (51) 2004444; fax (51) 2279512; e-mail isl@minbuza.nl; internet www.mfa.nl/isl -en; Ambassador Cornelis Wilhelmus Andreae.

Peru: Avda Principal 190, 4°, Urb. Santa Catalina, La Victoria, Lima; tel. (1) 4150660; fax (1) 4150689; e-mail info@nlgovlim.com; internet www.nlgovlim .com; Ambassador BAREND VAN DER HEIJDEN.

Philippines: Equitable PCI Bank Tower, 26th Floor, 8751 Paseo de Roxas, Makati City, Metro Manila; tel. (2) 7866666; fax (2) 7866600; e-mail man@ minbuza.nl; internet www.netherlandsembassy.ph; Ambassador Robert Brinks.

Poland: 00-468 Warsaw, ul. Kawalerii 10; tel. (22) 5591200; fax (22) 8402638; e-mail war@minbuza.nl; internet www.nlembassy.pl; Ambassador MARNIX KROP.

Portugal: Av. Infante Santo 43, 5°, 1399-011 Lisbon; tel. (21) 3914900; fax (21) 3966436; e-mail nlgovlis@netcabo.pt; internet www.emb-paisesbaixos .pt; Ambassador Robert Jan van Houtum.

Romania: 011823 Bucharest, Al. Alexandru 20; tel. (21) 2086030; fax (21) 2307620; e-mail bkr@minbuza.nl; internet www.olanda.ro; Ambassador JAAP L. WERNER.

Russian Federation: 125009 Moscow, Kalashnyi per. 6; tel. (495) 797-29-00; fax (495) 797-29-04; e-mail mos@minbuza.nl; internet www.netherlands -embassy.ru; Ambassador Jan-Paul Dirkse.

Saudi Arabia: POB 94307, Riyadh 11693; tel. (1) 488-0011; fax (1) 488-0544; e-mail riy@minbuza.nl; internet www.mfa.nl/riy-en; Ambassador NICOLAAS BEETS.

Senegal: 37 rue Jaques Bugnicourt, BP 3262, Dakar; tel. 33-849-0360; fax 33-821-7084; e-mail dak@minbuza.nl; internet www.nlambassadedakar.org; Ambassador Dr J. W. G. Jansing.

Serbia: 11000 Belgrade, Simina 29, POB 489; tel. (11) 2023900; fax (11) 2023999; e-mail info@nlembassy.org.yu; internet www.nlembassy.org.yu; Ambassador RONALD JACOBUS PETRUS MARIE VAN DARTEL.

Singapore: 541 Orchard Rd, 13-01 Liat Towers, Singapore 238881; tel. 67371155; fax 67371940; e-mail nlgovsin@singnet.com.sg; internet www.mfa .nl/sin; Ambassador Christiaan Cornelis Sanders.

Slovakia: Frana Krála 5, 811 05 Bratislava; tel. (2) 5262-5081; fax (2) 5249-1075; e-mail info@holandskoweb.com; internet www.holandskoweb.com; Ambassador ROB SWARTBOL.

Slovenia: 1000 Ljubljana, Palača Kapitelj, Polijanski nasip 6; tel. (1) 4201460; fax (1) 4201470; e-mail lju@minbuza.nl; internet www.netherlands-embassy .si; Ambassador J. C. M. Groffen.

South Africa: 825 Arcadia St, Arcadia, Pretoria 0083; POB 117, Pretoria 0001; tel. (12) 3443910; fax (12) 3439950; internet www.dutchembassy.co.za; Ambassador ROBERT GERARD DE VOS.

Spain: Avda del Comandante Franco 32, 28016 Madrid; tel. (91) 3537500; fax (91) 3537565; e-mail nlgovmad@telefonica.net; internet spanje.nlambassade .org; Ambassador Como van Hellenberg Hubar.

Sri Lanka: 25 Torrington Ave, Colombo 7; tel. (11) 2596914; fax (11) 2502855; e-mail col@minbuza.nl; internet www.hollandinsrilanka.org; Ambassador REYNOUT S. VAN DIJK.

Sudan: St 47, House No. 76, POB 391, Khartoum; tel. (183) 471200; fax (183) 471204; e-mail nlgovkha@mail.com; internet www.mfa.nl/kha; Ambassador J. H. M. Wolfs.

Suriname: Van Roseveltkade 5, POB 1877, Paramaribo; tel. 477211; fax 477792; e-mail prm@minbuza.nl; Ambassador TANYA VAN GOOL.

Sweden: Götgt. 16a, POB 15048, 104 65 Stockholm; tel. (8) 556-933-00; fax (8) 556-933-11; e-mail sto@minbuza.nl; internet www.nlemb.se; Ambassador Antoine François van Dongen.

Switzerland: Seftigenstr. 7, 3007 Bern; tel. 313508700; fax 313508710; e-mail ben@minbuza.nl; internet www.nlembassy.ch; Ambassador EDO HOFLAND.

Syria: BP 702, Immeuble Tello, rue al-Jala'a, Abou Roumaneh, Damascus; tel. (11) 3336871; fax (11) 3339369; e-mail dmc@minbuza.nl; Ambassador Désirée Bonis.

Tanzania: Umoja House, 4th Floor, Garden Ave, POB 9534, Dar es Salaam; tel. (22) 2110000; fax (22) 2110044; e-mail dar@minbuza.nl; internet tanzania .nlembassy.org; Ambassador KAREL VAN KESTEREN.

Thailand: 15 Soi Tonson, Thanon Ploenchit, Lumpini, Pathumwan, Bangkok 10330; tel. (2) 309-5200; fax (2) 309-5205; e-mail ban@minbuza.nl; internet www.mfa.nl/ban; Ambassador Pieter J. Th. Marres.

Trinidad and Tobago: Life of Barbados Bldg, 3rd Floor, 69–71 Edward St, POB 870, Port of Spain; tel. 625-1210; fax 625-1704; e-mail info@holland.tt; internet www.holland.tt; Ambassador H. P. P. M. HORBACH.

Tunisia: 6–8 rue Meycen, BP 47, Belvédère, 1082 Tunis; tel. (71) 797-724; fax (71) 785-557; e-mail tun@minbuza.nl; internet www.hollandembassy-tunisia .com; Ambassador Rita Dulci Rahman.

Turkey: Hollanda Cad. 3, 06550 Yıldız, Ankara; tel. (312) 4091800; fax (312) 4091898; e-mail ank@minbuza.nl; internet www.nl.org.tr; Ambassador P. M. KURPERSHOEK.

Uganda: Rwenzori Courts, 4th Floor, Plot 2, Nakasero Rd, POB 7728, Kampala; tel. (41) 2346000; fax (41) 2231861; e-mail kam@minbuza.nl; internet www.netherlandsembassyuganda.org; Ambassador Jeroen Verheul.

Ukraine: 01901 Kyiv, Kontraktova pl. 7; tel. (44) 490-82-00; fax (44) 490-82-09; e-mail kie@minbuza.nl; internet www.netherlands-embassy.com.ua; Ambassador RON KELLER.

United Arab Emirates: POB 46560, Al-Masood Tower, 6th Floor, Suite 6, Abu Dhabi; tel. (2) 6321920; fax (2) 6313158; e-mail abu@minbuza.nl; internet www.netherlands.ae; Ambassador Gilles Arnout Beschoor Plug.

United Kingdom: 38 Hyde Park Gate, London, SW7 5DP; tel. (20) 7590-3200; fax (20) 7225-0947; e-mail london@netherlands-embassy.org.uk; internet www.netherlands-embassy.org.uk; Ambassador PIETER WILLEM WALDECK.

United States of America: 4200 Linnean Ave, NW, Washington, DC 20008; tel. (202) 244-5300; fax (202) 362-3430; e-mail was@minbuza.nl; internet www.netherlands-embassy.org; Ambassador Christiaan M. J. Kröner.

Uruguay: Leyenda Patria 2880, Of. 202, 2°, Casilla 1519, 11300 Montevideo; tel. (2) 7112956; fax (2) 7113301; e-mail mtv@minbuza.nl; internet www .holanda.org.uy; Ambassador ROBERT H. MEYS.

Vatican City: Piazza della Città Leonina 9, 00193 Rome, Italy; tel. (06) 6868044; fax (06) 6879593; e-mail vat@minbuza.nl; Ambassador Monique P. A. Frank.

Venezuela: Edif. San Juan Bosco, 9°, San Juan Bosco con 2a Transversal de Altamira, Caracas; tel. (212) 263-3622; fax (212) 263-0462; e-mail car@ minbuza.nl; internet www.mfa.nl/car-es; Ambassador H. NIJENHUIS.

Viet Nam: Daeha Office Tower, 6th Floor, 360 Kim Ma, Ba Dinh District, Hanoi; tel. (4) 8315650; fax (4) 8315655; e-mail han@minbuza.nl; internet www.netherlands-embassy.org.vn; Ambassador André Haspels.

Yemen: POB 463, off 14th October St, San'a; tel. (1) 421800; fax 421035; e-mail holland@y.net.ye; internet www.holland.com.ye; Ambassador R. H. BUIKEMA.

Zambia: 5208 United Nations Ave, POB 31905, 10101 Lusaka; tel. (1) 253819; fax (1) 253733; e-mail lus@minbuza.nl; internet www .netherlandsembassy.org.zm; Ambassador Eduard J. M. Middeldorp.

Zimbabwe: 2 Arden Rd, Highlands, POB HG601, Harare; tel. (4) 776701; fax (4) 776700; e-mail nlgovhar@mweb.co.zw; Ambassador JOSEPH WETERINGS.

DIPLOMATIC MISSIONS OF NEW ZEALAND

United Nations: 1 United Nations Plaza, 25th Floor, New York, NY 10017; tel. (212) 826-1960; fax (212) 758-0827; e-mail nz@un.int; internet www .nzmissionny.org; Permanent Representative Rosemary Banks.

Argentina: Carlos Pellegrini 1427, 5°, C1011AAC Buenos Aires; tel. (11) 4328-0747; fax (11) 4328-0757; e-mail kiwiargentina@datamarkets.com.ar; internet www.nzembassy.com/buenosaires; Ambassador ANNA LOUISE DUNCAN.

Australia: Commonwealth Ave, Canberra, ACT 2600; tel. (2) 6270-4211; fax (2) 6273-3194; e-mail nzhccba@bigpond.net.au; internet www.nzembassy .com/australia; High Commissioner John Larkindale.

Belgium: 1 square de Meeûs, 7e étage, 1000 Brussels; tel. (2) 512-10-40; fax (2) 513-48-56; e-mail nzemb.brussels@skynet.be; internet www.nzembassy.com/ belgium; Ambassador PETER KENNEDY.

Brazil: SHIS, QI 09, Conj. 16, Casa 01, 71625-160 Brasília, DF; tel. (61) 3248-9900; fax (61) 3248-9916; e-mail zelandia@nwi.com.br; Ambassador Alison Mann.

Canada: Clarica Centre, 99 Bank St, Suite 727, Ottawa, ON K1P 6G3; tel. (613) 238-5991; fax (613) 238-5707; e-mail info@nzhcottawa.org; internet www.nzembassy.com/canada; High Commissioner KATHLEEN J. LACKEY.

Chile: El Golf 99, Of. 703, Las Condes, Santiago; tel. (2) 290-9800; fax (2) 458-0940; e-mail embajada@nzembassy.cl; internet www.nzembassy.com/ home.cfm?c = 16; Ambassador Nigel Fyfe.

China, People's Republic: 1 Ri Tan, Dong Er Jie, Chao Yang Qu, Beijing 100600; tel. (10) 65322731; fax (10) 65324317; e-mail nzemb@eastnet.com.cn; internet www.nzembassy.com/china; Ambassador ANTHONY PATRICK F. BROWNE.

Egypt: 8th Floor, North Tower, Nile City Bldg, Sharia Corniche en-Nil, Cairo (Boulac); tel. (2) 4619178; fax (2) 4619181; Ambassador Rene Wilson.

Fiji: Reserve Bank of Fiji Bldg, 10th Floor, Pratt St, POB 1378, Suva; tel. 3311422; fax 3300842; e-mail nzhc@connect.com.fj; High Commissioner CAROLINE MCDONALD (acting).

France: 7 ter rue Léonard de Vinci, 75116 Paris; tel. 1-45-01-43-43; fax 1-45-01-43-44; e-mail nzembassy.paris@fr.oleane.com; internet www.nzembassy .com/france; Ambassador Sarah Dennis.

Germany: Atrium, Friedrichstr. 60, 10117 Berlin; tel. (30) 206210; fax (30) 20621114; e-mail nzembassy.berlin@t-online.de; internet www.nzembassy .com/germany; Ambassador ALAN HOWARD COOK.

India: Sir Edmund Hillary Marg, Chanakyapuri, New Delhi 110 021; tel. (11) 26883170; fax (11) 26883165; e-mail nzhc@ndf.vsnl.net.in; internet www .nzembassy.com/home.cfm?c = 26; High Commissioner Rupert Holborow.

Indonesia: BRI II Bldg, 23rd Floor, Jalan Jenderal Sudirman, Kav. 44–46, Jakarta; tel. (21) 5709460; fax (21) 5709457; e-mail nzembjak@cbn.net.id; internet www.nzembassy.com/home.cfm?c = 41; Ambassador PHILLIP GIBSON.

Iran: POB 15875-4313, 34 North Golestan Complex, Cnr of 2nd Park Alley and Sosan St, Aghdasiyeh St, Niavaran, Tehran 11365; tel. (21) 22800289; fax (21) 22831673; e-mail newzealand@mavara.com; internet www.nzembassy .com/iran; Ambassador Hamish MacMaster.

Italy: Via Zara 28, 00198 Roma; tel. (06) 4417171; fax (06) 4402984; e-mail nzemb.rom@flashnet.it; internet www.nzembassy.com/italy; Ambassador LAWRENCE MARKES.

Japan: 20-40, Kamiyama-cho, Shibuya-ku, Tokyo 150-0047; tel. (3) 3467-2271; fax (3) 3467-2278; e-mail nzemb.tky@mail.com; internet www .nzembassy.com/japan; Ambassador Ian Kennedy.

Kiribati: POB 53, Bairiki, Tarawa; tel. 21400; fax 21402; e-mail nzhc@tskl .net.ki; High Commissioner CRAIG RICKIT.

Korea, Republic: Kyobo Bldg, 15th Floor, 1, 1-ga, Jongno, Jongno-gu, KPO Box 2258, Seoul 110-110; tel. (2) 3701-7700; fax (2) 3701-7701; e-mail nzembsel@kornet.net; internet www.nzembassy.com/korea; Ambassador Jane Coombs.

Malaysia: Menara IMC, 21st Floor, 8 Jalan Sultan Ismail, 50250 Kuala Lumpur; tel. (3) 20782533; fax (3) 20780387; e-mail nzhckl@po.jaring.my; High Commissioner DAVID KERSEY.

Mexico: Edif. Corporativo Polanco 4°, Jaime Balmes 8, Col. Polanco, Del. Miguel Hidalgo, 11510 México, DF; tel. (55) 5283-9460; fax (55) 5283-9480; e-mail kiwimexico@prodigy.net.mx; Ambassador Cecile Hillyer.

Netherlands: Eisenhowerlaan 77N, 2517 KK The Hague; tel. (70) 3469324; fax (70) 3632983; e-mail nzemb@xs4all.nl; internet www.nzembassy.com/ netherlands; Ambassador RACHEL FRY.

Papua New Guinea: Waigani Crescent, POB 1051, Waigani, NCD; tel. 3259444; fax 3250565; e-mail nzhcpom@dg.com.pg; High Commissioner Niels Holm.

Philippines: BPI Buendia Center, 23rd Floor, Sen. Gil J. Puyat Ave, POB 3228, MCPO, Makati City, Metro Manila; tel. (2) 8915358; fax (2) 8915353; e-mail nzmanila@nxdsl.com.ph; internet www.nzembassy.com/philippines; Ambassador DAVID PINE.

Poland: 00-536 Warsaw, Al. Ujazdowskie 51; tel. (22) 5210500; fax (22) 5210510; e-mail nzwsw@nzembassy.pl; Ambassador Philip Wallace Griffiths.

Russian Federation: 121069 Moscow, ul. Povarskaya 44; tel. (495) 956-35-79; fax (495) 956-35-83; e-mail nzembmos@umail.ru; internet www.nzembassy .com/home.cfm?c=42; Ambassador CHRISTOPHER J. ELDER.

Samoa: Beach Rd, POB 1876, Apia; tel. 21711; fax 20086; e-mail nzhcapia@ samoa.ws; High Commissioner Caroline Bilkey.

Saudi Arabia: POB 94397, Riyadh 11693; tel. (1) 488-7988; fax (1) 488-7912; e-mail info@nzembassy.org.sa; Ambassador TREVOR MATHESON.

Singapore: 391a Orchard Rd, Tower A, 15-06/10 Ngee Ann City, Singapore 238873; tel. 62359966; fax 67339924; e-mail enquiries@nz-high-com.org.sg; internet www.nzembassy.com/singapore; High Commissioner Dr Martin Wilfred Harvey.

Solomon Islands: Mendana Ave, POB 697, Honiara; tel. 21502; fax 22377; e-mail nzhicom@.solomon.com.sb; High Commissioner DEBORAH PANCKHURST.

South Africa: Block C, Hatfield Gardens, 1110 Arcadia St, Hatfield, Pretoria 0083; Private Bag X17, Hatfield 0028; tel. (12) 3428656; fax (12) 3428640; e-mail enquiries@nzhc.co.za; internet www.nzhc.co.za; High Commissioner Malcolm McGoun.

Spain: Pinar 7, 3°, 28006 Madrid; tel. (91) 5230226; fax (91) 5230171; e-mail embnuevazelanda@telefonica.net; internet www.nzembassy.com/spain; Ambassador GEOFFREY KENYON WARD.

Thailand: M Thai Tower, 14th Floor, All Seasons Place, 87 Thanon Witthayu, Lumpini, Pathumwan, Bangkok 10330; tel. (2) 254-2530; fax (2) 253-9045; e-mail nzembbkk@loxinfo.co.th; internet www.nzembassy.com/ home.cfm?c=21; Ambassador Brook Barrington.

Timor-Leste: Rua Alferes Duarte Arbiro, Lighthouse Area, Farol, Dili; fax 3324982; e-mail dili@mfat.gov.nz; Ambassador RUTH NUTTALL.

Tonga: cnr Taufa'ahau and Salote Rds, POB 830, Nuku'alofa; tel. 23122; fax 23487; e-mail nzhcnuk@kalianet.to; High Commissioner Christine Bogle.

Turkey: PK 162, İran Cad. 13/4, 06700 Kavaklıdere, Ankara; tel. (312) 4679054; fax (312) 4679013; e-mail nzembassyankara@ttnet.net.tr; internet www.nzembassy.com/turkey; Ambassador HAMISH COOPER.

United Kingdom: New Zealand House, 80 Haymarket, London, SW1Y 4TQ; tel. (20) 7930-8422; fax (20) 7839-4580; e-mail aboutnz@newzealandhc.org .uk; internet www.nzembassy.com/uk; High Commr Jonathan Hunt.

United States of America: 37 Observatory Circle, NW, Washington, DC 20008; tel. (202) 328-4800; fax (202) 667-5227; e-mail info@nzemb.org; internet www.nzembassy.com; Ambassador ROY FERGUSON.

Vanuatu: La Casa d'Andrea e Luciano, Rue Pierre Lamy St, Port Vila; tel. 22933; fax 22518; e-mail kiwi@vanuatu.com.vu; High Commissioner Jeff Langley.

Viet Nam: Level 5, 63 Ly Thai To, Hanoi; tel. (4) 8241481; fax (4) 8241480; e-mail nzembhan@fpt.vn; Ambassador JAMES KEMBER.

DIPLOMATIC MISSIONS OF NICARAGUA

United Nations: 820 Second Ave, Suite 801, New York, NY 10017; tel. (212) 490-7997; fax (212) 286-0815; e-mail nicaragua@un.int; internet www.un.int/ nicaragua; Permanent Representative Maria Rubiales de Chamorro.

Argentina: Avda Santa Fe 1845, 7°B, C1123AAA Buenos Aires; tel. (11) 4811-0973; e-mail embanic@fibertel.com.ar; Ambassador ZORAYA FABIOLA MASIS.

Austria: Ebendorferstr. 10/3/12, 1010 Vienna; tel. (1) 403-18-38; fax (1) 403-27-52; e-mail embanic-viena@aon.at; Ambassador Piero Dario Coen Montealegre (resident in Rome, Italy).

Belgium: 55 ave de Wolvendael, 1180 Brussels; tel. (2) 375-65-00; fax (2) 375-71-88; e-mail sky77706@skynet.be; Chargé d'affaires a.i. SANTIAGO URBINA GUERRERO.

Belize: 124 Barrack Rd, Belize City; tel. 223-2666; fax 223-0978; e-mail embanicbelize@btl.net; Ambassador Nora Gordon.

Brazil: SHIS, QL 16, Conj. 04, Casa 15, 71640-245 Brasília, DF; tel. (61) 3248-1115; fax (61) 3248-1120; e-mail embanibra@terra.com.br; Ambassador SARA MARÍA TÓRREZ RUIZ.

Chile: Zurich 255, Of. 111, Las Condes, Santiago; tel. (2) 234-1808; fax (2) 234-5170; e-mail embanic@vtr.net; Ambassador María Luisa Robleto Aguilar.

China (Taiwan): 3/F, Lane 62, Tien Mou West Road, Taipei 11156; tel. (2) 28749034; fax (2) 28749080; e-mail icaza@ms13.hinet.net; Ambassador WILLIAM TAPIA.

Colombia: Calle 108a, No 25-42, Bogotá, DC; tel. (1) 619-8934; fax (1) 612-6050; e-mail embnicaragua@007mundo.com; Chargé d'affaires a.i. Edgard José Genie Arevalo.

Costa Rica: Edif. Trianón, Avda Central 250, Barrio la California, Apdo 1382, 1000 San José; tel. 221-2884; fax 221-3036; e-mail embanic@sol.racsa .co.cr; Ambassador HAROLD FERNANDO RIVAS REYES.

Cuba: Calle 20, No 709, entre 7 y 9, Miramar, Havana; tel. (7) 204-1025; fax (7) 204-6323; e-mail embajnicc@enet.cu; Ambassador Luis Cabrera González.

Denmark: Kastelsvej 7, Ground Floor, 2100 Copenhagen Ø; tel. 35-55-48-70; fax 35-55-48-75; e-mail embajada@emb-nicaragua.dk; Ambassador DR RICARDO JOSÉ ALVARADO NOGUERA.

Dominican Republic: Edif. Metrópolis II, Apto D-O, Calle Eric Ekman, esq. Euclides Morillo, Arroyo Hondo, Santo Domingo, DN; tel. 563-2311; fax 565-7961; e-mail embanic-rd@codetel.net.do; Chargé d'affaires a.i. Corina García del Solar.

Ecuador: Edif. World Trade Center, Torre A, Avda 12 de Octubre 1942 con Avda Cordero, Quito; tel. (2) 224-4844; fax (2) 245-3413; Ambassador DONALD CASTILLO RIVAS (resident in Colombia).

El Salvador: Calle El Mirador y 93 Avda Norte 4814, Col. Escalón, San Salvador; tel. 2263-8770; fax 2263-2292; e-mail embanic@integra.com.sv; Ambassador Gilda María Bolt González.

Germany: Joachim-Karnatz-Allee 45, 10557 Berlin; tel. (30) 2064380; fax (30) 22487891; e-mail embajada.berlin@embanic.de; Chargé d'affaires a.i. KARLA LUZETTE BETETA BRENES.

Guatemala: 10a Avda 14-72, Zona 10, Guatemala City; tel. 2368-0785; fax 2337-4264; e-mail embaguat@terra.com.gt; Ambassador Silvio Mora Mora.

Honduras: Col. Tepeyac, Bloque M-1, Avda Choluteca 1130, Apdo 392, Tegucigalpa; tel. 231-1977; fax 231-1412; e-mail embanic@amnettgu.com; Ambassador PIERO COEN MONTEALEGRE.

Italy: Via Brescia 16, 00198 Roma; tel. (06) 8413471; fax (06) 85304079; e-mail embanicitalia@hotmail.com; Ambassador Piero Coen Montealegre.

Japan: Kowa Bldg, No. 38, Room 903, 9th Floor, 4-12-24, Nishi Azabu, Minato-ku, Tokyo 106; tel. (3) 3499-0400; fax (3) 3710-2028; e-mail nicjapan@gol.com; Ambassador SAÚL ARANA CASTELLÓN.

Mexico: Prado Norte 470, Col. Lomas de Chapultepec, Del. Miguel Hidalgo, 11000 México, DF; tel. (55) 5540-5625; fax (55) 5520-6961; e-mail embanic@prodigy.net.mx; Ambassador Horacio Brenes Icabalceta.

Netherlands: Statenlaan 81, 2582 GE, The Hague; tel. (70) 3225063; fax (70) 3508331; e-mail embajador@embanic.nl; Ambassador CARLOS ARGÜELLO GÓMEZ.

Panama: Quarry Heights, 16°, Ancón, Apdo 772, Zona 1, Panamá; tel. 211-2113; fax 211-2116; e-mail embapana@sinfo.net; Ambassador Antenor Alberto Ferrey Pernudi.

Peru: Avda Alvarez Calderón 738, San Isidro, Lima; tel. (1) 4223892; fax (1) 4223895; e-mail embanic@telefonica.net.pe; Ambassador TOMÁS WIGBERTO BORGE MARTÍNEZ.

Spain: Paseo de la Castellana 127, 1° b, 28046 Madrid; tel. (91) 5555510; fax (91) 4555737; e-mail augusto.zamora@orange.es; Ambassador Augusto C. Zamora Rodríguez.

Sweden: Sandhamnsgt. 40, 6th Floor, 115 28 Stockholm; tel. (8) 667-18-57; fax (8) 662-41-60; e-mail embajada.nicaragua@swipnet.se; Chargé d'affaires a.i. ALVARO BACA RODRÍGUEZ.

United Kingdom: Suite 31, Vicarage House, 58–60 Kensington Church St, London, W8 4DB; tel. (20) 7938-2373; fax (20) 7937-0952; e-mail embanic1@yahoo.co.uk; Ambassador Piero Paolo Coen Ubilla.

United States of America: 1627 New Hampshire Ave, NW, Washington, DC 20009; tel. (202) 387-4371; fax (202) 939-6545; e-mail nicaraguan.embassy@embanic.org; Ambassador ARTURO JOSÉ CRUZ SEQUEIRA.

Vatican City: Via Luigi Luciani 42/1, 00197 Rome, Italy; tel. (06) 32600265; fax (06) 3207249; e-mail embanicsantasede@tin.it; Ambassador José Cuadra Chamorro.

Venezuela: Avda El Paseo, Quinta Doña Dilia, Prados del Este, Caracas; tel. (212) 977-3289; fax (212) 977-3973; e-mail embanic@cantv.net; internet www.ibw.com.net; Ambassador RAMÓN ENRIQUE LEETS CASTILLO.

DIPLOMATIC MISSIONS OF NIGER

United Nations: 417 East 50th St, New York, NY 10022; tel. (212) 421-3260; fax (212) 753-6931; e-mail nigerun@aol.com; internet www.un.int/niger; Permanent Representative Aboubacar Ibrahim Abani.

Algeria: 54 rue Vercors Rostamia, Bouzaréah, Algiers; tel. (21) 78-89-21; fax (21) 78-97-13; Ambassador MOUSSA SANGARE.

Belgium: 78 ave F. D. Roosevelt, 1050 Brussels; tel. (2) 648-61-40; fax (2) 648-27-84; e-mail ambanigerbrux@skynet.be; Ambassador Abdou Abbary.

Benin: derrière l'Hôtel de la Plage, BP 352, Cotonou; tel. 21-31-56-65; Ambassador LOMPO SOULEYMANE.

Canada: 38 Blackburn Ave, Ottawa, ON K1N 8A3; tel. (613) 232-4291; fax (613) 230-9808; e-mail ambanigeracanada@rogers.com; internet www.ambanigeracanada.ca; Ambassador Nana Aïcha Mouctari Foumakoye.

China, People's Republic: 1-21 San Li Tun, Beijing 100600; tel. (10) 65324279; fax (10) 65327041; e-mail nigerbj@public.bta.net.cn; Ambassador ADAMOU BOUBAKAR.

Côte d'Ivoire: 23 ave Angoulvant, 01 BP 2743, Abidjan 01; tel. 21-26-28-14; fax 21-26-41-88; Ambassador Adam Abdoulaye Dan Maradi.

Egypt: 101 Sharia Pyramids, Cairo (Giza); tel. (2) 3865607; Ambassador MOULOUD AL-HOUSSEINI.

Ethiopia: Woreda 9, Kebele 23, POB 5791, Addis Ababa; tel. (11) 4651305; fax (11) 4651296; Ambassador Diamballa Maimouna.

France: 154 rue de Longchamp, 75116 Paris; tel. 1-45-04-80-60; fax 1-45-04-79-73; e-mail ambassadeniger@wanadoo.fr; internet www.ambassadeniger.org; Ambassador ADAMOU SEYDOU.

Germany: Machnower Str. 24, 14165 berlin; tel. (30) 80589660; fax (30) 80589662; e-mail ambaniger@t-online.de; Ambassador Djibo Ali Amina Bazindre.

Ghana: E104/3 Independence Ave, POB 2685, Accra; tel. (21) 224962; fax (21) 229011; Ambassador ABDOULKARIMOU SEINI.

Italy: Via Antonio Baiamonti 10, 00195 Roma; tel. (06) 3720164; fax (06) 3729013; Ambassador Fatouma Mireille Ausseil.

Kuwait: POB 44451, 32059 Hawalli, Salwa Block 12, St 6, Villa 183, Kuwait City; tel. 5652943; fax 5640478; Ambassador ASSOUMANE GUIAOURI.

Libya: POB 2251, Fachloun Area, Tripoli; tel. (21) 4443104; Ambassador Amadou Tidjani Ali.

Morocco: 14 bis, rue Jabal al-Ayachi, Agdal, Rabat; tel. (3) 7674615; fax (3) 7674629; Ambassador DIORI HAMANI RAMATOU.

Nigeria: 15 Adeola Odeku St, Victoria Island, PMB 2736, Lagos; tel. (1) 2612300; Ambassador Moussa Elhadji Ibrahim.

Saudi Arabia: POB 94334, Riyadh 11693; tel. (1) 464-2931; .

United States of America: 2204 R St, NW, Washington, DC 20008; tel. (202) 483-4224; fax (202) 483-3169; e-mail ambassadeniger@hotmail.com; internet www.nigerembassyusa.org; Ambassador Aminata Djibrilla Maiga Touré.

DIPLOMATIC MISSIONS OF NIGERIA

United Nations: 828 Second Ave, New York, NY 10017; tel. (212) 953-9130; fax (212) 697-1970; e-mail nigeria@un.int; Permanent Representative AMINU BASHIR WALI.

Algeria: BP 629, 27 bis rue Blaise Pascal, Algiers; tel. (21) 69-18-49; fax (21) 69-11-75; Ambassador Aliyu Mohammed.

Angola: Rua Houari Boumedienne 120, Miramar, CP 479, Luanda; tel. 222340089; Ambassador ADAMU UMAR.

Argentina: Juez Estrada 2746, Palermo, C1425CPD Buenos Aires; tel. (11) 4808-9245; fax (11) 4807-6423; e-mail info@nigerianembassy.org; internet nigerianembassy-argentina.org; Chargé d'affaires a.i. Inalegwu Victor Ogah.

Australia: POB 241, Civic Square, ACT 2608; tel. (2) 6282-7411; fax (2) 6282-8471; e-mail chancery@nigeria-can.org.au; internet www.nigeria-can.org.au; High Commissioner DR ICHA EMMANUEL ITUMA.

Austria: Nordbahnstr. 36/2/5, 1020 Vienna; tel. (1) 712-66-85; fax (1) 714-14-02; e-mail he@nigeriaembassyvienna.com; internet www.nigeriaembassyvienna.com; Chargé d'affaires a.i. Kenjika Linus Ekedede.

Bangladesh: House 9, Rd 1, Baridhara, Dhaka; tel. (2) 8817944; fax (2) 8817989; High Commissioner (vacant).

Belgium: 288 ave de Tervueren, 1150 Brussels; tel. (2) 762-52-00; fax (2) 762-37-63; e-mail nigeriabrussels@belgacom.net; internet www.nigeriabrussels.be; Ambassador Adekunle Oladokun Adeyanju.

Benin: ave de France, Marina, BP 2019, Cotonou; tel. 21-30-11-42; fax 21-30-18-79; Ambassador EZEKEIL O. OLADEJI.

Botswana: Plot 1086–92, Queens Rd, The Mall, POB 274, Gaborone; tel. 3913561; fax 3913738; High Commissioner Marius U. Offor.

Brazil: SEN, Av. das Nações, Lote 05, 70459-900 Brasília, DF; tel. (61) 3226-1717; fax (61) 3226-5192; e-mail admin@nigerianembassy-brazil.org; internet www.nigerianembassy-brazil.org; Ambassador KAYODE GARRICK.

Burkina Faso: rue de l'Hôpital Yalgado, 01 BP 132, Ouagadougou 01; tel. 50-36-30-15; Ambassador Ahmed Kashim.

Cameroon: Quartier Bastos, BP 448, Yaoundé; tel. 2223-5551; High Commissioner EDWIN ENOSAKHARE EDOBOR.

Canada: 295 Metcalfe St, Ottawa, ON K2P 1R9; tel. (613) 236-0522; fax (613) 236-0529; e-mail chancery@nigeriahcottawa.com; internet www.nigeriahcottawa.com; High Commissioner Ifeoma Jacinte Akabogu-Chinwuba (acting).

Central African Republic: ave des Martyrs, BP 1010, Bangui; tel. 61-40-97; fax 61-12-79; Ambassador A. A. ILEMIA.

Chad: 35 ave Charles de Gaulle, BP 752, N'Djamena; tel. 52-24-98; fax 52-30-92; e-mail nigndjam@intnet.td; Ambassador M. Argungu.

China, People's Republic: 2 Dong Wu Jie, San Li Tun, Beijing; tel. (10) 65323631; fax (10) 65321650; Ambassador JONATHAN OLUWOLE COKER.

Congo, Democratic Republic: 141 blvd du 30 juin, BP 1700, Kinshasa; tel. (81) 7005142; fax (81) 2616115; e-mail nigemb@jobantech.cd; Ambassador Dr Onuorah Jonikul Obodozie.

Congo, Republic: 11 blvd Lyauté, BP 790, Brazzaville; tel. 83-13-16; Ambassador GREG MBADIWE.

Côte d'Ivoire: Immeuble Maison du Nigéria, 35 blvd de la République, 01 BP 1906, Abidjan 01; tel. 20-22-30-82; fax 20-21-30-83; e-mail info@nigeriaembassy-ci.org; internet www.nigeriaembassy-ci.org; Ambassador Albert O. Soyombo.

Cuba: Avda 5, No 1401, entre 14 y 16, Miramar, Havana; tel. (7) 204-2898; fax (7) 204-2202; e-mail enigera@ceniai.inf.cu; Chargé d'affaires a.i. OZOEMANA OBIAJULU NWOBU.

Egypt: 13 Sharia Gabalaya, Cairo (Zamalek); tel. (2) 3406042; fax (2) 3403907; Ambassador Mohammed Ghali Omar.

Equatorial Guinea: 4 Paseo de los Cocoteros, Apdo 78, Malabo; tel. (09) 33-85; Chargé d'affaires a.i. A. ONAH.

Ethiopia: POB 1019, Addis Ababa; tel. (11) 1550644; Chargé d'affaires a.i. Chigozie Obi-Nnadozie.

France: 173 ave Victor Hugo, 75116 Paris; tel. 1-47-04-68-65; fax 1-47-04-47-54; e-mail embassy@nigeriafrance.com; internet www.nigeriafrance.com; Ambassador GODFREY BAYOUR PREWARE.

Gabon: ave du Président Léon-M'Ba, Quartier blvd Léon-M'Ba, BP 1191, Libreville; tel. 73-22-03; fax 73-29-14; e-mail nigeriamission@internetgabon.com; Ambassador Chief Ignatius H. Ajuru.

Gambia: 52 Garba Jalumpa Ave, Bakau, POB 630, Banjul; tel. 4495803; fax 4496456; e-mail nigeriahc@qanet.gm; High Commissioner MARIAM MUHAMMED.

Germany: Neue Jakobstr. 4, 10179 Berlin; tel. (30) 212300; fax (30) 21230212; e-mail info@nigeriaembassygermany.org; internet www.nigeriaembassygermany.org; Ambassador Abdulkadir bin Rimdap.

Ghana: 5 Tito Ave, POB 1548, Accra; tel. (21) 776158; fax (21) 774395; High Commissioner OLUTUNGI KOLAPO.

Greece: Odos Dolianis 65, Maroussi, 151 24 Athens; tel. (210) 8021168; fax (210) 8024208; e-mail ngrathen@otenet.gr; Ambassador Prof. Sunday Oluwadare Agbi.

Guinea: Corniche Sud, Quartier de Matam, BP 54, Conakry; tel. 30-46-13-41; fax 30-46-27-75; Ambassador ABDULKADIR SANI.

Hungary: 1022 Budapest, Árvácska u. 6; tel. (1) 212-2021; fax (1) 212-2025; e-mail embassy@nigerianembassy.hu; internet www.nigerianembassy.hu; Ambassador Adeola Adebisi Obileye.

India: Plot No. 4, Chandragupta Marg, Chanakyapuri, New Delhi 110 021; tel. (11) 24122142; fax (11) 24122138; e-mail nhcnder@vsnl.com; High Commissioner ABUBAKAR GARBA ABDULLAHI.

Indonesia: Jalan Taman Patra XIV/11–11a, Kuningan Timur, POB 3649, Jakarta Selatan 12950; tel. (21) 5260922; fax (21) 5260924; e-mail embnig@centrin.net.id; Ambassador Muhammed Buba Ahmed.

Iran: No. 9, Intifada Ave, 31st St, Tehran; tel. (21) 88774936; e-mail ngrembtehran@yahoo.com; Ambassador IBRAHIM GANYANA ABUBAKAR.

Iraq: 43/11/601 Hay al-Mansour, Baghdad; tel. (1) 541-3133; fax (1) 543-4513; Ambassador Ibrahim Mohammed.

Ireland: 56 Leeson Park, Dublin 6; tel. (1) 6604366; fax (1) 6604092; e-mail enquiries@nigerianembassy.ie; internet www.nigerianembassy.ie; Chargé d'affaires ONOCHIE B. AMOBI.

Israel: 34 Gordon St, Tel-Aviv 63414; tel. 3-5222144; fax 3-5237886; Ambassador Sam Azubuike Dada Olisa.

Italy: Via Orazio 14–18, 00193 Roma; tel. (06) 6896243; fax (06) 6832528; e-mail embassy@nigerian.it; Chargé d'affaires EDWARD DOLAPO OSUNMAKINDÈ.

Jamaica: 5 Waterloo Rd, POB 94, Kingston 10; tel. 926-6400; fax 968-7371; High Commissioner F. A. Ukonga.

Japan: 5-11-17, Shimo-Meguro, Meguro-ku, Tokyo 153-0064; tel. (3) 5721-5391; fax (3) 5721-5342; internet www.nigeriaembassy.jp; Ambassador YAHAYA TABARI ZARIA.

Kenya: Lenana Rd, Hurlingham, POB 30516, Nairobi; tel. (20) 564116; fax (20) 564117; High Commissioner N. Tapgun.

Korea, Democratic People's Republic: Munsudong, Taedongkang District, POB 535, Pyongyang; tel. (2) 3827558; fax (2) 3817293; Ambassador SULE BUBA.

Korea, Republic: 310-19, Dongbinggo-dong, Yeongsan-gu, Seoul; tel. (2) 797-2370; fax (2) 796-1848; e-mail chancery@nigerianembassy.or.kr; internet www.nigerianembassy.or.kr; Ambassador Abba A. Tijjani.

Kuwait: POB 6432, 32039 Hawalli, Surra, Area 1, St 14, House 24, Kuwait City; tel. 5320794; fax 5320834; Ambassador MUHAMMAD ADAMU JUMBA.

Liberia: Congotown, POB 366, Monrovia; tel. 227345; fax 226135; Ambassador Eineje Onobu.

Libya: POB 4417, Sharia Bashir al-Ibrahim, Tripoli; tel. (21) 4443038; Ambassador PROF. DANDATTI ABD AL-KADIR.

Malaysia: 85 Jalan Ampang Hilir, 55000 Kuala Lumpur; tel. (3) 42517843; fax (3) 42524302; e-mail chancerykl@nigeria.org.my; internet www.nigeria.org.my; High Commissioner Dr Wahab Olaseinde Dosunmu.

Mali: Badalabougou-est, BP 57, Bamako; tel. 221-53-28; fax 222-39-74; e-mail ngrbko@malinet.ml; Ambassador MOHAMMED SANI KANGIWA.

Mauritania: Ilot P9, BP 367, Nouakchott; tel. 525-23-04; fax 525-23-14; Ambassador Alhaji Bala Mohamed Sani.

Mexico: Paseo de las Palmas 1880, Col. Lomas de Chapultepec, Del. Miguel Hidalgo, 11000 México, DF; tel. (55) 5245-1487; fax (55) 5245-0105; e-mail nigembmx@att.net.mx; Chargé d'affaires a.i. CLEMENT ONOJA ADUKU.

Morocco: 70 ave Omar ibn al-Khattab, BP 347, Agdal, Rabat; tel. (3) 7671857; fax (3) 7672739; e-mail nigerianrabat@menara.ma; Ambassador Alhaji Abubakar Shehu Wurno.

Mozambique: Av. Kenneth Kaunda 821, CP 4693, Maputo; tel. 21490991; High Commissioner ALBERT G. PIUS OMOTAIO.

Namibia: 4 Omuramba Rd, Eros Park, POB 23547, Windhoek; tel. (61) 232103; fax (61) 221639; High Commissioner Okun Ayodeji.

Netherlands: Wagenaarweg 5, 2597 LL The Hague; tel. (70) 3501703; fax (70) 3551110; e-mail nigembassy@nigerianembassy.nl; internet www.nigerianembassy.nl; Chargé d'affaires a.i. NICHOLAS OLUSHEYE DAVIES.

Niger: rue Goudel, BP 11130, Niamey; tel. 20-73-24-10; fax 20-73-35-00; e-mail embnig@intnet.ne; Ambassador Dr Yakubu Kwari.

Pakistan: 132–135, Diplomatic Enclave 1, Isphani Rd, G-5/4, POB 1075, Islamabad; tel. (51) 2823542; fax (51) 2824104; e-mail nigeria@isb.comsats.net.pk; High Commissioner UMAR EL-GASH MAINA.

Philippines: 2211 Paraiso St, Dasmariñas Village, Makati City, 1221 Metro Manila; POB 3174, MCPO, Makati City, 1271 Metro Manila; tel. (2) 8439866; fax (2) 8439867; e-mail embassy@nigeriamanila.org; internet www.nigeriamanila.org; Chargé d'affaires a.i. Ndubuisi V. Amaku.

Poland: 02-952 Warsaw, ul. Wiertnicza 94; tel. (22) 8486944; fax (22) 8485379; e-mail info@nigeriaembassy.pl; internet www.nigeriaembassy.pl; Chargé d'affaires a.i. AYODEJI OLUKAYODE ROBERTS.

Portugal: Rue Fernão Mendes Pinto 50, Apdo 3146, 1400 Lisbon; tel. (21) 3016189; fax (21) 3018152; e-mail nigerlis@mail.telepac.pt; Ambassador Akatu A. Ella.

Romania: 010449 Bucharest, POB 1–305, Str. Gina Patrichi 9; tel. (21) 3128685; fax (21) 3120622; e-mail nigeremb@canad.ro; Ambassador A. B. MAGASHI.

Russian Federation: 121069 Moscow, ul. M. Nikitskaya 13; tel. (495) 290-37-83; fax (495) 956-28-25; e-mail ngrmosco@online.ru; Ambassador Air Cdre (retd) Dan Suleiman.

São Tomé and Príncipe: Av. Kwame Nkrumah, CP 1000, São Tomé; tel. 225404; fax 225406; e-mail nigeria@cstome.net; Ambassador SUNDAY DOGONYARO OON.

Saudi Arabia: POB 94386, Riyadh 11693; tel. (1) 482-3024; fax (1) 482-4134; e-mail nigeria@nigeriariyadh.com; internet www.nigeriariyadh.com; Ambassador Alhaji A. Garba Aminci.

Senegal: 8 ave Cheikh Anta Diop, BP 3129, Dakar; tel. 869-86-00; tel. 33-869-8600; fax 33-825-8136; e-mail info@nigeriandakar.sn; Ambassador AZUKA CECILIA UZOKA-EMEJULU.

Sierra Leone: 37 Siaka Stevens St, Freetown; tel. (22) 224224; fax (22) 2242474; High Commissioner Adamu A. Abbas.

Singapore: 08-02 Anson House, 72 Anson Rd, Singapore 079911; tel. 67321743; fax 67321742; e-mail highcommission@nigeriahc.org.sg; internet www.nigeriahc.org.sg; High Commissioner DR OZICHI J. ALIMOLE (acting).

South Africa: 971 Schoeman St, Arcadia, Pretoria 0083; POB 27332, Sunnyside 0132; tel. (12) 3420805; fax (12) 3421668; High Commissioner M Zanneh (acting).

Spain: Segre 28, 28002 Madrid; tel. (91) 5630911; fax (91) 5636320; e-mail nigerian-emb-sp@jet.es; internet www.nigeriainspain.org; Ambassador DR KINGSLEY SUNNY EBENYI.

Sudan: St 17, Sharia al-Mek Nimr, POB 1538, Khartoum; tel. (183) 779120; Ambassador Ibrahim Karli.

Sweden: Tyrgt. 8, POB 628, 101 32 Stockholm; tel. (8) 246-39-05; fax (8) 24-63-98; e-mail nigerian.embassy@swipnet.se; Ambassador FUNMILAYO A. ADEBO-KIENCKE.

Switzerland: Zieglerstr. 45, Postfach 574, 3007 Bern; tel. 313842600; fax 313842626; e-mail info@nigerianbern.org; internet www.nigerianbern.org; Ambassador Dr Martin I. Uhomoibhi.

Tanzania: 83 Haile Selassie Rd, POB 9214, Oyster Bay, Dar es Salaam; tel. (22) 2666000; fax (22) 2668947; e-mail nhc-dsm@raha.com; High Commissioner AHMED M. USMAN.

Thailand: 412 Thanon Sukhumvit 71, Prakhanong, Wattana, Bangkok 10110; tel. (2) 711-3076; fax (2) 392-6398; e-mail info@embnigeriabkk.com; Ambassador Umaru A. Sulaiman (designate).

Togo: 311 blvd du 13 janvier, BP 1189, Lomé; tel. 221-59-76; Ambassador BABA GANA ZANNA.

Trinidad and Tobago: 3 Maxwell-Phillip St, St Clair, Port of Spain; tel. 622-4002; fax 622-7162; e-mail nigerianpos@tstt.net.tt; High Commissioner Edward Agbe.

Turkey: Uğur Mumcu Sok. 56, 06700 Gaziosmanpaşa, Ankara; tel. (312) 4481077; fax (312) 4481082; Chargé d'affaires a.i. IBUKUN A. OLATIDOYE.

Uganda: 33 Nakasero Rd, POB 4338, Kampala; tel. (41) 4433691; fax (41) 4432543; e-mail nighicom-sgu@africaonline.co.ug; High Commissioner Chukudi Dixon Orike.

Ukraine: 01015 Kyiv, bulv. Panfiliovtsiv 36; tel. (44) 254-58-50; fax (44) 254-53-71; Ambassador IGNATIUS HEKAYRE AJURU.

United Kingdom: Nigeria House, 9 Northumberland Ave, London, WC2N 5BX; tel. (20) 7839-1244; fax (20) 7839-8746; e-mail chancery@nigeriahc.org.uk; internet www.nigeriahc.org.uk; High Commr Dr Dalhatu Sarki Tafida.

United States of America: 3519 International Court, NW, Washington, DC 20008; tel. (202) 986-8400; fax (202) 362-6541; e-mail babalola@nigeriaembassyusa.org; internet www.nigeriaembassyusa.org; Ambassador OLUWOLE ROTIMI.

Venezuela: Calle Chivacoa cruce con Calle Taría, Quinta Leticia, Urb. San Román, Apdo 62062, Chacao, Caracas 1060-A; tel. (212) 993-1520; fax (212) 993-7648; e-mail embnig@cantv.net; Ambassador A. Oyesola.

Zambia: 17 Broads Rd, Fairview, POB 32598, Lusaka; tel. (1) 229860; fax (1) 223791; High Commissioner Chief IBIRONKE O. VAUGHAN-ADEFOPE.

Zimbabwe: 36 Samora Machel Ave, POB 4742, Harare; tel. (4) 253900; Ambassador Anthony U. Osula.

DIPLOMATIC MISSIONS OF NORWAY

United Nations: 825 Third Ave, 39th Floor, New York, NY 10022; tel. (212) 421-0280; fax (212) 688-0554; e-mail delun@mfa.no; internet www.un.norway-un.org; Permanent Representative JOHAN LUDVIK LOVALD.

Afghanistan: St 15, Lane 4, Wazir Akbar Khan, Kabul; tel. (20) 2300899; e-mail emb.kabul@mfa.no; internet www.norway.org.af; Ambassador Jan Erik Leikvang.

Albania: Sky Tower, Rruga Dëshmorët e 4 Shkurtit 5; tel. (4) 256923; fax (4) 221507; e-mail embtia@mfa.no; Ambassador CARL SCHIØTZ WIBYE (resident in Skopje, former Yugoslav republic of Macedonia).

Angola: Rua de Benguela 17, Bairro Patrice Lumumba, CP 3835, Luanda; tel. 222449936; fax 222449248; e-mail emb.luanda@mfa.no; internet www.noruega.ao; Ambassador Arild R. Øyen.

Argentina: Carlos Pelegrini 1427, 2°, C1011AAC Buenos Aires; tel. (11) 4328-8717; fax (11) 4328-9048; e-mail emb.buenosaires@mfa.no; internet www.noruega.org.ar; Ambassador NILS HAUGSTVEIT.

Australia: 17 Hunter St, Yarralumla, ACT 2600; tel. (2) 6273-3444; fax (2) 6273-3669; e-mail emb.canberra@mfa.no; internet www.norway.org.au; Ambassador Lars A. Wensell.

Austria: Reisnerstr. 55–57, 1030 Vienna; tel. (1) 715-66-92; fax (1) 712-65-52; e-mail emb.vienna@mfa.no; internet www.norwegen.or.at; Ambassador BENGT OLAV JOHANSEN.

Azerbaijan: 1000 Baku, Nizami küç. 340, ISR Plaza, 11th floor; tel. (12) 497-43-25; fax (12) 497-37-98; e-mail emb.baku@mfa.no; internet www.norway.az; Ambassador Jon Ramberg.

Bangladesh: House 9, Rd 111, Gulshan, Dhaka 1212; tel. (2) 8816276; fax (2) 8823661; e-mail emb.dhaka@mfa.no; internet www.norway.org.bd/info/embassy.htm; Ambassador INGEBJØRG STØFRING.

Belgium: 17 rue Archimède, 2e étage, 1000 Brussels; tel. (2) 646-07-80; fax (2) 646-28-82; e-mail emb.brussels@mfa.no; internet www.norvege.be; Ambassador Jostein Helge Bernhardsen.

Bosnia and Herzegovina: 71000 Sarajevo, Ferhadija 20; tel. (33) 254000; fax (33) 666505; e-mail emb.sarajevo@mfa.no; internet www.norveska.ba; Ambassador JAN BRAATHU.

Brazil: SES, Av. das Nações, Quadra 807, Lote 28, 70418-900 Brasília, DF; tel. (61) 3443-8720; fax (61) 3443-2942; e-mail emb.brasilia@mfa.no; internet www.noruega.org.br; Ambassador Turid B. Rodrigues Eusébio.

Canada: 90 Sparks St, Suite 532, Ottawa, ON K1P 5B4; tel. (613) 238-6571; fax (613) 238-2765; e-mail emb.ottawa@mfa.no; internet www.emb-norway.ca; Ambassador TOR BERNTIN NAESS.

Chile: San Sebastián 2839, Of. 509, Casilla 2431, Santiago; tel. (2) 234-2888; fax (2) 234-2201; e-mail emb.santiago@mfa.no; internet www.noruega.cl; Ambassador Pål Moe.

China, People's Republic: 1 Dong Yi Jie, San Li Tun, Beijing 100600; tel. (10) 65322261; fax (10) 65322392; e-mail emb.beijing@mfa.no; internet www.norway.cn; Ambassador SVEIN OLE SAETHER.

Colombia: Edif. Fiducafé, 8°, Carrera 9, No 73-44, 8°, Bogotá, DC; tel. (1) 317-7851; fax (1) 317-7858; e-mail emb.bogota@mfa.no; internet www.noruega.org.co; Ambassador Martin Tore Bjørndal (resident in Venezuela).

Côte d'Ivoire: Immeuble N'Zarama, blvd Lagunaire, 01 BP 607, Abidjan 01; tel. 20-22-25-34; fax 20-21-91-99; e-mail emb.abidjan@mfa.no; internet www.norvege.ci; Ambassador ODD-EGIL ANDHØY.

Croatia: 10000 Zagreb, Petrinjska 9; tel. (1) 4922829; fax (1) 4922832; e-mail emb.zagreb@mfa.no; internet www.norwegianembassy.hr; Chargé d'affaires a.i. Jens Erik Grøndahl.

Czech Republic: Hellichova 1/458, 118 00 Prague 1; tel. 257323737; fax 257326827; e-mail emb.prague@mfa.no; internet www.noramb.cz; Ambassador PETER NICOLAY RAEDER.

Denmark: Amaliegade 39, 1256 Copenhagen K; tel. 33-14-01-24; fax 33-14-06-24; e-mail emb.copenhagen@mfa.no; internet www.norsk.dk; Ambassador Jørg Willy Bronebakk.

Egypt: 8 Sharia el-Gezirah, Cairo (Zamalek); tel. (2) 7353340; fax (2) 7370709; e-mail emb.cairo@mfa.no; internet www.norway-egypt.org; Ambassador LASSE SIGURD SEIM.

Eritrea: 11 173–1 St, POB 5801, Asmara; tel. (1) 122138; fax (1) 122180; internet www.norway.gov.er; Chargé d'affaires a.i. Arman Aardal.

Estonia: Harju 6, Tallinn 15054; tel. 627-1000; fax 627-1001; e-mail emb.tallinn@mfa.no; internet www.norra.ee; Ambassador STEIN VEGARD HAGEN.

Ethiopia: POB 8383, Addis Ababa; tel. (11) 3710799; fax (11) 3711255; e-mail emb.addisabeba@mfa.no; internet www.norway.org.et; Ambassador Jens-Petter Kjemprud.

Finland: Rehbinderintie 17, 00150 Helsinki; tel. (9) 6860180; fax (9) 657807; e-mail emb.helsinki@mfa.no; internet www.norja.fi; Ambassador LEIDULV NAMTVEDT.

France: 28 rue Bayard, 4e étage, 75008 Paris; tel. 1-53-67-04-00; fax 1-53-67-04-40; e-mail emb.paris@mfa.no; internet www.norvege.no; Ambassador Bjørn Skogmo.

Germany: Rauchstr. 1, 10787 Berlin; tel. (30) 505050; fax (30) 505055; e-mail emb.berlin@mfa.no; internet www.norwegen.no; Ambassador SVEN SVEDMAN.

Greece: Leoforos Vassilissis Sofias 23, 106 74 Athens; tel. (210) 7246173; fax (210) 7244989; e-mail emb.athens@mfa.no; internet www.norway.gr; Ambassador Sverre Stub.

Guatemala: Edif. Murano Center, 15°, Of. 1501, 14 Calle 3-51, Zona 10, Apdo 1764, Guatemala City; tel. 2366-5908; fax 2366-5928; e-mail ambgua@norad.no; internet www.noruega.org.gt; Chargé d'affaires a.i. TOM TYRIHJELL.

Hungary: 1015 Budapest, Ostrom u. 13, POB 32; tel. (1) 212-9400; fax (1) 212-9410; e-mail emb.budapest@mfa.no; internet www.norvegia.hu; Chargé d'affaires a.i. Kristin Marøy Stockman.

Iceland: Fjólugötu 17, 101 Reykjavík; tel. 5200700; fax 5529553; e-mail emb.reykjavik@mfa.no; internet www.noregur.is; Ambassador MARGIT F. TVEITEN.

India: 50c Shanti Path, Chanakyapuri, New Delhi 110 021; tel. (11) 41779200; fax (11) 41680145; e-mail emb.newdelhi@mfa.no; internet www.norwayemb.org.in; Ambassador Ann Ollestad.

Indonesia: Menara Rajawali, 25th Floor, Kawasan Mega Kuningan, Jakarta 12950; tel. (21) 5761523; fax (21) 5761537; e-mail emb.jakarta@mfa.no; internet www.norway.or.id/info/embassy.htm; Ambassador BJØRN BLOKHUS.

Iran: POB 19395-5398, Lavasani Ave 201, Tehran; tel. (21) 22291333; fax (21) 22292776; e-mail emb.tehran@mfa.no; internet www.norway-iran.org; Ambassador Roald Næss.

Ireland: 34 Molesworth St, Dublin 2; tel. (1) 6621800; fax (1) 6621890; e-mail emb.dublin@mfa.no; internet www.norway.ie; Ambassador TRULS HANEVOLD.

Israel: POB 17575, 13th Floor, Canion Ramat Aviv, 40 Einstein St, Tel-Aviv 69101; tel. 3-7441490; fax 3-7441498; e-mail emb.telaviv@mfa.no; internet www.norway.org.il; Ambassador Jakken Bjørn Lian.

Italy: Via delle Terme Deciane 7, 00153 Roma; tel. (06) 5717031; fax (06) 57170326; e-mail emb.rome@mfa.no; internet www.amb-norvegia.it; Ambassador EINAR MARENTIUS BULL.

Japan: 5-12-2, Minami Azabu, Minato-ku, Tokyo 106-0047; tel. (3) 3440-2611; fax (3) 3440-2620; e-mail emb.tokyo@mfa.no; internet www.norway.or.jp; Ambassador Åge Bernhard Grutle.

Jordan: POB 830510, Amman 11183; tel. (6) 5931646; fax (6) 5931650; e-mail emb.amman@mfa.no; internet www.norway.jo; Ambassador METTE RAVN.

Kenya: Lion Pl., 1st Floor, Wayiaki Way, POB 46363, 00100 Nairobi; tel. (20) 4251000; fax (20) 4451517; e-mail emb.nairobi@mfa.no; internet www.norway.or.ke; Ambassador Elisabeth Jacobsen.

Korea, Republic: 258-8, Itaewon-dong, Yeongsan-gu, Seoul 140-200; tel. (2) 795-6850; fax (2) 798-6072; e-mail emb.seoul@mfa.no; internet www.norway.or.kr; Ambassador DIDRIK TØNSETH.

Latvia: Zirgu iela 14, POB 1173, Rīga 1050; tel. 6781-4100; fax 6781-4108; e-mail emb.riga@mfa.no; internet www.norvegija.lv; Ambassador Nils Olav Stava.

Lebanon: POB 113-7001, Immeuble Dimashki, rue Bliss, Ras Beirut, Hamra, Beirut 1103 2150; tel. (1) 372977; fax (1) 372979; e-mail norleb@cyberia.net.lb; internet www.norway-lebanon.org; Chargé d'affaires a.i. AUD LISE NORHEIM.

Lithuania: Mėsinių g. 5/2, Vilnius 01133; tel. (5) 261-0000; fax (5) 261-0100; e-mail emb.vilnius@mfa.no; internet www.norvegija.lt; Ambassador Steinar Gil.

Macedonia, former Yugoslav Republic: 1000 Skopje, 8 Udarna brig. 2; tel. (2) 3129165; fax (2) 3111138; e-mail emb.skp@mfa.no; internet www.norway.org.mk; Ambassador CARL SCHIØTZ WIBYE.

Madagascar: Explorer Business Park, Bâtiment 2d, Antananarivo; tel. (20) 2230507; fax (20) 2237799; e-mail emb.antananarivo@mfa.no; internet www.amb-norvege.mg; Ambassador Hans Frederik Lehne.

Malawi: Plot 13–14, Arwa House, City Centre, Private Bag B323, Lilongwe 3; tel. 1774211; fax 1772845; e-mail emb.lilongwe@mfa.no; Ambassador GUNNAR FØRELAND.

Malaysia: Suite CD, 53rd Floor, Empire Tower, Jalan Tun Razak, 50400 Kuala Lumpur; tel. (3) 21750300; fax (3) 21750308; e-mail emb.kualalumpur@mfa.no; internet www.norway.org.my; Ambassador Arild Braastad.

Mexico: Avda de los Virreyes 1460, Col. Lomas Virreyes, Del. Miguel Hidalgo, 11000 México, DF; tel. (55) 5540-3486; fax (55) 5202-3019; e-mail emb.mexico@mfa.no; internet www.noruega.org.mx; Ambassador KNUT SOLEM.

Morocco: 9 rue Khénifra, BP 757, Agdal, 10006 Rabat; tel. (3) 7764084; fax (3) 7764088; e-mail emb.rabat@mfa.no; internet www.norvege.ma; Ambassador Arne Aasheim.

Mozambique: Av. Julius Nyerere 1162, CP 828, Maputo; tel. 21480100; fax 21480107; e-mail emb.maputo@mfa.no; internet www.norway.org.mz; Ambassador THORBJØRN GAUSTADSÆTHER.

Nepal: Surya Court, Pulchowk, Lalitpur, POB 20765, Kathmandu; tel. (1) 5545307; fax (1) 5545226; e-mail emb.kathmandu@mfa.no; internet www.norway.org.np; Ambassador Tore Toreng.

Netherlands: Lange Vijverberg 11, 2513 AC The Hague; tel. (70) 3117611; fax (70) 3659630; e-mail emb.hague@mfa.no; internet www.noorwegen.nl; Ambassador EVA BUGGE.

Nicaragua: Plaza España, Apdo 2090, Correo Central, Managua; tel. 266-4199; fax 266-3303; e-mail emb.managua@mfa.no; internet www.noruega.org.ni; Ambassador Kristen Christensen.

Nigeria: 3 Anifowoshe St, Victoria Island, PMB 2431, Lagos; tel. (1) 2618467; fax (1) 2618469; Ambassador TORE NEDREBO.

Pakistan: 25, St 19, F-6/2, Islamabad; tel. (51) 2279720; fax (51) 2279729; e-mail emb.islamabad@mfa.no; internet www.norway.org.pk; Ambassador Aud Marit Wiig.

Philippines: Petron Mega Plaza Bldg, 21st Floor, 358 Sen. Gil J. Puyat Ave, Makati City, 1209 Metro Manila; tel. (2) 8863245; fax (2) 8863384; e-mail emb.manila@mfa.no; internet www.norway.ph; Ambassador STÅLE TORSTEIN RISA.

Poland: 00-559 Warsaw, ul. Chopina 2a; tel. (22) 6964030; fax (22) 6280938; e-mail emb.warsaw@mfa.no; internet www.amb-norwegia.pl; Ambassador Knut Hauge.

Portugal: Av. D. Vasco da Gama 1, 1400-127 Lisbon; tel. (21) 3015344; fax (21) 3016158; e-mail emb.lisboa@mfa.no; internet www.noruega.org.pt; Ambassador INGA MAGISTAD.

Romania: 020463 Bucharest, Str. Dumbrava Roşie 4; tel. (21) 2100274; fax (21) 2100275; e-mail emb.bucharest@mfa.no; internet www.norvegia.ro; Ambassador Øystein Hovdkinn.

Russian Federation: 131940 Moscow, ul. Povarskaya 7; tel. (495) 933-14-10; fax (495) 933-14-11; e-mail emb.moscow@mfa.no; internet www.norvegia.ru; Ambassador ØYVIND NORDSLETTEN.

Saudi Arabia: POB 94380, Riyadh 11693; tel. (1) 488-1904; fax (1) 488-0854; e-mail emb.riyadh@mfa.no; internet www.al-norwige.org.sa; Ambassador Jan Bugge-Mahrt.

Serbia: 11000 Belgrade, Užička 43; tel. (11) 3670404; fax (11) 3690158; Ambassador HÅKON BLANKENBORG.

Singapore: 16 Raffles Quay, 44-01 Hong Leong Bldg, Singapore 048581; tel. 62207122; fax 62202191; e-mail emb.singapore@mfa.no; internet www.norway.sg; Ambassador Janne Julsrud.

Slovakia: Palisády 29, 811 06 Bratislava; tel. (2) 5910-0100; fax (2) 5910-0115; e-mail emb.bratislava@mfa.no; internet www.norway.sk; Ambassador BRIT LØVSETH.

Slovenia: 1000 Ljubljana, Ajdovščina 4/8; tel. (1) 3002140; fax (1) 3002150; Ambassador May Britt Brofoss.

South Africa: iParioli Bldg, A2, 1166 Park St, Hatfield, Pretoria 0083; POB 11612, Hatfield 0028; tel. (12) 3426100; fax (12) 3426099; e-mail emb.pretoria@mfa.no; internet www.norway.org.za; Ambassador TOR CHRISTIAN HILDAN.

Spain: Serrano 26, 28001 Madrid; tel. (91) 4363840; fax (91) 3190969; e-mail emb.madrid@mfa.no; internet www.noruega.es; Ambassador Per Ludvig Magnus.

Sri Lanka: 34 Ward Place, Colombo 7; tel. (11) 2469611; fax (11) 2695009; e-mail emb.colombo@mfa.no; internet www.norway.lk; Ambassador TORE HATTREM.

Sudan: St 49, House No. 63, POB 13096, Khartoum; tel. (183) 578336; fax (183) 577180; e-mail emb.khartoum@mfa.no; internet www.norway-sudan.org; Ambassador Fridtjov Thorkildsen.

Sweden: Skarpögt. 4, POB 27829, 115 27 Stockholm; tel. (8) 665-63-40; fax (8) 782-98-99; e-mail emb.stockholm@mfa.no; internet www.norge.se; Ambassador ODD LAURITZ FOSSEIDBRÅTEN.

Switzerland: Bubenbergpl. 10, Postfach 5264, 3011 Bern; tel. 313105555; fax 313105550; e-mail emb.bern@mfa.no; internet www.amb-norwegen.ch; Ambassador Lars Petter Forberg.

Syria: BP 7703, Immeuble 2, rue Shafei, Mezzeh Est, Damascus; tel. (11) 6122941; fax (11) 6131159; e-mail emb.damascus@mfa.no; internet www.norway.org.sy; Ambassador HANS WILHELM LONGVA.

Tanzania: 160/50 Mirambo St, POB 2646, Dar es Salaam; tel. (22) 2113366; fax (22) 2116564; e-mail emb.daressalaam@mfa.no; internet www.norway.go.tz; Ambassador Jon Lomøy.

Thailand: UBC II Bldg, 18th Floor, 591 Thanon Sukhumvit, Soi 33, Bangkok 10110; tel. (2) 204-6500; fax (2) 262-0218; e-mail emb.bangkok@mfa.no; internet www.emb-norway.or.th; Ambassador MERETTE FJELD BRATTESTED.

Tunisia: BP 124, Les Berges du Lac, 1053 Tunis; tel. (71) 861-777; fax (71) 961-080; e-mail emb.tunis@mfa.no; internet www.norvege-tunisie.org; Ambassador Per Kristian Pedersen.

Turkey: Kirkpinar Sok. 18, 06540 Çankaya, Ankara; tel. (312) 4058010; fax (312) 4430544; e-mail emb.ankara@mfa.no; internet www.norway.org.tr; Ambassador CECILIE LANDSVERK.

Uganda: 8a John Babiiha Ave, Kololo, POB 22770, Kampala; tel. (41) 4343621; fax (41) 4343936; e-mail emb.kampala@mfa.no; internet www.norway.go.ug; Ambassador Bjørg Schonhowd Leite.

Ukraine: 01901 Kyiv, vul. Striletska 15; tel. (44) 590-04-70; fax (44) 234-06-55; e-mail emb.kiev@mfa.no; internet www.norway.com.ua; Ambassador OLAV BERSTAD.

United Arab Emirates: POB 47270, Abu Dhabi; tel. (2) 6211221; fax (2) 6213313; e-mail emb.abudhabi@mfa.no; internet www.norway.ae; Ambassador Arne Rikter-Svendsen.

United Kingdom: 25 Belgrave Sq., London, SW1X 8QD; tel. (20) 7591-5500; fax (20) 7245-6993; e-mail emb.london@mfa.no; internet www.norway.org.uk; Ambassador BJARNE LINDSTRØM.

United States of America: 2720 34th St, NW, Washington, DC 20008; tel. (202) 333-6000; fax (202) 337-0870; e-mail emb.washington@mfa.no; internet www.norway.org; Ambassador Wegger Christian Strømmen.

Venezuela: Centro Lido, Torre A-92A, Avda Francisco de Miranda, El Rosal, Apdo 60532, Caracas 1060-A; tel. (212) 953-0269; fax (212) 953-6877; e-mail emb.caracas@mfa.no; internet www.noruega.org.ve; Ambassador MARTIN TORE BJØRNDAL.

Viet Nam: 10th Floor, Block B, Vincom City Towers, 191 Ba Trieu, Hanoi; tel. (4) 9742930; fax (4) 9743301; e-mail emb.hanoi@mfa.no; internet www .norway.org.vn; Ambassador Kjell Storløkken.

Zambia: cnr Birdcage Walk and Haile Selassie Ave, Longacres, POB 34570, 10101 Lusaka; tel. (1) 252188; fax (1) 253915; e-mail emb.lusaka@mfa.no; internet www.norway.org.zm; Ambassador TERJE VIGTEL.

Zimbabwe: 5 Lanark Rd, Belgravia, POB A510, Avondale, Harare; tel. (4) 252426; fax (4) 252430; e-mail emb.harare@mfa.no; internet www.norway .org.zw; Ambassador Per Gullik Stavnum.

DIPLOMATIC MISSIONS OF OMAN

United Nations: 866 United Nations Plaza, Suite 540, New York, NY 10017; tel. (212) 355-3505; fax (212) 644-0070; e-mail oman@un.int; Permanent Representative FUAD MUBARAK AL-HINAI.

Algeria: BP 201, 52 rue Djamel Eddine, el-Afghani, Bouzaréah, Algiers; tel. (21) 94-13-10; fax (21) 94-13-75; Ambassador Ali Abdullah al-Alawi.

Austria: Währingerstr. 2–4/24–25, 1090 Vienna; tel. (1) 310-86-43; fax (1) 310-72-68; e-mail embassy.oman@chello.at; Ambassador BADR MUHAMMAD ZAHIR AL-HINAI.

Bahrain: POB 26414, Bldg 37, Rd 1901, Diplomatic Area, Manama; tel. 17293663; fax 17293540; e-mail oman@batelco.com.bh; Ambassador Salim Ali Omar Bayaqoob.

Belgium: 40–42 ave Hermann Debroux, 4e étage, C2, 1160 Brussels; tel. (2) 679-70-15; fax (2) 534-79-64; e-mail omanembassy@europe.com; Ambassador SHEIKH GHAZI BIN SAID AL-BAHR AR-RAWAS.

Brunei: 35 Simpang 100, Kampong Pengkalan, Jalan Tungku Link, Gadong, Bandar Seri Begawan BE 3719; tel. 2446953; fax 2449646; e-mail omnembsb@brunet.bn; Ambassador Ahmad bin Mohammed bin Zaher Al-Hinai.

China, People's Republic: 6 Liang Ma He Nan Lu, San Li Tun, Beijing 100600; tel. (10) 65323692; fax (10) 65327185; Ambassador ABDULLAH SALEH AL-SAADII.

Djibouti: Djibouti; tel. 350852; Ambassador Saoud Salem Hassan al-Ansi.

Egypt: 52 Sharia el-Higaz, Mohandessin, Cairo; tel. (2) 3036011; fax (2) 3036464; Ambassador ABDULLAH BIN HAMED AL-BUSAIDI.

France: 50 ave d'Iéna, 75116 Paris; tel. 1-47-23-01-63; fax 1-47-23-77-10; Ambassador Jaifer Salim as-Said.

Germany: Clayallee 82, 14195 Berlin; tel. (30) 84416970; fax (30) 81005199; Ambassador KHALIFA ALI ISSA AL-HARTHI.

India: EP-10/11, Chandragupta Marg, Chankyapuri, New Delhi 110 021; tel. (11) 26885622; fax (11) 26885621; e-mail omandelhi@vsnl.com; Ambassador Mohammed bin Yousuf Shalwani.

Iran: No. 12, Tandis Alley, Africa Ave, Tehran; tel. (21) 22056831; fax (21) 22044672; Ambassador SHEIKH YAHYA BIN ABDULLAH.

Italy: Via della Camilluccia 625, 00135 Roma; tel. (06) 36300517; fax (06) 3296802; e-mail embassyoman@virgilio.it; Ambassador Said Nasser Mansour as-Sinawi al-Harthy.

Japan: 2-28-11, Sendagaya, Shibuya-ku, Tokyo 151-0051; tel. (3) 3402-0877; fax (3) 3404-1334; e-mail omanemb@gol.com; Ambassador KHALID BIN HASHIL BIN MOHAMMED AL-MUSLAHI.

Jordan: POB 20192, Amman 11110; tel. (6) 5686155; fax (6) 5689404; internet www.ca-oman.org.jo; Ambassador Musallam Ben Bakhit al-Barami.

Kazakhstan: 010000 Astana, Chubar sh-a, Novostroitelnaya 3; tel. (7172) 24-18-61; fax (7172) 24-18-63; Ambassador AHMED BIN NASSER AL-MAHRIZI.

Korea, Republic: 309-3, Dongbinggo-dong, Yeongsan-gu, Seoul; tel. (2) 790-2431; fax (2) 790-2430; e-mail omanembs@ppp.kornet.nm.kr; Ambassador Moussa Hamdan at-Tae.

Kuwait: POB 21975, 13080 Safat, al-Odeilia Block 3, St 3, Villa 25, Kuwait City; tel. 2561956; fax 2561963; Ambassador SAEED IBN ALI AL-KALBANI.

Malaysia: 6 Jalan Langgak Golf, off Jalan Tun Razak, 55000 Kuala Lumpur; tel. (3) 21452827; e-mail omanemb@po.jaring.my; Ambassador Aflah bin Suleiman Altaei.

Morocco: 21 rue Hamza, Agdal, 10000 Rabat; tel. (3) 7673788; fax (3) 7674567; Ambassador ABDULLAH BIN MUHAMMAD BIN ABDULLAH AL-FARISSI.

Netherlands: Nieuwe Parklaan 9, LA The Hague; tel. (70) 3615800; fax (70) 3605364; e-mail info@embassyofoman.nl; Ambassador Khadija Hassan Salman al-Lawati.

Pakistan: 53, St 48, F-8/4, POB 1194, Islamabad; tel. (51) 2254869; fax (51) 2255074; Ambassador MOHAAMAD BIN SAID BIN MOHAMMAD AL-LAWATI.

Qatar: POB 1525, 41 Ibn al-Qassim St, Villa 7, Doha; tel. 4931514; fax 4932278; e-mail oman_e126@hotmail.com; Ambassador Rashed bin Mubarak bin Rashed al-Ghelany.

Russian Federation: 109180 Moscow, Staromonetnii per. 14/1; tel. (495) 230-15-87; fax (495) 230-15-44; e-mail amoman@ipc.ru; Ambassador ABDULLAH BIN ZAHER AL-HUSSNI.

Saudi Arabia: POB 94381, Riyadh 11693; tel. (1) 482-3120; fax (1) 482-3738; Ambassador Hamad H. al-Mo'amary.

South Africa: 42 Nicholson St, Muckleneuk, Pretoria 0081; POB 2650, Brooklyn 0075; tel. (12) 3460808; fax (12) 3461660; e-mail sult-oman@ telkom.net; Ambassador. KHALID BIN SULAIMAN BIN ABDUL RAHMAN BA'OMAR.

Spain: Mirasierra Suite Hotel, hab. 416–17, Alfredo Marquerie 43, 28034 Madrid; tel. (91) 7277932; fax (91) 7277933; Ambassador Hilal B. Marhoon Salim Almamary.

Sudan: St 1, New Extension, POB 2839, Khartoum; tel. (183) 471606; fax (183) 471017; Ambassador SALIM BIN FANKHAR AL-SHANFARI.

Syria: BP 9635, rue Ghazzawi, Mezzeh Ouest, Damascus; tel. (11) 6110408; fax (11) 6110944; Ambassador Muhammad bin Salem bin Said ash-Shanfari.

Thailand: 82 Saeng Thong Thani Tower, 32nd Floor, Thanon Sathorn Nua, Bangkok 10500; tel. (2) 639-9380; fax (2) 639-9390; Ambassador HAFEEDH SALIM MOHAMED BA-OMAR.

Turkey: Mahatma Gandhi Cad. 63, 06700 Gaziosmanpaşa, Ankara; tel. (312) 4470630; fax (312) 4470632; e-mail omanembassy@yahoo.com; Ambassador Muhammad Nasser al-Wohaibi.

United Arab Emirates: POB 2517, Said bin Tahnon Sq., Al-Mushraf Area, Abu Dhabi; tel. (2) 4463333; fax (2) 4464633; Ambassador SHEIKH MUHAMMAD BIN ABDULLAH AL-QATABI.

United Kingdom: 167 Queen's Gate, London, SW7 5HE; tel. (20) 7225-0001; fax (20) 7589-2505; Ambassador Hussain Ali Abdullatif.

United States of America: 2535 Belmont Rd, NW, Washington, DC 20008; tel. (202) 387-1980; fax (202) 745-4933; Ambassador HUNAINA SULTAN AHMED AL-MUGHAIRY.

Yemen: POB 6163, 14th October St, al-Gala Quarter, Bldg 2, Khormaskar, San'a; tel. (1) 208874; fax (1) 204586; e-mail omanembassy@y.net.ye; Ambassador Abdullah bin Hamad al-Badi.

DIPLOMATIC MISSIONS OF PAKISTAN

United Nations: 8 East 65th St, New York, NY 10021; tel. (212) 879-8600; fax (212) 744-7348; e-mail pakistan@un.int; internet www.un.int/pakistan; Permanent Representative MUNIR AKRAM.

Afghanistan: 10 Nijat Watt Rd, Wazir Akbar Khan, Kabul; tel. (20) 2300911; fax (20) 2300912; e-mail embassy@pakembassykbl.com; Ambassador Tariq Aziz-ud-din Khan.

Algeria: Villa no 50, allée des Feuilles Vertes, Sidi Yahia, Hydra, Algiers; tel. (21) 54-96-61; fax (21) 54-96-60; e-mail ambpakistan@wissal.dz; Ambassador ZAFARULLAH SHAIKH.

Argentina: Gorostiaga 2176, C1426CTN Buenos Aires; tel. (11) 4775-1294; fax (11) 4776-1186; e-mail parepbaires@sinectis.com.ar; Ambassador Ishtiaq Hussain Andrabi.

Australia: POB 684, Mawson, ACT 2607; tel. (2) 6290-1676; fax (2) 6290-1073; e-mail parepcanberra@internode.on.net; internet www.pakistan.org .au; High Commissioner JALIL ABBAS JILANI.

Austria: Hofzeile 13, 1190 Vienna; tel. (1) 368-73-81; fax (1) 368-73-76; e-mail parepvienna@gmail.com; Ambassador Shahbaz Shahbaz.

Azerbaijan: 1000 Baku, Atatürk pr. 30; tel. (12) 436-08-39; fax (12) 436-08-41; e-mail parepbaku@artel.net.az; Ambassador ABDUL HAMID.

Bahrain: POB 563, Bldg 261, Rd 2807, Block 381, Segeiya, Manama; tel. 17244113; fax 17255960; e-mail parepbah@batelco.com.bh; internet www .pakistanembassy.com.bh; Ambassador Ikramullah Mehsud.

Bangladesh: House NE(C) 2, Rd 71, Gulshan Model Town, Dhaka 1212; tel. (2) 8825388; fax (2) 8850673; e-mail parepdka@citech-bd.com; High Commissioner ALAMGIR BABUR.

Belgium: 57 ave Delleur, 1170 Brussels; tel. (2) 673-80-07; fax (2) 675-83-94; e-mail parepbrussels@skynet.be; internet www.embassyofpakistan.be; Ambassador Saeed Khalid.

Bosnia and Herzegovina: 71000 Sarajevo, Emerika Bluma 17; tel. (33) 211836; fax (33) 211837; Ambassador SHIREEN MOIZ.

Brazil: SHIS, QL 12, Conj. 02, Casa 19, 71630-225 Brasília, DF; tel. (61) 3364-1632; fax (61) 3248-0246; e-mail parepbra@bruturbo.com; Ambassador Muhammad Haroon Shaukat.

Brunei: 8 Simpang 31, Jalan Bunga Jasmin, Beribi, Gadong, Bandar Seri Begawan; tel. 2424600; fax 2424603; e-mail hcpak@brunet.bn; internet www .brunet.bn/gov/emb/pakistan; High Commissioner MAJ.-GEN. (RETD) SYED HAIDAR JAWED.

Cambodia: 45 rue 310, Boeung Keng Kang 1, Phnom-Penh; tel. (23) 996890; fax (23) 992113; e-mail parep.cambodia@yahoo.com; Ambassador Mohammad Younis Khan.

Canada: 10 Range Rd, Ottawa, ON K1N 8J3; tel. (613) 238-7881; fax (613) 238-7296; e-mail parepottawa@rogers.com; internet www.pakmission.ca; High Commissioner MUSA JAVED CHOHAN.

China, People's Republic: 1 Dong Zhi Men Wai Dajie, San Li Tun, Beijing 100600; tel. (10) 65322504; fax (10) 65322715; e-mail pakrepbeijing@yahoo .com; internet www.embassyofpakistan-beijing.org.cn; Ambassador Salman Bashir.

Czech Republic: Páté Baterie 7/761, 162 00 Prague 6; tel. 233312868; fax 233312885; e-mail parepprague@gmail.com; Ambassador ATHAR MAHMOOD.

Denmark: Valeursvej 17, 2900 Hellerup; tel. 39-62-11-88; fax 39-40-10-70; e-mail parepcopenhagen@pakistan-embassy.dk; Ambassador Fawzia Mufti Abbas.

Egypt: 8 Sharia es-Salouli, Cairo (Dokki); tel. (2) 37487806; fax (2) 37480310; e-mail parepcairo@hotmail.com; Ambassador ARIF AYUB.

France: 18 rue Lord Byron, 75008 Paris; tel. 1-45-62-23-32; fax 1-45-62-89-15; e-mail pakemb_paris@gmail.com; Ambassador Asma Anisa.

Germany: Schaperstr. 29, 10719 Berlin; tel. (30) 212440; fax (30) 21244210; e-mail pakemb.berlin@t-online.de; Ambassador SHAHID AHMAD KAMAL.

Greece: Odos Loukianou 6, Kolonaki, 106 75 Athens; tel. (210) 7290122; fax (210) 7257641; e-mail info@pak-embassy.gr; internet www.pak-embassy.gr; Ambassador Iftikhar Hussain Kazmi.

Hungary: 1125 Budapest, Adonis u. 3A; tel. (1) 355-8017; fax (1) 375-1402; internet www.pakistanembassy.hu; .

India: 2/50g Shanti Path, Chanakyapuri, New Delhi 110 021; tel. (11) 26110601; fax (11) 26872339; e-mail pakhc@nda.vsnl.net.in; High Commissioner Shahid Malik.

Indonesia: Jalan Lembang 10, Menteng, Jakarta; tel. (21) 3144008; fax (21) 3103945; e-mail parepjakarta@link.net.id; Ambassador MAJ.-GEN. (RETD) ALI BAZ KHAN.

Iran: No. 1, Ahmed Eitmadzadeh Ave, Jamshidabad Shomali, Dr Fatemi Ave, Tehran 14118; tel. (21) 66941388; fax (21) 66944898; e-mail pareptehran@yahoo.com; Ambassador Iqbal Shafkat Saeed.

Iraq: 14/7/609 Hay al-Mansour, Baghdad; tel. (1) 542-5343; fax (1) 542-8707; e-mail pakembbag@yahoo.com; Ambassador (vacant).

Ireland: Ailesbury Villa, 1b Ailesbury Rd, Dublin 4; tel. (1) 2613032; fax (1) 2613007; e-mail parepdbn@yahoo.com; internet www.pakembassydublin .com; Ambassador Naghmana A. Hashmi.

Italy: Via della Camilluccia 682, 00135 Roma; tel. (06) 36301775; fax (06) 36301936; e-mail pacepromec@linet.it; Ambassador TASNIM ASLAM.

Japan: 2-14-9, Moto Azabu, Minato-ku, Tokyo 106-0046; tel. (3) 3454-4861; fax (3) 3457-0341; e-mail info@pakistanembassyjapan.com; internet www .pakistanembassyjapan.com; Ambassador Kamran Niaz.

Jordan: POB 1232, Amman 11118; tel. (6) 4622787; fax (6) 4611633; e-mail pakembjo@wanadoo.jo; Ambassador MUHAMMAD AKHTAR TUFAIL.

Kazakhstan: 050004 Almaty, Tulebayev 25; tel. (727) 273-15-02; fax (727) 273-13-00; e-mail parepalmaty@hotmail.com; Ambassador Irfan-ur-Rehman Raja.

Kenya: St Michel Rd, Westlands Ave, POB 30045, 00100 Nairobi; tel. (20) 4443911; fax (20) 4446507; e-mail parepnairobi@iwayafrica.com; internet www.pakistanafrica.org; High Commissioner IFTIKHAR A. ARIAN.

Korea, Democratic People's Republic: 23, Block 66, Munsudong, Taedong-kang District, Pyongyang; tel. (2) 3827479; fax 3817622; e-mail parep .pyongyang@kcckp.net; Ambassador Noorullah Khan.

Korea, Republic: 124-13, Itaewon-dong, Yeongsan-gu, Seoul 140-200; tel. (2) 796-8252; fax (2) 796-0313; Ambassador MURAD ALI.

Kuwait: POB 988, 13010 Safat, Jabriya, Police Station Rd, St 101, Plot 5, Block 11, Villa 7, Kuwait City; tel. 5327649; fax 5328013; e-mail pavepkw@

pakembkw.org; internet www.pakembkw.org; Ambassador Mohammad Aslam.

Kyrgyzstan: 720040 Bishkek, Serova Bayalinova 37; tel. (312) 62-17-11; fax (312) 66-15-50; e-mail parepbishkek@elcat.kg; Ambassador ALAM BROHI.

Lebanon: POB 135506, Immeuble Shell, 11e étage, Raoucheh, Beirut; tel. (1) 863041; fax (1) 864583; e-mail pakemblb@cyberia.net.lb; Ambassador Asma Aneesa.

Libya: POB 2169, Sharia Huzayfa bin al-Yaman, Manshiya bin Ashour, Tripoli; tel. (21) 3610937; fax (21) 3600412; e-mail pareptripoli@hotmail .com; Ambassador MUHAMMAD FAROOQ QARI.

Malaysia: 132 Jalan Ampang, 50450 Kuala Lumpur; tel. (3) 21618877; fax (3) 21645958; e-mail pahickl@gmail.com; internet www.pahickl.com; High Commissioner Maj.-Gen. (retd) Tahir Mahmud Qazi.

Maldives: G. Helengely, Lily Magu, Malé; tel. 3323005; fax 3321832; e-mail pahicmale@hotmail.com; High Commissioner MUHAMMAD ANWAR CHOHAN.

Mauritius: 9a Queen Mary Ave, Floreal, Port Louis; tel. 698-8501; fax 698-8405; e-mail pareportlouis@hotmail.com; High Commissioner Syed Hasan Javed.

Mexico: Hegel 512, Col. Chapultepec Morales, Del. Miguel Hidalgo, 11570 México, DF; tel. (55) 5203-3636; fax (55) 5203-9907; Ambassador ZEHRA AKBARI.

Morocco: 37 ave Ahmed Balafrej, Souissi, Rabat; tel. (3) 7631367; fax (3) 7631243; e-mail pareprabat@iam.net.ma; Ambassador Qazi Rizwan-ul-Haq Mahmood.

Myanmar: A4 Diplomatic Quarters, Pyay Rd, Dagon Township, Yangon; tel. (1) 222881; fax (1) 221147; e-mail parepygn@myanmar.com.mm; Ambassador QAZI M. KHALILULLAH.

Nepal: Pushpanjali, Maharajgunj, Chakrapath, POB 202, Kathmandu; tel. (1) 4374024; fax (1) 4374012; e-mail parepktm@wlink.com.np; Ambassador Sohail Amin.

Netherlands: Amaliastraat 8, 2514 JC The Hague; tel. (70) 3648948; fax (70) 3106047; e-mail info@embassyofpakistan.com; internet www .embassyofpakistan.com; Ambassador SIBTE YAHYA NAQVI.

New Zealand: 182 Onslow Rd, Khandallah, Wellington; tel. (4) 479-0026; fax (4) 479-4315; e-mail pakhcwellington@xtra.co.nz; High Commissioner Munawar Saeed Bhatti.

Niger: 90 rue YN 001, ave des Zarmakoye, Yantala Plateau, BP 10426, Niamey; tel. 20-75-32-57; fax 20-75-32-55; e-mail parepniamey@yahoo.com; internet www.brain.net.pk/˜farata; Ambassador (vacant).

Nigeria: 4 Molade Okoya-Thomas St, Victoria Island, POB 2450, Lagos; tel. (1) 613909; fax (1) 614822; Ambassador Khalid Durrani.

Norway: Eckersbergsgt. 20, 0244 Oslo; tel. 23-16-60-80; fax 22-55-50-97; e-mail info@pakistanembassy.no; internet www.pakistanembassy.no; Ambassador RAB NAWAZ KHAN.

Oman: POB 1302, Ruwi 112; tel. 24603439; fax 24697462; e-mail parepmuscat@gmail.com; Ambassador Sohail Amin.

Philippines: Alexander House, 6th Floor, 132 Amorsolo St, Legaspi Village, Makati City, Metro Manila; tel. (2) 8172776; fax (2) 8400229; e-mail pakrepmanila@yahoo.com; internet www.cpsctech.org/˜pkembphil; Ambassador MUHAMMAD NAEEM KHAN.

Poland: 02-516 Warsaw, ul. Starościńska 1/1–2; tel. (22) 8494808; fax (22) 8491160; e-mail parepwarsaw@wp.pl; Ambassador Seema Ilahi Baloch.

Portugal: Rua António Saldanha 46, 1400-021 Lisbon; tel. (21) 3009070; fax (21) 3013514; e-mail parep.lisbon.1@mail.telepac.pt; Ambassador FAUSIA M. SANA.

Qatar: POB 334, Diplomatic Area, Plot 30, West Bay, Doha; tel. 4832525; fax 4832227; e-mail parepqat@qatar.net.qa; Ambassador Muhammad Asghar Afridi.

Romania: 011352 Bucharest 1, Str. Barbu Delavrancea 22; tel. (21) 3187873; fax (21) 3187874; e-mail parepbuc@k.ro; Ambassador SANAULLAH.

Russian Federation: 123001 Moscow, ul. Sadovaya-Kudrinskaya 17; tel. (495) 254-97-91; fax (495) 956-90-97; e-mail parepmoscow@yahoo.com; internet www.pakistanembassy.ru; Ambassador Khalid Khattak.

Saudi Arabia: POB 94007, Riyadh 11693; tel. (1) 488-7272; fax (1) 488-7953; Ambassador ADM. (RETD) ADUL AZIZ MIRZA.

Senegal: Stèle Mermoz, Villa 7602, BP 2635, Dakar; tel. 33-824-6135; fax 33-824-6136; e-mail parepdakar@yahoo.com; Ambassador Abdul Malik Abdullah.

Serbia: 11000 Belgrade, bul. Kneza Aleksandra Karađorđevića 62; tel. (11) 2661676; fax (11) 2661667; e-mail ambpakistana@sbb.co.yu; internet www .pakistanembassy.org.yu; Ambassador MUHAMMAD NAWAZ CHAUDHRY.

Singapore: 1 Scotts Rd, 24-02/04 Shaw Centre, Singapore 228208; tel. 67376988; fax 67374096; e-mail parep@singnet.com.sg; internet www.parep .org.sg; High Commissioner Sajjad Ashraf.

Somalia: Via Afgoi, Km 5, POB 339, Mogadishu; tel. (1) 80856; .

South Africa: 312 Brooks St, Menlo Park, Pretoria 0181; POB 11803, Hatfield 0028; tel. (12) 3624072; fax (12) 3623967; e-mail pareppretoria@worldonline .co.za; High Commissioner Ashraf Qureshi.

Spain: Avda de Pio XII 11, 28016 Madrid; tel. (91) 3458995; fax (91) 3458158; e-mail cancilleria@embajada-pakistan.org; internet www.embajada -pakistan.org; Ambassador (vacant).

Sri Lanka: 211 De Saram Place, Colombo 10; tel. (11) 2696301; fax (11) 2695780; e-mail parepcolombo@sltnet.lk; High Commissioner Air Vice-Marshal (retd) Shahzad Aslam Chaudhry.

Sudan: Dr Mehmood Sharif St, House No. 13, Block 35, POB 1178, Khartoum; tel. (183) 265599; fax (183) 273777; e-mail parepkhartoum@ yahoo.com; Ambassador KHALID HUSSAIN YOUSFANI.

Sweden: Karlavägen 65, 1st Floor, POB 5872, 102 40 Stockholm; tel. (8) 20-33-00; fax (8) 24-92-33; e-mail info@pakistanembassy.se; internet www .pakistanembassy.se; Ambassador Shaheen Amin Gilani.

Switzerland: Bernastr. 47, 3005 Bern; tel. 313501790; fax 313501799; e-mail parepberne@bluewin.ch; Ambassador AYESHA RIYAZ.

Syria: BP 9284, rue al-Farabi, Mezzeh Est, Damascus; tel. (11) 6132694; fax (11) 6132662; e-mail parepdam@scs-net.org; Ambassador Munzer Shafiq.

Tajikistan: 734000 Dushanbe, Kuchai Dostoyevski 1–3, POB 55; tel. (372) 24-68-39; fax (372) 21-17-29; e-mail pareptaj@rs.tj; Ambassador KHALID USMAN QAISER.

Thailand: 31 Soi Nana Nua, Thanon Sukhumvit, Bangkok 10110; tel. (2) 253-0288; fax (2) 253-0290; e-mail parepbkk@ji-net.com; Ambassador Khateer Hassan Khan.

Tunisia: 35 rue Ali Ayari, al-Menzah IX, Tunis; tel. (71) 871-330; fax (71) 871-410; e-mail pareptunis@yahoo.com; Ambassador FAIZ MUHAMMAD KHOSO.

Turkey: İran Cad. 37, 06700 Gaziosmanpaşa, Ankara; tel. (312) 4271410; fax (312) 4671023; e-mail parepank@yahoo.com; Ambassador Lt-Gen. (retd) Syed Iftikhar Hussain Shah.

Turkmenistan: 744000 Aşgabat, ul. Garaşizlik 4/1; tel. (12) 48-21-28; fax (12) 48-21-30; e-mail parepashgabat@online.tm; Ambassador SAID AKBAR AFRIDI.

Ukraine: 01015 Kyiv, pr. Panfilovtsiv 7; tel. (44) 280-25-77; fax (44) 254-45-30; e-mail parepkyiv@mail.kar.net; Ambassador Ghazanfar Ali Khan.

United Arab Emirates: POB 846, Abu Dhabi; tel. (2) 4447800; fax (2) 4492076; e-mail pakem@emirates.net.ae; ; AHSAN ULLAH KHAN.

United Kingdom: 34–36 Lowndes Sq., London, SW1X 9JN; tel. (20) 7664-9200; fax (20) 7664-9224; e-mail pareplondon@supanet.com; internet www .pakmission-uk.gov.pk; High Commr Maleeha Lodhi.

United States of America: 3517 International Court, NW, Washington, DC 20008; tel. (202) 939-6200; fax (202) 387-0484; e-mail info@ embassyofpakistan.org; internet www.embassyofpakistan.org; Ambassador MAHMUD ALI DURRANI.

Uzbekistan: 100115 Tashkent, Kichik Halqa Yoli ko'ch. 15; tel. (71) 148-05-25; fax (71) 144-92-33; e-mail parepuzb@online.ru; Ambassador Sajjad Kamran.

Viet Nam: 44/2 Van Bao, Van Phuc Diplomatic Quarter, Hanoi; tel. (4) 7262251; fax (4) 7262253; e-mail parep-hanoi@hn.vnn.vn; Ambassador GHULAM RASOOL BALUCH.

Yemen: POB 2848, Ring Rd, off Haddah St, San'a; tel. (1) 248814; fax (1) 248866; e-mail pakembassy@yemen.net.ye; Ambassador Nawab Amir Abdul Rehman Nousherwani.

Zimbabwe: 314 Pipendale Rd, Barrowadalf, Harare; tel. (4) 720293; fax (4) 722446; e-mail pakhar@icon.zw; Ambassador RIFFAT IQBAL.

DIPLOMATIC MISSIONS OF PALAU

United Nations: 866 UN Plaza, Suite 575, New York, NY 10017; tel. (212) 813-0310; fax (212) 813-0317; e-mail mission@palauun.org; internet www .palauun.org; Permanent Representative Stuart Beck.

China (Taiwan): 5/F, 9 Lane 62, Tien Mou West Rd, Taipei 11156; tel. (2) 28765415; fax (2) 28760436; e-mail palau.embassy@msa.hinet.net; Chargé d'affaires a.i. LYDIA NGIRABLOSCH.

Japan: Rm 201, 1-1, Katamachi, Shinjuku-ku, Tokyo 160-0001; tel. (3) 3354-5500; Ambassador Daiziro Nakamura.

Philippines: Marbella Condominium II, Unit 101, Ground Floor, 2071 Roxas Blvd, Malate, Manila; tel. (2) 5221982; fax (2) 5210402; e-mail rop_piembassy@yahoo.com; Ambassador RAMON RECHEBEI.

United States of America: 1700 Pennsylvania Ave, NW, Suite 400, Washington, DC 20006; tel. (202) 452-6814; fax (202) 452-6281; e-mail info@palauembassy.com; internet www.palauembassy.com; Ambassador Hersey Kyota.

DIPLOMATIC MISSIONS OF PANAMA

United Nations: 866 United Nations Plaza, Suite 4030, New York, NY 10017; tel. (212) 421-5420; fax (212) 421-2694; e-mail emb@panama_msun.org; Permanent Representative RICARDO ALBERTO ARIAS.

Argentina: Santa Fe 1461, 1°, C1060ABA Buenos Aires; tel. (11) 4811-1254; fax (11) 4814-0450; e-mail epar@fibertel.com.ar; internet www .embajadadepanama.com.ar; Ambassador Olga Ivania Golcher de Manning.

Austria: Elisabethstr. 4–5/4/10, 1010 Vienna; tel. (1) 587-23-47; fax (1) 586-30-80; e-mail mail@empanvienna.co.at; Ambassador ISABEL DAMIÁN KAREKIDES.

Belgium: 18 blvd Général Jacques, 1050 Brussels; tel. (2) 649-07-29; fax (2) 648-92-16; e-mail embajada.panama@skynet.be; Ambassador Pablo Garrido Araúz.

Bolivia: Calle 10, 7853 Calacoto, Casilla 678, La Paz; tel. (2) 278-7334; fax (2) 279-7290; e-mail empanbol@ceibo.entelnet.bo; Ambassador AUGUSTO LUIS VILLARREAL AMARANTO.

Brazil: SHIS, QI 03, Conj. 09, Casa 11, 71605-290 Brasília, DF; tel. (61) 3248-7309; fax (61) 3248-2834; e-mail empanamabr@embaixada.brte.com.br; Ambassador Juan Bosco Bernal Yanis.

Canada: 130 Albert St, Suite 300, Ottawa, ON K1P 5G4; tel. (613) 236-7177; fax (613) 236-5775; e-mail embassyofpanama@gmail.com; Ambassador ROMY VÁSQUEZ DE GONZÁLEZ.

Chile: La Reconquista 640, Las Condes, Santiago; tel. (2) 202-6318; fax (2) 202-5439; e-mail embajada@panamachile.tie.cl; Ambassador Alejandro Young Downey.

China (Taiwan): 6/F, 111 Sung Kiang Rd, Taipei 10486; tel. (2) 25099189; fax (2) 25099801; Ambassador JULIO MOCK CÁRDENAS.

Colombia: Calle 92, No 7a-40, Bogotá, DC; tel. (1) 257-5058; fax (1) 257-5067; e-mail embpacol@cable.net.co; internet www.empacol.org; Ambassador Carlos R. Ozores Typaldos.

Costa Rica: Del San Pedro de Montes de Oca, Apdo 103, 2050 San José; tel. 257-3241; fax 257-4864; e-mail panaembacr@racsa.co.cr; Ambassador LUIS E. VERGARA.

Cuba: Calle 26, No 109, entre 1 y 3, Miramar, Havana; tel. (7) 204-0858; fax (7) 204-1674; e-mail panembacuba@ip.etecsa.cu; Ambassador Luis Antonio Gómez Pérez.

Dominican Republic: Benito Monción 255, Gazcue, Santo Domingo, DN; tel. 688-3789; fax 685-3665; e-mail emb.panam@codetel.net.do; Ambassador MIROSLAVA ROSAS DE MOTA.

Ecuador: Edif. ESPRO, 6°, Alpallana 505 y Whimper, Quito; tel. (2) 250-8856; fax (2) 256-5234; e-mail panaembaecuador@hotmail.com; Ambassador Olgalina Rodríguez de Quijada.

Egypt: POB 62, 4A Sharia Ibn Zanki, Cairo 11211 (Zamalek); tel. (2) 3400784; fax (2) 3411092; Chargé d'affaires a.i. ROY FRANCISCO LUNA GONZÁLEZ.

El Salvador: 203 Edif. Gran Plaza, Blvd El Hipódromo, Col. San Benito, San Salvador; tel. 2245-5410; fax 2245-5205; e-mail embpan@telesat.net; Ambassador Luis Enrique Torres Herrera.

France: 145 ave de Suffren, 75015 Paris; tel. 1-45-66-42-44; fax 1-45-67-99-43; e-mail panaemba.francia@wanadoo.fr; Ambassador OMAR JAÉN SUÁREZ.

Germany: Joachim-Karnatz-Allee 45, 10557 Berlin; tel. (30) 22605811; fax (30) 22605812; e-mail panaemba@t-online.de; Ambassador Darío E. Chirú Ochoa.

Greece: Odos Praxitelous & Odos II Merarchias 192, 185 35 Athens; tel. (210) 4286441; fax (210) 4286448; e-mail panpir5@otenet.gr; internet crewlicense@hotmail.com; Ambassador ANTONIO FOTIS TAQUIS OCHOA.

Guatemala: 12 Calle 2-65, Zona 14, Apdo 929A, Guatemala City; tel. 2366-3331; fax 2366-3338; e-mail panguate@hotmail.com; Ambassador Celso Gustavo Carrizo.

Haiti: 29 rue Capois, Park Hotel, face Champs Mars, Port-au-Prince; tel. 763-4960; Ambassador ALEXIS ROGELIO CABRERA.

Honduras: Edif. Palmira, 2º, Col. Palmira, Apdo 397, Tegucigalpa; tel. 239-5508; fax 232-8147; e-mail ephon@multivisionhn.net; Ambassador Robert Jované.

Hungary: 1016 Budapest, Mihály u. 15; tel. (1) 466-9817; e-mail embpanbu@freemail.c3.hu; .

India: 3-D, Palam Marg, Vasant Vihar, New Delhi 110 057; tel. (11) 26148268; fax (11) 26148261; e-mail panaind@bol.net.in; Ambassador Alberto J. Pinzón.

Indonesia: World Trade Center, 8th Floor, Jalan Jenderal Sudirman, Kav. 29–31, Jakarta 12920; tel. (21) 5711867; fax (21) 5711933; Ambassador RAÚL ANTONIO ENKILDSEN ARIAS.

Israel: 10 Rehov Hei Be'Iyar, Kikar Hamedina, Tel-Aviv 62998; tel. 3-6960849; fax 3-6910045; Ambassador Manuel Barletta Millan.

Italy: Viale Regina Margherita 239, 00198 Roma; tel. (06) 44252173; fax (06) 44252237; Ambassador EUDORO JAEN ESQUIVEL.

Jamaica: 1 St Lucia Ave, Spanish Court, Suite 26, Kingston 5; tel. 968-2928; fax 960-1618; Ambassador Ricardo Moreno.

Japan: Kowa Bldg, No. 38, Room 902, 4-12-24, Nishi Azabu, Minato-ku, Tokyo 106-0031; tel. (3) 3499-3741; fax (3) 5485-3548; e-mail panaemb@gol.com; internet www.embassyofpanamainjapan.org; Ambassador ALFREDO MARTIZ.

Korea, Republic: Northgate Bldg, 6th Floor, 66, Jeokseon-dong, Jongno-gu, Seoul; tel. (2) 734-8610; fax (2) 734-8613; e-mail panaemba@kornet.net; Ambassador Juan José Amado, III.

Mexico: Sócrates 339, Col. Polanco, Del. Miguel Hidalgo, 11560 México, DF; tel. (55) 5280-7857; fax (55) 5280-7586; e-mail informes@embpanamamexico.com; internet www.embpanamamexico.com; Ambassador RICARDO JOSÉ ALEMÁN ALFARO.

Nicaragua: Casa 93, Reparto Mántica, del Cuartel General de Bomberos 1 c. abajo, Apdo 1, Managua; tel. 266-2224; fax 266-8633; e-mail embdpma@ibw.com.ni; Ambassador Miguel Lecaro Bárcenas.

Paraguay: Carmen Soler 3912 y Radio Operadores del Chaco, Asunción; tel. (21) 21-1091; e-mail embapana@conexion.com.py; Ambassador GONZALO MONCADA LUNA.

Peru: Avda Alvarez Calderón 738, San Isidro, Lima 27; tel. (1) 4413652; fax (1) 4419323; e-mail panaemba@amauta.rcp.net.pe; Ambassador Roberto Díaz Herrera.

Philippines: 10th Floor, MARC 2000 Tower, 1973 Taft Ave and San Andres St, cnr Quirino Ave, Malate, 1004 Metro Manila; tel. (2) 5212790; fax (2) 5215755; e-mail panaembassy@i-manila.com.ph; Ambassador JUAN FELIPE PITTY.

Poland: 02-946 Warsaw, ul. Biedronki 13a; tel. (22) 6422143; fax (22) 6517616; e-mail panamaembassy@neostrada.pl; Ambassador Roko Ivan Setka Sagel.

Portugal: Av. Helen Keller 15, Lote C, 4º esq., 1400-197 Lisbon; tel. (21) 3642899; fax (21) 3644589; e-mail panemblisboa@netcabo.pt; Ambassador MINERVA LARA BATISTA.

Russian Federation: 119590 Moscow, ul. Mosfilmovskaya 50/1; tel. (495) 956-07-29; fax (495) 956-07-30; e-mail empanrus@aha.ru; Ambassador (vacant).

Singapore: 16 Raffles Quay, 41-06 Hong Leong Bldg, Singapore 048581; tel. 62218677; fax 62240892; e-mail general@panamaemb.org.sg; Ambassador EDUARDO A. REAL.

South Africa: Pretoria; Ambassador Roberto E. Cordovez Castilla.

Spain: Claudio Coello 86, 1º dcha, 28006 Madrid; tel. (91) 5765001; fax (91) 5767161; Ambassador HUMBERTO LÓPEZ TIRONE.

Sweden: Östermalmsgt. 59, POB 55547, 102 04 Stockholm; tel. (8) 662-65-35; fax (8) 662-89-91; Ambassador (vacant).

Syria: BP 2548, Apt 7, Immeuble az-Zein, rue al-Bizm, Malki, Damascus; tel. (11) 224743; Chargé d'affaires CARLOS A. DE GRACIA.

Thailand: 1168/37 Lumpini Tower Bldg, 16th Floor, Tungmahamek, Sathorn, Bangkok 10120; tel. (2) 679-7988; fax (2) 679-7991; e-mail embajada@panathai.com; internet www.panathai.com; Ambassador David Guardia Varela.

Trinidad and Tobago: Suite 6, 1A Dere St, Port of Spain; tel. 623-3435; fax 623-3440; e-mail embapatt@wow.net; Ambassador GERARDO MALONEY.

United Kingdom: 40 Hertford St, London, W1J 7SH; tel. (20) 7493-4646; fax (20) 7493-4333; e-mail panama1@btconnect.com; Ambassador Liliana Fernándes.

United States of America: 2862 McGill Terrace, NW, Washington, DC 20008; tel. (202) 483-1407; fax (202) 483-8413; e-mail info@embassyofpanama.org; internet www.embassyofpanama.org; Ambassador FEDERICO A. HUMBERT ARIAS.

Uruguay: Juan Benito Blanco 3388, Montevideo; tel. (2) 6230301; fax (2) 6230300; e-mail empanuru@netgate.com.uy; Ambassador Elvira Barrios Icaza.

Vatican City: Largo di Torre Argentina 11/28, 00186 Rome, Italy; tel. (06) 68809764; fax (06) 68809812; e-mail embapass@tiscalinet.it; Chargé d'affaires a.i. JAVIER FRANCISCO TORRES GONZÁLEZ.

Venezuela: Edif. Los Frailes, 6º, Calle La Guairita, Chuao, Apdo 1989, Caracas; tel. (212) 992-9093; fax (212) 992-8107; Ambassador Carmen Gabriela Menéndez González.

Viet Nam: 18th Floor, 44th St, Ly Thuong Kiet, Hanoi; tel. (4) 9365213; Ambassador LIZIA LU.

DIPLOMATIC MISSIONS OF PAPUA NEW GUINEA

United Nations: 201 East 42nd St, Suite 405, New York, NY 10017; tel. (212) 557-5001; fax (212) 557-5009; e-mail pngmission@pngun.org; Permanent Representative Robert Guba Aisi.

Australia: POB E6317, Kingston, ACT 2604; tel. (2) 6273-3322; fax (2) 6273-3732; internet www.pngcanberra.org; High Commissioner CHARLES W. LEPANI.

Belgium: 430 ave de Tervueren, 1150 Brussels; tel. (2) 779-06-09; fax (2) 772-70-88; e-mail kundu.brussels@skynet.be; Ambassador Isaac B. Lupari.

Canada: 130 Albert St, Suite 300, Ottawa, ON K1A 5G4; fax (613) 236-5775; High Commissioner EVAN J. PAKI.

China, People's Republic: 2-11-2 Tayuan Diplomatic Office Bldg, Beijing 100600; tel. (10) 65324312; fax (10) 65325483; e-mail kundu_beijing@pngembassy.org.cn; internet www.pngembassy.org.cn; Ambassador John Momis.

Fiji: Credit Corporation House, 3rd Floor, Government Bldgs, POB 2447, Suva; tel. 3304244; fax 3300178; e-mail kundufj@is.com.fj; High Commissioner PETER EAFEARE.

Indonesia: Panin Bank Centre, 6th Floor, Jalan Jenderal Sudirman 1, Jakarta 10270; tel. (21) 7251218; fax (21) 7201012; e-mail kdujkt@cbn.net.id; Ambassador Christopher Mero.

Japan: Mita Kokusai Bldg, Room 313, 3rd Floor, 1-4-28, Mita, Minato-ku, Tokyo 108; tel. (3) 3454-7801; fax (3) 3454-7275; e-mail png-tyo@nifty.ne.jp; Ambassador MICHAEL MAUE.

Korea, Republic: 36-1, Hannam 1-dong, Yeongsan-gu, Seoul; tel. (2) 798-9854; fax (2) 798-9856; e-mail pngembsl@ppp.kornet.nm.kr; Ambassador Kuma Aua.

Malaysia: 46 Jalan U Thant, 55000 Kuala Lumpur; tel. (3) 42575405; fax (3) 42576203; High Commissioner PETER P. MAGINDE.

New Zealand: 279 Willis St, POB 197, Wellington; tel. (4) 385-2474; fax (4) 385-2477; e-mail pngnz@globe.net.nz; High Commissioner Bernard Narokobi.

Philippines: 3rd Floor, Corinthian Plaza Condominium Bldg, cnr Paseo de Roxas and Gamboa St, Makati City, Metro Manila; tel. (2) 8113465; fax (2) 8113466; e-mail kundumnl@pngembmnl.com.ph; Ambassador DAMIEN DOMINIC GAMIANDU.

Solomon Islands: POB 1109, Honiara; tel. 20561; fax 20562; High Commissioner Parai Tamei.

United Kingdom: 3rd Floor, 14 Waterloo Pl., London, SW1R 4AR; tel. (20) 7930-0922; fax (20) 7930-0828; internet www.pnghighcomm.org.uk; High Commr JEAN L. KEKEDO.

United States of America: 1779 Massachusetts Ave, NW, Suite 805, Washington, DC 20036; tel. (202) 745-3680; fax (202) 745-3679; e-mail info@pngembassy.org; internet www.pngembassy.org; Ambassador Evan Jeremy Paki.

DIPLOMATIC MISSIONS OF PARAGUAY

United Nations: 211 East 43rd St, Suite 400, New York, NY 10017; tel. (212) 687-3490; fax (212) 818-1282; e-mail paraguay@un.int; Permanent Representative ELADIO LOIZAGA.

Argentina: Las Heras 2545, C1425ASC Buenos Aires; tel. (11) 4802-3826; fax (11) 4804-0437; Chargé d'affaires a.i. Myriam Celia Torres de Segovia.

Austria: Prinz-Eugen-Str. 18/1/2/7, 1040 Vienna; tel. (1) 505-46-74; fax (1) 941-98-98; e-mail embaparviena@chello.at; Chargé d'affaires a.i. NILDA FATIMA ACOSTA GARCETE.

Belgium: 475 ave Louise, BP 21, 1050 Brussels; tel. (2) 649-90-55; fax (2) 647-42-48; e-mail embapar@skynet.be; Chargé d'affaires a.i. Raúl José Vera Bogado.

Bolivia: Edif. Illimani II, 1°, Avda 6 de Agosto y Pedro Salazar, Casilla 882, La Paz; tel. (2) 243-3176; fax (2) 243-2201; e-mail embapar@acelerate.com; Ambassador NIMIA OVIEDO DE TORALES.

Brazil: SES, Av. das Nações, Quadra 811, Lote 42, 70427-900 Brasília, DF; tel. (61) 3242-3732; fax (61) 3242-4605; e-mail embapar-sec1@yawl.com.br; Ambassador Luis González Arias.

Canada: 151 Slater St, Suite 501, Ottawa, ON K1P 5H3; tel. (613) 567-1283; fax (613) 567-1679; e-mail consularsection@embassyofparaguay.ca; internet www.embassyofparaguay.ca; Ambassador JUAN ESTEBAN O. AGUIRRE MARTÍNEZ.

Chile: Huérfanos 886, 5°, Ofs 514–515, Santiago; tel. (2) 639-4640; fax (2) 633-4426; e-mail epychemb@entelchile.net; Ambassador Juan Andrés Cardozo Domínguez.

China (Taiwan): 7/F, 9-1 Lane 62, Tien Mou West Rd, Taipei 11156; tel. (2) 28736310; fax (2) 28736312; e-mail eptaipei@seed.net.tw; Ambassador RAMÓN ANTERO DÍAZ PEREIRA.

Colombia: Carrera 7, No 72-28, Of. 302, Bogotá, DC; tel. (1) 347-0322; e-mail emboy@etb-net-co; Ambassador Felipe Robertti.

Cuba: Calle 34, No 503, entre 5 y 7, Miramar, Havana; tel. (7) 204-0884; fax (7) 204-0883; e-mail cgphav@enet.cu; Chargé d'affaires a.i. AUGUSTO OCAMPOS CABALLERO.

Ecuador: Edif. Torre Sol Verde, 8°, Avda 12 de Octubre esq. Salazar, Apdo 17-03-139, Quito; tel. (2) 290-9005; fax (2) 290-9006; e-mail embapar@uio .telconet.net; Ambassador Felipe Mendoza Olovarrieta.

France: 1 rue St Dominique, 75007 Paris; tel. 1-42-22-85-05; fax 1-42-22-83-57; e-mail paraguay.ambassade@wanadoo.fr; internet www.mre.gov.py/ embaparfrancia; Ambassador LUIS FERNANDO AVALOS GIMÉNEZ.

Germany: Hardenbergstr. 12, 10623 Berlin; tel. (30) 31998612; fax (30) 31998617; e-mail embapyde@t-online.de; Ambassador Liliane Lebron de Wenger.

Italy: Via Firenze 43, Scala A int. 17, 00187 Roma; tel. (06) 4741715; fax (06) 4745473; e-mail ambaparoman@tiscali.it; Ambassador JORGE FIGUEREDO FRATTA.

Japan: 3-12-9, Kami-Osaki, Shinagawa-ku, Tokyo 141-0021; tel. (3) 5485-3101; fax (3) 5485-3103; e-mail embapar@gol.com; internet www.embapar .jp; Ambassador Isao Taoka.

Korea, Republic: Hannam Tower Annex Bldg, 3rd Floor, 730 Hannam-dong, Yeongsan-gu, Seoul; tel. (2) 792-8335; fax (2) 792-8334; e-mail pyemc2@ kornet.net; internet www.embaparcorea.org; Ambassador CEFERINO ADRIAN VALDEZ PERALTA.

Mexico: Homero 415, 1°, esq. Hegel, Col. Polanco, Del. Miguel Hidalgo, 11570 México, DF; tel. (55) 5545-0405; fax (55) 5531-9905; e-mail embapar@ prodigy.net.mx; Ambassador José Félix Fernández Estigarribia.

Peru: Alcanfores 1286, Miraflores, Lima; tel. (1) 4474762; fax (1) 4442391; e-mail embaparpe@terra.com.pe; Chargé d'affaires a.i. FELIPE SANTIADO JARA AGUERO.

Portugal: Av. Campo Grande 4, 7° dto, 1700-092 Lisbon; tel. (21) 7965907; fax (21) 7965905; e-mail embaparlisboa@mail.telepac.pt; Chargé d'affaires a.i. Luís Domingo Laino Guanes.

South Africa: 189 Strelitzia Rd, Waterkloof Heights, Pretoria 0181; POB 95774, Waterkloof 0145; tel. (12) 3471047; fax (12) 3470403; Chargé d'affaires a.i. ARNALDO R. SALAZAR.

Spain: Doctor Fleming 3, 1°, 28036 Madrid; tel. (91) 3082746; fax (91) 3085319; e-mail embapar@arrakis.es; Ambassador Oscar J. Cabello Sarubbi.

Switzerland: Kramgasse 58, Postfach 523, 3000 Bern 8; tel. 313123222; fax 313123432; e-mail embapar@embapar.ch; Chargé d'affaires RAÚL ALBERTO FLORENTÍN ANTOLA.

United Kingdom: 3rd Floor, 344 Kensington High St, London, W14 8NS; tel. (20) 7610-4180; fax (20) 7371-4279; e-mail embapar@btconnect.com; internet www.paraguayembassy.co.uk; Chargé d'affaires a.i. Maria Christina Acosta Alvarez.

United States of America: 2400 Massachusetts Ave, NW, Washington, DC 20008; tel. (202) 483-6960; fax (202) 234-4508; Ambassador JAMES SPALDING HELLMERS.

Uruguay: Blvr Artigas 1256, Montevideo; tel. (2) 7072138; fax (2) 7083682; e-mail embapur@netgate.com.uy; internet www.geocities.com/embapur; Ambassador Ana María Figueredo Amado.

Vatican City: Via Alpinismo 24, 4° int. 1, Rome, Italy; tel. (06) 39751368; fax (06) 39745063; e-mail pyssede@mclink.it; Ambassador GERÓNIMO NARVÁEZ TORRES.

Venezuela: Quinta Paraguay, Avda Principal Macaracuay 1960, entre Avda Cuicas y Carretera del Este, Caracas; tel. (212) 257-2747; fax (212) 257-7256; e-mail embaparven@cantv.net; Ambassador Federico González Franco.

DIPLOMATIC MISSIONS OF PERU

United Nations: 820 Second Ave, Suite 1600, New York, NY 10017; tel. (212) 687-3336; fax (212) 972-6975; e-mail peru@un.int; Permanent Representative JORGE VOTO-BERNALES.

Algeria: 20 ave Franklin Roosevelt, 1er étage, 16006 Algiers; tel. (21) 68-15-95; fax (21) 68-16-96; e-mail amb.perou@eepad.dz; Ambassador José Rafael Eduardo Beraún Araníbar.

Argentina: Avda del Libertador 1720, C1425AAQ Buenos Aires; tel. (11) 4802-2000; fax (11) 4802-5887; e-mail embperu@arnet.com.ar; Ambassador JUDITH DE LA MATA FERNÁNDEZ DE PUENTE.

Australia: POB 106, Red Hill, ACT 2603; tel. (2) 6273-7351; fax (2) 6273-7354; e-mail embassy@embaperu.org.au; internet www.embaperu.org.au; Ambassador Claudio de la Puente.

Austria: Gottfried-Keller-Gasse 2/1–2, 1030 Vienna; tel. (1) 713-43-77; fax (1) 712-77-04; e-mail embajada@embaperuaustria.at; internet www .embaperuaustria.at; Ambassador CARLOS ALBERTO HIGUEROS RAMOS.

Belgium: 179 ave de Tervueren, 1150 Brussels; tel. (2) 733-33-19; fax (2) 733-48-19; e-mail comunicaciones@embassy-of-peru.be; internet www.embaperu .be; Ambassador Jorge Valdez.

Bolivia: Calle F. Guachalla 300, Casilla 668, Sopocachi, La Paz; tel. (2) 244-1250; fax (2) 244-1240; e-mail embbol@caoba.entelnet.bo; Ambassador JUAN FERNANDO JAVIER ROJAS SAMANEZ.

Brazil: SES, Av. das Nações, Quadra 811, Lote 43, 70428-900 Brasília, DF; tel. (61) 3242-9933; fax (61) 3244-9344; e-mail embperu@embperu.org.br; internet www.embperu.org.br; Ambassador Hugo Claudio de Zela Martínez.

Bulgaria: Sofia, ul. F. Zh. Kyuri 17/2/2; tel. (2) 971-37-08; fax (2) 973-33-46; e-mail peru@mail.bol.bg; Chargé d'affaires JULIO VEGA ERAUSQUÍN.

Canada: 130 Albert St, Suite 1901, Ottawa, ON K1P 5G4; tel. (613) 238-1777; fax (613) 232-3062; e-mail emperuca@bellnet.ca; internet www .embassyofperu.ca; Ambassador Guillermo José Miguel Russo Checa.

Chile: Avda Andrés Bello 1751, Casilla 16277, Providencia, Santiago; tel. (2) 235-2356; fax (2) 235-8139; e-mail embstgo@entelchile.net; Ambassador HUGO OTERO LANZAROTTI.

China, People's Republic: 1-91 San Li Tun, Bangonglou, Beijing 100600; tel. (10) 65323477; fax (10) 65322178; e-mail embaperu-pekin@rree.gob.pe; internet www.embperu.cn.net; Ambassador Jesús J. Wu Luy.

Colombia: Calle 80A, No 6-50, Bogotá, DC; tel. (1) 257-0505; fax (1) 249-8581; e-mail embajadaperu@supercabletv.net.co; internet www .embajadadelperu.org.co; Ambassador JOSÉ ANTONIO MEIER ESPINOZA.

Costa Rica: Del Colegio de Igenieros y Arquitectos, 350 m al norte, Urb. Freses, Curridabat, Apdo 4248, 1000 San José; tel. 253-4671; fax 253-0457; e-mail embajadaperu.costarrica@gmail.com; Ambassador Oscar Alberto Gutiérrez La Madrid.

Cuba: Calle 30, No 107, entre 1 y 3, Miramar, Havana; tel. (7) 204-3570; fax (7) 204-2636; e-mail embaperu@embaperu.cu; Ambassador JUAN GERMÁN KOSTER KOSTER.

Czech Republic: Muchova 9, 160 00 Prague 6; tel. 224316210; fax 224314749; e-mail embaperu.praga@post.cz; Ambassador Alberto Efraín Salas Barahona.

Dominican Republic: Mayreni 31, Urbanización Los Cacicazgos, Santo Domingo, DN; tel. 482-3300; fax 482-3334; e-mail embaperu@verizon.net .do; Ambassador VICENTE ALEJANDRO AZULA DE LA GUERRA.

Ecuador: Avda República de El Salvador 495 e Irlanda, Apdo 17-07-9380, Quito; tel. (2) 246-8410; fax (2) 225-2560; e-mail embaperu-quito@rree.gob .pe; Ambassador Vicente Rojas Escalante.

Egypt: 8 Sharia Kamel esh-Shenawi, Cairo (Garden City); tel. (2) 3562973; fax (2) 3557985; Ambassador MANUEL VERAMENDI I. SERRA.

El Salvador: Avda Masferrer Norte 17p, Cumbres de la Escalafón, Col. Escalón, San Salvador; tel. 2275-5566; fax 2259-8082; e-mail embperu@ telesal.net; Ambassador Luis Juan Chuquihuara Chil.

Finland: Annankatu 31–33c 44, 00100 Helsinki; tel. (9) 7599400; fax (9) 75994040; e-mail embassy.peru@peruemb.inet.fi; Ambassador MANUEL PICASSO BOTTO.

France: 50 ave Kléber, 75116 Paris; tel. 1-53-70-42-00; fax 1-47-04-32-55; e-mail perou.ambassade@amb-perou.fr; internet www.amb-perou.fr; Ambassador Harry Belevan-McBride.

Germany: Mohrenstr. 42, 10117 Berlin; tel. (30) 2064103; fax (30) 20641077; e-mail gabinete@embaperu.de; internet www.botschaft-peru.de; Ambassador PROF. DR FEDERICO AUGUSTO KAUFFMANN DOIG.

Greece: Odos Semitelou 2, 115 28 Athens; tel. (210) 7792761; fax (210) 7792905; e-mail lepruate@compulink.gr; Ambassador Luis Felipe Gálvez Villarroel.

Guatemala: 5a Avda 13-46, Zona 9, Guatemala City; tel. 2331-8558; fax 2334-3744; e-mail leprugua@concyt.gob.gt; internet www.embajadaperu -guatemala.org; Ambassador ALFREDO JOSÉ CASTRO PÉREZ-CANETTO.

Honduras: Col. La Reforma, Calle Principal 2618, Tegucigalpa; tel. 221-0596; fax 236-6070; e-mail embajdadelperu@cablecolor.hn; Ambassador Gustavo Otero Zapata.

Hungary: 1023 Budapest, Vérhalom u. 12–16; tel. (1) 326-0984; fax (1) 326-1087; e-mail peru1@axelero.hu; internet www.peru.hu; Ambassador GUILLERMO RUSSO CHECA.

India: G-15 Maharani Bagh, New Delhi 110 065; tel. (11) 26312610; fax (11) 26312557; e-mail info@embaperuindia.com; internet www.embaperuindia .com; Ambassador Luis Hernandez.

Indonesia: Menara Rajawali, 12th Floor, Jalan Mega Kuningan, Lot 5.1, Kawasan Mega Kuningan, Jakarta 12950; tel. (21) 5761820; fax (21) 5761825; e-mail embaperu@cbn.net.id; Ambassador JUAN JOSÉ ALVAREZ VITA.

Israel: Rehov Medinat Hayehudim 60, Entrance A, 2nd Floor, Herzliya Pituach 46766; tel. 9-9578835; fax 9-9568495; e-mail emperu@012.net.il; Ambassador Luis Mendivil.

Italy: Via Francesco Siacci 2B, 00197 Roma; tel. (06) 80691510; fax (06) 80691777; e-mail emb.peru@aambasciataperu2.191.it; tel. www.ambasciataperu.it; Ambassador CARLOS ROCA CÁCERES.

Jamaica: 23 Barbados Ave, Kingston 5; tel. 920-5027; fax 920-4360; e-mail embaperu-kingston@rree.gob.pe; Ambassador Luis Sándiga Cabrera.

Japan: 4-100-1, Higashi, Shibuya-ku, Tokyo 150-0011; tel. (3) 3406-4243; fax (3) 3409-7589; e-mail embperutokyo@embperujapan.org; Ambassador HUGO PALMA.

Korea, Republic: Daeyungak Bldg, Suite 2002, 25-5, 1-ga, Jungmu-no, Jung-gu, Seoul 100-706; tel. (2) 757-1735; fax (2) 757-1738; e-mail lpruseul@uriel .net; Ambassador Doraliza López Bravo Vda de Ruíz.

Malaysia: Wisma Selangor Dredging, 6th Floor, South Block, 142A Jalan Ampang, 50450 Kuala Lumpur; tel. (3) 21633034; fax (3) 21633039; e-mail embperu@streamyx.com; Ambassador ALEJANDRO GORDILLO FERNÁNDEZ.

Mexico: Paseo de la Reforma 2601, Col. Lomas Reforma, Del. Miguel Hidalgo, 11000 México, DF; tel. (55) 5570-2443; fax (55) 5259-0530; e-mail embaperu@prodigy.net.mx; Ambassador Carlos Berninzón Devéscovi.

Morocco: 16 rue d'Ifrane, 10000 Rabat; tel. (3) 7723236; fax (3) 7702803; e-mail embajadadelperuenmarruecos@msn.com; Ambassador JORGE ABARCA DEL CARPIO.

Netherlands: Nassauplein 4, 2585 EA The Hague; tel. (70) 3653500; fax (70) 3651929; e-mail info@embassyofperu.nl; Chargé d'affaires a.i. Pedro Roberto Reategui Gamarra.

New Zealand: Cigna House, Level 8, 40 Mercer St, POB 2566, Wellington; tel. (4) 499-8087; fax (4) 499-8057; e-mail embassy.peru@xtra.co.nz; internet www.embassyofperu.org.nz; Ambassador CARLOS ZAPATA LÓPEZ.

Nicaragua: Las Cumbres, Casa D-13, contiguo a la Residencia del diputado Wilfredo Navarro Moreira, Apdo 211, Managua; tel. 266-8677; fax 266-1408; e-mail peru1@cablenet.com.ni; Ambassador Harry Gerardo Morris Abarco.

Panama: Edif. World Trade Center, 12°, Calle 53, Urb. Marbella, Apdo 4516, Panamá 5; tel. 223-1112; fax 269-6809; e-mail embaperu@pananet.com; Ambassador JOSÉ BARBA CABALLERO.

Paraguay: Feliciano Marecos 441, casi Agustín Barrios y España, Manorá, Casilla 433, Asunción; tel. (21) 60-0226; fax (21) 60-7327; e-mail embperu@ embperu.com.py; Ambassador Enrique Palacios Reyes.

Poland: 02-516 Warsaw, ul. Starościńska 1/3; tel. (22) 6468806; fax (22) 6468617; e-mail embperpl@atomnet.pl; internet www.perupol.pl; Ambassador JORGE DANTE FEDERICO CHÁVEZ SOTO.

Portugal: Rua Castilho 50, 4° dto, 1250-071 Lisbon; tel. (21) 3827470; fax (21) 3827479; e-mail embperuport@mail.telepac.pt; Ambassador Luzmila Zanabria Ishikawa.

Romania: 011346 Bucharest 1, Şos. Pavel Kiseleff 18; tel. (21) 2231956; fax (21) 2231088; e-mail embaperu@pcnet.ro; Ambassador ELARD ESCALA SANCHEZ-BARRETO.

Russian Federation: 121002 Moscow, Smolenskii bulv. 22/14/15; tel. (495) 248-27-66; fax (495) 230-20-00; e-mail leprumoscu@mtu-net.ru; Ambassador Dr Humberto Umeres Alvares.

Singapore: 390 Orchard Rd, 12-03 Palais Renaissance, Singapore 238871; tel. 67388595; fax 67388601; e-mail embperu@pacific.net.sg; internet www .embassyperu.org.sg; Ambassador J. ARTURO MONTOYA.

South Africa: Brooklyn Gardens Bldg, Block A, 1st Floor, 235 Veale St, Cnr Middel St, Nieuw Muckleneuk, Pretoria 0181; POB 907, Groenkloof 0027; tel. (12) 3468744; fax (12) 3468886; e-mail embaperu2@telkomsa.net; Ambassador Félix César Calderón.

Spain: Príncipe de Vergara 36, 5° dcha, 28001 Madrid; tel. (91) 4314242; fax (91) 5776861; e-mail lepru@embajadaperu.es; Ambassador JOSÉ LUIS PÉREZ SÁNCHEZ-CERRO.

Sweden: Brunnsgt. 21b, 2nd Floor, 111 38 Stockholm; tel. (8) 440-87-40; fax (8) 20-55-92; e-mail info@peruembassy.se; internet www.peruembassy.se; Chargé d'affaires a.i. Jorge Arturo Jarama Alvan.

Switzerland: Thunstr. 36, 3005 Bern; tel. 313518555; fax 313518570; e-mail infoperu@bluewin.ch; Ambassador ELIZABETH ASTETE RODRÍGUEZ.

Thailand: Glas Haus Bldg, 16th Floor, 1 Soi Sukhumvit 25, Khet Wattana, Bangkok 10110; tel. (2) 260-6243; fax (2) 260-6244; e-mail peru@peruthai.or .th; internet www.peru.org.pe; Ambassador Carlos Manuel Velasco Mendiola.

United Kingdom: 52 Sloane St, London, SW1X 9SP; tel. (20) 7235-1917; fax (20) 7235-4463; e-mail postmaster@peruembassy-uk.com; internet www .peruembassy-uk.com; Ambassador RICARDO LUNA MENDOZA.

United States of America: 1700 Massachusetts Ave, NW, Washington, DC 20036; tel. (202) 833-9860; fax (202) 659-8124; e-mail webadmin@ embassyofperu.us; internet www.peruvianembassy.us; Ambassador Felipe Ortiz de Zevallos Madueño.

Uruguay: Obligado 1384, 11300 Montevideo; tel. (2) 7076862; fax (2) 7077793; e-mail emba8@embaperu.org.uy; internet www.angelfire.com/ country/embaperu; Ambassador MAX DE LA FUENTE PREM.

Vatican City: Via di Porta Angelica 63, 00193 Rome, Italy; tel. (06) 68308535; fax (06) 6896059; e-mail embaperuva@tin.it; Ambassador Alfonso Dámaso Antonio Rivero Monsalve.

Venezuela: Andres Bello, 7°, Ofs 71-72 (Torre Oeste) y 73-74 (Torre Este), Maripérez, Caracas; tel. (212) 264-1483; fax (212) 265-7592; e-mail leprucaracas@cantv.net; Ambassador DR LUIS SANTA MARÍA CALDERÓN.

DIPLOMATIC MISSIONS OF PHILIPPINES

United Nations: 556 Fifth Ave, 5th Floor, New York, NY 10036; tel. (212) 764-1300; fax (212) 840-8602; e-mail misunphil@aol.com; internet www.un .int/phillipines; Permanent Representative Hilario G. Davide.

Argentina: Mariscal Ramón Castilla 3075/3085, C1425DZG Buenos Aires; tel. (11) 4807-3334; fax (11) 4804-1595; e-mail pheba@fibertel.com.ar; internet www.buenosairespe.com.ar; Chargé d'affaires a.i. EDGARDO R. MANUEL.

Australia: 1 Moonah Place, Yarralumla, Canberra, ACT 2600; tel. (2) 6273-2535; fax (2) 6273-3984; e-mail cbrpe@philembassy.org.au; internet www .philembassy.org.au; Ambassador Ernesto Hernandez de Leon.

Austria: Laurenzerberg 2, 1010 Vienna; tel. (1) 533-24-01; fax (1) 533-24-01-24; e-mail office@philippine-embassy.at; internet www.philippine-embassy .at; Ambassador LINGLINGAY LACANLALE.

Bahrain: POB 26681, Villa 992, Rd 3119, Area 331, Manama; tel. 17250990; fax 17258583; e-mail manamape@batelco.com.bh; Ambassador Eduardo Pablo M. Maglaya.

Bangladesh: House 6, Rd 101, Gulshan 2, Dhaka 1212; tel. (2) 9881590; fax (2) 8823686; e-mail philembl@citechco.net; Ambassador ZENAIDA TACORDA-RABAGO.

Belgium: 297 ave Molière, 1050 Brussels; tel. (2) 340-33-77; fax (2) 345-64-25; e-mail brussels@philembassy.be; Ambassador Cristina G. Ortega.

Brazil: SEN, Av. das Nações, Lote 01, 70431-900 Brasília, DF; tel. (61) 3223-5143; fax (61) 3226-7411; e-mail pg@persocom.com.br; Ambassador TERESITA V. G. BARSANA.

Brunei: 17 Simpang 126, Km 2, Jalan Tutong, Bandar Seri Begawan BA 2111; tel. 2241465; fax 2237707; e-mail bruneipe@brunet.bn; Ambassador Virginia H. Benavidez.

Cambodia: 33 rue 294, Khan Chamkarmon, Sangkat Tonle Bassac, BP 2018, Phnom-Penh; tel. (23) 215145; fax (23) 215143; e-mail phnompenhpe@online .com.kh; Ambassador LOURDES G. MORALES.

Canada: 130 Albert St, Suite 606, Ottawa, ON K1P 5G4; tel. (613) 233-1121; fax (613) 233-4165; e-mail embassy@philippineembassy.ca; internet philippineembassy.ca; Ambassador José S. Brillantes.

Chile: Félix de Amesti 367, Santiago; tel. (2) 208-1313; fax (2) 208-1400; e-mail santiagope@dfa.gov.ph; Ambassador MARÍA CONSUELO PUYAT-REYES.

China, People's Republic: 23 Xiu Shui Bei Jie, Jian Guo Men Wai, Beijing 100600; tel. (10) 65321872; fax (10) 65323761; e-mail main@philembassy -china.org; internet www.philembassy-china.org; Ambassador Sonia Brady.

Cuba: Avda 5, No 2207, esq. 24, Miramar, Havana; tel. (7) 204-1372; fax (7) 204-2915; e-mail philhavpe@enet.cu; Ambassador GEORGE B. REYES.

Czech Republic: Senovážné náměstí 8, 110 00 Prague 1; tel. 224216397; fax 224216390; e-mail praguepe@phembassy.cz; Ambassador Carmelita Rodríguez Salas.

Egypt: Villa 28, Sharia 200, Cairo (Degla Maadi); tel. (2) 25213062; fax (2) 25213048; e-mail cairope@dfa.gov.ph; Ambassador PETRONILA P. GARCIA.

France: 4 Hameau de Boulainvilliers, 75016 Paris; tel. 1-44-14-57-00; fax 1-46-47-56-00; e-mail ambaphilparis@wanadoo.fr; Ambassador José Abeto Zaide.

Germany: Uhlandstr. 97, 10715 Berlin; tel. (30) 8649500; fax (30) 8732551; e-mail info@philippine-embassy.de; internet www.philippine-embassy.de; Ambassador DELIA DOMINGO-ALBERT.

Greece: Odos Antheon 26, Palaio Psychiko, 154 52 Athens; tel. (210) 6721883; fax (210) 6721872; e-mail athensspe@otenet.gr; Ambassador Rigoberto D. Tiglao.

Hungary: 1026 Budapest, Gábor Áron u. 58; tel. (1) 391-4300; fax (1) 200-5528; e-mail phbuda@mail.datanet.hu; Ambassador ALEJANDRO D. DEL ROSARIO.

India: 50n Nyaya Marg, Chanakyapuri, New Delhi 110 021; tel. (11) 26889091; fax (11) 26876401; e-mail newdelhipe@bol.net.in; Ambassador Teresita V. Berner.

Indonesia: Jalan Imam Bonjol 6–8, Jakarta Pusat 10310; tel. (21) 3100334; fax (21) 3151167; e-mail phjkt@indo.net.id; Ambassador VIDAL E. QUEROL.

Iran: POB 19395-4797, 5 Khayyam St, Vali-e-Asr Ave, Tehran; tel. (21) 22668774; fax (21) 22668990; e-mail tehranpe@yahoo.com; internet www .philippine-embassy.ir; Ambassador Aladin Villacorte.

Iraq: POB 3236, 4/22/915 al-Jadriyah, Hay al-Jamiyah, Baghdad; tel. (1) 776-2696; fax (1) 719-3228; e-mail baghdadpe@dfa.gov.ph; Chargé d'affaires a.i. WILFREDO R. CUYUGAN.

Israel: Textile Centre Bldg, 13th Floor, 2 Kaufman St, Tel-Aviv 68012; tel. 3-5175263; fax 3-5102229; e-mail filembis@netvision.net.il; Ambassador Antonio C. Modena.

Italy: Viale delle Medaglie d'Oro 112–114, 00136 Roma; tel. (06) 39746621; fax (06) 39740872; e-mail philrepfao@libero.it; Ambassador PHILIPPE J. LHUILLIER.

Japan: 5-15-5, Roppongi, Minato-ku, Tokyo 106-8537; tel. (3) 5562-1600; fax (3) 5562-1603; e-mail info@tokyope.org; internet www.tokyope.org; Ambassador Domingo L. Siazon, Jr.

Jordan: POB 925207, Amman 11190; tel. (6) 5923748; fax (6) 5923744; e-mail ammanpe@wanadoo.jo; Ambassador JOSE DEL ROSARIO, Jr.

Korea, Republic: 34-44, Itaewon 1-dong, Yeongsan-gu, Seoul; tel. (2) 796-7387; fax (2) 796-0827; e-mail seoulpe@gmail.com; Ambassador Luis Teodoro Cruz.

Kuwait: POB 26288, 13123 Safat, Area 7, No. 103, Villa 503 Jabriya, Kuwait City; tel. 5349099; fax 5329319; e-mail kuwaitpe@dfa.gov.ph; internet www .philembassykuwait.gov.kw; Ambassador RICARDO M. ENDAYA.

Laos: Ban Saphanthong Kang, Sisattanak, BP 2415, Vientiane; tel. (21) 452490; fax (21) 452493; e-mail pelaopdr@laotel.com; Ambassador Elizabeth P. Buensuceso.

Lebanon: POB 136631, 1er et 2e étages, Immeuble Design, rue Abdullah Machnouk, Beirut; tel. (1) 791092; fax (1) 791095; e-mail beirutpe@cyberia .net.lb; Ambassador RAMONITO S. MARINO.

Libya: POB 12508, Km 7 Abu Nawas, Hay Andalus, Gargaresh, Tripoli; tel. (21) 4833966; fax (21) 4836158; e-mail tripoli_pe76@lttnet.net; Ambassador Bayani V. Mangibin.

Malaysia: 1 Changkat Kia Peng, 50450 Kuala Lumpur; tel. (3) 21484233; fax (3) 21483576; e-mail consular@philembassykl.org.my; internet www .philembassykl.org.my; Ambassador VICTORIANO M. LECAROS.

Mexico: Sierra Gorda 175, Col. Lomas de Chapultepec, Del. Miguel Hidalgo, 11000 México, DF; tel. (55) 5202-8456; fax (55) 5202-8403; e-mail ambamexi@att.net.mx; Ambassador Antonio Manuel Lagdameo Revilla.

Myanmar: 50 Saya San Rd, Bahan Township, Yangon; tel. (1) 558149; fax (1) 558154; e-mail phyangon@mptmail.net.mm; Ambassador PHOEBE ABAYA GOMEZ.

Netherlands: Laan Copes van Cattenburch 125, 2585 EZ The Hague; tel. (70) 3604820; fax (70) 3560030; e-mail ph@bart.nl; internet www.philembassy.nl; Ambassador Romeo A. Arguelles.

New Zealand: 50 Hobson St, Thorndon, POB 12-042, Wellington; tel. (4) 472-9848; fax (4) 472-5170; e-mail embassy@wellington-pe.co.nz; Ambassador DR BIENVENIDO V. TEJANO.

Nigeria: 16 Lake Chad Cres., cnr Kainji St, Maitama, Abuja; tel. (9) 4133649; fax (9) 4137650; Ambassador Masaranga R. Umpa.

Oman: POB 420, Madinat Qaboos 115; tel. 24605140; fax 24605176; e-mail muscatpe@omantel.net.om; Ambassador ACMAD D. OMAR.

Pakistan: House 20c, College Rd, F-7/2, Islamabad; tel. (51) 2824933; fax (51) 2653665; e-mail isdpe@isb.comsats.net.pk; Ambassador Jaime J. Yambao.

Palau: 2nd Flr, M. Ueki Bldg, Iyebukel Hamlet, POB 1497, Koror, PW 96940; tel. 488-5077; fax 488-6310; e-mail philkor@palaunet.com; Ambassador RAMONCITO MARIÑO.

Papua New Guinea: POB 5916, Boroko, NCD; tel. 3256577; fax 3231803; Ambassador Shirley Ho-Vicario.

Qatar: POB 24900, Doha; tel. 4831585; fax 4831595; e-mail dohape@qatar .net.qa; Ambassador ISAIAS FLORENDO BEGONIA.

Romania: 050453 Bucharest 5, Str. Carol Davila 105–107, 5th Floor, Rm 10–11; tel. (21) 3198252; fax (21) 3198253; e-mail bucharestpe@rdsmail.ro; Ambassador Teresita C. Daza.

Russian Federation: 121099 Moscow, Karmanitskii per. 6; tel. (495) 241-05-63; fax (495) 241-26-30; e-mail moscowpe@utsmail.ru; internet www.phil -embassy.ru; Ambassador ERNESTO V. LLAMAS.

Saudi Arabia: POB 94366, Riyadh 11693; tel. (1) 482-0507; fax (1) 488-3945; e-mail filembry@sbm.net.sa; Ambassador Antonio P. Villamor.

Singapore: 20 Nassim Rd, Singapore 258395; tel. 67373977; fax 67339544; e-mail php@pacific.net.sg; internet www.philippine-embassy.org.sg; Ambassador BELEN FULE-ANOTA.

South Africa: 54 Nicholson St, Muckleneuk, Pretoria 0181; POB 2562, Brooklyn Sq. 0075; tel. (12) 3460451; fax (12) 3460454; e-mail pretoriape@ mweb.co.za; internet mzone.mweb.co.za/residents/pretoriape/; Ambassador Virgilio A. Reyes, Jr.

Spain: Eresma 2, 28002 Madrid; tel. (91) 7823830; fax (91) 4116606; e-mail madridpe@terra.es; internet www.philmadrid.com; Ambassador JOSEPH DELANO BERNARDO Y MEDINA.

Sweden: Skeppsbron 20, 1st Floor, POB 2219, 103 15 Stockholm; tel. (8) 23-56-65; fax (8) 14-07-14; e-mail stockholm@philembassy.se; internet www .philembassy.se; Ambassador Maria Zeneida Angara Collinson.

Switzerland: Kirchenfeldstr. 73–75, 3005 Bern; tel. 313501717; fax 313522602; e-mail berne_pe@bluewin.ch; Ambassador MINERVA JEAN FALCON.

Thailand: 760 Thanon Sukhumvit, cnr Soi 30/1, Klongtan, Klongtoey, Bangkok 10110; tel. (2) 259-0139; fax (2) 259-2809; e-mail inquiry@ philembassy-bangkok.net; internet www.philembassy-bangkok.net; Ambassador Antonio V. Rodriguez.

Timor-Leste: Rooms 8–10, Hotel Turismo, Rua Direitos Humanos, Bidau Lecidere, Dili; tel. 33310408; fax 3310407; e-mail dilipe@dfa.gov.ph; Ambassador FARITA A. AGUILUCHO-ONG.

Turkey: Mahatma Gandhi Cad. 56, 06700 Gaziosmanpaşa, Ankara; tel. (312) 4465831; fax (312) 4465733; e-mail ankarape@dfa.gov.ph; Ambassador Bahnarim A. Guinomla.

779

United Arab Emirates: POB 3215, Plot 97, Villa 2, St 5, E-18/02, Abu Dhabi; tel. (2) 6415922; fax (2) 6412559; e-mail auhpe@emirates.net.ae; Ambassador LIBRAN N. CABACTULAN.

United Kingdom: 9a Palace Green, London, W8 4QE; tel. (20) 7937-1600; fax (20) 7937-2925; e-mail londonpe@dfa.gov.ph; internet www.philemb.org.uk; Ambassador Edgardo B. Espiritu.

United States of America: 1600 Massachusetts Ave, NW, Washington, DC 20036-2274; tel. (202) 467-9300; fax (202) 467-9417; e-mail info@philippineembassy-usa.org; internet www.philippineembassy-usa.org; Ambassador WILLY C. GAA.

Vatican City: Via Paolo VI 29, 00193 Rome, Italy; tel. (06) 68308020; fax (06) 6834076; e-mail vaticanpe@philamsee.mysam.it; Ambassador Leonida L. Vera.

Venezuela: 5a Transversal de Altamira, Quinta Filipinas, Altamira, Caracas 1060; tel. (212) 266-4725; fax (212) 266-6443; e-mail caracas@embassyph.com; Ambassador RONALD B. ALLAREY.

Viet Nam: 27b Tran Hung Dao, Hanoi; tel. (4) 9437873; fax (4) 9435760; e-mail hanoipe@dfa.gov.ph; Ambassador Estrella Berenguel.

DIPLOMATIC MISSIONS OF POLAND

United Nations: 9 East 66th St, New York, NY 10021; tel. (212) 744-2506; fax (212) 517-6771; e-mail poland@un.int; internet www.un.int/poland; Permanent Representative ANDRZEJ TOWPIK.

Albania: Rruga e Durrësit 123, Tirana; tel. (4) 234190; fax (4) 233364; e-mail polemb@albaniaonline.net; internet www.tirana.polemb.net; Ambassador (vacant).

Algeria: BP 60, 37 ave Mustafa Ali Khodja, el-Biar, Algiers; tel. (21) 92-25-53; fax (21) 92-14-35; e-mail marekmal@wissal.dz; Ambassador LIDIA MILKA-WIECZORKIEWICZ.

Angola: Rua Comandante N'zagi 21–23, Alvalade, CP 1340, Luanda; tel. 222323088; fax 222323086; e-mail embpol@netangola.com; internet www.luanda.polemb.net; Chargé d'affaires a.i. Piotr Myśliwiec.

Argentina: Marqués de Aguado 2870, C1425CEB Buenos Aires; tel. (11) 4802-9681; fax (11) 4802-9683; e-mail polemb@datamarkets.com.ar; Ambassador ZDZISŁAW JAN RYN.

Armenia: 0010 Yerevan, Hanrapetutiun St 44a; tel. (10) 54-24-93; fax (10) 54-24-98; e-mail armpolemb@ct.futuro.pl; internet www.erewan.polemb.net; Ambassador Tomasz Knothe.

Australia: 7 Turrana St, Yarralumla, ACT 2600; tel. (2) 6273-1208; fax (2) 6273-3184; e-mail embassy@poland.org.au; internet www.poland.org.au; Chargé d'affaires a.i. GRZEGORZ SOKOL.

Austria: Hietzinger Hauptstr. 42c, 1130 Vienna; tel. (1) 870-15-00-0; fax (1) 870-15-22-2; e-mail sekretariat@botschaftrp.at; internet www.wien.polemb.net; Chargé d'affaires a.i. Jarosław Dziedzic.

Azerbaijan: 1000 Baku, Icheri Şeher, Kichik Gala küç. 2; tel. (12) 492-01-14; fax (12) 492-02-14; e-mail embpol@azeurotel.com; internet www.baku.polemb.net; Ambassador KRYSZTOF KRAJEWSKI.

Belarus: 220034 Minsk, vul. Rumyantsava 6; tel. (17) 288-21-14; fax (17) 236-49-92; e-mail ambasada@minsk.polemb.net; internet www.minsk.polemb.net; Ambassador Henrik Litwin.

Belgium: 29 ave des Gaulois, 1040 Brussels; tel. (2) 739-01-51; fax (2) 736-18-81; internet www.bruksela.polemb.net; Ambassador SŁAWOMIR CZARLEWSKI.

Bosnia and Herzegovina: 71000 Sarajevo, Dola 13; tel. (33) 201142; fax (33) 233796; e-mail amsar@bih.net.ba; internet www.sarajewo.polemb.net; Ambassador Andrzej Tyszkiewicz.

Brazil: SES, Av. das Nações, Quadra 809, Lote 33, 70423-900 Brasília, DF; tel. (61) 3212-8000; fax (61) 3242-8543; e-mail embaixada@polonia.org.br; internet www.polonia.org.br; Ambassador JACEK JUNOSZA-KISIELEWSKI.

Bulgaria: 1000 Sofia, ul. Chan Krum 46; tel. (2) 987-26-10; fax (2) 987-29-39; e-mail polamba@internet-bg.net; internet www.sofia.polemb.net; Ambassador Andrzej Papierz.

Cambodia: 767 blvd Monivong, BP 58, Phnom-Penh; tel. (23) 217782; fax (23) 217781; e-mail emb.pol.pp@online.com.kh; internet www.phnompenh.polemb.net; Ambassador (vacant).

Canada: 443 Daly Ave, Ottawa, ON K1N 6H3; tel. (613) 789-0468; fax (613) 789-1218; e-mail ottawa@polishembassy.ca; internet www.polishembassy.ca; Ambassador Piotr Ogrodzinski.

Chile: Mar del Plata 2055, Santiago; tel. (2) 204-1213; fax (2) 204-9332; e-mail embajador.polonia@entelchile.net; internet www.polonia.cl; Ambassador JAROSIAW SPYRA.

China, People's Republic: 1 Ri Tan Lu, Jian Guo Men Wai, Chao Yang Qu, Beijing 100600; tel. (10) 65321235; fax (10) 65321745; e-mail polska@public2.bta.net.cn; internet www.pekin.polemb.net; Ambassador Krzysztof Szumski.

Colombia: Calle 104A, No 23-48, Bogotá, DC; tel. (1) 214-0400; fax (1) 214-0854; e-mail polemb@cable.net.co; internet www.bogota.polemb.net; Ambassador HENRYK KOBIEROWSKI.

Costa Rica: De la Iglesia Santa Teresita 300 m este, 3307, Barrio Escalante, Apdo 664, 2010 San José; tel. 234-7411; fax 234-7900; e-mail embajpolonia1@racsa.co.cr; internet www.polonia-emb-cr.com/indes.php; Ambassador Andrzej Braiter.

Croatia: 10000 Zagreb, Krležin Gvozd 3; tel. (1) 4899444; fax (1) 4834577; e-mail ambasada-polska@zg.t-com.hr; Chargé d'affaires a.i. DARIUSZ WIŚNIEWSKI.

Cuba: Calle G, No 452, esq. 19, Vedado, Havana; tel. (7) 833-2439; fax (7) 833-2442; e-mail havpolemb@ct.futuro.pl; internet www.embajadapolonia.cu; Chargé d'affaires a.i. Daniel Gromann.

Cyprus: POB 22743, 12–14 Kennedy Ave, 1087 Nicosia; tel. 22753784; fax 22751981; e-mail secretariat@polamb.org.cy; Ambassador ZBIGNIEW SZYMANSKI.

Czech Republic: Valdštejnská 8, 118 01 Prague 1; tel. 257530388; fax 257530135; e-mail ambrpczechy@mbox.vol.cz; internet www.prague.polemb.net; Ambassador Jan Pastwa.

Denmark: Richelieus Allé 12, 2900 Hellerup; tel. 39-46-77-00; fax 39-46-77-66; e-mail mail@ambpol.dk; internet www.copenhagen.polemb.net; Ambassador ADAM HALAMSKI.

Egypt: 5 Sharia el-Aziz Osman, Cairo (Zamalek); tel. (2) 7367456; fax (2) 7355427; e-mail secretary@kair.polemb.net; internet www.kair.polemb.net; Ambassador Jan Natkański.

Estonia: Suur-Karja 1, Tallinn 10140; tel. 627-8206; fax 644-5221; e-mail poola.info@mail.ee; internet www.tallinn.polemb.net; Ambassador TOMASZ CHIOŃ.

Ethiopia: Bole Sub-City, Kebele 3, House No. 2111, POB 27207, Addis Ababa; tel. (11) 6185401; fax (11) 6610000; e-mail polemb@ethionet.et; internet www.addisabeba.polemb.net; Chargé d'affaires a.i. Danuta Bolimowska.

Finland: Armas Lindgrenintie 21, 00570 Helsinki; tel. (9) 618280; fax (9) 6847477; e-mail amb.poland@helsinki.inet.fi; internet www.helsinki.polemb.net; Ambassador JOANNA HOFMAN.

France: 1–3 rue de Talleyrand, 75343 Paris Cedex 07; tel. 1-43-17-34-05; fax 1-43-17-35-07; e-mail info@ambassade.pologne.net; internet www.paris.polemb.net; Ambassador Tomasz Orłowski.

Georgia: 0108 Tbilisi, Zubalashvili 19; tel. (32) 92-03-98; fax (32) 92-03-97; e-mail ambpolgruzja@access.sanet.ge; internet www.tbilisi.polemb.net; Ambassador JACEK MULTANOWSKI.

Germany: Lassenstr. 19–21, 14193 Berlin; tel. (30) 223130; fax (30) 2213155; e-mail info@botschaft-polen.de; internet www.berlin.polemb.net; Ambassador Dr Marek Władysław Prawda.

Greece: Odos Chryssanthemon 22, Palaio Psychiko, 154 52 Athens; tel. (210) 6797700; fax (210) 6797711; e-mail info@poland-embassy.gr; internet www.poland-embassy.gr; Ambassador MICHAL KLINGER.

Hungary: 1068 Budapest, Városligeti fasor 16; tel. (1) 413-8200; fax (1) 351-1722; e-mail info@polishemb.hu; internet www.budapeszt.polemb.net; Ambassador Joanna Stempinska Urno.

India: 50M Shanti Path, Chanakyapuri, New Delhi 110 021; tel. (11) 41496900; fax (11) 26871914; e-mail polemb@airtelbroadband.in; internet www.newdelhi.polemb.net; Ambassador DR KRZYSZTOF MAJKA.

Indonesia: Jalan H. R. Rasuna Said, Kav. X, Blok IV/3, Jakarta Selatan 12950; tel. (21) 2525938; fax (21) 2525958; e-mail consular@polandembjak.org; internet www.jakarta.polemb.net; Ambassador Tomasz Łukaszuk.

Iran: POB 11365-3489, Africa Ave, Piruz St, No. 1/3, Tehran; tel. (21) 88787262; fax (21) 88788774; e-mail info@embpoltehran.com; internet www.embpoltehran.com; Ambassador WITOLD SMIDOWSKI.

Iraq: 22–24/60/904 Hay al-Wihda, Baghdad; tel. (1) 719-0297; fax (1) 719-0296; e-mail ambaspol@tlen.pl; Ambassador Edward Pietrzyk.

Ireland: 5 Ailesbury Rd, Ballsbridge, Dublin 4; tel. (1) 2830855; fax (1) 2698309; e-mail info@dublin.polemb.net; internet www.dublin.polemb.net; Ambassador TADEUSZ SZUMOWSKI.

Israel: 16 Soutine St, Tel-Aviv 64684; tel. 3-7253111; fax 3-5237806; e-mail embpol@netvision.net.il; internet www.telaviv.polemb.net; Ambassador Agnieszka Magdziak-Miszewska.

Italy: Via Pietro Paolo Rubens 20, 00197 Roma; tel. (06) 36204200; fax (06) 3217895; e-mail ufficio.stampa@ambasciatapolonia.it; internet www.rzym.polemb.net; Ambassador JERZY CHMIELEWSKI.

Japan: 2-13-5, Mita, Meguro-ku, Tokyo 153-0062; tel. (3) 5794-7020; fax (3) 5794-7024; e-mail polamb@poland.or.jp; internet www.tokio.polemb.net; Ambassador Marcin Rybicki.

Jordan: POB 942050, Amman 11194; tel. (6) 5512593; fax (6) 5512595; e-mail polemb@nol.com.jo; Ambassador ANDRZEJ BIERA.

Kazakhstan: 050059 Almaty, Jarkent 9; tel. (727) 258-16-17; fax (727) 258-15-50; e-mail ambpol@mail.kz; internet www.almaty.polemb.net; Ambassador (vacant).

Kenya: Kabarnet Rd, off Ngong Rd, Woodley, POB 30086, 00100 Nairobi; tel. (20) 3872811; fax (20) 3872814; e-mail ambnairo@kenyaweb.com; internet www.nairobi.polemb.net; Ambassador WOJCIECH JASINSKI.

Korea, Democratic People's Republic: Munsudong, Taedongkang District, Pyongyang; tel. (2) 3817327; fax (2) 3817634; e-mail phenian@polemb.net; Ambassador Roman Iwaszkiewicz.

Korea, Republic: 70, Sagan-dong, Jongno-gu, Seoul; tel. (2) 723-9681; fax (2) 723-9680; e-mail embassy@polandseoul.org; internet www.polandseoul.org; Ambassador MAREK CAIKA.

Kuwait: POB 5066, 13051 Safat, Jabriya, Plot 7, St 3, House 20, Kuwait City; tel. 5311571; fax 5311576; e-mail embassy@kuwejt.polemb.net; internet www.kuwejt.polemb.net; Ambassador Janusz Szwedo.

Laos: 263 Ban Thadeua, Km 3, quartier Wat Nak, BP 1106, Vientiane; tel. (21) 312940; fax (21) 312085; e-mail polembv@yahoo.com; internet www.vientiane.polemb.net; Chargé d'affaires DR TOMASZ GERLACH.

Latvia: Mednieku iela 6b, Rīga 1010; tel. 6703-1500; fax 6703-1549; e-mail ambpol@apollo.lv; internet www.ambpolriga.lv; Ambassador Maciej Klimczak.

Lebanon: POB 40-215, Immeuble Khalifa, ave Président Sulayman Franjiya 52, Baabda, Beirut; tel. (5) 924881; fax (5) 924882; e-mail polamb@cyberia.net.lb; Ambassador WALDEMAR MARKIEWICZ.

Libya: POB 519, Sharia ben Ashour 61, Tripoli; tel. (21) 3608569; fax (21) 3615199; e-mail poland@trypolis.polemb.net; internet www.trypolis.polemb.net; Ambassador Jósef Osas.

Lithuania: Smélio g. 20A, Vilnius 10323; tel. (5) 270-9001; fax (5) 270-9007; e-mail ampol@tdd.lt; internet www.polandembassy.lt; Ambassador JANUSZ SKOLIMOWSKI.

Luxembourg: 2 rue de Pulvermühl, 2356 Luxembourg; tel. 26-00-32; fax 26-68-75-54; e-mail ambapol@pt.lu; internet www.luksemburg.polemb.net; Ambassador Barbara Labuda.

Macedonia, former Yugoslav Republic: 1000 Skopje, Djuro Djakovic 50; tel. (2) 3112647; fax (2) 3119744; e-mail ambasada@skopje.polemb.net; internet www.skopje.polemb.net; Ambassador DARIUSZ KAROL BACHURA.

Malaysia: POB 10052, 50704 Kuala Lumpur; tel. (3) 42576733; fax (3) 42570123; e-mail info@ambasada.com.my; internet www.kualalumpur.polemb.net; Ambassador Eugeniosz Sawicki.

Mexico: Cracovia 40, Col. San Angel, Del. Alvaro Obregón, 01000 México, DF; tel. (55) 5550-4700; fax (55) 5616-0822; e-mail embajada@polonia.org.mx; internet www.polonia.org.mx; Chargé d'affaires a.i. JACEK GAWRYSZEWSKI.

Moldova: 2019 Chişinău, str. Grenoble 126; tel. (22) 28-59-50; fax (22) 28-90-00; e-mail polemb@mtc.md; internet www.kiszyniow.polemb.net; Ambassador Krzysztof Suprowicz.

Mongolia: Diplomatic Corps Bldg 95, Apartment 66, Ulan Bator (CPOB 1049); tel. (11) 320641; fax (11) 320576; e-mail polkonsulat@magicnet.mn; Ambassador ZBIGNIEW JERZY KULAK.

Montenegro: 81000 Podgorica, 8 Marta 72; tel. (81) 662442; fax (81) 662397; e-mail ambaspol@cg.yu; Chargé d'affaires Jarosław Lindenberg.

Morocco: 23 rue Oqbah, Agdal, BP 425, 10000 Rabat; tel. (3) 7771173; fax (3) 7775320; e-mail apologne@menara.ma; internet www.ambpologne.ma; Ambassador JOANNA WRONECKA.

Netherlands: Alexanderstraat 25, 2514 JM The Hague; tel. (70) 7990100; fax (70) 7990137; e-mail ambhaga@polamb.nl; internet www.haga.polamb.net; Ambassador Dr Janusz Stańczyk.

New Zealand: 17 Upland Rd, Kelburn, POB 10211, Wellington; tel. (4) 475-9453; fax (4) 475-9458; e-mail polishembassy@xtra.co.nz; internet poland.org.nz; Ambassador LECH MASTALERZ.

Nigeria: 16 Ona Cres., Maitama, Abuja; tel. (9) 4138280; fax (9) 4138281; e-mail poembabu@linkserve.com; internet www.abuja.polemb.net; Ambassador Grzegorz Walinski.

Norway: Olav Kyrres pl. 1, 0244 Oslo; tel. 24-11-08-50; fax 22-44-48-39; e-mail ambpol@online.no; internet www.oslo.polemb.net; Ambassador WOJCIECH LUDWIK KOLAŃCZYK.

Pakistan: St 24, G-5/4, Diplomatic Enclave 2, POB 1032, Islamabad; tel. (51) 2279491; fax (51) 2825442; e-mail polemb@isb.comsats.net.pk; Ambassador Wieslaw Kucharek.

Peru: Apdo 180174, Miraflores, Lima 18; tel. (1) 4713920; fax (1) 4714813; e-mail wojciech@amauta.rcp.net.pe; Ambassador PRZEMYSIAW MARZEC.

Portugal: Av. das Descobertas 2, 1400-092 Lisbon; tel. (21) 3012350; fax (21) 3041429; e-mail emb.polonia@mail.telepac.pt; internet www.lizbona.polemb.ne; Ambassador Katarzyna Skórzyńska.

Romania: 011821 Bucharest 1, Al. Alexandru 23; tel. (21) 2302330; fax (21) 2307832; e-mail ambasada@bukareszt.ro; Ambassador JACEK PALISZEWSKI.

Russian Federation: 123557 Moscow, ul. Klimashkina 4; tel. (495) 231-15-00; fax (495) 231-15-15; e-mail embassy@polandemb.ru; internet www.moskwa.polemb.net; Ambassador Jerzy Bahr.

Senegal: Villa 'Les Ailes', Fann Résidence, angle Corniche-Ouest, BP 343, Dakar; tel. 33-824-2354; fax 33-824-9526; e-mail ambassade.pl@sentoo.sn; internet www.ambassade-pologne.sn; Ambassador ANDRZEJ MICHAL LUPINA.

Serbia: 11000 Belgrade, Kneza Miloša 38; tel. (11) 2065318; fax (11) 3616939; e-mail ambrpfrj@eunet.yu; Ambassador Maciej Szymański.

Singapore: 435 Orchard Rd, 10-01/02 Wisma Atria, Singapore 238877; tel. 62359478; fax 62359479; e-mail polish_embassy@pacific.net.sg; internet www.singapore.polemb.net; Ambassador BOGUSLAW MARCIN MAJEWSKI.

Slovakia: Hummelova 4, 814 91 Bratislava; tel. (2) 5441-3175; fax (2) 5441-3184; e-mail bratampl@nextra.sk; internet www.polskevelvyslanectvo.sk; Chargé d'affaires a.i. Bogdan Wrzochalski.

Slovenia: 1000 Ljubljana, Bežigrad 10; tel. (1) 4364712; fax (1) 4362521; e-mail ambpol.si@siol.net; internet www.lublana.polemb.net; Ambassador PIOTR KASZUBA.

South Africa: 14 Amos St, Colbyn, Pretoria 0083; POB 12277, Queenswood 0121; tel. (12) 4302621; fax (12) 4302608; e-mail amb.pol@pixie.co.za; Ambassador Romuald Szuniewicz.

Spain: Guisando 23 bis, 28035 Madrid; tel. (91) 3736605; fax (91) 3736624; e-mail embajada@polonia.es; internet www.madrid.polemb.net; Chargé d'affaires a.i. BARBARA SOŚNICKA.

Sweden: Karlavägen 35, 114 31 Stockholm; tel. (8) 505-750-00; fax (8) 505-750-86; e-mail info.polen@tele2.se; internet www.sztokholm.polemb.net; Ambassador Michał Czyż.

Switzerland: Elfenstr. 20A, 3000 Bern 15; tel. 313580202; fax 313580216; e-mail polishemb@dial.eunet.ch; internet www.berno.polemb.net; Chargé d'affaires a.i. JERZY WIECZOREK.

Syria: BP 501, rue Baha Eddin Aita, Abou Roumaneh, Damascus; tel. (11) 3333010; fax (11) 3315318; e-mail damapol@scs-net.org; internet www.damaszek.polemb.net; Ambassador Jacek Chodorowicz.

Tanzania: 63 Alykhan Rd, Upanga, POB 2188, Dar es Salaam; tel. (22) 2115271; fax (22) 2115812; e-mail polamb@wingrouptz.com; Chargé d'affaires a.i. EUGENIUSZ RZEWUSKI.

Thailand: 100/81-82, Vongvanij Bldg b, 25th Floor, Thanon Phra Ram IX, Huaykwang, Bangkok 10310; tel. (2) 645-0367; fax (2) 645-0365; e-mail polemb@loxinfo.co.th; internet www.polemb.or.th; Ambassador Bogdan Goralczyk.

Tunisia: 5 Impasse no. 1, rue de Cordoue, El Manar I, Tunis; tel. (71) 873-837; fax (71) 872-987; e-mail amb.pologne@wanadoo.tn; internet www.tunis-polemb.net; Chargé d'affaires a.i. DARIUSZ SZEWCZYK.

Turkey: Atatürk Bul. 241, 06650 Kavaklıdere, Ankara; tel. (312) 4675619; fax (312) 4678963; e-mail polamb@superonline.com; internet www.polonya.org.tr; Chargé d'affaires a.i. Krzysztof Lewandowski.

Turkmenistan: 744005 Aşgabat, ul. Azadi 17A; tel. (12) 27-40-35; fax (12) 27-31-22; Ambassador MACIEJ LANG.

Ukraine: 01034 Kyiv, vul. Yaroslaviv Val 12; tel. (44) 230-07-00; fax (44) 270-63-36; e-mail ambasada@polska.com.ua; internet www.kijow.polemb.net; Ambassador Jacek Kluczkowski.

United Arab Emirates: POB 2334, Abu Dhabi; tel. (2) 4465200; fax (2) 4462967; e-mail polcon99@emirates.net.ae; internet www.plembassy.gov.ae; Ambassador ROMAN CHAKACZKIEWICZ.

United Kingdom: 47 Portland Pl., London, W1B 1JH; tel. (870) 774-2700; fax (20) 7291-3575; e-mail polishembassy@polishembassy.org.uk; internet www.london.polemb.net; Ambassador Barbara Tuge-Erecińska.

United States of America: 2640 16th St, NW, Washington, DC 20009; tel. (202) 234-3800; fax (202) 328-6271; e-mail polemb.info@earthlink.net; internet www.polandembassy.org; Ambassador ROBERT KUPIECKI.

Uruguay: Jorge Canning 2389, Casilla 1538, 11600 Montevideo; tel. (2) 4801313; fax (2) 4873389; e-mail ambmonte@netgate.com.uy; internet www.embajadapoloniauruguay.com; Ambassador Lech Zbigniew Kubiak.

Uzbekistan: 100084 Tashkent, Firdavsiy ko'ch. 66; tel. (71) 120-86-50; fax (71) 120-86-51; e-mail ambasada@bcc.com.uz; internet www.taszkent.polemb.net; Chargé d'affaires a.i. JERZY STANKIEWICZ.

Vatican City: Via dei Delfini 16/3, 00186 Rome, Italy; tel. (06) 6990958; fax (06) 6990978; e-mail polamb.wat@agora.it; Ambassador Hanna Suchocka.

Venezuela: Quinta Ambar, Final Avda Nicolás Copérnico, Sector Los Naranjos, Las Mercedes, Apdo 62293, Caracas; tel. (212) 991-1461; fax (212) 992-2164; e-mail ambcarac@ambasada.org.ve; internet www.caracas.polemb.net; Ambassador KRZYSZTOF JACEK HINZ.

Viet Nam: 3 Chua Mot Cot, Hanoi; tel. (4) 8452027; fax (4) 8236914; e-mail polamb@hn.vnn.vn; Ambassador Mirosław Gajewski.

Yemen: POB 16168, Haddah St, San'a; tel. (1) 413523; fax (1) 413647; e-mail polemb@y.net.ye; internet www.sana.polemb.net; Chargé d'affaires a.i. HENRYK PIASZCZYK.

Zimbabwe: 16 Cork Rd, Belgravia, POB 3932, Harare; tel. (4) 253442; fax (4) 253710; Ambassador Jan Wielinski.

DIPLOMATIC MISSIONS OF PORTUGAL

United Nations: 866 Second Ave, 9th Floor, New York, NY 10017; tel. (212) 759-9444; fax (212) 355-1124; e-mail portugal@un.int; internet www.un.int/portugal; Permanent Representative JOÃO MANUEL GUERRA SALGUEIRO.

Algeria: 4 rue Mohamed Khoudi, el-Biar, Algiers; tel. (21) 92-53-14; fax (21) 92-53-13; e-mail embportdz@yahoo.fr; Ambassador Luís de Almeida Sampaio.

Andorra: Carrer Prat de la Creu 59–65, 4°, Andorra la Vella AD500; tel. 805308; fax 869555; e-mail mail@andorra.dgaccp.pt; internet www.embaixadadeportugal.ad; Ambassador NUNO ANTÓNIO RIBEIRO DE BESSA LOPES.

Angola: Av. de Portugal 50, CP 1346, Luanda; tel. 222333027; fax 222390392; e-mail secretariado.emb@netcabo.co.ao; Ambassador Francisco Ribeiro Telles.

Argentina: Maipú 942, 17°, C1006ACN Buenos Aires; tel. (11) 4312-0187; fax (11) 4311-2586; e-mail mebpor@embajadaportugal.org.ar; Ambassador JOAQUIM JOSÉ LEMOS FERREIRA MARQUES.

Australia: 23 Culgoa Circuit, O'Malley, ACT 2606; tel. (2) 6290-1733; fax (2) 6290-1957; e-mail embport@internode.on.net; Ambassador Dr Antonio J. Mendes.

Austria: Opernring 3/1, 1010 Vienna; tel. (1) 586-75-36-0; fax (1) 586-75-36-99; e-mail portugal@portembassy.at; internet www.portembassy.at; Ambassador DR JOAQUIM RAFAEL CAIMOTO DUARTE.

Belgium: 55 ave de la Toison d'Or, 1060 Brussels; tel. (2) 533-07-00; fax (2) 539-07-73; e-mail ambassade.portugal@skynet.be; Ambassador Manuel Nuno Tavares de Sousa.

Brazil: SES Sul, Av. das Nações, Quadra 801, Lote 02, 70402-900 Brasília, DF; tel. (61) 3032-9600; fax (61) 3032-9642; e-mail embaixadaportugal@embaixadaportugal.org.br; internet www.embaixadadeportugal.org.br; Ambassador FRANCISCO MANUEL SEIXAS DA COSTA.

Bulgaria: 1504 Sofia, ul. Ivatz voyvoda 6; tel. (2) 943-36-67; fax (2) 943-30-89; e-mail embport@online.bg; Ambassador Mário Jesus dos Santos.

Canada: 645 Island Park Dr., Ottawa, ON K1Y 0B8; tel. (613) 729-0883; fax (613) 729-4236; e-mail embportugal@dgaccp.org; internet www.embportugal-ottawa.org; Ambassador JOÃO PEDRO DA SILVEIRA CARVALHO.

Cape Verde: Av. OUA, Achada de Santo António, CP 160, Praia, Santiago; tel. 2626097; fax 2613222; e-mail embport@cvtelecom.cv; internet www.consuladopt.cv; Ambassador Dr Graça Andersen Guimarães.

Chile: Nueva Tajamar 555, Torre Norte 16°, Las Condes, Santiago; tel. (2) 203-0542; fax (2) 203-0545; e-mail embaixada.portugal@entelchile.net; Ambassador LUÍS FILIPE DE MENDONÇA CRISTINA DE BARROS.

China, People's Republic: 8 San Li Tun Dong Wu Jie, Beijing 100600; tel. (10) 65323242; fax (10) 65324637; e-mail embport@public2.bta.net.cn; Ambassador Rui Quartin Santos.

Colombia: Carrera 12, No 93-37, Of. 302, Bogotá, DC; tel. (1) 622-1334; fax (1) 622-1134; e-mail embporbo@andinet.com; Ambassador AUGUSTO JOSÉ PESTANA SARAIVA PEIXOTO.

Congo, Democratic Republic: 270 ave des Aviateurs, BP 7775, Kinshasa; tel. (81) 5161277; e-mail ambassadeportugal@micronet.net; Ambassador Alfredo Manuel Silva Duarte Costa.

Croatia: 10000 Zagreb, trg ban J. Jelačića 5/2; tel. (1) 4882210; fax (1) 4920663; e-mail emb.port.zagreb@zg.htnet.hr; Ambassador LUÍS BARREIROS.

Cuba: Avda 7, No 2207, esq. 24, Miramar, Havana; tel. (7) 204-0149; fax (7) 204-2593; e-mail embport@enet.cu; Ambassador Mario Godinho de Matos.

Cyprus: Arch. Makarios III Ave 9, Severis Bldg, 5th Floor, POB 27407, 1645 Nicosia; tel. 22375131; fax 22756456; e-mail portembnic@cytanet.com.cy; Ambassador ANTONIO JORGE JACOB CARVALHO.

Czech Republic: Pevnostní 9, 160 00 Prague 6; tel. 257311230; fax 257311234; e-mail embport@mbox.vol.cz; internet www.embportugal.cz; Ambassador Fernando Manuel Oliveira de Castro Brandão.

Denmark: Toldbodgade 31, 1st Floor, 1253 Copenhagen K; tel. 33-13-13-01; fax 33-14-92-14; e-mail embport@get2net.dk; Ambassador JOSÉ BOUZA SERRANO.

Egypt: 1 Sharia es-Saleh Ayoub, Cairo (Zamalek); tel. (2) 7350779; fax (2) 7350790; e-mail embpcai@link.net; Ambassador Fernando Ramos Machado.

Estonia: Kohtu 10, Tallinn 10130; tel. 611-7468; fax 611-7467; e-mail emb.portugal.tallin@gmail.com; Ambassador ANA PAULA BAPTISTA GRADE ZACARIAS.

Ethiopia: Sheraton Addis, Taitu Street, POB 6002, Addis Ababa; tel. (11) 171717; fax (11) 173403; e-mail embportadis@hotmail.com; Ambassador Dr Vera Maria Fernandes.

Finland: Itäinen puistotie 11B, 00140 Helsinki; tel. (9) 68243713; fax (9) 663550; e-mail emb.port@portugal.fi; Ambassador JOÃO MANUEL DA CRUZ DA SILVA LEITÃO.

France: 3 rue de Noisiel, 75116 Paris; tel. 1-47-27-35-29; fax 1-44-05-94-02; e-mail mailto@embaixada-portugal-fr.org; internet www.embaixada-portugal-fr.org; Ambassador António Victor Martins Monteiro.

Germany: Zimmerstr. 56, 10117 Berlin; tel. (30) 590063500; fax (30) 590063600; e-mail mail@botschaftportugal.de; internet www.botschaftportugal.de; Ambassador JOSÉ CAETANO DE CAMPOS ANDRADA DA COSTA PEREIRA.

Greece: Leoforos Vassilissis Sofias 23, 106 74 Athens; tel. (210) 7290096; fax (210) 7245122; e-mail embportg@otenet.gr; Ambassador Carlos Neves Ferreira.

Guinea-Bissau: Av. Cidade de Lisboa, CP 76, 1021 Bissau; tel. 201261; fax 201269; e-mail embaixada@bissau.dgaccp.pt; Ambassador JOSÉ MANUEL SOARES B. PAIS MOREIRA.

Hungary: 1126 Budapest, Edifício C. Alkotás u. 53; tel. (1) 201-7617; fax (1) 201-7619; e-mail embport@axelero.hu; Ambassador Luís Filipe Castro Mendes.

India: 8 Olof Palme Marg, Vasant Vihar, New Delhi 110 057; tel. (11) 26142215; fax (11) 26152837; e-mail embportin@ndf.vsnl.net.in; internet www.embportindia.com; Ambassador JOAQUIM JOSÉ L. F. MARQUES CURTO.

Indonesia: Jalan Indramayu 2a, Menteng, Jakarta 10310; tel. (21) 31908030; fax (21) 31908031; e-mail embassyportugaljakarta@cbn.net.id; internet www.embassyportugaljakarta.or.id; Ambassador José Manuel Santos Braga.

Iran: No. 13, Rouzbeh Alley, Darrous, Hedayat St, Tehran; tel. (21) 22543237; fax (21) 22552668; e-mail portugal@myrlatak.com; Ambassador DR JOSÉ FERNANDO MOREIRA DA CUNHA.

Iraq: POB 2123, Alwiya, Baghdad; tel. (1) 541-3376; fax (1) 542-0845; Ambassador Francisco Domingos Garcia Falção Machado.

Ireland: 15 Leeson Park, Foxrock, Dublin 6; tel. (1) 4127040; fax (1) 4970299; e-mail embport@dublin.dgaccp.pt; Ambassador PAULO GUILHERME PIRES DE LIMA DE CASTILHO.

Israel: 12th Floor, 3 Daniel Frisch St, Tel-Aviv 64731; tel. 3-6956373; fax 3-6956366; e-mail eptel@012.net.il; Ambassador Josefina Reis Carvalho.

Italy: Viale Liegi 21–23, 00198 Roma; tel. (06) 844801; fax (06) 8417404; e-mail embport@embportroma.it; internet www.embportroma.it; Ambassador VASCO TAVEIRA DA CUNHA VALENTE.

Japan: Kamiura-Kojimachi Bldg, 5th Floor, 3-10-3, Kojimachi, Chiyoda-ku, Tokyo 102-0083; tel. (3) 5212-7322; fax (3) 5226-0616; e-mail tokyo .delegation@portugal.or.jp; internet www.portugal.or.jp; Ambassador João Pedro Zanatti.

Kenya: Reinsurance Plaza, 10th Floor, Aga Khan Walk, POB 34020, 00100 Nairobi; tel. (20) 313203; fax (20) 214711; e-mail embassy.nairobi@portugal .co.ke; Ambassador LUIS LORUÁO.

Korea, Republic: Wonseo Bldg, 2nd Floor, 171, Wonseo-dong, Jongno-gu, Seoul; tel. (2) 3675-2251; fax (2) 3675-2250; e-mail ambport@chollian.net; Ambassador Henrique Silveira Borges.

Latvia: Balasta Dambis 60, Oglu iela, Ķipsala, 1048 Rīga; tel. 6782-1926; fax 6733-4233; e-mail embporturiga@gmail.com; Ambassador JOÃO LUIS NIZA PINHEIRO.

Lithuania: Gedimino pr. 5, Vilnius 01103; tel. (5) 262-0511; fax (5) 262-0509; e-mail vilnius@embportugal.lt; Ambassador António Manuel Moreira Tanger Correa.

Luxembourg: 24 rue Guillaume Schneider, 2522 Luxembourg; tel. 46-61-90-1; fax 46-51-69; e-mail embport@pt.lu; Ambassador RUI ALFREDO DE VASCONCELOS FÉLIX ALVES.

Malta: Whitehall Mansions, 3rd Floor, Ta'Xbiex Seafront, Ta'Xbiex XBX 1026; tel. 21322924; fax 21322927; e-mail embportmalta@sapo.pt; Ambassador António Augusto Russo Dias.

Mexico: Avda Alpes 1370, Lomas de Chapultepec, Del. Miguel Hidalgo, 11000 México, DF; tel. (55) 5520-7897; fax (55) 5520-4688; e-mail embpomex@prodigy.net.mx; internet www.portugalenmexico.com.mx; Ambassador FRANCISCO DOMINGOS GARCÍA FALCÃO MACHADO.

Morocco: 5 rue Thami Lamdouar, Souissi, 10100 Rabat; tel. (3) 7756446; fax (3) 7756445; e-mail embport-rabat@hotmail.com; Ambassador João Rosa La.

Mozambique: Av. Julius Nyerere 720, CP 4696, Maputo; tel. 21490316; fax 21491172; e-mail embaixada@embpormaputo.org.mz; Ambassador JOSÉ JOAQUIM ESTEVES DOS SANTOS DE FREITAS FERRAZ.

Netherlands: Bazarstraat 21, 2518 AG The Hague; tel. (70) 3630217; fax (70) 3615589; e-mail info@portembassy.nl; Ambassador Júlio Francisco de Sales Mascarenhas.

Nigeria: 27B Gana St, Maitama, Abuja; tel. (9) 4137211; fax (9) 4137214; e-mail portemb@rosecom.net; Ambassador MARIA DE FÁTIMA DE PINA PERESTRELLO.

Norway: Josefinesgt. 37, 0244 Oslo; tel. 23-33-28-50; fax 22-56-43-55; e-mail portemb@frisurf.no; Ambassador João de Lima Pimentel.

Pakistan: 66, Main Margalla Rd, F-7/2, Islamabad; tel. (51) 2652491; fax (51) 2652492; e-mail portugal@isb.paknet.com.pk; Ambassador DR ANTONIO JOSÉ DA CAMARARA ROMALHO ORTIGÃO.

Peru: Calle Antequera 777, 3°, San Isidro, POB 3692, Lima 100; tel. (1) 4409905; fax (1) 4429655; e-mail limaportugal@hotmail.com; Ambassador Mário Alberto Lino da Silva.

Philippines: 17th Floor, Units C and D, Trafalgar Plaza, 105 H. V. de la Costa St, Salcedo Village, Makati City, Metro Manila; tel. (2) 8483789; fax (2) 8483791; Charge d'affaires a.i. LUÍS BRITO CAMARA.

Poland: 03-905 Warsaw, ul. Francuska 37; tel. (22) 5111010; fax (22) 5111013; e-mail embaixada@embport.internetdsl.pl; internet www .ambasadaportugalii.pl; Ambassador José Sequeira e Serpa.

Romania: 011815 Bucharest 1, Str. Paris 55; tel. (21) 2304136; fax (21) 2304117; e-mail secretariat@embportugal.ro; internet www.embportugal.ro; Ambassador ALEXANDRE VASSALO.

Russian Federation: 129010 Moscow, Botanicheskii per. 1; tel. (495) 981-34-10; fax (495) 981-34-16; e-mail embptrus@moscovo.dgaccp.pt; Ambassador Manuel Marcelo Montiero Curto.

São Tomé and Príncipe: Av. Marginal de 12 de Julho, CP 173, São Tomé; tel. 221130; fax 221190; e-mail eporstp@cstome.net; Ambassador FERNANDO JOSÉ RODRIGUES RAMOS MACHADO.

Saudi Arabia: POB 94328, Riyadh 11693; tel. (1) 462-2115; fax (1) 462-2105; e-mail portriade@nesma.net.sa; Ambassador Dr Henrique M. V. de Silveira Borges.

Senegal: 5 ave Carde, BP 281, Dakar; tel. 33-864-0317; fax 33-864-0322; e-mail ambportdakar@sentoo.sn; Ambassador ANTÓNIO AUGUSTO MONTENEGRO VIEIRA CARDOSO.

Serbia: 11040 Belgrade, Vladimira Gaćinovića 4; tel. (11) 2662895; fax (11) 2662892; e-mail embporbg@yubc.net; Ambassador Paulo Tiago Jerónimo da Silva.

Slovenia: 1000 Ljubljana, trg Republika 3/10; tel. (1) 4790540; fax (1) 4790550; Ambassador MARIA DO CARMO ALLEGRO DE MAGALHÃES.

South Africa: 599 Leyds St, Muckleneuk, Pretoria 0002; POB 27102, Sunnyside 0132; tel. (12) 3412340; fax (12) 3413975; e-mail portemb@ global.co.za; Ambassador Paulo Couto Barbosa.

Spain: Pinar 1, 28006 Madrid; tel. (91) 7824960; fax (91) 7824972; e-mail embmadrid@emb-portugal.es; internet www.embajadaportugal-madrid.org; Ambassador JOSÉ FILIPE MORAES CABRAL.

Sweden: Narvavägen 32, 2nd Floor, POB 10194, 100 55 Stockholm; tel. (8) 545-670-60; fax (8) 662-53-29; e-mail portugal@embassyportugal.se; internet www.embassyportugal.se; Ambassador José Carlos Júlio da Cruz Almeida.

Switzerland: Weltpoststr. 20, 3015 Bern; tel. 313528602; fax 313514432; e-mail embpt.berna@scber.dgaccp.pt; Ambassador EURICO JORGE HENRIQUES PAES.

Thailand: 26 Bush Lane, Thanon Charoenkrung, Bangkok 10500; tel. (2) 234-2123; fax (2) 238-4275; e-mail portemb@loxinfo.co.th; Ambassador António Felix Machado de Faria e Maya.

Timor-Leste: Edif. ACAIT, Av. Presidente Nicolau Lobato, Dili; tel. 3312533; fax 3312526; e-mail embaixada.portugal@embpor.tp; internet www.embpor.tp; Ambassador JOÃO RAMOS PINTO.

Tunisia: 2 rue Sufétula, Belvédère, 1002 Tunis; tel. (71) 893-981; fax (71) 791-008; e-mail embportunes@embport.intl.tn; Ambassador Maria Rita da Franca Sousa e Ferro Levy Gomes.

Turkey: Kuleli Sok. 26, 06700 Gaziosmanpaşa, Ankara; tel. (312) 4056028; fax (312) 4463670; e-mail embaixada@portugal.org.tr; Ambassador JOSÉ MANUEL DE CARVALHO LAMEIRAS.

Ukraine: 01901 Kyiv, vul. I. Fedorova 12/2; tel. (44) 287-58-61; fax (44) 230-26-25; e-mail geral@embport.kiev.ua; Ambassador José Manuel da Encarnação Pessanha Viegas.

United Kingdom: 11 Belgrave Sq., London, SW1X 8PP; tel. (20) 7235-5331; fax (20) 7235-0739; e-mail london@portembassy.co.uk; Ambassador ANTÓNIO NUNES DE CARVALHO SANTANA CARLOS.

United States of America: 2125 Kalorama Rd, NW, Washington, DC 20008; tel. (202) 328-8610; fax (202) 462-3726; internet www.portugalemb.org; Ambassador João de Vallera.

Uruguay: Avda Dr Francisco Soca 1128, Casilla 701, 11300 Montevideo; tel. (2) 7084061; fax (2) 7096456; e-mail embport@montevideu.dgaccp.pt; Ambassador LUISA BASTOS DE ALMEIDA.

Vatican City: Villa Lusa, Via S. Valentino 9, 00197 Rome, Italy; tel. (06) 8091581; fax (06) 8077585; e-mail embportugalvatican@tiscalinet.it; Ambassador João Alberto Bacelar da Rocha Páris.

Venezuela: Torre La Castellana, 3°, Avda Eugénio Mendoza, cruce con José Angel Lamas, La Castellana, Caracas 1062; tel. (212) 263-2529; fax (212) 266-4908; e-mail embajadaportugal@cantv.net; Ambassador JOÃO JOSÉ GOMES CAETANO DA SILVA.

Zimbabwe: 12 Harvey Brown Ave, Milton Park, Harare; tel. (4) 253023; fax (4) 253637; e-mail embport@harare.dgaccp.pt; Ambassador João Carlos Versteeg.

DIPLOMATIC MISSIONS OF QATAR

United Nations: 809 United Nations Plaza, 4th Floor, New York, NY 10017; tel. (212) 486-9335; fax (212) 758-4952; e-mail newyork@mofa.gov.qa; Permanent Representative NASSIR BIN ABDULAZIZ AL-NASSER.

Algeria: BP 348, 7 chemin Doudou Mokhtar, Algiers; tel. (21) 91-20-09; fax (21) 91-20-11; Ambassador Ali Mubarak Muhammad an-Nueimi.

Azerbaijan: 1000 Baku, pr. Aliyev; tel. (12) 496-78-00; fax (12) 496-78-01; .

Bahrain: POB 15105, Villa 814, Rd 3315, Area 333, Mahooz, Manama; tel. 17722922; fax 17740662; Ambassador Sheikh Abdullah bin Thamir ath-Thani.

Bangladesh: House 1, Rd 79/81, Gulshan 2, Dhaka 1212; tel. (2) 9887429; fax (2) 9896071; e-mail dhaka@mofa.gov.qa; Ambassador IBRAHIM MOHAMMAD A. AL-ABDULLA.

Belgium: 51 rue de la Vallée, 1000 Brussels; tel. (2) 223-11-55; fax (2) 223-11-66; internet www.qatarembassy.be; Ambassador Sheikh Meshal bin Hamad ath-Thani.

Brazil: SHIS, QL 20, Conj. 01, Casa 19, Lago Sul, 71650-115 Brasília, DF; tel. (61) 3366-1005; fax (61) 3366-1115; e-mail qatarbsb@embcatar.org.br; Ambassador JAMAL NASSER SULTAN AL-BADR.

China, People's Republic: A7 Liang Maqiao Diplomatic Compound, Chao Yang Qu, Beijing 100600; tel. (10) 6532231; fax (10) 65325274; e-mail beijing@mofa.gov.qa; Ambassador Abdulla A. al-Muftah.

Cuba: Hotel Nacional, 211, Havana; tel. (7) 33-3564; fax (7) 73-4700; Ambassador ALI BIN SAAD AL-KHARJI.

Cyprus: Nicosia; Ambassador Mubarak Abd ar-Rahman Mubarak an-Nasser.

Djibouti: Ambassador HADI NASSER MANSOUR AL-HAJIRI.

Egypt: 10 Sharia ath-Thamar, Midan an-Nasr, Madinet al-Mohandessin, Cairo; tel. (2) 7604693; fax (2) 7603618; e-mail cairo@mofa.gov.qa; Ambassador Muhammad bin Hamad al-Khalifa.

France: 1 rue de Tilsitt, 75008 Paris; tel. 1-45-51-90-71; fax 1-45-51-77-07; e-mail paris@mofa.gov.qa; internet www.qatarambassade.com; Ambassador MUHAMMAD JAHAM ABD AL-AZIZ AL-KUWARI.

Germany: Hagenstr. 56, 14193 Berlin; tel. (30) 862060; fax (30) 86206150; e-mail berlin@mofa.gov.qa; Ambassador Saleh Muhammad Saleh an-Nasif.

Hungary: 1026 Budapest, Gadonvi Geza u. 19; tel. (1) 392-1010; fax (1) 392-1019; e-mail qatarembassy@t-online.hu; Ambassador MUBARAK RASHID AL-BUAINEN.

India: EP-31A, Chandragupta Marg, Chanakyapuri, New Delhi 110 021; tel. (11) 26117988; fax (11) 26886080; e-mail newdelhi@mofa.gov.qa; Ambassador Hussan Mohammed Rafeh Alemadi.

Indonesia: Jalan Mega Kuningan Barat I, No. 7, Kawasan Mega Kuningan, Jakarta 12950; tel. (21) 2510751; fax (21) 2510754; e-mail qataremj@indosat.net.id; Ambassador YOUSEF KHALIFA AL-SADA.

Iran: POB 11365-1631, Africa Ave, Golazin Ave, Parke Davar, No. 4, Tehran; tel. (21) 22051255; fax (21) 22056023; e-mail tehran@mofa.gov.qa; Ambassador Dr Saleh Ibrahim al-Kawari.

Italy: Via Antonio Bosio 14, 00161 Roma; tel. (06) 44249450; fax (06) 44245273; e-mail info@qatarembassy.it; internet www.qatarembassy.it; Ambassador SOLTAN SAAD AL-MORAIKHI.

Japan: 2-3-28, Moto Azabu, Minato-ku, Tokyo 106-0046; tel. (3) 5475-0611; fax (3) 5475-0617; e-mail tokyo@mofa.gov.qa; Ambassador Reyad Ali al-Ansari.

Jordan: POB 831222, Amman 11183; tel. (6) 4659724; fax (6) 4659723; e-mail qataremb@index.com.jo; Ambassador MANA ABD AL-HADI AL-HAJRI.

Kazakhstan: 050000 Almaty; .

Korea, Republic: 309-5, Dongbinggo-dong, Yeongsan-gu, Seoul 140-817; tel. (2) 798-2444; fax (2) 790-1027; e-mail qatarseoul@hotmail.com; Ambassador AHMAD S. AL-MIDHADI.

Kuwait: POB 1825, 13019 Safat, Diiyah, Istiqlal St, Kuwait City; tel. 2523107; fax 2513604; e-mail kuwait@mofa.gov.qa; Ambassador Abd al-Aziz bin Saad al-Fehaid.

Lebanon: POB 11-6717, 1er étage, Immeuble Deebs, Shouran, Beirut; tel. (1) 865271; fax (1) 810460; e-mail beirut@mofa.gov.qa; Ambassador JABOR BIN ABDULLAH AS-SWAIDI.

Libya: POB 3506, Sharia ben Ashour, Tripoli; tel. (21) 4446660; Ambassador Saad Ben Ali al-Mahandy.

Malaysia: 113 Jalan Ampang Hilir, POB 13118, 55000 Kuala Lumpur; tel. (3) 42565552; fax (3) 42565553; e-mail qekl113@streamyx.com; Ambassador ABDULHAMEED MUBARAK AL-KUBAISI.

Mauritania: BP 609, Nouakchott; tel. 525-23-99; fax 525-68-87; e-mail nouakchoti@mofa.gov.qa; Ambassador Mohammed Kurdi Taleb al-Merri.

Morocco: 4 ave Tarik ibn Ziad, BP 1220, 10001 Rabat; tel. (3) 7765681; fax (3) 7765774; e-mail rabat@mofa.gov.qa; Ambassador SAQR MUBARAK AL-MANSOURI.

Netherlands: Borweg 7, 2597 LR The Hague; tel. (70) 4166666; fax (70) 4166660; e-mail info@embassyofqatar.nl; internet www.embassyofqatar.nl; Ambassador Saleh Abdullah al-Bouanin.

Oman: Diplomatic City, Jamiat ad-Dowal al-Arabiya St, Al-Khuwair, POB 802, Muscat 113; tel. 24691152; fax 24691156; Ambassador ABDULLAH BIN MUHAMMAD BIN KHALID AL-KHATIR.

Pakistan: 20, University Rd, Diplomatic Enclave, G-5/4, Islamabad; tel. (51) 2270833; fax (51) 2270207; e-mail islamabad@mofa.gov.qa; Ambassador Hamad Ali al-Henzab.

Philippines: 1398 Cabellero St, cnr Lumbang St, Dasmariñas Village, Makati City, Metro Manila; tel. (2) 8874944; fax (2) 8876406; e-mail gemanila2000@yahoo.com; Ambassador ABDULLAH AHMED YOUSIF AL-MUTAWA.

Romania: 011834 Bucharest, Str. Venezuela 10a; tel. (21) 2304741; fax (21) 2305446; e-mail qtr_ambassador@b.astral.ro; Ambassador Salem Abdullah Sultan al-Jaber.

Russian Federation: 117049 Moscow, ul. Korovii Val 7/196–198; tel. (495) 980-69-18; fax (495) 980-69-17; e-mail moscow@mofa.gov.qa; Ambassador SAAD MUHAMMAD SAAD AL-KOBAISI.

Saudi Arabia: POB 94353, Riyadh 11461; tel. (1) 482-5544; fax (1) 482-5394; Ambassador Ali Abdullah al-Mahmoud.

Senegal: 25 blvd Martin Luther King, BP 5150, Dakar; tel. 33-820-9559; fax 33-869-1012; Ambassador ALI ABDUL LATIF AHMED AL-MASALAMANI.

Singapore: c/o Shangri-La Hotel, 22 Orange Grove Rd, Rms 1832 & 1833, Singapore 258350; tel. 67373644; fax 62134021; Ambassador Rashid bin Ali Hassan al-Khater.

South Africa: 355 Charles St, Waterkloof, Pretoria 0181; Private Bag X13, Brooklyn Sq. 0075; tel. (12) 4521700; fax (12) 3466732; e-mail qatar-emb@lantic.net; Ambassador DR BASHIR ISSA AL-SHIRAWI.

Spain: Paseo de la Castellana 92, Hotel Villamagna, 28046 Madrid; tel. (91) 3106926; fax (91) 3104851; Ambassador Sheikh Fahad bin Awida ath-Thani.

Sri Lanka: 11 Rajakeeya Mawatha, Old Race Course Ave, Colombo 7; tel. (11) 2690440; fax (11) 2690443; Ambassador ALI HAMAD MUBARAK AL-MARRI.

Sudan: Elmanshia Block 92H, POB 223, Khartoum; tel. (183) 261113; fax (183) 261116; e-mail qatarembkht@yahoo.com; Ambassador Ali Hassan Abdullah al-Hamadi.

Syria: BP 4188, rue Ahmed Shouki, Abou Roumaneh, Damascus; e-mail damascus@mofa.gov.qa; tel. (11) 3336717; fax (11) 3342455; Ambassador MAJED GHANEM AL-ALI AL-MAADEED.

Thailand: Capital Tower, 14th Floor, All Seasons Place, 87/1 Thanon Witthayu, Lumpini, Pathumwan, Bangkok 10330; tel. (2) 660-1111; fax (2) 660-1122; e-mail info@qatarembassy.or.th; internet www.qatarembassy.or.th; Ambassador Abdalla Ibrahim Abdulrahman al-Hamar.

Tunisia: rue Alhadi Krai, Northern al-Omran Quarter, 1082 Tunis; tel. (71) 849-600; fax (71) 749-073; e-mail tunis@mofa.gov.qa; Ambassador SAAD BIN NASSER AL-HUMAIDI.

Turkey: Bakü Sok. 6, Diplomatik Site, Oran, Ankara; tel. (312) 4907274; fax (312) 4906757; e-mail ankara@mofa.gov.qa; Ambassador Abd ar-Razak Abd al-Ghani.

United Arab Emirates: POB 3503, 26th St, Al-Minaseer, Abu Dhabi; tel. (2) 4493300; fax (2) 4493311; e-mail abudhabi@mofa.gov.qa; Ambassador ABDULLAH M. AL-UTHMAN.

United Kingdom: 1 South Audley St, London, W1K 1NB; tel. (20) 7493-2200; fax (20) 7493-2661; Ambassador Khalid bin Rashid bin Salim al-Hamoudi al-Mansouri.

United States of America: 2555 M St, NW, Washington, DC 20037-1305; tel. (202) 274-1600; fax (202) 237-0061; e-mail info@qatarembassy.net; internet www.qatarembassy.net; Ambassador ALI BIN FAHAD AL-HAJRI.

Venezuela: Avda Principal Lomas El Mirador, Alto Claro, Municipio Baruta, Caracas; tel. (212) 909-7800; fax (212) 993-2917; e-mail qatarven@cantv.net; Ambassador Naser Rashid Muhammad A. an-Nuami.

Yemen: POB 19717, San'a; tel. (1) 304640; fax (1) 304645; e-mail sanaa@mofa.gov.qa; Ambassador JASIM ABU AL-INAYN.

DIPLOMATIC MISSIONS OF ROMANIA

United Nations: 573–577 Third Ave, New York, NY 10016; tel. (212) 682-3273; fax (212) 682-9746; e-mail romania@un.int; internet www.un.int/romania; Permanent Representative Mihnea Ioan Motoc.

Albania: Rruga Themistokli, Gjermeni 2, Tirana; tel. (4) 256071; fax (4) 256072; e-mail roemb@adanet.co.al; Chargé d'affaires GHEORGHE MICU.

Algeria: 24 rue Abri Arezki, Hydra, Algiers; tel. (21) 60-08-71; fax (21) 69-36-42; Ambassador Victor Mircea.

Angola: Rua Ramalho Ortigão 30, Alvalade, Luanda; tel. 222321076; e-mail ambromania@ebonet.net; Chargé d'affaires a.i. IACOB PRADA.

Argentina: Arroyo 962–970, C1007AAD Buenos Aires; tel. (11) 4326-5888; e-mail embarombue@rumania.org.ar; internet www.rumania.org.ar; Ambassador Ion Vilcu.

Armenia: Yerevan, Barbusse St 15; tel. (10) 27-53-32; fax (10) 22-75-47; e-mail ambrom@netsys.am; Ambassador RODINA CRINA PRUNARIU.

Australia: 4 Dalman Crescent, O'Malley, ACT 2606; tel. (2) 6286-2343; fax (2) 6286-2433; e-mail roembcbr@cyberone.com.au; internet canberra.mae .ro; Chargé d'affaires a. i. Florina Sava.

Austria: Prinz-Eugen-Str. 60, 1040 Vienna; tel. (1) 505-32-27; fax (1) 504-14-62; e-mail ambromviena@ambrom.at; internet viena.mae.ro; Chargé d'affaires a.i. ADRIANA LORETA STĂNESCU.

Azerbaijan: 1000 Baku, Hasan Aliyev küç. 125a; tel. (12) 465-63-78; fax (12) 456-60-76; e-mail rom_amb_baku@azdata.net; Ambassador Nicolae Ureche.

Belarus: 220035 Minsk, zav. Maskvina 4; tel. (17) 203-77-26; fax (17) 211-21-63; e-mail romania@nsys.by; Chargé d'affaires a.i. DUMITRU BADEA.

Belgium: 105 rue Gabrielle, 1180 Brussels; tel. (2) 345-26-80; fax (2) 346-23-45; e-mail secretariat@roumanieamb.be; internet bruxelles.mae.ro; Ambassador Dr Ion Jinga.

Bosnia and Herzegovina: 71000 Sarajevo, Tahtali sokak 13–15; tel. (33) 207447; fax (33) 668940; e-mail rumunska@bih.net.ba; Chargé d'affaires a.i. ADRIAN LĂRGEANU.

Brazil: SEN, Av. das Nações, Lote 06, 70456-900 Brasília, DF; tel. (61) 3226-0746; fax (61) 3226-6629; e-mail romenia@solar.com.br; Ambassador Mihai Zamfir.

Bulgaria: Sofia, bul. Mihai Eminescu 4; tel. (2) 971-28-58; fax (2) 973-34-12; e-mail ambsofro@vip.bg; internet sofia.mae.ro; Ambassador MIHAIL ROŞIANU.

Cameroon: Immeuble Dyna Immobilier, rue de Joseph Mballa Elounden, BP 6212, Yaoundé; tel. 2221-3986; Chargé d'affaires a.i. Mircea Boncu.

Canada: 655 Rideau St, Ottawa, ON K1N 6A3; tel. (613) 789-3709; fax (613) 789-4365; e-mail romania@romanian-embassy.com; internet ottawa.mae.ro; Ambassador ELENA STEFOI.

Chile: Benjamin 2955, Las Condes, Santiago; tel. (2) 231-1893; fax (2) 232-3441; e-mail embajada@rumania.tie.cl; internet www.rumania.cl; Ambassador Valentin Florea.

China, People's Republic: Ri Tan Lu, Dong Er Jie, Beijing 100600; tel. (10) 65323442; fax (10) 65325728; e-mail ambasada@roamb.link263.com; Ambassador VIOREL ISTICIOAIA-BUDURA.

Colombia: Carrera 7a, No 92-58, Bogotá, DC; tel. (1) 256-6438; fax (1) 256-6158; e-mail ambrombogota@etb.net.co; Ambassador Maria Sipos.

Croatia: 10000 Zagreb, Mlinarska 43; tel. (1) 4677550; fax (1) 4677854; e-mail veleposlanstvo.rumunjske@zg.t-com.hr; Ambassador OANA-CRISTINA POPA.

Cuba: Calle 21, No 307, Vedado, Havana; tel. (7) 33-3325; fax (7) 33-3324; e-mail erumania@ceniai.inf.cu; Ambassador Constantin Simirad.

Cyprus: POB 22210, 27 Pireos St, Strovolos, 2023 Nicosia; tel. 22495333; fax 22517383; e-mail rompol@cytanet.com.cy; Ambassador ANDREEA PASTARNAC.

Czech Republic: Nerudova 5, POB 87, 118 01 Prague 1; tel. 257534210; fax 257531017; e-mail embrprg@mbox.vol.cz; internet www.rouemb.cz; Chargé d'affaires a.i. Dan Adrian Balanescu.

Denmark: Strandagervej 27, 2900 Hellerup; tel. 39-40-71-77; fax 39-62-78-99; e-mail roemb@mail.tele.dk; internet copenhaga.mae.ro; Ambassador DR THEODOR PALEOLOGU.

Egypt: 6 El-Kamel Muhammad, Cairo (Zamalek); tel. (2) 27360107; fax (2) 27360851; e-mail roembegy@link.net; Ambassador Gheorghe Dumitru.

Ethiopia: Houses 9–10, Bole Kifle Ketema, Kebele 03, POB 2478, Addis Ababa; tel. (11) 6610156; fax (11) 6611191; e-mail roembaddis@ethionet.et; Chargé d'affaires a.i. GABRIEL BRANZARU.

Finland: Stenbäckinkatu 24, 00250 Helsinki; tel. (9) 2414414; fax (9) 2413272; e-mail romamb@clinet.fi; internet helsinki.mae.ro; Ambassador Lucian Fătu.

France: 5 rue de l'Exposition, 75007 Paris; tel. 1-47-05-10-46; fax 1-45-56-97-47; e-mail secretariat@amb-roumanie.fr; internet paris.mae.ro; Ambassador TEODOR BACONSCHI.

Georgia: Tbilisi, Lvovi 7; tel. (32) 38-53-10; fax (32) 38-52-10; e-mail roembtbl@caucasus.net; Ambassador Dan Mihai Bârliba.

Germany: Dorotheenstr. 62–66, 10117 Berlin; tel. (30) 21239202; fax (30) 21239399; e-mail office@rumaenische-botschaft.de; internet berlin.mae.ro; Ambassador BOGDAN MAZURU.

Greece: Odos Emmanuel Benaki 7, Palaio Psychiko, 154 52 Athens; tel. (210) 6728875; fax (210) 6728883; e-mail secretariat@romaniaemb.gr; internet www.atena.mae.ro; Ambassador George Ciamba.

Hungary: 1146 Budapest, Thököly u. 72; tel. (1) 384-0271; fax (1) 384-5535; e-mail postmaster@roembbud.axelero.net; Ambassador IRENY COMAROVSCHI.

India: A-47 Vasant Marg, Vasant Vihar, New Delhi 110 057; tel. (11) 26140447; fax (11) 26140611; e-mail embrom@touchtelindia.net; Ambassador Vasile Sofineti.

Indonesia: Jalan Teuku Cik Di Tiro, No. 42A, Menteng, Jakarta Pusat; tel. (21) 3900489; fax (21) 3106241; e-mail romind@cbn.net.id; Ambassador GHEORGHE VÎLCU.

Iran: 12 Fakhrabad Ave, Baharestan Ave, Tehran; tel. (21) 77539041; fax (21) 77535291; e-mail ambrotehran@parsonline.net; Chargé d'affaires a.i. Mircea Has.

Iraq: POB 2571, Arassat al-Hindia St, 452A/31/929 Hay Babel, Baghdad; tel. (1) 776-2860; fax (1) 776-7553; e-mail ambrobagd@yahoo.com; Ambassador MIHAI STUPARU.

Ireland: 26 Waterloo Rd, Dublin 4; tel. (1) 6681085; fax (1) 6681761; e-mail ambrom@eircom.net; internet dublin.mae.ro; Ambassador Silvia Stancu Davidoiu.

Israel: 24 Rehov Adam Hacohen, Tel-Aviv 64585; tel. 3-5230066; fax 3-5247379; e-mail rouembil@netvision.net.il; Ambassador VALERIA MARIANA STOICA.

Italy: Via Nicolo Tartaglia 36, 00197 Roma; tel. (06) 8084529; fax (06) 8084995; e-mail secretariat.ambasada@roembit.org; internet www.roembit .org; Ambassador Răzvan Victor Rusu.

Japan: 3-16-19, Nishi Azabu, Minato-ku, Tokyo 106-0031; tel. (3) 3479-0311; fax (3) 3479-0312; e-mail office@ambrom.jp; internet www.ambrom.jp; Ambassador AURELIAN NEAGU.

Jordan: POB 2869, 35 Madina Munawwara St, Amman; tel. (6) 5813423; fax (6) 5812521; e-mail roemb@batelco.jo; Ambassador Radu Onofrei.

Kazakhstan: 050010 Almaty, Pushkin 97; tel. (727) 261-57-72; fax (727) 258-83-17; e-mail amb@rom.ricc.kz; Ambassador EMIL RAPCEA.

Kenya: Gardenia Rd, Gigiri, POB 63240, Nairobi; tel. (20) 7123109; fax (20) 7122061; e-mail secretariat@romanianembassy.co.ke; Ambassador Mihail Constantin Coman.

Korea, Democratic People's Republic: Munhungdong, Taedongkang District, Pyongyang; tel. (2) 3827336; fax (2) 3817336; e-mail ambrophe@kcckp.net; Chargé d'affaires a.i. EUGEN POPA.

Korea, Republic: 1-42, UN Village, Hannam-dong, Yeongsan-gu, Seoul 140-210; tel. (2) 797-4924; fax (2) 794-3114; e-mail romemb@uriel.net; Chargé d'affaires a.i. Constantin Soare.

Kuwait: POB 11149, 35152 Dasmah, Keifan, Area 4, Moona St, House 34, Kuwait City; tel. 4845079; fax 4848929; e-mail ambsa@qualitynet.net; Ambassador CONSTANTIN VOLODEA NISTOR.

Lebanon: Route du Palais Presidentiel, Baabda, Beirut; tel. (5) 924848; fax (5) 924747; e-mail romembey@inco.com.lb; Ambassador Aurel Calin.

Libya: POB 5085, Sharia Ali bin Talib, Ben Ashour, Tripoli; tel. (21) 3615295; fax (21) 3607597; e-mail ambaromatrip@hotmail.com; Ambassador STAN NICULAE.

Lithuania: Vivulskio g. 19, Vilnius 03115; tel. (5) 231-0527; fax (5) 231-0652; e-mail ambromania@romania.lt; internet www.romania.lt; Ambassador Gheorghe Tokay.

Luxembourg: 41 blvd de la Pétrusse, 2320 Luxembourg; tel. 45-51-59; fax 45-51-63; e-mail ambroum@pt.lu; internet luxemburg.mae.ro; Ambassador VLAD TUDOR ALEXANDRESCU.

Macedonia, former Yugoslav Republic: 1000 Skopje, Rajko Zinzifov 42; tel. (2) 3228055; fax (2) 3228036; e-mail romanamb@on.net.mk; Ambassador Adrian Stefan Constantinescu.

Malaysia: 114 Jalan Damai, off Jalan Ampang, 55000 Kuala Lumpur; tel. (3) 21423172; fax (3) 21448713; e-mail roemb@streamyx.com; Ambassador PETRU PETRA.

Mexico: Sófocles 311, Col. Polanco, Del. Miguel Hidalgo, 11560 México, DF; tel. (55) 5280-0197; fax (55) 5280-0343; e-mail secretariat@rumania.org .mx; internet www.rumania.org.mx; Ambassador Manuela Vulpe.

Moldova: Chişinău, str. Bucureşti 66/1; tel. (22) 21-30-37; fax (22) 22-81-29; e-mail ambrom@moldnet.md; internet chisinau.mae.ro; Ambassador FILIP TEODORESCU.

Montenegro: 81000 Podgorica, Vukice Mitrovića 40; tel. (81) 618040; fax (81) 655081; Ambassador Mihail Florovici.

Morocco: 10 rue d'Ouezzane, Hassan, 10000 Rabat; tel. (3) 7724694; fax (3) 7700196; e-mail amb.roumanie@menara.ma; internet rabat.mae.ro; Ambassador VASILE POPOVICI.

Netherlands: Catsheuvel 55, 2517 KA The Hague; tel. (70) 3543796; fax (70) 3541587; e-mail sicrned@tip.nl; internet haga.mae.ro; Ambassador Călin Fabian.

Nigeria: Plot 498, Nelson Mandela St, Zone A4, Asokoro, POB 10376, Abuja; tel. (9) 3142304; fax (9) 3142306; e-mail romnig@gmail.com; Ambassador MARIAN PARJOL.

Norway: Oscarsgt. 51, 0244 Oslo; tel. 22-44-15-12; fax 22-43-16-74; e-mail embassy@romanianembassy.no; internet oslo.mae.ro; Ambassador Dr Cristian Istrate.

Pakistan: 13, St 88, G-6/3, Islamabad; tel. (51) 2826514; fax (51) 2826515; e-mail romania@isb.comsats.net.pk; Ambassador MIREEA HURMUZ.

Peru: Avda Jorge Basadre 690, San Isidro, Lima; tel. (1) 4224587; fax (1) 4210609; e-mail ambrom@terra.com.pe; Ambassador Ştefan Costin.

Philippines: 1216 Acacia Rd, Dasmariñas Village, Makati City, Metro Manila; tel. (2) 8439014; fax (2) 8439063; e-mail amaron@zpdee.net; Ambassador VALERIU GHEORGHE.

Poland: 00-559 Warsaw, ul. Chopina 10; tel. (22) 6283156; fax (22) 6285264; e-mail embassy@roembassy.com.pl; internet varsovia.mae.ro; Ambassador Gabriel Constantin Bărtaş.

Portugal: Rua de São Caetano a Lapa 5, 1200-828 Lisbon; tel. (21) 3968812; fax (21) 3960984; e-mail ambrom@mail.telepac.pt; internet lisabona.mae.ro; Ambassador GABRIEL GAFIŢA.

Qatar: POB 22511, Doha; tel. 4934848; fax 4934747; e-mail romamb@qatar .net.qa; Ambassador Adrian Măcelaru.

Russian Federation: 119590 Moscow, ul. Mosfilmovskaya 64; tel. (499) 143-04-24; fax (499) 143-04-49; e-mail ambasada@orc.ru; internet moscova.mae .ro; Ambassador MIHAIL GRIGORIE.

Senegal: rue A prolongée, point E, BP 3171, Dakar; tel. 33-825-2068; fax 33-824-9190; e-mail romania@sentoo.sn; Ambassador Simona Corlan-Ioan.

Serbia: 11000 Belgrade, Užička 10; tel. (11) 3675772; fax (11) 3675771; e-mail ambelgro@infosky.net; Ambassador ION MACOVEI.

Singapore: 48 Jalan Harom Setangkai, Singapore 258827; tel. 64683424; fax 64683425; e-mail comofrom@starhub.net.sg; Chargé d'affaires a.i. Silviu Ionescu.

Slovakia: Fraňa Krála 11, 811 05 Bratislava; tel. (2) 5249-1665; fax (2) 5244-4056; e-mail ro-embassy@ba.sknet.sk; internet bratislava.mae.ro; Chargé d'affaires a.i. GHEORGHE ANGHEL.

Slovenia: 1000 Ljubljana, Smrekarjeva 33 a; tel. (1) 5058294; fax (1) 5055432; e-mail embassy.of.romania@siol.net; internet ljubljana.mae.ro; Ambassador Dana Manuela Constantinescu.

South Africa: 117 Charles St, Brooklyn, Pretoria 0181; POB 11295, Hatfield 0028; tel. (12) 4606940; fax (12) 4606947; e-mail romembsa@global.co.za; Ambassador VALER GABRIEL PAUL POTRA.

Spain: Avda Alfonso XIII 157, 28016 Madrid; tel. (91) 3501881; fax (91) 3452917; e-mail secretariat@embajadaderumania.es; internet madrid.mae .ro; Ambassador Maria Ligor.

Sri Lanka: 14A Cambridge Terrace, Colombo 7; tel. (11) 2683421; fax (11) 2863422; e-mail romania@sltnet.lk; internet www.romania.lk; Chargé d'affaires a.i. IONEL GOMBOS.

Sudan: Kassala Rd, Plot No. 172–173, Kafouri Area, POB 1494, Khartoum North; tel. (185) 338114; fax (185) 341497; e-mail ambro_khartoum@ hotmail.com; Ambassador Dr Emil Ghitulescu.

Sweden: Östermalmsgt. 36, POB 26043, 100 41 Stockholm; tel. (8) 10-86-03; fax (8) 10-28-52; e-mail info@romanianembassy.se; internet stockholm.mae .ro; Ambassador VICTORIA POPESCU.

Switzerland: Kirchenfeldstr. 78, 3005 Bern; tel. 313523522; fax 313526455; e-mail roumanie.amb@befree.ch; internet berna.mae.ro; Ambassador Ionel Nicu Sava.

Syria: BP 4454, 8 rue Ibrahim Hanano, Damascus; tel. (11) 3327570; fax (11) 3327572; e-mail ro.dam@net.sy; Ambassador DANTOS FLORIN SANDOVETCH.

Thailand: 20/1 Soi Rajakhru, Phaholyothin Soi 5, Thanon Phaholyothin, Phayathai, Bangkok 10400; tel. (2) 617-1551; fax (2) 617-1113; e-mail romembnk@ksc.th.com; Ambassador Radu Gabriel Mateescu.

Tunisia: 18 ave d'Afrique, BP 57, al-Menzah V, 1004 Tunis; tel. (71) 766-926; fax (71) 767-695; e-mail amb.roumanie@planet.tn; internet www.ambassade -roumanie.intl.tn; Ambassador SORIN-MIHAIL TĂNĂSESCU.

Turkey: Bükreş Sok. 4, 06680 Çankaya, Ankara; tel. (312) 4271243; fax (312) 4271530; e-mail romanyabyk@dsl.ttnet.net.tr; Chargé d'affaires a.i. Petre Stoicescu.

Turkmenistan: 744000 Aşgabat, ul. Kusayeva 107; tel. (12) 34-76-55; fax (12) 34-76-20; e-mail ambromas@online.tm; Chargé d'affaires a.i. CIOCAN LAURENŢIU.

Ukraine: 01030 Kyiv, vul. M. Kotsyubynskoho 8; tel. (44) 234-00-40; fax (44) 235-20-25; e-mail romania@adamant.net; internet kiev.mae.ro; Ambassador Traian Laurenţiu Hristea.

United Arab Emirates: 9 POB 70416, Abu Dhabi; tel. (2) 4459919; fax (2) 4461143; e-mail romaniae@emirates.net.ae; Ambassador NIKOLAI JOYA.

United Kingdom: Arundel House, 4 Palace Green, London, W8 4QD; tel. (20) 7937-9666; fax (20) 7937-8069; e-mail roemb@roemb.co.uk; internet londra .mae.ro; Ambassador Ion Jinga.

United States of America: 1607 23rd St, NW, Washington, DC 20008; tel. (202) 232-4846; fax (202) 232-4748; e-mail info@roembus.org; internet www .roembus.org; Ambassador ADRIAN COSMIN VIERITA.

Uruguay: Echevarriarza 3452, Casilla 12040, 11000 Montevideo; tel. (2) 6220876; fax (2) 6220135; e-mail bcemontevideo@adinet.com.uy; Chargé d'affaires a.i. Gheorghe Petre.

Uzbekistan: 100000 Tashkent, Rejametov ko'ch. 44A; tel. (71) 152-63-55; fax (71) 120-75-67; e-mail romanian_embassy@sarkor.uz; Ambassador CONSTANTIN ALEXA.

Vatican City: Via Panama 92, 00198 Rome, Italy; tel. (06) 8541802; fax (06) 8554067; e-mail ambasciata@vatican.mae.ro; internet vatican.mae.ro; Ambassador Marius Gabriel Lazurca.

Venezuela: 4a Avda entre 8a y 9a Transversales, Quinta Guardatinajas 94-14, Altamira, Caracas; tel. (212) 261-9480; fax (212) 263-7161; e-mail ambasadaccs@cantv.net; Ambassador MARINEL IOANA.

Viet Nam: 5 Le Hong Phong, Hanoi; tel. (4) 8452014; fax (4) 8430922; e-mail rombcehan@fpt.vn; Ambassador Dumitru Olaru.

Zimbabwe: 105 Fourth St, POB 4797, Harare; tel. (4) 700853; fax (4) 725493; Chargé d'affaires a.i. LUMINITA FLORESCU.

DIPLOMATIC MISSIONS OF RUSSIA

United Nations: 136 East 67th St, New York, NY 10021; tel. (212) 861-4900; fax (212) 628-0252; e-mail rusun@un.int; internet www.un.int/russia; Permanent Representative Vitaly Churkin.

Afghanistan: House 63, Lane 5, St 15, Wazir Akbar Khan, Kabul; tel. (20) 2300500; e-mail rusembafg@neda.af; Ambassador ZAMIR N. KABULOV.

Albania: Rruga Asim Zeneli 5, Tirana; tel. (4) 256040; fax (4) 256046; e-mail rusemb@icc.al.eu.org; Ambassador Aleksandr L. Prishchepov.

Algeria: 7 chemin du Prince d'Annam, el-Biar, Algiers; tel. (21) 92-31-39; fax (21) 92-28-82; e-mail ambrussie@yandex.ru; internet www.ambrussie.gov.dz; Ambassador ALEKSANDR EGOROV.

Angola: Rua Houari Boumedienne 170, CP 3141, Luanda; tel. 222445028; fax 222445320; e-mail rusemb@netangola.com; Ambassador Andrei Kemarsky.

Argentina: Rodríguez Peña 1741, C1021ABK Buenos Aires; tel. (11) 4813-1552; fax (11) 4815-6293; e-mail embrusia@fibertel.com.ar; internet www .argentina.mid.ru; Ambassador YURI P. KORCHAGIN.

Armenia: 0015 Yerevan, Grigor Lusavorichi St 13a; tel. (10) 56-74-27; fax (10) 56-71-97; e-mail info@rusembassy.am; internet www.armenia.mid.ru; Ambassador Nikolai V. Pavlov.

Australia: 78 Canberra Ave, Griffith, ACT 2603; tel. (2) 6295-9033; fax (2) 6295-1847; e-mail rusembassy.australia@rambler.ru; internet www.australia .mid.ru; Ambassador ALEXANDER BLOKHIN.

Austria: Reisnerstr. 45–47, 1030 Vienna; tel. (1) 712-12-29; fax (1) 712-33-88; e-mail rusemb@chello.at; internet www.austria.mid.ru; Ambassador Stanislav V. Osadchiy.

Azerbaijan: 1022 Baku, Bakixanov küç. 17; tel. (12) 498-60-16; fax (12) 498-14-16; e-mail embrus@azdata.net; internet www.embrus-az.com; Ambassador VASILII N. ISTRATOV.

Bahrain: POB 26612, Manama; tel. 17725222; fax 17725921; e-mail rusemb@ batelco.com.bh; internet www.bahrain.mid.ru; Ambassador Yurii Antonov.

Bangladesh: NE(J) 9, Rd 79, Gulshan 2, Dhaka 1212; tel. (2) 8828147; fax (2) 8823735; e-mail info@rusdhaka.org; internet www.bangladesh.mid.ru; Ambassador GENNADII P. TROTSENKO.

Belarus: 220002 Minsk, vul. Staravilenskaya 48; tel. (17) 250-36-66; fax (17) 250-36-64; e-mail kira1130@yahoo.com; internet www.belarus.mid.ru; Ambassador Aleksandr A. Surikov.

Belgium: 66 ave de Fré, 1180 Brussels; tel. (2) 374-34-00; fax (2) 374-26-13; e-mail amrusbel@skynet.be; internet www.belgium.mid.ru; Ambassador VADIM B. LUKOV.

Benin: Zone résidentielle, ave de la Marina, face Hôtel du Port, BP 2013, Cotonou; tel. 21-31-28-34; fax 21-31-28-35; e-mail benamrus@leland.bj; internet www.benin.mid.ru; Ambassador Vladimir S. Timoshenko.

Bolivia: Calacoto, Avda Walter Guevara Arce 8129, La Paz; tel. (2) 278-6419; fax (2) 278-6531; e-mail embrusia@ceibo.entelnet.bo; Ambassador VLADIMIR L. KULIKOV.

Bosnia and Herzegovina: 71000 Sarajevo, Urjan Dedina 93–95; tel. (33) 668147; fax (33) 668148; e-mail rusembbih@lsinter.net; internet www .sarajevo.mid.ru; Ambassador Konstantin V. Shuvalov.

Botswana: Plot 4711, Tawana Close, POB 81, Gaborone; tel. 3953389; fax 3952930; e-mail embrus@info.bw; internet www.botswana.mid.ru; Ambassador IGOR S. LIAKIN-FROLOV.

Brazil: SES, Av. das Nações, Quadra 801, Lote A, 70476-900 Brasília, DF; tel. (61) 3223-3094; fax (61) 3226-7319; e-mail emb@embrus.brte.com.br; internet www.brazil.mid.ru; Ambassador Vladimir L. Tyurdenev.

Bulgaria: 1087 Sofia, ul. D. Tsankov 28; tel. (2) 963-16-63; fax (2) 963-41-03; e-mail info@russia.bg; internet www.russia.bg; Ambassador ANATOLII V. POTAPOV.

Burundi: 78 blvd de l'UPRONA, BP 1034, Bujumbura; tel. 22226098; fax 22222984; Ambassador Igor S. Liakin-Frolov.

Cambodia: 213 blvd Sothearos, Phnom-Penh; tel. (23) 210931; fax (23) 216776; e-mail russemba@online.com.kh; internet www.embrusscambodia .mid.ru; Ambassador VALERY TERESHCHENKO.

Cameroon: Quartier Bastos, BP 488, Yaoundé; tel. 2220-1714; fax 2220-7891; e-mail consrusse@camnet.cm; Ambassador Poulate Abdoulayev.

Canada: 285 Charlotte St, Ottawa, ON K1N 8L5; tel. (613) 235-4341; fax (613) 236-6342; e-mail rusemb@magma.ca; internet www.rusembcanada.mid .ru; Ambassador GEORGII MAMEDOV.

Cape Verde: Achada de Santo António, CP 31, Praia, Santiago; tel. 2622739; fax 2622738; e-mail embrus@cvtelecom.cv; Ambassador Vladimir E. Petukhov.

Central African Republic: ave du Président Gamal Abdel Nasser, BP 1405, Bangui; tel. 61-03-11; fax 61-56-45; e-mail ruscons@intent.cf; Ambassador IGOR P. LABUZOV.

Chad: 2 rue Adjutant Collin, BP 891, N'Djamena; tel. 51-57-19; fax 51-31-72; e-mail amrus@intnet.td; Ambassador Vladimir N. Martynov.

Chile: Cristobal Colón 4152, Las Condes, Santiago; tel. (2) 208-6254; fax (2) 206-8892; e-mail embajada@rusia.tie.cl; internet www.chile.mid.ru; Ambassador YURIY A. FILÁTOV.

China, People's Republic: 4 Dong Zhi Men Nei, Bei Zhong Jie, Beijing 100600; tel. (10) 65322051; fax (10) 65324851; e-mail embassy@russia.org.cn; internet www.russia.org.cn; Ambassador Sergei Sergeevich Razov.

Colombia: Carrera 4, No 75-02, Apdo Aéreo 90600, Bogotá, DC; tel. (1) 212-1881; fax (1) 210-4694; e-mail embajadarusia@cable.net.co; internet www .colombia.mid.ru; Ambassador VLADIMIR V. TRUJANOVSKI.

Congo, Democratic Republic: 80 ave de la Justice, BP 1143, Kinshasa 1; tel. (12) 33157; fax (12) 45575; Ambassador Valerii Gamaivne.

Congo, Republic: ave Félix Eboué, BP 2132, Brazzaville; tel. 81-19-23; fax 81-50-85; e-mail amrussie@ic.cd; internet www.congo.mid.ru; Ambassador MIKHAIL S. TSVIGUN.

Costa Rica: Curridabat, Lomas de Ayarco Sur, de la carretera a Cartago, 1a entrada, 100 m sur, Apdo 6340, 1000 San José; tel. 256-9181; fax 221-2054; e-mail emrusa@racsa.co.cr; Ambassador Valerii Dmitrievich Nikolayenko.

Côte d'Ivoire: BP 583, Riviera, Abidjan 01; tel. 22-43-09-59; fax 22-43-11-66; e-mail ambrus@globeaccess.net; Ambassador OLEG V. KOVALCHUK.

Croatia: 10000 Zagreb, Bosanska 44; tel. (1) 3755038; fax (1) 3755040; e-mail veleposlanstvo-ruske-federacije@zg.tel.hr; internet www.croatia.mid.ru; Ambassador Mikhail A. Konarovskii.

Cuba: Avda 5, No 6402, entre 62 y 66, Miramar, Havana; tel. (7) 204-2686; fax (7) 204-1038; e-mail embrusia@ceniai.inf.cu; Ambassador ANDREI VIKTOROVICH DIMITRIEV.

Cyprus: POB 21845, Ayios Prokopias St and Archbishop Makarios III Ave, Engomi, 2406 Nicosia; tel. 22774622; fax 22774854; e-mail russia1@cytanet .com.cy; internet www.cyprus.mid.ru; Ambassador Andrei A. Nesterenko.

Czech Republic: Pod kaštany 1, 160 00 Prague 6; tel. 233374100; fax 233377235; e-mail embrus@tiscali.cz; internet www.czech.mid.ru; Ambassador ALEKSEI L. FEDOTOV.

Denmark: Kristianiagade 5, 2100 Copenhagen Ø; tel. 35-42-55-85; fax 35-42-37-41; e-mail embrus@mail.dk; internet www.denmark.mid.ru; Ambassador Teimuraz O. Ramishvili.

Djibouti: BP 1913, Plateau du Marabout, Djibouti; tel. 350740; fax 355990; e-mail russiaemb@intnet.dj; Ambassador MIKHAIL TSVIGOUN.

Ecuador: Reina Victoria 462 y Ramón Roca, Quito; tel. (2) 256-6361; fax (2) 256-5531; e-mail embrusia@accessinter.net; Ambassador Valentin Bogomázov.

Egypt: 95 Sharia Giza, Cairo (Giza); tel. (2) 3489353; fax (2) 3609074; Ambassador MIKHAIL BOGDANOV.

Equatorial Guinea: Malabo; Ambassador Lev A. Vakhrameyev.

Eritrea: 21 Zobel St, POB 5667, Asmara; tel. (1) 127162; fax (1) 127164; e-mail rusemb@eol.com.er; Ambassador ALEXANDER OBLOV.

Estonia: Pikk 19, Tallinn 10133; tel. 646-4175; fax 646-4178; e-mail vensaat@ online.ee; internet www.rusemb.ee; Ambassador Nikolai N. Uspenskii.

Ethiopia: POB 1500, Addis Ababa; tel. (11) 6612060; fax (11) 6613795; e-mail russemb@ethionet.et; Ambassador MIKHAIL Y. AFANASIEV.

Finland: Tehtaankatu 1b, 00140 Helsinki; tel. (9) 661876; fax (9) 661006; e-mail rusembassy@co.inet.fi; internet www.rusembassy.fi; Ambassador Aleksandr Yu. Rumyantsev.

France: 40–50 blvd Lannes, 75116 Paris; tel. 1-45-04-05-50; fax 1-45-04-17-65; e-mail ambrus@orange.fr; internet www.france.mid.ru; Ambassador ALEKSANDR A. AVDEYEV.

Gabon: BP 3963, Libreville; tel. 72-48-69; fax 72-48-70; Ambassador Vsevolod Soukhov.

Georgia: 0162 Tbilisi, Chavchavadze 51; tel. (32) 91-24-06; fax (32) 91-27-38; e-mail russianembassy@caucasus.net; internet www.georgia.mid.ru; Ambassador VYACHESLAV YE. KOVALENKO.

Germany: Unter den Linden 63–65, 10117 Berlin; tel. (30) 2291110; fax (30) 2299397; e-mail info@russische-botschaft.de; internet www.russische -botschaft.de; Ambassador Vladimir V. Kotenev.

Ghana: 856/1 Ring Rd East, 13 Lane, POB 1634, Accra; tel. (21) 775611; fax (21) 772699; e-mail russia@4u.com.gh; internet www.ghana.mid.ru; Ambassador ANDREY V. POKROVSKIY.

Greece: Odos Nikiforou Litra 28, Palaio Psychiko, 154 52 Athens; tel. (210) 6725235; fax (210) 6479708; e-mail embraf@otenet.gr; internet www.greece .mid.ru; Ambassador Andrei Vdovin.

Guatemala: 2 Avenida 12-85, Zona 14, Guatemala City; tel. 2367-2765; fax 2367-2766; e-mail embrusia@guate.net.gt; internet www.guat.mid.ru; Ambassador VALERY NIKOLAENKO (resident in San José, Costa Rica).

Guinea: Matam-Port, km 9, BP 329, Conakry; tel. 30-40-52-22; fax 30-46-57-81; e-mail ambrus@biasy.net; Ambassador Dmitrii V. Malev.

Guinea-Bissau: Av. 14 de Novembro, CP 308, Bissau; tel. 251036; fax 251028; e-mail ambrus-gui@mirinet.net.gn; Chargé d'affaires a.i. VIACHELAV ROZHNOV.

Guyana: 3 Public Rd, Kitty, Georgetown; tel. 226-9773; fax 227-2975; e-mail embrus.guyana@mail.ru; internet www.rusembassyguyana.org.gy; Ambassador Vladimir S. Starikov.

Hungary: 1062 Budapest, Bajza u. 35; tel. (1) 302-5230; fax (1) 353-4164; internet www.hungary.mid.ru; Ambassador IGOR S. SAVOLSKII.

Iceland: Garastræti 33, 101 Reykjavík; tel. 5515156; fax 5620633; e-mail russemb@itn.is; internet www.iceland.mid.ru; Ambassador Viktor I. Tatarintsev.

India: Shanti Path, Chanakyapuri, New Delhi 110 021; tel. (11) 26873799; fax (11) 26876823; e-mail indrusem@del2.vsnl.net.in; internet www.india.mid .ru; Ambassador VYACHESLAV TRUBNIKOV.

Indonesia: Jalan H. R. Rasuna Said, Kav. X-6, Jakarta; tel. (21) 5222912; e-mail rusembjkt@uninet.net.id; internet www.indonesia.mid.ru; Ambassador Alexander A. Ivanov.

Iran: 39 Neauphle-le-Château Ave, Tehran; tel. (21) 66701161; fax (21) 66701652; e-mail rusembiran@parsonline.net; internet www.iran.mid.ru; Ambassador ALEKSANDR ALEXEYEVICH SADOVNIKOV.

Iraq: 4/5/605 Hay al-Mutanabi, Baghdad; tel. (1) 541-4749; fax (1) 543-4462; e-mail russian_embassy_in_iraq@land.ru; Ambassador Vladimir Chamov.

Ireland: 184–186 Orwell Rd, Dublin 14; tel. (1) 4922048; fax (1) 4923525; e-mail russiane@indigo.ie; internet www.ireland.mid.ru; Ambassador MIKHAIL YE. TIMOSHKIN.

Israel: 120 Rehov Hayarkon, Tel-Aviv 63573; tel. 3-5226736; fax 3-5226713; e-mail amb_ru@mail.netvision.net.il; internet www.russianembassy.org.il; Ambassador Gennadii Pavlovich Tarasov.

Italy: Via Gaeta 5, 00185 Roma; tel. (06) 4941680; fax (06) 491031; e-mail ambrus@ambrussia.it; internet www.ambrussia.com; Ambassador ALEXEI YU. MESHKOV.

Jamaica: 22 Norbrook Dr., Kingston 8; tel. 924-1048; fax 925-8290; e-mail rusembja@colis.com; Ambassador Eduard Malayan.

Japan: 2-1-1, Azabu-dai, Minato-ku, Tokyo 106-0041; tel. (3) 3583-4224; fax (3) 3505-0593; e-mail rosconsl@ma.kcom.ne.jp; internet www.russia-emb.jp; Ambassador MIKHAIL M. BELY.

Jordan: POB 2187, 22 Zahran St, Amman 11181; tel. (6) 4641158; fax (6) 4647448; e-mail rusembjo@mail.ru; internet www.jordan.mid.ru; Ambassador Aleksander Kalugin.

Kazakhstan: 010000 Astana, Barayev 4; tel. (7172) 22-24-83; fax (7172) 22-38-49; e-mail rfe@nursat.kz; internet www.rfembassy.kz; Ambassador MIKHAIL N. BOCHARNIKOV.

Kenya: Lenana Rd, POB 30049, Nairobi; tel. (20) 728700; fax (20) 721888; e-mail russemb@swiftkenya.com; Ambassador Valery Yegoshkin.

Korea, Democratic People's Republic: Sinyangdong, Central District, Pyongyang; tel. (2) 3823102; fax (2) 3813427; e-mail rusembdprk@yahoo.com; Ambassador VALERY SUKHININ.

Korea, Republic: 34-16, Jeong-dong, Jung-gu, Seoul 100-120; tel. (2) 318-2116; fax (2) 754-0417; e-mail rusemb@uriel.net; internet www.russian-embassy.org; Ambassador Gleb A. Ivashentsov.

Kuwait: POB 1765 Safat, Daya Diplomatic Area, Block 17, Kuwait City; tel. 2560427; fax 2524969; e-mail rospos@kuwait.net; Ambassador AZAMAT R. KULMUKHAMETOV.

Kyrgyzstan: 720040 Bishkek, Razzakova 17; tel. (312) 62-47-38; fax (312) 62-18-23; e-mail rusemb@elcat.kg; internet www.kyrgyz.mid.ru; Ambassador Valentin S. Vlasov.

Laos: Ban Thadeua, quartier Thaphalanxay, BP 490, Vientiane; tel. (21) 312222; fax (21) 312210; e-mail rusemb@laotel.com; Ambassador VLADIMIR PLOTNIKOV.

Latvia: Antonijas iela 2, Rīga 1010; tel. 6733-2151; fax 6783-0209; e-mail rusembas@delfi.lv; internet www.latvia.mid.ru; Ambassador Aleksandr Veshnyakov.

Lebanon: POB 5220, rue Mar Elias et-Tineh, Wata Mseitbeh, Beirut; tel. (1) 300041; fax (1) 303837; e-mail rusembei@cyberia.net.lb; internet www.lebanon.mid.ru; Ambassador SERGEI NIKOLAYEVICH BUKIN.

Liberia: Payne Ave, Sinkor, POB 2010, Monrovia; tel. 261304; Ambassador Andrey V. Pokrovskii.

Libya: POB 4792, Sharia Mustapha Kamel, Tripoli; tel. (21) 3330545; fax (21) 4446673; Ambassador VALERYIAN V. SHUVAYEV.

Lithuania: Latvių g. 53/54, Vilnius 08113; tel. (5) 272-1763; fax (5) 272-3877; e-mail post@rusemb.lt; internet www.rusemb.lt; Ambassador Boris A. Tsepov.

Luxembourg: Château de Beggen, 1719 Luxembourg; tel. 42-23-33; fax 42-23-34; e-mail ambruslu@pt.lu; internet www.ruslux.mid.ru; Ambassador EDUARD R. MALAYAN.

Macedonia, former Yugoslav Republic: 1000 Skopje, Pirinska 44; tel. (2) 3117160; fax (2) 3117808; e-mail embassy@russia.org.mk; internet www.russia.org.mk; Ambassador Vladimir Solotsinskii.

Madagascar: BP 4006, Ivandry-Ambohijatovo, 101 Antananarivo; tel. (20) 2242827; fax (20) 2242642; e-mail ambrusmad@wanadoo.mg; Ambassador VLADIMIR B. GONCHARENKO.

Malaysia: 263 Jalan Ampang, 50450 Kuala Lumpur; tel. (3) 42567252; fax (3) 42576091; e-mail ruemvvl@tm.net.my; internet www.malaysia.mid.ru; Ambassador Alexander A. Karchava.

Mali: BP 300, Niarela, Bamako; tel. 221-55-92; fax 221-99-26; Ambassador ANATOLII P. SMIRNOV.

Malta: Ariel House, 25 Anthony Schembri St, Kappara, San Ġwann SGN 08; tel. 21371905; fax 21372131; e-mail rusemb@onvol.net; internet www.malta.mid.ru; Ambassador Andrei E. Granovskii.

Mauritania: rue Abu Bakr, BP 221, Nouakchott; tel. 525-19-73; fax 525-52-96; e-mail ambruss@opt.mr; Ambassador LEONID V. ROGOV.

Mauritius: Queen Mary Ave, POB 10, Floreal, Port Louis; tel. 696-1545; fax 696-5027; e-mail rusemb.mu@intnet.mu; Ambassador Olga Ivanova.

Mexico: José Vasconcelos 204, Col. Hipódromo Condesa, Del. Cuauhtémoc, 06140 México, DF; tel. (55) 5273-1305; fax (55) 5273-1545; e-mail embrumex@mail.internet.com.mx; Ambassador VALERY I. MOROZOV.

Moldova: 2004 Chişinău, bd Ştefan cel Mare 153; tel. (22) 23-49-43; fax (22) 23-51-07; e-mail domino@mtc.md; internet www.moldova.mid.ru; Ambassador Valerii I. Kuzmin.

Mongolia: Enkh Taivny Gudamj 6-A, Ulan Bator (CPOB 661); tel. (11) 327191; fax (11) 327018; Ambassador BORIS ALEKSANDROVICH GOVORIN.

Montenegro: 81000 Podgorica, Veliše Mugoše 1; tel. (81) 272460; e-mail gencons.ru@cg.yu; Ambassador Yakov F. Gerasimov.

Morocco: km 4 route des Zaêrs, 10100 Rabat; tel. (3) 7753509; fax (3) 7753590; e-mail ambrus@iam.net.ma; internet www.morocco.mid.ru; Ambassador ALEXANDER TOKOVININ.

Mozambique: Av. Vladimir I. Lénine 2445, CP 4666, Maputo; tel. 21417372; fax 21417515; e-mail embrus@tvcabo.co.mz; internet www.mozambique.mid.ru; Ambassador Igor V. Popov.

Myanmar: 38 Sagawa Rd, Yangon; tel. (1) 241955; fax (1) 241953; e-mail rusinmyan@mptmail.net.mm; internet www.rusembmyanmar.org; Ambassador MIKHAIL M. MGELADZE.

Namibia: 4 Christian St, POB 3826, Windhoek; tel. (61) 228671; fax (61) 229061; Ambassador Nikolai M. Gribkov.

Nepal: Baluwatar, POB 123, Kathmandu; tel. (1) 4412155; fax (1) 4416571; e-mail ruspos@info.com.np; internet www.nepal.mid.ru; Ambassador ANDREI LEONIDOVICH TROFIMOV.

Netherlands: Andries Bickerweg 2, 2517 JP The Hague; tel. (70) 3451300; fax (70) 3617960; e-mail ambrusnl@euronet.nl; internet www.netherlands.mid.ru; Ambassador Kirill G. Gevorgiyan.

New Zealand: 57 Messines Rd, Karori, Wellington; tel. (4) 476-6113; fax (4) 476-3843; e-mail info@rus.co.nz; internet www.rus.co.nz; Ambassador MIKHAIL LYSENKO.

Nicaragua: Reparto Las Colinas, Calle Vista Alegre 214, Entre Avda Central y Paseo del Club, Apdo 249, Managua; tel. 276-0374; fax 276-0179; e-mail rossia@ibw.com.ni; Ambassador Igor Sergeevich Kondrashev.

Nigeria: 5 Walter Carrington Cres., Victoria Island, POB 2723, Lagos; tel. (1) 2613359; fax (1) 4619994; Ambassador GENNADY V. ILYITEHEV.

Norway: Drammensvn 74, 0244 Oslo; tel. 22-55-32-78; fax 22-55-00-70; e-mail rembassy@online.no; internet www.norway.mid.ru; Ambassador Sergei V. Andreev.

Oman: Shati al-Qurum, Way No. 3032, Surfait Compound, POB 80, Ruwi 112; tel. 24602894; fax 24604189; e-mail rusoman@omantel.net.om; Ambassador DR SERGEI E. EVANOV.

Pakistan: Khayaban-e-Suhrawardy, Diplomatic Enclave, Ramna 4, Islamabad; tel. (51) 2278670; fax (51) 2826552; e-mail russia2@comsats.net.pk; internet www.pakistan.mid.ru; Ambassador Sergey N. Peskov.

Panama: Torre IBC, 10°, Avda Manuel Espinosa Batista, Apdo 6-4697, El Dorado, Panamá; tel. 264-1408; fax 264-1588; e-mail emruspan@sinfo.net; Ambassador EVGENY ROSTISLAVOVICH VORONIN.

Peru: Avda Salaverry 3424, San Isidro, Lima 27; tel. (1) 2640036; fax (1) 2640130; e-mail embrusa@amauta.rcp.net.pe; Ambassador Mijaeil Troyanski.

Philippines: 1245 Acacia Rd, Dasmariñas Village, Makati City, Metro Manila; tel. (2) 8930190; fax (2) 8109614; e-mail RusEmb@i-manila.com.ph; Ambassador VITALIY VOROBIEV.

Poland: 00-761 Warsaw, ul. Belwederska 49; tel. (22) 6213453; fax (22) 6253016; e-mail rusemb_poland@mail.ru; internet www.poland.mid.ru; Ambassador Vladimir M. Grinin.

Portugal: Rua Visconde de Santarém 59, 1000-286 Lisbon; tel. (21) 8462423; fax (21) 8463008; e-mail mail@embaixadarussia.pt; internet www.portugal.mid.ru; Ambassador PAVEL F. PETROVSKII.

Qatar: POB 15404, Doha; tel. 4836231; fax 4836243; e-mail rusemb@qatar.net.qa; internet www.qatar.mid.ru; Ambassador Andrew V. Andreev.

Romania: 011341 Bucharest 1, Şos. Kiseleff 6; tel. (21) 2223170; fax (21) 2229450; e-mail rab@mb.roknet.ro; internet www.romania.mid.ru; Ambassador ALEKSANDR A. CHURILIN.

Rwanda: 19 ave de l'Armée, BP 40, Kigali; tel. 575286; fax 574818; e-mail ambruss@rwandatel1.rwanda1.com; Ambassador Mirgayas M. Shirinskii.

Saudi Arabia: POB 94308, Riyadh 11693; tel. (1) 481-1875; fax (1) 481-1890; Ambassador Igor A. MELIKHOV.

Senegal: ave Jean Jaurès, angle rue Carnot, BP 3180, Dakar; tel. 33-822-4821; fax 33-821-1372; e-mail ambrus@sentoo.sn; Ambassador Aleksandr A. Romanov.

Serbia: 11000 Belgrade, ul. Deligradska 32; tel. (11) 3611323; fax (11) 3611900; e-mail ambarusk@eunet.yu; Ambassador ALEKSANDR V. KONUZIN.

Seychelles: Le Niol, POB 632, St Louis, Mahé; tel. 266590; fax 266653; e-mail rfembsey@seychelles.net; Ambassador Alexander Vladimirov.

Singapore: 51 Nassim Rd, Singapore 258439; tel. 62351834; fax 67334780; e-mail rosposol@pacific.net.sg; internet www.singapore.mid.ru; Ambassador ANDREY N. ROZHKOV.

Slovakia: Godrova 4, 811 06 Bratislava; tel. (2) 5441-4436; fax (2) 5443-4910; e-mail embrus@chello.sk; internet www.slovakia.mid.ru; Ambassador Aleksandr I. Udaltsov.

Slovenia: 1000 Ljubljana, Tomšičeva 9; tel. (1) 4256875; fax (1) 4254141; e-mail ambrus.slo@siol.net; internet www.rus-slo.mid.ru; Ambassador MIKHAIL V. VANIN.

South Africa: 316 Brooks St, Menlo Park, Pretoria 0081; POB 6743, Pretoria 0001; tel. (12) 3621337; fax (12) 3620116; e-mail ruspospr@mweb.co.za; internet www.russianembassy.org.za; Ambassador Anatoly A. Makarov.

Spain: Velázquez 155, 28002 Madrid; tel. (91) 4110807; fax (91) 5629712; e-mail embrues@infonegocio.com; internet www.spain.mid.ru; Ambassador ALEKSANDR I. KUZNETSOV.

Sri Lanka: 62 Sir Ernest de Silva Mawatha, Colombo 7; tel. (11) 2573555; fax (11) 2574957; e-mail rusemb@itmin.net; internet www.sri-lanka.mid.ru; Ambassador Alexey L. Shebarshin.

Sudan: A10 St, B1, New Extension, POB 1161, Khartoum; tel. (183) 471042; fax (183) 471239; e-mail rfsudan@hotmail.com; Ambassador VALERII Y. SUKHIN.

Suriname: Anton Dragtenweg 7, POB 8127, Paramaribo; tel. 472387; Ambassador Pavel Sergiev.

Sweden: Gjörwellsgt. 31, 112 60 Stockholm; tel. (8) 13-04-41; fax (8) 618-27-03; e-mail rusembassy@telia.com; internet www.ryssland.se; Ambassador ALEKSANDR M. KADAKIN.

Switzerland: Brunnadernrain 37, 3006 Bern; tel. 313520566; fax 313525595; e-mail rusbotschaft@bluewin.ch; internet www.switzerland.mid.ru; Ambassador Igor B. Bratchikov.

Syria: rue Umar bin al-Khattab, ad-Dawi, Damascus; tel. (11) 4423155; fax (11) 4423182; e-mail rusemb@scs-net.org; Ambassador SERGEI KIRPICHENKO.

Tajikistan: 734000 Dushanbe, Kuchai Abu Ali ibni Sino 29/31; tel. (372) 235-70-65; fax (372) 235-88-06; e-mail rambtadjik@rambler.ru; internet www.rusembassy.tajnet.com; Ambassador Ramazan G. Abdulatipov.

Tanzania: Plot No. 73, Ali Hassan Mwinyi Rd, POB 1905, Dar es Salaam; tel. (22) 2666005; fax (22) 2666818; e-mail embruss@bol.co.tz; Ambassador LEONARD ALEKSEEVIC.

Thailand: 78 Thanon Sap, Bangrak, Bangkok 10500; tel. (2) 234-9824; fax (2) 237-8488; e-mail rusembbangkok@rambler.ru; internet www.thailand.mid.ru; Ambassador Yevgeny V. Afanasiev.

Tunisia: 4 rue Bergamotes, BP 48, El Manar I, 2092 Tunis; tel. (71) 882-446; fax (71) 882-478; e-mail ambrustn@mail.ru; internet www.tunisie.mid.ru; Ambassador ANDREI POLYAKOV.

Turkey: Karyağdı Sok. 5, 06692 Çankaya, Ankara; tel. (312) 4392122; fax (312) 4383952; e-mail rus-ankara@yandex.ru; internet www.turkey.mid.ru; Ambassador Vladimir E. Ivanovskii.

Turkmenistan: 744004 Aşgabat, pr. S. Türkmenbaşi 11; tel. (12) 35-39-57; fax (12) 39-84-66; e-mail emb-rus@online.tm; Ambassador IGOR A. BLATOV.

Uganda: 28 Malcolm X Ave, Kololo, POB 7022, Kampala; tel. (41) 4433676; fax (41) 4345798; Ambassador Valery I. Utkin.

Ukraine: 03049 Kyiv, Povitroflotskyi pr. 27; tel. (44) 244-09-63; fax (44) 246-34-69; e-mail embrus@public.icyb.kiev.ua; internet www.embrus.org.ua; Ambassador VIKTOR S. CHERNOMYRDIN.

United Arab Emirates: POB 8211, Abu Dhabi; tel. (2) 6721797; fax (2) 6728713; e-mail ruconsl@emirates.net.ae; Ambassador Sergei Yakovlev.

United Kingdom: 13 Kensington Palace Gdns, London, W8 4QX; tel. (20) 7229-6412; fax (20) 7727-8625; e-mail office@rusemblon.org; internet www.great-britain.mid.ru; Ambassador YURII V. FEDOTOV.

United States of America: 2650 Wisconsin Ave, NW, Washington, DC 20007; tel. (202) 298-5700; fax (202) 298-5735; e-mail rusembus@erols.com; internet www.russianembassy.org; Ambassador Yurii Viktorovich Ushakov.

Uruguay: Blvr España 2741, 11300 Montevideo; tel. (2) 7081884; fax (2) 7086597; e-mail embaru@montevideo.com.uy; internet www.uruguay.mid.ru; Ambassador SERGUEY N. KOSHKIN.

Uzbekistan: 100015 Tashkent, Nukus ko'ch. 83; tel. (71) 120-35-04; fax (71) 120-35-09; e-mail rusemb@albatros.uz; internet www.uzbekistan.mid.ru; Ambassador Farit M. Mukhametshin.

Vatican City: Via della Conciliazione 10, 00193 Rome, Italy; tel. (06) 6877078; fax (06) 6877168; Ambassador NIKOLAY SADCHIKOV.

Venezuela: Quinta Soyuz, Calle Las Lomas, Las Mercedes, Caracas; tel. (212) 993-4395; fax (212) 993-6526; e-mail rusemb95@infoline.wtfe.com; Ambassador Aleksei Ermakov.

Viet Nam: 191 La Thanh, Hanoi; tel. (4) 8336991; fax (4) 8336995; e-mail moscow.vietnam@hn.vnn.vn; Ambassador VADIM VIKTOROVICH SERAFIMOV.

Yemen: POB 1087, 26 September St, San'a; tel. (1) 278719; fax (1) 283142; e-mail remb@y.net.ye; Ambassador Alexander Zasypkin.

Zambia: Plot 6407, Diplomatic Triangle, POB 32355, 10101 Lusaka; tel. (1) 252120; fax (1) 253582; internet www.russianembassy.biz/zambia-lusaka.htm; Ambassador ANVAR AZIMOV.

Zimbabwe: 70 Fife Ave, POB 4250, Harare; tel. (4) 701957; fax (4) 700534; e-mail russemb@africaonline.co.zw; internet www.zimbabwe.mid.ru; Ambassador Sergei Kryukov.

DIPLOMATIC MISSIONS OF RWANDA

United Nations: 124 East 39th St, New York, NY 10016; tel. (212) 679-9010; fax (212) 679-9133; e-mail rwanda@un.int; Permanent Representative JOSEPH NSENGIMANA.

Belgium: 1 ave des Fleurs, 1150 Brussels; tel. (2) 763-07-21; fax (2) 763-07-53; e-mail ambarwanda@gmail.com; internet www.ambarwanda.be; Ambassador Joseph Bonesha.

Burundi: 24 ave du Zaïre, BP 400, Bujumbura; tel. 22223140; Ambassador JANVIER KANYAMASHULI.

Canada: 121 Sherwood Drive, Ottawa, ON K1Y 3V1; tel. (613) 569-5420; fax (613) 569-5421; e-mail generalinfo@ambarwaottawa.ca; internet www.ambarwaottawa.ca; Ambassador Edda Mukabagwiza.

China, People's Republic: 30 Xiu Shui Bei Jie, Jian Guo Men Wai, Beijing 100600; tel. (10) 65322193; fax (10) 65322006; e-mail ambarwda@public3.bta.net.cn; Ambassador BEN MATHIAS RUGANGAZI.

Egypt: 23 Sharia Babel, Mohandessin, Cairo (Dokki); tel. (2) 3350532; fax (2) 3351479; Ambassador Célestin Kabanda.

Ethiopia: Africa House, Woreda 17, Kebele 20, POB 5618, Addis Ababa; tel. (11) 6610300; fax (11) 6610411; Ambassador NYILINKINDI GASPARD.

France: 12 rue Jadin, 75017 Paris; tel. 1-42-27-36-31; fax 1-42-27-74-69; e-mail ambaparis@minaffet.gov.rw; Ambassador Emmanuel Ndagijimana (recalled Nov. 2006).

Germany: Jägerstr. 67–69, 10117 Berlin; tel. (30) 20916590; fax (30) 209165959; e-mail info@rwanda-botschaft.de; internet www.rwanda-botschaft.de; Ambassador EUGENE RICHARD GASANA.

India: 41 Paschimi Marg, Vasant Vihar, New Delhi 110 057; tel. (11) 51661604; fax (11) 51661605; e-mail ambadelhi@minaffet.gov.rw; Ambassador Lt-Gen. Kayumba Nyamwasa.

Japan: Kowa Bldg, No. 38, 4-12-24, Nishi Azabu, Minato-ku, Tokyo 106; tel. (3) 3486-7801; fax (3) 3409-2334; Ambassador EMILE RWAMASIRABO.

Kenya: International House, 12th Floor, Mama Ngina St, POB 48579, Nairobi; tel. (20) 560178; fax (20) 561932; Ambassador George William Kayonga.

Libya: POB 6677, Villa Ibrahim Musbah Missalati, Andalus, Tripoli; tel. (21) 72864; fax (21) 70317; Chargé d'affaires CHRISTOPHE HABIMANA.

Saudi Arabia: POB 94383, Riyadh 11693; tel. (1) 454-0808; fax (1) 456-1769; Ambassador Simon Insonere.

South Africa: 983 Schoeman St, Arcadia, Pretoria; POB 55224, Arcadia 0007; tel. (12) 3426536; fax (12) 3427106; e-mail ambapretoria@minaffet.gov.rw; Ambassador EUGÉNE MUNYAKAYANZA.

Tanzania: Plot 32, Ali Hassan Mwinyi Rd, POB 2918, Dar es Salaam; tel. (22) 2115889; fax (22) 2115888; e-mail ambadsm@minaffet.gov.rw; Ambassador Zephyr Mutanguha.

Uganda: 2 Nakaima Rd, POB 2468, Kampala; tel. (41) 4344045; fax (41) 4458547; Ambassador IGNACE KAMALI KAREGESA.

United Kingdom: 120–122 Seymour Pl., London, W1H 1NR; tel. (20) 7724-9832; fax (20) 7724-8642; e-mail uk@ambarwanda.org.uk; internet www.ambarwanda.org.uk; Ambassador Claver Gatete.

United States of America: 1714 New Hampshire Ave, NW, Washington, DC 20009; tel. (202) 232-2882; fax (202) 232-4544; e-mail rwandaembassy@rwandaembassy.org; internet www.rwandaembassy.org; Ambassador JAMES KIMONYO.

DIPLOMATIC MISSIONS OF SAINT CHRISTOPHER AND NEVIS

United Nations: 414 East 75th St, 5th Floor, New York, NY 10021; tel. (212) 535-1234; fax (212) 535-6854; e-mail sknmission@aol.com; internet www .stkittsnevis.org; Permanent Representative Delano Frank Bart.

Canada (see entry for Antigua and Barbuda).

China (Taiwan): 5/F, 9-1 Lane 62, Tien Mou West Rd, Taipei 11156; tel. (2) 28738252; fax (2) 28733246; Chargé d'affaires Jasmine Huggins.

Jamaica: 11A Opal Ave, Golden Acres, Red Hills, St Andrew; tel. 944-3861; fax 945-0105; High Commissioner CEDRIC HARPER.

United Kingdom: 2nd Floor, 10 Kensington Court, London, W8 5DL; tel. (20) 7937-9718; fax (20) 7937-7484; e-mail sknhighcomm@btconnect.com; High Commr James E. Williams.

United States of America: 3216 New Mexico Ave, NW, Washington DC 20016; tel. (202) 686-2636; fax (202) 686-5740; e-mail info@stkittsnevis.org; Ambassador (vacant).

DIPLOMATIC MISSIONS OF SAINT LUCIA

United Nations: 800 Second Ave, 9th Floor, New York, NY 10017; tel. (212) 697-9360; fax (212) 697-4993; e-mail slumission@aol.com; internet www.un .int/stlucia; Permanent Representative Anthony Bryan Severin.

Canada (see entry for Antigua and Barbuda).

United Kingdom: 1 Collingham Gdns, London, SW5 0HW; tel. (20) 7370-7123; fax (20) 7370-1905; e-mail hcslu@btconnect.com; High Commr Maura Felix (acting).

United States of America: OECS Bldg, 3216 New Mexico Ave, NW, Washington, DC 20016; tel. (202) 364-6792; fax (202) 364-6723; e-mail eofsaintlu@aol.com; Chargé d'affaires a.i. CLENIE GREER-LACASCADE.

DIPLOMATIC MISSIONS OF SAINT VINCENT AND THE GRENADINES

United Nations: 801 Second Ave, 21st Floor, New York, NY 10017; tel. (212) 687-4490; fax (212) 949-5946; e-mail stvg@un.int; Permanent Representative Camillo M. Gonsalves.

Canada (see entry for Antigua and Barbuda).

United Kingdom: 10 Kensington Court, London, W8 5DL; tel. (20) 7565-2874; fax (20) 7937-6040; e-mail info@svghighcom.co.uk; High Commr Cenio E. Lewis.

United States of America: 3216 New Mexico Ave, NW, Washington, DC 20016; tel. (202) 364-6730; fax (202) 364-6736; e-mail mail@embvsg.com; internet www.embvsg.com; Ambassador ELLSWORTH I. A. JOHN.

DIPLOMATIC MISSIONS OF SAMOA

United Nations: 800 Second Ave, Suite 400j, New York, NY 10017; tel. (212) 599-6196; fax (212) 599-0797; e-mail samoa@un.int; Permanent Representative Ali'ioaiga Feturi Elisaia.

Australia: POB 3274, Manuka, ACT 2603; tel. (2) 6286-5505; fax (2) 6286-5678; e-mail samoahcaussi@netspeed.com.au; High Commissioner LEIATAUA DR KILIFOTI S. ETEUATI.

Belgium: 20 ave de l'Orée, BP 4, 1050 Brussels; tel. (2) 660-84-54; fax (2) 675-03-36; e-mail samoaembassy@skynet.be; Ambassador Tuala Falani Chan Tung.

New Zealand: 1A Wesley Rd, Kelburn, POB 1430, Wellington; tel. (4) 472-0953; fax (4) 471-2479; e-mail shc@paradise.net.nz; High Commissioner ASI TUIATAGA J. F. BLAKELOCK.

United States of America: 800 Second Ave, Suite 800d, New York, NY 10017; tel. (212) 599-6196; fax (212) 599-0797; e-mail samoa@un.int; Ambassador Ali'ioaiga Feturi Elisaia.

DIPLOMATIC MISSIONS OF SAN MARINO

United Nations: 327 East 50th St, New York, NY 10022; tel. (212) 751-1234; fax (212) 751-1436; e-mail sanmarinoun@hotmail.com; Permanent Representative DANIELE BODINI.

Argentina: Avda Presidente Manuel Quintana 175, 1°a, C1014ACB Buenos Aires; tel. (11) 4815-3787; fax (11) 4815-9070; e-mail embajada@ consulatosanmarino.org.ar; Ambassador Stefano Pisa di Monterosa.

Austria: Dr-Karl-Lueger-Pl. 5, 1010 Vienna; tel. (1) 586-21-80; fax (1) 586-22-35; e-mail pfk@pfk.at; Ambassador GIOVANNI CONTI (resident in San Marino).

Belgium: 62 ave F. D. Roosevelt, 1050 Brussels; tel. (2) 644-22-24; fax (2) 644-20-57; e-mail ambrsm.bxl@scarlet.be; Ambassador Gian Nicola Filippi Balestra.

Egypt: 5 Sharia Ramez, Mohandessin, Cairo; tel. (2) 3602718; Ambassador GIACOMO MARIA UGOLINI.

France: 22 rue d'Artois, 75008 Paris; tel. 1-47-23-04-75; e-mail saint-marin@ wanadoo.fr; Ambassador Mario de Benedetti.

Italy: Via Eleonora Duse 35, 00197 Roma; tel. (06) 8072511; fax (06) 8070072; e-mail asmarino@ambrsm.it; Ambassador BARBARA PARA.

Japan: 3-5-1, Moto Azabu, Minato-ku, Tokyo 106-0046; tel. (3) 5414-7745; fax (3) 3405-6789; e-mail sanmarinoemb@tiscali.it; Ambassador Manlio Cadelo.

Spain: Padre de Jesús Ordóñez 18, 3°, 28002 Madrid; tel. (91) 5639000; fax (91) 5631931; e-mail sm_madrid@accessnet.es; Ambassador ENRICO MARIA PASQUINI.

Vatican City: Piazza G. Winckelmann 14, 00162 Rome, Italy; tel. (06) 86321798; fax (06) 8610814; e-mail amb-sanmarino@libero.it; Ambassador Giovanni Galassi.

DIPLOMATIC MISSIONS OF SÃO TOMÉ AND PRÍNCIPE

United Nations: 400 Park Ave, 7th Floor, New York, NY 10022; tel. (212) 317-0533; fax (212) 317-0580; e-mail stp@un.int; Chargé d'affaires a.i. OVIDIO MANUEL BARBOSA PEQUENO.

Angola: Rua Armindo de Andrade 173–175, Luanda; tel. 222345677; Ambassador Armindo Brito Fernandes.

Belgium: Square Montgomery, 175 ave de Tervueren, 1150 Brussels; tel. (2) 734-89-66; fax (2) 734-88-15; e-mail ambassade.sao.tome@skynet.be; Chargé d'affaires a.i. ARMINDO BRITO FERNANDES.

China (Taiwan): 10/F, 9-1 Lane 62, Tien Mou West Rd, Taipei 11156; tel. (2) 28766824; fax (2) 28766984; e-mail ladislaualmeida@yahoo.co.uk; Ambassador Ladislau d'Almeida.

Gabon: BP 489, Libreville; tel. 72-09-94; Ambassador URBINO JOSÉ GONHALVES BOTELÇO.

Portugal: Edif. EPAC 6°, Av. Gago Coutinho 26, 1000-017 Lisbon; tel. (21) 8461917; fax (21) 8461895; e-mail embstp@mail.telepac.pt; Ambassador Alda Alves de Melo dos Santos.

United States of America: 400 Park Ave, 7th floor, New York, NY 10022; tel. (212) 317-0580; e-mail stp@un.int; Ambassador OVIDIO MANUEL BARBOSA PEQUENO.

DIPLOMATIC MISSIONS OF SAUDI ARABIA

United Nations: 405 Lexington Ave, 56th Floor, New York, NY 10017; tel. (212) 697-4830; fax (212) 983-4895; e-mail saudi-mission@un.int; internet www.saudi-un-ny.org; Permanent Representative Fawzi bin Abd al-Majeed Shobokshi.

Afghanistan: Shash Darak (behind Eyes Office), Kabul; tel. (20) 2102064; e-mail ksa_kemb@hotmail.com; Ambassador GHURAM BIN SAID BIN MALHAN.

Albania: Bulevardi Dëshmorët e Kombit; tel. (4) 248306; e-mail embsaudarab@albaniaonline.net; Ambassador Abdullah S. al-Hamdan.

Algeria: 62 rue Med. Drafini, chemin de la Madeleine, Hydra, Algiers; tel. (21) 60-35-18; Ambassador DR SAMI BIN ABDULLAH BIN OTHMAN AS-SALIH.

Argentina: Marqués de Aguado 2881, C1425CEA Buenos Aires; tel. (11) 4802-3375; fax (11) 4806-1581; e-mail embasaudita@fibertel.com.ar; internet www.embajadasaudi.org; Ambassador Esam Abid ath-Thagafi.

Australia: POB 9162, Deakin, ACT 2600; tel. (2) 6282-6999; fax (2) 6282-8911; e-mail amb.auemb@mofa.gov.sa; internet www.saudiembassy.org.au; Ambassador HASSAN TALAT NAZER.

Austria: Formanekgasse 38, 1190 Vienna; tel. (1) 367-25-31; fax (1) 367-25-40; e-mail emb.saudiarabia.vienna@aon.at; Chargé d'affaires a.i. Abd ar-Rahman as-Suhaibani.

Azerbaijan: 1073 Baku, S. Dadashov küç. 44/2; tel. (12) 497-23-05; fax (12) 497-23-02; e-mail najdiahbaku@azereurotel.com; Ambassador ALI HASAN JAFAR.

Bahrain: POB 1085, Bldg 82, Rd 1702, Block 317, Diplomatic Area, Manama; tel. 17537722; fax 17533261; Ambassador Dr Abdullah bin Ibrahim el-Kuwaiz.

Bangladesh: House 12, Rd 92, Gulshan (North), Dhaka 1212; tel. (2) 889124; fax (2) 883616; Ambassador ABDULLAH MOHAMMAD AL-OBAID AL-NAMLA.

Belgium: 45 ave F. D. Roosevelt, 1050 Brussels; tel. (2) 649-20-44; fax (2) 647-24-92; e-mail beemb@mofa.gov.sa; Ambassador Abdullah bin Yahyua al-Mouallimi.

Bosnia and Herzegovina: 71000 Sarajevo, Koševo 44; tel. (33) 211861; fax (33) 212204; e-mail saudiembassy@epn.ba; Ambassador FAHAD BIN ABD AL-MUHSIN AL-ZEIDA.

Brazil: SHIS, QL 10, Conj. 09, Casa 20, 70471-900 Brasília, DF; tel. (61) 3248-3523; fax (61) 3284-1142; e-mail embsaud@terra.com.br; internet www.saudiembassy.org.br; Chargé d'affaires a.i. Hoda Omar Saleh al-Oyaidi.

Brunei: 1 Simpang 570, Kampong Salar, Jalan Muara, Bandar Seri Begawan BA 1429; tel. 2792821; fax 2792826; e-mail saudibru@brunet.bn; Ambassador ESAM BIN AHMED BIN JAMAL ABID AL-THAGAFI.

Burkina Faso: Ouagadougou; Ambassador Aid bin Muhammad ath-Thakfi.

Cameroon: rue 1951, Quartier Bastos, BP 1602, Yaoundé; tel. 2221-2675; fax 2220-6689; Ambassador AHMED HUSSEIN ALBEDEWI.

Canada: 201 Sussex Dr., Ottawa, ON K1N 1K6; tel. (613) 237-4100; fax (613) 237-0567; e-mail caemb@mofa.gov.sa; Ambassador Abdul Aziz H. I. as-Sowayegh.

Chad: Quartier Aéroport, rue Jander Miry, BP 974, N'Djamena; tel. 52-31-28; fax 52-33-28; e-mail najdiat.tchad@intnet.td; .

China, People's Republic: 1 Bei Xiao Jie, San Li Tun, Beijing 100600; tel. (10) 65324825; fax (10) 65325324; Ambassador Saleh bin Abdul-Aziz al-Hujylan.

Côte d'Ivoire: Plateau, Abidjan; Ambassador (vacant).

Cuba: Avda 5, No 8206, entre 82 y 84, Miramar, Havana; tel. (7) 204-1045; fax (7) 204-6401; e-mail erasdcu@ceniai.inf.cu; Ambassador Muhammad Mustafa Tleimidi.

Czech Republic: Na Hřebenkách 70, 150 00 Prague 5; tel. 257316597; fax 257316593; e-mail rse@saudi-embassy.cz; Ambassador PRINCEMANSOUR BIN KHALID BIN ABDULLAH AL-FARHAN AL-SAUD.

Denmark: Lille Strandvej 27, 2900 Hellerup; tel. 39-62-12-00; fax 39-62-60-09; e-mail embassy@saudiemb.dk; Ambassador Abd ar-Rahman Saad al-Hadlaq.

Djibouti: BP 1921, Djibouti; tel. 351645; fax 352284; Ambassador ABDULAZIZ MUHAMMAD AL-EIFAN.

Egypt: 2 Sharia Ahmad Nessim, Cairo (Giza); tel. (2) 3490775; Ambassador Hisham Mohi ed-Din an-Nazir.

Eritrea: POB 5599, Asmara; tel. (1) 120171; fax (1) 121027; Ambassador NASSER AR-RASHEIDAN.

France: 5 ave Hoche, 75008 Paris; tel. 1-56-79-40-00; fax 1-56-79-40-01; e-mail amb.arabiesaoudite@gmail.com; Ambassador Dr Muhammad bin Ismail al-Ashekh.

Germany: Kurfürstendamm 63, 10787 Berlin; tel. (30) 889250; fax (30) 88925179; Ambassador PROF. DR OSAMA ABD AL-MAJID ALI SHOBOKSHI.

Greece: Odos Marathonodromou 71, Palaio Psychiko, 154 52 Athens; tel. (210) 6716911; e-mail gremb@mofa.gov.sa; Chargé d'affaires a.i. Faleh Mohammad ar-Rahili.

Guinea: Quartier Camayenne, Commune de Dixinn, BP 611, Conakry; tel. 30-46-24-87; fax 30-46-58-84; e-mail gnemb@mofa.gov.sa; Chargé d'affaires a.i. MOHAMMAD MAHMOUD HILAL.

India: 2 Paschimi Marg, Vasant Vihar, New Delhi 110 057; tel. (11) 26144102; fax (11) 26144244; Ambassador Saleh M. al-Ghamdi.

Indonesia: Jalan M. T. Haryono, Kav. 27, Cawang Atas, Jakarta Timur; tel. (21) 8011533; fax (21) 3905864; e-mail idemb@mofa.gov.sa; Ambassador ABDULLAH BIN ABDULRAHMAN A'ALIM AL-KHAYYAT.

Iran: No. 1, Niloufar St, Boustan St, Pasdaran Ave, Tehran; tel. (21) 22288543; fax (21) 22294691; e-mail iremb@mofa.gov.sa; Ambassador Osama bin Ahmad as-Sanousi.

Italy: Via G. B. Pergolesi 9, 00198 Roma; tel. (06) 844851; fax (06) 8551781; e-mail ambasciata@arabia-saudita.it; internet www.arabia-saudita.it; Ambassador MUHAMMAD IBRAHIM AL-JARALLAH.

Japan: 1-8-4, Roppongi, Minato-ku, Tokyo 106-0032; tel. (3) 3589-5241; fax (3) 3589-5200; e-mail info@saudiembassy.or.jp; internet www.saudiembassy.or.jp; Ambassador Faisal Hassan Trad.

Jordan: POB 2133, 5th Circle, Jabal Amman; tel. (6) 5924154; fax (6) 4659853; e-mail joemb@mofa.gov.sa; Ambassador ABD AR-RAHMAN N. AL-OHALY.

Kazakhstan: 010000 Astana; tel. (727) 250-28-71; fax (727) 250-28-11; e-mail kzemb@mofa.gov.sa; Ambassador Hisham bin Abdel-Wahab Zaraa.

Kenya: Muthaiga Rd, POB 58297, Nairobi; tel. (20) 762781; fax (20) 760939; Ambassador NBEEL KHALAF A. ASHOUR.

Korea, Republic: 1-112, 2-ga, Sinmun-no, Jongno-gu, Seoul; tel. (2) 739-0631; fax (2) 732-3110; Ambassador Abdullah A al-A'ifan.

Kuwait: POB 20498, 13065 Safat, Istiqlal St, Kuwait City; tel. 2550021; fax 2420654; Ambassador ABD AL-AZIZ AL-FAYEZ.

Lebanon: POB 136144, Kuraitem, Beirut; tel. (1) 860351; fax (1) 861524; e-mail lbemb@mofa.gov.sa; Ambassador Abd al-Aziz Mahi ed-Din al-Khoja.

Libya: Sharia Kairouan 2, Tripoli; tel. (21) 30485; Chargé d'affaires MUHAMMAD HASSAN BANDAH.

Malaysia: Level 4, Wisma Chinese Chamber, 258 Jalan Ampang, 50450 Kuala Lumpur; tel. (3) 42579433; fax (3) 42578751; e-mail saembssy@tm.net.my; Ambassador Mohammed Reda Hussein Abu al-Hamayel.

Mali: Villa Bal Harbour, 28 Cité du Niger, BP 81, Bamako; tel. 221-25-28; fax 221-50-64; e-mail mlemb@mofa.gov.sa; Chargé d'affaires a.i. IMAD BIN AMEEN ELIAS.

Mauritania: Las Balmas, Zinat, BP 498, Nouakchott; tel. 525-26-33; fax 525-29-49; e-mail mremb@mofa.gov.sa; AmbassadorMohamed al Fadh el Issa.

Mexico: Paseo de las Palmas 2075, Col. Lomas de Chapultepec, Del. Miguel Hidalgo, 11000 México, DF; tel. (55) 5596-0173; fax (55) 5020-3160; e-mail saudiemb@prodigy.net.mx; Ambassador MUNEER IBRAHIM AL-BENJABI.

Morocco: 322 ave Imam Malik, km 6, route des Zaêrs, Rabat; tel. (3) 657789; fax (3) 7768587; e-mail ambassd@goodinfo.net.ma; Ambassador Dr Muhammad Abd ar-Rahman bin Abd al-Aziz Bachar.

Netherlands: Alexanderstraat 19, 2514 JM The Hague; tel. (70) 3614391; fax (70) 4276183; e-mail saudiembassy@casema.nl; Ambassador WALID A. AL-KHEREIJI.

Niger: route de Tillabery, BP 339, Niamey; tel. 20-75-32-15; fax 20-75-24-42; e-mail neemb@mofa.gov.sa; Ambassador Abdul Kareem Mohammad Al Maliki.

Nigeria: Plot 347H, off Adetokunbo Ademola Cres., Wuse 2, Abuja; tel. (9) 4131880; fax (9) 4134906; Ambassador ANWAR A. ABD-RABBUH.

Oman: Diplomatic City, Jamiat ad-Dowal al-Arabiya St, POB 1411, Ruwi 112; tel. 24601744; fax 24603540; e-mail omemb@mofa.gov.sa; Ambassador Abdullah bin Abd ar-Rahman Alim.

Pakistan: 14, Hill Rd, F-6/3, Islamabad; tel. (51) 2820156; fax (51) 2278816; Ambassador ALI S. AWADH ASSERI.

Philippines: Saudi Embassy Bldg, 389 Sen. Gil J. Puyat Ave Ext., Makati City, Metro Manila; tel. (2) 8909735; fax (2) 8953493; e-mail phemb@mofa.gov.sa; Ambassador Mohammad Ameen Wali.

Poland: 00-739 Warsaw, ul. Stępińska 55; tel. (22) 8400000; fax (22) 8405636; e-mail info@saudiembassy.pl; internet www.saudiembassy.pl; Ambassador NASSER BIN AHMED ALBRAIK.

Portugal: Av. do Restelo 42, 1400-315 Lisbon; tel. (21) 3041750; fax (21) 3014209; e-mail saudiembassy@netcabo.pt; Ambassador Muhammad ar-Rashid.

Qatar: POB 1255, Doha; tel. 4832030; fax 4832720; Ambassador AHMAD BIN ALI AL-QAHTANI.

Romania: 010501 Bucharest 1, Str. Polonă 6; tel. (21) 2109109; fax (21) 2107093; Chargé d'affaires Ahmad M. al-Zughaibi.

Russian Federation: 119121 Moscow, 3-i Neopalimovskii per. 3; tel. (495) 245-23-10; fax (495) 246-94-71; e-mail saudimoscow@yahoo.com; internet www.mofa.gov.sa/detail.asp?InServiceID=238; Chargé d'affaires a.i. GAZI SHERBINI.

Senegal: route Corniche-Ouest, face Olympique Club, BP 3109, Dakar; tel. 33-864-0141; fax 33-864-0130; e-mail snemb@mofa.gov.sa; Chargé d'affaires a.i. Fahd Nasser Al Bihairan.

Singapore: 40 Nassim Rd, Singapore 258449; tel. 67345878; fax 67385291; e-mail enquiries@saudiembassy.org.sg; internet www.saudiembassy.org.sg; Ambassador Dr Mohamad Amin Kurdi.

South Africa: 711 Duncan St, cnr Lunnon St, Hatfield, Pretoria 0083; POB 13930, Hatfield 0028; tel. (12) 3624230; fax (12) 3624239; Ambassador Mohammed Mahmoud Bin Ali al-Ali.

Spain: Dr Alvarez Sierra 3, 28033 Madrid; tel. (91) 3834300; fax (91) 3021145; e-mail info@arabiasaudi.org; internet www.arabiasaudi.org; Ambassador Prince Sa'ud bin Naif bin Abd al-Aziz as-Sa'ud.

Sri Lanka: 39 Sir Ernest de Silva Mawatha, Colombo 7; tel. (11) 2682087; fax (11) 2682088; e-mail lkemb@mofa.gov.sa; Ambassador Mohammed bin Mahmoud al-Ali.

Sudan: St 11, New Extension, Khartoum; tel. (183) 741938; Ambassador Sayed Mohammed Sibri Suliman.

Sweden: Sköldungagt. 5, POB 26073, 100 41 Stockholm; tel. (8) 23-88-00; fax (8) 796-99-56; Chargé d'affaires a.i. Mogbel as-Suraihi.

Switzerland: Kramburgstr. 12, 3006 Bern; tel. 313521555; fax 313514581; e-mail chemb@mofa.gov.sa; Chargé d'affaires a.i. Saud Abdullah Hassan Katib.

Syria: rue al-Jala'a, Abou Roumaneh, Damascus; tel. (11) 3334914; fax (11) 3337383; e-mail syemb@mofa.gov.sa; Ambassador (vacant).

Thailand: 82 Saeng Song Thani Bldg, 23rd Floor, Thanon Sathorn Nua, Bangrak, Bangkok 10500; tel. (2) 639-2960; fax (2) 639-2950; Ambassador Nabil H. H. Ashri.

Tunisia: blvd du 7 Novembre, Centre Urbain-Nord C, Mahrajène, 1080 Tunis; tel. (70) 728-666; fax (70) 728-440; Ambassador Ibrahim as-Saad al-Brahim.

Turkey: Turan Emeksiz Sok. 6, 06700 Gaziosmanpaşa, Ankara; tel. (312) 4685540; fax (312) 4274886; e-mail tremb@mofa.gov.sa; Ambassador Muhammad al-Hussaini ash-Sharif.

Turkmenistan: 744000 Aşgabat, ul. Yu. Emre 2/1, Imperial International Business Centre; tel. (12) 45-49-63; fax (12) 45-49-70; e-mail tmemb@mofa .gov.sa; Ambassador Abd al-Aziz Ibrahim al-Ghadeer.

Uganda: 3 Okurut Close, Kololo, POB 22558, Kampala; tel. (41) 4340614; fax (41) 4454017; Chargé d'affaires Majed Abdulrahman M. Martha al-Otaibi.

United Arab Emirates: POB 4057, Abu Dhabi; tel. (2) 4445700; fax (2) 4448491; Ambassador Dr Abdullah bin Muammar.

United Kingdom: 30 Charles St, London, W1J 5DZ; tel. (20) 7917-3000; fax (20) 7917-3330; e-mail ukemb@mofa.gov.sa; internet www.saudiembassy .org.uk; Ambassador Prince Muhammad bin Nawaf bin Abdulaziz.

United States of America: 601 New Hampshire Ave, NW, Washington, DC 20037; tel. (202) 342-3800; fax (202) 944-5983; e-mail info@saudiembassy .net; internet www.saudiembassy.net; Ambassador Adel din Ahmed al-Jubeir.

Uzbekistan: 100000 Tashkent; .

Venezuela: Calle Andrés Pietri, Quinta Makkah, Los Chorros, Caracas 1071; tel. (212) 239-0290; fax (212) 239-6494; e-mail saudiembassycaracas@cantv .net; Ambassador Judiya al-Hathal.

Yemen: POB 1184, Zuhara House, Hadda Rd, San'a; tel. (1) 240429; Ambassador Ali bin Muhammad al-Hamdan.

Zambia: 27bc Leopards Hill Rd, Kabulonga, POB 34411, 10101 Lusaka; tel. (1) 266861; fax (1) 266863; e-mail saudiemb@uudial.zm; Ambassador Talat Salem Radwan.

DIPLOMATIC MISSIONS OF SENEGAL

United Nations: 238 East 68th St, New York, NY 10021; tel. (212) 517-9030; fax (212) 517-3032; e-mail senegal.mission@yahoo.fr; internet www.un.int/ senegal; Permanent Representative Paul Badji.

Algeria: BP 720, 350 Parc Ben Omar Kouba, Alger-Gare, Algiers; tel. (21) 54-90-90; fax (21) 54-90-94; e-mail senegal@wissal.dz; Ambassador Papa Ousmane Seye.

Bahrain: Villa 25, Rd 33, Block 333, Mahooz, Manama; tel. 17821060; fax 17721650; Ambassador Mafode Ndong.

Belgium: 196 ave F. D. Roosevelt, 1050 Brussels; tel. (2) 673-00-97; fax (2) 675-04-60; e-mail senegal.ambassade@coditel.net; Ambassador (vacant).

Brazil: SEN, Av. das Nações, Lote 18, 70800-400 Brasília, DF; tel. (61) 3223-6110; fax (61) 3322-7822; e-mail senebrasilia@senebrasilia.com.br; internet www.senebrasilia.org.br; Ambassador Fodé Seck.

Burkina Faso: Immeuble Espace Fadima, ave de la Résistance du 17 Mai, 01 BP 3226, Ouagadougou 01; tel. 50-31-14-18; fax 50-31-14-01; Ambassador Cheikh Sylla.

Canada: 57 Marlborough Ave, Ottawa, ON K1N 8E8; tel. (613) 238-6392; fax (613) 238-2695; e-mail ambassn@sympatico.ca; Ambassador Issakha Mbacke.

Cape Verde: Rua Abílio Macedo, Plateau, CP 269, Praia, Santiago; tel. 2615621; fax 2612838; e-mail silcarneyni@hotmail.com; Ambassador Marième Ndiaye.

China, People's Republic: Diplomatic Office Bldg, 23 Dong Zhi Men Wai Da Jie, Beijing 100600; tel. (10) 65325035; fax (10) 65323730; Ambassador Gen. Pape Khalilou Fall.

Côte d'Ivoire: Immeuble Nabil Choucair, 6 rue du Commerce, 08 BP 2165, Abidjan 08; tel. 20-33-28-76; fax 20-32-50-39; Ambassador Moustapha Sène.

Egypt: 46 Sharia Abd al-Moneim Riad, Mohandessin, Cairo (Dokki); tel. (2) 3460946; fax (2) 3461039; e-mail mamadousow@hotmail.com; Ambassador Mamadou Sow.

Ethiopia: Africa Ave, POB 2581, Addis Ababa; tel. (11) 6611376; fax (11) 6610020; e-mail ambassene-addis@ethionet.et; Ambassador Amadou Kébé.

France: 14 ave Robert Schuman, 75007 Paris; tel. 1-47-05-39-45; fax 1-45-56-04-30; e-mail repsen@wanadoo.fr; internet www.ambassenparis.com; Ambassador Doudou Diop Salla.

Gabon: Quartier Sobraga, BP 3856, Libreville; tel. 77-42-67; fax 77-42-68; e-mail ambasengab@yahoo.fr; Ambassador Ibrahima Caba.

Gambia: 159 Kairaba Ave, POB 385, Banjul; tel. 4373752; fax 4373750; Ambassador Mamadou Fall.

Germany: Dessauerstr. 28–29, 10963 Berlin; tel. (30) 8562190; fax (30) 85621921; internet www.botschaft-senegal.de; Ambassador Cheikh Sylla.

Guinea: bâtiment 142, Coleah, Corniche Che Sud, BP 842, Conakry; tel. 30-44-61-32; fax 30-46-28-34; Ambassador Gen. Charles André Nelson.

Guinea-Bissau: Rua Omar Torrijos 43a, Bissau; tel. 212944; fax 201748; Ambassador Gen. Abdoulaye Dieng.

India: C-6/11, Vasant Vihar, New Delhi 110 057; tel. (11) 26147687; fax (11) 41662673; e-mail embassy@senindia.org; Ambassador Amadou Bocoum.

Iran: POB 19395-4743, 76 Sepand West St, Nejatollahi Ave, Tehran; tel. (21) 88881123; fax (21) 88805676; .

Italy: Via Giulia 66, 00186 Roma; tel. (06) 6872381; fax (06) 68219294; e-mail ambasenequiri@tiscali.it; Ambassador Papa Cheikh Saadibou Fall.

Japan: 1-3-4, Aobadai, Meguro-ku, Tokyo 153-0042; tel. (3) 3464-8451; fax (3) 3464-8452; e-mail senegal@senegal.jp; Ambassador Gabriel Alexandre Sar.

Kuwait: POB 23892, 13099 Safat, Rawdah, Block 3, St 35, House 9, Kuwait City; tel. 2573477; fax 2542044; e-mail senegal_embassy@yahoo.com; internet www.diplomatie.gouv.sn/maeuase/ambassene_koweit.htm; Ambassador Abdou Lahad Mbacke.

Liberia: Monrovia; Ambassador Moctar Traoré.

Libya: POB 6392, El-Arabia Gotchalle 246/5, Gargaresh, Tripoli; tel. (21) 4836090; fax (21) 4838955; e-mail ambassene.tripoli@stcc.presidence.sn; Chargé d'affaires a.i. Mamadou Diop.

Madagascar: Lot II R, 179b Ambohirakely, Betongolo, Antananarivo; tel. (20) 2252186; fax (20) 2252186; Ambassador César Coly.

Malaysia: 9 Lorong U Thant, off Jalan U Thant, 55000 Kuala Lumpur; tel. (3) 42567343; fax (3) 42563205; e-mail senamb_mal@yahoo.fr; Ambassador Abdel Kader Pierre Fall.

Mali: porte 341, rue 287, angle ave Nelson Mandela, BP 42, Bamako; tel. 221-08-59; fax 216-92-68; Ambassador Saoudatou Ndiaye Seck.

Mauritania: Villa 500, Tevragh Zeina, BP 2511, Nouakchott; tel. 525-72-90; fax 525-72-91; Ambassador Mahmoudou Cheikh Kane.

Morocco: 17 rue Cadi ben Hamadi Senhaji, Souissi, BP 365, 10000 Rabat; tel. (3) 7754171; fax (3) 7754149; e-mail ambassene@iam.net.ma; Ambassador Ibou Ndiaye.

Nigeria: 14 Kofo Abayomi Rd, Victoria Island, PMB 2197, Lagos; tel. (1) 2611722; Ambassador Amadou Thialaw Diop.

Qatar: Ibn Almoutas St, House 65, Dafna, Doha; tel. 4837644; fax 4838872; Ambassador Adama Sarr.

Russian Federation: 119049 Moscow, ul. Korovii Val 7/193–194; tel. (495) 230-20-72; fax (495) 230-20-63; Ambassador Maj.-Gen. Mountaga Diallo.

Saudi Arabia: POB 94352, Riyadh 11693; tel. (1) 488-0146; fax (1) 488-3804; Ambassador Mouhamadou Doudou Lo.

South Africa: Charles Manor, 57 Charles St, Baileys Muckleneuk, Pretoria 0181; POB 2948, Brooklyn Sq. 0075; tel. (12) 4605263; fax (12) 3465550; e-mail ambassenepta@telkomsa.za; Ambassador MAÏMOUNA DIOP SY.

Sweden: Birger Jarlsgt. 37, 3 tr., POB 7384, 111 45 Stockholm; tel. (8) 411-71-60; fax (8) 411-71-68; e-mail senegalembassy@telia.com; Ambassador Henri-Antoine Turpin.

Tunisia: 122 ave de la Liberté, Belvédère, Tunis; tel. (71) 802-397; fax (71) 780-770; internet www.ambasenegal.intl.tn; Ambassador ABDOURAHMANE SOW.

Turkey: İran Cad. 47/5, Gaziosmanpaşa, Ankara; tel. (312) 4663086; fax (312) 4272213; Chargé d'affaires a.i. Marcelline Pelevala Sylla.

United Kingdom: 39 Marloes Rd, London, W8 6LA; tel. (20) 7937-7237; fax (20) 7938-2546; e-mail senegalembassy@hotmail.co.uk; internet www .senegalembassy.co.uk; Ambassador ABDOU SOURANG.

United States of America: 2112 Wyoming Ave, NW, Washington, DC 20008; tel. (202) 234-0540; fax (202) 332-6315; Ambassador Dr Amadou Lamine Ba.

Vatican City: Via dei Monti Parioli 51, 00197 Rome, Italy; tel. (06) 3218892; fax (06) 3203624; e-mail senvat.iol.it; Ambassador FÉLIX OUDIANE.

DIPLOMATIC MISSIONS OF SERBIA

United Nations: 854 Fifth Ave, New York, NY 10021; tel. (212) 879-8700; fax (212) 879-8705; e-mail yugoslavia@un.int; internet www.un.int/serbia; Chargé d'Affaires Pavle Jevremovič.

Albania: Rruga Donika Kastrioti 9/1, Tirana; tel. (4) 232091; fax (4) 232089; e-mail ambatira@icc-al.org; internet www.tirana.mfa.gov.yu; Chargé d'affaires a.i. (vacant).

Algeria: BP 366, 7 rue des Frères Ben-hafid, Hydra, Algiers; tel. (21) 69-12-18; fax (21) 69-34-72; e-mail yuga@djazair-connect.com; Ambassador Vladimir Kohut.

Angola: Rua Comandante N'zagi 25–27, Alvalade, CP 3278, Luanda; tel. 222321421; fax 222321724; e-mail yugoemb@snet.co.ao; Ambassador DOBRIVOJ KACANSKI.

Argentina: Marcelo T. de Alvear 1705, C1060AAG Buenos Aires; tel. (11) 4812-9133; fax (11) 4812-1070; e-mail yuembaires@ciudad.com.ar; Chargé d'affaires a.i. Martin Simović.

Australia: POB 728, Mawson, ACT 2607; tel. (2) 6290-2630; fax (2) 6290-2631; e-mail serbembau@optusnet.com.au; Ambassador MILIVOJE GLISIC.

Austria: Rennweg 3, 1030 Vienna; tel. (1) 713-25-95; fax (1) 713-25-97; e-mail ambasada@amb.srbije.net; internet www.vienna.mfa.gov.yu; Ambassador Dragan Velikić.

Belarus: 220034 Minsk, vul. Rumyantseva 4; tel. (17) 284-29-84; fax (17) 233-92-26; e-mail embassy.minsk@mfa.gov.yu; internet www.ambasadasrbije .info; Ambassador SRECKO DJUKIĆ.

Belgium: 11 ave Emile de Mot, 1050 Brussels; tel. (2) 647-26-52; fax (2) 647-29-41; e-mail ambaserbie@skynet.be; Chargé d'affaires a.i. Aleksandar Tasic.

Bosnia and Herzegovina: 71000 Sarajevo, Obala Maka Dizdara 3A; tel. (33) 260080; fax (33) 221469; e-mail srbamba@bih.net.ba; Ambassador GRUJICA SPASOVIĆ.

Brazil: SES, Av. das Nações, Quadra 803, Lote 15, 70409-900 Brasília, DF; tel. (61) 3223-7272; fax (61) 3223-8462; e-mail embaixadaservia@terra.com .br; Ambassador Dušan Gajić.

Bulgaria: 1504 Sofia, ul. Veliko Tarnovo 3; tel. (2) 946-16-33; fax (2) 946-10-59; e-mail sofia@emb-serbia.com; internet www.emb-serbia.com; Ambassador (vacant).

Canada: 17 Blackburn Ave, Ottawa, ON K1N 8A2; tel. (613) 233-6289; fax (613) 233-7850; e-mail diplomat@yuemb.ca; Ambassador Dušan Bataković.

China, People's Republic: 1 Dong Liu Jie, San Li Tun, Beijing 100600; tel. (10) 65323516; fax (10) 65321207; e-mail ambjug@netchina.com.cn; internet www .embserbia.cn; Ambassador MIOMIR UDOVICKI.

Croatia: 10000 Zagreb, Pantovčak 245; tel. (1) 4579067; fax (1) 4573338; e-mail ambasada@ambasada-srbije.hr; Ambassador (vacant).

Cuba: Calle 42, No 115, entre 1 y 3, Miramar, Havana; tel. (7) 204-2488; fax (7) 204-2982; e-mail embyuhav@ceniai.inf.cu; Ambassador MILENA LUKOVIC JOVANOVIC.

Cyprus: 2 Vasilissis Olgas St, Engomi, 1903 Nicosia; tel. 22777511; fax 22775910; e-mail nicosia@scg.org.cy; internet www.serbia.org.cy; Ambassador Mirko Jelić.

Czech Republic: Mostecká 15, 118 00 Prague 1; tel. 257532075; fax 257533948; e-mail yuambacz@mbox.vol.cz; Ambassador VLADIMIR VEREŠ.

Denmark: Svanevænget 36, 2100 Copenhagen Ø; tel. 39-29-77-84; fax 39-29-79-19; e-mail serbianemb@city.dk; Ambassador Vida Ognjenović.

Egypt: 33 Sharia Mansour Muhammad, Cairo (Zamalek); tel. (2) 7354061; fax (2) 7353913; e-mail yugoemb_kairo@yahoo.com; Ambassador DEJAN VASILJEVIĆ.

Ethiopia: POB 1341, Addis Ababa; tel. (11) 5517804; fax (11) 5514192; e-mail serbembaddis@ethionet.et; Ambassador Ivan Zivković.

Finland: Kulosaarentie 36, 00570 Helsinki; tel. (9) 6848522; fax (9) 6848783; e-mail info.ambascghki@kolumbus.fi; internet www.kolumbus.fi/info .ambasghki; Ambassador VERA MAVRIĆ.

France: 54 rue Léonard de Vinci, 75116 Paris; tel. 1-40-72-24-17; fax 1-40-72-24-11; e-mail ambasadapariz@wanadoo.fr; internet www.amb-serbie.fr; Ambassador Predrag Simić.

Germany: Taubertstr. 18, 14193 Berlin; tel. (30) 8957700; fax (30) 8252206; e-mail info@botschaft-smg.de; internet www.konzulatiscg.de; Ambassador OGNJEN PRIBIĆEVIĆ.

Greece: Leoforos Vassilissis Sofias 106, 115 27 Athens; tel. (210) 7774344; internet www.embassyscg.gr; Ambassador Ljiljana Bacević.

Hungary: 1068 Budapest, Dózsa György u. 92 B; tel. (1) 322-9838; fax (1) 322-1438; e-mail ambjubp@mail.datanet.hu; internet budapest.mfa.gov.yu; Ambassador (vacant).

India: 3/50g Niti Marg, Chanakyapuri, New Delhi 110 021; tel. (11) 26873661; fax (11) 26885535; e-mail office@embassyofserbiadelhi.net.in; internet www.embassyofserbiadelhi.net.in; Ambassador Vuk Zugić.

Indonesia: Jalan Hos Cokroaminoto 109, Jakarta 10310; tel. (21) 3143560; fax (21) 3143613; Ambassador ZORAN KAZAZOVIĆ.

Iran: POB 11365-118, Velenjak Ave, 9th St, No. 12, Tehran 19858; tel. (21) 22412569; fax (21) 22402869; e-mail scgambateh@neda.net; Chargé d'affaires a.i. Fahrudin Mekić.

Iraq: 16/35/923 Hay Babel, Baghdad; tel. (1) 776-7887; fax (1) 717-1069; e-mail embscgb@warkaa.net; Ambassador NINO MALJEVIĆ.

Israel: 10 Bodenheimer St, Tel-Aviv 62008; tel. 3-6045535; fax 3-6049456; e-mail yuamb@netvision.net.il; internet www.embserbmont.co.il; Ambassador Miodrag Isakov.

Italy: Via dei Monti Parioli 20, 00197 Roma; tel. (06) 3200805; fax (06) 3200868; e-mail info@ambroma.com; Ambassador SANDA RAŠKOVIĆ-IVIĆ.

Japan: 4-7-24, Kita-Shinagawa, Shinagawa-ku, Tokyo 140-0001; tel. (3) 3447-3571; fax (3) 3447-3573; e-mail embassy@serbianembassy.jp; internet www.serbianembassy.jp; Ambassador Ivan Mrkic.

Kuwait: POB 20511, 13066 Safat, Jabriya, Block 7, St 12, Villa 3, Kuwait City; tel. 5327548; fax 5327568; e-mail embrskw@qualitynet.net; Chargé d'affaires a.i. ZLATAN MALTARIĆ.

Libya: POB 1087, 14–16 Sharia Turkia, Tripoli; tel. (21) 3330819; fax (21) 3334114; e-mail serbianembassy_tripoli@yahoo.com; Ambassador Dr Dusan Simeonovic.

Macedonia, former Yugoslav Republic: 1000 Skopje, Pitu Guli 8; tel. (2) 3129298; fax (2) 3129427; e-mail yuamb@unet.com.mk; Ambassador ZORAN POPOVIĆ.

Mexico: Montañas Rocallosas Oeste 515, Col. Lomas de Chapultepec, Del. Miguel Hidalgo, 11000 México, DF; tel. (55) 5520-0524; fax (55) 5520-9927; e-mail embajadaserbia@att.net.mx; Ambassador Milisav Paic.

Montenegro: 81000 Podgorica, Bulevar Svetog Petra Cetinjskog 1, Hotel Podgorica; tel. (81) 402500; fax (81) 402500; Ambassador ZORAN LUTOVAC.

Morocco: BP 5014, 23 ave Mehdi ben Barka, Souissi, 10105 Rabat; tel. (3) 7752201; fax (3) 753258; e-mail sermont@menara.ma; Ambassador Mehmed Becović.

Myanmar: 114A Inya Rd, POB 943, Yangon; tel. (1) 515282; fax (1) 504274; e-mail serbemb@yangon.net.mn; Chargé d'affaires a.i. DRAGAN JANEKOVIĆ.

Netherlands: Groot Hertoginnelaan 30, 2517 EG The Hague; tel. (70) 3632397; fax (70) 3602421; e-mail yuambanl@bart.nl; internet users.bart.nl/ ~yuambanl; Ambassador Radoslav Stojanović.

Nigeria: 11, Rio Negro Close, off Yedseram St, Cadastral Zone A6, Maitama District, Abuja; tel. (9) 4139492; fax (9) 4130078; e-mail mail@ambnig.com; Ambassador DRAGAN MRAOVIĆ.

Norway: Drammensvn 105, 0244 Oslo; tel. 23-08-68-58; fax 22-55-29-92; e-mail ambasada@serbianembassy.no; internet www.serbianembassy.no; Ambassador Vladislav Mladenović.

Peru: Carlos Porras Osores 360, Apdo 18-0392, San Isidro, Lima 27; Apdo 0392, Lima 18; tel. (1) 4212423; fax (1) 4212427; e-mail yugoembperu@amauta.rcp.net.pe; Ambassador GORAN MESIC.

Poland: 00-540 Warsaw, Al. Ujazdowskie 23/25; tel. (22) 6285161; fax (22) 6297173; e-mail yuabapl@zigzag.pl; Chargé d'affaires a.i. (vacant).

Portugal: Av. das Descobertas 12, 1400-092 Lisbon; tel. (21) 3015311; fax (21) 3015313; e-mail serviaemba@netcabo.pt; Ambassador DUŠKO LOPANDIĆ.

Romania: 010573 Bucharest 1, Calea Dorobanţilor 34; tel. (21) 2119871; fax (21) 2100175; e-mail ambiug@ines.ro; Ambassador Dušan Crnogorcević.

Russian Federation: 119285 Moscow, ul. Mosfilmovskaya 46; tel. (499) 147-41-06; fax (499) 147-41-04; e-mail ambasada@co.ru; Ambassador STANIMIR VUKIĆEVIĆ.

Slovakia: Búdková 38, 811 04 Bratislava; tel. (2) 5443-1927; fax (2) 5443-1933; e-mail info@embassyscg.sk; Ambassador Danko Prokić.

Slovenia: 1000 Ljubljana, Slomškova 1; tel. (1) 4380111; fax (1) 4342688; e-mail amba.srbije.lju@siol.net; Ambassador PREDRAG FILIPOV.

South Africa: 163 Marais St, Brooklyn, Pretoria; POB 13026, Hatfield 0028; tel. (12) 4605626; fax (12) 4606003; e-mail info@scgembassy.org.za; internet www.scgembassy.org.za; Ambassador Jovan Marić.

Spain: Velázquez 162, 28002 Madrid; tel. (91) 5635045; fax (91) 5630440; e-mail office@embajada-serbia.es; internet www.embajada-serbia.es; Ambassador JELA BAĆOVIĆ.

Sweden: Valhallavägen 70, POB 26209, 100 41 Stockholm; tel. (8) 21-84-36; fax (8) 21-84-95; e-mail serbiaemb@telia.com; Ambassador Prof. Dr Ninoslav D. Stojadinović.

Switzerland: Seminarstr. 5, 3006 Bern; tel. 313526353; fax 313514474; e-mail info@ambasadasrbije.ch; internet www.ambasadasrbije.ch; Ambassador DRAGAN MARŠIĆANIN.

Syria: BP 739, 18 rue al-Jala'a, Abou Roumaneh, Damascus; tel. (11) 3336222; fax (11) 3333690; e-mail ambasada@srbija-damask.org; internet www.srbija-damask.org; Chargé d'affaires Dr Gordana Aničić.

Tunisia: 4 rue de Libéria, Belvédère, 1002 Tunis; tel. (71) 783-057; fax (71) 796-482; e-mail amb.serbia@gnet.tn; Ambassador MILORAD JOVANOVIĆ.

Turkey: Paris Cad. 47, 06450 Kavaklıdere, Ankara; tel. (312) 4260236; fax (312) 4278345; e-mail embserank@tr.net; Ambassador Vladimir Curgus.

Ukraine: 04070 Kyiv, vul. Voloska 4; tel. (44) 425-60-60; fax (44) 425-60-47; e-mail ambars@optima.com.ua; Ambassador GORAN ALEKSIĆ.

United Kingdom: 28 Belgrave Sq., London, SW1X 8QB; tel. (20) 7235-9049; fax (20) 7235-7092; internet www.serbianembassy.org.uk; Chargé d'affaires Dragan Županjevac.

United States of America: 2134 Kalorama Rd, NW, Washington, DC 20008; tel. (202) 332-0333; fax (202) 332-3933; e-mail info@serbiaembusa.org; internet www.serbiaembusa.org; Ambassador DR IVAN VUJAĆIĆ.

Vatican City: Via dei Monti Parioli 20, 00197 Rome, Italy; tel. (06) 3200099; fax (06) 3204530; e-mail amb.serbia.vatican@ambroma.com; Ambassador Vladeta Janković.

Zambia: Independence Ave 5216, POB 33379, 10101 Lusaka; tel. (1) 250235; fax (1) 253889; e-mail serbianemba@zamnet.zm; Chargé d'affaires a.i. MIRKO MANOJLOVIC.

DIPLOMATIC MISSIONS OF SEYCHELLES

United Nations: 800 Second Ave, Rm 400c, New York, NY 10017; tel. (212) 972-1785; fax (212) 972-1786; e-mail seychelles@un.int; Permanent Representative Ronald Jean Jumeau.

France: 51 ave Mozart, 75016 Paris; tel. 1-42-30-57-47; fax 1-42-30-57-40; e-mail ambsey@aol.com; Ambassador CLAUDE MOREL.

United States of America: 800 Second Ave, Suite 900c, New York, NY 10017; tel. (212) 687-9766; fax (212) 972-1786; Ambassador Ronald Jean Jumeau.

DIPLOMATIC MISSIONS OF SIERRA LEONE

United Nations: 245 East 49th St, New York, NY 10017; tel. (212) 688-1656; fax (212) 688-4924; e-mail sierraleone@un.int; Permanent Representative JOE ROBERT PEMAGBI.

Belgium: 410 ave de Tervueren, 1150 Brussels; tel. (2) 771-00-53; fax (2) 771-82-30; e-mail sierraleoneembassy@brutele.be; Ambassador Fode M. Dabor.

China, People's Republic: 7 Dong Zhi Men Wai Dajie, Beijing 100600; tel. (10) 65322174; fax (10) 65323752; e-mail sejohnny@163bj.com; Ambassador SAHR E. JOHNNY.

Egypt Interests served by Saudi Arabia.

Ethiopia: POB 5619, Addis Ababa; tel. (11) 3710033; fax (11) 3711911; Ambassador IBRAHIM M. KAMARA.

Gambia: 67 Daniel Goddard St, Banjul; tel. 4228206; fax 4229819; e-mail mfodayyumkella@yahoo.co.uk; High Commissioner Mohammed Foday Yumkella.

Germany: Rheinallee 20, 53173 Bonn; tel. (228) 352001; fax (228) 364269; e-mail secretariat@sierraleone-embassy.de; internet www.sierraleone-embassy.de; Ambassador FODAY MOHAMED DURAMANY SEISAY.

Ghana: 83a Senchi St, Airport Residential Area, POB 55, Cantonments, Accra; tel. (21) 769190; fax (21) 769189; e-mail slhc@ighmail.com; High Commissioner Mokowa Adu- Gyamfi.

Guinea: Quartier Bellevue, face aux cases présidentielles, Commune de Dixinn, BP 625, Conakry; tel. 30-46-40-84; fax 30-41-23-64; Ambassador DR SHEKU B. SACCOH.

Iran: No. 10, Malek St, off Dr Shariati Ave, Tehran; tel. (21) 77502819; fax (21) 77529515; e-mail leone@nasim.net; Ambassador Haja Alari Cole.

Liberia: Tubman Blvd, POB 575, Monrovia; tel. 261301; Ambassador PATRICK J. FOYAH.

Libya: Tripoli; Ambassador el Hadj Mohammed Samura.

Nigeria: 31 Waziri Ibrahim St, Victoria Island, POB 2821, Lagos; tel. (1) 2614666; High Commissioner JOSEPH BLELL.

Russian Federation: 121615 Moscow, Rublevskoye shosse 26/1/58–59; tel. (495) 415-41-24; fax (495) 415-29-85; Ambassador Melrose Beyoh Kai-Banya.

Saudi Arabia: POB 94329, Riyadh 11693; tel. (1) 464-3982; fax (1) 464-3662; e-mail slembrdh@zajil.net; Ambassador ALHAJI AMADU DEEN TEJAN-SIE.

United Kingdom: 41 Eagle St, London, WC1R 4TL; tel. (20) 7404-0140; fax (20) 7430-9862; e-mail info@slhc-uk.org.uk; internet www.slhc-uk.org.uk; High Commr Melvin H. Chalobah.

United States of America: 1701 19th St, NW, Washington, DC 20009; tel. (202) 939-9261; fax (202) 483-1793; Ambassador BOCKARI KORTU STEVENS.

DIPLOMATIC MISSIONS OF SINGAPORE

United Nations: 231 East 51st St, New York, NY 10022; tel. (212) 826-0840; fax (212) 826-2964; e-mail singapore@un.int; internet www.mfa.gov.sg/newyork; Permanent Representative Vanu Gopala Menon.

Australia: 17 Forster Crescent, Yarralumla, ACT 2600; tel. (2) 6271-2000; fax (2) 6273-9823; e-mail singhc_cbr@sgmfa.gov.sg; internet www.mfa.gov.sg/canberra; High Commissioner EDDIE TEO.

Belgium: 198 ave F. D. Roosevelt, 1050 Brussels; tel. (2) 660-29-79; fax (2) 660-86-85; e-mail singemb_bru@sgmfa.gov.sg; internet www.mfa.gov.sg/brussels; Ambassador Anil Kumar Nayar.

Brunei: 8 Simpang 74, Jalan Subok, Bandar Seri Begawan; tel. 2262741; fax 2262743; e-mail singhc_bwn@sgmfa.gov.sg; internet www.mfa.gov.sg/brunei; High Commissioner JOSEPH K. H. KOH.

Cambodia: 129 blvd Norodom, Phnom-Penh; tel. (23) 221875; fax (23) 210862; e-mail singemb@online.com.kh; internet www.mfa.gov.sg/phnompenh; AmbassadorTan Yee Woan.

China, People's Republic: 1 Xiu Shui Bei Jie, Jian Guo Men Wai, Beijing 100600; tel. (10) 65323926; fax (10) 65322215; e-mail singemb_bej@sgmfa.gov.sg; internet www.mfa.gov.sg/beijing; Ambassador CHIN SIAT-YOON.

Egypt: 40 Sharia Babel, Cairo 11511 (Dokki); tel. (2) 37490468; fax (2) 37480562; e-mail singemb_cai@sgmfa.gov.sg; internet www.mfa.gov.sg/cairo; Ambassador Wong Kwok Pun.

France: 12 sq. de l'ave Foch, 75116 Paris; tel. 1-45-00-33-61; fax 1-45-00-61-79; e-mail singemb_par@sgmfa.gov.sg; internet www.mfa.gov.sg/paris; Ambassador BURHAN GAFOOR.

Germany: Friedrichstr. 200, 10117 Berlin; tel. (30) 2263430; fax (30) 22634355; e-mail singemb_ber@sgmfa.gov.sg; internet www.mfa.gov.sg/berlin; Ambassador A. Selverajah.

India: N-88 Panchsheel Park, New Delhi 110 017; tel. (11) 41019801; fax (11) 41019805; e-mail singhc_del@sgmfa.gov.sg; internet www.mfa.gov.sg/newdelhi; High CommissionerCALVIN EU MUN HOO.

Indonesia: Jalan H. R. Rasuna Said, Blok X/4, Kav. 2, Kuningan, Jakarta 12950; tel. (21) 5201489; fax (21) 5201486; e-mail singemb_jkt@sgmfa.gov.sg; internet www.mfa.gov.sg/jkt; Ambassador Ashok Mirpuri.

Japan: 5-12-3, Roppongi, Minato-ku, Tokyo 106-0032; tel. (3) 3586-9111; fax (3) 3582-1085; e-mail singemb@gol.com; internet www.mfa.gov.sg/tokyo; AmbassadorTAN CHIN TIONG.

Korea, Republic: Seoul Finance Bldg, 28th Floor, 84, 1-ga, Taepyeong-no, Jung-gu, Seoul 100-102; tel. (2) 774-2464; fax (2) 773-2465; e-mail singemb@unitel.co.kr; internet www.mfa.gov.sg/seoul; Ambassador Chua Thai Keong.

Laos: Unit 12, Ban Naxay, rue Nong Bong, Muang Sat Settha, Vientiane; tel. (21) 416860; fax (21) 416854; e-mail singemb_vte@sgmfa.gov.sg; internet www.mfa.gov.sg/vientiane; Ambassador BENJAMIN WILLIAM.

Malaysia: 209 Jalan Tun Razak, 50400 Kuala Lumpur; tel. (3) 21616277; fax (3) 21616343; e-mail singhc_kul@sgmfa.gov.sg; internet www.mfa.gov.sg/kl; High Commissioner T. Jasudasen.

Myanmar: 238 Dhamazedi Rd, Bahan Township, Yangon; tel. (1) 559001; fax (1) 559002; e-mail singemb_ygn@sgmfa.gov.sg; internet www.mfa.gov.sg/yangon; Ambassador ROBERT CHUA.

New Zealand: 17 Kabul St, Khandallah, POB 13140, Wellington; tel. (4) 470-0850; fax (4) 479-4066; e-mail singhc_wlg@sgmfa.gov.sg; internet www.mfa.gov.sg/wellington; High Commissioner Seetoh Hoy Cheng.

Philippines: Enterprise Center, Tower I, 35th Floor, 6766 Ayala Ave, cnr Paseo de Roxas, Makati City, Metro Manila; tel. (2) 7512345; fax (2) 7512346; e-mail singemb_mnl@sgmfa.gov.sg; internet www.mfa.gov.sg/manila; Ambassador LIM KHENG HUA.

Russian Federation: 121099 Moscow, per. Kamennoi Slobody 5; tel. (495) 241-39-13; fax (495) 241-78-95; e-mail singemb_mow@sgmfa.gov.sg; internet www.mfa.gov.sg/moscow; AmbassadorMichael Tay Cheow Ann.

Saudi Arabia: POB 94378, Riyadh 11693; tel. (1) 480-3855; fax (1) 483-0632; e-mail singemb_ruh@sgmfa.gov.sg; internet www.mfa.gov.sg/riyadh; Ambassador V. P. HIRUBALAN.

South Africa: 980 Schoeman St, Arcadia, Pretoria 0083; POB 11809, Hatfield 0028; tel. (12) 4306035; fax (12) 3424425; e-mail sporehc@mweb.co.za; High Commissioner Mohideen P. H. Rubin.

Thailand: 129 Thanon Sathorn Tai, Bangkok 10120; tel. (2) 286-2111; fax (2) 286-6966; e-mail singemb_bkk@sgmfa.gov.sg; internet www.mfa.gov.sg/bangkok; Ambassador PETER CHAN.

United Kingdom: 9 Wilton Cres., London, SW1X 8SP; tel. (20) 7235-8315; fax (20) 7245-6583; e-mail singhc_lon@sgmfa.gov.sg; internet www.mfa.gov.sg/london; High Commr Michael Eng Cheng Teo.

United States of America: 3501 International Pl., NW, Washington, DC 20008; tel. (202) 537-3100; fax (202) 537-0876; e-mail singemb_was@sgmfa.gov.sg; internet www.mfa.gov.sg/washington; Ambassador HENG CHEE CHAN.

Viet Nam: Pacific Place, Unit V804–808, 8th Floor, 83b, Ly Thuong Kiet, Hanoi; tel. (4) 9460808; fax (4) 9460821; e-mail singemb_hanoi@sgmfa.gov.sg; internet www.mfa.gov.sg/hanoi; Ambassador Lim Thuan Kuan.

DIPLOMATIC MISSIONS OF SLOVAKIA

United Nations: 801 Second Ave, 12th Floor, New York, NY 10017; tel. (212) 286-8418; fax (212) 286-8419; e-mail slovakia@un.int; internet www.un.int/slovakia; Permanent Representative PETER BURIAN.

Argentina: Figueroa Alcorta 3240, C1425CKY Buenos Aires; tel. (11) 4801-3917; fax (11) 4801-4654; e-mail embsl@fibertel.com.ar; Ambassador Vladimir Gracz.

Australia: 47 Culgoa Circuit, O'Malley, ACT 2606; tel. (2) 6290-1516; fax (2) 6290-1755; internet www.slovakemb-aust.org; Ambassador DR PETER PROCHACKA.

Austria: Armbrustergasse 24, 1190 Vienna; tel. (1) 318-90-55-20-0; fax (1) 318-90-55-20-8; e-mail slovakembassy@vienna.mfa.sk; internet www.vienna.mfa.sk; Ambassador Dr Peter Lizak.

Belarus: 220034 Minsk, vul. Platonova 1B; tel. (17) 285-29-99; fax (17) 283-68-48; e-mail slovemb@iptel.by; internet www.mzv.sk/minsk; Chargé d'affaires REHÁK ĽUBOMÍR.

Belgium: 195 ave Molière, 1050 Brussels; tel. (2) 346-40-45; fax (2) 346-63-85; e-mail emb.brussel@mzv.sk; Ambassador Peter Sopko.

Bosnia and Herzegovina: 71000 Sarajevo, Skopljanska 7; tel. (33) 716440; fax (33) 716410; e-mail emb.sarajevo@mzv.sk; internet www.sarajevo.mfa.sk; Ambassador MIROSLAV MOJŽITA.

Brazil: Av. das Nações, Quadra 805, Lote 21, 70414-900 Brasília, DF; tel. (61) 3443-1263; fax (61) 3443-1267; e-mail eslovaca@brasil. mfa.sk; Ambassador Marián Masarik.

Bulgaria: 1504 Sofia, bul. Ya. Sakazov 9; tel. (2) 942-92-10; fax (2) 942-92-35; e-mail embassy@sofia.mfa.sk; internet www.mzv.sk/sofia; Ambassador MICHAL KOTTMAN.

Canada: 50 Rideau Terrace, Ottawa, ON K1M 2A1; tel. (613) 749-4442; fax (613) 749-4989; e-mail ottawa@slovakembassy.ca; internet www.ottawa.mfa.sk; Ambassador Stanislav Opiela.

China, People's Republic: Ri Tan Lu, Jian Guo Men Wai, Beijing 100600; tel. (10) 65321531; fax (10) 65324814; e-mail slovak.emb.bj@svkmofabeijing.com; Ambassador ŽIGMUND BERTÓK.

Croatia: 10000 Zagreb, prilaz Đure Deželića 10; tel. (1) 4848941; fax (1) 4848942; e-mail slovak.emb@zg.htnet.hr; Ambassador Ján Báňas.

Cuba: Calle 66, No 521, entre 5B y 7, Miramar, Havana; tel. (7) 204-1884; fax (7) 204-1883; e-mail embeslovaca@enet.cu; Ambassador IVO HLAVACEK.

Cyprus: POB 21165, 4 Kalamatas St, 2002 Strovolos, Nicosia; tel. 22879681; fax 22311715; e-mail skembassy@cytanet.com.cy; Ambassador Anna Turenicova.

Czech Republic: Pod hradbami 1, 160 00 Prague 6; tel. 233113051; fax 233113054; e-mail skembassy@mfa.sk; Ambassador LADISLAV BALLEK.

Denmark: Vesterled 26–28, 2100 Copenhagen Ø; tel. 39-20-99-11; fax 39-20-99-13; e-mail embassy@copenhagen.mfa.sk; Ambassador Lubomír Golian.

Egypt: 3 Sharia Adel Hussein Rostom, Dokki, Cairo (Giza); tel. (2) 33358240; fax (2) 33355810; e-mail zukahira@tedata.net.eg; Ambassador PETER ZSOLDOS.

Finland: Annankatu 25, 00100 Helsinki; tel. (9) 68117810; fax (9) 68117820; e-mail skemb.hels@sci.fi; internet www.helsinki.mfa.sk; Ambassador Viera Štupáková.

France: 125 rue du Ranelagh, 75016 Paris; tel. 1-44-14-56-00; fax 1-42-88-76-53; e-mail paris@amb-slovaquie.fr; internet www.amb-slovaquie.fr; Ambassador JÁN KUDERJAVÝ.

Germany: Friedrichstr. 60, 10117 Berlin; tel. (30) 8892620; fax (30) 88926222; e-mail presse@botschaft-slowakei.de; internet www.berlin.mfa.sk; Ambassador Ivan Korčok.

Greece: Odos Georgiou Seferis 4, Palaio Psychiko, 154 52 Athens; tel. (210) 6771980; fax (210) 6771878; e-mail emb.athens@mzv.sk; internet www.mzv.sk/athens; Ambassador JÁN VODERADSKÝ.

Hungary: 1143 Budapest, Stefánia u. 22–24; tel. (1) 460-9010; fax (1) 460-9020; e-mail slovakem@matavnet.hu; Ambassador Juraj Migaš.

India: 50M Niti Marg, Chanakyapuri, New Delhi 110 021; tel. (11) 26889071; fax (11) 26877941; e-mail skdelhi@giasdl01.vsnl.net.in; Ambassador ALEXANDER ILASCIK.

Indonesia: Jalan Prof. Mohammed Yamin 29, POB 1368, Menteng, Jakarta Pusat 10310; tel. (21) 3101068; fax (21) 3101180; e-mail slovemby@indo.net.id; Ambassador Peter Holasek.

Iran: POB 19395-6341, 38 Sarlashgar Fallahi St, Tehran 19887; tel. (21) 22411164; fax (21) 22409719; e-mail svkemb@parsonline.sk; internet www.tehran.mfa.sk; Ambassador ANTON HAJDUK.

Iraq: 94/28/923 Hay Babel, Baghdad; tel. (1) 776-7367; fax (1) 776-7368; Ambassador Jozef Maréfka.

Ireland: 20 Clyde Rd, Ballsbridge, Dublin 4; tel. (1) 6600012; fax (1) 6600014; e-mail slovak@iol.ie; Ambassador JÁN GÁBOR.

Israel: POB 6459, 37 Jabotinsky St, Tel-Aviv 62287; tel. 3-5449119; fax 3-5449144; e-mail slovemb1@barak.net.il; Ambassador Milan Dubček.

Italy: Via dei Colli della Farnesina 144, 00194 Roma; tel. (06) 36715201; fax (06) 36715265; e-mail embassy@rome.mfa.sk; internet www.rome.mfa.sk; Ambassador STANISLAV VALLO.

Japan: POB 35, 2-16-14, Hiroo, Shibuya-ku, Tokyo 150-8691; tel. (3) 3400-8122; fax (3) 3406-6215; e-mail information@slovak-embassy.jp; internet www.embassy-avenue.jp/slovakia; Ambassador Peter Vršanský.

Kazakhstan: 010000 Astana, Mikroraion Karaotkel–2, 5; tel. (7172) 24-11-91; fax (7172) 24-20-48; e-mail zuastana1@post.sk; internet www.mzv.sk/astana; Ambassador DR DUŠAN PODHORSKÝ.

Kenya: Milimani Rd, POB 30204, Nairobi; tel. (20) 721896; fax (20) 721898; Ambassador Stefan Moravek.

Korea, Republic: 389-1, Hannam-dong, Yeongsan-gu, Seoul 140-210; tel. (2) 794-3981; fax (2) 794-3982; e-mail slovakemb@yahoo.com; Ambassador Pavel Hrmo.

Latvia: Smilšu iela 8, Rīga 1050; tel. 6781-4280; fax 6781-4290; e-mail embassy@slovakia.lv; Ambassador Ivan Špilda.

Libya: POB 5721, Gargaresh 3 Km, Hay Andalus, Tripoli; tel. (21) 4781388; fax (21) 4781387; e-mail slovembtrp@slovembtrp.com; Ambassador Ján Bóry.

Malaysia: 11 Jalan U Thant, 55000 Kuala Lumpur; tel. (3) 21150016; fax (3) 21150014; e-mail slovemb@tm.net.my; Ambassador Milan Lajčiak.

Mexico: Julio Verne 35, Col. Polanco, Del. Miguel Hidalgo, 11560 México, DF; tel. (55) 5280-6669; fax (55) 5280-6294; e-mail eslovaquia@prodigy.net.mx; Ambassador Marián Adamec.

Netherlands: Parkweg 1, 2585 JG The Hague; tel. (70) 4167777; fax (70) 4167783; e-mail embassy@haag.mfa.sk; internet www.haag.mfa.sk; Ambassador Oksana Tomová.

Nigeria: POB 1290, Lagos; tel. (1) 2621585; fax (1) 2612103; e-mail obeo.sk@micro.com.ng; Ambassador Vasil Hudák.

Norway: Thomas Heftyesgt. 24, 0244 Oslo; tel. 22-04-94-70; fax 22-04-94-74; e-mail slovakr@online.no; internet www.oslo.mfa.sk; Ambassador Dušan Rozbora.

Poland: 00-581 Warsaw, ul. Litewska 6; tel. (22) 5258110; fax (22) 5258122; e-mail embassy@varsava.mfa.sk; internet www.ambasada-slowacji.pl; Ambassador František Ružička.

Portugal: Av. Fontes Pereira de Melo 19, 7° dto, 1050-116 Lisbon; tel. (21) 3583300; fax (21) 3583309; e-mail emb.lisbon@mzv.sk; Ambassador Radomír Boháč.

Romania: 020977 Bucharest 2, Str. Oţetari 3; tel. (21) 3006100; fax (21) 3006101; e-mail embassy@bukurest.mfa.sk; internet www.bucharest.mfa.sk; Ambassador Hildegard Bunčáková.

Russian Federation: 123056 Moscow, ul. Yu. Fuchika 17/19; tel. (495) 250-10-70; fax (495) 250-15-91; e-mail embassy@moskva.mfa.sk; internet www.moscow.mfa.sk; Ambassador Dr Augustín Čisár.

Serbia: 11070 Belgrade, bul. Umetnosti 18; tel. (11) 2223800; fax (11) 2223820; e-mail embassy@belehrad.mfa.sk; Ambassador Igor Furdík.

Slovenia: 1000 Ljubljana, Tivolska cesta 4, POB 395; tel. (1) 4255425; fax (1) 4210524; e-mail embass@lublana.mfa.sk; internet lublana.mfa.sk; Ambassador Dr Roman Paldan.

South Africa: 930 Arcadia St, Pretoria 0083; POB 12736, Hatfield 0028; tel. (12) 3422051; fax (12) 3423688; e-mail slovakemb@telkomsa.net; internet www.mfa.sk/zu; Ambassador Pavol Ivan.

Spain: Pinar 20, 28006 Madrid; tel. (91) 5903861; fax (91) 5903868; e-mail mail@embajadaeslovaquia.es; Ambassador Ján Valko.

Sweden: Arsenalsgt. 2, 3rd Floor, POB 7183, 103 88 Stockholm; tel. (8) 545-039-60; fax (8) 545-039-69; e-mail slovakembassy@stockholm.mfa.sk; internet www.stockholm.mfa.sk; Ambassador Peter Kmec.

Switzerland: Thunstr. 99, 3006 Bern 1; tel. 313563930; fax 313563933; e-mail slovak@spectraweb.ch; internet www.bern.mfa.sk; Ambassador Štefan Schill.

Syria: BP 33115, 158 rue ash-Shafei, Mezzeh Est, Damascus; tel. (11) 6132114; fax (11) 6132598; e-mail slovemb@scs-net.org; internet www.damascus.mfa.sk; Ambassador Oldrich Hlaváček.

Thailand: 25/9-4, BKI/YWCA Bldg, 9th Floor, Thanon Sathorn Tai, Tungmahamek, Bangkok 10120; tel. (2) 677-3445; fax (2) 677-3447; e-mail slovakemb@actions.net; Ambassador Vasil Pytel.

Turkey: Atatürk Bul. 245, 06692 Kavaklıdere, Ankara; tel. (312) 4675075; fax (312) 4682689; e-mail emb.ankara@mzv.sk; Ambassador Vladimír Jakabčín.

Ukraine: 01901 Kyiv, vul. Yaroslaviv Val 34; tel. (44) 212-03-10; fax (44) 272-32-71; e-mail embassy@kiev.mfa.sk; internet www.slovakia.kiev.ua; Ambassador Urban Rusnák.

United Kingdom: 25 Kensington Palace Gdns, London, W8 4QY; tel. (20) 7313-6470; fax (20) 7313-6481; e-mail emb.london@mzv.sk; internet www.slovakembassy.co.uk; Ambassador Juraj Zervan.

United States of America: 3523 International Court, NW, Suite 210, Washington, DC 20008; tel. (202) 237-1054; fax (202) 237-6438; e-mail information@slovakembassy-us.org; internet www.slovakembassy-us.org; Ambassador Rastislav Kacer.

Uzbekistan: 100070 Tashkent, K. Beshyogoch ko'ch. 38; tel. (71) 120-68-52; fax (71) 120-68-51; e-mail slovakia@buzton.com; internet www.tashkent.mfa.sk; Ambassador Josef Mačisák.

Vatican City: Via dei Prati della Farnesina 57, 00194 Rome, Italy; tel. (06) 33221132; fax (06) 33219582; e-mail slovakemvat@libero.it; Ambassador Jozef Dravecký.

DIPLOMATIC MISSIONS OF SLOVENIA

United Nations: 600 Third Ave, 24th Floor, New York, NY 10016; tel. (212) 370-3007; fax (212) 370-1824; e-mail mny@mzz-dkp.gov.si; internet www.un.int/slovenia; Permanent Representative Sanja Štiglic.

Argentina: Santa Fe 846, 6°, C1059ABP Buenos Aires; tel. (11) 4894-0621; fax (11) 4312-8410; e-mail vba@mzz-dkp.gov.si; Ambassador Avguštin Vivod.

Australia: POB 284, Civic Square, Canberra, ACT 2608; tel. (2) 6243-4830; fax (2) 6243-4827; e-mail vca@gov.si; internet www.gov.si/mzz-dkp/veleposlanistva/eng/canberra; Chargé d'affaires a.i. Bojan Bertoncelj.

Austria: Nibelungengasse 13/3, 1010 Vienna; tel. (1) 586-13-09; fax (1) 586-12-65; e-mail vdu@gov.si; Ambassador Prof. Dr Ernest Petrič.

Belgium: 130A ave Louise, 1050 Brussels; tel. (2) 643-49-50; fax (2) 644-20-79; e-mail vbr@gov.si; internet www.gov.si/mzz-dkp/vbr/eng/index.html; Ambassador Borut Trekman.

Bosnia and Herzegovina: 71000 Sarajevo, Bentbaša 7; tel. (33) 271260; fax (33) 271270; e-mail vsa@gov.si; internet sarajevo.veleposlanistvo.si; Ambassador Nataša Vodušek.

Canada: 150 Metcalfe St, Suite 2200, Ottawa, ON K2P 1P1; tel. (613) 565-5781; fax (613) 565-5783; e-mail vot@gov.si; internet ottawa.embassy.si; Ambassador Tomaz Kunstelj.

China, People's Republic: Block F, 57 Ya Qu Yuan, King's Garden Villas, 18 Xiao Yun Lu, Chao Yang Qu, Beijing 100016; tel. (10) 64681030; fax (10) 64681040; e-mail vpe@gov.si; internet beijing.embassy.si; Ambassador Marjan Cencen.

Croatia: 10000 Zagreb, Savska cesta 41/II; tel. (1) 6311000; fax (1) 6177236; e-mail vzg@gov.si; Ambassador Milan Orožen Adamič.

Czech Republic: Pod hradbami 15, 160 41 Prague 6; tel. 233081211; fax 224314106; e-mail vpr@.gov.si; Ambassador Frank But.

Denmark: Amaliegade 6, 2nd Floor, 1256 Copenhagen K; tel. 33-73-01-20; fax 33-15-06-07; e-mail vkh@gov.si; internet kopenhagen.veleposlanistvo.si; Ambassador Rudolf Gabrovec.

Egypt: 6th Floor, 21 Sharia Soliman Abaza, Mohandessin, Cairo; tel. (2) 7491771; fax (2) 7497141; e-mail vka@gov.si; Ambassador Borut Mahnič.

Finland: Eteläesplanadi 24A, 00130 Helsinki; POB 9, 00101 Helsinki; tel. (9) 2289940; fax (9) 6944775; e-mail vhe@mzz-dkp.gov.si; Chargé d'affaires a.i. Jadran Hočevar.

France: 28 rue Bois-le-Vent, 75116 Paris; tel. 1-44-96-50-71; fax 1-45-24-67-05; e-mail vpa@gov.si; Ambassador Janez Šumrada.

Germany: Hausvogteipl. 3–4, 10117 Berlin; tel. (30) 2061450; fax (30) 20614570; e-mail vbn@mzz-dkp.gov.si; Ambassador Dragoljuba Benčina.

Greece: Odos Mavili 10, Palaio Psychiko, 154 52 Athens; tel. (210) 6775683; fax (210) 6775680; e-mail vat@mzz-dkp.gov.si; Ambassador Vladimir Kolmanič.

Hungary: 1025 Budapest, Cseppkö u. 68; tel. (1) 438-5600; fax (1) 325-9187; e-mail vbp@mzz-dkp.gov.si; Ambassador Andrej Gerenčer.

India: 46 Poorvi Marg, Vasant Vihar, New Delhi 110 057; tel. (11) 51662891; fax (11) 51662895; e-mail vnd@mzz-dkp.gov.si; Chargé d'affaires Miklavz Borštnik.

Iran: POB 19575-459, 30 Narenjestan 8th Alley, Pasdaran Ave, Tehran 19576; tel. (21) 22802223; fax (21) 22282131; e-mail vte@mzz-dkp.sigov.si; Chargé d'affaires a.i. Miljan Majhen.

Ireland: Morrison Chambers, 2nd Floor, 32 Nassau St, Dublin 2; tel. (1) 6705240; fax (1) 6705243; e-mail vdb@gov.si; internet dublin.veleposlanistvo.si; Ambassador Franc Mikša.

Israel: Top Tower, 50 Dizengoff St, POB 23245, Tel-Aviv 61231; tel. 3-6293563; fax 3-5282214; e-mail vta@mzz-dkp.gov.si; Chargé d'affaires a.i. Tatjana Miskova.

Italy: Via Leonardo Pisano 10, 00197 Roma; tel. (06) 80914310; fax (06) 8081471; e-mail vri@gov.si; Ambassador Andrej Capuder.

Japan: 7-5-15, Akasaka, Minato-ku, Tokyo 107-0052; tel. (3) 5570-6275; fax (3) 5570-6075; e-mail vto@mzz-dkp.gov.si; Ambassador Miran Čupkovič Skender.

Macedonia, former Yugoslav Republic: 1000 Skopje, Vodnjanska 42; tel. (2) 3178730; fax (2) 3176631; e-mail vsk@gov.si; Ambassador Alain Brian Bergant.

Montenegro: 81000 Podgorica, 13 Jula bb, PC Čelebić; tel. (81) 208020; fax (81) 237095; e-mail kpg@gov.si; Ambassador JERNEJ VIDETIČ.

Netherlands: Anna Paulownastraat 11, 2518 BA The Hague; tel. (70) 3108690; fax (70) 36266008; e-mail vhg@mzz-dkp.gov.si; internet hague .embassy.si; Ambassador Dr Tea Petrin.

Poland: 02-516 Warsaw, ul. Starościńska 1/23–24; tel. (22) 8498282; fax (22) 8484090; e-mail vvr@gov.si; Ambassador JOŽEF DROFENIK.

Portugal: Av. da Liberdade 49, 6° esq., 1250-139 Lisbon; tel. (21) 3423301; fax (21) 3423305; e-mail vli@gov.si; Ambassador Peter Andrej Bekeš.

Romania: Bucharest, Str. Puskin Alexandru 10, Sector 1; tel. (21) 3002780; fax (21) 3150927; e-mail vbk@gov.si; internet www.bukaresta .veleposlanistvo.si; Chargé d'affaires a.i. MARCEL KOPROL.

Russian Federation: 127006 Moscow, ul. M. Dmitrovka 14/1; tel. (503) 737-63-55; fax (495) 694-15-68; e-mail vmo@gov.si; internet moskva .veleposlanistvo.si; Ambassador Andrej Benedejčič.

Serbia: Belgrade, Pariska 15; tel. (11) 3038477; fax (11) 3288657; e-mail vbg@gov.si; Ambassador MIROSLAV LUCI.

Slovakia: Moyzesova 4, 813 15 Bratislava; tel. (2) 5726-7700; fax (2) 5245-0009; e-mail vbs@gov.si; Ambassador Maja Marija Lovrenčič Svetek.

Spain: Hermanos Bécquer 7, 2°, 28006 Madrid; tel. (91) 4116893; fax (91) 5646057; e-mail vma@gov.si; Ambassador PETER REBERC.

Sweden: Styrmansgt. 4, 1st Floor, 114 54 Stockholm; tel. (8) 545-65-885; fax (8) 662-92-74; e-mail vst@mzz-dkp.gov.si; Ambassador Vojislav Šuc.

Switzerland: Schwanengasse 9, 3011 Bern; tel. 313109000; fax 313124414; e-mail vbe@gov.si; internet bern.embassy.si; Chargé d'affaires a.i. BRANKO ZUPANC.

Turkey: Kırlangıç Sok. 36, 06700 Gaziosmanpaşa, Ankara; tel. (312) 4054221; fax (312) 4260216; e-mail van@gov.si; Ambassador Mitja Štrukelj.

Ukraine: 01030 Kyiv, vul. B. Khmelnytskoho 48; tel. (44) 585-23-31; fax 585-23-43; e-mail vki@gov.si; internet kijev.veleposlanistvo.si; Ambassador PRIMOŽ ŠELIGO.

United Kingdom: 10 Little College St, London, SW1P 3SH; tel. (20) 7222-5400; fax (20) 7222-5277; e-mail vlo@gov.si; internet london.embassy.si; Ambassador Iztok Mirošić.

United States of America: 2410 California St, NW, Washington, DC 20008; tel. (201) 667-5363; fax (202) 667-4563; e-mail vwa@gov.si; internet www .embassy.si/washington; Ambassador SAMUEL ŽBOGAR.

Vatican City: Via della Conciliazione 10, 00193 Rome, Italy; tel. (06) 6833009; fax (06) 68307942; e-mail vva@gov.si; Ambassador Ivan Rebernik.

DIPLOMATIC MISSIONS OF SOLOMON ISLANDS

United Nations: 800 Second Ave, Suite 400L, New York, NY 10017; tel. (212) 599-6193; fax (212) 661-8925; e-mail solomonislands@un.int; Permanent Representative COLIN D. BECK.

Australia: POB 256, Deakin West, ACT 2600; tel. (2) 6282-7030; fax (2) 6282-7040; e-mail info@solomon.emb.gov.au; High Commissioner Victor Ngele.

Belgium: 17 ave Edouard Lacomble, 1040 Brussels; tel. (2) 732-70-85; fax (2) 732-68-85; e-mail siembassy@compuserve.com; Ambassador JOSEPH MA'AHANUA.

China (Taiwan): 7/F, 9-1 Lane 62, Tien Mou West Rd, Taipei 11156; tel. (2) 28731168; fax (2) 28735224; e-mail embassy@solomons.org.tw; internet www.solomons.org.tw; Ambassador Beraki Jino.

Papua New Guinea: Port Moresby; e-mail sihicomm@daltron.com.pg; High Commissioner BERNARD BATA'ANISIA.

United States of America: 800 Second Ave, Suite 400l, New York, NY 10017; tel. (212) 599-6192; fax (212) 661-8925; e-mail simny@solomons.com; Ambassador Colin D. Beck.

DIPLOMATIC MISSIONS OF SOMALIA

United Nations: 425 East 61st St, Suite 702, New York, NY 10021; tel. (212) 688-9410; fax (212) 759-0651; e-mail somalianet@hotmail.com; internet www .iaed.org/somalia; Permanent Representative ELMI AHMED DUALE.

China, People's Republic: 2 San Li Tun Lu, Beijing 100600; tel. (10) 65321752; Ambassador Mohammed Ahmed Awil.

Djibouti: BP 549, Djibouti; tel. 353521; Ambassador MUSE HIRSI FAHIYE.

Egypt: 27 Sharia es-Somal, Cairo (Dokki), Giza; tel. (2) 3374577; Ambassador Abdalla Hassan Mahmoud.

Ethiopia: Bole Kifle Ketema, Kebele 20, House No. 588, POB 1643, Addis Ababa; tel. (11) 6180673; fax (11) 6180680; Ambassador ABDIKARIM FARAH.

France: 26 rue Dumont d'Urville, 75116 Paris; tel. 1-45-00-88-98; Ambassador Said Hajgi Mohamoud Farah.

India: A-7, Defence Colony, New Delhi 110 024; tel. (11) 24335026; e-mail mosman65@yahoo.com; Ambassador EBYAN MAHAMED SALAH.

Indonesia: Jalan Permata Hijau Raya Block T, No. 8, Kebayoran Lama, Jakarta Selatan 12210; tel. (21) 5321920; fax (21) 5494730; e-mail somalirep_jkt@yahoo.com; internet somaliembassyjkt.com; Ambassador Mohamud Olow Barow.

Iran: 1 Hadaiyan St, Mirzapour St, Dr Shariati Ave, Tehran; tel. (21) 22245146; e-mail safarian@hotmail.com; Chargé d'affaires a.i. KHALIFA AHMED SAHAL.

Italy: Via dei Villini 9, 00161 Roma; Chargé d'affaires Abscir Osman Hussein.

Kenya: POB 30769, Nairobi; tel. (20) 580165; fax (20) 581683; Ambassador MOHAMMED ALI NUR.

Kuwait: POB 22766, 13088 Safat, Bayan, St 1, Block 7, Villa 25, Kuwait City; tel. 5394795; fax 5394829; e-mail soamin1@hotmail.com; Ambassador Abdul Khadir Amin Sheikh Abubaker.

Nigeria: Plot 1270, off Adeola Odeka St, POB 6355, Lagos; tel. (1) 2611283; Ambassador M. S. HASSAN.

Oman: Mumtaz Street, Villa Hassan Jumaa Baker, POB 1767, Ruwi 112; tel. 24564412; fax 24564965; Ambassador Gen. Isma'il Qasim Naji.

Pakistan: 17, St 60, F-8/4, Islamabad; tel. (51) 2854733; fax (51) 2854733; Ambassador ABDISALAAM HAJI AHMAD LIBAN.

Qatar: POB 1948, Doha; tel. 4832771; fax 4834568; Ambassador Sharif Muhammad Omar.

Russian Federation: 117556 Moscow, Simferopolskii bulv. 7A /145; tel. (495) 317-06-22; e-mail somemb@nabad.org; Chargé d'affaires a.i. MOHAMED MOHAMED HANDULLE.

Saudi Arabia: POB 94372, Riyadh 11693; tel. (1) 464-3456; fax (1) 464-9705; Ambassador Abd ar-Rahman A. Hussein.

Sudan: St 23–25, New Extension, POB 1857, Khartoum; tel. (183) 744800; Ambassador PROF. MAHDI ABUKAR.

Syria: ave Ata Ayoubi, al-Afif, Damascus; Ambassador (vacant).

Tunisia: 6 rue Hadramout, Mutuelleville, Tunis; tel. (71) 289-505; Ambassador AHMAD ABDALLAH MUHAMMAD.

United Arab Emirates: POB 4155, Abu Dhabi; tel. (2) 6669700; fax (2) 6651580; e-mail somen@emirates.net.ae; Ambassador Hussein Muhammad Bullaleh.

Yemen: San'a; tel. (1) 208864; Ambassador HASSAN MOHAMED SIAD BARRE.

Zambia: G3/377a Kabulonga Rd, POB 34051, Lusaka; tel. (1) 262119; Ambassador Dr Oman Umal.

DIPLOMATIC MISSIONS OF SOUTH AFRICA

United Nations: 333 East 38th St, 9th Floor, New York, NY 10016; tel. (212) 213-5583; fax (212) 692-2498; e-mail soafun@worldnet.att.net; internet www .southafrica-newyork.net/pmun; Permanent Representative DUMISANI SHADRACK KUMALO.

Algeria: 30 rue Capitain Hocine Slimane, 16000 el-Biar, Algiers; tel. (21) 23-03-84; fax (21) 23-08-27; e-mail sae@medianet.dz; Ambassador Mzuvukile Maqethuka.

Angola: Edif. Maianga, 1° e 2° andar, Rua Kwamme Nkrumah 31, Largo da Maianga, CP 6212, Luanda; tel. 222330593; fax 222398730; e-mail saemb .ang@netangola.com; internet www.sambangola.info; Ambassador THEMBA M. N. KUBHEKA.

Argentina: Marcelo T. de Alvear 590, 8°, C1058AAF Buenos Aires; tel. (11) 4317-2900; fax (11) 4317-2951; e-mail embasa@ciudad.com.ar; internet www .sudafrica.org.ar; Ambassador Peter Goosen.

Australia: cnr State Circle and Rhodes Place, Yarralumla, ACT 2600; tel. (2) 6272-7365; fax (2) 6273-3543; e-mail info@sahc.org.au; internet www.sahc .org.au; High Commissioner ANTHONY MONGALO.

Austria: Sandgasse 33, 1190 Vienna; tel. (1) 320-64-93; fax (1) 320-64-93-51; e-mail vienna.ambassador@foreign.gov.za; internet www.saembvie.at; Ambassador Leslie Mabangambi Gumbi.

Belgium: 17–19 rue Montoyer, 1040 Brussels; tel. (2) 285-44-00; fax (2) 285-44-02; e-mail embassy@southafrica.be; internet www.southafrica.be; Ambassador DR ANIL SOOKLAL.

Benin: Marina Hotel, blvd de la Merina, 01 BP 1901, Cotonou; tel. 21-30-72-17; e-mail foreign@intnet.bj; Ambassador Sikose Ntombazana Mji.

Botswana: Plot 29, Queens Rd, Private Bag 00402, Gaborone; tel. 3904800; fax 3905501; e-mail sahcgabs@botsnet.bw; High Commissioner DIKGANG F. MOOPELOA.

Brazil: SES, Av. das Nações, Quadra 801, Lote 06, 70406-900 Brasília, DF; tel. (61) 3312-9500; fax (61) 3322-8491; e-mail saemb@solar.com.br; internet www.africadosul.org.br; Ambassador Lindiwe Daphne Zulu.

Canada: 15 Sussex Dr., Ottawa, ON K1M 1M8; tel. (613) 744-0330; fax (613) 741-1639; e-mail rsafrica@southafrica-canada.ca; internet www.southafrica-canada.ca; High Commissioner ABRAHAM SOKAYA NKOMO.

Chile: Avda 11 de Septiembre 2353, 16°, Torre San Ramón, Santiago; tel. (2) 231-2860; fax (2) 231-3185; e-mail info@embajada-sudafrica.cl; internet www.embajada-sudafrica.cl; Ambassador Victor Zazeraj.

China, People's Republic: 5 Dong Zhi Men Wai Dajie, Chao Yang Qu, Beijing 100600; tel. (10) 65320171; fax (10) 65327319; e-mail safrican@163bj.com; Ambassador NDUMISO NDIMA NTSHINGA.

Comoros: Itsandra Royal Hotel, Rm 112, Moroni; Ambassador Masilo Mabeta.

Congo, Democratic Republic: 77 ave Ngongo Lutete, BP 7829, Kinshasa-Gombe; tel. (88) 48287; fax (88) 04152; e-mail ambasud@ckt.cd; Ambassador REV. DR MOLEFE S. TSELE.

Côte d'Ivoire: Villa Marc André, rue Mgr René Kouassi, Cocody, 08 BP 1806, Abidjan 08; tel. 22-44-59-63; fax 22-44-74-50; e-mail ambafsudpol@aviso.ci; Ambassador G. Dumisani Gwadiso.

Cuba: Avda 5, No 4201, esq. 42, Miramar, Havana; tel. (7) 204-9671; fax (7) 204-1101; e-mail rsacuba@ceniai.inf.cu; internet www.sudafrica.cu; Ambassador THENJIWE ETHEL MTINTSO.

Czech Republic: Ruská 65, POB 133, 100 00 Prague 10; tel. 267311114; fax 267311395; e-mail saprague@nextra.cz; Ambassador Nomsa Qhamkile Dube.

Denmark: Gammel Vartov Vej 8, POB 128, 2900 Hellerup; tel. 39-18-01-55; fax 39-18-40-06; e-mail sa.embassy@southafrica.dk; internet www.southafrica.dk; Ambassador DOLANA FAITH MSIMANG.

Egypt: 6th Floor, 55 Rd 18, Maadi, Cairo; tel. (2) 23594365; fax (2) 3595015; e-mail saembcai@tedata.net.eg; internet saembassyinegypt.com; Ambassador Sonto Kudjoe.

Equatorial Guinea: Parque de las Avenidas de Africa s/n, POB 5, Malabo; tel. (09) 77-37; fax (09) 27-46; e-mail malabo@foreign.gov.za; Ambassador MOKGETHI MONAISA (resident in Gabon).

Eritrea: Intercontinental Hotel, Rm 101, Asmara; tel. (1) 150400; fax (1) 151940; e-mail saemb@eol.com.er; .

Ethiopia: POB 1091, Addis Ababa; tel. (11) 3713034; fax (11) 3711330; e-mail sa.embassy.addis@telecom.net.et; Ambassador CHRIS PEPANI.

Finland: Rahapajankatu 1a 5, 3rd Floor, 00160 Helsinki; tel. (9) 68603100; fax (9) 68603160; e-mail saembfin@welho.com; internet www.southafricanembassy.fi; Ambassador Bukelwa Gilberta Hans.

France: 59 quai d'Orsay, 75343 Paris Cedex 07; tel. 1-53-59-23-23; fax 1-53-59-23-68; e-mail info@afriquesud.net; internet www.afriquesud.net; Ambassador NOMASONTO MARY SIBANDA-THUSI.

Gabon: Immeuble les Arcades, 142 rue des Chavannes, BP 4063, Libreville; tel. 77-45-30; fax 77-45-36; e-mail saegabon@internetgabon.com; Ambassador Mahlomola Jomo Khasu.

Germany: Tiergartenstr. 18, 10785 Berlin; tel. (30) 220730; fax (30) 22073190; e-mail berlin.info@foreign.gov.za; internet www.suedafrika.org; Chargé d'affaires a.i. GEORGE HENRY JOHANNES.

Ghana: 10 Klotey Cres., Labone North, POB 298, Accra; tel. (21) 762380; fax (21) 762381; e-mail sahcgh@africaonline.com.gh; High Commissioner Dr R. S. Molekane.

Greece: Leoforos Kifissias 60, 151 25 Athens; tel. (210) 6106645; fax (210) 6106640; e-mail embassy@southafrica.gr; internet www.southafrica.gr; Ambassador MANDISA DONA MARASHA.

Hungary: 1026 Budapest, Gárdonyi Géza u. 17; tel. (1) 392-0999; fax (1) 200-7277; e-mail saemb@sa-embassy.hu; internet www.sa-embassy.hu; Ambassador Dr Duduzile M. Khoza.

India: B-18 Vasant Marg, Vasant Vihar, New Delhi 110 057; tel. (11) 26149411; fax (11) 26143605; e-mail highcommissioner@sahc-india.com; internet www.sahc-india.com; High Commissioner SEHLOHO FRANCIS MOLOI.

Indonesia: Suite 705, Wisma GKBI, Jalan Jenderal Sudirman 28, Jakarta 10210; tel. (21) 5740660; fax (21) 5740661; e-mail saembhom@centrin.net.id; internet www.southafricanembassy-jakarta.or.id; Ambassador Griffiths Memela.

Iran: POB 11365-7476, 5 Yekta St, Bagh-e-Ferdows, Vali-e-Asr Ave, Tehran; tel. (21) 22702866; fax (21) 22719516; e-mail saemb@neda.net; Ambassador YUSUF SALOOJEE.

Ireland: Alexandra House, 2nd Floor, Earlsfort Centre, Earlsfort Terrace, Dublin 2; tel. (1) 6615553; fax (1) 6615590; e-mail information@saedublin.com; Ambassador Devikarani Priscilla Sewpal Jana.

Israel: POB 7138, Top Tower, 16th Floor, 50 Dizengoff St, Tel-Aviv 61071; tel. 3-5252566; fax 3-5253230; e-mail admin@saemb.org.il; internet www.safis.co.il; Ambassador MAJ.-GEN. FUMANEKILE GQIBA.

Italy: Via Tanaro 14, 00198 Roma; tel. (06) 852541; fax (06) 85254301; e-mail sae2@sudafrica.it; internet www.sudafrica.it; Ambassador Lenin Magigwane Shope.

Jamaica: 15 Hillcrest Ave, Kingston 6; tel. 978-3160; fax 978-0339; e-mail sahc-jamaica@cwjamaica.com; High Commissioner FAITH DOREEN RADEBE.

Japan: Oriken Hirakawa Bldg, 2-1-1, Hirakawa-cho, Chiyoda-ku, Tokyo 102-0093; tel. (3) 3265-3366; fax (3) 3265-1108; e-mail rsatk-info@rsatk.com; internet www.rsatk.com; Ambassador Dr Baldwin Sipho Ngubane.

Jordan: POB 851508, Sweifiyeh 11185, Amman; tel. (6) 5921194; fax (6) 5920080; e-mail saembjor@index.com.jo; internet www.saembjor.com; Ambassador DR BOY GELDENHUYS.

Kazakhstan: 010000 Astana, Kabanbai batyr 6/1; tel. (7127) 259-82-60; fax (727) 259-82-59; e-mail almaty@foreign.gov.za; Ambassador Bekizizve Wisdom Gila.

Kenya: Roshanmaer Place, Lenana Rd, POB 42441, Nairobi; tel. (20) 2827100; fax (20) 2827219; e-mail sahc@africaonline.co.ke; High Commissioner TONY MSIMANGA.

Korea, Republic: 1-37, Hannam-dong, Yeongsan-gu, Seoul 140-210; tel. (2) 792-4855; fax (2) 792-4856; e-mail general@southafrica-embassy.or.kr; internet www.southafrica-embassy.or.kr; Ambassador Stefanus Johannes Schoeman.

Kuwait: POB 2262, 40173 Mishref, Salwa Block 10, St 1, Villa 91, Unit 3, Kuwait City; tel. 5617988; fax 5617917; e-mail saemb@southafricaq8.com; internet www.southafricaq8.com; Ambassador ASHRAF SULIMAN.

Lesotho: Lesotho Bank Tower, 10th Floor, Kingsway, Private Bag A266, Maseru 100; tel. 22325758; fax 22310128; e-mail sahcmas@leo.co.ls; High Commissioner William Leslie.

Madagascar: Villa Chandella, Lot Bonnet 38, Ivandry, BP 12101-05, 101 Antananarivo; tel. (20) 2243350; fax (20) 2243386; e-mail antananarivo@foreign.gov.za; Ambassador MOKGETHI SAMUEL MONAISA.

Malawi: Kang'ombe House, 3rd Floor, City Centre, POB 30043, Lilongwe 3; tel. 1773722; fax 1772571; e-mail sahc@malawi.net; High Commissioner N. M. Tsheole.

Malaysia: Menara HLA, Suite 22-01, 3 Jalan Kia Peng, 50450 Kuala Lumpur; tel. (3) 21688663; fax (3) 21643742; e-mail sahcadm@streamyx.com; High Commissioner S. NGOMBANE.

Mali: bât. Diarra, Hamdallaye, ACI-2000, BP 2015, Bamako; tel. 229-29-25; fax 229-29-26; e-mail bamako@foreign.gov.za; Ambassador W. T. Thabethe.

Mauritius: BAI Bldg, 4th Floor, 25 Pope Hennessy St, POB 908, Port Louis; tel. 212-6925; fax 212-6936; e-mail sahc@intnet.mu; High Commissioner MADUMANE M. MATABANE.

Mexico: Edif. Forum, 9°, Andrés Bello 10, Col. Polanco, Del. Miguel Hidalgo, 11560 México, DF; tel. (55) 5282-9260; e-mail safrica@prodigy.net.mx; Ambassador Mphakama Nyangweni Mbete.

Morocco: 34 rue Saâdiens, Rabat; tel. (3) 7706760; fax (3) 7724550; e-mail sudaf@menara.ma; Chargé d'affaires C. MOLLER.

Mozambique: Av. Eduardo Mondlane 41, CP 1120, Maputo; tel. 21493030; fax 21493029; e-mail sahc@tropical.co.mz; High Commissioner Thandi Lujabe-Rankoe.

Namibia: RSA House, cnr Jan Jonker and Nelson Mandela Aves, POB 23100, Windhoek; tel. (61) 229765; fax (61) 224140; Chargé d'affairs a.i. P. J. COETZEE.

Netherlands: Wassenaarseweg 40, 2596 CJ The Hague; tel. (70) 3924501; fax (70) 3460669; e-mail info@zuidafrika.nl; internet www.zuidafrika.nl; Ambassador Hlengiwe Buhle Mkhize.

Nigeria: 71 Usuma St, Maitama, Abuja; tel. (9) 4133862; fax (9) 4133829; e-mail sahcniga@rosecom.net; High Commissioner B. Sifingo.

Norway: Drammensvn 88c, POB 2822 Solli, 0204 Oslo; tel. 23-27-32-20; fax 22-44-39-75; e-mail info@saemboslo.no; internet www.saemboslo.no; Ambassador Ismail Coovadia.

Oman: Al-Harthy Complex, POB 231, Muscat 118; tel. 24694791; fax 24694792; e-mail southae@omantel.net.om; internet www.saembassymuscat.gov.om; Ambassador Yacoob Abba Omar.

Pakistan: House No. 48, Margalla Rd, Khayaban-e-Iqbal, F-8/2, Islamabad; tel. (51) 2262354; fax (51) 2250114; e-mail xhosa@isb.comsats.net.pk; internet www.southafrica.org.pk; High Commissioner Daniel Jabulani Mavimbela.

Peru: Edif. Real Tres, Avda Víctor Andres Belaúnde 147, Of. 801, Lima 27; tel. (1) 4409996; fax 4223881; e-mail saemb@amauta.rcp.net.pe; Ambassador Dr C. J. Streeter.

Poland: 00-675 Warsaw, ul. Koszykowa 54, IPC Business Centre, 6th floor; tel. (22) 6256228; fax (22) 6256270; e-mail warsaw.political@foreign.gov.za; internet www.southafrica.pl; Ambassador Fébé Charlene Potgieter-Gqubule.

Portugal: Av. Luís Bivar 10, 1069-024 Lisbon; tel. (21) 3192200; fax (21) 3535713; e-mail embsa@embaixada-africadosul.pt; internet www.embaixada-africadosul.pt; Ambassador Thandiwe Profit-McLean.

Qatar: POB 24744, Doha; tel. 4857111; fax 4835961; e-mail saembdoha@qatar.net.qa; Ambassador Dr Vincent Tiniza Zulu.

Romania: 010113 Bucharest, Str. Ştirbei Vodă 26–28, Sector 1; tel. (21) 3133725; fax (21) 3133795; Ambassador Johannes Hendrik Kotze.

Russian Federation: 123001 Moscow, Granatnyi per. 1/9; tel. (495) 540-11-77; fax (495) 540-11-78; e-mail moscow.ambassador@foreign.gov.za; internet saembassy.ru; Ambassador Dr B. W. J. Bheki Langa.

Rwanda: 1370 blvd de l'Umuganda, POB 6563, Kacyiru-Sud, Kigali; tel. 583185; fax 511760; e-mail saemkgl@rwanda1.com; internet www.saembassy-kigali.org.rw; Ambassador Dr Ezra M. Sigwela.

Saudi Arabia: POB 94006, Riyadh 11693; tel. (1) 456-2923; fax (1) 454-3718; e-mail saconsul@gmail.com; internet www.southafrica.com.sa; Ambassador Abd al-Hamid Khubair.

Senegal: Memoz SUD, Lotissement Ecole de Police, BP 21010, Dakar-Ponty; tel. 33-865-1959; fax 33-864-2359; e-mail ambafsud@sentoo.sn; internet www.saesenegal.info; Ambassador T. C. Majola-Embalo.

Singapore: 331 North Bridge Rd, 15/01-06 Odeon Towers, Singapore 188720; tel. 63393319; fax 63396658; e-mail singhc@foreign.gov.za; internet www.southafricahc.org.sg; High Commissioner Zanele Makina.

Spain: Claudio Coello 91, 28006 Madrid; tel. (91) 4363780; fax (91) 5777414; e-mail embassy@sudafrica.com; internet www.sudafrica.com; Ambassador Vusi Bruce Koloane.

Sri Lanka: Level 26, East Tower, World Trade Centre, Echelon Square, Colombo 1; tel. (11) 5635966; fax (11) 5505899; e-mail sahc_admin@sltnet.lk; High Commissioner Buyisiwe Maureen Pheto.

Sudan: St 11, House No. 16, Block B9, al-Amarat, POB 12137, Khartoum; tel. (183) 585301; fax (183) 585082; e-mail khartoum@foreign.gov.za; Ambassador Dr Manelisi Genge.

Swaziland: The New Mall, 2nd Floor, Dr Sishayi Rd, POB 2507, Mbabane; tel. 4044651; fax 4044335; e-mail sahc@africaonline.co.sz; High Commissioner Dr Mzolisi Mabude.

Sweden: Fleminggt. 20, 4th Floor, 112 26 Stockholm; tel. (8) 24-39-50; fax (8) 660-71-36; e-mail saemb@telia.com; internet www.southafricanemb.se; Ambassador Sophonia Raphulane Makgetla.

Switzerland: Alpenstr. 29, Postfach, 3000 Bern 6; tel. 313501313; fax 313501310; e-mail political@southafrica.ch; internet www.southafrica.ch; Ambassador Konji Sebati.

Syria: BP 9141, rue al-Ghazaoui, 7 Jadet Kouraish, Mezzeh Ouest, Damascus; tel. (11) 61351520; fax (11) 6111714; e-mail saembdam@ses-net.org; Ambassador Muhammad Dangor.

Tanzania: Plot 1338/1339, Mwaya Rd, Msaski, POB 10723, Dar es Salaam; tel. (22) 2601800; fax (22) 2600684; e-mail highcomm@sahc-tz.com; High Commissioner S. G. Mfenyana.

Thailand: M-Thai Tower, Floor 12A, All Seasons Place, 87 Thanon Witthayu, Prathumwan, Lumpini, Bangkok 10330; tel. (2) 250-9012; fax (2) 685-3500; e-mail saembbkk@loxinfo.co.th; internet www.saembbangkok.com; Ambassador Douglas Harvey Monro Gibson.

Tunisia: 7 rue Achtart, Nord Hilton, 1082 Tunis; tel. (71) 800-311; fax (71) 796-742; e-mail sa@emb-safrica.intl.tn; internet www.southafrica.intl.tn; Ambassador Daniel Nicholaas Meyer.

Turkey: Filistin Sok. 27, 06700 Gaziosmanpaşa, Ankara; tel. (312) 4464056; fax (312) 4466434; e-mail political@southafrica.org.tr; internet www.southafrica.org.tr; Ambassador Tebogo Joseph Seokolo.

Uganda: Plot 15A, Nakasero Rd, POB 22667, Kampala; tel. (41) 4343543; fax (41) 4348216; e-mail kampala.sahc@foreign.gov.za; High Commissioner Thanduyise Henry Chiliza.

Ukraine: 01004 Kyiv, vul. V. Vasylkivska 9/2, POB 7; tel. (44) 287-71-72; fax (44) 287-72-06; e-mail kiev.admin@foreign.gov.za; Ambassador Andries Venter.

United Arab Emirates: POB 29446, Abu Dhabi; tel. (2) 4473446; fax (2) 4473031; e-mail saemb@emirates.net.ae; internet www.southafrica.ae; Chargé d'affaires Mmutlane Samson Makena.

United Kingdom: South Africa House, Trafalgar Sq., London, WC2N 5DP; tel. (20) 7451-7299; fax (20) 7451-7284; e-mail webdesk@southafricahouse.com; internet www.southafricahouse.com; High Commr Dr Lindiwe Mabuza.

United States of America: 3051 Massachusetts Ave, NW, Washington, DC 20008; tel. (202) 232-4400; fax (202) 265-1607; e-mail info@saembassy.org; internet www.saembassy.org; Ambassador Barbara Masekela.

Uruguay: Echevarriarza 3335, Casilla 498, 11000 Montevideo; tel. (2) 6230161; fax (2) 6230066; e-mail safem@netgate.com.uy; Ambassador Peter Goosen (resident in Argentina).

Venezuela: Edif. Atrium ph-a, Sorocaima con Avda Venezuela, El Rosal, Chacoa, Apdo 2613, Caracas 1064; tel. (212) 952-0026; fax (212) 951-3613; e-mail embajador.caracas@foreign.gov.za; Ambassador Thami X. N. Ngwevela.

Viet Nam: 3rd Floor, Central Bldg, 31 Hai Ba Trung, Hanoi; tel. (4) 9362000; fax (4) 9361991; e-mail hanoi@foreign.gov.za; Ambassador Ratubatsi Super Moloi.

Zambia: D26, Cheetah Rd, Kabulonga, Private Bag W369, Lusaka; tel. (1) 260999; fax (1) 263001; e-mail sahcadmin@samnet.zm; High Commissioner Moses Mabokela Chikane.

Zimbabwe: 7 Elcombe Rd, Belgravia, POB A1654, Harare; tel. (4) 753147; fax (4) 749657; e-mail admin@saembassy.co.zw; Ambassador Mlungisi Makalima.

DIPLOMATIC MISSIONS OF SPAIN

United Nations: 823 United Nations Plaza, 9th Floor, New York, NY 10017; tel. (212) 661-1050; fax (212) 949-7247; e-mail spain@spainum.org; internet www.spainun.org; Permanent Representative Juan Antonio Yáñez-Barnuevo.

Afghanistan: House 274, 4R, St 15, Wazir Akbar Khan, Kabul; tel. (79) 9816349; e-mail embespaf@mail.mae.es; Ambassador José Turpín.

Albania: Rruga Skënderbej 43, Tirana; tel. (4) 274960; fax (4) 225383; e-mail emb.tirana@mae.es; Ambassador Manuel Montobbio de Balanzó.

Algeria: BP 142, 46 bis, rue Muhammad Chabane, el-Biar, Algiers; tel. (21) 92-27-13; fax (21) 92-27-19; e-mail emb.argel@mae.es; Ambassador Juan Bautista Leña Casas.

Andorra: Carrer Prat de la Creu 34, Andorra la Vella AD500; tel. 800030; fax 868500; e-mail embaspad@correo.mae.es; Ambassador Eugeni Bregolat Obiols.

Angola: Av. 4 de Fevereiro 95, 1° andar, CP 3061, Luanda; tel. 222391166; fax 222332884; e-mail emb.luanda@mae.es; Ambassador Francisco Javier Vallaure de Acha.

Argentina: Mariscal Ramón Castilla 2720, C1425DZB Buenos Aires; tel. (11) 4802-6031; fax (11) 4802-0719; Ambassador Rafael Estrella Pedrola.

Australia: POB 9076, Deakin, ACT 2600; tel. (2) 6273-3555; fax (2) 6273-3918; e-mail emb.canberra@mae.es; internet www.mae.es/Embajadas/Canberra/es/Home; Ambassador Antonio Cosano Pérez.

Austria: Argentinierstr. 34, 1040 Vienna; tel. (1) 505-57-88; fax (1) 505-57-88-25; e-mail embespat@mail.mae.es; internet www.mae.es/embajadas/viena/es; Ambassador Juan Manuel de Barandica y Luxán.

Belgium: 19 rue de la Science, 1040 Brussels; tel. (2) 230-03-40; fax (2) 230-93-80; e-mail ambespbe@mail.mae.es; internet www.mae.es/embajadas/bruselas; Ambassador Carlos Gómez-Múgica Sanz.

Bolivia: Avda 6 de Agosto 2827, Casilla 282, La Paz; tel. (2) 243-3518; fax (2) 211-3267; e-mail embespbo@correo.mae.es; Ambassador Juan Francisco Montalbán Carrasco.

Bosnia and Herzegovina: 71000 Sarajevo, Čekaluša 16; tel. (33) 278560; fax (33) 208758; Ambassador JOSÉ MARÍA CASTROVIEJO Y BOLÍBAR.

Brazil: SES, Av. das Nações, Quadra 811, Lote 44, 70429-900 Brasília, DF; tel. (61) 3244-2121; fax (61) 3242-1781; e-mail embespbr@correo.mae.es; Ambassador Ricardo Peidró Conde.

Bulgaria: 1087 Sofia, ul. Sheynovo 27; tel. (2) 943-30-32; fax (2) 946-12-01; e-mail embespbg@mail.mae.es; Ambassador FERNANDO ARIAS GONZALEZ.

Cameroon: blvd de l'URSS, Quartier Bastos, BP 877, Yaoundé; tel. 2220-3543; fax 2220-6491; e-mail embespcm@mail.mae.es; Ambassador María Jesús Alonso Jiménez.

Canada: 74 Stanley Ave, Ottawa, ON K1M 1P4; tel. (613) 747-2252; fax (613) 744-1224; e-mail emb.ottawa@mae.es; internet www.embaspain.ca; Ambassador MARIANO ALONSO-BURÓN Y ABERASTURI.

Chile: Avda Andrés Bello 1895, Casilla 16456, Providencia, Santiago; tel. (2) 235-2755; fax (2) 235-1049; e-mail embespcl@correo.mae.es; internet www.mae.es/embajadas/santiagodechile; Ambassador José Antonio Martínez de Villareal y Baena.

China, People's Republic: 9 San Li Tun Lu, Beijing 100600; tel. (10) 65323629; fax (10) 65323401; e-mail embesp@public.bta.net.cn; internet www.mae.es/embajadas/pekin; Ambassador CARLOS BLASCO VILLA.

Colombia: Calle 92, No 12-68, Apdo 90355, Bogotá, DC; tel. (1) 622-0090; fax (1) 621-0809; e-mail embespco@correo.mae.es; Ambassador Andrés Collado González.

Congo, Democratic Republic: blvd du 30 juin, Bldg Communauté Hellénique, Commune de la gombe, BP 8036, Kinshasa; tel. (81) 8843195; e-mail emb.kinshasa@mae.es; ; DR MIGUEL FERNÁNDEZ-PALACIOS MARTÍNEZ.

Costa Rica: Calle 32, Paseo Colón, Avda 2, Apdo 10150, 1000 San José; tel. 222-1933; fax 222-4180; e-mail embespcr@correo.mae.es; Ambassador Arturo Reig Tapia.

Côte d'Ivoire: impasse Abla Pokou, Cocody Danga Nord, 08 BP 876, Abidjan 08; tel. 22-44-48-50; fax 22-44-71-22; e-mail embespci@correo.mae.es; Ambassador FRANCISCO ELIAS DE TEJADA LOZANO.

Croatia: 10000 Zagreb, Tuškanac 21a; tel. (1) 4848950; fax (1) 4848711; e-mail emb.zagreb@mae.es; Ambassador Manuel Salazar Palma.

Cuba: Cárcel No 51, esq. Zulueta, Havana; tel. (7) 866-8025; fax (7) 866-8006; e-mail embespcu@correo.mae.es; Ambassador CARLOS ALONSO ZALDIVAR.

Cyprus: POB 28349, 32 Strovolos Ave, 2018 Strovolos, Nicosia; tel. 22450410; fax 22491291; e-mail enmora@cytanet.com.cy; Ambassador José Manuel Cervera de Góngora.

Czech Republic: Badeniho 401/4, 170 00 Prague 7; tel. 233097211; fax 233341770; e-mail embpraha@gts.cz; internet www.embajada-esp-praga.cz; Ambassador ANTONIO PEDAUYÉ Y GONZÁLEZ.

Denmark: Kristianiagade 21, 2100 Copenhagen Ø; tel. 35-42-47-00; fax 35-42-47-26; e-mail emb.copenhague@mae.es; internet www.mae.es/embajadas/copenhague; Ambassador Melitón Cardona Torres.

Dominican Republic: Avda Independencia 1205, Apdo 1468, Santo Domingo, DN; tel. 535-6500; fax 535-1595; e-mail embespdo@mail.mae.es; Ambassador MARÍA DE LA ALMUDENA MAZARRASA ALVEAR.

Ecuador: General Francisco Salazar E12-73 y Toledo (Sector La Floresta), Apdo 17-01-9322, Quito; tel. (2) 322-6296; fax (2) 322-7805; e-mail emb.quito@mae.es; internet www.embajadaespana.com.ec; Ambassador Juan María Alzina de Aguilar.

Egypt: 41 Sharia Ismail Muhammad, Cairo (Zamalek); tel. (2) 7356462; fax (2) 7352132; e-mail spainemb@startnet.com.eg; Ambassador ANTONIO LÓPEZ MARTÍNEZ.

El Salvador: Calle La Reforma 164 bis, Col. San Benito, San Salvador; tel. 2257-5700; fax 2298-0402; e-mail embespsv@correo.mae.es; internet www.mae.es/embajadas/sansalvador; Ambassador José Javier Gómez-Llera y García-Nava.

Equatorial Guinea: Parque de las Avenidas de Africa s/n, Malabo; tel. (09) 20-20; fax (09) 26-11; e-mail embespgq@correo.mae.es; Ambassador CARLOS ROBLES FRAGA.

Estonia: Liivalaia 13/15, 6th Floor, Tallinn 10118; tel. 667-6651; fax 631-3767; e-mail emb.tallinn@mae.es; internet www.mae.es/embajadas/tallin; Ambassador Eduardo Ibánes López-Dóriga.

Ethiopia: Entoto Ave, POB 2312, Addis Ababa; tel. (11) 1222544; fax (11) 1222541; e-mail emb.addisabeba@mae.es; Ambassador MARÍA DEL CARMEN DE LA PEÑA CORCUERA.

Finland: Kalliolinnantie 6, 00140 Helsinki; tel. (9) 6877080; fax (9) 660110; e-mail emb.helsinki@mae.es; internet www.mae.es/embajadas/helsinki/es/home; Ambassador Ricardo Zalcaín Jorge.

France: 22 ave Marceau, 75008 Paris; tel. 1-44-43-18-00; fax 1-47-23-59-55; e-mail emb.paris@mae.es; internet www.maec.es/subwebs/embajadas/paris; Ambassador FRANCISCO VILLAR Y ORTIZ DE URBINA.

Gabon: Immeuble Diamant, 2ème étage, blvd de l'Indépendance, BP 1157, Libreville; tel. 72-12-64; fax 74-88-73; e-mail ambespga@mail.mae.es; Ambassador Dr Ramiro Fernández Bachiller.

Germany: Lichtensteinallee 1, 10787 Berlin; tel. (30) 2540070; fax (30) 25799557; e-mail embespde@mail.mae.es; internet www.maec.es/subwebs/embajadas/berlin; Ambassador GABRIEL BUSQUETS APARICIO.

Ghana: Drake Ave Extension, Airport Residential Area, PMB KA44, Accra; tel. (21) 774004; fax (21) 776217; e-mail emb.accra@mae.es; Ambassador Jorge Montealegre Buire.

Greece: Odos D. Areapagitou 21, 117 42 Athens; tel. (210) 9213123; fax (210) 9213090; e-mail emb-esp@otenet.gr; Ambassador JUAN RÁMON MARTINEZ SALAZAR.

Guatemala: 6a Calle 6-48, Zona 9, Guatemala City; tel. 2379-3530; fax 2379-3533; e-mail emb.guatemala@mae.es; internet www.mae.es/embajadas/guatemala; Ambassador Juan López-Doriga Pérez.

Haiti: 54 rue Pacot, State Liles, BP 386, Port-au-Prince; tel. 245-4410; fax 245-3901; e-mail ampespht@mail.mae.es; Ambassador JUAN FERNÁNDEZ TRIGO.

Honduras: Col. Matamoros, Calle Santander 801, Apdo 3221, Tegucigalpa; tel. 236-6875; fax 236-8682; e-mail embesphn@correo.mae.es; Ambassador Augustín Núñez Martínez.

Hungary: 1067 Budapest, Kapás u. 11–15; tel. (1) 342-9992; fax (1) 351-0572; e-mail embesphu@mail.mae.es; Ambassador ANTONIO ORTIZ GARCIA.

India: 16 Sunder Nagar, New Delhi 110 003; tel. (11) 24359004; fax (11) 24359040; e-mail embspain@ndb.vsnl.net.in; Ambassador Don Rafael Conde de Saro.

Indonesia: Jalan H. Agus Salim 61, Jakarta 10350; tel. (21) 3142355; fax (21) 31935134; e-mail emb.yakarta@mae.es; Ambassador AURORA BERNÁLDEZ.

Iran: 76 Sarv St, Africa Ave, Tehran 19689; tel. (21) 88714575; fax (21) 88727082; e-mail embespir@mail.mae.es; Ambassador Antonio Pérez-Hernández y Torra.

Iraq: POB 2072, 50/1/609 al-Mansour, Baghdad; tel. (1) 542-4851; fax (1) 541-9857; Ambassador IGNACIO RUPÉREZ RUBIO.

Ireland: 17a Merlyn Park, Dublin 4; tel. (1) 2691640; fax (1) 2691854; e-mail emb.dublin.inf@maec.es; Ambassador Don José de Carvajal Salido.

Israel: Dubnov Tower, 18th Floor, 3 Daniel Frisch St, Tel-Aviv 64731; tel. 3-6958875; fax 3-6965217; e-mail embespil@mail.mae.es; Ambassador EUDALDO MIRAPEIX Y MARTÍNEZ (Baron of Abella).

Italy: Palazzo Borghese, Largo Fontanella Borghese 19, 00186 Roma; tel. (06) 6840401; fax (06) 6872256; e-mail ambespit@mail.mae.es; Ambassador D. Luis Calvo Merino.

Jamaica: Island Life Centre, 6th Floor, 8 St Lucia Ave, Kingston 5; tel. 929-5555; fax 929-8965; e-mail emb.kingston@mae.es; Ambassador JESÚS SILVA FERNÁNDEZ.

Japan: 1-3-29, Roppongi, Minato-ku, Tokyo 106-0032; tel. (3) 3583-8531; fax (3) 3582-8627; e-mail embespjp@mail.mae.es; internet www2.gol.com/users/esptokio; Ambassador Miguel Angel Carriedo Mompín.

Jordan: Zahran St, POB 454, Amman 11118; tel. (6) 4614166; fax (6) 4614173; e-mail embespjo@mail.mae.es; Ambassador MANUEL LORENZO GARCÍA-ORMAECHEA.

Kazakhstan: 010000 Astana, Kenesary 47/25; tel. (7172) 21-69-84; fax (7172) 20-03-17; e-mail emb.astana@maec.es; Ambassador Santiago Chamorro y González-Tablas.

Kenya: International House, 3rd Floor, Mama Ngina St, POB 45503, 00100 Nairobi; tel. (20) 226568; fax (20) 332858; Ambassador NICOLÁS MARTÍN CINTO.

Korea, Republic: 726-52, Hannam-dong, Yeongsan-gu, Seoul; tel. (2) 794-3581; fax (2) 796-8207; e-mail emb.seul@mae.es; internet www.mae.es/embajadas/seul/es/home; Ambassador Delfín Colomé Pujol.

Kuwait: POB 22207, 13083 Safat, Surra, Block 3, St 14, Villa 19, Kuwait City; tel. 5325827; fax 5325826; e-mail embespkw@mail.mae.es; Ambassador JESÚS CARLOS RIOSALIDO GAMBOTTI.

Latvia: Elizabetes iela 11, 3rd Floor, 1010 Rīga; tel. 6732-0281; fax 6732-5005; Ambassador Paulino González Fernández-Corugedo.

Lebanon: POB 11-3039, Palais Chehab, Hadath Antounie, Beirut; tel. (5) 464120; fax (5) 464030; e-mail embesplb@mail.mae.es; Ambassador MIGUEL BENZO PEREA.

Libya: POB 2302, Sharia el-Amir Abd al-Kader al-Jazairi 36, Tripoli; tel. (21) 3336797; fax (21) 4443743; e-mail emb.tripoli@mae.es; Ambassador Joaquín Antonio Pérez Villanueva y Tovar.

Lithuania: Algirdo g. 4, Vilnius 03220; tel. (5) 231-3961; fax (5) 231-3962; e-mail vilnius@mcx.es; 2004Ambassador JOSÉ LUÍS SOLANO GADEA.

Luxembourg: 4–6 blvd Emmanuel Servais, BP 290, 2012 Luxembourg; tel. 46-02-55; fax 46-12-88; e-mail emb.luxemburgo@mae.es; internet www.mae.es/embajadas/luxemburgo; Ambassador María Asunción Ansorena Conto.

Macedonia, former Yugoslav Republic: 1000 Skopje, 27 Mart 7; tel. (2) 3231002; fax (2) 3220612; e-mail ambspanija@mt.net.mk; Ambassador JOSÉ MANUEL PAZ Y AGÜERAS.

Malaysia: 200 Jalan Ampang, 50450 Kuala Lumpur; tel. (3) 21484868; fax (3) 21424582; e-mail embespmy@mail.mae.es; Ambassador José Ramón Barañano Fernández.

Mali: porte 81, rue 13, Badalabougou Est, BP 3230, Bamako; tel. 223-65-27; fax 223-65-24; e-mail emb.bamako@mae.es; Ambassador DR MARTA BETANZOS ROIG.

Malta: Whitehall Mansions, Ta'Xbiex Seafront, Ta'Xbiex XBX 1026; tel. 21317365; fax 21317362; e-mail emb.valletta@mae.es; Ambassador Marta Vilardell Coma.

Mauritania: BP 232, Nouakchott; tel. 525-20-80; fax 525-40-88; e-mail emb.nouakchott@mae.es; Ambassador ALEJANDRO POLANCO MATA.

Mexico: Galileo 114, esq. Horacio, Col. Polanco, Del. Miguel Hidalgo, 11550 México, DF; tel. (55) 5282-2271; fax (55) 5282-1520; e-mail embaes@prodigy.net.mx; Ambassador Carmelo Angulo Barturen.

Morocco: 3 rue Aïn Khalouiya, km 5.3, route des Zaêrs, Souissi, 10000 Rabat; tel. (3) 7633900; fax (3) 7630600; e-mail emb.rabat@maec.es; internet www.mae.es/Embajadas/Rabat; Ambassador D. LUIS PLANAS PUCHADES.

Mozambique: Rua Damião de Góis 347, CP 1331, Maputo; tel. 21492048; fax 21494769; e-mail emb.maputo@mae.es; Ambassador Juan Manuel Molina Lamothe.

Namibia: 58 Bismarck St, POB 21811, Windhoek-West; tel. (61) 223066; fax (61) 223046; e-mail emb.windhoek@mae.es; Ambassador MARÍA VICTORIA SCOLA PLIEGO.

Netherlands: Lange Voorhout 50, 2514 EG The Hague; tel. (70) 3024999; fax (70) 3617959; e-mail ambassade.spanje@worldonline.nl; internet www.mae.es/embajadas/lahaya; Ambassador Juan Prat y Coll.

Nicaragua: Avda Central 13, Las Colinas, Apdo 284, Managua; tel. 276-0966; fax 276-0937; e-mail embespni@correo.mae.es; internet www.mae.es/Embajadas/Managua; Ambassador JAIME LACADENA HIGUERA.

Nigeria: Plot 611, 8 Bobo Close, Maitama, PMB 5120, Abuja; tel. (9) 4137091; fax (9) 4137095; e-mail embespng@mail.mae.es; Ambassador Ángel Losada Fernández.

Norway: Oscarsgt. 35, 0244 Oslo; tel. 22-92-66-90; fax 22-55-98-22; e-mail embespno@mail.mae.es; internet www.mae.es/embajadas/oslo; Ambassador FERNANDO ALVARGONZÁLEZ SAN MARTÍN.

Oman: Shati al-Qurum, Way No. 2834, House No. 2573, POB 3492, Ruwi 112; tel. 24691101; fax 24698969; e-mail emb.mascate@mae.es; Ambassador Tomás Rodríguez-Pantoja Márquez.

Pakistan: St 6, G-5, Diplomatic Enclave 1, POB 1144, Islamabad; tel. (51) 2088777; fax (51) 2088774; e-mail embspain@dsl.net.pk; Ambassador JOSÉ MARÍA ROBLES FRAGA.

Panama: Calle 53 y Avda Perú (frente a la Plaza Porras), Apdo 1857, Panamá 1; tel. 227-5122; fax 227-6284; e-mail embesppa@correo.mae.es; Ambassador José Manuel López-Barrón de Labra.

Paraguay: Edif. S. Rafael, 5° y 6°, Yegros 437, Asunción; tel. (21) 49-0686; fax (21) 44-5394; e-mail embesppy@correo.mae.es; Chargé d'affaires a.i. MARTA DE BLAS MAYORDOMO.

Peru: Jorge Basadre 498, San Isidro, Lima 27; tel. (1) 2125155; fax (1) 4410084; e-mail embesppe@correo.mae.es; internet www.mae.es/embajadas/lima; Ambassador Julio Albi de la Cuesta.

Philippines: ACT Tower, 5th Floor, 135 Sen. Gil J. Puyat Ave, Makati City, 1200 Metro Manila; tel. (2) 8183561; fax (2) 8102885; e-mail embesphh@mail.mae.es; Ambassador LUIS ARIAS ROMERO.

Poland: 00-459 Warsaw, ul. Myśliwiecka 4; tel. (22) 5834000; fax (22) 6225408; e-mail embesppl@mail.mae.es; Ambassador Rafael Mendívil Peydro.

Portugal: Rua do Salitre 1, 1296-052 Lisbon; tel. (21) 3472381; fax (21) 3472384; e-mail emb.lisboa@mae.es; internet www.mae.es/embajadas/lisboa; Ambassador ENRIQUE PANÉS CALPE.

Romania: 011827 Bucharest, Str. Tirana 1; tel. (21) 2339190; fax (21) 2307626; e-mail embespro@mail.mae.es; internet www.spania.xnet.ro; Ambassador Juan Pablo García-Berdoy y Cerezo.

Russian Federation: 121069 Moscow, ul. B. Nikitskaya 50/8; tel. (495) 202-21-61; fax (495) 291-91-71; e-mail embespru@mail.mae.es; internet www.maec.es/embajadas/moscu; Ambassador FRANCISCO JAVIER ELORZA CAVENGT.

Saudi Arabia: POB 94347, Riyadh 11693; tel. (1) 488-0606; fax (1) 488-0420; e-mail embespsa@mail.mae.es; Ambassador Manuel Albert Fernández Kabad.

Senegal: 18–20 ave Nelson Mandela, BP 2091, Dakar; tel. 33-821-1178; fax 33-821-6845; e-mail ambespsn@mail.mae.es; Ambassador FERNANDO MORÁN CALVO-SOTELO.

Serbia: 11000 Belgrade, Prote Mateje 45; tel. (11) 3440231; fax (11) 3444203; e-mail embespyu@mail.mae.es; internet www.spanija.org.yu; Ambassador José Riera Siquier.

Singapore: 7 Temasek Blvd, 39-00 Suntec Tower 1, Singapore 038987; tel. 67259220; fax 63333025; Ambassador ANTONIO SÁNCHEZ JARA.

Slovakia: Prepoštská 10, 811 01 Bratislava; tel. (2) 5441-5724; fax (2) 5441-7565; e-mail embespsk@mail.mae.es; Ambassador Miguel Aguirre de Cárcer García del Arenal.

Slovenia: 1000 Ljubljana, Trnovski pristan 24; tel. (1) 4202330; fax (1) 4202333; e-mail emb.liubliana@maec.es; Ambassador CARMEN FONTES MUÑOZ.

South Africa: 337 Brooklyn Rd, Menlo Park, Pretoria 0181; POB 1633, Pretoria 0001; tel. (12) 4600123; fax (12) 4602290; e-mail emb.pretoria@mae.es; Ambassador Ramón Gil-Casaraes Satrústegui.

Sweden: Djurgårdsvägen 21, Djurgården, POB 10295, 100 55 Stockholm; tel. (8) 667-94-30; fax (8) 663-79-65; e-mail emb.estocolmo@mae.es; internet www.mae.es/embajadas/estocolmo; Ambassador ENRIQUE VIGUERA RUBIO.

Switzerland: Kalcheggweg 24, Postfach 99, 3000 Bern 15; tel. 313505252; fax 313505255; e-mail emb.berna@mae.es; internet www.mae.es/embajadas/berna/es/home; Ambassador Fernando Riquelme Lidón.

Syria: BP 392, rue ash-Shafi, Mezzeh Est, Damascus; tel. (11) 6132900; fax (11) 6132941; e-mail spainemda@net.sy; Ambassador JUAN RAMÓN SERRAT CUENCA-ROMERO.

Tanzania: 99b Kinondoni Rd, POB 842, Dar es Salaam; tel. (22) 2666936; fax (22) 2666938; e-mail embesptz@mail.mae.es; Ambassador Germán Zurita Sáenz de Navarrete.

Thailand: Lake Rajada Office Complex, 23rd Floor, 193 Thanon Rajadapisek, Klongtoey, Bangkok 10110; tel. (2) 661-8284; fax (2) 661-9220; e-mail emb.bangkok@mae.es; internet www.mae.es/embajadas/bangkok/es/home; Ambassador JUAN MANUEL LÓPEZ NADAL.

Tunisia: 22–24 ave Dr Ernest Conseil, Cité Jardin, 1002 Tunis; tel. (71) 782-217; fax (71) 786-267; e-mail emb.tunez@mae.es; Ambassador Juan Manuel Cabrera Hernández.

Turkey: Abdullah Cevdet Sok. 8, 06680 Çankaya, Ankara; tel. (312) 4380392; fax (312) 4426991; e-mail emb.ankara@mae.es; Ambassador LUIS FELIPE FERNÁNDEZ DE LA PEÑA.

Ukraine: 01901 Kyiv, vul. Zhoriva 46; tel. (44) 391-30-24; fax (44) 492-73-27; e-mail emb.kiev@maec.es; Ambassador Luis Javier Gil Catalina.

United Arab Emirates: POB 46474, Abu Dhabi; tel. (2) 6269544; fax (2) 6274978; e-mail emb.abudhabi@mae.es; Ambassador MANUEL PIÑEIRO.

United Kingdom: 39 Chesham Pl., London, SW1X 8SB; tel. (20) 7235-5555; fax (20) 7259-5392; e-mail embespuk@mail.mae.es; internet www.mae.es/embajadas/londres; Ambassador Carlos Miranda y Elío.

United States of America: 2375 Pennsylvania Ave, NW, Washington, DC 20037; tel. (202) 452-0100; fax (202) 833-5670; e-mail embespus@mail.mae.us; internet www.spainemb.org; Ambassador CARLOS WESTENDORP Y CABEZA.

Uruguay: Avda Libertad 2738, 11300 Montevideo; tel. (2) 7086010; fax (2) 7083291; e-mail embespuy@correo.mae.es; Ambassador Fernando Valderrama y de Pareja.

Vatican City: Palazzo di Spagna, Piazza di Spagna 57, 00187 Rome, Italy; tel. (06) 6784351; fax (06) 6784355; e-mail emb.santasede@mae.es; Ambassador FRANCISCO VÁZQUEZ Y VÁZQUEZ.

Venezuela: Avda Mohedano entre 1a y 2a Transversal, La Castellana, Caracas; tel. (212) 263-2855; fax (212) 261-0892; internet www.maec.es/embajadas/caracas; Ambassador Dámaso de Lario Ramírez.

Viet Nam: 15th Floor, Daeha Business Centre, 360 Kim Ma, Ba Dinh District, Hanoi; tel. (4) 7715207; fax (4) 7715206; e-mail embespvn@fpt.vn; Ambassador MARÍA SOLEDAD FUENTES GÓMEZ.

Zimbabwe: 16 Phillips Ave, Belgravia, POB 3300, Harare; tel. (4) 250740; fax (4) 795261; e-mail emb.harare@mae.es; Ambassador Santiago Martínez-Caro de la Concha-Castañeda.

DIPLOMATIC MISSIONS OF SRI LANKA

United Nations: 630 Third Ave, 20th Floor, New York, NY 10017; tel. (212) 986-7040; fax (212) 986-1838; e-mail srilanka@un.int; Permanent Representative PRASAD KARIYAWASAM.

Australia: 35 Empire Circuit, Forrest, ACT 2603; tel. (2) 6239-7041; fax (2) 6239-6166; e-mail admin@slhcaust.org; internet www.slhcaust.org; High Commissioner Kusumpala Balapatabendi.

Austria: Rainergasse 1/2/5, 1040 Vienna; tel. (1) 503-79-88; fax (1) 503-79-93; e-mail embassy.srilanka@etelnet.at; internet www.embassy.srilanka.at; Ambassador ARUNI YASHODHA WIJEWARDANE.

Bangladesh: House 4a, Rd 113, Gulshan Model Town, Dhaka 1212; tel. (2) 9896353; fax (2) 8823971; High Commissioner V. Krishnamoorthy.

Belgium: 27 rue Jules Lejeune, 1050 Brussels; tel. (2) 344-53-94; fax (2) 344-67-37; e-mail sri.lanka@skynet.be; Ambassador K. J. WEERASINGHE.

Brazil: SHIS, QI 09, Conj. 09, Casa 07, Lago Sul, 71625-090 Brasília DF; tel. (61) 3248-2701; fax (61) 3364-5430; e-mail lankaemb@yawl.com.br; Ambassador Swanda Hennedige Shantha Kottegoda.

Canada: 333 Laurier Ave West, Suite 1204, Ottawa, ON K1P 1C1; tel. (613) 233-8449; fax (613) 238-8448; e-mail slhcit@rogers.com; internet www.srilankahcottawa.org; High Commissioner WIJESINGHE JINASENA S. KARUNARATNE.

China, People's Republic: 3 Jian Hua Lu, Jian Guo Men Wai, Beijing 100600; tel. (10) 65321861; fax (10) 65325426; e-mail lkembj@public3.bta.cn.net; internet www.slemb.com; Ambassador Karunatilaka Amunugama.

Cuba: Calle 32, No 307, entre 3 y 5, Miramar, Havana; tel. (7) 204-2562; fax (7) 204-2183; e-mail sri.lanka@enet.cu; Ambassador LIYANAGE KIRITHI AMARASOMA SIGERA.

Egypt: POB 1157, 8 Sharia Sri Lanka, Cairo (Zamalek); tel. (2) 7350047; fax (2) 7367138; e-mail slembare@menanet.net; internet www.lankaemb-egypt.com; Ambassador W. Hettiarachchi.

France: 16 rue Spontini, 75016 Paris; tel. 1-55-73-31-31; fax 1-55-73-18-49; e-mail sl.france@wanadoo.fr; Ambassador CHITRANGANEE WAGISWARA.

Germany: Niklasstr. 19, 14163 Berlin; tel. (30) 80909749; fax (30) 80909757; e-mail info@srilanka-botschaft.de; internet www.srilanka-botschaft.de; Ambassador Tikiri Bandara Maduwegedera.

India: 27 Kautilya Marg, Chanakyapuri, New Delhi 110 021; tel. (11) 23010201; fax (11) 23793604; e-mail lankacom@del2.vsnl.net.in; High Commissioner C. ROMESH JAYASINGHE.

Indonesia: Jalan Diponegoro 70, Jakarta 10320; tel. (21) 3161886; fax (21) 3107962; e-mail lankaemb@rad.net.id; Ambassador Maj.-Gen. (retd) Nanda Mallawaarachchi.

Iran: 28 Golazin St, Africa Ave, Tehran; tel. (21) 22052688; fax (21) 22052149; e-mail emblanka@afranet.com; Ambassador MOHAMED MOHAMED ZUHAIR.

Israel: 4 Jean Jaures St, Tel-Aviv 63412; tel. 3-5277635; fax 3-5277634; Ambassador Tissa Wijeratne.

Italy: Via Adige 2, 00198 Roma; tel. (06) 8554560; fax (06) 84241670; e-mail slembassy@tiscali.it; Ambassador E. RODNEY M. PERERA.

Japan: 2-1-54, Takanawa, Minato-ku, Tokyo 108-0074; tel. (3) 3440-6911; fax (3) 3440-6914; e-mail tokyojp@lankaembassy.jp; internet www.lankaembassy.jp; Ambassador Ranjith Uyangoda.

Jordan: POB 830731, Amman 11183; tel. (6) 5820611; fax (6) 5820615; e-mail slemb@go.com.jo; Ambassador ADNRAYAS WICKRAMACHI MOHOTTALA.

Kenya: Lenana Rd, POB 48145 GPO, Nairobi; tel. (20) 572627; fax (20) 572141; e-mail slhckeny@africaonline.co.ke; internet www.lk/dipmissionf.html; High Commissioner Habeeb Mohammed Farook.

Korea, Republic: Kyobo Bldg, Rm 2002, 1-1, 1-ga, Jongno, Jongno-gu, Seoul 110-714; tel. (2) 735-2966; fax (2) 737-9577; e-mail lankaemb@chollian.net; Ambassador JOHN ASITHA IVON PERERA.

Kuwait: Jabriya, Block 10, St 107, Villa 1, Kuwait City; tel. 5339140; fax 5339154; e-mail lankaemb@qualitynet.net; internet www.slembkwt.org; Ambassador S. A. C. M. Zuhyle.

Lebanon: POB 175, Hazmieh, Mar-Takla, Beirut; tel. (5) 924765; fax (5) 924768; e-mail slemblbn@cyberia.net.lb; Ambassador MOHAMED MOHIDEEN AMANUL FAROUQUE.

Malaysia: 12 Jalan Keranji Dua, off Jalan Kedondong, Ampang Hilir, 55000 Kuala Lumpur; tel. (3) 42568987; fax (3) 42532497; e-mail slhicom@streamyx.com; internet www.slhc.com.my; High Commissioner (vacant).

Maldives: H. Sakeena Manzil, Medhuziyaaraiyh Magu, Malé 20-05; tel. 3322845; fax 3321652; e-mail highcom@dhivehinet.net.mv; High Commissioner MOHAMED ALI FAROOK.

Myanmar: 34 Taw Win Rd, POB 1150, Yangon; tel. (1) 222812; fax (1) 221509; e-mail srilankaemb@mpt.net.mm; Ambassador P. A. D. Samarasekera.

Nepal: 'Shah Villa', Chundevi Rd, Maharajgunj, POB 8802, Kathmandu; tel. (1) 4720623; fax (1) 4720128; e-mail embassy@srilanka.info.com.np; Ambassador SUMITH NAKANDALA.

Netherlands: Jacob de Graefflaan 2, 2517 JM The Hague; tel. (70) 3655910; fax (70) 3465596; e-mail mission@infolanka.nl; Ambassador Pamela Jayasekera Deen.

Norway: Nedre Vollgt. 3, 0158 Oslo; tel. 23-31-70-80; fax 23-31-70-90; e-mail embakont@online.no; internet www.srilanka.no; Ambassador ESALA RUWAN WEERAKOON.

Oman: POB 95, Madinat Qaboos 115; tel. 24697841; fax 24697336; e-mail lankaemb@omantel.net.om; Ambassador Mahroof Meerasahib.

Pakistan: 2C, St 55, F-6/4, Islamabad; tel. (51) 2828723; fax (51) 2828751; e-mail srilanka@isb.comsats.net.pk; High Commissioner WIJERATNE BANDARA DORAKUMBURKA.

Philippines: 2260 Avocado Ave, Dasmariñas Village, Makati City, Metro Manila; tel. and fax (2) 8439813; e-mail srilanka@bronline.com; Ambassador (vacant).

Poland: 02-665 Warsaw, Al. Wilanowska 313 A; tel. (22) 8535648; fax (22) 8435348; e-mail lankaemb@medianet.pl; internet www.srilankaembassy.pl; Ambassador CLARENCE FELICIAN CHINNIAH.

Qatar: 4 Al-Kharja St, POB 19705, Doha; tel. 4677627; fax 4674788; e-mail lankaemb@qatar.net.qa; Ambassador S. B. Atugoda.

Russian Federation: 129090 Moscow, ul. Shchepkina 24; tel. (495) 688-16-20; fax (495) 688-17-57; e-mail lankaemb@com2com.ru; Ambassador U. WEERATUNGA.

Saudi Arabia: POB 94360, Riyadh 11693; tel. (1) 460-8689; fax (1) 460-8846; e-mail lankaemb@shabakah.net.sa; Ambassador Adam Jaafar Sadiq.

Singapore: 13-07/12 Goldhill Plaza, 51 Newton Rd, Singapore 308900; tel. 62544595; fax 62507201; e-mail slhcs@lanka.com.sg; internet www.lanka.com.sg; High Commissioner WINITHKUMAR SHEHAN RATNAVALE.

South Africa: 410 Alexander St, Brooklyn, Pretoria 0181; tel. (12) 4607690; fax (12) 4607702; e-mail srilanka@global.co.za; internet www.srilanka.co.za; High Commissioner A. Rajakaruna.

Sweden: Strandvägen 39, POB 24055, 104 50 Stockholm; tel. (8) 663-65-23; fax (8) 660-00-89; e-mail slembassy@comhem.se; internet www.slembassy.se; Ambassador RANJITH PEMSIRI JAYASOORIYA.

Thailand: Ocean Tower II, 13th Floor, 75/6–7 Sukhumvit, Soi 19, Bangkok 10110; tel. (2) 261-1934; fax (2) 261-1936; e-mail slemb@ksc.th.com; Ambassador Jayaratna Banda Disanayaka.

United Arab Emirates: POB 46534, Abu Dhabi; tel. (2) 6426666; fax (2) 6428289; e-mail lankemba@emirates.net.ae; Ambassador MUHAMMAD NABAVI JUNAID.

United Kingdom: 13 Hyde Park Gdns, London, W2 2LU; tel. (20) 7262-1841; fax (20) 7262-7970; e-mail mail@slhc-london.co.uk; internet www.slhclondon.org; High Commr Kshenuka Senewiratne.

United States of America: 2148 Wyoming Ave, NW, Washington, DC 20008; tel. (202) 483-4025; fax (202) 232-7181; e-mail slembassy@usa.org; internet www.slembassyusa.org; Ambassador BERNARD ANTON BANDARA GOONETILLEKE.

Viet Nam: 55b Tran Phu, Ba Dinh District, Hanoi; tel. (4) 7341894; fax (4) 7341897; e-mail slembvn@fpt.vn; internet www.slembvn.org; Ambassador A. L. Ratnapala.

DIPLOMATIC MISSIONS OF SUDAN

United Nations: 655 Third Ave, Suite 500–510, New York, NY 10017; tel. (212) 573-6033; fax (212) 573-6160; e-mail sudan@un.int; Permanent Representative ABDALMAHMOOD ABDALHALEEM MOHAMAD.

Algeria: Algiers; tel. (21) 56-66-23; fax (21) 69-30-19; Ambassador Youcef Fadul Ahmed.

Austria: Reisnerstr. 29/5, 1030 Vienna; tel. (1) 710-23-43; fax (1) 710-23-46; e-mail sudanivienna@prioritytelecom.biz; Ambassador SAYED GALAL ED-DIN ES-SAYED AL-AMIN.

Bahrain: Villa 423, Rd 3614, Block 336, Manama; tel. 17717959; fax 17710113; e-mail sudanimanama@hotmail.com; Ambassador Bushra ash-Shaikh.

Belgium: 124 ave F. D. Roosevelt, 1050 Brussels; tel. (2) 647-94-94; fax (2) 648-34-99; e-mail sudanbx@yahoo.com; Ambassador NAJEIB EL-KHEIR ABDELWAHAB.

Brazil: SHIS, QI 11, Conj. 5, Casa 13, Lago Sul, 71635-050 Brasília, DF; tel. (61) 3248-4835; fax (61) 3248-4833; e-mail sdbrasilia@sudanbrasilia.org; internet www.sudanbrasilia.org; Ambassador Rahamtalla Mohamed Osman.

Canada: 354 Stewart St, Ottawa, ON K1N 6K8; tel. (613) 235-4000; fax (613) 235-6880; e-mail sudanembassy-canada@rogers.com; internet www .sudanembassy.ca; Ambassador DR FAIZA HASSAN TAHA ARMOUSA.

Central African Republic: ave de France, BP 1351, Bangui; tel. 61-38-21; Ambassador Dr Suleima Mohamed Mustapha.

Chad: rue de la Gendarmerie, BP 45, N'Djamena; tel. 52-43-59; e-mail amb .soudan@intnet.td; Ambassador ABDALLAH CHEIKH.

China, People's Republic: Bldg 27, San Li Tun, Beijing 100600; tel. (10) 65323715; fax (10) 65321280; e-mail mail@sudanembassychina.com; internet www.sudanembassychina.com; AmbassadorMirhgani Mohamed Salih.

Congo, Democratic Republic: 24 ave de l'Ouganda, Kinshasa; tel. (99) 37396; Chargé d'affaires a.i. ABDEL RA'OUF AMIR.

Djibouti: BP 4259, Djibouti; tel. 356404; fax 356662; Ambassador Osama Salahuddin.

Egypt: 4 Sharia el-Ibrahimi, Cairo (Garden City); tel. (2) 3545043; fax (2) 3542693; Ambassador MUHAMMAD HASSAN AL-HAJ.

Eritrea: Asmara; tel. (1) 202072; fax (1) 200760; e-mail sudanemb@eol.com .er; Ambassador Mohamed Al-Hassan.

Ethiopia: Kirkos, Kebele, POB 1110, Addis Ababa; tel. (11) 5516477; fax (11) 5519989; e-mail sudan.embassy@telecom.net.et; Ambassador ABU ZAID AL-HASSAN.

France: 11 rue Alfred Dehodencq, 75016 Paris; tel. 1-42-25-55-71; fax 1-54-63-66-73; e-mail ambassade-du-soudan@wanadoo.fr; internet www .ambassade-du-soudan.org; Ambassador Ahmed Hamid al-Faki.

Germany: Kurfürstendamm 151, 10709 Berlin; tel. (30) 8906980; fax (30) 89409693; e-mail poststelle@sudan-embassy.de; internet www .botschaftsudan.de; Ambassador DR BAHA AD-DIN HANAFI MANSOUR WAHEESH.

India: Plot No. 3, Shanti Path, Chanakyapuri, New Delhi 110 021; tel. (11) 26873785; fax (11) 26883758; e-mail sudandel@del3.vsnl.net.in; internet www.embassysudanindia.org; Ambassador Abdel Rahman Mohamed Bakhiet.

Indonesia: Mayapada Tower, 7th Floor, Suite 01, Jalan Jenderal Sudirman, Kav. 28, Jakarta 12920; tel. (21) 3908234; fax (21) 3908235; e-mail sudanind@cbn.net.id; Ambassador ABDEL G. A. RAHMAN HASSAN.

Iran: No. 17, Africa Ave, Zafar St, Kuchahi Nur, Tehran; tel. (21) 88781183; fax (21) 88792331; e-mail abdallasaahilmi@yahoo.com; internet www .sudanembassyir.com; Ambassador Abd al-Mahmoud Abd al-Halim.

Italy: Via Prati della Farnesina 57, 00194 Roma; tel. (06) 33222138; fax (06) 3340841; Ambassador RABIE HASSAN AHMED.

Japan: Chiyoda House, 7th Floor, 2-17-8, Nagata-cho, Chiyoda-ku, Tokyo 100-0014; tel. (3) 3506-7801; fax (3) 3506-7804; e-mail info@sudanembassy .jp; internet www.sudanembassy.jp; Ambassador Steven Kiliona Wondu.

Jordan: POB 3305, Bayader Wadi as-Seer, 7th Circle, Musa Irsheed at-Taib St, Amman 11181; tel. (6) 5854500; fax (6) 5854501; e-mail sudani@nets.com .jo; Ambassador MOHAMMAD OTHMAN MOHAMMAD SAEED.

Kenya: Minet-ICDC Bldg, 7th Floor, Mamlaka Rd, POB 48784, Nairobi; tel. (20) 720853; fax (20) 721015; Ambassador Omer el-Sheikh.

Korea, Republic: 653-24, Hannam-dong, Yeongsan-gu, Seoul; tel. (2) 793-8692; fax (2) 793-8693; e-mail sudansol@yahoo.com; Ambassador MOHAMMED SALAH ELDIN ABBAS.

Lebanon: POB 2504, Hamra, Beirut; tel. (1) 350057; fax (1) 353271; Ambassador Sayed Ahmad al-Bakhit.

Libya: POB 1076, Sharia Gargaresh, Tripoli; tel. (21) 4775387; fax (21) 4774781; e-mail sudtripoli@hotmail.com; internet www.sudtripoli.net; Ambassador OSMAN M. O. DIRAR.

Malaysia: 2a Persiaran Ampang, off Jalan Ru, 55000 Kuala Lumpur; tel. (3) 42569104; fax (3) 42568107; e-mail assalamiz@hotmail.com; Ambassador Abdel Rahman Hamzah Elraya.

Morocco: 5 ave Ghomara, Souissi, 10000 Rabat; tel. (3) 7752863; fax (3) 7752865; e-mail soudanirab@maghrebnet.net.ma; Ambassador YAHIA ABDELJALIL MAHMOUD.

Netherlands: Laan Copes van Cattenburch 81, 2585 EW The Hague; tel. (70) 3620939; fax (70) 3617975; e-mail sudan@tiscali.nl; Ambassador Abuelgasim Abdelwahid Sheikh Idris.

Nigeria: 2B Kofo Abayomi St, Victoria Island, POB 2428, Lagos; tel. (1) 2615889; Ambassador AHMED ALTIGANI SALEH.

Norway: Holtegt. 28, 0355 Oslo; tel. 22-60-33-55; fax 22-69-83-44; e-mail embassy@sudanoslo.com; Ambassador Mohamed Ali Eltom.

Oman: Diplomatic City, Al-Khuwair, POB 3971, Ruwi 112; tel. 24697875; fax 24699065; e-mail suanimt@gto.net.om; Ambassador ABD AR-RAHMAN MUHAMMAD BUKHEIT.

Pakistan: 1a, St 32, F-8/1, Islamabad; tel. (51) 2263926; fax (51) 2264404; e-mail sudanipk@isb.compol.com; Ambassador Dafaa Allah el-Haj Ali.

Qatar: POB 2999, Doha; tel. 4831474; fax 4833031; e-mail suemdoha@yahoo .com; Ambassador IBRAHIM ABDULLAH FAKIRI.

Romania: 011941 Bucharest 1, Str. Pictor Negulici 3; tel. (21) 2339189; fax (21) 2339188; e-mail sudanbuc@sudanembassy.ro; Ambassador Abdelaziz Marhoum Ahmed.

Russian Federation: 127006 Moscow, Uspenskii per. 4A; tel. (495) 299-54-61; fax (495) 299-33-42; e-mail sudmos@cityline.ru; Ambassador CHOL DENG ALAK.

Saudi Arabia: POB 94337, Riyadh 11693; tel. (1) 488-7979; fax (1) 488-7729; Ambassador Dr Muhammad Amin Abdullah al-Karb.

Senegal: 31 route de la Pyrotechnie, Mermoz, BP 15033, Dakar-Fann; tel. 33-824-9853; fax 33-824-9852; e-mail sudembse@sentoo.sn; Ambassador MAHMOUD HASSAN EL-AMIN.

Somalia: Via al-Mukarah, POB 552, Mogadishu; Chargé d'affaires a.i. Ali Hassan Ali.

South Africa: 1203 Pretorius St, Hatfield, Pretoria 0083; POB 25513, Monument Park 0105; tel. (12) 3424538; fax (12) 3424539; internet www .sudani.co.za; Ambassador KUOL ALOR.

Spain: Paseo de la Castellana 115, 11° izqda, 28046 Madrid; tel. (91) 4174903; fax (91) 5972516; e-mail sudani49@hotmail.com; Ambassador Eluzai Moga Yokwe.

Sweden: POB 26142, 100 41 Stockholm; Stockholmsvägen 33, 181 33 Lidingö; tel. (8) 611-77-80; fax (8) 611-77-82; e-mail sudanembassy@telia .com; Ambassador MOSES MOJWOK AKOL.

Syria: Damascus; tel. (11) 6111036; fax (11) 6112904; e-mail sud-emb@net .sy; Ambassador Abd ar-Rahman Derar.

Tanzania: 'Albaraka', 64 Ali Hassan Mwinyi Rd, POB 2266, Dar es Salaam; tel. (22) 2117641; fax (22) 2115811; e-mail sudan.emb.dar@raha.com; Ambassador ELMUGHIRA ALI OMAR.

Tunisia: 37 rue d'Afrique, al-Menzah V, 1008 Tunis; tel. (71) 231-322; fax (71) 751-756; e-mail contact@soudanembassy-tn.com; internet www .sudanembassy-tn.com; Ambassador Ismail Ahmed Ismail.

Turkey: Sancak Mah. 12 Cad. 16, 06550 Çankaya, Ankara; tel. (312) 4413885; fax (312) 4413886; e-mail ankara@mfa.gov.sd; Ambassador MUHAMMAD AL-HASSAN AHMED AL-HAJ.

United Arab Emirates: POB 4027, Abu Dhabi; tel. (2) 6666788; fax (2) 6654231; e-mail sudembll@emirates.net.ae; Ambassador Ahmad Mahjoub.

United Kingdom: 3 Cleveland Row, St James's, London, SW1A 1DD; tel. (20) 7839-8080; fax (20) 7839-7560; e-mail admin@sudanembassy.co.uk; internet www.sudanembassy.co.uk; Ambassador OMAR MUHAMMAD AHMAD SIDDIG.

United States of America: 2210 Massachusetts Ave, NW, Washington, DC 20008; tel. (202) 338-8565; fax (202) 667-2406; e-mail info@sudanembassy .org; internet www.sudanembassy.org; Chargé d'affaires a.i. Prof. John Ukec Lueth Ukec.

Yemen: POB 2561, 82 Abou al-Hassan al-Hamadani St, San'a; tel. (1) 265231; fax (1) 265234; Ambassador OMAR AS-SAID TAHA.

Zambia: 31 Ng'umbo Rd, Longacres, POB RW179X, 15200 Lusaka; tel. (1) 215570; fax (1) 40653; Ambassador Abdallah Khidir Bashir.

Zimbabwe: 4 Pascoe Ave, Harare; tel. (4) 700111; fax (4) 703450; e-mail sudan@africaonline.co.zw; internet www.sudaniharare.org.zw; Ambassador HASSAN AHMED FAGEERI.

DIPLOMATIC MISSIONS OF SURINAME

United Nations: 866 United Nations Plaza, Suite 320, New York, NY 10017; tel. (212) 826-0660; fax (212) 980-7029; e-mail suriname@un.int; internet www.un.int/suriname; Permanent Representative Henry Leonard MacDonald.

Belgium: 379 ave Louise, BP 20, 1050 Brussels; tel. (2) 640-11-72; fax (2) 646-39-62; e-mail sur.amb.bru@online.be; Ambassador GERHARD O. HIWAT.

Brazil: SHIS, QI 09, Conj. 08, Casa 24, 71625-080 Brasilia, DF; tel. (61) 3248-6706; fax (61) 3248-3791; e-mail surinameemb@terra.com.br; Ambassador Georgine Mavis Demon-Belgraef.

China, People's Republic: 1-3-31 Diplomatic Compound, Jian Guo Men Wai, Beijing 100600; tel. (10) 65322938; fax (10) 65322941; e-mail surembchina@hotmail.com; AmbassadorMOHAMED ISAAK SOEROKARSO.

Guyana: 171 Peter Rose and Crown Sts, Queenstown, Georgetown; tel. 226-7844; fax 225-0759; e-mail surnemb@gol.net.gy; Ambassador Manorma Soeknandan.

India: C-15 Malcha Marg, New Delhi 110 021; tel. (11) 26888543; fax (11) 26888450; e-mail embsurnd@vsnl.net; internet www.embsurnd.com; Ambassador K. BAJNATH.

Indonesia: Jalan Padalarang No. 9, Menteng, Jakarta Pusat 10310; tel. (21) 3154437; fax (21) 3154556; e-mail suramjkt@cbn.net.id; Ambassador Angelic C. Alihusain-del Castilho.

Netherlands: Alexander Gogelweg 2, 2517 JH The Hague; tel. (70) 3650844; fax (70) 3617445; e-mail ambassade.suriname@wxs.nl; Ambassador URMILA JOELLA.

South Africa: Suite No. 4, Groenkloof Forum Office Park, 57 George Storrar Drive, Groenkloof, 0181 Pretoria; POB 149, Pretoria; tel. (12) 3467627; fax (12) 3460802; e-mail embsur@lantic.net; Ambassador Edward Rudolf Braafheid.

Trinidad and Tobago: Tatil Bldg, 5th Floor, 11 Maraval Rd, Port of Spain; tel. 628-0704; fax 628-0086; e-mail surinameembassy@tstt.net.tt; Ambassador FIDELIA GRAAND-GALON.

United States of America: 4301 Connecticut Ave, NW, Suite 460, Washington, DC 20008; tel. (202) 244-7488; fax (202) 244-5878; e-mail esuriname@covad.net; internet www.surinameembassy.org; Ambassador Jacques R. C. Kross.

Venezuela: 4a Avda entre 7a y 8a Transversal, Quinta 41, Altamira, Caracas; Apdo 61140, Chacao, Caracas; tel. (212) 261-2724; fax (212) 263-9006; e-mail emsurl@cantv.net; Ambassador SAMUEL PAWIRONADI.

DIPLOMATIC MISSIONS OF SWAZILAND

United Nations: 408 East 50th St, New York, NY 10022; tel. (212) 371-8910; fax (212) 754-2755; e-mail swaziland@un.int; Permanent Representative Phesheya Mbongeni Dlamini.

Belgium: 188 ave Winston Churchill, 1180 Brussels; tel. (2) 347-47-71; fax (2) 347-46-23; Ambassador SOLOMON M. N. DLAMINI.

China (Taiwan): 10/F, 9 Lane 62, Tien Mou West Rd, Taipei 11156; tel. (2) 28725934; fax (2) 28726511; e-mail swazitpi@ms41.hinet.net; Ambassador Njabuliso Gwebu.

Kenya: Transnational Plaza, 3rd Floor, Mama Ngina St, POB 41887, Nairobi; tel. (20) 339231; fax (20) 330540; High Commissioner PRINCE SOLOMON MBILINI N. DLAMINI.

Malaysia: Suite 22-03 and 03 (A), Menara Citibank, 165 Jalan Ampang, 50450 Kuala Lumpur; tel. (3) 21632511; fax (3) 21633326; e-mail swazi@tm.net.my; High Commissioner Mpumelelo J. N. Hlope.

Mozambique: Av. Kwame Nkrumah, CP 4711, Maputo; tel. 21491601; fax 21492117; High Commissioner PRINCE TSHEKEDI.

South Africa: 715 Government Ave, Arcadia, Pretoria 0007; POB 14294, Hatfield 0028; tel. (12) 3441910; fax (12) 3430455; High Commissioner Phillip Nhlanhla Muntu Mswane.

United Kingdom: 20 Buckingham Gate, London, SW1E 6LB; tel. (20) 7630-6611; fax (20) 7630-6564; e-mail enquiries@swaziland.org.uk; High Commr MARY MADZANDZA KANYA.

United States of America: 1712 New Hampshire Ave, NW, Washington, DC 20009; tel. (202) 234-5002; fax (202) 234-8254; e-mail swaziland@compuserve.com; Ambassador Ephraim Mandlenkosi M. Hlophe.

DIPLOMATIC MISSIONS OF SWEDEN

United Nations: 1 Dag Hammarskjöld Plaza, 885 Second Ave, 46th Floor, New York, NY 10017; tel. (212) 583-2500; fax (212) 832-0389; e-mail sweden@un.int; internet www.un.int/sweden; Permanent Representative ANDERS LIDÉN.

Algeria: BP 263, rue Olof Palme, Nouveau Paradou, Hydra, Algiers; tel. (21) 54-83-33; fax (21) 54-83-34; e-mail ambassaden.alger@foreign.ministry.se; Ambassador Helena Nilsson-Lannegren.

Angola: Rua Garcia Neto 9, CP 1130, Miramar, Luanda; tel. 222440706; fax 222443460; e-mail Erik.Åberg@foreign.ministry.se; internet www.swedenabroad.com/luanda; Ambassador ERIK ÅBERG.

Argentina: Tacuari 147, 6°, C1071AAC Buenos Aires; tel. (11) 4329-0800; fax (11) 4342-1697; e-mail ambassaden.buenos-aires@foreign.ministery.ce; internet www.swedenabroad.com/buenosaires; Ambassador Arne Lennart Rodin.

Australia: 5 Turrana St, Yarralumla, ACT 2600; tel. (2) 6270-2700; fax (2) 6270-2755; e-mail sweden@iimetro.com.au; internet www.swedenabroad.com/canberra; Ambassador KARIN EHNBOM-PALMQUIST.

Austria: Obere Donaustr. 49–51, Postfach 18, 1025 Vienna; tel. (1) 217-53-0; fax (1) 217-53-370; e-mail ambassaden.wien@foreign.ministry.se; internet www.swedenabroad.com/wien; Ambassador Hans Lundborg.

Bangladesh: House 1, Rd 51, Gulshan 2, Dhaka 1212; tel. (2) 8833144; fax (2) 8823948; e-mail berth.abrahamsson@foreign.ministry.se; internet www.swedenabroad.com/dhaka; Ambassador BRITT FALKMAN HAGSTRÖM.

Belgium: 3 rue de Luxembourg, 1000 Brussels; tel. (2) 289-57-60; fax (2) 289-57-90; e-mail ambassaden.bryssel@foreign.ministry.se; internet www.swedenabroad.com/bryssel; Ambassador Magnus Robach.

Bosnia and Herzegovina: 71000 Sarajevo, Ferhadija 20; tel. (33) 276030; fax (33) 276060; e-mail ambassaden.sarajevo@foreign.ministry.se; internet www.swedenabroad.se/sarajevo; Ambassador LARS ERIK WINGREN.

Botswana: Development House, 4th Floor, The Mall, Private Bag 0017, Gaborone; tel. 3953912; fax 3953942; e-mail ambassaden.gaborone@foreign.ministry.se; internet www.swedenabroad.com/gaborone; Chargé d'affaires a.i. Marie Andersson de Frutos.

Brazil: SES, Av. das Nações, Quadra 807, Lote 29, 70419-900 Brasília, DF; tel. (61) 3442-5200; fax (61) 3443-1187; e-mail ambassaden.brasilia@foreign.ministry.se; internet www.suecia.org.br; Ambassador ANNIKA MARKOVIC.

Bulgaria: 1113 Sofia, ul. A. Nobel 4, POB 620; tel. (2) 930-19-60; fax (2) 973-37-95; e-mail ambassaden.sofia@foreign.ministry.se; internet www.swedenabroad.com/sofia; Ambassador Bertil Roth.

Canada: 377 Dalhousie St, Ottawa, ON K1N 9N8; tel. (613) 244-8200; fax (613) 241-2277; e-mail sweden.ottawa@foreign.ministry.se; internet www.swedishembassy.ca; Ambassador INGRID M. IREMARK.

Chile: Avda 11 de Septiembre 2353, 4°, Providencia; tel. (2) 940-1700; fax (2) 940-1730; e-mail ambassaden.santiago-de-chile@foreign.ministry.se; internet www.embajadasuecia.cl; Ambassador Maria Christina Lundqvist.

China, People's Republic: 3 Dong Zhi Men Wai Dajie, San Li Tun, Beijing 100600; tel. (10) 65329790; fax (10) 65325008; e-mail ambassaden.peking@foreign.ministry.se; internet www.swedenabroad.com/peking; Ambassador MIKAEL LINDSTRÖM.

Colombia: Calle 72-bis, No 5-83, 8°, Bogotá, DC; tel. (1) 325-6180; fax (1) 325-6181; e-mail embsueca@cable.net.co; internet www.swedenabroad.com/bogota; Ambassador Lena Nordström.

Congo, Democratic Republic: 93 ave Roi Baudouin, Commune de la gombe, BP 11096, Kinshasa; tel. (99) 8174289; fax (satellite) 870-600-147849; e-mail ambassaden.kinshasa@foreign.ministry.se; internet www.swedenabroad.com/kinshasa; Ambassador MAGNUS WERNSTEDT.

Croatia: 10000 Zagreb, Frankopanska 22; tel. (1) 4925100; fax (1) 4925125; e-mail swedish.embassy@zg.tel.hr; Ambassador Lars Fréden.

Cuba: Calle 34, No 510, entre 5 y 7, Miramar, Havana; tel. (7) 204-2831; fax (7) 204-1194; e-mail ambassaden.havanna@foreign.ministry.se; internet www.swedenabroad.com/havanna; Ambassador CHRISTER ELM.

Cyprus: POB 21621, 9 Archbishop Makarios Ave, Severis Bldg, Second Floor, 1065 Nicosia; tel. 22458088; fax 22374522; e-mail ambassaden.nicosia@foreign.ministry.se; internet www.swedenabroad.se/nicosia; Ambassador Ingemar Lindahl.

Czech Republic: Úvoz 13-Hradčany, POB 35, 160 12 Prague 6; tel. 220313200; fax 220313240; e-mail ambassaden.prag@foreign.ministry.se; Ambassador CATHERINE VON HEIDENSTAM.

Denmark: Skt Annæ Pl. 15a, 1250 Copenhagen K; tel. 33-36-03-70; fax 33-36-03-95; e-mail ambassaden.kopenhamn@foreign.ministry.se; internet www.swedenabroad.com/copenhagen; Ambassador Lars Grundberg.

Egypt: POB 131, 13 Sharia Muhammad Mazhar, Cairo (Zamalek); tel. (2) 7289200; fax (2) 7354357; e-mail ambassaden.kairo@foreign.ministry.se; internet www.embassyofsweden.org; Ambassador STIG ELVEMAR.

Estonia: Pikk 28, Tallinn 15055; tel. 640-5600; fax 640-5695; e-mail swedemb@neti.ee; internet www.sweden.ee; Ambassador Dag Hartelius.

Ethiopia: Ras Tessema Sefer, Woreda 3, Kebele 53, House No. 891, POB 1142, Addis Ababa; tel. (11) 5511255; fax (11) 5514558; e-mail ambassaden.addis-abeba@foreign.ministry.se; internet www.swedenabroad.com/addisabeba; Ambassador STAFFAN TILLANDER.

Finland: POB 329, 00171 Helsinki; Pohjoisesplanadi 7b, 00170 Helsinki; tel. (9) 6877660; fax (9) 655285; e-mail ambassaden.helsingfors@foreign.ministry.se; internet www.sverige.fi; Ambassador Eva Walder-Brundin.

France: 17 rue Barbet-de-Jouy, 75007 Paris; tel. 1-44-18-88-00; fax 1-44-18-88-40; e-mail info@amb-suede.fr; internet www.swedenabroad.com/paris; Ambassador GUNNAR LUND.

Germany: Rauchstr. 1, 10787 Berlin; tel. (30) 505060; fax (30) 50506789; e-mail ambassaden.berlin@foreign.ministry.se; internet www.swedenabroad.com/berlin; Ambassador Ruth Evelyn Jacoby.

Greece: Leoforos Vassileos Konstantinou 7, 106 74 Athens; tel. (210) 7266100; fax (210) 7266150; e-mail ambassaden.athens@foreign.ministry.se; internet www.swedenabroad.com/athen; Ambassador MÄRTEN GRUNDITZ.

Guatemala: 8a Avda 15-07, Zona 10, Guatemala City; tel. 2384-7300; fax 2384-7350; e-mail ambassaden.guatemala@foreign.ministry.se; internet www.swedenabroad.com/guatemala; Ambassador Ewa Werner Dahlin.

Hungary: 1146 Budapest, Ajtósi Dürer sor 27 A; tel. (1) 460-6020; fax (1) 460-6021; e-mail ambassaden.budapest@foreign.ministry.se; internet www.swedenabroad.com/budapest; Ambassador CECILIA BJÖRNER.

Iceland: POB 8136, 128 Reykjavík; Lágmúla 7, 108 Reykjavík; tel. 5201230; fax 5201235; e-mail embassy.reykjavik@foreign.ministry.se; internet www.swedenabroad.com/reykjavik; Ambassador Madeleine Ströje-Wilkens.

India: Nyaya Marg, Chanakyapuri, New Delhi 110 021; tel. (11) 24197100; fax (11) 26885401; e-mail ambassaden.new-delhi@foreign.ministry.se; internet www.swedenabroad.se/pages/start_21488.asp; Ambassador LARS-OLOF LINDGREN.

Indonesia: Menara Rajawali, 9th Floor, Jalan Mega Kuningan, Lot 5.1, Kawasan Mega Kuningan, Jakarta Selatan 12950; tel. (21) 55535900; fax (21) 5762691; e-mail ambassaden.jakarta@foreign.ministry.se; internet www.swedenabroad.com/jakarta; Ambassador Ann Marie Bolin Pennegård.

Iran: POB 19575-458, 2 Nastaran Ave, Pasdaran Ave, Tehran; tel. (21) 22296802; fax (21) 22296451; e-mail ambassaden.teheran@foreign.ministry.se; internet www.swedenabroad.com/tehran; Ambassador MAGNUS WERNSTEDT.

Ireland: Iveagh Court, Block E, 3rd Floor, Harcourt Rd, Dublin 2; tel. (1) 4744400; fax (1) 4744450; e-mail ambassaden.dublin@foreign.ministry.se; internet www.swedenabroad.com/dublin; Ambassador Claes Ljungdahl.

Israel: Asia House, 4 Rehov Weizman, Tel-Aviv 64239; tel. 3-6958111; fax 3-6958116; e-mail ambassaden.tel-aviv@foreign.ministry.se; internet www.swedenabroad.com/telaviv; Ambassador ELISABET BORSIIN BONNIER.

Italy: Piazza Rio de Janeiro 3, 00161 Roma; tel. (06) 441941; fax (06) 44194760; e-mail ambassaden.rom@foreign.ministry.se; internet www.swedenabroad.com/rome; Ambassador Anders Bjurner.

Japan: 1-10-3-100, Roppongi, Minato-ku, Tokyo 106-0032; tel. (3) 5562-5050; fax (3) 5562-9095; e-mail info@sweden.or.jp; internet www.sweden.or.jp; Ambassador STEFAN NOREÉN.

Jordan: POB 830536, 14 Ibrahim Ayoub St, 4th Circle, Jabal Amman 11183; tel. (6) 5901300; fax (6) 5930179; e-mail ambassaden.amman@foreign.ministry.se; internet www.swedenabroad.com/amman; Ambassador Tommy Arwitz.

Kenya: Lion Pl., 3rd Floor, Waiyaki Way, Westlands, POB 30600, 00100 Nairobi; tel. (20) 4234000; fax (20) 4452008; e-mail ambassaden.nairobi@foreign.ministry.se; internet www.swedenabroad.com/nairobi; Ambassador ANNA BRANDT.

Korea, Democratic People's Republic: Munsudung, Taedongkang District, Pyongyang; tel. (2) 3817485; fax (2) 3817663; e-mail ambassaden.pyongyang@foreign.ministry.se; Ambassador Mats Foyer.

Korea, Republic: Seoul Central Bldg, 12th Floor, 136, Seorin-dong, Jongno-gu, KPO Box 1154, Seoul 110-611; tel. (2) 3703-3700; fax (2) 3703-3701; e-mail embassy@swedemb.or.kr; internet www.swedenabroad.com/seoul; Ambassador LARS VARGÖ.

Latvia: A. Pumpura iela 8, Rīga 1010; tel. 6768-6600; fax 6768-6601; e-mail ambassaden.riga@foreign.ministry.se; internet www.swedenemb.lv; Ambassador Göran Håkansson.

Lithuania: Didžioji g. 16, Vilnius 01128; tel. (5) 268-5010; fax (5) 268-5030; e-mail ambassaden.vilnius@foreign.ministry.se; internet www.swedishembassy.lt; Ambassador MALIN KÄRRE.

Luxembourg: 2 rue Heinrich Heine, 1720 Luxembourg; tel. 26-64-61; fax 29-69-09; e-mail ambassaden.luxemburg@foreign.ministry.se; internet www.swedenabroad.com/luxembourg; Ambassador Agneta Söderman.

Macedonia, former Yugoslav Republic: 1000 Skopje, 8 Udarna Brigada 2; tel. (2) 3297800; fax (2) 3112065; e-mail swedembsk@mt.net.mk; Ambassador ULRIKA CRONENBERG-MOSSBERG.

Malaysia: Wisma Angkasa Raya, 6th Floor, 123 Jalan Ampang, 50450 Kuala Lumpur; tel. (3) 20522550; fax (3) 21486325; e-mail ambassaden.kuala-lumpur@foreign.ministry.se; internet www.swedenabroad.se/kualalumpur; Ambassador Helena Sångeland.

Mexico: Paseo de las Palmas 1375, Col. Lomas de Chapultepec, Del. Miguel Hidalgo, 11000 México, DF; tel. (55) 9178-5010; fax (55) 5540-3253; e-mail info@suecia.com.mx; internet www.suecia.com.mx; Ambassador ANNA LINDSTEDT.

Morocco: 159 ave John Kennedy, BP 428, Souissi, 10000 Rabat; tel. (3) 7633210; fax (3) 7758048; e-mail ambassaden.rabat@foreign.ministry.se; internet www.swedenabroad.com/rabat; Ambassador Klas Gierow.

Mozambique: Av. Julius Nyerere 1128, CP 338, Maputo; tel. 21480300; fax 21480390; e-mail ambasseden.maputo@foreign.ministry.se; internet www.swedenabroad.com/maputo; Ambassador TORVALD ÅKESSON.

Namibia: Sanlam Centre, 9th Floor, POB 23087, Windhoek; tel. (61) 2859111; fax (61) 2859222; e-mail ambassaden.windhoek@sida.se; Chargé d'affaires a.i. Lena Johansson Blomstrand.

Netherlands: Jan Willem Frisolaan 3, 2517, JS The Hague; tel. (70) 4120200; fax (70) 4120211; e-mail ambassaden.haag@foreign.ministry.se; internet www.swedenabroad.com/thehague; Ambassador HANS OSCAR MAGNUSSON.

Nicaragua: Plaza España, 1 c. abajo, 2 c. al lago y $\frac{1}{2}$ c. al oeste, Apdo 2307, Managua; tel. 255-8400; fax 266-6778; e-mail ambassaden.managua@foreign.ministry.se; internet www.swedenabroad.se/managua; scheduled to close in August 2008 Ambassador Eva Zetterberg.

Nigeria: PMB 569, Garki, Abuja; tel. (9) 3143399; fax (9) 3143398; e-mail ambassaden.abuja@foreign.ministry.se; internet www.swedenabroad.com/abuja; Ambassador LARS-OWE PERSSON.

Norway: Nobelsgt. 16, 0244 Oslo; tel. 24-11-42-00; fax 22-55-15-96; e-mail ambassaden.oslo@foreign.ministry.se; internet www.swedenabroad.com/oslo; Ambassador Michael Sahlin.

Pakistan: 4, St 5, F-6/3, Islamabad; tel. (51) 2828712; fax (51) 2825284; e-mail ambassaden.islamabad@foreign.ministry.se; internet www.swedenabroad.se/Start____28997.aspx; Ambassador ANNA KARIN ENESTRÖM.

Poland: 00-585 Warsaw, ul. Bagatela 3; tel. (22) 6408900; fax (22) 6408983; e-mail ambassaden.warszawa@foreign.ministry.se; internet www.swedishembassy.pl; Ambassador Tomas Bertelman.

Portugal: Rua Miguel Lupi 12, 2°, 1249-077 Lisbon; tel. (21) 3942260; fax (21) 3942261; e-mail ambassaden.lissabon@foreign.ministry.se; internet www.swedenabroad.com/lissabon; Ambassador MARIE GABRIELLA LINDHOLM.

Romania: 011343 Bucharest, Şos. Kiseleff 43, Sector 1; tel. (21) 4067100; fax (21) 4067124; e-mail ambassaden.bukarest@foreign.ministry.se; Ambassador Mats O. Åberg.

Russian Federation: 119590 Moscow, ul. Mosfilmovskaya 60; tel. (495) 937-92-00; fax (495) 937-92-02; e-mail moscow.sweinfo@foreign.ministry.se; internet www.swedenabroad.com/moscow; Ambassador JOHAN MOLANDER.

Saudi Arabia: POB 94382, Riyadh 11693; tel. (1) 488-3100; fax (1) 488-0604; e-mail ambassaden.riyadh@foreign.ministry.se; internet www.swedenabroad.se/riyadh; Ambassador Jan Thesleff.

Senegal: 18 rue Emile Zola, BP 6087, Dakar; tel. 33-849-0333; fax 33-849-0340; e-mail ambassaden.dakar@foreign.ministry.se; internet www.swedenabroad.com/dakar; Ambassador AGNETA BOHMAN.

Serbia: 11040 Belgrade, Ledi Pedzet 2, POB 5; tel. (11) 2069200; fax (11) 2069250; e-mail ambassaden.belgrad@foreign.ministry.se; internet www.swedenabroad.se/belgrad; Ambassador Nils Krister Bringéus.

Singapore: 111 Somerset Rd, 05-01 Singapore Power Bldg, Singapore 238164; tel. 64159200; fax 64159747; e-mail ambassaden.singapore@foreign.ministry.se; internet www.swedenabroad.com/singapore; Ambassador PÄR AHLBERGER.

Slovakia: Palisády 29, 4th Floor, 811 06 Bratislava; tel. (2) 5910-2200; fax (2) 5910-2233; e-mail ambassaden.bratislava@foreign.ministry.se; internet www.swedenabroad.com/bratislava; Ambassador Mikael Westerlind.

Slovenia: 1000 Ljubljana, Ajdovščina 4/8, POB 1680; tel. (1) 3000270; fax (1) 3000271; e-mail ambassaden.ljubljana@foreign.ministry.se; internet www.swedenabroad.com/ljubljana; Ambassador JOHN HAGARD.

South Africa: iParioli Bldg, 1166 Park St, Hatfield, Pretoria 0028; POB 13477, Hatfield 0028; tel. (12) 4266400; fax (12) 4266464; e-mail sweden@iafrica.com; internet www.swedenabroad.com/Sydafrika; Ambassador Anders Möllander.

Spain: Caracas 25, 28010 Madrid; tel. (91) 7022000; fax (91) 7022040; e-mail ambassaden.madrid@foreign.ministry.se; internet www.swedenabroad.com/Start_9935.aspx; Ambassador ANDERS RÖNQUIST.

Sri Lanka: 49 Bullers Lane, POB 1072, Colombo 7; tel. (11) 4795400; fax (11) 4795450; e-mail ambassaden.colombo@foreign.ministry.se; internet www.swedenabroad.com/colombo; Chargé d'affaires Börje Mattsson.

Switzerland: Bundesgasse 26, Postfach, 3001 Bern; tel. 313287000; fax 313287001; e-mail ambassaden.bern@foreign.ministry.se; internet www.swedenabroad.com/bern; Ambassador PER THÖRESSON.

Syria: BP 4266, Immeuble du Patriarcat Catholique, rue Chakib Arslan, Abou Roumaneh, Damascus; tel. (11) 33400700; fax (11) 3327749; e-mail ambassaden.damaskus@foreign.ministry.se; internet www.swedenabroad.com/damascus; Ambassador Catharina Kipp.

Tanzania: Mirambo St and Garden Ave, POB 9274, Dar es Salaam; tel. (22) 2196500; fax (22) 2196503; e-mail ambassaden.dar-es-salaam@foreign.ministry.se; internet www.swedenabroad.se/daressalaam; Ambassador STAFFAN HERRSTROM.

Thailand: First Pacific Place, 20th Floor, 140 Thanon Sukhumvit, Bangkok 10110; tel. (2) 263-7200; fax (2) 263-7260; e-mail ambassaden.bangkok@foreign.ministry.se; internet www.swedenabroad.com/bangkok; Ambassador Lennart Linnér.

Turkey: Katip Çelebi Sok. 7, 06692 Kavaklıdere, Ankara; tel. (312) 4554100; fax (312) 4554120; e-mail ambassaden.ankara@foreign.ministry.se; internet www.swedenabroad.com/ankara; Ambassador CHRISTER ASP.

Uganda: 24 Lumumba Ave, Nakasero, POB 22669, Kampala; tel. (41) 4340970; fax (41) 4340979; e-mail ambassaden.kampala@foreign.ministry.se; internet www.swedenabroad.com/kampala; Ambassador Anders Johnson.

Ukraine: 01901 Kyiv, vul. Ivana Franka 34/33; tel. (44) 494-42-70; fax (44) 494-42-71; e-mail ambassaden.kiev@foreign.ministry.se; internet www.swedenabroad.com/kiev; Ambassador JOHN-CHRISTER ÅHLANDER.

United Arab Emirates: POB 31867, Abu Dhabi; tel. (2) 6210162; fax (2) 6394941; e-mail ambassaden.abudhabi@foreign.ministry.se; internet www.swedenabroad.com/abudhabi; Ambassador Bruno S. Beijer.

United Kingdom: 11 Montagu Pl., London, W1H 2AL; tel. (20) 7917-6400; fax (20) 7724-4174; e-mail ambassaden.london@foreign.ministry.se; internet www.swedenabroad.com/london; Ambassador STAFFAN CARLSSON.

United States of America: 2900 K St, NW, Washington, DC 20007; tel. (202) 467-2600; fax (202) 467-2699; e-mail ambassaden.washington@foreign.ministry.se; internet www.swedenabroad.com/washington; Ambassador Jonas Hafström.

Viet Nam: 2 Nui Truc, Ba Dinh District, Hanoi; tel. (4) 7260400; fax (4) 8232195; e-mail ambassaden.hanoi@foreign.ministry.se; internet www.swedenabroad.com/hanoi; Ambassador ROLF BERGMAN.

Zambia: Haile Selassie Ave, POB 50264, 10101 Lusaka; tel. (1) 251711; fax (1) 254049; e-mail ambassaden.lusaka@foreign.ministry.se; internet www.swedenabroad.com/lusaka; Ambassador Lars Ronnås.

Zimbabwe: 32 Aberdeen Rd, Avondale, POB 4110, Harare; tel. (4) 302636; fax (4) 302236; e-mail ambassaden.harare@foreign.ministry.se; internet www.swedenabroad.com; Ambassador STEN RYLANDER.

DIPLOMATIC MISSIONS OF SWITZERLAND

United Nations: 633 Third Ave, 29th Floor, New York, NY 10017; tel. (212) 286-1540; fax (212) 286-1555; e-mail vertretung-un@nyc.rep.admin.ch; internet www.uno.admin.ch/sub_uno/e/uno.html; Permanent Representative Peter Maurer.

Albania: Rruga e Elbasanit 81, Tirana; tel. (4) 234888; fax (4) 234889; e-mail tir.vertretung@eda.admin.ch; internet www.eda.admin.ch/tirana; Ambassador YVANA ENZLER.

Algeria: BP 443, Paradou, 2 rue no 3, 16035 Hydra, Algiers; tel. (21) 60-04-22; fax (21) 60-98-54; e-mail vertretung@alg.rep.admin.ch; Ambassador Jean-Claude Richard.

Argentina: Avda Santa Fe 846, 10°, C1059ABP Buenos Aires; tel. (11) 4311-6491; fax (11) 4313-2998; e-mail vertretung@bue.rep.admin.ch; internet www.eda.admin.ch/buenosaires_emb/s/home.html; Chargé d'affaires a.i. ERIC ALAIN MAYORAZ.

Australia: 7 Melbourne Ave, Forrest, ACT 2603; tel. (2) 6162-8400; fax (2) 6273-3428; e-mail vertretung@can.rep.admin.ch; internet www.eda.admin.ch/australia; Ambassador Christian Mühlethaler.

Austria: Prinz-Eugen-Str. 7, 1030 Vienna; tel. (1) 795-05-0; fax (1) 795-05-21; e-mail vie.vertretung@eda.admin.ch; internet www.eda.admin.ch/wien; Ambassador DR OSCAR KNAPP.

Azerbaijan: 1000 Baku, Rasul Rza küç. 11/28–30; tel. (12) 598-53-14; fax (12) 498-15-43; e-mail baku.vertretung@eda.admin.ch; internet www.eda.admin.ch/baku; Ambassador Alain Guidetti.

Bangladesh: House 31B, Rd 18, Banani, Dhaka 1213; tel. (2) 8812874; fax (2) 8823872; Ambassador DR DORA RAPOLD.

Belgium: 26 rue de la Loi, BP 9, 1040 Brussels; tel. (2) 285-43-50; fax (2) 230-37-81; e-mail bru.vertretung@eda.admin.ch; internet www.eda.admin.ch/bruxelles; Ambassador Jean-Jacques de Dardel.

Bolivia: Calle 13, esq. Avda 14 de Setiembre, Obrajes, Casilla 9356, La Paz; tel. (2) 275-1001; fax (2) 214-0885; e-mail vertretung@paz.rep.admin.ch; Chargé d'affaires a.i. JACQUES GREMAUD.

Bosnia and Herzegovina: 71000 Sarajevo, Josipa Štadlera 15; tel. (33) 275850; fax (33) 570120; e-mail vertretung@sar.rep.admin.ch; internet www.eda.admin.ch/sarajevo; Ambassador Rolf Lenz.

Brazil: SES, Av. das Nações, Quadra 811, Lote 41, 70448-900 Brasília, DF; tel. (61) 3443-5500; fax (61) 3443-5711; e-mail vertretung@bra.rep.admin.ch; internet www.dfae.admin.ch/brasilia; Ambassador RUDOLF BAERFUSS.

Bulgaria: 1504 Sofia, ul. Shipka 33; tel. (2) 942-01-00; fax (2) 946-11-86; e-mail vertretung@sof.rep.admin.ch; Ambassador Thomas Feller.

Canada: 5 Marlborough Ave, Ottawa, ON K1N 8E6; tel. (613) 235-1837; fax (613) 563-1394; e-mail ott.vertretung@eda.admin.ch; internet www.eda.admin.ch/canada; Ambassador WERNER BAUMANN.

Chile: Avda Américo Vespucio Sur 100, 14°, Las Condes, Santiago; tel. (2) 263-4211; fax (2) 263-4094; e-mail vertretung@san.rep.admin.ch; internet www.eda.admin.ch/santiago; Ambassador André Regli.

China, People's Republic: 3 Dong Wu Jie, San Li Tun, Beijing 100600; tel. (10) 65322736; fax (10) 65324353; e-mail vertretung@bei.rep.admin.ch; Ambassador DANTE CANDIDO MARTINELLI.

Colombia: Carrera 9, No 74-08/1101, 11°, Bogotá, DC; tel. (1) 349-7230; fax (1) 349-7195; e-mail bog.vertretung@eda.admin.ch; internet www.eda.admin.ch/bogota; Ambassador Thomas Kupfer.

Costa Rica: Paseo Colón, Centro Colón, Apdo 895, 1007 San José; tel. 221-4829; fax 255-2831; e-mail sjc.vertretung@eda.admin.ch; Ambassador GABRIELA NÜTZI SULPIZIO.

Côte d'Ivoire: Immeuble Botreau Roussel, 28 ave Delafosse, Plateau, 01 BP 1914, Abidjan 01; tel. 20-21-17-21; fax 20-21-27-70; e-mail vertretung@abi.rep.admin.ch; Ambassador Johannes Kunz.

Croatia: 10000 Zagreb, Bogovićeva 3; tel. (1) 4810891; fax (1) 4810890; e-mail zag.vertretung@eda.admin.ch; Ambassador ERICH HERMANN PIRCHER.

Cuba: Avda 5, No 2005, entre 20 y 22, Miramar, Havana; tel. (7) 204-2611; fax (7) 204-1148; e-mail swissem@enet.cu; internet www.eda.admin.ch/havana; Ambassador Bertrand Louis.

Cyprus: 46 Themistocles Dervis St, Medcon Tower, 1066 Nicosia; POB 20739, 1663 Nicosia; tel. 22466800; fax 22766008; e-mail nic.vertretung@eda.admin.ch; internet www.eda.admin.ch/nicosia; Ambassador MARIANNE ENGLER.

Czech Republic: Pevnostní 7/588, POB 84, 162 01 Prague 6; tel. 220400611; fax 224311312; e-mail vertretung@pra.rep.admin.ch; Ambassador Jean-François Kammer.

Denmark: Amaliegade 14, 1256 Copenhagen K; tel. 33-14-17-96; fax 33-33-75-51; e-mail cop.vertretung@eda.admin.ch; internet www.eda.admin.ch/copenhagen; Ambassador ANDRÉ FAIVET.

Ecuador: Edif. Xerox, 2°, Amazonas 3617 y Juan Pablo Sanz, Apdo 17-11-4815, Quito; tel. (2) 243-4949; fax (2) 244-9314; e-mail qui.vertretung@eda.admin.ch; internet www.eda.admin.ch/quito; Ambassador Markus-Alexander Antonietti.

Egypt: POB 633, 10 Sharia Abd al-Khalek Sarwat, Cairo; tel. (2) 5758284; fax (2) 5745236; e-mail vertretung@cai.rep.admin.ch; internet www.eda.admin .ch/cairo; Ambassador CHARLES-EDOUARD HELD.

Ethiopia: Jimma Rd, Old Airport Area, POB 1106, Addis Ababa; tel. (11) 3711107; fax (11) 3712177; e-mail add.vertretung@eda.admin.ch; Ambassador Peter Reinhardt.

Finland: Uudenmaankatu 16A, 00120 Helsinki; tel. (9) 6229500; fax (9) 62295050; e-mail hel.vertretung@eda.admin.ch; internet www.eda.admin.ch/ helsinki; Ambassador JOSEF BUCHER.

France: 142 rue de Grenelle, 75007 Paris; tel. 1-49-55-67-00; fax 1-49-55-67-67; e-mail par.vertretung@eda.admin.ch; internet www.eda.admin.ch/paris; Ambassador Ulrich Lehner.

Georgia: 0114 Tbilisi, Krtsanisi 11; tel. (32) 75-30-01; fax (32) 75-30-06; e-mail tif.vertretung@eda.admin.ch; internet www.eda.admin.ch/tbilisi; Ambassador DR LORENZO AMBERG.

Germany: Otto-von-Bismarck-Allee 4a, 10557 Berlin; tel. (30) 3904000; fax (30) 3911030; e-mail ber.vertretung@eda.admin.ch; internet www.eda.admin .ch/berlin; Ambassador Dr Christian Blickenstorfer.

Ghana: Kanda Highway, North Ridge, POB 359, Accra; tel. (21) 228125; fax (21) 223583; e-mail acc.vertretung@eda.admin.ch; internet www.eda.admin .ch/accra; Ambassador GEORG ZUBLER.

Greece: Odos Iassiou 2, 115 21 Athens; tel. (210) 7230364; fax (210) 7249209; e-mail vertretung@ath.rep.admin.ch; internet www.eda.admin.ch/athens; Ambassador Paul Koller-Hauser.

Guatemala: Edif. Torre Internacional, 14°, 16 Calle 0-55, Zona 10, Apdo 1426, Guatemala City; tel. 2367-5520; fax 2367-5811; e-mail vertretung@gua .rep.admin.ch; Ambassador JEAN-PIERRE VILLARD.

Hungary: 1143 Budapest, Stefánia u. 107; tel. (1) 460-7040; fax (1) 343-9492; e-mail bud.vertretung@eda.admin.ch; internet www.swissembassy.hu; Ambassador Marc-André Salamin.

India: Nyaya Marg, Chanakyapuri, New Delhi 110 021; tel. (11) 26878372; fax (11) 26873093; e-mail ndh.vertretung@eda.admin.ch; Ambassador DOMINIQUE DREYER.

Indonesia: Jalan H. R. Rasuna Said, Kav. X-3/2, Kuningan, Jakarta Selatan 12950; tel. (21) 5256061; fax (21) 5202289; e-mail vertretung@jak.rep.admin .ch; internet www.eda.admin.ch/jakarta; Ambassador Bernardino Regazzoni.

Iran: POB 19395-4683, 13 Yasaman St, Cnr of Sharifi Manesh Ave, Elahieh, Tehran 19649; tel. (21) 22008333; fax (21) 22006002; e-mail vertretung@teh .rep.admin.ch; internet www.eda.admin.ch/tehran_emb; Ambassador PHILIPPE WELTI.

Iraq: 41/5/929, Masbah House, Alwiya, Baghdad; tel. (1) 719-3091; e-mail vertretung@bag.rep.admin.ch; Ambassador Martin Aeschbacher.

Ireland: 6 Ailesbury Rd, Dublin 4; tel. (1) 2186382; fax (1) 2830344; e-mail dubvertretung@eda.admin.ch; internet www.eda.admin.ch/dublin; Ambassador JOSEF DOSWALD.

Israel: POB 6068, 228 Rehov Hayarkon, Tel-Aviv 61060; tel. 3-5464455; fax 3-5464408; e-mail vertretung@tel.rep.admin.ch; internet www.eda.admin.ch/ telaviv; Ambassador Walter Haffner.

Italy: Via Barnaba Oriani 61, 00197 Roma; tel. (06) 809571; fax (06) 8088510; e-mail amsuisse@rom.rep.admin.ch; internet www.eda.admin.ch/roma; Ambassador BRUNO MAX SPINNER.

Japan: 5-9-12, Minami Azabu, Minato-ku, Tokyo 106-8589; tel. (3) 5449-8400; fax (3) 3473-6090; e-mail vertretung@tok.rep.admin.ch; internet www .eda.admin.ch/tokyo; Ambassador Paul Fivat.

Jordan: POB 5341, 19 Ibrahim Ayoub St, 4th Circle, Amman 11183; tel. (6) 5931416; fax (6) 5930685; e-mail amm.vertretung@eda.admin.ch; internet www.eda.admin.ch/amman; Ambassador PAUL WIDMER.

Kenya: International House, 7th Floor, Mama Ngina St, POB 30752, Nairobi; tel. (20) 228735; fax (20) 217388; e-mail nai.vertretung@eda.admin .ch; Ambassador George Martin.

Korea, Republic: 32-10, Songwol-dong, Jongno-gu, POB 2900, Seoul 110-101; tel. (2) 739-9511; fax (2) 737-9392; e-mail swissemb@elim.net; internet www .eda.admin.ch/seoul; Ambassador CHRISTIAN HAUSWIRTH.

Kosovo: 10060 Prishtina, Adrian Krasniqi 11; tel. (38) 248088; fax (38) 248078; e-mail pri.vertretung@eda.admin.ch; internet www.eda.admin.ch/ pristina; Ambassador Lukas Beglinger.

Kuwait: POB 23954, 13100 Safat, Qortuba, Block 2, St 1, Villa 122, Kuwait City; tel. 5340172; fax 5340176; e-mail vertretung@kow.rep.admin.ch; internet www.eda.admin.ch/kuwait; Ambassador MICHEL GOTTRET.

Latvia: Elizabetes iela 2, Rīga 1340; tel. 6733-8351; fax 6733-8354; e-mail vertretung@rig.rep.admin.ch; internet www.eda.admin.ch/riga; Ambassador Anne Bauty.

Lebanon: Immeuble Bourj al-Ghazal, ave Fouad Chehab, Achrafieh, Beirut; tel. (1) 324129; fax (1) 324167; e-mail bey.vertretung@eda.admin.ch; Ambassador FRANÇOIS BARRAS.

Libya: POB 439, Sharia al-Moussawer ben Maghzamah, off Sharia ben Ashour, Tripoli; tel. (21) 3614118; fax (21) 3614238; e-mail tri.vertretung@ eda.admin.ch; internet www.eda.admin.ch/tripoli; Ambassador Martin Aeschbacher.

Luxembourg: Immeuble Forum Royal, 25A blvd Royal, 3e étage, 2449 Luxembourg; tel. 22-74-74-1; fax 22-74-74-20; e-mail lux.vertretung@eda .admin.ch; internet www.eda.admin.ch/luxembourg; Ambassador PHILIPPE GUEX.

Macedonia, former Yugoslav Republic: 1000 Skopje, Maksim Gorki 19; tel. (2) 3103320; fax (2) 3103301; e-mail sko.vertretung@eda.admin.ch; internet www.eda.admin.ch/skopje; Ambassador Nicole Wyrsch.

Madagascar: Immeuble ARO, Solombavambahoaka, Frantsay 77, BP 118, 101 Antananarivo; tel. (20) 2262997; fax (20) 2228940; e-mail ant .vertretung@eda.admin.ch; internet www.eda.admin.ch/antananarivo; Chargé d'affaires a.i. BENOÎT GIRARDIN.

Malaysia: 16 Persiaran Madge, 55000 Kuala Lumpur; tel. (3) 21480622; fax (3) 21480935; e-mail kua.vertretung@eda.admin.ch; internet www.eda .admin.ch/kualalumpur; Ambassador Urs Stemmler.

Mexico: Paseo de las Palmas 405, 11°, Torre Óptima, Col. Lomas de Chapultepec, Del. Miguel Hidalgo, 11000 México, DF; tel. (55) 5520-3003; fax (55) 5520-8685; e-mail vertretung@mex.rep.admin.ch; internet www.eda .admin.ch/mexico_emb/s/home.html; Ambassador URS BREITER.

Morocco: square de Berkane, BP 169, 10001 Rabat; tel. (3) 7268030; fax (3) 7268040; e-mail rab.vertretung@eda.admin.ch; internet www.eda.admin.ch/ rabat; Ambassador Christian Dunant.

Mozambique: Av. Ahmed Sekou Touré 637, CP 135, Maputo; tel. 21315275; fax 21315276; e-mail map.vertretung@eda.admin.ch; internet www.eda .admin.ch/maputo; Ambassador RUDOLF BAERFUSS.

Netherlands: Lange Voorhout 42, 2514 EE The Hague; tel. (70) 3642831; fax (70) 3561238; e-mail hay.vertretung@eda.admin.ch; internet www.eda.admin .ch/denhaag; Ambassador Dominik Matthias Alder.

New Zealand: Panama House, 22 Panama St, POB 25004, Wellington; tel. (4) 472-1593; fax (4) 499-6302; e-mail vertretung@wel.rep.admin.ch; Ambassador DR BEAT NOBS.

Nigeria: 157 Adetokumbo Ademola Cres., Wuse II, Abuja; tel. (9) 4131081; fax (9) 4131089; e-mail abu.vertretung@eda.admin.ch; internet www.eda .admin.ch/abuja; Ambassador Pierre Helg.

Norway: Bygdøy allé 78, 0244 Oslo; tel. 22-43-05-90; fax 22-44-63-50; e-mail osl.vertretung@eda.admin.ch; internet www.eda.admin.ch/oslo; Ambassador KURT HÖCHNER.

Pakistan: St 6, G-5/4, Diplomatic Enclave, POB 1073, Islamabad; tel. (51) 2272991; fax (51) 2279286; e-mail vertretung@isl.rep.admin.ch; Ambassador Markus Peter.

Peru: Avda Salaverry 3240, San Isidro, Lima 27; tel. (1) 2640305; fax (1) 2641319; e-mail lana.llosa@eda.admin.ch; internet www.eda.admin.ch/lima; Ambassador BEAT LOELIGER.

Philippines: Equitable Bank Tower, 24th Floor, 8751 Paseo de Roxas, Makati City, 1226 Metro Manila; tel. (2) 7579000; fax (2) 7573718; e-mail man .vertretung@eda.admin.ch; internet www.eda.admin.ch/manila; Ambassador Peter Sutter.

Poland: 00-540 Warsaw, Al. Ujazdowskie 27; tel. (22) 6280481; fax (22) 6210548; e-mail var.vertretung@eda.admin.ch; internet www.eda.admin.ch/ warsaw; Ambassador HANS BÉNÉDICT DE CERJAT.

Portugal: Travessa do Jardim 17, 1350-185 Lisbon; tel. (21) 3944090; fax (21) 3955945; e-mail lis.vertretung@eda.admin.ch; internet www.eda.admin.ch/ lisbon; Ambassador Catherine Krieg Polejack.

Romania: 010626 Bucharest, Str. Grigore Alexandrescu 16–20; tel. (21) 2061600; fax (21) 2061620; e-mail vertretung@buc.rep.admin.ch; internet www.eda.admin.ch/bucarest; Ambassador LIVIO HÜRZELER.

Russian Federation: 101000 Moscow, per. Ogorodnoi Slobody 2/5; tel. (495) 258-38-30; fax (495) 621-21-83; e-mail mos.vertretung@eda.admin.ch; internet www.eda.admin.ch/moscow; Ambassador Erwin H. Hofer.

Saudi Arabia: POB 94311, Riyadh 11693; tel. (1) 488-1291; fax (1) 488-0632; e-mail vertretung@rya.rep.admin.ch; Ambassador MAURICE DARIER.

Senegal: rue René N'Diaye, angle rue Seydou, BP 1772, Dakar; tel. 33-823-0590; fax 33-822-3657; e-mail dak.vertretung@eda.admin.ch; internet www .eda.admin.ch/dakar; Ambassador Livio Hürzeler.

Serbia: 11000 Belgrade, Birčaninova 27; tel. (11) 3065820; fax (11) 2657253; e-mail vertretung@bel.rep.admin.ch; Ambassador WILHELM MEIER.

Singapore: 1 Swiss Club Link, Singapore 288162; tel. 64685788; fax 64668245; e-mail sin.vertretung@eda.admin.ch; internet www.eda.admin.ch/singapore; Ambassador Dr Daniel Woker.

Slovakia: Tolstého 9, 811 06 Bratislava; tel. (2) 5930-1111; fax (2) 5930-1100; e-mail vertretung@bts.rep.admin.ch; internet www.eda.admin.ch/bratislava; Ambassador JOSEF AREGGER.

Slovenia: 1000 Ljubljana, trg Republike 3/VI; tel. (1) 2008640; fax (1) 2008669; e-mail vertretung@lju.rep.admin.ch; internet www.eda.admin.ch/ljubljana; Ambassador Stefan Speck.

South Africa: 225 Veale St, Parc Nouveau, New Muckleneuk, Pretoria 0181; POB 2508, Brooklyn Sq. 0075; tel. (12) 4520660; fax (12) 3466605; e-mail vertretung@pre.rep.admin.ch; internet www.swissembassy.co.za; Ambassador VIKTOR CHRISTEN.

Spain: Núñez de Balboa 35a, 7°, 28001 Madrid; tel. (91) 4363960; fax (91) 4363980; e-mail vertretung@mad.rep.admin.ch; internet www.eda.admin.ch/madrid; Ambassador Armin Ritz.

Sri Lanka: 63 Gregory's Rd, POB 342, Colombo 7; tel. (11) 2695117; fax (11) 2695176; e-mail col.vertretung@eda.admin.ch; internet www.eda.admin.ch/colombo; Ambassador RUTH FLINT.

Sudan: St 15, House No. 7, Amarat, POB 1707, Khartoum; tel. (183) 471010; fax (183) 471115; e-mail vertretung@kha.rep.admin.ch; Ambassador Andrej Motyl.

Sweden: Valhallavägen 64, POB 26143, 100 41 Stockholm; tel. (8) 676-79-00; fax (8) 21-15-04; e-mail sto.vertretung@eda.admin.ch; internet www.eda .admin.ch/stockholm; Ambassador ROBERT REICH.

Syria: BP 234, 2 rue ash-Shafi, Mezzeh Est, Damascus; tel. (11) 6111972; fax (11) 6111976; e-mail dam.vertretung@eda.admin.ch; internet www.eda .admin.ch/damascus; Ambassador Jacques de Watteville.

Tanzania: 79 Kinondoni Rd/Mafinga St, POB 2454, Dar es Salaam; tel. (22) 2666008; fax (22) 2666736; e-mail dar.vertretung@eda.admin.ch; Ambassador EMMANUEL JENNI.

Thailand: 35 Thanon Witthayu, Lumpini, Pathumwan, Bangkok 10330; tel. (2) 253-0156; fax (2) 255-4481; e-mail ban.vertretung@eda.admin.ch; internet www.eda.admin.ch/bangkok_emb; Ambassador Rodolphe S. Imhoof.

Tunisia: BP 56, Les Berges du Lac, 1053 Tunis; tel. (71) 962-997; fax (71) 965-796; e-mail vertretung@tun.rep.admin.ch; Ambassador CHRISTIAN FAESSLER.

Turkey: Atatürk Bul. 247, 06692 Kavaklıdere, Ankara; tel. (312) 4675555; fax (312) 4671199; e-mail ank.vertretung@eda.admin.ch; internet www.eda .admin.ch/ankara; Ambassador Walter B. Gyger.

Turkmenistan: 744000 Aşgabat; Ambassador ALAN GIDETTI.

Ukraine: 01015 Kyiv, vul. Kozyatynska 12, POB 114; tel. (44) 281-61-28; fax (44) 280-14-48; e-mail kie.vertretung@eda.admin.ch; internet www.eda .admin.ch/kiev; Ambassador Georg Zubler.

United Arab Emirates: POB 46116, Abu Dhabi; tel. (2) 6274636; fax (2) 6269627; e-mail vertretung@adh.rep.admin.ch; internet www.eda.admin.ch/uae; Ambassador PETER VOGLER.

United Kingdom: 16–18 Montagu Pl., London, W1H 2BQ; tel. (20) 7616-6000; fax (20) 7724-7001; e-mail swissembassy@lon.rep.admin.ch; internet www.swissembassy.org.uk; Ambassador Alexis P. Lautenberg.

United States of America: 2900 Cathedral Ave, NW, Washington, DC 20008; tel. (202) 745-7900; fax (202) 387-2564; e-mail was.vertretung@eda.admin .ch; internet www.swissemb.org; Ambassador URS JOHANN ZISWILER.

Uruguay: Ing. Federico Abadie 2936/40, 11°, Casilla 12261, 11300 Montevideo; tel. (2) 7115545; fax (2) 7115031; e-mail vertretung@mtv.rep .admin.ch; internet www.eda.admin.ch/montevideo; Ambassador Michel Coquoz.

Uzbekistan: 100070 Tashkent, U. Nosyr ko'ch., tupik 1/4; tel. (71) 120-67-38; fax (71) 120-62-59; e-mail tas.vertretung@eda.admin.ch; internet www.eda .admin.ch/tashkent; Ambassador DR PETER BURKHARD.

Venezuela: Centro Letonia, Torre Ing-Bank, 15°, La Castellana, Apdo 62555, Chacao, Caracas 1060-A; tel. (212) 267-9585; fax (212) 267-7745; e-mail vertretung@car.rep.admin.ch; internet www.eda.admin.ch/caracas; Ambassador Armin Ritz.

Viet Nam: 44B Ly Thuong Kiet, 15th Floor, Hanoi; tel. (4) 9346589; fax (4) 9346591; e-mail vertretung@han.rep.admin.ch; internet www.eda.admin.ch/hanoi; Ambassador JEAN HUBERT LEBET.

Zimbabwe: 9 Lanark Rd, POB 3440, Harare; tel. (4) 703997; fax (4) 794925; e-mail har.vertretung@eda.admin.ch; Ambassador Marcel Stutz.

DIPLOMATIC MISSIONS OF SYRIA

United Nations: 820 Second Ave, 15th Floor, New York, NY 10017; tel. (212) 661-1313; fax (212) 867-3985; e-mail syria@un.int; internet www.syria-un .org; Permanent Representative BASHAR JA'AFARI.

Algeria: Domaine Tamzali, 11 chemin Abd al-Kader Gadouche, Hydra, Algiers; tel. (21) 91-20-26; fax (21) 91-20-30; Ambassador Numeir Wahib Ghanem.

Argentina: Callao 956, C1023AAP Buenos Aires; tel. (11) 4813-2113; fax (11) 4814-3211; Ambassador RIYAD AS-SINEH.

Armenia: 0019 Yerevan, Marshal Baghramian Ave 14; tel. (10) 52-40-36; fax (10) 54-52-19; e-mail syrem_ar@intertel.am; Chargé d'affaires a.i. Dr Mamoun Hariri.

Australia: 41 Culgoa Circuit, O'Malley, ACT 2606; tel. (2) 6218-5200; fax (2) 6218-5250; e-mail info@syrianembassy.org.au; internet www.syrianembassy .org.au; Ambassador TAMMAM SULAIMAN.

Austria: Daffingerstr. 4, 1030 Vienna; tel. (1) 533-46-33; fax (1) 533-46-32; e-mail vienna_embassy@syrianembassy.jet2web.at; Ambassador Muhammad Badi Khattab.

Bahrain: POB 11585, Villa 867, Rd 3315, Block 333, Malhouze, Manama; tel. 17722484; fax 17740380; e-mail syremb@batelco.com.bh; Ambassador SULEIMAN ADEL SARRA.

Belarus: 220049 Minsk, vul. Suvorova 2; tel. (17) 280-37-08; fax (17) 280-72-00; Ambassador Faruk Takh.

Belgium: 3 ave F. D. Roosevelt, 1050 Brussels; tel. (2) 648-01-35; fax (2) 646-40-18; e-mail ambsyrie@skynet.be; internet www.syrianembassy.be; Ambassador DR MUHAMMAD AYMAN SOUSAN.

Brazil: SEN, Av. das Nações, Lote 11, 70434-900 Brasília, DF; tel. (61) 3226-0970; fax (61) 3223-2595; e-mail embsiria@uol.com.br; Ambassador (vacant).

Bulgaria: 1087 Sofia, bul. Simeonovsko shose 13A; tel. (2) 962-45-80; fax (2) 962-53-89; Chargé d'affaires SADDIK SADDIKNI.

Canada: 151 Slater St, Suite 1000, Ottawa, ON K1P 5H3; tel. (613) 569-5556; fax (613) 569-3800; e-mail info@syrianembassy.ca; internet www .syrianembassy.ca; Ambassador Jamil Sakr.

Chile: Carmencita 111, Casilla 12, Correo 10, Santiago; tel. (2) 232-7471; Ambassador FARES CHAINE.

China, People's Republic: 6 Dong Si Jie, San Li Tun, Beijing 100600; tel. (10) 65321563; fax (10) 65321575; e-mail sy@syria.org.cn; internet www.syria.org .cn; Ambassador Mohammed Kheir al-Wadi.

Cuba: Avda 5, No 7402, entre 74 y 76, Miramar, Havana; tel. (7) 204-2266; fax (7) 204-2829; e-mail embsiria@ceniai.inf.cu; Ambassador SHAKER KHAYAT.

Cyprus: POB 21891, 24 Nikodimos Mylona St, Ayios Antonios, 1071 Nicosia; tel. 22817333; fax 22756963; e-mail syremb@cytanet.com.cy; Chargé d'affaires Nader Nader.

Czech Republic: Českomalínská 20/7, 160 00 Prague 6; tel. 224310952; fax 224317911; e-mail souria@volny.cz; Ambassador NADRA FAYEZ SAYYAF.

Egypt: 18 Sharia Abd ar-Rehim Sabry, POB 435, Cairo (Dokki); tel. (2) 3358806; fax (2) 3377020; Ambassador Yousuf al-Ahmad.

France: 20 rue Vaneau, 75007 Paris; tel. 1-40-62-61-00; fax 1-47-05-92-73; e-mail ambassade-syrie@wanadoo.fr; internet www.amb-syr.fr; Chargé d'affaires a.i. SHAGHAF KAYALI.

Germany: Rauchstr. 25, 10787 Berlin; tel. (30) 501770; fax (30) 50177311; e-mail info@syrianembassy.de; internet www.syrianembassy.de; Ambassador Hussein Omran.

Greece: Diamandidou 61, Palaio Psychiko, 154 52 Athens; tel. (210) 6725577; fax (210) 6716402; e-mail syrembas@otenet.gr; Ambassador SOUAD M. AL-AYOUBI.

Hungary: 1026 Budapest, Harangvirág u. 3; tel. (1) 200-8046; fax (1) 200-8048; e-mail hungary@syrianembassy.hu; Ambassador (vacant).

India: D-5/8, Vasant Vihar, New Delhi 110 057; tel. (11) 26140233; fax (11) 26143107; Ambassador FAHD SALIM.

Indonesia: Jalan Karang Asem I/8, Jakarta 12950; tel. (21) 5255991; fax (21) 5202511; Ambassador Mohamad Darwish Baladi.

Iran: 19 Iraj St, Africa Ave, Tehran; tel. (21) 22052780; fax (21) 22059409; e-mail syrambir@mail.dci.co.ir; Ambassador DR HAMED HASSAN.

Iraq: Baghdad; .

Italy: Piazza dell'Ara Coeli, 00186 Roma; tel. (06) 6749801; fax (06) 6794989; e-mail uffstampasyem@hotmail.it; Ambassador SAMIR NASER AL QASIR.

Japan: Homat Jade, 6-19-45, Akasaka, Minato-ku, Tokyo 107-0052; tel. (3) 3586-8977; fax (3) 3586-8979; Chargé d'affaires a.i. Rania al-Haj Ali.

Jordan: POB 1733, Amman 11118; tel. (6) 5920684; fax (6) 5920635; e-mail pbox@syrianembassy.jo; internet www.syrianembassy.jo; Ambassador ALI HAMOUD.

Korea, Democratic People's Republic: Munsudong, Taedongkang District, Pyongyang; tel. (2) 3827473; fax (2) 3817635; Chargé d'affaires a.i. Muhammad Adib al-Hani.

Kuwait: POB 25600, 13116 Safat, Kuwait City; tel. 5396560; fax 5396509; Ambassador ALI ABD AL-KARIM.

Kyrgyzstan: 720000 Bishkek; Ambassador Wahib Fadel.

Libya: POB 4219, Sharia Muhammad Rashid Reda 4, Tripoli (Relations Office); tel. (21) 3331783; Head MUNIR BORKHAN.

Malaysia: Suite 23-03, 23rd Floor, Menara Tan & Tan, 207 Jalan Tun Razak, 50400 Kuala Lumpur; tel. (3) 21634110; fax (3) 21634199; internet www .syrianembassy.com.my; Ambassador Lamia Merie Aasi.

Mauritania: Tevragh Zeina, BP 288, Nouakchott; tel. 525-27-54; fax 525-45-00; .

Morocco: km 5.2, route des Zaêrs, BP 5158, Souissi, Rabat; tel. (3) 7755551; fax (3) 7757522; Ambassador Nabih Ismail.

Nigeria: 25 Kofo Abayomi St, Victoria Island, Lagos; tel. (1) 2615860; Chargé d'affaires a.i. MUSTAFA HAJ-ALI.

Oman: Madinat Qaboos, Al-Ensharah Street, Villa No. 201, POB 85, Muscat 115; tel. 24697904; fax 24603895; e-mail syria@omantel.net.om; internet www.syrianembassy.gov.om; Ambassador Farouk Mahmoud Qaddour.

Pakistan: 30 Hill Rd, F-6/3, Islamabad; tel. (51) 2279470; fax (51) 2279472; Ambassador DR RIAD ISMAT.

Poland: 02-610 Warsaw, ul. Goszczyńskiego 30; tel. (22) 8484809; fax (22) 8491847; e-mail embsyria@palmyra.neostrada.pl; internet www.syrian -embassy.com; Chargé d'affaires a.i. Wissal Issa.

Qatar: POB 1257, Doha; tel. 4831844; fax 4832139; Ambassador DEEB ABU LATIF.

Romania: 010673 Bucharest, Bd. Lascar Catargiu 50; tel. (21) 3192467; fax (21) 3129554; Ambassador Dr Walid Ali Osman.

Russian Federation: 119034 Moscow, Mansurovskii per. 4; tel. (495) 203-15-21; fax (495) 956-31-91; Ambassador WAHIB AL-FADEL.

Saudi Arabia: POB 94323, Riyadh 11693; tel. (1) 482-6191; fax (1) 482-6196; Ambassador Muhammad Khalid at-Tall.

Senegal: rue 1, point E, angle blvd de l'Est, BP 498, Dakar; tel. 33-824-6277; fax 33-825-1755; Ambassador HAMZEH DAWALIBI.

Serbia: 11000 Belgrade, Aleksandra Stamboliskog 13; tel. (11) 2666124; fax (11) 2660221; e-mail syremb@net.yu; Ambassador Dr Majed Shadoud.

South Africa: 963 Schoeman St, Arcadia, Pretoria 0083; POB 12830, Hatfield 0028; tel. (12) 3424701; fax (12) 3424702; e-mail syriaemb@telkomsa.net; Chargé d'affaires a.i. DR M. KHODUR.

Spain: Plaza de Platerías Martínez 1, 1°, 28014 Madrid; tel. (91) 4203946; fax (91) 4202681; Ambassador Makram Obeid.

Sudan: St 3, New Extension, POB 1139, Khartoum; tel. (183) 471152; fax (183) 471066; Ambassador MOHAMMED AL-MAHAMEED.

Sweden: Narvavägen 32, POB 24262, 104 51 Stockholm; tel. (8) 660-88-10; fax (8) 660-88-05; internet www.syrianembassy.se; Ambassador Muhammad Bassam Hatem Imadi.

Tanzania: 246 Alykhan Rd, Upanga, POB 2442, Dar es Salaam; tel. (22) 2117656; fax (22) 2115860; Chargé d'affaires a.i. M. B. IMADI.

Tunisia: 119 Azzouz Ribai-Almanar 3, Tunis; tel. (71) 888-188; Ambassador Dr Sami Glaiel.

Turkey: Sedat Simavi Sok. 40, 06680 Çankaya, Ankara; tel. (312) 4409657; fax (312) 4385609; Ambassador KHALED RAAD.

Ukraine: 03050 Kyiv, vul. Biloruska 5; tel. (44) 489-55-51; fax (44) 483-97-88; e-mail syrian-emb@ukr.net; Chargé d'affaires a.i. Suleiman Abudiab.

United Arab Emirates: POB 4011, Abu Dhabi; tel. (2) 4448768; fax (2) 4449387; Ambassador DR RUSTUM AZ-ZOBI (vacant).

United Kingdom: 8 Belgrave Sq., London, SW1X 8PH; tel. (20) 7245-9012; fax (20) 7235-4621; e-mail info@syrianembassy.co.uk; internet www .syrianembassy.co.uk; Ambassador Dr Sami Khiyami.

United States of America: 2215 Wyoming Ave, NW, Washington, DC 20008; tel. (202) 232-6313; fax (202) 234-9548; e-mail info@syrembassy.net; internet www.syrianembassy.us; Chargé d'affaires a.i. IMAD MOUSTAPHA.

Venezuela: Avda Casiquiare, Quinta Damasco, Colinas de Bello Monte, Caracas; tel. (212) 753-5375; fax (212) 751-6146; Ambassador Mohammad Saleh Khafif.

Yemen: POB 494, Hadda Rd, Damascus St 1, San'a; tel. (1) 414891; Ambassador ABD AL-GHAFOUR SABOUNI.

DIPLOMATIC MISSIONS OF TAJIKISTAN

United Nations: 136 East 67th St, New York, NY 10021; tel. (212) 744-2196; fax (212) 472-7645; e-mail tajikistan@un.int; Permanent Representative Sirodjidin Mukhridinovich Aslov.

Afghanistan: House 41, St 10, Wazir Akbar Khan, Kabul; tel. (20) 2101080; fax (20) 2300392; e-mail kabultj@tojikistan.com; Ambassador FARKHOD MAHKAMOV.

Austria: Universitätsstr. 8/1a, 1090 Vienna; tel. (1) 409-82-66; fax (1) 409-82-66-14; e-mail tajikembassy@chello.at; internet www.tajikembassy.org; Ambassador Nuriddin T. Shamsov.

Belarus: 220050 Minsk, vul. Kirava 17; tel. (17) 222-37-98; fax (17) 227-76-13; e-mail tajikemb-belarus@mail.ru; Ambassador AMIRKHON SAFAROV.

Belgium: 363–365 ave Louise, BP 14, 1050 Brussels; tel. (2) 640-69-33; fax (2) 649-01-95; e-mail tajmin-belgium@skynet.be; internet www.taj-emb.be; Ambassador Saimumin S. Yatimov.

China, People's Republic: 5-1-41 Tayuan Diplomatic Office Bldg, Beijing 100600; tel. (10) 65322598; fax (10) 65323039; e-mail tjkemb@public2.bta.net .cn; Ambassador RASHID ALIMOV.

Germany: Otto-Suhr-Allee 84, 10585 Berlin; tel. (30) 3479300; fax (30) 34793029; e-mail info@botschaft-tadschikistan.de; Ambassador Imomudin M. Sattorov.

India: D-1/13, Vasant Vihar, New Delhi 110 057; tel. (11) 26154282; e-mail tajembindia@yahoo.com; Ambassador SALOHODDIN NASRIDDINOV.

Iran: 10 3rd Alley, Shahid Zeynali St, Tehran; tel. (21) 22299584; fax (21) 22291607; e-mail tajemb-iran@mail.ru; Ambassador Ramazan Mirzoyev.

Kazakhstan: 010000 Astana, Chubar sh-a, Marsovaya 15; tel. (7172) 24-09-29; e-mail embassy_tajic@kepter.kz; Ambassador BAHROM M. KHOLNAZAROV.

Kyrgyzstan: 720031 Bishkek, ul. Kara-Darinskaya 36; tel. (312) 51-23-43; fax (312) 51-14-64; e-mail tojsaforat@exnet.kg; Ambassador Makhmud N. Sobirov.

Pakistan: House 90, Main Double Rd, F-10/1, Islamabad; tel. (51) 2293462; fax (51) 2299710; e-mail tajemb_islamabad@inbox.ru; Ambassador SAIDBEK B. SIADOV.

Russian Federation: 103001 Moscow, Granatnyi per. 13; tel. (495) 290-38-46; fax (495) 291-89-98; e-mail embassy_moscow@tajikistan.ru; internet www .tajikistan.ru; Ambassador Abdulmajid S. Dostiyev.

Turkey: Cayhane Cad. 24, Gaziosmanpaşa, Ankara; tel. (312) 4461602; fax (312) 4463621; e-mail tajemb_turkey@inbox.ru; Ambassador SHUKHRAT M. SULTONOV.

Turkmenistan: 744000 Aşgabat, ul. Gurungan 19; tel. (12) 35-56-96; fax (12) 39-31-74; e-mail tadjemb_tm@mail.ru; Ambassador Kozidavlat Koimdodov.

United States of America: 1005 New Hampshire Ave, NW, Washington, DC 20037; tel. (202) 223-6090; fax (202) 223-6091; e-mail tajikistan@verizon.net; internet www.tjus.org; Ambassador ABDUJABBOR SHIRINOV.

Uzbekistan: 100000 Tashkent, A. Kahhor ko'ch., 6-chi tor, 61; tel. (71) 254-99-66; fax (71) 254-89-69; e-mail tajembuz@yandex.ru; Ambassador Bobokhon Makhmadov.

DIPLOMATIC MISSIONS OF TANZANIA

United Nations: 201 East 42nd St, 17th Floor, New York, NY 10017; tel. (212) 972-9160; fax (212) 682-5232; e-mail tzrepny@aol.com; Permanent Representative AUGUSTINE PHILIP MAHIGA.

Belgium: 72 ave F. D. Roosevelt, 1050 Brussels; tel. (2) 640-65-00; fax (2) 640-80-26; e-mail tanzania@skynet.be; Ambassador Simon U. R. Mlay.

Brazil: SHIS, QI 09, Conj. 16, Casa 20, Lago Sul, 71615-190, Brasília, DF; tel. (61) 3364-2629; fax (61) 3248-3361; e-mail tanrepbrasilia@yahoo.com.br; Ambassador JORAM MUKAMA BISWARO.

Burundi: 855 rue United Nations, BP 1653, Bujumbura; tel. 22248632; fax 22248637; e-mail tanzanrep@usan-bu.net; Ambassador Francis Mndolwa.

Canada: 50 Range Rd, Ottawa, ON K1N 8J4; tel. (613) 232-1500; fax (613) 232-5184; e-mail tzottawa@synapse.net; High Commissioner PETER ALLAN KALLAGHE.

China, People's Republic: 8 Liang Ma He Nan Lu, San Li Tun, Beijing 100600; tel. (10) 65321491; fax (10) 65324351; e-mail tzrep@tanzaniaembassy .org.cn; internet www.tanzaniaembassy.org.cn; Ambassador Omar Ramadhan Mapuri.

Congo, Democratic Republic: 142 blvd du 30 juin, BP 1612, Kinshasa; tel. (12) 81700; fax (12) 88081; e-mail amb.tanzanie@ic.cd; Ambassador GORDON LUHWANO NGILANGWA.

Egypt: 10 Anas Ibn Malek Street Mohandessin, Cairo; tel. (2) 3374286; fax (2) 3374155; Ambassador Muhammad A. Foum.

Ethiopia: POB 1077, Addis Ababa; tel. (11) 5511063; fax (11) 5517358; Ambassador MSUYA W. MANGACHI.

France: 13 ave Raymond Poincaré, 75116 Paris; tel. 1-53-70-63-66; fax 1-47-55-05-46; e-mail ambtanzanie@wanadoo.fr; internet www.amb-tanzanie.fr; Ambassador Hassan Omar Gumbo Kibelloh.

Germany: Eschenallee 11, 14050 Berlin; tel. (30) 3030800; fax (30) 30308020; e-mail info@tanzania-gov.de; internet www.tanzania-gov.de; Ambassador AHMADA RWEYEMAMU NGEMERA.

India: 10/1 Sav Priya Vihar, New Delhi 110 016; tel. (11) 26153148; fax (11) 26153289; e-mail tanzrep@del1.vsnl.net.in; High Commissioner Eva Lilian Nzaro.

Italy: Viale Cortina d'Ampezzo 185, 00135 Roma; tel. (06) 33485801; fax (06) 33485828; e-mail info@tanzania-gov.it; internet www.tanzania-gov.it; Ambassador ALI ABEID AMAN KARUME.

Japan: 4-21-9, Kami Yoga, Setagaya-ku, Tokyo 158-0098; tel. (3) 3425-4531; fax (3) 3425-7844; e-mail tzrepjp@tanzaniaembassy.or.jp; internet www .tanzaniaembassy.or.jp; Ambassador Elly E. E. Mtango.

Kenya: Continental House, Uhuru Highway, POB 47790, Nairobi; tel. (20) 331056; fax (20) 218269; e-mail tanzania@user.africaonline.co.ke; High Commissioner MAJ.-GEN. MIRISHO SAM HAGGAI SARAKIKYA.

Malawi: POB 922, Capital City, Lilongwe 3; tel. 1770150; fax 1770148; e-mail tanzanianhighcomm@tz.lilongwe.mw; High Commissioner Maj.-Gen. (retd) Makame Rashid.

Mozambique: Ujamaa House, Av. dos Mártires da Machava 852, CP 4515, Maputo; tel. 21490110; fax 21494782; e-mail ujamaa@zebra.eum.mz; High Commissioner ISSA MOHAMED ISSA.

Nigeria: 15 Yedseram St, Maitama, PMB 5125, Wuse, Abuja; tel. (9) 4132313; fax (9) 4132314; e-mail tanabuja@lytos.com; High Commissioner Cisco Mtiro (acting).

Russian Federation: 109017 Moscow, ul. Pyatnitskaya 33; tel. (495) 953-82-21; fax (495) 956-61-30; e-mail tzmos@wm.west.call.com; Ambassador PATRICK SEGEJA CHOKALA.

Saudi Arabia: POB 94320, Riyadh 11693; tel. (1) 454-2839; fax (1) 454-9660; e-mail tzriyad@deltasa.com; Ambassador Prof. A. A. Shareef.

South Africa: 822 George Ave, Arcadia, Pretoria 0007; POB 56572, Arcadia 0007; tel. (12) 3424393; fax (12) 4304383; e-mail thc@tanzania.org.za; internet www.tanzania.org.za; High Commissioner EMMANUEL A. MWAMBULUKUTU.

Sweden: Näsby Allé 6, 183 55 Täby; tel. (8) 732-24-30; fax (8) 732-24-32; e-mail mailbox@tanemb.se; internet www.tanemb.se; Ambassador Dr Ben Gwai Moses.

Uganda: 6 Kagera Rd, Nakasero, POB 5750, Kampala; tel. (41) 4456272; fax (41) 4343973; High Commissioner RAJAB H. GAMAHA.

United Kingdom: 3 Stratford Pl., London, WIC 1AS; tel. (20) 7569-1470; fax (20) 7491-3710; e-mail hom@tanzania-online.gov.uk; internet www.tanzania -online.gov.uk; High Commr Mwanaidi S. Maajar.

United States of America: 2139 R St, NW, Washington, DC 20008; tel. (202) 939-6125; fax (202) 797-7408; e-mail ubalozi@tanzaniaembassy-us.org; internet www.tanzaniaembassy-us.org; Ambassador OMBENI SEFUE.

Zambia: Ujamaa House, Plot 5200, United Nations Ave, POB 31219, 10101 Lusaka; tel. (1) 253222; fax (1) 254861; e-mail tzreplsk@zamnet.zm; High Commissioner George Mwanjabala.

Zimbabwe: Ujamaa House, 23 Baines Ave, POB 4841, Harare; tel. (4) 792714; fax (4) 792747; e-mail tanrep@icon.co.zw; Ambassador ADADI RAJABU.

DIPLOMATIC MISSIONS OF THAILAND

United Nations: 351 East 52nd St, New York, NY 10022; tel. (212) 754-2230; fax (212) 754-2535; e-mail thailand@un.int; Permanent Representative Don Pramudwinai.

Argentina: Vuelta de Obligado 1947, 12°, C1428ADC Buenos Aires; tel. (11) 4774-4415; fax (11) 4773-2447; e-mail thaiembargen@fibertel.com.ar; Ambassador ANUCHA OSATHANOND.

Australia: 111 Empire Circuit, Yarralumla, ACT 2600; tel. (2) 6273-1149; fax (2) 6273-1518; e-mail info@thaiembassy.org.au; internet www.thaiembassy .org.au; Ambassador Bandhit Sotipalalit.

Austria: Cottagegasse 48, 1180 Vienna; tel. (1) 478-33-35; fax (1) 478-29-07; e-mail thai.vn@embthai.telecom.at; Ambassador ADISAK PANUPONG.

Bahrain: POB 26475, Bldg 132, Rd 66, Block 360, Zinj Area, Manama; tel. 17246242; fax 17272714; e-mail thaimnm@mfa.go.th; internet www.mfa.go .th/web/1444.php?depid=269; Ambassador Suphat Chitranukroh.

Bangladesh: 18 & 20, Madani Ave, Baridhara, Dhaka 1212; tel. (2) 8812795; fax (2) 8854280; e-mail thaidac@mfa.go.th; internet www.thaidac.com; Ambassador CHALERMPOL THANCHITT.

Belgium: 2 square du Val de la Cambre, 1050 Brussels; tel. (2) 640-68-10; fax (2) 648-30-66; e-mail thaibxl@thaiembassy.be; internet www.thaiembassy.be; Ambassador Pisan Manawapat.

Brazil: SEN, Av. das Nações, Lote 10, 70433-900 Brasília, DF; tel. (61) 3224-6943; fax (61) 3223-7502; e-mail thaiemb@linkexpress.com.br; Ambassador SIREE BUNNAG.

Brunei: 2 Simpang 682, Jalan Tutong, Kampong Bunut, Bandar Seri Begawan BF 1320; tel. 2653108; fax 2653032; e-mail thaiemb@brunet.bn; Ambassador Sornsilp Polteja.

Cambodia: 196 Preah Norodom Blvd, Sangkat Tonle Bassac, Khan Chamkarmon, Phnom-Penh; tel. (23) 726306; fax (23) 726303; e-mail thaipn@mfa.go.th; internet www.thaiembassy.org/phnompenh; Ambassador VIRAPHAND VACHARATHIT.

Canada: 180 Island Park Dr., Ottawa, ON K1Y 0A2; tel. (613) 722-4444; fax (613) 722-6624; e-mail thaiott@magma.ca; internet www.thaiembottawa .org; Ambassador Snanchart Devahastin.

Chile: Avda Américo Vespucio 100, 15°, Las Condes, Santiago; tel. (2) 263-0710; fax (2) 263-0803; e-mail rte.santiago@vtr.net; internet www .thaiembassy.org/santiago; Ambassador VIMON KIDCHOP.

China, People's Republic: 40 Guang Hua Lu, Jian Guo Men Wai, Beijing 100600; tel. (10) 65321903; fax (10) 65321748; e-mail thaibej@public.bta.net .cn; internet www.thaiembbeij.org; Ambassador Rathakit Manathat.

Czech Republic: Romaina Rollanda 3, 160 00 Prague 6; tel. 220571435; fax 220570049; e-mail thaiemb@volny.cz; internet www.thaiembassy.cz; Ambassador THANARAT THANAPUTTI.

Denmark: Norgesmindevej 18, 2900 Hellerup; tel. 39-62-50-10; fax 39-62-50-59; e-mail mail@thai-embassy.dk; Ambassador Cholchineepan Chiranond.

Egypt: 9 Tiba St, Cairo (Dokki); tel. (2) 37603553; fax (2) 37605076; e-mail royalthai@link.net; internet www.thaiembassy.org/cairo; Ambassador NOPPADON THEPPITAK.

Finland: Eteläesplanadi 22c, 3rd Floor, 00130 Helsinki; tel. (9) 6122640; fax (9) 61226466; e-mail info@thaiembassy.fi; internet www.thaiembassy.fi; Ambassador Apichart Chinwanno (resident in Sweden).

France: 8 rue Greuze, 75116 Paris; tel. 1-56-26-50-50; fax 1-56-26-04-45; e-mail thaipar@wanadoo.fr; Ambassador THANA DUANGRATANA.

Germany: Lepsiusstr. 64–66, 12163 Berlin; tel. (30) 794810; fax (30) 79481511; e-mail general@thaiembassy.de; internet www.thaiembassy.de; Ambassador Sorayouth Prompoj.

Greece: Odos Marathonodromou & Odos Kyprou 25, Palaio Psychiko, 154 52 Athens; tel. (210) 6710155; fax (210) 6479508; e-mail thaiath@otenet.gr; Ambassador ASHA DVITIYANANDA.

Hungary: 1025 Budapest, Verecke u. 79; tel. (1) 438-4020; fax (1) 438-4023; e-mail thaiemba@mail.datanet.hu; internet www.thaiembassy.org/budapest; Ambassador Piamsak Milintachinda.

India: 56N Nyaya Marg, Chanakyapuri, New Delhi 110 021; tel. (11) 26118103; fax (11) 26872029; e-mail thaidel@mfa.go.th; internet www .thaiemb.org.in; Ambassador CHIRASAK THANESNANT.

Indonesia: Jalan Imam Bonjol 74, Jakarta 10310; tel. (21) 3904052; fax (21) 3107469; e-mail thaijkt@indo.net.id; internet www.thaiembassy.org/jakarta; Ambassador Akrasid Amatayakul.

Iran: POB 11495-111, 4 Esteghlal Alley, Baharestan Ave, Tehran; tel. (21) 77531433; fax (21) 77532022; e-mail info@thaiembassy-tehran.org; internet www.thaiembassy-tehran.org; Ambassador Suwit Saicheua.

Israel: 21 Shaul Hamelech Blvd, Tel-Aviv 64367; tel. 3-6958980; fax 3-6958991; e-mail thaisr@netvision.co.il; internet www.mfa.go.th/web/1315 .php?depid=210; Ambassador Kasivat Paruggamanont.

Italy: Via Nomentana 132, 00162 Roma; tel. (06) 86202051; fax (06) 86220555; e-mail thai.em.rome@wind.it.net; internet www.thaiembassy.org/rome; Ambassador Pradap Pibulsonggram.

Japan: 3-14-6, Kami Osaki, Shinagawa-ku, Tokyo 141-0021; tel. (3) 3447-2247; fax (3) 3442-6750; e-mail sathana@thaiembassy.jp; internet www .thaiembassy.jp; Ambassador Suvidhya Simaskul.

Jordan: POB 144329, Amman 11814; tel. (6) 5925410; fax (6) 5926109; e-mail thaibgw@mfa.go.th; Ambassador Isinthorn Sornvai.

Kenya: Ambassador House, Rose Ave, POB 58349, Nairobi; tel. (20) 2715243; fax (20) 2715801; e-mail thainbi@thainbi.or.ke; internet www .thaiembassy.org/nairobi; Ambassador Apichit Asatthawasi.

Korea, Democratic People's Republic: Pyongyang; Ambassador Nikhom Tantemsapya.

Korea, Republic: 653-7, Hannam-dong, Yeongsan-gu, Seoul 140-210; tel. (2) 795-3098; fax (2) 798-3448; e-mail rteseoul@kornet.net; internet www .thaiembassy.or.kr; Ambassador Vasin Teeravechyan.

Kuwait: POB 66647, 43757 Bayan, Block 6, St 8, Villa 1, Jabriya, Kuwait City; tel. 5317530; fax 5317532; e-mail thaiemkw@kems.net; Ambassador Dusit Chantasen.

Laos: ave Kaysone Phomvihane, Xaysettha, Vientiane; tel. (21) 214581; fax (21) 214580; e-mail thaivtn@mfa.go.th; internet www.thaiembassy.org/ vientiane; Ambassador Wiboon Khusakul.

Malaysia: 206 Jalan Ampang, 50450 Kuala Lumpur; tel. (3) 21488222; fax (3) 21486573; e-mail thaikl@pop1.jaring.my; internet www.mfa.go.th/web/1830 .php?depcode=23000100; Ambassador Piyawat Niyomrerks.

Mexico: Paseo de las Palmas 1610, Col. Lomas de Chapultepec, Del. Miguel Hidalgo, 11000 México, DF; tel. (55) 5540-4551; fax (55) 5540-4817; e-mail thaimex@prodigy.net.mx; internet www.thaiembmexico.co.nr; Ambassador Ravee Hongsaprabhas.

Morocco: 11 rue de Tiddes, BP 4436, Rabat; tel. (3) 7763328; fax (3) 7763920; e-mail thaima@menara.ma; Ambassador Akrasid Amatayakul.

Myanmar: 73 Manawhari St, Dagon Township, Yangon; tel. (1) 224647; fax (1) 225929; e-mail thaiygn@mfa.go.th; Ambassador Bansarn Bunnag.

Nepal: 167/4 Ward No. 3, Maharajgunj-Bansbari Rd, POB 3333, Kathmandu; tel. (1) 4371410; fax (1) 4371409; e-mail thaiemb@wlink.com.np; internet www.thaiembassy.org/kathmandu; Ambassador Vanvisa Thamrongnavasawat.

Netherlands: Laan Copes van Cattenburch 123, 2585 EZ The Hague; tel. (70) 3450766; fax (70) 3451929; e-mail thaihag@thaihag.demon.nl; internet www .thaiembassy.org/hague; Ambassador Suchitra Hiranprueck.

New Zealand: 2 Cook St, Karori, POB 17-226, Wellington; tel. (4) 476-8616; fax (4) 476-3677; e-mail thaiembassynz@xtra.co.nz; internet www .thaiembassynz.org.nz; Ambassador Oum Moalanon.

Nigeria: Plot 766, Panama St, Cadastral Zone A6, Maitama, Abuja; e-mail thaiabj@mfa.go.th; Ambassador N. Sathaporn.

Norway: Eilert Sundtsgt. 4, 0244 Oslo; tel. 22-12-86-60; fax 22-04-99-69; e-mail thaioslo@online.no; internet www.thaiembassy.no; Ambassador Jullapong Nonsrichai.

Oman: Shati al-Qurum, Villa No. 1339, Way No. 3017, POB 60, Ruwi 115; tel. 24602683; fax 24605714; e-mail thaimct@omantel.net.om; Ambassador Thinakorn Kanasuta.

Pakistan: 23, St 25, F-8/2, Islamabad; tel. (51) 5838245; fax (51) 5837422; e-mail thaiemb@dslplus.net.pk; internet www.mfa.go.th/web/1330 .php?depid=231; Ambassador Sukho Piromnam.

Philippines: 107 Rada St, Legaspi Village, Makati City, 1229 Metro Manila; tel. (2) 8154220; fax (2) 8154221; e-mail thaimnl@pacific.net.ph; Ambassador Kulkumut Singhara Na Ayudhya.

Poland: 00-790 Warsaw, ul. Willowa 7; tel. (22) 8492655; fax (22) 8492630; e-mail thaiemb@thaiemb.internetdsl.pl; Ambassador Thakur Phanit.

Portugal: Rua de Alcolena 12, 1400-005 Lisbon; tel. (21) 3014848; fax (21) 3018181; e-mail thai.lis@mail.telepac.pt; internet www.thaiembassy.org/ lisbon; Ambassador Kasivat Paruggamanont.

Qatar: POB 22474, Doha; tel. 4550715; fax 4550835; e-mail thaidoh@qatar .net.qa; internet www.thaiembqatar.com; Ambassador Suvat Chirapant.

Romania: 020953 Bucharest, Str. Vasile Conta 12; tel. (21) 3110031; fax (21) 3110044; e-mail thaibuh@speedmail.ro; Ambassador Rushda Thavaravej.

Russian Federation: 129090 Moscow, ul. B. Spasskaya 9; tel. (495) 608-08-17; fax (495) 290-96-59; e-mail thaiemb@nnt.ru; internet www .thaiembassymoscow.com; AmbassadorSuphot Dhirakaosal.

Saudi Arabia: POB 94359, Riyadh 11693; tel. (1) 488-1174; fax (1) 488-1179; e-mail thaiemryadsl@awalnet.net.sa; internet www.thaiembassy.org/riyadh; Chargé d'affaires a.i. Charn Jullamon.

Senegal: 10 rue Léon Gontran Damas, BP 3721, Dakar-Fann; tel. 33-869-3290; fax 33-824-8458; e-mail thaidkr@sentoo.sn; internet www.mfa.go.th/ web/2366.php; Ambassador Itti Ditbanjong.

Singapore: 370 Orchard Rd, Singapore 238870; tel. 67372158; fax 67320778; e-mail thaisgp@singnet.com.sg; internet www.thaiembassy.sg; Ambassador Nopadol Gunavibool.

South Africa: 428 cnr Hill and Pretorius Sts, Arcadia, Pretoria 0028; POB 12080, Hatfield 0083; tel. (12) 3424600; fax (12) 3424805; e-mail info@ thaiembassy.co.za; internet www.thaiembassy.co.za; Ambassador Domedej Bunnag.

Spain: Joaquín Costa 29, 28002 Madrid; tel. (91) 5632903; fax (91) 5640033; e-mail madthai@temb.e.telefonica.net; Ambassador Busba Bunnag.

Sri Lanka: Greenlanka Towers, 9th Floor, 46/46 Nawam Mawatha, Colombo 2; tel. (11) 2302500; fax (11) 2304511; e-mail thaicmb@sltnet.lk; internet www.thaiembassy.org/colombo; Ambassador Thinakorn Kanasuta.

Sweden: Floragt. 3, POB 26220, 100 40 Stockholm; tel. (8) 791-73-40; fax (8) 791-73-51; e-mail info@thaiembassy.se; internet www.thaiembassy.se; Ambassador Apichart Chinwanno.

Switzerland: Kirchstr. 56, 3097 Liebefeld-Bern; tel. 319703030; fax 319703035; e-mail thai.bern@bluewin.ch; Ambassador Chaiyong Satjipanon.

Timor-Leste: Av. de Portugal, Motael, Dili; tel. 3310609; fax 3322179; e-mail thaidli@mfa.go.th; Ambassador Wiwat Kunthonthien.

Turkey: Çankaya Cad. Kader Sok. 45/3–4, 06700 Gaziosmanpaşa, Ankara; tel. (312) 4673059; fax (312) 4277284; Ambassador Kanya Chaiman.

Turkmenistan: 744000 Aşgabat; Ambassador Kanya Chaiman.

United Arab Emirates: POB 47466, Abu Dhabi; tel. (2) 6421772; fax (2) 6421773; e-mail thaiauh@emirates.net.ae; Ambassador Karn Chiranond.

United Kingdom: 29–30 Queen's Gate, London, SW7 5JB; tel. (20) 7589-2944; fax (20) 7823-7492; e-mail thaiduto@btinternet.com; internet www .thaiembassyuk.org.uk; Ambassador Kitti Wasinondh.

United States of America: 1024 Wisconsin Ave, NW, Washington, DC 20007; tel. (202) 944-3600; fax (202) 944-3611; e-mail info@thaiembdc.org; internet www.thaiembdc.org; Ambassador Krit Garnjana-Goonchoor.

Viet Nam: 63–65 Hoang Dieu, Hanoi; tel. (4) 8235092; fax (4) 8235088; e-mail thaiemhn@netnam.org.vn; internet www.thaiembassy.org.vn; Ambassador Kittiphong Na Ranong.

DIPLOMATIC MISSIONS OF TIMOR-LESTE

United Nations: 866 Second Ave, 9th Floor, New York, NY 10017; tel. (212) 759-3675; fax (212) 759-4196; e-mail timor-leste@un.int; internet www.un .int/timor-leste; Permanent Representative Nelson Santos.

Australia: 25 Blaxland Crescent, Griffith, ACT 2603; tel. (2) 6260-8800; fax (2) 6239-7682; e-mail TL_Emb.Canberra@bigpond.com; Ambassador Hernani Filomena Coelho Da Silva.

Belgium: 12 ave de Cortenbergh, BP 198, 1040 Brussels; tel. (2) 280-00-96; fax (2) 280-02-77; Ambassador José António Amorim Dias.

China, People's Republic: Rm 156, Gold Island Diplomatic Compound, 1 Xi Ba He Nan Lu, Beijing 100028; tel. (10) 64403072; fax (10) 64403071; e-mail rdtlemb_beijing@yahoo.com; Ambassador Olimpio Maria Alves Gomes Miranda Branco.

Indonesia: Gedung Surya, 11th Floor, Jalan M. H. Thamrin, Kav. 9, Jakarta; tel. (21) 3902678; fax (21) 3902660; AmbassadorOlivio de Jesus Amaral.

Japan: Rokuban-cho House, 1/F, 3-4, Rokuban-cho, Chiyoda-ku, Tokyo 102-0085; tel. (3) 3238-0210; Ambassador Domingos Sarmento Alves.

Malaysia: 62 Jalan Ampang Hilir, 55000 Kuala Lumpur; tel. (3) 42562046; fax (3) 42562016; e-mail embaixada_tl_kl@yahoo.com; Ambassador Juvêncio de Jesus Martins.

Mozambique: Maputo; Chargé d'affaires a.i. Marina Alkatiri.

Portugal: Av. Infante Santo 17, 6°, 1350-175 Lisbon; tel. (21) 3933730; fax (21) 3933739; e-mail embaixada.rdtl@mail.telepac.pt; Ambassador MANUEL ABRANTES.

United States of America: 3415 Massachusetts Ave, NW, Washington, DC 20008; tel. (202) 965-1515; fax (202) 965-1517; e-mail embtlus@earthlink.net; Ambassador Jose Luis Guterres.

DIPLOMATIC MISSIONS OF TOGO

United Nations: 112 East 40th St, New York, NY 10016; tel. (212) 490-3455; fax (212) 983-6684; e-mail togo@un.int; e-mail onu@republicoftogo.com; Permanent Representative ROLAND YAO KPOTSRA.

Belgium: 264 ave de Tervueren, 1150 Brussels; tel. (2) 770-55-63; fax (2) 771-50-75; e-mail ambassade.togo@skynet.be; Ambassador Félix Kodjo Sagbo.

Canada: 12 Range Rd, Ottawa, ON K1N 8J3; tel. (613) 238-5916; fax (613) 235-6425; e-mail ambatogoca@hotmail.com; Ambassador BAWOUMONDOM AMELETE.

China, People's Republic: 11 Dong Zhi Men Wai Dajie, Beijing 100600; tel. (10) 65322202; fax (10) 65325884; Ambassador Nolana Ta-Ama.

Congo, Democratic Republic: 3 ave de la Vallée, BP 10117, Kinshasa; tel. (12) 30666; Ambassador MAMA GNOFAM.

Ethiopia: Addis Ababa; Ambassador Tilioufei Koffi Esaw.

France: 8 rue Alfred Roll, 75017 Paris; tel. 1-43-80-12-13; fax 1-43-80-06-05; e-mail france@ambassadetogo.org; internet www.ambassadetogo.org; Ambassador TCHAO SOTO BERE.

Gabon: BP 14160, Libreville; tel. 73-29-04; fax 73-32-61; Ambassador Ahlonko Koffi Aquereburu.

Germany: Grabbeallee 43, 13156 Berlin; tel. (30) 49908968; fax (30) 49908967; e-mail bbotschafttogo@web.de; internet www.botschaft-togo.de; Ambassador ESSOHANAM COMLA PAKA.

Ghana: Togo House, near Cantonments Circle, POB C120, Accra; tel. (21) 777950; fax (21) 765659; e-mail togamba@ighmail.com; Ambassador Jean-Pierre Gbikpi-Benissan.

Libya: POB 3420, Sharia Khaled ibn al-Walid, Tripoli; tel. (21) 4447551; fax (21) 3332423; Ambassador TCHAO SOTOU BERE.

Nigeria: 96 Awolowo Rd, SW Ikoyi, POB 1435, Lagos; tel. (1) 2617449; Ambassador Foli-Agbenozan Tettekpoe.

United States of America: 2208 Massachusetts Ave, NW, Washington, DC 20008; tel. (202) 234-4212; fax (202) 232-3190; Chargé d'affaires a.i. T. H. LOREMPO LANDJERGUE.

DIPLOMATIC MISSIONS OF TONGA

United Nations: 250 East 51st St, New York, NY 10022; tel. (917) 369-1025; fax (917) 369-1024; e-mail tongaunmission@aol.com; Permanent Representative Fekitamoeloa 'Utoikamanu.

China, People's Republic: Suite 3002, Embassy House, No. 18, Dong Zhi Men Wai Xiao Jie, Beijing 100027; tel. (10) 84499757; fax (10) 84499758; Ambassador EMELINE UHEINA TUITA.

United Kingdom: 36 Molyneux St, London, W1H 5BQ; tel. (20) 7724-5828; fax (20) 7723-9074; e-mail enquiries@tongahighcom.co.uk; High Commr Dr Sione Ngongo Kioa.

United States of America: 250 East 51st St, New York, NY 10022; tel. (917) 369-1025; fax (917) 369-1024; Ambassador FEKITAMOELOA 'UTOIKAMANU.

DIPLOMATIC MISSIONS OF TRINIDAD AND TOBAGO

United Nations: 820 Second Ave, 5th Floor, New York, NY 10017; tel. (212) 697-7620; fax (212) 682-3580; e-mail tto@un.int; Permanent Representative Philip R. A. Sealy.

Belgium: 14 ave de la Faisanderie, 1150 Brussels; tel. (2) 762-94-00; fax (2) 772-27-83; e-mail info@embtrinbago.be; Chargé d'affaires a.i. KEITH DE FREITAS.

Brazil: SHIS, QL 02, Conj. 02, Casa 01, 71665-028 Brasília, DF; tel. (61) 3365-1132; fax (61) 3365-1733; e-mail trinbago@terra.com.br; Ambassador Monica June Clement.

Canada: 200 First Ave, Ottawa, ON K1S 2G6; tel. (613) 232-2418; fax (613) 232-4349; e-mail ottawa@ttmissions.com; internet www.ttmissions.com; High Commissioner CAMILLE ROBINSON-REGIS.

India: 6/25 Shanti Niketan, New Delhi 110 021; tel. (11) 24118427; fax (11) 24118463; e-mail admin@hctt.org; High Commissioner Pundit Manideo Persad.

Jamaica: First Life Bldg, 3rd Floor, 60 Knutsford Blvd, Kingston 5; tel. 926-5730; fax 926-5801; High Commissioner YVONNE GITTENS-JOSEPH.

Nigeria: 3a Tiamiyu Savage St, Victoria Island, POB 6392, Marina, Lagos; tel. (1) 2612087; fax (1) 612732; High Commissioner Dr Harold Robertson.

South Africa: Pretoria 258 Lawley St, Waterkloof, 0181 Pretoria; POB 95872, Waterkloof, Pretoria 0145; tel. (12) 4609688; fax (12) 3467302; e-mail tthepretoria@telkomsa.net; High Commissioner DONNA MARINA CARTER.

United Kingdom: 42 Belgrave Sq., London, SW1X 8NT; tel. (20) 7245-9351; fax (20) 7823-1065; e-mail tthc.info@btconnect.net; High Commr Glenda P. Morean-Phillip.

United States of America: 1708 Massachusetts Ave, NW, Washington, DC 20036; tel. (202) 467-6490; fax (202) 785-3130; e-mail info@ttembwash.com; internet www.bordeglobal.com/ttembassy; Ambassador MARINA ANNETTE VALERE.

Venezuela: Quinta Serrana, 4a Avda entre 7 y 8 Transversales, Altamira, Caracas; tel. (212) 261-5796; fax (212) 261-9801; e-mail embassytt@cantv .net; Ambassador Razia Ali.

DIPLOMATIC MISSIONS OF TUNISIA

United Nations: 31 Beekman Pl., New York, NY 10022; tel. (212) 751-7503; fax (212) 751-0569; e-mail tunisia@un.int; internet www.tunisiaonline.com/ tunisia-un/index.html; Permanent Representative HABIB MANSOUR.

Algeria: 5 rue du Bois, Hydra, 16405 Algiers; tel. (21) 60-13-88; fax (21) 69-23-16; Ambassador Muhammad el-Fadhal Khalil.

Argentina: Ciudad de la Paz 3086, C1429ACD Buenos Aires; tel. (11) 4544-2618; fax (11) 4545-6369; e-mail atbuenosaires@infovia.com.ar; Ambassador FETHI MANAI.

Austria: Sieveringerstr. 187, 1190 Vienna; tel. (1) 581-52-81; fax (1) 581-55-92; e-mail at.vienne@aol.at; Ambassador Prof. Muhammad Daouas.

Bahrain: POB 26911, House 54, Rd 3601, Area 336, Manama; tel. 17714149; fax 17715702; e-mail atmanama@batelco.bh; Ambassador KHALED AZ-ZITOUNI.

Belgium: 278 ave de Tervueren, 1150 Brussels; tel. (2) 771-73-95; fax (2) 771-94-33; e-mail amb.detunisie@brutele.be; Ambassador Abdessalem Hetira.

Brazil: SHIS, QI 11, Conj. 01, Casa 23, 71625-210 Brasília, DF; tel. (61) 3248-7277; fax (61) 3248-7355; e-mail at.brasilia@terra.com.br; Ambassador SEIFEDDINE CHERIF.

Cameroon: rue de Rotary, Quartier Bastos, BP 6074, Yaoundé; tel. 2220-3368; fax 2221-0507; Chargé d'affaires a.i. Mohamed Nacer Kort.

Canada: 515 O'Connor St, Ottawa, ON K1S 3P8; tel. (613) 237-0330; fax (613) 237-7939; e-mail atottawa@comnet.ca; Ambassador MOULDI ESSAKRI.

China, People's Republic: 1 Dong Jie, San Li Tun, Beijing 100600; tel. (10) 65322435; fax (10) 65325818; e-mail at_beijing@public.netchina.com.cn; Ambassador DrMohamed Sahbi Basli.

Congo, Democratic Republic: 67–69 ave du Cercle, BP 1498, Kinshasa; tel. (12) 33167; e-mail atkinshasa@yahoo.fr; Ambassador (vacant).

Côte d'Ivoire: Immeuble Shell, ave Lamblin, 01 BP 3906, Abidjan 01; tel. 20-22-61-23; fax 20-22-61-24; Ambassador Zine El Abidine Terras.

Czech Republic: Nad Kostelem 8, 147 00 Prague 4; tel. 244460652; fax 244460825; e-mail atprague@vol.cz; Ambassador RADHOUANE LARIF.

Egypt: 26 Sharia el-Jazirah, Cairo (Zamalek); tel. (2) 3418962; Ambassador Ash-Shazli an-Nafati.

Ethiopia: Wereda 17, Kebele 19, Bole Rd, POB 100069, Addis Ababa; tel. (11) 6612063; fax (11) 6614568; Ambassador MUHAMMAD ADEL SMAOUI.

Finland: Liisankatu 14b 31, 00170 Helsinki; tel. (9) 6803960; fax (9) 68039610; e-mail at.helsinki@kolumbus.fi; Chargé d'affaires a.i. Tarek Ben Salem.

France: 25 rue Barbet-de-Jouy, 75007 Paris; tel. 1-45-55-95-98; fax 1-45-56-02-64; e-mail atn.paris@wanadoo.fr; internet www.amb-tunisie.fr; Ambassador RAOUF NAJJAR.

Gabon: BP 3844, Libreville; tel. 73-28-41; Ambassador Ezzedine Kerkeni.

Germany: Lindenallee 16, 14050 Berlin; tel. (30) 3641070; fax (30) 30820683; Ambassador MONCEF BEN ABDALLAH.

Greece: Odos Antheon & Odos Marathonodromou 2, Palaio Psychiko, 154 52 Athens; tel. (210) 6717590; fax (210) 6713432; e-mail atathina@otenet.gr; Ambassador Naceur Mestiri.

Hungary: 1025 Budapest, Pusztaszei u. 24 A; tel. (1) 336-1616; fax (1) 325-7291; e-mail at.budapest@axelero.hu; Chargé d'affaires ABDELWAHEB BOUZOUITA.

India: A-42 Vasant Marg, Vasant Vihar, New Delhi 110 057; tel. (11) 26145346; fax (11) 26145301; e-mail embtundelhi@dishnetdsl.net; Ambassador Raouf Chatti.

Indonesia: Wisma Dharmala Sakti, 11th Floor, Jalan Jenderal Sudirman 32, Jakarta 10220; tel. (21) 5703432; fax (21) 5700016; e-mail atjkt@uninet.net.id; Ambassador FAYCAL GOUIA.

Iran: No. 12, Shahid Dr Lavasani, Tehran; tel. (21) 22704161; e-mail at-teheran@safineh.net; Ambassador Hatem Essayem.

Iraq: 1/49/617 Hay al-Andalus, Baghdad; tel. (1) 542-0602; fax (1) 542-8585; Ambassador (vacant).

Italy: Via Asmara 7, 00199 Roma; tel. (06) 8603060; fax (06) 86218204; e-mail at.roma@tiscali.it; Ambassador Habib Mansour.

Japan: 3-6-6, Kudan-Minami, Chiyoda-ku, Tokyo 102-0074; tel. (3) 3511-6622; fax (3) 3511-6600; internet www.tunisia.or.jp; Ambassador NOUREDDINE HACHED.

Jordan: POB 17185, Amman 11195; tel. (6) 5922746; fax (6) 5922769; e-mail atamman@go.com.jo; Ambassador Salah ad-Din al-Jammali.

Korea, Republic: 1-17, Dongbinggo-dong, Yeongsan-gu, Seoul 140-809; tel. (2) 790-4334; fax (2) 790-4333; e-mail ambtnkor@kornet.net; Ambassador MUSTAPHA KHAMMARI.

Kuwait: POB 5976, 13060 Safat, Nuzha, Plot 2, Nuzha St, Villa 45, Kuwait City; tel. 2542144; fax 2528995; e-mail tunemrku@ncc.moc.kw; Ambassador Hichem Bayoudh.

Lebanon: Hazmieh, Mar-Takla, Beirut; tel. (5) 457431; fax (5) 950434; Ambassador NAZIHA ZARROUK.

Libya: POB 613, Sharia Bashir al-Ibrahim, Tripoli; tel. (21) 3331051; fax (21) 4447600; High Representative Muhammad B'rahem.

Mali: Quartier du Fleuve, Bamako; tel. 223-28-91; fax 222-17-55; Ambassador FARHAT CHEOUR.

Malta: Valletta Rd, Attard ATD 9052; tel. 21417070; fax 21413414; e-mail at.lavalette@maltanet.net; Ambassador Mohamed Ali Ghanzoui.

Mauritania: BP 681, Nouakchott; tel. 525-28-71; fax 525-18-27; Ambassador ABDEL WEHAB JEMAL.

Morocco: 6 ave de Fès et 1 rue d'Ifrane, 10000 Rabat; tel. (3) 7730636; fax (3) 7730637; Ambassador Salah Baccari.

Netherlands: Gentsestraat 98, 2587 HX The Hague; tel. (70) 3512251; fax (70) 3514323; e-mail ambassadetunisie@wanadoo.nl; Ambassador MUHAMMAD SALAH TEKAYA.

Norway: Haakon VIIs gt. 5b, 0161 Oslo; tel. 22-83-19-17; fax 22-83-24-12; e-mail at.oslo@online.no; Chargé d'affaires a.i. Nehrou al-Arbi.

Oman: Al-Ensharah Street, Way No. 1507, POB 220, Muscat 115; tel. 24603486; fax 24697778; Ambassador HAMMOUDA RIHANI.

Pakistan: 221, St 21, E-7, Islamabad; tel. (51) 2652781; fax (51) 2653564; Ambassador Souhier Dhaoudi.

Poland: 00-459 Warsaw, ul. Myśliwiecka 14; tel. (22) 6286330; fax (22) 6216298; e-mail at.varsovie@it.com.pl; Ambassador BÉCHIR CHEBAANE.

Portugal: Rua Rodrigo Rebelo 16, 1400-318 Lisbon; tel. (21) 3010330; fax (21) 3016817; e-mail at.lisbonne@netcabo.pt; Ambassador Muhammad Ridha Farhat.

Romania: 010517 Bucharest 1, Str. Mihai Eminescu 50–54, 4th Floor, Rm 10; tel. (21) 2101197; fax (21) 2101114; Ambassador SALOUA BAHRI.

Russian Federation: 113105 Moscow, ul. M. Nikitskaya 28/1; tel. (495) 291-28-58; fax (495) 291-75-88; Ambassador Muhammad Bellagi.

Saudi Arabia: POB 94368, Riyadh 11693; tel. (1) 488-7900; fax (1) 488-7641; Ambassador KACEM BOUSNINA.

Senegal: rue Alpha Hachamiyou Tall, BP 3127, Dakar; tel. 33-823-4747; fax 33-823-7204; Ambassador Jalel Lakhdar.

Serbia: 11000 Belgrade, Vase Pelagića 19; tel. (11) 3691961; fax (11) 3690642; e-mail at.belgr@eunet.yu; Ambassador HOURIA FERCHICHI.

South Africa: 850 Church St, Arcadia, Pretoria 0083; POB 56535, Arcadia 0007; tel. (12) 3426223; fax (12) 3426284; Ambassador Ali Goutali.

Spain: Avda Alfonso XIII 64–68, 28016 Madrid; tel. (91) 4473508; fax (91) 5938416; Ambassador HABIB M'BAREK.

Sudan: St 15, 35, al-Amarat, Khartoum; tel. (183) 487947; fax (183) 487950; e-mail at_khartoum@yahoo.fr; Ambassador Abdessalem Bouaïcha.

Sweden: Narvavägen 32, 1st Floor, POB 24030, 104 50 Stockholm; tel. (8) 545-855-20; fax (8) 662-19-75; e-mail at.stockholm@swipnet.se; Chargé d'affaires a.i. AMMAR AMARI.

Switzerland: Kirchenfeldstr. 63, 3005 Bern; tel. 313528226; fax 313510445; e-mail at.berne@bluewin.ch; Chargé d'affaires a.i. Muhammad Fawzi Blout.

Syria: BP 4114, 6 rue ash-Shafi, blvd Fahim, Mezzeh, Damascus; tel. (11) 6132700; fax (11) 6132704; e-mail at.damas@net.sy; Ambassador HEDI BEN NASR.

Turkey: Kuleli Sok. 12, 06700 Gaziosmanpaşa, Ankara; tel. (312) 4377812; fax (312) 4377100; e-mail at.ankara@superonline.com; Ambassador Ghazi Jomaa.

United Arab Emirates: POB 4166, Abu Dhabi; tel. (2) 6811331; fax (2) 6812707; e-mail ambtunad@emirates.net.ae; Ambassador MUHAMMAD AS-SEDIRI.

United Kingdom: 29 Prince's Gate, London, SW7 1QG; tel. (20) 7584-8117; fax (20) 7584-3205; Ambassador Hamida Mrabet Laâbidi.

United States of America: 1515 Massachusetts Ave, NW, Washington, DC 20005; tel. (202) 862-1850; fax (202) 862-1858; Ambassador MOHAMED NEJIB HACHANA.

Yemen: POB 2561, Diplomatic area, St No. 22, San'a; tel. (1) 240458; Ambassador (vacant).

Zimbabwe: Harare; tel. (4) 791570; fax (4) 727224; Ambassador HAMID ZAOUCHE.

DIPLOMATIC MISSIONS OF TURKEY

United Nations: 821 United Nations Plaza, 10th Floor, New York, NY 10017; tel. (212) 949-0150; fax (212) 949-0086; e-mail turkey@un.int; internet www.un.int/turkey; Permanent Representative Baki Ilkin.

Afghanistan: House 134, Shah Mahmoud Ghazi Khan St, Kabul; tel. (20) 2101581; fax (20) 2101579; e-mail etokdemir@mfa.gov.tr; Ambassador İSMAIL ETHEM TOKDEMIR.

Albania: Rruga Konferenca e Kavajes 31, Tirana; tel. (4) 233399; fax (4) 232719; e-mail turkemb@interalb.al; Ambassador Suphan Erkula.

Algeria: Villa Dar el-Ouard, chemin de la Rochelle, blvd Col Bougara, Algiers; tel. (21) 23-00-04; fax (21) 23-01-12; e-mail cezayir.be@mfa.gov.tr; Ambassador AHMET BIGALI.

Argentina: 11 de Septiembre 1382, C1426BKN Buenos Aires; tel. (11) 4788-3239; fax (11) 4784-9179; e-mail turquia@fibertel.com.ar; Ambassador Hayri Hayret Yalav.

Australia: 6 Moonah Place, Yarralumla, ACT 2600; tel. (2) 6234-0000; fax (2) 6273-4402; e-mail turkembs@bigpond.net.au; internet www.turkishembassy.org.au; Ambassador N. MURAT ERSAVCI.

Austria: Prinz-Eugen-Str. 40, 1040 Vienna; tel. (1) 505-73-38-0; fax (1) 505-36-60; e-mail tuerkische-botschaft@chello.at; internet www.tuerkischebotschaftwien.at; Ambassador Selim Yenel.

Azerbaijan: 1000 Baku, Khagani küç. 27; tel. (12) 444-73-20; fax (12) 444-73-55; e-mail bakube@artel.net.az; Ambassador HUSEYIN AVNI KARSLI.

Bahrain: POB 10821, Sehl Centre, 5th Floor, Bldg 81, Rd 1702, Area 317, Manama; tel. 17533448; fax 17536557; e-mail tcbahrbe@batelco.com.bh; Ambassador Khaldoun Othman.

Bangladesh: House 14A, Rd 62, Gulshan 2, Dhaka 1212; tel. (2) 8823536; fax (2) 8823873; e-mail dakkabe@citech-bd.com; Ambassador FERIT ERGIN.

Belarus: 220050 Minsk, vul. Valadarskaya 6; tel. (17) 227-13-83; fax (17) 227-27-46; e-mail trembassy@forenet.by; Ambassador Birnur Fertekligil.

Belgium: 4 rue Montoyer, 1000 Brussels; tel. (2) 513-40-95; fax (2) 514-07-48; e-mail info@turkey.be; internet www.turkey.be; Ambassador FUAT TANLAY.

Bosnia and Herzegovina: 71000 Sarajevo, Hamdije Kreševljakovića 5; tel. (33) 472437; fax (33) 445260; e-mail turksa@bih.net.ba; Ambassador Büllent Tulun.

Brazil: SES, Av. das Nações, Quadra 805, Lote 23, 70452-900 Brasília, DF; tel. (61) 3242-1850; fax (61) 3242-1448; e-mail turquia@conectanet.com.br; Ambassador AHMET GÜRKAN.

Bulgaria: 1087 Sofia, bul. V. Levski 80; tel. (2) 935-55-00; fax (2) 981-93-58; e-mail turkel@techno-link.com; Ambassador Haydar Berk.

Canada: 197 Wurtemburg St, Ottawa, ON K1N 8L9; tel. (613) 789-4044; fax (613) 789-3442; e-mail turkishottawa@mfa.gov.tr; internet www.turkishembassy.com; Ambassador AYDEMIR ERMAN.

Chile: Edif. Montolin, Of. 71, Monseñor Sotero Sanz 55, Providencia, Santiago; tel. (2) 231-8952; fax (2) 231-7762; e-mail embturquia@123.cl; Ambassador Aysenur Alpaslan.

China, People's Republic: 9 Dong Wu Jie, San Li Tun, Beijing 100600; tel. (10) 65322490; fax (10) 65325480; e-mail embassy@turkey.org.cn; internet www.turkey.org.cn; Ambassador OKTAY ÖZÜYE.

Congo, Democratic Republic: 18 ave Pumbu, BP 7817, Kinshasa; tel. (88) 01207; fax (88) 04740; e-mail tckinsbe@raga.net; Ambassador Mehmet Özyildiz.

Croatia: 10000 Zagreb, Masarykova 3/II; tel. (1) 4855200; fax (1) 4855606; e-mail turkishemb@zg.t-com.hr; Chargé d'affaires a.i. GÜL BÜYÜKERSEN ORAL.

Cuba: Avda 5, No 3805, entre 36 y 40, Miramar, Havana; tel. (7) 204-1205; fax (7) 204-2899; e-mail turkemb@ip.etecsa.cu; Ambassador Kandriye Sanivar Kizildeli.

Czech Republic: Na Ořechovce 69, 162 00 Prague 616; tel. 224311402; fax 224311279; e-mail turkembprague@ms.easynet.cz; Ambassador KORAY TARGAY.

Denmark: Rosbæksvej 15, 2100 Copenhagen Ø; tel. 39-20-27-88; fax 39-20-51-66; e-mail turkembassy@internet.dk; internet www.turkishembassy.dk; Ambassador Melih Mehmet Akat.

Egypt: 25 Sharia Felaki, Cairo (Bab el-Louk); tel. (2) 7963318; fax (2) 7958110; Ambassador ŞAFAK GÖKTÜRK.

Estonia: Narva mnt. 30, Tallinn 10152; tel. 627-2880; fax 627-2885; e-mail tallinn@turkishembassy.ee; Ambassador Fatma Sule Soysal.

Ethiopia: POB 1506, Addis Ababa; tel. (11) 6613161; fax (11) 6611688; e-mail turk.emb@ethionet.et; Ambassador ALI RIZA COLAK.

Finland: Puistokatu 1b A 3, 00140 Helsinki; tel. (9) 6811030; fax (9) 655011; e-mail turkish.embassy@welho.com; internet www.turkinsuurlahetysto.fi; Ambassador Reha Keskintepe.

France: 16 ave de Lamballe, 75016 Paris; tel. 1-53-92-71-12; fax 1-45-20-41-91; e-mail paris.be@mfa.gov.tr; Ambassador OSMAN KORUTÜRK.

Georgia: 0102 Tbilisi, D. Aghmashenebeli 61; tel. (32) 25-20-72; fax (32) 22-06-66; e-mail tiblisbe@dsl.ge; Ambassador Ertan Tezgor.

Germany: Rungestr. 9, 10179 Berlin; tel. (30) 275850; fax (30) 27590915; e-mail turk.em.berlin@t-online.de; internet www.tuerkischebotschaft.de; Ambassador MEHMET ALI IRTEMÇELIK.

Greece: Odos Vassileos Gheorghiou 8b, 106 74 Athens; tel. (210) 7263000; fax (210) 7229597; e-mail atina.be@mfa.gov.tr; Ambassador Ahmet Oğuz Çelikkol.

Hungary: 1062 Budapest, Andrássy u. 123; tel. (1) 344-5025; fax (1) 344-5143; e-mail budapest@turkishembassy.hu; Ambassador UMUR APAYDIN.

India: 50n Nyaya Marg, Chanakyapuri, New Delhi 110 021; tel. (11) 26889054; fax (11) 26881409; e-mail tembdelhi@mantraonline.com; Ambassador Hasan Gogus.

Indonesia: Jalan H. R. Rasuna Said, Kav. 1, Kuningan, Jakarta 12950; tel. (21) 5256250; fax (21) 5226056; e-mail cakartabe@telkom.net; Ambassador FERYAL ÇOTUR.

Iran: POB 11365-8758, 314 Ferdowsi Ave, Africa Ave, Tehran; tel. (21) 33118997; fax (21) 33117928; e-mail tctahranbe@parsonline.net; Ambassador Selim Kanaosmanoğlu.

Iraq: 2/8 al-Waziriyah, Baghdad; tel. (1) 422-0022; fax (1) 422-8353; Ambassador DERYA KAMBAY.

Ireland: 11 Clyde Rd, Dublin 4; tel. (1) 6685240; fax (1) 6685014; e-mail turkembassy@eircom.net; Ambassador Turan Morali.

Israel: 202 Rehov Hayarkon, Tel-Aviv 63405; tel. 3-5171731; fax 3-5176157; e-mail turqua2@netvision.net.il; Ambassador FERIDUN SINIRLIOĞLU.

Italy: Palazzo Gamberini, Via Palestro 28, 00185 Roma; tel. (06) 445941; fax (06) 4941526; e-mail roma.be@libero.it; internet www.ambasciataditurchia.it; Ambassador Sitki Ugur Ziyal.

Japan: 2-33-6, Jingumae, Shibuya-ku, Tokyo 150-0001; tel. (3) 3470-5131; fax (3) 3470-5136; e-mail embassy@turkey.jp; internet www.turkey.jp; Ambassador SERMET ATACANLI.

Jordan: POB 2062, Amman 11181; tel. (6) 4641251; fax (6) 4612353; e-mail ammanbe@nets.com.jo; Ambassador Ali Koprulu.

Kazakhstan: 050010 Almaty, Tole bi 29; tel. (727) 278-41-65; fax (727) 278-41-68; e-mail almatyturkbe@gmail.com; Ambassador TANER SEBEN.

Kenya: Gigiri Rd, off Limuru Rd, POB 64748, 00620 Nairobi; tel. (20) 7120404; fax (20) 7122778; e-mail tcbenair@accesskenya.com; internet www.turkishembassy.or.ke; Ambassador Levent Şahinkaya.

Korea, Republic: Vivien Corpn Bldg, 4th Floor, 4-52, Seobinggo-dong, Yeongsan-gu, Seoul; tel. (2) 794-0255; fax (2) 797-8546; e-mail tcseulbe@kornet.net; Ambassador DENIZ OZMEN.

Kuwait: POB 20627, 13067 Safat, Block 16, Plot 10, Istiqlal St, Kuwait City; tel. 2531785; fax 2560653; e-mail turkishembassykuwait@hotmail.com; internet www.turkish-embassy.org.kw; Ambassador Şakir Fakılı.

Kyrgyzstan: 720040 Bishkek, Moskovskaya 89; tel. (312) 62-23-54; fax (312) 66-05-19; e-mail biskbe@infotel.kg; Ambassador FATMA SERPIL ALPMAN.

Latvia: A. Pumpura iela 2, 1010 Rīga; tel. 6782-1600; fax 6732-0334; e-mail turkishembassy.riga@gmail.com; Ambassador Duray Polat.

Lebanon: POB 70-666, zone II, rue 1, Rabieh, Beirut; tel. (4) 520929; fax (4) 407557; e-mail trbebeyr@intracom.net.lb; Ambassador SAKIR TORUNLAR.

Libya: POB 947, Sharia Zaviya Dahmani, Tripoli; tel. (21) 3401140; fax (21) 3401146; e-mail trablusbe@yahoo.com; Ambassador Riza Erkmenoğlu.

Lithuania: Didžioji g. 37, Vilnius 01128; tel. (5) 264-9570; fax (5) 212-3277; e-mail turemvil@eunet.lt; Ambassador OGUZ ÖZGE.

Luxembourg: 49 rue Siggy vu Lëtzebuerg, 1933 Luxembourg; tel. 44-32-81; fax 44-32-81-34; e-mail ambtrlux@pt.lu; Chargé d'affaires a.i. Ihsan Sakarya.

Macedonia, former Yugoslav Republic: 1000 Skopje, Slavej Planina bb; tel. (2) 3113270; fax (2) 3117024; e-mail turkish@mol.com.mk; Ambassador TANER KARAKAŞ.

Malaysia: 118 Jalan U Thant, 55000 Kuala Lumpur; tel. (3) 42572225; fax (3) 42572227; e-mail turkbe@tm.net.my; Ambassador Barlas Ozener.

Mexico: Monte Líbano 885, Col. Lomas de Chapultepec, Del. Miguel Hidalgo, 11000 México, DF; tel. (55) 5282-5446; fax (55) 5282-4894; e-mail turkem@mail.internet.com.mx; Ambassador AHMET SEDAT BANGUOGLU.

Moldova: Chişinău, str. Valeriau Cupcea 60; tel. (22) 50-91-00; fax (22) 22-55-28; e-mail tremb@moldova.md; Ambassador Fatma Firat Topçuoğlu.

Mongolia: Enkh Taivny Örgön Chölöö 5, Ulan Bator (CPOB 1009); tel. (11) 311200; fax (11) 313992; Ambassador AHMET ASIM ARAR.

Morocco: 7 ave Abdelkrim Benjelloun, 10000 Rabat; tel. (3) 7661522; fax (3) 7660476; e-mail amb-tur-rabat@iam.net.ma; Ambassador Haluk Ilıcak.

Netherlands: Jan Evertstraat 15, 2514 BS The Hague; tel. (70) 3604912; fax (70) 3617969; e-mail turkishembassy@euronet.nl; Ambassador SELAHATTIN ALPAR.

New Zealand: 15–17 Murphy St, Level 8, POB 12-248, Wellington; tel. (4) 472-1292; fax (4) 472-1277; e-mail turkem@xtra.co.nz; Ambassador Ugur Ergun.

Nigeria: 3 Okunola Martins Close, Ikoyi, POB 56252, Lagos; tel. (1) 2691140; fax (1) 2693040; e-mail turkemb@infoweb.abs.net; Ambassador ÖMER SAHINKAYA.

Norway: Halvdan Svartesgt. 5, 0244 Oslo; tel. 22-12-87-50; fax 22-55-62-63; e-mail postmaster@oslo-turkish-embassy.com; Ambassador Mehmet Kazim Görkay.

Oman: Bldg No. 3270, Street No. 3042, Shati al-Qurum, POB 47, Mutrah 115; tel. 24697050; fax 24697053; e-mail turemmus@omantel.net.om; Ambassador ENGIN TÜRKER.

Pakistan: St 1, Diplomatic Enclave 1, Islamabad; tel. (51) 8319800; fax (51) 2278752; e-mail turkemb@dsl.net.pk; internet www.turkishembassy.org.pk; Ambassador Rauf Engin Soysal.

Philippines: 2268 Paraiso St, Dasmariñas Village, Makati City, Metro Manila; tel. (2) 8439705; fax (2) 8439702; Ambassador ADNAN BASAGA.

Poland: 02-622 Warsaw, ul. Malczewskiego 32; tel. (22) 6464323; fax (22) 6463757; e-mail turkemb@zigzag.pl; Ambassador (vacant).

Portugal: Av. das Descobertas 22, 1400-092 Lisbon; tel. (21) 3003110; fax (21) 3017934; e-mail info-turk@mail.telepac.pt; Ambassador ÖMER KAYA TÜRKMEN.

Qatar: POB 1977, Doha; tel. 4951300; fax 4951320; e-mail tcdohabe@qatar.net.qa; Ambassador Mithat Rende.

Romania: 010575 Bucharest, Calea Dorobanţilor 72; tel. (21) 2063700; fax (21) 2063737; e-mail bukres.be@mfa.gov.tr; Ambassador AYŞE SINIRLIOGLU.

Russian Federation: 119121 Moscow, 7-i Rostovskii per. 12; tel. (495) 956-55-95; fax (495) 956-55-97; e-mail turemb@co.ru; Ambassador Kurtuluş Taşkent.

Saudi Arabia: POB 94390, Riyadh 11693; tel. (1) 482-0101; fax (1) 488-7823; e-mail turkishembassy@sps.net.sa; Ambassador UGUR DOGAN.

Senegal: ave des Ambassadeurs, Fann Résidence, BP 6060, Etoile, Dakar; tel. 33-869-2542; fax 33-825-6977; e-mail trambdkr@sentoo.sn; Ambassador Ali Savut.

Serbia: 11000 Belgrade, Krunska 1; tel. (11) 3235431; fax (11) 3235433; e-mail turem@eunet.yu; Ambassador AHMET SUHA UMAR.

Singapore: 2 Shenton Way 10-03, SGX Centre 1, Singapore 068804; tel. 65333390; fax 65333360; e-mail turksin@singnet.com.sg; internet www.turkishembassy.org.sg; Ambassador Bülent Meriç.

Slovakia: Holubyho 11, 811 03 Bratislava; tel. (2) 5441-5504; fax (2) 5441-3145; e-mail testta@nextra.sk; Ambassador TUNÇ ÜGDÜL.

Slovenia: 1000 Ljubljana, Livarska 4; tel. (1) 2364150; fax (1) 4365240; e-mail vrtucije@siol.net; internet www.turkish-embassy.si; Ambassador Melek Sina Baydur.

Somalia: Via Km 6, POB 2833, Mogadishu; tel. (1) 81975; .

South Africa: 1067 Church St, Hatfield, Pretoria 0083; POB 56014, Arcadia 0007; tel. (12) 3426055; fax (12) 3426052; e-mail pretbe@global.co.za; internet www.turkishembassy.co.za; Ambassador Ferhat Ataman.

Spain: Rafael Calvo 18, 2°, 28010 Madrid; tel. (91) 3198111; fax (91) 3086602; e-mail info@tcmadridbe.org; internet www.tcmadridbe.org; Ambassador ENDER ARAT.

Sudan: St 29, 31, New Extension, POB 771, Khartoum; tel. (183) 794215; fax (183) 794218; e-mail trembkh@sudanmail.net; Ambassador Dr Ali Engin Oba.

Sweden: Dag Hammarskjölds Väg 20, POB 24105, 104 51 Stockholm; tel. (8) 23-08-40; fax (8) 663-55-14; e-mail turkbe@turkemb.se; internet www.turkemb.se; Ambassador NECIP EGÜZ.

Switzerland: Lombachweg 33, 3006 Bern; tel. 313597070; fax 313528819; e-mail tcbern@tr-botschaft.ch; internet www.tr-botschaft.ch; Ambassador Alev Kiliç.

Syria: BP 3738, 56–58 ave Ziad bin Abou Soufian, Damascus; tel. (11) 33501930; fax (11) 3339243; e-mail sambe@mfa.gov.tr; Ambassador KHALED CEVIK.

Tajikistan: 734019 Dushanbe, Khiyoboni Rudaki 17/2; tel. (372) 21-08-00; fax (372) 51-00-12; e-mail turemdus@tajik.net; Ambassador Akif Ayhan.

Thailand: 61/1 Soi Chatsan, Thanon Suthisarn, Huay Kwang, Bangkok 10310; tel. (2) 274-7262; fax (2) 274-7261; e-mail tcturkbe@mail.cscoms.com; Ambassador CINAR ALDEMIR.

Tunisia: 30 ave d'Afrique, BP 134, al-Menzah V, Tunis; tel. (71) 750-668; fax (71) 767-045; e-mail tunus.be@planet.tn; Ambassador Hüseyin Naci Akıncı.

Turkmenistan: 744007 Aşgabat, ul. Gerogly 9; tel. (12) 35-41-18; fax (12) 39-19-14; e-mail askabat.be@mfa.gov.tr; Ambassador HAKKI AKIL.

Ukraine: 01901 Kyiv, vul. Arsenalna 18; tel. (44) 281-07-51; fax (44) 285-64-23; e-mail kievbe@binet.com.ua; Ambassador Ali Bilge Cankorel.

United Arab Emirates: POB 3204, Abu Dhabi; tel. (2) 4454864; fax (2) 4452522; e-mail tcadbe@eim.ae; Ambassador UMUR APAYDIN.

United Kingdom: 43 Belgrave Sq., London, SW1X 8PA; tel. (20) 7393-0202; fax (20) 7393-0066; e-mail turkish.emb@btclick.com; internet www.turkishembassylondon.org; Ambassador Mehmet Yiğit Alpogan.

United States of America: 2525 Massachusetts Ave, NW, Washington, DC 20008; tel. (202) 612-6700; fax (202) 612-6744; e-mail contact@turkishembassy.org; internet www.turkishembassy.org; Ambassador NABI ŞENSOY.

Uzbekistan: 100000 Tashkent, Ya. G'ulomov ko'ch. 87; tel. (71) 133-03-00; fax (71) 113-03-33; e-mail turemb@bcc.com.uz; Ambassador Reshit Uman.

Vatican City: Via Lovanio 24/1, 00198 Rome, Italy; tel. (06) 85508601; fax (06) 85508660; e-mail vatibe@libero.it; Ambassador MUAMMER DOGAN AKDUR.

Venezuela: Calle Kemal Atatürk, Quinta Turquesa 6, Valle Arriba, Apdo 62078, Caracas 1060-A; tel. (212) 991-0075; fax (212) 992-0442; e-mail turquia@cantv.net; Ambassador Nihat Akyol.

Viet Nam: 4th Floor, North Star Bldg, 4 Da Truong, Hanoi; tel. (4) 8222460; fax (4) 8222458; e-mail turkeyhn@fpt.vn; Ambassador (vacant).

Yemen: POB 18371, as-Safiya, San'a; tel. (1) 241395; Ambassador Türel Özkaro.

DIPLOMATIC MISSIONS OF TURKMENISTAN

United Nations: 866 United Nations Plaza, Suite 424, New York, NY 10021; tel. (212) 486-8908; fax (212) 486-2521; e-mail turkmenistan@un.int; Permanent Representative AKSOLTAN T. ATAEVA.

Afghanistan: House 280, St 13, Lane 3, Wazir Akbar Khan, Kabul; tel. (20) 2300541; e-mail kabulemb@neda.af; Ambassador Aman Mohammady.

Armenia: 0028 Yerevan, Kievian St 19; tel. (10) 22-10-29; fax (10) 22-21-32; e-mail serdar@arminco.com; Ambassador KHIDIR SAPARLIYEV.

Austria: Argentinierstr. 22/11/EG, 1040 Vienna; tel. (1) 503-64-70; fax (1) 503-64-73; e-mail turkmenistan.botschaft@chello.at; Ambassador Esen Aydogdiyev.

Azerbaijan: Baku; tel. (12) 440-99-00; fax (12) 61-39-69; .

Belarus: 220050 Minsk, vul. Kirava 17; tel. (17) 222-34-27; fax (17) 222-33-67; Ambassador Ata Gundogdiyev.

Belgium: 106 blvd Reyers, 1030 Brussels; tel. (2) 648-18-74; fax (2) 648-19-06; e-mail turkmenistan@skynet.be; Ambassador KAKADJAN MOMMADOV.

China, People's Republic: King's Garden, Villa D-26, 18 Xiao Yuan Lu, Beijing; tel. (10) 65326975; fax (10) 65326976; e-mail China@a-1.net.cn; Ambassador (vacant).

France: 13 rue Picot, 75116 Paris; tel. 1-47-55-05-36; fax 1-47-55-05-68; e-mail turkmenamb@free.fr; Ambassador TCHARY G. NIYAZOV.

Germany: Langobardenallee 14, 14052 Berlin; tel. (30) 30102452; fax (30) 30102453; e-mail botschaft-turkmenistan@t-online.de; Ambassador Berdymurat Redjepov.

India: C-11, West End Colony, New Delhi 110 021; tel. (11) 24676526; fax (11) 24676527; e-mail turkmind@starith.net; Ambassador PARAHAT HOMMADOVICH DURDYEV.

Iran: No. 9, 5th Golestan St, Pasdaran Ave, Tehran; tel. (21) 22542178; fax (21) 22580432; e-mail tmnteh@afranet.com; Ambassador Murat Nazarov.

Kazakhstan: 010000 Astana, Otyrar 64; tel. (7172) 28-08-82; e-mail tm_emb@at.kz; Ambassador KURBANMUKHAMMED G. KASYMOV.

Pakistan: House 22a, Nazim-Ud-Din Rd, F-7/1, Islamabad; tel. (51) 2274913; fax (51) 2278790; e-mail turkmen@comsats.net.pk; Ambassador Sapor Berdiniyazov.

Russian Federation: 119019 Moscow, Filippovskii per. 22; tel. (495) 291-66-36; fax (495) 291-09-35; Ambassador KHALNAZAR A. AGAKHANOV.

Syria: Miset, 4097 Ruki ed-Din, 2e étage, Damascus; tel. (11) 2241834; fax (11) 3320905; .

Tajikistan: 734000 Dushanbe, Kuchai Chexov 22; tel. (372) 221-68-84; e-mail embturkm@tjinter.com; Ambassador AKHMED KURBANOV.

Turkey: Koza Sok. 28, 06700 Çankaya, Ankara; tel. (312) 4416122; fax (312) 4417125; e-mail tmankara@ttnet.net.tr; Ambassador Nurberdy Amanmuradov.

Ukraine: 01901 Kyiv, vul. Pushkinska 6; tel. (44) 229-34-49; fax (44) 229-30-34; e-mail ambturkm@ukrpack.net; Ambassador ARSLAN S. NEPESOV.

United Kingdom: 2nd Floor South, St George's House, 14–17 Wells St, London, W1P 3FP; tel. (20) 7255-1071; fax (20) 7323-9184; Ambassador Yazmurad Seryaev.

United States of America: 2207 Massachusetts Ave, NW, Washington, DC 20008; tel. (202) 588-1500; fax (202) 588-0697; e-mail turkmen@mindspring.com; internet www.turkmenistanembassy.org; Ambassador MERET BAIRAMOVICH ORAZOV.

Uzbekistan: 100000 Tashkent, 1-chi Katta Mirobod ko'ch. 10; tel. (71) 120-52-78; fax (71) 120-52-81; Ambassador Soltan Pirmuhamedov.

DIPLOMATIC MISSIONS OF TUVALU

United Nations: 800 Second Ave, Suite 400B, New York, N.Y. 10017; tel. (212) 490-0534; fax (212) 808-4975; Permanent Representative ENELE SOSENE SOPOAGA.

Fiji: 16 Gorrie St, POB 14449, Suva; tel. 3301355; fax 3308479; High Commissioner Tine Leuelu.

DIPLOMATIC MISSIONS OF UGANDA

United Nations: 336 East 45th St, New York, NY 10017; tel. (212) 949-0110; fax (212) 687-4517; e-mail ugandaamb@aol.com; internet www.un.int/uganda; Permanent Representative FRANCIS BUTAGIRA.

Australia: 7 Dunoon St, O'Malley, ACT 2606; tel. (2) 6286-1234; fax (2) 6286-1243; High Commissioner Dr Christopher James Lukabyo.

Belgium: 317 ave de Tervueren, 1150 Brussels; tel. (2) 762-58-25; fax (2) 763-04-38; e-mail ugembrus@brutele.be; Ambassador STEPHEN T. KAPIMPINA KATENTA-APUULI.

Canada: 231 Cobourg St, Ottawa, ON K1N 8J2; tel. (613) 789-7797; fax (613) 789-8909; internet ugandahighcommission.com; High Commissioner George M. Abola.

China, People's Republic: 5 Dong Jie, San Li Tun, Beijing 100600; tel. (10) 65321708; fax (10) 65322242; e-mail info@ugandaembassycn.org; internet www.ugandaembassycn.org; Ambassador CHARLES MADIBO WAGIDOSO.

Denmark: Sofievej 15, 2900 Hellerup; tel. 39-62-09-66; fax 39-61-01-48; e-mail info@ugandaembassy.dk; internet www.ugandaembassy.dk; Ambassador Joseph Tomusange.

Egypt: 66 Rd 10, Maadi, Cairo; tel. (2) 3802514; fax (2) 3802504; e-mail ugembco@link.net; Ambassador IBRAHIM MUKIIBI.

Ethiopia: Kirkos Kifle Ketema, Kebele 35, House No. 31, POB 5644, Addis Ababa; tel. (11) 5513088; fax (11) 5514355; Ambassador Edith Grace Ssempala.

France: 13 ave Raymond Poincaré, 75116 Paris; tel. 1-56-90-12-20; fax 1-45-05-21-22; e-mail uganda.embassy@club-internet.fr; Ambassador ELIZABETH PAULA NAPEYOK.

Germany: Axel-Springer-Str. 54a, 10117 Berlin; tel. (30) 24047556; fax (30) 24047557; e-mail ugembassy@yahoo.de; Ambassador Nyine Samson Bitahwa.

India: B-3/26, Vasant Vihar, New Delhi 110 057; tel. (11) 26144413; fax (11) 26144405; e-mail ughcom@ndb.vsnl.net.in; High Commissioner NIMISHA MADHVANI.

Iran: 3/F, 10 Malek St, Shariati Ave, Tehran; tel. (21) 77643335; fax (21) 77643337; e-mail uganda_teh@yahoo.com; Ambassador Dr Mohammad Ahmad Kissule.

Italy: Lungotevere dei Mellini 44, 1°, Scala Valadier int. B, 00193 Roma; tel. (06) 3225220; fax (06) 3213688; Ambassador DEO K. RWABITA.

Japan: 9-23 Hachiyamacho Shibuya-ku, Tokyo 150-0035; tel. (3) 3462-7107; fax (3) 3462-7108; e-mail ugabassy@hpo.net; internet www.uganda-embassy.jp; Ambassador Wasswa Biriggwa.

Kenya: Uganda House, 5th Floor, Kenyatta Ave, POB 60853, Nairobi; tel. (20) 4449096; fax (20) 4443772; High Commissioner BRIG. (RETD) MATAYO KYALIGONZA.

Libya: POB 80215, Sharia Jaraba, Tripoli; tel. (21) 3603083; fax (21) 3634471; e-mail ugembatp60@hotmail.com; internet www.ugandaembassy.org.ly; Ambassador Moses Sebunya.

Saudi Arabia: POB 94344, Riyadh 11693; tel. (1) 454-4910; fax (1) 454-9264; e-mail ugariyadh@hotmail.com; Ambassador IBRAHIM MUKAIBI.

South Africa: 882 Church St, Pretoria 0083; POB 12442, Hatfield 0083; tel. (12) 3426031; fax (12) 3426206; e-mail ugacomer@mweb.co.za; High Commissioner Kweronda Ruhemba.

Sudan: POB 2676, Khartoum; tel. (183) 158571; fax (183) 797868; e-mail ugembkht@hotmail.com; Ambassador MULL KATENDE.

Tanzania: Extelcom Bldg, 7th Floor, Samora Ave, POB 6237, Dar es Salaam; tel. (22) 2116754; fax (22) 2112974; High Commissioner Ibrahim Mukiibi.

United Kingdom: Uganda House, 58/59 Trafalgar Sq., London, WC2N 5DX; tel. (20) 7839-5783; fax (20) 7839-8925; internet www.ugandahighcommission.co.uk; High Commr JOAN KAKIMA NYAKATUURA RWABYOMERE.

United States of America: 5911 16th St, NW, Washington, DC 20011; tel. (202) 726-7100; fax (202) 726-1727; e-mail info@ugandaembassyus.org; internet www.ugandaembassy.com; Ambassador Perezi Karukubiro Kamunanwire.

DIPLOMATIC MISSIONS OF UKRAINE

United Nations: 220 East 51st St, New York, NY 10022; tel. (212) 759-7003; fax (212) 355-9455; e-mail mail@uamission.org; internet www.uamission.org; Permanent Representative YURIY A. SERGEEV.

Algeria: 19 rue des Frères Benhafid, Hydra, Algiers; tel. (21) 69-13-87; fax (21) 69-48-87; e-mail emb_dz@mfa.gov.ua; Ambassador Serhiy Borovyk.

Angola: Rua Companhia de Jesus 35, Miramar, Luanda; tel. 222447492; fax 222448467; e-mail emb_ao@mfa.gov.ua; Chargé d'affaires VOLODYMYR M. KOKHNO.

Argentina: Conde 1763, C1426AZI Buenos Aires; tel. (11) 4552-0657; fax (11) 4552-6771; e-mail embucra@embucra.com.ar; internet www.embucra.com.ar; Ambassador Oleksandr Nykonenko.

Armenia: 0037 Yerevan, Arabkir 29/5/1; tel. (10) 22-97-27; fax (10) 25-13-83; e-mail emb_am@mfa.gov.ua; internet www.mfa.gov.ua/armenia; Ambassador OLEKSANDR I. BOZHKO.

Australia: Level 12, St George Centre, 60 Marcus Clarke St, Canberra, ACT 2601; tel. (2) 6230-5789; fax (2) 6230-7298; e-mail ukremb@bigpond.com; internet www.ukremb.info; Ambassador Valentyn Adomaytis.

Austria: Naaffgasse 23, 1180 Vienna; tel. (1) 479-71-72; fax (1) 479-71-72-47; e-mail info@ukremb.at; internet www.ukremb.at; Ambassador VOLODYMYR YU. YELCHENKO.

Azerbaijan: 1069 Baku, Y. Vezirov küç. 49; tel. (12) 449-40-95; fax (12) 449-40-96; e-mail emb_az@mfa.gov.ua; internet www.mfa.gov.ua/azerbaijan; Ambassador Stepan V. Volkovetskiy.

Belarus: 220002 Minsk, vul. Staravilenskaya 51; tel. (17) 283-19-90; fax (17) 283-19-80; e-mail emb_by@mfa.gov.ua; internet www.belarus.mfa.gov.ua/belarus; Ambassador IHOR D. LIKHOVYI.

Belgium: 30–32 ave Albert Lancaster, 1180 Brussels; tel. (2) 379-21-00; fax (2) 379-21-79; e-mail embassy@ukraine.be; internet www.ukraine.be; Ambassador Yaroslav Koval.

Brazil: SHIS QI 05, Conj. 04, Casa 02, 71615-040 Brasília, DF; tel. (61) 3365-3889; fax (61) 3365-2127; e-mail brucremb@zaz.com.br; internet www.ucrania.org.br; Ambassador VOLODYMYR LAKOMOV.

Bulgaria: 1618 Sofia, Ovcha Kupel, ul. Boryana 29; tel. (2) 955-94-78; fax 955-52-47; e-mail puvrb@mail.bol.bg; internet www.mfa.gov.ua/bulgaria; Ambassador Viktor M. Kalnyk.

Canada: 310 Somerset St West, Ottawa, ON K2P 0J9; tel. (613) 230-2961; fax (613) 230-2400; e-mail emb_ca@ukremb.ca; internet www.ukremb.ca; Ambassador DR IHOR OSTASH.

China, People's Republic: 11 Dong Liu Jie, San Li Tun, Beijing 100600; tel. (10) 65324013; fax (10) 65326359; e-mail ukrembcn@public3.bta.net.cn; internet www.ukremb.cn; Ambassador Serhiy Oleksiyovych Kamyshev.

Croatia: 10000 Zagreb, Voćarska 52; tel. (1) 4616296; fax (1) 4633726; e-mail ukremb@zg.t-com.hr; Ambassador MARKIYAN R. LUBKIVSKY.

Cuba: Avda 5, No 4405, entre 44 y 46, Miramar, Havana; tel. (7) 204-2586; fax (7) 204-2341; e-mail cubukrem@ceniai.inf.cu; Ambassador Oleksandr Gnyedyh.

Cyprus: 10 Andrea Miaouli St, Makedonitissa, Engomi, 2415 Nicosia; tel. 22464380; fax 22464381; e-mail info@ukrembassy.com.cy; internet www.ukrembassy.com.cy; Chargé d'affaires a.i. ANATOLIY MALIUSKA.

Czech Republic: Charlese de Gaulla 29, 160 00 Prague 6; tel. 233342000; fax 233344366; e-mail emb_cz@mfa.gov.ua; internet www.ukrembassy.cz; Ambassador Ivan D. Kuleba.

Denmark: Toldbodgade 37A, 1st Floor, 1253 Copenhagen K; tel. 33-16-16-35; fax 33-16-00-74; e-mail embassy.ua@mail.tele.dk; internet www.ukraine-embassy.dk; Ambassador NATALIIA MYKOLAÏVNA ZARUDNA.

Egypt: 50 Sharia 83, Maadi, Cairo; tel. (2) 3786871; fax (2) 3786873; e-mail emb_eg@mfa.gov.ua; Ambassador Yevhen Mykytenko.

Estonia: Lahe 6, Tallinn 15170; tel. 601-5815; fax 601-5816; e-mail embukr@eol.ee; internet www.hot.ee/ukrembassy; Ambassador PAVLO O. KIRYAKOV.

Ethiopia: Woreda 17, Kebele 3, House No. 2116, POB 2358, Addis Ababa; tel. (11) 6611698; fax (11) 6621288; e-mail emb_et@mfa.gov.ua; Ambassador Vladyslav Demyanenko.

Finland: Vähäniityntie 9, 00570 Helsinki; tel. (9) 2289000; fax (9) 2289001; e-mail embassy@ukraine.fi; internet www.ukraine.fi; Ambassador OLEKSANDR MAIDANNYK.

France: 21 ave de Saxe, 75007 Paris; tel. 1-43-06-07-37; fax 1-43-06-02-94; e-mail ambassade-ukraine@wanadoo.fr; internet www.mfa.gov.ua/france; Ambassador Kostiatyn V. Tymochenko.

Georgia: 0160 Tbilisi, Oniashvili 75; tel. (32) 31-11-61; fax (32) 31-11-81; e-mail emb_ge@mfa.gov.ua; internet www.uaembassy.ge; Ambassador MYKOLA M. SPYS.

Germany: Albrechtstr. 26, 10117 Berlin; tel. (30) 288870; fax (30) 28887163; e-mail ukremb@t-online.de; internet www.mfa.gov.ua/germany; Ambassador Ihor Dolhov.

Greece: Odos Stefanou Delta 2–4, Filothei, 152 37 Athens; tel. (210) 6800230; fax (210) 6854154; e-mail ukrembas@otenet.gr; internet www.ukrembas.gr; Ambassador VALERIY TSYBUKH.

Guinea: Commune de Calum, Corniche Nord, Quartier Camayenne, BP 1350, Conakry; tel. 30-45-37-56; fax 30-45-37-95; e-mail ambgv@sotelgui.net .gn; Ambassador Oleksandr O. Shulha.

Hungary: 1143 Budapest, Stefania u. 77; tel. (1) 422-4122; fax (1) 220-9873; e-mail ukran.kovetseg@mail.datanet.hu; Ambassador DR YURIY MUSHKA.

India: E-1/8 Vasant Vihar, New Delhi 110 057; tel. (11) 26146041; fax (11) 26146043; e-mail embassy@bol.net.in; internet www.ukraineembassyindia .org; Chargé d'affaires a.i. Mischuk Mykola.

Indonesia: World Trade Center, 8th Floor, Jalan Jenderal Sudirman, Kav. 29–31, Jakarta 12920; tel. (21) 5211700; fax (21) 5211710; e-mail uaembas@ indo.net.id; Chargé d'affaires a.i. VALERIY KRAVCENKO.

Iran: 101 Vanak St, Vanak Sq., Tehran; tel. (21) 88034119; fax (21) 88007130; e-mail ir@mfa.gov.ua; Ambassador Ihor Lohinov.

Iraq: POB 15192, 20/1/609 al-Mansour, al-Yarmouk, Baghdad; tel. (1) 542-6677; e-mail emb_iq@mfa.gov.ua; Ambassador (vacant).

Ireland: 16 Elgin Rd, Dublin 4; tel. (1) 6685189; fax (1) 6697917; e-mail ukrembassy@eircom.net; internet www.mfa.gov.ua/ireland; Ambassador Borys M. Bazylevskiy.

Israel: 50 Yirmiyagu, Tel-Aviv 62594; tel. 3-6040242; fax 3-6042512; e-mail embukr@netvision.net.il; internet www.ukraine-embassy.co.il; Ambassador IHOR V. TIMOFEYEV.

Italy: Via Guido d'Arezzo 9, 00198 Roma; tel. (06) 8413345; fax (06) 8547539; e-mail segretaria@amb-ucraina.com; internet www.amb-ucraina.com; Ambassador Heorhiy V. Chernyavsky.

Japan: 3-15-6, Nishi Azabu, Minato-ku, Tokyo 106-0046; tel. (3) 5474-9770; fax (3) 5474-9772; e-mail ukremb@rose.ocn.ne.jp; internet ukremb-japan .gov.ua; Ambassador MYKOLA KULINICH.

Jordan: 6 Al-Umouma St, As-Sahl, Amman; tel. (6) 5922402; fax (6) 5922405; e-mail ukremb@nets.com.jo; Ambassador Ihor Dyachenko.

Kazakhstan: 010000 Astana, Auezova 57; tel. (7172) 32-60-42; fax (7172) 32-68-11; e-mail emb_kz@mfa.gov.ua; internet ukrembassy.kepter.kz; Ambassador MYKOLA F. SELIVON.

Korea, Republic: 1-97, Dongbinggo-dong, Yeongsan-gu, Seoul; tel. (2) 790-5696; fax (2) 790-5697; e-mail secretary@ukrembrk.com; internet www .ukrembrk.com; Ambassador Yurii Mushka.

Kuwait: POB 7588, 32096 Hawalli, Jabriya, Block 10, St 6, House 5, Kuwait City; tel. 5318507; fax 5318508; e-mail emb_kw@mfa.gov.ua; internet www .mfa.gov.ua/kuwait; Ambassador SERHIY A. PUSHARSKY.

Kyrgyzstan: 720040 Bishkek, bulv. Panfilova 150; tel. (312) 66-55-90; fax (312) 66-20-12; e-mail emb_kg@mfa.gov.ua; internet www.mfa.gov.ua/ kirgizia; Ambassador Volodymyr M. Tyahlo.

Latvia: Kalpaka bulv. 3, Rīga 1010; tel. 6724-3082; fax 6732-5583; e-mail embassy@ml.lv; Ambassador RAUL CHILACHAVA.

Lebanon: POB 431, Jardin al-Bacha, Jisr al-Bacha, Sin el-Fil, Beirut; tel. (1) 510527; fax (1) 510531; e-mail ukrembassy@inco.com.lb; Ambassador Boris Zharshok.

Libya: POB 4544, Sharia Dhil, Tripoli; tel. (21) 3608665; fax (21) 3608666; e-mail emb_ly@mfa.gov.ua; Ambassador OLEKSIY RYBAK.

Lithuania: Teatro g. 4, Vilnius 03107; tel. (5) 212-1536; fax (5) 212-0475; e-mail ukrembassy@post.5ci.lt; internet www.mfa.gov.ua/lithuania; Chargé d'affaires a.i. (vacant).

Macedonia, former Yugoslav Republic: 1000 Skopje, Pitu Guli 3; tel. (2) 3178120; e-mail ukrambas@mt.net.mk; Ambassador VITALIY MOSKALENKO.

Malaysia: Suite 22-02, 22nd Floor, Menara Tan & Tan, 207 Jalan Tun Razak, 50400 Kuala Lumpur; tel. (3) 21669552; fax (3) 21664371; e-mail emb_my@mfa.gov.ua; internet www.mfa.gov.ua/malaysia; Ambassador Oleksandr Shevchenko.

Mexico: Paseo de la Reforma 730, Col. Lomas de Chapultepec, Del. Miguel Hidalgo, 11000 México, DF; tel. (55) 5282-4085; fax (55) 5282-4768; e-mail ukrainembasy@mexis.com; Ambassador OLEKSII BRANASHKO.

Moldova: 2008 Chișinău, bul. Vasile Lupu 17; tel. (22) 58-21-51; fax (22) 58-51-08; e-mail emb_md@mfa.gov.ua; internet www.mfa.gov.ua/moldova; Ambassador Serhiy I. Pyrozhkov.

Morocco: rue Mouaouya ben Houdaig, Villa 212, Cité OLM, Souissi II, Rabat; tel. (3) 7657840; fax (3) 7754679; Ambassador VITALIY YOKHNA.

Netherlands: Zeestraat 78, 2518 AD The Hague; tel. (70) 3626095; fax (70) 3615565; e-mail embukr@wxs.nl; internet www.oekraine.com; Ambassador (vacant).

Nigeria: Plot 1273, Parakou Cres., off Nairobi St, Wuse II, Abuja; tel. (9) 5239577; fax (9) 5239578; e-mail emb_ng@mfa.gov.ua; internet www.mfa .gov.ua/nigeria; Ambassador OLEH M. SKOROPAD.

Norway: Arbinsgt. 4, 0253 Oslo; tel. 22-83-55-60; fax 22-83-55-57; e-mail embassy@ukremb.no; internet www.mfa.gov.ua/norway; Ambassador Ihor M. Sagach.

Pakistan: 20, St 18, F-6/2, Islamabad; tel. (51) 2274732; fax (51) 2274643; e-mail ukremb@isb.compol.com; Ambassador DR IGOR SERGIYOVYEH.

Peru: José Dellepiani 470, San Isidro, Lima; tel. (1) 2642884; fax (1) 2642892; e-mail emb_pe@mfa.gov.ua; internet www.mfa.gov.ua/peru; Chargé d'affaires a.i. Oleksii Liashenko.

Poland: 00-580 Warsaw, Al. J. Ch. Szucha 7; tel. (22) 6250127; fax (22) 6298103; e-mail emb_pl@mfa.gov.ua; internet www.mfa.gov.ua/poland; Ambassador OLEKSANDR F. MOTSYK.

Portugal: Av. das Descobertas 18, 1400-092 Lisbon; tel. (21) 3010043; fax (21) 3010059; e-mail emb_pt@mfaa.gov.ua; internet www.mfa.gov.ua/portugal; Ambassador Rostyslav Tronenko.

Romania: 010572 Bucharest, Bd. Aviatorilor 24, Sector 1; tel. (21) 2303660; fax (21) 2303661; e-mail emb_ukr@itcnet.ro; Ambassador YURIY MALKO.

Russian Federation: 103009 Moscow, Leontiyevskii per. 18; tel. (495) 629-35-42; fax (495) 629-46-81; e-mail emb_ru@mfa.gov.ua; internet www.mfa.gov .ua/russia; Ambassador Oleh O. Dyomin.

Serbia: 11000 Belgrade, bul. Oslobođenja 87; tel. (11) 3978987; fax (11) 3978998; internet www.mfa.gov.ua/serbia; Ambassador ANATOLIY OLYNYK.

Singapore: 50 Raffles Place, 16-05 Singapore Land Tower, Singapore 048623; tel. 65356550; fax 65352116; e-mail emb_sg@mfa.gov.ua; internet www .embassy-ukraine.com; Ambassador Dr Viktor Mashtabei.

Slovakia: Radvaňská 35, 811 01 Bratislava; tel. (2) 5920-2810; fax (2) 5441-2651; Ambassador INNA OHNYIVETS.

Slovenia: 1000 Ljubljana, Teslova 23, WTC; tel. (1) 4210604; fax (1) 4210603; e-mail emb_si@mfa.gov.ua; Ambassador Vadym V. Primachenko.

South Africa: 398 Marais St, Brooklyn, Pretoria 0181; POB 36463, Menlo Park 0102; tel. (12) 4601943; fax (12) 4601944; e-mail emb_za@mfa.gov.ua; Chargé d'affaires a.i. TETIANA SUSHKO.

Spain: Ronda de la Abubilla 52, 28043 Madrid; tel. (91) 7489360; fax (91) 3887178; e-mail emb_es@mfa.gov.ua; Ambassador Anatoliy A. Shcherba.

Sweden: Stjärnvägen 2A, 181 34 Lidingö; tel. (8) 731-76-90; fax (8) 731-56-90; e-mail ukraina.embassy@ukrainaemb.se; internet www.mfa.gov.ua/sweden; Ambassador ANATOLII PONOMARENKO.

Switzerland: Feldeggweg 5, 3005 Bern; tel. 313522316; fax 313516416; e-mail emb_ch@mfa.gov.ua; internet www.ukremb.ch; Chargé d'affaires a.i. Yan Omelchenko.

Syria: BP 33944, 14 rue as-Salam, Mezzeh Est, Damascus; tel. (11) 6113016; fax (11) 6121355; e-mail emb_sy@mfa.gov.ua; internet www.mfa.gov.ua/ syria; Chargé d'affaires a.i. MYKOLA KRAVCHENKO.

Thailand: 87 All Seasons Place, CRC Tower, 33rd Floor, Thanon Witthayu, Lumpini, Pathumwan, Bangkok 10330; tel. (2) 685-3216; fax (2) 685-3217; e-mail ukremb@thailand.truemail.co.th; internet www.ukremb.or.th; Chargé d'affaires a.i. Andriy Beshta.

Tunisia: 7 rue Saint Fulgence, Notre Dame, 1002 Tunis; tel. (71) 845-861; fax (71) 840-866; e-mail ambassade.ukraine@planet.tn; Ambassador VALERIY RYLACH.

Turkey: Sancak Mahallesi 206 Sok. 17, 06550 Çankaya, Ankara; tel. (312) 4415499; fax (312) 4406815; e-mail emb_tr@mfa.gov.ua; internet www.mfa .gov.ua/turkey; Ambassador Oleksandr Mischenko.

Turkmenistan: 744001 Aşgabat, ul. Azadi 49; tel. (12) 39-13-73; fax (12) 39-10-28; e-mail emb_tm@mfa.gov.ua; internet www.mfa.gov.ua/turkmenistan; Ambassador VIKTOR A. MAYKO.

United Arab Emirates: POB 45714, Abu Dhabi; tel. (2) 6327586; fax (2) 6327506; e-mail emb_ae@mfa.gov.ua; internet www.oae.mfa.gov.ua/oae; Ambassador Sergiy O. Pas'ko.

United Kingdom: 60 Holland Park, London, W11 3SJ; tel. (20) 7727-6312; fax (20) 7792-1708; e-mail emb_gb@mfa.gov.ua; internet www.ukremb.org.uk; Ambassador IHOR KHARCHENKO.

United States of America: 3350 M St, NW, Washington, DC 20007; tel. (202) 333-0606; fax (202) 333-0817; e-mail infolook@aol.com; internet www .ukraineinfo.us; Ambassador Oleh Shamshur.

Uzbekistan: 100000 Tashkent, Ya. G'ulomov ko'ch. 68; tel. (71) 236-08-12; fax (71) 233-10-89; e-mail emb_uz@mfa.gov.ua; internet www.ukraine.uz; Ambassador VYACHESLAV V. POKHVALSKY.

Vatican City: Via A. G. Barrili 68a, Int. 5, 00152 Rome, Italy; tel. (06) 39378800; fax (06) 45439216; e-mail emb_va@mfa.gov.ua; Ambassador Tetiana Izhevska.

Viet Nam: 6B Le Hong Phong, Hanoi; tel. (4) 7344484; fax (4) 7344497; e-mail emb_vn@mfa.gov.ua; internet www.mfa.gov.ua/vietnam; Ambassador PAVLO SULTANSKY.

DIPLOMATIC MISSIONS OF UNITED ARAB EMIRATES

United Nations: 747 Third Ave, 36th Floor, New York, NY 10017; tel. (212) 371-0480; fax (212) 371-4923; e-mail uae@un.int; Permanent Representative Ahmed Abdulrahman al-Jerman.

Afghanistan: Charahi Zambak, Wazir Akbar Khan, Kabul; tel. (20) 2101578; Ambassador ALI MUHAMMAD AL-SHAMSI.

Algeria: BP 165, Alger-Gare, 14 rue Muhammad Drarini, Hydra, Algiers; tel. (21) 69-25-74; fax (21) 69-37-70; Ambassador Ahmad al-Hosani.

Australia: 12 Bulwarra Close, O'Malley, ACT 2606; tel. (2) 6286-8802; fax (2) 6286-8804; e-mail uaeembassy@bigpond.com; internet www.uaeembassy.org.au; Ambassador DR SAEED MUHAMMAD ash-SHAMSI.

Austria: Peter-Jordan-Str. 66, 1190 Vienna; tel. (1) 368-14-55; fax (1) 368-44-85; e-mail emirats@aon.at; Ambassador Ahmad Rashid ad-Dosari.

Bahrain: POB 26505, Villa 221, Rd 4007, Area 340, Manama; tel. 17748333; fax 17717724; Ambassador ABD AL-AZIZ BIN HADEF ASH-SHAMSI.

Bangladesh: POB 6014, Dhaka 1212; tel. (2) 9882244; fax (2) 8823225; e-mail info@uaeembassydhaka.com; Ambassador Khalfan Battal al Mansouri.

Belgium: 73 ave F. D. Roosevelt, 1050 Brussels; tel. (2) 640-60-00; fax (2) 646-24-73; e-mail uae-embassy@skynet.be; internet www.uaeembassybrussels.be; Ambassador MUHAMMAD SALEM OBAID AS-SUWEIDI.

Brazil: SHIS, QI 05, Chácara 54, 71600-580 Brasília, DF; tel. (61) 3248-0717; fax (61) 3248-7543; e-mail uae@uae.org.br; internet www.uae.org.br; Ambassador Yousef Ali al-Usaimi.

Canada: World Exchange Plaza, 45 O'Connor St, Suite 1800, Ottawa, ON K1P 1A4; tel. (613) 565-7272; fax (613) 5658007; e-mail safara@uae-embassy.com; internet www.uae-embassy.com; Ambassador HASSAN MOHAMMED OBAID AS-SUWAIDI.

China, People's Republic: 1-9-1, Ta Yuan Diplomatic Office Bldg, Beijing; tel. (10) 65322112; AmbassadorMohammed Rashid Ali Al-Boot.

Djibouti: Djibouti; Ambassador SAÏD BEN HAMDAM BEN MUHAMMAD AN-NAGHI.

Egypt: 4 Sharia Ibn Sina, Cairo (Giza); tel. (2) 3609721; e-mail uaeembassyca@online.com.eg; Ambassador Ahmad az-Za'abi.

France: 2 blvd de la Tour Maubourg, 75007 Paris; tel. 1-44-34-02-00; fax 1-47-55-61-04; e-mail ambassade.emirats@wanadoo.fr; internet www.amb-emirats.fr; Ambassador SAIF SULTAN MUBARAK AL-ARYANI.

Germany: Hiroshimastr. 18–20, 10787 Berlin; tel. (30) 516516; fax (30) 51651900; e-mail uae@uaeembassy.de; internet www.uae-embassy.de; Ambassador Muhammad Ahmad al-Mahmud.

India: EP-12 Chandragupta Marg, New Delhi 110 021; tel. (11) 26872937; fax (11) 26873272; e-mail embassyabudhabi@bol.net.in; Chargé d'affaires ABDULLA JASSIM KASHWANI.

Indonesia: Jalan Prof. Dr Satrio, Kav. 16–17, Jakarta 12950; tel. (21) 5206518; fax (21) 5206526; e-mail uaeemb@rad.net.id; Ambassador Yousif Rashid Alshram.

Iran: POB 19395-4616, No. 355, Vahid Dastjerdi Ave, Vali-e-Asr Ave, Tehran; tel. (21) 88781333; fax (21) 88789084; e-mail uae_emb_thr@universalmail.com; Ambassador KHALIFA SHAHEEN AL-MERREE.

Iraq: 81/34/611 Hay al-Andalus (ad-Daoudi), Baghdad; tel. (1) 543-9174; fax (1) 543-9093; Chargé d'affaires Ahmad Abdullah bin Said.

Italy: Via della Camilluccia 492, 00135 Roma; tel. (06) 36306100; fax (06) 36306155; e-mail uaeroma@tin.it; Ambassador ABD AL-HAMID ABD AL-FATTAH KAZIM.

Japan: 9-10, Nanpeidai-cho, Shibuya-ku, Tokyo 150-0036; tel. (3) 5489-0804; fax (3) 5489-0813; e-mail info@uaeembassy.jp; internet www.uaeembassy.jp; Ambassador Saeed Ali al-Nowais.

Jordan: POB 2623, Jawdat Rashid Shama St, 5th Circle, Amman 11181; tel. (6) 5934780; fax (6) 5932666; Ambassador RAHMA HUSSAIN R. AZ-ZA'ABI.

Kazakhstan: 010000 Astana, pos. Zarechnyi, 70 let Oktyabrya 71; tel. (7172) 24-36-75; fax (7172) 24-36-76; e-mail emaratembassy_kz@yahoo.com; Ambassador Ibrahim Hassan Saif.

Korea, Republic: 5-5, Hannam-dong, Yeongsan-gu, Seoul; tel. (2) 790-3235; fax (2) 790-3238; Ambassador ABDULLAH MUHAMMADD AL-MAAINAH.

Kuwait: POB 1828, 13019 Safat, Plot 70, Istiqlal St, Kuwait City; tel. 2528544; fax 2526382; Ambassador Yousuf A. al-Ansari.

Lebanon: Immeuble Wafic Tanbara, Jnah, Beirut; tel. (1) 857000; fax (1) 857009; e-mail eembassy@uae.org.lb; Ambassador MUHAMMAD SULTAN AS-SOWAIDI.

Malaysia: 1 Gerbang Ampang Hilir, off Persiaran Ampang Hilir, 55000 Kuala Lumpur; tel. (3) 42535221; fax (3) 42535220; e-mail uaemal@tm.net.my; Ambassador Nasser Salman Alaboodi.

Mauritania: BP 6824, Nouakchott; tel. 525-10-98; fax 525-09-92; .

Morocco: 11 ave des Alaouines, 10000 Rabat; tel. (3) 7702085; fax (3) 7724145; e-mail emirabat@iam.net.ma; Ambassador Issaa Hamad Bushahab.

Netherlands: Eisenhowerlaan 130, 2517 KN The Hague; tel. (70) 3384370; fax (70) 3384373; e-mail info@uae-embassy.nl; internet www.uae-embassy.nl; Ambassador ALI THANI AS-SUWAIDI.

Oman: Diplomatic City, Al-Khuwair, POB 551, Muscat 111; tel. 24600302; fax 24604182; Ambassador Muhammad Ali Abd ar-Rahman al-Osaimi.

Pakistan: Plot No. 1-22, Quaid-e-Azam University Rd, Diplomatic Enclave, POB 1111, Islamabad; tel. (51) 2279052; fax (51) 2279063; e-mail uaeempk@isb.paknet.pk; Ambassador ALI MOHAMMED ASH-SHAMSI.

Philippines: Renaissance Bldg, 2nd Floor, 215 Sakedo St, Legaspi Village, Makati City, Metro Manila; tel. (2) 8173906; fax (2) 8183577; Ambassador Mohammed Ebrahim Abdullah al-Jowaid.

Qatar: POB 3099, 22 al-Markhiyah St, Khalifa Northern Town, Doha; tel. 4838880; fax 4836186; e-mail emarat@qatar.net.qa; Ambassador ABD AR-REDHA ABDULLAH KHOURI.

Russian Federation: 101000 Moscow, ul. U. Palme 4; tel. (499) 147-00-66; fax (495) 234-40-70; e-mail uae@col.ru; Ambassador Muhammad Ali al-Osaimi.

Saudi Arabia: POB 94385, Riyadh 11693; tel. (1) 482-9652; fax (1) 482-7504; Ambassador ISSA K. AL-HURAIMIL.

Singapore: 600 North Bridge Road, 09-01/05 Parkview Sq., Singapore 188778; tel. 62388206; fax 62380081; e-mail emarat@singnet.com.sg; internet www.uaeembassy-sg.com; Chargé d'affaires a.i. Asim Mirza Alrahmah.

Somalia: Via Afgoi, Km 5, Mogadishu; tel. (1) 23178; .

South Africa: 992 Arcadia St, Arcadia, Pretoria 0083; POB 57090, Arcadia 0007; tel. (12) 3427736; fax (12) 3427738; e-mail uae@mweb.co.za; Ambassador Ismael Obaid Yusuf al-Ali.

Spain: Capitán Haya 40, 28020 Madrid; tel. (91) 5701003; fax (91) 5715176; e-mail ambassadormadrid@uae.e.telefonica.net; Ambassador SULTAN MUHAMMAD AL-QORTASI AN-NOAIMI.

Sri Lanka: 44 Ernest de Silva Mawatha, Colombo 7; tel. (11) 2565052; fax (11) 2564104; Ambassador M. M. Mohamoud al-Mahmoud.

Sudan: St 3, New Extension, POB 1225, Khartoum; tel. (183) 744476; Ambassador ISA ABDULLAH AL-BASHAR.

Sweden: Norrlandsgt. 20, POB 7485, 103 92 Stockholm; tel. (8) 411-12-44; fax (8) 411-12-45; Chargé d'affaires a.i. Saeed Rashid O. Saif az-Zaabi.

Syria: Immeuble Housami, 62 rue Raouda, Damascus; Ambassador YOUSUF MUHAMMAD HUSSEIN AL-MADFA'AI.

Thailand: 82 Saeng Thong Thani Bldg, 25th Floor, Thanon Sathorn Nua, Bangkok 10500; tel. (2) 639-9820; fax (2) 639-9818; Ambassador Salim Issa Ali al-Kattam al-Zaabi.

Tunisia: 9 rue Achtart, Nord Hilton, Belvédère, 1002 Tunis; tel. (71) 788-888; fax (71) 788-777; e-mail emirates.embassy@planet.tn; Ambassador MUHAMMAD HAMAD OMRANE.

Turkey: Turan Güneş Bul. 15, Cad. 290, Sok. 3, Sancak Mah., Çankaya, Ankara; tel. (312) 4901414; fax (312) 4912333; e-mail uaeemb@uaeemb.net; internet www.uaeemb.net; Chargé d'affaires a.i. Ismail az-Zaabi.

Turkmenistan: 744000 Aşgabat, Khalifa Centre, pr. S. Türkmenbaşi 124; tel. (12) 45-69-15; fax (12) 45-69-16; Ambassador HASSAN ABDULLAH AL-ADHAB.

United Kingdom: 30 Princes Gate, London, SW7 1PT; tel. (20) 7581-1281; fax (20) 7581-9616; e-mail information@uaeembassyuk.net; internet www.uaeembassyuk.net; Ambassador Issa Saleh al-Gurg.

United States of America: 3422 International Court, NW, Washington, DC 20008; tel. (202) 243-2400; fax (202) 243-2432; e-mail info@uaeembassy-usa.org; internet www.uae-embassy.org; Ambassador (vacant).

Yemen: POB 2250, Ring Rd, San'a; tel. (1) 248777; Ambassador Ali Saif Sultan al-Awani.

818

DIPLOMATIC MISSIONS OF UNITED KINGDOM

United Nations: 1 Dag Hammarskjöld Plaza, 885 Second Ave, New York, NY 10017; tel. (212) 745-9200; fax (212) 745-9316; e-mail uk@un.int; internet www.ukun.org; Permanent Representative SIR JOHN SAWERS JOHN SAWERS.

Afghanistan: St 15, Roundabout Wazir Akbar Khan, POB 334, Kabul; tel. (70) 102000; fax (70) 102250; e-mail britishembassy.kabul@fco.gov.uk; internet www.britishembassy.gov.uk/afghanistan; Ambassador Sir Sherard Louis Cowper-Coles.

Albania: Rruga Skënderbej 12, Tirana; tel. (4) 234973; fax (4) 247697; e-mail information.tiran@fco.gov.uk; internet www.britishembassy.gov.uk/albania; Ambassador FRASER WILSON.

Algeria: 12 rue Slimane Amirate, Hydra, Algiers; tel. (21) 23-00-68; fax (21) 23-00-67; e-mail britishembassy.algiers@fco.gov.uk; internet www.britishembassy.gov.uk/algeria; Ambassador Andrew Henderson.

Angola: Rua Diogo Cão 4, CP 1244, Luanda; tel. 222334582; fax 222333331; e-mail ppa.luanda@fco.gov.uk; internet www.britishembassy.gov.uk/angola; Ambassador RALPH PUBLICOVER.

Antigua and Barbuda: British High Commission, Price Waterhouse Centre, 11 Old Parham Rd, POB 483, St John's; tel. 462-0008; fax 562-2124; e-mail britishc@candw.ag; Commissioner Terry Knight.

Argentina: Dr Luis Agote 2412, C1425EOF Buenos Aires; tel. (11) 4808-2200; fax (11) 4808-2274; e-mail askinformation.baires@fco.gov.uk; internet www.britain.org.ar; Ambassador DR JOHN HUGHES.

Armenia: 0019 Yerevan, Marshal Baghramian Ave 34; tel. (10) 26-43-01; fax (10) 26-43-18; e-mail enquiries.yerevan@fco.gov.uk; internet www.britishembassy.am; Ambassador Anthony Cantor.

Australia: Commonwealth Ave, Canberra, ACT 2600; tel. (2) 6270-6666; fax (2) 6273-3236; e-mail bhc.canberra@britaus.net; internet bhc.britaus.net/default.asp; High Commissioner HELEN LIDDELL.

Austria: Jaurèsgasse 12, 1030 Vienna; tel. (1) 716-13-0; fax (1) 716-13-29-99; e-mail info@britishembassy.at; internet www.britishembassy.at; Ambassador Simon John Meredith Smith.

Azerbaijan: 1010 Baku, Khagani küç. 45; tel. (12) 497-51-88; fax (12) 492-27-39; e-mail generalenquiries.baku@fco.gov.uk; internet www.britishembassy.az; Ambassador DR CAROLYN BROWNE.

Bahrain: POB 114, 21 Government Ave, Area 306, Manama; tel. 17574100; fax 17574161; e-mail bahrainchancery.bahrain@fco.gov.uk; internet www.britishembassy.gov.uk/bahrain; Ambassador Jamie Bowden.

Bangladesh: United Nations Rd, Baridhara, POB 6079, Dhaka 1212; tel. (2) 8822705; fax (2) 8826181; e-mail Dhaka.Chancery@fco.gov.uk; internet www.ukinbangladesh.org; High Commissioner ANWAR CHOWDHURY.

Barbados: Lower Collymore Rock, POB 676, Bridgetown; tel. 430-7800; fax 430-7813; e-mail britishhcb@sunbeach.net; internet www.britishhighcommission.gov.uk/barbados; High Commissioner Duncan John Rushworth Taylor.

Belarus: 220030 Minsk, vul. K. Marksa 37; tel. (17) 210-59-20; fax (17) 220-23-06; e-mail britinfo@nsys.by; internet www.britishembassy.gov.uk/belarus; Ambassador (vacant).

Belgium: 85 rue d'Arlon, 1040 Brussels; tel. (2) 287-62-11; fax (2) 287-63-60; e-mail info@britain.be; internet www.britishembassy.gov.uk/belgium; Ambassador Rachel Aron.

Belize: Embassy Sq., POB 91, Belmopan; tel. 822-2146; fax 822-2761; e-mail brithicom@btl.net; internet www.britishhighbze.com; High Commissioner JOHN YAPP.

Bolivia: Avda Arce 2732, Casilla 694, La Paz; tel. (2) 243-3424; fax (2) 243-1073; e-mail ppa@megalink.com; internet www.britishembassy.gov.uk/bolivia; Ambassador Nigel Baker.

Bosnia and Herzegovina: 71000 Sarajevo, Tina Ujevića 8; tel. (33) 444429; fax (33) 666131; e-mail britemb@bih.net.ba; internet www.britishembassy.gov.uk/bih; Ambassador MATTHEW JOHN RYCROFT.

Botswana: Plot 1079–1084, Main Mall, off Queens Rd, Private Bag 0023, Gaborone; tel. 3952841; fax 3956105; e-mail bhc@botsnet.bw; internet www.britishhighcommission.gov.uk/botswana; High Commissioner Francis (Frank) James Martin.

Brazil: SES, Quadra 801, Conj. K, Lote 08, 70408-900 Brasília, DF; tel. (61) 3329-2300; fax (61) 3329-2369; e-mail contato@reinounido.org.br; internet www.reinounido.org.br; Ambassador DR PETER COLLECOTT.

Brunei: POB 2197, Bandar Seri Begawan BS 8674; tel. 2222231; fax 2234315; e-mail brithc@brunet.bn; internet www.britishhighcommission.gov.uk/brunei; High Commissioner John Saville.

Bulgaria: 1000 Sofia, ul. Moskovska 9; tel. (2) 933-92-22; fax (2) 933-92-50; e-mail britembinf@mail.orbitel.bg; internet www.british-embassy.bg; Ambassador STEVE WILLIAMS.

Cambodia: 27–29 rue 75, Sangkat Sras Chak, Khan Daun Penh, Phnom-Penh; tel. (23) 427124; fax (23) 427125; e-mail britemb@online.com.kh; internet www.britishembassy.gov.uk/cambodia; Ambassador David George Reader.

Cameroon: ave Winston Churchill, BP 547, Yaoundé; tel. 2222-0545; fax 2222-0148; e-mail BHC.yaounde@fco.gov.uk; internet www.britcam.org; High Commissioner DAVID SYDNEY MADDICOTT.

Canada: 80 Elgin St, Ottawa, ON K1P 5K7; tel. (613) 237-1530; fax (613) 237-7980; e-mail generalenquiries@britainincanada.org; internet www.britainincanada.org; High Commissioner Anthony Joyce Cary.

Chile: Avda el Bosque Norte 0125, Casilla 72-D, Santiago; tel. (2) 370-4100; fax (2) 370-4180; e-mail embsan@britemb.cl; internet www.britemb.cl; Ambassador HOWARD DRAKE.

China, People's Republic: 11 Guang Hua Lu, Jian Guo Men Wai, Beijing 100600; tel. (10) 65321961; fax (10) 65321937; internet www.uk.cn; Ambassador William Geoffrey Ehrman.

Colombia: Edif. ING Barings, Carrera 9, No 76-49, 9°, Bogotá, DC; tel. (1) 317-6690; fax (1) 317-6265; e-mail ppa.bogota@fco.gov.uk; internet www.britain.gov.co; Ambassador HAYDON WARREN-GASH.

Congo, Democratic Republic: 83 ave Roi Baudouin, BP 8049, Kinshasa; tel. (81) 7150761; fax (81) 3464291; e-mail ambrit@ic.cd; Ambassador Nicholas Kay.

Costa Rica: Edif. Centro Colón, 11°, Apdo 815, 1007 San José; tel. 258-2025; fax 233-9938; e-mail britemb@racsa.co.cr; internet www.britishembassycr.com; Ambassador TOM KENNEDY.

Croatia: 10000 Zagreb, Ivana Lučića 4; tel. (1) 6009100; fax (1) 6009111; e-mail british.embassyzagreb@fco.gov.uk; internet www.britishembassy.gov.uk/croatia; Ambassador Sir John Ramsden.

Cuba: Calle 34, No 702/4, esq. 7 y 17, Miramar, Havana; tel. (7) 204-1771; fax (7) 204-8104; e-mail embrit@ceniai.inf.cu; internet www.britishembassy.gov.uk/cuba; Ambassador JOHN ANTHONY DEW.

Cyprus: POB 21978, Alexander Pallis St, 1587 Nicosia; tel. 22861100; fax 22861125; e-mail brithc.2@cytanet.com.cy; internet www.britishhighcommission.gov.uk/cyprus; High Commr Peter Joseph Millett.

Czech Republic: Thunovská 14, 118 00 Prague 1; tel. 257402111; fax 257402296; e-mail info@britain.cz; internet www.britain.cz; Ambassador LINDA JOY DUFFIELD.

Denmark: Kastelsvej 36–40, 2100 Copenhagen Ø; tel. 35-44-52-00; fax 35-44-52-93; e-mail enquiry.copenhagen@fco.gov.uk; internet www.britishembassy.dk; Ambassador David Frost.

Dominican Republic: Edif. Corominas Pepin, 7°, Avda 27 de Febrero 233, Santo Domingo, DN; tel. 472-7111; fax 472-7574; e-mail brit.emb.sadom@codeltel.net.do; internet www.britishembassy.gov.uk/dominicanrepublic; Ambassador IAN ALAN WORTHINGTON.

Ecuador: Edif. Citiplaza, 14°, Avda Naciones Unidas y República de El Salvador, Apdo 17-01-314, Quito; tel. (2) 297-0800; fax (2) 297-0809; e-mail consuio@uio.satnet.net; internet www.britembquito.org.ec; Ambassador Bernard Gerrard Whiteside.

Egypt: 7 Sharia Ahmad Ragheb, Cairo (Garden City); tel. (2) 7940852; fax (2) 7940859; e-mail info@britishembassy.org.eg; internet www.britishembassy.org.eg; Ambassador DOMINIC ASQUITH.

Eritrea: 66–68 Mariam Ghimbi St, POB 5584, Asmara; tel. (1) 120145; fax (1) 120104; e-mail asmara.enquiries@fco.gov.uk; Ambassador Nicholas Astbury.

Estonia: Wismari 6, Tallinn 10136; tel. 667-4700; fax 667-4755; e-mail information@britishembassy.ee; internet www.britishembassy.ee; Ambassador PETER CARTER.

Ethiopia: POB 858, Addis Ababa; tel. (11) 6612354; fax (11) 6610588; e-mail britishembassy.addisababa@fco.gov.uk; internet www.britishembassy.gov.uk/ethiopia; Ambassador Norman Ling.

Fiji: Victoria House, 47 Gladstone Rd, POB 1355, Suva; tel. 3229100; fax 3229132; e-mail publicdiplomacysuva@fco.gov.uk; internet www.britishhighcommission.gov.uk/fiji; High Commissioner ROGER SYKES.

Finland: Itäinen puistotie 17, 00140 Helsinki; tel. (9) 22865100; fax (9) 22865262; e-mail info.helsinki@fco.gov.uk; internet www.britishembassy.fi; Ambassador Dr Valerie Caton.

France: 35 rue du Faubourg St Honoré, 75383 Paris Cedex 08; tel. 1-44-51-31-00; fax 1-44-51-32-34; e-mail public.paris@fco.gov.uk; internet www.amb-grandebretagne.fr; Ambassador SIR PETER WESTMACOTT.

Gambia: 48 Atlantic Rd, Fajara, POB 507, Banjul; tel. 4495133; fax 4496134; e-mail bhcbanjul@fco.gov.uk; internet www.britishhighcommission.gov.uk/ thegambia; High Commissioner Philip Sinkinson.

Georgia: 0105 Tbilisi, Tavisuplebis Moedani 4; tel. (32) 27-47-47; fax (32) 27-47-92; e-mail british.embassy.tbilisi@fco.gov.uk; internet www .britishembassy.gov.uk/georgia; Ambassador DENIS KEEFE.

Germany: Wilhelmstr. 70–71, 10117 Berlin; tel. (30) 204570; fax (30) 20457594; e-mail info@britischebotschaft.de; internet www .britischebotschaft.de; Ambassador Sir Michael Arthur.

Ghana: Osu Link, off Gamel Abdul Nasser Ave, POB 296, Accra; tel. (21) 7010655; e-mail high.commission.accra@fco.gov.uk; internet www .britishhighcommission.gov.uk/ghana; High Commissioner DR NICHOLAS WESTCOTT.

Greece: Odos Ploutarchou 1, 106 75 Athens; tel. (210) 7272600; fax (210) 7272734; internet www.british-embassy.gr; Ambassador Simon Gass.

Guatemala: Edif. Torre Internacional, 11°, Avda de la Reforma, 16 Calle, Zona 10, Guatemala City; tel. 2367-5425; fax 2367-5430; e-mail embassy@ intelnett.com; Ambassador IAN N. HUGHES.

Guinea: BP 6729, Conakry; tel. 30-45-58-07; fax 30-45-60-20; e-mail britcon .oury@biasy.net; Ambassador John McManus.

Guyana: 44 Main St, POB 10849, Georgetown; tel. 226-5881; fax 225-0671; e-mail bhcguyana@networksgy.com; internet www.britishhighcommission .gov.uk/guyana; High Commissioner FRASER WILLIAM WHEELER.

Hungary: 1051 Budapest, Harmincad u. 6; tel. (1) 266-2888; fax (1) 266-0907; e-mail info@britemb.hu; internet www.britishembassy.hu; Ambassador Greg Dorey.

Iceland: POB 460, 121 Reykjavík; Laufásvegur 31, 101 Reykjavík; tel. 5505100; fax 5505105; e-mail postmaster@britishembassy.is; internet www .britishembassy.is; Ambassador ALPER (ALP) MEHMET.

India: Shantipath, Chanakyapuri, New Delhi 110 021; tel. (11) 26872161; fax (11) 26870065; e-mail postmaster.nedel@fco.gov.uk; internet www.ukinindia .com; High Commissioner Sir Richard Stagg.

Indonesia: Jalan M. H. Thamrin 75, Jakarta 10310; tel. (21) 3156264; fax (21) 3926263; e-mail commercial@dnet.net.id; internet www.britishembassy.gov .uk/indonesia; Ambassador CHARLES HUMFREY.

Iran: POB 11365-4474, 198 Ferdowsi Ave, Tehran 11344; tel. (21) 64052000; fax (21) 64052289; e-mail britishembassytehran@fco.gov.uk; internet www .britishembassy.gov.uk/iran; Ambassador Geoffrey Adams.

Iraq: c/o Iraq Policy Unit, Foreign and Commonwealth Office, London, SW1A 2AH, United Kingdom; tel. (20) 7008-1500; fax (20) 7008-4119; e-mail britembBaghdad@fco.gov.uk; internet www.britishembassy.gov.uk/iraq; Ambassador CHRISTOPHER PRENTICE.

Ireland: 29 Merrion Rd, Ballsbridge, Dublin 4; tel. (1) 2053700; fax (1) 2053885; e-mail chancery.dublx@fco.gov.uk; internet www.britishembassy .ie; Ambassador David Norman Reddaway.

Israel: 192 Rehov Hayarkon, Tel-Aviv 63405; tel. 3-7251222; fax 3-5278574; e-mail webmaster.telaviv@fco.gov.uk; internet www.britemb.org.il; Ambassador TOM R. V. PHILLIPS.

Italy: Via XX Settembre 80a, 00187 Roma; tel. (06) 42200001; fax (06) 42202333; e-mail romepoliticalsection@fco.gov.uk; internet www.britain.it; Ambassador Edward Chaplin.

Jamaica: 28 Trafalgar Rd, POB 575, Kingston 10; tel. 510-0700; fax 510-0737; e-mail bhc.kingston@fco.gov.uk; internet www.britishhighcommission.gov.uk/jamaica; High Commissioner JEREMY M. CRESSWELL.

Japan: 1, Ichiban-cho, Chiyoda-ku, Tokyo 102-8381; tel. (3) 5211-1100; fax (3) 5275-3164; e-mail embassy.tokyo@fco.gov.uk; internet www.uknow.or .jp; Ambassador Graham Fry.

Jordan: POB 87, Abdoun, Amman 11118; tel. (6) 5909200; fax (6) 5909279; e-mail info@britain.org.jo; internet www.britain.org.jo; Ambassador JAMES WATT.

Kazakhstan: 010000 Astana, Kosmonavtov 62, RENCO bldg; tel. (7172) 55-62-00; fax (7172) 55-62-11; e-mail britishembassy@mail.online.kz; internet www.britishembassy.kz; Ambassador Paul Brummell.

Kenya: Upper Hill Rd, POB 30465, 00100 Nairobi; tel. (20) 2844000; fax (20) 2844033; e-mail bhcinfo@jambo.co.ke; internet www.britishhighcommission .gov.uk/kenya; High Commissioner ADAM WOOD.

Korea, Democratic People's Republic: Munsudong Diplomatic Compound, Pyongyang; tel. (2) 3817980; fax (2) 3817985; e-mail postmaster.PYONX@ fco.gov.uk; Ambassador John Everard.

Korea, Republic: Taepyeongno 40, 4, Jeong-dong, Jung-gu, Seoul 100-120; tel. (2) 3210-5500; fax (2) 725-1738; e-mail bembassy@uk.or.kr; internet www.britishembassy.or.kr; Ambassador MARTIN UDEN.

Kosovo: 10000 Prishtina, Arbëri, Rruga Ismail Qemali 6; tel. (38) 254700; fax (38) 249799; e-mail britishoffice.pristina@fco.gov.uk; Ambassador Andrew Sparkes.

Kuwait: POB 2, 13001 Safat, Arabian Gulf St, Kuwait City; tel. 2594320; fax 2594339; e-mail kuwait.generalenquiries@fco.gov.uk; internet www .britishembassy-kuwait.org; Ambassador STUART LAING.

Latvia: J. Alunāna iela 5, Rīga 1010; tel. 6777-4700; fax 6777-4707; e-mail british.embassy@apollo.lv; internet www.britain.lv; Ambassador Richard Moon.

Lebanon: POB 11-471, Serail Hill, Beirut Central District, Beirut; tel. (1) 990400; fax (1) 990420; e-mail chancery@cyberia.net.lb; internet www .britishembassy.gov.uk/lebanon; Ambassador FRANCES GUY.

Libya: POB 4206, Tripoli; tel. (21) 3403644; fax (21) 3403648; e-mail tripoli .press@fco.gov.uk; internet www.britishembassy.gov.uk/libya; Ambassador Sir Vincent Fean.

Lithuania: Antakalnio g. 2, Vilnius 10308; tel. (5) 246-2900; fax (5) 246-2901; e-mail be-vilnius@britain.lt; internet www.britain.lt; Ambassador COLIN ROBERTS.

Luxembourg: 5 blvd Joseph II, 1840 Luxembourg; tel. 22-98-64; fax 22-98-67; e-mail britemb@internet.lu; internet www.britain.lu; Ambassador Peter Bateman.

Macedonia, former Yugoslav Republic: 1000 Skopje, Salvador Aljende 73; tel. (2) 3299299; fax (2) 3179726; e-mail britishembassyskopje@fco.gov.uk; internet www.britishembassy.gov.uk/macedonia; Ambassador ANDREW KEY.

Malawi: British High Commission Bldg, Capital Hill, POB 30042, Lilongwe 3; tel. 1772400; fax 1772657; e-mail bhclilongwe@fco.gov.uk; internet www .britishhighcommission.gov.uk/malawi; High Commissioner Richard Wildash.

Malaysia: 185 Jalan Ampang, 50450 Kuala Lumpur; tel. (3) 21702200; fax (3) 21702303; e-mail political.kualalumpur@fco.gov.uk; internet www.britain .org.my; High Commissioner BOYD MCCLEARY.

Malta: Whitehall Mansions, Ta'Xbiex Seafront, Ta'Xbiex XBX 1026; tel. 23230000; fax 23232216; e-mail bhcvalletta@fco.gov.uk; internet www .britishhighcommission.gov.uk/malta; High Commissioner Nicholas Archer.

Mauritius: Les Cascades Bldg, 7th Floor, Edith Cavell St, POB 1063, Port Louis; tel. 202-9400; fax 202-9408; e-mail bhc@intnet.mu; High Commissioner DR JOHN MURTON.

Mexico: Río Lerma 71, Col. Cuauhtémoc, Del. Cuauhtémoc, 06500 México, DF; tel. (55) 5242-8500; fax (55) 5242-8517; e-mail ukinmex@att.net.mx; internet www.embajadabritanica.com.mx; Ambassador Giles Paxman.

Moldova: 2012 Chişinău, str. N. Iorga 18; tel. (22) 22-59-02; fax (22) 25-18-59; e-mail enquiries.chisinau@fco.gov.uk; internet www.britishembassy.md; Ambassador JOHN BEYER.

Mongolia: Enkh Taivny Gudamj 30, Ulan Bator 13 (CPOB 703); tel. (11) 458133; fax (11) 458036; Ambassador (vacant).

Montenegro: 81000 Podgorica, bul. Svetog Petra Cetinjskog 149; tel. (81) 205460; fax (81) 205441; Ambassador KEVIN LYNE.

Morocco: 28 ave S.A.R. Sidi Muhammad, Souissi, Rabat; tel. (3) 72633333; fax (3) 7704531; e-mail generalenquiries.rabat@fco.gov.uk; internet www .britishembassy.gov.uk/morocco; Ambassador Charles Gray.

Mozambique: Av. Vladimir I. Lénine 310, CP 55, Maputo; tel. 21356000; fax 21356060; e-mail bhc.consular@tvcabo.co.mz; internet www .britishhighcommission.gov.uk/mozambique; High Commissioner ANDREW SOPER.

Myanmar: 80 Strand Rd, Kyauktada Township, Yangon; tel. (1) 370863; fax (1) 370866; e-mail chancery.Rangoon@fco.gov.uk; Ambassador Mark Canning.

Namibia: 116 Robert Mugabe Ave, POB 22202, Windhoek; tel. (61) 274800; fax (61) 228895; e-mail general.windhoek@fco.gov.uk; internet www .britishhighcommission.gov.uk/namibia; High Commissioner MARK BENSBERG.

Nepal: Lainchaur, POB 106, Kathmandu; tel. (1) 4410583; fax (1) 4411789; e-mail britemb@wlink.com.np; internet www.britishembassy.gov.uk/nepal; Ambassador Dr Andrew Hall.

Netherlands: Lange Voorhout 10, 2514 ED The Hague; tel. (70) 4270427; fax (70) 4270345; internet www.britain.nl; Ambassador LYN PARKER.

New Zealand: 44 Hill St, POB 1812, Wellington; tel. (4) 924-2888; fax (4) 473-4982; e-mail ppa.mailbox@fco.gov.uk; internet www.britain.org.nz; High Commissioner George Fergusson.

Nigeria: 19 Torren Close, off Mississippi St, Shehu Shagari Way, Maitama, Abuja; tel. (9) 4132010; fax (9) 4133552; e-mail information.abuja@fco.gov.uk; internet www.ukinnigeria.com; High Commissioner ROBERT DEWAR.

Norway: Thomas Heftyesgt. 8, 0264 Oslo; tel. 23-13-27-00; fax 23-13-27-41; e-mail britemb@online.no; internet www.britain.no; Ambassador David Powell.

Oman: POB 185, Mina al-Fahal 116; tel. 24609000; fax 24609010; e-mail enquiries.muscat@fco.gov.uk; internet www.britishembassy.gov.uk/oman; Ambassador DR NOEL GUCKIAN.

Pakistan: Diplomatic Enclave, Ramna 5, POB 1122, Islamabad; tel. (51) 2012000; fax (51) 2823439; e-mail bhcmedia@isb.comsats.net.pk; internet www.britainonline.org.pk; High Commissioner Robert Brinkley.

Panama: MMG Tower, 4°, Calle 53, Urb. Marbella, Apdo 0816-07946, Panamá 1; tel. 269-0866; fax 263-5138; e-mail britemb@cwpanama.net; internet www.britishembassy.gov.uk/panama; Ambassador RICHARD AUSTEN.

Papua New Guinea: Kiroki St, Locked Bag 212, Waigani 131, NCD; tel. 3251677; fax 3253547; e-mail bhcpng@datec.net.pg; internet www.britishhighcommission.gov.uk/papuanewguinea; High Commissioner David Dunn.

Peru: Torre Parque Mar, 22°, Avda José Larco 1301, Miraflores, Lima; tel. (1) 6173000; fax (1) 6173100; e-mail belima@fco.gov.uk; internet www.britemb.org.pe; Ambassador CATHERINE NETTLETON.

Philippines: Locsin Bldg, 15th–17th Floors, 6752 Ayala Ave, cnr Makati Ave, Makati City, 1226 Metro Manila; tel. (2) 5808700; fax (2) 8197206; e-mail uk@info.com.ph; internet www.britishembassy.gov.uk/philippines; Ambassador Peter Beckingham.

Poland: 00-556 Warsaw, Al. Róż 1; tel. (22) 3110000; fax (22) 3110311; e-mail info@britishembassy.pl; internet www.britishembassy.pl; Ambassador DAMIAN RODERIC (RIC) TODD.

Portugal: Rua de São Bernardo 33, 1249-082 Lisbon; tel. (21) 3924000; fax (21) 3924021; e-mail ppa@fco.gov.uk; internet www.uk-embassy.pt; Ambassador Alexander Ellis.

Qatar: POB 3, Doha; tel. 4962000; fax 4962086; e-mail consular_qatar@fco.gov.uk; internet www.britishembassy.gov.uk/qatar; Ambassador RODERICK IAN DRUMMOND.

Romania: 010463 Bucharest, Str. Jules Michelet 24; tel. (21) 2017200; fax (21) 2017299; e-mail press@bucharest.mail.fco.gov.uk; internet www.britishembassy.gov.uk/romania; Ambassador Robin Barnett.

Russian Federation: 121099 Moscow, Smolenskaya nab. 10; tel. (495) 956-72-00; fax (495) 956-72-01; e-mail moscow@britishembassy.ru; internet www.britaininrussia.ru; Ambassador SIR ANTHONY BRENTON.

Rwanda: Parcelle 1131, Blvd de l'Umuganda, Kacyiru, BP 576, Kigali; tel. 584098; fax 582044; e-mail embassy.kigali@fco.gov.uk; internet www.britishembassykigali.org.rw; Ambassador Nicholas Cannon.

Saint Lucia: Francis Compton Bldg, Waterfront, POB 227, Castries; tel. 452-2484; fax 453-1543; e-mail britishhc@candw.lc; High Commissioner DUNCAN JOHN RUSHWORTH TAYLOR (resident in Barbados).

Saudi Arabia: POB 94351, Riyadh 11693; tel. (1) 488-0077; fax (1) 488-1209; e-mail PressOffice.Riyadh@fco.gov.uk; internet www.britishembassy.gov.uk/saudiarabia; Ambassador William Patey.

Senegal: 20 rue du Dr Guillet, BP 6025, Dakar; tel. 33-823-7392; fax 33-823-2766; e-mail britembe@orange.sn; internet www.britishembassy.gov.uk/senegal; Ambassador CHRIS TROTT.

Serbia: 11000 Belgrade, Resavska 46; tel. (11) 3060900; fax (11) 3061077; e-mail belgrade.ppd@fco.gov.uk; internet www.britishembassy.gov.uk/serbia; Ambassador Stephen John Wordsworth.

Seychelles: 3rd Floor, Oliaji Trade Centre, POB 161, Victoria; tel. 283666; fax 283657; e-mail bhcvictoria@fco.gov.uk; internet www.bhcvictoria.sc; High Commissioner FERGUS COCHRANE-DYET.

Sierra Leone: 6 Spur Rd, Wilberforce, Freetown; tel. (22) 232565; fax (22) 232070; e-mail freetown.consular.enquiries@fco.gov.uk; internet www.britishhighcommission.gov.uk/sierraleone; High Commissioner Sarah MacIntosh.

Singapore: 100 Tanglin Rd, Singapore 247919; tel. 64244200; fax 64244218; e-mail commercial.singapore@fco.gov.uk; internet www.britain.org.sg; High Commissioner PAUL MADDEN.

Slovakia: Panská 16, 811 01 Bratislava; tel. (2) 5998-2000; fax (2) 5998-2237; e-mail bebra@internet.sk; internet www.britishembassy.sk; Ambassador Michael John Wyn Roberts.

Slovenia: 1000 Ljubljana, trg Republike 3/IV; tel. (1) 2003910; fax (1) 4250174; e-mail info@british-embassy.si; internet www.british-embassy.si; Ambassador TIM SIMMONS.

Solomon Islands: Telekom House, Mendana Ave, POB 676, Honiara; tel. 21705; fax 21549; e-mail bhc@solomon.com.sb; High Commissioner Richard John Lyne.

South Africa: 255 Hill St, Arcadia, Pretoria 0002; tel. (12) 4217500; fax (12) 4217555; e-mail media.pretoria@fco.gov.uk; internet www.britain.org.za; High Commissioner PAUL BOATENG.

Spain: Fernando el Santo 16, 28010 Madrid; tel. (91) 7008200; fax (91) 7008210; e-mail enquiries.madrid@fco.gov.uk; internet www.ukinspain.com; Ambassador Denise Mary Holt.

Sri Lanka: 190 Galle Rd, Kollupitiya, POB 1433, Colombo 3; tel. (11) 2437336; fax (11) 2430308; e-mail colombo.general@fco.gov.lk; internet www.britishhighcommission.gov.uk/srilanka; High Commissioner DR PETER HAYES.

Sudan: St 10, off Baladia St, POB 801, Khartoum; tel. (183) 777105; fax (183) 776457; e-mail Media.Khartoum@fco.gov.uk; internet www.britishembassy.gov.uk/sudan; Ambassador Ian Cliff.

Sweden: Skarpögt. 6–8, POB 27819, 115 93 Stockholm; tel. (8) 671-30-00; fax (8) 671-31-04; e-mail info@britishembassy.se; internet www.britishembassy.se; Ambassador ANDREW J. MITCHELL.

Switzerland: Thunstr. 50, 3000 Bern 15; tel. 313597700; fax 313597701; e-mail info@britain-in-switzerland.ch; internet www.britishembassy.ch; Ambassador Simon Featherstone.

Syria: BP 37, Immeuble Kotob, 11 rue Muhammad Kurd Ali, Malki, Damascus; tel. (11) 3739241; fax (11) 3921873; e-mail british.embassy.damascus@fco.gov.uk; internet www.britishembassy.gov.uk/syria; Ambassador SIMON COLLIS.

Tajikistan: 734002 Dushanbe, Kuchai M. Tursunzoda 65; tel. (372) 224-22-21; fax (372) 227-17-26; e-mail dushanbe.reception@fco.gov.uk; internet www.britishembassy.gov.uk/tajikistan; Ambassador Graeme Loten.

Tanzania: Umoja House, Garden Ave, POB 9200, Dar es Salaam; tel. (22) 2110101; fax (22) 2110102; e-mail bhc.dar@fco.gov.uk; internet www.britishhighcommission.gov.uk/tanzania; High Commissioner PHILIP PARHAM.

Thailand: 14 Thanon Witthayu, Lumpini, Pathumwan, Bangkok 10330; tel. (2) 305-8333; fax (2) 255-8619; e-mail info.bangkok@fco.gov.uk; internet www.britishembassy.gov.uk/Thailand; Ambassador Quinton Mark Quayle.

Trinidad and Tobago: 19 St Clair Circle, St Clair, POB 778, Port of Spain; tel. 622-2748; fax 622-4555; e-mail csbhc@tstt.net.tt; internet www.britishhighcommission.gov.uk/trinidadandtobago; High Commissioner ERIC JENKINSON.

Tunisia: rue du Lac Windermere, Les Berges du Lac, 1053 Tunis; tel. (71) 108-700; fax (71) 108-769; e-mail british.emb@planet.tn; internet www.britishembassy.gov.uk/tunisia; Ambassador Alan Goulty.

Turkey: Şehit Ersan Cad. 46/A, 06680 Çankaya, Ankara; tel. (312) 4553344; fax (312) 4553356; e-mail britembinf@fco.gov.uk; internet www.britishembassy.gov.uk/turkey; Ambassador NICK BAIRD.

Turkmenistan: 744001 Aşgabat, Four Points Ak Altin Hotel, 3rd Floor, Office Bldg; tel. (12) 36-34-62; fax (12) 36-34-65; e-mail beasb@online.tm; internet www.britishembassy.gov.uk/turkmenistan; Ambassador Peter Butcher.

Uganda: Plot 4, Windsor Loop Rd, POB 7070, Kampala; tel. (31) 4312000; fax (41) 4257304; e-mail bhcinfo@starcom.co.ug; internet www.britishhighcommission.gov.uk/uganda; High Commissioner FRANCOIS GORDON.

Ukraine: 01025 Kyiv, vul. Desyatynna 9; tel. (44) 490-36-60; fax (44) 490-36-62; e-mail ukembinf@sovamua.com; internet www.britishembassy.gov/ukraine; Ambassador Tim Barrow.

United Arab Emirates: POB 248, Abu Dhabi; tel. (2) 6101100; fax (2) 6101586; e-mail chancery.abudhabi@fco.gov.uk; internet www.britishembassy.gov.uk/uae; Ambassador EDWARD OAKDEN.

United States of America: 3100 Massachusetts Ave, NW, Washington, DC 20008; tel. (202) 588-7800; fax (202) 588-7870; e-mail washi@fco.gov.uk; internet www.britainusa.com; Ambassador Sir Nigel Sheinwald.

Uruguay: Marco Bruto 1073, Casilla 16024, 11300 Montevideo; tel. (2) 6223630; fax (2) 6227815; e-mail bemonte@internet.com.uy; internet www.britishembassy.org.uy; Ambassador DR HUGH SALVESSEN.

Uzbekistan: 100000 Tashkent, ul. Ya. G'ulomov ko'ch. 67; tel. (71) 120-78-52; fax (71) 120-65-49; e-mail brit@emb.uz; internet www.britishembassy .gov.uk/uzbekistan; Ambassador Iain Kelly.

Vatican City: Via XX Settembre 80A, 00187 Rome, Italy; tel. (06) 42204000; fax (06) 42204205; e-mail holysee@fco.gov.uk; internet www.britishembassy .gov.uk/vatican; Ambassador FRANCIS MARTIN-XAVIER CAMPBELL.

Venezuela: Torre La Castellana, 11°, Avda Principal La Castellana, Caracas 1061; tel. (212) 263-8411; fax (212) 267-1275; e-mail britishembassy@internet .ve; internet www.britain.org.ve; Ambassador Catherine Royle.

Viet Nam: Central Bldg, 4th Floor, 31 Hai Ba Trung, Hanoi; tel. (4) 9360500; fax (4) 9360561; e-mail behanoi@hn.vnn.vn; internet www.uk-vietnam.org; Ambassador MARK ANDREW GEOFFREY KENT.

Yemen: POB 1287, 938 Thaher Himiyar St, East Ring Rd, San'a; tel. (1) 302450; fax (1) 302454; e-mail britishembassysanaa@fco.gov.uk; internet www.britishembassy.gov.uk/yemen; Ambassador Tim Torlot.

Zambia: Plot 5201, Independence Ave, POB 50050, 15101 Ridgeway, Lusaka; tel. (1) 251133; fax (1) 253798; High Commissioner ALISTAIR HARRISON.

Zimbabwe: Corner House, cnr Samora Machel Ave and Leopold Takawira St, POB 4490, Harare; tel. (4) 772990; fax (4) 774617; e-mail consular .harare@fco.gov.uk; internet www.britishembassy.gov.uk/zimbabwe; Ambassador Dr Andrew Pocock.

DIPLOMATIC MISSIONS OF USA

United Nations: 799 United Nations Plaza, New York, NY 10017; tel. (212) 415-4000; fax (212) 415-4443; e-mail usa@un.int; internet www.un.int/usa; Permanent Representative ZALMAY KHALILZAD.

Afghanistan: Great Masoud Rd, Kabul; tel. (20) 2300436; fax (20) 2301364; e-mail usambassadorkabul@state.gov; internet kabul.usembassy.gov; Ambassador William Braucher Wood.

Albania: Rruga Elbasanit 103, Tirana; tel. (4) 247285; fax (4) 232222; e-mail wm_tirana@pd.state.gov; internet tirana.usembassy.gov; Ambassador DR JOHN L. WITHERS, II.

Algeria: BP 549, 4 chemin Cheikh Bachir El-Ibrahimi, el-Biar, 16000 Algiers; tel. (21) 69-12-55; fax (21) 69-39-79; e-mail algiers_webmaster@state.gov; internet algiers.usembassy.gov; Ambassador Robert S. Ford.

Angola: Rua Houari Boumedienne 32, Miramar, CP 6468, Luanda; tel. 222641000; fax 222641232; e-mail econusembassyluanda@yahoo.com; internet luanda.usembassy.gov; Ambassador DAN MOZENA.

Argentina: Avda Colombia 4300, C1425GMN Buenos Aires; tel. (11) 5777-4533; fax (11) 5777-4212; internet buenosaires.usembassy.gov; Ambassador Earl Anthony Wayne.

Armenia: 0082 Yerevan, American Ave 1; tel. (10) 46-47-00; fax (10) 46-47-42; e-mail usinfo@usa.am; internet yerevan.usembassy.gov; Chargé d'affaires a.i. JOSEPH PENNINGTON.

Australia: Moonah Place, Yarralumla, ACT 2600; tel. (2) 6214-5600; fax (2) 6214-5970; e-mail info@usembassy-australia.state.gov; internet canberra .usembassy.gov; Ambassador Robert D. McCallum, Jr.

Austria: Boltzmanngasse 16, 1090 Vienna; tel. (1) 313-39; fax (1) 310-06-82; e-mail embassy@usembassy.at; internet www.usembassy.at; Ambassador CHARLES A. GARGANO.

Azerbaijan: 1007 Baku, Azadlıq pr. 83; tel. (12) 498-03-36; fax (12) 465-66-71; internet azerbaijan.usembassy.gov; Ambassador Anne E. Derse.

Bahamas: Mosmar Bldg, Queen St, POB N-8197, Nassau; tel. 322-1181; fax 328-7838; e-mail embnas@state.gov; internet nassau.usembassy.gov; Ambassador NED L. SIEGEL.

Bahrain: POB 26431, Bldg 979, Rd 3119, Block 331, Zinj, Manama; tel. 17242700; fax 17270547; e-mail manamaconsular@state.gov; internet bahrain.usembassy.gov; Ambassador Joseph Adam Ereli.

Bangladesh: Madani Ave, Baridhara, POB 323, Dhaka 1212; tel. (2) 8824700; fax (2) 8823744; e-mail ustc@bangla.net; internet dhaka.usembassy.gov; Ambassador JAMES F. MORIARTY.

Barbados: Wildey Business Park, Wildey, POB 302, Bridgetown BB 14006; tel. 436-4950; fax 227-4073; internet bridgetown.usembassy.gov; Ambassador Mary Ourisman.

Belarus: 220002 Minsk, vul. Staravilenskaya 46; tel. (17) 210-12-83; fax (17) 234-78-53; e-mail webmaster@usembassy.minsk.by; internet www .usembassy.minsk.by; Ambassador KAREN B. STEWART.

Belgium: 27 blvd du Régent, 1000 Brussels; tel. (2) 508-21-11; fax (2) 511-21-60; internet brussels.usembassy.gov; Ambassador Sam Fox.

Belize: Floral Park Road, Belmopan; tel. 822-4011; fax 822-4012; e-mail embbelize@state.gov; internet belize.usembassy.gov; Ambassador ROBERT J. DIETER.

Benin: Carré 125, rue Caporal Anani Bernard, 01 BP 2012, Cotonou; tel. 21-30-06-50; fax 21-30-06-70; internet usembassy.state.gov/benin; Ambassador Gayleatha B. Brown.

Bolivia: Avda Arce 2780, Casilla 425, La Paz; tel. (2) 243-0251; fax (2) 243-3900; internet lapaz.usembassy.gov; Ambassador PHILIP S. GOLDBERG.

Bosnia and Herzegovina: 71000 Sarajevo, Alipašina 43; tel. (33) 445700; fax (33) 659722; e-mail bhopa@state.gov; internet sarajevo.usembassy.gov; Ambassador Charles L. English.

Botswana: Embassy Enclave, off Khama Cres., POB 90, Gaborone; tel. 3953982; fax 3956947; e-mail ircgaborone@state.gov; internet botswana .usembassy.gov; Ambassador KATHERINE H. CANAVAN.

Brazil: SES, Av. das Nações, Quadra 801, Lote 03, 70403-900 Brasília, DF; tel. (61) 3321-7000; fax (61) 3325-9136; e-mail ircbsb@state.gov; internet brasilia.usembassy.gov; Ambassador Clifford M. Sobel.

Brunei: Teck Guan Plaza, 3rd Floor, Jalan Sultan, Bandar Seri Begawan BS 8811; tel. 2220384; fax 2225293; e-mail amembassy_bsb@state.gov; internet bandar.usembassy.gov; Ambassador EMIL SKODON.

Bulgaria: 1407 Sofia, ul. Kozyak 16; tel. (2) 937-51-00; fax (2) 937-53-20; e-mail sofia@usembassy.bg; internet bulgaria.usembassy.gov; Ambassador John R. Beyrle.

Burkina Faso: 602 ave Raoul Follereau, Koulouba, 01 BP 35, Ouagadougou 01; tel. 50-30-67-23; fax 50-31-23-68; e-mail amembouaga@state.gov; internet ouagadougou.usembassy.gov; Ambassador JEANINE E. JACKSON.

Burundi: ave des Etats-Unis, BP 1720, Bujumbura; tel. 22223454; fax 22222926; e-mail jyellin@bujumbura.us-state.gov; internet burundi .usembassy.gov; Ambassador Patricia N. Moller.

Cambodia: 1 rue 96, Sangkat Wat Phnom, Khan Daun Penh, Phnom-Penh; tel. (23) 728000; fax (23) 728600; internet phnompenh.usembassy.gov; Ambassador JOSEPH A. MUSSOMELI.

Cameroon: rue Nachtigal, BP 817, Yaoundé; tel. 2223-1500; internet usembassy.state.gov/yaounde; Ambassador Janet E. Garvey.

Canada: 490 Sussex Dr., POB 866, Station B, Ottawa, ON K1P 5T1; tel. (613) 238-5335; fax (613) 688-3080; internet ottawa.usembassy.gov; Ambassador DAVID HORTON WILKINS.

Cape Verde: Rua Abílio Macedo 6, Praia, Santiago; tel. 2608900; fax 2611355; internet praia.usembassy.gov; Ambassador Roger Dwayne Pierce.

Central African Republic: ave David Dacko, BP 924, Bangui; tel. 61-02-00; fax 61-44-94; Ambassador FREDERICK B. COOK.

Chad: ave Félix Eboué, BP 413, N'Djamena; tel. 251-70-09; fax 251-56-54; e-mail YingraD@state.gov; internet chad.usembassy.gov; Ambassador Louis John Nigro, Jr.

Chile: Avda Andrés Bello 2800, Las Condes, Santiago; tel. (2) 232-2600; fax (2) 330-3710; internet www.usembassy.cl; Ambassador PAUL E. SIMONS.

China, People's Republic: 3 Xiu Shui Bei Jie, Jian Guo Men Wai, Beijing 100600; tel. (10) 65323831; fax (10) 65323178; internet beijing.usembassy -china.org.cn; Ambassador Clark Thorp Randt, Jr.

Colombia: Calle 22D-bis, No 47-51, Apdo Aéreo 3831, Bogotá, DC; tel. (1) 315-0811; fax (1) 315-2197; internet bogota.usembassy.gov; Ambassador WILLIAM R. BROWNFIELD.

Congo, Democratic Republic: 310 ave des Aviateurs, BP 397, Kinshasa; tel. (81) 5560151; fax (81) 5560173; e-mail AEKinshasaConsular@state.gov; internet kinshasa.usembassy.gov; Ambassador William John Garvelink.

Costa Rica: Calle 120 Avda 0, Pavas, Apdo 920, 1200 San José; tel. 519-2000; fax 220-2305; e-mail info@usembassy.or.cr; internet sanjose.usembassy.gov; Ambassador MARK LANGDALE.

Côte d'Ivoire: Cocody Riviera Golf, 01 BP 1712, Abidjan 01; tel. 22-49-40-00; fax 22-49-43-23; e-mail abjpress@state.gov; internet abidjan.usembassy.gov; Ambassador Wanda L. Nesbitt.

Croatia: 10010 Zagreb, Thomasa Jeffersona 2; tel. (1) 6612200; fax (1) 6612373; e-mail irc@usembassy.hr; internet www.zagreb.usembassy.gov; Ambassador ROBERT ANTHONY BRADTKE.

Cuba: Interests Section: Calzada, entre L y M, Vedado, Havana; tel. (7) 833-3551; fax (7) 833-1084; e-mail irchavana@state.org; internet havana .usinterestsection.gov; Principal Officer Michael E. Parmly.

Cyprus: Metochiou and Ploutarchou, Engomi, 2407 Nicosia; POB 24536, 1385 Nicosia; tel. 22393939; fax 22780944; e-mail consularnicosia@state.gov; internet cyprus.usembassy.gov; Ambassador RONALD L. SCHLICHER.

Czech Republic: Tržiště 15, 118 01 Prague 1; tel. 257022000; fax 257022809; e-mail webmaster@usembassy.cz; internet www.usembassy.cz; Ambassador Richard W. Graber.

Denmark: Dag Hammarskjölds Allé 24, 2100 Copenhagen Ø; tel. 33-41-71-00; fax 35-43-02-23; e-mail usembassycopenhagen@state.gov; internet www.usembassy.dk; Ambassador JAMES PALMER CAIN.

Djibouti: Villa Plateau du Serpent, blvd du Maréchal Joffre, BP 185, Djibouti; tel. 353995; fax 353940; e-mail amembadm@bow.intnet.dj; internet djibouti.usembassy.gov; Ambassador W. Stuart Symington.

Dominican Republic: César Nicolás Pensón, esq. Leopoldo Navarro, Santo Domingo, DN; tel. 221-2171; fax 685-6959; e-mail irc@usemb.gov.do; internet www.usemb.gov.do/index.htm; Ambassador P. ROBERT FANNIN.

Ecuador: Avda 12 de Octubre 1942 y Patria 120, Quito; tel. (2) 256-2890; fax (2) 250-2052; internet www.usembassy.org.ec; Ambassador Linda L. Jewell.

Egypt: 8 Sharia Kamal ed-Din Salah, Cairo (Garden City); tel. (2) 7973300; fax (2) 7973200; e-mail consularcairo@state.gov; internet cairo.usembassy.gov; Ambassador FRANCIS JOSEPH RICCIARDONE.

El Salvador: Blvd Santa Elena Sur, Antiguo Cuscatlán, San Salvador; tel. 2278-4444; fax 2278-1815; internet www.usinfo.org.sv; Ambassador Charles L. Glazer.

Equatorial Guinea: K-3, Carretera de Aeropuerto, Malabo; tel. (09) 88-95; fax (09) 88-94; e-mail usembassymalabo@yahoo.com; internet malabo.usembassy.gov; Ambassador DONALD C. JOHNSON.

Eritrea: POB 211, 179 Ala St, Asmara; tel. (1) 120004; fax (1) 127584; e-mail usembassyasmara@state.gov; internet asmara.usembassy.gov; Ambassador Ronald K. McMullen.

Estonia: Kentmanni 20, Tallinn 15099; tel. 668-8100; fax 668-8134; e-mail usasaatkond@state.gov; internet www.usemb.ee; Ambassador STANLEY DAVIS (DAVE) PHILLIPS.

Ethiopia: Entoto St, POB 1014, Addis Ababa; tel. (11) 5174000; fax (11) 5174001; e-mail pasaddis@state.gov; internet addisababa.usembassy.gov; Ambassador Donald Y. Yamamoto.

Fiji: 31 Loftus St, POB 218, Suva; tel. 3314466; fax 3308685; e-mail usembsuva@connect.com.fj; internet suva.usembassy.gov; Ambassador LARRY MILES DINGER.

Finland: Itäinen puistotie 14, 00140 Helsinki; tel. (9) 616250; fax (9) 6165135; e-mail webmaster@usembassy.fi; internet finland.usembassy.gov; Ambassador Marilyn Ware.

France: 2 ave Gabriel, 75382 Paris Cedex 08; tel. 1-43-12-22-22; fax 1-42-66-97-83; internet france.usembassy.gov; Ambassador CRAIG ROBERTS STAPLETON.

Gabon: blvd du Bord de Mer, BP 4000, Libreville; tel. 76-20-03; fax 74-55-07; e-mail clolibreville@state.gov; internet libreville.usembassy.gov; Ambassador R. Barrie Walkley.

Gambia: The White House, Kairaba Ave, Fajara, PMB 19, Banjul; tel. 4392856; fax 4392475; e-mail consularbanjul@state.gov; internet www.usembassybanjul.gm; Ambassador BARRY LEON WELLS.

Georgia: 0131 Tbilisi, G. Balanchine 11; tel. (32) 27-70-00; fax (32) 53-23-10; e-mail consulate-tbilisi@state.gov; internet georgia.usembassy.gov; Ambassador John F. Tefft.

Germany: Neustädtische Kirchestr. 4–5, 10117 Berlin; tel. (30) 2385174; fax (30) 83051215; internet germany.usembassy.gov; Ambassador WILLIAM ROBERT TIMKEN, Jr.

Ghana: Ring Rd East, POB 194, Accra; tel. (21) 775348; fax (21) 776008; e-mail prsaccra@pd.state.gov; internet accra.usembassy.gov; Ambassador Pamela Ethel Bridgewater.

Greece: Leoforos Vassilissis Sofias 91, 106 60 Athens; tel. (210) 7212951; fax (210) 7226724; e-mail usembassy@usembassy.gr; internet www.usembassy.gr; Ambassador DANIEL V. SPECKHARD.

Grenada: POB 54, St George's; tel. 444-1173; fax 444-4820; e-mail usemb_gd@caribsurf.com; Ambassador Mary Ourisman (resident in Barbados).

Guatemala: Avda de la Reforma 7-01, Zona 10, Guatemala City; tel. 2331-1541; fax 2331-8885; internet guatemala.usembassy.gov; Ambassador STEPHEN MCFARLAND (designate).

Guinea: Koloma, Ratoma, BP 603, Conakry; tel. 30-42-08-61; fax 30-42-08-73; e-mail Consularconkr@state.gov; internet conakry.usembassy.gov; Ambassador Phillip Carter, III.

Guyana: 100 Young and Duke Sts, POB 10507, Kingston, Georgetown; tel. 226-3938; fax 225-8497; internet georgetown.usembassy.gov; e-mail usembassy@hotmail.com; Chargé d'affaires a.i. KAREN WILLIAMS.

Haiti: 5 blvd Harry S Truman, BP 1761, Port-au-Prince; tel. 222-0200; fax 223-9038; internet haiti.usembassy.gov; Ambassador Janet A. Sanderson.

Honduras: Avda La Paz, Apdo 3453, Tegucigalpa; tel. 236-9320; fax 236-9037; internet honduras.usembassy.gov; Ambassador CHARLES A. FORD.

Hungary: 1054 Budapest, Szabadság tér 12; tel. (1) 475-4400; fax (1) 475-4764; e-mail postmaster@usembassy.hu; internet www.usembassy.hu; Ambassador April H. Foley.

Iceland: Laufásvegur 21, 101 Reykjavík; tel. 5629100; fax 5629110; e-mail reykjavikconsular@state.gov; internet iceland.usembassy.gov; Ambassador CAROL VAN VOORST.

India: Shanti Path, Chanakyapuri, New Delhi 110 021; tel. (11) 24198000; fax (11) 241900170; e-mail ndcentral@state.gov; internet newdelhi.usembassy.gov; Ambassador David Campbell Mulford.

Indonesia: Jalan Merdeka Selatan 4–5, Jakarta 10110; tel. (21) 34359000; fax (21) 34359922; e-mail jakconsul@state.gov; internet jakarta.usembassy.gov; Ambassador CAMERON R. HUME.

Iraq: APO AE 09316, Baghdad; e-mail BaghdadPressOffice@state.gov; internet iraq.usembassy.gov; Ambassador Ryan C. Crocker.

Ireland: 42 Elgin Rd, Ballsbridge, Dublin 4; tel. (1) 6688777; fax (1) 6689946; e-mail webmasterireland@state.gov; internet dublin.usembassy.gov; Ambassador THOMAS C. FOLEY.

Israel: 71 Hayarkon St, Tel-Aviv 63903; tel. 3-5197575; e-mail ac5@bezeqint.net; internet telaviv.usembassy.gov; Ambassador Richard H. Jones.

Italy: Palazzo Margherita, Via Vittorio Veneto 119A, 00187 Roma; tel. (06) 46741; fax (06) 46742217; internet italy.usembassy.gov; Ambassador RONALD P. SPOGLI.

Jamaica: 142 Old Hope Rd, Kingston 6; tel. 702-6000; e-mail opakgn@state.gov; internet kingston.usembassy.gov; Ambassador Brenda LaGrange Johnson.

Japan: 1-10-5, Akasaka, Minato-ku, Tokyo 107-8420; tel. (3) 3224-5000; fax (3) 3505-1862; internet tokyo.usembassy.gov; Ambassador THOMAS SCHIEFFER.

Jordan: POB 354, Amman 11118; tel. (6) 5906000; fax (6) 5920121; e-mail webmasterjordan@state.gov; internet www.usembassy-amman.org.jo; Ambassador David Hale.

Kazakhstan: 010010 Astana, Ak Bulak 4/23-22/3; tel. (7172) 70-21-00; fax (7172) 34-08-90; e-mail info@usembassy.kz; internet kazakhstan.usembassy.gov; Ambassador JOHN M. ORDWAY.

Kenya: United Nations Ave, POB 606, Village Market, 00621 Nairobi; tel. (20) 3636000; fax (20) 537810; e-mail ircnairobi@state.gov; internet nairobi.usembassy.gov; Ambassador Michael E. Ranneberger.

Korea, Republic: 32, Sejong-no, Jongno-gu, Seoul 110-710; tel. (2) 397-4114; fax (2) 735-3903; e-mail EmbassySeoulPA@state.gov; internet seoul.usembassy.gov; Ambassador ALEXANDER R. VERSHBOW.

Kosovo: 1000 Prishtina, Arbëri, Nazim Hikmet 30; tel. (38) 593000; fax (38) 549890; e-mail papristina@state.gov; internet www.pristina.usembassy.gov; Chargé d'affaires Tina S. Kaidanow.

Kuwait: POB 77, 13001 Safat, Bayan, Al-Masjed al-Aqsa St, Plot 14, Block 14, Kuwait City; tel. 2591001; fax 5380282; e-mail paskuwaitm@state.gov; internet kuwait.usembassy.gov; Ambassador DEBORAH K. JONES.

Kyrgyzstan: 720016 Bishkek, pr. Mira 171; tel. (312) 55-12-41; fax (312) 55-12-64; internet bishkek.usembassy.gov; Ambassador Marie L. Yovanovitch.

Laos: 19 rue Bartholonie, BP 114, That Dam, Vientiane; tel. (21) 267000; fax (21) 267190; e-mail khammanhpx@state.gov; internet vientiane.usembassy.gov; Ambassador RAVIC ROLF HUSO.

Latvia: Raiņa bulv. 7, Rīga 1510; tel. 6703-6206; fax 6722-2132; internet www.usembassy.lv; AmbassadorCharles W. Larson, Jr.

Lebanon: POB 70-840, Antélias; tel. (4) 542600; fax (4) 544136; e-mail pasbeirut@state.gov; internet lebanon.usembassy.gov; Chargé d'affaires a.i. MICHELE J. SISON.

Lesotho: 254 Kingsway, POB 333, Maseru 100; tel. 22312666; fax 22310116; e-mail infomaseru@state.gov; internet maseru.usembassy.gov; Ambassador Robert Nolan.

Liberia: 111 United Nations Dr., Mamba Point, POB 10-0098, Monrovia; tel. (7) 7054826; fax (7) 710370; e-mail ConsularMonrovia@state.gov; internet monrovia.usembassy.gov; Ambassador DONALD E. BOOTH.

Libya: Corinthia Bab Africa Hotel, Souq at-Tlat al-Qadim, Tripoli; tel. (21) 3351831; e-mail paotripoli@state.gov; internet libya.usembassy.gov; Chargé d'affaires a.i. John Christopher Stevens.

Lithuania: Akmenų g. 6, Vilnius 03106; tel. (5) 266-5300; fax (5) 266-5310; e-mail webemailvilnius@state.gov; internet vilnius.usembassy.gov; Ambassador JOHN A. CLOUD.

Luxembourg: 22 blvd Emmanuel Servais, 2535 Luxembourg; tel. 46-01-23; fax 46-14-01; internet luxembourg.usembassy.gov; Ambassador Ann Louise Wagner.

Macedonia, former Yugoslav Republic: 1000 Skopje, Ilindenska bb; tel. (2) 3116180; fax (2) 3117103; internet skopje.usembassy.gov; Ambassador GILLIAN ARLETTE MILOVANOVIĆ.

Madagascar: 14–16 rue Rainitovo, Antsahavola, BP 620, 101 Antananarivo; tel. (20) 2221257; fax (20) 2234539; internet www.usmission.mg; Ambassador R. Niels Marquardt.

Malawi: Area 40, Plot No. 18, 16 Jomo Kenyatta Rd, POB 30016, Lilongwe 3; tel. 1773166; fax 1770471; e-mail ConsularLilongwe@state.gov; internet lilongwe.usembassy.gov; Ambassador ALAN W. EASTHAM.

Malaysia: 376 Jalan Tun Razak, POB 10035, 50400 Kuala Lumpur; tel. (3) 21685000; fax (3) 21422207; e-mail klconsular@state.gov; internet www .usembassymalaysia.org.my; Ambassador James R. Keith.

Mali: ACI 2000, rue 243, porte 297, Bamako; tel. 270-23-00; fax 270-24-79; e-mail webmaster@usa.org.ml; internet mali.usembassy.gov; Ambassador TERENCE PATRICK McCULLEY.

Malta: Development House, 3rd Floor, St Anne St, Floriana FRN 9010; tel. 25614000; fax 21243229; e-mail usembmalta@state.gov; internet malta .usembassy.gov; Ambassador Molly Hering Bordonaro.

Marshall Islands: POB 1379, Majuro, MH 96960; tel. (247) 4011; fax (247) 4012; e-mail publicmajuro@state.gov; internet umajuro.usembassy.gov; Ambassador CLYDE BISHOP.

Mauritania: rue Abdallaye, BP 222, Nouakchott; tel. 525-26-60; fax 525-15-92; e-mail tayebho@state.gov; internet mauritania.usembassy.gov; Ambassador Mark M. Boulware.

Mauritius: Rogers House, 4th Floor, John F. Kennedy St, POB 544, Port Louis; tel. 208-4400; fax 208-9534; e-mail usembass@intnet.mu; internet mauritius.usembassy.gov; Ambassador CESAR BENITO CABRERA.

Mexico: Paseo de la Reforma 305, Del. Cuauhtémoc, 06500 México, DF; tel. (55) 5080-2000; fax (55) 5080-2150; internet www.usembassy-mexico.gov; Ambassador Antonio O. Garza, Jr.

Micronesia, Federated States: POB 1286, Kolonia, Pohnpei, FM 96941; tel. 320-2187; fax 320-2186; e-mail usembassy@mail.fm; internet www.fm/ usembassy; Ambassador MIRIAM K. HUGHES.

Moldova: 2009 Chişinău, str. Mateevici 103; tel. (22) 40-83-00; fax (22) 23-30-44; e-mail IRCChisinau@state.gov; internet moldova.usembassy.gov; Ambassador Michael D. Kirby.

Mongolia: Ikh Toiruu 59/1, Ulan Bator (CPOB 1021); tel. (11) 329095; fax (11) 320776; e-mail webmaster@us-mongolia.com; internet mongolia .usembassy.gov; Ambassador MARK C. MINTON.

Montenegro: 81000 Podgorica, Ljubljanska bb; tel. (81) 225417; fax (81) 241358; e-mail podgorica@state.gov; internet podgorica.usembassy.gov; Ambassador Roderick V. Moore.

Morocco: 2 ave de Muhammad el-Fassi, Rabat; tel. (3) 7762265; fax (3) 7765661; e-mail ircrabat@usembassy.ma; internet rabat.usembassy.gov; Ambassador THOMAS T. RILEY.

Mozambique: Av. Kenneth Kaunda 193, CP 783, Maputo; tel. 21492797; fax 21490114; e-mail consularmaputo@state.gov; internet www.usembassy -maputo.gov.mz; Ambassador William R. Steiger (designate).

Myanmar: 581 Merchant St, POB 521, Yangon; tel. (1) 379880; fax (1) 256018; e-mail info.rangoon@state.gov; internet rangoon.usembassy.gov; Chargé d'affaires SHARI VILLAROSA.

Namibia: 14 Lossen St, Ausspannplatz, PMB 12029, Windhoek 9000; tel. (61) 221601; fax (61) 229792; internet windhoek.usembassy.gov; Ambassador Gail Dennise Mathieu.

Nepal: Panipokhari, POB 295, Kathmandu; tel. (1) 4411179; fax (1) 4419963; e-mail usembktm@state.gov; internet nepal.usembassy.gov; Ambassador NANCY J. POWELL.

Netherlands: Lange Voorhout 102, 2514 EJ The Hague; tel. (70) 3102209; fax (70) 3102307; e-mail ircthehague@state.gov; internet thehague.usembassy .gov; Chargé d'affaires a.i. Michael Gallagher.

New Zealand: 29 Fitzherbert Terrace, POB 1190, Wellington; tel. (4) 462-6000; fax (4) 499-0490; internet wellington.usembassy.gov; Ambassador WILLIAM P. McCORMICK.

Nicaragua: Km 5½, Carretera Sur, Apdo 327, Managua; tel. 252-7100; fax 252-7300; e-mail consularmanagua@state.gov; internet managua.usembassy .gov; Ambassador Robert Callahan (designate).

Niger: rue des Ambassades, BP 11201, Niamey; tel. 20-73-31-69; fax 20-73-55-60; e-mail NiameyPASN@state.gov; internet niamey.usembassy.gov; Ambassador BERNADETTE MARY ALLEN.

Nigeria: 7 Plot 1075, Diplomatic Dr., Central District Area, Abuja; tel. (9) 4614000; fax (9) 4614036; e-mail ircabuja@state.gov; internet abuja .usembassy.gov; Ambassador Robin Renee Sanders.

Norway: Henrik Ibsensgate 48, 0244 Oslo; tel. 22-44-85-50; fax 22-43-07-77; e-mail oslo@usa.no; internet www.usa.no; Ambassador BENSON K. WHITNEY.

Oman: Jamiat ad-Dowal al-Arabiya St, Madinat Qaboos, POB 202, Muscat 115; tel. 24643400; fax 24699771; e-mail webmastermuscat@state.gov; internet oman.usembassy.gov; Ambassador Gary A. Grappo.

Pakistan: Diplomatic Enclave, Ramna 5, POB 1048, Islamabad; tel. (51) 2080000; fax (51) 2276427; e-mail webmasterisb@state.gov; internet islamabad.usembassy.gov; Ambassador ANNE WOODS PATTERSON.

Palau: POB 6028, Koror, PW 96940; tel. 488-2920; fax 488-2911; e-mail usembassykoror@palaunet.com; internet palau.usembassy.gov; Chargé d'affaires Mark Bezner.

Panama: Avda Balboa y Calle 38, Apdo 6959, Panamá 5; tel. 207-7000; fax 227-1964; e-mail panamaweb@state.gov; internet panama.usembassy.gov; Ambassador WILLIAM ALAN EATON BARBARA J. STEPHENSON (designate).

Papua New Guinea: Douglas St, POB 1492, Port Moresby; tel. 3211455; fax 3211593; e-mail png@state.gov; internet portmoresby.usembassy.gov; Ambassador Leslie V. Rowe.

Paraguay: Avda Mariscal López 1776, Casilla 402, Asunción; tel. (21) 21-3715; fax (21) 21-3728; e-mail paraguayusembassy@state.gov; internet asuncion.usembassy.gov; Ambassador JAMES CALDWELL CASON.

Peru: Avda La Encalada 17, Surco, Lima 33; tel. (1) 4343000; fax (1) 6182397; internet usembassy.state.gov/lima; Ambassador Peter Michael McKinley.

Philippines: 1201 Roxas Blvd, 1000 Metro Manila; tel. (2) 5286300; fax (2) 5223242; e-mail manila1@pd.state.gov; internet manila.usembassy.gov; Ambassador KRISTIE A. KENNEY.

Poland: 00-540 Warsaw, Al. Ujazdowskie 29/31; tel. (22) 6283041; fax (22) 6288298; internet poland.usembassy.gov; Ambassador Victor Henderson Ashe.

Portugal: Av. das Forças Armadas (Sete Rios), 1600-081 Lisbon; Apdo 43033, 1601-301 Lisbon; tel. (21) 7273300; fax (21) 7269109; e-mail reflisbon@state.gov; internet lisbon.usembassy.gov; Ambassador THOMAS F. STEPHENSON.

Qatar: 22nd February St, al-Luqta district, POB 2399, Doha; tel. 4884101; fax 4884298; e-mail pasdoha@state.gov; internet qatar.usembassy.gov; Ambassador Joseph LeBaron (designate).

Romania: 020942 Bucharest, Str. Tudor Arghezi 7–9; tel. (21) 2003300; fax (21) 2003442; internet www.usembassy.ro; Ambassador NICHOLAS TAUBMAN.

Russian Federation: 121099 Moscow, B. Devyatinskii per. 8; tel. (495) 728-50-00; fax (495) 728-50-90; e-mail pamoscow@pd.state.gov; internet moscow .usembassy.gov; Ambassador William J. Burns.

Rwanda: blvd de la Révolution, BP 28, Kigali; tel. 505601; fax 507143; e-mail irckigali@state.gov; internet kigali.usembassy.gov; Ambassador MICHAEL RAY ARIETTI.

Samoa: POB 3430, Apia; tel. 21631; fax 22030; e-mail usembassy@samoa .net; internet samoa.usembassy.gov; Chargé d'affaires George W. Colvin, Jr.

Saudi Arabia: POB 94309, Riyadh 11693; tel. (1) 488-3800; fax (1) 488-7360; e-mail riyadhniv@state.gov; internet riyadh.usembassy.gov; Ambassador FORD M. FRAKER.

Senegal: ave Jean XXIII, angle rue Kleber, BP 49, Dakar; tel. 33-823-4296; fax 33-823-5163; e-mail usadakar@state.gov; internet dakar.usembassy.gov; Ambassador Janice L. Jacobs.

Serbia: 11000 Belgrade, Kneza Miloša 50; tel. (11) 3619344; fax (11) 3615489; internet www.belgrade.usembassy.gov; Ambassador CAMERON MUNTER.

Sierra Leone: Leicester, Freetown; tel. (22) 515000; fax (22) 515355; e-mail TaylorJB2@state.gov; internet freetown.usembassy.gov; Ambassador June Carter Perry.

Singapore: 27 Napier Rd, Singapore 258508; tel. 64769100; fax 64769340; e-mail singaporeusembassy@state.gov; internet singapore.usembassy.gov; Ambassador PATRICIA LOUISE HERBOLD.

Slovakia: Hviezdoslavovo nám. 5, 811 02 Bratislava; tel. (2) 5443-3338; fax (2) 5443-0096; e-mail cons@usembassy-bratislava.sk; internet www.usembassy.sk; Ambassador Vincent Obsitnik.

Slovenia: 1000 Ljubljana, Prešernova cesta 31; tel. (1) 2005500; fax (1) 2005555; internet slovenia.usembassy.gov; Chargé d'affaires a.i. MARYRUTH COLEMAN.

South Africa: 877 Pretorius St, Arcadia, Pretoria 0083; POB 9536, Pretoria 0001; tel. (12) 4314000; fax (12) 3422299; e-mail embassypretoria@state.gov; internet southafrica.usembassy.gov; Ambassador Eric M. Bost.

Spain: Serrano 75, 28006 Madrid; tel. (91) 5872200; fax (91) 5872303; internet www.embusa.es; Ambassador EDUARDO AGUIRRE, Jr.

Sri Lanka: 210 Galle Rd, POB 106, Colombo 3; tel. (11) 2441272; fax (11) 2429070; internet srilanka.usembassy.gov; Ambassador Robert O. Blake.

Sudan: Ali Abd al-Latif St, POB 699, Khartoum; tel. (183) 774701; internet khartoum.usembassy.gov; Chargé d'affaires ALBERTO M. FERNANDEZ.

Suriname: Dr Sophie Redmondstraat 129, POB 1821, Paramaribo; tel. 472900; fax 425690; e-mail embuscen@sr.net; internet paramaribo.usembassy.gov; Ambassador Lisa Bobbie Schreiber Hughes.

Swaziland: 2350 Mbabane Pl., Mbabane; tel. 4046441; fax 4045959; internet mbabane.usembassy.gov; Ambassador MAURICE S. PARKER.

Sweden: Dag Hammarskjölds Väg 31, 115 89 Stockholm; tel. (8) 783-53-00; fax (8) 661-19-64; e-mail stockholmweb@state.gov; internet www.usemb.se; Ambassador Michael M. Wood.

Switzerland: Jubiläumsstr. 93, 3005 Bern; tel. 313577011; fax 313577320; internet bern.usembassy.gov; Ambassador PETER R. CONEWAY.

Syria: BP 29, 2 rue al-Mansour, Abou Roumaneh, Damascus; tel. (11) 33914444; fax (11) 33913999; e-mail damasweb-query@state.gov; internet syria.usembassy.gov; Chargé d'affaires Michael Corbin.

Tajikistan: 734019 Dushanbe, Khiyoboni I. Somoni 109A; tel. (372) 229-20-00; fax (372) 229-20-50; e-mail usembassydushanbe@state.gov; internet dushanbe.usembassy.gov; Ambassador TRACEY ANN JACOBSON.

Tanzania: 686 Old Bagamoyo Rd, Msasani, POB 9123, Dar es Salaam; tel. (22) 2668001; fax (22) 2668238; e-mail embassyd@state.gov; internet tanzania.usembassy.gov; Ambassador Mark Green.

Thailand: 95 Thanon Witthayu, Lumpini, Pathumwan, Bangkok 10330; tel. (2) 205-4000; fax (2) 254-1171; e-mail acsbkk@state.gov; internet bangkok.usembassy.gov; Ambassador ERIC G. JOHN.

Timor-Leste: Av. de Portugal, Praia dos Coqueiros, Dili; tel. 3324684; fax 3313206; e-mail larsonta@state.gov; Ambassador Hans G. Klemm.

Togo: rue Kouenou, angle rue 15 Beniglato, BP 852, Lomé; tel. 221-29-94; fax 221-79-52; e-mail RobertsonJJ2@state.gov; internet togo.usembassy.gov; Ambassador DAVID BERNARD DUNN.

Trinidad and Tobago: 15 Queen's Park West, POB 752, Port of Spain; tel. 622-6371; fax 625-5462; e-mail usispos@trinidad.net; internet trinidad.usembassy.gov; Ambassador Dr Roy L. Austin.

Tunisia: Les Berges du Lac, 1053 Tunis; tel. (71) 107-000; fax (71) 107-090; e-mail tuniswebsitecontact@state.gov; internet tunis.usembassy.gov; Ambassador ROBERT F. GODEC.

Turkey: Atatürk Bul. 110, 06100 Kavaklıdere, Ankara; tel. (312) 4555555; fax (312) 4670019; e-mail webmaster_ankara@state.gov; internet turkey.usembassy.gov; Ambassador Ross Wilson.

Turkmenistan: 744000 Aşgabat, ul. Pushkin 9; tel. (12) 35-00-45; fax (12) 39-26-14; e-mail irc-ashgabat@iatp.edu.tm; internet turkmenistan.usembassy.gov; Chargé d'affaires a.i. RICHARD E. HOAGLAND.

Uganda: Plot 1577, Ggaba Rd, POB 7007, Kampala; tel. (41) 4259791; fax (41) 4259794; e-mail KampalaWebContact@state.gov; internet kampala.usembassy.gov; Ambassador Steven A. Browning.

Ukraine: 01901 Kyiv, vul. Yu. Kotsyubynskoho 10; tel. (44) 490-40-00; fax (44) 490-40-85; e-mail press@usembassy.kiev.ua; internet kiev.usembassy.gov; Ambassador WILLIAM B. TAYLOR, Jr.

United Arab Emirates: POB 4009, Abu Dhabi; tel. (2) 4142200; fax (2) 4142469; e-mail webmasterabudhabi@state.gov; internet uae.usembassy.gov; Chargé d'affaires a.i. Martin R. Quinn.

United Kingdom: 24–32 Grosvenor Sq., London, W1A 1AE; tel. (20) 7499-9000; internet london.usembassy.gov; Ambassador ROBERT HOLMES TUTTLE.

Uruguay: Lauro Muller 1776, 11200 Montevideo; tel. (2) 4187777; fax (2) 4188611; e-mail webmastermvd@state.gov; internet uruguay.usembassy.gov; Ambassador Frank E. Baxter.

Uzbekistan: 100093 Tashkent, Moyqorghon ko'ch. 3, Yunusobod District; tel. (71) 120-54-50; fax (71) 120-54-48; e-mail consulartashkent@state.gov; internet www.usembassy.uz; Ambassador RICHARD B. NORLAND.

Vatican City: Villa Domiziana, Via delle Terme Deciane 26, 00153 Rome, Italy; tel. (06) 46743428; fax (06) 5758346; e-mail vaticaninfo@mail.usembassy.it; internet www.vatican.usembassy.gov; Ambassador Mary Ann Glendon.

Venezuela: Calle Suapure con Calle F, Colinas de Valle Arriba, Caracas; tel. (212) 975-6411; fax (212) 975-6710; e-mail embajada@state.gov; internet caracas.usembassy.gov; Ambassador PATRICK DENNIS DUDDY.

Viet Nam: 7 Lang Ha, Ba Dinh District, Hanoi; tel. (4) 7721500; fax (4) 7721510; e-mail irchanoi@state.gov; internet vietnam.usembassy.gov; Ambassador Michael W. Michalak.

Yemen: POB 22347, Sa'awan St, Sheraton Hotel District, San'a; tel. (1) 7552000; fax (1) 303182; e-mail consularsanaa@state.gov; internet yemen.usembassy.gov; Ambassador STEPHEN A. SECHE.

Zambia: cnr Independence and United Nations Aves, POB 31617, Lusaka; tel. (1) 250955; fax (1) 252225; internet zambia.usembassy.gov; Ambassador Carmen M. Martinez.

Zimbabwe: 172 Herbert Chitepo Ave, POB 3340, Harare; tel. (4) 758803; fax (4) 796488; e-mail hararepas@state.gov; internet harare.usembassy.gov; Ambassador JAMES D. McGEE.

DIPLOMATIC MISSIONS OF URUGUAY

United Nations: 866 United Nations Plaza, Suite 322, New York, NY 10017; tel. (212) 752-8240; fax (212) 593-0935; e-mail uruguay@un.int; internet www.un.int/uruguay; Permanent Representative Elbio O. Rosselli.

Argentina: Las Heras 1907, C1127AAB Buenos Aires; tel. (11) 4803-6030; fax (11) 4807-3050; e-mail embarou@impsat1.com.ar; internet www.embajadadeluruguay.com.ar; Ambassador FRANCISCO BUSTILLO BONASSO.

Australia: POB 5058, Kingston, ACT 2604; tel. (2) 6273-9100; fax (2) 6273-9099; e-mail urucan@iimetro.com.au; Chargé d'affaires a.i. Andrés Pelaez.

Austria: Palais Esterhazy, Wallnerstr. 4/3/17, 1010 Vienna; tel. (1) 535-66-36; fax (1) 535-66-18; e-mail uruvien@embuy.at; Ambassador JORGE PÉREZ OTERMIN.

Belgium: 22 ave F. D. Roosevelt, 1050 Brussels; tel. (2) 640-11-69; fax (2) 648-29-09; e-mail uruemb@skynet.be; Ambassador Dr Luis Alfredo Sica Bergara.

Bolivia: Edif. Monroy Velez, 7°, Calle 21, 8350 Calacoto, La Paz, La Paz; tel. (2) 279-1482; fax (2) 212-9413; e-mail urulivia@acelerate.com; Ambassador ZORRILLA DE SAN MARTÍN LLAMAS.

Brazil: SES, Av. das Nações, Quadra 803, Lote 14, 70450-900 Brasília, DF; tel. (61) 3322-1200; fax (61) 3322-6534; e-mail urubras@emburuguai.org.br; internet www.emburuguai.org.br; Ambassador Pedro Humberto Vaz Ramela.

Canada: 130 Albert St, Suite 1905, Ottawa, ON K1P 5G4; tel. (613) 234-2727; fax (613) 233-4670; e-mail embassy@embassyofuruguay.ca; internet embassyofuruguay.ca; Ambassador ALVARO MARCELO MOERZINGER PAGANI.

Chile: Avda Pedro de Valdivia 711, Santiago; tel. (2) 204-7988; fax (2) 274-4066; e-mail urusgo@uruguay.cl; internet www.uruguay.cl; Ambassador Juan Carlos Pita Alvariza.

China, People's Republic: 1-11-2 Tayuan Diplomatic Office Bldg, Beijing 100600; tel. (10) 65324445; fax (10) 65327375; e-mail urubei@public.bta.net.cn; Ambassador LUIS LEONARDO ALMAGRO LEMES.

Colombia: Carrera 9a, No 80-15, 11°, Apdo Aéreo 101466, Bogotá, DC; tel. (1) 235-2748; fax (1) 248-3734; e-mail urucolom@007mundo.com; Ambassador Silvia Lourdes Izquierdo Vila.

Costa Rica: Avda 14, Calles 35 y 37, Apdo 3448, 1000 San José; tel. 288-3424; fax 288-3070; e-mail embajrou@racsa.co.cr; Ambassador BRUGNINI GARCÍA LAGOS.

Cuba: Calle 14, No 506, entre 5 y 7, Miramar, Havana; tel. (7) 204-2311; fax (7) 204-2246; e-mail urucub@ceniai.inf.cu; Ambassador Jorge Ernesto Mazzarovich Severi.

Czech Republic: Muchova 9, 160 00 Prague 6; tel. 224314755; fax 224313780; e-mail urupra@urupra.cz; Ambassador (vacant).

Dominican Republic: Torre Ejecutiva Gapo, Local 401, Luis F. Thomen 110, Ensanche Evaristo Morales, Santo Domingo, DN; tel. 227-3475; fax 472-4231; e-mail embur@verizon.net.do; Ambassador Duncan Boris Croci de Mula.

Ecuador: Edif. Josueth González, 9°, Avda 6 de Diciembre 2816 y Paul Rivet, Apdo 17-12-282, Quito; tel. (2) 256-3762; fax (2) 256-3763; e-mail uruguay@embajada_uruguay.com.ec; Ambassador GUSTAVO VANERIO BALBELA.

Egypt: 6 Sharia Lotfallah, Cairo (Zamalek); tel. (2) 7353589; fax (2) 7368123; e-mail urugemb@idsc.gov.eg; Ambassador César Walter Ferrer Burle.

El Salvador: Edif. Gran Plaza 405, Blvd del Hipódromo, Col. San Benito, San Salvador; tel. 2279-1627; fax 2279-1626; Ambassador JULIO CÉSAR BENÍTEZ SÁENZ.

France: 15 rue Le Sueur, 75116 Paris; tel. 1-45-00-81-37; fax 1-45-01-25-17; e-mail amburuguay.urugalia@fr.oleane.com; internet www.amb-uruguay-france.com; Ambassador Héctor Gros Espiell.

Germany: Budapester Str. 39, 10787 Berlin; tel. (30) 2639016; fax (30) 26390170; e-mail urubrande@t-online.de; Ambassador PELAYO JOAQUÍN DÍAZ MUGUERZA.

Greece: Odos Likavitou I G, 106 72 Athens; tel. (210) 3602635; fax (210) 3613549; e-mail urugrec@otenet.gr; Ambassador Diana Espino de Papantonakis.

Guatemala: Edif. Plaza Marítima, 3°, Of. 341, 6a Avda 20-25, Zona 10, Guatemala City; tel. 2368-0810; fax 2333-7553; e-mail uruguate@guate.net; Ambassador ESTELLA RUBY ARMAND-UGON SEPÚLVEDA.

India: A-16/2 Vasant Vihar, New Delhi 110 057; tel. (11) 26151991; fax (11) 26144306; e-mail uruind@del3.vsnl.net.in; Ambassador William Ehlers.

Iran: 45 Shabnam Alley, Shahid Atefi Shargi St, Africa Ave, Tehran; tel. (21) 22052030; fax (21) 22053322; e-mail uruter@yahoo.com; Ambassador JOSÉ LUIS REMEDI ZUNINI.

Israel: POB 12244, G.R.A.P. Bldg, 1st Floor, 4 Shenkar St, Industrial Zone, Herzliya Pitauch 46733; tel. 9-9569611; fax 9-9515881; e-mail emrou@netvision.net.il; Ambassador Alfredo E. Cazes Alvarez.

Italy: Via Vittorio Veneto 183, 00187 Roma; tel. (06) 4821776; fax (06) 4823695; e-mail uruit@ambasciatauruguay.it; Ambassador RAMÓN CARLOS ABIN DE MARÍA.

Japan: Kowa Bldg, No. 38, Room 908, 4-12-24, Nishi Azabu, Minato-ku, Tokyo 106-0031; tel. (3) 3486-1888; fax (3) 3486-9872; e-mail urujap@luck.ocn.ne.jp; Ambassador Ana María Estévez Mercader.

Korea, Republic: 14F LIG Kangnam Bldg, 708-6 Yeoksam-dong, Gangnam-gu, Seoul; tel. (2) 6245-3179; fax (2) 6245-3181; e-mail uruseul@embrou.or.kr; Ambassador NELSON YEMIL CHABEN.

Lebanon: POB 2051, Centre Stella Marris, 7e étage, rue Banque du Liban, Jounieh; tel. (9) 636529; fax (9) 636531; e-mail uruliban@dm.net.lb; internet www.embauruguaybeirut.org; Ambassador Jorge Luis Jure.

Malaysia: 6th Floor, UBN Tower, 10 Jalan P. Ramlee, 50250 Kuala Lumpur; tel. (3) 20313669; fax (3) 20315669; e-mail urukuala@streamyx.com; Ambassador PABLO SADER.

Mexico: Hegel 149, 1°, Col. Chapultepec Morales, Del. Miguel Hidalgo, 11560 México, DF; tel. (55) 5531-4029; fax (55) 5545-3342; e-mail uruazte@ort.org.mx; Ambassador José Ignacio Korzeniak Pastorino.

Netherlands: Mauritskade 33, 2514 HD The Hague; tel. (70) 3609815; fax (70) 3562826; e-mail uruholan@wxs.nl; Ambassador DR CARLOS ANTONIO MORA MEDERO.

Panama: Edif. Los Delfines, Of. 8, Avda Balboa, Calle 50e Este, Apdo 8898, Panamá 5; tel. 264-2838; fax 264-8908; e-mail urupanam@cwpanama.net; Ambassador Domingo Francisco Schipani Brian.

Paraguay: Guido Boggiani 5832, 3°, Asunción; tel. (21) 66-4244; fax (21) 60-1335; e-mail embauru@telesurf.com.py; internet www.embajadauruguay.com.py; Ambassador CARLOS ERNESTO ORLANDO BONET.

Peru: José D. Anchorena 84, San Isidro, Lima; tel. (1) 2640099; fax (1) 2640112; e-mail uruinca@embajada-uruguay.com; Ambassador Juan José Arteaga Sáenz de Zumarán.

Poland: 02-516 Warsaw, ul. Rejtana 15/12; tel. (22) 8495040; fax (22) 6466887; e-mail urupol@urupol.ikp.pl; Ambassador (vacant).

Portugal: Rua Sampaio Pina 16, 2°, 1070-249 Lisbon; tel. (21) 3889265; fax (21) 3889245; e-mail urulusi@sapo.pt; Ambassador Gastón Lasarte.

Russian Federation: 119049 Moscow, ul. Mytnaya 3; tel. (495) 143-04-01; fax (495) 938-20-45; e-mail ururus@mrree.gub.uy; internet www.uruguay.org.ru; Ambassador JORGE ALBERTO MEYER LONG.

Saudi Arabia: POB 94346, Riyadh 11693; tel. (1) 462-0739; fax (1) 462-0648; e-mail ururia@nesma.net.sa; Ambassador Carlos A. Clulow.

South Africa: 301 MIB House, 3rd Floor, Hatfield Sq., 1119 Burnett St, Hatfield, Pretoria 0083; POB 3247, Pretoria 0001; tel. (12) 3626521; fax (12) 3626523; Ambassador GUILLERMO JOSÉ POMI BARIOLA.

Spain: Paseo del Pintor Rosales 32, 1°, 28008 Madrid; tel. (91) 7580475; fax (91) 5428177; e-mail urumatri@urumatri.com; Ambassador Ricardo González Arenas.

Sweden: Kommendörsgt. 35, POB 10114, 100 55 Stockholm; tel. (8) 660-31-96; fax (8) 665-31-66; e-mail urustoc@uruemb.se; Chargé d'affaires a.i. MERCEDES COROMINAS GALLOSO.

Switzerland: Kramgasse 63, 3011 Bern; tel. 313122226; fax 313112747; e-mail uruhelve@bluewin.ch; Ambassador Carlos Brugnini García Lagos.

United Kingdom: 2nd Floor, 140 Brompton Rd, London, SW3 1HY; tel. (20) 7589-8835; fax (20) 7581-9585; e-mail emburuguay@emburuguay.org.uk; Ambassador RICARDO VARELA.

United States of America: 1913 Eye St, NW, Washington, DC 20006; tel. (202) 331-1313; fax (202) 331-8142; e-mail uruwashi@uruwashi.org; internet www.uruwashi.org; Ambassador Carlos A. Gianelli Derois.

Vatican City: Via Antonio Gramsci 9/14, 00197 Rome, Italy; tel. (06) 3218904; fax (06) 3613249; e-mail uruvati@tin.it; Ambassador MARIO JUAN BOSCO CAYOTA ZAPPETTINI.

Venezuela: Torre Delta, 8°, Ofs A y B, Avda Francisco de Miranda, Altamira Sur, Apdo 60366, Caracas 1060-A; tel. (212) 261-7603; fax (212) 266-9233; e-mail uruvene@infoline.wtfe.com; Ambassador Juan José Arteaga Saenz de Zumarán.

DIPLOMATIC MISSIONS OF UZBEKISTAN

United Nations: 866 United Nations Plaza, Suite 326, New York, NY 10017; tel. (212) 486-4242; fax (212) 486-7998; e-mail uzbekistan@un.int; Permanent Representative ALISHER VOHIDOV.

Afghanistan: House 14, St 13, Wazir Akbar Khan, Kabul; tel. (20) 2300124; Ambassador Parvez Miriyevich Aliyev.

Austria: Poetzleinsdorferstr. 49, 1180 Vienna; tel. (1) 315-39-94; fax (1) 315-39-93; e-mail botschaft@usbekistan.at; internet www.usbekistan.at; Chargé d'affaires a.i. KADYRJAN YUSUPOV.

Azerbaijan: 1021 Baku, Patamdart, 1-chi Şosesi, 9-chi tor 437; tel. (12) 497-25-49; fax (12) 497-25-48; e-mail embuzb@azeronline.com; Ambassador Ismatilla R. Ergashev.

Belgium: 99 ave F. D. Roosevelt, 1050 Brussels; tel. (2) 672-88-44; fax (2) 672-39-46; Ambassador ISAN M. MUSTAFAEV.

China, People's Republic: 11 Bei Xiao Jie, San Li Tun, Beijing 100600; tel. (10) 65326305; fax (10) 65326304; e-mail Embassy@uzbekistan.cn; internet www.uzbekistan.cn; Ambassador Alisher A. Salahitdinov.

Egypt: 18 Sad el-Aali St, Cairo (Dokki); tel. (2) 3361723; fax (2) 3361722; Ambassador SOLIH R. INOGAMOV.

France: 22 rue d'Aguesseau, 75008 Paris; tel. 1-53-30-03-53; fax 1-53-30-03-54; e-mail contact@ouzbekistan.fr; internet www.ouzbekistan.fr; Ambassador Ravshanbek O. Olimov.

Germany: Perleberger Str. 62, 10559 Berlin; tel. (30) 3940980; fax (30) 39409862; e-mail botschaft@uzbekistan.de; internet www.uzbekistan.de; Ambassador BAKHTIYAR GULYAMOV.

India: EP-40 Dr S. Radhakrishnan Marg, Chanakyapuri, New Delhi 110 021; tel. (11) 24670774; fax (11) 24670773; e-mail uzembind@vsnl.com; internet www.uzbekembassy.in; Ambassador Prof. Saydakmal Saydakhmedovitch Saydaminov.

Indonesia: Menara Mulia, 24th Floor, Suite 2401, Jalan Jenderal Gatot Subroto, Kav. 9–11, Jakarta Selatan 12930; tel. (21) 5222581; fax (21) 5222582; e-mail registan@indo.net.id; Ambassador (vacant).

Iran: No. 6, Nastaran Alley, Boustan St, Pasdaran Ave; tel. (21) 22299780; fax (21) 22299158; Ambassador Ilham Solievich Akramov.

Israel: 35 Dvora Ha'Nevia St, Tel-Aviv 69350; tel. 3-6447746; fax 3-6447748; e-mail uzecon@barak-online.net; Ambassador FARHOD HAKIMOV.

Italy: Via Tolmino 12, 00198 Roma; tel. (06) 8542456; fax (06) 8541020; e-mail uzbembass@libero.it; Ambassador Zhahongir D. Ganiyev.

Japan: 5-11-8, Shimo-Meguro, Meguro-ku, Tokyo 153-0064; tel. (3) 3760-5625; fax (3) 3760-5950; Ambassador DR MIRSOBIT FOZILOVICH OCHILOV.

Kazakhstan: 050010 Almaty, Baribayeva 36; tel. (727) 291-02-35; fax (727) 291-10-55; Ambassador Turdikul S. Butayarov.

Korea, Republic: Diplomatic Center, Rm. 701, 1376-1, Seocho 2-dong, Seocho-gu, Seoul; tel. (2) 574-6554; fax (2) 578-0576; Ambassador VITALI V. FEN.

Kuwait: Kuwait City; Ambassador Abdurafik A. Hoshimov.

Kyrgyzstan: 720040 Bishkek, Tynystanova 213; tel. (312) 66-20-65; fax (312) 66-44-03; e-mail uzbembish@infotel.kg; Ambassador ZIYADULLA S. PULATKHOJAYEV.

Latvia: Elizabetes iela 11–11, Rīga 1010; tel. 6732-2424; fax 6732-2306; e-mail posoluz@apollo.lv; internet www.latvia.mfa.uz; Ambassador Kobiljon S. Nazarov.

Malaysia: Suite 6-03, 6th Floor, North Block The Ampang Walk, 218 Jalan Ampang, 50450 Kuala Lumpur; tel. (3) 21618100; e-mail uzbekemb@streamyx.com; Ambassador AYBEK KHASANOV.

Pakistan: 2, St 21, F-8/3, Kohistan Rd, Islamabad; tel. (51) 2264746; fax (51) 2261739; e-mail uzbekemb@isb.comsats.net.pk; Ambassador Oybek A. Usmanov.

Poland: 02-804 Warsaw, ul. Kraski 21; tel. (22) 8946230; fax (22) 8946231; e-mail info@uzbekistan.pl; internet www.uzbekistan.pl; Chargé d'affaires a.i. TIMUR RAHMANOV.

Russian Federation: 109017 Moscow, Pogorelskii per. 12; tel. (495) 230-00-76; fax (495) 238-89-18; e-mail info@uzembassy.ru; internet www.uzembassy.ru; Ambassador Bakhtiyor A. Islamov.

Saudi Arabia: POB 94008, Riyadh 11693; tel. (1) 263-5223; fax (1) 263-5105; Ambassador ULUGBEK A. ISROILOV.

Singapore: 5 Shenton Way 37-02, Rms 34 & 35, UIC Bldg, Singapore 068808; tel. 63251843; fax 63251844; e-mail uz-emb.sg@hotmail.com; Ambassador Alisher A. Kurmanov.

Spain: Madrid; .

Tajikistan: 734003 Dushanbe, Kuchai L. Sherali 15; tel. (372) 21-21-84; fax (372) 24-90-77; e-mail ruzintaj@rambler.ru; internet www.uzembassy-tadjik.mfa.uz; Ambassador Shoqosim I. Shoislomov.

Turkey: Sancak Mah. 211 Sok. 3, 06550 Çankaya, Ankara; tel. (312) 4413871; fax (312) 4427058; e-mail embankara@post.mfa.uz; Ambassador ULFAT S. KADYROV.

Turkmenistan: 744006 Aşgabat, ul. Gerogly 50 a; tel. (12) 33-10-55; fax (12) 34-23-37; Ambassador Alisher K. Kodirov.

Ukraine: 01901 Kyiv, vul. Volodymyrska 16; tel. (44) 501-50-00; fax 501-50-01; Ambassador ILHOM O. HAYDAROV.

United Kingdom: 41 Holland Park, London, W11 2RP; tel. (20) 7229-7679; fax (20) 7229-7029; e-mail info@uzbekembassy.org; internet www.uzbekembassy.org; Ambassador Otabek H. Akbarov.

United States of America: 1746 Massachusetts Ave, NW, Washington, DC 20036; tel. (202) 887-5300; fax (202) 293-6804; e-mail info@uzbekistan.org; internet www.uzbekistan.org; Ambassador ABDULAZIZ KOMILOV.

DIPLOMATIC MISSIONS OF VANUATU

United Nations: 866 United Nations Plaza, 3rd Floor, New York, NY 10017; tel. (212) 425-9600; fax (212) 425-9653; e-mail vanuatu@un.int; Permanent Representative Donald Kalpokas.

Belgium: 380 ave de Tervueren, 1150 Brussels; tel. (2) 771-74-94; e-mail info@embassyvanuatu.net; Ambassador ROY MICKEY JOY.

China, People's Republic: 3-1-11 San Li Tun Diplomatic Compound, Beijing; tel. (10) 65320337; fax (10) 65320336; e-mail vanuatuembassybj@yahoo.com.cn; internet www.vanuatuembassy.org.cn; AmbassadorLo Chi Wai.

DIPLOMATIC MISSIONS OF VENEZUELA

United Nations: 335 East 46th St, New York, NY 10017; tel. (212) 557-2055; fax (212) 557-3528; e-mail venezuela@un.int; internet www.un.int/venezuela; Permanent Representative JAVIER ARIAS ARIAS CÁRDENAS.

Algeria: BP 297, 3 impasse Ahmed Kara, Algiers; tel. (21) 69-38-46; fax (21) 69-35-55; Ambassador Michel Mujica Ricardo.

Antigua and Barbuda: Jasmine Court, Friar's Hill Rd, POB 1201, St John's; tel. 462-1574; fax 462-1570; e-mail embaveneantigua@yahoo.es; Ambassador JOSÉ LAURENCIO SILVA MÉNDEZ.

Argentina: Virrey Loreto 2035, C1426DXK Buenos Aires; tel. (11) 4788-4944; fax (11) 4784-4311; e-mail contacto@embavenarg.org; Ambassador Gen. (retd) Arévalo Enrique Méndez Romero.

Australia: 7 Culgoa Circuit, O'Malley, ACT 2606; tel. (2) 6290-2968; fax (2) 6290-2911; e-mail embaustralia@venezuela-emb-org.au; internet www.venezuela-emb.org.au; Chargé d'affaires a. i. NELSÓN DÁVILA LAMEDA.

Austria: Prinz-Eugen-Str. 72/1.OG/Steige 1/Top1.1, 1040 Vienna; tel. (1) 712-26-38; fax (1) 715-32-19; e-mail embajada@austria.gob.ve; internet www.austria.gob.ve; Chargé d'affaires a.i. Verónica Calcinari Van der Velde.

Barbados: Hastings, Main Rd, Christ Church; tel. 435-7619; fax 435-7830; e-mail embaven@sunbeach.net; internet www.geocities.com/embaven; Ambassador JUAN CARLOS VALDEZ.

Belarus: 220000 Minsk; tel. (17) 226-07-88; fax (17) 220-20-19; e-mail embavenbel@gmail.com; Chargé d'affaires Américo Díaz Nuñez.

Belgium: 10 ave F. D. Roosevelt, 1050 Brussels; tel. (2) 639-03-40; fax (2) 647-88-20; e-mail embajada@venezuela-eu.org; internet www.venezuela-eu.org; Ambassador DR ALEJANDRO ANTONIO FLEMING CABRERA.

Belize: 17 Orchid Garden St, POB 49, Belmopan; tel. 822-2384; fax 822-2022; e-mail embaven@bt1.net; Ambassador Omar José Valdivieso.

Bolivia: Edif. Illimani, 4°, Avda Arce, esq. Campos, Casilla 441, La Paz; tel. (2) 243-1365; fax (2) 243-2348; e-mail embvzla@caoba.telnet.bo; Ambassador JULIO AGOSTO MONTES PRADO.

Brazil: SES, Av. das Nações, Quadra 803, Lote 13, 70451-900 Brasília, DF; tel. (61) 3322-1011; fax (61) 3226-5633; e-mail emb@embvenezuela.org.br; internet www.embvenezuela.org.br; Ambassador Julio José García Montoya.

Bulgaria: 1087 Sofia, ul. Tulovo 1; tel. (2) 943-30-61; fax (2) 943-30-10; e-mail embavenez@mbox.digsys.bg; Ambassador BOANERGES SALAZAR.

Canada: 32 Range Rd, Ottawa, ON K1N 8J4; tel. (613) 235-5151; fax (613) 235-3205; e-mail info.canada@misionvenezuela.org; internet www.misionvenezuela.org; Chargé d'affaires a.i. José Antonio Rodríguez de la Sierra.

Chile: Bustos 2021, Providencia, Santiago; tel. (2) 225-0021; fax (2) 223-1170; e-mail emvenchi@entelchile.net; Ambassador MARÍA LOURDES URBANEJA DURANT.

China, People's Republic: 14 San Li Tun Lu, Beijing 100600; tel. (10) 65321295; fax (10) 65323817; e-mail embvenez@public.bta.net.cn; internet www.venezuela.org.cn; AmbassadorRocío Maneiro González.

Colombia: Carrera 11, No 87-51, 5°, Bogotá, DC; tel. (1) 640-1213; fax (1) 640-1242; e-mail embajada@embaven.org.co; internet www.embaven.org.co; Ambassador JOSÉ PÁVEL RONDÓN DAZA (recalled for consultations in Nov. 2007).

Costa Rica: Barrio Escalante, de la Iglesia de Santa Teresita 300 m este y 50 m norte, de la rotonda del Farolito 50 m sur, San José; tel. 234-0728; fax 253-1453; e-mail info@embavencr.com; internet www.embajadadevenezuelaencostarica.org; Ambassador (vacant).

Cuba: Avda 1601, No 5, entre 16 y 18, Miramar, Havana; tel. (7) 204-2612; fax (7) 204-2773; e-mail vencuba@enet.cu; Ambassador ALÍ RODRÍGUEZ ARAQUE.

Czech Republic: Sněmovní 9, 118 00 Prague 1; tel. 257534253; fax 257534257; e-mail embaven@vol.cz; internet www.embajada-venezuela.cz; Chargé d'affaires a.i. Luis Geronimo Sotillo Mendez.

Denmark: Toldbodgade 31, 3rd Floor, 1253 Copenhagen K; tel. 33-93-63-11; fax 33-37-76-59; e-mail emvendk@mail.dk; internet www.ve-ambassade.dk; Ambassador VICENTE EMILIO VALLENILLA.

Dominica: 20 Bath Rd, 3rd Floor, POB 770, Roseau; tel. 4483348; fax 4486198; e-mail embven@cwdom.dm; Ambassador Carmen Martínez de Grijalva.

Dominican Republic: Avda Anacoana 7, Mirador del Sur, Santo Domingo, DN; tel. 537-8578; fax 537-8780; e-mail embvenezuela@codetel.net.do; Ambassador FRANCISCO ALBERTO BELISARIO LANDIS.

Ecuador: Avda Los Cabildos 115, Apdo 17-01-688, Quito; tel. (2) 226-8636; fax (2) 246-6786; e-mail embavenecua@venezuela.org.ec; Ambassador Oscar Navas Tortolero.

Egypt: POB 1217, 15A Sharia Mansour Muhammad, Cairo (Zamalek); tel. (2) 7363517; fax (2) 7367373; e-mail eov@idsc.gov.eg; Ambassador VICTOR R. CARAZO.

El Salvador: 7a Calle Poniente, entre 75 y 77 Avda Norte, Col. Escalón, San Salvador; tel. 2263-3977; fax 2211-0027; e-mail embajadadevenezuela@telesal.net; Chargé d'affaires a.i. Waldimir Ruiz Tirado.

Ethiopia: Bole Kifle Ketama, Kebele 21, House No. 314–16, POB 1909, Addis Ababa; tel. (11) 6460601; fax (11) 5154162; Ambassador LUIS MARIANO JOUBERTT MATA.

Finland: Bulevardi 1a 62, 00100 Helsinki; tel. (9) 641522; fax (9) 640971; e-mail embavenefin@embavene.fi; internet www.embavene.fi; Chargé d'affaires a.i. Ernesto Navazio Mossucca.

France: 11 rue Copernic, 75116 Paris; tel. 1-45-53-29-98; fax 1-47-55-64-56; e-mail info@amb-venezuela.fr; internet www.embavenez-paris.com; Ambassador JESÚS ARNALDO PÉREZ.

Germany: Schillstr. 9–10, 10785 Berlin; tel. (30) 8322400; fax (30) 83224020; e-mail embavenez.berlin@botschaft-venezuela.de; internet www.botschaft -venezuela.de; Ambassador Blanca Nieves Portocarrero.

Greece: Odos Marathonodromou 19, Palaio Psychiko, 154 52 Athens; tel. (210) 6729169; fax (210) 6727464; internet users.hol.gr/~emvenath; Chargé d'affaires a.i. MARIA INES FONSECA.

Grenada: Upper Lucas St, POB 201, St George's; tel. 440-1721; fax 440-6657; e-mail embavengda@caribsurf.com; Ambassador Edna Figuera Cedeño.

Guatemala: Edif. Atlantis, Of. 601, 13 Calle 3-40, Zona 10, Apdo 152, Guatemala City; tel. 2366-9832; fax 2366-9838; e-mail embavene@concyt .gob.gt; Ambassador JENY FIGUEREDO FRÍAS.

Guyana: 296 Thomas St, South Cummingsburg, Georgetown; tel. 226-1543; fax 225-3241; e-mail embveguy@gol.net.gy; Ambassador Darío Morandy.

Haiti: blvd Harry S Truman, Cité de l'Exposition, BP 2158, Port-au-Prince; tel. 443-4127; fax 223-7672; e-mail embavenezhaiti@hainet.net; Ambassador PEDRO ANTONIO CANINO GONZÁLEZ.

Honduras: Col. Rubén Darío, 2116 Circuito Choluteca, Apdo 775, Tegucigalpa; tel. 232-1879; fax 232-1016; e-mail evenezue@multivisionhn .net; internet venezuelalabolivariana.com; Chargé d'affaires a.i. Claudio Sorio Fermín.

Hungary: 1023 Budapest, Vérhalom u. 12–16, I, 14; tel. (1) 326-0460; fax (1) 326-0450; e-mail embavenezhu@t-online.hu; Ambassador MARÍA TERESA GONZÁLEZ.

India: E-106 Malcha Marg, Chanakyapuri, New Delhi 110 021; tel. (11) 41680218; fax (11) 41750743; e-mail embavene@del2.vsnl.net.in; Ambassador Milena Santana-Ramírez.

Indonesia: Menara Mulia, 20th Floor, Suite 2005, Jalan Jenderal Gatot Subroto, Kav. 9–11, Jakarta Selatan 12930; tel. (21) 5227547; fax (21) 5227549; e-mail evenjakt@indo.net.id; Chargé d'affaires a.i. MARÍA VIRGINIA MENZONES LICCIONI.

Iran: POB 19395-7137, No. 26, Tandis St, Africa Ave, Tehran; tel. (21) 88715185; fax (21) 22053677; e-mail embajadavenezuela@emveniran.gob.ve; internet www.iran.gob.ve; Ambassador Arturo Anibal Gallegos Ramírez.

Israel: POB 2058, Beit Grap, 3rd Floor, 4 Rehov Shenkar, Herzliya Pituach 46120; tel. 9-9573363; fax 9-9580292; e-mail emven@netvision.net.il; Ambassador HÉCTOR QUINTERO (withdrawn in Aug. 2006).

Italy: Via Nicolò Tartaglia 11, 00197 Roma; tel. (06) 8079797; fax (06) 8084410; e-mail embaveit@iol.it; internet www.ambasciatadelvenezuela.it; Ambassador Rafael Alejandro Lacava Evangelista.

Jamaica: PCJ Bldg, 3rd Floor, 36 Trafalgar Rd, POB 26, Kingston 10; tel. 926-5510; fax 926-7442; e-mail embavene@n5.com.jm; Ambassador NOEL ENRIQUE MARTÍNEZ OCHOA.

Japan: Kowa Bldg, No. 38, Room 703, 4-12-24, Nishi Azabu, Minato-ku, Tokyo 106-0031; tel. (3) 3409-1501; fax (3) 3409-1505; e-mail embavene@ interlink.or.jp; Ambassador Seiko Luis Ishikawa Kobayashi.

Kenya: Ngong/Kabarnet Rd, POB 34477, Nairobi; tel. (20) 574646; fax (20) 337487; e-mail embavene@africaonline.co.ke; Ambassador MARÍA JACQUELINE MENDOZA.

Korea, Republic: 16th Floor, SC First Bank Bldg, 100 Gongpyeong-dong, Jongno-gu, 110-702 Seoul; tel. (2) 732-1546; fax (2) 732-1548; e-mail emvesel@soback.kornet.net; internet www.venezuelaemb.or.kr; Chargé d'affaires a.i. Wolfgang González.

Kuwait: POB 24440, 13105 Safat, Block 5, St 7, Area 356, Surra, Kuwait City; tel. 5324367; fax 5324368; e-mail embavene@qualitynet.net; Ambassador ELOY FERNÁNDEZ AZUAJE.

Lebanon: POB 603, Immeuble Baezevale House, 5e étage, Zalka, Beirut; tel. (1) 888701; fax (1) 900757; e-mail embavene@dm.net.lb; Ambassador Joel Ramón Pérez.

Libya: POB 2584, Sharia ben Ashour, Jamaa as-Sagaa Bridge, Tripoli; tel. (21) 3600408; fax (21) 3600407; Ambassador DAVID PARAVISINI.

Malaysia: Suite 20-05, 20th Floor, Menara Tan & Tan, 207 Jalan Tun Razak, 50400 Kuala Lumpur; tel. (3) 21633444; fax (3) 21636819; e-mail venezuela@ po.jaring.my; internet www.embavenezmalasia.org; Ambassador Manuel Antonio Guzman Hernández.

Mexico: Schiller 326, Col. Chapultepec Morales, Del. Miguel Hidalgo, 11570 México, DF; tel. (55) 5203-4233; fax (55) 5203-5072; e-mail embemve .mxmdf@mre.gob.ve; Ambassador ROY CHADERTON MATOS.

Morocco: 58 Lot OLM, Villa Yasmine, rue Capitaine Abdeslam el-Moudden el-Alami, Souissi, Rabat; tel. (3) 7650315; fax (3) 7650372; e-mail emvenez@ menara.ma; Ambassador Luisa Rebeca Sánchez Bello.

Namibia: Southern Life Tower, 3rd Floor, 39 Post St Mall, PMB 13353, Windhoek; tel. (61) 227905; fax (61) 227804; Chargé d'affaires a.i. JORGE JIMÉNEZ.

Netherlands: Nassaulaan 2, 2514 JS The Hague; tel. (70) 3651256; fax (70) 3656954; e-mail embvene@xs4all.nl; internet www.embven.nl; Ambassador Augustin Pérez Celis.

Nicaragua: Costado norte de la Iglesia Santo Domingo, Las Sierritas, Casa 27, Apdo 406, Managua; tel. (2) 72-0267; fax (2) 72-2265; e-mail embaveneznica@cablenet.com.ni; Chargé d'affaires a.i. PEDRO LUIS PENSO SÁNCHEZ.

Nigeria: 35b Adetokunbo Ademola St, Victoria Island, POB 3727, Lagos; tel. (1) 2611590; fax (1) 2617350; e-mail embavenez.nig@net.ng; Ambassador Alfredo Enrique Vargas.

Norway: Drammensvn 82, POB 2820 Solli, 0204 Oslo; tel. 22-43-06-60; fax 22-43-14-70; e-mail embajada@venezuela.no; Ambassador FRANCISCO VÉLEZ-VALERY.

Panama: Torre Hong Kong Bank, 5°, Avda Samuel Lewis, Apdo 661, Panamá 1; tel. 269-1014; fax 269-1916; e-mail embvenp@c-com.net.pa; Chargé d'affaires a.i. José Alfredo Guerrero Sosa.

Paraguay: Mariscal Estigarribia 1023 con Estados Unidos, Asunción; tel. (21) 66-4682; fax (21) 66-4683; e-mail bolivar@pla.net.py; internet www .embaven.org.py; Ambassador NORA MARGARITA URIBE TRUJILLO.

Peru: Avda Arequipa 298, Lima; tel. (1) 4334511; fax (1) 4331191; Ambassador Vice-Adm. Armando José Laguna Laguna.

Philippines: Unit 17A, Multinational Bancorporation Center, 6805 Ayala Ave, Makati City, Metro Manila 1226; tel. (2) 8452841; fax (2) 8452866; e-mail venezemb@info.com.ph; Chargé d'affaires a.i. MANUEL VICENTE PÉREZ ITURBE.

Poland: 02-516 Warsaw, ul. Rejtana 15/10–11; tel. (22) 6461846; fax (22) 6468761; e-mail embavenez.pl@qdnet.pl; Chargé d'affaires a.i. Ana Margarita Pino Pasquier.

Portugal: Av. Duque de Loulé 47, 4°, 1050-086 Lisbon; tel. (21) 3573803; fax (21) 3527421; e-mail embavenez@mail.telepac.pt; internet www .embavenezuela.pt; Ambassador LUCAS ENRIQUE RINCÓN ROMERO.

Romania: 011396 Bucharest 1, Str. G.D. Mirea, pictor 18; tel. (21) 2225874; fax (21) 2225073; e-mail embavero@pcnet.ro; Chargé d'affaires a.i. Margot J. Márquez García.

Russian Federation: 115127 Moscow, B. Karetnyi per. 13/15; tel. (495) 699-40-42; fax (495) 956-61-08; e-mail info@embaven.ru; internet www.embaven .ru; Ambassador DR ALEXIS RAFAEL NAVARRO ROJAS.

Saint Christopher and Nevis: Delisle St, POB 435, Basseterre; tel. 465-1078; fax 465-5452; e-mail frontado@caribsurf.com; Chargé d'affaires a.i. Nelson Manuel Camacho Rosales.

Saint Lucia: Vigie House, POB 494, Castries; tel. 452-4033; fax 453-6747; e-mail vembassy@candw.lc; Ambassador EDUARDO ALFONZO BARRANCO HERNÁNDEZ.

Saint Vincent and the Grenadines: Baynes Bros Bldg, Granby St, POB 852, Kingstown; tel. 456-1374; fax 457-1934; e-mail embavenezsanvicente@ vincysurf.com; Ambassador Tibisay Urdaneta Troconis.

Saudi Arabia: POB 94364, Riyadh 11693; tel. (1) 480-7141; fax (1) 480-0901; e-mail embvenar@embvenar.org.sa; Ambassador RAMÓN HERRERA NAVARRO.

Singapore: 3 Killiney Rd, 07–03 Winsland House I, Singapore 239519; tel. 64911172; fax 62353167; e-mail embassy@embavenez.org.sg; Chargé d'affaires a.i. Geomar Cattafi-Andrade.

South Africa: Hatfield Gables South Bldg, 1st Floor, Suite 4, 474 Hilda St, Pretoria 0083; POB 11821, Hatfield 0028; tel. (12) 3626593; fax (12) 3626591; e-mail embasudaf@icon.co.za; Ambassador ANTONIO MONTILLA-SALDIVIA.

Spain: Avda Capitán Haya 1, 13°, Edif. Eurocentro, 28020 Madrid; tel. (91) 5981200; fax (91) 5971583; e-mail embajada@espana.gob.ve; internet espana .gob.ve; Ambassador Alfredo Toro Hardy.

Suriname: Henck Arronstraat 23–25, POB 3001, Paramaribo; tel. 475401; fax 475602; e-mail embajador@suriname.gob.ve; internet www.suriname.gob .ve; Ambassador FRANCISCO DE JESÚS SIMANCAS.

Sweden: Engelbrektsgt. 35b, POB 26012, 100 41 Stockholm; tel. (8) 411-09-96; fax (8) 21-31-00; e-mail venezuela.embassy@chello.se; Ambassador Horacio Arteaga Acosta.

Switzerland: Schosshaldenstr. 1, Postfach 1005, 3000 Bern 23; tel. 313505757; fax 313505758; e-mail embavenez@greenmail.ch; internet www.embavenez -suiza.com; Chargé d'affaires a.i. FÁTIMA MAJZOUB EL-MAJZOUB.

Syria: BP 2403, Immeuble at-Tabbah, 5 rue Lisaneddin bin al-Khateb, place Rauda, Damascus; tel. (11) 3335356; fax (11) 3333203; e-mail embavenez@ net.sy; Ambassador Dia Nader al-Andari.

Trinidad and Tobago: 16 Victoria Ave, POB 1300, Port of Spain; tel. 627-9821; fax 624-2508; e-mail embaveneztt@carib-link.net; Ambassador VINICIO ROMERO MARTÍNEZ.

Turkey: Koza Sok. 91/3, 06700 Gaziosmanpaşa, Ankara; tel. (312) 4478131; fax (312) 4470711; e-mail embveank@tarassul.sy; Chargé d'affaires a.i. Raúl José Betancourt Seeland.

United Kingdom: 1 Cromwell Rd, London, SW7 2HW; tel. (20) 7584-4206; fax (20) 7589-8887; e-mail info@venezlon.co.uk; internet www.venezlon.co .uk; Ambassador SAMUEL MONCADA.

United States of America: 1099 30th St, NW, Washington, DC 20007; tel. (202) 342-2214; fax (202) 342-6820; e-mail apaiva@embavenez-us.org; internet www.embavenez-us.org; Ambassador Bernardo Alvarez Herrera.

Uruguay: Iturriaga 3589, esq. Tomás de Tezanos, Puerto Buceo, Montevideo; tel. (2) 6221262; fax (2) 6282530; e-mail embaven@adinet.com.uy; internet www.repbolvenezuela.com.uy; Ambassador FRANKLIN GONZÁLEZ.

Vatican City: Via Antonio Gramsci 14, 00197 Rome, Italy; tel. (06) 3225868; fax (06) 36001505; e-mail evidano@iol.it; Ambassador Iván Guillermo Rincón Urdaneta.

Viet Nam: 368 Lac Long Quan, Tay Ho District, Hanoi; tel. (4) 7588891; fax (4) 7588893; e-mail embavenezhanoi@yahoo.com; Ambassador JORGE JOSÉ RONDÓN UZCÁTEGUI.

DIPLOMATIC MISSIONS OF VIET NAM

United Nations: 866 United Nations Plaza, Suite 435, New York, NY 10017; tel. (212) 644-0594; fax (212) 644-5732; e-mail vietnamun@aol.com; internet www.un.int/vietnam; Permanent Representative Le Luong Minh.

Algeria: 30 rue de Chenoua, Hydra, Algiers; tel. (21) 69-27-52; fax (21) 69-37-78; e-mail sqvnaler@djazair-conn.ect.com; Ambassador VU VAN DU.

Angola: Rua Alexandre Peres 4, Maianga, CP 1774, Luanda; tel. 222390684; fax 222390369; e-mail dsqvnangola@netangola.com; Ambassador Nguyen Dinh.

Argentina: 11 de Septiembre 1442, C1426BKP Buenos Aires; tel. (11) 4783-1802; fax (11) 4782-0078; e-mail sqvnartn@fibertel.com.ar; Ambassador VAN LUNG THAI.

Australia: 6 Timbarra Crescent, O'Malley, ACT 2606; tel. (2) 6286-6059; fax (2) 6286-4534; e-mail vembassy@webone.com.au; internet www .vietnamembassy.org.au; Ambassador Nguyen Thanh Tan.

Austria: Félix-Mottl-Str. 20, 1190 Vienna; tel. (1) 368-07-55; fax (1) 368-07-54; e-mail embassy.vietnam@aon.at; Ambassador BA THAN NGUYEN.

Bangladesh: House 8, Rd 51, Gulshan 2, Dhaka 1212; tel. (2) 8854051; e-mail vietnam@citech-bd.com; internet www.vietnamembassy-bangladesh.org; Ambassador Nguyen Van That.

Belgium: 1 blvd Général Jacques, 1050 Brussels; tel. (2) 374-79-61; fax (2) 374-93-76; e-mail vnemb.brussels@skynet.be; Ambassador NGUYEN MANH DUNG.

Brazil: SHIS, QI 09, Conj. 10, Casa 01, Lago Sul, 71625-100 Brasília, DF; tel. (61) 3364-7856; fax (61) 3364-5836; e-mail embavina@yahoo.com; Ambassador Nguyen Thac Dinh.

Brunei: 9 Simpang 148-3, Jalan Telanai, Bandar Seri Begawan BA 2312; tel. 2456483; fax 2456485; e-mail vnembassy@yahoo.com; Ambassador HA HONG HAI.

Bulgaria: 1113 Sofia, ul. Zhetvarka 1; tel. (2) 963-26-09; fax (2) 963-36-58; e-mail dsqvnsofia@eml.cc; Ambassador Nguyen Van Dac.

Cambodia: 436 blvd Monivong, Phnom-Penh; tel. (23) 362741; fax (23) 427385; internet www.vietnamembassy-cambodia.org; Ambassador NGUYEN CHIEN THANG.

Canada: 470 Wilbrod St, Ottawa, ON K1M 6M8; tel. (613) 236-0772; fax (613) 236-2704; e-mail vietem@istar.ca; internet www.vietnamembassy -canada.ca; Ambassador Nguyen Duc Hung.

China, People's Republic: 32 Guang Hua Lu, Jian Guo Men Wai, Beijing 100600; tel. (10) 65321155; fax (10) 65325720; Ambassador TRAN VAN LUAT.

Cuba: Avda 5, No 1802, esq. 18, Miramar, Havana; tel. (7) 204-1502; fax (7) 204-1041; e-mail embaviet@ceniai.inf.cu; internet www.vietnamembassy -cuba.org; Ambassador Vu Chi Cong.

Czech Republic: Plzeňská 214/2578, 150 00 Prague 5; tel. 257211540; fax 257211792; Ambassador VUONG THUA PHONG.

Denmark: Bernstorffsvej 30c, 2900 Hellerup; tel. 39-18-39-32; fax 39-18-41-71; e-mail embvndk@hotmail.com; internet www.vietnamemb.dk; Ambassador Nguyen Xuan Hông.

Egypt: 8 Sharia Madina El Monawara, Cairo (Dokki); tel. (2) 7617309; fax (2) 3368612; e-mail vinaemb@intouch.com; Ambassador DUONG HUYNH LAP.

Finland: Aleksanterinkatu 15a, 5th Floor, 00100 Helsinki; tel. (9) 5626302; fax (9) 6229900; e-mail vietnamfinland@gmail.com; internet www .vietnamembassy-finland.org; Ambassador Tran Ngoc An.

France: 62–66 rue Boileau, 75016 Paris; tel. 1-44-14-64-00; fax 1-45-24-39-48; e-mail vnparis@club-internet.fr; Ambassador NGUYÊN DINH BIN.

Germany: Elsenstr. 3, 12435 Berlin; tel. (30) 53630108; fax (30) 53630200; e-mail info@vietnambotschaft.org; internet www.vietnambotschaft.org; Ambassador Duc Mau Tran.

Hungary: 1062 Budapest, Déhibáb u. 29; tel. (1) 342-5583; fax (1) 352-8798; e-mail su_quan@hu.inter.net; Ambassador DAO THI TAM.

India: 17 Kautilya Marg, Chanakyapuri, New Delhi 110 021; tel. (11) 23012123; fax (11) 23017714; e-mail sqdelhi@del3.vsnl.net.in; Ambassador Vu Quang Diem.

Indonesia: Jalan Teuku Umar 25, Jakarta; tel. (21) 3100358; fax (21) 3100359; e-mail embvnam@uninet.net.id; internet www.vietnamembassy-indonesia .org; Ambassador NGUYEN HUU DZUNG.

Iran: 6 East Ordibehesht, Mardani Sharestan, 8th St, Pey Syan St, M. Ardabili Vali-e-Asr Ave, Tehran; tel. (21) 22411670; fax (21) 22416045; e-mail dinh@mail.dci.co.ir; Ambassador Nguyen Van Hai.

Iraq: POB 15054, 71/34/611 Hay al-Mansour, Baghdad; tel. (1) 541-3409; fax (1) 541-1388; e-mail vietnam@uruklink.net; Ambassador NGUYEN QUANG KHAI.

Italy: Via di Bravetta 156–58, 00164 Roma; tel. (06) 66160726; fax (06) 66157520; e-mail vnemb.it@mofa.gov.vn; internet www.vnembassy.it; Ambassador Nguyen Van Nam.

Japan: 50-11, Moto Yoyogi-cho, Shibuya-ku, Tokyo 151-0062; tel. (3) 3466-3313; fax (3) 3466-3391; e-mail vnembasy@blue.ocn.ne.jp; internet www .vietnamembassy.jp; Ambassador NGUYEN PHU BINH.

Korea, Democratic People's Republic: Munsudong, Taedongkang District, Pyongyang; tel. (2) 3817353; fax (2) 3817632; Ambassador (vacant).

Korea, Republic: 28-58, Samcheong-dong, Jongno-gu, Seoul 140-210; tel. (2) 738-2318; fax (2) 739-2064; e-mail vndsq@yahoo.com; Ambassador PHAM TIEN VAN.

Laos: 85 23 rue Singha, Phonxay, Xaysettha, Vientiane; tel. (21) 413409; fax (21) 413379; e-mail dsqvn@laotel.com; internet www.mofa.gov.vn/vnemb.la; Ambassador Nguyen Huy Quang.

Libya: POB 587, Sharia Gargaresh, Tripoli; tel. (21) 4835587; fax (21) 4836962; e-mail dsqvnlib@yahoo.com; Ambassador DO BA KHOA.

Malaysia: 4 Jalan Persiaran Stonor, 50450 Kuala Lumpur; tel. (3) 21484036; fax (3) 21483270; e-mail daisevn@putra.net.my; internet www.mofa.gov.vn/ vnemb.my; Ambassador Hoang Trong Lap.

Mexico: Sierra Ventana 255, Col. Lomas de Chapultepec, Del. Miguel Hidalgo, 11000 México, DF; tel. (55) 5540-1632; fax (55) 5540-1612; e-mail vietnam.mx@mofa.gov.vn; Ambassador PHAM VAN QUE.

Mongolia: Enkh Taivny Örgön Chölöö 47, Ulan Bator (CPOB 670); tel. (11) 458917; fax (11) 458923; Ambassador Uong Huy Thanh.

Myanmar: 317–319 U Wisara Rd, Sanchaung Township, Yangon; tel. (1) 524656; fax (1) 524285; e-mail vnembmyr@bertech.net.mm; internet www .vietnamembassy-myanmar.org; Ambassador TRAN VAN TUNG.

Netherlands: Nassauplein 12, 2585 EB The Hague; tel. (70) 3648917; fax (70) 3648656; e-mail emviet@wanadoo.nl; Ambassador Hà Huy Thông.

New Zealand: Level 2, Grand Plimmer Tower, 2–6 Glimer Terrace, Wellington; tel. (4) 473-5912; fax (4) 473-5913; e-mail embassyvn@paradise .net.nz; Ambassador VUONG HAI NAM.

Pakistan: House 10a, Street 31, F-6/1, Islamabad; tel. (51) 2850581; fax (51) 2850582; Chargé d'affaires a.i. Nguyen Quang Thuc.

Panama: 52 José Gabriel Duque, La Cresta, Apdo 12434-6A, El Dorado, Panamá; tel. 264-2551; fax 265-6056; e-mail embavinapa@cwpanama.net; Ambassador NGHIEM XUAN LUONG.

Philippines: 670 Pablo Ocampo St, Malate, Metro Manila; tel. (2) 5216843; fax (2) 5260472; e-mail vnembph@yahoo.com; internet www .vietnamembassy-philippines.org; Ambassador Vu Xuan Truong.

Poland: 02-956 Warsaw, ul. Resorowa 36; tel. (22) 6516098; fax (22) 6516095; e-mail office@ambasadawietnamu.org; internet www.vietnamembassy -poland.org; AmbassadorNGUYEN VAN XUONG.

Romania: 020011 Bucharest, Str. C. A. Rosetti 35; tel. (21) 3111604; fax (21) 3121626; e-mail viethuru@b.astral.ro; internet www.vietnamembassy -romania.org; Ambassador Le Manh Hung.

Russian Federation: 119021 Moscow, ul. B. Pirogovskaya 13; tel. (495) 245-09-25; fax (495) 246-31-21; e-mail dsqvn@com2com.ru; AmbassadorNYUGEN VAN NGANG.

Singapore: 10 Leedon Park, Singapore 267887; tel. 64625938; fax 64625936; e-mail vnemb@singnet.com.sg; Ambassador Nguyen Trung Thanh.

South Africa: 87 Brooks St, Brooklyn, Pretoria 0181; POB 13692, Hatfield 0028; tel. (12) 3628119; fax (12) 3628115; e-mail embassy@vietnam.co.za; Ambassador DR TRAN DUY THI.

Spain: Arturo Soria 201, 1°a, 28043 Madrid; tel. (91) 5102867; fax (91) 4157067; e-mail claudiomes@yahoo.com; internet www.embavietnam -madrid.org; AmbassadorNguyen Xuan Phong.

Sweden: Örby Slottsvägen 26, 125 71 Älvsjö; tel. (8) 556-210-70; fax (8) 556-210-80; e-mail info@vietnamemb.se; internet www.vietnamemb.se; AmbassadorTRINH QUANG THANH.

Switzerland: Schlösslistr. 26, 3008 Bern; tel. 313887878; fax 313887879; e-mail info@vietnam-embassy.ch; internet www.vietnam-embassy.ch; AmbassadorNguyen Ngoc Son.

Thailand: 83/1 Thanon Witthayu, Lumpini, Pathumwan, Bangkok 10330; tel. (2) 251-3551; fax (2) 251-7203; e-mail vnembassy@bkk.a-net.net.th; Ambassador NGUYEN DUY HUNG.

Turkey: Çayhane Sok. 34, Gaziosmanpaşa, Ankara; tel. (312) 4468049; fax (312) 4465623; e-mail dsqvnturkey@yahoo.com; Ambassador Nguyen Sy Xung.

Ukraine: 01011 Kyiv, vul. Leskova 5; tel. (44) 254-45-89; fax (44) 294-80-87; e-mail dsq@dsqvn.kiev.ua; Ambassador NGUYEN VAN THANEM.

United Kingdom: 12–14 Victoria Rd, London, W8 5RD; tel. (20) 7937-1912; fax (20) 7937-6108; e-mail embassy@vietnamembassy.org.uk; internet www .vietnamembassy.org.uk; Ambassador Tran Quang Hoan.

United States of America: 1233 20th St, NW, Suite 400, Washington, DC 20036; tel. (202) 861-0737; fax (202) 861-0917; e-mail info@vietnamembassy .us; internet www.vietnamembassy-usa.org; Ambassador LE CONG PHUNG.

Uzbekistan: 100000 Tashkent, Sh. Rashidov ko'ch. 100; tel. (71) 134-03-93; fax (71) 120-62-65; e-mail dsqvntas@online.ru; Ambassador Do Van Dong.

DIPLOMATIC MISSIONS OF YEMEN

United Nations: 413 East 51st St, New York, NY 10022; tel. (212) 355-1730; fax (212) 750-9613; e-mail yemen@un.int; internet www.un.int/yemen; Permanent Representative ABDULLAH M. AS-SAIDI.

Algeria: 18 chemin Mahmoud Drarnine, Hydra, Algiers; tel. (21) 54-89-50; fax (21) 54-87-40; Ambassador Ahmad Abdullah Abd al-Elah.

Austria: Reisnerstr. 18–20, 1st Floor, Top 3–4, 1030 Vienna; tel. (1) 503-29-30; fax (1) 505-31-59; e-mail yemenembassy.vienna@aon.at; Ambassador DR AHMAD ALWAN MULHI AL-ALWANI.

Bahrain: Bldg 80, Rd 2802, Block 328, Umm al-Hassam, Manama; tel. 17822110; fax 17822078; Ambassador Dr Ali Mansour bin Muhammad.

Belgium: 114 ave F. D. Roosevelt, 1050 Brussels; tel. (2) 646-52-90; fax (2) 646-29-11; e-mail yemen@skynet.be; Ambassador ABD AL-WAHAB MUHAMMAD ASH-SHAWKANI.

Canada: 54 Chamberlain Ave, Ottawa, ON K1S 1V9; tel. (613) 729-6627; fax (613) 729-8915; e-mail info@yemenincanada.ca; internet www .yemenincanada.ca; Ambassador Dr Abdulla Abdulwali Nasher.

China, People's Republic: 5 Dong San Jie, San Li Tun, Beijing 100600; tel. (10) 65321558; fax (10) 65324305; e-mail info@embassyofyemen.net; internet www.embassyofyemen.net; Ambassador ABDULMALEK SULAIMAN M. AL-MUALEMI.

Cuba: Calle 16, No 503, entre 5 y 7, Miramar, Havana; tel. (7) 204-1506; fax (7) 204-1131; e-mail gamdan-hav@enet.cu; Ambassador Ahmed Ali Kalaz.

Czech Republic: Pod hradbami 5, 160 00 Prague 6; tel. 233331568; fax 233332204; e-mail yemenemb@seznam.cz; Ambassador AHMED SALEM AL-JABALI.

Djibouti: BP 194, Djibouti; tel. 352975; Ambassador Abdourab Ali As-Salafi.

Egypt: 28 Sharia Amean ar-Rafai, Cairo (Dokki); tel. (2) 3614224; fax (2) 3604815; Ambassador ABD AL-WALI ABD AL-WALITH.

Eritrea: POB 5566, Asmara; tel. (1) 114434; fax (1) 117921; Ambassador Dr Akram abd al-Marik al-Qabri.

Ethiopia: POB 664, Addis Ababa; Ambassador DR AMIN MUHAMMAD AL-YOUSFI.

France: 25 rue Georges Bizet, 75116 Paris; tel. 1-53-23-87-87; fax 1-47-23-69-41; e-mail ambyemenparis@easynet.fr; Ambassador Amir Salim al-Eidrous.

Germany: Budapester Str. 37, 10787 Berlin; tel. (30) 8973050; fax (30) 89730562; e-mail info@botschaft-jemen.de; internet www.botschaft-jemen .de; Ambassador DR MUHAMMAD LUTF MUHAMMAD AL-ERYANI.

Hungary: 1025 Budapest, Józsefhegyi u. 28-30, D/6; tel. (1) 212-3991; fax (1) 212-3883; e-mail al-yemen.al-saida@matavnet.hu; .

India: B-3/61, Safdarjung Enclave, New Delhi 110 029; tel. (11) 26179612; fax (11) 26179614; e-mail yemenembnd@yahoo.com; Ambassador MUSTAFA NUAMAN.

Indonesia: Jalan Yusuf Adiwinata 29, Menteng, Jakarta Pusat 10310; tel. (21) 3108029; fax (21) 3904946; e-mail yemenemb@rad.net.id; Ambassador Abdurahman Mohamed Hassan Al-Hothi.

Iran: Africa Ave, Golestan St, No. 15, Tehran; tel. (21) 22042701; e-mail yem .emb.ir@neda.net; Ambassador JAMAL ABDULLAH AS-SOLAL.

Iraq: 4/36/904 Hay al-Wahada, Baghdad; tel. (1) 718-6682; fax (1) 717-2318; .

Italy: Via Antonio Bosio 10, 00161 Roma; tel. (06) 44231679; fax (06) 44234763; e-mail info@yemenembassy.it; internet www.yemenembassy.it; Ambassador DR SHAYA MOHSIN MUHAMMAD ZINDANI.

Japan: Kowa Bldg, No. 38, Room 807, 4-12-24, Nishi Azabu, Minato-ku, Tokyo 106-0031; tel. (3) 3499-7151; fax (3) 3499-4577; Ambassador Marwan Abdulla Abdulwahab Noman.

Jordan: POB 3085, Prince Hashem Ben Al-Hussain St, Amman 11181; tel. (6) 5923771; fax (6) 5923773; Ambassador DR HUSSEIN TAHER BIN YAHYA.

Kenya: cnr Ngong and Kabarnet Rds, POB 44642, Nairobi; tel. (20) 564379; fax (20) 564394; Ambassador Ahmad Maysari.

Korea, Republic: 11-444, Hannam-dong, Yeongsan-gu, Seoul 140-210; tel. (2) 792-9883; fax (2) 792-9885; internet www.gpc.org.ye; Ambassador YAHYA AHMAD AL-WAZIR.

Kuwait: POB 7182, Al-Jabriya St, Kuwait City; tel. 5349416; fax 5349415; Ambassador Dr Ali al-Ahmadi.

Lebanon: Bir Hassan, Beirut; tel. (1) 852688; fax (1) 821610; Ambassador AHMAD ABDULLAH AL-BASHA.

Libya: POB 4839, Sharia Ubei ben Ka'ab 36, Tripoli; tel. (21) 607472; Ambassador Hussein Ali Hassan Sabah.

Malaysia: 7 Jalan Kedondong, off Jalan Ampang Hilir, 55000 Kuala Lumpur; tel. (3) 42511793; fax (3) 42511794; e-mail info@yemenembassykl .com; internet yemenembassykl.com; Ambassador DR ABDULLA MOHAMED ALI AL-MONTSER.

Mauritania: Tevragh Zeina, BP 4689, Nouakchott; tel. 525-55-91; fax 525-56-39; .

Morocco: 11 rue Abou-Hanifa, Agdal, 10000 Rabat; tel. (3) 7674306; fax (3) 7674769; e-mail yemenembassy@iam.net.ma; Ambassador AHMAD A. AL-BASHA.

Netherlands: Nassaulaan 2a, 2514 JS The Hague; tel. (70) 3653936; fax (70) 3563312; e-mail yemenembassy@planet.nl; internet www.yemenembassy.nl; Ambassador Naguib Ahmed Obeid Obeid.

Oman: Shati al-Qurum, Area 258, Way No. 2840, Bldg No. 2981, POB 105, Madinat Qaboos 115; tel. 24600815; fax 24605008; Ambassador ABD AR-RAHMAN KHAMIS UBAID.

Pakistan: 220, St 21, E-7, POB 1523, Islamabad 44000; tel. (51) 2653612; fax (51) 2653615; e-mail yemen22@isb.apollo.net.pk; Ambassador Abdul Elah Mohamed Hajar.

Poland: 03-941 Warsaw, ul. Zwycięzców 18; tel. (22) 6176025; fax (22) 6176022; e-mail biuro@ambasada-jemenu.pl; internet www.ambasada -jemenu.pl; Ambassador SHAIF BADR ABDULLAH QAID.

Qatar: POB 3318, Doha; tel. 4432555; fax 4429400; Ambassador Abd al-Malik Said.

Russian Federation: 119121 Moscow, 2-i Neopalimovskii per. 6; tel. (495) 246-15-40; fax (495) 230-23-05; Ambassador ABDULWAHAB MUHAMMAD ALI AL-RAWHANI.

Saudi Arabia: POB 94356, Riyadh 11693; tel. (1) 488-1769; fax (1) 488-1562; Ambassador Muhammad Ali Mohsen al-Ahwal.

Somalia: K4, Mogadishu; Ambassador AHMED HAMID ALI UMAR.

South Africa: 329 Main St, Waterkloof 0181; POB 13343, Hatfield 0028; tel. (12) 4250760; fax (12) 4250762; e-mail info@yemenembassy.org.za; internet www.yemenembassy.org.za; Chargé d'affaires a.i. Mohamed Jamil Muharram.

Spain: Paseo de la Castellana 117, 8°, 28046 Madrid; tel. (91) 4119950; fax (91) 5623865; e-mail secretaria@embajadayemen.es; internet www.embajadayemen.es; Chargé d'affaires a.i. ABDULRAHMAN KAMARAMI.

Sudan: St 11, New Extension, POB 1010, Khartoum; tel. (183) 743918; Ambassador Abdouljalil Azzouz.

Syria: Abou Roumaneh, Charkassieh, Damascus; Ambassador SALAH ALI AHEMD AL-ANSI.

Tanzania: 353 United Nations Rd, POB 349, Dar es Salaam; tel. (22) 2117650; fax (22) 2115924; Chargé d'affaires a.i. Mohamed Abdulla Almas.

Tunisia: rue Mouaouia ibn Soufiane, al-Menzah VI, Tunis; tel. (71) 237-933; Ambassador ABD AL-MALEK MANSOUR HASSAN.

Turkey: Fethiye Sok. 2, 06700 Gaziosmanpaşa, Ankara; tel. (312) 4462637; fax (312) 4461778; e-mail yemenemb@superonline.com; Ambassador Noria Abdullah al-Hamami.

United Arab Emirates: POB 2095, Abu Dhabi; tel. (2) 4448457; fax (2) 4447978; e-mail yemenemb@emirates.net.ae; Ambassador DR ABD AL-WAHID MUHAMMAD FAREA.

United Kingdom: 57 Cromwell Rd, London, SW7 2ED; tel. (20) 7584-6607; fax (20) 7589-3350; e-mail yemenembassy@btconnect.com; internet www.yemenembassy.org.uk; Ambassador Muhammad Taha Mustafa.

United States of America: 2319 Wyoming Ave, NW, Washington, DC 20008; tel. (202) 965-4760; fax (202) 337-2017; e-mail information@yemenembassy.org; internet www.yemenembassy.org; Ambassador ABDULWAHAB ABDULLA AL-HAJJRI.

DIPLOMATIC MISSIONS OF ZAMBIA

United Nations: 237 East 52nd St, New York, NY 10022; tel. (212) 888-5770; fax (212) 888-5213; e-mail zambia@un.int; internet www.un.int/zambia; Permanent Representative Lazarous Kapambwe.

Angola: Rua Rei Katyavala 106–108, CP 1496, Luanda; tel. 222331145; Ambassador MARINA NSINGO.

Belgium: 469 ave Molière, 1050 Brussels; tel. (2) 343-56-49; fax (2) 347-43-33; e-mail zambians_brussels@brutele.be; Chargé d'affaires a.i. Miyambo Sipangule.

Botswana: POB 362, Gaborone; tel. 3951951; fax 3953952; High Commissioner CECIL HOLMES.

Brazil: SHIS, QL 10, Conj. 6, Casa 10, Lago Sul, 71630-065 Brasília, DF; tel. (61) 3248-3494; e-mail zambiaembassybr@yahoo.com; Ambassador Albert M. Muchanga.

Canada: 151 Slater St, Suite 205, Ottawa, ON K1B 5H3; tel. (613) 232-4400; fax (613) 232-4410; e-mail embzamb@aol.com; High Commissioner DAVID CLIFFORD SAVIYE.

China, People's Republic: 5 Dong Si Jie, San Li Tun, Chao Yang Qu, Beijing 100600; tel. (10) 65321554; fax (10) 65321891; e-mail admin@zambiaembassy-beijing.com; internet www.zambiaembassy-beijing.com; Ambassador David Saviye.

Congo, Democratic Republic: 54–58 ave de l'Ecole, BP 1144, Kinshasa; tel. (81) 9999437; fax (88) 45106; e-mail ambazambia@ic.cd; Ambassador (vacant).

Egypt: 6 Abd ar-Rahman Hussein, Mohandessin, Cairo (Dokki); tel. (2) 7610282; fax (2) 7610833; Ambassador Cecil Almos Holmes.

Ethiopia: POB 1909, Addis Ababa; tel. (11) 3711302; fax (11) 3711566; Ambassador LAZAROUS KAPAMBWE.

France: 18 ave de Tourville, 75007 Paris; tel. 1-56-88-12-70; fax 1-56-88-03-50; e-mail zambianspars@wanadoo.fr; Ambassador Ian Sikazwe.

Germany: Axel-Springer Str. 54A, 10117 Berlin; tel. (30) 2062940; fax (30) 20629419; e-mail botschaftvonsambia@t-online.de; internet www.sambia-botschaft.de; Ambassador GEN. (RETD) GODWIN KINGSLEY CHINKULI.

India: D/54 Vasant Vihar, New Delhi 110 057; tel. (11) 26145883; fax (11) 26145764; e-mail zambiand@sify.com; High Commissioner S. K. Walubita.

Italy: Via Ennio Quirino Visconti 8, 00193 Roma; tel. (06) 36003590; fax (06) 97613035; Ambassador LUCY M. MUNGOMA.

Japan: 1-10-2, Ebara, Shinagawa-ku, Tokyo 142-0063; tel. (3) 3491-0121; fax (3) 3491-0123; e-mail emb@zambia.or.jp; internet www.zambia.or.jp; Ambassador Godfrey S. Simasiku.

Kenya: Nyerere Rd, POB 48741, Nairobi; tel. (20) 724850; fax (20) 718494; High Commissioner ENESS CHISHALA CHIYENGE.

Malawi: Area 40/2, City Centre, POB 30138, Lilongwe 3; tel. 1772100; fax 1774349; High Commissioner (vacant).

Mozambique: Av. Kenneth Kaunda 1286, CP 4655, Maputo; tel. 21492452; fax 21491893; e-mail zhcmmap@zebra.uem.mz; High Commissioner SIMON GABRIEL MWILA.

Namibia: 22 Sam Nujoma Dr., cnr Mandume Ndemufayo Rd, POB 22882, Windhoek; tel. (61) 237610; fax (61) 228162; e-mail zahico@iway.na; internet www.zahico.iway.na; High Commissioner Griffin Nyirongo.

Nigeria: 11 Keffi St, SW Ikoyi, PMB 6119, Lagos; High Commissioner B. N. NKUNIKA (acting).

Russian Federation: 129041 Moscow, pr. Mira 52a; tel. (495) 688-50-01; fax (495) 975-20-56; Ambassador Rev. Dr Peter L. Chintala.

South Africa: 570 Ziervogel St, Arcadia, Pretoria 0083; POB 12234, Hatfield 0028; tel. (12) 3261854; fax (12) 3262140; High Commissioner LESLIE SAINOT MBULA.

Sweden: Gårdsvägen 18, 3rd Floor, POB 3056, 169 03 Solna; tel. (8) 679-90-40; fax (8) 679-68-50; e-mail info@zambiaembassy.se; internet www.zambiaembassy.se; Ambassador Joyce Musenge.

Tanzania: 5–6 Ohio St/Sokoine Dr. Junction, POB 2525, Dar es Salaam; tel. (22) 2112977; e-mail zhcd@raha.com; High Commissioner JOHN KASHONKA CHITAFU.

United Kingdom: Zambia House, 2 Palace Gate, London, W8 5NG; tel. (20) 7589-6655; fax (20) 7581-1353; e-mail immzhcl@btconnect.com; internet www.zhcl.org.uk; High Commr Anderson Kaseba Chibwa.

United States of America: 2419 Massachusetts Ave, NW, Washington, DC 20008; tel. (202) 265-9717; fax (202) 332-0826; e-mail info@zambiainfo.org; internet www.zambiaembassy.org; Ambassador DR INONGE MBIKUSITA LEWANIKA.

Zimbabwe: Zambia House, cnr Union and Julius Nyerere Aves, POB 4698, Harare; tel. (4) 773777; fax (4) 773782; Ambassador Prof. E. C. Mumba.

DIPLOMATIC MISSIONS OF ZIMBABWE

United Nations: 128 East 56th St, New York, NY 10022; tel. (212) 980-9511; fax (212) 308-6705; e-mail zimbabwe@un.int; Permanent Representative T. J. B. BONIFACE GUWA CHIDYAUSIKU.

Angola: Edif. Secil, Av. 4 de Fevereiro 42, CP 428, Luanda; tel. 222311528; e-mail embzimbabwe@ebonet.net; Ambassador James Manzou.

Australia: 11 Culgoa Circuit, O'Malley, ACT 2606; tel. (2) 6286-2700; fax (2) 6290-1680; e-mail zimbabwe1@iimetro.com.au; Ambassador STEPHEN CHIKETA.

Austria: Strozzigasse 10/15, 1080 Vienna; tel. (1) 407-92-36; fax (1) 407-92-38; e-mail z.vien@chello.at; internet www.zimbabweembassyvienna.at; Ambassador Grace Tsitsi Mutandiro.

Belgium: 11 square Joséphine Charlotte, 1200 Brussels; tel. (2) 762-58-08; fax (2) 762-96-05; e-mail zimbrussels@skynet.be; Ambassador GIFT PUNUNGWE.

Botswana: Plot 8850, POB 1232, Gaborone; tel. 3914495; fax 3905863; Ambassador Thomas Mandigora.

Brazil: SHIS, QI 03, Conj. 10, Casa 13, Brasília, DF; tel. (61) 3365-4801; fax (61) 3365-4803; e-mail zimbrasilia@uol.com.br; internet www.zimbabue-brasilia.org.br; Ambassador THOMAS SUKUTAI BVUMA.

Canada: 332 Somerset St West, Ottawa, ON K2P 0J9; tel. (613) 237-4388; fax (613) 563-8269; e-mail zimembassy@bellnet.ca; internet www.zimbabweembassy.ca; Ambassador Florence Zano Chideya.

China, People's Republic: 7 Dong San Jie, San Li Tun, Beijing 100600; tel. (10) 65323795; fax (10) 65325383; e-mail zimbei@163.bj.com; Ambassador CHRISTOPHER HATIKURI MUTSVANGWA.

Cuba: Avda 3, No 1001, esq. a 10, Miramar, Havana; tel. (7) 204-2857; fax (7) 204-2720; e-mail zimhavana@yahoo.com; Ambassador Jevana Ben Maseko.

Egypt: 40 Sharia Ghaza, Mohandessin, Cairo; tel. (2) 3030404; fax (2) 3059741; e-mail zimcairo@thewayout.net; Ambassador AARON MABOYI-NCUBE.

Ethiopia: POB 5624, Addis Ababa; tel. (11) 6613877; fax (11) 6613476; e-mail zimbabwe.embassy@telecom.net.et; Ambassador Dr Andrew Hama Mtetwa.

France: 18 ave de Tourville, 75007 Paris; tel. 1-56-88-16-00; fax 1-56-88-16-09; e-mail zimparisweb@wanadoo.fr; Ambassador DAVID HAMADZIRIPI.

Germany: Kommandantenstr. 80, 10117 Berlin; tel. (30) 2062263; fax (30) 20455062; e-mail zimberlin@t-online.de; Ambassador Cuthbert Zhakata.

India: E 12/7, Vasant Vihar, New Delhi 110 057; tel. (11) 26140430; fax (11) 26154316; e-mail ambassador@zimdelhi.com; internet www.zimdelhi.com; Ambassador JONATHAN WUTAWUNASHE.

Iran: 24 Shad Avar St, Mogghadas Ardabili, Tehran; tel. (21) 22027553; fax (21) 22041109; e-mail zimbabwe@neda.net; Ambassador Stephen Cletus Chiketa.

Italy: Via Virgilio 8, 00193 Roma; tel. (06) 68308265; fax (06) 68308324; e-mail zimrome-wolit@tiscali.it; Ambassador MARY MARGARET MUCHADA.

Japan: 5-9-10, Shiroganedai, Minato-ku, Tokyo 108-0071; tel. (3) 3280-0331; fax (3) 3280-0466; e-mail zimtokyo@chive.ocn.ne.jp; Ambassador Stuart H. Comberbach.

Kenya: Minet-ICDC Bldg, 6th Floor, Mamlaka Rd, POB 30806, Nairobi; tel. (20) 721071; fax (20) 726503; Ambassador KELEBERT NKOMANI.

Kuwait: POB 36484, 24755 Salmiya, Kuwait City; tel. 5621517; fax 5621491; e-mail zimkuwait@hotmail.com; Ambassador Mark Grey Marongwe.

Malawi: POB 30187, Lilongwe 3; tel. 1774988; fax 1772382; e-mail zimhighcomllw@malawi.net; High Commissioner THANDIWE S. DUMBUTSHENA.

Malaysia: 124 Jalan Sembilan, Taman Ampang Utama, 68000 Ampang, Selangor Darul Ehsan; tel. (3) 42516779; fax (3) 42517252; e-mail zhck@tm.net.my; Ambassador Lucas Pande Tavaya.

Mozambique: Av. Kenneth Kaunda 816, CP 743, Maputo; tel. 21490404; fax 21492237; e-mail maro@isl.co.mz; Ambassador AGRIPA MUTAMBARA.

Namibia: cnr Independence Ave and Grimm St, POB 23056, Windhoek; tel. (61) 228134; fax (61) 226859; Ambassador Chipo Zindoga.

Nigeria: Abuja; tel. (9) 4611322; fax (9) 4611327; Ambassador DR JOHN SHUMBA MVUNDURA.

Russian Federation: 119121 Moscow, per. Serpov 6; tel. (495) 248-43-67; fax (495) 230-24-97; e-mail zimbabwe@rinet.ru; Ambassador Brig. (retd) Agrippah Mutambara.

South Africa: Zimbabwe House, 798 Merton St, Arcadia, Pretoria 0083; POB 55140, Arcadia 0007; tel. (12) 3425125; fax (12) 3425126; e-mail zimpret@lantic.net; Ambassador SIMON KHAYA MOYO.

Sweden: Herserudsvägen 5a, 7th Floor, 181 34 Lidingö; POB 3253, 103 65 Stockholm; tel. (8) 765-53-80; fax (8) 21-91-32; e-mail mbuya@stockholm.mail.telia.com; Ambassador Mary Sibusisiwe Mubi.

Tanzania: 2097 East Upanga, off Ali Hassan Mwinyi Rd, POB 20762, Dar es Salaam; tel. (22) 2116789; fax (22) 2112913; e-mail zimdares@cats-net.com; Ambassador J. M. SHAVA.

United Kingdom: Zimbabwe House, 429 Strand, London, WC2R 0QE; tel. (20) 7836-7755; fax (20) 7379-1167; e-mail zimlondon@yahoo.co.uk; Ambassador Gabriel Mharadze Machinga.

United States of America: 1608 New Hampshire Ave, NW, Washington, DC 20009; tel. (202) 332-7100; fax (202) 483-9326; e-mail info@zimbabwe-embassy.us; Ambassador MACHIVENYIKA TOBIAS MAPURANGA.

Zambia: 11058, Haile Selassie Ave, Longacres, POB 33491, 10101 Lusaka; tel. (1) 254012; fax (1) 227474; Ambassador Kosho Dube.

INDEX BY ORGANIZATION

INDEX BY NATIONALITY

Portugal

Qatar

Romania

United States

Uruguay

Uzbekistan

Vanuatu